ATIONS

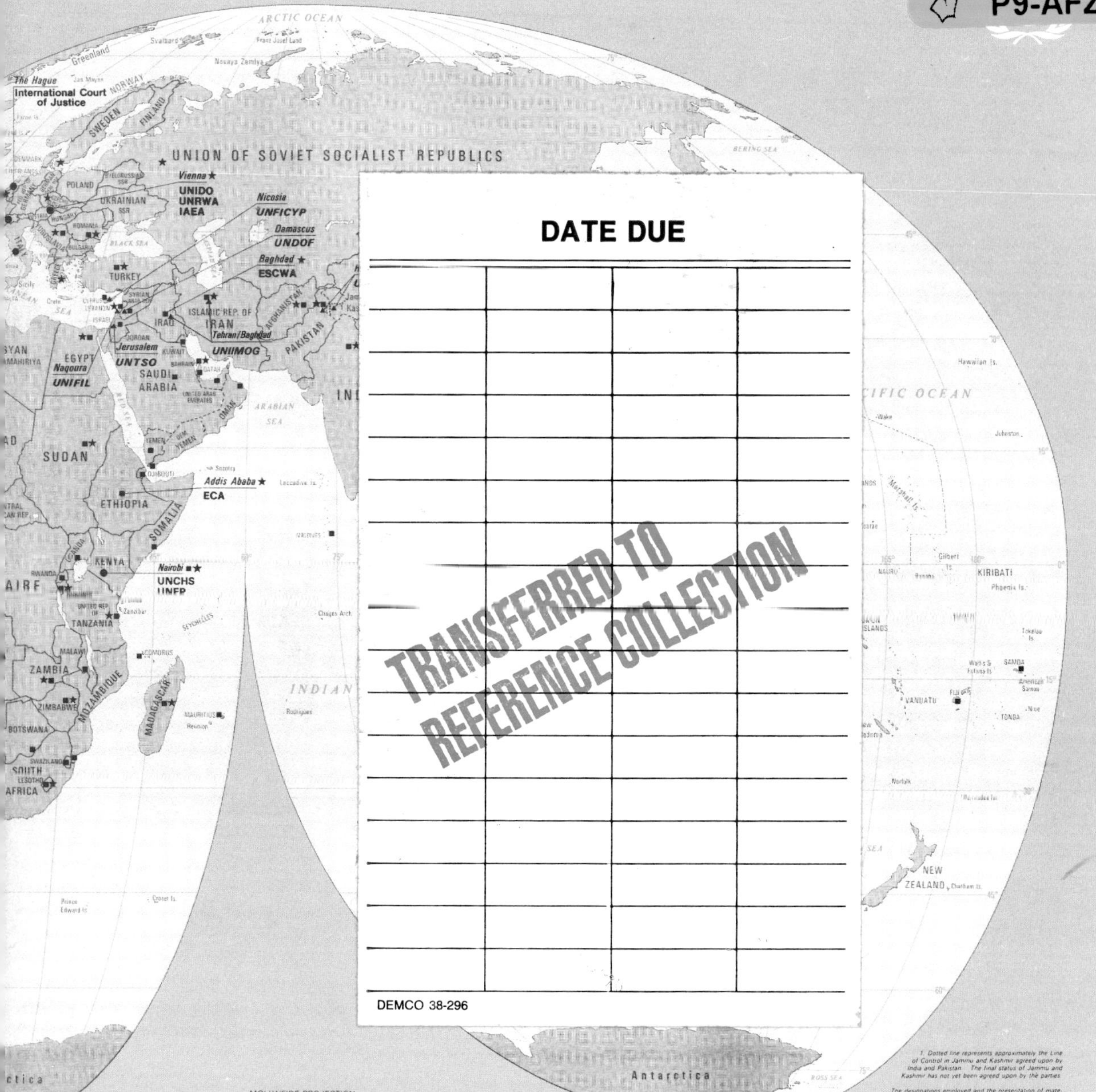

DATE DUE

DEMCO 38-296

MOLLWEIDE PROJECTION
Scale 1:75 000 000 (approximate)

The designations employed and the presentation of material on this map do not imply the expression of any opinion whatsoever on the part of the Secretariat of the United Nations concerning the legal status of any country, territory, city or area or of its authorities, or concerning the delimitation of its frontiers or boundaries.

1. Dotted line represents approximately the Line of Control in Jammu and Kashmir agreed upon by India and Pakistan. The final status of Jammu and Kashmir has not yet been agreed upon by the parties.

MAP NO. 3105 Rev. 10 UNITED NATIONS AUGUST 1989

MEMBERS OF THE UNITED NATIONS

Estimated population (mid-year 1988)	Name of country	Date of admission	Total area (square kilometres)	Estimated population (mid-year 1988)
487 000	Haiti	24 Oct. 1945	27 750	5 523 000
1 888 000	Honduras	17 Dec. 1945	112 088	4 802 000
2 866 000	Hungary	14 Dec. 1955	93 022	10 596 000
11 612 000	Iceland	19 Nov. 1946	103 000	249 500
10 402 400	India	30 Oct. 1945	3 287 590	797 000 000
687 000	Indonesia	28 Sep. 1950	1 904 569	174 951 000
15 608 183	Iran (Islamic Republic of)	24 Oct. 1945	1 648 000	52 779 000
7 869 000	Iraq	21 Dec. 1945	438 317	17 656 000
2 514 000	Ireland	14 Dec. 1955	70 284	3 538 000
5 129 516	Israel	11 May 1949	20 770	4 431 000
383 000	Italy	14 Dec. 1955	301 268	57 441 000
79 000	Jamaica	18 Sep. 1962	10 990	2 446 000
6 867 368	Japan	18 Dec. 1956	377 801	122 424 000
10 204 000	Jordan	14 Dec. 1955	97 740	3 943 000
51 897 000	Kenya	16 Dec. 1963	580 367	23 882 000
5 107 000	Kuwait	14 May 1963	17 818	1 958 000
620 000	Lao People's Democratic Republic	14 Dec. 1955	236 800	3 974 000
47 882 900	Lebanon	24 Oct. 1945	10 400	2 827 000
727 000	Lesotho	17 Oct. 1966	30 355	1 676 000
4 951 000	Liberia	2 Nov. 1945	111 369	2 508 000
55 874 000	Libyan Arab Jamahiriya	14 Dec. 1955	1 759 540	4 232 000
1 094 000	Luxembourg	24 Oct. 1945	2 586	374 000
812 000	Madagascar	20 Sep. 1960	587 041	11 238 000
16 666 340	Malawi	1 Dec. 1964	118 484	7 755 000
61 199 000	Malaysia	17 Sep. 1957	329 749	16 921 000
14 130 000	Maldives	21 Sep. 1965	298	202 000
10 013 000	Mali	28 Sep. 1960	1 240 192	8 918 000
100 000	Malta	1 Dec. 1964	316	347 000
8 681 000	Mauritania	27 Oct. 1961	1 025 520	1 916 000
5 071 000	Mauritius	24 Apr. 1968	2 040	1 077 000
945 000	Mexico	7 Nov. 1945	1 958 201	82 734 000
1 006 000	Mongolia	27 Oct. 1961	1 566 500	2 092 000

Name of country	Date of admission	Total area (square kilometres)	Estimated population (mid-year 1988)
Morocco	12 Nov. 1956	446 550	23 910 000
Mozambique	16 Sep. 1975	801 590	14 932 000
Myanmar	19 Apr. 1948	676 552	39 966 000
Nepal	14 Dec. 1955	140 797	18 234 000
Netherlands	10 Dec. 1945	40 844	14 757 948
New Zealand	24 Oct. 1945	268 676	3 292 300
Nicaragua	24 Oct. 1945	130 000	3 622 000
Niger	20 Sep. 1960	1 267 000	6 988 000
Nigeria	7 Oct. 1960	923 768	105 471 000
Norway	27 Nov. 1945	323 895	4 195 661
Oman	7 Oct. 1971	212 457	1 377 000
Pakistan	30 Sep. 1947	796 095	105 409 000
Panama	13 Nov. 1945	77 082	2 322 001
Papua New Guinea	10 Oct. 1975	462 840	3 561 000
Paraguay	24 Oct. 1945	406 752	4 039 000
Peru	31 Oct. 1945	1 285 216	21 255 900
Philippines	24 Oct. 1945	300 000	58 721 307
Poland	24 Oct. 1945	312 677	37 862 063
Portugal	14 Dec. 1955	92 389	10 408 000
Qatar	21 Sep. 1971	11 000	340 000
Romania	14 Dec. 1955	237 500	23 048 000
Rwanda	18 Sep. 1962	26 338	6 755 000
Saint Kitts and Nevis	23 Sep. 1983	261	48 000
Saint Lucia	18 Sep. 1979	622	133 000
Saint Vincent and the Grenadines	16 Sep. 1980	388	108 000
Samoa	15 Dec. 1976	2 831	167 000
Sao Tome and Principe	16 Sep. 1975	964	106 000
Saudi Arabia	24 Oct. 1945	2 149 690	14 016 000
Senegal	28 Sep. 1960	196 722	6 978 000
Seychelles	21 Sep. 1976	280	67 000
Sierra Leone	27 Sep. 1961	71 740	3 946 000
Singapore	21 Sep. 1965	618	2 641 000

Name of country	Date of admission	Total area (square kilometres)	Estimated population (mid-year 1988)
Solomon Islands	19 Sep. 1978	28 896	299 016
Somalia	20 Sep. 1960	637 657	7 106 000
South Africa	7 Nov. 1945	1 221 037	33 747 000
Spain	14 Dec. 1955	504 782	39 053 000
Sri Lanka	14 Dec. 1955	65 610	16 587 000
Sudan	12 Nov. 1956	2 505 813	23 797 000
Suriname	4 Dec. 1975	163 265	392 000
Swaziland	24 Sep. 1968	17 364	737 000
Sweden	19 Nov. 1946	449 964	8 436 486
Syrian Arab Republic	24 Oct. 1945	185 180	11 338 000
Thailand	16 Dec. 1946	513 115	54 536 000
Togo	20 Sep. 1960	56 785	3 247 000
Trinidad and Tobago	18 Sep. 1962	5 130	1 243 000
Tunisia	12 Nov. 1956	163 610	7 809 000
Turkey	24 Oct. 1945	779 452	52 422 000
Uganda	25 Oct. 1962	235 880	17 189 000
Ukrainian Soviet Socialist Republic	24 Oct. 1945	603 700	51 300 000
Union of Soviet Socialist Republics	24 Oct. 1945	22 402 200	283 682 000
United Arab Emirates	9 Dec. 1971	83 600	1 501 000
United Kingdom	24 Oct. 1945	244 100	57 077 000
United Republic of Tanzania	14 Dec. 1961	945 087	23 997 000
United States of America	24 Oct. 1945	9 372 614	246 329 000
Uruguay	18 Dec. 1945	177 414	3 059 545
Vanuatu	15 Sep. 1981	12 189	199 739
Venezuela	15 Nov. 1945	912 050	18 751 389
Viet Nam	20 Sep. 1977	331 689	64 227 000
Yemen	30 Sep. 1947	195 000	7 534 000
Yugoslavia	24 Oct. 1945	255 804	23 558 928
Zaire	20 Sep. 1960	2 345 409	33 458 000
Zambia	1 Dec. 1964	752 614	7 531 000
Zimbabwe	25 Aug. 1980	390 580	8 878 000

* Excluding Namibia.
1 United Nations estimate.
2 For 1987.
3 Excluding data for Jammu and Kashmir.
4 Including the figures of Byelorussian SSR and Ukrainian SSR.

The Encyclopedia
of
The United Nations
and
International Agreements

EDMUND JAN OSMAŃCZYK

The Encyclopedia of The United Nations and International Relations

Taylor and Francis 1990
New York – Philadelphia – London

First published 1985 by Taylor & Francis Inc.
Reprinted 1986
Second Edition published 1990

USA   Taylor & Francis Inc., 1900 Frost Road, Suite 101, Bristol, PA 19007

UK   Taylor & Francis, 4 John Street, London WC1N 2ET

Copyright © by Edmund Jan Osmańczyk 1990

Library of Congress Cataloging in Publication Data

Osmańczyk, Edmund Jan, 1913–1989
The Encyclopedia of the United Nations and International
Agreements/Edmund Jan Osmańczyk – 2nd edition   p.   cm.
Includes index.

ISBN 0-85066-833-6 $340.00
1. United Nations—Dictionaries.
2. International relations—Dictionaries   I. Title.
JX1977.08213   1990   341.23′03   dc20

British Library Cataloguing in Publication Data

Osmańczyk, Edmund Jan, 1913–1989
The Encyclopedia of the United Nations and International Agreements.
—2nd edition.
1. United Nations—History.
I. Title.
341.23′09

ISBN 0-85066-833-6

Published with the cooperation of the United Nations

Typeset in Times by Pindar Graphics Origination,
Scarborough, North Yorkshire.

Printed in Great Britain by
BPCC Wheatons Ltd
Exeter

CONTENTS

CONTENTS

Never more Auschwitz, never more Hiroshima.

John Paul II,
Hiroshima, Feb. 25, 1981

Observe good faith and justice toward all Nations. Cultivate peace and harmony with all.

George Washington,
Farewell Address

Between Nations as between people: respect for the rights of others makes peace.

Benito Juarez

To Aiko Ruta and to Szymon Jan
our grandchildren

INTRODUCTION OF THE SECRETARY-GENERAL OF THE UNITED NATIONS

In my introduction to the previous edition of this work, I noted that the United Nations had entered fully into the history of our time. It is now equally clear that the United Nations will be even more central to humankind's immediate future. As we stand before a new century, nations are more than ever economically, socially and politically interdependent, and this interdependence is accelerating.

Rapid advances in science, technology and communications systems in the second half of the Twentieth Century have reduced or eliminated the meaning of distance. The work of the United Nations and its specialized agencies grows increasingly prominent as ideological conflicts diminish and political barriers descend. The new pattern of international relations is energizing the multilateral pursuit of solutions for such world-wide problems as disease, drugs, human rights, debt, and the environment. These issues, peace-keeping and peace-making, the conclusion of international treaties, disarmament talks, economic co-operation – the entire gamut of subjects on the international agenda – are all the focus of increasing attention by Member States and of action by the World Organization.

Already available in Polish and Spanish, the first English language version of Edmund Jan Osmańczyk's *The Encyclopedia of the United Nations and International Agreements* was issued in 1985. On that occasion, I welcomed the availability of such a ready source of information as a valuable tool for research in international studies. The Second Edition, prepared just before the author's death in October 1989, brings the 1985 edition up to date with world events as witnessed in the United Nations. This constitutes another remarkable accomplishment in Mr. Osmańczyk's distinguished career as a parliamentarian, which culminated in his election in the summer of 1989 to the newly re-established Senate of his native Poland, and as a man of letters and journalist. It is most fortunate that scholars and students will have the benefit of his arduous efforts to document and assess the accomplishments of the Organization and to provoke insight into how it can be further strengthened.

I warmly welcome this posthumously published work of a most thoughtful analyst and supporter of the United Nations.

Javier PÉREZ DE CUÉLLAR
Secretary-General

FOREWORD, OR A FEW WORDS ON THE ENCYCLOPEDIA AND AUTHOR

The first English Encyclopedia of the UN System was published on the occasion of the 40th anniversary of the ratification of the Charter of the United Nations, Oct. 24, 1985.

During the first 40 years of the UN, perhaps the most inspiring yet most frustrating years in the history of human existence, many proposals were made to compile an encyclopedia of this type. We heard of them in the UN themselves as well as in institutions which do research on international relations and in publishing houses specializing in world affairs. As a UN official of rather lengthy service, and being also responsible for UN publications, I was constantly aware of both the substantive and commercial difficulties in bringing such projects into life.

In the UN Organization itself, besides the considerable economic problems of raising adequate funds for long-term research, such a project would have required the consensus of all members on entries, including those reflecting controversial problems debated in the UN System.

International institutions and publishers specializing in international affairs seemed to be unwilling to take up and objectively explain the growing number of problems examined in the UN System with the passage of time. The complexity and often controversial nature of the totality of international problems would have required a staff of specialists and many special research studies. The time estimates for the editorial work were too long, which would have made it a very costly publishing project.

Edmund Jan Osmańczyk, who was a journalist, has witnessed and recorded international events since 1932 and has systematically built an extensive archive that covers international events since 1918. This made it possible for him to compile a number of reference books covering international events of that period, gradually developing his main preoccupation with the UN System itself – as evidenced by the list of his published works dealing with international relations.

In a field as diversified and controversial as international relations one should always be able to find a nook omitted or a cranny simplified. But going through the entries as compiled here one could easily not only give the author the benefit of the doubt, but also acknowledge his evident effort not to edit the development of the UN System, but simply to follow it.

The following is not enough, of course. For the UN System arose and continues to develop in a nexus of bilateral and multilateral arrangements. Without guidance in these agreements it is impossible to understand the UN System and its role in world relations. Hence this is an encyclopedia of the UN System and international agreements.

The greatest challenge for a chronicler of any course of events is the attitude of the author towards them; not only a challenge, but also a test. How objective he is, is more often than not the ultimate test of the usefulness of his work. Here I do not hesitate to express the view that the author took exceptional care – and this could be challenged probably only by a few most scrutinizing and perfection-minded reviewers – not to express his own opinion in any entry but to quote or refer to an opinion of the UN body concerned or the opinions of dissenting groups.

The success of the first edition of this encyclopedia went far beyond the expectations. One has to remember that at the time of its publication in 1985 the UN Organization did not enjoy very high esteem among the public and governments. It took exceptional courage and foresight on the part of the author and publishers to undertake this project. They deserve highest congratulations.

How drastically the image of the UN has changed! The role of the Organization in ending Iran–Iraq war, in helping the USSR to withdraw from Afghanistan, in bringing freedom and democracy to Namibia – to mention only a few examples, and almost every day brings new ones – should make us aware that the UN is well and very much alive. This also should be a good reason to bring out the second, updated edition of this encyclopedia.

Osmańczyk was ahead of times when he launched this project. His strong belief in the UN and in multilateralism kept him active until the very last days of his life. Hence you are receiving now this new edition revised and expanded by him in the same spirit of total impartiality which guided him during the work on the first edition.

BOHDAN LEWANDOWSKI
Former UN Undersecretary General

OBITUARY

EDMUND J OSMAŃCZYK
born Jagielno, Silesia 10 August 1913
died Warsaw 4 October 1989

Edmund Osmańczyk was a versatile and accomplished author, journalist, parliamentarian and encyclopaedist who had a lifelong and unquenchable interest in international affairs. He spent most of his professional life outside his native Poland, working as a foreign and diplomatic correspondent for the Polish media. He worked in Europe, the USSR and North and Latin America and covered such important events as the storming of Berlin by the Russians and Poles in 1945, the Potsdam Conference, the Nuremberg Trials and many post-war Summit Conferences.

He was, par excellence, both Pole and European, looking forward eagerly to the day of the creation of a united Europe.

Born in 1913 in Silesia, the descendant of a Turkish soldier who had settled in Poland after being captured by the Poles at the Siege of Vienna in 1683, he was educated at a Gymnasium in Warsaw and at the Universities of Warsaw, Berlin and Bordeaux, where he studied history and journalism.

During the war he served in the Home Army, working for the clandestine radio station, and took part in the Warsaw uprising of 1944, which he later described as "the most tragic of all Polish insurrections". In January 1945 he was arrested in Krakow by the Gestapo but managed to escape from the transport taking him to a concentration camp. Soon after the liberation of Poland he joined the Polish regular army as a war correspondent and eventually entered Berlin with the First Polish Infantry Division.

From the publication, in 1946, of his book The Affairs of the Poles Osmańczyk's constant call was for Polish–German reconciliation as one of the essential steps towards the creation of a new, permanently conflict-free Europe. He rightly felt that in the age of nuclear weapons any future war in Europe would be an act of suicide and so from 1956 he appealed repeatedly for an improvement in East – West relations and for super-power disengagement in the continent's central heartland. He also strove staunchly to strengthen relations between the Poles living in Poland and those scattered abroad in the 13 million strong Polish diaspora.

Throughout the Seventies and Eighties – following his final return from postings abroad to work in Poland – he was a determined champion of human and civic rights for all his fellow citizens, regardless of political or religious affiliations, and an untiring advocate of political and economic reform as a long-standing independent member of the Polish Parliament (the Sejm).

He finished his parliamentary career as a Solidarity-sponsored senator (for his native Silesia) in the newly re-established Senate to which he was elected in summer 1989.

Edmund Osmańczyk, helped by his ever devoted wife Jolanta, wrote a number of useful and influential works, in Polish, Spanish and English, on Polish and international affairs and was author of 50 books. The most important of these is the Encyclopedia of the United Nations and International Agreements, Taylor & Francis Inc, published in 1985, of which he produced editions in all three languages. He was justifiably proud of this splendid work which he rightly considered to be his main literary achievement. At the time of his death he had just completed this updated and comprehensive second edition.

Edmund Jan Osmańczyk, author and politician, born Jagielno, Silesia 10 August 1913, Deputy to Sejm Warsaw 1952–61, 1969–85, President of Polish Copyright Association (ZAIKS) 1984–88, 1989 elected to the Senate of the Republic of Poland, married 1961 Jolanta Kimowicz (one daughter), died Warsaw 4 October 1989.

JAN CIECHANOWSKI

(Jan Ciechanowski, a Polish Historian, was a friend and colleague for over 20 years).

ACKNOWLEDGEMENTS

To my three American colleagues and friends during years, Robert R. Kenney, Basil Larthe and A. Chester Kisiel, I wish to state that without their help it would have been impossible to complete the English Encyclopedia. My thanks are also directed to my friend Bohdan Lewandowski for the same reason. Particular thanks are due to Jozef Goldblat from SIPRI and to the author of the indexes R. Szymon Ostrowski. Special thanks to my wife Jolanta who supplied constant aid, comfort and encouragement during the last two decades of a rather unusual "one man team" while working on different versions of this Encyclopedia, in Polish, Spanish and English. To Artur Zapalowski for his work on this second edition.

USER'S GUIDE

The *Encyclopedia of the United Nations and International Agreements* is a unique compendium of political, economic and social information. It offers in one volume material which would otherwise require a substantial collection of books and papers.

It contains data on the structure of the United Nations, its specialized agencies, and the many intergovernmental and nongovernmental organizations, international and regional, which cooperate with the United Nations

It also contains entries on several thousand international agreements, conventions and treaties, quoted in part or in their entirety, entered into in this century or the end of the last century.

Finally, it provides explanations of widely used political, economic, military, geographical and sociological terms, as well as terms used in diplomacy and international law.

The *Encyclopedia* is arranged in strict alphabetical order. Most entries conclude with a list of sources, to which readers are referred if they wish to pursue a topic further.

A key feature of the *Encyclopedia of the United Nations and International Agreements* is that it is fully cross-referenced. References are marked in the text or at the end of an entry with a $\triangleright$.

LAW OF CONCLUSION ON INTERNATIONAL AGREEMENTS. A part of the law of treaties, specifying which subjects of international law have the right to conclude international agreements, and which bodies of these subjects are established for this purpose. In the 19th century, in principle, the states were subjects of international law and in the case of federal states also the countries (states) belonging to the federation, but in a restricted sense, in the case of dependent states they were subjects of international law only with the consent of their protector. In the 20th century treaty competence has been fully received by inter-governmental international organizations (ius tractuum), and also by the Holy See and insurgents enjoying limited recognition. The $\triangleright$ Vienna Convention of the Law of Treaties of 1969, prepared by the Commission on International Law of the UN, is limited to regulating the treaty competence of states, leaving the competences "of other subjects of international law" unspecified in greater detail. The Convention in art. 7 states which state bodies are competent to conclude agreements.

H. CHIN, *The Capacity of International Organizations to Conclude Treaties and the Special Legal Aspect of the Treaties so concluded*, The Hague, 1966.

UN GENERAL ASSEMBLY PRESIDENT OF THE SESSION. The official title of chairmen of the UN General Assembly regular sessions elected by the Assembly to preside over such sessions in keeping with Art. 21 of the UN Charter and to exercise functions determined by the UN General Assembly rules of procedure. In case of Extraordinary Sessions the function of president is exercised as a rule by the president of regular sessions. The rules assign to the President the function of presiding over plenary sessions, putting motions to vote, announcing resolutions, etc., also, supervising the work of ancillary organs of the Assembly. President is assisted by 21 deputies also elected by the Assembly who, together with chairmen of seven main UN Committees, from the General Committee making decisions on procedural matters and not political ones.

The name of the presidents 1946–85 $\triangleright$ UN General Assembly Sessions. $\triangleright$ UN General Assembly.

UN. *Rules of Procedure of the General Assembly*, New York, 1972.

A

A. First letter of the Latin alphabet, currently an international symbol of atomic weapons (▷ ABC weapons).

AACHEN. AIX LA CHAPELLE OR BAD AACHEN. A city in the FRG near the Belgian and Dutch border, with French and German cultural monuments. Aachen Cathedral is included in the ▷ World Heritage UNESCO List. About 790, Charlemagne had the palace chapel constructed close to his castle in Aachen. This domed building, a combination of late classical art and Byzantine innovations, has had a lasting influence on architecture. It remains the symbol of the cultural renaissance which this illustrious king did so much to encourage. ▷ Aix La Chapelle Congress, 1818. See also ▷ Aix la Chapelle Treaty, 1748.

UNESCO. *A Legacy for All. The World's Major Natural, Cultural and Historic Sites*, Paris, 1984.

AAHO. ▷ Afro-Asian Housing Organization.

AALAND ISLANDS, OR ÅLAND ISLANDS OR AHVENANMAA ISLANDS. An archipelago of about 7000 islands and islets in the Baltic Sea between Sweden and Finland at the entrance to the Gulf of Bothnia. Area: 1,548 sq. km. Population, 1970 census, 21,010. Province of Finland.
Subject of international disputes in the 19th century between Russia and Finland, 1809, and between Russia and Great Britain and France, demilitarized and neutralized by the Paris Treaty of Mar. 30, 1856. Occupied in 1918 by Sweden and Germany; subject of debate in the League of Nations 1920–1921 (▷ Aaland Islands Convention, 1921). On Oct. 11, 1940 the USSR signed with Finland an agreement on total demilitarization of the islands and on establishment of a Soviet consulate for demilitarization control; integrated by the Finland –USSR Peace Treaty of Feb. 10, 1947. Sweden on Dec. 1, 1950 informed the UN Secretary General that it considered the League of Nations Convention of 1921 to be still in force. Finland renounced the Convention in 1951 and accorded a self-government status to the islanders.

L.A. PUNTILLA, *The Political History of Finland, 1809–1966*, Helsinki, 1974; FINLAND – SWEDEN (Aaland Islands), in: KEESING's *Border and Territorial Disputes*, London, 1988.

AALAND ISLANDS CONVENTION, 1921. Convention relating to the Non-fortification and neutralization of the Aaland Islands, signed in Geneva, Oct. 20, 1921 by the Governments of Denmark, Estonia, Finland, France, Germany, Italy, Latvia, Poland, Sweden and the UK. The highlights of the Convention: art. 2 describes the geographical points of the Aaland Islands including islets and reefs.

"No military or Naval establishments or base of operations, no military aircraft establishment or base of operations, and no other installation used for war purposes, shall be maintained or set up in the zone described in art. 2 (art. 3).

"The provisions of this Convention shall remain in force in spite of any changes that may take place in the present status quo in the Baltic Sea" (art. 8).
LNTS, Vol. 9, p. 217 and 219; M.G. SCHYBERGSON, *La position d'Aland pendant l'age historique*, Paris, 1919; League of Nations, *Aaland Islands. Documents*, Genève, 1920; *La question des Îles d'Aland (Octobre, 1920)*, Helsingfors, 1920; A. DANIELSON-KALMARI, *La question des Îles d'Aland de 1914 à 1920*, Paris, 1921; Report of Commission of Raporteurs on Aaland Island Questions, Apr. 16, 1921, in Council of League of Nations, B 7.21/68/106; *La question des Îles d'Aland*, 3 Vols., Stockholm, 1921; H.A. COLIJN, *La Decision de la Société des Nations concernant les Îles d'Aland*, Genève, 1921; J.O. SÖDERHJELM, *Demilitarisation et neutralisation des Îles d'Aland en 1856 et 1921*, Paris, 1928; P. MAURY, *La question des Îles d'Aland*, Paris, 1930; S. WAMBAUGH, *Plebiscites since the World War. With a Collection of Official Documents*, Vol. 2, Washington, 1933; T. SUONTAUSTA, "La situation juridique des Îles d'Aland", in *Zeitschrift für ausländisches öffentliches Recht und Völkerrecht*, Bd. 13, 1950; D.W. WAINHOUSE, *International Peace Observation. A History and Forecast*, Baltimore 1966.

AAPSO. ▷ Afro-Asian Peoples Solidarity Organization.

AARRO. ▷ Afro-Asian Rural Reconstruction Organisation.

ABANDONMENT. An international term of maritime law – formal (written) abandonment of a ship or a cargo by the ship-owner or cargo-owner, when sunk or damaged and in the case of insurance "abandonment of the insured interest to underwriters".

ABBREVIATIONS, INTERNATIONAL. Introduced in antiquity together with Phoenician, Greek and Latin writings; in the Middle Ages especially frequent in legal formulas; recorded alphabetically in dictionaries (*Declaratio de breviaturis* mid-14th century; *Modus legendi abbreviaturas in utroque iure* mid-15th century, with 68 editions 1478–1923; *Lexicon diplomaticum* of 1756, and others). In the 20th century the use in daily press and in broadcasting of both political e.g. "BENELUX" and technical e.g. "radar" international abbreviations became a widespread custom. English abbreviations of the names of some specialized UN agencies, e.g. UNESCO, became particularly widespread. See also ▷ Acronyms and abbreviations in the UN System.

A. CHASSANT, *Dictionnaire des abreviations latines et françaises*, Paris, 1846, ed. 5, 1884; A. CAPELLI, *Dizionario di abreviature latine et italiane*, ed. 3. Milano, 1929; C.C. MATTHIEWS, *A Dictionary of Abbreviations*, London, 1947; R.J. SCHWARTZ, *The Complete Dictionary of Abbreviations*, New York, 1955; W.O. BLUMSZTEJN, N.N. JERSHOV, J.W. SIEMIONOV, *Slovar anglyskiy i amierikanskiy sokrashcheniy*, Moskva, 1958; F.D. FAWCETT, *Encyclopedia of Initials and Abbreviations*, London, 1963; *Diccionario internacional de abreviaturas*, Rio de Janeiro, 1964; H. KOBLISCHKE, *Abkürzungsbuch. Abkürzungen-Kurzwörter-Zeichen-Symbole*, Leipzig, 1969; R. de SOLA, *Abbreviations Dictionary*, Amsterdam, 1978.

ABCD. Abbreviation used during World War II for the Allied Forces (American, British, Chinese and Dutch) taking part in the war against Japan.

ABC STATES. A Latin American denomination for three States – Argentina, Brazil, and Chile – which in 1914 offered their good offices in the conflict between Mexico and the United States; in 1915 the ABC States concluded a Treaty of Friendship and Settlement of All Disputes by an Arbitration Tribunal; the Treaty constituted one of the first steps aimed at establishing an international arbitration system, but it soon lost its importance considerably in view of many protracted disputes between Argentina and Chile and between Argentina and Brazil.

I. FABELA, *Documentos Historicos de la Revolución Mexicana: Carranza, Wilson y el ABC*, Mexico, DF, 1962; Ch.G FENWICK, *The OAS*, Washington, DC, 1963.

ABC WEAPONS. International term accepted after World War II in the UN for the three so-called weapons of mass destruction: atomic, bacteriological, and chemical, which are the subjects of separate international conventions concerning ▷ atomic weapons ▷ chemical and ▷ bacteriological weapons. On Dec. 5, 1966 the UN General Assembly recognized by 91 votes to 0, with 4 abstentions, Res. 2162B/XXI which states that "weapons of mass destruction constitute a danger to all of mankind and are incompatible with the accepted norms of civilization".

UN Yearbook 1966, pp. 23–24 and 27.

ABDICATION. The renouncing of power by an emperor, king or prince; in the 20th century the following rulers abdicated under the pressure of revolutionary movements: tsar Nikolas II of Russia, emperor William II of Germany, the rulers of Austria, Baden, Bavaria, Saxony, Württemberg; after World War II king Victor Emanuel III of Italy, Leopold III of Belgium, Michael of Romania, Fuad of Egypt, and Queen Wilhelmina in the Netherlands. In Great Britain a conflict between political and personal interests ended on Dec. 11, 1936 with the abdication of Edward VIII.
The Act of abdication signed by the Emperor William II in Amerongen, Holland on Nov. 28, 1918 read as follows:

"I hereby renounce forever the rights to the Crown of Prussia and the rights to the German Imperial Crown therewith bound up. At the same time I release all officials of the German Empire and of Prussia, as also all officers, non-commissioned officers, and the rank and file of the navy, the Prussian army, and the troops of the Federal contingents, of their oath of loyalty, which they took to me as their Emperor, King, and Commander-in-Chief. I expect of them that until the German Empire is ordered anew they will help those men who hold the actual power in Germany to protect the German people against the threatening dangers of anarchy, famine, and foreign domination. Given by our own hand and under our own seal, William."

The Documentary History of the German Revolution, in: *International Conciliation*, No. 137, April 1919, pp. 541–542.

ABGRENZUNG. (*German* = demarcation, separation). A term adopted by the world press in relation to the GDR policy of full formal separation of the GDR from the FRG and West Berlin in every aspect of international relations. The term first appeared in this sense in the speech of the newly elected First Secretary of the SED (German Socialist Party of Unity). E. Honecker, at the Eighth Congress of the SED in June 1971:

"This whole twaddle in the West about the so-called unity of the German nation and supposedly specific character of the relations between the GDR and the FRG is evidently intended to support those, whose policy still is to undermine the social and economic foundations of our Republic. The fundamental line of our Party is derived from the assumption that the whole process of the development and strengthening of our socialist State leads and must lead to the intensification of contradictions between us and the FRG, which goes the capitalist way, and – in view of this – to a constant deepening of the demarcation (Abgrenzung) process between both States in all realms of social life."

As a result of the Abgrenzung, the GDR telephone and post-rates for the FRG, which had been the same as domestic GDR rates, were as of July 1, 1971 replaced by rates obligatory to all dispatches to West European States. The next step in carrying out the Abgrenzung was the liquidation, on July 7, 1971 of the GDR Secretariat of State for West German Affairs (Staatssekretariat für Westdeutsche Fragen); this office had been established on Dec. 17, 1965 as the counterpart to the FRG Ministry of All-German Affairs (Ministerium für Gesamtdeutsche Fragen). Also the names of creative unions were changed to show their GDR affiliation, and the cars leaving the GDR had to replace their traditional D (Deutschland) sign by that of the DDR (Deutsche Demokratische Republik).

VIII Parteitag der SED, Berlin, 1971; D. BLUMEWITZ, "Rechtliche Probleme bei der Abgrenzung der beiden deutschen Staaten", in: *Jahrbuch für Ostrecht*, Juli 1971.

ABIDJAN. The capital (1975 census 951,211, 1985 estimate – 2 million) of the ▷ Côte d'Ivoire, West Africa on the South Atlantic, and a port on the Ebrié Lagoon of the Gulf of Guinea. An important international sea and airport and an intersection of motor roads to Ghana, Guinea, Upper Volta, Liberia, and Mali.

ABIDJAN DECLARATION, 1976. A Declaration adopted by the Economic and Social Council of the UN at Abidjan on Aug. 5, 1976. In the Declaration the Council:

Called for the speedy elimination of all forms of colonialism, neo-colonialism, foreign aggression and occupation, alien domination, racial discrimination and apartheid from the African continent and from wherever they existed and affirmed that this should continue to receive very high priority among the major preoccupations of the international community;
Determined that there was an imperative need to eliminate injustice and inequality which afflicted vast sections of humanity and to accelerate the development of developing countries;
Urged all countries and international organizations to give added impetus to the efforts of the international community towards achievement of the goals, targets and objectives of the development of developing countries through individual or collective action, taking fully into account the Declaration and the Programme of Action on the Establishment of a New International Economic Order, as well as the Charter of Economic Rights and Duties of States, the International Development Strategy for the Second United Nations Development Decade and General Assembly Res. 3362 (S-VII) on development and international economic co-operation;
Urged all countries and international organizations to pursue with the maximum sense of urgency the implementation of agreements reached within the United Nations system, including those reached at the fourth session of the United Nations Conference on Trade and Development and in other international conferences and fora, the search for further agreements and the widening of the existing ones where appropriate;
Reaffirmed the need to implement special measures or specific action adopted in favour of the most seriously affected, least developed, land-locked and island developing countries;
Expressed its concern over the critical nature of the problems of development in Africa, reflected by the large number of African countries identified as least developed or most seriously affected countries, and urged developed countries, developing countries in a position to do so and the appropriate organs of the United Nations system to increase assistance to these countries;
Affirmed the need to increase substantially the level of food production in developing countries, particularly those in Africa, and to extend adequate assistance to them for that purpose;
Urged all nations to display the necessary political will and place adequate resources at the disposal of the United Nations, in order to enable it to fulfil its role in the economic and social fields;

Finally declared that: the objective of eliminating injustice and inequality and of achieving international co-operation for the promotion of economic progress and better standards of life, as well as social advancement and the encouragement of respect for human rights and for fundamental freedoms for all without distinction, had yet to be achieved in large areas of the world; declared its adherence to the principles of national independence, sovereignty, and self-reliance and its faith in co-operation, dialogue and negotiation between developed and developing countries, based on a real political will to promote an equitable and just system of international economic relations in conformity with the principles of the United Nations Charter.

Yearbook of the UN, 1976, pp. 638–639.

ABM. ANTI-BALLISTIC MISSILE. An anti-missile system which was the subject of the ▷ SALT negotiations. The US–USSR treaty on the limitation of ABM, signed at Moscow on May 26, 1972, entered into force on Oct. 3, 1972. It foresees two regions of deployment of this weapon on each side, with not more than 100 rocket launchers and 100 anti-missiles in each region; it prohibits the transfer and installation of these systems as well as their elements on the territories of other states, and also developing ABM systems at sea and in the air. The supplementary protocol to this treaty, signed July 3, 1974 in Moscow and entered into force on May 24, 1976, obligates the sides to have only one region of deployment instead of two.
Art. 1 of the Treaty stated:

"1. Each Party undertakes to limit anti-ballistic missile (ABM) systems and to adopt other measures in accordance with the provisions of this Treaty.
2. Each Party undertakes not to deploy ABM systems for the defense of the territory of its country and not to provide a base for such a defense, and not to deploy ABM systems for defense of an individual region except as provided for in article III of this Treaty."

Art. 1 of the Protocol stated:

"1. Each Party shall be limited at any one time to a single area out of the two provided in article III of the Treaty for deployment of anti-ballistic missile (ABM) systems or its components and accordingly shall not exercise its right to deploy an ABM system or its components in the second of the two ABM system deployment areas permitted by article III of the Treaty, except as an exchange of one permitted area for the other in accordance with article II of this Protocol.
2. Accordingly, except as permitted by article II of this Protocol: the United States of America shall not deploy an ABM system or its components in the area centred on its capital, as permitted by article III (a) of the Treaty, and the Soviet Union shall not deploy an ABM system or its components in the deployment area of intercontinental ballistic missile (ICBM) silo launchers as permitted by article III(b) of the Treaty."

On Dec. 10, 1987 a joint American-Soviet special statement issued at the end of the Washington Gorbachev-Reagan Summit meeting made reference to the ABM Treaty:

"Taking into account the preparation of the Treaty on Strategic Offensive Arms, the leaders of the two countries also instructed their delegations in Geneva to work out an agreement that would commit the sides to observe the ABM Treaty, as signed in 1972, while conducting their research, development, and testing as required, which are permitted by the ABM Treaty, and not to withdraw from the ABM Treaty, for a specified period of time. Intensive discussions of strategic stability shall begin not later than three years before the end of the specified period, after which, in the event the sides have not agreed otherwise, each side will be free to decide its course of action. Such an agreement must have the same legal status as the Treaty on Strategic Offensive Arms, the ABM Treaty, and other similar, legally binding agreements. This agreement will be recorded in a mutually satisfactory manner. Therefore, they direct their delegations to address these issues on a priority basis.
The sides shall discuss ways to insure predictability in the development of the US-Soviet strategic relationship

under conditions of strategic stability, to reduce the risk of nuclear war".

The two sides did not agree how long the two sides must pledge to observe the ABM Treaty, whether until 1994 (USA) or 1997 (USSR), but both agreed to work out this issue.

J. GOLDBLAT, *Arms Control Agreements, A Handbook*, SIPRI, 1983, pp. 167–175 and 178–180. The New York Times, Dec. 11, 1987; R.L. GARTHOF, *Policy Versus the Law. The Reinterpretation of the ABM Treaty*, Washington DC, 1987; Zb. BRZEZINSKI, *Game Plan. How to Conduct the USA-Soviet Contest*, Boston, 1987; W.J. DURCH, *The ABM Treaty and Western Security*, New York, 1987; D. ROBERTSON, *Guide to Modern Defense and Strategy*, Detroit, 1988.

ABOLITIONISM. An international term for an 18th- and 19th-century social movement aimed at the abolition of ▷ slavery in Great Britain, the USA and other countries upholding Negro slavery.

H.J. NIEBOER, *Slavery as an Industrial System*. The Hague, 1900; R. COUPLAND, *The British Anti-Slavery Movement*, London, 1933; J.B. STEWART, *Holy Warriors. The Abolitionists and American Slavery*, New York, 1976.

ABOMINABLE SNOWMAN. ▷ Yeti.

ABORTION. ▷ Medical ethics.

ABROGATION. Annulment of agreement. ▷ Treaties termination.

ABSTINENCE. International societies and movements propagating forbearance from the use of alcohol and tobacco first emerged in the late 19th century among others the extant World Christian Women Temperance Union f. 1883, London; reg. with the UIA. Consultative Status ECOSOC and UNICEF. Publ.: Ribbon Bulletin.

Yearbook of International Organizations, 1986–87.

ABU DHABI CASE. A dispute between the sheikh of Abu Dhabi and British Petroleum Development Ltd. over the interpretation of the oil agreement concluded on Jan. 11, 1939. Two questions were involved: should the agreement refer only to the seabed of the territorial waters, or should it also cover the continental shelf beyond the territorial waters. The dispute was settled in Sept. 1951 by a British mediator chosen by both sides who replied "yes" to the first question and "no" to the second.

STRUPP-SCHLOCHAUER, *Wörterbuch der Völkerrechts*, Vol. 1, Berlin, 1960, pp. 9–10.

ABUJA. The future capital of Nigeria, in construction in 1988/89.

ABU MENA. A Libyan cultural monument included in the ▷ World Heritage UNESCO List. On the edge of the Libyan desert, from the 4th to the 8th centuries, a holy city grew up and prospered around the tomb of the martyr Abu Mena – St. Menas. Of this ancient place of pilgrimage there remain the ruins of workshops, monastery buildings, the baptistry and churches, evidence of the first contact between Egyptian and European architecture.

UNESCO. *A Legacy for All. The World's Major Natural, Cultural and Historic Sites*, Paris, 1984.

ABUSE OF RIGHT. An international term employed in domestic and international law. The use in bad faith (mala fide) of legal regulations or international conventions to the detriment of the other party; subject of international disputes, sometimes settled by arbitration tribunals.

M. SCERNI, *L'abuse di diritto nei rapporti internazionali*, Roma, 1930; H.C. GUTTRIDGE, "Abuse of rights", in: *Cambridge Law Journal*, 5 (1933); A.C. KISS, *L'abus de droit international*, Paris, 1953; J.D. ROULET, *Le caractère artificiel de la théorie de l'abus de droit en droit international public*, Paris, 1957; A. SCHULE, "Rechtsmissbrauch", in: STRUPP-SCHLOCHAUER, *Wörterbuch des Völkerrechts*, Berlin, 1962, Vol. III, pp. 69–71; G.D.S. TAYLOR, "The Content of the Rule Against Abuse of Rights in International Law", in: *British Year Book of International Law 1972–1973*, Oxford, 1975, pp. 323–352.

ABU SIMBEL. A site in ancient Nubia on the Nile River, presently in Egypt, close to the Sudanese frontier, famous for its temples devoted to the post-humous cult of pharaoh Ramses II and his wife Nefertari (*c.* 1250 BC), and also for its unique art treasures which, having been threatened with inundation due to the Aswan Dam construction, were eventually saved by the UNESCO. On June 22, 1959 the UNESCO Executive Council decided to start a world-wide campaign to rescue the colossal (10 and 20 m. high) statues flanking the entrances of the temples and the walls covered with bas-reliefs depicting religious and battle scenes. Thanks to the financial and technical help of some 50 member States of UNESCO, the Egyptian Government was able to start, on Nov. 16, 1963, the piecemeal raising of the statues and bas-reliefs rescuing i.a. the famous Faras mural paintings and placing them above the inundation level. The evacuation of the art treasures, a venture never seen before, was completed successfully in Aug. 1968. According to the UNESCO statement, "for the first time solidary international co-operation has been expressed in a moment of such importance to culture, owing to the idea that certain religious, historical and artistic monuments belong to the whole human race." Following the example of Abu Sumbel, the Peru Government launched in 1966 an international campaign to save from destruction the ▷ Machu Pichu ruins.

UN Monthly Chronicle No. 4, 1964, K. MICHAŁOW-SKI, *Faras*, Warsaw, 1967.

ABYSSINIAN–ITALIAN WAR, 1935–36. A name adopted for the military aggression of fascist Italy on Ethiopia, which started on Oct. 2, 1935 from the Italian colony of Somali and ended with the occupation of all of Abyssinia in May, 1936. The occupation lasted until Apr. 6, 1941, when Ethiopia was liberated by the British Expeditionary Corps, which forced the Italian occupant to surrender in Addis Ababa.

A.N. MANDELSTAM, *Le conflit Italo-Éthiopien devant la Société des Nations*, Paris, 1937.

ACABQ. Advisory Committee on Administrative and Budgetary Questions, est. 1946 by the Res. 14/I of the General Assembly, examines the budget of the UN and the administrative budgets of the specialized agencies. Reorganized by Res. 32/103 of 1977. Members of ACABQ (16) are appointed on the basis of geographical representations for 3 years with right to reappointment.

Yearbook of the United Nations, 1977.

ACADEMIC DEGREES. A subject of the International Agreement on Academic Degrees, signed at the Bolivar Congress in Caracas, July 17, 1911 by Bolivia, Colombia, Ecuador, Peru and Venezuela. After World War II subject of regional agreements. ▷ Scientific diplomas.

Tratados públicos y acuerdos internacionales de Venezuela, 1900–1920, Caracas, 1925, Vol. 2, pp. 19–31.

ACADEMIC FREEDOM. An international term for open scientific investigation of all data, protected by UNESCO.

ACADEMIES OF SCIENCES AND ARTS. Co-operation of scientific and artistic societies already existed during the Renaissance and Enlightenment, but in its organized form appeared for the first time in the 19th century. The first among such interstate societies was the Vienna Cartel of Scientific Societies (Gelehrtengesellschaften Kartell), founded in 1893, and comprising the Academies of Austria, Bavaria and Saxony. In 1899 the International Association of Academies (Association International des Academies) was created in Paris, but it did not outlive World War I. In 1919 the International Academic Union (Union Academique International), comprising academies of sciences and arts of several dozen countries, was established with headquarters in Brussels. In the interwar years the IAU was registered with the LN Secretariat and co-operated with its scientific and cultural organs; after World War II it became a member of the International Council of Philosophy and Arts, created by UNESCO; Publ. collective studies, such as the *Dictionnaire de la Terminologie du Droit International*, *Encyclopédie de l'Islam*, *Report on the Need for Publishing Dictionaries which do not Today Exist*, as well as special catalogues, such as *Catalogues Translationum et Commentariorum* or *Catalogues des Manuscrits Alchimiques Latins*.

Organizations reg. with the UIA:

European Organization of Academy of Sciences, f. 1960, Stockholm.
International Union of Academies, f. 1919, Brussels.
World Organization of National Colleges, Academies and Academic Associations of General Practitioners, Family Physicians, f. 1970, Chicago.

W. HISS, *Vorgeschichte des deutschen Kartells und der Internationaler Assoziation der Akademien*, Wien, 1902; *Yearbook of International Organizations*.

ACADEMY OF ASTRONAUTICS, INTERNATIONAL. F. 1960, Stockholm, by the Eleventh Congress of the International Astronautic Federation. Members: individuals elected for life. Publ. *Acta Astronautica*. Reg. with the UIA.

Yearbook of International Organizations.

ACADEMY OF AVIATION AND SPACE MEDICINE, INTERNATIONAL. F. 1959. Secretariat: Paris. Members: individuals in 36 countries. Reg. with the UIA.

Yearbook of International Organizations.

ACADEMY OF COMPARATIVE AND INTERNATIONAL LAW, INTER-AMERICAN. Academia Internacional Americana de Derecho Comparado e Internacional, est. 1938 in Havana by the ▷ Inter-American Bar Association, Washington, DC.

AIA Debates de Mesa Redonda 1948, 2 Vols. Havana, 1951.

ACADEMY OF INTERNATIONAL BUSINESS. F. 1959, Chicago USA, as Association for Education in National Business; present name adopted 1973. Members: academics, researchers, businessmen, postgraduate students in 36 countries. Publ. *Journal of International Business Studies* (twice a year). Reg. with the UIA.

Yearbook of International Organizations.

ACADEMY OF INTERNATIONAL LAW. Est. 1923 in The Hague by the Carnegie Foundation; a scientific institute dealing with the development of international law and related sciences. Each summer it organizes a series of lectures in English and French, conducted by scholars from all over the world, and publishes them in *Recueil des Cours de l'Académie de Droit International*; the first series, for 1923–39, comprises 76 volumes, the second was begun in 1946. The Academy's headquarters is the Palace of Peace in The Hague, which is also headquarters for the Association of Attenders and Alumni of The Hague Academy of International Law (AAA), est. 1923 and grouping over 500 members of the Association of International Law. The Academy organizes the Annual Congress of International Law. Fr.–Eng. Publ.: *Annuaire de l'AAA – Yearbook of the AAA*.

Documents relatifs à la création de l'Académie de Droit International de la Haye. La Haye, 1927.

ACADEMY OF INTERNATIONAL MILITARY HISTORY. F. 1965, Washington, DC., reg. with the UIA.

Yearbook of International Organizations.

ACADEMY OF POLITICAL SCIENCE AND CONSTITUTIONAL HISTORY. Académie internationale de science politique et d'histoire constitutionnelle, f. 1936 at the Sorbonne as the Institut International d'Histoire Politique et Constitutionnelle, present name adopted 1949. Membership limited to 100. Publ. *Revue internationale d'histoire politique et constitutionnelle* (since 1950), *Politique. Revue internationale des doctrines et des institutions* (since 1958). Reg. with the UIA.

Yearbook of International Organizations.

ACADEMY OF THE LATIN WORLD. Académie du Monde Latin, f. 1966 in Paris with the task of "developing spiritual exchange between the nations originating in Rome"; the Academy consists of 100 scholars from communities using Romance languages: French, Italian, Portuguese, Romanian and Spanish.

ACADEMY OF TOURISM, INTERNATIONAL. Académie international du tourisme, f. 1951, Monte Carlo. Membership limited to 60. Publ. *Dictionnaire touristique international*, *Revue* (quarterly). Reg. with the UIA.

Yearbook of International Organizations.

ACAST. Advisory Committee on the Application of Science and Technology for Development, est. in 1964 by the ECOSOC, whose members serve in their capacity as scientists and not as representatives of Governments. It is one of two standing UN bodies concerned exclusively with science and technology. The other is the ECOSOC Committee on Science and Technology for Development, CSTD which, unlike ACAST, consists of Government representatives. Both act as preparatory bodies for the UN Conference on Science and Technology for Development.

UN Chronicle, August–September 1978.

ACC. Administrative Committee on Coordination, est. 1946 by ECOSOC. Members: Secretary General of the UN and the executive heads of the specialized agencies and OAEA. Reorganized by the General Assembly Res. 32/197 of 1977.

Yearbook of the UN, 1977.

ACCESSION. International term – accession of new members to intergovernmental organizations, subject of international statutes or agreements. A Treaty of Accession to the European Communities was signed at Brussels on Jan. 22, 1972 by the six original member countries of the EEC (Belgium, France, FRG, Italy, Luxembourg and the Netherlands) and Denmark, the Irish Republic, Norway and the UK. Entered into force on Jan. 1, 1973. ▷ Admission to UN.

J. PAXTON, *A Dictionary of the EEC*, London, 1977, pp. 1–2.

ACCHAN. Allied Command Channel (previously CHANCOM), headquarters in Northwood near London, responsible to the Military Committee (chiefs of staff) of NATO along with Allied Command Europe (ACE) and Allied Command Atlantic (ACLANT).

ACCIDENTAL WAR. A military action provoked by events independent of the will of either side; one of the gravest issues deliberated in the UN and in talks between the atomic powers was how to safeguard against a war caused by the accidental explosion of nuclear or thermonuclear weapons.
In 1971 the USA and the USSR signed the so-called ▷ Nuclear Accidents Agreement. The parties undertake to notify each other immediately in the event of an accidental, unauthorized or any other unexplained incident involving a possible detonation of a nuclear weapon which could create a risk of the outbreak of nuclear war. France in 1976 and the United Kingdom in 1977 also signed the Nuclear Accidents Agreements with the USSR. The SALT Treaty 1979 extended the obligation of advance notification of missile launches.

J. GOLDBLAT, *Arms Control Agreements, A Handbook*, SIPRI, Stockholm, 1982, pp. 74–75; S. LODGAARD, K. BIRNBAUM, *Overcoming Threats to Europe*, SIPRI, Oxford, 1987; D. ROBERTSON, *Guide to Modern Defense and Strategy*, Detroit, 1988.

ACCIS. Advisory Committee for the Co-ordination of Information Systems, est. by the UN General Assembly Res. 37/226 of 1982, to facilitate access by Member States to UN information and to promote the improvement of the information infrastructure within the UN System. Hq. Palais des Nations, 1211 Geneva 10, Switzerland.

Yearbook of the UN, 1982.

ACCLAMATION. The acceptance or rejection of a motion or resolution by general applause or absence of protest instead of conducting a vote. Used in the UN, alongside "without vote" or by ▷ Consensus.

ACCOMMODATION BILL. A credit document obligating the drawer or his representative to unconditionally pay a specific person a stated sum of money in a designated time and place; two kinds are distinguished: (1) A personal a.b. or promissory note, which is an unconditional pledge to pay a specific sum of money in a fixed time and place to the payee, or to a person mentioned by first and last name, with the signature of the drawer and usually with the signature of two endorsers;
(2) A drawn a.b., which indicates the person (drawee) who is to pay a certain sum. The drawee of a drawn a.b. becomes the acceptor; subject of international private law, bill of exchange law concerning bills in international trade. Rules of a.b. law were formulated for the first time in the 9th century in Italy; in the 18th and 19th centuries similar a.b. laws existed in all states, but were only codified under the patronage of the UN. A Convention on adjusting certain collisions of laws relating to drawn a.b. and promissory notes, was signed in Geneva June 7, 1930; entered into force Sept. 1, 1932. Participants in the convention are Austria, Belgium, Denmark, Finland, France, Germany, Greece,

Hungary, India, Italy, Japan, Luxembourg, Monaco, the Netherlands Antilles, Norway, Poland, Portugal, Sweden, Switzerland, and the USSR. The Anglo-Saxon states did not join. The main principle of the convention: the law of the country in which payment of a drawn a.b. or promissory note is to be made resolves disputed issues.

LNTS, 1932; *Enzyklopädisches Lexikon für das Geld–, Bank und Börsenwesen*, Frankfurt am M. 1958.

ACCORDION. A subject of international co-operation. Organizations reg. with the UIA:

European Community of the Accordion, f. 1961, Brussels.
International Confederation of Accordionists, f. 1948, Surrey, UK, Championship.
World Accordion Organization, f. 1971, Retinne, Belgium.

Yearbook of International Organizations.

ACCOUNTANCY. A subject of international co-operation. Organizations reg. with the UIA:

Accounts Study Group of the EEC, f. 1960, London.
African Accounting Council, f. 1979, Kinshasa.
ASEAN Federation of Accounts, f. 1977, Bangkok.
Association of International Accountants, f. 1928, Billericay, Essex, UK. Publ. Accountant.
European Union of Public Accountants, f. 1951, Munich, FRG.
Consultative Status: Council of Europe. Publ. Lexique (8 languages).
Intergovernmental Working Group of Experts on International Standards of Accounting and Reporting, est. 1982, New York, N.Y. USA.
International Accounting Standards Committee, f. 1973, London.
International Affiliation of Independent Accounting Firms, f. 1978, Miami, Fl., USA.
International Coordination Committee for the Accountancy Profession, f. 1974, Dusseldorf, FRG.
Maghreb Commission of National Accounting and Statistics, f. 1964, Algiers.
International Council of Practitioners of the International Plan of Accounts, f. 1959, Brussels. Publ. *Revue International des Sciences Économique coordonnées.*

Yearbook of International Organizations.

ACCOUNTING INTERNATIONAL STANDARD. Subject of intergovernmental co-operation. An Intergovernmental Working Group of Experts on International Standards of Accounting and Reporting was est. by the ECOSOC Res. 1979/44 and 1982/67. The group is composed on the basis of geographical representation (Africa – 9, Asia – 7, Europe E. – 3, Latin America – 6, Europe W. and the other states – 9), the term lasts for 3 years with right to reappointment. Hq. New York.

Yearbook of the UN, 1979 and 1982.

ACCRA. The capital of Ghana: 1984 pop. census 964,879. A port on the Gulf of Guinea. Seat of organizations registered with the UIA: African Civil Aviation Commission, Association of African Universities, Office of International Transport Workers' Federation, UN Information Center.

ACCRA ASSEMBLY, THE. F. 1962, in Accra, Ghana, promoting the disarmament and denuclearization of Africa, Asia, Central Europe and Latin America. Publ. *Conclusions in the Accra Assembly*. Reg. with the UIA.

Yearbook of International Organizations.

ACCREDITATION. The act of authorizing a foreign envoy by a document of accreditation (a diplomatic representative of the I and II class) – by a Letter of Credence *lettre de créance*, (delegates to international organizations) – by letters of

accreditation stating the purpose of their mission (that of a diplomatic envoy, plenipotentiary, expert, or correspondent). According to international conventions, the Letter of Credence for an envoy is signed by the Head of the sending State and handed personally by the envoy to the Head of the receiving State (Chairman of the State Council, President or Monarch). The Letters of Credence are handed to the Heads of States only by the diplomats of the I (Ambassadors) and II (Ministers Plenipotentiary and Envoys Extraordinary) class; diplomats of the III class (*Chargés d'Affaires*) are accredited to Ministers of Foreign Affairs by Letters of Introduction (*lettres d'introduction*), signed by their Ministers of Foreign Affairs. For the accreditation of ▷ Consuls see ▷ Vienna Convention on Diplomatic Relations, 1961.

UNTS, Vol. 500.

ACCREDITATION TO THE UN. The presentation of Letters of Credence (lettres de créance) is required of diplomatic envoys representing their countries at the UN; they deposit their credentials with the UN Secretariat. Correspondents reporting UN affairs and technical personnel of permanent missions to the UN also have to be accredited.

Everyone's United Nations, New York, 1979, pp. 321–324, 344.

ACE. Allied Command Europe (previously SHAPE, Supreme Headquarters Allied Powers in Europe), headquarters in Casteau near Mons (Belgium), responsible for the defense of European territory with the exception of France, Iceland, UK and Portugal. Responsible to the Military Committee (chiefs of staff) of NATO. Operates along with Allied Command Atlantic (ACLANT) and Allied Channel Command (ACCHAN). Three regional areas of Western Europe are under the leadership of ACE–central, northern, and southern as well as the leadership of the so-called mobile forces (first readiness), which controls an organizationally separate military group, ACE Mobile Force.

ACETYLENE. A subject of international co-operation: Permanent International Committee on Acetylene, Oxy-Acetylene Welding and Allied Industries, f. 1923, Paris. Publ. *Bulletin*. Reg. with the UIA.

Yearbook of International Organizations.

ACID RAIN. An international term for ▷ air pollution from combustion fuel gases; subject of international pollution regulations. The emission of SO_2 and NO_X into the atmosphere from coal and oil-fired boilers in power plants and industrial installations is recognized as one of the main sources of environmental pollution. According to the IAEA Bulletin in the USA alone more than 50 million tons of SO_2 and NO_X gases will be released into the atmosphere each year up to 1990 by electric utilities and industrial boilers. The use of radiation processing for fuel gas clean-up technologies is recommended by the IAEA.

V. MARKOVIC, Electron Beam Processing of Combustion Fuel Gases, in: *IAEA Bulletin*, 1987, No 2; P. SHABECOFF, Acid Rain Sea Threat in: *New York Times*, April 27, 1988.

ACLANT. Allied Command Atlantic (previously SACLANT), headquarters in Norfolk, Va., USA, responsible to the Military Committee (chiefs of staff) NATO along with Allied Command Atlantic (ACE) and Allied Command Channel (ACCHAN).

ACOUSTICS. A subject of international co-operation. Organizations reg. with the UIA:

Acoustical Society of Scandinavia, f. 1954, Lyngby, Denmark.
International Commission on Acoustics, f. 1960, Rome.
World Acoustic Society, f. 1964, Tokyo.

Yearbook of International Organizations, 1986/87.

ACP STATES OF EEC. The African, Caribbean and Pacific countries participants in the ▷ Lomé Conventions 1975 and 1980 on co-operation with the European Economic Community.

J. PAXTON, *A Dictionary of the EEC*, London, 1978.

ACQUIRED IMMUNE DEFICIENCY SYNDROME. ▷ AIDS.

ACQUISITION OF TERRITORY. A legal or illegal gain of territory.

R.Y. JENNINGS, *Acquisition of Territory in International Law*, London, 1968.

ACRE. Anglo-Saxon measure of land = 4046.86 sq. meters.

ACRE. Brazilian federal state, on the borders of Peru and Bolivia. Area: 152,590 sq. km. Capital Rio Branco; state population 1970 est. 216,200. Acre was part of Bolivia since the Bolivian–Brazilian Treaty of Mar. 27, 1867; ceded to Brazil by Bolivia for 2 million pounds sterling on the strength of the Petropolis Treaty on Nov. 17, 1903. The delimitation of the 1565 km frontier with Peru was approved by the Brazilian–Peruvian Treaty of Rio de Janeiro on Sept. 8, 1909.

BARAO DE RIO BRANCO, *Questoes de Limites*, Rio de Janeiro, 1947, pp. 26–28 and 107–109; D. DE CARVALHO, "Questoes Acrenas", in: *Historia Diplomatica do Brasil*, São Paulo, 1959, pp. 217-233.

ACRONYM. An abbreviation created from the first letter of each major part of a compound name, e.g. ▷ FAO ▷, UNESCO, ▷ WHO.

ACRONYMS AND ABBREVIATIONS IN THE UN SYSTEM. A list of the principal officially recognized acronyms and abbreviations that may be used in United Nations documents, prepared by the Secretariat in: Arabic, Chinese, English, French, Russian and Spanish in Terminology Bulletin No 311 (ST/CS/SER.F/311/Rev. 1) and corrigenda on "Acronyms and abbreviations covering the United Nations system and other international organizations".

United Nations, Editorial Manual, New York, 1983, pp. 424–432.

ACROPOLIS. An historical Greek settlement or part of a city situated on its highest hill, the place of worship; the most famous in Athens, with ruins of temples devoted to Athene and Poseidon. In 1977 UNESCO published an appeal to UN Member States for financial, technical and material assistance to save the Athenian Acropolis, one of the outstanding cultural monuments of humanity, from further destruction. Included in the ▷ World Heritage UNESCO List.

UNESCO. A Legacy for All. *The World's Major Natural, Cultural and Historic Sites*, Paris, 1984.

ACSA. ▷ NATO.

ACTUARIES. A subject of international co-operation. Organizations reg. with the UIA:

Consultative Group of Actuaries of Countries of the EEC, f. 1978, London.
International Actuarial Association f. 1889, Brussels. Publ. *Bulletin*.

International Association Consulting Actuaries, f. 1968, New York.

Yearbook of International Organizations, 1986/87.

ACUPUNCTURE. A subject of international co-operation. Organizations reg. with the UIA:

Acupuncture International Association, f. 1949, St. Louis, USA.
International Council of Medical Acupuncture and Related Techniques, 1983, Brussels.
International Medical Alliance, f. 1961, Paris, Publ.: International Medical News.
International Society of Acupuncture, f. 1943, Paris. Publ. *Nouvelle revue internationale d'acupuncture*.
World Scientific Union of Acupuncture Physicians and Societies of Acupuncture, f. 1974, Marseilles, France.

R.H. BANNERMAN, "Acupuncture: the WHO View", in: *WHO World Health*, December 1979; *Yearbook of International Organizations*, 1986/87.

ADDIS ABABA. Capital of Ethiopia: 1984 pop. census 1.412.575. Seat of the Organization of African Unity (OAU) and the UN Economic Commission for Africa (ECA).

ADDIS ABABA DECLARATION, 1960. A name of the Final Act of the Second Conference of Independent African States at Addis Ababa, June 15–24, 1960. The Declaration initiated the establishment of the ▷ OAU.

D.S. ROTCHILD, *Toward Unity in Africa*, Washington, DC, 1960, p. 224; J. CONTRERAS GRANGUILLHOME, *El Panafricanismo*, Mexico, 1971, p. 384.

ADDIS ABABA DECLARATION, 1973. A Declaration on the General Policy of the Organization of African Unity, adopted by the Chiefs of State and governments of the independent African states on May 29, 1973 at Addis Ababa on the tenth anniversary of the OAU.

Y.E. AYOUTY, *The OAU after Ten Years*, New York, 1975.

ADDIS ABABA DECLARATION, 1985. A Declaration of the OAU summit meeting on July 21, 1985 in Addis Ababa on the economic situation related to the debt crisis and to the failure of the ▷ Lagos Plan of Action, 1980. A new five-year program, 1986–1990, provides: special action for the improvement of the food situation and agricultural development in Africa; measures for alleviating Africa's external debts burden; measures against the destabilization policy of South Africa on the economics of southern African States.

KEESING's *Contemporary Archive*, October, 1985.

ADDIS ABABA PLAN FOR AFRICAN EDUCATION, 1961. A plan for the years 1961–80 adopted by the UNESCO Conference on the Development of Education in Africa, held at Addis Ababa in May, 1961.

UN Yearbook 1961, pp. 610–611.

ADDIS ABABA TREATY, 1896. A peace treaty between Ethiopia and Italy, signed in Addis Ababa Oct. 26, 1896, ending the state of war between Italy and Ethiopia.

"Italy recognizes without reserve the absolute independence of the Ethiopian Empire as a sovereign and independent State." (Art. III).

Major Peace Treaties of Modern History, New York, 1967.

ADELA. Atlantic Development Group for Latin America. An investment corporation set up on Sept. 28, 1966 in Luxembourg by over 50 industrial and financial institutions of Western Europe,

Japan, Canada, and the USA, with an initial capital of US $40 million; its task consists in supplying research for private investment possibilities in Latin America and in extending technical and loan facilities to private investors (up to 50%). Headquarters: Luxembourg. Publ. *ADELA Information Bulletin*.

Yearbook of International Organizations, 1986–87.

ADEN. The biggest city and main port on the Gulf of Aden, from 1970 capital of South Yemen (1985 pop. census 265,326); a free port since 1950; since 1967 a common denomination for the territories dependent on Great Britain, called in the period 1859–1967 the Federation of South Arabia or South Arabia, and comprising (1) the city and port area under the name of the Aden Colony, and (2) Arabian sheikhdoms, emirates and sultanates situated between Yemen and the city of Aden, which in the 19th and 20th centuries concluded protectorate treaties with Great Britain; the eastern part of this area was called the Eastern Aden Protectorate, and the western the West Aden Protectorate. The whole area is claimed by North Yemen, officially since 1953 by a notification to the UN. Both the Aden Colony and the Aden Protectorates ceased to exist on Nov. 30, 1967 after the British army had been withdrawn and ▷ Yemen South proclaimed.

R.R. ROBINS, Legal Status of Aden Colony and Aden Protectorate, in: *American Journal of International Law*, 33 (1939); S. KING, *Imperial Outpost – Aden*, New York, 1964; J. PAGET, *Last Post: Aden 1964–1967*, London, 1969; *The Middle East and North Africa 1972–73*, London, 1972, pp. 789–792.

ADENAUER DOCTRINE. A doctrine formulated by the Chancellor of the FRG, K. Adenauer, Dec. 3, 1949 and reported in the American newspaper the *Cleveland Plain Dealer*. Adenauer requested the

"formation of European armed forces to which German soldiers should belong. ... The West must be strong enough to make it impossible for the USSR to move forward any further."

Adenauer developed this declaration at the meeting of the Main Board of the CDU in Königswinter, Dec. 9, 1949:

"The Germans should be represented in a European army on the same rights as are granted to other European nations. What is the greater danger: the Russian threat to the Western world or the existence of a contingent of German forces in connection with the armed forces of the other nations. The present tense relations between the powers should not be minimized, therefore the western powers should treat West Germany not as a desert, but as a densely populated country."

KEESING's *Contemporary Archive*, 1949.

ADEN, GULF OF. A western arm of the Arabian Sea, connected with the Red Sea, 885 km long. Territorial waters of Southern Yemen and the Somali Republic. A Convention for the Conservation of the Red Sea and Gulf of Aden Environment was signed in Febr. 1982 in Jeddah, Saudi Arabia. See also ▷ Red Sea.

ADHESION. An entrance to an open treaty by a State which did not sign it but is willing to comply with its general provisions (also called "accession") or with such a part of its provisions as defined in the declaration of adhesion (sometimes considered "adhesion" proper).

ADHESIVE MANUFACTURE. A subject of international co-operation: Association of European Adhesive Manufacturers, f. 1972, Dusseldorf, FRG. Reg. with the UIA.

Yearbook of International Organizations.

A

AD HOC UN COMMITTEES. Temporary subsidiary UN organs appointed ad hoc by the UN General Assembly, ECOSOC, and other organs, as provided by the UN Charter, with a view to considering specific questions; e.g. 1950 Ad Hoc Committee for World War II POWs; 1951 ECOSOC Ad Hoc Commission for international trade which submitted a report in 1955. Until 1956 the UN General Assembly considered many special issues through its Ad Hoc Political Committee in accordance with Rule 38 of its Rules of Procedure. After a change of the Rules in 1956, a permanent Special Political Committee was appointed.

Everyman's United Nations.

ADIGE. A river in northern Italy, *c.* 360 km long; flowing from ▷ UpperAdige, which till 1919 belonged to Austria.

AD INTERIM, *Latin* = provisional. A latin formula informing that a diplomat is carrying out his duties only on a provisional basis, e.g. chargé d'affaires ad interim.

ADIZ. ▷ Air Defense Identification Zone.

ADJACENT HIGH SEA WATERS. International term for waters of the high seas adjacent to the territorial sea, of indefinite breadth and thus differing from contiguous zones. Subject of international disputes and agreements relating to fisheries and the principles of conservation of living marine resources. Several Latin-American countries (Argentina and Panama, 1946; Chile and Peru, 1947; Costa Rica, 1948, Brazil and Honduras, 1950) issued unilateral declarations extending the rights of these countries to fishery zones up to 200 miles from the coast, thus creating zones of adjacent high sea waters which they reserved for themselves only. In 1952 Chile, Ecuador and Peru concluded an agreement on fisheries and conservation of living marine resources and extended their sovereign rights to 200-mile-wide belts at their shores. The Third Geneva Convention, 1958, on fishing and conservation of living resources of the high seas granted coastal states special privileges in respect to conservation of marine resources without precisely defining the breadth of adjacent waters on any area of the high sea which is adjacent to their territorial sea. The Geneva Convention does not use the term "contiguous zone" as did the first Geneva Convention, 1958, but "area of the high seas adjacent to territorial sea".
The ▷ Sea Law Convention in art. 135 defines the legal status of superjacent waters and air space.

T.K. OUDENDIJK, *Status and Extent of Adjacent Waters. A Historical Orientation*, Leiden, 1970; *The Law of Sea*, New York, 1983.

ADJUSTABLE PEG SYSTEM. An international stock exchange term, existing within the IMF currency exchange system until Aug. 15, 1971, when the dollar's convertibility into gold collapsed. The a.p.s. was designed to control the fluctuations at the exchange rate of IMF member countries' currencies, so that the fluctuations (the so-called intervention points) would not exceed 1% of the basic rate (e.g. 0.75% for EEC members). In 1970 the IMF considered increasing these fluctuations to 3% or even 5% (the so-called "wider band") and introducing the so-called "crawling peg" system of maintaining the value of currencies, which was to keep daily fluctuations within the limits of the "adjustable" or "wider band" systems – with the average exchange rate serving as a standard for transactions.

S. BRITTON, *The Price of Economic Freedom. A Guide to Flexible Exchange Rate*, London, 1970; A.D. CROCKETT, *International Money*, London, 1977.

AD LIMINA APOSTOLORUM. *Latin* = to the apostolic gates. A term used in the Catholic Church, at first describing pilgrimages to St Peter's and St Paul's graves in Rome; since 1585 official Vatican term for obligatory periodic reports of bishops to the Pope.

ADM. ▷ Atomic Demolition Munition.

ADMINISTRATION. A subject of international co-operation. Organizations reg. with the UIA:
African Research Center in Administration for Development, Tangiers, Morocco.
African Training and Research Centre in Administration for Development, f. 1934, Tangiers.
Arab Organization for Administrative Science, f. 1969, Cairo.
Asian Center for Development Administration, f. 1972, Kuala Lumpur.
Central American Institute of Public Administration, f. 1954, San Jose de Costa Rica. Publ. *Boletin de Documentos.*
Commonwealth Council for Educational Administration, f. 1970, Armidale, Australia.
Eastern Regional Organization for Public Administration, f. 1958, Manila. Consultative status: ECOSOC. Publ. *EROPA Review.*
International Association of Schools and Institutes of Administration, f. 1962, Publ. International Review of Administrative Sciences.
International Council for ▷ ADP in Government Administration, f. 1968, Seoul.
International Institute for Juridical and Administrative Terminology, f. 1960, Munich, FRG.
International Institute of Administrative Sciences, f. 1930, Brussels. Consultative status: ECOSOC, UNESCO. Publ. *International Review of Administrative Sciences.*
International Union of Local Authorities, f. 1913, The Hague.
Consultative Status: ECOSOC, WHO, UNESCO, UNICEF. Publ.: Bibliographia IULA.
Latin American Association of Public Administration, f. 1960, Mexico DF.
Latin American Centre for Development Administration, f. 1972, Caracas.
Maghreb Centre for Administrative Studies and Research, f. 1970, Algiers, Publ.: Integration.
World Institute on Communal Structures and Information on Local Administration, f. 1962, Roanne, France.

▷ UN Public Administration Programme.

Yearbook of International Organizations, 1986–87.

ADMINISTRATIVE COMMITTEE ON CO-ORDINATION. ▷ ACC.

ADMINISTRATIVE INTERNATIONAL LAW. A heterogeneous law controlling administrative problems: (a) international organizations; (b) internationalized territories; (c) multinational corporations.

Z.M. NEDJATI, T.E. TRICE, *English and Continental Systems of Administrative Law*, Amsterdam 1978.

ADMINISTRATIVE TRIBUNAL. ▷ UN Administrative Tribunal.

"ADMIRAL GRAF SPEE". A German battleship which, having been badly damaged on Dec. 13, 1939 in a battle with British cruisers at the Rio de la Plata estuary, took refuge in the neutral port of Montevideo where it was granted a 72-hour permission to stay; on Dec. 17, 1939 the battleship left the Uruguayan territorial waters and was sunk; its officers and crew, with the assistance of the German merchantship, *The Tacoma*, were transferred to Argentine vessels and carried to Buenos Aires to be interned according to art. 10 of the Hague Convention of July 29, 1899. For its part, the Uruguayan Government applied sanctions to *The Tacoma*. The Latin American States lodged both in Berlin and in London a joint protest in regard to the battle in the La Plata estuary, invoking the Panama Declaration of Oct. 3, 1939 on the establishment of the Security Zone in the Western Hemisphere, extending 300 miles from shore; the German and the British Governments replied that they did not recognize the unilateral Panama Declaration.

Libro Azul de la República Oriental del Uruguay, Antecedentes relativos al hundimiento del acorazado Admiral Graf Spee y a la internación del barco mercante Tacoma – Uruguayan Blue Book. The Documents Relating to the Sinking of the Admiral Graf Spee and the internment of the merchant vessel Tacoma, Montevideo, 1940.

ADMIRALTY ISLANDS. Group of 40 volcanic islands, 2070 sq. km, with *c.* 28,000 inhabitants (1974). Annexed by Germany 1884, occupied by Australia 1914, Australian League of Nations mandate 1920–42, occupied by Japan 1942–44; UN trusteeship under Australian administration 1944–75. Since 1975 part of Papua New Guinea.

P. RYAN (ed). *Encyclopaedia of Papua and New Guinea*, Melbourne, 1971.

ADMISSION OF NEW MEMBERS UN COMMITTEE. Est. of all the members of the Security Council, like the ▷ UN Experts on Rule and Procedure.

ADMISSION TO UN, Defined in Chapter 11, art. 4, of the UN Charter:

(1) "Membership in the United Nations is open to all peace-loving states which accept the obligations contained in the present Charter and, in the judgement of the organization, are able and willing to carry out these obligations."
(2) "The admission of any state to membership in the United Nations will be effected by a decision of the General Assembly upon the recommendation of the Security Council."

This requires ▷ unanimity of the Great Powers, and in the period of Cold War acted as an obstacle to the admission of new members (only 9 were admitted in 1945–54 compared to 16 in 1955 alone).

P.O. HUMBER, Admission to the UN, in *The British Yearbook of International Law 1947*, CIJ, 1948, p. 436; L. GARCIA ARIAS, El primer Dictamen del Tribunal Internacional de Justicia. Las condiciones de admision de un Estado como nuevo miembro de las NU, in: *Revista española de derecho internacional* No. 2, 1949; M.O. HUDSON, Conditions of Admission of a State to Membership in the UN, in *American Journal of International Law*, No. 43, 1949; J. ARCE, *Naciones Unidas: Admisión de nuevos Miembros*, México, DF, 1951; A.W. RUDZINSKI, Admission of New Members. The UN and LN, in: *International Conciliation*, No. 480, April. 1952, pp. 147–189. J.A. FROVEIN, Die VN und die Nichtmitglied Staaten, in: *Europa Archiv*, 1970.

ADOPTION. The acceptance of parental rights and duties in relation to an alien child or alien adult; the subject of multilateral international conventions since the first convention on adoptions had been drafted by the Hague Conference on Private International Law of 1965, earlier only bilateral agreements regulated cases when parties to adoption differed in nationality.

UN Department of Social Affairs, *Study on Adoption of Children*, New York, 1953; US Department of Health, Education and Welfare, Childrens Bureau, *Legislative Guides for the Termination of Parental Rights and Responsibilities and the Adoption of Children*, Washington, DC, 1964. Adoption from abroad. Western couples are turning to Asia and Latin America to fill cradles at home, in: *Newsweek*, June 6, 1988.

ADP SYSTEM. Automatic data processing system. A computer system of central government administrations; subject of an international convention signed on Aug. 2, 1968 by Australia, Belgium, Brazil, Canada, Chile, Denmark, Finland, France, the FRG, Israel, Japan, Korea (South), the Netherlands, Norway, Sweden, the UK, the US and Venezuela.

The organ of the convention is an intergovernmental organization registered by UIA: Intergovernmental Council for ADP.

Data for Development International Association, f. 1975, Marseilles, France Consultative Status: ECOSOC, UNESCO, UNDEP, UNEP. Publ. *Newsletter.*
Eurodata Foundation, f. 1976, London, Publ. *E.F. Yearbook.*
European Association of Information Services, f. 1970, London. Publ. *Newsidic.*
European Computing Services Association, f. 1975, Brussels.
Global Data Processing System, GDPS, f. 1970, by WMO, Geneva.
International Computing Centre, f. 1971, Geneva by the UN.
International Council for ADP in Government Administration, f. 1968, Seoul.
NATO Allied Data System Interoperability Agency, f. 1979, Brussels.

Yearbook of International Organizations, 1986–87.

ADR. An internationally accepted abbreviation of the European Agreement on the International Carriage of Dangerous Goods, 1968.

AD REFERENDUM. An international term used in the UN to indicate that (1) the international act signed by a diplomatic agent, whose full powers did not extend to all its provisions, would not be valid until after the approval of his government had been granted (art. 10 of the ▷ Vienna Convention on the Law of International Treaties, 1969); or that (2) the negotiated question has been, with the consent of the parties involved, postponed for further consideration.

ADRIA. The name of an oil pipe-line running from Hungary through Czechoslovakia to the Omisalj port (Krk Island, Yugoslavia) on the Adriatic Sea; built in 1975–78 pursuant to the inter-governmental agreement of the above-mentioned States. Capacity: 20 to 34 million tonnes.

ADRIANOPLE TREATY, 1829. A peace treaty between the Ottoman Empire and Russia, signed in Adrianople, Sept. 2 or 14, 1829.

Major Peace Treaties of Modern History, New York, 1967, Vol. II, pp. 931–942.

ADRIATIC SEA (*Latin*: Mare Adriaticum; *Serbian*: Jadransko More). An arm of the Mediterranean situated between the Balkan peninsula and the Apennine peninsula (separating Yugoslavia and Albania from Italy) extending *c.* 805 km. Area 132,000 sq. km. From 93.3 km to 225.3 km wide, with a maximum depth of 1250 m; average depth 240 m. Named after the Roman port Hadria which ceased to exist due to slime (today the city of Adria, situated between the lower Po and the Adige, is 25 km away from the Adriatic Sea). Fishing in the Adriatic for sardines, lobsters, tuna fish and mackerel is regulated by international agreements.

The International Geographic Encyclopedia and Atlas, London, 1979.

ADSIA. ▷ NATO.

AD VALOREM, *Latin* = according to value. An international term commonly accepted in tax and customs systems, fixing the amount of charges in relation to the real value of the object. In protective tariffs a charge many times higher than the real value of the object is often imposed.

ADVENTISTS, *Latin*: adventus = the arrival. A protestant religious group founded in 1831 in the USA by W. Miller, divided into the Seventh-Day Adventists observing Saturday, and the Millennium Adventists observing Sunday, both believing in the Second Advent of Christ; since 1863, organized into the General Conference of the Seventh-Day Adventists, with headquarters in Washington and churches in the majority of the states of the world; since 1945, reg. with the UIA. Publ. a weekly *Review and Herald.*

Yearbook of International Organizations.

ADVERTISING. A subject of international co-operation since the First World Congress of Advertising in Berlin, August 1929.
Organizations reg. with the UIA:

EEC Group of Advertisers Associations, f. 1960, Brussels.
European Association of Advertising Agencies, f. 1960, Brussels, Belgium.
European Community of Advertising Organizations, f. 1950, Paris.
European Group of TV Advertising, f. 1970, London.
International Advertising Association, f. 1954, New York. Consultative Status: ECOSOC, UNESCO. Publ. *IAA Airletter.*
International Association of Schools in Advertising, f. 1956, Paris.
International Federation of Advertising Clubs, f. 1949, Paris.
International Federation of Advertising Clubs, f. 1950, Lille, France, Publ. *Lettre d'information.*
International Federation of Advertising Managers Associations, f. 1960, Paris.
International Publishers Advertising Representatives Association, f. 1964, London. Publ. *Bulletin.*
International Union of Advertisers Associations, f. 1961, Brussels.
Screen Advertising World Associations Ltd. (SAWA), f. 1963, London.
World Federation of Advertisers, f. 1953, Brussels. Consultative Status: Council of Europe. Publ. *Inter-Contract.*

The International Convention to Facilitate the Importation of Commercial Samples and Advertising Material, was signed in Geneva, Nov. 7, 1952.

Yearbook of International Organizations, 1986–87; *The Europa Yearbook*, 1988; *A World Survey*, Vol. I, London, 1988.

ADVISORY COMMITTEE FOR THE CO-ORDINATION OF INFORMATION SYSTEMS. ▷ ACCIS.

ADVISORY COMMITTEE ON ADMINISTRATION AND BUDGETARY QUESTIONS. ▷ ACABQ.

ADVISORY OPINION. An international term for verdicts passed during 1919–45 by the Permanent Court of International Justice and later by the International Court of Justice on disputes and matters submitted to the former by the Assembly of the League of Nations and to the latter by the UN General Assembly; incorporated in art. 14 of the Covenant of the League of Nations of 1919 and also art. 96 of the UN Charter.

ADVOCATUS DEI. *Latin* = God's advocate. An international term used in the Roman Catholic Church during beatification or canonization proceedings the specific function of one of the counsels of the Roman Rota whose task is to promote the merits and virtues of the candidate for benediction or sainthood and present counter-arguments against the reservations put forward by the promoter of the faith, facetiously called ▷ Advocatus diaboli.

Codex Iuris Canonici, Vatican, 1985.

ADVOCATUS DIABOLI. *Latin* = devil's advocate. An international term used: (1) in the Roman Catholic Church the facetious definition of the function of the counsel of the Roman Rota, who in beatification or canonization proceedings is obligated to seek out the negative aspects in the character and life of the candidate for benediction or sainthood; (2) in public debate the defender of a bad cause for the purpose of provoking its opponents to better argumentation. *Codex Iuris Canonici*, canons 1999–2141.

AEGEAN SEA. An arm of the Mediterranean, 625 km long and 320 km wide. Territorial waters of Greece and Turkey. Connected by the Dardanelles with the Sea of Marmara and the Black Sea.
Subject of a Greek–Turkish dispute concerning the continental shelf and the rights of Greece and Turkey to explore and exploit the shelf; submitted on Aug. 10, 1976 by Greece to the ICJ. The ICJ on Dec. 19, 1978 ruled that in the case it was without jurisdiction.
Greece reiterated its continental shelf dispute to the arbitration of the ICJ, after the Turkish government on March 25, 1987 issued a permit to the state owned Turkish Petroleum Corporation for oil exploration in the Greek territorial waters around the islands Lesbos, Lemnos and Samothrace.
Since 1983 Greece has boycotted the NATO exercises in the Aegean Sea, but not bilateral British – Greek exercises.
New Greek – Turkish disputes over the continental shelves and the extent of coastal territorial waters started in mid- 1986 and in spring 1987.

Yearbook of the UN 1976, pp. 813–814; *UN Chronicle*, February 1979, p. 83; KEESING's *Record of World Events*, 1987, No. 5; Greece – Turkey, in: A.J. DAY ed., *Border and Territorial Disputes*, London, 1987; Greece – Turkey, in: KEESING's *Border and Territorial Disputes*, London, 1988.

AEROCASCO. An international term for aircraft insurance against damage incurred in crashes or inflicted on the ground. According to the Rome Aerial Navigation Conventions of 1933, aerocasco should be obligatory on all scheduled airlines. ▷ Air Rome Conventions.

M.D. JUGLAST, *La Convention de Rome du 7 Octobre*, 1952, Paris 1956.

AERONAUTICS. A subject of international co-operation. Organizations reg. with the UIA:

Commonwealth Advisory Aeronautical Research Council, f. 1946, London.
Ibero-American Institute of Aeronautic and Space Law and Commercial Aviation, f. 1964, Madrid.
International Aeronautical Federation, f. 1905, Paris. Consultative status: ECOSOC.
International Committee on Aeronautical Fatigue, f. 1952, Amsterdam.
International Council of the Aeronautical Sciences, f. 1967, Paris.

A.F. DORIAN, J. OSENTON, *Elsevier's Dictionary of Aeronautics*. In English/American (with definitions), French, Spanish, Italian, Portuguese and German, Amsterdam, 1964.

AEROSOL. A subject of international co-operation. Organizations reg. with the UIA:

EEC Committee of the Federation of European Aerosol Associations, f. 1968, Brussels.
European Association of Manufacturers of Aluminium Aerosol Cans, f. 1971, Frankfurt a. M, FRG.

A

Federation of European Aerosol Associations, f. 1959, Zurich. Publ. *Aerosol Bulletin*.

International Aerosol Association, f. 1957, Zurich. Publ. *IAA Information*.

International Society for Aerosols Medicine, f. 1974, Berlin, GDR.

Yearbook of International Organizations, 1986–87.

AEROSPACE. A subject of international co-operation. Organizations reg. with the UIA:

Aerospace Medical Association, f. 1929, Washington, DC, Publ. *Aviation Space and Environmental Medicine*.

European Association of Aerospace Manufacturers, f. 1950, Paris.

International Association of Machinists and Aerospace Workers, (IAM), f. 1888 as International Association of Machinists; name changed 1965, Washington, DC.

International Federation of Airworthiness, f. 1975, Ruislip, UK. Consultative Status: ICAO. Publ. *Airworthiness News*.

International Union, United Automobile, Aerospace and Agricultural Implement Workers of America (UAW), f. 1935, Detroit, Mich., USA.

Nato Advisory Group for Aerospace Research and Development, f. 1952, Neuilly-sur-Seine.

World Aerospace Education Organization, f. 1975, Dublin.

Yearbook of International Organizations, 1986–87.

AEROSTATES AND STRATOSTATES. An international term for lighter-than-air flying machines, such as gliders, balloons and zeppelins (cigar-shaped with one or more nacelles, provided with propeller engines and controls), as well as free balloons with hermetic cabins capable of rising into the stratosphere. The first noted glider flight was made by a Chinese in 196 BC. Almost 2000 years later on June 5, 1783, the Montgolfier brothers carried out the first balloon flight over Paris; in 1897 a Swede, S.A. Andree, attempted to reach the North Pole in the balloon "Ornen" ("Eagle") and after a 65-hour flight landed 800 km away from his target. Trying to reach the White Island, Andree and the whole crew perished. Their remains were found in 1930, and their notes and photos were published. In 1924 a dirigible German airship "Zeppelin" – named after the German airship designer, F. von Zeppelin (1838–1917), who had also founded the Zeppelin Werke in Friedrichshafen on Lake Constance – took off in Germany, crossed the North Atlantic, and landed in the USA; in 1926 a Scandinavian zeppelin "Norge" reached the North Pole; on May 27, 1931 a Swiss scientist and professor of physics at Zurich University, A. Piccard (1884–1962), accompanied by M. Kipfer, rose to the height of 15,781 m, and on Aug. 18, 1932, accompanied by M. Cosyns, he reached a height of 16,940 m (nota bene, in 1953, Cosyns also was the first to dive in a bathyscaphe to a depth of 3150 m). In 1934 a Soviet stratostate rose to 20,600 m, and in 1935 an American attained 22,066 m. During the Franco-Prussian War of 1870–71, aerostates were used in aerial warfare and during the Cold War stratostates also carried out diversionary actions. As a result, both types of flying machines provoked many international disputes (▷ Balloons).

P. BURCHARD, *Balloons: from Paper Bags to Skyhooks*, London, 1960; T. W. BILHORN, "Balloons for Scientific Research", in: *Astronautics and Aeronautics*, December 1965; L.T.C. ROLT, *The Aeronauts. A History of Ballooning 1783–1903*, London, 1966.

AFARS AND ISSAS. The Republic of ▷ Djibouti, formerly French Territory of Afars and Issas.

AFCENT. ▷ NORTHAG.

AFFIDAVIT. A statement in writing and upon oath made before an authorized home or foreign officer (e.g. a written declaration, upon which the issue of

visa is dependent, made before a consular officer to the effect that the declarant will pay the return ticket for the person he has invited from abroad), subject of international agreements.

AFGHANI. A monetary unit of Afghanistan 1 Af. = 100 puls, issued by the Afghanistan Bank since 1955.

AFGHANISTAN. Member of the UN. Democratic Republic of Afghanistan. State in SW Asia. Area: 636,266 sq. km. Pop. 1982 est. 16,347,000 (census 1979 – 13,051,000). Capital: Kabul with 377,715 inhabitants (587,643 metropolitan area) in 1976. GNP per capita in 1985: US $250. Border with the USSR, China, Pakistan and Iran. Border agreement with USSR signed 1946, demarcated 1948; with China 1963, demarcated 1964. Official languages: Afghan and Persian. Currency: 1 afghani weighing 10 grams of silver = 100 puls. National Day: May 27, independence anniversary, 1919. Since Nov. 19, 1946 Afghanistan has been a member of the UN and of all specialized agencies, except IMO, WIPO and GATT. Member of the ▷ Colombo Plan. A member of the Test Ban Treaty, Mar. 12, 1964; of the Nonproliferation Treaty, Feb 4, 1970; of the Sea-Bed Treaty, Apr. 22, 1971; and of the BW Convention, Mar. 26, 1975.

International relations: since 1747 an independent kingdom; in the 19th century, military conflicts with Great Britain, 1838–42 and 1878–80, resulted in an unfavorable shifting of the border being imposed on Afghanistan in 1893 to the so-called Durand line (present controversial border of Afghanistan with Pakistan); in 1895, on the basis of an English–Russian agreement, the border with India in the region of the Hindu Kush mountains was slightly shifted in favor of Afghanistan; in this way Russia became separated from India, and Afghanistan became a buffer state between the British colony of India and tsarist Russia. In World War I Afghanistan remained neutral; in 1919 a new military conflict broke out between Great Britain and Afghanistan, supported by Soviet Russia, ending with the recognition of Afghanistani independence by Great Britain and in a friendship treaty with the Russian FSSR in 1921; after another crisis in 1928–29, Afghanistan concluded an agreement with the USSR on neutrality and nonaggression in 1931. In the years 1934–36 Afghanistan was a member of the League of Nations. During World War II the country also remained neutral. After World War II it started a nonalignment policy, developing good relations with all neighbors and strengthening Afghanistani–Soviet relations (economic, technical and arms assistance, particularly for the airforce). Signatory of the Treaty on the Non-proliferation of Nuclear Weapons (1968). The Republic was proclaimed in June 1973. In Dec. 1978 an ▷ Afghanistan–USSR Friendship Treaty was signed in Moscow for 20 years. At the end of 1979 and beginning of 1980 the incursion of Soviet troops, formally on a request for military aid by the government of Afghanistan, according to the Afghanistani–Soviet Agreement, 1978, became subject of a resolution of the Security Council and then of the General Assembly, which demanded an "immediate, unconditional and total withdrawal of the foreign troops in Afghanistan", 104 votes for, 16 against (Afghanistan, Angola, the Byelorussian SSR, Bulgaria, Czechoslovakia, Ethiopia, Grenada, Cuba, Laos, Mongolia, Mozambique, the GDR, Poland, the Ukrainian SSR, South Yemen, the USSR) with 28 abstaining. In Feb., 1980 the ▷ Carrington Plan prompted negotiations.

An agreement, under Security Council aegis on non-interference of any Great Power in Afghanistan's internal affairs, linked with the withdrawal of

Soviet troops and the safe return of 2.5 million refugees from Pakistan, was not negotiated until 1985.

The proximity talks took place in Geneva between August 1985 and April 1988, with the intermediacy of the Personal Representative of the UN Secretariat Diego Cordovoz, Under Secretary General for Special Political Affairs. A Chronology of UN involvement in situations resulting from the Soviet military intervention in Afghanistan in late December 1979 was published in the *UN Chronicle*, 1988, as were the Bilateral Agreement between the Republic of Afghanistan and the Islamic Republic of Pakistan on the Principles of Mutual Relations in Particular on Non-Interference and Non-Intervention USA and USSR Declaration on International Guarantees; Bilateral Agreement between the Republic of Afghanistan and the Islamic Republic of Pakistan on the Voluntary Return of Refugees; Agreement on the Interrelationships for the Settlement of the Situation Relating to Afghanistan; and Annex: Memorandum of Understanding; all documents signed on April 14, 1988 in Geneva, were to go into effect, May 15, 1988. Complete Soviet withdrawal from Afghanistan beginning on May 15, 1988 was to end by Febr. 15, 1989. The Mujaheddin guerillas continued in late 1988 to attack the pro-Moscow regime and withdrawing Soviet troops.

J. HUMLIUM, *La géographie de l'Afghanistan. Étude d'un pays aride*, Copenhague, 1959; D.N. WILBER, *Afghanistan. A Bibliography*, New Haven, 1963; M.B. WATKINS, *Afghanistan. A land in Transition*, New York, 1964; N.M. GURIEWICZ, *Ekonomicheskoie rozwitie Afganistana*, Moscow, 1966; A.D. DAWYDOW, *Agrarnyi stroj Afganistana*, Moscow, 1967; R.T. ACHRAMOYICZ, *Afganistan 1961–1967*, Moscow, 1967; L.W. ADAMEC, *Afghanistan 1900–1923. A Diplomatic History*, Los Angeles, 1968; *The Kabul-Times Annual*, 1970; L. DUPRÉE, *Afghanistan*, Princeton, 1979; *UN Chronicle*, March 1980; K.P. MISRA (ed.), *Afghanistan in Crisis*, New York, 1981; A. BRADSHER, *Afghanistan and the Soviet Union*, Durham, 1982; A. ARNOLD, *Afghanistan. Two-Party Communism*, Stanford, 1983; S.S. BHARGAVA, *South Asian Security and Afghanistan*, Lexington, 1983; *UN Chronicle*, January, 1984, p. 22; *The Europa Year Book 1984*, Vol. I, pp. 1039–1050, London, 1984; J.J. COLLINS, *The Soviet Invasion of Afghanistan*, Toronto, 1986; O. ROY, *Islam and Resistance in Afghanistan*, London, 1986; M. URBAN, *War in Afghanistan*, London 1987; R. KLASS ed., *Afghanistan. The Great Game Revisited*, New York, 1988; *UN Chronicle*, June 1988, pp. 4–17; KEESING's *Record of World Events*, June, 1988.

AFGHANISTAN, IRAQ, IRAN AND TURKEY NONAGGRESSION TREATY, 1937, called Orient Pact, signed in Teheran, July 8, 1937 by the ministers of foreign relations, in spirit of the ▷ Briand-Kellogg Pact.

LNTS, Vol. 190, p. 21.

AFGHANISTAN-PAKISTAN AGREEMENTS 1988. ▷ Afghanistan.

AFGHANISTAN–PERSIA TREATIES 1921 AND 1927. The Treaty of Friendship between Afghanistan and Persia was signed at Teheran, on Jan. 22, 1927. The highlights of the Treaty:

"Art. I. From this day forward, sincere friendship and a permanent and cordial understanding shall be established between Persia and Afghanistan and their respective nationals.

Art. IX. The relations of cordial understanding between Persia and Afghanistan shall not be affected in the event of one of the High Contracting Parties becoming involved in a war with a third Power. But in this case the other Part shall undertake, in accordance with the rules of neutrality, not to favor this third Power in any respect.

Art. X. In order to emphasize the sincere friendship and mutual confidence existing between the Empire of Persia and the Kingdom of Afghanistan, the two Contracting Parties have decided, in conformity with international usage, to submit to arbitration all the difficulties arising between the two countries, of which a solution cannot be arrived at by diplomatic negotiations".

On Nov. 28, 1927, at Kabul Afghanistan and Persia signed a Treaty of Friendship and Security. The highlights of the Treaty:

"The Governments of Afghanistan and Persia,
Taking into consideration their material and intellectual relations and their geographical situation, and believing that from the standpoint of religious and moral homogeneity and from the standpoint of other needs, the present century requires and necessitates further engagements on the part of the two nations.
Being desirous of strengthening the friendly and fraternal ties already existing between them and of consolidating their sincere relations,
Have thought it necessary to conclude a treaty of friendship and security.
Art. 1. The basis of the relations between Persia and Afghanistan continues to be the Treaty of the first of Saratan, 1300, all of those provisions and articles remain in force.
Art. 2. Each of the Contracting Parties agrees to abstain from proceeding to attacks and aggressions against the other or from undertaking military expeditions on the territory of the other Party.
In case one of the Contracting Parties should be attacked by one or more third Powers, the other Contracting Party undertakes to remain neutral during the entire period of the conflict. Moreover, the attacked Party, on its part, regardless of all political, strategic or tactical advantages, shall not violate the neutrality of the other Party.
Art. 3. Each of the Contracting Parties agrees not to take part de facto or formally in any hostile operation which may be undertaken by one or more third Powers against the other Contracting Party, and not to enter into any political and military alliances and agreements directed against the independence, integrity or sovereignty of the other Party or which may cause to it political or military prejudices. The two Contracting Parties shall likewise abstain from taking part in a blockade or economic boycott which may be directed against one of them.
Art. 6. The two Contracting Parties agree that the settlement and liquidation of differences which may arise between them, and which it may not have been possible to settle by the ordinary diplomatic means, shall be effected in the manner provided for in the protocol annexed to this Treaty".

The Treaty entered into force on Dec. 28, 1927.

LNTS, Vol. XXXIII, No. 853, pp. 285–302; *European and Political Survey*, Vol. III, 1928, pp. 432–434.

AFGHANISTAN–SOVIET TREATIES. 1921 AND 1926. The first Afghan–Soviet treaty was signed on Feb. 28, 1921 at Moscow. On Aug. 31, 1926 at Paghman near Kabul Afghanistan and the USSR signed a Treaty of Neutrality and Mutual Non-Aggression. The highlights of the Treaty:

"Art. 1. In the event of war or military activity between the Contracting Parties and one or more third Powers, the Other Contracting Party undertakes to maintain neutrality towards the first.
Art. 2. Each of the Contracting Parties undertakes to abstain from any attack on the other and on the territories which are in its possession, and not to take any measures which might cause political or military prejudice to the other Contracting Party. In particular, each of the Contracting Parties obligates itself not to participate either in alliances or agreements of a military or political character directed against the other Contracting Party, nor in a financial or economic boycott or blockade aimed at the other Contracting Party. Moreover, in the event of hostile action by one or more third Powers against one of the Contracting Parties, the other Contracting Party undertakes not only not to support such action but to resist on its own territory such action and consequences flowing therefrom.
Art. 3. The High Contracting Parties, mutually acknowledging the sovereignty of the State, obligate themselves to abstain from all armed or unarmed interference in the internal affairs of the other Contracting Party and to refrain absolutely from co-operating or participating in any intervention on the part of one or more third Powers, undertaken against the other Contracting Party. The Contracting Parties shall not permit, and shall combat on their territory the formation and activity of groups and also resist the activity of individuals aimed at injuring the other Contracting Party, overthrowing its governmental regime, threatening its territorial integrity, or mobilizing or recruiting armed forces to be used against the other Contracting Party. Likewise both Parties shall not permit the passage or transport through their territories of armed forces, arms, munitions, military supplies or any kind of war materials directed against the other Contracting Party."

A Final Protocol was signed with the Treaty,

"to confirm, that at the moment of signing the abovementioned treaty, the Government of Afghanistan faithful to the principles of the treaty concluded on February 28, 1921, is not under any kind of obligations toward one or more States which might conflict with the treaty of neutrality and mutual nonaggression signed this day, August 31. He also declares in the name of his Government that the Government of the High State of Afghanistan confirms that during the entire period during which the said treaty of neutrality and mutual non-aggression is in force, it will not enter into any treaties or agreements which would conflict with the present treaty of neutrality and mutual non-aggression. The Government of the High State of Afghanistan expresses confidence that the friendly relations between the High State of Afghanistan and the Union of Socialist Soviet Republics will, on the basis of the treaties of Moscow of February 28, 1921 and of Paghman, of August 31, 1926, develop unalterably and serve the high aims of universal peace."

The Treaty with Protocol entered into force on Apr. 10, 1927.

Collections of Laws and Orders of the Workers' and Peasants' Government of the USSR, Part II, No. 3, January 20, 1928.

AFGHANISTAN–USSR FRIENDSHIP TREATY, 1978. A Treaty signed at Moscow on Dec. 5, 1978, by L.I. Brezhnev and N.M. Taraki; entered into force on Jan. 7, 1979. The text of the Treaty of Friendship, Good-Neighbourliness and Co-operation between the Union of Soviet Socialist Republics and the Democratic Republic of Afghanistan, is as follows:

"The Union of Soviet Socialist Republics and the Democratic Republic of Afghanistan.
Reaffirming fidelity to the purposes and principles of the Soviet-Afghan Treaties of 1921 and 1931, which laid the foundations for friendly and good-neighbourly relations between the Soviet and Afghan peoples and which respond to their fundamental national interests.
Desiring to consolidate in every way possible the friendship and all-round co-operation between the two countries,
Resolved to develop the social and economic achievements of the Soviet and Afghan peoples, to safeguard their security and independence and to work steadfastly for the unity of all forces striving for peace, national independence, democracy and social progress,
Expressing their firm determination to contribute to the consolidation of peace and security in Asia and throughout the world, to the development of relations between States and to the strengthening of fruitful and mutually beneficial co-operation in Asia, and attaching great importance to the further consolidation of the contractual and juridical basis of their mutual relations,
Reaffirming their fidelity to the purposes and principles of the Charter of the United Nations,
Have decided to conclude this Treaty of Friendship, Good-neighbourliness and Co-operation and have agreed as follows:
Art. 1. The High Contracting Parties solemnly declare their determination to consolidate and deepen the unshakable friendship between the two countries and to develop co-operation in all fields on the basis of equality of rights, respect for national sovereignty and territorial integrity, and non-interference in each other's internal affairs.
Art. 2. The High Contracting Parties shall take steps to consolidate and broaden the mutually beneficial co-operation between them in the economic field and the scientific and technological field. To that end, they shall develop and consolidate co-operation in the fields of industry, transport and communications, agriculture, the utilization of natural resources and the development of the power industry and in other economic fields and shall assist in the training of national personnel and in planning for the development of the national economy. The parties shall expand their trade on the basis of the principles of equality, mutual benefit and most-favoured-nation treatment.
Art. 3. The High Contracting Parties shall promote the development of co-operation and of the exchange of experience in the fields of science, culture, the arts, literature, education, health, the press, radio and television, the cinema, tourism and sports and in other fields.
The Parties shall encourage the expansion of co-operation between their organs of State power and public organizations, enterprises, and cultural and scientific institutions for the purpose of promoting a deeper knowledge of the life, work, experience and achievements of the peoples of the two countries.
Art. 4. The High Contracting Parties, acting in the spirit of the traditions of friendship and good-neighbourliness and in the spirit of the Charter of the United Nations shall consult with each other and shall, by agreement, take the necessary steps to safeguard the security, independence and territorial integrity of the two countries.
In the interest of strengthening their defensive capacity, the High Contracting Parties shall continue to develop their co-operation in the military field on the basis of the relevant agreements concluded between them.
Art. 5. The Union of Soviet Socialist Republics respects the policy of non-alignment pursued by the Democratic Republic of Afghanistan, that policy being an important factor for the maintenance of international peace and security. The Democratic Republic of Afghanistan respects the policy of peace pursued by the Union of Soviet Socialist Republics, aimed at strengthening friendship and co-operation with all countries and peoples.
Art. 6. Each of the High Contracting Parties solemnly declares that it will not enter into military or other alliances or participate in any groups of States or in actions or measures directed against the other Party.
Art. 7. The High Contracting Parties shall continue to do everything in their power for the defence of international peace and the security of peoples, for the intensification of the process of international detente, for its extension to all regions of the world, including Asia, for its realization in concrete forms of mutually beneficial co-operation between States and for the settlement of international disputes by peaceful means. The two Parties shall actively promote the cause of general and complete disarmament, including nuclear disarmament, under effective international control.
Art. 8. The High Contracting Parties shall promote the development of co-operation between Asian States, the establishment of relations of peace, good-neighbourliness and mutual trust between them and the creation of an effective system of security in Asia on the basis of the joint efforts of all the States of the continent.
Art. 9. The High Contracting Parties shall continue their steadfast struggle against the intrigues of the forces of aggression and for the final elimination of colonialism and racism in all their forms and manifestations.
The Parties shall co-operate with each other and with other peace-loving States in supporting the just struggle of peoples for their freedom, independence, sovereignty and social progress.
Art. 10. The High Contracting Parties shall consult with each other on all important international questions relating to the interests of the two countries.
Art. 11. The High Contracting Parties declare that their obligations under currently valid international treaties do not conflict with the provisions of this Treaty, and

they undertake not to conclude any international agreements inconsistent with this Treaty.

Art. 12. Questions that may arise between the High Contracting Parties with regard to the interpretation or application of any provision of this Treaty shall be settled on a bilateral basis, in a spirit of friendship and mutual understanding and respect.

Art. 13. This Treaty shall remain valid for a term of 20 years from the date of its entry into force.

Unless one of the High Contracting Parties, six months before the expiry of the above-mentioned term, declares its desire to terminate the Treaty, it shall be extended for an additional term of five years, and thereafter it shall be similarly extended until such time as one of the High Contracting Parties, six months before the expiry of the five-year term then in progress, gives notice in writing of its intention to terminate the Treaty.

Art. 14. If one of the High Contracting Parties, during the 20-year term of validity of the Treaty, wishes to terminate it before the expiry of the said term, it must, six months before the date on which it intends to terminate the Treaty, give the other High Contracting Party notice in writing of its desire to terminate the Treaty before the expiry of its term, and it may regard the Treaty as terminated as from the date so determined.

Art. 15. This Treaty is subject to ratification and shall enter into force on the date of the exchange of the instruments of ratification, which shall take place at Kabul. This Treaty has been drawn up in duplicate in the Russian and Dari languages, both texts being equally authentic".

"20-Year Treaty Moves Afghans Closer to Soviet. A Friendship Pact Calls for Military Co-operation", in: *New York Times*, Dec. 6, 1978; *Şbornik Wnieshniey Politiki*, Moscow, 1978.

AFLATOXIN. A substance produced by a corn fungus (Aspergillus flavus) which in regions of Asia and Africa causes the world's highest incidence of liver cancer. Subject of WHO research. At the end of the 1980's dangerous levels of aflatoxin have been found in the Corn Belt states of the United States.

S. KILMAN, Spreading Poison: Fungus in Corn Crop. A Potent Carcinogen Invades Food Supplies. In: *The Wall Street Journal*, February 23, 1989.

AFRICA. The second largest continent in the Eastern Hemisphere. Area: 30,244,050 sq. km including adjacent islands. Pop. 1970 – 343,000,000; est. 1980 – 412,000,000. In 1988 all African States were members of the United Nations, but not ▷ Namibia and ▷ Western Sahara. The last colonial problem is ▷ Apartheid.

The third Special Session of the General Assembly was convened from May 27th to June 1st, 1986 at UN Hqs. to address Africa's critical economic situation; adopted a five year Plan of Action for African Economic Recovery, 1986–1990.

See also ▷ OAU. In the 1980's all African States were represented at the Non-Aligned Movement, with the exception of South Africa. The World Bank has predicted that the population will increase from 460 mln in 1985 to 1.850 mln by 2050.

La URSS y los Paises de Africa 1945–1962. Documentos y materiales, Moscú, 1963, II Vls; E. SIK, *Histoire de l'Atlique Noire*, Budapest 1964; H. KITCHEN ed., *A Handbook of African Affairs*, New York, 1964; Institut Afriki Akademi Nauk SSSR, *Nezavisimye strany Afriki. Ekonomicheskie sotsial 'nye problemy*. Moskva, 1965; P.H. ADY, A.H. HASSLEWOOD, *Africa. Oxford Regional Economic Atlas*, Oxford 1965; F.H. BLASCO, *Africa, Tercer Mundo*, Barcelona, 1966; J. GANIAGE, H. DESCHAPS, O. GUITARD, *L'Afrique au XX Siècle*, Paris, 1966; R. DAVIDSON, *History of a Continent*, New York, 1967; R. OLIVER, *Africa since 1800*, Cambridge, 1967; *Neokapitalisticheskii put' razvitia stran Afriki*, Moskva, 1967; C. LEGUN (ed.), *Africa Contemporary Record. Annual Survey and Documents*, New York–London, since 1968/69; R. OLIVER, J.D. FAGE, *A Short History of Africa*, London, 1969; S. PARRIN, *Religion in Africa*, London, 1970; L.B. SOHN (ed.), *Basic Documents of African Regional Organizations*, New York, 1972; Ch.H. ALEKSANDROVICH, *The European–African

Confrontation*, Leyden, 1973; A.K. MENSAH-BROWN, *African International Legal History*, New York, 1975; A.A. MAZRUA, *Africa's International Relations*, Boulder, 1977; G.J. RUBINSHTEYN, *Afrika v Mirovom Khoziaystvye i Mezhdunarodnoy Torgovle*, Moscow, 1982; *Africa, South of the Sahara 1983–84*, London, 1984; *The Middle East and North Africa 1984*, London, 1984; UNESCO. *Africa and the Second World War*, Paris 1985; FAO. *African Agriculture. The Next 25 Years*, Rome, 1986; A.D. ROBERTS ed., *The Cambridge History of Africa*, 8 Vols., Cambridge, 1975–86; *UN Chronicle*, 1986, No. 4, pp. 9–20; D. RONEN ed., *Democracy and Pluralism in Africa*, Boulder Colo. 1986; J. RAVENHILL ed., *Africa in Economic Crisis*, New York, 1986; A. MAZRUN, *The Africans, A Triple Heritage*, Boston, 1986; OECD, *Directory of Development Research and Training Institutions in Africa*, Washington DC, 1987; E. KODJO, *Africa Tomorrow*, New York, 1987; *The Middle East and North Africa, 1987*, London, 1987; Z. ERGAS, *The African State in Transition*, New York, 1987; I.W. ZARTMAN, *International Relations in the New Africa*, Washington DC, 1987; J.S. WHITAKER, *How Can Africa Survive*, New York, 1988; UNESCO. *General History of Africa*, 8 Vols., Paris, 1980–1988; J. ILIFFE, *The African Poor*, New York, 1988.

AFRICA AND CUBA. In 1977 the Government of Angola approached the Government of Cuba for civil and military assistance against foreign intervention, mainly from South Africa. In 1978 the Government of Ethiopia requested similar assistance from Cuba in connection with the conflict with Somalia. In both cases Cuban army units responded by taking part in armed fighting, while groups of Cuban physicians, engineers and technicians assisted in civilian tasks. This Cuban involvement became a subject of international disputes in the UN (▷ Cuba). ▷ Africanization of Cuba, 1912.

P.S. FALK, *Cuba in Africa*, in: *Foreign Affairs*, Summer 1987.

AFRICA AND MADAGASCAR. In 1960, after Madagascar had attained independence, the Malagasy Republic became a member of the Francophonic Organization of African States (Organization Africaine et Malgache de Co-operation Economique, OAMCE).

AFRICA HORN. An international term for Egypt, Sudan, Ethiopia, Djibouti, and Somalia.

AFRICA IN THE UN. In 1945 there were only four signatories of the UN Charter among the African States: the Union of South Africa, Egypt, Ethiopia and Liberia; at that time all the remaining African countries were colonies or trusteeship territories administered by Belgium, France, Great Britain, Portugal and Spain. The Italian colonies in Africa after World War II were put under the UN Trusteeship Administration. In 1955, Libya attained independence and entered the UN; in 1956 – Morocco, Sudan and Tunisia; in 1957 – Ghana; in 1958 – Guinea; in 1960, which was called in the UN "The Year of Africa": Chad, Dahomey, Gabon, Upper Volta (at present Burkina Faso), Cameroon, Congo Brazzaville (at present the Congo Republic), Congo Leopoldville (at present Zaïre), Mali, Mauritania, Niger, Malagasy Republic, Central African Republic, Senegal, Togo, and Ivory Coast; in 1961 – Sierra Leone and Tanganyika; in 1962 – Algeria, Rwanda, Burundi, and Uganda; in 1963 – Zanzibar and Kenya; in 1964 – Malawi; in 1965 – Gambia; in 1967 – Botswana and Lesotho; in 1968 – Mauritius, Equatorial Guinea and Swaziland; in 1974 – Guinea Bissau; in 1975 – Mozambique; and in 1976 – Angola. After 1963 the African States were represented in the UN by such groupings as the Brazzaville Group or the Casablanca Group, both

differing about many questions. With the creation, in 1963, of the Organization of African States (OAS), its Secretariat began to co-ordinate initiatives of the African States in the UN. In 1964, a delegate from Ghana became – as the first representative of Africa – President of the UN General Assembly. Africa was twice represented in the UN Security Council during its first 15 years of existence – by Egypt (1946 and 1949–50) and Tunisia (1959–60). Since 1961, one representative of Africa is permanently elected to the Council. Africa has the strongest representation in the UN Decolonization Commission. The Economic Commission for Africa established by ECOSOC, has existed since 1958, and the African Development Bank – since 1964 (operating since 1966). The Commission since 1961, publishes the *Economic Bulletin for Africa* with an annex on African statistics. According to the data supplied by the Commission, Africa belongs to one of the poorest world regions, encompassing States with a yearly per capita income lower than US $100; out of 23 such States, 16 were in Africa: Botswana, Burundi, Chad, Dahomey, Ethiopia, Upper Volta, Guinea, Lesotho, Malawi, Mali, Niger, Rwanda, Somali, Sudan, Uganda and Tanzania.

On May 27–June 1, 1986 the General Assembly held a special session on the Economic Crisis in Africa and adopted by consensus the UN Program of Action for ▷ African Economic Recovery and Development 1986–1990.

The last colonial-type problems in Africa of concern to the UN are ▷ Apartheid and ▷ Namibia.

J.D. FAGE, *Atlas of African History*, London, 1958; Th. HOOVER Jr. *Africa in the UN*, New York, 1963; *UN Yearbook*, 1986; *UN Chronicle*, 1986.

AFRICAN-AMERICAN ORGANIZATIONS. ▷ Afro-American Organizations.

AFRICAN AND MALAGASY INDUSTRIAL PROPERTY OFFICE. F. 1962, Yaoundé, Cameroon. Intergovernmental institution of Benin, Cameroon, the Central African Rep., Chad, Congo, Gabon, Ivory Coast, Madagascar, Mauritania, Niger, Senegal, Togo, Upper Volta. Reg. with the UIA.

Yearbook of International Organizations.

AFRICAN AND MALAGASY ORGANIZATION FOR ECONOMIC CO-OPERATION. Organisation africaine et malgache de coopération économique (OAMCE), first regional intergovernmental economic organization of ten French-speaking African States, established at a summit meeting at Brazzaville, Dec. 15, 1960, converted 1961 to the ▷ African and Malagasy Union of Economic Co-operation (UAMCE).

Yearbook of International Organizations.

AFRICAN AND MALAGASY UNION OF DEVELOPMENT BANKS. Union africaine et malgache des banques pour le développement (UAMED), est. Sept. 13, 1962, Libréville, on signature of an agreement by the Chiefs of State of Cameroon, the Central African Republic, Congo, Dahomey, Gabon, Ivory Coast, Madagascar, Niger, Senegal, Togo and Upper Volta. Center for collection and distribution of documentation and for training and research and exchange of experience among member banks. Reg. with the UIA.

Yearbook of International Organizations.

AFRICAN AND MALAGASY UNION OF ECONOMIC CO-OPERATION. Union africaine et malgache de coopération économique

(UAMCE), regional intergovernmental African institution, 1961–1965, successor to the ▷ Afro-Malagasy Organisation for Economic Co-operation (OAMCE). In Feb. 1965 changed to the ▷ Common Afro-Malagasy Organisation (OCAM).
Yearbook of International Organizations.

AFRICAN AND MAURITIAN UNION OF DEVELOPMENT BANKS. Union africaine et mauricienne des banques pour le développement, f. 1962, Libréville, as Union africaine et malgache de banques pour le développement. Members: national central banks of 13 countries: Benin. Burkina Faso, Cameroon, the Central African Republic, Chad, Congo, Côte d'Ivoire, Gabon, Mauritius, Niger, Senegal, Togo, Zäire. Reg. with the UIA.
Yearbook of International Organizations, 1986–87.

AFRICAN, ASIAN, AND LATIN-AMERICAN SOLIDARITY CONFERENCE, 1966. Span. Conferencia de Solidaridad de los Pueblos de Asia, Africa y América Latina, 1966, also called Conference of Three Continents, held in Havana Jan. 3–14, 1966, ratified the General Havana Declaration of 1966 and four resolutions: political, economic, organizational and socio-cultural.

AFRICAN ASSOCIATION FOR PUBLIC ADMINISTRATION AND MANAGEMENT, f. 1971 in Addis Ababa, to promote the study of professional techniques and encourage the study of administrative problems. Publ. *Newsletter* (quarterly).
The Europa Yearbook, 1987. A World Survey Vol. I, London, 1988, p. 217.

AFRICAN CHARTER, 1961. Also called Casablanca Charter, 1961, adopted by governments of Egypt, Ghana, Guinea, Mali, Morocco and the interim government of the Algerian Republic as a conclusion of the conference of the then independent African states, Casablanca, Jan. 4–7, 1961; they proclaimed a determined struggle for the victory of freedom all over Africa and its unity, declared the will of the participating governments to liberate African territories which continued to be subject to foreign domination and announced their will to maintain their unity in thought and actions on the international forum with a view to safeguarding the independence, sovereignty and territorial inviolability of their countries and the consolidation of peace in the world through implementation of the policy of nonalignment.
The conference announced appointment of the African Advisory Assembly with four committees: political, cultural, military, economic and a Liaison Bureau. It was the first document of Pan-African solidarity of three Arab (Algeria, Egypt, Morocco) and three African States (Ghana, Guinea, Mali) which cleared the ground for the ▷ Charter of the Organization of African Unity (OAU), 1963.
M. LIONS, *Constitucionalismo y Democracia en la Africa Recien Independizada*, México, DF. 1964, pp. 161–162.

AFRICAN CHARTER ON HUMAN AND PEOPLE'S RIGHTS, 1986. Entered into force on Oct. 21, 1986. By 1988 it had been ratified by the following 34 states: Algeria, Benin, Botswana, Burkina Faso, Cape Verde, the Central African Republic, Chad, Comoro Islands, Congo, Egypt, Guinea, Guinea-Bissau, Equatorial Guinea, Gabon, The Gambia, Liberia, Libya, Mali, Mauritania, Niger, Nigeria, Rwanda, the Sahrawi Arab Democratic Republic, Sao Tomé and Principe, Senegal, Sierra Leone, Somalia, Sudan, Togo, Tunisia, Uganda, Tanzania, Zambia and Zimbabwe.
Under Article 30 of the Charter, in August 1987 the OAU elected the African Commission on Human Rights.

AFRICAN CHRISTIAN CHURCHES. An institution organized by the All-Africa Conference of Churches in 1958 to act as a fellowship of consultation and co-operation between the Christian Churches and National Christian Councils of America. Members: Churches and Christian Councils in 33 African countries. Publ. *AACC Bulletin* (quarterly), *AACC Newsletter* (monthly), Reports (in English and French). Reg. with the UIA.
Yearbook of International Organizations.

AFRICAN COMMISSION ON MEDIATION, CONCILIATION AND ARBITRATION. Est. by art. XIX of the Charter of the OAU at Addis Ababa and by a Protocol, signed at Cairo July 21, 1964. The Commission has jurisdiction over disputes between States only. A dispute may be referred to the Commission jointly by the parties, by a party to the dispute, by the OAU Council of Ministers or by the OAU Assembly of Heads of States and Government.
UNTS, Vol. 479, p. 39; *The Major International Treaties 1914–1973. A History and Guide with Texts*, London, 1974, pp. 488–490.

AFRICAN COMMITTEE OF ELEVEN. A name of a permanent committee for aid to national independence movements, created by the Third Conference of African Nations Mar. 30, 1961 held in Cairo, with headquarters in Dar-es-Salaam, since 1963 financed from the budget of the OAU.

AFRICAN COMMON MARKET. An organization for economic co-operation of Algeria, Egypt, Ghana, Guinea, Mali and Morocco; f. Cairo, Apr. 2, 1962; its activities ceased after the formation of the OAU, Mar 3, 1963, the function of co-ordination of economic co-operation being taken over, in keeping with the OAU Charter, by the OAU Economic–Social Commission which initiated research on Jan. 22, 1965 into possibilities of establishing an African Common Market.

AFRICAN CONFERENCE OF INDEPENDENT STATES, 1958. Held Apr. 15–22, 1958 in Accra, was the first African intergovernmental organization reg. in UIA; initiated the work on the creation of the ▷ OAU.

AFRICAN CO-OPERATION CHARTER, 1973. The Charter adopted in Abidjan, May, 1973, by the Conference of Economy and Finance Ministers; proclaimed extended inter-African co-operation in industry, agriculture, transport, communications and education and postulated liquidation of separate currency zones which continued to bind independent African states with former metropolitan powers and reduced the scope of their independent economic policies.

AFRICAN DECLARATION, 1967. A common position of African states on economic social matters, prepared July 1967 at Algiers, main points included in the ▷ Algiers Charter worked out by the Group of 77.

AFRICAN DEVELOPMENT BANK. F. 1963, in Abidjan, Côte d'Ivoire. Intergovernmental finance institution of Algeria, Benin, Botswana, Burundi, Cameroon, the Central African Rep., Chad, Congo, Côte d'Ivoire, Egypt, Ethiopia, Gabon, Gambia, Ghana, Guinea-Bissau, Guinea Equat., Kenya, Lesotho, Liberia, Libya, Malawi, Mali, Mauritania, Mauritius, Morocco, Niger, Nigeria, Rwanda, Senegal, Sierra Leone, Somalia, Sudan, Swaziland, Tanzania, Togo, Tunisia, Uganda, Upper Volta (now Burkina Faso), Zaïre, Zambia. Agreements with FAO, ILO, OAU, UNDP, UNESCO, UNCTAD, WHO, IMO and IBRD. The governments of 25 non-African Countries are also members. Publ. *ADB News, ADB Quarterly Review and Yearbook.*
In the 1980's joined by: Cape Verde, Comoros, Djibouti, Madagascar, Sao Tomé and Principe, Seychelles, and Zimbabwe. The Bank provides technical assistance, pre-investment studies and staff training, especially in agriculture, transport, publication, education and health.
The Europa Year Book 1984. A World Survey, Vol. I, pp. 92–93, London, 1984; *The Europa Yearbook 1987. A World Survey*, Vol. I, London, 1988, pp. 40–41; *Yearbook of International Organizations*, 1986–87.

AFRICAN DEVELOPMENT FUND. An institution for economic aid in capital expenditure, est. at the suggestion of the African Development Bank Nov. 29, 1972 in Abidjan, on the basis of a convention signed by representatives of 36 African states and 17 highly developed countries.
The ADF grants interest free loans to African Countries that are members of the ▷ African Development Bank, ADB, for projects with a service charge of 0.75% and with repayment over 50 years. In the 1980's 26 developed countries contributed to the ADF, 29% coming from the USA and Japan.
The Europa Yearbook 1987. A World Survey, Vol. I, pp. 40–41, London 1988.

AFRICAN ECONOMIC RECOVERY PLAN OF ACTION, 1986–1990. ▷ Africa.

AFRICAN EEC DECLARATION 1976. Elaborated and accepted on Feb. 23, 1976 in Luxembourg by the EEC Member States Declaration on Principles of Economic Relations between the European Economic Community and African Independent States.

AFRICAN ENTENTE. A name accepted for the Consultative Council of Dahomey, Côte d'Ivoire, Nigeria, and Upper Volta (now Burkina Faso) created in Abidjan Apr. 28, 1959 as Conseil de l'Entente pour la gestion des affairs communes, for the purpose of expanding interstate co-operation. Policy is determined at periodic conferences of heads of state with commissions of experts. Since June 8, 1966 Togo is also a member of the African Entente. Since 1972 the African Entente took part in the ▷ Franco-African Summit, but also held every year a summit meeting of the Conseil de l'entente.
KEESING's Record of World Events, April, 1985.

AFRICAN–FRENCH SUMMITS. ▷ Franco-African Summits.

AFRICAN GREAT LAKES COUNTRIES. ▷ Economic Community of the Great Lakes Countries.

AFRICAN INTEGRATION. Postulated by the OAU Charter, signed in Addis Ababa, May 2, 1963, implemented by OAU members; its first financial instrument was the ▷ African Development Bank.

AFRICAN INTELLECTUAL PROPERTY ORGANIZATION, f. 1962, Yaoundé (Cameroon). Established to succeed the African and Malagasy Industrial Property Office, on signature of an Agreement by the members of the African and Malagasy Union, (until its dissolution in 1985). Intergovernmental Organization of Benin, Burkina Faso, Cameroon, Central African Republic, Chad, Congo, Gabon, Côte d'Ivoire, Madagascar, Mauritania, Niger, Senegal, Togo. Agency of the OAU. Reg. with the UIA.

Yearbook of International Organizations, 1986–87.

AFRICAN INTERGOVERNMENTAL CONFERENCES. Initiated 1944–45 at ▷ Arab conferences of heads of state; joint Arabic and Black African conferences held since 1958 on the initiative of Ghana leader Kwame Nkrumah. Below is their chronological list covering the years 1958–85:

1958 – First Conference of Independent African States, held Apr. 15–22 at Accra and attended by Ethiopia, Ghana, Liberia, Libya, Morocco, Sudan, Tunisia, Egypt and observers: national liberation committees of Algeria, French Cameroon and Italian Somalia; adopted a declaration proclaiming solidary co-operation of African states in the UN forum; 11 other resolutions relating to liberation of subjugated territories.

1959 – Conference of Heads of State of Consultative Council – Dahomey, Upper Volta, Nigeria, Ivory Coast, held at Abidjan Apr. 28–29;

1960 – Second Conference of Independent states and seven non-independent territories; adopted a resolution on consolidation of peace and international security in keeping with the UN Charter; Bandung and Accra resolutions; a number of further resolutions among others on the establishment of an African Council for Economic Co-operation.

1960 – Preliminary Conference of heads of 11 states associated with France, held Abidjan, Oct. 25–26; Consultative Council of Dahomey, Upper Volta, Niger, Ivory Coast formed.

1960 – First Conference of the states of the ▷ Brazzaville Group in the capital of the Republic of Congo, Dec. 15–18, attended by 12 Francophonic states: Chad, Dahomey, Gabon, Upper Volta, Cameroon, the Republic of Congo, Mauritania, Niger, the Malagasy Republic, the Republic of Central Africa, Senegal and Ivory Coast; adopted preliminary resolutions on African Co-operation Organization for French-speaking states and a resolution on convening a Pan-African conference at Yaoundé, 1961;

1960 – First Integration Conference of Heads of State of Ghana, Guinea, and Mali, held at Conakry, Dec. 22–24, for the setting up of ▷ Union of African States.

1961 – Third Conference of Independent States of Africa held in Casablanca, Jan. 7, attended by heads of state from Ghana, Guinea, Libya, Mali, Morocco, the United Arab Republic, and the Interim Government of Algeria. Since other independent states refused to attend, those who did are called the – Casablanca Group; adopted African Charter establishing Pan-African Advisory Assembly, Pan-African Political, Economic and Cultural Committees as well as joint African Military Command. Also adopted were resolutions on Algeria, Palestine, Mauritania, Rwanda-Urundi, Congo, and on apartheid, the latter debated upon also by the Casablanca Group foreign ministers in Accra, Feb. 20–22, 1961;

1961 – Second Conference of Heads of State of Ghana, Guinea, and Mali, held in Accra, Apr. 26–29, concluded with the signing of the Charter of the Union of African States open to all other African states; the Charter went into force July 1, 1961.

1961 – Second Conference of the Brazzaville Group heads of state held Yaoundé, Mar. 27–30, founded African Malagasy Organization for Economic Cooperation (l'Organization afro-malgache de cooperation economique, OAMCE) and joint Society for Air Transport; adopted declaration on general policy of Member States of Afro-Malagasy Union;

1961 – Conference of Foreign Ministers of the Casablanca Group of states, held Cairo, May 3–5; adopted Protocol of the African Charter;

1961 – Pan-African Conference of Heads of State and Governments held in Monrovia, May 8–12, on the initiative of the 12 Brazzaville Group states, also attended by Ethiopia, Liberia, Libya, Nigeria, Sierra Leone, Somali, Togo, Tunisia, with the absence of the Casablanca Group. The 20 participating states came to be called the Monrovia Group; adopted 5 principles of peaceful coexistence of African states, dismissing as unrealistic the idea put forth by the Casablanca Group to build African unity through renouncement of sovereignty of individual states to the advantage of Pan-African supragovernmental political institutions;

1961 – Third Conference of Heads of State of the Brazzaville Group, held in Antamanarivo, Sept. 6–12, ending with the adoption and signing of Afro-Malagasy Defensive Union Charter and Pact, Afro-Malagasy Organization for Economic Co-operation Treaty, and Afro-Malagasy Union of Post and Telecommunications Convention;

1962 – Conference of Heads of State of the Monrovia Group, held Jan. 25–30 and boycotted by the Casablanca Group, which was invited to attend; prepared a preliminary African and Malagasy Republic Union Charter (L'Union Africaine et Malgache, UAM) and set up Finance Ministers Committee; adopted resolutions on Algeria, Congo, Angola, the South African Republic; established the Monrovia Group Secretariat at the UN; First UAM conference held at Bangi, Mar. 25–27; Second Conference held at Libreville, Sept. 10–13, where steps towards co-operation with the Casablanca Group were initiated;

1963 – First Assembly of Heads of Independent African States and Governments, held May 22–25, attended by 30 delegations of both Monrovia and Casablanca groups (Morocco did not attend because of its dispute over a coup d'etat with Mauritania and Togo); adopted the ▷ Charter of the Organization of African Unity and resolutions on decolonization, apartheid, attitude towards the UN, universal disarmament, and economic matters;

1963 – First Session of the OAU Ministers Council held at Dakar; First Special Session held at Addis Ababa, Nov. 18;

1963 – Third conference of Heads of UAM states, held at Ouagadougou, Upper Volta, admitted Rwanda as its 13th member; Fourth Conference held at Cotonou, Dahomey, July 27–30, decided to disband UAM group at the UN in connection with the setting up of OAU; admitted Togo as 14th member;

1964 – Meeting of Heads of State of Central and Equatorial Africa held at Fort-Lamy, Chad, attended by Chad, Gabon, Central African Republic, Cameroon and Republic of Congo; discussed proposal of setting up a customs and monetary union and economic co-operation; no final decision was taken;

1964 – OAU Conference held at Dar-es-Salaam, Tanganyika, Feb. 12–15; Second Special Session of Ministers Council for British intervention in Kenya, Uganda, and Tanganyika and border disputes of Somalia with Kenya and Ethiopia; Second Session of the Council held at Lagos, Nigeria, Feb. 24–29, attended by foreign ministers of 34 African states; Second Meeting of Heads of State from 33 countries (not attended by Democratic Republic of Congo), attended by UN Secretary General U Thant; Third Special Session of the Council held in Addis Ababa, Sept. 5–10, over the situation in the Democratic Republic of the Congo and South Rhodesia; Fourth Session called at New York, Dec. 15–21, over Belgian–American military intervention in Stanleyville;

1964 – Second Conference of Heads of UAM states at Dakar, Senegal, Feb. 15–18, decided to dissolve the Union and set up a new organization of an economic character: Afro-Malagasy Union for Economic Co-operation, l'Union africaine et malgache de coopération economique (UAMCE); First Session of UAMCE Foreign Ministers held at Nouakchott, the Mauritanian capital;

1965 – Conference of Heads of State of UAMCE countries held at Nouakchott, Feb. 10–12, resolved to replace the UAM with the Common Afro-Malagasy Organization (Organization Commune africaine et malgache, OCAM); First Extraordinary Conference of Heads of State of OCAM governments held at Abidjan following the diplomatic conflict of the Consultative Council (Dahomey, Upper Volta, Niger, Ivory Coast) with Ghana leader Kwame Nkrumah over their positive attitude towards Democratic Republic of the Congo led by Chombe. The Conference backed the Council and admitted the Democratic Republic to membership, which was opposed by Republic of the Congo (Brazzaville), Mauritania, and Cameroon. Congo-Brazzaville announced its intention to withdraw from OCAM; Mauritania withdrew from OCAM on July 7;

1965 – Conference of Heads of State of the Senegal River Riparian States, Mauritania, Mali, and Senegal (not attended by Guinea) held Saint-Louis, Feb. 13–15, set up the Inter-State Committee for the Senegal River States;

1965 – Meeting of Heads of State of Algeria, Ghana, Guinea and Mali held at Bamako and Conakry to draw up common lines of policy of states which chose a non-capitalist path of development towards the capitalist policy of OCAM states;

1965 – OAU Conference: Fourth Session of Council of Ministers held at Nairobi, Feb. 25–Mar. 9, to discuss key problems of Congo; Fifth Extraordinary Session of the Council of Ministers held at Lagos, June 10–13, over the controversy between OCAM states and Ghana as well as over the situation in Rhodesia; Third Assembly of Heads of State and Governments held at Accra Oct. 21–26 in which 8 out of 36 Member States did not take part because of their (Chad, Dahomey, Gabon, Upper Volta, Niger, Malagasy Republic, Togo, Ivory Coast) conflict with Ghana despite the meeting of Ghana President Kwame Nkrumah with the Consultative Council at Bamako, Oct. 13, during which he assured the Heads of State that Ghana would not grant asylum to political refugees from those countries. The refugee issue was one of the most controversial points of debate, as was Nkrumah's proposal for establishment of a Pan-African federal government; Sixth Extraordinary Session of the Consultative Council met at Addis Ababa, Dec. 3–5, to discuss the Rhodesian question. It recommended that OAU members break diplomatic relations with Great Britain; Conferences of Heads of State of Kenya, Tanzania and Uganda were held at Nairobi, Aug. 19–20 and at Mombasa, Aug. 31–Sept. 1. They discussed economic integration problems;

1966 – OCAM Conferences: First Conference of Foreign Ministers held at Tananarive, June 24–27, adopted OCAM Charter and examined the first draft for setting up a union of French-speaking states;

1966 – OAU Conference: Sixth Session of the Council of Ministers at Addis Ababa mostly devoted to South Rhodesia, annulled by majority decision the Sixth Extraordinary Session resolution on breaking diplomatic relations with Great Britain and as a result eight delegations abandoned the conference: Algeria, Guinea, Kenya, Republic of Congo, Mali, Tanzania, Somalia, the UAR; Fourth Assembly of Heads of State held at Addis Ababa, Oct. 5–9, with the president of Guinea absent;

1966 – Conference of Heads of Central and East African states held at Nairobi, Mar. 31–Apr. 2, attended by Ethiopia, Burundi, Kenya, the Democratic Republic of Congo, Malawi, Rwanda, Somalia, Sudan, Tanzania, Uganda, Zambia; main topics: economic integration and the problem of political refugees;

1966 – Conference of Heads of State of four members of the Consultative Council held at Abidjan, Apr. 6–7, devoted mainly to their conflict with Guinea. Next conference was held at Abidjan, June 7–8, and admitted Togo to membership; also discussed were economic integration problems and improvement of relations with Ghana;

1966 – Conference of Heads of Central and East African States: Kenya, Tanzania, and Uganda held at Nairobi, June 24–27, on economic integration;

1967 – Conference of Heads of Central and East African States held at Kinshasa, Feb. 12–14, attended by Burundi, Kenya, the Democratic Republic of Congo, the Republic of Congo (Brazzaville), the Central African Republic, Rwanda, Tanzania, Sudan, Uganda, and Zambia; adopted the Kinshasa Declaration on co-operation of participating states in collective security, economy, communications, and transport. The next conference was held at Kampala, Uganda, Dec. 15–16, dealing with implementation of the Kinshasa Declaration and the problem of white ▷ Mercenaries;

1967 – Conference of Heads of five African States: Algeria, Guinea, Mauritania, Tanzania and the UAR at Cairo (called also Meeting of Revolutionary States of

Africa) to deal with the Rhodesian issue and the international situation;

1967 – Fifth Assembly of Heads of State and Governments of the OAU at Kinshasa, Sept. 11–14, the Malawi delegation did not attend, criticized for its close relations with the Republic of South Africa; attended by UN Secretary General U Thant; adopted resolutions on settlement of internal African conflicts and eradication of colonialism;

1968 – Conference of Foreign Ministers of OCAM states at Niamey, Niger; also there on Jan. 19 – Conference of Heads of five States of Consultative Council; on Jan. 22–23 – Conference of Heads of OCAM States to discuss preparations for establishment of a Francophone community;

1968 – Conferences of Heads of State of Chad, Democratic Republic of Congo, and the Central African Republic held at Bangi, Feb. 1, to prepare establishment of the United States of Central Africa and at Fort-Lamy, Apr. 2, to sign a treaty on economic integration of participating states known as l'Union des Etats de l'Afrique Centrale (UAEC), open to other African states;

1968 – Conference of Heads of State of Senegal Riparian States held at Labe, Guinea, Mar. 24, ended with the signing of the Charter of Senegal Riparian States Organization (Organisation des Etats riveraines du Fleuve Senegal, (OERS), by Guinea, Mali, Mauritania, and Senegal;

1968 – OAU Conference: Conference of Council of Ministers at Addis Ababa, Feb. 20–24; meeting of Foreign Ministers held at Algiers, Sept. 3–12, Sixth Assembly of Heads of State and Governments at Algiers, Sept. 13–16 – celebration of the fifth anniversary of the OAU, attended by UN Secretary General U Thant as guest of honor;

1968 – Conference of Heads of State of Central and East African states held at Dar-es-Salaam, May 13–15, on regional economic co-operation;

1969 – Fourth Conference of Heads of State of OCAM, held at Kinshasa, Jan. 27–29;

1969 – OAU Conference: Twelfth Session of the Council of Ministers held at Addis Ababa, Feb. 17–22; also there thirteenth session, Aug. 27–Sept. 4, and on Sept. 6–10 – Sixth Assembly of Heads of State and Governments attended by UN Secretary General U Thant; adopted – among other things – a resolution extending the UN convention on political refugees, to African territory;

1969 – Francophone Conference at Niamey, Niger, Feb. 17–19, attended by 16 African states and 13 states from other continents;

1969 – Fifth Conference of Heads of State of Central and East Africa at Lusaka, Zambia, Apr. 14–16;

1970 – Sixth Conference of Heads of State of Central and East Africa at Khartoum; appointed a Sanctions Committee for monitoring the operation of African enterprises co-operating with the South African Republic and Rhodesia;

1970 – Conference of Heads of State of Senegal Riparian states held at Conakry; adopted decision to launch Mantanali dam project in Mali;

1970 – Conference of Heads of State of OCAM held at Yaoundé, Cameroon, Jan. 28–30, following admission of Mauritius to the organization renamed: Organization commune africaine, malgache et mauricienne (OCAMM);

1970 – Conference of Heads of State of West Africa held at Bamako, May 20–21, by seven member states of customs union of West African states (l'Union Douanière des Etats de l'Afrique de l'Ouest, UDEAD) founded in 1959; Dahomey, Upper Volta, Mali, Mauritania, Niger, Senegal, Ivory Coast affiliated since 1962 in monetary union, decided to establish an Economic Community of West Africa (Communauté économique de l'Afrique de l'Ouest, CEAO) the date of the formal signing of CEAO was scheduled for subsequent conference of heads of state, Nov. 1, 1971;

1971 – Annual Conference of Heads of OCAM states held at Fort-Lamy, Feb. 26, protesting against ever more outrageous interventions of European personages and political parties into the internal affairs of OCAM states;

1971 – Conference of Heads of OAU member states held at Addis Ababa, June 21–23; Conference of leaders of 14 Central and West African states held at Negadin; Conference of Heads of OERS (River

Senegal) states at Nouakchott ended with dissolution of the OERS;

1972 – Summit Meeting of the OAU held at Rabat, May 6–11, attended by 23 Heads of State and 18 representatives of Heads of State; elected N. Ekangahi from Cameroon as OAU Secretary General to succeed D. Telli from Guinea who resigned;

1972 – Summit Meeting of OCAM at Lome, May 25–27; Zaïre was absent;

1972 – Session of the Economic Community of West Africa, CEAO, at Bamako, June 6, initiated activity of the organization;

1973 – Meeting of presidents of Tanzania, Zambia, Zaïre held at Arusha, Tanzania, Feb. 3–6 on conflict between Zambia and Rhodesia;

1973 – Twentieth Session of the OAU Council of Ministers held at Addis Ababa, Feb. 5–9;

1973 – Second Conference of UN Economic Commission for Africa on relations of 30 African states with EEC (no agreement was reached) and development program for Africa until 1980 (resolutions adopted accordingly);

1973 – Conference of Heads of CEAO member states held at Abidjan, Apr. 16–17;

1973 – Tenth Conference of Heads of OCAM states held at Port-Louis, Mauritius, May 3–5;

1973 – First Conference of Economy and Finance Ministers of 37 African states held at Abidjan, May 9–13 (preceded by economic experts' conference at Addis Ababa, Apr. 27–30);

1973 – Tenth Anniversary Session of the OAU, held at Addis Ababa, May 24–26, attended by Heads of State and Governments;

1973 – OAU Conference held at Lagos, July 10–12, on relations with the EEC; adopted resolution on common front of OAU states in negotiations with the EEC;

1973 – Conference of leaders of Algeria, Morocco and Mauritania, held at Aghadir, Morocco, July 23–24, on ▷ Spanish Sahara;

1973 – Extraordinary Session of OCAM Council of Ministers held at Dakar, Aug. 9–10 on organizational reform;

1973 – Summit Conference of Chad, Upper Volta, Mali, Mauritania, Niger, Senegal held at Ouagadougou Sept. 11–12, on drought disaster;

1973 – Extraordinary Session of OAU Council of Ministers held at Addis Ababa, Nov. 19–21, on Middle East situation.

1974 – OAU Session on Middle East situation and Namibia.

1975 – OAU Extraordinary Session on Middle East situation, Namibia and Angola.

1976 – Extraordinary Session of the OAU on Angola situation.

1977 – Summit meeting of the OAU in Libreville, July 2 till 5; Conference on African future for the next 30 years and beyond, in Dakar, July 18 till 25;

1978 – Summit meeting of the OAU in Khartoum, in July;

1979 – Summit meeting of the OAU in Monrovia in July;

1980 – Summit meeting of the OAU in Free Town, in July;

1981 – Summit meeting of the OAU on Namibia, Ghana, Chad, in Freetown, in July;

1982 – Rump meeting in place of OAU Summit in Tripoli, Aug. 5–17, postponed because a boycott by 22 governments deprived it of a two-thirds quorum;

1982 – The Summit Meeting of the OAU in August in Tripoli was postponed after 19 members boycotted the meeting opposed to the dispute over the admission of the Sahrawi Arab Democratic Republic/SADR–Western Sahara/.

1983 – The 19th OAU Assembly of Heads of State met in June 1983 in Addis Ababa. The Assembly called for negotiation between the SADR and Morocco.

1984 – The 20th OAU Summit was held in November in Addis Ababa.

1985 – The West African Economic Community, CEAO, 10th Annual meeting in Brazzaville Oct. 17–19; and annual meeting in Lomé on Nov. 22–23; the 11th Franco-African summit in Bujumkura (Burundi) on Dec. 11–12; and the ▷ CEEAC summit in Brazzaville, Dec. 18.

1986 – On Febr. 12–13 the summit of the Conseil de l'entente ▷ African Entente was held in Yanoussoukro (Côte d'Ivoire); and the ▷ Lusophone African States summit meeting on Febr. 14–15 in Sao Tomé; Afro-

Asian Commemorative Session in Bandung, April 24–25; the Franco-African summit in Paris Dec. 11–13.

1987 – CEEAC summit Jan. 23–24; CEAO summit in Nouakchott, March 26–27; OAU in Addis Ababa on July 28–30, 1987 – OAU in Addis Ababa on July 24–26.

KEESING's *Contemporary Archive*, 1958–1984; KEESING's *Record of World Events*, 1985–1988.

AFRICANISTICS. An international term, for the study of things African, a subject of organized international co-operation.

Main Africanistic organizations reg. with the UIA:

African Museums Association, f. 1972 by The Livingstone Secretariat, Lusaka.

Association for the Taxonomic Study of Tropical African Flora, f. 1950, Uppsala (Sweden).

Association of African Geological Survey (Association des services géologiques africains), f. 1929, Paris.

Association of African Universities, f. 1967, Accra.

Historical Association of African Churches, f. 1962, Aberdeen (Great Britain).

International African Institute, f. 1926, London.

International African Law Association, f. 1959, Accra.

International Association for the Development of Documentation, Libraries and Archives in Africa, f. 1957, Dakar.

International Centre for African Sociology and Economic Documentation, f. 1961, Brussels.

International Congress of Africanists, f. 1962, Addis Ababa.

Society of African Culture (Société de Culture Africaine), f. 1957, Paris.

Standing Conference of African Universities Libraries, f. 1964, Nairobi.

West African Science Association, f. 1953, Freetown (Sierra Leone).

Yearbook of International Organizations.

AFRICANIZATION OF CUBA, 1912. A revolutionary political program of a group of Cuban Negroes proclaimed in Havana, 1912, together with the demand for withdrawal of US military forces from Cuban territory and for nationalization of all North-American property in Cuba (Cubanization of Cuba). ▷ Africa and Cuba.

AFRICAN LIBERATION DAY. First celebrated May 27, 1968 at UN Headquarters on the initiative of the OAU and African member states of the UN.

AFRICAN PETROLEUM PRODUCTION ASSOCIATION, est. on Jan. 26, 1987 in Lagos by African members of OPEC (Algeria, Gabon and Libya) and Angola, Benin, Cameroon and Egypt. On July 23–24, 1988 the first ministerial conference of APPA member states took place in Algiers (Algeria, Angola, Cameroon, Congo, Libya and Nigeria).

KEESING's *Record of World Events*, 1987.

AFRICAN POSTAL AGREEMENT, 1935. A colonial agreement founding the African Postal Union in the African dependencies of Great Britain, Belgium and Portugal. Signed in Pretoria, Oct. 30, 1935.

LNTS, Vol. 189, p. 41.

AFRICAN POSTAL UNION. Union Postale Africaine, est. Dec. 2, 1961 in Cairo by a Convention signed by the governments of Burundi, Egypt, Ghana, Guinea, Guinea-Bissau, Liberia, Libya, Mali, Mauritania, Somalia, Sudan, Zaïre.

Yearbook of International Organizations, 1986–87.

AFRICAN POSTS AND TELECOMMUNICATIONS UNION, f. 1975, Brazzaville, Congo. Members: governments of 12 countries: Benin, Burkina Faso, the Central African Republic, Chad, Congo, Côte d'Ivoire, Mali, Mauritania, Niger,

Rwanda, Senegal, Togo. Reg. with the UIA. Publ. *Revue UAPT*.

Yearbook of International Organizations, 1986–87.

AFRICAN SOLIDARITY FUND. A Fund est. Dec. 21, 1976 through an agreement of African Francophonic countries (Benin, Burkina Faso, Burundi, the Central African Republic, Chad, Côte d'Ivoire, Gabon, Mali, Mauritius, Rwanda, Senegal, Togo and Zaïre) with the French government, which undertook to cover 50% of the Fund.

Documentation Française, 1976; *Yearbook of International Organizations*, 1986–87.

AFRICAN TELECOMMUNICATION AGREEMENT, 1935. A colonial agreement founding the African Telecommunication Union in the African dependencies of Great Britain, Belgium and Portugal, signed in Pretoria, Oct. 30, 1935.

LNTS, Vol. 189, p. 51.

AFRICAN TRAINING AND RESEARCH CENTRE IN ADMINISTRATION FOR DEVELOPMENT, f. 1964 in Tangier, Morocco. Members: 29 African countries. Agreement with UNDP and UNESCO. Publ.*Cahiers Africains d'administration publique*, twice a year in English and French.

The Europa Yearbook 1987. A World Survey, Vol. 1, p. 217, London, 1988.

AFRICA'S DENUCLEARIZATION UN DECLARATION, 1965. The Organization of African Unity on July 21, 1964 solemnly announced a declaration on denuclearization of Africa and called on "all states to consider the African continent as a non-nuclear zone." The UN General Assembly on Dec 3, 1965 adopted Res. 2033/XX, relating to this Declaration:

"The General Assembly,
Believing in the vital necessity of saving contemporary and future generations from the scourge of a nuclear war,
Recalling its resolution 1652 (XVI) of Nov. 24, 1961, which called upon all Member States to refrain from testing, storing or transporting nuclear weapons in Africa and to consider and respect the continent as a denuclearized zone;
Recalling its resolution 2027 (XX) of Nov. 19, 1965 on the non-proliferation of nuclear weapons,
Observing that proposals for the establishment of denuclearized zones in various other areas of the world have also met with general approval,
Convinced that the denuclearization of various areas of the world would help to achieve the desired goal of prohibiting the use of nuclear weapons,
Considering that the Assembly of Heads of State and Government of the Organization of African Unity, at its first regular session, held at Cairo from 17 to 21 July 1964, issued a solemn declaration on the denuclearization of Africa in which the Heads of State and Government announced their readiness to undertake, in an international treaty to be concluded under the auspices of the United Nations, not to manufacture or acquire control of nuclear weapons,
Noting that this declaration on the denuclearization of Africa was endorsed by the Heads of State and Government of Non-Aligned countries in the Declaration issued on Oct. 10, 1964, at the close of their Second Conference, held at Cairo. Recognizing that the denuclearization of Africa would be a practical step towards the prevention of the further spread of nuclear weapons in the world and towards the achievements of general and complete disarmament and of the objectives of the United Nations,
1. Reaffirms its call upon all States to respect the continent of Africa as a nuclear-free zone;
2. Endorses the declaration on the denuclearization of Africa issued by the Heads of State and Government of African countries;

3. Calls upon all States to respect and abide by the aforementioned declaration;
4. Calls upon all States to refrain from the use, or the threat of use, of nuclear weapons on the African continent;
5. Calls upon all States to refrain from testing, manufacturing, using or deploying nuclear weapons on the continent of Africa, and from acquiring such weapons for taking any action which would compel African States to take similar action;
6. Urges those States possessing nuclear weapons and capability not to transfer nuclear weapons, scientific data or technological assistance to the national control of any State, either directly or indirectly, in any form which may be used to assist such States in the manufacture or use of nuclear weapons in Africa;
7. Expresses the hope that the African States will initiate studies, as they deem appropriate, with a view to implementing the denuclearization of Africa, and take the necessary measures through the Organization of African Unity to achieve this end;
8. Urges the African States to keep the United Nations informed of any further development in this regard;
9. Requests the Secretary-General to extend to the Organization of African unity such facilities and assistance as may be requested in order to achieve the aims of the present resolution".

UN Yearbook, 1965.

AFRIKAANS. Language of the Dutch colonists in South Africa, originating from the Dutch dialects of the 17th century, developed during the 19th century into a separate language (first newspaper 1875), and since 1915 the official language of the Union of South Africa. The attempt to introduce Afrikaans as a mandatory subject in schools for the non-white population caused a rebellion which resulted in strong repressions (June 1976 in Soweto) which were condemned by the UN General Assembly. See also ▷ Soweto Day. In July 1976 the South African administration annulled its decree on the obligatory teaching of Afrikaans.

E. ROSENTHAL, *Encyclopaedia of Southern Africa*, London, 1973.

AFRIKANERS. In the Boer language *Afrikaaners*. The official racist name for the white natives of South Africa, to distinguish them from dark-skinned Africans.

AFRO–AMERICAN ORGANIZATIONS. Organizations reg. with the UIA:

African-American Institute, f. 1953, New York.
Afro-American Cultural Foundation, f. 1918, White Plains, New York.
Afro-American Music Opportunities Association, f. 1969, Minneapolis, Minn., USA.
Afro-American Patrolmen's League, f. 1968, Chicago, USA.
Afro-American Society for International Relations, f. 1970, Washington DC, USA.
International Afro-American Museum, f. 1965, Detroit, USA.
Women's Africa Committee of the African–American Institute, f. 1954, Lexington, Ky., USA.

Yearbook of International Organizations, 1986–87.

AFRO–AMERICANS. North-American term for black US citizens accepted in the press and scientific literature in the 1980s.

Black-Americans or Afro-Americans, in: *The Concise Columbia Encyclopedia*, New York, 1983.

AFRO–ARABIC CONFERENCE, 1977. A summit meeting, Cairo, Mar. 1977, of chiefs of African and Arab states; Africa: Angola, Bechuana, Benin, Botswana, Burundi, the Central African Empire, Chad, Ethiopia, Gabon, Gambia, Ghana, Burkina Faso, Guinea, Guinea–Bissau, Equatorial Guinea, Cameroon, Kenya, the Comoros Islands, Congo, Lesotho, Liberia, Madagascar, Mali,

Mauritius, Mozambique, Niger, Nigeria, Rwanda, Senegal, Sierra Leone, Swaziland, Seychelles, Tanzania, Togo, Uganda, Sao Tomé and Principe, Zaïre, Zambia, Cape Verde, The Arab League was represented by: Algeria, Yemen, Saudi Arabia, Bahrain, Democratic Yemen, Egypt, Iraq, Jordan, Qatar, Kuwait, Lebanon, Libya, Mauretania, Morocco, Oman, Palestine (PLO), Sudan, Syria, Somalia, Tunisia, the United Arab Emirates. Adopted political and economical declarations stating the participants' "deep attachment to the principles of the nonaligned movement, peaceful co-existence and establishment of international economic order." Resolved that Arab and African leaders would meet every three years.

Document d'actualité internationale, No. 16–17, 1977.

AFRO–ASIA. An international political term used after World War II, introduced by solidarity conferences of African and Asian countries. The political and economic co-operation of these countries became a subject of international research. Delhi is headquarters for the Institute of Afro–Asian and World Affairs; publ. *Afro–Asian and World Affairs*; in Paris the information-analytical bulletin *Africasia* is published.

P. QUELLE, *Histoire de l'Afro–Asiatisme Jusqu'à Bandung: La Naissance du Thiers Monde*, Paris, 1965, p. 326.

AFRO–ASIAN HOUSING ORGANIZATION, AAHO, f. 1965, in Cairo, to promote Afro-Asian co-operation.

The Europa Yearbook 1987. A World Survey, Vol. 1, London, 1988.

AFRO–ASIAN INSTITUTE IN VIENNA, *Afro-Asiatisches Institut in Wien*, f. 1959 by Cardinal dr Franz König, Archbishop of Vienna. Publ. *Treffpunkte*.

AFRO–ASIAN ORGANIZATIONS. Reg. with the UIA:

Afro-Asian Federation for Tobacco Producers and Manufacturers, f. 1971, Cairo.
Afro-Asian Housing Organizations, f. 1965, Cairo.
Afro-Asian Institute for Co-operative and Labour Studies, f. 1965, Tel Aviv.
Afro-Asian Legal Consultative Committee, f. 1966, New Delhi.
Afro-Asian Organization for Economic Co-operation (AFRASEC), f. 1958, Cairo. Consultative status: ECOSOC, UNCTAD, UNIDO. Publ. *Afro-Asian Economic Review*.
Afro-Asian Pediatric Association, f. 1960, Karachi.
Afro-Asian Peoples Solidarity Organization (AAPSO), f. 1957, Cairo. Consultative status: ECOSOC. Publ. *Solidarity*.
Afro-Asian Rural Reconstruction Organization (AARRO), f. 1962, New Delhi. Publ. *Rural Reconstruction*.
Association of Schools of Public Health in Afro-Asian Regions, f. 1963, Manila, Philippines.
Federation of Afro-Asian Insurers and Reinsurers (FAIR), f. 1964, Cairo, Egypt. Consultative Status: ECOSOC, UNCTAD.
Organization of Afro-Asian–Latin-American Peoples Solidarity (OSPAAL), f. 1966, Havana. Publ. *Tricontinental Bulletin and Review*.
Permanent Bureau of Afro-Asian Writers, f. 1958, Cairo. Publ. *Lotus*.

Yearbook of International Organizations, 1986–87.

AFRO–ASIAN PEOPLES' SOLIDARITY ORGANIZATION, AAPSO. An inter-governmental institution, initiated May 2, 1954 at a Conference of Heads of Governments of Burma, Ceylon, India, Indonesia and Pakistan, held in Colombo, Ceylon; endorsed by the Bandung Conference, Apr. 18–24, 1955; in its present form since Jan. 1, 1958, headquarters Cairo; associates 69 countries of Asia and Africa (since 1967 debates not attended by the Chinese delegation). Reg. with the UIA. Aims: unite and co-ordinate struggle of Afro-Asian peoples against imperialism and colonialism, render assistance to national-liberation movements and ensure their economic, social and cultural development; implement and put into practice resolutions and recommendations adopted by conferences; promote and consolidate the Afro-Asian solidarity movement in all countries of both continents and act as permanent liaison body between different national solidarity movements.

Associated with AAPSO as observers are: OAU, Arab League, World Peace Council and other international and national organizations.

Organizations: Plenary Conference (twice a year), Council, Executive Committee, Permanent Secretariat, Asian and African Peoples' Solidarity Fund.

Official languages: Arabic, French, English. Publ.: *Afro-Asian Bulletin.*

Consultative status with ECOSOC, UNCTAD, UNESCO and UNIDO. Members: 82 African and Asian and 10 European associate members. Publ. *Socio-Economic Development and Progress* (quarterly).

Yearbook of International Organizations; The Europa Yearbook 1987. A World Survey, Vol. 1, p. 229, London, 1988.

AFRO-ASIAN RURAL RECONSTRUCTION ORGANIZATION, AARRO.
An inter-governmental institution est. 1962, New Delhi. Members: Algeria, Egypt, Ethiopia, Ghana, Kenya, Liberia, Morocco, Sierra Leone, Sudan, Tunisia; India, Iran, Iraq, Japan, Jordan, Korea S., Lebanon, Malaysia, the Philippines, Syria, Taiwan, the United Arab Emirates, Vietnam, Yemen DR.

Aims: "Develop understanding among members for a better appreciation of each other's problems and explore collectively opportunities for coordination of efforts for promoting welfare and eradication of hunger, thirst, illiteracy, disease and poverty among Afro-Asian rural people, thereby restructuring their rural communities and their rural economies and re-vitalizing their social life." Publ. *Rural Re-construction* Reg. with the UIA.

Yearbook of International Organizations; The Europa Yearbook 1987. A World Survey, Vol. 1, p. 216, London, 1988.

AFRO-ASIANS IN THE UN.
Since the first Afro-Asian Conference in 1955 in Bandung, African and Asian states began to express their solidarity at UN sessions in matters of decolonization and conditions of international trade.

F.S. BOUTROS, *La Groupe Afro-Asiatique dans le Cadre des Nations Unies*, Genève, 1963, p. 511; B. PFAHLBERG, *Zur Politik Afro-Asiatischer Staaten in den Vereinten Nationen, 1945–1960*, Baden-Baden, 1966.

AFRO-ASIAN SOLIDARITY CONFERENCES.
The first Conference - initiated by a summit conference between Burma, Ceylon, India, Indonesia and Pakistan, held in Colombo, Ceylon, Apr. 28–May 2, 1954 - was held in Bandung, Indonesia, and was attended by statesmen from twenty nine African and Asian countries: Afghanistan, Burma, Cambodia, Ceylon, China, Democratic Vietnam, Egypt, Ethiopia, the Gold Coast, India, Indonesia, Iran, Iraq, Japan, Jordan, Laos, Lebanon, Liberia, Libya, Nepal, Pakistan, the Philippines, the Republic of Vietnam, Saudi Arabia, Sudan, Syria, Thailand, Turkey, Yemen and leaders of liberation movements from Algeria, Cyprus, Malawi (then Nyassa), Tunisia and South-West Africa. The

Prime Minister of India, Jawaharlal Nehru, commented on the exceptional situation which had led to that conference: "Our countries represented here certainly differ much from one another, but they have one thing in common: they speak against the domination of Western powers on our continents." In its resolutions the conference condemned colonialism and demanded its complete liquidation; it demanded the universality of the UN. It adopted the ▷ Bandung Declaration which was aimed at securing universal peace and co-operation. Bandung gave rise to an international policy of ▷ Third World Nations and accelerated the disintegration of the colonial system; Second Afro-Asian Solidarity Conference was held in Cairo, Dec. 26, 1957–Jan. 1, 1958, where delegates from 44 Afro-Asian Solidarity National Committees resolved to establish a Permanent Secretariat of Afro-Asian Solidarity Conferences in Cairo; Third Conference was held in Cairo, Mar. 1961, while the fourth was held in Bandung in Apr., 1961. Aside from this, the Secretariat organized two special conferences to deal with economic matters held at Cairo, in Dec., 1958 and in May, 1960. Those two conferences created the Organization of Economic Co-operation of African and Asian States. In Apr., 1962, in Djakarta, a meeting was held of the representatives of states which attended the first Afro-Asian Solidarity Conference; they resolved to hold a "Bandung" of Heads of State, and invited all participants of Bandung I and all countries of Asia and Africa which had become independent in the period 1954–62, as well as Mongolia, South and North Korea, Cyprus, Kuwait, Western Samoa, the revolutionary government of Angola, and the leaders of liberation movements of Aden, South-West Africa and Southern Rhodesia. No agreement could be reached on the proposal to invite either the USSR, because of Chinese objections, or Malaysia because of Philippine and Indonesian objections. In 1964 the Soviet government again attempted to gain admittance to the proposed conference. However, Chinese opposition paralyzed preparations for Bandung II which failed to take place on either the first (Mar. 10, 1965), the second (June 29, 1965) or the third (Algiers, Nov. 5, 1965) scheduled dates. A meeting of 44 delegations from Afro-Asian states, called in Algiers between Oct. 30 and Nov. 1, 1965, decided to postpone Bandung II. However, the ▷ Afro-Asian Peoples Solidarity Organization (AAPSO) remained in Cairo.

On April 24–25, 1985 on the 30th anniversary of the ▷ Bandung Conference an Afro-Asian Conference to reestablish a true solidarity among Afro-Asian peoples took place in Bandung. The final declaration called for the negotiation of peaceful solutions in conflict areas.

G. MCTURNAU, *The Asian-African Conference*, Bandung, 1955; P.F. SMETS, *De Bandung a Moshi, Contribution à l'étude des Conférences Afro-Asiatique 1955–1963*, Bruxelles, 1964. 154 pp. KEESING's *Record of World Events*, March 1986.

AFRO-CUBAN CONFERENCE, 1976.
Summit meeting in Conakry, Guinea, Mar. 14, 1976 of the Heads of State of Angola, Guinea, Guinea-Bissau and Cuba.

KEESING's *Contemporary Archive*, 1976.

AFRO-MALAGASY ORGANIZATION FOR ECONOMIC CO-OPERATION.
Organization Africaine et Malgache de Co-opération Economique (OAMCE); regional inter-governmental economic organization of ten French-speaking African states, established at a summit meeting in Brazzaville on Dec. 15, 1960. Its name was changed in 1961 to ▷ African and Malagasy Union of Economic Co-operation (UAMCE).

AFRO-MALAGASY ORGANIZATIONS.
Reg. with the UIA:

African and Malagasy Coffee Organization, f. 1970, Paris.

African and Malagasy Council on Higher Education, f. 1968, Ougadougou.

African and Malagasy Industrial Property Office, f. 1962, Yaoundé.

African and Malagasy Union of Developments Bank, f. 1962, Yaoundé.

Agency for the Security of Aerial Navigation in Africa and Madagascar, f. 1959, Dakar.

Standing Technical Secretariat for the Conferences of Ministers of National Education in French-Speaking African and Malagasy States, f. 1968, Dakar.

Symposium of Episcopal Conferences of Africa and Madagascar, f. 1969, Accra.

Yearbook of International Organizations.

AGARD. ▷ NATO.

AGADIR.
A city (1981 pop. census: 248,800) and seaport on the Atlantic Ocean in south-western Morocco; the scene of a serious incident (on July 1, 1911) between France and Germany, which was started by a German cruiser occupying the seaport (in order to stress the Reich's interests in Morocco) and the German Reich invoking the provisions of the ▷ Algeciras Conference. The incident was ironed out by the Franco-German Agreement, of Nov. 4, 1911 guaranteeing to France full liberty in Morocco, but without detriment to economic interests of other Powers. The Agreement was abrogated by art. 141 of the ▷ Treaty of Versailles (1919). In 1960 destroyed by an earthquake.

Documents Diplomatique Français (1871–1914), 2e serie (1901–1911), Paris, 1930; F. HARTUNG, *Die Marokkokrise des Jahres 1911*, Berlin, 1927; H. CAMBON, *Histoire du Maroc*, Paris, 1952.

AGED ▷ Elderly and Aged.

AGFUND,
Arab Gulf Program for the UNDP, f. 1981 in Riyadh, Saudi Arabia to provide grants for projects carried out by UN organizations in the Arab Gulf Countries.

The Europa Yearbook 1987. A World Survey, Vol. 1, p. 217, London, 1988.

AGGIORNAMIENTO.
Italian = modernization; a giorno = in book-keeping the bringing of accounts up to the present day; an international term in the Roman Catholic Church referring to the adaptation of the Church to modern conditions; an expression used by John XXIII in the encyclical *Ad Petri cathedram* of June 29, 1959, in an Apostolic letter of Apr. 28, 1962, and at the opening of Vaticanum II, Oct. 11, 1962. The idea of accommodating the Church to the contemporary problems of the world, which continued to be supported by the successors of John XXIII.

N.J. WALSH, *Vatican City State*, Bibliography, Oxford, 1983.

AGGRESSION.
A term of international law denoting an attack of one or more states against another. The definition was subject of League of Nations' and UN work. A ban on aggression was introduced into international law by the ▷ Briand-Kellogg Treaty, 1928. First convention to deal with the definition of aggression was signed in London, July 3, 1933 on a Soviet initiative, drawn on the report on May 24, 1933 of the Disarmament Conference Security Committee (known as Politics Commission) which included a draft Convention with the Protocol. The Soviet Union recommended the signing to its neighbors (Afghanistan, Persia, Turkey, Romania, Poland, Latvia, Lithuania and Estonia), who signed on July 3, 1933; Finland

acceded on July 22, 1933 and Lithuania signed a bilateral treaty with the Soviet Union on July 5, 1933. The Soviet Union also signed a separate convention with Czechoslovakia, Romania, and Turkey, open for all states. The provisions are identical in all three conventions; all entered into force Oct. 20, 1933. See ▷ Aggression, Convention for the Definition of Aggression 1933.

In 1945, the Charter of International Military Tribunal at Nuremberg art. 6, p. 2 recognized as "crimes against peace" any "planning, preparing, and initiating of war aggression" which the UN International Law Commission acknowledged on July 29, 1950, as one of the principles of international law in the Nuremberg Provisions (▷ Nuremberg Principles).

In 1950 the Soviet Union submitted to the UN General Assembly a draft A/CL/608 of a universal convention to give a more specific definition of aggression. The motion was passed by the UN General Assembly Res. 378B/V of Nov. 17, 1950 to the International Law Committee. On Dec. 20, 1952 the UN General Assembly Res. 688/VII set up a Commission for the definition of aggression. Two years later Res. 895/IX of Dec. 4, 1954, confirmed by Res. 1181/XII of Nov. 29, 1957, established a new commission composed of 21 national delegates from Argentina, Bulgaria, Costa Rica, Cyprus, Czechoslovakia, Denmark, France, Ghana, Greece, Italy, Liberia, Mexico, The Netherlands, Nigeria, the Philippines, Poland, Taiwan, Tunisia, the UK, the USA, and the USSR.

The Commission held sessions at UN New York headquarters between Oct.–Nov. 1956, April 1959, April 1962, April 1965 and April 1967. On Dec. 18, 1967 the UN General Assembly adopted by a majority of votes (one against and 18 abstentions) Res. 2320/XII providing that the working-out of the definition of aggression would be of serious consequence to maintenance of international peace. A new commission composed of 34 experts on international law from countries appointed by the Chairman of the UN General Assembly: Algeria, Australia, Bulgaria, Canada, Colombia, Cyprus, Czechoslovakia, Egypt, Ecuador, Finland, France, Ghana, Guyana, Haiti, Indonesia, Italy, Mexico, Norway, the Malagasy Rep., Romania, Sierra Leone, Spain, Sudan, Syria, Turkey, Uganda, the UK, Uruguay, the USA, the USSR, Zaïre. The Commission debated in Geneva in June–July 1968 and in New York in Feb. 1969. On Apr. 3, 1973 a preliminary draft of the document was prepared in Geneva by a special committee. The Commission ended its activity on Apr. 12, 1974 by adopting the draft definition of aggression which was finally confirmed in UN General Assembly Res. 3314/XXIX of Dec. 14, 1974, ▷ Aggression, UN Definition 1974.

J.T. SHOTTWELL, *War as an Instrument of National Policy and its Renunciation in the Pact of Paris*, London, 1929; C. EAGLETON, "The Attempt to Define Aggression", in: *International Conciliation*, No. 264, 1930; R. VIGNOL, *Définition de l'agresseur dans la guerre*, Paris, 1933; E. SARRA, *L'aggressione internazionale*, Roma, 1946; S. GLUECK, *The Nuremberg Trial and Aggressive War*, London, 1947; G. LEIBHOLZ, "'Aggression' als zeitgeschichtliches Problem", in: *Vierteljahrshefte für Zeitgeschichte*, No. 6, 1958; J.D. CARTHY, E.J. EALING, *Historia Natural de la Agresión*, México DF, 1967; SIPRI, *World Armaments and Disarmament Yearbook* 1973, pp. 446–49, 462–65; "The Question of Defining Aggression", in: *UN Yearbook* 1973, pp. 780–786; and in: *UN Yearbook* 1974; "Aggression", in: E.J. OSMAŃCZYK, *Enciclopedia Mundial de las Relaciones Internacionales y Naciones Unidas*, México DF, 1976, pp. 32–34. R.L. BLEDSOE, B.A. BOCZEK, *The International Law Dictionary*, Oxford, 1987.

AGGRESSION, CONVENTION FOR THE DEFINITION OF AGGRESSION, 1933. A Convention signed on July 3, 1933, on the premises of the Soviet Embassy in London by representatives of eight nations. The text is as follows:

"The Central Executive Committee of the USSR, His Majesty the King of Afghanistan, the President of the Esthonian Republic, the President of the Latvian Republic, His Majesty the Shah of Persia, the President of the Polish Republic, His Majesty the King of Romania, and the President of the Turkish Republic. Impelled by the desire to strengthen the peace existing between their countries.

Believing that the Briand-Kellogg Pact /Pact of Paris/ to which they are signatories forbids all aggression.

Deeming it necessary in the interests of universal security to define as closely as possible the conception of aggression, in order to eliminate every pretext for its justification.

Declaring that every State has an equal right to independence, security, defense of its territory and free development of its State system.

Inspired by the desire in the interests of universal peace to assure all nations of the inviolability of the territory of their countries.

Considering it useful in the interests of universal peace to put into force as between their countries precise rules for the definition of aggression, pending the universal recognition of these rules.

Have decided for this purpose to conclude the present convention and have duly accredited: The Central Executive Committee of the USSR – Maxim Litvinov, People's Commissar for Foreign Affairs; His Majesty the King of Afghanistan – Ali Mohammed Khan, Minister of Education; the President of the Esthonian Republic – Dr Oscar Kallas, Envoy Extraordinary and Minister Plenipotentiary in London: the President of the Latvian Republic – Mr Waldemaras Salnais, Minister of Foreign Affairs; His Majesty the Shah of Persia – Fatolla-Khan Nury Esfendiary, Chargé d'Affaires in London; the President of the Polish Republic – M. Edouard Raczynski, Permanent Polish Representative to the League of Nations and Envoy Extraordinary and Minister Plenipotentiary; His Majesty the King of Romania – M. Nikolas Titulescu, Minister of Foreign Affairs; the President of the Turkish Republic, Towfik Rustu-Bey, Minister of Foreign Affairs.

Who have agreed upon the following provisions:

Article I. Each of the high contracting parties undertakes to recognize in its relations with each of the other parties, beginning with the day this convention enters into effect, the definition of aggressor outlined in the report of the Security Committee of May 24, 1933 (the Politic Report), at the Disarmament Conference, based upon the proposal of the Soviet delegation.

Article II. In accordance with the above, the aggressor in an international conflict, with due consideration to the agreements existing between the parties involved in the conflict, will be considered the State which will be the first to commit any of the following acts:

1. Declaration of war against another State;
2. Invasion by armed forces, even without a declaration of war, of the territory of another State;
3. An attack by armed land, naval or air forces, even without a declaration of war, upon the territory, naval vessels or aircraft of another State;
4. Naval blockade of the coasts or ports of another State;
5. Aid to armed bands formed on the territory of a State and invading the territory of another State, or refusal, despite demands on the part of the State subjected to attack to take all possible measures on its own territory to deprive the said bands of any aid and protection.

Article III. No considerations of a political, military, economic or any other nature can serve as an excuse or justification of aggression as specified in Article II (see below for explanation).

Article IV. This convention will be ratified by the high contracting parties in accordance with the laws of each of them.

Ratification papers will be deposited by each of the high contracting parties with the government of the USSR. As soon as ratification papers are deposited by two of the high contracting parties, the present convention enters into force between the said two parties. As each of the other high contracting parties deposits its ratification papers the convention will enter into force for it. Notice of each deposition of ratification papers will be immediately given to each of the signatories of this convention by the government of the USSR.

Article V. The present convention has been drawn up in eight copies, one of which is entrusted to each of the contracting parties, in confirmation of which the abovementioned representatives have signed the present convention and affixed their seal thereto."

On July 4, 1933, on the premises of the Soviet Embassy in London, a second Convention was signed by the USSR, Turkey, and the countries of the Little Entente (Czechoslovakia, Romania and Yugoslavia).

This convention is identical with the eight-power convention of July 3, 1933, except for Article IV, which reads as follows:

"The present convention is open for adherence by all other countries. Adherence will carry the same rights and obligations as in the case of the original signatories. Notification of adherence shall be made to the government of the Soviet Union which will immediately notify the other participants.

Appendix to art. III:

The high contracting parties which have signed the convention defining aggression, desirous, while retaining the complete inviolability of the absolute meaning of the rule formulated in Article III of the said convention, of giving certain indications permitting the determination of an aggressor, establish that none of the circumstances mentioned below may be used to justify any act of aggression in the sense of Article II of the said convention:

The internal position of any State, as for example: its political, economic or social structure; alleged shortcomings of its administration; disorder following upon strikes, revolutionary or counter-revolutionary movements, and civil war;

The international conduct of any State, as, for example: infringement or a threat of infringing the material or moral rights or interests of a foreign State or its citizens; rupture of diplomatic or economic relations; measures of economic or financial boycott; conflicts in the sphere of economic, financial or other obligations in connection with foreign governments; border incidents which do not fall under any of the cases of aggression indicated in Article II. At the same time the high contracting parties unanimously recognize that the present convention must in no case serve to justify the infringements of international law which might fall under the obligations included in the foregoing list."

Soviet Union Review. Special Supplement, July–August., 1933.

AGGRESSION, POLICY OF CONDEMNATION OF AGGRESSION BY THE AMERICAN REPUBLICS, 1890–1928. The policy of non-recognition of territorial acquisition obtained by means of war and condemnation of all aggression reflected in official inter-American documents:

1890, Recommendation of the First International American Conference, Apr. 18, 1890, adopted by Delegates of Bolivia, Brazil, Argentina, Colombia, Costa Rica, Ecuador, Guatemala, Haiti, Honduras, Mexico, Nicaragua, Paraguay, Peru, Salvador, Venezuela and the United States (Chile abstained from voting):

"First. That the principle of conquest shall not, during the continuance of the treaty of arbitration, be recognized as admissible under American public law.

"Second. That all cessions of territory made during the continuance of the treaty of arbitration shall be void if made under threats of war or in the presence of an armed force.

"Third. Any nation from which such cessions shall be exacted may demand that the validity of the cession so made shall be submitted to arbitration.

"Fourth. Any renunciation of the right to arbitration, made under the conditions named in the second section, shall be null and void."

1926, Project No. 30 of the American Institute of International Law, Oct. 1926;

"Conquest

"The American Republics . . . animated by the desire of preserving the peace and prosperity of the continent, for which it is indispensable that their mutual relations be based upon principles of justice and upon respect for law, solemnly declare as a fundamental concept of American international law, that, without criticizing territorial acquisitions effected in the past, and without reference to existing controversies –

"In the future territorial acquisitions obtained by means of war or under the menace of war or in presence of an armed force, to the detriment of any American Republic, shall not be lawful; and that

"Consequently territorial acquisitions effected in the future by these means can not be invoked as conferring title; and that

"Those obtained in the future by such means shall be considered null in fact and in law."

1928, Resolution of the Sixth International Conference of American States:

"Resolves:

"1. All aggression is considered illicit and as such is declared prohibited.

"2. The American States will employ all pacific means to settle conflicts which may arise between them."

Documents illustrating the origins of the policy of non-recognition of the American Republics, in: *International Conciliation*, No. 293, New York, October. 1933, pp. 461–477.

AGGRESSION, UN DEFINITION, 1974. A
definition adopted by the UN General Assembly Res. 3314/XXIX, Dec. 14, 1974. The text is as follows:

"The General Assembly,

Having considered the report of the Special Committee on the Question of Defining Aggression, established pursuant to its resolution 2330 /XXII/ of Dec. 18, 1967, covering the work of its seventh session held from Mar. 11 to Apr. 12, 1974, including the draft Definition of Aggression adopted by the Special Committee by Consensus and recommended for adoption by the General Assembly,

Deeply convinced that the adoption of the Definition of Aggression would contribute to the strengthening of international peace and security,

1. Approves the Definition of Aggression, the text of which is annexed to the present resolution;

2. Expresses its appreciation to the Special Committee on the Question of Defining Aggression for its work which resulted in the elaboration of the Definition of Aggression;

3. Calls upon all States to refrain from all acts of aggression and other uses of force contrary to the Charter of the United Nations and the Declaration on Principles of International Law concerning Friendly Relations and Co-operation among States in accordance with the Charter of the United Nations;

4. Calls the attention of the Security Council to the Definition of Aggression, as set out below, and recommends that it should as appropriate, take account of that Definition as guidance in determining, in accordance with the Charter, the existence of an act of aggression.

Annex. Definition of Aggression. The General Assembly,

Basing itself on the facts that one of the fundamental purposes of the United Nations is to maintain international peace and security and to take effective collective measures for the prevention and removal of threats to the peace, and for the suppression of acts of aggression or other breaches of the peace.

Recalling that the Security Council, in accordance with art. 39 of the Charter of the United Nations, shall determine the existence of any threat to the peace, breach of the peace or act of aggression and shall make recommendations, or decide what measures shall be taken in accordance with arts. 41 and 42, to maintain or restore international peace and security.

Recalling also the duty of States under the Charter to settle their international disputes by peaceful means in order not to endanger international peace, security and justice. Bearing in mind that nothing in this Definition shall be interpreted as in any way affecting the scope of the provisions of the Charter with respect to the functions and powers of the organs of the United Nations.

Considering also that, since aggression is the most serious and dangerous form of the illegal use of force, being fraught, in the conditions created by the existence of all types of weapons of mass destructions, with the possible threat of a world conflict and all its catastrophic consequences, aggression should be defined at the present integrity,

Reaffirming also that the territory of a State shall not be violated by being the object, even temporarily, of military occupation or of other measures of force taken by another State in contravention of the Charter, and that it shall not be the object of acquisition by another State resulting from such measures of the threat thereof. Reaffirming also the provisions of the Declaration on Principles of International Law concerning Friendly Relations and Co-operation among States in accordance with the Charter of the United Nations. Convinced that the adoption of a definition on aggression ought to have the effect of deterring a potential aggressor, would simplify the determination of acts of aggression and the implementation of measures to suppress them and would also facilitate the protection of the rights and lawful interests of, and the rendering of assistance to, the victim. Believing that, although the question whether an act of aggression has been committed must be considered in the light of all the circumstances of each particular case, it is nevertheless desirable to formulate basic principles as guidance for such determination.

Adopts the following Definition of Aggression:

Art. 1. Aggression is the use of armed force by a State against the sovereignty, territorial integrity or political independence of another State, or in any other manner inconsistent with the Charter of the United Nations, as set out in this Definition.

Explanatory note: In this Definition the term "State":
(a) is used without prejudice to questions of recognition or to whether a State is a member of the United Nations;
(b) includes the concept of a "group of States" where appropriate.

Art. 2. The first use of armed force by a State in contravention of the Charter shall constitute prima facie evidence of an act of aggression although the Security Council may, in conformity with the Charter conclude that a determination that an act of aggression has been committed would not be justified in the light of other relevant circumstances, including the fact that the act concerned or their consequences are not of sufficient gravity.

Art. 3. Any of the following acts, regardless of a declaration of war, shall, subject to and in accordance with the provisions of art. 2, qualify as an act of aggression:
(a) The invasion or attack by the armed forces of a State of the territory of another State, or any military occupation, however temporary, resulting from such invasion or attack, or any annexation by the use of force of the territory of another State or part thereof;
(b) Bombardment by the armed forces of a State against the territory of another State or the use of any weapons by a State against the territory of another State;
(c) The blockade of the ports or coasts of a State by the armed forces of another State;
(d) An attack by the armed forces of a State on the land, sea or air forces, or marine and air fleets of another State;
(e) The use of armed forces of one State which are within the territory of another State with the agreement of the receiving State, in contravention of the conditions provided for in the agreement or any extension of their presence in such territory beyond the termination of the agreement;
(f) The action of a State in allowing its territory, which it has placed at the disposal of another State, to be used by that other State for perpetrating an act of aggression against a third State;
(g) The sending by or on behalf of a State of armed bands, groups, irregulars or mercenaries, which carry out acts of armed force against another State of such gravity as to amount to the acts listed above, or its substantial involvement therein.

Art. 4. The acts enumerated above are not exhaustive and the Security Council may determine that other acts constitute aggression under the provisions of the Charter.

Art. 5. 1. No consideration of whatever nature, whether political, economic, military or otherwise, may serve as a justification for aggression.
2. A war of aggression is a crime against international peace. Aggression gives rise to international responsibility.
3. No territorial acquisition or special advantage resulting from aggression is or shall be recognized as lawful.

Art. 6. Nothing in this Definition shall be construed as in any way enlarging or diminishing the scope of the Charter, including its provisions concerning cases in which the use of force is lawful.

Art. 7. Nothing in this Definition, and in particular art. 3, could in any way prejudice the right to self-determination, freedom and independence, as derived from the Charter, of peoples forcibly deprived of that right and referred to in the Declaration on Principles of International Law concerning Friendly Relations and Co-operation among States in accordance with the Charter of the United Nations, particularly peoples under colonial and racist regimes or other forms of alien domination; nor the right of these peoples to struggle to that end and to seek and receive support, in accordance with the principles of the Charter and in conformity with the above-mentioned Declaration.

Art. 8. In their interpretation and application the above provisions are interrelated and each provision should be construed in the context of the other provisions." (Explanatory notes on arts. 3 and 5 are to be found in par. 20 of the report of the Special Committee on the Question of Defining Aggression (A)9619 and Corr. (1). Statements on the Definition are contained in pars. 9 and 10 of the report of the Sixth Committee (A9890).)

UN Yearbook 1974, pp. 846–848.

AGLINET. Union List of Serials, one of the information systems of the ▷ FAO.

AGING. ▷ Elderly and Aged.

AGM An abbreviation for air-to-ground missile.

AGRARIANISM. A doctrine claiming that agriculture constitutes the basis of national economy; developed in the interwar period in Central and East Europe; applied after World War II to colonial regions, and subsequently to the Third World countries.

AGRARIAN REFORM. The distribution of large private or state landownings among the landless and small-farm-holders in order to alter the agrarian structure; subject of international debates and UN recommendations. Res. 401/V of the General Assembly, Nov. 20, 1950 recommended that ECOSOC propose measures with a view to improving the living conditions of the rural populations and laid special emphasis on the institution of agrarian reform. ECOSOC studies gave rise to Res. 524/V of the UN General Assembly, Jan. 12, 1952, which acknowledged that the general program of agrarian reform requires large-scale investment and addressed all governments which wished to realize the reform program to pay special attention to the necessity of raising adequate funds. The UN General Assembly's further concern with the promotion of agrarian reform is reflected in Res. 625/VII of Dec. 21, 1952 and 826/IX of Dec. 11, 1954 as well as ECOSOC recommendations Res. 370/XIII of Sept. 7, 1951, 512/XVII of Apr. 30, 1954, 649B/XXIII of Dec. 2, 1957, and 712/XXVII of Apr. 17, 1961. Adopted on Dec. 5, 1959 on the initiative of Mexico was UN General Assembly Res. 1426/XIV recognizing the significance of changes in agrarian structure to many less-developed countries as well as Res. 1526/XV of Dec. 15, 1960 in which for the first time it recognized that agrarian reform very often is one of the basic factors of the general development of agriculture. Held in June–July 1966 was the First UN World Conference on Agrarian Reform which recommended unanimously that FAO should assist countries in planning and implementing the program of agricultural reform and also resolved to convene international conferences devoted to technological, social and economic aspects of agrarian reform. A World Conference on Agrarian Reform and Rural Development was held in Rome from July 12 to 20, 1979 under the auspices of the FAO. In the Declaration of Principles the Conference stated: (1) that a program of action on agrarian reform and rural development should be founded on guidelines and principles which included: recognition that the fundamental purpose of development was individual and social betterment, development of endogenous capabilities and improvement of the living standards of all peoples, especially the rural poor; every state's right to exercise full and permanent sovereignty over its natural resources and economic activities; use of foreign investments in accordance with national priorities; redistribution of national economic and political power, and fuller integration of rural areas into national development; application of appropriate population policies; mobilization of domestic resources; incentives for increased investment and production; equitable distribution and ecologically balanced and efficient use of land, water and other productive resources diversification of rural economic activities; mutually reinforcing links between agriculture and industrial development; participation of all rural people, including women and youth, in policy-making; efficient communications to improve understanding and awareness of problems at all levels; constant vigilance to ensure nonrecurrence of past concentration of resources in private hands or emergence of new forms of inequity; strengthening of international co-operation and increasing flows of financial and technical resources; intensifying efforts by governments to ensure world food security, overcome inequities and stabilize agricultural commodity trade; and strengthening technical co-operation and collective self-reliance among developing countries. (2) The Conference also invited international organizations, with FAO as the lead agency, to monitor agrarian reform and rural development, analyze and disseminate information, expand technical assistance activities, and assist in mobilizing resources. The UN General Assembly adopted the Declaration of Principles without vote (Res. 34/189 on Dec. 18, 1979).

Agrarian Reform with Particular References to Employment and Social Aspects, ILO Geneva, 1964, 164 pp.; O. DELGADO, *Reforma Agraria en América Latina. Processos y Perspectivas*, México DF, 1967, 766 pp.; *UN Yearbook* 1979, pp. 500–503; *UN Chronicle*, January, 1980, p. 67; *Everyone's United Nations*, New York, 1987.

AGREE TO DISAGREE. A mutual understanding in negotiations that in the specific case agreement has proved impossible in view of diametrically opposed positions of negotiating parties. In 1954 this term was used to define the result of the Berlin Conference of Four Powers on German unification.

AGRÉMENT. An initial consent of a state to receive a diplomatic representative appointed by another state. The consent is expressed in the form of agréementation. The refusal of agrément precludes accreditation and is a sign that the proposed person is considered a *persona non grata* in the receiving state.

J. MONTE-RADLOVIC, *Etiquette et Protocole*, Paris, 1956; R.L. BLEDSOE, B.A. BOCZEK, *The International Law Dictionary*, Oxford, 1987.

AGRICULTURAL DEVELOPMENT INTERNATIONAL FUND. ▷ IFAD.

AGRICULTURE. A subject of international co-operation. Organizations reg. with the UIA:

Asian Vegetable Research and Development Center, f. 1971, Tainan, Taiwan, Publ. *Annual Report*.
Association for the Advancement of Agricultural Sciences in Africa, f. 1968, Addis Ababa.
Committee of Agricultural Organizations in the EEC, f. 1958, Brussels.
Commonwealth Bureau of Agricultural Economics, f. 1960, Oxford, UK.
Consultative Group on International Agricultural Research, f. 1971, Washington, DC.
East African Agriculture and Forestry Research Organization (EARAFRO), f. 1948, Nairobi. Publ. *East African Agriculture and Forestry Journal*.
East African Agricultural Economics Society, f. 1967, Kampala, Uganda.
European Committee of Associations of Manufacturers and Agricultural Machines, f. 1959, Paris.
European Confederation of Agriculture, f. 1948, Paris.
European Society of Nuclear Methods in Agriculture, f. 1969, Wageningen, Netherlands. Consultative status: FAO, IAEA.
Food and Agricultural Organization of the UN (▷ FAO). General Union of Chambers of Commerce Industry and Agriculture for Arab Countries, f. 1951, Beirut. Publ. *The Arab Economic Report*.
Inter-American Institute of Agricultural Science of the OAS, f. 1942, San José de Costa Rica.
International Agricultural Aviation Center, f. 1958, The Hague, Consultative status: FAO. Publ. *Agricultural Aviation*.
International Agricultural Development Council, f. 1960, Durham, NC, USA.
International Association on Mechanization of Field Experiment f. 1964, Sollebal, Norway.
International Agricultural Co-operative, f. 1929, Rotterdam.
International Agricultural Exchange Association, f. 1963, Copenhagen.
International Center for Agricultural Education, f. 1958, Berne.
International Centre for Tropical Agriculture, CIAT (Centro Internacional de Agricultura Tropical), f. 1967 Cali. Publ.: *CIAT International*.
International Commission for Agricultural Industries, f. 1934, Paris, FAO.
International Commission of Agricultural Engineering, f. 1930, Paris. Consultative status: ECOSOC, UNESCO, FAO.
International Committee of Mastics in Agriculture, f. 1950, Paris.
International Committee of Scientific Management in Agriculture f. 1950, Paris.
International Confederation for Agriculture Credit, f. 1932, Zurich, FAO.
International Confederation of Technical Agricultural Engineers, f. 1930, Zurich. Publ. *La Technique Agricole*.
International Federation on Agricultural Journalists, f. 1959, Rome.
International Federation of Agricultural Executive, f. 1973, Paris.
International Federation of Agriculture Producers, f. 1946, Paris. Consultative status: ECOSOC, UNCTAD, FAO, ICO, WMO, UNICEF, OECD, Council of Europe.
International Federation of Organic Agriculture Movements, f. 1972, Huelgoat, France.
International Federation of Plantation, Agricultural and Allied Workers, f. 1959, Geneva.
International Institute of Tropical Agriculture, f. 1967, Itadan, Nigeria. Publ. *Research Highlights*.
International Liaison Center for Agricultural Machinery Distributors and Maintenance, f. 1953, The Hague.
International Movement of Catholic Agricultural and Rural Youth, f. 1954, Brussels.
International Secretariat of Catholic Technologists, Agriculturalists and Economists, f. 1951, Paris.
International Secretariat for Research on the History of Agricultural Implements, f. 1954, Copenhagen.
International Service for National Agricultural Research, f. 1980, The Hague.
International Working Group on Soilless Culture, f. 1955, Wageningen, Netherlands.
Royal Agricultural Society of the Commonwealth, f. 1957, London.

Scandinavian Agricultural Research Workers Association, f. 1918, Oslo.
Tropical Agricultural Research and Training Center, f. 1977 Turrialbo, Costa Rica.
World Federation of Agricultural Workers, f. 1921, Brussels. Publ. Landworkers.
See also ▷ Tropical Agriculture.

FAO, *Agriculture–Forward 2000*, Rome, 1981; *Yearbook of International Organizations*; *The Europa Yearbook 1988. A World Survey*, Vol. 1, London, 1988.

AGRICULTURE AND FOOD INDUSTRY IN THE CMEA SYSTEM. In May 1956 a special organisation, The Permanent Agricultural Commission, was created within the CMEA system, with the task of co-ordinating plans for agricultural production. In July 1963 The Permanent Commission of the Food Industry was formed, with headquarters in Sofia. By 1970 a division of labour was introduced in agriculture as well as in the food industry. The Twenty-Fifth Session of CMEA in Bucharest in July 1971 ratified the Comprehensive Program of CMEA which established the basic directions and tasks for the development of co-operation in both fields.
In 1988 the CMEA began discussing new methods of agricultural production and reshaping the food industry in the spirit of ▷ perestroika.

S. AUSCH, *Theory and Practice of CMEA Co-operation*, Budapest, 1972; J.F. BROWN, *Eastern Europe and Communist Rule*, Durham N.C., 1988; Z.A. MEDVEDEV, *Soviet Agriculture*, New York, 1988.

AGRICULTURE FUND. A financial institution est. 1931, called Fund A, created by the Bank for International Settlements, BIS, in Basel by a convention signed Aug. 21, 1931 by Great Britain, France, Hungary, Italy and Switzerland in reference to the resolutions of the ▷ Trianon Treaty, 1930.

AGRIS. An official name for the international Information System for the Agricultural Sciences and Technology, est. 1975 by FAO in Rome. AGRIS has two main purposes: (1) to provide fast information about the documentation on the development of individual agricultural sciences and technology; (2) to prepare complex issues, analyses, biographies etc. for national scientific information centers. The Abidjan Conference for Development in Africa, 1968, was the initiator of AGRIS. The Computerized Agricultural Research Information System ▷ CARIS is complementary to AGRIS.

FAO. *The State of Food and Agriculture. A Yearbook*, Rome, 1974 ff.

AGROMASH. International Society for Machines for Vegetable Growing, Horticulture and Viticulture, est. 1964 by agreement signed by the governments of Bulgaria and Hungary, in operation as of Mar. 1, 1965; in Jan., 1965 the USSR joined and on Jan. 1, 1973 the GDR. A new Charter of the International Agromash Society entered into force in 1973.

W.E. BUTLER (ed.), *A Source Book on Socialist International Organizations*, Alphen, 1978.

AGUDATH YISRAEL WORLD ORGANIZATION, *Hebrew*: Union of Israel. A Jewish organization created at the Congress of Orthodox Jews at Katowice in 1912; in the interwar period it was converted into a right-wing Jewish party taking part in Polish elections and being represented in Polish, Romanian, and Lithuanian parliaments; since 1949, represented in the Israeli parliament; maintains at the same time its status of an international organization; Reg. with the UIA.
Consultative Status with ECOSOC and UNESCO. Members: over 500.000 in 25 countries. Publ.

Hamodin (Jerusalem daily), *Jewish Observer* (New York monthly), *Jewish Tribune* (London weekly), *Jüdische Stimme* (Zürich monthly), and *La Voz Judia* (Buenos Aires monthly).

Yearbook of International Organizations; The Europa Yearbook 1987. A World Survey, Vol. 1, p. 246, London, 1988.

AGV, f. Avion à grand vitesse, acronym of the French airship industry, 1987.

Le Point, 16 III, 1987.

AIDE MEMOIRE. A note handed over or sent "*pro memoria*" after a diplomatic conversation to avoid misunderstanding in respect of statements made orally.

AID, INTERNATIONAL. An international term with diverse meanings: (1) defined by bilateral norms, international legal assistance; (2) defined by an international convention of 1977 for assistance to countries struck by natural catastrophes; (3) organized international economic or technical assistance, usually under UN auspices, for developing countries and also for saving cultural treasures (e.g. ▷ Abu Simbel).

AIDS. Acquired Immune Deficiency Syndrome. A new epidemic disease caused by a virus called since 1984 LAV/HTLV-III detected in blood, semen and saliva. Object of I International Conference on AIDS in Apr. 1985 in Atlanta.

Officially as of 9 December, 1987, 128 countries had reported a cumulative total of 72.004 cases of AIDS since the 1970's – about half the total AIDS cases estimated to have occurred to date (150,000).

The year 1988 was proclaimed by a World Summit of Ministers of Health in London, January, 1988, the Year of Communication and Co-operation about AIDS.

In May, 1988, the WHO reported the continued increase of AIDS cases officially reported to the WHO by 138 countries. The WHO estimates that between 5 and 10 million persons may currently be infected with ▷ HIV.

According to WHO prognoses, 1988, the number of new AIDS cases world-wide is expected to "rise steeply" in the years 1988–1992 with between 500.000 and three million new cases, mainly from age 20 to 49.

National committees which are essential for prevention and control were by 1987 set up in over 100 countries. The WHO has become the major financial supporter of AIDS control programs in the developing world.

The WHO conference on AIDS took place in Paris in June 1986.

The goals of the WHO Program on AIDS are: prevent HIV transmission, care for HIV infected people, unify national and international efforts against AIDS.

The Forty First WHO Assembly adopted on May 13, 1988 a Resolution on Avoidance of Discrimination to HIV-infected People and People with AIDS.

The Statistical data and prognosis 1981–1991:

1981–321 cases, 146 deaths
1987–22,000 cases, 14,000 deaths
1991–74,000 cases, 54,000 deaths

See also ▷ Hemophilia.

Newsweek, May 11th, 1987; *WHO, Health Statistics Annual*, 1987, Geneva, 1988; General Assembly pledges support for war against AIDS, in: *UN Chronicle*, March, 1988; Information of I Int. Conf. on AIDS. *WHO Chronicle*, No. 39, 198, pp. 98–103; *ICJ Newsletter*, April/June, 1988, p. 33; *Britannica World Data* 1987, Chicago, 1988, pp. 228–230.

AIDS PREVENTION, WHO LONDON DECLARATION, 1988. In January, 1988. a WHO World Summit of Ministers of Health took place in London and on Jan. 28, 1988, accepted by consensus the Final Document.

The World Summit of Ministers of Health on Programmes for AIDS Prevention, involving delegates from 148 countries representing the vast majority of the people of the world, makes the following declaration:
1. Since AIDS is a global problem that poses a serious threat to humanity, urgent action by all governments and people the world over is needed to implement WHO's Global AIDS Strategy as defined by the Fortieth World Health Assembly and supported by the United Nations General Assembly.
2. We shall do all in our power to ensure that our governments do indeed undertake such urgent action.
3. We undertake to devise national programmes to prevent and contain the spread of human immunodeficiency virus (HIV) infection as part of our countries' health systems. We commend to all governments the value of a high level coordinating committee to bring together all government sectors, and we shall involve to the fullest extent possible all governmental sectors and relevant nongovernmental organizations in the planning and implementation of such programmes in conformity with the Global AIDS Strategy.
4. We recognize that, particularly in the absence at present of a vaccine or cure for AIDS, the single most important component of national AIDS programmes is information and education because HIV transmission can be prevented through informed and responsible behaviour. In this respect, individuals, governments, the media and other sectors all have major roles to play in preventing the spread of HIV infection.
5. We consider that information and education programmes should be aimed at the general public and should take full account of social and cultural patterns, different lifestyles, and human and spiritual values. The same principles should apply equally to programmes directed towards specific groups, involving these groups as appropriate. These include groups such as:
– policy makers;
– health and social service workers at all levels;
– international travellers;
– persons whose practices may place them at increased risk of infection;
– the media;
– youth and those that work with them, especially teachers;
– community and religious leaders;
– potential blood donors; and
– those with HIV infections, their relatives and others concerned with their care, all of whom need appropriate counselling.
6. We emphasize the need in AIDS prevention programmes to protect human rights and human dignity. Discrimination against, and stigmatization of, HIV-infected people and people with AIDS and population groups undermine public health and must be avoided.
7. We urge the media to fulfil their important social responsibility to provide factual and balanced information to the general public on AIDS and on ways of preventing its spread.
8. We shall seek the involvement of all relevant governmental sectors and nongovernmental organizations in creating the supportive social environment needed to ensure the effective implementation of AIDS prevention programmes and humane care of affected individuals.
9. We shall impress on our governments the importance for national health of ensuring the availability of the human and financial resources, including health and social services with well-trained personnel, needed to carry out our national AIDS programmes, and in order to support informed and responsible behaviour.
10. In the spirit of United Nations General Assembly Resolution A/42/8, we appeal:
– to all appropriate organizations of the United Nations system, including the specialized agencies;
– to bilateral and multilateral agencies; and
– to nongovernmental and voluntary organizations to support the worldwide struggle against AIDS in conformity with WHO's global strategy.
11. We appeal in particular to these bodies to provide well-coordinated support to developing countries in

setting up and carrying out national AIDS programmes in the light of their needs. We recognize that these needs vary from country to country in the light of their epidemiological situation.
12. We also appeal to those involved in dealing with drug abuse to intensify their efforts in the spirit of the International Conference on Drug Abuse and Illicit Trafficking (Vienna, June, 1987) with a view to contributing to the reduction in the spread of HIV infection.
13. We call on the World Health Organization, through its Global Programme on AIDS, to continue to:
(i) exercise its mandate to direct and coordinate the worldwide effort against AIDS;
(ii) promote, encourage and support the worldwide collection and dissemination of accurate information on AIDS;
(iii) develop and issue guidelines on the planning, implementation, monitoring and evaluation of information and education programmes, including the related research and development, and ensure that these guidelines are updated and revised in the light of evolving experiences;
(iv) support countries in monitoring and evaluating preventive programmes, including information and education activities, and encourage wide dissemination of the findings in order to help countries to learn from the experiences of others;
(v) support and strengthen national programmes for the prevention and control of AIDS.
14. Following from this Summit, 1988 shall be a Year of Communication and Cooperation about AIDS in which we shall:
– open fully the channels of communication in each society so as to inform and educate more widely, broadly and intensively;
– strengthen the exchange of information and experience among all countries; and
– forge, through information and education and social leadership, a spirit of social tolerance.
15. We are convinced that, by promoting responsible behaviour and through international cooperation, we can and will begin *now to slow the spread of HIV infection.*

WHO Bulletin, February 11, 1988.

AIDS WORLD DAY. The WHO has proclaimed December 1, The World Day on AIDS.

WHO Bulletin, February, 1988.

AIFTA. ▷ Anglo-Irish Free Trade Agreement.

AIRBORNE TROOPS. An international military term for troops transported by aircraft or helicopter to the battlefield.

D. R. ROBERTSON, *Guide to Modern Defense and Strategy*, Detroit, 1988.

AIR BURST AND GROUND BURST. International military terms for a nuclear explosion in the air or near ground level ▷ Fall out.

D. ROBERTSON, *Guide to Modern Defense and Strategy*, Detroit, 1988.

AIRBUS. A jet-propelled airliner of medium range. Its construction was started in Western Europe in 1969 by France, the FRG, and Great Britain which soon abandoned the project. On Jan. 3, 1979 a new West European air consortium was established with the participation of Belgium, France, the FRG, Great Britain, Netherlands and Spain; its common task was to construct the A310 Airbus with 210 seats. The Airbus Industry was successful in the mid 1980's. In 1987 a four engine, 250-270 seat airliner called A 340 was launched. Aircraft sections are manufactured by Airbus Partners (Aerospatiale–France–37.9%, Deutsche Airbus –FRG–37.9%, British Aerospace–20%, Spanish Casa–4.2% and by associate members: Fokker, Netherlands and Belairbus, Belgium) then shipped to Toulouse, France for final assembly.

The USSR has since 1979 produced an airbus with 350 seats, named the IL86.

K. HAYWARD, *Airbus: Twenty Years of European Collaboration,* in: *International Affairs, Winter 1987–88; 1987 Britannica Book of the Year,* Chicago, 1988, p. 242; *Airbus Industries. The European Efforts,* in: *International Herald Tribune,* September 5, 1988.

AIR CHARTER. The transport of persons and goods, carried on outside of regular airline schedules by planes specially leased for groups of persons or a certain mass of goods, as a rule at lower costs than transport by passenger airlines. In 1971 the International Air Carriers Association (IACA) was founded with headquarters in Geneva, affiliating 16 transport companies of Canada, Denmark, France, Holland, Spain, Switzerland, USA and Yugoslavia; competing with IATA. Reg. with the UIA; also: Arab Air Carriers Operation, f. 1965, Beirut, Publ. *Arab Wings.*

Yearbook of International Organizations.

AIR CHICAGO CONVENTION, 1944. The Chicago Convention on International Civil Aviation, signed in Chicago. Dec. 7, 1944: modifying amendments were subsequently adopted at Montreal, May 27, 1947, June 7, 1954, May 21, 1961; New York, Mar. 12, 1971, and Vienna, July 7, 1971. The Convention ruled that "each contracting state agrees not to use civil aviation for any purpose inconsistent with the aims of this Convention".

Art. 4 aims to "create and preserve friendship and understanding among the nations and peoples of the world" (preamble).
Chapter Two provides rules of flight over territories of contracting states; art. 5: right of non-scheduled flight; art. 6: scheduled air services; art. 7: cabotage; art. 8: pilotless aircraft; art. 9: prohibited areas; art. 10: landing at customs airports; art. 11: applicability of air regulations; art. 12: air rules; art. 13: entry and clearance regulations; art. 14: prevention of the spread of diseases; art. 15: airport and similar charges; art. 16: search of aircraft.
Chapter Three provides rules relating to nationality of aircraft; art. 17: nationality of aircraft; art. 18: dual registration; art. 19: national laws governing registration; art. 20: display of marks; art. 21: report of registration.
Chapter Four provides measures to facilitate air navigation; art. 22: facilitation of formalities; art. 23: customs and immigration procedures; art. 24: customs duty; art. 25: aircraft in distress; art. 26: investigation of accidents; art. 27: exemption from seizure and patent claims; art. 28: air navigation facilities and standard systems.
Chapter Five provides conditions to be fulfilled with respect to aircraft; art. 29: documents carried in aircraft; art. 30: aircraft radio equipment; art. 31: certificate of airworthiness; art. 32: licenses of personnel; art. 33: recognition of certificates and licenses; art. 34: journey log books; art. 35: cargo restrictions; art. 36: photographic apparatus.
Chapter Six provides international standards and recommended practices; art. 37: adoption of international standards and procedures; art. 38: departures from international standards and procedures; art. 39: endorsement of certificates and licenses; art. 40: validity of the endorsed certificates and licenses; art. 41: recognition of existing standards of airworthiness; art. 42: recognition of existing standards of competency of personnel.
Chapters Seven to Twelve set up ▷ ICAO and specify its structure.
Chapters Fourteen and Nineteen relate to international air transport.
Final chapters Twenty to Twenty Three cover annexes, ratification, adherence, amendments, denunciation, definitions for the purpose of the Convention.

The Chicago Air Convention entered into force on June 6, 1945, amendments adopted in Montreal 1947, 1954, 1961 cover arts. 45, 48, 49, 61 relating to

organizational matters of ICAO, Cf. ▷ Air Law International.

UNTS, Vol. 15, pp. 296–475; E. PÉPIN, *Géographie de la circulation aérienne,* Paris, 1956.

AIR CONDITIONING. A subject of international co-operation. Organizations reg. with the UIA:

European Committee of the Air Handling and Air Conditioning Equipment Manufacturers (EUROVENT), f. 1959, Vienna.
International Confederation of Installers of Refrigeration and Air Conditioning Equipment, f. 1969, Paris.
International Mobile Air Conditioning Assistance, f. 1958, Burlingame, Calif., USA.
International Union of the Association of Heating, Ventilating and Air Conditioning Contractors, f. 1935, Paris.

Yearbook of International Organizations.

AIRCRAFT. An international term used in air law and in many treaties, according to the definition of art. I of the Air Hague Convention 1933:

"every apparatus which can maintain itself in the atmosphere through air resistance and designed for air navigation."

LNTS, 1933.

AIRCRAFT CARRIER. An international term used in treaties, according to the definition of art. 3 of the ▷ Washington Naval Treaty 1922:

The expression "aircraft carrier" includes any surface vessel of war, whatever its displacement, designed for the specific and exclusive purpose of carrying aircraft and so constructed that aircraft can be launched therefrom and landed thereon.

LNTS, Vol. 112, 1938, p. 71.

AIRCRAFT INDUSTRY. One of the great industries of international character in view of the development of international co-operation in this field and the role of airplanes in international travel. The first factories manufacturing airplane motors appeared in 1910–13: Breda, Breguet, Curtis, Devoitine, Dornier, Farman, Fokker, Nieuport, A.V. Ros, Short, Wright, and others. During World War I and after: Douglas, Focke-Wulf, de Havilland, Heinkel, Junkers, Messerschmidt; and the Soviet a.i. began its operations (designers: M.I. Guryevich, S.V. Ilyushin, A.S. Yakovlev, B.N. Yuryev, A.I. Mikoyan, A.N. Turpolev, and others). The air powers during the inter-war period were: France, Japan, the Reich, the USA, Great Britain, and Italy. After World War II the a.i. of Japan, the FRG and Italy was greatly limited up to 1956, after which both civilian as well as military construction began to develop. The main producers in the second half of the 20th century are the USA and USSR. The importance of the European a.i. was increased by the co-operation of France, the FRG, and Great Britain in the 1970s and 1980s.

AIR DEFENSE IDENTIFICATION ZONE. A zone established by some coastal states (USA, Canada) for security reasons, extending up to 300 miles beyond the territorial sea.

R. L. BLEDSOE, B. A. BOCZEK, *The International Law Dictionary,* Oxford, UK, 1987.

AIR FORCES. The strategic, air defence, tactical, naval, transport and auxiliary air forces. The first military reconnaissance aircraft were used in the war between Turkey and Italy, 1911–12; bomber aircraft in World War I in 1915; jet-propelled aircraft in World War II that ended in Aug. 1945 with the dropping of atomic bombs on ▷ Hiroshima and Nagasaki.

AIR GENEVA CONVENTION, 1948. A Convention adopted by the ICAO conference at Geneva, June 19, 1948, Convention on the International Recognition of Rights in Aircraft; entered into force on Sept. 17, 1953.
The text of art. I is as follows:

"(1) The Contracting States undertake to recognize:
(a) rights of property in aircraft:
(b) rights to acquire aircraft by purchase coupled with possession of the aircraft:
(c) rights to possession of aircraft under leases of six months or more;
(d) mortgages, hypotheques and similar rights in aircraft which are contractually created as security for payment of an indebtedness; provided that such rights
(i) have been constituted in accordance with the law of the contracting state in which the aircraft was registered as to nationality at the time of their constitution, and
(ii) are regularly recorded in a public record of the contracting state in which the aircraft is registered as to nationality. The regularity of successive recordings in different contracting states shall be determined in accordance with the law of the state where the aircraft was registered as to nationality at the time of each recording.
(2) Nothing in this convention shall prevent the recognition of any rights in aircraft under the law of any contracting state: but contracting states shall not admit or recognize any rights as taking priority over the rights mentioned in paragraph (1) of this Article."

UNTS, Vol. 310, p. 152.

AIR GUADALAJARA CONVENTION, 1961. A Supplementary Convention to the Warsaw Convention for the Unification of Certain Rules Relating to International Carriage by Air Performed by a Person Other than the Contracting Carrier, signed Guadalajara, Mexico, Sept. 18, 1961, went into effect May 1, 1964 (*UNTS,* vol. 500, p. 32). The Convention classified responsibilities regarding hire, charter, and interchangeable operation of aircraft of contracting and actual carriers by making the contracting carrier, subject to the Warsaw Convention, responsible for the entire carriage as provided for in the contract and persons other than the contracting partner, responsible only for their actual share of carriage.

O. RIESE, "Die internationale Luftprivatrechtskonferenz und das Charterabkommen von Guadalajara", 1961, in: *Zeitschrift für Luftrecht,* No. 11, 1962.

AIR GUATEMALA PROTOCOL, 1971. A Protocol signed by 21 countries in Guatemala on Feb. 9, 1971 and ratified at a Diplomatic Conference of 55 States, Mar. 8, 1981 revising the Air Warsaw Convention and the Air Hague Protocol on the standardization of rules of international air carriage. The Protocol supplements and changes the two previous treaties. The principle of complete responsibility of an airline company for the death or bodily injury to a passenger during boarding or disembarking of a plane, or on board was adopted, irrespective of whether the company is at fault. The limit of responsibility of the airline company was raised to US $100,000. Previously, under the Warsaw Convention, the maximum damages awarded were US $8,300; and under the Hague Protocol US $16,600. A second principle was accepted that a writ for damages as a result of death or bodily injury to a passenger could also be filed by the court of a state in which the injured party was a permanent resident, if the airline company had a representative in that country.

AIR HAGUE CONVENTION, 1933. An International Health Convention signed Apr. 12, 1933 concerning air navigation; official name only in French: Convention sanitaire internationale pour la navigation aérienne, which in part I made it mandatory for an airport to have a permanent medical staff and specified sanitary facilities; in part II the operating procedures in cases of plague, cholera, typhoid fever, smallpox and yellow fever and the measures to be taken after landing. The convention was modified in 1944 and 1946 in Washington.

LNTS, 1933; *UNTS*, 1946.

AIR HAGUE PROTOCOL, 1955. A document ratified at a diplomatic conference in The Hague, on Sept. 28, 1955, which changed the resolutions of the Warsaw Air Convention of 1929, i.a. by raising the limit of indemnity in the transport of people from US $8300 to 16,600 by simplifying transport documents and others; took effect Aug. 1, 1953.

AIR HOSTESSES. Organized by International Federation of Air Hostesses and Convoying Officers, Federation international des hôtesses et convoyeuses de l'air, f. 1970, Paris, reg. with the UIA.

Yearbook of International Organizations.

AIR-LAUNCHED CRUISE MISSILE, ALCM ▷ Cruise.

AIR LAW INTERNATIONAL. An international term coined at the International Aeronautical Congress, 1889, in Paris; discussed in the first international aeronautical organization established in 1905, the International Aeronautical Federation, FIA; the term defines a branch of international public and private law stemming from aircraft navigation rules as well as from a set of aeronautical rules and international principles. The first pioneer scientific work on international air law was announced in Paris in 1901 by a Frenchman, P.A.J. Fauchille (1858–1926) in *Revue Générale de Droit International Public,* under the title: *Le domaine aérien et le régime juridique des aérostats.* The 1902 Brussels conference of International Law was also devoted to the legal status of free balloons. The first interstate air agreement was the exchange of notes between the governments of France and the German Reich in Berlin, on July 26, 1913, stating that until the elaboration of a multilateral air convention the sides shall allow in their respective air spaces the aircraft of the other side on special conditions. The Convention international aérienne was prepared by the Paris Institute of International Law in 1906, stating that air space is open to trade and travel equally to the high seas. This draft was never approved by any country and the air bombardment during World War I resulted in the adoption immediately after the War of the principle ▷ *Cuius solum . . .* to the effect that "each state has full and exclusive sovereignty over its territory's air space", which was included in the Paris Aeronautical Convention of Oct. 13, 1919. As this was the first attempt to formulate general aeronautical international norms and principles, this convention may be considered a cradle of international air law. Following its pattern, the Ibero-American Convention on Air Navigation (Convención Ibero-Americana sobre Navegación Aerea) was prepared and signed in Madrid on Nov. 1, 1926, by Spain, Costa Rica, Mexico, Paraguay and the Dominican Republic. The Convention on Trade Navigation (Convención sobre Aviación Commercial) signed on Feb. 20, 1928 by 11 Latin American states during the Sixth International American Conference in Havana was of a different character; it was prepared in spite of the opposition presented by the United States and its purpose was to defend the Latin-American states against the unrestricted expansion of US air line routes in the Western Hemisphere. In turn, the Warsaw Aeronautical Convention of Oct. 12, 1929 on international aircraft transport, prepared by

CINA, came as a significant achievement, as did the conference in The Hague, where on Apr. 12, 1933, the so-called Hague Aeronautical Convention on Sanitary Conditions of Air Navigation (Convention international sanitaire de la navigation aérienne) was signed. This convention was replaced by the Washington Convention of Dec. 15, 1944. In Rome, on May 29, 1933 the so-called Rome Aeronautical Conventions on the Protection of Aircraft and on the Unification of Some of the Provisions on Damages Caused by Aircraft to Third Persons on the Ground were signed, the latter having been supplemented by the Brussels Protocol of Nov. 30, 1938. The last pre-war Convention to be signed was the one of Brussels of Nov. 29, 1938 on Assistance and Salvage of Aircraft at Sea; however, lacking a sufficient number of ratifications, it did not enter into force. Of the pre-war conventions the following are still in force: the Warsaw Convention, which was modified three times – on May 27, 1947, on June 7, 1954 and on May 21, 1961, and the Hague and Rome Conventions, modified on Nov. 28, 1955. In the years 1926–46, under the auspices of the League of Nations, the International Technical Committee of Experts in Aeronautical Legislation, CITEJA, was operating for the promotion of international air law; its functions were taken over in 1947 by the International Civil Aviation Organization "ICAO". During World War II the US and the UK started negotiations in London and Washington in 1943 on the preparation of a new aeronautical convention to replace the Paris Convention of 1919. The US pursued the internationalization of air routes because of the potentials for air transportation opened up by the War. Planning to use military cargo aircraft on their civil air routes after the War, the US government on Nov. 11, 1944 extended invitations to participate in the International Civil Aviation Conference in Chicago: the conference was held between Nov. 1 and Dec. 7, 1944, with the participation of 54 states (the USSR chose not to participate because of invitations extended to "fascists Spain and Portugal"). At the Conference there was a clash of different interpretations between states, above all between the US and the UK, but also between other European and Latin American states. The United States strove to pass a clause "on the privilege of friendly passage accorded by Nations", which de facto would open the air space of the world to those air powers having the means to establish a worldwide network of air routes. France opposed this provision. A compromise was realized and the following four treaties were adopted and included in the final act of the Chicago conference: (1) A Provisional Treaty on Civil Aviation, which allowed for the establishment of the Provisional Civil Aviation Organization on Aug. 15, 1945, i.e. 2 years earlier than the ICAO; (2) Convention on International Civil Aviation, also called the Chicago Aeronautical Convention of 1944, which replaced the Paris Convention of 1919 and of the Havana convention of 1928: (3) Treaty on the Transit of International Air Services; (4) Treaty on International Air Transportation. Other Conventions concluded between 1948 and 1971: The Geneva Convention of 1948 on the International Recognition of Rights Aboard Aircraft, signed on June 19, 1948; the Rome Convention of 1933 was replaced in 1952 by the Convention on Damages Caused on the Surface of the Earth to Third Persons by Alien Aircraft. At the Conference in The Hague in 1955 the Hague Protocol of 1955 was adopted together with recommendations to work out the question of chartering, renting and exploiting of aircraft; also recommended was the examination of the possibility of unifying international private air law and of regulating respective international dis-

putes. At the Conference in Tokyo on Oct. 14, 1963, the Convention on Crimes and Other Offences Committed on Board an Aircraft was adopted. However, because of the increasing incidence of ▷ air piracy during the decade 1961–70, this latter convention was considered insufficient and was substituted by the Hague Convention on Combating Unlawful Seizure of Aircraft of Dec. 16, 1970. The first legal act of the new decade was the Guatemala Air Protocol of Mar. 8, 1978 on further revision of the Warsaw Convention of 1929 and of the Hague Protocol of 1955. Apart from this, between 1955 and 1970 numerous regional aeronautical agreements were concluded, connected to the occurring integration processes, as e.g. the Paris Agreement of Apr. 30, 1956 on Irregular Air Transport within the EEC. With the launching of the first Sputnik on Oct. 4, 1957, ▷ outer space international law came into existence. Some publications on air law: *Revue Française de Droit Aérien, II Diritto Aero, Journal of Air Law and Commerce, Zeitschrift für Luftrecht und Weltraumrechtsfragen.*
Organizations reg. with the UIA: International Association of Lawyers, Jurists and Experts in Air Law, f. 1980, Ayr, UK.

II-e Conférence Internationale de Droit Privé Aérien 1929, Varsovie, 1930; J.W. GARBER, "International Regulation of Air Warfare", in *Air Law Review,* No. 3, 1932; A. AMBROSINI, *Corso di Diritto Aeronautico,* Vol. 2, Roma, 1933; J. KROELL, *Droit Internationale aérien,* Vol. II, Paris, 1936; D. GOEDHUIS, *Air law in the Making,* Hague, 1938; M. LEMOINE, *Traité de Droit Aérien,* Paris, 1947; P. CHAUVEAU, *Droit Aérien,* Paris, 1951; N. SHAWCROSS-BEAUMONT, *On Air Law,* London, 1952; M. DE GOFF, *Manuel de Droit Aérien (Droit Public),* Paris, 1954; ICAO Conférence Internationale de Droit Privé Aérien, La Haye, Sept., 1955; ICAO Doc. 7686-LC 140, 1956; A. MEYER, *International Luftfahrtabkommen,* Bd. 3, Berlin, 1953–57; E. PEPPIN, *L'enseignement du droit aérien dans le monde,* Montreal, 1958; H.A. WASSENBERGH, *Post-War International Civil Aviation Policy and the Law in the Air,* Hague, 1962; N. MATEOSCO MATTE, *Deux Frontieres Invisibles: de la Mer Territorial à l'Air "Territorial",* Paris, 1965; H.A. WASSENBERGH, *Aspects of air law and civil air policy in the seventies,* Amsterdam, 1970, p. 179; W.P. HEERE, *International Bibliography of Air Law 1900–1971,* Leiden, 1972; *Yearbook of International Organizations,* 1986–87.

AIR-LIFT. An international military term for transport of goods, equipment or troops over large distances to a territory cut off from the world by a natural disaster or a political blockade. See also ▷ Berlin Air-Lift 1948–1949.
D. ROBERTSON, *Guide to Modern Defense and Strategy,* Detroit, 1988.

AIRLINES, INTERNATIONAL. An international term, defined in art. 96 of the Chicago Air Convention 1944 as

"any industry of air transport offering or executing international air service", that is "executed in the air space of more than one state".

The beginning of regular a.i. service was in the period 1919–39, in Europe (London–Paris, 1919) and in North America. France 1919–26 initiated regular communication with her African colonies, Great Britain 1920–30, Belgium 1925–26; Holland and Great Britain with the Near and Middle East and S. Asia 1924–33; France with South America through Dakar–Recife. If, from 1919–30, development was slow, from 1930 it was extremely rapid; the airplane industry being one of the few branches of industry which was not impeded by the economic crisis. The number of civilian pilots of a.i. grew to 22,000 reg. in ICAO, of which half were in the USA where the number of passengers exceeded 1½ million in 1938 in comparison with 5780 in 1926, the first year of authorized passenger flights.

Organization reg. with the UIA: Airlines Worldwide Telecommunications and Information Service, f. 1949, Neuilly Sur Seine, France, Consultative Status: ECOSOC. ITO, UNCTAD.

R. CHAMBE, *Histoire de l'aviation*, Paris, 1958; *Yearbook of International Organizations*, 1986–87.

AIR-MAIL CORRESPONDENCE. A subject of international co-operation and conventions: UPU Agreement concerning Air-Mail Correspondence, July 17, 1952.

UNTS, Vol. 169, p. 3.

AIRMOBILE UNIT. An international military term for troops transported by helicopter directly to a battlefield.

D. ROBERTSON, *Guide to Modern Defense and Strategy*, Detroit, 1988.

AIR NAVIGATION INTERNATIONAL MAPS AND MARKS. An international term, introduced by the Paris Air Convention 1919, for strictly defined general maps binding in international air traffic, bearing the French title *Carte générale aéronautique internationale*; or specific maps with the French title *Carte normale aéronautique internationale*; as well as a universal system of air signals. The regulations are modified to meet the requirements of technological progress. ICAO rules now in force cover air navigation situational, topographic, and magnetic maps of 1 : 1 million or 1 : 500,000 scale.

AIR PARIS CONVENTION, 1919. A convention relating to the regulation of aerial navigation, full official name only in French: Convention internationale portant réglement de la navigation aérienne; approved by the Great Powers' Supreme Council on Sept. 27, 1919, signed on Oct. 13, 1919, entered into force on July 11, 1922, ratified by 33 states. The organ of the Paris Convention was the permanent International Commission for Navigation commonly known as CINA, seated in Paris, which made amendments and supplementary provisions to air norms and international principles.

Art. 1 recognized that "every Power has complete and exclusive sovereignty over the air space above its territory" understood as "including the national territory, both that of the mother country and of the colonies, and the territorial waters adjacent hitherto."

Art. 2 "Each contracting State undertakes in time of peace to accord freedom of innocent passage above its territory provided that the conditions laid down in the present Convention are observed".

Chapter Two provided for nationality of aircraft; Chapter Three – certificates of air-worthiness and competency; Chapter Four – admission to air navigation above foreign territory; Chapter Five – rules to be observed on departure under way and on landing; Chapter Six – prohibited transport; Chapter Seven – government aircraft; Chapter Eight – function of International Commission for Air Navigation (CINA); Chapter Nine – final provisions. The Convention was appended with annexes: A: registration marks; B: certificate of air-worthiness; C: log-books; D: signals, E: certificates and licences of the commanding officer, pilots, and crew; F: international aeronautical maps and ground marks for flying; G: collection and dissemination of statistical current and special meteorological information; H: customs.

The provisions of the Paris Convention were modified on Oct. 27, 1922 by First London Protocol (art. 5); June 30, 1923 by Second London Protocol (art. 34); June 15, 1929 by First Paris Protocol (arts. 3, 5, 7, 15, 34, 37, 41, 42); Dec. 11, 1929 by Second Paris Protocol (art. 43 and 44); and June 1, 1935 by

Brussels Protocol (Appendix H). The USA signed the Convention but did not ratify it; Brazil, China, Germany, Turkey, Hungary, the USSR did not accede.

On US initiative, the United Nations acceded in 1944 to the new ▷ Air Chicago Convention whose entry into force on June 6, 1945 annulled the Paris Air Convention of 1919.

A. ROPER, *La Convention internationale du 13 Octobre 1919 portant réglement de la navigation aérienne. Son origin, son application, son avenir*, Paris, 1920.

AIR PIRACY, HIJACKING. The abduction of civilian aircraft; a problem raised at the UN and in ICAO in the light of the growing number of seizures of civilian aircraft during 1961–70. The Tokyo ICAO Convention on Offences and Certain Other Acts Committed on Board Aircraft, of Sept. 14, 1963, proved to be insufficient. The International Conference on Aviation Law held in The Hague, Dec. 1–16, 1970, prepared – in keeping with recommendations of Res. 2551/XXIV of the UN General Assembly – a Convention on Unlawful Seizure of Aircraft signed by 49 states on Dec. 16, 1970, including France, Great Britain, the USA and the USSR.

The provisions of the Convention impose the obligation of "severe punishment (art. 2) of air piracy as it constitutes a hazard for persons and property and impairs confidence in the security of passenger air traffic; they refer exclusively to civilian airplanes. Under art. 3, item 2, the Convention does not apply to air force, police and custom service aircraft. Art. 4 determines that the state of the aircraft's registration or the state on whose territory the hijacked aircraft lands are competent to take punitive measures. All States parties to the convention are obliged to prosecute wrongdoers and deliver captives to states claiming them or to pass judgement on them in accordance with art. 2. Art. 8 provides for rules of extradition. Art. 9 imposes the obligation to render maximum assistance to passengers and crews of captured aircraft.

On Sept. 23, 1971, in Montreal 61 states signed a Convention on Suppression of Unlawful Acts Against Security of Civilian Aviation; entered into force on Jan. 26, 1972. According to the data provided by ICAO during 1960–70, 280 attempts of hijacking were made, 74 of them unsuccessful. In 1969 the record number of 57 aircraft were captured. During 30 months of 1970–72 over 90 persons were killed or injured as a result of air piracy. The first world 24-hour protest strike against hijacking was declared by the International Federation of Air Line Pilots Association (IFALPA) and was organized on June 19, 1972. The strike was joined by pilots of a majority of international airlines. On that day ICAO announced sanctions against States that grant ▷ asylum to hijackers (the immediate cause of the strike was the hijacking of a Czechoslovak airplane to the Federal Republic of Germany in which one pilot was shot and the other injured and the FRG refusal to deliver the hijackers to Czechoslovakia).

The ICAO Legal Committee in the fall of 1972 commenced work on a draft international convention on more effective suppression of air piracy and aimed to make more precise the Tokyo convention of 1963, the Hague convention of 1970 and the Montreal convention of 1971. In Nov., 1972 the US government, through mediation of the Swiss government informed the government of Cuba that it was ready to enter into negotiations proposed by Prime Minister Fidel Castro for a bilateral agreement on the suppression of air and sea piracy. Earlier on its own initiative, Cuba had started negotiations on similar matters with Canada and Mexico. On Aug. 15, 1973, the UN Security Council

adopted a resolution denouncing Israel for having used its Air Force to hijack a Libyan airliner from Lebanon four days earlier — the first case of hijacking by military aircraft.

A tragic hijacking of a Kuwaiti Airliner, 5–15, 1988, during which two hostages were killed, was the subject of a meeting of the Foreign Ministers of the EC in Luxembourg on April 25, 1988 and on April 29, 1988, of ICAO in Montreal, which ended with five recommendations:

(i) the formation of an international task force to investigate the Kuwaiti airliner hijacking;
(ii) the creation of a group of counter-terrorist experts to be on permanent stand-by to offer advice to any airport at which a hijacked airliner has landed;
(iii) mandatory guidelines for all nations on airport security;
(iv) a campaign to persuade all countries to sign the 1970 Hague Convention for the Suppression of Unlawful Seizure of Aircraft;
(v) a tightening up of the Hague Convention, specifically the provision binding governments not to allow a hijacked aircraft to take off.

R. GOLDSTEIN, "Convention de Tokio", in: *Revue Française de Droit Aérien*, No. 1, 1964; E. DU PONTAVICE, "La piraterie aérienne: notions et effects", in: *Revue Générale de l'Air et de l'Espace*, No. 3, 1969; Z. GALICKI, "Unlawful seizure of aircraft", in: *The Polish Year Book of International Law*, 1970, pp. 171–198; E. MACWHINNEY, *Aerial Piracy*, Leiden, 1971; Understanding between the US and Cuba on Hijacking Aircraft and Vessels, Washington-Havana, 15.11.1973, Washington, DC, 1973; E. MACWHINNEY, *The Illegal Diversion of Aircraft and International Law*, Leiden, 1975; *International Terrorism. Hearings. Subcommittee on Aviation House, on H.R. 13261, July 18–25, 1978*, Washington, DC, 1978, 392pp. KEESING's *Record of World Events*, May, 1988.

AIR POLLUTION. A world problem of the second half of the 20th century related to industrialization and the growing number of internal combustion engine vehicles; the subject of international conventions on the harmful impact of air pollution on the human organism as well as animal and plant life. The First European Congress on the Influence of Air Pollution on Plants met in 1968.

Under the auspices of the UN Economic European Commission and in collaboration with UNEP and WMO 35 European states signed (and 31 ratified) in November 1979, in Geneva a Convention on Long-range Transboundary Air Pollution, that came into effect on March 16, 1983, 21 member states of the Convention signed on July 9, 1986, an additional Protocol to "reduce until 1993 their national sulphur emissions of their transboundary fluxes by at least 30 per cent". The Protocol is also called the Club of the 30 Per Cent.

Organizations reg. with the UIA:

International Commission of Atmospheric Chemistry and Global Pollution, f. 1966, London.
International Union of Air Pollution Associations, f. 1964, Düsseldorf.

▷ Environmental protection.

A. WOLMAN, "Pollution as an International Issue", in: *Foreign Affairs*, Oct. 1968; *Air Pollution*. Proceedings of the First European Congress on the Influence of Air Pollution on Plants and Animals, Wageningen, 1968; *Air Quality Criteria and Guides for Urban Air Pollution*, Report of a WHO Experts Committee, Geneva, 1972; N.F. IZMIEROFF, *Control of Air Pollution in the USSR*, Geneva, 1973; *UN Air Pollution Across Boundaries*, New York, 1985; KEESING's *Contemporary Archives*, 1986, No 11.

AIRPORTS, INTERNATIONAL. The areas adapted for the takeoff and landing of airplanes in international traffic; the object of international aviation and sanitary conventions, establishing the conditions that must be fulfilled in order to receive planes of foreign lines and regulating the tariffs

(First Conference ICAO on Airports Charges, 1957). ICAO publ. *International Airport Charges and Documents relating to Airports*. After World War II the lighting system was unified under the International Calvert Airportlights System, based on the distribution of white, red and green lights to enable the pilot to descend at a constant angle between the take-off runway and the landing approach.

Organizations reg. with the UIA:

Airport Associations Co-ordinating Council (AACC), f. 1970, Geneva, Consultative status: ECOSOC, ICAO, IATA, IFALPA.
Airport Operators Council International (AOCI), f. 1970, Washington, DC, Publ. *Airport Highlights* (weekly).
International Civil Airport Association, ICAA, est. 1962, Paris; publ. *ICAA News, Airports and Ground Services* (weekly), and *Airports International* (quarterly). Consultative status: ECOSOC.
Western European Airports Association (WEAA), f. 1966, Brussels.
World Airport Technology (WAT), f. 1973, Paris.

P. DE LA PRADELLE, L. GALLEY, "Le statut des aérodromes", in: *Revue Française de Droit Aérien*, 1946; P. ROGUE, "The legal framework of airport operations", in *Journal of Air Law and Commerce*, 1952; R. MALEZIEUX, "Le nouveau régime de taxes et redevances sur les aérodromes ouverts à la circulation aérienne publique", in: *Revue Général de l'Air*, 1954; M. GUINCHARD, "Le problème de la classification des aérodromes", in: *Revue Française de Droit Aerien*, 1958; A.H. STRATFORD, *Airports and the Environment*, London, 1974; *Yearbook of International Organizations*.

AIR POWER. An international term for a state with considerable air forces, air transport and aircraft industry.

JANE's, *All the World's Aircraft*, British Annual; M. J. ARMITAGE, E. A. MASON, Lord CAMERON OF BALHOUSIE, *Air Power in the Nuclear Age*, 1945–84, London, 1985.

AIR ROME CONVENTIONS, 1933. The two conventions signed in Rome on May 29, 1933:

(1) On unification of certain principles relating to security seizure of aircraft (official name in French only: Convention pour l'unification de certaines règles relatives à la saisie conservatoire des aéroneufs) providing terms of seizure of aircraft by creditor and types of aircraft exempt from such sequestration (ones involved exclusively in state services including postal, commercial apart, operated within regular public services as well as indispensable for emergency and others employed to carry passengers and freight on profit lines except in case of debts drawn for the purpose of journey in point or during this journey).
(2) On unification of certain principles relating to damage inflicted by aircraft on the surface of the earth (official name in French only: Convention pour l'unification des certaines règles relatives aux dommages causés par les aéroneufs aux tiers à la surface) whose art. 2 ruled that damage caused by airborne aircraft to third persons or property on the ground give claim to compensation on the basis of simple establishment that such damage exists and has been caused by an aircraft. Additional Protocol signed Brussels, Sept. 30, 1938, specifying kinds of insurance against such damage; this convention and the Protocol were replaced Rome, Oct. 7, 1952, by one under the same title which introduced financial limitations of liability for damage but at the same time rights of states to demand that an aircraft be insured against such damage.

M. DE JUGLART, *La Convention de Rome du 7 Octobre, 1952*, Paris, 1956.

AIR SAFETY. A subject of international co-operation and conventions. Organizations reg. with the UIA:

Agency for the Security of Aerial Navigation in Africa and Madagascar, f. in Dakar, 1959.

Central American Air Safety Corporation, f. in Tegucigalpa, 1960.
European Organization for the Safety of Air Navigation (EUROCONTROL), f. in Brussels, 1960. Publ.: *EUROCONTROL Bulletin*.
International Air Safety Association (IASA), f. in Paris, 1952. Consultative status with ICAO, ITO, WMO; publ.: *Information Bulletin*.
International Federation of Air Traffic Controllers Association, f. in Geneva, 1961. Publ.: *The Controller*.
International Federation of Air Traffic Safety Electronic Associations, f. in London, 1972. Publ.: *Navaire*.

Yearbook of International Organizations.

AIR SERVICE INTERNATIONAL. An international term denoting, according to the definition of the Chicago Air Convention, 1944 (art. 96): every regular service performed by air ships in the air space of more than one state for the purpose of the public transport of passengers, mail, or freight; object of the International Air Services Transit Agreement signed Dec. 7, 1944 in Chicago, by which each Agreeing State granted to the other Agreeing States the following liberties for regular international air service: (1) the privilege of flying over its territory without landing, (2) the privilege of landing for non-commercial purposes, except that each State may limit flight to certain air corridors and landing to certain airports.

UNTS Vol 15, pp 296 475.

AIR SPACE. A subject of international law according to the definition of the Polish jurist, Prof. Cz. Berezowski:

"The place in which international relations in the field of aviation develop is the space directly encircling the earth, filled to a greater or lesser extent with air and bearing the name air space."

In the years 1902–14 legal theorists debated whether freedom of a.s. existed on the model of freedom of the open seas, but – in other opinions – the analogy to navigation on the seas is not complete, since the seas (and the air above them) are outside the territory of States, and a State and its inhabitants cannot be indifferent to what goes on above them. The principle of sovereignty of a state over its a.s. was formulated in the English Aerial Navigation Act, 1911, by France and Russia in 1913, and in the Declaration of Neutrality by Switzerland Aug. 4, 1914. World War I, with its examples of the military violation of the sovereignty of states by the invasion of their air space made it a foregone conclusion that air space would become an inseparable part of the territory of states and that a state would control its own air space. This found expression in the further development of international law; principally, in the so-called Paris Air Convention, 1919, which recognized "complete and exclusive sovereignty" (art. 1); and also in diverse interstate conflicts concerning the violation of a.s., as e.g. in the ▷ U2 case of 1960. However, the upper limit of air space for a long time remained the subject of debates between the supporters of the medieval principle ▷ Cuius solum ... and those in favor of separating a.s. from extraterrestrial interplanetary space, today commonly called ▷ outer space, which is assumed to start from the fourth outer layer of the earth's atmosphere, called the exosphere, extending to 800–1000 km above the surface of the earth. Though up to now no State has made claim to such a distant space, nonetheless it is theoretically assumed that the sovereign rights of States include not only the troposphere, whose height is dependent on geographical latitude and time of year (9–19 km), but also the stratosphere (50–85 km) as well as the ionosphere and exosphere, if air flight were technically possible there. Considered essential is acceptance of the principle that

a.s. is finite. The declaration of the representative of the Netherlands in the Department of State, 1939, that the sovereignty of this country over its a.s. reached to infinity is unique in the history of diplomacy. One of the first States to draft legislation on its sovereignty over its air space was the USSR in a directive of Jan. 17, 1921. Universally accepted in aviation law is the complete and exclusive authority of a state in the air space over its territory, territorial waters, and inland waters. In boundary treaties with neighbors the boundary line is divided not only vertically and into the earth, but also horizontally into air space. ▷ Air Law, ▷ Law of Outer Space.

J. SPIROPOULOS, *Der Luftraum*, Berlin, 1921; A. MAYER, *Le cabotage aérien*, Paris, 1948; P. DE GEOFFRE de la PRADELLE, *La frontière de l'air*, La Haye, 1954; C. BEREZOWSKI, *Międzynarodowe Prawo Lotnicze*, Warszawa, 1964.

AIR TARIFF WAR. A price war waged in the 1970s by companies not belonging to IATA with companies of IATA, which have maintained a uniform system of tariffs for 50 years. The crisis was caused by a British businessman, Freddie Laker, who in 1977 started a London–New York line at unusually low rates in comparison with the tariffs of IATA and achieved a considerable financial success. The abandonment by IATA of the system of uniform tariffs took place July 1, 1978, which resulted in a temporary sudden fall in rates and the intensification of free competition. Laker Airways did not have any ticket sales or reservations offices and provided no services or meals on its flights. Passengers purchased tickets on a "first-come, first-served" basis and paid for their tickets just before flight time. Laker Airways went into receivership in 1981; however, the air tariff war remained an unresolved issue in the 1980s.

AIR TRANSPORT. A subject of international co-operation and conventions. Organizations reg. with the UIA (not including ▷ IATA):

Arab Air Carriers Organization (AACO), f. 1965, Beirut. Publ. *Arab Wings*.
Commonwealth Air-Transport Council, f. 1945, London.
Institute of Air Transport, f. 1944, Paris.
International Air Carrier Association (IACA), f. 1971, Geneva. ICAO.
International Air Freight Agents'Association, f. 1958, JFK Airport, N.Y., USA.
International Federation of Independent Air Transport, f. 1946, Paris. Consultative status: ECOSOC, ICAO.
South Pacific Air Transport Council, f. 1946, Melbourne.

Yearbook of International Organizations.

AIR WAR. The only form of war for which no special international conventions are in force at present. In The Hague and Geneva Conventions there exist only vague references to other forms of war which also relate to air war. The Hague Declaration of 1899 prohibited the dropping of any projectiles or other explosive materials from balloons or other airships for a probationary period of five years. This was confirmed by the Second International Hague Peace Conference of 1907, but with the proviso si omnis; so it was not applied in World War I. In 1923 a group of experts in The Hague, at the initiative of the LN formulated the so-called Hague Rules of Air War, but they did not enter into force. International law experts decided that air war was covered by art. 25 of the Hague Statute on Land War of 1907, which prohibits the ▷ bombing of open cities and villages; also the Geneva Protocol of 1925, banning the use of chemical and bacteriological weapons.

'US Strategic Bombing Survey', in European War, Washington, DC, 1945; *Pacific War,* Washington, DC, 1946; R. CHAMBE, *Histoire de l'Aviation,* Paris, 1958.

AIR WARFARE RULES, or Hague Rules 1923. A project prepared by a League of Nations Commission of Jurists, representing military experts of France, Great Britain, Italy, Japan, Netherlands, and the US, at The Hague, Dec. 11, 1922–Feb. 19, 1923. They were never presented in the form of an international convention and never entered into force. The rules which should govern aerial bombardment are as follows:

Art. 22: Aerial bombardment for the purpose of terrorizing the civilian population, of destroying or damaging private property not of military character, or of injuring non-combatants is prohibited.
Art. 24: (1) Aerial bombardment is legitimate only when directed at a military objective, that is to say, an object of which the destruction or injury would constitute a distinct military advantage to the belligerent. (2) Such bombardment is legitimate only when directed exclusively at the following objectives: military forces; military works, military establishments or depots; factories constituting important and well-known centers engaged in the manufacture of arms, ammunition of distinctively military supplies; lines of communication or transportation used for military purposes.
(3) The bombardment of cities, towns, villages, dwellings or buildings not in the immediate neighborhood of the operations of land forces is prohibited. In cases where the objectives specified in par. 2 are so situated that they cannot be bombarded without the indiscriminate bombardment of the civilian population, the aircraft must abstain from bombardment.
(4) In the immediate neighborhood of the operations of land forces the bombardment of cities, towns, villages, dwellings or buildings is legitimate provided that there exists a reasonable presumption that the military concentration is sufficiently important to justify such bombardment, having regard to the danger thus caused to the civilian population.
(5) A belligerent state is liable to pay compensation for injuries to person or to property caused by the violation by any of its officers or forces of the provisions of this article.
▷ Bombing of open cities and villages.

International Conciliation, No. 248, New York, March 1929, pp. 161–162; R. L. BLEDSOE, B. A. BOCZEK, *The International Law Dictionary,* Oxford, 1987.

AIR WARSAW CONVENTION, 1929. A commonly used name for the Warsaw Convention; full official name only in French: Convention pour l'unification de certaines régles relatives au transport aérien international, i.e. for the unification of certain rules relating to international transport by air; signed Oct. 12, 1929 in Warsaw as the first international convention applying (art. 1, par. 1) "to all international transportation of persons, baggage, or goods performed by aircraft for hire. It shall apply equally to gratuitous transportation by aircraft performed by an air transportation enterprise."
The convention standardized passenger tickets, luggage tickets, air waybill, liability of the carrier and provisions relating to combined transportation. The convention with modifications is binding on all civil airlines belonging to ▷ IATA. Modifications: the Hague Protocol 1955, raising liability from US \$8300 to 16,600; the Guadalajara Convention, 1961, specifying freight carriage and the Guatemala Protocol, 1971, raising liability from US \$16,600 to 100,000.

D. GOEDHNIS, *La Convention de Varsovie,* La Haye, 1933; K.M. BAUMONT, "The Warsaw Convention of 1929 as amendable by the Hague Protocol, 1955", in: *Journal of Air Law and Commerce,* No. 22, 1955.

AIRWAY. An international term, defined in international agreements as an air route for transportation in the air of civilian passengers and cargo at definite altitudes between two controlled air traffic zones. These are 10 km (6.25 miles) wide for domestic and 20 km (12.5 miles) wide for international air traffic. Altitudes depend on the number of airways in a region.

AIX-LA-CHAPELLE CONGRESS, or AACHEN CONGRESS, 1818. A meeting of Austrian Emperor Francis I, Russian Tsar Alexander I, Frederick William III of Prussia and diplomats from these countries as well as England and France held Sept. 29–Nov. 21, 1818; set up conditions for withdrawal of foreign troops from post-Napoleonic France and a reduction of the contribution imposed on France included in the provisions of a convention signed on Oct. 9, 1818. France on Nov. 12, 1818 was admitted to the Holy Alliance endorsed by the Declaration of Nov. 15, 1818 which defined its aim as the maintenance of peace in Europe. The powers also declared their unconditional agreement to respect the principles of international law in their mutual relations as well as with other countries.

MARTENS: *Nouveau Recueil,* vol. IV, p. 549.

AIX-LA-CHAPELLE TREATY, 1748. The treaty which ended the Austrian Succession War, 1740–48.

AJMAN, one of the ▷ United Arab Emirates.

AKSUM OR AXUM. A town in northern Ethiopia, former capital of the country (*c.* first–eighth century AD); The Ethiopian cultural monument included in the ▷ World Heritage UNESCO List. The plateau of Aksum is dotted with ruins which recall the grandeur of Ethiopian civilization at the beginning of the Christian era. These monuments include votive thrones, stone seats venerated for 2000 years, and gigantic stelae which mark the burial places. Seven of the highest are carved in imitation of a facade several storeys high.

UNESCO. *A Legacy for All,* Paris, 1984.

"ALABAMA" CLAIMS. Damages sought by the USA from the UK for losses to the US merchant marine caused by the British-financed Confederate cruisers during the Civil War. A Tribunal in Geneva on Sept. 14, 1872, in accordance with the Washington Treaty, 1871, awarded US \$15.5 million for damage by the *Florida*, *Alabama* and *Shenandoah.*

E. REALE, *L'arbitrage international. Le règlement judiciaire du conflit l'Alabama,* Paris, 1929.

ALADI. ▷ Latin American Association of Integration.

ALALC. ▷ Latin American Free Trade Association.

ALAMOGORDO. A city (1978 est. pop. 22,900) in New Mexico, USA, founded in 1898 by the Southern Pacific Railway; during World War II and in the following decades an experimental base of the US Air Force (Holloman Air Force Base), used to test bombs and missiles. The first atom bomb was exploded June 16, 1945 near this city (White Sands Missile Range).
See also ▷ Manhattan Project.

D. ROBERTSON, *Guide to Modern Defense and Strategy.,* Detroit, 1988.

ALASKA. One of 2 non contiguous states of the USA.

Area: 1,530,700 sq. km. Population: 1880 – 33,426; 1900 – 63,592; 1950 – 128,643; 1958 – 210,000; 1985 – 521,000.

The Europa Yearbook. A World Survey, 1987, Vol. II, London, 1987.

ALASKA AGREEMENT, 1867. An American-–Russian Agreement concluded on Mar. 30, 1867 in Washington between the USA and Russia, signed by the Secretary of State, W.H. Seward and Ambassador E. de Stoeckel. Russia renounced Alaska for the sum of 7.2 million dollars in gold; therefore, initially, Alaska was called in the USA "the most expensive icebox" or "Seward's Ice-Box". Its borders with Canada were determined by the British–Russian convention of Feb. 28 (16), 1825. The border with Russia was demarcated by the Bering Sea and by the lines fixed in the agreement (art. 1). Arts. 2 and 3 guaranteed the rights of the Greek Orthodox communities and the right of option. The agreement was ratified in May and entered into force on June 20, 1897. Text only in English.

M. PONIATOWSKI, *Histoire de la Russie, de l'Amérique et de l'Alaska,* Paris, 1958; C.C. HULLEY, *Alaska: Past and Present,* 2nd edit., Portland, 1959; M. B. SHERWOOD (ed.), *Alaska and its History,* New York, 1967.

ALASKA BOUNDARY DISPUTE, 1896. A dispute between Canada and the USA which began after the discovery of gold in the Canadian Klondike; resolved in 1903 by a mixed commission consisting of two Americans, two Canadians and a representative of Great Britain.

ALBANIA. Member of the UN. People's Socialist Republic of Albania, Republika Popullore Socialiste e Shipörisö. State in SE Europe, on the Adriatic Sea coast of the Balkan Peninsula between Yugoslavia and Greece. Since Dec. 14, 1955 member of the UN and of the specialized agencies, FAO, IAEA, ITU, UNESCO, UNIDO, UPU, WHO and WMO. Albania was a member of ILO since 1920, and left it in 1967.
Area: 28,748 sq. km. Population: 1988 est. 3,140,000; 1960 census – 1,626,315. Capital: Tirana with 192,300 inhabitants 1976. GNP per capita 1986 US \$930. Border with Yugoslavia and Greece decided by the League of Nations Council in July 1923 (LN Doc. C.250, 1923). Official language: Albanian. Currency: 1 lek = 100 qintars. National Day: November 28/29, anniversary of the liberation, 1944. International relations: after nearly 450 years of Turkish occupation, proclamation of independence on Nov. 28, 1912, recognized by Great Powers on July 29, 1913; during World War I Albania was subject of inter-power contests and of partition plans between Greece and Yugoslavia (Secret London Agreement of Apr. 26, 1915), foiled by Albanian armed struggle, ended in a renewed recognition of Albanian independence by Great Powers in 1920. In the years 1914–25 monarchial system, 1925–28 republican, 1928–39 monarchial again. From Dec. 1, 1920 to Apr. 14, 1939 member of the League of Nations. Since 1926 connected by military alliance with Italy. Since Apr. 7, 1939 occupied by Italy, and, after its surrender on Sept. 3, 1943 – by Germany (Sept. 10, 1943–Nov. 29, 1944). The Anti-Fascist National Liberation Movement, organized by the Communist Party of Albania (f. on Jan. 8, 1941) formed on Nov. 29, 1944 a Temporary Government, recognized by Great Powers on Nov, 10, 1945. Its task was to carry out free elections, which took place on Dec. 2, 1945, and brought a sweeping victory (95% of votes) to the Democratic Front. On Jan. 11, 1946 the National Assembly proclaimed Albania a people's republic, which

brought about a breach of diplomatic relations with the UK and the USA, and a ▷ veto of both powers against admission of Albania to the UN. Beginning with Nov. 1948, the Communist Party of Albania changed its name to the Albanian Labor Party; along with it, the Albanian Democratic Front, a social-political mass organization, started its activities. Charter-member 1955 of the Warsaw Pact till Sept. 13, 1968, when the People's Assembly resolved a formal withdrawal from the Pact. Member of CMEA, relations with which practically do not exist since 1962, after Albania broke relations with USSR in 1961 in connection with Albania's declaration of sympathy for China. In 1977 Albania attacked the new leadership of China for the policy of rapprochement with the USA, which brought in July 1978 the end of Chinese aid to Albania. A railway line between Shköder, Albania and Titograd, capital of the Yugoslav republic of Montenegro was opened on Aug. 6, 1986.

On Aug. 28, 1987 Greece announced the formal end of the state of war with Albania, that had existed since 1940. On Oct. 17, 1987 in Tirana, Albania and Greece signed a cultural exchange agreement. On Sept. 16, 1987 Albania established diplomatic relations with the FRG and Yugoslavia on Dec. 11, 1987 Albania and the GDR decided to resume diplomatic relations. Establishment or re-establishment of diplomatic relations with Bolivia, Canada, Jordan and the Philippines also took place in 1987. Rumours of unrest, Jan. 1990.

K. FRASHERI, *History of Albania*, Tirana, 1965; N.C. PANO, *The People's Republic of Albania*, Baltimore, 1968; S. POLLO, *Histoire de l'Albanie des Origines à Nos Jours*, Roanne, 1974; R. MARMULLAKU, *Albania and the Albanians*, London, 1975; A. LOGORECI, *The Albanians: Europe's Forgotten Survivors*, London, 1977; P.R. PRIFFI, *Socialist Albania since 1944*, Cambridge, Mass., 1978; B. TOENNES, *Sonderfall Albania*, Munich, 1980; *The Europa Year Book 1984*, Vol. I, pp. 281–291, London, 1984. J. HALLIDAY, *The Artful Albania: The Memoirs of Enver Hoxha*, London, 1986. KEESING's *Contemporary Archive*, 1986.

ALBANIA DECLARATION, 1921. A Declaration by the governments of the British Empire, France, Italy and Japan in regard to Albania, signed in Paris, Nov. 9, 1921, reaffirming the frontiers of 1913.

LNTS, Vol. 12, p. 383.

ALBANIA–GREECE BORDER DISPUTES, called the Northern Epirus Question. The southern part of Albania, Northern Epirus, inhabited by ethnic Greeks, whose number was estimated before World War II at 300,000, was subject of Greek claims before and after World War II. In August 1987 Greece renounced all territorial claims to the region and on April 17, 1988 Albania and Greece signed in Ioamrino a cross-border trade agreement.

Albania-Greece, in: KEESING's *Border and Territorial Disputes*, London, 1987; *The International Herald Tribune*, April 18–19, 1988.

ALBANIAN GOLD. A name adopted for the 2338 kg of gold which were part of the reserves of the National Bank of Albania and 85% of which was owned by the Central Bank of Albania. It was deposited in Rome and removed to Germany in 1943, in 1945 confiscated by the Western Allies. They agreed, in Washington on Apr. 25, 1951, that the question should be resolved by an international commission appointed by the International Court of Justice; If the commission upheld the claims of Albania, the gold was to be handed over to Great Britain as part of its reparation payment. The arbiter, Prof. Sauser-Hall of Switzerland, ruled in favor of Albania on Feb. 20, 1953; Italy appealed to the International Court of Justice and demanded the gold for itself because it was the chief shareholder of the National Bank of Albania. The Court turned down the Italian claim on June 15, 1954.

CIJ, 1954.

ALBANIAN–ITALIAN TREATIES, 1927. Two treaties signed by Albania and Italy in 1927. The first was a Treaty for the Protection of the Political, Legal and Territorial Status Quo of Albania (Rome, Jan. 24, 1927). The second was a Treaty on the Mutual Security of the Contracting Parties Against External Aggression with Mutual Aid (Rome, Dec. 23, 1927).

LNTS, No. 1402 and 1616.

ALBANIA–YUGOSLAVIA BORDER DISPUTE, called the Kosovo Question. The autonomous region of Kosovo-Metchija within the republic of Serbia with a predominantly Albanian population (about 85% of its 1,486,000 inhabitants, 1981) was since 1949 subject of Albanian claims and a scene of border incidents and internal tensions. Since spring 1981 the hostility between Albanians and Serbs has been mounting, in spring 1988 the first negotiations were started between Albania and Yugoslavia.

Albania Yugoslavia (Kosovo), in: KEESING's *Border and Territorial Disputes*, London, 1987; *The Europa Yearbook. A World Survey 1988*, London, 1988.

ALCM. Air-Launched Cruise Missile, ▷ Cruise.

ALCOHOL. A subject of international co-operation. Organizations reg. with the UIA:

European Alcohol, Brandy and Spirit Union, f. 1959, Brussels.
Latin American Association of Producers of Alcoholic Beverages, f. 1971, Montevideo.

Yearbook of International Organizations.

ALCOHOLIC LIQUORS CONTRABAND. A subject of an international Convention for the Suppression of the Contraband Traffic in Alcoholic Liquors, signed in Helsingfors, Aug. 19, 1925 between Denmark, Estonia, Finland, Germany, Latvia, Lithuania, Norway, Poland, Sweden and the USSR; with Final Protocol and Additional Agreement (between Estonia, Finland, and the USSR). According to the Convention "beer and similar beverages with an alcoholic content of less than 12% shall not be regarded as alcoholic liquors," (art. 1).

LNTS, Vol. 42, p. 73.

ALCOHOLISM. An international problem caused by the increased production and consumption of alcohol. A WHO report of May 14, 1982, stated that the consumption of alcoholic beverages has risen considerably over the past 20 years, largely because the supply – of both home and imported brews – has increased. In the developing world in particular, beer production has soared. The production of beer shot up by leaps and bounds over two decades, the report says, increasing by 124% throughout the world. High as that is, the rise registered in the third world has been still higher. Over-all production jumped by some 500% in Asia, by 400% in Africa, thus "reaching the most distant villages", and by 200% in Latin America. "Some of this increase resulted from the establishment of subsidiary companies, joint ventures and licensing agreements with foreign corporations", the report says, adding that "the rate of beer production – and in some cases, wine production – has far outstripped population growth over the last 20 years." These trends, a "new signal for alarm", present governments with a dilemma, the report says. On the one hand, alcoholism and alcohol-related problems take a heavy toll on health. "The human costs are incalculable." On the other hand, the production and sales of alcoholic beverages create jobs. Above all, taxes on drink are a source of revenue. "Economically", the report states, "alcohol is an important commodity." As a result, "only a few countries have attempted to face this situation squarely". Many countries recognize the danger to health posed by alcohol but few have drawn up policies or programmes to combat the menace. The report asks governments to do so by putting health ahead of economic interests. Admitting that the "complete elimination of alcohol problems is nowhere feasible", the report says that "a more realistic goal would be the reduction of the extent, gravity and duration of problems". The regulation of alcohol production, the control of imports, the limiting of sales outlets and the banning of advertising are among measures with proven success in achieving those aims. Not only do alcohol-related problems place a heavy burden on the health services of most countries, but also, in the case of third-world nations, they may even threaten economic development.

Organizations reg. with the UIA:

International Association for Temperance Education, f. 1954, Leenwarden, Holland.
International Band of Hope Council, f. 1949, London.
International Catholic League Sobrietas, f. 1897, Freiburg Br., FRG.
International Council for the Prevention of Alcoholism, f. 1953, Washington, DC.
International Council on Alcohol and Addictions, f. 1907, New York ECOSOC (II), WHO, ILO.
International Doctors in Alcoholics Anonymous, f. 1939, Youngstown, Oh., USA.
International Federation of the Temperance Blue Cross Societies, f. 1890, Geneva.
International Good Templar Youth Federation, f. 1962, Gothenburg, Sweden.
Middle European Good Templar Youth Council, f. 1954, Königsfelden, Switzerland.
Scandinavian Union for Non-Alcoholic Traffic (Motorists Association), f. 1934, Stockholm.
World Christian Temperance Federation, f. 1960, Basel, Switzerland.
World Prohibition Federation, f. 1909, London.
World's Women's Christian Temperance Union, f. 1883, London.

UN Chronicle, July 1982, p. 96; *Yearbook of International Organizations*; D. WALSH, *Alcohol related medicosocial problems and their prevention*, WHO, Copenhagen, 1982. WHO, *Health Statistics Annual 1987*, Geneva 1988.

ALDABRA ATOLL. A natural site in the Seychelles, included in the ▷ World Heritage UNESCO List.

ALDERNEY. One of the islands of the Bailiwick of Guernsey, UK Crown dependencies in the English Channel. Area: 7.9 sq km. Population about 2,000 in 1985.

The Europa Yearbook 1988. A World Survey, Vol. II, London, 1988.

ALERT. In the UN System an international meteorological or seismographic emergency term.

ALEUTIAN ISLANDS. A chain of volcanic islands between the Alaskan Peninsula and Kamchatka, separating the Bering Sea from the Pacific Ocean. Area 37,840 sq. km with 8057 inhabitants (1970). Discovered by V. Bering (1741), and sold with Alaska to the USA (1867) by Russia. In June, 1942, Japan occupied Attu, Agattu and Kiska Islands.

They were recovered by the USA in May 1943 (Attu) and in Aug. 1943.

H.B. COLLINS, *Aleutian Islands; Their People and Natural History*, New York, 1945.

ALEXANDRIA. Al-Iskandariya. A city (1976 pop. 2,161,916) and the main port of Egypt. Main Allied naval base in the eastern part of the Mediterranean during World War II. The British armed forces left Alexandria in 1946. The city is the seat of the Alexandrian Patriarch of the Greek Orthodox Church, who is considered by the Eastern Orthodoxians to be the successor of St Mark the Evangelist.

ALEXANDROÚPOLIS. Bulgarian name: Dedéagatch. A seaport on the Gulf of Ainos, an inlet of the Aegean Sea in W. Thrace, Greece (1971 pop. 22,995). Occupied by Bulgaria in both World Wars. It was ceded to Greece by the Thrace Treaty, 1920, and the Paris Peace Treaty, 1947.

LNTS, Vol. 28, p. 233 and 235; *UNTS*, Vol. 41.

ALGAE, MARINE. A subject of international co-operation. World Association of Producers Marine Algae Extracts (Marinal International), f. 1976, Velisy, France. Reg. with the UIA.

In spring of 1988 a concentration of toxic algae killed thousands of fish in the Baltic and North Seas, Environmental experts blamed the sea pollution on industrial wastes surmising that the radiation released by the nuclear catastrophe in ▷ Chernobyl might also have been a factor.

Yearbook of International Organizations.

ALGECIRAS, CONFERENCE AND TREATY, 1906. A City in southern Spain, on the Bay of Algeciras opposite Gibraltar (1970 pop. 81,622). An international conference which took place from Jan. 15 to Apr. 7, 1906 with participants from: Austria, Belgium, France, Germany, Great Britain, Italy, Morocco, Netherlands, Portugal, Russia, Spain, Sweden and the USA. Its purpose was to alleviate the 1905 conflict between France and Germany over Morocco. On Apr. 7, 1906 the General Act of the International Conference in Algeciras, the Algeciras Treaty, was signed. The Treaty was meant to limit the influence of Germany in Morocco on behalf of France, whose protectorate over Morocco was recognized by Germany as late as 1912, in return for part of the French Congo.

A. TARDIEU, *La Conférence d'Algeciras. Histoire diplomatique de la crise marocaine 15 Janvier–7 Avril 1906*, vol. 1–3, Paris, 1909; *Documents Diplomatiques Français (1871–1914)*, 2e Série (1901–1911), Paris, 1930, *Major Peace Treaties of Modern History*, New York, 1967, pp. 1159–1195.

ALGERIA. Member of the UN. Democratic Peoples Republic of Algeria. El Djemhouria El Djazairia Eddemokratia Echaaba, République Algérienne Démocratique et Populaire. North-African state on the Mediterranean Sea, bordered by Tunisia, Libya, Niger, Mali, Mauritania, Western Sahara and Morocco. Since Oct. 10, 1962 member of the UN and of UN specialized organizations with exception of IFC and GATT. Member of the Arab League, OAU, OAPEC, OPEC and the Maghreb organization. A Trade and Co-operation Agreement with the EEC, 1976.

Area: 2,381,745 sq. km. Population, 1987 census: 22,971,558 (in 1977 nearly 17 mln). Capital Algiers 1983 census: 1,721,607 GNP per capita 1987 US $2,760. Official language: Arabic. Currency: 1 Algerian dinar = 100 centimes. National Day: July 5, Independence Day, 1962.

International relations: invaded by France 1830–37, declared French colonial territory 1848. On Nov. 1, 1954 the National Liberation Front (FLN) started an independence war, terminated on the whole in 1960 due to the recognition by General de Gaulle's government of the right of the Algerian people to independence; formally reaffirmed by referendum held in Algeria and metropolitan France on Jan. 6–8, 1961, and by the proclamation of independence of Algeria on July 5, 1962. The Algerian–French conflict was debated in the Security Council and in the UN General Assembly Session 1955–61, but the pro-Algerian UN resolutions were boycotted by France. In 1979–80 in dispute with Morocco. ▷ Polissario and ▷ Western Sahara.

In Feb. 1983 Algeria started to normalize frontier contacts with Morocco and in Mar. 1983 signed a Treaty of good neighbor relations with Tunisia.

On Aug. 7, 1987 the Algerian and Spanish Secretaries of Security signed an agreement to monitor the activities of Algerian dissidents in Spain and of Basque (ETA) separatists in Algeria. See also ▷ World Heritage UNESCO List.

Ch. FAVROD, *La révolution algérienne*, Paris, 1959; P. CORNET, *Le pétrole saharien*, Paris, 1961; D.C. GORDON, *The Passing of French Algeria*, London, 1965; F. BUY, *La République Algérienne*, Paris, 1965; H. BOURGES, *L'Algérie à l'épreuve de la décolonisation*, Paris, 1967; C. VIRATELLE, *L'Algérie algériennes*, Paris, 1970; J. MINCES, *L'Algérie indépendente*, Paris 1972; A. HORNE, *A Savage War of Peace: Algeria 1954–62*, London, 1977; P. LAFFONT, *Histoire de la France en Algerie*, Paris, 1980; Ch.A. JULIEN, Ch.R.AGERON, *Histoire de l'Algérie Contemporaine*, 2 vols., Paris, 1964–80; Ch.R. AGERON, *L'Algérie Algérienne de Napoléon III á de Gaulle*, Paris, 1980; *The Europa Year Book 1984. A World Survey*, Vol. I, pp. 1051–1064, London 1984. J. P. ENTELIS, *Algeria: The Revolution Institutionalized*, Boulder Colo., 1986; C. R. AGERON, *A History of Modern Algeria*, London, 1988; KEESING's *Record of World Events*, March, 1988.

ALGIERS. The capital of Algeria since 1962. Population: 1,721,607 in 1983; 2,442,300 in 1986. During World War II, from Nov., 1942 to Aug., 1944, the headquarters of the Allied Forces in North Africa and the seat of the French Committee for National Liberation. Seat of the All-African Women's Conference and Pan African Youth Movement. UN Information Center and ILO Regional Office.

KEESING's *Record of World Events*, 1987.

ALGIERS ECONOMIC ACTION PROGRAM OF NONALIGNED COUNTRIES, 1973. An action program for economic co-operation, adopted by the Fourth Conference of Heads of State or Government of Nonaligned Countries in Algiers, Sept. 5–9, 1973. The text is as follows:

"The Heads of State or Government reaffirm their belief that the primary responsibility for ensuring the rapid development of their countries rests with themselves. They declare their resolve to work towards attainment of individual and collective self-reliance in order to obtain their development goals. To that end they agree that continuous and coordinated efforts will be exerted at the national level to reduce unemployment, mass poverty, inequality of income distribution and economic dependence on the developed countries, and to mobilize all national resources for the integrated and balanced development of all sectors of the economy.

They have also decided that co-operation between developing countries should be expanded in the following specific directions:

I. In the interest of promoting trade among developing countries, each developing country should work towards the targets of doubling the rate of growth of its imports from other developing countries;

II. No developing country should accord to imports from developed countries more favourable treatment than that accorded to imports from developing countries.

III. Within the framework of the multilateral trade negotiations in GATT, developing countries should engage in a round of negotiations among themselves to promote intra-developing-country trade;

IV. To facilitate inter-regional trade, serious thought should be given to the possibility of establishing clearing and/or payment arrangements embracing the developing countries;

V. Developing countries should endeavour to deploy united aid funds to the maximum possible extent for procurement from other developing countries;

VI. Close co-operation and consultations should be established between the central banks of developing countries in order to promote greater monetary and financial co-operation between them and to study the possibility of creating a joint financial institution for that purpose;

VII. Institutional arrangements should be explored for employing surplus funds available in developing countries for financing projects with specific export orientation. These arrangements should be supported by developed countries and international financial institutions;

VIII. Projects in developing countries requiring foreign technical know-how should be supported to the maximum possible extent through the sharing and exchange of the technical know-how available within the developing countries themselves;

IX. Effective co-operation among the various existing organizations including those of the United Nations system, at the sub-regional, regional and inter-regional level, should be ensured with a view to intensifying the organizations future relations in all fields;

X. Co-operation should be established in the monetary field through the creation or adaptation at the regional or sub-regional level of agencies for co-operation therein;

XI. Credit relations should be developed on a preferential basis between developing countries;

XII. Developing countries should establish and strengthen producers' associations in respect of major commodities of importance to the world economy in order to halt the deterioration in their terms of trade, eliminate unhealthy competition, prevent harmful activities on the part of multinational corporations and strengthen their bargaining power;

XIII. Developing countries should take concerted action in the field of mass communications on the following lines in order to promote a greater interchange of ideas among themselves:

(a) Reorganize existing communication channels, which are the legacy of the colonial past and which have hampered free, direct and fast communication between them;

(b) Initiate joint action for the revision of existing multi-lateral agreements with a view to reviewing press cable rates and facilitating faster and cheaper inter-communication;

(c) Take urgent steps to expedite the process of collective ownership of communications satellites and evolve a code of conduct for directing their use;

(d) Promote increased contact between the mass media, universities, libraries, planning and research bodies and other institutions so as to enable developing countries to exchange experience and expertise and share ideas;

(e) Urge the Secretary-General of the United Nations to establish a special Chair of Non-alignment at the proposed United Nations University so as to facilitate research on the historical evolution and the present and future role of non-alignment in the changing world order. Developing countries should themselves promote similar studies in their universities and research institutions.

(f) Likewise establish at regional and inter-regional levels scientific and technical research institutes to study projects of national, regional and inter-regional interest among developing countries, and facilitate training of scientific and technical staff, inter alia through the granting of scholarships for training and advanced training.

XIV. Non-aligned countries should exchange and disseminate information concerning their mutual achievements in all fields through newspapers and periodicals, radio, television and the news media of their respective countries. They should formulate plans for sharing experience in this field, inter alia, through reciprocal visits of delegations from information media and through exchange of radio and television programmes, films, books, photographs, and through cultural events and art festivals.

I. Relations between developing and developed countries:

The Heads of States or Government solemnly reaffirm their determination to continue to work towards securing all the necessary conditions, both in their respective countries and in international relations, for their accelerated economic and social development and a higher standard of living for their peoples.

They call upon the international community to restore the development objective to its rightful place in the function of the United Nations system and to establish a new system of world economic relations based on equality and common interest of all countries which should co-operate to solve each other's problems, particularly by setting the following objectives:

1. The developing countries should secure the withdrawal of the reservations expressed by some developed countries at the time of the adoption of the International Development Strategy, and the fulfilment of the commitments assumed by them. Efforts should also be directed towards seeking new areas of agreement and widening the existing ones within a time-bound programme, to meet the increasing needs of the developing countries.

2. Those developed countries which have not so far implemented the Generalized System of Preferences should do so without further delay. Furthermore, the Generalized System of Preferences should be widened to include agricultural and other sensitive product of the developing countries, and the margin of preferences itself should be increased to improve the trade opportunities available to developing countries. The trend towards intensification and multiplication of non-tariff barriers, safeguards and other restrictive practices should be eliminated so that the developing countries obtain full benefit from the Generalized System of Preferences.

3. The liberalization of trade and the progressive removal of tariff barriers among developed countries should be accompanied by corresponding measures to safeguard the advantages enjoyed by developing countries under the Generalized System of Preferences.

4. Considering the importance of multilateral trade negotiations and the far reaching repercussions they will inevitably have on world trade, the developing countries should strive, at the preparatory and negotiating stages, for recognition of the principles of non-reciprocity, non-discrimination and preferential treatment in relations between developed and developing countries. Since the results of the multilateral trade negotiations will only begin to take effect after those negotiations have been concluded, it is of paramount importance that during this period no freeze is imposed on action in favour of the developing countries' trade and of its targets such as those fixed in the International Development Strategy.

5. Efforts should be made to build up the export potential of developing countries, particularly by the adoption of essential structural adjustments in the economies of developed countries conducive to a more rational international division of labour.

II. International Monetary and Financial Systems:

1. Developing countries should participate fully and on an equal footing in the formulation and application on an equitable and durable international monetary system.

2. The new international monetary system should take into account the interest of the international community as a whole on the basis of a new agreement taking into consideration the profound upheavals which have taken place since Bretton Woods. The principle of preferential treatment for developing countries should be applied in the new monetary arrangements.

3. The new monetary system should ensure effective participation by developing countries in the decision-making process through adoption of a voting quota system. It should ensure stable but flexible exchange rates so as to provide an environment conducive to the growth of the developing countries' trade. There should be adequate and orderly creation of liquidity to meet the global needs of trade through the additional allocation of special drawing rights (SDRs). A link should be established between special drawing rights (SDRs) and development financing in the interests of developing countries.

4. The international financial institutions should effectively play their role as development financing banks without resorting to political discrimination against countries. In addition, the resources released by disarmament should yield considerable funds for promoting the development of the developing countries.

5. The developed countries should accept a time-bound programme for the implementation of targets for the net flow of financial resources to developing countries. The official components of the net transfer of financial resources to the developing countries should be increased.

6. The adverse consequences for the current and future development of developing countries arising from the burden of external debt contracted on hard terms should be neutralized by appropriate international action. The World Bank should play an efficient role where it can do so in the settlement of the debt problems within the context of a policy of general measures taking account of the economic situation of the debtor countries and the origin of the foreign debt.

7. Appropriate measures should be taken to alleviate the heavy burden of debt-servicing, including the method of re-scheduling.

8. The international financial institutions should increasingly orient their lending policies to suit the emerging needs of developing countries.

9. The regional and subregional development banks will need to be provided with considerably greater resources in order to strengthen their operations and establish closer co-operation among themselves.

III. Transfer of Technology.

1. The provisions as regards the transfer of technology in the International Development Strategy will need to be implemented without delay, and the developing countries should take a joint stand on this question in international bodies.

2. Monopolistic practices, applied by transnational corporations through market-sharing and price-fixing, should be ended and the costs of transferring technology to developing countries reduced.

3. New international legislation for the transfer of technology to the developing countries on a preferential basis should be formulated, and an international code of conduct should be adopted and implemented without delay.

4. Urgent measures should be taken at both national and international levels to stop the brain-drain from developing to developed countries.

IV. Commodities.

The progress made towards the formulation of international commodity agreements has so far been extremely slow. The competent international bodies should give priority to this work. The problem of commodities like tea, which have suffered a continuous decline in price, should be dealt with expeditiously on the basis of global agreements.

V. Shipping

1. Developing countries should obtain the means for ensuring their ever-wider participation in freight and insurance operations in shipping so as to increase the volume and profitability of their trade and improve their balance of payments on a permanent basis.

2. The participation of the governments of developing countries concerned in consultations between liner conferences and shippers is essential, particularly in the matter of rate-fixing, surcharges and frequencies, and the quality of services which have a direct impact on the cost of foreign trade operations.

3. It is essential to formulate and apply a binding code of conduct for liner conferences, which should be prepared by the forthcoming United Nations Conference of plenipotentiaries and take fully into account the developing countries' special needs and problems.

VI. Environment

The additional cost of environmental programmes should not be allowed to stand in the way of the more basic development needs of developing countries. Any assistance in the environmental field provided to developing countries by the developed countries should be additional to whatever is already being provided as development assistance. The preoccupation of developed countries with environmental control ought not to lead to adverse effects on the flow of development assistance or on the trade of developing countries.

VII. Co-operation with Socialist Countries.

1. The socialist countries should consider incorporating in their development plans the export needs and possibilities of the non-aligned countries, in order to facilitate an increase in the proportion of imports of manufactured and semi-manufactured goods from the latter on a preferential basis.

2. Socialist countries should accord the most favourable terms for intensifying trade, economy, scientific and technical co-operation with non-aligned countries. Special action should be considered in the fields of transfer of technology and training of national personnel of developing countries. The non-aligned countries shall intensify information activities on opportunities for expanding trade and co-operation with the socialist countries through the establishment of joint committees, the exchange of delegations, the organization of fairs and exhibitions and increased collaboration between chambers of commerce and industry and other appropriate institutions.

The non-aligned countries shall encourage the development of scientific and technical co-production with the socialist countries, inter alia, through the conclusion of inter-governmental conventions, the establishment of the necessary joint bodies and the stimulation of relations between the organizations and institutions concerned.

VIII. Co-ordination

The Heads of State of Government reviewed the work carried out by the co-ordinators in pursuance of the Georgetown Action Programme, in the following fields:

1. Trade, industry and transport,
2. Financial and monetary co-operation,
3. Technology, know-how and technical assistance,
4. International co-operation for economic development.

They directed that the mandate of the co-ordinators should be extended until the next Conference of Heads of State or Government.

The Heads of State or Government welcomed the concrete work carried out by the co-ordinators, particularly in the field of trade, industry and transport and recommended that:

(a) A practical action programme based on the studies so far made should be undertaken;

(b) Further studies should continue for the final formulation of the project for inter-regional co-operation;

(c) Active involvement of the relevant organizations of the United Nations system should be sought for financial and technical support.

They agreed in principle to the proposal to set up a Development and Solidarity Fund to pool their excess resources in order to finance emergency projects and render long-term technical assistance to member countries of the Movement; They decided that a working party be established to urgently draw up a project and submit it to the next Ministerial Conference of Non-aligned Countries or, if necessary, to a special meeting of Ministers of Finance and Economy which could take place earlier.

The Heads of State or Government endorsed the following conclusions reached by a Committee of Experts from non-aligned countries appointed in pursuance of the Georgetown Programme of Action in regard to guidelines for foreign private investment:

I. All foreign private investment should be subject to prior authorization and to a system of centralized government control;

II. Care should be taken to ensure that foreign investment supplements the domestic effort and is consistent with national development plans, incorporates appropriate technology, leads to the further development of technology, generates employment, represents a net saving in foreign exchange, involves management that is decentralized from the parent company, etc.

III. Any reinvestment of profits made by foreign companies should be considered as new investment and subject to authorization by the recipient State;

IV. The purchase of existing national assets by foreign investors should be prohibited except in very special and justified cases.

V. Specific provisions should be established for all matters relating to remittances of profits.

VI. It is essential to exclude the possibility of receiving foreign investment in those sectors of the economy which can be considered strategic according to the conditions of each country, such as the extractive industries, commodity industries, public utilities, mass communications media, banking, insurance and marketing.

They further approved the following recommendations made by the Committee of Experts for purposes of regulating and controlling the operations and activities of multinational corporations:

I. The adoption of common rules in respect of multinational transnational companies;

II. Extension and support of the unrestricted application of the principle that any State effecting a nationalization in order to regain its natural resources is exercising a sovereign right;

III. Integration of such joint action within an overall strategy designed to bring about quantitative and qualitative changes in the system of economic and financial relations that subordinate the underdeveloped countries to the developed capitalist countries;

IV. Maintenance of close links with the group of 20 eminent persons convened by the United Nations to analyse this matter, in order to ensure that all economic, political and cultural variables, as well as variables having to do with international relations, are suitably treated, and also to ensure that the results of the group's work remain in line with the initial objectives set when it was established.

V. The establishment of an information centre on transnational companies with the aim of ensuring a free exchange of experience and information between non-aligned countries in order to facilitate the full and effective utilization of experience available in many non-aligned countries. Such a centre would be responsible for training personnel, providing services and carrying out research.

The Heads of State or Government decided that a group of experts should be nominated and entrusted with the task of preparing a specific study on this matter within a period of three months.

IX. Food Crisis

The Heads of State or Government urged that, in the context of the serious food crisis confronting vast areas and populations of the world, an emergency joint conference of FAO and UNCTAD should be convened at Ministerial level in order to formulate a programme of international co-operation to overcome the increasing shortage of food and other commodities and maintain stable prices.

They also considered it advisable that a conference of developing countries be convened on commodities with a view to developing an effective strategy for restructuring world trade and improving their bargaining power. The Heads of State or Government recommend that non-aligned countries should act as a catalytic force in the Group of 77 in order to increase the effectiveness and solidarity of the developing countries."

Conference on Economic Co-operation among Developing Countries. Declarations, Resolutions, Recommendations and Decisions adopted in the UN System, Mexico DF, 1976, Vol. B, pp. 486–500.

ALGIERS GROUP OF 77 CHARTER, 1967. The official name of the document adopted Oct. 24, 1967, in the capital of Algeria by the Conference of Ministers of Economy of Developing Countries, also called the Group of the 77. The text is as follows:

I. "The representatives of developing countries, united by common aspirations and the identity of their economic interests, and determined to pursue their joint efforts towards economic and social development, peace and prosperity,

Having reviewed the work of the international community for economic progress since the adoption of the Joint Declaration of Seventy-Seven Developing Countries at the conclusion of the first session of the United Nations Conference on Trade and Development in 1964,

Have decided to chart a common course of action as conceived in the African Declaration of Algiers, the Bangkok Declaration of Asian Countries and the Charter of Tequendama of Latin American countries, Deem it their duty to call the attention of the international community to the following facts:

The lot of more than a billion people of the developing world continues to deteriorate as a result of the trends in international economic relations;

The rate of economic growth of the developing world has slowed down and the disparity between it and the affluent world is widening;

While the developed countries are adding annually approximately 60 dollars to the per capita income of their people, the average increase of per capita income in the developing world amounts to less than 2 dollars per annum;

The share of the developing countries in total world exports declined from 27 per cent in 1963 to only 19.3 per cent in 1966. In the first half of the 1960s, total world exports grew at an average annual rate of 7.8 per cent and exports of developing countries, excluding oil exports, grew at an average rate of 4 per cent only. While the value of exports of manufactures from industrial countries increased between 1953/1954 and 1965/1966 by 65 billion dollars and from socialist countries by 10 billion dollars, the increase from developing countries amounted to only 3 billion dollars; The purchasing power of exports from developing countries has been steadily declining. In the mid-1960s the developing countries have been able to buy, for a given volume of their traditional exports, one-tenth less imports than at the beginning of this period. The loss in purchasing power amounted annually to approximately 2.5 billion dollars, which represents nearly half of the flow of external public financial resources to developing countries;

This has aggravated the problem of increasing indebtedness of developing countries. The external public debt alone has increased from 10 billion dollars in 1955 to 40 billion in 1966. While the debt service payments averaged half a billion dollars annually in the mid 1950s, these have already increased to 4 billion dollars and may offset the entire transfer of resources before the end of this decade if present trends continue; they already equal the entire amount of grants and grant-like contributions;

Although modern technology offers developing countries great possibilities to accelerate their economic development, its benefits are largely by-passing them due to its capital and skill intensive nature, and is drawing away from them such limited skills as are developed;

The virtual stagnation in the production of foodstuffs in developing countries, in contrast with the rapid increase in population, has aggravated the chronic conditions of under-nourishment and malnutrition and, combined with the distortion of production and trading patterns by artificial means, threatens to give rise to a grave crisis.

II. The concern over these economic and social trends and the joint efforts of developing countries to correct them have progressively led the international community to embark on a series of initiatives culminating in the Final Act adopted in 1964 by the first session of the United Nations Conference on Trade and Development; however, the promise held out by the Final Act has not been realized. In fact, in spite of the provisions of the Final Act of the first session; No new commodity agreement on primary products of interest to developing countries has been concluded;

The standstill has not been observed by the developed countries, and they have increased the degree of protection in many of those agricultural products in which developing countries are more efficient producers;

While the average prices for primary products exported from developing countries have decreased by 7 per cent since 1958; those for primary products exported from developed countries increased by 10 per cent in the same period;

Heavy fiscal charges continue to be levied on products of export interest to developing countries;

The proliferation and promotion of synthetic substitutes in developed countries has resulted in shrinking markets and falling prices for competing natural products produced by developing countries;

Insufficient progress has been made by developed countries in dismantling import tariffs on tropical products without prejudice to the interests of certain developing countries; Little or no progress has been achieved in the relaxation of quota restrictions that are applied particularly to industrial products imported from developing countries; nor did the situation improve for some temperature zone products whose

access to the developed countries is governed by restrictive measures and policies applied by the developed countries;

The implicit discrimination in tariff policies towards developing countries has been further intensified as a result of the process of economic integration among some developed countries and also as a consequence of the Kennedy Round of negotiations;

No progress has been made by developed socialist countries on the recommended transferability of credit balances held with them by developing countries;

The wide disparity between domestic selling prices of goods imported by socialist countries from developing countries and the import prices of such goods creates unfavourable conditions for increases in consumption and import of such goods from developing countries;

In spite of the unanimously agreed target of 1 per cent of national income of financial resources to be provided to developing countries, actual disbursements have levelled off in absolute terms and declined as a proportion of gross national product of developed countries. While in 1961 the flow of development financing to developing countries amounted to 0.87 per cent of gross national product of developed countries, it came down to 0.62 per cent in 1966;

With a few notable exceptions, the terms and conditions of development finance are becoming more and more onerous; the proportion of grants is declining; interest rates are increasing; repayment periods are shortening and development loans are becoming increasingly tied;

Discriminatory practices and arrangements in the field of shipping and increasing freight rates have aggravated further the balance-of-payments position and hindered the effort to promote the exports of developing countries.

III. The international community has an obligation to rectify these unfavourable trends and to create conditions under which all nations can enjoy economic and social well-being, and have the means to develop their respective resources to enable their peoples to lead a life free from want and fear.

In a world of increasing interdependence, peace, progress and freedom are common and indivisible. Consequently the development of developing countries will benefit the developed countries as well.

Developing countries reiterate that the primary responsibility for their development rests on them.

Developing countries are determined to contribute to one another's development.

However, a fuller mobilization and more effective utilization of domestic resources of developing countries is possible only with concomitant and effective international action.

Traditional approaches, isolated measures and limited concessions are not enough. The gravity of the problem calls for the urgent adoption of a global strategy for development requiring convergent measures on the part of both developed and developing countries.

The establishment of UNCTAD and the dialogue which has taken place within it constitute a step towards a new and dynamic trade and development policy. What is needed now is to move from the stage of deliberation to the plane of practical action.

Developing countries expect that the second session of the Conference will concentrate on a common endeavour for accelerated economic and social development. The agreement which has recently emerged on the basic issues to be negotiated reflects the general feeling in this respect.

To this end the representatives of developing countries at the Ministerial Meeting of the Group of 77 have considered carefully the present state of affairs and suggest the following programme of action as the most urgent and immediate step to be taken by the second session of the Conference."

The Declaration was followed by a detailed Program of Action, presenting problems of: raw materials, export of ready-made and semi-finished products, financing development, invisible trade, maritime transportation, trade policies, development of trade and economic integration of developing countries and problems of special means that should be applied by developed countries in dealing with developing countries.

UN Monthly Chronicle, No. 1, 1968; *Conference on Economic Co-operation among Developing Countries, Declarations, Resolutions, Recommendations and Decisions adopted in the UN System*. Mexico, DF, 1976, Vol. II, pp. 216–252.

ALGOL. An algorithmic language, name of the second major universal international language of automatic programming of digital computers; invented in 1958, extended in 1960; the first computer language was ▷ Fortran.

ALGOLOGY. A subject of international co-operation. International Commission for Algology, f. 1972, Berkeley, Calif., USA. Reg. with the UIA.

Yearbook of International Organizations.

ALIEN PROPERTY. Property belonging to alien persons or institutions, subject to seizure in wartime.

ALIENS' RIGHTS. Also called "foreigners' rights". A subject of international conventions and bilateral interstate agreements. In the understanding of international law, an alien is a person who is not a citizen of the state on the territory of which such a person resides, and has a citizenship of another state or states (▷ Dual nationality), or has no citizenship at all (▷ Apatridos). In international law and in the practice of states there exist (depending on conventions or agreements): aliens' rights identical with the rights of own citizens, aliens' rights restricted and aliens' rights privileged, unattainable for one's own citizens. Through military or diplomatic pressure colonial powers extorted special privileges for their citizens staying abroad, particularly as regards guarantees of property invested by them in an alien country.
The Second International American Conference held in Mexico between Oct. 22, 1901 and Jan. 31, 1902, prepared a Convention relative to Rights of Aliens, which in its art. 1 adopted a principle that aliens enjoy the same civic rights as citizens of the state; art. 2 states that states have no special obligations with respect to aliens and shall assume no special responsibility in their favor, nor shall respect any privileges for aliens; art. 3 adopted the principle that aliens shall be subject to the internal laws of a state and all disputes shall be resolved by internal courts. This convention was not ratified by the United States.
During the ▷ Bolivar Congress Bolivia, Colombia, Ecuador, Peru and Venezuela signed in Caracas, on July 18, 1911, an agreement on the Judicial Acts of Aliens.
In Havana, on Feb. 20, 1928, the governments of 21 American republics signed the ▷ Interamerican Convention on Status of Aliens. After World War II the United States concluded a bilateral pact with the majority of Latin American states, protecting the rights of private US businessmen who guaranteed full damages in case of nationalization or economic disturbances. However, when in 1966 the World Bank prepared the so-called Washington Convention on Resolution of Disputes Regarding Private Investments – by Jan. 1, 1970, 55 states had signed and ratified it, including 26 of the so-called "Third World states" – not a single Latin American state was in that number, viewing this convention as contradictory to art. 3 of the Convention of 1902, since the Washington Convention grants aliens the right to appeal to the courts of their native country and does not respect the jurisdiction of the courts of their country of residence or stay. In keeping with the international custom, an alien may enter the territory of a sovereign state only pursuant to the consent of such state's authorities. An alien shall be expelled from such country when, in accordance of

an accepted international principle, "the alien became a nuisance". Not all states recognize the right of ▷ asylum for aliens (foreign citizens); not all states apply the principle of ▷ extradition. Denmark, Finland, Norway and Sweden concluded in Stockholm on July 14, 1952, the Scandinavian Treaty on Aliens, who Arrived in the Territory of Their States in an Illegal Way (*UNTS*, Vol. 193, p. 47), and in Copenhagen, on Feb. 3, 1965, the same states and Iceland concluded the Scandinavian Treaty on Deported Persons (*UNTS*, Vol. 572, p. 105). The position of aliens under the International Covenant on Civil and Political Rights was elaborated in the General Comment on Position of Aliens by the European Human Rights Committee on Oct. 15, 1986.

Council of Europe, Information Sheet, No 21, Strasbourg, 1988, pp. 240–242. OAS, *Inter-American Treaties and Conventions*, Washington, DC, 1971, pp. 10, 24, 140. Treatment of Aliens, in: R.L. BLEDSOE, B.A. BOCZEK, *The International Law Dictionary*, Oxford, 1987.

ALIMONY. The means rendered by one person to another legally linked to the former and fully or partially unable to support himself or herself. The subject of an International Convention on Alimony Claims, signed on June 20, 1956 in New York by Brazil, the Central African Republic, Ceylon, Chile, Czechoslovakia, Denmark, Finland, France, the FRG, Guatemala, Haiti, Hungary, Israel (with a reservation), Italy, Monaco, Morocco, the Netherlands, Norway, Pakistan, Poland, Sweden (with a reservation), Upper Volta, Vatican City, and Yugoslavia. The purpose of the Convention: "to facilitate an alimony claim which a person residing on the territory of one of the contracting parties is entitled to put forward against another person being subject to the jurisdiction of the other contracting party" (art. 1). "This purpose is accomplished by each of the contracting parties acting as the sending and receiving organs" (art. 2). Arts. 3–7 establish the procedure of sending, receiving, and transmitting of the claims.

UNTS, 1956.

AL–ISKANNDRAIYA ▷ Alexandria.

ALLA ▷ NATO.

ALLENDE DOCTRINE, 1971. A term accepted in the world press for a principle put into effect in Chile by a decree of President S. Allende (1908–73) on Sept. 26, 1971 that a developing country has a just and proper right in the nationalization of foreign companies to deduct from the general sum paid in compensation an "excess profits tax", i.e. higher than 10%.

ALLERGOLOGY. A subject of international co-operation. Organizations reg. with the UIA:

Collegium International Allergologicum, f. 1954, Basel, Switzerland. Publ. *International Archives of Allergy and Applied Immunology*.
International Association of Allergology, f. 1945, Montreal.
International Allergy Association, f. 1953, New York.
Latin American Society of Allergology, f. 1960, Santiago de Chile.
Northern Society of Allergology, f. 1974, Copenhagen.

Yearbook of International Organizations.

ALLIANCE FOR PROGRESS OR ALIANZA PARA EL PROGRESSO. The official name of the Latin American integration system, initiated on Mar. 13, 1961 by President J.F. Kennedy's call "for a new Alliance for Progress", est. on Aug. 17, 1961 by the ▷ Punta del Este Charter, signed by 20 Latin

American Republics, Cuba being the only one abstaining, not having been invited to the Punta del Este Conference. The system working in the framework of the OAS, in co-operation with the Inter-American Development Bank IADB and the UN Economic Commission for Latin America. ECLA, was centralized in the ▷ Inter-American Economic and Social Council, IA-ECOSOC, which meets annually at ministers level. The permanent Executive Committee of the IA-ECOSOC was the Inter-American Committee on the Alliance for Progress, called in Spanish abbreviation CIAP (Commission Inter-American de Alianza para el Progresso) est. in Nov., 1963 by the Second Annual Meeting of IA-ECOSOC in Sao-Paulo, Brazil. In 1967 the Punta del Este Summit Meeting proclaimed a program towards a ▷ Latin American Free Trade Association LAFTA. The 1967 amendments to the ▷ OAS Charter, ratified in 1970, integrated the IA-ECOSOC as an institution of the OAS which deals with economic and social matters. The Alliance for Progress project formally ended in 1980.

Provisional Guide to Writing on the Alliance for Progress, PAU, Washington, DC, 1967; J. LEVINSON, J. DE ONIS, *The Alliance that Lost its Way. A Critical Report on the Alliance for Progress*, Chicago, 1971.

ALLIANCE FRANÇAISE. An association f. in Paris in 1883 to propagate – initially in the colonial territories only – the French language and cultural heritage. Its sui generis international counterpart is the French Cultural Union.

ALLIANCE OF THE RHINE. An alliance concluded on Aug. 14, 1658 by the King of France, Louis XIV, with the German Dukes of the provinces adjacent to France, of Moguntia, Trier, Cologne and Rhine-Palatinate, with the Dukes of Hesse, Brunswick and Lüneburg, and also with the King of Sweden as the Duke of Bremen and Lord of Wismar, in order to create an area of peace and mutual assistance. The Alliance was open both to "those who are Catholics and to those who belong to the Augsburg Confession"; it initiated the still existent French policy of linking West Germany to France. The Alliance, which had been concluded for three years, was renewed on Aug. 31, 1661 and on Jan. 25, 1663 when the Dukes of Wittenberg and Zweibrücken acceded thereto.

J. DUMONT, *Nouveau Recueil des Traités*, Amsterdam, La Haye, 1910.

ALLIANCES. The bi- or multi-lateral covenants obligating the parties to political, economic and military co-operation in the name of the common defense of joint interests and to render each other mutual assistance in certain specific cases defined in the a. (▷ Casus foederis). In the past alliances were divided into aggressive and defensive; after World War II aggressive a. were recognized in the judgments of the International Military Tribunal as conspiracies against peace and security, since their aim was aggression (e.g. The Berlin Pact, signed Sept. 27, 1940 in the capital of the III Reich by Japan, Germany, and Italy, which was joined Nov. 20, 1940 by Hungary, Nov. 23, 1940 by Romania, and March 1, 1941 by Bulgaria). In accordance with the principles of international law there exists only a. of a defensive character (e.g. the United Nations alliances made during World War II in the face of aggression).

S. ROSENNE, *United Nations Treaty Practice, Recueil des Cours de l'Académie de Droit International 86*, 1952; M. LACHS, "Les conventions multilatérales et les organisations internationales contemporaines", *Annuaire Français de Droit International 2*, 1956; S.M. WALT, *The Origins of Alliances*, New York, 1987.

ALLIED BANK COMMISSION. A Two Powers Commission est. Feb. 16, 1948 by UK and USA occupational authorities of Germany, with headquarters in Frankfurt a. Main, with the purpose of overseeing the introduction of a monetary reform and the creation of a separate banking system for West Germany and West Berlin. Dissolved Mar. 31, 1952.

ALLIED COMMAND EUROPE ALLIED COMMAND ATLANTIC AND ALLIED COMMAND CHANNEL. Three major ▷ NATO commands. See ▷ ACE ▷ ACCHAN ▷ ACLANT.

D. ROBERTSON, *Guide to Modern Defense and Strategy*, Detroit, 1988.

ALLIED COMMISSION FOR AUSTRIA. A Four Power Commission set up in Austria after World War II in keeping with the terms of the ▷ Declaration of the Defeat of Germany of June 5, 1945 as an organ of the allied monitoring system assembling France, Great Britain, the USA and USSR, operating through the Allied Council, Executive Committee, and military staff; its members appointed by the governments of the four powers. Active on the territory of Austria from July 4, 1945 till July 27, 1955 under an agreement signed in Vienna, July 4, 1945; headed by chief commanders of occupation troops; main aims of the Commission: implementation of the separation of Austria from Germany, establishment of central Austrian administration, preparation for the formation of an Austrian government in free elections. In this period Vienna remained under joint command of the four powers. The agreement expired on July 27, 1955 with the entry into force of the ▷ Austria State Treaty, signed in Vienna, May 15, 1955, by the four powers and Austria, which restored full sovereignty to Austria.

"Four Powers Agreement on the Machinery of Control in Austria, June 28, 1946", in: *International Legislation*, Vol. IX, No. 855; *Europa Archiv*, 1956; A.A. KLEIN, *Von 1945 bis zum Staatsvertrag von 1955*, Wien, 1969.

ALLIED COMMISSION FOR GERMAN ARMAMENTS CONTROL. An allied institution called into being by the Allied Council in 1919; its functions were turned over Jan. 31, 1927 to the Council of the League of Nations after the entry of Germany into the LN and its securing a permanent seat in the Council.

ALLIED CONTROL AUTHORITY, ACA. An inter-allied institution consisting of France, Great Britain, and the USA acting as a control body over West Berlin. Its functions were related to the special status of this territory which was determined after the war by the Quadripartite Agreement of the Great Powers on West Berlin. Military Missions were accredited to the ACA of those UN member states which in 1946 had been accredited to the Allied Control Council and were given permanent extraterritorial residences in West Berlin. ▷ Allied Military Missions in Berlin.

Documents on Germany under Occupation, 1945–1954, London, 1955.

ALLIED CONTROL COUNCIL FOR GERMANY. "The highest authority for matters concerning the whole of Germany", formed by France, the UK, USA and USSR, according to the Declaration on Germany's defeat, signed on June 5, 1945 in Berlin; the Powers were represented on the Council by their supreme commanders in Germany. The operation of the Council started on Aug. 30, 1945 and lasted till Mar. 20, 1948, when it was sus-

pended. The tasks of the Council were determined in the Declaration of Four Powers on Control Procedure in Germany, – a supplement to the Declaration on Germany's Defeat, which stated:

"The German armed forces on land, at sea and in the air have been completely defeated and have surrendered unconditionally and Germany, which bears responsibility of the war, is no longer capable of resisting the will of the victorious Powers.
The unconditional surrender of Germany has thereby been effected, and Germany has become subject to such requirements as may now or hereafter be imposed upon her.
There is no central Government or authority in Germany capable of accepting responsibility for the maintenance of order, the administration of the country and compliance with the requirements of the victorious Powers.
It is in these circumstances necessary, without prejudice to any subsequent decisions that may be taken respecting Germany, to make provision for the cessation of any further hostilities on the part of the German armed forces, for the maintenance of order in Germany and for the administration of the country, and to announce the immediate requirements with which Germany must comply.
The Representatives of the Supreme Commands of the United Kingdom, the United States of America, the Union of Soviet Socialist Republics and the French Republic, hereinafter called the "Allied Representatives", acting by authority of their respective Governments and in the interests of the United Nations, accordingly make the following Declaration: The Governments of the United Kingdom, the United States of America and the Union of Soviet Socialist Republics, and the Provisional Government of the French Republic, hereby assume supreme authority with respect to Germany, including all the powers possessed by the German Government, the High Command and any state, municipal, or local government or authority. The assumption, for the purposes stated above, of the said authority and powers does not effect the annexation of Germany.
The Governments of the United Kingdom, the United States of America and the Union of Soviet Socialist Republics, and the Provisional Government of the French Republic, will hereafter determine the boundaries of Germany or any part thereof and the status of Germany or of any area at present being part of German territory."

The Declaration on Control Procedure established the Council's organization: Co-ordination Committee and Control Staff were subjected to the Council; moreover, in order to keep in touch with governments of other countries, belonging to the UN, chiefly those interested in the occupation of Germany, allied military missions of those governments were attached to the Control Council.
The seat of the Council was Berlin W 35, Potsdamerstr. 186. The Secretariat of the Council was housed in Berlin W 35, Elsholtzstr. 32. The rulings of the Council were published in the official gazette: *Journal Officiel du Conseil de Controle en Allemagne*, published in four languages: French, Russian and English, as well as (non-obligatory text) in German. Up to 1950 19 issues came out, the first on Oct. 29, 1945, the nineteenth on Aug. 31, 1948. Apart from those issues, Supplement No. 1, which contained a collection of documents concerning Germany's defeat and the setting up of the Council. In 1945–49 members of the Council were successive supreme commanders of occupational forces: on behalf of the USSR Marshal G.K. Zhukov (1945–46), Marshal V.D. Sokolovsky (1946–49) and General V.I. Tshuikov (since 1949); on behalf of the USA General D.D. Eisenhower (1945–46), General M.T. McNarney (1946–47), General L.D. Clay (1947–49) and (formally) J. McCloy (since 1949); on behalf of Great Britain Marshal L. Montgomery (1945–46), Marshal S. Douglas (1946–47) and General B.H. Robertson (since 1947); on behalf of France General P. Koenig

(1945–49) and (formally) A. François-Poncet (since 1949). During the term of its operation, the Council examined 193 issues, 140 of which were approved unanimously. The elaboration of all current materials and of final drafts of resolutions was handled by the Co-ordination Committee, which supervised 10 directorates, divided into many departments and commissions: political, general, economic, finance, communication, legal, press, reparations, transport, POWs and Displaced persons directorates. On each level of the Council organization there was observed a system of elaboration used by representatives of the Four Powers. The Chairmanship in the Council and in each commission was alternated every month. The Chairman of the Council or of any of the commissions of the Council called and conducted meetings in the given month. After Mar. 20, 1948, in spite of formal rotation of Chairmen, no one exercised the right to call a Council meeting. The activity of the Council kept slackening from year to year. The last meeting of the Control Council for Germany was held on Mar. 20, 1948. The only sites in which representatives of the Four Powers have met since 1948 were: Berlin Centre of Air Security, responsible for the traffic of military and civilian planes, and the International Facility Office, responsible for passenger traffic. The agreement of the Four Powers on West Berlin of Aug., 1971, concluded in the building of the Control Council for Germany, actually closed the activities of the Four-Powers Council; however, the quadrilateral Berlin Centre of Air Security continued to control the three air corridors: American, British and French linking West Berlin with the West.
After the death on Aug. 17, 1987 of Rudolf Hess, the sole inmate of the Spandau War Crimes Prison, the four Allied prison governors decided to pull down the prison.

Journal Officiel du Conseil de Controle en Allemagne, Berlin, 1945–48; W. CORNIDES, "Der Kontrollrat", in: *Europa Archiv 1946–47*; D. STAPPERT, "Die Alliierte Kontrollbehörde in Deutschland", in: *Jahrbuch für Internationales und Ausländisches Öffentliches Recht*, 1948, pp. 139–159; E. OSMAŃCZYK, *Niemcy 1945–50* [Germany 1945–50], Warsaw, 1951; S. JAENICKE, *Der Abbau der Kontrollgesetzgebung*, Berlin W, 1952.

ALLIED COUNCIL FOR JAPAN. An organ of control over Japan established after World War II in keeping with the provisions of the Moscow conference of foreign ministers of the USA, Great Britain and the USSR (Dec. 16–26, 1945). Apart from the Powers mentioned above, the Council included China. The Council operated from Apr. 18, 1946, to Apr. 28, 1952, when it was suspended after the entry into force of the US Peace Treaty with Japan, signed in San Francisco, on Sept. 8, 1951.

M.E. CAMERON, *China, Japan and the Powers. A History of the Modern Far East*, New York, 1960; G. WINT (ed.), *Asia. A Handbook*, New York, 1966.

ALLIED HIGH COMMISSION FOR GERMANY, HICOG. A Commission created by a Treaty of three Western Powers in Washington on June 20, 1949, as an organ of France, the UK and the USA for the occupied zones of West Germany after suspension of the operations of the ▷ Allied Control Council for Germany. The task of the Commission was to exercise supreme allied authority in the Federal Republic of Germany after its formation on Sept. 6, 1949. All of the control powers which up to then were exercised by the supreme commanders of the armed forces of those powers in Germany were assumed Sept. 21, 1949 and performed to May 8, 1955 by three High Commissioners. When the activities of the Commission ceased they were appointed as ambassadors to the FRG.

E. PLISCHKE, H.J. HILLE, History of the Allied High Commission for Germany. Its Establishment, Structure and Procedures, New York, 1951; G. BÖHME, Der Alliierte Kontrolrat und die Alliierte Hohe Kommission. Das Kontrolsystem in Deutschland 1945–1951, Berlin W, 1971.

ALLIED MILITARY MISSIONS IN BERLIN, MISSIONS MILITAIRES ALLIÉES A BERLIN; SOYUZNYE VOYENNYE MISSYI V BER-LINIE. The official name of the missions of 15 UN member states accredited to the Allied Control Council for Germany in keeping with the declaration of the Four Powers on control procedures in Germany, signed June 5, 1945, in Berlin in the form of an amendment to the Berlin Declaration on the Defeat of Germany on that day. In early 1946 the following missions were accredited: Australian, Belgian, Brazilian, Canadian, Chinese, Czechoslovakian, Danish, Dutch, Greek, Indian, Luxembourgian, Norwegian, Polish, South African and Yugoslavian. They were assigned residence in Berlin where they remained after the termination of the Council's activities, Mar. 20, 1948, as Military Missions attached to commanders of Western sectors of Berlin; their status remained unchanged, also after the entry into force in 1971 of the four-party agreement on West Berlin.

Journal Officiel du Conseil de Contrôle, Apr. 30, 1946; The Allied Military Missions in Berlin 1945–1948, Berlin, 1949.

ALLIED STATES. An international term for states bound by military alliances; introduced in the 19th and 20th centuries into most peace treaties, apart from the separate concept of ▷ associated states.

ALLIES. The countries allied against the Central Powers during World War I; also known as the Entente or the Coalition. During World War II the majority of former Allies called themselves United Nations, whereas their adversaries (together with their satellites) were called the Axis States. ▷ Rome–Berlin–Tokyo Axis.

ALMA-ATA HEALTH DECLARATION, 1978. The WHO International Conference on Primary Health Care, in Alma-Ata, USSR, on Sept. 12, 1978 adopted the following Declaration:

"I. The conference strongly reaffirms that health, which is a state of complete physical, mental and social well-being, and not merely the absence of disease or infirmity, is a fundamental human right and that the attainment of the highest possible level of health is a most important world-wide social goal whose realization requires the action of many other social and economic sectors in addition to the health sector.
II. The existing gross inequality in the health status of the people, particularly between developed and developing countries as well as within countries, is politically, socially and economically unacceptable and is, therefore, of common concern to all countries.
III. Economic and social development, based on a New International Economic Order, is of basic importance to the fullest attainment of health for all and to the reduction of the gap between the health status of the developing and developed countries. The promotion and protection of the health of the people is essential to sustained economic and social development and contributes to a better quality of life and to world peace.
IV. The people have the right and duty to participate individually and collectively in the planning and implementation of their health care.
V. Governments have a responsibility for the health of their people which can be fulfilled only by the provision of adequate health and social measures. A main social target of governments, international organizations and the whole world community in the coming decades should be the attainment by all peoples of the world by

the year 2000 of a level of health that will permit them to lead a socially and economically productive life. Primary health care is the key to attaining this target as part of development in the spirit of social justice.
VI. Primary health care is essential health care based on practical, scientifically sound and socially acceptable methods and technology made universally accessible to individuals and families in the community through their full participation and at a cost that the community and country can afford to maintain at every stage of their development in the spirit of self-reliance and self-determination. It forms an integral part both of the country's health system, of which it is the central function and main focus, and of the overall social and economic development of the community. It is the first level of contact of individuals, the family and community with the national health system bringing health care as close as possible to where people live and work and constitutes the first element of a continuing health care process.
VII. Primary health care:
(1) reflects and evolves from the economic conditions and socio-cultural and political characteristics of the country and its communities, and is based on the application of the relevant results of social, biomedical and health services, research and public health experience;
(2) addresses the main health problems in the community, providing promotive, preventive, curative, and rehabilitative services accordingly;
(3) includes at least: education concerning prevailing health problems and the methods of preventing and controlling them; promotion of food supply and proper nutrition; an adequate supply of safe water and basic sanitation; maternal and child health care, including family planning; immunization against the major infectious diseases; prevention and control of locally endemic diseases; appropriate treatment of common diseases and injuries; and provision of essential drugs;
(4) involves, in addition to the health sector, all related sectors and aspects of national and community development, in particular agriculture, animal husbandry, food, industry, education, housing, public works, communications and other sectors; and demands the coordinated efforts of all those sectors;
(5) requires and promotes maximum community and individual self-reliance and participation in the planning, organization, operation and control of primary health care, making fullest use of local, national and other available resources, and to this end develops through appropriate education the ability of communities to participate;
(6) should be sustained by integrated, functional and mutually-supportive referral systems, leading to the progressive improvement of comprehensive health care for all, giving priority to those most in need;
(7) relies, at local and referral levels, on health workers, including physicians, nurses, midwives, auxiliaries and community workers as applicable, as well as traditional practitioners as needed, suitably trained socially and technically to work as a health team and to respond to the expressed health needs of the community.
VIII. All governments should formulate national policies, strategies and plans of action to launch and sustain primary health care as part of a comprehensive national health system and in coordination with other sectors. To this end, it will be necessary to exercise political will, to mobilize the country's resources and to use available external resources rationally.
IX. All countries should cooperate in a spirit of partnership and service to ensure primary health care for all people since the attainment of health by people in any one country directly concerns and benefits every other country. In this context the joint WHO/UNICEF report on primary health care constitutes a solid basis for the further development and operation of primary health care throughout the world.
X. An acceptable level of health for all the people of the world by the year 2000 can be attained through a fuller and better use of the world's resources, a considerable part of which is now spent on armaments and military conflicts. A genuine policy of independence, peace, detente and disarmament could and should release additional resources that could well be devoted to peaceful aims and in particular to the acceleration of social and economic development of which primary health care, as an essential part, should be allotted its proper share.

The International Conference on Primary Health Care calls for urgent and effective national and international action to develop and implement primary health care throughout the world and particularly in developing countries in a spirit of technical cooperation and in keeping with a New International Economic Order. It urges governments, WHO and UNICEF, and other international organizations, as well as multilateral and bilateral agencies, non-governmental organizations, funding agencies, all health workers and the whole world community to support national and international commitment to primary health care and to channel increased technical and financial support to it, particularly in developing countries. The Conference calls on all the aforementioned to collaborate in introducing, developing and maintaining primary health care in accordance with the spirit and content of this Declaration."

The Alma-Ata Declaration was reaffirmed by a Riga-USSR Meeting of 22 top level experts of the WHO, from March 22–28, 1988, and by the 41st World Health Assembly in Geneva from May 2–13, 1988.

World Health. The Magazine of the WHO, September, 1983, pp. 24–25.

ALMANACH DE GOTHA. A reference book published in French and German (*Gothaischer Kalender*) since 1764 at Gotha (Thuringia); a genealogical annual of European royal houses and noble families. The same publishing house issued genealogical annuals (*Genealogische Taschenbücher*) of the German families of counts since 1828, barons since 1848, and noblemen since 1900, as well as burghers since 1898 (*Genealogisches Handbuch der Bürgerlichen Familien*). In the interwar period the *Almanach*, apart from its genealogical section, commenced to publish diplomatic and statistical information on all states and international organizations.

Almanach de Gotha. Annuaire généalogique, diplomatique et statistique 1944, 181–2 année, Gotha, 1944.

AL PARI. The identical value of paper currency with the gold (silver) coin. In fact the real rate of exchange is above or below the al pari rate. Al pari also denotes the rate of exchange of securities when at par with their nominal value.

ALPHABETIZATION, UN UNIVERSAL PROGRAM OF. A campaign for universal alphabetization, unanimously adopted by the UN General Assembly on Dec. 11, 1963 by the Res. 1937/XVIII, after studying a UNESCO report which stated that more than 700 million persons aged over 15 (two-thirds of the entire world population) were illiterate, and that in some African, Latin-American and Asian countries 70–90% of the population were illiterate. The UN Program of 1966–69 was experimental in character and was based on the directions of the International Committee of Experts for Alphabetization, est. in 1964. The 1970 UNESCO General Conference appraised the experience that had been gained and worked out a world-wide program and campaign for universal alphabetization in the 1971–80 decade. The global illiteracy rate among persons 15 years of age and older dropped from 32.4% in 1970 to 28.9% in 1980. However, the absolute number of illiterate adults continued to increase from 742 million in 1970 to some 814 million in 1980.

UN Yearbook 1980, p. 1271.

ALPHABETS. The written symbols of speech sounds of different languages, or language groups, subject of international co-operation and research. Traces of first alphabetical writing are found in *c.* 1500 BC; in the 19th and 20th centuries new alphabet

A

systems were created (e.g. Somali writing, consisting of 29 signs) as well as writing based on different alphabets for scholastic purposes exclusively.

The Permanent International Committee of Linguists, f. 1939 in Paris. Publ. *Bibliographie Linguistique*; Reg. with the UIA.

J. FEVRIER, *Histoire de l'écriture*, Paris, 1948; D. DIRINGER, *The Alphabet*, London, 1951; M. COHEN, *La grande invention de l'écriture*, Paris, 1958; A. GIEYSZTOR, *Zarys dziejów pisma łacińskiego* (Outline of the History of Latin Alphabet), Warszawa, 1973; *Yearbook of International Organizations*.

ALPINISM. A subject of international co-operation. Organizations reg. with the UIA:

International Commission for Alpine Rescue, f. 1948, Gwatt, Thun, Switzerland.
International Union of Alpinist Associations, f. 1932, Geneva.

Yearbook of International Organizations.

ALPS. The highest mountains in West, Central, and South Europe, spread between the Gulf of Genoa and the Hungarian Plain in an area about 850 km long and 160 km wide, and running through Italy, France, Switzerland, Liechtenstein, the FRG, Austria and Yugoslavia; under international environmental protection and the sphere of activities of the International Union of Alpinist Associations.

The International Geographic Encyclopedia and Atlas, London, 1979.

AL'QAL'AH OF BENI HAMMAD. Algerian cultural monument, included in the ▷ World Heritage UNESCO List. In the Hodna mountains are the remains of an 11th century capital city with walls 7 km long, fortified gateways and the ruins of palaces, cisterns and the Great Mosque, whose minaret rises to a height of 25 m.

UNESCO. *The Protection of the World Cultural and Natural Heritage*, Paris, 1983.

ALSACE-LORRAINE. The eastern provinces of France annexed by Germany (1871–1918) under the Preliminaries of Peace, signed at Versailles on Feb. 26, 1871 by France and Germany and the Treaty of Frankfurt on May 10, 1871. French sovereignty was re-established on Nov. 11, 1918 and confirmed on June 28, 1919 in the Treaty of Versailles (section V, arts. 51–79, and the Annex). Both provinces were occupied by Germany in 1940, and annexed to the Third Reich. On Nov. 14, 1940, the German authorities demanded – under the threat of removal to Poland – that the French population move to the non-occupied part of France and the population of German extraction be registered on the German Volkslist. Alsace-Lorraine was liberated by French and American troops in Jan., 1945. In 1949 the FRG recognized French sovereignty over Alsace-Lorraine; at the same time a second boundary rectification was effected (in favor of France). The capital of Alsace, Strasbourg, is the seat of the Council of Europe.

E. SCHAEFFER, *L'Alsace et Lorraine 1940–45. Leur occupation en droit et en fait*, Paris, 1953; F. L'HUILLIER, *Histoire de l'Alsace*, Paris, 1955.

ALTA GRACIA CHARTER, 1964. The official name of a document adopted by the International Economic and Social Council (CIES) at its Second Annual Session, Feb. 26 – Mar. 6, 1964 at Alta Gracia health resort, Cordoba, Argentina by CIES ministers in the presence of a US observer. They adopted the Alta Gracia Charter as the standpoint of their governments for the first session of UNCTAD. The Charter was prepared by four sessions of experts in 1963; at Mar del Plata, San-

tiago de Chile, Sao Paulo and Brasilia. The main thesis of the Charter was as follows:

The present structure of international trade continues to widen the gap in the living standard of well-developed nations and the developing ones. ... This phenomenon, very frequent in the world, is particularly characteristic of Latin America. ... The conference ought to establish a new structure of international trade. ... The new structure should generally expand world exchange, favour integration through application of mechanisms and standards adequate to the trade among states being at the same level of development and a variety of economic organization systems.

The Charter closed with the statement that nothing in it was intended to favor Latin America exclusively. Everything which was debated at Alta Gracia also refers to the developing countries of Europe, Africa, Asia and Oceania.

G. CONNELL-SMITH, *The Inter-American System*, London, 1966, pp. 281–282.

ALTERNATE. A courtesy usage maintained among diplomatic representatives of equal rank on negotiating and signing bilateral treaties, consisting in showing mutual respect by (a) alternating the chairmanship of negotiations, (b) each contracting party being mentioned first in the preamble, text, and in the place for the signature of a treaty, in the copy which belongs to that party, (c) placing – the text of the treaty being bilingual and both languages being considered authentic – the language of each contracting party on the left side of the copy, (d) binding together the pages of each copy of the treaty by strings or ribbons showing national colors according to which of the parties the respective copy belongs, (e) alternating the states where the signature of the treaty and the exchange of the ratification instruments are carried out.

C. JORDAN, "Courtoisie internationale", in: *Répertoire de Droit International*, Paris, 1929.

ALTERUM TANTUM. An international principle stating that the rate interest of a debt cannot exceed the debt itself, and if the interest payer reaches the sum of the debt, he discontinues paying interest and returns only the debt within a given time; in practice not generally recognized, subject of international disputes. From *Latin* = twice as much.

ALUMINIUM. A subject of international co-operation. Organizations reg. with the UIA:

Aluminium Workers International Union, f. 1922, St Louis, USA.
European Aluminium Association, f. 1981, Düsseldorf, FRG.
European Wrought Aluminium Association, f. 1970, Zurich, Switzerland.
International Primary Aluminium Institute, f. 1972, London.

Yearbook of International Organizations, 1986–87; *The Europa Yearbook 1988. A World Survey*, Vol. I, London, 1988.

ALVENSLEBEN CONVENTION, 1863. A Russian–Prussian treaty signed in St Petersburg, Feb. 8, 1863 on the initiative of the chancellor of the German Reich, O. von Bismarck, through his special envoy, Gen. K. Alvensleben, and the Russian minister, Prince A.M. Gorchakov. The Treaty was directed against the January uprising in the Polish Congress Kingdom and empowered the armies of both sides to freely cross the border in pursuit of rebel units and to place captives before Russian military courts. England and France protested against the Convention as contrary to international law.

K. LUTOSLAWSKI, *Recueil des Acte Diplomatiques. Traités et Documents concernant Pologne*, Lausanne,

1918, Vol. 1, Doc. 321, p. 598; O. VON BISMARCK, *Gesammelte Werke*, Berlin, 1927, Vol. 4, p. 49.

ALVORADO ACT, 1988. A packet of 16 economic integration agreements, signed in Brasilia in the Presidential Palace, Alvorado on April 6, 1988 by the Presidents of Argentina, Brazil and Uruguay.

KEESING's *Record of World Events*, May, 1988.

AMAZON PACT 1978. ▷ Amazon River.

AMAZON RIVER. A South American river, 6275 km long. The Amazon and its basin comprise the greatest volume of fresh water in the world (2/3 of all fresh-water resources), link together the areas of eight South American States: Brazil, Bolivia, Peru, Colombia, Venezuela, Guyana, Suriname, and French Guiana (more than seven million sq. km, with a population of 8.5 million according to the 1975 data), and possess immeasurable natural resources (i.a., 1/3 of the forest area of the world). Since the 19th century, it has been the subject of international disputes in view of the USA (and also British and French) endeavors to internationalize not only the river itself, but also its basin, called also Amazonia.

On Oct. 31, 1853, the USA government officially requested of Brazil that the Amazon river be opened to international navigation; the request was granted. In 1922–45 the North Americans established many companies for the exploitation of rubber trees, such as the Amazon Corporation, the American Brazilian Exploration Corporation, the Canadian Amazon Corporation Ltd., and the Ford Amazon Company. In 1946 the Brazilian government requested that UNESCO set up an International Amazon Hydrographic Institute. As a result, experts from 10 countries, appointed by UNESCO, held four sessions – in Aug., 1947 in Belem (Brazil), in Dec., 1947 in Mexico City, in Apr., 1948 in Tingo Maria (Peru), and in May 1948 in Iquitos (Peru) where eventually a draft convention was worked out, envisaging the creation – as its principal organ – of an International Amazon Hydrographic Institute with an Executive Council consisting of the representatives of the Brazilian, Bolivian, Colombian, Peruvian and Venezuelan governments. The preparatory session was held in Paris, in Sept., 1948, at the headquarters of UNESCO, but – in view of the Brazilian Defense Council objections – no formal opening of the Institute was carried out. In 1964 the military government of Brazil concluded with the USA an agreement on producing photographic maps of the Amazon and its basin; similar agreements were concluded the same year with the USA by the governments of Peru, Colombia, Venezuela, and (in 1965) Bolivia. The photographic data obtained by the US Air Force were examined by the North American scientific institutes: USAID, Co-operative Research Foundation de Palo Alto (California), and Center of Amazon Research in Houston (Texas). In 1971 the construction of a Trans-Amazon Highway, 5700 km long, linking Recife, Altamira, Nova Brasilia, Rio Branco and Cruzeiro de Sul, and of a Belem-Brasilia Highway was launched. On July 3, 1978 the States of the Amazon basin: Bolivia, Brazil, Colombia, Ecuador, Guyana, Peru, Surinam and Venezuela signed in Brasilia the Amazon Pact with the aim of "harmonious development of the Amazon area and an equitable distribution of benefits". The Council of Amazon Co-operation is an organ of the Pact and gathers each year in a different capital of one of the member States. ▷ Belem, Amazonia Declaration. In 1985–1987 by unconstitutional presidential decrees foreign petroleum companies received licences, covering one third of the land inhabited by Indian tribes in Amazonia (▷ American Indians).

C.P. HASKINS, *The Amazon: The life history of a mighty river*, New York, 1943; *UN Bulletin*, April 15 and June 15, 1948; *Superintendencia do Plano da Valorizaçao Economica do Amazonia. Primeiro plano quinquenal*, Vol. 1–2, Rio de Janeiro, 1955–56; R. WILSON, "La Cuenca Amazónica. La Ocupación Extranjera y los Intereses Multinacionales", in: *Testimonio y Documento de El Dia*, México, DF, June 9–10, 1967; R.E. DICKINSON (ed.), *The Geophysiology of Amazonia. Vegetation and Climate Interactions*, UNO, New York, 1987; KEESING's *Record of World Events*, January, 1987.

AMBASSADOR. The highest class of a diplomatic representative since the Vienna Congress in 1815, confirmed by the Vienna Convention on Diplomatic Relations of 1961. It is usual that Chiefs of the Permanent Missions to the UN or other intergovernmental organizations in the UN System have the rank of ambassador. Another diplomatic custom is a nomination of non-permanent representatives for special missions as Ambassador-at-large.

S.E. NAHLIK, "Les classes diplomatiques personnelles", in: *Annuaire polonais des affaires internationales*, Varsovie, Vol. III, 1962, pp. 121–154.

AMERASIANS. An international term for people of Asian descent in the USA growing in number since 1980. A special group consists of some 15,000 Children of War, left in Vietnam by US servicemen and civilians, that are victims of discrimination in communist Vietnam and subject of negotiations between the US and Vietnam in 1988.

The Amerasians, in: *Newsweek*, March 14, 1988.

AMERICA. A continent in the Western Hemisphere, named in 1507 by German cartographer M. Waldseemüller (1480 1521) in his *Cosmopographiae universalis introductio* (1507) after the explorer Amerigo Vespucci; sometimes called the New World; geographically, it consists of South America, Central America and North America; politically of Latin America and the USA and Canada; area 42 million sq. km. Population *c.* 690 million inhabitants (1980). There are 26 independent states and 23 non-self-governing territories on the American continent; it also encompasses Greenland which is an integral part of Denmark. In 1951 the Council of European American Associations was established in Antwerp linking together 25 national associations for Euro-American co-operation; Publ. *News Letter* and *Why it is Important that Europe and America Should be Friends.*

A. ORTELIUS, *Catalogus Cartographorum*, Berlin, 1930; E.W. SHANAHAN, *South America. An Economic and Regional Geography with a Historical Chapter*, London, 1950; P. RIVET, *Les origines de l'homme americain*, Paris, 1957; G.B. SHAW, *Anglo-America; A Regional Geography*, New York, 1960; *America en cifras*, 1974; *The Europa Year Book 1984. A World Survey*, Vol. II, London, 1984.

AMERICA AND THE UN. All the independent American states took part in the San Francisco Conference of 1945, actively co-operated in drafting the UN Charter, and became original members of the UN. The basic differences between the USA and the Latin American States, which emerged at the Conference, were in relation to the right of ▷ veto of the Great Powers and the request that Latin America be granted one permanent seat on the UN Security Council. In 1962, Jamaica, Trinidad and Tobago achieved independence and entered the UN; in 1966 – Barbados and Guyana; in 1973 – the Bahamas; in 1974 – Grenada; in 1976 – Surinam; in 1978 – Dominica; in 1979 – St Vincent and the Grenadines; 1981 – Antigua and Barbuda, Belize. In the first decade of the UN American states constituted 40% of the entire UN membership, in 1980 less than 20%.

Main American affairs debated at the UN: the case of Guatemala in June–July 1954; the case of the Dominican Republic in 1960; the Cuban missile crisis from Oct. 1962 to Jan. 1963; the case of Chile after the military coup 1973; the case of Grenada 1983. Of all American states only Haiti was placed (in 1970) among the poorest states of the world, with an annual income per capita below US $100. The Central American conflicts in the last years of the 1980s were subject of diplomatic negotiations but not on an official UN level.

A. GARCIA ROBLES, *La Conferencia de San Francisco y su obra*, México, DF, 1946; J.A. HOUSTON, *Latin America and the UN*, New York, 1956; R.B. RUSSELL, J.E. MUTHER, *A History of the UN Charter. The Role of the US 1940–1945*, Washington, DC, 1958; UN, *The UN and Latin America. A collection of Basic Information Material about the World of the UN and the Related Agencies in Latin America*, New York, 1961; KEESING's *Record of World Events*, 1987–88.

AMERICA, DECLARATION OF THE PEOPLES OF AMERICA, 1961. Official name of a document adopted at the Extraordinary Session of the Inter-American Socio-Economic Council of the OAS, Aug. 17, 1961, in Punta del Este, by 20 votes cast by OAS members against one (Cuba); it proclaimed the objectives of the ▷ Alliance for Progress. The Declaration is a preamble to the ▷ Punta del Este Charter which specifies the provisions of the Alliance.

AMERICA, DECLARATION OF THE PRESIDENTS OF AMERICA, 1967. A document signed Apr. 14, 1967 at a conference held by 21 heads of Latin American governments in Punta del Este which proclaimed with the support of the US President, that during 1970–1985 "a Latin American common market will be created".

In Part II the declaration elaborates on the "program of activities": the principles of economic integration and industrial development of Latin America (Chapter I); multi-national actions concerning infrastructure (Chapter II); means of improvement of international trade in Latin America (Chapter III); modernization of life in rural areas and growth of farming production, mainly foodstuffs (Chapter IV); development of education, science and technology as well as intensification of health improvement projects (Chapter V). The Declaration expressed the need to "eliminate unnecessary military expenses".

Declaración de los Presidentes de América, PAU, Washington, DC, 1967.

AMERICA FIRST COMMITTEE. The official name of an American noninterventionist foreign policy pressure group which, during World War II, represented partisans of US isolationism. Founded in Sept., 1940 under the leadership of General R.E. Wood (from Sears, Roebuck and Co.). Charles A. Lindbergh, the pilot who crossed the Atlantic on his own in 1927 was i.a., the spokesman for the Committee. It had a membership of about 800,000. The Committee dissolved in Dec., 1941 after the Japanese attack on Pearl Harbor and declared itself in favor of active participation of all US citizens in the war.

W. JOHNSON, *The Battle Against Isolationism*, New York, 1944; W.S. COLE, *America First: the Battle Against Intervention 1940–41*, New York, 1953.

AMERICAN ACADEMY IN ROME, THE. An institution f. 1894 on the Janiculum in Rome, academic school of fine arts and classical studies, administered by a board of trustees in New York. N.Y. Publ.: *Memoirs, Papers and Monographs*.

AMERICAN ACADEMY OF POLITICAL AND SOCIAL SCIENCE. An institution f. 1889, Philadelphia, Pa. Publ. *The Annals* (bi-monthly) and *Proceedings of the Annual Meeting of the Academy*.

AMERICAN ASSEMBLY. The supreme organ of the Panamerican Congress, 1826, which prepared the ▷ Union, League and Permanent Confederation Treaty. Since 1950 Columbia University, New York, operates an institution called the American Assembly which prepares and publishes analyses of various aspects of US policy, usually foreign affairs.

A. DE LA PENA Y REYES, *El Congreso de Panamá y Algunos Otros Proyectos de Unión Hispano-Americana*, México, DF, 1926.

AMERICAN ASSOCIATION FOR THE ADVANCEMENT OF SCIENCE. Est. 1848, Washington DC, to foster ▷ Academic Freedom. Publ. *Science*.

AMERICAN–AUSTRIAN PEACE TREATY, 1921. A Treaty between the USA and Austria, signed Aug. 24, 1921, to establish secure and friendly relations between the two nations. The highlights of the Treaty are:

"The USA and Austria considering that the United States, acting in conjunction with its co-belligerents, entered into an Armistice with Austria–Hungary on November 3, 1918, in order that a Treaty of Peace might be concluded,

Considering that the former Austro–Hungarian Monarchy ceased to exist and was replaced in Austria by a republican Government;

Considering that the Treaty of St Germain-En-Laye to which Austria is a party was signed on September 10, 1919, and came into force according to the terms of its Article 381, but has not been ratified by the United States;

Considering that the Congress of the United States passed a Joint Resolution approved by the President July 2, 1921, which reads in part as follows:

Resolved by the Senate and House of Representatives of the United States of America in Congress assembled. ... That the state of war declared to exist between the Imperial and Royal Austro–Hungarian Government and the United States of America by the joint resolution of Congress approved December 7, 1917, is thereby declared at an end.

Sec. 4. That in making this declaration, and as a part of it, there are expressly reserved to the United States of America and its nationals any and all rights, privileges, indemnities, reparations or advantages, together with the right to enforce the same, to which it or they have become entitled under the terms of the armistice signed November 3, 1918, or any extension or modifications thereof; or which were acquired by or are in the possession of the United States of America by reason of its participation in the war or to which its nationals have thereby become rightfully entitled; or which, under the Treaty of St Germain-En-Laye or the Treaty of Trianon, have been stipulated for its or their benefit; or to which it is entitled as one of the principal Allied and Associated Powers; or to which it is entitled by virtue of any Act or Acts of Congress; or otherwise. ... Being desirous of establishing secure friendly relations between the two nations ... have agreed as follows:

Art. 1. Austria undertakes to accord to the United States and the United States shall have and enjoy all the rights, privileges, indemnities, reparations or advantages specified in the aforesaid Joint Resolution of the Congress of the United States of July 2, 1921, including all the rights and advantages stipulated for the benefit of the United States in the Treaty of St Germain-En-Laye which the United States shall fully enjoy notwithstanding the fact that such Treaty has not been ratified by the United States. The United States is availing itself of the rights and advantages stipulated in the provisions of that Treaty, will do so in a manner consistent with the rights accorded to Austria under such provisions.

Art. II. With a view to defining more particularly the obligations of Austria under the foregoing Article with respect to certain provisions in the Treaty of St Germain-En-Laye, it is understood and agreed between the High Contracting Parties:

(1) That the rights and advantages stipulated in that Treaty for the benefit of the United States which it is intended the United States shall have and enjoy, are those defined in Parts V, VI, VIII, IX, X, XI, XII and XIV.

(2) That the United States shall not be bound by the provisions of Part I of that Treaty nor by any provisions of that Treaty including those mentioned in paragraph (I) of this Article which related to the Covenant of the League of Nations, nor shall the United States be bound by any action taken by the League of Nations or by the Council or by the Assembly thereof, unless the United States shall expressly give its assent to such action.

(3) That the United States assumes no obligations under or with respect to the provisions of Part II, Part III, Part IV and Part XIII of that Treaty.

(4) That, while the United States is privileged to participate in the Reparation Commission, according to the terms of Part VIII of that Treaty and in any other commission established under the Treaty or under any agreement supplemental thereto, the United States is not bound to participate in any such commission unless it shall elect to do so.

(5) That the periods of time to which reference is made in Article 381 of the Treaty of St Germain-En-Laye shall run, with respect to any act or election on the part of the United States, from the date of the coming into force of the present Treaty."

Major Peace Treaties of Modern History, New York, 1967, pp. 2257–2262.

AMERICAN–BRITISH AGREEMENT, 1942. An agreement between the USA and the UN on the Principles applying to Mutual Aid in the Prosecution of the War Against Aggression, signed at Washington, DC, Feb. 23, 1942; Exchange of Notes, Sept. 3, 1942.

LNTS, Vol. 204, 1941–43, pp. 389–402.

AMERICAN BUREAU OF SHIPPING, ABS. An American classification association founded in 1867, registers approx. 1/5 of the world's merchant shipping.

AMERICAN–CHINESE TREATIES, 1844–1908. The Treaties signed by the USA and China. The first called Wan-hsien or Cushing Treaty, was signed at Wan-hsien port on the Yangtze River on July 3, 1844 and was a commercial treaty with an annexed Tariff of Duties. The Treaty of Tientsin was signed on June 26, 1858, supplemented in 1880 by the Treaty of Peking concerning Commercial Intercourse and Judicial Procedure; and finally suspended in 1903 by a Commercial Treaty with an Import Tariff Agreement signed in 1902.

The Emigration Treaty was signed 1894 and the Arbitration Convention in 1908. ▷ China–Washington Treaty 1922, and ▷ China–USA Friendship Treaty 1946.

W.M. MALLOY, *Treaties, Conventions ... between the USA and other Powers*, 4 Vols. Washington, DC, 1923–38.

AMERICAN COLONIZATION SOCIETY, 1816–1860. The organizer of re-settlement of freed Negroes from the USA to Africa; initiated the foundation of ▷ Liberia on the West Coast of Africa on the basis of an agreement, signed 1821 by the Society and a local African chief. The first freed American slaves settled in 1821 at Cape Mesurado.

H. HUBERICH, *The Political and Legislative History of Liberia*, Monrovia, 1947.

AMERICAN COMMITTEE ON DEPENDENT TERRITORIES. A Committee, est. Oct. 24, 1940

as the result of a decision made by the Second American Council of Ministers of Foreign Affairs in Havana Aug. 30, 1940 to take over the provisional administration of British, Dutch and French colonies in the Western Hemisphere. It was dissolved in 1945 and created again as an OAS specialized committee by the Ninth International Conference of American States at Bogota, on May 2, 1948 "to study the situation of colonies, possessions and occupied territories existing in America, whatever their feature, with a view to seeking pacific means of eliminating both colonialism and the occupation of American territories by extracontinental countries."

Novena Conferencia Internacional Americana, Actas y Documentos, Bogota, 1953, Vol. VI, pp. 304–306.

AMERICAN CONFERENCES AND CONGRESSES, 1826–89. The inter-American co-operation started in the 19th century with the following intergovernmental meetings, initiated, as a rule by Latin–American statesmen:

1826 – Panamerican Congress, Congreso de Panama, convened by S. Bolivar, the liberator of Colombia and commander-in-chief of Peru in his letter addressed to the governments of Colombia, Mexico, Central America, the United Provinces of Buenos Aires, Chile and Brazil on Feb. 7, 1824.

The Congress was held June 22–July 15, 1826 in Ciudad de Panama; taking part were delegates of: Greater Colombia (now the area of Colombia, Ecuador, Panama and Venezuela), Rep. of Central America (now the area of Costa Rica, Honduras, Nicaragua and El Salvador), Mexico, and Peru; delegates from Argentina, Brazil and Bolivia did not come "for material reasons"; Great Britain and Holland sent observers; signed was the ▷ Union, League and Permanent Confederation Treaty; the Supplementary Protocol attached to it determined that the permanent seat of the Congress would be "the settlement of Tacubaya not far from Mexico City" – the official name of the Congress: Congreso de Confederacion, often called Congreso de Tacubaya by historians.

1847–48 – Congress in Lima, Congreso de Lima, a meeting of the governments of Bolivia, Chile, Ecuador and New Grenada convened for the purpose of discussing the inter-American situation as a result of US aggression in Mexico and the conflict of Argentina with France and Great Britain; the Congress deliberated Dec. 11, 1847–Mar. 1, 1848 and ended with the signing of two treaties: Treaty of Union and Confederation of the Signatory States as well as the Treaty on Trade and Navigation and two conventions: consular and postal.

1856 – Continental Congress, Congreso Continental, meeting of the governments of Chile, Ecuador, and Peru, Aug. 10–Sept. 15, 1856 – Washington Congress, Congreso de Washington DC, meeting of the governments of Costa Rica, Guatemala, Honduras, Mexico, New Grenada, Peru, Salvador and Venezuela (in the presence of a US observer), in October in the US capital; concluded with the signing of an Allied Treaty on Common Defense against Foreign Aggressors, suggesting the creation of a Confederation of Hispanoamerican States.

1864–65 – Congress in Lima, II Congreso de Lima, conference of the governments of Argentina, Bolivia, Chile, Colombia, Ecuador, Guatemala, Panama, Peru, Salvador and Venezuela convened for the purpose of discussing the inter-American situation in face of the French invasion in Mexico, the re-incorporation of San Domingo and the occupation of the Peruvian islands Islas de Chinchas by Spain; the Congress deliberated Nov. 15, 1864–Mar. 12, 1865 in the Peruvian capital and concluded with the signing of two treaties: on post and on trade and navigation.

1877–79 – Juridical Congress in Lima, Congreso de Iurisconsultos de Lima, the first Latin–American conference of workers for the purpose of codifying international law Dec. 13, 1871–Dec. 27, 1879 in the capital of Peru with the participation of legal experts from the governments of Argentina, Bolivia, Chile, Costa Rica, Ecuador, Guatemala, Peru, Uruguay and Venezuela; not attending were experts from the US government, which stated that there is too great a difference between

US legislation and that of the Hispanic–American states." The work of the Congress initiated the codification of international law on the American continent.

1883 – Bolivarian Congress, Congreso Bolivariano, convened by the government of Venezuela in commemoration of the 100th anniversary of the birth of S. Bolivar, born Mar. 24, 1783 in Caracas; it was held July 24, 1883 in the capital of Venezuela with the participation of delegates of the governments of Argentina, Bolivia, Colombia, Mexico, Peru, Salvador, and Venezuela; the Congress appealed to the American Republics to introduce arbitration as "the only form of resolving conflicts between themselves". Two other anniversary Bolivarian Congresses were held in Panama in 1926 and 1958.

1888–89 – Juridical Congress in Montevideo, Congreso Juridico de Montevideo or Congreso Sudamericano, conference of legal experts of the governments of Argentina, Bolivia, Brazil, Chile, Paraguay, Peru, and Uruguay; the congress was convened at the initiative of the governments of Argentina and Uruguay and was held Aug. 25, 1888–Feb. 18, 1889; it made a significant contribution to the codification of international private law, protection of author's rights, protection of industrial property, international penal law, international civil law, and international commercial law.

J.M. JEPES, *Del Congreso de Panamá a la Conferencia de Caracas, 1826–1954*, 2 Vols., Caracas, 1955; *Congresos de Bolivar 1826–1926*, UPA/PAU Panama, 1927; J.M. SIERRA, *Derecho Internacional Público*, Mexico, DF, 1963, pp. 76–77.

AMERICAN CONTINENTAL SOLIDARITY DECLARATIONS, 1936–1940. The first manifestations of the solidarity of the American continent in the spirit of the ▷ Good Neighbor Doctrine were made in Dec. 1936 at Buenos Aires during the ▷ Interamerican Conference for the Maintenance of Peace.

The Eighth Interamerican Conference at Lima, in Dec., 1938 approved the Declaration of the Principles of Solidarity of America, called the ▷ Lima Declaration 1938. The Conference also made provision for Consultative Meetings of the Ministers of Foreign Affairs of all American Republics. The first meeting was held at Panama in Sept., 1939 and adopted a general declaration of neutrality, called the ▷ Panama Declaration 1939.

The Second Consultative Meeting was held at Havana on July 30, 1940 and adopted the Declaration of Reciprocal Assistance and Co-operation, called the ▷ Havana Declaration 1940.

CARNEGIE ENDOWMENT, *International Conferences of American States*. First Supplement 1933–40, Washington, DC, 1941; E.J. OSMAŃCZYK, *Enciclopedia Mundial de Relaciones Internacionales y Naciones Unidas*, México, DF, 1976, pp. 398–399, 412 and 417–418.

AMERICAN–CUBAN IMMIGRATION AGREEMENTS 1984 AND 1987. The first regulation on Cuban immigration was published in Havana and Washington in 1984. The Government of Cuba suspended the immigration understanding in May 1985, but restored it in November 1987. Under the new agreement Cuba agreed to accept the return of 2,746 Cuban nationals declared undesirable because they were either mentally ill, or had committed serious crimes in Cuba or in the United States after their arrival. Of those, 201 were returned before Cuba suspended the agreement. Most of those to be returned to Cuba were in Federal detention centers in Atlanta and Oakdale, Fla and in December 1987 started anti-deportation riots.

Under immigration regulations, up to 20,000 Cubans who do not have immediate family members in the United States are allowed to emigrate to the United States every year. In addition to that, an unlimited number of immediate family members are eligible and officials estimate them to number about 3,000 a year. A third category, those seeking political asylum, are believed to number about 3,500.

N.A. LEWIS, US and Havana Agreed to Restore Immigration Pact, in: *The New York Times*, November 21, 1987.

AMERICAN DECLARATION OF THE RIGHTS AND DUTIES OF MAN, 1948. A Declaration adopted by the Ninth International American Conference in Bogota, May 2, 1948, as Chapter XXX of the Final Act of the Conference. The text is as follows:

"Preamble. All men are born free and equal in dignity and in rights, and, being endowed by nature with reason and conscience, they should conduct themselves as brothers one to another. The fulfillment of duty by each individual is a prerequisite to the rights of all. Rights and duties are interrelated in every social and political activity of man. While rights exalt individual liberty, duties express the dignity of that liberty.

Duties of a juridical nature presuppose others of a moral nature which support them in principle and constitute their basis.

Inasmuch as spiritual development is the supreme end of human existence and the highest expression thereof, it is the duty of man to serve that end with all his strength and resources. Since culture is the highest social and historical expression of that spiritual development, it is the duty of man to preserve, practice and foster culture by every means within his power.

And, since moral conduct constitutes the noblest flowering of culture, it is the duty of every man always to hold it in high respect.

Chapter One. Rights. Art. 1. Every human being has the right to life, liberty and the security of his person.

Art. II. All persons are equal before the law and have the rights and duties established in this Declaration, without distinction as to race, sex, language, creed or any other factor.

Art. III. Every person has the right freely to profess a religious faith, and to manifest and practice it both in public and in private.

Art. IV. Every person has the right to freedom of investigation, of opinion, and of the expression and dissemination of ideas, by any medium whatsoever.

Art. V. Every person has the right to the protection of the law against abusive attacks upon his honor, his reputation, and his private and family life.

Art. VI. Every person has the right to establish a family, the basic element of society, and to receive protection therefor.

Art. VII. All women, during pregnancy and the nursing period, and all children, have the right to special protection, care and aid.

Art. VIII. Every person has the right to fix his residence within the territory of the State of which he is a national, to move about freely within such territory, and not to leave it except by his own will.

Art. IX. Every person has the right to the inviolability of his home.

Art. X. Every person has the right to the inviolability and transmission of his correspondence.

Art. XI. Every person has the right to the preservation of his health through sanitary and social measures relating to food, clothing, housing and medical care, to the extent permitted by public and community resources.

Art. XII. Every person has the right to an education, which should be based on the principles of liberty, morality and human solidarity.

Likewise every person has the right to an education that will prepare him to attain a decent life, to raise his standard of living and to be a useful member of society.

The right to an education includes the right to equality of opportunity in every case, in accordance with natural talents, merit and the desire to utilize the resources that the State or the community is in a position to provide.

Every person has the right to receive, free, at least a primary education.

Art. XIII. Every person has the right to take part in the cultural life of the community, to enjoy the arts, and to participate in the benefits that result from intellectual progress, especially scientific discoveries.

He likewise has the right to the protection of his moral and material interests as regards his inventions or any literary, scientific or artistic works of which he is the author.

Art. XIV. Every person has the right to work, under proper conditions, and to follow his vocation freely, insofar as existing conditions of employment permit.

Every person who works, has the right to receive such remuneration as will, in proportion to his capacity and skill, assure him a standard of living suitable for himself and for his family.

Art. XV. Every person has the right to leisure time, to wholesome recreation and to the opportunity for advantageous use of his free time to his spiritual, cultural and physical benefit.

Art. XVI. Every person has the right to social security which will protect him from the consequences of unemployment, old age and any disabilities arising from causes beyond his control that make it physically or mentally impossible for him to earn a living.

Art. XVII. Every person has the right to be recognized everywhere as a person having rights and obligations, and to enjoy the basic civil rights.

Art. XVIII. Every person may resort to the courts to ensure respect for his legal rights. There should likewise be available to him a simple, brief procedure whereby the courts will protect him from acts of authority that, to his prejudice, violate any fundamental constitutional rights.

Art. XIX. Every person has the right to the nationality to which he is entitled by law and to change it, if he so wishes, for the nationality of any other country that is willing to grant it to him.

Art. XX. Every person having legal capacity is entitled to participate in the government of his country, directly or through his representatives, and to take part in popular elections, which shall be by secret ballot, and shall be honest, periodic and free.

Art. XXI. Every person has the right to assemble peaceably with others in a formal public meeting or an informal gathering, in connection with matters of common interest of any nature.

Art. XXII. Every person has the right to associate with others to promote, exercise and protect his legitimate interests of a political, economic, religious, social, cultural, professional labor-union or other nature.

Art. XXIII. Every person has a right to own such private property as meets the essential needs of decent living and helps to maintain the dignity of the individual and of the home.

Art. XXIV. Every person has the right to submit respectful petitions to any competent authority, for reasons of either general or private interest, and the right to obtain a prompt decision thereon.

Art. XXV. No person may be deprived of his liberty except in the cases and according to the procedures established by pre-existing law.

No person may be deprived of liberty for non-fulfillment of obligations of a purely civil character.

Every individual who has been deprived of his liberty has the right to have the legality of his detention ascertained without delay by a court, and the right to be tried without undue delay, or, otherwise, to be released. He also has the right to humane treatment during the time he is in custody.

Art. XXVI. Every accused person is presumed to be innocent until proved guilty.

Every person accused of an offense has the right to be given an impartial and public hearing, and to be tried by courts previously established in accordance with preexisting laws, and not to receive cruel, infamous or unusual punishment.

Art. XXVII. Every person has the right, in case of pursuit not resulting from ordinary crimes, to seek and receive asylum in foreign territory, in accordance with the laws of each country and with international agreements.

Art. XXVIII. The rights of man are limited by the rights of others, by the security of all, and by the just demands of the general welfare and the advancement of democracy.

Chapter Two. Duties. Art. XXIX. It is the duty of the individual so to conduct himself in relation to others that each and every one may fully form and develop his personality.

Art. XXX. It is the duty of every person to aid, support, educate and protect his minor children, and it is the duty of children to honor their parents always and to aid, support and protect them when they need it.

Art. XXXI. It is the duty of every person to acquire at least an elementary education.

Art. XXXII. It is the duty of every person to vote in the popular elections of the country of which he is a national, when he is legally capable of doing so.

Art. XXXIII. It is the duty of every person to obey the law and other legitimate commands of the authorities of his country and those of the country in which he may be.

Art. XXXIV. It is the duty of every ablebodied person to render whatever civil and military service his country may require for its defense and preservation, and, in case of public disaster, to render such services as may be in his power. It is likewise his duty to hold any public office to which he may be elected by popular vote in the State of which he is a national.

Art. XXXV. It is the duty of every person to co-operate with the State and the community with respect to social security and welfare, in accordance with his ability and with existing circumstances.

Art. XXXVI. It is the duty of every person to pay the taxes established by law for the support of public services.

Art. XXXVII. It is the duty of every person to work, as far as his capacity and possibilities permit, in order to obtain the means of livelihood or to benefit his community.

Art. XXXVIII. It is the duty of every person to refrain from taking part in political activities that, according to law, are reserved exclusively to the citizens of the State in which he is an alien".

The conference recommended to the Inter-American Juridical Committee the preparation a draft Statute of an Inter-American Court to Protect the Rights of Man.

Novena Conferencia Internacional Americana, Actas y Documentos, Bogota, 1953, Vol. VI, pp. 289–297.

AMERICAN DEMOCRACY DOCTRINE, 1948. A Declaration on the Preservation and Defense of Democracy in America, adopted by the Ninth International Conference of American States, at Bogota, on May 2, 1948, as Chapter XXXII of the Final Act of the Conference. The text is as follows:

"Whereas:

In order to safeguard peace and maintain mutual respect among States, the present world situation requires that urgent measures be taken to prescribe the tactics of totalitarian domination that are irreconcilable with the tradition of the American nations, and to prevent agents serving international communism or any other totalitarian doctrine from seeking to distort the true and the free will of the peoples of this Continent,

The Republics represented at the Ninth International Conference of American States

Declare:

That, by its anti-democratic nature and its interventionist tendency, the political activity of international communism or any other totalitarian doctrine is incompatible with the concept of American freedom, which rests upon two undeniable postulates: the dignity of man as an individual and the sovereignty of the nation as a State;

Reiterate:

The faith that the peoples of the New World have placed in the ideal and in the reality of democracy, under the protection of which they shall achieve social justice, offering to all increasingly broader opportunities to enjoy the spiritual and material benefits that are the guarantee of civilization and the heritage of mankind;

Condemn:

In the name of international law, interference by any foreign power, or by any political organization serving the interests of a foreign power, in the public life of the nations of the American Continent; and

Resolve:

(1) To reaffirm their decision to maintain and further an effective social and economic policy for the purpose of raising the standard of living of their peoples; and their conviction that only under a system founded upon a guarantee of the essential freedoms and rights of the individual is it possible to attain this goal.

(2) To condemn the methods of every system tending to suppress political and civil rights and liberties, and in

particular the action of international communism or any other totalitarian doctrine.

(3) To adopt, within their respective territories and in accordance with their respective constitutional provisions, the measures necessary to eradicate and prevent activities directed, assisted or instigated by foreign governments, organizations or individuals tending to overthrow their institutions by violence, to foment disorder in their domestic political life or to disturb, by means of pressure, subversive propaganda, threats or by any other means, the free and sovereign right of their peoples to govern themselves in accordance with their democratic aspirations.

(4) To proceed with a full exchange of information concerning any of the aforementioned activities that are carried on within their respective jurisdictions".

Novena Conferencia Internacional Americana, Actas y Documentos, Bogota, 1953, Vol. VI, pp. 303–304.

AMERICAN–GERMAN PEACE TREATY, 1921.
A treaty between the USA and Germany signed in Berlin on Aug. 25, 1921 to restore friendly relations existing between the two nations prior to the outbreak of War.

The text is as follows:

"Germany and the United States of America considering that the United States, acting in conjunction with its cobelligerents, entered into an Armistice with Germany on November 11, 1918, in order that a Treaty of Peace might be concluded; considering that the Treaty of Versailles was signed on June 28, 1919, and came into force according to the terms of its Article 440, but has not been ratified by the United States; considering that the Congress of the United States passed a Joint Resolution, approved by the President July 2, 1921, which reads in part as follows:

Resolved by the Senate and House of Representatives of the United States of America in Congress assembled, that the state of war declared to exist between the Imperial German Government and the United States of America by the joint resolution of Congress approved April 6, 1917 is hereby declared at an end.

Sec. 2. That in making this declaration, and as a part of it, there are expressly reserved to the United States of America and its nationals any and all rights, privileges, indemnities, reparations, or advantages, together with the right to enforce the same, to which it or they have become entitled under the terms of the armistice signed November 11, 1918 or any extensions or modifications thereof; or which were acquired by or are in the possession of the United States of America by reason of its participation in the war or to which its nationals have thereby become rightfully entitled; or which, under the Treaty of Versailles, have been stipulated for its or their benefit; or to which it is entitled as one of the principal Allied and Associated powers; or to which it is entitled by virtue of any Act or Acts of Congress; or otherwise.

Sec. 5. All property of the Imperial German Government, or its successor or successors, and of all German nationals, which was, on April 6, 1917, in or has since that date come into the possession or under control of, or has been the subject of a demand by the United States of America or of any of its officers, agents, or employees, from any source or by any agency whatsoever, and all property of the Imperial and Royal Austro–Hungarian Government, or its successor or successors, and of all Austro–Hungarian nationals which was on Dec. 7, 1917, in or has since that date come into the possession or under control of, or has been the subject of a demand by the United States of America or any of its officers, agents, or employees, from any source or by any agency whatsoever, shall be retained by the United States of America and no disposition thereof made, except as shall have been heretofore or specifically hereafter shall be provided by law until such time as the Imperial German Government and the Imperial and Royal Austro–Hungarian Government, or their successor or successors, shall have respectively made suitable provision for the satisfaction of all claims against said Governments, respectively, of all persons, wheresoever domiciled, who owe permanent allegiance to the United States of America and who have suffered, through the acts of the Imperial German Government, or its agents, or the Imperial and Royal Austro–Hungarian Government, or its agents,

since July 31, 1914, loss, damage, or injury to their persons or property, directly or indirectly, whether through the ownership of shares of stock in German, Austro–Hungarian, American, or other corporations, or in consequence of hostilities or of any operations of war, or otherwise, and also shall have granted to persons owing permanent allegiance to the United States of America most-favored-nation treatment, whether the same be national or otherwise, in all matters affecting residence, business, profession, trade, navigation, commerce and industrial property, rights, and until the Imperial German Government and the Imperial and Royal Austro–Hungarian Government, or their successor or successors, shall have respectively confirmed to the United States of America all fines, forfeitures, penalties, and seizures imposed or made by the United States of America during the war, whether in respect to the property of the Imperial German Government or German nationals or the Imperial and Royal Austro–Hungarian Government of Austro–Hungarian nationals, and shall have waived any and all pecuniary claims against the United States of America.

Being desirous of restoring the friendly relations existing between the two nations prior to the outbreak of war; Have for that purpose appointed their plenipotentiaries: The President of the German Empire, Dr. Friedrich Rosen, Minister of Foreign Affairs, and the President of the United States of America; Ellis Loring Dresel, Commissioner of the United States of America to Germany;

Who, having communicated their full powers, found to be in good and due form, have agreed as follows:

Art. 1. Germany undertakes to accord to the United States, and the United States shall have and enjoy, all the rights, privileges, indemnities, reparations or advantages specified in the aforesaid Joint Resolution of the Congress of the United States of July 2, 1921 including all the rights and advantages stipulated for the benefit of the United States in the Treaty of Versailles which the United States shall fully enjoy notwithstanding the fact that such Treaty has not been ratified by the United States.

Art. II. With a view to defining more particularly the obligations of Germany under the foregoing Article with respect to certain provisions in the Treaty of Versailles, it is understood and agreed between the High Contracting Parties:

(1) That the rights and advantages stipulated in that Treaty for the benefit of the United States, which it is intended the United States shall have and enjoy, are those defined in Section I, of Part IV, and Parts V, VI, VIII, IX, X, XI, XII, XIV and XV.

The United States in availing itself of the rights and advantages stipulated in the provisions of that Treaty mentioned in this paragraph will do so in a manner consistent with the rights accorded to Germany under such provisions.

(2) That the United States shall not be bound by the provisions of Part I of that Treaty, nor by any provisions of that Treaty including those mentioned in paragraph (1) of this Article, which related to the Covenant of the League of Nations, nor shall the United States be bound by any action taken by the League of Nations, or by the Council or by the Assembly thereof, unless the United States shall expressly give its assent to such action.

(3) That the United States assumes no obligations under or with respect to the provisions of Part II, Part III, Sections 2 to 8 inclusive of Part IV, and Part XIII of that Treaty.

(4) That, while the United States is privileged to participate in the Reparation Commission, according to the terms of Part VIII of that Treaty, and in any other Commission established under the Treaty or under any agreement supplemental thereto, the United States is not bound to participate in any such commission unless it shall elect to do so.

(5) That the periods of time to which reference is made in Art. 440 of the Treaty of Versailles shall run, with respect to any act or election on the part of the United States, from the date of the coming into force of the present Treaty.

Art. III. The present Treaty shall be ratified in accordance with the constitutional forms of the High Contracting Parties and shall take effect immediately on the exchange of ratifications which shall take place as soon as possible at Berlin. In witness whereof, the

respective plenipotentiaries have signed this Treaty and have hereunto affixed their seals. By a proclamation of the President signed November 14, 1921, war between the United States and Germany was declared to have terminated July 2, 1921."

Major Peace Treaties of Modern History, New York, 1967, pp. 2261–2264.

AMERICAN–GERMAN PROGRAM. ▷ German-American Youth Exchange Program.

AMERICAN–HUNGARIAN PEACE TREATY, 1921.
A treaty between the USA and Hungary, signed Aug. 29, 1918, to establish secure and friendly relations between the two nations. The highlights of the treaty:

"The USA and Hungary considering that the United States, acting in conjunction with its co-belligerents, entered into an armistice with Austria–Hungary on November, 3, 1918, in order that a Treaty of Peace might be concluded:

Considering that the former Austro–Hungarian Monarchy ceased to exist and was replaced in Hungary by a national Hungarian Government;

Considering that the Treaty of Trianon to which Hungary is a party was signed on June 4, 1920, and came into force according to the terms of its Article 364, but has not been ratified by the United States;

Considering that the Congress of the United States passed a Joint Resolution, approved by the President July 2, 1921, which reads in part as follows:

Resolved by the Senate and House of Representatives of the United States of America in Congress assembled, That the state of war declared to exist between the Imperial and Royal Austro–Hungarian Government and the United States of America by the joint resolution of Congress approved December 7, 1917, is hereby declared at an end, Have agreed as follows:

Art. 1. Hungary undertakes to accord to the United States, and the United States shall have and enjoy, all the rights, privileges, indemnities, reparations or advantages specified in the aforesaid Joint Resolution of the Congress of the United States of July 2, 1921, including all the rights and advantages stipulated for the benefit of the United States in the Treaty of Trianon which the United States shall fully enjoy notwithstanding the fact that such Treaty has not been ratified by the United States. The United States, in availing itself of the rights and advantages stipulated in the provisions of that Treaty, will do so in a manner consistent with the rights accorded to Hungary under such provisions."

Major Peace Treaties of Modern History, New York, 1967, pp. 2265–2268.

AMERICAN INDIAN MOVEMENT.
American Indian civil rights organization, f. 1968. In 1973 organized occupation of the Bureau of Indian Affairs in Washington DC and also of the historical site ▷ Wounded Knee. Participated in the UN Treaty Conference in Geneva 1977 to demand review of 300 treaties between Indian Committees and the USA.

KEESING's *Contemporary Archive*, 1973.

AMERICAN INDIANS.
In the 20th century protected under terms of international conventions following genocidal extermination of entire tribes in the colonial era. The First Convention was signed at the 8th International American Conference, Lima, Dec. 27, 1938 on introduction of permanent study of the situation of Indian settlements existing in various American countries; the Conference resolved to convene the 1st Inter-American Congress on Indian Life in Patzcuaro, Mexico, April 1940; the Congress was institutionalized by an international convention with the Inter-American Indian Institute as its organ for co-operation with national Indian institutes. From 1948 the Institute has the status of a specialized organ with the Organization of American States and acts as a standing committee of the Inter-American Indian Congress, head-

quarters Mexico City. Publ.: *America Indigena, Anuario Indigenista* and studies. The Convention was ratified by governments of Bolivia, Brazil, Ecuador, Guatemala, Honduras, Colombia, Mexico, Peru, El Salvador, the USA and Venezuela. The Second Conference was held in Cuzco, Peru, June–July 1949; The Third in La Paz, Bolivia, Aug. 1954; Fourth in Guatemala City, May 1959; Fifth in Quito, Ecuador, Oct. 1964; Sixth in Patzcuaro, Mexico, April 1968; Seventh in Brasilia, Aug. 1972 and every four years since. The first all-American Indian conference was held under UNESCO auspices, in the Palace of Nations in Geneva, Sept. 20–23, 1977. Brazil and Colombia did not allow Indian delegations to attend the Conference.

On the initiative of Latin American states an ILO conference on June 26, 1957 adopted a Convention No. 107 on Protection of Aborigines preceded by preparation in 1953 by the ILO of an Andean Indians Program for seven million Indians living in the Andes; two pilot units were set up in Bolivia and Peru. The program covered: in Argentina–Abrapampa, Cienaga Grande and Puesto Grande, Jujuy; in Bolivia–Pillapi, Playa Verde, Paracaya, Cotaca, Otavi, Illica, Adapez and Tarija; in Chile–Molina, Coapa, Putre, Belen and Arica; in Ecuador–Candar, Chimborazo, Cotopaxi, Imbambura, Tungarahua; in Colombia–Silvia and Tierradentro; in Peru–Cuyochico, Chuquito, Camicachu, Huancayo, Pampa Cangallo, Taraco and Vicos. Excluded from the Program were Brazil and Paraguay. The Program drew for technical assistance on the American Indians Fund, a post-1968 organization founded by the OAS to sponsor educational and technical projects in Indian settlements. The Fifth Congress in Patzcuaro, 1968, revealed the murder of *c.* 100,000 Indians in the Brazilian state of Mato Grosso, mostly by means of TB injections or food poisonings, or else killings, in order to seize oil grounds so far immune as part of Indian reservations. The crime of genocide was committed by employees of a state Office for the Protection of Indians (SIP). In July 1973 *Newsweek* reported that none of the 58 accused of acts of Indian extermination and appropriation of $62 million worth of property had been put on trial. The Brazilian government dissolved SIP and replaced it by FUNAI, National Indian Fund, whose chairman Antonio Cotrini resigned, 1972, because of the institution's extermination policy towards Indians. From early 1965, during construction of the Trans-Amazonian Highway, the Indian population in Amazonia fell from 200,000 to far below 100,000. The position of the Brazilian government was represented by FUNAI chairman, Gen. J. Bandeira de Melo, who claimed that assistance for Indians could not stand in the way of the country's development; his views triggered public protest from 84 Brazilian academics. *Newsweek*'s report concluded that the fortunes of Indians in Brazil and the USA were not likely to become a concern of all until their way of life was a historical curiosity. The Brazilian Interior Minister assured the Congress about a new status for Indians being framed to secure their survival.

In Feb. 1973 similar policies of extermination were disclosed in Paraguay: the local Council of Bishops and ethnographers all over the world lodged protests; the West German weekly *Der Spiegel* reported round-ups and extermination of the Indian Ache tribe in Paraguay and seizure of territories reserved for Indians because under local law the land went to the state if not inhabited or tilled by Indians. The campaign was aimed at decimation of Indians and was a deliberate, planned genocide of the Indian population.

International Commission for Inquiry into the Crimes of the Chilean Junta at its 1st session, Hel-

sinki, March 21–24, 1974 found that the junta had abrogated all civil rights for the Indian Mapuche tribe and had launched an extermination campaign. The Indian population in USA dropped to 20,000 in 1910 and grew to 625,000 in 1920–70. Many Indians left rural reservations and moved to towns. US Indians continue to belong to the worst-off strata of US society; their life expectancy is 44 years compared with 71 for white citizens.

At the end of 1985 the Paraguayan Episcopal Conference protested against an "institutional genocide" of Paraguayan Indians by mercenaries of the landowners with knowledge of the police.

In 1985–86 one third of the land inhabited by Indian tribes in Amazonia was penetrated by Canadian and British oil companies acting on the basis of a 1985 presidential decree granting prospecting licences to search for minerals on Indian reserves. On February 24, 1989, a meeting of Brazilian Indians in Altamira protested against the Transamazonian Highway, and a big dam planned to be built on the Xing River. The meeting was also attended by Indians from Mexico, USA and Canada and received a message of spiritual solidarity from the Pope John Paul II.

Inter-American Conferences, Supplement 1938–1942, Washington, DC, 1943; A.N. LOCKWOOD, *Indians of the Andes: Technical Assistance on the Altiplano*, New York, 1956; F. LANGENHOVE, "Le problème de la protection des populations aborigènes aux Nations Unies", in *Recueil des Cours de l'Académie de Droit International*, 69/1956; ILO, *El Programa Andino*, Ginebra, 1959; *Conferencias Especializadas Interamericanas*, Washington, DC, 1965; "Brazil's vanishing Indians", in: *Newsweek*, July 3, 1972, p. 12; Ch. VAHNECKE, "Génocide et Ethnocide des Indiens d'Amérique Latine", in: *Le Monde*, No. 8589, Aug. 26, 1971; "Paraguay Tollwütige Ratten", in: *Der Spiegel*, 1972, No. 33, pp. 68–69; KEESING's *Record of World Events*, 1986; KEESING's *Record of World Events*, 1987; M. SIMONS, The Amazon's Savvy Indians, in: *The New York Times Magazine* of February 26, 1989.

AMERICAN INTERNATIONAL CONFERENCES, AIC, 1889–1954. The official name of 10 international conferences which were held mainly on the initiative of the USA; the eleventh AIC scheduled for 1959 was not convened.

The First AIC was held in Washington, Oct. 2, 1889–Apr. 19, 1890, with the participation of 18 American states (the Dominican Rep. did not participate); in the US capital it established the ▷ Commercial Bureau of American Republics and worked out the International Convention on arbitration, signed Apr. 20, 1890 by Bolivia, Brazil, Ecuador, Guatemala, Honduras, Nicaragua, Salvador, Uruguay, the USA and Venezuela. The Convention was never ratified by any of the signatories.

The Second AIC was held in Mexico City, Oct. 22, 1901–Feb. 20, 1902 with the participation of all of the American states; it resolved the participation of the American republics in the Hague Convention (1899) on the peaceful resolution of international conflicts.

The Third AIC was held in Rio de Janeiro, July 21–Aug. 26, 1906 with the participation of 19 American states out of 21 existing ones (for the first time Cuba and Panama were present; Haiti and Venezuela did not participate). The AIC worked out for the II Hague Peace Conference (1907) the plan of a Convention on Limitation of the Use of Force in Collection of Foreign Debts of States.

The Fourth AIC was held in Buenos Aires, July 12–Aug. 30, 1910 with the participation of all of the American states except Bolivia; resolved to replace the ▷ Commercial Bureau of American Republics with an institution called the ▷ Panamerican Union.

The Fifth AIC was held in Santiago de Chile, March 25–May 3, 1923 with the absence of Bolivia, Mexico and Peru. The AIC worked out and ratified the ▷ Inter-American Treaty to avoid or prevent conflicts between the American states, known as the Gondra Treaty ▷ (Gondra Doctrine).

The Sixth was held in Havana, Feb. 16–22, 1928 with the participation of all the American states, ratified the ▷ Bustamente Code and worked out a new convention for the Panamerican Union.

The Seventh AIC was held in Montevideo, Dec. 3–26, 1933 with the absence of Costa Rica; worked out and approved the Convention of Rights and Duties of American states, with Additional Protocol and the No-Intervention Convention.

The Eighth AIC was held in Lima, Dec. 19–27, 1938, with the participation of all the American states; worked out and approved the Lima Declaration on the Principles of American Solidarity and Declaration of American Principles.

The Ninth AIC was held in Bogota, Mar. 30–May 2, 1948 with the participation of all the American states; worked out and approved the OPA Charter, Bogota Pact, Declaration on the Rights of Man and the Treaty on American Economic Co-operation.

The Tenth AIC was held in Caracas, Mar. 1–28, 1954 with the absence of Costa Rica. The AIC worked out and approved Anti-Communist Declaration.

The Eleventh AIC was scheduled and prepared 1959 and 1960 in Quito but postponed sine anno.

Conferencias Americanas Internacionales 1889–1936, Washington, DC, 1938, also in English; *Novena Conferencia Interamericana, Actas y Documentos*, Vol. VIII, Bogota, 1953; *Decima Conferencia Interamericana, Actas y Documentos*, Vol. VI, Washington, DC, 1956; *América y sus Problemas Economicos y Sociales. Materiales preparados para la Undecima Conferencia Interamericana*, Quito, 1960; *The Inter-American Conference, Quito, Secretaria General, Preparación del Pais Sede*, Quito, 1960; S. GUY INMAN, *Inter-American Conferences 1826–1954. History and Problems*, Washington, DC, 1965.

AMERICAN INTERNATIONAL LAW. A controversial term, disseminated by some American scientists before and after World War I, rejected by others, not accepted by the United Nations. "In fact", said American scholar M.J. Sierra, "there's nothing to justify the existence of American international law as an independent branch of international law."

A. ALVAREZ, *Le Droit International Américain*, Paris, 1910; C. SANCHEZ Y SANCHEZ, *Derecho Internacional Público Americano*, Ciudad Trujillo, 1943; J.M. YPPES, *Createur du Droit Internationale Americain–Alejandro Alvarez*, Paris, 1936; J.M. SIERRA, *Derecho International Público*, México, DF, 1963, pp. 69–70; M.A. GOMEZ DE LA TORRE, *Derecho Constitucional Interamericano*, Quito, 1964, Vol. II.

AMERICAN–IRANIAN AGREEMENT, 1959. An Agreement of Co-operation between Iran and the United States, signed at Washington DC, March 3, 1959. The highlights of the Agreement are:

"Art. I. The Imperial Government of Iran is determined to resist aggression. In case of aggression against Iran, the Government of the United States of America, in accordance with the Constitution of the United States of America, will take such appropriate action, as may be mutually agreed upon and as is envisaged in the Joint Resolution to Promote Peace and Stability in the Middle East, in order to assist the Government of Iran at its request.

Art. II. The Government of the United States of America, in accordance with the Mutual Security Act of 1954, as amended, and related laws of the United States of America, and with applicable agreements heretofore or hereafter entered into between the Government of the United States of America and the Government of

Iran, reaffirms that it will continue to furnish the Government of Iran such military and economic assistance as may be mutually agreed upon between the Government of the United States of America and the Government of Iran, in order to assist the Government of Iran in the preservation of its national independence and integrity and in the effective promotion of its economic development.
Art. III. The Imperial Government of Iran undertakes to utilize such military and economic assistance as may be provided by the Government of the United States of America in a manner consonant with the aims and purposes set forth by the Governments associated in the Declaration signed at London on July 28, 1958, and for the purpose of effectively promoting the economic development of Iran and of preserving its national independence and integrity.
Art. IV. The Government of the United States of America and the Government of Iran will cooperate with the other Governments associated in the Declaration signed at London on July 28, 1958, in order to prepare and participate in such defensive arrangements as may be mutually agreed to be desirable, subject to the other applicable provisions of this Agreement.
Art. V. The provisions of the present Agreement do not affect the co-operation between the two Governments as envisaged in other international agreements or arrangements.
Art. VI. This Agreement shall enter into force upon the date of its signature and shall continue in force until one year after the receipt by either Government of written notice of the intention of the other Government to terminate the Agreement".

UST 10, part. 2, p. 314; J.A.S. GRENVILLE (ed.), *The Major International Treaties 1914–1973*, London, 1974, pp. 345–346.

AMERICAN–JAPANESE TREATY, 1960. The Treaty of Mutual Co-operation and Security between the USA and Japan, signed at Washington, Jan. 19, 1960; read as follows:

"The United States of America and Japan,
Desiring to strengthen the bonds of peace and friendship traditionally existing between them, and to uphold the principles of democracy, individual liberty, and the rule of law;
Desiring further to encourage closer economic co-operation between them and to promote conditions of economic stability and well-being in their countries;
Reaffirming their faith in the purposes and principles of the Charter of the United Nations, and their desire to live in peace with all peoples and all Governments;
Recognizing that they have the inherent right of individual or collective self-defense as affirmed in the Charter of the United Nations;
Considering that they have a common concern in the maintenance of international peace and security in the Far East;
Having resolved to conclude a Treaty of Mutual-Co-operation and Security;
Therefore agree as follows:
Art. I. The parties undertake, as set forth in the Charter of the United Nations, to settle any international disputes, in which they may be involved by peaceful means in such a manner that international peace and security and justice are not endangered and to refrain in their international relations from the threat or use of force against the territorial integrity or political independence of any State, or in any other manner inconsistent with the purposes of the United Nations.
The parties will endeavor in concert with other peace-loving countries to strengthen the United Nations so that its mission of maintaining international peace and security may be discharged more effectively.
Art. II. The parties will contribute toward the further development of peaceful and friendly international relations by strengthening their free institutions, by bringing about a better understanding of the principles upon which these institutions are founded, and by promoting conditions of stability and well-being. They will seek to eliminate conflict in their international economic policies and will encourage economic collaboration between them.
Art. III. The parties, individually and in co-operation with each other, by means of continuous and effective selfhelp and mutual aid will maintain and develop subject to their constitutional provisions, their capacities to resist armed attack.
Art. IV. The parties will consult together from time to time regarding the implementation of this Treaty, and, at the request of either party, whenever the security of Japan or international peace and security in the Far East is threatened.
Art. V. Each party recognizes that an armed attack against either party in the territories under the administration of Japan would be dangerous to its own peace and safety and declares that it would act to meet the common danger in accordance with its constitutional provisions and processes. Any such armed attack and all measures taken as a result thereof shall be immediately reported to the Security Council of the United Nations in accordance with the provisions of Art. 51 of the Charter. Such measures shall be terminated when the Security Council has taken the measures necessary to restore and maintain international peace and security.
Art. VI. For the purpose of contributing to the security of Japan and the maintenance of international peace and security in the Far East, the United States of America is granted the use by its land, air and naval forces of facilities and areas in Japan.
The use of these facilities and areas as well as the status of United States armed forces in Japan shall be governed by a separate agreement, replacing the Administrative Agreement under Art. III of the Security Treaty between the United States of America and Japan, signed at Tokyo on February 28, 1952, as amended, and by such other arrangements as may be agreed upon.
Art. VII. This Treaty does not affect and shall not be interpreted as affecting in any way the rights and obligations of the parties under the Charter of the United Nations or the responsibility of the United Nations for the maintenance of international peace and security.
Art. VIII. This Treaty shall be ratified by the United States of America and Japan in accordance with their respective constitutional processes and will enter into force on the date on which the instruments of ratification thereof have been exchanged by them in Tokyo.
Art. IX. The Security Treaty between the United States of America and Japan signed at the city of San Francisco on September 8, 1951, shall expire upon the entering into force of this Treaty.
Art. X. This Treaty shall remain in force until in the opinion of the Governments of the United States of America and Japan there shall have come into force such United Nations arrangements as will satisfactorily provide for the maintenance of international peace and security in the Japan area.
However, after the Treaty has been in force for ten years, either party may give notice to the other party of its intention to terminate the Treaty, in which case the Treaty shall terminate one year after such notice has been given".

UST II, pp. 1632, 1652, 2160; J.A.S. GRENVILLE (ed.), *The Major International Treaties 1914–1973. A History and Guide with Texts*, London, 1974, pp. 343–345.

AMERICAN LANGUAGE. English language of the United States of America, called General American as spoken by the great majority of the inhabitants of North America. In autumn 1979 the Oxford University in England established the department of the American language. In the opinion of experts British English dominated in the League of Nations, but in the United Nations – the American.

L.V. BERREY, M. VAN DEN BARK (eds), *The American Thesaurus of Slang*, New York, 1948; *Websters New World Dictionary of the American Language*, New York, 1970; E. EHRLICH, S.B. FLEXNER, G. CARRUTH, J.M. WATKINS, *Oxford American Dictionary*, New York, 1982; R.L. CHAPMAN (ed), *New Dictionary of American Slang*, New York, 1988.

AMERICAN NATIONS HERITAGE PROTECTION, 1976. A Convention on the Protection of the Archeological, Historical and Artistic Heritage of the American Nations, adopted at San Salvador on June 16, 1976 by the OAS General Assembly. The text is as follows:

"The Governments of the Member States of the Organization of American States, having seen the continuous looting and plundering of the native cultural heritage suffered by the countries of the hemisphere, particularly the Latin American countries; and considering that such acts of pillage have damaged and reduced the archeological, historical, and artistic wealth, through which the national character of their peoples is expressed; finding that there is a basic obligation to transmit to coming generations the legacy of their cultural heritage; that this heritage can only be protected and preserved through mutual appreciation and respect for such properties, within a framework of the soundest inter American co-operation; and that the member states have repeatedly demonstrated their willingness to establish standards for the protection and surveillance of the archeological, historical, and artistic heritage, declare: that it is essential to take steps, at both the national and international levels, for the most effective protection and retrieval of cultural treasures, and have agreed upon the following:
Art. 1: The purpose of this Convention is to identify, register, protect, and safeguard the property making up the cultural heritage of the American nations in order:
(a) to prevent illegal exportation or importation of cultural property; and
(b) to promote cooperation among the American states for mutual awareness and appreciation of their cultural property.
Art. 2: The cultural property referred to in the preceding article is that included in the following categories:
(a) Monuments, objects, fragments of ruined buildings, and archeological materials belonging to American cultures existing prior to contact with European culture, as well as the remains of human beings, fauna, and flora related to such cultures;
(b) Monuments, buildings, objects of an artistic, utilitarian, and ethnological nature, whole or in fragments, from the colonial era and the nineteenth Century;
(c) Libraries and archives; incunabula and manuscripts; books and other publications, iconographies, maps and documents published before 1850;
(d) All objects originating after 1850 that the States Parties have recorded as cultural property, provided that they have given notice of such registration to the other parties to the treaty;
(e) All cultural property that any of the States Parties specifically declares to be included within the scope of this convention.
Art. 3: The cultural property included in the above article shall receive maximum protection at the international level, and its exportation and importation shall be considered unlawful, except when the state owning it authorizes its exportation for purposes of promoting knowledge of national cultures.
Art. 4: Any disagreement between the parties to this Convention, regarding application of the definitions and categories of art. 2 to specific property, shall be resolved definitively by the inter-American Council for Education, Science, and Culture, CIECC, following an opinion by the Inter-American Committee on Culture.
Art. 5: The cultural heritage of each state consists of property mentioned in art. 2, found or created in its territory and legally acquired items of foreign origin.
Art. 6: The control exercised by each state over its cultural heritage and any actions that may be taken to reclaim items belonging to it are imprescriptible.
Art. 7: Regulations on ownership of cultural property and its transfer within the territory of each state shall be governed by domestic legislation. With a view to preventing unlawful trade in such goods, the following measures shall be encouraged:
(a) Registration of collections and of transfer of cultural property subject to protection;
(b) Registration of transactions carried out by establishments engaged in the sale and purchase of such property;
(c) Prohibition of imports of cultural property from other states without appropriate certificate and authorization.
Art. 8: Each state is responsible for identifying, registering, protecting, preserving, and safeguarding its cul-

tural heritage; in fulfillment of these functions each state undertakes to encourage;
(a) Preparation, in accordance with its respective constitutional standards, of rules and legislative provisions required for effective protection of this heritage from destruction resulting from neglect or inadequate preservation work;
(b) Establishment of technical organs entrusted specifically with the protection and safeguarding of cultural property;
(c) Establishment and maintenance of an inventory and record of cultural property, to make it possible to identify and locate it;
(d) The establishment and development of museums, libraries, archives, and other centers for the protection and preservation of cultural property;
(e) The delimitation and protection of archeological sites and places of historical and artistic interest;
(f) Exploration, excavation, investigation, and preservation of archeological sites and objects by scientific institutions, in collaboration with the national agency in charge of the archeological heritage.
Art. 9: Each State Party shall prevent by all available means any unlawful excavation in its territory or any removal of cultural property therefrom."

OAS General Report 1976, Washington, DC, 1977.

AMERICAN–POLISH FRIENDSHIP TREATY, 1931.
A Treaty signed June 15, 1931 in Washington under the name: Treaty of Friendship, Commerce and Consular Rights between the United States and Poland. The highlights of the Treaty are:

"Art. I, The nationals of each of the High Contracting Parties shall be permitted to enter, travel and reside in the territories of the other; to exercise liberty of conscience and freedom of worship; to engage in professional, scientific, religious, philanthropic, manufacturing and commercial work of every kind; to carry on every form of commercial activity which is not forbidden by the local law; to own, and erect and lease and occupy appropriate buildings and to lease lands for residential, scientific, religious, philanthropic, manufacturing, commercial and mortuary purposes; to employ agents of their choice; and generally the said nationals shall be permitted, upon submitting themselves to all local laws and regulations duly established, to enjoy all of the foregoing privileges and to do anything incidental to or necessary for the enjoyment of these privileges, upon the same terms as nationals of the state of residence, except as otherwise provided by laws of either High Contracting Party in force at the time of the signature of this Treaty. In so far as the laws of either High Contracting Party in force in the time of the signature of this Treaty do not permit nationals of the other Party to enjoy any of the foregoing privileges upon the same terms as the nationals of the state of residence, they shall enjoy, on condition of reciprocity, as favourable treatment as nationals of the most favored nation."
"Art. III. The dwellings, warehouses, manufactories, shops, and other places of business, and all premises thereto appertaining of the nationals of each of the High Contracting Parties in the territories of the other, used for any purposes set forth in art. I, shall be respected. It shall not be allowable to make a domiciliary visit to, or search of, any such buildings and premises, or there to examine and inspect books, papers or accounts, except under the conditions and in conformity with the forms prescribed by the laws, ordinances and regulations for nationals."
Art. IV. Set forth in great detail "the freedom of trade and navigation between the two Parties".

In a note of July 5, 1957, the American Party proposed deletion of art. IV or optional annulment of the Treaty. The reply of the Polish Party was transmitted in a note of Aug. 26, 1957.

LNTS, 1931; *Recueil de documents*, Warsaw, 1957.

AMERICAN POLITICAL SCIENCE ASSOCIATION.
F. 1903, Washington, DC, publ. *The American Political Science Review* (bi-monthly). Prints annually a list of doctoral dissertations in Political Science in preparation at American Universities.

AMERICAN PRINCIPLES DECLARATION, 1942.
The Third Inter-American Consultative Meeting of the Ministers of Foreign Affairs at Rio de Janeiro, Jan. 15–28, 1942, adopted a Declaration on American Principles. The text is as follows:

"A. Reiteration of a Principle of American Law.
Whereas:
(1) In accordance with its historical, racial, political and juridical tradition, there is and can be no room in America for the so-called racial, linguistic or religious 'minorities' and
(2) In accordance with this concept, Resolutions 27 and 28 approved at the Pan-American Conference in Lima in 1938, confirm the principle that residents who, according to domestic law, are considered aliens, cannot claim collectively the condition of minorities, individually, however, they will continue to enjoy the rights to which they are entitled.
The Third Meeting of the Ministers of Foreign Affairs of the American Republics, declares:
That it reiterates the principle of American Public Law, according to which aliens residing in an American state are subject to the jurisdiction of that State, and the Governments and Agencies of the countries of which such aliens are nationals cannot lawfully interfere, directly or indirectly, in domestic affairs or the purpose of controlling the status or activities of such aliens.
B. Continental Solidarity in Observance of Treaties.
Whereas:
(1) The concept of solidarity, in addition to embodying altruistic sentiments held in common, includes that of co-operation so necessary to forestall obstacles which may prejudice the maintenance of that principle, or the re-establishment of harmony when weakened or disrupted by the adoption of measures contrary to the dictates of international law and morality;
(2) This solidarity must be translated into facts in order to become a living reality. Since from a philosophical concept it has developed into an historic affirmation through repeated and frequent reaffirmations in international agreements freely agreed upon;
(3) Respect for the pledged word in international treaties rests upon incontestable juridical principles as well as on precepts of morality in accordance with the maxim of canon law; Pacta sunt servanda;
(4) Such agreements, whether bilateral or multilateral, must not be modified or nullified unilaterally, except as otherwise provided as in the case of denunciation clearly authorized by the parties;
(5) Only thus can peace, inspired by the common welfare of the peoples be founded on an enduring basis, as proclaimed at the meeting in Havana;
(6) Or peaceful relations among peoples would be practically impossible in the absence of strict observance of all pacts solemnly celebrated which have met all the formalities provided for in the laws of the High Contracting Parties in order to render them juridically effective.
The Third Meeting of the Ministers of Foreign Affairs of the American Republics declares:
(1) That should the Government of an American nation violate an agreement or a treaty duly perfected by two or more American Republics or should there be reason to believe that a violation which might disturb the peace or solidarity of the Americas is being contemplated, any American State may initiate the consultation contemplated in Resolution 17 of Havana with the object of agreeing upon the measures to be taken.
(2) That the Government desiring to initiate the consultation and propose a Meeting of the Ministers of Foreign Affairs of the American Republics or their representatives, shall communicate with the Governing Board of the Pan-American Union specifying in detail the subjects to be considered as well as the approximate date on which the meeting should take place.
C. The Good Neighbour Policy.
Whereas:
(1) Relations among nations, if they are to have foundations which will assure an international order under law, must be based on the essential and universal principle of justice;
(2) The standard proclaimed and observed by the US of America to the effect that its international policy must be founded on the 'good neighbour' is a general criterion of right and a source of guidance in the relations between States, and this well-conceived policy prescribes respect for the fundamental rights of States

as well as co-operation between them for the welfare of international society; and
(3) This policy has been one of the elements contributing to the present solidarity of the Americas and their joint co-operation in the solution of outstanding problems of the continent.
The Third Meeting of the Ministers of Foreign Affairs of the American Republics declares:
That the principle that international conduct must be inspired by the policy of the good neighbour is a norm of international law of the American Continent.
D. Post-war Problems.
Whereas:
(1) World peace must be based on the principles of respect for law, of justice and co-operation which inspire the nations of America and which have been expressed at Inter-American Meetings held from 1889 to date;
(2) A new order of peace must be supported by economic principles which will ensure equitable and lasting international trade with equal opportunities for all Nations;
(3) Collective security must be founded not only on political institutions but also on just, effective and liberal economic systems;
(4) It is indispensable to undertake the immediate study of the basis for this new economic and political order; and
(5) It is an imperative necessity for the countries of America to increase their productive capacity; to secure, from their international trade, returns which will permit them adequately to remunerate labor and improve the standard of living of workers to protect and preserve the health of their peoples and develop their civilization and culture".

Conferencias Interamericanas. Primer Suplemento 1938–1942, Washington, DC, 1943, pp. 98–99.

AMERICAN REPUBLICS INTERNATIONAL UNION, 1890.
An institution, est. Apr. 14, 1890 by the First International American Conference in Washington with the aim to promptly collect and make available data relating to trade. Its function was taken over in 1891 by the ▷ Commercial Bureau of the American Republics.

AMERICAN REVOLUTION, 1775–83.
The independence movement of thirteen British colonies in North America (New Hampshire, Massachussets, Rhode Island, Connecticut, New York, New Jersey, Pennsylvania, Delaware, Maryland, Virginia, North Carolina, South Carolina and Georgia). The ▷ Continental Congress adopted the ▷ Declaration of Independence on July 4, 1776.

Ch. WARD, *The American Revolution*, 2 Vls., New York, 1952; J.R. ALDEN, *The American Revolution, 1775–83*, New York, 1954.

AMERICAN SAMOA.
Part of the Samoa Islands chain in the South Pacific, administered by the US Department of Interior. Area: 196.8 sq. km. Population: 1980 census: 32,297. Capital: Pago Pago – 3,075 habitants on Tutuila Island. Great Britain and Germany renounced in favor of the US all rights over the islands east of longitude 171°W under the Tripartite Treaty of Nov. 7, 1899, ratified Feb. 19, 1900. In 1980 the Territory elected a non-voting delegate to US Congress.

J.W. PRATT, *America's Colonial Experiment: How the United States Gained, Governed and in Part Gave Away a Colonial Empire*, New York, 1950; *The World Almanac*, New York, 1980; *The Europa Yearbook 1988. A World Survey*, Vol. II, London, 1988.

AMERICAN SENATE UNITED NATIONS RESOLUTIONS, 1943.
Two resolutions: (1) a bipartisan Ball–Burton–Hatch–Hill resolution calling for the creation of a United Nations agency with special funds for relief and rehabilitation and with own military force; defeated by the Senate, replaced by (2) Connally Resolution, sponsored by

Senator Tom Connally of Texas in Nov., 1943, generally supporting the idea of US participation in a World Organization of the United Nations.

AMERICAN SOCIETY OF INTERNATIONAL LAW, ASIL. A society f. 1905 in Washington, DC. Publ. since 1905 *American Journal of International Law* (a monthly), and since 1912 also *Revista Americana de Derecho Internacional.* Reg. with the UIA.

Yearbook of International Organizations.

AMERICAN–SOVIET AGREEMENTS, 1957–81. The following is a list of bilateral agreements, treaties, protocols, memoranda of understanding as well as joint communiqués and simultaneous statements:

(1) On Jan. 27, 1957 was signed an Agreement on Co-operation in the fields of Science, Technology, Education and Culture; renewed periodically.
(2) On June 20, 1963, was signed at Geneva a US–Soviet Memorandum of Understanding, regarding the establishment of a direct telecommunications link; entered into force the same day. ▷ Hot line.
(3) On Apr. 20, 1964, simultaneous statements were made in Washington and Moscow by the US President L.B. Johnson and the Soviet Prime Minister N.S. Khrushchev on the reduction of fissionable material production (plutonium and enriched uranium).
(4) On Sept. 30, 1971, was signed at Washington an Agreement on measures to reduce the risk of outbreak of nuclear war, called – Nuclear Accidents Agreement; entered into force the same day.
(5) On Sept. 30, 1971 was signed also at Washington a Hot Line Modernization Agreement; entered into force the same day; amended on Apr. 29, 1975.
During the official visit to the USSR by President R.M. Nixon, May 22–30, 1972, (▷ Moscow Communiqué 1972) further agreements were signed:
(6) On May 25, 1972, was signed at Moscow the Agreement on the Prevention of Incidents on and over the High Seas, providing for measures to assure the safety of navigation of the US and the USSR ships and flight of their military aircraft over the high seas. Entered into force the day of signature. An Additional Protocol was signed on May 22, 1973 at Washington.
(7) On May 26, 1972 was signed at Moscow a Treaty on the Limitation of Anti-Ballistic Missile System, called SALT II ABM Treaty, prohibiting the deployment of ▷ ABM systems on the whole territory of both countries or of an individual region, except as expressly permitted; and limiting the number of ABM launchers (100) and ABM interceptor missiles (100) in each ABM deployment area. Entered into force on Oct. 3, 1972. Additional Protocol was signed in Moscow on July 3, 1974 and entered into force on May 25, 1976.
(8) On May 26, 1972 was signed at Moscow the Interim Agreement on Certain Measures with Respect to the limitation of Strategic Offensive Arms, called ▷ SALT I Agreement, providing for a freeze on the aggregate number of fixed land-based intercontinental ballistic missile launchers and ballistic missile launchers on modern submarines; and limiting by an annexed Protocol the number of ballistic missile launchers on submarines. The Agreement entered into force on Oct. 3, 1972.
(9) On May 29, 1972 was signed at Moscow the Agreement on ▷ American–Soviet Basic Principles, accepting "in common determination that in the nuclear age there is no alternative to conducting their mutual relations on the basis of peaceful coexistence."
(10) On May 29, 1972 was signed at Moscow a provisional Agreement on some means of limitation of offensive strategic armaments, ▷ ICBM type.
(11) On May 29, 1972 was signed at Moscow an agreement to make manned space flights more secure, to resume works on devices for docking Soviet and American space vessels and laboratories. (▷ Apollo-Soyuz).
(12) On May 29, 1972 were signed at Moscow agreements: on co-operation for the protection of the natural environment; on the establishment of a Joint Commission for Trade; on scientific and technical co-operation and the establishment of a standing commission for scientific and technical co-operation; and
(13) On Dec. 21, 1972, at Geneva was signed a Memorandum of Understanding regarding the establishment of a US–USSR Standing Consultative Commission to promote the objectives of the SALT I ABM Treaty, 1972; the SALT I Interim Agreement 1971 and the Nuclear Accident Agreement 1971. An Additional Protocol was signed in May 1973 in Geneva.
During the visit of L. Brezhnev to the USA, in May 1973 further agreements were signed in Washington:
(14) Agreement on annual educational, scientific and artistic exchange.
(15) Agreement on prevention of double taxation of persons and firms conducting business in one of the countries by the other country.
(16) Agreement concerning agriculture and food (exchange of information about production, methods of husbandry, mechanization of field work, etc.).
(17) Agreement on oceanographic research (mainly co-operation in exploration of sea and ocean beds).
(18) Agreement on transportation (exchange of experts and information about major areas of transportation by road, railway, sea and air).
(19) Joint Statement concerning limitation of a potential danger to mankind arising from the possible invention of new types of warfare "mindful that progress in science and technology in the fields related to the environments around us, to the impact on climate inclusively may create new possibilities to use means of acting on the natural environment for warlike purposes; in recognition of the fact that such use when made would have broad, long-term and serious influence detrimental to human welfare, that appropriate use of scientific and technical progress might lead to an improvement in the interaction between man and nature – they voice for most effective and possible steps to be taken in favor of eliminating the threat to the natural environment".
(20) Joint Communiqué: I. Progress in the improvement of Soviet–American relations, II. Further limitation of strategic armaments and other problems of disarmament, III. Progress in the settlement of international problems, IV. Trade and economic relations, V. Progress in other spheres of bilateral relations: (energy, co-operation in space research, protection of natural environment, cultural exchange, new consulates to be opened in New York and Kiev.).
(21) On June 21, 1973 at Washington was signed an Agreement on Basic Principles of Negotiations on the Further Limitation of Strategic Offensive Arms.
(22) On June, 22, 1973 was signed at Washington an Agreement on the Prevention of Nuclear War, called ▷ Nuclear War Prevention Treaty 1973; entered into force on the day of signature.
(23) On July 3, 1974 was signed at Moscow by L.I. Brezhnev and R. Nixon, who went to the USSR June 2–July 3, 1974, a Treaty on the Limitation of Underground Nuclear Weapon Tests, called Threshold Test Ban Treaty, prohibiting to both sides for five years, from Mar. 31, 1976, "any underground nuclear tests beyond 150 kilotons". Not entered into force by Jan., 1981.
(24) On Nov. 24, 1974, at Vladivostok was signed by the President of the USA and the Prime Minister of the USSR a Statement on the Question of Further Limitations of Strategic Offensive Arms, called Vladivostok Agreement.
(25) On May 28, 1976 was signed at Moscow and Washington the Treaty on Underground Nuclear Explosions for Peaceful Purposes, called Nuclear Peaceful Explosions Treaty. Not entered into force by Jan., 1981.
(26) On June 18, 1979 was signed at Vienna the Treaty on the Limitation of Strategic Offensive Arms, with Protocol called SALT II Treaty (▷ SALT II Documents); not entered into force by Jan., 1981.
(27) On June 18, 1979 was signed at Vienna a Joint Statement of Principles and Basic Guidelines for Subsequent Negotiations on the Limitations of Strategic Arms.

Documents on Disarmament 1964: SIPRI, *World Armaments and Disarmament Yearbook 1980*, London, 1980; J. GOLDBLAT, *Arms Control Agreements. A Handbook,* New York, 1983.

AMERICAN–SOVIET BASIC PRINCIPLES, 1972. The Joint Declaration by the USA and USSR on Basic Principles of Reciprocal Relations, signed at Moscow on May 29, 1972, adopted "in common determination that in the nuclear age there is no alternative to conducting their mutual relations on the basis of peaceful coexistence." read as follows:

"The United States of America and the Union of Soviet Socialist Republics,
Guided by their obligations under the Charter of the United Nations and by a desire to strengthen peaceful relations with each other and to place these relations on the firmest possible basis;
Aware of the need to make every effort to remove the threat of war and to create conditions which promote the reduction of tensions in the World and the strengthening of universal security and international co-operation;
Believing that improvement of United States-Soviet relations and their mutually advantageous development in such areas as economics, science and culture will meet these objectives and contribute to better mutual understanding and business-like co-operation, without in any way prejudicing the interests of third countries;
Conscious that these objectives reflect the interests of the peoples of both countries.
Have agreed as follows:
First. They will proceed from the common determination that in the nuclear age there is no alternative to conducting their mutual relations on the basis of peaceful coexistence.
Differences in ideology and in the social systems of the USA and the USSR, are not obstacles to the bilateral development of normal relations based on the principles of sovereignty, equality, non-interference in internal affairs and mutual advantage.
Second. The USA and the USSR attach major importance to preventing the development of situations capable of causing a dangerous exacerbation of their relations. Therefore, they will do their utmost to avoid military confrontations and to prevent the outbreak of nuclear war. They will always exercise restraint in their mutual relations, and will be prepared to negotiate and settle differences by peaceful means. Discussions and negotiations on outstanding issues will be conducted in a spirit of reciprocity, mutual accommodation and mutual benefit.
Both sides recognize that efforts to obtain unilateral advantage at the expense of the other, directly or indirectly ... are inconsistent with these objectives. The prerequisites for maintaining and strengthening peaceful relations between the USA and the USSR, are the recognition of the security interests of the parties based on the principle of equality and the renunciation of the use or threat of force.
Third. The USA and the USSR have a special responsibility ... as do other countries which are permanent members of the United Nations Security Council, to do everything in their power so that conflicts or situations will not arise which would serve to increase international tensions. Accordingly they will seek to promote conditions in which all countries will live in peace and security and will not be subject to outside interference in their internal affairs.
Fourth. The USA and the USSR intend to widen the juridical basis of their mutual relations and to exert the necessary efforts so that bilateral agreements which they have concluded and multilateral treaties and agreements to which they are jointly parties are faithfully implemented.
Fifth. The USA and the USSR reaffirm their readiness to continue the practice of exchanging views on problems of mutual interest, and, when necessary to conduct such exchanges at the highest level, including meetings between leaders of the two countries.
The two Governments welcome and will facilitate an increase in productive contacts between representatives of the legislative bodies of the two countries.
Sixth. The parties will continue their efforts to limit armaments on a bilateral as well as on a multilateral basis. They will continue to make special efforts to limit strategic armaments. Whenever possible, they will conclude concrete agreements aimed at achieving these purposes.
The USA and the USSR regard as the ultimate objective of their efforts the achievement of general and complete disarmament and the establishment of an effective system on international security in accordance with the purposes and principles of the United Nations.

Seventh. The USA and the USSR regard commercial and economic ties as an important and necessary element in the strengthening of their bilateral relations and thus will actively promote the growth of such ties. They will facilitate co-operation between the relevant organizations and enterprises of the two countries and the conclusion of appropriate agreements and contracts, including long-term ones. The two countries will contribute to the improvement of maritime and air communications between them.
Eighth. The two sides consider it timely and useful to develop mutual contacts and co-operation in the fields of science and technology. Where suitable, the USA and the USSR will conclude appropriate agreements dealing with concrete co-operation in these fields.
Ninth. The two sides reaffirm their intention to deepen cultural ties with one another and to encourage fuller familiarization with each other's cultural values. They will promote improved conditions for cultural exchanges and tourism.
Tenth. The USA and the USSR will seek to ensure that their ties and co-operation in all the above-mentioned fields and in any others in their mutual interest are built on a firm and long-term basis. To give a permanent character to these efforts, they will establish in all fields where this is feasible joint commissions or other joint bodies.
Eleventh. The USA and the USSR make no claim for themselves and would not recognize the claims of anyone else to any special rights or advantages in world affairs. They recognize the sovereign equality of all States.
The development of United States-Soviet relations is not directed against third countries and their interests.
Twelfth. The basic principles set forth in this Document do not affect any obligations with respect to other countries earlier assumed by the USA and the USSR."

US State Department Bulletin, May 1972.

AMERICAN–SOVIET CULTURAL AGREEMENTS, 1985–86, signed by Ronald Reagan and Michail Gorbachev in Geneva, Nov. 14, 1985. Another two agreements were signed on Dec. 13, 1985: on academic exchange and on exchange of art exhibitions; and on Aug. 5, 1986 on 13 educational, cultural and scientific exchanges.

KEESING's *Record of World Events*, 1987, No 3.

AMERICAN–SOVIET TREATIES, 1941–45. Following the German aggression against the USSR on June 21, 1941, American-Soviet negotiations were started by envoys of the US President to Moscow, H. Hopkins, on July 30, 1941, and A. Harriman, Sept. 28, 1941. As a result, on Oct. 1, 1941, the American-Soviet Protocol on 1 billion dollar credit for the USSR was agreed in Moscow under the ▷ Lend-Lease Act. Preliminary provisions for mutual assistance were set up through exchange of notes on Feb. 13, 20 and 23, 1941; finally, signed on June 11, 1942 in Washington by the Governments of the USA and the USSR, was the Treaty on mutual assistance in the war against aggression, patterned on an identical treaty, signed Feb. 23, 1942, by Great Britain and the USA. The major provision was to delay payment for mutual services and defense material until after the war; however, the payment "should not hamper the trade between the two states but contribute to the growth in world economic relations". All subsequent American-Soviet treaties were part of multilateral, tripartite agreements with Great Britain. (▷ Teheran Conference 1943, ▷ Yalta Declaration 1945 and ▷ Potsdam Agreement 1945).

Vnieshnaia politika Sovietskogo Soyuza v Pieriod Otchestviennoy Voyni, Moskva, 1944; *Foreign Aid of the US Government 1940–1951*, Washington, DC, 1955.

AMERICAN–SPANISH PEACE TREATY, 1898. A Treaty between the USA and Spain signed in Washington, DC, Aug. 12, 1898. The text is as follows:

"Art. I. Spain relinquishes all claim of sovereignty over and title to Cuba. And as the island is, upon its evacuation by Spain, to be occupied by the United States, the United States will, so long as such occupation shall last, assume and discharge the obligations that may under international law result from the fact of its occupation, for the protection of life and property.
Art. II. Spain cedes to the United States the island of Porto Rico and other islands now under Spanish sovereignty in the West Indies, and the Island of Guam in the Marianas or Ladrones.
Art. III. Spain cedes to the United States the archipelago known as the Philippine Islands ... The United States will pay to Spain the sum of twenty million dollars ($20,000,000) within three months after the exchange of the ratifications of the present treaty.
Art. IV. The United States will, for the term of ten years from the date of the exchange of the ratifications of the present treaty, admit Spanish ships and merchandise to the ports of the Philippine Islands on the same terms as ships and merchandise of the United States.
Art. V. The United States will, upon the signature of the present Treaty, send back to Spain, at its own cost, the Spanish soldiers taken as prisoners of war on the capture of Manila by the American forces. The arms of the soldiers in question shall be restored to them.
Spain will, upon the exchange of the ratifications of the present treaty, proceed to evacuate the Philippines as well as the island of Guam, on terms similar to those agreed upon by the Commissioners appointed to arrange for the evaluation of Porto Rico and other islands in the West Indies, under the Protocol of August 12, 1898, which is to continue in force till its provisions are completely executed ...
Art. VI. Spain will, upon the signature of the present treaty, release all prisoners of war ...
Reciprocally, the United States will release all persons made prisoners of war by the American forces ..."

Major Peace Treaties of Modern History, New York, 1967, pp. 853–855.

AMERICAN UNION, 1826. First Latin American integration initiated by S. Bolivar under the ▷ Union, League and Permanent Confederation Treaty 1826.

AMERICAN WARS. The most important armed conflicts in the western hemisphere in the 19th and 20th centuries were as follows:

1800–24:	Wars of independence of the states of Latin America.
1812–15:	English–American war.
1824–25:	War of Argentina and Uruguay against Brazil.
1835:	War between Bolivia and Peru.
1842:	Defensive war of Costa Rica against the invasion of F. Morazan.
1846–48:	US war against Mexico.
1851–52:	Argentina's war against Brazil and Uruguay.
1855–60:	Defensive war of Nicaragua against the invasion of W. Walker.
1857:	Defensive war of Costa Rica against the invasion of W. Walker.
1861–65:	Civil War in USA.
1861–67:	War of Mexico against the invasion of Maximilian I.
1863:	War of El Salvador with Honduras and Guatemala.
1864–70:	War of Argentina, Brazil, and Uruguay against Paraguay.
1866:	Defensive war of Chile and Peru against Spain.
1867:	War of El Salvador with Honduras and Guatemala.
1879–84:	War of the Pacific.
1886–88:	Insurrection of Cuba against Spain.
1887–1902:	Civil war in Colombia.
1890:	War of El Salvador with Honduras and Guatemala.
1894–1907:	War of Honduras with Nicaragua.
1895–98:	Insurrection of Cuba against Spain.
1898:	US–Spanish war.
1899–1901:	US–Philippines war.
1901–03:	"Rubber war" between Bolivia and Brazil.
1902–03:	Military conflict of England, Italy, and Germany with Venezuela ("Execution of debts").
1910–17:	Civil war in Mexico with US military interventions.
1912–33:	American–Nicaraguan military conflict.
1916–24:	Military US intervention in the Dominican Republic.
1917–18:	American–German war.
1929–39:	War of Ecuador with Peru.
1932–35:	War between Brazil and Paraguay.
1940–42:	War of Ecuador with Peru.
1941–45:	American–Japanese war.
1942–45:	American–German war.
1954:	US military intervention in Guatemala.
1956–59:	Civil war in Cuba.
1965–66:	US military intervention in the Dominican Republic.
1969:	"Soccer war" between El Salvador and Honduras.
1973:	State of war in Chile.
1979:	Civil war in Nicaragua.
1980:	Civil war in El Salvador.
1982:	"Falklands–Malvinas War" between UK and Argentina.
1983:	Military actions by contras based in Honduras and other Central American Countries against Nicaragua. US military intervention in Grenada.

T.H. WILLIAMS, *The History of the American Wars* from 1745 to 1918, New York 1981.

AMERICAN WAY OF LIFE. International term since 1936. During the Presidential election 1936 the Republican candidate Alf Landon campaigning against F.D. Roosevelt's New Deal coined the slogan: "Save the American Way of Life".

AMGOT. Allied Military Government of Occupied Territories; American–British military administration in North Italy during World War II (Dec. 10, 1943–Dec. 31, 1945).

AMIENS. City in northern France, historical capital of Picardy. The Cathedral of Notre Dame (built 1220–1280) included in the ▷ World Heritage UNESCO List is the largest Gothic cathedral in France. Through the irresistible upward surge of its architecture, this 13th-century cathedral was a precursor of the later techniques of the flamboyant Gothic style. It was also influential on account of its sculpture, with an immense display of statues and bas-reliefs, among which the large image of Christ, known as "le Beau Dieu", acquired immediate fame and was widely imitated.

UNESCO, *A Legacy for All*, Paris, 1984.

AMMUNITION. Projectiles of every kind used for military purposes, some of them controlled by international conventions (for instance ▷ Dumdum bullets).

AMNESTY. An act of pardon by a legislative authority, revoking not only the punishment but also the offence; an international custom since the Middle Ages consisting in inserting the amnesty clause into a peace treaty, applied to all persons who were imprisoned during a war for political reasons. After World War II such a clause was introduced into the Peace Treaties with Bulgaria (art. 3), Finland (art. 7), Romania (art. 4), and Hungary (art. 3).

P.F. SIMON, "La clause d'amnistie dans les traités de la paix", in: *Revue générale de droit international public*, No. 26, 1919; R. LEMKIN, *Amnestia*, Warsaw, 1936.

AMNESTY DECLARATION IN GREECE AND TURKEY, 1923. An international document signed in Lausanne July 24, 1923, by the governments of the British Empire, France, Greece, Italy, Japan, Romania and Turkey, proclaiming that "full and complete amnesty shall be granted by the Turkish Government and by the Greek Government (after the signing of Peace Treaty) for all crimes or offences committed from Aug. 1, 1914 to Nov. 20, 1922."

LNTS, Vol. 36, p. 147.

AMNESTY INTERNATIONAL. An international organization reg. with the UIA, f. 1961, London. An independent worldwide movement working impartially for the release of all prisoners of conscience, fair and prompt trials for all political prisoners, and the abolition of torture and the death penalty; financed by donations. Members: 42 national sections with over 3,000 local groups; over 500,000 individuals in 150 countries. Nobel Peace Prize, 1977. Consultative status: ECOSOC, UNESCO, Council of Europe, OAU, OAS. Publ. *Amnesty International Newsletter* (monthly), *Annual Report* and *Chronicle of Current Events* (bi-monthly).

B. MARCHAL, "Amnesty International a dix ans", in: *Le Monde*, October 6, 1971: *The Europa Year Book 1984. A World Survey*, vol. 1, p. 260, London, 1984.

"AMOCO CADIZ". An American supertanker, flying the Liberian flag, which on Mar. 16, 1978 was wrecked off the Breton coast and polluted a 200 km stretch of the English Channel and French maritime coastal waters by leaking 224,000 tons of oil. The spill, the greatest of its kind and remembered under the name of "ecological bomb", inflicted material damage upon Brittany amounting to more than US $30 million.
A Chicago court, on Febr. 11, 1987 recognized for the first time an oil company's responsibility for the damages caused by its oil tanker, ordering Standard Oil of Indiana to pay $85 million in damages and occured interest to the French government and Breton syndicates for "Amoco Cadiz" damages.

D. FAIRSHALL, Ph. JORDAN, *Black Tide Rising: The Wreck of the* Amoco Cadiz, London, 1980; *The International Herald Tribune*, February 12, 1987; KEESING's *Record of World Events*, June, 1988.

AMOEBIASIS. *Entamoeba histolytica.* A subject of international actions, under the aegis of WHO, against the spread of amoebic dysentery, called the poor people's disease, prevalent in certain zones of South East Asia, East and West Africa, Mexico and the north-west part of South America.

B. SEPULVEDA, "Amoeba: companion or killer", in: *World Health*, March, 1984.

AMORTIZATION. An international term used in LN and UN statistics: value of consumed capital goods at a given time. After World War II the accelerated amortization method was used in many countries. It consisted of shortening the period of amortization of capital goods, thus providing additional means for financing investments.

AMORTIZATIONS LAW. A historic name given to legal provisions that have been issued since the 18th century in England and later in France, Germany and Italy; since the 16th century also the name for the Acts of the Polish Seym (Diet) limiting the rights of the church to purchase freely land estates, because canon law prohibited the resale of church estates to private persons, a fact significantly reducing the turnover of land.

AMPÈRE. Symbol: A. An international unit of electric current, introduced by the International Electrical Congress in Chicago, 1793; defined by the General Conference of Weights and Measures (CGPM), 1948, as follows:

"The ampère is that constant current which, if maintained in two straight parallel conductors of infinite length, of negligible circular cross-section, and placed 1 metre apart in vacuum, would produce between these conductors a force equal to 2×10^{-7} newton per metre of length."

Since 1960 one of the base units of the International System of Units (▷ SI).

AMPHETAMINES. ▷ Drugs of abuse related pharmacologically to cocaine, called also stimulants.

UN Chronicle, May, 1987.

AMRAAM. Advanced Mechanic Range Air-to-Air Missile. A US missile, 1987, which guides itself to the target with its own radar.

AMRITSAR. City and district in the Punjab state NW India. Area of the district: 5,123 sq km. Population: 1985 est. over 3 million. The holy city of the Sikhs with the sacred Golden Temple; in the early XIX century center of the independent Sikh empire in the present territories of India and Pakistan. In April 1919 scene of a massacre by the British colonial troops. On April 30, 1986, one day after the proclamation in the Golden Temple of the independent Sikh state ▷ Khalistan, the Punjab police and commandos entered the Golden Temple killing one person and detaining hundreds of Sikhs.

The International Geographic Encyclopedia, London, 1979; KEESING's *Contemporary Archive*, 1986, No 8.

AMSTERDAM. The official capital (1986 pop. 938,920) of the Netherlands since 1814; occupied by Germany from 1940 to 1945, liberated by the Allies in Apr., 1945. The seat of 22 international organizations registered with the UIA, e.g. European Marketing Council, International Bureau of Fiscal Documentation, World Chess Federation.

Yearbook of International Organizations.

AMSTERDAM, INTERNATIONAL, THE. A generally accepted term in the international workers' movement for the International Federation of Trade Unions, Fédération Syndicale Internationale (FSI), existing from 1919 to 1939, founded in Amsterdam and having its headquarters there, connected with the Socialist International. It was officially dissolved in 1945, and its functions were taken over in 1949 by the International Confederation of Free Trade Unions, which came into being after the split in the ▷ Trade Unions. Eight Congresses of FSI were held: in Amsterdam 1919, in Rome 1922, in Vienna 1924, in Paris 1927, in Stockholm 1930, in Brussels 1933, in London 1936 and in Zurich 1939.

J. PRICE, *International Labour Movement*, London, 1965.

AMSTERDAM ISLAND OR NEW AMSTERDAM. A volcanic subarctic island, near the SE coast of Africa, 60 sq. km. Since 1950 the base of a French scientific research station (32 staff); part of the ▷ French Southern and Antarctic Territories.

Expéditions Polaires Français. Études et Rapports, Paris, 1945–59.

AMTORG. Amerykanskaya Torgovla = American Trade. The AMTORG Trading Corporation. A Soviet stock company set up in New York as a result of a fusion of two other Soviet companies in the USA: Product Exchange Corporation and Arcos America Inc.; Reg. on May 25, 1924 as the representatives of all Soviet import and export companies for trade with the USA; it was, up to the time of diplomatic recognition of the USSR by the USA (1933), the only Soviet institution in the USA. At present it acts as a broker between American companies and financial institutions on the one side, and Soviet foreign trade companies on the other. The activities of ▷ ARCOS Ltd. in Great Britain are similar.

AMU DARYA. The largest river in Central Asia (flows through Tadjikistan, Uzbekistan and Turkmenistan), 2575 km long, with a river-basin of 466,200 sq. km. Owing to the Kara-Kum Canal system, completed in 1962, the irrigation of the adjacent desert areas has become possible. Part of Amu-Darya forms the USSR border with Afghanistan; it flows to the Aral Sea. The subject of the Afghan–Soviet Agreement of 1946.

AMUR RIVER. One of the great rivers of the world; 4375 km long; rising in China (Chinese name: Heilung-kiang) and constituting a 1609 km long boundary with the USSR. Subject to Chinese–Russian treaties of 1689, 1858 and 1860, and to Chinese–Soviet Agreement on Scientific Co-operation of 1956–58.

ANAD, AGRÉMENT DE NON-AGGRESSION ET DEFENSE, Non Aggression and Defence Aid Agreement, between Togo and the ▷ West African Economic Community (ECOWAS) countries, signed 1979.

ANALGESIC OR PAIN RELIEVER. ▷ Heroin.

ANALOGUE COMPUTATION. A subject of international co-operation. Organizations reg. with the UIA:

Five International Associations Co-ordinating Committee, f. 1970 in Paris by delegates of: International Association for Analogue Computation, International Federation of Automatic Control, International Federation of Information on Processing, International Federation of Operational Research and International Measurement Confederation.
International Association for Analogue Computation, f. 1955, Brussels, Publ. *Scientific Review*.

Yearbook of International Organizations.

ANARCHISM. A utopian social and political trend which developed on a large scale in the 19th century, opposing all state organizations as a spontaneous protest against capitalist social relations and aiming at the creation of a stateless system through revolution, prepared by conspiracies and acts of terror; under the influence of English anarchists this trend appeared on the international arena with the secret International Brotherhood, which together with the Russian anarchist International Alliance of Socialist Democracy, formed in 1868 under the leadership of M.A. Bakunin organized the First International Congress of Anarchists held in 1877 in Brussels, the Second in The Hague in 1907. Anarchist terrorist activities in 1880–90, mainly directed against heads of state, resulted in the conclusion of treaties, first in Europe and then in America, on international police co-operation in combatting the anarchist movement. At the Second International American Conference in Mexico City, 1901–02 – all of the governments of the American republics with the exception of Brazil and Venezuela signed on Jan. 28, 1902 a Treaty for the Extradition of Criminals and for Protection against Anarchism; for lack of ratification it never entered into force. During the interwar period the anarchist movements main organizations were in Spain and in Latin America. After World War II an International Federation of Anarchists, with headquarters in London organized since 1949 International Congresses in Western Europe.

A. SEDGENT, G. HARMEL, *Histoire de l'anarchie*, Paris, 1948; S.D.H. COLE, *A History of Socialist Thought, Marxism and Anarchism 1850–1890*, London, 1954; J. PEIRATS, *Los anarquistas en la crisis politica de España*, Buenos Aires, 1964; V. ALBA, *Historia del movimiento obrero en América Latina*, Mexico, DF, 1964; S.M. LIPSET, S.S. WOLIN, *The Berkeley Student Revolt: Facts and Interpretation*, New York, 1965; P. AVRICH, *The Russian Anarchists*, Princeton, 1967; L. COMBY, *L'histoire du mouvement anarchiste*, Paris, 1972; G. BARTSCH, *Anarchismus in Deutschland (1955–73)*, 4 vols. Hannover, 1972–73.

ANATOMY. A subject of international co-operation. Organizations reg. with the UIA:

European Association of Veterinary Anatomists, f. 1963, Ghent., Belgium.
International Anatomical Nomenclature Confederation, f. 1976, London.
International Committee on Veterinary Anatomical Nomenclature, f. 1957, Vienna.
International Federation of Associations of Anatomists, f. 1905, Paris.
Pan-American Association of Anatomy, f. 1966, Sao Paulo, Brazil.
World Association of Veterinary Anatomists, f. 1955, Zurich.

Yearbook of International Organizations.

ANCA. ▷ NATO.

ANCOM. ▷ Andean Common Market.

ANCON TREATY, 1883. A Peace Treaty concluded in the Peruvian city of Ancón near Lima on Oct. 20, 1883, which ended the Chilean–Peruvian war, also called the Pacific War, granting the region of Arica to Chile.

V.A. BELAUNDE, *The Treaty of Ancón in the Light of International Law*, London, 1922.

"ANCONA". A passenger steamship of Italian Ocean Lines, sunk Nov. 7, 1915 during a voyage to the USA by an Austro-Hungarian submarine (*c.* 200 persons died); subject of dispute between USA and Austro-Hungarian governments caused by the death of many US citizens during the torpedoing of the ship. The sinking of the *Ancona*, the ▷ *Arabic*, the ▷ *Lusitania* and other ships had an influence on US public opinion and the US entering World War I.

"Notenwechsel zwischen den Vereinigten Staaten von Amerika und Österreich-Ungarn", in: *Zeitschrift für Völkerrecht*, No. 9, 1916.

ANDAMAN ISLANDS. Indian territory separating the Bengal Bay and Andaman Sea. Area: 6,495 sq km; subject of maritime border agreements between India and ▷ Burma, 1987.

ANDAMAN SEA. An arm of the ▷ Indian Ocean separated by the Andaman Islands, formed by a range of submarine mountains, from the ▷ Bengal Bay, included in the Indian Ocean Zone of Peace.

UN Chronicle, April, 1983.

ANDEAN COMMON MARKET, ANCOM. A project est. by the ▷ Andean Pact 1969, revitalized by the ▷ Andean Group in the late 1980s.

KEESING's *Record of World Events*, 1988.

ANDEAN DEVELOPMENT CORPORATION. A Corporation est. 1968 with headquarters in Caracas by an Agreement, signed in Bogota, Feb. 7, 1968 by the governments of Bolivia, Chile, Colombia, Ecuador, Peru and Venezuela, which came into force on Jan. 30, 1970. ▷ Andean Group.

UNTS, Vol. 778, pp. 256–298; *CEMLA Boletin Mensual*, No. 3, 1968, pp. 151–160.

ANDEAN GROUP. An integrative union of Andean states: Bolivia, Chile, Colombia, Ecuador, Peru and Venezuela, whose Heads of State on Aug. 16, 1966 signed in the capital of Colombia the Bogota Declaration on Economic Co-operation and Mutual Assistance. The first convention was an agreement on co-operation in petrochemistry, signed Oct. 26, 1967 in Bogota. Then on May 26, 1969 in Cartagena the ▷ Andean Pact was signed, called the Cartagena Treaty, 1969, whose organ became the ▷ Andean Development Corporation. The group represents a territory of 5.7 million sq. km with a pop. of 80 million (1978) and natural resources such as tin, zinc, copper, petroleum, lead and silver.

"Convenio Constitutivo de la Corporación Andina de Fomento", in: *CEMLA Boletin Mensual*, México, DF, March, 1968; pp. 151–160; T. WYRWA, *Les Républiques Andines (Bolivie, Chili, Colombie, Ecuator, Pérou, Venezuela)*, Paris, 1972; D. MORAVETZ, *The Andean Group*, Cambridge, 1974; *Legislación económica y social de los Paises-miembros del Grupo Andino*, Lima, 1971–1980; *The Europa Year Book 1984. A World Survey*, Vol. I, pp. 94–95, London, 1984.

ANDEAN PACT, OR CARTAGENA TREATY, 1969. The pact on the Andean Common Market, signed on May 16, 1969 in Cartagena by Bolivia, Chile, Ecuador, Colombia, Peru and on Feb. 10, 1973, by Venezuela. Chile resigned from the Pact on Oct. 30, 1976.

Acuerdo de Cartagena, Lima, 1969.

ANDEAN PARLIAMENT. ▷ Parliament of the Andean Group.

ANDORRA. Les Vallées d'Andorre – Los Valles de Andorra. Not a member of the UN. The co-principality of Andorra in the Pyrenees is co-governed by France and Spain. Area: 465 sq. km. 1988 pop. 51,400. Capital: Andorre La Veille 1987 pop. 16,200. Official language: Catalan. Currency: French and Spanish currencies. Andorra belongs only to one specialized UN agency, the UPU. National Day: 26th of October.
International relations: In 803 the French King Louis I ceded part of his suzerainty to the Spanish Bishop of Urgel. In 1278 Andorra was placed under the joint suzerainty (paréage) of the Comte de Foix and of the Bishop of Urgel. The rights of the house of Foix passed by marriage to that of Béarn, in 1580 to the French Crown and subsequently to the president of the French Republic. The co-rulers of the principality of Andorra are: the Viguier français and the Viguier Episcopal. Andorra is not sovereign; its relations with France and, through the Bishop, with the city of Urgel are of a feudal--legal and not legal–international character; thus it has no right to conclude any international agreements, or to participate in inter-governmental organizations or operations. The attempts to conclude treaties with Spain in 1841 on Spanish fugitives and in 1863 on demarcation of the Andorran–Spanish border were annulled by the French feudal lords. Andorran passports are visaed by French "viguier", and France exercises diplomatic care of Andorrans abroad and represents their interests in international trade. In 1950 in the conflict of Andorra Radio with European radio stations on violation of the convention on wave frequency, complaints were addressed to the French government, which made Andorra conform to international rules. In 1951, however, the Spanish government signed on behalf of Andorra the ▷ WMO Convention, and in 1954 The Hague Convention on Protection of Cultural Values, which brought about protests of France considering itself to be the only state representative of Andorra. In 1967 a visit was paid to Andorra by its superior lords: President of France, General Charles de Gaulle and Bishop of Urgel, Dr R. Iglesias Navarri. In foreign trade France is traditionally the main partner, while after World War II, the Americans account for most of the tourism. Every second year Andorra effects payment of 960 francs to the Treasury of France, and of 960 pesetas to the treasury of the Bishop of Urgel.

R. TOURENG, *Statut juridique des Vallées d'Andorre*, Toulouse, 1939; J. CORTES PEYZET, *Geografia e Historia de Andorra*, Barcelona, 1945; J.M. VIDAL Y GUITART, *Instituciones politicas y sociales de Andorra*, Madrid, 1949; CH. ROUSSEAU, *Les Vallées d'Andorre. Une survivance féodale dans le monde contemporain*, La Haye, 1958; *The Europa Year Book 1984.* Vol. I, pp. 292–294, London, 1984.

ANDREAS BELLO AGREEMENT, 1970. An interstate agreement of Bolivia, Chile, Ecuador, Colombia, Peru and Venezuela on co-operation in the field of education, science and culture. The permanent organ of the Agreement is an annual meeting of ministers of education. The Meeting and the Agreement are named after Venezuelan writer, Andreas Bello (1781–1865). The Executive Secretariat headquarters is in Lima and the Andean Regional Center for Research and Promotion of Rural Education is in La Paz, Bolivia.

ANESTHESIOLOGY. The science of producing the loss of feeling or sensation; the subject of organized international co-operation since 1949, that is, the date of the I Latino-American Congress on Anesthesiology in Buenos Aires. Organizations reg. with the UIA:

International Association of French-Speaking Anesthesists–Reanimateurs, Association internationale des anesthesistes–reanimateurs d'expression française, f. 1963, Paris.
Latin–American Confederation of Societies of Anesthesia, Confederacion Latino–Americana de Sociedades de Anestesiologia (CLASA), f. 1963, Rio de Janeiro.
Scandinavian Society of Anesthesiologists, linking together not only Scandinavian, but also foreign anesthesiologists, f. 1950, Aarhus (Denmark); publ. a quarterly: *Acta Anaesthesiologica Scandinavica*.
World Federation of Societies of Anaesthesiologists, f. 1955, Seattle (USA).

Yearbook of International Organizations.

ANF. Atlantic Nuclear Forces, inter-allied nuclear forces designed by the UK in NATO 1964; they were to take the place of the Multilateral Forces (MLF) promoted by the USA. This project brought forth the opposition of France and was criticized by other NATO countries. ANF saw a decrease of FRG influence in NATO and a strengthening of the role of the UK through an increased participation of British armed forces and giving it, besides USA and France, the right of veto in matters concerning the use of nuclear weapons. The project was not accepted by the Council of NATO.

KEESING's *Contemporary Archive*, 1964.

ANGARY. A term of customary maritime law for the right of requisition (*ius angariae*) of the maritime, land or aerial means of transportation belonging to a neutral state by a belligerent to make the blockade of an enemy more efficient. The states affected by angary must be fully compensated. The requisitioned ships fly the flag of the requisitioning state, but the crew must not be forced into rendering further service abroad. The right of angary was applied by the belligerents both in World Wars I and II.

C.L. BULLOCK, "Angary", in: *The British Yearbook of International Law*, 1922, pp. 99–129; "Rights and Duties of Neutral States in Naval and Aerial War", in: *American Journal of International Law*, No. 33, 1939; J.L. DE ARCARRAGA, *El derecho de angaria*, Mexico, DF, J. LE CLEZE, *Les mesures coercitives sur les sources de commerce étrangers. Angarie Embargo Arrêt de Prince*, Paris. 1949. R.L. BLEDSOE, B.A. BOCZEK, *The International Law Dictionary*, Oxford, 1987.

ANGIOLOGY. A subject of international co-operation:
International Union of Angiology, f. 1958, Paris. Publ. *Angiologie*. Reg. with the UIA.

Yearbook of International Organizations.

ANGKOR. The capital of Khmer kings. Abandoned in about 1430, the great city (103 sq. km) with a vast complex of sandstone and brick temples and monuments lay at the mercy of the jungle till the 20th century. A restoration initiated by the French Angkor Conservancy in the 1960s was halted by the internal war in Kampuchea since 1972. UNESCO is calling for special protection for this important monument of ▷ World heritage. In April 1982 in the UN Headquarters in New York under the sponsorship of UNESCO an exhibit of more than 50 color photomurals of Angkor produced by the National Geographic Society of the US was presented.

UN Chronicle, June 1982, pp. 107–109.

ANGLICAN COMMUNION. Document declaring mutual loyalty accepted by the ▷ Lambeth Conference of 1930 as "a fellowship, within the One Holy Catholic and Apostolic Church, of those duly constituted Dioceses, Provinces or Regional Churches in communion with the See of Canterbury, which have the following characteristics in common: (a) they uphold and propagate the Catholic and Apostolic faith and order as they are generally set forth in the Book of Common Prayer, as authorized in their several Churches; (b) they are particular or national Churches, and, as such, promote within each of their territories a national expression of Christian faith, life and worship; and (c) they are bound together not by a central legislative and executive authority, but by mutual loyalty sustained through the common counsel of the Bishops in conference". Members of the Anglican Communion are:
The Church of England.
The Episcopal Church in Scotland.
The Church in Ireland.
The Church in Wales.
The Protestant Episcopal Church in the United States.
The Anglican Church of Canada.
The Church of India, Pakistan, Burma, and Ceylon.
The Church of England in Australia.
The Church of the Province of New Zealand.
The Church of the Province of South Africa.
The Church in the Province of the West Indies.
Nippon Sei Ko Kai (Japan Holy Catholic Church).
Chung Hua Sheng Kung Hui (The Holy Catholic Church in China).
The Church of the Province of West Africa.
The Church of the Province of Central Africa.
The Jerusalem Archbishopric (with responsibilities extending from Iran to the Sudan).
The Church of the Province of East Africa.
The Church of Uganda, Rwanda, and Burundi.
Episcopal Church of Brazil.

Representatives of the Anglican Communion initiated the ▷ World Council of Churches and took part in the ecumenical movement.
Observers from the Anglican Communion took part in the ▷ Vaticanum II.

J.C. WAND ed., *The Anglican Communion*, London, 1948.

ANGLO–AMERICAN 'SPECIAL RELATION-SHIP'. An international term coined during World War II by Winston Churchill.

W. ROSER, L.H. BULL, *The 'Special Relationship': Anglo-American Relations since 1945*, Oxford, 1986; R. BULLEN, M.E. PELLY eds., *The London Conferences, Anglo-American Relations and Cold War Strategy January-June 1950*, London, 1987; T.J. BOTTI, *The Forging of the Anglo-American Nuclear Alliance 1948–58*, London, 1987.

ANGLO–IRANIAN OIL COMPANY CASE, 1951. A case presented to the ICJ by the UK on May 26, 1951. The subject was one of the largest oil companies in the world in the period 1901–51; founded in 1909 as the Anglo–Persian Oil Co. Ltd. and endowed with an oil franchise for 60 years which included almost the whole of Iran's territory, except for the northern provinces; the 1909 franchise was replaced in 1935 by an agreement once again for 60 years, which was annulled in 1951 by the expropriation decree and the nationalization of all Iranian oil fields. The British government brought the case of the company before the International Court of Justice which, on July 22, 1951, decided that it had no jurisdiction to deal with the dispute. On Aug. 5, 1954, the new government of Iran repealed the nationalization act of 1951 and concluded a new agreement changed in 1954 and in 1973, when the Iranian oil industry came totally under the control of the National Iranian Oil Company.

ICJ, 1951; KEESING's *Contemporary Archive*, 1951.

ANGLO–IRISH AGREEMENT, 1985. ▷ Hillsborough Accord.

ANGLO–IRISH CONFERENCE. The Anglo-Irish Intergovernmental Conference, an institution established by the ▷ Anglo-Irish Agreement of Nov. 1985. During the meetings held in Belfast, Dublin or London the current problems of the community in Northern Ireland are discussed.

KEESING's *Record of World Events*, 1985–90.

ANGLO–IRISH FREE TRADE AGREEMENT, AIFTA, signed 1965 in London came into force on July 1, 1966.

Britain. *An Official Handbook*, London 1966; D. BUTLER, G. BUTLER, *British Political Facts 1900–1985*, London, 1986.

ANGLO–JAPANESE ALLIANCE, 1902. An alliance signed Jan. 30, 1902 in London, renewed and expanded Aug. 12, 1905 and July 23, 1911. In fulfillment of the obligations arising from the alliance, Japan entered World War I on Aug. 23, 1914 on the British side. Formally, the Anglo–Japanese Alliance came to an end on Aug 17, 1923, along with the entry into force of the ▷ Pacific Treaty 1921.

D. BUTLER, J. FREEMAN, *British Political Facts 1900–1960*, London, 1963.

ANGLO–RUSSIAN CONVENTION 1908. An agreement between Great Britain and Tsarist Russia which partioned Iran into two spheres of influence: British over South Iran, Russian over North Iran.

F. KAZEMZADEH, *Russia and Britain in Persia 1864–1914*, New Haven, 1967.

ANGLO–SAXONS. An international historical term for Germanic settlers of England in the 5th and 6th century. In the world press of the 19th and 20th century broadened to include any person of British stock. See also ▷ WASP.

J. CAMPBELL ed., The Anglo-Saxons, Ithaca 1982.

ANGLO–SAXON LAW. An international term for legal rules and customs worded in English.

ANGLO–SOVIET TRADE AGREEMENT, 1921. The first commercial agreement of the Soviet Union with a capitalistic state, signed at London, Mar. 16, 1921.

J.A.S. GRENVILLE, *The Major International Treaties 1914–1973. A History and Guide with Texts*, London, 1974, pp. 140–141.

ANGOLA. Member of the UN. People's Republic of Angola, Republica Popular do Angola. State in south-west Africa on the Atlantic Ocean. Area: 1,246,700 sq. km. Pop.: 1987 est. 9,243,000 (1970 census: 5,673,046). Capital: Luanda with 1977 est. 500,000 inhabitants, GNP per capita 1984 US $302. Bordering with Zaïre, Zambia and Namibia. Boundary agreements with Zaïre July 22, 1977; with Zambia June 11, 1891; with Namibia Dec 30, 1886. Official language: Portuguese, Currency: 1 kwanza = 100 lwei. National Day: Dec. 11, independence anniversary, 1975. Member of the UN since Dec. 1, 1976. Member of ILO, UNESCO, WHO, ITU, FAO, ICAO, WMO, IMO, WIPO, IFAD and UNIDO. Member of the Organization of African Unity.
Member of Lomé Convention since 1985.
International relations: Angola was formally a Portuguese colony from May 12, 1886 (separated from the Congo) to Oct. 20, 1954 (statute of "overseas province"). The new statute was not accepted by the UN. On Mar. 10, 1961 the UN Security Council, and on Apr. 20, 1961 the UN General Assembly, with Res. 1603/XV, decided that the case of Angola should be solved according to the UN Declaration on Colonialism; on Jan. 30, 1962 the General Assembly, Res. 1742/XV, expressed regret that Portugal refused to co-operate.
In April 1962 the Patriotic Front for National Liberation of Angola formed a revolutionary government of the Republic of Angola in exile, recognized by the Organization of African Unity and the Conference of Solidarity of Africa and Asia. The UN subcommission (Bolivia, Dahomey, Finland, Malaysia and Sudan) informed the Assembly in late 1962 that "the situation in Angola constitutes a hard problem for the UN." On Dec. 3, 1963 the General Assembly 1913/XVIII (91 votes in favor, 2 against – Portugal and the Republic of South Africa) recommended to the Security Council immediate consideration of the "Angola case."
Since 1966 the UN remained in permanent touch with the liberation movements. In May 1971 the parliament of Portugal granted Angola and Mozambique the status of a "country" which has the right to decide on its internal affairs under supervision of a governor general. In 1972 guerilla warfare took place on the major part of Angolan territory. In May 1974, after the army took power in Portugal, negotiations were started on granting independence to Angola, and ended in Nov. 1975 in a proclamation of independence. Normalization of relations with Portugal followed. In permanent border clashes with troops of the Republic of South Africa operating from the territory of Namibia. The UN Council for Namibia protested since 1978

against the illegal South African military bases located in northern Namibia and against the attacks from these bases on the Namibian refugee camps 250 km inside Angola territory.

The UN Secretary General visited Angola and Namibia in August 1983. In 1984 the linkage of withdrawal of South African troops from Namibia with the withdrawal of Cuban troops from Angola was a precondition of peace on the Angola–Namibia frontier, not resolved until Jan. 1985.

On Jan. 1, 1988 Cuba had 40,000 troops stationed in Angola. Since March 1975 when the first Cuban troops arrived there the estimated number of Cuban casualties has come to 1,000.

Angola, Cuba, South Africa and Namibia's SWAPO started first negotiations, initiated by Angolan, Cuban and US experts in Luanda in January 1988, continued in March 1988 in Luanda and by the US–South Africa negotiations in Geneva.

F. WOHLGEMUTH, *The Portuguese Territories and the UN*, New York, 1963; A. EHNMARK, P. WAESTBERG, *Angola and Mozambique. The Case against Portugal*, New York, 1964; R. DAVEZIES, *Les Angolais*, Paris, 1965; R.H. CHILCOTE, *Portuguese Africa*, Prentice Hall, 1967; B. DAVIDSON, *In the Eye of the Storm. Angola's People*, London, 1972; G.J. BENDER, *Angola under the Portuguese*, London, 1979; *UN Chronicle*, June 1978; *The Europa Yearbook, 1984*, Vol. 1, pp. 1065–1075, London, 1984; K. SOMMERVILLE, *Angola, Politics, Economics and Society*, London, 1986; I. HODGES, *Angola to the 1990's: The Potential for Recovery*, London, 1987; R. KAPUSCINSKI, *Another Day of Life*, San Diego, 1987.

ANGOLA–CUBA DECLARATION, 1984. A Declaration signed on Mar. 19, 1984 at Havana by the President of Angola, José Eduardo Dos Santos, and the Cuban Premier Fidel Castro. They signed an agreement on the withdrawal of Cuban forces from Angola after the withdrawal of South African troops from Angola and Namibia, and after strict application of UN Security Council Res. 435 on the achievement of independence of Namibia.

ANGOLA, ZAÏRE AND ZAMBIA NONAGGRESSION PACT, 1979. An agreement signed in Ndola (Zambia) Oct. 14, 1979 by the Presidents of Angola, Zaïre, and Zambia, forbidding the signatory states to make their territory available for subversive activities or any attack directed against the remaining countries. On that same day a treaty was concluded on strengthening economic co-operation, especially in transport and communications.

KEESING's *Contemporary Archive*, 1979.

ANGSTRÖM. An angström unit, a unit of length, mainly of light, applied to X-rays, equal to 10^{-10} m; named after the Swedish physicist, A.J. Angström (1814–74).

ANGUILLA ISLANDS. British West Indies, one of the Leeward Islands. Area: 90.7 sq. km. Pop.: 6700 in 1988. Capital: The Valley. Formally part of the Associated States of St Kitts–Nevis–Anguilla, but since Feb. 10, 1976 a self-governing British colony under the Anguilla Order.

By the Anguilla Act of December 1980 Anguilla is separated from the State of St Christopher (St Kitts) – Nevis Anguilla and as a British separate dependency is administered under the Anguilla Constitution Order of 1983. Member of the Organization of Eastern Caribbean States, 1984.

Report of the St Kitts, Anguilla Constitutional Conference 1966, London, 1966; Sir F. PHILLIPS, *Freedom in the Caribbean*, New York, 1977; *The Europa Year Book 1984. A World Survey*, Vol. I, pp. 1233–1234, London, 1984.

ANIMAL DISEASES. A subject of international co-operation and agreements:
International Convention between Austria, Belgium, Bulgaria, Czechoslovakia, France, Greece, Italy, Latvia, the Netherlands, Poland, Romania, Spain, Switzerland, Turkey, and the USSR for the Campaign against Diseases of Animals, signed in Geneva, Feb. 20, 1935.
International Office for dealing with Contagious Diseases of Animals, f. 1924 in Paris, by Agreement between the Governments of Argentina, Belgium, Brazil, Bulgaria, Czechoslovakia, Guatemala, Hungary, Italy, Luxembourg, Morocco, Mexico, Monaco, the Netherlands, Peru, Poland, Portugal, Romania, Siam, Sweden, Switzerland and Tunis, signed Jan. 25, 1924.

LNTS, Vol. 57, p. 135; Vol. 186, p. 173.

ANIMALS. A subject of international co-operation. Organizations reg. with the UIA:

Commonwealth Bureau of Animal Breeding and Genetics, Oxford, UK.
Commonwealth Bureau of Animal Health, New Haw, UK.
Euromarket Fed. of Animal Protein and Traders, f. 1961, Hamburg, FRG.
European Association for Animal Production, f. 1949, Rome, Publ. *Livestock Production Science*.
Inter-African Bureau for Animal Resources, f. 1976, Nairobi.
International Association Against Painful Experiments on Animals, f. 1969, London. Consultative status: ECOSOC.
International Center on Laboratory Animals, f. 1956, Oslo. Consultative status: WHO.
International Confederation for Recording the Productivity of Milk Animals, f. 1951, Rouen, France.
International Defender of Animals, f. 1958, Hialeah, USA.
International Laboratory for Research on Animal Diseases, f. 1973, Nairobi.
International Meeting of Animal Nutrition Experts, f. 1959, Barcelona.
International Society for Animal Blood Group Research, f. 1964, Cambridge, UK. Publ. *Animal Blood Group and Biochemical Genetics*.
International Society for the Protection of Animals, f. 1959, London.
International Standing Committee on Physiology and Pathology of Animal Reproduction (including artificial insemination), f. 1948, London.
International Veterinary Association for Animal Production, f. 1951, Madrid, Publ. *Zootechnia*.
Nordic Council for Animal Protection, f. 1962, Oslo.
Nordic Society Against Painful Experiments on Animals, f. 1882, Stockholm.
Regional International Organization of Plant Protection and Animal Health, f. 1953, San Salvador.
Section on Experimental Psychology and Animal Behavior of the International Union of Biological Sciences, f. 1965, New York.
World Association for Animal Production, f. 1965, Rome. Organizer of World Conferences on animal production (every 3–5 years).
World Blue Chain for the Protection of Animals and Nature, f. 1964, Brussels. Publ. *La Chaine*
World Federation for the Protection of Animals, f. 1950, Zurich. Publ. *Animalia*.
World Small Animal Veterinary Association, f. 1960, Oak Park, Ill., USA.

FAO. *Animal Health Yearbook*, Rome, 1957; R. FRIEDMAN, ed. *The Animal Rights Movement and Scientific Experimentation*, Oxford, 1987; *Yearbook of International Organizations*.

ANKARA. The capital (1985 pop. 2,231,533) of the Republic of Turkey since 1923. The seat of the Central Treaty Organization (CENTO), Mediterranean Social Science Research Council, UN Information Center and ILO Regional Office.

Yearbook of International Organizations.

ANKARA AGREEMENT, 1963. An association convention between Turkey and the European Economic Community, signed Sept. 12, 1963 in Ankara.

KEESING's *Contemporary Archive*, 1963.

ANKARA TREATY, 1921. An international agreement, signed on Oct. 20, 1921 in Ankara between France and Turkey, which established peace between the two countries. The borderline between Turkey and French Syria, determined by the Ankara Treaty, was approved by the Treaty concluded in Lausanne in 1923 (art. 3, item 1).

LNTS, 1923.

ANKARA TREATY, 1953. Treaty of Friendship and Collaboration between Greece, Turkey and Yugoslavia, signed in Ankara Feb. 28, 1953. It was supplemented by the ▷ Balkan Pact 1954.

UNTS, 1953.

ANNAM. A former state in central Vietnam, conquered in the 19th century by the French, from 1887 to 1954 part of the Union of Indochina.

ANNEXATION. An international term for taking possession of part or all of foreign territory by force (▷ debellation) or under threat of the use of force; in the past recognized as the law of war; in the 20th century in opposition to the principles of International Law, especially the right to self-determination of nations; in opposition to the UN Charter. The first international act not to recognize annexation was the ▷ Decree of Peace 1917.

J.W. GARNER, Non-recognition of illegal territorial annexations and claims to sovereignty", in: *American Journal of International Law*, No. 30, 1936; T. STARK, "La conquête en Droit International Contemporain" in *Recueil de Travaux Scientifiques des Polonais internés en Suisse*, Vol. 2, Rappersville, 1944; R. LANGER, *Seizure of Territory. The Stimson Doctrine and Related Principles in Legal Theory and Diplomatic Practice*. Baltimore, 1947; H. WEHRBERG, *Krieg und Eroberung im Wandel des Völkerrechts*, Stuttgart, 1953.

ANNIHILATION. An international military term introduced in relation to the arms of mass destruction; cessation of all life and destruction of all goods.

ANNUARIO PONTIFICIO. The annual published by the Vatican; contains data on the Roman Catholic Church administrative units, institutions and diplomatic relations of the Vatican with other states and international organizations.

ANSCHLUSS. *German = annexation.* A term accepted by the world press for the 19th-century Pan-German program of German and Austrian nationalist organizations for uniting Austria with Germany. In 1919, on the strength of art. 80 of the ▷ Versailles Treaty, Germany recognized the independence of Austria as inviolable and that this independence could be altered only by permission of the council of the League of Nations. On Oct. 4, 1922, in the Geneva Protocol, Austria renounced the right to Anschluss. The Third Reich violated the Treaty's resolutions, on Mar. 15, 1938 by annexing Austria to Germany, which was recognized as illegal action in the ▷ Moscow Declaration 1943 and annulled by the ▷ Potsdam Agreement 1945. The Austria State Treaty 1955 prohibits political and economic Anschluss. ▷ Austria.

F. GEHL, *Austria, Germany and the Anschluss 1931–1938*, London, 1963.

ANTARCTICA. A continent in the southern hemisphere; area: 14,425,000 sq. km; in the 19th and 20th centuries subject of international research and since the end of World War I subject of international dispute concerning the right to individual parts of this hitherto "no-man's-land". The territorial claims of Argentina (Antartida Argentina), Australia (Australian Antarctic Territory), Chile (Antartica Chilena), France (Terre Adélie), New Zealand (Ross Dependency), Norway (Dronning Maud Land), and the UK (British Antarctic Territory) are not recognized by the USA and the USSR. In the sector between 90°W and 150°W no formal claims have been made. During the International Geophysical Year (IGY) from Jan. 1, 1957 to Dec. 31, 1958 twelve nations (Australia, Argentina, Belgium, Chile, France, Japan, New Zealand, Norway, South Africa, UK, USA, USSR) maintained 65 stations in Antarctica. After the IGY the same 12 nations signed the ▷ Antarctic Treaty, 1959. Since 1961–62 air connections with the USA and USSR. There is no indigenous population, only visitors to the scientific bases. The major bases south of latitude 60° are as follows:

	Latitude	Longitude
ARGENTINA		
Belgrano II	77°52′S	34°37′W
Belgrano III	77°54′S	45°59′W
Brown	64°53′S	62°53′W
Esperanza	63°24′S	56°59′W
Marambio	64°14′S	56°43′W
Orcadas	60°45′S	44°43′W
Primavera	64°09′S	60°57′W
San Martin	68°07′S	67°08′W
AUSTRALIA		
Casey	66°17′S	110°32′E
Davis	68°35′S	77°58′E
Mawson	67°36′S	62°52′E
CHILE		
Arturo Prat	62°30′S	59°41′W
Bernardo O'Higgins	63°19′S	57°54′W
Rodolfo Marsh	62°12′S	58°54′W
FRANCE		
Dumont d'Urville	66°40′S	140°01′E
FEDERAL REPUBLIC OF GERMANY		
Georg von Neumayer	70°37′S	8°22′W
JAPAN		
Mizuho	70°42′S	44°20′E
Syowa	69°00′S	39°35′E
NEW ZEALAND		
Scott	77°51′S	166°45′E
POLAND		
Arctowski	62°09′S	58°28′W
SOUTH AFRICA		
Sanae	70°18′S	2°24′W
USSR		
Bellingshausen	62°12′S	58°58′W
Leningradskaya	69°30′S	159°23′E
Mirny	66°33′S	93°01′E
Molodezhnaya	67°40′S	45°51′E
Novolazarevskaya	70°46′S	11°50′E
Russkaya	74°46′S	136°52′W
Vostok	78°28′S	106°48′E
UNITED KINGDOM		
Faraday	65°15′S	64°16′W
Halley	75°31′S	26°58′W
New Halley	75°35′S	26°40′W
Rothera	67°34′S	68°08′W
Signy	60°43′S	45°36′W
UNITED STATES		
South Pole	South Pole	
McMurdo	77°51′S	166°40′W
Palmer	64°46′S	64°03′W

Acceding states to the Treaty: Brazil, Bulgaria, Czechoslovakia, Denmark, the FRG, the GDR, India, Italy, the Netherlands, Papua, New Guinea, Peru, Poland, Romania, Spain and Uruguay.

A consultative status was granted to Brazil, the FRG, India and Poland. They are active in the Antarctic research stations. The Antarctic Treaty, Consultative Meetings are dedicated to the protection of the Antarctic environment and wildlife.

The 11th Consultative Meeting of signatories of the Treaty was held in Buenos Aires in June–July 1981 and convoked Special Consultative Sessions on mineral exploitation, held in June 1982 and January 1983 in Wellington, in July 1983 in Bonn, in January 1984 in Washington DC, and in May 1984 in Tokyo.

The 12th Consultative Meeting was held in Canberra in September 1983.

The UN General Assembly Res. 38/77 of December 15, 1983, adopted without vote, affirmed the conviction "that in the interest of all mankind, Antarctica should continue forever to be used exclusively for peaceful purposes, and that it should not become the scene or object of international disputes".

In relation to the General Assembly Res. 38/77 of Dec. 10, 1983, the Secretary General presented to the First Committee 1984 and 1985 a comprehensive study of all questions concerning Antarctica and the Antarctica Treaty:

The highlights of the study:

Geography: According to the report, Antarctica, the southernmost continent, consists of the area around the South Pole, its adjacent ice shelf, the southern extremities of the Indian, Atlantic and Pacific oceans (the so-called southern ocean) and various islands. Some 13.9 million square kilometres in area, of which 98 per cent is a permanent ice cap, Antarctica covers one tenth of the earth's surface. Seventy per cent of the world's fresh water is stored in the ice cap, the report states.

Legal and political aspects: Since the beginning of the twentieth century, seven nations – Australia, Argentina, Chile, France, New Zealand, Norway and the United Kingdom – have made territorial claims to parts of Antarctica. The claims are based on various legal grounds, including discovery, occupation, contiguity, inherited rights, geological affinity and geographical proximity, formal acts of taking possession and administrative acts.

By the mid-1950s, increasing tensions over the sovereignty issue and the active involvement in Antarctica of such non-claimant States as the USSR and the United States led to the awareness that an international agreement for the area was urgent to avoid a world-wide confrontation. Activities connected with the International Geophysical Year (IGY) in 1957–1958 paved the way for negotiations to make Antarctica a zone of peace.

On the initiative of the United States, the 12 countries which had participated in IGY – Argentina, Australia, Belgium, Chile, France, Japan, New Zealand, Norway, South Africa, USSR, United Kingdom and United States – agreed to conclude a treaty aimed at preserving the continent for international scientific research to be used only for peaceful purposes. The Treaty, signed in 1959, entered into force in June 1961 after the original 12 Parties ratified it.

Since then, 20 more States have acceded to the Treaty: Brazil, Bulgaria, China, Czechoslovakia, Cuba, Denmark, Finland, German Democratic Republic, Federal Republic of Germany, Hungary, India, Italy, Netherlands, Papua New Guinea, Peru, Poland, Romania, Spain, Sweden and Uruguay.

The Treaty stipulates in the preamble that "it is in the interest of all mankind that Antarctica shall continue forever to be used exclusively for peaceful purposes and shall not become the scene or object of international discord". Under article I the Treaty prohibits any military activity on the continent, such as establishing military personnel or equipment is permitted only to support scientific research or for other peaceful purposes.

The Treaty requires exchange of information regarding plans for scientific research and provides for exchange of scientific personnel.

To ensure compliance with its provisions, the Treaty establishes a comprehensive system of on-site inspection with complete access to all areas and installations in Antarctica. According to the Secretary-General's report: "The system of observation and inspection is one of the vital elements in the Treaty for assuring its operation in accordance with its terms. The Consultative Parties are convinced that it contributes significantly to the effectiveness of the Treaty and the realization of its principles and objectives, the most important of which is preservation of peace in Antarctica."

Inspections have been carried out by New Zealand, Australia, the United Kingdom, Argentina and the United States. None has uncovered violations of Treaty provisions, according to the Secretary-General.

Sovereignty: The report clearly indicates that the Treaty does not settle the issue of territorial sovereignty. Rather, it freezes the *status quo* by providing, in article IV, that nothing contained in the Treaty shall be interpreted as a renunciation of previously asserted rights of or claims to territorial sovereignty in Antarctica; as a renunciation or diminution of any basis of claim to territorial sovereignty in Antarctica which any Contracting Party may have; or as prejudicing the position of any Contracting Party regarding its recognition or non-recognition of any other State's right of or claim or basis of claim to territorial sovereignty in Antarctica.

Article IV also states that no acts or activities taking place while the Treaty is in force shall be a basis for asserting, supporting or denying a claim to territorial sovereignty in Antarctica or create any rights of sovereignty on the continent. No new claim, or enlargement of an existing claim, shall be asserted while the Treaty is in force.

Consultative meetings: A mechanism in the form of a system of biennial Consultative Meetings has been set up for exchange of information, consultations, consideration and formulation to further the principles and objectives of the Treaty. (The thirteenth Consultative Meeting was held in Brussels in October 1985.)

The Treaty is open for accession by any United Nations Member State, or by any other State which may be invited to accede to the Treaty with the consent of all the Consultative Parties. However, full participation in the work of the Consultative Meetings is accorded to original Parties to the Treaty and those Contracting Parties which demonstrate their interest in the region by conducting substantial scientific research there. So far, Brazil, China, the Federal Republic of Germany, India, Poland and Uruguay have acquired consultative status. Acceding Parties without consultative status have been invited to participate as observers in the work of the Consultative Meetings since 1983. As of 1984, nonconsultative Parties have also been invited to attend as observers to negotiations on a proposed Antarctic mineral resource régime.

"Proof of interest in the form of substantial research activity may be regarded by some as a high entrance fee", the report states. However, Treaty Parties believe that such a requirement for consultative status "helps create a more professional approach", the Secretary-General reports. it is noted, however, that that requirement does not apply to the original Treaty Parties, not all of which have continuing research programmes in Antarctica.

Nuclear-weapon-free zone: Since the Antarctic Treaty was signed in 1959, the area has been free from militarization of any kind, including nuclear weapons, the report states. Compared with subsequent international agreements establishing nuclear-weapon-free zones, the Antarctic Treaty is unique in that it enjoys the concurring support of all five nuclear-weapon Powers. It has been noted that the Treaty thus represents an important example of co-operation between the Soviet Union and the United States in the field of arms control.

Environmental protection: The Antarctic exerts a critical influence on oceanic and atmospheric circulation, and thus on the global climate, the report observes. At the same time, Antarctic ecosystems are extremely vulnerable to disturbance. Since 1961, environmental protection of Antarctica has been a central issue in the Consultative Meetings. Approval of the 1964 Agreed Measures for the Conservation of Antarctic Fauna and Flora was the first significant step in that direction. Governments proclaimed the continent a special conservation area and agreed to take action to mimimize

harmful interference with the normal living conditions of native mammals and birds.
Because of the unique structure of the Antarctic ecosystem and the complex interactions between different species competing for food consisting mainly of krill (a small crustacean living in Antarctic waters), the report notes that an "ecosystem conservation standard" was required to manage the continent's living resources. In that regard, the 1982 Convention on the Conservation of Antarctic Marine Living Resources represents an "interesting development in international law". Consultative Party negotiations also resulted in the 1972 Convention for the Conservation of Antarctic Seals.
The 1946 International Convention for the Regulation of Whaling, which set global quotas for catching whales, has helped to drastically reduce whaling in Antarctic waters, the report notes.
Mineral resources: "The hidden mineral wealth of Antarctica has been a subject of interest for many years", the report states. It has still to be proved that there are any mineral resources worth exploiting, but in recent years interest in the economic potential of the continent has increased. "As a result", the Secretary-General declares, "concern for and tensions over the fate of the world's last unexploited continent are rising rapidly."
There are recorded "occurrences" (presence, often in minute quantities) of a wide range of minerals in Antarctica, including iron, coal, copper, molybdenum, gold, silver, chromium, nickel, cobalt, platinum, lead, zinc, tin, manganese, titanium and uranium. Because of the harsh environment, lack of infrastructure, tremendous transportation problems and high cost, there has been little minerals exploration activity until recently.
The mineral resources question "revives an old problem of claims for territorial sovereignty in Antarctica and non-recognition of such claims, because claimant States assert ownership over resources in their claims, while non-claimant States argue for freedom of access. The possibility of unilateral actions by both sides, and therefore of conflicts, is quite real and should not be discounted", the report states. In that respect, the possibility of Antarctic mineral resources raises the question of the need for elaboration of an international régime for management of exploration and exploitation of potential resources.
Problems raised by emerging interest in the economic potential of Antarctic mineral resources revolve around one main issue: how such resources should be managed. Supporters of one approach insist on discussion of the matter in a global forum, preferably established by the United Nations, to ensure that exploration and exploitation is carried out for the benefit of all mankind. Others, while acknowledging the need for an open international approach, favour consideration of the question within the framework of the Antarctic Treaty. In their view, the Treaty puts to rest the sovereignty issue; furthermore, the long presence in Antarctica of countries which have invested large resources should not be ignored.
The report notes that the Antarctic Treaty makes no special reference to mineral resources. However, the Consultative Parties have recorded their view that it would be "ironic" not to allow them to address the question of exploration and exploitation of those resources once it became an urgent issue of public concern.
The question was first raised infomally in 1970, at the Sixth Consultative Meeting; two years later, participants in the Seventh Consultative Meeting, "noting technological developments in polar mineral exploration", decided to put the matter on the agenda. By 1977, the question was a major issue before the Consultative Parties, according to the Secretary-General. Consultative Parties were called on to refrain from exploration and exploitation of Antarctic mineral resources while working towards a régime covering such activities.
By 1981, the Consultative Parties decided that the question of elaborating a régime had become sufficiently urgent to convene a Special Consultative Meeting on the subject. Since then, negotiations have proceeded within the framework.
The Consultative Parties, by Recommendation XI-1 adopted at the eleventh Consultative Meeting in 1981, agreed that the régime should apply to all mineral resource activities on the continent and adjacent offshore areas "but without encroachment on the deep-sea bed," and that it should include procedures for adherence by other than Consultative Parties.

During the 1983 UN debates the representatives of the non-members of the Antarctica Treaty raised the "Antarctic question" on the basis of the ▷ Law of the Sea Conventions Rule, that all seabeds are the common heritage of Man.
In January 1986 the international environmentalist organization ▷ Greenpeace started a campaign to make: Antarctica a World Heritage Park for Future Generations.
In 1981 the voting members of the Antarctic Treaty started negotiations on a régime of exploitation of minerals in Antarctica. A special session was held in Rio de Janeiro in February–March 1986. The report was a basis for the UN General Assembly Res. 40/156 in 1986.
The 30 Antarctic Treaty countries adopted on June 2, 1988 a Convention on the Regulation of Antarctic Mineral Resource Activities and a set of rules on the extraction of its oil (estimated at 48 billion barrels), gas and mineral deposits. The convention will come into force after ratification by 16 out of the 20 full Treaty member States.

Expéditions Polaires Françaises, Études et Rapports, Paris, 1948–59; E.W.H. CHRISTIE, *The Antarctic Problems*, London, 1951; P.A. TOMA, "Soviet Attitude towards the Acquisition of Territorial Sovereignty in the Antarctic", in *American Journal of International Law*, No. 50, 1956; C.W. JENKS, "An international regime for Antarctica", in *International Affairs*, No. 32, 1956; W.I. LEBEDEV, *Antarktika*, Moskva, 1957; I.V. MUNCH, "Völkerrechtsfragen der Antarktis", in: *Archiv der Völkerrechts*, No. 7, 1958–59; E.H. ARCHIDALE, "Claims to Antarctica", in *Yearbook of World Affairs*, No. 12, 1958; A.J. TAUBENFELD, *A Treaty for Antarctica*, New York, 1961, 68 pp.; T. HATHERTONED, *Antarctica*, New York, 1965, 511 pp; R. LEWIS, *La Antártida. Un Continente dedicado a la Ciencia*, México, DF, 1968, 212 pp; SIPRI, *World Armaments and Disarmament Yearbooks*, 1971, 1972 and 1980; F.M. AUBUM, "Offshore oil and gas in Antarctica", in: *German Yearbook of International Law*, 1977, pp. 139–173; E. PORTEK, *Antarctica*, New York 1978; *UN Chronicle*, 1986. No 2, pp. 68–75; P. BECK, *The International Politics of Antarctica*, London, 1986; KEESING's Contemporary Archive, 1986; KEESING's *Record of World Events*, 1986 and 1988; *Antarctica: The Next Decade*, Report of a Study Group Chaired by Sir Anthony Parsons, Cambridge, 1987; *The Economist*, May 7, 1988.

ANTARCTIC CIRCLE. An international geographical term for an imaginary circle 66°30′ S lat. where both the sun during the Summer solstice, c. June 22, and the midnight sun can be seen.

ANTARCTIC PENINSULA. A mountain region of West Antarctica, named Palmer Land in 1820; present name since 1964 by international agreement. Rights to the territory are claimed by Great Britain since 1832, Argentina, 1940, Chile, 1942.

ANTARCTIC TERRITORY, AUSTRALIAN. Established by the Australian Antarctic Territory Act, 1933, lying between 45°E and 136°E, and between 142°E and 160°E. Area: 6,120,000 sq. km. Three permanent Australian Research Stations: Casey, Davis and Mawson.

The Europa Yearbook, 1988. *A World Survey*, Vol. II, London, 1988.

ANTARCTIC TERRITORY, BRITISH. A British colony created on March 3, 1962 consists of all islands and territories south of latitude 60°S, between longitudes 20° and 80°W; includes the South Orkney Islands, the South Shetland Islands, and the Antarctic Peninsula. The island of South Georgia and the South Sandwich Islands were integrated by the dependencies of the ▷ Falkland Islands. Area: 1,710,000 sq. km. Habitants: scientists and personnel of the British Antarctic Survey Stations.

The Europa Yearbook, 1988. *A World Survey*, Vol. II, London, 1988.

ANTARCTIC TREATY, 1959. The Antarctic Treaty between Argentina, Australia, Belgium, Chile, France, Japan, New Zealand, Norway, Union of South Africa, the USSR, the UK and the USA, signed in Washington, DC., Dec. 1, 1959. Came into force on June 23, 1961. The text is as follows:
"The Governments of Argentina, Australia, Belgium, Chile, the French Republic, Japan, New Zealand, Norway, the Union of South Africa, the Union of Soviet Socialist Republics, the United Kingdom of Great Britain and Northern Ireland, and the United States of America.
Recognizing that it is in the interest of all mankind that Antarctica shall continue forever to be used exclusively for peaceful purposes and shall not become the scene or object of international discord;
Acknowledging the substantial contributions to scientific knowledge resulting from international cooperation in scientific investigation in Antarctica;
Convinced that the establishment of a firm foundation for the continuation and development of such cooperation on the basis of freedom of scientific investigation in Antarctica as applied during the International Geophysical Year accords with the interests of science and the progress of all mankind; Convinced also that a treaty ensuring the use of Antarctica for peaceful purposes only and the continuance of international harmony in Antarctica will further the purposes and principles embodied in the Charter of the United Nations;
Have agreed as follows:
Art. I(1) Antarctica shall be used for peaceful purposes only. There shall be prohibited, inter alia, any measures of a military nature, such as the establishment of military bases and fortifications, the carrying out of military manoeuvres, as well as the testing of any type of weapons.
(2) The present Treaty shall not prevent the use of military personnel or equipment for scientific research or for any other peaceful purpose.
Art. II. Freedom of scientific investigation in Antarctica and cooperation toward that end, as applied during the International Geophysical Year, shall continue, subject to the provisions of the present Treaty.
Art. III(1) In order to promote international cooperation in scientific investigation in Antarctica, as provided for in art. II of the present Treaty, the Contracting Parties agree that, to the greatest extent feasible and practicable:
(a) information regarding plans for scientific programs in Antarctica shall be exchanged to permit maximum economy and efficiency of operations;
(b) scientific personnel shall be exchanged in Antarctica between expeditions and stations;
(c) scientific observations and results from Antarctica shall be exchanged and made freely available.
(2) In implementing this art., every encouragement shall be given to the establishment of cooperative working relations with those Specialized Agencies of the United Nations and other international organizations having a scientific or technical interest in Antarctica.
Art. IV(1) Nothing contained in the present Treaty shall be interpreted as:
(a) a renunciation by any Contracting Party of previously asserted rights of or claims to territorial sovereignty in Antarctica;
(b) a renunciation or diminution by any Contracting Party of any basis of claim to territorial sovereignty in Antarctica which it may have whether as a result of its activities or those of its nationals in Antarctica, or otherwise;
(c) prejudicing the position of any Contracting Party as regards its recognition or non-recognition of any other State's right of or claim or basis of claim to territorial sovereignty in Antarctica.
(2) No acts or activities taking place while the present Treaty is in force shall constitute a basis for asserting, supporting or denying a claim to territorial sovereignty

in Antarctica. No new claim, or enlargement of an existing claim, to territorial sovereignty in Antarctica shall be asserted while the present Treaty is in force.

Art. V(1) Any nuclear explosions in Antarctica and the disposal there of radioactive waste material shall be prohibited.

(2) In the event of the conclusion of international agreements concerning the use of nuclear energy, including nuclear explosions and the disposal of radioactive waste material to which all of the Contracting Parties whose representatives are entitled to participate in the meetings provided for under art. IX are parties, the rules established under such agreements shall apply in Antarctica.

Art. VI. The provisions of the present Treaty shall apply to the area south of 60° South Latitude, including all ice shelves but nothing in the present Treaty shall prejudice or in any way affect the rights, or the exercise of the rights, of any State under international law with regard to the high seas within that area.

Art. VII(1) In order to promote the objectives and ensure the observance of the provisions of the present Treaty, each Contracting Party whose representatives are entitled to participate in the meetings referred to in Art. IX of the Treaty shall have the right to designate observers to carry out any inspection provided for by the present art. Observers shall be nationals of the Contracting Parties which designate them. The names of observers shall be communicated to every other Contracting Party having the right to designate observers, and like notice shall be given of the termination of their appointment.

(2) Each observer designated in accordance with the provisions of paragraph 1 of this article shall have complete freedom of access at any time to any or all areas of Antarctica.

(3) All areas of Antarctica, including all stations, installations and equipment within those areas, and all ships and aircraft at points of discharging or embarking cargoes or personnel in Antarctica, shall be open at all times to inspection by any observers designated in accordance with paragraph 1 of this article.

(4) Aerial observation may be carried out at any time over any or all areas of Antarctica by any of the Contracting Parties having the right to designate observers.

(5) Each Contracting Party shall, at the time when the present Treaty enters into force for it, inform the other Contracting Parties, and thereafter shall give them notice in advance, of

(a) all expeditions to and within Antarctica, on the part of its ships or nationals, and all expeditions to Antarctica organized in or proceeding from its territory;

(b) all stations in Antarctica occupied by its nationals; and

(c) any military personnel or equipment intended to be introduced by it into Antarctica subject to the conditions prescribed in paragraph 2 of Article I of the present Treaty.

Art. VIII(1) In order to facilitate the exercise of their functions under the present Treaty, and without prejudice to the respective positions of the Contracting Parties relating to jurisdiction over all other persons in Antarctica, observers designated under paragraph 1 of art. VII and scientific personnel exchanged under subparagraph 1 (b) of art. III of the Treaty, and members of the staffs accompanying any such persons, shall be subject only to the jurisdiction of the Contracting Party of which they are nationals in respect of all acts or omissions occurring while they are in Antarctica for the purpose of exercising their functions.

(2) Without prejudice to the provisions of paragraph 1 of this art., and pending the adoption of measures in pursuance of subparagraph 1(e) of art. IX, the Contracting Parties concerned in any case of dispute with regard to the exercise of jurisdiction in Antarctica shall immediately consult together with a view to reaching a mutually acceptable solution.

Art. IX(1) Representatives of the Contracting Parties named in the preamble to the present Treaty shall meet at the City of Canberra within two months after the date of entry into force of the Treaty, and thereafter at suitable intervals and places, for the purpose of exchanging information, consulting together on matters of common interest pertaining to Antarctica and formulating and considering, and recommending to their Governments, measures in furtherance of the principles

and objectives of the Treaty, including measures regarding:

(a) use of Antarctica for peaceful purposes only;

(b) facilitation of scientific research in Antarctica;

(c) facilitation of international scientific cooperation in Antarctica;

(d) facilitation of the exercise of the rights of inspection provided for in art. VII of the Treaty;

(e) questions relating to the exercise of jurisdiction in Antarctica.

(2) Each Contracting Party which has become a party to the present Treaty by accession under art. XIII shall be entitled to appoint representatives to participate in the meetings referred to in paragraph 1 of the present Article, during such time as that Contracting Party demonstrates its interest in Antarctica by conducting substantial scientific research activity there, such as the establishment of a scientific station or the despatch of a scientific expedition.

(3) Reports from the observers referred to in art. VII of the present Treaty shall be transmitted to the representatives of the Contracting Parties participating in the meetings referred to in paragraph 1 of the present Article.

(4) The measures referred to in paragraph 1 of this Article shall become effective when approved by all the Contracting Parties whose representatives were entitled to participate in the meetings held to consider those measures.

(5) Any or all of the rights established in the present Treaty may be exercised as from the date of entry into force of the Treaty whether or not any measures facilitating the exercise of such rights have been proposed, considered or approved as provided in this Article.

Art. X. Each of the Contracting Parties undertakes to exert appropriate efforts, consistent with the Charter of the United Nations, to the end that no one engages in any activity in Antarctica contrary to the principles or purposes of the present Treaty.

Art. XI(1) If any dispute arises between two or more of the Contracting Parties concerning the interpretation or application of the present Treaty, those Contracting Parties shall consult among themselves with a view to having the dispute resolved by negotiation, inquiry, mediation, conciliation, arbitration, judicial settlement or other peaceful means of their own choice.

(2) Any dispute of this character not so resolved shall, with the consent, in each case, of all parties to the dispute, be referred to the International Court of Justice for settlement; but failure to reach agreement on reference to the International Court shall not absolve parties to the dispute from the responsibility of continuing to seek to resolve it by any of the various peaceful means referred to in paragraph 1 of this Article.

Art. XII(1)(a) The present Treaty may be modified or amended at any time by unanimous agreement of the Contracting Parties whose representatives are entitled to participate in the meetings provided for under art. IX. Any such modification or amendment shall enter into force when the depositary Government has received notice from all such Contracting Parties that they have ratified it.

(b) Such modification or amendment shall thereafter enter into force as to any other Contracting Party when notice or ratification by it has been received by the depositary Government. Any such Contracting Party from which no notice of ratification is received within a period of two years from the date of entry into force of the modification or amendment in accordance with the provisions of subparagraph 1(a) of this art. shall be deemed to have withdrawn from the present Treaty on the date of the expiration of such period.

(2)(a) If after the expiration of thirty years from the date of entry into force of the present Treaty, any of the Contracting Parties whose representatives are entitled to participate in the meetings provided for under art. IX so requests by a communication addressed to the depositary Government, a Conference of all the Contracting Parties shall be held as soon as practicable to review the operation of the Treaty.

(b) Any modification or amendment to the present Treaty which is approved at such a Conference by a majority of the Contracting Parties there represented, including a majority of those whose representatives are entitled to participate in the meetings provided for under art. IX, shall be communicated by the depositary Government to all the Contracting Parties immediately

after the termination of the Conference and shall enter into force in accordance with the provisions of paragraph 1 of the present Article.

(c) If any such modification or amendment has not entered into force in accordance with the provisions of subparagraph 1(a) of this art. within a period of two years after the date of its communication to all the Contracting Parties, any Contracting Party may at any time after the expiration of that period give notice to the depositary Government of its withdrawal from the present Treaty; and such withdrawal shall take effect two years after the receipt of the notice by the depositary Government.

Art. XIII(1) The present Treaty shall be subject to ratification by the signatory States. It shall be open for accession by any State which is a Member of the United Nations, or by any other State which may be invited to accede to the Treaty with the consent of all the Contracting Parties whose representatives are entitled to participate in the meetings provided for under art. IX of the Treaty.

(2) Ratification of or accession to the present Treaty shall be effected by each State in accordance with its constitutional processes.

(3) Instruments of ratification and instruments of accession shall be deposited with the Government of the United States of America, hereby designated as the depositary Government.

(4) The depositary Government shall inform all signatory and acceding States of the date of each deposit of any instrument or accession, and the date of entry into force of the Treaty and of any modification or amendment thereto.

(5) Upon the deposit of instruments of ratification by all the signatory States, the present Treaty shall enter into force for those States and for States which have deposited instruments of accession. Thereafter the Treaty shall enter into force for any acceding State upon the deposit of its instrument of accession.

(6) The present Treaty shall be registered by the depositary Government pursuant to Article 102 of the Charter of the United Nations.

Art. XIV. The present Treaty, done in the English, French, Russian and Spanish languages, each version being equally authentic, shall be deposited in the archives of the Government of the United States of America, which shall transmit duly certified copies thereof to the Governments of the signatory and acceding States.

In witness whereof, the undersigned Plenipotentiaries, duly authorized, have signed the present Treaty.

Done at Washington this first day of December, one thousand nine hundred and fifty-nine."

The Treaty was ratified until Jan. 1, 1987, by 33 countries.

UNTS, vol. 402, pp. 72–85; 1988, p. 461. J.D. MYHRE, *The Antarctic Treaty System: Politics, Law and Diplomacy*, London, 1986; G.D. TRIGGS (ed.), *The Antarctic Treaty Regime: Law, Environment and Resources*, Cambridge, 1987; *SIPRI Yearbook*.

ANTARTIDA ARGENTINA ▷ Antarctica.

ANTARTIDA CHILENA ▷ Antarctica.

ANTHONY ISLAND. A tiny island which forms the southernmost tip of the Queen Charlotte Islands in British Columbia, included in the ▷ World Heritage UNESCO List. The remains of a village, now abandoned for over a hundred years, are to be found here. It belonged to the Haida, a tribe of hunters and fishermen who inhabited this small island to the north-north-west of Vancouver. They have now died out, but in a magnificent natural environment are preserved the masterpieces they left behind: heraldic totem and mortuary poles which are among the finest examples of the magical arts of primitive peoples.

UNESCO, *The Protection of the World Cultural and Natural Heritage*, Paris, 1983.

ANTHROPOLOGY. The scientific study of man, a subject of permanent international co-operation since 1845 when the First International Congress on

Anthropology took place in Paris. Organizations reg. with the UIA:

Association for Social Anthropology in Oceania, f. 1960, University of Wisconsin, USA.
International Bureau of Differential Anthropology, f. 1950, Geneva; publ. *Anthropologie Différentielle et Sciences des Types Constitutionnels Humains.*
International Committee for the Anthropology of Food and Food Habits, f. 1960, Paris.
International Union of Anthropology and Ethnological Sciences, f. 1948, W. Berlin.

Yearbook of International Organizations; Ch. SEYMOUR-SMITH, *Macmillan Dictionary of Anthropology*, London, 1987.

ANTHROPOSOPHY. A subject of international co-operation: General Anthroposophical Society, f. 1923, Dornach, Switzerland. Reg. with the UIA.

Yearbook of International Organizations.

ANTI-BALLISTIC MISSILE. ▷ ABM.

ANTIBIOTICS. A subject of international co-operation: International Center of Information on Antibiotics, f. 1961, Liège, Belgium. Publ. *ICIA Information Bulletin.* Reg. with the UIA.

Yearbook of International Organizations.

ANTI-CLERICALISM. A social movement in Europe directed against the clergy's influence on state affairs, began in the 12th century and expanded in the 18th and 19th centuries in Western Europe and Latin America; in the 20th century in Russia and Mexico. The call of French anti-clericalist Republicans against clerical Royalists was Leon Gambetta's: *"Le cléricalisme, voilà l'ennemi!"* ("Clericalism is the enemy!"). At the same time the fight against Catholic Church influence in Germany was called ▷ Kulturkampf. The Catholic Church with radical decisions of the Second Vatican Council (Oct. 11, 1962–Dec. 8, 1965) opened a new era in the relations between the Church and states, reflected also in the UN system. See ▷ Pacem in Terris.

A. DEBIDOUR, *Histoire des rapports de l'église et l'état en France de 1789 à 1870*, Paris, 1898; E. FAGUET, *L'anti-cléricalisme*, Paris, 1906; J. KISSLING, *Geschichte des Kulturkampfes im Deutschen Reich*, Berlin, 1929; J. LLOYD MECHAN, *Church and State in Latin America*, New York, 1934; E.J. HUGHES, *The Church and the Liberal Society*, London, 1944; W.V. D'ANTONIO, F.B. PIKE, *Religion, Revolution and Reform*, New York, 1964; W.M. ABBOTT (ed.), *The Documents of Vatican II*, London, 1966.

ANTI-COMINTERN PACT, 1936. A Pact signed Nov. 25, 1936 in Berlin for five years by ministers of foreign affairs of the Third Reich and Japan, with the purpose of organizing together the fight against the Communist International (▷ Komintern). Italy joined the Pact Nov. 6, 1937, Hungary and Manchuria, Feb. 24, 1939; Spain, Mar. 27, 1939. The Protocol Supplement stated that the signatories would not only co-operate in the exchange of information on the activities of the Comintern, but would also undertake "severe action against those who directly or indirectly, at home or abroad, remain in the service of the Comintern or provide aid for its destructive activities". After the outbreak of World War II, the Anti-Comintern Pact was joined by: Bulgaria, Denmark, Finland, Romania and the governments of Croatia, Slovakia, and China in Nanking. The Pact was extended Nov. 25, 1941 for another five years. In 1939–40 the Anti-Comintern Pact became the basis for further military alliances between Germany, Italy and Japan: May 22, 1939 the alliance of Germany and Italy,

called the Steel Pact, and Nov. 27, 1940 the Pact of Three, which was a supplement to the Steel Pact.

Warum Krieg mit Stalin? Das Rotbuch der Antikomintern, Berlin, 1941; BRUNS-GRETSCHANINOV, *Politische Verträge*, Bd. 3, Berlin, 1936–42; "Das Geheime Abkommen zum Antikominternpakt. Dokumentation", in: *Vierteljahreshefte für Zeitgeschichte*, No. 2, 1954.

ANTI-COMMUNISM. An international term for the fight against communist ideology. A subject of concerted international actions since the middle of the 19th century when, following the publication in 1848 of the Communist Manifesto by K. Marx and F. Engels, an international agreement was concluded between the political forces of the European Powers on co-operation in prosecuting the advocates of communist ideas. In 1936 the Third Reich, Japan and Italy established an anti-communist intergovernmental organization – the ▷ Anti-Comintern Pact. After World War II anti-communist doctrines were basis for bi- and multilateral agreements in Western Europe, South-East Asia, Africa and the Americas. The OAS Council of Ministers of Foreign Affairs of 21 American States in Punta del Este adopted on Jan. 1, 1961 with one vote in opposition (Cuba), a resolution entitled the Offensive of Communism in America, proclaiming that "the assumptions of communism are incompatible with the American system".

OAS General Report, 1961, Washington, DC, 1962.

ANTI-DUMPING TARIFFS. The tariffs and customs regulations against ▷ Dumping. The GATT elaborated an Anti-Dumping Code and the EEC the Anti-Dumping Regulations.

K. JUNCKERSTORFF, *Anti-dumping Recht Texte. Erläuterungen. Dokumentation*, Berlin, 1974, p. 462; J. PAXTON, *A Dictionary of the EEC*, London, 1977, p. 6.

ANTI-FASCISM. An international movement, which arose between the wars, branding fascism as an aggressive racist ideology dangerous to peace and the cultural values of the world. Anti-fascism played an important role in European resistance during World War II as the platform of the United Nations fight against the Axis states, which consequently gave the UN Charter an anti-fascist and anti-racist character. After the war the UN General Assembly often took a stand against the rebirth of fascism. ▷ Nazi and Fascist Postwar Activities and the UN.

L. VALIANI, *Dall' antifascismo alla resistenza*, Roma, 1959.

ANTIGUA AND BARBUDA. Member of the UN. Part of the West Indies Constitutional Monarchy, with the British sovereign as Head of State, represented by the Governor General. Area: 441.6 sq. km. Population est, 1986, 81,500 (census 1960 – 54,000; 1970 – 65,525). Capital: St Johns with 25,000 inhabitants, 1979. Currency: one East Caribbean dollar = 100 cents. GNP per capita 1987 US$2,570. Official language: English. National Day: Nov. 1, Independence Day, 1981. Member of the UN, Nov. 11, 1981 and of its specialised agencies, save IDA, UPU, WMO, WIPO and UNIDO. Member of the Organization of Eastern Caribbean States (OECS). As member of the OECS supported the invasion by the USA of Grenada in Oct. 1983. On March 30, 1987, Antigua and Barbuda became the 94th contracting party to the ▷ GATT.

M. PROUDFOOT, *Britain and the US in the Caribbean*, London, 1984; *The Europa Year Book 1984. A World Survey*, Vol. I, pp. 1078–1081, London, 1984.

ANTIGUA GUATEMALA. A town in central Guatemala, in colonial times capital of Spanish Guatemala; a cultural monument, included in the ▷ World Heritage UNESCO List. Wreathed columns and pilasters, and a profusion of animal and vegetable motifs in stucco on façades and altarpieces, provide luxuriant decoration for the architecture of this former capital which has all too often been a victim of earthquakes.

UNESCO. *The Protection of World Cultural and Natural Heritage*, Paris, 1983.

ANTI-MILITARISM. A pacifist trend, sometimes connected with the refusal of compulsory military service for humanitarian or religious reasons (conscientious objectors). A periodical, *Antimilitarismus Information*, appears in Frankfurt am Main (FRG).

ANTI-NUCLEAR MOVEMENT. Since 1948, a world movement initiated by Albert Einstein, Frederic Joliot-Curie, Leopold Infeld, Linus Pauling and other atomic scientists.

W. RÜDIG, *Anti-Nuclear Movements, A World Survey*, London, 1987.

ANTI-PERSONNEL WEAPONS. An international term for conventional delayed-action weapons, high-velocity small arms, incendiary weapons, cluster bombs (BU), chemical warfare bomblets, mines and minelets, laser weapons, fuel–air explosives, uranium projectiles, etc.; a subject of international humanitarian law.

M. LUMSDEN, *Anti-Personnel Weapons*, SIPRI, London, 1978, p. 299.

ANTIPODES. An international geographical term for places separated by half the circumference of the Earth (180°), the parts of the globe diametrically opposite.

ANTI-SATELLITE SYSTEM. ▷ ASAT.

ANTI-SEMITISM. An international term for enmity to ▷ Jews promoted for centuries by arguments of religious, social, nationalistic or racial character; expressed by economic boycott, expulsions, ▷ pogroms, ▷ genocide; the fight against anti-Semitism and against the propaganda of anti-Semitism, which is the subject of organized international co-operation, has been expressed, i.a., in international conventions and resolutions of the UN General Assembly on Racism and anti-Semitism. In the 20th century anti-Semitism became the basis for legally binding discrimination in two States: The Third Reich and Italy. In the Third Reich, legislation was passed by the Reichstag at a session in Nuremberg, on Sept. 15, 1935 (Nuremberg Anti-Semitic Laws) on the Reich's citizenship, and "protection of the German blood and honour", but the Reich's nationals of Jewish descent were put practically beyond the protection of law, ▷ Kristallnacht, ▷ Holocaust, ▷ Endlösung. In Italy, the Manifesto of Race (Manifesto della Razza), issued on July 14, 1938 by B. Mussolini, stated in point 9 that "Jews do not belong to the Italian race". The international fight against anti-Semitism was initiated in the 19th century by the international labor movement. On Jan. 28, 1960, the UN Commission on Human Rights, having discussed anti-Semitic excesses, the devastation of Jewish cemeteries, and the profanation of synagogues in the FRG, condemned "all present-day forms of anti-Semitism and other forms of racial and religious hatred". On Oct. 28, 1965, the Vatican II Ecumenical Council, in its Declaration on the Attitude of the Church towards the Non-Christian Religions, repealed the centuries-old doctrine of the

Church that the Jewish nation had been responsible for the death of Christ: "... that what had happened [to Christ] during his Passion cannot in any case be blamed upon all Jews which lived then or upon Jews living today ... moreover, the Church regrets acts of hatred and persecution, and demonstrations of anti-Semitism, which at any time in the past and in whatever form were manifested against the Jews". During the first papal visit to a synagogue in Rome on April 13, 1986, Pope John Paul II condemned all forms of antisemitism. On Feb. 10, 1989, a Vatican Declaration on the Church and Racism condemned all forms of racism and Antisemitism in particular: "If anti-Semitism has been the most tragic form that racist ideology has assumed in our century, with the horrors of the Jewish Holocaust, it has unfortunately not yet entirely disappeared. As if some had nothing to learn from the crimes of the past, certain organizations, with branches in many countries, keep alive the anti-Semitic racist myth, with the support of networks of publications.

Terrorist acts which have Jewish persons or symbols as their target have multiplied in recent years and show the radicalism of such groups. Anti-Zionism – which is not of the same order, since it questions the State of Israel and its policies – serves at times as a screen for anti-Semitism, feeding on it and leading to it. Furthermore, some countries impose undue harassments and restrictions on the free emigrations of Jews".

P.W. MASSING, *Rehearsal for Destruction. A Study of Political Antisemitism in Imperial Germany*, New York, 1949; *UN Review*, 296/1960, pp. 31–33; R.H. PHELPS, *Before Hitler Came*, in: *The Journal of Modern History*, No 3, 1963; J. PARKES, *Anti-Semitism: A Concise History*, Chicago, 1964, 205 pp.; W.M. ABBOTT (ed.), *The Documents of Vatican II*, London, 1966; L. PRETTI, *Imperio Fascista. Africani ed Ebrai*, Rome, 1968; L. POLIAKOV, *The History of Antisemitism*, 2 Vols, London, 1974; B. LEWIS, *Semites and Antisemites*, New York, 1986; KEESING's *Contemporary Archive*, 1986; The New York Times, Feb. 11, 1989.

ANTI-SLAVERY SOCIETY FOR THE PROTECTION OF HUMAN RIGHTS. F. 1839, London, as the British and Foreign Anti-Slavery Society; amalgamated in 1909 with the Aborigines Protection Society (f. 1837), since then under the present name. Consultative status ECOSOC, on ILO Special List. Publ. *The Anti-Slavery Reporter* and *Aborigines Friend* (irregularly). Reg. with the UIA.

Yearbook of International Organizations.

ANTI-SUBMARINE WARFARE. ▷ Submarines. ▷ ASW.

ANTI-TRANSFER DOCTRINE, 1811–1940. An inter-American term for a principle proclaimed by the US Congress, on Jan. 15, 1811, that in the Western Hemisphere the transfer of colonial rights from one state to another is prohibited; strengthened during World War II by a resolution of the Council of Ministers of Foreign Affairs of the American Republics in Havana, on Aug. 30, 1940, to accept temporary administration over European colonies and possessions by the USA, which excluded the possibility of transferring the rights of France and Holland to Germany.

International American Conferences. First Supplement 1938–43, Washington, DC, 1943, pp. 151–152.

ANTI-TRUST ACT, 1890. The first anti-trust legislation adopted by the US Congress on July 2, 1890, called the Sherman Anti-Trust Act (Senator John Sherman, Rep., 1823–1900). The text of the bill is as follows:

SEC. 1. Every contract, combination in the form of trust or otherwise; or conspiracy, in restraint of trade or commerce among the several States, or with foreign nations, is hereby declared to be illegal. Every person who shall make any such contract or engage in any such combination or conspiracy, shall be deemed guilty of a misdemeanor, and, on conviction thereof, shall be punished by fine not exceeding five thousand dollars, or by imprisonment not exceeding one year, or by both said punishments, in the discretion of the court.
SEC. 2. Every person who shall monopolize, or attempt to monopolize, or combine or conspire with any other person or persons, to monopolize any part of the trade or commerce among the several States, or with foreign nations, shall be deemed guilty of a misdemeanor, and, on conviction thereof, shall be punished by fine not exceeding five thousand dollars, or by imprisonment not exceeding one year, or by both said punishments, in the discretion of the court.
SEC. 3. Every contract, combination in form of trust or otherwise, or conspiracy, in restraint of trade or commerce in any Territory of the United States or of the District of Columbia, or in restraint of trade or commerce between any such Territory and another, or between any such Territory or Territories and any State or States or the District of Columbia, or with foreign nations, or between the District of Columbia and any State or States or foreign nations, is hereby declared illegal. Every person who shall make any such contract or engage in any such combination or conspiracy, shall be deemed guilty of a misdemeanor, and, on conviction thereof, shall be punished by fine not exceeding five thousand dollars, or by imprisonment not exceeding one year, or by both said punishments, in the discretion of the court.
SEC. 4. The several circuit courts of the United States are hereby invested with jurisdiction to prevent and restrain violations of this act; and it shall be the duty of the several district attorneys of the United States, in their respective districts, under the direction of the Attorney-General, to institute proceedings in equity to prevent and restrain such violations. Such proceedings may be by way of petition setting forth the case and praying that such violation shall be enjoined or otherwise prohibited. When the parties complained of shall have been duly notified of such petition the courts shall proceed, as soon as may be, to the hearing and determination of the case; and pending such petition and before final decrees, the court may at any time make such temporary restraining order or prohibition as shall be deemed just in the premises.
SEC. 5. Whenever it shall appear to the court before which any proceeding under Section four of this act may be pending, that the ends of justice require that other parties should be brought before the court, the court may cause them to be summoned, whether they reside in the district in which the court is held or not; and subpoenas to that end may be served in any district by the marshal thereof.
SEC. 6. Any property owned under any contract or by any combination, or pursuant to any conspiracy (and being the subject thereof) mentioned in section one of this act, and being in the course of transportation from one State to another, or to a foreign country, shall be forfeited to the United States, and may be seized and condemned by like proceedings as those provided by law for the forfeiture, seizure, and condemnation of property imported into the United States contrary to law.
SEC. 7. Any person who shall be injured in his business or property by any other person or corporation by reason of anything forbidden or declared to be unlawful by this act, may sue therefor in any circuit court of the United States in the district in which the defendant resides or is found, without respect to the amount in controversy, and shall recover threefold the damages by him sustained, and the costs of suit, including a reasonable attorney's fee.
SEC. 8. That the word "person", or "persons", wherever used in this act shall be deemed to include corporations and associations existing under or authorized by the laws of either the United States, the laws of any of the Territories, the laws of any State, or the laws of any foreign country.

The Sherman Anti-Trust Law 1890 was amended by the Clayton Anti-Trust Law of 1914, the Capper-Volstead Act of 1922, the National Recovery Act of 1933 and 1936, the Miller-Tydings Act of 1937, and the Reed-Bulwinkle Act of 1948. The impact of the American anti-trust legislation was important after World War II in regional economic integrations of the West, especially in the rules of competition policy in the European Economic Community. ▷ Code of multinational companies.

W.L. FUGATE, *Foreign Commerce and the Anti-Trust Law*, Boston, 1973.

ANZAC. Australia and New Zealand Army Corps; the armed forces of both these states, united under one supreme command according to the ANZAC Pact signed in Jan. 1944; in 1951 integrated within ▷ ANZUS.

H.V. EVATT, *Foreign Policy of Australia*, Sydney, 1945.

ANZUK. Abbreviation for three states: Australia, New Zealand, and the United Kingdom; the name of a military alliance of the United Kingdom with Australia, New Zealand, Malaysia, and Singapore, which entered into force on Nov. 1, 1971 as a military body of the British Commonwealth in the Australasia region for the defense of Malaysia and Singapore. In Dec. 1972, Australia and New Zealand decided to withdraw their armed forces from Malaysia and Singapore, and the latter expressed its wish to obtain the status of a neutral state.

SIPRI, *World Armaments and Disarmament Yearbook 1973*, pp. 78–79.

ANZUS. A security treaty between Australia, New-Zealand and the USA, signed on Sept. 1, 1951 at San Francisco, named after the initial letters of the signatory states. Entered into force on April 29, 1952. The organs of the Pact: the Anzus Council comprising Ministers of Foreign Affairs (or their deputies) of the signatory states and Military Representatives accredited to the Council. The text is as follows:

"The Parties to this Treaty,
Reaffirming their faith in the purposes and principles of the Charter of the United Nations and their desire to live in peace with all peoples and all Governments, and desiring to strengthen the fabric and peace in the Pacific Area,
Noting that the United States already has arrangements pursuant to which its Armed Forces are stationed in the Philippines, and has Armed Forces and administrative responsibilities in the Ryukyus, and upon the coming into force of the Japanese Peace Treaty may also station armed forces in and about Japan to assist in the preservation of peace and security in the Japan area,
Recognizing that Australia and New Zealand as members of the British Commonwealth of Nations have military obligations outside as well as within the Pacific Area,
Desiring further to co-ordinate their efforts for collective defense for the preservation of peace and security pending the development of a more comprehensive system of regional security in the Pacific Area,
Therefore declare and agree as follows:
Art. 1. The Parties undertake, as set forth in the Charter of the United Nations, to settle any international disputes in which they may be involved by peaceful means in such a manner that international peace and security and justice are not endangered and to refrain in their international relations from the threat or use of force in any manner inconsistent with the purposes of the United Nations.
Art. 2. In order more effectively to achieve the objective of this Treaty the Parties separately and jointly by means of continuous and effective self-help and mutual aid will maintain and develop their individual and collective capacity to resist armed attack.
Art. 3. The Parties will consult together whenever in the opinion of any of them the territorial integrity, political

independence or security of any of the Parties is threatened in the Pacific.

Art. 4. Each Party recognizes that an armed attack in the Pacific Area on any of the Parties would be dangerous to its own peace and safety and declares that it would act to meet the common danger in accordance with its constitutional processes.

Any such armed attack and all measures taken as a result thereof shall be immediately reported to the Security Council of the United Nations. Such measures shall be terminated when the Security Council has taken the measures necessary to restore and maintain international peace and security.

Art. 5. For the purpose of art. 4, an armed attack on any of the Parties is deemed to include an armed attack on the metropolitan territory of any of the Parties, or on the island territories under its jurisdiction in the Pacific or on its Armed Forces, public vessels or aircraft in the Pacific.

Art. 6. This Treaty does not affect and shall not be interpreted as affecting in any way the rights and obligations of the Parties under the Charter of the United Nations or the responsibility of the United Nations for the maintenance of international peace and security.

Art. 7. The Parties hereby establish a Council, consisting of their Foreign Ministers or their Deputies, to consider matters concerning the implementation of this Treaty. The Council should be so organized as to be able to meet at any time.

Art. 8. Pending the development of a more comprehensive system of regional security in the Pacific Area and the development by the United Nations of more effective means to maintain international peace and security, the Council, established by art. 7, is authorized to maintain a consultative relationship with States, Regional Organizations Associations of States or other authorities in the Pacific Area in position to further the purposes of this Treaty and to contribute to the security of that Area.

Art. 9. This Treaty shall be ratified by the Parties in accordance with their respective constitutional processes. The instruments of ratification shall be deposited as soon as possible with the Government of Australia, which will notify each of the other signatories of such deposit. The treaty shall enter into force as soon as the ratifications of the signatories have been deposited.

Art. 10. This Treaty shall remain in force indefinitely. Any Party may cease to be a member of the Council established by art. 7 one year after notice has been given to the Government of Australia, which will inform the Governments of the other Parties of the deposit of such notice.

Art. 11. This Treaty in the English language shall be deposited in the archives of the Government of Australia. Duly certified copies thereof will be transmitted by that Government to the Governments of each of the other signatories."

From 1954 till 1972 it operated in close contact with the ▷ SEATO. On Nov. 27, and Dec. 8, 1972, Australia and New Zealand announced that they would reduce their armed forces and restrict their participation in ANZUS and SEATO, and also in ▷ ANZUK. In October 1976, the ANZUS States conducted maneuvres of its forces under the cryptonym 'Kangaroo II'. In the 1980s the ANZUS States staged exercises in the Indian Ocean off Western Australia and "expressed themselves satisfied with the continued high degree of co-operation and consultation".

UNTS, Vol. 131, pp. 84–88; N. HARPER, D. SISSONS, *Australia and the UN*, New York, 1959, pp. 115–126; J.G. STARKE, *The ANZUS Treaty Alliance*, Melbourne, 1966; *The Far East and Australia 1974*, London, 1974, pp. 92–93; *Department of State Bulletin*, Vol. 80, No. 2037, IV, 1980; *The Europa Year Book 1984. A World Survey*, Vol. I, p. 96, London, 1984; H.S. ALBINSKI, *ANZUS: The United States and Pacific Security*, New York, 1987; D. ROBERTSON, *Guide to Modern Defense and Strategy*, Detroit, 1988.

AOZOU STRIP. ▷ Chad.

APARTHEID. *Afrikaans* = "separation". An international term for the racial policy of the Republic of South Africa based on segregation according to the color of one's skin; inhuman acts ensuing from this policy were condemned by the UN General Assembly on Dec. 12, 1966 (Res. 2184/XXI) and on Dec. 16, 1966 (Res. 2202/XXI) as "crimes against humanity" and on Nov. 26, 1968 (Res. 3291/XXIII) as crimes not subject to statutory limitations similarly to War Crimes. The National Party governing in South Africa introduced there between 1949 and 1957, on behalf of the population of European descent (20%), a total segregation of the non-European population (of African as well as Asiatic descent) according to the concept stated by the South African Prime Minister, J.S. Strijdom, that "either the whites will consolidate their domination, or the blacks theirs". The official form of segregation is expressed in the Racial Register of the Population of the Republic of South Africa and the provisions of the Apartheid Statute which may be characterized, for instance, by its art. 12: "It is against the law for a white to drink tea together with a black in any tea-room in the Republic of South Africa, unless they have received a special permission to do so". In 1949–60, the UN General Assembly repeatedly requested the government of South Africa to put an end to the policy of Apartheid as being contradictory to the principles of the UN Charter. On Nov. 28, 1961, the UN General Assembly, by 97 votes for and 2 against (South Africa and Portugal), condemned Apartheid and stated that it "brought about international tension and its continuance constitutes a serious danger to peace and international security". On Nov. 6, 1962, the UN General Assembly, with 67 votes for and 16 against (Austria, Belgium, Canada, Great Britain, Greece, France, Ireland, Japan, Luxembourg, Netherlands, New Zealand, Portugal, South Africa, Spain, Turkey and the USA) and 27 abstaining, recommended to the UN member states that they should break their diplomatic relations with South Africa, close their seaports to the vessels flying the South African flag and their airports to the airplanes of the South African Airways, boycott South African goods, and introduce embargo on any armaments for South Africa. The provisions have proved to be ineffective since the USA, Great Britain, the FRG and Japan are the main trading and political partners of South Africa. Also further resolutions of the UN General Assembly, adopted in 1963–83, have been ineffective, moreover the reports of the Special Commission on Apartheid have disclosed that the racial terror in South Africa and in Namibia, occupied by South Africa, is still growing. The ILO and UNESCO also adopted several resolutions on Apartheid. In June 1971, the OAU Assembly of Heads of State and government in Addis Ababa discussed the proposals by the government of Ivory Coast, of Apr. 1971, that the OAU states should establish diplomatic relations with South Africa in spite of the racial system of Apartheid reigning there. In open voting, 26 states pronounced themselves against the proposal, six for (Gabon, Lesotho, Malawi, Mauritius, the Malagasy Republic and Ivory Coast), and five abstained (Dahomey, Upper Volta, Niger, Swaziland and Togo). In the 1980s the UN continued its efforts to aid the people of South Africa, their national liberation movement and victims of Apartheid. The General Assembly in every session urged contribution to the UN Trust Fund for South Africa, to the UN Educational and Training Program for South Africa as well to the UN Program of Assistance to South African Student Refugees. The Special Committee Against Apartheid continued to review the Apartheid policies in South Africa. The Security Council and the General Assembly also dealt with aspects of South Africa's relations with the neighbouring states of Angola, Lesotho, Mozambique and Zambia.

The year 1982 was proclaimed by the UN as an International Year of Mobilization of Sanctions against South Africa.

Dec. 14, 1982 the UN General Assembly unanimously condemned the South African raid against Lesotho on Dec. 9, 1982 against the homes of alleged African National Congress members residential area of Lesotho, which resulted in the death of 42 people, 30 of whom were reported to be South African refugees.

On March 2, 1984 a ten-year Agreement on Non-aggression and Good Neighbourliness was signed by the South African Prime Minister and President of Mozambique.

Apartheid, Déclaration Concernant la Politique de Apartheid de la République Sudafricaine et programme de l'OIT pour l'Élimination de l'Apartheid dans le Domaine du Travail, Geneva, 1964; *Estudio del Examen del Apartheid por las NU*, New York, 1967; *UNESCO "Apartheid" – its Effects on Education, Science, Culture and Information*, Paris, 1967; *El Apartheid y el tratado a los presos en Sudáfrica. Declaraciones y testimonios jurados de las NU*, New York, 1968; *La Anatomía del Apartheid, Preguntas y Respuestas sobre las NU y la Discriminación Racial en Sudáfrica*, México, DF, 1968; *The Laws of Armed Conflict*, Leiden, 1973, pp. 703–709; *UN Yearbook 1980*, pp. 194–260; *UN Chronicle*, November 1983; M.A. UHLIG, *Apartheid in Crisis*, New York, 1986.

APARTHEID, CRIME OF APARTHEID, CONVENTION, 1973. The International Convention on the Suppression and Punishment of the Crime of Apartheid, adopted by the UN General Assembly, with Res. 3068/XXVIII, Nov. 30, 1973; came into force July 18, 1976. The text is as follows:

"The States Parties to the present Convention,
Recalling the provisions of the Charter of the United Nations, in which all Members pledged themselves to take joint and separate action in co-operation with the Organization for the achievement of universal respect for, and observance of, human rights and fundamental freedoms for all without distinction as to race, sex, language or religion.
Considering the Universal Declaration of Human Rights, which states that all Human beings are born free and equal in dignity and rights and that everyone is entitled to all the rights and freedoms set forth in the Declaration, without distinction of kind, such as race, colour or national origin,
Considering the Declaration on the Granting of Independence to Colonial Countries and Peoples, in which the General Assembly stated that the process of liberation is irresistible and irreversible and that, in the interests of human dignity, progress and justice, an end must be put to colonialism and all practices of segregation and discrimination associated therewith.
Observing that, in accordance with the International Convention on the Elimination of All forms of Racial Discrimination, States particularly condemn racial segregation and apartheid and undertake to prevent, prohibit and eradicate all practices of this nature in territories under their jurisdiction,
Observing that, in the Convention on the Prevention and Punishment of the Crime of Genocide, certain acts which may also be qualified as acts of apartheid constitute a crime under international law.
Observing that, in the Convention on the Non-Applicability of Statutory Limitations to War Crimes and Crimes Against Humanity, "in-human acts resulting from the policy of apartheid" are qualified as crimes against humanity,
Observing that the General Assembly of the United Nations has adopted a number of resolutions in which the policies and practices of apartheid are condemned as a crime against humanity.
Observing that the Security Council has emphasized that apartheid, its continued intensification and expansion, seriously disturbs and threatens international peace and security,

Convinced that an International Convention on the Suppression and Punishment of the Crime of Apartheid would make it possible to take more effective measures at the international and national levels with a view to the suppression and punishment of the apartheid,
Have agreed as follows:

Art. I.(1) The States Parties to the present Convention declare that apartheid is a crime against humanity and that inhuman acts resulting from the policies of apartheid and similar policies and practices of racial segregation and discrimination, as defined in article II of the Convention, are crimes violating the principles of international law, in particular the purposes and principles of the Charter of the United Nations, and constituting a serious threat to international peace and security.

(2) The States Parties to the present Convention declare criminal those organizations, institutions and individuals committing the crime of apartheid.

Art. II. For the purpose of the present Convention, the term "the crime of apartheid", which shall include similar policies and practices of racial segregation and discrimination as practised in southern Africa, shall apply to the following inhuman acts committed for the purpose of establishing and maintaining domination by one racial group of persons over any other racial group of persons and systematically oppressing them:

(a) Denial to a member or members of a racial group or groups of the right to life and liberty of person:

(i) By murder of members of a racial group or groups;

(ii) By the infliction upon the members of a racial group or groups of serious bodily or mental harm by the infringement of their freedom or dignity, or by subjecting them to torture or to cruel, inhuman or degrading treatment or punishment;

(iii) By arbitrary arrest and illegal imprisonment of the members of a racial group or groups;

(b) Deliberate imposition on a racial group or groups of living conditions calculated to cause its or their physical destruction in whole or part;

(c) Any legislative measures and other measures calculated to prevent a racial group or groups from participation in the political, social, economic and cultural life of the country and the deliberate creation of conditions preventing the full development of such a group or groups, in particular by denying to members of a racial group or groups basic human rights and freedoms, including the right to work, the right to form organized trade unions, the right to education, the right to leave and to return to their country, the right to a nationality, the right to freedom of opinion and expression, and the right to freedom of peaceful assembly and association,

(d) Any measures, including legislative measures, designed to divide the population along racial lines by the creation of separate reserves and ghettos for the members of a racial group or groups, the prohibition of mixed marriages among members of various racial groups, the expropriation of landed property belonging to a racial group or groups or to members thereof;

(e) Exploitation of the labour of the members of a racial group or groups, in particular by submitting them to forced labour;

(f) Persecution of organizations and persons, by depriving them of fundamental rights and freedoms, because they oppose apartheid.

Art. III. International criminal responsibility shall apply, irrespective of the motive involved, to individuals, members of organizations and institutions and representatives of the State, whether residing in the territory of the State in which the acts are perpetrated or in some other State, whenever they:

(a) Commit, participate in, directly incite or conspire in the commission of the acts mentioned in article II of the present Convention;

(b) Directly abet, encourage or cooperate in the commission of the crime of apartheid.

Art. IV. The States Parties to the present Convention undertake:

(a) To adopt any legislative or other measures necessary to suppress as well as to prevent any encouragement of the crime of apartheid and similar segregationist policies or their manifestations and to punish persons guilty of that crime;

(b) To adopt legislative, judicial and administrative measures to prosecute, bring to trial and punish in accordance with their jurisdiction persons responsible for, or accused of, the acts defined in art. II of the present

Convention, whether or not such persons reside in the territory of the State in which the acts are committed or are nationals of that State or of some other State or are stateless persons.

Art. V. Persons charged with the acts enumerated in article II of the present Convention may be tried by a competent tribunal of any State Party to the Convention which may acquire jurisdiction over the person of the accused or by an international penal tribunal having jurisdiction with respect to those States Parties which shall have accepted its jurisdiction.

Art. VI. To States Parties to the present Convention undertake to accept and carry out in accordance with the Charter of the United Nations the decisions taken by the Security Council aimed at the prevention, suppression and punishment of the crime of apartheid, and to co-operate in the implementation of decisions adopted by other competent organs of the United Nations with a view to achieving the purposes of the Convention.

Art. VII.(1) The States Parties to the present Convention undertake to submit periodic reports to the group established under art. IX on the legislative, judicial, administrative or other measures that they have adopted and that give effect to the provisions of the Convention.

(2) Copies of the reports shall be transmitted through the Secretary-General of the United Nations to the Special Committee on Apartheid.

Art. VIII. Any State Party to the present Convention may call upon any competent organ of the United Nations to take such action under the Charter of the United Nations as it considers appropriate for the prevention and suppression of the crime of apartheid.

Art. IX.(1) The Chairman of the Commission on Human Rights shall appoint a group consisting of three members of the Commission on Human Rights, who are also representatives of joint States Parties to the present Convention, to consider reports submitted by States Parties in accordance with art. VII.

(2) If, among the members of the Commission on Human Rights, there are no representatives of States Parties to the present Convention or if there are fewer than three such representatives, the Secretary-General of the United Nations shall, after consulting all States Parties to the Convention, designate a representative of the State Party or representatives of the States Parties which are not members of the Commission on Human Rights to take part in the work of the group established in accordance with paragraph I of this article, until such time as representatives of the States Parties to the Convention are elected to the Commission on Human Rights.

(3) The group may meet for a period of not more than five days, either before the opening or after the closing of the session of the Commission on Human Rights, to consider the reports submitted in accordance with art. VII.

Art. X.(1) The States Parties to the present Convention empower the Commission on Human Rights:

(a) To request United Nations organs, when transmitting copies of petitions under art. 15 of the International Convention on the Elimination of All Forms of Racial Discrimination, to draw its attention to complaints concerning acts which are enumerated in art. II of the present Convention;

(b) To prepare, on the basis of reports from competent organs of the United Nations and periodic reports from States Parties to the present Convention, a list of individuals, organizations, institutions and representatives of States which are alleged to be responsible for the crimes enumerated in article II of the Convention, as well as those against whom legal proceedings have been undertaken by States Parties to the Convention;

(c) To request information from the competent United Nations organs concerning measures taken by the authorities responsible for the administration of Trust and Non-Self-Governing Territories, and all other Territories to which General Assembly resolution 1514/XV of December 14, 1960 applies, with regard to such individuals alleged to be responsible for crimes under article II of the Convention who are believed to be under their territorial and administrative jurisdiction.

(2) Pending the achievement of the objectives of the Declaration on the Granting of Independence to Colonial Countries and Peoples, contained in General Assembly resolution 1514/XV, the provisions of the present Convention shall in no way limit the right of

petition granted to those peoples by other international instruments or by the United Nations and its specialized agencies.

Art. XI.(1) Acts enumerated in article II of the present Convention shall not be considered political crimes for the purpose of extradition.

(2) The States Parties to the present Convention undertake in such cases to grant extradition in accordance with their legislation and with the treaties in force.

Art. XII. Disputes between States Parties arising out of the interpretation, application or implementation of the present Convention which have not been settled by negotiation shall, at the request of the States Parties to the dispute, be brought before the International Court of Justice, save where the parties to the dispute have agreed on some other form of settlement.

Art. XIII. The present Convention is open for signature by all States. Any State which does not sign the Convention before its entry into force may accede to it.

Art. XIV.(1) The present Convention is subject to ratification. Instruments of ratification shall be deposited with the Secretary-General of the United Nations.

(2) Accession shall be effected by the deposits of an instrument of accession with the Secretary-General of the United Nations.

Art. XV.(1) The present Convention shall enter into force on the thirtieth day after the date of the deposit with the Secretary-General of the United Nations of the twentieth instrument of ratification or instrument of accession.

Art. XVI. A State Party may denounce the present Convention by written notification to the Secretary-General of the United Nations. Denunciation shall take effect one year after the date of receipt of the notification by the Secretary-General.

Art. XVII.(1) A request for the revision of this Convention may be made at any time by any State Party by means of a notification in writing addressed to the Secretary-General of the United Nations.

(2) The General Assembly of the United Nations shall decide upon the steps, if any, to be taken in respect of such request.

Art. XVIII. The Secretary-General of the United Nations shall inform all States of the following particulars:

(a) Signatures, ratifications and accessions under article XIII and article XIV;

(b) The date of entry into force of the present Convention under article XV;

(c) Denunciations under article XVI;

(d) Notifications under article XVII.

Art. XIX.(1) The present Convention of which the Chinese, English, French, Russian and Spanish texts are equally authentic, shall be deposited in the archives of the United Nations.

(2) The Secretary General of the United Nations shall transmit certified copies of the present Convention to all States".

UN Yearbook 1973; *UN Chronicle Aug.–Sept., 1976*, p. 29.

APATRIDOS. An international term for persons without citizenship of any state; ▷ Stateless persons.

M.C. HERNANDEZ, *Los Apatridas*, La Habana, 1945.

APOLLO. The US governmental outer-space program (1961–73) envisaging, i.a., the construction of a space vehicle for three persons (Project Apollo), the eleventh variant of which first landed on the moon on July 20, 1969. The expedition was preceded by an eight-year experimental period of launching the following spacecraft: Mercury, Gemini, Ranger, Surveyor, Lunar Orbiter, and finally Apollo 1 which burned on the ground, on Jan. 22, 1967, together with three cosmonauts: V. Grissom, M. White, and R. Chaffee. The subsequent experimental space flights were carried out on Apollo 7–10, of which the Apollo 8–10 expeditions reached the moon's vicinity. The manned moon expeditions following the Apollo 11 flight were also carried out in space vehicles of the Apollo type. In July 1973, the Houston Center for space flights witnessed the beginning of a series of American–Soviet astronaut encounters which ended in a common flight, in mid-1975, of the American (Apollo) and Soviet (Soyuz) space vehicles.

Apollo–Soyuz. Test Project, Houston, 1975.

APOLLO–SOYUZ. The name of the first international space flight in history, organized by the governments of the USA and the USSR on July 17, 1975, when two space ships linked up: American Apollo under the command of astronauts T. Stafford and D. Sleyton, and Soviet Soyuz 19 under the command of A. Leonov and V. Kubashov. After a two-day link-up and the carrying out of joint experiments, the ships separated and returned to earth.

Apollo–Soyuz. Test Project, Houston, 1975.

APOSTOLATE. A subject of international cooperation. Organizations reg. with the UIA:

Apostleship of Prayer, f. 1849, Rome.
International Military Apostolate, f. 1967, Kornenburg, Austria.
International Movement of Apostolate in Middle and Upper Classes, f. 1963, Rome.
International Movement of Apostolate of Children, f. 1962, Paris.
World Catholic Federation for the Biblical Apostolate, f. 1969, Rome. Publ. *The Biblical Apostolate*.

Yearbook of International Organizations.

APOSTOLIC ADMINISTRATORS. An office in the Roman Catholic Church, defined by art. 248, para 2 and art. 312–318 of the Code of Canonical Law (*Codex Iuris Canonici*), managers of dioceses established as temporary administrative units as distinct from episcopal dioceses managed by resident bishops.

Annuario Pontificio 1979, p. 1459.

APOSTOLIC DELEGATE. A title of the head of the standing foreign committee of the Apostolic See, who does not represent the Pope in any specific state but who, nevertheless, performs diplomatic functions to a limited extent. A title distinct from Nuncio, introduced in this form in *Motu proprio* of Paul VI on June 24, 1969.

APOSTOLIC SEE OR HOLY SEE. *Latin: Sedes Apostolica.* An international term used in the Catholic Church to denote its seat in Vatican City; the supreme authority of the pope in the whole Church with all of its executive institutions (Roman Curia); a separate subject of international law, inseparably connected with the Vatican. A.S. makes the supreme decisions on matters of faith, the Vatican state on internal and external political affairs of the Church.

APPEASEMENT. An international term for a policy of alleviating tension at any cost. Created before the World War II, giving origin to the ▷ Munich Agreement, 1938.

M. GILBERT, *The Roots of Appeasement*, London, 1966; D. ROBERTSON, *Guide to Modern Defense and Strategy*, Detroit, 1988.

APPROPRIATE TECHNOLOGY ▷ Technological progress.

AQABA. A gulf in the north-eastern arm of the Red Sea, also the name (Al 'Aqabah) of the only seaport of Jordan and site where Israel, after the 1949 ceasefire, built its seaport Eilat; the subject of Israel–Arabian dispute since 1948 when Egypt cut off the access of Israeli merchant ships and navy to the Aqaba Gulf by closing the Tiran Strait and, simul-

taneously, the Suez Canal. Twice, in Nov., 1956 and June 1967, Israeli armed forces seized the Arabian coast up to ▷ Sharm-al-Sheik, occupying the Arabian territory and closing the Aqaba Gulf to Arabian merchant ships. According to the opinion submitted to the UN General Assembly by the UN Secretary-General, Dag Hammarskjöld, both the Aqaba Gulf and Tiran Strait had been always an universally recognized sea line, accessible to the shipping of all states. This has been also indirectly confirmed by art. 16 of the 1958 Geneva Convention on ▷ Territorial Sea in its section 4 on the ▷ Straits. In preliminary negotiations, led by a representative of the UN, Egypt and Jordan expressed their readiness to recognize Israel's right to free navigation in the Aqaba Gulf and Tiran Strait provided that Israel's armed forces would be withdrawn from the territories occupied on June 5, 1967. ▷ Camp David Agreement, 1978.

L.M. BLOOMFIELD, *Egypt, Israel and the Gulf of Akaba in International Law*, London, 1957; B. SELAK, "A consideration of the legal status of the Gulf of Akaba", in: *American Journal of International Law*, Vol. 52, 1958; A. MELAMID, "Legal status of the Gulf of Akaba", in: *American Journal of International Law*, Vol. 53, 1959.

AQSA. Al-Aqsa Mosque in Jerusalem, a holy place for Moslems, situated in the Old City, on the hill of Moria, the subject of Arabian–Israeli dispute since 1967. On Apr. 11, 1982 an Israeli soldier in uniform burst into the square in front of the Al-Aqsa Mosque and opened fire with a rifle on a crowd of Moslem worshippers. That incident and the violent disturbances that followed it led to a call by Morocco and Iraq for a meeting of the Security Council. Israel condemned the incident in the Mosque, attributing it to the deranged actions of one man. On Apr. 20, 1982 a draft resolution, presented by Jordan, Iraq, Morocco and Uganda, expressed its deep concern over the criminal act of shooting worshippers and affirmed once more that the Geneva Convention relative to the Protection of Civilian Persons in Time of War, 1949, was applicable to all territories occupied by Israel since 1967, including Jerusalem. The vote was 14 in favor (China, France, Guyana, Ireland, Japan, Jordan, Panama, Poland, Spain, Togo, Uganda, the USSR, the United Kingdom, Zaïre) to one against (the United States) with no abstentions. Because of the veto by the United States, the draft resolution was not adopted.

UN Chronicle, June 1982, p. 25.

ARAB BANK FOR ECONOMIC DEVELOPMENT IN AFRICA. Banque arabe pour le développement économique, BADED, est. by an Agreement, signed in Cairo on Feb. 18, 1974, between the governments of 18 Arab States (Algeria, Bahrain, Egypt, Iraq, Jordan, Kuwait, Lebanon, Libya, Mauritania, Morocco, Oman, Palestine, Qatar, Saudi Arabia, Sudan, Syria, Tunisia and the United Arab Emirates); came into force on Sept. 16, 1974. Headquarters: Khartoum.

The Europa Year Book 1984. A World Survey, Vol. I, pp. 97–98, London, 1984.

ARAB CONFERENCES, 1944–84. The first solidarity conferences of the heads of the Arab states were held during World War II in reaction to Great Britain's policy of preparing the formation of the State of Israel by granting to the Jewish Agency in 1942 unlimited rights to settle and purchase property in Palestine. In Aug., 1943 the chiefs of state of the governments of Egypt and Iraq resolved to create the ▷ League of Arab States. In 1944, as a result of diplomatic preparations, from 25 Sept. to 7 Oct. in Alexandria, the first meeting was held of

the heads of the governments of Egypt, Iraq, Lebanon, Saudi Arabia, Transjordan, and Yemen, who drafted and signed a Protocol which formed the organizational Committee of the League, composed of the representatives of the above states at the ministerial level and also a Palestinian observer. This Committee, meeting in Cairo, ended its work on the Pact of the League, Mar. 3, 1945, following which, Mar. 22, 1945, the heads of the above states signed the Pact there.

1950 – In Cairo, on June 17, the Heads of State of Egypt, Lebanon, Saudi Arabia, Syria, and Yemen signed a Defensive Pact, which was joined on Feb. 2, 1951 by Iraq and on Feb. 16, 1952 by Jordan (expanded in 1956).
1956 – In Cairo, on Mar. 6–12, the Heads of State of Egypt, Saudi Arabia, and Syria deliberated on the situation created by the intensification of the war in Algeria by France and an increase in French supplies of arms for Israel. Resolutions were passed which aimed at extending to other states treaties on immediate mutual assistance in the event of armed attack by Israel, concluded Oct. 20, 1955 by Egypt and Syria and Oct. 27, 1955 by Egypt and Saudi Arabia. As a result of diplomatic moves Syria on Apr. 21, 1956 signed a defensive treaty with Jordan and Apr. 21, 1956 Yemen with Egypt and Saudi Arabia. Due to the armed conflict of Great Britain, France and Israel with Egypt in Oct., 1956 in connection with the Suez Canal, a conference of the Heads of State of the members of the Defensive pact of 1950 was held Nov. 6 15, 1956 which resolved to expand it. In its new form, signed Nov. 15, 1956, the Pact of Collective Security introduced automatic mutual assistance in case of attack by Great Britain, France or Israel and created a permanent Military Committee.
1957 – In Cairo, on Feb. 25–28, a meeting of the Heads of State of Egypt, Jordan, Saudi Arabia, and Syria set the Arab conditions for ending the Suez conflict.
1958 – In Tangiers, on Apr. 28–30, a conference of the Heads of State of the Maghreb countries on assistance for Algeria in her war with France. Then June 17–20 a conference of the same states was held in Tunis, which resolved to create a permanent secretariat of the Maghreb.
1961 – In Rabat, on Mar. 1, a meeting of the Heads of Government of the Maghreb states on the question of Algerian–French negotiations.
1963 – In Cairo, on Apr. 16, a meeting of the Heads of Government of Egypt, Iraq, and Syria and the proclamation of the federation of these states as the United Arab Republic.
1964 – In Cairo, Jan. 13–16, on the initiative of the UAR the First Conference of the Heads of State and Governments of the members of the Arab League; it was resolved to undertake the planned resolution of inter-Arab conflicts and adopt common principles of struggle with imperialism and the aggressive policies of Israel. The Second Conference at the summit was held in the same year, Sept. 5–11, in Alexandria; the main subjects: the Palestine question, joint military co-operation of the armies of the Arab states as part of the Pact of Collective Security, the construction of dams on the river Yarmuk in Jordan.
1965 – In Casablanca, the Third Conference at the summit, on Sept. 17, with the absence of Tunisia; drafted and adopted as an annex to the Charter of the League of Arab States was a Pact of Solidarity, which in art. 6 defined the principles of the relations between the member states.
1966 – In Cairo, the Fourth Conference at the summit, Mar. 14–17, revealed an internal crisis within the League and no concrete decisions were made.
1967 – In Khartoum, Aug. 29–Sept. 2, resolved "not to recognize the state of Israel and not to interfere in the question of the Palestinians".
1969 – In Rabat, the Fifteenth Conference at the summit, Dec. 21–23, with the participation of all 14 member countries of the League and a representative of the Palestine Liberation Organization continued to reveal the existence of significant differences on the question of the conflict with Israel and on the matter of a design for a united Palestine state to be formed from the occupied territory of Jordan, from the territory of Israel and Gaza (supporters: Algeria, Iraq, Kuwait, Morocco, Tunisia, and Saudi Arabia; opponents:

Egypt, Jordan, Libya, Sudan). On the last day the meeting was boycotted by the delegates of Iraq, Syria, and South Yemen, and, as a result, for the first time no final joint statement was announced. In the same year, a meeting was held in Tripoli on Dec. 26, of the heads of government of Egypt, Libya, and Sudan with the task of preparing a federation of those countries, which was declared in the Tripoli Charter signed on that day.

1970 – A conference of the Heads of Government of Libya, Sudan and Egypt in Cairo, Nov. 4–8, which ended with a proclamation of the Arab Federation of those three states. On Nov. 27, Syria joined the Federation.

1971 – A conference on the Jordan–Palestine crisis, Apr. 10–15, in Cairo; a meeting of the Heads of State of Egypt, Libya, Syria, Yemen, and South Yemen, July 30, in Tripoli on the same question.

1972 – A conference of the Heads of Government of Egypt, Lybia, and Syria in Tobruk, Bengazhi, and Tripoli on the question of the structure of the Arab Federation.

1973 – A conference in Benghazi of the foreign ministers of 28 Moslem states (15 Arabian, 8 African, and 5 Asiatic) on the question of protection of oppressed Moslems in Israel and in the Philippines; and a conference, Aug. 23–24, in Agadir of the leaders of Algeria, Morocco, and Mauritania on the question of the so-called Spanish Sahara. In the fall, Nov. 26–28, an Algerian summit conference was held with the participation of 10 Presidents (Algeria, Egypt, Iraq, Lebanon, Mauritania, Sudan, Syria, Tunisia, Yemen and South Yemen), 4 emirs (Bahrain, Kuwait, Qatar, and the United Arab Emirates), 2 kings (Morocco and Saudi Arabia), 1 sultan (Oman), and the leader of the Palestinian Resistance Movement. Not participating was the king of Jordan, which was represented at the conference by the chairman of the king's cabinet. A summit conference was held in Cairo, Dec. 15–16, 1973.

1974 – The Seventh Session of the Council of the League of Arab States at the summit in Rabat recognized the Palestine Liberation Organization as the sole representative of the Palestine nation.

1975 – A summit conference scheduled to take place in Mogadir, June 20, was not held due to disputes connected with the civil war in Lebanon.

1976 – A conference of the governors of the Arab central banks in Baghdad, Feb. 20–22, created the Arab Monetary Fund to begin operations in Apr. 1977.

1977 – An extraordinary session of the League of Arab States, Nov. 12–14, in Tunis.

1978 – A boycott of a regular session of the Council of the League in Cairo, Mar. 27–29, by Algeria, Iraq, Libya, Syria, and South Yemen due to the policy of Egypt. The Camp David agreement of Egypt with Israel resulted in the conference of the Council of the League of Nov. 2–5 in Baghdad being held without Egypt.

1979 – A Conference of the Council of the League on the question of Egypt's signing of a peace treaty with Israel. It was resolved to withdraw all of the institutions of the League from Cairo.

1980 – Conferences of the Council of the League on the question of Egypt–Libya and Israel–Lebanon conflicts.

1981 – In Feb.–June economic summit meeting of the Gulf Co-operation Council. In Aug. in Aden the Tripartite summit of South Yemen, Libya and Ethiopia. Signature of tripartite treaty of friendship and co-operation. In Nov. Arab League summit meeting.

1982 – In May–July the Gulf Co-operation Council initiative to unify Arab position in Iran–Iraq conflict. In Sept. the Arab League summit meeting in Fez and the Fez Declaration.

1983 – In Feb.–Oct. meetings of the Gulf Co-operation Council on Iran–Iraq war, Israeli–Lebanon conflict and the factional strife within the PLO. In Nov. summit meeting in Doha, Qatar.

1984 – In Nov. summit meeting in Kuwait of the Gulf Co-operation Council.

KEESING's *Contemporary Archive*, 1944–85.

ARAB EAST, THE. An international term for the territory of 13 Arab countries (Bahrain, Egypt, Iraq, Jordan, Kuwait, Lebanon, North Yemen, Oman, Qatar, Saudi Arabia, Syria, South Yemen and the United Arab Emirates), divided by Israel. The territory had in 1988 a population of over 110

million with an absolute majority speaking a common language (Arabic), a common religion (Islam), and half of the world's proven oil reserves.

A Survey of the Arab East, in: *The Economist*, February 6–12, 1988.

ARAB ECONOMIC UNITY. An Arab states integration convention, prepared 1957–62 at the Arab League's suggestion, signed in 1962 by Egypt, Jordan, Kuwait, Morocco and Syria, 1963 by Iraq and Yemen, 1968 by Sudan. Its executive body is the Council of the Arab Economic Unity, from 1965 acting towards forming the ▷ Arab States Common Market.

ARAB FEDERATIONS. The international federations of Arab countries, supported by the Pan–Arabic movement since the end of the fifties in the following forms:

The Union of Egypt with Syria, est. Feb. 1, 1958 under the name ▷ United Arab Republic (UAR); Sept. 28, 1961, as the result of a military coup d'état, Syria resigned from the Union.

The Iraqi–Jordanian Federation, proclaimed Feb. 14, 1958 by the Hachemite monarchs of both states under the name Arab Federal State; dissolved July 1958 by the revolution in Iraq, which overthrew the monarchy and proclaimed a republic. The Conference of United Arab States, est. Mar. 8, 1958 as a step towards an agreement between the UAR and Yemen; dissolved Dec. 25, 1961 after the earlier (Sept. 28, 1961) resignation of Syria from the UAR. The official reason for this was the publication of an anti-socialist poem 1961, criticizing UAR policy, whose author was the ruler of Yemen, imam Ahmad ibn Yahya. The Federation of Egypt, Syria and Iraq, whose establishment was agreed on Apr. 17, 1963 in a treaty stating the principles of conducting a general referendum on this matter; was not put into effect because of an internal crisis in Syria. The Presidential Union of Egypt (UAR) with Iraq, existed in the form of the Egyptian–Iraqi Presidential Council May 25, 1964–July 1, 1968, when an administration opposed to the Union came into power in Iraq, following a coup d'état. The Arab Federation of Egypt, Libya, Sudan and Syria, initiated Dec. 26, 1969 when heads of the three first states (without Syria) signed the Tripoli Charter, which established the principles of close co-operation in the political, military and economic fields, confirmed Nov. 8, 1970 by these states and Nov. 27, 1970 by the government of Syria. Formally the Federation was created, in the absence of the head of state of Sudan, by Egypt, Libya and Syria, Apr. 17, 1971 through the Benghazi Treaty. Sudan announced that it would join at a later date.

The Union of Egypt and Libya, proclaimed Aug. 2, 1972 by the heads of these states (after consultations in Tobruk and Benghazi) as a "complete union" under the name United Arab Republic. It was to be put into effect in stages until Sept. 1, 1973, when a plebiscite was to decide about the unification. Because of differing opinions as to the political system of the new state, the plebiscite was not carried through.

The Union of Libya with Tunisia, proclaimed Jan. 12, 1974 by presidents Qadhafi and Bourguiba, under the name Arab Islamic Republic. It was not put into effect because of internal opposition in Tunisia.

Union of Political Leadership of Egypt, Sudan and Syria was proclaimed Feb. 28, 1977 in Khartoum; was not put in effect because of Egypt–Israel rapprochement 1978/79.

ARAB FUND FOR ECONOMIC AND SOCIAL DEVELOPMENT, AFSED. Est. in 1968 by the Economic Council of the Arab League; in operation since 1973. Members: Algeria, Bahrain, Djibouti, Egypt, Iraq, Jordan, Kuwait, Lebanon, Libya, Mauritania, Morocco, Oman, PLO, Qatar, Saudi Arabia, Somalia, Sudan, Syria, Tunisia, the United Arab Emirates, the Yemen Arab Republic, the Yemen People's Democratic Republic.

The Europa Year Book 1984. A World Survey, Vol. I, p. 99, London, 1984.

ARAB GULF PROGRAM FOR THE UNDP. ▷ AGFUND.

ARAB HIGHER POSTAL INSTITUTE FOR PROFESSIONAL TRAINING. The Institution est. 1956, Baghdad, by the ▷ Arab Postal Union.

ARABIA. Jazirat al Arab = Island of the Arabs or Arabian peninsula in SW Asia, bounded on the West by the Gulf of Aqaba and the Red Sea, on the south by the Gulf of Aden and the Arabian Sea, on the east by the Gulf of Oman and the Persian Gulf, on the north by Iraq and Jordan. Area: 2,590,000 sq. km. Est. pop. 17,000,000 (1970). Rich in oil deposits. Politically divided into eight states: Bahrain, Kuwait, Oman, Qatar, Saudi Arabia, Southern Yemen, the United Arab Emirates and Yemen. Sphere of British influence during the 19th and 20th centuries up to the withdrawal of British military forces from the Persian Gulf and Red Sea in the 1960s.

G. ANTONIUS, *The Arab Awakening*, London, 1938; E. ROSSI, *Documenti sul Origine e gli Sviluppi della Questione Araba* (1875–1944), Roma, 1944; J.J. BERRELY, *La Péninsule arabique*, Paris, 1959; J.B. KELLY, *Arabia, the Gulf and the West*, London, 1980; T. NIBLOCK (ed.), *Social and Economic Development in the Arab Gulf*, London, 1980; M.A. HAMEED, *Arabia Imperiled: The Security Implications of the Arab Gulf States*, London, 1986.

ARABIAN SEA. The NW section of the India Ocean, bounded by India, Pakistan, Iran, the Arabian peninsula and the Horn of Africa. International trade route.

ARABIC LANGUAGE. The Arab Member States of the UN since 1978 print the main UN documents in Arabic. The Arabic language is spoken by over 100,000,000 people in Arab States.

UN Chronicle, Jan. 1978, pp. 96–97.

"ARABIC" THE, name of British passenger steamship sunk with passengers (among them US citizens) Aug. 19, 1915 near Ireland by a German submarine; subject of dispute between the governments of USA and the German Reich, as also the sinking of the ▷ *Ancona* and the ▷ *Lusitania*.

ARAB INTEGRATION. Initiated by art. 2 of the Arab League Pact, Mar. 22, 1945, spans economic, financial, transport and communications spheres. Questions of Arab integration were dealt with from June, 1950 by the League's Economic Council which provided an Agreement on Economic Unity of the Arab States signed June 3, 1957, in force from Apr. 30, 1964 on ratification by first four states: Kuwait – Sept. 9, 1962; Egypt – May 25, 1963; Iraq – Jan. 30, 1964; and Syria – Feb. 22, 1964. Ratified by Jordan, June 1, 1964. In 1965, Economic Council decision to set up Arab Common Market to ensure, in keeping with the Agreement, free traffic in persons, articles, services and capital. Publ. by the Centre of Economic, Financial and Social Studies and Documentation in Beirut is a monthly on current affairs of Arab integration: *L'economie et les finances de Pays Arabes*.

ARAB INTERGOVERNMENTAL ORGANIZATIONS. Reg. with the UIA:

Arab Air Carriers Organization, f. 1969, Beirut.
Arab Bank for Economic Development in Africa, f. 1974, Khartoum.
Arab Organization for Administrative Sciences, f. 1969, Cairo.
Arab Organization for Standardization and Metrology, f. 1965, Cairo.
Arab Postal Union, f. 1954, Amman.
Arab States Broadcasting Union, f. 1969, Cairo.

Arab Tourism Union, f. 1954, Cairo.
Civil Aviation Council of Arab States, f. 1967, Cairo.
Council of Arab Economic Unity, f. 1957, Cairo.
Federation of Arab Republics, est. 1971, Heliopolis, Egypt.
League of Arab States, f. 1945, Cairo.
Organization of Arab Petroleum Exporting Countries, OAPEC, f. 1968, Kuwait.

Yearbook of International Organizations.

ARAB–ISRAELI WARS. Armed conflicts between Arab states and Israel:
Dec., 1947–July, 1949, the first war after the UN decision on Palestine partition on Nov. 29, 1948.
The June, 1967 war, called the Six-Day War.
The October 1973 war, called the Yom Kippur War.

SIPRI *World Armaments and Disarmament Yearbook,* 1968, pp. 61–65, 135, 414–428; H. WAGNER, *Der Arabisch–Israelische Konflikt im Völkerrecht,* Berlin, 1971; *World Politics and the Arab–Israeli Conflict,* Oxford, 1979.

ARAB LEAGUE. ▷ League of Arab States.

ARAB MARITIME PETROLEUM TRANSPORT COMPANY. Est. 1977 in Kuwait by the Organization of Arab Petroleum Exporting Countries OAPEC, with the task of building a tanker fleet that would carry export oil of OAPEC members in amounts that by 1985 were to exceed 40% of total export.

ARAB MILITARY ASSISTANCE. Formally exists in the framework of the ▷ League of Arab States, in its subsidiary bodies: the Arab Defense Council, f. 1959, and the Unified Arab Command, f. 1964.

ARAB MONETARY FUND. Est. 1975 by the Arabic central banks on the initiative of the Arab League and OAPEC with the task of supporting in Arabic countries the development of industry not connected with the extraction and refining of petroleum. The agreement entered into force Feb. 2, 1977. Members: Algeria, Bahrain, Egypt, Iraq, Jordan, Kuwait, Lebanon, Libya, Mauritania, Morocco, Oman, the PLO, Qatar, Saudi Arabia, Somalia, Sudan, Syria, Tunisia, the United Arab Emirates, the Yemen Arab Republic, the Yemen People's Democratic Republic.

The Europa Year Book 1984. A World Survey, Vol. I, pp. 100–101, London, 1984.

ARAB, OCCUPIED TERRITORIES. An international term, used in the UN system. Areas occupied since 1967 by Israel. They include the ▷ West Bank ▷ Gaza Strip ▷ Golan Heights and the Eastern portion of ▷ Jerusalem.

UN Chronicle, Oct. 1983, pp. 3–11.

ARAB POSTAL UNION. F. 1954, Cairo, under the aegis of League of Arab States. Members: Postal administration of Algeria, Bahrain, Egypt, Iraq, Jordan, Kuwait, Lebanon, Libya, Mauritania, Morocco, Oman, Palestine, Qatar, Saudi Arabia, Somalia, Sudan, Tunis, the UAE, the Yemen Dem. Rep., and the Yemen Rep. Publ. *News of the UPU.* Est. 1956 in Baghdad the Arab Higher Postal Institute for Professional Training.

ARAB STATES INDUSTRIAL DEVELOPMENT CENTRE. F. 1968, Cairo. An intergovernmental institution of Algeria, Arab Emirates, Bahrain, Egypt, Iraq, Jordan, Kuwait, Lebanon, Libya, Morocco, Oman, Qatar, Saudi Arabia, Sudan, Syria, Tunis, the Yemen Dem. Rep., the Yemen Rep. Associated Members: Abu Dhabi, Al Sharjah, Dubai, Ras Al-Khaima. Publ. *Bulletin* (Arabic and French). Reg. with the UIA.

Yearbook of International Organizations.

ARAB STATES IN THE UN. In 1945 the Arabic states in the UN were: Egypt, Iraq, Lebanon, Saudi Arabia and Syria; in 1947 – Yemen. Those states had formed earlier, in 1945, the Arab League, which obtained the right of permanent presence in the UN and in UN specialized agencies. In 1953 Jordan and Libya were admitted to the UN; in 1956 – Morocco, Tunisia, Sudan; in 1962 – Algeria; in 1963 – Kuwait; in 1967 – South Yemen; in 1972 – Bahrain, Oman, Qatar and the United Arab Emirates; and thus the number of Arabic states in the UN reached 18. The main problem of UN debates and mediations is the conflict of Arab states with Israel. ▷ Arab–Israeli wars.

ARAB UNIONS ▷ Arab Federations.

ARBITRAL AWARDS. A subject of international conventions:
Convention for the Execution of Foreign Arbitral Awards, signed in Geneva, Sept. 26, 1927; entered into force on July 25, 1929; ratified by Austria, Belgium, Czechoslovakia, Denmark, Estonia, Finland, France, Germany, Greece, India, Ireland, Israel, Italy, Japan, Luxembourg, Malta, Mauritius, the Netherlands, New Zealand, Portugal, Romania, Spain, Sweden, Thailand, the UK and Yugoslavia. The Treaty was also signed but not ratified by Bolivia, Nicaragua, Peru, the Rep. of Korea, Uganda. Convention on the Recognition and Enforcement of Foreign Arbitral Awards held at New York, June 10, 1958, entered into force on June 7, 1959. Ratified by Austria, Botswana, Bulgaria, Byelorussian SSR, the Central African Republic, Ceylon, Czechoslovakia, Ecuador, Egypt, the FRG, Finland, France, Ghana, Greece, Hungary, India, Israel, Italy, Japan, the Khmer Rep., Madagascar, Mexico, Morocco, the Netherlands, Niger, Nigeria, Norway, the Philippines, Poland, Romania, Sweden, Switzerland, Syria, Tanzania, Thailand, Trinidad and Tobago, Tunisia, Ukrainian SSR, the USSR and the USA. The Treaty was also signed but not ratified by Argentina, Belgium, Costa Rica, El Salvador, Jordan, Luxembourg, Monaco and Pakistan.

ARBITRATION. An institution of international law, the subject of multilateral conventions. Arbitration and conciliatory courts were called as early as in ancient and medieval times; they expanded in the 19th century to become international institutions, starting with the Peace Conferences in The Hague in 1899 and 1907, which prepared conventions on peaceful settlement of international disputes. According to these Conventions:

"The aim of international arbitration is to resolve disputes between the States by judges of their choice and on the basis of the observance of law; from submitting to arbitration the obligation ensues to submit in good faith to the decision."

The earlier provisions on international arbitration are contained in art. 12 of the Final Act of the 1885 Berlin Conference and in arts. 116–118 of the Algeciras General Act. Also the II Hague Conference, 1907, introduced the principles of international arbitration into the Convention on the Pacific Settlement of International Disputes recommending that the member states conclude arbitration treaties "either due to the already existing disputes, or for disputes that may arise" (art. 39). Both Conventions established the Permanent Court of Arbitration with its seat in The Hague, where in the Bureau of the Court all arbitration pacts are registered. In the 19th and 20th centuries ad hoc Courts of Arbitration were also set up by force of multi- or bilateral agreements. The Covenant of the League of Nations, adopted (in 1919) after World War I, provided in art. 12 that, should any dispute arise between the members of the League, "they will submit the matter either to arbitration or judicial settlement …". It was also on the initiative of the LN that the Geneva Protocol (on arbitration clauses) of Oct. 24, 1923 was adopted; it never entered into force as only one State had ratified it. On Sept. 26, 1928, the LN Assembly adopted a resolution recommending arbitration agreements according to the Geneva General Act on the Pacific Settlement of International Disputes (enclosed to the resolution). After World War II the UN Charter, in arts. 2, 14, 33 and 36, directly or indirectly, recommended the peaceful settlement of disputes by negotiation, mediation and arbitration. Since 1948, the United Nations has published *Recueil des Sentences Arbitrales.* One of the precedent cases of arbitration was the so-called ▷ Alabama Claims case, resolved by the Court of Arbitration in Washington, composed of representatives of the United States and Great Britain, and also of Switzerland, Brazil and Italy, which laid down the so-called Washington Rules on the rights and duties of neutral states at sea in wartime in the American region.
On Aug. 2, 1952, the UN International Law Commission adopted a draft Arbitration Code. Having acquainted itself with the opinions submitted by governments, the Commission worked out in 1958 draft rules of arbitration proceedings. On Nov. 4, 1958, the UN General Assembly instructed the Commission to work out a draft treaty on international arbitration, based on those rules. Regional arbitration obligations integrated the treaty of Bogota, 1948, and the statute of the ▷ Organization of African Unity.
A chronological survey of political international arbitrations, worked out by A.N. Stuyt, contains 231 arbitration cases examined in 1749–1899, 177 in 1900–39, and 21 in 1950–71. The oldest form of non-political arbitration is maritime arbitration, a section of commercial arbitration, organized by Lloyd's of London, operating in conformity with English Law which was accepted in the majority of the maritime traffic documents by subscribing to a relevant clause. In the socialist states there were national maritime arbitration courts, such as the Maritime Arbitration Commission (Morskaya Arbitralnaya Komisya) set up in 1930 at the All-Union Commercial Chamber of the USSR; or the Council of Arbitrators established in 1949 at the Polish Chamber of Foreign Trade; there was also an International Arbitration Court for Maritime and Inland Navigation in Gdynia, which was set up in the pursuance of the agreement between the Polish, Czechoslovakian and East German Chambers of Foreign Trade in 1959. The chairmen of the national Chambers of Commerce exercise in turn the chairmanship of the Court for a term of one year. Commercial arbitration is regulated by many international treaties applied to settling disputes arising from the interpretation of contracts concluded by physical or legal persons of two or more states. On the initiative of the LN, a Protocol on Arbitration Clauses was signed at Geneva (Sept. 24, 1923), which provided that they may be included by the contracting parties into their contracts under the condition that such contracts are recognized by the law of their home states as commercial obligations. After World War II, the ECOSOC initiated in 1958 a UN Conference on International Commercial Arbitration, which adopted two conventions:

1. The Convention on the Recognition and Enforcement of Foreign Arbitral Awards, signed on July 10, 1958 in New York. Participants: Austria, Bulgaria, Byelorussian SSR, Cambodia, the Central African Republic, Ceylon, Czechoslovakia, Ecuador, Finland, France, the Federal Republic of Germany, Hungary, India, Israel, Japan, Malagasy Republic, Romania, Sweden, Tanganyika, Tanzania, Thailand, Ukrainian SSR, the United Arab Republic, the USSR.
2. The Convention on International Commercial Arbitration, signed on Apr. 21, 1961 at Geneva.

In 1962 the socialist countries signed the Convention on the General Delivery Terms of Goods between the organizations of CMEA states, and other documents regulating specific domains of economic, scientific and technical co-operation between those states.

The member states of the CMEA signed on May 26, 1972 in Moscow the Convention on the Arbitral Settlement of Disputes Resulting from the Economic, Scientific and Technical Co-operation. This Convention initiated a process of unification of economic arbitration in the member states of the CMEA with respect to the arbitration courts of the respective national Chambers of Foreign Trade. The Complex Program adopted at the XXV Session of the CMEA resolved "to extend the rights of the national arbitration organs for foreign trade by placing under their jurisdiction civil law disputes arising out of the carrying out of various forms of economic, scientific and technical co-operation between the member states of the CMEA; to extend the exchange of information (including the exchange of arbitral decisions) between the arbitration organs of the member states of the CMEA; to bring and unify the settling of questions procedure in the national arbitration organs at the chambers of commerce of the CMEA member states."

Since 1957, an Anglo-French collection of European and American (of the NATO states) arbitration laws appeared in Paris under the title *Arbitrage International Commercial*. In the USA, the American Arbitration Association publishes, since 1927, the *Yearbook of Commercial Arbitration*.

In Vienna on June 21, 1985, the UN Commission on International Trade Law (UNCITRAL) adopted a model law on international commercial arbitration. The highlights of the model law:

● Provides a liberal framework that offers disputing parties a broad scope for agreeing on the rules of procedure – allowing them, for example, to refer in their contracts to the standard procedures suitable for their trade or branch of industry. Where such agreement is lacking, it gives wide discretion to the arbitrators regarding the conduct of the proceeding – including rules for taking evidence. This effectively excludes the use of inappropriate local rules of a court or arbitral procedure and it limits the extent of any intervention of local courts where the arbitral proceedings are taking place;
● Has only a few mandatory rules, intended to ensure fairness and equal treatment of the disputing parties, and provide freedom and discretion for arbitration;
● Contains supplementary provisions to assist in arbitration where parties concerned have not agreed on procedural rules;
● Has provisions on recognition and enforcement of arbitral awards which apply irrespective of the country where the award was made. Whereas the 1958 New York Convention dealt only with foreign awards, the new model law no longer makes such a territorial distinction, instead drawing a new line on more substantive grounds determined by whether an arbitration is international or not.

A. LAPRADELLE, N. POLITIS, *Recueil des Arbitrages internationaux*, Vol. I, pour l'années 1798–1855, Paris, 1905; Vol. II, pour l'années 1856–1872, Paris, 1924; R.J.N. BAKER, *The Geneva Protocol for the Pacific Settlement of Disputes*, London, 1925; S. DOTREMONT, *L'arbitrage internationale et la Conseil de la SdN*, Genève, 1929; M. FARAGGI, *L'Acte Général de l'Arbitrage*, Paris, 1935; A.M. STUYT, *Survey of International Arbitrations, 1794–1939*, London, 1939; UN Systematic Survey of Treaties for the Pacific Settlement of International *Arbitrations Disputes*, 1928–48, Vol. 3, New York, 1949; K.S. CARLSTON, "World court opinion", in: *Interna-*

tional Arbitration Journal, No. 5, 1951, *Boletin de las NU*, No. 5, 1952, pp. 322–325; "L'heure de conciliation comme mode de réglement pacifique des litiges", in: *European Yearbook, 1957*; M.J. SIERRA, *Derecho International Público*, México, DF, 1963, pp. 439–449; I.A. KOROVIN, *Derecho Internacional Público*, México, DF, 1963, pp. 384–388; *UN Survey of Treaty Provisions for the Pacific Settlement of International Disputes 1949–62*, Vol. 5, New York, 1966; O.R. YOUNG, *The Intermediaries: Third Parties in International Crisis*, Princeton, 1967; ONU, *La Comisión de Derecho Internacional y su obra*, New York, 1967, pp. 41–44 and 81–90; A.M. ALEXANDER, *Survey of International Arbitrations, 1794–1970*, Leiden, 1972; *UN Chronicle*, 1985, No 5, p. 57; R.L. BLEDSOE, B.A. BOCZEK, *The International Law Dictionary*, Oxford, 1987.

ARBITRATION COURT OF UPPER SILESIA – TRIBUNAL D'ARBITRAGE POUR LA HAUTE SILESIE, 1923–1937.
A Court formed under the terms of the ▷ Upper Silesia Convention of May 15, 1922; headquarters, Beuthen–Bytom for 15 years. Active from June 23, 1923 till July 15, 1937 as an arbitrating organ for physical and legal persons within the Upper Silesia Convention with the aim of arbitrating private legal disputes such as may ensue from the application of the Convention; it also issued permits for crossing the border which were recognized by both sides. Established at the Court was the Conciliatory Commission for Citizenship composed of three justices: the chairman, appointed by the League of Nations Council (G. Kaeckenbeck, Belgium), a justice appointed by the Polish government (1923–33 J. Kalużniacki succeeded by B. Stelmachowski), a justice appointed by the Reich government (1923–33 H. Schneider; 1933–35 L. Herwegen succeeded by A. von Steinacker). A special feature of the Court in terms of international law was that it heard cases where private persons sued the state, though in practice these related mostly to property disputes between members of the German minority and the Polish state.

G. KAECKENBECK, *Sammlung von Entscheidungen des Schiedsgerichts für Oberschlesien, 1922–1937*, Berlin, 1937; G. KAECKENBECK, *The International Experiment of Upper Silesia*, London, 1942.

ARBITRATION LATIN AMERICAN TREATY – TRATADO DE ARBITRAJE OBLIGATORIO DE LOS ESTADOS LATINOAMERICANOS, 1902.
A Treaty on Obligatory Arbitration of Latin American States, 1902, signed on Jan. 29, 1902, in the capital of Mexico, during the Second International American Conference, by the governments of Argentina, Bolivia, the Dominican Republic, Guatemala, Mexico, Paraguay, Peru, Salvador and Uruguay. Referring to art. 26 of the Hague Convention of 1899 concerning peaceful resolution of international conflicts, the signatories assumed the obligation "to submit for resolution to mediators all disputes which exist or are likely to occur and can be solved in a diplomatic way". The Convention entered into force on Jan. 31, 1903, being ratified by 6 out of 9 signatories: Salvador on May 28, 1902, Guatemala on Aug. 2, 1902, Uruguay on Jan. 31, 1903, Mexico on Apr. 18, 1903, the Dominican Republic on Sept. 30, 1904 and Peru on Oct. 10, 1904. The Convention is deposited with Mexico.

Tratados y Convenciones Interamericanos de Paz, PAU, Washington DC, 1961, pp. 1–4.

ARBITRATION, PERMANENT COURT OF, LA COUR PERMANENTE D'ARBITRAGE.
A court est. on July 29, 1889 in The Hague, by art. 20–29 of the Convention for the Pacific Settlement of International Disputes and art. 41–50 of the revision of that Convention, Oct. 18, 1907. Members: governments of 72 states. Each state may designate 4 qualified persons for terms of 6 years as

members of the Court. The Court facilitates the solution of international differences by arbitration or conciliation or enquiry. Publ. *Annual Report*.

K.S. CARLSTON, *The Process of International Arbitration*, New York, 1946; J.P.A. FRANÇOIS, "La Cour Permanente d'Arbitrage, son origine, sa jurisprudence, son avenir", in: *Recueil des Cours de l'Académie de Droit International*, No. 87, 1955; L.L. SIMPSON, H. FOX, *International Arbitration: Law and Practice*, London, 1959.

ARBITRATION RULES OF UNCITRAL.
The UN Commission on International Trade Law on Apr. 28, 1976 approved a set of rules for optional use in ad hoc arbitration relating to international trade, as well as model arbitration clauses. The UNCITRAL Arbitration Rules, prepared by the UN Secretariat, comprised 41 articles in four sections. The UN General Assembly by Res. 31/98 on Dec. 15, 1976, adopted them by consensus.

"Recognizing the value of arbitration as a method of settling disputes arising in the context of international commercial relations,
Convinced that the establishment of rules for ad hoc arbitration that are acceptable in countries with different legal, social and economic systems would significantly contribute to the development of harmonious international economic relations.
(1) Recommends the use of the Arbitration Rules of the UNCITRAL in the settlement of disputes arising in the context of international commercial relations, particularly by reference to the Arbitration Rules in commercial contracts;
(2) Requests the Secretary-General to arrange for the widest possible distribution of the Arbitration Rules."

The UNCITRAL Arbitration Rules comprised 41 articles divided into four sections.

Section I, containing introductory rules, dealt with the scope of the application of the Rules, the delivery of notices and the calculation of periods of time. It also contained specific provisions concerning notice of arbitration and the representation and assistance of parties.

Section II concerned the composition and appointment of arbitral tribunals, which were to consist of one of three arbitrators, and contained provisions regarding challenging and replacement of arbitrators.

Section III dealt with arbitral proceedings: the presentation of evidence and oral arguments and the exchange of written pleadings. Included were rules concerning the place of arbitration, the languages to be used, statements of claim and of defense, pleas as to the jurisdiction of an arbitral tribunal, interim measures of protection, hearings, expert witnesses, default and the waiver of rules. The Rules would allow for the continuation of arbitral proceedings despite the failure of a party to take requisite actions within prescribed periods of time.

Section IV contained provisions concerning the award – its form, effect, interpretation and correction – and the costs of the arbitral proceedings. It further dealt with the question of the law applicable to the substance of the dispute: arbitrators were to apply the law designated by the parties. Any award or other decision was to be made in accordance with the terms of the contract in question.

Yearbook of the UN 1976, pp. 825–826.

ARC AND SÉNAS.
Natural sites of France, included in the ▷ World Heritage UNESCO List.

ARCHEOLOGY.
A subject of international co-operation. Organizations reg. with the UIA.

International Association for Classical Archeology, f. 1945, Rome. Publ. *Fasti Archaeologici* (annual).
International Institute for Ligurian Studies, f. 1947, Rome. Publ. *Revista de Estudios Ligures*.

International UNESCO Committee on Monuments, Artistic and Historical Sites and Archeological Excavations, f. 1946, Paris.
International Union of Prehistoric Sciences, f. 1932, Geneva.

G.E. DANIEL, *A Hundred Years of Archeology*, London, 1950; *Yearbook of International Organizations*; R. WHITEHOUSE, *Dictionary of Archeology*, London 1986; *UNESCO, Recent Archeological Discoveries in India*, Paris, 1986; *UNESCO, Recent Archeological Discoveries in Japan*, Paris, 1987.

ARCHERY. An Olympic sport since 1900, organized in the International Archery Federation (FITA), f. 1931, York, UK. Organizes World Championship Tournaments and Olympic Games. Recognized by the International Olympic Committee. Publ. *FITA Information*. Reg. with the UIA.

Yearbook of International Organizations.

ARCHIPELAGO. A subject of the ▷ Sea Law Convention, 1982 (Part IV Archipelagic States).

R.L. BLEDSOE, B.A. BOCZEK, *The International Law Dictionary*, Oxford, 1987.

ARCHISYST. An international information and research system on architecture, initiated in 1975 by the Twelfth International Congress of the Union of Architects. In Jan., 1976 the system became operative in Madrid under the sponsorship of the Union.

Yearbook of International Organizations.

ARCHITECTURE. A subject of international co-operation. Organizations reg. with the UIA:

Central American Union of Associations of Engineers and Architects, f. 1958, San Jose de Costa-Rica.
Commonwealth Association of Architects, f. 1963, London.
Commonwealth Board of Architectural Education, f. 1966, London.
International Council of the Architects of Historical Monuments, f. 1954, Brussels.
International Federation of Landscape Architects, f. 1948, Lisbon.
International Union of Architects, f. 1948, Paris, ECOSOC, UNESCO (A), WHO, ILO. Publ. *Bulletin*.
International Union of Women Architects, f. 1963, Paris.
Panamerican Federation of Architects Associations, f. 1920, Montevideo.

Yearbook of International Organizations; W. SANDERSON, *International Handbook of Contemporary Developments in Architecture*, New York 1981; C. ERDER, *Our Architectural Heritage From Consciousness to Conservation*, UNESCO, Paris, 1986.

ARCHIVES. A subject of international co-operation and agreements (Rome Convention signed Mar. 16, 1922). Organizations reg. with the UIA

International Council on Archives, ICA, f. 1948, Paris, under the auspices of UNESCO. Consultative status: UNESCO, ECOSOC. Publ. *Archivum* (annual).
International Federation of Film Archives, f. 1938, Paris. Publ. *International Index to Film Periodicals*.

Guide international des archives: Europe, Paris, 1934; *The National Archives of Latin America*, New York, 1945; E. POSNER, *American State Archives*, New York, 1964; *Yearbook of International Organizations*; L. BELL, B. FAYE, *La concepción de los Edificios de Archivos en países tropicales*, UNESCO, Paris, 1980 (also in French).

ARCHIVES OF THE UN. A UN Secretariat service, est. 1946 for the "storage of outdated UN documents, which are to be constantly available".

ARCOS LTD. All Russian Co-operative Society Limited, est. June 11, 1920 in London as a private firm with limited obligations in accordance with English legislation; with the purpose of expanding trade between the USSR and Great Britain. In 1927 subject of diplomatic conflict resulting from occupation of the ARCOS office by the British police. Since the establishment of diplomatic relations between the UK and the USSR in 1929, ARCOS continues to play the role of mediator between Soviet foreign trade centers and British private firms. In the USA a similar role is played by ▷ AMTORG Trading Corporation.

ARCTIC CIRCLE. An international geographical term for an imaginary circle 66°.30'N where both the sun during the winter solstice and the midnight sun can be seen.

ARCTIC INSTITUTE OF NORTH AMERICA, f. 1945, Calgary, Alberta. Publ. *Arctic, Information North*.

ARCTIC OCEAN. Also called the Frozen Ocean. The smallest ocean, 13,986,000 sq. km, centered around the North Pole, within the Arctic Circle; exchanges water with the Atlantic Ocean through the Greenland Sea. International research started 1926 with the Amundsen–Ellsworth flight over the Arctic basin.

ARCTIC, THE OR ARCTIC REGION. The northern polar region encompassing the Arctic Ocean with its islands (Wrangel, N. Siberia, Severnaya Zemlya, Franz Josef Land, Novaya Zemlya, Spitsbergen, Bear, Jan Mayen, Greenland and Arctic Archipelago), and the northern peripheries of North America, north-east Asia and Europe. Area: *c.* 26,500,000 sq. km of which *c.* 14,000,000 sq. km is occupied by seas. Pop.: about 50,000 residents (Eskimos, Lapps, Samoyeds, and Chukchies). The subject of several international disputes. between Denmark, Great Britain, Netherlands, Norway, Sweden, the USSR over Spitsbergen Archipelago, from 1912 to 1920; between Denmark and the USA, till 1916, over south-western Greenland; between Canada and the USA, from 1918 to 1925, over the Arctic Archipelago; between Canada, the USA and the USSR over Wrangel Island, from 1921 to 1924; between Norway and the USSR over Franz Josef Land, from 1920 to 1926; and between Denmark and Norway over eastern Greenland from 1921 to 1933. As for neighboring states, claims have been submitted to the following "polar sectors" running between meridians to the North Pole: Denmark to the sector between 10°E and 60°W; Finland to the sector between 31°E and 32°4'35"; Canada to the sector between 60°W and 141°W; Norway to the sector between 10°E and 32°4'35"; the USA to the sector between 141°W and 169°W; the USSR to the sector between 168°49'30"W and 32°4'35"E (which means that the claims of the USA and USSR overlap the same territory). The decision of the Permanent Court of International Justice in the case concerning the legal status of eastern Greenland of Apr. 5, 1933 (PCIJ Series A/B, No. 53), and the decision of the nine states concerning Spitsbergen (the Paris Treaty of 1920) settled the main disputes over this region. After World War II a new controversy was created by US military bases on the Arctic Archipelago and in north-western Greenland. In 1958, during the disarmament negotiations, the USSR proposed that international air control over the Arctic Regions be established; no agreement was achieved. In May 1973, the International Congress on Oil, Petroleum and Natural Gas took place at Le Havre, with the participation of the interested governments (i.e. Great Britain, France, Japan, the USA and USSR), technical and environmental experts, and representatives of the indigenous Eskimo population. Since 1953, the *Arctic Bibliography* appears yearly in the USA, and since 1948, a periodical, *Arctic*, has been published. Since July 1976, the USA and USSR conduct joint scientific research in the Arctic.

J.B. SCOTT, "Arctic Exploration and International Law", in: *American Journal of International Law*, 3/1909; A.B. DOBROWOLSKI, *Wyprawy Polarne*, Warsaw, 1925; L. SEGAL, *Conquest of the Arctic*, London, 1939; N.N. ZUBOV, *V tsentre Arktiki*, Moscow, 1948; R. DOLLOT, "Le Droit International des espaces polaires", in: *Recueil des Cours de l'Académie de Droit International*, No. 75, 1949; T. ARMSTRONG, *The Northern Sea Route: Soviet Exploration of the North East Passage*, London, 1952; G. KIMBLE, D. GOOD, *Geography of the Northlands*, New York, 1955; O. SVARLIEN, "The legal aspect of the Arctic", in: *American Journal of International Law*, July 1958; R.D. HAYTON, "Polar problems and International Law", in: *American Journal of International Law*, 52/1958; F.T. FISHER, ed. *Man living in the Arctic*, New York, 1961; J.E. SATER, *The Arctic Basin*, London, 1963; A.D. PHARAND, "Innocent passage in the Arctic", in: *Canadian Yearbook of International Law*, 1968; B. LOPEZ, *Arctic Dreams, Imagination and Desire in Northern Landscape*, New York, 1987.

ARE. An international area unit = 100 square meters, or approx. 119.60 square yards.

ARECIBO. A town in Puerto Rico, where since Nov. 1974 the largest radiotelescope in the world has been operating, constructed by the American organization ▷ NASA, with the task of transmitting specific signals to the Universe, informing other civilizations assuming that they exist, of life on earth.

ARFA. ▷ NATO.

ARGENTINA. Member of the UN. Republic of Argentina, Republica Argentina. State in South America on the Atlantic Ocean. Area: 2,808,602 sq. km. Pop., 1986 estimate: 31,030,000 (1960 census – 20,009,000. Capital: Buenos Aires (to be moved to Viedma-Carmen by 1995); 1980 census 2,908,001, metropolitan area 6,802,222. GNP per capita, 1985, US $2,350. Bordering on Chile, Bolivia, Paraguay, Brazil and Uruguay. (a border agreement on territorial coasts of La Plata on Nov. 3, 1973). The Arctic Sector of Argentina officially comprises the Falklands – Malvinas, South Orcadas (Orkneys), South Georgias, South Sandwich Islands and the sovereign territories of Argentina in the Antarctic. Official language: Spanish. Currency: 1 austral = 100 cents. National Day: 25 May, anniversary of the independence revolution, 1810. Since Oct. 24, 1945 Member of the UN and of all specialized agencies, including GATT since 1967. A Member of the OAS since Jan. 14, 1956. A member of the Antarctic Treaty on June 23, 1961; of the Outer Space Treaty on Mar. 26, 1969; of the BW Convention on Nov. 27, 1979. Signed a Non-Preferential Agreement with the EEC 1972; also, 1972, signed the Tlatelolco Treaty. International relations: Argentina was a possession of the Spanish crown until the declaration of independence 1813; in the first half of the 19th century Argentina did not conduct an active foreign policy and did not participate in the Latin–American conferences of 1826, 1847/48, 1856, 1865. Argentina participated in Inter-American Conferences since 1889/90, except the conference in 1928. During World War I it stayed neutral. In 1919–20 and 1933–39 it was a member of the League of Nations. In Jan., 1936 the President of the USA, F.D. Roosevelt, visited Buenos Aires. In 1940, at the Second Conference of Ministers of Foreign Affairs of American Republics in Havana, Argentina declared itself against any action directed against ▷ Axis states; also in Jan.,

1942, at the Third Conference in Rio de Janeiro, Argentina opposed (together with Chile) the recommendation of breaking diplomatic relations with those states. In 1944 it came to an open crisis with the USA and a breach of relations with the USA, Mexico, and most of the Latin–American states. In Feb., 1945 Argentina refused to participate in the Inter-American Conference on War and Peace Problems in Chapultepec; on Feb. 11, 1945 the USA published Memorandum 4756, named *Blue Papers on Nazi influences in Argentina*; Mexico made a similar declaration on Mar. 19, 1945. Finally, on Mar. 27, 1945 Argentina declared war on the Reich and on Japan, and on Apr. 4, 1945 it joined the resolutions passed in Chapultepec. On Apr. 9, 1945 diplomatic relations, which had been broken in 1944, were resumed with the American states, which, on Apr. 16, 1945, at the UN Conference in San Francisco, recommended the admission of Argentina to the UN; which took place on Apr. 29, 1945 by a majority of votes, against four (Czechoslovakia, Greece, Yugoslavia and the USSR). Consequently, on Oct. 24, 1945 Argentina became one of the charter members of the UN. In 1946 Argentina refused to conform to the resolution of the UN General Assembly to break relations with Franco's Spain. On June 22–23, 1960 the UN Security Council considered the complaint of Argentina against Israel concerning the kidnapping of the German Nazi war criminal, A. Eichmann, from the territory of Argentina, and transporting him to Israel. In 1979 it concluded an agreement with Brazil on the use of Rio Paraguay waters for dams in Argentina and Brazil (▷ Corpus and ▷ Itaipu). In 1982 in military conflict with the UK over the ▷ Falklands–Malvinas Islands. In Jan. 1984 the new civilian government of president Raul Alfonsin signed a declaration on peace and friendship with Chile.

On July 29, 1986, President Alfonsino and President Sarney of Brazil signed in Buenos Aires an agreement liberalizing trade between the two countries and envisaged an integration process towards a common market.

On April 6, 1988, Argentina signed 16 integration agreements with Brazil and Uruguay (▷ Alvorado Act, 1988).

See also ▷ World Heritage UNESCO List.

E. PALACIO, *Historia de la Argentina*, 2 Vols., Buenos Aires 1957; F.F. MC GARM, *Argentina. The US and the Inter-American System 1880–1914*, New York, 1957; *UN Review*, No. 301, 1960; A. CONIL PAZ, G. FERRARI, *Politica exterior de Argentina 1930–1962*, Buenos Aires, 1964; A. FERRER, *Argentina*, New York, 1969; H.S. FENS, *The Argentine Republic*, Newton Abbot, 1973; C.M. VILAS, *La dominación imperialiste en Argentina*, Buenos Aires, 1974; *UN Chronicle*, May and June 1982; A.E. BRAILOVSKY, *Historia de las crisis argentinas, 1880–1982. Un sacrificio inutil*, Buenos Aires, 1982; *The Europa Year Book 1984. A World Survey*, Vol. I, pp. 1082–1100, London, 1984; G.W. WYNIA, *Argentina: Illusions and Realities*, New York, 1986; R. CRASSWELLER, *Peron and the Enigmas of Argentina*, New York, 1987.

ARGYROTHECOLOGISTS CLUB, THE. An International Society of Money Box Collectors, f. 1957, Almelo, Netherlands. Reg. with the UIA.

Yearbook of International Organizations.

ARIANA. A district of Geneva in which the Palace of Nations was built for headquarters of the League of Nations; since June 11, 1946 European headquarters of the UN on the basis of the Ariana Agreement, signed in Berne by the government of Switzerland and on July 1, 1946 in New York by the Secretary-General of the UN. (▷ League of Nations Geneva Headquarters).

UNTS, Vol. 1, 1946/47, pp. 153–154.

ARIANE. A space rocket, launched on Sept. 15, 1987, at Kouron, French Guiana, by the European Space Agency

Europe Takes the Lead in Space, in *NEWSWEEK*, Sept. 28, 1987; KEESING's *Record of World Events*, October, 1987.

ARIANISM. An international term for a body of theological views professed by the priest Arius (*c.* 256–336) of Alexandria, known from fragments of his work *Thalei,* which did not recognize the divine nature of Jesus Christ and thus also rejected the dogma of the Holy Trinity (Antitrinitarianism). The Council of Nice in 325 condemned it as heresy, which was confirmed by the Council of Constantinople in 381. A. lasted in Europe to the 7th century and was revived in the 16th–17th centuries, i.a. in Poland (Polish Brethren) and in the 18th century in England. Presently A. teachings are professed by ▷ Jehovah's Witnesses.

J.H. NEWMAN, *The Arians of the Fourth Century*, London, 1895; S. KOT, *Ideologia polityczna i spoleczna Braci Polskich zwanych Arianami*, Warszawa, 1932; L. CHMAJ, *Bracia Polscy*, Warszawa, 1957; *Yearbook of International Organizations.*

ARICA. A city and port in N. Chile (1980 pop. 118,500) on the Pacific Ocean; on the Peruvian border; since 1929 in the port there is a free zone with Chilean and Peruvian custom houses. See also ▷ Tacna and Arica.

ARID EARTH. An international term for land made desolate as a rule due to deforestation; one of the international problems of the human environment. In Dec. 1970 in Mexico a world colloquium on a.e. was organized by the Institute Mexicano de Zonas Aridas, under UNESCO auspices. Organizations reg. with the UIA:

Arab Center for the Studies of Arid Zones and Dry Lands, f. 1971, Damascus, Syria. Members: national organizations in 20 Arab countries.
International Centre for Agricultural Research in Dry Areas, f. 1977, Aleppo, Syria. Publ. *ICARDA Research Highlights.*
International Crop Research Institute for the Semi-Arid Tropics, f. 1972, Patancheru, India. Publ. *Annual Report.*
B. GIBBONS, "Do we treat our soil like dirt?" in: *National Geographic*, September, 1984, pp. 350–390; *The Europa Yearbook*, 1988. *A World Survey*, Vol. I, London, 1988.

ARISCHE ABSTAMMUNG. *German* = Aryan descent. An international term for a racial doctrine introduced in 1935 by the Nuremberg laws in the Third Reich, derived from Sanskrit ("arya" = noble, or "aryan" = lord), which was to indicate "the purity of German blood" in Third Reich nationals. Since 1933, admission to the Nazi Party – the NSDAP, and to the German civil service, was possible only to those who had proved that no "racially alien blood (Semitic, Hamitic, Negro or Mongolian)" had flowed in the veins of their ancestors. Art. 3 of the Law on Civil Service of Apr. 7, 1933, was commonly known as the "Arier-paragraph". ▷ Aryans.

J. NOAKES, G. PRIDHAM, *Documents on Nazism 1919–1945*, London, 1974.

ARKHANGELSK or ARCHANGEL. A city (1986 pop. 412,000) and port on the Dvina estuary to the White Sea in the USSR. In 1941–45, a naval port where British and US shipments landed with ▷ lend-lease materials.

"ARKTIKA", a Soviet atomic ice-breaker which, as the first surface ship in the history of navigation, reached the North Pole on Aug. 17, 1977.

ARLES. City in south-central France, in Provence. The Roman and Romanesque Monuments of Arles are included in the ▷ World Heritage UNESCO List. The monuments remaining from the first period (from the first century BC to the fifth century AD) include one of the oldest Roman amphitheatres. From the second period (from the 9th to the 13th centuries) is a church with its cloister, a centre of artistic activity which extended its influence throughout southern France.

UNESCO. *The Protection of the World Cultural and Natural Heritage*, Paris, 1983.

ARMAGEDDON. According to the Apocalypse (16, 14–16) the place of the final battle between Good and Evil on the Day of the Last Judgment. An international term for a bloody, destructive war waged by both sides with the aim of achieving a total solution.

M.S. SHERRY, *The Rise of American Airpower: The Creation of Armageddon*, London, 1987.

ARMAMENTS. The major subject of international negotiations in the 20th century between powers and in international organizations: after World War I in the LN, since 1945 under the auspices of the UN. During the interwar period the matter of reduction of armaments at sea was the subject of conferences between the powers. After World War II, according to data compiled by the appropriate UN committees and by special groups of experts, the armaments race continues unabated. In 1947, two years after World War II, the total expenditures of the states of all continents amounted to the sum of 30 billion dollars; in 1962 they exceeded 120, in 1965, 180, and in 1981 they reached 620 billion, representing 6% of world output. The armaments expenditures of the world for the period 1946–75 amounted to 7 trillion dollars (according to SIPRI). The XXV Session of the UN General Assembly unanimously resolved to call upon a Group of Experts to compile a report on the "economic and social consequences of the arms race and its exceedingly harmful influence on the peace and security of the world ...". The report was made public on Oct. 20, 1971 by UN Secretary General U Thant. The *UN Chronicle* 1982 stated:

In 1980, world military expenditure was as much as 500 billion dollars or approximately $110 for every man, woman and child on earth.
Each year for the past 30 years, five to eight per cent of the world's total output has been allocated to the military. Something approaching 50,000 nuclear warheads are now deployed and their combined explosive yield is about one million times greater than the bomb dropped on the city of Hiroshima in 1945. The co-existence of high rates of military spending and high rates of economic growth does not indicate a causal linkage between armament and development.
The arms race and development are in a competitive relationship. Military outlays by definition reflect consumption of resources and not an input into investment.
The international trade in arms is of major economic as well as political significance. It is estimated that more than 26 billion dollars is annually spent on the arms traffic, by both developed and developing countries.
At the same time, there are about 570 million people in various parts of the world who are malnourished. 800 million are illiterate. 1500 million have little or no access to medical services. 250 million children do not go to school. In financial terms, world military expenditures are some 19 times as large as all the official development assistance provided by the States belonging to the Organization for Economic Co-operation and Development in 1980.

Arms Museums

In the absence of disarmament measures and given the current state of international tensions the introduction of a new generation of more deadly and expensive weapons may well add further to military expenditure. If we assume a 2 per cent annual rate of increase, which is modest by historical standards, this will mean total expenditure of some 743 billion dollars even at today's prices by the year 2000; assuming a 3 per cent rate of increase, the corresponding figure would be 903 billion dollars."

According to SIPRI the world military expenditure in constant price figures was in 1975 – $508 310 million, 1980 – $563 542, 1983 – $636 790.

In 1986, the USA for the first time in 10 years reduced military spending.

The figures on military expenditures were available in the 1980s only for 60% of the world's nations. The SIPRI Yearbook, gives no figures for Chinese and Soviet spending.

See also ▷ Disarmament.

League of Nations Armaments Yearbook, Geneva, 1923-39; *Yearbook 1971; UN Report on the Economic and Social Consequences of the Armistice*, New York, 1971; *UN Chronicle*, June, 1982, p. 56; SIPRI, *World Armaments and Disarmament Yearbook*, Stockholm–London, 1983–84; *Armaments or Disarmament, SIPRI Summary 1984*, Stockholm, 1984; *International Institute for Strategy Studies, The Military Balance 1983–84*, London, 1984; SIPRI *The Arms Race and Arms Control* 1984, London, Philadelphia, 1984, pp. 52–164; *World Military Expenditures*, 1977–1986, in: *SIPRI Yearbook*, 1987, Oxford 1987; IISS, *The Military Balance*, 1987–1988, London, 1988.

ARMCO-1. An expert system for nuclear arms control.

A.M. DIN (ed.), *Arms and Artificial Intelligence. Weapons and Arms Control Applications of Advanced Computing*, SIPRI, Oxford, 1987.

ARMED CONFLICTS LAW. An international term, popularized in the second half of the 20th century, designating the practice of law based on the assumption that aggresive war is a crime against peace and humanity (e.g. the ▷ Nuremberg Trial 1945–46 and the ▷ Aggression, UN definition), as opposed to the previous "law of war", which until the ▷ Briand Kellogg Treaty of 1928, recognized the legitimacy of war.

ARMED FORCES. A subject of conventions of international law in the 19th and 20th centuries. The first, signed in Brussels in 1874, considered as part of the regular army volunteer and militia units wearing an identifying emblem and openly bearing arms. The majority of the signatories did not ratify this convention. The First International Hague Peace Conference, 1899, concerned the laws and customs of land war and its principles took effect after the Second Peace Conference with the Fourth Hague Convention 1907, to which was appended the Hague Statute. During World War II the governments of the Axis powers did not recognize members of the resistance movement as part of the armed forces as was demanded by the Allies based on the ▷ Martens Clause added to the Fourth Hague Convention 1907. This question was resolved by the First and Third Geneva Conventions 1949 on the treatment of wounded, ill, and war prisoners and on extending protection to civilians as well as members of the resistance movement. The first neutral state, which in 1944 recognized units of the resistance movement as part of the regular army, was Switzerland (in reference to occupied France).

J. KAEGAN, *World Armies*, London, 1979.

ARMENIAN CHURCH. Called the Armenian–Georgian Church. One of the Eastern Christian Churches, from the 5th century independent from Rome, basing itself on the doctrine of Monophysitism, retaining the Old Armenian language in the national liturgy. The head of the Armenian church is the patriarch; whose seat is in the St Egmiadzim monastery, near Mount Ararat. His subordinates are the patriarchs of Cilicia, Jerusalem and Istanbul. The Armenian Church patriarch Vasgen I visited the Vatican in 1970, which resulted in a mutual declaration of Pope Paul VI and the Armenian Church superior, concerning the need of Christianity participating in efforts towards global détente.

P. DULAURIER, *Histoire de dogmes, traditions et liturgie de l'Église Arménienne Orientale*, Paris, 1855; *Armianskaia Apostolskaia Tserkov*, Vol. 2, Moscow, 1970.

ARMENIANS. A people living mostly in Armenia in the USSR; during 1915–20 subject to extermination in Turkey. The League of Nations was in charge of matters concerning the fate of Armenian refugees fleeing from Turkish rule. In total about 3 million Armenians died and 1.2 million were forced to emigrate.

See ▷ Nagorno-Karabakh Autonomous Region.

C.F. LEHMAN-HAUPT, *Armenian einst und jetzt*, Berlin, 1931; D. VAVE, *Der Lachende Diplomat*, Leipzig, 1938, pp. 220–230; J. MISSAKIN, *A searchlight on the Armenian question*, 1878–1950, Boston, 1950; S.R. SONYEL, *The Ottoman Armenians: Victims of Great Power Diplomacy*, London, 1987.

ARMENIAN SOVIET SOCIALIST REPUBLIC. Haikakan Sovetakan Sotzialistakan Respublika, Armyenskaya Sovietskaya Sotsyalisticheskaya Respublika. A constituent republic since 1936 of the USSR in the South Caucasus bordering on Turkey, Iran, Azerbaidzhan and Georgia. Area: 29,785 sq. km. Population: 1988 estim. 3,459,500, 1986 (birth rate 24.0, and death rate 5.7) comprising 89.7% Armenians, 5.3% Azeris, 2.3% Russians and 1.7% Kurds. Capital: Yerevan 1,168,300 inhabitants 1987. Official languages: Armenian and Russian. Currency: Soviet ruble = 100 kopeks. National Day: Nov. 7, anniversary of the Oct. Revolution, 1917. International relations: in 1639 divided between Persia and Turkey; in 1828, after the Russian–Persian war, East Armenia became part of the Russian empire by virtue of the Turkmenian agreement. West Armenia remained in Turkey. In Oct. 1918 Turkey invaded East Armenia, but withdrew its troops in Nov. 1918, giving way to English and American troops. Soviet authority was established in Dec. 1920. Since 1936 a Soviet Republic.

After the pogrom of Armenians by Azeris in the city of Sumgait on Febr. 28, 1988, the regional parliament in the Azerbaidzhan province Nagorny Karabakh formally voted for transfer of the territory to Armenia. New demonstrations of Armenians took place on March 13, 1988.

R. GROUSSET, *Histoire de l'Arménie*, Paris, 1948; M. SHAGINVAN, *A Journey through Soviet Armenia*, Moscow, 1954; N. KURKIYAN, *A History of Armenia*, New York, 1958; A. ASLANYAN, A. BAGDASARIAN, *L'Arménie Soviétique*, Moscow, 1972; *The Europa Year Book 1984. A World Survey*, Vol. I, pp. 909–910, London, 1984.

ARMISTICE. An agreement between combatants which leads to a general cease-fire. A capitulary armistice, resulting from the surrender of one of the sides, is synonymous with the ending of war. Arts. 36–41 of the Hague Convention Respecting the Laws and Customs of War on Land, 1907, determined:

"A cease-fire halts military operations with the mutual agreement of the combatants" and may be "general or local"; it should be "officially announced and in the proper time-limit to the competent authorities and the military" and enters into force "immediately upon notification." The resumption of military operations may take place immediately in the event of a "serious violation" of the armistice, but not by "individuals acting on their own initiative": such persons should be punished, and the damages caused by them compensated.

E. CLUNET, "Suspension d'armes. Armistice. Préliminaires de paix", in: *Journal du droit international*, 46/1919; M. SIBERT, "L'armistice", in: *Revue général de droit international*, 40/1933; R. BERNARD, *L'armistice dans les guerres internationales*, Paris, 1947; H.W. LEWIS. "The nature and scope of the armistice agreement", in: *American Journal of International Law*, 50/1956; R.L. BLEDSOE, B.A. BOCTEK, *The International Law Dictionary*, Oxford, 1987.

ARMOURED FIGHTING VEHICLE, AFW. An international military term for vehicles transporting infantry to the battlefield.

D. ROBERTSON, *Guide to Modern Defense and Strategy*, Detroit, 1988.

ARMS. A subject of international studies and statistics. The London International Institute for Strategic Studies, publ. since 1960 *The Military Balance*. The Stockholm International Peace Research Institute, since 1968, publ. *SIPRI World Armaments and Disarmament Yearbook*.

J. TURNER and SIPRI, *Arms in the 1980s. New Development in the Global Arms Race*, London, 1985.

ARMS AND ARTIFICIAL INTELLIGENCE. An international term since the 1980s for the application of artificial intelligence in modern weapon systems; an essential ingredient in projects such as the ▷ SDI.

A.M. DIN (ed.), *Arms and Artificial Intelligence – Weapon and Arms Control Applications of Advanced Computing*, SIPRI, Oxford, 1987.

ARMS CONTROL. A subject of multilateral agreements. ▷ Disarmament.

SIPRI, *Prospects for Arms Control in the Ocean*, Stockholm, 1972; SIPRI, *Arms Control: A Survey and Appraisal of Multilateral Agreements*, London, 1978; J. GOLDBLAT, *Agreements for Arms Control. A Critical Survey*, New York, 1982; G. SEGAL, *Arms Control in Asia*, New York, 1987; Major Multilateral Arms Control Agreements, in: *SIPRI Yearbook*, 1987, Oxford 1987; J. GOLDBLAT, Multilateral Arms Control Efforts, in: *SIPRI Yearbook*, 1987, Oxford, 1988, pp. 384–408; D. ROBERTSON, *Guide to Modern Defense and Strategy*, Detroit, 1988.

ARMS EMBARGO. An international term for multilateral agreements prohibiting export of arms to a specified country or countries during a war or in peace-time. The UN General Assembly imposed 1977 the arms embargo to ▷ South Africa.

UN Chronicle, Apr., 1980, p. 24.

ARMS INSPECTION. An international term in disarmament agreements. First defined in a memorandum of understanding to the American–Soviet Agreement, 1987, on medium and short range weapons. A number of missile production installations in the USA and Western Europe and in the USSR and Eastern Europe are open to inspection in the years 1987–2000.

The Summit: Arms Inspection, Locations of Sites Named in Arms Agreement in: *The New York Times*, December 11, 1987.

ARMS MUSEUMS. A subject of international cooperation: International Association of Arms

Museums and Military History, f. 1957, London. Reg. with the UIA.

Yearbook of International Organizations.

ARMS RACE. The steadily growing military expenditures for conventional arms, and after World War II also for nuclear, chemical and biological arms. In the decade 1970–79 the competition between the US and USSR absorbed about 60% of global military spending and their NATO and Warsaw Pact allies another 20% of the world total. The staggering cost, according to the UN:

World military spending:
1981: $600 billion
1985: $870 billion
2000: $1 trillion?
Nuclear weapons: More than 50,000 nuclear warheads in the world. Explosive power: 1 million times greater than the Hiroshima atomic bomb.
Conventional forces: Consume some 80 per cent of all military spending. Used in more than 150 wars since World War II killing over 20 million people, mostly in developing countries.
Research: Some 25 per cent of the world's 3 million scientists and engineers are engaged in military work.
Labour: There are 60–80 million people employed in military activities worldwide.
Arms production: Active arms producers have emerged in developing countries in the past 15 years. In 1970 they produced $68 million worth of weapons; in 1984, $635 million. Total world output: $200 billion in 1986.

UN Report on the Economic and Social Consequences of the Arms Race, New York 1971. SIPRI, *The Arms Race and Arms Control,* Stockholm, 1984; *UN Chronicle,* September 1988; M. EVANGELISTA, *Innovation and the Arms Race: How the USA and the USSR Develop New Military Technologies,* Ithaca, NY, 1988; Ch.R. MORRIS, *Iron Destinies, Lost Opportunities: The Arms Race Between the USA and the USSR, 1945–1987,* New York, 1988; D. ROBERTSON, *Guide to Modern Defense and Strategy,* Detroit, 1988.

ARMS TRADE INTERNATIONAL. Subject of an international convention concluded by the Allied Powers in Paris on Sept. 10, 1919; the first convention introduced international control over the arms trade in specific dependent territories of Africa and Asia; the second, drafted on the initiative of the League of Nations, introduced universal regulations on international arms trade and control of munitions and military equipment. The Convention was signed in Geneva on June 17, 1925 and remains in force. The ▷ Non-Proliferation Treaty of July 27, 1968, pertains specifically to arms trade in the field of nuclear weapons. In 1980 the UN Secretary-General estimated that more than 26 billion dollars is annually traded in the arms traffic, by both developed and developing countries.
According to SIPRI the 20 largest Third World major-weapon importing countries, 1979–83, were: Syria, Libya, Iraq, Egypt, Saudi Arabia, India, Israel, Cuba, Argentina, South Yemen, Algeria, Morocco, Vietnam, South Korea, Peru, Taiwan, Indonesia, Jordan, Pakistan, Kuwait. The value of major conventional weapons imported by Third World countries between 1971 and 1985 was quadruple the amount for the previous two decades. The largest major-weapon exporting countries were, and still are: the USSR, the USA, France, the UK, the FRG, China and Italy, for more than US$ 30 billion in 1986.
The International Conference on the Relationship between Disarmament and Development held in New York from Aug. 24 to Sept. 11, 1987, in its Final Document adopted by consensus states that the developing countries accounted for over two thirds of all arms imports, with almost half going to Iraq, Egypt, India, Syria, and Saudi Arabia.

SIPRI, *World Armaments,* Stockholm, 1974; J.R. FOX, *Arming America,* Boston, 1974; SIPRI, *World Arma-*

ments and Disarmament Yearbook, 1968–85; U. RA'ANAN (ed.), *Arms Transfer to the Third World,* West View, London, 1979; A.T. PIERRE, *Arms Transfer and American Foreign Policy,* New York, 1980; SIPRI, *The Arms Race and Arms Control 1984,* London, Philadelphia, 1984, pp. 95–109; M. BRZOSKA, Th. OHLSON, *Arms Trade to the Third World, 1971–85,* SIPRI, Oxford, 1987; R. LEGER SIVARD, *World Military and Social Expenditures, 1987–88,* Washington DC, 1987; *UN Chronicle,* November, 1987; *SIPRI Yearbook,* 1987, Oxford, 1988, pp. 181–295.

ARMS TRANSFER. An international term for global value arms transactions, including large-scale training programs (approximately 15 per cent of the global value of arms). According to UN estimates, world arms transfers measured in constant 1982 dollars, grew from $26.8 billion in 1973 to a peak of $38 billion in 1981 and 1982 and declined to 32.4 billion in 1984.

UN Chronicle, November, 1987.

ARMY AND THE MILITARY. An international term for military forces and persons serving in all branches of armed forces which come under international conventions.

ARMY SERVICE OF ALIENS. A subject of ▷ Aliens Rights, controlled by the internal law of a state on whose territory the alien resides, by international law and bilateral interstate agreements. There are no uniform norms concerning service of aliens; they are dependent on the legislation of a state and whether it has compulsory military service for its citizens and permanent residents, e.g. in Denmark from Nov. 8, 1912; in the USA from May 18, 1917, the law partially changed July 9, 1918, Sept. 16, 1940, June 24, 1948 and June 19, 1951; in France from Apr. 12, 1939; and from Nov. 4, 1953 army service obligatory for each person of draft age residing permanently in France for longer than a year in response to a similar law in the USA, 1951; in the FRG from July 21, 1956 applicable to foreign citizens on the principle of mutuality, stateless persons by the order of FRG authorities. The effort to work out a uniform convention on this matter by the LN Conference on Aliens, 1929 failed. The Panamerican Convention on the Status of Aliens of Feb. 20, 1928, in art. 3 prohibited the calling of aliens into the army, but did permit calling them to labor in the case of natural catastrophes. The USA ratified this convention but with a basic reservation to art. 3. After World War II the EEC states attempted without success to formulate uniform norms concerning service of aliens. The Convention on Aliens and the Convention on Citizenship were signed Dec. 13, 1955 without the article on service of aliens.

LN Doc. C 36 M 21, 1929, II; European Treaty Series, No. 19.

AROLSEN. A city in Hessen, FRG, where, in 1945, the Allied Control Council for Germany established an information center on persons who had been imprisoned in Nazi concentration and other camps during World War II. On June 6, 1955, an agreement was signed in Bonn between the UK, France, the FRG, Israel, Luxembourg, the Netherlands and the USA establishing an International Commission on International Information Service, based in the Arolsen Center. The archives of the Bureau contain a collection – unique in the world – of documents concerning concentration camps (Department I), the situation of foreigners in the III Reich and the situation of forced labor workers (Departments II and IV). A separate department contains archives concerning children taken to the Reich for Germanization ▷ (*Lebensborn*). The Historical

Department embraces general archives, and especially decrees and regulations of the III Reich organs responsible for the administration of concentration camps, statistical data, documents containing rules of employing forced labor et cetera.
Of special significance is the central register. It contains 42 million cards classified in accordance with an alphabetic and phonetic key embracing personal data of 14 million people.

UNTS, Vol. 219; A. DE COCATRIX, "Service International de Recherche Arolsen", in: *Bulletin of the General Commission for Investigating Nazi Crimes in Poland,* Vol. XXIX, Warsaw, 1979.

ARPEL. Asociación de Asistencia Recíproca Petroléros Estatal Latinoamericana – Association for Mutual Assistance of the Latin American Petroleum State Enterprises, f. in 1965 in Lima (Peru) by the following state companies: Argentinian – Yacimientos Petrolíferos Fiscales (YPF), Bolivian – Yacimientos Petrolíferos Fiscales Bolivianos (YPFB), Brazilian – Petroles Brasileiro (PETROBRAS), Chilean – Empresa Nacional Petrolera (ENAP), Mexican – Petroleos Mexicanos (PEMEX), Paraguayan – Administración Nacional de Combustibles Alcool y Petroleos (ANCAP), Peruvian – Empresa Petrolera Fiscal del Perú (EPP), Uruguayan – Administración Nacional de Combustibles, Alcool y Portland (MININDUSTRIA), Venezuelan – Corporación Venezoelana Petroleo (VCP); it has a consultative status to the ECOSOC. Headquarters: Montevideo (Uruguay). Reg. with the UIA.

Yearbook of International Organizations.

ARRANGEMENT. An international term for inter-governmental agreements dealing with matters of lesser importance, or supplements to earlier acts.

ARRAS CONGRESS, 1435. The first summit of European kings and princes held in Arras (France) caused by the need to reestablish internal peace in France torn by a conflict between Charles VII and Philip the Good, Duke of Burgundy; considered to be the first international congress.

ARREST CONVENTION, 1952. ▷ Maritime Law Conventions, 1882–1978.

ARRÊT DE MARCHANDISE. A confiscation of merchandise. An international term for confiscation and sale of the enemy's merchandise found on ships of neutral states; used in World Wars I and II.

ARRÊT DE PRINCE. A "detention of the prince". An international term for preventive detention of ships of a state with which an armed conflict is expected.

ARSENIC. A subject of international co-operation: Arsenic Development Committee, f. 1962, Paris. Reg. with the UIA.

Yearbook of International Organizations.

ART, subject of international co-operation. Organizations reg. with the UIA:

International Academy of Social and Moral Sciences, Arts and Letters, f. 1972, Cologne, FRG.
International Association for Crafts and the Teaching of Art, f. 1938, Brussels.
International Association of Art Critics, f. 1949, Paris. Consultative status: UNESCO, ECOSOC.
International Association of Art, Painting, Sculpture, Graphic Art, f. 1954, Paris. Consultative status: UNESCO, ECOSOC. Publ. *Art.*
International Center of Medieval Art, f. 1956, New York. Publ. *Gesta.*

International Committee for the Diffusion of Arts and Literature through the Cinema, f. 1930, Paris.
International Committee on the History of Art, f. 1930, Madrid. Publ. *Répertoire d'Art et d'Archéologie* (annual).
International Confederation of Art Dealers, f. 1936, Brusssels.
International Council of the Museum of Modern Art, f. 1953, New York.
International Federation of Films on Art, f. 1945, Paris.
International Institute for Conservation of Historic and Artistic Works, f. 1950, London. Publ. *Studies in Conservation.*
International Institute of Arts and Letters, 1931, Zurich. Publ. *History of the World Arts.*
International Literary and Artistic Association, f. 1878, Paris. Consultative status: UNESCO, ECOSOC, Council of Europe. Publ. *Bulletin.*
International Organization for the Protection by Works of Art, f. 1974, Montpellier, France.
International Society for Education through Art, f. 1952, Paris.
International Society of Art and Psychopathology, f. 1959, Paris. Publ. *Confinia Psychiatrica.*
International Society Performing Arts Administrators, f. 1961, Houston, USA.
International Union for the Protection of Literary and Artistic Works, f. 1886, Geneva. Publ. *Le Droit d'Auteur and Copyright* (monthly).
World Academy of Art and Science, f. 1960, New York. Publ. *WAAS Newsletter.*

Yearbook of International Organizations, 1986–87; The Europa Yearbook, 1988. A World Survey, Vol. 1, London, 1988.

ART CLUB OF THE UN. A club founded in 1949 by UN Secretariat personnel; arranges annual exhibitions of graphic art and sculpture by artists from all over the world, the proceeds from which go to UNICEF.

ART-DRAIN. An international term that appeared towards the end of the sixties (compare ▷ Braindrain), for growing international commerce by antique dealers of works of art that were stolen and smuggled abroad, which caused an efflux of works of art from financially weak countries to the more affluent ones. In Nov., 1970, as part of the campaign for ▷ cultural property protection, UNESCO drew up and unanimously passed an International Convention on the Prevention of Export, Import and Transit of Stolen Works of Art. The convention has not come into force because of an insufficient number of ratifications.

P. SCHNEIDER, "Art-drain?" in: *Die Weltwoche,* Zürich, 1972.

ARTHURIAN SOCIETY INTERNATIONAL. A Society f. 1948, Nottingham University, UK, for promoting international study of the Arthurian legends of the Round Table. Publ. *Bibliographical Bulletin* (annual). Reg. with the UIA.

Yearbook of International Organizations.

ARTIFICIAL PROCREATION. An international term, a subject of international research and discussion on legal problems. The Committee of Experts on Medical Research on Human Beings and the Ad Hoc Committee of Experts on Progress in Bio-Medicine of the Council of Europe in 1987, elaborated a set of principles covering scope, definitions, and general conditions for the use of artificial procreation techniques, storage of gametes and embryos, donation of gametes and embryos, determination of maternity and paternity, surrogate motherhood, acts and procedures carried out on embryos.
The Committee of Ministers is preparing for 1989 a Recommendation to Member States on Medical Research of Artificial Procreation.

Council of Europe, Information Sheet No 21, Strasbourg, 1988, pp. 109–110.

ARTISTS INTERNATIONAL ORGANIZATIONS. Reg. with the UIA:

International Artists Co-operation, f. 1972, Friedrichsfeld, FRG.
International Society of Christian Artists, f. 1951, Zurich.
Union of Latin Writers and Artists, f. 1957, Paris.

Yearbook of International Organizations.

ART OBJECTS, WORKS OF ART, OBJETS D'ART. An international term for objects covered by international conventions on protection of works of art. The UN General Assembly, on Dec. 13, 1973 with the Res. 3187/XXVIII decided by 113 votes with 17 abstentions that the colonial powers which removed from their colonies works of art which are part of the cultural heritage of a given country should return them without charge in the shortest possible period of time. Reaffirmed by the UN General Assembly Res. 32/8, Nov. 16, 1977. ▷ Cultural property return.

UN Yearbook, 1973 and 1974.

ARUBA. Island in the Leeward Islands group of the ▷ Netherlands Antilles. Area: 193 sq. km. Population 1988 estim. 62,500, Capital Oranjestad. Administered as part of ▷ Curaçao. Since Jan. 1, 1986, autonomous status with elected parliament, member of the federation of The Netherlands Antilles, Official language: Dutch, common language: Papiamento. In 1996 will be granted full independence.

KEESING's *Record of World Events,* 1986, No 4; *The Europa Yearbook,* 1988. *A World Survey,* Vol. II, London, 1988

ARUSHA. A city (1985 pop. 1,183,000) in northeastern Tanzania where, on July 26, 1968, the Arusha Convention was signed, concluded between the EEC and three African states: Kenya, Tanzania, and Uganda. The convention, having expired in Jan., 1975, has been replaced by the ▷ Lomé Convention of 1975.

European Committee Yearbook, 1969.

ARYANS. An international term for people speaking one of the Indo-European (Indo-Iranian) languages. A term abused by the German nationalists in the interwar period for racist purposes (▷ Arische Abstammung).

ASAT. Anti-Satellite System developed in the 1980s for destroying, damaging or disturbing the normal functioning of, or changing the trajectory of, artificial Earth satellites; first by the US, since then, in 1985–86 by the USSR. In the US, according to the SIPRI trend is "to focus on ground based lasers . . . under the SDI program for ASAT applications".

SIPRI Yearbook, 1987, Oxford, 1988, pp. 67–68; D. ROBERTSON, *Guide to Modern Defense and Strategy,* Detroit, 1988.

ASBM. An abbreviation for air-to-surface ballistic missile.

ASCENSION ISLAND. A part since 1922 of the British St Helena colony in the South Atlantic, north-west of St Helena, area: 88.1 sq. km. Population December, 1987, excluding British Military personnel: 1,007 (St. Helenians 649, UK nationals 200, US nationals 143, others 15). US missile and satellite tracking station.

B. STONEHOUSE, *Wideawake Island (Ascension),* London, 1960.

ASEAN. Association of South East Asian Nations. An intergovernmental organization, of Indonesia, Malaysia, the Philippines, Singapore and Thailand (observer Papua New Guinea) f. 1967 in Bangkok to support economic and cultural co-operation; it is composed of foreign ministers who meet at irregular intervals in the capitals of member states. It has one permanent committee with headquarters in Singapore which meets monthly and 10 special committees: in Bangkok – navigation; in Djakarta – food, tourism, and science and technology; in Kuala Lumpur – transport, communication and telecommunication, mass media, and finances; in Manila – trade and industry; in Singapore – civil aviation. In Mar., 1977 the member states began work on the preparation of a Common Market and an understanding on the question of trade preferences. The Ninth Conference of Ministers of Foreign Affairs of Indonesia, Malaysia, the Philippines, Singapore and Thailand, July 24–26, 1976 in Manila proposed a plan for transforming south-east Asia into a "zone of peace, freedom, and neutrality". First Summit Conference of the member states was held in 1976. On Mar. 7, 1980 ASEAN signed in Brussels a co-operation agreement with the European Common Market. In July 1981 ASEAN sponsored a regional UN Conference on Kampuchea demanding the withdrawal of Vietnamese troops from Kampuchea. The first ASEAN–EEC meeting took place in Bangkok on Oct. 17–18, 1985. Publ.: *Annual Report, ASEAN Newsletter* (monthly) and *ASEAN Journal* (quarterly). An ASEAN–EEC Business Council was est. in December 1983.

"Five South East Asia Nations Seek to Create Neutral Zone", in: *International Herald Tribune,* May 16, 1975; J. WONG, *ASEAN Economics in Perspective,* London, 1979; D.K. CRONE, *The ASEAN states,* New York, 1983; S. HARRIS, B. BRIDGES, *European Interests in ASEAN,* London, 1983; *The Europa Year Book 1984. A World Survey,* Vol. I, pp. 105–107, London, 1984; W. ROSTOW, *The United States and the Regional Organizations of Asia and the Pacific, 1945–1985,* Austin, Tex., 1986.

ASFIS. Aquatic Sciences and Fisheries Information System, one of the information systems of the ▷ FAO.

ASHANTI. The traditional Ashanti buildings in central Ghana, included in the ▷ World Heritage UNESCO List, are the only remaining architectural evidence of the great Ashanti civilization of Ghana which reached its apogee in the 18th century. Many palaces and shrines have been restored since 1960. Their walls are covered with paintings.

UNESCO. *A Legacy for All,* Paris, 1984.

ASHKENAZIM. Hebrew: 'Ashkenas = Germany. One of the three major divisions of the Jews (two others: ▷ Oriental Jews, and ▷ Sephardim). The Ashkenazim are the Jewish communities comprising Eastern, Central and Northern European Jews. Ashkenazim language: Yiddish. The Chief Rabbi has his headquarters in Jerusalem and together with the Sephardic Chief Rabbi, is member of the Supreme ▷ Rabbinacal Council. See also ▷ Jews.

Yearbook of International Organizations, 1986–87; The Europa Yearbook 1988. A World Survey, Vol. I, London, 1988.

ASHMORE ISLANDS. Australian territories in the Timor Sea, annexed by the British Empire 1878, small and uninhabited, consisting of sand and coral. In 1983 declared a national nature reserve.

The Europa Yearbook 1988. A World Survey, Vol. II, London, 1988.

ASIA. The largest continent of the world; forming together with Europe a land mass called Eurasia. Area: 44,390,010 sq. km. Pop. about: 2,558,000,000 (1980), that is, about 58% of the world's population. Politically, divided into 40 independent states and 6 non-self-governing territories. Organization reg. with the UIA:
International Union for Oriental and Asian Studies, f. 1951, Paris, France.

J. HERBERT, *Asie*, Paris, 1959; D. WILSON, *Asia Awaked. A Continent in Transition*, London, 1970; *Asia and the International System*, Cambridge, Mass., 1972; *UN Demographic Yearbook. 1980; The Europa Year Book 1984. A World Survey*, 2 Vols., London, 1984; R.A. SCALAPINO, Asia's Future, in: *Foreign Affairs*, Fall, 1987 *Yearbook of International Organizations, 1986–87; The Europa Yearbook*, 1988. *A World Survey*, Vol. I, London, 1988.

ASIA GORBACHEV PLAN 1988. The Soviet government proposal, announced on Sept. 16, 1988 in Krasnoyarsk by Mikhail Gorbachev. This is a Reuter's summary of the seven points in the Asian Plan:
1. The Soviet Union will not increase its nuclear weapons in the Asia-Pacific region and calls on the United States and other nuclear powers to freeze their deployments there.
2. Major naval powers in the region are invited to hold talks on the nonincrease of naval forces.
3. The Soviet Union proposes multilateral talks on lowering confrontation at the points where the coasts of China, Japan, North and South Korea, and the Soviet Union converge. The talks would focus on reducing the strength and activity of those countries' air and naval forces.
4. The Soviet Navy will stop using Cam Ranh Bay for its fleet if the United States scraps its bases in the Philippines.
5. Measures should be taken to prevent incidents in Asian-Pacific seas and airspace. These could be based on accords already worked out between the Soviet Union and Britain, the United States and Japan.
6. The Soviet Union proposes an international conference on making the Indian Ocean a zone of peace to be held by 1990.
7. A 'negotiating mechanism' should be created for talks on Asian-Pacific security. This could be begun by the Soviet Union, the United States and China, permanent members of the United Nations Security Council.

International Herald Tribune, September 17–18, 1988.

ASIA IN THE UNITED NATIONS. On Oct. 24, 1945, only five Asian states entered the UN: China, India, Iran, Iraq and the Philippines. They were followed by Afghanistan and Thailand (1946); Pakistan (1947); Burma (1948); Indonesia (1950); Cambodia, Ceylon, Laos, and Nepal (1955); Japan (1956); Malaysia (1957); Mongolia (1961); the Maldive Islands and Singapore (1965). From 1949 to 1972 Taiwan represented China in all organs and specialized organizations of the UN: this was challenged and put to the vote at each UN General Assembly. In 1976 Vietnam was admitted; the two Korean States remained outside UN membership. Asian issues discussed in the UN (in chronological order):
(1) Jan.–May, 1946; Iran's request for the withdrawal of Soviet armed forces from North Iran, stationed there since 1942 (were withdrawn on Apr. 2, 1946).
(2) Jan.–Feb., 1946; July, 1947–Dec., 1949; Indonesia's complaints of armed interventions by the Netherlands (ceased with the achieving of independence by Indonesia on Dec. 27, 1949).

(3) Autumn, 1948–Jan., 1967; Pakistan–Indian dispute over ▷ Kashmir and Janmmu.
(4) Aug., 1948–Aug., 1949; the question of ▷ Hyderabad.
(5) Mar., 1953–Oct., 1954; Burma's complaints against Taiwan of being invaded by the Chiang Kaishek mercenary armies.
(6) May–Aug., 1954; the question of Thailand.
(7) Aug., 1954–Nov., 1955; the question of western New Guinea.
(8) Aug., 1954–Aug., 1955; the question of 15 American airman serving with the UN Armed Forces in South Korea, who had been in China as prisoners of War (they were released after UN Secretary General Dag Hammarskjöld visited Peking).
(9) July 1958–Jan., 1962; the question of Western Samoa.
(10) Nov., 1958–July, 1962; the dispute between Cambodia and Thailand over the temple of ▷ Preah Vihear.
(11) Aug.–Nov., 1961; the complaints of Laos against North Vietnam over boundary incidents.
(12) 1959; Tibet's complaint against China.
(13) 1961; the question of Portuguese Timor.
(14) Dec., 1961; Portuguese protest against the incorporation by India of ▷ Goa, Daman and Diu.
(15) Aug.–Sept., 1963; dispute between Malaysia and Indonesia.
(16) Aug.–Dec., 1963; protest of the Afro-Asian states against the persecution of Buddhists in South Vietnam.
(17) Apr., 1964; Cambodia's protests against armed intervention by South Vietnam.
(18) Jan., 1979; Cambodia's complaint against Vietnam over armed intervention.
(19) Feb.–Mar., 1979; Vietnam's complaint against China concerning the invasion by Chinese armed forces.
(20) Sept., 1979–1986; the question of Kampuchea representation.

A 1970 UN list enumerating the 23 poorest states of the world, with a yearly national income per head below US $100, included 8 states from the region of Asia and Oceania: Afghanistan, Bhutan, Yemen, Laos, the Maldive Islands, Nepal, Sikkim, Western Samoa.

G. MYRDAL, *Asian Drama: An Inquiry into the Poverty of Nations*, New York, 1967; M. HASAD (ed.), *Basic Documents of Asian Regional Organizations*, 8 Vols., New York, 1974–1980.

ASIA MINOR. A peninsula, part of the Republic of Turkey in Western Asia. Area: 647,500 sq. km.

M. OSWARD, *Asia Minor*, London, 1958.

ASIAN–AFRICAN LEGAL CONSULTATIVE COMMITTEE. An intergovernmental organization, est. 1956, with headquarters in Delhi, by: Burma, Ceylon, Egypt, Ghana, India, Indonesia, Iraq, Iran, Japan, Jordan, Kenya, Kuwait, Malaya, Nepal, Nigeria, Pakistan, the Philippines, Sierra Leone, Syria, Thailand. Besides dealing with legal advice in international law matters, it expresses the position of its member states on questions debated by the UN Commission on International Law. Reg. with the UIA.

Yearbook of International Organizations.

ASIAN AND PACIFIC COUNCIL. An intergovernmental organization, f. in Seoul in 1966 with headquarters in Bangkok, by: Australia, Japan, Malaysia, New Zealand, the Philippines, South Korea, South Vietnam, Taiwan and Thailand for the co-ordination and development of economic, social, cultural and technological co-operation. The Council holds annual sessions, attending the Ministers of Foreign Affairs. Laos is associated with the Council as a permanent observer.

Yearbook of International Organizations.

ASIAN AND PACIFIC DEVELOPMENT CENTRE. F. 1980 in Kuala Lumpur, replacing: the Asian and Pacific Centre for Women, Asian and

Pacific Development Institute, Asian and Pacific Development Administration Centre, Development and Social Welfare Centre.

The Europa Year Book 1984. A World Survey, Vol. I, p. 25, London, 1984.

ASIAN BANGKOK DECLARATION, 1967. A document drafted by the Asian states, members of the Group of 77, in July, 1967 in the capital of Thailand; a declaration on the economic problems of the developing countries. The principal points of the declaration were included, Oct., 1967, in the ▷ Algiers Group of 77 Charter.

ASIAN CHARTER FOR HEALTH DEVELOPMENT, 1980. A Charter signed by the governments of Bangladesh, India, Sri Lanka, Thailand, and WHO Feb. 15, 1980 and open to other countries of the region. The purposes of the Charter, as set out in art. 1, are:
"To serve as the declaration of principles and expression of the consensus of the people and the governments of the countries on common health problems considered by them as having high priority and requiring urgent and concerted action, and to focus national, regional and international attention on these needs;
To facilitate and rationalize the mobilization, provision and utilization of adequate national funds and resources to tackle priority health problems;
To promote inter-country consultation and collaboration and to foster close international co-operation, and
To provide a common basis for formulating health plans, programs and projects in the best way possible, within the framework of national, regional and global development policies.
The Charter in no way infringes the inalienable sovereignty of the Member States. It establishes only their endorsement of those priority health areas which they jointly consider important for health development in the context of overall socio-economic development."

"Charter for Health Development: a Milestone for WHOs South-East Asia Region", in: *WHO Chronicle*, No. 5, 1980.

ASIAN CLEARING UNION. A financial union to promote the use of domestic currencies in foreign trade, f. 1974 by the central banks of Bangladesh, Burma, India, Iran, Nepal, Pakistan and Sri Lanka. The Union's agent: Bank Mahrazi, Teheran. Publ. *Annual Report, Newsletter*/monthly.

The Europa Year Book 1984. A World Survey, Vol. I, p. 25, London, 1984.

ASIAN CONFERENCES. The regional conferences after World War II initiated by the UN, with the participation of all the member states of ▷ UN Economic Commission for Asia and the Far East as well as the members of UNESCO. Up to 1985 no international political conference of all of the Asian states was held, despite the suggestion of the USSR, 1975, for convening an Asian Conference on Security and Co-operation.

ASIAN CULTURAL CENTRE FOR UNESCO. f. 1971, Tokyo. Publ.: *Asian Culture* (quarterly) and *Asian Book Development* (quarterly).

ASIAN DEVELOPMENT BANK. Intergovernmental finance institution, est. Dec. 4, 1965 in Manila by the Conference of Plenipotentiaries of the Governments of 27 states: Afghanistan, Australia, Belgium, Cambodia, Canada, Ceylon, China, Denmark, the FRG, India, Iran, Italy, Japan, South Korea, Malaysia, Nepal, the Netherlands, New Zealand, Pakistan, the Philippines, Singapore, Thailand, the UK, the USA, South Vietnam and Western Samoa. The Conference adopted an Agreement est. the AD Bank; entered into force on Aug. 22, 1966. The Bank commenced operations Dec. 19, 1966 in Manila. Publ. *ADB Quarterly Review* and *ADB Annual Report*.

UNTS, Vol. 571, p. 123; *The Europa Year Book 1984. A World Survey*, Vol. I, pp. 102–104, London, 1984. KEESING's *Record of World Events*, 1987, No. 6.

ASIAN DOLLARS. An international term for US dollars deposited in South Asian countries, especially in Hong Kong, Japan and Singapore.

A.K. BHATTAEKARYA, *The Asian Dollar Market*, New York, 1977.

ASIAN–ECONOMIC DEVELOPMENT FUND, AEDF. A US institution est. 1956 by the US Congress providing Presidential Economic Aid to Cambodia, Laos, South Vietnam and Thailand in the framework of the US Mutual Security Program.

ASIAN FREE TRADE ZONE. F. 1975 by the Bangkok Agreement, signed by Bangladesh, India, South Korea, Laos and Sri Lanka, which entered into force in 1976.

ASIAN INDUSTRIAL DEVELOPMENT COUNCIL. An intergovernmental institution f. 1966, Bangkok, of Afghanistan, Australia, Bhutan, Brunei, Burma, China, the Cook Islands, Fiji, Hong Kong, India, Indonesia, Iran, Japan, Kampuchea, South Korea, Laos, Malaysia, Mongolia, Nauru, Nepal, New Zealand, Pakistan, Papua-New Guinea, the Philippines, Western Samoa, Singapore, the Solomon Islands, Sri Lanka, Thailand, Tonga, Vietnam. Publ. *Asian Industrial Development News*. Reg. with the UIA.

Yearbook of International Organizations.

ASIAN INTERGOVERNMENTAL ORGANIZATIONS. The organizations reg. with the UIA:

Asian African Legal Consultative Committee, est. 1956, New Delhi.
Asian Development Bank, est. 1966, Manila.
Asian Highway Co-ordinating Committee, est. 1964, Bangkok.
Asian Industrial Development Council, est. 1966, Bangkok.
Asian-Oceanic Postal Union, est. 1962, Manila.
Asian Productivity Organization, est. 1961, Tokyo.
Colombo Plan for Co-operative Economic Development in South and South-east Asia, est. 1950, Colombo.
Council of Ministers for Asian Co-operation, est. 1966, Bangkok.
South East Asian Ministers of Education Conference, est. 1965, Bangkok.
South East Asia Treaty Organization (SEATO), est. 1954, Bangkok.

Yearbook of International Organizations.

ASIAN MONETARY UNIT, AMU. An accounting unit 1 AMU = 1 SDR, created in Dec. 1974 by the Asia Clearing Union, associating the central banks of Bangladesh, India, Iran, Nepal, Pakistan and Sri Lanka.

J. ASHHEIM, Y.S. PARK, *Artificial Currency Units*, Princeton, 1976.

ASIAN–OCEANIC POSTAL UNION. An intergovernmental institution, est. on Apr. 1, 1962 by the Governments of: Australia, Bangladesh (1975) China, India, Indonesia, Japan, South Korea, Laos, New Zealand, the Philippines and Thailand. Convention revised during 1965, 1970 and 1975 congresses. Publ. *Annual Report*. Reg. with the UIA.

Yearbook of International Organizations.

ASIAN PRODUCTIVITY ORGANIZATION, APO. An intergovernmental institution uniting India, Japan, Nepal, Pakistan, the Philippines, South Korea, Taiwan and Thailand. The Convention was signed in Manila on Apr. 14, 1961. Came into force May 11, 1961.

"The objective of Organization is, by mutual co-operation, to increase productivity in the countries of Asia" (art. 1).

UNTS, Vol. 422, p. 101.

ASIAN WARS. The most important armed conflicts in Asia in the 20th century:

1899–1901:	Boxer rebellion in China.
1904–05:	Russo–Japanese war.
1924–49:	Civil war in China.
1929:	Sino–Soviet military conflict.
1931–45:	War of Japan against China.
1939:	War of Japan against Mongolia.
1941–45:	War of Japan against Britain, Holland, and the US.
1942–45:	Vietnamese war against Japan.
1945:	War of the USSR against Japan.
1946–54:	Vietnamese war against France.
1946–49:	War of liberation of Indonesia against Holland.
1946–73:	Indochina wars.
1947:	Military conflict between India and Pakistan over Kashmir.
1950–53:	Korean war.
1961–73:	Vietnamese war.
1971–72:	Armed conflict between India and Pakistan.
1972:	Civil war in East Pakistan (Bangladesh).
1975:	Civil war in Timor.
1979:	Civil war in Afghanistan.
1980:	Civil war in Kampuchea.
1980–1988:	Iran–Iraq war.

ASIA–PACIFIC TRANSPORT AND COMMUNICATION DECADE, 1985–1994, proclaimed by the General Assembly Res. 19/227 adopted without a vote on Dec. 18, 1984.

UN Chronicle, January, 1985.

ASIATIC COLLECTIVE SECURITY SYSTEM. An international term for a projected collective security pact for Asia, put forward by the USSR May, 1969, expanded Mar. 14, 1972 and Mar. 23, 1972.

KEESING's *Contemporary Archive*, 1969 and 1972.

ASM. An abbreviation for air-to-surface missile.

ASPAC. The Asian and Pacific Council. An intergovernmental organization set up in Seoul in 1966 by Australia, Japan, Malaysia, New Zealand, the Philippines, South Korea, South Vietnam, Taiwan, Thailand for the co-ordination and development of economic, social, cultural and technological co-operation of the states concerned. Headquarters in Bangkok. The Council holds sessions of the Ministers of Foreign Affairs once a year, each time in a different capital of one of the member states, as a rule in June–July. Laos is associated with the Council as a permanent observer.

Yearbook of International Organizations.

ASPEN INSTITUTE FOR HUMAN STUDIES. f. 1972 in Aspen, Colorado, an American institute with branches in France, Italy and West Berlin.

The Economist, December 28, 1987.

ASROC. Anti-submarine rocket. An international naval term for a ship-launched, rocket-boosted coventional torpedo or nuclear depth bomb fired against submarines.

ASSET. Abstract of Selected Solar Energy Technology. A journal (10 issues per year) publ. since 1979 by Tata Energy Institute (TERI) in New Delhi, dedicated to ▷ Solar energy, bioconversion energy, wind energy, energy storage and their socioeconomic and environmental aspects. In co-operation with United Nations University, Tokyo.

ASSIMILATION. A term used in the UN System for the absorption process of alien nationalities by a society; a source of international disputes and conflicts when a state imposes a policy of assimilation upon its minorities, aimed at their denationalization; the reverse process to assimilation is called ▷ dissimilation.

ASSISTANCE AND SALVAGE CONVENTION, 1910. ▷ Maritime law conventions.

ASSOCIATED STATES. An international term used in peace treaties in contrast to ▷ allied states; it indicates those states which participated in wars outside of alliances, e.g. the USA during World War I. At the request of US President W.W. Wilson it found expression in a formula often repeated in the Treaty of Versailles: "allied and associated powers". A similar formula is found in art. 88 of the Italian Peace Treaty of Feb. 10, 1947. In organizations of economic integration another differentiation is adopted: "member states and associated states".

ASSOCIATIONS, INTERNATIONAL. A subject of international co-operation. Organizations reg. with the UIA:

Federation of International Associations Established in Belgium, f. 1949, Brussels.
Union of International Associations (UIA), f. 1907, Brussels. Consultative status: ECOSOC, UNESCO, ILO. Information center on intergovernmental and non-governmental organizations.
From 1950 the UIA under aegis of the UN publishes the *Yearbook of International Organizations.*

Encyclopedia of Associations, Detroit, 1988.

ASSURANCE OF NUCLEAR SUPPLY, IAEA COMMITTEE. ▷ CAS.

ASSURED DESTRUCTION. ▷ MAD.

ASTEROIDS. ▷ Planets.

ASTHMOLOGY. A subject of international co-operation. Organization reg. with the UIA:

Association of Asthmology (INTERASTHMA), f. 1954, Pamplona, Spain. Publ. *Allergologia et Immunopathologia*.

Yearbook of International Organizations.

ASTROLOGY. A subject of international co-operation. Organization reg. with the UIA:

International Society for Astrological Research, f. 1968, Oxford (USA). Publ. *Journal of Astrological Research*.

Yearbook of International Organizations.

ASTRONAUTICS. A subject of international co-operation. Organizations reg. with the UIA:

International Academy of Astronautics, f. 1960, Paris. Publ. *Acta Astronautica*.
International Astronautical Federation, f. 1960, Paris. Consultative status of ECOSOC, UNESCO, ITU, WHO, WMO, Publ. *Acta Astronautica*.

Yearbook of International Organizations.

ASTRONOMICAL CALENDAR. A subject of international co-operation, co-ordinated by the

Federation of Astronomical and Geophysical Services under the auspices of the International Astronomical Union; establishes data for succeeding decades concerning the location of planets and stars essential for the scientific exploration of space and space voyages.

ASTRONOMICAL SIGNS. The oldest international signs for planets, moon phases, zodiac signs and others, in the form of ideograms universally accepted since ancient times.

ASTRONOMICAL UNIT. A unit of length equal to the mean radius of the Earth's orbit, about 92,900,000 miles.

ASTRONOMY. A subject of international co-operation. Organizations reg. with the UIA:

Central Bureau for Astronautical Telegrams, f. 1919, Cambridge, Mass., USA.
Federation of Astronomical and Geophysical Services, f. 1956, Hailsham, E. Sussex, UK.
International Astronomical Union, f. 1919, Athens. Consultative status: ITU, WMO.
International Informative Bureau on Astronomical Ephemerides, f. 1970, Paris.
Inter-Union Commission on Frequency Allocations for Radio Astronomy and Space Science, f. 1960, Appleton Laboratory, Dirton Park, Slough, UK.

Yearbook of International Organizations; V. ILLINGWORTH, *Dictionary of Astronomy*, London 1986.

ASUNCIÓN. The capital of Paraguay. A city and port (1979 pop. *c.* 481,700) on the Paraguay river. The seat of the Pan-American Medical Confederation and a UN Information Centre.

Yearbook of International Organizations.

ASW. Anti-submarine warfare. A strategic weapon against submarine vessels of any kind; one of the weapons included in the ▷ SALT negotiations.

D. ROBERTSON, *Guide to Modern Defense and Strategy*, Detroit, 1988.

ASWAN, HIGH DAM. A large dam on the Nile in southern Egypt, close to city Aswan (or Asuan) at the First Cataract. In 1956, the financing of its construction produced an international crisis between Great Britain and the USA on the one side, and Egypt on the other. The first two states (after the evacuation of the British forces from the Suez Canal zone, cancelled their financial credits for the construction of the dam. Egypt counteracted by nationalizing the Suez Canal. The USSR then granted Egypt credits and technical assistance; the construction of the High Dam, 114.4 m high and 3602.4 m long, started in 1960, was completed in 1970; the dam's reservoir formed Lake Nasser, allowed the irrigation of about 800,000 hectares and provided Egypt with electric power from a hydroelectric plant generating 2400 megawatts. Lake Nasser (area 5180 sq. m), one of the world's largest artificial reservoirs, has a storage capacity of *c.* 157 billion cu m. The first Aswan Dam, the so-called Low Dam, was constructed by the British in 1898–1902, with a hydroelectric plant generating 350 megawatts; it is situated 6 km to the north of the High Dam. As the historical site of ▷ Abu Simbel was to be inundated by the High Dam, UNESCO organized the evacuation of the Abu Simbel art treasures to higher ground as ▷ World Heritage.

UNESCO, *Patrimoine Culturel de l'Humanité*, No. 3, 1974; UNESCO, *Temples and Tombs of Ancient Nubia*, Paris, 1987.

ASYLUM. The granting of refuge to an alien who, for racial or political reasons, is exposed to persecution, imprisonment or death in his own state. Diplomatic asylum is refuge in an exterritorial alien representation. Territorial asylum is refuge on the territory of an alien state with the latter's permission. Included into regional treaties, mainly Latin American, and into international conventions. ▷ Inter-American Asylum Conventions 1928–54. The European Parliamentary Assembly on March 17, 1988, adopted a Resolution on the Right of Asylum.

See also ▷ Migration, and ▷ Refugees.

E. HAMBRO, "New trends in the law of extradition and asylum", in: *Western Political Quarterly*, 1952; G. MORA, *International Law and Asylum as a Human Right*, London, 1956; OAS Treaties Series, No. 34, Washington DC, 1967; L.N. GALONSKAIA, *Pravo ubezhishcha*, Moscow, 1968. *Cuestion del Asilo Diplomatico. Informe del Secretario General de las NU, A/10139, Part I, of 2 IX 1975, and Part II, of 22 IX 1975.* R.L. BLEDSOE, B.A. BOCZEK, *The International Law Dictionary*, Oxford, 1987; Council of Europe, *Human Rights, Information Sheet No. 21*, Strasbourg, 1988, pp. 220–224.

ASYLUM POLICY AND ASYLUM SEEKERS. Two international terms of the 1980s. The European Parliament on June 19, 1987, adopted a Resolution on the Asylum Policy of certain Member States. The text is as follows:
The European Parliament.
(a) whereas the ad hoc working party set up by the Council in London on October 20, 1986, to co-ordinate visa and asylum policy (TREVI group) met on April 28, 1987, and against the wish expressed by the European Parliament in its resolution of March 12, 1987, took decisions concerning visa and asylum policy without first hearing the Parliament's views, thereby violating elementary democratic convention,
(b) whereas the TREVI group agreed that the Member States should pool information on the transit countries and potential first countries of asylum of asylum-seekers, allow them across their frontiers only if they have obtained valid travel permits and visas in their countries of origin prior to departure, and refuse them visas or even transit permits, making it virtually impossible for them to avail themselves of the right of asylum
(c) having regard to the flagrant violations of human rights and international law perpetrated by border officials, who, in particular at Amsterdam, Frankfurt, Copenhagen and London airports, are forcibly returning ever increasing numbers of asylum-seekers to the countries through which they have passed previously or even those countries from which they have had to flee,
(d) whereas detention cells for asylum-seekers without entry permits have been set up at Schiphol and Zaventem airports,
(e) whereas in certain Member States asylum-seekers who have managed to flee with counterfeit documents are being prosecuted in increasing numbers for forgery, etc.,
(f) whereas certain Member States, by fining airlines and making them pay the costs of flying asylum-seekers back, are forcing them to require their staff in the main countries of origin concerned – often local people – to check the validity and authenticity of passports and visas before check-in,
(g) having regard to the inhumane treatment deliberately meted out to asylum-seekers in reception centres in certain Member States in the hope of deterring them,
(1) Calls on the Member States to desist from such treatment, which aggravates the de facto and de jure position of potential asylum-seekers and those already in the country;
(2) Urges the Member States in particular not to devolve sovereign responsibilities to transport companies such as airlines;
(3) Stresses the need for all potential asylum-seekers to be able to submit their applications under satisfactory circumstances in a Member State so that a procedure that satisfies the requirements of the rule of law can be conducted;
(4) Stresses that erosion of the right not to be turned away by action that makes it impossible for potential applicants for asylum even to enter the country of their choice constitutes a breach of international law and an intolerable weakening of the principle that the state should be governed by the rule of law;
(5) Believes a narrow interpretation of the term "first country of asylum" to be unacceptable;
(6) Calls on the Member States not to impose any unilateral restrictions on asylum, to improve and streamline the asylum procedure by devoting greater manpower and resources to it and to work constructively for the adoption of the proposal for a directly announced by the Commission, without which the goal of a single internal market cannot be achieved;
(7) Calls on the Commission immediately, and in consultation with it, to appoint one of Parliament's Members as the Community spokesman on matters of asylum; this spokesman will take part without further delay in the work of the relevant bodies, work within the Commission and be able to report directly to both the Commission and Parliament on his or her own initiative;
(8) Instructs its President to forward this resolution to the Commission and Council and the governments of the Member States.

Council of Europe, Human Rights, Information Sheet No. 21, Strasbourg, 1988, pp. 234–235.

ASYMMETRY. An international term used in the 1970s to describe the US concept for a "balanced", that is, "asymmetric" reduction of armed forces in Europe (▷ MBFR); for instance, if one US division is to be withdrawn from Europe to the USA, that is, to a distance of 5000 km, then, according to the Western strategists, the USSR should withdraw five divisions to a distance of about 1000 km, or 500 km from Central and Eastern Europe; a matter discussed during the Vienna disarmament negotiations (1973–83). On July 16, 1988, the Warsaw Pact States called for a reduction of conventional forces in Europe whereby asymetry would be eliminated followed by a 26% reduction of troop levels and creation of "low-armament zones" along frontlines.

KEESING's *Record of World Events*, August, 1988.

ATA-BOOK. An international term for forms standardized by the Brussels Customs Convention on Condition Clearance of Goods (so-called ATA Convention) of Dec. 6, 1961 simplifying the customs-free import of commercial samples and advertising materials (in accordance with the Geneva Convention on this matter of Nov. 7, 1952) and the customs-free importation of goods in transit. Many states belonging to the ATA Convention do not recognize ATA Book in postal transactions (ATA is a French-English official abbreviation of Admission Temporaire–Temporary Admission).

ATCA ▷ NATO.

ATHEISM. A doctrine rejecting the existence of God or of any other supernatural power; it found its political reflection in the 18th- and 19th-century revolutionary doctrines and the contemporary international free-thinking movements. In 1892 an Italian scholar of religions, A. Palomba, introduced in his work *L'ateismo scientifico* the term "scientific atheism" which was to become, in the 20th century, a part of the scientific philosophy of life propagated mainly by the Marxists.

F. MAUTNER, *Der Ateismus und seine Geschichte im Abendlande*, Berlin, 1920–23, 4 vols.; J. LAIRD, *Theism and Cosmology*, London, 1940–41, 2 vols.; I.O. CAMERIAN (ed.), *Osnovy nauchnogo ateizma*, Moskva, 1961; H. LEY, *Geschichte der Aufklärung und des Atheismus*, Berlin, 1966. G. STEIN, The Encyclopedia of Unbelief, 2 Vls., New York 1985. D.V. POSPIELOVSKY, *A History of Marxist–Leninist Atheism and Soviet Anti-religious Policies*, 3 Vls, London, 1987.

"ATHEN". The name of a British passenger ship which, while making for the USA, was the first to be sunk by German submarines during World War II (on Sept. 3, 1939). More than 100 persons, many of them Americans, perished with the ship. The Third Reich denied its responsibility for the sinking; however, the Nuremberg Trial, which uncovered evidence that the sinking of *Athen* had been carried out by the German submarine U30, pronounced the deed a war crime.

Internationaler Militärgerichtshof, *Der Prozess gegen die Hauptkriegsverbrecher 1947–1949*, Vol. 5, p. 300; Vol. 13, p. 529; Vol. 17, p. 372; Vol. 32, p. 83; Vol. 35, pp. 35, 314, 330; Vol. 36, p. 3.

ATHENS. The capital of Greece (1971 pop. 867,023, metropolitan area 2,540,241). Its oldest part situated on the hills of Acropolis has been recognized by UNESCO as a cultural monument for the whole of humanity. ▷ Urbanization.

UNESCO, *Patrimoine Culturel de l'Humanité*, No. 3, 1974.

ATHENS CSCE CONFERENCE, 1984 ▷ Peaceful Settlement of International Disputes.

ATHENS CSCE JURIST AND DIPLOMATS MEETING, 1984. Held in Athens, March 21–April 30, 1984. A meeting of 120 jurists and diplomats from 35 CSCE countries discussed without result a generally acceptable method for the peaceful settlement of international disputes. The discussion was based on a Swiss draft plan from an international meeting in 1978 in Montreux.

KEESING's *Contempory Archive*, 1986, No. 12.

ATHIS. Appropriate Technology for Health Information System, one of the information systems of the ▷ WHO.

ATHLETICS. A subject of international co-operation. Organizations reg. with the UIA:

European Athletic Association, f 1969, Paris.
International Amateur Athletic Federation, f. 1912, London, recognized by the International Olympic Committee. Publ. *IAAF Bulletin, IAAF World Record Book*.
South American Association of Athletic Referees, f. 1967, Santiago de Chile.
South American Athletic Confederation, f. 1918, Lima.

Yearbook of International Organizations.

ATHOS OR AKTE. An independent state of Monks of the Order of St Basil of the Orthodox Eastern Church in north-east Greece. Area: 335 sq. km with a community of 20 monasteries built *c.* 963 at the altitude of 2035 m. The Holy Community has had an independent statute for more than ten centuries. A woman or a female animal has never visited the Community.

R.M. DAWKIM, *The Monks of Athos*, London, 1936; E. AMAND, *La Presqu'ile des Caloyers: Le Mont Athos*, Paris, 1955; P. SHERRAND, *Athos, the Moun-tain of Silence*, London, 1960. "Mount Athos", in: *National Geographic*, December, 1983.

ATLANTIC. The ocean between Europe and Africa in the east, and North and South America in the west, 82,362,000 sq. km; fisheries in its north-western, north-eastern and south-western regions are regulated by a number of international agreements.

ATLANTIC ALLIANCE. The alliance of North America and Western European states created by the North Atlantic Pact (▷ NATO) signed in Washington, 1949. Since 1962 publ. *Atlantic Community Quarterly*.

D.P. CALLEO, *Beyond American Hegemony: The Future of the Western Alliance*, New York 1987; S.M. WALT, *The Origins of the Alliance*, Ithaca, 1987.

ATLANTIC BLUE RIBAND. An award conferred since 1938 by a special international committee on vessels with motor propulsion for the highest speed–distance ratio on one of five Atlantic routes connecting south and north Europe with the USA and Canada. The first steamship to cross the Atlantic was the American ship *Savannah* which did so in 29 days, 4 hours in May 1819 along the Savannah–Liverpool route; the British ship *Great Western* took 15 days in Apr., 1838. Until 1970 the award had been granted 45 times. Since 1952 the record for passenger ships has belonged to the *United States*, which covered the distance from Ambrose Light to Bishop's Rock in 3 days, 12 hours, 12 minutes; since 1962 the record for freighters has belonged to the *American Challenger*, which covered the same route in 4 days, 20 hours, 50 minutes.

ATLANTIC CABLE. The first oceanic cable between Europe and America was laid by the British vessel *Agamemnon* and the USS *Niagara* between Valentia Bay, Ireland and Trinity Bay, Newfoundland in 1857, a distance of 1640 nautical miles. On Aug. 17, 1858 the first message was cabled:

"Europe and America are united by telegraph. Glory to God in the highest. On earth peace and good-will toward men."

C. BRIGHT, *The Story of the Atlantic Cable*, New York, 1903.

ATLANTIC CHARTER, 1941. A joint declaration of the US president Franklin Delano Roosevelt (1882–1945) and the British Prime Minister Winston S. Churchill (1874–1965), signed on Aug. 14, 1941 on board the warship *Prince of Wales* in the Atlantic, near Newfoundland Island. The Atlantic Charter was the first "common program of purposes and principles" of the United Nations, 1942. Its main purpose was that ... "all nations of the World ... must come to the abandonment of the use of force."

The full text of the Atlantic Charter is as follows:

"Joint declaration of the President of the United States of America and the Prime Minister, Mr. Churchill, representing His Majesty's Government in the United Kingdom, being met together, deem it right to make known certain common principles in the national policies of their respective countries on which they base their hopes for a better future for the world.
First, their countries seek no aggrandizement, territorial or other;
Second, they desire to see no territorial changes that do not accord with the freely expressed wishes of the peoples concerned;
Third, they respect the right of all peoples to choose the form of government under which they will live; and they wish to see sovereign rights and self-government re-stored to those who have been forcibly deprived of them;
Fourth, they will endeavor, with due respect for their existing obligations, to further the enjoyment by all States, great or small, victor or vanquished, of access, on equal terms, to the trade and to the raw materials of the world which are needed for their economic prosperity;
Fifth, they desire to bring about the fullest collaboration between all nations in the economic field with the object of securing, for all, improved labor standards, economic advancement and social security;
Sixth, after the final destruction of the Nazi tyranny, they hope to see established a peace which will afford to all nations the means of dwelling in safety within their own boundaries, and which will afford assurance that all the men in all the lands may live out their lives in freedom from fear and want;
Seventh, such a peace should enable all men to traverse the high seas and oceans without hindrance;
Eighth, they believe that all of the nations of the world, for realistic as well as spiritual reasons must come to the abandonment of the use of force. Since no future peace can be maintained if land, sea or air armaments continue to be employed by nations which threaten, or may threaten, aggression outside of their frontiers, they believe, pending the establishment of a wider and permanent system of general security, that the disarmament of such nations is essential. They will likewise aid and encourage all other practicable measures which will lighten for peace-loving peoples the crushing burden of armaments."

Yearbook of the UN, 1946–47, p. 2.

ATLANTIC INSTITUTE FOR INTERNATIONAL AFFAIRS. f. 1954, Paris. Members: national associations in the NATO countries.

The Europa Yearbook 1988. A World Survey, Vol. I, London, 1988.

ATLANTIC NUCLEAR FORCE ▷ ANF.

ATLANTIC PACIFIC CANAL PROJECTS. The first specific plan for constructing a canal connecting the Atlantic and Pacific Oceans, through Nicaragua, was drawn up in 1826 by experts of the US State Department (Henry Clay Project) and was appended to the USA–Nicaragua Treaty (1849; not ratified) and to the Treaty between the USA and Great Britain (Clayton–Bulwer Treaty), signed in Washington on Apr. 19, 1850, concerning neutralization of the future canal: "No one will have exclusive control over the aforementioned canal. No fortifications will be erected." Earlier, on Dec. 12, 1846, the USA had signed a Treaty with New Granada (Colombia) in Bogota under which the government of New Granada guaranteed the government of the USA that "The right to passage or transit through the Isthmus of Panama by any means of communication existing presently or which will exist in the future will be without charge and free for the citizens and government of the USA." On the basis of this Treaty, the USA built a railroad between the two oceans in the years 1850–55. In the second half of the 19th century, the opinion of the US Senate and its Special Committee (ISTHM Committee) was divided between supporters of a canal through Nicaragua and a canal through the Isthmus of Panama. In 1880 Colombia signed a contract with a French firm, Compagnie Universelle du Canal Interoceanique de Panama, directed by the constructor of the Suez Canal, F. de Lesseps, granting for 99 years the exclusive right to construct and make use of the interocean canal through the Colombian province of Panama. The construction, which began in 1881, was halted in 1889. The French firm declared bankruptcy, resulting in one of the biggest international financial scandals of the 19th century. On Nov. 18, 1901 the USA signed a new Treaty with Great Britain (Hay–Panncefote Treaty) under which Great

Britain ceded her rights under the Clayton–Bulwer Treaty. The USA then separated Panama from Colombia through a coup d'état in that province, which on Nov. 3, 1903 proclaimed the Republic of Panama. Following this, the USA on Nov. 18, 1903 signed a Treaty with the new state under which the USA received the right to a 100-year lease of an area called the Panama Canal-Zone, with an area of 1400 sq. km, and the right to station armed forces. The Treaty entered into force on Feb. 23, 1904 following ratification by the US Senate (66 votes to 14). The domination of the USA over the entire Central American isthmus was confirmed in 1916 by a Treaty between Nicaragua and the USA (Bryan–Chamorro Treaty) under which the USA was granted the right to the year 2015 to build a canal along the route San Juan river–Lake Nicaragua–Rivas isthmus and to build American naval bases on islands in the Gulf of Fonseca.

This Treaty was immediately denounced before the Court of Justice of Central America by Costa Rica, as being in violation of her sovereign rights to the San Juan border river, and by El Salvador and Honduras, as violating their sovereign rights to the Gulf of Fonseca. The Court handed down a verdict against the USA and Nicaragua. The refusal of the USA to recognize this verdict resulted in a suspension of the Court's activities.

As a result of the 1964 crises in US–Panama relations, the Latin-American press began to promote the idea of internationalizing the Panama Canal and all future Latin-American canals under the patronage of the UN or OAS. On Sept. 22, 1964 the US President L.B. Johnson signed a bill, which was passed by Congress, requesting that studies be made on the possibilities of constructing a Latin-American canal at sea-level in three versions: a second canal through Panama in the province of Darien; a canal running along the border between Nicaragua and Costa Rica; and a canal through Colombia. The method of construction was to be traditional excavation or by using nuclear energy, the so-called Plowshare Project developed by the US Atomic Energy Commission. With this aim in mind the USA concluded the following treaties: in 1965 with Nicaragua and in 1966 with Panama and Colombia, allowing surveying studies after 1970 (carried on since 1971). A Colombian plan for an interocean canal through Chaco province was debated by the Colombian Congress in 1964, and surveying was carried out by the Ministry of Public Works (1966–68) with technical assistance from the UN, France and the USA in an area 175 km long and 16 km wide, from the delta of the Atrato river in the Gulf on Uraba to the shores of the Pacific, the highest elevation on this route being 310 m. US experts worked under the guidelines established by the US Congress, while the participation of French experts was the result of a visit by General Charles de Gaulle to Colombia in 1964 and his promise of assistance, especially in hydrographic studies. As part of the UN Development Program, UN experts in 1967 studied the eventual economic effects on Chaco province of constructing a canal and utilizing dams for hydroelectric power plants. The studies were concluded in the 1970s.

J. KLETTE, *From Atlantic to Pacific: A New Interocean Canal*, New York, 1967.

ATLANTIC PEACE ZONE. The General Assembly on Oct. 27, 1986 adopted Res. 41/11 proposed by Brazil, declaring "the Atlantic Ocean, in the region between Africa and South America a zone of peace and co-operation of the South Atlantic" (124 in favour, one (USA) against, eight abstentions: Belgium, France, the FRG, Italy, Japan, Luxembourg, the Netherlands and Portugal, 25 absent).

UN Chronicle, November 1986.

ATLANTIC UNION MOVEMENT. The organizations reg. with the UIA, promoting co-operation between the West European countries and North America:

Council of European American Associations, f. 1951, Antwerp (Belgium). Publ. *Newsletter* and *Why it is important that Europe and America should be Friends*.
International Movement for Atlantic Union, f. 1958, Paris and Washington, DC. Publ. *Freedom and Union*.

Yearbook of International Organizations.

ATLANTIC WALL. A chain of German field fortifications on the Atlantic coast from the Pyrenees on the Spanish–French frontier to Kirkenes in North Norway; about 4000 km long, with *c.* 6000 bunkers built 1941–44 by foreign forced labor. After the Allied invasion of Normandy on June 6, 1944 the German Army withdrew from the Atlantic Wall. At the Nuremberg International Military Trial, 1945–46 documents were presented on inhumane labor conditions for foreign workers during the Atlantic Wall construction.

International Military Trial, Vol. 16, pp. 22–493, 522.

ATLAS. A set of maps universally accepted since the publication 1585–95 by the Flemish cartographer Gerhardus Mercator (1512–94) of a collection of geographic maps entitled *Atlas sive cosmographicae meditationes de fabrica mundi et fabricati*, with a drawing on the title page of the mythical titan Atlas, brother of Prometheus, supporting the globe. The development of ▷ Cartography is a subject of international co-operation: in the International Geographical Union there is a Commission for National Atlases. Since 1950 the UN Cartographic Office is preparing the International Map of the World on the 1:1.000.000 scale. See ▷ Cartography of the UN.

PH. LEE PHILLIPS, *A List of Geographical Atlases in the Library of Congress,* Washington, DC, 1909–1920; C.E. LEGEAR, *A List of Geographical Atlases in the Library of Congress,* Washington, DC, 1958–; ST. LESZCZYCKI, *National and Regional Atlases,* Warsaw, 1964; RAND McNALLY, *The New International Atlas,* Chicago–New York 1980; T. CAMPBELL, *Early Maps,* New York 1981; THE HARPER ATLAS OF WORLD HISTORY, New York 1987.

ATM, Antitactical Missile Defense. A military system discussed in the mid 1980s–in the NATO.

Zb. BRZEZINSKI, *Game Plan. How to Conduct the US–Soviet Contest,* Boston, 1987.

ATMOSPHERE. A subject of international co-operation. Organizations reg. with the UIA:

International Association of Meteorology and Atmospheric Physics, f. 1919, Brussels. Publ. *New Bulletin.*
International Atmospheric Radiation Committee, f. 1970. Munich (FRG).

Yearbook of International Organizations.

ATMOSPHERE, INTERNATIONAL STANDARD. A conventional dependence of mean pressure magnitudes, air density and temperature on the altitude above sea level at medium latitudes, recognized as an international standard for the testing of aircraft, aircraft engines and missiles in various heat and pressure conditions. The standard is determined by assuming the existence of fixed conditions (dry air not changing its composition with the change of altitude; defined pressure at sea level and temperature). Atmospheric research was conducted at the initiative of UNESCO and sponsored by the International Council of Scientific Unions and the WMO within the framework of the

General Atmospheric Research Program (GARP), initiated in 1967.

COSPAR, *International Reference Atmosphere,* Paris, 1965.

"ATOM FOR PEACE". A United States international program formulated by President Dwight Eisenhower, calling for the creation of the ▷ International Atomic Energy Agency, IAEA.

ATOMIC ATMOSPHERIC TESTS. The first atomic atmospheric test took place in 1946 over the ▷ Bikini Atoll; afterwards until the 1980's the majority were carried out in the Pacific region, by the USA in the ▷ Marshall Islands area, by the UK on Malden and ▷ Christmas Islands, and by France on ▷ Muroroa Atoll.

KEESING's *Record of World Events,* 1986, No. 2.

ATOMIC BOMB. An international military term since August 1945 (▷ Hiroshima and Nagasaki), replaced in 1950s by the term ▷ Nuclear Weapons, after invention of the ▷ Hydrogen bomb.

R. RHODES, *The Making of the Atomic Bomb,* New York 1987; D. ROBERTSON, *Guide to Modern Defense and Strategy,* Detroit 1988.

ATOMIC COSMIC TESTS. A subject of international test ban agreements, ▷ Outerspace Moscow Treaty, 1963.

ATOMIC DEMOLITION MUNITION, ADM. An international military NATO term for nuclear mines buried before Warsaw Pact troop lines on the FRG frontier with Czechoslovakia and the GDR.

D. ROBERTSON, *Guide to Modern Defense and Strategy,* Detroit, 1988.

ATOMIC DIPLOMACY. An international term from the 1950s for the foreign policy of atomic powers and superpower nations. See also ▷ Brinkmanship.

D. ROBERTSON, *Guide to Modern Defense and Strategy,* Detroit, 1988.

ATOMIC ENERGY. A subject of international co-operation. Organizations reg. with the UIA:

European Atomic Energy Society, f. 1954, London
European Atomic Energy Commission (▷ EURATOM).
European Atomic Forum, f. 1960, Paris.
Nordic Institute for Theoretical Atomic Physics, f. 1957, Copenhagen.
Nuclear Research Dubna Joint Institute, f. 1956, Dubua, USSR.

Yearbook of International Organizations. B. GOLDSCHMIDT, *The Atomic Complex. A Worldwide Political History of Nuclear Energy,* La Grange Park, Illinois, 1982.

ATOMIC ENERGY AND THE UN. The first resolution of the UN General Assembly, Res. 1/I of 24 Jan., 1946, concerned the establishment of the Atomic Energy Commission with the task of fostering the utilization of atomic energy solely for peaceful purposes. The initiators of the establishment of the Commission were the United States, Canada, and Great Britain on Nov. 15, 1945 in the joint so-called Washington Declaration, 1945. However, work of the UN Commission was paralyzed by a basic dispute between the USA, which proposed that control over the mining and utilization of uranium in the entire world be handed over to a special atomic agency, and the USSR, which came out in favor of exercising this control through the UN Security Council. Moreover, the USSR on June 4, 1946 suggested the signing of the International Convention on the Prohibition of the Production of

Atomic Bombs and the destruction of those existing within 90 days; this motion was rejected. In 1949 the first Soviet atomic bomb was exploded, in 1952 a British, in 1960 a French, in 1964 a Chinese. From then on in the UN there were no further discussions either on the control of uranium or on a convention on its prohibition, but on the ▷ non-proliferation of atomic weapons and on the ▷ denuclearization of certain regions of the world, as well as on universal ▷ disarmament and the possibilities of the peaceful use of atomic energy for the economic development of the world. In 1955–57 the UN created the International Atomic Energy Agency (▷ IAEA) as one of its related agencies; in 1957 in West Europe an international regional agency was created ▷ EURATOM, in Eastern Europe ▷ Dubna. Other organizations reg. with the UIA:

European Atomic Energy Society, 1954, headquarters in Vienna; co-ordinates the national commissions of Austria, Belgium, Denmark, France, the FRG, Great Britain, Holland, Norway, Portugal, Spain, Sweden, Switzerland.
European Atomic Forum (FORATOM), f. 1960, headquarters in Paris, has an advisory statute IAEA, affiliates 15 countries of Western Europe and Scandinavia.

In 1955, 1958, 1964 and 1970 meetings of the UN International Conference on Peaceful Uses of Atomic Energy took place in Geneva. The multivolumed reports from the conferences were published in English and French. See also ▷ Soviet proposal on atomic energy 1947.

UN Yearbooks 1946–85.

ATOMIC ENERGY COMMISSION OF THE UN ▷ UNEAC.

ATOMIC ENERGY WASHINGTON DECLARATION, 1945.
A declaration by the President of the USA, Harry S. Truman, the Prime Minister of the UK, C.R. Attlee, and the Prime Minister of Canada, W.L. Mackenzie King, relating to atomic energy; signed in Washington, DC Nov. 15, 1945:

"The President of the United States, the Prime Minister of the United Kingdom, and the Prime Minister of Canada, have issued the following statement:
(1) We recognize that the application of recent scientific discoveries to the methods and practice of war has placed at the disposal of mankind means of destruction hitherto unknown, against which there can be no adequate military defense, and in the employment of which no single nation can in fact have a monopoly.
(2) We declare to emphasize that the responsibility for devising means to ensure that the new discoveries shall be used for the benefit of mankind, instead of as a means of destruction, rests not on our nations alone, but upon the whole civilized world. Nevertheless, the progress that we have made in the development and use of atomic energy demands that we take an initiative in the matter, and we have accordingly met together to consider the possibility of international action:
(a) To prevent use of atomic energy for destructive purposes;
(b) To promote the use of recent and future advances in scientific knowledge, particularly in the utilization of atomic energy, for peaceful and humanitarian ends.
(3) We are aware that the only complete protection for the civilized world from the destructive use of scientific knowledge lies in the prevention of war. No system of safeguards that can be devised will of itself provide an effective guarantee against production of atomic weapons by a nation bent on aggression. Nor can we ignore the possibility of the development of other weapons, or of new methods of warfare, which may constitute as great a threat to civilization as the military use of atomic energy.
(4) Representing as we do, the three countries which possess the knowledge essential to the use of atomic energy, we declare at the outset our willingness as a first contribution, to proceed with the exchange of fundamental scientific information and the interchange of

scientists and scientific literature for peaceful ends with any nation that will fully reciprocate.
(5) We believe that the fruits of scientific research should be made available to all nations, and that freedom of investigation and free interchange of ideas are essential to the progress of knowledge. In pursuance of this policy, the basic scientific information essential to the development of atomic energy for peaceful purposes has already been made available to the world. It is our intention that all further information of this character that may become available from time to time shall be similarly treated. We trust that other nations will adopt the same policy, thereby creating an atmosphere of reciprocal confidence in which political agreement and co-operation will flourish.
(6) We have considered the question of the disclosure of detailed information concerning the practical industrial application of atomic energy. The military exploitation of atomic energy depends, in large part, upon the same methods and processes as would be required for industrial uses. We are not convinced that the spreading of the specialized information regarding the practical application of atomic energy, before it is possible to devise effective, reciprocal, and enforceable safeguards acceptable to all nations, would contribute to a constructive solution of the problem of the atomic bomb. On the contrary, we think it might have the opposite effect. We are, however, prepared to share, on a reciprocal basis with others of the United Nations, detailed information concerning the practical industrial application of atomic energy just as soon as effective enforceable safeguards against its use for destructive purposes can be devised.
(7) In order to attain the most effective means of entirely eliminating the use of atomic energy for destructive purposes and promoting its widest use for industrial and humanitarian purposes, we are of the opinion that at the earliest practicable date a Commission should be set up under the United Nations Organization to prepare recommendations for submission to the Organization.
The Commission should be instructed to proceed with the utmost dispatch and should be authorized to submit recommendations from time to time dealing with separate phases of its work.
In particular the Commission should make specific proposals:
(a) For extending between all nations the exchange of basic scientific information for peaceful ends,
(b) For control of atomic energy to the extent necessary to ensure its use only for peaceful purposes,
(c) For the elimination from national armaments of atomic weapons and of all other major weapons adaptable to mass destruction,
(d) For effective safeguards by way of inspection and other means to protect complying states against the hazards of violations and evasions.
(8) The work of the Commission should proceed by separate stages, the successful completion of each one of which will develop the necessary confidence of the world before the next stage is undertaken. Specifically, it is considered that the Commission might well devote its attention first to the wide exchange of scientists and scientific information, and as a second stage to the development of full knowledge concerning natural resources of raw materials.
(9) Faced with the terrible realities of the application of science to destruction, every nation will realize more urgently than before the overwhelming need to maintain the rule of law among nations and to banish the scourge of war from the earth. This can only be brought about by giving wholehearted support to the United Nations Organization, and by consolidating and extending its authority, thus creating conditions of mutual trust in which all peoples will be free to devote themselves to the arts of peace. It is our firm resolve to work without reservation to achieve those ends."

UNTS, vol. 3, pp. 124–128.

ATOMIC POWERS
The states which carried out nuclear bomb tests; in chronological order: USA – on July 16, 1945, USSR – Sept. 22, 1949, Great Britain – Feb. 26, 1952, France – Feb. 13, 1960, People's Republic of China – Oct. 16, 1966. The first three atomic powers signed on Aug. 5, 1963 an agreement on the ban of nuclear weapon tests in the

atmosphere, in space, and under water (▷ Moscow Nuclear Test Treaty), and on July 1, 1968 the agreement on ▷ non-proliferation of nuclear weapons. On May 18, 1974, India carried out an underground nuclear test. In June 1975, with the USA protesting, Brazil concluded an agreement with the Federal Republic of Germany on construction of installations which would allow Brazil "to use nuclear explosions for peaceful purposes."

B. GOLDSCHMIDT, *The Atomic Complex. A Worldwide Political History of Nuclear Energy*, La Grange Park, Illinois, 1982.

ATOMIC RADIATION.
A radioactive contamination of the atmosphere by radioactive fall-out occurs during nuclear bomb explosions or in the case of an accident to atomic reactors causing pollution of the earth's atmosphere and then land and sea surfaces to a degree dangerous to man and nature. Subject of international research under the aegis of the UN. The UN General Assembly, with the Res. 913/X, Dec. 3, 1955, established the UN Scientific Committee on the Effects of Atomic Radiations; at the same time it charged the WMO to record the level of radioactivity in the atmosphere on a continual basis and to make reports. On Dec. 17, 1965 the UN General Assembly, with the Res. 2078/XX instructed the Committee to continue its work for the purpose of "more precisely ascertaining the level and effects of radiation coming from all sources". The Committee in close co-operation with WMO, FAO and IAEA made its first report in 1966 and submits succeeding ones every four years. The UN General Assembly, with the Res. 2113/XXI, Dec. 17, 1966, expressed its recognition for the work of the Committee and the WMO and recommended its continuation. The IAEA publishes periodic scientific reports on the biological effects of atomic radiation.

UN Yearbook, 1955, 1965, 1966; *UN Review*, No. 1. 1956, and No. 5, 1959; *Report of the UN Scientific Committee on the Effects of Atomic Radiation*, UN, New York, 1958, 1966 and 1970; *Methods of Radiochemical Analysis*, FAO, Rome, 1959; *Radioactive Materials in Food and Agriculture*, FAO, Rome, 1960; *Agricultural and Public Health Aspects of Radioactive Contamination in Normal and Emergency Situations*, FAO, IAEA, WHO, Rome, 1966; *Manual on Radiation Protection in Hospitals*, Geneva, 1974; S. GLASSTONE, P.J. DOLAN, *Effects of Nuclear Weapons*, Washington, DC, 1977; SIPRI, *Nuclear Radiation in Warfare*, Stockholm, 1981.

ATOMIC STALEMATE.
An international term, adopted from chess terminology, for a position which constitutes a draw; first appeared in 1957, when it became apparent that not only the USA, but also the USSR in case of atomic war, had nuclear resources capable of destroying the opponent; this resulted in a revision of strategic doctrines. ▷ MAD.

ATOMIC TESTS VETERANS ASSOCIATIONS.
Organizations of the US and UK exservicemen and civilians who took part in atomic tests in the Pacific region: the US National Association of Atomic Test Veterans, est. 1979 and the British Nuclear Test Veterans Association, est. 1983. Both organizations claimed compensation for all members who had suffered from radiation linked illness.

KEESING's *Record of World Events*, 1986, No. 2.

ATOMIC UMBRELLA.
Also called the Gromyko Plan. A political–military term used in the UN, formulated for the first time on Nov. 26, 1962 by the foreign minister of the USSR, A.A. Gromyko, in a proposal submitted to the UN Disarmament Com-

mittee on universal and total disarmament. It stipulated that in the second stage of disarmament, the USA and USSR would retain a limited number of intercontinental rockets as well as anti-ballistic and anti-aircraft weapons which would comprise a special "atomic umbrella" that would deter any military provocations. The idea was also included in the second Soviet proposal of Feb. 4, 1964 which proposed that retaining of the "atomic umbrella" in the third stage of universal disarmament.

ATOMIC UNDERGROUND TESTS. A subject of international agreement.

ATOMIC UNDERWATER TESTS. A subject of test ban agreement.

ATOMIC WAR ▷ Nuclear war.

ATOMIC WEAPONS. The first weapons of mass destruction. ▷ Nuclear arms.

ATTACHÉ. A person attached to a diplomatic representation as a military, commercial, scientific, press, cultural or any other expert. According to their function, they enjoy different status within the diplomatic hierarchy (from the rank approaching that of a Counsellor to the lowest classes of diplomatic functionaries). ▷ Vienna Convention on Diplomatic Relations, 1961.

ATTENTATENKLAUSEL ▷ Belgian Clause.

AUDIENCE. (1) A diplomatic term for an official interview granted by the head or other government representative of the receiving state to a foreign diplomatic envoy; (2) A judicial term for a hearing in a court as, for instance, in the International Court of Justice (arts. 46, 47, 66, 67 of the ICJ Statute and art. 85 of the ICJ Rules of Procedure).

AUDIOLOGY. A subject of international co-operation. Org. reg. with the UIA:

International Society of Audiology, f. 1952, London. Publ. *Audiology, Journal of Auditory Communication.*
International Association of Physicians in Audiology, f. 1980, London, UK. Publ.: *Bulletin.*

Yearbook of International Organizations, 1986–87.

AUDIOPHONOLOGY. A subject of international co-operation. Organizations reg. with the UIA:

European Association of Audiophonological Centers, f. 1970, Lyon, France.
International Office for Audiophonology, f. 1967, Brussels.

Yearbook of International Organizations, 1986–87.

AUDIO-VISUAL MEDIA. A subject of international co-operation. Organizations reg. with the UIA:

European Audio-Visual Committee, f. 1973, Antwerp, Belgium.
International Association for Art and Audio-Visual Techniques, f. 1970, Venice.
International Association for the Study and Promotion of Audio-Visual and Structure – Global Methods, f. 1965, Brussels. Publ. *Langue et culture.*
International Audio-Visual Technical Center, f. 1960, Antwerp, Belgium.
International Federation of Audio-Visual Workers Union, f. 1975, London.
International Institute for Music, Dance and Theater in the Audio-Visual Media, f. 1969, Vienna.

Yearbook of International Organizations.

AUDITING. A subject of international co-operation. Organizations reg. with the UIA:

Institute of Internal Auditors, f. 1941, New York. Publ. *Auditing News and Reports.*
International Federation of Audit Bureaus of Circulation, f. 1933, Madrid. Publ. *Circulation Auditing around the World.*
International Organization of Supreme Audit Institutions, f. 1953, Vienna, ECOSOC(II). Publ. *INTOSAI Documents.*

Yearbook of International Organizations, 1986–87.

AUDITORS ▷ UN Board of Auditors.

AUGSBURG RELIGIOUS PEACE TREATY, 1555. A settlement between German Emperor Charles V and German princes, signed Sept. 25, 1555, about secularization of their lands, recognizing the rights of practitioners of the Augsburg Confession (the Lutherans) as equal with those of the Roman Catholics but banning other denominations arising from the Reformation, whose followers were allowed to emigrate; it de facto introduced the principle ▷ *Cuius regio eius religio,* which was not included in the original German text of the Treaty but appeared later in an anonymous commentary.

K. BRANDT, *Der Augsburger Religiöse Friede vom 25 September 1555,* Berlin, 1927.

AU PAIR. International term, French: "on equal terms". (1) An agreement with equal gain; (2) In Anglo-Saxon countries name of status of foreign girls living with English families in order to learn English; subject of international agreements (first, 1924, UK with Switzerland) and rules. ▷ Au pair placement. In 1987 US law limited household help by foreigners.

R. RHEINHOLD, Au pair crisis, in: *International Herald Tribune,* May 20, 1987.

AU PAIR PLACEMENT. A subject of a European Agreement, signed in Strasbourg, Nov. 24, 1969, came into force on May 30, 1971. The Preamble and the main points of the Agreement are as follows:

"The member States of the Council of Europe, signatory hereto,
Considering that the aim of the Council of Europe is to achieve greater unity between its Members, in particular for the purpose of facilitating their social progress;
Noting that in Europe more and more young persons, especially girls, are going abroad to be placed au pair;
Considering that, without wishing to make any critical assessment of this widespread practice, it is advisable to define and standardise, in all member states, the conditions governing such au pair placement;
Considering that au pair placement constitutes in member states an important social problem with legal, moral, cultural and economic implications, which transcends national boundaries and thereby takes on a European complexion;
Considering that persons placed au pair belong neither to the student category nor to the worker category but to a special category which has features of both, and that therefore it is useful to make appropriate arrangements for them;
Acknowledging more particularly the need to give persons placed au pair adequate social protection inspired by the principles laid down in the European Social Charter;
Considering that many of these persons are minors deprived for a long period of the support of their families, and that as such they should receive special protection relating to the material or moral conditions found in the receiving country;
Considering that only the public authorities can fully ensure and supervise the implementation of these principles;
Being convinced of the need for such co-ordination within the framework of the Council of Europe,
Have agreed as follows:
Art. 1. Each Contracting Party undertakes to promote in its territory to the greatest extent possible the implementation of the provisions of this Agreement.

Art. 2.(1) Au pair placement is the temporary reception by families, in exchange for certain services, of young foreigners who come to improve their linguistic and possibly professional knowledge as well as their general culture by acquiring a better knowledge of the country where they are received.
(2) Such young foreigners are hereinafter called "persons placed au pair".
Art. 3. Placement au pair, which shall initially be for a period not exceeding one year, may, however, be extended to permit of a maximum stay of two years.
Art. 4.(1) The person placed au pair shall not be less than 17 or more than 30 years of age.
(2) Nevertheless, exceptions to the upper age limit may be granted by the competent authority of the receiving country in individual cases when justified.
Art. 5. The person placed au pair shall have a medical certificate established less than three months before placement, declaring that person's general state of health.
Art. 6.(1) The rights and obligations of the person au pair and the receiving family, as those rights and obligations are defined in this Agreement, shall be the subject of an agreement in writing to be concluded between the parties in question, in the form of a single document or of an exchange of letters, preferably before the person placed au pair leaves the country in which that person was resident and at least during the first week of the placement.
(2) A copy of the agreement referred to in the preceding paragraph shall be lodged in the receiving country with the competent authority or the organization chosen by this authority.
Art. 7. The agreement referred to in Art. 6 shall specify inter alia the manner in which the person placed au pair is to share the life of the receiving family, while at the same time enjoying a certain degree of independence.
Art. 8.(1) The person placed au pair shall receive board and lodging from the receiving family and, where possible, shall occupy a separate room.
(2) The person placed au pair shall be given adequate time to attend language courses as well as for cultural and professional improvement; every facility as regards the arrangement of working hours shall be accorded to this end.
(3) The person placed au pair shall have at least one full free day per week, not less than one such free day in every month being a Sunday, and shall have full opportunity to take part in religious worship.
(4) The person placed au pair shall receive a certain sum of money, as pocket money, the amount of which and the intervals at which it is paid shall be determined by the agreement referred to in Art. 6.
Art. 9. A person placed au pair shall render the receiving family services consisting in participation in day-to-day family duties. The time effectively occupied in such services shall generally not be more than five hours per day."

UNTS, Vol. 788, pp. 260–285.

AUSCHWITZ-BIRKENAU. A concentration camp existing from May 20, 1940 to Jan. 27, 1945 in the suburb of the district city of Oświecim (the Cracow district). The largest of all German concentration camps, established during World War II on Polish territory. Official German name: Konzentrationslager Auschwitz-Birkenau. Close to the mother camp (the so-called Stammlager), called Auschwitz I, a second camp was built in Brzezinka (German Birkenau), called Auschwitz II, as well as a complex, called Aussenlager-Auschwitz III, composed of about 40 branch camps of different sizes. The camp was initially created for Poles, who from June 14, 1940 to June 6, 1941 were its sole inmates, after which Czechs were brought in. Following the declaration of war against the Soviet Union, H. Himmler ordered R. Höss to construct gas chambers. Also in 1941 the first transports of Jews and Soviet prisoners – mainly political commissars arrived. The localization of the camp was, according to Höss, decided upon by reason of the damp mist swept marshy terrain, where, as in Dachau, life had for thousands of years succumbed to death. Auschwitz was an extermination camp for millions of Jews (▷ Endlösung), Poles (▷ German Penal Law for Poles and Jews), Russians (▷ Kommissarbefehl), ▷ Gypsies and 25 other nationalities. Four million were killed, the majority with the poison gas ▷ Zyklon B. The name of the camp has become the international symbol of Nazi genocide. After the war the camp was converted into a museum of martyrdom, under the protection of an International Auschwitz Committee established in 1955, with headquarters till 1962 in Vienna, moved afterwards to Warsaw. Publ. *Auschwitz Reports* (*Zeszyty Oświecimskie*). The present-day city of Oświecim maintains close co-operation with Hiroshima. On July 7, 1972, Auschwitz was visited by UN Secretary-General Kurt Waldheim, and on June 12, 1979 by Pope John Paul II. In 1980 the UNESCO World Heritage Committee put Auschwitz-Birkenau on the list of the world's most important sites. On Dec. 10, 1985, Human Rights Day, in UN Hqs, Secretary General Javier Perez de Cuellar opened a photo exhibition entitled "Auschwitz. A Crime Against Mankind". The exposition organized by the International Auschwitz Committee came to the United States under the sponsorship of the UN Center for Human Rights. On the 43rd Anniversary of the Liberation of the Camp two Nobel Peace Prize Winners, Elie Wiesel (USA), a former Auschwitz prisoner and Lech Wałesa (Poland) leader of the then outlawed "Solidarity" pledged to "proclaim to the World that human beings are worthy of hope". See ▷ World Heritage UNESCO List.

The Trial of German Major War Criminals, Proceedings of the IMT Sitting at Nuremberg, 42 Vols (Auschwitz case in vols. 2, 4, 5, 8, 11, 14, 16, 20 and 22), London, 1946–1948; S. SZMAGLEWSKA, *Dymy nad Birkenau* (Smoke over Birkenau), Warsaw, 1946; C. RAITLINGER, *The Final Solution*, London, 1953; B. BAUM, *Widerstand in Auschwitz*. Berlin, 1957; Lord E.F. RUSSEL, *The Scourge of the Swastika*, London, 1958; R.R. HOESS, *Commandant of Auschwitz*, London, 1959; H.G. ADLER, H. LANGBEIN, E. LIGGENS-REINER, *Auschwitz. Zeugnisse und Berichte*, Frankfurt a.M., 1962; F.K. LESCH, *Pater Maximilian Kolbe*, Würzburg, 1964; B. NAUMAN, *Auschwitz. Bericht über die Strafsache gegen Mulka*, Frankfurt a.M., 1965; H. LANGBEIN, *Der Auschwitz Prozess. Eine Dokumentation*, 2 vols, Vienna, 1965; K. SMOLEN, *Auschwitz 1940–1945*, Oświecim, 1966; J. LUKOWSKI, *Bibliografia obozu koncentracyjnego Oświęcim-Brzezinka 1945–1965*, Warsaw, 1968; K. DUNIN, *La résistance dans les camps de concentration nazis*, Warsaw, 1972; H. LANGBEIN, *Menschen in Auschwitz*, Vienna, 1973; J. GARLINSKI, *Fighting Auschwitz*, Greenwich Conn., 1975; *Auschwitz. Hoja Vernichtungslager*, Warsaw, 1977; W. KIELAR, *Anus Mundi*, London, 1979; M. GILBERT, *Auschwitz and the Allies*, New York, 1981; UNESCO. *The Protection of the World Cultural and Natural Heritage*, Paris, 1983, UNESCO, *A Legacy for All*, Paris, 1984. *UN Chronicle*, 1986, No. 2.

AUSGLEICH. *German* = equalization. An international term for the equalization of rights of Hungary and Austria through a compromise concluded on Dec. 21, 1867 by the emperor of Austria, Franz Joseph I, with Hungary, which established the political union of both states in the form of the Dual Monarchy of Austria–Hungary.

H. WICKHAM STEED, *The Hapsburg Monarchy*, London, 1919; E. ZÖLLNER, *Geschichte Österreichs*, Wien, 1966.

AUSTRALASIA. An indefinite geographical term for regions to the south of Asia – as far as the Antarctic. The term is sometimes replaced by that of Oceania, used most often in Australia for the areas outside the Australian continent and New Zealand, and in its adjectival form for indigenous cultures in the Polynesia region.

J. RONAYNE, *Science and Technology in Australasia, Antarctica and the Pacific Islands*, London 1988.

AUSTRALIA. Member of the UN. Commonwealth of Australia. Federal state on the smallest continent between the Indian and Pacific Oceans. Area: 7,686,801 sq. km. Pop. 1988 est. 16,531,000 (1947 census 7,579,358). Capital since 1927 Canberra with 241,000 inhabitants est. 1980 (Australian Capital Territory). Territories under Australian jurisdiction: Adélie Lands, Ashmor and Cartier Islands, Australian Antarctic Territory, Christmas Islands, and Norfolk Islands (▷ New Guinea). GNP per capita 1987 US $10,900. Official language: English. Currency: 1 Australian dollar = 100 cents. National day: Jan. 28, Australia Day, 1788. Original Member of the UN since Oct. 24, 1945 and of all specialized agencies. Member of the Commonwealth, OECD, Colombo Plan and SEATO. A member of the Antarctic Treaty, June 23, 1961; of the Outer Space Treaty, Mar. 26, 1969; of the Non-Proliferation Treaty, Jan. 23, 1973; of the Sea-Bed Treaty, Jan 23, 1973; the BW Convention, Nov. 27, 1979.

International relations: Australia was a British colony from 1770 to 1900. On Jan 1, 1901 six former colonies, now states, were federated under the name Commonwealth of Australia: New South Wales, Victoria, Queensland, South Australia, Western Australia and Tasmania; on Jan. 1, 1911 also the Northern Territory. During World Wars I and II active on the Allied, United Nations, side (▷ ANZAC, ▷ ANZUS). Participated in the Korean and Vietnam Wars. Member of the League of Nations 1919–39.

In May 1983 Australia called for denuclearization of the South Pacific and protested to France against nuclear test explosions at Mururoa Atoll. See also ▷ World Heritage UNESCO List.

N. HARPER, D. SISSIONS, *Australia and the UN*, New York, 1959; J. ZUBRZYCKI, *Immigrants in Australia*, Melbourne, 1960; A.P. ELKIN, *The Australian Aborigines*, Sydney, 1961; P. COLEMAN (ed.), *Australian Civilization*, Melbourne, 1962; T.R. REESE, *Australia in the XXth Century*, New York, 1964; T.B. MILLAR, *Australia's Defence*, Melbourne, 1965; J.D.B. MILLER, *Australia*, London, 1966; A. WATT, *The Evolution of Australian Foreign Policy 1938–1965*, London, 1967; *The Modern Encyclopaedia of Australia and New Zealand*, Sydney, 1967; A.A. GUBER, K.V. MALAYOVSKI (eds.), *Australia i Okeania. Istoria i Sovremiennost*, Moskva, 1970; C. FOSTER, *Australian Economic Development in the XXth Century*, London, 1970; J. COGHILL, *Australia's Mineral Wealth*, London, 1973; D. BUTTLER, *The Canberra Model. Essays on Australian Government*, London, 1974; W.A. WYNES, *Executive and Judicial Powers in Australia*, Sydney, 1976; H.S. ALBINSKI, *The Australian–American Society Relationship*, London, 1982; H. COXON, *Australian Official Publications*, Oxford, 1981; *The Europa Year Book 1984. A World Survey*. Vol. I pp. 1101–1128, London, 1984.

AUSTRALIAN ANTARCTIC TERRITORY ▷ Antarctic Territory, Australian.

AUSTRALIAN BALLOT. An international term for secret voting, first introduced in parliamentary elections in Australia 1880, in United States 1888. ▷ Election.

AUSTRALIAN INSTITUTE OF INTERNATIONAL AFFAIRS, f. 1933, Canberra, with branches in all states. Publ. *Australia in World Affairs* (six vols. 1951–1980), *Australian Outlook*.

AUSTRIA. Member of the UN. Republic of Austria. Republik Oesterreich. Central European State, bordered by the FRG, Czechoslovakia, Hungary, Yugoslavia, Italy, Switzerland and Liechtenstein. Area: 83,855 sq. km. Pop. 1982 est. 7,570,000 (1971 census 7,491,000). Capital: Vienna with 1,614,841 inhabitants, 1971. GNP per capita 1987 US $11,970. Official language: German. Currency: 1 schilling = 100 groschen. National Day: Oct. 26, Parliament Act of Perpetual Neutrality, 1955. Member of the UN since Mar. 14, 1955 and of all UN specialized agencies, Member of the EFTA, 1959 and of the Test Ban Treaty, July 17, 1964; the Outer Space Treaty, Feb. 26, 1968; the Non-Proliferation Treaty, June 27, 1969; a Preferential Agreement with the EEC, 1973; the Sea-Bed Treaty, Aug. 10, 1973; the BW Convention, Oct. 5, 1977.

International relations: after six centuries of Habsburg rule 1282–1918, the Saint-Germain-en-Laye Treaty, 1919, gave Austria its present borders and forbade the confederation with the German Reich (▷ Anschluss). On Mar. 13, 1938 Nazi Germany occupied Austria. During World War II the Great Powers declared the Anschluss of 1938 as illegal (▷ Allied Commission for Austria) divided, after the war, into four zones of occupation until May 15, 1955, when an ▷ Austria State Treaty with France, Great Britain, USA and USSR restored full sovereignty to Austria, but under the condition of Perpetual Neutrality.

The Austrian government elaborated since then a foreign policy of "active neutrality" presented also on the UN forum. An Austrian statesman, Dr Kurt Waldheim, was UN Secretary-General from 1971 to 1981. After the election of the former UN Secretary General Dr Kurt Waldheim as President of Austria in June 1986, allegations continued to be made in the international community as to his wartime record during the Second World War. On April 17, 1987 the US Justice Department placed Dr Waldheim on a "watch" list preventing him from entering the USA as a private citizen.

S. VEROSTA, *Die internationale Stellung Oesterreichs 1938 bis 1947; Eine Sammlung von Erklärungen und Verträgen*, Wien, 1947; S. ANDREEV, "Uregulirovanie avstriskogo voprosa – vazhnaya zadacha v bor'be za ukreplenie mira v Evrope", in: *Mezhdunarodnaya Zhisn'*, No. 5, 1955; Ch. CHAMMONT, "La neutralité de l'Autriche et les Nations Unies", in: *Annuaire Francaise de Droit International*, 1955; J.L. KUNZ, "Austria's Permanent Neutrality", in: *American Journal of International Law*, No. 50, 1956; A. VERDROSS, "Austria's Neutrality and the UN", in: *American Journal of International Law*, No. 50, 1956; A. SCHARF, *Oesterreichs Erneuerung 1945–1955. Das erste Jahrzehnt der Zweiten Republik*, Wien, 1956; W. GOLDINGER, *Geschichte der Republik Oesterreich*, Wien, 1962; W.B. BANDER, *Austria between East and West, 1945–1955*, Stanford, 1966; Gen BETHOUART, *La bataille pour l'Autriche*, Paris, 1966; W. STRASSER, *Oesterreich und die Vereinten Nationen 1955–1965*, Wien, 1967; S.I. VOROSHILOV, *Rozhdeni vtoroy respubliki Avstri*, Leningrad, 1968; *Das Oesterreichische Buch 1971–1972*, Wien, 1972; E. BARKER, *Austria 1918–1972*, London, 1973; *Republic of Austria 1945–1975*, Vienna, 1976; K. SOTRIFFR, *Greater Austria: 100 years of Intellectual and Social Life from 1800 to the present Time*, Vienna, 1982; *The Europa Year Book 1984. A World Survey*, Vol. I, pp. 297–314, London, 1984. A.K. CRONIN, *Great Power Politics and the Struggle Over Austria, 1945–1955*, London, 1986; J.L. SZIRTES, *Austrian Foreign Policy, 1945–1985*, Vienna 1986; F.I. CARSTEN, *The First Austrian Republic 1918–1938*, Alderskol, 1986.

AUSTRIA HOUSE ▷ Habsburg Empire.

AUSTRIA–ITALY BORDER DISPUTE, called the South Tyrol Question. The Italian region of South Tyrol in the province of ▷ Bolzano, in the autonomous region of Trentino ▷ Upper Adiga, with a predominantly German-speaking population, on the Italian Alpine border with Austria was a subject of border disputes before World War II between Mussolini's Italy and Hitler's Germany,

A

that were resolved by a "final and complete solution" of the question of ▷ Upper Adiga on June 23, 1939 (Hitler–Mussolini South Tyrol Agreement); and again after World War II on Sept. 5, 1946 in Paris by Austrian Foreign Minister Dr Karl Gruber and the Italian Prime Minister Alvido de Gaspari. The non-realization of the Agreement has opened new negotiations on the initiative of the UN General Assembly, 1960 and on July 17, 1971 a new agreement was signed by Austria and Italy and came into effect on Oct. 27, 1971.

Austria–Italy (South Tyrol), in: KEESING's *Border and Territorial Disputes*, London, 1987.

AUSTRIA–MOSCOW DECLARATION, 1943. A
document published at Moscow, Oct. 31, 1943 in the name of the Three Big Powers, which read as follows:

"The Government of the United Kingdom, the Union of Soviet Socialist Republics, and the United States have agreed that Austria, the first free country to fall a victim to Nazi aggression, shall be liberated from German domination. They regard the annexation imposed upon Austria by Germany's penetration of March. 15, 1938, as null and void. They consider themselves as in no way bound by any changes effected in Austria since that date. They declare that they wish to see re-established a free and independent Austria, and thereby to open the way for the Austrian people themselves, as well as those neighbouring States which will be faced with similar problems, to find that political and economic security which is the only basis for lasting peace.
Austria is reminded however that she has a responsibility which she cannot evade for participation in the war on the side of Hitlerite Germany, and that in the final settlement account will inevitably be taken of her own contribution to her liberation."

A Decade of American Foreign Policy. Basic Documents 1941–1949, Washington, DC, 1950.

AUSTRIAN GOLD AGREEMENT, 1947. A
protocol relating to the restitution to Austria of its gold looted by Germany, signed in London, Nov. 4, 1947 by the UK, USA and Austria.

UNTS, Vol. 93, pp. 61–65.

AUSTRIAN SUCCESSION WAR, 1740–1748 ▷
Aix la Chapelle Treaty 1748.

AUSTRIA SAINT-GERMAIN PEACE TREATY, 1919. A Treaty between the Allied Powers (France, Great Britain, Italy, Japan, and USA) and the Associated Powers (Belgium, China, Cuba, Czechoslovakia, Greece, Nicaragua, Poland, Portugal, Romania, the Serb-Croat-Slovene state, Siam) on the one part and Austria on the other part, signed in Saint-Germain-en-Laye, Sept. 10, 1919. The highlights of the Treaty:

Part I of the Treaty is the Covenant of the League of Nations (arts. 1 to 26 and Annex).
Part II Frontiers of Austria (arts. 27 to 35).
Part III Political clauses for Europe (arts. 36 to 94):
"Austria renounces in favor of Italy all rights and title over the territory of the former Austro-Hungarian Monarchy, situated beyond the frontiers of Austria laid down in art. 27 ... " (art. 36).
"Austria ... recognizes the complete independence of the Serb-Croat-Slovene State" (art. 46).
"Austria renounces ... in favor of Romania all rights and title over such portion of the former Duchy of Bukowina as lies within the frontiers of Romania which may ultimately be fixed by the Principal Allied and Associated Powers" (art. 59).
"Austria undertakes to assure full and complete protection of life and liberty to all inhabitants of Austria without distinction of birth, nationality, language, race or religion." (Section V, Protection of Minorities, art. 63).
"Every person possessing rights of citizenship (pertinenza) in territory which formed part of the territories

of the former Austro-Hungarian Monarchy shall obtain ipso facto to the exclusion of Austrian nationality the nationality of the state exercising over such territory" (art. 70).
Part IV, Austrian interests outside Europe (arts. 95 to 117) relating to Morocco, Egypt, Siam and China.
Part V, Military, Naval and Air Clauses (arts. 118 to 159).
Part VI, Prisoners of War and Graves (arts. 160 to 172).
Part VII, Penalties (arts. 173–176).
Art. 173. "The Austrian Government recognises the right of the Allied and Associated Powers to bring before military tribunals persons accused of having committed acts in violation of the laws and customs of war. Such persons shall, if found guilty, be sentenced to punishments laid down by law. This provision will apply notwithstanding any proceedings or prosecutions before a tribunal in Austria or in the territory of her allies.
The Austrian Government shall hand over to the Allied and Associated Powers, or to such one of them as shall so request all persons accused of having committed an act in violation of the laws and customs of war, who are specified either by name or by the rank, office or employment which they held under the Austrian authorities."
Art. 174. "Persons guilty of criminal acts against the nationals of one of the Allied and Associated Powers will be brought before the military tribunals of that Power. Persons guilty of criminal acts against the nationals of more than one of the Allied and Associated Powers will be brought before military tribunals composed of members of the military tribunals of the Powers concerned.
In every case the accused will be entitled to name his own counsel."
Part VIII, Reparation (arts. 177–196).
Part IX, Financial Clauses (arts. 197–216).
Part X, Commercial Relations (arts. 217–275).
Part XI, Aerial Navigation (arts. 276–283).
Part XII, Ports, Waterways and Railways (arts 284 to 331):
Art. 290. "The nationals of any of the Allied and Associated Powers as well as their vessels and property shall enjoy in all Austrian ports and the one inland navigation route of Austria the same treatment in all respects as Austrian nationals, vessels, and property.
In particular, the vessels of any one of the Allied or Associated Powers shall be entitled to transport goods of any description, and passengers, to or from any ports or places in Austrian territory to which Austrian vessels may have access, under conditions which shall not be more onerous than those applied in the case of national vessels; they shall be treated on a footing of equality with national vessels as regards port and harbour facilities and charges of every description, including facilities for stationing, loading and unloading, and duties and charges of tonnage, harbor, pilotage, lighthouse, quarantine, and all analogous duties and charges of whatsoever nature, levied in the name of or for the profit of the Government, public functionaries, private individuals, corporations or establishments of any kind.
In the event of Austria, granting a preferential régime to any of the Allied or Associated Powers or to any other foreign Power this régime shall be extended immediately and unconditionally to all the Allied and Associated Powers. There shall be no impediment to the movement of persons or vessels other than those arising from prescriptions concerning customs, police, sanitation, emigration and immigration, and those relating to the import and export of prohibited goods. Such regulations must be reasonable and uniform and must not impede traffic unnecessarily."
Art. 291. "The following river is declared international: the Danube from Ulm; together with all navigable parts of this river system which naturally provide more than one state with access to the sea, with or without transhipment from one vessel to another, as well as the portion of the course of the Morava (March) and the Thaya (Theiss) forming the frontier between Czechoslovakia and Austria, and lateral canals and channels constructed either to duplicate or to improve naturally navigable sections of the specified river system or to connect two naturally navigable sections of the same river.

The same shall apply to the Rhine–Danube navigable waterway, should such a waterway be constructed, under the conditions laid down in Article 308.
Any part of the above-mentioned river system which is not included in the general definition may be declared international by an agreement between the riparian States."
Art. 292. "On the waterways declared to be international in the preceding Article, the nationals, property and flags of all Powers shall be treated on a footing of perfect equality, no distinction being made to the detriment of the nationals, property or flag of any power between them and the nationals, property or flag of the riparian state itself or of the most-favoured-nation."
Part XIII (Part XIII of the Treaty of Versailles: the International Labour Office, ILO).
Part XIV, Miscellaneous Provisions (arts. 373 to 381).

Major Peace Treaties of Modern History, New York, 1967, pp. 1535–1726.

AUSTRIA STATE TREATY, 1955. A State Treaty
(with Annexes and Maps) for the Re-establishment of an Independent and Democratic Austria, signed in Vienna, May 15, 1955, by the USSR, UK, USA, France and Austria. The text of the Preamble and of Part I Political and Territorial Clauses, is as follows:

"Art. 1. Re-establishment of Austria as a Free and Independent State.
The Allied and Associated Powers recognize that Austria is re-established as a sovereign, independent and democratic State.
Art. 2. Maintenance of Austria's Independence.
The Allied and Associated Powers declare that they will respect the independence and territorial integrity of Austria as established under the present Treaty.
Art. 3. Recognition by Germany of Austrian Independence.
The Allied and Associated Powers will incorporate in the German Peace Treaty provisions for securing from Germany the recognition of Austria's sovereignty and independence and the renunciation by Germany of all territorial and political claims in respect of Austria and Austrian territory.
Art. 4. Prohibition of Anschluss.
(1) The Allied and Associated Powers declare that political or economic union between Austria and Germany is prohibited. Austria fully recognizes its responsibilities in this matter and shall not enter into political or economic union with Germany in any form whatsoever.
(2) In order to prevent such union Austria shall not conclude any agreement with Germany, nor do any act, not take any measures likely, directly or indirectly, to promote political or economic union with Germany, or to impair its territorial integrity or political or economic independence. Austria further undertakes to prevent within its territory any act likely, directly or indirectly, to promote such union and shall prevent the existence, resurgence and activities of any organizations having as their aim political or economic union with Germany, and Pan-German propaganda in favor of union with Germany.
Art. 5. Frontiers of Austria.
The frontiers of Austria shall be those existing on 1st January, 1938.
Art. 6. Human Rights
(1) Austria shall take all measures necessary to secure to all persons under Austrian jurisdiction, without distinction as to race, sex, language or religion, the enjoyment of human rights and of the fundamental freedoms, including freedom of expression, of press and publication, of religious worship, of political opinion and of public meeting.
(2) Austria further undertakes that the laws in force in Austria shall not, either in their content or in their application, discriminate or entail any discrimination between persons of Austrian nationality on the grounds of their race, sex, language, or religion, whether in reference to their persons, property, business, professional or financial interests, status, political or civil rights or any other matters.
Art. 7. Rights of the Slovene and Croat Minorities
(1) Austrian nationals of the Slovene and Croat minorities in Carinthia, Burgenland and Styria shall enjoy the same rights on equal terms as all other Austrian nationals, including the right to their own

organizations, meetings and press in their own language.
(2) They are entitled to elementary instruction in the Slovene or Croat language and to a proportional number of their own secondary schools; in this connection school curricula shall be reviewed and a section of the Inspectorate of Education shall be established for Slovene and Croat schools.
(3) In the administrative and judicial districts of Carinthia, Burgenland and Styria, where there are Slovene, Croat or mixed populations, the Slovene or Croat language shall be accepted as an official language in addition to German. In such districts topographical terminology and inscriptions shall be in the Slovene or Croat language as well as in German.
(4) Austrian nationals of the Slovene and Croat minorities in Carinthia, Burgenland and Styria shall participate in the cultural, administrative and judicial systems in these territories on equal terms with other Austrian nationals.
(5) The activity or organizations whose aim is to deprive the Croat or Slovene population of their minority character or rights shall be prohibited.
Art. 8. Democratic Institutions
Austria shall have a democratic government based on elections by secret ballot and shall guarantee to all citizens free, equal and universal suffrage as well as the right to be elected to public office without discrimination as to race, sex, language, religion or political opinion.
Art. 9. Dissolution of Nazi Organizations
(1) Austria shall complete the measures already begun by the enactment of appropriate legislation approved by the Allied Commission for Austria, to destroy the National Socialist Party and its affiliated and supervised organizations, including political, military and para-military organizations, on Austrian territory. Austria shall also continue the efforts to eliminate from Austrian political, economic and cultural life all traces of Nazism, to ensure that the above-mentioned organizations are not revived in any form, and to prevent all Nazi and militarist activity and propaganda in Austria.
(2) Austria undertakes to dissolve all Fascist-type organizations existing on its territory, political, military and para-military and likewise any other organizations carrying on activities hostile to any United Nation or which intend to deprive the people of their democratic rights.
Austria undertakes not to permit, under threat of penal punishment which shall be immediately determined in accordance with procedures established by Austrian Law, the existence and the activity on Austrian territory of the above-mentioned organizations.
Art. 10. Special Clauses on Legislation
(1) Austria undertakes to maintain and continue to implement the principles contained in the laws and legal measures adopted by the Austrian Government and Parliament since 1st May, 1945, and approved by the Allied Commission for Austria, aimed at liquidation of the remnants of the Nazi regime and at the re-establishment of the democratic system, and to complete the legislative and administrative measures already taken or begun since 1st May, 1945, to codify and give effect to the principles set out in arts. 6, 8 and 9 of the present Treaty, and insofar as she has not yet done so to repeal or amend all legislative and administrative measures adopted between 5th March, 1933 and 30th April, 1945, which conflict with the principles set forth in arts. 6, 8 and 9.
(2) Austria further undertakes to maintain the law of 3rd April, 1919, concerning the House of Habsburg-Lorraine.
Art. 11. Recognition of Peace Treaties
Austria undertakes to recognize the full force of the Treaties of Peace with Italy, Romania, Bulgaria, Hungary, and Finland, and other agreements or arrangements which have been or will be reached by the Allied and Associated Powers in respect of Germany and Japan for the restoration of peace."
Part II relates to Military and Air Clauses, Part III to Withdrawal of Allied Forces, Part IV to Claims Arising out of War, Part V to Property, Rights and Interests, Part VI to General Economic Relations, Part VII to Settlement of Disputes, Part VIII to Miscellaneous Economic Provisions, Part IX to Final Clauses.
Came into force on July 27, 1955.

UNTS, Vol. 217, pp. 225–379.

AUSTRO-GERMAN ALLIANCE, 1873–1918. A military alliance, negotiated Oct. 7, 1873 in Vienna; put an end to German–Austrian disputes and conflicts. The Dual Alliance was preceded, Aug. 23, 1866, by the Peace of Prague, ending the war between Austria and Prussia, and then by a defensive alliance obligating both sides to joint defense in case of attack by Russia and to "sympathetic neutrality" in case of attack by another power. The Dual Alliance took effect Oct. 21, 1879, but was not made public until Feb. 3, 1888. Extended Mar. 22, 1883 and June 2, 1902, it lasted until the fall of both monarchies in 1918. It was the foundation of the Austro–German–Italian Triple Alliance (formed 1879–82) and the alliance of central powers.

A.F. PRIEBRAM, *Die Politischen Geheimverträge Österreich-Ungarn 1879–1914*, Wien, 1920.

AUSTRO-HUNGARY. *German:* Österreich-Ungarn. The name of the Austrian-Hungarian Union 1867–1918 after both countries gained equality (▷ *Ausgleich*) in the Hapsburg empire.

B. AUERBACH, *L'Autriche et la Hongrie pendant la guerre depuis le débat des hostilités jusqu'à la fin de la monarchie (août 1914–novembre 1918)*, Paris, 1925; A. GLAISE-HOLSTENAU, *Die Katastrophe. Die Zertrümmerung Österreich-Ungarns und das werden der Nachfolgestaaten*, Wien, 1929; A.J. MAY, *The Habsburg Monarchy 1867–1914*, Cambridge, 1951.

AUSTRO-PRUSSIAN PEACE TREATY, 1866. A Treaty signed in Prague Aug. 23, 1866, after the Battle of Sadova. Austria accepted the hegemony of Prussia in Germany ("a new organization of Germany", art. IV).

H. FRIEDJUNG, *Der Kampf um die Vorherrschaft in Deutschland, 1859–66*, Berlin, 1913; J.A.R. MARRIOT, C.G.K. HEVER, *The Evolution of Prussia*, Oxford, 1946.

AUSTRO-SLAVISM. A political current propagated in the Austrian Empire between 1846 and 1848 in opposition to Pan-Slavism; its main proponents, the Czechs, K. Havlicek-Borovsky and F. Palacky, arranged in Prague, between June 2 and 12, 1848, a Slavonic Congress composed of 340 representatives of the Slavonic groups living in Austria. A Manifesto to the Peoples of Europe, drawn up by F. Palacky and published by the Congress, set forth a program of Austro-Slavism, which expressed the readiness of the Slavonic nationalities for reconciliation with the Hapsburg monarchy. The Hapsburgs disregarded these suggestions, opting instead for the Austro-Hungarian dualistic system.

A. FISCHEL, *Der Panslavismus bis zum Weltkrieg*, Berlin, 1919.

AUTHORIZATION. In international relations a certificate warranting that the person is authorized by his government to represent it before a foreign government or at an international conference or to sign an international treaty; subject to international conventions, e.g., the Vienna Convention on the Law of Treaties.

AUTOCASCO. An international term for insurance against the total loss of, or material damage to, the motor-car.

AUTOCEPHALIA. An international term originated in Byzantium for the independence of a national Church from any commanding center outside the borders of the country. The Orthodox Churches called autocephalous are not subject to foreign jurisdiction; dependent only in canonical matters, but not administratively, subject to the ecumenical patriarch in Constantinople. In 1980 there were 14 autocephalous churches, with patriarchs: in Alexandria, Athens, Belgrade, Damascus, Bucharest, Constantinople, Jerusalem, Moscow, Nicosia, Prague, Tbilisi, Tirana, Sofia, and Warsaw.

AUTO-DA-FÉ. Act of the Faith. An international term for a ceremony from the times of the Spanish or Portuguese Inquisition; euphemistic name of the Italian Inquisition's judgement (in the 15th–18th centuries) condemning books or heretics to be burnt at the stake; in the 20th century – the burning of progressive books by fascist dictatorships (1933 – in Germany, 1973 – in Chile).

AUTOMATIC DATA PROCESSING. ▷ ADP System.

AUTOMATICS. A subject of international co-operation, reg. with the UIA:

Five International Associations Co-ordinating Committee (FIACC) f. 1970, Budapest. Publ. *Automatics, Bibliography of Automatic Control, FIACC Information Bulletin.* Five members of the FIACC:
Intergovernmental Council for Automatic Data Processing, ADP, f. 1968, Edinburgh. Publ. *ICADP Information.*
International Association for Analogue Computation, f. 1955, Brussels, Publ. *Quarterly Scientific Review.*
International Federation of Automatic Control, f. 1957, Geneva. Consultative Status: UNIDO, UNESCO, ECOSOC. Publ. *Journal Automatica.*
International Federation for Information Processing, f. 1959, Geneva. Consultative Status: UNESCO, ECOSOC, Publ. *IFIP Summary. Congress and Conferences Proceedings.*
International Federation of Operational Research Societies, f. 1959, Geneva.
International Measurement Confederation, f. 1961, Budapest. Publ. *Acta IMEKO, IMEKO Bulletin.*

W.E. CLASON, *Elsevier's Dictionary of Automatic Control*. In English/American, French, German and Russian. Amsterdam, 1963, p. 211; *Yearbook of International Organizations.*

AUTOMATION, INDUSTRIAL. Subject of international co-operation and study by the UN Economic Commission for Europe, ECE, through the Working Party on Engineering Industries and Automation.

ILO Automation, *Work Organization and Occupational Stress*, Geneva, 1984; *Production and Use of Industrial Robots*, UN Publications, New York, 1984.

AUTOMOBILE INDUSTRY. One of the largest international mass production industries since the beginning of the 20th century; in 1905 production was 80,000 units, and by 1910 it was 2,155,000; developed first in Europe and the USA; annual production reached 33 million in 1935; after World War II a.i. also developed in Asia (mainly in Japan) and in Latin America. Production included in international statistics shows a tremendous leap of the a.i. of Japan and the FRG 1950–70; the USSR began its great leap during 1971–80. World automobile manufacturing up to 1970 was concentrated more than 80% in the USA, Canada and West Europe. In 1970 a group of six EEC states passed the USA in the manufacture of passenger cars, producing 8,017,000, i.e. 35% of world production (1965 – 5,444,000), while the USA produced 6,550,000, i.e. 29%. In third place was Japan with 3,179,000 (1965 – 696,000). In fourth place Great Britain – 1,641,000. Within the EEC in 1970 the greatest producer was the FRG – 3,528,000, then France – 2,458,000, Italy – 1,720,000, and the Benelux countries – 900,000.
In Latin America the production of automobiles began more or less 10 years after World War II. In 1959 production there amounted to 29,400 passen-

A

ger cars and 31,500 trucks, while imports in the same year totalled 68,400 passenger cars and 66,400 trucks. In 1960 production grew correspondingly to 117,300 and 171,900 and imports to 85,400 and 67,100; in 1969 591,000 passenger cars and 267,000 trucks were produced, while imports were 55,200 and 40,100; In 1980 1,428,300 passenger cars and 765,100 trucks were produced and for 1985 – 2,099,000 and 1,127,000 were anticipated. The main markets are Brazil, Mexico, Argentina, and Venezuela. By 1980 the total number of passenger cars in Latin America reached 21 million, and *c.* 10 million trucks.

Within CMEA the a.i. of the member states co-operate on the basis of bi- and multilateral agreements, i.a. in Sept. 1971 Czechoslovakia, Romania and the USSR signed an agreement concerning the production of some groups of trucks with a large capacity; Yugoslavia participates on the basis of a separate agreement with the USSR. Co-operation also exists in the category of passenger cars and buses, i.a. multilateral agreements between Bulgaria, Czechoslovakia, Hungary, Poland, Yugoslavia and the USSR as well as bilateral agreements Poland–Hungary, Hungary–USSR, Poland–Bulgaria, Czechoslovakia–GDR and trilateral agreements: Bulgaria–Czechoslovakia–Poland and GDR–Poland–Hungary. Organizations reg. with the UIA.

Committee of Common Market Automobile Constructors, f. 1972, Brussels, Belgium.
International Bureau of Automobile Manufacturers, f. 1919, Paris, France. Consultative Status: ECOSOC. Publ. *Yearbook of the Automobile Industry.*
International Organization for Motor Trade and Repairs, f. 1947, Rijswijk, The Netherlands. Publ. *Newsletters.*
Liaison Committee for the Motor Industry in the EEC Countries, f. 1957, Brussels, Belgium.

G. SCHUURMANS STEKHOVEN, *Elsevier's Automobile Dictionary*. In English-American (with some definitions), French, Italian, Spanish, Portuguese, German, Russian and Japanese, Amsterdam 1960 and 1974; K. KONDO, *Elsevier's Dictionary of Automobile Engineering*. In English, German, French,

AUTOMOBILE TRAFFIC. A subject of international conventions since 1909, permanent organized international co-operation and international statistics, which since 1913 record the output of the car industry. International norms were introduced by the International Convention on Car Traffic. Convention internationale relative a la circulation des automobiles, signed in Paris on Oct. 11, 1909; it included the first four traffic signs ("obstacle signs" – "signaux d'obstacles", ditch, curve, tracks crossing and intersection); modified in Paris on Apr. 24, 1926 it is still valid. The titles of the first eight articles:

Art. 1: conditions which should be met by cars to be admitted to traffic on public roads; art. 2: conditions for the driver; art. 3: issuance and recognition of international road certificate during a temporary stay abroad; art. 4: distribution of licence plates; art. 5: warning devices (horn and headlights); art. 6: special regulations for tricars ("cyclonettes") and motorcycles; art. 7: passing and overtaking of other vehicles; art. 8: conditions of distribution of traffic signs on roads.

The first countries which signed the convention of 1909 and obtained the letter-symbols for their cars' origin by Annex C were the following: Austria – A, Belgium – B, Switzerland – CH, Germany – D, Spain – E, France – F, England – GB, Greece – GR, Hungary – H, Italy – I, Monaco – MC, Montenegro – MN, Holland – NL, Portugal – P, Russia – R, Romania – RM, Sweden – S, Serbia – SB, and the USA – US.

On Mar. 30, 1931 a Convention on taxing of foreign mechanical vehicles was signed in Geneva. On Dec. 15, 1943 all American Republics signed in Washington, DC a Convention on the Regulation of Inter-American Automotive Traffic; entered into force on July 25, 1944. A Central American Agreement on Highway Traffic was signed by Costa Rica, El Salvador, Guatemala, Honduras, and Nicaragua, on June 10, 1958 in Tegucigalpa; entered into force Dec. 17, 1959.

International car rallies were first held in 1894, and in 1904 the International Automobile Federation (FIA), in Paris, was called into being; since 1948 it has an advisory status to ECOSOC. All international car rallies and races on fixed distances such as Monte Carlo Rally, Safari, Races across the Continents, etc., are held under the patronage of FIA. Other organizations reg. with the UIA:

Inter-American Federation of Automobile Clubs, 1941, Buenos Aires; ECOSOC status.
International Driving Tests Committee, f. 1956, Rijswijk, The Netherlands, Consultative Status: ECOSOC.
International Permanent Office of Automobile Constructors, 1919, Paris; ECOSOC status.
Union of Technical Assistance for Motor Vehicle and Road Traffic, f. 1978, Geneva, Switzerland. Consultative Status: ECOSOC.
World Touring and Automobile Organization, 1950, London; ECOSOC status. Publ. *International Road Safety* and *Traffic Review.*

OAS Treaty Series, Washington, DC, 1943; *Bulletin Informativo*, ODECA, August 15, 1961; *Yearbook of International Organizations*, 1986–87.

AUTOSTOP. An international term for free motor-car transport of persons who indicate by wayside signs that they wish to be picked up and given a lift to a specific place; a custom which has become common in the majority of countries in the second half of the 20th century; in several European countries it is subject to traffic regulations (special identity cards for youths when on holiday); recommended by the International Tourism Organization.

AVERAGE. An international term for any loss incurred by a ship or cargo at sea; a subject of international law which recognizes General Average (not particular) as an institution of the law of the sea, following the tradition of the ancient Rhodian Sea Law as set forth in the Roman Digest (Lex Rhodia e iactu). The Rules of General Average, which consist in apportionment of loss caused by international damage to part of a ship or cargo in the interest of common safety or salvage of life and property, have been expounded in the ▷ York–Antwerp Rules of 1890, 1924 and 1950. The formula *franco d'avarie* in an insurance policy stands for insurance against loss incurred by a ship at sea, caused by a general average sacrifice.

AVIATION. A subject of international law and organized international co-operation since 1889, i.e. I International Aeronautical Congress in Paris. Aviation was defined as "the art of rising in the air and moving in any direction." The history of motor powered aviation (after glider and balloon flights in previous centuries) began on Dec. 17, 1903, when the American brothers Orville (1871–1948) and Wilbur (1867–1912) Wright, made a series of successful flights at Kitty Hawk (USA) for a distance of 36–284 m in 12–59 seconds in an airplane having a 16 hp motor. In 1909 the Frenchman L. Bleriot (1872–1936) was the first to fly over the English Channel, from Calais to Dover, initiating international flights. In 1919 the Englishman Alcock together with A. Brown started flights over oceans, flying from Newfoundland to Ireland; 1925 the Soviet pilot M.N. Gromov opened the air connec-

tion between Moscow and W. Europe, covering the route Moscow–Paris–Rome–Moscow; 1926 the Pole B. Orlinski opened the connection between Europe and Japan by flying Warsaw–Tokyo–Warsaw; May 12, 1927 the American C. Lindbergh initiated the intercontinental route New York-- Paris, covering in a Ryan plane "Spirit of Saint Louis", with a radial motor of 220 hp (160 kW) 5905 km, in 33.6 hours, alone, without radio contact; 1928 the Englishman C. Kingsford-Smith flew from America to Australia. In 1931 the one-eyed American W. Boos made the first flight around the world together with an observer; in 1933 alone, in a Lockheed plane "Winnie Mae" equipped with automatic pilot, he covered some 25,000 km in 7 days, 8 hours and 49 minutes. In June 1937 three Soviet fliers, W.P. Chkalov, G.F. Baydokov, and A.W. Bielakov, flew in a northerly direction from Moscow to Vancouver; and in July 1937 M.M. Gromov with two comrades made a record flight without landing, flying from Moscow over the pole to Riverside (Calif.) 10,645 km in 62 hours, 15 minutes. Just before the outbreak of World War II the jet plane HC 178 constructed by the German designer E.H. Heinkel made the first test flight in the Reich. In the interwar period aviation ministries were established in a number of countries: in Great Britain 1924, Italy 1926, the Third Reich 1934. During World War II the development of the airplane radar coincided with long-distance rocket launchers, and the appearance of the first helicopters. After World War II, civil air communication grew rapidly as a result of the employment of turbojet and turbo-prop motors; 1955 the first supersonic planes, whose introduction to civil communication was planned for the decade 1960–70 by France and Great Britain with the ▷ Concorde and USSR TU-144; the Concorde and TU-144 were shown in 1971 at the Paris Air Exhibition; the USA gave up the construction of the supersonic planes, SST, by a decision of Congress, which refused to give further funds in view of disturbances to the natural environment.

Organizations reg. with the UIA:

African Civil Aviation Association, f. 1969, Accra, Ghana.
Air Line Employees Association International, f. 1951, Chicago, USA.
Air Line Pilots Association International, f. 1931, Washington, DC.
Airlines Staff International Association, f. 1947, Paris.
Arab Carriers Air Organization, f. 1956, Beirut, Lebanon. Publ.: *Arab Wings.*
Arab Civil Aviation Council, f. 1965, Rabat, Morocco. Publ.: *Annual Review.*
Association of African Airlines, f. 1968, Nairobi.
Association of European Airlines, f. 1952, Brussels.
Central American Air Safety Services Corporation, f. 1950, Tegucigalpa.
East African Airways Corporation, f. 1946, Nairobi.
European Airlines Research Bureau, f. 1952, Brussels.
European Civil Aviation Conference, f. 1954, Paris.
European Organization for Civil Aviation Electronics, f. 1963, Paris.
European Organization for the Safety of Air Navigation, EUROCONTROL, f. 1960, by the EEC States, Brussels. Publ. *EUROCONTROL Bulletin.*
Flight Safety Foundation, f. 1945, Arlington Va. USA, Publ. *Accident Prevention Bulletin, Pilot Safety.*
Ibero-American Institute of Aeronautic and Space Law and Commercial Aviation, f. 1964, Madrid, Spain. Consultative Status: ECOSOC. Publ. *Revista del Instituto Iberoamericano de Derecho Aeronáutico y del Espacio.*
Institute of Air Transport, f. 1944, Paris, Publ. *ITA Bulletin.*
International Academy of Aviation and Space Medicine, f. 1959, Brussels.
International Aeronautical Federation, Federation aeronautique internationale, FAI, f. 1905, Paris. Consultative Status ECOSOC. Recognized by ICAO and

IOC. Certification of world records, regulating international aeronautical sporting events.

International Agricultural Aviation Center, f. 1958, The Hague. Publ. *Agricultural Aviation.*

International Airline Navigators Council, IANC, f. 1950, Zurich: Consultative Status WMO, ECOSOC, ICAO. Publ. *Newsletters.*

International Association of Aircraft Brokers and Agents, f. 1951, Copenhagen.

International Civil Airports Association, ICAA, f. 1962, Paris.

International Council of the Aeronautical Sciences, f. 1957, New York.

International Council of Aircraft Owner and Pilot Associations, f. 1964, Washington, DC.

International Federation of Aeronautical and Astronautical Journalists, f. 1961, Paris.

International Federation of Aero-Philatelic Societies, f. 1951, Heverlec, Leuven, Belgium.

International Federation of Air Line Pilots Association, f. 1948, London. Consultative Status ECOSOC, ICAO, WHO.

International Federation of Air Traffic Controllers Associations, f. 1961, Amsterdam.

International Federation of Airworthiness, f. 1961, Kingston Hill, Surrey, UK.

International Federation of Independent Air Transport, f. 1946, Paris.

International Maritime Pilots Association, f. 1970, London, UK. Consultative Status: ECOSOC, IMO. Publ.: *Coast Line News.*

International Safety Association, f. 1952, Paris.

International Society of Aviation Writers, f. 1956, Ottawa.

International Union of Aviation Insurers, f. 1934, London.

Latin American Civil Aviation Commission, f. 1973, Lima, Peru. Publ.: *Reports.*

Orient Airlines Association, f. 1966, Manila.

Scandinavian Airlines System, SAS, f. 1951, Stockholm.

South Pacific Air Transport Council, f. 1946, Melbourne.

Western European Association for Aviation Psychology, f. 1956, Brussels.

World Airlines Clubs Association, f. 1966, Frankfurt am Main (FRG).

The ABC Travel Guide Ltd, World Time Center in Dunstable Beds, UK, publishes monthly an *ABC World Airways Guide* and *ABC Cargo Guide and Directory* and *General Information Supplement,* containing timetables for all civil airlines, both those affiliated and non-affiliated with IATA, ticket prices and cargoes, reservation codes, etc. In Great Britain an annual *Jane's All the World's Aircraft* is published.

E. PEPIN, *Géographie de la Circulation Aérienne,* Paris, 1956; Ch. GIBBS-SMITH, *The Aeroplane: an Historical Survey of Its Origin and Development,* New York, 1960; D. ROLFE, *Airplanes of the World 1940–1960.* New York, 1962; T.N. VIDELA ESCALADA, *Aeronautical Law,* Germantown Md., 1979; *Yearbook of International Organizations, 1986–87.*

AVIATION INSURANCE. The insurance encumbering national and international airlines engaged in the air transport of passengers and cargo, regulated by international rules established by IATA.

AVIATION NORMS AND PRINCIPLES, INTERNATIONAL. A comprehensive expression for the international regulations defined in the Chicago Convention on International Civil Aviation, signed on Dec. 27, 1944, art. 37 concerning: (a) communications systems and facilities for the flight crew together with ground markings; (b) characteristic features of airports and airstrips; (c) flight rules and methods for controlling air traffic; (d) licensing operating and mechanical personnel; (e) airworthiness of planes; (f) registration and identification of airplanes; (g) collection and exchange of meteorological information; (h) log-books; (i) maps and flight plans; (j) customs and immigration formalities; (k) airplanes in danger and investigations in case of accidents as well as all other problems connected with safety, regularity, and efficiency of air travel which may arise. According to the Convention, in view of technological improvements ICAO should periodically make changes in the established international norms and operating procedures. ▷ Air Chicago Convention, 1944.

UNTS, Vol. 15, 1949, pp. 296–475.

AVOIRDUPOIS. ▷ Ounce; ▷ Pound International.

AVULSION. An international term for a rapid territorial change caused by a new course of a river. See also ▷ Chamizal.

R.L. BLEDSOE, B.A. BOCZEK, *The International Law Dictionary,* Oxford, UK, 1987.

AWACS. The Airborne Warning and Control System; the name of the American electronic equipment on board of aircraft, which permits remote detecting and watching of alien aircraft.

AWASH. The valley in the Wallo ana Harrar area in Ethiopia, where in 1974 was discovered the first of the known skeletons of an early type of man, known as Australopithecus, dating back some 3 million years. The skeleton was that of a young female of twenty years of age, and was given the name Lucy. The paleontological Ethiopian sites of the Awash and ▷ Omo valleys were included in the ▷ World Heritage UNESCO List.

UNESCO. *The Protection of the World Cultural and Natural Heritage,* Paris, 1983.

AXIS STATES. An international term for Nazi Germany and Fascist Italy (▷ Rome-Berlin Axis), later after formation of a war alliance of the above with Japan, known as the Rome-Berlin-Tokyo Axis for Italy, Germany and Japan (▷ Anti-Comintern Pact 1936).

E. WISKEMAN, *The Rome–Berlin Axis. A Study on the Relations between Hitler and Mussolini,* London, 1966.

AYACUCHO DECLARATION, 1974. The official name of the Declaration of the governments of Argentina, Chile, Bolivia, Columbia, Ecuador, Panama, Peru and Venezuela, adopted in Lima on Dec. 9, 1974, the 150th anniversary of the Battle of Ayacucho, Dec. 9, 1824, when Agentinian, Bolivian, Chilean, Peruvian and Venezuelan troops, under the command of Simon Bolivar, annihilated the Spanish army.

"Declaración de Ayacucho 1974" (full text in Spanish) in: E.J. OSMAŃCZYK, *Enciclopedia Mundial de Relaciones Internacionales y Naciones Unidas,* México, DF, 1976, pp. 381–382.

AYATOLLAH. Arabic: "giving divine signs". In the Shiite religion the name of a scholar with the authority to interpret the rules of the Koran for the faithful. In Iran during 1978–79 the authority of ayatollah Khomeini brought about the fall of the monarchy and the proclamation of an Iranian Moslem Republic.

W.H. FORBIS, *Fall of the Peacock Throne,* New York, 1979.

AZAD-KASHMIR. Border territory of Pakistan with China and India (area: 11,639 sq. km. Population: 1,980,000 census 1981), subject of Pakistanian conflicts with India over ▷ Kashmir and with China over ▷ Ladakh.

The Europa Yearbook 1988. A World Survey, Vol. II, London, 1988.

AZERBAIDZHAN SOVIET SOCIALIST REPUBLIC, founded April 28, 1920, since Dec. 30, 1922 part of the USSR. Area: 86,600 sq. km. Population: 6,921,000, estim. 1988; comprising 78.1% Azeris, 7.9% Armenians and 7.9% Russians. The Republic encompasses the Nakhichevan Autonomous Republic and the ▷ Nagorno-Karabakhskaya Autonomous oblast, with strong Armenian national groups, subject of conflict with the ▷ Armenian Soviet Socialist Republic, 1988–89.

The Europa Yearbook 1988. A World Survey, Vol. II, 1988. London.

AZORES. Port. Acores. An archipelago of 9 Portuguese islands in the Atlantic Ocean 1448 km west of Portugal. The nine islands are: south-east Sao Miguel and Santa Maria; central group: Terceira, Pico, Fayal, Sao Jorge, Graciosa; north-west: Flores and Corvo. Sao Miguel, Terceira and Pico are the largest. Area: 2344 sq. km. Population 251,352 (1981). Divided into 3 provinces, the names of which are derived from their main ports: Angra do Heroismo (on the island of Terceira), Horta (on the island of Faial) and Ponta Delgada (on the island of Sao Miguel). During World War II, on Oct. 12, 1943, the UK and the USA acquired for a period of 4 years the right to use the Azores as their maritime and air bases; the agreement of Oct. 1, 1947 allowed the USA to build a permanent military base on the Terceira island, and, on Sept. 6, 1951, the USA rights within the NATO system were extended over the whole archipelago; renewed Dec. 10, 1983. On Dec. 13–14, 1971, a summit meeting between the President of France, G. Pompidou, and the President of the USA, R. Nixon, took place in the Azores. On Sept. 4, 1976, Portugal granted the Azores limited self-government.

O. RIBEIRO, *Portugal, O Mediterraneo e o Atlantico. Estudio geografico,* Lisboa, 1963; *The Europa Year Book 1984. A World Survey,* Vol. I, p. 135, London, 1984.

B

BAASISM. An international term for a socio-political Arab independence movement known by the Arab abbreviation for the Socialist Party for Arab Rebirth (al-Baas). Established 1940 in Syria under the catchword Unity, Freedom, Socialism. This movement, organizationally modelled on the system of masonic lodges, also gained influence outside Syria, above all in Iraq and also in Jordan, Algeria and Libya.

P. SEALE, *The Struggle for Syria. A Study of Post War Arab Politics 1945–1958*, London, 1965.

BAC, BRITISH AIRCRAFT CORPORATION. The largest industrial aircraft company in the UK, orig. 1959/60 from the merger of the aircraft plants of Bristol, English Electric and Vickers Armstrong. In 1962 it signed a contract with the French ▷ Sud-Aviation company for the joint construction of a supersonic passenger plane, the ▷ Concorde.

BACCALAUREATE OFFICE, INTERNATIONAL. An international organization, f. in Geneva in 1968 which plans the curricula and university entrance examination (International Baccalaureate) common to multinational schools throughout the world and acceptable to universities in all countries. Publ. *The International Baccalaureate; General Guide to the International Baccalaureate*. Consultative status: ECOSOC, UNESCO.

Yearbook of International Organizations, 1986–87.

BACKFIRE BOMBER. The American name of the Soviet swingwing supersonic bomber TU-22M with a combat radius of 6000 km. In March 1977 the US Government proposed that the USSR ban the Soviet Backfire in return for a ban on the US subsonic missile, called Cruise. In June 1979 a Soviet Statement was handed by the USSR President to the US President that the TU-22M is a medium-range bomber, that the USSR does not intend to give this bomber an inter-continental capability and pledges to limit its production. ▷ SALT.

SIPRI, *World Armaments and Disarmament 1980*, London, 1980, p. 477.

BACTERIOLOGICAL AND CHEMICAL WEAPONS. ▷ B and C Arms.

BACTERIOLOGY. Subject of international co-operation. International organization reg. with the UIA:

International Committee on Systematic Bacteriology, f. 1930 in Paris. Publ. *International Journal of Systematic Bacteriology*.

Yearbook of International Organizations.

BAGHDAD. The capital of Iraq (since 1920), on the Tigris River (1982 pop. 4,038,000). The seat of International Council on Archives and UN Information Center.

The Europa Yearbook, 1987; A World Survey, London, 1987.

BAGHDAD PACT, 1955–59. A pact concluded by Turkey and Iraq on Jan. 24, 1955 in Baghdad, on the initiative of the UK and the USA. It was expanded in the same year to include the UK (Apr. 4); Pakistan (Sept. 23); and Iran (Nov. 3). From Jan 1, 1956 the USA sent observers. The Pact concerned co-operation between the armies of the signatory states and formed a link in the system of western military blocks. After July 1958 the headquarters was moved to Ankara. On Mar. 24, 1959 Iraq left the organization and in Aug. 1959 the name was changed to the Central Treaty Organization, ▷ CENTO.

BAHA'I INTERNATIONAL COMMUNITY. An international religious organization whose founder in 1844 was Bah the Herald (1819–50). Aims: to promulgate the unity of the human race and eliminate prejudice of race, class and creed. Baha'i World Center is in Haifa Israel. Representatives at UN, with UNEP for Africa and for Europe. Consultative status with ECOSOC and UNICEF. Publ. *The Baha'i World*.

Yearbook of International Organizations.

BAHAMAS. Member of the UN. The Commonwealth of the Bahamas. State consisting of 700 islands and islets and about 2400 cays in the Atlantic Ocean, between the south-east coast of Florida, USA, and Haiti. Principal islands: New Providence, Grand Bahama, Andros, Eleuthera and Aruba. Area: 13,939 sq. km. Pop. 1986 census 236,171 (1970 census: 168,812). Capital: Nassau with 1980 est. 92,000 inhabitants. Currency: One Bahamian dollar = 100 cents. GNP per capita in 1987: US $10,320. Official language: English. National day: July 10, independence anniversary, 1973. Since Sept. 18, 1973 member of the UN and all its specialized agencies, save IDA and IFAD. A member of the Test Ban Treaty, July 16, 1976; the Outer Space Treaty, Aug. 11, 1976; the Tlatelolco Treaty, Apr. 26, 1977; the Non-proliferation Treaty, Aug. 11, 1976. The USA has a naval and air base on the Bahamas, taken on lease in 1942 from Great Britain for 99 years. A signatory of the Lomé Conventions of 1975 and of 1980.

International relations: between 1783–1963 British colony, since Jan. 7, 1964 with autonomous status, not recognized by the UN Commission for Decolonization. In 1969 the Bahamas obtained autonomy limited by the responsibility of the Governor for defense, internal security and foreign affairs. The Bahamas obtained full independence on June 30, 1973.

A constitutional monarchy with the British sovereign as Head of State, represented by the Governor-General.

M.A. CRATON, *A History of the Bahamas*, London, 1962; *UN Yearbook* 1967 and 1973; P. ABURY, *The Story of the Bahamas*, London 1975; *Everyone's United Nations*, New York, 1979; *The Europa Year Book 1984. A World Survey*, Vol. I, pp. 1129–1135, London, 1984.

BAHIA DE COCHINOS. ▷ Bay of Pigs.

BAHRAIN. Member of the UN. Sheikdom of Bahrain. State in the archipelago of Bahrain in the Arabian Gulf, between the Qatar peninsula and the coast of Saudi Arabia. The two main islands: Bahrain or Aval and Alcmuharraq. Area: 698.3 sq. km. Pop. 1988 est. 480,000 (1971 census: 216,815). Capital and chief port: Manama with 122,000 inhabitants, 1981. GNP per capita, 1987 US $8,110. Currency: 1 Bahrain dinar = 100 fils. Official language: Arabic. National Day: Aug. 15, indepen-

dence anniversary, 1971. Bahrain joined the Arab League on Sept. 11, 1971. Admitted into the UN on Sept. 21, 1971. Bahrain is a member of all UN specialized agencies save IFC, IDA, WIPO and IFAD.

International relations: from 1861 to 1971, by an agreement of 1861, Bahrain was a protectorate of Great Britain. In 1968 Great Britain decided to withdraw its troops "East of Suez" by 1971. In Mar. 1970 at the request of the Iranian and UK governments the UN Secretary General sent a personal representative to Bahrain to ascertain the wishes of the people. In his report, he stated on Apr. 30, 1970, that the large majority of the people of Bahrain wished to gain recognition of their identity in a fully independent and sovereign state. The Security Council on May 11, 1970, at the request of Iran and the UK, unanimously endorsed the report and both Iran and the UK accepted the conclusions of the UN Secretary-General. On Aug. 15, 1971 Bahrain concluded a new friendship treaty with Great Britain, cancelling previous agreements of 1861, 1882 and 1892 on Great Britain's obligation to defend Bahrain. In December 1971 Bahrain concluded an agreement with USA, through which the US Middle East Fleet took over former British military naval bases on the territory of Bahrain. Founder-Member, 1981 of the Co-operation Council for the Arab States of the Gulf, GCC.

M. TWEEDY, *Bahrain and the Persian Gulf*, Ipswich, 1952; J.H.D. BELGRAVE, *Welcome to Bahrain*, 5th edn, Panama, 1965; A.M. HAKIMA, *The Rise and Development of Bahrain and Kuwait*, Beirut, 1965; S.B. MILES, *The Countries and Tribes of the Persian Gulf*, London, 1970; M.G. RUMAIHI, *Bahrain: Social and Political Change since the First World War*, London, 1976; *Everyone's United Nations*, New York, 1979. *The Europa Year Book 1984. A World Survey*, Vol. I, pp. 1136–1142, London, 1984.

BAHR-PLAN, 1969. An international term for a four-stage plan for détente in Europe presented by the West German politician Egon Bahr, b. 1922, on Jan. 9, 1969, to the director of the Foreign Policy Research Institute in Philadelphia, W. Hahn. Publ. in the spring of 1973 by the periodical *Orbis*, it became the subject of controversial commentaries in the West European press in view of the role of Bahr as the personal advisor of the leader of the Social Democratic party, Willy Brandt (b. 1913, in 1968/69 Minister of Foreign Affairs in the CDU/CSU–SPD coalition government and 1970–82 chancellor of the FRG government). The Bahr Plan was to be made up of four stages: (1) normalization of relations with the GDR; (2) conclusion by the FRG of a non-aggression treaty with the states of East Europe and recognition of the existing boundaries; (3) a 30–50% reduction of the armed forces of the USA and USSR in the FRG and the GDR; (4) creation of a collective security system in Europe with the exclusion of the nuclear powers the USA, the USSR, France and the UK and the dissolution of NATO and the Warsaw Pact Organization.

Le Monde, No. 8894, Aug. 18, 1973.

BAHT. A monetary unit of Thailand; one baht = 100 stang; issued by the Bank of Thailand.

BAILIFFS. Internationally organized in International Union of Bailiffs and Law Officers, f. 1952 in Paris. Members in W. European countries. Aims: to maintain professional independence and rights. Publ. *La revue des huissiers de justice*. Reg. with the UIA. Consulative status, Council of Europe.

Yearbook of International Organizations, 1986– 87.

BAILIWICK OF GUERNSEY. Islands of the UK Crown Dependencies in the English Channel: ▷

Alderney, Brechou (area 0.6 sq. km) and Lihou (area: 0.2 sq. km) leased by the Crown, Herm (area 2.0 sq. km), leased by the state of Guernsey, Jethou (area: 0.2 sq. km) leased by the Crown and ▷ Sark.

The Europa Yearbook, 1987. A World Survey, Vol. II, London, 1988.

BAISSE. A French international term. A drop in the prices of securities or of commodities quoted on the stock-market; the opposite of ▷ *hausse*.

BAJA CALIFORNIA OR LOWER CALIFOR-NIA. A peninsula in NW Mexico, separating the Gulf of California from the Pacific. Area: 143,790 sq. km. Pop. 1,508,280 (est. 1980). Occupied by US Forces during the Mexican War, 1847–48.

BAKER PLAN, 1985. A proposal on debt and development financing by the US Secretary of the Treasury, James Baker, on Oct. 8, 1985, at a Seoul IMF–BANK meeting.

KESSING's *Record of World Events*, 1986, No. 1 and No. 2.

BAKERY AND CONFECTIONERY. A subject of international co-operation: organizations reg. with the UIA:

Association of National Bakery and Confectionery Federations of the EEC, f. 1960, Brussels.
Bakery and Confectionery Worker's International Union, f. 1886, Washington, DC.
International Union of Bakers and Confectioners, f. 1954, Vienna.
International Union of Master Bakers, f. 1924, Paris. Publ. *Revue internationale de boulangerie.*

Yearbook of International Organizations.

BALANCE OF PAYMENTS. An international term for the monetary claims and obligations of a given country in relation to other states, as a rule, during one fiscal year. In a wider sense, a term defining the relationship of goods and services produced by a given country for domestic use and exports, to imported domestic goods and services consumed by the population. The balance of payments can be roughly reduced to: favorable surplus of income, adverse surplus of expenses. It is the subject of constant analysis in international organizations as well as economic and credit institutions, together with ▷ trade balance and ▷ clearing.

N.S. FIELAKE, *What is the Balance of Payments?*, Boston, 1976; J. ALVES, *The Balance of Payments. A Glossary of Terms*, Washington, DC, 1979.

BALANCE OF POWER. An international term for the 16th century English doctrine that the maintenance of peace depends on not allowing a situation to arise in which one power achieves domination over others. A peaceful *sui generis* of the doctrine of B. of P. was introduced to the UN Charter with the principle ▷ unanimity of the great powers in the Security Council, where no Power is able to dominate.

D. ROBERTSON, *Guide to Modern Defense and Strategy*, Detroit, 1988.

BALANCE OF TERROR. International term of the nuclear age relating to East-West nuclear competition. See also ▷ Deterrence, and ▷ MAD.

A.J.C. EDWARDS, *Nuclear Weapons, The Balance of Terror, The Quest for Peace*, London, 1986; D. ROBERTSON, *Guide to Modern Defense and Strategy*, Detroit, 1988.

BALANCE OF TRADE. An international term designating the relation between values of exported and imported goods. If it has an export surplus, the balance of trade is called active (positive); if it has an

import surplus – passive (negative). International credit institutions recording the balance of trade of particular countries evaluate it together with ▷ balance of payments and ▷ foreign balance.

BALEARIC ISLANDS. Archipelago in the western Mediterranean, Spanish province Baleares, area: 5014 sq. km.; pop. 685,088 census 1981; the main islands: Majorca, Minorca, Ibiza, Formentera; capital: Palma de Majorca. Occupied by British troops: 1708–56, 1763–82, 1798–1902; bases of Italian fascist troops 1936–39.

B. WHELPTON, *The Baleares*, London, 1952; *Îles Baleares*, Paris, 1953; *The International Geographic Encyclopaedia and Atlas*, London, 1979.

BALFOUR DECLARATION, 1917. A Declaration contained in a letter of the UK Minister of Foreign Affairs, A.J. Balfour on Nov. 2, 1917 to A.G. Rothschild, the representative of ▷ Zionism:

Dear Lord Rothschild, I have much pleasure in conveying to you, behalf of His Majesty's Government, the following declaration of sympathy with Jewish Zionist aspirations which has been submitted to, and approved by, the Cabinet. His Majesty's Government view with favour the establishment in Palestine of a national home for the Jewish people, and will use their best endeavours to facilitate the achievement of this object, it being clearly understood that nothing shall be done which may prejudice the civil and religious rights of existing non-Jewish communities in Palestine, or the rights and political status enjoyed by Jews in any other country. I shall be grateful to you if you would bring this declaration to the knowledge of the Zionist Federation. Sincerely yours, Arthur James Balfour.

This letter became the cornerstone of the state of Israel and initiated the emigration, planned and organized by the Jewish Agency, (▷ Jews), of Jews from the entire world to Palestine.

A.J. BALFOUR, *Opinions and Agreements*, London, 1927; H.M. SACHAR, *Modern Jewish History*, New York, 1958.

BALKAN. A peninsula in south-eastern Europe, bounded by the Black Sea, Sea of Marmara, Aegean Sea, Mediterranean Sea, Ionian Sea and Adriatic Sea. Area: 518,000 sq. km. Divided between Albania, continental Greece, Bulgaria, European Turkey, most of Yugoslavia and south-eastern Romania.

B.M. JANKOVIC, *The Balkans in International Affairs*, London, 1987.

BALKAN ALLIANCE, 1954. ▷ Balkan Pact, 1954.

BALKAN ALLIANCES, 1912 AND 1913. Two separate treaties:
(1) Alliance of Mar. 13, 1912 between Bulgaria and Serbia and the military convention of Aug. 29, 1912; the alliance was joined by Montenegro on the date of conclusion. It was directed against Austria–Hungary in case it attacked Serbia;
(2) Alliance of May 5, 1913 between Serbia and Greece, extended June 1, 1913 by a military convention. It was directed against Bulgaria which, after a dispute over Macedonia, started the Second Balkan War, June 29–Aug. 10, 1913.

H. BATOWSKI, "The Failure of the Balkan Alliance of 1912", in: *Balkan Studies*, Salonika, 1966, pp. 111–122.

BALKAN CONFERENCES, 1976 AND 1984. Two intergovernmental meetings devoted to comprehensive co-operation: first between Albania, Bulgaria, Greece, Turkey, and Yugoslavia, held Jan. 25–Feb. 5, 1976 in Athens; second between Bulgaria, Greece, Romania, Turkey and Yugoslavia held in Jan. 1984 in Athens.

KEESING's *Contemporary Archive*, 1976 and 1984.

BALKAN CONFERENCE, 1988. The first meeting of foreign ministers of six Balkan countries (Albania, Bulgaria, Greece, Romania, Turkey and Yugoslavia) took place in Belgrade, on Febr. 24–26, 1988. A joint communiqué warranted further meetings on economic, security, humanitarian, cultural and technological issues and 'when appropriate conditions exist a summit meeting of Balkan heads of states'.

KEESING's *Record of World Events*, March 1988.

BALKAN ENTENTE, 1934. An international term for an agreement concluded on Feb. 9, 1934 in Athens by Greece, Romania, Turkey and Yugoslavia valid for seven years. It was supplemented on Nov. 2, 1934 in Ankara by an organizational statute and an advisory economic council statute. The four Balkan states pledged to guarantee the mutual "security of all Balkan boundaries" (art. 1), obligated themselves to "co-ordinate all dispositions which would have to be taken in the face of events that could affect their interests ..." and obligated themselves "not to take any political action toward any other Balkan country, which is not a member of the present pact, without previous mutual consultation, nor to incur any political obligation without the consent of the remaining agreeing parties" (art. 2).
The following bilateral relations existed between the members of the Pact: between Romania and Yugoslavia, through treaties within the ▷ Entente, Little; between Greece and Yugoslavia, a Pact of Friendship, Conciliation, and Legal Procedure concluded in Belgrade, Mar. 27, 1929; extended Feb. 18, 1934 for another five years; between Yugoslavia and Turkey, a Treaty of Friendship, Nonaggression, Legal Procedure and Conciliation concluded in Belgrade, Nov. 27, 1933, for five years; between Greece and Romania, a pact of nonaggression and arbitration concluded for ten years in Geneva on Mar. 21, 1928 for 10 years; between Greece and Turkey a Treaty of Friendship, Neutrality, Conciliation and Arbitration in Ankara, Oct. 30, 1930, superseded there by a Pact of Sincere Agreement, Sept. 14, 1933, including mutual border guarantees and the responsibility for mutual consultation in the international field, supplemented May 27, 1938 in Athens by a further Treaty of Friendly Neutrality in Case of Unprovoked Aggression; between Romania and Turkey a Treaty of Friendship, Nonaggression, Arbitration and Conciliation concluded in Ankara, Oct. 17, 1933 for 10 years. However, remaining outside the Balkan Entente were Albania, Bulgaria and Hungary. The influence of France on the Balkan Entente was expressed through treaties concluded by her within the Little Entente System with Yugoslavia and Romania as well as through a Treaty of Friendship, Conciliation, and Arbitration with Turkey, concluded Feb. 3, 1930, superseded by a Treaty of Friendship, July 4, 1938. France did not sign any political treaty with Greece. Germany and Italy had certain influence on the Balkan Entente directly through the Treaty of Friendship between Germany and Turkey concluded for an unlimited time in Ankara, Mar. 3, 1924, supplemented by a Treaty of Arbitration and Conciliation concluded there May 16, 1929 for 10 years, and through the Treaty of Neutrality, Conciliation and Legal Procedure between Italy and Turkey concluded in Rome, May 30, 1928, extended May 25, 1932 for 10 years. Indirectly Germany and Italy influenced the Balkan Entente through treaties of Bulgaria and Hungary with the states belonging to it: through a Treaty of Friendship between Bulgaria and Turkey

(no time-limit) concluded in Ankara, Oct. 18, 1925, and through a Treaty of Neutrality, Conciliation, Legal Procedure and Arbitration concluded there Mar. 6, 1919 (renewed for 5 years), and also through a Treaty of Friendship between Turkey and Hungary (no time-limit) concluded in Ankara, Dec. 8, 1923 and a Treaty of Neutrality, Conciliation and Arbitration concluded Jan 5, 1929. The Balkan Entente disintegrated in 1938–40 as a result of the breakdown of the Versailles system, whose first sign in the Balkans was a treaty concluded in Salonika, July 31, 1938, between the Entente and Bulgaria, permitting her remilitarization and thereby annulling the resolutions of the ▷ Neuilly-sur-Seine Peace Treaty 1919.

LNTS, Vol. 153; M. PANDEFF, "The Balkan entente treaties", in: *American Journal of International Law*, No. 48, 1954.

BALKAN PACT, 1954 OR BLED TREATY, 1954. A Treaty of Alliance, Political Co-operation and Mutual Assistance between Greece, Turkey and Yugoslavia, signed in Bled, Aug. 9, 1954, supplementing the ▷ Ankara Treaty 1953. The text read as follows:

"Art. 1. The Contracting Parties undertake to settle any international dispute in which they may become involved by peaceful means in conformity with the provisions of the Charter of the United Nations and to refrain in their international relations from threatening to use or using force in any way which would be incompatible with the purposes of the United Nations.
Art. 2. The Contracting Parties agree that any armed aggression against one or more of them on any part of their territory shall be deemed to constitute aggression against all of them and, the Contracting Parties, exercising the right of individual or collective self-defence recognized by Art. 51 of the Charter of the United Nations, shall accordingly, individually and collectively assist the attacked Party or Parties by immediately taking, by common agreement, all measures, including the use of armed forces, which they consider necessary for effective defence.
Without prejudice to art. VII of this Treaty, the Contracting Parties bind themselves not to conclude peace or to make any other arrangement with the aggressor without prior common agreement among themselves.
Art. III. In order to ensure the attainment of the objects of this Treaty in a regular and effective manner, the Contracting Parties pledge themselves to assist one another with a view to maintaining and strengthening their capacity for defence.
Art. IV. With a view to ensuring the effective application of this Treaty it is hereby decided as follows:
(1) A Permanent Council shall be formed, to be composed of the Ministers of Foreign Affairs and of any other members of the Governments of the Contracting Parties whose presence may be desirable in the light of the exigencies of the situation and the nature of the matters to be discussed. The Permanent Council shall meet regularly twice yearly."

The Treaty entered into force on May 21, 1955, for 20 years.

UNTS, Vol. 211, pp. 241–243; *UNTS*, Vol. 167, pp. 25–27; KEESING's *Contemporary Archive*, 1953 and 1954.

BALKAN QUESTION. An international term for disputes and conflicts on the Balkan peninsula in the 19th and early 20th centuries resulting from liberation movements and the struggle of Balkan peoples and the rivalry between Austria, France, Russia, the German Empire and Great Britain over influence in this region as the Ottoman Empire was declining; subject of international conferences and treaties most of all between Turkey (Ottoman Empire) and Russia, Austria or other powers, e.g.: Adrianople Peace of Sept. 7, 1829; Paris Peace of Mar. 3, 1856; Berlin Peace of July 13, 1878; Balkan Treaties of Alliance 1912/13; Bucharest Peace of

Aug. 10, 1913; and Constantinople Peace of Sept. 29, 1913. A clash between Austria and Southern Slavs culminated in shots fired at Archduke Ferdinand in Sarajevo, June 28, 1914, and precipitated World War I.
A serious problem after World War I was the resettlement of the Turkish population from Greece and subsequently Fascist pressure, exerted on Balkan states by Italy and the Third Reich, which provoked the Balkan Entente and military conflicts of Italy with Albania, Germany with Yugoslavia and Greece. Bulgaria and Romania supported the Axis countries. Turkey remained neutral.

R.W. SETON-WATSON, *The Rise of Nationality in the Balkans*, London. 1917.

BALKAN RAILROAD. An international railroad line connecting Austria, Hungary, Yugoslavia, and Italy; belongs to the Danube, Sawa, Adriatic Railroad Company and operates by virtue of a Convention signed in Rome, Mar. 29, 1923 by the above states.

LNTS, Vol. 23, p. 336.

BALKANS. The major mountain range of the Balkan Peninsula from East Yugoslavia via central Bulgaria to the Black Sea, 565 km long.

The International Geographic Encyclopedia and Atlas, London, 1979.

BALKANS: PROBLEMS IN THE UN. After World War II a UN Commission on the Balkans 1947–51, observed the disputes and conflicts of some Balkan states in connection with the civil war in Greece. ▷ UNSCOB.
In 1958 Yugoslavia presented to the UN a plan for a Balkan ▷ denuclearized zone.
The first summit meeting of the south-eastern European foreign ministers took place in Athens on Jan 31–Feb. 5, 1976; represented were: Bulgaria, Greece, Romania, Turkey, and Yugoslavia. Only Albania refused to participate. The meeting had the aim of increasing co-operation in the fields of economics, environmental protection, communications, transport, and tourism. The proposals discussed were submitted to all of the governments of the Balkan states (including Albania). The Romanian parliament on Dec. 19, 1976 made the following appeal:

"Assuming the importance of establishing zones of peace and cooperation in Europe, we make an appeal to the states and nations of the Balkans to increase their efforts and actions to develop bilateral and multilateral relations in this region, transforming the Balkans into a zone of good-neighborliness and cooperation free of nuclear weapons."

International organization reg. with the UIA:

International Association of South East European Studies, f. 1963 in Bucharest.

P.L. HORECKY, *Southeastern Europe, A Guide to Basic Publications*, Chicago, 1969; *Südosteuropa Bibliographie*, Vols. I–V, Oldenburg, 1959–76; R. PETKOVIC, *Balkan ui 'bure baruta ui 'zona mira'* (Balkans not a "powder barrel", but also not a "peace zone"), Zagreb, 1978.

BALKAN WARS, 1912–13. The name of two wars waged on the Balkan Peninsula, preceded by alliances made before the first Balkan War by Bulgaria with Serbia, Greece and Montenegro, with the active role of Russian diplomacy, for the purpose of armed action against Turkey and liberating the Balkan territories, above all Macedonia. The first Balkan War, declared against Turkey on Oct. 18, 1912, ended with the defeat of Turkey, which on the basis of the London Peace Treaty concluded on May 30, 1913, ceded to the Balkan allies its

European territories along the lines Enez-Midye (with the exception of Albania, whose fate was to be determined by the powers and which, on Nov. 28, 1912 proclaimed its independence). The second Balkan War was waged against Bulgaria by Greece, Serbia, and Montenegro, and in its second phase also by Romania and Turkey; started June 29, 1913, with the attack of Bulgarian forces on the armies of Serbia and Greece; the war was concluded on Aug. 10, 1913 with the Bucharest Peace Treaty between Bulgaria and Montenegro, Greece, Serbia and Romania, as a result of which Bulgaria lost southern Dobruja to Romania, the southern half of Macedonia and part of western Thrace to Greece, as well as nearly all of northern Macedonia to Serbia. The Treaty of Constantinople between Bulgaria and Turkey on Sept. 16, 1913 returned Adrianopolian Thrace to the latter.

E.C. HELNREICH, *The Diplomacy of the Balkan Wars*, London, 1938.

BALLET. A subject of international co-operation. Organization reg. with the UIA:

International Ballet Competition, since 1960 organized every other year in July in Varna (Bulgaria). The age limit being 28, it is a review of young ballet dancers of the East and West.

Yearbook of International Organizations.

BALLISTIC MISSILE EARLY WARNING SYSTEM, BMEWS. The American and British Distant Early Warning system based on three special radar stations, two in Canada, one in England.

D. ROBERTSON, *Guide to Modern Defense and Strategy*, Detroit, 1988.

BALLISTIC MISSILES. An international term for short-range (tactical) and long-range (strategic) missiles propelled by a rocket or turbojet engine, fitted with a classical or nuclear warhead and having a self-steering mechanism. The first missiles of this type were the V1 and V2 rockets in World War II, then developed by the USA and USSR in various types of various classes (land–land, land–air, air–land, land–sea, and sea–sea). Subject of ▷ SALT negotiations, defined as a missile which follows a ballistic trajectory, part of which is outside the Earth's atmosphere, when thrust is terminated. Military acronym: BMD, Ballistic Missile Defence.

J. GOLDBLAT, *Arms Control Agreements. A Handbook*, New York, 1983. D. ROBERTSON, *Guide to Modern Defense and Strategy*, Detroit, 1988.

BALLOON. The first air ship, subject of two international conventions, 1899 and 1907: the IVth Hague Declaration prohibiting for a term of 5 years the launching of projectiles and explosives from balloons, signed July 29, 1899 in The Hague and the XIVth Hague Declaration prohibiting the discharge of projectiles and explosive materials from balloons, signed Sept. 18, 1907 in The Hague, in effect "until the time of the convocation of the III Peace Conference in The Hague". The signatory states: Argentina, Austria–Hungary, Bolivia, Brazil, Belgium, Bulgaria, China, Colombia, Cuba, Dominican Republic, Ecuador, Ethiopia, Finland, Great Britain, Greece, Haiti, Holland, Liberia, Luxembourg, Nicaragua, Norway, Panama, Persia, Peru, Siam, Switzerland, Turkey, the USA and Uruguay.
International organizations reg. with the UIA:
International Society of Balloonpost Specialists, The Hague, Netherlands.
Scientific Ballooning and Radiations Monitoring Organization, Saint-Maur, France.

C.H. GIBBS-SMITH, *Ballooning*, London, 1948; D. SCHINDLER, J. TOMAN (eds) *The Law of Armed Conflicts*, Leiden, 1973, pp. 133–138. *Yearbook of International Organizations*, 1986–87.

BALLOON AND YACHT COMPETITIONS.
International competitions of free-floating balloons with a volume of 2200 m³ for the cup named after J.G. Bennett, publisher of the *New York Herald* and initiator of the competitions. International competitions for the J.G. Bennett cup were held annually from 1905 to 1938 with the exception of the years of World War I. After World War II they were renewed in 1983.

D.C. SEITZ, *The James Gordon Bennetts*, New York, 1928.

BALLOON INCIDENTS, 1953–56.
An international term for diversionary operations carried out with the help of balloons. A subject of an exchange of notes and protests in the UN. In 1953, balloons were launched on a mass scale from Western Germany with propaganda leaflets despite the notes of protest by the government of Czechoslovakia. The operation was expanded to Hungary, Romania and the USSR, to an extent which threatened internal air communications. On Jan. 1, 1956 a Czech passenger plane collided with a balloon in Slovakia, resulting in the death of 22 persons. On Jan. 21, 1956 and Feb. 6, 1956 similar accidents befell Hungarian fighters and on Aug. 3, 1956 a Polish fighter. Protest notes were lodged by the government of the USSR on Feb. 4 and 18 and Mar. 24, 1956 to the government of the USA, as were similar notes by the governments of Romania and Hungary on Feb. 8, 1956, and Poland on Feb. 11, 1956. In addition to these notes of protest, Albania and Czechoslovakia formally protested to the UN on Feb. 7, 1956. The government of Sweden on Mar. 6, 1956, in a note to the government of the USA, stated that the flights of balloons were against international law and violated Sweden's sovereignty and air space. In a note to the government of Norway, Sweden demanded that the launching of balloons from naval bases on its territory be stopped. The US halted the balloon operation in Feb. 1956 against the USSR and in Oct. 1956 against Czechoslovakia, Hungary, Poland and Romania.

W. GÓRALCZYK, A. SKOWROŃSKI, "Amerykanska 'akcja balonowa' w świetle prawa miedzynarodowego" [American Balloon Action in the Light of International Law] in: *Sprawy Miedzynarodowe*, No. 4, 1956; V. MARCHETTI, J.D. MARKS, *The CIA and the Cult of Intelligence*, New York, 1975, pp. 166–167.

BALNEOLOGY AND CLIMATOTHERAPY.
A subject of organized international co-operation. Organization reg. with the UIA:
International Society of Medical Hydrology and Climatology, f. 1921; Coimbra, Portugal. Publ.: *Archives of Medical Hydrology*.

International Federation of Thermalism and Climatism, f. 1947 in Yverdon-les-Bains, (Switzerland).

Yearbook of International Organizations, 1986–87.

BALTAFRICA AND UNIAFRICA.
An international commercial shipping line connecting European Baltic ports with the ports of west and east Africa, serviced by vessels of the German Democratic Republic and Poland.

BALTAMERICA.
An international commercial shipping line connecting the European Baltic ports with the ports of Latin America, serviced by the vessels of the GDR, Poland and the USSR. The line connecting Cuban ports with the European Baltic ports is serviced by vessels of Czechoslovakia, Cuba, GDR, Poland and the USSR.

BALTIC AND NORTH SEA CONVENTIONS, 1907–08.
Three international agreements concluded in the years 1907–08:
(1) German–Russian Convention, signed on Oct. 29, 1907, aiming at guaranteeing status quo in the Baltic Sea, among others, it also dealt with the status of ▷ Aaland Islands;
(2) German–Russian–Danish–Swedish Convention, signed on Apr. 23, 1908, guaranteeing status quo in the Baltic Sea;
(3) English–French–Dutch–German–Swedish Convention also signed on Apr. 23, 1908, guaranteeing status quo in the North Sea.

BALTIC CLUB.
A mercantile institution, f. 1823 in London, which established the rules and regulations for the largest mercantile and shipping exchange in the world, the ▷ Baltic Mercantile and Shipping Exchange.

F.E. HYDE, *Shipping Enterprises and Management 1830–1939*, London, 1967.

BALTIC CODE.
A set of international rules prepared by the seven states bordering on the Baltic Sea (Denmark, the FRG, Finland, the GDR, Poland, Sweden and the USSR) in order to create a comprehensive system of protecting the maritime environment and to establish rules for utilizing the Baltic. The first normative acts of the Baltic Code were the Baltic Conventions; the first of them, called the ▷ Baltic Gdansk Convention of 1973, refers to the protection of fishing and living resources of the Baltic; the second, the ▷ Baltic Helsinki Convention of 1974, signed Mar. 22, 1974, provides for the protection of the environment of the Baltic Sea and the area (The Convention on the Protection of the Environment of the Baltic Sea and Area). The Permanent Commission for the Protection of the Environment of the Baltic Sea is an organ of the Helsinki Convention.

BALTIC CONFERENCES, 1920–25.
The six conferences of some of the Baltic states:
(1) in Riga in Aug. 1920 with the participation of Poland, Estonia, Finland, Lithuania, and Latvia;
(2) in Helsinki in July 1921 with the participation of the ministers of foreign affairs of Poland, Estonia, Finland, and Latvia;
(3) in Warsaw in March 1922 with the participation of the ministers of foreign affairs of these same states, ending with the signing on March 17 of a political treaty, to which two interpretative declarations were appended on Apr. 29, 1922.

Three further conferences took place with the participation of these same states: in Riga in Mar. 1923, in Warsaw in Feb., 1924 and in Helsinki in Jan., 1925, at which on Jan. 17 a Protocol closing the conference and a Conciliatory-Arbitration Convention was signed.

BALTIC CONVENTIONS, 1925–29.
An international term for four conventions relating to the Baltic Sea:
(1) Conciliatory and Arbitrating Convention, signed on Feb. 17, 1925 in Helsinki by Estonia, Finland, Latvia and Poland;
(2) Geodetic Convention, signed Dec. 31, 1925 by Denmark, Estonia, Germany, Finland, Lithuania, Latvia, Poland and Sweden which established for 12 years the Baltic Geodetic Commission;
(3) Convention on the Suppression of Contraband of Alcoholic Articles, signed on Aug. 19, 1925 by Denmark, Estonia, Germany, Finland, Latvia, Lithuania, Norway, Poland, Sweden and USSR;
(4) Baltic Agreement on Flatfish Catches on the Baltic, signed on Dec. 17, 1929, by all Baltic countries.

LNTS, 1925, 1929.

BALTIC ENTENTE. L'ENTENTE BALTIQUE.
An international term for a tripartite alliance of Estonia, Lithuania, and Latvia, concluded in Kovno, 1924; attempts to extend it to Finland and Poland failed because of the Lithuanian–Polish conflict. In Apr., 1934 Estonia came out in favor of drafting an international agreement along the lines of the ▷ Locarno treaties for the purpose of guaranteeing the independence of Estonia, Lithuania, and Latvia by Finland, Germany, Poland, and the USSR. In view of the disputed Polish–Lithuanian problem concerning Vilnius, stipulations of the signatories in accordance with art. 19 of the Covenant of the LN were anticipated. Negotiations held in Kovno in July, 1934 led to the signing in Geneva on Sept. 12, 1934 by Estonia, Lithuania and Latvia of a Baltic States Co-operation Treaty, art. 1 of which obligated the parties to continual mutual consultations and support in all matters of common interest, while art. 2 formed a Council of Ministers of Foreign Affairs, which was supposed to meet at least twice a year. The treaty together with a Declaration on Good Mutual Understanding and Co-operation was to be binding for 10 years. Up to 1940, 11 sessions of the Council were held; at the 10th in Kovno (Feb., 1939) and 11th in Tallin (Mar., 1939) neutrality in case of war was agreed upon based on the so-called Stockholm principles of the neutrality of states. At the last session in Riga, Mar. 14–16, 1940, the correctness of the policy of neutrality was confirmed. On July 10, 1940 the pact was dissolved by a declaration of the governments of the three signatories. See ▷ Eastern Pact.

LNTS, Vol. 154, p. 93; B. KAZLAUKAS, *L'Entente Baltique*, Paris, 1939; *The Formation of the Baltic States*, Cambridge, 1959.

BALTIC GDANSK CONVENTION, 1973.
A convention adopted Nov. 13, 1973 by the governments of Denmark, Finland, FRG, GDR, Poland, Sweden and USSR, initiating the formation of the ▷ Baltic Code. The Baltic Gdansk Convention relates to fishing and protection of living reserves of the Baltic Sea. The Convention's chief organ is the Baltic Sea Fishing Commission, est. 1974 in Warsaw, for overseeing protection of the living resources of the Baltic Sea. The Conference on Fishing and Conservation of the Living Resources in the Baltic Sea and the Belts, at Gdansk, Sept., 1973, expresses the hope that the member states will take all necessary measures on a national basis, to protect the Baltic resources, until such time as international regulatory measures are put into practice. The Conference turned to the International Council for the Exploration of the Sea with a request to analyze the state of exploitation of the stocks of herring, sprat, cod and flatfish (flounder) in the Baltic Sea and to advise as to regulation which might be used for approaching optimum yield of the stocks of the said species.

Final Act of the Conference on Fishing at Gdansk, Gdansk, 1973.

BALTIC GEODETIC CONVENTION. ▷ Baltic Conventions, 1925–1929.

BALTIC HELSINKI CONFERENCE, 1974.
The Diplomatic Conference on the Protection of the Marine Environment of the Baltic Sea Area was held in Helsinki Mar. 18–22, 1974. Delegations from Denmark, Finland, FRG, GDR, Poland, Sweden and the USSR adopted the text of the ▷ Baltic Helsinki Convention. The Conference also adopted seven Resolutions:

(1) Application by other states of special rules for ships operating in the Baltic Sea area (invites IMCO to adopt

a recommendation on the application by states other than the Contracting Parties of special rules for ships operating in the Baltic Sea area);

(2) Facilities for the reception of residues of oil and other noxious substances, sewage and garbage;

(3) Navigation of commercial ships through the entrances to the Baltic Sea;

(4) Development of a uniform position reporting system for commercial ships within the Baltic Sea area;

(5) Safety of navigation;

(6) Application of art. 21 (Relations to other Conventions) to future treaties; and

(7) Interim Commission.

Final Act of the Diplomatic Conference, Helsinki, 1974.

BALTIC HELSINKI CONVENTION, 1974. A Convention adopted Mar. 22, 1974 by the ▷ Baltic Helsinki Conference of seven Baltic states: Denmark, Finland, FRG, GDR, Poland, Sweden and the USSR. The highlights of the Convention on the Protection of the Marine Environment:

"Art. 3. Fundamental principles and obligations

(1) The Contracting Parties shall individually or jointly take all appropriate legislative, administrative or other relevant measures in order to prevent and abate pollution and to protect and enhance the marine environment of the Baltic Sea Area.

(2) The Contracting Parties shall use their best endeavours to ensure that the implementation of the present Convention shall not cause an increase in the pollution of sea areas outside the Baltic Sea Area.

Art. 4. Application. (1) The present Convention shall apply to the protection of the marine environment of the Baltic Sea Area which comprises the water-body and the sea-bed including their living resources and other forms of marine life.

(2) Without prejudice to the sovereign rights in regard to their territorial sea, each Contracting Party shall implement the provisions of the Present Convention within its territorial sea through its national authorities.

(3) While the provisions of the present Convention do not apply to internal waters, which are under the sovereignty of each Contracting Party, the Contracting Parties undertake, without prejudice to their sovereign rights, to ensure that the purposes of the present Convention will be obtained in these waters.

(4) The present Convention shall not apply to any warship, naval auxiliary, military aircraft or other ship and aircraft owned or operated by a State and used, for the time being, only on government non-commercial service.

However, each Contracting Party shall ensure, by the adoption of appropriate measures not impairing the operations or operational capabilities of such ships and aircraft owned or operated by it, that such ships and aircraft act in a manner consistent, so far as is reasonable and practicable, with the present Convention.

Art. 5. Hazardous substances. The Contracting Parties undertake to counteract the introduction whether airborne, waterborne or otherwise, into the Baltic Sea Area of hazardous substances as specified in Annex I of the present Convention.

Art. 6. Principles and obligations concerning land-based pollution

(1) The Contracting Parties shall take all appropriate measures to control and minimize land-based pollution of the marine environment of the Baltic Sea Area.

(2) In particular, the Contracting Parties shall take all appropriate measures to control and strictly limit pollution by noxious substances and materials in accordance with Annex II of the present Convention. To this end they shall, inter alia, as appropriate co-operate in the development and adoption of specific programmes, guidelines, standards or regulations concerning discharges, environmental quality, and products containing such substances and materials and their use.

(3) The substances and materials listed in Annex II of the present Convention shall not be introduced into the marine environment of the Baltic Sea Area in significant quantities without a prior special permit, which may be periodically reviewed, by the appropriate national authority.

(4) The appropriate national authority will inform the Commission referred to in Article 12 of the present Convention of the quantity, quality and way of discharge if it considers that significant quantities of

substances and materials listed in Annex II of the present Convention were discharged.

(5) The Contracting Parties shall endeavour to establish and adopt common criteria for issuing permits for discharges.

(6) To control and minimize pollution of the Baltic Sea Area by harmful substances the Contracting Parties shall, in addition to the provisions of Article 5 of the present Convention, aim at attaining the goals and applying the criteria enumerated in Annex III of the present Convention.

(7) If the discharge from a watercourse, flowing through the territories of two or more Contracting Parties or forming a boundary between them, is liable to cause pollution of the marine environment of the Baltic Sea Area, the Contracting Parties concerned shall in common take appropriate measures in order to prevent and abate such pollution.

(8) The Contracting Parties shall endeavour to use best practicable means in order to minimize the airborne pollution of the Baltic Sea Area by noxious substances.

Art. 7. Prevention of pollution from ships.

(1) In order to protect the Baltic Sea Area from pollution by deliberate, negligent or accidental release of oil, harmful substances other than oil, and by the discharge of sewage and garbage from ships, the Contracting Parties shall take measures as set out in Annex IV of the present Convention.

(2) The Contracting Parties shall develop and apply uniform requirements for the capacity and location of facilities for the reception of residues of oil, harmful substances other than oil, including sewage and garbage, taking into account inter alia the special needs of passenger ships and combination carriers.

Art. 8. Pleasure craft. The Contracting Parties shall in addition to implementing those provisions of the present Convention which can appropriately be applied to pleasure craft, take special measures in order to abate harmful effects on the marine environment of the Baltic Sea Area of pleasure craft activities. The measures shall inter alia deal with adequate reception facilities for wastes from pleasure craft.

Art. 9. Prevention of dumping (1) The Contracting Parties shall, subject to Paragraphs 2 and 4 of this Article, prohibit dumping in the Baltic Sea Area.

(2) Dumping of dredged spoils shall be subject to a prior special permit by the appropriate national authority in accordance with the provisions of Annex V of the present Convention.

(3) Each Contracting Party undertakes to ensure compliance with the provisions of this Article by vessels and aircraft:

(a) registered in its territory or flying its flag;

(b) loading, within its territory or territorial sea, matter which is to be dumped; or

(c) believed to be engaged in dumping within its territorial sea.

(4) The provisions of this Article shall not apply when the safety of human life or of a vessel or aircraft at sea is threatened by the complete destruction or total loss of the vessel or aircraft, or in any case which constitutes a danger to human life, if dumping appears to be the only way of averting the threat and if there is every probability that the damage consequent upon such dumping will be less than would otherwise occur. Such dumping shall be so conducted as to minimize the likelihood of damage to human or marine life.

(5) Dumping made under the provisions of Paragraph 4 of this Article shall be reported and dealt with in accordance with Annex VI of the present Convention and shall also be reported forthwith to the Commission referred to in Article 12 of the present Convention in accordance with the provisions of Regulation 4 of Annex V of the present Convention.

(6) In case of dumping suspected to be in contravention of the provisions of this Article the Contracting Parties shall co-operate in investigating the matter in accordance with Regulation 2 of Annex IV of the present Convention.

Art. 10. Exploration and exploitation of the sea-bed and its subsoil. Each Contracting Party shall take all appropriate measures in order to prevent pollution of the marine environment of the Baltic Sea Area resulting from exploration or exploitation of its part of the sea-bed and its subsoil or from any associated activities thereon. It shall also ensure equipment is at hand to start an immediate abatement of pollution in that area.

Art. 11. Co-operation in combatting marine pollution. The Contracting Parties shall take measures and co-operate as set out in Annex VI of the present Convention in order to eliminate or minimize pollution of the Baltic Sea Area by oil or other harmful substances.

Art. 12. Institutional and organizational framework.

(1) The Baltic Marine Environment Protection Commission, hereinafter referred to as 'the Commission', is hereby established for the purposes of the present Convention.

(2) The chairmanship of the Commission shall be given to each Contracting Party in turn in alphabetical order of the names of the States in the English language.

The Chairman shall serve for a period of two years, and cannot during the period of his chairmanship serve as representative of his country ...

Art. 13. The duties of the Commission

The duties of the Commission shall be:

(a) To keep the implementation of the present Convention under continuous observation;

(b) To make recommendations on measures relating to the purposes of the present Convention; ...

Art. 16. Scientific and technological co-operation.

(1) The Contracting Parties undertake directly, or when appropriate through competent regional or other international organizations, to co-operate in the fields of science, technology and other research, and to exchange data as well as other scientific information for the purposes of the present Convention ...

Art. 17. Responsibility for damage. The Contracting Parties undertake, as soon as possible, jointly to develop and accept rules concerning responsibility for damage resulting from acts or omissions in contravention of the present Convention, including, inter alia, limits of responsibility, criteria and procedures for the determination of liability and available remedies.

Art. 18. Settlement of disputes (1) In case of a dispute between Contracting Parties as to the interpretation or application of the present Convention, they should seek a solution by negotiation. If the Parties concerned cannot reach agreement they should seek the good offices of or jointly request the mediation by a third Contracting Party, a qualified international organization or a qualified person.

(2) If the Parties concerned have not been able to resolve their dispute through negotiation or have been unable to agree on measures as described above, such disputes shall be, upon common agreement, submitted to an ad-hoc arbitration tribunal, to a permanent arbitration tribunal, or to the International Court of Justice.

Art. 19. Safeguard of certain freedoms. Nothing in the present Convention shall be construed as infringing upon the freedom of navigation, fishing, marine scientific research and other legitimate uses of the high seas, as well as upon the right of innocent passage through the territorial sea.

Art. 20. Status of Annexes. The Annexes attached to the present Convention form an integral part of the Convention.

Art. 21. Relations to other Conventions. The provisions of the present Convention shall be without prejudice to the rights and obligations of the Contracting Parties under treaties concluded previously as well as under treaties which may be concluded in the future, furthering and developing the general principles of the Law of the Sea that the present Convention is based upon and in particular provisions concerning the prevention of pollution of the marine environment.

Art. 22. Revision of the Convention. A conference for the purpose of a general revision of the present Convention may be convened with the consent of the Contracting Parties or at the request of the Commission."

Final Act of the Diplomatic Conference on the Protection of the Marine Environment, Helsinki, 1974; L. GELBERG, "Rechtsprobleme des Schutzes der lebenden Ressourcen in der Ostsee", in: *Jahrbuch für Internationales Recht*, 1975, pp. 204–222.

BALTIC INSTITUTE, INSTYTUT BAŁTYCKI. A scientific research association f. in 1925 in Toruń devoted to studies of the Baltic Sea region with particular consideration of Polish–German and Polish–Scandinavian relations; since 1945 its headquarters are in Gdańsk.

BALTIC MERCANTILE AND SHIPPING EXCHANGE. THE BALTIC. The world's largest chartering institution f. in the 17th century in London, modernized by ▷ Baltic Club in 1824 and ever since known as The Baltic; headquarters in St. Mary Axe, London EC3. Since World War II, charters aircraft; also acts as an exchange of oleaginous seed and grain.

BALTIC PACT, 1934. ▷ Baltic entente.

BALTIC PEOPLES. An international term since the II World War for the Estonians, Latvians and Lithuanians, whose states were occupied by Soviet troops 1939–1941, then by Nazi German troops, and since 1944 incorporated into the Soviet Union, not recognized by the majority of Western European and Western Hemisphere countries. The European Parliamentary Assembly adopted on Jan. 28, 1987, Resolution 872 (1987) on the situation of Baltic Peoples.
The text is as follows:
The Assembly,
(1) Considering that Article 1 of both the International Covenant on Civil and Political Rights and the International Covenant on Economic, Social and Cultural Rights proclaims the right of peoples to self-determination, and that the Soviet Union is a Contracting Party thereto;
(2) Considering that Principle VIII of the Final Act of the Conference on Security and Co-operation in Europe guarantees the right of peoples to self-determination and also their right, in full freedom, to determine, when and as they wish, their internal and external political status;
(3) Recalling that the incorporation of the three Baltic States into the Soviet Union was and still is a flagrant violation of the right to self-determination of peoples, and that it remains unrecognised by the great majority of European states and many members of the international community;
(4) Considering that the elimination of the international problems created by this incorporation demands solutions on the basis of the international obligations entered into by the Soviet Union and other members of the international community;
(5) Having noted and deplored serious violations of human rights, including freedom of religion, committed by the Soviet Union authorities in the three Baltic states;
(6) Deploring the fact that, as a result of forced immigration into their area, the Baltic peoples are brought under pressure to assimilate, and that the lack of possibilities for education and cultural expression of their own is leading towards the loss of national identity;
(7) Recalling the Resolution adopted by the European Parliament on January 13, 1983, concerning the situation in Estonia, Latvia and Lithuania;
(8) Believing that, politically, a solution of the Baltic problem can best be sought in the wider framework of East–West relations, in particular relations between the two superpowers;
(9) Considering that an improvement of those relations could make it easier effectively to raise the question of these countries' fate notably in the framework of the CSCE, the aim of which, by means of the endeavours of all European states, is to overcome East–West antagonisms while respecting the right of each to freely determine its political, economic, social and cultural systems in accordance with the wishes of its population;
(10) Noting that some of the principles governing mutual relations between the states participating in the CSCE take note of the territorial demarcation inherited at the end of hostilities in 1945 (inviolability of frontiers, territorial integrity) without,

however, freezing the situation or sanctioning the European status quo;
(11) Emphasising that the Helsinki Final Act expressly provides for the possibility of changing frontiers, in accordance with international law, by peaceful means and by agreement;
(12) Emphasising that, in the field of human rights, the states participating in the CSCE cannot invoke the principle of national sovereignty in order to prevent discussion of respect for these rights;
(13) Appeals to the Government of the Soviet Union to respect the rights to self-determination and the human rights in the Baltic states;
(14) Invites the governments of member states of the Council of Europe at the CSCE Conference in Vienna and, if need be, at further CSCE meetings to draw the attention of participating states to the serious violations of human rights and the right to self-determination in the three Baltic states.

Council of Europe, Human Rights, *Information Sheet No. 2*, pp. 168–169.

BALTIC SALMON COMMISSION. An intergovernmental institution created 1963 by an understanding between the governments of Denmark, FRG, Poland, and Sweden with the task of defining rational limits of catches and controlling the stocking of the Baltic with this species. The Commission does not have a permanent seat; it is located in turn in the capitals of the member states during the term of office of the chairman from a given state.

BALTIC SEA. An arm of the Atlantic Ocean indenting northern Europe connected with the North Sea via Danish Belts and the Kiel Canal. The Baltic sea area is defined by the Baltic Helsinki Convention 1974 as follows:
"The Baltic Sea proper with the Gulf of Bothnia, the Gulf of Finland and the entrance to the Baltic Sea bounded by the parallel of the Skaw in the Skagerrak at 57°44′8″N. It does not include internal waters of the Baltic States."
Surface area 385,000 sq. km, average depth: 86 m. Since 1970 the seven Baltic Countries (Denmark, Finland, FRG, GDR, Poland, Sweden and the USSR) have been working on a joint research project aimed at eliminating dangerous pollution of Baltic sea waters and sea bottom. Since 1973 the Baltic Sea Diplomatic Conference has been preparing a ▷ Baltic Code. On Feb. 16, 1988, Norway, the USSR and Sweden signed a preliminary accord on boundaries in the Baltic Sea, discussed since 1967.

C.R. PUSTO, "Le Statut Juridique de la Mer Baltique a partir du 19 siècle", in: *Recueil de l'Académie de Droit International*, Nos. 52 and 53, 1953; L. GELBERG, *Maritime Cooperation of the Baltic States*, Wroclaw, 1981. KEESING's *Record of World Events*, February, 1988.

BALTIC SEA OF PEACE. An international term introduced in 1967 by the interparliamentary meetings of Denmark, Poland, GDR, Finland, Sweden and the USSR, held traditionally in Rostock, the major East German port.

Appel adressé aux parlements et aux gouvernements des États riverains de la Mer Baltique relatif à la protection de la Mer Baltique, Rostock-Warnemünde, July 12, 1972.

BALTIC STATES. In the period between the World Wars an international term for three states: ▷ Estonia, ▷ Lithuania and ▷ Latvia. After World War II the term indicated all states of the Baltic area when dealing with problems of the Baltic.

V.S. VARDYS, R.J. MISIUNAS, *The Baltic States in Peace and War, 1917–1945*, Pittsburg, 1978; L. GELBERG, *Problemy Prawne Współpracy Państw*

Baltyckich [Juridical Problems of Co-operation of the Baltic States], Gdańsk, 1976.

BALTIC STATES AGREEMENT, 1922. A political agreement between Estonia, Finland, Latvia and Poland, signed in Warsaw on Mar. 17, 1922, mutually acknowledging Peace Treaties signed by the named states with Russia: by Estonia on Feb. 2, 1920, by Latvia on Aug. 11, 1921, by Finland on Oct. 14, 1920, and by Poland ▷ Riga Peace Treaty with Russia, Ukraine and Byelorussia on Mar. 18, 1921.

LNTS, Vol. 11, p. 167.

BALTIC STATES CONVENTION ON ARBITRATION. ▷ Baltic conventions, 1923–29.

BALTIC STATES CONVENTION ON BILLS OF EXCHANGE, 1938. A convention signed in Kaunas on Apr. 9, 1938 by Estonia, Lithuania and Latvia on a uniform law for bills of exchange.

LNTS, Vol. 191, p. 119.

BALTIC STATES CONVENTION ON CHEQUES, 1938. A convention signed in Kaunas on Apr. 9, 1938 by Estonia, Lithuania and Latvia on a uniform law for cheques.

LNTS, Vol. 191, p. 165.

BALTIC STATES CONVENTION ON GEODESY, 1925. ▷ Baltic conventions, 1925–29.

BALTIC STATES CONVENTION ON JUDGMENTS, 1935. A convention signed in Kaunas, on Nov. 14, 1935 by Estonia, Lithuania, Latvia regarding reciprocal recognition and enforcement of judgments in criminal matters.

LNTS, Vol. 166, p. 87.

BALTIC STATES CO-OPERATION TREATY, 1934. ▷ Baltic entente.

BALUCHISTAN. A land in Asia located in Pakistan and Iran on the Arabian Sea and Gulf of Oman. Since 1970 the Baluchistanis in Pakistan have been demanding autonomy; in 1972 disturbances took place; in Jan., 1973 the government of Pakistan, which charged Iraq with supplying weapons to the Baluchistan separatist movement, took military action. In the spring of 1977 the separatist Pakhtunistan tribes, which are an absolute majority in the western part of Pakistan, i.e. in the border province of Baluchistan, began demonstrations. These tribes, separated 1883 by the so-called ▷ Durand Line, live for the most part in Afghanistan, which claims a right to the western part of Pakistan, called Pakhtunistan.

BALZAN FOUNDATION. An Italian–Swiss foundation named after Eugenio Balzan (1890–1953), editor of the Italian daily paper *Coriere de la Serra*, based on his property bequeathed to a foundation of the Nobel Prize type "for contribution to the peace of mankind and the brotherhood of peoples." The first prize was granted to the Nobel Foundation in 1962, and the second to the Pope John XXIII in 1963.

BAM. BAYKALSKO-AMURSKAYA MAGISTRALIA. The Baykal–Amur Railroad. A railway line in the south-eastern Siberian USSR between the Baykal Lake and Pacific Ocean; 3145 km long. The construction of the electric line began in 1975; finished on Sept. 29, 1984.
The BAM line made it possible to begin a program of geological development of the region (coal, iron

B

ore and copper) for the years 1985–1995. The region encompasses 1.5 mil sq. km.

BAMAKO. The capital of Mali. Population 1976 census: 404,022. Seat of organizations reg. with the UIA:

International African Migratory Locust Organization.
Union of National Radio and TV Organizations of Africa.
West African Federation of Association for the Advancement of Handicapped Persons.

Yearbook of International Organizations, 1986–87.

BAMBOO CURTAIN. A catch-phrase used in relation to communist countries of Asia, in the sense identical to that of the ▷ Iron Curtain in Europe.

BANACH MATHEMATICAL CENTER. The Stefan Banach International Mathematical Center for Raising Research Qualifications, f. 1972 in Warsaw. Members: Academies of Sciences of Bulgaria, Czechoslovakia, GDR, Hungary, Poland, Romania and the USSR. Reg. with the UIA.

Yearbook of International Organizations.

BANANAS. One of the basic agricultural products of tropical countries, object of international conventions. The greatest producers of bananas in the world are: Brazil more than 30%, India *c.* 17%, Ecuador *c.* 12%, followed by Colombia, Ivory Coast, Somalia, Honduras, Trinidad and Tobago, Guatemala and the Netherlands Antilles. In 1963 in La Lima (Honduras) the Federation of Workers of the Banana Industry in Latin America and the Caribbees, Federación de los Trabajadores en la Industria de Platano de América Latina y del Caribe (FETIBALC), was established; reg. with the UIA. The greatest consumers of American bananas are the USA and Canada, of African–Western Europe. The largest banana company is United Bonds in New York, former (to 1970) United Fruit Company (UFC). The operations of UFS were debated 1954 in the UN during the debate on the situation in Guatemala. United Bonds represents 35% of the banana trade, Standard Fruit 25% and Del Monte 19%. The producers in 1974 initiated the so-called "banana war" to change their terms of trade. Ecuador, Colombia, Costa Rica, Guatemala, Honduras, Nicaragua, and Panama on Sept. 17, 1974 established the Unión of Banana Exporting States, Unión de Paises Exportadores de Banana, UPEB. In March, 1977 the UPEB states (without Ecuador) formed the banana export company COMUBANA. In the EEC system the ▷ STABEX includes bananas in the ACP countries.

CH.D. KEPNER, J.H. SOOTHILL, *El imperio del banano; las compañas bananeras contra la soberanía de las naciones del Caribe,* 2 Vols, Havana, 1961; F. VILLAGRAN KRAMER, *Intergración Económica Centroamericana,* Guatemala, 1967, pp. 291–292; CEPAL, *Estudio Económico de América Latina 1966,* New York, 1968, pp. 390–392, *Yearbook of International Organizations.*

B AND C ARMS, BACTERIOLOGICAL (BIOLOGICAL) AND CHEMICAL WEAPONS. Weapons of mass destruction utilizing lethal poisonous substances that act on the organism as well as weapons using infectious bacteria and their toxins to create epidemics and communicable illnesses; one of the most threatening international problems for humanity of the 20th century in the judgment of UN Secretary-General "in certain respects more dangerous than atomic weapons" (U Thant on Sept. 15, 1968). The use of B and C arms is contrary to common international law in accordance with the principle *Armas bella non veneris geri* (war is waged with weapons, not poisons); despite

this it was used in the 30 years' war in the poisoning of wells, condemned as a crime, and also in infecting with smallpox germs, which was first used for genocidal purposes against the Indians in 1763 in New Scotland by the British officer J.A. Amherst. The first formal prohibitions on using chemical weapons were introduced by the Brussels Declaration, 1874 and the Hague Conventions of 1889 and 1907. They were violated by Germany on Apr. 22, 1915 at Ypres in Belgium, which changed the character of World War I, in which for the first time poisonous chemical substances (shells with poisonous asphyxiating, blinding gases) were used on a mass scale (*c.* 125,000 tons), and the number of casualties exceeded 1.3 million soldiers, including *c.* 100,000 killed. In 1922 the Washington Conference on disarmament formulated a new convention prohibiting B and C weapons, but the signatories did not ratify it. On June 17, 1925 on the initiative of the LN was signed the Geneva Protocol for the Prohibition of the Use in War of Asphyxiating, Poisonous or Other Gases and of Bacteriological Methods of Warfare (based on the Washington Convention, 1922, but without the proviso *si omnes*). The Geneva Protocol was ratified by the majority of the European states (France and the USSR in 1926, Great Britain in 1927, Germany and Poland in 1929) as well as those of America (with the exception of the USA). In 1935–36 Italy used in Ethiopia ▷ yperite (mustard gas) and during World War II Germany used asphyxiating gases ▷ *Zyklon B* for genocidal operations in the extermination camps and besides this produced other kinds of B and C arms, as did Japan, using them in the war with China; this was condemned on June 6, 1942 by the US president F.D. Roosevelt, warning Japan, and then on June 9, 1943 warning also Germany, that the USA would make reprisals. The issue of B and C arms was examined by the International Military Tribunal in Nuremburg and Tokyo, 1946–48 (▷ plague). In the UN the problem of B and C arms came up in the Security Council on July 20, 1952 during the war in Korea, but the notion was rejected. On Dec. 5, 1966 the UN General Assembly stated its unanimous opinion on the issue of B and C arms in Res. 2162/XXI that:

"… Recalling that the Geneva Protocol 1925 has been signed and adopted and is recognized by many States … calls for strict observance by all States of the principles and objectives of the Protocol and condemns all actions contrary to this objective … [and] invites all States to accede to the Geneva Protocol of June 17, 1925."

Then on Dec. 20, 1968 the UN General Assembly in Res. 2454 A/XXIII confirmed the recommendation of Res. 2162 B/XXI and requested UN experts to draft a report on the effects of the eventual use of these weapons, which was completed and published by the UN Secretary-General on July 1, 1969. The final conclusions of the report are as follows:

"The general conclusion of the report can thus be summed up in a few lines. Were these weapons ever to be used on a large scale in war, no one could predict how enduring the effects would be, and how they would affect the structure of society and the environment in which we live. This overriding danger would apply as much to the country which initiated the use of these weapons as to the one which had been attacked, regardless of what protective measures it might have taken in parallel with its development of an offensive capability. A particular danger also derives from the fact that any country could develop or acquire, in one way or another, a capability in this type of warfare, despite the fact that this could prove costly. The danger of the proliferation of this class of weapons applies as much to the developing as it does to developed countries.
"The momentum of the arms race would clearly decrease if the production of these weapons were effectively and unconditionally banned. Their use, which could cause an enormous loss of human life, has already

been condemned and prohibited by international agreements, in particular the Geneva Protocol of 1925, and, more recently, in resolutions of the General Assembly of the United Nations. The prospects for general and complete disarmament under effective international control, and hence for peace throughout the world, would brighten significantly if the development, production and stockpiling of chemical and bacteriological (biological) agents intended for purposes of war were to end and if they were eliminated from all military arsenals.
"If this were to happen, there would be a general lessening of international fear and tension. It is the hope of the authors that this report will contribute to public awareness of the profoundly dangerous results if these weapons were ever used, and that an aroused public will demand and receive assurances that governments are working for the earliest effective elimination of chemical and bacteriological (biological) weapons.
"I have given the study prepared by the consultant experts my earnest consideration and I have decided to accept their unanimous report in its entirety, and to transmit it to the General Assembly, the Security Council, the Eighteen-Nation Committee on Disarmament and to the Governments of Member States, as the report called for by resolution 2454 A(XXIII). I also feel it incumbent upon me, in the hope that further action will be taken to deal with the threat posed by the existence of these weapons, to urge that the Members of the United Nations undertake the following measures in the interests of enhancing the security of the peoples of the world:
(1) To renew the appeal to all States to accede to the Geneva Protocol of 1925;
(2) To make a clear affirmation that the prohibition contained in the Geneva Protocol applies to the use in war of all chemical, bacteriological and biological agents (including tear gas and other harassing agents) which now exist or which may be developed in the future;
(3) To call upon all countries to reach agreement to halt the development, production and stockpiling of all chemical and bacteriological (biological) agents for purposes of war and to achieve their effective elimination from the arsenal of weapons."

On Dec. 16, 1969 the UN General Assembly adopted the following declaration:

"The General Assembly,
Considering that chemical and biological methods of warfare have always been viewed with horror and been justly condemned by the international community,
Considering that the methods of warfare are inherently reprehensible because their effects are often uncontrollable and unpredictable and may be injurious without distinction to combatants and non-combatants and because any use would entail a serious risk of escalation,
Recalling that successive international instruments have prohibited or sought to prevent the use of such methods of warfare,
Noting specifically in this regard that:
(a) The majority of States then in existence adhered to the Protocol for the Prohibition of the Use in War of Asphyxiating, Poisonous or Other Gases, and of Bacteriological Methods of Warfare, signed at Geneva on June 17, 1925,
(b) Since then, further States have become Parties to that Protocol,
(c) Still other States have declared that they will abide by its principles and objectives,
(d) These principles and objectives have commanded broad respect in the practice of States,
(e) The General Assembly, without any dissenting vote, has called for the strict observance by all States of the principles and objectives of the Geneva Protocol,
Recognizing therefore, in the light of all the above circumstances, that the Geneva Protocol embodies the generally recognized rules of international law prohibiting the use in international armed conflicts of all biological and chemical methods of warfare, regardless of any technical developments, mindful of the report of the Secretary-General, prepared with the assistance of the Group of Consultant Experts, appointed by him under General Assembly Res. 2454 A(XXIII) of 20 December 1968, and entitled 'Chemical and Bacteriological (Biological) Weapons and the Effects of their Possible use'.

Considering that this report and the foreword to it by the Secretary-General add further urgency for an affirmation of these rules and for dispelling, for the future, any uncertainty as to their scope and, by such affirmation, to assure the effectiveness of the rules and to enable all States to demonstrate their determination to comply with them. Declares as contrary to the generally recognized rules of international law, as embodied in the Protocol for the Prohibition of the Use in War of Asphyxiating, Poisonous or Other Gases, and of Bacteriological Methods of Warfare, signed at Geneva on 17 June 1925, the use in international armed conflict of:
(a) Any chemical agents of warfare – chemical substances, whether gaseous, liquid or solid – which might be employed because of their direct toxic effects on man, animals or plants;
(b) Any biological agents of warfare – living organisms, whatever their nature, or infective material derived from them – which are intended to cause disease or death in man, animals or plants, and which depend for their effects on their ability to multiply in the person, animal or plant attacked."

Simultaneously the UK submitted to the UN Disarmament Committee in Geneva the plan of a convention supported by the USA on prohibition of the production and use of bacteriological weapons. The USSR and the socialist countries demanded the coupling of the prohibition of B weapons with the prohibition of C weapons, but in view of the opposition of the western powers submitted a compromise proposal on Apr. 15, 1971, which enabled the Commission on Sept. 30, 1971 to present to the UN General Assembly a new plan for a Treaty on the Prohibition of the Production and Stockpiling of B weapons and Toxic substances. The UN General Assembly on Dec. 16, 1971 approved the Convention of the Prohibition of the Development, Production and Stockpiling of Bacteriological (Biological) and Toxic Weapons and on Their Destruction, 100 votes without opposition with the abstention of France and in the absence of the Chinese People's Republic delegation during the time of voting. The Convention entered into force on Mar. 26, 1975 after ratification by the twenty-second Party, including the governments designated as Depositaries – the UK, the USA and the USSR. This Convention is called in the UN the ▷ BW Convention 1972. At a conference of the Disarmament Committee in Geneva on Mar. 28, 1973 Bulgaria, Byelorussian SSR, Czechoslovakia, Mongolia, Poland, Romania, Ukrainian SSR, and the USSR presented a proposal for a convention on the Prohibition of Research, Production and Stockpiling of Chemical Weapons and on Their Destruction. The Disarmament Committee continued to discuss the project in 1979–80. The Review Conference of the Parties to the 1971 Convention, attended by 53 of the 67 states parties and by eight of the 37 states which had signed, but had not yet ratified the document, concluded on Mar. 21, 1980 that a second review conference should be held in Geneva at the request of a majority of the state parties not earlier than 1985 and not later than 1990.

E.S. FARROW, *Gas Warfare*, New York, 1920; J.H. ROTSHILD, *Tomorrow's Weapons. Chemical and Biological*, New York, 1964; S.M. HERSCH, *Chemical and Biological Warfare*, New York, 1968; R. CLARKE, *We All Fall Down. The Prospect of Biological and Chemical Warfare*, London, 1968; *Chemical and Bacteriological (Biological) Weapons and the Effects of their Possible Use*, UN New York, 1972; *The Problem of Chemical and Biological Warfare. CB Weapons Today*, SIPRI, Stockholm, 1973; *UN Chronicle*, May 1980.

BANAT. A land situated between the Danube, Cisa, Marusha and southern Carpathians; subject of international disputes; until World War I within the Kingdom of Hungary; by virtue of the Peace Treaty of Trianon, 1920, a smaller part of Banat was ceded to Yugoslavia, a larger part to Romania;

nine villages remained within Hungary; the drawing of the final boundaries took place Nov. 24, 1923.

J. RADONITCH, *Le Banat*, Paris, 1919; V.V. TILEA, *Actiunea diplomatica a Romanici 1919–1920*, Sibiu, 1929; M. JOVANOVIC, *Staranje zajednicke drzave SHS*, 3 Vols., Beograd, 1930.

BANCO CENTRAL DO BRASIL. ▷ Banco do Brasil SA.

BANCO DE DESARROLLO DEL CARIBE. CARIBBEAN DEVELOPMENT BANK. Intergovernmental institution, established by an agreement, signed on Oct. 18, 1969, entered into force on Jan. 25, 1970. Members: Antigua, Bahamas, Barbados, Belize, Cayman, Colombia, Dominica, Grenada, Guayana, Jamaica, Montserrat, St Kitts, Nevis, Anguilla, St Lucia, St Vincent, Trinidad-Tobago, Turks Caicos, Venezuela, Virgin Islands and two non-regional states: Canada and the USA. Publ. *Annual Report*. Reg. with the UIA.

Yearbook of International Organizations

BANCO DE LA NACION ARGENTINA. A governmental institution, f. in 1891 in Buenos Aires. A state credit bank of agriculture, industry and trade. As an international trade bank it has branch offices in Bolivia, Brazil, Paraguay, Uruguay and the USA, and agencies in Bogota, Caracas, Lima, London, Madrid, Mexico, Paris, Quito, Rome and Santiago de Chile.

BANCO DO BRASIL SA. A governmental institution, f. in 1808 in Rio de Janeiro. From 1970 Central Office in Brasilia, 57.8% owned by the Federal Government; abroad, acts as the State Treasury financial agent. The exchange operations of the Banco Central do Brasil are regulated by the Banco do Brasil. The foreign trade policy of the government – the issue of export and import licences – is administered by the Foreign Trade Department of the Banco do Brasil. Offices abroad in: Argentina, Bolivia, Chile, France, FRG, Italy, Japan, Mexico, Netherlands, Panama, Paraguay, Portugal, the UK, Uruguay and the USA.

BANCOR. International monetary unit proposed by J.M. Keynes during the Monetary Conference in Bretton Woods, 1943.

BANCROFT TREATIES, 1867–72. Conventions concluded by the USA with other states on the citizenship of immigrants, naturalized after at least a five-year stay in the United States. Initiated by G. Bancroft, USA envoy to Berlin (1867–74), with treaties concluded with German member states of the Reich. Similar Bancroft Treaties were later concluded by the USA with Belgium 1868, Sweden and Norway 1869, Great Britain 1870, Austria-Hungary 1870, Denmark 1872, Haiti 1902, Peru 1907, Portugal 1907, Bulgaria 1923, Czechoslovakia 1928, and Albania 1932.

A. DZIAŁOSZYNSKI, *Die Bancroft Verträge*, Dissertation Universitatis Vratislaviae, Breslau, 1913.

BAND AID ▷ Hunger.

BANDUNG. The capital of West Java province, Indonesia (1983 pop. 1,566,700); from 1810 until Dec. 1949, headquarters of the Netherlands East India Colonial Dutch Administration. Site of the ▷ Bandung Conference.

The Europa Yearbook, 1987, A World Survey, London, 1987.

BANDUNG CONFERENCE AND DECLARATION, 1955. The first Afro-Asian Solidarity Con-

ference, initiated by a summit meeting of the Prime Ministers of Burma, Ceylon, India, Indonesia and Pakistan held in Calcutta and Kandy, Apr. 28–May 2, 1954, was celebrated in Bandung, Indonesia, Apr. 18–24, 1955, attended by 29 delegations: Afghanistan, Burma, Cambodia, Ceylon, China, Egypt, Ethiopia, Gold Coast, India, Indonesia, Iran, Iraq, Japan, Jordan, Laos, Lebanon, Liberia, Libya, Nepal, Pakistan, Philippines, Saudi Arabia, Sudan, Syria, Thailand, Turkey, Dem. Rep. of Vietnam, State of Vietnam and Yemen. The Final Communiqué of the Bandung Conference adopted on Apr. 24, 1955 is as follows:

"The Asian–African Conference considered problems of common interest and concern to countries of Asia and Africa and discussed ways and means by which their people could achieve fuller economic, cultural and political co-operation.
A. Economic Cooperation.
(1) The Asian–African Conference recognized the urgency of promoting economic development in the Asian–African region. There was general desire for economic cooperation among the participating countries on the basis of mutual interest and respect for national sovereignty. The proposals with regard to economic cooperation within the participating countries do not preclude either the desirability or the need for cooperation with countries outside the region, including the investment of foreign capital. It was further recognized that the assistance being received by certain participating countries from outside the region, through international or under bilateral arrangements, had made a valuable contribution to the implementation of their development programmes.
Final Communiqué.
(2) The participating countries agreed to provide technical assistance to one another, to the maximum extent practicable, in the form of: experts, trainees, pilot projects and equipment for demonstration purposes; exchange of know-how and establishment of national, and where possible, regional training and research institutes for imparting technical knowledge and skills in cooperation with the existing international agencies.
(3) The Asian–African Conference recommended: the early establishment of the Special United Nations Fund for Economic Development; the allocation by the International Bank for Reconstruction and Development of a greater part of its resources to Asian–African countries; the early establishment of the International Finance Corporation which should include in its activities the undertaking of equity investment, and encouragement to the promotion of joint ventures among Asian–African countries in so far as this will promote their common interest.
(4) The Asian–African Conference recognized the vital need for stabilizing commodity trade in the region. The principle of enlarging the scope of multilateral trade and payments was accepted. However, it was recognized that some countries would have to take recourse to bilateral trade arrangements in view of their prevailing economic conditions.
(5) The Asian–African Conference recommended that collective action be taken by participating countries for stabilizing the international prices of and demand for primary commodities through bilateral and multilateral arrangements, and that as far as practicable and desirable, they should adopt a unified approach on the subject in the United Nations Permanent Advisory Commission on International Commodity Trade and other international forums.
(6) The Asian–African Conference further recommended that: Asian–African countries should diversify their export trade by processing their raw material, wherever economically feasible, before export; intraregional trade fairs should be promoted and encouragement given to the exchange of trade delegations and groups of businessmen; exchange of information and of samples should be encouraged with a view to promoting intraregional trade and normal facilities should be provided for transit trade of land-locked countries.
(7) The Asian–African Conference attached considerable importance to shipping and expressed concern that shipping lines reviewed from time to time their freight rates, often to the detriment of participating countries. It recommended a study of this problem, and collective

action thereafter, to induce the shipping lines to adopt a more reasonable attitude. It was suggested that a study of railway freight of transit trade may be made.

(8) The Asian–African Conference agreed that encouragement should be given to the establishment of national and regional banks and insurance companies.

(9) The Asian–African Conference felt that exchange of information on matters relating to oil, such as remittance of profits and taxation, might eventually lead to the formulation of common policies.

(10) The Asian–African Conference emphasized the particular significance of the development of nuclear energy for peaceful purposes, for the Asian–African countries. The Conference welcomed the initiative of the Powers principally concerned in offering to make available information regarding the use of atomic energy for peaceful purposes; urged the speedy establishment of the International Atomic Energy Agency which should provide for adequate representation of the Asian–African countries on the executive authority of the Agency; and recommended to the Asian and African Governments to take full advantage of the training and other facilities in the peaceful uses of atomic energy offered by the countries sponsoring such programmes.

(11) The Asian–African Conference agreed to the appointment of Liaison Officers in participating countries, to be nominated by their respective national Governments, for the exchange of information and ideas on matters of mutual interest. It recommended that fuller use should be made of the existing international organizations, and participating countries who were not members of such international organizations, but were eligible, should secure membership.

(12) The Asian–African Conference recommended that there should be prior consultation of participating countries in international forums with a view, as far as possible, to furthering their mutual economic interest. It is, however, not intended to form a regional bloc.

B. Cultural Cooperation

(1) The Asian–African Conference was convinced that among the most powerful means of promoting understanding among nations is the development of cultural cooperation. Asia and Africa have been the cradle of great religions and civilizations which have enriched other cultures and civilizations while themselves being enriched in the process. Thus the cultures of Asia and Africa are based on spiritual and universal foundations. Unfortunately contacts among Asian and African countries were interrupted during the past centuries. The people of Asia and Africa are now animated by a keen and sincere desire to renew their old cultural contacts and develop new ones in the context of the modern world. All participating Governments at the Conference reiterated their determination to work for closer cultural cooperation.

(2) The Asian–African Conference took note of the fact that the existence of colonialism in many parts of Asia and Africa in whatever form it may be not only prevents cultural cooperation but also suppresses the national cultures of the people. Some colonial powers have denied to their dependent peoples basic rights in the sphere of education and culture which hampers the development of their personality and also prevents cultural intercourse with other Asian and African peoples. This is particularly true in the case of Tunisia, Algeria and Morocco, where the basic right of the people to study their own language and culture has been suppressed. Similar discrimination has been practised against African and coloured people in some parts of the Continent of Africa. The Conference felt that these policies amount to a denial of the fundamental rights of man, impede cultural advancement in this region and also hamper cultural cooperation on the wider international plane. The Conference condemned such a denial of fundamental rights in the sphere of education and culture in some parts of Asia and Africa by this and other forms of cultural suppression.

In particular, the Conference condemned racialism as a means of cultural suppression.

(3) It was not from any sense of exclusiveness or rivalry with other groups of nations and other civilisations and cultures that the Conference viewed the development of cultural cooperation among Asian and African countries. True to the age-old tradition of tolerance and universality, the Conference believed that Asian and African cultural cooperation should be developed in the larger context of world cooperation.

Side by side with the development of Asian–African cultural cooperation the countries of Asia and Africa desire to develop cultural contacts with others. This would enrich their own culture and would also help in the promotion of world peace and understanding.

(4) There are many countries in Asia and Africa which have not yet been able to develop their educational, scientific and technical institutions. The Conference recommended that countries in Asia and Africa which are more fortunately placed in this respect should give facilities for the admission of students and trainees from such countries to their institutions. Such facilities should also be made available to the Asian and African people in Africa to whom opportunities for acquiring higher education are at present denied.

(5) The Asian–African Conference felt that the promotion of cultural cooperation among countries of Asia and Africa should be directed towards:
(I) the acquisition of knowledge of each other's country;
(II) mutual cultural exchange, and
(III) exchange of information.

(6) The Asian–African Conference was of the opinion that at this stage the best results in cultural cooperation would be achieved by pursuing bilateral arrangements to implement its recommendations and by each country taking action on its own, wherever possible and feasible.

C. Human Rights and Self-determination

(1) The Asian–African Conference declared its full support of the fundamental principles of Human Rights as set forth in the Charter of the United Nations and took note of the Universal Declaration of Human Rights as a common standard of achievement for all peoples and all nations.

The Conference declared its full support of the principles of self-determination of peoples and nations as set forth in the Charter of the United Nations and took note of the United Nations resolutions on the rights of peoples and nations to self-determination, which is a pre-requisite of the full enjoyment of all fundamental Human Rights.

(2) The Asian–African Conference deplored the policies and practices of racial segregation and discrimination which form the basis of government and human relations in large regions of Africa and in other parts of the world. Such conduct is not only a gross violation of human rights, but also a denial of the fundamental values of civilisation and the dignity of man. The Conference extended its warm sympathy and support for the courageous stand taken by the victims of racial discrimination, especially by the peoples of African and Indian and Pakistani origin in South Africa; applauded all those who sustain their cause, re-affirmed the determination of Asian–African peoples to eradicate every trace of racialism that might exist in their own countries; and pledged to use its full moral influence to guard against the danger of falling victims to the same evil in their struggle to eradicate it.

D. Problems of Dependent Peoples

(1) The Asian–African Conference discussed the problems of dependent peoples and colonialism and the evils arising from the subjection of peoples to alien subjugations, domination and exploitation.

The Conference is agreed:
(a) in declaring that colonialism in all its manifestations is an evil which should speedily be brought to an end;
(b) in affirming that the subjection of peoples to alien subjugation, domination and exploitation constitutes a denial of fundamental human rights, is contrary to the Charter of the United Nations and is an impediment to the promotion of world peace and cooperation;
(c) in declaring its support of the cause of freedom and independence for all such people, and
(d) in calling upon the powers concerned to grant freedom and independence to such peoples.

(2) In view of the unsettled situation in North Africa and of the persisting denial to the peoples of North Africa of their right to self-determination, the Asian–African Conference declared its support of the rights of the people of Algeria, Morocco and Tunisia to self-determination and independence and urged the French Government to bring about a peaceful settlement of the issue without delay.

E. Other Problems

(1) In view of the existing tension in the Middle East, caused by the situation in Palestine and of the danger of

that tension to world peace, the Asian–African Conference declared its support of the rights of the Arab people of Palestine and called for the implementation of the United Nations Resolutions on Palestine and the achievement of the peaceful settlement of the Palestine question.

(2) The Asian–African Conference, in the context of its expressed attitude on the abolition of colonialism, supported the position of Indonesia in the case of West Irian based on the relevant agreements between Indonesia and the Netherlands.

The Asian–African Conference urged the Netherlands Government to reopen negotiations as soon as possible, to implement their obligations under the above-mentioned agreements and expressed the earnest hope that the United Nations would assist the parties concerned in finding a peaceful solution to the dispute.

(3) The Asian–African conference supported the position of Yemen in the case of Aden and the Southern parts of Yemen known as the Protectorates and urged the parties concerned to arrive at a peaceful settlement of the dispute.

F. Promotion of World Peace and Cooperation

(1) The Asian–African Conference, taking note of the fact that several States have still not been admitted to the United Nations, considered that for effective cooperation for world peace, membership in the United Nations should be universal, called on the Security Council to support the admission of all those States which are qualified for membership in terms of the Charter. In the opinion of the Asian–African Conference, the following among participating countries, viz: Cambodia, Ceylon, Japan, Jordan, Libya, Nepal, a unified Vietnam were so qualified. The Conference considered that the representation of the countries of the Asian–African region on the Security Council, in relation to the principle of equitable geographical distribution, was inadequate. It expressed the view that as regards the distribution of the non-permanent seats, the Asian–African countries which, under the arrangement arrived at in London in 1946, are precluded from being elected, should be enabled to serve on the Security Council, so that they might make a more effective contribution to the maintenance of international peace and security.

(2) The Asian–African Conference having considered the dangerous situation of international tension existing and the risks confronting the whole human race from the outbreak of global war in which the destructive power of all types of armaments, including nuclear and thermonuclear weapons, would be employed, invited the attention of all nations to the terrible consequences that would follow if such a war were to break out.

The Conference considered that disarmament and the prohibition of the production, experimentation and use of nuclear and thermonuclear weapons of war are imperative to save mankind and civilization from the fear and prospect of wholesale destruction.

It considered that the nations of Asia and Africa assembled here have a duty towards humanity and civilization to proclaim their support for disarmament and for the prohibition of these weapons and to appeal to nations principally concerned and to world opinion, to bring about such disarmament and prohibition.

The Conference considered that effective international control should be established and maintained to implement such disarmament and prohibition and that speedy and determined efforts should be made to this end.

Pending the total prohibition of the manufacture of nuclear and thermonuclear weapons, this Conference appealed to all the powers concerned to reach agreement to suspend experiments with such weapons.

The Conference declared that universal disarmament is an absolute necessity for the preservation of peace and requested the United Nations to continue its efforts and appealed to all concerned speedily to bring about the regulation, limitation, control and reduction of all armed forces and armaments, including the prohibition of the production, experimentation and use of all weapons of mass destruction, and to establish effective international control to this end.

G. Declaration on the Promotion of World Peace and Cooperation

The Asian–African Conference gave anxious thought to the question of world peace and cooperation. It viewed with deep concern the present state of international tension with its danger of an atomic world war. The problem of peace is correlative with the problem of international security. In this connection, all States should cooperate, especially through the United Nations, in bringing about the reduction of armaments and the elimination of nuclear weapons under effective international control. In this way, international peace can be promoted and nuclear energy may be used exclusively for peaceful purposes. This would help answer the needs particularly of Asia and Africa, for what they urgently require are social progress and better standards of life in larger freedom. Freedom and peace are interdependent. The right of self-determination must be enjoyed by all peoples, and freedom and independence must be granted, with the least possible delay, to those who are still dependent peoples. Indeed, all nations should have the right freely to choose their own political and economic systems and their own way of life, in conformity with the purposes and principles of the Charter of the United Nations.

Free from mistrust and fear, and with confidence and goodwill towards each other, nations should practise tolerance and live together in peace with one another as good neighbours and develop friendly cooperation on the basis of the following principles:

(1) Respect for fundamental human rights and for the purposes and principles of the Charter of the United Nations.

(2) Respect for the sovereignty and territorial integrity of all nations.

(3) Recognition of the equality of all races and of the equality of all nations large and small.

(4) Abstention from intervention or interference in the internal affairs of another country.

(5) Respect for the right of each nation to defend itself singly or collectively, in conformity with the Charter of the United Nations.

(6)(a) Abstention from the use of arrangements of collective defence to serve the particular interests of any of the big powers.

(b) Abstention by any country from exerting pressures on other countries.

(7) Refraining from acts or threats of aggression or the use of force against the territorial integrity or political independence of any country.

(8) Settlement of all international disputes by peaceful means, such as negotiation, conciliation, arbitration or judicial settlement as well as other peaceful means of the parties' own choice, in conformity with the Charter of the United Nations.

(9) Promotion of mutual interests and cooperation.

(10) Respect for justice and international obligations. The Asian–African Conference declared its conviction that friendly cooperation in accordance with these principles would effectively contribute to the maintenance and promotion of international peace and security, while cooperation in the economic, social and cultural fields would help bring about the common prosperity and well-being of all.

The Asian–African Conference recommended that the five sponsoring countries consider the convening of the next meeting of the Conference, in consultation with the participating countries."

On April 23–25, 1985, in Bandung, delegations from 80 Asian and African countries commemorated the Bandung Declaration.

Asia–Africa Speaks from Bandung, Djakarta, 1955, pp. 161–171; G. KAHIN, *The Asian–African Conference Bandung*, Ithaca, 1956. KEESING's *Record of World Events*, 1986, No. 3.

BANGALORE DECLARATION 1986 ▷ South Asian Association for Regional Co-operations.

BANGKOK. The capital of Thailand since 1782, city on the eastern bank of Chao Phraya River, near the Gulf of Siam (1986 pop. 5,446,708). Headquarters of 26 international organizations reg. with the UIA as Asian Highway Co-ordinating Committee, International Rice Commission, Asian–Pacific Council, Asian Industrial Development Council, Council of Ministers for Asian Economic Co-operation, Indo-Pacific Fishing Council, Pepper Community, World Fellowship of Buddhists.

Yearbook of International Organizations.

BANGLADESH. Member of the UN. People's Republic of Bangladesh. South Asiatic state on the Bay of Bengal, bordered by India and Burma. Area: 143,998, sq. km. Pop. 1987 est. 105,868,000, 1974 census: 71,316,517. Capital: Dacca with 3,458,000 inhabitants in 1981. GNP in 1987, US $160. Official languages: Bengali and English. Currency: 1 taka = 100 poisha. National Day: Mar. 26, Independence Day, 1971. Member of the UN since June 11, 1974 and of all UN specialized agencies. Member of the Colombo Plan, 1950; of the Non-Proliferation Treaty, 1979, and of the ENMOD Convention, 1979.

International relations: in 19th century, part of the British Empire in India until 1947 when India and ▷ Pakistan achieved independence. After Aug. 15, 1947 the country was the Eastern Province of Pakistan called East Pakistan. Internal disputes between East and West Pakistan provoked, on Mar. 26, 1971, a civil war, which ended on Dec. 13, 1971 with the victory of the separatist movement. The People's Republic of Bangladesh was proclaimed by the Constitution, which came into force on Dec. 16, 1972. The UN relief operation helped pave the way for rehabilitation of the war-shattered economy of Bangladesh. In 1977, dispute with India over the ▷ Farakka Dam. An Agreement with India on the sharing of Ganges water was signed in Nov., 1977 and in Nov., 1982. See also ▷ World Heritage UNESCO List.

S.C. KASHYAP (ed.), *Bangladesh: Background and Perspectives*, New Delhi, 1971; B.N. MEHRISH, *War Crimes and Genocide. The Trial of Pakistani War Criminals*, New Delhi, 1972; R. CHOWDBURY, *The Genesis of Bangladesh*, London, 1972; A.R. KHAN, *The Economy of Bangladesh*, London, 1972; M. AYOOB, K. SUBRAHMANYAN, *The Liberation War*, New Delhi, 1972; PH. GAVI, *Le Triangle Indien. De Bandoengen a Bangla Desh*, Paris, 1972; L. CHEN, *Disaster in Bangladesh. Health Crisis in Developing Nation*, London, 1973; *Everyone's United Nations*, New York, 1979; *The Europa Year Book 1984. A World Survey*, Vol. I, pp. 1143–1157, London, 1984.

BANISHMENT. An international term – known since ancient times – for temporary or permanent expulsion from a country for political reasons or for a transgression. In the 20th century applied only to political adversaries, mostly in Latin America, with the reservation that the exile must obtain ▷ asylum in another state.

BANJUL. The capital of Gambia, formerly Bathurst. Population 1983 census: 44,188, metropolitan area 145,692. Headquarters of organization reg. by the UIA.
Islamic Peace Committee.

Yearbook of International Organizations, 1986–87.

BANK. An international term for institutions conducting financial transactions, dealing mainly with credit and investments. The term comes from Italian banca = desk, denoting money exchange places in ancient harbors. Banks of emission are usually called – central banks, deposit and endorsement banks – commercial banks, and long-term credit banks – investment banks. The first intergovernmental bank was established in Basel in 1930, the Bank for International Settlements, BIS.

J. WHITE, *Regional Development Banks*, New York, 1972; THOMSON's *Dictionary of Banking*, London, 1974; J. RICCI, *Elsevier's Banking Dictionary*, in English, American, French, Italian, Spanish, Dutch and German, Amsterdam, 1979; *Who Owns What in World Banking?: A Guide to the Subsidiary and Affiliated Interests of the World's Major Banks*, London, 1983; *Who is Where in World Banking?*, London, 1983.

BANK DRUG MONEY ACCOUNTS. An international term for bank accounts held by persons suspected of major drug offences. The USA and UK initiated in 1984 the so called Mutual Legal Assistance Treaties with off shore banking centres such as the Bahamas, the British Virgin Islands, the Cayman Islands and others, the treaties giving US and UK law enforcement officials broad access to previously secret bank records.

Wall Street Journal, July 3, 1986.

BANK FOR INTERNATIONAL SETTLEMENTS, BIS. An intergovernmental institution established on the basis of international convention, signed at The Hague on Jan. 20, 1930, by the governments of France, Germany, Great Britain, Italy, Japan and Switzerland, as a joint stock company. The task of the Bank, with headquarters in Basel, Switzerland, is to support the co-operation between central banks for the purpose of developing additional simplifications in international financial operations and to act as a trustee or agent with regard to international financial settlements entrusted to it under agreements with the parties concerned (art. 3 of the Statutes). Stockholders of BIS are organized in the form of a joint stock company and comprise the central banks of the European states with the exception of the State Bank of the USSR and the Spanish Central Bank.

Main functions: the purchase and sale of coins and gold bars for its account or those of the central banks, and making other transactions in gold, foreign currencies, bonds, etc. for the central banks. Co-operates with the IMF. The Bank is an agent of OECD and a depositary of the European Coal and Steel Community, ECSC. Publ. *BIS Information Yearbook*. The ten central banks of the highly developed capitalist states formed in 1961 the ▷ Group of Ten, which usually holds its periodic sessions in the headquarters of BIS. An unusual incident in the history of BIS was the decision of the UN Conference made at ▷ Bretton Woods in 1944, to dissolve the Bank as soon as the IMF came into being because of BIS supposed collaboration with the Third Reich, for which insufficient proof was presented. After World War II and the formation of the IMF, the decision of Bretton Woods was cancelled.

LNTS, Vol. 104, pp. 445–447; G.U. PAPI, *The First Twenty Years of the BIS*, Roma, 1951; R. AUSBOIN, *La Banque des Règlements Internationaux, 1930–1955*, Basel, 1955; A.J. PEASLEE, *International Governmental Organizations, Constitutional Documents*, The Hague, 1961; *The Europa Year Book 1984. A World Survey*, Vol. I, p. 108, London, 1984.

BANK HOLIDAY. An international term for a weekday on which banks are closed, subject of international information because of international bank transactions. An international bank calendar is published annually, giving information on a particular country's bank holidays other than weekends, or Fridays in Moslem countries. In case of drastic fluctuations in foreign-exchange dealings additional bank holidays may be introduced to protect banks from excessive payments. The *ABC World Airways Guide* publishes in Part One a world list of bank and public holidays.

BANK OF CENTRAL AFRICAN STATES, BEAC. Banque des États de l'Afrique Centrale. Intergovernmental finance institution of Cameroon, Central African Republic, Chad, Congo and Gabon, established in 1955 in Paris. Publ. *Études et statistique*.

B

Yearbook of International Organizations.

BANK OF CHINA. A governmental financial institution, established in 1912 in Peking. From 1949 state merchant international bank with 15 branches: 12 in China, one in Hong Kong, one in London and one in Singapore.

K.H. HSIAO, *Money and Monetary Policy in Communist China*, New York, 1971.

BANK OF EUROPE. A project of a central bank for integrated West Europe, discussed by the finance ministers of the EEC as of June 1988.

A Central Bank for Europe, The Economist, June 25, 1988.

BANK OF GENES. An institution which, according to the recommendations of the 1972 Stockholm Conference on Protection of Man's Environment, should collect seeds of the most valuable plants and also secure, in the interest of mankind, natural reservations protecting specific breeds and species of animals and of microorganisms. The organizing of the Bank of Genes is within the plans of the UN Programs for Protection of Man's Environment.

BANK OF INDIA. A governmental financial institution, established in 1906 in Bombay, India; nationalized on July 19, 1969. Merchant international state bank with 753 branches in India and Birmingham, Hong Kong, Djakarta, Karachi, Leeds, London, Manchester, Nairobi, Paris, Singapore and Wembley. Subsidiary: Bank of India (Nigeria) Ltd.

BANK OF ISLAM. A governmental financial institution of Iran, founded in 1979 in Teheran for inland credit transactions, which, according to Koranic laws, does not admit interest on loans, and charges the borrowers a small commission only for bank services. It has branch offices in major cities of Iran.

BANK OF JAPAN, NIPPON SINKO. A financial Japanese institution under governmental control, established in 1882 in Tokyo. A merchant international bank with 33 branches in Japan and representative offices in London and New York. Fifty-five per cent of the shares belong to the Central Bank of Japan.

BANK OF NEW ZEALAND. A state-owned merchant international bank established in 1861 in Wellington, with 212 branches in New Zealand, two in Australia, six in Fiji and three in the UK. Representative offices in Tokyo and Singapore.

BANK OF THE UNITED STATES. A historical name of the first national bank created by the US Congress, existed 1791–1811; and the second, 1816–1836, replaced by a system of state banks and private banks on the basis of the National Bank Act of 1863; since 1913 ▷ Federal Reserve System.

The Federal Reserve System: Purposes and Functions, Washington DC, 1963.

BANK PRIVACY. In past centuries the custom of not disclosing bank accounts; since the 19th century in many European and American countries legal protection of privacy on the customer's request. In some countries the custom is not binding for revenue offices. Foreign capital is placed under the authority of the state in which the deposit was made. The rules of securing bank privacy and conditions on which information might be disclosed to other states, are not internationally uniform.

S. SICHTERMANN, *Bankgeheimnis und Bankauskunft*, Frankfurt a.M., 1966.

BANKRUPTCY. An international term for a declaration of insolvency by a financial institution or business firm, subject of international bilateral and regional agreements securing the interests of a country on a reciprocity principle. In 1933, during the world crisis, Denmark, Finland, Iceland, Norway and Sweden signed on Nov. 7, 1933 the ▷ Scandinavian Bankruptcy Convention.

LNTS, Vol. 155, p. 115.

BANKS AND BANKERS ORGANIZATIONS. International organizations reg. with the UIA:

African and Malagasy Union of Development Banks, f. 1962, Yaoundé. Members: Development Banks of Cameroon, Central African Republic, Congo, Dahomey, Gabon, Ivory Coast, Madagascar, Senegal, Togo, Upper Volta;
American Confederation of Bank Employees, f. 1955, Montevideo;
Banking Federation of the EEC, f. 1960, Brussels;
Centre for Latin American Monetary Studies, CEMLA, f. 1949, Mexico DF. Consultative status in ECOSOC; joins programs with the IMF and Inter-American Development Bank. Members: central banks of all Latin American Republics. Publ.: *CEMLA Bulletin*;
Committee of West African Banks, f. 1959, Ouagadougou, Upper Volta;
European Banks Advisory Committee, f. 1963, Brussels;
International Bankers Associations, f. 1968, Washington DC. Publ.: *International Bankers* and *Interbank*;
International Banking Research Institute, f. 1951, Copenhagen;
International Bank Note Society, f. 1961, Raleigh, NC, USA. Publ.: *Paper Money*;
International Savings Banks Institute, f. 1924, New York. Consultative status in ECOSOC, UNIDO, FAO, UNCTAD, Publ.: *Savings Bank International*;
Latin American Association of Development Financing Institutions, ALIDE, f. 1968, Lima, Peru. Consultative Status: ECOSOC, FAO, UNCTAD, UNIDO, OAS, LAES, IICA. Publ.: *Boletin Informativo*, ALIDE.
Latin American Banking Federation, f. 1965, Bogota.
Nordic Bank Employees' Union, f. 1923, Bergström, Sweden;
Union of Arab Banks, f. 1972, Cairo;
Union of French and Arab Banks, f. 1971, Neuilly-sur-Seine, France.

Yearbook of International Organizations, 1986–87; *Bankers Almanac and Yearbook*.

BANKS OF ARGENTINA. State banks are: Banco Central de la Republica Argentina, Banco de la Nación Argentina and Banco Industrial de la Republica Argentina. Private banks are: Banco de Galicia y Buenos Aires, Banco de Italia y Rio de la Plata, Banco Espanol del Rio de la Plata Ltd, Banco Popular Argentino and Nuevo Banco Italiano.

R.A. CAIROLI, *El nuevo sistema bancario Argentino*, Buenos Aires, 1974.

BANKS OF BELGIUM. The central bank is Banque Nationale de Belgique, f. 1850, whose shares since 1937 are half-owned by the state. The three largest commercial banks are: Banque de la Société Générale de Belgique, Banque de Bruxelles-Lambert, and Kreditbank. Besides this a number of banks conduct business abroad, i.a. Banque Belge pour l'Étranger, f. 1935; Banque du Commerce, S.A. – Handelsbank, NV, f. 1893; Banque Italo-Belge SA, f. 1911; Banque Lambert, f. 1946; Continental Bank SA, f. 1914; Banque de Paris et des Pays Bas Belgique SA, f. 1872; Crédit Foncier International, f. 1959; Internationale Handels en Diamantbank NV, f. 1960; United California Bank SA, f. 1848. Investment banks: Société Nationale de

Crédit a l'Industrie, f. 1919; Instituté de Réescompte et de Garantie, f. 1939 and Société Nationale d'Investissement, f. 1962.

A.P. TIMMERMAN, *Les banques en Belgique 1946–1968*, Groeninghe, 1969; H.S. GEIS, *Struktur des Bankwesen in Belgien*, Frankfurt am M., 1969.

BANKS OF FRANCE. The central bank is Banque de France. Three large state deposit banks Banque Nationale de Paris, ▷ Crédit Lyonnais and Société Générale together make up 52% of all of the assets of French banks. Besides them there are private deposit banks: Crédit Industriel et Commercial and Crédit Commercial de France. The financing of development and founding of new companies is handled by banks d'affaires headed by Banque de Paris et des Pays Bas and Banque de l'Indochine et de Suez and Crédit du Nord. A special variety of banks d'affaires are old private banks so-called Haute Banque: Banque Lazard Freres, Banque Rothschild, Banque Worms, Banque Neuflize, Schlumberger, Mallet. National and semi-national banks with a special status are: Banque Française du Commerce Extérieur, financing foreign trade, Crédit Foncier de France, granting mortgage loans, Caisse des Dépôts et Consignations, storing the deposits of savings institutions, insurance societies, and pension funds. Association Professionnelle des Banques has been in operation since 1871.

M. NETTER, *Les institutions monétaires en France*, Paris, 1973; A. CHAINEAU, *Mécanisme et politique monétaire: économie du système bancaire français*, Paris, 1973; J.P. GAULLIER, *Le système bancaire français*, Paris, 1975; *Newsweek*, May 16, 1986, p. 48.

BANKS OF FRG. The central bank of issue is ▷ Deutsche Bundesbank, f. Aug. 1, 1957 as the result of a merger of the central national banks *(Länder-Banken)* created after World War II, the central bank of West Berlin and Bank Deutscher Länder, headquarters in Frankfurt am Main. The large banking companies which continued after World War II and encompass – in accordance with the regulations of the occupying authorities – only some lands *(Länder)*, on the basis of the laws of Mar. 29, 1952 and Dec. 24, 1957, were ultimately formed as successor institutions of the former great private banking groups of the Reich with an international scope; these are: (1) Commerzbank AG, operating 1870–1945 as Commerzbank, under the present name since Jan. 1, 1957, headquarters in Düsseldorf, Frankfurt am Main and Hamburg, has 636 branches and in West Berlin operates as Berliner Commerzbank; (2) Deutsche Bank Aktiengesellschaft, existing 1870–1945 as Deutsche Bank, under the present name since Jan. 1, 1957, headquarters in Frankfurt am Main and Düsseldorf, has 900 branches, exists in West Berlin as Disconto Bank; (3) Dresdner Bank Aktiengeselschaft existing 1872–1945 as Dresdner Bank, under the present name since Jan. 1, 1957, headquarters in Frankfurt am Main, Düsseldorf and Hamburg, has 672 branches, exists in West Berlin as Bank für Handel und Industrie. Besides these three main banking groups included among the dominant banks are: Bayerische Hypotheken und Wechsel Bank, f. 1835, headquarters in Munich.

Enzyklopädisches Lexikon für das Geld, Bank und Börsenwesen, Frankfurt am M., 1968; DEUTSCHE BUNDESBANK, *Instruments of Monetary Policy in the FRG*, Frankfurt am M., 1971.

BANKS OF ISRAEL. Since 1954 the state bank of issue is Bank of Israel (up to 1954 the bank of issue was Bank Leumi le Israel). The largest commercial banks with foreign branches are: Bank Leumi le Israel, Israel Discount Bank, Bank Hapoalim and First International Bank of Israel.

M. HETH, *Banking Institutions in Israel*, Jerusalem, 1966.

BANKS OF JAPAN. The central state bank of issue in Nippon Ginho, Bank of Japan, f. 1882; it has 32 branches, headquarters in Tokyo. Since 1985 five great Japanese banks are the world's biggest creditors: Dai-Ichi Kangyo Bank, Fuji Bank, Sumitomo Bank, Mitsubishi Bank, Sanwa Bank. Besides private banks, an important role in Japan is played by state credit institutions such as: Central Bank of Commercial and Industrial Corporation, Central Co-operative Bank, ▷ The Export–Import Bank of Japan, Housing Loan Corporation, The Japan Development Bank, The Overseas Economic Co-operation Fund, People's Finance Corporation, Small Business Finance Corporation. In addition 12 foreign banks operate in Japan, mainly American and British. The leading organization of banks in Japan is the Federation of Bankers Associations of Japan, f. 1945 in Tokyo. Publ. *Banking System in Japan*.

BANK OF JAPAN, *Money and Banking in Japan*, Tokyo, 1973; *Newsweek*, May 16, 1986, p. 48.

BANKS OF LUXEMBOURG. The state bank of issue is Caisse d'Espargné de l'Etat, Banque de l'Etat, f. 1850. Commercial and deposit banks with international transactions are i.a. Banque du Benelux, La Luxembourgoise SA, Banque Commerciale SA, Banque Continentale du Luxembourg SA, Banque Nordeurope and Commerz International SA.

U. MEIER, *Struktur des Bankwesens in Luxemburg*, Frankfurt am M., 1975; J. DARGENT, *Luxembourg, an International Financial Centre*, Luxembourg, 1972.

BANKS OF SCANDINAVIA. The central banks of issue are: Denmark National Bank, Soumen Pankki Finlands Bank, Norges Bank and Sveriges Riksbank. The main commercial banks for overseas transactions are: in Denmark – Kjobenshavens Handelsbank SA, f. 1873, in Finland – Postipankki, Domestic and International Commercial Banking and Giroservice, f. 1887; in Norway – Christiania Bank of Kreditkasse, f. 1848 and Den Norske Creditbank, f. 1857, Oslo Handelsbank, f. 1917; in Sweden – Skandinaviska Enskilda Banken, f. 1972 and Svenska Handelsbanken, f. 1871.

By a decision of the Nordic Council of Dec. 4, 1975 a Scandinavian Investment Bank was created by the governments of Denmark, Finland, Iceland, Norway and Sweden with an initial capital of 400 millions ▷ SDR. The bank began its operations on Jan. 1, 1977.

FEDERATION OF DANISH BANKS, *The Danish Banking System*, Copenhagen, 1976; L. EIDE, *The Norwegian Credit and Monetary Systems*, Oslo, 1973.

BANKS OF SOUTH AFRICA. The central bank of issue is the South African Bank, f. 1920 as a joint stock company; has 906 stockholders, none of whom can have more shares than can be bought for the sum of 10,000 rands. The main deposit bank is The Standard Bank of South Africa, Ltd., in Johannesburg. The majority of commercial banks are affiliated with overseas banks: Bank of Lisboa and South Africa, Ltd., f. 1965 in Pretoria; Barclays National Bank, Ltd., in Johannesburg; First National City Bank (South Africa), Ltd., in Johannesburg; French Bank of Southern Africa, Ltd., f. 1949 as a branch of the Paris Banque de l'Indochine; The South African Bank of Athens, Ltd., f. 1948 in Johannesburg. Publ. *The South African Banker*. By a decision of the government from Dec., 1973 all of the foreign banks were obligated to sell 50% of their shares to the state to the end of 1983.

E. ROSENTHAL, *Encyclopedia of Southern Africa*, London, 1973.

BANKS OF SPAIN. Besides the central issuing Banco de Espana, the main commercial and investment banks with foreign ties are: Banco Central, f. in Madrid 1919; Banco de Bilbao, f. 1857 in Bilbao; Banco Exterior de Credito, f. 1929 in Madrid; Banco Hispano–Americano, f. 1900 in Madrid; Banco Comercial Transatlantico (former Banco Aleman Transatlantico), f. 1950 in Barcelona; Banco Intercontinental Espanol (Bankinter), f. 1965 in Madrid, affiliated with the Bank of America National Trust.

R. MARTINEZ CORTINA, *Credito y banco en España*, Madrid, 1971.

BANKS OF SWITZERLAND. The central state bank of issue is Banque Nationale Suisse, f. 1907, with headquarters in Berne and Zurich. Three large banks dominate: Union des Banques Suisses (Schweizerische Bankgesellschaft), f. 1862 in Zurich; Schweizerische Kreditanstalt (Crédit Suisse), f. 1865 in Zurich and Schweizerischer Bankverein (Société de Banque Suisse), f. 1872 in Basel. Besides these included among the leading banks are: Swiss Volksbank (Banque Populaire Suisse), f. 1869 in Geneva, Compagnie de Gestion et de Banque, f. 1956 in Geneva, Crédit Foncier Vaudois, f. 1858 in Lausanne, Genossenschaftlische Zentralbank, f. 1927 in Basel and Schweizersiche Hypotheken und Handelsbank, f. 1889 in Solothurn. The leading organization of Swiss banks is Association Suisse des Banquiers with headquarters in Basel.

E. BROMEIER, *Struktur des Bankwesens in der Schweiz*, Frankfurt am M., 1968; W. BROWNE's *Complete Guide to Swiss Banks*, New York, 1976.

BANKS OF THE NETHERLANDS. The central bank is Nederlandsche Bank NV, f. 1814 and since 1863 the bank of issue; 1948 nationalized through the purchase of all of its shares. The main commercial banks: Algemeine Bank Nederland NV, and Amsterdam-Rotterdam Bank NV, which represents two-thirds of the assets of commercial banks. Besides this there are: Indonesische Overzeese Bank NV, f. 1965 in Amsterdam and Nederlandsche Middenstandbank NV, f. 1927 in Amsterdam. Light industry is financed by Cooperative Centrale Raiffeisen Bank en Aangesloten Banken, f. 1898 with headquarters in Utrecht.

BANKS OF THE UK. The central state bank of issue is the Bank of England f. 1694, headquarters in London. It has the exclusive right of issue since 1844; it was nationalized in 1946. Still formally remaining banks of issue are the National Bank of Scotland and the Royal Bank of Scotland, Ltd., but they can meet their needs for banknotes and specie only with the banknotes and specie of the Bank of England, though in 1971 in Scotland 160 million pounds sterling issued by the Bank of Scotland in denominations of 1, 20, 50 and 100 pound notes were still in circulation. Four great banks dominate: Barclays Bank Ltd., Lloyds Bank Ltd., Midland Bank Ltd. and National Westminster Bank Ltd., which on Jan 1, 1970 absorbed the National Financial Bank previously included among the Big Five. Besides this Big Four included among the leading banks are: Australia and New Zealand Bank Ltd., Bank of London and South America Ltd., British Linen Bank, The Chartered Bank, Clydesdale Bank Ltd., Cooperative Bank, Coutts and Co, Eastern Bank Ltd., The English, Scottish and Australian Bank Ltd., Glyn, Mills Co, Ionian Bank Ltd., Lloyds Bank Europe Ltd., Lombard Banking, Mercantile Bank Ltd., Midland and International Bank, The National Bank Ltd., National and Commercial Banking Group Ltd., National and Grindlays Bank Ltd., Reliance Bank Ltd., The Standard Bank Ltd., Standard Bank of East Africa Ltd., Westminster Foreign Bank Ltd., Williams Geecons Bank Ltd. and Yorkshire Bank Ltd.

The central bank of the USSR, Moscow Narodny Bank Ltd., also has an office in London. There are 11 banking organizations, among which the most important and oldest is The Institute of Bankers, f. 1879 in London, has *c.* 75,000 national and foreign members. Publ. the bimonthly *Journal*.

R. PRINGLE, *A Guide to Banking in Britain*, London, 1973; J. GRADY, *British Banking 1960–85*, London, 1986.

BANKS OF THE USA. The central state financial institution of the USA with the right of issue is the Federal Reserve System, created in 1913 and composed of a seven-man Board of Governors in Washington, 12 regional banks of issue (Regional Federal Reserve Banks) with 24 branches and 40% of the National Banks and State Banks. Headquarters of the banks of Federal Reserve System are in Boston, New York, Philadelphia, Cleveland, Richmond, Atlanta, Chicago, St Louis, Minneapolis, Kansas City, Dallas, and San Francisco. US federal international commercial banks are ▷ Export-Import Bank of the US, f. 1934 and ▷ First Washington Securities Corporation, f. 1970. Among the major incorporated banks are three large banks of international scope: Chase Manhattan Bank, Bank of America National Trust and Savings Association and Citibank, formerly First National City Bank of New York. Also included among the main banks are: American Bank and Trust Company, American Security Bank, Bankers Trust Company, Bank of Hawaii, Bank of New York, Brown Brothers, Central Pacific Bank, Chemical New York Trust Company, Bank of Honolulu, City National Bank and Trust Co of Chicago, Cleveland Trust Co., Continental Illinois National Bank and Trust Co. of Chicago, First Federal Savings and Loan Association of Chicago, First Hawaian Bank, Harriman and Co, Hawaii National Bank, Irving Trust Co., Liberty Bank, Manufacturers Hanover Trust Co, Marine Midland Grace Trust Co of New York, Mellon National Bank and Trust Co, Morgan Guaranty Trust Co of New York, Philadelphia National Bank, The Riggs National Bank, Seattle First National Bank, Security Pacific National Bank, Wells Fargo Bank. The total number of commercial incorporated banks is more than 14,000. The leading organization of banks affiliating 97% of the banks is The American Bankers' Association, f. 1875, with headquarters in New York. The New York daily, *American Banker* publishes twice a year a list of the 300 largest US commercial banks in order of assets. On June 3, 1976 there were 89 banks in the USA with deposits of more than $1 billion, among which 11 had deposits of more than $10 billion:

Bank of America (San Francisco)	56,586,753,000
Citibank NA	45,912,508,000
Chase Manhattan Bank	35,196,619,000
Manufacturers Hanover Trust Co.	23,454,514,000
Chemical Bank	19,179,237,000
Morgan Guaranty Trust Co.	18,936,312,000
Continental Illinois	15,648,352,000
Bankers Trust Co.	15,519,728,000
First National Bank of Chicago	13,379,295,000
Security Pacific National Bank	12,442,318,000
Wells Fargo Bank	10,221,255,000

In 1985 the Citibank NA assets have reached 136 billion in US $ and Bank of America 106 billion.

E.W. READ, *Commercial Banking*, Englewood Cliffs, 1976; J.M. CULBERTSON, *Money and Banking*, New York, 1977; H. GUNTHER, *Banking in the US*,

B

London, 1977; *Newsweek*, The New Superbanks, May, 16, 1986; J.A. FRIEDE, *Banking on the World: The Politics of American International Finance*, New York 1987.

BANKS OF THE USSR. The central bank of the USSR is the USSR State Bank – Gosbank SSSR. Since 1959 the central credit bank is Stroybank, which took over the functions of previously existing banks specializing in credits: industrial (Prombank), agricultural (Sielkhozbank) and building (Cekombank). The bank handling foreign trade and international financial transactions is Vnyeshtorgbank, f. in 1922. Subsidiary role is performed by ▷ Moscow Narodny Bank, Ltd., operating exclusively abroad. In order to facilitate financial transactions with capitalist countries, according to legal regulations valid in those countries, the USSR set up a network of their own banks in Western Europe: Moscow Narodny Bank in London, f. in 1919, with a branch office in Beirut since 1963; ▷ Banque Commerciale pour l'Europe du Nord, in Paris, f. in 1921; Voschod Bank in Zurich, f. in 1960, and Ost-West Handelsbank AG in Frankfurt am Main, f. in 1971.

P.R. GREGORY, R.C. STUART, *Soviet Economic Structure and Performance*, New York, 1981.

BANNED ARMS. An expression for various weapons used in armed conflicts in different epochs. The effort to eliminate weapons regarded as particularly inhuman in a given epoch has already appeared in the Middle Ages, e.g. the Church ban on the use of catapults and bows in the 13th century. In the 19th century the first St Petersburg Declaration of 1868 attempted to introduce limitations in the development of artillery weapons. The Hague Statute, appended to the Second Hague Convention of 1899 and in altered form to the Fourth Hague Convention, 1907, and the Third Hague Convention, 1899, introduced a ban on poisonous weapons and bullets that inflict tearing wounds (so-called dum-dum bullets) or in any other way increase the suffering of the wounded. The Hague Declaration of 1899, and the Geneva Protocol of 1925, initiated the ban on ▷ B and C arms. An initial step on the road to the ban of nuclear weapons was the ratification by the UN General Assembly on Dec. 7, 1970, Res. 2660/XXV, of a Treaty banning the placing of nuclear weapons and other weapons of mass destruction on the sea-bed and ocean floor by the Treaty on the Denuclearization of Seabeds. In Feb., 1974 Sweden submitted in the UN a proposal for a convention banning both ▷ napalm and weapons of the ▷ CBU type, delayed-action munition, fragmentation weapons, incendiary weapons and the like.

SIPRI, *World Armaments and Disarmament Yearbook*, 1968–85.

BANQUE COMMERCIALE POUR L'EUROPE DU NORD, EUROBANK. A governmental financial institution of the USSR, established in 1921 in Paris. From 1972 has had additional name Eurobank. Merchant international bank. Shareholders: State Bank of the USSR and Bank for Foreign Trade of the USSR. Correspondents in London and New York: all principal banks.

BANTU INTERLACUSTRINE. A name common to black mountain inhabitants of the Victoria, Kyoga, Albert, Edward, and Tanganyika lakes region; also to family of languages spoken there: Cheva, Ganda, Herero, Kwena, Lamba, Luba, Lembwe, Nyanja, Shona, Swahili, Umbudu and Zulu. Swahili is the most popular. "*Bantu*" literally means "people" in these languages.

M. BRYAN, *The Bantu Languages of Africa*, London, 1959.

BANTU LINE. African term of the linguistic frontier of the Bantu communities, defined south from Mount Cameroon on the West coast to the north of the Congo River, Victoria Lake, Tana River, north of Mombassa.

BANTU HOMELANDS. Administrative regions of South Africa. A racist term introduced by the South African administration in 1951 by the Bantu Authorities Act; The Promotion of Bantu Self Government Act, 1959; the Constitution of Transho, 1963; and the Bantu Homelands Constitution Act, 1971. The "Bantu areas" intended only for the Black population granted "self government" were ▷ Bophuthatswana, ▷ Ciskei, and ▷ Leboeva in 1972, Gazanhulu and ▷ Kwa Zulu in 1973, Owaqua 1974 and Kwa Ndebele 1977 and "independence" ▷ Transkei 1976, ▷ Bophuthatswana 1977, ▷ Venda, 1979 and ▷ Ciskei 1981. The South African Black population, excluded from participation in central government demonstrated in the 1970s, and in the 1980s, claiming that they would never accept the "independence" from South Africa. The General Assembly, on Nov. 28, 1985, in Res. 3411 D/XXX condemned South Africa's establishment of Bantu Homelands with 99 votes for, and 8 abstentions (Belgium, France, the FRG, Italy, Luxembourg, Netherlands, UK, USA).
Of eleven Bantu-Homelands only four (Bophuthatswana, Ciskei, Transkei and Venda) were granted "self-government". Area of all homelands: 162.510 sq km. Population (1980): 11,980,930. A 1987 International Commission of Jurists Report, stated that "the human rights records of most of the homelands are even worse than that of South Africa ... any political dissent is harshly suppressed, political detainees – often only minors – are brutally tortured by the police".

ICJ Newsletter, No. 32, 1987, pp. 42–43; *The Europa Yearbook*, 1988. *A World Survey*, Vol. II, London 1988.

BANTU PEOPLES. Communities in Southern Africa, belonging to three different linguistic groups: Bantu, Khosian and Bergdama.

BANTUSTAN. A discriminating racial term, introduced by the 1913 Land Act of South African government, granting the white community (19% of the total population) 87% of state territory and leaving the remaining 13% to the non-white majority (81% of the total population). These isolated reservations were officially named Bantustans and renamed Homelands in 1968. Their purpose is to preserve division of Africans into tribes according to their place of habitation during white conquest. The General Assembly, Nov. 28, 1975 in the Res. 3411 D/XXX condemned South Africa's establishment of Bantustans with 99 votes for and 8 abstaining (Belgium, France, FRG, Great Britain, Italy, Luxembourg, Netherlands, USA). ▷ Bophushatswana; Transkei.

CH.R. HILL, *Bantustans. The Fragmentation of South Africa*, London, 1964. Paper for the UN: "Bantustans", in: *Sechab*, Official organ of the National Congress of South Africa, 1976.

BAOR ▷ British Army of the Rhine.

BAPTISTS. Members of a world-wide religious community, the majority concentrated in the USA. Organizations reg. with the UIA:

Baptist World Alliance, f. 1905, Washington, DC, European Office: London. "A voluntary and fraternal organization for promoting fellowship and co-operation among Baptists; serves as an agency of commun-

ication between Baptists; a forum for study and discussion of doctrines and practice; a channel of co-operation in extending help to each other and those in need; an agency for promotion of evangelism and education; a vigilant force for safeguarding religious liberty and other God-given rights; a sponsor of regional and world-wide gatherings for the furtherance of the gospel."
Consultative status: ECOSOC. Members: Union (106) totalling 27,017,100 members in 78 countries (1976).
Asian Baptist Fellowship, f. 1972. Publ. *Asian Baptist News*.
European Baptist Federation, f. 1950, London. Publ. *The European Baptist*.
European Baptist Mission, f. 1954, Bad Hamburg, FRG, Publ. *EBM Information*.
Pan-American Union of Baptist Men, f. 1968, Yazoo City, Miss., USA.
Scandinavian Independent Baptist Union, f. 1872, Tidaholm, Sweden.

A.C. UNDERWOOD, *A History of English Baptists*, London 1947; R.G. TORBERT, *A History of the Baptists*, New York, 1955; W.S. HUDSON, *Baptist Concept of the Church*, London, 1959; *Yearbook of International Organizations*, 1986–87.

BARBADOS. Member of the UN. Island state in the West Indies in the Atlantic Ocean, east of St Vincent in the Windward Islands. Area: 430 sq. km. Pop. 1987 census: 253,881 (1970 census: 238,141). Capital: Bridgetown with 7,517 inhabitants, 1980. GNP per capita, 1987 , US $4668. Official language: English. Currency: Barbados dollar = 100 cents. National Day: 30th Nov., independence anniversary 1966.
From Dec. 9, 1966 member of the UN and a member of all UN specialized agencies except IAEA, and IDA; member of the Caribbean Free Trade Association and of the Inter-American Development Bank from Mar. 19, 1969.
International relations: from 1625 to 1958 was a British colony; from 1958 to 1962 member of the Federation of West Indies; 1962–66 organizer of the unrealized East Caribbean Federation. Until 1966 listed by the UN General Assembly as non-self-governing territory. On Nov. 30, 1966 Barbados obtained independence within the British Commonwealth. In October 1983 Barbados troops supported the US invasion of Grenada.

D.P. STARKEY, *Commercial Geography of Barbados*, Indiana University Press, 1961; M.J. CHANDLERS, *A Guide to Records in Barbados*, University of the West Indies, 1965; CEPAL, *Estudio Económico de América Latina 1966*, New York, 1968; F.A. HOYOZ, *Barbados. A History from the Amerindians to Independence*, London, 1978; *Everyone's United Nations*, New York, 1979; *The Europa Year Book 1984. A World Survey*, Vol. I, pp. 1158–1163, London, 1984.

BARBAROSSA PLAN, 1940. A secret directive No. 21 of Adolf Hitler, Dec. 18, 1940, ordering the German General Staff to prepare aggression against the USSR; carried out on June 23, 1941; revealed at the ▷ Nuremberg War Criminals Trial, 1945–46. Directive No. 21 began with the following preamble:

"German armed forces must prepare, even before ending the war with England, to destroy Soviet Russia in a lightning campaign (Barbarossa Plan).
Preparations which require a longer time should be begun if they have not started immediately and end by May 15, 1941. Particular emphasis must be placed on maintaining secret the intention of striking the East.
General objective: the masses of Russian armed forces located in the western part of Russia must be destroyed in bold operations through deep wedges of panzer forces and we must not allow units capable of fighting to withdraw to the deep spaces of the Russian territory."

P. ZHILIN, *Plan Barbarossa*, Moskva, 1971.

BARBARY STATES. An international term from 16th to 19th century for the piratical states in North Africa (Tripolitania, Tunisia, Algeria and Morocco); organizer of piracy in Mediterranean region.

BARBITURATES ▷ Depressants.

BARBUDA. ▷ Antigua and Barbuda.

BARCELONA. A city in Spain, (1981 pop. census. 1,754,900), major city of Catalonia, since the 17th century the center of Catalonian separatism; since 1934 the capital of Catalonian Republic.

The Europa Yearbook 1987, *A World Survey*, London 1987.

BARCELONA TRANSIT CONFERENCE, 1921. A Conference under the aegis of the League of Nations on land, water and maritime transport, Mar.–Apr. 1921. It drew up and signed, Apr. 20, 1921 three Barcelona Conventions:
(1) Statute on Freedom of Transit.
(2) Convention and Statute on the Arrangement for Navigation Routes of International Importance.
(3) Convention on the Right to Flag for State of No Access to Sea.
The documents were signed by 40 states and ratified by 38.

LNTS, 1921.

BARCELONA TRACTION, LIGHT AND POWER COMPANY CASE. A case brought before the International Court of Justice by Belgium against a foreign company. Proceedings concerning the Canadian Barcelona Traction Company, bankrupted in Spain in 1948, were first instituted by Belgium in 1958, the application stating that the share capital belonged largely to Belgian nationals. Belgium claimed compensation on the grounds that the manner in which the company had been bankrupted and its assets subsequently disposed of by the Spanish authorities was contrary to international law. These proceedings were discontinued in 1961 to allow negotiations to take place. No settlement was, however, reached and, on June 19, 1972, Belgium submitted a new application, asking the Court to declare that Spain was under an obligation to Belgium to make reparation for damage caused to the Belgian shareholders. Spain raised four preliminary objections, of which two were dismissed and two joined to the merits by a Judgment of July 24, 1964. After proceedings during which extended time-limits were granted at the parties' request, the Court gave its decision on Feb. 5, 1970. In its Judgment, the Court addressed itself to the question of the right of Belgium to exercise diplomatic protection of shareholders in a company incorporated in Canada, the measures complained of having been taken in relation not to any Belgian nationals as such but to the company itself. In this field, the Court said, international law had to refer to those rules generally accepted by internal legal systems. An injury to a shareholder's interests resulting from an injury to the rights of a company was insufficient to found a claim. Where it was a question of an unlawful act committed against a company representing foreign capital, the general rule of international law authorized solely the national state of the company to exercise diplomatic protection. The Court considered that there were no special circumstances in the case as a result of which that general rule should not take effect. Nor, in view of the fact that the national state of the company was able to act, did any considerations of equity confer a right of action on Belgium.

Accordingly, the Court found that the applicant lacked *jus standi* and, by 15 votes to 1, rejected the claim.

Everyone's United Nations, New York, 1979, pp. 316–317.

BARENTS SEA. An arm of the Atlantic Ocean, north of Norway, and east of the USSR. Its ports such as Murmansk are ice-free all year. The dispute between Norway and the USSR over boundaries on the Barents Sea was by 1988 still unresolved.

The International Geographic Encyclopaedia and Atlas, London, 1979; H.O. BERGESENI, A. MOE, W. OSTRENG, *Soviet Oil and Security in the Barents Sea,* London 1987.

BARILOCHE FOUNDATION. Argentinian institute promoting development of scientific research. In 1976, on the initiative of the Bariloche Foundation, a model of world economic development was elaborated, following the example of the ▷ Club of Rome Report, the so-called ▷ Herrera Report 1976.

BAR LAWYERS. International organizations reg. with the UIA:

All Asia Bar Association, f. 1981., Kochi, Japan.
Arab Lawyers Union, f. 1958, Cairo, Egypt.
Consultative Committee of Bar Associations of the EEC, f. 1960, Brussels.
Inter-American Bar Association, f. 1940, Washington, DC. Publ. *Newsletter.*
Inter-American Bar Foundation, f. 1957, Washington, DC.
International Association of Democratic Lawyers, f. 1946, Brussels, Belgium. Publ. *International Review of Contemporary Law.*
International Bar Association, f. 1947, London. Consultative statute of ECOSOC Publ. *International Bar Journal.*
International Federation of Women Lawyers, f. 1944, Brussels, Belgium.
Internatonal Union of Lawyers, f. 1927, Paris, France. Publ. *Bulletin* (quarterly).
Joint Council of Nordic Lawyers Association, f. 1970, Helsinki, Finland.
World Association of Lawyers, f. 1975, Washington DC, USA.
Young Lawyer's International Association, f. 1962, Brussels, Belgium, Publ. *Gazette.*

KIME's *International Law Directory. A List of Legal Practitioners in Most of the Principal Towns Throughout the World Together wiuth General Legal Informations and Telegraphic Code,* London 1987 (Ninety-Fifth Year). *Yearbook of International Organizations,* 1986–87; *The Europa Yearbook,* 1988, *A World Survey,* Vol. I, London 1988.

BARLEY. One of the main agricultural products included in UN international statistics. The world production exceeded 150.4 million tons in 1972. Main producers; the USSR, the USA, France and the UK. Since 1951 FAO publishes annual data on world barley supplies according to its brands, entitled *World Catalogue of Genetic Stocks: Barley.*

B.D. HARTONG, *Elsevier's Dictionary of Barley, Malting and Brewing.* In German, English, French, Danish, Italian and Spanish, Amsterdam, 1961.

BARN. A special unit employed in nuclear physics to express effective cross-section (▷ SI).

BAROTSELAND. A province of Zambia, of about 126,000 sq. km area, subject of international conflict solved on Oct. 24, 1964 in favor of Zambia.

BARUCH PLAN, 1946. A US plan for internationalizing atomic energy submitted to the UN Atomic Energy Commission by the US representative, chairman of the US Atomic Energy Com-

mission Bernard Baruch, on Jun. 14, 1946. The Baruch Plan was composed of 14 points describing the powers of the International Office for Atomic Energy Development, including control on the entire globe not only of all production of atomic energy, but also mines of fissionable materials. The Baruch Plan assumed the cessation of the production of nuclear weapons by abolishing the right of veto of the powers in the UN Security Council regarding decisions of the proposed Agency. The text of the 14 points is as follows:

"(1) General. The Authority should set up a thorough plan for control of the field of atomic energy, through various forms of ownership, dominion, licenses, operation, inspection, research, and management by competent personnel. After this is provided for, there should be as little interference as may be with the economic plans and the present private, corporate, and State relationships in the several countries involved.
(2) Raw Materials. The authority should have as one of its earliest purposes to obtain and maintain complete and accurate information of world supplies of uranium and thorium and to bring them under its dominion. The precise pattern of control for various types of deposits of such materials will have to depend upon the geological, mining, refining, and economic facts involved in different situations. The Authority should conduct continuous surveys so that it will have the most complete knowledge of the world geology of uranium and thorium. Only after all current information on world sources of uranium and thorium is known to us all can equitable plans be made for their production, refining, and distribution.
(3) Primary Production Plants. The Authority should exercise complete managerial control of the production of fissionable materials. This means that it should control and operate all plants producing fissionable materials in dangerous quantities and must own and control the product of these plants.
(4) Atomic Explosives. The Authority should be given sole and exclusive right to conduct research in the field of atomic explosives. Research activities in the field of atomic explosives are essential in order that the Authority may keep in the forefront of knowledge in the field of atomic energy and fulfil the objective of preventing illicit manufacture of bombs. Only by maintaining its position as the best-informed agency will the Authority be able to determine the line between intrinsically dangerous and nondangerous activities.
(5) Strategic Distribution of Activities and Materials. The activities entrusted exclusively to the Authority because they are intrinsically dangerous to security should be distributed throughout the world. Similarly stockpiles of raw materials and fissionable materials should not be centralized.
(6) Nondangerous Activities. A function of the Authority should be promotion of the peacetime benefits of atomic energy. Atomic research (except in explosives), the use of research reactors, the production of radioactive tracers by means of nondangerous reactors, the use of such tracers, and to some extent the production of power, should be open to nations and their citizens under reasonable licensing arrangements from the Authority. Denatured materials, whose use we know also requires suitable safeguards, should be furnished for such purposes by the Authority under lease or other arrangement. Denaturing seems to have been overestimated by the public as a safety measure.
(7) Definition of Dangerous and Nondangerous Activities. Although a reasonable dividing line can be drawn between dangerous and nondangerous activities, it is not hard and fast. Provision should, therefore, be made to assure constant re-examination of the questions and to permit revision of the dividing line as changing conditions and new discoveries may require.
(8) Operations of Dangerous Activities. Any plant dealing with uranium or thorium after it once reaches the potential of dangerous use must be not only subject to the most rigorous and competent inspection by the Authority, but its actual operation shall be under the management, supervision, and control of the Authority.
(9) Inspection. By assigning intrinsically dangerous activities exclusively to the Authority, the difficulties of inspection are reduced. If the Authority, is the only agency which may lawfully conduct dangerous

B

activities, then visible operation by others than the Authority will constitute an unambiguous danger signal. Inspection will also occur in connection with the licensing functions of the Authority.

(10) Freedom of Access. Adequate ingress and egress for all qualified representatives of the Authority must be assured. Many of the inspection activities of the Authority should grow out of, and be incidental to, its other functions. Important measures of inspection will be associated with the tight control of raw materials, for this is a keystone of the plan. The continuing activities of prospecting, survey, and research in relation to raw materials will be designed not only to serve the affirmative development functions of the Authority but also to assure that no surreptitious operations are conducted in the raw-materials field by nations or their citizens.

(11) Personnel. The personnel of the Authority should be recruited on a basis of proved competence but also so far as possible on an international basis.

(12) Progress by Stages. A primary step in the creation of the system of control is the setting forth, in comprehensive terms, of the functions, responsibilities, powers, and limitations of the Authority. Once a charter for the Authority has been adopted, the Authority and the system of control for which it will be responsible will require time to become fully organized and effective. The plan of control will, therefore, have to come into effect in successive stages. These should be specifically fixed in the charter or means should be otherwise set forth in the charter for transitions from one stage to another, as contemplated in the resolution of the United Nations Assembly which created this Commission.

(13) Disclosures. In the deliberations of the United Nations Commission on Atomic Energy, the United States is prepared to make available the information essential to a reasonable understanding of the proposals which it advocates. Further disclosures must be dependent, in the interests of all, upon the effective ratification of the treaty. When the Authority is actually created, the United States will join the other nations in making available the further information essential to that organization for the performance of its functions. As the successive stages of international control are reached, the United States will be prepared to yield, to the extent required by each stage, national control of activities in this field to the Authority.

(14) International Control. There will be questions about the extent of control to be allowed to national bodies, when the Authority is established. Purely national authorities for control and development of atomic energy should to the extent necessary for the effective operation of the Authority be subordinate to it. This is neither an endorsement nor a disapproval of the creation of national authorities. The Commission should evolve a clear demarcation of the scope of duties and responsibilities of such national authorities."

The B.P. was rejected by the USSR representative A. Gromyko as contrary to the sovereignty of the member states of the UN. These proposals "are of such a character that in reality such an authority would be independent of the Security Council and would have almost full autonomy. This cannot be reconciled with the Charter of the United Nations". Mr Gromyko stressed that "when the Charter of the United Nations was prepared by the conference at San Francisco, the question of sovereignty was one of the most important questions considered. This principle of sovereignty is one of the cornerstones on which the United Nations structure is built; if this were touched the whole existence and future of the United Nations would be threatened."

Mr Gromyko declared further that the United States proposals also "change entirely the meaning of Article 51 of the Charter". On the question of the voting procedure in the Security Council, Mr Gromyko said: "On this question also I should like to make again clear the position of the Soviet Union that we cannot accept any proposals that would undermine in any degree the principle of the unanimity of the permanent members of the Security Council in the maintenance of peace and security."

In conclusion Mr Gromyko said: "The United States proposals, referring to United States Memorandum No. 3, in their present form cannot be accepted in any way by the Soviet Union either as a whole or in separate parts."

Baruch on Apr. 10, 1947 resigned from the chairmanship of the American AEC, and in his place the President of the US nominated D. Lilienthal, who somewhat modified the B.P., but even this plan, called the Lilienthal Plan, was not supported by the majority of the members of the UN Commission. ▷ Gromyko Plan 1946.

The Department of State Bulletin, No. 364, June 23, 1946; "The Control of Atomic Energy. Proposals before the UN Atomic Energy Commission", in: *International Conciliation*, No. 423, September, 1946, pp. 308–432.

BASELINE OF THE TERRITORIAL SEA. The ▷ Sea Law Convention, 1982 (Art. 5–7) defined the normal baseline for measuring the breadth of the territorial sea and of the mouth of a river flowing directly into the sea.

R.L. BLEDSOE, B.A. BOCZEK, *The International Law Dictionary*, Oxford, UK 1987.

BASIC. A ▷ Programming language for personal computers. Acronim of Beginners All-Purpose Symbolic Code. Authors: John Kemeny and Thomas Kurtz at Dartmouth College, 1967.

BASKETBALL. Subject of international co-operation. Reg. with the UIA.

Arab Gulf Basketball Association, f. 1980, Manama, Bahrain.
International Amateur Basketball Federation, f. 1932, Munich, FRG. Recognized by International Olympic Committee. Publ.: *Basketball International News*.
Asian Basketball Confederation, f. 1960, Seoul.

Yearbook of International Organizations, 1986–87.

BASQUES. Inhabitants of a country called in the Basque language Eushalerria or Euskadi. French – Basques, Spanish – Bascos. A people residing in the West Pyrenees, in France in the department Bas Pyrenee and in Spain in the provinces of Alva, Guipuzcoa, Viscaya and part of Navarra. In 1976 there were *c*. 1.6 million Basques in the world, mainly in Spain, where they originally had complete autonomy; this was suspended in 1932 by the monarchistic Spanish Cortes, restored 1936 by the Spanish Republic, liquidated 1937 by the fascist army of General Franco. The struggle of the Basque people against the dictatorship of General Franco was carried on by an underground organization, ETA (Euskadi Ta Astahusana = Basque Country and Freedom), which in 1972 began to co-operate with the French-Basque organization E (Eubata = "Ocean Gale"). In Madrid on Dec. 20, 1973 members of ETA blew up a car carrying the premier of Spain, admiral Carrero Blanco, which led to new arrests of Basque patriots. In Oct. 1975 the execution of three members of ETA at the order of General Franco led to world protests and debates in the UN. In 1978, as a result of the restitution of the constitutional monarchy, the Basques gained autonomy, which ETA did not recognize.

In autumn 1984 the extradition to Spain by France of three Basques, suspected of being members of ETA, set off anti-French violence in the Spanish Basque country. In July 1987 first talks of Spanish Interior Ministry officials with ETA were held in Algeria.

J. CARO BAROJA, *Los Vascos*, Madrid, 1958; G. SNEATH, *Your Guide to the Basque Country of France and Spain*, London, 1966; *UN Monthly Chronicle*, Nov., 1975. *International Herald Tribune*, October 1, 1984; R.

COLLINS, *The Basques*, London, 1986; KEESING's *Record of World Events*, September 1987.

BASSAS DA INDIA ▷ Madagascar.

BASUTO. A South African tribe (about 800,000), living in Lesotho (formerly Basutoland) and in Northern Transvaal.

E. ROSENTHAL, *Encyclopaedia of Southern Africa*, London, 1973.

BASUTOLAND. ▷ Lesotho.

BATAVIA. Republic of Batavia, Commonwealth of Batavia, name of a Dutch state. At the suggestion of Napoleonic France, it was transformed in 1798 into the Republic of Batavia and in 1805 into Commonwealth of Batavia and in June 1806 again into the Kingdom of Holland, but under the rule of Napoleon's brother, Louis.

BATTELLE MEMORIAL INSTITUTE. Founded 1925 in Columbus, Ohio, USA, under the terms of the will of Gordon Battelle; a private industrial research organization in metallurgy and mineral industries; European laboratories in Wiesbaden, FRG and Geneva; since 1963 consultative status ECOSOC. Publ. Technical books and papers. Reg. with the UIA.

Yearbook of International Organizations.

BATTLE ACT, 1951. Name adopted in Anglo-Saxon press for action of US Congress of May 22, 1951 on Mutual Defence Assistance Control Act, which introduced the automatic application of an ▷ embargo on supplies of military and strategic materials to countries acknowledged by the US government as constituting a threat to the safety of the USA. The bill prohibited granting foreign aid to those countries, and also to countries selling the named materials to countries covered by the American embargo. ▷ United States foreign aid.

BATTLE OF BERLIN, 1945. The final battle of World War II, Apr. 16–May 2, 1945. Berlin was captured by the Red Army of the USSR; the only allied army that participated directly in the battle of the city was the Polish Army, capturing the Siegassäule in Tiergarten, the center of Berlin.

S. KOMORNICKI, *Poles in the Battle of Berlin*, Warsaw, 1967; G.K. ZHUKOV, *Wspominanya y Razmyshlenya*, Moskva, 1969; E.J. OSMAŃCZYK, *Chwalebna wyprawa na Berlin*, Warszawa, 1970.

BATTLE OF BRITAIN, 1940. The defensive operations of the Royal Airforce (RAF) on Aug. 13–Oct. 31, 1940, against assaults by German Luftwaffe designed as preparation for Third Reich's invasion of the British Isles. Luftwaffe lost 1733 aircraft; the RAF, 733. The victorious defense of Great Britain, decisive to the further course of warfare, was thus commented on by Prime Minister W.S. Churchill in the House of Commons on Aug. 28, 1940:

"Never in the field of human conflict was so much owed by so many to so few."

D. EGGENBERGER, *Dictionary of Battles. From 1479 N.C. to the Present*, London, 1967; B. ARCT, *Polish Wings in the West: The Battle of Britain*, Warsaw, 1971.

BATTLE OF CORREGIDOR, 1945. On Feb. 15–28, 1945 the US paratroopers supported by an amphibious assault force recaptured from Japanese troops the fortified Corregidor Island at the entrance to Manila Bay, near Bataan Peninsula of Luzon Island, Philippines. The opening of Manila

Bay for Allied shipping hastened the liberation of the Philippines.

S. WOODBURN-KIRBY ed., *The War Against Japan*, 5 vol., 1957–69.

BATTLE OF EL ALAMEIN, 1942. A decisive British victory in World War II, in North Africa over the German army, near Egyptian town of El Alamein on the Mediterranean Sea. The battle between the British army under the command of Gen. B.L. Montgomery and German and Italian troops commanded by Field Marshal E. Rommel, started on Oct. 23 and ended on Nov. 2, 1942 with total retreat of Germans.

VISCOUNT MONTGOMERY, *Memoirs*, London, 1958: C. BARNETT, *The Battle of El Alamein: Decision in the Desert*, London, 1964.

BATTLE OF MIDWAY. ▷ Midway.

BATTLE OF STALINGRAD. A decisive strategic operation on the German–Russian front during World War II, which took place on the Volga near Stalingrad (present Volgograd) Aug. 17, 1942–Feb. 2, 1943. It ended with the encirclement and capture of most of the 300,000 strong German army.

A.M. SAMSONOV, *Stalingradskaya Opieratsya*, Moskva, 1960; A.I. YEREMIENKO, *Opieratsya nad Volgu*, Moskva, 1962.

BAUXITE. A subject of inter-governmental co-operation. Reg. with the UIA:

International Bauxite Association, f. 1974 in Kingston, Jamaica, by the ten bauxite-producing countries: Australia, Dominican Republic, Ghana, Guinea, Guyana, Haiti, Indonesia, Jamaica, Sierra Leone, Surinam and Yugoslavia, representing about 82% of total World production and about 80% of export.

Yearbook of International Organizations

BAYKONUR. The Soviet cosmodrome located in a region 47° longitude north, and 65° latitude east, in Western Siberia. Space flights were started from Baykonur on Apr. 12, 1961 by Y.A. Gagarin (1934–68).

K. SAWYER, Baikonur: *The Shore of the Universe*, in: *International Herald Tribune*, July 21, 1988.

BAY OF PIGS OR BAHIA DE COCHINOS INVASION, 1961. An attempted invasion of Cuba by about 1500 CIA trained and US Army supported Cuban exiles who on April 17, 1961 landed in the Bahia de Cochinos (Bay of Pigs). The majority of guerrillas (1,113) was captured by the Cuban army and on Dec. 23, 1962 exchanged for 53 million dollars worth of medicine and food from the Cuban community in Florida.

R.F. LIGHT, C. MARZANI, *Cuba vs the CIA*, New York 1961; K. MEYER, T. SZULC, *The Cuban Invasion. The Chronicle of a Disaster*, New York, 1962; J.L. MASSO, Cuba: 17 de Abril, México DF, 1962; P. WYDEN, *Bay of Pigs: The Untold Story*, New York, London 1979; T. SZULC, *Fidel. A Critical Portrait*, New York, 1987; T. HIGGINS, *The Perfect Failure: Kennedy, Eisenhover and the CIA at the Bay of Pigs*, New York 1987.

BAYS. A subject of the ▷ Sea Law Convention 1982 (Art. 10).

R.L. BLEDSOE, B.A. BOCZEK, *The International Law Dictionary*, Oxford, UK, 1987.

BAZOOKA. Antitank US Army rocket launcher since 1943.

BEAGLE CHANNEL. A waterway dividing Chile and Tierra del Fuego between Fire Island and the Hoste and Navarino islands joining the Atlantic and Pacific Ocean. Discovered 1830 by a British surveying ship *Beagle*, which was carrying Charles Darwin around the world. Beagle channel was the subject of a dispute between Argentina and Chile over sovereign rights since 1881. In 1977 British arbitration settled in Chile's favor the question of all rights to the islands of Picton, Lennox and Nueva on the Atlantic side of the Channel entrance. Argentina rejected this decision on Feb. 2, 1978. Chile appealed to the International Court of Justice. In 1979 both sides turned to Pope John Paul II to assist in arbitration.

On Oct. 4, 1984 Argentina and Chile accepted John Paul II's arbitration, that the islands of Picton, Lennox and Nueva be confirmed as Chilean territory, but in the Atlantic Ocean Chilean sovereignty should extend only to a 12 mile zone from the islands, while beyond this point Argentina should have jurisdiction up to 200 miles. It reflected the so-called bi-oceanic principle whereby Argentina controls Atlantic waters and Chile controls Pacific waters of the tip of South America.

The Europa Year Book. A World Survey, Vol. I, p. 1083, London, 1984; KEESING's *Contemporary Archive*, 1984.

BEANS. One of the basic food articles in Latin America, where is has the same importance as rice in Southern Asia, subject of international statistics analyzed by the UN Economic Commission for Latin America. According to figures of the Commission, the biggest producer and consumer of black beans is Brazil, producing exclusively for its own use more than 25 kg per capita. The second place is taken by Mexico.

"Situación actual y perspectivas del comercio de los frijoles en los paises de la ALALC", in: *Notas sobre de economia y el desarrollo de América Latina de la CEPAL*, No. 106, June 1, 1972.

BEARINGS INDUSTRY. A subject of an agreement between the governments of Bulgaria, Czechoslovakia, FRG, Hungary, and Poland, signed Apr. 25, 1964 in Moscow; on the basis of this agreement, as well as the Statute appended to the Agreement, the Organization for Co-operation of the Bearings Industry, OCBI, was formed within the CMEA system. The headquarters of the permanent Secretariat of OCBI is Warsaw. The agreement entered into force on July 2, 1964. The depositary of the Agreement is Poland. Signed in Moscow on Dec. 27, 1970 was the Protocol on the character and forms of co-operation between CMEA and OCBI.

W.E. BUTLER (ed.), *A Source Book on Socialist International Organizations*, Alphen aan den Rijn, 1978, pp. 373–386.

BEARS. A subject of International Agreement to Protect Polar Bears, signed in Nov. 1973 by the governments of Denmark, Canada, Norway, the USA and the USSR. The agreement prohibits hunting, killing or catching polar bears, except in cases strictly specified in the agreement.

LNTS, 1974.

BEAUFORT'S SCALE. International scale of wind velocity, initially established without instruments, according only to descriptions of 12 phases of growing wind velocity on land and at sea. These descriptions were made in 1806 on the basis of experience by the British admiral Sir Francis Beaufort (1774–1857) beginning with a windless ocean calm and ending with a hurricane force 12, "that which no canvas could withstand". In 1874 the scale was accepted by the International Meteorological Commission, IMC, and supplemented with a metrical measurement of wind velocity. In 1939 the IMC elaborated this twelve point International Beaufort Scale, commonly accepted in the world with the exception of the Anglo-Saxon countries, which expanded it to 17 degrees (maximum wind velocity 126–136 m per second).

The 1939 internationally accepted description of the Beaufort Scale is as follows:

0.	Calm	wind speed 0–1
1.	Light air	wind speed 1–3
2.	Light breeze	wind speed 4–7
3.	Gentle breeze	wind speed 8–12
4.	Moderate breeze	wind speed 13–16
5.	Fresh breeze	wind speed 17–21
6.	Strong breeze	wind speed 21–27
7.	Moderate gale	wind speed 28–33
8.	Fresh gale	wind speed 34–40
9.	Strong gale	wind speed 41–48
10.	Whole gale	wind speed 49–56
11.	Storm	wind speed 57–65
12.	Hurricane	wind speed more than 65

The American description as used by the US Weather Bureau is as follows:

Calm	less than wind speed 2
Light	less than wind speed 7
Gentle	wind speed between 8 and 12
Moderate	wind speed between 13 and 18
Fresh	wind speed between 19 and 24
Strong	wind speed between 25 and 38
Gale	wind speed between 39 and 54
Whole gale	wind speed between 55 and 92
Hurricane	wind speed between 93 and 136

W.E.K. MIDDLETON, A.F. SPILHAUS, *Meteorological Instruments*, London, 1953.

BECHUANALAND. Until 1966 a British Protectorate listed by the UN General Assembly as non-self-governing territory. ▷ Botswana.

BEER AND BREWERIES. Subjects of international co-operation; organizations reg. with the UIA:

Continental Brewery Centre, f. 1948, Rotterdam, Netherlands, The European Brewery Convention, 1948.
EFTA Brewing Industry Committee, f. 1962, Vienna, Austria.
European Community of Associations of the Wholesale Beer Trade for the EEC countries, f. 1959, Bottelare, Belgium.
International Beer Tasting Society, f. 1956, Newport Beach, Calif. USA.
International Union of United Brewery, Flour, Cereal, Soft Drink and Distillery Workers of America, f. 1886, Cincinatti, Ohio, USA.
Working Committee of Common Market Brewers, f. 1958, Brussels, Belgium.

Yearbook of International Organizations, 1986–87.

BEES. Subject of international co-operation. Organizations reg. with the UIA:

Bee Research Associations, f. 1949, London. Publ.: *Journal of Agricultural Research*.
International Commission for Bee Botany, f. 1951, Bures-sur-Yvete, France.
International Federation of Beekeepers Association, APIMONDIA, f. 1949, Rome, Italy. Consultative Status: ECOSOÇ, FAO, UNCTAD. Publ.: Apiacta.

Yearbook of International Organizations, 1986–87.

B

BEIRUT. The capital of Lebanon. Population 1985 estimated: 1,500,000. Seat of 13 international organizations, reg. with the UIA, among others: Arab Air Carriers Organization; Arab Iron–Steel Union; Middle East Council of Churches; UN Information Center; World Muslim Congress.

Yearbook of International Organizations, 1986–87.

BELAU. ▷ Palau or Belau.

BELEM AMAZONIA DECLARATION, 1980. A declaration adopted at Belem, Brazil on Oct. 24, 1980 by Bolivia, Brazil, Colombia, Ecuador, Guyana, Peru, Surinam and Venezuela, the signatories of the Amazon Pact 1978, proclaiming that the development of the Amazon region and protection of its environment are inseparable and involve the exclusive responsibility of the Amazon countries, represented by the Amazon Co-operative Council. ▷ Amazon River.

Yearbook of International Organizations.

BELFAST. Capital of Northern Ireland, on Belfast Lough, an inlet of the North Channel of the Irish Sea. Population in 1985 est. 301,600. Since the 19th century it has been a site of social–religious conflicts between Catholics and Protestants; since 1921 subject of disputes between the Irish Republic and the United Kingdom.

D.J. OVEN, *History of Belfast*, 1921; W.D. FLACKERS, *Northern Ireland Political Directory 1968–1983*, London, 1983. *The Europa Yearbook 1987, A World Survey*, London, 1987.

BELGIAN CLAUSE. A principle of international law stating that persons who commit homicidal assault on the head of an alien state shall not be granted asylum as political refugees; the term was coined due to the fact that Belgium was the first to introduce such a clause into its national legislation on Mar. 22, 1856, which was later adopted by the majority of European states.

H. GRÜTZNER, 'Attentatenklausel', in: *STRUPP-SCHLOCHAUER Wörterbuch des Völkerrechts*, Vol. I, pp. 109–120, Berlin, 1960; R.L. BLEDSOE, B.A. BOCZEK, *The International Law Dictionary*, Oxford, 1987.

BELGIAN CONGO. Until 1960 African territory listed by the UN General Assembly as a non-self-governing country. ▷ Zaïre.

BELGIAN NEUTRALITY, 1839–1940. The London Protocol of Apr. 19, 1839, decided that Belgium would be "an independent and for ever neutral State." After the violation of Belgian neutrality by Germany in World War I the Belgian Kingdom signed in Aug. 1920 a military defense convention with France. On May 22, 1926 a collective treaty of the signatories of the London Protocol declared the Protocol as abrogated. After the remilitarization of ▷ Rhineland, Mar. 7, 1936, Belgium announced its return to neutrality in Oct. 1936, but after the second violation of Belgian neutrality by Germany in May 1940, Belgium decided after World War II to join the defense treaties of the Western Powers: the ▷ Brussels Treaty 1948 and the ▷ NATO 1949.

MARTENS, *Nouveau Recueil*, Vol. XVI, p. 770; F.W. GHILLANY, *Europäische Chronik*, Leipzig, 1865, Vol. 1, p. 48; *LNTS*, 1926 and 1936, *UNTS*, 1948 and 1949.

BELGIUM. Member of the UN. Kingdom of Belgium. Royaume de Belgique, Koninkrijk Belgie. State in western Europe on the North Sea. Area: 30,519 sq. km. Pop.: 9,860,000 inhabitants in 1987. Capital: Brussels with 994,774 inhabitants in 1981.

Borders with France, Luxembourg, the FRG and Holland; frontiers established by the London Treaty, 1831, confirmed by the Versailles Treaty, 1919; minor adjustments of the frontier with the FRG in 1950. Official languages: Flemish *c.* 56% and French *c.* 33% of the population. GNP per capita in 1980: US $12180. Currency: Belgian franc and Luxembourg franc. National Day: July, 21, Independence Day.

In 1919–39 a member of the League of Nations; since Oct. 24, 1945 a member of the UN and all specialized UN organizations; member of the Rhine Navigation Committee, 1815, Customs Union with Luxembourg, 1921, Bank of International Settlements, 1930; Economic Union BENELUX, 1948; West European Union, 1948; NATO, 1949; European Council, 1949; EEC, 1958, and all EEC organizations and OECD, 1961.

International relations: on Oct. 4, 1839 Belgium's independence was proclaimed and its secession from Holland and the guarantee of Belgium's "perpetual neutrality" by the London Treaty of Nov. 15, 1831 by Austria, Prussia, Russia and Great Britain, confirmed by the Versailles Treaty, June 28, 1919, and the Franco-British Declaration of Apr. 24, 1937; Belgium's neutrality was twice violated by the German Reich – in 1914 and 1940. After World War II Belgium abandoned perpetual neutrality and joined the Western European economic, political and military organizations.

Belgium, after France, Switzerland and Great Britain, is the headquarters of the largest number (more than 370) international organizations reg. in the UN Secretariat; they comprise the Federation of International Associations in Belgium, *Fédération des Associations internationales ètablies en Belgique* with headquarters in Brussels; periodically publ. *Guide pratique a l'usage des organizations internationales établies en Belgique.*

Since Oct. 1980 Flanders, the Flemish-speaking northern half of Belgium and Wallonia, the French-speaking southern half, have their own regional assemblies and executives, which take control over cultural matters, public health, regional economy and urban projects (about 10% of the national budget). The military and foreign affairs, finance and education remain in the power of national parliament, and government. Brussels an overwhelmingly French-speaking city but entirely situated in Flemish-speaking territory has special bilingual legal status. The linguistic conflicts between the Flemish and Walloons flared up in 1983. The new immigration law valid since Jan. 1, 1988 determines that asylum seekers will be turned back at the border if their identification or travel documents are not in order.

The Royal Institute of International Relations, f. 1947, Brussels. Publ.: *Studio Diplomatica. La 'Belgique et les Nations Unies*, New York, 1958; F.G. EYCK, *The Benelux Countries, An Historical Survey*, Toronto, 1959; IRRI, *Les Conséquences d'ordre interne de la participation de la Belgique aux organisations internationales*, Bruxelles, 1964; *Documents Relatifs au Statut International de la Belgique depuis 1830*; 3 Vols., Bruxelles, 1964; E. FODOR, *Belgium and Luxembourg 1970*, London, 1970; *Everyone's United Nations*, New York, 1979; *The Europa Year Book 1984. A World Survey*, Vol. I, pp. 315–336, London, 1984; R.L. BLEDSOE, B.A. BOCZEK, *The International Law Dictionary*, Oxford, 1987.

BELGRADE. The capital of Yugoslavia (population 1981 census: 1,470,073), since 1929, at the confluence of the Danube and Sava Rivers. The seat of the International Esperantic Scientific Association, of the International Institute for the Science of Sintering. The Association of Writers in Esperanto; International Society of Esperantists Architects and

Builders, International League of Blind Esperantists. Reg. by the UIA.

Yearbook of International Organizations, 1986–87. The Europa Yearbook 1987, A World Survey, London 1987.

BELGRADE CSCE MEETING, 1977–78. The representatives of the participating States of the Conference on Security and Co-operation in Europe (▷ Helsinki Conference 1973–75) met at Belgrade from June 15 to Aug. 5, 1977 to organize the Belgrade Meeting, which took place from Oct. 4, 1977 to Mar. 9 1978. The Concluding Document read as follows:

"The representatives of the participating States of the Conference on Security and Co-operation in Europe, appointed by the Ministers of Foreign Affairs of these States, met at Belgrade from 4 October 1977 to 9 March 1978 in accordance with the provisions of the Final Act relating to the Follow-up to the Conference.

The participants received a message from the President of the Socialist Federal Republic of Yugoslavia, Josip Broz Tito, and were addressed by Mr. Milos Minić, Vice-President of the Federal Executive Council and Federal Secretary for Foreign Affairs of the Socialist Federal Republic of Yugoslavia. Contributions were made by the following non-participating Mediterranean States: Algeria, Egypt, Israel, Lebanon, Morocco, Syria and Tunisia.

The representatives of the participating States stressed the importance they attach to détente, which has continued since the adoption of the Final Act in spite of difficulties and obstacles encountered. In this context they underlined the role of the CSCE, the implementation of the provisions of the Final Act being essential for the development of this process.

The representatives of the participating States held a thorough exchange of views both on the implementation of the provisions of the Final Act and of the tasks defined by the Conference, as well as, in the context of the questions dealt with by the latter, on the deepening of their mutual relations, the improvement of security and the development of co-operation in Europe, and the development of the process of détente in the future. The representatives of the participating States stressed the political importance of the Conference on Security and Co-operation in Europe and reaffirmed the resolve of their Governments, to implement fully, unilaterally, bilaterally and multilaterally, all the provisions of the Final Act.

It was recognized that the exchange of views constitutes in itself a valuable contribution towards the achievement of the aims set by the CSCE, although different views were expressed as to the degree of implementation of the Final Act reached so far.

They also examined proposals concerning the above questions and the definition of the appropriate modalities for the holding of other meetings in conformity with the provisions of the chapter of the Final Act concerning the Follow-up to the Conference.

Consensus was not reached on a number of proposals submitted to the meeting.

In conformity with the relevant provisions of the Final Act and with their resolve to continue the multilateral process initiated by the CSCE, the participating States will hold further meetings among their representatives. The second of these meetings will be held in Madrid commencing Tuesday, 11 November 1980.

A preparatory meeting will be held in Madrid commencing Tuesday, 9 September 1980, to decide on appropriate modalities for the main Madrid Meeting. This will be done on the basis of the Final Act as well as of the other relevant documents adopted during the process of the CSCE.

It was also agreed to hold, within the framework of the Follow-up to the CSCE, the meetings of experts of the participating States indicated below.

In conformity with the mandate contained in the Final Act and according to the proposal made to this effect by the Government of Switzerland a meeting of experts will be convened at Montreux on 31 October 1978, charged with pursuing the examination and elaboration of a generally acceptable method for peaceful settlement of disputes aimed at complementing existing methods.

Upon the invitation of the Government of the Federal Republic of Germany, the meeting of experts envisaged in the Final Act in order to prepare a "Scientific Forum" will take place in Bonn starting on 20 June 1978. Representatives of UNESCO and the United Nations Economic Commission for Europe shall be invited to state their views.

Upon the invitation of the Government of Malta, a meeting of experts on the Mediterranean will be convened on 13 February 1979 in Valletta. Its mandate will be, within the framework of the Mediterranean Chapter of the Final Act, to consider the possibilities and means of promoting concrete initiatives for mutually beneficial co-operation concerning various economic, scientific and cultural fields, in addition to other initiatives relating to the above subjects already under way. The non-participating Mediterranean States will be invited to contribute to the work of this meeting. Questions relating to security will be discussed at the Madrid Meeting. The duration of the meetings of experts should not exceed 4–6 weeks. They will draw up conclusions and recommendations and send their reports to the Governments of the participating States. The results of these meetings will be taken into account, as appropriate, at the Madrid Meeting.

All the above-mentioned meetings will be held in conformity with paragraph 4 of the chapter on 'Follow-up to the Conference' of the Final Act.

The Government of the Socialist Federal Republic of Yugoslavia is requested to transmit the present document to the Secretary-General of the United Nations, to the Director-General of UNESCO and to the Executive Secretary of the United Nations Economic Commission for Europe. The Government of the Socialist Federal Republic of Yugoslavia is also requested to transmit the present document to the Governments of the Mediterranean non-participating States. The representatives of the participating States expressed their profound gratitude to the people and Government of the Socialist Federal Republic of Yugoslavia for the excellent organization of the Belgrade Meeting and the warm hospitality extended to the delegations which participated in the Meeting."

A.D. ROTFELD, *From Helsinki to Madrid. Documents*, Warsaw, 1984, pp. 213–217.

BELGRADE SOVIET-YUGOSLAV DECLARATION, 1988. ▷ Soviet-Yugoslav Declaration.

BELIZE. Member of the UN. Independent state in Central America on the Caribbean Sea. Belize bordered by Guatemala and Mexico. Area: 22,965 sq. km. Pop. in 1987: 176,000 (1970 census 119,863). Capital: Belmopan with *c.* 5800 inhabitants, 1980. Main city: Belize City with 39,877 inhabitants, 1980. Official language: English. Currency: 1 Belize dollar = 100 cents. GNP per capita 1986 US $1170. National Day: September 21, Independence Day, 1981. Since Sept. 25, 1981 member of the UN by a recorded vote of 144 in favor of 1 against (Guatemala). Member of all specialized UN agencies, save IAEA ICAO, WHO, IMO and WIPO. International relations: In the 18th century Belize was part of the Spanish Central American possession, but was occupied by the British settlers from Jamaica. British Colony 1862–1981 called British Honduras. Independent Sept. 15, 1981. Guatemala has claimed the territory since 1821. In 1981 Belize rejected all Guatemala claims. Belize was supported against Guatemala claims in Nov. 1982 by the CARICOM states and in Oct. 1983, again by the UK.

A reform of the ▷ Charter of OAS by the Protocol of Cartagena 1985, opened to Belize the possibility of OAS membership after 1990.

On April 29–30, 1987 in Miami representatives of Belize–UK–Guatemala first discussed the future of Belize.

FR. ASTURIAS, *Belice*, Guatemala, 1941; J.L. MENDOZA, *Britain and her Treaties on Belize*, Guatemala, 1946; L.M. BLOOMFIELD, *The British Honduras–Guatemala Dispute*, Toronto, 1963; W.J. BIANCHI, *Belize. The Controversy between Guatemala and Great Britain*, New York, 1959; R.A. HUMPHREYSJ, *The Diplomatic History of British Hon-*

duras 1638–1901, London, 1961; D.A. WADDELL, *British Honduras: A Historical and Contemporary Survey*, London, 1961; I. FABELA, *Belice, Defensa de los Derechos de México*, México, DF, 1964; *British Honduras UN Economic Report 1963*, Belize City, 1964; M. TOLEDANO, *Guatemala, Monografía Sociológica*, México, DF, 1965; D. DOBSON, *A History of Belize*, Belize City, 1973; C.H. GRANT, *The Making of Modern Belize*, London, 1976; *Everyone's United Nations*, New York, 1979, pp. 276, 308. *UN Chronicle*, January 1980 and November 1981, pp. 7–8; *The Europa Year Book 1984. A World Survey*, Vol. I, pp. 1164–1168, London, 1984.

BELLIGERENT. Term of international law. A state which is at war with another state or states. The Third Meeting of Foreign Ministers of American Republics adopted on Jan. 28, 1942 the principle that "within the framework of their solidarity the American republics do not consider as a belligerent party any American state which is or will be at war with any non-American state."

By adopting this doctrine Latin-American states which remain non-aligned were relieved of all restrictions in their normal relations with the USA.

International American Conferences. First Supplement 1938–1942. Washington, DC, 1942.

BELLIGERENT OCCUPATION ▷ Occupied Territories.

BELLO ANDREAS. ▷ Andreas Bello Agreement, 1970.

BELLUM IUSTUM ET INIUSTUM. *Latin*: "a just war and unjust war". An international term which appeared in the Middle Ages, distinguishing wars as just and unjust.
(Saint Augustine, 354–430, bishop of Hippo in Roman Africa).

B.deSOLAGES, *La théologie de la guerre juste*, Paris, 1947; M. WALZER, *Just and Unjust Wars*, London, 1977.

BELMOPAN. The capital of Belize (1985 pop. 4,500). Since 1986 site of the University College of Belize.

J. PAXTON ed., *The Statesman's Yearbook 1987–1988*, London, 1987.

BELORUSSIA. ▷ Byelorussia.

BELSEN BERGEN. German concentration camp during World War II in Lower Saxony (now FRG) north-west of Celle, where some 48,000 victims of German fascism were killed. Liberated by the British Apr. 15, 1945. Organization reg. with the UIA: World Federation of the Bergen Belsen Associations, f. in Apr. 1945 to perpetuate the memory of the Martyrs of Bergen Belsen and all other victims of the Nazi Holocaust. Headquarters in New York, USA.

T. NIZIELSKI, *Belsen-Bergen 1943–1945*. Warszawa, 1971; *The Trial of German Major War Criminals. Proceedings of the IMT Sitting at Nuremberg*, 42 Vols., London, 1946–1958, Vol. II, p. 313.

BELUGA. *Huso huso.* A Black Sea fish protected by international convention.

UNTS, Vol. 377, p. 203.

BELZEC. Nazi death camp in east Poland, that between Nov. 1, 1941 and June 30, 1943, claimed more than 600,000 lives.

Y. ARAD, Belzec, Sobibor, Treblinka, Bloomington, Indiana, 1987.

BENELUX. Belgium, Netherlands, Luxembourg. A common name adopted on Sept. 5, 1944 in

London by the governments in exile of Belgium, Holland, and Luxembourg as an expression of their aspirations toward integration "in order that from the moment of liberation of the territories" a permanent customs union of these three states might be formed. The Benelux Customs Convention 1944 and the Hague Protocol 1947 took effect Jan. 1, 1948. The Benelux Economic Union entailing free movement of persons, goods, capital and services was established by a Treaty signed in The Hague, Feb. 3, 1958 in accordance with the London Customs Convention 1944 and The Hague Protocol 1947. This union implies:

"(a) the co-ordination of economic, financial and social policies; (b) the pursuit of a joint policy in economic relations with third countries and regarding payments related thereto" (art. 1).

The Treaty came into force Nov. 1, 1960 valid for 50 years. Organization: Committee of Ministers, Consultative Inter-parliamentary Council, Council of the Economic Union, General Secretariat, Economic and Social Consultative Council and Special Committees. Pub. quarterly review *Benelux and Textes de Base*. The Benelux Economic Union publ. *Benelux Texte de Base, Benelux Periodical* (quarterly) and *Info-Benelux* (monthly).

UNTS, Vol. 381, p. 260; R.C. RILEY, G.J. ASHWORTH, *Benelux: An Economic Geography*, New York, 1975.

BENES-SIKORSKI CONFEDERATION PACT 1942. ▷ Czechoslovak-Polish Agreement.

BENE-ISRAEL. ▷ Jews.

BENGAL. A region in India and Bangladesh on the Bay of Bengal. In 1765 the British took over the rule of Bengal from one Mogul empire. In 1905 efforts were made to have the area divided into East Bengal with an Islamic majority and West Bengal with a Hindu majority. The administrative division of Bengal recommended by Lord Curzon was opposed by the Bengal unification movement. Official partition did not take place until 1947 when West Bengal became a province of India and East Bengal became East Pakistan. On Apr. 27, 1971 East Pakistan declared its independence and proclaimed the Republic of ▷ Bangladesh.

R. CHOWDHURY, *The Genesis of Bangladesh*, London, 1972.

BENGAL BAY OF. An arm of the Indian Ocean, 2,200 km long and 1,610 km wide, bordered by Sri Lanka, India, Bangladesh, Burma, Andaman Islands and Thailand; subject of maritime border agreements (▷ Burma).

BENGHAZI DECLARATION, 1971 The official name of an agreement among the Heads of State of Libya, Egypt, and Syria concerning the formation of an Arabic Federation whose aim was to create "one Arabian socialist society". Signed Apr. 19, 1971 in Benghazi. The treaty did not enter into force.

BENGUELA RAILWAY. An international railroad, linking the post Lobito on the Angolan coast with mineral-rich areas in Zaïre and Zambia, subject of an agreement between Angola, Mozambique, Zambia and Zaïre, April 16, 1987 in Luanda.

KEESING's *Record of World Events*, June 1987.

BENIN. Member of the UN. People's Republic of Benin. République Populaire du Benin. West African state on the Gulf of Guinea, bordering on Togo, Upper Volta, Niger and Nigeria. Area:

B

112,622 sq. km. Pop. 1988 est. 4,400,000. Capital: Porto Novo with 104,000 inhabitants, 1975, GNP per capita in 1986 US $270. Currency: 1 franc CFA = 100 centimes. Official language: French. National Day: Nov. 30, Proclamation of the Socialist Revolution, 1974.

Member of the UN since Sept. 20, 1960 and of UN specialized agencies, with the exception of the IAEA. Member of OAU, ACP state of EEC. A signatory of the Yaundé Conventions of 1963 and of the Lomé Conventions of 1975 and 1980.

International relations: under the name Dahomey occupied by France in the last two decades of the 19th century; in 1899 it became part of French West Africa; in 1946 it became an autonomous state within the French Union and in 1958 a member of the French Community: independent since Aug. 1, 1960. In August, September and October 1988 disastrous floods caused substantial material damages, and loss of human lives. The UN decided to provide special assistance to Benin (GA. Res. 43/211 of Dec. 20, 1988).

See also ▷ World Heritage UNESCO List.

J. SERRAU, *Le développement á la base au Dahomey et au Sénégal*, Paris, 1966; M.A. STELE, *Naissance d'un état noir. L'évolution politique et constitutionnelle du Dahomey de la colonisation á nos jours*, Paris, 1969; D. RONEN, *Dahomey: Between Tradition and Modernity*, Ithaca, 1975; *Everyone's United Nations*, New York, 1979; *The Europa Year Book 1984. A World Survey*, Vol. I, pp. 1169–1177, London, 1984.

BENITO JUAREZ PRIZE. Founded by Mexico in 1967, annual artistic and scientific award for creators coming from Latin America; first prize winners were: Ecuadorian writer B. Carion, Brazilian architect O. Niemeyer, and Argentinian biochemist L. Leboir.

BENZENE. A toxic liquid, subject of the international ILO Convention, 1977 on Protection Against Hazards of Poisoning Arising From Benzene.

ILO Conventions and Recommendations, 1919–1981, Geneva, 1982.

BENZODIAZEPINES. ▷ Tranquilizers.

BERARD–JORDAN AGREEMENT, 1939. A French–Spanish agreement concluded on Feb. 25, 1939 between France and the General Franco regime in Burgos; named after the agreement signatories who conducted negotiations, Senator L. Berard and General F. Jordan. The government of France recognized the regime of General Franco, followed by Great Britain (Feb. 27, 1939) and the USA (Apr. 7, 1939). The Agreement guaranteed to the government of General Franco the return of the Spanish state treasury sent to France, as well as ships and battleships which had taken shelter in French ports, and the cessation of anti-Franco propaganda.

C.A. COLLIARD, *Droit international et histoire diplomatique*, Paris, 1950.

BERING SEA. An arm of the Pacific Ocean, between Siberia and Alaska connected with the Atlantic Ocean by the Bering Strait. Area: 2,274,220 sq. km. Explored 1733–41 by Danish sailor Vitus Bering (1680–1741). In 1911 Great Britain, Japan, Russia and USA signed an agreement prohibiting pelagic sealing in the Bering Sea.

After the USA in March 1983 imposed a 200 mile exclusive economic zone in the Bering Sea, the USSR and the USA claimed jurisdiction of adjacent areas and initiated, 1984, talks on the demarcation of the Maritime boundary in this region.

Ekspiediciya Bieringa. Sbornik dokumentov, Moscow, 1941; KEESING's *Record of World Events*, 1987, No. 3.

BERING STRAIT. Strait between the continents of Eurasia and North America, connects the Chukcha Sea and Bering Sea; at its narrowest part separates the USA from the USSR by 35 km which fact after World War II gave rise in both states to plans for constructing a bridge over the Bering Straits: in 1948 an American plan; in 1960 a Soviet one. In 1968 an American society was formed for the construction of a "bridge of peace" between the continents.

W. SIOSKIN, "Most nad prolivem Beringa", in: *SSha-Economia, Politika, Idieologuia*, No. 12, Moscow, 1973.

BERLIN. German city, former capital of Prussia, 1709–1945, and of the Reich, 1871–1945; divided on June 7, 1945, as an outcome of World War II into four occupation sectors: Eastern: Soviet; and Western: American, English and French. Since Oct. 7, 1949 the Eastern part has been the capital of GDR. The status of West Berlin was determined by the ▷ Berlin Agreement, 1971.

International relations: as the capital of Prussia it was occupied by Austrian forces 1757, Russian forces 1760, French forces 1806–08 and 1812–13. Site of revolution in 1848. Site of ▷ Berlin Congress 1878 and ▷ Berlin Congress 1885. On Nov. 9, 1918, the revolution in Berlin introduced a republican system, changed to fascist on Jan. 30, 1933; abolished by unconditional surrender of Berlin on May 2, 1945 to the Red Army, with units of the 1st Army of Polish Forces co-operating in conquering Berlin. Former capital of Prussia and the Reich was divided into four occupation sectors by virtue of inter-power agreements: London Protocol on Berlin of Sept. 12, 1944; Agreement on Administration of Great Berlin of June 5, 1945; ▷ Potsdam Agreement of Aug. 2, 1945. Common administrative and control authority of allied powers became institutionalized in ▷ Berlin Allied Komendantura consisting of military commanders of four occupation sectors, operating from July 11, 1945 to July 1, 1948, the date of the last common session of the four commanders. In consequence of the introduction of a separate currency reform on June 23, 1948 by Western powers, the four-power system of Great Berlin practically stopped functioning. The new monetary unit, West Mark in West Germany, and West Mark with B overprint in West Berlin, cut off West Germany and West Berlin economically from the Soviet zone of Germany and the Soviet sector in Berlin. On June 24, 1948 the Soviet side introduced the monetary separation of areas under its control.

During the period from July 1948 to Sept. 1949, Western powers prepared a new occupation status for West Germany (▷ Germany, Federal Republic of Germany), and also for their West Berlin sectors. The military commanders initiated on Dec. 21, 1948 the operation of the trilateral American–English–French headquarters of West Berlin. Contacts of the Soviet commander with the commanders of Western sectors started in summer 1949, according to recommendations settled in Paris on May 23 to June 20, 1949 by ministers of foreign affairs of the four powers. The system worked-out confirmed that Berlin still remained a four-power problem. The ▷ Berlin blockade, as a problem dangerous for peace, was transferred by the Western powers to the forum of the UN Security Council and the UN General Assembly in Sept. and Nov. 1948. The USSR vetoed the Berlin case as contradictory to provisions of the UN Charter which excluded German affairs from UN competence (▷ Clause on Enemy States in UN Charter; ▷ Berlin Blockade in

the UN). On Nov. 10, 1958 the government of the USSR suggested to the Western powers a normalization of relations between Berlin, capital of the GDR, and West Berlin; in 1962 it proposed the change of West Berlin status to a demilitarized city, or a free city under UN patronage. The Western powers rejected both proposals. Attempts at incorporating West Berlin by the FRG as a federal "Land" ("Land Berlin") in 1949–71 were paralyzed each time by the objection of the four powers. The items of the constitution of the FRG of 1949 and that of West Berlin of 1950, stating that West Berlin is a "Land" of the FRG, were not acknowledged by any of the powers. Some federal laws of the FRG can be valid in West Berlin only on the condition that they are passed by the Senate of West Berlin. The idea to make West Berlin the capital of the FRG government and parliament (for this reason, among others, the ▷ Reichstag had been rebuilt) was not supported by any of the Great Powers. On Aug. 13, 1961 the Warsaw Treaty states, at the suggestion of GDR, decided unanimously on a complete separation of West Berlin in a form, in which "customarily, frontiers are made between sovereign states." For this purpose a border wall was built, the so-called "Berlin Wall". Earlier the special character of West Berlin was acknowledged by declarations of NATO on Dec. 16, 1958; later by those of Nov. 15, 1967. In a different form, by art. 6 of the USSR–GDR Treaty of June 12, 1964, which stated that "High Negotiating Parties consider West Berlin to be a politically independent, administrative unit." Similarly, art. 8 of the Polish People's Republic–GDR Treaty of Mar. 15, 1967, as well as other agreements of Warsaw Pact countries with the GDR, consistently stated that "High Negotiating Parties consider West Berlin to be a separate political unit." On May 25, 1967 commanders of the Western sectors of Berlin reminded, in a letter to the Head Mayor of West Berlin, that "West Berlin is not a Land of the FRG and cannot be governed by FRG authorities." On Apr. 13, 1968 the government of the GDR introduced the obligation, beginning with June 1, 1968, of having GDR visas for inhabitants of West Berlin travelling to the GDR or to its Capital, Berlin. Previously, family visiting was allowed according to the agreement between the Senate of West Berlin and the GDR of Dec. 17, 1963, only at the holiday season, from Dec. 18, 1963 to Jan. 5, 1964. Similar agreements were signed for the seasons of Christmas, Easter and Whitsuntide in the years 1964–66. In 1969, the government of the GDR suspended passenger traffic between West Berlin and the GDR capital, and introduced a ban on crossing the GDR to West Berlin for government officials of the FRG. At the time from Feb. 20, 1970 to Sept. 3, 1971, the four powers responsible for the status of West Berlin started negotiations on a new status, which would allow a normalization of West Berlin relations with the GDR and the FRG. The negotiations started on Feb. 8, 1971 between the government of the GDR and the Senate of West Berlin. A respective skeleton agreement was signed on Sept. 3, 1971. In the four-page Final Protocol the following was stated in point 1:

"By the present protocol the four governments enact the quadrilateral agreement, which, similarly as this protocol, does not contravene quadrilateral agreements or resolutions concluded or passed earlier."

That is generally interpreted as upholding of the validity of the Potsdam Agreement provisions on ▷ responsibility of the four powers. The West Berlin administration is managed by the Senate, elected by the population from among candidates put up by political parties. The activity of the Senate is supervised by the ▷ Allied Control Authority and is limited in internal and external relations by agreements of the four powers.

On Aug. 11, 1973 the Allied Control Authority of Western powers definitely rejected the proposal, submitted in 1970 by the Senate and Deputy Chamber of West Berlin, on calling a Constitutional Tribunal, which would pass judgement on arguments concerning the interpretation of laws valid in West Berlin. Thus the Western powers maintained the local, and not federal, character of West Berlin legislation. In late May 1973, a Consulate General of the USSR was opened in West Berlin, according to the four-power agreement of 1971. On June 27, 1973 the USSR addressed a letter to the UN Secretary-General informing him that West Berlin would be represented at the UN by the FRG under observation of the provisions of the quadrilateral Berlin agreement, and, in particular, that Western sectors of Berlin are not a part of the FRG; that the USA, France and Great Britain retain responsibility for West Berlin representation as regards city security and status; that the FRG can represent West Berlin as far as other matters are concerned on the forum of international organizations mentioned in the four-power agreement. On July 22, 1974 the government of the FRG, with the consent of Western powers, transferred the seat of the FRG Federal Office for Environmental Protection from the FRG to West Berlin, which was found by the USSR to be a violation against the quadrilateral agreement. The new metropolitan status of Berlin was formally acknowledged by the establishment of diplomatic representations to the government of the GDR in Berlin, by an absolute majority of UN member states together with the five great powers, 1972–74. That process ended in the signing on Mar. 14, 1974 in Bonn of a Protocol on the opening of permanent legations of the GDR in Bonn and of the FRG in Berlin.

Statistical data: Area of Berlin – 883.1 sq. km (West Berlin 480.1 sq. km included). Pop.: according to census 1985 in East and West 3,762,984 (East – 1,902,900, West – 1,860,084). Historical development of Berlin population: in 1709 it numbered 57,000 inhabitants; 1800 – 172,000; 1871 – 913,000; 1900 – 2,700,000; 1925 – 4,000,000; according to census of May 17, 1939 – 4,338,000 inhabitants, including 1,982,000 men and 2,356,000 women, July 12, 1945 – about 2,807,000; according to census of Oct. 29, 1946 – 3,132,000 including 1,266,000 men and 1,866,000 women.

The capital of the GDR is the seat of many institutions of CMEA countries. The USSR contribution to Berlin's liberation from fascism has been memorized by monuments of the Soviet Soldier in the quarters of Treptov (Soviet Sector) and Tiergarten (British Sector); the Polish contribution by the monument of the Polish soldier and German antifascist in the quarter of Friedrichshain (Soviet Sector).

On June 23, 1988 the United States, Great Britain and France ended a postwar monopoly of three airlines (Panamerican, British Airlines and Air France) flying to West Berlin. They awarded landing rights to American Airlines, Trans World Airlines and Lufthansa (in co-operation with Air France). The air traffic between West Berlin and nine major West European cities in 1988 was about 700 round-trip flights a week.

On the 25th Anniversary of the erection of the Berlin Wall a demonstration took place in West Berlin against the "monument of inhumanity" in the opinion of the FRG Chancellor H. Kohl. President Ronald Reagan on May 8, 1987 in West Berlin and on Aug. 8, 1987 in Washington DC demanded the demolition of the Berlin Wall. On Nov. 9, 1989, the East German government, pressured by street demonstrations calling for greater democracy and the renunciation of power by the Communist Party, opened the country's borders, prompting the spontaneous destruction of parts of the Berlin Wall by jubilant crowds and the official opening of a score of new border crossings, including one at the Brandenburg Gate, symbolic heart of Berlin.

Berlin in Zahlen 1946–47, Berlin, 1949; *Documents on Germany under Occupation 1945–54*, London, 1955; *Documents on the Status of Berlin 1944–59*, München, 1959; J. RSHEWSKI, *Westberlin. Ein politisches Gebilde sui generis*, Moskau, 1971; R.M. SCHLUSSER, *The Berlin Crisis of 1961*, Baltimore, 1981; J. PAXTON (ed.), *The Statesman's Year-Book*, 1987–88, London 1987; I.D. HENDRY, M.C. WOOD, *The Legal Status of Berlin*, Cambridge, UK, 1987; N. GELB, *The Berlin Wall*, New York, 1987; KEESING's *Contemporary Archive* 1986, No. 8 and 1987, No. 8; M. SIMMONS, *Berlin: The Dispossessed City*, London, 1988; *International Herald Tribune*, June 28, 1988; KEESING's *Record of World Events*, Nov., Dec., 1989.

BERLIN AGREEMENT, 1971. The Four Power agreement, signed in Berlin, Sept. 3, 1971. The text is as follows:

"The Governments of the Union of Soviet Socialist Republics, the United Kingdom of Great Britain and Northern Ireland, the United States of America and the French Republic, Represented by their Ambassadors, who held a series of meetings in the building formerly occupied by the Allied Control Council in the American Sector of Berlin, Acting on the basis of their quadripartite rights and responsibilities, and of the corresponding wartime and postwar agreements and decisions of the Four Powers, which are not affected,
Taking into account the existing situation in the relevant area,
Guided by the desire to contribute to practical improvements of the situation,
Without prejudice to their legal positions,
Have agreed on the following:
Part I. General provisions.
(1) The Four Governments will strive to promote the elimination of tension and the prevention of complications in the relevant area.
(2) The four Governments, taking into account their obligations under the Charter of the United Nations, agree that there shall be no use or threat of force in the area and that disputes shall be settled solely by peaceful means.
(3) The four Governments will mutually respect their individual and joint rights and responsibilities, which remain unchanged.
(4) The four Governments agree that, irrespective of the differences in legal views, the situation which has developed in the area, and as it is defined in this Agreement as well as in the other agreements referred to in this Agreement, shall not be changed unilaterally.
Part II. Provisions relating to the Western Sectors of Berlin.
A. The Government of the Union of Soviet Socialist Republics declares that transit traffic by road, rail and waterways through the territory of the German Democratic Republic of civilian persons and goods between the Western Sectors of Berlin and the Federal Republic of Germany will be unimpeded; that such traffic will be facilitated so as to take place in the most simple and expeditious manner; and that it will receive preferential treatment. Detailed arrangements concerning this civilian traffic, as set forth in Annex I, will be agreed by the competent German authorities.
B. The Governments of the French Republic, the United Kingdom and the United States of America declare that the ties between the Western Sectors of Berlin and the Federal Republic of Germany will be maintained and developed, taking into account that these Sectors continue not to be a constituent part of the Federal Republic of Germany and not to be governed by it. Detailed arrangements concerning the relationship between the Western Sectors of Berlin and the Federal Republic of Germany are set forth in Annex II.
C. The Government of the Union of Soviet Socialist Republics declares that communications between the Western Sectors of Berlin and areas bordering on these Sectors and those areas of the German Democratic Republic which do not border on these Sectors will be improved. Permanent residents of the Western Sectors of Berlin will be able to travel to and visit such areas for compassionate, family, religious, cultural or commercial reasons, or as tourists, under conditions comparable to those applying to other persons entering these areas. The problems of the small enclaves, including Steinstuecken, and of other small areas may be solved by exchange of territory. Detailed arrangements concerning travel, communications and the exchange of territory, as set forth in Annex III, will be agreed by the competent German authorities.
D. Representation abroad of the interests of the Western Sectors of Berlin and consular activities of the Union of Soviet Socialist Republics in the Western Sectors of Berlin can be exercised as set forth in Annex IV.
Part III. Final provisions.
This Quadripartite Agreement will enter into force on the date specified in a Final Quadripartite Protocol to be concluded when the measures envisaged in Part II of this Quadripartite Agreement and in its Annexes have been agreed. Done at the building formerly occupied by the Allied Control Council in the American Sector of Berlin, this third day of September, 1971, in four originals, each in the Russian, English and French languages, all texts being equally authentic.
Annex I. The Government of the Union of Soviet Socialist Republics, with reference to Part II(A) of the Quadripartite Agreement of this date and after consultation and agreement with the Government of the German Democratic Republic, has the honor to inform the Governments of the French Republic, the United Kingdom and the United States of America that:
(1) Transit traffic by road, rail and waterways through the territory of the German Democratic Republic of civilian persons and goods between the Western Sectors of Berlin and the Federal Republic of Germany will be facilitated and unimpeded. It will receive the most simple, expeditious and preferential treatment provided by international practice.
(2) Accordingly,
(a) Conveyances sealed before departure may be used for the transport of civilian goods by road, rail and waterways between the Western Sectors of Berlin and the Federal Republic of Germany. Inspection procedures will be limited to the inspection of seals and accompanying documents.
(b) With regard to conveyances which cannot be sealed, such as open trucks, inspection procedures will be limited to the inspection of accompanying documents. In special cases where there is sufficient reason to suspect that unsealed conveyances contain either material intended for dissemination along the designated routes or persons or material put on board along these routes, the content of unsealed conveyances may be inspected. Procedures for dealing with such cases will be agreed by the competent German authorities.
(c) Through trains and buses may be used for travel between the Western Sectors of Berlin and the Federal Republic of Germany. Inspection procedures will not include any formalities other than identification of persons.
(d) Persons identified as through travellers using individual vehicles between the Western Sectors of Berlin and the Federal Republic of Germany on routes designated for through traffic will be able to proceed to their destinations without paying individual tolls and fees for the use of the transit routes. Procedures applied for such travellers shall not involve delay. The travellers, their vehicles and personal baggage will not be subject to search, detention or exclusion from use of the designated routes, except in special cases, as may be agreed by the competent German authorities, where there is sufficient reason to suspect that misuse of the transit routes is intended for purposes not related to direct travel to and from the Western Sectors of Berlin and contrary to generally applicable regulations concerning public order.
(e) Appropriate compensation for fees and tolls and for other costs related to traffic on the communication routes between the Western Sectors of Berlin and the Federal Republic of Germany, including the maintenance of adequate routes, facilities and installations used for such traffic, may be made in the form of an annual lump sum paid to the German Democratic Republic by the Federal Republic of Germany.

(3) Arrangements implementing and supplementing the provisions of paragraphs 1 and 2 above will be agreed by the competent German authorities.

Annex II. The Governments of the French Republic, the United Kingdom and the United States of America, with reference to Part II/B of the Quadripartite Agreement of this date and after consultation with the Government of the Federal Republic of Germany, have the honor to inform the Government of the Union of Soviet Socialist Republics that:

(1) They declare, in the exercise of their rights and responsibilities, that the ties between the Western Sectors of Berlin and the Federal Republic of Germany will be maintained and developed, taking into account that these Sectors continue not to be a constituent part of the Federal Republic of Germany and not to be governed by it. The provisions of the Basic Law of the Federal Republic of Germany and of the Constitution operative in the Western Sectors of Berlin which contradict the above have been suspended and continue not to be in effect.

(2) The Federal President, the Federal Government, the Bundesversammlung, the Bundesrat and the Bundestag, including their Committees and Fraktionen, as well as other state bodies of the Federal Republic of Germany will not perform in the Western Sectors of Berlin constitutional or official acts which contradict the provisions of Paragraph 1.

(3) The Government of the Federal Republic of Germany will be represented in the Western Sector of Berlin to the authorities of the three Governments and to the Senate by a permanent liaison agency.

Annex III. The Government of the Union of Soviet Socialist Republics, with reference to Part II(C) of the Quadripartite Agreement of this date and after consultation and agreement with the Government of the German Democratic Republic, has the honor to inform the Governments of the French Republic, the United Kingdom and the United States of America that:

(1) Communications between the Western Sectors of Berlin and areas bordering on these Sectors and those areas of the German Democratic Republic which do not border on these Sectors will be improved.

(2) Permanent residents of the Western Sectors of Berlin will be able to travel to and visit such areas for compassionate, family, religious, cultural or commercial reasons, or as tourists, under conditions comparable to those applying to other persons entering these areas. In order to facilitate visits and travel, as described above, by permanent residents of the Western Sectors of Berlin, additional crossing points will be opened.

(3) The problems of the small enclaves, including Steinstuecken, and of other small areas may be solved by exchange of territory.

(4) Telephonic, telegraphic, transport and other external communications of the Western Sectors of Berlin will be expanded.

(5) Arrangements implementing and supplementing the provisions of Paragraphs 1 to 4 above will be agreed by the competent German authorities.

Annex IVA. The Governments of the French Republic, the United Kingdom and the United States of America, with reference to Part II(D) of the Quadripartite Agreement of this date and after consultation with the Government of the Federal Republic of Germany, have the honor to inform the Government of the Union of Soviet Socialist Republics that:

(1) The Governments of the French Republic, the United Kingdom and the United States of America maintain their rights and responsibilities relating to the representation abroad of the interests of the Western Sectors of Berlin and their permanent residents, including those rights and responsibilities concerning matters of security and status, both in international organizations and in relations with other countries.

(2) Without prejudice to the above and provided that matters of security and status are not affected, they have agreed that:

(a) The Federal Republic of Germany may perform consular services for permanent residents of the Western Sectors of Berlin.

(b) In accordance with established procedures, international agreements and arrangements entered into by the Federal Republic of Germany may be extended to the Western Sectors of Berlin provided that the extension of such agreements and arrangements is specified in each case.

(c) The Federal Republic of Germany may represent the interests of the Western Sectors of Berlin in international organizations and international conferences.

(d) Permanent residents of the Western Sectors of Berlin may participate jointly with participants from the Federal Republic of Germany in international exchanges and exhibitions. Meetings of international organizations and international conferences as well as exhibitions with international participation may be held in the Western Sectors of Berlin. Invitations will be issued by the Senate or jointly by the Federal Republic of Germany and the Senate.

(3) The three Governments authorize the establishment of a Consulate General of the USSR in the Western Sectors of Berlin accredited to the appropriate authorities of the three Governments in accordance with the usual procedures applied in those Sectors, for the purpose of performing consular services, subject to provisions set forth in a separate document of this date.

Annex IVB. The Government of the Union of Soviet Socialist Republics, with reference to Part II(D) of the Quadripartite Agreement of this date and to the communication of the Governments of the French Republic, the United Kingdom and the United States of America with regard to the representation abroad of the interests of the Western Sectors of Berlin and their permanent residents has the honor to inform the Governments of the French Republic, the United Kingdom and the United States of America that:

(1) The Government of the Union of Soviet Socialist Republics takes note of the fact that the three Governments maintain their rights and responsibilities relating to the representation abroad of the interests of the Western Sectors of Berlin and their permanent residents, including those rights and responsibilities concerning matters of security and status, both in international organizations and in relations with other countries.

(2) Provided that matters of security and status are not affected, for its part it will raise no objection to:

(a) the performance by the Federal Republic of Germany of consular services for permanent residents of the Western Sectors of Berlin;

(b) in accordance with established procedures, the extension to the Western Sectors of Berlin of international agreements and arrangements entered into by the Federal Republic of Germany provided that the extension of such agreements and arrangements is specified in each case;

(c) the representation of the interests of the Western Sectors of Berlin by the Federal Republic of Germany in international organizations and international conferences;

(d) the participation jointly with participants from the Federal Republic of Germany of permanent residents of the Western Sectors of Berlin in international Sectors of meetings or international conferences as well as exhibitions with international participation, taking into account that invitations will be issued by the Senate or jointly by the Federal Republic of Germany and the Senate.

(3) The Government of the Union of Soviet Socialist Republics takes note of the fact that the three Governments have given their consent to the establishment of a Consulate General of the USSR in the Western Sectors of Berlin. It will be accredited to the appropriate authorities of the three Governments, for purposes and subject to provisions described in their communications and as set forth in a separate document of this date."

Four Power Berlin Agreement, Berlin, 1971.

BERLIN AIRLIFT, 1948–49. The US and British Air Force airlift of food and other supplies between the American and British occupation zone of Germany and West Berlin, during the ▷ Berlin Crisis, called also Berlin Blockade.

BERLIN ALLIED KOMENDANTURA, COMMANDANCE ALLIÉE DE BERLIN, MEZHSOYUZHNICHESKAYA KOMYENDANTURA BERLINA, ALLIIERTE KOMMANDANTUR FÜR BERLIN. Inter-allied institution formed July 7, 1945 on the basis of an agreement of the allied powers on the quadripartite administration of the former capital of the Reich (▷ Germany, Declar-

ation on the Defeat). According to the agreement the Komendantura was composed of the four allied military commanders in Berlin (commanders of the city), who successively for 15 days performed the functions of the Commander of Berlin. The Commander governed all sectors of Berlin, except that decisions on the solution of fundamental issues and problems relating to all sectors had to be made unanimously by all four commanders. The orders and instructions of the Commander of Berlin were published in Russian, English, French and German and were submitted to the mayor of Berlin with the obligation to implement them in all sectors of the city. The Allied Komendantura was subordinated to the ▷ Allied Control Council for Germany. The main headquarters of the Komendantura were in the American sector. The first session of the Komendantura was held July 11, 1945 under the chairmanship of the Russian commander. Up to June 16, 1948, when the Komendantura suspended its activities, 97 sessions were held (1945 – 22, 1946 – 35, 1947 – 28, 1948 – 12), at which, despite increasingly stormy debates, nearly 1200 decisions were made unanimously. Most fruitful was the period to October 1946, i.e. up to the elections which resulted in the victory of parties supported by the western powers: SPD – 48.7%, CDU – 22.2% and FDP – 9.3%, while the pro-Soviet SED received 19.8%. Differences in the Komendantura, as in the Allied Control Council for Germany, were a reflection of the crisis within the allied coalition. The direct reason for the suspension of the operations of the Komendantura was the walkout from its session July 16, 1948 by the American military commander in Berlin, Col. F. Howley. On Dec. 21, 1948 the three commanders of the western sectors officially began tripartite sessions of the Komendantura, which resulted in the creation of a separate administration unit with special status called West Berlin and a separate tripartite ▷ Allied Control Authority. The separate international status of West Berlin was confirmed by an understanding between the four powers on this issue Sept., 1971 (▷ Berlin Agreement 1971).

Documents on Germany under Occupation, 1945–1954, London, 1955.

BERLIN BLOCKADE 1948–49 IN THE UN. On Sept. 29, 1948, France, the United Kingdom, and the United States drew the attention of the UN Security Council to the serious situation which had arisen "as the result of the unilateral imposition by the Government of the USSR of restrictions on transport and communications between the Western zones of occupation in Germany and Berlin."

The Security Council considered this question at several meetings beginning Oct. 4, 1948. The USSR questioned the Council's competence, and, after the question was placed on the Council's agenda, the USSR and the Ukrainian SSR announced that they would not take part in the discussion. Between Oct. and May 1949, a number of Council members informally considered ways of solving the problem and later submitted a draft resolution, which was vetoed by the Soviet Union. In addition, the Council President set up a Technical Committee on Currency Problems and Trade in Berlin but it was unable to work out an acceptable solution.

On May 4, 1949, following informal conversations at the UN between the representatives of the four powers, the Secretary-General was requested by France, the United Kingdom, and the United States to notify the Security Council that an agreement had been concluded between them and the USSR, removing as of May 12, 1949 all restrictions imposed by both sides since Mar. 1, 1948, on communications, transport, and trade between Germany and their respective zones of occupation in Germany, and between those zones themselves.

Everyman's United Nations. New York, 1964, pp. 161–162.

BERLIN CONFERENCE. ▷ Potsdam Conference, 1945.

BERLIN CONGRESS AND TREATY, 1878. A treaty between Austria–Hungary, France, Germany, Italy, Turkey, Russia and the UK to settle the Balkan problems. Principal decisions included recognition of Serbia, Montenegro and Romania as independent states; threefold division of Bulgaria; assignment of Bosnia and Hercegovina to Austria–Hungary; and revision of the Greek-Turkish border. It revised the ▷ San Stefano Peace Treaty.

Major Peace Treaties of Modern History, Vol. II, pp. 976–997, New York, 1967.

BERLIN CONGRESS, 1885. An intergovernmental meeting also known as the West African Conference of Berlin, held on the initiative of the King of Belgium, Leopold II, in Berlin in Jan.–Feb. 1885, on the Congo, internationalization of the Congo and Niger rivers and the final partitioning of unoccupied African territories; attended by Great Britain, Austria–Hungary, Belgium, Denmark, France, Spain, Holland, Luxembourg, Germany, Norway, Portugal, Russia, Sweden, Turkey, USA, Italy. The Final Act was signed on Feb. 22, 1885 concerning the development of trade and civilization, granting the colonial powers freedom of trade and navigation in the Congo River catchment area which was recognized as a neutral territory; also adopted as an international norm was the ▷ res nullius status of the African territories. The Congress accepted the abolition of ▷ slavery, prompted by shortage of workforce on the Western Coast of Africa, depopulated by the three-centuries-long export trade of slave labor to North and South America. The Final Act, called the Berlin General Act, was ratified by all European states in 1885 and by the USA in 1886.

Reichsgesetzblatt 1885, Teil II (with translations), C.A. COLLIARD, *Droit international et histoire diplomatique*, Paris, 1950; *Major Peace Treaties of Modern History*, New York, 1967, Vol. II, pp. 1081–1099.

BERLIN DECLARATION ON REUNIFICATION OF GERMANY, 1957. A Declaration by the Foreign Minister of the FRG and the British, US and French Ambassadors on Germany, European Security and Disarmament, made in West Berlin on July 29, 1957, read as follows:

"Twelve years have elapsed since the end of the war in Europe. The hopes of the peoples of the world for the establishment of a basis for a just and lasting peace have nevertheless not been fulfilled. One of the basic reasons for the failure to reach a settlement is the continued division of Germany, which is a grave injustice to the German people and the major source of international tension in Europe.

The Governments of France, the United Kingdom, and the United States, which share with the Soviet Union responsibility for the reunification of Germany and the conclusion of a peace treaty, and the Government of the Federal Republic of Germany, as the only Government qualified to speak for the German people as a whole, wish to declare their views on these questions, including the question of European security, and the principles which motivate their policies in this regard:

(1) A European settlement must be based on freedom and justice. Every nation has the right to determine its own way of life in freedom, to determine for itself its political, economic, and social system, and to provide for its security with due regard to the legitimate

interests of other nations. Justice requires that the German people be allowed to re-establish their national unity on the basis of this fundamental right.

(2) The reunification of Germany remains the joint responsibility of the four Powers who in 1945 assumed supreme authority in Germany, a responsibility which was reaffirmed in the Directive issued by the four Heads of Government in Geneva in July 1955. At the same time, the achievement of German reunification requires the active co-operation of the German people as a whole under conditions ensuring the free expression of their will.

(3) The unnatural division of Germany and of its capital, Berlin, is a continuing source of international tension. So long as Germany remains divided there can be no German peace treaty and no assurance of stability in Europe. The reunification of Germany in Freedom is not only an elementary requirement of justice for the German people, but is the only sound basis of a lasting settlement in Europe.

(4) Only a freely elected all-German Government can undertake on behalf of a reunified Germany obligations which will inspire confidence on the part of other countries, and which will be considered just and binding in the future by the people of Germany themselves.

(5) Such a Government can only be established through free elections throughout Germany for an all-German National Assembly.

(6) There should be no discrimination against a reunified Germany. Its freedom and security should not be prejudiced by an imposed status of neutralisation or demilitarisation. Its Government should be free to determine its foreign policy and to decide on its international associations. It should not be deprived of the right recognized in the Charter of the United Nations for all nations to participate in collective measures of self-defence.

(7) Re-establishment of the national unity of Germany in accordance with the freely expressed wishes of the German people would not in itself constitute a threat to Germany's neighbours, nor would it prejudice their security. Nevertheless, so as to meet any preoccupation which other Governments may have in this respect, appropriate arrangements, linked with German reunification, should be made which would take into account the legitimate security interests of all the countries concerned. It was for this reason that, at the Geneva Foreign Ministers' Conference, the Western Powers made proposals for a treaty of assurance on the reunification of Germany.

(8) The Western Powers have never required as a condition of German reunification that a reunified Germany should join the North Atlantic Treaty Organisation. It will be for the people of a reunified Germany themselves to determine, through their freely elected Government, whether they wish to share in the benefits and obligations of the Treaty.

(9) If the all-German Government, in the exercise of its free choice, should elect to join NATO, the Western Powers after consultation with other members of NATO are prepared to offer on a basis of reciprocity, to the Government of the Soviet Union and the Governments of other countries of Eastern Europe which would become parties to a European security arrangement, assurances of a significant and far-reaching character. The Western Powers are also prepared, as part of a mutually acceptable European security arrangement, to give assurance that, in the event of a reunified Germany choosing to join NATO, they would not take military advantage as a result of the withdrawal of Soviet forces.

(10) But the Western Powers could not contemplate that the existence of NATO itself should constitute the subject of negotiations.

(11) The reunification of Germany accompanied by the conclusion of European security arrangements would facilitate the achievement of a comprehensive disarmament agreement. Conversely, if a beginning could be made toward effective measures of partial disarmament, this would contribute to the settlement of outstanding major political problems such as the reunification of Germany. Initial steps in the field of disarmament should lead to a comprehensive disarmament agreement which presupposes prior solution of the problem of German reunification. The Western Powers do not intend to enter into any agreement on disarmament which would prejudice the reunification of Germany.

(12) Any measures of disarmament applicable to Europe must have the consent of the European nations concerned, and take into account the link between European security and German reunification. The four Governments continue to hope that the Soviet Government will come to recognize that it is not in its own interest to maintain the present division of Germany. The Western Powers are ready to discuss all these questions with the Soviet Union at any time that there is a reasonable prospect of making progress. At such time, there will be many points relating to the procedure for German reunification and the terms of a treaty of assurance which will be worked out by detailed negotiation.

In advance of serious negotiations, the Western Powers, cannot finally determine their attitude on all points, Nor can they contemplate in advance the making of concessions to which there is no present likelihood of response from the Soviet side. If negotiations are to be fruitful, both sides must approach them in a spirit of accommodation and flexibility. Through this declaration the Western Powers, in full accord with the Federal Republic, wish again to manifest their sincere desire to enter into negotiations with the Soviet Union in order to reach a European settlement, and to give evidence that the paramount objective of their policy is the attainment of a just and lasting peace."

Selected Documents on Germany and the Question of Berlin 1944–1961, HMSO, London, December, 1961, pp. 276–278.

BERLIN DECREE OF NAPOLEON, 1806. A decree issued Nov. 21, 1806 in Berlin by Napoleon I announcing that the British Isles were under blockade and calling for a "defence against English commerce." In art. 11 he defined the conditions of the blockade.

MARTENS, *Nouveau Recueil Général*, Vol. I, p. 439.

BERLIN GENERAL ACT. ▷ Berlin Congress, 1885.

BERLIN LONDON DECLARATION, 1977. A Joint Declaration of the Heads of State and Government of the US, France, the UK and the FRG on Berlin, at London, on May 9, 1977. The text is as follows:

"The four heads of state and of government of France, the United States, the United Kingdom and the FRG have reviewed questions relating to the situation in Germany and particularly Berlin.

The four governments expressed their satisfaction at the positive effect which the Quadripartite Agreement of 3 September 1971 has had on the situation in and around Berlin. They agreed that the strict observance and full implementation of the Agreement, which are indispensable to the continued improvement of the situation, are essential to the strengthening of détente, the maintenance of security and the development of co-operation throughout Europe. The governments of France, the United States and the United Kingdom noted that *détente* would be seriously threatened if any one of the four signatory powers to the Quadripartite Agreement were not to respect fully the undertakings confirmed by the signatory powers in the Agreement and in the Quadripartite Declaration of November 1972. The three Powers recalled that the Quadripartite Agreement was based explicitly on the fact that quadripartite rights and responsibilities and the corresponding wartime and post-war four Power agreements and decisions were not affected. They reaffirmed that this status of the special area of Berlin could not be modified unilaterally. The three Powers will continue to reject all attempts to put in question the rights and responsibilities which France, the United States, the United Kingdom and the Soviet Union retain relating to Germany as a whole and to all four sectors of Berlin. The four governments recalled that one of the essential elements in the Quadripartite Agreement is the affirmation that the ties between the Western Sectors of Berlin and the FRG should be maintained and developed in accordance with the relevant provisions of the Agreement. This conforms with the interests and wishes of the people directly concerned. In this regard, the three Powers took special note of efforts by the Federal

B

Republic of Germany, taking into account the provisions of the Quadripartite Agreement relevant to its responsibilities for representing the interests of the Western Sectors of Berlin to profit from the practical benefits of East–West relations.

The four governments pledged their cooperation in maintaining a political situation conducive to the vitality and prosperity of the Western Sectors of Berlin. The three Powers expressed their appreciation of the efforts of the Federal Republic of Germany and the Senate of Berlin to ensure that the Western Sectors remain an attractive place in which to invest and to work. They reaffirmed their commitment to the city's security, which is an indispensable prerequisite for its economic and social development."

Presidential Documents, No. 20, May 16, 1977.

BERLIN WALL. ▷ Berlin.

BERLIN–ROME AXIS. ▷ Rome–Berlin–Tokyo Axis.

BERMUDA. A group of over 300 islands in the Atlantic Ocean. Area 53.8 sq. km. 1985 pop. 57,145; capital: Hamilton 1985 pop. ca. 3000. GNP per capita 1986 US $1800. Currency: one Bermuda dollar = 100 cents.
International relations: a non-autonomous territory 1684–1968; from June 8, 1968 a special statute of a British colony with representative government. The population elect a parliament which selects an Executive Council that performs certain functions along with the governor. The UN Committee on Decolonization regarded the changes in the colonial statute of Bermuda as unsatisfactory and insisted on granting complete independence to the population of Bermuda. Member UPU, ITU, and WHO. Under a 99-year lease, operates a US naval and air force base. The racial riots in the 1970s were quelled by British troops in Dec. 1978.

W.E.S. ZUILL, *Bermuda Today*, New York, 1958; H.T. DVER, *The Next 20 Years, Report on the Development Plans for Bermuda*, Hamilton, 1963; H.C. WILKINSON, *Bermuda from Sail to Steam*, London, 1973; *Everyone's United Nations*, New York, 1979; S.J. HAYWARD, V. HOLT GOMEZ, W. STERRER, *Bermuda's Delicate Balance: People and the Environment*, Hamilton, 1981; *The Europa Year Book 1984. A World Survey*, Vol. I, pp. 1235–1238, London, 1984; J. PAXTON (ed.), *The Statesman's Year-Book, 1987–88*, London, 1987.

BERMUDA TELECOMMUNICATIONS AGREEMENT, 1945. A convention signed by Australia, Canada, India, New Zealand, Southern Rhodesia, Union of South Africa, the UK and the USA in Bermuda on Dec. 4, 1945.

UNTS, Vol. 9, pp. 101–119.

BERNE. The capital (1986 pop. 138,574) since 1848 of Switzerland. The seat of the Universal Postal Union ▷ UPU and twenty other international organizations reg. with UIA.

W. JUKER, *Berne: the Portrait of a Town*, Berne, 1953. *The Europa Yearbook 1987. A World Survey*, London, 1987.

BERNE CONVENTION, 1886. An International Convention on the Protection of Literacy and Artistic Works, signed in Berne on 9 Sept. 1886, and subsequently revised: Paris, 1896; Berlin, 1908; Berne, 1914; Rome, 1928; Rome, 1941; Brussels, 1948; Stockholm, 1967. The contracting states form a union for the protection of the rights of authors over literary and artistic works, defined by art. 2 as:

"any production in the literary, scientific or artistic domain, whatever may be the mode or form of its reproduction, such as books, pamphlets, and other writings; dramatic or dramatico-musical works, choreographic works and entertainments in dumb show, the acting form of which is fixed in writing or otherwise; musical compositions with or without words; works of drawing, painting, architecture, sculpture, engraving and lithography; illustrations, geographical charts, plans, sketches and plastic works relative to geography, topography, architecture or science. Translations, adaptations, arrangements of music and other reproductions in an altered form of a literary or artistic work, as well as collections of different works, shall be protected as original works without prejudice to the rights of the author of original works."

▷ Copyright.

British and Foreign State Papers, Vol. 77, p. 22, and Vol. 88, p. 36; *LNTS*, Vol. 1, p. 217 and 243; Vol. 123, p. 233; *UNTS*, Vol. 331, p. 217 and 828, p. 9 and p. 221; S. RICKETSON, *The Berne Convention of the Protection of Literary and Artistic Works, 1886–1986*, London, 1988.

BERNE CSCE MEETING ON HUMAN CONTACTS, 1985. A ▷ CSCE forum of experts on human contacts took place on April 15–May 27 in Berne and ended without any agreement.

KEESING's *Contemporary Archive*, 1986.

BERNE UNION. ▷ WIPO.

BESSARABIA. A region in southeastern Europe, divided between the Moldavian SSR and the Ukrainian SSR; subject of international disputes in the 17th century between Poland and Turkey, and between Russia and Turkey in the 18th century. From 1812 to 1917 Bessarabia was a province of Russia. Incorporated by Romania in Apr. 1918, acknowledged by the Chief Allied and Associated Powers, France, Japan, Italy and Great Britain on Oct. 30, 1920. The USA made its opinion subject to consultation with Russian FSSR, Russia notified the chief powers on Nov. 1, 1920 that it cannot acknowledge the agreement concerning Bessarabia, concluded without participation of the RFSSR, to have any legal force. Bessarabia was returned to the Soviet Union on June 28, 1940 after a USSR–Romanian agreement, which was confirmed in the Peace Treaty with Romania on Feb. 10, 1947. Under the USSR–Romanian agreement of Aug. 2, 1940, the western part of Bessarabia was incorporated into the Moldavian SSR while its northeastern part was incorporated by the Ukrainian SSR.

Istorija Ukrainskoji SSR, Kiev, 1953; *Romania–Soviet Union (Bessarabia)*, in: A.J. DAY (ed.), *Border and Territorial Disputes*, London, 1987.

BHUTAN. Member of the UN. Kingdom in the eastern Himalayas. Bhutan is bordered by India, China (Tibet) and Sikkim. Area: 47,600 sq. km. Pop.: 1988 est. 1,400,000 (1963 census 931,514). Capital: Thimphu with 8,992 inhabitants, 1977. GNP per capita 1987 US $160. Currency: one ngultrum = 100 chetrum. Official language: Dzongkha. National Day: installation of the first hereditary King of Bhutan on Dec. 17, 1907.
On Sept. 21, 1971 Bhutan was admitted to the UN after having applied for membership since 1965; member of all specialized UN agencies, save IFC, WMO, IMO and WIPO; since 1962 member of the Colombo Plan, and since 1972 the UN Economic and Social Commission for Asia and the Pacific, ESCAP.
International relations: Bhutan become a monarchy in 1774 under British protectorate, confirmed by agreements of Nov. 1865 and Jan. 1910; since Aug. 8, 1949 it has been linked with India by Friendship Treaty, signed in New Delhi, allowing India to represent Bhutan abroad. According to art. 2 of the Friendship Treaty: "The government of India will not interfere in internal administrative affairs of Bhutan. The government of Bhutan, on its part, agrees to consult the government of India as regards its foreign relations." Bhutan maintains only two permanent diplomatic missions: in Calcutta, to the government of India, and in New York to the UN. Bhutan granted asylum to about 4000 Tibetan refugees under the condition of acceptance by them of Bhutanese citizenship.

P.P. KARAN, W.M. JENKINS, *The Himalayan Kingdoms*, Princeton, 1963; P.P. KARAN, *Bhutan, A Physical and Cultural Geography*, Lexington, 1967; V.H. COELHO, *Sikkim and Bhutan*, New Delhi, 1970; *Facts about Bhutan*, Kalimpong, 1974; L.E. ROSE: *The Politics of Bhutan*, Cornell, 1977; N. RUSTOUYI, *Bhutan. The Dragon Kingdom in Crisis*, Oxford, 1978; *The Europa Year Book 1984. A World Survey*, Vol. I, pp. 1178–1183, London, 1984.

BIAFRA. Region in south-eastern Nigeria. Area about 75,000 sq. km. Civil war territory 1967–70, stemming from separatist movements of the Ibo tribe, discriminated against by the government, which was exploited by the foreign oil concerns (Nigerian Gulf Oil, Mobil Oil, Royal Dutch, Shell, SAFRAP). These latter supported the proclamation on May 30, 1967, of the "Independent and Sovereign Republic of Biafra, faithful to the Commonwealth", by the governor of the Eastern Region of Nigeria, Lt. Col. Odumegwu Ojukwu. At first, the capital was at Enugu (till Oct. 30, 1967), then in Umuahia (till Apr. 22, 1969), and in the final phase of war, in Oweria.
A few days after the escape from Biafra of the government chief, O. Ojukwu, on Jan. 12, 1970, the commander of the Biafran forces signed in Lagos the act of surrender to Col. Gowon's government of central Nigeria. During the conflict the Nigerian government in the UN General Assembly accused Portugal, Rhodesia and the Republic of South Africa of active help rendered from their territories to secessionists. Officially, only two states acknowledged Biafra as an Independent and Sovereign Republic – Tanzania on Apr. 13, 1968 and Gabon on May 8, 1968.

KEESING's *Contemporary Archive*, 1967–70; D. JACOBS, *The Brutality of Nations*, New York, 1987.

BIALOVIEZA. One of the largest European forest and animal preserves, 1165 sq. km, property of the kings of Poland, occupied by Prussia 1795, by Russia 1807, restored to Poland 1921, divided between Poland and Byelorussian SSR, 1945.
The Bialovieza National Park, situated on the watershed dividing the catchment area of the Baltic Sea from that of the Black Sea, with extremely ancient forest (contains 56 species of mammals including bison and wild horses and 200 species of birds) is included in the ▷ World Heritage UNESCO List.

O. HEDOMAN, *Dzieje Puszczy Bialowieskiej w Polsce przedrozbiorowej*, Kraków, 1939; J.I. KAPINSKI, *Puszcza Bialowieska*, Warszawa, 1953;

BIBLE. A subject of international research and promotion. Organizations reg. with the UIA:

International Association of Biblists and Orientalists, f. 1967, Ravenna, Italy. Publ. *Biblia Revuo in Esperanto*.
International Bible Reading Association, f. 1882, London.
International Bible Students Association, f. 1914, London.
International Organization for the Study of the Old Testament, f. 1950, Cambridge, UK.
Pontifical Biblical Commission, f. 1902, Rome, Italy.
Pontifical Biblical Institute, f. 1909, Rome, Italy. Publ. *Biblica, Orientalia, Acta PIB*.
Society for the Study of the New Testament, f. 1938, Old Aberdeen, UK.

United Bible Societies, f. 1946, Haywards Heath, UK, Consultative status: UNESCO. Publ. *World Report* (monthly) and *The Bible Translator* (quarterly).
World Catholic Federation for the Biblical Apostolate, f. 1969, Rome.
Watch Tower Bible and Tract Society, f. 1872, New York. Publ. *Jehovah's Witnesses* and *The Watchtower*.
Organized Bible Schools, private gratuitous schools and classes.
Yearbook of International Organizations, 1986–87.

BIBLICISTS. One of the Protestant Christian religious groups who believe that independent study of the Bible will lead to discovery of the principles of Christian faith; formed in the 19th century in the USA; has adherents in the majority of the states of Europe and America. Its first international organization was est. 1872 by the ▷ Jehovah's Witnesses.

BIBLIOGRAPHIC UN INFORMATION SYSTEM. ▷ UNBIS.

BIBLIOGRAPHY. A subject of international co-operation. Organizations reg. with the UIA:
Inter-American Bibliographical and Library Association, f. 1930, Washington. Publ. *Doors to Latin America* (quarterly).
International Office for Universal Bibliographic Control, f. 1973, London, UK. Publ. *International Standard Bibliographical Descriptions*.
International Society for Classical Bibliography, f. 1923, Paris. Publ. *L'Année Philologique*.
UNISIST International Centre for Bibliographic Descriptions, UNIBID, f. 1976, Paris, France. Publ. *Reference Manual for Machine Readable Bibliographic Descriptions*.
F. BOWERS, *Principles of Bibliographical Description*, London, 1949; *Yearbook of International Organizations*, 1986–87.

BIBLIOPHILES. International term for book collectors. The international organization reg. with the UIA:
International Association of Bibliophiles, Association Internationale de bibliophilie, AIB, f. 1963, Paris. Publ. together with Syndicat national de la librairie ancienne et moderne, a quarterly Bulletin du Bibliophilie (First edition in 1834). The bulletins of major national associations in international co-operation:
Almanask Bibliofila, Moscow, since 1974.
La Bibliofilia. Rivista di Storia del libro e di Bibliografia, Rome, since 1899.
Biblis, Føreningen før bokhantwersk, arsbok, Stockholm.
Biblos. Österreichische Zeitschrift für Buch-und Bibliotheks-wesen, Dokumentation, Bibliographie und Bibliophilie, Vienna, since 1952.
Bibliofil, Warsaw, since 1987.
Marginalien, Zeitschrift für Buchkunst und Bibliophilie, Berlin DDR, since 1954.
Philobiblon. Eine Vieseteljahr-schrift für Buch-und Graphik-sammler, Hamburg, since 1957.
Bibliofil, Warsaw, Poland, Autumn 1987.

BIBLIOTHECONOMY. An international term introduced by UNESCO for a library science disseminated by UNESCO along with the knowledge of documentation, called the science of documentation and the scientific keeping of archives. In May 1972 an international meeting took place at UNESCO headquarters, Paris, devoted to bibliotheconomy.
UNESCO Courier, 1972.

BICYCLE. A subject of international co-operation. Organizations reg. with UIA:
European Fellowship of the Wholesale Bicycle Trade, f. 1976, Ratinger, FRG.
International Bicycle Touring Society, f. 1964, La Jolla, Calif., USA.

International Esperantist Cyclist Movement, f. 1980, Leverwijk, Netherlands. Publ. *BEMI-Revus*.
Joint Committee of Bicycle Manufacturers, f. 1978, Coventry, UK.
Yearbook of International Organizations, 1986–87.

BIDONVILLE. ▷ Slums.

BIENNALE. *Italian*: "two-yearly". An international term introduced in 1895 in Venice for exhibitions of contemporary painting every two years, which were first exclusively Italian and then, after World War II, international. The biennial international presentation of various forms of art has been universally accepted, e.g. in Poland an International Biennale Poster Exhibition is held in Warsaw and an International Biennale Graphic Exhibition in Cracow, in June of each odd-numbered year.

"BIG BANG". An international term in anglo-american journalism for the collapse of the dollar on the New York, London and Tokyo Stock exchanges on October 27, 1987.
KEESING's *Record of World Events*, February, 1988.

BIG BROTHER. An international term for the role of the Soviet superpower in relations with other communist ruled countries.
H. CARRERE D'ENCAUSE, *Big Brother: The Soviet Union and Soviet Europe*, New York, 1987.

BIG FIVE. An international term, adopted after World War I at the Conference at Versailles, 1919, for the Allied powers: France, Japan, the USA, Great Britain and Italy; after World War II used in relation to five great powers having special status in the UN Security Council: China, France, the USA, Great Britain and the USSR.

BIG FOUR. An international term, adopted after World War II to denote powers occupying German territory: France, the UK, the USA, and the USSR.

BIG POWERS OR GREAT POWERS IN THE UN. In the UN Charter arts. 23 and 27 determined the special status to be enjoyed by five allied powers during World War II: China, France, the UK, the USA, and the USSR. They were granted permanent seats in the Security Council and the right to make resolutions in the Security Council, conditional upon their unanimity in all matters apart from those of procedure. This indicates the obligation of unanimity between the Big Powers on all questions vital for the maintenance of peace and security. Decisions restricted to the exclusive competence of the Security Council were taken over by the UN General Assembly under UN General Assembly Res. 377/V 1950 called Uniting for Peace. Influence of the USA in the General Assembly diminished during 1955–60 in the face of the growing power of the Third World states. The differences that arose in the 1960s between France and the USA changed the structure of the Western Powers bloc; similarly the return of the Chinese People's Republic to its seat in the Security Council in 1972 introduced a new element of permanent representation of all Big Powers in the UN. The General Assembly twice appealed to the Big Powers for unanimity: Nov. 3, 1948 during the Berlin crisis and Nov. 6, 1962 on the question of halting nuclear tests. Until 1985 no summit meeting of the Great Powers took place in the UN headquarters.
A. GARCIA ROBLES, *La Conferencia de San Francisco y su Obra*, Mexico, DF, 1946; H. KRAMER, *Grossmächte und die Weltpolitik 1789 bis 1945*, München, 1952; J.G. STOESSINGER, *The UN and the Superpowers: United States–Soviet Union Interaction in the UN*, New York, 1965.

BIG POWERS SUPREME COUNCIL. Conseil Suprême des Hautes Puissances, the highest organ of the Versailles Conference, composed of the Heads of State of France, Great Britain, Italy, Japan and the USA, which was also supposed to meet after the Conference to make important decisions of the Allied and Associated Powers; its functions were de facto taken over by ▷ Conference of Ambassadors.

BIG STICK DIPLOMACY. An international term, derived from the US President Theodore Roosevelt's (1858–1919), phrase in a speech made in New York, 1912:
"Speak softly and carry a big stick, you will go far."
K. BEALE, *Theodore Roosevelt and the Rise of America to World Power*, New York, 1956.

BIKINI. An atoll (*c.* 5.2 sq. km) in the Pacific Ocean. One of the Ralik Chain in the ▷ Marshall Islands, it comprises 36 islets on a reef 20.2 km long. On June 30, 1946 an experimental drop, called operation Crossroad, of an atomic bomb from a US Air Force Plane "Dave's Dream" was made on Japanese, German, and US anchored ships earmarked for destruction, as well as other inanimate and living objects, animals and plants.
On July 25, 1946 the first underwater atomic explosion took place in one of the lagoons of the atoll. Subsequent drops of 23 US atomic and hydrogen bombs took place between 1954 and 1958. Several islands in the atoll were vaporized out of existence. The population of Bikini was evacuated in the spring of 1946 to the island of Rongerik, 130 miles from Bikini, and then to Kili Island 500 miles southeast of Bikini. In 1970, scientists judged the main island of Bikini to be sufficiently free of lingering radiation for human habitation, and 140 Bikinians went back to homes built for them by the government.
But in 1978, after new radiological surveys of the island, the scientists decided that they had been wrong. Bikini was evacuated again.
Bikini was taken from Japan by US forces in World War II and came under US administration in 1945 as part of the Trust Territory of the Pacific Islands, otherwise known as Micronesia, a UN trusteeship. In March 1985 the USA pledged to meet the cost of $50 million of replacing radioactive topsoil and food crops to render Bikini atoll safe for habitation.
J.M. WEISGALL, "The Nuclear Nomads of Bikini Atoll", in: *Foreign Policy*, No. 39, 1980, pp. 74–98; KEESING's *Record of World Events*, 1986, No. 2; J.B. BLAIR, Bikini, in: *National Geographic*, June 1986.

BILATERAL AGREEMENTS. An international term for the oldest form of international written agreements concluded between two countries; known already in antiquity. Up to the 19th century they were, primarily, peace and trade treaties; since the Vienna Congress of 1815 they cover ever more fields of co-operation. In the second half of the 20th century they acquire more frequently the character not only of "country–country" agreements, but of "country–international organization", particularly as regards technical assistance. Simultaneously, a certain limitation has occurred in their number through multilateral treaties, connected with integration processes. The supporters of multilateralism against bilateralism in the UN system became specialized financial UN agencies such as IBRD and IMF.
J. BASDEVANT, "La conclusion et la rédaction des traités et des documents diplomatiques autres que les traités" in: *Recueil des Cours de l'Académie de Droit International*, 1926.

B

BILDERBERG GROUP CONFERENCES. Annual conference, reg. with the UIA, est. in 1954 at the invitation of Prince Bernhard of the Netherlands at the Hotel de Bilderberg in Oosterbeck, Netherlands. The political, economic and military problems of Europe are discussed by statesmen, scholars, businessmen and labor leaders from the NATO countries.

R. ERINGER, *The Global Manipulations*, Bristol, 1980; *The Economist*, December 28, 1987.

BILHARZIASIS. An intestinal parasitic tropical disease, called "snail fever" under WHO control, especially at the chemotherapy center in Tanga, Tanganyika.

BILINGUAL EDUCATION ACT, 1985. New regulation in the USA for bilingual education of minority groups in local schools; applying in 80% to Hispanics, announced in Washington DC on Sept. 26, 1985.

KEESING's *Contemporary Archive*, 1986.

BILLIARDS. A subject of international co-operation. Organizations reg. with the UIA:

African and Near East Billiards Confederation, f. 1972, Khartoum.
Asian Billiards Confederation, f. 1973, Osaka.
European Billiards Confederation, f. 1958, Brussels. Publ. *Le Billard*.
North American Billiards Confederation, f. 1972, San Jose, Calif.
South American Billiards Confederation, f. 1959, La Plata.
World Billiards Union, f. 1959, Barcelona.

Yearbook of International Organizations.

BILLS OF EXCHANGE. A subject of Conventions and similar instruments relating to international payments.
The rules of bills of exchange law were first formulated in Italy in the 9th century; in the 18th and 19th centuries similar bills of exchange laws existed in all countries. The codification of the laws began with the Treaty on International Commercial Law, signed at Montevideo, Feb. 12, 1889, ratified by Argentina, Bolivia, Colombia, Paraguay, Peru and Uruguay; arts. 26–34 contain the Laws on bills of exchange.
A convention on the Unification of the Law relating to Bills of Exchange and Promissory Notes and Uniform Regulation, was prepared by The Hague Conference, July 23, 1912, but did not enter into force. During the Second Hague Conference on July 23, 1912, a Treaty on the unification of bills of exchange law was signed by 17 European and 10 American states, replacing Napoleon's Code of Commerce which had been in use since 1807. Although the Treaty was not ratified by any state, its provisions entered a number of national legislations. After World War I the codification work was taken up by the Cuban internationalist A.S. Bustamente (arts. 263–273 on Contracts and Bill of Exchange of the ▷ Bustamente Code); and by the International Chamber of Commerce under the patronage of the League of Nations, which organized congresses in Rome in 1923, Brussels in 1925, Stockholm in 1927 and Geneva in 1930, where a Convention on Uniform Law for Bills of Exchange and Promissory Notes was elaborated, signed in Geneva on June 7, 1930, entering into force on Jan. 1, 1934. The main principle of the Convention was that the law of the country where a drawn or own bill of exchange is paid is decisive in controversial cases. The Convention was ratified by Austria, Belgium, Brazil, Denmark, Finland, France, Germany, Greece, Hungary, Italy, Japan, Luxembourg, Monaco, Netherlands, Norway,

Poland, Portugal, Sweden, Switzerland and the USSR; without ratification signed by Colombia, Czechoslovakia, Ecuador, Peru, Spain, Turkey and Yugoslavia.
Convention for the Settlement of Certain Conflicts of Laws in Connection with Bills of Exchange and Promissory Notes, was signed at Geneva, June 7, 1930; entered into force Jan. 1, 1934, ratified and signed as above.
Convention of the Stamp Laws in Connection with Bills of Exchange and Promissory Notes, was signed at Geneva, June 7, 1930 and entered into force on Jan. 1, 1934. It was ratified by Australia, Austria, Belgium, Brazil, Cyprus, Denmark, Finland, France, Germany, Hungary, Ireland, Italy, Japan, Luxembourg, Malaysia, Malta, Monaco, Netherlands, Norway, Poland, Portugal, Sweden, Switzerland, Uganda, the UK, and the USSR; not ratified but signed by Colombia, Czechoslovakia, Ecuador, Peru, Spain, Turkey, Yugoslavia.
The Treaty on International Commercial Terrestrial Law was signed at Montevideo, Mar. 19, 1940, includes (arts. 23–39) rules on Bills of Exchange.
The Inter-American Convention on Conflict of Laws Concerning Bills of Exchange, Promissory Notes and Invoices was signed in Panama, Jan. 30, 1975 by Brazil, Colombia, Costa Rica, Chile, Ecuador, El Salvador, Guatemala, Honduras, Nicaragua, Panama, Peru, Uruguay and Venezuela.
The Institute for Latin American Integration of the Inter-American Development Bank prepared in 1968 a Draft Uniform Law for Latin America on Commercial Documents, setting forth rules with respect to bills of exchange, promissory notes, checks, exchange invoices.
The Anglo-Saxon states did not participate, preserving their own legislation on these matters under the British Bills of Exchange and American Negotiable Instruments Law (amended in some US states since 1957 under the name: Uniform Commercial Code).
The Congress of International Private Law in Rome initiated in July 1950 work on the codification of English and American provisions with the uniform European ones.
The UN Commission on International Trade Law, UNCITRAL, adopted on Aug. 14, 1987, in Vienna a draft Convention on International Bills of Exchange and International Promissory Notes and a Legal Guide on Drawing up International Contracts for Construction of Industrial Works. The 91-article draft Convention established world wide legal rules for new bills of exchange and promissory notes which trading parties and banks could use in their credit or financing transactions.

LNTS, Vol. 143, p. 259, p. 319 and 339; *American Journal of International Law*, Vol. 37, 1943; M. MEGRAH, F.R. RYDER, *Bills of Exchange*, London, 1972; *OAS Treaty Series* No. 40, Washington, DC, 1975; *Publication of the OAS*, Ser. G. V, c-d-1589; *UN Chronicle*, November 1987.

BILLS OF LADING. The main document in sea trade, issued by the carrier or his representative as proof of the acceptance of a cargo for the purpose of loading it on ship or as proof of loading completed (bill of lading received or bill of lading shipped), secured by regulations in case of accident, resale, etc. A subject of international convention whose drafting was initiated by a Conference on bills of lading in Copenhagen 1913. The work was continued by the International Sea Committee which produced the Convention on the Unification of Certain Rules of Law Relating the Bills of Lading signed on Aug. 25, 1924, in Brussels. A Protocol to

amend the Brussels Convention 1924 was signed in Brussels on Feb. 23, 1968. The definition of bills of lading was passed by the XIII Congress of the International Chamber of Commerce in Lisbon 1953, in the introduction to the ▷ Incoterms:

"... The term 'bill of lading' is a shipped bill of lading, issued by or on behalf of the carrier, and is evidence of a contract of carriage as well as proof of delivery of the goods on board the vessel; a bill of lading may be either freight prepaid or freight payable at destination. In the former case the document is usually not obtainable until freight has been paid."

Register of Texts of Conventions and other Instruments concerning International Trade Law, Vol. I, UN, New York, 1973; M.M. BOYD, *Scrutton on Charter-parties and Bills of Lading*, London, 1974; J. WALENSLEY, *A Dictionary of International Finance*, London, 1979.

BILLS OF LADING CONVENTIONS, 1924–68. ▷ Maritime law conventions.

BIMETALISM. An international term for a monetary system in which two metals, silver and gold, are simultaneously the basis for establishing monetary parity; this system required the fixing of an exchange relationship between the two metals and recognizing it as constant; recognized by ▷ Latin Monetary Union, and generally accepted throughout the world up to World War I. During the second half of the 20th century there was a departure from bimetalism in connection with a significant fall in the price of silver and the acceptance of gold parity for most currencies; the relation of the value of gold to silver was 1 : 15 or 1 : 16. The German Reich in 1871 was the first to liquidate bimetalism by changing to the gold standard; all the West European states followed and introduced a prohibition against the unlimited minting of silver coins, except France which, after being flooded by these coins, was compelled in 1876 to devalue the silver 5 franc coin, (however, they retained their value in Latin America and Indo China); ▷ gold and ▷ silver.

F.A. WALKER, *International Bimetalism*, London, 1896; J.L. LAUGHLIN, *History of Bimetalism in the United States*, New York, 1897; H.P. WILLIS, *A History of the Latin Monetary Union*, New York, 1901.

BINARY CHEMICAL WEAPONS. An international military term for a shell or other device with two chemicals of relatively low toxicity which mix and react while the device is being delivered to the target, the reaction product being a supertoxic chemical warfare agent, such as nerve gas.

J. GOLDBLAT, *Arms Control Agreements. A Handbook*, New York, 1983, p. 311; R. LEGER SILVARD, *World Military and Social Expenditures, 1987–88*, Washington DC, 1987.

BIOCHEMISTRY. A subject of international co-operation. Organizations reg. with the UIA:

Andean Federation for Pharmacy and Biochemistry, f. 1975, Lima, Peru.
Asian and Pacific Federation of Clinical Biochemistry, f. 1982, Surabaya, Indonesia.
Biochemistry Commission of International Union of Biological Sciences, f. 1919, Paris.
Bioelectrochemical Society, f. 1960, Rome, Italy, Publ. *Bioelectrochemistry and Bioenergetics*.
European Society of Comparative Physiology and Biochemistry, f. 1978, Liège, Belgium. Publ. *Newsletter*.
Federation of European Biochemical Societies, f. 1964, Utrecht, Netherlands.
International Society for Biochemical Pharmacology, f. 1963, Rome.
International Union of Biochemistry, f. 1955, Miami.
Pan American Association of Biochemical Societies, f. 1969, Richmond VA, USA.
Panamerican Federation of Pharmacy and Biochemistry, f. 1976, San Juan, Puerto Rico.

World Association of Veterinary Physiologists, Pharmacologists and Biochemists, f. 1973, Charbonmeres-les-Bains, France.

Yearbook of International Organizations, 1986–87.

BIOENERGETICS. A subject of international co-operation. Organizations registered with the UIA:

International Federation of Hand Therapists, Philadelphia, PA., USA.
International Institute for Bioenergetic Analysis, f. 1956, New York, USA.
Joint Bioenergetics Group, f. 1976, Nashville, Tenn., USA.

Yearbook of International Organizations, 1986–87.

BIOGRAPHY, INTERNATIONAL. The collections of biographies of outstanding personalities of various nationalities, a subject of international co-operation.

The first dictionary of this kind was published in London in 1849 by Black's the publishing house, entitled *Who's Who: An Annual Biographical Dictionary*, with which is incorporated *Men and Women of the Time*. In the 19th century, international and national biographical dictionaries gained wide popularity, their estimated number running to 2500–3000 titles in various languages. Aside from Black, other leading publications in the Anglophone world include: *The International Who's Who*, publ. London, Europa Publications, annually, since 1935; *The International Yearbook and Statesmen's Who's Who*, publ. London, *Burke's Peerage*, since 1953; and *World Biography*, publ. New York Institute for Research in Biography, since 1940.

The editors of these dictionaries arrange the proportion of names listed according to occupations for individual countries; sent annually to these persons and authorized by them, the texts are printed as biographical data. There are many regional biographical dictionaries such as *Who's Who in Latin-America*, publ. Stanford (USA) in three editions: 1935, 1946, 1947; *The Asia Who's Who*, publ. Hongkong, 1957. National dictionaries are the most numerous, e.g., *Who's Who in America: A Biographical Dictionary of Notable Living Men and Women*, publ. Chicago, since 1899 with a supplement *Who Was Who in America*. Others are primarily of historical significance, e.g., *Biographical Directory of the American Congress, 1774–1961*. The first *Who's Who in the United Nations* was printed at the end of the *UN Yearbook* 1947–48, pp. 1077–1091. Organization registered with the UIA:

International Biographical Association (IBA), f. 1970, Cambridge, UK. Publ. *IBA Magazine*; *Biographical Directory*.

J.K. ZAWODNY, *Guide to the Study of International Relations*, San Francisco, 1966, *Encyclopedia of World Biography*, 12 Vols., New York, 1973; *Yearbook of International Organizations*, 1986–87.

BIOLOGICAL AGENTS. An international term defined by the World Health Organization 1969 in a report on the health aspects of chemical and biological weapons (▷ BW Convention 1972) as those agents that depend for their effects on multiplication within the target organism, and are intended for use in war to cause disease or death in man, animals or plants.

J. GOLDBLAT, *Arms Control Agreements; A Handbook*, New York, 1983, p. 47.

BIOLOGICAL CONVENTION. ▷ Biological Weapons; ▷ BW Convention.

BIOLOGICAL WEAPONS. An international term, subject of the convention on the Prohibition of the Development, Production and Stockpiling of Bacteriological and Toxic Weapons and their Destruction, called Biological Convention or ▷ BW Convention, entered into force on March 26, 1975. In March 1980 the 103 signatories including Three Great Powers: UK, USA, USSR but not France and China, who are not party to the BW Convention held the first review conference, and the second in Sept. 1986 in Geneva. The third review conference to be held not later than 1991.

KEESING's *Record of World Events*, 1987, No. 5; D. ROBERTSON, *Guide to Modern Defense and Strategy*, Detroit, 1988.

BIOLOGY. A subject of international co-operation. Organizations reg. with the UIA:

Association for the Introduction of New Biological Nomenclature, f. 1971, Kalmthout, Belgium.
Asian Association for Biology Education, f. 1905, Katugostota, Sri Lanka.
Baltic Marine Biologists, f. 1968, Lysekil, Sweden.
Council for Biology in Human Affairs, f. 1970, San Diego, Calif.
Committee for European Marine Biological Symposia, f. 1966, Padora, Italy.
Craniofacial Biology Group, f. 1961, Chicago.
European Association of Editors of Biological Periodicals (European Life Science Editors, ELSE), f. 1967, Amsterdam. Publ. *ELSE Newsletter*.
European Molecular Biology Conference, f. 1969, Geneva.
European Molecular Biology Organization (EMBO), f. 1964, Geneva.
European Society for Radiation Biology, f. 1959, Brussels.
International Association for Biological Oceanography, f. 1968, Copenhagen.
International Association for Medicine and Biology of Environment, f. 1971, Paris.
International Association of Biological Standardization, f. 1955, Ilford, Essex.
International Association of Human Biologists, f. 1967, Porto Alegre.
International Centre for Biological Research, fl. 1952, Geneva.
International Committee for Standardization in Human Biology, f. 1968, Brussels.
International Congress of Systematic and Evolutionary Biology, f. 1973, Baltimore.
International Federation of Cell Biology, f. 1972, Toronto, Canada. Publ. *Cell Biology International Reports*.
International Photobiology Association, f. 1928 (present name since 1976), Epalignes, s/Lausanne, Switzerland.
International Society for Chronobiology, f. 1937, Minneapolis, MN, USA. Publ. *Chronobiologica*.
International Society of Development Biologists, f. 1950, Helsinki.
International Society of Mathematical Biology, f. 1962, Paris.
International Union of Biological Sciences, f. 1919, Paris. Consultative statute: WHO, FAO. Publ. *Newsletters*.
Latin American Association of Societies of Nuclear Biology and Medicine, f. 1961, Santiago de Chile.
Mediterranean Association for Marine Biology and Oceanology, f. 1964, Naples.
Nordic Council for Marine Biology, f. 1956, Bergen.
Special Committee for the International Biological Program, f. 1963, London.
World Federation of Nuclear Medicine and Biology, f. 1974, Tokyo.

G. HAENSCH, G. HABERKAMP DE ANTON, *Dictionary of Biology*. In English, German, French and Spanish, Amsterdam, 1976; *Yearbook of International Organizations*, 1986–87.

BIOMECHANICS. A subject of international co-operation. Organization reg. with the UIA:

European Society of Biomechanics, f. 1976, Nijmegen, Netherlands.

Yearbook of International Organizations, 1986–87.

BIO-MEDICINE. A subject of international co-operation. Organizations reg. with the UIA:

European Underseas Bio-Medical Society, f. 1971, Alverstoke, Hants, UK.
International Federation for Medical and Biological Engineering, f. 1959, Ottawa, Canada. Consultative Status: ECOSOC, WHO, UNIDO. Publ. *Medical and Biological Engineering and Computing*.
International Institute of Bio-medical Engineering, f. 1961, Paris.
International Society for Biological Medicine, Hamburg, FRG.
International Society for Biomedical Research on Alcoholism, f. 1982, Berne, Switzerland.
Nordic Committee for Biomedical Technology, Helsinki, Finland.

Yearbook of International Organizations, 1986–87.

BIOMETEOROLOGY. A subject of international co-operation. Organization reg. with the UIA:

International Society of Biometeorology, f. 1956, Zurich. Consultative status with UNESCO, FAO, WHO, WMO. Publ. *International Journal of Biometeorology*.

Yearbook of International Organizations.

BIOMETRICS. A subject of international co-operation. Organization reg. with the UIA:

Biometric Society, f. 1947, Colorado State University, USA. Consultative status: WHO, ESOSOC. Publ. *Biometrics*.

Yearbook of International Organizations, 1986–87.

BIONICS. An international term introduced in 1960 at an international conference of scientists in Dayton (USA), for work on the borderline of the biological sciences, technology, and mathematics which utilizes the principles of the structure and working of living organisms in the construction of various technical instruments, e.g. the creation of technical and economical information systems or the creation of large hierarchically guided systems.

BIOPHYSICS. A subject of international co-operation. Organizations reg. with the UIA:

CMEA Coordinating Centre for Biophysics, Moscow, USSR.
International Commission of Biophysics of Communication and Control Processes, Tübingen, Germany FR.
International Commission on Education and Development in Biophysics, Staffordshire, UK.
International Commission on Radiation and Environmental Biophysics, Stockholm, Sweden.
International Union for Pure and Applied Biophysics, f. 1961, Cambridge, UK.

Yearbook of International Organizations, 1986–87.

BIOSPHERE. A subject of international co-operation. Organizations reg. with the UIA:

Informatics and Biosphere, f. 1971, Paris.
International Coordinating Council of the Programme on Man and the Biosphere, f. 1974 under the aegis of UNESCO, Paris.

Yearbook of International Organizations.

BIOSPHERE AND MAN. The name of a UNESCO Program, adopted by the 18th Session of the UNESCO General Conference, 1974, with the purpose of developing a basis within the natural and social sciences for the rational use and conservation of the resources of the biosphere and for the improvement of the global relationship between man and the environment. The UNESCO International Coordinating Council of the Program on Man and Biosphere started its work in Paris in 1974–75.

UNESCO Courier, 1975.

B

BIOSTATICS. A subject of international co-operation. Organization reg. with the UIA:

Inter-American centre of Biostatics, f. 1952, Santiago de Chile, Chile.

Yearbook of International Organizations.

BIOTECHNOLOGY. A subject of international co-operation and multinational research by biotechnological companies in the 1970s and 1980s. Organizations reg. with the UIA:

European Federation of Biotechnology, f. 1980, London.
International Organization for Biotechnology and Bioengineering, Cambridge, UK.

The Genetic Alternative. A Survey of Biotechnology, in: *The Economist*, April 30–May 8, 1988; *Yearbook of International Organizations*, 1988.

BIPARTISAN FOREIGN POLICY. An American term for the common foreign policy of the Republican and Democratic parties in the US Congress; a custom observed for almost half a century under Republican and Democratic presidents alike, abandoned since the Vietnam War.

H. KISSINGER, C. VANCE, Bipartisan Objectives for American Foreign Policy, in: *Foreign Affairs*, Summer 1988.

BIPOLARITY. A political theory, according to which the world is absolutely divided into two superpower spheres of influence – the American and the Soviet. The theory came into being after WW II, and is now gradually being abandoned.

D. ROBERTSON, *Guide to Modern Defense and Strategy*, Detroit, 1988.

BIRDS. Subject of an international Convention on the Protection of Birds Useful to Agriculture, signed Mar. 19, 1902, Paris. Organizations reg. with the UIA:

International Bird Rescue Centre, f. 1971, Berkeley, Calif.
International Committee on Avian Anatomical Nomenclature, f. 1957, Omaha NE, USA. Publ. *Nomina Anatomica Avium*.
International Council for Bird Preservation ICBP, est. 1922 at the initiative of IOC, London: joins scholars of 60 countries and biannually arranges the International Bird Preservation Conferences. Runs the International Wildfowl Research Bureau, IWRB. Publ.: *Bulletin of the ICBP* and *Newsletter of IWRB*.
International Ornithological Congress, IOC, f. 1884, Oxford, Great Britain, affiliates institutions of 34 countries.
International Waterfowl Research Bureau, f. 1947, Simbridge, UK. Representatives from FAO, UNESCO, UNEP.
Joint Anti-Locust and Anti-Aviarian Organization, f. 1965, Dakar.
World Veterinary Poultry Association, f. 1959, Huntingdon, UK. Publ. *Avian Pathology*.

Yearbook of International Organizations, 1986–87.

BIRTH CONTROL. ▷ Family planning.

BIRTH RATE. An international term for ▷ vital statistics.

BIS. ▷ Bank for International Settlements.

BISMARCK ARCHIPELAGO. An island group in the south-west Pacific, a part of Papua New Guinea. A German Reich protectorate 1884–1914; mandated by the League of Nations to Australia 1920–41; occupied by Japan 1942–48.
The main islands: Admiralty (now Manus with 1986 pop. 29,900), New Britain (now divided into East New Britain with 1986 pop. (154,200 and West New Britain with 107,700), New Ireland (1986 pop. 77,200). Total area: 58,200 sq km.

BI-ZONE. Official name for economic fusion of the American and English zones of occupied Germany combined May 29, 1947; the next stage in 1948 was the Tri-Zone, integrating the French Zone, changed Sept., 1949 into the Federal Republic of Germany.

"The American–British Agreement on the Economic Fusion of their Zones of Occupation in Germany", in: *US Department of State Bulletin*, No. 389, Dec. 15, 1946.

BJÖRKO TREATY, 1905. An agreement between the Emperor of the Reich, Wilhelm II, and the Tsar of Russia, Nicholas II, signed in Björko in Finland on July 24, 1905, obligating both sides to mutual help in case Germany or Russia were attacked "in Europe" by other European powers.

BLACK FRIDAY. An international term for serious financial crisis and panic on the stock exchange. In the United States Friday, Sept. 24, 1869 and Friday, Sept. 19, 1873, were the days of financial panic on the gold market. The panic on the American and European stock exchanges on Friday, Oct. 25, 1929 was also called "Black Friday" or "krach". On Sept. 11, 1987 the ▷ Dow Jones Industrial Average droped 86.61 points, but there was no panic.

See also ▷ World Economic Crisis, 1929–1939.

BLACK LIST. An international term for: (1) a list of criminal offenders, drug dealers, slave traders and pirates wanted by ▷ Interpol; (2) a list of persons or institutions breaking away from a boycott of another state or group of states, compiled by the boycotting party with the purpose of applying discriminating measures against those listed; e.g., when enforcing the 1961 boycott of Cuba, the US began making out black lists of trading ships and their captains which docked at Cuban ports, at the same time prohibiting admission of these ships into US ports or disembarkation of their captains in the US.

BLACK MARKET. An international term for illegal speculation in goods, precious metals, foreign currency, etc. at prices generally higher than official ones. The only institution which observes, analyzes, and annually publishes data on prices on the black market in most countries of the world is the Pick Publishing Corporation in New York, directed since 1945 by F. Pick. From 1945–67 it published the monthly *Picks World Currency Report*. In 1951, 1953, 1954, and 1955 it published a special yearly, *Black Market Yearbook*. Data on Black Markets are also contained in *Picks Currency Yearbook*, which has appeared each year since 1955.

BLACK POWER OR POWER FOR THE BLACKS. Initially an American term coined in June 1966 in the State of Mississippi during a Negro March (author of the motto Black Power was the leader of Student Non-violent Coordinating Committee, Stokely Carmichael). During the XIX Olympic Games some members of the USA team, who were spokesmen of Black Power, greeted the stadium with a black glove which brought about their expulsion from the Games. In Aug., 1969 the national conference of Black Power followers declared a program for setting up within the USA a "separate, free and independent" New African Republic, to cover five states: Mississippi, Louisiana, Georgia, Alabama and South Carolina, with 615,000 sq. km and 16.1 million pop. (1970).

BLACK RIBBON DAY. An international solidarity movement of Central and East European emigrant communities to commemorate the Nazi–Soviet pact of August 23, 1939 signed by J. Ribbentrop and W. Molotov under which the two totalitarian powers divided Europe between them and which allowed Hitler to start World War II. The solidarity movement fights for peace and freedom; for the self-determination of nations and elimination of military or political domination or influence of any nation by Soviet communism; against the threat to, or violation of fundamental rights and freedoms in various territories by Soviet communism. Among the rights and freedoms threatened or violated are: "freedom of conscience and religion; of thought, belief, opinion and expession; of peaceful assembly; of association. Freedom to move within a country, to emigrate from it or to re-enter it. Right to life, liberty and security; to own private property; to vote in elections for representative govenments".

International Black Ribbon Day Committee, Toronto, Ontario, Canada with offices in Austria, England, France, FRG, the Netherlands and Sweden.

E. GIERAT, *Kalendarz Polonii Swiatowej*, Bethlehem, USA, 1988.

BLACK SEA. An inland sea between Europe and Asia, 413,365 sq. km; 1210 km long, from 120 to 560 km wide; connected by the Bosporus, the Sea of Marmara and the Dardanelles with the Mediterranean Sea; bounded by the USSR, Romania, Bulgaria, and Turkey. Through the Kerch Strait it is connected with the Sea of Azov. A subject of international conventions. ▷ Bosporus.

K. ZEMANEK, 'Schwarzes Meer', in: *Strupp-Schlochauer Wörterbuch des Völkerrechts*, Vol. 3, pp. 222–224, Berlin, 1962.

BLACK SEPTEMBER. A Palestine Liberation group, formed after Sept., 1970, when a significant number of Palestinian partisans were killed in Amman in a conflict with the Jordanian army. The group decided to revenge the death of its soldiers by applying terrorist methods against the government of Jordan as well as in its continuing struggle with Israel. The first action of the Black September organization was the assassination in Cairo of the premier of Jordan, Wasfi-et-Tella on Oct. 2, 1971, and, shortly thereafter, the wounding of the Jordanian ambassador in London. The most notorious action of Black September was the seizure of Israeli hostages in the Olympic village in Munich on Sept. 5, 1972 during the Olympic games, ending with the massacre of the Israelis and most of the Palestinians, caused by the Bavarian police. Three Palestinians, who came out alive, were released from jail on Oct. 29, 1972 and transported to Libya as the result of the hijacking of a Lufthansa plane by other members of Black September. In Mar. 1973 members of Black September assassinated three Western diplomats in the Saudi Arabian Embassy in Khartoum, Sudan. Palestinian liberation organizations have distanced themselves from the terrorist activities of Black September.

C. DOBSON, *Septembre Noir*, Paris, 1975.

BLINDNESS. A subject of the WHO Program for the Prevention of Blindness, concentrated on four diseases: trachoma, onchocersiasis, xerophthalmia and cataract. See also ▷ Cataract. Organizations reg. with the UIA:

International Agency for the Prevention of Blindness, f. 1929, The Hague. Consultative status: UNICEF, WHO, ECOSOC, UNESCO, ILO; Publ. *WCWB Newsletters*.
International Blind Sports Association, f. 1981, Berlin, GDR. Publ. *Blind Sports*.

International Catholic Committee on the Blind, f. 1974, Sancerre, France.

International Committee of Crusade for the Blind, f. 1957, Paris.

International Federation of the Blind, f. 1964, New York. Publ. *Braille International*.

International League of Blind Esperantists, f. 1950, Ancona, Italy.

Royal Commonwealth Society for the Blind, f. 1950, London.

World Blind Union, f. 1984, Paris, France (with offices in Africa, Asia, Europe, Latin and North America, Middle East). Consultative Status: ECOSOC, UNESCO, ILO, WHO, UNICEF, WIPO, CIDA. Publ. *The World Blind*.

World Council for the Welfare of the Blind, f. 1951, Paris.

World of Health, Jan. 1983; *Yearbook of International Organizations*, 1986–87.

BLITZKRIEG. German "lightning war". An international term for a war doctrine implemented by Germany during the initial campaigns of World War II. This doctrine assumed that in ▷ total war there is the need for lightning-like results achieved by massed and unexpected air and armored strikes. The Blitzkrieg conception assured the III Reich successes only during the initial stages of the war, but failed completely under conditions of an equal balance of forces and the absence of the element of surprise (from the battle of Moscow). The theoretical foundations of the doctrine were the ideas advanced by the Italian General Douhet (war is waged by the airforce), the British General Fuller (the backbone of the army is armor supported by the airforce), and the German General Ludendorff (the total waging of war).

E. LUDENDORFF, *Der totale Krieg*, Berlin, 1935; G. FOSTER, *Totaler Krieg und Blitzkrieg*, Berlin, 1967; P. H. VIGOR, *Soviet Blitzkrieg Theory*, London, 1983; D. ROBERTSON, *Guide to Modern Defense and Strategy*, Detroit, 1988.

BLOCH DOCTRINE OF THE WAR OF THE FUTURE, 1893. A thesis "that the future of war is not fighting, but famine, not the slaying of men but the bankruptcy of nations and the break up of whole social organizations." The author was a Polish economist, Jan Gotlib Bloch (1836–1902). His book *Przyszla wojna, jej techniczne, ekonomiczne i polityczne przyczyny i skutki* [The War of the Future in its Technical, Economic and Political Relations], edited in six volumes, in Warsaw 1893–1897, was translated into Russian 1897, French 1898, English 1899, German and Spanish 1900 and was a bestseller of the *fin de siécle* in Europe and the USA. This book made a profound impression on the Tsar of Russia and induced him to convoke the first International Hague Peace Conference in 1899.

International Conciliation, New York, 1916, p. 4.

BLOCKADE. An international term for shutting off access to a certain state or cutting it off from communication with the world for the purpose of compelling it peacefully, or by war, to accept certain imposed conditions, or for the purpose of bringing about the breakdown of the economic system and the collapse of the government. An instrument of ▷ intervention. Peaceful blockade consists of placing warships outside the ports of a second state and patrolling the coasts. A war blockade is usually combined with the mining of territorial waters of a second state and shelling of the coasts. The first international document mentioning blockade is the Declaration Respecting Maritime Law, signed Apr. 16, 1856 by the signatories of the Paris Treaty, which ended the Crimean War, 1853–56. In the Declaration p. 4 established the principle: "In order to be valid a blockade must be effective, that means the disposal of sufficient forces in order to shut off the enemy's access to the coast." The second document is the Declaration concerning the Laws of Naval War, signed Feb. 26, 1909 in London by Austria–Hungary, France, Great Britain, Germany, Holland, Italy, Japan, Russia, Spain and the USA, which in chapter 1 (arts. 1–21) established the principles of "blockade during time of war."

A peaceful sea or land blockade, if it does not result from international sanctions, is an act of aggression contrary to contemporary international law. Also an act of intervention is economic blockade which has the aim of bringing about the economic breakdown of a given state, usually supported by a so-called invisible blockade, consisting of persuading large banks not to grant credits and impeding international financial transactions.

A HOGAN, *Pacific Blockade*, London, 1908; H. FALCKE, *Le blocus pacifique*, Paris, 1919; A.H. WASHBARN, "The Legality of the Pacific Blockade", in: *Columbia Law Review*, No. 21, 1921; E. TARLE, *Le blocus continental et le royaume d'Italie*, Paris, 1928. B. de JOUVENEL, *Napoleon et l'économie dirigée. Le blocus continental*, Paris, 1942; L. GABRIEL ROBINET, *Le blocus à travers l'histoire*, Paris, 1943; S.E.D. ROWSON, "Modern blockades, some legal aspects", in: *The British Yearbook of International Law*, 1946; C.G. FENWICK, "The quarantine against Cuba, legal or illegal?" in: *American Journal of International Law*, July 1963; A.L. KOLODKIN, "Morskaia blokada i sovremennoe pravo", in: *Sovetskoe gosudarstvo i pravo, 1963–64*; D. SCHINDLER, J. TOMAN, *The Law of Armed Conflicts*, Leiden, 1973, pp. 567–570 and 623–627; R.L. BLEDSOE, B.A. BOCZEK, *The International Law Dictionary*, Oxford, 1987; D. ROBERTSON, *Guide to Modern Defense and Strategy*, Detroit, 1988.

BLOEMFONTEIN. Judicial capital of the South African Republic and capital of the Orange Free State. Population, 1985, census: city, 104,381; Metropolitan Area, 232,984.

BLOOD, HUMAN AND ITS DERIVATIVES. The subjects of international co-operation and agreements, defined as therapeutic substances of human origin:

The European Agreement on the Exchange of Therapeutic Substances of Human Origin, signed in Paris, Dec. 15, 1958, by the governments of Austria, Belgium, Denmark, France, FRG, Greece, Iceland, Italy, Luxembourg, Netherlands, Norway, Sweden, Turkey and UK, came into force Jan. 1, 1959. Organizations reg. with the UIA:

European Bank of Frozen Blood of Rare Groups, f. 1969, Amsterdam, Netherlands (f. by the Council of Europe).

International Federation of Blood Donors Organizations, f. 1955, Dôle, France. Publ. *FIODS Revue*.

International Federation of Bloodgivers' Organisations, f. 1955, Luxembourg. Publ.: *Le don universel de sang*;

International Society of Blood Transfusion, f. 1937, Paris. Consultative status: WHO, ECOSOC, Publ.: *Vox Sanguinis*.

Pan American Federation for Voluntary Bloodgiving, f. 1971, Rio de Janeiro, Brazil.

UNTS, Vol. 351, p. 159; *Yearbook of International Organizations*, 1986–87.

BLUE BERETS. An international term for UN armed forces which, regardless of their national uniforms, all use blue berets or helmets as headgear.

UN The Blue Helmets: A Review of United Nations Peace-Keeping, New York, 1985.

BLUE CROSS. Old symbol of the anti-alcohol and drugs societies. Organization reg. with the UIA:

International Federation of Blue Cross Societies, f. 1877, Geneva, Switzerland.

Yearbook of International Organizations, 1986–87; *The Europa Yearbook 1988. A World Survey*, Vol. I, London, 1988.

BLUE JEANS. An international term for American workers' overalls of the 19th century which became a world-wide youth fashion in the second half of the 20th century. Subject of international trademark agreements.

BMD. ▷ Ballistic missile defence.

BMEWS. ▷ Ballistic Missile Early Warning System.

BOARD OF AUDITORS. ▷ UN Board of Auditors.

BOAT PEOPLE. International term of the 1980s for the Vietnamese refugees, fleeing by boat to Brunei, Indonesia, Malaysia, Singapore, Hong Kong, subject of a special conference in Bangkok organized by ASEAN in July 1988.

BOBSLEIGH. A subject of international co-operation; branch of sport recognized by the international Olympic Committee. Organizations reg. with the UIA:

International Bobsleigh Federation, f. 1973, Munich, FRG.

International Bobsleighing and Tobogganing Federation, f. 1923, Paris.

Yearbook of International Organizations.

DOCCE. A subject of international co-operation; branch of sport recognized by the International Olympic Committee, though the game is not featured in Olympic Sports. Organization reg. with the UIA:

International Bocce Federation, f. 1946, Torino, Italy.

Yearbook of International Organizations.

BODYBUILDING. A subject of international co-operation; reg. with the UIA:

International Federation of Bodybuilders, f. 1946, Montreal, Canada. Publ. *Muscle Builders, Power Magazine*.

Yearbook of International Organizations.

BOERS. *Dutch* = peasants. A name adopted in the 19th century by colonists of Dutch origin who settled in South Africa in the 17th century and who, with the support of British colonists, formed in the second half of the 19th century the Republics of Transvaal and Orania, and in 1899–1902 waged war against Great Britain, the so-called Boer War, ending with the acceptance of the supremacy of Great Britain. In the 20th century they adopted the name Afrikaaners and formed the racist Republic of South Africa based on the principles of ▷ apartheid.

T. PAKENHAM, *The Boer War*, New York, 1979.

BOGOTA. The capital of Colombia (since 1830) (1985 pop. census, 3,982,941). The seat of Inter-American Export Promotion Committee, Inter-American Institute of Agricultural Sciences, Latin-American Banking Federation, Latin-American Confederation of Religious Orders, Latin-American Episcopal Council (CELAM), UN Information Center.

Yearbook of International Organizations, The Europa Yearbook 1987. A World Survey, London, 1987.

B

BOGOTA ACT, 1960. A program drawn up by 19 American Republics to improve the social and economic development of Latin America within the ▷ Pan-American Operation. It was commissioned Sept. 24, 1958 by a meeting of foreign ministers of OAS from a special committee, Comité de las 21 de la OEA which, after additional sessions in Washington, Jan.–Mar., 1959 and in Buenos Aires, Apr. 1959, submitted their results, among others a postulate to set up the ▷ Inter-American Development Bank to the seventh OAS meeting at San José de Costa Rica, Aug. 1960. In Bogota in Sept. 1960 the Committee met to frame the final draft program. The delegation of the Cuban Revolutionary Government made the viability of the program conditional on creation of a Latin-American Development Fund of US \$30 billion. The proposal was opposed by the USA, Chile, Ecuador, Guatemala, Honduras, Colombia, Costa Rica, Nicaragua, Panama, Paraguay, Peru, and Uruguay. The Program for Social Improvement and Economic Development with the Pan-American Operation, Sept. 12, 1960 was adopted by 19 votes, with Cuba dissenting. The Act of Bogota recommended the application of measures with a view to:

(1) social improvement in the form of a broader, more just distribution of land, credits for farms, a reform of tax systems, colonization of virgin lands, extension of production and expansion of road construction;
(2) improvement of the housing situation and public services through assistance for private construction industry and credits for public units;
(3) improvement of general and vocational schooling systems through development of modern teaching methods in order to eliminate illiteracy;
(4) improvement of public health through extended national and local health service, installation of water mains, fighting malaria and intensification of complete nourishment for lower classes;
(5) mobilization of natural resources to increase incomes;
(6) economic development through strengthening of credit institutions for small and medium-size private industrial and agricultural enterprises.

Also recommended to the Inter-American Development Bank was the possible management of the Inter-American Special Fund for Social Development. The Bogota Program inspired the ▷ Alliance for Progress.

Acta de Bogota, Bogota, 1960; C. CASTILLA, *El Panamericanismo*, Buenos Aires, 1961.

BOGOTA CONFERENCE, 1948. ▷ American International Conferences.

BOGOTA DECLARATION, 1966. A Declaration of the Heads of Governments of Chile, Colombia, Ecuador, Peru and Venezuela adopted at Bogota on Aug. 16, 1966. It concerned the economic integration of the ▷ Andean Group.

Acta de Bogota 1966, Bogota, 1966; E.J. OSMAŃCZYK, *Enciclopedia Mundial de Relaciones Internacionales y Naciones Unidas*, Madrid–Mexico, 1976, p. 385.

BOGOTA DECLARATION, 1973. A Declaration of Ministers of Foreign Affairs of Latin American Republics, adopted at Bogota, on Nov. 16, 1973, relating to the "new dialogue" with the United States, initiated by the Secretary of State, H.A. Kissinger.

Recueil de Documents, No. 11, 1973.

BOGOTA DECLARATION, 1976. ▷ Geostationary orbit.

BOGOTA ECONOMIC AGREEMENT 1948. The first inter-American economic co-operation agreement, signed by all 21 American Republics at Bogota, on May 2, 1948, at the Ninth International Conference of American States; did not enter into force, ratified only by Costa Rica, Honduras and Panama.

PAU, *International Conferences of American States. Second Supplement 1942–54*, Washington, DC, 1958.

BOGOTA PACT, 1948, OR PACT OF BOGOTA. The official name of the American Treaty on Pacific Settlement signed at the Inter-American Conference held in Bogota on Apr. 30, 1948 by 21 American republics (Argentina, Bolivia, Ecuador, Nicaragua, Paraguay, Peru and the USA with reservation clauses). The Pact, considered as a major instrument of the Inter-American system, was ratified by only seven states: Mexico – Nov. 23, 1948; Costa Rica – May 6, 1949; Honduras – Feb. 7, 1950; Nicaragua – May 26, 1950 (with reservation clause); Haiti – Mar. 29, 1951; Panama – Apr. 25, 1951 and Uruguay – Sept. 1, 1955. The treaty was registered with the UN on May 13, 1949. The text is as follows:

"In the name of their peoples, the Governments represented at the Ninth International Conference of American States have resolved, in fulfilment of Article 23 of the Charter of the Organization of American States, to conclude the following Treaty:

Chapter one General Obligation to Settle Disputes by Pacific Means.

Art. I. The High Contracting Parties, solemnly reaffirming their commitments made in earlier international conventions and declarations, as well as in the Charter of the United Nations, agree to refrain from the threat of the use of force, or from any other means of coercion for the settlement of their controversies, and to have recourse at all times to pacific procedures.

Art. II. The High Contracting Parties recognize the obligation to settle international controversies by regional pacific procedures before referring them to the Security Council of the United Nations.

Consequently, in the event that a controversy arises between two or more signatory States which, in the opinion of the parties, cannot be settled by direct negotiations through the usual diplomatic channels, the parties bind themselves to use the procedures established in the present Treaty, in the manner and under the conditions provided for in the following articles, or, alternatively, such special procedures as, in their opinion, will permit them to arrive at a solution.

Art. III. The order of the pacific procedures established in the present Treaty does not signify that the parties may not have recourse to the procedure which they consider most appropriate in each case, or that they should use all these procedures, or that any of them have preference over others except as expressly provided.

Art. IV. Once any pacific procedure has been initiated, whether by agreement between the parties or in fulfilment of the present Treaty or a previous pact, no other procedure may be commenced until that procedure is concluded.

Art. V. The aforesaid procedures may not be applied to matters which, by their nature, are within the domestic jurisdiction of the State. If the parties are not in agreement as to whether the controversy concerns a matter of domestic jurisdiction, this preliminary question shall be submitted to decision by the International Court of Justice, at the request of any of the parties.

Art. VI. The aforesaid procedures, furthermore, may not be applied to matters already settled by arrangement between the parties, or by arbitral award or by decision of an international court, or which are governed by agreements or treaties in force on the date of the conclusion of the present Treaty.

Art. VII. The High Contracting Parties bind themselves not to make diplomatic representations in order to protect their nationals, or to refer a controversy to a court of international jurisdiction for that purpose, when the said nationals have had available the means to place their case before competent domestic courts of the respective State.

Art. VIII. Neither recourse to pacific means for the solution of controversies, nor the recommendations of their use, shall, in the case of an armed attack, be ground for delaying the exercise of the right of individual or collective self-defense, as provided for in the Charter of the United Nations.

Chapter two. Procedures of Good Offices and Mediation.

Art. IX. The procedure of good offices consists in the attempts by one or more American Governments not parties to the controversy, or by one or more eminent citizens of any American State which is not a party to the controversy, to bring the parties together, so as to make it possible for them to reach an adequate solution between themselves.

Art. X. Once the parties have been brought together and have resumed direct negotiations, no further action is to be taken by the States or citizens that have offered their good offices or have accepted an invitation to offer them; they may, however, by agreement between the parties, be present at the negotiations.

Art. XI. The procedure of mediation consists in the submission of the controversy to one or more American Governments not parties to the controversy, or to one or more eminent citizens of any American State not a party to the controversy. In either case, the mediator or mediators shall be chosen by mutual agreement between the parties.

Art. XII. The functions of the mediator or mediators shall be to assist the parties in the settlement of controversies in the simplest and most direct manner, avoiding formalities and seeking an acceptable solution. No report shall be made by the mediator and, so far as he is concerned, the proceedings shall be wholly confidential.

Art. XIII. In the event that the High Contracting Parties have agreed to the procedure of mediation but are unable to reach an agreement within two months on the selection of the mediator or mediators, or no solution to the controversy has been reached within five months after mediation has begun, the parties shall have recourse without delay to any one of the other procedures of peaceful settlement established in the present Treaty.

Art. XIV. The High Contracting Parties may offer their mediation, either individually or jointly, but they agree not to do so while the controversy is in process of settlement by any of the other procedures established in the present Treaty.

Chapter three. Procedure of Investigation and Conciliation.

Art. XV. The procedure of investigation and conciliation consists in the submission of the controversy to a Commission of Investigation and Conciliation, which shall be established in accordance with the provisions established in subsequent articles of the present Treaty, and which shall function within the limitations prescribed therein.

Art. XVI. The party initiating the procedure of investigation and conciliation shall request the Council of the Organization of American States to convoke the Commission of Investigation and Conciliation. The Council for its part shall take immediate steps to convoke it.

Once the request to convoke the Commission has been received, the controversy between the parties shall immediately be suspended, and the parties shall refrain from any act that might make conciliation more difficult. To that end, at the request of one of the parties, the Council of the Organization of American States may, pending the convocation of the Commission, make appropriate recommendations to the parties.

Art. XVII. Each of the High Contracting Parties may appoint, by means of a bilateral agreement consisting of a simple exchange of notes with each of the other signatories, two members of the Commission of Investigation and Conciliation, only one of whom may be its own nationality. The fifth member, who shall perform the functions of Chairman, shall be selected immediately by common agreement of the members thus appointed. Any one of the contracting parties may remove members whom it has appointed, whether nationals or aliens; at the same time it shall appoint the successor. If this is not done, the removal shall be considered as not having been made. The appointments and substitutions shall be registered with the Pan American Union, which shall endeavor to ensure that the commissions maintain their full complement of five members.

Art. XVIII. Without prejudice to the provisions of the foregoing article, the Pan American Union shall draw

up a permanent panel of American conciliators, to be made up as follows:
(a) Each of the High Contracting Parties shall appoint, for three-year periods, two of their nationals who enjoy the highest reputation for fairness, competence and integrity.
(b) The Pan American Union shall request of the candidates, notice of their formal acceptance, and it shall place on the panel of conciliators the names of the persons who so notify it.
(c) The Governments may, at any time, fill vacancies occurring among their appointees; and they may reappoint their members.
Art. XIX. In the event that a controversy should arise between two or more American States that have not appointed the Commission referred to in Art. XVII, the following procedure shall be observed:
(a) Each party shall designate two members from the permanent panel of American conciliators, who are not of the same nationality as the appointing party.
(b) These four members shall in turn choose a fifth member, from the permanent panel, not of the nationality of either party.
(c) If, within a period of 30 days following the notification of their selection, the four members are unable to agree upon a fifth member, they shall each separately list the conciliators composing the permanent panel; in order to find their preference, and upon comparison of the lists so prepared, the one who first receives a majority of votes shall be declared elected. The person so elected shall perform the duties of Chairman of the Commission.
Art. XX. In convening the Commission of Investigation and Conciliation, the Council of the Organization of American States shall determine the place where the Commission shall meet. Thereafter, the Commission may determine the place or places in which it is to function, taking into account the best facilities for the performance of its work.
Art. XXI. When more than two States are involved in the same controversy, the States that hold similar points of view shall be entitled to increase the number of conciliators in order that all parties may have equal representation. The Chairman shall be elected in the manner set forth in Art. XIX.
Art. XXII. It shall be the duty of the Commission of Investigation and Conciliation to clarify the points in dispute between the parties and to endeavor to bring about an agreement between them upon mutually acceptable terms. The Commission shall institute such investigations of the facts involved in the controversy as it may deem necessary for the purpose of proposing acceptable bases of settlement.
Art. XXIII. It shall be the duty of the parties to facilitate the work of the Commission and to supply it, to the fullest extent possible, with all useful documents and information, and also to use the means at their disposal to enable the Commission to summon and hear witnesses or experts and perform other tasks in the territories of the parties, in conformity with their laws.
Art. XXIV. During the proceedings before the Commission, the parties shall be represented by plenipotentiary delegates or by agents, who shall serve as intermediaries between them and the Commission. The parties and the Commission may use the services of technical advisers and experts.
Art. XXV. The Commission shall conclude its work within a period of six months from the date of its installation; but the parties may, by mutual agreement, extend the period.
Art. XXVI. If, in the opinion of the parties, the controversy relates exclusively to questions of fact, the Commission shall limit itself to investigating such questions, and shall conclude its activities with an appropriate report.
Art. XXVII. If an agreement is reached by conciliation, the final report of the Commission shall be limited to the text of the agreement and shall be published after its transmittal to the parties, unless the parties decide otherwise. If no agreement is reached, the final report shall contain a summary of the work of the Commission; it shall be delivered to the parties, and shall be published after the expiration of six months unless the parties decide otherwise. In both cases, the final report shall be adopted by a majority vote.
Art. XXVIII. The reports and conclusions of the Commission of Investigation and Conciliation shall not be binding upon the parties, either with respect to the statement of facts or in regard to questions of law, and they shall have no other character than that of recommendations submitted for the consideration of the parties in order to facilitate a friendly settlement of the controversy.
Art. XXIX. The Commission of Investigation and Conciliation shall transmit to each of the parties, as well as to the Pan American Union, certified copies of the minutes of its proceedings. These minutes shall not be published unless the parties so decide.
Art. XXX. Each member of the Commission shall receive financial remuneration, the amount of which shall be fixed by agreement between the parties. If the parties do not agree thereon, the Council of the Organization shall determine the remuneration. Each government shall pay its own expenses and an equal share of the common expenses of the Commission, including the aforementioned remunerations.
Chapter four. Judicial Procedure.
Art. XXXI. In conformity with Art. 36, par. 2, of the Statute of the International Court of Justice, the High Contracting Parties declare that they recognize, in relation to any other American State, the jurisdiction of the Court as compulsory ipso facto, without the necessity of any special agreement so long as the present Treaty is in force, in all disputes of a juridical nature that arise among them concerning:
(a) The interpretation of a treaty;
(b) Any question of international law;
(c) The existence of any fact which, if established, would constitute the breach of an international obligation; or
(d) The nature or extent of the reparation to be made for the breach of an international obligation.
Art. XXXII. When the conciliation procedure previously established in the present Treaty or by agreement of the parties does not lead to a solution, and the said parties have not agreed upon an arbitral procedure, either of them shall be entitled to have recourse to the International Court of Justice in the manner prescribed in Art. 40 of the Statute thereof. The Court shall have compulsory jurisdiction in accordance with Art. 36, par. 1, of the said Statute.
Art. XXXIII. If the parties fail to agree as to whether the Court has jurisdiction over the controversy, the Court itself shall first decide that question.
Art. XXXIV. If the Court, for the reasons set forth in Arts. V, VI and VII of this Treaty, declares itself to be without jurisdiction to hear the controversy, such controversy shall be declared ended.
Art. XXXV. If the Court for any other reason declares itself to be without jurisdiction to hear and adjudge the controversy, the High Contracting Parties obligate themselves to submit it to arbitration, in accordance with the provisions of Chapter Five of this Treaty.
Art. XXXVI. In the case of controversies submitted to the judicial procedure to which this Treaty refers, the decision shall devolve upon the full Court, or, if the parties so request, upon a special chamber in conformity with Art. 26 of the Statute of the Court. The parties may agree, moreover, to have the controversy decided ex aequo et bono.
Art. XXXVII. The procedure to be followed by the Court shall be that established in the Statute thereof.
Chapter five. Procedure of Arbitration.
Art. XXXVIII. Notwithstanding the provisions of Chapter Four of this Treaty, the High Contracting Parties may, if they so agree, submit to arbitration differences of any kind, whether juridical or not, that have arisen or may arise in the future between them.
Art. XXXIX. The Arbitral Tribunal to which a controversy is to be submitted shall, in the cases contemplated in Arts. XXXV and XXXVIII of the present Treaty, be constituted in the following manner, unless there exists an agreement to the contrary.
Art. XL. (1) Within a period of two months after notification of the decision of the Court in the case provided for in Art. XXXV, each party shall name one arbiter of recognized competence in questions of international law and of the highest integrity, and shall transmit the designation to the Council of the Organization. At the same time, each party shall present to the Council a list of 10 jurists chosen from among those on the general panel of members of the Permanent Court of Arbitration of The Hague who do not belong to its national group and who are willing to be members of the Arbitral Tribunal.
(2) The Council of the Organization shall, within the month following the presentation of the lists, proceed to establish the Arbitral Tribunal in the following manner:
(a) If the lists presented by the parties contain three names in common, such persons, together with the two directly named by the parties, shall constitute the Arbitral Tribunal.
(b) In case these lists contain more than three names in common, the three arbiters needed to complete the Tribunal shall be selected by lot.
(c) In the circumstances envisaged in the two preceding clauses, the five arbiters designated shall chose one of their number as presiding officer.
(d) If the lists contain only two names in common, such candidates and the two arbiters directly selected by the parties shall by common agreement choose the fifth arbiter, who shall preside over the Tribunal. The choice shall devolve upon a jurist on the aforesaid general panel of the Permanent Court of Arbitration of The Hague who has not been included in the lists drawn up by the parties.
(e) If the lists contain only one name in common, that person shall be a member of the Tribunal, and another name shall be chosen by lot from among the 18 jurists remaining on the above-mentioned lists. The presiding officer shall be elected in accordance with the procedure established in the preceding clause.
(f) If the lists contain no names in common, one arbiter shall be chosen by lot from each of the lists; and the fifth arbiter, who shall act as presiding officer, shall be chosen in the manner previously indicated.
(g) If the four arbiters cannot agree upon a fifth arbiter within one month after the Council of the Organization has notified them of their appointment, each of them shall separately arrange the list of jurists in the order of their preference and, after comparison of the lists so formed, the person who first obtains a majority vote shall be declared elected.
Art. XLI. The parties may by mutual agreement establish the Tribunal in the manner they deem most appropriate; they may even select a single arbiter, designating in such case a chief of state, an eminent jurist, or any court of justice in which the parties have mutual confidence.
Art. XLII. When more than two States are involved in the same controversy, the States defending the same interests shall be considered as a single party. If they have opposing interests they shall have the right to increase the number of arbiters so that all parties may have equal representation. The presiding officer shall be selected by the method established in Art. XL.
Art. XLIII. The parties shall in each case draw up a special agreement clearly defining the specific matter that is the subject of the controversy, the seat of the Tribunal, the rules of procedure to be observed, the period within which the award is to be handed down and such other conditions as they may agree upon among themselves.
If the special agreement cannot be drawn up within three months after the date of the installation of the Tribunal, it shall be drawn up by the International Court of Justice through summary procedure, and shall be binding upon the parties.
Art. XLIV. The parties may be represented before the Arbitral Tribunal by such persons as they may designate.
Art. XLV. If one of the parties fails to designate its arbiter and present its list of candidates within the period provided for in Art. XL, the other party shall have the right to request the Council of the Organization to establish the Arbitral Tribunal. The Council shall immediately urge the delinquent party to fulfill its obligations within and additional period of 15 days, after which time the Council itself shall establish the Tribunal in the following manner:
(a) It shall select a name by lot from the list presented by the petitioning party.
(b) It shall choose, by absolute majority vote, two jurists from the general panel of the Permanent Court of Arbitration of the Hague who do not belong to the national group of any of the parties.
(c) The three persons so designated, together with the one directly chosen by the petitioning party, shall select the fifth arbiter, who shall act as presiding officer, in the manner provided for in Art. XL.
(d) Once the Tribunal is installed, the procedure established in Art. XLIII shall be followed.

Art. XLVI. The award shall be accompanied by a supporting opinion, shall be adopted by a majority vote and shall be published after notification thereof has been given to the parties. The dissenting arbiter or arbiters shall have the right to state the grounds for their dissent.

The award, once it is duly handed down and made known to the parties, shall settle the controversy definitively, shall not be subject to appeal and shall be carried out immediately.

Art. XLVII. Any differences that arise in regard to the interpretation or execution of the award shall be submitted to the decision of the Arbitral Tribunal that rendered the award.

Art. XLVIII. Within a year after notification thereof, the award shall be subject to review by the same Tribunal at the request of one of the parties, provided a previously existing fact is discovered unknown to the Tribunal and to the party requesting the review, and provided the Tribunal is of the opinion that such fact might have a decisive influence on the award.

Art. XLIX. Every member of the Tribunal shall receive financial remuneration, the amount of which shall be fixed by agreement between the parties. If the parties do not agree on the amount, the Council of the Organization shall determine the remuneration. Each government shall pay its own expenses and an equal share of the common expenses of the Tribunal, including the aforementioned remuneration.

Chapter six. Fulfillment of Decisions.

Art. L. If one of the High Contracting Parties should fail to carry out the obligations imposed upon it by a decision of the International Court of Justice or by an arbitral award, the other party or parties concerned shall, before resorting to the Security Council of the United Nations, propose a Meeting of Consultation of Ministers of Foreign Affairs to agree upon appropriate measures to ensure the fulfillment of the judicial decision or arbitral award.

Chapter seven. Advisory Opinions.

Art. LI. The parties concerned in the solution of a controversy may, by agreement, petition the General Assembly or the Security Council of the United Nations to request an advisory opinion of the International Court of Justice on any juridical question.

The petition shall be made through the Council of the Organization of American States.

Chapter eight. Final Provisions.

Art. LII. The present Treaty shall be ratified by the High Contracting Parties in Accordance with their constitutional procedures. The original instrument shall be deposited in the Pan American Union, which shall transmit an authentic certified copy to each government for the purpose of ratification. The instruments of ratification shall be deposited in the archives of the Pan American Union, which shall notify the signatory governments of the deposit. Such notification shall be considered as an exchange of ratifications.

Art. LIII. This Treaty shall come into effect between the High Contracting Parties in the order in which they deposit their respective ratifications.

Art. LIV. Any American State which is not a signatory to the present Treaty, or which has made reservations thereto, may adhere to it, or may withdraw its reservations in whole or in part, by transmitting an official instrument to the Pan American Union, which shall notify the other High Contracting Parties in the manner herein established.

Art. LV. Should any of the High Contracting Parties make reservations concerning the present Treaty, such reservations shall, with respect to the State that makes them, apply to all signatory States on the basis of reciprocity.

Art. LVI. The present Treaty shall remain in force indefinitely, but may be denounced upon one year's notice, at the end of which period it shall cease to be in force with respect to the State denouncing it, but shall continue in force for the remaining signatories. The denunciation shall be addressed to the Pan American Union, which shall transmit it to the other Contracting Parties.

The denunciation shall have no effect with respect to pending procedures initiated prior to the transmission of the particular notification.

Art. LVII. The present Treaty shall be registered with the Secretariat of the United Nations through the Pan American Union.

Art. LVIII. As this Treaty comes into effect through the successive ratifications of the High Contracting Parties, the following Treaties, Conventions and Protocols shall cease to be in force with respect to such parties:
Treaty to Avoid or Prevent Conflicts between the American States, of May 3, 1923;
General Convention of Inter-American Conciliation, of January 5, 1929;
General Treaty of Inter-American Arbitration and Additional Protocol of Progressive Arbitration, of January 5, 1929;
Additional Protocol to the General Convention of Inter-American Conciliation, of December 26, 1933;
Anti-War Treaty of Non-Aggression and Conciliation, of October 10, 1933;
Convention to Coordinate, Extend and Assure the Fulfillment of the Existing Treaties between the American States, of December 23, 1936;
Inter-American Treaty of Good Offices and Mediation, of December 23, 1936 and
Treaty on the Prevention of Controversies, of December 23, 1936.

Art. LIX. The provisions of the foregoing article shall not apply to procedures already initiated or agreed upon in accordance with any of the above-mentioned international instruments.

Art. LX. The present Treaty shall be called the 'Pact of Bogota'.

In witness whereof, the undersigned Plenipotentiaries, having deposited their full powers, found to be in good and due form, sign the present Treaty, in the name of their respective governments, on the dates appearing below their signatures.

Done at the city of Bogota, in four texts, in the English, French, Portuguese and Spanish languages respectively, on the thirtieth day of April, of the year one thousand nine hundred and forty-eight."

Novena Conferencia Internacional Americana. Actas y Documentos, Bogota, 1948, Vol. VI, pp. 83–92; W. SANDERS, "Bogota Conference", in: *International Conciliation*, No. 442, June 1948, pp. 383–417.

BOGS. Marshlands under international protection as the living environment for ▷ waterfowl.

BOHEMIA. A historical land in Czechoslovakia, inhabited by the Czechs. From the 8th to the early 14th century center of the Przemyslid monarchy, from 1526 part of the Habsburg Empire, as of 1919 constitutes the western half of Czechoslovakia.

BOHEMIAN AND MORAVIAN PROTECTORATE. *German*: Protektorat Böhmens und Mährens. The name of the western part of the territory of Czechoslovakia occupied by the III Reich from Mar. 16, 1939 to May 5, 1945. The German Protectors of Bohemia and Moravia, K. von Neurath (1939–43) and W. Frick (1943–45) were sentenced by the International Military Tribunal in Nuremberg in Nov. 1946, for war crimes committed in the territories administered by them. Nuremberg War Criminals Trial 1945–46.

V. MASTNY, *The Czechs Under Nazi Rule*, New York, 1971.

BOILERS. A subject of international co-operation. Organization reg. with the UIA:

Association of European Manufacturers of Instantaneous Gas Water Heaters and Wall-Hung Boilers, f. 1958, Brussels, Belgium.
European Committee for Boilermaking and Kindred Steel Structures, f. 1951, Paris.
European Committee of Boiler Vessel and Pipework Manufacturers, f. 1951, Düsseldorf, FRG.
European Heating Boilers Association, f. 1980, Hagen, FRG.

Yearbook of International Organizations, 1986–87.

BOLIVAR. A monetary unit of Venezuela; one bolivar = 100 centimos; issued by the Banco Central de Venezuela.

BOLIVAR CONGRESS, 1883. ▷ American Conferences and Congresses, 1826–89.

BOLIVAR CONGRESS, 1911. The Congress of the Bolivar states: Bolivia, Colombia, Ecuador, Peru and Venezuela in Caracas, July 1911, on the occasion of the 100th anniversary of Venezuelan independence. The Congress adopted 13 Inter-American conventions:
Agreement on Literary and Artistic Property, Agreement on Academic Degrees, Agreement on Telegraphs, Agreement on Internal Commotions and Neutrality, Agreement on Extradition, Agreement on Patents and Privileges of Invention, Agreement on Road and Waterways, Agreement on Commercial Relations, Consular Latin American Convention, Agreement on the Judicial Acts of Aliens, Agreement on the History of the Liberator, Agreement on Publication of Unpublished Documents, Postal Agreement.

J.M. YEPES, *Del Congreso de Panamá a la Conferencia de Caracas 1826–1954*, Caracas, 1955, Vol. 2, pp. 71–78.

BOLIVAR DECLARATION, 1983. A declaration of the Latin-American States on the 200th anniversary of Simon Bolivar's birthday, in Caracas, on July 23, 1983.

BOLIVAR PRIZE. The Simon Bolivar international UNESCO prize for activity in accordance with Bolivar's ideals, founded by Venezuela. The prize was instituted to commemorate the 200th anniversary of Bolivar's birth, 24 July 1983, on which day it was awarded for the first time to the King of Spain, Juan I, and Nelson R. Mandela, the leader of the African National Congress imprisoned 1962–1990 for anti-apartheid activities in South Africa.

BOLIVIA. Member of the UN. República de Bolivia. Republic of Bolivia. South American land-locked state, bordering on Chile, Peru, Brazil, Paraguay, and Argentina. Area: 1,098,580 sq. km. Pop.: 1987 est. 6,796,000 (1970 census 4,931,000). Legal capital and seat of the judiciary – Sucre, 68,426 inhabitants (1980 est); seat of the government – La Paz, 719,780 inhabitants (1980 est.). GNP per capita in 1987 – US $570. Official language: Spanish. Currency: 1 boliviano = 100 centavos. National Day: Aug. 6, Independence Day, 1825.

Founding member of UN on Oct. 24, 1945, member of all UN specialized agencies, with the exception of GATT and WIPO; founding member of OAS; member of ALALC with privileged status (ALALC Res. 171/CMI, 175/VI and 176/VI); member of Andean Corporation for Development (until Dec. 19, 1980). International relations: from 1535 Pizzaro's conquest to 1809 resistance of the people against the occupying Spanish administration and conflicts between administration, colonial oligarchy and the monarchical rule in Madrid. On Aug. 6, 1825 a meeting of representatives of the province held in Chuquisaca declared an independent republic – Republica Bolivara, soon changed into the present state; 1836–39 Peruvian Bolivian confederation; 1879–83 wars with Chile, ended formally with a Peace Treaty 1904. Border with Brazil delineated twice: under the treaty of Mar. 27, 1867, which granted Bolivia the region of Acre (c. 193,000 sq. km) and under the Petropolis Treaty of Nov. 17, 1903 by which Bolivia conceded almost all of Acre (191,000 sq. km). The Treaty of Petropolis was supplemented Dec. 29, 1928 with an agreement regulating ownership of 13 islands in the border River Madeira. Border with Paraguay set up by the Treaty of Peace, Friendship and Borders of June 21,

1938 and Arbitration Protocol of Oct. 10, 1938. The border with Chile was set up under the Treaty of Peace, Friendship and Trade of Oct. 20, 1904; with Argentina under treaties of 1889 and 1925. During World War I, until 1917, Bolivia remained neutral, then broke relations with Germany after the USA joined the war against Germany. Founding member of the League of Nations, waged wars 1928–29 and 1932–35, over ▷ Gran Chaco with Paraguay, which ended with the Peace Treaty in 1938. The war was debated by the LN. In 1944 Bolivia declared war against Germany and Japan. In 1961 Bolivia broke diplomatic relations with Chile and lodged a complaint with the OAS concerning the River ▷ Lauca. The OAS Council adjudicated in favor of Chile, provoking a Bolivian boycott of that organization lasting until Jan 21, 1965. From Mar. 23 to Oct. 8, 1967 a national liberation organization called Ejercito de Liberacion Nacional de Bolivia, formed and headed by an Argentinian Che Guevara, was active in the region of Nacaguacu; it was crushed on Oct. 8, 1967. Its leader was wounded, taken prisoner and shot 24 hours later on orders from La Paz at a primary school in the village of Higueros by a junior officer of Military Force, B.M. Ternà, pursuant to the orders of Colonel A. Selich and Major M. Ayoroa, who stated they had received such orders from the chief of State General R. Barrientos and Chief of Armed Forces, General J. Ovando. In 1973–74 the Bolivian government resumed its claims for access to the Pacific in the region of the northern province of Chile bordering on Peru. In Mar., 1979 Peru granted Bolivia a free trade zone in Antofagasta and Inquique, the ports of the Pacific. In Feb., 1983 Bolivia extradited to France the war criminal Klaus Barbie, called the "butcher of Lyon". Because of its geographical location (c. 3400 m above sea level) La Paz is the permanent seat of the Latin-American Council for Cosmic Radiation and Physical Interplanetary Space (LARCEF, f. 1958). In April 1987 official negotiations of the foreign relations ministers of Bolivia and Chile on Bolivia's access to the Pacific took place in Montevideo. See also ▷ World Heritage UNESCO list.

Anuario Geográfico y Estadistico de la República de Bolivia, 1950; Informe de la Misión de Asistenciá Técnica de las NU a Bolivia 1950, New York, 1951; G. FRANKOWITCH, *El Pensamiento Boliviano en el siglo XX,* México, DF, 1956; CEPAL, *El Desarrollo Económico de Bolivia,* Santiago de Chile, 1958; M. LE FOY, *The Chaco Dispute and the League of Nations,* New York, 1961; *Everyman's United Nations,* New York, 1964; A. URQUIDI, *El Feudalismo en América y la Reforma Agraria Boliviana,* Cochabamba, 1966; A. CANALES, *Mito y realidad de la industrialización boliviana,* Cochabamba, 1966; C.H. ZONDAG, *The Bolivian Economy 1952–1965, The Revolution and its Aftermath,* New York, 1966; R.F. ABADIE-AICAR-DIE, *Economia y Sociedad de Bolivia en el siglo XX, El Antiguo Régimen,* Montevideo, 1967; J.D. BARTON, *A Short History of Bolivia,* La Paz, 1968; *El Diario de Che Guevara. Prologo de Fidel Castro.* La Habana, 1968; W. GUTENBERG-TICHAUER, *Bibliografia Boliviana 1966,* La Paz, 1968; J.V. FIFER, *Bolivia: Land Location and Politics Since 1825,* CUP, 1972; R. DEBRAY, *La Guerrilla du Che,* Paris, 1974; V. MARCHETTI, J.D. MARKS, *The CIA and the Cult of Intelligence,* New York, 1975, pp. 139–145; L. GUILLERMO, *A History of the Bolivian Labour Movement 1848–1971,* 1977; *The Europa Year Book 1984. A World Survey,* Vol. I, pp. 1184–1196, London, 1984.

BOLZANO. An Italian (since 1919) city and province in Trentino Alto Adiga (South Tirol). The status of the German-speaking element in the Province of Bolzano (Bozen) was subject of Res. 1497/XV and of Res. 1661/XVII in the 1960 and 1961 sessions of the UN General Assembly. ▷

Upper Adiga. See also ▷ Austria–Italy Border Dispute.

UN Yearbook, 1960. p. 179 and 1961, pp. 140–144.

BOMBER. An international military term since World War II for aircraft used in World War I and II for strategic bombardment of the enemy's military targets, industrial areas and civilian population, subject of international agreements. The first intercontinental bomber was produced in 1948 by the USA and in 1955 by the USSR; a new strategic bomber by the USA in 1985, by the USSR in 1987; the supersonic bomber by the USA in 1960, by the USSR in 1975; the long range fighter bomber by the USA in 1972, by the USSR in 1976; and in 1987 USA produced the ▷ Stealth Bomber.

R. LEGER SILVARD, *World Military and Social Expenditures, 1987–88,* Washington DC, 1987.

BOMBING OF OPEN CITIES AND VILLAGES. Military operations contrary to international law, subject of international law. The Hague Conventions of 1899 and 1907 prohibited the attack and bombardment by land and naval artillery of undefended urban and rural buildings and also "dropping missiles and explosive materials from balloons or other analogous new airships." The first bombs dropped from an airplane fell in May 1914 on a railroad line in northern Mexico at the order of Pancho Villa, in whose employ was the builder of the first bombers, the US citizen Lester Ponce Barlow. During World War I the Germans began the air bombing of many open cities. In 1923 a League of Nations Commission of Military Jurists elaborated the Rules of Air Warfare, declaring "the bombardment of cities, towns, villages, dwellings or buildings not in the immediate neighborhood of the operations of land forces as prohibited." During World War II the Germans used it on a mass scale, first testing its air force in the Spanish Civil War (1936–39), where a Nazi unit called the Condor Legion took part in the war on the side of General Franco (▷ Guernica). A World Conference for Action on the Bombardment of Open Towns and the Restoration of Peace was held in Paris, July 23–24, 1938, in relation with the Spanish Civil War.

N. SLOUTZKI, "Le bombardement des villes ouvertes", in: *Revue de droit international des sciences diplomatiques et politiques,* No. 24, 1923; *International Conciliation, Documents for the Year 1938,* pp. 344–348; L. NURICK, "Aerial bombardment, theory and practice", in: *American Journal of International Law,* No. 39, 1945; J.M. SPAIGHT, *Air Power and War Rights,* London, 1947; MING-MIN PEN, "Les bombardements aériens et la population civile depuis la seconde guerre mondiale", in: *Revue général de l'Air,* No. 4, 5, 1952; E. SPETZLER, *Luftkrieg und Menschlichkeit,* 1957.

BONA FIDES. *Latin* = "in good faith". An international term for the basic principle of the acts of international law, which are exclusively those of *bonae fidei,* as distinct from principles underlying the acts of internal law, which are those of *stricti iuris* and *bonae fidei.* The second basic principle of international law, namely that of *pacta sunt servanda,* is derived from the *bonae fidei principle.* The principle that states shall fulfill in good faith obligations assumed by them has been formulated in the Declaration on Principles of International Law Concerning Friendly Relations and Co-operation Among States, adopted on Oct. 24, 1970 by the UN General Assembly. The reverse is *mala fides.*

G. SCHWARZENBERGER, "The fundamental principles of international law", in: *Recueil des Cours de l'Academie de Droit International,* No. 87, 1955.

BONAIRE. Island in the Leeward Islands group in the ▷ Netherlands Antilles. Area: 290.1 sq km. Population: 1985 estim. 10,200. Since Jan. 1, 1986 special status with ▷ Curaçao.

BONDED ZONE. An international term for the separated area of a seaport or airport where uncleared goods are stored awaiting further transit or non-immediate sale or, in case of raw materials, for processing by local factories or those of a foreign consignee.

BONDS. An international term for a formal certificate of indebtedness issued by state or city, government or financial organizations, national and international (Eurocurrency bonds). The international bond market has been dominated in the 1980s by Japanese, Swiss, American and British and West European Banks. Foreign bonds free from taxes imposed on domestic bonds are attractive to foreign investors. See also ▷ UN Bonds.

P. O'HAGEN, Bonds as a Source of LDC Finance, in *Economic Impact, 1988–83.*

BONES. A subject of international co-operation and conventions. An international Agreement relating to the Exportation of Bones was signed in Geneva on July 11, 1928 and a Protocol on Sept. 1, 1929 between Austria, Belgium, Bulgaria, Czechoslovakia, Denmark, Finland, France, Germany, Great Britain, Hungary, Italy, Luxembourg, Netherlands, Norway, Poland, Romania, Serbo-Croat-Slovene State, Sweden, Switzerland and Turkey stated that "... the export of raw and dried bones ... shall not be subjected ... to any prohibition or restriction ..." (art. 1)

LNTS, Vol. 95, p. 378.

BONN. The capital of the FRG on the Rhine (1985 pop. 292,600). The decision to make Bonn the temporary capital of the FRG was taken on May 10, 1949 in the West German Parliamentary Council by a vote of 33 for Bonn and 29 against, by those who supported Frankfurt am Main (the West German Council was the organ which prepared the institutionalization of the FRG, which took place Sept. 7, 1949). Bonn in 1949 had less than 100,000 residents, in 1980 more than 300,000. It is the seat of the International Council for Environmental Law, Intergovernmental Committee of European Migration and the ILO Office.

Yearbook of International Organizations; The Europa Yearbook 1987. A World Survey, London, 1987.

BONN AGREEMENTS, 1952. An international term, commonly used to describe treaties concluded in Bonn, May 26, 1952, by three Western powers with the Federal Republic of Germany. The first was called the General Bonn Agreement and the second the Military Bonn Agreement on the Rights and Duties of Foreign Military Forces Deployed in the Federal Republic of Germany; the third, the Financial Bonn Agreement on Regulation of Financial Matters between the German Federal Republic and Western powers and the fourth, the Bonn Agreement on Regulation of Issues and Problems Arising from the War and Occupation. Apart from these, 10 other documents on specific problems are amended thereto and form an integral part of the Bonn Agreements. The General Bonn Agreement anticipated the end of the occupational status of the Federal Republic of Germany after the Treaty on Defense of the European Community had entered into force; this did not take place due to the fact that the Parliament of France did not ratify this Treaty, a decision taken on Aug. 30, 1954. As a result, the General Bonn Agreement was substituted by the Paris Protocol of Oct. 23, 1954, which in art. 1 terminated the occupational status of the Federal Republic of Germany, preserving, at the same time, in art. 2 and in keeping with the Potsdam agreement, the responsibility of the four big powers "for Germany as a whole."

W. CORNIDES and H. VOLLE, *Die internationalen Verhandlungen über die Schaffung der Europäischen Verteidigungsgemeinschaft. Die Vertragswerke von Bonn und Paris vom Mai 1952*, Frankfurt am, M., 1952; W. CORNIDES, *Die Welmächte und Deutschland. Geschichte der jüngsten Vergangenheit 1945–1955*, Frankfurt am, M., 1957; H. KUTSCHER, "Bonner Verträge vom 26.V.1952 in der Fassung des Parisers Protokolls vom 23 October 1954", in: *STRUPP-SCHLOCHAUER Wörterbuch des Völkerrechts*, Berlin, 1960, Vol. 1, pp. 224–233.

BONN FOUR GROUP. A permanent inter-allied institution for all-German affairs and West Berlin, established in Bonn after the FRG joined NATO May 8, 1955. Members of the group are ambassadors of the three western powers and a high official of the Bonn ministry of foreign affairs. US Secretary of State W.F. Rogers June 8, 1972, in commenting on the new statute for West Berlin, stated that the operation of this statute would be a subject of continual observation by the Bonn Four Group.

BONN–PARIS–MADRID AXIS. An international term coined by Madrid daily *El Pais* for the new group inside NATO with its own conception of disarmament negotiations with the USSR.

J.L. CERIAN, Bonn–Paris–Madrid Aje, in: *El Pais*, March 10, 1988.

BOOKS. A subject of international co-operation. Organizations reg. with the UIA:

Book Publishers Group of EEC, f. 1967, Brussels, Belgium.
IBBY Documentation Centre on Books For and About Handicapped Children, Hosle, Norway.
International Association for Past and Present History of the Art of Printing (Gutenberg Society), f. 1901, Mainz, FRG.
International Association of Bibliphiles, f. 1963, Paris.
International Board on Books for Young People, f. 1953, Zurich. Consultative status: UNESCO, ECOSOC. Publ. *Bookbird*.
International Book Committee, f. 1973, Paris. Consultative status: UNESCO.
International Community of Booksellers Associations, f. 1956, Vienna.
International League of Antiquarian Booksellers, f. 1948, Amsterdam. Publ. *International Directory*.
Regional Centre for the Promotion of Books in Latin America and the Caribbean, f. 1971, Bogota, Colombia. Publ. *News on Books*.
UNESCO Latin American Book Development Centre, f. 1962, Bogota, Colombia.
UNESCO Regional Book Development Centre for Africa South of the Saraha, est. 1962, Yaounde, Cameroon.
UNESCO Regional Office for Book Development in Asia and the Pacific, est. 1958, Karachi, Pakistan. Publ. *Asia Pacific Book News*.

Yearbook of International Organizations, 1986–87.

BOOKSELLERS. A subject of international co-operation as early as in antiquity, organized in a modern way after the passing of the Berne Convention in 1886 on editorial rights' protection. International organizations reg. with the UIA:

Booksellers International. International Publishers Association, f. 1896, Geneva, Switzerland. Consultative Status: UNESCO, ECOSOC, WIPO (observer status). Publ. *Bulletin*.
International Association of Wholesale Newspaper, Periodical and Book Distributors, f. in 1955, Cologne; publ. *Der Neue Vertrieb*.

International Board on Books for Young People, f. in 1952, Vienna. Advisory status UNESCO.
International Booksellers Federation, f. 1956, Vienna, Austria. Consultative Status: ECOSOC, ENESCO. Publ. *IBF Bulletin*; *Book, Book Trade and Society*.
International Community of Booksellers Association, f. in 1956, Delf (Holland). Advisory status UNESCO.
International League of Antiquarian Booksellers, f. in 1947 in Brussels; publ. *Dictionary for the Antiquarian Book Trade*, 1953; *Rules* 1957; *International Directory* 1965, and others;

Moreover, International Book Fairs are held in many countries, among others, each spring in Warsaw (Poland), and each fall in Frankfurt am Main (FRG). An International Exhibition of Editorial Art named Internationale Buchausstellung, IBA is held since 1959 every 5 years in Leipzig (GDR).

Yearbook of International Organizations, 1986–87.

BOOK YEAR, INTERNATIONAL, 1972. According to a decision of the sixteenth General Conference Session of UNESCO, 1972 the International Book Year was proclaimed in order to promote reading and the development of libraries, particularly in Asia, Africa and Latin America, where, though inhabited by 80% of world population, only 25% of books published throughout the world are sold. The International Book Year was preceded by four regional UNESCO conferences devoted to promotion of reading: Asian in Tokyo in May 1966, African in Accra in Feb. 1968, Latin American in Bogota in Sept. 1969 and Arab in Cairo in Dec. 1971. The Report on the International Book Year was presented at the Seventeenth UNESCO General Conference Session in 1973. According to UNESCO data, book production remains highly uneven in the world: Africa for 10% of potential readers brings out less than 2% of the total number of books, Latin America for 5% about 2%, Asia for 56% only 20%. Other regions publish for 30% of the population 76% of books, 75% of which come out in Europe, the USA and the USSR.

BOPHUTHATSWANA. One of the South African ▷ Bantu Homelands, created in 1972 with "self government" and on Dec. 6, 1977 declared an "independent republic" by South Africa, not recognized by the United Nations or by any government other than that of the South African government. The General Assembly on Nov. 28, 1985 generally condemned South Africa's establishment of Bantu Homelands. Area: 44,000 sq km. Population: 1980 census: 1,300,000 (excluding 1,200,000 Botswana residents in South Africa); 1985 census: 1,740,600 (1,460,000). Capital: Mmabatho.

The Europa Yearbook 1988. A World Survey, Vol. II, London, 1988.

BORAH PLAN TO OUTLAW WAR, 1923. Introduced on Feb. 13, 1923 as a resolution in the US Senate, by Senator W.E. Borah (1865–1940). The text is as follows:

"That it is the view of the Senate of the United States that war between nations should be outlawed as an institution or means for the settlement of international controversies by making it a public crime under the law of nations and that every nation should be encouraged by solemn agreement or treaty to bind itself to indict and punish its own international war breeders or instigators and war profiteers under powers similar to those conferred upon our Congress under Art. I, Section 8, of our Federal Constitution which clothes the Congress with the power to define and punish offenses against the law of nations."

S.O. LAWINSON, *Outlawry of War, A Plan to Outlaw War*, Washington, DC, 1922; W.E. BORAH, *Public Opinion Outlaws War*, Washington, DC, 1924; *International Conciliation*, No. 208, March 1925, pp. 94–97; Q.

WRIGHT, "The outlawry of war", in: *American Journal of International Law*, No. 1, 1925, pp. 76–103.

BORDER DISPUTES. ▷ Frontier Litigation; ▷ Frontier Inviolability.

BORDERLAND INTEGRATION. A Latin-American term, introduced in the Bogota Declaration of States of the ▷ Andean Group, on Aug. 16, 1966. First agreement on borderland integration in Latin America, Acta de Rumichaca, signed by Ecuador and Colombia, Mar. 12, 1966. The program of borderland integration provides for joint planning of agricultural and power production, exchange of services and joint sanitary control.

Acta de Rumichaca 1966, Bogota, 1966; *Acta de Bogota 1966*, Bogota, 1966; E.J. OSMAŃCZYK, *Enciclopedia Mundial de Relaciones Internacionales y Naciones Unidas*, Madrid–Mexico, 1976, p. 653.

BORNHOLM. A Danish island in the Baltic Sea; area 588 sq. km; (1986 pop. 47,039); subject of an interntional dispute in the 17th century between the Hanseatic League, Sweden, and Denmark; in 1860 the Treaty of Copenhagen returned the island to Denmark. Occupied by the Germans, Apr. 11, 1940 to Apr. 9, 1945, when it was liberated by the Soviet army; ceded by the USSR to Denmark on May 11, 1945.

J. PAXTON (ed.), *The Stateman's Yearbook 1987–88*, London, 1987.

BOROBUDUR OR BOROBODO. The site on Java of a great Buddhist temple of the 7th–8th century. An international campaign to save this monument, which belongs to the cultural heritage of all mankind, was undertaken by UNESCO with the formation of a special Committee for Borobudur operating on the same principle as the previous UNESCO Committee on ▷ Abu Simbel. At the end of 1973 UNESCO signed a contract with the government of Indonesia on the work of conservation and up to 1982 spent 17 million US dollars on it. On Jan. 21, 1985 three Muslim fundamentalists demonstrating for an Islamic State placed nine bombs which exploded in the temple.

KEESING's *Record of World Events*, March 1986.

BOSNIA AND HERZEGOVINA. Balkan lands conquered by Turkey in the 15th century. In 1878 the Congress of Berlin ceded Bosnia and Herzegovina to Austria–Hungary against the desire of the population demanding independence. On Dec. 1, 1918 Bosnia and Herzegovina became part of the Kingdom of Serbia, Croatia and Slovenia (SHS), which in 1929 took the name Yugoslavia. During World War II, when the Germans and Italians occupied Yugoslavia in Apr., 1941, three separate states were formed to replace it: ▷ Serbia, ▷ Montenegro and ▷ Croatia. Bosnia and Herzegovina were annexed to Croatia; one of the main areas of partisan campaigns in Yugoslavia; liberated in May 1945 and since Nov. 29, 1945 one of the six federal republics of Yugoslavia.

R.W. SETON-WATSON, *The Role of Bosnia in International Politics, 1875–1914*, London, 1932.

BOSPORUS. The strait between the Marmara and the Black Sea, 32 km long, and 640 m wide. The Bosporus Bridge in Istanbul between European and Asian Turkey, 1074.8 m long, was opened 1973. Subject of international conventions on the organization of ▷ straits of July 24, 1923, signed in Lausanne and July 20, 1936, signed in Montreux by Bulgaria, France, Great Britain, Greece, Japan,

Romania, Turkey, Yugoslavia, and the USSR. ▷ Dardanelles.

BOSRA. The ancient Syrian city of Busra at the junction of the routes from the Arabian Gulf and the Mediterranean, included in the ▷ World Heritage UNESCO List, was a powerful city during the Hellenistic and Roman periods. The most astonishing of its monuments is the 2nd-century theatre which is magnificently preserved thanks to the Arab fortress surrounding it.

UNESCO. *A Legacy for All*, Paris, 1984.

BOTANY. A subject of international co-operation. Organizations reg. with the UIA:

International Association of Botanical and Mycological Societies, f. 1981, Bochum, FRG.
International Association of Botanic Gardens, f. 1954, Paris;
International Botanical Congress, f. 1900, Paris;
International Commission for Bee Botany, f. 1951, Leamington, UK.
International Organization of Paleobotany, f. 1954, London, UK. Publ. *IOP Newsletter*.
Organization for Flora Neotropica, f. 1964, Bronx NY, USA. Consultative Status: ECOSOC, UNESCO. Publ. *Flora of the Tropical American Region*.

Yearbook of International Organizations, 1986–87.

BOTSWANA. Member of the UN. Republic of Botswana. A Southern African State, bordering on Namibia, Zambia, Zimbabwe and Republic of South Africa. Area: 582,000 sq. km. Pop. 1989 est. 1,200,000 (1971 census 630,370). Capital: Gaborone with 59,657 inhabitants, 1981. GNP per capita in 1987 US $1,030. Official language: English and Setswana. Currency: 1 pula = 100 thebe. National Day: Sept. 30, Independence Day, 1966. Member of the UN since Oct. 7, 1966 and of all UN specialized agencies save IMO, IAEA and WIPO. Member of OAU, ACP state of EEC. A signatory of the Lomé Conventions of 1975 and 1980.
International relations: British protectorate, called Bechuanaland from 1884 to 1965, when Britain granted it internal self-government. On Sept. 30, 1966 Botswana was granted full independence within the Commonwealth. In Jan. 1977 the Security Council condemned all acts of provocation and harassment committed by Southern Rhodesia against Botswana. In Dec. 1977 the UN General Assembly called upon all states and international organizations concerned to respond to the appeals to provide assistance on a generous scale to Botswana's three-year development projects. In May 1983 Botswana established diplomatic relations with Zimbabwe.

UN Monthly Chronicle, No. 10, 1967, pp. 37–38, *Botswana: Resources and Development*, Pretoria, 1970; A. SILLERY, *Botswana. A Short Political History*, London, 1974; *UN Yearbook* 1977; C. STEVENS, *Ford Aid and the Developing World*, London, 1979; *The Europa Year Book 1984. A World Survey*, Vol. I, pp. 1197–1199, London, 1984.

BOTTLING. A subject of international co-operation. Organization reg. with the UIA:

International Technical Center of Bottling, f. 1960, Paris.

Yearbook of International Organizations.

BOUGAINVILLE. The largest island of the Solomons Archipelago. Area: 9,300 sq km; 1986 pop. 154,500. Part of ▷ Papua New Guinea (as North Solomons provinces). A German colony 1889–1914, Australian 1914–20, then, with New Guinea, a mandated territory of the League of Nations entrusted to Australia; 1942–45 under Japanese occupation; 1946–75 an Australian territ-

ory held under UN mandate. An agreement on a maritime border between the North Solomon province and Choiseul Island and Shortland Island, was signed in June 1987 by the Governments of Papua New Guinea and the ▷ Solomon Islands.

The Europa Yearbook 1987. A World Survey, London, 1987; J. PAXTON (ed.), *The Stateman's Yearbook, 1987–88*, London, 1987.

BOULDER "UNITED NATIONS". A yearly academic conference on World affairs, organized since 1947 by Boulder University's governing body every Easter Holiday in Boulder, Colorado.

The Economist, December 8, 1987.

BOULOGNE CONFERENCE, 1920. A conference of the members of ▷ Entente, held in Boulogne-sur-Seine, June 21–22, 1920 to deal with the amount and distribution of reparations and the demilitarization of Germany; the result was a preliminary agreement on the acceptance of a reparation of 269 billion DM in gold paid by 1962. The conference was called by the decision of the ▷ Hythe Conference, 1920; its subject-matter being further dealt with at the ▷ Spa Conference, 1920.

BOUNDARIES. ▷ Frontier Litigation; ▷ Frontiers, Inviolability of.

BOURKINA FASSO ▷ Burkina Faso.

BOVINE MEAT. Subject of international conventions. The ▷ Tokyo Round in the November 1979 accepted an Agreement on Bovine Meat. See also ▷ Meat.

BOWLING. A subject of international co-operation. Organization reg. with the UIA:

International Bowling Board, f. 1905, Bournemouth UK.

Yearbook of International Organizations.

BOXER PROTOCOL, 1901. The peace agreement between China and the Great Powers (Austria–Hungary, Belgium, France, Germany, Great Britain, Italy, Japan, the Netherlands, the United States, Russia and Spain), signed in Peking Sept. 7, 1901, after an uprising in China against the domination of foreigners 1899/1900, especially Germans and Japanese; organized by a secret organization I-ho-cüen (a fist in the name of peace and justice); crushed by joint American, British, French, German and Japanese forces. Highlights of the Protocol:

The Plenipotentiaries of Germany, Austria–Hungary, Belgium, Spain, the United States, France, Great Britain, Italy, Japan, the Netherlands, Russia, and the Plenipotentiaries of China have met for the purpose of declaring that China has complied with the conditions laid down in the note of 22nd December, 1900, and which were accepted in their entirety by His Majesty the Emperor of China in a Decree dated the 27th December, 1900.
Art. I.(1) By an Imperial Edict of the 9th June last, Tsai-Feng, Prince of the First Rank, Chün, was appointed Ambassador of His Majesty the Emperor of China, and directed in that capacity to convey to His Majesty the German Emperor the expression of the regrets of His Majesty the Emperor of China and of the Chinese Government at the assassination of his Excellency the late Baron von Ketteler, German Minister. Prince Chün left Peking on the 12th July last to carry out the orders which had been given him.
(2) The Chinese Government has stated that it will erect on the spot of the assassination of his Excellency the late Baron von Ketteler, commemorative monument worthy of the rank of the deceased, and bearing an inscription in the Latin, German, and Chinese languages which shall express the regrets of His Majesty the Emperor of China for the murder committed. The

Chinese Plenipotentiaries have informed his Excellency the German Plenipotentiary, in a letter dated the 22nd July last, that an arch of the whole width of the street would be erected on the said spot, and that work on it was begun on the 25th June last.
Art. II.(1) Imperial Edicts of the 13th and 21st February, 1901, inflicted the following punishments on the principal authors of the attempts and of the crimes committed against the foreign governments and their nationals:
Tsa-Li, Prince Tuan, and Tsai-Lan, Duke Fu-kuo, were sentenced to be brought before the Autumnal Court of Assize for execution, and it was agreed that if the Emperor saw fit to grant them their lives, they should be exiled to Turkestan, and there imprisoned for life, without the possibility of commutation of these punishments.
Tsai Hsun, Prince Chuang, Ying-Nien, President of the Court of Censors, and Chao Shu-chiao, President of the Board of Punishments, were condemned to commit suicide.
Yu Hsien, Governor of Shansi, Chi Hsui, President of the Board of Rites, and Hsu Cheng-yu, formerly Senior Vice-President of the Board of Punishments, were condemned to death. Posthumous degradation was inflicted on Kang Yi, Assistant Grand Secretary, President of the Board of Works, Hsu Tung, Grand Secretary, and Li Ping-heng, former Governor-General of Szuchuan.
An Imperial Edict of the 13th February last rehabilitated the memories of Hsu Yung-yi, President of the Board of War; Li-Shan, President of the Board of Works; Hsu Ching Cheng, Senior Vice-President of the Board of Civil Office; Lien Yuan, Vice-Chancellor of the Grand Council; and Yuan Chang, Vice-President of the Court of Sacrifices, who had been put to death for having protested against the outrageous breaches of international law of last year. Prince Chuang committed suicide on the 21st February last; Ying Nien and Chao-Shu-chiao on the 24th February; Yu Hsien was executed on the 22nd February; Chi Hsiu and Hsü Cheng-Yu on the 26th February; Tung Fu-hsiang, General in Kan-su, had been deprived of his office by Imperial Edict of the 13th February last, pending the determination of the final punishment to be inflicted on him.
The Imperial Edicts, dated the 29th April and 19th August, 1901, have inflicted various punishments on the provincial officials convicted of the crimes and outrages of last summer.
(2) An Imperial Edict, promulgated the 19th August, 1901, ordered the suspension of official examinations for five years in all cities where foreigners were massacred or submitted to cruel treatment.
Art. III. So as to make honourable reparation for the assassination of Mr Sugiyama, Chancellor of the Japanese Legation, His Majesty the Emperor of China, by an Imperial Edict of the 18th June, 1901, appointed Na T'ung, Vice-President of the Board of Finances, to be his Envoy Extraordinary, and specially directed him to convey to His Majesty the Emperor of Japan the expression of the regrets of His Majesty the Emperor of China and of His Government at the assassination of Mr Sugiyama.
Art. IV. The Chinese Government has agreed to erect an expiatory monument in each of the foreign or international cemeteries which were desecrated, and in which the tombs were destroyed. It has been agreed with the Representatives of the Powers that the Legations interested shall settle the dates for the erection of these monuments, China bearing all the expenses thereof, estimated at 10,000 taels, for the cemeteries at Peking and in its neighbourhood, and at 5,000 taels for the cemeteries in the provinces. The amounts have been paid, and the list of these cemeteries is inclosed herewith.
Art. V. China has agreed to prohibit the importation into its territory of arms and ammunition, as well as of materials exclusively used for the manufacture of arms and ammunition. An Imperial Edict has been issued on the 25th August, forbidding said importation for a term of two years. New Edicts may be issued subsequently extending this by other successive terms of two years in case of necessity recognized by the Powers.
Art. VI. By an Imperial Edict dated the 29th May, 1901, His Majesty the Emperor of China agreed to pay the Powers an indemnity of 450,000,000 of Haikwan taels. This sum represents the total amount of the indemnities

B

for States, Companies, or Societies, private individuals and Chinese, referred to in Article 6 of the note of the 22nd December, 1900.

(1) These 450,000,000 taels constitute a gold debt calculated at the rate of the Haikwan tael to the gold currency of each country, as indicated below:

Marks	3.055
Austro-Hungary crown	3.595
Gold dollar	0.843
Francs	3.740
£ sterling	3 s
Yen	1.407
Netherlands florin	1.796
Gold rouble (17.434 dolias fine)	1.412.

This sum in gold shall bear interest at 4 per cent per annum, and the capital shall be reimbursed by China in thirty-nine years in the manner indicated in the annexed plan of amortization. Capital and interest shall be payable in gold or at the rates of exchange corresponding to the dates at which the different payments fall due. The amortization shall commence the 1st January, 1902, and shall finish at the end of the year 1940. The amortizations are payable annually, the first payment being fixed on the 1st January, 1903. Interest shall run from the 1st July, 1901, but the Chinese Government shall have the right to pay off within a term of three years, beginning January 1902, the arrears of the first six months ending the 31st December, 1901, on condition, however, that it pays compound interest at the rate of 4 per cent, a year on the sums the payment of which shall have been thus deferred. Interest shall be payable semi-annually, the first payment being fixed on the 1st July, 1902.

(2) The service of the debt shall take place in Shanghai in the following manner: Each Power shall be represented by a Delegate on a Commission of bankers authorized to receive the amount of interest and amortization which shall be paid to it by the Chinese authorities designated for that purpose, to divide it among the interested parties, and to give a receipt for the same.

(3) The Chinese Government shall deliver to the Doyen of the Diplomatic Corps at Peking a bond for the lump sum, which shall subsequently be converted into fractional bonds bearing the signature of the Delegates of the Chinese Government designated for that purpose. This operation and all those relating to issuing of the bonds shall be performed by the above-mentioned Commission, in accordance with the instructions which the Powers shall send their Delegates.

(4) The proceeds of the revenues assigned to the payment of the bonds shall be paid monthly to the Commission.

(5) The revenues assigned as security for the bonds are the following: (a) The balance of the revenues of the Imperial Maritime Customs, after payment of the interest and amortization of preceding loans secured on these revenues, plus the proceeds of the raising to 5 per cent, effective of the present tariff of maritime imports, including articles until now on the free list, but exempting rice, foreign cereals, and flour, gold and silver bullion and coin. (b) The revenues of the native Customs, administered in the open ports by the Imperial Maritime Customs. (c) The total revenues of the salt gabelle, exclusive of the fraction previously set aside for other foreign loans.

(6) The raising of the present tariff on imports to 5 per cent, effective, is agreed to on the conditions mentioned below. It shall be put in force two months after the signing of the present Protocol, and no exceptions shall be made except for merchandize in transit not more than ten days after the said signing."

P.H. CLEMENTS. *An Outline of the Politics and Diplomacy of China and the Powers 1894–1902*, New York, 1915; H. CLEMENTS, *The Boxers' Rebellion*, London, 1915; W.M. MALLOY, *Treaties, Conventions, International Acts, Protocols and Agreements between the USA and other Powers*, Vols. 1–4, Washington, DC, 1923–38, Vol. 1; *Major Peace Treaties of Modern History*, New York, 1967, pp. 1135–1143.

BOXING. A subject of international co-operation. A branch of sport recognized by the International Olympic Committee, 1904, first in seven classes, in 1920 in eight, 1954 in nine, and since 1980 in ten classes:

flyweight, 112 lb;
bantamweight, 119 lb;
featherweight, 125 lb;
lightweight, 132 lb;
light welterweight, 139 lb;
welterweight, 147 lb;
light middleweight, 156 lb;
middleweight, 165 lb;
light heavyweight, 178 lb;
heavyweight, over 178 lb;

Organizations reg. with the UIA:

European Amateur Boxing Association, f. 1970, The Hague.
International Amateur Boxing Association, f. 1946, Moscow. Publ. *Rules for International Matches*.
World Boxing Association, f. 1920, Louisville KY, USA.
World Boxing Council, f. 1963, Mexico DF, Mexico. Publ. *Bulletin*.

N.S. FLEISCHER (ed.), *Ring Record Book and Boxing Encyclopedia*, New York, 1960; *Yearbook of International Organizations*, 1986–87.

BOYANA. A village in Western Bulgaria, 8 km south of Sofia. The Boyana Church is included in the ▷ World Heritage UNESCO List. This is a group of three churches joined to each other, all three having the form of a Greek cross and with decorated facades. The first, to the east, dates from the 10th and 11th centuries. The one to the west, which dates from the 19th century, marks the "Bulgarian revival" after 400 years of foreign occupation. The church in the center, built around 1250, contains frescoes which are both realistic and mystical and display a marvellous serenity.

UNESCO. *The Protection of the World Cultural and Natural Heritage*, Paris, 1983.

BOYCOTT. An international term for an organized action in abstaining from or preventing a person or a group of persons, a nation or a state from participating in the life of the international community or part of it; e.g., in international trade. The first such action was taken in Ireland in 1880 where leaseholders of the landed estates run by C.C. Boycott stopped all professional and social links with him. Boycott is also practised in international intercourse as a weapon in economic and political competition; it is applied for defensive (e.g. boycott of an invader) as well as aggressive reasons (e.g. economic boycott) which in UN terminology is called economic aggression.

S.P. SEFERIADES, "Réflexions sur le Boycottage", in: *Droit International*, Paris, 1912; E. CLARK, *Boycotts and Peace. A Report by Committee on Economic Sanctions*, London, 1932; S. MATSUMOTO, *The Historical Development of Chinese Boycott (1834–1925)*, London, 1933; S. JENZOWSKI, *Die Chinesisch–Japanischen Boykotfälle als völkerrechtliches Problem*, Berlin, 1939; W.J. LAMBERS, "Das Ostembargo", in: *Dokumente*, 1956, No. 21; H. LAUTERPACHT, "Boycott in International Relations", in: *The British Yearbook of International Law*, 1933.

BRACEROS. *Spanish* = "workers, day-laborers". An international term for Mexicans seeking work in the United States; from 1968 the US government has applied severe measures against braceros – 150,000 were arrested and expelled to Mexico, in 1969 – 201,000, in 1970– 389,000. In 1978/79, USA and Mexican governments began talks on the issue of a general solution to the problem. The US Aliens Bill of June 26, 1984 with amnesty for about six million 'illegal' migrants in the US has not satisfied the Hispanic migrants, while the Immigration Bill also established the employer penalty provision.

J. BUSTAMENTE, *Braceros*, Mexico, DF, 1972.

BRADLEY DOCTRINE. A doctrine formulated by US Senator Bill Bradley in October, 1987:

"A society governed by a centralized, one-party state that insists on dictatorial control is inherently unstable. History teaches that instability and great military power are a dangerous combination. That is why Soviet power has been such a problem for the rest of the world, especially for Eastern Europe."

A. M. ROSENTHAL, The Bradley Doctrine, in: *The New York Times*, October 27, 1987.

BRAIN. A subject of international co-operation. Organizations reg. with the UIA:

European Brain and Behaviour Society, f. 1969, London.
International Brain Research Organization, f. 1960, Paris. Consultative status: UNESCO, WHO, ECOSOC. Publ. *IBRD News*.
International Cerebral Palsy Society, f. 1954, London.
International Study Group on Cerebral Circulation, f. 1962, Graz, Austria.

Yearbook of International Organizations, 1986–87.

BRAIN-DRAIN. An international term for the emigration of highly qualified people, mainly from less developed countries to the industrialized ones to take advantage of better financial opportunities and better facilities in which to work. After World War II the brain-drain occurred mostly from Europe to the USA and, when economic and political stabilization considerably decreased the number of those willing to leave Europe, the brain-drain switched to Third World countries. A meeting was convened in Aug., 1962 in Geneva to discuss the effects of the brain-drain on Africa, Latin America and Asia. On Dec. 13, 1967 the Economic and Financial Committee of the UN General Assembly resolved to carry on detailed investigations on the problem of emigration of highly qualified people from poor countries to the rich ones. The UN General Assembly ratified Resolutions on the question: 2320/XXII of Dec. 15, 1967; 2417/XXIII of Dec. 17, 1968; 3017/XXVII of Dec. 18, 1972.

US NATIONAL SCIENCE FOUNDATION. *Scientists and Engineers from Abroad, 1962–1964*, Washington, DC, 1967; PAHO. *Migration of Health Personnel, Scientists and Engineers from Latin America*, Washington, DC, 1967; *The Brain-drain, Report of Working Group on Migration*, London, 1967; *The Brain-Drain into the United States: A Staff Study for the Research and Technical Programs Subcommittee of the Committee on Government Operations*, Washington, DC, 1967; "The brain-drain, foreign aid for US", in: *US News and World Report*, May 22, 1967; "Le 'brain-drain' ou la fuite des 'cerveux' vers le pays les plus riches", in: *Documents d'Actualité*, No. 125, March 1968; *The International Migration of High-Level Manpower: Its Impact on the Development Process*, New York, 1972; J.W. BHAGWATI, M. PARTINGTON, *Taxing the Brain Drain: A Proposal*, Amsterdam, 1976; *Notas sobre economia y el desarrollo de América Latina*, CEPAL No. 182, 16.1.1975; *UN Chronicle*, January 1978; UNITAR, *The Brain Drain: Emigration and Return*, New York, 1978: *UN Chronicle*, October 1982.

BRAINS TRUST. An international term for a group of intellectuals acting as advisers to a program of development: coined by US President, F.D. Roosevelt, 1933.

BRAIN-WASH. A cold-war term adopted by the world press in 1951 for the Chinese method of "thought reforming" (*ssuhsiang kaitsao*) through intensive indoctrination of a determined world outlook.

BRANDT COMMISSION REPORT, 1980. A report entitled "North–South: A Programme for

Survival", published at the beginning of 1980 by the Independent Commission on International Development Issues, chaired by the former Chancellor of the FRG, Nobel Peace Prize Winner, Willy Brandt and consisting of 11 persons from the Group of 77, representing the South and 9 persons from OECD countries, representing the North. The Report suggests ways of promoting adequate solutions to the problems involved in development and in attacking absolute poverty. The second report about the financial situation and the debts of southern states was published on Feb. 9, 1983.

North–South: A Programme for Survival, Cambridge, 1980; *UN Chronicle*, June 1980: KEESING's *Contemporary Archive*, 1983.

BRANDWEIN. ▷ Cognac.

BRASILIA. The capital of Brazil (since 1960); city and federal district with 1,176,908 resident population (1980 census).

BRATISLAVA. The capital, on the Danube River, of the Federal State of Slovakia, from 1918; city with 340,902 resident population, 1975.

BRAVO RIVER AND COLORADO RIVER, RIO BRAVO Y RIO COLORADO. Two border rivers of Mexico and the USA internationalized 1853; subject of disputes and American Mexican treaties in 1889, 1905, 1933, 1944, 1965, 1967, and 1973. The Rio Bravo, also called Rio Grande, changed its riverbed in the 19th century and separated from the Mexican part of its territory, called ▷ Chamizal. The dispute over Chamizal ended in 1967. The dispute on the utilization of the waters of Rio Colorado for industrial purposes, which began in 1961, ended with the Treaty of Aug. 30, 1973.

A. GARCIA ROBLES, *El Mundo de la Postguerra*, Mexico, DF, 1946, Vol. II, pp. 459–460; *International Navigable Waterways*, UPA, Washington, DC, 1975.

BRAZIL. Member of the UN. República Federative do Brasil. Federal Republic of Brazil. State in South America on the Atlantic Ocean. Bordering on all the South American countries except Chile and Ecuador. Area: 8,511,965 sq. km. Pop. 1987 est. 141,450,000; 1970 census: 93,139,037; 1980 census: 119,070,865. Capital: Brasilia with 1,176,908 inhabitants, 1980. GNP per capita in 1987 US $2020. Official language: Portuguese. Currency: 1 new cruzado = 100 centavos. National Day: Sept. 7, Independence Day, 1822.
Original member of the League of Nations 1919. During World War II on the side of United Nations. Original member of the UN and of all UN specialized agencies. Member of the OAS. Member of the Tlatelolco Treaty.
International relations: discovered on Apr. 22, 1500 by the Portuguese, became a Portuguese colony. Independent Kingdom proclaimed on Sept. 7, 1822; since Nov. 15, 1889 a republic (Republic of the United States of Brazil); present name (Federative Republic of Brazil) since Nov. 10, 1967. Demarcation of frontiers with Colombia by the Treaties and Agreements of 1853, 1907, 1928 and 1930; with Venezuela by the Treaties and Agreements of 1859, 1891, 1904, 1907 and 1931; with British Guiana in 1904, with Dutch Guiana in 1906; with French Guiana in 1900 and in 1955; with Uruguay by the Treaty of Oct. 12, 1851; with Argentina by arbitration Agreement on Feb. 6, 1895; with Paraguay by the Treaty of Dec. 25, 1850; with Bolivia by the Treaties of Mar. 27, 1867, of Nov. 17, 1903 and of Dec. 29, 1928; with Peru by a Treaty of 1851. During World War I Brazil declared war on Germany on Oct. 26, 1917. The capital of Brazil until 1960 was Rio de Janeiro, since then Brasilia.

Brazil's debts of over US $91 billion were on top of the world list in 1984, before Mexico – US $85 billion and Argentina over US $40 billion. In October 1987 in the Goiana Radiotherapy Institute a radiation leak, second in severity to the ▷ Chernobyl disaster occurred, contaminating thousands of people over a 310 sq km area. On April 6, 1988 Brazil signed 16 integration agreements with Argentina and Uruguay (▷ Alvorado Act, 1988). See also ▷ World Heritage UNESCO List.

R.B. DE MORAES, *Bibliographia Brasiliana 1504–1900*, 2 Vols, Rio de Janeiro, 1958: D. DE CARVALHO, *Historia diplomatica do Brasil*, São Paulo, 1959: J.J. FAUST, *Une Amérique pour demain*, Paris, 1966; E.B. BURNS, *A History of Brazil*, New York, 1971; P. RAINE, *Brazil: Awaking Giant*, Washington, DC, 1974; P. MCDONOUGH, *Power and Ideology in Brazil*, Princeton, 1981; W.E. SEICHER ed., *Brazil in the International system*, Boulder, 1981; W.G. TYLER, *The Brazilian Industrial Economy*, Aldershot, 1981; *The Europa Year Book 1984. A World Survey*, Vol. I, pp. 1208–1232, London, 1984; T.E. SKIDMORE, *The Politics of Military Rule in Brazil 1964–1985*, Boston, 1988; KEESING's *Record of World Events*, April, 1988.

BRAZILIAN DOCTRINE OF FLEXIBLE BOUNDARIES, 1974. A doctrine also called the doctrine of "living boundaries", asserting that the boundaries of a state move forward or recede depending on the demographic vitality of the country. The doctrine was formulated in 1974 by Gen. Golbera de Conto e Silva, justified in a work of the director of the department of boundaries in the Brazilian ministry of foreign affairs, T. Soares, promoting planned colonization combined with the purchase of lands on bordering states by Brazilians, and, as a consequence, changing the old ethnic boundary to a new one, which permits Brazil to make demands for a suitable change in political boundaries. The doctrine of "flexible boundaries" had been implemented by Brazil in the 19th century: 1852 from Uruguay 43,000 sq. km, 1859 from Venezuela 150,000 sq. km, 1867 from Bolivia 160,000 sq. km, 1871 from Paraguay 60,000 sq. km, 1885 from Argentina 30,000 sq. km, 1901 from Guiana 60,000 sq. km, 1903 from Bolivia 191, 000 sq. km and from Colombia 127,000 sq. km, and in 1904 from Guiana 13,500 sq. km, in total 834,000 sq. km. The justification of the Brazilian doctrine by T. Soares:

"A country-continent such as Brazil, a true empire without a crown, has a definite mission to fulfill. In order to fulfill it well our boundaries must be live ... "

T. SOARES, *Historia de fronteiras do Brasil*, Rio de Janeiro, 1974.

BRAZZAVILLE. Capital of Congo (since 1958); city (1983 pop. census 456,383). The seat of the African Postal Telecommunications Union and a WHO Regional Office.

The Europa Yearbook, 1987. A World Survey, London, 1987; J. PAXTON (ed.), *The Statesman's Yearbook, 1987–88*, London, 1987.

BRAZZAVILLE GROUP, GROUPE DE BRAZZAVILLE. Official name of the francophonic states of Africa after a Conference on Dec. 15–19, 1960 in Brazzaville, of the chiefs of state of Cameroon, Central African Republic, Chad, Dahomey, Congo, Gabon, Ivory Coast, Mauritania, Niger, Republic of Congo (now Zaïre), Republic of Malagasy and Upper Volta (now Burkina Faso). The chiefs of state of the Brazzaville Group met again in Yaoundé Mar. 26–28, 1961 and created the Afro-Malagasy Organization for Economic Co-operation, OCAM.

M. LYONS, *Constitucionalismo y Democracia en el Africa Recien Independizada*, pp. 170–173, Mexico, DF, 1964.

BREAD. A subject of international co-operation. Organizations reg. with the UIA:

Bread for the World, f. 1973, New York.
Committee of Bread Yeast Manufacturers of the EEC, f. 1959, Paris.
International Association of the Bread Industry, f. 1956, Paris.

Yearbook of International Organizations, 1986–87.

BREASTFEEDING. A subject of international co-operation and promotion. Organization reg. with the UIA:

International Baby Food Action Network, f. 1979, Geneva, Switzerland (with offices) in America and Asia.
La Leche League International, f. 1956, Franklin Park, Ill., USA. Aims: give help and encouragement to those mothers who want to nurse their babies. Publ. books, brochures, pamphlets in different languages.

The 41st WHO Assembly in Geneva, May 2–13, 1988 accepted the status of implementation of the International Code of Marketing of Breast-milk substitutes.

M. CARBALLO, "Breastfeeding: the natural option", in: *World Health*, Aug.–Sept., 1979, pp. 29–31. *WHO Press*, April 25, 1988.

BREASTFEEDING WHO PROMOTION. The WHO Special Program of Research Development and Research Training in Human Reproduction promoted breastfeeding as a natural contraceptive. The nursing of a baby helps postpone the next pregnancy and "prevent more pregnancies than any other contraceptive method."

I. SHAH, J. KHANNA, Natural Contraceptive, in: *World Health*, November, 1987.

BRECHOU, one of the islands of the ▷ Bailiwick of Guernsey, UK Crown Dependency.

BRENNER PASS. Italian–Austrian border mountain pass in the Alps, until 1914 completely belonging to Austria; from 1919 in large part belonged to Italy, which led to the resettlement of the German-speaking population; in 1934 when Austria was threatened with ▷ Anschluss by the III Reich, Italy sent its army to Brenner Pass threatening armed opposition. On May 3, 1938, after the Anschluss, Hitler on an official visit was formally welcomed at Brenner Pass by Mussolini. Railroad line between Austria and Italy built in 1867.

KEESING's *Contemporary Archive* 1938.

BREST-LITOVSK TREATIES, 1918. Two Peace Treaties signed by Austria, Hungary and Germany, one with Soviet Russia, second with the Ukrainian People's Republic and Soviet Russia; first on Feb. 9, 1918, second on Mar. 3, 1918, both at Brest-Litovsk (today Brest in the Byelorussian SSR near the Polish border). Both treaties came into force on Mar. 15, 1918.
The highlights of the Treaty of Peace between the Central Powers and Russia:

"Art. 1. The Central Powers and Russia declare the state of war between them to be terminated and are resolved henceforth to live in peace and friendship with one another.
Art. 5. Russia will, without delay, carry out the full demobilization of her army inclusive of those units recently organized by the present government.
Furthermore, Russia will either bring her warships into Russian ports and there detain them until the day of the conclusion of a general peace, or disarm them forthwith. Warships of the States which continue in the state of war with the Powers of the Quadruple Alliance, in so far as they are within Russian sovereignty, will be treated as Russian warships.
The barred zone in the Arctic Ocean continues as such until the conclusion of a general peace. In the Baltic Sea, and as far as Russian power extends within the Black

B

Sea, removal of the mines will be proceeded with at once. Merchant navigation within these maritime regions is free and will be resumed at once. Mixed commissions will be organized to formulate the more detailed regulations, especially to inform merchant ships with regard to restricted lanes. The navigation lanes are always to be kept free from floating mines.
Art. 6. Russia obligates herself to conclude peace at once with the Ukrainian People's Republic and to recognize the treaty of peace between that State and the Powers of the Quadruple Alliance. The Ukrainian territory will, without delay, be cleared of Russian troops and the Russian Red Guard. Russia is to put an end to all agitation or propaganda against the Government or the public institutions of the Ukrainian People's Republic.
Esthonia and Livonia will likewise, without delay, be cleared of Russian troops and the Russian Red Guard. The eastern boundary of Esthonia runs, in general, along the river Narwa. The eastern boundary of Livonia crosses, in general, Lakes Peipus and Pskow, to the southwestern corner of the latter, then across Lake Luban in the direction of Livenhof on the Dvina. Esthonia and Livonia will be occupied by a German police force until security is insured by proper national institutions and until public order has been established. Russia will liberate at once all arrested or deported inhabitants of Esthonia and Livonia, and insures the safe return of all deported Esthonians and Livonians. Finland and the Aaland Islands will immediately be cleared of Russian troops and the Russian Red Guard, and the Finnish ports of the Russian fleet and of the Russian naval forces. So long as the ice prevents the transfer of warships into Russian ports, only limited forces will remain on board the warships. Russia is to put an end to all agitation or propaganda against the government or the public institutions of Finland. The fortresses built on the Aaland Islands are to be removed as soon as possible. As regards the permanent non-fortification of these islands as well as their further treatment in respect to military and technical navigation matters, a special agreement is to be concluded between Germany, Finland, Russia, and Sweden; there exists an understanding to the effect that, upon Germany's desire, still other countries bordering upon the Baltic Sea would be consulted in this matter.
Art. 7. In view of the fact that Persia and Afghanistan are free and independent states, the contracting parties obligate themselves to respect the political and economic independence and the territorial integrity of these States.
Art. 10. Diplomatic and consular relations between the contracting parties will be resumed immediately upon the ratification of the treaty of peace."

The Peace Treaty with the Ukrainian People's Republic, ceded to the Ukraine part of Galicia, Bukowina and the Chelm district.
Soviet Russia recognized the independence of the Ukraine and Finland, and ceded the control over Estonia, Latvia, Lithuania and the Kingdom of Poland to Germany, and Batum and Kass to Turkey-Ardahan.
Both Peace Treaties were annulled by Germany at the request of Western powers, included in the truce act signed in Compiègne on Nov. 11, 1918; and also by Russia on Nov. 13, 1918; apart from that declared null and void by art. 116 of the Versailles Peace Treaty 1919.

Proceedings of the Brest-Litovsk Peace Conference, Nov. 22, 1917–Mar. 3, 1918, Washington, DC, 1918; V. JOHN, Brest-Litovsk Verhandlungen und Friedensverträge in Osten 1917 bis 1918, Berlin, 1937; J.W. WHEELER-BENNET, Brest Litovsk. The Forgotten Peace, Mar. 1918, London, 1958; TH. SHIEDER, "Brest-Litovsk. Friede von 1918", in: STRUPP – SCHLOCHAUER Wörterbuch des Völkerrechts, Berlin, 1960, Bd. I, pp. 245–247.

BRETON LANGUAGE. A subject of international protection. Organization reg. with the UIA:

International Committee for Protection of the Breton Language, f. 1975, Brussels.

Yearbook of International Organizations.

BRETTON WOODS CONFERENCE AND AGREEMENTS, 1944. The first UN Monetary and Financial Conference held July 1–22, 1944, in the health resort of Bretton Woods, White Mountains, New Hampshire, USA, attended by 45 states: Australia, Belgium, Bolivia, Brazil, Canada, Chile, China, Colombia, Costa Rica, Cuba, Czechoslovakia, Denmark, Dominican Republic, Ecuador, Egypt, Ethiopia, Philippines, France, Greece, Guatemala, Haiti, Holland, Honduras, India, Iraq, Iran, Ireland, Liberia, Luxembourg, Mexico, Nicaragua, Norway, New Zealand, Panama, Paraguay, Peru, Poland, Republic of South Africa, Salvador, the UK, Uruguay, the USA, the USSR, Yugoslavia and Venezuela. Two conventions were signed on July 22, 1944 setting up International Monetary Fund ▷ IMF, and International Bank for Reconstruction and Development ▷ IBRD.

J. VINER, Two Plans for International Monetary Specialization, London, 1943; J. VINER, The Bretton Woods Agreement, London, 1944; R. MOSSE, Le système monétaire de Bretton Woods et les grands problèmes de l'après-guerre, Paris, 1948; Everyone's United Nations, New York, 1979, pp. 364, 366; COMMONWEALTH STUDY GROUP, Towards a New Bretton Woods. Challenges to the World Financial Trading System, London, 1983.

BREVE. *Latin: brevis* = short. In the Roman Catholic Church an official papal letter addressed to particular persons, churches or church or secular institutions on strictly defined matters concerning the recipients alone. Since 1967 *breve* of lesser importance have been handled by a special office of the Papal Secretariat of State; since 1973 *breve* of greater importance have been sent by the Chancellary of Apostolic Letters.

BREZHNEV DOCTRINE, 1968. After the Soviet Army together with Bulgarian, Hungarian, Polish and GDR troops intervened in Czechoslovakia, 1968, the First Secretary of the CPSU, Leonid Brezhnev announced publicly that the USSR had the right "to protect Communist regimes even if it means the use of force". This doctrine was in 1970 repeated by L. Brezhnev in Budapest as a doctrine of limited sovereignty (▷ Brezhnev Doctrine 1970). But in April 1987 during a visit in Budapest, Yegor K. Ligachev member of the CP SU Politburo stated:

"Each individual country (of the Warsaw Pact) can act independently. In the past it used to be said that the orchestra was conducted by Moscow and that everybody else listened. That is no longer the case".

See also ▷ *Gorbachev Doctrine on Warsaw Pact Countries*, 1987.

Ph. TANBMAN, Soviet Won't Push Policy on Allies, in: *New York Times*, Nov. 5, 1987.

BREZHNEV DOCTRINE, 1970. A doctrine on limited sovereignty of the socialist countries in relation to international interests of socialism, called Brezhnev doctrine by the Western press after a speech of L. Brezhnev, General Secretary of the USSR Communist Party Central Committee on April 4, 1970, in Budapest. The doctrine was occasioned by the Soviet invasion of Czechoslovakia in 1968. Brezhnev claimed the right of the USSR to intervene "when internal and external forces that are hostile to socialism try to turn the development of some socialist country towards the restoration of a capitalist regime, when socialism in that country and the socialist community as a whole is threatened." In a common communiqué signed in Moscow on July 7, 1971, L. Brezhnev and G. Marchais, General Secretary of the French Communist Party stated, that a doctrine on limited sovereignty is not acceptable to Soviet and French

communists. See also ▷ *Gorbachev Doctrine*, 1987 and also ▷ *Belgrade Soviet–Yugoslav Declaration*, 1988.

Documentation Française, 1971; L'Humanité, July 8, 1971.

BRIAND–KELLOGG TREATY OR PARIS PACT, 1928. The first multi-lateral international treaty condemning war. The General Treaty for Renunciation of War as an Instrument of National Policy was signed in Paris, Aug. 27, 1928, by the governments of Belgium, Czechoslovakia, France, Germany, Great Britain, Italy, Japan, Poland, and the USA. Ratification was deposited in Washington by all the States signatories, July 25, 1929. Accession, 1928/29; Afghanistan, Albania, Austria, Bulgaria, Chile, China, Costa Rica, Cuba, Danzig (Free City), Denmark, Dominican Republic, Egypt, Ethiopia, Estonia, Finland, Greece, Guatemala, Haiti, Honduras, Hungary, Iceland, Latvia, Liberia, Lithuania, Luxembourg, Mexico, Netherlands, Nicaragua, Norway, Panama, Paraguay, Peru, Persia, Portugal, Romania, Serbo-Croat-Slovene State, Siam, Spain, Sweden Switzerland, Turkey, the USSR and Venezuela. The Treaty is composed of a preamble and three articles, the third one specifying terms of ratification and entry into force. Here are the first two articles:

"Art. 1. The High Contracting Parties solemnly declare in the names of their respective peoples that they condemn recourse to war for the solution of international controversies, and renounce it as an instrument of national policy in their relations with one another.
Art. 2. The High Contracting Parties agree that the settlement or solution of all disputes or conflicts of whatever nature or of whichever origin they may be, which may arise among them, shall never be sought except by pacific means."

The architects of the treaty were French Foreign Minister A. Briand and American Secretary of State F.B. Kellogg; at first on the French initiative (June 1927) it was designed as a French–American Treaty of Friendship and Renouncement of War, but the USA proposed to give it the status of an open multilateral agreement; won support of the Soviet Union on whose initiative (Feb. 9, 1929) a Protocol was signed in Moscow on the immediate entry into force of the provisions of that treaty, the signatories being Estonia, Latvia, Poland, Romania, and USSR and subsequently and separately Lithuania, Persia and Turkey. Referring to the Briand–Kellogg Treaty, USSR signed a convention with its neighbors in 1933 on definition of ▷ aggression. The Briand–Kellogg Treaty permitted a peaceful settlement of a dispute in the Sino-Soviet conflict over the Manchurian railway line, in 1929.

LNTS, Vol. 94, pp. 57–64, UNTS, No. 796; D.N. MILLER, The Peace Pact of Paris, New York, 1928; J.T. SHOTWELL, "The Pact of Paris, Historical Commentary. Text of Treaty and Related Documents", in: International Conciliation, No. 243, Oct. 1928; Treaty for the Renunciation of War, Washington, 1933; International Conciliation, No. 293, New York, October 1933, pp. 357–480; C.P. ANDERSON, "Harmonizing the League of Nations covenant with the peace pact", in: American Journal of International Law, Jan. 1933, pp. 105–109.

BRIBERY AND CORRUPTION IN INTERNATIONAL RELATIONS. The UN General Assembly adopted on Dec. 15, 1976, Res. 3514/XXX:

"The UN General Assembly condemn all corrupt practices, including bribery by transnational and other corporations, their intermediaries and others involved in violation of the laws and regulations of the host countries."

UN Chronicle, January 1976, p. 99; January 1977, pp. 50–51 and 99.

BRIDGE, CARD GAME. A subject of international co-operation. Organizations reg. with the UIA:

European Bridge League, f. 1947, Geneva.
International Bridge Academy, f. 1963, New York.
International Bridgepress Association, f. 1958, Oslo.
World Bridge Federation, f. 1958, Antwerp, Belgium, organizes from 1968 every four years Bridge World Olympics.

E. CULBERTSON, *The Contract Bridge Blue Book*, New York, 1930; J.A. CUDDON, *Dictionary of Sport and Games*, London, 1980; *Yearbook of International Organizations; Yearbook of International Organizations*, 1986–87.

BRIDGES, TUNNELS AND TURNPIKES. A subject of international co-operation. Organizations reg. with the UIA:

International Association for Bridge and Structural Engineering, f. 1929, Zurich, Switzerland. Publ. *Bolletin*.
International Bridge, Tunnel and Turnpike Association, f. 1932, Washington, DC. Publ. Tollways (monthly).

Yearbook of International Organizations, 1986–87.

BRIGADES INTERNATIONAL. Anti-Fascist combat squads of volunteers from 54 countries, fighting in the Spanish civil war in 1936–39 on the side of the Republican People's Army against the rebellious forces of General Franco and German and Italian units supporting Franco. The following brigades existed: German-Austrian (XI), Italian (XII), Polish (XIII, Jaroslaw Dabrowski Brigade), French (XIV), English–American (XV), and Balkan–Czechoslovak (129). A great role, as organizers and leaders, was played in the international brigades by prominent activists in the workers' movement such as P. Togliatti, P. Nenni and L. Longo.

L. LONGO, *Le Brigate internazionali*, Roma, 1972.

BRILL. *Sopthalmus rhombus.* A fish under the protection of an international convention.

UNTS, Vol. 321, p. 199.

BRINKMANSHIP. An international term taken from the cold war language of the 1950's, related to ▷ Atomic Diplomacy and ▷ On the Brink of War.

D. ROBERTSON, *Guide to Modern Defense and Strategy*, Detroit, 1988.

BRISTOL CHANNEL. A bay cutting into the south-west coast of Great Britain; separating Wales from south-west England, inlet of the Atlantic Ocean, 135 km long and from 8 to 80.5 km wide. Subject of an international dispute caused by the collision there of two ships in 1927, raising the issue of whether it belonged to the territorial waters of Great Britain or whether it was part of the North Sea.

BRITISH ANTARCTIC TERRITORY ▷ Antarctic Territory, British.

BRITISH ARMY OF THE RHINE, BAOR. The British land forces in North West Germany within the framework of NATO.

D. ROBERTSON, *Guide to Modern Defense and Strategy*, Detroit, 1988.

BRITISH ASIANS. An international term for inhabitants of former British colonies in Africa of Hindu or Pakistani origin who were granted British citizenship and were encouraged to settle in British dominions in Africa. Subject of an international dispute in Aug., 1972 when the leader of Uganda, General Amin, ordered about 50,000 British Asians, living in Uganda and engaged mostly in trade, to leave the country within 90 days.

BRITISH–CHINA TREATIES. Great Britain established relations with China on special conditions through the Peking Treaty of 1860, leasing for 99 years a part of Shantung peninsula called Hong Kong New Territories, on July 1, 1898. England was also a signatory of the Peking Protocol of Sept. 7, 1901; (▷ Boxer Protocol).

MAC MURRAY, *Treaties and Agreements with and Concerning China 1894–1919*, New York, 1921.

BRITISH COUNCIL. Governmental institution, established 1934 under the name British Committee for Relations with Other Countries as a private association, under the present name since 1940, when the royal statute gained legal status and the privilege of benefiting from government subsidies and the secretary of foreign affairs became obligated to represent the interests of the British Council. Works to improve the friendly relations of Great Britain with other countries and to develop cultural relations with them, i.e. through popularizing the English language. The head office of the British Council is in London. It has branches in the majority of countries of the world. Publ. *The British Council Annual Report*.

BRITISH EMPIRE. The historical name of the overseas territories under the rule of the British monarch during three centuries before 1914; changed to the British Commonwealth of Nations by the Statute of Westminster, 1931.

BRITISH–FRENCH GUARANTEE AGREEMENT, 1919. An agreement concluded in Paris on the day of signing the Treaty of Versailles on June 28, 1919, by France and Great Britain along with a similar one between France and the USA. The highlights of the agreement are:

Art. 1. guaranteed immediate British or American assistance to France in case Germany violated the provisions of the Treaty of Versailles (arts. 42–44) concerning demilitarization of the Rhineland.
Art. 2. conditioned both treaties' entry into force on their ratification by the signatory states.

Since the USA did not ratify the Treaty of Versailles, ratification of the French–USA Treaty and the French–British Treaty became superfluous. France faced a political crisis, because she had not managed to ensure her claims to the frontier along the left bank of the Rhine at the Conference of Versailles; and since American and British guarantees were not fulfilled, remilitarization of the Rhineland by the Third Reich in 1936 was made possible.

Documents on British Foreign Policy 1919–1939, London, 1947.

BRITISH–FRENCH–TURKISH AGREEMENT, 1939. A Mutual Assistance Treaty, signed Oct. 19, 1939 at Ankara.

Documents on British Foreign Policy 1919–1939, London, 1947.

BRITISH GUARANTEE TO POLAND, 1939. A statement by the Prime Minister A. Neville Chamberlain (1869–1940) in the House of Commons concerning the guarantee to Poland, Mar. 31, 1939:

"The Right Hon. Gentleman the Leader of the Opposition asked me this morning whether I could make a statement as to the European situation. As I said this morning, His Majesty's Government have no official confirmation of the rumours of any projected attack and they must not, therefore, be taken as accepting them as true.

I am glad to take this opportunity of stating again the general policy of His Majesty's Government. They have constantly advocated the adjustment, by way of free negotiation between the parties concerned, of any differences that may arise between them. They consider that this is the natural and proper course where differences exist. In their opinion there should be no question incapable of solution by peaceful means, and they would see no justification for the substitution of force or threats of force for the method of negotiation.

As the House is aware, certain consultations are now proceeding with other Governments. In order to make perfectly clear the position of His Majesty's Government in the meantime before those consultations are concluded, I now have to inform the House that during that period, in the event of any action with clearly threatened Polish independence, and which the Polish Government accordingly considered it vital to resist with their national force, His Majesty's Government would feel themselves bound at once to lend the Polish Government all support in their power. They have given the Polish Government an assurance to this effect. I may add that the French Government have authorized me to make it plain that they stand in the same position in this matter as to His Majesty's Government."

E.L. WOODWARD, R. BUTLER (eds.), *Documents on British Foreign Policy 1919–1939*, London, 1948, Vol. 4, Doc. 582.

BRITISH GUIANA. A British colony 1814–1966. ▷ Guiana.

M. SWAN, *British Guiana*, London, 1957.

BRITISH HONDURAS. A British colony 1884–1973. ▷ Belize.

BRITISH IMPERIAL CONFERENCES, 1909–37. The official name of the meetings of the government of Great Britain and representatives of the dominions and colonies of the British Empire in 1909, 1911, 1917, 1918, 1921, 1923, 1926, 1929, 1930, 1932, 1933, 1935 and 1937. Previously the meetings were called Colonial conferences, and then Meetings of the Prime Ministers of the British Commonwealth.

BRITISH INDIAN OCEAN TERRITORY. Since 1965 official name of a British colony, consisting of the Chagos Archipelago (formerly a dependency of Mauritius) and up to June 1976, the Aldabra, Farguhar and Desroches Islands, which returned to the Seychelles. The Chagos Archipelago includes the coral atoll ▷ Diego Garcia. Area: 54,400 sq. km. There is no permanent population.

The Statesman's Yearbook 1979–1980, p. 1052. *The Europa Yearbook. A World Survey, 1988, Vol. II*, London, 1988.

BRITISH–IRAQI TREATY OF ALLIANCE, 1930. A Treaty signed on June 30, 1930 in Baghdad, with Annex and Exchange of Notes. The text of the Art. 1 is as follows:

"Art. 1. There shall be perpetual peace and friendship between His Britannic Majesty and His Majesty the King of Iraq.
There shall be established between the High Contracting Parties a close alliance in consecration of their friendship, their cordial understanding and their good relations, and there shall be full and frank consultation between them in all matters of foreign policy which may affect their common interests.
Each of the High Contracting Parties undertakes not to adopt in foreign countries an attitude which is inconsistent with the alliance or might create difficulties for the other party thereto."

LNTS, Vol. 132, 1932, pp. 364–371.

BRITISH–IRISH PEACE TREATY, 1921. Signed Dec. 6, 1921 in London between the Free Irish State and Great Britain. Under Art. 11 it determined that

"Northern Ireland shall not be subject to the rule of the Parliament and Government of the Free Irish State."

Documents on British Foreign Policy 1919–1939, London, 1947.

BRITISH–LIBYAN ALLIANCE TREATY, 1953.
A Treaty signed in London on July 29, 1953; defined the Alliance in Art. 3:

"Should either High Contracting Party become engaged in war or armed conflict, the other High Contracting Party will ... immediately come to his aid as a measure of collective defence. In the event of an imminent menace of hostilities involving either of the High Contracting Parties they will immediately concert together the necessary measures of defence."

J.A.S. GRENVILLE, *The Major International Treaties 1914–1973. A History and Guide with Texts*, London, 1974, pp. 506–507.

BRITISH PETROLEUM. ▷ Abu Dhabi case.

BRITISH–POLISH PACT OF MUTUAL ASSISTANCE, 1939.
A Pact signed in London on Aug. 25, 1939. The Pact was of a defense alliance nature in which the two Parties made the commitment that in the case of aggression of "any European power whatsoever" against any of the Parties, the other Party "shall immediately render all assistance and support being at its power to the Party being in hostilities" and "shall not conclude an armistice or a peace treaty otherwise than on mutual agreement." Concluded for a duration of five years; included a top secret protocol explaining that the term "any European power whatsoever" refers exclusively to the Third Reich, and the possibilities of different aggressive actions of "any European power whatsoever" provided for in art. 2 refer to acts of potential aggression against Gdansk, Belgium, Holland and the Baltic States, Lithuania, Latvia and Estonia.

On Nov. 7, 1939, the pact was amended with a pact on military credits; with an exchange of notes of Oct. 12 and 25, 1939 on the use of Polish merchant fleet in hostilities; on Nov. 18, 1939, with a pact on the Polish navy; on July 18, 1940 with a pact on military co-operation between Poland and Great Britain and on Aug. 5, 1940, with a military pact signed by W. Sikorski and W.S. Churchill.

LNTS, Vol. V, 1939; E.L. WOODWARD (ed.), *Documents on British Foreign Policy 1919–1939*, London, 1947; K. LAPTER, "Les garanties anglaises accordées à la Pologne en 1939", in: *Annuaire Polonais des Affairs Internationales*, Varsovie, 1961, pp. 192–221; W.W. KULSKI, "The Anglo-Polish agreement of August 25th, 1939", in: *The Polish Review*, New York. No. 1–2, 1976.

BRITISH SOUTH AFRICA COMPANY.
A British colonial institution established in 1889 by Cecil Rhodes extending British rule over the Central African region, called after 1895 Rhodesia. The Company administrated Southern Rhodesia until 1923, and Northern Rhodesia until 1924, but retained all mineral rights. In 1965 the Company merged with an associated company of the Anglo-American Corporation into a holding company: Charter Consolidated Ltd.

BRITISH–SOVIET TREATIES, 1941–42.
Two treaties: Treaty on Joint War Activities of 1941 and Treaty of Alliance of 1942. The first Treaty was signed in Moscow on July 12, 1941 and concerned the joint activities of the government of the USSR and of the government of Great Britain in wartime against Germany. In two articles it stated that both Parties "undertake to render each other all forms of assistance and support" and shall not conclude any

armistice or peace treaty "unless on mutual agreement." The treaty entered into force at the moment of signature.

This Treaty was substituted by the Treaty of Alliance in the War against Hitlerite Germany and Her Associates in Europe and of Collaboration and Mutual Assistance thereafter between the UK and the USSR, which was signed in London on May 26, 1942. The text is as follows:

"Art. I. In virtue of the alliance established between the United Kingdom and the Union of Soviet Socialist Republics the High Contracting Parties mutually undertake to afford one another military and other assistance and support of all kinds in the war against Germany and all those States which are associated with her in acts of aggression in Europe.
Art. II. The High Contracting Parties undertake not to enter into any negotiations with the Hitlerite Government or any other Government in Germany that does not early renounce all aggressive intentions, and not to negotiate or conclude except by mutual consent any armistice or peace treaty with Germany or any other State associated with her in acts of aggression in Europe.
Art. III.(1) The High Contracting Parties declare their desire to unite with other like-minded States in adopting proposals for common action to preserve peace and resist aggression in the postwar period.
(2) Pending the adoption of such proposals, they will after the termination of hostilities take all the measures in their power to render impossible a repetition of aggression and violation of the peace by Germany or any of the States associated with her in acts of aggression in Europe.
Art. IV. Should one of the High Contracting Parties during the post-war period become involved in hostilities with Germany or any of the States mentioned in Article III(2) in consequence of an attack by that State against that Party, the other High Contracting Party will at once give to the Contracting Party so involved in hostilities all the military and other support and assistance in his power. This Article shall remain in force until the High Contracting Parties, by mutual agreement, shall recognise that it is superseded by the adoption of the proposals contemplated in Article III(1). In default of the adoption of such proposals, it shall remain in force for a period of twenty years, and thereafter until terminated by either High Contracting Party, as provided in Article VIII.
Art. V. The High Contracting Parties, having regard to the interests of the security of each of them, agree to work together in close and friendly collaboration after the re-establishment of peace for the organization of security and economic prosperity in Europe. They will take into account the interests of the United Nations in these objects, and they will act in accordance with the two principles of not seeking territorial aggrandisement for themselves and of non-interference in the internal affairs of other States.
Art. VI. The High Contracting Parties agree to render one another all possible economic assistance after the war.
Art. VII. Each High Contracting Party undertakes not to conclude any alliance and not to take part in any coalition directed against the other High Contracting Party." The treaty entered into force on July 4, 1942 and lasted 20 years; it was renounced by the Soviet Union on May 7, 1955, "due to the fact that Great Britain participated in re-militarization of West Germany and that the Federal Republic of Germany had been allowed into NATO."

Great Britain Treaty Series, No. 2, 1942; *LNTS*, Vol. 204, 1941–43, pp. 353–362.

BRITISH–TRANSJORDANIAN ALLIANCE TREATY, 1948.
A Treaty signed in London on Mar. 15, 1948; defined the alliance in art. 3: "Should either High Contracting Party become engaged in war ... other High Contracting Party will ... immediately come to his aid as a measure of collective defence."

J.A.S. GRENVILLE, *The Major International Treaties 1914–1973. A History and Guide with Texts*, London, 1974, pp. 504–506.

BRITISH VIRGIN ISLANDS ▷ Virgin Islands, British.

BROADCASTING.
A subject of international agreements and co-operation: Organizations reg. with the UIA:

Arab States Broadcasting Union, f. 1969, Cairo. Consultative status; ITU. Publ. *Arab Broadcast*.
Asian Broadcasting Union, f. 1964, Tokyo, and Sydney. Consultative status: UNESCO, ECOSOC, FAO.
Commonwealth Broadcasting Association, f. 1945, London. Publ. *Combroad*.
European Broadcasting Union (Eurovision), f. 1950, Geneva and Brussels. Consultative status: FAO, ILO, ITU, WHO. Publ. *The EBU Review. Canal of Europe*.
Inter-American Association of Broadcasters, f. 1946, Montevideo, Consultative status: ECOSOC, UNESCO, ITU, OAS.
Intergovernmental Committee of the International Convention of Rome for the Protection of Performers, Producers of Phonograms and Broadcasting Organizations, f. 1961, Geneva. Consultative status: UNESCO, ILO, WIPO.
International Broadcasting Institute, f. 1967, London.
International Christian Broadcasters, f. 1965, Chicago, USA.

See also ▷ Broadcasting European Convention, ▷ Broadcasting in the Cause of Peace, ▷ Broadcasting Stations, ▷ Phonograms.

E. KATZ, *Broadcasting in the Third World*, London, 1978; R. HOGGART, J. MORGAN, *The Future of Broadcasting*, London, 1982; E. ETZIOND-HALEVY, *National Broadcasting under Siege. A Comparative Study of Australia, Britain, Israel and West Germany*, London 1987.

Yearbook of International Organizations, 1986–87.

BROADCASTING EUROPEAN CONVENTION, 1933.
An agreement signed in Lucerne, on June 19, 1933 by the governments of Austria, Belgium, Czechoslovakia, Denmark, Estonia, France, Germany, Great Britain, Iceland, Ireland, Italy, Latvia, Norway, Poland, Portugal, Romania Spain, Switzerland, the USSR, Vatican and Yugoslavia, with the Lucerne Plan annexed thereto and a Final Protocol. The Lucerne Plan indicated the frequencies of all European broadcasting stations. Revised 1949 and 1979.

LNTS, Vol. 154, p. 133.

BROADCASTING IN THE CAUSE OF PEACE.
A subject of the International Convention concerning the Radio Service in the Cause of Peace, signed on Sept. 23, 1936 in Geneva. The highlights of the Convention:

"Art. 3. The High Contracting Parties mutually undertake to prohibit and, if occasion arises, to stop without delay within their respective territories any transmission likely to harm good international understanding by statements the incorrectness of which is or ought to be known to the persons responsible for the broadcast.
They further mutually undertake to ensure that any transmission likely to harm good international understanding by incorrect statements shall be rectified at the earliest possible moment by the most effective means, even if the incorrectness has become apparent only after the broadcast has taken place.
Art. 4. The High Contracting Parties mutually undertake to ensure, especially in time of crisis, that stations within their respective territories shall broadcast information concerning international relations the accuracy of which shall have been verified – and that by all means within their power – by the persons responsible for broadcasting the information."

LNTS, Vol. 186, pp. 302–303.

BROADCASTING STATIONS OUTSIDE NATIONAL TERRITORIES.
A subject of the

ITU Radio Regulations and of the European Agreement for the Prevention of Broadcast transmitted from Stations outside National Territories, signed on Jan. 22, 1965 by Belgium, Denmark, France, FRG, Greece, Ireland, Italy, Luxemburg, the Netherlands, Norway, Sweden and the UK. The highlights of the Agreement:

"The member states of the Council of Europe signatory hereto,
Considering that the Radio Regulations annexed to the International Telecommunication Convention prohibit the establishment and use of broadcasting stations on board ships, aircraft or any other floating or airborne objects outside national territories;
Considering also the desirability of providing for the possibility of preventing the establishment and use of broadcasting stations on objects affixed to or supported by the bed of the sea outside national territories;
Have agreed as follows:
Art. 1. This Agreement is concerned with broadcasting stations which are installed or maintained on board ships, aircraft, or any other floating or airborne objects and which, outside national territories, transmit broadcasts intended for reception or capable of being received, wholly or in part, within the territory of any Contracting Party, or which cause harmful interference to any radio-communication service operating under the authority of a Contracting Party in accordance with the Radio Regulations.
Art. 2. Each Contracting Party undertakes to take appropriate steps to make punishable as offences, in accordance with its domestic law, the establishment or operation of broadcasting stations referred to in Art. 1, as well as acts of collaboration knowingly performed."
European Treaty Series, No. 53.

BROKERS. A subject of international co-operation. Organizations reg. with the UIA:
Federation of National Association of Ship Brokers and Agents, f. 1959, London. Consultative Status: UNCTAD, EFTA, OECD.
International Association of Aircraft Brokers and Agents, f. 1951, Paris.
International Union of Commercial Agents and Brokers, f. 1953, Amsterdam.
Yearbook of International Organizations

BRONCHO-ESOPHAGOLOGY AND PNEUMOLOGY. A subject of international co-operation. Organizations reg. with the UIA:
International Bronchoesophagological Society, f. 1951, Philadelphia, Pa.
International Broncho-Pneumology Association, f. 1951, Paris. Publ. *Les bronches*.
Pan-American Association of Oto-Rhino-Laryngology and Broncho-Esophagology, f. 1946, Los Angeles, Calif.
Yearbook of International Organizations.

BRT. BRUTTO REGISTER TONNAGE. An international term for ship gross volume unit (net ▷ NRт). ▷ Register tonnage.

BRUNDTLAND UN COMMISSION REPORT, 1988. A UN Commission on economic and political conditions of environmental protection, was working in 1987 guided by the Prime Minister of Norway, Gro Harlem Brundtland. The resulting 374 page report, called the Brundtland Report, 1988 presented massive evidence that environmental survival is unthinkable without development and that development is impossible to sustain if the environment is destroyed and no resources are left for growth.
"Sustainable development" is the answer – growth that respects environmental constraints.
To reach it, more and better development aid is necessary. A larger portion of development assistance should be invested in the environment: reforestation, soil conservation, small-scale agriculture.

Small projects with maximum grass-roots participation should be favoured.
The World Bank must make a fundamental commitment to sustainable development. Both the Bank and the International Monetary Fund should fully incorporate sustainability considerations. But no single blueprint of sustainable development can be found for the whole planet. Each nation will have to work on its own. Environmental concerns must be integrated into political and economic decision-making, because in the real world all those issues are tightly interlocked. "The planet is not neatly compartmentalized anymore", the report states.
Economy and ecology are also interlocked.
Ecosystems do not respect national boundaries – water and air pollution move through borders; nuclear accidents can threaten entire regions.
Environmental stresses are linked one to another – deforestation provokes soil erosion; air pollution kills forests.
Environmental and economic problems are linked to many social and political factors. For example, rapid population growth, which has a tremendous impact on environment and development, is driven partly by the status of women in society.
The report analyses how poverty and "unsustainable growth" threaten the environment.
It also studies in depth – in an integrated manner and from the vantage point of sustainable development – population, food security, energy, urbanization, industry, trade, technology, the institutional and legal changes that are needed, and species and ecosystems, which it considers resources for development.
Throughout, it makes general recommendations for change. Three recommendations, however, are very specific.
An independent body should be set up to assess global risks. It should be made up mostly of NGOs, scientific organs and industry groups. This is needed, "given to the politically sensitive nature" of the subject, the Commission stated.
A universal declaration on environmental protection and sustainable development, followed by a convention, should be prepared under UN auspices. The General Assembly should transform the report into a UN Programme on Sustainable Development, organize regional conferences, and later an international conference.
See also ▷ Environmental UN perspective, 1988. ▷ Environmental Protection.
UN Chronicle, March, 1988, p. 38.

BRUNEI DARUSSALAM. Member of the UN. A state in the north-western part of the island of Borneo on the South China Sea; area: 5,765 sq. km; pop.: 1988 est.: 226,300, among which 54% are Malayans, 26% Chinese. Official languages: Malay and English. Capital: Bandar Sevi Begawan, GNP per capita 1988 US $15,400. Currency: one Brunei dollar = 100 cents. National Day: January 1, Independence Day, 1984.
Member of the UN from Sept. 20, 1984 and ICAO, WHO, ITU, WMO, IMO. Member of the ASEAN and the Commonwealth. International relations: Sultanate under British protectorate from 1888 to 1983. Great Britain did not agree that Brunei become part of Malaysia, 1963, remaining a non-autonomous territory under the authority of the British High Commissioner. In Nov. 1971 the British government transferred complete administrative authority to the Sultan, retaining the exclusive right to represent Brunei in foreign affairs. In Nov. 1976, in the UN, 88 states adopted a resolution demanding the granting of full sovereignty to Brunei. The Sultan and Great Britain signed in London, Jan. 7, 1979, a treaty under which

Brunei became a fully sovereign and independent state in 1984.
UN Yearbook 1976; *Everyone's United Nations*, New York, 1979; *The Europa Year Book 1984. A World Survey*. Vol. I, pp. 1268–1272, London, 1984.

BRUSHWARE. A subject of international co-operation. Organization reg. with the UIA:
EEC European Brushware Federation, f. 1958, Brussels.
Yearbook of International Organizations.

BRUSSELS. The capital of Belgium (1985 pop. 976,538 metropolitan area), since 1830, on the Senne River; it is the seat of NATO, of the Council of Ministers of the European Communities and of c. 370 international organizations reg. with the UIA, organized in the Fédération des Associations International Etablies en Belgique, which publishes a *Guide pratique a l'usage des organisations internationaux établies en Belgique*.
Yearbook of International Organizations. J. PAXTON (ed.), *The Stateman's Yearbook 1987–88*, London, 1987

BRUSSELS CONVENTIONS. ▷ Maritime Brussels Conventions.

BRUSSELS DECLARATION, 1874. Draft of a Declaration concerning the laws of war, adopted by the Brussels International Conference on Aug. 27, 1874.

BRUSSELS TREATY, 1948, AND PROTOCOLS, 1954. Called also West-Pact 1948. The Treaty on Economic, Social and Cultural Co-operation and on Collective Defense, signed in Brussels on Mar. 17, 1948 by the governments of Belgium, France, the Netherlands, Luxembourg and Great Britain, thus bringing into being the Western European Union, to which on force of the additional Protocol of Oct. 23, 1954, the German Federal Republic and Italy were accepted under special conditions, annulled in June 1980. (▷ Western European Union Agency for the Control of Armaments). The Brussels Treaty provided for close co-operation of signatories in the military, economic and political fields and was forerunner of NATO. The initiator of the Brussels Treaty was the Labor Government of Great Britain, whose Foreign Secretary E. Bevin (1881–1951), set forth in the House of Commons on Jan. 28, 1948 the draft of the alliance as the first step towards a "united Western Europe". One month after the conclusion of the Brussels Treaty the Western European countries commenced negotiations with the United States for an enlarged military pact, which was signed Apr. 4, 1949 under the name North Atlantic Treaty, by Belgium, Canada, Denmark, France, Iceland, Italy, Luxembourg, the Netherlands, Norway, Portugal, the UK and the USA. In Feb., 1952 Greece and Turkey adhered to the Treaty, and May 8, 1955 the Federal Republic of Germany. The text of the treaty is as follows:

"His Royal Highness the Prince Regent of Belgium, the President of the French Republic, President of the French Union, Her Royal Highness the Grand Duchess of Luxembourg, Her Majesty the Queen of the Netherlands and His Majesty the King of Great Britain, Ireland and the British Dominions beyond the Seas, resolved;
To reaffirm their faith in fundamental human rights, in the dignity and worth of the human person and in the other ideals proclaimed in the Charter of the United Nations;
To fortify and preserve the principles of democracy, personal freedom and political liberty, the constitutional traditions and the rule of law, which are their common heritage;

To strengthen, with these aims in view, the economic, social and cultural ties by which they are already united;

To cooperate loyally and to coordinate their efforts to create in Western Europe a firm basis for European economic recovery;

To afford assistance to each other, in accordance with the Charter of the United Nations, in maintaining international peace and security and in resisting any policy of aggression;

To take such steps as may be held to be necessary in the event of a renewal by Germany of a policy of aggression;

To associate progressively in the pursuance of these aims other States inspired by the same ideals and animated by the like determination;

Desiring for these purposes to conclude a treaty for collaboration in economic, social and cultural matters and for collective self-defence;

Art. 1. Convinced of the close community of their interests and of the necessity of uniting in order to promote the economic recovery of Europe, the High Contracting Parties will so organize and coordinate their economic activities as to produce the best possible results, by the elimination of conflict in their economic policies, the coordination of production and the development of commercial exchanges.

The cooperation provided for in the preceding paragraph, which will be effected through the Consultative Council referred to in Article VII as well as through other bodies, shall not involve any duplication of, or prejudice to, the work of other economic organizations in which the High Contracting Parties are or may be represented but shall on the contrary assist the work of those organizations.

Art. II. The High Contracting Parties will make every effort in common, both by direct consultation and in specialized agencies, to promote the attainment of a higher standard of living by their peoples and to develop on corresponding lines the social and other related services of their countries. The High Contracting Parties will consult with the object of achieving the earliest possible application of recommendations of immediate practical interest, relating to social matters, adopted with their approval in the specialized agencies. They will endeavour to conclude as soon as possible conventions with each other in the sphere of social security.

Art. III. The High Contracting Parties will make every effort in common to lead their peoples towards a better understanding of the principles which form the basis of their common civilization and to promote cultural exchanges by conventions between themselves or by other means.

Art. IV. If any of the High Contracting Parties should be the object of an armed attack in Europe, the other High Contracting Parties will, in accordance with the provisions of Article 51 of the Charter of the United Nations, afford the Party so attacked all the military and other aid and assistance in their power.

Art. V. All measures taken as a result of the preceding Article shall be immediately reported to the Security Council. They shall be terminated as soon as the Security Council has taken the measures necessary to maintain or restore international peace and security.

The present Treaty does not prejudice in any way the obligations of the High Contracting Parties under the provisions of the Charter of the United Nations. It shall not be interpreted as affecting in any way the authority and responsibility of the Security Council under the Charter to take at any time such action as it deems necessary in order to maintain or restore international peace and security.

Art. VI. The High Contracting Parties declare, each so far as he is concerned, that none of the international engagements now in force between him and any other of the High Contracting Parties or any third State is in conflict with the provisions of the present Treaty.

None of the High Contracting Parties will conclude any alliance or participate in any coalition directed against any other of the High Contracting Parties.

Art. VII. For the purpose of consulting together on all the questions dealt with in the present Treaty, the High Contracting Parties will create a Consultative Council, which shall be so organized as to be able to exercise its functions continuously. The Council shall meet at such times as it shall deem fit.

At the request at any of the High Contracting Parties, the Council shall be immediately convened in order to

permit the High Contracting Parties to consult with regard to any situation which may constitute a threat to peace, in whatever area this threat should arise; with regard to the attitude to be adopted and the steps to be taken in case of renewal by Germany of an aggressive policy; or with regard to any situation constituting a danger to economic stability.

Art. VIII. In pursuance of their determination to settle disputes only by peaceful means, the High Contracting Parties will apply to disputes between themselves the following provisions:

The High Contracting Parties will, while the present Treaty remains in force, settle all disputes falling within the scope of Article 36, paragraph 2, of the Statute of the International Court of Justice by referring them to the Court, subject only, in the case of each of them, to any reservation already made by that Party when accepting this clause for compulsory jurisdiction to the extent that Party may maintain the reservation.

In addition, the High Contracting Parties will submit to conciliation all disputes outside the scope of Article 36, paragraph 2, of the Statute of the International Court of Justice. In the case of a mixed dispute involving both questions for which conciliation is appropriate and other questions for which judicial settlement is appropriate, any Party to the dispute shall have the right to insist that the judicial settlement of the legal questions shall precede conciliation.

The preceding provisions of this Article in no way affect the application of relevant provisions or agreements prescribing some other method of pacific settlement.

Art. IX. The High Contracting Parties may, by agreement, invite any other State to accede to the present Treaty on condition to be agreed between them and the State so invited. Any State so invited may become a Party to the Treaty by depositing an instrument of accession with the Belgian Government. The Belgian Government will inform each of the High Contracting Parties of the deposit of each instrument of accession.

Art. X. The present Treaty shall be ratified and the instruments of ratification shall be deposited as soon as possible with the Belgian Government.

It shall enter into force on the date of the deposit of the last instrument of ratification and shall thereafter remain in force for fifty years.

After the expiry of the period of fifty years, each of the High Contracting Parties shall have the right to cease to be a party thereto provided that he shall have previously given one year's notice of denunciation to the Belgian Government. The Belgian Government shall inform the Governments of the other High Contracting Parties of the deposit of each instrument of ratification and of signing the present Treaty and each notice of denunciation."

C.A. COLLIARD, *Droit international et l'histoire diplomatique*, Paris, 1950; LORD ISMAY, *NATO. The First Five Years 1949–1954*, Paris, 1954, pp. 3–12.

BRYAN–CHAMORRO TREATY, 1916. A Treaty concluded between the United States and Nicaragua, signed in 1916 by Secretary of State W.J. Bryan (1860–1925) and Minister of Foreign Affairs E. Chamorro (1871–1960); granted the USA the right, for a period of 99 years, to build an interocean canal across the territory of Nicaragua and Fonseca Bay; contested by Costa Rica and El Salvador in the Central American Court of Justice as being contradictory to the sovereign rights of these states, upheld by the Court in its verdict that "Fonseca Bay forms a territorial part of three coastal states: Costa Rica, El Salvador and Nicaragua."

W.M. MALLOY, *Treaties, Conventions ... and Agreements between the US and other Powers 1910–1923*, Vol. 3, Washington, 1923; J.I. MECHAN, *The US and Inter-American Security 1889–1960*, Austin, 1967, pp. 514–515.

BRYAN TREATIES, 1914. The name of treaties signed in 1914 between the USA and 30 states to serve "the system of cooling-off tensions", prepared by Secretary of State W.J. Bryan (1860–1925) and consisting of the obligation assumed by states-signatories that in case of aggravation of any

dispute they would not attempt to settle it by force prior to termination of a "cooling-off period" specified in the treaty. Extracts from the text of the Bryan Treaty for the Advancement of Peace, signed Sept. 15, 1914:

"The President of the United States of America and the President of the French Republic, desiring to strengthen the friendly relations which unite their two countries and to serve the cause of general peace, have decided to conclude a treaty for these purposes ...

Art. 1. Any disputes arising between the Government of the United States of America and the Government of the French Republic, of whatever nature they may be, shall, when ordinary diplomatic proceedings have failed and the High Contracting Parties do not have recourse to arbitration, be submitted for investigation and report to a Permanent International Commission constituted in the manner prescribed in the following article.

The High Contracting Parties agree not to resort, with respect to each other, to any act of force during the investigation to be made by the Commission and before its report is handed in."

PH. C. JESSUP, "The US and Treaties for the Avoidance of War", in: *International Conciliation*, No. 239, April 1928, pp. 179–243.

BRYGGEN OF BERGEN. A cultural site of Norway, included in the ▷ World Heritage UNESCO List. The houses of Bryggen, with their gabled fronts, large courtyards and stone cellars, bespeak the austere elegance of this old trading city whose prosperity lasted 800 years, right up to the beginning of this century.

UNESCO. *The Protection of the World Cultural and Natural Heritage*, Paris, 1983.

BTW CONVENTION ▷ BW Convention.

BUCHAREST. The capital of Romania from 1861, on the Dimbovita River, a tributary of the Danube. (1986 pop. 1,989,823). The seat of the Balkan Medical Union, International Association of South-East European Studies, UN Information Center.

Yearbook of International Organizations. The Europa Yearbook 1987. A World Survey, London 1987.

BUCHAREST ACTION PLAN, 1974. The official name of a resolution adopted in Bucharest Aug. 30, 1974, by the III World Population Conference. ▷ World Population Conferences, 1954–1984.

BUCHAREST APPEAL, 1976. A document passed on Nov. 26, 1976 in Bucharest by leaders of the Warsaw Pact States, calling upon the signatories of the Helsinki Final Act, Aug. 2, 1975 to pledge themselves not to be the first to use nuclear weapons against one another.

Preamble and the first main items of the draft of the agreement:

"States participating in the Conference on Security and Co-operation in Europe, named further the High Negotiating Parties, inspired by purposes and resolutions of the Final Act of this Conference;

Wishing to undertake a new common action aiming at consolidation of confidence among them, decreasing a military confrontation and contributing to disarmament;

Expressing their will to act in line with the purposes and rules of the UN Charter;

Determined to prevent the use or threat of using nuclear weapons against one another;

Aiming at contributing to the decrease of the threat of nuclear war in Europe and in all the world, undertake the obligation:

Art. 1. Not to use, as the first, nuclear weapons against one another on land, sea, in the air and in space.

Art. 2. The obligation provided for in Art. 1 covers not only the territory of the states, but also their armed forces, regardless of the world region where they might be stationed.

Art. 3. The agreement is open for signing to each state which had signed on 1st August, 1975 in Helsinki the Final Act of the Conference on Security and Cooperation in Europe."

New Times, Moscow, Dec., 1976.

BUCHAREST CLUB. International organization reg. with the UIA, f. 1972, Lugano, Switzerland. Aims: open a Euro-African dialogue to achieve closer unity in the examination of problems pertaining to the future.

Yearbook of International Organizations.

BUCHAREST DECLARATION, 1966. A Declaration on consolidation of peace and security in Europe, signed on July 5, 1966 in Bucharest, by the member States of the Warsaw Treaty: Bulgaria, Czechoslovakia, GDR, Poland, Romania, Hungary and the USSR. The Declaration contains an analysis of relations in Europe, "where the effects of World War II have not yet been eradicated, and where tensions persist in inter-State relations. States signatories of the Declaration consider it necessary to take measures aimed at a turn towards detente in Europe and at consolidation of security and the development of co-operation among European States. These measures should be implemented, primarily, along the following lines:

(1) Development of good neighborly relations according to the rule of peaceful coexistence of States having different social systems, and by expanding economic relations, scientific and cultural co-operation; (2) Simultaneous dissolution of the existing military alliances, NATO and Warsaw Treaty, which should be substituted by a system of European security; (3) Piecemeal moves aimed at dispelling tension such as closing down of military bases, withdrawal of foreign forces from territories of other States, reducing military forces of both German states, creation of atom-free zones; (4) Eliminating the possibility of FRG access to nuclear weapons; (5) Acknowledgement of inviolability of frontiers in Europe, including the Oder-Neisse frontier and the frontier between both German States; (6) Peaceful settlement of the German problem, primarily, the recognition of the fact of the existence of the two German States – GDR and FRG; (7) Calling an all-European conference on problems of ensuring security in Europe and all-European cooperation, which might further the setting up of a collective security system in Europe."

New Times, Moscow, July 1966.

BUCHAREST TREATIES, 1812, 1886, 1913, 1918. Five Balkan states peace and alliance treaties:

(1) Peace Treaty between Russia and Turkey of May 16–28, 1812, establishing the frontier along the river Prut and granting autonomy to Serbia;
(2) Peace Treaty between Bulgaria and Serbia of Feb. 19–Mar. 3, 1886, ending the war on the principle of the status quo;
(3) Peace Treaty between Greece and Montenegro, Romania, Serbia and Bulgaria of July 28–Aug. 10, 1913; Turkey refused to participate in this treaty, though she participated in the initial negotiations held in London on May 30, 1913; Bulgaria concluded a separate border-line treaty with Turkey, the so called Peace of Constantinople;
(4) Alliance Treaty between Romania and France, Russia, Italy and Great Britain of Aug. 4–17, 1916, bringing Romania into the Entente;
(5) Peace Treaty between Romania and Austro-Hungary, Bulgaria, Germany and Turkey of May 7, 1918; Romania gave up South Dobrudja to Bulgaria, granted the German Reich a concession for exploitation of crude oil for 50 years, won support for her claims to Bessarabia. This treaty was annulled by the Bessarabia Treaty of 1919.

K. STRUPP, *Ausgewählte diplomatische Aktenstücke zur orientalischen Frage*, Gotha, 1916.

BUCHENWALD. A German concentration camp north of Weimar, est. in Mar., 1937, liquidated in Apr., 1945. A subject of the Nuremberg Trial. The first prisoners were members of national minorities in the III Reich (Jews, Lusiatian Serbs, Poles and German anti-fascists). In all 240,000 prisoners of various nationalities passed through the camp. After the liberation of the camp by the US Army, the entire German population of nearby Weimar was forced to march through the camp.

The Trial of German Major War Criminals. Proceedings of the IMT Sitting at Nuremberg, 42 Vols, London, 1946–1948, Vols. 1, 2, 4, 5, 9, 10, 11, 12, 15 and 20. *Buchenwald Mahnung und Verpflichtung. Dokumente und Berichte* Berlin, 1983.

BUDAPEST. The capital of Hungary, (1986 pop. 2,075,990). Seat of 10 international organizations reg. with the UIA; among others: the Danube Commission, International Bureau of Tourism Youth Exchange, World Federation of Democratic Youth.

Yearbook of International Organizations. The Europa Yearbook 1987. A World Survey, London 1987.

BUDAPEST APPEAL, 1969. A Declaration signed on Mar. 17, 1969 in Budapest by the member states of the Warsaw Pact. An appeal to all European countries on preparing and implementing an all-European conference on security and co-operation proposed in the ▷ Bucharest Declaration of 1966. Most of the European States responded favorably to the Budapest Appeal, and the government of Finland declared its willingness to co-operate in preparing the Conference on Security and Co-operation in Europe (▷ Helsinki Conference) which was approved by the signatory-countries of the Appeal at the Conference of Ministers of Foreign Affairs in Prague on Oct. 31, 1969.

Recueil des documents, Varsovie, March, 1969.

BUDAPEST CSCE CULTURAL FORUM 1985. A ▷ CSCE forum on cultural creations, discrimination and co-operation took place on Oct. 15–Nov. 25, 1985 in Budapest and ended without any agreement.

KEESING's *Contemporary Archive*, 1986.

BUDDHISM. The religion of the followers of Gautama Buddha (c. 563–483 BC). The organization reg. with the UIA is: the World Fellowship of Buddhists, f. in 1950, Bangkok. Aims: work for the peace and welfare of peoples in accordance with the teaching of the Buddha. Regional centers in over 60 countries. Publ. *WFB Review*. Suborganization: World Fellowship of Buddhist Youth, f. 1972, Bangkok.

E.N. BREWSTER, *The Life of Gotama the Buddha*, London, 1926; E.J. THOMAS (ed.), *The Road to Nirvana*, London, 1950; C.H. HAMILTON, *Buddhism, a Religion of Infinite Compassion*, London, 1952; E. CONZE, *A Short History of Buddhism*, London 1960; S. HANAYAMA, *Bibliography on Buddhism*, London, 1961; D. IKEDA, *The Living Buddha. An Interpretive Biography*, Tokyo, 1976; D. IKEDA, *The Flower of Chinese Buddhism*, New York 1986. *Experience: Buddhist Practice for Oneself and for Others*, in: *Soka Gakkai News*, November 1987.

BUDGET OF THE LEAGUE OF NATIONS. The budget of the LN was based on the contributions of member states according to area, population, and economic potential. For simplification the "contributory unit" was accepted equal to 32,086.71 Swiss fr. in gold. In 1931, when the composition of the LN was the most numerous, the division of 986 "contributory units" among 54 states was a follows:

Albania	1	Honduras	1
Argentina	29	India	56
Australia	27	Ireland	10
Austria	8	Italy	60
Belgium	18	Japan	60
Bolivia	4	Latvia	3
Bulgaria	5	Liberia	1
Canada	35	Lithuania	4
Chile	14	Luxembourg	1
China	46	Nicaragua	1
Colombia	6	Norway	8
Czechoslovakia	29	New Zealand	10
Denmark	12	Panama	1
Estonia	8	Poland	32
Ethiopia	2	Salvador	1
Finland	10	Siam	9
France	79	Spain	40
Great Britain	105	Sweden	18
Germany	79	Switzerland	17
Greece	7	Union of S.Africa	15
Guatemala	20	Uruguay	7
Haiti	1	Venezuela	5
Holland	23	Yugoslavia	20

The budget for 1931 amounted to 31.6 million francs in gold, of which: for the Secretariat and specialized organizations – 17, for ILO – 8.6, for the Permanent Tribunal of International Justice – 2.6, for retirement – 1 million.

The League Year to Year, 1931.

BUDGET OF THE UN. The UN Secretary-General prepares the budget estimates for the Organization. The Budget was prepared annually until 1974, and since then the Organization has had a biennial program budget which is drafted in the framework of a four-year medium-term plan. The new system was adopted by the Assembly in 1973 in order to provide member states with a comprehensive picture of the nature, scope and objectives of the programs of activity of the Organization and of the resources required for the fulfillment of these objectives.

The plan was introduced in response to an Assembly resolution calling for the development of an integrated system of long-term planning on a program basis so as to improve programming and budgetary processes and to ensure the most rational use of available resources. The program budget provides a full description of the programs of activity of each organizational unit of the Secretariat, including their components, their legislative basis, their objectives and the related resource requirements. This new approach replaced a budget system in which specific amounts were approved annually for expenditure categories such as staff costs and printing rather than programs of activity.

Submitted by the Secretary-General in even-numbered years, the plan is reviewed by the Committee for Program and Coordination, a body composed of representatives of 21 states which reports to the Assembly through the Economic and Social Council. The plan was approved by the Assembly in 1976 for the 1978–81 period and divided the activities of the Organization into 29 major programs and approximately 325 subprograms in the political, economic, social, legal and other fields. The proposed program budget is submitted to the Assembly by the Secretary-General in odd-numbered years. It is reviewed by the Advisory Committee on Administrative and Budgetary Questions (ACABQ), a standing committee of the Assembly composed of 16 experts chosen with a view to geographical balance (there were nine experts from 1946 to 1961, 12 through 1971 and 13 through 1977). The recommendations of the ACABQ are examined by the Fifth Committee (Administrative and Budgetary) of the Assembly. The Assembly itself acts on the recommendations of the Fifth Committee in adopting or revising the budget. In even-numbered years the budget is revised as necessary to take into account such factors as inflation, change in rates of currency exchange, and Assembly decisions on new activities.

In its first 32 years the membership of the United Nations almost trebled and the number and scope of its activities greatly increased, as is reflected in part by a nearly 23-fold increase in its regular budget for a single year between 1946 and 1977. In 1977, the Assembly appropriated $985,913,300 for the regular budget for the two-year period 1978–79. The figure is exclusive of any supplement or reduction which the Assembly might subsequently approve. The total appropriations, including initial appropriation and subsequent supplement or reduction, for the regular budget of the United Nations for each year or two-year period from 1946 through 1985 were as follows:

Year	Gross budget US $
1946	$19,390,000
1947	28,616,568
1948	39,285,736
1949	43,204,080
1950	44,520,773
1951	48,925,500
1952	50,547,660
1953	49,869,450
1954	48,528,980
1955	50,228,000
1956	50,683,350
1957	53,174,700
1958	61,121,900
1959	61,657,100
1960	65,734,900
1961	71,649,300
1962	85,818,220
1963	92,876,550
1964	102,948,977
1965	108,472,800
1966	121,080,530
1967	133,084,000
1968	141,787,750
1969	156,967,300
1970	168,956,950
1971	194,627,800
1972	208,650,200
1973	233,820,374
1974–75	612,550,000
1976–77	789,488,900
1978–79	811,795,100
1980–81	1,267,793,200
1982–83	1,506,241,800
1984–85	1,587,159,800

Assessments on member states constitute the main source of funds under the regular budget. They are made in accordance with a scale adopted by the Assembly on the recommendation of its Committee on Contributions. How much each state shall pay is calculated primarily on the basis of its total national income in relation to that of other states. However, for countries with low per capita income, a category which includes many of the developing countries, a national income is adjusted downward by a special allowance formula. In addition, there is a maximum assessment of 25% of the budget (payable by the United States) and a minimum assessment of 0.01% (payable by 67 out of a total of 149 member states and amounting to $40,296 net each for 1978). The minimum contribution had been 0.02% until it was lowered by the Assembly to 0.01% effective in 1978. Although the scale of assessments is normally revised every three years, the scale which the Assembly approved in 1977 was for 1978 and 1979 only. The Contributions Committee, in 1976, had recommended a scale covering 1977–79, but the Assembly approved it for 1977 only, after a number of member states objected to the way it had been formulated. In approving the 1977 scale the Assembly established additional criteria for drawing up future scales, asking the Contributions Committee to consider such factors as "the continuing disparity between the economies of developed and develop-

ing countries" and methods to avoid excessive rate changes from one scale to the next. The Contributions Committee took those factors into account in drawing up the 1978–79 scale which, for member states of the United Nations, the Assembly approved without change.

Under the scale of assessments for 1984–85, the following 18 countries contributed more than 1% to the budget

Country	%
USA	25.00
USSR	11.10
Japan	9.58
Germany, Federal Rep.	8.31
France	6.26
United Kingdom	4.46
Italy	3.45
Canada	3.28
Australia	1.83
Spain	1.70
Netherlands	1.63
China	1.62
Ukrainian SSR	1.46
GDR	1.39
Sweden	1.31
Brazil	1.27
Poland	1.24
Belgium	1.22

The list of countries contributing more than 1% will be changed in the author's proofs in Nov. 89 and the 1990-1991 budget provided.

The regular budget of the United Nations, to which these assessments apply, covers the administrative and other expenses of the central Secretariat and the other principal organs of the United Nations, both at headquarters and throughout the world. All member states are also assessed, in accordance with a modified version of the basic scale, for the costs of the United Nations Emergency Force (UNEF) and the United Nations Disengagement Observer Force (UNDOF) in the Middle East. The Assembly appropriated $76,321,000 for UNEF for the year beginning Oct. 25, 1977 and $11,611,871 for UNDOF from Oct. 25, 1977 to May 31, 1978. Many other United Nations activities are financed by voluntary contributions outside the regular budget. The main programs in this category, with their expenditure in 1976, are as follows: United Nations Development Program ($535 million); United Nations Children's Fund ($113 million); United Nations Relief and Works Agency for Palestine Refugees in the Near East ($115 million); voluntary funds administered by the United Nations High Commissioner for Refugees ($90 million); United Nations Fund for Population Activities ($76 million); and United Nations Institute for Training and Research ($2 million).

Total expenditure of all organizations in the United Nation's system, including the United Nations and the separately financed specialized agencies, exceeded $2700 million in 1977.

The 1980–81 budget provided for gross appropriation as follows:

	$ c
(1) Over-all policy-making, direction and co-ordination	25,113,400
(2) Political and Security Council affairs; peace-keeping activities	59,258,000
(3) Political affairs, trusteeship and decolonization	13,584,200
(4) Policy-making organs (economic and social activities)	7,073,900
(5) Office of the Director-General for Development and International Economic Co-operation	3,850,400
(6) Department of International Economic and Social Affairs	40,035,800
(7) Department of Technical Co-operation for Development	13,110,000
(8) Office of Secretariat Services for Economic and Social Matters	2,500,200
(9) Transnational corporations	7,298,100
(10) Economic Commission for Europa	24,137,300
(11) Economic and Social Commission for Asia and the Pacific	23,056,100
(12) Economic Commission for Latin America	32,455,800
(13) Economic Commission for Africa	27,120,300
(14) Economic Commission for Western Asia	14,393,500
(15) United Nations Conference on Trade and Development	50,069,600
(16) International Trade Center	8,370,500
(17) United Nations Industrial Development Organization	70,117,200
(18) United Nations Environment Program	10,678,200
(19) United Nations Center for Human Settlements (Habitat)	7,598,400
(20) International drug control	5,904,200
(21) Office of the United Nations High Commissioner for Refugees	25,740,600
(22) Office of the United Nations Disaster Relief Co-ordinator	4,762,200
(23) Human rights	9,689,900
(24) Regular program of technical co-operation	27,248,100
(25) International Court of Justice	7,573,200
(26) Legal activities	10,049,000
(27) Department of Public Information	46,226,300
(28) Administrative, management and general services	213,008,400
(29) Conference and library services	190,416,800
(30) United Nations bond issue	17,056,000
(31) Staff assessment	184,604,300
(32) Construction, alteration, improvement and major maintenance of premises	65,693,300

The great problem of the UN budget in the 1980s is the growing number of UN members not paying the regular budget contribution.

See also ▷ Debtors of the UN; ▷ Financial Crises of the UN 1985–86.

Everyone's United Nations, New York, 1979, pp. 339–342; *Programme Budget for the Biennium 1984–85*, UN, New York, 1984; *UN Secretariat's Budget Crisis*, in: KEESING's *Record of World Events*, April 1988.

BUENOS AIRES. The capital of Argentina, (1980 pop. census 2,922,829, metropolitan area: 9,969,826). Seat of 39 international organizations reg. with the UIA, among others: the Latin-American Integration Institute; Latin-American Confederation of Tourist Organizations; Latin-American Social Science Council; Latin-American Railways Association; UN Information Center.

Yearbook of International Organizations. The Europa Yearbook 1987. A World Survey, London 1987.

BUENOS AIRES ACTION PLAN, 1978. The official name for the final document of the UN Conference on Technical Co-operation among Developing Countries, in Buenos Aires, Sept., 1978, called by the UNDP, with 138 countries participating. The action plan formulates in 28 points the purposes and forms of technical co-operation of Third World countries within the ▷ New International Economic Order.

BUENOS AIRES CONFERENCE, 1910. ▷ American International Conferences.

BUENOS AIRES CONFERENCE, 1938. ▷ Inter-American Conference for the Maintenance of Peace.

BUENOS AIRES PEACE TREATY, 1938. ▷ Chaco Peace Treaty.

BUFFER STATE. An international term, introduced by the French statesman, A.F. Thiers. A definition of a state which separates two potentially conflicting powers. In the 19th-century Afghanistan, for example, was considered to be a buffer state separating tsarist Russia from British India; in the 20th century, in the post-Versailles period, examples were Czechoslovakia and Poland, separating the USSR from Germany.

BUFFER STOCK. An international term, used in the UN system, for stockpiles from which commodities are bought or sold whenever necessary to maintain relative stability of supply and prices. ▷ commodity agreements.

UN Chronicle, Oct., 1982, p. 46.

BUFFER STOCKS FUND. An international fund postulated by the Conference of Developing Countries on Raw Materials, held Feb. 3–8, 1975 at Dakar to establish a Special Fund to finance buffer stocks of raw materials and primary commodities exported by developing countries; established by the Conference of Ministers of Foreign Affairs of the Nonaligned Countries in Lima, Aug. 30, 1975.

BUFFER ZONE. An International term for a territorial strip separating two military forces in conflict after the suspension of arms, sometimes under jurisdiction of UN Forces.

BUILDING. A subject of international co-operation. Organizations reg. with the UIA:

European Federation of Building Joinery Manufacturers, f. 1957, Paris.
European Union of Independent Building Contractors, f. 1958, Brussels.
International Association of Building Companies, f. 1953, Heverlec, Belgium.
International Council for Building Research, Studies and Documentation, f. 1953, Rotterdam, Netherlands. Consultative status: UNESCO, ECOSOC, Publ. Building Research and Practice.
International European Construction Federation, f. 1905, Paris. Consultative status: ECOSOC, ILO, EEC.
International Union of Building Centres, f. 1958, London.

C.J. VAN MANSUM, *Elsevier's Dictionary of Building Construction*. In English/American, French, Dutch, and German, Amsterdam, 1979; *Yearbook of International Organizations*.

BULGARIA. Member of the UN. Narodna Republika Bulgaria, People's Republic of Bulgaria. European state on the Balkan Peninsula, bordered by the Black Sea, Romania, Yugoslavia, Greece, and European Turkey. Area: 110,119 sq. km. Population 1985 census: 8,942,000, (1975 census – 8,727,771). Capital: Sofia, 1,047,920 inhabitants 1980. GNP per capita in 1987 – US $5676. Currency: one lev = 100 stotinki. Official language: Bulgarian. National Day: Sept. 9, Liberation Day, 1944. Member of the League of Nations from 1926 to 1939, member of UN since Dec. 14, 1955 and all UN specialized agencies, except GATT, IDA, IMF, IFAD, IFC, and BANK/IBRD: founding member of Warsaw Treaty Organization and CMEA.
International relations: from 1361 to 1878 under Turkish rule, 1878–1908 autonomous princedoms within the Ottoman Empire. Proclaimed independent monarchy Oct. 5, 1908. In World War I fought on the side of Central States and, as a result of their defeat, lost part of its territory to Greece (Balkan Agreement concluded with Greece in Salonika, July 31, 1938), Yugoslavia (Pact of Eternal Friendship signed in Belgrade Jan. 25, 1937), and Romania, with whom a final borderline was established in the Kraiova Treaty 1940. In World War II Bulgaria joined the ▷ Anticomintern. Nov. 25, 1941 and

fought on the side of the Axis countries. The Soviet army entered Bulgaria on Sept. 5, 1944 and withdrew in Dec. 1947. On Oct. 28, 1944 a formal truce was signed between Bulgaria and the USSR, the UK and the USA. A Peace Treaty was concluded with the Allied powers in Paris on Feb. 10, 1947. Abolition of the monarchy and proclamation of the Bulgarian People's Republic was carried out on Sept. 8, 1947. On Mar. 18, 1948 Bulgaria signed a Treaty of Friendship and Mutual Assistance with the USSR for 20 years, renewed for an additional 20 years in Mar., 1968. In Mar., 1949 Bulgaria was accused by Australia before the UN General Assembly of violating the Paris Peace Treaty of 1947 by reducing the civil rights of clergy exclusively to religious matters. Bulgaria dismissed the accusation and refused to admit the UN Investigation Commission. See also ▷ World Heritage UNESCO List.

UN Yearbook 1949; Le développement social et économique de la Bulgarie 1944–1964, Sofia, 1964; R. RUSINOW, *Bulgaria: Land, Economy, Culture*, Sofia, 1965; M.V. PUNDEFF, *Bulgaria: A Bibliographic Guide of the Library of Congress*, Washington DC, 1965; N. TODOROV, *Bulgaria: Historical and Geographical Outline*, Sofia, 1965; *Kratka Bylgarska Enciklopediya*, t. 1–5, Sofia, 1963–69; J.F. BROWN, *Bulgaria under Communist Rule*, London, 1970; G.R. FEIVEL, *Growth and Reforms in Centrally Planned Economies; the Lessons of the Bulgarian Experience*, New York, 1977; *Everyone's United Nations*, New York, 1979; *The Europa Year Book 1984. A World Survey*, Vol. I, pp. 337–353, London, 1984. R.J. CRAMPTON, *A Short History of Modern Bulgaria*, Cambridge, 1987.

BULGARIAN NATIONAL BANK. Bulgarska Narodna Banka. F. 1879, in 1947 took over all the commercial banks of the country. A central bank responsible for issuing currency, also plays an important part in the management of the economy.

BULGARIA PEACE TREATY 1947. A Treaty signed in Paris, Feb. 10, 1947. The texts of the Preamble and of the first three articles are as follows:

"The USSR, the UK, the USA, Australia, the Byelorussian SSR, Czechoslovakia, Greece, India, New Zealand, the Ukrainian SSR, the Union of South Africa and Yugoslavia, as the States which are at war with Bulgaria and actively waged war against the European enemy states with substantial military forces, hereinafter referred to as the Allied and Associated Powers, of the one part,
and Bulgaria, of the other part;
Whereas Bulgaria, having become an ally of Germany and having participated on her side in the war against the USSR, the UK, the USA and other United Nations, bears her share of responsibility for this war;
Whereas, however, Bulgaria, having ceased military operations against the United Nations, broke off relations with Germany, and, having concluded on October 28, 1944, an Armistice with the Governments of the Union of Soviet Socialist Republics, the United Kingdom and the United States of America, acting on behalf of all the United Nations at war with Bulgaria, took an active part in the war against Germany; and
Whereas the Allied and Associated Powers and Bulgaria are desirous of concluding a treaty of peace, which, conforming to the principles of justice, will settle questions still outstanding as a result of the events hereinbefore recited and form the basis of friendly relations between them, thereby enabling the Allied and Associated Powers to support Bulgaria's application to become a member of the United Nations and also to adhere to any Convention concluded under the auspices of the United Nations;
Have therefore agreed to declare the cessation of the state of war and for this purpose to conclude the present Treaty of Peace, and have accordingly appointed the undersigned Plenipotentiaries who, after presentation of their full powers, found in good and due form, have agreed on the following provisions:

Art. 1. The frontiers of Bulgaria, as shown on the map annexed to the present Treaty (Annex I), shall be those which existed on January 1, 1941.
Art. 2. Bulgaria shall take all measures necessary to secure to all persons under Bulgarian jurisdiction, without distinction as to race, sex, language or religion, the enjoyment of human rights and of the fundamental freedoms, including freedom of expression, of press and publication, of religious worship, of political opinion and of public meeting.
Art. 3. Bulgaria, which in accordance with the Armistice Agreement has taken measures to set free, irrespective of citizenship and nationality, all persons held in confinement on account of their activities in favour of, or because of their sympathies with, the United Nations or because of their racial origin, and to repeal discriminatory legislation and restrictions imposed thereunder, shall complete these measures and shall in future not take any measures or enact any laws which would be incompatible with the purposes set forth in this Article."

Came into force on Sept. 15, 1947 upon the deposit with the Government of the USSR of the instruments of ratification by the USSR, the UK and the USA, in accordance with art. 38.

UNTS, Vol. 41, pp. 21–133.

BULGARIAN-POLISH FRIENDSHIP TREATY, 1948. Treaty of Friendship, Co-operation and Mutual Assistance between the Bulgarian Peoples Republic and the Polish Republic, signed at Warsaw, May 29, 1948. The text is as follows:

"Art. 1. The High Contracting Parties undertake to apply all means at their disposal for the purpose of preventing the repetition of aggression on the part of Germany directly or in some other form;
The High Contracting Parties shall participate in the spirit of widest cooperation in all international actions aiming at preserving world peace and security and shall contribute their share in the realization of these noble tasks;
Art. 2. Should one of the High Contracting Parties become the object of aggression on the part of Germany, or any other country which would unite with Germany directly or in some other form, the other High Contracting Party shall immediately afford the other Party military and other assistance with all the means at it's disposal;
Art. 3. The High Contracting Parties undertake not to conclude any alliance and not to participate in any action directed against the other High Contracting Party;
Art. 4. The High Contracting Parties shall confer upon all important international questions which may concern the interests of both countries and in the first place their security, territorial integrity and problems of peace and international cooperation;
Art. 5. The High Contracting Parties shall promote and strengthen mutual economic and cultural relations with the purpose of bringing about the general development of the two countries;
Art. 6. The provisions of the present Treaty shall in no way interfere with the obligations undertaken by the High Contracting Parties towards third countries and shall be fulfilled in accordance with the Charter of the United Nations."

Recueils de documents, Warsaw, No. 6, 1948, pp. 299–302; US Department of States, *Documents and State Papers*, No. 4, July 1948, pp. 248–249.

BULLA. A name adopted by the Catholic Church for a solemn Papal writ, e.g. in the Middle Ages a writ confirming the election of a Roman emperor, the nomination of church princes or announcing anniversaries or holidays. It always had a lead seal affixed called a *bulla*, hence the name of the whole document. A subject of international trade in connection with the occurrence of private collections, called *bullaria* and due to the fact that a great many counterfeits occurred in the market in the 19th century; the canon law code, CC 2360, imposed a penalty of anathema on forgers of *bulla*. An extraordinary *bulla* in the history of international rela-

B

tions was the one by Pope Alexander VI, *Inter caerera divinea*, of May 4, 1493, dividing the newly discovered territories in the Western Hemisphere between Spain and Portugal; it was approved with amendments in the ▷ Tordesillas Treaty.

Bullarium Magnum Romanum, Torino, 1857.

BULLETS. An international legal issue since the Declaration banning the use of explosive and incendiary missiles weighing less than 400 grams, signed in Petersburg, Nov. 9, 1868 (▷ Saint Petersburg Declaration, 1868). The Second Declaration banning the use of gas missiles, The Hague, July 29, 1899, coincided with the Third Hague Declaration banning the use of bullets which expand or flatten on impact (mushroom) inflicting tearing wounds, or the dum-dum bullets employed by the British colonial army from 1895 in India and the Sudan; used in 1939 in Ethiopia by Fascist Italy. In 1980 the UN discussed a Convention forbidding plastic shrapnel which is more dangerous than dum-dums and undetectable by X-rays.

H. KRAUSE, "Geschosse", in: *Strupp-Schlochauer Wörterbuch des Völkerrechts*, Berlin, 1960, Bd. 1, pp. 674–675.

BULLFIGHTING. *Spanish: Corrida de Toro.* A popular Spanish spectacle during which a bull is usually killed, also popular in other Latin-American countries. A subject of international actions opposing corrida de toros in the name of ▷ animal protection. Organization reg. with the UIA:
International Council Against Bullfighting, f. 1963, London. Member of World Federation for the Protection of Animals.

Yearbook of International Organizations.

BULLIONISM. An international term coined in Europe in the 15th and 16th centuries. A theory that the resources of gold and silver, calculated according to their weight, are decisive for the wealth of a country, and for the equilibrium of its ▷ balance of payments.

BULLION SYSTEM. An international term for a system of accepting gold or silver coins by their weight, just as with gold and silver bullion. Each year Samuel Montagu and Co. Ltd., London, publishes an analysis of the gold trade by its weight entitled *Annual Bullion Review*.

BURAIM. An oil-bearing region on the border of Oman and Abu Dhabi, member of United Arabian Emirates; a subject of military incidents 1952–55, between the protectors of both sultanates, Great Britain and Saudi Arabia. In view of British military intervention, the conflict ended in withdrawal of Saudi Arabian troops, which had entered Buraim in 1952.

BURDEN SHARING. An international term first used by ▷ NATO in the 1970s for the difference between the US and West European participation in the cost of common defense. In the 1980s also applied to the Warsaw Pact.

D. ROBERTSON, *Guide to Modern Defense and Strategy*, Detroit, 1988.

BUREAUCRACY INTERNATIONAL AND IN THE UN SYSTEM. International term, subject of international and UN research. See also ▷ Geographical Representation; ▷ Nomenklatura.

D. BEETHAM, *Bureaucracy*, London, 1987.

BUREAU OF NONALIGNED STATES. Bureau des pays non-alignés. A permanent institution of the Conference of Nonaligned States operating

between conferences, and evaluating the implementation of resolutions and decisions of summit meetings or those at the ministerial level. Seat: Algiers.

BURGES SHALE SITE. A Canadian natural monument included in the ▷ World Heritage UNESCO List. The site in British Columbia provides evidence of a complete era of evolution at the beginning of the mid-Cambrian period, more than 500 million years ago. These shale fossils have brought to light a previously unimagined number and variety of soft-bodied marine forms of life dating from the beginning of multi-cellular animal life on earth.

World Cultural Heritage, *Information Bulletin*, Paris, 1984.

BURKINA FASO. Member of the UN. Formerly Upper Volta. African state, bordering on Mali, Niger, Benin, Togo, Ghana and Ivory Coast. Area: 247,200 sq. km. Pop.: 1988 est. 8,530,000 (1975 census: 5,638,203; 1970 – 5,380,000; 1965 – 4,858,000). Capital city: Ouagadougou with 247,877 inhabitants (1980). GNP per capita (1986): US $150. Currency: CFA Franc = 100 centimes. Official language: French. National Day: Aug. 5, Independence Day, 1960.
Since Sept. 20, 1960 member of the UN and all its specialized agencies except IAEA and WMO. Member of OAU, OCAM, West African Common Market. A Signatory of the Yaoundé Conventions of 1963 and of 1969; and of the Lomé Conventions of 1975 and of 1980. An ACP state of the EEC.
International relations: 1897–1904: French protectorate; 1904 incorporated to French West Africa; granted autonomy within the French Union in 1958; independence proclaimed Aug. 5, 1960. Involved in border disputes with Mali since 1960; negotiations in the years 1961–74; border incidents 1974–76. On Sept. 16, 1983 the two countries agreed to submit the territorial dispute to the International Court of Justice. The border demarcation judgement of the IOJ, on Dec. 22, 1986 was accepted by both sides and came into effect at the end of 1987. The disputed area was divided into roughly equal parts on both sides.

E.P. SKINNER, *The Mossi of the Upper Volta. The Political Development of a Sudanese People*, Stanford, 1964; P.H. LIPPENS, *La République de Haute-Volta*, Paris, 1972; *The Europa Year Book 1984. A World Survey*, Vol. II, pp. 2638–2647, London, 1984; *Burkina Faso – Mali*, in: A.J. DAY (ed.), *Border and Territorial Disputes*, London, 1987, pp. 105–110.

BURMA–REPUBLIC OF CHINA DISPUTE 1953–54. At the request of Burma, the UN General Assembly on Mar. 31, 1953, included in the agenda the item "Complaint by the Union of Burma regarding aggression against it by the Government of the Republic of China."
The situation as described by Burma was that in 1950 Kuomintang troops had crossed the border into Burma. They had refused to submit to disarmament and internment, and engagements had taken place between them and the Burmese army. By 1953 the number of Kuomintang troops had grown to about 12,000.
The representative of China replied that the so-called aggression against Burma was not an idea of the Chinese Government and that the army led by General Li Mi was no longer part of the regular forces of the Republic of China. On Apr. 23, 1953, the General Assembly adopted a resolution by which, i.a., it deplored the presence of foreign troops in Burma and condemned their hostile acts against that country, declared that these foreign

forces must be disarmed and either agree to internment or leave Burma forthwith.
On Oct. 29, 1954 the Assembly adopted a resolution which: (1) noted with satisfaction that nearly 7000 persons had been evacuated from Burma; (2) expressed its appreciation of the efforts of the United States and Thailand in achieving the evacuation. The rest of the foreign forces left Burma in 1956.

Everyman's United Nations, New York, 1979, pp. 122–123.

BURMA ROAD. A 1.145 km long mountainous road between S. China and Burma built 1937–38, during WWII a vital artery for US military supplies to Chang Kai Shek's China, supported by a supply Ledo Road (810 km) constructed by Allied forces in 1944 between Lashio in Burma and Ledo in India.

U NU, *Burma Under the Japanese*, New York, 1954.

BURN INJURIES. A subject of international co-operation. Organization reg. with the UIA:
International Society for Burn Injuries, f. 1965, Edinburgh, UK. Consultative status: WHO.

Yearbook of International Organizations.

BURUNDI. Member of the UN. Republic of Burundi, République du Burundi. East central African state, bordering on Rwanda, Tanzania, on Lake Tanganyika and on Zaïre. Area: 27,834 sq. km. Pop.: 1988 est. 5,130,000 (1959 census 2,213,280; 1979 census 4,111,310). Capital: Bujumbura with 157,000 inhabitants 1980. GNP per capita 1986 US $240. Currency: one franc du Burundi = 100 centimes. Official languages: Kierundi and French. National Day: July 1, Independence Day, 1962.
Member of the UN and the UN specialized agencies with exception of IAEA and WMO. Member of OAU. ACP state of EEC.
International relations: occupied by the German Reich in 1890 and incorporated into German East Africa. Occupied 1916 by Belgian forces and together with Rwanda, under the name Ruanda–Urundi became part of the League of Nations Mandate, 1919–46. In 1946 became a UN trust territory administrated by Belgium until 1962, when Burundi became an independent Kingdom (Republic since Sept., 1966). A monetary and customs union with Rwanda, signed in Apr. 1962 in Addis Ababa, was dissolved Sept. 30, 1964. In the tragic civil war in 1971–72 between the Ba-Hutu (84%) and the influential Tutsi ethnic group (15%) about 120,000 persons were killed.

R. LEMARCHAM, *Rwanda and Burundi*, London, 1970; G. MPOZARA, *La République du Burundi*, Paris, 1971; T.P. MELADY, *Burundi: The Tragic Years*, New York, 1974; W. WEINSTEIN, *Historical Dictionary of Burundi*, Metuchen, 1976. *The Europa Year Book 1984. A World Survey*, Vol. I, pp. 1284–1291, London, 1984.

BURUNDI, RWANDA AND ZAÏRE ECONOMIC COMMUNITY. Communauté économique des pays des grands lacs, CEPGL. The official French name for the Economic Community of the Great Lakes States, established in fall 1976 by force of an agreement between the heads of the respective states. It is an institution open to all African states of the Great Lakes region. Seat: Gisenye (Rwanda).

BUSHMEN. A native people of the south-western part of Africa, annihilated like the ▷ Hottentots in the 19th century by the German colonialists. The last families are living in Namibia and Botswana.

BUSINESS ADMINISTRATION. A subject of international co-operation. Organizations reg. with the UIA:

Academy of International Business, f. 1959, Chicago, USA, Publ. *Journal of International Engineers Studies.*
Business and Industry Advisory Committee to OECD, f. 1962, Paris.
Central American Institute for Business Administration, f. 1963, Managua.
European Institute of Business Administration, f. 1958, Fontainebleau.
International Christian Union of Business Executives, f. 1949, Brussels.
International Society for Business Education, f. 1901, Zurich.

Yearbook of International Organizations.

BUSINESS OF AMERICA IS BUSINESS. A doctrine of US President Calvin Coolidge, proclaimed Jan 27, 1925, meaning that the first US Government obligation to the economy is to aid American private business, at home and abroad.

C. COOLIDGE, *The Autobiography*, New York, 1929; C.M. FUESS, *Calvin Coolidge*, New York, 1940.

BUSTAMANTE CODE OF PRIVATE INTERNATIONAL LAW, 1928. The official name of the codification of private international law initiated by a Cuban lawyer and statesman Antonio Sanchez de Bustamante (1865–1951). The Code was adopted by the Sixth International American Conference in Havana on Feb. 20, 1928 and officially designated as the "Bustamante Code". It was ratified by 15 Latin American countries. The General Rules of the Code entered into force in 1930. The text is as follows:

"General rules.

Art. 1. Foreigners belonging to any of the contracting States enjoy, in the territory of the others the same civil rights as are granted to nationals. Each contracting State may, for reasons of public order, refuse or subordinate to special conditions, the exercise of certain civil rights by the nationals of the remaining States and any of the latter States may in such cases refuse or subordinate to special conditions the same exercise to the nationals of the former.

Art. 2. Foreigners belonging to any of the contracting States shall also enjoy in the territory of the others identical individual guarantees with those of nationals, except as limited in each of them by the Constitution and the laws.
Identical individual guarantees do not include, unless especially provided in the domestic legislation, the exercise of public functions, the right of suffrage, and other political rights.

Art. 3. For the exercise of civil rights and the enjoyment of identical individual guarantees, the laws and regulations in force in each contracting State are deemed to be divided into the three following classes:
I. Those applying to persons by reason of their domicile or their nationality and following them even when they go to another country, termed personal or of an internal public order.
II. Those binding alike upon all persons residing in the territory, whether or not they are nationals, termed territorial, local, or of an international public order.
III. Those applying only through the expression, interpretation, or presumption of the will of the parties or of one of them, termed voluntary or of a private order.

Art. 4. Constitutional precepts are of an international public order.

Art. 5. All rules of individual and collective protection, established by political and administrative law, are also of an international public order, except in case of express provisions therein enacted to the contrary.

Art. 6. In all cases not provided for in this Code each one of the contracting States shall apply its own definition to the juridical institutions or relationships corresponding to the groups of laws mentioned in article 3.

Art. 7. Each contracting State shall apply as personal law that of the domicile or that of the nationality or that which its domestic legislation may have prescribed, or may hereafter prescribe.

Art. 8. The rights acquired under the rules of this Code shall have full extraterritorial force in the contracting States, except when any of their effects or consequences is in conflict with a rule of an international public order.
Book I. International Civil Law. Title I. Persons.
Chapter I. Nationality and Naturalization.

Art. 9. Each contracting party shall apply its own law for the determination of the nationality of origin of any individual or juristic person and of its acquisition, loss and recuperation thereafter, either within or without its territory, whenever one of the nationalities in controversy is that of the said State. In all other cases the provisions established in the remaining articles of this chapter shall apply.

Art. 10. In questions relating to nationality of origin in which the State in which they are raised is not interested, the law of that one of the nationalities in issue in which the person concerned has his domicile shall be applied.

Art. 11. In the absence of that domicile, the principles accepted by the law of the trial court shall be applied in the case mentioned in the preceding article.

Art. 12. Questions concerning individual acquisition of a new nationality shall be determined in accordance with the law of the nationality which is supposed to be acquired.

Art. 13. In collective naturalizations, in case of the independence of a State, the law of the acquiring or new State shall apply, if it has established in the territory an effective sovereignty which has been recognized by the State trying the issue, and in the absence thereof that of the old State all without prejudice to the contractual stipulations between the two interested States, which shall always have preference.

Art. 14. In the case of loss of nationality, the law of the lost nationality should be applied.

Art. 15. Resumption of nationality is controlled by the law of the nationality which is resumed.

Art. 16. The nationality of origin of corporations and foundations shall be determined by the law of the State which authorizes or approves them.

Art. 17. The nationality or origin of associations shall be the nationality of the country in which they are constituted, and therein they shall be registered or recorded if such requisite is demanded by the local legislation.

Art. 18. Unincorporated civil, commercial, or industrial societies or companies shall have the nationality provided by the articles of association, or, in an applicable case, that of the place where its principal management or governing body is habitually located.

Art. 19. With respect to stock corporations, nationality shall be determined by the articles of incorporation or, in an applicable case, by the law of the place where the general meeting of shareholders is normally held, and in the absence thereof, by the law of the place where its principal governing of administrative board or council is located.

Art. 20. Change of nationality of corporations, foundations, associations and partnerships, except in cases of change of territorial sovereignty, should be subject to the conditions required by their old law and by the new. In case of change in the territorial sovereignty, owing to independence, the rule established in Article 13 for collective naturalizations shall apply.

Art. 21. The provisions of Article 9, in so far as they concern juristic persons, and those of Articles 16 and 20, shall not be applied in the contracting States which do not ascribe nationality to juristic persons.
Chapter II. Domicile.

Art. 22. The concept, acquisition, loss and recovery of general or special domicile of natural or juristic persons shall be governed by the territorial law.

Art. 23. The domicile of diplomatic officers and that of individuals temporarily residing abroad in the employment or commission of their Government or for scientific or artistic studies, will be the last one they had in their national territory.

Art. 24. The legal domicile of the head of the family extends to the wife and children, except children who have reached their majority or have been emancipated, and that of the tutor or guardian extends to the minors or incapables under his guardianship unless otherwise provided by the personal legislation of those to whom the domicile of another is ascribed.

Art. 25. Questions relating to change of domicile of natural or juridical persons shall be determinated in accordance with the law of the Court, if it is that of one of the interested States, otherwise they shall be determined by the law of the place in which it is alleged they have acquired their domicile.

Art. 26. For persons having no domicile the place of their residence or, where they may happen to be, shall be considered as such.
Chapter III. Birth, extinction, and consequences of civil personality. Section I – Individual persons.

Art. 27. The capacity of individual persons is governed by the personal law, with the exception of the restrictions established for its exercise by this Code or by local laws.

Art. 28. Personal law shall be applied for the purpose of deciding whether birth determines personality and whether the unborn child is to be deemed as born for all purposes favorable to him, as well as for the purpose of viability and the effects of priority of birth in the case of double or multiple childbirth.

Art. 29. The presumptions of survivorship or simultaneous death, in the absence of proof, are governed by the personal law of each of the deceased persons in so far as their respective estates are concerned.

Art. 30. Each State shall apply its own legislation for the purpose of declaring that civil personality is extinguished by the natural death of individual persons and the disappearance or official dissolution of juristic persons, as well as for the purpose of deciding whether minority, insanity or imbecility deaf-dumbness, prodigality, and civil interdiction are only restrictions upon the status of persons permitting the existence of rights and even certain obligations.
Section II. – Juristic persons.

Art. 31. Each contracting State, as a juristic person, has full capacity to acquire and exercise civil rights and to assume obligations of the same character within the territory of the others, without restrictions other than those expressly established by the local law.

Art. 32. The concept and recognition of juristic persons shall be governed by territorial law.

Art. 33. Excepting the restrictions provided in the two preceding articles, the civil capacity of corporations is governed by the law which has created or recognized them; that of foundations by the rules of their institution, approved by the proper authority if required by their national laws and that of associations by their constitutions upon like conditions.

Art. 34. With the same restrictions, the civil capacity of civil, commercial or industrial partnerships is governed by the provisions relating to the contract of partnership.

Art. 35. The local law applies for the purpose of escheat in respect to the property of juristic persons which have ceased to exist, unless otherwise provided for in their by-laws, charters, or in the law in force for associations.
Chapter IV. Marriage and Divorce. Section I. – Legal conditions which must precede the celebration of matrimony.

Art. 36. The parties thereto shall be subject to their personal law in so far as it relates to their capacity to celebrate the marriage, the parents' consent or advice, the impediments and their dispensation.

Art. 37. Foreigners must show, before marrying, that they have complied with the conditions provided by their personal laws in respect of the provisions of the preceding article. They may do so by a certificate issued by their diplomatic or consular officers or by any other means deemed sufficient by the local authority, which shall have full liberty of determining in every case.

Art. 38. Local legislation is applicable to foreigners in respect to the impediments which it establishes as indispensable, to the form of consent, to the binding or non binding force of the betrothal, to the opposition to the marriage, the obligation of notifying impediments and the civil consequences of a false notice, to the form of preliminary procedure, and to the authority who may be competent to perform the ceremony.

Art. 39. The liability or non liability for breach of promise of marriage or for the publication of banns in such case is governed by the common personal law of the parties and in the absence thereof by the local law.

Art. 40. The contracting States are not obliged to recognize a marriage celebrated in any one of them by their nationals or by foreigners, which is in conflict with their provisions relative to the necessity of dissolution of a former marriage, to the degree of consanguinity or affinity, in respect to which there exists an absolute impediment, to the prohibition of marriage established in respect to those guilty of adultery by reason of which the marriage of one of them has been dissolved, to the same prohibition in respect to the one guilty of an attempt against the life of one of the spouses for the

purpose of marrying the survivor, and to any other inexcusable grounds of annulment.
Section II. – The form of marriage.
Art. 41. A marriage shall be held valid everywhere in respect to its form it if has been celebrated in the manner prescribed as valid by the laws of the country where it has taken place. However the States whose legislation prescribes a religious ceremony may refuse to recognize the validity or marriages entered into by their nationals abroad without the observance of that form.
Art. 42. In the countries where the law admits thereof, marriages entered into by foreigners before the diplomatic or consular agents of both contractants shall be subject to their personal law without prejudice to the application thereto of the provisions of Article 40.
Section III. – Effects of marriage in respect to the persons of the spouses.
Art. 43. The personal law of the spouses shall be applied, and, if different, that of the husband, in what concerns the respective duties of protection and obedience, the obligation or non obligation of the wife to follow the husband when he changes his residence, the disposal and administration of their joint property and all other special effects of marriage.
Art. 44. The personal law of the wife will govern the disposal and administration of her own property and her appearance in trial.
Art. 45. The obligation of the spouses to live together and be faithful to and help each other is subject to the territorial law.
Art. 46. A local law which deprives the marriage of a bigamist of civil effects is also imperatische applied.
Section IV. – Nullity of Marriage and its effects.
Art. 47. The nullity of marriage should be governed by the law to which the intrinsic or extrinsic condition which gives rise to it is subject.
Art. 48. Coercion, fear, and abduction as causes of nullity of marriage are governed by the law of the place of solemnization.
Art. 49. The personal law of the spouses if it is the same, otherwise that of the spouse who acted in good faith, and in the absence of both conditions that of the male, shall apply in respect to the rules regarding the care of the children of void marriages in cases in which the parents cannot or do not wish to stipulate anything on the subject.
Art. 50. The same personal law shall be applied to all other civil effects of a void marriage, except those which it must produce in respect to the property of the spouses, which shall follow the law of the matrimonial economic regime.
Art. 51. The rules fixing the judicial effects of the action of nullity are of an international public order.
Section V. – Separation and divorce.
Art. 52. The right to separation and divorce is regulated by the law of the matrimonial domicile, but it cannot be founded on causes prior to the acquisition of said domicile, if they are not authorized with equal effect by the personal law of both spouses.
Art. 53. Each contracting State has the right to permit or recognize, or not, the divorce or new marriage of persons divorced abroad, in cases, with effects or for causes which are not admitted by their personal law.
Art. 54. The causes of divorce and separation shall be subject to the law of the place in which they are sought, if the married couple are domiciled there.
Art. 55. The law of the court before which the litigation is pending determines the judicial consequences of the action and terms of the judgment in respect to the spouses and the children.
Art. 56. Separation and divorce, obtained in conformity with the preceding articles, produce their civil effects in accordance with the legislation of the court which grants them, in the other contracting States, saving the provisions of Article 53.
Chapter V. Paternity and Filiation.
Art. 57. Rules concerning the presumption of legitimacy and its conditions, those conferring the right to the name, and those which determine the evidence of filiation and regulate the inheritance of the child are rules of an internal public order, the personal law of the child if different from that of the father being applied.
Art. 58. The rules granting rights of inheritance to legitimated children partake of the same character but in this case the personal law of the father is applied.
Art. 59. The rule which gives the legitimate child the right to maintenance is of an international public order.
Art. 60. The capacity to legitimate is governed by the personal law of the father, and the capacity to be legitimated by the personal law of the child, legitimation requiring the concurrence of the conditions prescribed by both.
Art. 61. A prohibition against legitimation of children not simply natural is of an international public order.
Art. 62. The consequences of legitimation and the action to impugn it are subject to the personal law of the child.
Art. 63. Investigation of paternity, maternity and prohibition thereof are regulated by territorial law.
Art. 64. The rules prescribing the required conditions for acknowledgement, compelling it in certain cases, establishing the actions necessary for the purpose, granting or refusing the family name and fixing the causes of nullity, are subject to the personal law of the child.
Art. 65. The inheritance rights of illegitimate children are subject to the personal law of the father and those of illegitimate parents are subject to the personal law of the child.
Art. 66. The form and circumstances of acknowledging illegitimate children are subordinated to the territorial law.
Chapter VI. Maintenance among relatives.
Art. 67. The legal concept of maintenance, the order in which it is to be provided, the manner of furnishing it, and the extinction of that right shall be subject to the personal law of the one to be maintained.
Art. 68. The provisions establishing the duty to provide maintenance, its quantity, reduction or increase the time at which it is due, and the manner in which it is to be provided, as well as those forbidding the renunciation and the assignment of that right, are of an international public order.
Chapter VII. Paternal power.
Art. 69. The existence and general extent of paternal power in respect to person and property, as well as the cause of its extinction and recovery, and the limitation, by reason of a new marriage of the right to punish, are subject to the personal law of the child.
Art. 70. The existence of the right of usufruct and all other rules applicable to the different classes of his private property are also subject to the personal law of the child, whatever the nature of the property or the place where it is situated may be.
Art. 71. The provisions of the preceding article are to be applied in foreign territory without prejudice to the rights of third parties which may be granted by local law and the local provisions in respect to publicity and specialty of mortgage securities.
Art. 72. Provisions which determine the kind and limits of the right of the father to correct and punish and his recourse to the authorities, as well as provisions depriving him of power by reason of incapacity, absence or by judgment of a court, are of an international public order.
Chapter VIII. Adoption.
Art. 73. The capacity to adopt and to be adopted and the conditions and limitations of adoption are subject to the personal law of each of the interested persons.
Art. 74. The effects of adoption are regulated by the personal law of the adopting party in so far as his estate is concerned, and by that of the adopted one in respect to the name, the rights and duties which he retains regarding his natural family, as well as to his estate in regard to the adopting person.
Art. 75. Either one of the interested persons may repudiate the adoption in accordance with the provisions of his personal law.
Art. 76. Provisions regulating in this matter the right to maintenance, as well as provisions establishing solemn forms for the act of adoption, are of an international public order.
Art. 77. The provisions of the four preceding articles will not apply to States whose legislations do not recognize adoption.
Chapter IX. Absence.
Art. 78. Provisional measures in the case of absence are of an international public order.
Art. 79. Notwithstanding the provisions of the preceding article, the representation of the person whose absence is presumed shall be designated in accordance with his personal law.
Art. 80. The personal law of the absence determines who is competent to institute an action requesting such declaration and establishes the order and conditions of the administrators.
Art. 81. The local law shall be applied for the purpose of deciding when the declaration of absence is made and takes effect and when and how the administration of the property of the absentee shall terminate as well as the obligation and manner of rendering accounts.
Art. 82. Everything relating to the presumption of death of the absentee and his eventual rights is regulated by his personal law.
Art. 83. A declaration of absence or of its presumption as well as its cessation and that of presumption of death of the absentee have extraterritorial force, including what has reference to the appointment and powers of the administrators.
Chapter X. Guardianship.
Art. 84. The personal law of the minor or incapacitated person shall be applied to what concerns the object of the guardianship or curatorship, its organization, and its different classes.
Art. 85. The same law is to be observed in respect to the appointment of an ancillary guardian.
Art. 86. To incapacities and excuses concerning guardianship, curatorship, and ancillary guardianship must be simultaneously applied the personal laws of the guardian, curator, or ancillary guardian and of the minor or incapacitated person.
Art. 87. The security to be furnished by the guardian or curator and the rules for the exercise of guardianship are subject to the personal law of the minor or incapacitated person. If the security is a mortgage or a pledge, it is to be furnished in the manner prescribed by the local law.
Art. 88. Obligations relating to accountings, except responsibilities of a penal nature, which are territorial, are also governed by the personal law of the minor or incapacitated person.
Art. 89. In respect to registration of guardianships, the local and the personal laws of the guardian or curator and of the minor or incapacitated person shall be simultaneously applied.
Art. 90. The precepts which compel the public prosecutor or any other local functionary to request the declarations of incapacity of insane and deaf-mutes and those fixing the procedure to be followed for that declaration are of an international public order.
Art. 91. Rules establishing the consequences of interdiction are also of an international public order.
Art. 92. The declaration of incapacity and interdiction have extraterritorial force.
Art. 93. Local law shall be applied to the obligation of the guardian or curator to support the minor or incapacitated person and to the power to correct the latter only to a moderate degree.
Art. 94. The capacity to be a member of a family council is regulated by the personal law of the interested person.
Art. 95. The special incapacities and the organization, functioning, rights and duties of the family council, are subject to the personal law of the ward.
Art. 96. The proceedings and resolutions of the family council shall in all cases conform with the forms and solemnities prescribed by the law of the place in which it meets.
Art. 97. Contracting states which have as personal law that of domicile, may demand, on transferring the domicile of incapacitated persons from one country to another, that the guardianship or curatorship be ratified or that the guardian or tutor be reappointed.
Chapter XI. Prodigality.
Art. 98. A spendthrift decree and its effects are subject to the personal law of the spendthrift.
Art. 99. Notwithstanding the provisions of the preceding article, the law of the domicile shall not be applied to a spendthrift decree respecting parties whose national law ignores this institution.
Art. 100. A spendthrift decree made in one of the contracting States shall have extraterritorial force in respect to the others in so far as the local law may permit it.
Chapter XII. Emancipation and majority.
Art. 101. The rules applicable to emancipation and majority are the ones established by the personal legislation of the interested persons.
Art. 102. However, the local legislation may be declared applicable to majority as a requisite for electing the nationality of said legislation.
Chapter XIII. Civil registry.

Art. 103. Provisions relating to the civil registry are territorial, except in respect to the register kept by consular or diplomatic agents. The stipulations of this article do not affect the rights of another State in legal relations under international public law.

Art. 104. A literal and formal certificate of each inscription relating to a national of any of the contracting States, made in the civil registry of another, shall be sent gratuitously and through diplomatic channels to the country of the interested person.

Title II. Property. Chapter I. Classification of property.

Art. 105. All property of whatever description, is subject to the law of the place where it is situated.

Art. 106. For the purposes of the preceding article, as regards personal property of a corporal nature and of all titles representative of debts of any kind, account shall be taken of the place of their ordinary or normal situation.

Art. 107. The situation of debts is determined by the place in which they should be paid, and, if that is not fixed, by the domicile of the debtor.

Art. 108. Industrial property, copyrights, and all other similar rights of an economic nature which authorize the exercise of certain activities granted by law, are considered to be situated where they have been formally registered.

Art. 109. Concessions are deemed to be situated where they have been legally acquired.

Art. 110. In the absence of any other rule and also in the cases not provided for in this Code, it shall be understood that personal property of every kind is situated in the domicile of its owner, or if he be absent, in that of the property holder.

Art. 111. From the provision of the preceding article are excepted things given as pledge, which are considered as situated in the domicile of the person in whose possession they have been placed.

Art. 112. The territorial law shall be always applied for the purpose of distinguishing between personal and real property, without prejudice to rights acquired by third parties.

Art. 113. The other legal classifications and qualifications of property are subject to the same territorial law.

Chapter II. Possession.

Art. 114. Inalienable family property exempt from encumbrances and attachments is governed by the law of the place. However, the nationals of a contracting State in which that kind of property is not admitted or regulated shall not be able to hold it or organize it in another, except in so far as it does not injure their necessary heirs.

Art. 115. Copyrights and industrial property shall be governed by the provisions of the special international conventions at present in force or concluded in the future. In the absence thereof, their acquisition, registration, and enjoyment shall remain subject to the local law which grants them.

Art. 116. Each contracting State has the power to subject to special rules as respects foreigners, property in mines, in fishing and coasting vessels, in industries in territorial waters and in the maritime zone, and the acquisition and enjoyment of concessions and works of public utility and public service.

Art. 117. The general rules relating to property and the manner of acquiring it or alienating it inter vivos, including those applicable to treasure trove, as well as those governing the waters of public and private domain and the use thereof, are of an international public order.

Chapter III. Community of property.

Article 118. The community of property is governed in general by the agreement or will of the parties and in the absence thereof by the law of the place. Its place shall be the domicile of the community in the absence of an agreement to the contrary.

Art. 119. The local law shall be always applied, exclusively, to the right of requesting a division of the thing held in common and to the forms and conditions of its exercise.

Art. 120. Provisions relative to surveying and marking and the right to inclose rural properties, as well as those relating to ruined buildings and trees threatening to fall, are of an international public order.

Chapter IV. Possession.

Art. 121. Possession and its effects are governed by local law.

Art. 122. The modes of acquiring possession are governed by the law applicable to each in accordance with its nature.

Art. 123. The means and procedure to be employed in order to maintain the possession of a holder disquieted, disturbed, or dispossessed by judicial measures or resolution or in consequence thereof are determined by the law of the court.

Chapter V. Usufruct, use, and habitation.

Art. 124. When the usufruct is established by mandate of the law of a contracting State, the said law shall govern it obligatorily.

Art. 125. If it has been established by the will of private persons as manifested in acts inter vivos or mortis causa, the law of the act or that of the succession shall be respectively applied.

Art. 126. If it springs from prescription, it shall be subject to the local law which establishes.

Art. 127. The precept which does or does not excuse the usufructuary father from furnishing security depends upon the personal law of the child.

Art. 128. The requiring of security by the surviving spouse for the hereditary usufruct and the obligation of the usufructuary to pay certain legacies or hereditary debts are subordinated to the law of the succession.

Art. 129. The rules defining the usufruct and the forms of its establishment, those fixing the legal causes which extinguish it, and that which limits it to a certain number of years for peoples, corporations or partnerships are of an international public order.

Art. 130. Use and habitation are governed by the will of the party or parties who establish them.

Chapter VI. Servitudes.

Art. 131. The local law shall be applied to the concept and classification of servitudes, to the noncontractual ways of acquiring them and extinguishing them, and to the rights and obligations in this case of the owners of the dominant and servient lands.

Art. 132. The servitudes of accontractual or voluntary origin are subject to the law of the instrument or juridical relationship which creates them.

Art. 133. From the provision of the preceding article are excepted community of pasturage on public lands and the redemption of the use of wood and all other products of the mountains of private ownership which are subject to the territorial law.

Art. 134. The rules applicable to legal servitudes imposed in the interest or for the use of private persons are of a private order.

Art. 135. Territorial law should be applied to the concept and enumeration of legal servitudes and to the nonconventional regulation of those relating to waters, passage, party walls, light and prospect drainage of buildings, and distances and intermediate works for constructions and plantation.

Chapter VII. Registries of property.

Art. 136. Provisions establishing and regulating them and imposing them as necessary as regards third persons are of an international public order.

Art. 137. There shall be recorded in the registries of property of each of the contracting States the recordable documents or titles executed in another and having valid force in the former in accordance with this Code, and executory judgments which under this Code are given effect in the State to which the registry belongs, or which have in it the force of res adjudicata.

Art. 138. Provisions relating to legal mortgages in favor of the State, provinces, or towns are of an international public order.

Art. 139. The legal lien which some laws concede in benefit of certain individual persons, shall be enforceable only when the personal law agrees with the law of the place in which the property thereby affected is situated.

Title III. Various modes of acquisition.

Chapter I. General rule.

Art. 140. The local law is applied to the modes of acquisition regarding which there are no provisions to the contrary in this Code.

Chapter II. Gifts.

Art. 141. Whenever they are of contractual origin they shall remain subject for their perfection and effects inter vivos to the general rules of contracts.

Art. 142. The capacity of both the donor and donee shall be subject to the respective personal law of each of them.

Art. 143. Gifts which are to take effect on the death of the donor shall partake of the nature of testamentary provisions and shall be governed by the international rules established in this Code for testamentary succession.

Chapter III. Successions in general.

Art. 144. Successions, both intestate and testamentary, including the order of descent, the quantum of the rights of descent and the intrinsic validity of the provisions, shall be governed, except as hereinafter provided, by the personal law of the person from whom the rights are derived, whatever may be the nature of the estate and the place where it is found.

Art. 145. The precept by which the rights to the estate of a person are transmitted from the moment of his death is of an international public order.

Chapter IV. Wills.

Art. 146. The capacity to devise by will is regulated by the personal law of the testator.

Art. 147. The territorial law shall be applied to the rules established by each State for the purpose of showing that an insane testator acted in a lucid interval.

Art. 148. Provisions forbidding a joint or a holographic or a nuncupative will, and those which declare it to be a purely personal act are of an international public order.

Art. 149. Rules relating to the form of private papers relating to wills and concerning the nullity of a will made under duress of force, deceit, or fraud, are also of an international public order.

Art. 150. The rules on the form of wills are of an international public order, except those concerning a will made in a foreign country, and military and maritime wills, when made abroad.

Art. 151. The procedure, conditions, and effects of the revocation of a will are subject to the personal law of the testator, but the presumption of revocation is determined by the local law.

Chapter V. Inheritance.

Art. 152. The capacity to inherit by will or without it is regulated by the personal law of the heir or legates.

Art. 153. Notwithstanding the provision of the preceding article, the incapacities to inherit which contracting States consider as such, are of an international public order.

Art. 154. The appointment and substitution of heirs shall be according to the personal law of the testator.

Art. 155. The local law shall, nevertheless, be applied to the prohibition of fideicommissary substitutions beyond the second degree, or those made in favor of persons not living at the time of the death of the testator, and of those involving a perpetual prohibition against alienation.

Art. 156. The appointment and powers of testamentary executors depend upon the personal law of the deceased and should be recognized in each one of the contracting States in accordance with the law.

Art. 157. In case of intestate estates, in which the law designates the State as heir in the absence of others, the personal law of the person from which the right is derived shall be applied; but if it is designated as occupant of res nullius, the local law shall be applied.

Art. 158. The precautions which are to be taken when the widow is pregnant shall be in accordance with the provisions of the legislation of the place where she happens to be.

Art. 159. The formalities required in order to accept the inheritance with benefit of inventory or for the purpose of using the right of deliberating shall be subject to the law of the place where the succession is opened; and this is sufficient to produce their extraterritorial effects.

Art. 160. The rule referring to the unlimited undivided preservation of the inheritance or establishing a provisional partition, is of an international public order.

Art. 161. The capacity to solicit and carry into effect a division is subject to the personal law of the heir.

Art. 162. The appointment and powers of the auditor or partitioner depend upon the personal law of the person from whom the title is derived.

Art. 163. The payment of hereditary debts is subordinated to the same law. However, the creditors who have security of a real nature may realize on it in accordance with the law controlling said security.

Title IV. Obligations and contracts.

Chapter I. Obligations in general.

Art. 164. The concept and classification of obligations are subject to the territorial law.

Art. 165. Obligations arising from the operation of law are governed by the law which has created them.

Art. 166. Those obligations arising from contracts have force of law as between the Contracting Parties and should be discharged in accordance with the terms thereof with the exception of the limitations established by this Code.

Art. 167. Those arising from crimes or offences are subject to the same law as the crime or offence from which they arise.

Art. 168. Those arising from actions or omissions involving guilt or negligence not punishable by law shall be governed by the law of the place in which the negligence or guilt giving rise to them was incurred.

Art. 169. The nature and effect of the various classes of obligations, as well as the extinction thereof, are governed by the law of the obligation in question.

Art. 170. Notwithstanding the provisions of the preceding article, the local law regulates the conditions of payment and the money in which payment shall be made.

Article 171. The law of the place also determines who is to cover the judicial costs for enforcing payment and regulates them.

Art. 172. The evidence relative to obligations is subject, so far as its admission and value is concerned, to the law governing the obligation itself.

Art. 173. Objection to the certainty of the place where a private instrument was executed, if having any bearing on its validity, may be made at any time by a third party prejudiced thereby, and the burden of proof shall be on him who makes it.

Art. 174. The presumption of res judicata by a foreign judgment shall be admissible whenever the judgment fulfils the necessary requirements for its execution within the territory, in conformity with the present Code.

Chapter II. Contracts in general.

Art. 175. The rules which prevent the conclusion of contracts, clauses, and conditions in conflict with the law, morality, and public policy, and the one which forbids the taking of an oath and regards the latter as void, are of an international public order.

Art. 176. The rules which determine the capacity or incapacity to give consent depend upon the personal law of each Contracting Party.

Art. 177. The territorial law shall be applied to mistake, violence, intimidation, and fraud, in connection with consent.

Art. 178. Every rule which prohibits as the subject matter of contracts, services contrary to law and good morals and things placed outside the field of trade, is also territorial.

Art. 179. Provisions which refer to unlawful matters in contracts are of an international public order.

Art. 180. The law of the place of the contract and that of its execution shall be applied simultaneously to the necessity of executing a public indenture or document for the purpose of giving effect to certain agreements and to that of reducing them to writing.

Art. 181. The rescission of contracts by reason of incapacity or absence is determined by the personal law of the absentee or incapacitated person.

Art. 182. The other causes of rescission and the form and effects thereof are subordinated to the territorial law.

Art. 183. Provisions relating to the nullity of contracts shall be subject to the law upon which the cause of nullity depends.

Art. 184. The interpretation of contracts should be effected, as a general rule, in accordance with the law by which they are governed.

However, when that law is in dispute and should appear from the implied will of the parties the legislation provided for in that case in Articles 185 and 186 shall be presumptively applied, although it may result in applying to the contract a different law as a consequence of the interpretation of the will of the parties.

Art. 185. Aside from the rules already established and those which may be hereafter laid down for special cases, in contracts of accession, the law of the one proposing or preparing them is presumed to be accepted, in the absence of an expressed or implied consent.

Art. 186. In all other contracts and in the case provided for in the preceding article, the personal law common to the Contracting Parties shall be first applied, and in the absence of such law there shall be applied that of the place where the contract was concluded.

Chapter III. Contracts relating to property in respect to marriage.

Art. 187. This contract is governed by the personal law common to the Parties, and in the absence thereof by that of the first matrimonial domicile.

The same laws determine in that order, the supplemental legal control in the absence of stipulation.

Art. 188. The precept which forbids the making of marriage settlements during wedlock or modification of same, or which alters the control of property by changes of nationality or of domicile after marriage are of an international public order.

Art. 189. Those relating to the enforcement of laws and good morals, to the effects of marriage settlements affecting third parties, and the solemn form thereof are of the same character.

Art. 190. The will of the parties regulates the law applicable to gifts by reason of marriage, except in respect to their capacity, to the safeguard of lawful rights of heirship, and to the nullity thereof during wedlock, all of which is subordinated to the general law governing marriage as long as it does not affect international public order.

Art. 191. Provisions regarding dowry and paraphernalia depend on the personal law of the wife.

Art. 192. The rule which repudiates the inalienableness of dowries is of an international public order.

Art. 193. A prohibition against renouncing the conjugal partnership during marriage is of an international public order.

Chapter IV. Sale, assignment, and exchange.

Art. 194. Provisions relating to compulsory alienation for purposes of public utility are of an international public order.

Art. 195. It is the same with provisions fixing the effects of possession and registration among various acquirers and those referring to the right of legal redemption.

Chapter V. Leases.

Art. 196. In respect to leases of things, the territorial law should be applied to such measures as are intended to protect the interest of third parties and the rights and duties of the purchaser of leased real estate.

Art. 197. In so far as the contract for services is concerned, the rule which prevents the making of such contracts for life or for more than a certain time, is of an international public order.

Art. 198. Legislation relating to accidents of labor and social protection of the laborer is also territorial.

Art. 199. Special and local laws and regulations are territorial as regards carriers by water, land, and air.

Chapter VI. Annuities.

Art. 200. The territorial law is applied to the determination of the concept and classes of annuities, the redeemable character and prescription thereof, and the real action arising therefrom.

Art. 201. In respect to emphyteutic annuities (censos enfiteuticos), provisions fixing the conditions and formalities, prescribing an acknowledgement every certain number of years, and forbidding subemphyteusis, are also territorial.

Art. 202. In case of transferable annuities (censos consignativos), the rule forbidding that payment in fuuits may consist of an aliquot part of the products of the land subject to the annuity is of an international public order.

Art. 203. The same is the character of the demand that the land subject to the annuity be appraised, in the case of reservative annuities.

Chapter VII. Partnership.

Art. 204. Laws requiring a lawful object, solemn forms, and an inventory when there is real estate, are territorial.

Chapter VIII. Loans.

Art. 205. Local law is applied to the necessity of an express agreement for interest and the rate thereof.

Chapter IX. Bailment.

Art. 206. Provisions relating to necessary bailments and attachments are territorial.

Chapter X. Aleatory contracts.

Art. 207. The effects of capacity in actions arising out of gambling contracts are determined by the personal law of the interested party.

Art. 208. The local law defines lottery contracts (de suerte) and determines the games of chance and the betting which are permitted or forbidden.

Art. 209. A provision which declares null and void an annuity constituted on the life of a person deceased at the time of its creation, or at a time when he was suffering from an incurable disease, is territorial.

Chapter XI. Compromise and arbitration.

Art. 210. Provisions forbidding compromise or arbitration of certain matters are territorial.

Art. 211. The extent and effects of the arbitration and the authority of res judicata of the compromise also depend upon the territorial law.

Chapter XII. Security.

Art. 212. A rule forbidding the surety to assume a greater liability than that of the principal debtor is of an international public order.

Art. 213. To the same class belong the provisions relating to legal or judicial security.

Chapter XIII. Pledge, mortgage, and antichresis.

Art. 214. The provision forbidding the creditor to appropriate to himself the chattels received by him as pledge or mortgage is territorial.

Art. 215. The precepts fixing the essential requirements of the pledge contract are also territorial, and they must be complied with when the thing which is pledged is taken to a place where such requirements are different from those required when the contract was executed.

Art. 216. The provisions by virtue of which the pledge is to remain in the possession of the creditor or of a third party, the one which requires as against strangers that a certain date be expressed in a public instrument, and the one which fixes the procedure for the alienation of the pledge, are also territorial.

Art. 217. The special rules and regulations of pawn shops and analogous public establishments are territorially binding in respect to all transactions made with them.

Art. 218. The provisions fixing the objects, conditions, requisites, extent, and recording of the mortgage contract are territorial.

Art. 219. A prohibition against the creditor acquiring the property of the real estate involved in the antichresis, for default in payment of the debt, is also territorial.

Chapter XIV. Quasi-contracts.

Art. 220. The conduct of another's business is regulated by the law of the place in which it is effected.

Art. 221. The collection of that which is not due is subject to the common personal law of the parties and in the absence thereof, to that of the place in which the payment was made.

Art. 222. The other quasi-contracts are subject to the law which regulates the legal institution which gives rise to them.

Chapter XV. Concurrence and preference of debts.

Art. 223. When concurrent obligations have no real character and are subject to one and the same law the latter shall also regulate the preference of said obligations.

Art. 224. In respect to those which are guaranteed by a real action, the law of the place of the guaranty shall apply.

Art. 225. Aside from the cases provided for in the preceding articles, the law of the trial court should be applied to the preference of debts.

Art. 226. When the question is simultaneously presented in more than one court of different States, it shall be determined in accordance with the law of that one which actually has under its jurisdiction the property or money which is to render the preference effective.

Chapter XVI. Prescription.

Art. 227. Acquisitive prescription of both real and personal property is governed by the law of the place where they are situated.

Art. 228. If personal property should change situation during the period of prescription, the latter shall be governed by the law of the place where it is at the moment the period required is completed.

Art. 229. Extinctive prescription of personal actions is governed by the law to which the obligation which is to be extinguished is subject.

Art. 230. Extinctive prescription of real actions is governed by the law of the place where the object to which it refers is situated.

Art. 231. If in the case provided for in the proceding article personal property has changed its location during the period of prescription, the law of the place where the property is found at the completion of the time there specified for prescription shall apply.

Book II. International commercial law.

Title I. Merchants and commerce in general.

Chapter I. Merchants.

Art. 232. The capacity to engage in commerce and to become party to commercial acts and contracts, is regulated by the personal law of each interested person.

Art. 233. To the same personal law are subordinated incapacities and their cessation.
Art. 234. The law of the place where the business is carried on should be applied in the measures for publicity necessary to the effect that persons incapacitated therefor may engage in it through their representatives, and married women by themselves.
Art. 235. The local law should be applied to the incompatibility to engage in commerce of public servants and of commercial agents and brokers.
Art. 236. Every incompatibility for commerce resulting from laws or special provisions in force in any territory shall be governed by the law of the same.
Art. 237. The said incompatibility, in so far as diplomatic and consular agents are concerned, shall be measured by the law of the State appointing them. The country where they reside has also the right to forbid them to engage in commerce.
Art. 238. The partnership contract or, in an applicable case, the law to which such contract may be subject, is applied to the prohibition against general or silent partners engaging in commercial transactions, or in certain classes of them, on their own account or on that of others.
Chapter II. The quality of merchants and acts of commerce.
Art. 239. For all purposes of a public character, the quality of merchants is governed by the law of the place where the act has taken place or where the trade in question has been carried on.
Art. 240. The form of contracts and commercial acts is subject to the territorial law.
Chapter III. Commercial registry.
Art. 241. Provisions relating to the recording in the commercial registry of foreign merchants and partnerships are territorial.
Art. 242. Rules fixing the effect of recording in said registry the credits or rights of third parties have the same character.
Chapter IV. Places and houses of commercial traffic and official quotation of public securities and commercial paper payable to bearer.
Art. 243. Provisions relating to the places and exchanges for the official quotation of public securities and documents payable to bearer are of an international public order.
Chapter V. General provisions relating to commercial contracts.
Art. 244. The general rules provided for civil contracts in Chapter II, Title IV, Book I, of this Code shall be applied to commercial contracts.
Art. 245. Contracts by correspondence shall be complete only when the conditions prescribed for the purpose by the legislation of all the contracting parties have been duly complied with.
Art. 246. Provisions relating to unlawful contracts and terms of grace, courtesy, and others of a similar nature are of an international public order.
Title II. Special commercial contracts.
Chapter I. Commercial companies.
Art. 247. The commercial character of a collective or silent partnership is determined by the law to which the articles of partnership are subject, and in the absence thereof, by the law of the place where it has its commercial domicile. If those laws do not distinguish between commercial and civil societies, the law of the country where the question is submitted to the courts shall be applied.
Art. 248. The commercial character of a corporation depends upon the law provided in the articles of association; in the absence of such provision, upon the law of the place where the general meetings of shareholders are held, and in the absence thereof, the law of the place where its board of directors is normally located.
If the said laws should not distinguish between commercial and civil societies, the said corporation shall have either character according to whether it is or not registered in the commercial registry of the country where the question is to be judicially determined. In the absence of a commercial registry, the local law of the latter country shall be applied.
Art. 249. Questions relative to the constitution and manner of operation of commercial societies and the liability of the members thereof are subject to the articles of association or, in an applicable case, to the law governing such articles.
Art. 250. The issue of shares and obligations in one of the contracting States, the forms and guarantees of publicity and the liability of managers of agencies and branch offices in respect to third persons are subject to the territorial law.
Art. 251. Laws subordinating the partnership to a special regime by reason of its transactions are also territorial.
Art. 252. Commercial partnerships duly constituted in a contracting State will enjoy the same juristic personality in the other contracting States except for the limitations of territorial law.
Art. 253. Provisions referring to the creation, operation, and privilege of banks of issue and discount, general warehouse, companies, and other similar companies, are territorial.
Chapter II. Commercial commission.
Art. 254. Provisions relating to the form of an urgent sale by a commission merchant to save as far as possible the value of the articles of the commission are of an international public order.
Art. 255. The obligations of the factor are subject to the law of the commercial domicile of the principal.
Chapter III. Commercial deposit and loans.
Art. 256. The non civil liabilities of a depositary are governed by the law of the place where the deposit is made.
Art. 257. The rate of freedom of commercial interests is of an international public order.
Art. 258. Provisions relating to loans upon collateral of quotable securities made in the exchange through the intervention of a duly authorized broker or official functionary, are territorial.
Chapter IV. Land transportation.
Art. 259. In cases of international transportation there is only one contract, governed by the proper law corresponding to it according to its nature.
Art. 260. Time limits and formalities for the exercise of actions arising out of this contract but not provided for therein are governed by the law of the locality where the facts took place.
Chapter V. Contracts of insurance.
Art. 261. The contract of fire insurance is governed by the law of the place where the thing insured is located at the time of its execution.
Art. 262. All other contracts of insurance follow the general rule, being regulated by the personal law common to the parties, or in the absence thereof, by the law of the place where the contract of insurance was executed; but the external formalities for proving facts or omissions necessary to the exercise or preservation of actions or rights are subject to the law of the locality where the act or omission which gives rise to them took place.
Chapter VI. Contracts and bills of exchange and similar commercial instruments.
Art. 263. The forms of the order, indorsement, suretyship, intervention of honor, acceptance, and protest of a bill of exchange, are subject to the law of the locality in which each one of those acts takes place.
Art. 264. In the absence of expressed or implied agreement, the legal relations between the drawer and the payee are governed by the law of the place where the bill is drawn.
Art. 265. Likewise, the obligations and rights existing between the acceptor and the holder are regulated by the law of the place in which the acceptance was made.
Art. 266. In the same hypothesis, the legal effects produced by indorsement between indorser and indorsee depend upon the law of the place where the bill has been indorsed.
Art. 267. The greater or lesser extent of the obligations of each indorser does not alter the original rights and duties of the drawer and the payee.
Art. 268. Guaranty (aval), in the same conditions, is governed by the law of the place in which it is furnished.
Art. 269. The legal effects of acceptance by intervention are regulated, in the absence of agreement by the law of the place in which the third party intervenes.
Art. 270. The time limits and formalities for acceptance, payment, and protest, are subject to the local law.
Art. 271. The rules of this chapter are applicable to local drafts (libranzas), duebills, promissory notes and orders or checks.
Chapter VII. Forgery, robbery, larceny, or loss of public securities and negotiable instruments.
Art. 272. Provisions relating to the forgery, robbery, theft or loss of credit documents and bonds payable to bearer, are of an international public order.
Art. 273. The adoption of the measures established by the law of the locality in which the fact takes place does not excuse the interested parties from taking all other measures established by the law of the place in which those documents and securities are negotiated, and by that of the place of their payment.
Title III. Maritime and air commerce.
Chapter I. Ships and aircraft.
Art. 274. The nationality of ships is proved by the navigation licence and the certificate of registration and has the flag as an apparent distinctive symbol.
Art. 275. The law of the flag governs the forms of publicity required for the transfer of property in a ship.
Art. 276. The power of judicial attachment and sale of a ship, whether or not it is loaded and cleared, should be subject to the law of the place where it is situated.
Art. 277. The rights of the creditors after the sale of the ship, and their extinguishment, are regulated by the law of the flag.
Art. 278. Maritime hypothecation, privileges, and real guaranties, constituted in accordance with the law of the flag, have extraterritorial effect even in those countries the legislation of which does not recognize nor regulate such hypothecation.
Art. 279. The powers and obligations of the master and the liability of the proprietors and ship's husbands for their acts are also subject to the law of the flag.
Art. 280. The recognition of the ship, the request for a pilot, and the sanitary police depend upon the territorial law.
Art. 281. The obligations of the officers and seamen and the internal order of the vessel are subject to the law of the flag.
Art. 282. The preceding provisions of this chapter are also applicable to aircraft.
Art. 283. The rules on nationality of the proprietors of ships and aircraft and ship's husbands, as well as of officers and crew, are of an international public order.
Art. 284. Provisions relating to the nationality of ships and aircraft for river, lake, and coastwise commerce, or commerce between certain points of the territory of the contracting States, as well as for fishing and other submarine exploitations in the territorial sea, also are of an international public order.
Chapter II. Special contracts of maritime and aerial commerce.
Art. 285. The charter party, if not a contract of adhesion, shall be governed by the law of the place of departure of the merchandise.
The acts of execution of the contract shall be subject to the law of the place where they are performed.
Art. 286. The powers of the captain in respect to loans on bottomry bond are determined by the law of the flag.
Art. 287. The contract of a bottomry bond, except as otherwise by agreement, is subject to the law of the place in which the loan is made.
Art. 288. In order to determine whether the average is particular or general and the proportion in which the vessel and cargo are to contribute therefor, the law of the flag is applied.
Art. 289. A fortuitous collision in territorial waters or in the national air is subject to the law of the flag if common to colliding vessels.
Art. 290. In the same case, if the flags are different the law of the place is applied.
Art. 291. The same local law is in every case applied to wrongful collisions in territorial waters or in the national air.
Art. 292. To a fortuitous or wrongful collision in the open sea or air is applied the law of the flag if all the ships or aircraft carry the same one.
Art. 293. If that is not the case, the collision shall be regulated by the flag of the ship or aircraft struck if the collision has been wrongful.
Art. 294. In the cases of fortuitous collision on the high sea or in the open air between vessels or aircraft of different flags, each shall bear one half of the sum total of the damage apportioned in accordance with the law of one of them, and the other half apportioned in accordance with the law of the other.
Title IV. Prescription.
Art. 295. Prescription of actions arising from contracts and commercial acts shall be subject to the rule established in this Code in respect to civil actions.
Book III. International penal law.

Chapter I. Penal laws.

Art. 296. Penal laws are binding on all persons residing in the territory, without other exceptions than those established in this chapter.

Art. 297. The head of each of the contracting States is exempt from the penal laws of the others when he is in the territory of the latter.

Art. 298. The diplomatic representatives of the contracting States in each of the others, together with their foreign personnel, and the members of the families of the former who are living in his company enjoy the same exemption.

Art. 299. Nor are the penal laws of the State applicable to offenses committed within the field of military operations when it authorizes the passage of an army of another contracting State through its territory, except offenses not legally connected with said army.

Art. 300. The same exemption is applied to offenses committed on board foreign war vessels or aircraft while in territorial waters or in the national air.

Art. 301. The same is the case in respect to offenses committed in territorial waters or in the national air, on foreign merchant vessels or aircraft, if they have no relation with the country and its inhabitants and do not disturb its tranquillity.

Art. 302. When the acts of which an offense is composed take place in different contracting States, each State may punish the act committed within its jurisdiction, if it by itself constitutes a punishable act.

In the contrary case, preference shall be given to the right of the local sovereignty where the offense has been committed.

Art. 303. In case of related offenses committed in the territories of more than one contracting State, only the one committed in its own territory shall be subject to the penal law of each.

Art. 304. No contracting State shall apply in its territory the penal laws of the others.

Chapter II. Offenses committed in a foreign contracting State.

Art. 305. Those committing an offense against the internal or external security of a contracting State or against its public credit, whatever the nationality or domicile of the delinquent person, are subject in a foreign country to the penal laws of each contracting State.

Art. 306. Every national of a contracting State or every foreigner domiciled therein who commits in a foreign country an offense against the independence of that State remains subject to its penal laws.

Art. 307. Moreover, those persons are subject to the penal laws of the foreign State in which they are apprehended and tried who have committed outside its territory an offense, such as white slavery, which said contracting State has bound itself by an international agreement to repress.

Chapter III. Offenses committed outside the national territory.

Art. 308. Piracy, trade in negroes and slave traffic, white slavery, the destruction or injury of submarine cables, and all other offenses of a similar nature against international law committed on the high seas, in the open air, and on territory not yet organized into a State, shall be punished by the captor in accordance with the penal laws of the latter.

Art. 309. In cases of wrongful collision on the high seas or in the air, between ships or aircraft carrying different colors, the penal law of the victim shall be applied.

Chapter IV. Sundry questions.

Art. 310. For the legal concept of reiteration or recidivism will be taken into account the judgment rendered in a foreign contracting State, with the exception of the cases in which same is contrary to local law.

Art. 311. The penalty of civil interdiction shall have effect in each of the other States upon the previous compliance with the formalities of registration or publication which may be required by the legislation of such State.

Art. 312. Prescription of an offense is subordinated to the law of the State having cognizance thereof.

Art. 313. Prescription of the penalty is governed by the law of the State which has imposed it.

Book IV. International law of procedure.

Title I. General rules.

Art. 314. The law of each contracting State determines the competence of courts, as well as their organization, the forms of procedure and of execution of judgments, and the appeals from their decisions.

Art. 315. No contracting State shall organize or maintain in its territory special tribunals for members of the other contracting States.

Art. 316. Competence ratione loci is subordinated, in the order of international relations, to the law of the contracting State which establishes it.

Art. 317. Competence ratione materiae and ratione personae, in the order of international relations should not be based by the contracting States on the status as nationals or foreigners of the interested parties, to the prejudice of the latter.

Title II. Competence.

Chapter I. General rules concerning competence in civil and commercial matters.

Art. 318. The judge competent in the first place to take cognizance of suits arising from the exercise of civil and commercial actions of all kinds shall be the one to whom the litigants expressly or implicitly submit themselves, provided that one of them at least is a national of the contracting State to which the judge belongs or has his domicile therein, and in the absence of local laws to the contrary.

The submission in real or mixed actions involving real property shall not be possible if the law where the property is situated forbids it.

Art. 319. The submission can be made only to a judge having ordinary jurisdiction to take cognizance of a similar class of cases in the same degree.

Art. 320. In no case shall the parties be able to submit themselves expressly or impliedly for relief to any judge or court other than that to whom is subordinated according to local laws the one who took cognizance of the suit in the first instance.

Art. 321. By express submission shall be understood the submission made by the interested parties in clearly and conclusively renouncing their own court and unmistakably designating the judge to whom they submit themselves.

Art. 322. Implied submission shall be understood to have been made by the plaintiff from the fact of applying to the judge in filing the complaint, and by the defendant from the fact of his having after entering his appearance in the suit, filed any plea unless it is for the purpose of denying jurisdiction. No submission can be implied when the suit is proceeded with as in default.

Art. 323. Outside the cases of express or implied submissions, without prejudice to local laws to the contrary, the judge competent for hearing personal causes shall be the one of the place where the obligation is to be performed, and in the absence thereof, the one of the domicile or nationality of the defendants and subsidiarily that of their residence.

Art. 324. For the exercise of real actions in respect to personal property, the judge of the place where the property is situated shall be competent, and if it is not known by the plaintiff, then the judge of the domicile, and in the absence thereof. the one of the residence of the defendant.

Art. 325. For the exercise of real actions in respect to real property, and for that of mixed actions to determine boundary and partition of common property, the competent judge shall be the one where the property is situated.

Art. 326. If in the cases to which the two preceding articles refer there is any property situated in more than one of the contracting States, recourse may be had to the judges of any of them, unless prohibited, as to immovables, by the law of their situation.

Art. 327. In cases relating to the probate of wills or to intestate estates, the competent court will be that of the place in which the deceased had his last domicile.

Art. 328. In insolvency and bankruptcy proceedings, when the debtor has acted voluntarily, the judge of the domicile of the latter shall be the one competent.

Art. 329. In insolvency or bankruptcy proceedings brought by the creditors, the competent judge shall be the one of any of the places who has cognizance of the claim which gives rise to them, preference being given, if among them, to that of the domicile of the debtor if the majority of the creditors demand it.

Art. 330. In respect to acts of voluntary jurisdiction, saving also the case of submission without prejudice to local laws to the contrary, the competent judge shall be the one of the place where the person instituting it has or has had his domicile, or if none, his residence.

Art. 331. Respecting acts of voluntary jurisdiction in commercial matters, apart from the case of submission, without prejudice to local laws to the contrary, the competent judge shall be the one of the place where the obligation should be performed or, in the absence thereof, the one of the place where the event giving rise to them occurred.

Art. 332. Within each contracting State, the preferable competence of several judges shall be in conformity with their national law.

Chapter II. Exceptions to the general rules of competence in respect to civil and commercial matters.

Art. 333. The judges and courts of each contracting State shall be incompetent to take cognizance of civil or commercial cases to which the other contracting States or their heads are defendant parties, if the action is a personal one, except in case of express submission or of counter-claims.

Art. 334. In the same case and with the same exception, they shall be incompetent when real actions are exercised, if the contracting State or its head has acted on the case as such and in its public character, when the provisions of the last paragraph of Article 318 shall be applied.

Art. 335. If the foreign contracting State or its head has acted as an individual or private person, the judges or courts shall be competent to take cognizance of the cases where real or mixed actions are brought, if such competence belongs to them in respect to foreign individuals in conformity with this Code.

Art. 336. The rule of the preceding article shall be applicable to universal causes (juicios universales e.g., distribution of a bankrupt's or decedent's effects), whatever the character in which the contracting foreign State or its head intervenes in them.

Art. 337. The provisions established in proceding articles shall be applied to foreign diplomatic agents and to the commanders of war vessels or aircraft.

Art. 338. Foreign consuls shall not be exempt from the civil jurisdiction of the judges and courts of the country in which the act, except in respect to their official acts.

Art. 339. In no case can judges or courts adopt coercive or other measures which have to be executed within the legations or consulates or their archives, nor in respect to diplomatic or consular correspondence, without the consent of the respective diplomatic or consular agents.

Chapter III. General rules of competence in penal matters.

Art. 340. The judges and courts of the contracting State in which crimes or misdemeanors have been committed are competent to take cognizance of and pass judgment upon them.

Art. 341. Competence extends to all other crimes and misdemeanors to which the penal law of the State is to be applied in conformity with the provisions of this Code.

Art. 342. It also extends to crimes or misdemeanors committed in a foreign country by national officials enjoying the benefit of immunity.

Chapter IV. Exceptions to the general rules of competence in penal matters.

Art. 343. Persons and crimes and misdemeanors to which the penal law of the respective State does not extend are not subject, in penal matters, to the competence of the judges and courts of the contracting States.

Title III. Extradition.

Art. 344. In order to render effective the international judicial competence in penal matters, each of the contracting States shall accede to the request of any of the others for the delivery of persons convicted or accused of crime, if in conformity with the provisions of this title, subject to the dispositions of the international treaties and conventions containing a list of penal infractions which authorize the extradition.

Art. 345. The contracting States are not obliged to hand over their own nationals. The nation which refuses to give up one of its citizens shall try him.

Art. 346. Whenever before the receipt of the request, a person accused or convicted has committed an offense in the country from which his delivery is requested, the said delivery may be postponed until he is tried and has served sentence.

Art. 347. If various contracting States should request the extradition of a delinquent for the same offense, he should be delivered to that one in whose territory the offense has been committed.

Art. 348. In case the extradition is requested for different acts, the preference shall belong to the contracting State in whose territory the most grievous offense has been committed, according to the legislation of the State upon which the request was made.

Art. 349. If all the acts imputed should be equally grave, the preference shall be given to the contracting State which first presents the request for extradition. If all have applied simultaneously, the State upon which the request was made shall decide, but the preference should be given to the State of origin, or in the absence thereof to that of the domicile, of the accused, if such State is among those requesting extradition.

Art. 350. The foregoing rules in respect to preference shall not be applicable if the contracting State is obligated toward a third one, by reason of treaties in force prior to the adoption of this Code to establish a different method.

Art. 351. In order to grant extradition it is necessary that the offense has been committed in the territory of the State requesting it, or that its penal laws are applicable to it in accordance with the provisions of Book III of this Code.

Art. 352. Extradition extends to persons accused or convicted as principals, accomplices, or abettors of a consummated offense.

Art. 353. It is necessary that the act which gives rise to the extradition be a criminal offense in the legislation of the State making the request and in that upon which it is made.

Art. 354. It shall be likewise necessary that the penalty attached to the alleged acts, according to their provisional or final description by the competent judge or court of the State requesting the extradition is not less than one year of deprivation of liberty, and that the arrest or detention of the accused has been ordered or decided upon, in case final sentence has not been delivered. The sentence should be deprivation of liberty.

Art. 355. Political offenses and acts related thereto, as defined by the requested State, are excluded from extradition.

Art. 356. Nor shall it be granted, if it is shown that the request for extradition has been in fact made for the purpose of trying or punishing the accused for an offense of a political character in accordance with the same definition.

Art. 357. Homicide or murder of the head of a contracting State or of any other person who exercises authority in said State, shall not be deemed a political offense nor an act related thereto.

Art. 358. Extradition shall not be granted if the person demanded has already been tried and acquitted or served his sentence, or is awaiting trial, in the territory of the requested State for the offense upon which the request is based.

Art. 359. Not should extradition be granted if the offense or the penalty is already barred by limitation by the laws of the requesting or requested State.

Art. 360. In all cases in which the legislation of the requested State prevents extradition it is an indispensable requirement that such legislation be enacted before the commission of the crime.

Art. 361. Consuls general, consuls, vice consuls, or consular agents may request the arrest and delivery on board of a vessel or aircraft of their country of the officers, sailors, or members of the crew of its war or merchant ships or aircraft who may have deserted therefrom.

Art. 362. For the purposes of the preceding article, they shall exhibit to the proper local authority delivering also to it an authenticated copy thereof, the register of the ship or aircraft, the crew list, or any other official document upon which the request is founded.

Art. 363. In adjoining countries special rules may be agreed upon for extradition in the regions or localities of the boundary.

Art. 364. The request for extradition should be made through agents duly authorized for this purpose by the laws of the petitioning State.

Art. 365. Together with the final request for extradition the following should be submitted:

(1) A sentence of conviction of a warrant or order of arrest or a document of equal force, or one which obliges the interested party to appear periodically before the criminal court, together with such parts of the record in the case as furnish proof or at least some reasonable evidence of the guilt of the person in question.

(2) The filiation of the person whose extradition is requested, or such marks or circumstances as may serve to identify him.

(3) An authenticated copy of the provisions establishing the legal definition of the act which gives rise to the request for extradition, describing the participation imputed therein to the defendant, and prescribing the penalty applicable.

Art. 366. The extradition may be requested by telegraph and, in that case, the documents mentioned in the preceding article shall be presented to the requesting country or to its legation or consulate general in the requesting country, within two months following the detention of the accused. Otherwise he shall be set at liberty.

Art. 367. Moreover, if the requesting State does not dispose of the person demanded within three months following his being placed at its disposal, he shall be set at liberty.

Art. 368. The person detained may use, in the State to which the request for extradition is made, all legal means provided for its nationals for the purpose of regaining their freedom, basing the exercise thereof on the provisions of this Code.

Art. 369. The person detained may also thereafter use the legal remedies which are considered proper in the State which requests the extradition, against the qualifications and resolutions upon which the latter is founded.

Art. 370. The delivery should be made together with all the effects found in the possession of the person demanded whether as proceeds of the alleged crime or whether to be used as evidence in so far as practicable in accordance with the laws of the State effecting the delivery and duly respecting the rights of third persons.

Art. 371. The delivery of the effects referred to in the preceding article can be made, if requested by the State requesting the extradition, even though the detained person dies on escapes before it is effected.

Art. 372. The expenses of detention and delivery shall be borne by the requesting State, but the latter shall not, in the meanwhile, have to defray any expenses for the services rendered by the public paid employees of the government from which extradition is requested.

Art. 373. The charge for the services of such public employees or officers as receive only fees or perquisites shall not exceed their customary fees for their acts or services under the laws of the country in which they reside.

Art. 374. All liability arising from the fact of a provisional detention shall rest upon the requesting State.

Art. 375. The passage of the extradited person and his custodians through the territory of a third contracting State shall be permitted upon presentation of the original document which allows the extradition, or of an authenticated copy thereof.

Art. 376. A State which obtains extradition of an accused who is afterwards acquitted shall be obliged to communicate to the State which granted it an authenticated copy of the judgment.

Art. 377. The person delivered cannot be detained in prison nor tried by the contracting State to which he is delivered for an offense different from the one giving rise to the extradition and committed prior thereto, unless it is done with the consent of the requested State, or unless the extradited person remains free in the territory of the former for three months after his trial and acquital for the offense which gave rise to the extradition, or after having served the sentence of deprivation of liberty imposed upon him.

Art. 378. In no case shall the death penalty be imposed or executed for the offense upon which the extradition is founded.

Art. 379. Whenever allowance for temporary detention is proper, it shall be computed from the time of the detention of the extradited person in the State to which the request was made.

Art. 380. The detained person shall be set free if the requesting State does not present the request for extradition in a reasonable period, within the least time possible after temporary arrest, taking into account the distance and facilities of postal communication between the two countries.

Art. 381. If the extradition of a person has been refused, a second request on account of the same crime cannot be made.

Title IV. The right to appear in court and its modalities.

Art. 382. The nationals of each contracting State shall enjoy in each of the others the benefit of having counsel assigned to them upon the same conditions as natives.

Art. 383. No difference shall be made between nationals and foreigners in the contracting States in respect to giving security for judgment.

Art. 384. Aliens belonging to a contracting State may exercise in the others public rights of action in matters of a penal nature upon the same conditions as the nationals.

Art. 385. Nor shall those aliens be required to furnish security when exercising a private right of action in cases in which it is not required from nationals.

Art. 386. None of the contracting States shall require from the nationals of another the security judicio sisti nor the onus probandi in cases where they are not required from its own nationals.

Art. 387. No provisional attachments, bail, or any other measures of a similar nature shall be authorized in respect to the nationals of the contracting States by reason merely of their being foreigners.

Title V. Letters requisitorial or letters rogatory.

Art. 388. Every judicial step which a contracting State has to take in another shall be effected by means of letters requisitorial or letters rogatory, transmitted through the diplomatic channel. Nevertheless, the contracting States may agree upon or accept as between themselves any other form of transmission in respect to civil or criminal matters.

Art. 389. The judge issuing the letters requisitorial is to decide as to his own competence and the legality and propriety of the act or evidence, without prejudice to the jurisdiction of the judge to whom said letters are addressed.

Art. 390. The judge to whom such letters requisitorial are sent shall decide as to his own competence ratione materiae in respect to the act which he is requested to perform.

Art. 391. The one receiving the letters requisitorial or letters rogatory should comply, as to the object thereof, with the law of the one issuing the same, and as to the manner of discharging the request he should comply with his own law.

Art. 392. The letters requisitorial will be written in the language of the State which sent them and will be accompanied by a translation in the language of the State to which they are addressed, said translation to be duly certified by a sworn public translator.

Art. 393. Parties interested in the execution of letters requisitorial and rogatory of a private nature should give powers of attorney, being responsible for the expenses incurred by the same and by the investigations made.

Title VI. Exceptions having an international character.

Art. 394. *Litispendencia* by reason of a suit in another of the contracting States may be pleaded in civil matters when the judgment rendered in one of them is to take effect in the other as res judicata.

Art. 395. In criminal cases the plea of *litispendencia* by reason of a cause pending in another contracting state shall not lie.

Art. 396. The plea of res judicata founded on a judgment of another contracting party shall lie only when the judgment has been rendered in the presence of the parties or their legal representatives, and no question founded on the provisions of this Code has arisen as to the competence of the foreign court.

Art. 397. In all cases of juridical relations subject to this Code, questions of competence founded on its precepts may be addressed to the jurisdiction of the Court.

Title VII. Evidence.

Chapter I. General provisions in respect to evidence.

Art. 398. The law governing the offense or the legal relation constituting the subject of the civil or commercial suit determines upon whom the burden of proof rests.

Art. 399. In order to determine the modes of proof which may be used in each case, the law of the place in which the act or fact to be proved has taken place shall apply except those which are not authorized by the law of the place in which the suit is instituted.

Art. 400. The form of the evidence is regulated by the law in force in the place where it is taken.

Art. 401. The weight of the evidence depends on the law of the judge.

Art. 402. Documents executed in each of the contracting States shall have in the others the same value in

court as those executed therein, if they fulfill the following requirements:
(1) That the subject matter of the act or contract in question is lawful and permitted by the laws of the country where it is executed and of that where it is used.
(2) That the contracting parties have ability and capacity to bind themselves in conformity with their personal law.
(3) That in the execution thereof the forms and formalities established in the country where the acts or contracts have been executed have been observed.
(4) That the document is authenticated and contains the other requisites necessary to this authenticity in the place where it is used.
Art. 403. The executory force of a document is subordinated to the local law.
Art. 404. The capacity of witnesses and challenging thereof depend upon the law to which the legal relation constituting the object of the suit is subject.
Art. 405. The form of the oath shall conform to the law of the judge or court before whom it is administered, and its validity is subject to the law governing the fact in respect to which the oath is taken.
Art. 406. The presumptions derived from an act are subject to the law of the place where the act giving rise to them occurs.
Art. 407. Circumstantial evidence is subject to the law of the judge or court.
Chapter II. Special rules on evidence of foreign laws.
Art. 408. The judge and courts of each contracting State shall apply ex officio, in suitable cases, the laws of the others, without prejudice to the means of proof referred to in this chapter.
Art. 409. The party invoking the application of the law of any contracting State in one of the others, or dissenting from it, may show the text thereof, force and sense, by means of a certificate subscribed by two practicing lawyers of the country whose legislation is in question, which certificate shall be duly authenticated.
Art. 410. In the absence of proof, or if the judge or the court deems it insufficient for any reason, they may request ex officio before deciding, through the diplomatic channel, that the State whose legislation is in question furnish a report on the text, force and sense of the applicable law.
Art. 411. Each contracting State binds itself to furnish to the others, as soon as possible, the information referred to in the preceding article, which information should come from its Supreme Court, or from some one of its divisions or sections, or from the State Attorney, or from the Department or Ministry of Justice.
Title VIII. Appeal for annulment.
Art. 412. In every contracting State where the appeal for annulment or other similar institution exists it may be interposed for the infraction, erroneous interpretation, or improper application of a law of another contracting State, upon the same conditions and in the same cases as in respect to the national law.
Art. 413. The rules established in Chapter II of the preceding title shall be applicable to the appeal for annulment, although the inferior judge or the lower court may have already applied them.
Title IX. Bankruptcy or insolvency.
Chapter I. Unity of bankruptcy or insolvency.
Art. 414. If the insolvent or bankrupt creditor has only one civil or commercial domicile, there can be only one preventive proceeding in insolvency or bankruptcy, or one suspension of payments, or a composition (quita y espera) in respect of all his assets and his liabilities in the contracting States.
Art. 415. If one and the same person or partnership should have in more than one contracting State various commercial establishments entirely separate economically, there may be as many suits for preventive proceeding in bankruptcy as there are commercial establishments.
Chapter II. Universality of bankruptcy or insolvency, and their effects.
Art. 416. A decree establishing the capacity of the bankrupt or insolvent, has extraterritorial effect in each of the contracting States, upon the previous compliance with the formalities of registration or publication which may be required by the legislation of each State.
Art. 417. A decree of bankruptcy or insolvency, rendered in one of the contracting States, shall be executed in others in the cases and manner established in this code in respect to judicial resolutions, but it shall have the effect of res. judicata from the moment it is made final, as to the persons which it is to affect.
Art. 418. The powers and functions of the trustees appointed in one of the contracting States in accordance with the provisions of this code shall have extraterritorial effect in the others, without the necessity of any local proceeding.
Art. 419. The retroactive effect of a declaration of bankruptcy or insolvency and the annulment of certain acts in consequence of those judgments shall be determined by the law thereof and shall be applicable to the territory of all the other contracting States.
Art. 420. Real actions and rights of the same nature shall continue to be subject, notwithstanding the declaration in bankruptcy or insolvency, to the law of the situation of the things affected thereby and to the competence of the judges of the place in which they are found.
Chapter III. Agreement and rehabilitation.
Art. 421. The agreement among the creditors and the bankrupt or insolvent shall have extraterritorial effect in the other contracting States, saving the right to a real action by the creditors who may not have accepted.
Art. 422. The rehabilitation of the bankrupt has also extraterritorial validity in the other contracting States, as soon as the judicial resolution by which it is ordered becomes final, and in conformity with its terms.
Title X. Execution of judgments rendered by foreign courts.
Chapter I. Civil matters.
Art. 423. Every civil or contentious administrative judgment rendered in one of the contracting States shall have force and may be executed in the others if it combines the following conditions:
(1) That the judge of the court which has rendered it have competence to take cognizance of the matter and to pass judgment upon it, in accordance with the rules of this Code.
(2) That the parties have been summoned for the trial either personally or through their legal representative.
(3) That the judgment does not conflict with the public policy or the public laws of the country in which its execution is sought;
(4) That it is executory in the State in which it was rendered.
(5) That it be authoritatively translated by an official functionary or interpreter of the State in which it is to be executed, if the language employed in the latter is different.
(6) That the document in which it is contained fulfills the requirements necessary in order to be considered as authentic in the State from which it proceeds, and those which the legislation of the State in which the execution of the judgment is sought requires for authenticity.
Art. 424. The execution of the judgment should be requested from a competent judge or tribunal in order to carry it into effect, after complying with the formalities required by the internal legislation.
Art. 425. In the case referred to in the preceding article, every recourse against the judicial resolution granted by the laws of that State in respect to final judgments rendered in a declarative action of greater import shall be granted.
Art. 426. The judge or tribunal from whom the execution is requested shall, before decreeing or denying it, and for a term of twenty days, hear the party against whom it is directed as well as the prosecuting attorney.
Art. 427. The summons of the party who should be heard shall be made by means of letters requisitorial or letters rogatory, in accordance with the provisions of this Code if he has his domicile in a foreign country and lacks sufficient representation in the country, or in the form established by the local law if he has his domicile in the requested State.
Art. 428. After the term fixed for appearance by the judge or the court, the case shall be proceeded with whether or not the party summoned has appeared.
Art. 429. If the execution is denied, the judgment shall be returned to the party who presented it.
Art. 430. When the execution of judgment is granted, the former shall be subject to the procedure determined by the law of the judge or the court for its own judgments.
Art. 431. Final judgments rendered by a contracting State which by reason of their pronouncements are not to be executed shall have in the other States the effects of res judicata if they fulfill the conditions provided for that purpose by this Code, except those relating to their execution.
Art. 432. The procedure and effects regulated in the proceding articles shall be applied in the contracting States to awards made in any of them by arbitrators or friendly compositors, whenever the case to which they refer can be the subject of a compromise in accordance with the legislation of the country where the execution is requested.
Art. 433. The same procedure shall be also applied in respect to civil judgments rendered in any of the contracting States by an international tribunal when referring to private persons or interests.
Chapter II. Acts of voluntary jurisdiction.
Art. 434. The provisions made in acts of voluntary jurisdiction regarding commercial matters by judge or tribunals of a contracting State or by its consular agents shall be executed in the others in accordance with the procedure and the manner indicated in the preceding article.
Art. 435. The resolutions adopted in acts of voluntary jurisdiction in civil matters in a contracting State shall be accepted by the others if they fulfill the conditions required by this Code for the validity of documents executed in a foreign country and were rendered by a competent judge or tribunal, and they shall in consequence have extraterritorial validity.
Chapter III. Penal matters.
Art. 436. No contracting State shall execute the judgments rendered in one of the others in penal matters in respect to the sanctions of that class which they impose.
Art. 437. They may, however, execute the said judgments in respect to civil liability and the effects thereof upon the property of the convicted person if they have been rendered by a competent judge or tribunal in accordance with this Code and upon a hearing of the interested party and if the other conditions of form and procedure established by the first chapter of this title have been complied with.

A.S. DE BUSTAMANTE, *Tratado de derecho internacionial privado*, Habana, 1896; *LNTS*, Vol. 84, pp. 111–381; *International Conferences of American States 1889–1928*, Washington, DC, 1931.

BUS TRANSPORT. Subject of an international agreement, signed on Dec. 5, 1970 in Berlin by the governments of Czechoslovakia, GDR, Poland, Hungary and the USSR. It came into force on Sept. 3, 1971.

UNTS, Vol. 802, p. 5.

BUTCHERY. A subject of international co-operation. Organizations reg. with the UIA:

EEC Committee of Butchery Organizations, f. 1959, Brussels. International Confederation of the Butchers and Delicatessen Trade, f. 1946, Zürich, Switzerland.

Yearbook of International Organizations, 1986–87; *The Europa Yearbook 1988. A World Survey*, Vol. I, London, 1988.

BUTTER. The production and trade of butter is the subject of organized international co-operation under the patronage of the FAO. In the EEC there is a Commission for Butter, which regulates the quota system and manages subsidies of exports.

BUY AMERICAN ACT, 1930. A bill passed in 1930 by the US Congress in connection with the great economic crisis; it introduced restrictions in the importation of agricultural and industrial products and established privileges for domestic manufacturers. In 1977/78 some US states restored the validity of the privileges, or introduced new restrictions in the importation of steel, glass, shoes and other manufactured products.

BW CONVENTION, 1972. The Convention on the Prohibition of the Development, Production and Stockpiling of Bacteriological (Biological) and Toxin Weapons and on their Destruction adopted by Res. 2829 of the UN General Assembly, and signed in London, Moscow and Washington on Apr. 10, 1972 by the majority of UN Members. The BW Convention was not signed or signed (s) but not ratified until 1984 by the following states: Algeria, Bahamas, Bangladesh, Botswana (s), Burma (s), Burundi (s), Cameroon, Central African Republic (s), Chad, (s), Colombia (s), Egypt (s), El Salvador (s), Equatorial Guinea, France, Gabon (s), Gambia (s), Germany, Federal Republic of (s), Grenada, Guinea, Guyana (s), Haiti (s), Indonesia (s), Iraq (s), Israel, Ivory Coast (s), Japan, (s), Kampuchea (s), Korean Republic (s), Liberia (s), Libya, Liechtenstein, Madagascar (s), Malawi (s), Malaysia (s), Maldives, Mali (s), Mauritania, Morocco (s), Nepal (s), Peru (s), Somali (s), Sudan, Suriname, Swaziland, Syria (s), Tanzania (s), Trinidad and Tobago, Tuvalu, Uganda, United Arab Emirates (s), Upper Volta (now Burkina Faso), Western Samoa, Yemen Arab Republic (s), Zambia.

The text of the Resolution and of the Convention is as follows:

"The General Assembly,

Recalling its resolution 2662 (XXV) of 7 December, 1970, Convinced of the importance and urgency of eliminating from the arsenals of States, through effective measures, such dangerous weapons of mass destruction as those using chemical or bacteriological (biological) agents.

Having considered the report of the Conference of the Committee on Disarmament dated 6 October, 1971, and being appreciative of its work on the draft Convention on the Prohibition of the Development, Production and Stockpiling of Bacteriological (Biological) and Toxic Weapons and on Their Destruction, annexed to the report.

Recognizing the important significance of the Protocol for the Prohibition of the Use in War of Asphyxiating, Poisonous or Other Gases, and of Bacteriological Methods of Warfare, signed at Geneva on 17 June, 1925, and conscious also of the contribution which the said Protocol has already made, and continues to make, to mitigating the horrors of war.

Noting that the Convention provides for the parties to reaffirm their adherence to the principles and objectives of that Protocol and to call upon all States to comply strictly with them.

Further noting that nothing in the Convention shall be interpreted as in any way limiting or detracting from the obligations assumed by any State under the Geneva Protocol.

Determined, for the sake of all mankind, to exclude completely the possibility of bacteriological (Biological) agents and toxins being used as weapons.

Recognizing that an agreement on the prohibition of bacteriological (biological) and toxin weapons represents a first possible step towards the achievement of agreement on effective measures also for the prohibition of the development, production and stockpiling of chemical weapons.

Noting that the Convention contains an affirmation of the recognized objective of effective prohibition of chemical weapons and, to this end, an undertaking to continue negotiations in good faith with a view to reaching early agreement on effective measures for the prohibition of their development, production and stockpiling and for their destruction, and on appropriate measures concerning equipment and means of delivery specifically designed for the production or use of chemical agents for weapons purposes.

Convinced that the implementation of measures in the field of disarmament should release substantial additional resources, which should promote economic and social development, particularly in the developing countries.

Convinced that the Convention will contribute to the realization of the purposes and principles of the Charter of the United Nations.

(1) Commends the Convention on the Prohibition of the Development, Production and Stockpiling of Bacteriological (Biological) and Toxin Weapons and on Their Destruction, the text of which is annexed to the present resolution;

(2) Requests the depositary Governments to open the Convention for signature and ratification at the earliest possible date;

(3) Expresses the hope for the widest possible adherence to the Convention.

Annex: Convention on the Prohibition of the Development, Production and Stockpiling of Bacteriological (Biological) and Toxin Weapons and on Their Destruction.

The States Parties to this Convention,

Determined to act with a view to achieving effective progress towards general and complete disarmament, including the prohibition and elimination of all types of weapons of mass destruction, and convinced that the prohibition of the development, production and stockpiling of chemical and bacteriological (biological) weapons and their elimination, through effective measures, will facilitate the achievement of general and complete disarmament under strict and effective international control,

Recognizing the important significance of the Protocol for the Prohibition of the Use in War of Asphyxiating, Poisonous or Other Gases, and of Bacteriological Methods of Warfare, signed at Geneva on 17 June, 1925, and conscious also of the contribution which the said Protocol has already made, and continues to make, to mitigating the horrors of war. Reaffirming their adherence to the principles and objectives of that Protocol and calling upon all States to comply strictly with them.

Recalling that the General Assembly of the United Nations has repeatedly condemned all actions contrary to the principles and objectives of the Geneva Protocol of 17 June, 1925.

Desiring to contribute to the strengthening of confidence between peoples and the general improvement of the international atmosphere.

Desiring also to contribute to the realization of the purposes and principles of the Charter of the United Nations.

Convinced of the importance and urgency of eliminating from the arsenals of States, through effective measures, such dangerous weapons of mass destruction as those using chemical or bacteriological (biological) agents.

Recognizing that an agreement on the prohibition of bacteriological (biological) and toxin weapons represents a first possible step towards the achievement of agreement on effective measures also for the prohibition of the development, production and stockpiling of chemical weapons, and determined to continue negotiations to that end.

Determined, for the sake of all mankind, to exclude completely the possibility of bacteriological (biological) agents and toxins being used as weapons.

Convinced that such use would be repugnant to the conscience of mankind and that no effort should be spared to minimize this risk.

Have agreed as follows:

Art. 1. Each State Party to this Convention undertakes never in any circumstances to develop, produce, stockpile or otherwise acquire or retain:

(1) Microbial or other biological agents, or toxins whatever their origin or method of production, of types and in quantities that have no jurisdiction for prophylactic, protective or other peaceful purposes;

(2) Weapons, equipment or means of delivery designed to use such agents or toxins for hostile purposes or in armed conflict.

Art. 2. Each State Party to this Convention undertakes to destroy, or to divert to peaceful purposes, as soon as possible but not later than nine months after the entry into force of the Convention, all agents, toxins, weapons, equipment and means of delivery specified in article 1 of the Convention, which are in its possession or under its jurisdiction or control. In implementing the provisions of this article all necessary safety precautions shall be observed to protect populations and the environment.

Art. 3. Each State Party to this Convention undertakes not to transfer to any recipient whatsoever, directly or indirectly, and not in any way to assist, encourage, or induce any State, group of States or international organizations to manufacture or otherwise acquire any of the agents, toxins, weapons, equipment or means of delivery specified in article 1 of the Convention.

Art. 4. Each State Party to this Convention shall, in accordance with its constitutional processes, take any necessary measures to prohibit and prevent the development, production, stockpiling, acquisition or retention of the agents, toxins, weapons, equipment and means of delivery specified in article 1 of the Convention, within the territory of such State, under its jurisdiction or under its control anywhere.

Art. 5. The States Parties to this Convention undertake to consult one another and to co-operate in solving any problems which may arise in relation to the objective of, or in the application of the provisions of, the Convention. Consultation and co-operation pursuant to this article may also be undertaken through appropriate international procedures within the framework of the United Nations and in accordance with its Charter.

Art. 6.(1) Any State Party to this Convention which finds that any other State Party is acting in breach of obligations deriving from the provisions of the Convention may lodge a complaint with the Security Council of the United Nations. Such a complaint should include all possible evidence confirming its validity, as well as a request for its consideration by the Security Council.

(2) Each State Party to this Convention undertakes to co-operate in carrying out any investigation which the Security Council may initiate, in accordance with the provisions of the Charter of the United Nations, on the basis of the complaint received by the Council. The Security Council shall inform the States Parties to the Convention of the results of the investigation.

Art. 7. Each State Party to this Convention undertakes to provide or support assistance, in accordance with the United Nations Charter, to any Party to the Convention which so requests, if the Security Council decides that such Party has been exposed to danger as a result of violation of the Convention.

Art. 8. Nothing in this Convention shall be interpreted as in any way limiting or detracting from the obligations assumed by any State under the Protocol for the Prohibition of the Use in War of Asphyxiating, Poisonous or Other Gases, and of Bacteriological Methods of Warfare, signed at Geneva on 17 June, 1925.

Art. 9. Each State Party to this Convention affirms the recognized objective of effective prohibition of chemical weapons and, to this end, undertakes to continue negotiations in good faith with a view to reaching early agreement on effective measures for the prohibition of their development, production and stockpiling and for their destruction, and on appropriate measures concerning equipment and means of delivery specifically designed for the production or use of chemical agents for weapons purposes.

Art. 10.(1) The States Parties to this Convention undertake to facilitate, and have the right to participate in, the fullest possible exchange of equipment, materials and scientific and technological information for the use of bacteriological (biological) agents and toxins for peaceful purposes. Parties to the Convention in a position to do so shall also co-operate in contributing individually or together with other States or international organizations to the further development and application of scientific discoveries in the field of bacteriology (biology) for the prevention of disease, or for other peaceful purposes.

(2) This Convention shall be implemented in a manner designed to avoid hampering the economic or technological development of States Parties to the Convention or international co-operation in the field of peaceful bacteriological (biological) activities, including the international exchange of bacteriological (biological) agents and toxins and equipment for the processing, use or production of bacteriological (biological) agents and toxins for peaceful purposes in accordance with the provisions of the Convention.

Art. 11. Any State Party may propose amendments to this Convention. Amendments shall enter into force for each State Party accepting the amendments upon their acceptance by a majority of the States Parties to the Convention and thereafter for each remaining State Party or the date of acceptance by it.

Art. 12. Five years after the entry into force of this Convention, or earlier if it is requested by a majority of Parties to the Convention by submitting a proposal to this effect to the Depository Governments, a conference of States Parties to the Convention shall be held at Geneva, Switzerland, to review the operation of the Convention, with a view to assuring that the purposes of the preamble and the provisions of the Convention, including the provisions concerning negotiations on chemical weapons, are being realized. Such review shall take into account any new scientific and technological developments relevant to the Convention.

Art. 13.(1) This Convention shall be of unlimited duration.

(2) Each State Party to this Convention shall in exercising its national sovereignty have the right to withdraw from the Convention if it decides that extraordinary events, related to the subject matter of the Convention, have jeopardized the supreme interests of its country. It shall give notice of such withdrawal to all other States Parties to the Convention and to the United Nations Security Council three months in advance. Such notice shall include a statement of the extraordinary events it regards as having jeopardized its supreme interests.

Art. 14.(1) This Convention shall be open to all States for signature. Any State which does not sign the Convention before its entry into force in accordance with paragraph 3 of this article may accede to it at any time.

(2) This Convention shall be subject to ratification by signatory States. Instruments of ratification and instruments of accession shall be deposited with the Governments of the Union of Soviet Socialist Republics, the United Kingdom of Great Britain and Northern Ireland and the United States of America, which are hereby designated the Depository Governments.

(3) This Convention shall enter into force after the deposit of instruments of ratification by twenty-two Governments, including the Governments designated as Depositories of the Convention.

(4) For States whose instruments of ratification or accession are deposited subsequent to the entry into force of this Convention, it shall enter into force on the date of the deposit of their instruments of ratification or accession.

(5) The Depository Governments shall promptly inform all signatory and acceding States of the date of each signature, the date of deposit of each instrument of ratification or of accession and the date of the entry into force of this Convention, and of the receipt of other notices.

(6) This convention shall be registered by the Depository Governments pursuant to Article 102 of the Charter of the United Nations.

Art. 15. This Convention, the Chinese, English, French, Russian and Spanish texts of which are equally authentic, shall be deposited in the archives of the Depository Governments. Duly certified copies of the Convention shall be transmitted by the Depository Governments to the Governments of the signatory and acceding States."

The Convention entered into force in 1975. In September 1986 the Review Conference of the parties to the BW Convention took place. The final Declaration of the Conference classified documents regarding the scope of the prohibition (of the possession of biological and toxic weapons) which had arisen as a result of advances in the biological field since 1972. By January 1, 1987 the Convention had been ratified by 107 countries. See also ▷ Biological Weapons.

Recueil de documents, Varsovie, December 12, 1971; *UN Yearbook*, 1971; J. GOLDBLAT, *Arms Control Agreements; A Handbook*, New York, 1983, pp. 100–102, 163–165, 251–281; J. GOLDBLAT, *Strengthening the Convention*, in: *Transnational Perspectives*, Geneva, Nr. 3, 1986: J. GOLDBLAT, *The Review of the BW Conventions*, in *SIPRI Yearbook 1987*, Oxford, 1987; J. PAXTON (ed.), *The Statesman's Yearbook 1987–88*, London, 1987.

BYELORUSSIA. Member of the UN. Byelorussian Soviet Socialist Republic. European federated state of the USSR, bordering on Poland, Latvia, Lithuania, Russian SFSR and the Ukraine. Area: 207,600 sq. km. Pop. 1983 census: 9,806,000. (79.4% Byelorussians, 11.9% Russians, 4.2% Poles, 2.4% Ukrainians and 1.4% Jews, 1979 census). Capital: Minsk with 1,405,000 inhabitants 1983. Official languages: Byelorussian and Russian. Currency: one Soviet rouble = 100 kopeks. National Day: Nov. 7, October Revolution Day, 1917.

Original member of the UN since Oct. 24, 1945 and of the UN specialized agencies, with the exception of: FAO, IBRD, IMF, IFC, GATT, IDA, IMO, IFAD.

International relations: part of the Kingdom of Lithuania–Poland from 1569 to 1795; in the Russian Empire until 1917; divided by the Riga Treaty 1921 between Poland and USSR. Occupied by the Germans 1941–44. New frontier with Poland 1945.

UNTS, Vol. 10, pp. 194–197; G.T. KOVALEVSKI, Y.G. RAKOV (eds.), *Byelorusskaya SSR, An outline of Her Economic Geography*, Minsk, 1953; N.P. VAKAR, *A Bibliographical Guide to Byelorussia*, Harvard University Press, 1956; *Byelorusskaya SSR*, Moskva, 1959; J.P. BROVKA, *Mezhdunarodnaya pravosubyektnost Byelorusskoy SSR*, Minsk, 1967; *Everyone's United Nations*, New York, 1979; *The International Geographic Encyclopedia and Atlas*, London, 1979; *The Europa Year Book 1984. A World Survey*, Vol. I, pp. 913–914, London, 1984.

BYEZHENTSY. *Russian*: "fugitives, refugees". An international term which appeared at the end of World War I for war refugees from revolutionary Russia called also "White Russians" (▷ Nansen passport). In the League of Nations the English word "refugees" was introduced. During World War II the American term ▷ displaced persons became accepted, but in the UN replaced with the English ▷ Refugees.

F. NANSEN, *Russland und der Friede*, Zurich, 1923; S.P. LADAS, *Exchange of Minorities*, New York, 1932; J.H. SIMPSON, *The Refugee Problem*, London, 1939; P. FRINGS, *Das internationale Flüchtlingsproblem, 1919–1950*, Frankfurt am M., 1951; M.J. PROUDFOOT, *European Refugees 1919–1952*, New York, 1957.

BYZANTINE STUDIES. Subject of international co-operation. Organization reg. with the UIA:

International Association for Byzantine Studies, f. 1948, Athens. Publ. *Bulletin d'information*. Members: National Committees and individuals in Austria, Belgium, Brazil, Bulgaria, Canada, Chile, Cyprus, Czechoslovakia, Denmark, France, the FRG, the GDR, Greece, Hungary, Italy, Japan, Lebanon, the Netherlands, Poland, Romania, Sweden, Switzerland, Turkey, the UK, the USSR and Yugoslavia. Organizes International Congresses of Byzantine Studies in co-operation with the International Federation of the Societies of Classical Studies.

S. RUNCIMAN, *Byzantine Civilization*, London, 1933; L. BRÉHIER, *Le Monde Byzantine*, 3 Vols., Paris, 1947–1950; G. OSTROGORSKY, *Geschichte des byzantinischen Staates*, Berlin, 1952; J.M. HUSSEY, *The Byzantine World*, London, 1957. *Yearbook of International Organizations*.

C

CABINDA. Angolan enclave in west Africa in the Atlantic Ocean, north of the mouth of the Congo river between Zaïre and the Republic of Congo. Area: 7270 sq. km. Pop.: 1980 est. 95,000 (census 1960 – 58,547). After the discovery of oil in 1957, exploitation was undertaken by the American company Gulf Oil of Cabinda. In 1975, despite efforts to organize a separatist state, Cabinda became part of the People's Republic of Angola. In 1976 Gulf Oil of Cabinda paid the government of Angola US$ 120 million in back taxes and acquired the right to further exploitation.

The Europa Year Book. A World Survey, Vol. I, p. 1068, London, 1984.

CABLE. A subject of international protection and agreements. The first Convention on the Protection of Submarine Cables was signed on Mar. 14, 1884. Organization reg. with the UIA:
International Cable Protection Committee, f. 1958 in London. Publ. *Trawling and Submarine Cables*.
Yearbook of International Organizations.

CABOTAGE. An international term for coastal navigation as well as commercial navigation between ports of one sea, so-called Small Sea Cabotage or between many seas – Great Sea Cabotage; cabotage between river ports has the name River Cabotage, and the transport of goods and passengers between airports of one country Air Cabotage.

CADMIUM. Subject of international co-operation. Organization reg. with the UIA:
Cadmium Association, f. 1976, London. Members: companies concerned with the production of cadmium except those of North America. Affiliate of the Zinc Development Association in close liaison with the North American Cadmium Council.
Yearbook of International Organizations 1986/87; The Europa Yearbook 1988. A World Survey, Vol. I, London 1988.

CAIRO. The capital of Egypt (Pop. 1976 census 5.074.016; 1986 metropolitan area, called Great Cairo, over 10 million) since 969; city with 5,750,000 inhabitants in 1975. During World War II Cairo was the Allied headquarters. In 1943 the site of the ▷ Cairo Conference. Seat of 25 international organizations reg. with the UIA. Cairo was the seat of the League of Arab States until 1979, in which year, after the Egypt–Israeli Peace Treaty, the League transferred all offices to Tunisia.
Yearbook of International Organizations. Europa Yearbook 1987. A World Survey, London 1987; J. PAXTON, *The Statesman's Yearbook 1987/88*, London 1988.

CAIRO CONFERENCE, 1943. A summit meeting in Cairo, Nov., 1943, of the President of the USA, F.D. Roosevelt, with the Prime Minister of the UK W.S. Churchill and the President of China, Chang-Kai-shek.

H. FEIS, *China Tangle: the American Effort in China from Pearl Harbour to the Marshall Mission*, New York, 1953.

CAIRO CONFERENCES, 1956 AND 1957. Three summit meetings of the chiefs of state of Egypt, Syria, and Saudi Arabia in Cairo on Mar. 6–12, 1956 on Jan. 18–19 and on Feb. 25–28, 1957 in connection with the ▷ Suez Canal crisis.

CALCUTTA. Capital of India until 1931, replaced by New Delhi. The largest urban agglomeration of India. Population, 1981, census: 9.194.018.
Europa Yearbook. A World Survey, 1987, London, 1987.

CALENDAR OF THE FRENCH REVOLUTION. Proclaimed by the National Committee of France on Oct. 5, 1793, annulled by Napoleon on Jan. 1, 1806. One year consisted of 12 months of 30 days each, beginning with the September equinox; 5 days were added at the end of the year (6 days on leap years). The first month of the year, consisting of 30 days from Sept. to Oct. was called *Vendémaire*, the second (Oct.–Nov. days) *Brumaire*, the third (Nov.–Dec. days) *Frimaire*, the fourth (Dec.–Jan. days) *Nivose*, the fifth (Jan.–Feb. days) *Pluviôse*, the sixth (Feb.–Mar. days) *Sentôse*, the seventh (Mar.–Apr. days) *Germinal*, the eighth (Apr.–May days) *Floréal*, the ninth (May–June days) *Arairial*, the tenth (June–July days) *Messidor*, the eleventh (July–Aug. days) *Thermidor* and the twelfth (Aug.–Sept. days) *Fructidor*. *Thermidor* became an international term, being the month when terror in France was ended by the National Convent, by which M.F. Robespierre and his collaborators were arrested on *Thermidor* 9 (Aug. 27, 1794) and sentenced to death by guillotine, executed a day later. In Brumaire the military *coup d'état* of Napoleon took place (Nov. 9–10, 1799). The annulment of the Revolution calendar and reinstatement of the Roman Catholic calendar (Julian) was a step towards an agreement between Napoleon and Pope Pius VII, with whom Napoleon concluded a concordat on Aug. 15, 1806.

J. GODECHOT, *Les institutions de la France sous la Révolution et l'Empire*, Paris, 1951.

CALENDAR WORLD REFORM. The subject of international co-operation for establishment of a perpetual calendar with four equal quarters of 91 days during one year plus one Worldsday.
Organizations reg. with the UIA:
Calendar Reform Foundation, f. 1962, Washington. International World Calendar Association, f. 1930, New York. Consultative status: ECOSOC. Publ. *World Calendar Reform.*
Yearbook of International Organizations.

CALIFORNIA CHURCH FOUNDATIONS. A Church property belonging to foundations in California administered 1767–1821 by Spain and subsequently by Mexico and from 1870 the subject of claims which began in 1853, by the San Francisco archbishops to share the incomes of the foundations. These were twice heard by the Court of Arbitration, on Nov. 11, 1875 and Oct. 14, 1902. Both cases were decided against Mexico, which had to pay US $904,000 damages to the archbishopric for the years 1848–69 and the same amount for the years 1870–1902 when the dispute ended.

E. DESCAMP, *Les fondations californiennes et la question de la chose jugée en droit international*. Paris, 1902; H.J. HALLIER, "Kalifornischer Kirchengüter-Streit", in: *Strupp-Schlochauer Wörterbuch des Völkerrechts*, Vol. 2, Berlin, 1961, pp. 181–182.

CALL MONEY. A common banking term, denoting short-term cash deposits or deposits payable on demand.

CALVINISM. An international term for one of the main doctrines of ▷ Protestantism (besides ▷ Lutheranism and ▷ Zwinglianism), formulated by the Swiss reformer, J. Calvin (1609–64), in the work *Christianae religionis institutio* (1636) stating that people are foreordained by God to be saved or condemned (the doctrine of predestination) and introducing a rigoristic ethic, which became the basis for Puritan civilization. Calvinists take part in the international ecumenical movement.

F. WENDEL, *Calvin: sources et évolution de sa pensée religieuse*, Genève, 1950; J.T. McNEILL, *The History and Character of Calvinism*, London, 1954.

CALVO DOCTRINE, 1868. A general principle of international law formulated by the Argentinian diplomat and historian, G. Calvo, that the state cannot agree to accept responsibility for losses incurred by aliens as the result of a civil war or uprising, since this would introduce "unjustified inequality in the rights of native citizens and aliens." An alien should be treated as a native citizen responsible to local courts and laws. "The diplomatic protection of private aliens is an instrument of pressure applied by strong states against weaker ones." Since the end of the 19th century in certain Latin American states the "*Calvo proviso*" has become binding in contracts made with persons or private foreign companies. In Mexico the Calvo clause was included in the Constitution of 1817, art. 27.

G. CALVO, *El derecho internacional y práctico*, Buenos Aires, 1868; K. LIPSTEIN, "The Place of Calvo Clause in International Law" in: *The British Yearbook of International Law*, 1945; D.R. SHEA, *The Calvo Clause*, London, 1955. R.L. BLEDSOE, B.A. BOCZEK, *The International Law Dictionary*, Oxford, 1987

CAMBODIA. An historical name of the Khmer Empire in South-east Asia on the Gulf of Siam, between the Kingdom of Siam, Laos and Vietnam; 1854–1953 part of French Indochina; name of independent state 1954 to 1975, replaced by the Khmer Republic of ▷ Kampuchea.

F. PONCHARD, *Cambodia Year Zero*, London, 1978.

CAMELOT PROJECT, 1964. A code name of a system of sociological research carried out from Dec., 1964, commissioned by the US Special Operation Research Office (SORO) at a number of scientific centers in Argentina, Bolivia, Brazil, Chile, Dominicana, Colombia, El Salvador, and Peru, aimed at establishing the nature of social tensions and possibilities of outbreak of civil war or mounting of guerilla movements in Latin American countries. Findings were submitted to US Senate in a joint report called Pax Americana.

H. PACHECO, "Proyectos Secretos y Ciencias Sociales" (Camelot), in: *El Día*, México, DF, February 26, 1968, p. 5; V. MARCHETTI, J.D. MARKS, *The CIA and the Cult of Intelligence*, New York, 1945, pp. 40–41.

CAMEROON. Member of the UN. République du Cameroun. Republic of Cameroon. West African State on the Atlantic Coast, bounded by Nigeria, Chad, Central African Republic, Congo, Gabon and Equatorial Guinea; Area: 475,441 sq. km. Pop.: 1987 est. 10,927,000 (1976 census 7,663,246). Capital: Yaoundé with 313,706 inhabitants, 1976. GNP per capita in 1987 US $960. Official languages: French and English. Currency: 1 franc CFA = 100

C

centimes. National Day: Jan. 1, Independence Day, 1960.

Member of the UN since Sept. 20, 1960 and of the UN specialized agencies. Member of the OAU. ACP state of EEC. A signatory of the Lomé Conventions of 1975 and of 1980.

International relations: a German colony 1884–1916 (Kamerun); during World War I it was occupied by French and English troops and divided in 1919 between French and British administration as League of Nations mandates. In 1946 they became UN trusteeship territories. In French East Cameroon full independence was proclaimed on Jan. 1, 1960, while in British West Cameroon in a plebiscite on Feb. 1961 the northern provinces decided to join Nigeria and the southern provinces, East Cameroon. Unification took place on Oct. 1, 1961 as the Federal Republic of Cameroon. Renamed as the bilingual and pluricultural United Republic of Cameroon by a national referendum on May 20, 1972, the name changed to the Republic of Cameroon in Jan. 1984. Involved in border disputes with Nigeria since 1961 after the transfer of Northern Cameroon to Nigeria. A maritime border agreement was signed on May 31, 1975, but not ratified by Nigeria. A Nigeria-Cameroon joint commission was established on April 21, 1983. Border incidents took place in 1981, 1983 and 1987.

See also ▷ World Heritage UNESCO List.

UN Bulletin, No. 4 and No. 8, 1949; *UN Yearbook* 1960; *UN Review,* No. 3, 1961; E. MWENG, *Histoire du Cameroun,* Paris, 1963; D.E. CARDINIER, *Cameroun: UN Challenge to French Policy,* New York, 1963; V.T. LE VINE, *The Cameroons: From Mandate to Independence,* Los Angeles, 1964; A. BOCKEL, *L'administration camerounaise,* Paris, 1971; V.T. LE VINE, *The Cameroon Federal Republic,* Cornell University Press, 1971; A. DEBEL, *Cameroun d'aujourd'hui,* Paris, 1977; *Everyone's United Nations,* New York, 1979; J.F. BAYART, *L'État au Cameroun,*- Paris, 1980; *The Europa Year Book 1984. A World Survey,* Vol. II, pp. 1307–1319, London, 1984. *Cameroon-Nigeria,* in: A.J. DAY ed., *Border and Territorial Disputes,* London, 1987, pp. 111–113.

CAMEROON (BRITISH) TRUSTEESHIP AGREEMENT, 1946. Approved by the UN General Assembly on Dec. 13, 1946.

UNTS, Vol. 8, pp. 119–133.

CAMEROON (FRENCH) TRUSTEESHIP AGREEMENT, 1946. Approved by the UN General Assembly on Dec. 13, 1946.

UNTS, Vol. 8, pp. 135–149.

CAMP DAVID. One of the summer residences of US Presidents, in the state of Maryland. The site (in Sept. 25–27, 1959) of the first summit meeting between US President D. Eisenhower and Soviet Premier N.S. Khrushchev. Honorary residence in June 1973 of Soviet Communist Party General Secretary L.I. Brezhnev during his visit in USA. The site in Sept. 1978 of negotiations between US President J. Carter, Egyptian President A. Sadat, and Israeli Prime Minister M. Begin.

CAMP DAVID AGREEMENT, 1978. The final act of the negotiations between the US President J. Carter, the Egyptian President A. Sadat and the Israeli Prime Minister M. Begin in Sept. 1978 at Camp David. The text is as follows:

Framework for the conclusion of a peace treaty between Egypt and Israel.
In order to achieve peace between them Israel and Egypt agree to negotiate in good faith with a goal of concluding within three months of the signing of this framework a peace treaty between them.
It is agreed that:

The site of the negotiations will be under a United Nations flag at a location or locations to be mutually agreed. All of the principles of UN Res. 242 will apply in this Resolution of the dispute between Israel and Egypt.
Unless otherwise mutually agreed terms of the peace treaty will be implemented between two and three years after the peace treaty is signed.
The following matters are agreed between the parties:
(a) the full exercise of Egyptian sovereignty up to the internationally recognized border between Egypt and mandated Palestine;
(b) the withdrawal of Israeli armed forces from the Sinai;
(c) the use of airfields left by the Israelis near El Arishi Rafahi Ras en Nageb and Sharm el Sheikh for civilian purposes only including possible commercial use by all nations;
(d) the right of free passage by ships of Israel through by Egypt and Jordan and
(f) the stationing of military forces listed below.
Stationing of forces:
No more than one division (mechanized or infantry) of Egyptian armed forces will be stationed within an area lying approximately 50 kilometers east of the Gulf of Suez and the Suez Canal.
Only United Nations forces and civil police equipped with light weapons to perform normal police functions will be stationed within an area lying west of the international border and the Gulf of Aqaba varying in width from 20 kilometers to 40 kilometers.
In the area within 3 kilometers east of the international border there will be Israeli limited military forces not to exceed four infantry battalions and United Nations observers.
Border patrol units not to exceed three battalions will supplement the civil police in maintaining order in the area not included above.
The exact demarcation of the above areas will be as decided during the peace negotiations.
Early warning stations may exist to insure compliance with the terms of the agreement.
United nations forces will be stationed: (a) in part of the area in the Sinai lying within about 20 kilometers of the Mediterranean Sea and adjacent to the international border and (b) in the Sharm el Sheikh area to ensure freedom of passage through the Strait of Tirani and these forces will not be removed unless such removal is approved by the Security Council of the United Nations with a unanimous vote of the five permanent members.
After a peace treaty is signed and after the interim withdrawal is complete, normal relations will be established between Egypt and Israel including full recognition including diplomatic economic and cultural relations termination of economic boycotts and barriers to the free movement of goods and people and mutual protection of citizens by the due process of law. Between three months and nine months after the signing of the peace treaty all Israeli forces will withdraw east of a line extending from a point east of El Arish to Ras Muhammad. The exact location of this line to be determined by mutual agreement. (Signed by Sadat and Begin with Carter signing as a witness).
Muhammad Anwar al Sadat President of the Arab Republic of Egypt and Menachem Begin Prime Minister of Israel met with Jimmy Carter President of the United States of America at Camp David from Sept. 5 to Sept. 17, 1978 and have agreed on the following framework for peace in the Middle East.
They invite other parties to the Arab–Israeli conflict to adhere to it.
The search for peace in the Middle East must be guided by the following:
The agreed basis for a peaceful settlement of the conflict the Security Council Resolution 242 in all its parts.
After four wars during 30 years, despite intensive human efforts, the Middle East, which is the cradle of civilization and the birthplace of three great religions, does not yet enjoy the blessings of peace. The people of the Middle East yearn for peace so that the vast human and natural resources of the region can be turned to the pursuits of peace and so that this area can become a model for co-existence and co-operation among nations.
The historic initiative of President Sadat in visiting Jerusalem and the reception accorded to him by the Parliament government and people of Israel and the

reciprocal visit of Prime Minister to Ismailia the peace proposals made by both leaders as well as the warm reception of these missions by the peoples of both countries have created an unprecedented opportunity for peace which must not be lost if this generation and future generations are to be spared the tragedies of war. The provisions of the Charter of the United Nations and the other accepted norms of international law and legitimacy now provide accepted standards for the conduct of relations among all states.
To achieve a relationship of peace in the spirit of art. 2 of the United Nations Charter future negotiations between Israel and any neighbor prepared to negotiate peace and security with it are necessary for the purpose of carrying out all the provisions and principles of Res. 242 and Res. 338.
Peace requires respect for the sovereignty territorial integrity and political independence of every state in the area and their right to live in peace within secure and recognized boundaries free from threats or acts of force. Progress toward that goal can accelerate movement toward a new era of reconciliation in the Middle East marked by co-operation in promoting economic development in maintaining stability and in assuring security.
Security is enhanced by a relationship of peace and by co-operation between nations which enjoy normal relations. In addition under the terms of peace treaties the parties can on the basis of reciprocity agree to special security arrangements such as demilitarized zones limited armaments areas early warning stations the presence of international forces liaison agreed measures for monitoring and other arrangements that they agree are useful.
Taking these factors into account the parties are determined to reach a just comprehensive and durable settlement of the Middle East conflict through the conclusion of peace treaties based on Security Council Resolutions 242 and 338 in all their parts. Their purpose is to achieve peace and good neighborly relations. They recognize that for peace to endure it must involve all those who have been most deeply affected by the conflict. They therefore agree that this framework as appropriate is intended by them to constitute a basis for peace not only between Egypt and Israeli but also between Israel and each of its other neighbors which is prepared to negotiate peace with Israel on this basis. With that objective in mind they have agreed to proceed as follows:
A. *West Bank and Gaza:*
Egypt, Israel, Jordan and the representations of the Palestinian people should participate in negotiations on the resolution of the Palestinian problem in all its aspects. To achieve that objective negotiations relating to the West Bank and Gaza should proceed in three stages:
(a) Egypt and Israel agree that in order to ensure a peaceful and orderly transfer of authority and taking into account the security concerns of all the parties there should be transitional arrangements for the West Bank and Gaza for a period not exceeding five years. In order to provide full autonomy to the inhabitants under these arrangements the Israeli military government and its civilian administration will be withdrawn as soon as a self-governing authority has been freely elected by the inhabitants of these areas to replace the existing military government. To negotiate the details of a transitional arrangement the government of Jordan will be invited to join the negotiations on the basis of this framework. These new arrangements should give due consideration both to the principle of self-government by the inhabitants of these territories and to the legitimate security concerns of the parties involved.
(b) Egypt, Israel and Jordan will agree on the modalities for establishing the elected self-governing authority in the West Bank and Gaza. The Delegations of Egypt and Jordan may include Palestinians from the West Bank and Gaza or other Palestinians as mutually agreed. The parties will negotiate an agreement which will define the powers and responsibilities of the self-governing authority to be exercised in the West Bank and Gaza. A withdrawal of Israeli armed forces will take place and there will be a redeployment of the remaining Israeli forces into specified security locations. The agreement will also include arrangements for assuring internal and external security and public order. A strong local police force will be established which may include Jordanian citizens. In addition

Israeli and Jordanian forces will participate in joint patrols and in the manning of control posts to assure the security of the borders.

(c) When the self-Governing authority (administrative council) in the West Bank and Gaza is established and inaugurated the transitional period of five years will begin. As soon as possible but not later than the third year after the beginning of the transitional period negotiations will take place to determine the final status of the West Bank and Gaza and its relationship with its neighbors and to conclude a peace treaty between Israel and Jordan by the end of the transitional period. These negotiations will be conducted between Egypt, Israel, Jordan and the elected representatives of the inhabitants of the West Bank and Gaza. Two separate but related committees will be convened one committee consisting of representatives of the four parties which will negotiate and agree on the final status of the West Bank and Gaza and its relationship with its neighbors and the second committee consisting of representatives of Israel and representatives of Jordan to be joined by the elected representatives of the inhabitants of the West Bank and Gaza to negotiate the peace treaty between Israel and Jordan taking into account the agreement reached on the final status of the West Bank and Gaza. The negotiations shall be based on all the provisions and principles of UN Security Council Resolution 242. The negotiations will resolve among other matters the location of the boundaries and the nature of the security arrangements. The solution from the negotiations must also recognize the legitimate rights of the Palestinian people and their just requirements. In this way the Palestinians will participate in the determination of their own future through

(1)(a) The negotiations among Egypt, Israel, Jordan and the representatives of the inhabitants of the West Bank and Gaza to agree on the final status of the West Bank and Gaza and other outstanding issues by the end of the transitional period.

(b) Submitting their agreement to a vote by the elected representatives of the inhabitants of the West Bank and Gaza.

(c) Providing for the elected representatives of the inhabitants of the West Bank and Gaza to decide how they shall govern themselves consistent with the provisions of their agreement.

(d) Participating as stated above in the work of the committee negotiating the peace treaty between Israel and Jordan.

(2) All necessary measures will be taken and provisions made to assure the security of Israel and its neighbors during the transitional period and beyond. To assist in providing such security a strong local police force will be constituted by the self-governing authority. It will be composed of inhabitants of the West Bank and Gaza. The police will maintain continuing liaison on internal security matters with the designated Israeli Jordanian and Egyptian officers.

(3) During the transitional period representatives of Egypt, Israel, Jordan and the self-governing authority will constitute a continuing committee to decide by agreement on the modalities of admission of persons displaced from the West Bank and Gaza in 1967, together with necessary measures to prevent disruption and disorder. Other matters of common concern may also be dealt with by this committee.

(4) Egypt and Israel will work with each other and with other interested parties to establish agreed procedures for a prompt just and permanent implementation of the resolution of the refugee problem.

B. *Egypt–Israel*:

(1) Egypt and Israel undertake not to resort to the threat or the use of force to settle disputes. Any disputes shall be settled by peaceful means in accordance with the provisions of art. 33 of the Charter of the United Nations.

(2) In order to achieve peace between them the parties agree to negotiate in good faith with a goal of concluding within three months from the signing of this framework a peace treaty between them while inviting the other parties to the conflict to proceed simultaneously to negotiate and conclude similar peace treaties with a view to achieving a comprehensive peace in the area. The framework for the conclusion of a Peace Treaty between Egypt and Israel will govern the peace negotiations between them. The parties will agree on the modalities and the timetable for the implementation of their obligations under the treaty.

C. *Associated Principles*:

(1) Egypt and Israel state that the principles and provisions described below should apply to peace treaties between Israel and each of its neighbors Egypt, Jordan, Syria and Lebanon.

(2) Signatories shall establish among themselves relationships normal to states at peace with one another. To this end they should undertake to abide by all the provisions of the Charter of the United Nations. Steps to be taken in this respect include:

(a) Full recognition

(b) Abolishing economic boycotts

(c) Guaranteeing that under their jurisdiction the citizens of the other parties shall enjoy the protection of the due process of law.

(3) Signatories should explore possibilities for economic development in the context of final peace treaties with the objective of contributing to the atmosphere of peace co-operation and friendship which is their common goal.

(4) Claims Commissions may be established for the mutual settlement of all financial claims.

(5) The United States shall be invited to participate in the talks on matters related to the modalities of the implementation of the agreements and working out the timetable for the carrying out of the obligations of the parties.

(6) The United Nations Security Council shall be requested to endorse the peace treaties and ensure that their provisions shall not be violated. The permanent members of the Security Council shall be requested to underwrite the peace treaties and ensure respect for their provisions. They shall also be requested to conform their policies and actions with the undertakings contained in this framework."

▷ Egypt–Israel Peace Treaty, 1979.

US State Department Bulletin, September, 1978. M.J. KAMEL, *The Camp David Accords: a Testimony by Sadat's Foreign Minister*, London, 1987. W.B. QUANDT ed., *The Years after Camp David*, Washington DC 1988.

CAMPING AND CARAVANNING. A subject of international co-operation. Organization reg. with the UIA:

International Federation of Camping and Caravanning, f. 1932, Brussels. Publ. *Information Bulletin*.

Yearbook of International Organizations.

CAMPIONE D'ITALIA. Italian enclave of the province of Como in Switzerland at Lake Lugano; united with Switzerland by a customs union; property of a monastery until 1871, then secularized; has its own administrative statute that does not obligate its inhabitants to pay any taxes except a lump sum for water, which caused it to become an international center of gambling casinos and headquarters of several thousand foreign firms seeking to avoid taxes. A similar tax oasis for international holding companies is Liechtenstein.

CAMPO FORMIO TREATY, 1797. A peace treaty between Austria and France, signed in Campo Formio, Italy on Oct. 17, 1797.

Major Peace Treaties of Modern History, 1648–1967, New York, 1967, Vol. I, pp. 433–444.

CANAAN. The ancient name for ▷ Palestine.

CANADA. Member of the UN. Dominion of Canada. Country in North America bounded by the Atlantic, the Arctic Sea, the Pacific, and the USA. Area: 9,920,974 sq. km. Pop.: 1987 est. 25,861,000 (1851 census: 2,436,000; 1901: 5,371,000; 1951: 14,000,000; 1971: 21,568,000; 1981: 24,343,000). Capital: Ottawa with 737,000 inhabitants, 1983. GNP per capita (1987): US $15,080. Nationality census 1961: British 7,996,000; French – 5,540,000; German – 1,049,000; Ukrainian – 473,000; Italian – 450,000; Dutch – 429,000; Polish – 323,000; Indian and Eskimo – 220,000; Jewish – 173,000; Nor-

wegian – 148,000; Hungarian – 106,000; Danish – 85,000; Czech and Slovak – 73,000; Yugoslav – 68,000; Belgian – 60,000, Finnish – 59,000; Chinese – 58,000; Greek – 56,900; Romanian – 43,000; Negro – 32,000; Muslim – 30,000; Japanese – 29,000; Lithuanian – 27,000; no admitted nationality – 210,000 (in 1969 the number of Indians was 244,000 and of Eskimos – 17,000). Official languages English and French. Currency: 1 Canadian dollar = 100 cents. National Day: July 1, anniversary of proclamation of confederation, 1867.

Canada was a founding member of the League of Nations 1919–39 and among the United Nations during World War II. Founding member of UN since Oct. 24, 1945 and all its specialized agencies. Member of NATO and the OECD. Joint Defense Treaty with the USA signed on May 12, 1953, whose organ is a Permanent Board on Defense. Canada signed the Partial Nuclear Test Ban Treaty on Jan. 28, 1964; the Outer Space Treaty on Oct. 10, 1967; the Non-Proliferation Treaty on Jan. 8, 1969; the Sea-Bed Treaty on May 17, 1972; and the BW Convention on Sept. 18, 1972. Canada participates in International Control Commissions; attended, alongside the USA, the European Conference on Security and Co-operation 1975 and signed the ▷ Helsinki Final Act, 1975.

International relations: 1605–1763 French colony; 1763–1867 British colony; 1867–1953 British dominion. Since 1953 sovereign kingdom within the British Commonwealth in personal union with the Queen of the United Kingdom as Queen of Canada and Head of the Commonwealth. Canada is a constitutional kingdom with a parliament and government headed by a prime minister, pursuing domestic and foreign policies of her own. In World War I among the Allies. Its border with the USA on the St Lawrence River was disputed in the 19th century because of British intervention in North America in 1812 and following the activities of the United Delimitation Commission, set up by the Jay Treaty, 1794. New commissions which were appointed as a result of the Gent Peace Treaty, 1814, settled only part of the border. Further sections of the border were delineated by later treaties of July 22, 1892 and May 21, 1910. The issue was closed finally by the Washington Treaty of Feb. 24, 1925 which appointed a Permanent Mixed Border Commission.

The Canadian Institute of International Affairs, f. 1928, Toronto Ont., Publ.: International Journal (quarterly).

See also ▷ World Heritage UNESCO List.

F.X. GARNEAU, *Histoire du Canada Français*, Vols. 1–2, Paris, 1928; G. IRELAND, *Boundaries, Possessions and Conflicts in Central and North America and the Caribbean*, New York, 1941; G.P. GLAZER-BROOK, *A History of Canadian External Relations*, Toronto, 1950; C. DE BONNAULT, *Histoire du Canada Français*, Paris, 1950; B. HUTCHINSON, *Canada, Tomorrow's Giant*, New York, 1955; T.H. HOWARD, Z. MCINNIS, *Canada and the UN*, New York, 1957; J.B. BREBNER, *North Atlantic Triangle: The Interplay of Canada, the United States and Great Britain*, New York, 1958; V.S. LANCTOT, *Histoire du Canada. Des origines au régime royal*, Montreal, 1960; G.W. WILSON, *Canada: An Appraisal of its Needs and Resources*, New York, 1965; C. CLARK, *Canada, The Uneasy Neighbour*, New York, 1965; *Canada and the UN 1945–1965*, Ottawa, 1966; *Encyclopaedia Canadiana*, 10 Vols., Ottawa, 1967; *Canada One Hundred 1867–1967*, Ottawa, 1967; P.E. TRUDEAU, *Federalism and the Canadians*, Ottawa, 1968; I. LUMSDEN, *The Americanization of Canada*, Toronto, 1970; R. COOK, *French-Canadian Nationalism*, Toronto, 1970; D.C. THOMPSON, R.F. SWANSON, *Canadian Foreign Policy: Options and Perspectives*, Toronto, 1971; R. BOTHWELL, I. DRUMMOND, J. ENGLISH, *Canada since 1945: Power, Politics and Provincialism*, Toronto, 1981; *The Europa Year Book 1984. A World Survey*, Vol. II, pp. 1320–1348, London, 1984. D.V. VERNEY, *Three Civilizations, Two Cul-*

C

tures, One State: Canada's Political Traditions, London, 1986. P. WONNACOTT, The United States and Canada. The Quest for Free Trade, Washington DC., 1987.

CANADIAN INSTITUTE FOR INTERNATIONAL PEACE AND SECURITY, f. 1985 at Montebello, Canada.

CANADIAN INSTITUTE OF INTERNATIONAL AFFAIRS. An institution f. 1928 in Toronto, affiliated with the Royal Institute of International Affairs, London. Publ. *International Journal* (quarterly), *Contemporary Affairs, Canada in World Affairs.*

CANALS, INTERNATIONAL. At present there is no international code which uniformly defines the status of international canals, straits or rivers. The internationalization or neutralization of canals began on Oct. 29, 1888 with the Istanbul Convention on the ▷ Suez Canal statute (▷ Suez Treaty 1888); next was the Declaration of the Government of Greece on the Corinth Canal statute, 1893; the Declaration of the US government on the Panama Canal statute; and arts. 380–386 of the Versailles Treaty, 1919 defined the organization of the Kiel Canal. In international practice "the right of harmless passage" through canals is limited only in time of war.

V. BÖHMERT, "Kanäle", in: *Strupp-Schlochauer Wörterbuch des Völkerrechts,* Vol. 2, Berlin, 1961, pp. 187–190; P.D.BARABOLIY, L.A. IVANASHCHENKO, D.N. KOLESNIK, *Mezhdunarodnopravovoi rezhim vazhnieyshij prolivov i kanalov,* Moskva, 1965; *Rios y Canales Navegables Internacionales. Aspectos financieros e institucionales de su desarrollo. Informe sobre el Simposio realizado en Buenos Aires* (Nov. 30–Dec. 4, 1970) UNITAR, Buenos Aires, 1971; *International Navigable Waterways,* UNITAR, New York, 1975.

CANARY ISLANDS. Seven Spanish islands on the Atlantic Ocean near Western Sahara; constitute two provinces: Las Palmas (area 4,072 sq. km; pop. 1981 census 756,353) and Santa Cruz de Tenerife (area 3,170 sq. km; pop. 1981 census 688,273).

The Europa Yearbook 1987. A World Survey, London 1987.

CANBERRA. The capital of Australia (1984 pop. 264,300) from 1913 (previously the central authorities of the country were located in Melbourne and Sydney). The seat of the ANZUS Council.

The Europa Yearbook. 1987. A World Survey, London 1987.

CANCER. A subject of international co-operation. Organizations reg. with the UIA:

Cancer International Research Co-operative (CANCIRCO), f. 1961, New York. Publ. *Concern for Cancer* (series of leaflets).
European Association for Cancer Research, f. 1968, Copenhagen.
European Institute of Cancerology, f. 1961, Brussels.
European Institute of Ecology and Cancerology, f. 1965, Brussels.
European Organization for Research on Treatment of Cancer, f. 1963, Zurich.
The International Agency for Research on Cancer, IARC, f. 1968 by the WHO in Lyon, Publ.: Research in Cancer Epidemiology.
International Medical Sports Federation for Aid to Cancer Research, f. 1970, Béziers, France.
International Study Group for the Detection and Prevention of Cancer, f. 1971, Varazers, Belgium.
International Union Against Cancer, f. 1935, Geneva. Consultative status: WHO, ECOSOC. Publ. *International Journal of Cancer.*

Pan American Cancer Cytology Society, f. 1957, Melville, NY, USA. Publ. *Cancer Cytology.*
Scandinavian Cancer Union, f. 1970, Stockholm.

In 1980 the CIRC started a world-wide cancer surveillance system under the aegis of WHO.

J. WATERHOUSE, C. MUIR (eds.), *Cancer Incidence in Five Continents,* CIRC, 3 Vols., Lyon, 1976. WHO, *Health Statistics Annual 1987,* Geneva 1988.

CANDELA. Symbol: cd. An international unit of luminous intensity, defined by the General Conference of Weights and Measures, CGPM 1948 (new version 1967), as follows:

"The candela is the luminous intensity, in the perpendicular direction, of a surface of 1/600,000 square metre of a black body at the temperature of freezing platinum under a pressure of 101,325 newtons per square metre."

Since 1960 one of the base units of the International System of Units (▷ SI).

CANE SUGAR. ▷ Sugar.

CANNABIS. A common name of Indian hemp, →Marijuana, →Hashish, kif, maconha, a subject of studies of the UN Commission on Narcotic Drugs.

UN Yearbook 1961, pp. 381–382.

CANOEING. An Olympic branch of sport since 1936. Organization reg. with the UIA and recognized by the International Olympic Committee:

International Canoe Federation, f. 1924, reconstituted 1948, Stockholm; organizes international competitions. Publ. *ICF Bulletin.*

Yearbook of International Organizations.

CANON LAW. The law of the Catholic Church, arranged in the Code of Canon Law, Codex Iuris Canonici, announced in the *bulla Providentissima Mater Ecclesia* of the Pope Benedictus XV on May 17, 1917, which entered into force on May 10, 1918. It is the codification of the old Provisions included in the *Corpus Iuris Canonici* and in numerous papal ordinances. Some of its rules, in particular in the final Book V, *De Belictis e Poenis,* on offences and punishment, intervenes into internal affairs of States, as e.g. ▷ excommunication (canons 2257–2267) being the cause of international conflicts in the past as well as in the present. In 1963 Pope John XXIII initiated work on a new code of canon law. In Pampeluna (Spain) in Nov., 1976, an International Congress on the revision of canon law was held. Deliberations focused on a draft new code of canon law composed of 1440 paragraphs, divided into 7 parts and reflecting the decisions taken by the Vatican II ecumenical council. The new Canon Law was published on Jan. 25, 1983. The Canon Law is also a subject of international research; reg. with the UIA: International Association for the Study of Canon Law, f. 1973, Rome.

B. SAGMULLER, *Lehrbuch des Katholischen Kirchenrechts,* Tübingen, 1928; P. BOURNIER, G. LE BRAS, *Histoire des Collections canoniques en Occident,* 2 Vols., Paris, 1931–32; *Codex iuris Canonici,* Vaticano, 1930; 1948; 1983.

CAPE CANAVERAL. The main US launching site for artificial earth satellites and cosmic flights located on the East coast of central Florida. In 1964–72 called Cape Kennedy, reverted to its original name by a decision of Congress, which gave to the launching center in Cape Canaveral the name The John F. Kennedy Manned Space Flight Center of the National Astronautics and Space Administration. ▷ ICBM. The test range, (complex 16) at Cape Canaveral, was opened to inspection for 13 yrs by American-Soviet agreement, Dec. 10, 1987

like 21 other sites in the USA. (In the USSR 77, in Western Europe 12, in Eastern Europe 7).

The New York Times, Dec. 11, 1987.

CAPETOWN. Legislative capital of the South African Republic, and capital of the Cape Province, a port on the Atlantic coast. Pop. 1985 census: city 776,617; Metropolitan Area 1,911,521.

CAPE VERDE. Member of the UN. República de Cabo Verde. Republic of Cape Verde. African state. Two groups of islands in the Atlantic Ocean about 480 km west of Senegal, Barlavento or Windward in the north (Sao Vicente, Santo Antao, Sao Nicolau, Santa Lucia, Sal, Boa Vista, Branco and Raso) and Sotavente or Leeward in the south (Sao Tiago, Maio, Fogo, Brava, Rei and Rombo). Area: 4033 sq. km. 1980 census: 296,093, 1987 est. 343,000. Capital: Praia (Sao Tiago) with 35,000 inhabitants, est. 1979. GNP per capita in 1987: US $500. Official language: Portuguese. Currency: I escudo do Cabo Verde = 100 centavos. National Day: July 5, independence anniversary, 1975. Member of the UN, Sept. 17, 1975. Member of FAO, WHO, ITU, WMO, IMCO. Member of all UN specialized agencies save IFC, WIPO, GATT, IAEA, and OAU. International relations: Portuguese colony since 1587: "provincia de ultramar" (overseas province) of Portugal 1951–75, with Portuguese citizenship since 1961. In 1963 started a guerrilla war of the Partido Africano da Independencia da Guinea e Cabo Verde, PAIGCV, recognized by the UN and OAU. On Dec. 30, 1974 the Portuguese Revolutionary Government transferred power to a transitional government; full independence was proclaimed July 5, 1975. Since 1976 common judicial system with Guinea-Bissau. In 1975–76 a drought destroyed most of the country's crops. The UN General Secretary made a general appeal to the international community to provide assistance to Cape Verde. On February 23, 1985 Cape Verde and Gabon concluded a Treaty of Friendship and Co-Operation.

Cabo Verde, Lisboa, 1961; *UN Yearbook* 1963, 1965, 1975, 1976, 1977; *Everyone's United Nations,* New York, 1979. *The Europa Year Book 1984 A World Survey,* Vol. II, pp. 1349–1352, London, 1984.

CAPITAL–INTENSIVE. An international term, used in the UN system, describes a method of production which uses relatively more capital and capital goods (e.g. machinery) than labor per unit produced.

UN Chronicle, October 1982, p. 46.

CAPITALISM. An international term denoting a socio-economic order which developed in the 19th and 20th centuries; object of international studies.

W. SOMBART, *Der moderne Kapitalismus,* Berlin, 1924–27; P.M. SWEEZY, *The Theory of Capitalist Development,* New York, 1942; J.A. SCHUMPETER, *History of Economic Analysis,* New York, 1954; A.A. BERLE, *The 20th Century Capitalist Revolution,* New York, 1954; J.K. GALBRAITH, *The Affluent Society,* New York, 1958; M. BEAUD, *A History of Capitalism,* London, 1983; A. BUICK, J. CRUMP, *State Capitalism,* London, 1986.

CAPITAL PUNISHMENT. For a long time the subject of controversies and international action. The first abolitionist movements occurred in Europe in the 18th century. The first two states which temporarily repealed the death penalty were Tuscany and Austria in 1786. K. Marx supported abolition in 1853 in an article in the *New York Herald Tribune.* In the 19th century capital punishment was repealed by Greece – 1862, Colombia – 1869, San Marino, Romania, and Venezuela – 1864,

Holland – 1870, Switzerland – 1874, Italy and Brazil – 1899. In the 20th century many states repealed and restored capital punishment (e.g. Austria – 1919 and 1950). In the UN, debate on the issue began in 1946 during the period of the formulation of the Universal Declaration of Human Rights, when Yugoslavia, Poland, and the USSR came out in favor of universal repeal of capital punishment in peacetime. The majority of states voted against the proposal.

The International Convention on Civil and Political Rights of 1966, in part III art. 6, lays down that in those states where abolition did not come into force capital punishment should be applied only in case of the most serious crimes, in accordance with the law in effect during the time when the crime was committed and with the regulations of the Pact and Convention or preventing and punishing the crime of genocide. The death penalty can be carried out as a result of a legally valid sentence and no person below the age of 18 or pregnant can be sentenced to death. The right to life, which is proclaimed in the UN Human Rights Declaration, as well as in other conventions on human rights, is not formulated in such a manner as would imply the necessity of abolition. The issue was studied by the UN International Law Commission, ILC, which periodically (1956, 1967, and 1973) publishes the opinions of the governments of member states and legal institutions. In 1970 according to a report of the ILC 11 states of Latin America did not apply capital punishment; in Europe: Austria, Denmark, Finland, FRG, the UK (with the exception of Northern Ireland), Holland, Norway, Portugal, San Marino, Switzerland, Sweden; in the USA the Supreme Court in June, 1972 recognized the illegality of capital punishment regardless of individual state laws. In Australia and Mexico some federal states have repealed while others have retained it. As a rule, repeal stemmed from internal social conditions, resulting from the recognition that application of the death penalty did not reduce crime and stimulated the search for other means to achieve the same end. The third report of the ILC submitted to the Council of ECOSOC in Mar. 1973 noted the tendency to restore capital punishment, which was favored by the majority of UN member states.

Capital Punishment, UN New York, 1967; F.A. ALLEN, "Capital punishment", in: *Encyclopedia of the Social Sciences*, 1968; I.Z. ANASHIM, *Smertnaia kazn' v kapitalisticheskih stranah*, Moskva, 1971; CH. BLACK JR., *Capital Punishment*, New York, 1975; *UN Chronicle*, January, 1978, pp.80–81.

CAPITOL HILL. The seat of the US Congress (House and Senate) of the Supreme Court of the United States and of the Library of Congress, in Washington DC.

S. BROWN, *History of the United States Capitol*, Washington DC, 1903; J. DUFFIELD, W. KRAMER, C. SHEPPARD, *Washington DC, The Complete Guide*, New York, 1987.

CAPITULATION. A treaty between two warring sides, one of which admits defeat and sets the terms of its surrender or throws itself at the mercy of the enemy (unconditional surrender).

Art. XXXV. of the Hague Statutes of Laws and Practices of Land War, constituting an addendum to the IVth Hague Convention of 1907 stipulates that:

"In capitulations decided between the agreeing sides the rules of military honor must be taken into consideration. The concluded capitulations must be strictly observed by both sides."

See also ▷ Germany's Unconditional Surrender, 1945; ▷ Japan's Unconditional Surrender, 1945.

CAPITULATIONS IN CONSULAR JURISDICTION. An arrangement allowing for execution of consular jurisdiction in alien countries by consuls (called jurisdictional consuls) over nationals of their own countries or third states. Began in 1535 by Turkey with respect to France, it was later also applied by other European states before annullment by Turkey in 1914 and later formally voided by the Lausanne Peace Treaty of 1923. Was also applied by European states and the USA in Egypt and the Far East.

R.L. BLEDSOE, B.A. BOCZEK, *The International Law Dictionary*, Oxford, 1987.

CARACAS. The capital of Venezuela (1986 pop. 3,184,958) from 1811. The seat of the Latin-American Economic System, ▷ SELA.

The Europa Yearbook 1987. A World Survey, London, 1987.

CARAT. *Greek*: keration = carob bean, fruit of *Ceratonia siliqua*, weight – 3.5 grains. An international term for the (1) amount of gold content in alloys; essayed at mints: (fine) pure gold – 24 c., top standard – 23 c., second – 18 c., third – 13 c.; (2) unit of weight in gemstones, unified in 1907 by International Bureau of Weights and Measures as 200 milligrames (metric system). In Great Britain – 205 milligrames until 1971.

CARBONARISM. An international movement of freedom fighters against absolute governments, initiated in Italy at the turn of the 19th and 20th centuries (secret organization Carboneria); spread quickly in Spain, France and Poland.

R. SORIGA, *La Societa secreta, l'emigrazione politica e i primi meti per l'independenza*, Roma, 1942.

CARDENAS DOCTRINE, 1938. Principle of international law formulated on Sept. 10, 1938 by the President of Mexico, General L. Cardenas, that on the American continent the rights of natives and aliens are equal. Cardenas at that time was carrying out the nationalization of the petroleum industry in Mexico. ▷ Calvo doctrine.

L. CARDENAS, *Discurso pronunciado en la inauguración del Congreso Internacional contra la Guerra*, México, DF, 1938; "Discussion of Mexican Oil Problem" in: *International Conciliation*, New York, 1938.

CARDINALS COLLEGE. The Sacred College of Cardinals was, in the first centuries of the Church, a group of close advisers and assistants of the Pope as the bishop of the city of Rome, composed of deacons and presbyters (priests) appointed by the Pope and bishops of suburban dioceses (in the immediate neighborhood of Rome); formally established as council with a dean – always the cardinal bishop of Ostia and a cardinal camerlingo who is an administrator of the materials goods of the Holy See. From 1050 (after the stormy election of Nicolaus II) the College has the right to elect the Pope. From the 12th century the Pope appoints cardinals from outside Rome to sit on the College. Till the 15th century their number could not exceed 30, until Sixtus V raised the maximum strength to 70 members (Dec. 3, 1586): six cardinal bishops, 50 cardinal priests, and 14 cardinal deacons. John XXIII raised the total number of cardinals to 85 and Paul VI to 120. Cardinals are appointed by the Pope in the consistories; the signs of their rank are a scarlet robe (*purpuriari*) and a red cap (since 1591). Cardinals are granted the official title of "eminence" (since 1630) and citizenship of the Vatican City State (the Lateran Treaty, art. 21). John XXIII granted every cardinal the title of

bishop (*Motu proprio*, Apr. 15, 1962) and Paul VI limited to 80 the age of cardinals sitting on the Conclave or executing any functions in the Roman Curia (*Motu proprio*, Nov. 21, 1970).

G.D. KITTLER, *The Papal Princess: A History of the Sacred College of Cardinals*, New York, 1960.

CARDIOLOGY. A subject of international co-operation. Organizations reg. with the UIA:

Asian–Pacific Society of Cardiology, f. 1956, Jakarta.
Association of European Pediatric Cardiologists, f. 1964, Louven, Belgium.
European Society of Cardiology, f. 1950, Brussels.
European Society of Cardiovascular surgery, f. 1951, Zurich.
Inter–American Society of Cardiology, f. 1964, Mexico DF.
International Cardiology Federation, f. 1960, Geneva.
International Cardiovascular Society, f. 1950, Boston, Mass.
International Society of Cardiology, f. 1950, Geneva. Publ. *ICS Bulletin*.

Yearbook of International Organizations.

CARDIO-VASCULAR DISEASES. A subject of international combined pathological and epidemiological studies under the aegis of the WHO. According to WHO, coronary death rates for males aged 30 to 69, for whom the disease is "much more common" than for females, indicate overall trends in the 1980's: on the one hand, a decrease in mortality of: between 30 and 40 per cent in Australia, Canada and the United States, about 25 per cent in Belgium and Japan, between 15 and 24 per cent in Finland, Malta, the Netherlands, and New Zealand, between 10 and 14 per cent in France, Luxembourg, Portugal, and the United Kingdom (England, Wales, Scotland only), and to 9 per cent in Austria, Denmark, the Federal Republic of Germany, Iceland, Norway, Sweden, Switzerland and the United Kingdom (Ireland).

And on the other hand, an increase in mortality of up to 25 per cent in Bulgaria, Czechoslovakia, and Greece, between 25 to 40 per cent in Hungary, Poland and Yugoslavia, and over 50 per cent in Romania and Spain.

WHO, *World Health Statistics Annual 1987*, Geneva 1988.

CARE. Co-operative for American Relief Everywhere, est. 1945 with seat in New York; until 1952 called the Co-operative for American Remittance to Europe. US philanthropic organization. Since 1982 ▷ CARE International.

Yearbook of International Organizations.

CARE INTERNATIONAL f, 1945 as Co-operative for American Relief Everywhere, est. in 1982 Paris by CARE USA, CARE Canada, CARE Germany, CARE Italy, CARE France, CARE Britain and CARE Norway. Publ.: *Annual Report.*

CARGO VESSELS, MERCHANT FLEET, MERCHANTMEN. Subjects of international conventions and international statistics which register cargo vessels launched each year. A Convention on measurements of the cargo capacity of vessels operating on inland seas was concluded in Paris on Nov. 27, 1925 by Austria, Belgium, Bulgaria, Czechoslovakia, Finland, France, Greece, Spain, Holland, Germany, the Serbo-Croatian–Slovenian State, Poland, Romania, Switzerland, Great Britain and the USSR. The term "cargo ships" embraces all vessels designed for any economic activity. The Brussels Sea Conventions of 1926 related to private and state-owned sea-going merchant vessels. A Scandinavian convention on ships was signed in Copenhagen on Jan. 28, 1926 by Denmark,

Finland, Iceland, Norway and Sweden. A Convention on tonnage measurement of cargo vessels was signed in Warsaw on Apr. 16, 1934 by Australia, India, Canada, New Zealand, Poland and Great Britain and came into force on June 26, 1936. The League of Nations specified international regulations on tonnage measurements of vessels' tonnage which came into force, together with the Convention on Standardization of Tonnage signed on June 10, 1947. The Geneva Convention on the High Seas unified rules concerning cargo vessels; all such ships in international traffic are subject to registration carried out by special classifying associations. The chief shipping document is the Certificate of Registry or a temporary certificate of flag. Other documents, certificate of safety, list of crew, passengers, cargo, log book, were specified by Convention on Facilitation of International Sea Traffic. An International Convention on the Limitation of Liability of Shipowners was signed in Brussels on Oct. 10, 1957. CMEA members signed an Agreement on Co-operation in Technological Supervision of Ships and Their Classification in Warsaw on Dec. 15, 1961.

Organizations reg. with the UIA:

International Cargo Handling Co-ordinating Association, f. 1952, London. Consultative status with: ECOSOC, UNCTAD, FAO, ILO, ICAO, and IMCO. Publ. *ICHCA Monthly Journal*;
East African Cargo Handling Services, f. 1963, Mombasa.

Yearbook of International Organizations.

CARIBBEAN AGREEMENT, 1946. Concluded between the governments of France, Netherlands, the UK and the USA for the establishment of the ▷ Caribbean Committee signed in Washington on Oct. 30, 1946.

UNTS, Vol. 27, pp. 78–102.

CARIBBEAN BASIN INITIATIVE, 1983. ▷ CARICOM.

CARIBBEAN COMMITTEE. Est. 1942 by the UK and the USA; assumed guardianship over French and Dutch dominions in the Caribbean area. Membership expanded in 1946 to include France and Netherlands to the Caribbean Treaty, 1946. It was dissolved in 1959.

CARIBBEAN COMMON MARKET. Instituted on Aug. 1, 1973 by a decision of the Heads of Government of 12 member states of the ▷ Caribbean Free Trade Association, CARIFTA, and the Bahamas, at a Conference in Port of Spain on Oct. 9–14, 1972 by way of transforming the Free Trade Zone into a Common Market, representing the interests of the Commonwealth not only in economic customs and financial matters, but also in international negotiations with other regional Common Market Territories. The principal organs of the Common Market are the Heads of Government Conference, the Common Market Council at Ministerial level and the Secretariat.

CARIBBEAN COMMUNITY, CARICOM. A common market of four Caribbean states: Barbados, Guyana, Jamaica, and Trinidad and Tobago, created on Aug. 1, 1973 on the basis of a Treaty signed on July 4, 1973 in Chaguaramas, Trinidad. The Community is an association open to the remaining members of the ▷ Caribbean Free Trade Association CARIFTA. On Apr. 17, 1974 the Treaty of Chaguaramas was signed by Belize, Dominica, Grenada, St Lucia, St Vincent and Montserrat; on July 4, 1974 by Antigua; and on July 26, 1974 by the Associated States of St Kitts–Nevis–Anguilla. CARICOM co-ordinates the

foreign policies of independent member states, organizes certain common services and oversees the economic integration of the Caribbean Common Market. The leading organ of the Community is a conference of heads of government and its main institutions are: The Caribbean Development Bank, the Shipping Council and the Caribbean Investment Association. The summit meetings of CARICOM took place on Nov. 16 to 18, 1982 in Ocho Rios, Jamaica. The Final Communiqué, called the Ocho Rios Declaration, stated, that the heads of government noted that the conflicts in Central America were in large part due to past failures to correct deep-seated social and economic problems. In Oct. 1983 an emergency summit meeting of CARICOM condemned the military *coup d'état* in Grenada and temporarily suspended Grenada's membership. A Caribbean basin initiative of the USA known as Caribbean Basin Economic Recovery Act of 1983 failed to stimulate economic growth, as also the Nassau Understanding of the CARICOM summit held in Barbados, July 4–7, 1984. The sixth CARICOM summit held in Barbados, July 1–4, 1985 was attended by all 13 member states: Antigua and Barbuda, Bahamas, Barbados, Belize, Dominica, Grenada, Guyana, Jamaica, Montserrat, St. Kitts and Nevis, St. Lucia, St. Vincent and the Grenadines, Trinidad and Tobago. Haiti and the Dominican Republic have an observer status at ministerial meetings. In July 4–6, 1986 a meeting of the heads of 13 member governments in Georgetown decided to introduce industrial programming and to establish an Export Credit Facility System. The ninth summit of CARICOM took place in St. John's, Antigua and Barbuda on July 7–8, 1988. Publ. bi-monthly *CARICOM Perspective* and bi-annual *CARICOM Bibliography*.

A.W. AXLINE, *Caribbean Integration*, New York, 1979; A.J. PAYNE, *The Politics of the Caribbean Community 1961–79*, Manchester, 1980; *The Europa Year Book 1984. A World Survey*, Vol. I, pp. 110–111, London, 1984; KEESING's *Contemporary Archive*, 1985; KEESING's *Contemporary Archive, 1986*, No. 12; G.K. LEWIS, *Main Currents in Caribbean Thought. The Historical Evolution of Caribbean Society in its Ideological Aspects, 1492–1900*, Baltimore, Md., 1987.

CARIBBEAN DEVELOPMENT AND CO-OPERATION COMMITTEE. A permanent body of the Economic Commission for Latin America (ECLA), established in 1975 to promote social and economic development and stimulate better co-ordination within the Caribbean subregion. In its first session in Havana in Oct.–Nov., 1975 the Committee adopted the Declaration of Havana. In Mar., 1977 the Committee met in Santo Domingo and

"reaffirmed the principle of permanent sovereignty over natural resources and reiterated the need for political will for active participation in programmes on horizontal co-operation and for strengthening co-operation in schemes for the subregion with respect to the different economic and social systems prevailing in the region."

UN Chronicle, April, 1977, p. 40.

CARIBBEAN DEVELOPMENT BANK. An intergovernmental finance institution f. 1970, in Barbados by Antigua, the Bahamas, Barbados, Cayman, Colombia, Dominica, Grenada, Guyana, Jamaica, Montserrat, St Kitts–Nevis–Anguilla, St Lucia, St Vincent, Trinidad and Tobago, Turks and Caicos, Venezuela, Virgin UK and two non-regional states: Canada and the UK. Publ. *Annual Report*.

UNTS, Vol. 172, 1970; p. 217; *Yearbook of International Organizations*.

CARIBBEAN FOOD AND NUTRITION INSTITUTE. An intergovernmental institution, f. in

1967 in Kingston, under the auspices of FAO, PAHO and WHO, with facilities provided by the governments of Jamaica and of Trinidad and Tobago and the University of the West Indies. Members: the 17 English speaking countries of the Caribbean: Antigua, the Bahamas, Barbados, Belize, Bermuda, Cayman, Dominica, Grenada, Guyana, Montserrat, St Kitts, St Lucia, St Vincent, Trinidad and Tobago, Turks and Caicos, and the Virgin Islands (UK). Publ. *Cajanus (bi-monthly), Protein Food for the Caribbean*.

Yearbook of International Organizations.

CARIBBEAN FREE TRADE ASSOCIATION, CARIFTA. Established by an intergovernmental agreement, signed in Antigua on Apr. 30, 1968, by governments of Antigua, Barbados, Guyana, Trinidad and Tobago; came into force on May 1, 1968. The objectives are: "to promote the expansion and diversification by trade in the Area of the Association." On June 29, 1968 it was joined by Dominica, Grenada, St Kitts–Nevis–Anguilla, St Lucia and St Vincent. Jamaica and Montserrat followed. Replaced 1973 by the ▷ Caribbean community. CARICOM.

UNTS, Vol. 772, pp. 4–144.

CARIBBEAN ISLANDS, DISPUTED. Islands in the Caribbean Sea which are the subject of international disputes: the USA occupies the Swan islands (Great Swan, Little Swan) near Honduras, which lays claim to them; the USA also occupies the Corn islands (Great Corn and Little Corn) off the coast of Nicaragua, which in 1914 was forced to lease these islands to the USA for 99 years. In the area between Nicaragua and Jamaica there are four coral reefs: Quita Sueno Bank, Roncador Bank, Serrana Bank, and Serranilla Bank, which are claimed by Colombia and Honduras. In the region between Jamaica and Haiti is Navassa island, on which the USA has reserved for itself the right to build a lighthouse.

CARIBBEAN METEOROLOGICAL SERVICE. Established on Dec. 8, 1965 by an agreement adopted in Port of Spain by the Caribbean Meteorological Council.

UNTS, Vol. 600, p. 162.

CARIBBEAN ORGANIZATION. Functioned 1961–65 as a successor to the Caribbean Committee (1946–61). It was created by a convention signed on June 21, 1960 in Washington by the governments of France, Netherlands, the UK and the USA on economic, social and cultural co-operation of all of the territories in the Caribbean region which were administered by the signatory states; came into force on Sept. 6, 1961. In June 1965 it formally suspended its activities. Headquarters of the Secretariat was San Juan de Puerto Rico. Publ. a periodical, *The Caribbean and Current Caribbean Bibliography*.

CARIBBEAN SEA. Named after the Carib Indians, it is an arm of the Atlantic Ocean, on the Central American isthmus between the West Indies and South America and linked to the Gulf of Mexico by the Yucatan Channel. Area: 1,942,500 sq. km. Dominated by the Spanish navy in the 16th–17th centuries together with British, Danish, Dutch and French colonial expeditions; from the 19th century control passed to the US navy. The opening of the Panama Canal in 1914 changed the strategic importance of the sea in the Western Hemisphere.

G. ARCINIEGAS, *Caribbean: Sea of the New World*, New York, 1946.

CARIBBEAN STATES COMMITTEE ON DEVELOPMENT AND CO-OPERATION. Est. Nov. 1, 1975 in Port of Spain on the initiative of ECLA as an intergovernmental organ of the Bahamas, Barbados, Cuba, Dominican Republic, Grenada, Guyana, Haiti, Jamaica, and Trinidad and Tobago to formulate economic projects, establish regional industries, prepare a common customs policy, expand fishing, sea transport and communications and to determine common positions at the Conference on the Law of the Sea and in the ▷ SELA.

CARIBBEES. Political name for the region of the Caribbean Sea including the Greater Antilles (Cuba, Haiti, Puerto Rico, Jamaica), Lesser Antilles (Guadeloupe, San Domingo, Martinique, St Lucia, St Vincent, Grenada, Barbados, Netherlands Antilles, Trinidad and Tobago). The region was the subject of controversy and armed conflict in the 19th century involving France, Spain, the Netherlands, Great Britain and the USA. During World War II the USA and the UK created the Caribbean Committee in 1942, which France and the Netherlands also joined in 1946. The purpose of the Committee was united military policy in time of war and then common policy in the UN in the Committee on Non-self-governing Territories. It was abolished in 1959 as a result of decolonization as independence had been gained by a majority of the main islands: Haiti 1804, Dominican Republic 1821, Cuba 1891 (1902), Jamaica, Trinidad and Tobago 1962; and Barbados 1966. On the initiative of the UN Economic Commission for Latin America, ECLA, on Nov. 1, 1975, the Committee for the Development and Co-operation of the Caribbean States was formed.

The Caribbean Who, What, Why?, London, 1965; F.M. ANDIC, T.G. MATHEWS, *The Caribbean in Transition*, Puerto Rico, 1965, L. COMITAS, *Caribbeana 1900–1965; A Topical Bibliography*, Washington, DC, 1968; R.D. CRASSWELLER, *The Caribbean Community. Changing Societies and US Policy*, New York, 1972; T. THEBERS (ed.), *The Soviet Sea Power in Caribbean. Political and Strategic Implications*, Washington, DC, 1972; "Ampliación del proceso de integración del Caribe", in: *Boletin Económico de América Latina*, No. 1, 1974; pp. 79–85. *The International Geographic Encyclopedia and Atlas*, London, 1979, p. 135.

CARICOM. ▷ Caribbean Community.

CARIFTA. ▷ Caribbean Free Trade Association.

CARINTHIA. *German:* Kärnten. A federal state in Austria bordering on Yugoslavia and Italy; area: 9531 sq. km. Pop. 525,758 (census 1971). Subject of an international dispute at the Versailles Conference, 1919, resolved by a plebiscite on Oct. 10, 1920 in favor of Austria, which received 59% of the votes of the population. This was confirmed by the Conference of Ambassadors on Mar. 26, 1921. The Slovenian minority, 1924–39 belonged to the Union of National Minorities in Europe. In late 1972 bilingual signs were introduced in the 205 localities (out of 2900) which had a Slovenian majority. This led to protests and anti-Slovenian campaigns by Austrian nationalistic organizations, and diplomatic protests from Yugoslavia.

F. KOVACIC, *La question de Prekomurje, de la Styrie et de la Carinthie*, Paris, 1919; CARINTHIACUS, *The Position of the Slovenes under Austria compared with that of the German Minority in the Serb-Croat-Slovenic Kingdom*, Ljubljana, 1925; S. SCHEICHELBAUER, *Die Nationalpolitische Entwicklung in Kärnten*, Klagenfurt, 1930; S. WAMBAUGH, *Plebiscites since the World War. With a Collection of Official Documents*, Washington, DC, 1933; KEESING's *Record of World Events*, March 1988.

CARIS. Computerized Agricultural Research Information System, established in Rome, 1973 attached to FAO as a supplement to the ▷ AGRIS; collects information from *c.* 1300 institutions and research stations throughout the world and supplies up to 75,000 research projects with information material by means of the most modern telecommunication equipment.

FAO Information, June, 1973.

CARITAS INTERNATIONALIS. The International Conference of Catholic Charities, est. in Rome 1951 succeeding a charitable organization of the Roman Catholic Church dating from 1924. Reg. with the UIA, has consultative status with ECOSOC, FAO, UNICEF and UNEF and is affiliated with Catholic charitable organizations throughout the world. Publ. *Caritas Internationalis News Bulletin*.

Yearbook of International Organizations.

CARNEGIE ENDOWMENT FOR INTERNATIONAL PEACE. Est. Dec. 14, 1910, in New York, with a gift of US $10,000,000 from Andrew Carnegie (1835–1919), American industrialist and philanthropist, also benefactor of Palace of Peace in The Hague (1903), Carnegie Foundation for the Advancement of Teaching (1905) and over 2000 libraries. Andrew Carnegie wrote in a letter of Dec. 14, 1910, creating The Carnegie Peace Fund:

"The crime of war is inherent, since it decides not in favor of the right, but always of the strong. The nation is criminal that refuses arbitration and drives its adversary to a tribunal which knows nothing of righteous judgment."

The Endowment is not a membership organization; and does not operate as a grant-making foundation, but conducts its own programs of research, investigation, publication, education and training. It is reg. with the UIA and has a consultative status with ECOSOC. Publ. *International Conciliation.*

A Manual of the Public Benefaction of Andrew Carnegie, New York, 1919; "The Carnegie Endowment for International Peace; 1910–1945", in: *International Conciliation*, No. 417, January, 1946, pp. 5–39.

CARNET DE PASSAGE. *French* = certificate of passage. Name of a customs pass for trucks carrying goods in transit without the payment of any customs duties.

CAROLINE ISLANDS. Part of the Federate State of ▷ Micronesia, together with the Marshall Islands and the Marianas Islands. Formerly a Spanish possession, they were sold by Spain to Germany on June 30, 1899; mandated by the League of Nations to Japan 1920; and since Apr. 2, 1947 held by the US under UN trusteeship; they have been represented in the Congress of Micronesia since 1965.

CARPATHIAN MOUNTAINS. Major mountain system of Central and East Europe (1495 km) linking the Alps with the Balkans. On the Polish-Czechoslovak border comprises the Beskids and Tatra, subject of international border disputes (▷ Jaworzyna). The Ukrainian part of Southern Carpathians extends into Romania as the Transylvanian Alps.

The International Geographic Encyclopedia and Atlas, London, 1979.

CARPETS. A subject of research and promotion by the International Trade Center, UNCTAD/GATT, Geneva.

ITC, *Major Markets and Suppliers for Hand-Knotted Carpets*, 3 Vols., Geneva, 1981–83; *Hand-Knotted Carpets in FRG and Italy*, Geneva, 1984.

CAR PHONES AGREEMENT, 1987. All European Community Countries except Greece and Luxembourg signed Sept. 2, 1987 in Brussels an agreement allowing international calls on a common frequency to be made from car telephones as of 1991.

CARRANZA DOCTRINE, 1918. A set of principles of foreign policy accepted in inter-American relations, formulated in 1918 in the annual message to the Congress of Mexico by President V. Carranza:

"The ideas guiding the international politics of Mexico are clear and sincere. They can be reduced to proclaiming; that no State may intervene in whatsoever form and for whatsoever reason in the internal affairs of other States. All should strictly and without exception subordinate themselves to the principle of universal non-intervention; that no person may demand a better situation than the citizens of the country in which he has settled, nor make his alien status a claim to protection and privileges: natives and aliens should be treated equally by the sovereign authorities of the State in which they live; and, finally, that this set of principles is the result of far-reaching changes in the present concept of diplomacy. It cannot serve the protection of private interests, nor use for these purposes the armed forces and majesty of the State. Neither can it serve to exert pressure on the governments of weaker States for the purpose of introducing amendments to laws which are not convenient to the citizens of the powers. Diplomacy should serve the general interests of civilization and the establishment of universal brotherhood."

I. FABELA, *Intervención*, México, DF, 1959, pp. 90–101.

CARRIAGE AND PASSENGERS CONVENTION, 1961. ▷ Maritime Law Conventions.

CARRIAGE NUCLEAR MATERIAL CONVENTION, 1971. ▷ Maritime Law Conventions.

CARRIAGE OF GOODS BY SEA. The subject of a draft convention, prepared by the Working Group on International Shipping Legislation of UNCTAD and presented to interested international organizations for comments and proposals in 1976. The UN General Assembly by Res. 31/100 on Dec. 15, 1976 decided to convene the UN Conference on the Carriage of Goods by Sea, held on Mar. 6–31, 1978 in Hamburg. The Conference approved the Convention on Carriage of Goods by Sea, called officially the Hamburg Rules, 1978. ▷ Bill of lading.

Yearbook of the UN 1976, pp. 822–825; K. GRÖNFERS, "The Hamburg rules – failure or success?" in: *Journal of Business Law*, London, October 1978; C.M. SCHMITTHOF, "New rules relating to bills of lading", in: *Export*, London, May 1978; *UN Chronicle*, January 1979, p. 80–81.

CARRIAGE OF PASSENGERS BY SEA. A subject of the International Draft Convention for the Unification of Certain Rules relating to the Carriage of Passengers by Sea, voted at Brussels, on Oct. 7, 1957 by Argentina, Australia, Belgium, Brazil, Canada, Denmark, Finland, France, Germany, Great Britain, Greece, India, Iran, Israel, Italy, Japan, the Netherlands, Norway, Peru, Poland, Spain, Switzerland, Vatican City, Venezuela and Yugoslavia. The highlights of the Convention are:

"Art. 2. This Convention shall apply to any international carriage if either the ship flies the flag of a contracting State or if, according to the agreements of

C

the parties, the place of departure or destination is in the territory of Contracting State.

Art. 3. The carrier, his servants and agents shall exercise due diligence to make and keep the ship seaworthy and properly manned, equipped and supplied at all times during the carriage, and in all other respects to secure the safety of the passengers.

Art. 4.(1) The carrier shall be liable for any damage suffered as a result of the death of, or personal injury to the passenger when the damage has occurred in the course of the carriage, if the damage arises from the fault or neglect of the carrier or of his servants or agents acting within the scope of their employment.

(2) The fault or neglect of the carrier, his servants and agents shall be presumed, unless the contrary is proved, if the death or personal injury arises from or in connection with ship-wreck, collision, stranding, explosion or fire.

(3) Except as provided in paragraph 2 of this article, the burden of proving the fault or neglect of the carrier, his servants or agents shall be on the claimant.

Art. 5. If the carrier proves that the death of, or personal injury to the passenger was caused or contributed to by the fault or neglect of the passenger, the Court may, in accordance with the provisions of its own law, exonerate the carrier wholly or partly from his liability.

Art. 6. The liability of the carrier for the death of or personal injury to a passenger shall in no case exceed 250,000 Francs."

Jahrbuch für Internationales Recht, 1959, pp. 189–191.

CARRINGTON PLAN, 1980. A proposal by Britain's Foreign Secretary, Lord Carrington, on Feb. 22, 1979, that Afghanistan be neutralized under international guarantee; endorsed by the European Community foreign ministers. The USSR declared its willingness to withdraw its troops when the West ended its interference in Afghanistan. The US reacted with a declaration that it is willing to guarantee "a neutral and nonaligned Afghanistan Government."

KEESING's *Contemporary Archive*, 1979.

CARS. ▷ Automobile industry.

CARTAGENA AGREEMENT, 1969. A subregional integration agreement of the ▷ Andean group, signed on May 26, 1969 in Bogota by the governments of Bolivia, Chile, Ecuador and Peru, approved by the Free Trade Association of Latin America, Res. 179 of July 9, 1969; which came into force on Oct. 16, 1969. The term Cartagena Agreement refers to the tradition of Simon Bolivar who, in 1813, proclaimed a Manifesto from Cartagena, calling for unity of Andean countries. The organ of the agreement is the Commission for the Cartagena Agreement, Commission del Acuerdo de Cartagena with headquarters in Lima. It convenes three times a year, and on June 8, 1970 created the Andean Development Corporation, Corporación Andina de Formento, headquarters in Caracas. The Agreement was amended in 1978 by the Protocol of Arequipa. In 1981 Ecuador temporarily suspended its membership. Chile withdrew on Oct. 30, 1976. On Aug. 17, 1982 a summit meeting of the Chiefs of States of Latin America was held in Cartagena.

INTAL. *Derecho de integración*, Buenos Aires, 1969; ASIL, *International Legal Material*, Washington, DC, Vol. IX, 1970; KEESING's *Contemporary Archive*, 1982. *The Europa Year Book 1984. A World Survey*, Vol. I, pp. 94–95, London, 1984.

CARTAGENA PROTOCOL, 1985. New rules on Organization of American States membership, accepted by a special OAS meeting in Cartagena, Colombia on Dec. 5, 1985. Art. 8 of the ▷ Charter of OAS, 1948 was to be replaced in 1990, stipulating the eligibility of all independent states which were members of the UN as of Dec. 10, 1985 (Belize and Guyana) and of certain non autonomous territories (Bermuda, Guadeloupe, French Guiana, Mar-

tinique, Montserrat but not the Falkland/Malvinas Islands).

The Protocol required ratification by two thirds of the 31 member states.

KEESING's *Contemporary Archive*, 1986.

CARTEL. A monopolistic agreement between firms in the same branch of production for the purpose of gaining control of the market and controlling prices; in many states such arrangements are forbidden (i.a. in the USA and in the EEC states). The first international cartel appeared in 1867 by virtue of an agreement between French and German salt companies. Companies belonging to the cartel had the same sales offices. In July 1972, the Court of Justice of the EEC states in Luxembourg levelled fines of half a million dollars against nine West European paint manufacturers for violating the anti-trust resolutions of the EEC Rome Treaty (arts. 85 and 86). Commodity cartels are defensive international institutions of raw material exporting states which establish prices for them in strict relationship to the prices for industrial articles set by the cartels of the highly industrialized states. The first successful defense was the appearance of ▷ OPEC the commodity cartel of the oil-exporting states.

R.L. BLEDSOE, B.A. BOCZEK, *The International Law Dictionary*, Oxford, 1987.

CARTER'S DOCTRINE OF PEACE, 1979. Announced in Congress on June 19, 1979, by the US President Jimmy Carter, the day after signing with L. Brezhnev in Vienna the SALT II Treaty, reading as follows:

"The truth of the atomic age is that the United States and the Soviet Union must live in peace, for otherwise we shall not live at all. Since the beginning of history the fate of peoples and nations was determined by alternating periods of war and peace. Now this principle must be rejected for ever. When nations have at their disposal thousands of nuclear weapons, and each of them alone can lead to unimaginable destruction – there is no place for the former alternating cycle of wars and peace. There can only be – peace ..."

Congressional Record, June 19, 1979.

CARTER'S NEAR EAST DOCTRINE, 1978. A statement of the US President J. Carter on Jan. 4, 1978, in Aswan (Egypt) during a summit meeting with President Anwar Sadat:

"We believe that there are certain principles, fundamentally, which must be observed before a just and a comprehensive peace can be achieved. First, true peace must be based on normal relations among the parties to the peace. Peace means more than just an end to belligerency. Second, there must be withdrawal by Israel from territories occupied in 1967 and agreement on secure and recognized borders for all parties in the context of normal and peaceful relations in accordance with UN Res. 242 and 338. And third, there must be a resolution of the Palestinian problem in all its aspects. The problem must recognize the legitimate rights of the Palestinian people and enable the Palestinians to participate in the determination of their own future."

US Department of State Bulletin, January 4, 1978.

CARTER'S PERSIAN GULF DOCTRINE, 1980. A statement of the US President J. Carter on Jan. 16, 1980 in the State of the Union Address to the second session of the 96th Congress, Jan. 23, 1980:

"An attempt by an outside force to gain control of the Persian Gulf region will be regarded as an assault on the vital interests of the United States. And such assault will be repelled by use of any means necessary, including military force."

The statement was a reaction to the Soviet military presence since Dec., 1979 in ▷ Afghanistan, com-

mented on by J. Carter in the State of the Union Address as follows:

"We superpowers also have a responsibility to exercise restraint in the use of military power. The integrity and the independence of weaker nations must not be threatened. But now the Soviet Union has taken a radical and aggressive new step. It is using its great military power against a relatively defenseless nation. The implications of the Soviet invasion of Afghanistan could pose the most serious threat to world peace since the Second World War."

Congressional Record, January, 16, 1980; Zb. BRZEZINSKI, *Game Plan. How to Conduct the US–Soviet Contest*, Boston, 1987.

CARTHAGE. Ancient city-state whose ruins, located in present Tunisia *c.* 16 km north-east of Tunis, became the subject of international archaeological investigations in the 19th and 20th centuries. The government of Tunisia together with UNESCO on May 19, 1972 announced an international campaign to save the archaeological treasures on the model of a similar campaign organized by UNESCO in Nubia to save ▷ Abu Simbel. The archaeological site of Carthage is included in the ▷ World Heritage UNESCO List. Along the coast among the modern villas and in the fields lie the ruins of the great Roman city, the capital of the province of Africa. Also to be seen are the charred remains of the capital of the fallen Carthaginian Empire.

O. MELTZER, *Geschichte der Karthagener*, 3 Vols. Berlin, 1879–1913; G. PICARD, *Le Monde de Carthage*, Paris, 1956. UNESCO, *A Legacy for All*, Paris, 1984.

CARTHAGE–ROME PEACE TREATY, 1985. On Feb. 5, 1985 the mayors of Carthage (Tunis) and Rome (Italy) signed a peace treaty, officially ending the state of war dating from the Punic Wars of 246–146 BC.

KEESING's *Contemporary Archive*, 1986, No. 9.

CARTOGRAPHY. Subject of international co-operation.

Organizations reg. with the USA:

African Association of Cartography, f. 1976, Algiers, Algeria.
European Cartographic Association, f. 1959, Perth, Australia. Publ.: *International Yearbook of Cartography, Multilingual Dictionary, ICA Bibliography*.
Inter-African Committee on Cartography, Maps, Survey, f. 1983, Lagos, Nigeria.

See also ▷ *Map of the World*.

R.V. TOOLEY, *A History of Cartography*, London, 1969; *Yearbook of International Organizations*, 1986/87; *The Europa Yearbook 1988. A World Survey*, Vol. I, London, 1988.

CARTOGRAPHY OF THE UN. One of the fields of ECOSOC. The first study by ECOSOC experts was presented on Mar. 21, 1949 at the UN Cartography Conference in Lake Success (USA). It stated the following:

"Large sources of energy and food and better means of communication are becoming ever more necessary for the advances of civilization. It can be achieved in different ways, but in each case it can be accelerated and made less expensive by means of adequate maps .... Actually, we know very little about our world nowadays. UN interests extend to the entire world, but a reasonable solution of world problems is unfeasible without precise information on three-fourths of the globe's surface.... Over 2 per cent of the globe's surface is shown in maps on 1 : 25,000 scale, for such maps are essential for designing development programmes and their administration. It is doubtful whether more than 25 per cent of the surface of our globe has been covered by maps on 1 : 300,000 or 1 : 250,000 scale, or larger, compiled on the basis of air photographs or systematic regional studies. Except for some European countries, and very limited zones of other states, the present level of studies and geographic maps is far from what allows full development and economic use of natural resources." In 1950 the UN Cartographic Office was organized at UN Headquarters; task of preparing a world map on the 1 : 1,000,000 scale. In 1955 the UN for the first time published The International Map of the World on the Million Scale (Doc. 57.1.9) since re-issued each year with up-to-date political borders of states and dependent countries. All editions have the note: Borders shown in this map are not in all cases of final character, therefore their reproduction does not imply that the UN supports or approves of them."

Since 1951 the UN has published *World Cartography–Cartographie Mondiale*; reports of Regional Cartographic Conferences: Latin America, 1958; Asia and the Far East, 1955, 1958, 1961, 1964 and 1970; Africa, 1965; Europe, 1962. In Sept., 1967 the First Conference on Unification of Geographic Names in World Cartography was held in Geneva.

UN Bulletin, July 14, 1948; *UN Technical Conference on the International Map of the World*, 2 Vols., New York, 1950; *UN Yearbook*, 1963, pp. 407–408; *UN Monthly Chronicle*, October, 1967.

CAS, COMMITTEE ON ASSURANCE OF SUPPLY. An IAEA body est. in 1980, open to all IAEA member states, to consider and advise on "ways and means in which supplies of nuclear material, equipment and technology and fuel cycle service could be assured on a more predictable and longterm basis in accordance with mutually acceptable considerations of nonproliferation; and the IAEA role and responsibility in relation to threats".

United Nations Handbook, Wellington, 1986.

CASABLANCA. The largest city and main port of Morocco on the Atlantic Ocean (1981 pop. 2,553,300). In 1907 occupied by France, object of The Hague mediation. Site of summit conferences: (1) January 14–24, 1943 of US President F.D. Roosevelt and the Prime Minister of Great Britain W.S. Churchill, who determined that in the summer of 1943 they would begin the invasion of Italy (▷ Casablanca Conference 1943); (2) in January 1961 the meeting of the chiefs of state and governments of Ghana, Guinea, Mali, Morocco, Egypt and the temporary government of the Algerian Republic, which created the so-called ▷ Casablanca Group and announced the ▷ African Charter.

CH. DE BOECK, *La sentence arbitrale de La Haye*, Paris, 1909; G. GIDEL, "L'arbitrage de Casablanca", in: *Revue générale de droit international*, No. 17, 1910; *The Europa Yearbook*, 1987; *A World Survey*, London 1987.

CASABLANCA CONFERENCE, 1943. A meeting between Winston S. Churchill and Franklin D. Roosevelt, also attended by Chiefs-of-Staff, navy commanders and political advisers in Casablanca, Morocco, Jan. 14–26, 1943, following the Allied troops' landing in North Africa (Oct. 8, 1942). The main object was to determine future joint policy and strategy. Major decisions included: adoption of military plans against Germany, Italy and Japan for the year 1943; timing of the summer 1943 landing of Allied troops in Italy (after the end of the North African campaign). Also discussed were the American and British attitudes to the French national liberation movement and French colonies in Africa; Churchill and Roosevelt had talks with General de Gaulle, not then recognized by the USA as leader of "France Libre" and with General Giraud, who had essential command of French forces in North Africa. Roosevelt demanded that

the war be fought until the unconditional surrender of Germany. Both western leaders suggested a meeting of the so-called Big Three to Joseph V. Stalin, the first of which took place at the ▷ Teheran Conference, 1943.

A Decade of American Foreign Policy. Basic Documents 1941–1949, Washington, DC, 1950.

CASABLANCA GROUP. Algeria, Egypt and Morocco as well as Ghana, Guinea and Mali which in Jan., 1961 at a Conference of Heads of State in Casablanca jointly initiated the struggle for the unity of Africa. In succeeding years the Casablanca Group concentrated its efforts on the establishment of the Organization for African Unity.

CASA DE LAS AMERICAS. *Spanish*: Home of the Americas. An institution established in 1960 in Havana by the Revolutionary Government of Cuba as a center of cultural and artistic co-operation of the nations of Latin America; Casa de las Americas awards annual prizes for short stories, novels, poetry essays and theatrical plays; each year it also organizes the Festival of Latin American Theaters in Havana.

CASH-AND-CARRY CLAUSE. A clause of the US Neutrality Act 1939, stating that all American goods to belligerent countries could be shipped only on foreign ships, upon payment in the USA.

CASTELLANO, EL. *Spanish*: Castilian language of the inhabitants of the Spanish province of Castile, official language of Spain. The Spanish Constitution of 1978 in Art. 3 states that:

"Castilian is the official Spanish state language. All Spaniards have the obligation to know it and the right to use it. The remaining Spanish languages are also official in their autonomous communities in accordance with their statutes. The richness and diversity of the linguistic diversities of Spain are a cultural inheritance which should be an object of particular respect and protection."

Among the Spanish languages mentioned in the constitutional statute on autonomous communities besides Castilian are included: Basque, Galician and Catalonian.

CASTLES. A subject of inter-governmental co-operation. Organization reg. with the UIA:

International Castles Institute, f. 1949, Zurich. Consultative status with UNESCO, Council of Europe. Publ. *Bulletin*.

Yearbook of International Organizations.

CASUS BELLI. *Latin* = "cause for war". An international term used either for justifying the beginning of war or for threatening war based on the infringement of the rights or interests of a given power which might constitute a *casus belli*. The concept is not recognized by the UN, which obligates members to solve disputes solely by peaceful means.

CASUS FOEDERIS. = An international term for a fact, event or situation defined in a treaty of alliance generating the obligations of the parties (e.g. granting of aid for the purpose of common defense in case of aggression).

CATALOGUES INTERNATIONAL. An information bank on scientific and technical literature, set up under the auspices of UNESCO, FAO, WHO and other UN specialized agencies. The first international convention was negotiated in 1905 and concerned scientific literature.

CATALAN LANGUAGE. ▷ Spanish language.

CATALONIA. A historical region in Spain, subject of international dispute between France and Spain in the Middle Ages and later in 1640–59, 1694–97 and 1808–1913. Area: 31,930 sq. km; 1981 pop. census 5,958,208. Capital: Barcelona; 1981 census 1,754,900. A region of conflict within Spain, caused by rebellions of the Catalans demanding autonomy or even separation from Spain, 1919–22. Statute of autonomy granted Sept. 1932 by the Spanish Republic; proclamation of an independent Catalan republic, Oct. 1934; Dec. 20, 1934 the Spanish government abrogated the autonomous status of Catalonia; after the Civil War 1936–39 absolute loss of Catalan self-government; new separatist movements triggered after World War II. In 1977–79 the autonomy of Catalonia was re-established in the form of Catalan government under its historical name Generali-tatu. The first Catalian Parliament was elected in Mar. 1980 for four years.

J. TRUETA RASPALI, *The Spirit of Catalonia*, New York, 1946; F. SOLDEVILA, *Historia de España*, Barcelona, 1959; J. VICENS VIVES, *Historia social y económica de España*, Barcelona, 1959; P. VILAR, *La Catalogne dans l'Espagne moderne. Recherches sur les fondements économiques des structures nationales*, 3 Vols. Paris, 1962, Barcelona, 1964–66; J.W. ELLIOT, *The Revolt of the Catalans*, London, 1963; C. SEMPRUN-MAURA, *Révolution et Contre-Révolution en Catalogne*, Paris, 1974; *The Europa Yearbook*, 1987; *A World Survey*, London, 1987.

CATALYTIC WAR. An international military term for "a small nuclear engagement or the use of nuclear weapons by a minor nuclear power".

D. ROBERTSON, *Guide to Modern Defense and Strategy*, Detroit, 1988.

CATARACT. Latin: 'waterfall: An eye disease, subject of international research integrated with the WHO Program for the Prevention of Blindness. According to 1988 WHO estimates, cataract accounts for 50% of the world's 28 million cases of blindness.

Cataract, in: *WHO In Point of Facts*, No. 60, 1988.

CATHOLICISM. Christian religious moral and social doctrine. The concept of Catholicism came into use after the Council of Trent (1545–63) to distinguish it from ▷ Protestantism.

O. GORE, *Catholicism and Roman Catholicism*, London, 1923; K. ADAM, *Das Wesen des Katholizismus*, Düsseldorf, 1957; Y.M.J. CONGAR, *Sainte Église*, Paris, 1963.

CATHOLIC INTERNATIONAL ORGANIZATIONS. Organizations reg. with the UIA:

Apostleship of the See, f. 1922, Rome.
Asian Committee for People's Organizations, f. 1971, Manila.
Catholic Committee for Intra-European Migration, f. 1960, Geneva.
Catholic European Study, f. 1956, Strasbourg, France.
Catholic International Association of Teachers, f. 1965, Geneva.
Catholic International Education Office, f. 1952, Brussels. Consultative Status with ECOSOC, UNESCO, UNICEF, Council of Europe.
Catholic International Federation for Physical and Sports Education, f. 1911, Paris.
Catholic International Union for Social Services, f. 1925, Brussels. Consultative status with ECOSOC, UNESCO, UNICEF, FAO, ILO, Council of Europe.
Catholic Media Council, f. 1969, Aachen, FRG.
Conference of International Catholic Organizations, f. 1927, Fribourg, Switzerland.
European Association for Catholic Adult Education, f. 1963, Bonn, FRG.

Inter-American Confederation of Catholic Education, f. 1945, Bogota. Consultative status with UNESCO, OAS.

International Catholic Association for Radio and TV, f. 1928, Brussels. Consultative status with UNESCO, FAO, Council of Europe.

International Catholic Centre for UNESCO, f. 1952, Paris.

International Catholic Child Bureau, f. 1948, Geneva. Consultative status with ECOSOC, UNESCO, UNICEF.

International Catholic Committee of the Blind, f. 1974, Sancerre, France.

International Catholic Confederation of Hospitals, f. 1951, Brussels.

International Catholic Conference of Scouting, f. 1948, Brussels.

International Catholic Film Organization, f. 1928, Brussels. Consultative status: UNESCO.

International Catholic Girls Society, f. 1897, Fribourg, Switzerland.

International Catholic League Sobrietas, f. 1897, Breisgau, FRG.

International Catholic Migration Commission, f. 1951, Geneva. Consultative status: ECOSOC, UNICEF, ILO.

International Catholic Union Rural Association, f. 1964, Rome. Consultative status with FAO.

International Catholic Union of the Middle Classes, f. 1956, Brussels.

International Catholic Union of the Press, f. 1927, Geneva. Consultative status with ECOSOC, UNESCO.

International Center "Humane Vitae", f. 1908, Paris.

International Council of Catholic Men, f. 1948, headquarters in Vatican City.

International Committee of Catholic Nurses, f. 1933, Brussels. Consultative status with WHO, UNICEF, ECOSOC, UNESCO.

International Federation of Associations of Catholic Doctors, f. 1936, Brussels.

International Federation of Catholic Parochial Youth Communities, f. 1961, Antwerp, Belgium.

International Federation of Catholic Pharmacists, f. 1963, Paris.

International Federation of Catholic Press, f. 1928, Geneva.

International Federation of Catholic Universities, f. 1948, Paris. Consultative status with UNESCO, ECOSOC.

International Federation of Rural Adult Catholic Movements, f. 1964, Brussels. Consultative status with UNESCO.

International Movement of Apostolate of Children, f. 1962, Paris.

International Movement of Catholic Agricultural and Rural Youth, f. 1954, Leuven, Belgium.

International Secretariat of Catholic Technologists, Agriculturalists and Economists, f. 1951, Paris.

International Young Catholic Students, f. 1964, Paris. Consultative status with UNESCO, ECOSOC.

Legion of Mary, f. 1921, Dublin.

Opus Dei, f. 1928, Rome.

Organization of Catholic Universities in Latin America, f. 1953, Buenos Aires.

Pax Christi International, f. 1945, The Hague. Consultative status with ECOSOC.

Pax Romana, International Catholic Movement for Intellectual and Cultural Affairs, f. 1947, Fribourg, Switzerland. Consultative status with UNESCO.

Pax Romana International Movement of Catholic Students, f. 1921, Fribourg, Switzerland. Consultative status with ECOSOC, UNESCO.

Service for Documentation and Study, f. 1964, Rome.

St Jean's International Alliance, f. 1911, Geneva. Consultative status: ECOSOC, UNESCO, ILO.

SODEPAX, f. 1968, Geneva.

World Organization of Former Students of Catholic Teaching, f. 1967, Rome.

World Catholic Federation on the Biblical Apostolate, f. 1969, Stuttgart.

World Federation of Catholic Youth, f. 1968, Brussels. Consultative status with ECOSOC, UNESCO, UNICEF, Council of Europe, OAS.

World Union of Catholic Philosophical Societies, f. 1948, Washington, DC.

World Union of Catholic Teachers, f. 1910, Rome. Consultative status with UNESCO.

World Union of Catholic Women's Organizations, f. 1910, Paris. Consultative status with ECOSOC, UNESCO, UNICEF, FAO, ILO.

Yearbook of International Organizations.

CATHOLIC–MOSLEM MEETING, 1976. The first meeting in history, arranged by Libya and the Vatican, held Feb. 1–5, 1976 in Tripoli, of high representatives of both religious denominations with the participation of several hundred observers. Participating in the meeting from the Moslem side – chairman of the Libyan Council, Colonel M. Gadafi, and from the Roman Catholic side – Cardinal S. Pignedoli, chairman of the Vatican Secretariat for Non-Christian Religions, on behalf of whom the Moslems were assured "of the feelings of guilt and pity for all the bad, indignant and insulting things that had been said in the past about God's praiseworthy Prophet Mohammed." On this occasion Colonel M. Gadafi was given a Papal invitation to make an official visit to the Vatican. The meeting was not attended by the representatives of Protestant Churches. The agenda included four major topics: religion as the ideology of life; common provisions of Islam and Christianity and their converging points; social justice as "the fruit of faith in God"; and what should be done to overcome mutual prejudice and to reconstruct confidence between the two religions.

CATHOLIC–ORTHODOX PATMOS DIALOGUE, 1980. The first dialogue of Roman Catholic and Eastern Orthodox theologians, since the schism of 1054, took place in May–June 1980 on the Greek island of Patmos outside the monastery of Saint John the Divine. The heads of delegations were Cardinal Johannes Willebrand, the Catholic archbishop of Utrecht, Netherlands, and Metropolitan Meliton of Chalcedon, Turkey. The dialogue was initiated by Pope John Paul II and Ecumenical Patriarch Dimitrios I, in Istanbul, 1979.

CATHOLIC SOCIAL DOCTRINES. The views of the Roman Catholic Church on social questions. Catholic social doctrine dates back to the early 19th century, although its first seeds originated in concepts of earlier Roman Catholic philosophers and thinkers, especially Thomas Aquinas. The 19th century witnessed their elaboration in the face of the industrial revolution occurring in European countries. The first systematic pronouncement of the official Roman Catholic Church position on social questions was Pope Leo XIII's encyclical Rerum Novarum (1891), which was developed in Pope Pius XI's Quadragesimo anno (1931): the former threatened to excommunicate those Catholics who endorsed socialist ideas and belonged to socialist organizations; the latter stated that "socialism cannot be reconciled with the dogmas of Roman Catholic Church" and that "one cannot be both a good Catholic and a good socialist at the same time." It also warned Catholics against any form of co-operation with proponents of socialism, which was reiterated by Pope Pius XII, who, in his Easter letter of 1942, condemned Marxism and communism and in 1949 imposed a decree of the Congregation of the Holy Office providing that it is unlawful for Catholics to enter into any co-operation with Marxists, including peace movements, and that any Catholic doing so must be excommunicated. The social doctrines contained in these documents approved of capitalism and its socio-economic system based on the principle of indivisibility of private property and confined themselves to appeals for the alleviation of social poverty in the name of social solidarism. The gradual departure of the Church from these positions started with the pontificate of John XXIII (1958–63). Contem-porary modifications of the Catholic social doctrine can be found in John XXIII's encyclicals ▷ *Mater et magistra* (1961) ▷ *Pacem in Terris* (1963) and Pope Paul VI's ▷ *Populorum progressio* (1967); they are directed towards recognition of the right of societies to control the property system on behalf of the struggle against socio-economic injustices. A similar approach was taken by the Second Vatican Council, whose *Gaudium et spes* declared that "all people, believers or not, should contribute their effort to the proper construction of the world in which they live together, which is of course impossible without broader and reasonable dialogue." In his encyclical *Octagesima adveniens* (1971) Pope Paul VI recommended a dialogue with all people of goodwill in the search for a program of "social, political and economic changes which are urgently required in many cases." This process seems to be epitomized in ten points defining the problems of justice in the world, adopted by a plenary conference of the episcopate of Brazil in Rio de Janeiro, July 1971:

"The situation of injustice in the world results from the fact of the existence of imperialism and colonialism. The situation of the population which lives on the margin of social life, especially the peasants and the poor, is close to the situation of slavery. The policy with regard to the people who live on the margin of social life, expressed by the limitation or outright abolition of human rights calls for counteraction for the good of the nation. Social unrest in backward countries results from the domination of the privileged elite to the detriment of the masses. The power of big international concerns leads to exploitation of socially and economically backward countries. This arouses a fatalistic attitude among men deprived of the possibility of medical treatment or attainment of knowledge, those who lack help to counter this situation. Injustice is also a result of rapid modernization of industry which entails unemployment. This distortion of economic models developed in such a way that the whole burden of development and lowered pay falls on the most handicapped classes. The fact of the existence of unjust structures maintains inequality of the right to culture. Systematically liquidated are all movements represented by trade unions and associations."

One symptomatic expression of views typical for South American Catholicism which often goes beyond the framework of official social doctrine of Roman Catholicism are concepts professed by the Brazilian Archbishop of Olinda y Recife, Dom Helder Camera in a Polish catholic weekly, 1971:

"When I ponder and study our situation in Latin America, in countries on the road of development, it occurs to me ever more clearly that solutions to our problems are not to be found by the capitalist or neocapitalist way. It is my conviction as a believer that the solutions are to be sought by way of socialization. I am not afraid of this word, even more, I would say these solutions must be sought through socialism."

In Dec. 1977, Pope Paul VI approved the theses of Iustitia et Pax Commission entitled: Universal destination of landed property.

In 1980, Pope John Paul II in Turin, and during his visits in Africa and Brazil condemned ▷ Consumerism. On Sept. 15, 1981 the encyclical ▷ Laborem exercens was published.

In 1983 the catholic bishops of the USA, France and FRG published their standpoint on nuclear war ▷ Theology of Liberation.

Acta Apostolicae Sedis 1891, 1931, 1963, 1966; "Octagesima adveniens", in: *Osservatore Romano*, May 15, 1971; *Tygodnik Powszechny*, August 29, 1971.

CATTLE. A subject of international co-operation. Organizations reg. with the UIA:

Cattle and Meat Economic Community, f. 1970, Ougadougou, Burkina Faso.

European Cattle and Meat Trade Union, f. 1952, Paris.

Inter-American Confederation of Cattlemen, f. 1964, Panama City.
World Jersey Cattle Bureau, f. 1951, London.
Yearbook of International Organizations.

CAUCASUS. A region and mountain system in south-east European USSR from the Kuban River on the Black Sea to the Apsheron peninsula on the Caspian Sea, 1205 km long, a divide between Europe and Asia. During World War II occupied by German forces July 1942–Feb. 1943. Politically the region is divided into three federal socialist soviet republics (Armenia, Azerbaijan and Georgia), seven autonomous republics and four autonomous districts.

CAYMAN BRAC. ▷ Cayman Islands.

CAYMAN ISLANDS. An archipelago in the Caribbean Sea, about 200 miles north-west of Jamaica, dependent territory of the UK; consists of Grand Cayman, Little Cayman and Cayman Brac. Total area: 260 sq. km. Pop.: 1985 20,300 (Grand Cayman – 16,600, Little Cayman – 1,630, Cayman Brac – 70). Capital: George Town – 8,900. GNP per capita 1987 US $9000. Currency 1 Cayman Islands dollar = 100 cents. On July 4, 1959 made a Crown colony, since 1972 with its own Governor. The government of the Caymans Island signed on July 3, 1986 with the USA and the UK a Mutual Legal Assistance Treaty which gave US law-enforcement broad official access to local bank records.

Wall Street Journal, July 3, 1986; J. PAXTON ed., *The Statesman's Yearbook, 1987–88*, London 1987; J. BROOKS ed., *1988 South American Handbook. Including Caribbean, Mexico Central and South America*, Bath, England, 1987.

CBU. Cluster Bomb Unit. A special explosive tested during American raids in Laos, composed of 250 bullets which disperse horizontally at explosion and themselves explode when stepped upon. One B-52 bomber took some 1000 CBUs (c. 250,000 bullets) which produced a danger area of several hundred square metres.

CBW. Chemical and biological warfare prohibited by the Geneva Protocol 1925, since 1983 a subject of negotiations of the Chemical Warfare Convention, CWC.

J.P. ROBINSON, *Chemical-Biological Warfare. A Selected Bibliography*, Los Angeles, 1979; D. ROBERTSON, *Guide to Modern Defense and Strategy*, London 1987; *SIPRI Yearbook 1987*, Oxford 1988, pp. 97–99.

CC. *Corps Consulaire*, Consular Staff. An internationally accepted French term referring to consular personnel or staff accredited in a given country. After World War I used world-wide to designate motor vehicles belonging to consulates and their employees, who benefit from the privileges defined in the Vienna Consular Convention, 1963.

CD. *Corps Diplomatique* – Diplomatic Staff. An internationally accepted French term for the diplomatic community accredited in a given country. After World War I used throughout the world to designate motor vehicles belonging to diplomatic missions and their members who benefit from the privileges defined in the Vienna Diplomatic Convention, 1961.

CEAO, Communauté économique d'Afrique Occidentale ▷ West African Economic Community.

CECON. Comisión Especial de Consulta y Negociación, Special Commission for Consultations and Negotiations, established on the initiative of the Latin states, members of OAS in July 1970 as one of the permanent organs of the Inter-American Economic Social Council (IESC). The aim of the activity of CECON is to provide advisory and professional assistance in commercial and financial negotiations with the USA carried out by Latin member states of OAS. Annual plenary sessions of the Commission take place in Punta del Este (Uruguay). Reports are published in OAS *Yearbooks.*

CEDEL. Centrale de Livraison de Valeurs Mobilieres, an interbanking computerized system for ▷ Eurobonds delivery, est. 1970 in Luxembourg. Members: financial institutions of Western Europe.

H.C. DONNERSTAG, *The Eurobond Market*, London, 1975; *Instruction to CEDEL Participants*, Luxembourg, 1977; J. WALMSLEY, *A Dictionary of International Finance*, London, 1979.

CEDI. A monetary unit of Ghana; one cedi = 100 reseawas; issued by the Bank of Ghana.

CEEAC. Communauté économique des états de l'Afrique Centrale ▷ Central African Economic Community.

CELADE. Centro Latinoamericano de Demografía, Latin-American Demographic Center. An inter-governmental institution founded in Aug., 1957 under the auspices of the UN by governments of Argentina, Colombia, Costa Rica, Mexico, Nicaragua, Panama, El Salvador and Venezuela with headquarters in Santiago and a regional bureau in San José. Publ. *Boletín Demográfico*, and studies.

CEPAL, *Notas sobre la economia y el desarrollo de América Latina*, No. 188, 1975.

CELAM. ▷ Council of the Espiscopate of Latin America.

CELL BIOLOGY. A subject of international co-operation. Organizations reg. with the UIA:

European Cell Biology Organization, f. 1969, Leiden, Netherlands.
International Cell Research Organization, f. 1962, Paris. Consultative status: UNESCO, ECOSOC, UNEP.
International Federation of Cell Biology, f. 1947, London. Publ. *Cell Biology International Reports.*
Nordic Society for Cell Biology, f. 1960, Oslo.

Yearbook of International Organizations.

CELLULOSE. One of the basic raw materials of the textile, paper and chemical industries and also explosives. A subject of international co-operation and statistics. Main producers are: Canada, Finland, Japan, Sweden, the USA and the USSR. Within CMEA there is an agreement signed July 2, 1972 between the governments of Bulgaria, GDR, Hungary, Poland and USSR on co-operation in the great cellulose combines in Ust Ilimsk (USSR). Organizations reg. with the UIA:

European Liaison Committee for Pulp and Paper, f. 1956, Paris.
European Confederation of the Pulp, Paper and Board Industry, f. 1963, Brussels.

Yearbook of International Organizations.

CELPA. El Centro Experimental para el Lanzamiento de Proyectiles Autopropulsados, The Experimental Center for Launching Self-Propelled Rockets, acting since 1969 under the aegis of the UN in Mar del Plata in Argentina.

CELSIUS SCALE. ▷ Temperature.

CELTIC LEAGUE. An international organization of the Celtic national movements in Brittany, Cornwall, Ireland, Isle of Man, Shetland, Wales and abroad, f. 1961, Dublin. Publ. *Carn* (quarterly) and studies: *The Celt in the Seventies*, Dublin, 1971; *The Celtic Experience*, Dublin, 1972. Reg. with the UIA.

F. DELANEY, *The Celts*, London, 1986; *Yearbook of International Organizations.*

CEMENT. A subject of international co-operation. Organization reg. with the UIA:

European Cement Association, f. 1947, Paris.

Yearbook of International Organizations.

CEMETERIES OF FOREIGN SOLDIERS. In accordance with the Geneva Convention 1949 under international protection. The obligation of care for them was introduced into the ▷ Versailles Peace Treaty after World War I, and after World War II, into the Paris Peace Treaties. (▷ Paris Peace Conference 1946). Separate bilateral treaties in the name of the British Commonwealth were made by the UK with all countries in which there are cemeteries of soldiers of the Commonwealth who fell in World War II.

CEMLA. Centro de Estudios Monetarios Latinoamericanos, Latin American Center for the Study of Currencies. A scientific–research institution of the central banks of Latin America, f. 1952, in Mexico City. Publ.: *CEMLA Boletín* and many analyses and studies.

CENCOM. Abbreviation of Central Command, since 1970's a USA military term for any headquarters and planning staff of military groups in action.
D. ROBERTSON, *Guide to Modern Defense and Strategy*, Detroit, 1988.

CENSORSHIP. An international term for state control over publications and entertainment, introduced in ancient Rome and applied to this day in various social orders by secular, civil, or military authorities or religious institutions, hence the definition as civil, military, or church censorship. Appears in two forms: preventive censorship requiring the presentation of the object of control to censorship before displaying it to the public and disciplinary censorship, punishing with confiscation, fine, or imprisonment (separately or jointly) persons who have published in whatever form a work in conflict with the prevailing laws or customs in a given country. During World War I the extraordinary legislation (the Espionage Act of 1917, the Enemy Act of 1917, the Sabotage Act of 1918 and the Sedition Act of 1919) empowered the US Administration to test the First Amendment; as also during World War II the Office of Censorship, abolished in 1945.
A UNESCO commission on international news, in a 1980 report recommended: "Censorship or arbitrary control of information should be abolished."

G.S. SNYDER, *The Right to be Informed: Censorship in the United States*, New York, 1968.

CENTARE. An international area unit = 1 square meter, or approx. 10.76 square feet.

CENTER FOR THE STUDY OF DEMOCRATIC INSTITUTIONS. An organization f. in 1953 in Santa Barbara, Calif. USA, with the task of studying the activities of democratic institutions in the USA and other states as instruments for the guaranteeing of peace; in 1965 the Center was the organizer of the Conference ▷ *Pacem in Terris*. Publ. since 1983, *New Perspectives* (quarterly).

Yearbook of International Organizations.

CENTIGRAM. An international mass and weight unit = 0.01 gram, or approx. 0.154 grain.

CENTILITER. An international capacity unit = 0.01 liter, or approx. 0.6 cubic inch, or 0.338 fluid ounce.

CENTIMETER. An international length unit = 0.01 meter or approx. 0.39 inch. Square centimeter = 0.0001 square meter, or approx. 0.155 square inch.

CENTNAR. A Latin unit of measure in the Middle Ages, accepted in the second half of the 19th century in Europe as = 50 kg (metric centnar). Retained in the Anglo-Saxon world as a unit of measure called English centnar = 50.802 kg or American centnar = 45.39 kg, and is divided into 100 English or American pounds.

CENTO, CENTRAL TREATY ORGANIZATION, 1955–79. An institution of the ▷ Baghdad Pact, signed by Turkey and Iraq on Feb. 24, 1955, UK Apr. 4, 1955, Pakistan Sept. 23, 1955 and Iran Nov. 3, 1955. The USA became a member of the CENTO Economic Committee and Counter-Subversion Committee in Apr., 1956, the Military Committee in Mar., 1957 and the Scientific Committee in May 1961. In Mar., 1959 the USA signed bilateral defense treaties with Iran, Pakistan and Turkey in Ankara. The original headquarters was in Baghdad, but after the withdrawal of Iraq in July 1958, since October 1958 it is located in Ankara. In Mar., 1979 Iran, Pakistan and Turkey left CENTO. On Sept. 26, 1979 with the closing of its headquarters in Sahara, CENTO officially ceased to operate.

World Armaments and Disarmament. Sipri Yearbook 1980, London, 1980, p.798.

CENTRAL AFRICAN CUSTOMS AND ECONOMIC UNION. Intergovernmental institution est. on Dec. 8, 1964 in Brazzaville by a treaty signed by Cameroon, the Central African Republic, Chad, Congo and Gabon, which entered into force Jan. 1, 1966. The Treaty was revised in Yaounde on Dec. 8, 1974 by Cameroon, Central African Republic, Central Congo and Gabon. Chad withdrew from the Union in Apr., 1968. Publ. *Journal Officiel* (twice a year) and *Le Défi* (quarterly).

Yearbook of International Organizations.

CENTRAL AFRICAN ECONOMIC COMMUNITY. An integration institution of ten Central African states, established by an intergovernmental agreement, signed on Oct. 18, 1983. The second ordinary summit was held in Yaounde on Jan. 23–24, 1986, attended by the heads of state or government of Burundi, Cameroon, Chad, Congo, Equatorial Guinea, Rwanda, São Tomé and Principe and Zaire. Angola as an observer.

KEESING's *Contemporary Archive.*

CENTRAL AFRICAN EMPIRE. The official name between 1977 and 1979 of the ▷ Central African Republic.

CENTRAL AFRICAN REPUBLIC. Member of the UN. Landlocked state in central Africa, bordered by Chad, Sudan, Zaïre, Congo and

Cameroon. Area: 622,984 sq. km. Pop. 1986 est. 2,860,000. Capital: Bangui with 301,793 inhabitants 1975. GNP per capita 1986 US $290. Currency: 1 franc CFA = 100 centimes. Official language: French. National Day: Aug. 13, Independence Day, 1960.

Member of the UN since Sept. 20, 1960 and UN specialized agencies, with the exception of IAEA, IFC and IMO. Member of OAU, OCAM and an ACP state of EEC. In 1968 was member of the ▷ Central African States Union. A signatory of the Yaounde Conventions of 1963 and of 1969 and of the Lomé Conventions of 1975 and 1980.

International relations: a territory in the region of the Ubangi river, called Ubangi Shari, was occupied by France in 1887; remained French colony until 1946 and was part of French Equatorial Africa (Chad, Congo Brazzaville, Gabon and Ubangi Shari) from 1946 to 1958. From Dec. 1, 1958 a member state of the French Community and achieved full independence on Aug. 13, 1960. The president of the republic, Jean Bedel Bokassa, appointed president for life on Feb. 5, 1972, proclaimed the Central African Empire on Dec. 4, 1977 with himself as Emperor Bokassa I. He was dethroned on Oct. 15, 1979. In Oct. 1982 a visit in Bangui by President G. Mitterrand normalized the relations with France.

The Europa Year Book 1984. A World Survey. Vol. I, pp. 1353–1361, London, 1984.

CENTRAL AFRICAN STATES UNION. Union des etats d'Afrique Centrale. Est. in Apr., 1968 by an agreement on economic co-operation signed in Bangui on Feb. 1, 1968 by the Heads of State of Chad, Congo (Kinshasa) and the Central African Republic but dissolved in Dec. 1968.

Documentation Française. Paris, 1968.

CENTRAL AMERICA. A geological region between the Isthmus of Tehuantepec and the Isthmus of Panama, separating the Caribbean Sea from the Pacific Ocean. Includes the territories of Belize, Costa Rica, El Salvador, Guatemala, Honduras, Nicaragua and one state of Mexico but excludes Panama. Area: 715,875 sq. km. During colonial times there were two administrative formations: Capitania de Guatemala, which included the present republic of Guatemala, Honduras and El Salvador; and La Audiencia de Panama, which included Costa Rica, Nicaragua and Panama. At the beginning of the 19th century Panama united with Colombia and did not enter the Central American Confederation of 1830–38. At US suggestion the International Central American Bureau was founded in 1907 as an inter-governmental organization of Central American states and the USA. The bureau was dissolved 1956, when states of this region began economic, military and political integration under US supervision. See ▷ Contadora Group. On June 12, 1988 the UN General Assembly approved a US$300 million plan for the economic reactivation of Central America.

R.N. ADAMS, *Cultural Surveys of Panama, Nicaragua, Guatemala, El Salvador, Honduras,* London, 1957; H. SCHOOLEY, *Conflict in Central America,* London, 1987: C. KRAUSS, *Revolution in Central America?* in: *Foreign Affairs,* No. 3, 1987; J. BROOKS ed., 1988, *The South American Handbook. Including the Caribbean, Mexico, Central and South America,* Bath, England, 1987; KEESING's *Record of World Events,* June, 1988.

CENTRAL AMERICA AND PANAMA. In the 20th century universally accepted name after the separation of Panama from Colombia in 1903 for the Central American isthmus.

CENTRAL AMERICAN ADVANCED SCHOOL FOR PUBLIC ADMINISTRATION. Escuela Superior de Administración Pública de América Central, ESAPAC, est. 1957 on the basis of an agreement between the UN and the governments of Costa Rica, El Salvador, Guatemala, Honduras and Nicaragua, signed in Guatemala City on Feb. 22, 1957. This was replaced by the agreement on the establishment of the Central American Institute of Public Administration, ICAP on Feb. 17, 1967.

UNTS, Vol. 274, p. 98; OAS, *Inter-American Treaties and Conventions,* Washington, DC, 1971, p. 211.

CENTRAL AMERICAN AGREEMENT ON ROAD VEHICLES, 1956. A regional agreement between Costa Rica, El Salvador, Guatemala, Honduras and Nicaragua on the temporary importation of road vehicles, signed in San Salvador, Nov. 8, 1956.

UNTS, Vol. 470, p. 170.

CENTRAL AMERICAN AIR NAVIGATION SERVICE CONVENTION, 1960. An agreement between Costa Rica, El Salvador, Guatemala, Honduras and Nicaragua, signed in Tegucigalpa on Feb. 26, 1960. Came into force Nov. 8, 1961.

UNTS, Vol. 418, p. 171.

CENTRAL AMERICAN BANK FOR ECONOMIC INTEGRATION. An intergovernmental finance institution est. in 1961 by agreement between Costa Rica, El Salvador, Guatemala, Honduras and Nicaragua, signed in Managua on Dec. 13, 1960. Its aims are:

"to promote the economic intergration and balanced economic development of the Member Countries, to study and promote the investment opportunity ... to make or participate in long-and-medium term loans. [The Bank is] an international juridical person."

The agreement came into force on May 8, 1961; the bank has its headquarters in Tegucigalpa.

UNTS, Vol. 455, p. 216.

CENTRAL AMERICAN CLEARING HOUSE. An organization est. in 1961 by the Central Banks of Costa Rica, El Salvador, Honduras, Guatemala and Nicaragua, related to the ▷ Common Market of Central America and to the ▷ Central American Bank for Economic Integration.

CENTRAL AMERICAN COMMON MARKET. ▷ Common Market of Central America.

CENTRAL AMERICAN CONFEDERATION, CONFEDERACION CENTRO-AMERICANA, 1842. A term for the union of the states of El Salvador, Guatemala, Honduras and Nicaragua which was created in the capital of Guatemala on Oct. 7, 1842 and broke up in 1845.

CENTRAL AMERICAN CONFERENCES. The First Conference on Central American Affairs was held Dec. 4, 1922–Feb. 7, 1923 in Washington, DC. It approved the Central American Peace and Amity General Treaty (▷ Central American Treaties); the Convention for the establishment of the ▷ Central American International Tribunal; Convention for the ▷ Central American Limitation of Armaments, Convention for the establishment of Permanent Central American Commissions, Convention on ▷ Extradition, Convention relative to the preparation of projects of Electoral Legislation (▷ Election Law), Convention for the Unification of Protective Laws for Workmen and Laborers, Convention for the Establishment of Stations for Agricultural Experiments and Animal Industries, Convention for Reciprocal Exchange of Central American

Students, Convention on the Practice of the Liberal Professions, Convention for the Establishment of Free Trade, Convention for the establishment of the International Commission of Inquiry.

The Second Central American Conference was held in Guatemala City in April, 1934; approved the Central American Fraternity Treaty (▷ Central American Treaties) and the Central American Extradition Convention.

After World War II the General Secretariat of Organization of Central American States and the Committee for Economic Co-operation of the Central American Isthmus organizes meetings and specialized conferences of the Central American States, Publ. *Boletín Informativo ODECA.*

Conference on Central American Affairs, Washington, DC, 1923; Carnegie Endowment, *International Legislation, 1922–1945*, Vols. 1–9, Washington, DC, 1945.

CENTRAL AMERICAN COURT OF JUSTICE. The first international court of justice, established by a Convention between Costa Rica, El Salvador, Guatemala, Honduras and Nicaragua. The seat of the CACJ was Cartago, Costa Rica, 1909–18.

Annales de la CACJ, 1908–18; A. GARCIA ROBLES, *El Mundo de la Postguerra*, México, DF, 1946; M. SEARA VAZQUEZ, *Tratado General de la Organización Internacional*, México, DF, 1974.

CENTRAL-AMERICAN DECLARATION, 1963. A Declaration prepared and signed on Mar. 19, 1963 in San José by the presidents of Central American republics and Panama. A meeting took place on the same day with the US President, John Kennedy. The Declaration included a promise that the states of the region would strive for full economic integration in the spirit of the principles of the ▷ Alliance for Progress and on the basis of ▷ Representative democracy.

CENTRAL AMERICAN DEFENCE COUNCIL. A Council with headquarters in Guatemala City. Est. by an agreement between Costa Rica, El Salvador, Guatemala, Honduras, Nicaragua and Panama, which was signed in Guatemala City on Dec. 14, 1963 and came into force on May 18, 1964. An except from the Preamble states:

"The Contracting Parties considering that the Republics of the Central American Isthmus base their institutions on the democratic system, in which they find complete satisfaction for the ideals of a better life, and that joint action is required in order to preserve forces which are attempting to destroy it by violence."

UNTS. Vol. 507, pp. 156–168.

CENTRAL AMERICAN ECONOMIC COUNCIL. CONSEJO ECONOMICO CENTROAMERICANO. The main institution of the General Treaty on ▷ Central American Economic Integration, 1960.

CENTRAL AMERICAN ECONOMIC INTEGRATION. Initiated in 1949 by the UN Economic Commission for Latin America, ECLA. The aims were approved in May, 1951 by Central American governments. In Aug. 1952 ministers of finance of Guatemala, Honduras, Costa Rica, Nicaragua and El Salvador formed the ECLA Committee of Economic Co-operation. The first legal act of Central American integration is the Multilateral Free Trade and Central American Economic Integration Treaty concluded on June 10, 1958,

"with a view to creating customs union between their respective territories as soon as conditions are favourable" (art. 1).

The Treaty came into force on June 2, 1959.

The next step was the Tripartite Treaty on Economic Association (El Salvador, Guatemala, Honduras) signed on Feb. 6, 1960, also General Treaty on Central American Economic Integration signed on Dec. 13, 1960. This General Treaty between Costa Rica, El Salvador, Guatemala, Honduras and Nicaragua was signed in Managua on Dec. 13, 1960 and came into force with regard to El Salvador, Guatemala and Nicaragua on June 4, 1961; to Honduras on Apr. 27, 1962, and Costa Rica on Nov. 16, 1962.

"The Contracting States agree to establish among themselves a common market, within a period of not more than five years ... " (art. 1).

A Protocol consisting of a List of Merchandise Subject to Temporary Exceptions was signed on Nov. 16, 1962; and another Protocol (Central American Uniform Customs Code) was signed Dec. 13, 1963. The Second Protocol to the Agreement was signed on Nov. 5, 1965, and came into force on Jan. 27, 1968.

Other integration agreements:

Central American Agreement on Highway Traffic, signed on June 10, 1958; entered into force on Dec. 17, 1959.

Central American Agreement on Uniform Road Signs, signed on June 10, 1958, entered into force Oct. 31, 1963.

Central American Agreement on Equalization of Import Charges, signed on Sept. 1, 1959, entered into force on Sept. 29, 1960; with eight Protocols, signed 1959, 1960, 1962, 1963, 1964, 1965 and 1967.

An agreement establishing the Central American Bank for Economic Integration, signed Dec. 13, 1960; came into force on May 8, 1961.

An agreement establishing the Central American Corporation of Air Navigation Service (COCESMA), signed Feb. 26, 1960, came into force on Nov. 8, 1961.

A Central American Agreement on Basic Unification of Education, signed on June 22, 1962, came into force on Oct. 31, 1963.

An Agreement on the Practice of Professions and Recognition of University Studies, signed on June 22, 1962; came into force on July 7, 1964.

A Central American Agreement on Fiscal Incentives to Industrial Development, signed on July 31, 1962; came into force on Mar. 23, 1969.

A Protocol of San José on Emergency Measures to Protect the Balance of Payments, signed in June 1968, came into force on Nov. 9, 1968.

A Protocol of Limón on Basic Cereal Grains, signed on Oct. 28, 1965, came into force on Oct. 14, 1967.

A Treaty on Telecommunications, signed on April 26, 1966, came into force on Nov. 18, 1966.

An agreement on the establishment of the Central American Institute of Public Administration, signed on Feb. 17, 1967.

A Multilateral Treaty on Social Security, signed on Oct. 14, 1967.

A Central American Treaty for the Protection of Industrial Property, signed on June 1, 1968.

UNTS, Vol. 455, p. 70; *Instruments Relating to the Economic Integration of Latin America*, Washington, DC, 1968; *La Cooperación Económica Multilateral en América Latina*. Vol. 1. *Textos y documentos*. México, DF. 1961; *Economic Integration Treaties of Central America*, Guatemala, March 1964; F. VILLAGRAN KRAMER, *Integración Económica Centroamericana*, Guatemala, 1967; *Instruments relating to the Economic Integration of Latin America*, Washington, DC, 1968.

CENTRAL AMERICAN EDUCATION UNIFICATION, 1962. An agreement on basic unification of education, signed in San Salvador on June 22, 1962 by Costa Rica, El Salvador, Guatemala, Honduras and Nicaragua, came into force on Oct. 31, 1963.

UNTS, Vol. 770, pp. 247–306; *Boletín Informativo ODECA*, San Salvador, No. 28, 1962.

CENTRAL AMERICAN FRATERNITY TREATY, 1934. ▷ Central American Treaties.

CENTRAL AMERICAN IMPORT DUTIES AGREEMENT, 1959. An Agreement between Costa Rica, El Salvador, Guatemala, Honduras and Nicaragua on the Equalization of Import Duties and Charges (with Schedules and Protocol concerning a Central American Preferential Tariff) which was signed in San José on Sept. 1, 1959. A Protocol to this Agreement was signed in Managua on Dec. 13, 1960.

UNTS, Vol. 454, p. 289.

CENTRAL AMERICAN INSTITUTE OF PUBLIC ADMINISTRATION, INSTITUTO CENTROAMERICANO DE ADMINISTRACIÓN PÚBLICA, IPAC. An Institute est. by an Agreement, signed in San José on Feb. 17, 1967 by the governments of Costa Rica, El Salvador, Guatemala, Honduras, Nicaragua and Panama replacing the Agreement of 1957 on ▷ ESAPAC. Publ. *Boletín de Documentos*. Reg. with the UIA.

OAS, *Inter-American Treaties and Conventions*, Washington, DC, 1971, p. 211; *Yearbook of International Organizations*.

CENTRAL AMERICAN INTERNATIONAL INQUIRY COMMISSIONS, 1923–53. Institutions 1923–53, est. by the Conference on Central American Affairs in a Convention signed by Costa Rica, El Salvador, Guatemala, Honduras, Nicaragua and the USA, at Washington on Feb. 7, 1923. They came into force on June 13, 1925. Denunciation by Honduras on Mar. 26, 1953.

The American Journal of International Law, Vol. 17, No. 2, Apr., 1923.

CENTRAL AMERICAN INTERNATIONAL TRIBUNAL. A Tribunal est. by a Convention with Protocol, signed in Washington, on Feb. 7, 1923, at the Central American Affairs Conference 1922/23; ratified by Costa Rica, Guatemala, Honduras and Nicaragua; denounced by Honduras on Mar. 26, 1953 and not ratified by El Salvador; remains in force as long as at least three signatories remain members.

Conference on Central American Affairs, Washington, DC, 1923.

CENTRAL AMERICAN LIMITATION OF ARMAMENTS, 1923. A Convention for the Limitation of Armaments was signed in Washington, DC, on Feb. 7, 1923 at the Conference on Central American Affairs by Costa Rica, El Salvador, Guatemala, Honduras and Nicaragua. It came into force on Mar. 10, 1925; denounced by Honduras on Mar. 26, 1953.

The American Journal of International Law, Vol. 17, No. 2, Apr. 1923; *Conference on Central American Affairs*, Washington, DC, 1923.

CENTRAL AMERICAN MONETARY STABILIZATION FUND, FONDO CENTROAMERICANO DE ESTABILIZACIÓN MONETARIA. A Fund est. 1968 in Tegucigalpa by the Central American Bank for Economic Integration and the Central American Monetary Council.

CENTRAL AMERICAN MONETARY UNION, UNION MONETARIA CENTROAMERICANA. Est. by the Central Banks of Costa Rica, El Salvador, Guatemala, Honduras and Nicaragua on Feb. 25, 1964 in San Salvador, under the aegis of the Central American Economic Council and of the Central American Bank of Economic Integration.

C

CENTRAL AMERICAN NON-RECOGNITION OF REVOLUTIONARY GOVERNMENTS DOCTRINE, 1907. A subject of a Convention of Central American Republics, 1907, which declared:

"The Governments of the high contracting parties shall not recognize any other government which may come into power in any of the five Republics as a consequence of a *coup d'état* or of a revolution against the recognized government, so long as the freely elected representatives of the people thereof have not constitutionally reorganized the country."

American Journal of International Law, Supplement 1908, p. 229.

CENTRAL AMERICAN PARLIAMENT. An idea supported by the ▷ Esquipulas Declaration, 1986 of the heads of state of five Central American countries.

CENTRAL AMERICAN RESEARCH INSTITUTE FOR INDUSTRY. INSTITUTO CENTROAMERICANO DE INVESTIGACIÓN DE TECNOLOGÍA INDUSTRIAL. An Institute est. Jan. 20, 1956 on signature of a Convention by the governments of Costa Rica, El Salvador, Guatemala, Honduras and Nicaragua; came into force on the date of signature. Headquarters in Guatemala City.

A.J. PEASLEE, *International Intergovernmental Organizations*, 2 Vols., The Hague, 1961; *Yearbook of International Organizations*.

CENTRAL AMERICAN ROAD TRAFFIC AGREEMENT, 1958. An agreement between Costa Rica, El Salvador, Guatemala, Honduras and Nicaragua on Road Traffic, signed in Tegucigalpa on June 10, 1958.

"While reserving its jurisdiction over the use of its own roads each Contracting State agrees to the use of its roads for international traffic under the condition set out in this Agreement" (art. 1).

UNTS, Vol. 454, p. 146.

CENTRAL AMERICAN STATES ORGANIZATION. ▷ ODECA.

CENTRAL AMERICAN TREATIES, 1923–67. A chronological list of regional Treaties of the Central American governments since 1923 is as follows:

Central American Peace and Amity General Treaty 1923, approved by the First Conference on Central American Affairs and signed by Costa Rica, El Salvador, Guatemala, Honduras and Nicaragua in Washington, DC on Feb. 7, 1923. It came into force on May 26, 1925 and is no longer in effect as it was denounced by Costa Rica on Dec. 23, 1935, by El Salvador on Dec. 26, 1935 and by Honduras on Mar. 26, 1953.
Central American Fraternity Treaty, 1934, signed at the Second Central American Conference in Guatemala City on Apr. 12, 1934 by Costa Rica, El Salvador, Guatemala, Honduras and Nicaragua.
Multilateral Free Trade and Central America in Integration Treaty 1958, signed on June 10, 1958 in Tegucigalpa by the governments of Guatemala, Honduras, Costa Rica, Nicaragua and El Salvador together with a convention on economic integration and road signs and traffic agreements. Replaced on Dec. 13, 1960, with the General Treaty ▷ Central American Economic Integration.
Treaty on Economic Association or the Tripartite Treaty 1960, signed at Guatemala City, on Feb. 6, 1960 by El Salvador, Guatemala and Honduras. It came into force on Apr. 27, 1960.
Central American Telecommunication Treaty 1966, between Costa Rica, El Salvador, Guatemala, Honduras and Nicaragua, signed in Managua on Apr. 26, 1966; came into force on Nov. 18, 1966, establishing a Central American Telecommunication System with a Regional Technical Telecommunications Commission.
Multilateral Treaty on Social Security 1967, signed at San José, on Oct. 14, 1967.

Inter-American Treaties and Conventions, Washington DC, 1971.

CENTRAL AMERICAN UNION COVENANT, 1921. A covenant signed in San José de Costa Rica, on Jan 19, 1921, by the governments of Costa Rica, El Salvador, Guatemala and Honduras determined to "unite in a perpetual and indissoluble union … the Federation of Central America" (art. 1).

LNTS, Vol. 2, p. 9.

CENTRAL AMERICAN UNITED PROVINCES, PROVINCIAS UNIDAS DEL CENTRO DE AMÉRICA. In 1823 the Congress of Central America proclaimed the independence of the territories of the colonial Capitania General de Guatemala and the Federation of the Central American United Provinces with a capital in Guatemala City. The Federation ended with the proclamations of independence: of Nicaragua in Apr. 1838, of Costa Rica and Honduras in Nov. 1838, of Guatemala in Apr. 1839 and of El Salvador in Jan. 1841.

CENTRAL BANK OF THE WEST AFRICAN STATES. Banque centrale des États de l'Afrique de l'ouest. An Intergovernmental finance institution of Benin f. 1955 in Dakar, by the Ivory Coast, Niger, Senegal, Togo, Upper Volta.

CENTRAL BANKS. An international term for state banks of issue which have a monopoly in their countries on the issue of money and the financing and control of other financial institutions. According to the definition of IMF the function of central banks is

"acting as a credit and fiscal agent of the government, storing part of the reserves of commercial banks, storing and administering the national reserves of gold and foreign currencies, exercising a monopoly on the issue of banknotes and the eventual control of credits."

In 1920 the I International Financial Conference in Brussels convened by the LN recommended the creation of central banks in all countries. The first state central bank was created in 1921 in the USSR, the central bank of Canada was nationalized in 1938, France nationalized hers in 1945, the UK in 1946 and the Netherlands in 1948.

H. AUFRICHT, *Legislación Comparada del Banco Central*, México, DF, 1964; T. TAMAGNA, *Central Banking in Latin America*, New York, 1965; *The Bankers Almanac and Year Book*, London.

CENTRAL COMMAND. ▷ CENCOM.

CENTRAL EUROPE. The Disarmament Conference in Vienna in Nov. 1973 declared that the concept of Central Europe includes: Belgium, Czechoslovakia, the FRG, the GDR, Holland, Luxembourg and Poland. The geographical concept also includes Austria.

P.L. HORECKY, *East Central Europe, A Guide to Basic Publications*, Chicago, 1969.

CENTRAL FRONT. An International military term for the border between the FRG and GDR, as the possible main battlefield between NATO and Warsaw Pact armies.

D. ROBERTSON, *Guide to Modern Defense and Strategy*, Detroit, 1988.

CENTRAL INTELLIGENCE AGENCY. ▷ Intelligence Service. ▷ CIA.

CENTRALLY PLANNED ECONOMIES. An international term used in the UN system, for those economies in which the government is dominant in ownership of productive factors and in control of economic processes.

UN Chronicle, October 1982, p. 46.

CENTRAL STATES. A group of four powers: Germany, Austria–Hungary, Turkey and Bulgaria forming a coalition in World War I against the Allies. The coalition was initiated in 1879 by the Dual Alliance of Austria–Hungary and the German Empire. The name referred to the central geographical position of Germany and Austria in Europe.

CEOA. ▷ NATO.

CERAMICS. A subject of international co-operation. Organizations reg. with the UIA:

Common Market Liaison Bureau for the Ceramic Industries, f. 1962, Brussels.
European Ceramic Association, f. 1948, Paris.
European Federation of Ceramic Sanitary-Ware Manufacturers, f. 1954, Milan, Italy.
International Academy of Ceramics, f. 1953, Zurich. Consultative status: with UNESCO. Publ. *Céramique*.
Rei Cretariae Romanae Fautores, Association of Roman Ceramic Archaeologists, f. 1957, Zurich.

Yearbook of International Organizations; *International Trade Center UNCTAD/GATT, Unglazed and Glazed Ceramic Tiles. A Market Survey*, Geneva, 1983. *The Europa Yearbook 1988. A World Survey*, Vol. I, London, 1988.

CEREALS. A subject of international co-operation. Organizations reg. with the UIA:

Cereals Agricultural Co-operative Group of the EEC, f. 1959, Marksem, Belgium.
Federation of Nordic Cereal Societies, f. 1931, Lyngby, Denmark.
International Association for Cereal Chemistry, f. 1958, Schwechat, Austria.
International Union of United Brevery, Flour Cereal, Soft Drink and Distillery Workers of America, f. 1886, Cincinnati, USA.
Union of Cereal Storage Firms in the EEC, f. 1969, Bonn.

The American Republics signed a Protocol of Limón on Basic Cereals Grains on Oct. 14, 1967.

Instruments relating to the Economic Integration of Latin America, Washington, DC, 1968; *UN Chronicle*, July 1982, p. 97, *Yearbook of International Organizations*. FAO published bi-monthly *Cereals*.

CEREBRO-VASCULAR DISEASES. A subject of international studies under the aegis of the WHO. According to WHO statistics the death rate in 1987 ranged from 26 per 100,000 pop. (Sri Lanka) to 44 Guatemala, 46 Kuwait, 58 Canada, 60 USA, 66 Switzerland, 80 France, 98 New Zealand, 104 England, 113 Japan, 151 Greece, 187 Hungary, 194 Czechoslovakia to a high of 255 in Bulgaria.
WHO Health Statistics Annual 1987, Geneva, 1988.

CEREMONIES AT SEA. Traditional customs at sea: saluting upon the meeting of ships, rendering of honors, raising and lowering of flags, etc., defined by the Protocol of Aix-la-Chapelle, 1818, and the regulation of ship étiquette.

CERN, CENTRE EUROPÉENNE POUR LA RECHERCHE NUCLEAIRE, EUROPEAN CENTER OF ATOMIC RESEARCH. The Center was planned and est. 1950–54 on the initiative of UNESCO as an intergovernmental institution of the Paris Convention of July 1, 1953, signed by Denmark, France, Greece, the Netherlands, Norway, Sweden, Switzerland and Yugoslavia. It has the task of "developing inter-European co-operation in the field of purely scientific atomic research." Also joining the Convention were: Austria, Italy, the FRG and the UK. A new revised Convention took effect on Jan. 17, 1971. A laboratory complex called CERN was constructed near Geneva with synchro-cyclotronic and synchro-

Chad

protonic accelerators. From 1955 publ. *CERN Courrier* and *CERN Annuaire*.

The Scope and Activities of CERN, Geneva, 1954.

CERTIFICATE. An international term in shipping and foreign trade for all affidavits attesting to ships and goods, their origin and insurance.

CESSATION OF HOSTILITY. An international term for reciprocal cessation of war operations between the belligerent states.

Dictionnaire de la terminologie du droit international, Paris, 1960.

CESSION. An international term in international law for the transfer of sovereignty over a territory by the owner-state to another state; in civil law for an agreement on the transfer of debts or specific rights to another person or institution; in the banking system for a form of clearing.

CESSION OF STATE TERRITORY. A legal act of giving up sovereignty over a territory by one state for the benefit of another. Usually such renunciation forms part of a peace treaty (for instance, Austria–Hungary in the Treaty of Versailles ceded parts of its territory in favor of Czechoslovakia, Poland and Yugoslavia). Another form is an agreement against payment (for instance, the USA bought Alaska in 1867 from Russia and in 1916, a part of the Virgin Islands from Denmark). There is no international rule requiring that cession of state territory be effected solely through a peace treaty and this is of essential importance to the validity, for example, of the boundaries of the GDR and FRG, which have been exclusively established by way of bilateral agreements with neighboring states.

D. SCHWARZENBERG, "Title to territory: response to a challenge", in *American Journal of International Law*, 1957; R.L. BLEDSOE, B.A. BOCZEK, *The International Law Dictionary*, Oxford, 1987.

CESSION TREATY, 1920. A border agreement signed on Aug. 9, 1920 in Sèvres by the Main Allied and Associated Powers with cession states of post-Austrian territories, Czechoslovakia, Yugoslavia and Romania. Poland, which came under the Cession Treaty, did not sign it because of Eastern Galicia, found the agreement invalid and protested against its registration on Jan. 9, 1922 in the Secretariat of the League of Nations sub. No. 203.

CETIS, CENTRE DE TRANSFORMATIONS DES INFORMATIONS SCIENTIFIQUES, CENTER FOR THE PROCESSING OF SCIENTIFIC INFORMATION. An intergovernmental institution est. in 1958 in Brussels as the main information center of Western Europe operating in close connection with the European Energy Community ▷ EURATOM.

CEUTA AND MELILLA. Two ports on the Mediterranean coast of Morocco, which have been Spanish enclaves since 1580. Ceuta is located opposite Gibraltar. Area: 18 sq. km and 70,864 inhabitants (1980); and Melilla located to the east of Ceuta, area 14 sq. km with *c.* 58,449 inhabitants 1980. In 1961 Morocco made official claims to both enclaves and in 1975 gained the support of the UN Committee on Decolonization as well as the OAU. In Oct. 1978 Morocco officially renewed its claims, and the Spanish government once again firmly rejected them. Belonging to the enclaves are two small towns between Ceuta and Melilla: Penon de Velez de la Gomera and Villa Sanjurio, as well as the uninhabited island of Chafarinas. On Jan. 1, 1986 Ceuta and Mellila as Spanish cities joined, with

status of free ports, the European Community. In Nov. 1986 Muslim leaders demanded Muslim administration in the enclave; in Mar. 1987 King Hassan of Morocco supported the Muslim claims.

Europa Yearbook 1987. A World Survey, London, 1987.

CEYLON. Island in the Indian Ocean, separated from India by the Palk strait, width 53 km. Length of the island 435 km, width 225 km. Area 65,610 sq. km. Ceylon means "island of the Singhalese." The Singhalese name ▷ Sri Lanka was officially introduced on May 22, 1972 as the name of the Republic, means "large and beautiful island."

CHACO PEACE TREATY, 1938. A Treaty between Bolivia and Paraguay, signed in Buenos Aires on July 21, 1938 which ended the ▷ Chaco War. The highlights of the Treaty were:

"Art. 1. Peace between the Republics of Paraguay and Bolivia (Bolivia and Paraguay) is re-established.
Art. 2. The dividing line in the Chaco between Bolivia and Paraguay (Paraguay and Bolivia) will be that determined by the Presidents of the Republics of Argentina, Chile, United States of America, United States of Brazil, Peru and Uruguay in their capacity as arbitrators in equity, who acting ex aequo et bono will give their arbitral award in accordance with this and the following clauses.
(a) The arbitral award will fix the northern dividing line in the Chaco in the zone comprised between the line of the Peace Conference presented May 27, 1938 and the line of the Paraguayan counter-proposal presented to the consideration of the Peace Conference June 24, 1938, from the meridian of Fort 27 of November, i.e. approximately meridian 61° 55′ west of Greenwich, to the eastern limit of the zone, excluding the littoral on the Paraguay River south of the mouth of the Araguaia
(b) The arbitral award will likewise fix the western dividing line in the Chaco between the Pilcomayo River and the inter-section of the meridian of Fort 27 of November, i.e., approximately 61° 55′ west of Greenwich with the line of the award in the north referred to in the previous paragraph.
(c) The said line will not go on the Pilcomayo River more to the east than Pozo Hondo, nor to the west further than any point on the line which, starting from D'Orbigny, was fixed by the Neutral Military Commission as intermediary between the maximum positions reached by the belligerent armies at the suspension of fire on June 14, 1935.
Art. 10. The Republics of Bolivia and Paraguay renewing the non-aggression pact stipulated in the Protocol of June 12, 1935 solemnly obligate themselves not to make war on each other nor to use force, directly or indirectly, as a means of solution of any present or future difference ...".

The Chaco Peace Conference, July 1, 1935–January 23, 1939, Washington, DC, 1940; *Major Peace Treaties of Modern History*, New York, 1967, pp. 2397–2402.

CHACO WAR. A war between Bolivia and Paraguay, after a long history of rival claims to the Chaco Boreal region of ▷ Gran Chaco 1879, 1887, 1894, 1907 and 1928, when the International Conference of American States on Good Services and Arbitration created a special committee, the so-called McCoy Committee, composed of representatives of Colombia, Cuba, Mexico and Uruguay under the chairmanship of General Frank R. McCoy of the USA, which, during the period Mar. 13-Sept. 21, 1929 was able to lessen the conflict and re-establish diplomatic relations between Bolivia and Paraguay. It also gained the consent of both states for the est. of a Neutral Commission composed of the representatives of the same states as the McCoy Committee, whose draft was to be a proposal for a nonaggression pact. As the work on the pact was being completed, Bolivia on July 21, 1932 charged Paraguay before the League of Nations Council with aggression in the region of Lake Chuquisaca. On May 10, 1933 Paraguay

formally declared war on Bolivia. The League Council on July 19, 1933 convened a commission to investigate the Paraguayan–Bolivian conflict (France, Mexico, Spain, the UK and Uruguay). It began work on Nov. 3, 1933 in Montevideo and concluded on Mar. 14, 1934 with a draft plan for a peace treaty, which was not accepted by any of the sides. On Nov. 24, 1934 the LN Assembly created a Commission composed of five LN member states (Argentina, Brazil, Chile, Peru and Uruguay) and the USA, which convened a Peace Conference in Montevideo. This ended with a Protocol of Peace signed July 21, 1935 in Buenos Aires by Bolivia and Paraguay, as well as a Treaty of Peace, Friendship and Borders, signed July 21, 1938 (see ▷ Chaco Peace Treaty, 1938).

L. FUR, *Le Conflit de Chaco Boreal*, Paris, 1934; A. RAMIREZ, *Position juridique de Chaco Boreal*, Paris, 1935; "Différend entre Bolivie et Paraguay", in: *SdN Journal Officiel Supplément Spécial*, No. 132 and 134; I. GORDON, *Boundaries, Possessions and Conflicts in South America*, Boston, 1939; *La Conferencia de Paz del Chaco 1935–1939. Compilación de Documentos*, Buenos Aires, 1939; C.J. FERNANDEZ, *La Guerra de Chaco*, Buenos Aires, 1955; R. AYALA MOREINA, *Por que no ganamos la Guerra del Chaco?*, La Paz, 1959; D.H. ZOOK, *The Conflict of the Chaco*, New York, 1961.

CHAD. Member of the UN. Republic of Chad, République du Tchad. A Central African land-locked state, bounded by Sudan, the Central African Republic, Cameroon, Nigeria, Niger and Libya. Area: 1,284,000 sq. km. Pop. 1988 est. 5,400,000 (1975 census: 4,029,917). Capital: N'djamena (formerly Fort Lamy) with 303,000 inhabitants, 1979. GNP per capita 1987 US $150. Currency: one franc CFA = 100 centimes. Official language: French. National Day, Jan. 11, Independence Day, 1960.
Since Sept. 18, 1960 member of the UN and of the UN specialized agencies with the exception of IAEA, IFC, IMO and UNIDO. Member of OAU. ACP state of EEC.
International relations: occupied by France 1890–1913. French colony, part of French Equatorial Africa until Nov. 28, 1958. Autonomous state within the French Community; became independent on Aug. 11, 1960. Involved in border disputes with ▷ Nigeria; and with Libya since 1973 about the so-called Aouzou strip annexed by Libya in Sept. 1975. During the civil war, 1980 Libyan forces invited to Chad by a provisional government occupied a great part of Chad. In Nov., 1981 a neutral Inter-African force was installed by the OAU to end the Libyan–Chad conflict. The neutral forces ended the mission on June 30, 1982.
In August 1983 a de facto partition of Chad along the 16th parallel took place following the intervention of French troops in the South and of the Libyan troops in the North. On Sept. 17, 1984 France and Libya announced a mutual phased withdrawal of their troops from Chad. In Aug. 1987 Libyan forces were repulsed from the town of Aouzou by Chadian forces supported by French military logistical advisors. On Oct. 3, 1988 Chad formally ended war with Libya over the Aouzou Strip.
The GA Res. 43/205 of Dec. 20, 1988 decided:

"To contribute, in co-operation with the United Nations Development Programme, to the preparation of a development plan for Chad for 1989–1992;
To continue to assess, in close collaboration with the humanitarian agencies concerned, the humanitarian needs, particularly in the areas of food and health, of the displaced populations;
To mobilize special humanitarian assistance for persons who have suffered as a result of the war, natural calamities and disasters, and for the resettlement of displaced persons."

143

J. LE CORNEC, *Histoire Politique du Tchad de 1900 à 1962*, Paris, 1963; *L'essentiel sur le Tchad*, N'djamena, 1972; *UN Chronicle*, March, 1978, pp. 5–6; R. WESTEBBE, *Chad. Development, Potential and Constraints*, Washington, DC, 1974; *Everyone's United Nations*, New York, 1979; V. THOMPSON, R. ADOLFF, *Conflict in Chad*, London, 1981; *The Europa Year Book 1984. A World Survey*, Vol. II, pp. 1362–1369, London, 1984; *Documentation Française*, Paris, 1984; Chad-Libya, in A.J. DAY ed., *Border and Territorial Disputes*, London, 1987, pp. 113–117; *UN Resolutions and Decisions adopted by the General Assembly during the First Part of its Forty-Third Session, From 20 September to 22 December 1988*, New York, 1989, p. 309.

CHAD, LAKE. A body of water of central Africa, bordering on Chad, Cameroon and Nigeria and subject of a convention signed in May 1964 in Fort Lamy and in Aug. 1968 in Lagos. The organ of the convention is the permanent Lake Chad Basin Commission in N'djamena. The size of the Lake changes seasonally from 10.360 to 25.900 sq. km.

The Europa Yearbook, 1988. A World Survey, Vol. I, London 1988.

CHAGOS ARCHIPELAGO. An islands group in the Indian Ocean, since 1965 a part of the British Indian Ocean Territory, formerly a dependency of Mauritius. ▷ Diego Garcia Island.

CHAIN STORES. A subject of international co-operation. Organizations reg. with the UIA:

European Chain-Stores Association, f. 1965, Brussels.
International Association of Chain Stores, f. 1953, Paris. Publ. *Newsletter*.

Yearbook of International Organizations.

CHALDEAN CHURCH. The Uniates, in communion with the Roman Catholic Church (union of 1552 confirmed 1672, 1771, 1778) headed by the patriarch of Babylon, headquarters in Mosul, Iraq, now in Baghdad. Close to 200,000 adherents in Iraq, smaller communities in Iran.

R. ETTELDORF, *The Catholic Church in the Middle East*, London, 1959.

CHALLENGE. A name of international airplane sports races, organized 1928–34 every two years by Britain, Czechoslovakia, France, Germany, Italy, Poland and Switzerland under the aegis of the International Aviation Federation, Federation Aerienne International (FAI), which existed from 1925 to 1939; the full French name was: Challenge internationale de tourisme. The country whose representative won the FAI cup was the organizer of the next races. The first was organized in 1928 by the Aeroclub of France in a course of about 2000 km; the victor was the German K. Lusser. The second – 1930 in Germany – was on a route of about 7500 km through Central Europe; the winner was the German H. Morzig. The third – 1932 in Germany – on a Central European route of 7360 km; the winners were Poles, F. Zwirko and S. Wigura in a plane of Polish construction, a RWD-6. The fourth – 1934 in Poland – on a Europe–African course more than 9500 km; the winner was a Pole, J. Bajan in a RWD-9. In Aug. 1935 it was decided to suspend the races, officially due to excessive costs. From 1972 in Poland the International Friendship Rallies (Memorial to Zwirko and Wigura) take place.

CHALLENGER. ▷ Space-Shuttle.

CHAMBER OF COMMERCE. Institutions whose aim is to protect the interests of firms engaged in foreign and other trade and to develop them in the international arena. In June 1933 the I International. Congress of Chambers of Commerce was held. Organizations reg. with the UIA:

Chamber of Commerce of the USA, f. 1912, Washington, DC; advisory status with ECOSOC; Publ. *Washington Report* and *Nation's Business*.
Federation of Commonwealth Chambers of Commerce, f. 1911 as British Imperial Council of Commerce; present name since 1963, London; Publ. *Economic Geography of the Commonwealth*.
General Union of Chambers of Commerce, Industry and Agriculture for Arab Countries, f. 1951, Beirut; Publ. *The Arab Economic Report*.
European Chambers of Commerce Group for Trade with Latin America, f. 1962, Brussels; an EEC institution.
International Chamber of Commerce, ICC, f. 1920 by the resolutions of the International Trade Conference, which was held in 1919 in Atlantic City; Consultative status with ECOSOC, FAO, ICAO, ITU, IMCO, IAEA, OECD and UNESCO. Its institutions are the Court of Arbitration, International Council on Advertising Practice, International Bureau of Chambers of Commerce and ICC Commission on Asian and Far-Eastern Affairs, Paris, with branches in Geneva and Bangkok. Publ. *Yearbook*, *The ICC at Work* and the monthly *ICC News* and many directories such as *Guide to ICC Arbitration*, *Double Taxation in the Atlantic Community* and *Towards Maximum Efficiency in Transport*. In the Warsaw Pact states Chambers of Foreign Commerce are in operation.

Yearbook of International Organizations.

CHAMBORD CHATEAU. ▷ Château and Estate of Chambord.

CHAMIZAL. Mexican border territory, from 1864 until 1967 the subject of a dispute between Mexico and the USA as a result of a change in the bed of the Rio Grande river (Rio Bravo del Norte) and occupation of the former river bed by the US, in spite of the fact that the International Arbitration Commission appointed by both parties in 1911 adjudged that Chamizal belonged to Mexico. Talks resumed in 1962 when US President J.F. Kennedy stated that non-acceptance of the commission's pronouncement had been a mistake. This led to the formal transfer of Chamizal back to Mexico on Oct. 20, 1967. In Chamizal, west Texas, USA, a National Memorial commemorates the peaceful settlement of the 99-year border dispute.

El Chamizal, México, Presidencia de la República. Octobre 1967.

CHAMPAGNE. Name for a sparkling white wine, patented by France in the Versailles Treaty, 1919, for its exclusive use in international trade. Hence for example the Germans had to introduce their own term: Sekt.

CHANCOM. Channel Command. Within the framework of NATO the officer responsible for the defense of the Channel region.

CHANNEL ISLANDS. An ancient part of the French Duchy de Normandie belonging to the Crown of England. The main islands: Jersey, with 1986 pop. 80,212 and Guersney with 1986 pop. 55,482 with dependencies: Guernsey-Alderney, Brechou, Great Sark, Herm, Jethou, Lihou and Little Sark. The official languages are French and English. Area: 194.3 sq. km. In World War II occupied 1940–44 by Germany.

R.M. LOCKLEY. *The Channel Islands*, London, 1968; C. CRUICKSHANK, *The German Occupation of the Channel Islands*, London, 1975; V. COYCH, *The Channel Islands. A New Study*, Newton Abbot, 1977; N. JEE, *The Landscape of the Channel Islands*, Chichester, 1982; *The Europa Year Book 1984*. Vol. I, pp. 1003–1008, London, 1984; J. PAXTON ed., *The Statesman's Yearbook 1987–88*, London, 1987.

CHAPULTEPEC ACT, 1945. Signed in Mexico City in Chapultepec Palace on Mar. 3, 1945 as the final act of Inter-American Conference for Problems of War and Peace. It was the first document in the inter-American system to approve the principle of using sanctions against aggressors and the principle of condemning all assailants, both from the American continent and outside. The Declaration of Mutual American Assistance and Solidarity and its recommendations were given the name Act of Chapultepec. The Declaration was signed by Argentina, Bolivia, Brazil, Chile, Dominicana, Ecuador, Guatemala, Haiti, Honduras, Colombia, Costa Rica, Cuba, Mexico, Nicaragua, Panama, Paraguay, Peru, El Salvador, Uruguay, Venezuela and the USA. Argentina acceded on Apr. 4, 1945. The text is as follows:

"Declaration on Reciprocal Assistance and American Solidarity by the Governments Represented at the Inter-American Conference on War and Peace
Whereas:
(1) The peoples of the Americas, animated by a profound love of justice, remain sincerely devoted to the principles of international law:
(2) It is their desire that such principles, notwithstanding the present difficult circumstances, may prevail with greater force in future international relations:
(3) The Inter-American Conferences have repeatedly proclaimed certain fundamental principles, but these must be reaffirmed and proclaimed at a time when the juridical bases of the community of nations are being established:
(4) The new situation in the world makes more imperative than ever the union and solidarity of the American peoples, for the defense of their rights and the maintenance of international peace:
(5) The American States have been incorporating in their international law, since 1890, by means of conventions, resolutions and declarations, the following principles:
(a) The proscription of territorial conquest and the non-recognition of all acquisitions made by force (First International Conference of American States, 1890).
(b) The condemnation of intervention by a State in the internal or external affairs of another (Seventh International Conference of American States, 1933, and Inter-American Conference for the Maintenance of Peace, 1936).
(c) The recognition that every war or threat of war affects directly or indirectly all civilized peoples, and endangers the great principles of liberty and justice which constitute the American ideal and the standard of its international policy (Inter-American Conference for the Maintenance of Peace, 1936).
(d) The procedure of mutual consultation in order to find means of peaceful co-operation in the event of war or threat of war between American countries (Inter-American Conference for the Maintenance of Peace, 1936).
(e) The recognition that every act susceptible of disturbing the peace of America affects each and every one of them and justifies the initiation of the procedure of consultation (Inter-American Conference for the Maintenance of Peace, 1936).
(f) That any difference or dispute between the American nations, whatever its nature or origin, shall be settled by the methods of conciliation, or unrestricted arbitration, or through the operation of international justice (Inter-American Conference for the Maintenance of Peace, 1936).
(g) The recognition that respect for the personality, sovereignty and independence of each American State constitutes the essence of international order sustained by continental solidarity, which historically has been expressed and sustained by declarations and treaties in force (Eighth International Conference of American States, 1938).
(h) The affirmation that respect for and the faithful observance of treaties constitutes the indispensable rule for the development of peaceful relations between States, and treaties can only be revised by agreement of the contracting parties (Declaration of American Principles, Eighth International Conference of American States, 1938).

(i) That in case the peace, security or territorial integrity of any American republic is threatened by acts of any nature that may impair them, they proclaim their common concern and their determination to make effective their solidarity, co-ordinating their respective sovereign will by means of the procedure of consultation, using the measures which in each case the circumstances may make advisable (Declaration of Lima, Eighth International Conference of American States, 1938).

(j) That any attempt on the part of a non-American State against the integrity or inviolability of the territory, the sovereignty or the political independence of an American State be considered as an act of aggression against all the American States (Declaration of the Second Meeting of the Ministers of Foreign Affairs, Habana, 1940).

(6) The furtherance of these principles, which the American States have practiced in order to secure peace and solidarity between the nations of the continent, constitutes an effective means of contributing to the general system of world security and of facilitating its establishment: and

(7) The security and solidarity of the continent are affected to the same extent by an act of aggression against any of the American States by a non-American State, as by an American State against one or more American States.

Part I, Declaration, The Government Represented at the Inter-American Conference on War and Peace Declare:

First. That all sovereign States are juridically equal amongst themselves.

Second. That every State has the right to the respect of its individuality and independence, on the part of the other members of the international community.

Third. That every attack of a State against the integrity or the inviolability of territory, or against the sovereignty or political independence of an American State, shall, conformably to Part III hereof, be considered as an act of aggression against the other States which sign this declaration. In any case, invasion by armed forces of one State into the territory of another trespassing boundaries established by treaty and demarcated in accordance there with shall constitute an act of aggression.

Fourth. That in case acts of aggression occur or there may be reasons to believe that an aggression is being prepared by any other State against the integrity and inviolability of territory, or against the sovereignty or political independence of an American State, the States signatory to this declaration will consult amongst themselves in order to agree upon measures it may be advisable to take.

Fifth. That during the war, and until the treaty recommended in Part II hereof is concluded, the signatories of this declaration recognize that such threats and acts of aggression as indicated in paragraphs Third and Fourth above constitute an interference with the war effort of the United Nations, calling for such procedures, within the scope of their constitutional powers of a general nature and for war, as may be found necessary, including:

recall of chiefs of diplomatic missions;
breaking of diplomatic relations;
breaking of consular relations;
breaking of postal, telegraphic, telephonic, radio-telephonic relations;
interruption of economic, commercial and financial relations;
use of armed force to prevent or repeal aggression.

Sixth. That the principles and procedure contained in this declaration shall become effective immediately, inasmuch as any act of aggression or threat of aggression during the present state of war interferes with the war effort of the United Nations to obtain victory. Henceforth, and with the view that the principles and procedure herein stipulated shall conform with the constitutional principles of each republic, the respective Governments shall take the necessary steps to perfect this instrument on order that it shall be in force at all times.

Part II. Recommendation. The Inter-American Conference on Problems of War and Peace

Recommends:

That for the purpose of meeting threats or acts of aggression against any American republic following the establishment of peace, the Governments of the American republics should consider the conclusion, in accordance with their constitutional processes, of a treaty establishing procedures whereby such threats or acts may be met by:

The use, by all or some of the signatories of said treaty of any one or more of the following measures:
recall of chiefs of diplomatic missions;
breaking of diplomatic relations;
breaking of consular relations;
breaking of postal, telegraphic, telephonic, radio-telephonic relations;
interruption of economic, commercial and financial relations;
use of armed force to prevent or repeal aggression.

Part III. This declaration and recommendation provide for a regional arrangement for dealing with matters relating to the maintenance of international peace and security as are appropriate for regional action in this hemisphere and said arrangements and the activities and procedures referred to therein shall be consistent with the purposes and principles of the general international organization, when established. This declaration and recommendation shall be known as the Act of Chapultepec."

The regional treaty mentioned in Part III was signed on Sept. 2, 1947 and is known as the ▷ Inter-American Treaty of Reciprocal Assistance. That section of the Chapultepec Act regarding regional treaties was used as a model for the ▷ United Nations Charter.

US Department of State Bulletin, No. 297, Mar. 4, 1945; *Acta Final de la Conferencia de las Problemas de Guerra y de la Paz*, Washington, DC, 1945; P.L. MOLINAR *Aprobación del Acta de Chapultepec y la Carta de las NU*, Buenos Aires, 1946; A. DE ROSENZWEIG, *El Acta de Chapultepec*, México, DF, 1946.

CHAPULTEPEC CONFERENCE, 1945.

The Inter-American Conference on War and Peace, Conferencia Interamericana sobre Problema de la Guerra y de la Paz held on Feb. 21–Mar. 8, 1945 in the historic Chapultepec Castle in Mexico City; elaborated and confirmed the following:

Agreement on Mutual Aid and American Solidarity, named ▷ Chapultepec Act.
Economic Charter of the Americas, Carta Economica de las Americas.
Charter of the Woman and Child, Carta de la Mujer y de Nino.
Declaration of Mexico on Essential Normative Rules in Relations Between States, Declaration de Mexico sobre principios como normatives de las relaciones entre los Estados.
Declaration of Social Principles of the Americas, Declaración de Principios Sociales de Americas.
Recommendations on the Constitution of a Permanent Military Organism. Recomendacion sobre constitucion de un organismo militar permanente.
Recommendations on Freedom of Information, Recomendacion sobre libertad de informacion.

Besides, the Conference passed a number of resolutions, among others, on armament control, on the need of setting up an International General Organization (UNO), on including the rules of international law in the law, on international protection of human rights against racial discrimination, on reorganization, consolidation and improvement of the international system, on the international system of preserving peace, on development of transportation and industry, on trade in basic raw materials. These resolutions anticipated the standpoint of American states on the Conference in San Francisco in 1945, and a number of initiatives on the forum of UN and of UN specialized organizations.

Final Act of the Chapultepec Conference, Washington, DC, 1945; A. GARCIA ROBLES, *El Mundo de la Postguerra*, 2 Vols., México, DF, 1946.

CHARGE D'AFFAIRES.

French phrase meaning one who performs the duties of the head of a diplomatic mission in his absence (▷ Ad interim) in accordance with the regulations of the Diplomatic Convention of Vienna, 1961. In the diplomatic convention of the Congress of Vienna, 1815, Chargés d'affaires were diplomats appointed not by the head of state but by the minister of foreign affairs, and for that reason were given the title Chargé d'affaires à pied, vel en titre or ad hoc.

R.L. BLEDSOE, B.A. BOCZEK, *The International Law Dictionary*, Oxford, 1987.

CHARITY.

A subject of international co-operation. Organizations reg. with the UIA:

Brothers of Hope, Frères des espérance, f. 1971, Paris.
Brothers to all Men, Frères de nos Frères, f. 1965, Paris.
International Association of Charities of St Vincent, f. 1933, Brussels.
Comitas Internationalis (International Conference of Catholic Charities), f. 1951, Rome. Consultative status with ECOSOC, UNESCO, FAO, UNICEF, ILO.
World Brotherhood, Fraternité Mondiale, f. 1950, Geneva. Consultative status with UNESCO.

Yearbook of International Organizations.

CHARTER AGREEMENTS.

Concern carriage by sea of specified goods; specific agreements are drawn up by appropriate international organizations, one of the first, concluded at the Baltic International Maritime Coal Charter Conference 1921 framed forms of agreements for charter of, among other commodities sugar, salt, ores, grain, scrap, artificial fertilizers. In 1926 the Baltic Wood Charter, concerning shipment of wood on the Baltic was signed.

CHARTER FLIGHTS.

International term for non-scheduled flights booked for the purpose of transporting a group of people organized by any institution whatsoever, at rates generally lower than the mandatory tariff of IATA for regular flights.

J. BES, *Chartering Practice. Analysis of Charter Parties*, Amsterdam, 1960.

CHARTER FOR HEALTH DEVELOPMENT. ▷

Asian Charter for Health Development, 1980.

CHARTER OF AFRICAN AND MALAGASY COMMON ORGANIZATION, OCAM, 1966.

Signed in Tananarive on June 27, 1966, by the governments of Cameroon, the Central African Republic, Chad, Congo, Dahomey, Gabon, Ivory Coast, Malagasy Republic, Niger, Rwanda, Senegal, Togo, Upper Volta and Zaïre, which came into force on Dec. 28, 1967. The text is as follows:

"The Heads of African and Malagasy States and Governments, assembled at Tananarive from 25 to 28 June, 1966.

Desiring to provide solid foundations for African unity, True to the spirit, principles and objectives of the Charter of the United Nations and the Charter of the Organization of African Unity.

Considering the decision of the Conference of the Heads of African and Malagasy States, held at Noukchott in February, 1965.

Considering the historical, economic, social and cultural bonds existing between their respective countries.

Considering the need to harmonize their economic, social and cultural policies for the purpose of maintaining conditions for progress and security,

Have agreed as follows:

Art. 1. The High Contracting Parties do by this Charter establish an organization to be known as the African and Malagasy Common Organization, OCAM. This Organization shall be open to any independent and sovereign African State that requests admission and accepts the provisions of this Charter.

The admission of a new member to the OCAM shall require a unanimous decision of the members of the Organization.

Art. 2. The OCAM is based on the solidarity which unites its members. In the spirit of the Organization of African Unity, its purpose is to strengthen co-operation and solidarity between the African and Malagasy States in order to accelerate their economic, social, technical and cultural development.

Art. 3. For this purpose, the Organization shall seek to harmonize the action of Member States in the economic, social, technical and cultural fields, to co-ordinate their development programmes, and to facilitate foreign policy consultations between them, with due respect for the sovereignty and fundamental options of each Member State.

Art. 4. The institutions and organs of the Organization shall be:
– The Conference of Heads of State and Government;
– the Council of Ministers;
– the Administrative General Secretariat.

Art. 5. The Conference of Heads of State and Government shall be the supreme authority of the Organization. It shall consist of the Heads of State and Government of the Member States or their duly authorized representatives.

Art. 6. The Conference shall consider questions of common interest and take its decisions in accordance with the provisions of this Charter and the rules of procedure of the Conference.

Art. 7. The Conference of Heads of State and Government shall meet once a year in regular session. The Conference shall meet in special session at the request of a Member State and subject to the formal approval of two thirds of the members of the Organization.

The agenda of a special session shall contain, in principle, only the questions for which the Conference has been convened.

Art. 8. The Conference shall formulate and adopt its own rules of procedure.

Art. 9. Each Member State shall have one vote. Any Member State may be represented by another Member State, which shall have the right to vote at the place specified in the proxy. A Member State may be represented by only one other Member State. Two thirds of the Member States of the Organization shall constitute a quorum.

Any decision taken under the conditions of a quorum or required majority shall be binding on all Member States.

Art. 10. The Council of Ministers shall consist of the Ministers for Foreign Affairs of the Member States, or of such other Ministers as may be designated by the Governments of the Member States.

It shall meet once a year in regular session.

The regular session shall be held a few days before the annual regular session of the Conference of Heads of State and Government and in the same place.

Art. 11. The Council shall meet in special session at the request of a Member State and subject to the formal approval of two thirds of the Members of the Organization. The agenda of a special session of the Council shall contain only the questions for which the Council has been convened.

Art. 12. The Council of Ministers shall be responsible to the Conference of Heads of State and Government. It shall be responsible for preparing for that Conference, shall take cognizance of any matter referred to it by the Conference, and shall ensure that the decisions of the Conference are implemented.

It shall ensure that the Member States co-operate with each other in accordance with the instructions of the Conference of Heads of State and Government, in conformity with this Charter.

Art. 13. Each Member State shall have one vote.

Any Member State may be represented by another Member State.

Two thirds of the Member States shall constitute a quorum.

Art. 14. The Council shall formulate and adopt its own rules of procedure.

Art. 15. The African and Malagasy Common Organization shall have an Administrative General Secretariat, with its headquarters at Yaounde, Federal Republic of Cameroon.

The Administrative General Secretariat shall be appointed for two years by the Conference of Heads of State and Government on the recommendation of the Council of Ministers. His term of office may be renewed.

Art. 16. Under the authority of the President of the Conference, the Administrative Secretary-General shall be responsible for the administrative functioning of the various organs of the Organization.

The rules of procedure of the Conference of Heads of State shall specify the conditions in which another person may replace the Administrative Secretary-General if he is incapacitated, or if a vacancy occurs.

Art. 17. The Administrative General Secretariat shall be divided into departments corresponding to the main fields of activity of the Organization.

It shall supervise the activities of joint enterprises, particularly the multinational airline, Air-Afrique, and the African and Malagasy Postal and Telecommunications Union.

Art. 18. The Conference may dismiss the Administrative Secretary-General in the same manner as it appoints him, when the proper functioning of the Organization warrants it.

Art. 19. The conditions governing the employment of the staff of the Administrative General Secretariat shall be defined in a Convention to be concluded between the Member States of the Organization.

Art. 20. The budget of the Organization, to be prepared by the Administrative Secretary-General, shall be approved by the Conference of Heads of State and Government on the recommendation of the Council of Ministers.

It shall be financed by the contributions of the Member States, to be determined on the basis of the net amount of their respective operational budgets.

However, the contribution of a Member State may not exceed 20 per cent of the annual regular budget of the Organization. The Member States agree to pay their respective contributions regularly at the specified time.

Art. 21. This Charter shall be ratified or approved by the signatory States in accordance with their constitutional procedures.

The original instrument shall be deposited with the Government of the Federal Republic of Cameroon, which shall notify the deposit thereof to all signatory States.

Art. 22. This Charter shall enter into force upon receipt by the Government of the Federal Republic of Cameroon of the instruments of ratification or approval of two thirds of the signatory States.

Art. 23. After it has been duly ratified or approved, this Charter shall be registered with the United Nations Secretariat by the Government of the Federal Republic of Cameroon, in accordance with Article 102 of the Charter of the United Nations.

Art. 24. Any decision concerning the interpretation of this Charter must be taken by a two-thirds majority of the Member States of the Organization.

Art. 25. The Administrative Secretary-General may accept, on behalf of the Organization, any gifts, contributions, or bequests to the Organization, subject to the approval of the Council of Ministers. They shall be taken over by the budget of the Organization.

Art. 26. A convention between the Member States shall define the privileges and immunities to be granted to the staff of the Administrative General Secretariat.

Art. 27. Any State that wishes to withdraw from the Organization shall so inform the Administrative General Secretariat in writing.

The latter shall notify the Member States.

One year after such notification, this Charter shall cease to apply to that State, which will consequently no longer be a member of the Organization.

Art. 28. This Charter may be amended or revised if a Member State sends a written request to that effect to the Administrative General Secretariat.

The draft amendment or revision shall not be submitted to the Conference until all the Member States have been duly informed and one year has elapsed since the date of submission of the amendment.

The amendment or revision shall not become effective until it has been ratified or approved by two thirds of the Member States of the Organization."

UNTS, Vol. 637, pp. 249–261.

CHARTER OF AFRICAN AND MALAGASY UNION, AMU, 1961.
Signed on Dec. 12, 1961 in Tananarive by the governments of Chad, Cameroon, Dahomey (now Benin), Gabon, Upper Volta (now Burkina Faso), Democratic Republic of Congo (now Zaïre), Mauritania, Niger, Malagasy Republic, the Central African Republic, Senegal, Ivory Coast, each of them belonging to the ▷ Brazzaville Group of French-speaking states. In

1962 the Charter was signed by Guinea, Rwanda and Togo. The main point of the Charter was as follows:

"The African and Malagasy Union is a union of independent and sovereign states open to all independent African states. In keeping with the principle of solidarity AMU aims to organize co-operation among its members at all levels of foreign policy with a view to consolidate solidarity, guarantee collective security, promote progress and maintain peace in Africa, Madagascar and worldwide."

Arts 3–6 of the Charter appointed as organs of the AMU: the Conference of Heads of State and Government, meetings of ministers, the AMU secretariat affiliated with the UN, the secretariat general seated in Cotonou, Dahomey, the African–Malagasy Organization for Economic Co-operation, the Defensive Pact Organization and Postal and Telecommunications Union.

M. LIONS, *Constitucionalismo y Democracia en el Africa Recien Independizada*, México, DF, 1964, pp. 170–173.

CHARTER OF AFRICAN STATES UNION, 1961.
Signed on Apr. 28, 1961 by the governments of Ghana, Guinea and Mali in Accra in order to create a nucleus for the United States of Africa: work out a common orientation in domestic policies to bring about "complete decolonization through a change in the structures inherited after the colonial regime and arrangement of exploitation of national resources to the benefit of the people"; rehabilitate and develop African culture and establish joint defence. The Conference of Heads of State was made the supreme organ of the Union which dissolved in 1965, following a change of Ghana's government.

"Charter for the OAS", in: *International Organization*, Vol. XVI, 1962; J. CONTRERAS, *El Panafricanismo*, México, DF, 1971, pp. 341–344.

CHARTER OF ALLIANCE OF PROGRESS. ▷ PUNTA DEL ESTE CHARTER, 1961.

CHARTER OF COUNCIL FOR MUTUAL ECONOMIC ASSISTANCE, CMEA, 1959.
Signed in Sofia on Dec. 14, 1959 by the governments of the USSR, Albania, Bulgaria, Czechoslovakia, Hungary, the GDR, Poland and Romania. The text is as follows:

"The Governments of the People's Republic of Albania, the People's Republic of Bulgaria, the Hungarian People's Republic, the German Democratic Republic, the Polish People's Republic, the Romanian People's Republic, the Union of Soviet Socialist Republics and the Czechoslovak Republic,

Bearing in mind that the economic co-operation which is successfully taking place between their countries helps to promote the most rational development of the national economy, to raise the level of living of the people and to strengthen the unity and solidarity of those countries;

Determined to continue the development of comprehensive economic co-operation based on consistent implementation of the international socialist division of labour in the interests of the building of socialism and communism in their countries and the maintenance of lasting peace throughout the world;

Convinced that the development of economic co-operation between their countries contributes to the achievement of the purposes set forth in the Charter of the United Nations;

Affirming their readiness to develop economic relations with all countries, irrespective of their social and political structure, on the basis of equality, mutual advantage and non-intervention in each other's domestic affairs;

Recognizing the increasing importance of the part played by the Council for Mutual Economic Assistance in the organizing of economic co-operation between their countries,

Have agreed, to these ends, to adopt the present Charter.

Art. I(1) The purpose of the Council for Mutual Economic Assistance is to promote, by uniting and co-ordinating the efforts of the member countries of the Council, the planned development of the national economies and the acceleration of the economic and technical progress of those countries, the raising of the level of industrialization of the countries with a less-developed industry, and a continual growth in the productivity, together with a steady increase in the well-being of the peoples, of the member countries of the Council.

(2) The Council for Mutual Economic Assistance is based on the principle of the sovereign equality of all the member countries of the Council.

Economic and scientific-technical co-operation between the member countries of the Council shall take place in accordance with the principles of complete equality of rights, respect for sovereignty and national interest, mutual advantage and friendly mutual aid.

Art. II.(1) The original members of the Council for Mutual Economic Assistance shall be the countries which have signed and ratified the present Charter.

(2) Membership in the Council shall be open to other European countries which subscribe to the purpose and principles of the Council and declare that they agree to accept the obligations contained in the present Charter. New members shall be admitted by a decision of the Session of the Council, on the basis of official requests by countries for their admission to membership in the Council.

(3) Any member country of the Council may leave the Council, after notifying the depositary of the present Charter to that effect. Such notice shall take effect six months after its receipt by the depositary. Upon receiving such notice, the depositary shall inform the member countries of the Council thereof.

(4) The member countries of the Council agree:

(a) To ensure implementation of the recommendations, accepted by them, of organs of the Council;

(b) To render to the Council and its officers the necessary assistance in the execution of the duties laid upon them by the present Charter;

(c) To make available to the Council the material and information essential to the fulfilment of the tasks entrusted to it;

(d) To keep the Council informed of progress in the implementation of the recommendations adopted in the Council.

Art. III.(1) In conformity with the purposes and principles set forth in Art. I of the present Charter, the Council for Mutual Economic Assistance shall:

(a) Organize:

Comprehensive economic and scientific-technical co-operation among the member countries of the Council, with a view to the most rational use of their natural resources and the more rapid development of their productive forces;

The preparation of recommendations on the most important questions in the economic relations resulting from the plans for the development of the national economies of the member countries of the Council, for the purpose of co-ordinating those plans;

The study of economic problems which are of interest to the member countries of the Council:

(b) Assist the member countries of the Council in the preparation and execution of joint measures regarding: The development of industry and agriculture in the member countries of the Council, based on consistent implementation of the international socialist division of labour and on specialization and co-operation in production; The development of transport, for the primary purpose of ensuring the conveyance of the increasing volume of export-import and transit freight between member countries of the Council; The most effective use of the capital invested by member countries of the Council in projects to be carried out on the basis of joint participation. The development of the exchange of goods and services between member countries of the Council and with other countries; The exchange of experience in the matter of scientific-technical achievements and advanced methods of production;

(c) Undertake other action required for achieving the purposes of the Council.

(2) The Council for Mutual Economic Assistance, through its organs acting within their competence, is authorized to adopt recommendations and decisions in accordance with the present Charter.

Art. IV.(1) Recommendations shall be adopted on questions of economic and scientific-technical co-operation. Such recommendations shall be communicated to the member countries of the Council for consideration. Recommendations adopted by member countries of the Council shall be implemented by them through decisions of the Governments or competent authorities of those countries, in conformity with their laws.

(2) Decisions shall be adopted on organizational and procedural questions. Such decisions shall take effect, unless it is specified otherwise in them, from the date on which the record of the meeting of the Council organ concerned is signed.

(3) All recommendations and decisions of the Council shall be adopted only with the consent of the member countries concerned, each country being entitled to state its interest in any question under consideration by the Council. Recommendations and decisions shall not apply to countries which state that they have no interest in the question at issue. Nevertheless, each such country may subsequently associate itself with the recommendations and decisions adopted by the remaining member countries of the Council.

Art. V.(1) For the discharge of the functions and the exercise of the powers mentioned in article III of the present Charter, the Council for Mutual Economic Assistance shall have the following principal organs:

The Session of the Council,

The Conference of representatives of the countries in the Council,

The Standing Commissions,

The Secretariat.

(2) Other organs may be established, as necessary, in conformity with the present Charter.

Art. VI.(1) The Session of the Council shall be the highest organ of the Council for Mutual Economic Assistance. It shall be authorized to discuss all questions falling within the competence of the Council, and to adopt recommendations and decisions in accordance with the present Charter.

(2) The Session of the Council shall consist of delegations from all the member countries of the Council. The composition of the delegation of each country shall be determined by the Government of the country concerned.

(3) The regular sessions of the Council shall be convened twice a year in the capital of each member country of the Council in turn, under the chairmanship of the head of the delegation of the country in which the session is held.

(4) A special session of the Council may be convened at the request or with the consent of not less than one third of the member countries of the Council.

(5) The Session of the Council shall:

(a) Consider:

Proposals on questions of economic and scientific-technical co-operation submitted by member countries of the Council, as well as by the Conference of representatives of the countries in the Council, the Standing Commissions and the Secretariat of the Council; The report of the Secretariat of the Council on the activity of the Council;

(b) Determine the course of action of the other organs of the Council, and the main questions for the agenda of the next session of the Council;

(c) Perform such other functions as may be found necessary for achieving the purposes of the Council.

(6) The Session of the Council is authorized to establish such organs as it may consider necessary for the discharge of the functions entrusted to the Council.

(7) The Session of the Council shall establish its own rules of procedure.

Art. VII.(1) The Conference of representatives of the countries in the Council for Mutual Economic Assistance shall consist of representatives of all member countries of the Council, one for each country. The representative of a country in the Council shall have, at the headquarters of the Secretariat of the Council, a deputy together with the necessary number of advisers and other staff. The deputy, when so authorized by the representative, shall perform the functions of representative in the Conference.

(2) The Conference shall hold its meetings as necessary.

(3) Within its field of competence, the Conference shall have the right to adopt recommendations and decisions in conformity with the present Charter. The Conference may also submit proposals for consideration by the Session of the Council.

(4) The Conference shall:

(a) Consider proposals from the member countries of the Council, the Standing Commissions and the Secretariat of the Council regarding the implementation of the recommendations and decisions of the Session of the Council, as well as other questions connected with economic and scientific-technical co-operation which need to be settled in the period between sessions of the Council;

(b) Engage in preliminary discussion, where necessary, of the proposals made be member countries of the Council, by the Standing Commissions and by the Secretariat of the Council regarding items for the agenda of the next session of the Council;

(c) Co-ordinate the work of the Standing Commissions of the Council, and study their reports on the work completed and on future activities;

(d) Approve:

The personnel and budget of the Secretariat of the Council, and the report of the Secretariat on the operation of the budget;

The regulation for the Standing Commissions and Secretariat of the Council;

(e) Establish control organs for supervising the financial activity of the Secretariat of the Council;

(f) Perform other functions arising from the present Charter and from the recommendations and decisions of the Session of the Council;

(5) The Conference may set up auxiliary organs for preparatory work in regard to items of the agenda.

(6) The Conference shall establish its own rule of procedure.

Art. VIII.(1) Standing Commissions of the Council for Mutual Economic Assistance shall be set up by the Session of the Council for the purpose of promoting the further development of economic relations between the member countries of the Council and organizing comprehensive economic and scientific-technical co-operation in the various sectors of the national economies of those countries. The regulations for the Standing Commissions shall be approved by the Conference of representatives of the countries in the Council.

(2) Each member country of the Council shall appoint its representatives to the Standing Commissions.

(3) The Standing Commissions shall have the right, within their field of competence, to adopt recommendations and decisions in conformity with the present Charter. The Commissions may also submit proposals for consideration by the Session of the Council and the Conference of Representatives of the countries in the Council.

(4) The Standing Commissions shall work out measures and prepare proposals for implementing the economic and scientific-technical co-operation mentioned in paragraph 1 of this article; they shall also perform other functions arising from the present Charter and from the recommendations and decisions of the Session of the Council and of the Conference of representatives of the countries in the Council. The Standing Commissions shall submit to the Conference of representatives of the countries in the Council annual reports on the work done and on their future activities.

(5) The meetings of the Standing Commissions shall, as a rule, be held at their permanent headquarters, which shall be designated by the session of the Council.

(6) The Standing Commissions may establish auxiliary organs, as necessary. The composition and terms of reference of such organs, and their place of meeting, shall be determined by the Commissions.

(7) Each Standing Commission shall have a secretariat, headed by the secretary of the Commission. The establishment pertaining to the secretariat of a Commission shall be a part of the Secretariat of the Council and shall be maintained from the budget of the Council.

(8) The Standing Commissions shall establish their own rules of procedure.

Art. IX.(1) The Secretariat of the Council for Mutual Economic Assistance shall consist of the Secretary of the Council, his deputies and such personnel as may be required for the performance of the functions entrusted to the Secretariat. The Secretary and his deputies shall be appointed by the Session of the Council and shall direct the work of the Secretariat of the Council. The personnel of the Secretariat shall be recruited from citizens of the member countries of the Council, in accordance with the regulations for the Secretariat of the Council.

The Secretary of the Council shall be the chief officer of the Council. He shall represent the Council vis-a-vis officials and organizations of the member countries of the Council and other countries, and vis-a-vis international organizations. The Secretary of the Council may authorize his deputies, as well as other members of the Secretariat to act on his behalf.

The Secretary and his deputies may take part in all meetings of the organs of the Council.

(2) The Secretariat of the Council shall:

(a) Submit a report on the Council's activity to the regular session of the Council:

(b) Assist in the preparation and conduct of meetings of the Session of the Council, the Conference of representatives of the countries in the Council and the Standing Commissions of the Council, and of meetings convened by decision of those organs of the Council;

(c) Prepare, when so instructed by the Session of the Council or by the Conference of representativeness of the countries in the Council, economic surveys and studies on the basis of material submitted by member countries of the Council, and publish material on questions regarding economic and scientific-technical co-operation between those countries;

(d) Prepare:

Proposals concerning the work of the Council, for consideration in the appropriate organs of the Council; Information and guidance on questions involved in economic and scientific-technical co-operation between member countries of the Council;

(e) Organize, jointly with the Standing Commissions of the Council, the preparation of draft multilateral agreements on questions arising from economic and scientific-technical co-operation, on the basis of recommendations and decisions adopted by the session of the Council and by the Conference of represenatives of the countries in the Council;

(f) Undertake other action arising out of the present Charter, the recommendations and decisions adopted in the Council, and the regulations for the Secretariat of the Council.

(3) The Secretary of the Council, his deputies and the personnel of the Secretariat, when fulfilling the duties entrusted to them, act as international officials.

(4) The headquarters of the Secretariat of the Council shall be in Moscow.

Art. X. The Council for Mutual Economic Assistance may invite countries which are not members of the Council to take part in the work of the organs of the Council.

The conditions under which the representatives of such countries may participate in the work of the organs of the Council shall be determined by the Council in agreement with the countries concerned.

Art. XI. The Council for Mutual Economic Assistance may establish and maintain relations with the economic organizations of the United Nations and with other international organizations.

The nature and form of such relations shall be determined by the Council in agreement with the international organizations concerned.

Art. XII.(1) The member countries of the Council for Mutual Economic Assistance shall bear the cost of maintaining the Secretariat and of financing its activity. The share of this cost falling to each member country shall be determined by the Session of the Council. Other financial questions shall be dealt with by the Conference of representatives of the countries in the Council.

(2) The Secretariat of the Council shall submit to the Conference of Representatives of the countries in the Council a report on the operation of the budget for each calendar year.

(3) The maintenance expenses of participants in the meetings of the Session of the Council, the Conference of representatives of the countries in the Council and the Standing Commissions of the Council, and in all meetings held within the framework of the Council, shall be borne by the country sending its representatives to those meetings.

(4) The expense involved in the servicing of the meetings mentioned in paragraph 3 of this article shall be borne by the country in which those meetings are held.

Art. XIII.(1) The Council for Mutual Economic Assistance shall enjoy, on the territories of all member countries of the Council, the legal capacity essential to the performance of its functions and the achievement of its purposes.

(2) The Council, as also the representatives of the member countries of the Council and the officers of the Council, shall enjoy, on the territory of each of those countries, the privileges and immunities which are necessary for the performance of the functions and the achievements of the purposes set forth in the present Charter.

(3) The legal capacity, privileges and immunities mentioned in this article shall be defined in a special Convention.

(4) The provisions of the present Charter shall not affect the rights and obligations of the member countries of the Council arising out of their membership of other international organizations, or out of international treaties which they have concluded.

Art. XIV. The official languages of the Council for Mutual Economic Assistance shall be the languages of all the member countries of the Council.

The working language of the Council shall be Russian.

Art. XV.(1) The present Charter shall be ratified by the signatory countries, in accordance with their constitutional procedure.

(2) The instruments of ratification shall be deposited with the depositary of the present Charter.

(3) The present Charter shall enter into force immediately after the deposit of instruments of ratification by all the countries which have signed the Charter, and the depositary shall notify those countries thereof.

(4) With respect to each country which in accordance with Article II, paragraph 2, is admitted to membership in the Council for Mutual Economic Assistance and which ratifies the Charter, this Charter shall enter into force from the date of the deposit by such country of its instrument of ratification of the Charter, and the depositary shall notify the other member countries of the Council thereof.

Art. XVI. Each member country of the Council for Mutual Economic Assistance may make proposals for the amendment of the present Charter.

Amendments to the Charter, when approved by the Session of the Council, shall come into force immediately after the ratifications of those amendments have been deposited with the depositary by all member countries of the Council.

Art. XVII. This Charter has been drawn up in a single copy, in the Russian language. It shall be deposited with the Government of the Union of Soviet Socialist Republics, which shall send certified true copies of the Charter to the Governments of all the other member countries of the Council and shall notify those Governments, and the Secretary of the Council, of the deposit of the instruments of ratification with the Government of the USSR.

In witness whereof the representatives of the Government of the member countries of the Council for Mutual Economic Assistance have signed the present Charter.

UNTS, Vol. 368, pp. 264–282.

CHARTER OF ECONOMIC RIGHTS AND DUTIES OF STATES, 1974. Adopted by the UN Geneva Assembly Res. 328/XXIX on Dec. 12, 1974 by 120 countries for, 6 against (Belgium, Denmark, FRG, Luxembourg the UK and the USA) and 10 abstentions (Austria, Canada, France, Ireland, Israel, Italy, Japan, the Netherlands, Norway and Spain). The idea of the Charter was presented in the Third UNCTAD Session, on Apr. 19, 1972 in Santiago de Chile by the president of Mexico, Luis Echeverria. The text is as follows:

"Preamble.

The General Assembly, reaffirming the fundamental purposes of United Nations, in particular the maintenance of international peace and security, the development of friendly relations among nations and the achievement of international co-operation in solving international problems in the economic and social fields. Affirming the need for strengthening international co-operation in these fields. Reaffirming further the need for strengthening international co-operation for development. Declaring that it is a funda-

mental purpose of the present Charter to promote the establishment of the new international economic order, based on equity, sovereign equality, independence, common interest and co-operation among all States, irrespective of their economic and social systems. Desirous of contributing to the creation of conditions for: (a) The attainment of wider prosperity among all countries and of higher standards of living for all peoples; (b) The promotion by the entire international community of the economic and social progress of all countries, especially developing countries; (c) The encouragement of co-operation, on the basis of mutual advantage and equitable benefits for all peace-loving States which are willing to carry out the provisions of the present Charter, in the economic, trade, scientific and technical fields, regardless of political, economic or social systems; (d) The overcoming of main obstacles in the way of the economic development of the developing countries; (e) The acceleration of the economic growth of developing countries with a view to bridging the economic gap between developing and developed countries; (f) The protection, preservation and enhancement of the environment.

Mindful of the need to establish and maintain a just and equitable economic and social order through: (a) The achievement of more rational and equitable international economic relations and the encouragement of structural changes in the world economy; (b) The creation of conditions which permit the further expansion of trade and intensification of economic co-operation among all nations; (c) The strengthening of the economic independence of developing countries; (d) The establishment and promotion of international economic relations, taking into account the agreed differences in the development of the developing countries and their specific needs. Determined to promote collective economic security for development, in particular of the developing countries, with strict respect for the sovereign equality of each State and through the co-operation of the entire international community. Considering that genuine co-operation among States, based on joint consideration of and concerted action regarding international economic problems, is essential for fulfilling the international community's common desire to achieve a just and rational development of all parts of the world. Stressing the importance of ensuring appropriate conditions for the conduct of normal economic relations among all States, irrespective of differences in social and economic systems, and for the full respect of the rights of all peoples, as well as strengthening instruments of international economic co-operation as a means for the consolidation of peace for the benefit of all. Convinced of the need to develop a system of international economic relations on the basis of sovereign equality, mutual and equitable benefit and the close inter-relationship of the interests of all States. Reiterating that the responsibility for the development of every country rests primarily upon itself but that concomitant and effective international co-operation is an essential factor for the full achievement of its own development goals. Firmly convinced of the urgent need to evolve a substantially improved system of international economic relations. Solemnly adopts the present Charter of Economic Rights and Duties of States.

Chapter I. Fundamentals of International Economic Relations.

Economic as well as political and other relations among States shall be governed, inter alia, by the following principles: (a) Sovereignty, territorial integrity and political independence of States; (b) Sovereign equality of all States; (c) Non-aggression; (d) Non-intervention; (e) Mutual and equitable benefit; (f) Peaceful coexistence; (g) Equal rights and self-determination of peoples; (h) Peaceful settlement of disputes; (i) Remedying of injustices which have been brought about by force and which deprive a nation of natural means necessary for its normal development; (j) Fulfilment in good faith of international obligations; (k) Respect for human rights and fundamental freedoms; (l) No attempt to seek hegemony and spheres of influence; (m) Promotion of international social justice; (n) International co-operation for development; (o) Free access to and from the sea by land-locked countries within the framework of the above principles.

Chapter II. Economic Rights and Duties of States.

Art. 1. Every State has the sovereign and inalienable right to choose its economic system as well as its political, social and cultural systems in accordance with the will of its people, without outside interference, coercion or threat in any form whatsoever.

Art. 2.(1) Every State has and shall freely exercise full permanent sovereignty, including possession, use and disposal, over all its wealth, natural resources and economic activities.

(2) Each State has the right: (a) To regulate and exercise authority over foreign investment within its national jurisdiction in accordance with its laws and regulations and in conformity with its national objectives and priorities. No State shall be compelled to grant preferential treatment to foreign investment; (b) To regulate and supervise the activities of transnational corporations within its natural jurisdiction and take measures to ensure that such activities comply with its laws, rules, and regulations and conform with its economic and social policies. Transnational corporations shall not intervene in the internal affairs of a host State. Every State should, with full regard for its sovereign rights, co-operate with other States in the exercise of the right set forth in this subparagraph; (c) To nationalize, expropriate or transfer ownership of foreign property, in which case appropriate compensation should be paid by the State adopting such measures, taking into account its relevant laws and regulations and all circumstances that the State considers pertinent. In any case where the question of compensation gives rise to a controversy, it shall be settled under the domestic law of the nationalizing State and by its tribunals, unless it is freely and mutually agreed by all States concerned that other peaceful means be sought on the basis of the sovereign equality of States and in accordance with the principle of free choice of means.

Art. 3. In the exploitation of natural resources shared by two or more countries, each State must co-operate on the basis of a system of information and prior consultations in order to achieve optimum use of such resources without causing damage to the legitimate interest of others.

Art. 4. Every State has the right to engage in international trade and other forms of economic co-operation, irrespective of any differences in political, economic and social systems. No State shall be subjected to discrimination of any kind based solely on such differences. In the pursuit of international trade and other forms of economic co-operation, every State is free to choose the forms of organization of its foreign economic relations and to enter into bilateral and multilateral arrangements consistent with its international obligations and with the needs of international economic co-operation.

Art. 5. All States have the right to associate in organizations of primary commodity producers in order to develop their national economies, to achieve stable financing to their development and, in pursuance of their aims, to assist in the promotion of sustained growth of the world economy, in particular accelerating the development of developing countries. Correspondingly all States have the duty to respect that right by refraining from applying economic and political measures that would limit it.

Art. 6. It is the duty of States to contribute to the development of international trade of goods, particularly by means of arrangements and by the conclusion of long-term multilateral commodity agreements, where appropriate and taking into account the interests of producers and consumers. All States share the responsibility to promote the regular flow and access of all commercial goods traded at stable remunerative and equitable prices, thus contributing to the equitable development of the world economy, taking into account, in particular, the interests of developing countries.

Art. 7. Every State has the primary responsibility to promote the economic, social and cultural development of its people. To this end, each State has the right and the responsibility to choose its means and goals of development, fully to mobilize and use its resource, to implement progressive economic and social reforms and to ensure the full participation of its people in the process and benefits of development. All States have the duty, individually and collectively, to co-operate in eliminating obstacles that hinder such mobilization and use.

Art. 8. States should co-operate in facilitating more rational and equitable international economic relations and in encouraging structural changes in the context of a balanced world economy in harmony with the needs and interests of all countries, especially developing countries, and should take appropriate measures to this end.

Art. 9. All States have the responsibility to co-operate in the economic, social, cultural, scientific and technological fields for the promotion of economic and social progress throughout the world, especially that of the developing countries.

Art. 10. All States are juridically equal and, as equal members of the international community, have the right to participate fully and effectively in the international decision-making process in the solution of world economic, financial and monetary problems, inter alia, through the appropriate international organizations in accordance with their existing and evolving rules, and to share equitably in the benefits resulting there from.

Art. 11. All States should co-operate strengthen and continuously improve the efficiency of international organizations in implementing measures to stimulate the general economic progress of all countries, particularly of developing countries, and therefore should co-operate to adapt them, when appropriate to the changing needs of international economic co-operation.

Art. 12.(1) States have the right, in agreement with the parties concerned, to participate in subregional, regional and inter-regional co-operation in the pursuit of their economic and social development. All States engaged in such co-operation have the duty to ensure that the policies of those groupings to which they belong correspond to the provisions of the present Charter and are outward-looking, consistent with their international obligations and with the needs of international economic co-operation, and have full regard for the legitimate interests of third countries, especially developing countries.

(2) In the case of groupings to which the States concerned have transferred or may transfer certain competences as regards matters that come within the scope of the present Charter, its provisions shall also apply to those groupings in regard to such matters, consistent with the responsibilities of such States as members of such groupings. Those States shall co-operate in the observance by the groupings of the provisions of this Charter.

Art. 13.(1) Every State has the right to benefit from the advances and developments in science and technology, for the acceleration of its economic and social development.

(2) All States should promote international scientific and technological co-operation and the transfer of technology with proper regard for all legitimate interests including, inter alia, the rights and duties of holders, suppliers and recipients of technology. In particular, all States should facilitate the access of developing countries to the achievements of modern science and technology, the transfer of technology and the creation of indigenous technology for the benefit of the developing countries in forms and in accordance with procedures which are suited to their economies and their needs.

(3) Accordingly, developed countries should co-operate with the developing countries in the establishment strengthening and development of their scientific and technological infra-structures and their scientific research and technological activities so as to help to expand and transform the economies of developing countries.

(4) All States should co-operate in research with a view to evolving further internationally accepted guidelines or regulations for the transfer of technology, taking fully into account the interests of developing countries.

Art. 14. Every State has the duty to co-operate in promoting a steady and increasing expansion and liberalization of world trade and an improvement in the welfare and living standards of all peoples, in particular those of developing countries. Accordingly all States should co-operate, inter alia, towards the progressive dismantling of obstacles to trade and the improvement of the international framework for the conduct of world trade and, to these ends, co-ordinated efforts shall be made to solve in an equitable way the trade problems of all countries, taking into account the specific trade problems of the developing countries. In this connection, States shall take measures aimed at securing additional benefits for the international trade of developing countries so as to achieve a substantial increase in their foreign exchange earnings, the diversification of their exports, the acceleration of the rate of growth of their trade, taking into account their development needs, and improvement in the possibilities for these countries to participate in the expansion of world trade and a balance more favourable to developing countries in the sharing of the advantages resulting from this expansion, through, in the largest possible measure, a substantial improvement in the conditions of access for the products of interest to the developing countries, and wherever appropriate, measures designed to attain stable, equitable and remunerative prices for primary products.

Art. 15. All States have the duty to promote the achievement of general and complete disarmament under effective international control and to utilize the resources released by effective disarmament measures for the economic and social development of countries, allocating a substantial portion of such resources as additional means for the development needs of developing countries.

Art. 16.(1) It is the right and duty of all States, individually and collectively, to eliminate colonialism, apartheid, racial discrimination, neo-colonialism and all forms of foreign aggression, occupation and domination, and the economic and social consequences thereof, as a prerequisite for development. States which practise such coercive policies are economically responsible to the countries, territories and peoples affected for the restitution and full compensation for the exploitation and depletion of, and damages to, the natural and all other resources of those countries, territories and peoples. It is the duty of all States to extend assistance to them.

(2) No State has the right to promote or encourage investments that may constitute an obstacle to the liberation of a territory occupied by force.

Art. 17. International co-operation for development is the shared goal and common duty of all States. Every State should co-operate with the efforts of developing countries to accelerate their economic and social development by providing favourable external conditions and by extending active assistance to them, consistent with their development needs and objectives, with strict respect for the sovereign equality of States and free of any conditions derogating from their sovereignty.

Art. 18. Developed countries should extend, improve and enlarge the system of generalized non-reciprocal and non-discriminatory tariff preferences to developing countries, consistent with the relevant agreed conclusions and relevant decisions as adopted on this subject, into the framework of the competent international organizations. Developed countries should also give serious consideration to the adoption of other differential measures in areas where this is feasible and appropriate and in ways which will provide special and more favourable treatment, in order to meet the trade and development needs of the developing countries and in the conduct of international economic relations the developed countries should endeavour to avoid measures having a negative effect on the development of the national economies of the developing countries, as promoted by generalized tariff preferences and other generally agreed differential measures in their favour.

Art. 19. With a view to accelerating the economic growth of developing countries and bridging the economic gap between developed and developing countries, developed countries should grant generalized preferential non-reciprocal and non-discriminatory treatment to developing countries in those fields of international economic co-operation where it may be feasible.

Art. 20. Developing countries should in their efforts to increase their overall trade, give due attention to the possibility of expanding their trade with socialist countries, by granting to these countries conditions for trade not inferior to those granted normally to the developed market economy countries.

Art. 21. Developing countries should endeavour to promote expansion of their mutual trade and to this end may, in accordance with the existing and evolving provisions and procedures of international agreements where applicable, grant trade preferences to other developing countries without being obliged to extend such preferences to developed countries, provided these arrangements do not constitute an impediment to general trade liberalization and expansion.

Art. 22.(1) All States should respond to the generally recognized or mutually agreed development needs and objectives of developing countries by promoting increased net flows of real resources to the developing countries from all sources, taking into account any obligations and commitments undertaken by the States concerned, in order to reinforce the efforts of developing countries to accelerate their economic and social development.

(2) In this context, consistent with the aims and objectives mentioned above and taking into account any obligations and commitments undertaken in this regard, it should be their endeavour to increase the net amount in financial flows from official sources to developing countries and to improve the terms and conditions thereof.

(3) The flow of development assistance resources should include economic and technical assistance.

Art. 23. To enhance the effective mobilization of their own resources, the developing countries should strengthen their economic co-operation and expand their mutual trade so as to accelerate their economic and social development. All countries, especially developed countries, individually as well as through the competent international organizations of which they are members, should provide appropriate and effective support and co-operation.

Art. 24. All States have the duty to conduct their mutual economic relations in a manner which takes into account the interests of other countries. In particular, all States should avoid prejudicing the interests of developing countries.

Art. 25. In furtherance of world economic development the international community, especially its developed members, shall pay special attention to the particular needs and problems of the least developed among the developing countries, of land-locked developing countries and also island developing countries, with a view to helping them to overcome their particular difficulties and thus contribute to their economic and social development.

Art. 26. All States have the duty to coexist in tolerance and live together in peace, irrespective of differences in political, economic, social and cultural systems, and to facilitate trade between States having different economic and social systems. International trade should be conducted without prejudice to generalized non-discriminatory and non-reciprocal preferences in favour of developing countries, on the basis of mutual advantage, equitable benefits and the exchange of most-favoured-nation treatment.

Art. 27.(1) Every State has the right to enjoy fully the benefits of world invisible trade and to engage in the expansion of such trade.

(2) World invisible trade, based on efficiency and mutual and equitable benefit, furthering the expansion of the world economy, is the common goal of all States. The role of developing countries in world invisible trade should be enhanced and strengthened consistent with the above objectives, particular attention being paid to the special needs of developing countries.

(3) All States should co-operate with developing countries in their endeavours to increase their capacity to earn foreign exchange from invisible transactions, in accordance with the potential and needs of each developing country consistent with the objectives mentioned above.

Art. 28. All States have the duty to co-operate in achieving adjustments in the prices of exports of developing countries in relation to prices of their imports so as to promote just and equitable terms of trade for them, in a manner which is remunerative for producers and equitable for producers and consumers.

Chapter III. Common responsibilities towards the international community.

Art. 29. The sea-bed and ocean floor and the subsoil thereof, beyond the limits of national jurisdiction, as well as the resources of the area, are the common heritage of mankind. On the basis of the principles adopted by the General Assembly in Res. 2749(XXV) of Dec. 17, 1970, all States shall ensure that the exploration of the area and exploitation of its resources are carried out exclusively for peaceful purposes and that the benefits derived therefrom are shared equitably by all States, taking into account the particular interests and needs of developing countries; an international regime applying to the area and its resources and including appropriate international machinery to give effect to its provisions shall be established by an international treaty of a universal character, generally agreed upon.

Art. 30. The protection, preservation and enhancement of the environment for the present and future generations is the responsibility of all States. All States shall endeavour to establish their own environmental and developmental policies in conformity with such responsibility. The environmental policies of all States should enhance and not adversely affect the present and future development potential of developing countries. All States have the responsibility to ensure that activities within their jurisdiction or control do not cause damage to the environment of other States or of areas beyond the limits of national jurisdiction. All States should co-operate in evolving international norms and regulations in the field of the environment.

Chapter IV. Final provisions.

Art. 31. All States have the duty to contribute to the balanced expansion of the world economy, taking duly into account the close inter-relationship between the well-being of the developed countries and the growth and development of the developing countries, and the fact that the prosperity of the international community as a whole depends upon the prosperity of its constituent parts.

Art. 32. No State may use or encourage the use of economic, political or any other type of measures to coerce another State in order to obtain from it the subordination of the exercise of its sovereign rights.

Art. 33. (1) Nothing in the present Charter shall be construed as impairing or derogating from the provisions of the Charter of the United Nations or actions taken in pursuance thereof.

(2) In their interpretation and application, the provisions of the present Charter are inter-related and each provision should be construed in the context of the other provisions.

Art. 34. An item on the Charter of Economic Rights and Duties of States shall be included in the agenda of the General Assembly at its thirtieth session, and thereafter on the agenda of every fifth session. In this way a systematic and comprehensive consideration of the implementation of the Charter, covering both progress achieved and any improvements and additions which might become necessary, would be carried out and appropriate measures recommended. Such considerations should take into account the evolution of all the economic, social, legal and other factors related to the principles upon which the present Charter is based and on its purpose."

Report of Working Group on Charter of Economic Rights and Duties of States, Geneva, 4–22 February 1974 and Mexico 10–28 June, 1974; *UN Year Book 1974*, pp. 381–401; *UN Monthly Chronicle*, January 1975, pp. 121–132.

CHARTER OF INTERNATIONAL MILITARY TRIBUNAL, IMT, 1945.

Adopted by the Big Four Powers at London on Aug. 8, 1945. The text is as follows:

"1. Constitution of the International Military Tribunal.

Art. 1. In pursuance of the Agreement signed on the 8th August, 1945, by the Government of the United Kingdom of Great Britain and Northern Ireland, the Government of the United States of America, the Provisional Government of the French Republic and the Government of the Union of Soviet Socialist Republics, there shall be established an International Military Tribunal (hereinafter called 'the Tribunal') for the just and prompt trial and punishment of the major war criminals of the European Axis.

Art. 2. The Tribunal shall consist of four members, each with an alternate. One member and one alternate shall be appointed by each of the Signatories. The alternates shall, so far as they are able, be present at all sessions of the Tribunal. In case of illness of any member of the Tribunal or his incapacity for some other reason to fulfil his functions, his alternate shall take his place.

Art. 3. Neither the Tribunal, its members nor their alternates can be challenged by the prosecution, or by the Defendants of their Counsel. Each Signatory may replace its member of the Tribunal or his alternate for reasons of health or for other good reasons, except that no replacement may take place during a Trial, other than by an alternate.

Art. 4. (a) The presence of all four members of the Tribunal or the alternate for any absent member shall be necessary to constitute the quorum.

(b) The members of the Tribunal shall, before any trial begins, agree among themselves upon the selection from their number of a President, and the President shall hold office during that trial, or as many otherwise be agreed by a vote of not less than three members. The principle of rotation of presidency for successive trials is agreed. If, however, a session of the Tribunal takes place on the territory of one of the four Signatories, the representative of that Signatory on the Tribunal shall preside.

(c) Save as aforesaid the Tribunal shall take decisions by a majority vote and in case the votes are evenly divided, the vote of the President shall be decisive: provided always that convictions and sentences shall only be imposed by affirmative votes of at least three members of the Tribunal.

Art. 5. In case of need and depending on the number of the matters to be tried, other Tribunals may be set up; and the establishment, functions, and procedure of each Tribunal shall be identical and shall be governed by this Charter.

II. Jurisdiction and General Principles.

Art. 6. The Tribunal established by the Agreement referred to in Art. 1. hereof for the trial and punishment of the major war criminals of the European Axis countries, whether as individuals or as members of organizations, committed any of the following crimes. The following acts, or any of them, are crimes within the jurisdiction of the Tribunal for which there shall be individual responsiblity:

(a) Crimes against peace: namely, planning, preparation, initiation or waging of a war of aggression, or a war in violation of international treaties, agreements or assurances, or participation in a common plan or conspiracy for the accomplishment of any of the foregoing;

(b) War crimes: namely, violations of the laws or customs of war. Such violations shall include but not be limited to, murder, ill-treatment or deportation to slave labour or for any other purpose of civilian population of or in occupied territory, murder or ill-treatment of prisoners of war or persons on the seas, killing of hostages, plunder of public or private property, wanton destruction of cities, towns or villages, or devastation not justified by military necessity;

(c) Crimes against humanity: namely, murder, extermination, enslavement, deportation, and other inhumane acts committed against any civilian population, before or during the war; or persecutions on political, racial or religious grounds in execution of or in connection with any crime within the jurisdiction of the Tribunal, whether or not in violation of the domestic law of the country where perpetrated. Leaders, organisers, instigators and accomplices participating in the formulation or execution of a common plan or conspiracy to commit any of the foregoing crimes are responsible for all acts performed by any persons in execution of such plan.

Art. 7. The official position of defendants, whether as Heads of State or responsible officials in Government Departments, shall not be considered as freeing them from responsibility or mitigating punishment.

Art. 8. The fact that the Defendant acted pursuant to order of his Government or of a superior shall not free him from responsibility, but may be considered in mitigation of punishment if the Tribunal determines that justice so requires.

Art. 9. At the trial of any individual member of any group or organisation the Tribunal may declare (in connection with any act of which the individual may be convicted) that the group or organisation of which the individual was a member was a criminal organisation. After receipt of the Indictment the Tribunal shall give such notice as it thinks fit that the prosecution intends to ask the Tribunal to make such declaration and any member of the Tribunal to make such declaration and any member of the organisation will be entitled to apply to the Tribunal for leave to be heard by the Tribunal upon the question of the criminal character of the organisation. The Tribunal shall have power to allow or reject the application. If the application is allowed, the Tribunal may direct in what manner the applicants shall be represented and heard.

Art. 10. In cases where a group or organisation is declared criminal by the Tribunal, the competent national authority of any Signatory shall have the right to bring individuals to trial for membership therein before national, military or occupation courts. In any such case the criminal nature of the group or organisation is considered proved and shall not be questioned.

Art. 11. Any person convicted by the Tribunal may be charged before a national, military or occupation court, referred to in Article 10 of this Charter, with a crime other than of membership in a criminal group or organisation and such court may, after convicting him, impose upon him punishment independent of and additional to the punishment imposed by the Tribunal for participation in the criminal activities of such group or organisation.

Art. 12. The Tribunal shall have the right to take proceedings against a person charged with crimes set out in Article 6 of this Charter in his absence, if he has not been found or if the Tribunal, for any reason, finds it necessary, in the interests of justic, to conduct the hearing in his absence.

Art. 13. The Tribunal shall draw up rules for its procedure. These rules shall not be inconsistent with the provisions of this Charter.

III. Committee for the Investigation and Prosecution of Major War Criminals.

Art. 14. Each Signatory shall appoint a Chief Prosecutor for the Investigation of the charges against and the prosecution of major war criminals.

The Chief Prosecutors shall act as a committee for the following purposes:

(a) to agree upon a plan of the individual work of each of the Chief Prosecutors and his staff,

(b) to settle the final designation of major war criminals to be tried by the Tribunal,

(c) to approve the Indictment and the documents to be submitted therewith,

(d) to lodge the Indictment and the accompanying documents with the Tribunal,

(e) to draw up and recommend to the Tribunal for its approval draft rules of procedure, contemplated by Article 13 of this Charter. The Tribunal shall have power to accept, with or without amendments, or to reject, the rules so recommended. The Committee shall act in all the above matters by a majority vote and shall appoint a Chairman as may be convenient and in accordance with the principle of rotation: provided that if there is an equal division of vote concerning the designation of a Defendant to be tried by the Tribunal, or the crimes with which he shall be charged, that proposal will be adopted which was made by the party which proposed that the particular Defendant be tried, or the particular charges be preferred against him.

Art. 15. The Chief Prosecutors shall individually, and acting in collaboration with one another, also undertake the following duties:

(a) investigation, collection and production before or at the Trial of all necessary evidence,

(b) the preparation of the Indictment for approval by the Committee in accordance with paragraph (c) of Article 14, hereof,

(c) the preliminary examination of all necessary witnesses and of the Defendants,

(d) to act as prosecutor at the Trial,

(e) to appoint representatives to carry out such duties as may be assigned to them,

(f) to undertake such other matters as may appear necessary to them for the purposes of the preparation for and conduct of the Trial.

It is understood that no witness or Defendant detained by any Signatory shall be taken out of the possession of that Signatory without its assent.

IV. Fair Trial for Defendants.

Art. 16. In order to ensure fair trail for the Defendants, the following procedure shall be followed:

(a) The Indictment shall include full particulars specifying in detail the charges against the Defendents. A copy of the Indictment and of all the documents lodged with the Indictment, translated into a language which he understands, shall be furnished to the Defendant at a reasonable time before the Trial,

(b) During any preliminary examination or trial of a Defendant he shall have the right to give any explanation relevant to the charges made against him.

(c) A preliminary examination of a Defendant and his Trial shall be conducted in, or translated into, a language which the Defendant understands.

(d) A Defendant shall have the right to conduct his own defence before the Tribunal or to have the assistance of Counsel,

(e) A Defendant shall have the right through himself or through his Counsel to present evidence at the Trial in support of his defence, and to cross-examine any witness called by the Prosecution.

V. Powers of the Tribunal and Conduct of the Trial

Art. 17. The Tribunal shall have the power:

(a) to summon witnesses to the Trial and to require their attendance and testimony and to put questions to them.

(b) to interrogate any Defendant,

(c) to require the production of documents and other evidentiary material,

(d) to administer oaths to witnesses,

(e) to appoint officers for the carrying out of any task designated by the Tribunal including the power to have evidence taken on commission.

Art. 18. The Tribunal shall:

(a) confine the Trial strictly to an expeditious hearing of the issues raised by the charges,

(b) take strict measures to prevent any action which will cause unreasonable delay, and rule out irrelevant issues and statements of any kind whatsoever,

(c) deal summarily with any contumacy, imposing appropriate punishment, including exclusion of any Defendant or his Counsel from some or all further proceedings, but without prejudice to the determination of the charges,

Art. 19. The Tribunal shall not be bound by technical rules of evidence. It shall adopt and apply to the greatest possible extent expeditious and non-technical procedure, and shall admit any evidence which it deems to have probative value.

Art. 20. The Tribunal may require to be informed of the nature of any evidence before it is offered so that it may rule upon the relevance thereof.

Art. 21. The Tribunal shall not require proof of facts of common knowledge but shall take judicial notice thereof. It shall also take judicial notice of official governmental documents and reports of the United Nations, including the acts and documents of the committees set up in the various Allied countries for the investigation of war crimes and the records and findings of military or other Tribunals of any of the United Nations.

Art. 22. The permanent seat of the Tribunal shall be in Berlin. The first meetings of the members of the Tribunal and of the Chief Prosecutors shall be held at Berlin in a place to be designated by the Control Council for Germany. The first trial shall be held at Nuremberg, and any subsequent trials shall be held at such places as the Tribunal may decide.

Art. 23. One or more of the Chief Prosecutors may take part in the prosecution at each Trial. The function of any Chief Prosecutor may be discharged by him personally, or by any person or persons authorized by him.

The function of Counsel for a Defendant may be discharged at the Defendant's request by any Counsel professionally qualified to conduct cases before the Courts of his own country, or by any other person who may be specially authorised thereto by the Tribunal.

Art 24. The proceedings at the Trial shall take the following course:

(a) The Indictment shall be read in court.

(b) The Tribunal shall ask each Defendant whether he pleads 'guilty' or 'not guilty'.

(c) The Prosecution shall make an opening statement.

(d) The Tribunal shall ask the Prosecution and the Defence what evidence (if any) they wish to submit to the Tribunal, and the Tribunal shall rule upon the admissibility of any such evidence.

(e) The witnesses for the Prosecution shall be examined and after that the witnesses for the Defence. Thereafter such rebutting evidence as may be held by the Tribunal to be admissible shall be called by either the Prosecution or the Defence.

(f) The Tribunal may put any question to any witness and to any Defendant, at any time.

(g) The Prosecution and the Defence shall interrogate and may cross-examine any witnesses and any Defendant who gives testimony.

(h) The Defence shall address the court.

(i) The Prosecution shall address the court.

(j) Each Defendant may make a statement to the Tribunal.

(k) The Tribunal shall deliver judgement and pronounce sentence.

Art. 25. All official documents shall be produced, and all court proceedings conducted, in English, French and Russian, and in the language of the Defendant. So much of the record and of the proceedings may also be translated into the language of any country in which the Tribunal is sitting, as the Tribunal considers desirable in the interests of justice and public opinion.

VI. Judgement and Sentence.

Art. 26. The Judgement of the Tribunal as to the guilt or the innocence of any Defendant shall give the reasons on which it is based, and shall be final and not subject to review.

Art. 27. The Tribunal shall have the right to impose upon a Defendant, on conviction, death or such other punishment as shall be determined by it to be just.

Art. 28. In addition to any punishment imposed by it, the Tribunal shall have the right to deprive the convicted person of any stolen property and order its delivery to the Control Council for Germany.

Art. 29. In case of guilt, sentences shall be carried out in accordance with the orders of the Control Council for Germany, which may at any time reduce or otherwise alter the sentences, but may not increase the severity thereof. If the Control Council for Germany, after any Defendant has been convicted and sentenced, discovers fresh evidence which, in its opinion, would found a fresh charge against him, the Council shall report accordingly to the Committee established under Article 14 hereof for such action as they may consider proper, having regard to the interests of justice.

VII. Expenses.

Art. 30. The expenses of the Tribunal and of the Trials, shall be charged by the Signatories against the funds allotted for maintenance of the Control Council for Germany."

The Trial of German Major War Criminals. Proceedings of the IMT Sitting at Nuremberg, Germany, London, 1946, Vol. 1.

CHARTER OF ORGANIZATION OF AFRICAN UNITY, OAU, 1963. Adopted by a Summit Conference of Independent African States in Addis Ababa and signed on May 25, 1963 by the Heads of African State and governments of Algeria, Burundi, Cameroon, the Central African Republic, Chad, Congo (Brazzaville), Congo (Leopoldville), Dahomey, Ethiopia, Gabon, Ghana, Guinea, Ivory Coast, Liberia, Libya, Madagascar, Mali, Mauritania, Morocco, Niger, Nigeria, Rwanda, Senegal, Sierra Leone, Somalia, Sudan, Tanganyika, Togo, Tunisia, Uganda, the United Arab Republic and Upper Volta. The text is as follows:

"We, the Heads of African States and Governments assembled in the City of Addis Ababa, Ethiopia;

Convinced that it is the inalienable right of all people to control their own destiny;

Conscious of the fact that freedom, equality, justice and dignity are essential objectives for the achievement of the legitimate aspirations of the African peoples;

Conscious of our responsibility to harness the natural and human resources of our continent for the total advancement of our peoples in spheres of human endeavor;

Inspired by a common determination to promote understanding among our peoples and co-operation among our States in response to the aspirations of our peoples for brotherhood and solidarity, in a larger unity transcending ethnic and national differences;

Convinced that, in order to translate this determination into dynamic force in the cause of human progress, conditions for peace and security must be established and maintained;

Determined to safeguard and consolidate the hard-won independence as well as the sovereignty and territorial integrity of our States, and to fight against neo-colonialism in all its forms;

Dedicated to the general progress of Africa;

Persuaded that the Charter of the United Nations and the Universal Declaration of Human Rights, to the principles of which we reaffirm our adherence, provide a solid foundation for peaceful and positive co-operation among states;

Desirous that all African States should henceforth unite so that the welfare and well-being of their peoples can be assured;

Resolved to reinforce the links between our states by establishing and strenthening common institutions;

Have agreed to the present Charter.

Art. I.(1) The High Contracting Parties do by the present Charter establish an Organization to be known as the Organization of African Unity.

(2) The Organization shall include the Continental African States, Madagascar and other Islands surrounding Africa.

Art. II.(1) The Organization shall have the following purposes:

(a) to promote the unity and solidarity of the African States;

(b) to coordinate and intensify their co-operation and efforts to achieve a better life for the peoples of Africa;

(c) to defend their sovereignty, their territorial integrity and independence;

(d) to eradicate all forms of colonialism from Africa; and

(e) to promote international co-operation, having due regard to the Charter of the United Nations and the Universal Declaration of Human Rights.

(2) To these ends, the Member States shall coordinate and harmonise their general policies, especially in the following fields:

(a) political and diplomatic co-operation;

(b) economic co-operation, including transport and communications;

(c) educational and cultural co-operation;

(d) health, sanitation, and nutritional co-operation;

(e) scientific and technical co-operation; and

(f) co-operation for defence and security.

Art. III. The Member States, in pursuit of the purposes stated in Article II, solemnly affirm and declare their adherence to the following principles:

(1) the sovereign equality of all Member States;

(2) non-interference in the internal affairs of States;

(3) respect for the sovereignty and territorial integrity of each State and for its inalienable right to independent existence;

(4) peaceful settlement of disputes by negotiation, mediation, conciliation or arbitration;

(5) unreserved condemnation, in all its forms, of political assassination as well as of subversive activities on the part of neighbouring States or any other State;

(6) absolute dedication to the total emancipation of the African territories which are still dependent;

(7) affirmation of a policy of non-alignment with regard to all blocs.

Art. IV. Each independent sovereign African State shall be entitled to become a Member of the Organization.

Art. V. All Member States shall enjoy equal rights and have equal duties.

Art. VI. The Member States pledge themselves to observe scrupulously the principles enumerated in Article III of the present Charter.

Art. VII. The Organization shall accomplish its purposes through the following principal institutions:

(1) The Assembly of Heads of State and Government;

(2) the Council of Ministers;

(3) the General Secretariat;

(4) the Commission of Mediation, Conciliation and Arbitration.

Art. VIII. The Assembly of Heads of State and Government shall be the supreme organ of the Organization. It shall, subject to the provisions of this Charter, discuss matters of common concern to Africa with a view to co-ordinating and harmonising the general policy of the Organization. It may in addition review the structure, functions and acts of all the organs and any specialized agencies which may be created in accordance with the present Charter.

Art. IX. The Assembly shall be composed of the Heads of State and Government or their duly accredited representatives and it shall meet at least once a year. At the request of any Member State and on approval by a two-thirds majority of the Member States, the Assembly shall meet in extraordinary session.

Art. X.(1) Each Member State shall have one vote.

(2) All resolutions shall be determined by a two-thirds majority of the Members of the Organization.

(3) Questions of procedure shall require a simple majority. Whether or not a question is one of procedure shall be determined by a simple majority of all Member States of the Organization.

(4) Two-thirds of the total membership of the Organization shall form a quorum at any meeting of the Assembly.

Art. XI. The Assembly shall have the power to determine its own rules of procedure.

Art. XII.(1) The Council of Ministers shall consist of Foreign Ministers or such other Ministers as are designated by the Governments of Member States.

(2) The Council of Ministers shall meet at least twice a year. When requested by any Member State and approved by two-thirds of all Member States, it shall meet in extra-ordinary session.

Art. XIII.(1) The Council of Ministers shall be responsible to the Assembly of Heads of State and Government. It shall be entrusted with the responsibility of preparing conferences of the Assembly.

(2) It shall take cognisance of any matter referred to it by the Assembly. It shall be entrusted with the implementation of the decision of the Assembly of Heads of State, and Government. It shall co-ordinate inter-African cooperation in accordance with the instruction of the Assembly and in conformity with Article II (2) of the present Charter.

Art. XIV.(1) Each Member State shall have one vote.

(2) All resolutions shall be determined by a simple majority of the members of the Council of Ministers.

(3) Two-thirds of the total membership of the Council of Ministers shall form a quorum for any meeting of the Council.

Art. XV. The Council shall have the power to determine its own rules of procedure.

Art. XVI. There shall be an Administrative Secretary-General of the Organization, who shall be appointed by the Assembly of Heads of State and Government. The Administrative Secretary-General shall direct the affairs of the Secretariat.

Art. XVII. There shall be one or more Assistant Secretaries-General of the Organization, who shall be appointed by the Assembly of Heads of State and Government.

Art. XVIII. The functions and conditions of services of the Secretary-General, of the Assistant Secretaries-General and other employees of the Secretariat shall be governed by the provisions of this Charter and the regulations approved by the Assembly of Heads of State and Government.

(1) In the performance of their duties the Administrative Secretary-General and the staff shall not seek or receive instructions from any government or from any other authority external to the Organization. They shall refrain from any action which might reflect on their position as international officials responsible only to the Organization.

(2) Each member of the Organization undertakes to respect the exclusive character of the responsibilities of the Administrative Secretary-General and the Staff and not to seek to influence them in the discharge of their responsibilities.

Art. XIX. Member States pledge to settle all disputes among themselves by peaceful means and, to this end decide to establish a Commission of Mediation, Conciliation and Arbitration, the composition of which and conditions of service shall be defined by a separate Protocol to be approved by the Assembly of Heads of State and Government. Said Protocol shall be regarded as forming an integral part of the present Charter.

Art. XX. The Assembly shall establish such Specialized Commissions as it may deem necessary, including the following:

(1) Economic and Social Commission;

(2) Educational and Cultural Commission;

(3) Health, Sanitation and Nutrition Commission;

(4) Defence Commission;

(5) Scientific, Technical and Research Commission.

Art. XXI. Each Specialized Commission referred to in Article XX shall be composed of the Ministers concerned or other Ministers of Plenipotentiaries designated by the Governments of the Member States.

Art. XXII. The functions of the Specialized Commissions shall be carried out in accordance with the provisions of the present Charter and of the regulations approved by the Council of Ministers.

Art. XXIII. The budget of the Organization prepared by the Administrative Secretary-General shall be approved by the Council of Ministers. The budget shall be provided by contributions from Member States in accordance with the scale of assessment of the United Nations; provided, however, that no Member State

shall be assessed an amount exceeding twenty percent of the yearly regular budget of the Organization. The Member States agree to pay their respective contributions regularly.

Art. XXIV.(1) This Charter shall be open for signature to all independent sovereign African States and shall be ratified by the signatory States in accordance with their respective constitutional processes.

(2) The original instrument, done, if possible in African languages, in English and French, all texts being equally authentic, shall be deposited with the Government of Ethiopia which shall transmit certified copies thereof to all independent sovereign African States.

(3) Instruments of ratification shall be deposited with the Government of Ethiopia, which shall notify all signatories of each such deposit.

Art. XXV. This Charter shall, after due ratification, be registered with the Secretariat of the United Nations through the Government of Ethiopia in conformity with Article 102 of the Charter of United Nations.

Art. XXVI. The Charter shall be registered with the Secretariat of the United Nations.

Art. XXVII. Any question which may arise concerning the interpretation of this Charter shall be decided by a vote of two-thirds of the Assembly of Heads of State and Government of the Organization.

Art. XXVIII.(1) Any independent sovereign African State may at any time notify the Administrative Secretary-General of its intention to adhere or accede to this Charter.

(2) The Administrative Secretary-General shall, on receipt of such notification, communicate a copy of it to all the Member States. Admission shall be decided by a simple majority of the Member States. The decision of each Member State shall be transmitted to the Administrative Secretary-General, who shall, upon receipt of the required number of votes, communicate the decision to the State concerned.

Art. XXIX. The working languages of the Organization and all its institutions shall be, if possible, African languages, English and French.

Art. XXX. The Administrative Secretary-General may accept on behalf of the Organization gifts, bequests and other donations made to the Organization, provided that this is approved by the council of Ministers.

Art. XXXI. The Council of Ministers shall decide on the privileges and immunities to be accorded to the personnel of the Secretariat in the respective territories of the Member States.

Art. XXXII. Any State which desires to renounce its membership shall forward a written notification to the Administrative Secretary-General. At the end of one year from the date of such notification, if not withdrawn, the Charter shall cease to apply with respect to the renouncing State, which shall thereby cease to belong to the Organization.

Art. XXXIII. This Charter may be amended or revised if any Member State makes a written request to the Administrative Secretary-General to that effect; provided, however, that the proposed amendment is not submitted to the Assembly for consideration until all the Member States have been duly notified of it and a period of one year has elapsed. Such an amendment shall not be effective unless approved by at least two-thirds of all the Member States.

In faith whereof, We, the Heads of African State and Government have signed this Charter."

B. GOUTROS GHALI, "The Addis Ababa Charter", in: *International Conciliation*, Jan., 1964; T.O. ELIAS, "The Charter of the OUA", in: *American Journal of International Law*, No. 2, 1965.

CHARTER OF ORGANIZATION OF AMERICAN STATES, OAS, 1948, AND PROTOCOL, 1967. The constitution of the Organización de Estados Americanos OEA, drafted by the IX International Conference of American States in Bogotá (Mar. 30–May 2, 1948) and the supplementary Protocol signed Mar. 27, 1967 in Buenos Aires. The Charter was based on a plan for an "organic pact" prepared by the Executive Council of the ▷ Pan-American Union and submitted to the governments of the American Republics on Apr. 10, 1946; passed Apr. 30, 1948 and came into force on Dec. 13, 1951 after ratification by all states participating in the conference, though Guatemala, Peru and the USA made provisions: Guatemala – that the Charter does not infringe on its rights to ▷ Belize; Peru – that it continues to regard the ▷ Chapultepec Act of 1945 as in effect; the USA – that the Charter does not violate any of the laws of the US Federal Constitution. The following States were founders of OAS: Argentina, Bolivia, Brazil, Chile, Colombia, Costa Rica, Cuba, the Dominican Republic, Ecuador, Guatemala, Haiti, Honduras, Paraguay, Peru, El Salvador, Uruguay, the USA and Venezuela. In 1962 the revolutionary government of Cuba was barred from participation in OAS meetings; in Dec. 1966 Barbados was admitted, in June 1969, Jamaica, and in Feb. 1967, Trinidad and Tobago. In the 1960s a conflict took place between a majority of the American States and the USA concerning the interpretation of the Charter; the USA wanted to give the OAS the character of a military-police alliance, while the Latin States aimed at making it a vehicle for economic, scientific and technical co-operation and assistance in social reforms. At the II Special International Conference in Nov. 1965 in Rio de Janeiro both sides recognized the need for a reform of the Charter. The III Special International Conference on this question held in Buenos Aires, Feb. 15–27, 1967, resulted in the passage of a number of amendments relating to changes in the organization and competence of OAS organs, but in the main devoted to the economic and social tasks of OAS. The document signed Feb. 27, 1967, by all American Republics, officially called the Buenos Aires Protocol of 1967, entered into force Feb. 27, 1970. Following are the main parts of the OAS Charter of Apr. 30, 1948 with the amendments introduced by the Buenos Aires Protocol of Feb. 27, 1967:

"In the Name of Their Peoples, the States Represented at the Ninth International Conference of American States. Convinced that the historic mission of America is to offer to man a land of liberty, and a favorable environment for the development of his personality and the realization of his just aspirations;

Conscious that this mission has already inspired numerous agreements, whose essential value lies in the desire of the American peoples to live together in peace, and, through their mutual understanding and respect for the sovereignty of each one, to provide for the betterment of all, in independence, in equality and under law;

Confident that the true significance of American solidarity and good neighborliness can only mean the consolidation on this continent, within the framework of democratic institutions, of a system of individual liberty and social justice based on respect for the essential rights of man;

Persuaded that their welfare and their contribution to the progress and the civilization of the world will increasingly require intensive continental co-operation;

Resolved to persevere in the noble undertaking that humanity has conferred upon the United Nations, whose principles and purposes they solemnly reaffirm;

Convinced that juridical organization is a necessary condition for security and peace founded on moral order and on justice; and

In accordance with Resolution IX of the Inter-American Conference on Problems of War and Peace, held at Mexico City, have agreed upon the following.

Part One. Chapter I. Nature and Purposes.

Art. 1. The American States establish by this Charter the international organization that they have developed to achieve an order of peace and justice, to promote their solidarity, to strengthen their collaboration, and to defend their sovereignty, their territorial integrity, and their independence. Within the United Nations, the Organization of American States is a regional agency.

Art. 2. The Organization of American States, in order to put into practice the principles on which it is founded and to fulfill is regional obligations under the Charter of the United Nations, proclaims the following essential purposes:

(a) To strengthen the peace and security of the continent;

(b) To prevent possible causes of difficulties and to ensure the pacific settlement of disputes that may arise among the Member States;

(c) To provide for common action on the part of those States in the event of aggression;

(d) To seek the solution of political, juridical, and economic problems that may arise among them; and

(e) To promote, by co-operative action, their economic, social, and cultural development.

Chapter II. Principles.

Art. 3. The American States reaffirm the following principles:

(a) International law is the standard of conduct of States in their reciprocal relations;

(b) International order consists essentially of respect for the personality, sovereignty, and independence of States, and the faithful fulfilment of obligations derived from treaties and other sources of international law;

(c) Good faith shall govern the relations between States;

(d) The solidarity of the American States and the high aims which are sought through it require the political organization of those States on the basis of the effective exercise of representative democracy;

(e) The American States condemn was of aggression: victory does not give rights;

(f) An act of aggression against one American State is an act of aggression against all the other American States;

(g) Controversies of an international character arising between two or more American States shall be settled by peaceful procedures;

(h) Social justice and social security are bases of lasting peace;

(i) Economic co-operation is essential to the common welfare and prosperity of the peoples of the continent;

(j) The American States proclaim the fundamental rights of the individual without distinction as to race, nationality, creed, or sex;

(k) The spiritual unity of the continent is based on respect for the cultural values of the American countries and requires their close co-operation for the high purposes of civilization;

(l) The education of peoples should be directed toward justice, freedom, and peace.

Chapter III. Members.

Art. 4. All American States that ratify the present Charter are Members of the Organization.

Art. 5. Any new political entity that arises from the union of several Member States and that, as such, ratifies the present Charter, shall become a Member of the Organization. The entry of the new political entity into the Organization shall result in the loss of membership of each one of the States which constitute it.

Art. 6. Any other independent American State that desires to become a Member of the Organization should so indicate by means of a note addressed to the Secretary-General, in which it declares that it is willing to sign and ratify the Charter of the Organization and to accept all the obligations inherent in membership, especially those relating to collective security expressly set forth in Articles 27 and 28 of the Charter.

Art. 7. The General Assembly, upon the recommendation of the Permanent Council of the Organization, shall determine whether it is appropriate that the Secretary-General be authorized to permit the applicant State to sign the Charter and to accept the deposit of the Permanent Council and the decision of the General Assembly shall require the affirmative vote of two thirds of the Member States.

Art. 8. The Permanent Council shall not make any recommendation nor shall the General Assembly take any decision with respect to a request for admission on the part of a political entity whose territory became subject, in whole or in part, prior to Dec. 18, 1964, the date set by the First Special Inter-American Conference, to litigation or claim between an extracontinental country and one or more Member States of the Organization, until the dispute has been ended by some peaceful procedure.

Chapter IV. Fundamental Rights and Duties of States.

Art. 9. States are juridically equal, enjoy equal rights and equal capacity to exercise these rights, and have equal duties. The rights of each State depend not upon its power to ensure the exercise thereof, but upon the mere fact of its existence as a person under international law.

Art. 10. Every American State has the duty to respect the rights enjoyed by every other State in accordance with international law.

Art. 11. The fundamental rights of States may not be impaired in any manner whatsoever.

Art. 12. The political existence of the State is independent of recognition by other States. Even before being recognized, the State has the right to defend its integrity and independence, to provide for its preservation and prosperity, and consequently to organize itself as it sees fit, to legislate concerning its interests, to administer its services, and to determine the jurisdiction and competence of its courts. The exercise of these rights is limited only by the exercise of the rights of other States in accordance with international law.

Art. 13. Recognition implies that the State granting it accepts the personability of the new State, with all the rights and duties that international law prescribes for the two States.

Art. 14. The right of each State to protect itself and to live its own life does not authorize it to commit unjust acts against another State.

Art. 15. The jurisdiction of States within the limits of their national territory is exercised equally over all the inhabitants, whether nationals or aliens.

Art. 16. Each State has the right to develop its cultural, political, and economic life freely and naturally. In this free development, the State shall respect the rights of the individual and the principles of universal morality.

Art. 17. Respect for and the faithful observance of treaties constitute standards for the development of peaceful relations among States. International treaties and agreements should be public.

Art. 18. No State or group of States has the right to intervene, directly or indirectly, for any reason whatever, in the internal or external affairs of any other State. The foregoing principle prohibits not only armed force but also any other form of interference or attempted threat against the personality of the State or against its political, economic, and cultural elements.

Art. 19. No State may use or encourage the use of coercive measures of an economic or political character in order to force the sovereign will of another State and obtain from it advantages of any kind.

Art. 20. The territory of a State is inviolable; it may not be the object, even temporarily, of military occupation or of other measures of force taken by another State, directly or indirectly, on any grounds whatever. No territorial acquisitions or special advantages obtained either by force or by other means of coercion shall be recognized.

Art. 21. The American States bind themselves in their international relations not to have recourse to the use of force, except in the case of self-defense in accordance with existing treaties or in fulfillment thereof.

Art. 22. Measures adopted for the maintenance of peace and security in accordance with existing treaties do not constitute a violation of the principles set forth in Articles 18 and 20.

Chapter V. Pacific Settlement of Disputes.

Art. 23. All international disputes that may arise between American States shall be submitted to the peaceful procedures set forth in this Charter, before being referred to the Security Council of the United Nations.

Art. 24. The following are peaceful procedures: direct negotiation, good offices, mediation, investigation and conciliation, judicial settlement, arbitration, and those which the parties to the dispute may especially agree upon at any time.

Art. 25. In the event that a dispute arises between two or more American States which, in the opinion of one of them, cannot be settled through the usual diplomatic channels, the parties shall agree on some other peaceful procedure that will enable them to reach a solution.

Art. 26. A special treaty will establish adequate procedures for the pacific settlement of disputes and will determine the appropriate means for their application, so that no dispute between American States shall fail of definitive settlement within a reasonable period.

Chapter VI. Collective Security.

Art. 27. Every act of aggression by a State against the territorial integrity or the inviolability of the territory or against the sovereignty or political independence of an American State shall be considered an act of aggression against the other American States.

Art. 28. If the inviolability or the integrity of the territory or the sovereignty or political independence of any

American State should be affected by an armed attack or by an act of aggression that is not an armed attack, or by an extra-continental conflict, or by a conflict between two or more American States, or by any other fact or situation that might endanger the peace of America, the American States, in furtherance of the principles of continental solidarity or collective self-defense, shall apply the measures and procedures established in the special treaties on the subject.

Chapter VII. Economic Standards.

Art. 29. The Member States, inspired by the principles of inter-American solidarity and co-operation, pledge themselves to a united effort to ensure social justice in the Hemisphere and dynamic and balanced economic development for their peoples, as conditions essential to peace and security.

Art. 30. The Member States pledge themselves to mobilize their own national human and material resources through suitable programs, and recognize the importance of operating within an efficient domestic structure, as fundamental conditions for their economic and social progress and for assuring effective inter-American cooperation.

Art. 31. To accelerate their economic and social development, in accordance with their own methods and procedures and within the framework of the democratic principles and the institutions of the inter-American system, the Member States agree to dedicate every effort to achieve the following basic goals:

(a) Substantial and self-sustained increase in the per capita national product;

(b) Equitable distribution of national income;

(c) Adequate and equitable systems of taxation;

(d) Modernization of rural life and reforms leading to equitable and efficient land-tenure systems, increased agricultural productivity, expanded use of undeveloped land, diversification of production; and improved processing and marketing systems for agricultural products; and the strengthening and expansion of facilities to attain these ends;

(e) Accelerated and diversified industrialization, especially of capital and intermediate goods;

(f) Stability in the domestic price levels, compatible with sustained economic development and the attainment of social justice;

(g) Fair wages, employment opportunities, and acceptable working conditions for all;

(h) Rapid eradication of illiteracy and expansion of educational opportunities for all;

(i) Protection of man's potential through the extension and application of modern medical science;

(j) Proper nutrition, especially through the acceleration of national efforts to increase the production and availability of food;

(k) Adequate housing for all sectors of the population;

(l) Urban conditions that offer the opportunity for a healthful, productive, and full life;

(m) Promotion of private initiative and investment in harmony with action in the public sector; and

(n) Expansion and diversification of exports.

Art. 32. In order to attain the objectives set forth in this Chapter, the Member States agree to co-operate with one another, in the broadest spirit of inter-American solidarity, as far as their resources may permit and their laws may provide.

Art. 33. To attain balanced and sustained development as soon as feasible, the Member States agree that the resources made available from time to time by each, in accordance with the preceding Article, should be provided under flexible conditions and in support of the national and multinational programs and efforts undertaken to meet the needs of the assisted country, giving special attention to the relatively less-developed countries.

They will seek, under similar conditions and for similar purposes, financial and technical co-operation from sources outside the Hemisphere and from international institutions.

Art. 34. The Member States should make every effort to avoid policies, actions, or measures that have serious adverse effects on the economic or social development of another Member State.

Art. 35. The Member States agree to join together in seeking a solution to urgent or critical problems that may arise whenever the economic development or stability of any Member State is seriously affected by conditions that cannot be remedied through the efforts of that State.

Art. 36. The Member States shall extend among themselves the benefits of science and technology by encouraging the exchange and utilization of scientific and technical knowledge in accordance with existing treaties and national laws.

Art. 37 The Member States, recognizing the close interdependence between foreign trade and economic and social development, should make individual and united efforts to bring about the following:

(a) Reduction or elimination, by importing countries, of tariff and non-tariff barriers that affect the exports of the Members of the Organization, except when such barriers are applied in order to diversify the economic structure, to speed up the development of the less-developed Member States, or to intensify their process of economic integration, or when they are related to national security or to the needs for economic balance;

(b) Maintenance of continuity in their economic and social development by means of:

(i) Improved conditions for trade in basic commodities through international agreements, where appropriate; orderly marketing procedures that avoid the disruption of markets; and other measures designed to promote the expansion of markets, and to obtain dependable incomes for producers, adequate and dependable supplies for consumers, and stable prices that are both remunerative to producers and fair to consumers;

(ii) Improved international financial co-operation and the adoption of other means for lessening the adverse impact of sharp fluctuations in export earnings experienced by the countries exporting basic commodities;

and

(iii) Diversification of exports and expansion of export opportunities for manufactured and semimanufactured products from the developing countries by promoting and strengthening national and multinational institutions and arrangements established for these purposes.

Art. 38. The Member States reaffirm the principle that when the more-developed countries grant concessions in international trade agreements that lower or eliminate tariffs or other barriers to foreign trade so that they benefit the less-developed countries, they should not expect reciprocal concessions from those countries that are incompatible with their economic development, financial, and trade needs.

Art. 39. The Member States, in order to accelerate their economic development, regional integration, and the expansion and improvement of the conditions of their commerce, shall promote improvement and coordination of transportation and communication in the developing countries and among the Member States.

Art. 40. The Member States recognize that integration of the developing countries of the Hemisphere is one of the objectives of the inter-American system and, therefore, shall orient their efforts to take the necessary measures to accelerate the integration process, with a view to establishing a Latin American common market in the shortest possible time.

Art. 41. In order to strengthen and accelerate integration in all its aspects, the Member States agree to give adequate priority to the preparation and carrying out of multinational projects and to their financing, as well as to encourage economic and financial institutions of the inter-American system to continue giving their broadest support to regional integration institutions and programs.

Art. 42. The Member States agree that technical and financial co-operation that seeks to promote regional economic integration should be based on the principle of harmonious, balanced, and efficient development, with particular attention to the relatively less-developed countries, so that it may be a decisive factor that will enable them to promote, with their own efforts, the improved development of their infrastructure programs, new lines of production, and export diversification.

Chapter VIII. Social Standards.

Art. 43. The Member States, convinced that man can only achieve the full realization of his aspirations within a just social order, along with economic development and true peace, agree to dedicate every effort to the application of the following principles and mechanisms:

(a) All human beings, without distinction as to race, sex, nationality, creed, or social condition, have a right to material well-being and to their spiritual development, under circumstances of liberty, dignity, equality of opportunity, and economic security.

(b) Work is a right and a social duty, it gives dignity to the one who performs it, and it should be performed under conditions including a system of fair wages, that ensure life, health, and a decent standard of living for the worker and his family, both during his working years and in his old age, or when any circumstance deprives him of the possibility of working;

(c) Employers and workers, both rural and urban, have the right to associate themselves freely for the defense and promotion of their interests, including the right to collective bargaining and the workers' right to strike, and recognition of the juridical personality of associations and the protection of their freedom and independence, all in accordance with applicable laws;

(d) Fair and efficient systems and procedures for consultation and collaboration among the sectors of production, with due regard for safeguarding the interests of the entire society;

(e) The operation of systems of public administration, banking and credit, enterprise, and distribution and sales, in such a way, in harmony with the private sector, as to meet the requirements and interests of the community;

(f) The incorporation and increasing participation of the marginal sectors of the population, in both rural and urban areas, in the economic, social, civic, cultural, and political life of the nation, in order to achieve the full integration of the national comunity, acceleration of the process of social mobility, and the consolidation of the democratic system. The encouragement of all efforts of popular promotion and co-operation that have as their purpose the development and progress of the community;

(g) Recognition of the importance of the contribution of organizations such as labor unions, co-operatives, and cultural, professional, business, neighborhood, and community associations to the life of the society and to the development process;

(h) Development of an efficient social security policy; and

(i) Adequate provision for all persons to have due legal aid in order to secure their rights.

Art. 44. The Member States recognize that, in order to facilitate the process of Latin American regional integration, it is necessary to harmonize the social legislation of the developing countries, especially in the labor and social security fields, so that the rights of the workers shall be equally protected, and they agree to make the greatest efforts possible to achieve this goal.

Chapter IX. Educational, Scientific, and Cultural Standards.

Art. 45. The Member States will give primary importance within their development plans to the encouragement of education, science, and culture, oriented toward the overall improvement of the individual, and as a foundation for democracy, social justice, and progress.

Art. 46. The Member States will co-operate with one another to meet their educational needs, to promote scientific research, and to encourage technological progress. They consider themselves individually and jointly bound to preserve and enrich the cultural heritage of the American peoples.

Art. 47. The Member States will exert the greatest efforts, in accordance with their constitutional processes, to ensure the effective exercise of the right to education, on the following bases:

(a) Elementary education, compulsory for children of school age, shall also be offered to all others who can benefit from it. When provided by the State it shall be without charge;

(b) Middle-level education shall be extended progressively to as much of the population as possible, with a view to social imrovement. It shall be diversified in such a way that it meets the development needs of each country without prejudice to providing a general education; and

(c) Higher education shall be available to all, provided that, in order to maintain its high level, the corresponding regulatory or academic standards are met.

Art. 48. The Member States will give special attention to the eradication of illiteracy, will strengthen adult and vocational education systems, and will ensure that the benefits of culture will be available to the entire population. They will promote the use of all information media to fulfil these aims.

Art. 49. The Member States will develop science and technology through educational research institutions and through expanded information programs. They will organize their co-operation in these fields efficiently and will substantially increase exchange of knowledge, in accordance with national objectives and laws and with treaties in force.

Art. 50. The Member States, with due respect for the individuality of each of them, agree to promote cultural exchange as an effective means of consolidating inter-American understanding; and they recognize that regional integration programs should be strengthened by close ties in the fields of education, science, and culture.

Part two

Chapter X. The Organs.

Art. 51. The Organization of American States accomplishes its purposes by means of:

(a) The General Assembly;

(b) The Meeting of Consultation of Ministers of Foreign Affairs;

(c) The Councils;

(d) The Inter-American Juridical Committee;

(e) The Inter-American Commission on Human Rights;

(f) The General Secretariat;

(g) The Specialized Conferences; and

(h) The Specialized Organizations.

There may be established, in addition to those provided for in the Charter and in accordance with the provisions thereof, such subsidiary organs, agencies, and other entities as are considered necessary.

Chapter XI. The General Assembly.

Art. 52. The General Assembly is the supreme organ of the Organization of American States. It has as its principal powers, in addition to such others as are assigned to it by the Charter, the following:

(a) To decide the general action and policy of the Organization, determine the structure and functions of its organs, and consider any matter relating to friendly relations among the American States;

(b) To establish measures for coordinating the activities of the organs, agencies, and entities of the Organization among themselves and such activities with those of the other institutions of the inter-American system;

(c) To strengthen and coordinate co-operation with the United Nations and its specialized agencies;

(d) To promote collaboration, especially in the economic, social, and cultural fields, with other international organizations whose purposes are similar to those of the Organization of American States;

(e) To approve the program-budget of the Organization and determine the quotas of the Member States;

(f) To consider the annual and special reports that shall be presented to it by the organs, agencies, and entities of the inter-American system;

(g) To adopt general standards to govern the operations of the General Secretariat; and

(h) To adopt its own rules of procedure and, by a two-thirds vote, its agenda.

The General Assembly shall exercise its powers in accordance with the provisions of the Charter and of other inter-American treaties.

Art. 53. The General Assembly shall establish the bases for fixing the quota that each Government is to contribute to the maintenance of the Organization, taking into account the ability to pay of the respective countries and their determination to contribute in an equitable manner. Decisions on budgetary matters require the approval of two thirds of the Member States.

Art. 54. All Member States have the right to be represented in the General Assembly. Each State has the right to one vote.

Art. 55. The General Assembly shall convene annually during the period determined by the rules of procedure and at a place selected in accordance with the principle of rotation. At each regular session the date and place of the next regular session shall be determined, in accordance with the rules of procedure.

If for any reason the General Assembly cannot be held at the place chosen, it shall meet at the General Secretariat, unless one of the Member States should make a timely offer of a site in its territory, in which case the Permanent Council of the Organization may agree that the General Assembly will meet in that place.

Art. 56. In Special circumstances and with the approval of two thirds of the Member States, the Permanent Council shall convoke a special session of the General Assembly.

Art. 57. Decisions of the General Assembly shall be adopted by the affirmative vote of an absolute majority of the Member States, except in those cases that require a two-thirds vote as provided in the Charter or as may be provided by the General Assembly in its rules of procedure.

Art. 58. There shall be a Preparatory Committee of the General Assembly, composed of representatives of all the Member States, which shall:

(a) Prepare the draft agenda of each session of the General Assembly;

(b) Review the proposed program-budget and the draft resolution on quotas, and present to the General Assembly a report thereon containing the recommendations it considers appropriate; and

(c) Carry out such other functions as the General Assembly may assign to it.

The draft agenda and the report shall, in due course, be transmitted to the Governments of the Member States.

Chapter XII. The Meeting of Consultation of Ministers of Foreign Affairs.

Art. 59. The Meeting of Consultation of Ministers of Foreign Affairs shall be held in order to consider problems of an urgent nature and of common interest to the American States, and to serve as the Organ of Consultation.

Art. 60. Any Member State may request that a Meeting of Consultation be called. The request shall be addressed to the Permanent Council of the Organization, which shall decide by an absolute majority whether a meeting should be held.

Art. 61. The agenda and regulations of the Meeting of Consultation shall be prepared by the Permanent Council of the Organization and submitted to the Member States for consideration.

Art. 62. If, for exceptional reasons, a Minister of Foreign Affairs is unable to attend the meeting, he shall be represented by a special delegate.

Art. 63. In case of an armed attack within the territory of an American State or within the region of security delimited by treaties in force, a Meeting of Consultation shall be held without delay. Such Meeting shall be called immediately by the Chairman of the Permanent Council of the Organization, who shall at the same time call a meeting of the Council itself.

Art. 64. An Advisory Defense Committee shall be established to advise the Organ of Consultation on problems of military co-operation that may arise in connection with the application of existing special treaties on collective security.

Art. 65. The Advisory Defense Committee shall be composed of the highest military authorities of the American States participating in the Meeting of Consultation, Under exceptional circumstances the Governments may appoint substitutes. Each State shall be entitled to one vote.

Art. 66. The Advisory Defense Committee shall be convoked under the same conditions as the Organ of Consultation, when the latter deals with matters relating to defense against aggression.

Art. 67. The Committee shall also meet when the General Assembly or the Meeting of Consultation or the Governments, by a two-thirds majority of the Member States, assign to it technical studies or reports on specific subjects.

Chapter XIII. The Councils of the Organization Common Provisions.

Art. 68. The Permanent Council of the Organization, the Inter-American Economic and Social Council, and the Inter-American Council for Education, Science, and Culture are directly responsible to the General Assembly and each has the authority granted to it in the Charter and other inter-American instruments, as well as the functions assigned to it by the General Assembly and the Meeting of consultation of Ministers of Foreign Affairs.

Art. 69. All Member States have the right to be represented on each of the Councils. Each State has the right to one vote.

Art. 70. The Councils may, within the limits of the Charter and other inter-American instruments, make recommendations on matters within their authority.

Art. 71. The Councils, on matters within their respective competence, may present to the General Assembly studies and proposals, drafts of international instruments, and proposals on the holding of specialized conferences, on the creation, modification, or elimination of specialized organizations and other inter-American agencies, as well as on the coordination of their activities. The Councils may also present studies, proposals, and drafts of international instruments to the Specialized Conferences.

Art. 72. Each Council may, in urgent cases, convoke Specialized Conferences on matters within its competence, after consulting with the Member States and without having to resort to the procedure provided for in Article 128.

Art. 73. The Councils, to the extent of their ability, and with the co-operation of the General Secretariat, shall render to the Governments such specialized services as the latter may request.

Art. 74. Each Council has the authority to require the other Councils, as well as the subsidiary organs and agencies responsible to them, to provide it with information and advisory services on matters within their respective spheres of competence. The Councils may also request the same services from the other agencies of the inter-American system.

Art. 75. With the prior approval of the General Assembly, The Councils may establish the subsidiary organs and the agencies that they consider advisable for the better performance of their duties. When the General Assembly is not in session, the aforesaid organs or agencies may be established provisionally by the corresponding council. In constituting the membership of these bodies, the Councils, insofar as possible, shall follow the criteria of rotation and equitable geographic representation.

Art. 76. The Councils may hold meetings in any Member State, when they find it advisable and with the prior consent of the Government concerned.

Art. 77. Each Council shall prepare its own statutes and submit them to the General Assembly for approval. It shall approve its own rules of procedure and those of its subsidiary organs, agencies, and committees.

Chapter XIV.

Art. 78. The Permanent Council of the Organization is composed of one representative of each Member State, especially appointed by the respective Government, with the rank of ambassador. Each Government may accredit an acting representative, as well as such alternates and advisers as it considers necessary.

Art. 79. The offices of Chairman of the Permanent Council shall be held by each of the representatives, in turn, following the alphabetic order in Spanish of the names of their respective countries. The office of Vice-Chairman shall be filled in the same way, following reverse alphabetic order. The Chairman and the Vice-Chairman shall hold office for a term of not more than six months, which shall be determined by the statutes.

Art. 80. Within the limits of the Charter and of inter-American treaties and agreements, the Permanent Council takes cognizance of any matter referred to it by the General Assembly or the Meeting of Consultation of Ministers of Foreign Affairs.

Art. 81. The Permanent Council shall serve provisionally as the Organ of Consultation when the circumstances contemplated in Article 63 of this Charter arise.

Art. 82. The Permanent Council shall keep vigilance over the maintenance of friendly relations among the Member States, and for that purpose shall effectively assist them in the peaceful settlement of their disputes, in accordance with the following provisions.

Art. 83. To assist the Permanent Council in the exercise of these powers, an Inter-American Committee on Peaceful Settlement shall be established, which shall function as a subsidiary organ of the Council. The statutes of the Committee shall be prepared by the Council and approved by the General Assembly.

Art. 84. The parties to a dispute may resort to the Permanent Council to obtain its good offices. In such a case the Council shall have authority to assist the parties and to recommend the procedures it considers suitable for the peaceful settlement of the dispute.

If the parties so wish, the Chairman of the Council shall refer the dispute directly to the Inter-American Committee on Peaceful Settlement.

Art. 85. In the exercise of these powers, the Permanent Council through the Inter-American Committee on Peaceful Settlement or by any other means, may ascertain the facts in the dispute, and may do so in the territory of any of the parties with the consent of the Government concerned.

Art. 86. Any party to a dispute in which none of the peaceful procedures set forth in Article 24 of the Charter is being followed may appeal to the Permanent Council to take cognizance of the dispute.

The Council shall immediately refer the request to the Inter-American Committee on Peaceful Settlement, which shall consider whether or not the matter is within its competence and, if it deems it appropriate, shall offer its goods offices to the other party or parties. Once these are accepted, the Inter-American Committee on Peaceful Settlement may assist the parties and recommend the procedures that it considers suitable for the peaceful settlement of the dispute.

In the exercise of these powers, the Committee may carry out an investigation of the facts in the dispute, and may do so in the territory of any of the parties with the consent of the Government concerned.

Art. 87. If one of the parties should refuse the offer, the Inter-American Committee on Peaceful Settlement shall limit itself to informing the Permanent Council, without prejudice to its taking steps to restore relations between the parties, if they were interrupted, or to reestablish harmony between them.

Art. 88. Once such a report is received, the Permanent Council may make suggestions for bringing the parties together for the purpose of Article 87 and, if it considers it necessary, it may urge the parties to avoid any action that might aggravate the dispute.

If one of the parties should continue to refuse the good offices of the Inter-American Committee on Peaceful Settlement or of the Council, the Council shall limit itself to submitting a report to the General Assembly.

Art. 89. The Permanent council, in the exercise of these functions, shall take its decisions by an affirmative vote of two thirds of its members, excluding the parties to the dispute, except for such decisions as the rules of procedure provide shall be adopted by a simple majority.

Art. 90. In performing their functions with respect to the peaceful settlement of disputes, the Permanent Council and the Inter-American Committee on Peaceful Settlement shall observe the provisions of the Charter and the principles and standards of international law, as well as take into account the existence of treaties in force between the parties.

Art. 91. The Permanent Council shall also:

(a) Carry out those decisions of the General Assembly or of the Meeting of Consultation of Ministers of Foreign Affairs the implementation of which has not been assigned to any other body;

(b) Watch over the observance of the standards governing the operation of the General Secretariat and, when the General Assembly is not in session, adopt provisions of a regulatory nature that enable the General Secretariat to carry out its administrative functions;

(c) Act as the Preparatory Committee of the General Assembly in accordance with the terms of Article 58 of the Charter, unless the General Assembly should decide otherwise;

(d) Prepare, at the request of the Member States and with the co-operation of the appropriate organs of the Organization, draft agreements to promote and facilitate co-operation between the Organization of American States and the Untied Nations or between the Organization and other American agencies of recognized international standing. These draft agreements shall be submitted to the General Assembly for approval;

(e) Submit recommendations to the General Assembly with regard to the functioning of the Organization and the coordination of its subsidiary organs, agencies, and committees;

(f) Present to the General Assembly any observations it may have regarding the reports of the Inter-American Juridical Committee and the Inter-American Commission on Human Rights; and

(g) Perform the other functions assigned to it in the Charter.

Art. 92. The Permanent Council and the General Secretariat shall have the same seat.

Chapter XV. The Inter-American Economic and Social Council.

Art. 93. The Inter-American Economic and Social Council is composed of one principal representative, of the highest rank, of each Member State, especially appointed by the respective Government.

Art. 94. The purpose of the Inter-American Economic and Social Council is to promote co-operation among the American countries in order to attain accelerated economic and social development, in accordance with the standards set forth in Chapters VII and VIII.

Art. 95. To achieve its purpose the Inter-American Economic and Social Council shall:

(a) Recommend programs and courses of action and periodically study and evaluate the efforts undertaken by the Member States;

(b) Promote and coordinate all economic and social activities of the Organization;

(c) Coordinate its activities with those of the other Councils of the Organization;

(d) Establish co-operative relations with the corresponding organs of the United Nations and with other national and international agencies, especially with regard to coordination of inter-American technical assistance programs; and

(e) Promote the solution of the cases contemplated in Article 35 of the Charter, establishing the appropriate procedure.

Art. 96. The Inter-American Economic and Social Council shall hold at least one meeting each year at the ministerial level. It shall also meet when convoked by the General Assembly, the Meeting of Consultation of Ministers of Foreign Affairs, at its own initiative, or for the cases contemplated in Article 35 of the Charter.

Art. 97. The Inter-American Economic and Social Council shall have a Permanent Executive Committee, composed of a Chairman and no less than seven other members, elected by the Council for terms to be established in the statutes of the Council. Each member shall have the right to one vote. The principles of equitable geographic representation and of rotation shall be taken into account, insofar as possible, in the election of members. The Permanent Executive Committee represents all of the Member States of the Organization.

Art. 98. The Permanent Executive Committee shall perform the tasks assigned to it by the Inter-American Economic and Social Council, in accordance with the general standards established by the Council.

Chapter XVI. The Inter-American Council for Education, Science, and Culture.

Art. 99. The Inter-American Council for Education, Science, and Culture is composed of one principal representative, of the highest rank, of each Member State, especially appointed by the respective Government.

Art. 100. The purpose of the Inter-American Council for Education, Science, and Culture is to promote friendly relations and mutual understanding between the peoples of the Americas through educational, scientific, and cultural cooperation and exchange between Member States, in order to raise the cultural level of the peoples, reaffirm their dignity as individuals, prepare them fully for the tasks of progress, and strengthen the devotion to peace, democracy, and social justice that has characterized their evolution.

Art. 101. To accomplish its purpose the Inter-American Council for Education, Science, and Culture shall:

(a) Promote and coordinate the educational, scientific, and cultural activities of the Organization;

(b) Adopt or recommend pertinent measures to give effect to the standards contained in Chapter IX of the Charter;

(c) Support individual or collective efforts of the Member States to improve and extend education at all levels, giving special attention to efforts directed toward community development;

(d) Recommend and encourage the adoption of special educational programs directed toward integrating all sectors of the population into their respective national cultures;

(e) Stimulate and support scientific and technological education and research, especially when these relate to national development plans;

(f) Foster the exchange of professors, research workers, technicians, and students, as well as of study materials; and encourage the conclusion of bilateral or multilateral agreements on the progressive coordination of curricula at all educational levels and on the validity and equivalence of certificates and degrees;

(g) Promote the education of the American peoples with a view to harmonious international relations and a better understanding of the historical and cultural origins of the Americas, in order to stress and preserve their common values and destiny;

(h) Systematically encourage intellectual and artistic creativity, the exchange of cultural works and folklore, as well as the interrelationships of the different cultural regions of the Americas;

(i) Foster co-operation and technical assistance for protecting, preserving, and increasing the cultural heritage of the Hemisphere;

(j) Coordinate its activities with those of the other Councils. In harmony with the Inter-American Economic and Social Council, encourage the interrelationship of programs for promoting education, science, and culture with national development and regional integration programs;

(k) Establish co-operative relations with the corresponding organs of the United Nations and with other national and international bodies;

(l) Strengthen the civic conscience of the American peoples, as one of the bases for the effective exercise of democracy and for the observance of the rights and duties of man;

(m) Recommend appropriate procedures for intensifying integration of the developing countries of the Hemisphere by means of efforts and programs in the fields of education, science, and culture; and

(n) Study and evaluate periodically the efforts made by the Member States in the fields of education, science, and culture.

Art. 102. The Inter-American Council for Education, Science, and Culture shall hold at least one meeting each year at the ministerial level. It shall also meet when convoked by the General Assembly, by the Meeting of Consultation of Ministers of Foreign Affairs, or at its own initiative.

Art. 103. The Inter-American Council for Education, Science, and Culture shall have a Permanent Executive Committee, composed of a Chairman and no less than seven other members, elected by the Council. Each member shall have the right to one vote. The principles of equitable geographic representation and of rotation shall be taken into account, insofar as possible. in the election of members. The Permanent Executive Committee represents all of the Member States of the Organization.

Art. 104. The Permanent Executive Committee shall perform the tasks assigned to it by the Inter-American Council for Education, Science, and Culture, in accordance with the general standards established by the Council.

Art. 105. The purpose of the Inter-American Juridical Committee is to serve the Organization as an advisory body on juridical matters; to promote the progressive development and the codification of international law; and to study juridical problems related to the integration of the developing countries of the Hemisphere and, insofar as may appear desirable, the possibility of attaining uniformity in their legislation.

Art. 106. The Inter-American Juridical Committee shall undertake the studies and preparatory work assigned to it by the General Assembly, the meeting of Consultation of Ministers of Foreign Affairs, or the Councils of the Organization. It may also, on its own initiative, undertake such studies and preparatory work as it considers advisable, and suggest the holding of specialized juridical conferences.

Art. 107. The Inter-American Juridical Committee shall be composed of eleven jurists, nationals of Member States, elected by the General Assembly for a period of four years from panels of three candidates presented by Member States. In the election, a system shall be used that takes into account partial replacement of membership and, insofar as possible, equitable geographic representation. No two members of the Committee may be nationals of the same State. Vacancies that occur shall be filled in the manner set forth above.

Art. 108. The Inter-American Juridical Committee represents all of the Member States of the Organization, and has the broadest possible technical autonomy.

Art. 109. The Inter-American Juridical Committee shall establish co-operative relations with universities, institutes, and other teaching centers, as well as with national and international committees and entities devoted to study, research, teaching, or dissemination of information on juridical matters of international interest.

Art. 110. The Inter-American Juridical Committee shall draft its statutes, which shall be submitted to the General Assembly for approval.

The Committee shall adopt its own rules of procedure.

Art. 111. The seat of Inter-American Juridical Committee shall be the city of Rio de Janeiro, but in special cases the Committee may meet at any other place that may be designated, after consultation with the Member State concerned.

Chapter XVIII. The Inter-American Commission on Human Rights.

Art. 112. There shall be an Inter-American Commission on Human Rights, whose principal function shall be to promote the observance and protection of human rights and to serve as a consultative organ of the Organization in these matters. An Inter-American convention on human rights shall determine the structure, competence, and procedure of this Commission, as well as those of other organs responsible for these matters.

Chapter XIX. The General Secretariat.

Art. 113. The General Secretariat is the central and permanent organ of the Organization of American States. It shall perform the functions assigned to it in the Charter, in other inter-American treaties and agreements, and by the General Assembly, and shall carry out the duties entrusted to it by the General Assembly, the Meeting of Consultation of Ministers of Foreign Affairs, or the Councils.

Art. 114. The Secretary-General of the Organization shall be elected by the General Assembly for a five-year term and may not be reelected more than once or succeeded by a person of the same nationality. In the event that the office of Secretary-General becomes vacant, the Assistant Secretary-General shall assume his duties until the General Assembly shall elect a new Secretary-General for a full term.

Art. 115. The Secretary-General shall direct the General Secretariat, be the legal representative thereof, and, notwithstanding the provisions of Article 91(b), be responsible to the General Assembly for the proper fulfillment of the obligations and functions of the General Secretariat.

Art. 116. The Secretary-General, or his representative, participates with voice but without vote in all meetings of the Organization.

Art. 117. The General Secretariat shall promote economic, social, juridicial, educational, scientific, and cultural relations among all the Member States of the Organization, in keeping with the actions and policies decided upon by the General Assembly and with the pertinent decisions of the Councils.

Art. 118. The General Secretariat shall also perform the following functions:

(a) Transmit ex officio to the Member States notice of the convocation of the General Assembly, the Meeting of Consultation of Ministers of Foreign Affairs, the Inter-American Economic and Social Council, the Inter-American Council for Education, Science, and Culture, and the Specialized Conferences;

(b) Advise the other organs, when appropriate, in the preparation of agenda and rules of procedure;

(c) Prepare the proposed program-budget of the Organization on the basis of programs adopted by the Councils, agencies, and entities whose expenses should be included in the program-budget and, after consultation with the Councils or their permanent committees, submit it to the Preparatory Committee of the General Assembly and then to the Assembly itself;

(d) Provide, on a permanent basis, adequate secretariat services for the General Assembly and the other organs, and carry out their directives and assignments. To the extent of its ability, provide services for the other meetings of the Organization;

(e) Serve as custodian of the documents and archives of the Inter-American Conferences, the General Assembly, the Meetings of Consultation of Ministers of Foreign Affairs, the Councils, and the Specialized Conferences;

(f) Serve as depository of inter-American treaties and agreements, as well as of the instruments of ratification thereof;

(g) Submit to the General Assembly at each regular session an annual report on the activities of the Organization and its financial condition; and

(h) Establish relations of co-operation, in accordance with decisions reached by the General Assembly or the Councils, with the Specialized Organizations as well as other national and international organizations.

Art. 119. The Secretary-General shall:

(a) Establish such offices of the General Secretariat as are necessary to accomplish its purposes; and

(b) Determine the number of officers and employees of the General Secretariat, appoint them, regulate their powers and duties, and fix their renumeration.

The Secretary-General shall exercise this authority in accordance with such general standards and budgetary provisions as may be established by the General Assembly.

Art. 120. The Assistant Secretary-General shall be elected by the General Assembly for a five-year term and may not be reelected more than once or succeeded by a person of the same nationality. In the event that the office of Assistant Secretary-General becomes vacant, the Permanent Council shall elect a substitute to hold that office until the General Assembly shall elect a new Assistant Secretary-General for a full term.

Art. 121. The Assistant Secretary-General shall be the Secretary of the Permanent Council. He shall serve as advisory officer to the Secretary-General and shall act as his delegate in all matters that the Secretary-General may entrust to him. During the temporary absence or disability of the Secretary-General, the Assistant Secretary-General shall perform his functions.

The Secretary-General and the Assistant Secretary-General shall be of different nationalities.

Art. 122. The General Assembly, by a two-thirds vote of the Member States, may remove the Secretary-General or the Assistant Secretary-General, or both, whenever the proper functioning of the Organization so demands.

Art. 123. The Secretary-General shall appoint, with the approval of the respective Council, the Executive Secretary for Economic and Social Affairs and the Executive Secretary for Education, Science, and Culture, who shall also be the secretaries of the respective Councils.

Art. 124. In the performance of their duties, the Secretary-General and the personnel of the Secretariat shall not seek or receive instructions from any Government or from any authority outside the Organization, and shall refrain from any action that may be incompatible with their position as international officers responsible only to the Organization.

Art. 125. The Member States pledge themselves to respect the exclusively international character of the Secretary-General and the personnel of the General Secretariat, and not to seek to influence them in the discharge of their duties.

Art. 126. In selecting the personnel of the General Secretariat, first consideration shall be given to efficiency, competence, and integrity; but at the same time, in the recruitment of personnel of all ranks, importance shall be given to the necessity of obtaining as wide a geographic representation as possible.

Art. 127. The seat of the General Secretariat is the city of Washington.

Chapter XX. The Specialized Conferences.

Art. 128. The specialized Conferences are inter-governmental meetings to deal with special technical matters or to develop specific aspects of inter-American co-operation. They shall be held when either the General Assembly or the Meeting of Consultation of Ministers of Foreign Affairs so decides, on its own initiative or at the request of one of the Councils or Specialized Organizations.

Art. 129. The Agenda and rules of procedure of the Specialized Conferences shall be prepared by the Councils or Specialized Organizations concerned and shall be submitted to the Governments of the Member States for consideration.

Chapter XXI. The Specialized Organizations.

Art. 130. For the purposes of the present Charter, Inter-American Specialized Organizations are the intergovernmental organizations established by multilateral agreements and having specific functions with respect to technical matters of common interest to the American States.

Art. 131. The General Secretariat shall maintain a register of the organizations that fulfil the conditions set forth in the foreign Article, as determined by the General Assembly after a report from the Council concerned.

Art. 132. The Specialized Organizations shall enjoy the fullest technical autonomy, but they shall take into account the recommendations of the General Assembly and of the Councils, in accordance with the provisions of the Charter.

Art. 133. The Specialized Organizations shall transmit to the General Assembly annual reports on the progress of their work and on their annual budgets and expenses.

Art. 134. Relations that should exist between the Specialized Organizations and the Organization shall be defined by means of agreements concluded between each organization and the Secretary-General, with the authorization of the General Assembly.

Art. 135. The Specialized Organizations shall establish cooperative relations with world agencies of the same character in order to coordinate their activities. In concluding agreements with international agencies of a worldwide character, the Inter-American Specialized Organizations shall preserve their identity and their status as integral parts of the Organization of American States, even when they perform regional functions of international agencies.

Art. 136. In determining the location of the Specialized Organizations consideration shall be given to the interest of all of the Member States and to the desirability of selecting the seats of these organizations on the basis of a geographic representation as equitable as possible.

Part three

Chapter XXII. The United Nations.

Art. 137. None of the provisions of this Charter shall be construed as impairing the rights and obligations of the Member States under the Charter of the United Nations.

Chapter XXIII. Miscellaneous Provisions.

Art. 138. Attendance at meetings of the permanent organs of the Organization of American States or at the conferences and meetings provided for in the Charter, or held under the auspices of the Organization, shall be in accordance with the multilateral character of the aforesaid organs, conferences, and meetings and shall not depend on the bilateral relations between the Government of any Member State and the Government of the host country.

Art. 139. The Organization of American States shall enjoy in the territory of each Member such legal capacity, privileges, and immunities as are necessary for the exercise of its functions and the accomplishment of its purposes.

Art. 140. The representatives of the Member States on the organs of the Organization, the personnel of their delegations, as well as the Secretary-General and the Assistant Secretary-General shall enjoy the privileges and immunities corresponding to their positions and necessary for the independent performance of their duties.

Art. 141. The juridical status of the Specialized Organizations and the privileges and immunities that should be granted to them and to their personnel, as well as to the officials of the General Secretariat, shall be determined in a multilateral agreement. The foregoing shall not preclude, when it is considered necessary, the concluding of bilateral agreements.

Art. 142. Correspondence of the Organization of American States, including printed matter and parcels, bearing the frank thereof, shall be carried free of charge in the mails of the Member States.

Art. 143. The Organization of American States does not allow any restriction based on race, creed, or sex, with respect to eligibility to participate in the activities of the Organization and to hold positions therein.

Chapter XXIV. Ratification and Entry Into Force.

Art. 144. The present Charter shall remain open for signature by the American States and shall be ratified in accordance with their respective constitutional procedures. The original instrument, the Spanish, English, Portuguese, and French texts of which are equally authentic, shall be deposited with the General Secretariat, which shall transmit certified copies thereof to the Governments for purposes of ratification. The instruments of ratification shall be deposited with the General Secretariat, which shall notify the signatory States of such deposit.

Art. 145. The present Charter shall enter into force among the ratifying States when two thirds of the signatory States have deposited their ratifications. It shall enter into force with respect to the remaining States in the order in which they deposit their ratifications.

Art. 146. The present Charter shall be registered with the Secretariat of the United Nations through the General Secretariat.

Art. 147. Amendments to the present Charter may be adopted only at a General Assembly convened for that purpose. Amendments shall enter into force in accordance with the terms and the procedure set forth in Article 145.

Art. 148. The present Charter shall remain in force indefinitely, but may be denounced by any Member State upon written notification to the General Secretariat, which shall communicate to all the others each notice of denunciation received. After two years from the date on which the General Secretariat receives a notice of denunciation, the present Charter shall cease to be in force with respect to the denouncing State, which shall cease to belong to the Organization after it has fulfilled the obligations arising from the present Charter.

Chapter XXV. Transitory Provisions.

Art. 149. The Inter-American Committee on the Alliance for Progress shall act as the permanent executive committee of the Inter-American Economic and Social Council as long as the Alliance is in operation.

Art. 150. Until the inter-American convention on human rights, referred to in Chapter XVIII, enters into force, the present Inter-American Commissions on Human Rights shall keep vigilance over the observance of human rights."

Reservations Made at the Time of Ratifying the Charter of 1948.

Guatemala

None of the stipulations of the present Charter of the Organization of American States may be considered as an impediment to Guatemala's assertion of its rights over the territory of Belize by such means as at anytime it may deem advisable.

Peru

With the reservation that the principles of inter-American solidarity and co-operation and essentially those set forth in the preamble and declarations of the Act of Chapultepec constitute standards for the mutual relations between the American States and juridical bases of the Inter-American system.

United States

That the Senate give its advice and consent to ratification of the Charter with the reservation that none of its provisions shall be considered as enlarging the powers of the Federal Government of the United States or limiting the powers of the several states of the Federal Union with respect to any matters recognized under the Constitution as being within the reserved powers of the several states.

Declarations Made at the Time of Signing the Protocol.

Ecuador

The Delegation of Ecuador, drawing its inspiration from the devotion of the people and the Government of Ecuador to peace and law, states for the record that the provisions approved with respect to peaceful settlement of disputes do not carry out the purpose of Resolution XIII of the Second Special Inter-American Conference, and that the Permanent Council has not been given sufficient powers to aid the Member States effectively in the peaceful settlement of their disputes. The Delegation of Ecuador signs this Protocol of Amendment to the Charter of the Organization of American States in the understanding that none of its provisions in any way limits the right of the Member States to take their disputes, whatever their nature and the subject they deal with, to the Organization, so that it may assist the parties and recommend the suitable procedures for peaceful settlement thereof.

Panama

The Delegation of Panama, upon signing the Protocol of Amendment to the Charter of the Organization of American States, states that it does so in the understanding that none of its provisions limits or in any way impedes the right of Panama to bring before the Organization any conflict or dispute that may have arisen with another Member State to which a just solution has not been given within a reasonable period after applying, without positive results, any of the procedures for peaceful settlement set forth in Article 21 of the present Charter.

Argentina

On signing the present Protocol, the Argentine Republic reiterates its firm conviction that the amendments introduced in the Charter of the OAS do not duly cover the requirements of the Organization, inasmuch as its basic instrument should contain, in addition to the organic economic, social, and cultural standards, the essential provisions that would make the security system of the Hemisphere effective."

Art. 8 of the Charter was changed by the ▷ Cartagena Protocol, 1985, opening the possibility of membership after five years for Belize and Guyana.

Inter-American Juridical Yearbook, Washington, DC, 1949; *Novena Conferencia Internacional Americana Actas y Documentos*, Bogota, 1953; *The American Journal of International Law*, Vol. 64, No. 10, Oct. 5, 1970; *Charter of the OAS as amended by the Protocol of Buenos Aires in 1960*, OAS Treaty Series, Washington, DC, 1970.

CHARTER OF ORGANIZATION OF CENTRAL AMERICAN STATES, 1962. Organización de Estados Centroamericanos. ODECA, The Charter was signed in Panama City on Dec. 12, 1962 by the governments of Costa Rica, Honduras, Guatemala, Nicaragua and El Salvador and called under Art. 30, the San Salvador Charter; came into force on Mar. 30, 1965. The text is as follows:

"The Governments of Costa Rica, Nicaragua, Honduras, El Salvador and Guatemala,

Considering:

That it is necessary to provide the five States with a more effective instrument by establishing organs which will ensure their economic and social progress, remove the barriers which divide them, bring about steady improvement in the living conditions of their peoples, ensure industrial stability and growth, and strengthen Central American solidarity,

Therefore:

The above-mentioned Governments have decided to replace the Charter signed at San Salvador, in the Republic of El Salvador on 14 October 1951 by the following Charter of the Organization of Central American States:

Art 1. Costa Rica, Nicaragua, Honduras, El Salvador and Guatemala constitute an economic and political community which aspires to achieve the integration of Central America. It is for this purpose that the Organization of Central American States (OCAS) has been established.

Art. 2. The following organs shall be established in order to give effect to the purposes of the Organization of Central American States:

(a) The Meeting of Heads of State;
(b) The Conference of Ministers for Foreign Affairs;
(c) The Executive Council;
(d) The Legislative Council;
(e) The Central American Court of Justice;
(f) The Central American Economic Council;
(g) The Cultural and Educational Council; and
(h) The Central American Defence Council.

Art. 3. The Organization of Central American States is based on the principles of the United Nations Charter and the Charter of Organization of American States.

Art. 4. The Conference of Ministers for Foreign Affairs shall meet in regular session once a year and in special session whenever not less than three of their number deem it necessary.

Art. 5. In the Conference of Ministers for Foreign Affairs, each Member State shall have only one vote. Decisions on questions of substance shall be adopted unanimously. Where doubt exists whether a question is one of substance or of procedure, the matter will be settled by unanimous vote.

Art. 6. The Conference of Ministers for Foreign Affairs may establish such subsidiary organs as it deems appropriate for the study of various problems.

The seats of the various subsidiary organs shall be chosen on the basis of equitable geographical distribution and in accordance with the needs which have led to the establishment of the said organs.

Art. 7. The Executive Council shall be composed of the Ministers for Foreign Affairs or their specially authorized representatives. It shall be responsible for the legal representation of the Organization.

Art. 8. The Executive Council shall be presided over by one of its members. The Presidency shall rotate each year among the States Members of the Organizations. The Council shall hold regular meetings once a week and shall hold special meetings when convoked by the President.

Art. 9. The Executive Council shall be responsible for directing and co-ordinating the policy of the Organization with a view to the accomplishment of its purposes. The Council shall appoint a Secretary and the necessary staff in order to ensure the proper functioning of the administrative services. It shall for that purpose adopt appropriate rules defining their obligations.

The Council shall be the channel of communication between the organs and Member States.

Art. 10. The legislative Council shall be composed of three representatives of the legislative authority of each Member State.

The Council shall give advice and act as an organ of consultation in legislative matters. It shall also study the possibility of unifying the legislation of the Central American States.

Art. 11. The Council shall, in accordance with its own rules, establish such working committees as it deems appropriate.

Art. 12. The Legislative Council shall meet in regular session each year, starting on 15 September, and in special session whenever it is convoked by the Executive Council at the request of at least two Governments of Member States.

Art. 13. The adoption of resolutions and recommendations by the Council shall require the affirmative vote of a majority of its members.

Art. 14. The Central American Court of Justice shall be composed of the Presidents of the Judiciary of the Member States.

Art. 15. The Central American Court of Justice shall have the following functions:

(a) To hear such legal disputes arising between Member States as the latter submit to it by agreement;
(b) To formulate and express opinions on schemes for the unification of Central American legislation when requested to do so by the Conference of Ministers for Foreign Affairs or the Executive Council.

Art. 16. The Central American Court of Justice shall meet whenever it deems it necessary or is convoked by the Executive Council.

Art. 17. The Central American Economic Council shall be composed of the Ministers of Economics of the Member States and shall be responsible for the planning, co-ordination and execution of Central American economic integration.

All Central American economic integration agencies shall form part of the Council.

Art. 18. The Economic Council shall, on the basis of the reports of the various agencies connected with the Central American Economic Integration Programme, submit a comprehensive annual report on its work to the Executive Council for the information of the Conference of Ministers for Foreign Affairs.

Art. 19. The Cultural and Educational Council shall be composed of the Ministers of Education of the Member States or their representatives.

Art. 20. The Cultural and Educational Council shall have the following functions:

(a) To promote educational, scientific and cultural exchanges among Member States;
(b) To conduct studies of the state of education, science and culture in the region;
(c) To co-ordinate efforts to achieve uniformity in the educational systems of Central America;
(d) To report on its activities to the Conference of Ministers for Foreign Affairs through the Executive Council of the Organization.

Art. 21. The Defence Council shall be composed of the Ministers of Defence or officials of equivalent rank and functions of the Member States.

Art. 22. The Defence Council shall act as an organ of consultation in matters of regional defence and shall endeavour to ensure the collective security of Member States. It shall report on its activities to the Conference of Ministers for Foreign Affairs through the Executive Council.

Art. 23. Any Member State may, through the Executive Council, propose a meeting of the organs or of ministers of other departments to deal with matters affecting Central America.

Art. 24. The Organization shall not function in such a way as to interfere with the internal systems of States, and nothing in the provisions of this Charter shall prejudice observance of and compliance with the constitutional rules of the various States or be interpreted in such a way as to impair the rights and obligations of the Central American States or such special positions as any one of them may have adopted through specific reservations in existing treaties or agreements.

Art. 25. This Charter shall be ratified by the Central American States as soon as possible in accordance with their respective constitutional procedures.

It shall be registered with the Secretariat of the United Nations in accordance with Article 102 of the Charter of the United Nations.

Art. 26. Each of the organs provided for in this Charter shall draw up its own rules.

Art. 27. The organs shall, save as otherwise provided, meet at the seat of the Organization.

Art. 28. The original of this Charter shall be deposited with the Office of the Organization, which shall transmit certified true copies thereof to the Ministers for Foreign Affairs of the Member States.

The instruments of ratification shall be deposited with the Office of the Organization, which shall notify the Ministries of Foreign Affairs of the Member States of each deposit.

Art. 29. This Charter shall enter into force on the date of the deposit of the instruments of ratification of the five Member States.

Art. 30. This Convention on the Organization of Central American States shall retain the name "San Salvador Charter."

UNTS, Vol, 552, pp, 24–36.

CHARTER OF UNITED NATIONS, 1945. ▷ United Nations Charter.

CHARTRES. A city in north-west France, in Orléanais, on the Eure River. The Chartres Cathedral is included in the ▷ World Heritage UNESCO List. Taking as their starting point the already existing Romanesque doorway, whose columns in the form of statues are world-famous, the architects at the beginning of the 13th century constructed a building which marks the triumph of Gothic art, an art of vertical line and light. The 173 stained-glass windows, all dating from before 1240, have a total area of more than 2000 sq. m, and form the largest extant collection of stained-glass from that period.

UNESCO. *A Legacy for All*, Paris, 1984.

CHATEAU AND ESTATE OF CHAMBORD. French cultural monument 48 km south of Orleans and 4 km from the left bank of the Loire, included in the ▷ World Heritage UNESCO List. Chambord stands in a park of more than 5000 hectares. When it was finished, in 1541, it was called "one of the miracles of the world". It continues to fascinate because of the paradoxical nature of the aesthetic approach, the most innovative features of which have provided a point of reference for architects up to the present day.

World Cultural Heritage. Information Bulletin, Paris, 1983.

CHATTAM HOUSE. The headquarters of the Royal Institute of International Affairs in London, f. 1920 as the British Institute of International Affairs; present name and headquarters since 1923.

B. WEIRREB, C. HIBBERT eds., *The London Encyclopedia*, London, 1983.

CHECKS OR CHEQUES. An international term for written instructions in a specific form to pay the bearer or a specific person a sum of money stated in figures and words or as a transfer from the account of issue to a specific account. In the first case it is an uncrossed check and in the second a clearance check. On the initiative of the League of Nations an International Conference on Foreign Exchange and Cheque Law took place in Geneva in Mar., 1931. It was then established that "the law of the country in which payment is made will determine to whom a cheque may be written out."

(1). Convention providing for a Uniform Law for Cheques, signed at Geneva, Mar. 19, 1931; came into force on Jan. 1, 1934; ratified by Austria, Belgium, Brazil, Denmark, Finland, France, Germany, Greece, Hungary, Indonesia, Italy, Japan, Luxemburg, Monaco, Netherlands, Nicaragua, Norway, Poland, Portugal, Sweden, Switzerland. It was signed by Czechoslovakia, Ecuador, Mexico, Romania, Spain, Turkey and Yugoslavia.

(2). Convention for the Settlement of Certain Conflicts of Laws in Connection with Cheques, signed at Geneva, Mar. 19, 1931, came into force on Jan. 1, 1934; ratified and signed by the same states as above.

Convention on the Stamp Laws in Connection with Cheques, signed at Geneva Mar. 19, 1931; entered into force on Nov. 10, 1933; ratified and signed by the same states as above.

LNTS, Vol. 143, pp. 9, 357, and 409.

CHEESES. A subject of international co-operation and of the Stresa Convention on Cheeses, 1951. Organizations reg. with the UIA:

EEC Association of the Processed Cheese Industry, f. 1914, Brussels.

Permanent Council of the International Convention for the use of Appellations of Origin and Denomination of Cheeses, signed in Stresa, June 1, 1951. Secretariat in Rome.

Yearbook of International Organizations.

"CHELUSKIN". The Soviet ice-breaker (7500 BRT) which in 1933 was the first to navigate the northern route from Murmansk to the Bering Sea; broken up by ice floes in the Chukotsk Sea Feb. 13, 1934; the crew was rescued by air.

CHEMICAL DISARMAMENT. Intergovernmental talks on a treaty to ban chemical and biological warfare had begun in 1968, but negotiations started under the auspices of the UN Conference on Disarmament on Febr. 5, 1985 in Geneva and during the 1986-session on Jan. 28, 1986. Before, on Jan. 15, 1986, M. Gorbachev, Secretary General of the CP USSR in his nuclear arms elimination proposals supported the "total elimination of chemical weapons".

SIPRI, *The Problem of Chemical and Biological Warfare: CB Disarmament Negotiations 1920–1970*, Stockholm, 1971; SIPRI, *Chemical Weapons: Destruction and Conversion*, London, 1980; J. GOLDBLAT, *Chemical Disarmament. From the Ban on Use to a Ban on Possession Background Paper Canadian Institute for International Peace and Security*, No. 17, February, 1988.

CHEMICAL ELEMENTS. Substances constituting matter, which appear in nature, or in the case of those with an atomic number greater than that of Uranium (92), are artificially derived through nuclear reactions. Since 1889 (The Table of D.I. Mendelyeeff) chemical elements are designated with international symbols, the majority derived from Latin names. Subject of organized international co-operation in international institutes for nuclear research.

CHEMICAL SAFETY. INTERNATIONAL WHO PROGRAM. A WHO action which in collaboration with FAO, ILO and UNEP, started at the beginning of 1980 in Europe where half the world's chemical industry is concentrated. Toxic chemicals reach the environment at all stages of manufacture, during transportation, and in the use and disposal of waste products. They can affect the air man breathes, the water he drinks and the food he eats. Workers employed in industry and agriculture may run special risks. A major element of the WHO Program is technical co-operation in many environmental health aspects of toxic chemicals, surveillance and control. The aim is to reduce health dangers as far as possible.

CHEMICAL WARFARE. Known since 429 BC when during the siege of the city of Platea the Spartans used enormous pots of sulphur, pitch and burning charcoal. In the Middle Ages stink pots were used while modern chemical warfare dates from the second part of 19th century with industrial production of ▷ asphyxiating gases. The St Petersburg Declaration 1868 was against incendiary or fulminating substances and the Hague Declarations 1899 against poison gases. Chemical weapons were used by Germany during the I World War, Japan during the II World War, the USA in Vietnam (▷ Defoliation) and ▷ Iraq against Iran. See also ▷ CBW.

E.K. FRADKIN, "Chemical warfare: its possibilities and probabilities", in: *International Conciliation*, No. 248, New York, March, 1929, pp. 113–192. SIPRI, *Yearbook 1987*, Oxford, 1988, pp. 97–115. D. ROBERTSON, *Guide to Modern Defense and Strategy*, Detroit, 1988.

CHEMICAL WEAPON FREE ZONE IN CENTRAL EUROPE. A project adopted in April 1982 by the Independence Commission for Disarmament and Security (▷ Olof Palme Commission) and supported generally by the political parties of the GDR and FRG; discussed also in other regions of the World.

R. TRAPP, *Chemical Weapons Free Zones?*, SIPRI, Stockholm, 1987.

CHEMICAL WEAPONS. The chemical substances which might be used in war because of their toxic properties are the subject of negotiations in the UN primarily concerning biological weapons (▷ B and C Arms). After the ▷ BW Convention, 1972, separate negotiations took place in the Committee on Disarmament for a convention that would prohibit chemical weapons and this was also the subject of negotiations between the USA and the USSR. This was in accordance with the UN General Assembly Resolutions 2827A/XXVI, 2933/XXVII, 3077/XXVIII, 3256/XXIX, 3465/XXX, 31/65, 32/77, S-10/2, 33/59A and 33/71H.

The Conference of the Committee on Disarmament, 1972–79, discussed a comprehensive ban on chemical weapons in one move and a step-by-step approach; national and international verification measures; production, stockpiling, destruction of stockpiles, and other provisions.

In June 1979 SIPRI convened an international symposium on chemical weapons in Stockholm, which was attended by 30 experts from 14 countries. The secretariat of the Committee on Disarmament prepared a compilation of material on chemical warfare resulting from the Conference of the Committee on Disarmament working papers and statements.

A joint USA–USSR report on progress in the bilateral negotiations on the prohibition of chemical weapons was published on Aug. 7, 1979 (Doc. CD/48) stressing "the great importance attached to the elaboration of a convention by the UN General Assembly and the Committe on Disarmament."

On Jan. 10, 1984 the Warsaw Pact States presented to the NATO States a proposal on elimination of chemical weapons in Europe.

On March 22, 1986 the Security Council condemned Iraq for violating the Geneva Protocol 1925 forbidding the use of chemical weapons.

On May 22, 1986 in Brussels NATO defence ministers approved US plans to resume the production of chemical weapons.

According to SIPRI, 1987, the following countries, outside of NATO and the Warsaw Pact, probably have toxic gas weapons: Afghanistan, China, Egypt, Ethiopia, India, Iraq, Israel, Libya, Pakistan, South Africa, Syria, Thailand and Vietnam. See also ▷ Chemical Disarmament.

R. HANSLIAN, *Der Chemische Krieg*, Berlin, 1937; H. OCHSNER, "History of German Chemical Warfare in World War II", in: *US Chemical Corps Historical Study*, No. 2, 1949; B.Z. KLEBER, D. BIRDSELL, *The Chemical Warfare Service: Chemicals in Combat*, 3 Vols., Washington, DC, 1966; SIPRI. *The Problem of Chemical and Biological Warfare*, 4 Vols., Stockholm, 1971; SIPRI, *Chemical Weapons: Destruction and conversion. Current Disarmament Problems*. London, 1980, J. GOLDBLAT, *Arms Control Agreements. A Handbook*, New York, 1983; J. PERRY ROBINSON, *Chemical Warfare Arms Control: General Principles*, SIPRI, London, Philadelphia, 1984; A THOMAS, J. PERRY ROBINSON, *Effects of Chemical Warfare. A Selective Review and Bibliography of British State Papers*, SIPRI, London, Philadelphia, 1984; R. TRAPP, J. PERRY ROBINSON, *Detoxification of Chemical Warfare Contamination*, SIPRI, London, Philadelphia, 1984. Medical expert reports use of chemical weapons in Iran-Iraq war, in: *UN Chronicle*, 1985, No. 5, pp. 24–26. SIPRI, *World Armament and Disarmament 1987*, Oxford, 1987; R. TRAPP ed., *Chemical Weapon Free Zone*, SIPRI, Oxford, 1987. *UN Chronicle* June, 1988, pp. 24–26. SIPRI *Yearbook 1987*, Oxford, 1988, pp. 97–115.

CHEMICAL WEAPONS PARIS DECLARATION 1989. A Declaration of the International Conference of 140 Nations states parties to the ▷ Geneva Protocol of 1925 and other interested states, adopted in Paris Jan.11.1989. The text of the last three paragraphs of the Declaration reads as follows:

"(4) The states participating are gravely concerned by the growing danger posed to international peace and security by the risk of the use of chemical weapons as long as such weapons remain and are spread: In this context, they stress the need for the early conclusion and entry into force of the convention, which will be established on a nondiscriminatory basis. They deem it necessary, in the meantime, for each state to exercise restraint and to act responsibly in accordance with the purpose of the present declaration. (5) The participating states confirm their full support for the United Nations in the discharge of its indispensible role, in conformity with its charter. They affirm that the United Nations provides a framework and an instrument enabling the international community to exercise vigilance with respect to the prohibition of the use of chemical weapons. They confirm their support for appropriate and effective steps taken by the United Nations in this respect in conformity with its charter. They further reaffirm their full support for the Secretary General in carrying out his responsibilities for investigations in the event of alleged violations of the Geneva Protocol. They express their wish for early completion of the work undertaken to strengthen the efficiency of existing procedures and call for the cooperation of all states, in order to facilitate the action of the Secretary General. (6) The participating States, recalling the final document of the first special session of the United Nations General Assembly devoted to disarmament in 1978, underline the need to pursue with determination their efforts to secure general and complete disarmament under effective international control, so as to ensure the right of all states to peace and security".

The Conference was called at the initiative of the United States and France in relation to the ▷ Iraq-Iran war 1980–88 and because of concerns raised over alleged Libyan plans to produce poison gas at Rabta, 40 miles southwest of Tripoli. See also ▷ Poison Gas.

KEESING'S *Record of World Events*, No. 1, 1989.

CHEMISTRY. A subject of international co-operation. Organizations reg. with the UIA:

European Council of Chemical Manufacturers Federation, f. 1960, Brussels, Belgium.
European Federation of Chemical Engineering, f. 1953, London.
European Society for the Chemical Processing of Irradiated Fuels (EUROCHEMIC), est. July 20, 1957, Brussels by the convention signed by the governments of Austria, Belgium, Denmark, France, Italy, Luxembourg, Netherlands, Norway, Portugal, Sweden, Switzerland and Turkey. The atomic centre is Mol, Belgium.
International Association for Cereal Chemistry, f. 1958, London.
International Union of Pure and Applied Chemistry (IUPAC), f. 1951, Basel (Switzerland). Publ. *Journal of Pure and Applied Chemistry*.
Permanent International Bureau of Analytical Chemistry of Human and Animal Food (PIBAC), f. 1912, Paris. Intergovernmental organization of Argentina, France, Greece, Hungary, Israel, Mexico, Portugal and Uruguay. Publ. *Annales des falsifications et de l'expertise chimique*.

A.F. DORIAN, *Elsevier's Dictionary of Industrial Chemistry*. In English American (with definitions), French, Spanish, Italian, Dutch and German. Amsterdam, 1964. *Yearbook of International Organizations 1986/87; The Europa Yearbook 1988. A World Survey*, Vol. I, London, 1988.

CHERNOBYL. A Soviet nuclear plant in Ukraine, 80 miles north of Kiev; the breakdown and explosion on April 25, 1986 initiated radio-active fallout in the Eastern, Central, Western Europe, Scandinavia and Balkan countries. After Chernobyl the first international agreement on prompt exchange of information in case of a nuclear accident, was signed in Helsinki on Jan. 7, 1987 between Finland and the USSR. In 1987 the IAEA initiated a global radiation monitoring programme to improve international cooperation in curbing the environmental consequences of post-accident radiation.

KEESING'S *Contemporary Archives*; *Newsweek*, May 12, 1986. B. RAMBERG, *Learning from Chernobyl, in: Foreign Affairs*, Winchester, 1986/87; IAEA, *Convention on Early Notification of a Nuclear Accident or Radiological Emergency*, Vienna, 1986; B. RAMBERG, *Global Nuclear Energy Risks. The Search for Preventive Medicine*, Boulder, Colo., 1986; A. PETROSYANTS, *The Soviet Union and the Development of Nuclear Power. An overview of plans and the Chernobyl accident, in: IAEA Bulletin*, Autumn 1986; H. BLIX, *The Post-Chernobyl Outlook for Nuclear Power, in: IAEA Bulletin*, Autumn 1986: A. SALO, *Information Exchange after Chernobyl, in: IAEA Bulletin*, Autumn 1986; IAEA and Chernobyl, *in: IAEA Bulletin*, Winter 1986; "OBSERVER" Correspondents, *Chernobyl. The End of the Nuclear Dream*, London, 1987. SIPRI *Yearbook 1987*, Oxford 1988, pp. 425–432. *IAEA Newsbriefs*, June 1, 1988.

CHESS. A subject of international co-operation. Organizations reg. with the UIA:

World Chess Federation, FIDE, f. 1927, Česke Budejovice; publ. *Result Sheets*.
International Esperantists Chess League, f. 1951, Prässebo, Sweden;
International Braille Chess Association, f. 1951, London; Publ. *Information Bulletin*;

FIDE organizes world chess team championships, called the Chess Olympics. The first international chess tournament was held in London in 1851 and won by A. Anderson (Germany), who in 1858 was defeated by P. Morphy (USA). Since 1889 regular world championships have been organized where the current world champion selects his opponent. During 1886–1946 there were only five world champions who won the title that way: W. Steinitz (Germany) 1886–94; E. Lasker (Germany) 1894–1921; J. Capablanca (Cuba) 1921–28; A.A. Alechine (France) 1927–35 and 1937–46; M. Euwe (the Netherlands) 1935 and 1937.

In 1948 a new multi-stage system of elimination was started that included regional and inter-regional tournaments; on basis of this principle the world championship has been won by: M.M. Botvinnik (USSR) 1948–55, 1958–60, and 1961–62; W.W. Smyslov (USSR) 1957–58; M.N. Tal (USSR) 1960–61; T.T. Petrosian (USSR) 1962–69; B.W. Spasski (USSR) 1969–72; R. Fisher (USA) 1972–75; A. Karpov (USSR) since 1975.

Yearbook of International Organizations.

CHETNIKS. In *Serbian* = fighters, partisans. An historical name of Serbian partisans in struggles with the Turks in the 19th century. In the interwar period members of nationalistic Yugoslav monarchist organizations; 1941–45 organized by General Drazha Michailovich (1893–1946) as units loyal to the king in exile and opposing the people's partisan forces of J. Broz Tito. In May 1944 D. Michailovich was dismissed by King Peter from his position as minister of defense and commander of the armed forces, while the government of Great Britain withdrew its mission in the Chetnik command headquarters (replaced by a US mission in Aug., 1944); arrested Mar., 13, 1946, sentenced to death, and shot July 16, 1946; posthumously decorated in secret by US President Harry Truman with the American Distinguished Service Cross, which was revealed in 1965. The trial of D. Michailovich was the object of an exchange of notes between the governments of the USA and Yugoslavia. The US Government demanded the admission of the testimony of 20 American pilots shot down over Yugoslavia who owed their lives to the Chetniks. The Yugoslav government replied that the people's partisan forces had saved the lives of more than 2000 American pilots.

The Trial of Drazha Michailovich, Belgrade, 1946; D. MARTIN, *Ally Betrayed: The Uncensored Story of Tito and Mikhailovich*, Englewood Cliffs, N.J., 1946; F. MACLEAN, *Eastern Approaches*, London, 1950. V. DEDIJER, *History of Yugoslavia*, New York, 1974. M. J. MILAZZO, *The Chetnik Movement and the Yugoslav Resistance*, Baltimore, 1985 and 1986.

CHICANOS. The colloquial name adopted in the USA for citizens of Mexican and Indian descent, mainly living in former North provinces of Mexico, now the American states of California, Arizona, Colorado, Texas, Nevada, New Mexico and Utah. According to statistical data of the US National Census Bureau for 1970, the number of US citizens of Mexican descent, amounted to 9.3 million, half of which were below the age of 20.7, whereas the national average age was 28.1, making Mexican Americans the ethnic goup with the lowest average age and the highest birth rate.

A group of US citizens of Mexican and Indian descent submitted a petition on June 18, 1968 to the OAS requesting the appointment of a subcommission of human rights to investigate discrimination applied by the US government toward the native population of the above-named states, contrary to the provisions of the American– Mexican Guadalupe–Hidalgo Treaty of Feb. 22, 1848, which obligated the USA to respect the rights of the autochthonous population. In June 1972 an inter-governmental American–Mexican commission for Chicanos was called, in consequence of talks held in Washington by the President of Mexico, L. Echeverria, and the US President, R. Nixon. In 1979 problems of the Chicanos were discussed during the meeting of the President of Mexico, L. Portillo, with the American President J. Carter and 1983 during the meeting of the President of Mexico Leon de la Madrid with the American President R. Reagan.

J.H. BURMA (ed.), *Mexican American in the United States*, New York, 1970; W. MOQUIN (ed.), *A Documentary History of the Mexican Americans*, New York, 1971; Z.A. KRUSZEWSKI, *Chicanos. Native Americans. Territorial Minority*, New Jersey, 1972; M. S. MEIER, F. RIVERA, *Chicanos. A History of Mexican Americans,* New York, 1972; H. COY, *Chicano Roots Go Deep*, New York, 1975; G. SMITH Jr., "The Mexican Americans", in: *National Geographic*; June, 1980; Z.A. KRUSZEWSKI, R.L. HOUGH, J. ORNSTEIN-GALICIA, *Politics and Society in the Southwest. Ethnicity and Chicano Pluralism*, Westview Press, 1982.

CHICKEN WAR. An international term for a 1963 commercial dispute between the US and the European Common Market on discriminatory tariffs imposed on the American export of poultry to Europe. After the US President threatened with retaliatory tariffs, the chicken war was resolved by the GATT Kennedy Round negotiations.

CHILD ABUSE. An international term for child molestation, a subject of international actions against a dramatic increase in the number of cases, reported to the WHO and CIOMS. The first International Conference on Child Abuse, under the aegis of WHO and CIOMS took place on Dec. 4–6, 1985 in Berne.

J. CREWDSON, *By Silence Betrayed: Sexual Abuse of Children in America*, Boston, 1988.

CHILD ALLOWANCES. An international term for family allowances paid for children. A subject of international bilateral and multilateral agreements. In Helsinki, Aug. 28, 1951, the governments of Finland, Iceland, Norway and Sweden signed a convention on the mutual recognition of family allowance payments for children.

UNTS, vol. 198, p. 18.

CHILD, DECLARATION OF THE RIGHTS OF, 1959. A Declaration prepared by ECOSOC, adopted unanimously by the UN General Assembly Res. 1386/XIV on Nov. 20, 1959; elaborates in detail ten fundamental rights of the child. The text is as follows:

"Whereas the peoples of the United Nations have, in the Charter, reaffirmed their faith in fundamental human rights and in the dignity and worth of the human person, and have determined to promote social progress and better standards of life and larger freedom, Whereas the United Nations has, in the Universal Declaration of Human Rights, proclaimed that everyone is entitled to all the rights and freedoms set forth therein, without distinction of any kind, such as race, colour, sex, language, religion, political or other opinion, national or social origin, property, birth or other status. Whereas the child by reason of physical and mental immaturity, needs special safeguards and care, including appropriate legal protection, before as well as after birth. Whereas the need for such special safeguards has been stated in the Geneva Declaration of the Rights of the Child of 1924, and recognized in the Universal Declaration of Human Rights and in the statutes of specialized agencies and international organizations concerned with the welfare of children. Whereas mankind owes to the child the best it has to give. Now therefore, The General Assembly, proclaims this Declaration of the Rights of the Child to the end that he may have a happy childhood and enjoy for his own good for the good of society rights and freedoms herein set forth, and calls upon parents, upon men and women as individuals, and upon voluntary organizations, local authorities and national Governments to recognize these rights and strive for their observance by legislative and other measures progressively taken in accordance with the following principles:
Principle 1. The child shall enjoy all the rights set forth in this Declaration. Every child, without any exception whatsoever, shall be entitled to these rights, without distinction or discrimination on account of race, colour, sex, language, religion, political or social origin, property, birth or other status whether of himself or his family.
Principle 2. The child shall enjoy special protection, and shall be given opportunities and facilities, by law and other means, to enable him to develop physically, mentally, morally, spiritually and socially in a healthy and normal manner and in conditions of freedom and dignity. In the enactment of laws for this purpose, the best interests of the child shall be the paramount considerations.
Principle 3. The child shall be entitled from his birth to a name and a nationality.
Principle 4. The child shall enjoy benefits of social security. He shall be entitled to grow and develop in health; to this end, special care and protection shall be provided both to him and to his mother, including adequate pre-natal and post-natal care. The child shall have the right to adequate nutrition, housing, recreation and medical services.
Principle 5. The child who is physically, mentally or socially handicapped shall be given the special treatment, education and care required by his particular condition.
Principle 6. The child, for the full and harmonious development of his personality, needs love and understanding. He shall, wherever possible, grow up in the care and under the responsibility of his parents, and in any case, in an atmosphere of affection and of moral and material security; a child of tender years shall not save in exceptional circumstances, be separated from his mother. Society and the public authorities shall have the duty to extend particular care to children without a family and to those without adequate means of support. Payment of state and other assistance towards the maintenance of children of large families is desirable.
Principle 7. The child is entitled to receive education, which shall be free and compulsory, at least in the elementary stages. He shall be given an education which will promote his general culture, and enable him, on a basis of equal opportunity, to develop his abilities, his individual judgement, and his sense of moral and social responsibility, and to become a useful member of society. The best interests of the child shall be the guiding principle of those responsible for his education and guidance; that responsibility lies in the first place with his parents. The child shall have full opportunity for play and recreation, which should be directed to the same purposes as education; society and the public authorities shall endeavour to promote the enjoyment of his rights.
Principle 8. The child shall in all circumstances be among the first to receive protection and relief.
Principle 9. The child shall be protected against all form of neglect, cruelty and exploitation. He shall not be the subject of traffic, in any form. The child shall not be admitted to employment before an appropriate minimum age; he shall in no case be caused or permitted to engage in any occupation or employment which would prejudice his health or education, or interfere with his physical, mental or moral development. The child shall be protected from practices which may foster racial, religious and any other form of discrimination. He shall be brought up in a spirit of understanding, tolerance, friendship among peoples, peace and universal brotherhood, and in full consciousness that his energy and talents should be devoted to the service of his fellow men."

UN Yearbook 1959, pp. 192–199.

CHILD EXPLOITATION. An international term for commercial or industrial exploitation of child labour and related traffic in children. The European Parliamentary Assembly adopted on Oct. 6, 1987 Recommendation 1065 (1987) on the traffic in children and other forms of child exploitation. The text is as follows:

The Assembly,
(1) Considering that children have the right to be brought up in a secure and humane way, and that society has an obligation to protect them and look after their interests;
(2) Appalled by the international trade in children for such purposes as prostitution, pornography, slavery, illegal adoption, etc.;
(3) Referring to its Recommendation Lo44 (1986) on international crime, in which it recommends that the Committee of Ministers invite the governments of member states to co-operate in a study of and action against the trade in children;
(4) Considering that children have the same right as all human beings to enjoy an environment which affords them security, health and physical integrity, and that they must be treated humanely, that society has a duty to provide them with protection, to monitor observance of their rights and to afford them equality of opportunity;
(5) Bearing in mind its Recommendation 874 (1979) on a European Charter on the Rights of the Child, covering a number of aspects ranging from legal status to medical and social protection;
(6) Considering that it is essential that member states, as a matter of urgency, take the following measures:
(a) sign and ratify, insofar as they have not yet done so, the following conventions:
(i) the Convention for the suppression of the traffic in persons and the exploitation of the prostitution of others (United Nations Treaty Series No. 1342, opened for signature at Lake Success, New York, on March 21, 1950);
(ii) the European Convention on the Adoption of Children (1967);
(iii) The Hague Convention on jurisdiction, applicable law and recognition of decrees relating to adoption;
(iv) Convention No. 138 of the International Labour Organisation, on the minimum age for employment;
(v) the European Social Charter, with particular reference to Article 7 concerning the right of children and adolescents to protection;
(b) support in the United Nations General Assembly the draft declaration on social and legal principles relating to the protection and welfare of children, with special reference to foster placement and adoption, nationally and internationally;
(c) seek safeguards and improve all practices in the case of international adoptions, inter alia:
(i) by the elaboration of a code of conduct and guidelines for individuals and agencies proposing to undertake the interstate movement of unaccompanied minors;
(ii) by regulating that, in interstate adoption, placements should be made through competent authorities or agencies, with the application of safeguards and standards equivalent to those existing in respect of national adoption;
(iii) by regulating that in no case should the placement result in improper financial gain for those involved;
(d) promote and encourage a wide-ranging campaign of public information concerning the sale of and traffic in children, and the exploitation of child labour.
(e) inform educators and youth of the rights of the child, and incorporate human rights education in school curricula at all levels;
(f) promote the undertaking of judicious research programmes at national and international levels to analyse the forms, conditions and structures of the sale and traffic of children;
(g) enact strict laws and regulations to combat child pornography and harmonise member states' relevant legislation;
(h) promote and pursue a policy directed at meeting the needs of abandoned and street children;
(i) condemn any policy of commercial and industrial competition based on exploitation of child labour, and ensure that the activities of national and international agencies working in the field of development are designed in such a way as to have a positive effect of the rights and interests of children throughout the world;
(j) take measures to guarantee children working in conformity with Article 7 of the European Social Charter decent living and working conditions;
(k) increase public surveillance of such children, for instance by improving the labour inspectorate, appointing ombudsmen to protect their rights, providing for education and training in the workplace, and introducing additional welfare measures concerning their health and diet.
(7) Recommends that the Committee of Ministers instruct the European Committee on Crime Problems (CDPC) to study the traffic in children and other forms of exploitation of children as a priority matter in the light of the proposal made above.

Council of Europe, Human Rights, Information Sheet No 21, pp. 177–179 and 230–231.

C

CHILD LABOUR. An international term, subject of ILO Conventions and Recommendations on the protection of children at work and social legislation of the majority of UN Member States. On June 16, 1987 the European Parliament adopted a Resolution on Child Labour:

The European Parliament
– having regard to the motion for a resolution tabled by Mrs Van Hemeldonck on child labour (Doc. B2-87/86),
– having regard to the Conventions and Recommendations of the International Labour Organization on the protection of children at work and especially to Conventions Nos 5, 33, 59, 60 and 138 and Recommendation No 146,
– having regard to social legislation in the Member States on child labour and the social objectives of the EEC Treaty,
– having regard to its resolution of March 9, 1987 on compliance with and the consolidation of international labour standards,
– having regard to the report of the Committee on Social Affairs and Employment (Doc. A2-67/87);
(1) Believes that the ethical aspect of child labour are pre-eminent, since such labour affects the child's health, physical and intellectual development, education and, ultimately, personal development and that the use of children in the production process is a challenge to the conscience of the world and should therefore be abolished;
(2) Points out, however, that other aspects of the problem, such as the direct relationship between child labour and the educational system, unemployment, movements of migrant workers (particularly the education of migrant worker's children) and the rise in the underground economy cannot be left aside;
(3) Considers that the root cause of child labour must be dealt with by means of measures to create employment and eliminate poverty;
(4) Believes that steps must be taken in the area of economic, social and educational policy to guarantee that the right to education and vocational training can be exercised in practice, as these are conditions without which the child's or young person's personality, cannot develop freely and equality of opportunity in access to employment cannot be furthered;
(5) Rejects all policies aimed at achieving competitiveness between Community countries by lowering labour costs through the use of child labour and points out that increasingly frequent infringements of labour law protecting minors are being observed in certain Member States;
(6) Expresses the deep concern at the fact that the rise in the underground economy in the Member States and the emerging trend towards moving productive activity into worker's homes leads to increased use of unpaid child labour and prevents any check being carried out into health and safety conditions in the working environment;
(7) Expresses its repugnance at the high frequency of occupational accidents among child workers;
(8) Points out, furthermore, that child labour in the Third World countries is a structural factor closely related to their poverty, although it considers that it would be difficult to put an end to such a situation, urges the Community to approach this issue in the context of its development programmes and, in its relations with third countries, to safeguard workers' living conditions in society and their rights, which are an integral part of democracy and of Europe's actual cultural identity;
(9) Consequently calls on the Commission to submit a proposal for a directive harmonizing national legislations on child labour;
(10) Stresses that such a directive should contain flexible provisions along the following lines:
(a) Employment, whether contractual or non-contractual, of young persons under 16 years of age should, as a general rule, be strictly forbidden and obligatory schooling should continue until this age,
(b) Exception should be made for casual and light work compatible with schooling, particularly in the context of the family or a family business, and for work in enterprises and vocational training establishments as an integral part of training. For both these cases, the directive will define the nature of such work at the limits within which it can, on an exceptional basis, be permitted, and the appropriate authorities should adopt

measures to prevent abuses and lay down appropriate penalties,
(c) Exception should also be made for the employment of minors in public entertainment (cinema, theatre, radio, television) where their participation is essential. In such cases the employment contract should be concluded by the young person's parents or legal representatives, with the express agreement of the young person concerned and the approval of the appropriate labour authority,
(d) For young persons between 16 and 18 years of age the employment contract should require the authorization of the parents or legal representatives, except where the young person concerned has, for all other purposes, been authorized to lead an independent life,
(e) For young persons between 16 and 18 years of age nightwork, underground work and the working of overtime should be prohibited. In addition there should be a prohibition on noisome and hazardous occupations and all those which can endanger the physical and mental health, the safety and moral well being of the adolescent. In order to identify these types of occupations and lay down conditions in which young people may engage in them with full safeguards for their health, safety and moral well-being, the national authority should carry out consultations with the appropriate employers' and workers' organizations,
(f) For young persons between 16 and 18 years, time spent with the employer's consent in vocational training during normal working hours should count as working time within the limits of maximum hours. Intervals for rest should also be prescribed,
(g) Full capacity to enter into contracts and perform all kinds of work should begin at 18 years of age;
(11) Calls on the appropriate authorities in the Community countries to ensure that the provisions governing child labour are complied with, conferring wider powers on and allowing greater scope for action to labour inspectorates and strengthening the system of penalties where necessary;
(12) Pending the drafting of the appropriate directive, urges those Community Member States which have not yet done so to ratify ILO Convention No 138 as well as Conventions Nos 13, 16, 77, 78, 79, 90 and 124;
(13) Instructs its President to forward this resolution to the Commission, Council and the governments of the Member States and the Director-General of the International Labour Organization.

Council of Europe, Human Rights. Information Sheet No 21, Strasbourg, 1988, pp. 230–231.

CHILD MORTALITY. A subject of international statistics. Child mortality figures and projections are published and analized by the WHO in connection with WHO Expanded Program of ▷ Immunization. The WHO figures and projections for the years 1950–2000 of child mortality between the ages of 0 and 5 (per thousand):

	1950–1955	1980–1985	1985–2000
WORLD TOTAL	240	118	83
More developed countries	73	19	13
Less developed countries	281	134	94
Africa	322	182	132
Latin America	189	88	61
East Asia	248	50	28
Southeastern Asia	244	111	67
Southern Asia	327	177	125
Western Asia	307	115	65

WHO Features, March, 1988.

CHILDREN. A subject of international conventions aimed at children's protection, and providing the basis for ▷ Children's Rights. Specialized UN organization for Children is ▷ UNICEF.
International organizations reg. with UIA:

Children's International Summer Villages, f. 1951, Newcastle-upon-Tyne, UK. Consultative status with UNESCO.
Children's Medical Relief International f. 1967, New York.
European Office for Youth and Children, f. 1949, Brussels, Consultative status with ECOSOC.

European Union for Child Psychiatry, f. 1954, Vienna.
Inter-American Children's Institute, f. 1919, Montevideo, by 2nd Pan-American Congress for the Child (1st Congress held 1916); until 1955 known as Instituto Americano Internacional de Protección a la Infancia. Publ. *Boletin.*
International Association for Child Psychiatry and Allied Professions, f. 1948, London. Consultative status with UNESCO, WHO. Publ. *International Yearbook of Child Psychiatry.*
International Association for Children's and Youth Theatres, f. 1965, Paris, Publ. *Théâtre Enfance et Jeunesse* (quarterly in English and French).
International Association of Dentistry for Children, f. 1969, London Publ. *Journal.*
International Association of Workers for Maladjusted Children, f. 1951, Paris. Consultative Status UNESCO, ECOSOC.
International Catholic Child Bureau, f. 1948, Geneva, Consultative status with UNICEF, UNESCO and ECOSOC. Publ. *Études Pédagogiques.*
International Centre of Films for Children and Young People, f. 1957, Paris. Consultative status with UNESCO. Publ. *News.*
International Children's Centre, f. 1950, Paris, under UNESCO auspices, as intergovernmental organization; financed by UNESCO (35%) and French government (65%); serves UN specialized agencies and UN member states as centre of co-ordination of research on medico-social problems of children. Publ. *Le Courrier, L'Enfant en milieu tropical.*
International Committee of Children's and Adolescents' Movements (ICCAM), f. 1957, Budapest. Publ. *ICCAM Information* (quarterly in English, French and Spanish).
International Council for Children's Play, f. 1959, Stuttgart.
International Federation of Children's Communities, f. 1948, Trogen, Switzerland. Consultative status with UNESCO, ECOSOC. Publ. *Documents.*
International Help for Children, f. 1947, London. Publ. *Annual Report.*
International Institute for Children's Literature and Reading Research, f. 1965, Vienna. Consultative status with UNESCO. Publ. *Bookbird.*
International League for Child and Adult Education, f. 1947, Paris. Consultative Status UNESCO, ECOSOC.
International Movement of Apostolate of Children, f. 1962, Catholic Organization, Paris.
International Union for Child Welfare, f. 1920, Geneva. Consultative status with UNESCO, ECOSOC and UNICEF. Publ. *International Child Welfare Review* (quarterly).
Non-Governmental Organizations Committee on UNICEF, f. 1949, New York, Publ. *NGO UNICEF Newsletter.*
SOS Children's Villages, f. 1964, Vienna; takes care of abandoned children. Consultative status with ECOSOC. Publ. *SOS Messenger.*
World Council for Gifted Children, f. 1975, London.
World Missions to Children, f. 1946, Grants Pass, Oregon, USA.
World Organization for Early Childhood Education, f. 1948, Paris. Consultative status with UNESCO, UNICEF, ECOSOC. Publ. *International Journal of Early Childhood.*

UNICEF, a Report on the State of the World's Children", in: *UN Chronicle,* February, 1983, pp. 57–81; *Yearbook of International Organizations.*

CHILDREN'S DAY, INTERNATIONAL. Celebrated since 1955, the date varying from one UN member state to another, mostly on June 1; declared Dec. 14, 1954 by the UN General Assembly and defined as the day of universal brotherhood and understanding among children; dedicated to the spread of ideas and aims of the UN Charter in the interest of the children of the world.

CHILDREN'S ORDER OF THE SMILE. Granted by children in Poland since 1968 to adult friends of the youngest, internationalized by a UNICEF decision connected with the International Year of the Child 1979, since then granted in all UN member countries.

CHILDREN'S RIGHTS. A subject of international declarations specifying fundamental and universal principles of children's rights. The first of these was the so-called Geneva Declaration adopted on the initiative of the League of Nations in 1924; the second the ▷ Child, Declaration of the Rights of, 1959. By order of the Assembly, ECOSOC carries out studies to determine to what extent the principles drawn up in the 1959 Declaration are reflected in domestic legislations of UN member states. According to a study of the ILO, 1986 the exact number of working children under age 15 is unknown, but it is estimated that the figure around the World could range from 50 million to almost 200 million.

A draft of the Convention on Rights of the Child was elaborated 1984–1986 by the UN Commission on Human Rights.

UN Review, Nov., 1959 and December, 1959; UN Chronicle, November, 1982. *UN Chronicle,* May 1984, March 1985; *UN Chronicle,* November 1986, p. 116.

CHILE. Member of the UN. República de Chile. A country in South America on the Pacific Ocean. Area: 756,626 sq. km with Easter Island, excluding sectors of the Antarctic to which Chile asserted claims in 1940, causing disputes with Argentina, Bolivia, Peru and the UK; boundary with Bolivia established in 1883, with Peru in 1929, and with Argentina in 1966 after British arbitration with the exception of the problem of the ▷ Beagle Channel. Pop.: 1988 est. 12,748,498 (1970 census: 8,884,768) including métis – 65%, Creole – 25% and Indian – 5%. Capital: Santiago with 3,448,000 inhabitants 1975. Official language: Spanish. GNP per capita 1987: US $1,310. Currency: 1 peso = 100 centavos. National Day: Dec. 18, anniversary of declaration of independence, 1810.

Member of the League of Nations 1920–28. Original member since Oct. 24, 1945 of the UN and all its specialized agencies. Member of the OAS, ALALC and the Tlatelolco Treaty.

International relations: Spanish colony 1557–1810; from Sept. 18, 1810, when independence was proclaimed until Mar. 18, 1818 in a national liberation war with Spain; proclamation of the republic in 1866; 1879–83 war with Bolivia and Peru known as the War of the Pacific, won by Chile. Its territory was enlarged by the Bolivian province of Antofagosta which cut Bolivia off from the Pacific (on Apr. 28, 1968 Chile offered its ports to Bolivia should the latter form its own commercial fleet) and the Peruvian provinces of Tacna and Arica which brought about the so-called Tacna–Arica controversy which was settled (1929) through the arbitration of US President Herbert C. Hoover: Chile retained Arica and returned Tacna to Peru. A dispute with Bolivia over the river ▷ Lauca. In World War I Chile remained neutral. During World War II on the side of the Allied nations. In April 1950 Chilean President G.G. Videla concluded a military pact with USA which provided for common defence of the Strait of Magellan and the northern parts of Chile rich in copper deposits and also granted the USA a military base on Easter Island. On July 23–24, 1970 Chilean President S. Allende met in Salta, a town on the Argentine–Chilean border, with Argentine President A. Lanuss to draw up ▷ the Salta Declaration. On Aug. 24–Sept. 3, 1971 President Allende visited Ecuador, Colombia, and Peru and in December 1972 – Mexico, Cuba, Algeria, and the USSR. Argentine President A. Lanuss visited Chile on Oct. 16–18, 1971 and Cuban Premier Fidel Castro on Sept. 11–Dec. 4, 1971, his visit having been preceded by the Chilean Foreign Minister's Clodomiro Almeyda talks in Havana July 25–Aug. 2, 1972 which concluded with the first Chilean–Cuban Joint Declaration. Since the Popular Front assumed power in Chile in 1970, the country became a target of an economic and financial blockade imposed by the USA against which President S. Allende lodged a complaint at the UN General Assembly on Dec. 8, 1972. In the fall of 1973, the problems of Chile were debated in the UN Security Council and General Assembly in connection with the military coup of General A. Pinochet Ugarte on Sept. 11, 1973 in which President Salvador Allende (1908–73) was murdered. Tribute to him was paid by the UN General Assembly on Sept. 18, 1973. Other issues on the UN agenda were the shelling of the commercial vessel *Playa Larga* flying the Cuban flag in the vicinity of Valparaiso and the wave of terror against the Chilean population and political activists. UN Secretary General Kurt Waldheim spoke in defense of those suffering this terror. UNESCO protested against the burning of books, destruction of libraries and cultural centers, and against the devastation of the apartment and collections of Nobel Prize winner Pablo Neruda (1904–73) on the day of his death in Santiago on Sept. 23, 1973. On Feb. 21, 1974 UN Human Rights Commission in New York heard the account of the widow of the late President S. Allende of the crimes and terror spread by Chilean military junta. The UN Human Rights Commission, denied entry to Chile in 1975 by the junta, condemned the regime for the institutionalization of torture and violation of basic human rights in 1975 and in subsequent years. In Jan., 1979 a charge was heard at the American court in Washington against former chief of security forces General Contrares and his two subordinates for the murder in Washington, DC on Sept. 21, 1976 of Chilean emigré Orlando Leterier on the order of General Pinochet. They were found guilty and their extradition was demanded, which the Chilean junta refused. As a result, on May 15, 1979, the USA announced a temporary withdrawal of its ambassador to Chile. On Dec. 9. 1975 the UN General Assembly adopted Res. 3448 and 3452/XXX and on Dec. 16, 1976 Res. 31/124 on the protection of human rights in Chile.

The dispute with Argentina over the ▷ Beagle Channel came to an end on Jan. 23, 1984 at a meeting of the Vatican Secretary of State Agostino Cassaroli with the Argentinian and Chilean Foreign ministers by the signing of a Treaty of Peace and Friendship and with preparation of a final Treaty on the Beagle Canal; signed on Dec. 8, 1984 in the Vatican. On Oct. 23, 1986 Chile extended its territorial waters from 12 to 24 miles.

In Febr. 1987 the USA on the basis of new evidence requested the extradition of the murderer of Orlando Letelier. On Dec. 14, 1989 a new president was democratically elected, bringing an end to the Pinochet regime.

Informe de la Mision Económica de las NU en Chile 1949–1950, New York, 1952; J. EYZAGUIRRE, *Fisonomia histórica de Chile*, México, DF, 1948; Institut Latinskoi Ameriki, *Chili, Politika, Ekonomika i Kultura*,, Moskva 1965; J. EYZAGUIRRE, *Breve historia de las fronteras de Chile*, Santiago, 1965; G. GAIL, *The Political System of Chile*, Boston, 1966; L. CORTES, J. FUENTES, *Diccionario Politico de Chile 1810–1966*, Santiago, 1967; A.G. FRANK, *Capitalism and Underdevelopment in Latin America: Historical Studies of Chile and Brazil*, New York, 1967; E.G. LABARCA, *Chile al Rojo*, Santiago, 1971; S.F. LAU, *The Chilean Response to Foreign Investment*, London, 1972; J. PETRAS, H.Z. MERINO, *Peasants in Revolt: A Chilean Case Study*, Houston, 1972; S. ALLENDE, *Chile's Road to Socialism*, Harmondsworth, 1973; G. MACEOIN, *No Peaceful Way: Chile Struggle for Dignity*, New York, 1974; A. TOURAINE, *Vie et mort du Chili Populaire*, Paris, 1974; M.A. URIBE, *Le Livre Noir de l'intervention américaine au Chili*, Paris, 1974; P.M. SIGMUND, *The Overthrow of Allende and the Politics of Chile 1964–1976*, Pittsburgh, 1977; J.

SOEDERMAN, *The Disappearance of Arrested Persons in Chile*, Helsinki, 1978; B. LOVEMAN, *Chile: The Legacy of Hispanic Capitalism*, New York, 1979; *UN Chronicle*, January, 1979, pp. 60–61, March, 1979, pp. 34–35; *Everyone's United Nations*, New York, 1979, pp. 249–250; M. LASAGA, *The Copper Industry in the Chilean Economy*, Aldershot, 1981; *The Europa Yearbook, 1984. A World Survey*, Vol. II, pp. 1370–1384, London, 1984. D. KAY, *Chileans in Exile*, London, 1987; J. TIMERMAN, *Chile: Death in the South*, New York, 1987; O. MILLAS, D O'HIGGINS. *Allende, Páginas de la Historia de Chile*, Madrid, 1987.

CHILE FUND. ▷ Tortures.

CHILE, INTERNATIONAL COMMISSION OF ENQUIRY INTO THE CRIMES OF THE MILITARY JUNTA IN CHILE. Comision Internacional Investigadora de los crimenes de la Junta Militar en Chile. Convened at the initiative of Scandinavian parliamentarians and composed of 70 representatives from 40 countries. The first session was held in Dipoli, Finland, Mar. 21–24, 1974; the second July 26–27, 1974 in the Danish Parliament in Copenhagen; the third took place in Mexico City, Feb 18–21, 1975, inaugurated by the President of Mexico, L. Echeverria; the fourth in Feb., 1978 in Algiers; the following years in Athens, Stockholm, Copenhagen and Helsinki. The collected documentary evidence was passed on by the Commission to the governments and parliaments of the UN member states and to the UN General Secretary.

The Crimes of the Chilean Military Junta in the Light of Chilean and International Law, Helsinki, 1974.

CHINA, PEOPLE'S REPUBLIC OF CHINA. Member of the UN and permanent member of the UN Security Council. Chung-Hua Jen-Min Kung-Ho Kuo. Area: 9,597,230 sq. km, including Taiwan. Population 1985 census: 1.036 million. The birthrate 10.81 per 1.000 was the lowest since 1949. (1953 census–582,603,000). According to official statistics 94% of the population is of Han (Chinese) nationality. Capital: Beijing with *c.* 9,335,000 inhabitants in 1976. GNP per capita in 1986: US $250. Currency: 1 yuan = 10 jiao = 10 fen. Length of the land frontiers *c.* 20,000 km, of which 7500 km are with the USSR and *c.* 14,000 km coastline. China borders upon the USSR (delimitation negotiations 1964, 1969, 1971, 1977–85 not concluded), Mongolia, North Korea, Vietnam, Laos, Burma, India (border disputes), Bhutan, Nepal, Pakistan and Afghanistan. Official language: Chinese han yu whose writing is difficult to learn; therefore, in 1959 a system for transcribing Chinese symbols into a phonetic alphabet was devised, called Pinyin, as the first step toward simplifying the teaching of Chinese in accordance with the thesis of Chou-En-lai that the use the Roman alphabet, Arabic numerals or the Christian calendar is a natural unifying tendency throughout the world. On Mar. 23, 1972 the Chairman of the Academy of Sciences Ku-mo-jo came out in favor of gradually replacing Chinese ideographic writing (containing some 50,000 symbols) with the Roman alphabet: "This reform will be consonant with a common world trend toward the Latinization of alphabets." The Pinyin transcription in the Roman alphabet was adopted on Jan 1, 1979. Currency: yuan. National Day: Oct. 1, anniversary of the proclamation of the Chinese People's Republic, 1949. Member of the UN and of all specialized organizations. Signatory of the Tlatelolco Treaty.

International relations: after many centuries of trade and diplomatic contacts with the states of Asia, Africa and Europe, the Chinese empire in 1839 was defeated by Great Britain in the so-called ▷ Opium wars, as a result of which China lost ▷ Hong Kong and opened her ports for British factories (▷ Open door policy) and also agreed to permit Britain to carry on an unrestricted opium trade in China. In 1895–96 China lost a war with Japan, which occupied Korea and Taiwan; in 1900 as a result of the so-called Boxer Rebellion the colonial powers intervened militarily in China. ▷ Boxer Protocol 1901.

China was proclaimed a republic in 1912, which initiated a period of civil wars and Japanese military intervention. On Sept. 18, 1931 Japan began the occupation of ▷ Manchuria and then proceeded to conquer outlying Chinese provinces; on July 26, 1937, without a declaration of war the next invasion began, which by the fall of 1937 had conquered a significant part of the country with Beijing, Tientsin, Nanking, Canton, Shanghai, Wuhan; on Aug. 21, 1937 China signed a non-aggression treaty with the USSR. The Council of the League of Nations on Oct. 6 and Dec. 15, 1937 condemned Japanese aggression. During World War II China waged a war of liberation against Japan.

On Oct. 1, 1949 the Chinese People's Republic was proclaimed, and the Kuomintang government of Chiang Kai-shek with US assistance made the island of Taiwan the seat of the Chinese Republic, which until 1975 represented China in the UN. During the ▷ Korean War, 1950–53, volunteers from the Chinese People's Republic fought UN forces and the Chinese People's Republic in 1954 participated in the signing of an armistice in Korea in Geneva on July 22, 1954. In Jan., 1955 UN Secretary-General Dag Hammarskjold visited Beijing for the first time. In the same year the Chinese People's Republic participated in the Afro-Asian Solidarity Conference in Bandung. In 1969 Sino-Soviet border incidents occurred on the ▷ Ussuri river. The UN General Assembly on Oct. 25, 1971 passed a resolution on the representation of China in the United Nations by 76 votes in favor (with 35 against and 17 abstentions). The Assembly recognized that:

"the representatives of the Chinese People's Republic are the sole legal representatives of China in the United Nations and that the Chinese People's Republic is one of the five permanent members of the Security Council."

The Assembly then resolved: (1) "to return to the Chinese People's Republic all her rights"; (2) "to recognize the representatives of her government as the sole legal representatives of China in the United Nations" and in accordance with this (3) "to exclude the representatives of Chiang Kai-shek from their illegally held seat in the United Nations and from all organizations connected with the United Nations." In Feb., 1972 the President of the USA, R. Nixon, visited Mao Tse-tung.

The Constitution ratified in Sept. 1954 by the People's Congress was replaced by a new one of Jan. 17, 1975, Art. 1 of which states that: "the Chinese People's Republic is a socialist country based on the dictatorship of the proletariat, led by the working class in alliance with the peasantry." The new Constitution in its preamble states that China will "never be a super-power and will always oppose the hegemonistic aspirations of the great powers." The Peace Treaty between the Chinese People's Republic and Japan was signed on Aug. 12, 1978, (▷ China–Japan Peace Treaty 1978). Since the Conference on Korea and Indochina in Geneva the Chinese PR has maintained continual diplomatic contacts with the USA through ambassadorial talks in Switzerland 1954–57, in Warsaw 1957–69 and in Paris 1970–71, in March 1973 Trade and Information Bureaus were opened in Beijing and Washington; in Jan., 1979 diplomatic relations on the embassy level were established. In Feb., 1979 Vice-Premier Teng visited President Jimmy Carter

and in Jan., 1984 the Prime Minister Ihao Ziyan visited President Ronald Reagan in Washington, DC. In Mar., 1979 Chinese armed forces undertook military action in the border region of Vietnam, which the government of the Chinese People's Republic officially called a "punitive expedition". Sino-Vietnamese peace talks began in Apr., 1979. In May, 1980 Sino-Indian negotiations were reopened. On July 1, 1980 US President J. Carter met the Chairman of the Chinese Communist Party and Prime Minister Hua-Kuo-feng in Tokyo. On Oct. 24, 1979 the Chinese Press Agency Sinhua published the first list of twenty Chinese nuclear explosions during the period Oct. 16, 1964–Mar. 15, 1978 and a list of eight Chinese Earth satellites placed in orbit Sept. 24, 1970–Jan. 1, 1978. In formal relations with the EEC since Sept. 1976 (an ambassador of the Chinese PR is accredited to the European Communities). A signatory of a five-year Trade Agreement with the EEC in April 1978. In 1984 China agreed with the UK on a new status in 1997 of ▷ Hong Kong. In the 1980's China has emerged as a significant commercial arms merchant.

In July 1986 submitted application to join GATT. Member of the Asian Development Bank since 1986. On Jan. 15, 1986 China rejected the "so-called non-aggression treaty" proposed by the USSR over many years, saying that no accord could be reached as long as Soviet troops were in Afghanistan and the USSR supported the Vietnamese military intervention in Kampuchea.

In Febr., 1987 China and the Soviet Union reopened border talks, first since Nov. 1979. Involved in border disputes with ▷ Vietnam, 1987 and 1988, and with the Philippines and Vietnam over the ▷ Spratly Islands. On June 4, 1989 pro-democracy student protests, which had been going on since April were brutally crushed by the People's Army, resulting in several thousand casualties.

China–USA relations 1949–1984:

1949–People's Republic of China proclaimed by Mao Tse-tung. not recognized by the USA. Chiang Kai-shek flees to Taiwan. The Republic of China delegation, supported by the USA, represents China in the UN until 1971.
1950–President H. Truman sends US Forces to Korea and the Seventh Fleet to protect Taiwan.
1951–China enters the Korean War.
1953–End of the Korean War.
1954–Chou En-lai and John Foster Dulles in Geneva during the Indochina Conference.
1957–Mao proclaims that "US imperialism is a paper tiger".
1965–US bombing of North Vietnam prompts China to step up its aid to North Vietnam.
1969–President R. Nixon suspends Seventh Fleet patrols in the Taiwan Strait.
1971–A US ping-pong team on Chinese invitation play in Beijing. Henry Kissinger flies in secret to Beijing.
1972–President R. Nixon meets the Chairman Mao Tse-tung in Beijing. The United States "acknowledges that all Chinese on either side of the Taiwan Strait maintain there is but one China and that Taiwan is a part of China".
1975–President G. Ford visits China.
1979–President J. Carter recognizes the People's Republic of China and ends recognition of the Republic of China in Taiwan.
Deng Xiaoping visits USA.
1982–In American–Chinese communiqué China says it will "strive for a peaceful solution to the Taiwan question", and the US says it "intends to reduce gradually its sales of arms to Taiwan".
1983–President R. Reagan approves the sale of high-technical items to China.
1984–Chinese Prime Minister Zhao Ziyang visits Washington, DC, President R. Reagan visits Beijing.
Chinese-Soviet relations 1949–1989:
1949–Oct. 1 proclamation of the People's Republic of China; December–January 1950 Mao in Moscow.

1954–Chinese-Soviet Treaty on Co-operation; Mao-Khrushchev summit in Beijing.
1957–Mao attends 21st Congress of CPSU, but leaves Moscow after clashing with Khrushchev over Soviet pre-eminence in the Communist movement.
1959–second Mao-Khrushchev summit in Beijing.
1961–22nd Congress of CPSU, open conflict with the Chinese Party.
1963–end of Soviet aid to China.
1964-1969–border clashes.
1967–Ambassadors withdrawn.
1976–death of Mao.
1980–ambassadors reinstated.
1982–China expresses willingness to normalize relations with the USSR under three conditions: the withdrawal of Soviet troops and missiles from the Chinese border, the withdrawal of Soviet troops from Afghanistan and the end of Soviet support for the Vietnamese army in Cambodia.
1983–border crossing reopens; trade agreement.
1985–meeting of Chinese Deputy Prime Minister Li Pang and M. S. Gorbachev occasioned by the funeral of First Secretary K. U. Chernenko.
1987–high-level Chinese–Soviet talks in Moscow.
1989–February, Soviet Foreign Minister visits China; May, Chinese–Soviet summit in Beijing.
See also ▷ World Heritage UNESCO List.

Harvard Bibliographical Guide on Modern China, vol. 1; *Selected Chinese Books and Documents, 1898–1937*, vol. 2; *Works in Western Languages*, Cambridge Mass., 1949–50; *The Chinese–Russian Frontier*, Baltimore, 1951; P. BERTON, E. WU, *Contemporary China: A Research Guide*, Stanford, 1967; A.S. MOZESIK, *China Representation in the UN*, New York, 1967; D.M. JOHNSTON, H. CHIU, *Agreements of the People's Republic of China 1947–67*, Harvard, 1968; *Documents of China Relations with South and South-East Asia 1949–1962*, New York, 1968; B.D. LERKIN, *China and Africa 1949–70, The Foreign Policy of the People's Republic of China*, Berkeley, 1971; A.A. MUSOT-SOWA, *Problemy industrializatsyi Kitayskoi Narodnoy Riespubliki*, Moskva, 1971; *UN Yearbook 1971*; D.W. KLEIN, A.B. CLARK, *Biographic Dictionary of Chinese Communism 1921–1965*, 2 Vols, Harvard, 1972; "Istoria Rusko-Kitaiskoy granitsi", in: *Mezhdunarodnaya zhizn*, No. 6, 1972; A.A. STAHNKE, *China's Trade with the West*, London, 1972; V. GLUNIN, A. GREGOREV, K. KUKUTSIN, W. NIKIFOROV, *Istoria sovremennogo Kitaya 1917–1970*, Moskva, 1972; B.S.J. WENG, *Beijing's UN Policy, Continuity and Change*, New York, 1972; W. CHAI (ed.), *The Foreign Relations of the People's Republic of China*, New York, 1972; E. SNOW, *The Long Revolution*, London, 1973; K.S. KAROL, *La deuxième révolution chinoise*, Paris, 1974; J.M. COHEN, *People's China and International Law*, Princeton, 1974; A. DOAK BARNOFT, *China's Transition to the Post Mao Era*, Washington, DC, 1975; S. GINSBURG, C.F. PINKELE, *The Sino-Soviet Territorial Dispute 1949–1964*, New York, 1978; F.M. KAPLAN, J.M. SOBIN, S. ANDORS, *Encyclopaedia of China Today*, London, 1979; V. LOUIS, *The Coming Decline of the Chinese Empire*, New York, 1979; B. BRUGGED (ed.), *China since the Gang of Four*, London, 1980; B. STAIGER, *China*, Gubingen, 1980; D. BONAVIA, *The Chinese*, New York, 1980; G. GEGAL, *The China Factor: Beijing and the Superpowers*, London, 1981; R. GARSIDE, *Coming Alive: China after Mao*, New York, 1981; R. BERNSTEIN, *From the Center of the Earth: The Search of the Truth about China*, Boston, 1982; E. MASI, *China Winter: Workers, Mandarins, and the Purge of the Gang of Four*, New York, 1982; *The Cambridge Encyclopaedia of China*, CUP, 1982; L. BIANCO, *The Origins of the Chinese Revolutions 1915-49*, New York, 1982; J. PAXTON (ed.), *The Statesman's Yearbook 1983–84*, London 1983; CHU-YUAN CHENG, *China's Economic Development: Growth and Structural Change*, Boulder, 1983; "Reagan Goes to China. Special Report", in: *Newsweek*, April 30, 1984; *The Europa Yearbook 1984. A World Survey*, Vol. II, pp. 1385–1419, London, 1984. T. B. TANG, *Science and Technology in China*, London, 1984; A. J. DAY, ed., *China and the Soviet Union 1949-1984*, London, 1985; KEESING's *Contemporary Archive*, August 1985; J. KING FAIRBANK, *The Great Chinese Revolution, 1800-1985*, New York, 1986; J. K. FAIRBANKS, A FENERWERKER, *The Cambridge History of China*, Cambridge, Vls. 13, 1986;

R. MEDVEDEV, *China and the Superpowers*, Oxford, 1986; Y. SONG, *On China's Concept of Security*, Geneva, 1986; M. OKSENBURG, *China's 13th Party Congress*, in: *Problems of Communism*, November-December 1987; W. BARTKE ed., *Who's Who in the People's Republic of China*, New York, 1987; H. HARDING, *China's Second Revolution, Reforms after Mao*, Washington DC, 1988; S.A.M. ADSHEAD, *China in World History*, London, 1988; SIPRI, *Yearbook 1987*, Oxford, 1988, pp. 37–43.

CHINA–FRG NUCLEAR TREATY, 1984. The treaty on bilateral peaceful use of nuclear energy between China and the Federal Republic of Germany was signed on May 9, 1984 in Bonn.

CHINA–GERMAN TREATIES. In 1861, Prussia, and in 1871 the German Reich concluded agreements with China on establishing diplomatic relations to ensure the same privileges as those granted in the British–Chinese ▷ Peking Peace Treaty of 1860. On 6 Mar., 1898 the German Reich concluded a treaty with China on lease of the coast of Ciaoczou Bay for 99 years. The German Reich was also a signatory of the Peking Protocol of 7 Sept., 1901, ▷ Boxer Protocol.

CHINA, GREAT WALL OF. The largest fortification in the world, 2415 km long, built BC and AD in China from Kansu province to Itopeh province on the Yellow Sea. A tapestry with a contemporary view of the Great Wall was offered by the Government of the People's Republic of China to the UN in 1976 and now decorates the Delegates Lounge at UN headquarters, New York.

CHINA–JAPAN DECLARATION, 1972. The first document after World War II on normalization of the relations between China and Japan, signed Sept. 29, 1972 in Peking by the Prime Minister of ChPR, Chou-En-lai and Prime Minister of Japan, K. Tanaka.

CHINA–JAPAN PEACE TREATY, 1952. The Treaty of Peace (with Protocol, exchange of notes and agreed minutes), between the Republic of China (▷ Taiwan) and Japan signed in Taipei, April 28, 1952. The text is as follows:

"Art. I. The state of war between the Republic of China and Japan is terminated as from the date on which the present Treaty enters into force.
Art. II. It is recognized that under Article 2 of the Treaty of Peace with Japan signed at the city of San Francisco in the United States of America on Sept. 8, 1951 (hereinafter referred as the San Francisco Treaty), Japan has renounced all right, title and claim to Taiwan (Formosa) and Penghu (the Pescadores) as well as the Spratly Islands and the Paracel Islands.
Art. III. The disposition of property of Japan and of its nationals in Taiwan (Formosa) and Penghu (the Pescadores), and their claims, including debts, against the authorities of the Republic of China in Taiwan (Formosa) and Penghu (the Pescadores) and the residents thereof, and the disposition in Japan of property of such authorities and residents and their claims, including debts, against Japan and its nationals, shall be the subject of special arrangements between the Government of the Republic of China and the Government of Japan. The terms nationals and residents whenever used in the present Treaty include juridical persons.
Art. IV. It is recognized that all treaties, conventions and agreements concluded before December 9, 1941, between China and Japan have become null and void as a consequence of the war.
Art. V. It is recognized that under the provisions of Article 10 of the San Francisco Treaty, Japan has renounced all special rights and interests in China, including all benefits and privileges resulting from the provisions of the final Protocol signed at Peking on Sept. 7, 1901, and all annexes, notes and documents supplementary thereto, and has agreed to the abroga-

tion in respect to Japan of the said protocol, annexes, notes and documents.
Art. V(a) The Republic of China and Japan will be guided by the principles of Article 2 of the Charter of the United Nations in their mutual relations.
(b) The Republic of China and Japan will co-operate in accordance with the the principles of the Charter of the United Nations and, in particular, will promote their common welfare through friendly co-operation in the economic field.
Art. VII. The Republic of China and Japan will endeavor to conclude, as soon as possible, a treaty or agreement to place their trading, maritime and other commercial relations on a stable and friendly basis.
Art. VIII. The Republic of China and Japan will endeavor to conclude, as soon as possible, an agreement relating to civil air transport.
Art. IX. The Republic of China and Japan will endeavour to conclude, as soon as possible, an agreement providing for the regulation of limitation of fishing and the conservation and development of fisheries on the high seas.
Art. X. For the purposes of the present Treaty, nationals of the Republic of China shall be deemed to include all the inhabitants and former inhabitants of Taiwan (Formosa) and Penghu (the Pescadores) and their descendants who are of the Chinese nationality in accordance with the laws and regulations which have been or may hereafter be enforced by the Republic of China and Taiwan (Formosa) and Penghu (the Pescadores); and juridical persons of the Republic of China shall be deemed to include all those registered under the laws and regulations which have been or may hereafter be enforced by the Republic of China in Taiwan (Formosa) and Penghu (the Pescadores).
Art. XI. Unless otherwise provided for in the present Treaty and the documents supplementary thereto, any problem arising between the Republic of China and Japan as a result of the existence of a state of war shall be settled in accordance with the relevant provisions of the San Francisco Treaty.
Art. XII. Any dispute that may arise out of the interpretation or application of the present Treaty shall be settled by negotiation or by other pacific means.
Art. XIII. The present Treaty shall be ratified and the instruments of ratification shall be exchanged at Taipei as soon as possible. The present Treaty shall enter into force as from the date on which such instruments of ratification are exchanged.
Art. XIV. The present Treaty shall be in the Chinese, Japanese and English languages. In case of any divergence of interpretation, the English text shall prevail".

UNTS, Vol. 138, pp. 38–42.

CHINA–JAPAN PEACE TREATY, 1978. The Treaty of Peace and Understanding between the People's Republic of China and Japan, signed on Aug. 12, 1978 in Peking and formally implemented in Tokyo on Oct. 23, 1978. The text is as follows:

"Japan and the People's Republic of China, recalling with satisfaction that since the government of Japan and the government of the People's Republic of China issued a joint communique in Peking on Sept. 29, 1972, the friendly relations between the two governments and the peoples of the two countries have developed greatly on a new basis. Conforming that the above mentioned joint communique constitutes the basis of the relations of peace and friendship between the two countries and that the principles enunciated in the joint communique should be strictly observed. Confirming that the principles of the Charter of the UN should be fully respected,
Hoping to contribute to peace and stability in Asia and in the world,
For the purpose of solidifying and developing the relations of peace and friendship between the two countries,
Have resolved to conclude a Treaty of Peace and Friendship and have agreed as follows:
Art. I, 1. The contracting parties shall develop relations of perpetual peace and friendship between the two countries on the basis of the principles of mutual respect for sovereignty and territorial integrity, mutual non-aggression, non-interference in each other's internal affairs, equality and mutual benefit and peaceful co-existence.

The contracting parties confirm that in conformity with the foregoing principles and the principles of the charter of the United Nations, they shall in their mutual relations settle all disputes by peaceful means and shall refrain from the use or threat of force.
Art. 2. The contracting parties declare that neither of them should seek hegemony in the Asia–Pacific region or in any other region and that each is opposed to efforts by any other country or group of countries to establish such hegemony.
Art. 3. The contracting parties shall, in the good neighborly and friendly spirit and in conformity with the principle of equality and mutual benefit and non-interference in each other's internal affairs, endeavor to further develop economic and cultural relations between the two countries and to promote exchanges between the peoples of the two countries.
Art. 4. The present treaty shall not affect the position of either contracting party regarding its relations with third countries.
Art. 5. The present treaty shall be ratified and shall enter into force on the date of the exchange of instruments of ratification which shall take place at Tokio. The present treaty shall remain in force for ten years and thereafter shall continue to be in force until terminated in accordance with the provisions of paragraph 2.
Either contracting party may, by giving one year's written notice to the other contracting party, terminate the present treaty at the end of the initial ten-year period or at any time thereafter.
In witness whereof the respective plenipotentiaries have signed the present treaty and have affixed thereto their seals. Done in duplicate, in the Japanese and Chinese languages, both texts being equally authentic, at Peking, this twelfth day of Aug., 1978".

UNTS, 1978.

CHINA–JAPAN TREATIES, 1871–1895. The first agreement between China and Japan was a Trade Treaty called the Treaty of Tientsin, signed 1877 with a Japanese Tariff annexed to the Treaty; amended by an Agreement of Peking and appended Guarantee, signed 1874. The Convention of Tientsin signed 1885 related to Korea was not ratified by Japan.
The Japanese–Chinese Korea War 1894–1895 terminated with the ▷ Shimonoseki Peace Treaty 1895.

MARTENS, *Nouveau Recueil Général*, 2 serie, Göttingen, 1907; MACMURRAY, *Treaties and Agreements with and concerning China 1894–1919*, New York, 1921.

CHINANDOGA CONVENTION, 1842. A Convention establishing the ▷ Central American Confederation, signed at the former capital of the Central American Union Chinandoga, Nicaragua, on Mar. 17, 1842.

TH.L. KARNES, *The Failure of Union: Central America 1824–1960*, Chapel Hill, N.J., 1961.

CHINA REPUBLIC. Member of the UN 1945–1971. Republic of China, proclaimed 1931. ▷ People's Republic of China, and ▷ Taiwan.

CHINA–RUSSIA AGREEMENTS AND TREATIES, 1727–1901. The following agreements and treaties were signed:

(1) On Oct. 21, 1727 in Nerchinsk, establishing new borders between both empires, terms of commercial exchange; on building of an Orthodox church in Peking; assuming the rule that military deserters from China will be pursued in Russia, and those from Russia will be hanged in China. Exchange of ratification documents took place on June 14, 1728 on the river Kiachta, therefore the name Kiachta Agreement. A Supplementary Treaty of Kiachta was signed 1768.
(2) Aigun Agreement, in Aigun on Amur on May 28, 1858, by Governor-General of Russian Eastern Siberia, General N.N. Muraviov and by the commander of the Chinese forces on Manchurian Amur, Prince J. Chan; tracing out the border between the two states on the Amur river. According to art. 1, the left bank of Amur

to the estuary, beginning from the river Argun, belongs to Russia, while the right bank up the river to the Ussuri river belongs to China. The territory and small localities between Ussuri and the sea will remain common property until the conclusion of the agreement on delimitation. Shipping on the rivers Amur, Sungari and Ussuri is prohibited to other countries.
(3) Treaty of ▷ Tientsin 1838.
(4) Peking Agreement of Oct. 14, 1860 granting Russia the coastal province Haishenvei, the present Coastal Land, where the port city of Vladivostok was built.
(5) Treaty of St. Petersburg 1881.
(6) Chinese–Russian secret agreement of Sept. 8, 1896, on a defensive alliance against Japanese aggression, allowing Russia the rights of construction and exploitation of the Eastern Railway to Vladivostok, financed through the Chinese–Russian Bank, which was founded on Sept. 8, 1896.
(7) On Sept. 7, 1901 Russia was a party to the final protocol concerning the Boxer Rebellion. ▷ Boxer Protocol 1901.
(8) Agreement relative to Manchuria 1902.
(9) Agreement with the Chinese Eastern Railway Company, 1908, supplemented 1909.
(10) Sungasi River Customs Regulations Protocol 1910.

Sbornik dogovorov i drugikh dokumentov po istoryi mezhdunarodnikh otnosheniy na Dal'nem Vostokie 1842–1925, Moskva, 1927; *Sbornik dogovorov Rossyi s drugimi gosudarstvami 1856–1917*, Moskva, 1952. M. PONIATOWSKI, *Histoire de la Russie, d'Amerique et de l'Alasca*, Paris, 1958.

CHINA-SOVIET AGREEMENTS 1984–1989.
After border clashes in 1969 the first agreements between China and the USSR were signed during an official visit of the Soviet First Deputy Premier I. Arkhipov in Beijing, providing for: increased economic and technical co-operation, an expansion of scientific and technological exchanges and the establishment of a Sino-Soviet joint committee to promote economic, trade, scientific and technological co-operation. The first agreements on the boundary east of Mongolia (about 2800 km long) were signed on Oct. 31, 1988 after 2 years of negotiations.

KEESING's *Contemporary Archive*, March 1985.

CHINA–SOVIET TREATIES, 1945 AND 1950.
Two treaties on friendship and mutual aid:

(1) The Treaty signed on Aug. 14, 1945. It obligated both sides in art. 1 to common war against Japan till victory; in art. 3 to common concern in preventing Japan from resumed aggression; in art. 5 to mutual non-interference in each party's home affairs; in art. 6 to mutual aid in reconstruction of war damages. The following Protocols were attached to the Treaty:
(a) on setting up, after the liberation of Eastern Provinces of China, joint Chinese–Soviet management of the Manchuria railway for the thirty years of the Treaty's validity;
(b) on taking over of civilian administration of Port Arthur by China for common Chinese–Soviet use and exclusive access to the naval port for battleships of China and the USSR, the latter undertaking the obligation of military defense of Port Arthur;
(c) on proclaiming by China of Talien (Dalnij) a free port where the USSR would possess docks and warehouses;
(d) on collaboration of Chinese and Soviet commands in the territory of Eastern China in military operations against Japan. Moreover, on the occasion of concluding the Treaty, notes were exchanged concerning the granting of independence to Outer Mongolia, provided its population chose independence in plebiscite (that followed by 98.4% of votes on Oct. 20, 1945).
(2) The Treaty of 1945, after the revolution in China, was on Feb. 14, 1950 replaced by the Treaty on Friendship, Alliance and Mutual Aid between the USSR and the People's Republic of China, signed at Moscow on Feb. 14, 1950. Came into force on Apr. 11, 1950. The text is as follows:
"The Presidium of the Supreme Soviet of the Union of Soviet Socialist Republics and the Central People's Government of the People's Republic of China,

Being determined, by strengthening friendship and co-operation between the Union of Soviet Socialist Republics and the People's Republic of China, jointly to prevent the revival of Japanese imperialism and the repetition of aggression on the part of Japan or of any other State that might in any way join with Japan in acts of aggression,
Being anxious to promote a lasting peace and general security in the Far East and throughout the world in accordance with the purposes and principles of the United Nations,
Being firmly convinced that the strengthening of good-neighbourly and friendly relations between the Union of Soviet Socialist Republics and the People's Republic of China is in accordance with the fundamental interests of the peoples of the Soviet Union and China. Have decided for this purpose to conclude the present Treaty and have appointed as their plenipotentiaries:
The Presidium of the Supreme Soviet of the Union of Soviet Socialist Republics: Andrei Yanaurevich Vyshinsky, Minister of Foreign Affairs of the USSR;
The Central People's Government of the People's Republic of China: Chou En-lai, Chairman of the State Administrative Council and Minister of Foreign Affairs of China.
The two plenipotentiary representatives, having exchanged their full powers, found in good and due form, have agreed as follows:
Art. 1. The two Contracting Parties undertake to carry out jointly all necessary measures within their power to prevent a repetition of aggression and breach of the peace by Japan or any other State which might directly or indirectly joint with Japan in acts of aggression. Should either of the Contracting Parties be attacked by Japan or by States allied with Japan and thus find itself in a state of war, the other Contracting Party shall immediately extend military and other assistance with all the means at its disposal.
The Contracting Parties likewise declare that they are prepared to participate, in a spirit of sincere co-operation, in all international action designed to safeguard peace and security throughout the world, and will devote all their energies to the speediest realization of these aims.
Art. 2. The two Contracting Parties undertake, by common agreement, to strive for the conclusion at the earliest possible date, in conjunction with the other Powers which were their Allies during the Second World War, of a Peace Treaty with Japan.
Art. 3. Neither of the Contracting Parties shall enter into any alliance directed against the other Party, or participate in any coalition or in any action or measures directed against the other Party.
Art. 4. The two Contracting Parties shall consult together on all important international questions involving the common interests of the Soviet Union and China, with a view to strengthening peace and universal security.
Art. 5. The two Contracting Parties undertake, in a spirit of friendship and co-operation and in accordance with the principles of equal rights, mutual interests, mutual respect for State sovereignty and territorial integrity, and non-intervention in the domestic affairs of the other Party, to develop and strengthen the economic and cultural ties between the Soviet Union and China, to render each other all possible economic assistance and to effect the necessary economic co-operation.
Art. 6. This Treaty shall come into force immediately upon ratification; the exchange of the instruments of ratification shall take place at Peking.
This Treaty shall remain in force for thirty years. If neither of the Contracting Parties gives notice one year before the expiration of the said period that it wishes to denounce the Treaty, it shall remain in force for a further five years and shall thereafter be continued in force in accordance with this provision."

The following were attached to the Treaty:
(a) agreement on Chinese Changun railway line and on Port Arthur and Talien (Dalnij);
(b) agreement on granting credits by the USSR to the Chinese People's Republic. This agreement was confirmed during the visit of the party-government delegation of China to Moscow, Aug. 17, to Oct. 16, 1952, and that of the USSR to Peking, Sept. 29 to Oct. 12, 1954, when further agreements were concluded:

(a) on withdrawal of the USSR troops from Port Arthur; (b) on turning over to the Chinese People's Republic of the USSR shares in Chinese–Soviet mixed companies; (c) on scientific-technical co-operation; (d) on construction of a common railway line connecting both countries along the route Lanczon–Urumc zi–Alma Ata; (e) on construction by the Chinese People's Republic, Mongolian People's Republic and the USSR of a railway line Czinin–Ulan Bator.
A year before the treaty's expiry in an interview for *Time* magazine, Jan. 19, 1979, L. Brezhnev said:
"Now and again statements are heard from Peking alleging that the Sino–Soviet Treaty of Friendship, Alliance and Mutual Assistance concluded in 1950 'has lost all significance', has become a 'mere sheet of paper', and so on. Apparently the Chinese leaders are provoking us to abrogate this treaty. I can say that we shall not give in to provocation. We shall never tear up of our own will a document that epitomizes friendship between the peoples of the USSR and China. But should the Peking leaders take such a step, they would have to bear the entire onus of responsibility before the people of their country, before the forces of peace and progress all over the world.'
In April, 1979 Sinhua, the official Chinese news agency, issued a communique in which it stated:
"The Treaty of Friendship, Alliance and Mutual Assistance which was signed between the PRC and the USSR in Moscow, February 14, 1950, and entered into force April 11 of the same year, will expire April 11, 1980. In view of changes in the international situation and the fact that this treaty has long ceased to exist except in name owing to violations for which the Chinese side is not responsible, the Permanent Committee of the All Chinese Assembly of People's Representatives at its VII Session held April 3, 1979, resolved not to extend the aforementioned treaty beyond the term of its validity. This decision was transmitted to the Soviet side on April 3, 1979, by the Minister for Foreign Affairs of the PRC, Huang Hua, who met with the ambassador of the USSR to China. J. Shtsherbakov, and again presented concrete positions of the Chinese Government in view of which the differences in principal questions between China and the Soviet Union should not hamper maintenance and development of normal interstate relations on the basis of five principles of mutual respect for sovereignty and territorial integrity, mutual non-aggression, non-interference into internal affairs, equality and mutual benefit as well as peaceful coexistence. The Chinese Government proposed that negotiations be held between China and the Soviet Union in order to settle the open questions and improve relations between the two countries."
In reply TASS, the official Soviet news agency, published the following statement:
"On April 3, 1979, the government of the People's Republic of China announced that it does not intend to prolong the Treaty of Friendship, Alliance and Mutual Assistance between the Soviet Union and the People's Republic of China concluded in 1950, which expires in April, 1980, although the treaty itself provides that by mutual consent expressed by the two sides it may be extended. In an attempt to justify this hostile act the Chinese side resorts to gross insinuations which, as a result, calls for a reiteration of the actual state of affairs. The Treaty of Friendship, Alliance and Mutual Assistance between the USSR and the PRC was signed at a time when the Chinese people was in urgent need of assistance and support to defend its revolutionary gains and to meet the objectives of economic and cultural construction facing it.
True to its international duties, fulfilling honestly the obligations arising from the treaty by the USSR from the very beginning resolutely and consistently stood in defence of the interests of the PRC in the international arena, effectively helped the young people's republic fend off the attempts to interfere into its affairs launched by imperialist forces. Soviet troops sent to the PRC at its request relentlessly defended the country against raid of hostile air forces. The existence of the Sino–Soviet Treaty of 1950 played a decisive role also in thwarting an open imperialist aggression against the PRC during the 1950–53 war in Korea as well as during the so-called Taiwan crisis of 1958.
The assistance in creating new and reconstructing old instruments in the People's Republic of China, in

mapping out and preparing deposits of useful minerals, the development of relations in the fields of science and culture, etc. was also a result of the 1950 treaty being implemented and Sino–Soviet co-operation agreement concluded on its basis and concerning many fields. All this was highly appreciated and favorably estimated by the Chinese side.

Now, the one-sided actions of Peking in announcing that the treaty of 1950 has lost its significance, by no means can be reconciled with numerous declarations to maintain regular relations with the Soviet Union.

While rejecting in 1971 Soviet proposals to conclude a treaty on non-use in force and in 1973 a proposal to sign a treaty of non-aggression, the government of China explained that there was apparently no need to conclude such treaties as the Treaty of Friendship, Alliance and Mutual Assistance between the USSR and the PRC which remained in force.

At present, by a Chinese move this treaty is also losing its validity. This and other moves of the Chinese leadership irrefutably show that it intentionally aims to continue entangling and impairing Sino–Soviet relations. The change in Peking's position toward the Treaty of Friendship, Alliance and Mutual Assistance between the USSR and the PRC – from total approval and active implementation to abrogation – is closely related to the decadent policy purposed by the Chinese leadership ever more determined by big power and hegemonistic tendencies and a negligent attitude toward other countries and peoples, animosity toward everything that leads to strengthening peace and international security and stands in the way of its plans to rule the world. To what extent the policy practiced by Peking equals adventurism, how low it has sunk in the betrayal of the interests of socialism has been shown by the ignominious aggression unleashed by China against the Socialist Republic of Vietnam. As to the Soviet Union, its attitude toward the Treaty of Friendship, Alliance and Mutual Assistance with the PRC has always been univocal and consistent. It stems from the standpoint of principle adopted by the Soviet Union with regard to treaties it has concluded and obligations it has assumed, unconditionally implemented by the Soviet Union.

The force and effectiveness of the Sino–Soviet Treaty of 1950 arose from the fact that it rendered the inflexible will of the two great nations to live in peace and friendship. Therefore there may be no doubt as to the decision on abrogating the treaty being made in spite of the will and interests of the Chinese people.

In the Soviet Union great admiration for the Chinese people, for its history and culture has always prevailed. There are no objective reasons to alienate and, all the more so, to move our nations towards confrontation. No effort made by enemies of the Chinese–Soviet friendship, no attempt to erase from the memory of the masses and to undo all the favorable aspects that have accumulated over the years of fraternal cooperation between the two countries, to put up a dam of hostility between the Soviet Union and the PRC, will yield the anticipated result.

The Soviet side declares that entire responsibility for rupturing the Treaty of Friendship, Alliance and Mutual Assistance between the USSR and the PRC falls upon the Chinese side. This Soviet Union will draw, of course, appropriate conclusions from the Chinese side's conduct."

D.M. JOHNSTON, H. CHIN, *Agreements of the People's Republic of China 1947–67*, Harvard, 1968.

CHINA'S THREE WORLDS THEORY. A doctrine announced by the delegate of the Chinese People's Republic, Teng Siao-ping, at the VI Special Session of the UN General Assembly, 1974, in New York; then presented at the XI Congress of the Chinese Communist Party, 1977, as the ideological explanation of Chinese foreign policy, formulated by Mao Tse-tung in 1974, as follows:

"In my opinion the USA and USSR compromise the first world. Intermediate powers, as e.g. Japan, Europe and Canada, belong to the second world. We are the third world. The third world has a tremendous number of people. With the exception of Japan all of Asia belongs to the third world. All of Africa belongs to the third world as well as Latin America."

In 1977 the Albanian Communist Party came out against this theory, which was also criticized by the Communist Party of the Soviet Union and other Marxist–Leninist parties, with the slogan: "There are no three worlds, only two: the old and the new."

CHINA TRADE CO-ORDINATING COMMITTEE, CHINCOM. An intergovernmental institution with headquarters in London which regulates economic relations with the Chinese People's Republic. It was founded in Nov. 1949 and consisted of NATO states. In 1951 the FRG and Japan joined CHINCOM. ▷ COCOM and CHINCOM.

CHINA–USA FRIENDSHIP TREATY, 1946. Treaty of Friendship, Commerce and Navigation between the Republic of China and the United States of America, signed on Nov. 4, 1946; ratifications exchanged and entered into force on Nov. 30, 1948. The text of the Preamble and of art. 1 is as follows:

"The Republic of China and the United States of America, desirous of strengthening the bond of peace and the ties of friendship which have happily long prevailed between the two countries by arrangements designed to promote friendly intercourse between their respective territories through provisions responsive to the spiritual, cultural, economic and commercial aspirations of the peoples thereof, have resolved to conclude a Treaty of Friendship, Commerce and Navigation.

Art. 1. There shall be constant peace and firm and lasting friendship between the Republic of China and the United States of America.

Art. 2. The Government of each High Contracting Party shall have the right to send to the Government of the other High Contracting Party duly accredited diplomatic representatives, who shall be received and, upon the basis of reciprocity, shall enjoy in the territories of such other High Contracting Party the rights, privileges, exemptions and immunities accorded under generally recognized principles of international law."

UNTS, 1946.

CHINA–WASHINGTON TREATY, 1922. Treaty relating to Principles and Policies to be followed in matters concerning China, signed in Washington, Feb. 6, 1922, by the governments of the USA, Belgium, the British Empire, France, Italy, Japan, the Netherlands, Portugal and China.

LNTS, Vol. 38, p, 281 and 282.

CHINCOM. ▷ China Trade Co-ordinating Committee.

CHINESE. Chinese is one of the official ▷ languages of the UN. Since Jan. 17, 1974 it has been one of the five working languages of the Security Council and the UN General Assembly.

CHINESE CONCESSIONS. An international term for concessions imposed upon China by European colonial states providing privileges for settlement of their citizens, first by the Nanking Treaty of Aug. 29, 1842 followed by other similar treaties; also provided for formation in Peking 1860 of extra-territorial legations quarters and international commercial settlements. Liquidated under pressure from revolutionary forces 1917–22, the last disappearing in 1927. Liquidated earlier or concurrently were similar concessions gained in the 19th century by colonial powers in Egypt, Japan, Morocco and Turkey. Those in Cairo ceased to exist in 1949 and in the Suez canal zone in 1956.

V.K.W. KOO, *The Status of Aliens in China*, London, 1912; W.R. FISHEL, *The End of Extraterritoriality in China*, London, 1952; J.K. FAIRBANK, *Trade and Diplomacy on the China Coast. The Opening of the Treaty Ports 1842–1854*, 2 Vols., London, 1953.

CHINESE CULTURAL REVOLUTION. An international term for a controversial return to dogmatic communist doctrine in People's China in the years 1966–69, ordered by Chairman Mao to combat the ▷ Hundred Flowers Doctrine.

Y. YIANG, *Six Chapters from My Life 'Downunder'*, Hong Kong, 1983; J. SAHPIRO, L. HENS, *Cold Winds, Warm Winds: Intellectual Life in China Today*, Middletown Ont., 1986; G. YUAN, *Born Red: A Chronicle of the Cultural Revolution*, Stanford, Calif. 1987.

CHINESE DOCTRINE OF ONE HUNDRED FLOWERS, 1956. An international term for a Chinese doctrine of multidirectionality in socialist thought, formulated by Mao Tse-tung on May 2, 1956: "Let one hundred flowers bloom, let one hundred schools compete with one another."

R. MACQFARUHAR (ed.), *The Hundred Flowers*, London, 1960.

CHINESE DOCTRINE OF TWO SUPERPOWERS, 1977. An international term for an idea attributed to Mao Tse-tung that besides the capitalistic and socialistic countries two superpowers exist in the world, the USA and the USSR, among which the more dangerous is the USSR, and hence the struggle should be concentrated against the latter in concert with the less dangerous powers. ▷ China's Three Worlds Theory.

CHINESE IMMIGRATION IN USA. A subject of Sino–American disputes in the 19th and 20th centuries since 1854 when large groups of Chinese came to settle in California. Governments of both countries concluded the Burlingame Treaty, 1864, granting Chinese emigrants the most-favored-nation clause but not naturalization. Another agreement, Nov. 17, 1880, sought to reduce Chinese influx to the USA; the flow was arrested completely for ten years by a resolution of Congress, May 6, 1882, called the Chinese Exclusion Act, later prolonged for further decades; repealed Dec. 17, 1943 (Repeal of Chinese Exclusion Laws. Public Law 199).

CHING-CHUN. ▷ Manchuria.

CHOLERA. Subject of International Health Regulations. "... the incubation period of cholera is five days" (art. 62 of IHR). The requirement of a cholera vaccination certificates for travellers has been removed from the WHO ▷ International Health Regulation. In 1987 only 8 countries continue to require one. In WHO opinion "experience has shown that cholera is not a major public health problem in a country or a community that has a properly organized programme for the control of diarrhoeal diseases."

UNTS, Vol. 764, pp. 52–60; *WHO Features*, May 1987, Nr. 107.

CHOPIN COMPETITIONS INTERNATIONAL. The international piano competitions organized by Poland. I International Chopin Competition took place in 1927; from then every five years (with an interruption caused by World War II), always in Warsaw in the Philharmonic Building. The candidates to the Warsaw Chopin Competition are chosen in national competitions by National Chopin Committees. In the USA the organizer of the national competition is the Chopin Foundation of San Francisco, initiated by the Polish Arts and Culture Foundation. Prize winners 1927–80 were (name and sequence of prize),

I – 1927: Lev Oborin (USSR), Stanislaw Szpinalski (Poland).
II – 1932: Alexandre Uminski (France), Imre Ungar (Hungary), Boleslaw Kon (Poland).
III – 1937: Jakub Zak (USSR), Roza Tamarkina (USSR), Witold Malcuzynski (Poland).
IV – 1949: Halina Czerny-Stefanska (Poland), Bella Davidovitch (USSR) ex aequo, Barbara Hesse-Bukowska (Poland), Waldemar Maciszewski (Poland).
V – 1955: Adam Harasiewicz (Poland), Vladimir Ashkenazy (USSR), Fu Cung (China).
VI – 1960: Maurizio Pollini (Italy), Irina Zaricka (USSR), Tania Aszot-Harutunian (Iran).
VII – 1965: Martha Argerich (Argentina), Artur Moreira-Lima (Brazil), Marta Sosinska (Poland).
VIII – 1970: Garrick Ohlsson (USA), Mitsuko Uchida (Japan), Piotr Paleczny (Poland).
IX – 1975: Krystian Zimerman (Poland), Dina Joffie (USSR), Tatiana Fiedkin (USSR).
X – 1980: Thai Son Oang (Vietnam), Tatiana Shebanova (USSR), Arutium Papazjan (USSR).
XI – 1985: Stanislav Bunin (USSR), Marc Laforêt (France), Krzysztof Jablonski (Poland).

CHORNAYA SOTNYA. Russian = "black hundreds". An international term for extreme right fighting squads, used for terrifying national or ethnic minorities with pogroms and murdering political opponents. The name originated in Tsarist Russia after 1905, when the police organized ▷ terrorist squads from the outcasts of society which provoked incidents and organized pogroms of the Armenian and Jewish population. ▷ Death squads.

CHRISTIAN-DEMOCRATIC AND CONSERVATIVE PARTIES. National political organizations set up in Europe and Latin America in parliamentary democracies. In 1978 two international groups were founded: ▷ European Democratic Union and ▷ Euro-right.

M. PRELOT, G. LESENGER, *Histoire des idées politiques*, Paris, 1978, pp. 730–750.

CHRISTIAN INTERNATIONAL ORGANIZATIONS. Common name for religious non-Catholic organizations, reg. with the UIA:

All African Conference of Churches, f. 1958, Nairobi.
Alliance of the Reformed Churches throughout the World Holding the Presbyterian Order, f. 1875, Geneva.
Baptist World Alliance, f. 1905, Washington.
Christian Family Movement, f. 1957, Montevideo.
Christian Peace Conference, f. 1958, Prague.
Churches Committee on Migrant Workers in Western Europe, f. 1964, Geneva.
Church of Christ Scientist, f. 1879, Boston.
Conference of European Churches, f. 1959, Geneva.
Commission of the Churches on International Affairs, f. 1946, Geneva.
Eirene, International Christian Service for Peace, f. 1957, Bonn.
Friends World Committee for Consultation (Quakers), f. 1937, London.
General Conference of Seventh-Day Adventists, f. 1863, Washington.
Girls Brigade, The, f. 1902, London.
International Association for Liberal Christianity and Religious Freedom, f. 1900, The Hague.
International Consultative Committee of Organizations for Christian–Jewish Co-operation, f. 1955, London.
International Council of Christian Churches European Alliance, f. 1957, Amsterdam.
International Fellowship of Reconciliation, f. 1919, Brussels.
International Hebrew Christian Alliance, f. 1925, London.
International Inter-Church Film Centre, f. 1955, Hilversum, Holland.
International League of Religious Socialists, f. 1922, Bentveld (Holland), with branches in Denmark, Finland, France, FRG, Norway and Switzerland.
International Organization of Good Templars, f. 1851, New York.

International Organization for the Study of the Old Testament, f. 1950, Cambridge, G. Britain.
International Union of Liberal Christian Women, f. 1910, The Hague.
Lutheran World Federation, f. 1947, Geneva.
Society for African Church History, f. 1921, Nsukka, Nigeria.
The Salvation Army, f. 1865, London.
Toc H Women's Association (League of Women Helpers), f. 1922, London.
Union of Latin American Evangelical Youth, f. 1941, Montevideo.
Watch Tower Bible and Tract Society (Jehovah's Witnesses), f. 1872, New York.
World Council of Churches, f. 1948, Geneva.
World Federation of Methodist Women, f. 1939, Geneva.
World Methodist Council, f. 1881, Geneva.
World Student Christian Federation, f. 1965, Geneva.
World Christian Endeavour Union, f. 1895, Columbus, Ohio, USA.
World's Woman's Christian Temperance Union, f. 1883, London.

Yearbook of International Organizations.

R. HARRIES, *Christianity and War in a Nuclear Age,* London, 1987.

CHRISTIAN RELIGIOUS COURTS IN ISRAEL. In the Israeli system of religious courts the Christian Religious Courts in Jerusalem have exclusive jurisdiction in matters of marriage and divorce and other matter of personal status of Christians who are Israeli citizens or residents (94.151 population 1983 census).

The Europa Yearbook 1987. A World Survey, London 1987.

CHRISTIAN SCIENTISTS. The followers of the Scientific ▷ Church of Christ.

CHRISTIANS FOR SOCIALISM. CRISTOS PARA EL SOCIALISMO. An Iberian–American Catholic social movement, professing the ▷ theology of liberation. Born in the 1960s among the young clergy of Latin America turned radical in the face of growing poverty of the Latin masses and the successes of the Cuban revolution. Symbol of the movement became a professor of theology at the Catholic University in Bogota, who fell in a partisan action in Colombia, Father Camilo Torres (▷ Encuentros Latino-americanos de Camilo Torres). The spiritual leader of the movement became the bishop of the Mexican diocese of Cuernavaca, Father Mendez Arceo, who proclaimed in 1972 that "for our world, retarded in its socio-economic development, there is no other solution except socialism". The First Latin-American Congress, Christians for Socialism, took place in Santiago de Chile in Apr., 1972. The movement expanded to Spain, Portugal, and Italy. Not promoted by the Holy See.

CHRISTIAN TRADE UNIONS, INTERNATIONAL FEDERATION OF, IFCTU. Established 1920 with seat in Brussels, includes 54 countries in Europe, Africa, and Latin America as well as 11 international federations of various professions. In 1968 changed its name to ▷ World Confederation of Labour. Advisory status (A) with ECOSOC.

Yearbook of International Organizations.

CHRISTIAN WORLD PEACE CONFERENCE, 1983. A Conference of Christian Churches held in April 1983 at Stockholm dedicated to problem of life and peace.

CHRISTMAS ISLAND. An island in the Polynesians, Line Islands. The largest atoll in the Pacific. Area: 575 sq. km. 1968 pop.: 367. Since 1919 a part of the British colony of ▷ Gilbert and Ellice

Islands. The US claims sovereignty over Christmas Island, but the UN Decolonization Committee did not accept either the British colonial status nor the US claims. Site of British nuclear tests in 1957 and 1958 and US tests in 1962. The island is inhabited. Since July 12, 1979 part of the Republic of ▷ Kiribati.

E. BAILEY, *The Christmas Islands Story,* London, 1977; J. PAXTON ed., *The Statesman's Yearbook 1987–88,* London, 1987.

CHRISTMAS ISLAND. An island south of Java in the Indian Ocean. Area: 155.4 sq. km. Annexed in 1888 by Great Britain, part of the ▷ Straits Settlements in 1889. Since 1958 under Australian administration.

CHRONOLOGY, INTERNATIONAL. The first permanent description of international events, published annually since 1759 in London, is *The Annual Register of World Events.* The second, also published in London since 1864, is *The Statesman's Yearbook.* Published continuously since 1868 in New York is *The World Almanac and Book of Facts.* After World War I, since 1921 the American Foreign Policy Association in New York has published a description of world events with commentary, entitled *Foreign Policy Bulletin: An Analysis of Current International Events*; since 1925 the London Royal Institute of International Affairs has published an annual, *Survey of International Affairs*; since 1931 in London the first daily chronicle of world events has appeared in the form of numbered cards, which were compiled into a yearbook and mailed to subscribers as Keesing's *Contemporary Archives: Weekly Diary of World Events with Index,* published simultaneously in Vienna in German as Keesing's *Archiv der Gegenwart*; since 1932 a similar world chronology of each day began to appear in New York in the form of a yearbook, *The New International Yearbook: A Compendium of the World's Progress for the Year.* After World War II, from 1945 The Royal Institute of International Events, as well as a 1947 *Chronology of the Second World War,* and, since 1945, has published a monthly, *The World Today*; in France since 1944 Agence International de Documentation Pharos has published *Les Archives International Pharos,* and also since 1944 a bureau, the Direction de la Documentation has published a quarterly, *La Documentation Française*; since 1946 Press Université de France has published *Bulletin analitique de documentation politique, économique et social contemporaine*; since 1947 the London Institute of World Affairs has published *Yearbook of World Affairs*; since 1951 in Poland *Dokumentacja prasowa* has appeared modelled on Kessing (from 1971 called *Kronika*); since 1957 Moskyevski Institut Sprav Myezhdunarodnyey has published *Mezhdunarodni vezhogodnik.* In addition, regional chronologies have appeared: e.g. since 1947 Brookings Institution in Washington has published *Major Problems of US Foreign Policy: A Study Guide.* Since 1955 in Delhi, *Asian Recorder: A Weekly Digest of Outstanding Asian Events with Index*; since 1961 in Delhi, *African Diary: Weekly Diary of African Events with Index*; since 1962 in Delhi, *African Recorder: A Fortnightly Record of African Events with Index.* There are also many chronological analyses in various languages for specific periods in the history of countries and regions of the world: e.g. *Chronology of International Events and Treaties, Jan. 1, 1920–Dec. 31, 1925.* Compiled by V. Boulter, London, 1928; *A Buchkreis-Chronik: Urzeit bis 1900,* Nürnberg, 1933. *Politik des 20 Jahrhunderts, Weltgeschichte 1901–1936,* Nürnberg, 1937, supplemented 1939, 1940 and 1941, two Vols. *Die Jahre 1937–1938; Das Jahr 1939; Das Jahr*

1940; Weltgeschichte der Nachkriegszeit 1945–1957. In Spain the Edición Nacional publ. the *Documentación española* and the Instituto de Cultura Hispánica publ. since 1962 *Annuario Iberoamericano,* since 1963 *Documentación Iberoamericana* and since 1970 *Síntesis Informativa Iberoamericana.*

CHUNNEL. A term created in 1960 by combining the English words channel and tunnel, to define the tunnel under the English Channel on the route Dover–Calais, then under consideration by the governments of Great Britain and France. Construction of the tunnel had first been considered in the early 19th century. Preliminary diplomatic talks in 1870 were followed on 24 June 1872 by exchange of notes between France and Great Britain, and by appointment of an international commission, the works of which ended in a common protocol of May 30 1876. The commission recommended the construction of a railway tunnel. Later financial associations were set up in France and Great Britain (such as Channel Tunnel Co. Ltd.) to aid investment in the construction. The latter was started in 1881 but was interrupted on 1 July 1882 because of the objection of the British War Office. Attempts to revise the position of Great Britain in 1929/30 failed in view of the opinion of the parliamentary commission that the development of air transportation made the tunnel needless. Only the rapid development of car tourism in the second half of the 20th century re-aroused interests in French and English financial circles, which brought about a resumption of international diplomatic talks. On 20 Oct. 1972, an international English–French agreement was concluded regarding rules and dates of tunnel construction: 52 km long, 36 of which would be under the Channel, with two main lanes of 6.85 m diameter for two-way railway transport, and one auxiliary lane of 4.5 m diameter. Time of the ride from London to Paris: 3 hours and 40 minutes. The British–French agreement was signed on 17 Nov., 1973. The agreement of Nov., 1973, ratified in 1974 by the French Parliament, was cancelled by the British Parliament on 21 Jan., 1975 (285 votes against 218). In Jan. 1986 President F. Mitterand and Prime Minister M. Thatcher agreed to build in the years 1987–1993 the Chunnel. The Treaty was signed on Febr. 12, 1986 in Canterbury.
See also ▷ Eurotunnel.

L. OPPEHNEIM, "Der Tunnel unter dem Armelkanal und das Völkerrecht", in: *Zeitschrift für Völkerrecht,* No. 2, 1908; R. ROBIN, "Le tunnel sur La Manche et le droit de gens", in: *Revue générale de droit public,* No. 15, 1908; P.H. GAIN, *La question du tunnel sous La Manche,* Nancy, 1932; G. MARSTON, "Some legal problems of the Channel Tunnel scheme, 1874–1883", in: *The British Year Book of International Law 1974–1975,* Oxford, 1977, pp. 299–300. KEESING's *Record of World Events,* 1986, No. 2.

CHURCH AND STATE. An international term for relations between religious associations and states, changing throughout centuries, source of international conflicts, bi- and multilateral disputes and treaties (▷ Concordat). In the 20th century formation of universal division of Church and State; the opposite tendency observed in ▷ Islamic Republics. ▷ Separation of Church and State.

CHURCH OF CHRIST, SCIENTIST. Called also Christian Science Church. A religious organization of an American Christian Group, f. 1879 by Mary Baker Eddy (1821–1910) in Boston, USA. From 1892 called the First Church of Christ Scientist. Includes national churches in 55 countries, holds international meetings. Reg. with UIA. Publ. daily *The Christian Science Monitor,* monthly *The Herald of Christian Science,* and *Christian Science Quarterly.*

M. BAKER-EDDY, *Manual of the Mother Church,* Boston, 1908; E. MARY RAMSAY, *Christian Science and its Discovery,* Boston, 1963.

CHURCH OF ENGLAND. One of the Protestant churches est. 1534 (Act of Supremacy) as a national church, headed by the sovereign as "the only supreme head on earth of the Church of England" regardless of sex and age (from 1946 Queen Elizabeth II). Internally divided into adherents of High Church, Low Church, and Broad Church; worshippers in Commonwealth countries and USA; accepted name – Anglicanism; Catholic elements from Anglo-Catholic Oxford Movement; religious capital – Canterbury (Great Britain), former seat of Catholic primate of England. Councils held since 1867 every 10 years in London, residence of the Archbishop of Canterbury, called Lambeth Conferences.

Yearbook of International Organizations, 1973.

CHURCH STATE. *Latin:* Patrimonium Sancti Petri. The name of the state of the Roman Catholic Church. It comprised many enclaves in the territory of Italy. Subject to the secular rule of the Pope; existing from 728 to 1870, when all of the Church enclaves were integrated into the United Kingdom of Italy with the exception of the area of the Vatican, where the royal decree of guaranty of May 13, 1871 permitted the Church to retain its sovereign rights; which was not recognized by Pius IX (and his successors to Pius XI), who regarded himself as "a prisoner of the Vatican". This state of affairs was liquidated by the Lateran Treaty of the Apostolic See with Italy which gave the Vatican a mutually recognized statute of a sovereign state on Feb. 11, 1929.

J.L. KUNZ, "The status of the Holy See in international law", in: *American Journal of International Law,* No. 46, 1952.

CIA. ▷ Intelligence Service.

CIEC ▷ Conference on International Economic Cooperation.

CIESZYN OR TESIN. A city on the border of Poland and Czechoslovakia, subject of a Polish–Czech conflict in 1919, resolved by a decision of the Conference of Ambassadors, July 28, 1920 which divided the city into a Polish part (Cieszyn) and a Czech part (Tesin). The treaty between Poland and Czechoslovakia on the community of Cieszyn signed Dec. 21, 1920 was in force from Apr. 25, 1931. Within the borders of Poland from Oct. 11, 1938 to Sept. 1, 1939 as a result of the ▷ Munich Agreement, 1938. After the war the division of Cieszyn of 1920 into a Polish and Czech part was resumed.

LNTS, Vol. 5, p. 49.

CIF. English abbreviation of "cost, insurance, freight . . ., named port of destination". One of the international formulas of trade. ▷ Incoterms, 1953.

INCOTERMS, Paris, 1976.

CIF PRICES, FOB PRICES. An international term meaning that:
(1) CIF price includes, besides the value of the goods, also its cost of loading, transport, and insurance to the port of the purchaser or its delivery to the addressee;
(2) FOB price includes only the value of the goods delivered to the coast of the seller to shipside in a designated port.

D.M. SASSOON, *CIF and FOB Contracts,* London, 1975.

CIJ. A French abbreviation for Cour international de Justice, International Court of Justice, ICJ. Documents and publications of the Court are signed with the first or the second abbreviation, depending on the language in which they are printed.

CILSS. Permanent Inter-State Committee on Drought Control in the ▷ Sahel, f. 1980. See also ▷ Drought.

CINA. A French abbreviation used in the League of Nations for the Commission internationale de la navigation aerienne, International Commission of Air Navigation, commonly accepted in the League of Nations and by international airlines for the permanent organ of the Paris Air Convention of Oct. 13, 1919, which in chapter VIII, art. 34 specifically defined the tasks and aims of the Commission. It began its work on the date when the Convention took effect, July 11, 1922. Continued to 1945, the year when its functions were assumed by ▷ ICAO. A special feature of the Commission composed of 33 signatories to the Convention, was that formally the votes of five powers (of which the USA did not ratify the Convention) outweighed every decision of the remaining members (art. 37). The resolutions of art. 34 were modified by: London Protocol of June 30, 1923; I Paris Protocol of June 15, 1929 and II Paris Protocol of Dec. 11, 1929. CINA took the initiative for unifying air maps, on which one of its special commissions worked from June 1923.

CINCCHAN. Commander-in-Chief Channel. Leading the combined armed forces of Channel la Manche (NATO) besides SACEUR (Supreme Commander of Combined Armed Forces in Europe) and SACLANT (Supreme Commander of Joint Armed Forces in the Atlantic). In principle he is one of the deputies of SACEUR or the British deputy of SACLANT.

CINMEN. A Chinese island, formerly Wu-moi, near the south-east shore of China, in Taiwan Strait (Formosa), 25 km off the town of Sheming (Xiamen, formerly Amoy), Fukien province. From 1949 occupied by Chiang Kai-shek troops and fortified with US aid; from Aug., 1954 till Feb., 1955 shelled by the artillery of the People's Republic of China from Sheming; in Jan.–Feb. 1955 the Chinese army liberated the islands Tachin and Manchu in Taiwan Strait, but fortified Cinmen remained in the hands of Chiang Kai-shek. Shelling from land was continued sporadically in subsequent years. In July 1976 USA withdrew all its troops from Cinmen and Manchu, acknowledging the islands as insignificant for US military presence in Taiwan Strait.

CINTERFOR. Centro Interamericano de Investigación y Documentación sobre Formación Profesional, Interamerican Center of Research and Documentation on Professional Education. An inter-governmental institution, est. on Sept. 17, 1963 under the auspices of ILO with headquarters in Montevideo, treaty with the governments of Argentina, Brazil, Chile, Costa Rica, Guatemala, Mexico, Panama, Peru, Trinidad and Tobago, Venezuela. Publ.: *Boletín, Documentación and CINTERFOR Legislación.*

Yearbook of International Organizations.

CIPHER. An international term for a text written in code that is supposed to be incomprehensible to strangers unfamiliar with the code of the sender,

C

used in strictly secret military, commercial, and diplomatic correspondence. The sending of coded messages in international trade is permitted under the International Telegraphic Statute signed 1949 in Paris and the International Telegraphic Convention signed 1952 in Paris.

D. KAHN, *The Codebreakers*, New York, 1967; J. A. BILEWICZ, *Secret Language, Communicating in Codes and Ciphrers*, London, 1976; R. A. WOYTAK, *The Origins of the Ultra-Secret Code in Poland 1937–1938, in: The Polish Review*, New York No. 3, 1978.

CIS. International Occupational Safety and Health Information Centre, an information center of the ▷ ILO.

CISKEI. One of the South African ▷ Bantu Homelands, declared independent as The Republic of, on Dec. 4, 1981, not recognized by any other government than that of the South African Republic; divided by the towns East London and King William's Town in Eastern Cape from the border of Transkei, divided the Xhosa people of Ciskei and Transkei. Area: 8,500 sq km. Population (1981): 660,000 (de iure population: 2,100,000). See also ▷ South Africa.

Europa Yearbook, Vol. II, London, 1987.

CITEJA. A French abbreviation used in the League of Nations for the Comité international technique d'experts juridiques aériens, International Technical Committee of Air Experts, est. 1924 under the auspices of LN, in continual connection with ▷ CINA; this committee, though not universal in its composition due to the absence of experts from China, Germany, the USA and the USSR, worked out several air norms and international principles which became part of international air law. Disbanded along with other institutions of the LN 1946/47. Its functions were assumed in May 1947 by the Legal Committee of ▷ ICAO.

CITIZENSHIP, NATIONALITY. An international term with no international definition since it defines an institution of internal law of every state. A subject of international conventions on collision of citizenship laws of individual countries, beginning with the Hague Convention of Apr. 12, 1930. A subject of international provision of art. 15 of Universal Declaration of Human Rights, Dec. 10, 1948, that every man has the right to a citizenship. The UN Commission for International Law debated in 1954 on the establishment of "International citizenship" in connection with the problem of persons with no citizenship (▷ Stateless persons) but the idea was dismissed on legal grounds: UN not being a "supra-state" organization (A/CN. 4/8 Mar. 11, 1954, pp. 11–12). The UN General Assembly in Dec., 1982 decided to re-establish in 1985 a Working Group on elaborating an official version of the draft on the human rights of individuals who are not citizens of the country where they live.

M.O. HUDSON (ed.), *International Legislation*, Washington DC, 1936, pp. 359–374; H.F. PANKHUYS, *The Role of Nationality in International Law*, London, 1959; *UN Chronicle*, February 1983, p. 101; R. L. BLEDSOE, B. A. BOCZEK, *The International Law Dictionary*, Oxford, 1987.

CITRUS FRUITS. Oranges, tangerines, lemons, grapefruits and others, subject of international co-operation under FAO auspices. Organizations reg. with the UIA:

International Organization of Citrus Virologists, f. 1957, Campinas Brazil, affiliating more than 200 scientists from 41 countries. Organizes Congresses every 3 years. Publ. *Citrus Virus Diseases*.

International Society for Citriculture, f. 1970, Tel Aviv. Liaison Committee for Mediterranean Citrus Fruits Culture, f. 1954, Madrid.
Maghreb States Committee for Citrus Fruits, est. 1971, Algiers, by the governments of Algeria, Morocco and Tunisia.

Yearbook of International Organizations.

CIVIL AND POLITICAL RIGHTS, INTERNATIONAL COVENANT ON, 1966. An intergovernmental convention belonging to ▷ Human Rights Covenants, prepared by the Human Rights Committee of the UN between 1949 and 1954, re-edited by the 3rd Committee of the UN General Assembly, which on Dec. 16, 1966 adopted its text with the Res. 2200/XXI. The Additional Protocol was adopted with 66 positive votes, 2 negative and 38 abstaining. For text ▷ Human Rights, International Convention on Civil and Political Rights.

UN Yearbook 1966, pp. 406–488.

CIVIL AVIATION. An international term for communication, economic and sports aviation, subject of international conventions and regulations. The leading organizations of civil aviation are ▷ ICAO and ▷ IATA. The Air Rome Convention on International Civil Aviation was signed on Sept. 15, 1962 in Rome. ▷ Air law.

CIVIL AVIATION STANDARDS AND PROCEDURES, INTERNATIONAL. A general term referring to art. 37 of the ▷ Air Chicago Convention 1944, international regulations for: (a) system of communication and facilities for air navigation including ground markings, (b) characteristic features of airports and airfields, (c) aviation rules and methods for controlling air traffic, (d) the issuance of licenses to operational and mechanical personnel, (e) the readiness of aircraft for flight, (f) registration and identification of aircraft, (g) the collection and exchange of meteorological information, (h) logbooks, (i) maps and aviation planes, (j) customs and immigration formalities, (k) aircraft in danger and investigation in case of accidents as well as all other problems connected with safety, regularity, and efficiency of air navigation, which may be required from time to time. In the spirit of the Convention, as technology is continually improved, ICAO at regular intervals makes changes in the established international norms and procedures.

P. CHAVEAU, *Droit aérien*, Paris, 1951; A. MEYER, *Internationale Luftfahrtabkommen*, 3 Vols. Berlin, 1953–57; C.N. SHAWCROSS, *Air Law*, London, 1966.

CIVIL DEFENCE. An international military term, controversial in the nuclear era. Subject of international co-operation. Organization reg. with the UIA:

International Civil Defence Organization, f. 1931, Geneva, Switzerland, Publ.: International Civil Defence.

Yearbook of International Organizations, 1986/87; The Europa Yearbook 1988. A World Survey, Vol. I, London, 1988; D. ROBERTSON, *Guide to Modern Defense and Strategy*, Detroit, USA, 1988.

CIVIL DEFENCE ACT, 1951. First American law providing a program of civil defence against atomic attack, passed in Congress on Jan. 2, 1951.

CIVILIAN EVACUATION. An international term for deportation in a state of emergency or state of war, of the civilian population, a subject of international law.

T. L. CROSBY, *The Impact of Civilian Evacuation in the Second World War*, Dover, N.H., 1986.

CIVILIAN MORALE. An international military term during World War II for a nation's will to resist; controversial in the nuclear era.

D. ROBERTSON, *Guide to Modern Defense and Strategy*, Detroit, 1988.

CIVILIAN PERSONS PROTECTION IN TIME OF WAR. The international legal rules to protect civilians were codified in the Fourth Geneva Convention on the Protection of Civilian Population in Time of War, Aug. 12, 1949. It focused on the right of states to establish, in agreement with the enemy, security zones for the wounded, sick, handicapped persons, pregnant women, mothers with children under seven and all children under fifteen; protection of civilian hospitals and free shipment of supplies for the population. The convention also determined the treatment of protected and interned persons. It did not provide a definition of civilian persons. Draft definitions prepared by the International Red Cross in 1949, 1956 and 1971 have not yet been adopted by any international convention of the UN General Assembly. Further studies on "respecting human rights in time of warfare" have been initiated since 1969. The Twentieth International Conference of the Red Cross held in Vienna in Oct., 1965 adopted by the Declaration on the Protection of Civilian Population against the Dangers of Indiscriminate Warfare. Draft Rules for diminishing the dangers for civilian populations were prepared by the International Committee of the Red Cross in Sept., 1956. Art. 4 of the Rules provides the following definition of civilian population:

"Civilian population consists of persons not included in one or the other of the following categories:
(a) members of armed forces or auxiliary forces or complementary organizations,
(b) persons who do not belong to any of the categories mentioned above, nevertheless, are involved in warfare."

The Basic Rules of the Protection of Civilian Population were adopted on Dec. 9, 1970, in Res. 2675/XXV of the UN General Assembly by 109 votes for and no vote against. The Geneva Diplomatic Conference, Feb. 20–Mar. 29, 1974, was devoted to the preparation of a new convention on the protection of civilian population in time of war and in the end adopted a preliminary draft. Organization reg. with the UIA:

International Civil Defense Organization called ▷ Geneva Zone, f. 1931, Geneva.

Yearbook of International Organizations.

CIVILIANS. An international term for persons not involved in military service in wartime; subject to an international convention on Civilian Persons Conventions in Time of War.

CIVILIZED NATIONS. An anachronistic international term of the colonial era, preserved in art. 38 of the Statutes of International Tribunal of Justice (taken over from the statutes of the Permanent International Tribunal of Justice), not in line with the spirit of the UN or of contemporary international law, which is of a universal character.

CIVILIZED STATE. An international term since Immanuel Kant "zum ewigen Frieden" (1795) for the rule of law within nations and between nations.

S. S. RAMPHAL, *Justice World-Wide: The Rule of Law in an Interdependent World, in: International Jurist Commission Newsletter No 34*, 1987.

CIVIL LAW. *Latin: ius civile.* A branch of the law which determines relations governing property and some aspects of personal relations between equal subjects of the law, provided for in international private law; it is divided into two separate systems: (1) civil law, which is generally a private law; (2) civil law, which is mostly public law governing relations both between citizens and between state institutions and between such institutions and citizens. The *Codex Iuris Civilis Justiniani* (533–535) exerted the greatest influence on the development of civil law as well as the *Codex Civil de Napoleon* of 1804. The ▷ Civil procedure is made uniform under international conventions.

The First South American Congress on Private International Law in Montevideo, 1888–89, adopted a Treaty on International Civil Law, with Additional Protocol, signed and ratified by Argentina, Bolivia, Paraguay, Peru and Uruguay.

P.J. EDER, *Comparative Survey of Anglo-American and Latin American Civil Law*, Boston, 1950; M.A. VIEIRA (ed.), *Tratados de Montevideo 1888–1889*, Montevideo, 1959.

CIVIL LIABILITY FOR NUCLEAR DAMAGE ▷ Nuclear Accident Convention, 1986.

CIVIL MILITARY ACTION. An international term for the participation of armed forces in salvage actions due to natural disasters, in particular earthquakes and floods; commonly used in the world after World War II; in numerous countries expanded to include public works, such as construction of roads and bridges, deforestation of colonized territories and also sanitary actions frequently on the initiative of international or regional organizatons.

CIVIL PROCEDURE. The subject of international co-operation and agreements. The first convention relating to Civil Procedure was signed at the IV Conference on Private International Law on July 17, 1905. A Protocol concerning the Adhesion of States not represented at the IV Conference was signed in The Hague on July 4, 1924. The second international Convention was signed on Mar. 1, 1954 in The Hague by the Governments of Austria, Belgium, Denmark, Finland, France, the FRG, Great Britain, Italy, Luxembourg, Netherlands, Norway, Portugal, Spain, Sweden and Switzerland. The Convention in Chapter I defined Service of writs and extra-judicial documents, in Chapter II, Letters rogatory, in III Security for costs and penalties by foreign plaintiffs, in IV Free legal aid, in V Free issue of extracts from registers of births, marriages and deaths and in VII Final provisions.

DE MARTENS, *Nouveau Recueil*...3-eme serie, tome II, p, 243; *LNTS*, Vol. 51, p, 279; *UNTS*, Vol. 286, p. 265.

CIVIL RIGHTS. A subject of international conventions and pacts. The first convention on protection against voidance of civil rights was prepared at the IV International Private Law Conference of July 17, 1905; the Report on accession to the Convention by states not represented at the IV Conference was signed in The Hague, Dec. 28, 1923. The US Congress created in 1957 the US Commission on Civil Rights.

CIVIL RIGHTS ACTS. The name of legislation passed by US Congress during the years 1957–68 which eliminated limitations in civil rights, particularly those applying to the black, red and half-breed population. The first act of 1957 appointed election committees to determine whether citizens were not deprived of their right to vote due to their race, color, nationality or religion. The act of 1960 conferred on the federal jurisdiction the right to interfere should a state contest voting rights of any group of citizens. The act of 1964 granted every citizen free access to all public utilities. The act of

1965 introduced a ban on subordinating citizens' voting rights to their writing and reading skills. The act of 1968 provided for severe penalties to be inflicted on those who prevented citizens from enjoying the right to vote and also prohibited any kind of discrimination with respect to house or apartment purchase.

CH.J. ANTIEU, *Federal Civil Rights Acts*, Washington DC, 1971.

CIVIL SERVANTS, INTERNATIONAL. An international term defined in art. 5 of the UN Convention on Privileges and Immunities of Feb. 13, 1946, to name a group of UN staff, the International Court of Justice and specialized organizations personnel who enjoy diplomatic immunities and privileges in UN member states. The first group of international clerical personnel formed in the 2nd half of the 19th century; in 1856 in the European Commission for the Danube, 1863 in the World Postal Union, 1875 in the International Weight and Measure Bureau. Up to 1914 there were 33 international organizations of this kind employing international clerical workers and the number of full-time international workers totalled about 100 persons, the majority of them being Swiss nationals. In the interwar period the staff expanded to 2000 persons, again mostly Swiss, as a result of the fact that Geneva was selected for the headquarters of the League of Nations. A rapid growth of the number of international civil servants was observed after World War II in UN institutions and specialized organizations as well as over 110 other intergovernmental organizations. Estimates for 1970 give a number between 30,000 and 40,000 persons. The rights and obligations of international civil servants are determined by many acts issued by the UN Secretariat which also serve as a pattern for other inter-governmental institutions.

S. BASDEVANT, *Les Fonctionnaires Internationaux*, Paris, 1931; C.W. JANKS, "Co-ordination in international organizations", in: *The British Year Book of International Law*, 1951; *The Handbook on the Legal Status, Privileges and Immunities of the UN*, New York, 1952; C. MC CORRNICK, *Protection of International Personnel Abroad: Law and Practice*, New York, 1952; F.R. SCOTT "The world's civil service", in: *International Conciliation*, No. 496, January, 1954, pp. 259–320; *Rapport sur les normes de conduite requises des fonctionnaires internationaux. Comité Consultatif de la fonction internationale publique des Nations Unies*, New York, 1954; E. KORDT, P. CAUDEMET, E. KERN, *Der Europäische Beamte*, Bonn, 1955; A.C. BREYCHA-VAUTHIER, *Le Fonctionnaire international*, Paris, 1959; T.M. GAUDEMET, "The status of international civil servants in national law", in: *Revue internationale des sciences administratives*, No. 25, 1959; E. KERN, "On the establishment of an European civil service", in: *Revue internationale des sciences administratives*, No. 25, 1959.

CIVIL STATUS RECORDS. A subject of international conventions. Convention between Belgium, France, Luxembourg, Netherlands, Switzerland and Turkey, concerning the issue of certain extracts from civil status records to be sent abroad, signed in Paris on Sept. 27, 1956.

UNTS, Vol. 299, p. 211.

CIVIL STRIFE. A subject of international conventions: ▷ Inter-American Conventions concerning the Duties and Rights of States in the event of Civil Strife, 1928, ▷ Inter-American Convention on Rights and Duties of States, 1933, ▷ Charter of the Organization of American States, 1948.

CIVIL WAR. A political struggle for power in a state carried on by regular or partisan military forces; subject of international law in connection

with the threat of civil war to the interests of other states and the problem of recognizing or not recognizing the government of the victor in a civil war. The Geneva Convention on the protection of war victims of Aug. 12, 1949, in art. III also provides for the obligation to render assistance to the victims of a civil war.

H. WEHBERG, "La guerre civile et le droit international", in: *Recueil des Cours de l'Academie de Droit International*, No. 63, 1938; D. SCHINDLER, "Völkerrecht im Bürgerkrieg", in: *Neue Schweizer Rundschau, 1937–38*; F. SIORDET, "Les Conventions de Geneve et la guerre civile", in: *Revue internationale de la Croix-Rouges*, 1950; J. SIOTIS, *Le droit de guerre et le conflicts armes d'un caractere non-international*, Paris, 1958; R. PINTO, "Les régles du droit international concernant la guerre civile", in: *Recueil des Cours de l'Academie de Droit International*, 1966: E. CASTREN, *Civil War*, Helsinki, 1966; R.A. FALK (ed.), *The International Law of Civil War*, Baltimore, 1971; J. NORTON MOORE (ed.), *Law and Civil War in the Modern World*, Baltimore, 1975; A.V. LOMBARDI, *Bürgerkrieg und Völkerrecht*, Berlin, 1976.

CLADES. Centro Latinoamericano de Documentation Económica y Social, Latin American Center of Economic and Social Documentation, est. 1973, seat in Santiago de Chile attached to the UN Economic Commission for Latin America ECLA. Publ. index and summaries of all documents of ECLA from 1970 under the title *CLADINDEX*.

CLASSIFICATION BY BROAD ECONOMIC CATEGORIES, CBEB. An international term introduced by the UN for definition of the economic potential of states through a set of general demographic and economic data.

CLASSIFICATION CLAUSE. An international term for a clause binding on ship insurance companies that makes the amount of insurance fee dependent on the ship's class or the degree of reliance on the Classification Society which classifies the ship.

CLASSIFICATION SOCIETIES. An international term for institutions formally assessing the quality of ships and their class, which consist of representatives of shipowners, shipbuilding industry, insurance companies and chambers of commerce. Classification societies are international institutions. The oldest of them are: Lloyds Register of Shipping, 17th century, in London, French Bureau Veritas 1838 in Antwerp, now in Paris; Italian Registro Italiano Navale 1860 in Genoa; The American Bureau of Shipping 1862 in New York; Scandinavian Det Norske Veritas 1864 in Oslo; German Germanischer Lloyd 1867 in Hamburg, Japanese Teikoku (Nipon) Kaiji Kyokai 1899 in Tokyo; Morskoy Registr SSSR in Leningrad 1923 (since 1953 named Registr Soyuza SSSR); Polish Ships Register (PRS) in Gdansk 1946. Organization reg. with the UIA:

International Association of Classification Societies (IACS), f. in 1968 in Washington, DC.

Yearbook of International Organizations.

CLASSIFICATORY DOCUMENTS. An international term in maritime navigation for a set of documents specified by international conventions that the authorized shipping agencies have made measurements, tests, and classificational studies of seafaring or inland vessels.

CLAUSE. An international term for a stipulation in an international agreement or treaty.
See also ▷ Optional Clause.

CLAUSE OF PRICE REVISION. A clause in the international trade licence contracts setting rules of

C

pricing particular components of orders along with their delivery on the basis of current world prices. It is based on the pattern of the General Conditions of Delivery and Assembly of Plants and Machines in Import and Export, together with the Clause of Price Revision.

CLAUSE ON ENEMY STATES IN UN CHARTER. An international term for a clause which has effects in international law in relation to the former states of the Axis and their satellites, contained in arts. 53 and 107 of the ▷ United Nations Charter.

D. BLUMENWITZ, *Feindstaatenklauseln. Die Friedensordnung der Sieger*, München, 1972; K. KRAKAU, *Feindstaatenklauseln und Rechtslage Deutschlands nach den Ostverträgen*, Hamburg, 1975.

CLAUSEWITZ DOCTRINE, 1831. An international term for a doctrine formulated by the Prussian military theorist general Karl von Clausevitz (1780–1831), that:

"war is nothing other than a continuation of politics by other means" ["Der Krieg ist nichts anders als die Fortsetzung der Politik mit anderen Mitteln"].

KARL von CLAUSEWITZ, *Vom Kriege*, Berlin, 1832; D. ROBERTSON, *Guide to Modern Defense and Strategy*, Detroit, 1988.

CLAYTON–BULVER TREATY, 1850. A treaty concluded in Washington on Apr. 19, 1850 between Great Britain and the USA, on the transoceanic canal, signed by J.M. Clayton for the USA and H.L. Bulver for Great Britain, officially named Convention Concerning a Shipcanal Connecting the Atlantic and Pacific Oceans. It guaranteed neutrality of the Isthmus of Panama, together with the Panama and Tehuantepec Isthmus and obligated both sides to free shipping on the Panama Canal. The Treaty was concluded on the initiative of Great Britain and concerned the agreement between the USA and Colombia of Dec. 12, 1846 granting the US the right to build a canal in the Colombian province of Panama.

W.M. MALLOY, *Treaties, Conventions... between the USA and other Powers*, Vol. 1, 1776–1909, Washington DC, 1910, p. 659.

CLEAR. Clearing-House for Thesaurus and Classification, one of the information centres of ▷ UNESCO.

CLEARAGE. International term – operations connected with customs clearance and port formalities at a ship's entry or departure or when a ship passes through an international canal; the principle is that fees for clearage are collected from the number of cubic meters of the ship's cargo capacity.

CLEARING. The forms of settlement of financial accounts between banks or between countries (above all, bilateral, but they can also be multi-sided within the framework of interstate treaties). Clearing as a system for the settlement of financial accounts between states was universally accepted in 1929. The clearing of financial accounts is made according to official exchange rates or rates agreed upon in one or many currencies; depending on the treaty, the clearing account can be balanced with gold, foreign exchange or the supply of certain goods. The first bilateral clearing agreement was reached Oct. 14, 1931 between Switzerland and Hungary.

G. JACCARD, *De l'incidence juridique du clearing sur le rapport entre acheteurs et vendeurs*, Paris, 1935; *Société des Nations, Enquête sur les accords de clearing*, Genève, 1935, A. BOGLAVI, *I Regolamenti inter-*

nazionali mediante compensazione (Clearing), Roma, 1943.

CLEARING HOUSES. An international term for banking institutions performing only clearing functions between banks connected with all kinds of payments. Each bank belonging to a clearing house has its plenipotentiaries in it. The accounts' operations performed by clearing houses facilitate and expedite non-cash turnover. The first clearing houses were established in London as early as the 18th century.

CLEARING ORGANIZATION. International Organization reg. with the UIA:

Asian Clearing Union, intergovernmental institution of Bangladesh, India, Iran, Nepal, Pakistan, Sri Lanka, est. on signature Dec. 19, 1970 of the Kabul Declaration of the Council of Ministers for Asian Economic Co-operation.

The Union commenced operations on Nov. 1, 1975. Headquarters Teheran. West African Clearing House, est. on Mar. 14, 1975, Lagos, on signature of Agreement by Governors of Central Banks of Gambia, Ghana, Liberia, Nigeria and Sierra Leone and by the Central Bank of West African States. Headquarters in Dakar.

Yearbook of International Organizations.

CLERICALISM. An international term for the aspiration of churches, particularly the Catholic Church, to occupy or control directly or indirectly the key positions of secular power, or by other methods to determine social and economic policies, etc. Clericalism was most strongly visible in various epochs in Italy, Spain, Portugal, Poland. ▷ Anti-clericalism.

N.A. RESHETNIKOV, *Klerikalizm*, Moscow, 1965; J. CONNELLY ULLMAN, *La Semana Tragica. Estudio sobre las causas socio-económicas del anticlericalismo en España (1898–1912)*, Barcelona, 1972.

CLEVELAND DOCTRINE. An international term for a thesis of the US President Grover Cleveland (1837–1908) developing the ▷ Monroe doctrine and ▷ Grant doctrine that the existing European colonies in the Western Hemisphere cannot be expanded; formulated in a speech to Congress Dec. 17, 1895 in connection with the dispute between Great Britain and Venezuela on the frontiers of British Guiana, which Great Britain wished to change to its advantage.

CONGRESSIONAL RECORD, *Message of the President of the US, Dec. 17, 1895*, Washington, DC, 1895; R.M. McELROY, *Grover Cleveland*, 2 Vols., New York, 1923.

CLIENT STATE. An international term for a state, some of whose rights (e.g. carrying on foreign policy or administering finances and tarifs) are subordinate to another state.

CLIMATE, GLOBAL PROTECTION. Subject of GA Res. 43/53 of Dec. 6, 1988, on Protection of Global Climate for Present and Future Generations of Mankind:

"The General Assembly, welcoming with appreciation the initiative taken by the Government of Malta in proposing for consideration by the Assembly the item entitled "Conservation of Climate as Part of the Common Heritage of Mankind".
Concerned that certain human activities could change global climate patterns, threatening present and future generations with potentially severe economic and social consequences.
Noting with concern that the emerging evidence indicates that continued growth in atmospheric concentrations of "greenhouse" gases could produce global warming with eventual rise in sea levels, whose

effects could be disastrous for Mankind if timely steps are not taken at all levels.
Recognizing the need for additional research and scientific studies into all sources and causes of climate change.
Concerned also that emissions of certain substances are depleting the ozone layer and thereby exposing the earth's surface to increased ultra-violet radiation, which may pose a threat, inter alia, to human health, agricultural productivity and animal and marine life, and reaffirming in this context the appeal, contained in its resolution 42/182 of 11 December 1987, to all states that have not yet done so to consider becoming parties to the 1985 Vienna Convention for the Protection of the Ozone Layer and its related 1987 Montreal Protocol as soon as possible.
Welcoming the convening in 1990 of the Second World Climate Conference.
Urges Governments, intergovernmental and non-governmental organizations and scientific institutions to treat climate change as a priority issue, to undertake and promote specific, co-operative action-oriented programmes and research so as to increase understanding of all sources and causes of climate change, including its regional aspects and specific time-frames as well as the cause and effect relationship of human activities and climate, and to contribute, as appropriate, with human and financial resources to efforts to protect the global climate.
Calls upon all relevant organizations and programmes of the United Nations system to support the work of the intergovernmental Panel on Climate Change.

UN Resolutions and Decisions adopted by the General Assembly during the First Part of its Forty-Third Session, from 20 September to 22 December 1988, New York 1989, pp. 263–265.

CLIMATOLOGY. A subject of international co-operation. Organizations reg. with the UIA:

International Federation of Thermalism and Climatism, f. 1947, St. Gallen, Switzerland.
International Society of Medical Hydrology and Climatology, f. 1921, London. Publ. *Archives*.

C.C. WALLEN, *Climates of Northern and Western Europe*, Amsterdam, 1970; R.A. BRYSON, F.K. HARE, *Climates of North America*, Amsterdam, 1974; C.C. WALLEN (ed.), *Climates of Central and Southern Europe*, Amsterdam, 1977; P.E. LYDOLPH, *Climates of the Soviet Union*, Amsterdam, 1977; W. SCHWERDTFEGER (ed.), *Climates of Central and South America*, Amsterdam, 1977; L.A. FRAKES. *Climates Throughout Geologic Time*, Amsterdam, 1979; *Yearbook of International Organizations.*

CLUB OF PARIS. An international financial committee of 13 states (USA and Canada, Denmark, France, FRG, Italy, Japan, the Netherlands, Norway, Spain, Sweden, Switzerland and the UK), meeting periodically since 1971 in Paris for the purpose of negotiating international financial agreements or moratoria with highly indebted countries. "An international forum for the rescheduling of service on debts granted or guaranteed by official bilateral creditors". (IMF definition).

S. STRAUGE, *International Monetary Relations 1959–71*, London, 1976. *IMF Survey*, Sept. 30, 1986.

CLUB OF ROME. International organization for research on mankind's economic–social development, composed of economists, sociologists, political scientists and industrialists from Western Europe, USA and Japan; reg. with the UIA as the Club of Rome, Le Club de Rome; f. 1968, Rome; but with office headquarters in Institute Batelle, Geneva, Publ.: monthly *Prosthetics International*. In Apr. 1968 on the initiative of Italian industrialist Dr A. Paccei, a meeting held in Rome's Academia dei Lincei discussed development of industrial civilization of the contemporary world, attended by 30 academics and economists from Western

Europe, USA and Japan who decided to set up a permanent group called the Club of Rome composed of no more than 100 members. In 1970, on the initiative of the Club, with financial support of the Volkswagen Foundation, West European and American academics from Massachusetts Institute of Technology (MIT) began work on a forecast of mankind's development until the year 2001, whose findings were publ. summer 1972 in a report, *Limits of Growth* (of world population). The authors claimed the present pattern of demographic increase and industrial growth will lead not to the equality of all peoples but to deepening the gap between the rich and the poor. The Club's second report – *Mankind at the Turning Point* – publ. 1974, pointed out that disproportions in living standards between the developing and the developed countries would increase from 5:1 in 1975 to 8:1 in 2025; at the same time exhaustion of most of power resources was predicted; complete pollution of inland waters, and famine expected to take lives of *c.* 500 million children up to 15 years of age. The Report proposed a number of alternatives to alleviate food and energy crisis. Third Report – *Reshaping the International Order* (economic) – publ. autumn 1976, called for equal development opportunities for the Third World, immediate establishment of a fund of international solidarity with the poorest countries with annual national income per capita lower than $200, setting up of an international central bank, international organization for energy, world disarmament agency, and granting wider prerogatives for UNCTAD. The Third Report was worked out at Club's session in Algiers attended for the first time by representatives of socialist and Third World countries. The Fourth Report was dedicated to the world energy crisis, and the Fifth was dedicated to the ▷ Microelectronic Revolution.

J. DELAUNAY, *Halte a la croissance. Enquête sur le Club de Rome*, Paris, 1972; D.L. MEADOWS, D.L. MEADOWS, J. RANDERS, W.W. BEHRENS III, *The Limits of Growth. A Report for the Club of Rome's Projects the Predicament of Mankind*, New York, 1972; H. COLE, C. FREEMAN, M. JAHOOLA, *L'anti-Malthus*, Paris, 1974; CLUB OF ROME, *Microelectronics and Society. For Better or for Worse*, Tokyo, 1982; A. KING, *The Club of Rome. Reaffirmation of a Mission*, in: *Interdisciplinary Science Review*, No 1, 1986; B. SCHNEIDER, *The Barefoot Revolution: A Report to the Club of Rome*, London, 1988.

CLUB OF THE 30 PER CENT ▷ Air Pollution.

CLUB OF VIENNA. The name of an annual Conference of the leading international commercial banks of Western Europe, since 1957 in the capital of Austria.

CMEA. The official English abbreviation for the ▷ Council for Mutual Economic Assistance. In Western press the abbreviation COMECON is accepted.

H.W. SHELLER, *Comecon and the Politics of Integration*, London, 1972; H. WILCOX, *Comecon and the Politics of Integration*, New York, 1972; J. WILCZYN-SKI, *Technology in Comecon*, London, 1974; J.M.P. Van BRABANT, *Essays on Planning, Trade and Integration in Eastern Europe*, Rotterdam, 1974; N.V. BAUTINA, *CMEA Today*, Moscow, 1975; R. SZAW-LOWSKI, *The System of International Organizations of the Communist Countries*, Leiden, 1976; R. BYSTRICKI, *Le droit de l'intégration économique socialiste*, Geneva, 1979; G. SHAVONE, *The Instruments of Comecon*, London, 1981.

CMEA ASSISTANCE FUND FOR THE DEVELOPING NATIONS. A Fund created on Apr. 11, 1973 by a decision of the Council of the International Investment Bank for the purpose of expanding economic relations between the developing countries and members of the fund, which are member countries of CMEA. The total value of the fund composed of transfer roubles as well as exchangeable currencies was fixed at 1 billion transfer roubles. The fund began its activities on Jan. 1, 1974. It is also open to other countries.

CMEA–EEC RELATIONS 1980–1989. The first contact between CMEA and the EEC took place in 1980. After six years first talks on the establishment of relations were held on Sept. 22–24, 1986, in Geneva. See also ▷ East-West.

KEESING's *Record of World Events*, January, 1987.

CMEA INSTITUTE. An international Institute for Economic Problems of the Socialist World System, Mezhdunarodnyi institut ekonomicheskikh problem mirovoy socyalisticheskoy sistyemy. A scientific research institute of CMEA, established by a decision of the Council of the Executive Committee, which on July 24, 1970 ratified the Statute of the Institute, whose headquarters are in Moscow. Official languages are the languages of all of the CMEA member countries; Russian is the working language. The studies of the Institute are guided by a Scientific Council. The director of the Institute is appointed by the Council for 5 years, his deputy for 4 years. According to p 3 of art. III works published in the name of the Institute should reflect "various points of view within the area of all of the problems elaborated in the Institute." The Institute is empowered to establish direct scientific contacts with international scientific institutions and those of the CMEA states.

CMR. A French abbreviation for Convention de Marchandises par Route, universally accepted by participants in the Convention concerning the Agreement on the International Transport of Goods by Road, signed on May 19, 1955 in Geneva.

COAL. A subject of international agreements defined in Annex I of the Treaty constituting the ▷ European Coal and Steel Community. One of the main raw materials of power and chemical industries; world deposits are estimated at 42% of total power resources, more than ▷ Crude oil (39%), peat, natural gas and water energy (19%); subject of international conventions and co-operation. Major deposits of coal and lignite are found in the USA, the USSR, the Chinese People's Republic, the Republic of South Africa, Poland, the FRG, India and Canada. Leading producers: the USA, the USSR, the UK, the FRG, Poland, the Chinese People's Republic, France, Japan, India, the Republic of South Africa. World coal production according to UN statistical data: 1950 – 1430 million t; 1960 – 1970 million t; 1970 – 2240 million t; 1975 – 2412 million t; 1980 – 2612 million t. In the two decades, 1950–70, not all the countries increased coal output, while some of them like France, the FRG and Great Britain considerably reduced production, which brought adverse repercussion in the following decade during the energy crisis. During the interwar period an international convention concerning coke was concluded in 1936, and in 1938/39 a British–German cartel was being prepared. After World War II the European Coal and Steel Community was formed. Since May 1956 a Permanent Commission for Coal Industry operates within CMEA, with its seat in Warsaw; it co-ordinates co-operation in mechanization and automation of mining in hard coal and lignite strip mines; in designing and construction of mines: in the optimum methods of briquette forming work safety, and others; also as regards methods of using coal for organic synthesis, and of using electronic calculating machines for planning and organizing of brigades to familiarize them with the most up-to-date methods of coal output in single member-countries of the CMEA. The comprehensive CMEA program of 1971 assumed, according to the suggestion of Poland, "the possibility of creating, by common effort, in the territory of Polish People's Republic of additional production capacities for power coal", and likewise in the territory of Mongolia, where considerable deposits of coal are suitable for long-term strip mining.

The Coal Committee is attached to the European Economic Commission of the UN, operating under the auspices of international symposia and devoted to long-range development trends in coal production and use.

Organizations reg. with the UIA:

European Coal Merchants Union, Union européenne des négociants en combustibles (EUROCOM), f. 1953, Lausanne (Switzerland); it associates national companies of Austria, Belgium, France, Spain, Holland, Luxembourg, the FRG, Switzerland and Great Britain; publishes *EUROCOM Bulletin*.
International Standing Committee of Carboniferous Congresses, f. 1927, Warsaw.
Western European Coal Producers Association, Comité d'étude des producteurs de charbon d'Europe occidentale (CEPCEO), f. 1953, Brussels; it associates producers groups of Belgium, Holland and the FRG.

W. ASHWORTH, *The History of the British Coal Industry, 1946–1982*, Oxford, 1986. *Yearbook of International Organizations*.

COALITION. An international term for an alliance of several states; the term identified with the ▷ Entente during World War I. During World War II used to denote all the states fighting against Germany and her satellites, called the anti-Hitlerite coalition, and from 1942 the Great Coalition.

COASTAL TRADE. An international term for the customary right of commercial vessels to carry out limited trade operations in their ports of call; subject of international conventions and clauses in trade agreements. ▷ Line shipping.

COBOL. The abbreviation for Common Business Oriented Language, one of the computer languages such as ▷ ALGOL or ▷ FORTRAN, "common language for industrial – commercial purposes."

COCA. *Erythroxylon coca.* The cocaine shrub whose leaves contain 0.25–1.31% cocaine and thus the cultivation of coca shrubs in Australia, South America, Ceylon, India, Indonesia, and Cameroons is an international problem (▷ Narcotics). In 1967 ECOSOC Res. 1105/XL established the Consultative Group on Coca Leaf Problems.

W. E. CARTER, *Coca in Bolivia*, Oxford, 1987.

COCA-COLA. One of the few internationally-known non-alcoholic beverages. A refreshment drink whose manufacture in most countries is organized by one concern, which has the patent for Coca-Cola production. The name includes the two basic ingredients of the drink from which it is produced: leaves of South American cocaine trees, called coca (*Erythroxylon coca*) and nuts of cola trees (cola), containing caffeine, growing in Brazil, India, Africa and other tropical regions. In 1973 the American company, Coca-Cola, Inc., had branch offices or was selling the Coca-cola extract to factories in 137 countries (in 1939 in 40 countries) including Bulgaria, the Chinese People's Republic, Czechoslovakia, Hungary, Poland, Yugoslavia and the USSR. Coca-Cola was invented in 1886 by the pharmacist J.S. Pemberton from Atlanta (USA),

C

where since 1892 the headquarters of the Coca-Cola Co. are located. Up to 1960 the Coca-Cola Co. produced refreshment drinks only, since 1960, to a large extent also fruit juices and coffee and tea extracts, since 1970 also chemical remedies to fight environmental pollution.

COCAINE. The principal alkaloid of the leaves of *Erythroxylon coca*, having the chemical formula $C_{17}H_{21}NO_4$; subject of international ▷ Opium Conventions 1912, and 1925. According to WHO reports, 1985, cocaine abuse has reached epidemic levels in North and South America and is rapidly spreading in parts of Europe and South-East Asia.

WHO Press Release, 1985, 2689; D. PACINI, CH. FRANQUEMONT, *Coca and Cocaine Effects on People and Policy in Latin America*, Cambridge, Mass., 1986; *WHO, Adverse Health Consequences of Cocaine Abuse*, Geneva, 1987; F. CASTILLO, *Los Jinetes de la Cocaína*, Bogota, 1988.

COCADOLLAR. Latin American term for money coming from illegal narcotic trade.

COCHIN CHINA. The Portuguese name for the East coast of Indochina dating back to 16th century, adopted in the 19th century by the colonial French administration of the territory of Vietnam; in official use by France between 1867 and 1949.

J. VIAL, *Les premières années de la Cochinchine, colonie française*, Paris, 1874.

COCOA. The seeds of the fruits of the tree *Theobroma cacao*; main raw material of chocolate (Indian *chocotatl* = "foaming water", name of an Indian drink from cocoa seeds), also used in the pharmaceutical and cosmetic industries; subject of an international convention. Main producers: Africa (Ghana, Guinea, Nigeria, Ivory Coast, Cameroon) 75% and Latin America (Brazil, Dominican Republic, Ecuador) 25% of world production. Object of continuous studies by FAO. In Sept. 1963 the UN World Cocoa Conference took place in Geneva, which established a working group to formulate an International Cocoa Agreement and the World Cocoa Organization on the model of the World Coffee Organization. From 1965 this work was taken over by UNCTAD, but the proposals of 1966, 1967, and 1968 were not approved; only in May of 1971 did the session of UNCTAD agree on a proposed understanding, which came about as a result of a significant fall in prices. In October 1972 the UNCTAD Cocoa Conference in Geneva of 55 exporting and importing countries worked out the final text of the agreement, which came into force on Apr. 30, 1973 after ratification by countries representing 80% of the export and countries representing 70% of the import. The mechanism of this agreement is based on a system of minimal and maximum prices, export quotas and buffer reserves. The minimum price of the cocoa bean was set with great resistance by the importers and the absolute objection of the USA at the level of 23 cents per pound, the maximum at 32 cents per pound. The total basic export quota for the member countries was set at the level of 1,580,000 tons, among which for Ghana – 580,900 t., Nigeria – 307,800 t., Ivory Coast – 224,000 t., Brazil – 200,600 t., Cameroon – 126,000 t., Dominican Republic – 47,000 t., Guinea – 38,700 t., Togo – 20,000 t., Mexico – 27,000 t. Simultaneously the level of buffer reserves was set at the level of 250,000 t. In the event that prices level at 24 cents per pound, the export quotas would be 90% of the basic export quota; the level of 24–26 cents per pound export quotas would increase to 95% of the basic quota; while at the level of 26–27.5 cents per pound export quotas would be 100% of the basic quota. In the

event of a further increase in prices from 27.5 cents to 30 cents per pound all export limitation would be removed. The sale of cocoa beans from buffer reserves would begin at the price of 31 cents per pound. The agreement, which ensures the stabilization of prices for cocoa beans, is an instrument safeguarding the interests of exports and importers in case of insufficient production or overproduction. The former occurred in the decade 1962–72, when prices exceeded 31 cents per pound. The organ of the Convention is the International Cocoa Council.
Organizations reg. with the UIA:

Cocoa Producers' Alliance, est. in May, 1962 with the ratification of an agreement signed in Jan., 1962 in Abijan, by Brazil, Ghana, Cameroons, Nigeria, Togo, and the Ivory Coast; establishes the export quotas for the member states; headquarters in Lagos.
International Cocoa Trade Federation, f. 1962, London.
International Office of Cocoa and Chocolate, f. 1930, Brussels. Publishes a quarterly, *Cocoa Statistics*.
International Institute of Agricultural Sciences in San José del Costa Rica. Publ. *Cocoa Bulletin* and a bibliography of works on cocoa.

In the EEC system ▷ STABEX included cocoa in the ACP states. A destabilization of the cocoa market in the 1980's resulting in price instability paralyzed the 1980 International Cocoa Agreement and the UN Cocoa Conference, held in Geneva on Febr. 10–March 4, 1986. A new International Cocoa Agreement came into effect on Febr. 1, 1987, valid until Jan. 31, 1990 for the 60 producers and consumer members of the ICA.

C.A. KRUG, E. QUARTEY-PAPAFIO, *World Cocoa Survey*, Rome, 1964. *UN Chronicle*, November, 1986, p. 119; KEESING's *Contemporary Archive*, 1986; KEESING's *Contemporary Archive*, July 1987.

COCOM AND CHINCOM. English abbreviations for Co-ordinating Committee for East–West Trade Policy and China Trade Co-ordinating Committee, with headquarters in Paris and London; names of two institutions of Western powers, which regulate economic relations the first with the Warsaw Pact countries; the second with People's China called into being in Jan., 1950 to replace the Consultative Group founded in Nov., 1949, which consisted of the NATO states. In 1951 Japan and the FRG joined COCOM and CHINCOM. Both organizations laid down three International Lists of Commodities, Strict Embargo List, Qualitative Control List and Surveillance List, modified now and again, and introduced a control system of granting permits for imports IC/DU, Import Certificate (Delivery Unification).

"Der Geheime COCOM Club", in: *Die Zeit*, Hamburg, December, 1983. KEESING's *Contemporary Archive*, May, 985.

COCONUTS. One of raw materials covered by organized international co-operation. In 1970 the UN Economic Commission for Asia and the Far East, ECAFE, by Res. 95/XXV, called into being the Asian Coconut Community.

COCOS (KEELING) ISLANDS. Two atolls with 27 coral islets in the Indian Ocean, 2255 km southeast of Ceylon. Area: 14.2 sq. km. Pop. 1982 census 546 inhabitants. British Crown possession since 1857, placed under Australian administration on Nov. 23, 1955; a part of the Australian Antarctic Territory.

J.M. HOLMES, *Australian Open North*, Sydney, 1963; *The Europa Year Book 1984. A World Survey*, Vol. I, p. 1126, London, 1984.

COD. *Gadus callarius*. A fish protected by the International Fish Convention (▷ Fishery).

UNTS, Vol. 231, p. 199.

CODE. An international term also called telegraphic code. A universally accepted name for a set of international abbreviations which in most economical form facilitate commercial transactions, bank orders, reservation of transport, etc. The most well-known codes are the ABC Code, Bentley's Code, and Unicode. A separate set of abbreviations formulated by ICAO forms the civil aviation code.

CODE OF CRIMES AGAINST THE PEACE AND SECURITY OF MANKIND. A new name of the Draft of ▷ Code of Offences against the Peace and Security of Mankind; adopted by the International Law Commission during the 39th session, May 4–July 17, in Geneva. On Dec. 9, 1988 the GA Res. 43/164 adopted by 137 votes, to 5 (France, the FRG, Israel, the UK, and the US), with 13 abstentions, decided to include in the provisional agenda of its forty-fourth session (1989/1990) the item entitled "Draft Code of Crimes against the Peace and Security of Mankind".

UN Chronicle, November, 1987. *UN Resolutions and Decisions adopted by the General Assembly during the First Part of its Forty-Third Session, from 20 September to 22 December 1988*. New York 1989, pp. 542–544.

CODE OF OFFENSES AGAINST PEACE AND SECURITY OF MANKIND. The draft prepared during 1949–54 by order of the UN General Assembly Res. 177/II, Nov. 21, 1949, by the UN Commission of International Law on the basis of the Nuremberg Principles and the verdict of the Nuremberg Trials. The Commission consciously confined the range of the Code to offenses of political character that are a threat to the peace and security of mankind and ruled out other kinds of offense, such as: ▷ slavery, ▷ sea and air piracy, counterfeit of monies or devastation of ▷ submarine cables. The Commission also resolved that the Code deals exclusively with responsibility of definite persons and not abstract institutions. The Commission refrained from determining the procedure of the Code's application in recognition of the fact that until the International Penal Court is founded the draft may be referred to by national courts. The Commission did not go so far as to specify definite penalties for particular offenses, leaving the question open to courts. The UN General Assembly at its Session held in 1954, in view of the dependence of the Code's adoption on the definition of aggression, resolved to adjourn the debate on the Code, to the moment when a Special Committee of the UN General Assembly takes up the question, under Res. 1186/XII Dec. 1, 1957. Such definition was adopted in Res. 3314/XXIX of Dec. 14, 1974 (▷ Aggression, UN Definition). The UN General Assembly on Dec. 16, 1978 and on Dec. 4, 1979 invited the member states to submit comments and observations to the Draft Code of Offenses against the Peace and Security of Mankind.

UN Chronicle, January, 1979, p. 82.

CODE OF TRANSFER OF TECHNOLOGY. On the initiative of the UNCTAD Conference 1976 an international group of experts at special sessions under UN auspices 1976–79 formulated a Code of Transfer of Technology. Due to the opposition of highly industrialized states against the obligatory character of the Code from the standpoint of international law, the work was suspended *sine die*.

CODES INTERNATIONAL. International term introduced by the International Standard Organization, ISO, for a standardized system of abbreviating frequently used names, e.g. periodicals and complete editions, also a name accepted for various systems of transmitting texts in the form of visual signals (semaphore and flag alphabets), by teletype, radio communication and others; existing code books permit the coding, decoding and transmission of code sequences manually or mechanically.

COD FISH WAR. Name adopted by the world press for successive arguments between Great Britain and Iceland over the enlargement by the latter of territorial waters and limitation of the fishing rights of British cutters. The first cod war took place in 1958 on the enlargement of a 4-mile shelf to 12 nautical miles. The second in 1972–73 on the enlargement of the Icelandic coastal zone to 50 miles. ▷ Iceland.

CODIFICATION. An international term for unified legal norms in the universally binding system obtained through a comprehensive arrangement of a given realm of legal relations; known in the Middle Ages (Justinian codifications done in the 6th century, Consolado del mare of the 13th century and others). The first private codification was rendered by an English lawyer, J. Bentham, in 1789 in the treatise entitled *The Principles of Morals and Legislation.* The first state codification is Chapter VI of the Constitution of the French Republic 1791. In the 20th century individual and collective codification works have prepared ground for international codifications and regional codifications, which are elaborated under the entry ▷ International law. The Statute of the UN International Law Commission defines codification in a twofold manner: (1) the definition of formulae and systematization of principles of international law in fields already covered by broad international practice of states, precedents and tenets; (2) gradual development of international law through preparation of draft conventions concluded by states in matters not yet arranged or insufficiently developed.

P. FIORE, *Le Droit international codifié et sa sanction juridique*, Paris, 1890; A. ALVAREZ, *Le Droit international de l'avenir. Plan Général de codification de Droit international*, Paris, 1920; *Actes de la Conférence pour la codification de Droit international*, Paris, 1932; *Bibliography on the Codification of International Law*, UN Doc. A/AC 10/6, 1947; *Historical Survey of Development of International Law and its Codification by International Conferences*, UN Doc. Int. A/AC 10/5, 1947; *Survey of International Law in Relation to the Work of Codification of the International Law Commission*, UN Doc. A/CN 4/1, 1948; H.J. RUNGE, *Die Kodifikationsversuche der Internationaler Rechtskommision der Vereinten Nationen*, Hamburg, 1952; D. DANOLET, *Les Conférences des Nations Unies pour la Codification du Droit International*, Paris, 1968.

COFACE. Companie Francaise pour l'Assurance du Commerce Exterieure, export credit insurance company under the aegis of the French Government, est. 1946.

The Export Credit Financing Systems in OECD Member Countries, OECD, Paris, 1976.

COFFEE. A subject of international co-operation and agreements. The first International Coffee Agreement was signed 1950. The International Coffee Pact 1958 has est. International Coffee Organization ICO, in London with International Coffee Fund, 1967 Members 42 coffee exporting countries: Benin, Bolivia, Brazil, Burundi, Cameroon, the Central African Republic, Colombia, Congo, Costa Rica, the Dominican Republic, Ecuador, Ethiopia, Gabon, Ghana, Guatemala, Guinea, Haiti, Honduras, India, Indonesia, Ivory Coast, Jamaica, Kenya, Liberia, Madagascar, Mexico, Nicaragua, Nigeria, Panama, Paraguay, Papua-New Guinea, Peru, Rwanda, El Salvador, Sierra Leone, Tanzania, Timor, Togo, Trinidad and Tobago, Uganda and Venezuela and 21 coffee importing countries: Australia, Belgium, Canada, Cyprus, Czechoslovakia, Denmark, Finland, France, the FRG, Ireland, the Netherlands, New Zealand, Norway, Portugal, Spain, Sweden, Switzerland, the UK, the USA and Yugoslavia). The regional organizations reg. with the UIA:

Afro-Malgasy Coffee Organization, f. 1960, Paris.
Association for the Coffee Trade and Industry in the EEC, f. 1961, in Antwerp.
Central American Coffee Board, f. 1975 in Caracas.
European Coffee Bureau, f. 1959 in Brussels.
European Federation of Coffee Roasters Associations, f. 1967 in Milan.
Inter-African Coffee Organization, f. 1960, Paris.
International Scientific Association of Coffee, f. 1965 in Paris.
Pan American Coffee Bureau, f. 1970 in New York.

In the EEC system the ▷ STABEX included Coffee in the ACP states.

Annual Coffee Statistics of the Panamerican Coffee Office, ICO Bulletin; CEPAL, *El café en América Latina, Problemas de la Productividad y Perspectivas*, 2 Vols., Santiago de Chile, 1958–60; C.A. KRUG, R.A. DE POERCK, *World Coffee Survey*, Roma, 1968; Pan-American Coffee Bureau, *Annual Coffee Statistics; Yearbook of International Organizations.*

COFFI. Communication Frequency and Facility Information System, information system of the ▷ ICAO.

COGNAC. A French brandy name patented by France in the Versailles Treaty, 1919, for its exclusive use in international trade. ▷ Wine. Thus e.g. the Germans had to introduce their own new name Brandwein, the English brandy.

COKE. A subject of co-operation and international conventions. In the years 1937–40 there existed in London the International Coke Association, an organ of the International Convention on Coke. After World War II the mining of coking coal and the production of coke came within the definition of the treaty on European Coal and Steel Community and also treaties negotiated within CMEA.

COLD WAR. An international term for a state of tension between the capitalistic Powers and the USSR. Introduced by the American Senator B. Baruch in a speech made in Colombia S. Carolina on Apr. 16, 1947, popularized that year in a book by the American publicist W. Lipmann entitled *Cold War.* According to the opinion of J.K. Galbraith the cold war in 1946–66 was in close relation to the development of industry, which expressed itself in the arms race, while the next impulses were found in the space race. A new wave of a cold war after a period of ▷ detente started in the 1980s.

W. LIPPMAN, *The Cold War. A study in US Foreign Policy*, New York, 1947; CARTON DE WIART, *Chronique de Guerre Froide 1947–1949*, Bruxelles, 1950; *Defence in the Cold War*, London, 1950; F. HONIG, "The Cold War as instrument of policy", in: *The Yearbook of World Affairs*, 1953; J.P. WARBURG, "Cold War tragedy", in: *The Western Political Quarterly*, 1954; R. VERGNAUD, "La guerre froide", in: *Revue général de droit international public*, 1958; D. FLEMING, *The Cold War. A Book of Documents*, New York, 1966; G. CONNEL SMITH, *The Interamerican System*, New York, 1966; A. FONTAINE, *Histoire de la Guerre Froide*, Paris, 1966; J.K. GALBRAIGHT, *New Industrial State*, New York, 1967; L.J. HALLE, *The Cold War as History*, New York, 1967; W. LAFEBER, *America, Russia and the Cold War 1945–1966*, New York, 1967; CH.O. LERCHE JR., *The Cold War and after*, Englewood Cliffs, 1967; P. SEABURY, *The Rise and Decline of the Cold War 1945–1966*; New York, 1967; D. REES, *The Age of Containment. The Cold War 1945–1965*, London, 1967; R. FRELEK, *Historia zimnej wojny*, Warszawa, 1970; A. IRIYE, *The Cold War in Asia*, Englewood Cliffs, 1974; C.L. SULZBERGER, *The Coldest War; Russia's Game in China*, New York, 1974; E.P. THOMPSON, *Beyond the Cold War: A New Approach to the Arms Race and Nuclear Annihilation*, New York, 1982; GEORGE F. KENNAN, *The Nuclear Delusion: Soviet–American Relations in the Atomic Age*, New York, 1982; N. CHOMSKY, *Towards a New Cold War*, New York, 1982; H. THOMAS, *Armed Truce; The Beginning of the Cold War 1945–46*, London, 1987; F.J. HARBUTT, *The Iron Curtain, Churchill, America and the Origin of the Cold War*, Oxford, 1987; W. W. ROSTOW, *On Ending the Cold War*, in: *Foreign Affairs*, Spring 1987; *Sollicitudo Rei Socialis. Encyclical letter of the Supreme Pontiff John Paul II for the Twentieth Anniversary of Populorum Progressio*, London, 1988, p. 34; D. ROBERTSON, *Guide to Modern Defense and Strategy*, Detroit, 1988; R. H. ULLMAN, *Ending the Cold War, in: Foreign Policy*, Fall 1988; Ch. SIMPSON Blowback, *America's Recruitment of Nazis and its Effects on the Cold War*, New York, 1988.

COLLABORATION ▷ Wartime Collaboration.

COLLECTIVE DEFENCE. An international term introduced by the Pact of the League of Nations of 1919 for an obligation assumed by the members of the League of Nations to co-operate and render support in the case when "one of the members resorts to war counter to the duties provided for in arts. 12, 13, or 15". This system failed in confrontation with the policy of aggression exercised by Japan in Italy and the Third Reich. In effect, after World War II the United Nations Charter introduced a system of collective security, providing for immediate acts of repression within the frames of the United Nations in emergency cases.

COLLECTIVE LEGITIMIZATION. An international term for those UN resolutions which favor specific legal tenets, e.g., the rights of nations to nationalize their natural resources, to effect social reforms tailored to their needs, or resolutions taking a positive position in a dispute (e.g. that between Namibia and the Republic of South Africa) to back one side. By the fact that support for a legal tenet is rendered, or a side is taken, by the international community, such as the UN, collective legitimization of important moral and political tenets is thereby expressed.

I.L. CLAUDE, "Collective legitimization as a political function of the UN", in: *International Organization*, No. 3, 1966.

COLLECTIVE SECURITY. An international term from the interwar period, originating from the preamble of the Covenant of the League of Nations, which obligated all nations to solidarity "for their peace and security". The League of Nations in 1927 convened a Security Commission whose aim was to prepare an international convention for strengthening collective security. Simultaneously, the USA and France brought about the signing in 1928 of the ▷ Briand–Kellog Treaty. The great economic crisis which followed shortly thereafter, as well as the great political crisis, paralyzed the efforts of the League of Nations. At that time the idea of creating a system of collective security was presented by the USSR in a speech of M.M. Litvinov at the XVI Session of the LN, Aug. 1, 1936, on the indivisibility of peace. During World War II the ▷ Atlantic Charter signed on Aug. 14, 1941 and supported by the USSR Sept. 24, 1941 announced in art. 8 that in the future a "system of universal security would be created". The International Conference on War and Peace in Mexico City in its final Declaration,

Mar. 3, 1945, proposed a "general system of world security" which should contain regional international security systems. The principles of the Covenant of the Arab League, signed in Cairo, Mar. 22, 1945, were formulated in a similar spirit. The ▷ United Nations Charter signed on June 26, 1945 in San Francisco created the framework for world and regional systems of collective security.

P.F. BRUGIERE, *La sécurité collective 1919–1946*, Paris, 1946; L.M. GOODRICH, *The UN and the Maintenance of International Peace and Security*, London, 1955; E. KURGANOV, E. NIKOLAEV, "Chto predstavlyaet soboy tak nazivaemia "programma vzaymnogo obezpiecheniya bezopasnosti", in: *Mezhdunarodnaza Zhizn*, 1956; H. KELSEN, *Collective Security in International Law*, London, 1957; F. VAN LANGEHOVE, *La crise du système de sécurité collective des Nations Unies*, Bruxelles, 1958; A. GARCIA ROBLES, "La seguridad colectiva", in: *El Continente Americano*, México, DF, 1960; J. LARUSY, (ed.), *From Collective Security to Preventive Diplomacy*, New York, 1965; M.L. FINKELSTEIN, *Collective Security*, San Francisco, 1966; *World Armaments and Disarmament SIPRI Yearbook 1984*, London, Philadelphia 1984, p. 590; D. ROBERTSON, *Guide to Modern Defence and Strategy*, Detroit, 1988.

COLLECTIVIZATION. An international term for farm collectivization under state pressure, introduced in the USSR in the 1930's and in Czechoslovakia, Bulgaria, East Germany, Hungary, Poland, Romania and Yugoslavia after World War II.

R. CONQUEST, *The Harvest of Sorrow: Soviet Collectivization and Terror-Famine*, New York, 1986; R. SERBYN, B. KRAVCHENKO eds., *Famine in the Ukraine 1932–1933*, Edmonton, 1986.

COLLEGE OF EUROPE. f. 1973 in Brugge, Belgium as the educational institution of the European Community.

COLLISION AT SEA. A subject of international agreement. The International Conference on Safety of Life at Sea, drew up and approved the International Regulations for Presenting Collisions at Sea on June 10, 1948 in London. These Regulations are annexed to the Final Act of the Conference.

UNTS, Vol. 191, p. 3; S. MANKABADY, *Collision at Sea. A Guide to the Legal Consequences*, Amsterdam, 1978.

COLLISION CIVIL JURISDICTION CONVENTION, 1952. ▷ Maritime Law Conventions, 1882–1978.

COLLISION CONVENTION, 1910. ▷ Maritime Law Conventions, 1882–1978.

COLLISION NORM. An international term for a rule of international private law indicating a legal system in which one should seek a legal solution for an event containing a foreign element.

COLLOQUIUM OPOLE. An international meeting of scholars in history, sociology, and international law, organized from 1974 annually by the Silesian Institute in Opole. The first session took place Jan. 16–18, 1974 under the chairmanship of Prof. Jozef Kokot (1916–75) on the subject of the consequences of the normalization of relations of Czechoslovakia and Poland with the Federal Republic of Germany.

COLOMBIA. Member of the UN. República de Colombia. Republic of Colombia. State on the Pacific and the Caribbean in the north-western part of South America. Bounded by Panama, Venezuela, Brazil, Peru and Ecuador. Area:

1,141,748 sq. km. Pop. 1987 est. 29,500,000 (1905 census; 4,143,000; 1918: 5,696,000; 1938: 8,701,000; 1951: 11,228,000; 1967: 19,215,000; 1973: 22,551,000). Capital city: Bogota with 4,055,900 inhabitants 1979. GNP per capita in 1987 US $1240. Currency: one peso = 100 centavos. Official language: Spanish. National Day: July 20, proclamation of independence, 1810.
Founding member of the UN since Oct. 24, 1945 and all its specialized agencies; founding member of OAS; member of ALALC; member of Tlatelolco Treaty; member of SELA.
International relations: 1564–1810 Spanish colony called Nueva Grenada; 1810–19 liberation war ended with proclamation, Dec. 18, 1819, of Republica de la Gran Colombia, Republic of Great Colombia which included, besides the present territory the territory of Venezuela till 1829, Ecuador till 1830, and Panama till 1903. Present name since 1886. Following the Panamian separatist movement, the Republic of Panama was founded; by way of compensation the US government agreed, under a treaty signed in Bogota, Apr. 6, 1914, to pay Colombia 25 million dollars; the treaty was ratified by both parties in 1919. During World War I on the Allied side, 1919–38 member of League of Nations which examined the Colombian dispute with Peru over ▷ Leticia Trapezium 1932–35. During World War II among United Nations. In 1950–53 the only Latin-American country to take active part in Korean war. In 1957 520 Colombian troops took part in armed operations of the UN in the Suez Canal Zone. Heads of state of Ecuador and Colombia on Mar. 12, 1966 signed a treaty on integration of borderland known as Acta Rumichaca, and Bogota Declaration 1966. In 1967 Chile, Bolivia, Ecuador, Peru, Venezuela and Colombia formed the ▷ Andean Group. In the 1980's the terrorism of the ▷ narcotraficantes resulted in some 11,000 murders every year.
See also ▷ World Heritage UNESCO List.

El Desarrollo Económico de Colombia, CEPAL, Santiago, 1956; M. NIEDERGANG, *Les Vingt Amériques Latines*, Paris, 1962; A. RIVADENEIRA VARGA, *Historia Constitucional de Colombia*, Bogota, 1962; P.M. HOLT, *Colombia Today and Tomorrow*, New York, 1964; *Fiscal Survey of Colombia*, BIRD Baltimore, 1965; M. AGUILERA, *La legislación y el derecho en Colombia*, Bogota, 1965; S.W. WURFEL, *Foreign Enterprise in Colombia. Laws and Policies*, Chapel Hill, 1965; W.P. MCGREEWEY, *An Economic History of Colombia 1845–1930*, Oxford, 1970; *The Europa Year Book 1984. A World Survey*, Vol. II, pp. 1423–1437, London, 1984; B. M. BAGLEY, *Colombia and The Wars on Drugs, in: Foreign Affairs*, Fall 1988.

COLOMBO. The capital of Sri Lanka from 1948. City and port on the Indian Ocean with 643,000 inhabitants (1984). The seat of the Colombo Plan, International Federation for Planned Parenthood, UN Information Center.

Yearbook of International Organizations.
Europa Yearbook 1987. A World Survey, London, 1987.

COLOMBO PLAN, 1950. An organization created in Jan., 1950 by the Ministers of Foreign Affairs of the British Commonwealth of Nations deliberating in Colombo on Ceylon. They established the Colombo Plan for Co-operative Economic Development in South and South-East Asia, whose permanent organ since May 1950 is the Colombo Plan Council for Technical Co-operation in South and South-East Asia, composed of representatives of the governments of Afghanistan, Australia, Burma, Bhutan, Cambodia, Canada, Ceylon, India, Indonesia, Iran, Japan, Laos, Malaysia, Maldives, Nepal, New Zealand, Pakistan, Philippines, Singapore, Thailand, the UK, the USA, and Vietnam. The UN has a permanent observer in the

Council. The headquarters of the secretariat and of the Council is Colombo.

J.R.E. CARR-GREGG. *The Colombo Plan*, New York, 1951; A. BASH, "The Colombo Plan. A case of regional economic co-operation", in: *International Organization*, 1955; F. BENHAM, *The Colombo Plan and Other Essays*, London, 1956; L.P. SINGH, *The Colombo Plan: Some Political Aspects*, Vancouver, 1963; R.S. WIRIODJATMODIO, *Der Gedanke der Blockfreiheit in Südostasien. Geschichte und Deutung der Solidaritätskonferenzen der Colombo-Staaten 1954–61*, Stuttgart, 1964. *The Colombo Plan Annual Report*, London, 1952–71 and Colombo, 1972 ff.

COLONIAL AGREEMENTS. The first international act which sanctioned the colonial division of the globe by European states was the ▷ Tordesillas Treaty, 1494. The process of colonial conquests reached its apogee in the General Act of the ▷ Berlin Congress 1885. From the Berlin Congress and up to the outbreak of World War I the following colonial agreements were concluded:

(1) English–Italian Mediterranean Agreement of Feb. 12, 1887 guaranteeing, among others the colonial status quo in North Africa;
(2) Suez Agreement of 1889;
(3) Heligoland–Zanzibar Agreement of July 1, 1890, German–English, solving the argument over equatorial Africa in favor of Great Britain (art. 11) in exchange for German control of Heligoland island. (art. 12);
(4) London Agreement, English–German, on Angola, of Aug. 30, 1898, concerning the secretly planned division of Portuguese colonies in Africa between the Reich and Great Britain; not implemented;
(5) Madrid Agreement, Spanish–German, of Feb. 12, 1899, on cession of Caroline Islands and Mariana Islands (except for Guam) in the Pacific to the Reich for 25 million pesos;
(6) London Agreement, English–French, of Mar. 21, 1899, on Sudan, dividing the interest zones;
(7) London Convention, English–German, of Nov. 14, 1899 on division of the Samo archipelago islands among the Reich, the USA and Great Britain;
(8) Mediterranean Agreement, signed in Rome on Dec. 16, 1900, French–Italian, after the war of Italy against Ethiopia, on division of interests in the Cyrenaica, Tripoli and Morocco;
(9) English–Japanese Agreement of Jan. 30, 1902, on division of interests in Korea and China;
(10) Vereeniging Peace of May 13, 1903, ending the Boer war in South Africa by subjecting the latter to Great Britain's authority;
(11) French–British Agreement of Apr. 8, 1904, known as ▷ Entente cordiale;
(12) English–Spanish Agreement of Oct. 3, 1904 on interests of both countries in Algeria and Morocco;
(13) London English–Japanese Alliance of Aug. 12, 1905, which was to guarantee colonial possessions and interest zones of Japan and Great Britain, supplemented and extended on July 13, 1911, and valid till Dec. 13, 1921, when it was replaced by the Washington 4-power Agreement with France and the USA participating;
(14) Algeciras Act, signed on April 7, 1906 by Austro-Hungary, Belgium, France, Spain, Holland, Morocco, Germany, Portugal, Russia, Sweden, the USA and Great Britain;
(15) Petersburg Agreement, English–French of Aug. 31, 1907 on division of interests in Afghanistan, Persia and Tibet;
(16) Berlin Agreement, French–German, of Feb. 9, 1909 on Morocco;
(17) Petersburg Agreement, German–Russian, of Aug. 19, 1911 on construction of ▷ Baghdad railway and on interest zones in Persia;
(18) Berlin Agreement, French–German, of Nov. 4, 1911 on division of interests in Congo and Morocco;
(19) Lausanne Peace between Turkey and Italy, signed on Oct. 18, 1913, turning over Cyrenaica and Tripoli to Italy. The quasi-colonial agreements also include most of the agreements of European powers and the USA with Asian countries, such as the final Protocol of the Boxer Rebellion 1901, Nanking Treaty 1842, Thimonoseki Treaty 1895, Tien Tsin Treaty 1858, Yedo Treaty 1858, Yokohama Treaty 1854, Indochina Treaties 19th century, as well as some USA treaties, such as

Hay–Pauncefote Treaty, Hay–Varilla Treaty concerning Panama or Treaties on Cuba and Puerto Rico.

After World War I the rules of colonialism established at the Berlin Congress of 1885 for Africa were expanded to cover other world regions by the Saint-Germain Convention 1919; simultaneously, the colonial system ensuring to powers a free penetration of conquered regions was sanctioned by the mandate system of the League of Nations. In 1920 two-thirds of mankind, i.e. 1250 million of 1875 million people then alive, were living in colonies with full approval of the League of Nations.

Only after World War II did the UN Charter, owing to its anti-fascist character, entirely eliminate the term "colonies", contained in the Pact of the League of Nations. The UN Charter introduces a new concept of ▷ trusteeship territories, with the stipulation imposed that colonies be granted independence as soon as possible. This initiated the process of ▷ decolonization by the UN.

The colonial area, which covered in 1945 36,000,000 sq. km with 663,000,000 people living in dependence on 12 colonial powers: Australia, Belgium, Denmark, Spain, Holland, Japan, New Zealand, the Union of South Africa, Great Britain and the USA, dwindled by 1960 to an area of 13,000,080 sq. km with 83,000,000 people. In the 15 years that followed, a further considerable decrease of the number of colonies occurred. In 1974/75 the possessions of Portugal: Angola, Guinea-Bissau, and Mozambique became decolonized.

In 1984/85 the main unsolved colonial problems remained: ▷ Namibia and the "homelands" vel "bantustans" of ▷ South Africa.

A. ZIMMERMAN, *Die Kolonialreiche der Grossmächte, 1871–1916*, Berlin, 1916; F. SCHACK, *Das Deutsche Kolonialrecht in seiner Entwicklung bis zum Weltkrieg*, Berlin, 1923; E. MORESCO, "Les rapports de droit public entre la metropole et les colonies domaines et autres territoires d'autre-mer", in: *Recueil des Cours de l'Academie de Droit International*, No. 55, 1936; E.M. VAN ASBECK, "Le regime de Etrangers dans les colonies", in: *Recueil des Cours de l'Académie de Droit International*, No. 61, 1937; G. HARDZ, *La politique coloniale et le partage de la terre au 19e et 20e siècles*, Paris, 1937; S.R. SERTOLI, *Storia e politica coloniale italiana 1869–1935*, Messina, 1938; M.E. TOWNSEND, C.H. PEAKE, *European Colonial Expansion since 1871*, Chicago, 1941; F.N. VAN ASBECK, "Le statut actuel des pays non-autonomes d'autre mer", in: *Recueil des Cours de l'Académie de Droit International*, No. 71, 1947; "International Responsibility for Colonial Peoples. The UN and Chapter XI of the Charter", in: *International Conciliation*, No. 458, February, 1950; M.L. BEVEL, *Le Dictionnaire Colonial*, Bruxelles, 1955.

COLONIAL CLAUSE. An international term for application of agreements signed by colonial powers to territories under their rule.

Clause fédérale et clause coloniale, Rapport du Secrétaire Général, UN Doc. E/1721. 19 VI 1950; "Colonial Clauses and Federal Clauses in UN Multilateral Instruments", in: *American Journal of International Law*, No. 45, 1951.

COLONIALISM. An international term for the policy of enslaving some countries by others, differently justified in different centuries; modern European colonialism dates back to the 15th–16th centuries, following geographic discoveries.

T.R. ADAM, *Modern Colonialism*, London, 1955; D.S. FIELDHOUSE, *The Colonial Empires*, London, 1982; D. S. FIELDHOUSE, *Colonialism 1870–1945*, London 1983.

COLONIAL WARS. An international term founded at the beginning of the modern era connected with the conquest of overseas territories by the colonial powers of Europe and later also by the United States and Japan. In the 19th and 20th centuries major colonial wars occurred in Africa and Asia: waged by France 1830–47 and 1954–62 against Algeria and 1862–1908 and 1954–62 against Indochina; by Italy against Ethiopia, Eritrea and Somalia in 1880–90 and against Ethiopia in 1935–36; by England against Afghanistan 1838–1919, Burma in 1824–26; China (the ▷ opium wars), India in 1857–58 and against the Boers in South Africa 1899–1902; by Japan against ▷ Manchuria and ▷ China 1931–45.

C.D. LANNOY, H. VAN DER LINDEN, *Histoire de l'expansion coloniale des peuples européens*, 3 Vols., Paris, 1907–21.

COLON SALVADORIAN. A monetary unit of El Salvador. 1 colon = 100 centos; issued by the Banco Central de Reserva de El Salvador.

COLOUR. Subject of international co-operation. Organizations reg. with UIA:

European Committee of Print, Printing Ink and Artists Colours Manufacturers Association, f. 1951, Brussels, Belgium.
International Colour Association, f. 1967, Soesteberg, Netherlands.
International Commission for Fashion and Textile Colours, f. 1963, Neuilly-sur-Seine, France.
Nordic Committee for Oil and Colour, Industry, f. 1970, Copenhagen, Denmark.

Yearbook of International Organizations, 1986/87; The Europa Yearbook 1988. A World Survey, Vol. I, London, 1988.

"COLUMBIA". ▷ Space Shuttle.

COLUMBIA RIVER TREATY, 1961. A Treaty signed in Jan. 1961 by Canada and the USA; ratified in Sept., 1964, supplemented with protocols of Jan. 1964. It sets proportions of water to be used from the river as a source of energy, with reference to the American–Canadian Agreement on border waterways 1909. The validity of the Treaty is at least 60 years and its organ is the Permanent Engineering Board.

COLUMBUS DAY. Oct. 12, celebrated in the United States since the end of the 19th century (in other American states since 1917) as "the day of discovering a new world" (Dia del Descubrimiento del Nuevo Mundo) to commemorate Oct. 12, 1492, when three ships – *Santa Maria*, *Pinta* and *Niña* – with a crew of 90 men under the command of Christopher Columbus (1451–1506) sailing from the Spanish harbor of Palos on Aug. 3, 1492 reached the Western Hemisphere at the island of Buanahani, called by Columbus San Salvador in the Bahamas archipelago, also known as Watling.

COLUMBUS LIBRARY. A Panamerican Library est. 1902 by the II International American Conference in Washington as a library of the Panamerican Union with the task of collecting, storing, and cataloging bibliographic materials about the American continent as well as serving the American governments and national libraries with information, technical help, etc. From 1959 the Columbus Library is almost exclusively concerned with co-operation in technical programs.

COLUMBUS MEMORIAL. A subject of international governmental resolutions taken at International American Conferences of 1923, 1928, 1933, 1936, 1938, 1954 on the joint project to erect a memorial statue to Christopher Columbus (1451–1506), discoverer of the New World, in the form of a lighthouse on the island of San Salvador but not until extracontinental colonialism is completely ousted from the Western Hemisphere. In the face of the persistence of the French, Dutch and the British on the American continent the construction of the memorial was postponed. The matter is raised traditionally once a year on the occasion of ▷ Columbus Day.

COMBATANTS. An international term for soldiers of regular army or irregular forces taking part in battle, protected by international martial law ▷ Partisan War.

COMBUSTION ENGINES. A subject of international co-operation. Organizations reg. with the UIA:

European Builders of Internal Combustion Engines and Electric Locomotives, f. 1966, Paris.
International Council on Combustion Engines (CIMAC), f. 1951, Paris. Publ.: *Lexicon of Technical Terms of the Internal Combustion Engine and Gas Turbine Industries* in 6 languages.

Yearbook of International Organizations.

COMECON. ▷ CMEA.

COMEX. Commodity Exchange of New York, f. 1933 in New York, trade center for metals.

COMINTERN ▷ Komintern.

COMISCO. Committee of International Socialistic Conferences, est. 1946, transformed in 1951 into the ▷ Socialist International.

COMITAS GENTIUM. ▷ Comity of Nations.

COMITEXTIL. An official abbreviation of the Co-ordinating Committee of the Textile Industry in the EEC.

COMITY OF NATIONS, COURTOISIE INTERNATIONALE. An international term introduced at the Vienna Congress, 1815, to define the obligation to apply old Roman Comitas gentium in diplomatic relations.

Comity in: *The International Law Dictionary*, Oxford, 1987.

COMMERCE INTERNATIONAL PROTECTION. A subject of international agreements ensuring free trade to neutral states during a war. An International Union of Trade Protection in Case of War existed from 1856 to 1909.

COMMERCIAL AND TRADE NAMES PROTECTION. A subject of international conventions: ▷ Inter-American Trade Mark Conventions, and ▷ WIPO.

COMMERCIAL ARBITRATION. A subject of international conventions; applied to settling disputes arising from the interpretation of contracts concluded by physical or legal persons of two or more states. On the initiative of the LN, a Protocol on Arbitration Clauses was signed at Geneva, Sept. 24, 1923, which provided that they may be included by the contracting parties in their contracts under the condition that such contracts are recognized by the law of their home states as commercial obligations. The Protocol entered into force on July 28, 1924. The following states have deposited their ratifications or accession: Albania, Austria, Belgium, Brazil, Czechoslovakia, Denmark, Estonia, Finland, France, Germany, Greece, India, Iraq, Ireland, Israel, Italy, Japan, Luxembourg, Malta, Mauritius, Monaco, the Netherlands, New Zealand, Norway, Poland, Portugal, Romania,

Spain, Sweden, Switzerland, Thailand, the UK, and Yugoslavia. States that have signed the Protocols have not deposited their ratifications: Bolivia, Chile, Latvia, Liechtenstein, Lithuania, Nicaragua, Panama, Paraguay, Peru, Republic of Korea, El Salvador, Uganda and Uruguay (*LNTS*, vol. XXVII, p. 158).

The ▷ Bustamente Code, 1928, includes (arts. 210, 211 and 423–435) rules on commercial arbitration; also the Treaty on International Procedural Law, 1940 (arts. 5–15).

After World War II the International Law Association formulated Rules on International Commercial Arbitration (▷ Copenhagen Rules 1950) and the Inter-American Council of Jurists approved in 1956 at Mexico City a Draft Uniform Law of Inter-American Commercial Arbitration, which includes provisions on the validity, effectiveness and enforcement of arbitration. (OAS Official Records, Ser. 1/VI 1, CIJ-91, p. 52).

The International Chamber of Commerce elaborated 1955 Rules of Conciliation and Arbitration (ICC Publication of June 1, 1955). The International Institute for the Unification of Private Law prepared with the Legal Committee of the Council of Europe a Draft Uniform Law on Arbitration in Respect of International Relations of Private Law (*UNIDROIT Yearbook, 1957*, p. 134). The Institute of International Law adopted at Amsterdam (1957) and Neuchatel (1959) articles on the freedom of parties to decide to submit a dispute to arbitration and the place of arbitration (*Annuaire de l'Institut de Droit International*, 1959, Vol. 48, p. 372). The UN Economic Commission for Asia and the Far East published in 1966 Rules for International Commercial Arbitration and Standards and the UN Economic Commission for Europe published Jan. 20, 1966, Arbitration Rules. The Inter-American Juridical Committee prepared, Oct. 5, 1967 a Draft Convention on International Commercial Arbitration (OAS Official Records, Ser. 1/VI 1, CIJ-91, p. 42). The Inter-American Arbitration Commission published Apr. 1, 1969, Rules of Procedure (Doc. AAA-19-2M-6-69). ECOSOC initiated in 1958 a UN Conference on International Commercial Arbitration, which drafted two conventions. The Convention on the Recognition and Enforcement of Foreign Arbitral Awards, done on July 10, 1958 in New York. (▷ Arbitral Awards).

The European Convention on International Commercial Arbitration, signed on Apr. 21, 1961 at Geneva; entered into force on Jan. 7, 1964; ratified by Austria, Bulgaria, the Byelorussian SSR, Cuba, Czechoslovakia, the FRG, France, Hungary, Italy, Poland, Romania, the Ukrainian SSR, the USSR, Upper Volta and Yugoslavia. States that have signed the Convention but have not deposited their ratifications: Belgium, Denmark, Finland, Spain, Turkey. The Convention applies (art. 1) to arbitration agreements concluded for the purpose of settling disputes arising from international trade between physical or legal persons having, when concluding the agreement, their habitual place or residence or their seat in different contracting states (*UNTS*, Vol. 484, p. 364). The governments of the member states of the Council of Paris signed at Paris, Dec. 17, 1962, an Agreement relating to the Application of the European Convention on International Commercial Arbitration 1961 (*UNTS*, Vol. 523, p. 43) and at Strasbourg, Jan. 20, 1966, a European Convention Providing a Uniform Law on Arbitration. The member states of the CMEA signed on May 26, 1972 in Moscow the Convention on the Settlement by arbitration of Disputes Resulting from Economic, Scientific and Technical Co-operation.

In 1957 an Anglo-French collection of European and American (of the NATO states) arbitration

laws began appearing in Paris under the title, Arbitrage International Commercial. In the USA, the American Arbitration Association publish since 1927, the *Yearbook of Commercial Arbitration*. Since 1962, that is, from the date CMEA member states signed the Convention on the General Delivery Terms of Goods between the Organizations of CMEA states, and other documents regulating specific domains of economic, scientific and technical co-operation between those states, a process began toward the unification of economic arbitration with respect to the arbitration courts of the respective national Chambers of Foreign Trade. The complex program adopted at the XXV Session of the CMEA resolved

"to extend the rights of the national arbitration organs for foreign trade by placing under their jurisdiction civil law disputes arising out of the carrying out of various forms of economic, scientific and technical co-operation between the member States of the CMEA; to extend the exchange of information (including the exchange of arbitral decisions) between the arbitration organs of the member States of the CMEA; and to bring and unify the settling of questions of procedure in the national arbitration organs at the chambers of commerce of the CMEA member States."

Fields of Commercial Arbitration include ▷ Investment disputes settlement and ▷ Maritime arbitration.

COMMERCIAL BUREAU OF THE AMERICAN REPUBLICS. Name of the first panamerican organization created by the I International American Conference 1889–1890, seat in Washington; changed its name 1902 to International Bureau of the American Republics, which in 1910 was changed into ▷ Pan-american Union.

COMMERCIAL CODE. ▷ Code.

COMMERCIAL FIRMS IN UNITED NATIONS DOCUMENTS AND PUBLICATIONS. The names of commercial firms and industrial enterprises (hereinafter referred to as 'firms') other than research organizations and government-operated undertakings may not be mentioned in official United Nations documents and publications, except that:

(a) If the author of a paper or article reproduced in a United Nations document or publication is affiliated with a firm, he may, where appropriate, be so identified in the note or footnote designating the author;

(b) A firm may be identified by name where it is given credit for a photograph or figure used with its permission, it being understood that the photograph or figure may not be used if it implies endorsement or criticism of the firm by the United Nations;

(c) When reference is made to a process that bears a firm name, the process may be designated by name;

(d) When a legislative body requests the Secretary-General to prepare a study on a specific question (such as apartheid or transnational corporations) that must by its nature involve reference to specific firms, the names may be mentioned.

The names of firms should be obliterated from photographs and other artwork reproduced in United Nations documents or publications, except in cases where they are used by express permission of the firms under the exception given above.

When, for any acceptable reason, the name of a firm is given in a document or publication, the document or publication should, in appropriate cases, bear a disclaimer (normally in a explanatory note) to the effect that mention of any firm or licensed process does not imply endorsement by the United Nations.

Exceptions to the rule other than those stated above may be made only with the express permission of the Chairman of the Publications Board.

United Nations Editorial Manual, New York, 1983, p. 502.

COMMERCIAL PAPER COLLECTION. An international term defined by the International Chamber of Commerce in Uniform Rules for the Collection of Commercial Paper, adopted on May 14, 1967. The general provisions and definitions are as follows:

"(a) These provisions and definitions and the following articles apply to all collections of commercial paper and are binding upon all parties thereto unless otherwise expressly agreed or unless contrary to the provisions of a national, state or local law and/or regulations which cannot be departed from.

(b) For the purpose of such provisions, definitions and articles:

(i) 'commercial paper' consists of clean remittances and documentary remittances. 'Clean remittances' means items consisting of one or more bills of exchange, whether already accepted or not, promissory notes, cheques, receipts, or other similar documents for obtaining the payment of money (there being neither invoices, shipping documents, documents of title, or other similar documents whatsoever attached to the said items). 'Documentary remittances' means all other commercial paper, with documents attached to be delivered against payment, acceptance, trust receipt or other letter of commitment, free or on other terms and conditions.

(ii) The 'parties thereto' are the principal who entrusts the operation of collection to his bank (the customer), the said bank (the remitting bank), and the correspondent commissioned by the remitting bank to see to the acceptance or collection of the commercial paper (the collecting bank).

(iii) The 'drawee' is the party specified in the remittance letter as the one to whom the commercial paper is to be presented.

(c) All commercial paper sent for collection must be accompanied by a remittance letter giving complete and precise instructions. Banks are only permitted to act upon the instructions given in such remittance letter. If the collecting bank cannot, for any reason, comply with the instructions given in the remittance letter received by it, it must advise the remitting bank immediately."

Register of Texts of Conventions and Other Instruments Concerning International Trade Law, UN, New York, Vol. I, p. 239.

COMMERCIAL SAMPLES. Subject of the International Convention to Facilitate the Importation of Commercial Samples and Advertising Material, signed in Geneva on Nov. 7, 1953.

UNTS, Vol. 221, p. 255.

COMMERCIAL SATELLITE CORPORATION. ▷ COMSAT.

COMMISSION OF EUROPEAN COMMUNITIES. The main organ of the ▷ European Economic Community, EEC, which was created at a joint session of representatives of member states of the EEC for a period of four years.

J. PAXTON, *A Dictionary of the EEC*, London, 1978, pp. 44–45.

COMMISSION ON CONVENTIONAL ARMAMENTS. An organ of the UN created 13 Feb., 1947 on the basis of Res. 18 of the Security Council; composed of representatives of all of the member states of the Security Council; transformed Jan. 11, 1952 together with the Atomic Energy Commission into the ▷ UN Disarmament Commission.

COMMITTEE OF EXPERTS ON RULE AND PROCEDURE ▷ UN Experts on Rule and Procedure.

COMMITTEE OF RESPONSIBILITIES, 1919–20. The Committee was the organ of the Paris Peace Conference 1919–20 and consisted of 15 Allied experts in international law, therefore, also called the Committee of 15. It operated from Jan. until June 1919, under the Chairmanship of the US Secretary of State R. Lansing (1864–1928). The Committee prepared part VII of the Versailles Treaty (▷ Sanctions). For the first time in history, the rules of responsibility for encroaching on laws and customs of war, as well as a list of war crimes, were elaborated. The Committee made a list of war criminals and established a system of punishing them. The Committee of Responsibilities stated that persons, regardless of the positions they hold, should be punished if they have committed any of the 32 war crimes. These are:
(1) murder, mass killing and systematic terrorism; (2) killing of hostages; (3) torturing of civilians; (4) deliberate starving of civilian population; (5) acts of violence of all kinds; (6) compulsory prostitution; (7) deportation of civilian population; (8) internment of civilian population in inhuman conditions; (9) compulsory work for the enemy's benefit; (10) aiming at assuming sovereign authority during a military occupation; (11) compulsory drafting of recruits in occupied territories, (12) aiming at depriving the population in occupied territories of citizenship; (13) robbery of property; (14) illegal seizures and contributions; (15) destroying property; (16) devaluation of money, minting of forged coins; (17) infliction of collective punishments; (18) damaging and devastating property; (19) deliberate bombardment of open cities; (20) destruction of monuments and buildings of historical value or those serving charitable purposes; (21) sinking of cargo and passenger ships without previous warning to apply life-saving measures; (22) sinking of fishing boats; (23) deliberate bombardment of hospitals; (24) violation of Red Cross rules; (25) use of poison gases; (26) attacking and sinking hospital ships; (27) use of prohibited types of missiles; (28) refusal to take prisoners of war (giving "pardon"); (29) maltreatment of the wounded and the POWs; (30) forcing POWs to perform labor prohibited by the law of nations; (31) violation of the white flag; (32) contamination of wells.
The Committee, while making it clear that the list is tentative, demanded convening the Supreme Tribunal for trying war crimes, both civilian and military, consisting of judges of the Big Powers (3 from each) and of the Allied States (1 from each). Two American members of the Committee, J. Brown Scott and R. Lansing, declared against the rule of trying heads of state, and against punishment for the crimes which are a violation of war customs. The Committee of Responsibilities also published a list of 895 German war criminals, headed by former Emperor Wilhelm II, again with a reservation made by the Americans, although Wilhelm II was, among others, the author of two formulations concerning war crimes:
(1) In 1900, in an address to German soldiers going to China he declared:

"When it comes to fighting, remember, not to give pardon, not to take prisoners of war. Whoever falls in your hands must die. Exactly as a thousand years ago, when the Huns led by Attila acquired terrifying renown in tradition and history, make the name of Germans so known in China that, for a thousand years to come, no Chinese dares scowl at a German."

(2) In a letter addressed to the Austrian Emperor, Franz Joseph, on the day of the outbreak of World War I, Wilhelm wrote:

"We must drown everything in a sea of blood and fire. We must kill men and women, old people and children, we cannot spare a house or a tree. Only by systematic terror, which can terrify the degenerated French nation, can we put an end to the war sooner than in two months, whereas by observing humanitarian respects the war will drag for a couple of years."

The opposition of US delegates in the Committee of Responsibilities, and a similar attitude of the chairman of the peace conference, US President W. Wilson, account for a greatly attenuated tone of the Committee's formulations, included in the Versailles Treaty, although the Treaty provided for the convening of a Tribunal and demanding from Holland the extradition of Wilhelm II for trial. The convening of the Tribunal did not materialize, and Holland did not extradite the former Emperor. The so-called ▷ Leipzig Processes, arranged by the Government of the Reich in 1920–22, were a mockery of the administration of justice: only one trial ended in sentencing for a few years' imprisonment of a certain number of non-commissioned officers and junior officers for robbery on the front line.

S. GEEL, *War Criminals and Punishment*, New York, 1944; F. BAUER, *Die Kriegsverbrecher vor Gericht*, Zürich, 1945.

COMMITTEE OF TEN. A Committee created in 1959 by the four great powers with members from five Warsaw Pact states: Bulgaria, Czechoslovakia, Poland, Romania and the USSR and five NATO states: Canada, France, Italy, the UK and the USA. ▷ Disarmament.

COMMITTEE ON APPLICATION FOR REVIEW OF ADMINISTRATIVE TRIBUNAL JUDGEMENTS ▷ UN Administrative Tribunal.

COMMITTEE ON CONTEMPORARY DANGER. A Committee est. on 11 Nov., 1976 in Washington by a group of American politicians (John Connally, Douglas Dillon, Paul Nitze, David Packard, Eugen Rostov, Dean Rusk and others) with the task of warning American society against the "danger of ▷ *détente*."

COMMITTEE ON DEVELOPMENT AND CO-OPERATION OF CARIBBEAN STATES. A Committee created on Nov. 1, 1975 in Port of Spain on the initiative of ECLA as an intergovernmental organ of Bahamas, Barbados, Cuba, the Dominican Republic, Grenada, Guiana, Haiti, Jamaica and Trinidad and Tobago with the task of formulating economic projects, establishing regional industries, preparing a common customs policy, expanding fishing, sea transport and communications, determining common positions at the conference on law of the sea and in ▷ SELA.

COMMITTEE ON FOREIGN AFFAIRS. An international term for a parliamentary institution created for the purpose of controlling foreign policy and in some countries also for setting its directions, as in the US House of Representatives and Senate.

COMMITTEE ON NON-GOVERNMENTAL ORGANIZATIONS. A Committee created in 1946 by ECOSOC concerned with processing applications of individual non-governmental organizations, NGOs, for consultative status with ECOSOC, as well as relating the activities of NGOs to the work of the Council.

Yearbook of International Organizations.

COMMITTEE ON THE ADMISSION OF NEW MEMBERS ▷ Admission of New Members.

COMMODITY. An international term used in the UN system, generally understood to mean unprocessed minerals or agricultural products. In general use, it can mean any article of commerce.

FAO. *Commodity Review. A Yearbook*, Rome, 1961 ff;. UN Dag Hammarskjöld Library, *Commodities 1970–1979, A Selective Bibliography*, New York, 1980; *UN Chronicle*, October 1982, p. 40; *UN Yearbook of International Commodity Statistics*, 1984.

COMMODITY AGREEMENTS. An international term used in the UN system for multilateral arrangements between consumer and producer nations to stabilize supplies and prices of individual commodities.

UN Chronicle, October 1982, p. 46.

COMMODITY CREDIT CORPORATION. A US international financial institution, created in 1933 with the task of assisting US agriculture. From 1940 to 1950 financed these successive transactions ▷ Lend Lease Act ▷ UNRRA and ▷ Marshall Plan.

COMMODITY EXCHANGE. An international term for an institution of an international character in which buying selling transactions of mass goods are carried on, often determining the world price for a given product. Special commodity exchanges deal only with trading in one raw material, e.g. grain exchanges in Antwerp, Chicago, New York, Rotterdam, Winnipeg; cotton in London and Calcutta; coffee in London and New York.

E. MALINWOOD (ed.), *Economic Growth and Resources*, London, 1979.

COMMODITY SALE. A subject of international conventions since 1914 and unification efforts of laws governing such sales and since 1968 subject of discussion by the UN Commission on International Trade Law, UNCITRAL.

COMMON AFRO–MALAGASY ORGANISATION, ORGANIZATION COMMUNE AFRICAINE ET MAURICIENNE, OCAM. An intergovernmental institution est. Feb. 1965 in Nouakchott as successor to the ▷ African and Malagasy Union of Economic Co-operation, UAMCE. The ▷ Charter of the African and–Malagasy Common Organization with political and economic responsibilities was signed on Dec. 27, 1966 in Tananarive and came into force Dec. 28, 1967. At the summit conference at Bangui, 1974 the Heads of State decided that OCAM should promote co-operation between member states only in the economic, technical and cultural fields, and not in political matters. Publ. *Chronique mensuelle* (monthly), *Nations nouvelles* (bi-monthly) and *Bulletin statistique* (quarterly). It is reg. with the UIA.

Yearbook of International Organizations.

COMMON LAW. An international term for the legal system in Anglo-Saxon countries including both common unwritten law as well as national law.

COMMON MARKET. An international term used in the UN system for a territory of several or a dozen or more states free of tariff and passport barriers for their citizens and products, affording the possibility of free movement of persons, goods, services and capital. Common markets are the result of the creation of a free trade zone and customs union; its further stage of development is an economic union leading to a standardized currency, tax, and social system for the purpose of achieving complete economic integration. The first common market est. after World War II was the EEC, but the term generally includes any customs union which eliminates all trade barriers within the group and fixes a common external tariff on imports from non-member countries.

UN Chronicle, October 1982, p. 46.

COMMON MARKET LAW. All treaties, agreements, conventions and rules of the European Communities.

A. CAMPBELL, D. THOMPSON, *Common Market Law, Texts and Commentaries*, London, 1962.

COMMON MARKET OF ARAB STATES. A market proclaimed on Dec. 13, 1964 by the Cairo Convention signed by the governments of Egypt, Iraq, Jordan, Kuwait and Syria. Kuwait did not ratify the convention. It became effective formally on Jan. 1, 1965, but actually on Jan. 1, 1971, when Iraq, Syria and Egypt started organizing a Common Market without the participation of the other states.

COMMON MARKET OF CENTRAL AMERICA. A market initiated in 1958 by the Multilateral Treaty on Free Trade and Economic Integration of Central America. It became an institution in 1960 under the General Treaty on Central American Economic Integration for Costa Rica, Guatemala, Honduras, Nicaragua and El Salvador. The organs of the Common Market are: the Economic Council composed of ministers of economy and the Executive Committee having a common Secretariat with the Bank of Central American Economic Integration. See ▷ Central American economic integration.

COMMONWEALTH INSTITUTE. F. 1887 as the Imperial Institute in London with a comprehensive library and Resource Center. Open to the general public.

B. WEIRREB, C. HIBBERT eds., *The London Encyclopedia*, London 1983.

COMMONWEALTH OF NATIONS. The British Commonwealth was first defined by the Imperial Conference of 1926 as a group of

"autonomous communities within the British Empire, equal in status, in no way subordinate one to another in any aspect of their domestic or foreign affairs, though united by a common allegiance to the Crown, and freely associated as members of the British Commonwealth of Nations."

The name "British Commonwealth" replaces "British Empire" formally in the ▷ Westminster Statute 1931. The qualifying adjective "British" was omitted for the first time in the Declaration of London, Apr. 27, 1949 which was issued by a meeting of British Commonwealth Prime Ministers:

"the prime ministers ... hereby declare that they remain as free and equal members of the Commonwealth of Nations freely co-operating in the pursuit of peace, liberty and progress."

The Queen is Head of the Commonwealth. The Commonwealth Secretariat, est. in London in 1965, is the central co-ordinating organization and has consultative status at the UN General Assembly.
Members 1931: Australia, Canada, Great Britain, Irish Free State, Newfoundland, New Zealand and South Africa.
Members 1984 (with their dates of independence): the United Kingdom, Canada, July 1, 1867; Australia, Jan. 1, 1901; New Zealand, Sept. 26, 1907; India, Aug. 15, 1947, became a Republic on Jan. 26, 1950; Sri Lanka, Feb. 4, 1948 (Republic on May 22, 1972); Ghana, Mar. 6, 1957 (Republic on July 1, 1960); Malaysia, Aug. 31, 1957 as Federa-

tion of Malaya, Sept. 16, 1963 as Federation of Malaysia; Cyprus, Aug. 16, 1960 (Republic on independence); Nigeria, Oct. 1, 1960 (Republic on Oct. 1, 1963); Sierra Leone, Apr. 27, 1961 (Republic on Apr. 19, 1971); Tanzania–Tanganyika, Dec. 9, 1961 (Republic on Dec. 9, 1962); Zanzibar, Dec. 10, 1963 (Republic on independence), United Republic of Tanganyika and Zanzibar, Apr. 26, 1964; renamed Tanzania, Oct. 29, 1964; Western Samoa, Jan. 1, 1962; Jamaica, Aug. 6, 1962; Trinidad and Tobago, Aug. 31, 1962 (Republic on Aug. 1, 1976); Uganda, Oct. 9, 1962 (Republic on Sept. 8, 1967; second Republic, Jan. 25, 1971); Kenya, Dec. 12, 1963 (Republic on Dec. 12, 1964); Malawi, July 6, 1964 (Republic on July 6, 1966); Malta, Sept. 21, 1964 (Republic on Dec. 13, 1974); Zambia, Oct. 24, 1964 (Republic on independence); Gambia, Feb. 18, 1965 (Republic on Apr. 24, 1970); Singapore, Sept. 16, 1963 as a state in the Federation of Malaysia, Aug. 9, 1965 as an independent state and republic not part of Malaysia; Guyana, May 26, 1966 (Republic on Feb. 23, 1970); Botswana, Sept. 30, 1966 (Republic on independence); Lesotho, Oct. 4, 1966; Barbados, Nov. 30, 1966; Nauru, Jan. 31, 1968 (Republic on independence); Mauritius, Mar. 12, 1968; Swaziland, Sept. 6, 1968; Tonga, June 4, 1970; Fiji, Oct. 10, 1970; Bangladesh seceded from Pakistan, Dec. 16, 1971, recognized by the United Kingdom, Feb. 4, 1972; Bahamas, July 10, 1973; Grenada, Feb. 7, 1974; Papua New Guinea, Sept. 16, 1975; Seychelles, June 29, 1976 (Republic on independence); Solomon Islands, July 7, 1978; Tuvalu, Oct. 1, 1978; Dominica, Nov. 3, 1978 (Republic on independence); Zimbabwe, Apr. 18, 1980; Vanuatu, July 1980; Brunei, Jan. 1, 1984.
Organization reg. with the UIA:

English-Speaking Union of the Commonwealth, f. 1918, London, UK. Publ.: *Comord*.

See also ▷ *Nassau Commonwealth Declaration*, 1985.

The Cambridge History of the British Empire, 8 Vols., Cambridge, 1929 ff.; *Economic Survey of the Colonial Territories*, London, 1952 ff.; W.H. MAXWELL, *A Legal Bibliography of the British Commonwealth of Nations*, London, 1956; K.C. WHEARE, *Constitutional Structure of the Commonwealth*, Oxford, 1960; K. BRADLEY, *The Living Commonwealth*, London, 1962; A.D. PATTERSON, *Handbook of Commonwealth Organizations*, London, 1965; M. BALL, *The Open Commonwealth*, Duke University Press, 1971; H.D. HALL, *Commonwealth: A History of the British Commonwealth*, London, 1971; D.T. INGRAN, *The Imperfect Commonwealth*, London, 1977; A. WALKER, *New Look at the Commonwealth*, Oxford, 1977; J. CHADWICK, *The Unofficial Commonwealth*, London, 1982; D. JUDD, P. SLINN, *The Evolution of the Modern Commonwealth 1902–1980*, London, 1982; N. MANSERGH, *The Commonwealth Experience*, 2 Vols., London, 1982; *The Europa Year Book 1984. A World Survey*, Vol. 1 pp. 116–122, London, 1984; *The Commonwealth Yearbook 1987*, London, 1987; R.J. MOORE, *Making the New Commonwealth*, Oxford, 1987; *Yearbook of International Organizations 1986/87*; *The Europa Yearbook 1988. A World Survey*, Vol I, London, 1988.

COMMONWEALTH PARLIAMENTARY ASSOCIATION. The Empire Parliamentary Association was founded in 1911 and accepted its present name in 1931. Its members are national, provincial and territorial parliaments, its general secretariat is in London. Publ. *The Parliamentarian*. Reg. with the UIA.

Yearbook of International Organizations.

COMMONWEALTH SECRETARIAT. The Secretariat was est. in June 1965 in London with headquarters at Marlborough House, by the Commonwealth Prime Ministers' Meeting. It has observer status of the UN General Assembly. The functions of the Secretariat were defined as follows:

"(4) The Secretary-General and his staff should approach their task bearing in mind that the Commonwealth is an association which enables countries in different regions of the world, consisting of a variety of races and representing a number of interests and points of view, to exchange opinions in a friendly, informal and intimate atmosphere. The organization and functions of the Commonwealth Secretariat should be so designed as to assist in supporting the building on these fundamental elements in the Commonwealth association. At the same time the Commonwealth is not a formal organization. It does not encroach on the sovereignty of individual members. Nor does it require its members to seek to reach collective decisions or to take united action. Experience has proved that there are advantages in such informality.
It enables its members to adapt their procedures to meet changing circumstances; conversely there would be disadvantages in establishing too formal procedures and institutions in the association.
General Considerations
(5) Both the Secretary-General and his staff should be seen to be the servants of Commonwealth countries collectively. They derive their functions from the authority of Commonwealth Heads of Government; and in the discharge of his responsibilities in this connection the Secretary-General should have access to Heads of Government, who will indicate the appropriate channels of communication to them.
(6) The secretariat should not arrogate to itself executive functions. At the same time it should have, and develop, a relationship with other intra-Commonwealth bodies.
(7) The Secretariat should have a constructive role to play. At the same time it should operate initially on a modest footing; and its staff and functions should be left to expand pragmatically in the light of experience, subject always to the approval of Governments.
(8) Against this background and in the expectation that, as its contacts spread, the Secretariat could expect to receive increasing calls on its resources, the various functions which it will exercise fall under the following broad headings; international affairs, economic affairs and general and administrative functions.
International Affairs
(9) Consultation is the life blood of the Commonwealth association. At their Meeting in July 1964, the Commonwealth Prime Ministers expressed the view that on matters of major international importance a fuller exchange of views could very appropriately be promoted on an increasingly multilateral basis through the agency of the Secretariat. They were particularly anxious to ensure that there should be opportunity for fuller participation by all member countries in the normal process of Commonwealth consultation. At the same time they showed themselves conscious of the importance of maintaining the unwritten conventions which have always determined those processes. The Secretary-General will observe the same conventions and act in the same spirit.
(10) In so far as Commonwealth Governments agree that the Secretariat should discharge any specific task, it will be fully at their disposal. In general, however, its purpose will be to serve them by facilitating and promoting consultation on matters of common concern. To this end, subject to the general principles set out in paragraphs 12 and 13 below, the Secretary-General will arrange to prepare and circulate papers on international questions of common concern to all Commonwealth Governments where he considers it useful to do so. It may also prove helpful if, in consultation with the Governments concerned, he arranges occasional meetings of officials of member Governments for the exchange of information and views on agreed subjects. Such meetings might on occasion, if member Governments agreed, take place in various Commonwealth capitals or elsewhere.
(11) The general principles which the Secretary-General will observe are set out in the following paragraphs.
(12) The functions of the Secretariat are envisaged as being inter alia the dissemination of factual information to member countries on matters of common concern. 'Factual' information cannot be precisely defined; but, provided that the Secretary-General proceeds with circumspection in the exercise of this function, he is authorized, where he thinks it useful to do so, to prepare and circulate, either on his own

initiative or at the request of a member Government, papers on international questions of common concern, provided that these papers do not propagate any particular sectional or partisan points of view, contain no policy judgments or recommendations by the Secretariat and do not touch upon the internal affairs of a member country or disputes or serious differences between two or more member countries. In addition, the Secretary-General will, on the request of a member Government, circulate papers submitted by that Government on international questions of common concern, provided that, if these touch upon the internal affairs of member countries or disputes between two or more member countries, they will not be circulated without prior concurrence of the country or countries concerned. The Secretary-General has discretion to refuse to prepare or circulate any paper, whatever its origin which in his view propagates any sectional or partisan point of view or would for any other reason be liable to be offensive to any member country or countries.

(13) The position of the remaining dependent territories within the Commonwealth is one matter which continues to command lively interest among member countries. The Secretariat could play a role in this field; and it might circulate to member Government balanced papers on the constitutional advance of the remaining territories or on their progress towards independence, on the understanding that the responsible member Governments would always be closely consulted in the preparation of the papers.

(14) The Secretariat will be guided by the principles outlined in the preceding paragraphs because it is important that it should develop as a unifying element within the Commonwealth. But, provided that it begins modestly and remains careful not to trespass on the independence and sovereignty of the member Governments whose servant it will be, it will be possible for it to grow in the spirit of the Commonwealth association itself. All Commonwealth Governments wish to contribute to this process and will be ready to assist the Secretary-General in every possible way. In particular the Secretary-General will from the outset establish close relations with Commonwealth Governments and with their representatives in London: and governments will arrange to keep the development of the Secretariat's functions under regular review, by means of an annual report on its work. By these means the Secretariat will gradually accumulate, with the passage of time, a body of knowledge and experience which will contribute to an even closer understanding among member Governments on these major international issues which are of common and continuing concern to all the members of the Commonwealth.

Economic Affairs.

(15) The Secretariat will discharge several valuable roles in the economic field, the more important of which are outlined in the following paragraphs. Several intra-Commonwealth bodies are already actively at work in this field, and their relationship to the Secretariat is to be examined in accordance with the arrangements set out in paragraphs 23 to 26.

(16) The Secretary-General will initiate, collate and distribute to member Governments material bearing not only on economic problems, but also on special and cultural issues in respect of which the potential value of this work could be considerable. He is authorized to follow up the specialized factual reports of the various agencies already in work in these fields by promoting wider ranging studies on, e.g., the inter-relationship of agricultural and industrial growth in the new Commonwealth. In this connection the Secretary-General may implement such tasks by commissioning, with the limits prescribed by his approved budget, specialist studies from outside expert sources rather than by engaging additional permanent staff.

(17) Apart from servicing meetings of the various Commonwealth economic bodies, the Secretariat may, as appropriate, be represented at meetings of these specialized agencies in order to keep in close touch with their activities; and it will also keep in touch with the various United Nations agencies whose work in Commonwealth countries will on occasion be of direct concern to it.

(18) In connection with the general economic aspects of the Secretariat's work, the proposals advanced at the last meeting of Commonwealth Prime Ministers for the initiation of joint Commonwealth Development Projects in individual Commonwealth countries are relevant. The passage from the 1964 communique read: 'In particular they considered a proposal that development projects might be launched in individual Commonwealth countries which would be implemented by various members acting in close collaboration and contributing whatever resources – in men, money, materials and technical expertise – they could most appropriately provide. Such projects, which would be additional to the support which Commonwealth countries already provide to the United Nations Special Fund and Expanded Programme of Technical Assistance, could be directed to a member of different purposes – the improvement of agricultural production and the development of natural resources through extension services, training and research; the enlargement of professional and technical training; the development of new industries; and so forth. But they would all be inspired by the common purpose of promoting the development of the Commonwealth by a co-ordinated programme of joint or bilateral projects. The British Government said that they would be prepared to make a substantial contribution to projects of this kind within their expanding programme of development aid. The other member Governments expressed support for the objective of the proposal and agreed that further consideration should be given to the basis on which such a programme might be established.'

(19) As regards the Secretariat's general functions and, in particular, its activities in the economic field, it is important that nothing should be done which might disturb the existing channels of economic and technical assistance to member countries or duplicate the present bilateral and multilateral link. The functions of the Secretariat in connection with the Commonwealth Development Projects are therefore expert and advisory and will not detract from the right of member countries to determine their own aid and development programmes.

(20) Subject to these basic considerations the Secretariat will be able to play a valuable part in assisting member Governments at their request, in advancing, and obtaining support for, development projects and technical assistance in a variety of fields on a multilateral Commonwealth basis, as appropriate. It will also help in the expeditious processing of requests for such assistance made by one Commonwealth country to another. In this connection, it will prepare and make available to Commonwealth Governments up-to-date information on the possibility of securing aid and technical assistance in various fields from individual countries of the Commonwealth.

(21) Thus the Secretariat, by accumulating a reliable body of knowledge on the aid potential of the Commonwealth to which member countries can usefully have recourse for the purpose of promoting their own development, will enable Commonwealth countries generally to co-operate to the maximum extent possible in promoting the economic development of all.

(22) In general, the Secretary-General, in discharging his functions in this field of economic and related affairs, will be guided by the principles set down in paragraphs 12 and 13.

Proposed Review of Intra-Commonwealth Organizations

(23) A comprehensive review of existing intra-Commonwealth organizations concerned with economic and related affairs will be carried out, in view of the changing nature of the Commonwealth and of the fact that the multiplicity of organizations working in these fields has created problems of staff and finance.

(24) The main purpose of this review will be to examine whether existing work on economic and related affairs is being unnecessarily duplicated; how far the activities of the Specialized Agencies of the United Nations now supersede those of existing intra-Commonwealth bodies; what Commonwealth bodies might usefully be absorbed within the Secretariat; which have functions so specialized that they cannot profitably be so absorbed; and how close co-operation between these latter and the Secretariat, particularly in the light of the needs of the changing Commonwealth, can most effectively be achieved.

(25) In order to secure an impartial appraisal and to protect the future relationship between the Secretariat and other Commonwealth organizations this review will be carried out by a small committee, appointed by Commonwealth Governments, under an independent Chairman. In order to safeguard the Secretary-General's position he will not be a member of the Committee. Nevertheless, he will have the right to be present or to be represented throughout the proceedings of the Committee and to participate in its discussions. The Commonwealth organizations concerned will, of course, have the right to submit evidence to the Committee.

(26) Pending the outcome on the review the Secretariat and the Commonwealth Economic Committee will work in the closest consultation. Again without prejudice to the review, the Secretariat will take over from the Commonwealth Relations Office as soon as convenient the secretariat functions which that Department at present carries out on behalf of the Commonwealth Liaison Committee.

Servicing of Commonwealth Meetings

(27) The Secretariat, operating as the visible servant of the Commonwealth association, will carry out the task of servicing future meetings of Commonwealth Heads of Government and, where appropriate, other Ministerial and official meetings open to all members of the Commonwealth. The Secretariat will be able to rely on the host country for such secretariat help as it cannot itself provide and for assistance in matters of accommodation, hospitality, transport and the like.

(28) The Secretariat will service the annual conferences of the Commonwealth Economic Consultative Council and meetings of the Commonwealth Liaison Committee. The more technical or specialized organizations, e.g. the Commonwealth Education Conference, the Commonwealth Education Liaison Committee or the Commonwealth Telecommunications Board will, pending the proposed review of Commonwealth organizations, continue to organize their own meetings.

(29) As regards Meetings of Prime Ministers the Secretary-General will henceforth serve as Secretary-General to each Meeting. Subject to the principles set out in paragraphs 12 and 13 above, his duties will include the preparation, collation and circulation of papers on agenda items, together with such background papers as appear appropriate; the production of minutes, and, with the assistance of the host Government, the general organization of the Meeting.

(30) As to the preparation of the agenda itself, the Secretary-General will be responsible for coordinating this process in the light of such direct discussions as Commonwealth Heads of Government may find convenient. Heads of Government will maintain the practice whereby the provisional agenda is drawn up, after consultation among themselves, in the form of a list of broad headings for discussion and they also reserve to themselves decisions on the timing and location of their Meetings.

(31) In consonance with the above functions of the Secretariat, its administrative organization will be as follows.

(32) The Chief Officer of the Secretariat will be the Secretary-General, and all members of the staff of the Secretariat will be responsible only to him.

(33) The Secretary-General will be appointed by Commonwealth Heads of Government collectively. He will be a man of high standing, equivalent in rank to a Senior High Commissioner. A significant part of his duties will be visiting member countries of the Commonwealth.

(34) The Deputy Secretaries-General will be appointed by Commonwealth Heads of Government acting through their representatives in London. One Deputy Secretary-General will have the necessary qualifications and special responsibilities for economic matters and should deal, on request, with development projects. As the work of the Secretariat expands, it may become necessary to appoint a second Deputy Secretary-General who will be primarily concerned with the other functions of the Secretariat.

(35) The paramount consideration in the selection of staff and in the determination of conditions of service will be the necessity of securing the highest standards of efficiency, competence and integrity, due regard being paid to the importance of recruiting the staff on as wide a geographical basis as possible within the Commonwealth. The Secretary-General will have discretion, in the light of the above considerations, to appoint senior staff to the service of the Secretariat from among panels of names submitted by Commonwealth Governments, who need not feel themselves limited to Government servants in submitting nominations.

(36) The Secretary-General has authority to make appointments of junior staff, subject to the approved budgetary limitations.

(37) All persons appointed to the staff of the Secretariat must be subject to clearance to the extent that their own Governments raise no objection to their suitability for employment. All members of the Secretariat, whatever their origin, must be strictly impartial in the discharge of their functions and place loyalty to the Commonwealth as a whole above all other considerations.

(38) Senior officers, including the Secretary-General and Deputy Secretaries-General, will be appointed in the first instance for not more than five years and preferably not less than three in order to ensure continuity of administration. In determining the period of tenure of other individual officers. The Secretary-General will no doubt wish to have a complete change of senior staff at any one time.

(39) The British Government will introduce legislation in order to give the Secretariat a legal personality under United Kingdom law and to accord to the Secretariat and its staff the immunities and privileges which are set out in Annex A.

(40) Other Commonwealth Governments will take steps to accord corresponding immunities and privileges to the staff of the Secretariat when visiting their territories, subject to whatever constitutional processes are required.

(41) The cost of the Secretariat will be borne in agreed shares by Commonwealth Governments; the scale of contributions is set out as follows:

	Per cent		Per cent
Australia	10.4	Malawi	1.5
Britain	30.0	Malta	1.5
Canada	20.8	New Zealand	2.5
Ceylon	1.5	Nigeria	1.5
Cyprus	1.5	Pakistan	2.4
Gambia	1.5	Sierra Leone	1.5
Ghana	1.5	Tanzania	1.5
India	11.4	Trinidad and	
Jamaica	1.5	Tobago	1.5
Kenya	1.5	Uganda	1.5
Malaysia	1.5	Zambia	1.5
			100.0

(42) The annual budget will be considered by the Commonwealth High Commissioners in London or their representatives, together with a United Kingdom representative, meeting as a Finance Committee. The budget will then be submitted to Commonwealth Governments for their approval. The Senior Commonwealth High Commissioner in London or a representative of the British Government will be responsible for convening the Finance Committee as necessary."

K.C. WHEARE, *Constitutional Structure of the Commonwealth*, Oxford, 1961; *Handbook of Commonwealth Organizations*, Methuen, 1965; P. STREETER, H. KORBET, *Commonwealth Policy in a Global Context*, London, 1971; A.J. PEASLEE (ed.), *International Governmental Organizations*, The Hague, 1974, pp. 290–299. *Yearbook of the Commonwealth*, London, 1983.

COMMUNICATION. An international term, subject of international co-operation and agreements▷ Broadcasting, ▷ Satellite Telecommunication, ▷ Telecommunication, ▷ Transport. In the years 1945–1965 the operational activities of the UN in the field of transport and communications were concentrated on technical assistance, fellowship, training courses and seminars, pilot projects and administration projects. A Working Group on Direct Broadcast Satellites was set up in 1965. The satellite system was feasible technologically by 1975. A Transport and Communications Decade in Africa, 1978–1988, recommended by UN Economic Council for Africa was adopted by UN General Assembly Res. 32/160 of Dec. 19, 1977. The Acapulco Conference in Jan. 1982 of the UNESCO International Program for the Development of Communications established 1981, approved financial support for the establishment of a Pan-African News Agency and an Asia-Pacific News Network:

and in Dec. 1982 in Paris Latin-American Feature Agency. A ▷ Communications World Year 1983 recognized "the fundamental importance of the communications infrastructure as an essential element in the economic and social development of all countries."

Everyman's United Nations, 1945–1965, New York, 1968; *Everyman's United Nations, 1966–1970*, New York, 1971; *Yearbook of the United Nations 1971*, pp. 597 and 601; and 1980, pp.1023–1024.

COMMUNICATIONS DEVELOPMENT. ▷ IPDC

COMMUNICATIONS LAW, INTERNATIONAL. All legal regulations related to international transportation and communications, including the international law on: roads, motor vehicles, railroads, shipping, post, telecommunication, transmission of electric power and fuels, transit etc.; subject of international conventions and bilateral agreements; subject of co-operation among intergovernmental organizations since 1874, the date of establishing UPU.

COMMUNICATIONS WORLD YEAR, 1983. The year 1983 was proclaimed as the World Communications Year by the UN General Assembly on Nov. 19, 1981.

Report by the International Commission for the Study of Communication. *Many Voices. One World. Communication and Society Today and Tommorrow*. London, 1980: *UN Chronicle*, January. 1982, p.29.

COMMUNIQUÉ. An international term denoting official information made public by a government or governments of two or more states; treated as official document or, in case of inter-government communication, as an international legal act.

COMMUNISM. An international term for an ideology advocated in the 19th and 20th centuries, foundations of which were laid by K. Marx (1813–83) and F. Engels (1820–95). A social system and socio-political international movement.

W. SWORAKOWSKI (ed.), *World Communist Movement. Selective Chronology 1848–1957*, Washington, DC, 1960; W. SWORAKOWSKI (ed.), *World Communism. A Selected Annotated Bibliography*, Washington, DC, 1963; C.D. KERNIG, *Marxism, Communism and Western Society. A Comparative Encyclopedia*, New York, 1972; R.H. McNEAL ed., *Resolutions and Decisions of the Communist Party of the Soviet Union*, 5 Vols., Toronto, 1974–1982; L. SHAPIRO, *The Russian Revolution of 1917. The Origin of Modern Communism*, New York, 1984; R.F. STARR ed., *Yearbook of International Communist Affairs 1987*, Stanford, 1987; Zb. BRZEZINSKI, *The Grand Failure: The Birth and Death of Communism in the Twentieth Century*, New York, 1989; J. SHELTON, *Gorbachev's Desperate Pursuit of Credit in Western Financial Markets*, New York, 1989.

COMMUNIST AND WORKERS' PARTIES. Names adopted after World War II by the international workers' movement to indicate Marxist--Leninist parties bearing different, historically founded names, such as the Communist Party of the Soviet Union, France, Greece, etc.; however, the Polish United Workers' Party, the Hungarian Socialist Workers' Party, etc. During 1947–56 the parties operated a permanent organ, Informburo. Since that time representatives of communist and workers' parties have held occasional meetings on selected world problems.

The First World Conference of Communist and Workers' Parties was held Nov. 16–19, 1957, at which 64 Marxist-Leninist national organizations were represented: (in brackets names other than

Communist Party): Albania, Algeria, Argentina, Australia, Austria, Belgium, Bolivia, Brazil, Bulgaria, Canada (the Progressive Workers' Party of Canada), Ceylon, Chile, China, Colombia, Cuba (the People's Socialist Party of Cuba), Costa Rica (the Popular Vanguard Party), Czechoslovakia, Denmark, Dominica (the People's Socialist Party of the Republic of Dominica), Ecuador, Finland, the Federal Republic of Germany (the Communist Party of Germany), the German Democratic Republic (the Socialist Unity Party of Germany), Great Britain, Greece, Guatemala (the Guatemala Labor Party), Honduras, Hungary (the Hungarian Socialist Workers' Party,) Jordan, Democratic People's Republic of Korea (the Korean Workers' Party), Luxembourg, Malaysia (the Communist Party of Malaya), Morocco (the Party of Liberation and Socialism), Mexico, Mongolia (the Mongolian People's Revolutionary Party), the Netherlands, Norway, New Zealand, Panama (the People's Party of Panama), Paraguay, Peru, Poland (the Polish United Workers' Party), Portugal, Romania, Spain, Sweden, Switzerland (the Swiss Workers' Party), Syria and Lebanon, Tunisia, Turkey, the USSR, Uruguay, Venezuela, Democratic Republic of Vietnam, (the Vietnamese Workers' Party). At the Conference views were expressed on the international situation and an ideological declaration, as well as the Peace Manifesto 1957 were adopted.

The Second World Conference of communist and workers' parties held in Moscow in 1960 was attended by members of 81 Marxist-Leninist national organizations; of all parties represented at the First Conference only the Yugoslav delegation was missing. Apart from the 63 delegations that participated in the First Conference, another 15 delegations of communist parties (or those called otherwise) joined the Conference: Burma, Cyprus (the Progressive Party of the Working People), Guadeloupe, Haiti (the Haitian Party of Popular Accord), Iceland (the Icelandic Labor Alliance), Iran (the People's Party of Iran), Northern Ireland, Lebanon, Martinique, Nepal, Nicaragua (the Nicaraguan Socialist Party), East Pakistan, Puerto Rico, Reunion, El Salvador, Sudan, the Union of South Africa, the USA. The Second Conference also adopted the Peace Appeal to Peoples of the World called the Moscow Appeal 1960.

The Third Conference was held in Moscow, June 5–17, 1969 and was attended by 75 Marxist–Leninist national organizations. Of the Parties taking part in the First or Second Conference the following communist and workers' parties were missing: Albania, Burma, China, the People's Democratic Republic of Korea, Nepal, Thailand, the Democratic Republic of Vietnam and Yugoslavia; the Communist Party of Lesotho was there for the first time. The Conference was preceded by a preparatory meeting in Budapest, Mar. 1968, with the participation of 67 communist and workers' parties. Two points were on the agenda: (1). aims of the struggle against imperialism at its present stage and joint actions by communist and workers' parties and all anti-imperialist forces; (2). the centennial of V.I. Lenin's birth. Under these headings two documents were adopted and a decision was made to call a World Anti-Imperialist Congress. The first of the two documents containing four bulky chapters was not signed by the delegations of Dominica, Great Britain and Norway and the delegations of Austria, Italy, Reunion and San Marino signed only one chapter of the document and formulated a joint program for the struggle against imperialism. The other document of Lenin's Centennial was adopted unanimously. During the years 1970–86 no world conference of communist and workers' parties was held. The number of party members in the World was in 1986 – 82,2 million, in

1987 – 89,8 million (44 million in China, 18.5 million in the USSR, 3.6 million Romania, 2.5 million North Korea, 2.3 million GDR, 2.2 million Yugoslavia, 2.1 million Poland, 1.7 million Czechoslovakia, 0.9 million Bulgaria). Communist parties were active in 78 states. A checklist of Communist Parties is published since 1976 by the "*Yearbook on International Communist Affairs*"; since 1981 published jointly with "*Problems of Communism*". Both publications also publish information on major ▷ Communist Front International Organizations.

The New Times, Moscow 1957–86; R.J. ALEXANDER, *Communism in Latin America*, New Brunswick, N.J., 1969. W.S. SWORAKOWSKI (ed.), *World Communism. A Handbook 1918–1965*, Stanford, 1973; *Yearbook on International Communist Affairs*, 5 Vols., Stanford 1976–80. *Hoover Institute Yearbook 1987*: CH. HOBDAY, *Communist and Marxist Parties of the World*, London, 1986; R.F. STARR ed., *Yearbook of International Communist Affairs 1986*, 20th eds., Stanford, 1986.

COMMUNIST AND WORKERS' PARTIES OF ARAB STATES DECLARATION, 1979. Announced in Damascus on Jan. 13, 1979, criticizing the policy of the United States, Israel and China in the Arab region and claiming that it aims at weakening the Arab national liberation movement. In the opinion of the session's participants, the Camp David accords of 1978 support the establishment of facilities for spreading the political, economic and military hegemony of the United States over the whole region, providing them with control over the oil deposits of the Arab States to the detriment of the Arab national liberation movement and conducting an imperialist policy in the Middle East in order to undermine international detente. The declaration ends with a statement that the workers' and communist parties of the Arab states are of the opinion that for attaining victory a universal, progressive Arab front should be established, uniting communists, BAAS-ists, nasserists, socialists, nationalists and other progressive forces, as well as all Arab revolutionary forces, on the basis of the principle of respecting the organizational independence, political and ideological sovereignty of each of those groupings.

COMMUNIST FRONT INTERNATIONAL ORGANIZATIONS. After World War II the communist world movement embraced the following major organizations:
1945 – Women's International Democratic Federation, with hq. in East Berlin. World Federation of Democratic Youth, with hq. in Budapest.
1946 – International Association of Democratic Lawyers, with hq. in Brussels. International Organization of Journalists, with hq. in Prague. International Radio and Television Organization, with hq. in Prague. International Union of Students, with hq. in Prague. World Federation of Scientific Workers, with hq. in East Berlin. World Federation of Teachers' Unions, with hq. in East Berlin.
1950 – World Peace Council, with hq. in Helsinki.
1951 – International Federation of Resistance Movements, with hq. in Vienna.
1957 – Afro-Asian People's Solidarity Organization, with hq. in Cairo. International Institute for Peace, with hq. in Vienna.

1958 – Christian Peace Conference, with hq. in Prague.
1964 – Berlin Conference of European Catholics, with hq. in East Berlin.
1966 – Organization of Solidarity of the Peoples of Africa, Asia and Latin America, with hq. in Havana.
1970 – Asian Buddhist Conference for Peace, with hq. in Ulan Bator

H. TIMMERMAN, *The Decline of the World Communist Movement: Moscow, Beijing and Communist Parties in the West*, Boulder, Col., 1987; W. SPAULDING, *Communist Fronts in 1987, in: Problems of Communism*, January-February, 1988.

COMMUNIST INTERNATIONAL. The ▷ International

COMMUNIST MANIFESTO, 1848. The original German title: Manifest der Kommunistischen Partei. An ideological declaration of communists, written by K. Marx (1818–83) and F. Engels (1820–95) at the request of the Second Congress of the Communists' Union of Nov.–Dec., 1847, published in German in London in Feb., 1848; the same year in Polish, and then in Danish, Flemish, French and Italian, in 1850 in English in London, in 1869 in Russian; the decades to come saw the translation of the Communist Manifesto into almost all world languages

K. MARX, *Manifesto of the Communist Party*, London, 1946.

COMMUNIST YOUTH INTERNATIONAL. A communist organization, f. 1919 in Berlin. Section of the Third ▷ International. The governing organ was the Congress of the Communist Youth International which held six sessions: in 1919, 1921, 1922, 1924, 1928 and 1935. The Communist Youth International was dissolved in 1943, together with the Communist International.

COMMUTATION. An international term for a theory concerning the rapprochement of contradictory systems: capitalism and socialism by means of common social reforms; a variation of the theory of ▷ Convergence.

COMNET. International Network of Centres for Documentation on Communication Research and Policies, one of the ▷ UNESCO Information Systems.

COMOROS. Member of the UN. État Comorien; Comor State. Comoro islands in the Indian Ocean, between African mainland (Mozambique coast) and Madagascar. Area: 2,236 sq. km. Pop. 1987 est. 422,500 inhabitants. Capital: Moroni (Grand Comore) with 16,000 inhabitants 1980. GNP per capita 1986: US $280. Currency: one franc CFA = 100 centimes. Official languages: Kiswahili and French. National Day: Nov. 12, Day of UN Membership, 1975.
Member of the UN and all its specialized agencies save IFC, IMO and WIPO. OAU and Lomé Convention 1975 (since 1977) and 1980; an ACP State of EEC.
International relations: all islands were a possession of the king of Mayotte, who ceded them to France in the 19th century. Occupied by British troops 1940–44. Autonomy within the French Union, 1946. French overseas territory, 1958, internal self-government 1968. On Dec. 22, 1974 in the referendum the Moslem population of Grand Comore, Anjouan and Mohili voted 95.56% for independence, but 65% of the Catholic inhabitants of Mayotte against independence. The Comoran Chamber of Deputies on July 6, 1975 proclaimed

independence of the whole group; recognized by the UN General Assembly on Nov. 12, 1975. A new referendum on Mayotte was held on Feb. 8 and April 11, 1976; again the majority preferred to retain links with France. The Comoros claim the whole Comoros Archipelago as national territory, including the island of ▷ Mayotte. The dispute with France over Mayotte was a subject of discussion in the UN General Assembly and UN Security Council in 1974, 1976, 1979 and at the OAU Assembly in 1980 and 1986. The UN took the side of the OAU in supporting the sovereignty of the Comoros over Mayotte.

Everyman's United Nations, New York 1979; *The Europa Year Book 1984. A World Survey*, Vol. II, pp. 1438–1441, London, 1984; Comoros – France (Mayotte), in: A.J. DAY ed., *Border and Territorial Disputes*, London, 1987, pp. 117–125.

COMPARATIVE LAW. An international term for a field including mostly civil law, but also penal and other; subject of international comparative studies aimed at a unified civil law that might replace international private law and of continuing international co-operation. Organizations reg. with the UIA:

The International Society for Teaching Comparative Law, f. 1960, Paris; appointed in 1961 the International Faculty for the Teaching of Comparative Law, seated in Strassbourg; arranges congresses.

The International Association of Legal Sciences, f. 1950, Brussels. Consultative Status with UNESCO. Publ. *Revue de droit international et de legislation comparé.*

Latin American Institute of Comparative Law, f. 1963, Mexico City.

Yearbook of International Organizations.

COMPENSATION. An international term in international law to make up for one's loss; in international trade levelling of debt by agreement theoretically conducted without resorting to money but by means of specific commodities, services rendered or raw materials in exchange for other commodities, services or raw materials. Variations of compensation trade are the English terms "barter" or "counter purchase", consisting in paying the debt by means of products manufactured on imported machinery (e.g. in exchange for textile machines–textiles).

COMPENSATION CHAMBERS. An international term for banking institutions performing exclusively clearing functions between banks as regards all kinds of liabilities, facilitating and legalizing non-cash turnovers. The staff of such chambers is composed of the plenipotentiaries of banks belonging to it. The first chambers were established in London in the mid-18th century.

COMPENSATORY FINANCING. A program of the IMF which offers loans to countries suffering temporary shortfalls in income due to temporary falls in prices of commodities
UN Chronicle, October. 1982, p. 46.

COMPETENCE. An international term for the range of authorization and power needed to arrive at solutions and decisions; in international law equivalent to jurisdiction of different attributes such as advisory competence, e.g. under art. 96 of the UN Charter conferred on the International Court of Justice; exclusive competence (cited in art. 15, item 8, of the Covenants of the League of Nations); domestic competence of state (cited in art. 2, item 7, of the UN Charter); territorial competence.

C

COMPETITION RULES IN THE EEC. A code of rules governing competition contained in arts. 85–89 of the ▷ Rome Treaty, 1957.

COMPIÈGNE. A city in northern France on the Oise River (1975 pop. 37,699). Historical place where Joan of Arc was captured by the Burgundians, 1430. On Nov. 11, 1918 at the forest at Compiègne on a railroad siding of the Paris-Brussels line in a parlor car of the commander of the French army, Marshal F. Foch, the signing of the surrender of Germany took place by the representatives of the armed forces of the Reich. There also, on June 22, 1940, France signed its surrender to the III Reich, after which the historic parlor car was transported to Germany, where in April 1945 it was destroyed upon Hitler's order. Earlier, on Aug. 30, 1944 Compiègne was liberated by the Allies.

CH. MANGIN. *Comment fini la guerre*, Paris. 1921.

COMPULSORY JURISDICTION. An international term, synonim of ▷ jus cogens, defined in Art. 36 of the ▷ International Court of Justice Statute. 47 UN Member States have accepted until 1985 the Compulsory Jurisdiction of the Court (1954–32; 1964–39; 1974–45).

About 160 bilateral and trilateral treaties ranging from commerce to consular relations involving at least 64 states contain clauses relating to the jurisdiction of the Court in contentious proceeding. About 87 multilateral treaties mostly universal or regional in scope, dealing with specific topics, ranging from copyright narcotics to refugees, refer to the Court for decision, in dispute concerning the application or interpretation of the treaties.

On Jan. 18, 1985 the USA which have accepted the compulsory jurisdiction of the Court informed the Registrar of the ICJ that it had decided not to participate in further Court proceedings in the case initiated by Nicaragua concerning military and paramilitary activities in and against Nicaragua. The UN Chronicle presented the case as follows:

While appearance before the Court by the Parties concerned is assumed, the absence of a party does not mean that the Court is therefore unable to act. Such a contingency is envisaged in Art. 53 of the Statute of the Court, by which the other party may call upon the Court to decide in favour of its claim. Before doing so, the Court has a duty to satisfy itself that the claim "is well founded in fact and law".

The proceedings, according to the United States announcement, "are a misuse of the Court for political purposes", and the Court lacks jurisdiction and competence over such a case.

The President of the Court was informed on Jan. 22 by the Agent of Nicaragua that his Government maintained its application and availed itself of the rights provided for in Art. 53 of the Court's Statute.

The Court fixed the following time-limits for written proceedings: memorial of Nicaragua, April 30, 1985; counter-memorial of the United States, May 31. The subsequent procedure, including fixing of a date for oral proceedings, was reserved for a further decision. (*Press Release IC/432*).

The Court had ruled on Nov. 26 by 11 votes to one that it had jurisdiction in the case on the basis of either Art. 36 (i.e. compulsory jurisdiction) or the 1956 Treaty of Friendship, Commerce and Navigation between the United States and Nicaragua. (The Charter provides that, in the case of doubt, it is for the Court itself to decide whether it has jurisdiction, and that each member of the United Nations undertakes to comply with the decision of the Court.) The Court also ruled by unanimity that the present case was admissible (see *UN Chronicle* 1984, No. 9).

The United States said the decision was "contrary to law and fact". "The haste with which the Court proceeded to a judgement on these issues", the United States said "only adds to the impression that the Court is determined to find in favour of Nicaragua in this case". It said the conflict in Central America was not a narrow legal dispute; "it is an inherently political

problem that is not appropriate for judicial resolution." The Court was "never intended to resolve issues of collective security and self-defense".

The United States said "much of the evidence that would establish Nicaragua's aggression against its neighbours is of a highly sensitive intelligence character. We will not risk United States national security by presenting such sensitive material in public or before a Court that includes two judges from Warsaw Pact nations."

The United States said it was taking steps to clarify its acceptance of compulsory jurisdiction, to make explicit that cases of this nature were not proper for adjudication by the Court.

The Court, in provisional measures indicated in an Order on May 10, 1984, had ruled that Nicaragua's right to sovereignty and political independence should not be jeopardized by any military or paramilitary activities, and that the United States should cease restricting access to and from Nicaragua's ports, particularly through the laying of mines.

UN Chronicle, 1985, No. 1, pp. 8-9.

COMPULSORY LICENSING OF JOURNALISTS. ▷ Freedom of the press. ▷ Journalists Compulsory Licensing.

COMPUTATION CENTER, INTERNATIONAL. An organization est. in Rome in 1981 under the aegis of UNESCO, on the basis of a Convention, signed in Paris, on Dec. 6, 1951 which came into force on Nov. 28, 1961. The Center has a triple function: scientific research, education, consultative and computation service (art. 2).

UNTS, Vol. 425, p. 61.

COMPUTER LANGUAGES. An international term for various systems of programming computers such as ▷ ALGOL, ▷ COBOL, ▷ FORTRAN, ▷ IPL; ▷ Basic; ▷ PASCAL.

COMPUTERS. An international term for automatic calculating machines recording and processing coded information in sets of symbols of numbers, letters, or conventional signs. The first computer appeared in 1944 in the USA; included in international statistics in the 2nd half of the 20th century, they became one of the essential measurements of technological progress in particular countries. The electronic computer was first used in nuclear weapons in 1946 in the USA and in 1951 in the USSR. The dominant producer of computers in the world is the USA. American firms also dominate the West European market – IBM, Control Data, Honeywell – General Electric (in co-operation in France with Machines Bull, and in Italy with the computer division of Olivetti); and RCA which until the fall of 1971 (when it suspended production) co-operated with Siemens in the FRG and West Berlin. In the USA in mid-1971 68.6% of the installed computers were IBM equipment; in Europe 57%.

On May 6, 1971 the European Union published the so-called Chapman Report on European co-operation in the field of military and civilian computers, according to which:

"There is still a desire in Europe to retain independence from America – and not at all for chauvinistic or anti-American reasons. The true argument for gaining European control over our own market is as follows: if we do not do this, then: (a) the entire technique of management will become an appendage to the American system, for these are precisely American computers and American computer "language" will push us in this direction; (b) dependence on the American computer industry and the use e.g. in education of an exclusively American system of programming – to all intents and purposes IBM – will lead to our losing control over the content of the education of youth."

At the end of 1972 the International Commission on Co-operation of the Socialist Countries in the field of electronic calculation technology at its session in Warsaw decided to create a standardized system of electronic calculating machines, in the CMEA states called RYAD (series in Russian) since it is based on a series of computers of increasing calculating capacity. Specialization of the CMEA countries in the production of computers was established Hungary – mini computer R-10; Bulgaria – R-20; Czechoslovakia – R-20A; Poland – a computer of medium size, R-30; GDR – the larger R-40; USSR – the largest, R-50 and R-60.

Organizations reg. with the UIA:

Computation Centre of the Equatorial African States. est. 1959, Brazzaville.

European Computer Manufacturers Association (ECMA), est. 1961, Geneva; unites Belgium, France, the FRG, G. Britain, Holland, Ireland, Italy, Sweden, Switzerland; publ. *ECMA Standards* and the yearbook, *Memento*.

International Association for Analogue Computation (ASIC), est. 1955, Brussels; unites scientists from 32 states.

International Computation Centre – Intergovernmental Bureau for Information, est. 1958 under the aegis of UNESCO, Rome; publ. *ICC Bulletin, ICC Newsletters* and *International Repertory of Computation on Laboratories*.

International Organization for the Study of Ancient Languages through Computers, Organisation international pour l'etude des langues anciens par ordinateur, est. 1975, Liège (Belgium).

The Applied Computer Research Center in Phoenix, USA, publ. 1980–1988, a yearbook: *Computer Literature Index*, and since 1988 a quarterly *Computer Literature Index*.

W.E. CLASON, *Elsevier's Dictionary of Computers, Automatic Control and Data Processing*, Amsterdam, 1971; A. JONES, *The Computer Revolution*, London, 1986; *Yearbook of International Organizations, 1986/87*; *The Europa Yearbook 1988. A World Survey*, Vol. I, London, 1988. D.M. HILDEBRANDT, *Computing Information Directory. A Comprehensive Guide to the Computing Literature*, Washington.

COMSAT, COMMERCIAL SATELLITE CORPORATION. An American telecommunication corporation est. in 1963 which officially represents the USA in the ▷ INTELSAT, where it plays the leading role as the main constructor and co-ordinator of telecommunication services of artificial earth satellites: Intelsat I – 1965, connecting the USA with Europe and S America; Intelsat II – 1967, link for the northern half of the globe from the Atlantic coast of Africa to Australia; Intelsat III – 1968, for the second half of the globe. The Control Center of COMSAT is in Washington, DC.

COMUNBANA. An official shortened Spanish commercial name for a multi-national company exporting bananas, Comercializadora Multinacional de Banana, est. in Mar. 1977, by the Union of Banana Exporting Countries, UPEB, affiliating the Dominican Republic, Guatemala, Honduras, Colombia, Costa Rica and Panama.

CONCENTRATION CAMPS. An international term, introduced at the end of 1900 by a proclamation of Lord Kitchener (1850–1916) during the South African War (1899–1902), establishing concentration camps for Boer families. Over 150,000 women and children were imprisoned and over 20,000 died. After World War I, Germany organized the first concentration camps in 1919 for Polish Silesian insurgents in Cottbus Sachsen. The first Nazi concentration camp was established in Mar. 1933 in Dachau and after in Sachsenhausen, Flossenburg, Buchenwald, Bergen-Belsen, Mauthausen, and Theresienstadt in Austria; and a women's camp in Ravensbrück, and during World War II in all countries occupied by the German army; condemned as a crime against Humanity by the Nuremberg Trial, 1946. ▷ Arolsen.

H. KÜHNRICH, *Der KZ-Staat, Rolle und Entwicklung der faschistischen Konzentrationslager 1933 bis 1945*, Berlin, 1960; O. WORMSER-MIGOT, *Le système concentrationnaire Nazi, 1933–1945*, Paris, 1968; E. KOGON, *Der SS-Staat. Das System der deutschen Konzentrationslager*, München, 1974; *Vorläufiges Verzeichnis der Konzentrationslager deren Aussenkommandos, sowie andere Haftstätten unter dem Reichsfuhrer-SS in Deutschland und deutsch besetzen Gebieten 1933–1945*, Arolsen, 1979; CZ. PILICHOWSKI, *Es Gibt keine Verjährung*, Warsaw, 1980; K. DUNIN-WASOWICZ, *Resistance in the Nazi Concentration Camps 1933–1945*, Warsaw, 1982.

CONCESSION. An international term for political or economical grants by a state to another state or aliens permitting activity which is not allowed for the general public because of legal restrictions, professional requirements, policy of protection of state interests or interested pressure groups; agreements granting foreign firms the right to exploit local natural resources in return for a specified equivalent, e.g. mining or oil concessions; political agreements e.g. ▷ Chinese concessions.

P. DEVELLE, *La concession en droit international public*, Paris, 1936; "Concession, agreements and nationalization", in: *American Journal of International Law*, Vol 52, 1958; K. STRUPP-SCHLOCHAUER, *Wörterbuch des Volkerrechts, Konzession*, Berlin, 1961, Vol. 2.

CONCILIATION. An international term for conciliatory proceedings, peaceful settlement of international disputes through setting up special conciliatory organs and courts. This practice saw its development in the early 20th century within the system of conciliatory agreements concluded by the USA (the so-called Bryan Treaties); the First Hague Convention of 1907, while recommending conciliation, did not define it. This was done by the General Act of 1928 (arts. 1–16). There are permanent or ad hoc conciliatory commissions established to study disputes and present governments with suggestions concerning their settlement. The parties in a dispute are not bound by these suggestions which, from the legal point of view, are merely recommendations. ▷ Inquiry and conciliation.

Dictionnaire de la terminologie de droit international, Paris, 1960; R.L. BLEDSOE, B.A. BOCZEK, *The International Law Dictionary*, Oxford, 1987.

CONCLAVE. In the Roman Catholic Church the precise meaning refers to a secluded place (*cum clave* – under key*) where in a period from 15 to 20 days after the death of a Pope the ▷ Cardinals College gathers for the purpose of electing a new Pope. Initially this selection was made by the Roman community, then by the clergy and people of Rome, sometimes with the intervention of secular rulers; from 1059 by virtue of the directive In nomine Domini of Nicholas II the election of the Pope was exclusively entrusted to the cardinals and precisely defined (the form of voting, the requirement of two-thirds of the votes) in the apostolic constitution *Licet de evitanda* of Alexander III in 1179. That form of the conclave, made more precise and perfected through the centuries, has lasted to the present time. Pius X in the constitution *Commissum nobis* (Jan, 1904) codified all legislation concerning the conclave. Pius XII in the constitution Vacantis Apostolici Sedis (Dec. 8, 1945) introduced the requirement of two-thirds plus 1 vote, and Paul VI in the constitution *Romano Pontifici eligendo* (Oct. 1, 1975) fixed the number of electors at up to 120

and, within the framework of the whole set of rules concerning the course of conclave established three possible forms for the selection of a Pope at a conclave by acclamation, by compromise, and the most frequently used – by voting. The place of the selection of the Pope is the Sistine Chapel.

CONCLUSUM. An international term for a diplomatic note summing up the negotiations held or a joint memorandum of the two sides listing the partial accords reached; usually with desiderata on further negotiations.

CONCORDAT. An international term for an agreement reached by the Apostolic See with other states; it defines the conditions under which the Church can exist and operate within a given state. Some states in concordat recognize Catholicism as the state religion; in Europe: Ireland, Italy to 1979. (Poland before the war), in America: Bolivia, Colombia, Costa Rica, the Dominican Republic, Ecuador, Guatemala, Haiti, Paraguay and Peru. Concordats signed since 1922 are published in *Acta Apostolicae Sedis*.

CONCORDE. An intercontinental supersonic passenger plane of British–French co-production (▷ BAC and ▷ SUD-Aviation) on the basis of the de Gaulle-Macmillan agreement of Nov. 29, 1962, first tested on Mar. 2, 1969 in Toulouse, introduced into regular air service of Air France and British Airways Jan. 21, 1976. Speed 2200 km/h. Length of plane 61.74 m, width of wings 25.56 m, height 11.32 m, weight 183.4 tons, range 6300 km, seats 100 passengers. The first readiness to purchase Concorde planes was announced by the American airline PANAM, June 5, 1963, but they withdrew from the agreement Jan. 31, 1973, like other American airlines under the influence of a campaign in the USA claiming that supersonic planes cause ecological damage, and for this reason the US government withheld credits for the construction of American supersonic planes. In 1973 it granted permission for Concorde planes to land in New York and Washington after long negotiations at the highest level. The lack of orders forced the governments of France and the UK on Nov. 2, 1976 to end production with an output of 16 Concordes. The cost of planning and constructing 16 planes was 32 billion French francs. British-French losses were estimated at 17.1 billion French francs (around 4 billion US dollars).

CONDITIO SINE QUA NON. *Latin* = "indispensable condition" An international term in international agreements for a preliminary condition agreed to by both parties, eg capitulatio of one party as conditio sine qua non of a truce.

CONDL. Collection of Nuclear Data Libraries, one of the information systems of the ▷ IAEA.

CONDOM. ▷ Population Council.

CONDOMINIUM. An international term used in the 19th century referring to the common administration of two or more powers over a common territory; e.g. Austria and Prussia over Schleswig 1864–66; France and the USA over the Pacific Islands Canton and Enderbury; France and the UK over the New Hebrides. According to the relation of Richard Nixon, the Soviet leader Leonid Brezhnev during the Summit in June 1973, in ▷ Camp David, suggested in private conversation a USA-USSR condominium "against the Chinese and without regard to the sensitivities of allies... We the Europeans, we the white must unite to control them

because in the future they are going to be a superpower". (Nixon relation to C.L. Sulzberger).

C.L. SULZBERGER, "How Brezhnev Offered to 'Split the World' With Nixon, in: *The New York Times*, July 27, 1987; R.L. BLEDSOE, B.A. BOCZEK, *The International Law Dictionary*, Oxford, 1987.

CONDOM RECOMMENDATION AND DISTRIBUTION, WHO SPECIAL, PROGRAM ON AIDS. WHO official recommendation, Dec. 1987 urging governments around the world to carefully consider the prevention of AIDS by condoms in school education programs and an obligatory distribution of condoms to prisoners to prevent infection, and initiating rehabilitation programs for intravenous drug-users. The WHO, stating that "the problem of AIDS in prison has received insufficient attention in many parts of the world", demanded, that prisoners with AIDS – like all other persons suffering from AIDS – should be shown "compassion", and even be allowed early release to "die in dignity and freedom"; condom distribution in prisons should be considered to help prevent HIV infection; prison staff should be informed and educated about HIV infection and AIDS.

(In 17 states of Western Europe according to official records the total prison pop, 1987 was approximately 270,000.)

WHO Press Release, No. 33, Dec. 14, 1987.

CONDOR LEGION. German name of armed intervention units of the III Reich operating on General Franco's side during the Civil War 1936–39 in Spain, partly as instruction personnel; chiefly in the air force: transport aircraft and bomber squadrons, which considerably destroyed Bilbao, Madrid and ▷ Guernica. Over 5500 German troops took part in operations of the Condor Legion; losses 420.

K.H. VÖLKER, *Die deutsche Luftwaffe 1933–1939*, Hamburg, 1967.

CONFEDERATION OR CONFEDERACY. An international term for a union of states in which aims are realized not through one common organ, as it is the case with federation, but through individual organs of authority of each of the states separately. Confederations were formed, i.a. in: USA 1776–87 and 1861–65; Switzerland 1291–1741 and 1815–65 and Germany 1815–65; in the Kingdom of Poland the term confederation referred to estates' unions (nobility, clergy, townsfolk) periodically united for attaining political or economic privileges. During World War II the immigrant governments of Czechoslovakia and Poland planned to establish an interstate confederation of Czechoslovakia and Poland after the war (▷ Czechoslovak–Polish Agreements 1940–43).

A. NEWINO, *The American States During and After the Revolution 1775–1785*, New York, 1924; E.M. COULTER, *The Confederate States of America 1861–1865, A History of the South*, New York, 1950; R.L. BLEDSOE, B.A. BOCZEK, *The International Law Dictionary*, Oxford, 1987.

CONFERENCE, INTERNATIONAL. ▷ Congresses and conferences international.

CONFEDERATION OF EUROPE. ▷ European Confederation.

CONFERENCE OF AMBASSADORS. An institution est. by the Big Powers in the 19th century composed of their ambassadors, meeting in a chosen capital city and framing decisions of international significance for summit conferences or taking international decisions as recommended by their governments. The following is a list of conferences of ambassadors held to consider problems in various parts of the world:

1815–18   Paris; following the Vienna Congress, 1815, the conference was active as a monitoring body for the execution of the peace treaty.

1830–2   London: attended by Austria, France, Prussia, Russia and the UK, to consider the question of Belgium.

1860–1   Paris: Syria
1869   Paris: Crete
1876–77   Constantinople: the Balkans
1880   Madrid: Morocco
1883   London: navigation on the Danube.
1884   Berlin: the Congo
1896   Istanbul: the Ottoman Empire.
1900   Peking: the Boxer rebellion.
1912–13   London: the Balkans.

After World War I the Conference was re-established in Jan., 1920 by the chief Allied Powers, France, Italy, Japan, the UK and the USA, as their permanent organ for assessment and joint decision-making, composed of ambassadors accredited to Paris. Since the USA did not ratify the Treaty of Versailles, the US ambassador attended as an observer. Its activities ceased formally in 1935, following the violation of part 5 of the Versailles Treaty by Germany. The provisions of the Conference of Ambassadors were published in the LN collection of treaties and international obligations. During World War II Conferences of the Ambassadors of the UK, USA and USSR arranged for summit meetings and councils of foreign ministers. A Conference of Ambassadors of the three Western Powers, with a representative of the government of the Federal Republic of Germany, has held sporadic meetings in Bonn since 1952.

R. OPIC, *Search for Peace Settlements*, London, 1951.

CONFERENCE OF NUCLEAR EXPERTS. An international organization, generally called the ▷ London Club.

CONFERENCE ON INTERNATIONAL ECONOMIC CO-OPERATION, CIEC, 1975–1977. Official name of the North-South Conference. See ▷ North-South.

CONFERENCE ON SECURITY AND CO-OPERATION IN EUROPE. The Conference, est. 1973, called in the beginning ▷ Helsinki Conference, 1973–75, adopted the ▷ Helsinki Final Act, 1975. On its basis have been held the ▷ Belgrade, 1977–1978 Conference, ▷ Madrid Conference, 1980–1983, the ▷ Stockholm Conference, 1984–1986, and the ▷ Vienna Conference, 1986, as well as special meetings ▷ Athens CSCE Jurist and Diplomats Meeting, 1984; ▷ Venice CSCE Meeting on Mediterranean, 1984: ▷ Ottawa CSCE Meeting on Human Rights, 1985, ▷ Budapest CSCE Cultural Meeting, 1986, ▷ Berne CSCE Meeting, 1986.
The Vienna CSCE follow-up conference took place from Nov. 4, 1986 to Nov. 20, 1987.

KEESING's *Record of World Events*, Feb. 1988.

CONFISCATION. An international term for appropriation by authority or forfeit to the public domain or for seizure of printed matter to prevent its dissemination. In international trade confiscation is a duty of a state when the smuggling of narcotics is detected.

CONFLICT LIMITATION INTERNATIONAL. An international term for UN resolutions and international management, bargaining and negotiations to limit a local, regional or global conflict.

L.N. RAGARAJAN, *The Limitation of Conflict: A Theory of Bargaining and Negotiation*, London, 1985.

CONFLICT OF LAWS. An international term of the private international law.

"Conflict of Laws", in: *The International Law Dictionary*, Oxford, 1987.

CONFUCIANISM. A religion and ideology of the feudal states of China, based on the philosophical and social doctrines of the Chinese thinker Confucius, Kung tu-tzu (c. 551–479 B.C.); official ideology under the Han dynasty in the 2nd century B.C. and under the Sung dynasty in the 12th century A.D.; denounced in China at the turn of 1973/74.

L.S. HSY, *The Political Philosophy of Confucianism*, London, 1975; J. CHING, *Confucianism and Christianity – A Comparative Study*, Tokyo-New York, 1978.

CONGO. Member of the UN. République Populaire du Congo, People's Republic of the Congo. In 1960–71 called Congo (Brazzaville) at the UN as distinguished from Congo (Kinshasa), presently Zaïre. State in Central Africa on the Atlantic. Bordering on Gabon, Cameroon, the Central African Republic, Zaïre and Angola. Area: 342,000 sq. km. Pop. 1988 est. 2,270,000 (1974 census: 1,300,120). Capital city: Brazzaville with 422,402 inhabitants 1980. GNP per capita 1986 US $1040. Currency: one CFA franc = 100 centimes. Official language: French. National Day: Aug. 15, Independence Day, 1960.
Member of UN since Sept. 20, 1960 and all UN specialized agencies except IAEA; member of OCAM, UDEAC and OAU. A signatory of the Yaoundé Conventions of 1963 and 1969, and of the Lomé Conventions of 1975 and 1980.
International relations: in 1885 frontier demarcated with Portuguese colony of Angola, also known as Portuguese Congo, and in 1887 with the Belgian Congo; in 1891 entire territory occupied by France, termed Central Congo, in 1910 incorporated into French Equatorial Africa; colonial status since 1946, when it became an overseas French territory with a parliament of its own and representatives in the French parliament. In Nov. 1958 became a republic within the French Community. Independent state since Aug. 15, 1960. In Dec. 1969 the revolutionary movement changed the name to the People's Republic of Congo. In May 1981 Congo signed a 20-year Treaty of Friendship and Co-operation with the Soviet Union.

A.M. WOIGRET, *Histoire et sociologie politique de la République de Congo*, Paris, 1963; S. AMIN, C. COQUERY, *Histoire Économique du Congo 1880–1968*, Paris, 1969; *Everyone's United Nations*, New York, 1979. *The Europa Year Book 1984. A World Survey*, Vol. II, pp. 1442–1451, London, 1984; B. URQUHART, *A Life in Peace and War*, New York, 1987.

CONGO (BRAZZAVILLE). Official name of Congo in the UN, 1960–71.

CONGO (KINSHASA). Official name of Zaïre in the UN, 1966–71.

CONGO (LEOPOLDVILLE). Official name of Zaïre, in the UN, 1960–66.

CONGO, PORTUGUESE. Colonial name of ▷ Angola.

CONGREGATIONALISTS. The followers of the oldest free Protestant church, recognizing no other higher authority; est. 1581 in Norfolk by Father Robert Brown; in the form of services conducted by the Congregation of the Faithful; persecuted by Elizabeth I, they emigrated to Holland and then to North America in 1620 as the Pilgrim Fathers; in 1891 organized in the International Congregationalist Council; from 1925 among the pioneers of the Ecumenical Movement. ▷ World Council of Churches. The Congregational Church is a founding member of the World Council of Churches.

Yearbook of International Organizations.

CONGREGATION FOR THE DOCTRINE OF THE FAITH. *Sacra Congregatio pro Doctrina Fidei.* The highest ranking Congregation of the Roman Curia whose task is to supervise the true purity of the faith in the Church and protect it from errors, earlier ▷ Congregation for the Holy Office, changed in the spirit of the recommendations of Vatican Council II by Paul VI in Motu proprio of Dec. 7, 1965. Decisions of CDF are made collegially and take effect only after ratification by the Pope.

CONGREGATION FOR THE EVANGELIZATION OF NATIONS. *Sacra Congregatio pro Gentium Evangelisatione.* One of the main Congregations of the ▷ Roman Curia, existing from 1622, missionary organization of the Church called Congregation for the Propagation of the Faith. The new constitution and name was received in 1967 in accordance with the recommendations of the Vatican Council II. Its aim is to initiate and co-ordinate the missionary activities of the Church in countries where there still exists no stabilized administration and hierarchy of the Roman Catholic Church.

CONGREGATION FOR THE HOLY OFFICE. *Congregatio Sancti Officii.* The supreme congregation in the Roman Curia, 1542–1965, responsible for the security of the purity of faith, morality and suppression of heresy, established by the constitution of July 21, 1542 by Pope Paul III as the Universal Congregation of ▷ Inquisition of which it became a synonym. Called *Sanctum officium* in the 19th century reformed by Pius X through Sapienti Consilio constitution. Transformed into ▷ Congregation for the Doctrine of the Faith in 1965.

CONGRESS. An international term used commonly with reference to international congresses. In both the Americas a common name of a bicameral parliament; introduced officially 1789 by the US Constitution on the initiative of the ▷ Continental Congress; in the 19th century adopted by the majority of Latin American constitutions.

R.U. SOEHLERT, J.B. SAYRE, *The United States Congress.* A Bilbiography, London, 1982; M.McCUBBINS, T. SULLIVAN, *Congress: The Structure and Policy*, Cambridge, 1987; D.B. FASCELL, "Congress and Arms Control", in: *Foreign Affairs*, Spring, 1987.

CONGRESSES AND CONFERENCES, INTERNATIONAL. An international term used for all kinds of international and interorganizational meetings, conferences, deliberations. In the 19th century it was the practice to give the name "congress" to political meetings, and "conference" – to meetings of scientists; in the 20th century the opposite; English speakers universally termed congresses as well as conferences "Congresses", which was reflected in a register of all meetings of this type kept since 1907 by the ▷ Union of International Associations (UIA) in Brussels, annually publishing *International Congress Calendar*. Due to the tremendous development of international co-operation, the number of international congresses and conferences grows each year and the task of the UIA is to co-ordinate the terms and provide technical assistance. The ▷ Arras Congress, 1435 and the ▷ Westphalia Peace, 1648 have been recognised as the first international congresses. After World War II, according to the Vienna formula, only those states have the right to participate in intergovernmental conferences which belong to the UN or to one of its specialized agencies. Reg. with the Secretariat besides the UIA is: International Association of Congress Centres, est. 1958, seat in Lausanne.

The main center of international conferences is New York with about 4000 such meetings held annually, followed by Geneva, Brussels and Vienna. Organization reg. with the UIA:
International Congresses and Convention Association, f. 1963, Amsterdam, Netherlands. Publ.: *ICCA News* (bi-monthly).

Yearbook of International Organizations, 1986/87; The Europa Yearbook 1968. A World Survey, Vol. I, London, 1986.

CONGRESS OF CENTRAL AMERICAN CONGRESSES. Congreso de los Congresos de Centroamerica. The parliament of Central America, consisting of delegates from Guatemala, Honduras, Costa Rica, Nicaragua and Salvador; since 1967 it has met once a year (in February, as a rule), alternating meeting sites. It has an advisory status to the Organization of Central American States. ODECA.

CONGRUA PORTIO. An international term of the Catholic Church for the calculation of incomes required for maintenance of central church offices in the Holy See, obtained either out of voluntary donations of worshippers or out of state contributions as provided for in a concordat with the state.

CONSENSUS. *Latin* = agreement. In international relations concord between states, preceding the working out of an international agreement or rule, according to the Roman law principle that *consensus facit legem* (concord makes law). The method of consensus was often adopted by the UN in the decades after 1960 when UN membership, enlarged by the group of the Third World states, lacked clear domination by any one group of states enjoying a two-thirds majority. This created the necessity of often adjusting different viewpoints and avoiding voting in order to protect positions of particular interest to one group which could be rejected by another group. Negotiations were extended until an unopposed wording was fixed. This sometimes led to a watering down of resolutions and to compromised positions, but it also facilitated the adoption of many decisions of basic significance to the development of general international law. In Dec., 1972, while the Helsinki Conference on Security and Co-operation in Europe was being prepared, it was accepted that "procedural decisions shall be taken on the basis of consensus", and that "once they have been taken, they shall not be altered otherwise than on the basis of consensus"; at the same time the following definition was approved.

"It is understood that the principle of consensus means the lack of any objection constituting an obstacle to the adoption of a resolution being under consideration."

The practice of seeking to reach decisions by consensus was considered irreplaceable in the present state of international relations by Amadou Mahtar M'Bow, Director-General of the United Nations Educational, Scientific and Cultural Organization (UNESCO).

"It is to the practice of consensus that we owe the adoption of resolutions as important as those of the sixth and seventh special sessions of the United Nations General Assembly, relating to the concept of the 'new international economic order.' This concept appears to be increasingly the focal point of the reflections and work of the various institutions of the United Nations system. Indeed, in recent years the search for a consensus has become in practice the habitual working method of the General Assembly, the Economic and Social Council, and other United Nations bodies, commissions and committees."

The same is true for the United Nations Conference on Trade and Development (UNCTAD) and the major international conferences held in recent times. The practice is also tending to become established in the deliberative organs of the specialized agencies: for example, it worked satisfactorily at the nineteenth session of the General Conference of UNESCO.

While the dictionary defines consensus as the "collective but not unanimous opinion of a number of persons", this term is used in the organizations of the United Nations system in a slightly different sense, and it is significant that it denotes both a process of negotiation and its result. What is being referred to is a practice designed to achieve the elaboration of a text by means of negotiation, and its adoption without taking a vote. The founders of the United Nations system adopted the view point of the traditional parliamentary system, based on the majority rule. The General Assembly reaches its decisions by a majority of the Members present and voting, except when it discusses the "important questions" listed in Article 18 (para. 2) of the United Nations Charter, which are the only ones to require a two-thirds majority. Other United Nations organs also observe the majority rule, although with the important exception of the Security Council, where there is not only the requirement of a specified majority (an affirmative vote by nine members out of 15) but also that of the affirmative vote of all the permanent members. The deliberative organs of the specialized agencies also make decisions by a majority, either simple or otherwise specified, depending on the case.

It was in 1964 – as a result, moreover, of chance circumstances – that consensus appeared in the United Nations as a deliberately sought-out method of work; at the time, it made it possible to avoid a crisis which would have been heavily fraught with consequences.

The nineteenth session of the General Assembly opened at a time when the conflict between member states over the financing of peace-keeping operations (operations in the Congo and Suez) had reached its height. Some states, in particular the United States, considered that the Assembly could make the financing of these operations the responsibility of all member states. In consequence, states which refused to pay their pro-rata contribution became liable to the provisions of art. 19 of the Charter, which lays down that a Member which is "in arrears in the payment of its financial contributions to the Organization shall have no vote in the General Assembly if the amount of its arrears equals or exceeds the amount of the contributions due from it for the preceding two full years".

On the other hand, other states, including the USSR and France, contested the obligatory nature of the contributions required from them to finance peace-keeping operations, hence the applicability of art. 19 in the case of arrears arising from a failure to pay these contributions.

The United States called for the application of art. 19, whereas the USSR threatened to withdraw if it were applied. In those circumstances, the only way of avoiding a crisis was to give up voting. At the opening meeting the Secretary-General, U Thant, therefore made the following statement:

"In view of the differences of opinion which have arisen among member states regarding the conduct of the nineteenth session of the General Assembly, I have been in consultation with several delegations for the past week with the sole purpose of avoiding a confrontation. In this connexion, I may mention that there is an understanding to the effect that issues other than those that can be disposed of without objection will not be raised while the general debate proceeds."

Thus by this procedure the Assembly settled a number of urgent questions on which it was essential that it should take a decision by voting (for example the adoption of the budget and the election of Council members). Decisions were taken after consultations, the results of which, read out by the President, were declared to be adopted where no opposition was manifested.

Born of the serious financial crisis which shook the United Nations between 1960 and 1965, the practice of consensus subsequently spread, on the one hand to bodies entrusted with difficult negotiations in the economic field – for instance UNCTAD – and on the other hand to bodies which manage funds constituted from voluntary contributions, such as the Governing Council of the United Nations Development Programme. At the first session of UNCTAD, in 1964, its Secretary-General, Raul Prebisch, said that:

"There is obviously no immediate practical purpose in adopting recommendations by a simple majority of the developing countries but without the favourable votes of the developed countries, when the execution of those recommendations depends on their acceptance by the latter."

Thus the way in which international assemblies operate can be distinguished from parliamentary methods, and more closely resembles the technique of diplomatic conferences. When the agenda contains an item whose importance and controversial nature justify an attempt to settle it by consensus, a discussion begins, which is rarely anything else than a series of monologues in which member states and groups of states recall their position. The draft resolutions submitted towards the end of the discussion may express positions which are frequently highly divergent. The next stage is that of negotiation. That may take very varied forms, ranging from small meetings held behind closed doors, without any record, to action by regional groups, which begin by trying each to achieve a common position internally, and then negotiate with the other groups through authorized representatives specially appointed for the purpose. Alongside regional groups, the so-called Group of 77 frequently plays a vital part, since in fact it consists of all the developing countries, i.e. at present more than 100, out of the 151 member states of the United Nations. Numerous questions are in fact settled by negotiations involving three participating bodies: the Group of 77, the group made up of industrial countries having a market economy (generally called the Western group, even though countries such as Japan, Australia and New Zealand are members of it), and the group made up of the socialist countries.

A technique frequently used is the "contact group", comprising representatives nominated by regional groups. Sometimes contact groups are open to any delegation wishing to join. Very frequently adoption is followed by statements by delegations, either in order to formulate reservations on secondary points or to give an interpretation of the text, in whole or in part. It is not rare to hear a delegation state that it falls in with the consensus from a desire for conciliation, but that if the text had been voted, it would have abstained. There is no doubt that statements of this kind may weaken the scope of the consensus.

While therefore it clearly differs in its results from unanimity, which presupposes the absence of any contrary opinion, consensus is still further removed from unanimity on account of the process by which it is reached. A unanimous vote implies to begin with an agreement on essentials, or at least the absence of deep divergences between the participants. It usually occurs after a regular discussion, and adoption or rejection of amendments. Consensus, on the other hand, implies negotiation, and exists only through negotiation. It is the result of patient efforts, reciprocal concessions, and compromises from positions which appear at the outset to be incompatible.

Is it possible to form an over-all judgement on the value and utility of the practice of consensus? In the present state of international relations it seems to me irreplaceable. It has admittedly its limitations. It is a process which is slow and difficult, which frequently turns back on itself, and is often exasperating for all those who have to take part in it or follow it, whether delegates, members of the Secretariat, or the press. In many cases it results – this is the very nature of compromise – in solutions which satisfy neither states which desire radical change, nor those which would prefer to abide by the status quo ante; it gives the minority a weight which it would not have if the issue had to be settled by a vote. It is not easy to strike a balance between the justified desire to reach an agreement, and the equally justified desire to avoid a situation in which the minority would have a virtual right of veto. It is here, moreover, that the consensus system finds its limits, since assuming that a small minority of powerful states is firmly opposed to any agreement on a text, a return to the voting procedure would make it possible to reach a decision which would be perfectly valid in law. But in any case, whatever its legal value, a decision opposed by even a few major powers or a substantial minority of states is more than likely, if not to remain a dead letter, at least not to take full effect.

When applied to the definition and adoption of the broad lines of a general policy, or of standard-setting texts, consensus also makes it possible to produce compromise texts which attract broader adherence than if they had been voted by a majority. Thus what counts in the process, over and above the result obtained, i.e. a kind of common denominator of the different positions concerned, is the recognition of the basic principle whereby today, in an international organization, any kind of decision-making, if it is to be effective, must be not the formal expression of a majority, but the result of a negotiation which safeguards basic principles, opens up new prospects and makes possible subsequent progress. During the 41st Session of the General Assembly the majority of issues was decided by consensus (159 : 314).

J.S. TEJA. "Expansion of the Security Council and its Consensus Procedure", in: *Netherlands International Law*, 1969, Vol. XVI; A.M. M'BOW, *De la concertation au consensus. L'UNESCO et la solidarité des nations*, Paris, 1979; J. STONE, *Conflict Through Consensus: United Nations Approaches to Aggression*, Baltimore, 1985.

CONSERVATION OF ARTISTIC WORKS. A subject of international co-operation. Organization reg. with UIA:

International Institute for Conservation of Historic and Artistic Works, f. 1950, London.

Yearbook of International Organizations.

CONSILIUM PRO LAICIS. The official name of the Council for the Laity created on Jan. 6, 1967 on the initiative of Vatican II by Pope John XXIII; reorganized by Pope Paul VI as *Pontificum Consilium pro Laicis*. Members of the Papal Council are mostly laity; their jurisdiction includes the mission of the laity in the Church as well as questions relating to the discipline of lay members as such.

CONSILIUM PRO PUBLICIS ECLESIAE. The official name from Mar. 18, 1967 of the reorganized Vatican secretariat of state to which are subordinated the papal nunciatures and all other diplomatic agencies of the Church State.

CONSISTORY. An international term for the Papal Consistory, the public or private council of cardinals under the leadership of the Pope discussing matters connected with management of Church government; or for the Consistory of bishops the ▷ Roman Curia; or the Consistory in Protestant churches – the executive organ of a synod, the leading administrative authority.

CONSOLAT DE MAR (*It.*) Name of the collection of medieval customary laws of the sea recorded in Barcelona in the 13th and 14th centuries in a book entitled *Libre del Consolat*; the source of the international law of the sea referred to in the Paris Declaration on the Sea of 1856. The first printed edition was published in the Catalan and Spanish languages in 1791 under the title *Código de las costumbres marítimas de Barcelona*.

Consolat de Mar, Roma, 1954; W. PREISER, "Consolat de Mar", in: *STRUPP-SCHLOCHAUER Wörterbuch des Völkerrechts*, Berlin, 1960, Vol. I, pp. 299–300.

CONSTANCE, LAKE OF. German Konstanz- or Boden-see. Lake in Central Europe, 67.6 km long, bordered by Austria, Switzerland and the FRG; area: 538.7 sq. km; subject of international agreement between Austria, and the FRG and Switzerland regulating the withdrawal of water from Lake Constance (with Final Protocol), signed in Berne, April 30, 1966.

"Each riparian State shall, in withdrawing water, endeavour to take due account of the legitimate interests of the other riparian States" (art. 1,b).

UNTS, Vol. 620, p. 198.

CONSTANTINOPLE. A former capital of the Byzantine Empire and of the Ottoman Empire to 1923, when Ankara became the new capital of Turkey. Occupied by the Allies 1918 to 1923. In 1930 denominated Istambul.

CONSTANTINOPLE CONVENTION, 1888. ▷ Suez Canal.

CONSTANTINOPLE PEACE TREATIES, 1833 AND 1879. Between the Ottoman Empire and Russia signed in Constantinople on June 26, 1833 and on Jan. 27, 1879.

Major Peace Treaties of Modern History, New York, 1967, Vol. II, pp. 943–945 and 999–1004.

CONSTANTINOPLE PEACE TREATY, 1913. A Treaty concluded by Albania, Bulgaria, Montenegro, Greece and Serbia with Turkey on Sept. 29, 1913 after the Balkan wars; introduced a new territorial division in the Balkans. On Nov. 14, 1913 Greece concluded a separate peace treaty with Turkey, demarcating a new frontier on the Maritza river.

CONSTELLATIONS. An international term for 88 star systems with boundaries agreed upon in 1922 by the International Astronomical Union; the object of standardized Latin nomenclature.

CONSTITUTION. A state's major legal document defining, i.a., its relation to the international community of states. After World War II a trend began to incorporate provisions of the United Nations Charter in one form or another in state constitutions. The same is true of the Universal Declaration of Human Rights and some other international conventions, e.g. on the duty to fight racism, discrimination of any kind, non-application of the statute of limitations to war crimes, etc.

J.A. PEASLEE, *Constitutions of Nations*, Vol. I, *Africa*, The Hague, 1965; Vol. 2, *Asia, Australia and Oceania*, 1966; Vol. 3, *Europe*, 1968; Vol. 4, *The Americas*, 1970; M. KAMMEN, *A Machine that Would Go Off Itself: The Constitution in American Culture*, New York, 1988.

CONSTITUTIONAL LAW. A subject of international law, of comparative studies and also a subject of disputes regarding its relation to international law.

CONSUETUDO EST SERVANDA. *Latin* "customs should be maintained". An international term for a tenet of international law which regards accepted customs as equally obligatory as international agreements (▷ *Pacta Sunt Servanda*).

CONSUL. One of the oldest international terms which in modern times describes a non-diplomatic representative of a state sent to another state in order to protect the interests of his state and its nationals; his tasks may be restricted to one or two fields: (economy, administration, law, commercial land, water and air transportation) in keeping with the ▷ Vienna Convention on Consular Relations of 1963. A separate consular institution, under Chapter III of the Convention, is the honorary consul.

W.E. BECKETTŁ, "Consular immunities", in: *The British Yearbook of International Law*, 1929; A. VERDIER, *Manuel pratique des consulats*, Paris, 1946; G.H. STUART (ed.), *American Diplomatic and Consular Practice*, New York, 1952; G. ZAMPAGLIONE, *Manuele di Diritto Consolare*, Roma, 1958; C. LIBERA, "Le fondement juridique des privilèges et immunités consulaires", in: *Revue générale de droit international public*, 1959; H. OHLENDORF. H. LOTTIG, *Konsularrecht. Sammlung uber Recht und Befugnisse ausländischer Konsulen in der Bundesrepublik Deutschland, insbesondere in der Freien Hansestadt Hamburg*, 1960; A. MARESCO, *Las relaciones consulares*, Madrid, 1974.

CONSULAR AGENT. An international term for the lowest (fourth) rank of a consular representative, in accordance with the ▷ Vienna Convention on Consular Relations, 1963.

CONSULAR CORPS, CC. An international term for all consuls in a given city or country; headed by a dean.

CONSULAR HAVANA CONVENTION, 1928. A Convention on consular agents, prepared and adopted by the Sixth International Conference of American States in Havana on Apr. 20, 1928, ratified by Brazil, the Dominican Republic, Ecuador, Haiti, Colombia, Cuba, Mexico, Nicaragua, Panama, Peru, El Salvador, Uruguay and the USA. The Convention was not ratified by Argentina, Bolivia, Chile, Costa Rica, Guatemala, Honduras, Paraguay, Venezuela. It came into force on Sept. 30, 1929.

LNTS, Vol. 155, p. 289.

CONSULAR LATIN-AMERICAN CONVENTION 1911. A convention on consular functions, signed on July 18, 1911 in Caracas, ratified by governments of Bolivia, Ecuador, Colombia, Peru, and Venezuela. First multilateral convention in the history of consular law.

CONSULAR LAW. A branch of common international law; a set of legal rules and norms defining the status and functions of consular officers as well as the organizational forms of consular service. Codification of consular law, begun in the 19th century, resulted in the draft of the so-called Venice Convention of 1896; ▷ Consular Latin-American Convention 1911; regional, Pan-american ▷ Consular Havana Convention 1928 and in 1932 the ▷ Harvard Consular Research. The UN special conference for consular law adopted the ▷ Vienna Convention on Consular Relations of 1963, but it has not been ratified, i.a., by the Warsaw Pact states. The EEC countries prepared a Draft European Convention on Consular Functions in 1964.

CONSULAR VIENNA CONFERENCE, 1963. The UN Consular Conference held at the Neue Hofburg in Vienna, from Mar. 4 to Apr. 22, 1963, elaborated and adopted in accordance with UN General Assembly Res. 1685/XVI, the ▷ Vienna Convention on Consular Relations 1963, the Optional Protocol concerning Acquisition of Nationality, the Optional Protocol concerning the Compulsory Settlement of Disputes, the Final Act and three Resolutions annexed to the Act. The Governments of 92 states were represented at the Conference: Albania, Algeria, Argentina, Australia, Austria, Belgium, Brazil, Bulgaria, Burundi, Byelorussian SSR, Cambodia, Ceylon, Chad, Chile, China Republic (Taiwan), Colombia, Congo, Congo (Zaïre), Costa Rica, Cuba, Czechoslovakia, Denmark, the Dominican Republic, Ecuador, Ethiopia, Finland, France, the FRG, Ghana, Greece, Guinea, Honduras, Hungary, India, Indonesia, Iran, Iraq, Ireland, Israel, Italy, Japan, Jordan, Korea South, Kuwait, Laos, Lebanon, Liberia, Libya, Liechtenstein, Luxembourg, Madagascar, Malaya, Mali, Mexico, Mongolla, Morocco, the Netherlands, New Zealand, Nigeria, Norway, Pakistan, Panama, Peru, Philippines, Poland, Portugal, Romania, Rwanda, El Salvador, San Marino, Saudi Arabia, Sierra Leone, South Africa, Spain, Sweden, Switzerland, Syria, Thailand, Tunisia, Turkey, the UAR, the UK, Ukrainian SSR, Upper Volta (now Burkina Faso), Uruguay, the USSR, Vatican, Venezuela, Vietnam Republic and Yugoslavia.

UN Conference on Consular Relations, Official Records, Vols. I and II, New York, 1963/64.

CONSULTATION. An international term for seeking advice of other states or international organizations, e.g. the UN, in order to find a solution of an international problem, also offering mediatory services to conflicting parties. Within the UN system, advisory status is also conferred on specialized international non-governmental organizations or institutions, consultations are conducted, for the most part privately, at special conferences held under UN auspices or that of UN agencies.

CONSULTATIONS ON LAW QUESTIONS OF COMECON STATES. A permanent body of the Council of Mutual Economic Assistance established in Sept. 1970 aimed at regulating and codifying legal forms of economic and trade cooperation among member states. At the consultations states worked on international norms of public and private law (civil and commercial).

CONSUMERISM. An international term for the way of life in highly developed countries, subject of moral and philosophic disputes. Pope John Paul II, on April 14, 1980 in Turin, Italy, linked violence to consumerism:

"Men kill in homes, in offices, in universities ... Incidents of this type have happened before, but today it has become a system of countries of great technical progress and wellbeing that foster what is usually called consumerism."

Osservatore Romano, April 15, 1980.

CONSUMER PROTECTION. An international term for governmental policies to ensure that goods produced by manufacturers are safe for use; subject of General Assembly Res. 39/248.

Guidelines for Consumer Protection
Following is the full text of General Assembly res. 248, approved without a vote on April 9, 1985 at the resumed thirty-ninth session, by which the Assembly adopted the Guidelines for Consumer Protection:
The General Assembly
Recalling Economic and Social Council resolution 1981/82 of 23 July, 1981, in which the Council requested the Secretary-General to continue consultations on consumer protection with a view to elaborating a set of general guidelines for consumer protection, taking particularly into account the needs of the developing countries.
Recalling further General Assembly resolution 38/147 of 19 December, 1983.
Noting Economic and Social Council resolution 1984/63 of 26 July 1984.
(1) Decides to adopt the guidelines for consumer protection annexed to the present resolution.
(2) Requests the Secretary-General to disseminate the guidelines to Governments and other interested parties.
(3) Requests all United Nations organizations that elaborate guidelines and related documents on specific areas relevant to consumer protection to distribute them to the appropriate bodies of individual States.
Guidelines for Consumer Protection
I. Objectives
(1) Taking into account the interests and needs of consumers in all countries, particularly those in developing countries, recognizing that consumers often face imbalances in economic terms, educational levels, and bargaining power, and bearing in mind that consumers should have the right of access to non-hazardous products, as well as of promoting just, equitable and sustainable economic and social development, these guidelines for consumer protection have the following objectives:
(a) To assist countries in achieving or maintaining adequate protection for their population as consumers.
(b) To facilitate production and distribution patterns responsive to the needs and desires of consumers.
(c) To encourage high levels of ethical conduct for those engaged in the production and distribution of goods and services to consumers.
(d) To assist countries in curbing abusive business practices by all enterprises at the national and international levels which adversely affect consumers.
(e) To facilitate the development of independent consumer groups.
(f) To further international co-operation in the field of consumer protection.
(g) To encourage the development of market conditions which provide consumers with greater choice at lower prices.
II. General principles
(2) Governments should develop, strengthen or maintain a strong consumer protection policy, taking into account the guidelines set out below. In so doing, each Government must set its own priorities for the protection of consumers in accordance with the economic and social circumstances of the country, and the needs of its population, and bearing in mind the costs and benefits of proposed measures.
(3) The legitimate needs which the guidelines are intended to meet are the following:
(a) The protection of consumers from hazards to their health and safety.
(b) The promotion and protection of the economic interests of consumers.
(c) Access of consumers to adequate information to enable them to make informed choices according to individual wishes and needs.
(d) Consumer education.
(e) Availability of effective consumer redress.

(f) Freedom to form consumer and other relevant groups or organizations and the opportunity of such organizations to present their views in decision-making processes affecting them.
(4) Governments should provide or maintain adequate infrastructure to develop, implement and monitor consumer protection policies. Special care should be taken to ensure that measures for consumer protection are implemented for the benefit of all sectors of the population, particularly the rural population.
(5) All enterprises should obey the relevant laws and regulations of the countries in which they do business. They should also conform to the appropriate provisions of international standards for consumer protection to which the competent authorities of the country in question have agreed. (Hereinafter references to international standards in the guidelines should be viewed in the context of this paragraph.)
(6) The potential positive role of universities and public and private enterprises in research should be considered when developing consumer protection policies.
III. Guidelines
(7) The following guidelines should apply both to home-produced goods and services and to imports.
(8) In applying any procedures or regulations for consumer protection, due regard should be given to ensuring that they do not become barriers to international trade and that they are consistent with international trade obligations.
A. Physical safety
(9) Governments should adopt or encourage the adoption of appropriate measures, including legal systems, safety regulations, national or international standards, voluntary standards and the maintenance of safety records to ensure that products are safe for either intended or normally foreseeable use.
(10) Appropriate policies should ensure that goods produced by manufacturers are safe for either intended or normally foreseeable use. Those responsible for bringing goods to the market, in particular suppliers, exporters, importers, retailers and the like (hereinafter referred to as distributors), should ensure that while in their care these goods are not rendered unsafe through improper handling or storage and that while in their care they do not become hazardous through improper handling or storage. Consumers should be instructed in the proper use of goods and should be informed of the risks involved in intended or normally foreseeable use. Vital safety information should be conveyed to consumers by internationally understandable symbols wherever possible.
(11) Appropriate policies should ensure that if manufacturers or distributors become aware of unforeseen hazards after products are placed on the market, they should notify the relevant authorities and, as appropriate, the public without delay. Governments should also consider ways of ensuring that consumers are properly informed of such hazards.
(12) Governments should, where appropriate, adopt policies under which, if a product is found to be seriously defective and/or to constitute a substantial and severe hazard even when properly used, manufacturers and/or distributors should recall it and replace or modify it, or substitute another product for it; if it is not possible to do this within a reasonable length of time, the consumer should be adequately compensated.
(B) Promotion and protection of consumers' economic interests
(13) Government policies should seek to enable consumers to obtain optimum benefit from their economic resources. They should also seek to achieve the goals of satisfactory production and performance standards, adequate distribution methods, fair business practices, informative marketing and effective protection against practices which could adversely affect the economic interests of consumers and the exercise of choice in the market-place.
(14) Governments should intensify their efforts to prevent practices which are damaging to the economic interests of consumers through ensuring that manufacturers, distributors and others involved in the provision of goods and services adhere to established laws and mandatory standards. Consumer organizations should be encouraged to monitor adverse practices, such as the adulteration of foods, false or misleading claims in marketing and service frauds.
(15) Governments should develop, strengthen or maintain, as the case may be, measures relating to the control

of restrictive and other abusive business practices which may be harmful to consumers, including means for the enforcement of such measures. In this connection, Governments should be guided by their commitment to the Set of Multilaterally Agreed Equitable Principles and Rules for the Control of Restrictive Business Practices adopted by the General Assembly in resolution 35/63 of 5 December 1980.

(16) Governments should adopt or maintain policies that make clear the responsibility of the producer to ensure that goods meet reasonable demands of durability, utility and reliability, and are suited to the purpose for which they are intended, and that the seller should see that these requirements are met. Similar policies should apply to the provision of services.

(17) Governments should encourage fair and effective competition in order to provide consumers with the greatest range of choice among products and services at the lowest cost.

(18) Governments should, where appropriate, see to it that manufacturers and/or retailers ensure adequate availability of reliable after-sales service and spare parts.

(19) Consumers should be protected from such contractual abuses as one-sided standard contracts, exclusion of essential rights in contracts, and unconscionable conditions of credit by sellers.

(20) Promotional marketing and sales practices should be guided by the principle of fair treatment of consumers and should meet legal requirements. This requires the provision of the information necessary to enable consumers to take informed and independent decisions, as well as measures to ensure that the information provided is accurate.

(21) Governments should encourage all concerned to participate in the free flow of accurate information on all aspects of consumer products.

(22) Governments should, within their own national context, encourage the formulation and implementation by business, in co-operation with consumer organizations, of codes of marketing and other business practices to ensure adequate consumer protection. Voluntary agreements may also be established jointly by business, consumer organizations and other interested parties. These codes should receive adequate publicity.

(23) Governments should regularly review legislation pertaining to weights and measures and assess the adequacy of the machinery for its enforcement.

(C) Standards for the safety and quality of consumer goods and services

(24) Governments should, as appropriate, formulate or promote the elaboration and implementation of standards, voluntary and other, at the national and international levels for the safety and quality of goods and services and give them appropriate publicity. National standards and regulations for product safety and quality should be reviewed from time to time, in order to ensure that they conform, where possible, to generally accepted international standards.

(25) Where a standard lower than the generally accepted international standard is being applied because of local economic conditions, every effort should be made to raise that standard as soon as possible.

(26) Governments should encourage and ensure the availability of facilities to test and certify the safety, quality and performance of essential consumer goods and services.

(D) Distribution facilities for essential consumer goods and services

(27) Governments should, where appropriate, consider:
(a) Adopting or maintaining policies to ensure the efficient distribution of goods and services to consumers; where appropriate, specific policies should be considered to ensure the distribution of essential goods and services where this distribution is endangered, as could be the case particularly in rural areas. Such policies could include assistance for the creation of adequate storage and retail facilities in rural centres, incentives for consumer self-help and better control of the conditions under which essential goods and services are provided in rural areas.
(b) Encouraging the establishment of consumer co-operatives and related trading activities, as well as information about them, especially in rural areas.

(E) Measures enabling consumers to obtain redress

(28) Governments should establish or maintain legal and/or administrative measures to enable consumers

or, as appropriate, relevant organizations to obtain redress through formal or informal procedures that are expeditious, fair, inexpensive and accessible. Such procedures should take particular account of the needs of low-income consumers.

(29) Governments should encourage all enterprises to resolve consumer disputes in a fair, expeditious and informal manner, and to establish voluntary mechanisms, including advisory services and informal complaints procedures, which can provide assistance to consumers.

(30) Information on available redress and other dispute-resolving procedures should be made available to consumers.

(F) Education and information programmes

(31) Governments should develop or encourage the development of general consumer education and information programmes, bearing in mind the cultural traditions of the people concerned. The aim of such programmes should be to enable people to act as discriminating consumers, capable of making an informed choice of goods and services, and conscious of their rights and responsibilities. In developing such programmes, special attention should be given to the needs of disadvantaged consumers, in both rural and urban areas, including low-income consumers and those with low or non-existent literacy levels.

(32) Consumer education should, where appropriate, become an integral part of the basic curriculum of the educational system, preferably as a component of existing subjects.

(33) Consumer education and information programmes should cover such important aspects of consumer protection as the following:
(a) Health, nutrition, prevention of food-borne diseases and food adulteration.
(b) Product hazards.
(c) Product labelling.
(d) Relevant legislation, how to obtain redress, and agencies and organizations for consumer protection.
(e) Information on weights and measures, prices, quality, credit conditions and availability of basic necessities; and
(f) As appropriate, pollution and environment.

(34) Governments should encourage consumer organizations and other interested groups, including the media, to undertake education and information programmes, particularly for the benefit of low-income consumer groups in rural and urban areas.

(35) Business should, where appropriate, undertake or participate in factual and relevant consumer education and information programmes.

(36) Bearing in mind the need to reach rural consumers and illiterate consumers, Governments should, as appropriate, develop or encourage the development of consumer information programmes in the mass media.

(37) Governments should organize or encourage training programmes for educators, mass media professionals and consumer advisers, to enable them to participate in carrying out consumer information and education programmes.

(G) Measures relating to specific areas

(38) In advancing consumer interests, particularly in developing countries, Governments should, where appropriate, give priority to areas of essential concern for the health of the consumer, such as food, water and pharmaceuticals. Policies should be adopted or maintained for product quality control, adequate and secure distribution facilities, standardized international labelling and information, as well as education and research programmes in these areas. Government guidelines in regard to specific areas should be developed in the context of the present document.

(39) *Food.* When formulating national policies and plans with regard to food, Governments should take into account the need of all consumers for food security and should support and, as far as possible adopt standards from the Food and Agriculture Organization of the United Nations and the World Health Organization Codex Alimentarius or, in their absence, other generally accepted international food standards. Governments should maintain, develop or improve food safety measures, including, *inter alia*, safety criteria, food standards and dietary requirements and effective monitoring, inspection and evaluation mechanisms.

(40) *Water.* Governments should, within the goals and targets set for the International Drinking Water Supply and Sanitation Decade, formulate, maintain or

strengthen national policies to improve the supply, distribution and quality of water for drinking. Due regard should be paid to the choice of appropriate levels of service, quality and technology, the need for education programmes and the importance of community participation.

(41) *Pharmaceuticals.* Governments should develop or maintain adequate standards, provisions and appropriate regulatory systems for ensuring the quality and appropriate use of pharmaceuticals through integrated national drug policies which could address, *inter alia*, procurement, distribution, production, licensing arrangements, registration systems and the availability of reliable information on pharmaceuticals. In so doing, Governments should take special account of the work and recommendations of the World Health Organization on pharmaceuticals. For relevant products the use of that organization's Certification Scheme on the Quality of Pharmaceuticals Products Moving in International Commerce and other international information systems on pharmaceuticals should be encouraged. Measures should also be taken, as appropriate, to promote the use of international non-proprietary names (INNs) for drugs, drawing on the work done by the World Health Organization.

(42) In addition to the priority areas indicated above, Governments should adopt appropriate measures in other areas, such as pesticides and chemicals in regard, where relevant, to their use, production and storage, taking into account such relevant health and environmental information as Governments may require producers to provide and include in the labelling of products.

IV. International co-operation

(43) Governments should, especially in a regional or subregional context:
(a) Develop, review, maintain or strengthen, as appropriate, mechanisms for the exchange of information on national policies and measures in the field of consumer protection.
(b) Co-operate or encourage co-operation in the implementation of consumer protection policies to achieve greater results within existing resources. Examples of such co-operation could be collaboration in the setting up or joint use of testing facilities, common testing procedures, exchange of consumer information and education programmes, joint training programmes and joint elaboration of regulations.
(c) Co-operate to improve the conditions under which essential goods are offered to consumers, giving due regard to both price and quality. Such co-operation could include joint procurement of essential goods, exchange of information on different procurement possibilities and agreements on regional product specifications.

(44) Governments should develop or strengthen information links regarding products which have been banned, withdrawn or severely restricted in order to enable other importing countries to protect themselves adequately against the harmful effects of such products.

(45) Governments should work to ensure that the quality of products, and information relating to such products, does not vary from country to country in a way that would have detrimental effects on consumers.

(46) Governments should work to ensure that policies and measures for consumer protection are implemented with due regard to their not becoming barriers to international trade, and that they are consistent with international trade obligations.

The consumer protection movement is presented by the Consumer Federation of America and the International Organization of Consumers Unions based in The Hague.

Organization reg. with the UIA:
International Organization of Consumer's Union, f. 1947, Rijswijk, Netherlands. Publ.: Newsletter.
UN Chronicle, No. 5, 1985; *Yearbook of International Organizations*, 1986/87; *The Europa Yearbook 1988. A World Survey*, Vol. I, London, 1988.

CONTADORA GROUP. The foreign ministers of Colombia, Mexico, Panama and Venezuela, who since their first meeting on the Panamian island Contadora in Jan. 1983 are seeking peaceful settlements to the regional conflicts of Central America. On July 17, 1983 the Presidents of Colombia, Mexico and Venezuela after a summit meeting in

Continental Congress Declaration of Rights and Grievances, 1774

Cancún, Mexico, proclaimed the Cancún Declaration as a general program for the countries of Central America that could lead, region-wide, to: effective control of the arms race, an end of arms traffic, the elimination of foreign advisers, the creation of demilitarized zones, prohibition of other forms of interference in the internal affairs of countries of the region.

The UN Secretary General J. Perez de Cuellar on Dec. 21, 1983 stated that the UN should give "the most honest support to the Contadora efforts." On Oct. 26, 1984 the UN General Assembly supported the peace efforts of the Contadora Group.

In Jan. 1984 in Panama City the foreign ministers of Nicaragua, El Salvador, Honduras, Guatemala and Costa Rica signed a preliminary agreement sponsored by the Contadora Group, on an inventory of each country's military strength and possibilities of eventual reduction to create a reasonable balance of power in the region. Another agreement was reached in Oct. 1984 also in Spain. On July 28, 1985, Argentina, Brazil, Peru and Uruguay formed a support group known as the Lima Group for the Contadora efforts, which since August 10, 1988 also includes Ecuador. On June 6, 1986 in Panama City the Contadora and Lima Groups elaborated a new peace proposal, rejected by Costa Rica and El Salvador. In September 1986 at the UN Hqs. both groups initiated a study of a peace proposal put forward by Mexico and an Action Plan of the President of Costa Rica Ricardo Arias, presented to the UN General Assembly, and discussed the Plan on Dec. 8, 1986 with US President R. Reagan. In March 1987 the US Senate approved the Costa Rican plan by 97 votes to one, and the Contadora and Lima Groups in a Buenos Aires meeting on April 13-16, 1987 supported the Plan. On October 13, 1987 President R. Arias was awarded the 1987 Nobel Peace Prize for his 'outstanding contribution to the possible return of stability and peace to a region long torn by strife and civil war'. A provisional 60 day cease fire agreement was concluded by Nicaragua's Sandinist government and the contras between April 12 and 15.

"Contadora: Peace Process in Central America" in: *UN Chronicle*, No. 3, 1984, pp. 9-12. Security Council reaffirms support for Contadora efforts in: *UN Chronicle, 1985*, No. 5, pp. 16-21; B.M. BAGLEY, *Contadora and the Diplomacy of Peace in Central America*, Boulder, Col., 1987; *SIPRI Yearbook 1987*, Oxford 1988, pp. 401-404; KEESING's *Record of World Events*, 1988.

CONTAINERS. An international term for transportation equipment, defined in the Customs Conventions of 1956 and 1972, capable of transporting cargo from a sender to a receiver. The containerization initiated by the USA during World War II was extended to sea, land and air transport and resulted in the construction of container ports and stations as well as pneumatic underground and ground-level lines for the transport of wheat, building materials, etc. A special kind are LASH Containers (Lighter-Aboard-Ship), loaded one on top of the other on large barge ships in the shape of a cigar box, which is then lowered into the water near the port of destination and makes its way there either under its own power or with the help of tugs. Subject of a Geneva Customs Convention on containers and a Protocol, signed on May 18, 1956 in Geneva, establishing conditions for the temporary importation of containers exempt from customs payments as well as import bans and restrictions, and also the technical conditions imposed on containers carrying cargo in transit; signatories of the Convention: Albania, Austria, Belgium, Bulgaria, the Byelorussian SSR, Czechoslovakia, Denmark, Finland, France, the FRG, Great Britain, Greece, Holland, Hungary, Iceland, Ireland, Italy, Luxembourg,

Norway, Poland, Portugal, Romania, Sweden, Switzerland, Spain, Turkey, the Ukrainian SSR, the USA and the USSR. The first ship with containers sailed the New York-Amsterdam route in 1966. In 1967 the European association of dockyard workers formed an international organization for the normalization of containers ▷ Intercontainer. In 1980 the number of containers in the world exceeded 2 million, of which 60% were the property of firms leasing containers.

Organizations reg. with the UIA:
Coordinating CMEA Centre for Container Transport, f. 1972, Moscow, USSR.
European Container Glass Federation, f. 1977, Brussels, Belgium.
European Container Manufacturers Committee, f. 1969, Brussels, Belgium.
European Glass Containers Manufacturers Committee, f. 1951, London, UK.
Joint Container Utilization CMEA Board for International Transport, f. 1974, Bucharest, Romania.
International Container Bureau, f. 1933, Paris, France. Publ.: Containers (quarterly).

Yearbook of International Organizations, 1986/87; *The Europa Yearbook 1988*, Vol. I, London, 1988. *A World Survey*.

CONTAINMENT DOCTRINE, 1947. Also called Kennan doctrine, since it was formulated in an article published in the American *Foreign Affairs* 1947, signed with the letter "X", later discovered to be the pseudonym of George Kennan, former counsellor to the US embassy in Moscow 1945 and later US ambassador to the USSR 1952-53. Its content:

"The leading principle of the foreign policy of the USA toward the USSR must be patient and long-calculated containment of Russian expansive tendencies."

"The sources of Soviet conduct", by Mr. X, in *Foreign Affairs*, July, 1947. T.L. DEIBEL, L. GADDIS (eds.) *Containment Concept and Policy*, New York, 1985; Containment: 40 Years Later, *in: Foreign Affairs*, Spring, 1987; G.K. KENNAN, Containment Then and Now, *in: Foreign Affairs*, Spring, 1987; D. ROBERTSON, *Guide to Modern Defense and Strategy*, Detroit, 1988.

CONTESTATORES. An international term for members of a social movement questioning the social order, protesting and demanding changes; the term used, i.a., for those priests, who after the Vatican II Council (▷ Ecumenical councils) in a number of countries called for more rapid and deeper reforms in the Church.

CONTINENTAL CONGRESS 1774-1789. The official name of the first American legislative organ in the period of breaking away from the Crown rule from Sept. 5, 1774 to the introduction of the US Constitution June 21, 1788. Formally ceased to exist when its functions were assumed by the first post-constitutional Congress, 1789. The Continental Congress proclaimed the ▷ United States Declaration of Independence, July 4, 1776.

W.C. FORD (ed.), *Journal of the Continental Congress*, Washington, DC, 1904-37, 34 Vols.; L. MONTROSS, *The Reluctant Rebels: the Story of the Continental Congress, 1774-1789*, New York, 1950.

CONTINENTAL CONGRESS DECLARATION OF RIGHTS AND GRIEVANCES, 1774. A Declaration accepted by the delegates to the First Continental Congress in Philadelphia on Oct. 14, 1774:

"Whereas, since the close of the last war, the British parliament, claiming a power of right to bind the people of America by statute in all cases whatsoever, hath, in some acts expressly imposed taxes on them, and in others, under various pretences, but in fact for the purpose of raising a revenue, hath imposed rates and duties payable in these colonies, established a board of

commissioners with unconstitutional powers, and extended the jurisdiction of courts of Admiralty not only for collecting the said duties, but for the trial of causes merely arising within the body of a county.

And whereas, in consequence of other statutes, judges who before held only estates at will in their offices, have been made dependent on the Crown alone for their salaries, and standing armies kept in times of peace.

And it has lately been resolved in Parliament, that by force of a statute made in the thirty-fifth year of the reign of king Henry the Eighth, colonists may be transported to England, and tried there upon accusations for treason and misprisions, or concealments of treasons committed in the colonies; and by a late statute, such trials have been directed in cases therein mentioned.

And whereas, in the last session of Parliament, three statutes were made ... (the Boston Port Act, the Massachusetts Government Act, the Administration of Justice Act), and another statute was then made (the Quebec Act) ... All which statutes are impolitic, unjust, and cruel, as well as unconstitutional, and most dangerous and destructive of American Rights.

And whereas, Assemblies have been frequently dissolved, contrary to the rights of the people, when they attempted to deliberate on grievances; and their dutiful, humble, loyal and reasonable petitions to the crown for redress, have been repeatedly treated with contempt, by His Majesty's ministers of state:

The good people of the several Colonies of New-Hampshire, Massachusetts-bay, Rhode-island and Providence plantations, Connecticut, New-York, New-Jersey, Pennsylvania, Newcastle Kent and Sussex on Delaware, Maryland, Virginia, North-Carolina, and South-Carolina, justly alarmed at these arbitrary proceedings of parliament and administration, have severally elected, constituted, and appointed deputies to meet, and sit in general Congress, in the city of Philadelphia, in order to obtain such establishment, as that their religion, laws, and liberties, may not be subverted: Whereupon the deputies so appointed being now assembled, in a full and free representation of these Colonies, taking into their most serious consideration the best means of attaining the ends aforesaid, do in the first place, as Englishmen their ancestors in like cases have usually done, for asserting and vindicating their rights and liberties, declare,

That the inhabitants of the English Colonies in North America, by the immutable laws of nature, the principles of the English constitution, and the several charters or compacts, have the following Rights:
Resolved, N.C.D.
1. That they are entitled to life, liberty, and property, and they have never ceded to any sovereign power whatever, a right to dispose of either without their consent.
2. That our ancestors, who first settled these colonies, were at the time of their emigration from the mother country, entitled to all the rights, liberties, and immunities of free and natural-born subjects within the realm of England.
3. That by such emigration they by no means forfeited, surrendered, or lost any of those rights, but that they were, and their descendants now are entitled to the exercise and enjoyment of all such of them, as their local and other circumstances enable them to exercise and enjoy.
4. That the foundation of English liberty, and of all free government, is a right in the people to participate in their legislative council: and as the English colonists are not represented, and from their local and other circumstances, cannot properly be represented in the British parliament, they are entitled to a free and exclusive power of legislation in their several provincial legislatures, where their right of representation can alone be preserved, in all cases of taxation and internal polity, subject only to the negative of their sovereign, in such manner as has been heretofore used and accustomed. But, from the necessity of the case, and a regard to the mutual interest of both countries, we cheerfully consent to the operation of such acts of the British parliament, as are bona fide restrained to the regulation of our external commerce, for the purpose of securing the commercial advantages of the whole empire to the mother country, and the commercial benefits of its respective members excluding every idea of taxation, internal or external, for raising a revenue on the subjects in America without their consent.

5. That the respective colonies are entitled to the common law of England, and more especially to the great and inestimable privilege of being tried by their peers of the vicinage, according to the course of that law.

6. That they are entitled to the benefit of such of the English statutes, as existed at the time of their colonization; and which they have, by experience, respectively found to be applicable to their several local and other circumstances.

7. That these, his majesty's colonies, are likewise entitled to all the immunities and privileges granted and confirmed to them by royal charters, or secured by their several codes of provisional laws.

8. That they have a right peaceably to assemble, consider of their grievances, and petition the King; and that all prosecutions, prohibitory proclamations, and commitments for the same, are illegal.

9. That the keeping of a Standing army in these colonies, in times of peace, without the consent of the legislature of that colony in which such army is kept, is against the law.

10. It is indispensably necessary to good government, and rendered essential by the English constitution, that the constituent branches of the legislature be independent of each other; that, therefore, the exercise of legislative power in several colonies, by a council appointed during pleasure, by the crown, is unconstitutional, dangerous, and destructive to the freedom of American legislation. All and each of which the aforesaid deputies, in behalf of themselves, and their constituents, do claim, demand, and insist on, as their indubitable rights and liberties; which cannot be legally taken from them, altered or abridged by any power whatever, without their own consent, by their representatives in their several provincial legislatures. In the course of our inquiry, we find many infringments and violations of the foregoing rights, which, from an ardent desire that harmony and mutual intercourse of affection and interest may be restored, we pass over for the present, and proceed to state such acts and measures as have been adopted since the last war, which demonstrate a system formed to enslave America."

W.C. FORD (ed.), *Journal of Continental Congress 1774–1789*, 34 Vols., Washington, DC. 1904–1937.

CONTINENTAL SHELF. An international term, defined by the Convention on the Continental Shelf, 1958, as follows:

"the seabed and subsoil of the submarine areas adjacent to the coast but outside the area of the territorial sea, to a depth of 200 metres or, beyond that limit, to where the depth of the superjacent waters admits of the exploitation of the natural resources of the said areas; the seabed and subsoil of similar submarine areas adjacent to the coast of islands" (art. 1).
"The Coastal State exercises over the Continental Shelf sovereign rights for the purpose of exploring it and exploiting its natural resources" (art. 2, p. 1).
"The rights of the coastal State over the Continental Shelf do not affect the legal status of the superjacent waters at high seas, or that of the airspace above those waters" (art. 3).
"Where the same Continental Shelf is adjacent to the territories of two or more States whose coasts are opposite each other, the boundary of the Continental Shelf, appertaining to such States, shall be determined by agreement between them. In the absence of agreement . . . the boundary is the median line, every point of which is equidistant from the nearest points of the baselines from which the breadth of the territorial sea is measured" (art 6, p. 1).

The Convention on the Continental Shelf was signed in Geneva on Apr. 29, 1958, by the governments of Afghanistan, Argentine, Australia, Bolivia, Byelorussia, Canada, Ceylon, Chile, China Republic (Taiwan), Colombia, Costa Rica, Cuba, Czechoslovakia, Denmark, the Dominican Republic, Ecuador, Finland, the FRG, Ghana, Guatemala, Haiti, Iceland, Indonesia, Iran, Ireland, Israel, Lebanon, Liberia, Nepal, the Netherlands, New Zealand, Pakistan, Panama, Peru, Poland, Portugal, Switzerland, Thailand, Tunisia, Ukraine, the UK, Uruguay, the USA, the

USSR, Venezuela and Yugoslavia; came into force on June10, 1964.
"In accordance with the provisions of art. 716 of the ▷ Sea Law Convention 1982, a Commission on the Limits of the Continental Shelf beyond 200 nautical miles shall be established within 18 months after the date of entry into force of this Convention. The Commission shall consist of 21 members who shall be experts in the field of geology, geophysics or hydrography, elected by States Parties to this Convention from among their nationals, having due regard to the need to ensure equitable geographical representation, who shall serve in their personal capacities."

A dispute concerning the delimitation of the continental shelf between Libya and Malta was presented 1982 by those two States to the International Court of Justice. The judgment took place on March 21, 1984.

The depth of continental shelf was proclaimed at 200 metres in 1985 by: Argentina, Australia, the Bahamas, Brazil, Canada, Colombia, Cuba, Cyprus, Denmark, Ecuador, Egypt, Fiji, Finland, France, E. Germany, W. Germany, Greece, Honduras, Italy, Ivory Coast, Liberia, Malaysia, Malta, Morocco, Nicaragua, Nigeria, Norway, Oman, Papua New Guinea, Portugal, Romania, S. Africa, Soviet Union, Sudan, Sweden, Syria, Thailand, Tonga, Trinidad and Tobago, UK, USA, Uruguay, Venezuela, N. Yemen, S. Yemen and Yugoslavia.

ICJ, *Case Concerning the Continental Shelf (Libyan Arab Jamahiriya-Malta) Judgment of 21 March 1984*, The Hague, 1984; KEESING's *Contemporary Archive*, November, 1985.

CONTINUITY OF STATES. An international term related to the principle of international law that the changes of constitutions or in government 'do not affect the existence of the state'.

R.L. BLEDSOE, B.A. BOCZEK, *The International Law Dictionary*, Oxford, UK, 1987.

CONTINUOUS VOYAGE ▷ Contraband of War.

CONTRABAND. An international term for trafficking, smuggling; also anything smuggled.

CONTRABAND CONVENTION, 1925. An antialcoholic convention signed by all Baltic States on Aug. 19, 1925, in Helsinki.

LNTS, Vol. 42, p. 73.

CONTRABAND OF WAR. An international term from the 19th century for illegal supply of goods covered by an embargo to a hostile state or group of states; subject of international treaties since Apr. 16, 1856, the date of the Paris Declaration on Maritime Law. A term of wartime law of the sea to describe secret transportation of goods during a wartime blockade that may help the enemy in waging war. In keeping with the international convention, ships flying the flag of a neutral state may carry everything apart from contraband of war; in fact, what is contraband of war and what is not is ruled on by the side that declared the war blockade and an embargo on specific materials, in accordance with what the London Conference of the Law of the Sea (1908–09) in its declaration recognized as the absolute contraband: supply of all kinds of military materials, starting with armaments and ending with uniforms; relative contraband: foodstuffs, gold, currency, clothing, fuels and informative materials; however, most raw materials are not considered contraband. This division was not recognized during World War I and II and the term contraband was expanded during World War II to include other material. The UK using blockade at sea against the

Axis states, issued to neutral states' ships that voluntarily submitted to inspection in specified sea ports appropriate certificates, called Navycert, certifying that they did not carry contraband of war, and thus that there were no grounds for confiscating the neutral ship.

J.B. MOORE, "La Contrebande de guerre", in: *Revue de droit international et de législation comparée*, No. 44, 1911; G.G. FITZMAURICE, "Some aspects of modern contraband control and the law of prize", in: *The British Yearbook of International Law*, 22/1945; A. VANDAUX, *Blockade und Gegengblockade. Handelspolitische Sicherung der Schweizerischen Ein-und Ausfuhr im zweiten Weltkrieg*, Zürich, 1948; *Continuous Voyage, Doctrine of, in:* R.L. BLEDSOE, B.A. BOCZEK, *The International Law Dictionary*, Oxford, 1987.

CONTRACT. An international term in civil law for a unanimous statement of the will of two or more parties to attain a specific legal effect.

CONTRAS. ▷ Nicaragua.

CONTRAT SOCIAL. *French* = "social agreement". An international term created by J.J. Rousseau (1712–78) in a work of that title whose first edition was burned in Geneva in 1762 as heretical.

CONTRE-LETTRE. French = "anti-letter". An international term for a confidential annex to a nonconfidential agreement, mainly commercial, changing or annulling one or more provisions of the agreement; in keeping with international law contre-lettre cannot be in conflict with the rights of third countries.

CONTRIBUTION AGREEMENT, 1919. An Agreement between the USA, Belgium, the British Empire, China, Cuba, France, Greece, Italy, Japan, Nicaragua, Panama, Poland, Portugal, Romania, the Serb-Croat-Slovene State, Siam and the Czecho-Slovak State, with regard to the contributions to the cost of liberation of the territories of the former Austro-Hungarian Monarchy, signed in Saint-Germain-en-Laye, Sept. 10, 1919;

"Poland, Romania, the Serb-Croat-Slovene State and the Czecho-Slovak State, as States to which territory of the former Austro-Hungarian Monarchy is transferred or States arising from the dismemberment of that Monarchy, severally agree to pay, as a contribution towards the expenses of liberating the said territories, sums not exceeding in the aggregate the equivalent of 1,500,000,000 francs gold, the gold franc be taken as of the weight and fineness of gold as enacted by law on Jan. 1, 1914" (art 1).
"The amount due as above by each State for liberation . . . shall be set off against the approved claims, if any, of these States for reparation" (art. 3).

On Dec. 8, 1919 a Declaration of the Allied and Associated Powers was signed at Paris, modifying arts. 4 and 5 concerning the issue of contribution bonds.

LNTS, Vol. 2, pp. 35 and 43.

CONTROL COUNCIL FOR GERMANY. "The highest authority for matters concerning the whole of Germany", formed by France, the UK, the USA and the USSR, according to the Declaration on the defeat of Germany. The powers were represented on the Council by their Supreme Commanders in Germany. The operation of the Council started on Aug. 30, 1945 and lasted until 20 Mar., 1948, when it was suspended. The tasks of the Council were determined in the Declaration on Control Procedure: the Co-ordination Committee and the Control Staff were subject to the Council; moreover in order to keep in touch with governments of other countries, chiefly those interested in the occupation of Germany, allied military missions of those governments were attached to the Control Council. The seat of the Council was Berlin W. 35, Potsdamerstr. 186. The rulings of the Council were published in the official gazette: *Journal Officiel du Conseil de Controle en Allemagne*, published in 4 languages: French, Russian and English, as well as (non-obligatory text) in German. Up to 1950 19 issues came out, the first on Oct. 29, 1945, the nineteenth on Aug. 31, 1948. Apart from those issues, there was Supplement No. 1, which contained a collection of documents concerning Germany's defeat and the setting up of the Council. In 1945–49 members of the Council were successive supreme commanders of occupational forces: on behalf of France General P. Koenig (1945–49) and (formally) A. François-Poncet (since 1949); on behalf of Great Britain Marshal L. Montgomery (1945–46), Marshal S. Douglas (1946–47) and General B.H. Robertson (since 1947); on behalf of the USA General D.D. Eisenhower (1945–46), General M.T. McNarney)1946–47), General L.D. Clay (1947–49) and (formally) J. McCloy (since 1949); on behalf of the USSR Marshal G.K. Zhukov (1945–46), Marshal V.D. Sokolovsky (1946–49) and General V.I.Tshuikov (since 1949). During the term of its operation, the Council examined 193 issues, 140 of which were approved unanimously. The elaboration of all current materials and of final drafts of resolutions was handled by the Co-ordination Committee, which supervised 10 directorates, divided into many departments and commissions: the political, general, economic, finance, communication, legal, press, reparations, transport, POWs and Displaced Persons directorates. On each level of the Council organization there was observed a system of elaboration used by representatives of the Four Powers.

The chairmanship in the Council and in each commission was alternated every month. The Chairman of the Council or of any of the commissions of the Council called and conducted meetings in the given month. After Mar. 20, 1948, in spite of formal rotation of Chairmen, no one exercised the right to call a Council meeting. The activity of the Council kept slackening from year to year. The last meeting of the Control Council for Germany was held on Mar. 20, 1948. The only sites in which representatives of the Four Powers have met since 1948 were: the Berlin Center of Air Security, responsible for the traffic of military and civilian planes, and the International Facility Office, responsible for passenger traffic. The agreement of the Four Powers on West Berlin of Aug., 1971, concluded in the building of the Control Council for Germany, actually closed the activities of the Four-Powers Council, however, the quadrilateral Berlin Center of Air Security still remained in operation as well as the Spandau Prison with Rudolf Hess (▷ Nuremberg War Criminals Trial 1945–46), which following his death in 1987 has been earmarked for demolition.

Journal Officiel du Conseil de Contrôle en Allemagne, Berlin 1945–1948; D. STAPPERT, "Die Allierte Kontrollbehörde in Deutschland", in: *Jahrbuch für Internationales und Ausländisches Öffentliches Recht*, 1948, pp. 139–159; E. OSMAŃCZYK, *Niemcy 1945–1950* (Germany 1945–1950), Warsaw, 1951.

CONTROL, INTERNATIONAL. An international term for an activity of an international organ specified in an international agreement aimed at finding out whether subjects of international law comply with the duties they assumed. International control is one of the most difficult problems connected with execution of treaties, pacts, conventions and also occurs in arbitration or trusteeship; a key issue of disarmament and de-nuclearization. In keeping with art. 2 of the UN Charter, states should "fulfill in good faith the obligations assumed by them." In concluding an agreement, a state observes its provisions due to the principle ▷ *pacta sunt servanta* and its own Constitution, which includes basic provisions for the binding character of international agreements. In concluding agreements, specific provisions included therein may provide for a system of control over their implementation, as e.g. the treaty on de-nuclearization of Latin America (▷ Tlatelolco Treaty), which recognized the need of an International Safeguard System necessary for peaceful utilization of nuclear energy. The means of control, are among others: information, reports periodically made by states, concerning the implementation of an agreement's provisions, field studies including inspections, or visitations made by organs of the states-parties (e.g. inspection of merchant vessels by naval ships aimed at eradicating slave trade in accordance with a treaty of 1862) or by international organs, but always performed with the consent of the state on the territory of which such studies are to be performed (e.g. the commissions of safeguarding the implementation of armistice and truce agreements in Korea of 1953 and in Indochina of 1954). Field studies are used in exceptional cases due to the fact that it is an inevitable violation of the sovereignty of the state concerned. The space age for the first time in the history of mankind gave an opportunity for organizing international control from satellites, both with regard to the Earth as well as with regard to the other celestial bodies.

N. KAASIK, *Le Contrôle en Droit International*, Paris, 1933; P. VERTHOUD, *Le Contrôle International de l'exécution des conventions collectives*, Paris, 1946; L. KOPPELMANAS, "Le contrôle international", in: *Recueil des Cours de l'Académie de Droit International*, 77/1950; J. STONE, *Legal Control of International conflict*, London, 1954; R.H. CORY Jr., "International inspections: from proposals to realization", in: *International Organization*, 13/1959; M. LACHS, *The Law of Outer Space. An Experience in Contemporary Law Making*, London, 1972.

CONVENTION. An international term for an international agreement, bi- or multilateral. Conventions may be open or closed to other states which have not participated in their preparation.

CONVENTIONAL ARMS. An international term for all arms used by military forces, excluding nuclear, chemical and biological weapons. At the end of the 1980's the modernization of the conventional arms by civilian and military high-technologies has sharply increased the range of conventional weapons such as close combat weapons, artillery, mines, helicopters and tanks. The most revolutionary innovation, presented since 1986 are according to SIPRI the fibre-optic guided missiles (▷ FCS-M and POLYPHEM).

The conventional arms control negotiations between NATO and the Warsaw Pact started in the 1970's in Stockholm and Vienna (▷ MBFR). In 1987 Poland initiated discussion on the possibility of disarmament in the field of conventional arms (▷ Jaruzelski Plan).

F. BARNABY, *Non-nuclear defence of Europe*, SIPRI, London, Philadelphia, 1984; *ISSS. The Military Balance 1986–1987*, London, 1986; R.B. KILLEBREW, *Conventional Defence and Total Deterrence Assessing NATO Strategies Options*, Wilmington, Del., 1986; *Conventional Weapons Technology*, in: *SIPRI Yearbook 1987*, Oxford, 1987; D. ROBERTSON, *Guide to Modern Defense and Strategy*, Detroit, 1988; *SIPRI Yearbook 1987*, Oxford, 1988, pp. 85–95.

CONVENTIONAL ARMS OGARKOV DOCTRINE, 1984. The opinion of the Soviet Marshal N.V. Ogarkov, published on May 9, 1984, that instead of a continuing nuclear statemate, another war is likely to be fought with enhanced conventional forces equipped with the newest technology. "You do not have to be a military man or a scientist to realize that a further build-up of nuclear weapons is becoming senseless." But the rapid changes in conventional arms, such as unmanned aircraft cruise missiles with conventional warheads and new electronic control systems increase sharply the destructive potential of conventional weapons, bringing them closer to weapons of mass destruction in terms of effectiveness. The sharply increased range of conventional weapons makes it possible to immediately extend active combat operations not just to the border regions but to the whole country's territory, which was not possible in past wars. The rapid growth of technology could produce "even more destructive and previously unknown types of weapons"; work on these new types of weapons is already in progress in a number of countries. "Their development is a reality of the very near future."

Krasnaya Zvezda, May 9, 1984; *The International Herald Tribune*, October 3, 1984; Zb. BRZEZINSKI, *Game Plan, How to Conduct the US-Soviet Contest*, Boston, 1987.

CONVENTIONAL STABILITY TALKS. Negotiations, replacing after 15 years the ▷ MBFR, started in Vienna on March 6, 1989.

CONVERGENCE, *Latin*: "convergentio", international term – controversial theories of automatic rapprochement of different economic systems such as socialism and capitalism under the influence of the same development in modern science and technology.

W.W. ROSTOW, *Stages of Economic Growth. A Non-Communist Manifesto*, New York, 1960.

CONVERTIBILITY. An international term for the free exchange of a local currency for foreign ones by private individuals, companies, or financial institutions without government control.

J. GOLD, *The International Monetary Fund's Concept of Convertibility*, Washington, DC, 1971.

CONVERTIBLE CURRENCY OR "HARD CURRENCY". An international term used in the UN system for any currency which may be exchanged for gold, silver or other currencies without restriction. Convertible currencies are based on sound, usually developed and industrialized economies as well as substantial holdings of international reserve assets (gold, US dollars, and SDRs). Unconvertible or "soft currencies" are usually only used locally in the countries of issue.

UN Chronicle, October, 1982, p. 46.

CONVICTS ▷ Transfer of Convicts.

CONVOY. An international term for a protective escort of a cargo carried on land or for an armed escort – warships and aircraft – protecting commercial vessels on seas and oceans during warfare or blockade. A subject of international legal disputes, especially on marine convoys of nonaligned, neutral states; not yet settled by an international convention guaranteeing free passage.

COOK ISLANDS. A group of islands in the South Pacific, south-east of Samoa, self-governing New Zealand overseas territory; area 234 sq. km, pop. 1981 census 17,227. Capital: Avarua on Ravotonga Island. A British protectorate since 1888; annexed by New Zealand on June 11, 1901; internal self-government since Aug. 4, 1965, in 'free association' with New Zealand. Member of three UN specialized agencies: FAO, ICAO and WHO.

Encyclopaedia of New Zealand, 3 Vols, Wellington, 1966; *The Europa Year Book 1984. A World Survey*, Vol. II, pp. 2136–2138, London, 1984; J. PAXTON (ed), *The Statesman's Yearbook 1987–88*, London, 1987.

COOLIDGE DOCTRINE, 1922. International.
term – an interventionist principle formulated against the ▷ Calvo doctrine by the President of the USA, C. Coolidge (1872–1933), in a speech to Congress April 25, 1922:

"It is ... well established that our Government has certain rights over and certain duties toward our own citizens and their property, wherever they may be located. The person and the property of a citizen are a part of the general domain of the nation, even when abroad."

J.W. GANTENBEIN (ed.), *The Evolution of our Latinoamerican Policy, A Documentary Record*, New York, 1950.

CO-OPERATION COUNCIL FOR THE ARAB STATES OF THE GULF. An intergovernmental
institution, called the Gulf Co-operation Council, GCC. est. on May 25, 1981 by Bahrain, Kuwait, Oman, Qatar, Saudi Arabia and the United Arab Emirates.

The Europa Year Book 1984. A World Survey, Vol. I, p. 125, London, 1984.

CO-OPERATION INTERNATIONAL YEAR, 1965. In 1961 the premier of India, J. Nehru, came
before the UN General Assembly with the idea of organizing an international year of co-operation justifying it by the fact that:

"little is known and little is said about existing international co-operation, while much is said about each conflict, and so the opinion prevails in the world that conflicts predominate and that we live on a volcano. It is true that we live in a world of conflicts, but without doubt simultaneously the co-operation of nations and peoples is continually growing."

The UN General Assembly, Res. 1907/XVIII, unanimously resolved to proclaim 1965 as the International Year of Co-operation for the purpose of spreading knowledge of the dimensions and significance of everyday co-operation in the common interest of humanity. The Assembly on Dec. 7, 1966 with appreciation accepted the report on the course of the year.

UN Yearbook 1961–66.

CO-OPERATION OF STATES. A subject of
international law. A Declaration on Principles of International Law concerning Friendly Relations and Co-operation Among States, adopted Oct. 24, 1970 by the UN General Assembly provides that: "States have the duty to co-operate with one another irrespective of the differences in their political, economic and social systems" and specifies principles and duties to that end.

UN Yearbook 1970.

CO-OPERATIVISM. An international term for a
social-economic movement initiated in the 19th century, developed on a world scale in the 20th century; organizes consumers and producers co-operatives, called work co-operatives. The UN General Assembly emphasized in Res. 2479/XXIII of Dec. 20, 1968 the highly beneficial role of the co-operative movement in economic and social development.
Organizations reg. with the UIA:

Co-operative Alliance, f. 1895, London; regional offices in Delhi and Moshi (Tanzania), permanent representative to the UN in New York; Consultative Status UNESCO, ECOSOC, FAO, ILO, IAEA, UNIDO and UNICEF; in 1972 it was associated in 59 countries with 268 million co-operative members, 132 million of which in Europe, about 80 million in Asia, about 53 million in America, 1.4 million in Oceania and 1 million in Africa. In Europe, the biggest number of co-operative members was in the USSR – 58 million, in the UK – 12.5 million, Romania – 9 million, Poland – 8.2 million, France – 5.4 million, Italy – 4.9 million, Hungary – 3.6 million, Sweden – 2.9 million, Czechoslovakia – 2.6 million, Austria – 2.1 million. Consumers co-operatives made up for 42% of all cooperatives, followed by credit, agricultural, work, craftsman, housing, fisheries and various other co-operatives. It organizes Congresses, at one of which in 1972 for the first time the problem of ▷ multi-national corporations was debated; other topics discussed were: the attitude of co-operativism to supranational economic communities and the role of the international co-operative movement in the Development Decade. Publ. *International Co-operation, Review of International Banks and Finance Institutions, Directory of Co-operative Colleges, Schools and University Institutes*, and others.

European Community of Consumers Co-operatives, EURO-COOP, f. 1957, Brussels.
International Raiffeisen Union, f. 1968, Neuwied, FRG.
International Co-operative Alliance, f. 1986, Geneva, Switzerland. Publ. Review of International Co-operations (quarterly).
International Co-operative Women's Guild, f. 1921, Vienna.
Organization of the Co-operatives of America, f. 1963, San Juan de Puerto Rico

Yearbook of International Organizations 1986/87; The Europa Yearbook 1988. A World Survey, Vol. I, London, 1988.

COORDINATING COMMITTEE CONTROLLING EAST–WEST TRADE.▷ COCOM and
CHINCOM.

COPAN. The Maya site of Copan at the eastern tip
of Honduras, included in the ▷ World Heritage UNESCO List; examples of the religious architecture of the Maya civilization.

World Cultural Heritage, UNESCO Information Bulletin, No. 18, May 1982.

COPENHAGEN. The capital of Denmark 1986
pop. 626,889, metropolitan area: 1,351,999, since 1443, built on East Sjaelland and North Amager islands and on the Øresund. Occupied by Nazi Germany 1940–45. Seat of 37 international organizations reg. with the UIA. Seat of the intergovernmental Baltic Maritime Conference.

The International Geographic Encyclopedia and Atlas, London, 1979, pp.180–181; *Yearbook of International Organizations*. J. PAXTON (ed), *The Statesman's Yearbook 1987–88*, London 1987.

COPENHAGEN MARITIME RADIO CONVENTION, 1948. The European Regional Convention
for the Maritime Mobile Radio Service (with ▷ Copenhagen Plan, statements, resolutions and recommendations), signed in Copenhagen on Sept. 17, 1948.

UNTS, Vol. 97, pp. 31–120.

COPENHAGEN PLAN, 1948. Provided for the
frequency division among radio stations in the European radiophonic zone; enclosure to the European Radiophonic Convention, signed on Sept. 15, 1948 in Copenhagen. It became effective, together with the Convention, on Mar. 15, 1950. A new division was elaborated in 1975 in Geneva and was enacted on Nov. 23, 1978, named the ▷ Geneva Plan 1978.

COPENHAGEN RULES, 1950. An international
term for rules of international commercial arbitration formulated by the International Law Association in Copenhagen 1950. The rules deal with the initiation of arbitration proceedings, the composition of the arbitral tribunal, the formal requirements for submission to arbitration, the place where the arbitration is to be held, and the procedure to be followed. The rules also concern the content and form of the award majority voting by the Tribunal, the period within which the Tribunal must give the award, the cost of arbitration, the secrecy to be observed by the arbitrators, the finality of the award, and possible revisions by the arbitrators of their award.

Report on the Forty Fourth Conference of the ILA, Copenhagen 1950; *Register of Texts of Conventions and other Instruments Concerning International Trade Law*, Vol. II, UN, New York, 1973.

COPERNICUS' PRINCIPLE. An international
term for a thesis stating that bad money drives out good, formulated in a work by Nicholas Copernicus entitled, *On the minting of money* [*Monetae cudendae ratio*], written in the years 1519–26 for Sigismund the Old. In England it was accepted and announced in a royal proclamation, 1560, and henceforth known as Gresham's law.

COPERNICUS YEAR, 1973. The 500th anniver-
sary of the birth of the Polish astronomer, Nicholas Copernicus, was celebrated worldwide under the aegis of UNESCO, as the International Copernicus Year. Main celebrations were held in Poland, under the patronage of the Polish Academy of Science. On Feb. 19, 1972 in UNESCO headquarters in Paris a scientific session was held. The Apr. 1973 issue of the 14-language periodical, *The UNESCO Courier*, was devoted to the anniversary of Copernicus.

COPESCO PLAN. A scheme worked out under
UNESCO auspices on the initiative of Peru to save the Peruvian pre-Colombian monuments of Machu Picchu, Cuzco, Puno and Desaguadero.

COPMEC. Committee of Small and Medium Sized
Commercial Enterprises of the EEC countries.

COPPER. One of the basic raw materials for metal-
lurgical industries and the subject of international co-operation and conventions. The first international agreement was in 1887; the first copper cartel was formed in 1935 by concerns of Western Europe and Canada, which concluded an agreement on exports limitation. After World War II copper mines were the main reason for conflicts in the Katanga province of the Congo, where the Belgian Union Minière du Haute Katanga operated. Copper was also at the root of a USA–Chile dispute in connection with the nationalization of American copper concerns in Chile, passed unanimously by the Chilean Congress on July 10, 1971. Leading producers: the USA, Chile, Zambia, the USSR, Canada, Congo, Peru, Mexico, Japan, Australia. Organizations reg. with the UIA:

International Copper Development Council, CIDEC, f. 1961, Geneva.
International Wrought Copper Council, f. 1953, London.
International Copper Research Association, ICRA, f. 1959, members are big companies: American Brass, American Metal Climax, American Smelting and Refining Corporation, Anaconda, Betty, Hochschild, Kennecott, Road Selection Trust; headquarters: New York and Geneva.
Intergovernmental Council of Copper Exporting Countries, CIPEC, f. June 7, 1967 in Lusaka by the governments of Chile, Peru, Zaïre and Zambia for protection of common interests; headquarters Lima.

Yearbook of International Organizations 1986/87; The Europa Yearbook 1988. A World Survey, Vol. I, London, 1988.

COPPERBELT. Name of a massive copper deposit in north-central Zambia, discovered after World War I; one of the richest mining regions in the world.

COPRODUCTION. An international term for a modern form of international economic co-operation developed especially after World War II within emergent economic regions; from about 1965 also between companies from different regions with differing social systems, e.g. coproduction in the car or film industry. Considered by UNCTAD to be an important factor in the development of Third World countries.

COPTIC CHURCH. One of the Eastern Christian churches, established in the 5th century in Egypt; doctrinal basis is Monophysitism, liturgical language–Coptic and Arabic; preserved many early Christian rites (e.g. baptism through immersion). There exist two independent Coptic Orthodox Patriarchists in Egypt and in Ethiopia. A small percentage of Coptic church believers remain in union with the Roman Catholic Church and are subject to the Latin Alexandrian Patriarch in Cairo.

R. STROTHMANN, *Die Koptische Kirche in der Neuzeit,* Berlin, 932, W.H. WORRELL, *A Short Account of the Copts,* London, 1945.

COPYLEFT. A public license enabling computer users to copy and distribute software free of usual copyright charges. The author of the Copyleft concept, Richard W. Stallman, a programmer at M.I.T. Artificial Intelligence Laboratory believes that "it is impossible to do anything without copying something that has come before" and that intellectual property protection imposes limits on human knowledge in the name of personal gain. Stallman's programs are subject to no such restrictions. The concept of free software raises considerable controversy.

J. MARKOFF, *One Man's Fight for Free Software, The New York Times,* January 11, 1989.

COPYRIGHT. The law governing the protection of intellectual property and the subject of international conventions. The first country to introduce copyright was England, 1709, where the so-called Queen Anne's Statute was passed and included provisions on the growth of culture by granting authors copyright of their printed works for a specified period of time. The US Constitution 1787 empowers Congress, 'to promote the progress of science and useful arts by securing for limited times to authors and inventors the exclusive right to their respective writing and discoveries. The first French Republican Constitution of Sept. 3, 1791 stated:

"Authors of any kind of written works, music composers, painters and drawing artists who make pictures and drawings, are to enjoy an exclusive lifelong right to sell their works, to put them for sale, to diffuse them throughout the territory of the Republic and to determine to whom they belong as a whole or in part."

The progress in domestic legislation in this matter did not solve the problem of international editorial and literary piracy in Europe and America in the 19th century. As late as Sept. 9, 1886, the First International Conference on Copyright in Berne drafted the first Convention on artistic and literary copyright, called the ▷ Berne Convention and established the International Association for the Protection of Literary and Artistic Works; the convention was modified and amended in 1893 in Paris, 1908 in Berlin, 1928 in Rome, 1948 in Brussels, 1961 in Rome and 1967 in Stockholm (▷ WIPO). In the international system of the League of Nations, the Institute of Intellectual Cooperation, established in 1929, acted as a patron to the Berne Convention. In the UN system this part is performed by UNESCO which established the Copyright Committee of Experts to prepare a Universal Convention on Copyright. After having held three sessions: 1947 and 1949 in Paris and in 1950 in Washington the Inter-Governmental Conference on Copyright was held in Geneva, 1952, adopted the ▷ Copyright Universal Convention and established the Inter-Governmental Committee for Copyright. The Geneva Convention came into force on Sept. 16, 1956; it guarantees citizens of other member states of the convention, on the basis of reciprocity, copyright equivalent to that granted to those states' nationals. The Universal Convention on Copyright was revised in Paris, July 24, 1971, and came into force on July 10, 1974; it introduced exclusive copyright also covering audio-visual means of reproduction (film, theater, radio, television). The Convention also determined principles of copyright expiration (▷ *Post mortem auctoris*).

In the 1980's television broadcasting by satellites created new copyright problems especially when emission and reception did not take place in the same state. The International Confederation of Societies of Authors and Composers, CISAC, at its meeting in Sydney in April 1987 adopted the following regulations: "The responsibility for granting the necessary licences to broadcast programmes is always that of the Society of the originating country. A relation should be established between the originating country and the originating organization".

"The originating organization is the natural or corporate person who decides what programmes the signals transmitted by him or under his responsibility shall carry".

From April 1986 the US is limiting trade preferences for developing countries that do not protect US intellectual property.

On the American continents only Brazil and Canada acceded to the Berne Convention of 1886. However, out of the regional ▷ Inter-american Copyright Conventions on Literary, Scientific and Artistic Works, signed in Montevideo (1889), Mexico (1902), Rio de Janeiro (1906) Buenos Aires (1910), Havana (1928) and Washington (1946) none proved to be successful. In 1976, 68 states were members of the 1952 Geneva Convention. Agreements in the area of copyright, in 1989, include:
the Rome Convention for the Protection of Performers, Producers of Phonograms and Broadcasting Organizations;
the Convention for the Protection of Producers of Phonograms Against Unauthorized Duplication of Their Phonograms;
the Convention Relating to Distribution of Programs Carrying Signals Transmitted by Satellite; and six Inter-American Copyright Conventions.

There is a periodical devoted to copyright – *Inter-auteur.* Since 1956 continuing documentation is collected by UNESCO, in Copyright Law and Treaties of the World. Since Jan. 1974 the UNESCO Information Center for Copyright publishes the *Bulletin du Centre d'information sur le droit d'auteur.* Organizations reg. with the UIA:

Intergovernmental Copyright Committee, f. 1952, Paris, under the auspices of UNESCO.
International Bureau for Mechanical Reproduction, f. 1929, Paris;
International Conference of Societies of Authors and Composers, f. 1926, Paris.

International Copyright Society, f. 1954, Paris, to study the development of copyright. Consultative Status UNESCO.
International Federation of Societies of Authors and Composers, f. 1937, Havana.
International Literary and Artistic Association, f. 1878, Paris. Consultative status UNESCO.
International Union for the Protection of Literary and Artistic Works, est. 1886, Geneva, operates the International Bureau for the Protection of Industrial, Literary and Artistic Property (▷ WIPO), in contact with UNESCO. Publ. *Droit d'Auteur.*

UN Bulletin, September 15, 1952, pp. 361–362; D. DAVIES, *The Copyright Act 1956,* London, 1956; *World Copyright Encyclopaedia,* 4 Vols., Leiden, 1956, Supplement 1959.

COPYRIGHT OF THE UN PUBLICATIONS. The majority of United Nations documentation is in the public domain, only some publications are copyrighted by the UN. In these cases there may be obligatory royalty payment due to the Organization and a written permission for any extensive reproduction of United Nations materials, in hardcopy, microfiche or databases format, should be obtained from the Secretary, Publications Board, United Nations, New York, N.Y. 10017.

United Nations Publications, 1988, p. 4.

COPYRIGHT UNIVERSAL CONVENTION, 1952. A Convention signed in Geneva on Sept. 6, 1952, by the governments of Andorra, Argentina, Australia, Belgium, Brazil, Canada, Chile, Cuba, Denmark, Finland, France, the GDR, Guatemala, Haiti, Honduras, India, Ireland, Israel, Italy, Japan, Liberia, Luxembourg, Mexico, Monaco, Nicaragua, Norway, the Netherlands, Peru, Portugal, El Salvador, San Marino, Spain, Sweden, Switzerland, the UK, Uruguay, the USA, Vatican and Yugoslavia. Came into force with three Protocols on Sept. 16, 1955.

The texts of the main Articles are as follows:

"The Contracting States,
Moved by the desire to assure in all countries copyright protection of literary, scientific and artistic works.
Convinced that a system of copyright protection appropriate to all nations of the world and expressed in a universal convention, additional to, and without impairing international systems already in force, will ensure respect for the rights of the individual and encourage the development of literature, the sciences and the arts,
Persuaded that such a universal copyright system will facilitate a wider dissemination of works of the human mind and increase international understanding,
Have agreed as follows:
Art. I. Each Contracting State undertakes to provide for the adequate and effective protection of the rights of authors and other copyright proprietors in literary, scientific and artistic works, including writings, musical, dramatic and cinematographic works, and paintings, engravings and sculpture.
Art. II.(1) Published works of nationals of any Contracting State and works first published in that State shall enjoy in each other Contracting State the same protection as that other State accords to works of its nationals first published in its own territory.
(2) Unpublished works of nationals of each Contracting State shall enjoy in each other Contracting State the same protection as that other State accords to unpublished works of its own nationals.
(3) For the purpose of this Convention any Contracting State may, by domestic legislation, assimilate to its own nationals any person domiciled in that State.
Art. III.(1) Any Contracting State, which, under its domestic law, requires as a condition of copyright, compliance with formalities such as deposit, registration, notice, notarial certificates, payment of fees or manufacture of publication in that contracting State, shall regard these requirements as satisfied with respect to all works protected in accordance with this Convention and first published outside its territory and the author of which is not one of its nationals, if from the

time of the first publication all the copies of the work published with the authority of the author or other copyright proprietor bear the symbol C accompanied by the name of the copyright proprietor and the year of first publication placed in such manner and location as to give reasonable notice of claim of copyright.
(2) The provisions of paragraph 1 of this article shall not preclude any Contracting State from requiring formalities or other conditions for the acquisition and enjoyment of copyright in respect of works first published in its territory or works of its nationals wherever published.
(3) The provisions of paragraph 1 of this article shall not preclude any Contracting State from providing that a person seeking judicial relief must, in bringing the action, comply with procedural requirements, such as that the complainant must appear through domestic counsel or that the complainant must deposit with the court or an administrative office or both, a copy of the work involved in the litigation; provided that failure to comply with such requirements shall not effect the validity of the copyright, nor shall any such requirement be imposed upon a national of another Contracting State if such requirement is not imposed on nationals of the State in which protection is claimed.
(4) In each Contracting State there shall be legal means of protecting without formalities the unpublished works of nationals of other Contracting States.
(5) If a Contracting State grants protection for more than one term of copyright and the first term is for a period longer than one of the minimum periods prescribed in article IV, such State shall not be required to comply with the provisions of paragraph 1 of this article III in respect of the second or any subsequent term of copyright.
Art. IV.(1) The duration of protection of a work shall be governed, in accordance with the provision of article II and this article, by the law of the Contracting State in which protection is claimed.
(2) The term of protection for works protected under this Convention shall not be less than the life of the author and 25 years after his death. However, any Contracting State which, on the effective date of this Convention in that State, has limited this term for certain classes of works to a period computed from the first publication of the work, shall be entitled to maintain these exceptions and to extend them to other classes of works. For all these classes the term of protection shall not be less than 25 years from the date of first publication.
Any Contracting State which, upon the effective date of this convention in that State, does not compute the term of protection upon the basis of the life of the author, shall be entitled to compute the term of protection from the date of the first publication of the work or from its registration prior to publication, as the case may be, provided the term of protection shall not be less than 25 years from the date of first publication or from its registration or from its registration prior to publication, as the case may be. If the legislation of a Contracting State grants two or more successive terms of protection, the duration of the first term shall not be less than one of the minimum periods specified above.
(3) The provisions of paragraph 2 of this article shall not apply to photographic works or to works of applied art; provided, however, that the term of protection in those Contracting States which protect photographic works, or works of applied art in so far as they are protected as artistic works, shall not be less than ten years for each of said classes of works.
(4) No Contracting State shall be obliged to grant protection to a work for a period longer than that fixed for the class of works to which the work in question belongs, in the case of unpublished works by the law of the Contracting State of which the author is a national, and in the case of published works by the law of the Contracting State in which the work has been first published.
For the purposes of the application of the preceding provision, if the law of any Contracting State grants two or more successive terms of protection, the period of protection of that State shall be considered to be the aggregate of those terms. However, if a specified work is not protected by such State during the second or any subsequent term for any reason, the other Contracting States shall not be obliged to protect it during the second or any subsequent term.
(5) For the purposes of the application of paragraph 4 of this article, the work of a national of a Contracting State, first published in a non-Contracting State, shall be treated as though first published in the Contracting State of which the author is a national.
(6) For the purposes of the application of paragraph 4 of this article, in case of simultaneous publication in two or more Contracting States, the work shall be treated as though first published in the State which affords the shortest term; any work published shall be considered as having been published simultaneously in said Contracting States.
Art. V.(1) Copyright shall include the exclusive right of the author to make, publish, and authorize the making and publication of translations of works protected under the Convention.
(2) However, any Contracting State may, by its domestic legislation, restrict the right of translation of writings, but only subject to the following provisions: If, after the expiration of a period of seven years from the date of the first publication of a writing, a translation of such writing has not been published in the national language or languages, as the case may be, of the Contracting State, by the owner of the right of translation or with his authorization, any national of such Contracting State may obtain a non-exclusive licence from the competent authority thereof to translate the work and publish the work so translated in any of the national languages in which it has not been published; provided that such national, in accordance with the procedure of the State concerned establishes either that he has requested, and been denied, authorization by the proprietor of the right to make and publish the translation, or that, after due diligence on his part, he was unable to find the owner of the right. A licence may also be granted on the same conditions if all previous editions of a translation in such language are out of point.
If the owner of the right of translation cannot be found, then the applicant for a licence shall send copies of his application to the publisher whose name appears on the work and, if the nationality of the owner of the right of translation is known, to the diplomatic or consular representative of the State of which such owner is a national, or to the organization which may have been designated by the government of that State. The licence shall not be granted before the expiration of a period of two months from the date of the dispatch of the copies of the application.
Due provision shall be made by domestic legislation to assure to the owner of the right of translation a compensation which is just and conforms to international standards, to assure payment and transmittal of such compensation, and to assure a correct translation of the work. The original title and the name of the author of the work shall be printed on all copies of the published translation. The licence shall be valid only for publication of the translation in the territory of the Contracting State where it has been applied for. Copies so published may be imported and sold in another Contracting State if one of the national languages of such other State is the same language as that into which the work has been so translated, and if the domestic law in such other State makes provision of such licences and does not prohibit such importation and sale. Where the foregoing conditions do not exist, the importation and sale of such copies in a Contracting State shall be governed by its domestic law and its agreements. The licence shall not be transferred by the licence.
The licence shall not be granted when the author has withdrawn from circulation all copies of the work.
Art. VI. 'Publication', as used in this Convention, means the reproduction in tangible form and the general distribution to the public of copies of a work from which it can be read or otherwise visually perceived.
Art. VII. This convention shall not apply to works or rights in works which, at the effective date of the Convention in a Contracting State where protection is claimed, are permanently in the public domain in the said Contracting State.
Art. VIII.(1) This Convention, which shall bear the date of September 6, 1952, shall be deposited with the Director-General of the United Nations Educational, Scientific and Cultural Organization and shall remain open for signature by all States for a period of 120 days after that date. It shall be subject to ratification or acceptance by the signatory States.
(2) Any State which has not signed this Convention may accede thereto."

In the United States the first Copyright Act adopted by Congress 1909, was revised in 1976 and put into force Jan. 1, 1978. The revised Copyright Act forbade unlimited photocopying.

UNTS, vol. 216, p. 132.

CORDILLERAS. Spanish = little string. International geographical term for any extensive group of mountains. In North and South America, the chain of mountains from Alaska to Nicaragua and from Panama to Cape Horn, called also Cordilleras de los Andes.

CORDOBA. A monetary unit of Nicaragua; one cordoba = 100 centavos; issued by the Banco Central de Nicaragua.

CORDON SANITAIRE. French "sanitary cordon". An international term accepted during the Congress of Vienna in 1815 to define the preventive measures which were to isolate France from the possibility of a return to Bonapartism or to the progressive forces of the French Revolution. This term appeared again at the Versailles Conference in 1919 after the victory in Russia of the October Revolution, when the neighbors of Soviet Russia were assigned the role of isolating her from the rest of the world.

CORFU. An island on the Ionian Sea. The Corfu Straits or Corfu Channel separate the island from the Greek and Albanian coasts. Area: 641 sq. km. Pop. 1971 census: 92,833. It is known for three international events: (1) proclamation of the Croatian and Slovenian Kriska declaration, June 20, 1917; (2) international Corfu incident examined by League of Nations involving slaying of five Italian officers, members of an international. Commission delimitating the Greek-Albanian border on Aug. 23, 1923, by Greek border guards; the Italian regime bombed, Aug. 29, and Aug. 31 occupied the island in retaliation; League of Nations Council persuaded Italy to evacuate Corfu; (3) Corfu Straits were the scene of international incident considered by the UN Security Council and International Court of Justice between Albania and Great Britain. A British warship collided with an Albanian mine on Oct. 22, 1946. Pronouncement in favour of Albania was made on Mar. 25, 1948.

Minutes of the XXVI Session of the Council of the League of Nations Geneva, 1923; A. LAWRENCE LOWEL, *The Corfu Crisis, the Council of the League of Nations and Corfu*, London, 1923; S. NICOGLU, *L'affaire de Corfou et la Société des Nations*, Paris, 1925; L. GARCIA ARIAS, "El primer caso ante el Tribunal Internacional de Justicia: El Caso del Canal Corfu", in: *Revista Española de Derecho Internacional*, No. 1, 1948, No. 2, 1949; R.J. WILHELM, "La réalisation du droit par la force ou la menace des armes, Considérations de la Cour internationale de Justice sur l'affaire du détroit de Corfou", in: *Schweizerisches Jahrbuch für Internationales Recht*, 1958.

CORFU DECLARATION 1917 ▷ Yugoslav Independence Declaration 1917.

CORINTH CANAL. A canal in Greece, 32 km long, and 6.4–12.9 km wide, transversing the Isthmus of Corinth, joins the Aegean Sea with the Ionian Sea; constructed 1881–93; during World War II occupied by the German army, which in withdrawing destroyed its installations; rebuilt 1948 and opened to international navigation.

E.C.R. HADFIELD, *Canals of the World*, London, 1964.

CORPORATE STATE MOVEMENT. An international term for a socio-economic policy recommending that professional groups, associating on equal footing employers and employees, embark upon joint development of the national economy; the Catholic corporate movement was propagated in the following encyclicals: Pope Leo XII's *Rerum Novarum* 1891 and Pope Pius XII's *Quadragesimo Anno* 1931; operated in Austria 1934–38; the total, Fascist corporate state was introduced by the Fascist regime in Italy 1923–38, Third Reich 1933–45; democratic corporate movement: from 1934 in Switzerland – Fribourg canton, from 1924 in Luxembourg.

B. MUSSOLINI, *Le Stato corporativo*, Roma, 1936.

CORPORATION. ▷ Transnational Corporations.

CORPUS. A place on the Argentine–Paraguay border on the river Parana 300 km from the border of Argentina with Brazil where a great Argentinian–Paraguayan hydroelectric project is located with a power of 2600 megawatts, 10,000 less than a Brazilian hydroelectric plant constructed on the same river on the Brazilian–Paraguayan border in ▷ Itaipú. The power of the hydroelectric plant Corpus is dependent on damming the waters of the Itapui, this became the subject of long Argentina–Brazil negotiations, terminating with an agreement in 1980.

CORPUS IURIS CANONICI. *Latin* = "collection of canonical laws". The name of the first sets of Church laws published from 1580, superseded in 1917 by *Codex Juris Canonici* ▷ Canon Law.

CORPUS IURIS CIVILIS. *Latin* = "a collection of civil laws". The name for a collection of Roman laws codified in the 6th century by emperor Justinian.

CORRECTION, INTERNATIONAL RIGHT OF. A subject of international agreement. The Convention on the International Right of Correction (of false or distorted news or reports) was signed in New York on 31 Mar. 1953 by the governments of Argentina, Chile, Ecuador, Egypt, El Salvador, Ethiopia, France, Guatemala, Paraguay and Peru. Accessions: Cuba (1954), the United Arab Republic (1955), Yugoslavia (1956) and Sierra Leone (1963); came into force on 24 Aug. 1962.

UNTS, vol. 435, p. 192.

CORROSION. A subject of international co-operation on the prevention of corrosion. Organizations reg. with the UIA:

European Federation of Corrosion, f. 1955, Paris with the task of conducting studies and research on prevention of corrosion, combines scientific institutions from Western Europe and Yugoslavia.
International Corrosion Committee of International Water Supply Association, IWSA, f. 1964, London.

Within the framework of the CMEA seven member states: Bulgaria, Czechoslovakia, the GDR, Poland, Romania, Hungary and the USSR initiated joint research in 1966 on the development of the theory of corrosion and protection of metals by means of metallic coating with the application of electrochemical and chemical methods.

Yearbook of International Organizations.

CORRUPTION. An international term for practices such as fraud, sale of offices, granting of public contracts and other grants by governmental institutions or international concerns to high officials in foreign countries for monetary awards with a view to political or financial benefits, in the latter case chiefly contracts for sales of arms. In 1976 affairs involving the American aviation companies Lockheed and Boeing were revealed by Senator F. Church's special US Senate commission. Known under several regional names: *bak-sheesh* in the Balkans and Middle East; *dash* in Africa; *pot de vin* in France; *soborno* in Spain, but *mordida* in Mexico; *bustarella* in Italy; *Schmiergeld* in German; *Vzyatka* in Russia.

R. WILLIAMS, *Political Corruption in Africa*, Aldershot, UK, 1987.

CORSICA. French island in the Mediterranean Sea, a department of Metropolitan France. Area: 8,700.5 sq. km. Population 289,842 (census 1975), 246,000 (census 1985). Principal towns: Bastio and Ajaccio. International relations: ceded by Genoa, 1768, to France. In 1794 in union with the British crown, recovered by Napoleon in 1796 and guaranteed as French possession 1815 by the Congress of Vienna. In World War II occupied by Italian and German troops from Nov. 1942 to Oct. 1943. In the 1980's two separatist organizations were outlawed following terrorist bombing: Front de liberation nationale de la Corse (FLNC) and Mouvement Corse pour l'autodétermination (MCA).
See also ▷ Mafia.

J. CHIARI, *Corsica Isle*, London, 1960.

COR UNUM. *Latin* = "one heart". The name of the Papal Council, *Pontificium consilium Cor Unum de Humana et Christiana Progresione Fovenda*, appointed in 1971 by Pope Paul VI, with the following tasks:

"co-ordination of initiatives of Catholic organizations serving the development of man; serving bishops and persons performing public functions; mediating through institutions of social welfare; caring for a just distribution of material values; maintaining contracts with separated brothers to carry out common aid activities; facilitating communication between Catholic organizations and international institutions; aiming at securing aid for development; serving through the Church with effective and rapid aid to people afflicted by natural calamities and disasters; undertaking and implementing special charitable activities conducted each time in response to a suggestion submitted by the Pope."

The Cor Unum has since 1971 co-ordinated the ▷ Catholic International Organizations.

COSA NOSTRA, LA. *Italian* = "our affair". An international term for the Sicilian-Neapolitan mafia which after World War I extended its influences to the United States and there assumed control of the trade in alcohol in the years of prohibition, 1920–33, and then narcotics, gambling casinos and some branches of industry and commerce. The object of investigations of special commissions of the US Senate, 1950–51 and 1958.
On the basis of the Racketeer-Influenced and Corrupt Organizations Act of 1970, the federal Grand Jury in Manhattan, on Nov. 19, 1986 and on March 13, 1987 convicted the heads of the mafia families of New York (Gambino, Genovese, Colombo, Lucchese and Bonnano) and dismantled the ruling council of La Cosa Nostra.

F. SONDERN, *Brotherhood of Evil: the Mafia*, New York, 1959. KEESING's *Record of World Events*, 1987.

COSMETOLOGY. A subject of international co-operation. Organization reg. with the UIA:

International Committee for Aesthetics and Cosmetology, CIDESCO, f. 1946, Brussels; organizer of annual CIDESCO Congresses.

Yearbook of International Organizations.

COSMONAUTS. A subject of international Agreement on Rescuing Cosmonauts, ratified unanimously by the UN General Assembly on Dec. 19, 1967 with Res. 2345/XXII and signed Apr. 22, 1968 in Moscow, London and Washington by the governments of the UK, USA, USSR. The agreement stipulates i.a. that in case of a forced landing of a cosmonaut or space vehicle the country which launched this vehicle or the Secretary-General of the UN should be immediately notified; it defines the procedures for rescuing cosmonauts on the open sea as well as for the return of the cosmonauts and space vehicles to the country of origin, and the settling of costs connected with this operation. The agreement took effect on Mar. 5, 1970, after having been ratified by 45 states, among them the USA and USSR.

UN Yearbook 1967, UN Monthly Chronicle No. 1, 1968 p. 20–24, No. 5, p. 60.

COSMOS. ▷ Outer Space.

COSMOVISION. A transmission to Earth by artificial communications satellites of television broadcasts through a so-called point-to-point system. The first intercontinental Cosmovision satellite broadcasts covered the Olympic Games, Mexico, 1968.

COSPAR. Committee for Space Research, created in 1958 by the International Council for the Unification of Science under the auspices of UNESCO, Paris. Reg. with the UIA.

Yearbook of International Organizations.

COSTA RICA. Member of the UN. República de Costa Rica. Republic of Costa Rica State in Central America, on the Caribbean Sea and Pacific Ocean. Area: 51,060 sq. km. Pop. in 1987: c. 2,781,000 (according to censuses: 1892 – 243,000; 1927 – 471,000; 1950 – 800,000; 1963 – 1,336,000; 1973 – 1,871,000). Capital: San José with 890,000 inhabitants 1983. GNP per capita in 1987: US $1610. Currency one colone = 100 centimes. Official language: Spanish. National Day: Sept. 15, Independence Day, 1821.
Founding member of the League of Nations, 1919–39. Founding member of the UN on Oct. 24, 1945 and of all UN special organizations with the exception of IMCO and GATT. Member of OAS. Member of OCAS and of the Common Market of Central America. Signatory of the Tlatelolco Treaty.
International relations: from 1564 to 1821 a Spanish colony; independence was proclaimed on Sept. 15, 1821; from 1823 to 1838 in the Federation of Central America. The proclamation of the Republic occurred 10 years after the dissolution of the Federation, Aug. 30, 1848. In 1858 at war with Nicaragua. During World War I and II on the side of the USA. In 1948–49 in conflict with Nicaragua, ended with the signing of a Pact of Friendship on Feb. 24, 1949. Again in conflict with Nicaragua in 1955, ended with the signing of a Treaty of Friendship on Jan. 9, 1956. Costa Rica is the only country in Latin America which, since 1948 has had no armed forces, only police and border units. In 1979 Costa Rica supported anti-Somoza forces in Nicaragua. In 1982 an Anti-Terrorist Brigade was created with military aid and counter-insurgency training provided by Israel. In Jan. 1984 the use of American soldiers in construction projects financed by the USA along the Costa Rican border with Nicaragua was suspended.
See also ▷ World Heritage UNESCO List.

M. NIEDERGANG, *Les 20 Amériques latines*, Paris, 1962; F.D. PARKER, *The Centralamerican Republics*,

London, 1964, J.P. BALL, *Crisis in Costa Rica*, London 1971; R. BIESANZ, *The Costa Ricans*, Hemel Hempstead, 1982; *The Europa Yearbook 1984. A World Survey*, Vol. II, pp. 1452–1462, London, 1984.

COST OF LIVING. Index of the general price level in one country; important for UN comparative economic statistics.

CÔTE D'IVOIRE.. Member of the UN. République de la Côte d'Ivoire. Republic of the Ivory Coast. West African state on the Gulf of Guinea of the Atlantic Ocean, bounded by Liberia, Guinea, Mali, Burkina Faso and Ghana. Area: 322,462 sq. km. Pop. 1986 est. 10,160,000 (1975 census: 6,709,600). Capital: Abidjan with 951,216 inhabitants 1979. GNP per capita 1980 US $1150. Currency: one franc CFA = 100 centimes. Official language: French. National Day: Dec 7, Independence Day, 1960.

Member of the UN since Sept. 26, 1960 and of all UN specialized agencies. Member of the Conseil d'entente and of OAU.

International relations: French colony 1842–1958, part of French West Africa; 1958–59 autonomous state of the French Community; became independent on Aug. 7, 1960. In 1967 in dispute with Guinea; in 1969 with Ghana. The Treaty of Co-operation with Ghana signed 1971. A signatory of the Yaoundé conventions of 1963 and of 1969 and of the Lomé conventions of 1975 and 1980.

▷ Ivory Coast.

A. ZOLBERG. *One Party Government in the Ivory Coast*, Princeton, 1964; L.F. BLOJIN, *Bereg Slanovoi Kosti, Ekonomichno-geograficheskaya kharakteristika*, Moskva, 1967; B. HOLAS, *Industries et cultures en Côte d'Ivoire*, Abidjan, 1979; *La Côte d'Ivoire en chiffre*, Abidjan, 1979; *The Europa Year Book 1984. A World Survey*, Vol. II, pp. 1775–1786, London, 1984. KEESING's *Record of World Events*, 1986, No. 6.

COTTON. A subject of intergovernmental conventions and international co-operation. Organizations reg. with the IUA:

EUROCOTTON, Committee of the Cotton and Allied Textile Industries of the EEC, f. 1961, Brussels.
International Cotton Advisory Committee, f. 1939, Washington, DC. Relations with FAO and OAS. Publ. Monthly Review in English, French and Spanish. Members: governments of 46 countries.
International Federation of Cotton and Allied Textile Industries, f. 1904, Zurich, Switzerland. Consultative status with ECOSOC, FAO, UNCTAD. Publ. *News-letter*.
International Institute for Cotton, f. 1966, Brussels. Members: cotton-exporting countries: Brazil, Greece, India, Mexico, Spain, Tanzania and Uganda.

Yearbook of International Organizations.

COUNCIL FOR MUTUAL ECONOMIC ASSIST-ANCE, CMEA. The international economic organization of socialist countries called in the West COMECON, est. Jan. 1949 by a Convention signed by Albania, Bulgaria, Czechoslovakia, the GDR, Poland, Romania, Hungary and the USSR; Albania withdrew in 1962; Mongolian People's Republic admitted in July 1962; Yugoslavia signed an agreement on participation in the work of CMEA organs on the principle of equal rights and mutual benefits in matters of mutual interest, Sept. 17, 1964; the Republic of Cuba admitted in 1972; the Democratic Republic of Vietnam, admitted in 1972; in the following years Angola, Ethiopia, Iraq, North Korea, Laos, Mexico and Vietnam signed co-operation agreements. The statute of CMEA, adopted in Sofia, Dec. 14, 1959, entered into force Apr. 13, 1960; granted the status of permanent observer at

UN sessions and works under UN General Assembly Res. 3209/XXIX of Oct. 11, 1974.
Chief organs: Sessions of the Council, Executive Committee, f. June, 1962, Moscow; active since June, 1962 is the CMEA Standardization Institute; since July, 1962, Conference of Heads of the Office of Water Economy and Bureau of the Executive Committee for Common Questions of Economic Planning; since Dec., 1962, Co-ordination Bureau for Sea Freight; since Oct., 1963, Conference of Shipowning Enterprises; also operating are 21 Permanent Commissions: since June, 1958 Permanent Commission for Construction, headquarters Berlin; since Mar. 1958, permanent Commission for Economic Questions, Moscow; since June, 1958, Permanent Commission for Power, Moscow; since July, 1963, Permanent Commission for Geology, Ulan Bator; since May, 1956, Permanent Commission for Foreign Trade, Moscow; since June, 1962, Permanent Commission for Coordination of Scientific and Technical Research, Moscow; since May 1956, Permanent Commission for Machine Building Industry, Prague; since June, 1962, Permanent Standardization Commission, Berlin; since July, 1960, Permanent Commission for Peaceful Uses of Nuclear Energy, Moscow; since May, 1956, Permanent Commission for Chemical Industry, Berlin; since May, 1956, Permanent Commission for Ferrous Metals Industry, Moscow; since July, 1963, Permanent Commission for Light Industry, Prague; since May, 1956, Permanent Commission for Non-Ferrous Metals Industry, Budapest; since May, 1956, Permanent Commission for Oil and Gas Industry, Budapest; since July, 1963, Permanent Commission for Radio and Electonics Industry, Budapest; since July, 1963, Permanent Commission for Food Industry, Sofia; since May, 1956, Permanent Commission for Coal Industry, Warsaw; since May, 1956, Permanent Agricultural Commission, Sofia; since June, 1952, Permanent Commission for Statistics, Moscow; since Oct., 1971, Permanent Commission for Telecommunications, Moscow; since June, 1958, Permanent Commission for Transport, Moscow; since Dec., 1962, Permanent Commission for Finance and Currency, Moscow, Operating within the Council are General Terms of Assemblage, General Terms of Technical Service and General Terms of Supply of Spare Parts and others.
A uniform system of submitting disputes for arbitration by conference of Arbitration Courts is held every two years (the Courts are affiliated with Chambers of Foreign Commerce of member countries); a uniform system of liability of sellers for defects of goods supplied by them; a uniform system of legal standard norms – General Terms of Supply in CMEA – regulating economic exchange between members, modified Jan. 1, 1980. In 1971–72 work began on a system of legal norms for individual branches of forwarding and transport.
Other permanent bodies of CMEA:
Council of members' representatives for legal matters, f. May 1970; Council of heads of patent institutions, since 1960; Council of heads of water economy organs, since 1962; Council of internal trade ministers, since 1976; Standardization Institute; International Institute for Economic Problems of World Socialist System; International Investment Bank; International Bank for Economic Co-operation; International Centre for Scientific--Technical Information; Central Disposition Board for Joint Power Systems, Common Railway Truck of CMEA; and branch organizations: Inter--atominstrument, Interatomenergo, Interchim, Interelektro, Intermetal, Intershipnik, Interetilmash. The CMEA statute expresses readiness to develop economic relations with all countries irrespective of their state and social systems in keeping

with the principle of equal rights, mutual benefits and non-interference in internal affairs. This fundamental principle was confirmed and consolidated in the comprehensive program of socialist economic integration of CMEA countries adopted at the 25th Session of CMEA on July 29, 1971. CMEA co-operates with 20 international organizations within the UN system, chiefly with ECOSOC, UN Economic Commission for Europe, FAO, ILO, UNCTAD, UNIDO, particularly in the field of ass-istance to the developing countries both by training experts and through technical assistance in the construction of projects of significance to national economy. An agreement between the Soviet government and CMEA regulating questions relating to the headquarters of CMEA bodies in the Soviet Union and providing for the immunity of premises, financial problems, permanent agencies (enjoy the same privileges and immunities as diplomatic representations), transit and sojourns and other matters was signed in Moscow on Dec. 7, 1961 and entered into force on Mar. 1, 1962. Analogous agreements were signed (and came into force) between CMEA and other members: Bulgaria, Oct. 26, 1962; Czechoslovakia, Sept. 3, 1962; GDR, Feb. 14, 1963; Polish People's Republic, July 1, 1962; and Hungary, May 10, 1963. On its 30th anniversary CMEA held a solemn session in Moscow and adopted a declaration whose concluding passages covered the following program for the decade 1980–90:

"Member states of CMEA believe that in the coming decade the mainlines of their co-opeation should be aimed at: comprehensive accelaration of scientific-tech-nical progress; satisfaction of rational demand for raw materials–fuels and energy, plant, equipment and modern technologies; improvement of supply of the population with foodstuffs and industrial goods of common use; creation of an effective and technically efficient network of transport between CMEA members in accordance with the growing requirements of their national economies and comprehensive co-operation."

To this end CMEA members co-ordinate national economic plans, lay down an accepted plan of mul-tilateral integration measures as well as bilateral long-range programs of specialization and co-operation in production for 1981–90.
A special problem is the establishment of inter-national relations between CMEA and EEC.
In 1981-85 the national income of the CMEA countries had risen by 18 per cent, with an 18 per cent rise in aggregate industrial output and one of 11 per cent in aggregate agricultural output.
The 39th session held in Havana, on Oct. 29–31, 1984 started a drafting of the comprehensive program for scientific and technical progress for a period of 15–20 years, beyond the year 2000. The 40th session held in Warsaw, on June 25–27, 1985 put out a proposal for the establishment of relations between CMEA and the EEC.
On Nov. 4, 1986 during the Session of CMEA, and with its support Bulgaria, Czechoslovakia, the GDR, and Hungary concluded bilateral inter-govern-mental agreements on the development of production and scientific and technical ties with enterprises in the Soviet Union (Poland had previously signed in Moscow the first agreement of this kind).
At the session, held on Nov 3–5 in Bucharest, 10 full CMEA members were represented with Yugoslavia as an associate member and Afghanistan, Angola, Ethiopia, Laos, Nicaragua, and South Yemen as observers.
The 42nd special session of CMEA in Moscow, on Dec. 18, 1986, accepted a Comprehensive Program initiated by M. Gorbachev, General Secretary of the CPSU, with five priority areas of co-operation

'for the creation and utilization of fundamentally new types of machinery and technology' in the fields of: electronics, automatization, nuclear power, raw materials and bio-engineering.

On Nov. 14, 1987 a special session in Moscow of the CMEA decided to promote currency convertibility and special aid to Cuba and Mongolia and Vietnam, the non-European countries.

In a joint declaration, signed in Luxembourg on June 25, 1988 the European Communities and the CMEA formally recognized each other and agreed to exchange ambassadors.

See also ▷ CMEA-EEC relations 1980–1989.

The Vienna Institute for Comparative Economic Studies publishes on the basis of the CMEA countries and comparable western statistics the biennial Yearbook on COMECON Current Foreign Trade Data and COMECON Data.

A. KORBONSKI, "COMECON", in: *International Conciliation*, No. 549, September. 1964, pp. 3-62; S. AUSCH, *Theory and Practice of CMEA Corporation*, Budapest, 1972; A. WASILKOWSKI, "Legal regulations of economic relations within the CMEA", in: *Polish Yearbook of International Law 1972–1973*, Wroclaw, 1974; J.P. ZHURAVLEV, *Mezhshdunarodniye Sviazi Sovieta Economicheskoi Wzaimopomoshi*, Moskva, 1979. M. MARRESE, J. VANOUS, *Soviet Subsidization of Trade with Eastern Europe*, Berhelen, 1983; V. SOBELL, *The Red Market: Industrial Co-operation and Specialization in COMECON*, Aldershot, 1984; KEESING's *Contemporary Archive*, July, 1985 and March 1987. *A Complex Programme for Scientific Technical Progress of CMEA Member States Until the Year 2000*, Moscow, 1985; W.V. WALLACE, A.R. CLARKE, *COMECON, Trade and the West*, London, 1986; G.B. KOCHETKOV, V. PAVERCHEV, V.M. SERGEEV, *Artificial Intelligence and Disarmament, in: Arms and Artificial Intelligence*, SIPRI, Oxford, 1987. KEESING's *Record of World Events*, March, 1988. KEESING's *Record of World Events*, No. 9, 1988.

COUNCIL FOR PUBLIC AFFAIRS OF THE CATHOLIC CHURCH. *Consilium pro Publicis Ecclesiae Negottis*, also called Congregation for Extra-ordinary Affairs of the Church, originally an office of ▷ Roman Curia, established for political contacts with France by Paul V in 1793, then reorganized in 1814 by Pius VII. After the apostolic constitution of Paul VI on Aug. 15, 1967, a section of the Secretariat of the Apostolic See, connected i.a. with the person of the prefect, who handles contacts with governments and supervises the diplomatic representatives of the Apostolic See in all countries. In approximation the counterpart of the minister of foreign affairs in civilian governments.

COUNCIL OF ARAB ECONOMIC UNITY. An intergovernmental organ for the implementation of the Arab Convention for Arab Economic Unity, drafted on the initiative of the Arab League in 1957–62 and signed in 1962 by Egypt, Jordan, Kuwait, Morocco and Syria, in 1963 by Iraq and Yemen, in 1968 by Sudan and by Somalia in 1970. On Aug. 13, 1964 the Council decided to establish the Common Market of Arab States.

COUNCIL OF ASIA INDUSTRIAL DEVELOPMENT. An intergovernmental organization of 24 states: Afghanistan, Australia, Brunei, Burma, Ceylon, Chinese People's Republic, Hong Kong, India, Indonesia, Iran, Japan, Cambodia, South Korea, Laos, Malaysia, Mongolia, Nepal, New Zealand, Pakistan, the Philippines, Western Samoa, Singapore, Thailand and Vietnam; founded in 1966, with headquarters in Bangkok, on recommendation of the UN Economic Commission for Asia and the Far East, ECAFE. Its task is to synchronize development plans of member countries. Publishes Asian Industrial Development News.

Yearbook of International Organizations.

COUNCIL OF CONSTANCE, 1414–1418. One of the 21 councils recognized by the Catholic Church as universal. In the history of international law it has particular significance due to a doctrinal dispute filed by the Polish delegation against the Teutonic Order, whether under the pretext of proselytism, the armed invasion of lands of non-believers is permitted, and thus a dispute aiming at the limitation of *ius ad bellum* just wars in accordance with the thesis of Stanislaw of Skalbmierz and Pawel Wlodkowic called Paulus Vladimiri, who preceeded Grotius by two centuries in the formulation of the principles "*de bellis iustis.*" Wlodkowic's opponent at the Council, the German Dominican J. Falkenberg, defended the unrestricted right of the Teutonic Order to exterminate pagans and charged Poland with co-operating with the pagans and combatting the Teutonic Knights. Poland received the complete support of its position at the Commission of Councils as well as by the College of Cardinals and nations, but the plan accepted by the Commission for ratification by the general session of the Council was pigeonholed, so the Polish thesis did not become a legally-binding doctrine of the Church. The Polish–Teutonic dispute was settled by means of a legal compromise, not through the doctrinal process.

Acta concilii Constansis, vol. 4, 1896–1928; S. BELCH, *Paulus Vladimiri and His Doctrine*, The Hague, 1965.

COUNCIL OF ENTENTE. An intergovernmental institution of Dahomey (now Benin), Upper Volta (now Burkina Faso), Niger, Togo and Ivory Coast (now Côte d'Ivoire), founded on May 29, 1959, with headquarters of its Secretariat General in Abidjan. The Council co-ordinates the foreign policy of its member states, unifies the systems of public administration, such as courts, press, telecommunications, public works etc, has its own development credit system.

COUNCIL OF EUROPE, 1949. The statute of the Council of Europe was signed in London by the governments of Belgium, Denmark, France, Ireland, Italy, Luxembourg, the Netherlands, Norway, Sweden and the UK on May 5, 1949; came into force Aug. 3, 1949. Art. 1 states that the Council's aim is

"to achieve a greater unity between its members for the purpose of safeguarding and realizing the ideals and principles which are their common heritage and facilitating their economic and social progress, this aim shall be pursued .. by discussion of questions of common concern and by agreements and common actions".

Art. 1 (d) excludes "matters relating to national defence".

The Council of Europe publ. in The Hague, *The European Yearbook*, 1955, ff.; a quarterly *Forum*, from 1978; *Yearbook on the Convention of Human Rights*, from 1958.

UNTS, Vol. 87, pp. 103–129. C. COOK J. PAXTON, *European Political Facts 1918–1975*, London 1975; *Guide to the Council of Europe*, Strasbourg, 1982. *Council of Europe, Human Rights Information Sheet No. 21*, November 1986–October 1987, Strasbourg, 1988.

COUNCIL OF FOREIGN MINISTERS OF THE BIG POWERS. A council established by a decision of the Heads of States and governments of the USA, the UK and the USSR on Feb. 11, 1945 at the Yalta Conference "as the permanent tripartite mechanism", expanded by the Potsdam Treaty of Aug. 2, 1945, when the foreign ministers of five states were invited to take part in the conference, these being:

the members of the UN Security Council, i.e. also China and France.

Documents on Germany 1944–1959, Washington, DC, 1959.

COUNCIL OF FOUR. A name adopted during the Versailles Conference in 1919 for debates of government heads of the Big Four: USA President W. Wilson, and Prime Ministers: G. Clemenceau of France, Lloyd George of Great Britain, and A. Orlando of Italy.

P. MANTOUN, *Les délibérations du Conseil des Quatre*, 2 Vols., Paris, 1955.

COUNCIL OF THE AMERICAS. American–Canadian organization, founded in 1965, with headquarters in New York, aimed at protecting the investments of private banks and industrial corporations of the USA in Latin America and Canada. In 1970 Council of the Americas associated 210 financial institutions and enterprises, representing 85% of private American and Canadian investments in Latin American states for the amount of about 13 billion dollars.

COUNCIL OF THE EPISCOPATE OF LATIN AMERICA. CONSEJO EPISCOPAL LATINO-AMERICANO, CELAM. The leading regional organization of the hierarchy of the Roman Catholic Church in Latin America, est. on the recommendation of the Apostolic See on Sept. 2, 1955 in Rio de Janeiro; seat in Bogota; reg. with the UIA; studies socio-religious problems of the region and co-ordinates the activity of the Church. Each national episcopate is represented in the Council by one bishop and his proxy with the right of one vote. Publ. the monthly *Boletin CELAM*. Organizes the periodic conferences of CELAM, the first of which took place in Bogota; the second in Medelin (Colombia) with the participation of Paul VI; the third in Puebla (Mexico) with the participation of Pope John Paul II.

Yearbook of International Organizations.

COUNCIL ON FOREIGN RELATIONS. The CFR was f. New York in 1921 to study the international aspects of American political economic and strategic problems. It operates an international affairs fellowship program. Publ. *Foreign Affairs* (quarterly), *American Foreign Relations* (annual).

COUNTERFEIT GOODS. A subject of intergovernmental co-operation on efficient measures to combat trade in counterfeit goods. The GATT together with WIPO decided in 1986 in the framework of the ▷ Uruguay Round to examine the relevant provisions for national legislation in international trade in counterfeit goods.

T. ABU-GHAZALEZ, The GATT and Intellectual Property, in: *Economic Impact*, 1988/3.

COUNTERFEITING CURRENCY. The subject of the International Convention for the Suppression of Counterfeiting, signed in Geneva on Apr. 20, 1929, and ratified in the following years by 64 countries; came into force Feb. 22, 1931.

LNTS, Vol. 112, pp. 371 and 395; V.V. PELLA, *La co-opération des États dans la lutte contre le faux monnayage. Rapport à la Société des Nations*, Paris, 1927; *Actes de la III-e Conférence internationale pour l'unification du Droit Pénal*, Bruxelles, 1931; R. LEMKIN, 'Monety falszywe' in: *Encyklopedia Nauk Politycznych*, Warszawa, 1938; S.M. COLE, *Counterfeit*, London, 1955; M.T. BLOOM, *Money of Their Own*, London, 1957

COUNTER FORCE, COUNTER GOVERNMENT, COUNTER VALUE. Three strategic terms

C

for thermonuclear strikes depending on the basic aim in a "limited nuclear war":
(1) a strike destroying the strategic rockets of the opponent;
(2) a strike destroying the governmental apparatus of the opponent;
(3) a strike destroying everything that has essential value for the opponent: large cities, centers of industry, transport, culture and science.

COUNTERINSURGENCY DOCTRINE. A US political and military XIX and XXth century doctrine, supporting the idea of the ▷ Big Stick Diplomacy.

L.A. CABLE, *Conflict of Myths: The Development of American Counterinsurgency Doctrine and the Vietnam War*, New York, 1986.

COUNTERVAILING STRATEGY ▷ Schlesinger Nuclear War Doctrine.

COUNTRY UNDER FOREIGN RULE. An international term used in the UN System for countries under colonial domination or foreign occupation.

UN Chronicle, May 1980, p. 29.

COUP D'ÉTAT. French international term for a take-over of the government by force; in Latin America the Spanish term *golpe de estado* is used.

S.R. DAVID, *Third World coup d'état and International Security*, Baltimore, MD, 1987.

COURSE-INDICATING RADIO. Radio stations constructed on the coast with the task of assisting ships to fix their position by receiving signals from two radio beacons separated from each other. A subject of international co-operation and regulations.

COVENTRY. A city in central England, bombed for 11 hours on Nov. 13, 1940 by the German airforce (i.a. the 14th century cathedral of St Michael). Coventry became one of the symbols of destruction of World War II. Pop. 1981 census: 314,124.

COVERT ACTION OR OPERATIONS. An international term for secret direct interventions into the internal affairs of a foreign country.

J. PRADOS, *The President's Secret Wars: CIA and Pentagon Covert Operations Since World War II*, New York, 1986; G. TREVERTON, *Covert Action: The Limits of Intervention in the Postwar World*, New York, 1987; J. MARSHALL, P. SCOTT, J. HUNTER, *The Iran-Contra Connection: Secret Teams and Covert Operations in the Reagan Era*, Boston, 1987.

CPJI. Fr. abbrev. Cour Permanente de Justice Internationale, Permanent Court of International Justice; Eng. abbrev. PCIJ. The documents and publications of the Court are signed with the first or the second abbreviation, depending on the language in which they are printed.

CPPS.. Comision Permanente del Pacifico (Permanent South Pacific Commission) ▷ South Pacific Commission.

CRABS. *Cancer pugurus*. Sea creatures, subject of international protection (▷ Scandinavian Fishery Conventions).

CRACOW. Polish: Kraków. The capital of Polish Kings from the 14th to 18th century. City in southern Poland, on the Vistula. After the partitions of Poland the Congress of Vienna 1815, created a Republic of Cracow under the protectorate of Russia, Prussia and Austria, integrated by

Austria 1846. In 1978 UNESCO placed Cracow on the list of monuments of human heritage.
The historic center of Cracow is included in the ▷ World Heritage UNESCO List. Cracow is just as it was originally planned in 1257, with its vast market square around which are the buildings symbolizing the three powers of the city – the tower of the Town Hall, the Church of the Virgin Mary and the Cloth Market. Overlooking the city, on the Wavel hill, stand the imposing buildings of the Royal Castle and the cathedral, where valuable objects from the past are kept.

S. KIENIEWICZ, "The Free State of Cracow 1815–1846", in: *The Slavonic and East European Review*, London, 1947/48, pp. 69–89. *Cracow: World's Culture Heritage*, Warsaw, 1982. UNESCO, *A Legacy for All*, Paris, 1984.

CRAFTS. A subject of international co-operation. Organizations reg. with the UIA:

Council of Nordic Master-Craftsmen, f. 1912, Stockholm.
International Association for Crafts and Teaching of Art, f. 1938, Brussels.
International Association of Crafts and Small and Medium-Sized Enterprises, f. 1947, Berne, Switzerland. Consultative status with ECOSOC, UNIDO, ILO, Council of Europe.
International Crafts Center, f. 1972, Paris.
Union of Craft-industries and Trade in the EEC, f. 1959, Brussels.
World Crafts Union, f. 1964, New York. Consultative status with ECOSOC, UNCTAD, UNESCO, UNIDO. Publ. *Bulletin*.

Yearbook of International Organizations.

CRAIOVA TREATY, 1940. The Bulgarian–Romanian border treaty, signed on Sept. 7, 1940 in the Romanian city of Craiova. On the strength of the Craiova Treaty, the province of South Dobrudsha, which had been turned over by Bulgaria to Romania by the ▷ Neuilly Peace Treaty of 1919, was returned to Bulgaria. The Paris Peace Treaty of 1947 confirmed the validity of the Craiova Treaty, stating, that "borders of Bulgaria remain as they were on Jan. 1, 1941."

Weltgeschichte der Gegenwart in Dokumenten, Essen, 1936-1942; S.D. SPECTOR, *Romania at the Paris Peace Conference*, London, 1962.

CRASH. An international economic term for bankruptcy, insolvency; since May 9, 1873, when the Vienna Stock Exchange suspended trading due to the bankruptcy of a number of commercial banks and companies; used again after the crash of the largest stock exchange in New York, on "Black Friday", Oct. 13, 1929.

J.K. GALBRAITH, *The Great Crash*, London, 1955.

CRAYFISH. A subject of international co-operation. Organization reg. with the UIA:

International Association of Astacology, f. 1972, University of Kuopio, Finland. Aim: promoting study of freshwater crayfish.

Yearbook of International Organizations.

CREDENTIAL LETTER. French = *Lettre de crédence*. An international term for a title or claim to credit or accreditation letter.

CREDIBILITY GAP. An international term for the public opinion's distrust of a state leader's veracity or in international relations for crisis in talks resulting from one party's growing distrust of the assurances made by the other party.

CREDIT. An international term, defined by the International Chamber of Commerce in Uniform

Customs and Practice for Documentary Credits, adopted in Nov. 1962, as follows;

"General Provisions and Definitions: (a) These provisions and definitions and the following articles apply to all documentary credits and are binding upon all parties thereto unless otherwise expressly agreed.
(b) For the purposes of such provisions, definitions and articles the expressions 'documentary credit(s)' and 'credit(s)' used therein mean any arrangement, however named or described, whereby a bank (the issuing bank), acting at the request and in accordance with the instructions of a customer (the applicant for the credit) is to make payment to or to the order of a third party (the beneficiary) or is to pay, accept or authorises such payments to be made or such drafts to be paid, accepted or negotiated by another bank, against stipulated documents and compliance with stipulated terms and conditions.
(c) Credits, by their nature, are separate transactions from the sales or other contracts on which they may be based on banks are in no way concerned with or bound by such contracts.
(d) Credit instructions and the credits themselves must be complete and precise and, in order to guard against confusion and misunderstanding, issuing banks should discourage any attempt by the applicant for the credit to include excessive detail.
(e) When the bank first entitles to avail itself of an option it enjoys under the following articles, its decision shall be binding upon all the parties concerned.
(f) A beneficiary can in no case avail himself of the contractual relationship existing between banks or between the applicant for the credit and the issuing bank.
Art. 1. Credits may be either: (a) revocable, or (b) irrevocable. All credits, therefore, should clearly indicate whether they are revocable or irrevocable.
In the absence of such indication the credit shall be deemed to be revocable, even though an expiry date is stipulated.
Art. 2. A revocable credit does not constitute a legally binding undertaking between the bank or banks concerned and the beneficiary because such a credit may be modified or cancelled at any moment without notice to the beneficiary. When, however, a revocable credit has been transmitted to and made available at a branch or other bank, its modification or cancellation shall become effective only upon receipt of notice thereof by such branch or other bank and shall not affect the right of that branch or other bank to be reimbursed for any payment, acceptance or negotiation made by it prior to receipt of such notice.
Art. 3. An irrevocable credit is a definite undertaking on the part of an issuing bank and constitutes the engagement of that bank to the beneficiary or, as the case may be, to the beneficiary and bona fide holders of drafts drawn and/or documents presented thereunder, that the provisions for payment, acceptance of negotiation contained in the credit will be duly fulfilled, provided that all the terms and conditions of the credit are complied with.
An irrevocable credit may be advised to a beneficiary through another bank without engagement on the part of that other bank (the advising bank), but when an issuing bank authorizes another bank to confirm its irrevocable credit and the latter does so, such confirmation constitutes a definite undertaking on the part of the confirming bank either that the provisions for payment or acceptance will be duly fulfilled or, in the case of a credit available by negotiation of drafts, that the confirming bank will negotiate drafts without recourse to drawer.
Such undertakings can neither be modified nor cancelled without the agreement of all concerned."

Register of Texts of Conventions and Other Instruments Concerning International Trade Law, UN, New York, Vol. I, p. 229–230.

CREDIT CARD. An international term for a system of personal cards authorising purchase on credit, first established in 1950 in the USA (▷ Diners Club International) accepted in the 1980s in all countries.

CREDIT EXPORT. An international term for credits granted by national financial institutions to foreign states or foreign companies and firms. Credit export occurs when an increased demand is observed abroad and a number of factors such as exchange rates of currencies, direct production costs and export prices on current production for export (determined by credits) etc, yield greater profit abroad than at home.

CREDIT INSURANCE. An international term for insurance covering tradesmen and manufacturers against losses resulting from credited delivery of products as well as credit insurance related to foreign trade credit grants; introduced in the second half of the 19th century, most often applied in the second half of the 20th century.

CREDIT LYONNAIS. A French state bank f. 1863 in Lyon; one of private international commercial banks until 1945; from Jan. 1, 1946 state commercial bank with headquarters in Paris and branches all over the world. In 1980 fifth on the list of world banks.

CREDIT MARKETS. An international term for markets for monies sold as commodities at interest: (a) money markets for generally short-term transactions: (b) capital markets for mainly medium- and long-term investment credits. After World War II the major credit markets were New York and London, followed by Zurich, Paris, Frankfurt am Main, and Amsterdam; in Asia Tokyo and Hongkong. A traditional form of credit was the granting of loans in local currency. In the second half of the 20th century a new phenomenon appeared on credit markets: the granting of loans in the currency of a third state (▷ Eurodollar). The euro-currency market was formed in Western Europe.

CREMATION, CREMATORIES. An international term for the burning of corpses, a custom known since antiquity, spread in the 19th century in Europe and America with the construction of many crematories, condemned by the Catholic Church in 1886 and subject to excommunication, condemnation annulled in 1964 on the initiative of Pope John XXIII. During World War II, Germany built gigantic crematories in many concentration camps where they cremated up to 24,000 corpses in 24 hours; at the Nuremberg trial of war criminals crematories became a symbol of genocide. The first international organization, the International and Universal Federation of Cremation Societies, operated from 1919 to 1925. Organization reg. with the UIA:

International Cremation Federation f. 1937, Stockholm; it associates national cremation societies of Argentina, Australia, Austria, Belgium, Czechoslovakia, Denmark, France, the FRG, the GDR, Holland, Norway, New Zealand, Switzerland, Sweden, the UK, USA, Yugoslavia and Zimbabwe; it organizes congresses every 3 years; Publ. *Pharos*.

H. LANGBEIN, *Der Auschwitz Prozess, Eine Dokumentation*, 2 Vols., Wien, 1965.

CREOLE. An international term for a descendant of European settlers in America cultivating language and culture of their ancestors, Black Creole – Negro born in South America, descendant of Negroes brought from Africa.

CREST. An official abbreviation of the EEC Committee of Scientific and Technological Research.

CRIMEAN ASTROPHYSICAL OBSERVATORY ▷ Observations.

CRIMEAN WAR 1853–1856. The military conflict of 1853–56 between Russia and Turkey, the latter supported by its allies: France, the Kingdom of Sar-

dinia and Great Britain; the war was waged mainly in the Crimea, where Turkey captured Sevastopol, and also in the Caucasus, where Russia captured Karsu; it ended in the Paris Peace Pact of Apr., 1856; amended (arts. 11, 13, 14) on Mar. 13, 1871.

V. DE GUICHEN, *La guerre de Crimée 1853–1856 et l'attitude des puissances européennes*, Paris, 1936; G.D. HENDERSON, *Crimean War Diplomacy*, London, 1947; V. BESTUZHEV, *Krymskaya voyna 1853–1856*, Moskva, 1956.

CRIMEN LAESAE HUMANITATIS. *Latin* = crime offending humanity. A travesty of the medieval principle that high treason is a crime (crimen laesae maiestatis), used on Oct. 16, 1972 to define the criminal character of colonialism, in the Fourth Committee of the UN General Assembly, by A. Cabral, head of the African Party for the Independence of Guinea-Bissau and the Cape Verde Islands (PAIGC). The principle was later recalled in the UN when A. Cabral was killed on Jan. 22, 1973 on the order of Portuguese colonialists.

CRIME PREVENTION. A subject of international co-operation and conventions. In 1950 the UN General Assembly authorized the convening every five years of a congress on Crime Prevention and the Treatment of Offenders.

"The First Crime Congress approved a set of Standard Minimum Rules for the Treatment of Prisoners, which was approved by the Economic and Social Council in 1957. In December 1979, the General Assembly approved a Code of Conduct for Law Enforcement Officials, prepared by the Economic and Social Council's Committee on Crime Prevention and Control, and it recommended that Governments incorporate it into national legislation and practice. The General Assembly's Special Committee against Apartheid regularly throws the spotlight on the situation of political prisoners in South Africa. Work is continuing on a draft code of medical ethics in connection with the torture of imprisoned persons, a draft body of principles for the protection of all persons under any form of detention or imprisonment, and draft guidelines on procedures for determining whether adequate grounds exist for detaining persons on the grounds of mental ill-health"

The Sixth UN Congress held in Caracas from Aug. 25, to Sept. 5, 1980, with the theme "Crime prevention and the quality of Life". was attended by more than 1000 participants from 101 countries. The Caracas Declaration on Crime Prevention which embodied a preamble and 10 principles stated that it was essential to review traditional crime prevention strategies based exclusively on legal criteria and advocated that crime prevention and criminal justice be considered in the context of economic development, political systems, social and cultural values and social change, as well as in the context of the ▷ New international economic order.

The Seventh Crime Prevention Congress took place in 1985 in Milan, Italy, and adopted a Milan Plan of Action, Guiding Principles for Crime Prevention and Criminal Justice, Basic Principle on the independence of the Judiciary, Model Agreement on the Transfer of Foreign Prisoners, Recommendation on the Treatment of Foreign Prisoners the UN Standard Minimum Rules for the Administration of Juvenile Justice, and 25 resolutions.

UN Yearbook 1950, UN Chronicle, November, 1980, p. 46–47 and November, 1982, p. 47. *UN Chronicle*, 1985, No. 8, pp. 38–46; *UN International Review of Criminal Policy*, New York, 1986 (issued irregularly since 1946).

CRIMES AGAINST HUMANITY. An international term used in the UN, defined in an agreement between France, the UK, the USA and the USSR on the persecution and punishment of the

major war criminals, signed Aug. 8, 1945 in London; Crimes against humanity:

"murder, extermination, enslavement, deportation and other inhumane acts against any civilian population before or during war; or persecution on political, racial or religious grounds in execution of or in connection with any crime within the jurisdiction of the domestic law of the country where perpetrated" (art. 6 of Charter of the IMT).

A subject of the UN Declaration banning the use of atomic weapons, 1961, which recognized such use a crime against humanity; also subject to Convention on Non-applicability of the Statutory Limitation to War Crimes against Humanity.

Questions of Punishment of War Criminal and of Persons who have Commited Crimes against Humanity, UN, New York, 1966; A. KLAFKOWSKI, *L'imprescriptibilité des crimes de guerre en l'Allemagne Federal, au regard du droit international*, Poznan, 1970.

CRIMES AGAINST LAW OF NATIONS. An international term for slavery, traffic in people, narcotics, maritime and aeronautical piracy and other acts of terrorism. Other variations of the crimes against the law of nations are ▷ crimes against humanity.

CRIMES AGAINST PEACE. An international term for crimes of warmongering, provoking and waging aggressive wars. The first statesman to be charged with a crime against peace was the emperor of France, Napoleon Bonaparte, in the Vienna Congress Declaration of March 13, 1815:

"Napoleon Bonaparte has placed himself outside the scope of social and civic relations as an enemy of mankind, violated the world peace and has exposed himself to the liability of a public repression."

The second head of state to be put under the charge of crimes against peace was the emperor of the German Reich, Wilhelm Hohenzollern, as stated in Art. 227 of the Versailles Treaty:

"The Allied and Associated States place Wilhelm II, former German emperor, under public prosecution charged with the gravest outrage against international morals and the sacred importance of treaties."

In World War II the list of war criminals included: the leaders of the Axis states – Germany, Italy and Japan. Adolf Hitler committed suicide, Benito Mussolini was hanged before trial, Hirohito after the unconditional surrender of Japan was excluded from the list of criminals against peace by the United States. The term crimes against peace was defined in the Agreement between France, the USA, the UK and the USSR on prosecution of top war criminals, signed on Aug. 8, 1945, in London, which defined crimes against peace as the planning, preparation, initiation or waging of an aggressive war or of a war in violation of treaties, agreements or international guarantees, or co-operation in planning or conspiracy aimed at committing one of the aforementioned acts. Crimes against peace have been defined in detail in the verdict of the International Military Court in Nuremberg and in the ▷ Nuremberg Principles.

F.H. MAUGHAM, *UN and War Crimes*, New York, 1951.

CRIMES AGAINST THE PEACE AND SECURITY OF MANKIND. An international term, defined 1987 in the draft ▷ Code of Crimes against the Peace and Security of Mankind.

UN Chronicle, November, 1987.

CRIMES AND TREATMENT OF DELINQUENTS, PREVENTION OF. An international term introduced by ECOSOC. In accordance with Res. 155/VII/C/ ECOSOC of Aug. 13, 1948, a

C

Meeting of Specialized Agencies and Non-Governmental Organizations Interested in the Prevention of Crime and the Treatment of Offenders was held in Paris on Oct. 15–16, 1948, which shortly thereafter became a permanent institution financed by the United Nations and meeting every 2 years since 1950. The UN General Assembly in Res. 415/V of Dec. 1, 1950 integrated the International Penal and Penitentiary Commission (IPPC, f. 1872) under whose patronage Congresses were held every 5 years on prevention of crimes and treatment of delinquents (First in Geneva in 1955; Second in Tokyo in 1970). The penitentiary issues formed the subject of a debate in the UN Human Rights Committee in 1946–1948, which found its expression in art. 5 of the Universal Declaration of Human Rights. On the basis of this article, the UN General Assembly in 1949 issued an absolute ban on bodily punishment in trusteeship territories. In 1955 the Geneva Congress formulated the UN Minimum Rules on Treatment of Prisoners. These rules were accepted in 1957 by ECOSOC and recommended to United Nations member states. They prohibit the use of all kinds of bodily punishment, imprisonment in dungeons as well as other inhuman or degrading methods of treatment of prisoners. In 1967 the United Nations established the Far East Institute on Treatment of Delinquents in Tokyo; in 1968 the UN Institute for Investigation of Social Defence in Rome; both institutes were established for the purpose of "stimulating the activity of the United Nations with regard to issues concerning prevention of crimes and treatment of delinquents." Organizations reg. with the UIA:

International Penal and Penitentiary Foundation, f. 1951, Brussels. Publ. various studies such as: *New Psychological Methods for the Treatment of Prisoners*, 1963. International Society of Social Defence, f. 1947, Paris, Consultative status with ECOSOC. Publ.: *Bulletin de la Société internationale de défense sociale*.

United Nations and the Human Rights, New York, 1968; *The UN Review*, No. 303, 1960; *UN Yearbook 1963*, pp. 310–314; *UN Monthly Chronicle*, No. 8, 1965; L.N. GALIENSKAYA, *Miezhdunarodnaya bor'ba z priestupnostyiu*, Moscow, 1972; *UN Chronicle*, January 1978.

CRIMINAL COURT, INTERNATIONAL.

A permanent institution projected by the League of Nations in connection with the definition of the three types of war crimes specified by the Versailles Treaty 1919: offense of international morality (later called by the UN ▷ crimes against humanity), offense of the sacred importance of the inviolability of treaties (in the UN ▷ crimes against peace) and acts contradictory to the rules and customs of war (in the UN ▷ war crimes UN Resolutions). The Third Committee of the League of Nations in 1920 prepared a draft on the International Criminal Court and circulated it for opinions to international legal associations.

From among them, the international Association of Penal Law voiced in favor of establishing the Penal Court within the Permanent Court of International Justice and of drawing up a Constitution for such a Court (the so-called project of Professor V.V. Pelli of 1927) as well as preparing, together with the Association of International Law and the Interparliamentary Union, a draft International Penal Code (the so-called project, of V.V. Pelli of 1935). In Geneva, on Nov. 16, 1937, a Convention on the establishment of the International Criminal Court was signed by the governments of Belgium, Bulgaria, Cuba, Czechoslovakia, France, Greece, Spain, Monaco, the Netherlands, Romania, Turkey, the USSR and Yugoslavia. It did not enter into force due to the lack of a sufficient number of ratifications.

After World War II these projects were transmitted to the United Nations and were considered during preparatory work on a constitution for an International Military Court. However, the idea of establishing a Penal Court within the International Court of Justice was finally rejected in 1949. The UN General Assembly under Res. 260-B/III of Dec. 9, 1948, and 489/V of Dec. 12, 1950, initiated work on establishing an international body of justice for the prosecution of individuals accused of the crime of genocide and other crimes against peace and security of peoples. On Dec. 12, 1950, the UN General Assembly appointed a special Commission which in 1951 prepared a draft constitution for an International Criminal Court. The opinions furnished by some governments, and recommendations of the UN General Assembly expressed in Res. 687/V, were the basis for the revision of the draft and for further drafts submitted in 1954 and 1957, on which the General Assembly expressed its view in Res. 898/IX of Dec. 14, 1954 and 1187/XII of Dec. 11, 1957, when it was decided to postpone further debate on international penal jurisdiction until work was completed on the definition of ▷ aggression (which was done in 1976) and the Code of Crimes against Peace and Security of Peoples (which had not been completed by 1985).

CRIMINAL LAW, INTERNATIONAL.

A subject of international co-operation, dedicated to the prevention of crimes international in character, like ▷ Crimes against Humanity, ▷ War crimes, ▷ Slavery, ▷ Traffic in Women and Children, ▷ Narcotics, and others.

A.N. TRAJNIN, *The Hitlerite Responsibility under the Criminal Law*, London, 1945; V. BART DE SCHUTTER, C. ELIAERTS, *Bibliography on International Criminal Law*, Leiden, 1972.

CRIMINOLOGY.

A subject of international co-operation. Organization reg. with the UIA:

International Society of Criminology, f. 1934, Paris, as Society of Criminological Science, present name since Jan. 1949. Consultative Status with ECOSOC, UNESCO, WHO. Publ. Selected Documentation on Criminology and International Annals of Criminology. The Society est. 1969 in Montreal by agreement with the Université de Montreal an International Centre for Comparative Criminology which publ. *Criminologie* and studies.

J.A. ADLER, *Elsevier's Dictionary of Criminal Science. In English/American, French, Italian, Spanish, Portuguese, Dutch, Swedish and German*, Amsterdam, 1960; M.E. WOLFGANG, R.M. FIGLIO, T.P. THORNBERRY, *Criminology Index*. 2 Vols., Amsterdam, 1975. J.R. NASH, *Encyclopedia of World Crime, Criminal Justice, Criminology and Law Enforcement*, Wilmete, Illinois, 1989.

CRISIS.

▷ World Economic Crisis.

CROATIA.

Hrvatska. A federal unit of Yugoslavia. Area: 56,538 sq. km. Pop., 1981 census: 4,601,469. Croatia includes Croatia proper, Slavonia, Dalmatia and most of Istria; capital: Zagreb. A Balkan country, under the government of the Hungarian dynasty from the 12th century then the Hapsburgs (with an interruption 1805–14); from Dec. 1, 1918 part of the Kingdom of Serbs, Croats, and Slovenes (SHS), which took the name Yugoslavia in 1929. The Germans, Italians and Hungarians occupied Croatia and on Apr. 10, 1941 established the so-called Independent Croatian State (Nezavisna Drzava Hrvatska – NDH) with a fascist administration. The anti-fascist resistance movement in Croatia directed by the Communist Party of Yugoslavia caused an armed uprising in July 1941 and partisan struggles continued during the entire period of occupation. Liberated in May 1945 by the Yugoslav National Liberation Army. On Nov. 29, 1945 it became one of the six federal republics of Yugoslavia.

V. BOGDANOV, *Historia politickih stranaka u Hrvatskoi*, Zagreb, 1958.

CROWCASS.

Criminal of War Commission. An intergovernmental institution, est. in Oct. 1943 in London by the representatives of 17 Allied nations, without the USSR. The aim of CROWCASS was to put on a list the war criminals in occupied countries in Europe and to ensure their detection, apprehension, trial and punishment. A subcommission was established for the Far East territories occupied by Japan. See ▷ Crimes against Humanity.

CROZET ISLANDS.

An archipelago of five larger (Apostles, Pig, Penguins, Possession and Eastern Islands) and 15 tiny islands; with a total area of 300 sq. km; since 1964 French meteorological and scientific station on Possession Island (28 members); part of the ▷ French Southern and Antarctic Territories.

CRUDE OIL.

A basic raw material of the petroleum and petro-chemical industry; subject since 1933 of international co-operation, international conventions, international statistics and also international disputes. The industrial extraction and refining of crude oil for oil lamps, oils and greases began in 1862, and only 8 years later the first large American oil company Standard Oil was formed, which began to search for oil in the Middle East and was followed by other American, British, Dutch, French and Italian companies, whose competitive struggle had an influence on international relations both in the years 1870–1914 as well as after World War I and World War II.

The reserves of crude oil were estimated for the first time in 1920 by the US Geological Department at 43,055 million barrels. World production in 1900 came to 149,137 barrels, of which 75,780 were produced by Russia, the USA 63,621 and the rest by the British Indies, Dutch Indies, Japan, Peru, Romania and others. In 1913 production increased to 385,345, of which the USA – 248,446; Russia – 62,834 and the rest – the above mentioned countries and Argentina, Iraq, Egypt, Mexico, Trinidad, Sarawak. In 1920 production exceeded 1000 million barrels. After World War I, rich sources of crude oil were discovered in Latin America, where Mexico in 1938 was the first to nationalize the petroleum industry. In 1971 the known and proven reserves of crude oil were appraised at 50–60 billion barrels and in fact estimated at 200–500 billion tons. World production, which in 1960 exceeded 1 billion, reached 2.3 billion tons in 1970 and 4 billion tons in 1980. The main producers in 1960–80 were: the USA, USSR, Venezuela, Kuwait, Saudi Arabia, Iran, Iraq, Libya, Algeria, Indonesia, Mexico, Abu Dhabi, Nigeria, Romania, Qatar. In the Warsaw Pact countries more than 80% of crude oil is produced by the USSR; in Latin America the main producers are Venezuela and Mexico. Dominant in the Middle East are Kuwait, the United Arab Emirates and Saudi Arabia. The floor of the Mediterranean Sea has become a new region for crude oil exploration. With the growing industrialization of the world, the importance of crude oil as one of the main sources of energy has grown with each decade. On the one hand this has led to competition among the world petroleum companies to secure regions of exploration for themselves, and on the other it has resulted in the organization of the oil-exporting states in unified action against the international cartels of the world oil companies. On Dec. 27, 1970 OPEC, at the

Cuba

session in Caracas, resolved to cancel the contracts of the oil-importing states and negotiate a uniform increase in posted prices. On Feb. 14, 1971 an agreement between the oil-producing states united in OPEC and the oil-importing states was signed in Teheran on a general price increase of 30% for Persian Gulf crude. Then, on Feb. 14, 1971, the governments of Algeria, Saudi Arabia, Libya and Iraq at a conference in Tripoli, based on the Teheran oil agreement, resolved to raise the price from US $2.55 to US $3.75 per barrel. The negotiations of these governments with the West European importers – France, the FRG, Italy, the Netherlands, Spain, and the UK – led to the signing of an agreement on Apr. 2, 1971 in Tripoli, guaranteeing the supply of oil at a price of US $3.45 per barrel up to 1976. This agreement was already revised in the fall of 1973 in connection with the Middle East crisis and the raising of the price for oil by the Arab states to more than US $10 per barrel.

In 1969–72 basically all of the disputes and conflicts ended with concessions by the world companies, whose united front was first broken in July 1972, when, against the background of the nationalization of the Iraq Petroleum Company, five oil companies withdrew from the suggested boycott of Arab oil: Deminex FRG, Japan Petroleum, Development Corporation, Hispano oil, and Osterreichische Mineralverwaltung AG, called the Zürich Group, since negotiations were held in the Secretariat of the Group in Zurich.

Shortly thereafter on Aug. 21–25, 1972, at an intergovernmental Conference in Caracas of the oil-producing and exporting states of Latin America (Argentina, Bolivia, Brazil, Chile, the Dominican Republic, Ecuador, Guyana, Jamaica, Colombia, Costa Rica, Uruguay and Venezuela) an intergovernmental secretariat for petroleum and natural gas and a regional organization for energy and the oil market of Latin America were formed with the task of co-ordinating the oil policies of the 16 states. The Conference supported the Venezuelan plan submitted to OPEC for having OPEC create an International Oil Bank, which would make the OPEC member states independent from conducting oil transactions through the banks of the highly developed states. The five of the Arab states from the Persian Gulf region belonging to OPEC (Abu Dhabi, Iraq, Kuwait, Qatar and Saudi Arabia) concluded an agreement on Oct. 11, 1972 with 10 Western oil companies, which, in order to maintain their interests in the region, had to agree to give the five above states a 51% share in their concessions and full legal supervision over the concessions. The rapidly increasing price of oil directed the attention of the world companies to reserves located under sea beds, as e.g. in southern Asia, where during the Vietnam War intensive exploration was conducted, resulting in 1968–69 in the discovery of large reserves of crude oil under sea beds in the following regions: around the entire Indochina peninsula, along the south coast of China, Taiwan in the north-easterly direction through the eastern China Sea to Japan and along the coast of Korea. In 1970 the governments of Japan, South Korea and the Chiang Kai-shek regime of Taiwan granted concessions to American and Japanese oil companies, which resulted in a dispute between Japan and Taiwan over the right to the archipelago of uninhabited islands and their territorial waters, located 150–200 km north-east of Taiwan (called in Chinese Tiaoyu, in Japanese Senkaku), where crude oil was discovered. Taiwan placed its flag on the islands and granted a concession to the American Pacific Gulf Company; the Japanese reacted to this by removing the flags and granting the concession to the Japanese Mitsubishi Company. The Chinese People's Republic protested against both the

decisions of Japan and Taiwan, claiming sovereignty over Taiwan and its territorial waters. At the same time, the Chinese People's Republic announced its claims to all discoveries of oil and gas on the Chinese territorial shelf. The dispute was not resolved and neither was the second dispute between South Korea and Japan, over their concurrent granting of concessions to various American companies to explore for oil on the sea bed located between Korea and Japan. Simultaneously, Thailand and Cambodia announced claims to some islands near South Vietnam. The American oil companies received rights from Indonesia under the condition of granting the government of Indonesia 60–70% of the profits. This higher-than-average rate was due to the discovery that supposedly all of Indonesia is situated on a huge pool of offshore petroleum. At the end of the 1970s, the international oil companies began negotiations on exploration of the Chinese continental shelf. On June 22, 1971 the government of the UK announced that exploration of offshore waters of the North Sea had revealed tremendous reserves of crude oil and natural gas, following which the British goverment began to grant drilling concessions over an area of c. 20,000 million sq. km. Similar reserves were discovered under the coastal offshore waters of Norway. The major licences were granted to Shell Oil Company and British Petroleum Company. In the 1960's the USSR also concentrated a significant part of its drilling operations on the beds of the Black and Caspian Seas.

On Oct. 17, 1973 the Arab countries announced in Kuwait that they would use the oil weapon as a means of pressure in the conflict with Israel. And then, in the following months up to Jan. 1974, they gradually reduced the production of crude oil by 30% and placed an embargo on the supply of oil to states with a pro-Israel policy, leading to an energy crisis, especially in the USA and Western Europe. In 1979 the fall of the monarchy in Iran shut off the supply of Iranian oil to Israel and the Republic of South Africa. OPEC raised the price of crude oil to US $23.50 per barrel. In 1980 the intensification of the energy crisis made the production and supply of crude oil from the Middle East a great problem for Western Europe, Japan, and the USA.

The decline of daily crude oil consumption in the years:

	1973	1979	1983
USA	16,870	17,910	14,705
W. Europe	15,155	15,000	12,190
Japan	5,960	5,485	4,360

The USA petroleum reserves, insignificant in 1973 reached 430 million barrels in 1983, with a goal of 750 million barrels for 1990.

In October 1987 the ▷ UNESCAP decided that stringent oil conservation measures should be taken soon by governments in the Asia-Pacific region. Alternative energy sources must be developed since, at the current consumption rate, the region's known oil reserve will be exhausted in less than 16 years. A regional energy plan for 1990–1995 urging those measures was approved in Bangkok in October by a committee of UNESCAP, the United Nations Economic and Social Commission for Asia and the Pacific.

G.B. MOODY, *Petroleum Exploration Handbook*, New York, 1961; J.A. CLARK, *The Chronological History of the Petroleum and Natural Gas Industries*, New York, 1963; CH. TUGENDHAT, *Oil, the Biggest Business*, London, 1968; M. ADELMAN, *The World Petroleum Market*, Baltimore, 1975; Oil and Energy. *UN Chronicle*, March 1983, p. 90. A Special Report in: *International Herald Tribune*, October 18, 1984.

CRUISE. An American supersonic rocket armed with conventional or atomic warheads, launched from sea or air for a distance up to 3400 km. See also ▷ SLBM and ▷ SLCM.

R.K. BETTS, *Cruise Missiles: Technology, Strategy, Politics*, Oxford, Mass., 1982. D. ROBERTSON, *Guide to Modern Defense and Strategy*, Detroit, 1988.

CRUSADES. An international name for a series of wars between the European Christians and the Arab Muslims for the purpose of recovering the Holy Sepulchre at Jerusalem initiated and promoted by the Papacy from 1095 until the mid-15th century. In the 20th century calls for anti-communist intervention after the October Revolution 1917 in Russia were termed Crusades.

A. GIEYSZTOR, "The Genesis of the Crusades: The Encyclical of Sergius IV (1009–1012)", in: *Medievalia et Humanistica*, 1948 and 1950; S. RUNCIMAN, The History of the Crusades, Cambridge, 1954; H.E. MEYER, *Bibliographie zur Geschichte der Kreuzzuge*, Heidelberg, 1960.

CRUZEIRO. A monetary unit of Brazil; one cruzeiro = 100 centavos; issued by the Banco Central de Brasil.

CRYSTALLOGRAPHY. A subject of international co-operation. Organization reg with the UIA:

International Union of Crystallography, f. 1947, London. Publ. *Acta Crystallographica* (English, French, German, Russian), *Journal of Applied Crystallography* (English, French, German, Russian), *Structure Reports* (English), *International Tables for X-ray Crystallography* (English), *World Directory of Crystallographers*.

Yearbook of International Organizations.

CSCE ▷ Conference on Security and Cooperation of Europe.

CSTD. ▷ ACAST.

CUBA. Member of the UN. Republic of Cuba. República de Cuba. State in Central America, in the Antilles, the Caribbean. Area (the Islands of Cuba and Pines plus some 1600 surrounding islets): 110,922 sq. km. Pop. 1986 est. 10,240,000 (1899 census: 1,572,000; 1907: 2,048,000; 1919: 2,889,000; 1943: 4,778,000; 1953: 5,829,000; 1970: 8,569,000). Capital city: Havana with 1,951,000 inhabitants (1982). GNP per capita (1979): US $1410. Currency: 1 peso = 100 centavos. Official language: Spanish. National Day: Jan. 1, Liberation Day, 1959.

Founding member of the League of Nations 1919–39, member of UN since Oct. 24, 1945 and all its specialized agencies except BANK/IBRD, IMF, IDA, IFC; member of CMEA (since July 1972). International relations: 1515–1819 Spanish colony; 1810–37 with self-government and representation at Spanish Cortes; again Spanish dependency under colonial administration in civil war, 1865–78, which ended with restoration of self-government and representation at Cortes as well as gradual abolition of slavery 1880–86. In 1895 Spain suspended constitutional rights provoking a rebellion for independence, which ended with US intervention and the American–Spanish war. In the Paris Treaty of Dec. 10, 1898 Spain renounced its rights to Puerto Rico, the Philippines, the Isle of Guam and the rights to Cuba, entrusting the USA with protection of its inhabitants on Jan. 1, 1899. From Jan. 1, 1899 to May 20, 1902 Cuba remained under US military administration. The Cuban Assembly working Nov. 5, 1900–June 21, 1901 on a Constitution of the Republic of Cuba, was forced by the USA to include in the Constitution the so-called Platt Amendment, which tied Cuba to the USA by a Provision granting the USA the right to intervene in Cuban internal affairs and a military base for 99 years at Guantanamo. The intervention clause in the Platt Amendment was abandoned on May 29, 1934 by the US President Franklin Delano Roosevelt, but the Guantanamo statute has remained unchanged. In World Wars I and II on the Allies side. One year after overthrowing the Batista dictatorship by the Revolutionary Government under Fidel Castro on Jan. 1, 1959 the US government started an economic boycott of Cuba. On Apr. 21, 1961 anti-Castro emigrants supported by the CIA attempted an invasion of Cuba ▷ Bay of Pigs or Bahia de Cochinos. On May 1, 1961 the Cuban government announced a policy of socialist reconstruction. On Jan. 31, 1962 the Cuban government was expelled from the OAS and all its specialized agencies. In two years all Latin-American States, except Mexico, broke off diplomatic, consular and trade relations with Cuba. On Oct. 22–28, 1962 the issue of construction of Soviet missile-launching-pads on Cuba initiated the Cuba Missile Crisis 1962. In 1963–64 Venezuela and in 1967 Colombia accused Cuba of threatening peace in the Western Hemisphere before the UN Security Council. In 1963–72 Cuba put the case of its economic boycott before the UN. In Spring 1973 the USA and Cuba concluded an agreement on the joint suppression of air and sea piracy, later joined by Canada and Mexico. (▷ Cuba-USA Understanding on Hijacking, 1973). In 1976 Cuba rendered military and civil aid to Angola in its struggle for independence and in 1977 to Ethiopia in its conflict with Somalia. On Feb. 28, 1978 Cuba extended its fishing zone to 200 sea miles, followed by a US–Cuban treaty of fisheries, signed in Havana, Apr. 27, 1977. The Cuban Liberation organization, Movimiento de 26 Julio, founded by Fidel Castro, was transformed in July, 1961, together with other groupings, into a Revolutionary Organization and in 1962 into the United Party of Socialist Revolution, which on Oct. 3, 1965 was changed into the Communist Party of Cuba. On May 1, 1973 Fidel Castro stated that Cuba would not return to OAS but was ready to participate in the founding of a regional organization in the Caribbean, not to be seated in Washington, which would promote the interests of Latin-American and Caribbean states.

In Nov. 1981 high-level talks took place between Cuba and the USA but in Apr., 1982 US sanctions against Cuban economy were tightened. During the ▷ Falkland Islands/Malvinas crisis in the fall of 1982 Cuba supported Argentina in the UN General Assembly Committee on Decolonization. Cuba in 1984 signed an agreement on the withdrawal of Cuban forces from Angola after the withdrawal of South African troops from Angola and Namibia, and on strict application of UN Security Council Res. 435 on the achievement of independence of Namibia. ▷ Angola – Cuba Declaration 1984. See also ▷ Africa and Cuba. ▷ World Heritage UNESCO List.

Tratados, convenios celebrados por la República de Cuba desde 1916 a 1929, La Habana, 1929; *Tratados, convenios desde 1930*; R.H. FITZGIBBON, *Cuba and the United States 1900–1935*, New York, 1935; *Tratados, convenios y convenciones celebrados por la República de Cuba desde 1903 a 1914*, La Habana, 1936; F.P. SAURANSA, *Bibliografia Cubana*, La Habana, 1945; P.M. SWEEZY, *Anatomy of a Revolution*, New York, 1960; H.L. MATTHEWS, *The Cuban Story*, New York, 1961; K. MEYER, T. SZULC, *The Cuban Invasion; The Chronicle of a Disaster*, New York, 1962; D.L. LASSON, *The Cuban Crisis of 1962. Selected Documents and Chronology*, Boston, 1963; *Tratados bilaterales de Cuba 1902–1963*, La Habana, 1963; H.B. JOHN, *Los Estados Unidos contra Cuba*, 2 Vols, La Habana, 1964; M. LEMIDEL, *Les États Unies et la Révolution Cubaine 1959–1964*, Paris, 1968; *Compendio de tratados bilaterales*, La Habana, 1971; *Constitución de la República de Cuba*, La Habana, 1976; C. BLASIER, C. MESA (eds), *Cuba in the World*, Pittsburgh, 1979; *The Europa Yearbook 1984. A World Survey*, Vol. II, pp. 1463–1476, London 1984. T. SZULC, *Fidel A Critical Portrait*, New York, 1986; W.S. SMITH, *The Closest of Enemies. A Personal and Diplomatic History of US–Cuban Relations Since 1957*, New York, 1987; M. H. MORLEY, *Imperial State and Revolution: The United States and Cuba, 1952–1986*, New York, 1988.

CUBA AND PUERTO RICO TREATY, 1898. A Treaty also called the Paris peace treaty, concluded between the USA and Spain on Dec. 10, 1898 after the war of Apr. 25–Aug. 12, 1898, won by the USA; according to art. 7, Spain renounced all rights to Cuba, and ceded to the USA the rights to Puerto Rico together with the islands of Culebra, Culebrita, Vieques, and the island of Guam (art. 2), as well as the Philippines against 20 million dollars (art. 3). The Treaty became effective on Apr. 11, 1899; confirmed by the friendship agreement of July 3, 1902.

W.M. MALLOY, *Treaties, Conventions ... between the USA and other Powers*, Washington, DC, 1910, Vol. 2.

CUBAN-AMERICAN AGREEMENTS 1980's ▷ American-Cuban Immigration Agreements 1984 and 1987.

CUBAN MISSILE CRISIS, 1962. A conflict between the USA and the USSR threatening nuclear confrontation, Oct. 22–28, 1962, over the question of principle concerning Soviet intermediate missile launchers in Cuba. Dramatic negotiations concluded with compromise on Nov. 2, 1962 when the Soviet Union undertook not to supply Cuba with missiles and the USA not to interfere with socialist Cuba. The crisis was a turning point in international relations in that any conflict between nuclear powers posed a danger of nuclear confrontation.

On the 25th anniversary of the missile crisis an American-Soviet Harvard Symposium took place in Cambridge, Massachusetts.

On Jan. 28, 1989 Soviet officials disclosed that Soviet nuclear warheads had already been deployed to Cuba in 1962 and could be fired at American cities.

J. DANIEL, J.G. HUBBEL, *Strike in the West. The Complex Story of the Cuban Crisis*, New York, 1963; "Dokumentation zur Kubakrise 1962", in: *Jahrbuch für Internationales Recht 1965*, pp. 476–502; T. SZULC, *Latin America*, New York, 1966, pp. 109–113; *Newsweek*, January 20, 1975; B.J. BERNSTEIN, "Kennedy and the Cuban Missile Crisis: was this crisis necessary?", in: *The Washington Post*, Oct. 2, 1975; D. DETZER, *The Brink, The Cuban Missile Crisis, 1962*, New York, 1979. E. PACE, *Dean Rusk Reveals Ploy Prepared by Kennedy Over Cuba*, in: *New York Times*, August 30, 1987; J.C. BLIGHT, J.S. NYE Jr., D.A. WELCH, The Cuban Missile Crisis Revisited, in: *Foreign Affairs*, Fall, 1987; R. BERNSTEIN, Meeting Sheds New Light on Cuban Missile Crisis, in: *The New York Times*, October 14, 1987; R.L. BLEDSOE, B.A. BOCZEK, *The International Law Dictionary*, Oxford, 1987; D. ROBERTSON, *Guide to Modern Defense and Strategy*, Detroit, 1988; R.L. GARTHOFF, *Cuban Missile Crisis, The Soviet Story*, in: *Foreign Policy*, Fall, 1988; S. BUNDY, *Danger and Survival: Choices about the bomb in the first 50 years*, New York, 1988. *New York Times 29 and 30 January 1989.*

CUBA–USA TREATIES, 1903. Five years after the ▷ Cuba and Puerto Rico Treaty, 1898, with Spain, the United States signed with Cuba two treaties on May 23, 1903: (1) a political covenant called the Permanent Treaty, embodying the ▷ Platt Amendment, and (2) an economic agreement called the Reciprocity Treaty. Both treaties came into force on Dec. 27, 1903.

C.E. CHAPMAN, *A History of the Cuban Republic*, New York, 1927; P.S. WRIGHT, *The Cuban Situation and our Treaty Relations*, Washington, DC, 1931; J.A. LITERAS, "Relations between Cuba and the US", in: *International Conciliation*, No. 296, January. 1934.

CUBA–USA UNDERSTANDING ON HIJACKING, 1973. The text of the four articles of the agreement published on Feb. 15, 1973 at Havana and Washington is as follows:

"The Government of the United States of America and the Government of the Republic of Cuba, on the bases of equality and strict reciprocity, agree:

First: Any person who hereafter seizes, removes, appropriates or diverts from its normal route or activities an aircraft or vessel registered under the laws of one of the parties and brings it to the territory of the other party shall be considered to have committed an offense and therefore shall either be returned to the party of registry of the aircraft or vessel to be tried by the courts of that party in conformity with its laws or be brought before the courts of the party whose territory he reached for trial in conformity with its laws for the offense punishable by the most severe penalty according to the circumstances and the seriousness of the acts to which this article refers. In addition, the party whose territory is reached by the aircraft or vessel shall take all necessary steps to facilitate without delay the continuation of the journey of the passengers and crew innocent of the hijacking of the aircraft or vessel in question, with their belongings, including any funds obtained by extortion or other illegal means, or the return of the foregoing to the territory of the first party; likewise, it shall take all steps to protect the physical integrity of the aircraft or vessel and all goods, carried with it, including any funds obtained by extortion or other illegal means, and the physical integrity of the passengers and crew innocent of the hijacking, and their belongings, while they are in its territory as a consequence of or in connection with the acts to which this article refers.

In the event that the offenses referred to above are not punishable under the laws existing in the country to which the persons committing them arrived, the party in question shall be obligated, except in the case of minor offenses, to return the persons who have committed such acts, in accordance with the applicable legal procedures, to the territory of the other party to be tried by its courts in conformity with its laws.

Second: Each party shall try with a view to severe punishment in accordance with its laws any person who, within its territory, hereafter conspires to promote, or promotes, or prepares, or directs, or forms part of an expedition which from its territory or any other place carries out acts of violence or depredation against aircraft or vessels of any kind or registration coming from or going to the territory of the other party or who, within its territory, hereafter conspires to promote, or promotes, or prepares, or directs, or forms part of an expedition which from its territory or any other place carries out such acts or other similar unlawful acts in the territory of the other party.

Third: Each party shall apply strictly its own laws to any national of the other party who, coming from the territory of the other party, enters its territory, violating its laws as well as national and international requirements pertaining to immigration, health, customs and the like.

Fourth: The party in whose territory the perpetrators of the acts described in art. 1 may take into consideration any extenuating or mitigating circumstances in those cases in which the persons responsible for the acts were being sought for strictly political reasons and were in real and imminent danger of death without a viable alternative for leaving the country, provided there was no financial extortion or physical injury to the members of the crew, passengers, or other persons in connection with the hijacking."

The Department of State Bulletin, No. 1758, March 5, 1973.

CUBIC CENTIMETER. An international volume unit = 0.000001 cubic meter, or approx. 0.061 cubic inch.

CUIUS REGIO, EIUS RELIGIO. *Latin*: "he whose country it is, decides its religion"; European international term in modern times, expression of the principle adopted in the ▷ Augsburg Religious, Peace Treaty of, 1555.

CUIUS SOLUM, EIUS COELUM. *Latin*: = "he who has the land, has the sky". A doctrine adopted in international law for a view expressed in 13th-century *Pandectum Voetus* (publ. in Venice, 1541); "*Cuius est solum, eius debat esse usque ad coelum ut his et infra, quo vivant coelum*" interpreted until the first launching of Artificial Earth Satellites (1957) either as unlimited right to ▷ Outer space, or to certain layers of ▷ Air space.

CULTURAL AGGRESSION. An international term first mentioned during the annual UNESCO session in Nairobi, 1976, in connection with the debate concerning the forms of mass media information in the world; denoting the imposing of foreign cultural patterns mainly through radio, film and television. Delegates of Africa accused the BBC and Voice of America among others of conducting "permanent cultural aggression" round the clock by giving Third World listeners information selected by London and Washington, "imposing patterns of western culture at the cost of our own, diverting the attention of our peoples from the problems of Africa." ▷ New International Information Order.

CULTURAL AND NATURAL HERITAGE PROTECTION. An action conducted under the auspices of UNESCO since 1972 by the Committee for World Heritage in co-operation with the Center (in Rome) of Studies on the Protection and Restoration of Cultural Values of the International Council for the Protection of Monuments and Historic Sites, ICOMOS and the International Union for the Protection of Nature and its Resources, UICN. ▷ World Heritage UNESCO List.

CULTURAL AND SOCIAL CENTER FOR THE ASIAN AND PACIFIC REGION. A center est. 1968 by agreement between the governments of Australia, Japan, South Korea, Malaysia, New Zealand, Philippines, Taiwan, Thailand and Republic of Vietnam, signed in Canberra on Aug. 1, 1968. Specialized organization of ASPAC.

"The purpose of the Centre is to promote friendly relations and mutual understanding among the peoples of the Asian and Pacific Regions through the furtherance of collaboration in cultural and related social fields" (art. 2).

UNTS, Vol. 653, p. 427.

CULTURAL CO-OPERATION, INTERNATIONAL. A subject of bilateral and multilateral agreements, conventions, treaties in the 20th century. The League of Nations International Institute of Intellectual Co-operation published in Paris, 1938, *Recueil des accords intellectuels, 1919–1938*. Following World War II, UNESCO published a collection of cultural agreements in English and French, in the form of loose-leaf publications.

An international exchange of cultural goods and services is a subject of bi- and multi-lateral agreements.

The Inter-American Convention on promotion of cultural relations was signed in Buenos Aires on Oct. 23, 1936.

LNTS, Vol. 188, p. 125.

CULTURAL DEVELOPMENT WORLD DECADE, 1988–1997. On Dec. 8, 1986 the UN General Assembly and UNESCO called for the observance of a World Decade for Cultural Development from Jan. 1, 1988 to Dec. 3, 1997. The Plan of Action presented the four major objectives assigned to the Decade:
– acknowledgement of the cultural dimension of development;
– affirmation and enrichment of cultural identities;
– broadening participation in culture;
– promotion of international cultural cooperation.

UNESCO, *Launching of the World Decade for Cultural Development*, Paris, 1988.

CULTURAL FUND OF THE NORDIC COUNTRIES. A fund est. 1966 by a treaty between the governments of Denmark, Finland, Iceland, Norway and Sweden with the task of supporting cultural co-operation of the Nordic states; signed on Oct. 3, 1966 in Copenhagen; came into force July 1, 1967. Contributions to the fund are as follows: 37% from Sweden, 23% from Denmark, 22% from Finland, 17% from Norway and 1% from Iceland.

UNTS, Vol. 610, p. 174.

CULTURAL HAGUE CONVENTION, 1954. A Convention elaborated by UNESCO and signed in The Hague on May 14, 1954. Full name International Convention on Protection of Cultural Property during a War. ▷ Cultural Property Protection.

CULTURAL PROPERTY PROTECTION. A subject of international co-operation and agreements. The principles concerning protection of cultural property during armed conflict were set down in the Conventions of The Hague of 1899 and 1907 and in the Washington Pact of Apr. 15, 1935. A special Conference convened by UNESCO for the purpose of drawing up and adopting the Convention for the Protection of Cultural Property in the Event of Armed Conflict and Regulation for the Execution of the said Convention and Protocol, was held in The Hague, Apr. 21–May 14, 1954. The Convention signed May 14, 1954 came into force on Aug. 7, 1956. The text of the first ten Articles of the Convention is as follows:

"Art. 1. For the purposes of the present Convention, the term "cultural property" shall cover, irrespective of origin or ownership:
(a) movable or immovable property of great importance to the cultural heritage of every people, such as monuments of architecture, art or history, whether religious or secular; archeological sites; groups of buildings which, as a whole, are of historical or artistic interest; works of art; manuscripts, books and other objects of artistic, historical or archaeological interest; as well as scientific collections and important collections of books or archives or of reproductions of the property defined above;
(b) buildings whose main and effective purpose is to preserve or exhibit the movable cultural property defined in sub-paragraph (a) such as museums, large libraries and depositories of archives, and refuges intended to shelter, in the event of armed conflict, the movable cultural property defined in sub-paragraph (a);
(c) centres containing a large amount of cultural property as defined in sub-paragraphs (a) and (b), to be known as 'centres containing monuments'.
Art. 2. For the purposes of the present Convention, the protection of cultural property shall comprise the safeguarding of and respect for such property.
Art. 3. The High Contracting Parties undertake to prepare in time of peace for the safeguarding of cultural property situated within their own territory against the foreseeable effects of an armed conflict, by taking such measures as they consider appropriate.

Art. 4.(1) The High Contracting Parties undertake to respect cultural property situated within their own territory as well as within the territory of other High Contracting Parties by refraining from any use of the property and its immediate surroundings or of the appliances in use for its protection for purposes which are likely to expose it to destruction or damage in the event of armed conflict; and by refraining from any act of hostility directed against such property.
(2) The obligations mentioned in paragraph 1 of the present Article may be waived only in cases where military necessity imperatively requires such a waiver.
(3) The High Contracting Parties further undertake to prohibit, prevent and, if necessary, put a stop to any form of theft, pillage or misappropriation of, and any acts of vandalism directed against, cultural property. They shall refrain from requisitioning movable cultural property situated in the territory of another High Contracting Party.
(4) They shall refrain from any act directed by way of reprisals against cultural property.
(5) No High Contracting Party may evade the obligations incumbent upon it under the present Article, by reason of the fact that the latter has not applied the measures of safeguard referred to in Article 3.
Art. 5.(1) Any High Contracting Party in occupation of the whole or part of the territory of another High Contracting Party shall as far as possible support the competent national authorities of the occupied country in safeguarding and preserving its cultural property.
(2) Should it prove necessary to take measures to preserve cultural property situated in occupied territory and damage by military operations, and should the competent national authorities be unable to take such measures, the Occupying Power shall, as far as possible, and in close co-operation with such authorities, take the most necessary measures of preservation.
(3) Any High Contracting Party whose government is considered their legitimate government by members of a resistance movement, shall, if possible, draw their attention to the obligation to comply with those provisions of the Convention dealing with respect for cultural property.
Art. 6. In accordance with the provisions of Article 16, cultural property may bear a distinctive emblem so as to facilitate its recognition.
Art. 7.(1) The High Contracting Parties undertake to introduce in time of peace into their military regulations or instructions such provisions as may ensure observance of the present Convention, and to foster in the members of their armed forces a spirit of respect for the culture and cultural property of all peoples.
(2) The High Contracting Parties undertake to plan or establish in peacetime, within their armed forces, services or specialist personnel whose purpose will be to secure respect for cultural property and to co-operate with the civilian authorities responsible for safeguarding it.
Art. 8.(1) There may be placed under special protection a limited number of refuges intended to shelter movable cultural property in the event of armed conflict, of centres containing monuments and other immovable cultural property of very great importance, provided that they:
(a) are situated at an adequate distance form any large industrial centre or from any important military objective constituting a vulnerable point, such as, for example, an aerodrome, broadcasting station, establishment engaged upon work of national defence, a port or railway station of relative importance or a main line of communication;
(b) are not used for military purposes.
(2) A refuge for movable cultural property may also be placed under special protection, whatever its location, if it is so constructed that, in all probability, it will not be damaged by bombs.
(3) A centre containing monuments shall be deemed to be of use for military purposes whenever it is used for the movement of military personnel or material, even in transit. The same shall apply whenever activities directly connected with military operations, the stationing of military personnel, or the production of war material are carried on within the centre.
(4) The guarding of cultural property mentioned in paragraph 1 above by armed custodians specially empowered to do so, or the presence, in the vicinity of such cultural property, of police forces normally responsible

C

for the maintenance of public order shall not be deemed to be use for military purposes.

(5) If any cultural property mentioned in paragraph 1 of the present Article is situated near an important military objective as defined in the said paragraph, it may nevertheless be placed under special protection if the High Contracting Party asking for that protection undertakes, in the event of armed conflict, to make no use of the objective and particularly, in the case of a port, railway station or aerodrome, to divert all traffic therefrom. In that event, such diversion shall be prepared in time of peace.

(6) Special protection is granted to cultural property by its entry in the "International Register of Cultural Property under Special Protection." This entry shall only be made, in accordance with the provisions of the present Convention and under the conditions provided for in the Regulations for the execution of the Convention.

Art. 9. The High Contracting Parties undertake to ensure the immunity of cultural property under special protection by refraining, from the time of entry in the International Register, from any act of hostility directed against such property and, except for the cases provided for in paragraph 5 of Article 8, from any use of such property or its surroundings for military purposes.

Art. 10. During an armed conflict, cultural property under special protection shall be marked with the distinctive emblem described in Article 16, and shall be open to international control as provided for in the Regulations for the execution of the Convention."

In 1970 the General Conference of the UNESCO adopted a Convention on the Means of Prohibiting the Illicit Import, Export and Transfer of Ownership of Cultural Property.

On Nov. 21, 1986 the General Assembly called on States to pursue bilateral agreements to prepare inventories of their cultural property and to adopt the necessary protective legislation with regard to their own heritage and that of other nations.

UNTS, Vol. 249, pp. 242–248; *UN Chronicle*, March, 1980, p. 76; *UN Chronicle*, 1986, No 1, pp. 19–20.

CULTURAL PROPERTY RETURN OR RECONSTRUCTION.
A problem of the return of cultural treasures to the country of their origin, presented by the Director General of UNESCO, Amadou Mahtar M'Bow in an appeal to governments and world public opinion on June 7, 1978:

"The genius of each nation finds its most noble expression in the cultural heritage, since through the centuries it has been made up of the work of its architects, sculptors, painters, engravers and goldsmiths – all those creators of form who knew how to give a work a concrete character of manifold beauty and uniqueness. Due to historical turmoils many countries have been deprived of a priceless part of their heritage in which their identity is contained."

The General Director of UNESCO appealed to countries to conclude bilateral agreements on the return of cultural treasures, supported by long-term loans, deposits, selling and donating works to those institutions interested in fostering an equitable international exchange.

Countries which still have not done so should ratify and implement the Convention which would effectively put an end to the illegal smuggling of artistic and archaeological objects. In A.M. M'Bow's opinion, countries which have been stripped of their irreplaceable masterpieces have the right to demand their return. They know that the calling of art is its universality. They are aware that art speaks about their history, their truth, that it is not only their history. They are pleased that other nations in the world can study and take delight in the work of their ancestors. They know that for centuries some works have been intimately connected with their soil and roots, from which they emerged and which no power is able to sever. These nations demand the return of their art treasures, those which are most representative of their culture, those works to which they attach the most importance and whose absence, for psychological reasons, is unbearable to them.

The UN General Assembly in its XXXIII session debated the UNESCO motion on point (c) entitled The Protection and Further Development of Cultural Treasures.

The UN General Assembly adopted on Nov. 29, 1979, without a vote, Res. 34/64 under which it invited member states to take all necessary steps for the return or restitution of cultural property to the countries of its origin and also invited all governments to accede to the Convention on the Means of Prohibiting and Prevention of the Illicit Import, Export and Transfer of Ownership of Cultural Property, 1970. On Nov. 23, 1981 the UN General Assembly invited all governments to co-operate with the Intergovernmental Committee for Promoting the Return of Cultural Property to its Country of Origin or its Restitution in Case of Illicit Appropriation.

On Nov. 21, 1986 in the debate in the General Assembly on illicit traffic in cultural property many member states (Iraq, Nepal, Oman, Ecuador, Peru, Syria) declared that no real progress had been made and no genuine response had been elicited on the return of cultural property to its original owners.

UN Yearbook 1969; UN Chronicle, February, 1982; January, 1984; *UN Chronicle*, 1986, No 1, pp. 19–20.

CULTURE.
International term used in the UN system for the field covered by the activities of ▷ UNESCO.

CURAÇAO.
Island in the Dutch West Indies, part of the ▷ Netherlands Antilles. Area: 461 sq km. Population 1985 estimate 172,000. Since Jan. 1, 1986 autonomy with elected parliament of representatives of the population of Cucaçao (14 seats) and of the islands Bonaire (3), Saba (1), St. Eustatius (1) and St. Maarten (3).

In 1996 will be granted full independence.

See also ▷ Aruba.

CURIA ROMANA.
▷ Roman Curia

CURRENCIES OF THE WORLD.
For thousands of years different means of payment were used depending, on what in a given period was regarded as the most valuable metals or products. From 3000 BC to the 19th century these were most often copper, silver, as well as gold, which became the foundation of currencies in the 19th and beginning of the 20th century. After World Wars I and II the period of duration of currencies based on the gold standard, became ever shorter (this applied only to paper banknotes, not gold coins). The number of freely exchangeable hard currencies shrank. In 1970 these were: American dollar, Argentinian peso, Austrian schilling, Belgian franc, Canadian dollar, Hondurian lempira, Lebanese pound, Liberian dollar, Mexican peso, Panamanian balboa, Saudi rial, Spanish peseta, Swedish krona, Swiss franc. Many other hard currencies, among them French franc, Dutch gulden, Japanese yen, English pound, were subject to exchange controlled by the state. From Aug. 15, 1971, the date when the USA suspended the convertibility of the dollar into gold, the number of freely exchangeable hard currencies diminished. This was also related to the fact that the majority of states did not permit the export of gold, while only the following states permitted the unlimited export of their currency abroad in 1975: Argentina, Belgium, Bolivia, Canada, Congo, Costa Rica, Ecuador, France, the FRG, Great Britain, Guatemala, Haiti, Honduras, Laos, Lebanon, Liberia, Luxembourg, Mexico, Nicaragua, Pakistan, Panama, Peru, Portugal, Saudi Arabia, Switzerland, the USA, Uruguay, Venezuela. The possession of foreign currencies was only permitted in the following countries in 1975: Afghanistan, Argentina, Australia, Austria, Belgium, Bolivia, Canada, Ecuador, Finland, the FRG, Greece, Holland, Haiti, Honduras, Hong Kong, Kuwait, Laos, Lebanon, Liberia, Mexico, Panama, Peru, Poland, Saudi Arabia, Switzerland, Taiwan, the USA, Uruguay, Venezuela. The majority of world currencies were grouped in ▷ Monetary Areas or other integrative systems of financial co-operation. Not officially connected with any system in 1975 were the currencies of: Afghanistan, Argentina, Brazil, Burma, Burundi, Cambodia, Congo, Egypt, Ethiopia, Guinea, Indonesia, Iraq, Iran, Israel, Japan, Laos, Lebanon, Nepal, Paraguay, Peru, Rhodesia, Rwanda, Somalia, South Korea, Saudi Arabia, Spain, Sudan, Syria, Taiwan, Thailand, Tunisia, Uruguay, Yugoslavia. An annual analysis of all of the currencies of the world has been published since 1945 by Pick Publishing Corp. in New York. Current information and analyses are published by: Agence Economique et Financiere Paris; *The Economist*, London; *Finanz und Wirtschaft*, Zurich; *Financial Times*, London; *Journal of Commerce*, New York; *Northern Miner*, Toronto; Pick's *Currency Report*, New York; *Vereinigter Wirtschaftsdienst*, Frankfurt am Main; *Wall Street Journal*, New York; in addition several international banks make analyses of currency markets for their clients, such as Bank Leu and Co. A.G. in Zurich, Barclay's Bank in London and others. The American International Investment Corporation. publ. in San Francisco from 1963 *World Currencies Charts*. ▷ SDR.

See also ▷ Exchange Rate.

F. PICK *Currency Yearbook*, New York, 1968; *Valiuty stran mira. Spravochnik*, Moskva, 1970; P. BERGER, *La monnaie et ses mécanismes*, Paris, 1970; A. CHAINEAU, *Mécanisme et politique monétaire*, Paris, 1971; F. PICK, R. SEDILLOT, *All the Money of the World. A Chronicle of Currency Values*, New York, 1971.

CURRENCY SNAKE.
An international term for exchange regulations introduced by the EEC countries in Apr., 1972. These countries undertook to maintain the mutual exchange rates of their currencies within a band of 1.125% below or above the central rate. This band was twice as narrow as that permitted by the IMF. In this way the currency exchange rates of this group could jointly fluctuate in relation to third currencies in a snakelike movement, moving upwards or downwards within the band of the "tunnel" created by the wider limits of the IMF. When three floating exchange rates were introduced in the spring of 1973 the EEC currency snake "came out of its tunnel". Snake members have included at various times all EEC countries, plus Austria, Norway, Sweden and the UK – as associates. On Mar. 13, 1979 the currency snake was superseded by the ▷ European Monetary System; the band of fluctuations in exchange rates was expanded to 2.25% above and below the central rate. All of the EEC countries joined the system except the UK.

CURZON LINE.
An international term for a proposed demarcation line on the river Bug suggested to the Supreme Council of the Powers after World War I as the eastern border of Poland by the British Minister of Foreign Affairs, Lord George Nathaniel Curzon of Kedleston (1859–1925), and accepted by the Council on Dec. 8, 1919 as a provisional line. A truce signed during the Polish–Soviet war, 1920, stipulated that Polish forces were

to withdraw to the C.L. The basis for drawing up the C.L. was the nationality factor. The Polish government which had lands east of the Bug under its administration rejected the decision of the Council, but half a year later when Soviet authority took over administration of those lands and as a result of a counter-offensive, the Red Army crossed the Bug and approached the Vistula, premier W. Grabski on July 10, 1920 signed an agreement with the Western Powers in Spa agreeing to the C.L. The further development of war events cancelled this agreement and ultimately the Polish–Soviet border was established by a bilateral treaty: ▷ Riga Peace Treaty, 1921. During World War II the USSR returned to the concept of the C.L. as the Soviet–Polish border and met with complete support 1943–44 from Great Britain, France and the USA, which became the source of a severe crisis in the relations of the Polish emigré governments with Great Britain and the USA which on July 5, 1945 withdrew their recognition of the emigré government and recognized the Temporary Government of National Unity in Warsaw.

Documents concerning the origin of the concept of the C.L. are contained in a reference publication of the Versailles Conference entitled *Recueil des Acts de Conférence*, Paris 1922–1934, Vol. IVC(2), p. 129 ff. German-Soviet Non-Aggression Pact, 1939.

EARL OF RONALDSHAY, The Life of Lord Curzon, London, 1928, II. NICOLSON, *Curzon, The Last Phase, 1919–1925*, London, 1930.

CUSTOMS. An indirect tax periodically levied by the state in the form of specified duty on importation, exportation and transportation of commodities. A subject of international conventions and subject of codification procedures to unify the provisions and forms of customs tax.

There exist several divisions of customs, depending on the criteria accepted. From the point of view of the goal, customs are divided into fiscal customs (providing the state's treasury with income) and economic customs (in order to influence the economic policy of foreign trade). The economic customs include: control customs, protective customs, prohibitionary customs, anti-dumping customs, preferential customs, retortive customs and war-time customs. From the point of view of the control of commodity traffic, customs are divided into import customs and export customs. Depending on the method of levying customs fees, customs duties are divided into ad valorem customs and specific customs.

International trade gave rise to customs as early as in antiquity. Customs were in common use in the period of protectionism and colonialism from the 14th to the mid-19th century. Income yield on customs was so large that colonial powers imposed their customs policy upon dominated states, and in return for credits they assumed the role of a cashier of customs duties for a specific number of years. International co-operation with regard to establishing customs rules began in the second half of the 19th century in the wake of the spread of free trade in the capitalist system and the need for simplification of rules on imports, exports and transportation of goods. The first customs convention on establishment of an International Union for Publication of Customs Tariffs was signed in Brussels on July 5, 1890, also modified in Brussels on Dec. 16, 1949. ▷ Customs tariffs.

In accordance with international law, foreign commodities are subject to customs at the moment they cross the frontier and are called customs commodities that the importer has to re-purchase by paying customs fees or send back after paying storage dues and possible customs operation fees. Numerous Latin-American countries (e.g. Brazil) do not allow commodities to be reloaded on a ship if an importer fails to pay customs duties; rather, the cargo is sequestered by putting it under the hammer, to cover the costs of customs clearance. On the basis of international law and custom, diplomatic missions, consular posts, special missions, United Nations agencies and their personnel and other staff who, on the basis of agreements, legal acts or commonly recognized custom, have the same right as the aforementioned, are all exempted from customs dues on importation, exportation and transportation of commodities (English: duty-free, French: exempt de droits de douane, Spanish: libre de derechos aduaneros). Generally, the rule of reciprocity is applied in such cases in interstate relations. Each state regulates the customs clearance rules on persons and goods in accordance with its laws and regulations. As a rule, items exempted from customs fees have to be registered and have to be listed in customs certificates.

Customs Co-operation Council, *Comparative Study of Customs Procedures*, Brussels, 1964; R.L. BLEDSOE, B.A. BOCZEK, *The International Law Dictionary*, Oxford, 1987.

CUSTOMS AREA. An international term for an area covered by a uniform customs system, not necessarily in line with the territory of one member state of a multi-state customs union (e.g. Benelux), or a state having a duty free zone or zones.

CUSTOMS BARRIER. An international term for a protectionist customs policy of a state with the aim of protecting national industries; depending on general level of customs dues in the customs tarrifs of country, one can speak of countries with high customs barriers or low customs barriers.

CUSTOMS CLEARANCE. An international term for an office of state administration at points of frontier crossing, competent and authorized to control imported, exported and transported goods, to impose and collect customs duties and customs performance fees and to confiscate commodities bearing false marks (i.e. those that do not arrive from the sending country as specified, which is against international customs and conventions) or on which there is a ban on exportation or importation.

CUSTOMS CONDITIONAL CLEARANCE. An international term stipulated for in customs conventions; the customs-free importation of certain goods either for a limited time (e.g. motor vehicles, packaging, exhibitions) or in transit, assuming exportation in a specific time or the payment of customs duties in accordance with the international guarantee system.

CUSTOMS IN CMEA SYSTEM. Defined by an agreement on co-operation and mutual assistance in customs matters, signed on July 5, 1962 in Berlin. Entered into force for Bulgaria, the GDR and USSR – May 8, 1963, for Poland – May 12, 1963, for Hungary – July 7, 1963, for Czechoslovakia – Aug. 14, 1963, for Mongolia – Sept. 7, 1963 and Romania – Jan. 29, 1964. The purpose of the agreement is i.a. the gradual standardization of customs regulations and the development and use of standardized customs documents. The customs offices of the signatories grant each other mutual assistance gratuitously. The depositary of the agreement is the GDR.

CUSTOMS INTERNATIONAL CONVENTIONS. A subject of international customs law since the first convention concluded between Holland and Sweden on Oct. 12, 1697, in which the parties gave each other ▷ most-favoured nation status and also since the economic treaty concluded between Great Britain and Portugal on Dec. 27, 1703 on mutual ▷ preferences, after the name of the British Ambassador in Lisbon, John Methuen, called the Methuen Treaty of 1703; in the Peace Treaty signed in Utrecht in 1713 there were also principles on the most-favored treatment clause similar to those defined in the General Agreement on Tariffs and Trade, GATT. International customs rules are the result of inter-governmental conventions on the foundation of international customs organizations, codification and simplification of customs regulations, and framing of uniform tariffs for definite raw materials as well as lifting of customs barriers within economic and regional integration schemes.

The first Convention which made common the practice of Publication of Tariffs, was signed in Brussels July 5, 1890.

In Madrid was signed Apr. 14, 1891 the Agreement on the Suppression of False Certificates of Origin of Goods which introduced as one of the international functions of customs offices of member states the confiscation of goods falsely bearing the name of the contracting parties as the point of their origin. A Convention Lifting Customs Duties for Goods in Transit was signed June 20, 1921 at Barcelona. International Convention Relating to the Simplification of Customs Formalities was signed after World War I in Geneva, Nov. 3, 1923, where participating states undertook to introduce many simplifications and adopted certain general rules for publication of their own customs regulations. Further conventions appeared after World War II on the initiative of the UN General Assembly, which in 1951 ordered an inquiry into the possibilities of uniformization and further simplification of customs formalities.

The first UN Conference to deal with these matters in consultation with GATT and UNESCO was held in New York, in the summer of 1954, and issued the Final Act of the UN Conference on Customs Formalities for the Temporary Importation of Private Road Motor Vehicles and For Tourism with Additional Protocol – all signed New York, July 4, 1954. Further conventions prepared under UN auspices were:

Customs Convention on Containers, Customs Convention on the Temporary Importation of Commercial Road Vehicles, signed Geneva, May 18, 1956; Customs Convention on the International Transport of Goods under Cover of ▷ TIR Books, signed Geneva Jan. 15, 1959; Customs Convention on the Temporary Importation of Packings signed Brussels, Oct. 6, 1960; European Convention on Customs Treatment of ▷ Pallets Used in International Transport, signed Geneva, Dec. 9, 1960; Customs Convention Concerning Facilities for the Importation of Goods for Display of Use at Exhibitions, Fairs, Meetings or Similar Events, signed Brussels, June 8, 1961; Customs Convention on the Temporary Importation of Professional Equipment, signed Brussels, June 8, 1961; Customs Convention on the ▷ ATA-Book for the Temporary Admission of Goods, ATA Convention, signed Brussels, Dec. 6, 1961.

Organizations reg. with the UIA:

Customs Cooperation Council, est. in Brussels, Dec. 15, 1950 by an international convention that entered into force on Nov. 4, 1952; concluded by 32 states of Western Europe, Africa, Asia and Australasia. Publ. *Bulletin* and numerous studies.

International Union for the Publication of Customs Tariffs, est. July 5, 1890, Brussels by 72 states. Publ. *Bulletin International des Douanes* in English, French, Spanish, German and Italian.

DE MARTENS, *Nouveau Recueil Général de Traités*, 2-ème série, tome XVI, p. 532 and tome XVIII, p. 558;

C

LNTS, Vol. 107, p. 564, Vol. 111, p. 421; *UNTS*, Vol. 72, pp. 3–23; *Comparative Study of Customs Procedures*, Brussels, 1964; *Yearbook of International Organizations*, 1986/87; *The Europa Yearbook 1988. A World Survey*, Vol. I, London, 1988.

CUSTOMS IN THE INTER-AMERICAN SYSTEM. The establishment of the Commercial Bureau of American States in Washington by the government of the United States began the unification and simplification of customs rules on importation, exportation and transportation in the western hemisphere (1890). The Bureau had the task of publishing all information on customs tariffs, rules and regulations of respective seaports as well as trade statistics. The US government suggested to the members of the First Inter-American Conference (1890) the establishment of a Customs Union, but the Latin-American states in fact accepted only the idea. At the Second Inter-American Conference (1901–1902), the Pan-American Customs Conference was drafted; its task was the unification of existing customs rules. At the Third Conference (1906), a Customs Section was established at the Commercial Bureau; at the Fourth Conference (1910) and at the Fifth Conference (1923) unified customs and consular regulations and rules were elaborated; at the Sixth Conference (1928) the Pan-American Commission for Simplification and Standardization of Consular Procedure in Commercial Relations was established; at the Seventh Conference (1933) a group of experts was called for drafting a uniform customs procedure in seaports. In the crisis years of 1931–39 debates were held at numerous inter-American conferences on the abolishment of high customs barriers and liberalization of inter-American trade. New efforts were taken at the Economic Conference of the OAS held in Buenos Aires in 1957; these ended with the signing of a Treaty on the establishment of the Latin-American Association of Free Trade, ALALC, in Montevideo on Feb. 18, 1960 and of the General Treaty on Economic Integration of Central America, Nov. 13, 1960. The gradual abolishment of customs barriers had not ended by 1989.

CUSTOMS NOMENCLATURES. A subject of international conventions. Codification of customs nomenclatures was started in 1932 by a League of Nations Committee of Experts in the form of a draft of unified customs nomenclatures which, however, was not adopted. After World War II four systems of international customs nomenclatures were formulated:

(1) The UN Standard International Trade Classification (SITC) announced by the UN in 1950; divided into 56 groups, 177 sub-groups and 1312 commodity items;
(2) Nomenclature de Bruxelles (the Brussels Nomenclature), formulated in 1950 in the Brussels Convention of Benelux states, Denmark, Finland, France, Great Britain, Italy, Norway and Sweden; divided into 21 sections, 99 commodity groups and 1097 commodity items; the International Customs Office (Bureau International Douane) with headquarters in Brussels is an organ of the Convention;
(3) The Uniform Commodity Nomenclature of Foreign Trade of CMEA member states announced in 1962 by the Council of Mutual Economic Assistance; divided into 9 chapters, 58 groups, 307 sub-groups and about 4000 commodity items;
(4) NAUCA – Nomenclature Aduanera Unificada Centro-Americana – applied by Costa Rica, Guatemala, Honduras, Nicaragua, Panama and El Salvador.

The Brussels Nomenclature is most often used. In 1972 it was used for customs tariffs by over 110 states, among them almost all European states (together with territories and provinces on other continents or islands), except for CMEA member states, which use the uniform nomenclature of CMEA adopted in 1962, as do all African states.
In South America the Brussels Nomenclature is used by Bolivia, Brazil, Chile, Colombia, Cuba, Ecuador, Jamaica, Haiti, Mexico, Paraguay, Peru, Surinam and Uruguay.
On the Asian continent the Brussels Nomenclature is used by: Afghanistan, Cambodia, Ceylon, Cyprus, India, Indonesia, Iraq, Iran, Israel, Japan, Jordan, People's Democratic Republic of Korea, South Korea, Laos, Lebanon, Malaysia, Pakistan, the Philippines, Saudi Arabia, Syria, Thailand, Turkey, South Vietnam. The Brussels Nomenclature is also used by Australia, New Zealand and Fiji. Except for the four nomenclatures mentioned above, other systems of customs nomenclatures arranged in individual national patterns are also used in the customs tariffs of 30 countries (on all continents). National systems are used: in Europe – by Albania; in Africa – Ethiopia; in America by Barbados, Canada, Dominica, Ecuador, Paraguay, Trinidad and Tobago and the USA; in Asia – Afghanistan, Burma, India, Indonesia, Iran, Kuwait, Nepal and South Yemen.
The SITC nomenclature is used by: Guyana, Jamaica and Singapore.

CUSTOMS OTTAWA AGREEMENTS, 1932. A name given to the customs agreements adopted at the Ottawa Imperial Economic Conference, July 21–Aug. 20, 1932, introducing a system of ▷ preferences in trade relations among the countries of the British Commonwealth, called the imperial preferences. Under the Ottawa agreements specific commodities in a given Commonwealth country were either duty-free or duty was reduced in their importation to Great Britain. The problem of preferences granted to New Zealand became the issue of special clause in the Luxembourg Treaty of 1971.

CUSTOMS PERMIT BOOK. An international term for a document issued by an authorized international association for motor vehicles and trailers for the purpose of facilitating international road transport by granting temporary licences for the duty-free importation of goods by vehicle in accordance with the Geneva Customs Convention on the temporary importation of goods by road transport of May 18, 1956. The regulations of the custom permit book state that the international language is French, but a translation into the language of the issuing country may be appended to the book by the issuing country.

CUSTOMS TARIFFS. The lists of customs fees levied by respective states for specified commodities at their importation, exportation or transit and lists of commodities that are fully or partially exempted from customs fees, and lists of goods whose importation, exportation or transit is prohibited in a given country. Subject of international conventions on unification and simplification of customs tariffs or on lowering such tariffs with regard to specific commodities. Customs tariffs initially used to be of the so-called one-column kind, i.e. the level of tariffs was the same for all countries. In the 20th century, due to customs wars, the Cold War and also due to the GATT, two-column lists are in use, including two types of tariffs: lower for commodities from countries enjoying the ▷ most favoured IMF clause, or the so-called "treaty countries", and higher for commodities from all other countries, the so-called "non-treaty countries", or the multi-column lists of customs tariffs that also include preferential tariffs used, i.a., by Great Britain in trade relations with other Commonwealth countries, or occasional tariffs. Fiscal custom tariffs, applying unified customs tariffs (as differentiated by the type of commodity) to the entire territory of a state, were introduced in Europe in the 14th–17th centuries (first in France), and only in the 20th century did they start applying to the common customs territory of several states.
As regards the Western Hemisphere, the problem of customs tariffs was discussed without any effect at the International American Conference from 1889–90 to 1954; since 1960, customs tariffs have been an exclusive internal problem of each Latin-American state within the framework of Latin-American integration and sub-regional integration. Customs tariffs of the United States have always been an issue of global importance because of the country's significant role in international trade. Customs tariffs in the USA are being promoted by the US Congress, which has created a number of customs barriers on the basis of relevant US legislation, introducing additional customs duties for commodities already covered by customs tariffs and on goods previously exempted from such duties. With the exception of the period between 1934 and 1945, all legislation passed by the US Congress did not refer to goods from the Soviet Union, as the country had been boycotted by the United States since 1917. One of the anti-Soviet laws passed by the Congress in 1921 was the so-called Anti-dumping Act. In the period of the world economic crisis of 1933, the ▷ Smoot-Hawley Tariff Act 1930 was made more severe by adopting an autarchic amendment recommending the purchase of only American-made products, the so-called Buy-American Act. During World War I there was the Trading-with-the-Enemy Act of 1917 in the United States, introducing a strict ban on trade with Germany and her allies. A similar act was in force during World War II. In 1948 for strategic reasons an official embargo was placed on goods produced in Eastern Europe and exports to those countries were controlled on the basis of the Export Control Act of 1949. In 1950 the Cannon Amendment and Kem Act expanded the embargo and increased the control of trade by means of the Mutual Defense Assistance Control Act of 1951, adopted by the US Congress, and called, in short the Battle Act (after the name of its sponsor), amended in 1954. A system of ▷ licences was also introduced. The Trading-with-the-Enemy Act adopted during the Korean War in 1951 also remained in force after the war, as did the customs law PL 480, called the Agricultural Trade and Development Act of 1954, making it impossible for the Warsaw Pact states to purchase agricultural products. In 1971 the Western Powers made the first steps to open up trade with communist countries, but not with the People's Democratic Republic of Korea, the Democratic Republic of Vietnam or Cuba, which were still included under the law of 1951 and 1954. All the above customs restrictions were imposed upon all NATO allies, since 1949 through a special mechanism of the Co-ordinating Committee for East Trade and China Trade Co-ordinating Committee (▷ COCOM and CHINCOM) The departure from this policy (but not with regard to all countries) began on Aug. 16, 1954 with a revision of the embargo lists, continued in 1958 and 1964. With regard to Poland, the lifting of restrictions on the purchase of agricultural products was made in 1957–58, and in Nov., 1960 Poland was granted the most-favored nation treatment in its exports, which was annulled in Jan., 1982. Such a clause was granted to Yugoslavia in 1950 and in 1964 to Romania.
Apart from customs barriers, non-tariff barriers are also applied, which put a total ban on specific exports to a country for security reasons, sanitary rules or special laws. The Buy-American Act of 1971 prohibits US public authorities from purchas-

ing foreign goods if their prices are lower by a certain percentage than prices for similar domestic goods; or in the case of American customs rules that impose customs fees on foreign chemical products on the basis of generally higher prices of products made in the USA (i.e. on the basis of selling price). These two forms of non-tariff barriers became a subject of debate in the ▷ Nixon Round.

CUSTOMS CO-OPERATION COUNCIL, *Comparative Study of Customs Procedure*, Brussels, 1964.

CUSTOMS TEMPORARY ADMISSION. An international term for duty-free admission (importation) of specific goods for a temporary period, provided for in customs conventions (e.g. motor vehicles, wrappings, exhibits) or for transit, anticipating that after a given date, such goods will be removed from the country or customs dues paid in keeping with the international system of guarantees.

Yearbook of International Organizations.

CUSTOMS UNIONS. An international term for customs integration of two or more countries into one customs area; conclusion of a customs union means abolishment of customs for imports, exports and transit of goods to those countries in the customs-integrated area, which also have a common trade policy. This would mean in particular the establishment of a uniform customs barrier in relation to third countries.

In the 19th century German states on the initiative of Prussia began negotiations on a customs union, which, after conclusion of many sub-regional agreements, led to the forming of a Prussian–German Customs Union (Preussisch-Deutscher Zollverein) on Jan. 1, 1834. The four duchies not included in the Union: Brunswick, Hanover, Oldenburg and Schaumburg-Lippe, formed a separate customs union on Jan. 1, 1836, named the Tax Union (Steuerverein). The Austrian–Prussian Customs and Trade Treaty was signed on Apr. 4, 1854 in Berlin. Those customs unions broke up in 1866, but in 1871–88 the entire German Reich became one customs area (free cities of Bremen and Hamburg were the last ones to join it). Austria formed a customs union with Hungary in 1867. After World War I the Versailles Treaty established a customs union between Poland and Gdansk, signed on June 26, 1919. On Jan. 25, 1921 a customs union was concluded between Luxembourg and Belgium, and on Mar. 29, 1923, between Switzerland and Liechtenstein. On Mar. 19, 1931 a protocol was signed in Vienna concerning the establishment of a customs union between the German Reich and Austria. That was considered by the Western powers as an attempt at ▷ Anschluss, contradictory to the ▷ Saint Germain-en-Laye Austria Peace Treaty of 1919, and to the ▷ Geneva Protocol of Oct. 2, 1924, which obligated Austria to non-conclusion of political and economic agreements with the German Reich. The issue was brought up before the League of Nations, which, on the basis of a ruling of the Permanent International Tribunal in The Hague, Sept. 5, 1931, stating the inconsistency of the Vienna Protocol of 1931 with the Geneva Protocol of 1922, ordered the annulment of the Austrian–German customs union.

The attempts of the USA since 1889–90 to form a customs union with Latin-American countries have failed.

After World War II the European Customs Union Study Group was called into being in Paris in Sept. 1947, and the Benelux countries were the first participants of the new customs union of 1948.

On Mar. 25, 1957 the EEC countries established a customs union in accordance with the Rome Treaty.

In 1959 two African customs unions were set up:
(1) that of West Africa, L'Union Douanière de l'Occident de l'Afrique, which covers Dahomey, Upper Volta now – Burkina Faso, the Malagasy Republic, Mali, Mauritania, Niger, Senegal, Togo, the Ivory Coast, and
(2) that of Central Africa, l'Union Douanière et Economique de l'Afrique Centrale, which covers Chad, Gabon, Congo, and the Central African Republic. The customs union of Central Africa has been in operation since 1960.

J. VINER, *The Customs Union Issue*, New York, 1950.

CUSTOMS WAR. An international term for foreign trade conflict between two countries or a group of countries, mutually impeding commercial exchange by raising customs rates; it often has the character of an economic boycott or economic war. After World War I, Western powers applied a boycott of goods in relation to USSR products, to which the USSR reacted with dumping. The provision of Art. 286 of the Versailles Treaty, which from July 15, 1922 to July 15, 1925 obligated Germany as part of war reparations to let in duty-free raw materials and articles produced in the area of Silesia that had been granted to Poland, indirectly initiated a German–Polish custom war. After July 15, 1925 the Germans issued a ban on coal imports from Poland. Poland's response was a retaliatory decree introducing customs barriers for a number of German products, which was followed in turn by a German list. In this way, in summer and fall of 1925 considerable customs barriers were set up which checked the development of Polish–German trade relations till Mar., 1934. The customs war ended after the German–Polish declaration on non-aggression on Jan. 31, 1934 by way of a special decree, named Protocol on Normalization of Economic Relations, signed on Mar. 7, 1934 in Warsaw.

H. SOKULSKI, "Wojna celna Rzeszy przeciw Polsce 1925–1934 [German Customs War against Poland 1924–1934]", in: *Sprawy Miedzynarodowe*, Warsaw, No. 9, 1955.

CYBERNETICS. A subject of organized international co-operation since June 1956 when the First International Congress on Cybernetics was held in Namur (Belgium). Organizations reg. with the UIA:

International Association for Cybernetics, f. Jan. 7, 1957 Namur, Belgium, as a permanent organ of the International Congress of Cybernetics, with the task of developing and co ordinating co-operation of scientists and firms producing cybernetic machinery; unites 500 scientists and 100 firms from 35 countries. Publ. *Cybernetics.*
International Society of Cybernetic Medicine, f. 1969, Naples, Italy.
World Cybernetic Federation, f. 1971, Namur, Belgium, by the Sixth International Congress of Cybernetics with the task of collecting and disseminating information on the accomplishments in the area of cybernetics reached by scientists from the entire world.
World Organization of General Systems and Cybernetics, f. 1969, Lytham St. Annes, England. Publ.: International Journal of Cybernetics and Systems.

Yearbook of International Organizations, 1986/87; The Europa Yearbook 1988. A World Survey, Vol. I, London, 1988.

CYCLING. A subject of international co-operation. Organizations reg. with the UIA:

International Association of Organizers of Cycle Competitions (AOICC), f. 1958, Paris.

International Cycling Union (UCI), f. 1900, Geneva. Publ.: *Le monde cycliste*. Recognized by the International Olympic Committee.
International Federation of Professional Cycling (FICP), f. 1965, Brussels.
International Union of Cycle and Motor-Cycle Trade and Repair, f. 1958, Bielefeld, FRG.

Yearbook of International Organizations.

CYNOLOGY. A subject of international co-operation. Organization reg. with the UIA:

International Federation of Kennel Clubs, Federation cynologique internationale, FCI, f. 1911, Thuin, Belgium: unites national committees and clubs from 36 states.

Yearbook of International Organizations.

CYPRUS, REPUBLIC OF. Member of the UN. An island in the Mediterranean Sea, 60 km south of Turkey and 100 km west of Syria. Area: 9251 sq. km. Pop. 1987 est. 680,400 (1973 census: 631,778, of whom 498,511 were Greek Orthodox, 116,000 Turkish Moslems and 17,267 others). Capital: Nicosia with 125,100 inhabitants in 1980. GNP per capita in 1987: US $5,210. Official languages: Greek and Turkish. Currency: one Cyprus pound = 1000 mils. National Day: Oct. 1, Independence Day, 1960.

On Sept. 20, 1960 Cyprus became a member of the UN and all specialized agencies. Member of the Commonwealth and the Council of Europe.

International relations: in 1193 Cyprus became a possession of the king of France and in 1489 it was subject to Venice. 1571–1878 it was part of the Ottoman Empire, then a Treaty between Great Britain and Turkey signed in Istanbul on June 4, 1878 placed Cyprus under British administration. On Nov. 5, 1914 it was annexed by Great Britain. Proclaimed a Royal colony on May 1, 1925. The movement for independence which started at that time changed into a struggle between the Greek and Turkish populations. Archbishop Makarios III, head of the Orthodox Church on Cyprus, who supported aspirations to unify Cyprus with Greece, was deported to England in 1956–57. As a result of Greek–Turkish negotiations in Zurich at the end of 1958 and beginning of 1959 a Treaty was signed on Feb. 19, 1959 in London between the governments of Greece, Turkey and the UK and representatives of the Greek and Turkish populations. The Republic of Cyprus was proclaimed on Aug. 16, 1960, with the UK retaining sovereign rights over its military bases on the island.

The President of the Republic, archbishop Makarios III, made a visit to the UN and spoke before the UN General Assembly on June 7, 1962. The Security Council on Oct. 27, 1963 examined a charge of the government of Cyprus concerning Turkish efforts to alter the conditions of the Zurich–London treaties. On Dec. 23, 1963 an armed conflict broke out between the Greek and Turkish populations, which led to the intervention of British, Greek and Turkish forces. The UN Armed Forces for Cyprus, UNFICYP, formed by the Security Council on Mar. 4, 1964, arrived in Cyprus on Mar. 27, 1964 in a force of 7000 troops from Austria, Canada, Denmark, Finland, New Zealand, Sweden and the UK. On Apr. 4, 1964 the government of Cyprus repudiated the Zurich accords with Greece and Turkey. Under UN pressure a cease-fire was put into effect in the fall of 1964; new conflicts broke out 1966–67, when Greek and Turkish forces arrived in Cyprus. From this time, besides the UNFICYP contingent, Greek, Turkish and British forces have all been stationed on the island as well as units of the Greek Cypriot and Turkish Cypriot police forces and units of the Greek Cypriot National Guard. In view of continual tensions, the UN Security Council every 6 months extends the presence of UNFICYP. On July 19, 1974 the Greek National Guard in conspiracy with the military junta in Greece attempted a *coup d'état*, which resulted in a dangerous crisis. On July 20, 1974 the Turkish troops invaded the island and occupied 40% of the northern part of Cyprus. The Greek population in this region (over 200,000 people) fled to the south. The new civilian government established in Greece accepted the recommendations of the UN Security Council of July 22, 1974. On Feb. 13, 1975 the Turkish northern administration proclaimed a Turkish Cypriot Federated State not recognized by President Makarios and the Greek government. The *de facto* partition of Cyprus between two different administrations, Greek and Turkish, was formally institutionalized on Nov. 15, 1983 by the proclamation of the sovereign, independent Turkish Republic of Northern Cyprus, TRNC. On Nov. 18, 1983 UN Security Council Res. 541/83 condemned by 13 votes to one (Pakistan) with one abstention (Jordan) the declaration of Turkish Cypriot authorities as incompatible with the 1960 agreement. In 1984 the Cyprus Government's conciliatory proposals that the Turkish Cypriots should be allowed to administer 25% of the island, on condition that the declaration of TRNC would be withdrawn – was rejected by the Turkish separatists. See also ▷ World Heritage UNESCO List.

D. ALSTOS, *Cyprus in History*, London 1955; D. ALSTOS, *Cyprus Guerrilla*, Nicosia, 1962; A. EMILIANIDES, *The Zurich and London Agreements and the Cyprus Republic*, Athens, 1962; CH. FOLEY, *Legacy of Strife, Cyprus from Rebellion in Civil War*, London, 1964; J. STENEGER, *The UN Forces in Cyprus*, Columbus, 1966; S. KYRIAKDEES, *Cyprus, Constitutionalism and Crisis Government*, Philadelphia, 1968; H. KOSUT, *Cyprus 1946–1968*, New York, 1970; P.N. VANEZIS MACARIOS, *Faith and Power*, New York, 1972; F. CROUZET, *Le conflit de Chypre*, 1946–49, Vol. 2, Paris, 1974, T. EHRLICH, *Cyprus 1958–67*, New York, 1974; N. KRANIDTIS, *The Cyprus Problem. The Proposed Solutions on the Concept of the Independent and Sovereign State*, Athens, 1975; Z. STAVRINIDES, *The Cyprus Conflict*, Nicosia, 1976; K.C. MARKIDES, *The Rise and Fall of the Cyprus Republik*, Yale, 1977; P.S. POLYVION, *Cyprus, Conflict and Negotiations, 1960–1980*, London, 1980; R. DESIKTASH, *The Cyprus Triangle*, London, 1982; K. HALIL, *The Rape of Cyprus*, London, 1982; *UN Chronicle*, January, 1984, p. 73; *The Europa Yearbook 1984. A World Survey*, Vol. I, pp. 354–370, London, 1984; *Cyprus Question, in:* A.J. DAY ed., *Border and Territoria Disputes*, London, 1987.

CYTOLOGY. A subject of international co-operation. Organizations reg. with the UIA:

International Academy of Cytology, f. 1957, New York; unites scientists from America, Asia and Europe; Publ. *Acta Cytologica*
International Cell Research Organization, ICRO, f. 1962, London, on the initiative of UNESCO.
International Committee for Histochemistry and Cytochemistry, f. 1960, Paris.
International Society for Cell Biology, ISBC, f. 1923, Liége, Belgium. Under the name International Society for Experimental Cytology, present name since 1947; unites biologists from the entire world. Publ. *Annual Review of Cytology* and *Experimental Cell Research.*

Yearbook of International Organizations.

CZECHOSLOVAK–AUSTRIAN TREATY, 1922. A Treaty signed in Vienna on Mar. 15, 1922. The highlights of the Treaty:

Art. 2 – The two States mutually guarantee their territories as fixed by the Treaties of Peace referred to in Article 1; and, with a view to maintaining peace and safeguarding the integrity of these territories, they undertake to afford each other mutual political and diplomatic support.
Art. 3 – Each State undertakes to remain neutral should the other be compelled to defend itself against attack.
Art. 4 – Both States undertake not to tolerate on their territories any political or military organization directed against the integrity and security of the other Contracting Party. They agree to work together and afford each other mutual aid against any plans or attempts to restore the former regime, either as regards foreign and domestic policy, or in respect of the form of the State and of Government. The competent authorities of both States shall afford each other mutual assistance in effectively combating secret intrigues having this object.

LNTS, No. 257.

CZECHOSLOVAK CORPS IN RUSSIA, 1914–18. Formation composed of Czech and Slovak prisoners of war taken in Russia on the Austro-Hungarian front. In 1918 they amounted to two divisions (about 50,000 troops), part of which in Siberia opposed the Revolution. After the defeat of Kolchak's White army, the corps was evacuated to Czechoslovakia.

CZECHOSLOVAK CORPS IN THE USSR, 1942–44. A military corps formed of Czechs and Slovaks, from Feb. 1942 in Buzuluk near Kuibyshev under the command of Colonel L. Svoboda by an agreement between the provisional Czechoslovak government in exile in London and the Soviet Union on Sept. 27, 1941. Its first battalion fought in the Battle of Sokolovo near Kharkov on Mar. 8, 1942, and its first independent brigade took part in the relief of Kiev, Apr. 1, 1944. In Sept.–Nov., 1944 a corps of 16,000 troops fought at Slovakian Dukla Pass and crossed it on Oct. 6, 1944. The date is celebrated in Czechoslovakia as the Day of the Czechoslovak People's Army.

E. P. HOYT, *The Army Without a Country*, New York, 1967.

CZECHO-SLOVAK DECLARATION OF INDEPENDENCE, 1918. A Declaration adopted by the Provisional Government on Oct. 28, 1918 in Paris, signed by Thomas G. Masaryk (1850–1937) and Eduard Beneš (1884–1948). The Declaration of Independence of the Czecho-Slovak Nation read as follows:

"At this grave moment, when the Hohenzollerns are offering peace in order to stop the victorious advance of the allied armies and to prevent the dismemberment of Austria–Hungary and Turkey, and when the Hapsburgs are promising the federalization of the Empire and autonomy to the dissatisfied nationalities committed to their rule we, the Czecho-Slovak National Council, recognized by the allied and American Governments as the Provisional Government of the Czechoslovak State and nation, in complete accord with the declaration of the Czech deputies made in Prague on January 6, 1918, and realizing that federalization and, still more, autonomy, means nothing under a Hapsburg dynasty, do hereby make and declare this our declaration of independence. We do this because of our belief that no people should be forced to live under a sovereignty they do not recognize and because of our knowledge and firm conviction that our nation cannot freely develop in a Hapsburg mock federation, which is only a new form of the denationalizing oppression under which we have suffered for the past 300 years. We consider freedom to be the first prerequisite for federalization, and believe that the free nations of central and eastern Europe may easily federate should they find it necessary.
We make this declaration on the basis of our historic and natural right. We have been an independent State since the seventh century, and in 1526, as an independent State, consisting of Bohemia, Moravia, and Silesia, we joined with Austria and Hungary in a defensive union against the Turkish danger. We have never voluntarily surrendered our rights as an independent State in this confederation. The Hapsburgs broke their compact with our nation by illegally transgressing our rights and violating the constitution of our State, which they had pledged themselves to uphold, and we therefore refuse longer to remain a part of Austria–Hungary in any form.
We claim the right of Bohemia to be reunited with her Slovak brethren of Slovakia, once a part of our national State, later torn from our national body, and fifty years ago incorporated in the Hungarian State of the Magyars, who, by their unspeakable violence and ruthless oppression of their subject races, have lost all moral and human right to rule anybody but themselves.
The world knows the history of our struggle against the Hapsburg oppression, intensified and systematized by the Austro-Hungarian dualistic compromise of 1867. This dualism is only a shameless organization of brute force and exploitation of the majority by the minority; it is a political conspiracy of the Germans and Magyars against our own as well as the other Slav and the Latin nations of the monarchy. The world knows the justice of our claims, which the Hapsburgs themselves dared not deny. Francis Joseph in the most solemn manner repeatedly recognized the sovereign rights of our nation. The Germans and Magyars opposed this recognition, and Austria-Hungary, bowing before the Pan-Germans, became a colony of Germany and, as her vanguard to the East, provoked the last Balkan conflict, as well as the present world war, which was begun by the Hapsburgs alone without the consent of the representatives of the people.
We cannot and will not continue to live under the direct or indirect rule of the violators of Belgium, France, and Serbia, the would-be murderers of Russia and Rumania, the murderers of tens of thousands of civilians and soldiers of our blood, and the accomplices in numberless unspeakable crimes committed in this war against humanity by the two degenerate and irresponsible dynasties. We will not remain a part of a State which has no justification for existence and which, refusing to accept the fundamental principles of modern world-organization, remains only an artificial and immoral political structure, hindering every movement toward democratic and social progress. The Hapsburg dynasty, weighed down by a huge inheritance of error and crime, is a perpetual menace to the peace of the world, and we deem it our duty toward humanity and civilization to aid in bringing about its downfall and destruction.
We reject the sacrilegious assertion that the power of the Hapsburg and Hohenzollern dynasties is of divine origin; we refuse to recognize the divine right of kings. Our nation elected the Hapsburgs to the throne of Bohemia of its own free will and by the same right deposes them. We hereby declare the Hapsburg dynasty unworthy of leading our nation, and deny all of their claims to rule in the Czecho-Slovak Land, which we here and now declare shall henceforth be a free and independent people and nation. We accept and shall adhere to the ideals of modern democracy, as they have been the ideals of our nation for centuries. We accept the American principles as laid down by President Wilson; the principles of liberated mankind – of the actual equality of nations – and of governments deriving all their just power from the consent of the governed. We, the nation of Comenius, cannot but accept these principles expressed in the American Declaration of Independence, the principles of Lincoln, and of the declaration of the rights of man and of the citizen. For these principles our nation shed its blood in the memorable Hussite Wars 500 years ago; for these same principles, beside her allies, our nation is shedding its blood today in Russia, Italy, and France.
We shall outline only the main principles of the Constitution of the Czecho-Slovak Nation; the final decision as to the constitution itself falls to the legally chosen representatives of the liberated and united people.
The Czecho-Slovak State shall be a republic. In constant endeavor for progress it will guarantee complete freedom of conscience, religion and science, literature and art, speech, the press, and the right of assembly and petition. The Church shall be separated from the State. Our democracy shall rest on universal suffrage; women shall be placed on an equal footing with men, politically, socially, and culturally. The rights of the minority shall be safeguarded by proportional representation; national minorities shall enjoy equal rights. The government shall be parliamentary in form and shall

recognize the principles of initiative and referendum. The standing army will be replaced by militia.

The Czecho-Slovak Nation will carry out far-reaching social and economic reforms; the large estates will be redeemed for home colonization; patents of nobility will be abolished. Our nation will assume its part of the Austro-Hungarian prewar public debt; the debts for this war we leave to those who incurred them.

In its foreign policy the Czecho-Slovak Nation will accept its full share of responsibility in the reorganization of Eastern Europe. It accepts fully the democratic and social principle of nationality and subscribes to the doctrine that all covenants and treaties shall be entered into openly and frankly without secret diplomacy.

Our constitution shall provide an efficient, rational and just government, which will exclude all special privileges and prohibit class legislation.

Democracy has defeated theocratic autocracy. Militarism is overcome – democracy is victorious; on the basis of democracy mankind will be recognized. The forces of darkness have served the victory of light – the longed-for age of humanity is dawning.

We believe in democracy – we believe in liberty – and liberty evermore."

The Official US Bulletin, October 19, 1918.

CZECHOSLOVAK–FRENCH FRIENDSHIP TREATY, 1924.

A Treaty signed on Mar. 4, 1924 in Paris. The highlights of the Treaty:

Art. 3 – The High Contracting Parties, being fully in agreement as to the importance, for the maintenance of the world's peace, of the political principles laid down in Article 88 of the Treaty of Peace of St. Germain-en-Laye of September 10, 1919, and in the Protocols of Geneva, dated October 4, 1922, of which instruments they both are signatories,

Undertake to consult each other as to the measures to be taken in case there should be any danger of an infraction of these principles.

Art. 4. – The High Contracting Parties, having special regard to the declarations made by the Conference of Ambassadors on February 3, 1920, and April 1, 1921, on which their policy will continue to be based, and to the declaration made on November 10, 1921, by the Hungarian Government to the Allied diplomatic representatives,

Undertake to consult each other in case their interests are threatened by a failure to observe the principles laid down in the aforesaid declarations.

Art. 5 – The High Contracting Parties solemnly declare that they are in complete agreement as to the necessity, for the maintenance of peace, of taking common action in the event of any attempt to restore the Hohenzollern dynasty in Germany, and they undertake to consult each other in such a contingency.

LNTS, No. 588.

CZECHOSLOVAK–FRENCH LOCARNO TREATY, 1925.

A Treaty signed on Oct. 16, 1925 in Locarno. The highlights of the Treaty:

Art. 1 – In the event of Czechoslovakia or France suffering from a failure to observe the undertakings arrived at this day between them and Germany with a view to the maintenance of general peace, France, and reciprocally Czechoslovakia, acting in application of Article 16 of the Covenant of the League of Nations, undertake to lend each other immediate aid and assistance, if such a failure is accompanied by an unprovoked recourse to arms.

In the event of the Council of the League of Nations, when dealing with a question brought before it in accordance with the said undertakings, being unable to suceed in making its report accepted by all its members other than the representatives of the Parties to the dispute, and in the event of Czechoslovakia or France being attacked without provocation, France, or reciprocally Czechoslovakia, acting in application of Article 15, paragraph 7, of the Covenant of the League of Nations, will immediately lend aid and assistance.

LNTS, No. 594.

CZECHOSLOVAK–FRENCH MILITARY TREATY, 1926.

A treaty on French military aid to Czechoslovakia and on enforcement of the terms of the Locarno Pact on the part of Germany with

reference to frontiers and arbitration, signed on Sept. 14, 1926 in Paris.

LNTS, No. 1298.

CZECHOSLOVAKIA.

Member of the UN. Československá Socialistická Republika. Czechoslovakian Socialist Republic. A state in Central Europe. Frontiers with the USSR, Hungary, Austria, the FRG, GDR and Poland. Official Languages: Czech and Slovak. Area: 127,896 sq. km. Pop. 15,478,000 on Dec. 31, 1987 (census of 1970: 14,344,987). Nationalities: 9,600,000 Czechs, 4,513,000 Slovaks, 595,000 Hungarians, 293,000 Gypsies, 78,000 Germans, 78,000 Poles, and 60,000 Ukrainians and Russians. Capital: Prague with 1,182,862 inhabitants in 1980. GNP per capita in 1985: US $8700. Currency: one koruna = 100 haler. National Day: May 9, Liberation Day, 1945; and Oct. 28, Proclamation of the Republic, 1918.

A founding member of the UN since Oct. 24, 1945. A member of all specialized UN organizations with the exception of IBRD, IDA, IMF and IFC. A member of the Warsaw Pact and CMEA.

International relations: the common history of Bohemia and Slovakia, 1526–1918 in the Austrian Empire and (from 1867) the Austro-Hungarian Monarchy, resulted in a common struggle for independence. During World War I, representatives of both nations came out in support of the Allied side against the Central Powers and signed the Pittsburgh Agreement in 1917; as a result of this Agreement, on Oct. 28, 1918 they proclaimed in Paris their joint independence from Austria (▷ Czecho-Slovak Declaration of Independence) and on Nov. 14, 1918 formed the government of the Republic of Czechoslovakia. In 1920–21 Czechoslovakia entered a political–military alliance with Yugoslavia and Romania, forming together with them the so-called Little Entente, and in 1924 with France. On May 16, 1935 signed a Pact on Mutual Assistance with the USSR. A founding member of the League of Nations, 1918–38. Withdrew from the League when, by the Munich Pact of Sept. 30, 1938, she was compelled to cede the Sudeten part of her country to the III Reich. Occupied by Nazi Germany from Mar. 15, 1939 to May 5, 1945 (Czech territory formed the ▷ Bohemian and Moravian Protectorate, while Slovakia was an independent state under the protection of the Reich). Through her representatives in London, Czechoslovakia during World War II signed a treaty with the USSR on friendship, mutual assistance, and co-operation after the war, on Dec. 12, 1943. An Agreement concerning the final demarcation of the State frontier between Poland and Czechoslovakia was signed on June 13, 1958 in Warsaw together with a treaty on legal relations at the Polish–Czechoslovak frontier and on co-operation and mutual assistance in frontier matters. On Aug. 20, 1968 five members of the Warsaw Pact (the USSR, Bulgaria, the GDR, Poland, and Hungary) made a decision to intervene in Czechoslovakia, stating that they had taken this decision:

"... in view of the threat which had arisen to the socialist order in Czechoslovakia from counter-revolutionary forces which are in collusion with external forces hostile to socialism ... This decision is completely in accord with the right of states to individual and collective self-protection provided for in allied treaties concluded between brotherly socialist states."

This military intervention became the subject of a dispute in the UN. The Resolution of the Security Council of Aug. 23, 1968 against the presence of military forces of the Warsaw Pact was passed by 10 votes in favor but was not implemented due to the veto of the USSR. Abstaining were Algeria, India and Pakistan; Hungary and the USSR voted

against. On July 26, 1968 in Moscow the above-mentioned states of the Warsaw Pact signed an agreement with the government of Czechoslovakia. On Jan. 1, 1969 the Republic of Czechoslovakia became the Federation of the Czech Socialist Republic and the Socialist Republic of Slovakia. In May, 1970 signed a 20-year Treaty of Friendship, Co-operation and Mutual Assistance with the USSR. In Dec. 1973 the Czechoslovak-FRG Treaty was signed; ratified in July 1974. The normalization of relations with the Vatican began in 1978 with the formal recognition for the first time by the Vatican of the 1918 frontiers of Czechoslovakia and a change on Jan. 10, 1978 of the boundaries of Catholic dioceses, which up to then did not include wholly Czechoslovakian territory, for part of them, as before World War I, belonged to Hungarian, Polish and Romanian dioceses. Following massive street demonstrations, which led to the resignation of the hardline Communist government, and the abolition of the Communist Party's leading role, a largely non-Communist coalition government was formed on December 10, 1989. Earlier, Czechoslovakia had condemned the 1968 invasion by Warsaw Pact forces, as had the countries whose troops took part, and suggested the dissolution of COMECON. The new President, Vaclav Havel proposed that the next USA–USSR summit take place in Prague, and offered to mediate in the Middle East conflict.

UNTS, Vol. 354, p. 221 and Vol. 830, p. 148; *Dokumenty ceskoslovenske zahraniecni politiky 1945–1960*, Praha, 1961; *Sovietsko–Czeskoslovatskie otnoshenia vo vremia Velikoi Otiechestviennoi voiny. Dokumenty i materiali 1941–1945*, Moskva, 1960; V. KNAPP, Z. MLYNAR, *La Tchécoslovaquie*, Paris, 1965; *Slovenske Narodne powstanie. Dokumenty*, Bratislava, 1966, 1220 pp.; *Nemci a Slovensko 1944. Dokumenty*, Bratislava, 1971, J. KREJCI, *Social Change and Stratification in Postwar Czechoslovakia*, London, 1972; V.S. MAMATAY, R. LUZA (eds.), *A History of the Czechoslovak Republic 1914–1948*, Princeton, 1973; A.H. HERMAN, *A History of the Czechs*, London, 1975; C.M. NOWAK, *Czechoslovak–Polish Relations 1918–1938*, Stanford, 1976; *Socialist Czechoslovakia*, Prague, 1976; W.V. WALLAS, *Czechoslovakia*, London, 1977; F.D. EIDLIN, *The Logic of Normalization*, New York, 1980; *The Europa Yearbook 1984. A World Survey*, Vol. I, pp. 371–389, London, 1984; J. BUGAJSKI, *Czechoslovakia Charter 77' Decade of Dissidents*, New York, 1988; KEESING's *Record of World Events*, Dec. 1989.

CZECHOSLOVAKIA–FRG AGREEMENT, 1973.

A Treaty initialled in Bonn on Apr. 21, 1973, and signed on Dec. 21, 1973 in Prague. The Treaty was ratified by both Parties and came into force July 19, 1974. The Treaty is annexed with a letter from the Minister of Foreign Affairs of Czechoslovakia to the Minister of Foreign Affairs of the Federal Republic of Germany on the non-prescription of war crimes, and with two letters exchanged between them expressing their intention to consult each other whenever the provisions should be extended to cover West Berlin "stemming from the implementation of art. V of the present agreement, in accordance with the agreement between the Four Powers of Sept. 3, 1971, in keeping with the adopted procedure".

UNTS, 1973; O. KIMMINICH, "Der Prager Vertrag", in: *Jahrbuch für Internationales Recht*, 1975, pp. 62–91.

CZECHOSLOVAK–POLISH AGREEMENTS, 1940 AND 1943.

Two agreements concluded by the governments in exile of Poland, headed by Gen. W. Sikorski, and of Czechoslovakia, headed by E. Beneš, during World War II in London. The first Treaty on co-operation during and after the war was signed on Nov. 11, 1940 and became the basis for negotiations, concluded with a Treaty on a future Polish–Czechoslovak confederation of states. It was signed on Jan. 23, 1942, with the aim at pursuing a common foreign, military, economic, financial, social, communication, postal and telegraph policy. The confederation was meant to be open to other states. Following the German aggression against the USSR, the Czechoslovak–Soviet treaty was concluded on Dec. 12, 1943 in Moscow. The Treaty was open to Poland but was never acceded to by the London government. Post-war relations between Poland and Czechoslovakia developed independently of the wartime agreements.

P. WANDYCZ, *Polish–Czechoslovak Confederation and the Great Powers 1940–1943*, Bloomington, 1956.

CZECHOSLOVAK–ROMANIAN FRIENDSHIP TREATY, 1921. A Treaty signed on May 27, 1921 in Bucharest, renewed June 14, 1923 and June 17, 1926. The highlights of the Treaty:

"Art. 1. In case of an unprovoked attack on the part of Hungary against one of the High Contracting Parties, the other Party agrees to assist in the defense of the Party attacked, in the manner laid down by the arrangement provided for in Art. 2 of the present Convention.
Art. 2. The competent technical authorities of the Czechoslovak Republic and Romania shall decide by mutual agreement and in a Military Convention to be concluded, upon the provisions necessary for the execution of the present Convention."

LNTS, No. 155, 455 and 1288.

CZECHOSLOVAK–SOVIET FRIENDSHIP TREATY 1943. A Treaty signed on Dec. 12, 1943 in Moscow. It was an extension of the Soviet–Czechoslovak Treaty of June 16, 1935, as well as of the London treaty of June 18, 1941 concerning common tasks in the war against the Third Reich; it obligated both sides to friendly co-operation during the war and after (arts. 1 and 4) and forbade the conclusion of any pact aimed against the other signatory. The Protocol annexed to the agreement provided for the possibility of joining the pact by "a third state bordering upon the USSR and Czechoslovakia". The country in question was Poland, which was directly mentioned in one of the Teheran Declarations of 1943. The Czechoslovak–Soviet Treaty was supplemented on May 8, 1944 with an agreement determining the rights of the Red Army in Czechoslovakia in consequence of military operations.

British and Foreign State Papers, London, 1943; *Sovietsko–Czeskoslovenskie otnoshenya ve vremia Vielikoy Otchestviennoy Woiny. Dokumenty 1941–45*, Moskva, 1960.

CZECHOSLOVAK – SOVIET FRIENDSHIP TREATY, 1970. The Treaty of Friendship, Cooperation and Mutual Aid between the Czechoslovak Socialist Republic and the USSR was signed on May 6, 1970 in Prague and read as follows:

"The Union of Soviet Socialist Republics and the Czechoslovak Socialist Republic,
Affirming their fidelity to the aims and principles of the Soviet–Czechoslovak Treaty of Friendship, Mutual Aid and Post-War Co-operation, concluded on December 12, 1943, and extended on November 27, 1963, a treaty that played a historic role in the development of friendly relations between the peoples of the two States and laid a solid foundation for the further strengthening of fraternal friendship and all-round cooperation between them;
Profoundly convinced that the indestructible friendship between the Union of Soviet Socialist Republics and the Czechoslovak Socialist Republic, which was cemented in the joint struggle against Fascism and has received further deepening in the years of the construction of socialism and communism, as well as the fraternal mutual assistance and all-round co-operation between them, based on the teachings of Marxism–Leninism and the immutable principles of socialist internationalism, correspond to the fundamental interests of the peoples of both countries and of the entire socialist commonwealth;
Affirming that the support, strengthening and defense of the socialist gains achieved at the cost of the heroic efforts and selfless labour of each people are the common internationalist duty of the socialist countries;
Consistently, and steadfastly favouring the strengthening of the unity and solidarity of all countries of the socialist commonwealth, based on the community of their social systems and ultimate goals;
Firmly resolved strictly to observe the obligations stemming from the May 14, 1955 Warsaw Treaty of Friendship, Co-operation and Mutual Aid;
Stating the economic co-operation between the two States facilitates their development, as well as the further improvement of the international socialist division of labour and socialist economic integration within the framework of the Council for Mutual Economic Aid;
Expressing the firm intention to promote the cause of strengthening peace and security in Europe and throughout the world, to oppose imperialism, revanchism and militarism; Guided by the goals and principles proclaimed in the United Nations Charter;
Taking into account the achievements of socialist and communist construction in the two countries, the present situation and the prospects for all-round co-operation, as well as the changes that have taken place in Europe and throughout the world since the conclusion of the Treaty of December 12, 1943;
Have agreed on the following:
Art. 1. In accordance with the principles of socialist internationalism, the High Contracting Parties will continue to strengthen the eternal, indestructible friendship between the peoples of the Union of Soviet Socialist Republics and the Czechoslovak Socialist Republic, to develop all-round co-operation between the two countries and to give each other fraternal assistance and support, basing their actions on mutual respect for State sovereignty and independence, on equal rights and non-interference in one another's internal affairs.
Art. 2. The High Contracting Parties will continue, proceeding from the principles of friendly mutual assistance and the international socialist division of labour, to develop and deepen mutually advantageous bilateral and multilateral economic, scientific and technical co-operation with the aim of developing their national economies, achieving the highest possible scientific and technical level and efficiency of social production, and increasing the material well-being of the working people of their countries. The two sides will promote the further development of economic ties and co-operation and the socialist economic integration of the member countries of the Council for Mutual Economic Aid.
Art. 3. The High Contracting Parties will continue to develop and expand co-operation between the two countries in the fields of science and culture, education, literature and the arts, the press, radio, motion pictures, television, public health, tourism and physical culture and in other fields.
Art. 4. The High Contracting Parties will continue to facilitate the expansion of co-operation and direct ties between the bodies of State authority and the public organizations of the working people, with the aim of achieving a deeper mutual familiarization and a closer drawing together between the peoples of the two States.
Art. 5. The High Contracting Parties, expressing their unswerving determination to proceed along the path of the construction of socialism and communism, will take the necessary steps to defend the socialist gains of the peoples and the security and independence of the two countries, will strive to develop all-round relations among the States of the socialist commonwealth, and will act in a spirit of the con-solidation of the unity, friendship and fraternity of these States.
Art. 6. The High Contracting Parties proceed from the assumption that the Munich Pact of September 29, 1938, was signed under the threat of aggressive war and the use of force against Czechoslovakia, that it was a component part of Hitlerite Germany's criminal conspiracy against peace and was a flagrant violation of the basic norms of international law, and hence was invalid from the very outset, with all the consequences stemming therefrom.
Art. 7. The High Contracting Parties, consistently pursuing a policy of the peaceful coexistence of States with different social systems, will exert every effort for the defence of international peace and the security of the peoples against encroachments by the aggressive forces of imperialism and reaction, for the relaxation of international tension, the cessation of the arms race and the achievement of general and complete disarmament, the final liquidation of colonialism in all its forms and manifestations, and the giving of support to countries that have been liberated from colonial domination and are marching along the path of strengthening national independence and sovereignty.
Art. 8. The High Contracting Parties will jointly strive to improve the situation and to ensure peace in Europe, to strengthen and develop co-operation among the European States, to establish good-neighbour relations among them and to create an effective system of European security on the basis of the collective efforts of all European States.
Art. 9. The High Contracting Parties declare that one of the main preconditions for ensuring European security is the immutability of the State borders that were formed in Europe after the Second World War. They express their firm resolve, jointly with the other Member States of the May 14, 1955, Warsaw Treaty of Friendship, Co-operation and Mutual Aid and in accordance with this Treaty, to ensure the inviolability of the borders of the Member States of this Treaty and to take all necessary steps to prevent aggression on the part of any forces of militarism and revanchism and to rebuff the aggressor.
Art. 10. In the event that one of the High Contracting Parties is subjected to an armed attack by any State or group of States, the other Contracting Party, regarding this as an attack against itself, will immediately give the first party all possible assistance, including military aid, and will also give it support with all means at its disposal, by way of implementing the right to individual or collective self-defense in accordance with Art. 51 of the United Nations Charter.
The High Contracting Parties will without delay inform the United Nations Security Council of steps taken on the basis of this Art., and they will act in accordance with the provisions of the United Nations Charter.
Art. 11. The High Contracting Parties will inform each other and consult on all important international questions affecting their interests and will act on the basis of common positions agreed upon in accordance with the interests of both States.
Art. 12. The High Contracting Parties declare that their obligations under existing international treaties are not at variance with the provisions of this Treaty.
Art. 13. This Treaty is subject to ratification and will enter into force on the day of the exchange of instruments of ratification, which will be conducted in Moscow in a very short time.
Art. 14. This Treaty is concluded for a period of twenty years and will be automatically extended every five years thereafter, if neither of the High Contracting Parties gives notice that it is denouncing the Treaty twelve months before the expiration of the current period."

J.A.S. GRENVILLE, *The Major International Treaties 1914–1979. A History and Guide with Texts*, London, 1974, pp. 374–376.

CZECHOSLOVAK–SOVIET PACT OF MUTUAL ASSISTANCE, 1935. A Pact signed in Prague on May 16, 1935, related to preparations for the Eastern Pact, in close connection with the ▷ French–Soviet Pact of Mutual Assistance, signed on May 2, 1935 in Paris, as expressed by the identical formulation of arts. 1–3, with the reservation that Soviet assistance will follow assistance granted by France. It came into force for 5 years on June 9, 1935.

C.A. COLLIARD, *Droit international et histoire diplomatique*, Paris, 1950.

CZECHOSLOVAK–YUGOSLAV FRIENDSHIP TREATY, 1922. An Agreement between Czechoslovakia and the Kingdom of Serbs, Croats, and Slovenes, signed on Aug. 31, 1922 in Belgrade, on common security against aggression and preservation of their political status quo in Europe.

LNTS, No. 354.

CZECH SOCIALIST REPUBLIC. A federal state in the western part of Czechoslovakia. Area: 78,853 sq. km. Pop. 1980 est. 10,600,000. Capital: Prague. ▷ Czechoslovakia. ▷ Slovak Socialist Republic.

D

DAB. *Limanda.* A flatfish, subject of the ▷ Scandinavian Fishery Convention 1937, concerning the preservation of dab.

DAC. Development Assistance Committee of the OECD meeting in Paris as a forum of principal contributing countries, who consult on all aspects of their assistance policies, bilateral and multilateral aid programs and about the amount and nature of their contributions.

UN Chronicle, October, 1982, p. 47.

DACCA ▷ **DHAKA.**

DACHAU. German city (Bavaria, FRG), on the Amper River, near which, one of the first Nazi concentration camps was established in Feb., 1933; existed until Apr., 1945 with 130 hard labor camps and about 160,000 prisoners, of whom 66,000 were murdered, of various nationalities from European countries occupied by German troops. Liberated by the US Army on Apr. 28, 1945. On Oct. 16, 1946 in the Crematory of Dachau were burned the cadavers of major German war criminals, condemned to death, and hanged in Nuremberg during the night of 15–16 Oct. The ashes were scattered in an unknown place. Organization reg. with the UIA: International Dachau Committee, f. 1958, Brussels, Belgium. Publ.: *Bulletin.*

The Trial of German Major War Criminals, Proceedings of the IMT Sitting at Nurembert, 42 Vols. London 1946–48, Vols. 1, 2, 3, 4, 8, 11, 12, 15, 20 and 21; B.C. ANDRUS, *The Infamous of Nuremberg,* New York, 1969; P. Berben, *The Official History 1933-1945,* London 1975. *Yearbook of International Organizations, 1986/87; The Europa Yearbook 1988. A World Survey,* Vol. I, London 1988.

DAG HAMMARSKJÖLD FOUNDATION. f. 1962, Uppsala, to provide nationals of the developing Third World countries with an opportunity to discuss in seminars and conferences issues related to the legal, economic and social problems of international development. Publ biannnually.: *Development Dialogue.*

DAG HAMMARSKJÖLD LIBRARY.▷ Hammarskjöld Dag Library, ▷ UN Libraries.

DAHOMEY. A historical name of a African territory on the Gulf of Guinea dominated since the 17th century by an ethnic group named Dahomey or Fon. The name was used during the French colonial period 1880–1960 and by the Republic of Dahomey which gained independence on Aug. 1, 1960; in 1975 was officially changed to ▷ Benin.

DAIRYING ▷ **MILK**

"DAISY CUTTER" The name of a 15,000 pound bomb exploding seven feet above the ground, used by US Air Forces in the Vietnam war to clear jungle areas.

DU PUY, C. JOHNSON, G.P. HAYES eds., *Dictionary of Military Terms; A Guide to Warfare and Military Institutions,* New York 1986.

DAKAR. The capital of Senegal (1979 pop. estimate 978,553), since 1960, and a port on Cape Verde Peninsula on the Atlantic Ocean, 1942–45 occupied by the US forces. 1959–60 capital of the Federation of ▷ Mali. Headquarters of the: African Civil Aviation Association, Afro-Mauritian Cultural Institute, African Trade Union Confederation, Central Bank of West African States, International Association for the Development of Documentation, Libraries and Archives, African ILO Office, Joint Anti-Locust and Anti-Aviarian Organization, Organization for Development of the Senegal River, Standing Technical Secretariat of the Conference of Ministers of National Education of the French-Speaking African-Malagasy States, UNESCO Office, Union of National Radio and TV Organizations of Africa, UN Information Centre, West African Monetary Union.

Yearbook of International Organizations. J. PAXTON ed., *The Statesman's Yearbook 1987-88,* London 1987.

DAKAR ANTI-APARTHEID MEETING, 1987. First meeting of the members of the African National Congress outlawed in South Africa with 50 whites, members of anti-apartheid liberal movements in South Africa, in the capital of Senegal from 10 to 12 July 1987. The common statement noted "a shared commitment towards the removal of the apartheid system and the building of a united South Africa. The main area of concern arose over the ANC's resolve to maintain and intensify the armed struggle".

International Herald Tribune, July 13, 1987.

DAKAR DECLARATION, 1975. A Declaration on raw materials and primary commodities, adopted by the First Conference of Developing Countries on Raw Materials, held Feb. 3–8, 1975 in Dakar. The text is as follows:

"The developing countries, meeting in Dakar on 4–8 February on the initiative of the Fourth Summit Conference of Non-Aligned Countries, carried out a detailed analysis of the fundamental problems of raw materials and development in the light of recent trends in international economic relations, and taking into account the decisions of the Sixth Special Session of the United Nations Assembly on raw materials and development.

They noted the trends in the international economic situation, which was marked by the perpetuation of inequalities in economic relations, imperialist domination, neo-colonialist exploitation and a total lack of solutions to the basic problems of the developing countries.

Determined to pursue together and in unity a joint action to broaden the irreversible process which has been initiated in international economic relations and which has opened the way for the developing countries to put an end to their position of dependence vis-à-vis imperialism.

Convinced that the only way for them to achieve full and complete economic emancipation is to recover and control their natural resources and wealth and the means of economic development in order to secure the economic, social and cultural progress of their peoples.

Decide, in accordance with the principles and objectives of the Declarations and Programmes of Action of the Fourth Summit Conference of Non-Aligned Countries and the Sixth Special Session of the United Nations General Assembly, on the basis of a common course of action, to adopt the following declaration:

(1.) The present structure of international trade, which had its origins in imperialist and colonialist exploitation, and which has continued in force up to the present day, in most cases through various forms of neo-colonialism, needs to be replaced by a new international economic order based on principles of justice and equity, designed to safeguard the common interests of

all peoples, to correct present injustices and to prevent the occurrence of further injustices. The profound crisis now affecting the international economic system has once again demonstrated the breakdown of traditional mechanisms, and with it the particular vulnerability of the economies of developing countries. It cannot be denied that the structure and organization of world import and export trade operate for the most part to the advantage of developed countries. A powerful weapon which the developing countries can use to change this state of affairs is to defend their natural resources and to grasp the fact (as they are in fact doing) that it is only by combining their forces to strengthen their negotiating power that they will ever succeed in obtaining their rights to just and equitable treatment, something for which our peoples have lived and fought for centuries. Despite innumerable efforts at international level to tackle the problems which confront developing countries which export primary products, no perceptible progress has in fact been made for several decades in solving any aspect of the primary products problem. (2.) According to the views imposed by the industrialized capitalist countries concerning world trade in primary products, the free working of the primary products markets should normally ensure an optimum distribution of the world resources, and the rising trend of demand in the industrialized countries for exports of primary products from developing countries should stimulate the economic growth of this latter group of countries. This would have been the case if favourable conditions had been created, especially with regard to free access to the markets of the developed countries and the marketing of primary products, but the developing countries have, in the performance of this function of suppliers of raw materials to the industrialized countries, run into other obstacles imposed on them.

(3.) The framework and organization of commodity trade, and especially the marketing and distribution systems for individual commodities prevailing at present, were developed in the nineteenth century by colonial powers and are wholly inadequate today as instruments of economic change and advancement. Under such systems, transnational corporations control the production of and trade in many primary commodities, particularly through the exercise of bargaining power against a large number of weak competing sellers in developing countries. World commodity markets experience a chronic instability which arises through sudden and substantial shifts in the balance of world supply and demand as well as through excessive speculative activities encouraged by the lack of adequate regulation of these markets.

(4.) The fact that developing countries have been denied adequate participation in the determination of the international prices of their export commodities has led to a permanent transfer of real resources from developing to developed countries, because the benefits from the improvements in productivity in the production of primary commodities and raw materials are transferred to developed consumer countries rather than translated into higher earnings for commodity producers, in marked contrast with what occurs in developed countries where improvements in productivity result in higher profits for those countries. Furthermore the low level of commodity prices has stimulated an excessive consumption and considerable waste of scarce raw materials in the affluent countries, resulting in the rapid depletion of non-renewable resources.

(5.) The repeated MFN tariff reductions in the postwar period which resulted from trade negotiations in GATT covered mostly industrial products traded mainly between developed countries. Moreover efforts towards the liberalization of international trade tended to ignore non-tariff barriers, which more particularly affect raw or semi-processed primary commodities of export interest to developing counties, and also left unresolved the problem of tariff escalation, which greatly hampers the trade of developing countries.

(6.) In addition, developed countries or groupings of developed countries spent on the subsidization of their domestic production of primary commodities competing with those exported by developing countries a much larger amount than that allocated to official development assistance to developing countries. Moreover, they have violated the principles adopted in the framework of the GATT and have failed to meet their obligations under the International Development Strategy with regard to the readjustments of their respective economies. As a result, their self-sufficiency ratios for most of these commodities increased substantially, and in some cases surpluses became available for dumping on third countries' markets, thus reducing the export outlets available to producer developing countries.

(7.) At the same time considerable research and development efforts were undertaken, in particular by transnational corporations–partly financed out of the excess profits they had made by controlling the exploitation and marketing of the natural resources of the developing countries–and led to the large-scale production of synthetics and substitutes which displaced in well-protected markets the natural products exported by developing countries.

(8) The fast growth of developed countries was partly financed through an international monetary system tailored to their needs, allowing inflationary trends to affect not only their domestic economies but also international trade. Developing countries, being the weakest partners in this trade, were those who suffered most from inflation. Moreover, speculative monetary activities by transnational corporations contributed significantly to the destabilization of the international monetary system. The monetary instability and devaluation of the early 1970s affected adversely the currency reserves held by developing countries.

(9.) The above constraints imposed on the commodity trade of developing countries have resulted in a persistent long-term deterioration in their terms of trade, despite occasional improvements such as those which occurred at the beginning of the fifties or recently in 1973 and at the beginning of 1974. The sudden increase in commodity prices which occurred in 1973 and part of 1974, however, was due to exceptional circumstances and to an increase in demand as a hedge against inflation and exchange-rate changes rather than to any conscious international policy. Furthermore, this rise in commodity prices was uneven among the various commodities, the prices of some important commodities having actually remained stagnant or decreased in real terms.

(10.) Finally, this increase in commodity prices, including oil prices, followed a long period of deterioration in the terms of trade of the developing countries.

(11.) The prices of several major commodities have begun to decline significantly, leading to a further deterioration in the terms of trade of developing countries. There is also a real possibility that other commodities may also experience a decline in prices, given the likelihood that developed countries will take measures to reduce their imports of many of these commodities as part of their strategy of dividing the developing countries.

(12.) Ever rising freight rates and the failure by the Liner Conference in most cases to grant promotional freight rates in respect of primary commodities of export interest to the developing countries have further impeded export promotion, particularly in countries which are land-locked and geographically handicapped.

(13.) The high rates of inflation generated within the economies of the industrialized developed countries have been exported to the economies of the developing countries by raising their import bills to unbearable limits. The balance-of-payments difficulties already being experienced by many developing countries have been seriously aggravated by, inter alia, the enormous increase in the cost of imports of food, fertilizers, capital equipment and fuel and in the cost of transport, ocean freight services and insurance, and the implementation of the development plans of developing countries facing such difficulties has been seriously impeded. In this respect the land-locked developing countries are in a very difficult position, which certainly deserves special attention in view of the special problems with which these countries are confronted.

(14.) Finally, the potential mineral resources of the seabed, the ocean floor and the sub-soil thereof outside the limits of national jurisdiction, the extraction of which might become a reality towards 1985, threaten seriously to reduce the export earnings of developing countries, particularly given the danger that the exploitation of these resources may be undertaken under a regime which will not fully safeguard the interests of the producer developing countries concerned.

(15.) The fundamental problem remains the same: developing countries still depend on their commodity exports for 75 to 80 per cent of their foreign exchange earnings. The process of their development is still largely dependent upon external factors, i.e. the demand from the developed countries for their export commodities.

(16.) There is no price support at just and remunerative levels in the world market for primary commodities, in marked contrast to the systems operating in the domestic markets of the developed countries in favour of their own farmers. Finally, the existing system of organization of the world food trade has been unable to meet the essential requirements of food-deficient developing countries.

(17) By the middle of the second United Nations Development Decade, the first measures for the implementation of the International Strategy which were to be taken by developed countries have not yet been applied, or in some cases even agreed upon. The lack of action by developed countries to tackle the commodity problem of the developing countries is particularly apparent in the following areas:

1. Non-implementation of the provisions of the International Development Stragegy for the Second United Nations Developent Decade concerning world trade in commodities, and concerning the reduction and elimination of duties and other barriers to imports of primary products, including those in processed and semi-processed form, of export interest to developing countries;
2. Failure of the international community to establish comprehensive international arrangements on most individual commodities owing to the intransigence of developed countries;
3. Non-implementation of resolutions adopted in UNCTAD and other forums with respect to pricing policy and access to markets and the increasing trend towards protectionism in developed countries;
4. Failure of the recent round of intensive intergovernmental consultations on individual commodities, pursuant to resolution 83(III) of the United Nations Conference on Trade and Development and resolution 7(VII) of the UNCTAD Committee on Commodities, to achieve concrete results.
5. Long delay in the commencement of the multilateral trade negotiations and in the implementation of the provisions of the Tokyo Declaration, which referred inter alia to (i) the need to secure additional benefits for the international trade of developing countries so as to achieve a substantial increase in their foreign exchange earnings, the diversification of their exports, and the acceleration of the growth of their trade, and (ii) the need to treat tropical products as a special and priority sector;

(18) To this must be added the anarchial exploitation by the multinational corporations and the misuse and squandering of non-renewable raw materials by the developed countries, which constitute a threat to the indispensable conservation of the natural resources needed for promoting development and satisfying in the long term the real needs of mankind as a whole.

At the same time the food deficit in the developing countries, caused by the economic policies pursued by the developed countries, which aggravate the dependent position and accentuate the external disequilibrium and under-development of the developing countries make an effective contribution to the long-term solution of the world food problem.

The developed countries should undertake action to alleviate the position of the deficit developing countries, making both food supplies and also adequate technical and financial aid available to them, the latter being directed in particular to developing countries enjoying comparative advantages so that they may expand as far as possible their local production of food. This action must however in no way hamper the production and exports of developing countries which are traditional exporters of food.

(19.) Given this lack of adequate action by the international community owing to the lack of political will on the part of developed countries, there is an urgent need for the developing countries to change their traditional approach to negotiations with the developed countries, hitherto consisting in the presentation of a list of requests to the developed countries and an appeal to their political good will, which in reality was seldom forthcoming. To achieve this change, the developing countries must undertake common action to strengthen their bargaining position in relation to the developed countries. It is more imperative than ever for the developing countries to take practical steps to strengthen economic co-operation among themselves on the lines of the Programme of Action adopted by the Fourth Summit Conference of Non-Aligned Countries in September 1973 and to agree on a common strategy and on specific lines of action in the field of raw materials and other primary commodities, based on the principle of relying first and foremost on themselves and their own resources to obtain the means for their own development and to establish a new international economic order.

(20.) The causes of the current economic crisis are rooted in the colonial past of many developing countries, characterized by centuries of uninhibited exploitation of their natural resources. Although colonialism is disappearing, economic exploitation of the developing countries by the developed countries continues to be a major obstacle to the even and balanced development of all countries. The developing countries, which have 70% of the world's population, generate only 30 per cent of the world's income, and the gap between the developed and the developing countries continues to widen.

(21.) Moreover, some peoples, still victims of direct colonialism or racism, are deprived of their fundamental rights to sovereignty and independence and any possibility of development. On the other hand, many countries are still subject to imperialist domination and neo-colonialist exploitation, which constitute a reality and a serious obstacle to their independence.

(22.) The inequities and weaknesses of the present economic system are particularly glaring in the conduct of world trade in raw material. Those who control the levers of the price mechanism have successfully denied to the producers of a number of raw materials their due profit from their labour and from their natural endowment, while they have themselves continued to make excessive profits by charging high prices for the finished products.

(23.) The prevailing economic order, and the international division of labour on which it depends, have been based essentially on the exploitation and processing by industrialized countries of the raw materials produced by developing countries and on the enjoyment of the value added which determines both the final overall price and the unfair terms of trade resulting therefrom. To these must be added the further profits accruing from the processes of marketing, financing, freight and insurance.

(24.) Consequently, the only possibility of correcting this economic order and such a division of labour lies essentially in transferring to the developing countries the job of processing the raw materials they produce in their own national territories, so that they may be able to derive maximum benefit from their potential wealth and improve their real terms of trade with developed countries.

(25.) For this reason, when the developing countries meet at Algiers from the 15th to 18th February 1975 for the Ministerial Conference of the Group of 77, they will have to decide on concerted action and follow the same line if they are to acquire a larger share in world industrial output by processing and upgrading their raw materials within their own frontiers and by this means helping to establish new forms of international industrial co-operation.

(26) That is why the Algiers Ministerial Conference marks a decisive step forward for developing countries in the preparation for the Second General Conference of UNIDO which is to be held at Lima from the 12th to the 26th March, and during which a Declaration will be made and a plan of action for industrialization adopted by the international community in line with the principles for the establishment of a new international economic order.

(27.) Recent events have shown that traditional ideas about international trade conflict with reality, for they are based on an increasingly outmoded conception of international specialization. This conception is simply that trade relations depend on factors with which the various countries participating in international trade are endowed. Based as it is on a false assumption, it disregards some essential features of present-day economic reality.

(28.) These events have thrust into prominence the reality of interdependence of all members of the international community and have made it clear that a few developed countries can no longer decide the community's fate. This realization led to the convening of a special session of the General Assembly devoted exclusively to the problems of raw materials and development, and to the adoption of the historic Declaration and Programme of Action on the establishment of a new international economic order, whose provisions must be implemented as a matter of urgency.

The Sixth Special Session of the United Nations General Assembly on raw materials and development has set in motion an irreversible process in international relations and made it possible to reaffirm the intention of developing countries to engage in dialogue, to concert policies and to co-operate in order to establish new economic relations between Members of the international community. This necessary shift in international relations obliges developed countries to take full cognisance of economic and political facts in the world today and to accept precise commitments to assume their responsibilities within the framework of the inevitable alterations which must be made for the establishment of a new international economic order.

(29.) Considering that there is now a general tendency among developing countries to mobilise and more rationally exploit their natural resources, these countries undertake to advance along the road towards the complete eradication of their economic dependence on imperialism, to develop their economies, their science and their technology, to achieve prosperity in their countries, to systematically improve the lives of their people, to achieve complete economic independence, social justice and political sovereignty and to eliminate inequalities between nations in international relations, and so to establish a new international economic order.

(30.) The new international economic order must be based on the principles of equality and equity, and conceived in the common interest for the benefit of all the peoples of the world. It entails reversal of the existing trends in world economy in which structural changes are necessary and inevitable. The introduction of the new international economic order, which must provide for the broadest possible co-operation between all States in eliminating the existing disparities and securing prosperity for all, is a prerequisite for the establishment of a new type of economic relations based on respect of the right of every State to exercises permanent sovereignty over its natural resources and to dispose of them freely.

(31.) The principles set out in the Charter of the Economic Rights and Obligations of States must be fully implemented. Consequently, it is the right and duty of all states, individually and collectively, to eliminate colonialism, apartheid, racial discrimination, neo-colonialism and all forms of foreign aggression, occupation and domination, and the economic and social consequences thereof, as a prerequisite for development. States which practice such coercive polices are economically responsible to the countries, territories and peoples affected for the restitution and full compensation for the exploitation and depletion of, and damage to, the natural and all other resources of those countries, territories and peoples. It is the duty of all states to extend assistance to them."

Conference on Economic Co-operation among Developing Countries. Declarations, Resolutions, Recommendations and Decisions, adopted in the UN System. México, DF, 1976, Vol. 3, pp. 511–523.

DALAI LAMA. *Mongolian:* dalai "ocean", *Tibetan:* bla-ma "older". The highest spiritual rank of ▷ Lamaism. The flight of the 14th Dalai Lama from Tibet to India became the subject of a UN debate on Oct. 21, 1959. On Oct. 5, 1989 the Dalai Lama was awarded the Nobel Peace Prize for his efforts to find a peaceful solution to the problems of Tibet.

DAMASCUS. The capital of Syria (1981 pop. census 1,251,028). The Old City of Damascus is included in the ▷ World Heritage UNESCO List. The Great Mosque of the Umayyads, constructed between 705 and 716 A.D., is surrounded by the

walls of the Temple of Jupiter which was built in the 3rd century on the site of another sanctuary whose origins went back to the 11th century B.C. The area surrounding the Mosque is an extremely valuable part of the heritage of Islam.

UNESCO. *A Legacy for All*, Paris, 1984. J. PAXTON ed., *The Statesman's Yearbook 1987-88.* London 1987.

DANCE. A subject of international co-operation. Organizations reg. with the UIA:

Imperial Society of Teachers of Dancing, f. 1904, London. Publ. *Dance.*
International Association of Margaret Morris Movement (Recreational Dance), f. 1939, Edinburgh.
International Dancing Council, f. 1973, Paris. consultative status: UNESCO. Publ. *Le monde de la Danse.*
International Institute for Music, Dance and Theatre in the Audio-Visual Media, 1969, Vienna.
International Council of Ballroom Dancing, f. 1950, Edinburgh.

Yearbook of International Organizations.

DANGEROUS GOODS. An international term for explosive, caustic and malodorous substances transported in keeping with international conventions, i.a. Accord européen relatif au transport international des marchandises dangereuses par route, ADR. This European agreement on road transportation was signed on Sept. 30, 1957, in Geneva

UNTS, Vol. 619, p. 798. *UN Transport of Dangerous Goods,* New York, 1986.

DANISH STRAITS. A common name of a chain of straits: Kattegat, Skagerrak, Oresund, Store Baelt, and Little Baelt connecting the Baltic Sea with the North Sea. Internationalized by the Treaty of Copenhagen, 1857, open to navigation by both merchant and war vessels with the exception of the years of World Wars I and II, when they were mined. The unilateral decisions by Denmark in 1938 and 1951 limiting the right of free passage for warships was nullified by a Convention on the question of territorial sea and its adjacent zone, 1958. In 1924 the USSR made the proposal, supported after World War II by Poland and the GDR, to limit passage through D.S. for warships to ships of the Baltic States; rejected by NATO.

E. WOLGAST, "Zur Frage der Kogsundrinne und der Ostsee Eingäge", in: *Zeitschrift für öffentliches Recht,* No. 5, 1926; E. BRUEL, *International Straits,* London, 1947; R.R. BAXTER, "Passage of ships through international waterways in time of war," in: *The British Yearbook of International Law,* 1954.

DANUBE AND DANUBE COMMISSION. An international river of central and south eastern Europe; 2850 km. long, flowing from the FRG through Austria, Bulgaria, Czechoslovakia, Hungary, Yugoslavia, and Romania, where the south arm of the delta forms the border between Romania and the USSR. A drainage basin of 828,800 sq. km. The international status of the Danube was established for the first time in art. 17 of the Treaty of Paris, signed on Mar. 30, 1856, when the European Commission for Navigation on the Danube was created. Later confirmed by the treaties of 1865, 1871, 1881, and 1883. After World War I, in accordance with arts. 327–364 of the Versailles Treaty, 12 states (Austria, Belgium, Bulgaria, Czechoslovakia, France, Greece, Germany, Hungary, Italy, Romania, the UK and Yugoslavia) on July 23, 1921 signed, in Paris, a Convention which created the International Commission for the Danube, which dealt with the river from the Ulm to the Black Sea. On Nov. 14, 1936, Germany withdrew (on the occasion of her renunciation of the Versailles Treaty) and in 1938 Austria followed suit.

On Aug. 18, 1938, in Sinaia, Romania, an Agreement was signed which revised the Convention in such a way that Germany once again joined. On Dec. 12, 1946 the Council of Ministers of Foreign Affairs of the Four Powers recommended the drafting of a new convention on the international status of navigation on the Danube. On Aug. 18, 1948, Bulgaria, Czechoslovakia, Hungary, Romania, the Ukrainian SSR and USSR signed, in Belgrade, a new Convention according to which "Navigation on the Danube will be free and open for citizens, for commercial vessels and for the goods of all states on the principle of equality ..." (art. 1); execution of the Convention is supervised by the Danube Commission (arts. 5–19), with headquarters in Budapest. It went into effect on May 11, 1949.

Danube Commission publ.: *Summary Reports and Documents, Guidebook for Sailors, Regulations for Navigation on the Danube, Mileage Chart of the Danube, Collection of Internal Laws Concerning Navigation on Danube, Radio Codes for Navigation in the Danube, Danube Hydrological Yearbook* and *Danube Statistical Bulletin.*

LNTS, Vol. 26, p. 177; H. HAINAL, *Le droit du Danube international,* Paris, 1929; H.A. SMITH, "The Danube", in: *Yearbook of World Affairs 1950;* W. WEGENER, *Die Internationale Donau,* Wien, 1956, *Le Danube,* Paris, 1956; W. LOGUNOF, *Sovremienniy mezhdunarodniy riezhim Dunaya,* Moskva, 1956; UNITAR, *International Navigable Waterways,* New York, 1975.

DANUBE-BLACK SEA CANAL. A 61 km. waterway linking the Danube River from Cernavoda with the Black Sea near the Constanta seaport, built by Romania 1973–84, allows heavy-barge traffic to flow unimpeded as far as Austria and West Germany.

"Romania's Danube Connection", in: *Newsweek,* January 30, 1984.

DARDANELLES. The Turkish straits connecting the Marmara Sea with the Aegean Sea, internationalized since 1833; coastline fortified by Germany at the beginning of World War I; place of a battle at Gallipoli between a British–French expeditionary fleet and Turkish forces 1915. Toward the end of the war, on Jan. 8, 1918, the US President Woodrow Wilson in point 12 of his ▷ Fourteen Points stipulated:

"The Dardanelles should be permanently open as a free route for vessels and commerce of all states on the basis of international guarantees."

▷ Wilson's Fourteen Points.

This was agreed upon by Bulgaria, Czechoslovakia, France, Greece, Italy, Japan, Romania and the USSR on the one hand, and Turkey on the other on July 24, 1923, in Lausanne:

"The High Contracting Parties agree to recognize and declare the principle of freedom of transit and of navigation by sea and by air on the Strait of the Dardanelles, the Sea of Mamara and the Bosphorous ..." (art. I).

The Convention was replaced by the Dardanelles Montreux Convention on Mar. 20, 1936.

LNTS, Vol. 28, pp. 119–137; J. ABREVARA, *La Conférence de Montreux et le régime des détroits,* Paris, 1938; M. SOKOLNICKI, *The Turkish Straits,* Beirut, 1950; *Major Peace Treaties of Modern History,* New York, 967, pp. 2369–2383.

DARE. Data Retrieval System for Social Science. A computer system on the administration of information in the field of social sciences designed by the Documentation Centre of UNESCO.

DAR ES SALAAM. The capital of Tanzania (1985 pop. estimate 1,183,000). Since 1964, former capital

D

of Tanganyika (1961) and main port on the arm of the Indian Ocean. Summer residence (1866) of the Sultan of Zanzibar. Occupied by German colonial forces, 1887, was capital of German East Africa, 1891–1914. Headquarters of the All African Trade Union Federation, East African Directorate of Civil Aviation, ILO Office and UN Office.

Yearbook of International Organizations. J. PAXTON ed., *The Statesman's Yearbook 1987-88*, London 1987.

DAR ES SALAAM OAU DECLARATION, 1975. The final act of the Extraordinary Conference of the Foreign Ministers of the Organization of African Unity on the situation in South Africa and Rhodesia (Zimbabwe), which was held on Apr. 11, 1975 in Dar es Salaam. It was approved by the OAU Summit Conference on July 31, 1975 in Kampala.

DARIEN NATIONAL PARK. A Panamanian natural monument, included in the ▷ World Heritage UNESCO List. The Darien National Park is situated at the junction of South America and Central America. It covers more than 500,000 hectares and contains a fantastic variety of ecosystems, habitats and vegetable and animal species. It is the home of the Chocos and the Kunas, native peoples who live off the forest just as their ancestors did before the arrival of Christopher Colombus.

World Cultural Heritage. Information Bulletin, Paris, 1983.

DARPA. Advanced Research Projects Agency of the US defense system, f. Febr. 1958 together with the Department of Defence Office of Research and Enginering with the simultaneous reorganization of the National Advisory Committee for Aeronautics into the National Aeronautics and Space Administration ▷ NASA; founded in reaction to the launching of ▷ Sputnik on Oct. 4, 1957.

S.I. ÄKERSTEN, *The Strategic Computing Program, in Arms and Artificial Intelligence*, SIPRI, Oxford, 1987.

DARTMOUTH MEETING. ▷ Torgau.

DARWIN FOUNDATION. ▷ Galapagos Islands.

DATA BANK. International term for information centers.

DATA PROCESSING. ▷ Information processing.

DATA RETRIEVAL SYSTEM. ▷ DARE.

DATE LINE, INTERNATIONAL. An international term for a hypothetical line running along the 180° meridian admitting certain deviations to include Aleutian Islands and Alaska as well as some Pacific islands and Australia; customarily adopted by sailors and flyers as the most appropriate place to set the date back by one day when sailing or flying westward, e.g. from Wednesday, Mar. 22 to Tuesday, Mar. 21; or to set the date ahead by one day when going eastward, e.g. from Tuesday, Mar. 21 to Wednesday, Mar. 22. Therefore, travellers from Asia to America lose one day, and gain one day when they travel back. The international date line has never been subject to international conventions; however, it has become an international custom.

DAWES PLAN, 1924. A plan adopted on Apr. 9, 1924, by the International Reparations Commission and on Aug. 16 of the same year by governments of the Great Powers; came into force on Sept. 1, 1924; it concerned payment of war reparations by Germany after World War I. The plan was prepared by a Committee of Experts selected on Nov. 30,

1923, headed by an American financier and politician G. Dawes. Under the Dawes Plan payment of the reparations imposed on Germany in keeping with the Treaty of Versailles was to be split into long-term instalments and take into account the degree of reconstruction of Germany's industrial potential which enabled that country to fulfill its financial commitments. To this end the UK and USA granted Germany a credit to the amount of 800 million DM in gold to keep the German currency stable and to initiate development of German industry. In 1929 the Dawes Plan was replaced with the ▷ Young Plan.

R. RAAB, "Der Dawes Plan und seine Durchführung", in: *Zehn Jahre Versailles*, Berlin, 1929, Bd. 1; CH. G. DAWES, *A Journal of Reparations*, New York, 1939; H. COING, "Dawes Plan," in: *STRUPP-SCHLOCHAUER, Wörterbuch des Völkerrechts*, Berlin, 1960, Bd. 1, pp. 314–317.

DAYLIGHT SAVING TIME. An international term for the prolongation of solar lighting power in the afternoon and evening by setting ahead clocks by one or two hours in Summer. First adopted in the USA during World War 1, accepted later by the majority of European countries and the USSR.

DAYS FREE FROM WORK. A subject of international ILO conventions ensuring a minimum annual amount of days free from work to the gainfully employed according to sex and age.

D-DAY. A code name of the invasion day of German-occupied France by Allied Forces on June 6, 1944.

DEAD SEA-MEDITERRANEAN SEA CANAL. A controversial international project, debated 1980 by the Israeli government. The proposed waterway has the form of a canal in the Gaza Strip, then of a 50 mile long tunnel (15 feet in diameter) and again a canal with hydroelectric energy obtained due to the difference of altitudes between the two seas (Dead Sea is 1300 feet below sea level). Egypt protested against any change in the Gaza Strip occupied by Israel from 1967. Jordan, whose frontier with Israel lies on the Dead Sea, rejected the Israeli plan. On Dec. 16, 1981 the UN General Assembly adopted Res. B61150, by a recorded vote of 139 in favour 2 against (Israel, USA) with 4 abstentions, demanded that Israel cease forthwith implementation of its canal project linking the Mediterranean and the Dead Sea. On Oct. 11, 1984 a team of UN experts, who visited Jordan, reported that the canal could damage Jordan's agriculture and mineral production. On July 1, 1985 the Secretary General was informed by an Israeli verbal note, that on June 11, 1985 the Mediterranean Dead Sea Corporation had been instructed to "cease forthwith all work related to the canal". On Dec. 10, 1985, The General Assembly adopted by a recorded vote of 150 in favour to one against (Israel) Res. 40/167 asking the Secretary General to monitor one new Dead Sea Canal development "on a continuing basis", and also stipulating that it would resume consideration of the subject in case activities by Israel relating to that canal were resumed.

The Economist, September 6, 1980, p. 31; *UN Chronicle*, February, 1982, p. 27; *International Herald Tribune*, October 12, 1984. *UN Chronicle*, 1986, No. 2, p. 49.

DEAD SEA SCROLLS. An international term for leather and papyrus manuscripts discovered in 1947 and after in caves on the northwestern shore of the Dead Sea, near the ruins of the Khirbet Qumran and the Wilderness of Judaea. The over 2000-year-old documents are most important to the early history of Judaism and Christianity, because some

of them contain the oldest known versions of passages from the Old Testament.

J.T. MILIK, *Ten Years of Discovery in the Wilderness of Judaea*, Chicago, 1959. G. VERNES, *The Dead Sea Scrolls in English*, London, 1962; R. DE VAUX, *L'archéologie et les manuscrits de la mer Morte*, Paris, 1963; M.YIZHAR, *Bibliography of Hebraes Publications on the Dead Sea Scrolls, 1948–1964*, Jerusalem, 1965; *UN Chronicle*, Jan., 1984, p. 36.

DEAF-MUTES LANGUAGE. A UNESCO term for the language of deaf-mutes used at World Congresses of Deaf-Mutes held every four years since 1951 by the World Federation of the Deaf. Unlike lip-reading or sign-language, it is international and permits the holding of congresses without interpreters. A project of a *Dictionnaire international de gestes* was begun in 1971 under the auspices of UNESCO.

DEAFNESS. A subject of international co-operation. Organizations reg. with the UIA:
Commonwealth Society for the Deaf, f. 1959, London.
European Federation of the Association of Teachers for the Deaf, f. 1969, Brussels.
International Lutheran Deaf Association, f. 1971, St. Louis.
International Sound Foundation Society, f. 1967, Ottawa.
World Federation of the Deaf, f. 1951, Rome, as World Federation of the Deaf-Mutes, present name adopted 1953. Aims: social rehabilitation of the deaf. Consultative status with: ECOSOC, UNESCO. Official relations with WHO, ILO Special List. Members: National organizations. Publ. *La voix du Silence* (quarterly in French and English)

Yearbook of International Organizations.

DEALIGNMENT. An international term for a new global concensus based on a respect for pluralism and political and social diversity, coined in the late 1980's at the forum of The United Nations University.

M. KALDOR, R. FALK, eds., *Dealignment A New Foreign Policy Perspective*, Oxford, UK, 1987.

DEATH. A subject of international research and co-operation on a legal definition of death. In 1968 Harvard University initiated international research of new criteria for the determination of death. The following criteria were adopted: (1.) The complete and permanent absence of consciousness; (2.) Permanent absence of spontaneous respiration; (3.) The absence of any reaction to external stimuli and reflexes of any kind; (4.) Atomy of all muscles; (5.) The cessation of body temperature regulation; (6.) The maintenance of vascular tonicity only through the administration of vascular analeptics; and (7.) Complete and permanent absence of spontaneous or induced cerebral electrical activity. A legal concept of death of the Institute of Government and Law of the Soviet Academy of Sciences states: "Human death is to be determined not as the interruption of cardiac activity, but as the irreversible cessation of cardiac activity and the nervous electrical activity of the brain." Two Russian experts represent the opinion that to arrive at a final definition of the concept of death will require physicians and lawyers to work together. In their opinion, a preliminary version might look like this: "The death of an individual shall be considered to be the complete and irreversible cessation of cerebral cortex function resulting from the death of the brain cells, and shall be determined by a series of methods, devised in accordance with the latest medical science, which clearly and unequivocally prove that death has occurred." All legal consequences associated with the death of the individual will begin to have effect at precisely that moment.

M. KOVALEV, I. VERMEL, "The legal definition of death," in: *Socialist Law*, No. 7, Moscow, 1982; *World Health*, November, 1982. R. PLANT, C. PRITCH-ARD, *Life and Death Issues, Ethical Dilemma in Medicine and Social Work*, London, 1987.

DEATH CERTIFICATES. ▷ UN International Office for Death Certificates.

DEATH SQUADS. A right wing terrorist organization in El Salvador responsible for killings of thousands of Salvadorians during the years 1980–84; a subject of international protests, also on the UN forum.

"The Death Squads" in: *Newsweek*, January 16, 1984.

DEATH TRADE. An international term from the 1920's for the international arms trade.
See also ▷ Arms Trade International.

M. BRZOSKA, Th. OHLSEN, *Arms Transfer to the Third World 1971-85*, Oxford, 1987.

DEBIT. French "sales", "outlet". An international term for governmental permission to import and distribute foreign periodicals and books.

DEBT HAVANA CONFERENCE 1985 ▷ Havana Debt Conference 1985.

DEBTORS OF THE UNITED NATIONS. A report of the UN on Nov. 20, 1987 stated that the United Nations is owed a total of $877 million by its Members. The biggest debtors were: US – $414.2 million, USSR – $225 million, Poland – $18 million, GDR – $17 million, Brazil – $16 million, Czechoslovakia – $9 million. On Sept. 13, 1988 President R. Reagan ordered the release of US$44,000,000 in outstanding dues to the UN and a payment of US$144,000,000 for the fiscal year 1988/89.

DEBTS OF DEVELOPING COUNTRIES. ▷ Foreign debts.

DEBTS REPORTING SYSTEM, DRS ▷ Foreign Debts.

DECIGRAM. International mass and weight unit = 0.10 gram, or approx. 1.543 grains.

DECILITER. International capacity unit = 0.10 liter, or approx. 6.1 cubic inches, or 0.18 pint (dry) or 0.21 pint (liquid).

DECIMAL UNIVERSAL CLASSIFICATION. An international decimal system for classifying books in public libraries, initiated in 1876 by the work of the American librarian M. Dewey, called Decimal Classification, accepted and developed into a universal classification system 1905–33 by the International Institute of Bibliography in Brussels; since then in common use. The principle of the decimal system is that the whole of catalogued publications is divided into 10 main divisions designated by symbols from 0 to 9. By adding additional numbers from 0 to 9 to the main symbols divisions of a second degree are obtained, which are designated by two digits (e.g. 01, 02, 03, etc.). Further subdivisions are obtained in the same manner, thus extending the symbols as need arises to several or even a dozen or more digits. An extended example:

6	applied sciences	621 3	electrical engineering
62	engineering	621 39	telecommunications
621	machine construction	621 396	radio communications

R. DEBUC, *La Classification Décimale Universalle, CDU. Manual pratique d'utilisation*, Paris, 1965.

DECIMETER. An international length unit = 0.1 meter, or approx. 3.94 inches.

DECISTORE. An international volume unit = 0.10 cubic meter, or approx. 3.53 cubic ft.

DECLARATION. An international term in the UN system applied to legal statements made by governments or groups of governments; in the UN it refers to unanimously agreed statements, in contrast to resolutions which are adopted by a majority of votes.

DECLARATION OF WAR. ▷ War declaration.

DECOLONIZATION. An international term in the UN system for the process of liquidation of the colonial system in the world and creating independent states from the former dependent territories, accepted in the UN since 1960, i.e. from the date of the adoption by the UN General Assembly on Dec. 14, 1960 by 89 votes for, none against and 9 abstentions (Australia, Belgium, the Dominican Republic, France, Portugal, South Africa, Spain, the UK and the USA) a Declaration, proposed by N. Krushchev, of the USSR, on the Granting of Independence to Colonial Countries. One year later on Nov. 27, 1961 the Special Committee for the realization of the Declaration on the Granting of Independence to Colonial Countries and Peoples, commonly known as the Committee on Decolonization was established by UN General Assembly Res. 1654/XVI. Since that time the UN General Assembly each year debates the problem of the realization of the terms of the Declaration and passes further resolutions (i.a. Res. 1805 and 1810/XVII, 1956/XVIII, 2105/XX, 2189/XXI, 2288/XXII, calling for complete world decolonization). The UN Decolonization Committee, composed of representatives from 24 states, is now made up of 22 states, following the withdrawal in 1971 of Italy, the UK and USA and the admission of the Chinese People's Republic. On Nov. 2, 1972 the UN General Assembly passed by 99 votes to 5 (France, Portugal, South Africa, the UK and USA) a resolution asserting i.a. that the further retention of colonialism constitutes a threat to peace and security. On Dec. 12, 1980 the UN General Assembly held a special meeting to commemorate the twentieth anniversary of the adoption of the Declaration on the Granting of Independence to Colonial Countries and Peoples and adopted an Action Plan for Full Elimination of Colonialism. ▷ Colonial agreements, ▷ Independence to Colonial countries, UN Declaration 1960. ▷ Right of People to Peace, Declaration 1984.

H. LABOURET, *Colonisation, Colonialisme, Décolonialisme*, Paris, 1952; JV.J. AVARIN, *Raspad kolonialnoi sistemy*, Moskva, 1957; V.J VASILIEVA, *Raspad kolonialnoi sistemy imperializma*, Moskva, 1958; N.A. CHALFIN, *Sozdaniie i raspad britanskoi kolonialnoi imperii*, Moskva, 1961; KWAME NKRUMAH, *Consciencism, Philosophy and Ideology for Decolonization and Development with Particular Reference to the African Revolution*, London, 1964; S.C. STEWART, *The Rise and Fall of Western Colonialism; A Historical Survey from the early XIX Century to the Present*, New York, 1964; W. WAINHOUSE, *The UN and the End of Colonialism*, New York, 1964; E.D. MODZHANSKAJA, *Raspad kolonialnoi sistemy i*

ideologiia imperializma, Moskva, 1965; *The United Nations and decolonization*, UN, New York, 1965; H. GRIMEL, *Decolonization: the British, French, Dutch and Belgian Empires, 1919–1963*, Colorado, 1965; E.V. ALBERTINI, *Dekolonisation, Die Diskussion ueber Verwaltung und Zukunft der Kolonien, 1919 bis 1960*, Köln, 1966; J. BERGUE, *La descolonización del Mundo*, México, DF. 1968; Y. EL-AYOUTY, *The UN and Decolonization: The Role of Afro-Asia*, The Hague, 1971; "28 Years of Decolonization", in: *The UNESCO Courier*, November, 1973; *UN Chronicle*, February, 1981, pp. 23–27; November, 1982, pp. 49–58; December, 1983, pp. 69–70. CHINWEIZU, *Decolonising the African Mind*, London, 1987. *UN Resolutions and Decisions adopted by the General Assembly during the First Part of its Forty Third Session, from 20 September to 22 December, 1988*. p. 76.

DECORATIONS, INTERNATIONAL. National civil and military orders obtainable by foreigners (French Legion of Honor) or medals of international organizations (Anniversary medals); ▷ Killed in the Service of the United Nations.

DECREE OF PEACE, 1917. A revolutionary Russian decree, issued immediately after the seizure of power by the Petrograd workers headed by the Bolshevik Party; adopted unanimously at a Meeting of the All-Russian Convention of Soviets of Workers', Soldiers' and Peasants' Deputies, held on Oct. 26 (Nov. 8), 1917 in Petersburg; edited by W.I. Lenin, announced next day in the 208th issue of the Moscow daily *Izvestia*. The text is as follows:

"The Workers' and Peasants' Governments, created by the revolution of October 24th and 25th (November 6th and 7th), and based on the Soviet of Workers', Soldiers' and Peasants' Deputies, proposes to all warring peoples and their Governments to begin immediately negotiations for a just and democratic peace.

An overwhelming majority of the exhausted, wearied, and war-tortured workers and the labouring classes of all the warring countries are longing for a just and democratic peace – a peace which in the most definite and insistent manner was demanded by Russian workers and peasants after the overthrow of the Tsar's monarchy. Such a peace the Government considers to be an immediate peace without annexations (i.e., without seizure of foreign territory, without the forcible annexation of foreign nationalities) and without indemnities.

The Government of Russia proposes to all warring peoples immediately to conclude such a peace. It expresses it readiness to take at once without the slightest delay, all the decisive steps until the final confirmation of all terms of such a peace by the plenipotentiary conventions of the representatives of all countries and all nations.

By annexation or seizure of foreign territory the Government understands, in accordance with the legal consciousness of democracy in general, and of labouring classes in particular, any addition to a large or powerful state of a small or weak nationality, without the definitely, clearly, and voluntarily expressed consent and desire of this nationality, regardless of when this forcible addition took place, regardless also of how developed or how backward is the nation forcibly attacked or forcibly retained within the frontiers of a given state, and finally regardless of the fact whether this nation is located in Europe or in distant lands beyond the seas.

If any nation whatsoever is retained within the frontiers of a certain state by force, if it is not given the right of free voting in accordance with its desire, regardless of the fact whether such desire was expressed in the press, in people's assemblies, in decisions of political parties, or rebellions and insurrections against national oppression, such plebiscite to take place under the condition of the complete removal of the armies of the annexing or the more powerful nation; if the weaker nation is not given the opportunity to decide the question of the forms of its national existence, then its adjoining is an annexation, that is, seizure – violence.

The Government considers it to be the greatest crime against humanity to continue the war for the sake of dividing among the powerful and rich nations the

D

weaker nationalities which were seized by them, and the Government solemnly states its readiness to sign immediately the terms of peace which will end this war, on the basis of the above stated conditions, equally just for all nationalities without exception. At the same time the Government announces that it does not consider the above-stated conditions of peace as in the nature of an ultimatum, that is, it is ready to consider any other terms of peace, insisting, however, that such be proposed as soon as possible by any one of the warring countries and on condition of the most definite clarity and absolute exclusion of any ambiguousness, or any secrecy when proposing the terms of peace.

The Government abolishes secret diplomacy and on its part expresses the firm intention to carry on all negotiations absolutely openly before all the people, and immediately begin to publish in full the secret treaties concluded or confirmed by the Government of landowners and capitalists from February up to November 7th, 1917. The Government abrogates absolutely and immediately all the provisions of these secret treaties in as much as they were intended in the majority of cases for the purpose of securing profits and privileges for Russian landowners and capitalists and retaining or increasing the annexations by the Great-Russians.

While addressing the proposal to the Governments and peoples of all countries to start immediately open negotiations for the conclusion of peace, the Government expresses its readiness to carry on these negotiations by written communications, by telegraph, as well as by parleys of the representatives of various countries, or at a conference of such representatives. To facilitate such negotiations the Government appoints a plenipotentiary representative in neutral countries.

The Government proposes to all the Governments and peoples of all the warring countries to conclude an armistice immediately; at the same time, it considers desirable that this armistice should be concluded for a period of not less than three months – that is, a period during which it would be fully possible to terminate the negotiations for peace with the participation of the representatives of all peoples and nationalities drawn into the war or compelled to participate in it, as well as to call the plenipotentiary conventions of people's representatives of all countries for the final ratification of the terms of peace.

While addressing this proposal of peace to the Governments and peoples of all the warring countries, the Provisional Workers' and Peasants' Government of Russia appeals also in particular to the class-conscious workers of the three most forward nations of the world and the largest states participating in the present war – England, France, and Germany. The workers of these countries have been of the greatest service to the cause of progress and socialism. We have the great example of the Chartist movement in England, several revolutions which were of universal historic importance accomplished by the French proletariat, and finally the heroic struggle against the exclusive law in Germany and the prolonged, stubborn, disciplined work – a work setting an example for the workers of the whole world – of creating mass proletarian organisations in Gemany. All these examples of proletarian heroism and historic creative work serve as a guarantee that the workers of the above-mentioned countries understand the duties which devolve upon them now in the cause of the liberation of humanity from the horrors of war and its consequences, a cause which these workers by their resolute and energetic activity will help us to bring to a successful end – the cause of peace, and, together with this, the cause of the liberation of the labouring and exploited."

The Soviet Union and Peace, New York, 1929, pp. 22–25.

DEDÉAGACH. ▷ Alexandróupolis.

DE FACTO. *Latin:* "really, in fact". An international term in the UN system meaning that a given state, government, or border, though not recognized legally, really exists in fact.

DE FACTO GOVERNMENT. A state government formed by a *fait accompli* and exercising power in a state despite the fact that it has not been recognized either in the country by way of plebiscite, elections

or referendum, or outside the country by other governments or inter-governmental organizations; a subject of international doctrines (▷ Estrada doctrine).

J. SPIROPOULOS, *Die de facto Regierung im Völkerrecht*, Berlin, 1926; F.L. SCHUMANN, "De facto government," in: *Encyclopedia of the Social Sciences*, 1931–1937: E. WOLF, "La validité des actes d'un gouvernement de fait", in: *Revue du droit public et de la science politique*, No. 68, 1952: W. SCHUMAN, "De facto-Regierung", in: *STRUPP-SCHLOCHAUER, Wörterbuch des Völkerrechts*, Bd. 1, Berlin, 1960, pp. 317–321.

DEFENCE BOARD. ▷ Interamerican Defence Board.

DEFENCE COUNCIL. ▷ Central American Defence Council.

DEFENCE INTELLIGENCE AGENCY, DIA. One of the three US ▷ intelligence services (with the CIA and National Security Agency).

D. ROBERTSON, *Guide to Modern Defense and Strategy*, Detroit, 1988.

DEFINITION INTERNATIONAL. The explicit characterization of a concept or subject established by an intergovernmental agreement, treaty, or convention, or by an international organization, or by an international scientific institution reg. with the UIA. Example: a definition formulated by WHO in 1972 of the term ▷ physician.

DEFLATION. An economic term in the UN system. The opposite of ▷ inflation. Deflation consists in reducing the amount of money in circulation: used for the purpose of reducing excessive market demand.

DEFOLIATION. An international term for destruction of foliage by chemical means used for the first time in the Vietnam war; a subject of international protests against means of destruction of nature and tragic effects of the poisoning caused by defoliants.

The New York Times, May 31, 1979.

DE GAULLE DOCTRINE, 1958. A pan-European concept of long-range construction of "*l'Europe des Patries ... d'Atlantic jusqu'Ural*" (a Europe of Fatherlands ... from the Atlantic to the Ural Mountains) since, in the conviction of General Charles de Gaulle (1890–1970):

"... it is Europe from the Atlantic to the Ural Mountains, the whole of Europe that determines the destiny of the world. If the peoples of Europe, whichever side of the Curtain they are on, wanted to establish concord among themselves, peace would be secured. If, however, Europe remains divided into two opposed factions, sooner or later a war will destroy the human race. The responsibility of Europe is greater than any time before."

Documentation française, Paris, 1958 and 1959.

DEHYDRATORS. Subject of international co-operation. Organization reg. with the UIA: European Dehydrators Association, f. 1960, Paris, France.

Yearbook of International Organizations, 1986/87; The Europa Yearbook 1988. A World Survey, Vol. I, London 1988.

DE JURE. An international term meaning that a state, government, or boundary has been recognized by a second state on the basis of law.

DEKAGRAM. A mass and weight unit of the metric system: 1 dekagram = 10 grams; US equivalent 0.353 ounce.

DEKALITER. A capacity unit of the metric system: 1 dekaliter = 10 liter; English equivalent: 0.35 cubic feet; US equivalent 1.14 pecks or 2.64 gallons.

DEKAMETER. A length unit of the metric system: 1 dekameter = 10 meters; US equivalent 32.81 feet.

DEKASTORE. A volume unit of the metric system: 1 dekastore = 10 cubic meters; US equivalent 13.10 cubic yards.

DELAWARE. One of the smallest states in USA located on the Atlantic coast; area 5238 sq. km; pop. *c.* 500,000 (1970); capital – Dover; major city – Wilmington; since 1899 has the most liberal state legislation concerning large American and international concerns (various tax reductions) and, as a result, over 70,000 corporations are registered in this state, including over half of the top hundred. American, British, West German and Japanese corporations. Delaware has become an international synonym of extremely favorable conditions for the growth of big business.

DELAWARE INDIAN TREATY, 1778. A peace treaty "made and entered into by Commissioners for, and on behalf of the United States of North America of the one part and Deputies and Chief-Men of the Delaware Nation of the other part", signed on Sept. 17, 1778 in Fort Pitt.

Major Peace Treaties of Modern History, New York, 1967, Vol. I, pp. 669–672.

DELEGATIONS TO THE UN. The official name of the permanent diplomatic missions of UN member states accredited by the UN Secretary-General and having a specific diplomatic status. In 1946–56 the protocol section of the UN Secretariat annually published a list of accredited member delegations together with the composition of all UN General Assembly Committees, entitled permanent Missions to the UN. From 1956 they are called Delegations to the UN. The statute of a delegation to the UN is established by the ▷ Vienna Convention on the Representation of States in their Relations with International Organizations, 1975.

Delegations to the UN, New York, 1980.

DELHI, union territory the second urban agglomeration of India, after ▷ Calcutta. Population: 1981, census; 5,714,000.
See also ▷ New Delhi.

DELICTUM IURIS GENTIUM. *Latin* = "a crime against the law of nations". An international term for the principle that the breaking of international law is a crime.

DELIMITATION. The precise demarcation of two states or territories, carried out as a rule by Delimitation Commissions. The legal subcommittee of the Committee on the Peaceful Uses of Outer-Space discussed since 1987 ▷ Outer Space Delimitation in relation to international agreements on territorial, maritime and airspace delimitation.
See also ▷ Geostationary Orbit.

DELINQUENCY. In the UN system an international term for violation of international law or an act prohibited by international law committed by one state to the detriment of another state or group of states, requiring compensation determined by the practice of international life providing for direct or indirect responsibility of states, which implies the obligation to repair damages. Since the Hague Peace Conference of 1907 subject to codification aimed at formulating unified, universal rules of international law in dealing with particular acts of international delinquency. Draft conventions to this end were prepared, i.e. 1925 by the American Institute of International Law, at the request of the Pan-American Union and 1930 by the German International Law Society. The League of Nations initiated codification work at the Geneva Conference on Codification of International Law in 1929. The UN General Assembly took a stance in this matter in Res. 799/VIII of Dec. 7, 1953.

A. DECENCIERE-FERRANDIERE, *La Responsabilité des états a raison des dommages subis par des etrangers*, Paris, 1925; C. EAGELTON, *The Responsibility of States in International Law*, London, 1928; P.A. ZANNES, *La responsabilité internationale des états pour les actes de négligence*, Paris, 1952; F.V. GARCIA-AMADOR, *State Responsibility in the Light of the International Law*, No. 49, 1955; A. SCHÜLE, "Delikt Völkerrechtlich", in: STRUPP-SCHLOCHAUER, *Wörterbuch des Völkerrechts*, Berlin, 1960, Bd. 1, pp. 326–339; G.W. BORODIN, J.G. LACHOV, *Mezhdunarodnoye sotrudnichestvo v borbie o ugodornoy priestupnostiu. Problemy dieyatielnosti OON v oblasti predieprieshdieniya priestupnosti i obrashcheniya s pravomanishatielami*, Moskva, 1983.

DELINQUENTS TREATMENT. ▷ Crimes and treatment of delinquents.

DEMARCATION. A line establishing and delimiting by treaty the border between two states.

DÉMARCHE. In diplomatic language an oral objection, warning, the statement of an opposing position.

DÉMENTI. An official denial by a government spokesman or in the form of a communiqué or note of inaccurate information given to the public.

DEMILITARIZATION. An international term for the prohibition or limitation of, armed forces, war materials, armaments factories in a given territory, e.g. demilitarization of ▷ Rhineland after World War I.

DEMILITATION. Latin: *debellatio* = conquest. An international term for conquest by armed force and the complete subordination of the territory of the conquered state to the conquerors, e.g. III Reich and Prussia on May 5, 1945 to the Allied powers.

L.M. BENTIVIGLIO, *La "Debellatio" nel Dirito Internazionale*, Roma, 1948; J. SYMONIDES, "*Zawojowanie w klasycznym i współczesnym prawie miedzynarodowym*" (*Conquest in classical and contemporary international law*), in: *Wojskowy Przeglad Prawniczy*, Warszawa, No. 4, 1967.

DEMOCRACY. An international term indicating people's rule having several meanings depending on the class of the people who rule. In the period when the state was dominated by the gentry (second half of the 15th and 16th centuries) noblemen's democracy existed; in the 18th century forms of bourgeois democracy. A democracy of indirect character where people determine their rights and obligations through the legislative organs they elect is called ▷ representative democracy. Democracy of direct character where fundamental rights and obligations are determined by way of general ▷ referendum by all people eligible to vote is in Switzerland. In the 20th century as many states entered the path to socialism their forms of government are called ▷ "socialist democracy" or ▷ "people's democracy".

C. FARRAR, *The Origins of Democratic Thinking*, Cambridge, UK 1988.

DEMOGRAPHIC EXPLOSION. An international term in the UN system for the historically unprecedented rapid growth of the world's population in the second half of the 20th century. According to UN predictions the growth rate of world population in the 20th century will triple to exceed 6.3 billion people. In 1976 demographers discerned a significant weakening of the demographic explosion and a new phenomenon which they called population implosion, asserting that the world birth rate fell from 1.9% in 1970 to 1.64% in 1975 and will certainly fall below 1% by 1985, resulting in the dissemination of birth control devices as well as the permission of abortions in states inhabited by 64% of the world's population.

THE AMERICAN ASSEMBLY, *The Population Dilemma*, New York, 1963.

DEMOGRAPHY. An international term coined by the French scholar A. Guillard, author of *Éléments de statistique humaine ou démographie comparée*, 1855.
According to the UN Demographic Dictionary, "demography is a science whose aim is to study the number, structure and growth of world population from principally the quantitative point of view."
A subject of international conventions on the application of UN established rules of general censuses; subject of demographic studies carried out by the UN and specialized organizations. UN demographic activities were started by the Population Commission of the UN General Assembly in 1947 supported by the UN Trusteeship Fund for Demographic Activities, established in 1963 by ECOSOC. Since 1949 the UN has published the *UN Demographic Yearbook*; besides, since 1952/53 two periodicals devoted to demography: *Population Bulletin* and *Population and Vital Statistics Reports*. In 1948–85 the UN has also issued several dozen volumes of studies and reports. The bibliography of UN demographic publications is contained in the *Demographic Yearbook*. On the American continents UN demographic activities were started earlier, at the First Demographic Congress on Oct. 12–20, 1944, held in Mexico City. The Congress appointed the Inter-American Demographic Committee in Washington. A demographic boom in Latin America, the greatest in the world, necessitated the establishment of a special Latin American Demographic Center, Centro Latinoamericano de Demografia, CELADE, sponsored by the UN Social and Economic Commission for Latin America, CEPAL and organizing annual seminars and symposia. In 1968 on the initiative of OAS, a Conference dealing with the problems of demography and economic development of Latin America was held in Santiago.
Organizations reg. with the UIA:

European Centre for Population Studies, est. 1953 in Paris as an extragovernmental organization of demographic centers of Austria, Belgium, Denmark, Finland, France, Italy, Spain, the Netherlands, Norway, Portugal, Switzerland, Sweden and the UK. Publ. *Etudes Européens de Population*;
International Union for the Scientific Study of the Population, est. 1928, Liège. Consultative status with ECOSOC and UNESCO. Publ. *Le Demograph, The Materials of Demography*.
Latin American Demographic Centre CELADE, est. 1957, Santiago, as a chapter of Universidad de Chile. Publ. *Informes*.

A. GARCIA ROBLES, *El Mundo de la Postguerra*, México, DF, 1946, Vol. I, pp. 195–203; *Dictionnaire démographique multilingue*, UN, New York, 1958; A. SAUVY, *De Malthus à Mao Tse-Tung*, Paris, 1958; M. REINHARD, A. ARMENGAUD, *Histoire Gènèrale de la Population Mondiale*, Paris 1961; A. MATNELART, *Manual de Análisis Demográfico. Un Ejemplo de Investigación en un País Latinoamericano*, Santiago, 1964; *Population Dilemma in Latin America*, Washington, DC, 1966; *UNESCO Situación Demográfica, Económica, Social y Educativa de América Latina*, Buenos Aires, 1968; D.J. VALENT'EV (ed.), *Marksistoleninskaia teoriia demografii*, Moskva, 1971; B. BERENSON (ed.), *La politique démographique des pays developpées*, edit. Paris, 1974; "Asian demographic problems", in: *Asia 1975, Far-Eastern Economic Review Yearbook*, Hongkong, 1975.

DEMONTAGE. An international term for the disassembling of factories as a result of war reparations and their transport to the country receiving war reparation. Germany during World Wars I and II applied demontage, based on the so-called right to war prizes. After World War II, as a result of the demilitarization of occupied Germany demanded by the Potsdam Conference on Aug. 2, 1945, demontage or destruction of German war industry was carried out in the four zones of occupation.

DEMURRAGE. An international term in the sea law, for the obligation to pay charges for the late delivery of goods to shipside or unloading from shipboard. Included in contracts on the transport by sea is a so called "lien clause" which ensures the captain of a vessel rights to freight charges, stand still and demurrage charges, due to the confiscation of a cargo:

"The Captain has an absolute lien upon the cargo for all freight and demurrage."

MOCATTA, MUSTILL, BOYD, *Scrutton on Charter parties and Bills of Lading*, London, 1974; M.J. MUSTILL, *Pseudo-Demurrage and the Arrived Ship*, Stockholm, 1974.

DENATURING. An international term for artificial conversion of human food into animal feed, mixing, for example, flour with fish meal.

DENATIONALIZATION ▷ Expatriation.

DENAZIFICATION. An international term for methods used after World War II to eliminate Nazism in occupied Germany; a procedure introduced by the military occupation authorities of the Four Powers of keeping with the rules set by the ▷ Control Council for Germany: Act No. 1 of Sept. 20, 1945 concerning elimination of Nazi laws from German legislation; No. 2 of Oct. 10, 1945 on the dissolution of all Nazi organizations; No. 10 of Dec. 20, 1945 on the system of punishing war criminals; also in keeping with the Council's guideline; No. 25 of Dec. 25, 1945 on elimination of NSDAP members from public offices and No. 38 which determined five degrees of crime and German denazification courts to be appointed. Separate and different executive rules were made for each of the occupation zones.

E. OSMAŃCZYK, *Niemcy 1945–1950* [Germany 1945–1950], Warsaw, 1951. T. BOWER, *The Paperclip Conspiration*, New York, 1988; Ch. SIMPSON, BLOWBACK, *America's Recruitment of Nazis and its Effects on the Cold War*, New York 1988.

DENGUE FEVER. A contagious illness caused by a filtrable virus carried by mosquitos (*Aedes aegypti*), subject of the International Convention on Mutual Protection against Dengue Fever, signed on July 25, 1934 in Athens by Bulgaria, Egypt, France, Germany, Greece, Italy, Romania, Spain, Turkey, Yugoslavia, the UK and the USSR.

LNTS, Vol. 177, p. 59.

DENMARK. Member of the UN. Kongeriget Danmark, Kingdom of Denmark. Scandinavian

D

country in north-east Europe on the Jutland Peninsula and comprising several hundred neighboring islands in the Baltic (most prominent: Sjaelland, Fyn, Laaland, Bornholm, Falster). Bordering on the FRG with the frontier provided for in the Versailles Treaty and resulting from plebiscite in ▷ Schleswig. Outlying Danish territory spans the Faroe Islands in the Atlantic and since June 5, 1953 ▷ Greenland. Area: 43,080 sq. km. Pop. Jan. 1983: 5,116,467 (1970 census: 4,937,579). Capital: Copenhagen with 1,377,064 inhabitants (1982). GNP per capita in 1987: US $14,930. Official language: Danish. Currency: one krona = 100 ore. National Day: April 16, Birthday of the Monarch, Margrethe II, 1940.

Original member of the UN since Oct. 24, 1945 and member of all UN specialized agencies. Member of NATO 1949, Nordic Council 1953, EFTA 1961, EEC 1972.

International relations: in 1865 at war with Austria and Prussia which annexed the princedoms of Schleswig-Holstein and Lauenburg. In 1920 after a plebiscite North Schleswig was restored to Denmark. The Danish national minority in South Schleswig took an active part, 1924–39, alongside Poles, Lusatian Serbs, Frisians and Lithuanians, in the Union of National Minorities in Germany. Member of the League of Nations in 1920–40. In World War II occupied by the Third Reich (Apr. 9, 1940–May 5, 1945). Under treaty with the USA of Apr. 27, 1951 obliged to join in the military defense of Greenland. Exchange of notes constituting an Agreement concerning the delimitation of the borderline between Denmark and the FRG in the Flensborg Fiord Area, signed on Oct. 22 and 28, 1970 in Copenhagen, and Supplementary Protocol, signed on Aug. 25, 1971 in Flensborg, and on Sept. 14, 1971 in Abenra. The State Library in Copenhagen publ. *Dania Polyglotta. Annual bibliography of Books in Foreign Languages printed in Denmark*; the Ministry of Foreign Relations, publ. every year *Denmark: An Official Handbook* and *Danish Foreign Office Journal*. The Danish Institute (Danske Selskab) f. 1940 to stimulate cultural relations between Denmark and other countries. Publ.: *Musical Denmark* (annually).

In Dec. 1982 the Danish Government suspended Denmark's contribution to NATO's "flexible response" nuclear strategy. On Oct. 17, 1986 the Aliens Act stated that immigrants seeking asylum without valid visas for Denmark could be refused entry unless they were travelling directly from a country where they were exposed to persecution or their lives were at risk.

B. OUTZE (ed.), *Denmark During the German Occupation*, Copenhagen, 1946; J. DANSTRUP, *History of Denmark*, Copenhagen, 1949; N.J. HAAGERUP, *Denmark and the UN*, New York, 1956; P. LAURING, *A History of Denmark*, Copenhagen, 1960; H. HESTRUP, *From Occupied to Ally: The Danish Resistance Movement*, Copenhagen, 1963; E. MILLER, *Governments and Politics in Denmark*, Boston, 1968; *UNTS*, Vol. 871, 1973, pp. 183–192; R. PETROV, *The Bitter Years. The Invasion and Occupation of Denmark and Norway*, New York, 1974; *The Europa Year Book 1984. A World Survey*, Vol. I, pp. 390–409, London, 1984. *KEESING's Record of World Events*, 1987.

DENTISTRY. A subject of international co-operation. Organizations reg. with the UIA:
American Dental Society of Europe, f. 1873, Rigi-Lucerne, Switzerland. Publ. *Lloydia* (quarterly).
Arab Dental Federation, f. 1969, Cairo, Egypt.
Asian Pacific Dental Federation, f. 1955, Sydney. Publ.: *Newsletter*.
Dentists' Liaison Committee for the EEC, f. 1960, London.
East African Dental Association, f. 1943, Nairobi. Publ. *Newsletter*.

European Orthodontic Society, f. 1907, London. Publ.: *Transactions*.
Group of Francophone Dentists' Associations, f. 1971, Paris.
International Association for Dental Research, f. 1920, Chicago. Publ. *Journal of Dental Research*.
International Association of Dental Students, f. 1951, London. Publ. *Newsletter*.
International Association of Dentistry for Children, f. 1969, London. Publ. *Journal*.
International Dental Federation, f. 1900, London. consultative status ECOSOC, WHO, Council of Europe. Secretariats: South Pacific Dental Secretariat, Secretariat for Dental Health in Africa, (Dakar and Nairobi). Publ. *International Dental Journal* (quarterly).
Latin American Association of Dental Schools, f. 1960, Guatemala. Publ. *ALAFO Journal*.
Scandinavian Dental Association, f. 1866, Oslo.

Yearbook of International Organizations.

DENUCLEARIZATION. An international term for a ban on placing on land, sea, air or in outer space any nuclear weapons or equipment for their manufacture or for making any experiments with these weapons. During the XII Session of the UN General Assembly, Oct. 2, 1957, Poland proposed the creation of a non-nuclear zone in Central Europe (▷ Rapacki Plan). The idea of ▷ denuclearized zones was implemented in other regions of the world. In addition, a draft of the ▷ Sea-Bed, Treaty on Denuclearization of, was signed in Moscow, Feb. 11, 1971.

DENUCLEARIZED ZONES. Called also Atomic Free Zones or Nuclear Weapon Free Zones. The UN General Assembly with Res. 3261/XXIX, Dec. 9, 1974, decided to undertake a comprehensive study of the question of nuclear-weapon-free zones and its aspects. The study prepared by an Ad Hoc Group of Qualified Governmental Experts in co-operation with the IAEA presented a number of principles for the denuclearized zones:
(a) Obligations relating to the establishment of nuclear-weapon-free zones may be assumed not only by groups of states, including entire continents or large geographical regions, but also by smaller groups of states and even individual countries;
(b) Nuclear-weapon-free zone arrangements must ensure that the zone would be, and would remain, effectively free of all nuclear weapons;
(c) The initiative for the creation of a nuclear-weapon-free zone should come from states within the region concerned, and participation must be voluntary;
(d) Whenever a zone is intended to embrace a region, the participation of all militarily significant states, and preferably all states, in that region would enhance the effectiveness of the zone;
(e) The zone arrangements must contain an effective system of verification to ensure full compliance with the agreed obligations;
(f) The arrangements should promote the economic, scientific, and technological development of the members of the zone through international co-operation on all peaceful uses of nuclear energy;
(g) The treaty establishing the zone should be of unlimited duration;
(h) States members of a zone should not exercise control over nuclear weapons outside the zone, although some experts felt that part of a state could also be included in a nuclear-weapon-free zone and that, in this case, the nuclear-weapon-free status would be applied only to the part of its territory which is situated within the boundary of the zone;
(i) Most experts noted that any arrangements for the establishment of a zone must provide for

appropriate guarantees by the nuclear-weapon states not to use or threaten to use nuclear weapons against members of the zone. Other experts believed, however, that while such undertakings could contribute to the effectiveness of a zone, they should not be considered a prerequisite for the establishment of a nuclear-weapon-free zone but should instead be considered on a case-by-case basis. The UN General Assembly Res. 3472/XXX of Dec. 11, 1975 defined the principles as follows:
"In every case of a nuclear-weapon-free zone that has been recognized as such by the General Assembly, all nuclear-weapon states shall undertake or reaffirm, in a solemn international instrument having full legally binding force, such as a treaty, a convention or a protocol, the following obligations:
(a) To respect in all its parts the statute of total absence of nuclear weapons defined in the treaty or convention which serves as the constitutive instrument of the zone;
(b) To refrain from contributing in any way to the performance in the territories forming part of the zone of acts which involve a violation of the aforesaid treaty or convention;
(c) To refrain from using or threatening to use nuclear weapons against the states included in the zone.
The above definitions in no way impair the resolutions which the General Assembly has adopted or may adopt with regard to specific cases of nuclear-weapon-free zones nor the rights emanating for the Member States from such resolutions."

The order of precedence of drafts on regional denuclearized zones is as follows:
The *European* denuclearized zones, initiated by the government of Poland on behalf of which on Oct. 2, 1957, minister for foreign affairs, Adam Rapacki, presented at the XII UN General Assembly Session a draft concerning creation of denuclearized zones in Central Europe, also called the ▷ Rapacki Plan. An important element of the draft was a ban on the use of nuclear weapons against the countries in the zone. European denuclearized zones – apart from the Polish proposal of 1957–were proposed by Yugoslavia in 1958, including the Balkans and Italy (▷ Tito Plan), in 1959 backed by Romania and in 1960 by the USSR; and Finland in 1963 concerning Scandinavian states (▷ Kekkonen Plans).

The *African* denuclearized zone. On Nov. 24, 1961, the UN General Assembly by the Res. 1652/XVI adopted by 55 votes for with 44 votes abstaining called on the member-states "to refrain from starting or continuing in Africa nuclear tests in any form; to refrain from using the territory, territorial waters and air space over Africa to carry out nuclear tests, stockpile or transport nuclear weapons; to consider the African continent a denuclearized zone and to respect it as such." In 1962 in Accra, Ghana, was established an organization called the Accra Assembly which aimed to support the idea of the denuclearization of Africa. In view of the fact that: heads of the governments of OAU member-states at the session in Cairo, June 17–21, 1964, made a declaration concerning denuclearization of Africa and expressed their readiness to assume an obligation, in the form of an international treaty supervised by the UN, not to produce and possess nuclear weapons as well as that the declaration won support of heads of governments of non-aligned states by a statement made on Oct. 10, 1964, in Cairo, the UN General Assembly on Dec. 3, 1965, adopted the Res. 2033/XX by 105 votes (France, Republic of South Africa and Portugal abstained) resolving to call on "all states to consider the African continent a denuclearized zone".

The *Latin American* denuclearized zones. On Nov. 8, 1962, the government of Brazil called on the General Assembly Political Commission to study a possibility of denuclearizing Latin America, however, in December of the same year it withdrew the suggestion. On Apr. 29, 1963, at the initiative of

220

the Mexican president, Lopez Mateos, the presidents of Bolivia, Brazil, Chile, Ecuador and Mexico announced a joint declaration on the need to denuclearize Latin America. The UN General Assembly in the Res. 1911/XVIII of Nov. 27, 1963, rendered support for the idea contained in the declaration of the five presidents. On Nov. 27, 1964, in the capital of Mexico the commission for denuclearization of Latin America (Commission Preparatoria para la Desnuclearización de América Latina – COPREDAL) started its activities. Its work, which took 2 years, was crowned with the ▷ Tlatelolco Treaty, signed on Feb. 14, 1967 in Mexico City, concerning establishment of the Latin American denuclearized zone. The UN General Assembly in the Res. 2286/XXII of Dec. 5, 1967 by 82 votes for and no votes against (28 abstained) adopted the treaty and advised the member-states to respect fully its provisions.

The *Middle East* denuclearized zone. The UN General Assembly in Dec. 1974 on the request of Iran and Egypt request commended the idea of establishing a nuclear-weapon-free zone in the Middle East with Res. 3263/XXIX. Israel postulated to convene a regional conference on the matter.

The *South Asia* denuclearized zone. In Sept., 1974 Pakistan and in Oct., 1975 Bangladesh presented to the UN General Assembly a Plan for a South Asian denuclearized zone. In July 1975 the South Pacific Forum of Heads of Government of the independent and self-governing member states agreed to keep the region free from the risk of nuclear contamination. In June 1981 the UN Disarmament Commission recommended the strengthening of the existing nuclear-weapon-free zones and the establishment of other nuclear-weapon-free zones and of zones of peace. In 1981 Bulgaria proposed a Balkan Nuclear Weapon-Free Zone. In October 1987 in Murmansk the Soviet leader M. Gorbachev supported the Kekkonen Plan for a Nordic denuclearized zone. In February 1988 the foreign ministers of the six Balkan states discussed the question of the Balkan Nuclear Weapon-Free Zone as well as a chemical weapon free zone.

In 1986 North Korea proposed to make the Korean peninsula a nuclear weapon free zone.

In 1986 the foreign ministers of the ASEAN states group suggested a Southeast Asian nuclear weapon free zone.

The 42nd session, 1987, of the UN General Assembly decided that the Conference on the establishment of the Indian Ocean Nuclear Weapon-Free Zone will be held in 1990.

On Dec. 7, 1988, the GA Res. 43/65 urged all parties to establish a nuclear free zone in the region of the Middle East (adopted without vote); the GA Res. 43/66 urged once again the states of South Asia to continue to make all possible efforts to establish a nuclear free zone in South Asia (adopted by 116 votes to 3 (Bhutan, India, Mauritius) and 39 abstentions); and the GA Res. 43/71 renewed its call to consider and respect the continent of Africa and its surrounding areas as a nuclear free zone (adopted with 151 votes and 4 abstentions).

See ▷ Outer Space.

See ▷ Antarctica.

UN Yearbook 1957, 1963, 1964, 1965, 1967; A. RAPACKI: "Polish Plan of denuclearization of Europe after 5 years", in: *Foreign Affairs*; January, 1967; A. GARCIA ROBLES, *La desnuclearización de América Latina*, México, DF, 1967; *UN Chronicle*, August, 1981, pp. 17–18; D. PITT, S. THOMPSON (eds.), *Nuclear Free Zones*, Cambridge, Mass., 1987. *UN Resolutions and decisions adopted by the General Assembly during the First Part of its Forty-Third Session, From 20 September to 22 December 1988*, New York 1989, p. 122.

DEPARTMENT OF STATE. Since 1789 the official name of the US ministry of foreign affairs, answerable directly to the President; implements US foreign policy, initiates and coordinates ▷ United States foreign aid and ▷ Mutual Security Program; headed by the Secretary of State.

A 2 volume compilation of US Department of State Reports on Contemporary Political and Economical Conditions, Government Personnel and Policies, Political Parties, Religions, History, Education, Press, Radio and TV, Climate, and other characteristics of selected countries of the World: together with Travel Alerts, Passport and Visa Information, World Health Information for Travellers, Customs and Duty Tips for Returning Residents and World Climate Highlights: *Countries of the World and Their Leaders Yearbook 1987 (Afghanistan–Zimbabwe)* was published in Detroit in 1987.

T.H. LAV, *The Foreign Service of the United States*, Washington, DC, 1925.

DEPARTMENT STORES. A subject of international co-operation. Organizations reg. with the UIA:

International Association of Department Stores, f. 1928, Paris with the sponsorship of the International Management Institute, Geneva. Publ. *Retail News Letter* (monthly) and *Studies*.

H. PASDERMADYIAN, *The Department Store. Its Origins, Evolution and Economics*, Paris, 1962.

DEPENDENCIES. An international term in the UN system for all colonial and trust territories not possessing independence, dependent on the state fulfilling administrative functions over them, subject of studies of the UN Committee on Decolonization.

R.L. BLEDSOE, B.A. BOCZEK, *The International Law Dictionary*, Oxford, 1987.

DEPORTATION. An international term for the compulsory removing of population from a territory menaced by military operations, natural disasters, nuclear tests or war, by terrorist actions, also used by an occupying power against the civilian population on the grounds that their activity is harmful to that country, or that their safety is endangered for whatever reasons, or that their work is required in another country. The mass deportation during the World War II in occupied German territories was condemned as a war crime by the Nuremberg Trial 1945–46. A special form of deportation is ▷ Banishment.

The Trial of German Major War Criminals. Proceedings of the IMT Sitting at Nuremberg, 42 Vols, London, 1946–48, Vol. 2, p. 295–311. Vol. 4, p. 325, Vol. 5, p. 265, Vol. 7, p.227 and Vol. 12, p. 170. R. CONQUEST, *The Nation Killers: Soviet Deportation of Nationalities*, London, 1970.

DEPOSITORY. An international term for a state which has assumed the obligation of safe-keeping the original documents of a multilateral treaty and all of the other obligations resulting from this fact.

DEPRESSANTS. An international term for barbiturates or their close pharmacological relatives, capable of producing psychological dependence, since 1980's under international control as a kind of drugs of abuse.

UN Chronicle, May 1987.

DEPRESSION. An international economic term for the post-crisis phase of stagnation in trade and production. The reverse of prosperity. In the United States major depressions, called also panics took place in 1836, 1856, 1893, 1907 and 1929. The last panic called the Great Depression or Great Panic was the severest stock market and financial crash, as

a result of which "one third of a nation was ill-housed, ill-clad and ill-nourished" as stated in the US Congress on Jan. 20, 1937 by President F.D. Roosevelt.

DERATIZATION. A subject of international health conventions since 1905, in connection with the fact that rats are the carriers of ▷ plague. The conventions made mandatory the permanent deratization of sea and air ports as well as ocean vessels and airplanes, which must possess a standardized WHO certificate or an exemption in special cases, Deratting Certificate, Deratting Exemption Certificate. Mandatory deratization also applies to some other rodents, especially mice. The Health Conventions also require special protection of contents against rodents.

DERELICTION. An international term for the unilateral renouncement of sovereign rights to a territory without ▷ cession of any other state's territory. Such instances took place in the colonial period (Santa Lucia Island, Antilles, 18th century; Bay of Delagos, Portuguese East Africa, 19th century; Palmas Island, 20th century). The Federal Republic of Germany Tribunal, Bundesgerichtshof, in its verdict of Jan. 18, 1956 declared the separation of Austria from the former German Reich after World War II to be an act of dereliction – its decision is considered a false interpretation of the Act of Allied Powers concerning voidance of the annexation of Austria by the III Reich on Mar. 13, 1938.

E. MENZEL, "Dereliktion", in: *STRUPP-SCHLO-CHAUER Wörterbuch des Völkerrechts*, Bd. 1, Berlin, 1960, pp. 346–348.

DERMATOLOGY. A subject of international co-operation. Organizations reg. with the UIA:

Ibero-Latin-American College of Dermatology, f. 1948, Lisbon. Publ. *Dermatología Ibero-Latino-Americana* (quarterly).
International League of Dermatological Societies, f. 1957, Stockholm. Official relations with WHO.
International Society of Tropical Dermatology, f. 1958, New York, Publ. *International Journal of Dermatology*.

Yearbook of International Organizations.

DESALINIZATION, ▷ Water desalinization.

DESERTERS. Soldiers who willfully leave their military unit (in full consciousness of the severe punishments for desertion pronounced by military courts) either for the purpose of temporarily or permanently evading further military service, or during wartime going over to the side of the enemy, or taking refuge in a neutral country; subject of international legal disputes, since not all states treat deserters alike. Neutral states which are obligated to intern military units taking refuge on their territories do not have the same obligation with respect to deserters whom they may leave at liberty (e.g. in Sweden American deserters from Vietnam). A separate disputed problem is the treatment of war prisoners who refuse to return to their country as deserters (e.g. after the cease-fire in Korea).

CH. ALPHAUD, "L'expulsion des déserteurs et l'extradition depuisée", in: *Revue du droit international privé*, 1910; L. B. SHAPIRO, "Repatriation of Deserters", in: *The British Yearbook of International Law*, 1952.

DESERTIFICATION. A subject of international control in desert and semi-desert regions of Africa (▷ Sahel), Central Asia and North America (Mexico and the USA).

... In conformity with the Charter of the United Nations, a number of resolutions by the United

D

Nations General Assembly have addressed these problems. The First All-African Seminar on the Human Environment, convened in August 1971 under the auspices of the Economic Commission for Africa, ECA, made specific recommendations for steps to be taken to combat the spread of deserts in Africa. At the third session of the ECA Conference of Ministers, Res. 264/XII on desertification drew attention to this menace recommending that ECA take steps in collaboration with the international community to seek solutions to the problems. The UN General Assembly Res. 3202/S-VI of 1 May 1974 recommended that the international community undertake concrete and speedy measures to arrest desertification. The ECOSOC Res. 1878/LVII of 16 July 1974 requested all the concerned organizations of the UN system to pursue a broad attack on the drought problem. The UN General Assembly then decided, by Res. 3337/XXIX of 17 Dec. 1974, to initiate concerted international action and decided to convene a UN Conference on Desertification, between Aug. 19 and Sept. 9, 1977 in Nairobi.

The UN General Assembly on Dec. 15, 1978 adopted the Plan of Action to Combat Desertification and took note of the establishment of the Consultative Group for Desertification. The highlights of the Plan are as follows:

"... More than one-third of the earth's land area is arid. Much of it has become desert since the dawn of civilization, and many vulnerable areas are even now being turned into desert. This process has intensified in recent decades, and threatens the future of 628 million people, or that 14 per cent of the world's population who live in the drylands; of this number, between 50 and 78 million people are affected directly by decreases in productivity associated with current desertification processes. In the past half century, on the southern edge of the Sahara alone, as much as 650,000 square kilometres of once productive land has become desert. Drought represents a recurrent menace in various parts of the world. The Sahellan drought of 1968–1973 and its tragic effect on the peoples of that region drew world attention to the chronic problems of human survival and development on the desert margins.

... Desertification is the diminution or destruction of the biological potential of the land, and can lead ultimately to desert-like conditions. It is an aspect of the widespread deterioration of ecosystems, and has diminished or destroyed the biological potential, i.e. plant and animal production, for multiple use purposes at a time when increased productivity is needed to support growing populations in quest of development. Important factors in contemporary society – the struggle for development and the effort to increase food production, and to adapt and apply modern technologies, set against a background of population growth and demographic change – interlock in a network of cause and effect. Progress in development, planned population growth and improvements in all types of biological production and relevant technologies must therefore be integrated. The deterioration of productive ecosystems is an obvious and serious threat to human progress. In general, the quest for ever greater productivity has intensified exploitation and has carried disturbance by man into less productive and more fragile lands. Over-exploitation gives rise to degradation of vegetation, soil and water, the three elements which serve as a natural foundation for human existence. In exceptionally fragile ecosystems, such as those on the desert margins, the loss of biological productivity through the degradation of plant, animal, soil and water resources can easily become irreversible, and permanently reduce their capacity to support human life. Desertification is a self-accelerating process, feeding on itself, and as it advances, rehabilitation costs rise exponentially. Action to combat desertification is required urgently before the costs of rehabilitation rise beyond practical possibility or before the opportunity to act is lost forever.

... The basic principles guiding the present Plan of Action are:

(a) All action shall be consistent with the provision of the Charter of the United Nations;
(b) A central theme will be the immediate adaptation and application of existing knowledge, particularly in the implementation of urgent corrective measures against desertification, in educating the people of the

affected communities to an awareness of the problem, and instituting training programmes in collaboration with international Organizations such as the Permanent Inter-State Committee on Drought Control in the Sahel, the UNESCO through its Man and the Biosphere Program, the FAO through its programme on Ecological Management of Arid and Semi-Arid Rangelands;
(c) improved land use, calling for assessment, planning and sound management on the basis of the application of known ecological principles to areas subject to desertification, is a key to success in combating desertification;
(d) improved land use should recognize the inevitability of periodic climatic drought in dry lands and their generally low natural biological potential;
(e) Integrated land use measures should be directed at the restoration of vegetation cover on marginal land, making particular use of adapted species of plants and animals;
(f) When the restoration of vegetation requires the relaxation of human pressures, temporary compensatory measures should be taken to provide alternative supplies of food and fuel;
(g) The plan is to be carried out as an effective, comprehensive and co-ordinated action programme against desertification, including the building up of local and national scientific, technological and administrative facilities in the areas concerned;
(h) All measures are to be primarily directed toward the wellbeing and development of the peoples affected by, or vulnerable to, desertification;
(i) Efforts should be consistent with, and form part of, wider programmes for development and social progress;
(j) Implementation is based on the recognition of socio-economic, cultural and ecological variety in the vulnerable areas, and the overriding need for a positive and flexible response;
(k) Additional research to clarify a number of fundamental problems for the solution of which the requisite scientific knowledge is not yet available, should be consistent with strengthening the scientific and technological capability of the affected areas;
(l) Traditional use as food, fuel or other products of wild species of plants and animals which often do not appear in the national marketing statistics should be regarded as an important resource and fully investigated;
(m) Implementation calls for the pooling of the resources of the United Nations system in launching the Plan and carrying out an integrated and world wide programme of development, research and application of science and technology to solve the special problems of desertification;
(n) Land and water management should take into account a number of ecological principles:
(i) Lands need to be managed as ecological wholes (e.g. an entire watershed, the total of plant and animal communities, an area viewed as a complex of micro topographies);
(ii) The use of dry lands should be carefully timed to confirm with fluctuations in climatic conditions;
(iii) The use of land should be carefully allocated so as to give optimum sustained productivity; its use must be fitted to its capabilities;
(o) Particular attention should be given to the utilization of local experience, knowledge and expertise in the implementation of the recommendations of the Plan at the national level in the countries concerned;
(p) While populations currently affected by desertification urgently require short-term relief measures, long-term amelioration should not be delayed, since the cost of prevention is less than that of cure;
(q) Attention should be given to the assessment of secondary environmental problems which may be triggered by measures intended to remedy desertification, as well as the effects of development activities undertaken outside the affected areas;
(r) Attention should be paid to providing adequate facilities and housing for people living in new conditions created by programmes which combat desertification;
(s) Attention should be paid to the judicious conservation and use of water resources in each region, including fair and equitable sharing of the waters of international rivers, lakes and underground aquifers, and inter-basin transfer of surplus water where this is en-

vironmentally sound and is necessary to prevent desertification;
(t) The productivity of all available renewable resources, including forest, wildlife and fisheries, should be optimized and managed on a sustainable yield basis."

An Environmental Conference in Sept. 1987 in Bangkok adopted recommendations to help save Asia from becoming a desert plagued region.

Report of the UN Conference on Desertification, Nairobi, 1977; *UN Chronicle,* November, 1982, p. 44. *UN Chronicle,* November 1986, p. 102.

DESERT LOCUST. ▷ Locust.

DESIGN ▷ Industrial Designs or models.

DESTABILIZING. An international term for a diversionary economic–political method directed from abroad whose aim is to lead to economic chaos, government collapse, and the introduction of a dictatorship.

DÉTENTE. *French* = relaxation. An international term for easing of tension in international relations or between blocs of states. On Dec. 19, 1977 with Res. 32/155 the UN General Assembly adopted by consensus (not accepted by Albania and China) the Declaration on the Deepening and Consolidation of International Détente. In Sept. 1983 former US President R. Nixon formulated the doctrine that "the real peace must be based on détente with deterrence."

J.N. AQUISTAPACE, *Dictionnaire de la politique,* Paris, 1966; *UN Chronicle,* January, 1978, p. 83; R. NIXON, *Real Peace. A Strategy for the West,* New York, 1983. R.I. GARTHOFF, *Détente and Confrontation: American–Soviet Relations from Nixon to Reagan,* Washington DC, 1985. R.W. STEVENSON, *The Rise and Fall of Detente. Relaxation of Tension in US–Soviet Relations 1953–84,* London 1985. D. ROBERTSON, *Guide to Modern Defense and Strategy,* Detroit 1988.

DETENTION AND IMPRISONMENT ▷ Protection of all persons under any form of Detention or Imprisonment, Principles 1988.

DETERGENTS. Subject of the European Agreement on the Restriction of the Use of Certain Detergents in Washing and Cleaning Products, signed on Sept. 16, 1968 in Strasbourg; came into force Feb. 16, 1971.

UNTS, Vol. 788, pp. 182–188; G. CARRIERE, *Lexicon of Detergents, Cosmetics and Toiletries.* In English, French, Spanish, Italian, Portuguese, German, Dutch and Swedish.

DETERRENCE. A military doctrine of restraining the opponent through fear of the results of initiating an atomic war, assuming maximum or minimum deterrent depending on one's own atomic weapons' potential.
See also ▷ Extended Deterrence.

Ch. BERTRAM, *The Future of Strategic Deterrence,* London 1981; P. BOBBIT, *Democracy and Deterrence,* London 1987; B. BUZAN ed., *The International Politics of Deterrence,* New York 1987; J. FINNIS, J.M. BOYLE, G. GRISER, *Nuclear Deterrence. Morality and Realism,* Oxford 1987; Zb. BRZEZINSKI, H.A. KISSINGER, F.C. INKLÉ, A. WOHLSTETTER, *Discriminate Deterrence Won't Leave Europe Dangling,* in: International Herald Tribune, February 24, 1988; C. WEINBERGER, *Arms Reduction and Deterrence,* in Foreign Affairs, Spring, 1988; D. ROBERTSON, *Guide to Modern Defense and Strategy,* Detroit 1988.

DEUTSCHE BUNDESBANK. A state bank est. 1957 with headquarters in Frankfurt am Main;

Development International Strategy for the 1980s

central bank of emission of the FRG, created to replace Bank Deutscher Länder est. 1948.

Enzyklopädisches Lexikon für das Geld, Bank un Börsenwesen, Frankfurt a. M., 1968, Bd. I, pp. 358–380.

DEUTSCHE MARK. A monetary unit of the FRG; one deutsche Mark = 100 pfennigs issued by the Deutsche Bundesbank.

DEUTSCHER BUND, 1815–1866. *German =* German Confederation. A federation created on June 8, 1815 at the Congress of Vienna; it included Austria, Bavaria, Prussia, Württemberg and all the other German kingdoms and duchies up to 1866, when the Austro–Prussian conflict, the so-called Prusso–German Seven Weeks War (June 7–July 26, 1866) resulted in the break-up of the Confederation.

J.L. KLÜBER, *Akten des Wiener Kongresses*, 9 Vols. Erlangen, 1815–1835; C.A. COLLIARD, *Droit international et histoire diplomatique*, Paris, 1950, p. 187; A.J.P. TAYLOR, *The Struggle for Mastery in Europe, 1848–1918*, London, 1954.

DEVALUATION. An international term for the statutory lowering by government decision of the value of domestic currency with regard to gold or foreign currencies. ▷ Revaluation.

DEVELOPING, DEVELOPED AND HIGHLY DEVELOPED COUNTRIES. Three international terms used in the UN system to classify countries in terms of their economic level. Developing countries are those in which large segments of the economy are still comparatively undeveloped and the majority of the population very poor, although there are wide variations of gross national products (GNP) and per capita income.
The least developed countries were defined by the UN General Assembly as countries with per capita GNPs of US $100 a year or less. Under other UN criteria manufacturing accounts for less than 10% of their GNP and their literacy rates are 20% or less. Most developing countries have economies based on exports of raw materials, and their infrastructures (transportation, social services, educational system etc.) are inadequate for their needs.
A subsidiary body of the ▷ UNCTAD is the Committee on Economic Cooperation among Developing Countries which initiated a Global System of Trade Preferences among Developing Countries, a Trade Information System, the establishment of export credit and export credit guarantee schemes, etc. The Fourth Conference of Nonaligned Countries in Algiers, 5–9 Sept. 1973, adopted a Res. on Special Measures in Favour of the Least Developed Among the Developing Countries, requesting the speedy implementation of various resolutions adopted by the UN and its related organizations in favour of the Least Developed Countries. ▷ Economic and Social World Development. The GA Res. 43/186 decided to convene the Second UN Conference on the Least Developed Countries at a high level in Paris in September 1990.

Conference on Economic Co-operation among Developing Countries: Declarations, Resolutions, Recommendations and Decisions adopted in the UN System, Mexico, DF, 1976; THE WORLD BANK, *World Development Report 1980*, Washington, DC, 1980; "The world economy in crisis", in: *UN Chronicle*, June 1982, pp. 32–57; *UN Chronicle*, October, 1982, pp. 44–47; *UN Chronicle*, December, 1983, pp. 83–84; D. TUSSIE, *The Less Developed Countries and the World Trading System: A Challenge to the GATT*, London, 1987; OECD. *Directory of Development Research and Training Institutions in Africa*, Washington DC, 1987.

DEVELOPMENT. International term in the UN system for all cultural, economic and social problems arising from the relative backwardness of the ▷ Third World.

H.W. ARDNT, *Economic Development. The History of An Idea*, Chicago, Ill., USA, 1988.

DEVELOPMENT ASSISTANCE COMMITTEE. ▷ DAC.

DEVELOPMENT BANK OF CENTRAL AFRICAN STATES. An intergovernmental finance institution of Cameroon, the Central African Republic, Chad, Congo, Gabon and Kuwait, est. 1975 in Bangui.

DEVELOPMENT BANKS. The regional development finance institutions are: the ▷ African Development Bank, ▷ African and Mauritian Union of Development Banks, ▷ Asian Development Bank, ▷ Caribbean Development Bank, ▷ Development Bank of Central African States, ▷ Islamic Development Bank.

T. SCHARF, M.C. SHETTY, *Dictionary of Development Banking*. In English (with definitions), French and German. Amsterdam, 1972; *Yearbook of International Organizations 1986/87*.

DEVELOPMENT DECADES. In the UN system 10 year periods for which targets for development are set and reviewed by the UN General Assembly to measure progress. The first Development Decade was the 1960s, the second the 1970s and the third is the 1980s. ▷ Development International Strategy for the 1980s.

"Third Development Decade: The Showdown", in: *UN Chronicle*, No. 4, 1984, pp. 1–16.

DEVELOPMENT FINANCE. An international term in the UN system for the money needed to finance economic and social growth of developing countries. The funds come primarily from trade and domestic savings. The non-oil exporting countries in the developing category got over 80% of their funds from domestic sources. A negative phenomenon for investment policy is the permanent flow of capital from developing countries. In the opinion of UN experts billions of US dollars annually take flight abroad from the non-oil exporting countries of the Third World, especially from Latin America. Foreign aid – in the opinion of UN experts – though it provides only a small part of the funds spent on development, is important. It usually brings valuable technology and skills to bear on development problems and eases the payment burdens imposed by the need for imports from developed countries. Despite the general recognition of the important role of foreign aid, however, there has been less and less of it over the last decade.
In setting targets for financial flows in the 1970s, the International Development Strategy had envisaged the developed countries would provide 1% of their GNP as public and private finance. Seven-tenths of this (or 0.7% of GNP) was to be official development assistance on concessional terms. Except for a few European countries, neither target has been met.
When talking of development it often seems that a great deal of money will be necessary to make a major dent in the world's poverty. This is indeed true. But to get some perspective on the amounts necessary we must compare them to what is being spent today on, for instance, arms. The 21-member Brandt Commission on International Development Issues pointed out in its December 1979 report that:

(1) The military expenditure of only half a day would suffice to finance the whole malaria eradication programme of the World Health Organization, and less would be needed to conquer river blindness, which is still the scourge of millions.
(2) A modern tank costs about one million dollars; that amount could improve storage facilities for 100,000 tons of rice and thus save 4000 tons or more annually (one person can live on just over a pound of rice a day). The same sum of money could provide 1000 classrooms for 30,000 children.
(3) For the price of one jet fighter (20 million dollars) one could set up about 40,000 village pharmacies.
(4) One-half of 1% of one year's world military expenditure would pay for all the farm equipment needed to increase food production and approach self-sufficiency in food-deficit low-income countries by 1990.

UN Chronicle, October, 1982, p. 44.

DEVELOPMENT INTERNATIONAL STRATEGY FOR THE 1980s. The Sixth Conference of Heads of State or Government of Non-Aligned Countries Sept. 3–9, 1979 in Havana, in the Final Declaration, points 93–105, postulated for the 1980s a new international development strategy:

"(93) The Heads of State or Government assessed the progress made in the fulfilment of the goals and objectives and the implementation of the policy measures of the Strategy for the Second UN Development Decade. They were of the view that in spite of the likely fulfilment at the global level of some of the quantitative targets of goals made possible mainly due to the domestic and collective self-reliance efforts of the developing countries, most of the objectives of the Strategy had remained unfulfilled and policy measures addressed to the developed countries had remained unimplemented. The gap between the developed and the developing countries had widened instead of being reduced and the position of the developing countries in the world economy had become precarious and their prospects of development uncertain. The grave situation facing the least developed countries had become all the more precarious and progress in combatting poverty, disease, malnutrition and illiteracy remained inadequate. This was due to the nature of the present world economic crisis, the persistent refusal of most of the developed countries to accept the imperative of restructuring the present world economic order and their inflexible policies concerning the legitimate demands of the non-aligned and other developing countries and persistent efforts of imperialism, colonialism and neo-colonialism, racism, including Zionism, apartheid, exploitation, power politics and all forms and manifestations of foreign occupation, domination and hegemony to, exploit and dominate developing countries.
(94) The Heads of State or Government reaffirmed the validity of the guidelines for the formulation of the International Development Strategy for the 1980s given at the Ministerial Meeting at Havana and endorsed by the Conference of Foreign Ministers of Non-Aligned Countries in Belgrade and noted that they had been broadly reflected in the resolution adopted by the General Assembly at its thirty-third session on the preparation for a New International Development Strategy. They called upon the non-aligned and other developing countries represented in the Preparatory Committee for the New International Development Strategy to make every effort to see that these guidelines were fully reflected during the process of the detailed formulation of the Strategy.
(95) The Heads of State or Government expressed their grave concern at the total lack of progress so far in the formulation of the Strategy and the inability of the Preparatory Committee to submit a preliminary draft of the New International Development Strategy to the General Assembly at its forthcoming session, as envisaged in General Assembly resolution 35/193. They noted that the stalemate reached in the formulation of the Strategy was primarily due to the attempt of the developed countries to go back on the agreement reached on the principles and objectives of the Strategy, their reluctance to accept quantitative targets of goals and means and to negotiate commitments on adoption of policy measures, and their attempt to impose upon developing countries patterns of development and

223

concepts of interdependence which are designed to perpetuate dependence and domination.

(96) The Heads of State or Government warned that there was a real danger of the international community giving up a planned and strategic approach to organizing international development co-operation and reverting to the ad hoc basis of such co-operation which prevailed during the decades of the 1950s and 1960s and placing it on the basis of an *ad hoc* approach where the developed countries will always have the upper hand.

(97) They, therefore, called upon the non-aligned and other developing countries to devote the time available between now and the forthcoming special session of the General Assembly to complete the formulation of the Strategy in time for its adoption by the special session and take into account in the formulation of this Strategy ongoing and future negotiations.

(98) The Heads of State or Government considered that as a vast undertaking involving the entire international community and as a tool for achieving the objectives of the New International Economic Order, the new Strategy inter alia should:
– within the framework of viable, consistent, specific and both qualitative and quantitative goals and objectives, define the role and agreed commitment of all countries expressed in quantified terms and in an agreed time-frame form the adoption and implementation of policy measures to achieve the goals and objectives of the Strategy;
– establish an average rate of growth for developing countries as a group during the Decade at a level commensurate with the need to reduce substantially the present income gap between developed and developing countries by the end of the century, which will warrant the establishment of a target for over-all growth of developing countries at a level higher than that for the Second United Nations Development Decade;
– seek to achieve a breakthrough in the resolution of major issues which are subjects of negotiation in the context of the efforts for the establishment of the New International Economic Order;
– incorporate the comprehensive new programme for the least developed among developing countries adopted at UNCTAD V as improved upon in the light of experience.

(99) The Heads of State or Government considered it basic that the New International Development Strategy should contribute to the developing countries' exercise of sovereignty and control over their natural resources and economic activities, as well as to creating conditions for efficient national exploitation of their resources, with a view to accelerating their development efforts.

(100) The Conference stressed that the New International Development Strategy should fully take into account the fact that imperialism, colonialism, neo-colonialism, apartheid, racism, including Zionism, foreign aggression and domination, the occupation of territories by force, and all other manifestations of exploitation constitute basic obstacles to the emancipation and development of the developing countries and peoples and should therefore be eliminated without delay.

(101) The Heads of State or Government considered that the special session of the General Assembly of the United Nations in 1980 should review the implementation of the New International Economic Order and take effective measures to promote its establishment. It should in particular conclude the negotiations, resolve the outstanding issues relating to the International Development Strategy for the Third United Nations Development Decade, so as it could be adopted at the session.

(102) The Heads of State or Government considered it necessary for the special session to produce results commensurate to both the graveness of the moment and the significance of the problems.

(103) The Heads of State or Government called on the Governments of the developed countries to reexamine, bearing in mind the need to establish the New International Economic Order, their political positions on most important international economic problems, so as to enable the special session of the General Assembly to adopt effective guidelines.

(104) The Heads of State or Government considered that the world economic crisis and the difficult economic situation faced by the developing countries, the limited advances in the negotiations for the establish-

ment of the New International Economic Order fully justifies that the special session should be held at a political level appropriate to the gravity of these problems.

(105) The Conference also endorsed the recommendation of the Belgrade Ministerial Conference of Non-Aligned Countries and the Colombo Ministerial Meeting of the Co-ordinating Bureau that a ministerial meeting of the Group of 77 should be held prior to the special session of the General Assembly with a view to preparing common positions and platforms of the non-aligned and other developing countries."

In the opinion of the UN Chronicle, Apr. 1984: "after two decades of sustained growth in the 1960s and 1970s, developing countries have suffered a setback in the 1980s. Stagnation and decline have replaced economic growth in many of the developing countries. Their per capita incomes have declined in the three years. International economic co-operation has been eroding. Economic recovery in the developed world will not be sufficient to restore momentum to the poor countries, unless concrete steps are taken to ease their exports, and increase the flow of resources for the developments".

During the autumn 1984 session of the UN General Assembly, the International Development Strategy for the 1980's was a major issue of the debates.

Review of International Affairs, Belgrade, October 1979; J.W. LEWELL, J.A. MATHIESON, "Priorities for a third development decade", in: *Setting National Priorities: Agenda for the 1980s*, Washington, DC, 1980; *UN Chronicle*, April 1980, p. 32, March 1981, p. 42, October 1982, pp. 44–47, April 1984, pp. 1–16.

DEVELOPMENT, UN PROGRAM OF ACTION ON SUSTAINABLE DEVELOPMENT ▷ Environmental Protection.

DHAKA. Capital of Bangladesh. Pop. 1981 census 3.340.312. Capital of the XVIII century Muslim state of Bengal.

DIABETES. A subject of international research. Organizations reg. with the UIA:

European Association for the study of Diabetes, est. 1965, Umea (Sweden). Publ. *Diabetologia*.
International Diabetes Federation, est. 1949, London; Scandinavian Society for the Study of Diabetes, est. 1967, Airhus (Denmark).

Yearbook of International Organizations.

DIAMONDS. One of the basic resources for the drilling and jewelry-making industries; subject of international conventions. Major producers of 96% of world output in total: Zaïre (over 60%), South Africa (c. 14%), Ghana (c. 11%) and Angola, Namibia, Sierra Leone. The first international concern was founded in 1888. The Diamond Trading Corporation was established in 1928. Its headquarters were located in London, where the diamond exchange handles 90% of all world contracts. The main diamond cutting center is located in Antwerp.
Organizations reg. with the UIA:

Universal Alliance of Diamond Workers, Alliance universelle des ouvriers diamentaires, est. 1905, Antwerp; affiliates national unions of South Africa, Belgium, France, The Netherlands, Israel and the UK. Publ. *Bulletin*.
World Federation of Diamond Bourses, Federation mondiale des bourses de diamants, est. 1968, Antwerp.

T. GREEN, *The World of Diamonds*, London, 1983; *Yearbook of International Organizations*.

DIASPORA. An international term for national or religious minorities scattered throughout the world far from their homeland or origins; historically the term appeared for the first time in the Bible in

reference to the dispersal of the Jews (Letter of Jacob the Apostate, 1, 1).

DICKENSON BAY AGREEMENT, 1965. The official name of the Treaty of Caribbean Free Trade Association, signed on Dec. 15, 1965, in Dickenson Bay, by the Heads of Government of Antigua, Barbados and Guyana; came into force Dec. 30, 1966; modified by the Caribbean Conference on Oct. 28, 1967 in Bridgetown.

M. SEARA VAZQUEZ, *Tratado General de la Organización Internacional*, México, DF, pp. 872–873.

DICTIONARIES, INTERNATIONAL. International lexicographic term for bilingual and multilingual dictionaries. The United Nations publishes the *Terminology Bulletin and Multilingual* (of UN official languages) *Dictionaries of Terms Used in Subject of Documents and Other Materials Relevant to United Nations Programs and Activities*.
See also ▷ UNBIS Thesaurus.

WEBSTER's *Third New International Dictionary*, New York, 1966.

DIEGO GARCIA ISLAND. A part of the ▷ Chagos Archipelago in the Indian Ocean, British possession since 1794, situated on a strategic point between Africa and Sumatra, c. 1000 sea miles south of India. In Feb. 1974 the UK ceded naval and air bases to the United States; India and the USSR protested, recalling UN General Assembly Res. 2832/XXVI of Dec. 12, 1971 on proclamation of the Indian Ocean as a zone of peace. The first UK–US leasing agreement for 50 years was signed in 1965, three years before ▷ Mauritius attained independence and all inhabitants were relocated to Mauritius. The remainder of the Chagos Archipelago was included in the agreement of 1974. The Mauritius Government called the UK–USA agreements "a fraud and an illegal act, contrary to the resolutions of the UN", and demanded the demilitarization of Diego Garcia and its incorporation together with Mauritius into an "Indian Ocean Zone of Peace".

UN Monthly Chronicle, January 1972; SIPRI, *World Armament and Disarmament Yearbook*, 1973, pp. 74–89; 1974, pp. 20–23; J.D. BATTERSBY, *Mauritius Stresses Claim to Diego Garcia*, in: New York Times, Jan. 4, 1988.

DILLON ROUND. The fifth round (1960–61) of GATT deliberations on the problem of customs duties; begun on the initiative of the Under-Secretary of State of the USA, Douglas Dillon. ▷ Kennedy round and ▷ Tokyo round.

A. SCHONFIELD, *International Economic Relations of the Western World 1959–71*, London, 1976.

DINAR ALGERIAN. A monetary unit of Algeria; one dinar = 100 centimes; introduced Apr. 10, 1964 in place of Algerian franc; issued by the Banque Centrale d'Algérie.

DINAR IRAQUI. A monetary unit of Iraq; one dinar = 1000 fils; issued by the Central Bank of Iraq.

DINAR ISLAMIC An accounting unit accepted since 1974 by the Arabic central banks on the basis that one Islamic dinar = 1 SDR.

DINAR JORDANIAN. A monetary unit of Jordan; one dinar = 1000 fils; first issued July 1, 1950 by the Central Bank of Jordan.

DINAR KUWAITI. A monetary unit of Kuwait; one dinar = 1000 fils; first issued, replacing the Gulf rupee, Apr. 1, 1961 by the Central Bank of Kuwait.

DINAR LIBYAN. A monetary unit of Libya; one dinar = 1000 dirhams; issued by the Central Bank of Libya.

DINAR OF SOUTH YEMEN. A currency unit of the People's Democratic Republic of Yemen; one dinar = 1000 fils; issued by the National Bank of Yemen.

DINAR TUNISIAN. A monetary unit of Tunisia; one dinar = 1000 millimes; issued by the Banque Centrale de Tunesie.

DINAR YUGOSLAVIAN. A monetary unit of Yugoslavia; one dinar = 100 paras; issued by the Narodna Banka Yugoslaviye.

DINERS CLUB INTERNATIONAL. The first American travel and entertainment credit card system, established 1950, accepted 1980 in over 150 countries.

DINOSAUR PROVINCIAL PARK. A Canadian natural site, included in the ▷ World Heritage UNESCO List. In Alberta, amidst the luxuriant vegetation of the terraces of the Red Deer River, birds and deer abound. Seventy million years ago, however, there were many large reptiles, the remains of about 60 different species of which have been found. From a 24-kilometer-long stretch of the river, more than 300 specimens of dinosaurs have been removed.

UNESCO. *A Legacy for All*, Paris, 1984.

DIPHTHERIA ▷ Immunization.

DIPLOMACY, INTERNATIONAL. (1) Diplomatic activity of member states in international organizations; (2) ▷ Good Offices of the UN; (3) Activity in developing international co-operation carried on by UN functionaries and UN specialized agencies. A common synonym for international diplomacy is multilateral diplomacy.

Dictionnaire Diplomatique, Paris, 1960, Vol. VI; G.L. BEST, *Diplomacy in the UN*, Ann Arbor, 1962; T. MOUSSA, *Diplomatie contemporaine, Guide bibliographique*, Genève, 1964; B. SEN, *A Diplomatic Handbook of International Law and Practice*, The Hague, 1964; *Diplomatya Sotsialisma*, Moskva, 1973; H. NICOLSON, *La diplomacia*, Mexico, DF, 1975.

DIPLOMAS. A subject of international agreements on reciprocal recognition of professional or semi-professional diplomas. In the EEC countries there exists from Dec. 1976 a mutual recognition of ▷ Scientific diplomas.

DIPLOMATIC ACADEMY, INTERNATIONAL. Académie diplomatique internationale, f. 1926 in Paris. Its members are the Heads of States, ministers of foreign affairs and ambassadors, representing 91 countries. Publ.: *Dictionnaire diplomatique* (since 1933). It is reg. with the UIA.

Yearbook of International Organizations.

DIPLOMATIC AGENTS. An international law term for state representatives to foreign governments and to world or regional international organizations, in ranks determined by the Diplomatic Convention. A subject of the New York Conventions on Prevention and Punishment of Crimes against Internationally Protected Persons, including Diplomatic Agents, 1973.

DIPLOMATIC ASYLUM CONVENTION, 1954. A Latin American Convention, signed in Caracas on Mar. 28, 1954, at the Tenth Inter-American Conference by Brazil, Costa Rica, the Dominican Republic, Ecuador, Guatemala. Haiti (renounced on Aug. 1, 1967), Honduras, Mexico, Nicaragua, Panama, Paraguay, Peru, El Salvador, Uruguay and Venezuela. The convention came into force on Dec. 29, 1954.

The text of the 24 main Articles is as follows:

"The governments of the Member States of the Organization of American States, desirous of concluding a Convention on Diplomatic Asylum, have agreed to the following articles:

Art. 1. Asylum granted in legations, war vessels, and military camps or aircraft, to persons being sought for political reasons or for political offences shall be respected by the territorial State in accordance with the provisions of this Convention.

For the purposes of this Convention, a legation is any seat of a regular diplomatic mission, the residence of chiefs of mission, and the premises provided by them for the dwelling places of asylees when the number of the latter exceeds the normal capacity of the buildings. War vessels or military aircraft that may be temporarily in shipyards, arsenals, or shops for repair may not constitute a place of asylum.

Art. 2. Every State has the right to grant asylum; but it is not obligated to do so or to state its reasons for refusing it.

Art. 3. It is not lawful to grant asylum to persons who, at the time of requesting it, are under indictment or on trial for common offences or have been convicted by competent regular courts and have not served the respective sentence, nor to deserters from land, sea and air forces, save when the acts giving rise to the request for asylum, whatever the case may be, are clearly of a political nature.

Persons included in the foregoing paragraph who de facto enter a place that is suitable as an asylum shall be invited to leave or, as the case may be, shall be surrendered to the local authorities, who may not try them for political offences committed prior to the time of the surrender.

Art. 4. It shall rest with the State granting asylum to determine the nature of the offense or the motives for the persecution.

Art. 5. Asylum may not be granted except in urgent cases and for the period of time strictly necessary for the asylee to depart from the country with the guarantees granted by the Government of the territorial State, to the end that his life, liberty, or personal integrity may not be endangered, or that the asylee's safety is ensured in some other way.

Art. 6. Urgent cases are understood to be those, among others in which the individual is being sought by persons or mobs over whom the authorities have lost control, or by the authorities themselves, and is in danger of being deprived of his life or liberty because of political persecution and cannot, without risk, ensure his safety in any other way.

Art. 7. If a case of urgency is involved, it shall rest with the State granting asylum to determine the degree of urgency of the case.

Art. 8. The diplomatic representative, commander of a warship, military camp, or military airship, shall, as soon as possible after asylum has been granted, report the fact to the Minister of Foreign Affairs of the territorial State, or to the local administrative authority if the case arose outside the Capital.

Art. 9. The official furnishing asylum shall take into account the information furnished to him by the territorial government in forming his judgment as to the nature of the offense or the existence of related common crimes; but this decision to continue the asylum or to demand a safe-conduct for the asylee shall be respected.

Art. 10. The fact that the Government of the territorial State is not recognized by the State granting asylum shall not prejudice the application of the present Convention, and no act carried out by virtue of this Convention shall imply recognition.

Art. 11. The government of the territorial State may, at any time, demand that the asylee be withdrawn from the country, for which purpose the said State shall grant a safe-conduct and the guarantees stipulated in article 5.

Art. 12. Once asylum has been granted, the State granting asylum may request that the asylee be allowed to depart for foreign territory, and the territorial State is under obligation to grant immediately, except in case of force majeure, the necessary guarantees referred to in Article 5, as well as the corresponding safe-conduct.

Art. 13. In the cases referred to in the preceding articles the State granting asylum may require that the guarantees be given in writing, and may take into account, in determining the rapidity of the journey, the actual conditions of danger involved in the departure of the asylee.

The State granting asylum has the right to transfer the asylee out of the country. The territorial State may point out the preferable route for the departure of the asylee, but this does not imply determining the country of destination.

If the asylum is granted on board a warship or military airship, departure may be made therein, but complying with the previous requisite of obtaining the appropriate safe-conduct.

Art. 14. The State granting asylum cannot be held responsible for the prolongation of asylum caused by the need for obtaining the information required to determine whether or not the said asylum is proper, or whether there are circumstances that might endanger safety of the asylee during the journey to a foreign country.

Art. 15. When, in order to transfer an asylee to another country it may be necessary to traverse the territory of a State that is a party to this Convention, transit shall be authorized by the latter, the only requisite being the presentation, through diplomatic channels, of a safe conduct, duly countersigned and bearing a notation of his status as asylee by the diplomatic mission that granted asylum.

En route, the asylee shall be considered under the protection of the State granting asylum.

Art. 16. Asylees may not be landed at any point in the territorial State or at any place near thereto, except for the exigencies of transportation.

Art. 17. Once the departure of the asylee has been carried out, the State granting asylum is not bound to settle him in its territory; but it may not return him to his country of origin, unless this is the express wish of the asylee. If the territorial State informs the official granting asylum of its intention to request the subsequent extradition of the asylee, this shall not prejudice the application of any provision of the present Convention. In that event, the asylee shall remain in the territory of the State granting asylum until such time as the formal request for extradition is received, in accordance with the jurisdical principles governing that institution in the State granting asylum. Preventive surveillance over the asylee may not exceed thirty days.

Payment of the expenses incurred by such transfer and of preventive control shall devolve upon the requesting State.

Art. 18. The official furnishing asylum may not allow the asylee to perform acts contrary to the public peace or to interfere in the internal politics of the territorial State.

Art. 19. If as a consequence of a rupture of diplomatic relations the diplomatic representative who granted asylum must leave the territorial State, he shall abandon it with the asylees. If this is not possible for reasons independent of the wish of the asylee or the diplomatic representative, he must surrender them to the diplomatic mission of a third State, which is a party to this Convention, under the guarantees established in the Convention. If this is also not possible, he shall surrender them to a State that is not a party to this Convention and that agrees to maintain the asylum. The territorial state is to respect the said asylum.

Art. 20. Diplomatic asylum shall not be subject to reciprocity. Every person is under its protection, whatever his nationality.

Art. 21. The present Convention shall be open for signature by the Member States of the Organization of American States and shall be ratified by the signatory States in accordance with their respective constitutional procedures.

Art. 22. The original instrument, whose texts in the English, French, Spanish, and Portuguese languages are equally authentic, shall be deposited in the Pan-American Union, which shall send certified copies to the governments for the purpose of ratification. The instruments of ratification shall be deposited in the Pan

D

American Union, and the said organization shall notify the signatory governments of the said deposit.
Art. 23. The present Convention shall enter into force among the States that ratify it in the order in which their respective ratifications are deposited.
Art. 24. The present Convention shall remain in force indefinitely, but may be denounced by any of the signatory States by giving advance notice of one year, at the end of which period it shall cease to have effect for the denouncing State, remaining in force, however, among the remaining signatory States."

PAU Treaty Series No. 18, 1961.

DIPLOMATIC CEREMONIAL. An international term for forms of behavior in various official situations established by diplomatic protocol of the representative of a foreign state in accordance with his rank and time of residence in a given state as well as in accordance with the customs of a given country, and also the ceremony of receiving envoys or official foreign guests, carrying on talks and signing treaties established by diplomatic protocol and international or local custom.

Dictionnaire de la terminologie du droit international, Paris, 1960; J.R. WOOD, J. SERRES, *Diplomatic Ceremonial and Protocol: Principles, Procedures and Practices,* London, 1970.

DIPLOMATIC CONFERENCES. An international term for international meetings to codify international law, initiated at the Diplomatic Conference in Berne, 1892; within the UN – an institution of the International Law Commission for codification of conventions.

DIPLOMATIC CORPS. French = Corps Diplomatique (CD). An international term for all diplomats accredited in a given country; headed by a dean.

DIPLOMATIC CORRESPONDENCE AND DOCUMENTS. The subject of the ▷ Vienna Convention on Diplomatic Relations, 1961.

E. DENZA, *Diplomatic Law. Commentary on Vienna Convention,* New York, 1976.

DIPLOMATIC COURIER. An official travelling messenger bearing sealed diplomatic mail, subject of international convention on diplomatic immunities, rights and duties of diplomatic couriers; aside from a diplomatic passport they are equipped with a courier's letter specifying the number of pouches with diplomatic mail as recommended by League of Nations Commission for Transport and Transit, Paris, Oct. 21, 1920. In 1982 the UN International Law Commission adopted the first draft articles on the topic of the status of the diplomatic courier and the diplomatic bag not accompanied by diplomatic courier.

UN Chronicle, October, 1982, pp. 24–25.

DIPLOMATIC HAVANA CONVENTION, 1928.
A Convention on Diplomatic Officers, signed on Feb. 20, 1928 in Havana, during the Sixth International Conference of American States and ratified by Brazil, Chile, Colombia, Costa Rica, Cuba, Dominicana, Ecuador, Haiti, Mexico, Nicaragua, Panama, Peru, Uruguay, and Venezuela; it was not ratified by Argentina, Bolivia, Guatemala, Honduras, Paraguay and the USA. It came into force on Mar. 21, 1929.

C.A. COLLIARD, *Droit international et Histoire diplomatique,* Paris, 1950.

DIPLOMATIC IMMUNITIES. A subject convened by the UN General Assembly Res. 1450/XIV of Dec. 7, 1959, held at the Neue Hofburg in Vienna, from Mar. 2 to Apr. 14, 1961 with the

official name: UN Conference on Diplomatic Intercourse and Immunities. The governments of 81 States were represented. The Conference prepared the ▷ Vienna Convention on Diplomatic Relations 1961, Final Act of the Conference, Optional Protocol concerning Acquisition of Nationality and Optional Protocol concerning the Compulsory Settlement of Disputes.

UNTS, Vol. 500, pp. 212–218.

DIPLOMATIC LAW. A branch of common international law; a set of legal rules and norms defining the status and functions of diplomatic agents as well as the organizational forms of diplomatic service. The first modern legal act to this end was the Vienna Regulation of 1815. The first regional agreement was the Havana Diplomatic Convention of 1928. The main contemporary sources of diplomatic law are the ▷ Vienna Convention on Diplomatic Relations of 1961, the Vienna Convention on Special Missions of 1969, the Convention on the Prevention and Punishment of Crimes against Internationally Protected Persons, including Diplomatic Agents, the ▷ Vienna Convention on the Representation of States in Their Relations with International Organizations of a Universal Character of 1975, set for the first time permanent norms on diplomatic relations with universal international organizations.

J.L. DEPETRE, *Derecho Diplomático,* México, DF, 1952; M. CAHIER, *Derecho Diplomático Contemporaneo,* Madrid–México, 1965; *UN Conference on Diplomatic Relations and Immunities in Vienna,* 2 Vols., New York, 1963; E. SATOW, *A Guide to Diplomatic Practice,* London, 1968; E. DENZA, *Diplomatic Law, Commentary on the Vienna Convention on Diplomatic Relations,* New York –London, 1976.

DIPLOMATIC MAIL. An international term for sealed containers carried by ▷ Diplomatic couriers to or from posts abroad, subject of international conventions on diplomatic privileges and immunities, which ensure that the diplomatic mail will not be opened or delayed or destroyed. In each diplomatic shipment a courier's warrant is obligatory, specifying packages transported by the courier.

DIPLOMATIC MISSION. A permanent or ad hoc official representation to the government of an alien state or to an inter-governmental organization. The first document defining the status of a diplomatic mission was the Vienna Rule of 1815; at present it is the Viennese Diplomatic Convention of 1961. A diplomatic mission is a one-person office representing the state through an ambassador, envoy or chargé d'affaires. Acts of violence against diplomatic missions are the subject of the ▷ Vienna Convention on Diplomatic Relations of 1961, the ▷ Vienna Convention on Consular Relations of 1963 and the New York Convention on Prevention and Punishment of Crimes against Internationally Protected Persons including Diplomatic Agents, 1973. On Nov. 13, 1981 the UN General Assembly adopted a Res. 35/168 strongly condemning acts of violence against diplomatic and consular missions and representatives as well as missions and representatives of inter-governmental organizations. On Dec. 9, 1988 the GA Res. 43/167 on Diplomatic and Consular Missions was adopted without a vote:

"Alarmed by the repeated acts of violence against diplomatic and consular representatives, as well as against representatives to international intergovernmental organizations and officials of such organizations, which endanger or take innocent lives and seriously impede the normal work of such representatives and officials ...

Strongly condemns acts of violence against diplomatic and consular missions and representatives, as well as against missions and representatives to international intergovernmental organizations and officials of such organizations, and emphasizes that such acts can never be justified;
Urges States to observe, implement and enforce the principles and rules of international law governing diplomatic and consular relations and, in particular to ensure, in conformity with their international obligations, the protection, security and safety of such missions, representatives and officials as mentioned in paragraph 2 above officially present in territories under their jurisdiction, including practical measures to prohibit in their territories illegal activities of persons, groups and organizations that encourage, instigate, organize or engage in the perpetration of acts against the security and safety of such missions, representatives and officials."

UN Chronicle, January 1982, p. 42; December, 1983, p. 76; *UN Resolutions and Decisions adopted by the General Assembly during the first Part of its Forty-Third Session, from 20 September to 22 December 1988,* New York 1989, pp. 573–575.

DIPLOMATIC NEGOTIATIONS. An international term, international legal means of settlement of disputes, conclusion of bi- and multilateral agreements and drawing up of international regulations. The concept of the peaceful settlement of disputes was institutionalized in the 20th century through negotiations in various international Conventions such as ▷ Briand–Kellog Treaty, or the ▷ United Nations Charter; the norms of negotiations were codified by ▷ Vienna Convention on the Law of International Treaties, 1969.

H. NICOLSON, *The Evolution of Diplomatic Methods,* Glasgow, 1954; H. NICOLSON, *The Diplomacy,* Oxford, 1958; H.J. MORGENTHAU, *Politics among Nations,* New York, 1967.

DIPLOMATIC POUCH. A sealed pouch with ▷ diplomatic mail.

DIPLOMATIC PROTECTION. An activity performed by states to protect their nationals abroad and secure their interests; subject to international conventions aimed at providing nationals with diplomatic protection by neutral states during wars; also, an issue of international conflicts when it is applied to armed forces or persons not accredited diplomats but private nationals of alien states.

A. BORCHARD, *The Diplomatic Protection of Citizens Abroad and the Law of International Claims,* London, 1915; A. BORCHARD, *Les principes de la protection diplomatique des nationaux à l'étranger,* Leiden, 1924; E.J.S. CASTREN, "Some consideration upon the conception, development and importance of diplomatic protection", in: *Jahrbuch für Internationales Recht,* 1962, pp. 37–47.

DIPLOMATIC PROTOCOL. Also called diplomatic ceremonial. A collection of norms concerning contacts of diplomats with state authorities or intergovernmental organizations to which they are accredited, codified by the Vienna Congress, 1815, the so-called ▷ Vienna Rules, modernized by the ▷ Vienna Convention on Diplomatic Relations, 1961.

DIPLOMATIC RELATIONS, DISCONTINUATION OR SUSPENSION. Two international terms for two forms of manifesting the significance of a conflict or dispute between two states: (1) discontinuation is the most severe form usually applied with respect to a state recognized as the aggressor or in the case of a serious diplomatic incident (e.g. offence to a head of state, devastation of a diplomatic mission or assault on members of staff); (2) suspension is the form usually used in the case when an unfriendly government comes to power or in the case of hostile demonstrations preventing from the diplomatic mission in the discharging its normal activities. Resumption of relations with regard to (1) requires the repetition of the whole procedure of their establishment, whereas the state of suspension can be lifted automatically by consent of the two parties on again accrediting their diplomats. The ▷ Vienna Convention on Diplomatic Relations of Apr. 18, 1961 in arts. 43–45, obligates the states discontinuing diplomatic relations to return diplomatic representatives to their countries and to respect premises of diplomatic missions, their property and archives. It is a commonly accepted custom for a neutral diplomatic mission in such country to extend care over the premises of a mission whose work has been suspended.

DIPLOMATIC RESIDENCE. A subject of the ▷ Vienna Convention on Diplomatic Relations, 1961.

E. DENZA, *Diplomatic Law*, New York, 1976.

DIPLOMATS. The persons empowered by a state or an intergovernmental organization to settle issues with other states or intergovernmental institutions. On the initiative of the UN in 1973 a plan was developed for a Convention on the Prevention and Punishment of Crimes Against Diplomatic Representatives and Persons Having the Right to International Protection. In Havana, Feb. 20, 1928, 21 American republics signed the Inter-American Convention on diplomats which i.a. states that:

"foreign diplomats cannot participate in the internal or external politics of the state in which they perform their functions."

LNTS, Vol. 155, p. 265; J. CAMBON, *Le diplomate*, Paris, 1926; M.H. CARDOW, "Diplomats", in: *International Co-operation*, New York, 1962; J.E. HARR, *The Professional Diplomat*, London, 1969.

DIRECTORIES, INTERNATIONAL. Directories of universities, scientific associations, cultural institutions, communication, transportation research institutes, libraries, museums, theatres etc., object of international bibliography of special directories (e.g. *International Bibliography of Book Trade and Librarianship*).

C.A. MARLOW ed., *The Directory of Directories 1988*. An Annotated Guide to Over 10,000 Business and Industrial Directories, Professional and Scientific Rosters, Directory Data Bases and Other Lists and Guides of All Kinds, 2 Vols, Detroit, 1988.

DIRHAM. A monetary unit of Morocco; one dirham = 100 centimes; issued from Oct. 17, 1959 by the Banque du Maroc replacing the Moroccan franc.

DIRHAM. A monetary unit of the United Arab Emirates; one dirham = 100 fils; issued on May 19, 1973 by the United Arab Emirates Currency Board in Abu Dhabi Town, replacing the Bahrain dinar and the Dubai riyal.

DISABLED PERSONS UN DECADE OF, 1983–1992. After the International Year of Disabled Persons, 1981, the General Assembly proclaimed 1983–1992 the UN Decade of Disabled Persons, based on the World Program of Action concerning Disabled Persons, 1982. The first results according to a UNESCO report 1987, is the integration in many countries of disabled young people into ordinary education. Subject of the GA Res. 43/98 of December 8, 1988.

The Courier, July 1987. UN Resolutions and Decisions Adopted by the General Assembly During the First part of its Forty-Third Session, from 20 September to 22 December 1988. pp. 335–339.

DISABLED REHABILITATION. A subject of international co-operation. In 1981 the International Year of Disabled Persons was observed under the aegis of the UN General Assembly. Organizations reg. with the UIA:

Committee for Rehabilitation of the Disabled in Africa, f. 1917, Kampala.
Council of World Organizations Interested in the Handicapped, f. 1953, New York. Sponsored by the UN.
International Federation of Disabled Workmen and Civilian Cripples, f. 1953, Olten, Switzerland. Publ. *Bulletin* (quarterly).
International Sports Organization for the Disabled, f. 1961, Paris.
Rehabilitation International, f. 1922, International Society for Rehabilitation of the Disabled, official name since 1929, New York. Consultative status ECOSOC, WHO, UNICEF, ILO and UNESCO. Publ. *International Rehabilitation Review* (quarterly).

Compendium on the Activities of World Organizations Interested in the Handicapped, New York, 1975; Ph. WOOD, E.M. BADLEY, *People with Disabilities. Their Problems and needs*, New York, 1981; *UN Chronicle* January, 1980 p. 71, February, 1982, p. 50 and November, 1982 p. 47; *Yearbook of International Organizations*.

DISAPPEARED PERSONS FOR POLITICAL REASONS. A subject of UN investigations. In 1980 the UN Commission on Human Rights appointed a Working Group on Enforced or Involuntary Disappearance to investigate persistent reports of the disappearances for political reasons of persons in the following 22 countries: Argentina, Bolivia, Brazil, Chile, Cyprus, El Salvador, Ethiopia, Guatemala, Guinea, Honduras, Indonesia, Iran, Lesotho, Mexico, Nicaragua, thePhilippines, South Africa and Namibia, Sri Lanka, Uganda, Uruguay, Zaïre. A continued vigilance of the ongoing violations of human rights in those countries was ordered by the UN General Assembly in the following years.

UN Chronicle, March, 1980, pp. 73–74 and April, 1982 pp. 31–33.

DISARMAMENT. In the UN system the term disarmament covers: (1) complete and universal disarmament; (2) limitation and reduction of armaments; (3) arms control.
The first states which mutually limited their armaments by treaty were Colombia and Peru, 1829, and two years later Peru and Bolivia and Argentina with Brazil.
The first international organization which began a campaign for disarmament was the ▷ Interparliamentary Union, 1889. The first international Conference on this subject was the First International Hague Peace Conference, 1899 which adopted a resolution suggesting that the states of Europe limit their armed forces and expenditures for armaments. The Second International Hague Peace Conference, 1907, made a non-binding recommendation to "study the question of disarmament". After World War I the League of Nations Covenant in arts. 1, 8 and 23 recognized the need to "limit to a minimum" national land, sea, and air armaments. In 1927 the LN Committee of Experts drew up a list of "expenditures required for national defence," suggesting the minimizing of military budgets. The first disarmament treaty was drafted by the Washington Conference on the Limitation of Armaments, 1921/22, with the participation of France, Italy, Japan, the UK and USA, a treaty on the limitation of naval armaments which was not ratified. In 1927 in Geneva, Japan, the UK and the USA could not reach agreement on cruisers and submarines. Two London Conferences (with the Washington participants) were devoted to the problems of limiting naval armaments (▷ London Naval Treaties). The

first, Apr. 21, 1930, obligated the signatories for five years not to increase the tonnage of ships of the line; introduced quantitative and qualitative limitations with respect to submarines; established parity for fleets of cruisers, destroyers, and submarines on a mutual basis between the UK, USA, and Japan; finally, it obligated submarines to adhere to the same norms of international sea law as surface ships. The second Conference from Dec. 9, 1935 to March 25, 1936, from which Japan and Italy withdrew and the remaining powers signed an open treaty which was joined by the USSR, concerned the qualitative limitation of naval armaments. This treaty was rendered void by World War II. The I World Disarmament Conference was prepared by the LN 1926–31 and was held – preceded by an appeal of the LN Assembly Nov. 29, 1931 to suspend the arms race for one year – in Geneva from Feb. 2, 1932 to Nov. 21, 1934, when it was adjourned sine die (formally the LN Council suspended the activity of the Conference Jan. 22, 1936). Taking part were the members of the LN and the USA and USSR. The subject of the meeting was collective security, the definition of aggression, stages of disarmament and instruments of reconciliation and control; Oct. 14, 1933 the III Reich withdrew from participation in the sessions and with its policy of remilitarization paralyzed further efforts by the Conference. Twelve years later, Dec. 14, 1946, the UN General Assembly, Res. 41/I on the Principles which govern the General Control and Reduction of Armaments, and Res. 42/I on the Information which UN member states should supply on their armed forces, began its efforts in the direction of disarmament. Both resolutions reflected the ideas of the I Session of the UN General Assembly Oct. 29, 1946, which concerned outlawing atomic weapons, destroying existing stockpiles, and proceeding to a general reduction of armaments.
The organs created by the UN for the purpose of studying and submitting proposals concerning disarmament included the Atomic Energy Commission and the Committee on Conventional Armaments. In 1952 the UN General Assembly replaced both Commissions with one Disarmament Commission, directly accountable to the Security Council on whose recommendations it formulated proposals for treaties – on control, limitation and mutual reduction of all armed forces and kinds of weapons; on effective international nuclear control for the purpose of introducing a ban on nuclear weapons and using nuclear power exclusively for peaceful purposes; on eliminating all weapons of mass destruction. In this period negotiations were taken over by the Subcommittee of the Five Powers in the Disarmament Commission. Differences in the position of the respective powers diminished, but they continued to be serious, especially regarding gradual nuclear disarmament, the limitation of conventional weapons, and on an international system of control and inspection. In 1959 the Treaty on the Demilitarization of Antartica was signed in Washington. On Sept. 18, 1959 the premier of the USSR, N.S. Khrushchev, submitted to the UN General Assembly a general proposal for universal and complete disarmament. The UN General Assembly Res. 1378/XIV, Nov. 20, 1959, unanimously affirmed that this question was the most important problem facing humanity and expressed the hope that ways could be found toward universal disarmament and effective international control. On Sept. 20, 1961 the ▷ Disarmament Negotiations Principles, 1961, obligatory to all disarmament negotiations were presented by the USA and USSR to all UN member States. On Nov. 24, 1961, the UN General Assembly Res. 1653/XVI, adopted with 55 voices in favor, 20 against, and 26 abstentions a Declaration Prohibiting the Use of Nuclear

Weapons. At the same time the USA and USSR reached agreement on the creation of the Disarmament Committee composed of 18 states: Brazil, Bulgaria, Burma, Canada, Czechoslovakia, Ethiopia, France, India, Italy, Mexico, Nigeria, Poland, Romania, Sweden, the UAR, the UK, the USA and the USSR. This Committee, which submitted reports on its work to the Assembly and the Disarmament Commission, began its meetings in Geneva in Mar., 1962 with the absence of France, which stated that it wished to first discuss the above problems with other powers, a form of protest by General Charles de Gaulle against the USA–USSR dialogue. A World Congress for Universal Disarmament was held in Moscow July 9–14, 1962, previously on Mar. 18 1962 the USSR submitted to the Commission an 18-point proposal of a plan for universal disarmament, proposing three stages of disarmament: with an ▷ Atomic umbrella in stages I and II and the creation of a new UN special disarmament organization. On April. 18, 1962 the USA submitted its counterproposal to the Commission. One of the main problems was the question of banning of tests of nuclear weapons. In accordance with the recommendations of the UN General Assembly of June 20, 1962 direct communications between Moscow and Washington were installed (called the "hot-line"), and in July, 1962 the UK, USA and USSR drafted the ▷ Nuclear Weapons Tests Ban Moscow Treaty in the Atmosphere, Outer Space and Under Water, signed on Aug. 5, 1963 in Moscow and later signed by more than 100 states. Remaining open were the questions of underground tests and the joining of the treaty by two nuclear powers not participating in the negotiations: France and the People's Republic of China. The UN General Assembly, Res. 1884/XVIII then called for the formulation of a ban on the placement of weapons of mass destruction in earth orbit. The Assembly Dec. 5, 1966 adopted three Res. A, B and C/XXI concerning universal and complete disarmament: Res. A called for the drafting by experts of a report on the eventual consequences of the use of nuclear weapons (Dec. 19, 1967 the UN Gen. Ass., Res. 2342/XXII accepted the report); Res. B. recommended strict adherence to the Geneva Protocol on the prohibition of chemical and bacteriological weapons and the signing of the Protocol by the remaining states; Res. C. recommended that the Commission continue its work. The first disarmament achievement of the space age was the signing on Jan. 27, 1967 of the Outer Space Treaty. Then the Assembly began a campaign on behalf of the Treaty on the Non-proliferation of Nuclear Weapons, Res. 2149/XXI, Nov. 4, 1966, Res. 2135 A and B/XXI, Nov. 17, Res. 2346/XXII, Dec. 19, 1967. As a result, from Apr. 24 to June 12, 1968 a resumed Session of the UN General Assembly was held devoted to this Treaty, whose simultaneous signing in London, Moscow, and Washington took place July 1, 1968. Previously on June 19, 1968 the Security Council adopted a resolution concerning a guarantee for non-nuclear states, who met in Geneva between Aug. 22 and Sept. 28, 1968 to discuss the problems of their own security. In Mexico in 1968 the first regional treaty on a denuclearized zone the ▷ Tlatelolco Treaty was signed. At the XXIII Session of the UN General Assembly, Dec. 20, 1968, there was a request for a report by experts on the effects of the use of bacteriological and chemical weapons (the report was published July 1, 1969). In 1969 the Committee of 18 was expanded to include Argentina, Hungary, Japan, Mongolia, Morocco, the Netherlands, Pakistan and Yugoslavia, and from Aug. 26, 1969 was renamed the Conference of the Committee on Disarmament. In 1975 membership of the Committee was increased to 31. From Nov., 1969 the USA

and USSR began discussions on the subject of the limitation of strategic armaments, which were continued in succeeding years (▷ SALT). In Sept., 1970 a group of Nobel peace prize laureates submitted to the UN General Assembly, Res. 2602E/XXIV proclaiming the decade 1971–80 the Disarmament Decade. After reaching agreement on the Treaty on Denuclearization of the Sea Bed, 1971, and the Treaty on the Prohibition of Bacteriological Weapons, 1971, the work of the Disarmament Committee in Geneva in 1972/73 concentrated on the following issues: the complete halting of nuclear test explosions, including underground ones; a ban on nuclear and chemical weapons; the creation of nuclear-free zones; the complete demilitarization of the sea-bed; removal of foreign military bases and the reduction of armed forces and military expenditures.

In accordance with a decision of the X Special Session of the UN General Assembly on Disarmament, 1978, the Disarmament Committee was expanded from 31 to 40 members, and the system of rotating chairmanship of the work of the Committee by the USA and USSR was eliminated. Among the five Great Powers France participated in its first conference as a new member Jan. 24, 1979 after 16 years of boycotting the Geneva talks, while China looked on as an observer. France announced a plan for creating an International Agency for Satellite Observation of Disarmament Agreements.

The joint Soviet–American communiqué on the visit of the US President, Richard Nixon to the USSR and the ▷ ABM treaty signed by L. I. Brezhnev and R. Nixon and the agreement on ICBMs, part of which was entitled Questions of Disarmament, was announced May 30, 1972. The negotiations of 17 states of East and West Europe, Canada and the USA on the "mutual reduction of armed forces and armaments and the steps connected with this in Central Europe" (▷ MURFAAMCE) began in Vienna, Oct. 30, 1973. They were preceded by the Vienna preparatory consultations of 19 states, Jan. 31; June 28, 1973, which agreed that:

"The issue of the mutual reduction of armed forces and armaments as well as the steps connected with this in Central Europe will be examined during the course of negotiation. The general purpose of the negotiations is to lead to the creation of more stabilized relations and to strengthen peace and security in Europe; during the negotiations agreement should be reached on conducting them in such a way as to ensure the most effective and painstaking approach to the examination of the matters under discussion considering their complex nature; specific resolutions should be precisely formulated as to extent and time so that from every aspect and at every moment they would be in keeping with the principle of not being prejudicial to the security of any of the sides. It was also resolved that each question relating to the subject of negotiations can, during the course of negotiations, be placed under debate by any one of those states which will make the indispensable decisions. This does not violate the rights of all participants to submit and disseminate documents on the subject of the discussions."

These negotiations were continued in succeeding years parallel with the American-Soviet negotiations 1973–79 in Geneva (▷ SALT).

In Oct., 1977 the USSR at a meeting of the Belgrade signatories of the ▷ Helsinki Final Act proposed: the conclusion of a Treaty Renouncing the Right to be the First to Use Nuclear Weapons Against Each Other by the Participating States; suspending the provisions of the Warsaw Pact and Atlantic Pact, making it possible to expand the number of members of both military alliances; limiting the size of maneuvres to 50,000 – 60,000 troops, since military exercises on a larger scale "arouse suspicion and sometimes look like military demonstrations."

The X Special Session of the UN General Assembly, May 23–June 30, 1978 was devoted exclusively to the question of disarmament. It accepted the ▷ Disarmament UN Declaration and Program of Action. In 1979 the UN General Assembly adopted resolutions on: nuclear disarmament, cessation of nuclear weapon tests, non-use of nuclear weapons, nuclear weapon-free zones, non-proliferation of nuclear weapons, prohibition of chemical weapons, prohibition of radiological weapons, prohibition of new weapons of mass destruction, prohibition of inhumane conventional weapons, reduction of military expenditures, disarmament and development, disarmament and international security, disarmament machinery, confidence building measures, Indian Ocean as a zone of Peace and declared the decade of the 1980s as the Second Disarmament Decade.

In 1979 the American Soviet SALT II Agreement was also concluded.

The UN General Assembly during the 1980 Session adopted a Declaration on the 1980's as the Second Disarmament Decade. The UN Institute for Disarmament Research was established in 1980 in Geneva.

A Soviet proposal on Feb. 3, 1982 for a two-third cut by 1990 in the US and Soviet arsenals of medium-range nuclear weapons deployed in Europe was rejected by the USA. The UN Second Special Session of the General Assembly devoted exclusively to disarmament problems was held in New York from June 7 to July 10, 1982. The Chinese People's Republic submitted to the Session, on June 21, 1982, a proposal that if the USA and USSR will reduce their nuclear arsenals by 50% China will be ready to join all the other nuclear states in reducing its arsenals in reasonable proportion. On Dec. 13, 1982, the UN General Assembly adopted a resolution calling upon all nuclear weapons states to agree to a freeze on nuclear weapons. On June 14, 1983 Sweden submitted to the UN Committee on Disarmament a draft treaty banning nuclear weapon test explosions in all environments. The situation in Europe was changed in 1983/84 by the NATO decision to install the Pershing II missiles in the FRG and other West European countries, followed by the Warsaw Pact member states decision on the deployment of SS 20 missiles on the territory of the GDR and Czechoslovakia. In 1984 the UN Conference on the peaceful uses of nuclear energy was postponed for 1986 because of disagreement on its agenda. In Feb. 1985 the UN Conference on Disarmament started talks in Geneva – on a world-wide ban of ▷ Chemical weapons, continued in 1986 and 1987. The unilateral reduction of Soviet forces in East Germany, Czechoslovakia and Hungary (50,000 troops and 5,000 tanks) took place in two stages: the first in April 1989 and the second in 1990.

TH. NIEMEYER, Handbuch des Abrüstungsproblems, 3. Bnd., Berlin, 1929; C. LOOSLI-USTERI, Geschichte der Konferenz für die Herabsetzung und die Begrenzug der Rüstungen, Zürich, 1940; Ch.W.HARRINGTON, The Problem of Disarmament in the UN, Geneva, 1950; Historical Survey of the Activities of the League of Nations 1920–1937, UN Doc. A/AC 50/2, 1951; H. VOLLE, Probleme der internationaler Abrüstung. Eine Darstellung der Bemühungen der Vereinten Nationen 1945–1955. Dokumente und Berichte des Europa-Archiv, Frankfurt am M., 1956; Y. COLLARD, Le Désarmement. Étude et Bibliographie sur les Efforts des Nations Unies, La Haye, 1958; B. DEXTER, The Years of Opportunity. The League of Nations 1920–26, New York, 1967; UNESCO Répertoire internationale des institutions specialisées dans les recherches sur la paix et le désarmement, Paris, 1967; Arms Control and Disarmament Agency; Documents on Disarmament, Washington, DC 1968; The United Nations and Disarmament, 1945–1965, New York, 1968; V.M. JAITSMAN, SSSR i problema razoruzheniya 1945–1959.

Istoriia mezhdunarodnyj peregovorov, Moskva, 1970; E. FORNDRANE, *Probleme der internationaler Abrüstung, Die internationale Bemühungen und kooperative Rüstungssteuerung 1962–1968*, Frankfurt am M., 1970; SIPRI, *Yearbooks of World Armaments and Disarmament 1961–1984; Disarmament 1945–70*, UN, New York, 1970; *US Arms Control and Disarmament Agency*, Washington, DC, 1970; A. GARCIA ROBLES, "Mesures de désarmement dans les zones particulieres: Le Traité visant l'interdiction des armes nucleaires en Amérique Latine", in: *Recueil des Cours*, Vol. 1/1971; O.W. BOGDANOV, *Razoruzhenie-garantiya mira. Mezhdunarodno-pravovye problemy*, Moskva, 1972; SIPRI, *Strategic Arms Limitation*, Stockholm, 1972, 2 Vols.; SIPRI, *The Implementation of International Disarmament Agreements*, Stockholm, 1973; *Disarmament: A Select Bibliography 1969–1972*, UN New York, 1973; *Disarmament and Development*, UN New York, 1973; *Report of the Ad Hoc Committee on the World Disarmament Conference*, UN New York, 1975; *UN Chronicle*, July, 1978, p. 134; J. MARSTENSON, "A Review of Progress in Disarmament: 1975–1980", in: *IAEA Bulletin*, August, 1980, pp. 87–90; *UN Chronicle*, June, 1982, p. 49 and September, 1982, p. 3; J.H. BARSON, I. RYNKICHI, *Arms Control. A New Approach to International Security*, Cambridge Mass., 1983; "Disarmament: Four New Studies", in: *UN Chronicle*, 1985, No 1, pp. 39–42; *The United Nations and Disarmament: 1945–1985*, New York, 1985; *The United Nations Disarmament Yearbook*, New York, 1985 (issued since 1976 irregularly); *Disarmament: A Periodic Review by the United Nations*, New York, 1986 (issued irregularly since 1978).

DISARMAMENT AND DEVELOPMENT. The UN International Conference on the Relationship between Disarmament and Development, held in New York from Aug. 24 to Sept. 11, 1987, adopted by consensus its Final Document, which in its preamble describes disarmament and development as two of the most urgent challenges facing the contemporary World, as "two pillars" on which enduring international peace and security can be built. The conference, at which delegations of 120 governments were present was boycotted by the USA as "an additional forum for Soviet propaganda".
See also ▷ Perez de Cuellar Triangular Doctrine, 1987.

UN Chronicle, November 1987; KEESING's *Record of World Events*, May 1988. .

DISARMAMENT CAMPAIGN, WORLD, f. 1980, London. Reg. with the UIA; an international organization to encourage governments to end the arms race.

The Europa Yearbook 1988. A World Survey, Vol. I, London, 1988.

DISARMAMENT DECLARATION OF THE UN, 1980. The UN General Assembly adopted on Dec. 3, 1980, without vote, the following declaration:

"Declaration of the 1980s as the Second Disarmament Decade
I. General
(1) In proclaiming the decade of the 1970s as the first United Nations Disarmament Decade, the General Assembly, in its resolution 2602E/XXIV/ of 16 December 1969, enumerated its objectives as follows:
(a) All Governments should intensify without delay their concerted and concentrated efforts for effective measures relating to the cessation of the nuclear arms race at an early date and to nuclear disarmament and the elimination of other weapons of mass destruction, and for a treaty on general and complete disarmament under strict and effective international control;
(b) Consideration should be given to channelling a substantial part of the resources freed by measures in the field of disarmament to promote the economic development of developing countries and, in particular, their scientific and technological progress.
(2) Although these objectives were reiterated by the General Assembly in later sessions, the first Disarmament Decade ended without their accomplishment. While it is true that some limited agreements were reached, effective measures relating to the cessation of the nuclear arms race at an early date and to nuclear disarmament have continued to elude man's grasp. Furthermore, no progress has been made in channelling for the purpose of economic and social development any amount of the enormous resources which are wasted on the unproductive arms race.
(3) Through the Final Document of the Tenth Special Session of the General Assembly, contained in resolution S-10/2 of 30 June 1978, which was adopted by consensus, the Assembly, after expressing its conviction that disarmament and arms limitation, particularly in the nuclear field, were essential for the prevention of the danger of nuclear war, for the strengthening of international peace and security and for the economic and social advancement of all peoples, laid down a Programme of Action enumerating the specific measures of disarmament which should be implemented over the next few years.
(4) In spite of the positive and encouraging outcome of the special session devoted to disarmament, the decade of the 1980s has started with ominous signs of deterioration in the international situation. International peace and security are threatened by the use or threat of use of force against the sovereignty, national independence and territorial integrity of States, by military intervention and occupation, hegemonism, interference in the internal affairs of States, the denial of the right of self-determination of peoples and nations under colonial and alien domination, and by the further escalation of the arms race and efforts to achieve military superiority. It is clear that, if the emerging trend continues and meaningful efforts are not made to check and reverse it, international tensions will be further exacerbated and the danger of war will be greater than foreseen at the time of the special session on disarmament. In this connexion, it is pertinent to recall that in the Final Document the General Assembly emphasized that, on the one hand, the arms race in all its aspects runs counter to efforts to achieve further relaxation of international tension to establish a viable system of international peace and security and, on the other, that peace and security must be based on strict respect for the principles of the Charter of the United Nations. It is ironic that, while intensive discussions are under way in various forums on global economic problems and on the depletion of resources available for coping with present international economic problems, military expenditures by major military Powers are reaching ever higher levels, involving the greater diversion of resources that could have helped to promote the well-being of all peoples.
(5) The close relationship between disarmament and development was also underscored in the Final Document, which stated that the resources released as a result of the implementation of disarmament measures should be devoted to the economic and social development of all nations and contribute to the bridging of the economic gap between developed and developing countries. It is, therefore, only appropriate that, simultaneously with the proclamation of the Third United Nations Development Decade and the launching of the global round of negotiations, the 1980s should be declared as the Second Disarmament Decade.
II. Goals and principles
(6) The goals of the Second Disarmament Decade should be conceived in the context of the ultimate objective of the efforts of States in the disarmament process, which is general and complete disarmament under effective international control, as elaborated in the Final Document.
(7) Consistent with this overall objective, the goals of the Second Disarmament Decade should be the following:
(a) Halting and reversing the arms race, particularly the nuclear arms race;
(b) Concluding and implementing effective agreements on disarmament, particularly nuclear disarmament, which will contribute significantly to the achievement of general and complete disarmament under effective international control;
(c) Developing on an equitable basis the limited results obtained in the field of disarmament in the 1970s in accordance with the provisions of the Final Document;
(d) Strengthening international peace and security in accordance with the Charter of the United Nations;
(e) Making available a substantial part of the resources released by disarmament measures to promote the attainment of the objectives of the Third United Nations Development Decade and, in particular, the economic and social development of developing countries, so as to accelerate the progress towards the new international economic order.
(8) The disarmament process and the activities during the Second Disarmament Decade should be in accordance with the fundamental principles enshrined in the Final Document and should be carried out in such a balanced and equitable manner as to ensure the right of each State to security through the adoption of appropriate measures, taking into account the importance of nuclear disarmament and conventional disarmament, the special responsibility of the States of regional situations and the necessity for adequate measures of verification. At each stage, the objective should be undiminished security at the lowest possible level of armaments and military forces.
(9) Progress in disarmament should be accompanied by the strengthening of the peace-making and peace-keeping functions of the United Nations in accordance with the Charter.
III. Activities
A. General.
(10) The decade of the 1980s should witness renewed intensification by all Governments and the United Nations of their efforts to reach agreement and to implement effective measures that will lead to discernible progress towards the goal of general and complete disarmament under effective international control. In this connexion, special attention should be focused on certain identifiable elements in the Programme of Action as adopted by the General Assembly at its tenth special session which should, as minimum, be accomplished during the Second Disarmament Decade both through negotiations in the multilateral negotiating forum, the Committee on Disarmament, and in other appropriate forums. Adequate methods and procedures of verification should be considered in the context of international disarmament negotiations.
B. Comprehensive programme of disarmament
(11) Having been recognized as an important element in an international disarmament strategy, the comprehensive programme of disarmament should be elaborated with the utmost urgency. The Committee on Disarmament should expedite its work on the elaboration of the programme with a view to its adoption no later than at the second special session of the General Assembly devoted to disarmament, scheduled for 1982.
C. Priorities
(12) The accomplishment of those specific measures of disarmament which have been identified in the Final Document as worthy of priority negotiations by the multilateral negotiating organ would create a very favourable international climate for the second special session of the General Assembly devoted to disarmament. All efforts should be exerted, therefore, by the Committee on Disarmament urgently to negotiate with a view to reaching agreement, and to submit agreed texts where possible before the second special session devoted to disarmament on:
(a) a comprehensive nuclear-test-ban treaty;
(b) A treaty on the prohibition of the development, production and stockpiling of all chemical weapons and their destruction;
(c) A treaty on the prohibition of the development, production and use of radiological weapons;
(d) Effective international arrangements to assure non-nuclear-weapon States against the use or threat of use of nuclear weapons, taking into account all proposals and suggestions that have been made in this regard.
(13) The same priority should be given to the following measures which are dealt with outside the Committee on Disarmament:
(a) Ratification of the Treaty on the Limitation of Strategic Offensive Arms (SALT II) and commencement of negotiations for a SALT III agreement;
(b) Ratification of Additional Protocol I of the Treaty for the Prohibition of Nuclear Weapons in Latin America (Treaty of Tlatelolco);
(c) Signature and ratification of the agreement negotiated by the United Nations Conference on Prohibitions or Restrictions of Use of Certain Conventional Weapons Which May Be Deemed to Be Excessively Injurious or to Have Indiscriminate Effects;

(d) Achievement of an agreement on mutual reduction of armed forces and armaments and associated measures in central Europe;

(e) Negotiations on effective confidence-building measures and disarmament measures in Europe among the States participating in the Conference on Security and Cooperation in Europe, taking into account initiatives and proposals to this effect;

(f) Achievement of a more stable situation in Europe at a lower level of military potential on the basis of approximate equality and parity by agreement on appropriate mutual reduction and limitation of armaments and armed forces in accordance with paragraph 82 of the Final Document, which would contribute to the strengthening of security in Europe and constitute a significant step towards enhancing international peace and security.

(14) Other priority measures that should be pursued as rapidly as possible during the Second Disarmament Decade include:

(a) Significant progress towards the achievement of nuclear disarmament, which will require urgent negotiation of agreements at appropriate stages and with adequate measures of verification satisfactory to the States concerned for:

(i) Cessation of the qualitative improvement and development of nuclear-weapon systems;

(ii) Cessation of the production of all types of nuclear weapons and their means of delivery, and of the production of fissionable material for weapons purposes;

(iii) A comprehensive, phased programme with agreed time-frames, whenever feasible, for progressive and balanced reduction of stockpiles of nuclear weapons and their means of delivery, leading to their ultimate and complete elimination at the earliest possible time;

(b) Prevention of the emergence of new types of weapons of mass destruction and new systems of such weapons;

(c) Further strategic arms limitation negotiations between the two parties, leading to agreed significant reductions of, and qualitative limitations on, strategic arms. These should constitute an important step in the direction of nuclear disarmament and, ultimately, of the establishment of a world free of such weapons;

(d) Further steps to develop an international consensus to prevent the proliferation of nuclear weapons in accordance with the provisions of paragraphs 65 to 71 of the Final Document;

(e) Strengthening of the existing nuclear-weapon-free zone and establishment of other nuclear-weapon-free zones in accordance with the relevant paragraphs of the Final Document;

(f) Establishment of zones of peace in accordance with the relevant provisions of the Final Document;

(g) Measures to secure the avoidance of the use of nuclear weapons, the prevention of nuclear war and related objectives, where possible through international agreement, bearing in mind various proposals designed to secure these objectives and in accordance with paragraphs 57 and 58 of the Final Document, and thereby to ensure that the survival of mankind is not endangered;

(h) Further steps to prohibit military or any other hostile use of environmental modification techniques;

(i) Multilateral regional and bilateral measures on the limitation and reduction of conventional weapons and armed forces, in accordance with the relevant provisions of the Final Document;

(j) Reduction of military expenditures;

(k) Confidence-building measures, taking into account the particular conditions and requirements of different regions, with a view to strengthening the security of States.

D. Disarmament and development

(15) Peace and development are indivisible. During the Second Disarmament Decade, utmost efforts should be made towards the implementation of the specific measures whereby disarmament will contribute effectively to economic and social development and thus facilitate the full and early realization of the new international economic order. To this end, renewed efforts should be made to reach agreement on the reduction of military expenditures and the reallocation of resources from military purposes to economic and social development, especially for the benefit of developing countries.

(16) Efforts should also be made to strengthen international co-operation for the promotion of the transfer and utilization of nuclear technology for economic and social development, especially in the developing countries, taking into account the provisions of all relevant paragraphs of the Final Document, in particular to ensure the success of the United Nations Conference for the Promotion of International Co-operation in the Peaceful Uses of Nuclear Energy, to be convened in principle by 1983, as decided upon in General Assembly resolution 34/63 of 29 November 1979, as well as other promotional activities in this field in the United Nations system, including those within the framework of the International Atomic Energy Agency.

E. Disarmament and international security

(17) An essential condition for progress in the field of disarmament is the preservation and strengthening of international peace and security and the promotion of confidence among States. Nuclear weapons pose the greatest danger to mankind and to the survival of civilization. It is essential to halt and reverse the nuclear arms race in all its aspects in order to avert the danger of war involving nuclear weapons. The ultimate goal in this context is the complete elimination of nuclear weapons. Significant progress in nuclear disarmament would be facilitated both by parallel political and international legal measures to strengthen the security of States and by progress in the limitation and reduction of armed forces and conventional armaments of the nuclear-weapon States and other States in the regions concerned.

(18) All States Members of the United Nations have, in the Final Document, reaffirmed their full commitment to the purposes of the Charter of the United Nations and their obligation strictly to observe its principles as well as other relevant and generally accepted principles of international law relating to the maintenance of international peace and security. Disarmament, relaxation of international tension, respect for the right to self-determination and national independence, the right to self-determination and national independence, sovereignty and territorial integrity of States, the peaceful settlement of disputes in accordance with the Charter and the strengthening of international peace and security are directly related to each other. Progress in any of these spheres has a beneficial effect on all of them; in turn, failure in one sphere has negative effects on others. In the decade of the 1980s, all Governments. In particular the most advanced military Powers, should therefore take such steps as will contribute to the widening of trust among nations of the world as well as in the various regions. This implies a commitment on the part of all States to avoid actions likely to increase tension or create new areas of threats to international peace and security and, in their relationship with other countries, strictly to respect the sovereignty and territorial integrity of States, and the right of peoples under colonial or foreign domination to self-determination and national independence.

F. Public awareness

(19) As stated in paragraph 15 of the Final Document, it is essential that not only Governments but also the peoples of the world recognize and understand the dangers in the present world armaments situation, so that world public opinion will be mobilized on behalf of peace and disarmament. This will be of great importance to the strengthening of international peace and security, the just and peaceful resolution of disputes and conflicts and effective disarmament.

(20) In the course of the decade of the 1980s, therefore, governmental and non-governmental information organs of Member States and those of the United Nations and the specialized agencies, as well as non-governmental organizations, should, as appropriate, undertake further programmes of information relating to the danger of the armaments race as well as to disarmament efforts and negotiations and their results, particularly by means of annual activities conducted in connexion with Disarmament Week. These actions should constitute a large-scale programme further to alert world opinion to the danger of war in general and of nuclear war in particular. In keeping with its central role and primary responsibility in the sphere of disarmament, the United Nations, in particular its Centre for Disarmament, should intensify and co-ordinate its programme of publications, audio-visual materials, co-operation with non-governmental organizations and

relations with the media. Among its activities, the United Nations should also, in the course of the Second Disarmament Decade, sponsor seminars in the different regions of the world at which issues relating to world disarmament, in general, and to the particular region, especially, will be extensively discussed.

G. Studies

(21) As part of the process of facilitating the consideration of issues in the field of disarmament, studies on specific questions should be undertaken on the decision of the General Assembly, when necessary for preparing the ground for negotiations or reaching agreement. Also, studies pursued under the auspices of the United Nations, in particular by the United Nations Institute for Disarmament Research established by Assembly resolution 34/83M of 11 December 1979 within the framework of the United Nations Institute for Training and Research, could bring a useful contribution to the knowledge and exploration of disarmament problems, especially in the long term.

H. Implementation, review and appraisal

(22) In the accomplishment of the activities earmarked for the Second Disarmament Decade, all Governments, particularly the most advanced military Powers, should make an effective contribution. The United Nations should continue to play a central role. The Committee on Disarmament should fully discharge its responsibility as the single multilateral disarmament negotiating body. The General Assembly should, at its annual sessions and, in particular, at its second special session devoted to disarmament to be held in 1982, make an effective contribution to the pursuit of the goals of disarmament.

(23) It is pertinent also to recall that paragraphs 121 and 122 of the Final Document stated:

(a) That bilateral and regional disarmament negotiations may also play an important role and could facilitate the negotiation of multilateral agreements in the field of disarmament;

(b) That at the earliest appropriate time, a world disarmament conference should be convened with universal participation and with adequate preparation.

(24) In order to ensure a co-ordinated approach and to consider the implementation of the Declaration of the 1980s as the Second Disarmament Decade, this question should be included in the agenda of the second special session of the General Assembly devoted to disarmament, envisaged for 1982.

(25) In addition, the General Assembly will undertake at its fortieth session, in 1985, a review and appraisal, through the Disarmament Commission, of progress in the implementation of the measures identified in the present Declaration."

The UN Institute for Disarmament Research was established in 1980 in Geneva.

Yearbook of the United Nations 1980, New York, 1983, pp. 101–104.

DISARMAMENT NEGOTATIONS PRINCIPLES, 1961. A statement containing agreed principles as a basis for multilateral negotiations on disarmament was issued jointly by the USSR and the United States on 20 September 1961 for circulation to all United Nations Members.

This statement followed an exchange of views between the representatives of the two Governments on questions relating to disarmament and to the resumption of negotiations in an appropriate body, the composition of which was to be decided on. The exchange of views took place at meetings held in Washington, Moscow and New York–in June, July and September 1961–in accordance with statements made by the two Governments in the General Assembly's First Committee on March 30, 1961 and in compliance with an Assembly Res. 1617/XV of April 21, 1961.

In their joint statement, the USSR and the United States recommended the following principles:

(1) The goal of negotiations is to achieve agreement on a programme which will ensure that (a) disarmament is general and complete and war is no longer an instrument for settling international problems and (b) such disarmament is accompanied by the establishment of reliable procedures for the peaceful settlement of dis-

putes and effective arrangements for the maintenance of peace in accordance with the principles of the United Nations Charter.
(2) The programme for general and complete disarmament shall ensure that: States will have at their disposal only those non-nuclear armaments, forces, facilities, and establishments as are agreed to be necessary to maintain internal order and protect the personal security of citizens; and that States shall support and provide agreed manpower for a United Nations peace force.
(3) To this end, the programme for general and complete disarmament shall contain the necessary provisions, with respect to the military establishment of every nation, for: (*a*) disbanding of armed forces, dismantling of military establishments, including bases, and cessation of the production of armaments as well as their liquidation or conversion to peaceful uses; (*b*) elimination of all stockpiles of nuclear, chemical, bacteriological and other weapons of mass destruction and cessation of the production of such weapons; (*c*) elimination of all means of delivery of weapons of mass destruction; (*d*) abolishment of the organization and institutions designed to organize the military effort of States, cessation of military training and closing of all military training institutions; and (*e*) discontinuance of military expenditures.
(4) The disarmament programme should be implemented in an agreed sequence, by stages, until it is completed with each measure and stage carried out within specified time-limits. Transition to a subsequent stage in the process of disarmament should take place upon a review of the implementation of measures included in the preceding stage and upon a decision that all such measures have been implemented and verified and that any additional verification arrangements required for measures in the next stage are, when appropriate, ready to operate.
(5) All measures of general and complete disarmament should be balanced so that at no stage of the implementation of the treaty could any State or group of States gain military advantage and so that security is ensured equally for all.
(6) All disarmament measures should be implemented from beginning to end under such strict and effective international control as would provide firm assurance that all parties are honouring their obligations. During and after the implementation of general and complete disarmament, the most thorough control should be exercised, the nature and extent of such control depending on the requirements for verification of the disarmament measures being carried out in each stage. To implement control over the inspection of disarmament, an International Disarmament Organization including all parties to the agreement should be created within the framework of the United Nations. This International Disarmament Organization and its inspectors should be assured unrestricted access without veto to all places as necessary for the purpose of effective verification.
(7) Progress in disarmament should be accompanied by measures to strengthen institutions for maintaining peace and the settlement of international disputes by peaceful means. During and after the implementation of the programme of general and complete disarmament, there should be taken, in accordance with the principles of the United Nations Charter, the necessary measures to maintain international peace and security, including the obligation of States to place at the disposal of the United Nations agreed manpower necessary for an international peace force to be equipped with agreed types of armaments. Arrangements for the use of this force should ensure that the United Nations can effectively deter or suppress any threat or use of arms in violation of the purposes and principles of the United Nations.
(8) States participating in the negotiations should seek to achieve and implement the widest possible agreement at the earliest possible date. Efforts should continue without interruption until agreement upon the total programme has been achieved, and efforts to ensure early agreement on and implementation of measures of disarmament should be undertaken without prejudicing progress on agreement on the total programme and in such a way that those measures would facilitate and form part of that programme.

On Sept. 20, 1961, John J. McCloy and V. A. Zorin, who had represented the United States and the USSR, respectively, in the exchange of views on disarmament, exchanged letters on the question of control. The document is also called the McCloy-Zorin Principles. Since 1961 this document is obligatory for all UN Members in all disarmament negotiations.

Yearbook of the United Nations 1961, New York, 1962, pp. 10–11.

DISARMAMENT UN DECLARATION AND PROGRAM OF ACTION, 1978. The General Assembly held its Tenth Special Session Devoted to Disarmament from May. 23–July 1, at the UN Headquarters. The Assembly adopted by concensus on June 30, a Final Document consisting of an Introduction, a Declaration, a Programme of Action, and recommendations concerning the international machinery for disarmament negotiations. The text of the Final Document reads:

"The General Assembly,
Alarmed by the threat to the very survival of mankind posed by the existence of nuclear weapons and the continuing arms race, and recalling the devastation inflicted by all wars,
Convinced that disarmament and arms limitation, particularly in the nuclear field, are essential for the prevention of the danger of nuclear war and the strengthening of international peace and security and for the economic and social advancement of all peoples, thus facilitating the achievement of the new international economic order,
Having resolved to lay the foundations of an international disarmament strategy which, through co-ordinated and persevering efforts in which the United Nations should play a more effective role, aims at general and complete disarmament under effective international control,
Adopts the following Final Document of this special session of the General Assembly devoted to disarmament:
I. Introduction
(1) Attainment of the objective of security, which is an inseparable element of peace, has always been one of the most profound aspirations of humanity. States have for a long time sought to maintain their security through the possession of arms. Admittedly, their survival has, in certain cases, effectively depended on whether they could count on appropriate means of defence. Yet the accumulation of weapons, particularly nuclear weapons, today constitutes much more a threat than a protection for the future of mankind. The times has therefore come to put an end to this situation, to abandon the use of force in international relations and to seek security in disarmament, that is to say, through a gradual but effective process beginning with a reduction in the present level of armaments. The ending of the arms race and the achievement of real disarmament are tasks of primary importance and urgency. To meet this historic challenge is in the political and economic interests of all the nations and peoples of the world as well as in the interests of ensuring their genuine security and peaceful future.
(2) Unless its avenues are closed the continued arms race means a growing threat to international peace and security and even to the very survival of mankind. The nuclear and conventional arms build-up threatens to stall the efforts aimed at reaching the goals of development, to become an obstacle on the road of achieving the new international economic order and to hinder the solution of other vital problems facing mankind.
(3) Dynamic development of detente, encompassing all spheres of international relations in all regions of the world, with the participation of all countries, would create conditions conducive to the efforts of States to end the arms race, which has engulfed the world, thus reducing the danger of war. Progress on detente and progress on disarmament mutually complement and strengthen each other.
(4) The Disarmament Decade solemnly declared in 1969 by the United Nations is coming to an end. Unfortunately, the objectives established on that occasion by the General Assembly appear to be as far away today as they were then, or even further because the arms race is not diminishing but increasing and outstrips by far the efforts to curb it. While it is true that some limited agreements have been reached, "effective measures relating to the cessation of the nuclear arms race at an early date to nuclear disarmament" continue to elude man's grasp. Yet the implementation of such measures is urgently required. There has not been either any real progress that might lead to the conclusion of a treaty on general and complete disarmament under effective international control. Furthermore, it has not been possible to free any amount, however modest, of the enormous resources, both material and human, that are wasted on the unproductive and spiralling arms race, and which should be made available for the purpose of economic and social development, especially since such a race "places a great burden on both the developing and the developed countries."
(5) The Members of the United Nations are fully aware of the conviction of their peoples, that the question of general and complete disarmament is of utmost importance and that peace, security and economic and social development are indivisible and have therefore recognized that the corresponding obligations and responsibilities are universal.
(6) Thus a powerful current of opinion has gradually formed, leading to the convening of what will go down in the annals of the United Nations as the first special session of the General Assembly devoted entirely to disarmament.
(7) The outcome of this special session, whose deliberations have to a large extent been facilitated by the five sessions of the Preparatory Committee which preceded it, is the present Final Document. This introduction serves as a preface to the document which comprises also the following three sections: a Declaration, a Programme of Action and recommendations concerning the international machinery for disarmament negotiations.
(8) While the final objective of the efforts of all States should continue to be general and complete disarmament under effective international control, the immediate goal is that of the elimination of the danger of a nuclear war and the implementation of measures to halt and reverse the arms race and clear the path to towards a lasting peace. Negotiations on the entire range of those issues should be based on the strict observance of the purposes and principles enshrined in the Charter of the United Nations in the field of disarmament and reflecting the vital interests of all the peoples of the world in this sphere. The aim of the Declaration is to review and assess the existing situation, outline the objectives and the priority tasks and set forth fundamental principles for disarmament negotiations.
(9) For disarmament, the aims and purposes of which the Declaration proclaims to become a reality it was essential to agree on a series of specific disarmament measures, selected by common accord as those on which there is a consensus to the effect that their subsequent realization in the short term appears to be feasible. There is also a need to prepare through agreed procedures a comprehensive disarmament programme. That programme, passing through all the necessary stages, should lead to general and complete disarmament under effective international control. Procedures for watching over the fulfilment of the obligations thus assumed had also to be agreed upon. That is the purpose of the Programme of Action.
(10) Although the decisive factor for achieving real measures of disarmament is the "political will" of States, and especially of those possessing nuclear weapons, a significant role can also be played by the effective functioning of an appropriate international machinery designed to deal with the problems of disarmament in its various aspects. Consequently, it would be necessary that the two kinds of organs required to that end, the deliberative and the negotiating organs, have the appropriate organization and procedures that would be most conducive to obtaining constructive results. The fourth and last section of the Final Document has been prepared with that end in view.
II. Declaration
(11) Mankind today is confronted with an unprecedented threat of self-extinction arising from the massive and competitive accumulation of the most destructive weapons ever produced. Existing arsenals of nuclear weapons alone are more than sufficient to destroy all life on earth. Failure of efforts to halt and reverse the arms race, in particular the nuclear arms race, increases the danger of the proliferation of nuclear weapons. Yet the arms race continues. Military budgets are constantly growing, with enormous consumption of human and

material resources. The increase in weapons, especially nuclear weapons, far from helping to strengthen international security, on the contrary weakens it. The vast stock-piles and tremendous build-up of arms and armed forces and the competition for qualitative refinement of weapons of all kinds to which scientific resources and technological advances are diverted, pose incalculable threats to peace. This situation both reflects and aggravates international tensions, sharpens conflicts, in various regions of the world, hinders the process of detente, exacerbates the differences between opposing military alliances, jeopardizes the security of all States, heightens the sense of insecurity among all States, including the non-nuclear weapon States, and increases the threat of nuclear war.

(12) The arms race, particularly in its nuclear aspect, runs counter to efforts to achieve further relaxation of international tension, to establish international relations based on peaceful coexistence and trust between all States, and to develop broad international co-operation and understanding. The arms race impedes the realization of the purposes, and is incompatible with the principles, of the Charter of the United Nations, especially respect for sovereignty, refraining from the threat or use of force against the territorial integrity or political independence of any State, peaceful settlement of disputes and non-intervention and non-interference in the internal affairs of States. It also adversely affects the rights of peoples freely to determine their systems of social and economic development and hinders the struggle for self-determination and the elimination of colonial rule, racial or foreign domination or occupation. Indeed, the massive accumulation or armaments and the acquisition of armaments technology by racist regimes, as well as their possible acquisition of nuclear weapons, present a challenging and increasingly dangerous obstacle to a world community faced with the urgent need to disarm. It is therefore, essential for purposes of disarmament to prevent any further acqusition of arms or arms technology by such regimes, especially through strict adherence by all States to relevant decisions of the Security Council.

(13) Enduring international peace and security cannot be built on the accumulation of weaponry by military alliances nor be sustained by a precarious balance of deterrence of doctrines of strategic superiority. Genuine and lasting peace can only be created through the effective implementation of the security system provided for in the Charter of the United Nations and the speedy and substantial reduction of arms and armed forces, by international agreement and mutual example leading ultimately to general and complete disarmament under effective international control. At the same time, the causes of the arms race and threats to peace must be reduced and to this end effective action should be taken to eliminate tensions and settle disputes by peaceful means.

(14) Since the process of disarmament affects the vital security interests of all States, they must all be actively concerned with the contribution to the measures of disarmament and arms limitations, which have an essential part to play in maintaining and strengthening international security. Therefore the role and responsibility of the United Nations in the sphere of disarmament, in accordance with its Charter, must be strengthened.

(15) It is essential that not only Governments but also the peoples of the world recognize and understand the dangers in the present situation. In order that an international conscience may develop and that world public opinion may exercise a positive influence, the United Nations should increase the dissemination of information on the armaments race and disarmament with the full co-operation of Member States.

(16) In a world of finite resources there is a close relationship between expenditure on armaments and economic and social development. Military expenditures are reaching ever higher levels, the highest percentage of which can be attributed to the nuclear weapon States and most of their allies, with prospects of further expansion and the danger of further increases in the expenditures of other countries. The hundreds of billions of dollars spent as annually on the manufacture or improvement of weapons are in sombre and dramatic contrast to the want and poverty in which two-thirds of the world's population live. This colossal waste of resources is even more serious in that it diverts to military purposes not only material but also technical and human resources which are urgently needed for development in all countries, particularly in the developing countries. Thus, the economic and social consequences of the arms race are so detrimental that its continuation is obviously incompatible with the implementation of the new international economic order based on justice, equity and co-operation. Consequently, resources released as a result of the implementation of disarmament measures should be used in a manner which will help to promote the well-being of all peoples and to improve the economic conditions of the developing countries.

(17) Disarmament has thus become an imperative and most urgent task facing the international community. No real progress has been made so far in the crucial field of the reduction of armaments. However, certain positive changes in international relations in some areas of the world provide some encouragement.

Agreements have been reached that have been important in limiting certain weapons or eliminating them altogether, as in the case of the Convention on the Prohibition of the Development, Production and Stockpiling of Bacteriological (Biological) and Toxin Weapons and on Their Destruction, and excluding particular areas from the arms race. The fact remains that these agreements relate only to measures of limited restraint while the arms race continues. These partial measures have done little to bring the world closer to the goal of general and complete disarmament. For more than a decade there have been no negotiations leading to a treaty on general and complete disarmament. The pressing need now is to translate into practical terms the provisions of this Final Document and to proceed along the road of binding and effective international agreements in the field of disarmament.

(18) Removing the threat of a world war – a nuclear war – is the most acute and urgent task of the present day. Mankind is confronted with a choice: we must halt the arms race and proceed to disarmament or face annihilation.

(19) The ultimate objective of the efforts of States in the disarmament process is general and complete disarmament under effective international control.

The principal goals of disarmament are to ensure the survival of mankind and to eliminate the danger of war, in particular nuclear war, to ensure that war is no longer an instrument for settling international disputes and that the use and the threat of force are eliminated from international life, as provided for in the Charter of the United Nations.

Progress towards this objective requires the conclusion and implementation of agreements on the cessation of the arms race and on genuine measures of disarmament taking into account the need of States to protect their security.

(20) Among such measures, effective measures of nuclear disarmament and the prevention of nuclear war have the highest priority. To this end, it is imperative to remove the threat of nuclear weapons, to halt and reverse the nuclear arms race until the total elimination of nuclear weapons and their delivery systems has been achieved, and to prevent the proliferation of nuclear weapons. At the same time, other measures designed to prevent the outbreak of nuclear war and to lessen the danger of the threat or use of nuclear weapons should be taken.

(21) Along with these, agreements or other effective measures should be adopted to prohibit or prevent the development, production or use of other weapons of mass destruction. In this context, an agreement on elimination of all chemical weapons should be concluded as a matter of high priority.

(22) Together with negotiations on nuclear disarmament measures, negotiations should be carried out on the balanced reduction of armed forces and of conventional armaments, based on the principle of undiminished security of the parties with a view to promoting or enhancing stability at a lower military level, taking into account the need of all States to protect their security. These negotiations should be conducted with particular emphasis on armed forces and conventional weapons of nuclear-weapon States and other militarily significant countries. There should also be negotiations on the limitation of international transfer of conventional weapons, based, in particular, on the same principle, and taking into account the inalienable right to self-determination and independence of peoples under colonial or foreign domination and the obligations of States to respect that right, in accordance with the Charter of the United Nations and the Declaration on Principles of International Law concerning Friendly Relations and Co-operation among States, as well as the need of recipient States to protec their security.

(23) Further international action should be taken to prohibit or restrict for humanitarian reasons the use of specific conventional weapons, including those which may be excessively injurious, cause unnecessary suffering or have indiscriminate effects.

(24) Collateral measures in both the nuclear and conventional fields, together with other measures specifically designed to build confidence, should be undertaken in order to contribute to the creation of favourable conditions for the adoption of additional disarmament measures and to further relaxation of international tension.

(25) Negotiations and measures in the field of disarmament shall be guided by the fundamental principles set forth below.

(26) All States Members of the United Nations reaffirm their full commitment to the purposes of the Charter of the United Nations and their obligation strictly to observe its principles as well as other relevant and generally accepted principles of international law relating to the maintenance of international peace and security.

They stress the special importance of refraining from the threat or use of force against the sovereignty, territorial integrity or political independence of any State, or against peoples under colonial or foreign domination seeking to exercise their right to self-determination and to achieve independence; non-intervention and non-interference in the internal affairs of other States; the inviolability of international frontiers; and the peaceful settlement of disputes, having regard to the inherent right of States to individual and collective self-defence in accordance with the Charter.

(27) In accordance with the Charter, the United Nations has a central role and primary responsibility in the sphere of disarmament. In order effectively to discharge this role and facilitate and encourage all measures in this field, the United Nations should be kept appropriately informed of all steps in this field, whether unilateral, bilateral, regional or multilateral, without prejudice to the progress of negotiations.

(28) All the peoples of the world have a vital interest in the success of disarmament negotiations. Consequently, all States have the duty to contribute to efforts in the field of disarmament. All States have the right to participate in disarmament negotiations. They have the right to participate on an equal footing in those multilateral disarmament negotiations which have a direct bearing on their national security. While disarmament is the responsibility of all States, the nuclear-weapon States have the primary responsibility for nuclear disarmament, and, together with other militarily significant States for halting and reversing the arms race. It is therefore important to secure their active participation.

(29) The adoption of disarmament measures should take place in such an equitable and balanced manner as to ensure the right of each State to security and that no individual State or group of States may obtain advantages over others at any stage. At each stage the objective should be undiminished security at the lowest possible level of armaments and military forces.

(30) An acceptable balance of mutual responsibilities and obligations for nuclear and non-nuclear-weapon States should be strictly observed.

(31) Disarmament and arms limitation agreements should provide for adequate measures of verification satisfactory to all parties concerned in order to create the necessary confidence and ensure that they are being observed by all parties. The form and modalities of the verification to be provided for in any specific agreement depend upon and should be determined by the purposes, scope and nature of the agreement. Agreements should provide for the participation of parties directly or through the United Nations system in the verification process. Where appropriate, a combination of several methods of verification as well as other compliances procedures should be employed.

(32) All States, and in particular nuclear weapon States, should consider various proposals designed to secure the avoidance of the use of nuclear weapons, and the prevention of nuclear war. In this context, while

noting the declarations made by nuclear-weapon States, effective arrangements, as appropriate, to assure non-nuclear-weapon States against the use or the threat of use of nuclear weapons could strengthen the security of those States and international peace and security.

(33) The establishment of nuclear-weapon-free-zones on the basis of agreements or arrangements freely arrived at among the States of the zone concerned, and the full compliance with those agreements or arrangements, thus ensuring that the zones are genuinely free from nuclear weapons, and respect for such zones by nuclear weapon States, constitute an important disarmament measure.

(34) Disarmament, relaxation of international tension, respect for the right to self-determination and national independence, the peaceful settlement of disputes in accordance with the Charter of the United Nations and the strengthening of international peace and security are directly related to each other. Progress in any of these spheres has a beneficial effect on all of them: in turn, failure in one sphere has negative effects on others.

(35) There is also a close relationship between disarmament and development. Progress in the former would help greatly to the realization of the latter. Therefore resources released as a result of the implementation of disarmament measures should be devoted to economic and social development of all nations and contribute to the bridging of the economic gap between developed and developing countries.

(36) Non-proliferation of nuclear weapons is a matter of universal concern. Measures of disarmament must be consistent with the inalienable right of all States, without discrimination, to develop, acquire and use nuclear technology, equipment and materials for the peaceful use of nuclear energy and to determine their peaceful nuclear programmes in accordance with their national priorities, needs and interests, bearing in mind the need to prevent the proliferation of nuclear weapons. International cooperation in the peaceful uses of nuclear energy should be conducted under agreed and appropriate international safeguards applied on a non-discriminatory basis.

(37) Significant progress in disarmament, including nuclear disarmament, would be facilitated by parallel measures to strengthen the security of States and to improve in general the international situation.

(38) Negotiations on partial measures of disarmament should be conducted concurrently with negotiations on more comprehensive measures and should be followed by negotiations leading to a treaty on general and complete disarmament under effective international control.

(39) Qualitative and quantitative disarmament measures are both important for a halting the arms race. Efforts to that end must include negotiations on the limitation and cessation of the qualitative improvement of armaments, especially weapons of mass destruction and the development of new means of warfare so that ultimately scientific and technological achievements may be used solely for peaceful purposes, also contribute to the attainment of that goal.

(40) Universality of disarmament agreements helps create confidence among States. When multilateral agreements in the field of disarmament are negotiated, every effort should be made to ensure that they are universally acceptable. The full compliance of all parties with the provisions contained in such agreements would also contribute to the attainment of that goal.

(41) In order to create favourable conditions for success in the disarmament process, all States should strictly abide by the provisions of the Charter of the United Nations, refrain from actions which might adversely affect efforts in the field of disarmament, and display a constructive approach to negotiations and the political will to reach agreements. There are certain negotiations on disarmament under way at different levels, the early and successful completion of which could contribute to limiting the arms race. Unilateral measures of arms limitation or reduction could also contribute to the attainment of that goal.

(42) Since prompt measures should be taken in order to halt and reverse the arms race, Member States hereby declare that they will respect the above-stated objectives and principles and make every effort faithfully to carry out the Programme of Action set forth in Section III below.

III. Programme of Action

(43) Progress towards the goal of general and complete disarmament can be achieved through the implementation of a programme of action on disarmament, in accordance with the goals and principles established in the Declaration on disarmament. The present Programme of Action contains priorities and measures in the field of disarmament that States should undertake as a matter of urgency with a view to halting and reversing the arms race and to giving the necessary impetus to efforts designed to achieve genuine disarmament leading to general and complete disarmament under effective international control.

(44) The present Programme of Action enumerates the specific measures of disarmament which should be implemented over the next few years, as well as other measures and studies to prepare the way for future negotiations and for progress toward general and complete disarmament.

(45) Priorities in disarmament negotiations shall be: nuclear weapons; other weapons of mass destruction, including chemical weapons; conventional weapons, including any which may be deemed to be excessively injurious or to have indiscriminate effects; and reduction of armed forces.

(46) Nothing should preclude States from conducting negotiations on all priority items concurrently.

(47) Nuclear weapons pose the greatest danger to mankind and to the survival of civilization. It is essential to halt and reverse the nuclear arms race in all its aspects in order to avert the danger of war involving nuclear weapons. The ultimate goal in this context is the complete elimination of nuclear weapons.

(48) In the task of achieving the goals of nuclear disarmament, all the nuclear-weapon States, in particular those among them which possess the most important nuclear arsenals, bear a special responsibility.

(49) The process of nuclear disarmament should be carried out in such a way, and requires measures to ensure, that the security of all States is guaranteed at progressively lower levels of nuclear armaments, taking into account the relative qualitative and quantitative importance of the existing arsenals of the nuclear-weapon States and other States concerned.

(50) The achievement of nuclear disarmament will require urgent negotiation of agreements at appropriate stages and with adequate measures of verification satisfactory to the States concerned for:
– cessation of the qualitative improvement and development of nuclear-weapon systems;
– cessation of the production of all types of nuclear weapons and their means of delivery, and the production of fissionable material for weapons purposes;
– a comprehensive phased programme with agreed time-frames, whenever feasible, for progressive and balanced reduction of stockpiles of nuclear weapons and their means of delivery, leading to their ultimate and complete elimination at the earliest possible time.
Consideration can be given in the course of the negotiations to mutual and agreed limitation or prohibition, without prejudice to the security of any State, of any types of nuclear armaments.

(51) The cessation of nuclear-weapon testing by all States within the framework of an effective nuclear disarmament process would be in the interest of mankind. It would make a significant contribution to the above aim of ending the qualitative improvement of nuclear weapons and the development of new types of such weapons and of preventing the proliferation of nuclear weapons. In this context the negotiations now in progress on a "treaty prohibiting nuclear-weapon tests, and a protocol covering nuclear explosions for peaceful purposes, which would be an integral part of the treaty," should be concluded urgently and the result submitted for full consideration by the multilateral negotiating body with a view to the submission of a draft treaty to the General Assembly at the earliest possible date. All efforts should be made by the negotiating parties to achieve an agreement which, following General Assembly endorsement, could attract the widest possible adherence. In this context, various views were expressed by non-nuclear-weapon States that, pending the conclusion of this treaty, the world community would be encouraged if all the nuclear-weapon States refrained from testing nuclear

weapons. In this connection, some nuclear-weapon States expressed different views.

(52) The Union of Soviet Socialist Republics and the United States of America should conclude at the earliest possible date the agreement they have been pursuing for several years in the second series of the strategic arms limitation talks (SALT II). They are invited to transmit in good time the text of the agreement to the General Assembly. It should be followed promptly by further strategic arms limitation negotiations between the two parties, leading to agreed significant reductions of, and qualitative limitations on, strategic arms. It should constitute an important step in the direction of nuclear disarmament and ultimately of establishment of a world free of such weapons.

(53) The process of nuclear disarmament described in the paragraph on this subject should be expedited by the urgent and vigorous pursuit to a successful conclusion of ongoing negotiations and the urgent initiation of further negotiations among the nuclear-weapon States.

(54) Significant progress in nuclear disarmament would be facilitated both by parallel political or international legal measures to strengthen the security of States and by progress in the limitation and reduction of armed forces and conventional armaments of the nuclear-weapon States and other States in the regions concerned.

(55) Real progress in the field of nuclear disarmament could create an atmosphere conducive to progress in conventional disarmament on a world-wide basis.

(56) The most effective guarantee against the danger of nuclear weapons is nuclear disarmament and the complete elimination of nuclear weapons.

(57) Pending the achievement of this goal, for which negotiations should be vigorously pursued, and bearing in mind the devastating results which nuclear war would have on belligerents and non-belligerents alike, the nuclear-weapon States have special responsibilities to undertake measures aimed at preventing the outbreak of nuclear war, and of the use of force in international relations, subject to the provisions of the Charter of the United Nations, including the use of nuclear weapons.

(58) In this context, all States and in particular nuclear-weapon States should consider as soon as possible various proposals designed to secure the avoidance of the use of nuclear weapons, the prevention of nuclear war and related objectives, where possible through international agreement and thereby ensure that the survival of mankind is not endangered. All States should actively participate in efforts to bring about conditions in international relations among States in which a code of peaceful conduct of nations in international affairs could be agreed and which would preclude the use or threat of use of nuclear weapons.

(59) In the same context, the nuclear weapon States are called upon to take steps to assure the non-nuclear-weapon-States against the use or threat of use of nuclear weapons. The General Assembly notes the declarations made by the nuclear-weapon States and urges them to pursue efforts to conclude as appropriate effective arrangements to assure non-nuclear-weapon States against the use or threat of use of nuclear weapons.

(60) The establishment of nuclear-weapon-free zones on the basis of arrangements freely arrived at among the States of the region concerned, constitutes an important disarmament measure.

(61) The process of establishing such zones in different parts of the world should be encouraged with the ultimate objective of achieving a world entirely free of nuclear weapons. In the process of establishing such zones the characteristics of each region should be taken into account. The States participating in such zones should undertake to comply full with all the objectives, purposes and principles of the agreements or arrangements establishing the zones, thus ensuring that they are genuinely free from nuclear weapons.

(62) With respect to such zones, the nuclear-weapon States in turn are called upon to give undertakings, the modalities of which are to be negotiated with the competent authority of each zone, in particular:
(a) to respect strictly the status of the nuclear-weapon-free zone;
(b) to refrain from the use or threat of use of nuclear weapons against the States of the zone.

(63) In the light of existing conditions, and without prejudices to other measures which may be considered in other regions, the following measures are especially desirable:
(a) Adoption by the States concerned of all relevant measures to ensure the full application of the Treaty for the Prohibition of Nuclear Weapons in Latin America (Treaty of Tlatelolco), taking into account the views expressed at the special session of the adherence to it.
(b) Signature and ratification of the Additional Protocols of the Treaty for the Prohibition of Nuclear Weapons in Latin America (Treaty of Tlatelolco) by the States entitled to become parties to those instruments which have not yet done so;
(c) In Africa, where the Organization of African Unity has affirmed a decision for the denuclearization of the region, the Security Council shall take appropriate effective steps whenever necessary to prevent the frustration of this objective;
(d) The serious consideration of the practical and urgent steps, as described in the paragraphs above, required for the implementation of the proposal to establish a nuclear-weapon-free zone in the Middle East in accordance with the relevant General Assembly resolutions where all parties directly concerned have expressed their support for the concept and where the danger of nuclear-weapon proliferation exists. The establishment of a nuclear-weapon-free zone in the Middle East would greatly enhance international peace and security. Pending the establishment of such a zone in the region, States of the region should solemnly declare that they will refrain on a reciprocal basis from producing, acquiring, or in any other way, possessing nuclear weapons and nuclear explosive devices, and from permitting the stationing of nuclear weapons on their territory by any third party and agree to place all their nuclear activities under International Atomic Energy Agency safeguards. Consideration should be given to a Security Council role in advancing the establishment of a Middle East nuclear-weapon-free zone;
(e) All States in the region of South Asia have expressed their determination of keeping their countries free of nuclear weapons. No action should be taken by them which might deviate from that objective. In this context, the question of establishing a nuclear-weapon-free zone in South Asia has been dealt with in several resolutions of the General Assembly which is keeping the subject under consideration.
(64) The establishment of zones of peace in various regions of the world, under appropriate conditions, to be clearly defined and determined freely by the States concerned in the zone and the principles of the Charter of the United Nations, and in conformity with international law, can contribute to strengthening the security of States within such zones and to international peace and security as a whole.
In this regard, the General Assembly notes the proposals for the establishment of zones of peace, inter alia in:
(a) South-East Asia where States in the region have expressed interest in the establishment of such a zone, in conformity with their views;
(b) Indian Ocean, taking into account the deliberations of the General Assembly and its relevant resolutions and the need to ensure the maintenance of peace and security in the region.
(65) It is imperative as an integral part of the effort to halt and reverse the arms race, to prevent the proliferation of nuclear weapons. The goal of nuclear non-proliferation is on the one hand to prevent the emergence of any additional nuclear-weapon States beside the existing five nuclear-weapon States, and on the other progressively to reduce and eventually eliminate nuclear weapons altogether. This involves obligations and responsibilities on the part of both nuclear-weapon States and non-nuclear weapon States, the former undertaking to stop the nuclear-arms race and to achieve disarmament by urgent application of measures outlined in the relevant paragraphs of this Document, and all States undertaking to prevent the spread of nuclear weapons.
(66) Effective measures can and should be taken at the national level and through international agreements to minimize the danger of the proliferation of nuclear weapons without jeopardizing energy supplies or the development of nuclear energy for peaceful purposes. Therefore, the nuclear-weapon States and the non-nuclear-weapon States should take joint further steps to develop an international consensus of ways and means, on a universal and non-discriminatory basis, to prevent the proliferation of nuclear weapons.
(67) Full implementation of all the provisions of existing instruments on non-proliferation, such as the Treaty on the Non-Proliferation of Nuclear Weapons and/or the Treaty for the Prohibition of Nuclear Weapons in Latin America (Treaty of Tlatelolco) by States parties to those instruments will be an important contribution to this end. Adherence to such instruments has increased in recent years and the hope has been expressed by the parties that this trend might continue.
(68) Non-proliferation measures should not jeopardize the full exercise of the inalienable rights of all States to apply and develop their programmes for the peaceful uses of nuclear energy for economic and social development in conformity with their priorities, interests and needs. All States should also have access to, and be free to acquire technology, equipment and materials for peaceful uses of nuclear energy, taking into account the particular needs of the developing countries. International co-operation in this field should be under agreed and appropriate international safeguards applied through the International Atomic Energy Agency on a non-discriminatory basis in order to prevent effectively proliferation of nuclear weapons.
(69) Each country's choices and decisions in the field of the peaceful uses of nuclear energy should be respected without jeopardizing their respective fuel cycle policies or international co-operation, agreements, and contracts for the peaceful use of nuclear energy provided that agreed safeguard measures mentioned above are applied.
(70) In accordance with the principles and provisions of Resolution 32/50, international co-operation for the promotion of the transfer and utilization of nuclear technology for economic and social development, especially in the developing countries, should be strengthened.
(71) Efforts should be made to conclude the work of the International Nuclear Fuel Cycle Evaluation strictly in accordance with the objectives set out in the final communiqué of its Organizing Conference.
(72) All States should adhere to the Protocol for the Prohibition of the Use in War of Asphyxiating, Poisonous or Other Gases, and of Bacteriological Methods of Warfare.
(73) All States which have not yet done so should consider adhering to the Convention on the Prohibition of the Development, Production and Stockpiling of Bacteriological (Biological) and Toxin Weapons and on Their Destruction.
(74) States should also consider the possibility of adhering to multilateral agreements concluded so far in the disarmament field which are mentioned below in this section.
(75) The complete and effective prohibition of the development, production and stockpiling of all chemical weapons and their destruction represent one of the most urgent measures of disarmament. Consequently, conclusion of a convention to this end, on which negotiations have been going on for several years, is one of the most urgent tasks of multi-lateral negotiations. After its conclusion, all States should contribute to ensuring the broadest possible application of the convention though its early signature and ratification.
(76) A convention should be concluded prohibiting the development, production, stockpiling and use of radiological weapons.
(77) In order to help prevent a qualitative arms race and so that scientific and technological achievements may ultimately be used solely for peaceful purposes, effective measures should be taken to avoid the danger and prevent the emergence of new types of weapons of mass destruction based on new scientific principles and achievements. Efforts should be appropriately pursued aiming at the prohibition of such new types and new systems of weapons of mass destruction. Specific agreements could be concluded on particular types of new weapons of mass destruction which may be identified. This question should be kept under continuing review.
(78) The Committee on Disarmament should keep under review the need for a further prohibition of military or any other hostile use of environmental modification techniques in order to eliminate the dangers to mankind from such use.
(79) In order to promote the peaceful use of and to avoid an arms race on the sea bed and the ocean floor and the sub-soil thereof, the Committee on Disarmament is requested – in consultation with the States parties to the Treaty on the Prohibition of the Emplacement of Nuclear Weapons and Other Weapons of Mass Destruction on the Sea-Bed and the Ocean Floor and the Subsoil Thereof, and taking into account the proposals made during the 1977 Review Conference and any relevant technological developments – to proceed promptly with the consideration of further measures in the field of disarmament for the prevention of an arms race in that environment.
(80) In order to prevent an arms race in outer space, further measures should be taken and appropriate international negotiations be held in accordance with the spirit of the Treaty on Principles Governing the Activities of States in the Exploration and Use of Outer Space including the Moon and Other Celestial Bodies.
(81) Together with negotiations on nuclear disarmament measures, the limitation and gradual reduction of armed forces and conventional weapons should be resolutely pursued within the framework of progress towards general and complete disarmament. States with the largest military arsenals have a special responsibility in pursuing the process of conventional armaments reductions.
(82) In particular the achievement of a more stable situation in Europe at a lower level of military potential on the basis of approximate equality and parity, as well as on the basis of undiminished security of all States with full respect for security interests and independence of States outside military alliances, by agreement on appropriate mutual reductions and limitations would contribute to the strengthening of security in Europe and constitute a significant step towards enhancing international peace and security. Current efforts to this end should be continued most energetically.
(83) Agreements or other measures should be resolutely pursued on a bilateral, regional and multilateral basis with the aim of strengthening peace and security at a lower level of forces, by the limitation and reduction of armed forces and of conventional weapons, taking into account the need of States to protect their security, bearing in mind the inherent right to self-defence embodied in the Charter of the United Nations and without prejudice to the principle of equal rights and self-determination of peoples in accordance with the Charter, and the need to ensure balance at each stage an undiminished security of all States. Such measures might include those in the following two paragraphs.
(84) Bilateral, regional and multilateral consultations and conferences where appropriate conditions exist with the participation of all the countries concerned for the consideration of different aspects of conventional disarmament, such as the initiative envisaged in the Declaration of Ayacucho subscribed in 1974 by eight Latin American countries.
(85) Consultations should be carried out among major arms supplier and recipient countries on the limitation of all types of international transfer of conventional weapons, based, in particular, on the principle of undiminished security of the parties with a view to promoting or enhancing stability at a lower military level, taking into account the need of all States to protect their security as well as the inalienable right to self-determination and independence of peoples under colonial or foreign domination and the obligations of States to respect that right, in accordance with the Charter of the United Nations and the Declaration on Principles of International Law concerning Friendly Relations and Co-operation Among States.
(86) The 1979 United Nations Conference on Prohibitions or Restrictions of Use of Certain Conventional Weapons which may be Deemed to be Excessively Injurious or to have Indiscriminate Effects should seek agreement, in the light of humanitarian and military considerations, on the prohibition or restriction of use of certain unnecessary suffering or which may have indiscriminate effects. The conference should consider specific categories of such weapons, including those which were the subject-matter of previously conducted discussions.
(87) All States are called upon to contribute towards carrying out this task.
(88) The result of the conference should be considered by all States and especially producer States, in regard to

the question of the transfer of such weapons to other States.

(89) Gradual reduction of military budgets on a mutually agreed basis, for example, in absolute figures or in terms of percentage points, particularly by nuclear-weapon States and other militarily significant States would be a measure that would contribute to the curbing of the arms race, and would increase the possibilities of reallocation of resources now being used for military purposed to economic and social development, particularly for the benefit of the developing countries. The basis for implementing this measure will have to be agreed by all participating States and will require ways and means of its implementation acceptable to all of them, taking account of the problems involved in assessing the relative significance of reductions as among different States and with due regard to the proposals of States on all the aspects of reduction of military budgets.

(90) The General Assembly should continue to consider what concrete steps should be taken to facilitate the reduction of military budgets bearing in mind the relevant proposals and documents of the United Nations on this question.

(91) In order to facilitate the conclusion and effective implementation of disarmament agreements and to create confidence, States should accept appropriate provisions for verification in such agreements.

(92) In the context of international disarmament negotiations, the problem of verification should be further examined and adequate methods and procedures in this field be considered. Every effort should be made to develop appropriate methods and procedures which are non-discriminatory and which do not unduly interfere with the internal affairs of other States or jeopardize their economic and social development.

(93) In order to facilitate the process of disarmament, it is necessary to take measures and pursue policies to strengthen international peace and security and to build confidence among States. Commitment to confidence-building measures could significantly contribute to preparing for further progress in disarmament. For this purpose, measures such as the following and other measures yet to be agreed, should be undertaken:

1. The prevention of attacks which take place by accident, miscalculation or communications failure by taking steps to improve communications between Governments, particularly in areas of tension, by the establishment of "hot lines" and other methods of reducing the risk of conflict.

2. States should assess the possible implications of their military research and development for existing agreements as well as for further efforts in the field of disarmament.

3. The Secretary-General shall periodically submit reports to the General Assembly on the economic and social consequences of the arms race and its extremely harmful effects on world peace and security.

(94) In view of the relationship between expenditure on armaments and economic and social development and the necessity to release real resources now being used for military purposes to economic and social development in the world, particularly for the benefit of the developing countries, the Secretary-General should, with the assistance of a group of qualified governmental experts appointed by him, initiate an expert study on the relationship between disarmament and development. The Secretary-General should submit an interim report on the subject to the General Assembly at its thirty-fourth session and submit the final results to the Assembly at its thirty-sixth session for subsequent action.

(95) The expert study should have the terms of reference contained in the report of the Ad Hoc Group on the Relationship between Disarmament and Development appointed by the Secretary-General in accordance with General Assembly resolution 32/88 A of 12 December 1977. It should investigate the three main areas listed in the report, bearing in mind the United Nations studies previously carried out. The study should be made in the context of how disarmament can contribute to the establishment of the new international economic order. The study should be forward-looking and policy-oriented and place special emphasis on both the desirability of a reallocation, following disarmament measures, of resources now being used for military purposes to economic and social develop-

ment, particularly for the benefit of the developing countries and the substantive feasibility of such a reallocation. A principal aim should be to produce results that could effectively guide the formulation of practical measures to reallocate those resources at the local, national, regional and international levels.

(96) Taking further steps in the field of disarmament and other measures aimed at promoting international peace and security would be facilitated by carrying out studies by the Secretary-General in this field with appropriate assistance from governmental or consultant experts.

(97) The Secretary-General shall, with the assistance of consultant experts, appointed by him, continue the study of the interrelationship between disarmament and international security and submit it to the thirty-fourth session of the General Assembly, as requested in resolution A/RES/32/87C.

(98) The thirty-third and subsequent sessions of the General Assembly should determine the specific guidelines for carrying out studies, taking into account the proposals already submitted including those made by individual countries at the special session, as well as other proposals which can be introduced later in this field. In doing so, the General Assembly would take into consideration a report on these matters prepared by the Secretary-General.

(99) In order to mobilize world public opinion on behalf of disarmament, the specific measures set forth below, designed to increase the dissemination of information about the armaments race and the efforts to halt and reverse it, should be adopted.

(100) Governmental and non-governmental information organs and those of the United Nations and its specialized agencies should give priority to the preparation and distribution of printed and audiovisual material relating to the danger represented by the armaments race as well as to the disarmament efforts and negotiations on specific disarmament measures.

(101) In particular, publicity should be given to the final documents of the special session.

(102) The General Assembly proclaims a week starting 24 October, the day of the foundation of the United Nations, as a week devoted to fostering the objectives of disarmament.

(103) To encourage study and research on disarmament, the United Nations Centre for Disarmament should intensify its activities in the presentation of information concerning the armaments race and disarmament. Also, the United Nations Educational, Scientific and Cultural Organization (UNESCO), is urged to intensify its activities aimed at facilitating research and publications on disarmament, related to its fields of competence, especially in developing countries, and should disseminate the results of such research.

(104) Throughout this process of disseminating information about the developments in the disarmament field of all countries, there should be increased participation by non-governmental organizations concerned with the matter, through closer liaison between them and the United Nations.

(105) Member States should be encouraged to ensure a better flow of information with regard to the various aspects of disarmament to avoid dissemination of false and tendentious information concerning armaments and to concentrate on the danger of escalation of the armaments race and on the need for general and complete disarmament under effective international control.

(106) With a view to contributing to a greater understanding and awareness of the problems created by the armaments race and of the need for disarmament, Governments and governmental and non-governmental international organizations are urged to take steps to develop programmes of education for disarmament and peace studies at all levels.

(107) The General Assembly welcomes the initiative of the United Nations Educational, Scientific and Cultural Organization in planning to hold a world congress on disarmament education and, in this connexion, urges that organization to step up its programme aimed at the development of disarmament education as a distinct field of study through the preparation, inter alia, of teachers' guides, textbooks, readers and audio-visual materials. Member States should take all possible measures to encourage the incorporation of such materials in the curricula of their educational institutes.

(108) In order to promote expertise in disarmament in more Member States, particularly in the developing countries, the General Assembly decides to establish a programme of fellowships on disarmament. The Secretary-General, taking into account the proposal submitted to the special session, should prepare guidelines for the programme. He should also submit the financial requirements of 20 fellowships at the thirty-third regular session of the General Assembly, for inclusion in the regular budget of the United Nations bearing in mind the savings that can be made within the existing budgetary appropriations.

(109) Implementation of these priorities should lead to general and complete disarmament under effective international control, which remains the ultimate goal of all efforts exerted in the field of disarmament. Negotiations on general and complete disarmament shall be conducted concurrently with negotiations on partial measures on disarmament. With this purpose in mind, the Committee on Disarmament will undertake the elaboration of a comprehensive programme of disarmament encompassing all measures thought to be advisable in order to ensure that the goal of general and complete disarmament under effective international control becomes a reality in a world in which international peace and security prevail and in which the new international economic order is strengthened and consolidated. The comprehensive programme should appropriate procedures for ensuring that the General Assembly is kept fully informed of the progress of the negotiations including an appraisal of the situation when appropriate and, in particular, a continuing review of the implementation of the programme.

(110) Progress in disarmament should be accompanied by measures to strengthen institutions for maintaining peace and the settlement of international disputes by peaceful means. During and after the implementation of the programme of general and complete disarmament, there should be taken, in accordance with the principles of the United Nations Charter, the necessary measures to maintain international peace and security, including the obligation of States to place at the disposal of the United Nations agreed manpower necessary for an international peace force to be equipped with agreed types of armaments. Arrangements for the use of this force should ensure that the United Nations can effectively deter or suppress any threat or use of arms in violation of the purpose and principles of the United Nations.

(111) General and complete disarmament under strict and effective international control shall permit States to have at their disposal only those non-nuclear forces, armaments facilities and establishments as are agreed to be necessary to maintain internal order and to protect the personal security of citizens and in order that States shall support and provide agreed manpower for a United Nations peace force.

(112) In addition to the several questions dealt with in this Programme of Action, there are a few others of fundamental importance, on which, because of the complexity of the issues involved and the short time at the disposal of the special session, it has proved impossible to reach satisfactory agreed conclusions. For those reasons they are treated only in very general terms and, in a few instances, even not treated at all in the Programme.

It should be stressed, however, that a number of concrete approaches to deal with such questions emerged from the exchange of views carried out in the General Assembly which will undoubtedly facilitate the continuation of the study and negotiation of the problems involved in the competent disarmament organs.

IV. Machinery

(113) While disarmament, particularly in the nuclear field, has become a necessity for the survival of mankind and for the elimination of the danger of nuclear war, little progress has been made since the end of the Second World War. In addition to the need to exercise political will, the international machinery should be utilized more effectively and also improved to enable implementation of the Programme of Action and help the United Nations to fulfil its role in the field of disarmament.

In spite of the best efforts of the international community, adequate results have not been produced with the existing machinery. There is, therefore, an urgent need that existing disarmament machinery be revitalized and forums appropriately constituted for disarmament deliberations and negotiations with a better representative character.

For maximum effectiveness, two kinds of bodies are required in the field of disarmament – deliberative and negotiating. All Member States should be represented on the former, whereas the latter, for the sake of convenience, should have a relatively small membership.

(114) The United Nation, in accordance with the Charter, has a central role and primary responsibility in the sphere of disarmament. Accordingly, it should play a more active role in this field, and in order to discharge its functions effectively, the United Nations should facilitate and encourage all disarmament measures – unilateral, bilateral, regional or multilateral; and be kept duly informed through the General Assembly, or any other appropriate United Nations channel reaching all Members of the Organization, of all disarmement efforts outside its aegis without prejudice to the progress of negotiations.

(115) The General Assembly has been and should remain the main deliberative organ of the United Nations in the field of disarmament and should make every effort to facilitate the implementation of disarmament measures.

An item entitled "Review of the implementation of the recommendations and decisions adopted by the General Assembly at its tenth special session" shall be included in the provisional agenda of the thirty-third and subsequent sessions of the General Assembly.

(116) Draft multilateral disarmament conventions should be subjected to the normal procedures applicable in the law of treaties. Those submitted to the General Assembly for its commendation should be subject to full review by the Assembly.

(117) The First Committee of the General Assembly should deal in the future only with questions of disarmament and related international security questions.

(118) The General Assembly establishes, as successor to the Commission originally established by resolution 502(V), a Disarmament Commission composed of all Members of the United Nations.

The General Assembly decides that:

(a) The Disarmament Commission shall be a deliberative body, a subsidiary organ of the General Assembly, the function of which shall be to consider and make recommendations of various problems in the field of disarmament and to follow up the relevant decisions and recommendations of the special session devoted to disarmament. The Disarmament Commission should, inter alia, consider the elements of a comprehensive programme for disarmament to be submitted as recommendations to the General Assembly and, through it, to the negotiating body, the Committee on Disarmament;

(b) The Disarmament Commission shall function under the rules of procedure relating to the committees of the General Assembly with such modifications as the Commission may deem necessary and shall make every effort to ensure that, in so far as possible, decisions on substantive issues be adopted by consensus;

(c) The Disarmament Commission shall report annually to the General Assembly. It will submit for the consideration by the thirty-third session of the General Assembly a report on organizational matters. In 1979, the Disarmament Commission will meet for a period not exceeding four weeks, the dates to be decided at the thirty-third session of the General Assembly;

(d) The Secretary-General shall furnish such experts, staff and services as are necessary for the effective accomplishment of the Commission's functions.

(119) A second special session of the General Assembly devoted to disarmament should be held on a date to be decided by the General Assembly at its thirty-third session.

(120) The General Assembly is conscious of the work that has been done by the international negotiating body that has been meeting since March 14, 1962 as well as the considerable and urgent work that remains to be accomplished in the field of disarmament.

The General Assembly is deeply aware of the continuing requirement for single multilateral disarmament negotiating forum of limited size taking decisions on the basis of consensus. It attaches great importance to the participation of all the nuclear-weapon States in an appropriately constituted negotiating body: the Committee on Disarmament.

The General Assembly welcomes the agreement reached following appropriate consultations among the member States during the Special Session of the General Assembly Devoted to Disarmament that the Committee on Disarmament will be open to the nuclear-weapon States, and 32 to 35 other States to be chosen in consultation with the President of the thirty-second session of the General Assembly; that the membership of the Committee on Disarmament will be reviewed at regular intervals; that the Committee on Disarmament will be convened in Geneva not later than January 1979 by the country whose name appears first in the alphabetical list of membership; and that the Committee on Disarmament will:

(a) Conduct its work by consensus;

(b) Adopt its own rules of procedure;

(c) Request the Secretary-General of the United Nations, following consultations with the Committee on Disarmament, to appoint the Secretary of the Committee, who shall also act as his personal representative, to assist the Committee and its Chairman in organizing the business and timetables of the Committee;

(d) Rotate the chairmanship of the Committee among all its members on a monthly basis;

(e) Adopt its own agenda taking into account the recommendations made to it by the General Assembly and the proposals presented by the members of the Committee;

(f) Submit a report to the General Assembly annually, or more frequently as appropriate, and provide its formal and other relevant documents to the Member States of the United Nations on a regular basis;

(g) Make arrangements for interested States, not members of the Committee, to submit to the Committee written proposals or working documents on measures of disarmament that are the subject of negotiation in the Committee and to participate in the discussion of the subject matter of such proposals or working documents;

(h) Invite States not members of the Committee, upon their request, to express views in the Committee when the particular concerns of those States are under discussion;

(i) Open its plenary meetings to the public unless otherwise decided.

(121) Bilateral and regional disarmament negotiations may also play an important role and could facilitate negotiations of multilateral agreements in the field of disarmament.

(122) At the earliest appropriate time, a world disarmament conference should be convened with universal participation and with adequate preparation.

(123) In order to enable the United Nations to continue to fulfil its role in the field of disarmament and to carry out the additional tasks assigned to it by this special session, the United Nations Centre for Disarmament should be adequately strengthened and its research and information functions accordingly extended.

The Centre should also take account fully of the possibilities offered by the United Nations specialized agencies and other institutions and programmes within the United Nations system with regard to studies and information on disarmament. The Centre should also increase contacts with non-governmental organizations and research institutions in view of the valuable role they play in the field of disarmament. This role could be encouraged also in other ways that may be considered as appropriate.

(124) The Secretary-General is requested to set up an advisory board of eminent persons, selected on the basis of their personal expertise and taking into account the principle of equitable geographical representation, to advise him on various aspects of studies to be made under the auspices of the United Nations in the field of disarmament and arms limitation, including a programme of such studies.

(125) The General Assembly notes with satisfaction that the active participation of the Member States in the consideration of the agenda items of the special session and the proposals and suggestions submitted by them and reflected to a considerable extent in the Final Document have made a valuable contribution to the work of the special session and to its positive conclusion.

Since a number of those proposals and suggestions, which have become an integral part of the work of the special session, deserve to be studied further and more thoroughly, taking into consideration the many relevant comments and observations made both in the general debate of the plenary and the deliberations of the Ad Hoc Committee, the Secretary-General is requested to transmit, together with this Final Document, to the appropriate deliberative and negotiating organs dealing with the questions of disarmament all the official records of the special session of the General Assembly devoted to disarmament, in accordance with the recommendations which the Assembly may adopt at its thirty-third session. Some of the proposals put forth for consideration of the special session of the Assembly are listed below:

(a) Text of the decision of the Central Committee of the Romanian Communist Party concerning Romania's position on disarmament and, in particular, on nuclear disarmament, adopted on 9 May 1978 (A)/s-10(14);

(b) Views of the Swiss Government on problems to be discussed at the tenth special session of the General Assembly (A)S-10/AC.1(2);

(c) Proposals of the Union of Soviet Socialist Republics on practical measures for ending the arms race (A)S-10/AC.1(4);

(d) Memorandum from France concerning the establishment of an International Satellite Monitoring Agency (A)S-10/AC.1(7);

(e) Memorandum from France concerning the establishment of an International Institute for Disarmament Research (A)S-10/AC.1(8);

(f) Proposal by Sri Lanka for the establishment of a World Disarmament Authority (A)S-10/AC.1(9).

(g) Working paper submitted by the Federal Republic of Germany entitled 'Contribution to the seismological verification of a comprehensive test ban' (A)S-10/AC.1(12);

(h) Working paper submitted by the Federal Republic of Germany entitled 'Invitation to attend an international chemical-weapon verification workshop in the Federal Republic of Germany' (A)S-10/AC.1(13);

(i) Working paper on disarmament submitted by China (A)S-10/AC.1(17);

(j) Working paper submitted by the Federal Republic of Germany concerning zones of confidence; building measures as a first step towards the preparation of a world-wide convention on confidence-building measures (A)S-10/AC.1(20);

(k) Proposal by Ireland for a study of the possibility of establishing a system of incentives to promote arms control and disarmament (A)S-10/AC.1(21);

(l) Working paper submitted by Romania concerning a synthesis of the proposals in the field of disarmament (A)S-10/AC.1(23);

(m) Proposal by the United States of America on the establishment of a United Nations Peace-keeping Reserve and on confidence-building measures and stabilizing measures in various regions, including notification of manoeuvres, invitation of observers to manoeuvres, and United Nations machinery to study and promote such measures (A)S-10/AC.1(24);

(n) Proposal by Uruguay on the possibility of establishing a polemological agency (A)-10/AC.1(25);

(o) Proposal by Belgium, Canada, Denmark, Germany, Federal Republic of, Ireland, Italy, Japan, Luxembourg, the Netherlands, New Zealand, Norway, Sweden, the United Kingdom of Great Britain and Northern Ireland and the United States of America on the strengthening of the security role of the United Nations in the peaceful settlement of disputes and peacekeeping (A)S-10/AC.1(26) and Corr. (1) and (2);

(p) Memorandum from France concerning the establishment of an International Disarmament Fund for Development (A)S-10/AC.1(28);

(q) Proposal by Norway entitled 'Evaluation of the impact of new weapons on arms control and disarmament efforts' (A)S-10AC.1(31);

(r) A verbal note transmitting the text, signed in Washington on 22 June 1978, by the Ministers for Foreign Affairs of Argentina, Bolivia, Chile, Colombia, Ecuador, Panama, Peru and Venezuela, reaffirming the principles of the Declaration of Ayacucho with respect to the limitation of conventional weapons (A)S-10/AC.1(34);

(s) Memorandum from Liberia entitled 'Declaration of a new philosophy on disarmament' (A)S-10/AC.1(35);

(t) Statements made by the representatives of China on 22 June 1978 on the draft Final Document of the tenth special session (A)S-10/AC.1(36);

(u) Proposal by the President of Cyprus for the total demilitarization and disarmament of the Republic of Cyprus and implementation of the resolutions of the United Nations (A)S-10/AC.1(39);

(v) Proposal by Costa Rica on economic and social incentives to halt the arms race (A)S-10/AC.1(40);

(w) Amendments submitted by China to the draft Final Document of the tenth special session (A)S-10/AC.1(L.2) to (L.4), (A)S-10/AC.1(L.7) and (L.8);

(x) Proposals by Canada for the implementation of a strategy of suffocation of the nuclear arms race (A)S-10/AC.1(L.6);

(y) Draft resolution submitted by Cyprus, Ethiopia and India on the urgent need for cessation of further testing of nuclear weapons (A)S-10/AC.1(L10);

(z) Draft resolution submitted by Ethiopia and India on the non-use of nuclear weapons and prevention of nuclear war (A)S-10/AC.1(L11);

(aa) Proposal by the non-aligned countries on the establishment of a zone of peace in the Mediterranean (A)S-10/AC.1(37), para. (72);

(bb) Proposal by the Government of Senegal for a tax on military budgets (A)S-10/AC.1(37), para. (101);

(cc) Proposal by Austria for the transmission to Member States of working paper A/AC.187/109 and the ascertainment of their views on the subject of verification (A)S-10/AC.1(37), para. (113);

(dd) Proposal by the non-aligned countries for the dismantling of foreign military bases from foreign territories and withdrawal of foreign troops from foreign territories (A)S-10/AC.1(37), para. (126);

(ee) Proposal by Mexico for the opening, on a provisional basis, of an Ad Hoc account in the United Nations Development Programme to use for development the funds which may be released as a result of disarmament measures (A)S-10/AC.1(37), para. (141);

(ff) Proposal by Italy on the role of the Security Council in the field of disarmament in accordance with Article 26 of the United Nations Charter (A)S-10/AC.1(37), para. (179);

(gg) Proposal by the Netherlands for a study on the establishment of an international disarmament organization (A)S-10/AC.1(37), para. (186).

(126) In adopting this Final Document, the States Members of the United Nations solemnly reaffirm their determination to work for general and complete disarmament and to make further collective efforts aimed at strengthening peace and international security; eliminating the threat of war, particularly nuclear war; implementing practical measures aimed at halting and reversing the arms race; strengthening the procedures for the peaceful settlement of disputes; and reducing military expenditures and utilizing the resources thus released in a manner which will help to promote the well-being of all peoples and to improve the economic conditions of the developing countries.

(127) The General Assembly expresses its satisfaction that the proposals submitted to its special session devoted to disarmament and the deliberations thereon have made it possible to reaffirm and define in this Final Document fundamental principles, goals, priorities and procedures for the implementation of the above purposes, either in the Declaration or the Programme of Action or in both. The Assembly also welcomes the important decisions agreed upon regarding the deliberative and negotiating machinery and is confident that these organs will discharge their functions in an effective manner.

(128) Finally, it should be borne in mind that the number of States that participated in the general debate, as well as the high level of representation and the depth and scope of that debate, are unprecedented in the history of disarmament efforts. Several Heads of State or Government addressed the General Assembly. In addition, other Heads of State or Government sent messages and expressed their good wishes for the success of the special session of the Assembly. Several high officials of specialized agencies and other institutions and programmes within the United Nations system and spokesmen of 25 non-governmental organizations and six research institutes also made valuable contributions to the proceedings of the session. It must be emphasized, more-over, that the special session marks not the end but rather the beginning of a new phase of the efforts of the United Nations in the field of disarmament.

(129) The General Assembly is convinced that the discussions of the disarmament problems at the special session and its Final Document will attract the attention of all peoples, further mobilize world public opinion and provide a powerful impetus for the cause of disarmament."

UN Chronicle, July, 1978.

DISARMAMENT UN INSTITUTE. ▷ UNIDIR.

DISARMAMENT WORLD CONFERENCE. The idea of a World Disarmament Conference was raised for the first time in resolutions concerning disarmament at the XXth Session of the UN General Assembly, 1965. On Dec. 16, 1971, the UN General Assembly charged the UN Secretary-General to take a poll on this issue among the member states. The results were submitted to the UN General Assembly on Oct. 4, 1972, and after debating them in the Political Committee 78 states expressed themselves in favor of calling a World Conference. Earlier during his visit to Moscow, US President R. Nixon issued a joint communiqué with Soviet leader L. Brezhnev, stating that "the convening of a World Disarmament Conference at a suitable time could play a positive role."

In accordance with Res. 29/30/XXVII the chairman of the UN General Assembly appointed, in Dec. 1972, the members of the Preparatory Committee for a World Disarmament Conference, reserving five places for the permanent members of the Security Council, among whom the Chinese Peoples Republic and the USA did not participate in the work of the Committee, whereas France, the UK and the USSR did. The appointed members of the Committee were: Algeria, Argentina, Austria, Belgium, Brazil, Bulgaria, Burundi, Chile, Czechoslovakia, Egypt, Ethiopia, Hungary, India, Indonesia, Iran, Italy, Japan, Lebanon, Liberia, Mongolia, Morocco, the Netherlands, Nigeria, Pakistan, Peru, Philippines, Poland, Romania, Spain, Sri Lanka, Sweden, Tunisia, Turkey, Venezuela, Zaïre and Zambia. The position of the USA was that:

"The General Assembly should state by way of a consensus that a World Disarmament Conference could play a role in the disarmament process at a suitable time."

The position of the Chinese People's Republic was that:

"A World Conference can be called only if two introductory conditions for creating a disarmament climate are fulfilled: renouncement of the use of nuclear weapons by all powers; the liquidation of all foreign military bases."

UN Yearbook, 1972.

DISASTER RELIEF, INTERNATIONAL. A subject of UN co-ordinated efforts. The UN General Assembly Res. 2816/XXVI, Dec. 14, 1971 established in Geneva the Office of UN Disaster Relief Co-ordinator, UNDRO, as a body authorized to mobilize, direct and co-ordinate the relief activities of the various units of the UN system (FAO, UNDP, UNICEF, UNEP, UNHCR, UNESCO, WHO, WMO and ITU) and the assistance given by inter-governmental and non-governmental organizations and the voluntary agencies in response to requests from countries stricken by natural catastrophes. The Trust Fund of UNDRO helps cover unforeseen expenses in connection with disaster relief operations. A World Voluntary Service Corps in the event of Natural Disaster, was started 1971 in Paris as a non-governmental organization. Reg. with the UIA. An annual international prize of $50,000 for outstanding contribution to disaster prevention was announced on July 3, 1986 by the UNDRO on the basis of a $1 million endowment made by the Japanese philanthropist R. Sasakawa. The award is to be known as Sasakawa–UNDRO Disaster Prevention Award.

S. GREEN, *International Disaster Relief. Towards a Responsible System*, New York, 1978; *UN Chronicle*, March 1982, p. 67 and October, 1983, p. 57; *Yearbook of International Organizations; UN Chronicle*, January, 1984, pp. 43–44; *UN Chronicle*, November 1986; P. MACALISTER-SMITH, "International Humanitarian Assistance. Disaster Relief Actions", in: *International Law and Organization*, Dordrecht, 1985.

DISCOUNT HOUSE. An international banking term, an institution of the ▷ discount market. Also a special shop selling at reduced prices.

DISCOUNT MARKET. In Anglo-Saxon countries the short-term money market, or market for discounting bills.

W. M. SCAUMNEL, *The London Discount Market*, London, 1968.

DISCOUNT RATE. An international banking term for a fee for lending money. In international financial systems, an important element of central bank agreements.

In 1986 Japan reduced the DR from 5 to 4.5 percent, and effective Nov. 1, to 3 per cent; West Germany from 4.5 to 3.5 per cent; USA from 7.5 to 7 and then to 5.5 per cent, the lowest point since 1977.

KEESING's *Record of World Events*, January, 1987.

DISCOVERER. American artificial earth satellite; Discoverer was launched into orbit on Feb. 28, 1959. Previous American artificial satellites: ▷ Explorer and ▷ Vanguard.

DISCOVERIES. An international colonial term for discoveries of unknown territories, subject of international law in connection with the annexation by the discoverers of these lands for their monarch or state.

D.J. BOORSTIN, *The Discoverers, A History of Man's Search to Know His World and Himself*, New York, 1983; R.L. BLEDSOE, B.A. BOCZEK, *The International Law Dictionary*, Oxford, 1987.

DISCOVERY LAW. ▷ Law of discovery.

DISCRIMINATION. An international term for deprivation of individuals, groups of persons or whole communities within a society divided into certain social classes of equitable social, political or economic rights; persecution due to ethnic origin, nationality, world view or other social factors; in international relations – the treatment of a state or a group of states as inferior to all other states and the encroachment upon their rights immanent to the customs of commonly acceptable principles of international law. The UN Charter rules out racial, political, religious, etc. discrimination from international relations under arts 6; 62, para. 2; 73, para. 6. The UN General Assembly Res. 103/I of Nov. 19, 1946 was the first to denounce racism and all forms of racial discrimination. On Jan. 14, 1947, the UN Commission on Human Rights established a sub-commission to deal with prevention of discrimination of ▷ minorities; it conducted world studies on the situation of various minorities. In 1948 the ▷ Human Rights, Universal Declaration of, denounced all forms of racial and other discrimination. The UN General Assembly on many occasions manifested its standpoint of principle in this matter and reaffirmed it in Res. 1798/XVI of Dec., 1961, condemning racial discrimination and segregation. In 1963 on the initiative of African states, the ECOSOC prepared a declaration on discrimination and denounced colonialism as the

D

major source of discrimination; also demanded was total decolonization.

On Mar. 7, 1966, the Convention on the Elimination of All Forms of Racial Discrimination, prepared by the UN, was signed in New York. On Dec. 18, 1967, the UN General Assembly adopted Res. 2331/XXII denouncing free dissemination of the Nazi ideology in the FRG as well as racial discrimination in Rhodesia and apartheid in the Republic of South Africa.

In the Pan-American system there is a resolution in force adopted by the Pan-American Conference on War and Peace (the ▷ Chapultepec Conference, 1945) declaring racial and religious discrimination inadmissible.

In Geneva the ILO adopted the Convention on discrimination in employment and the exercise of professional activities, signed on June 25, 1958.

Acta Final de la Conferencia de Chapultepec, México DF, 1945; *UN Bulletin,* December 1, 1946; *UN Study of Discrimination in the Matter of Education,* New York, 1957; *UN Study of Discrimination in the Matter of Religion and Religious Practices,* New York, 1960; H. SANTA CRUZ, *Study of Discrimination in the Matter of Political Rights,* New York, 1962; *The United Nations and the Human Rights,* New York, 1968; *Report of the Committee on the Elimination of Racial Discrimination,* New York, 1975.

DISEASES. A subject of international control, research, statistics and conventions, intermediate nomenclature was recommended by the International Commission for the Decennial Revision of International Nomenclature of Diseases in Paris, 1929. As early as the 17th century, attempts had been made to classify diseases and causes of death. In 1853 the first International Statistical Congress, meeting in Brussels, decided to create "une nomenclature uniforme des causes de decés applicable a tous les pays". This was one of the first examples of international co-operation in the field of health. From that date until 1929, the international nomenclature was periodically revised and updated, but continued to be restricted to causes of death. In 1948 the Conference for the sixth revision, the first to be held under the auspices of the WHO, modified the nomenclature so that it could be used also for the classification of morbidity data. Since then, the international classification has been amplified to keep pace with progress in statistics and, above all, in medicine. In 1980 the ninth revision of the International Classification of Diseases and several other volumes have been established in order to facilitate the collection of data and to improve comparability between data from different sources. The WHO, at the request of a number of countries, has prepared a classification of procedures in medicine; it includes procedures used in medical diagnosis, laboratories, prophylaxis, surgery and radiology (both diagnostic and therapeutic), as well as drugs, medicaments and biological agents (vaccines, etc.). In addition, three adaptations of the international classification have been created for use by specialists; the first deals with oncology and allows tumors to be classified by their topography, morphology and behavior; the second concerns dentistry and stomatology and the third is an extended classification of eye diseases. Similar adaptations are proposed in fields such as ear, nose and throat diseases, dermatology and childhood disorders. Finally, a classification of impairments, disabilities and handicaps has been prepared. In many countries, use of the international classification poses considerable problems on account of its complexity and of the lack of medical personnel capable of using it to advantage. Simplified lists have therefore been established to allow the reporting of health information by non-medical personnel. A world campaign against epidemic diseases, spread through contagion, is directed by the WHO. International Sanitary Regulations passed by the WHO introduced the international obligation of preventive vaccination for persons travelling abroad, International Certificate of Vaccination against smallpox, yellow fever, cholera and other infectious diseases. In Dec., 1972 a permanent 24-hour worldwide telex information system on the outbreak of infectious illnesses in all member states and other territories was put into operation at WHO Geneva Headquarters: Genève Telex 28150. In 1978 the WHO started a Diarrhoeal Disease Control program to combat one of the leading causes of illness and death in the developing world. In 1980 the population of children aged under five in Africa, Latin America and Asia (excluding China) was estimated at 338 million; the number of diarrhoeal disease episodes at 774 million to a billion; and the number of diarrhoeal deaths at 4.6 million. The WHO also organizes a worldwide control of diseases like ▷ bilharziasis, ▷ cardio-vascular diseases, ▷ leprosy, ▷ malaria, ▷ tuberculosis, ▷ polio, ▷ trachoma and venereal diseases (▷ STD). ▷ occupational diseases.

Organizations reg. with the UIA:

International Epidemiological Association, f. 1954, Baltimore.
International Society for the Study of Diseases of the Colon and Rectum (Hedrologicum Collegium), f. 1961, Milan.
International Society for the Study of Infectious and Parasitic Diseases, est. 1966, Turin (Italy). International Congress held every two years.
Organization for Co-ordination in Control of Epidemic Diseases in Central Africa, est. 1963, Yaounde. Publ. *Bulletin.*
World Association of Veterinary Microbiologists, Immunologists and Specialists in Infectious Diseases, est. 1967, Maison-Alfort (France).

LNTS, Vol. 154, pp. 395–399; *Yearbook of International Organizations.*

DISENGAGEMENT. An international term in the UN system for the initial process of easing of tension, a term used since 1955 in reference to plans designed to lessen tensions between blocs of states, as e.g. ▷ Rapacki Plan.

DISINSECTIZATION. A subject of international sanitary conventions in connection with international air travel and the possibility of transporting insects that could bring contagious diseases, above all malaria and the like; International Health Rules, IHR, provide for disinsectization of certain areas including sea- and air-ports, ships and planes, and land vehicles. The use of airplanes to disinsectize mosquito areas or those threatened by locusts was begun on a wide scale in 1930–31 in the USA and USSR; became the subject of FAO action from 1951. International air rescue action organized in 1954 by FAO against invasion of locusts in North Africa was successful.

Since the 1980's insect control at air and sea-ports and the disinsection of aircraft is practised all over the world to prevent the international spread of insect-borne diseases. The ICAO, the IATA as well as national health administrations are collaborating with WHO in this effort.

International Health Regulations (1969), WHO Geneva 1971, arts. 1, 15, 19, 26, 55, 58, 60, 61, 74, 80, 81, 96; Insects and Disease, in: *WHO In Point of Facts,* Geneva No 61, 1988.

DISPENSATION. (1) Exemption of citizens by a lawmaker from the obligation to adhere to a certain law; (2) An exemption by the Pope or a bishop from the duty of a Church member to adhere to one of the laws or rules of the Church.

DISPLACED NATION IN A DISPLACED STATE. An international term related to Poland, which after WW II had lost in the East a great part of her territory to the Soviet Union, and gained a new frontier in the West. (▷ Oder-Neisse). The Polish population from the territories in the USSR was repatriated to Poland as was a large number of Polish ▷ displaced persons from Germany. The majority of the repatriated Poles settled in Western Poland from where in accordance with the ▷ Potsdam Agreement 1945 of the Great Powers, the German population was resettled to Germany.

DISPLACED PERSONS. Official international designation for citizens of countries occupied by Nazi Germany who as a result of the vicissitudes of World War II found themselves outside their homeland and wanted either to be repatriated or to emigrate further. Displaced persons, whose number in the spring of 1945 was estimated in Europe at *c.* 10 million mainly in the area of occupied Germany, were located in special camps which were maintained in the American and British zones until 1949; care over displaced persons was exercised by UNRRA.

H. REUT-NICOLUSSI, "Displaced persons and International law", in: *Recueil des Cours,* 1948, II, pp. 5–68.

DISPUTES, INTERNATIONAL. A subject of international co-operation imposing an obligation to resolve international disputes only by peaceful means as the prerequisite for maintaining peace and security; a principle of international law universally in force since 1899, the date of the Hague conventions, stating that all disputes and international conflicts should be solved by peaceful means; introduced after World War I into the League of Nations Covenant (arts. 12, 15 and 17) and into the Geneva Protocol of Oct. 2, 1924. The League of Nations on Sept. 26, 1928 approved the General Act on the principles of peaceful resolution of international disputes. After World War II these principles were included in the Charter of the United Nations, 1945, (Chapter IV); they are reaffirmed in numerous bilateral and multilateral pacts. At present, apart from the Constitution of the International Court of Justice, the Geneva General Act of 1928 in the wording given to it by Res. 268/III of April 28, 1949, of the UN General Assembly is of particular significance:

"The principle that States shall resolve their disputes by peaceful means..." has been defined in the Declaration on the Principles of International Law, adopted by the UN General Assembly on Oct. 24, 1970. It is also one of the major principles adopted by the Conference on Security and Co-operation in Europe in 1975. (▷ Helsinki Final Act).

E.A. JELF, "Justiciable disputes", in: *Transactions of Grotius Society,* 1921; H. LAMBERPRECHT, "The doctrine of non-justiciable disputes in international law", in: *Economica,* 1928; M. HABICHT, *Post-War Treaties for the Pacific Settlement of International Disputes,* Cambridge, Mass., 1931; L.G. SOHN, "Exclusion of political disputes from judical settlement", in: *American Journal of International Law,* No. 4, October, 1944.

DISSIDENTS. An international term for groups organised in more than 1000 national, regional or international movements of political., religious or social character, demanding changes in the social order. The Byelorussian and Ukrainian dissidents call themselves "inakodumcy".

H.H. DESENHARDT, *Revolutionary and Dissident Movements of the World.* An International Guide, London, 1987; J. ZAPRUDNIK, "Inakodumstwo" na Białorusi, in: *Nowa Koalicja, New Coalition,* Nr 4, 1987.

J. BUGAJSKI, M. POLLACK, East European Dissidents, in: *Problems of Communism*, March–April, 1988.

DISSIMILATION. An international term for a process of voluntary or forced isolation of persons not accepted by a certain society. In 1933 the racist legislation of the III Reich imposed compulsory dissimilation on Germans of Jewish extraction, which led to protests in the League of Nations and a sharp debate at the Congress of National Minorities in Geneva in the fall of 1933. Similar racist dissimilation legislation was introduced after World War II by the Republic of South Africa in its policy of ▷ apartheid, opposed by the UN. Besides racist dissimilative processes imposed on some groups of people history records national movements in favor of dissimilation, e.g. in the 19th century, Irish in the British Kingdom, Slavs under the Prussian occupation.

DISTRICT OF COLUMBIA. The US Federal district on the north-east bank of the Potomac river, co-extensive with the capital of the United States, the city of ▷ Washington, DC, established by Congress 1791 after two Federal States, Virginia and Maryland, granted land on both sides of the Potomac together with Alexandria and George-town. Alexandria returned in 1846 to Virginia; Georgetown was incorporated into the city of Washington 1878, and since then the capital of the United States comprises the entire area of the District of Columbia (180 sq. km.).

L.F. SCHMECKBIER, *The District of Columbia*, Washington, DC, 1928.

DIVERSION. An international term referring to enemy operations in peace or war that aim at weakening the opponent through political disturbances or rioting, economic sabotage, the spreading of alarming news (▷ psychological war), etc. Modern military forms of diversion and anti-diversion developed during World War II and in regional wars.

DIVINERS. Persons with the psychotronic ability to discover by means of a diviners' rod (a metal rod or a branch usually of hazel, *Hamamelis virginiana*) underground water streams, mineral deposits, buried minerals. The development of international scientific research on psychotronics resulted in the organizing of diviners internationally. The I International Congress was held in 1974.
In the years 1913–33 there existed the International Association for the Study of Divining based in Berlin, which published *Zeitschrift für Wünschelrutenforschung*. In 1974 the First International Congress of Diviners was held in Tashkent, USSR. ▷ Psychotronics.

W.B. GIBSON, "Radiestesia", in: *The Complete Illustrated Book of the Physic Sciences*, London, 1969; *Yearbook of International Organizations*.

DIVORCES AND SEPARATIONS. A subject of international family law, included in a Convention signed in The Hague on April 21, 1902, concerning regulation of legislation and jurisdiction with regard to divorce and separation from bed and table. It adopted the following principle:

"Art. 1: Spouses can file a suit for divorce only in the case when both the legislation in force in their homeland, and the legislation binding in the place the suit is filed, recognizes divorce. The same refers to separation."

The Convention provided only for cases when both spouses had the same citizenship. With the considerable increase in marriages and divorces among people of different nationality and the existence of states that do not recognize nationality as the criterion in such cases, the Hague Conference on International Private Law at its IXth Session held in 1960 began work on a revision of the convention of 1902, finalized at its XIth Session in 1969, elaborating a new Hague Convention on the Recognition of Marriages and Separations and introducing a number of important changes, of which first and foremost recognized the jurisdiction of "the state of regular stay" or "of the state of domicile", and the possibility of spouses having multiple nationality. Its art. 1, para. 1, states the following:

"The Convention shall be applicable for the recognition of divorces and separations in a Contracting State, which have been granted in another Contracting State after holding – officially recognized in the latter State – court or other proceedings, which are in that State legally effective."

Divorces in Europe are allowed in all countries except Portugal and Spain. In Italy the government attempted in 1969 to annul the divorce law by means of a referendum, but 59% of Italian citizens voiced their support for keeping the divorce law in force. According to international statistics for 1972, the highest divorce rate per 1000 people was noted in the USA – 3.70, USSR – 2.60, Hungary – 2.30, the GDR – 2.00, Sweden – 1.87, Czechoslovakia – 1.80, Great Britain – 1.47, Austria – 1.34, the FRG – 1.31, Canada – 1.24, Poland – 1.13.

DE MARTENS, *Nouveau Recueil*, 2me série, tome XXXI, p. 715; *LNTS*, Vol, 51, p. 215. L. PARKINSON, *Separation, Divorce and Families*, London, 1987.

DJAKARTA OR JAKARTA. Formerly Batavia. The capital of Indonesia (1980 pop. census 6,503,449) city and port on Djakarta Bay, f. 1619. In 1945 under the new name proclaimed the capital of independent Indonesia. Headquarters of international organizations reg. with the UIA: Asian Pacific Coconut Community, Asian Pacific Society of Cardiology, Association of South East Asian Nations, International Islamic Organization and Organization of Asian News Agencies.

J. PAXTON ed., *The Statesman's Yearbook 1987-88*, London, 1987; *Yearbook of International Organizations*

DJIBOUTI. Member of the UN. An African state bounded on the north-east by the Gulf of Aden, south-east by Somalia and then by Ethiopia. Area: 21,783 sq. km. Pop. 1988 est.: 484,000 (47% Somali, 37% Afar, 8% European and 6% Arab). Capital Djibouti with 150,000 inhabitants 1981. GNP per capita 1984: US $760. Currency: one Djibouti Franc = 100 centimes. National Day: June 27, Independence Day 1977.
Member of the UN, Sept 18, 1977 and of specialized organizations of the UN with the exception of UNESCO, UNIDO, WIPO and GATT. Member of the OAU, the Arab League and an ACP State of EEC.
International relations: colonial territory of France under the name Somalie Française, in 1958 autonomous territory in the Communauté Française, gained independence 1977. In 1981 Djibouti signed separate Treaties of Friendship and Cooperation with Ethiopia, Kenya, Somalia and Sudan.

J. P. POINSOT, *Djibouti et la Côte française de Somalie*, Paris, 1965; V. THOMPSON, R. ADLOFF, *Djibouti and the Horn of Africa*, Stanford, 1967; *The Europa Year Book 1984. A World Survey*, Vol. II, pp. 1477–1480, London, 1984.

DJOUDJ NATIONAL BIRD SANCTUARY. The Senegal natural monument, included in the ▷ World Heritage UNESCO List. Situated in the delta of the Senegal River, 16,000 hectares of lakes, pools, river backwaters, canals and streams provide a natural habitat for 1,500,000 water birds (pelicans, herons, spoon-bills, egrets, cormorants, etc.) and also for manatees and crocodiles.

World Cultural Heritage, *Information Bulletin*, Paris, 1983.

DNA. Deoxyribonucleic acid or Nucleic Acid, found in the nuclei of animal and plant cells. Subject of international research ▷ (Genetic Engineering).

DOBRUDJA. A Romanian–Bulgarian border province, subject of international disputes; in the 19th century between Turkey, Bulgaria and Romania; under the Berlin Treaty, July 13, 1878, divided between Romania and Bulgaria; then after the invasion of Bulgaria by Romania ceded in whole to Romania by the Treaty of Bucharest, Aug. 10, 1913; in 1918 divided by the Central Powers between Romania and Bulgaria; again ceded to Romania by the Peace Treaty with Bulgaria; signed Nov. 27, 1919 in Neuilly. This Treaty was revised by the Treaty of Craiova, Sept. 7, 1940, ceding the southern part of Dobrudja to Bulgaria with the obligation for the mutual resettlement of minorities, which was implemented and became the basis for recognizing the boundary drawn by the Treaty of Craiova by the Paris Peace Treaty, Feb. 10, 1947.

E. B. VALEV, *Bolgariya*, Moskva, 1957.

DOCPAL. Latin American Population Documentation System, one of the information systems of the ▷ UN Economic Commission for Latin America and the Caribbean.

DOCTOR'S OATH. ▷ Hippocratic Oath.

DOCTRINA GUARANI. ▷ Guarani Indians.

DOCTRINE. A philosophical term designating the assumptions of some field of knowledge or beliefs; in international politics used as a synonym for a program of action of a state or group of states in diverse areas of international relations, elevated to the rank of a political doctrine.

DOCUMENTATION. A subject of international co-operation. Organizations reg. with the UIA:

European Documentation and Information Center, f. 1958. Madrid.
International Association of Documentalists and Information Officers, f. 1962, Paris.
International Center for African Social and Economic Documentation, f. 1961, Brussels. Publ. *Bibliographical Index*.
International Committee for the Publication of Documents on European History, f. 1968, Mainz (FRG).
International Committee for Social Sciences Documentation, f. 1950 in Paris. Publ. *International Bibliography* (annual), *International Political Science Abstracts* (quarterly).
International Federation for Documentation, f. 1895. The Hague. Consultative status: UNESCO, ECOSOC. Publ. *International Forum on Information and Documentation Quarterly*.
International Micrographic Congress, f. 1973, Del Mar, Calif., USA. Publ. *Newsletter*.
Service for Documentation and Study, f. 1964, Rome. Publ. *Bulletin*.
World Office of Information on Environmental Problem. f. 1971, Paris.
See also ▷ commercial firm in UN documents.
See also ▷ UNESCO Information Systems.

Th. D. DIMITROV, *World Bibliography of International Documentation 2 Vls.*, New York, 1981; *Yearbook of International Organizations*.

DOCUMENTATION UN REGULATION. The General Assembly and the ECOSOC have established the general principle that reports and studies submitted to them and their subsidiary

bodies should be action-oriented and concise and should not exceed 32 single-spaced pages in length (equivalent to 44 one-and-one-half spaced pages or 60 double-spaced pages). The Secretary General has directed that henceforth documents originating in the Secretariat for submission to United Nations organs and bodies shall not exceed 24 single spaced pages or 45 double-spaced pages).
Any exception to the rule must be accepted by the Under-Secretary-General for Conference Services.
United Nations Editorial Manual, New York, 1783, pp. 512–513.

DOCUMENTS OF THE UNITED NATIONS. Material officially issued under a United Nations document symbol, regardless of the form of reproduction. In practice, the term is applied mainly to material offset from typescript and issued under a mast-head.
A "Daily List of Documents" is issued as a separate document.
United Nations Editorial Manual, New York, 1983, p. 4.

DOCUMENTS SYMBOLS OF THE UNITED NATIONS. Symbols of UN documents are composed of capital letters combined with figures, usually arabic numerals. The basic elements of the principal organs of the UN are:
A/- General Assembly
E/- ECOSOC
S/- Security Council
T/- Trusteeship Council
ST- Secretariat
List of United Nations Document Series Symbols (ST/ LIB/SER. B/5/Rev.3/UN Publication, Sales No. E.79.I.3; United Nations Editorial Manual, New York, 1983, p. 10–14.

DODECANESE. A group of Greek islands between Asia Minor and Crete in the Aegean Sea; the two largest are: Rhodos and Samos. Area: 2663 sq. km. Pop. 1971 census: 121,017. The Dodecanese have been the subject of disputes between Greece and Italy since the Italian–Turkish war 1911 (known as the Libyan war), when they were occupied by Italy and Turkey. Under the terms of a treaty with Italy, signed in Lausanne on July 24, 1923, Turkey renounced its claims to the Dodecanese in favor of Italy. They were occupied by Germany during World War II, 1943–45 and returned to Greece on Feb. 10, 1947 under the terms of the Italian peace treaty.
Executive Committee of the Inhabitants of the Dodecanese. White Book. The Dodecanese Resolutions and Documents concerning the Dodecanese 1912–1919, London, 1919; A. TSALAKIS, *Le Dodecanese, étude de Droit international*, Alexandrie, 1928; J. CASAVIS, *Italy and the Unredeemed Islands of Greece*, London, 1935; J. ROUČEK, "The legal aspects of sovereignty over the Dodecanese", in: *American Journal of International Law*, No. 10, 1944.

DOGMA. *Greek* = "provision binding on everyone". An international term inherited from ancient times when it indicated a statement by supreme authorities of city-states; commonly used in the Catholic church to name the basic provisions of the religion. Controversies concerning dogmas as well as a controversy concerning dogmatism of the pope brought about a split in the Christian church; the gap was widened by a controversy concerning infallibility of the pope announced July 18, 1870 by the Vatican Council in Constitutio Dogmatica I de ecclesia Christi, Chapter IV of *De Romani Pontificis infallibili magisterio*, which stated that when the pope pronounces as head of the Church (ex cathedra loquitur) in the matter of faith or morals

(de fide vel moribus) he is infallible and he who objects shall be doomed (anathema sit).
Collectio Lacensis VII, Freiburg in Br., 1890.

DOGS. A subject of international co-operation. Organizations reg. with UIA:
International Sled Dog Racing Association, f. 1966, Ontario.
International Union of Dog Clubs, f. 1976, Chernex Vt.
Kennel Clubs International federation, f. 1911, Thuin, Belgium, with aims to "encourage, protect and defend cynology and the raising of purebreed dogs." Members: national Kennel Clubs.
Yearbook of International Organizations.

DOLLAR. American or US dollar, US$. A monetary unit of the United States of America; one dollar = 100 cents; issued by the Federal Reserve System. In the years 1946–68 the dollar standard was synonymous with the ▷ gold standard. In accordance with art. 1 of the Statue of the IMF,
"the standard of the currency of each IMF member country will be expressed in gold as common denominator or in American dollars of such weight and fineness as were in force on July 1, 1944, i.e. 35 dol. per ounce as established in the USA in 1934."
After Feb. 21, 1968, when a two-tiered price of gold was introduced, official and free-market, and the member states of the IMF in fact continued to fix the exchange rates of their currencies in relation to the dollar, the dollar standard became a great problem for the monetary systems of members of the IMF, since the currencies of those states became directly dependent on the US balance of payments (which General de Gaulle had warned of several times), which was in chronic deficit, greatly intensified by the Vietnam war years with a simultaneously rapid shrinking gold reserve. The dollar standard was finally unilaterally abolished by the USA on Aug. 16, 1971 by the exchangeability of dollars for gold. In December 1987 the dollar dropped to its lowest level since the 1940's.
A.H. HANSEN, *The Dollar and the International Monetary System*, New York, 1965; M. FRIEDMAN, A. JACOBSON, *A Monetary History of the US $ 1867–1967*, Oxford, 1972; C.F. BERGSTEN, *The Dilemmas of the Dollar*, New York, 1979.

DOLLAR, AUSTRALIAN. A monetary unit of Australia; one dollar = 100 cents; introduced Feb. 14, 1966 in place of the Australian pound, issued by the Reserve Bank of Australia.

DOLLAR, BRUNEIAN. A monetary unit of Brunei; one dollar = 100 cents.

DOLLAR, CANADIAN. A monetary unit of Canada; one dollar = 100 cents; issued by the Bank of Canada.

DOLLAR, ETHIOPIAN. A monetary unit of Ethiopia; one dollar = 100 cents; issued by the National Bank of Ethiopia.

DOLLAR, HONG KONG. A monetary unit of Hong Kong; one dollar = 100 cents; issued by the Hong Kong and Shanghai Banking Corporation (79%), by Chartered Bank (13%), by the Mercantile Bank (1%), the rest (7%) by the Financial Secretary of the Government but only in one dollar banknotes and subsidiary coins.

DOLLAR, JAMAICAN. A monetary unit of Jamaica; one dollar = 100 cents; introduced Sept. 8, 1969 in place of the Jamaican pound; issued by the Bank of Jamaica.

DOLLAR, LIBERIAN. A monetary unit of Liberia; one dollar = 100 cents; at par with the US dollar from Jan. 1, 1944. The name "Liberian dollar" is only a formal term of the North American banknotes used in Liberia, under the supervision 1944–75 of The Bank of Monrovia, a subsidiary of the First National City Bank of New York, and from 1975 by the National Bank of Liberia, a Central Bank with the right to issue limited coins of 1, 5, 10, 25, 50 cents and one dollar but not paper money.

DOLLAR, NEW ZEALAND. A monetary unit of New Zealand; one dollar = 100 cents; issued by the Reserve Bank of New Zealand.

DOLLAR, SINGAPORE. A monetary unit of Singapore; one dollar = 100 cents; issued by the Monetary Authority of Singapore replacing the Malayan dollar June 12, 1967.

DOLLAR STANDARD. ▷ Dollar.

DOLLAR, TAIWAN. A monetary unit of Taiwan; one dollar = 100 cents; issued by the Central Bank of China in Taipei, Taiwan.

DOLLAR, TRINIDAD AND TOBAGO. A monetary unit of Trinidad and Tobago; one dollar = 100 cents; introduced April 1979 in place of Trinidad and Tobago pound; issued by the Central Bank of Trinidad and Tobago.

DOLLAR, ZIMBABWE. A monetary unit of Zimbabwe; one dollar = 100 cents, issued by the Reserve Bank of Zimbabwe replacing the Rhodesian dollar in 1980.

DOMESTIC JURISDICTION OF STATES. An international term for matters excluded from intervention and "which are essentially within the domestic jurisdiction of any state" in keeping with art. 7, para. 2 of the UN Charter, except for UN action taken in cases of threats to peace, breaches of peace and acts of aggression (the UN Charter, Chapter VII). The term was introduced in 1919 by the Covenant of the League of Nations in art. 15, para. 8.

DOMICILE. An international term for place of origin; in international private law indicates the law of the State in which the person resides; contrary to nationality, related to the law of the state of which the person is a national (*Lex domicili and Lex patriae*). Some States, Anglo-Saxon among them, divide domicile of origin from domicile of choice. France, for instance, differentiates between domicile and séjour (place of residence and place of sojourn).
A.S. BUSTAMANTE. *La Nacionalidad y el Domicilio*, La Habana, 1928; B. SCHNEIDER, *Le Domicile international*, Neuchâtel, 1973; E.D. GRANE, "Domicile, nationality and the proper law of the person", in: *German Yearbook of International Law*, 1976, pp. 254–277.

DOMINANCE. A synonim of ▷ Hegemonism.

DOMINICA. Member of the UN. Commonwealth of Dominica. The largest of the Windward Islands of the West Indies, between Martinique and Guadeloupe. Area: 750.6 sq. km. Pop. 1987 census: 94,191 (1970 census: 70,513). Capital Roseau with 8,346 inhabitants 1981. Official language: English. GNP per capita 1986: US $1210. Currency: since Jan. 1, 1979 there are three legal currencies: the East Caribbean dollar, the French franc, and the British pound sterling. National Day: Nov. 3, Independence Day, 1978.

A member of the UN from Nov. 17, 1978. Member of all UN specialized agencies: save ICAO, IAEA, GATT, WIPO and ITU. Member of the Commonwealth, OAS, CARICOM and is an ACP state of EEC. International relations: a British possession from 1805; a member of the Federation of the West Indies 1958–62; an associated state of Britain 1967–78; an independent republic as the Commonwealth of Dominica on Nov. 3, 1978.

Commonwealth of Dominica, HMSO, London, 1979; *The Europa Yearbook 1984. A World Survey*, Vol. II, pp. 1481–1485, London, 1984.

DOMINICAN REPUBLIC. Member of the UN. República Dominicana. Caribbean State on the eastern part of the island of Hispaniola, bounded in the west by Haiti. Area: 48,072 sq. km. Pop. 1987 est. 6,700,000 (1970 census: 4,006,005; 1981 census: 5,647,977). Capital: Santo Domingo (1936–61 called Ciudad Trujillo) with 817,067 inhabitants, 1981. GNP per capita in 1986: US $710. Official language: Spanish. Currency: one Dominican peso = 100 centavos. National Day: Nov. 30, Independence Day, 1821.

Original member of the UN since Oct. 25, 1945 and of UN specialized agencies save WIPO. Member of OAS and the Tlatelolco Treaty.

International relations: Spanish colony 1511–1795; ceded to France. First independence proclamation Nov. 30, 1821; invaded and occupied by the Haitians 1824–44; second proclamation Feb. 27, 1844. Occupied by US marines 1916–24, under US fiscal control until 1941, again occupied by US marines from Apr. to Sept. 1965. Formally the US troops were incorporated by the OAS into an Inter-American Peace Force. In 1973 and 1975 guerilla forces of Dominican émigrées landed on the coast, both times unsuccessfully.

A. VAN VYNEN, A. THOMPSON Jr., *La No-Intervención. Sus Normas y su Significado en las Americas*, Buenos Aires, 1959; T. SZULC, *Dominican Diary*, New York, 1965; J. BOSCH, *The Unfinished Experiment: Democracy in the Dominican Republic*, New York, 1965; M. NIEDERGANG, *La Révolucion de Saint-Domingue*, Paris, 1966; A. DE LA ROSA, *Las finanzas de Santo Domingo y el control americano*, Santo Domingo, 1969; J. SLATER, *Intervention and Negotiation. The US and the Dominican Revolution*, New York, 1970; J.C. ESTRELLA, *La moneda, la banca y las finanzas en la República Dominicana*, 2 Vols. Santiago, 1971; *The Dominican Republic: Rebellion and Depression*, London, 1973; *The Europa Year Book 1984. A World Survey*, Vol. II, pp. 1486–1497, London, 1984. J. KNIPPERS BLACK, *The Dominican Republic: Politics and Development in an Unsovereign State*, Winchester, Mass., 1986.

DOMINIUM. *Latin* = "under rule." An international term introduced for the first time by Great Britain, 1867, in the constitution given to Canada to define its autonomous status; extended after 1907 to other former British colonies when they received autonomy within the British Commonwealth (Australia, Ceylon, Nigeria, New Zealand, Republic of South Africa, Sierra Leone).

DOMINO THEORY. A political–strategic doctrine put forward by some members of the government of the USA to justify military engagement of the USA in South-east Asia after the withdrawal of France from Indochina 1954–55, based on the assumption that on the principle of a chain reaction, like dominos, the states of the region one after the other would become communist. In 1989 the term was used to denote the renunciation of communism by successive East European nations.

D. ROBERTSON, *Guide to Modern Defense and Strategy*, Detroit, 1988.

DOM-TOM. French abbreviation for Departments et territoires d'outre mer – "Overseas Departments and Territories". Francophonic term for overseas possessions of France.

DONG. A monetary unit of Vietnam; one dong = 100 sau; issued by the Banque de l'Etat de la Republique Democratique de Vietnam in Hanoi, replacing the Indochinese Piastre, July 20, 1954. During the war years in Vietnam the South Vietnam piastre, issued by the Bank of Vietnam in Saigon, was circulated in the south, and the Gia Phong dong, issued by the Provisional Revolutionary Government, was circulated in the north. With the nationalization of all banks after the war one monetary system was established in 1976 for a unified Vietnam.

DOPING. An international term in sport for improvement of a competitor's performance by psychological stimuli (encouragement) or chemical (narcotics); the latter combatted by the International Olympic Committee and other international sports institutions.

DOTATION CARNEGIE POUR LA PAIX INTERNATIONALE. ▷ Carnegie Endowment for International Peace.

DOUBLE ZERO OPTION OR ZERO-ZERO OPTION. An international military term coined in the 1980's during USA-USSR nuclear disarmament negotiations. First, in 1981 President Ronald Reagan proposed a Zero Option under which the US ▷ Pershing II and Soviet SS-20 missile would be withdrawn from Europe. The USSR rejected the Zero Option, but in 1987 stated its readiness to discuss a global ▷ INF ban, whereupon the European NATO countries demanded the withdrawal of Short Range INF, in which the superiority of the USSR in Europe was absolute. This demand was called Double Zero Option. Accepted by the USSR during 1987-88 negotiations, was a basis of the Reagan-Gorbachev summits in Washington DC 1987 and Moscow 1988.

D. ROBERTSON, *Guide to Modern Defense and Strategy*, Detroit, 1988.

DOW–JONES AVERAGES. One of the American price indexes, published since 1883 by the Dow Jones Company financial news bulletin. The founders: Charles H. Dow (1851–1902) and Edward D. Jones (1856–1920).

G.W. BISHOP, JR., *Charles H. Dow and the Dow Theory*, New York, 1960.

DOWNING STREET. A street in London whose No. 10 is the residence of British Prime Ministers and the seat of the Foreign Ministry and Treasury; name used in international relations to designate the policies of the British government or its foreign policy.

B. WEINREB, Ch. HIBBERT, *The , London Encyclopedia*, London, 1983.

DRACHMA. A monetary unit of Greece; one drachma = 100 lepta; issued by the Banque de Grèce.

DRAGO DOCTRINE, 1902. A principle of international law which excludes the use of force in the collection of monies loaned to a state. In 1902 Argentina was under threat of armed force from Germany, Italy, and the UK because of non-

payment of debts incurred with them by Argentina. The foreign minister of Argentina, L. M. Drago (1859–1921) requested the US government to supplement the Monroe Doctrine with a statement that the intervention of non-American states in the internal affairs of American states for the purpose of collecting debts would not be permitted. In 1907 on the initiative of the US ambassador, H. Porter (1837–1921), the Hague Conference drafted the Convention on Limitation of the Employment of Force for the Recovery of Contract Debts based on the Drago doctrine, art. 1 of which reads: "The High Parties pledge themselves not to resort to the use of force for the recovery of loans granted . . . and to submit disputes to the Permanent Court of International Justice."

L.M. DRAGO, "Les emprunts d'états et leurs rapports avec la politique internationale," in: *Revue générale de droit international public*, No. 14, 1907; H.A. MOULIN, *La doctrine de Drago*, Paris, 1908; J. FABELA, *Las Doctrinas Monroe y Drago*, México, DF, 1957.

DRAGOMAN. An official interpreter at a diplomatic post or consulate in the Near or Middle East who should not be Moslem; special legal status. Now the name is given to tourist guides.

DRAINAGE BASINS. A subject of international co-operation and conventions under the aegis of the UN system.

A. GARRETSON, R. HAYTON (eds), *The Law of International Drainage Basins*, New York, 1967.

DRANG NACH OSTEN. *German* = "Drive toward the east." A designation for German expansion in Slavic lands, especially prevalent in the history of Prussia and the Reich, 1870–1945. ("The Czech Nation formed a Slav bulwark against the Drang nach Osten" – a slogan of Nazi propaganda 1938 during the ▷ Sudeten Crisis).

F.L. CARSTEN, The Origins of Prussia, London, 1954; *Germanska expansiva v Tsentralnoy i Vostochnoy Yewropie, Sbornik Statiey po istorii tak nazywayenogo "Dranga nach Osten"*, Moskva, 1965. W.L. SHIRER, *The Nightmare Years 1930–1940*, New York, 1983.

DRAWBACKS. An international term for repayments of the customs duties paid on imported materials when the materials – processed or in the same form – are re-exported. A state concession designed to raise competitiveness.

S.E. STIEGELER (ed), *A Dictionary of Economics and Business*, London, 1986.

DRAWING RIGHTS. A statutory exchange transaction within the International Monetary Fund, members' purchases (i.e. drawings) from the IMF of the currencies of other member states for the equivalent amounts of their own currencies specified by the Fund regulations. Due to growing international trade the floating of international currencies proved to be insufficient; therefore, the IMF introduced in the 1950s apart from the drawing rights, the system of special agreements called Stand-By Arrangements, which are credit promissory notes or "protective credits". When this too proved insufficient, the IMF introduced the Special Drawing Rights, called in abbreviation ▷ SDR.

DREIBUND, 1882. *German* = "Triple Alliance". A secret treaty concluded between Austria-Hungary, Germany and Italy in Vienna on May. 20, 1882. Under its terms:

Art. 2 provided that Austria–Hungary and Germany should render military assistance to Italy in case of French attack; the same applied to Italy in case of French attack against Germany.

D

Art. 3 provided that if any of the signatories were involved in hostilities with other powers it would be treated as casus foederis by the other signatories.

Art. 4 provided for benevolent non-involvement of the signatories towards a signatory who waged war against any power threatening its interests.

The treaty was renewed on Feb. 20, 1887 and on June 6, 1891 was supplemented with a clause relating to the Balkan Peninsula and African colonies; again prolonged June 28, 1902 and Dec 5, 1912. In keeping with these terms Italy remained "benevolently non-involved" after German declaration of war against France Aug. 3, 1914. However, after the London Conference of the Allies, Apr. 26, 1915 Italy withdrew from the Triple Alliance (May 3, 1915) and declared war against Austria–Hungary, May 23, 1915, and against Germany, Aug. 28, 1916.

A.F. PRIBRAM, *Die politische Geheimverträge Osterreich-Ungarns 1879–1914*, Vol. 1, p. 128; Wien, 1920.

DRINKING WATER. An international term for water safe for human consumption. A subject of international co-operation. The International Drinking Water Supply and Sanitation Decade, 1981–1990, was launched at a special meeting of the UN General Assembly on Nov. 10, 1980, following a recommendation by the UN Water conference at Mar del Plata in 1977. The development of municipal sanitation includes waterworks, filters and canalization. From 1980 to 1983 safe drinking water was provided for an estimated 345 million people in developing countries according to a 1985 UN report on "Progress in the attainment of the goals of the International Drinking Water Supply and Sanitation Decade.

Strategies for extending and improving potable water supply during the decade of the 1980s, PAHO, Washington, 1979; *UN Chronicle*, April, 1979, p. 54. *UN Chronicle*, 1985, No. 5, pp. 50–51.

DROIT D'ARRÊT French = "the right of detention". An international term for the right of a country at war to detain and search neutral ships

DROIT DE CHAPELLE. A privilege of the ambassador to his own religious shrine in the embassy area when public exercise of his religion is not permitted in the receiving state.

E. DENSA, *Diplomatic Law*, New York, 1976, p. 86.

DRÔLE DE GUERRE. *French* = "funny war." An international term from World War II. The name for a war without military actions, such as France and Britain experienced after declaring war on The German III Reich Sept. 3, 1939 until the time of the attack of Nazi armed forces May 10, 1940 on France and the Battle of Britain Aug. 13, 1940. *German*: Sitzkrieg.

T. SCHACHTMAN, *The Phony War 1939–1940*, New York, 1982.

"DROPSHOT". Cryptonym of a strategic American plan for war with the USSR, deliberated in 1952. ▷ Truman Atom Threat, 1952.

DROUGHT. A subject of international control: Interstate Permanent Committee for Drought Control in the Sahelian Zone, est. Sept. 12, 1974 in Ougadougou, Upper Volta (now Burkina Faso), by a convention signed by heads of state of Chad, Gambia, Mali, Mauritania, Niger, Senegal, Upper Volta on Dec. 22, 1973. It came into force on July 1, 1974; organizes all African efforts against ▷ desertification. The UN General Assembly on Dec. 5, 1980, appealed to the international community to provide all the necessary humanitarian assistance to the countries of the Horn of Africa which were still

suffering from the deleterious effects of the successive years of drought. On Dec. 20, 1983, the UN General Assembly Res. 38/199 called for special measures for concerted international action and substantial and sustained levels of resources to promote the actions against the "scourges that ravage the African continent".

The 24 African countries most affected by drought, facing food shortage, listed by FAO 1984, are: Angola (interior affected); Benin (officially declared "disaster area"); Botswana (three years of consecutive drought); Cape Verde (has suffered from severe drought since 1968); Central African Republic (cereal production 22 per cent below normal level); Chad (two consecutive years of drought, compounded by many years of civil strife); Ethiopia (3,400,000 people affected by drought); Gambia (cereal production 50 per cent below normal); Ghana (hydro-electric service reduced to three days a week; drought exacerbated by arrival of thousands of Ghanians from Nigeria); Guinea (500,000 people acutely affected; compounded by recent earthquakes); Guinea-Bissau (North and Northeast); Lesotho (50 per cent of the population in need of emergency food supplies; two consecutive seasons of drought); Mali (three million people affected); Mauritania (thousands of nomads fled into Senegal and Mali, cattle nearing decimation); Mozambique (thousands have died); Sao Tome and Principe (countrywide); Senegal (interior and Northern regions worst hit); Somalia (exacerbated by large-scale presence of refugees); Swaziland (drought has persisted for two years); Tanzania (rinderpest and grain borer outbreaks); Togo (last year's rains were late and erratic); Upper Volta – now Burkina Faso (crop production 13 per cent below normal); Zambia (two years of consecutive drought); Zimbabwe (two years of consecutive drought, compounded by arrival of thousands of Mozambican victims). In 1980 the Governments of Burkina Faso, Chad, Gambia, Mali, Niger, Mauretania and Senegal established the Permanent Inter-State Committee on Drought in the Sahel. In 1984 the Governments of Ethiopia, Kenya, Somalia, Sudan and Uganda established the Permanent Inter-Government Authority on Drought and Development in East Africa.

The IFAD fund for sub-Saharan countries (Ethiopia, Ghana, Kenya, Mali, Mauritania, Niger, Senegal and Sudan) for 1986 amounted to $129 million.

Organizations reg. with the UIA:
Intergovernmental Authority on Drought and Development, f. 1986 Djibouti, Members: Djibouti, Ethiopia, Kenya, Somalia, Sudan, Uganda.
Drought Control in the Sahel, f. 1973, Ouagadougou, Burkina Faso. Members: Burkina Faso, Cape Verde, Chad, The Gambia, Guinea, Bissau, Mali, Mauritania, Niger, Senegal.

UN Chronicle, March, 1981, pp. 49–50 and March, 1982, p. 57 and March, 1984, pp. 1–28. *The Europa Yearbook 1983. A World Survey*, Vol. I, London, 1988.

DRUG ABUSE AND ILLICIT TRAFFICKING, INTERNATIONAL DAY AGAINST. Declared on Dec. 11, 1988 by the UN General Assembly, to be observed each year on June 26.

DRUG CONTROL CHRONICLE 1909–1989.
1909–The first international conference on narcotics of 13 nations (Opium Commission in China) took place in Shanghai.
1912–The First International Opium Convention signed in The Hague, entered into force in 1915.
1920–The League of Nations established an Advisory Committee on Traffic in Opium and other Dangerous Drugs.

1925–The second International Opium Convention, adopted in Geneva, entered into force 1926.
1931–The Convention for Limiting the Manufacture and Regulating the Distribution of Narcotic Drugs, signed in Geneva, entered into force in 1933.
1936–The Convention for the Suppression of the Illicit Traffic in Dangerous Drugs, signed in Geneva, entered into force in 1939.
1946–The Commission on Narcotic Drugs, established by the UN as a functional commission of the ECOSOC.
1953–UN Protocol for Limiting and Regulating the Cultivation of the Poppy Plant, the Production of, International and Wholesale Trade in and Use of Opium, entered into force in 1963.
1961–The Single Convention on Narcotic Drugs, signed on March 31, 1961, entered into force on Dec. 13, 1964.
1971–The Convention on Psychotropic Substances, adopted by WHO General Assembly, entered into force on Aug. 16, 1976.
1972–A Protocol amending the Single Convention on Narcotic Drugs, entered into force on Aug. 8, 1975.
1981–The UN General Assembly adopted an International Drug Abuse Control Strategy and a five-year, 1982–86 Action Program.
1984–The UN General Assembly adopted by Res. 39/142 a Declaration on the Control of Trafficking and Drug Abuse.
1987–A UN International Conference on Drug Abuse and Illicit Trafficking was held in Vienna on June 17–26.
The principal document prepared by the UN before the Conference was a 'Comprehensive Multi-disciplinary Outline of Future Activities in Drug Abuse Control'.

UN Chronicle, May, 1987.

DRUG CONTROL WITHIN THE UN SYSTEM. The Commission on Narcotic Drugs, a functional commission of ECOSOC is the main policy-making body concerned with international drug control within the UN system. The Commission, which consists of 30 member states elected by ECOSOC, is entrusted with specific functions attributed to it by the provisions of the international treaties on narcotic drugs and psychotropic substances. By virtue of the same treaties, the International Narcotics Control Board (INCB), assisted by its own secretariat, is an independent treaty organ composed of 13 members who are elected by ECOSOC on the basis of "their competence, impartiality and disinterestedness" and exercises a number of control functions entrusted to it by these treaties. In addition, specific functions in the implementation of the international conventions are also entrusted by the treaties to the UN Secretary-General, who carries them out through the UN Division of Narcotic Drugs, which also serves as the permanent secretariat of the Commission on Narcotic Drugs. Although not entrusted with any control functions by virtue of the international treaties, the UN Fund for Drug Abuse Control, UNFDAC, created in 1971, plays an important role in complementing the international treaty system by financing programs and projects aimed at supporting international and national drug control, which are executed by the Division of Narcotic Drugs and the specialized agencies of the UN family, including, i.a., the World Health Organization. WHO itself also is entrusted by these treaties with specific functions which are important and closely related to the work of the Commission on Narcotic Drugs. According to WHO estimates, in 1965–70 drug addiction in the USA and Western Europe had reached epidemic proportions. The UN Commission was alerted and recommendations to help governments prevent new forms of drug dependence were worked out. UNESCO launched a campaign against drug abuse by young people. Annual reports are published by the WHO Expert Committee on Drug Dependence. Organizations reg. with the UIA include:

European Society for the Study of Drug Toxicity, f. 1962, Berne.
Institute for the Study of Drug Dependence, f. 1907, London. Consultative status with ECOSOC and ILO. Publ. Drugs and Society.
International Commission on Alcohol, Drugs and Traffic Safety, f. 1962, Stockholm.

▷ Narcotics, ▷ Tranquillizers.

H.L. MAY, "Narcotic Drug Control. Development of international action and the establishment of supervision under the UN", in: *International Conciliation*, No. 441, pp. 303–380, May, 1948; *WHO Chronicle*, January, 1978; *UN Chronicle*, November, 1982, p. 47; *Yearbook of International Organizations*.

DRUG DEPENDENCE. A special form of drug addiction caused by the use of certain non narcotic drugs, in large doses for the purpose of becoming intoxicated. In the second half of the 20th century this form of drug addiction became quite widespread, especially in the Americas and in Europe. As a result of studies made by WHO in the 1970s the UN Commission on Narcotics formulated recommendations for the governments of UN member states on methods of combatting drug dependence.

R.B. FISHER, G.A. CHRISTIE, *A Dictionary of Drugs*, London, 1979.

DRUG SMUGGLING. One of the world problems in the last decades of the XX century; subject of international customs regulations. In 1987 the IMO prepared interim guidelines to help ship-owners, seafarers and others involved in shipping prevent illicit drug smuggling by sea, including tips on identifying some common drugs of abuse and people who may be using them.

UN Chronicle, May, 1987, p. VI.

DRUGS OF ABUSE. An international term, a subject of international conventions. The most widely abused drugs: ▷ Amphetamines, ▷ Cocaine, ▷ Depressants, ▷ Hallucinogens, ▷ Hashish, ▷ Heroin, ▷ Inhalants, ▷ LSD 25, ▷ Marijuana, ▷ Mescaline.
In July 1986 the USA and Brazil extended an agreement on fighting drug trafficking by including a programme for the prevention of drug addiction and the rehabilitation of addicts.

UN Chronicle, May, 1987; WHO, *The Rational Use of Drugs*, Geneva, 1987.

DRUZE OR DRUSE. A hill people living in Lebanon, Syria and Israel, numbering about 200,000 in the 1980's in majority Muslims or Christians. In 1963 a system of Druze Courts was founded in Jerusalem with exclusive jurisdiction in matters of marriage or divorce or other matters of personal status for the Israeli citizens or residents. In Israel the 1983 population census noted 65,861 Druzes.

N. BURON, F. MASSEY, *Druze History*, London, 1952; *The Europa Yearbook 1987. A World Survey*, London, 1987.

"DRUZHBA". *Russian* = "friendship". The name of an oil pipeline (4655 km) constructed 1960–64 within CMEA, running from the Soviet Union (3004 km), through Poland (675 km), Czechoslovakia (836 km), the GDR (27 km) and Hungary (123 km); supplies oil from the Volga–Ural Oil Basin (Tatar ASSR) to Mozysh (Byelorussia) from

where it forks, one leg going to Poland (Plock Plant) and GDR (Schwedt), the other to Hungary (Shazhalombatta) and Czechoslovakia (Zaluzhi).

DRY LANDS ▷ Arid Earth.

DSB. ▷ Narcotics.

DUAL-KEY SYSTEM. An international military term since the 1950's for a system applying to US nuclear weapons based in European NATO countries, which requires that two different keys be used to launch a nuclear missile, thus neither the US nor the NATO country in question can act independently of one another.

D. ROBERTSON, *Guide to Modern Defense and Strategy*, Detroit, 1988.

DUAL NATIONALITY. A Subject of international agreements since 1868, the first of the so-called ▷ Bancroft Treaties. Dual or multiple nationality was a result of changing domicile or cession and lack of conscious or unconscious renouncement of the previous or subsequent nationality which, under art. 5 of the Hague Convention of Apr. 12, 1930 on some questions of conflicting legislation related to nationality, should not be recognized by third countries. There are, however, countries in and outside of Europe that fully or with partial limitations recognize dual or multiple nationality, mostly for political or economic reasons (e.g. the Federal Republic of Germany and many states of Latin America). Therefore, West European states concluded the Convention of Strasbourg, May, 6, 1963, on the limitation of cases of multiple nationality. A controversy between West and East German lawyers was stirred by the verdict passed by the Senate of the Federal Constitutional Tribunal of FRG, July 31, 1973, concerning the interpretation of the treaty concluded between the FRG and the GDR which, in the context of nationality, provides under art. 16 and art. 116 of the Basic Law of the FRG (Grundgesetz der BRD), that "the German State nationality is simultaneously the nationality of the Federal Republic of Germany" which indicates that "not only nationals of the Federal Republic of Germany are German nationals" and when "a German national shall be in the sphere of State protection of the system of the FRG he shall enjoy full rights to protection by the Tribunal of the FRG and shall be guaranteed fundamental rights included in the Basic Law." Such an interpretation indicates, in practice, that all alien nationals that have had any time in the past "the German State nationality," thus particularly nationals of the GDR, are subject to laws of the FRG.

American Journal of International Law, 1964, p. 563; *Das Parlament*, Bonn, September, 1973. R.L. BLEDSOE, B.A. BOCZEK, *The International Law Dictionary*, Oxford, 1987.

DUBAI. A sheikdom, one of the former Trucial States, part of the federation of ▷ United Arab Emirates.

DUBLIN. Capital of the Republic of Ireland. Population 1981 census: 915,115.

DUBNA. A town in the Russian SFSR, Moscow area, in the Dubna river estuary of the Volga; est. pop. (1976) 50,000; since 1956 headquarters of ▷ Nuclear Research Dubna Joint Institute of CMEA of which it became a synonym in international academic quarters.

DUBROVNIK. A city of Croatia, Yugoslavia. The old City is included in the ▷ World Heritage

UNESCO List. Inside the walls of the former capital of the Republic of Ragusa are preserved all the districts built there successively since its foundation in the 7th century. They contain private and public, religious and civil buildings of remarkable splendour.

UNESCO. *A Legacy for All*, Paris, 1984.

DUE DILIGENCE. A international term introduced by the so-called ▷ Washington Rules 1871 on the obligation of neutral governments in an armed conflict to exercise "due diligence" so that ships carrying arms would not sail from their ports; repeated in the British–American Treaty of May 8, 1871; henceforth an English formula used in international conventions, but despite many attempts still not defined in a way formally recognized; subject of conflicting interpretation. ▷ Neutrality at sea.

"Devoirs internationaux des États Neutres. Règles de Washington", in: *Annuaire de l'Institut de Droit International*, 1877; *Dictionnaire de la terminologie du Droit international*, Paris, 1960; H. BLOMEYER, "Due diligence", in: *STRUPP-SCHLOCHAUER Wörterbuch des Völkerrechts*, Berlin, 1960, Bd. I, pp. 401–402. R.L. BLEDSOE, B.A. BOCZEK, *The International Law Dictionary*, Oxford, 1987.

DULLES DOCTRINE, 1949. A US strategic program formulated 1949 by the ideologist of the Republican Party, later Secretary of State in the years 1952–59, J.F. Dulles proposing the gradual repelling (roll-back) of the USSR from positions gained through the victory in World War II by threatening it with "on the brink of war." In 1952 Dulles was one of the co-authors of the ▷ Liberation doctrine, which he abandoned Oct. 21, 1956.

J. F. DULLES, *War and Peace*, New York, 1950.

DUMBARTON OAKS CONFERENCE AND PROPOSALS, 1944. A preliminary meeting on the establishment of the United Nations, held Aug. 21–Oct. 7, 1944, in the estate of Dumbarton Oaks in suburban Washington, DC; at the first stage, Aug. 21–Sept. 28, the UK, US and USSR representatives (William Cadogan, Edward R. Stettinius and Andrei Gromyko) considered the problems of war with Germany; during the second stage, Sept. 29–Oct. 7, the Chinese, UK and US representatives discussed war with Japan. Simultaneously a group of experts appointed by the big powers framed the Dumbarton Oaks Proposals for the General International Organization which was accepted Oct. 7, 1944 and provided a point for departure for the preparation of the UN Charter signed at the UN Conference of San Francisco, 1945. The text of the first four Chapters is as follows:

"Proposals for the Establishment of a General International Organization
There should be established an international organization under the title of The United Nations, the Charter of which should contain provisions necessary to give effect to the proposals which follow.
Chapter I. Purposes
The purposes of the Organization should be:
(1) To maintain international peace and security; and to that end to take effective collective measures for the prevention and removal of threat to the peace and the suppression of acts of aggression or other breaches of the peace, and to bring about by peaceful means adjustment or settlement of international disputes which may lead to a breach of the peace;
(2) To develop friendly relations among nations and to take other appropriate measures to strengthen universal peace;
(3) To achieve international co-operation in the solution of international economic, social and other humanitarian problems; and
(4) To afford a centre for harmonizing the actions of nations in the achievement of these common ends.

Chapter II. Principles

In pursuit of the purposes mentioned in Chapter I the Organization and its members should act in accordance with the following principles:

(1) The Organization is based on the principle of the sovereign equality of all peaceloving states.

(2) All members of the Organization undertake, in order to ensure to all of them the rights and benefits resulting from membership in the Organization, to fulfill the obligations assumed by them in accordance with the Charter.

(3) All members of the Organization shall settle their disputes by peaceful means in such a manner that international peace and security are not endangered.

(4) All members of the Organization shall refrain in their international relations from the threat or use of force in any manner inconsistent with the purposes of the Organization.

(5) All members of the Organization shall give every assistance to the Organization in any action undertaken by it in accordance with the provisions of the Charter.

(6) All members of the Organization shall refrain from giving assistance to any state against which preventive or enforcement action is being undertaken by the Organization.

The organization should ensure that states not members of the Organization act in accordance with these principles so far as may be necessary for the maintenance of international peace and security.

Chaper III. Membership

Membership of the Organization should be open to all peace-loving states.

Chapter IV. Principal Organs

(1) The Organization should have as its principal organs: (a) A General Assembly; (b) A Security Council; (c) An International Court of Justice; and (d) A Secretariat.

(2) The Organization should have such subsidiary agencies as may be found necessary.

Chapter V. The General Assembly; Chapter VI. The Security Council; Chapter VII. An International Court of Justice; Chapter VIII. Arrangements for the Maintenance of International Peace and Security, Including Prevention and Suppression for Aggression; Chapter IX. Arrangements for International Economic and Social Co-operation; Chapter X. Secretariat; Chapter XI. Amendments; Chapter XII. Transitional Arrangements.

Dumbarton Oaks Documents on International Organizations. US Department of State, Washington, DC, Oct. 9, 1944; P.E. CORBERT, *The Dumbarton Oaks Plan*, New York, 1944; E. BORCHARD, "The Dumbarton Oaks Conference", in: *American Journal of International Law*, No. 39, 1945; A. GARCIA ROBLES, *El Mundo de la Postguerra*, México DF, 1946, Vol. 1, pp. 41–44 and 78–85, Vol. II, pp. 136–143; *Postwar Foreign Policy Preparation 1939–1945*, Washington, DC, 1949, pp. 301–340; G. CONNELL-SMITH, *The Interamerican System*, New York, 1966; *Sovietskiy Soyuz na mezhdunarodnikh konfierentsiyakh 1941–1945. Konfierentsiya w Dumbarton Okse 21 VIII-28 IX 1944. Sbornik Dokumentov*, Moskva, 1978.

DUM-DUM. A rifle bullet that shatters in the body of the victim either due to a notch on the cross of the casing of the bullet or a percussion cap with mercury located within the bullet; produced for the first time in the locality of Dum-Dum near Calcutta in the second half of the 19th century, prohibited by the Second Hague Conference, Declaration of July 29, 1899.

DUMPING. An international term for the sale of goods in foreign markets below prevailing price levels to dispose of surpluses. Dumping was used very frequently in the interwar period. On Oct. 22, 1930 the government of the USSR announced that in view of increases in customs duties in many countries of Europe it was adopting dumping. Japan followed with a similar announcement Nov. 18, 1931. The UK and other countries of Europe passed anti-dumping laws, introducing the obligation to raise the price of goods to the level of local prices. After World War II this was condemned by GATT. However, a new phenomenon of currency dumping appeared, consisting of lowering the exchange rate of one's own currency below its real value, which promoted an increase in exports. GATT recognized as quasi-dumping the offering of goods on foreign markets above the costs of their production but below the costs of production of the importing countries, defining this by the formula "market disruption." The legislation of many countries permits the use of special customs charges, so-called anti-dumping tariffs as a protection against dumping.

Anti-Dumping Legislation, GATT, Geneva, 1970; *Anti-Dumping Actions and the GATT System*, London, 1977.

DUMPING LONDON CONVENTION, 1972 ▷ Radioactivity of the Deep Sea.

DUMPING OF WASTES. An international term, a subject of the 1972 London Convention on the Prevention of Marine Pollution by Dumping of Nuclear Waste at Sea (▷ Marine Pollution), and consultative meetings.

KEESING's *Contemporary Archive*, 1986.

DUNKIRK, DUNKERQUE. A port city in northern France on the North Sea; port of the evacuation of the British expeditionary force and part of the French army to Great Britain May 28–June 4, 1940; place of the signing of the French-British alliance on Mar. 4, 1947, called the ▷ Dunkirk Treaty.

DUNKIRK TREATY, 1947. A British–French Treaty of Alliance and Mutual Assistance concluded for 50 years, signed on Mar. 4, 1947 in the French port city of Dunkirk. Ratified by France on July 18, and by the UK on Oct. 8, 1947. In signing the treaty the ministers of foreign affairs of both states made a joint declaration, expressing the desire that the four powers occupying Germany should conclude a quadripartite treaty establishing the conditions and manner of disarmament and demilitarization of Germany. The first three articles stated that mutual assistance should be rendered in cases of violation of the peace by German aggression against one of the parties, or the non-fulfillment by Germany of the obligations resulting from the unconditional surrender of Germany. Art. 4 obligated both sides to on-going consultation on the question of problems concerning their economic relations. Art. 5 stated that the parties would make

no alliance or take any part in any coalition directed against one of them. The Treaty was extended to the BENELUX countries under the ▷ Brussels Treaty, 1948.

H. FISCHER-WOLLPERT, "Der Vertrag von Dünkirchen", in: *Europa Archiv, 1946–1947; UNTS 1947*; P. BARANDON, *"Von Dünkirchen zum Atlantikpakt"*, in: *Die Friedenswarte, 1950–51;* C.A. COLLIARD, *Droit international et Histoire Diplomatique*, Paris, 1950; A. LEPOITIER, *Dunkerque*, Paris, 1975; N. HANNAM, *Dunkirk. The Necessary Myth*, London, 1980.

DURAND LINE. A frontier between Afghanistan and British India demarcated in 1893 by Sir Mortimer Durand, 2240 km long, from North Gilgit to Kuh-i-Malik Siah in the north-west frontier mountains, established by Great Britain leaving, on the Pakistani side, the district of ▷ Pakhtunistan; since 1947, following the inception of independent Pakistan, subject of border disputes.

W. BARTIN, *India's North-West Frontier*, London 1939.

DURMITOR NATIONAL PARK. A Yugoslavian natural monument, included in the ▷ World Heritage UNESCO List. The Park covers the 61 km of the Canyon of the River Tara.

World Cultural Heritage. *UNESCO Information Bulletin*. No. 18, May 1982.

DUTCH GUIANA. ▷ Suriname.

DUTCH WEST INDIA COMPANY. Trading and colonizing company, 1621–1791, chartered by the State-General of the Netherlands, founded in 1624 Fort Amsterdam on Manhattan Island, which after the British-Dutch War 1664–67 was renamed ▷ New York, and is today the seat of the United Nations.

W.R. MANKMAN, *De West-Indische Compagnie*, Amsterdam, 1947.

DUTY-FREE SHOPS. An international term coined at Irish Shannon airport in 1947 to name sales to passengers in transit of special Irish merchandise (wool, English cloth, Irish whiskey) free of tax and duty; a new form of foreign trade soon adopted by all airports as well as some seaports, bus and railroad stations.

DVINA. The name of two rivers: (1) the Northern Dvina in North European USSR, rises in Veliki Ustyng and empties into Dvina Bay, an arm of the White Sea, 750 km long; (2) the Western Dvina in north-west European USSR, rising in the Valdai Hills, flows through Byelorussia and Latvia into the Gulf of Riga, an arm of the Baltic Sea, 1020 km long; during the years 1921–39 the Western Dvina was a border river between Poland and the USSR; the conditions of navigation, rafting; and others were defined by annex No. 5 to art. II of the ▷ Riga Peace Treaty of Mar. 18, 1921.

E

EAAFRO. ▷ East African Agriculture and Forestry Research Organization.

EACSO. ▷ East African Common Services Organization.

EAGGF. ▷ European Agriculture Fund.

EARTH. One of the planets of the Solar System, subject of international co-operation in the study of human life on Earth as well as exploration of space. The International Union of Geodesy and Geophysics is affiliated with the International Association of Seismology and Physics of the Earth's Interior and the International Association of Volcanology and Chemistry of the Earth's Interior.

D.H. HALL, *History of the Earth Sciences, during the Scientific and Industrial Revolution,* Amsterdam, 1979; *Yearbook of International Organizations;* UNESCO, *Man's Dependence on the Earth,* Paris 1987.

EARTH DAY 1970 and 1990. The first Earth Day hailed as the birthday of environmentalism was observed only in the USA, April 22, 1970. On the same day in 1990 the event was organised by the USA on an international basis.

The New York Times, February 8, 1989.

EARTHQUAKE. Seismic catastrophe, subject of international observation through systems of warning and aid. Since 1935 the energy of earthquakes is measured by a scale of magnitude worked out by C.F. Richter (▷ Richter's scale). The most violent earthquake in recent times took place in Chile 1960; 8.8 magnitude on the Richter scale, i.e. over 10,000 times more energy than the atomic bomb dropped on Hiroshima. The annual number of earthquakes registered by seismographs is *c.* 50,000. Organizations reg. with the UIA:

International Association for Earthquake Engineering, f. 1963, Tokyo, Japan.
International Association of Seismology and Physics of the Earth's Interior, f. 1901, Strasbourg. Members from 80 countries. Publ.; *Travaux Scientifiques.*
International Commission on Earthquake Hazard, f. 1986, Ottawa, Canada.
International Information Center, f. 1965, Honolulu, USA. Publ. Reports.
International Seismological Centre, f. 1964, London, UK. Consultative Status: UNESCO, WMO. Publ.: *Bibliography of Seismology.*

See also ▷ Seismology. ▷ Disaster Relief.

A. GUTENBERG, C.F. RICHTER, *Seismicity of the Earth and Associated Phenomena,* London, 1954; B.A. BOLT, *Nuclear Explosions and Earthquakes: The Parted Veil,* San Francisco, 1976; E.S. HUSEBYE, S. MYKKLTUEIT eds., *Identification of Seismic Sources – Earthquake or Underground Explosions,* NATO, Dordrecht, 1981. *Yearbook of International Organizations, 1986/87; The Europa Yearbook 1988. A World Survey,* Vol. I, London, 1988.

EARTH SATELLITES, ARTIFICIAL. An international term for all kinds of objects launched into orbit around the Earth; the subject of the international convention on the peaceful use of outer space under the terms of which the Secretary-General of the UN records all artificial earth satellites. On Oct. 4, 1957 the USSR opened the space age with first artificial earth satellite Sputnik I.

The number of a.e.s. grew quickly. In the first decade, 1957–67, the number of satellites launched into orbit exceeded 1000. The need to work out a Convention on possible damage caused by debris falling to Earth became obvious. ▷ Space objects convention 1971. ▷ Outer Space Exploration.

EAST AFRICA CO-OPERATION TREATIES, 1961 AND 1967. The first treaty signed in Dec., 1961 in Nairobi by the heads of government of Kenya, Tanganyika and Uganda, established the ▷ East African Common Services Organisation, EACSO; the second signed on June 6, 1967 in Nairobi came into effect on Dec. 1, 1967, established in place of EACSO the ▷ East African Community.

EAST AFRICA MEDICAL RESEARCH COUNCIL. A research institution established on Dec. 1, 1967 by a treaty of co-operation signed by Kenya, Tanzania and Uganda with administrative headquarters at Arusha. It has centers for general medical research in Amani, Tanzania; Leprosy Research Center in Alupe Busia, Kenya; Institute for Malaria and Vector-borne Diseases in Mwanza, Tanzania; trypanosomiasis in Tororo, Uganda; tuberculosis in Nairobi, Kenya; Virus Research Institute in Entebbe, Uganda. Reg. with the UIA.

Yearbook of International Organizations.

EAST AFRICAN AGRICULTURE AND FORESTRY RESEARCH ORGANIZATION, EAAFRO. An intergovernmental institution est. 1948 as a successor to the East African Agricultural Research Station, operating since 1927, and the East African Agricultural Research Institute, existing since 1944; an intergovernmental organization of Kenya, Tanzania and Uganda, headquarters in Arusha. Publ. *East African Agricultural and Forestry Journal* and *Record on Research.*

Yearbook of International Organizations.

EAST AFRICAN COMMON MARKET. An intergovernmental organization est. on Dec. 1, 1967 as the main organ of the ▷ East African Community. The ▷ East African Development Bank provides financial and technical assistance in the promotion of industrial development of the community of Kenya, Tanzania and Uganda.

EAST AFRICAN COMMON SERVICES ORGANIZATION, EACSO. An intergovernmental organization est. in Dec., 1961 in Nairobi by the East African Co-operation Treaty, responsible for communication, finance, commerce, industrial and labor co-operation and for social and research services.

EAST AFRICAN COMMUNITY. A common market between Kenya, Tanzania and Uganda, est. on Dec. 1, 1967 by the East Africa Co-operation Treaty 1967; replacing the ▷ East African Common Services Organizations. Headquarters Kampala. Reg. with the UIA.

Yearbook of International Organizations.

EAST AFRICAN DEVELOPMENT BANK. An intergovernmental institution, est. in 1967 in Nairobi by Kenya, Tanzania and Uganda. Associated with the African Development Bank, Barclays Bank International, Commercial Bank of Africa.

EAST AFRICAN INDUSTRIAL LICENSING COUNCIL. An intergovernmental institution of Kenya, Tanzania and Uganda, est. in 1953 in Arusha. Reg. with the UIA.

Yearbook of International Organizations.

EAST AND WEST BENGAL. ▷ Bengal.

EAST CARIBBEAN CURRENCY AUTHORITY. An intergovernmental institution, est. on Jan. 1, 1965, by a treaty which introduced a common currency unit (East Caribbean dollar), signed by representatives of governors of eight Caribbean islands: Antigua, Barbados, Dominica, Grenada, Montserrat, St Christopher-Nevis-Anguilla, St Lucia and St Vincent.

EASTER ISLAND. *Polyneysian:* Rapa Nui, *Spanish:* Isla de Pascua. A volcanic island in the South Pacific, 3540 km west of Chile. Area: 119 Sq. km. Discovered on Easter Sunday 1722. A subject of international disputes between Spain and France in the 18th century; annexed formally by Chile in 1888; since 1951 it has been a US naval and air base. The Thor Heyerdahl expedition, 1956–57, produced new information on the history and culture of the island.

Population 1988 est. 2,000 inhabitants of Polyneysian stock and some American military personnel supervising the installation of technological equipment for an emergency landing site for the US space shuttle, being built by NASA on the basis of a Chile-USA agreement signed on Aug. 2, 1985. A Committee for the Defence of Peace and Easter Island has protested against the $15 million military US investment in the Island's airstrip.

Since 1986 the Island is open to international tourism.

A. METREAUX, *The Ethnology of Easter Island,* London, 1940; T. HEYERDAHL, *Aku-aku; the Secret of Easter Island,* London, 1958; KEESING's *Contemporary Archive,* September 1985.

EASTERN AFRICAN NATIONAL SHIPPING LINE. An intergovernmental organization, est. in 1966 in Dar-es-Salaam. Members: governments of Kenya, Uganda, Zambia and the Southern Line Ltd. Regular shipping services between East Africa and foreign countries.

EASTERN CHURCHES. Christian churches in the East which became independent during the development of Christianity. The Eastern Churches consist of many Orthodox churches and churches which split in the 5th–6th centuries in the wake of debates on the Nature of Christ. These are the Monophysite churches (a doctrine recognizing only one – divine – nature of Christ), among which are: the Armenian, Ethiopic, Jacobinic, Coptic Churches, as well as those called Nestorian: Chaldean and Siro-Mulabrian (a doctrine recognizing two persons in Christ – divine and human, and as a result rejecting the cult of Mary as the Mother of God); part of the Eastern churches remain in union with Rome; accepting the Catholic doctrine and the supremacy of the Pope, while only retaining their own ritual in the liturgy and their own legislation in their internal church discipline.

R. A. KLOSTERMANN, *Probleme der Ostkirche,* Göttingen, 1955; R. JANIN, *L'église orientale et les rites orientaux,* Paris, 1955; M. LACKO, "Churches of Eastern Rite in North America", in: *Unitas,* 1964.

EASTERN EUROPE. An international term, geographically integrating the European part of the

E

Soviet Union; in the United Nations represented by Eastern European States: Bulgaria, the Byelorussian SSR, Czechoslovakia, the German Democratic Republic, Hungary, Poland, Romania, the Ukrainian SSR, the USSR, Yugoslavia".

D. R. SHANOR, *Soviet Europe*, New York 1975; CH. JONES, *Soviet Influence in Eastern Europe: Political Autonomy and the Warsaw Pact*, New York 1980; W. SUKIENNICKI, *East Central Europe During World War I: From Foreign Domination to National Independence*, Boulder, Col., 1984; *UN Chronicle* No. 10/11, 1985, p. 113; L. GORDON, *Eroding Empire: Western Relations with Eastern Europe*, Washington DC, 1987; G. GATI, *Gorbachev and Eastern Europe*, in *Foreign Affairs*, Summer 1987; W. H. IVERS, The US and Eastern Europe, in: *Foreign Affairs*, Summer 1987; J. STROYNOWSKI ed., *Who's Who in the Socialist Countries of Europe: Albania, Bulgaria, CSSR, GDR, Hungary, Poland, Romania, Yugoslavia*, New York, 1988; B. KAMINSKI, R. W. JANES, Economic Rationale for Eastern Europe's Third World Policy, in: *Problems of Communism*, March-April 1988; Z. BRZEZINSKI Special Address, in *Problems of Communism*, May–August 1988; J. F. BROWN, *Eastern Europe and Communist Rule*, Durham N.C., 1988; Ch. GATTI, Eastern Europe on its own, in *Foreign Affairs*, No 1, 1989; W. E. GRIFFITH Ed., *Central and Eastern Europe and the West*, Boulder, Colorado 1989.

EASTERN PACT, 1934. The common name of agreements drafted in the 1930s aimed at securing territorial status quo in Eastern Europe. The idea was mooted by French Foreign Minister J.L. Barthou who, during his visit to Warsaw, Poland, April 1934 put forward a concept of "East Locarno", a system of pacts guaranteeing the status quo in Eastern Europe modelled on Locarno Pact of 1925 which guaranteed the status quo in Western Europe. The initiative was prompted by international tensions following Hitler's takeover of Germany on Jan. 30, 1933, the announcement of the policy of retaliation and Germany's withdrawal from the League of Nations on Oct. 20, 1933. After multilateral diplomatic consultations including a meeting in Geneva, May 18–19, 1934 with the Soviet foreign minister M. Litvinov, the French submitted in July 1934 drafts of three agreements: a regional pact of mutual assistance between Czechoslovakia, Germany, Poland, the USSR, and the Baltic states (Latvia, Lithuania, Estonia and Finland); a French–Soviet agreement covering French obligations towards the USSR ensuing from a regional pact and French obligations towards the USSR ensuing from the Locarno Pact; and a general pact covering both the Locarno Pact and the above agreements with reference to the principles of the League of Nations. The Eastern Pact project was never implemented because of Germany's refusal to endorse it on Sept. 10, 1934. For Germany the terms of the Pact would prevent the possibility of frontier revisions in Eastern Europe.

Documents on German Foreign Policy, 1918–1945, Series C, 1933–1937, Vols. 2 and 3, Washington, DC, 1949–1962; B. MEISSNER, *Das Ostpaktsystem, Dokumentenzusammenstellung,* Hamburg, 1951.

EASTERN QUESTION. In the 19th century ▷ Balkan Question. After World War I related to the new central-eastern European states, Czechoslovakia and Poland.

EAST INDIA COMPANIES. Three European associations for direct trade with the East Indies and the Far East, 1600–1858 established in the 17th and 18th centuries by England, the United Provinces (Dutch), France, Denmark, Scotland, Spain, Austria and Sweden, known as the English East India Company, Dutch East India Company and French East India Company (Compagnie des Indes Orientales).

E. COTTON, *East Indiamen*, London, 1949; K. M. PANIKKAR, *Survey of Indian History*, London, 1960; C. R. BOXER, *The Dutch Seaborne Empire 1600–1800*, London, 1965.

EAST INDIA COMPANY, BRITISH. Company for trade with Asia, 1600–1858, chartered by the British Crown.

EAST INDIA COMPANY, DUTCH. Company for trade and colonization in the Far East, 1602–1798, chartered by the States-General of the Netherlands.

EAST INDIA COMPANY, FRENCH. Company for trade in South Asia and North America, 1664–1769, chartered by the Kings of France.

EAST INDIES. A name used in Europe since the 16th century for South East Asia (India, Ceylon, the Indochina Peninsula, Indonesia and the Malayan Archipelago).

EAST PRUSSIA. A province in the German Reich, the boundaries of which were defined in art. 28 of the Versailles Treaty, June 28, 1919. In accordance with arts. 94–98 plebiscites were organized in the East Prussian Provinces of Warmia, Masuria and Powisle on Aug. 11, 1920. On Apr. 21, 1921 a Convention was signed in Paris between Poland, the Free City of Gdansk and Germany concerning innocent transit between East Prussia and the rest of Germany, in keeping with art. 89 of the Versailles Treaty and of the Polish–Gdansk Convention, signed in Paris on Nov. 9, 1920. Poland granted Germany:

"Free transit for persons, commodities, ships, vessels, wheeled transportation means railroad cars, for postal traffic and telecommunication in transit between East Prussia and the rest of Germany through the territory (including territorial waters) released by Germany for the benefit of Poland on the grounds of the Versailles Treaty."

The convention, containing 107 articles, introduced privileged traffic on 10 railroad lines, operative till Aug. 31, 1939. The demands of the Third Reich made in the spring of 1939 regarding an uncontrolled highway and a railroad line running through Polish territory and linking the Reich with East Prussia were turned down by Poland. After World War II, under the Potsdam Treaty of Aug. 2, 1945 the territory of East Prussia was divided. The smaller north eastern part was ceded to the Soviet Union while the larger was ceded to Poland.

J. ANCEL (ed.), *La Pologne et la Prusse Oriental,* Paris, 1933; K. SMOGORZEWSKI, "East Prussia (Ostpreussen)", in: *Encyclopaedia Britannica*, Vol. 7, p. 88, Chicago, 1973.

EAST RIVER. A tidal strait, 25.7 km long and 183–1220 m wide, between Upper New York Bay and Long Island Sound; in New York City separating Manhattan Island and the Bronx from Brooklyn and Queens. Since Oct. 24, 1952 the UN Headquarters is situated on the East River.

EAST TIMOR. ▷ Timor island.

EAST–WEST. An age-old international term, which after World War II became a synonym of world division. In The Hague the International Center for Documentation and Information, INTERDOC, publishes a monthly in English entitled *East West CONTACTS, Relations between Communist World and Western World, Ideology – Politics – Economics – Culture*. Also in The Hague the East–West Institute publishes partly in English and partly in German a monthly entitled *Economic*

East–West Relations. The first contacts between CMEA and EEC were established in the 1970's. In March 1981 the EEC officially expressed a willingness to negotiate on the subject of relations with CMEA. In June 1985 the CMEA invited EEC representatives to visit CMEA headquarters in Moscow. The talks started in 1986/87. The negotiations on legal, economic and political aspects of CMEA–EEC co-operation were complicated by the different structures of both integration systems. The CMEA and EEC are not comparable organizations (CMEA with headquarters in Moscow is not a European regional organism like the EEC) and differ in attitude towards the Generalized System of Preferences of the UNCTAD, the Common Fund for Commodities etc. A major economic and political problem of the end of the 20th century is the disproportion of technological development between East and West.

S. VERNY, CEE–CAEM: le problème de la reconaissance mutuelle, in *Courrier des Pays de l'Est,* April 1986; M.D. SHULMAN, ed., *East-West Tensions in the Third World*, New York, 1986; L.E. BIRDZEL, Jr., *How the West Grew Rich: The Economic Transformation of the Industrial World*, New York, 1987; R.M. CUTLER, Harmonizing EEC-CMEA relations: never the twain shall meet? in: *International Affairs*, Nr 2, 1987; J. WINIECKI, *Economic Prospects East and West*, London 1987.

EAST–WEST AGREEMENT ON THE PROTECTION OF HUMAN RIGHTS, 1989. The final document of the Vienna meeting of the Conference on Security and Cooperation in Europe, adopted Jan. 16, 1989. The highlights of the Agreement:
On terrorism:
"The participating states unreservedly condemn as criminal all acts, methods and practices of terrorism, wherever and by whomever committed . . . and agree that terrorism cannot be justified under any circumstances . . . Convinced of the need to combine measures at a national level with reinforced international cooperation, the participating states express these intentions:
To pursue a policy of firmness in response to terrorist demands;
To reinforce and develop bilateral and multilateral cooperation among themselves in order to prevent and combat terrorism;
To prevent on their territories illegal activities of persons, groups or organizations that instigate, organize or engage in the perpetration of acts of terrorism or subversive or other activities directed toward the violent overthrow of the regime of another participating state;
To insure the extradition or prosecution of persons implicated in terrorist acts."
On Dignity of the Human Person:
"They expressed their determination to guarantee the effective exercise of human rights and fundamental freedoms, all of which derive from the inherent dignity of the human person and are essential for his free and full development.
In this context they will:
Develop their laws, regulations and policies in the field of civil, political, economic, social, cultural and other human rights and fundamental freedoms and put them into practice in order to guarantee the effective exercise of these rights and freedoms;
Publish and disseminate the text of the Final Act of the Madrid Concluding Document and of the present Document as well as those of any relevant international instruments in the field of human rights . . . to make them known as widely as possible and to render them accessible to all individuals in their countries, in particular through public library systems;

Publish and make accessible all laws, regulations and procedures relating to human rights and freedoms;

Respect the right of their citizens to contribute actively, individually or in association with others to the promotion and protection of human rights and fundamental freedom.

Insure human rights and fundamental freedoms to everyone within their territory and subject to their jurisdiction, without distinction of any kind such as race, color, sex, language, religion, political or other opinion, national or social origin, property, birth or other status."

On Equal Rights:

"The participating states confirm their determination to insure equal rights of men and women. Accordingly, they will take all measures necessary, including legislative measures, to promote equally effective participation of men and women in political, economic, social and cultural life.

In order to insure the freedom of the individual to profess and practice religion or belief, the states will: Take effective measures to prevent and eliminate discrimination against individuals or communities on the grounds of religion or belief in the recognition, exercise and enjoyment of human rights and fundamental freedoms in all fields of civil, political, economic, social and cultural life and to insure effective equality between believers and nonbelievers; Foster a climate of mutual tolerance and respect between believers of different communities as well as between believers and nonbelievers;

Respect the right of these religious communities to establish and maintain freely accessible places of worship or assembly; to organize themselves according to their own hierarchical and institutional structure; and to select, appoint and replace their personnel in accordance with their respective requirements and standards as well as with any freely accepted arrangement between them and their state;

Respect the right of everyone to give and receive religious education in the language of his choice, whether individually or in association.

They will protect and create conditions for the promotion of the ethnic, cultural, linguistic and religious identity of national minorities on their territory. They will respect the free exercise of rights by persons belonging to such minorities and insure their full equality with others.

The participating states will respect fully the right of everyone to freedom of movement and residence within the borders of each state and to leave any country including his own, and to return to his country."

On Trade, Health and Energy:

"The participating states recognize the importance of favorable business conditions for the development of trade between them. They will facilitate direct contacts between business people, potential buyers and end-users, including on-site contacts relevant to the business being transacted.

The participating states will develop their cooperation in medical and related sciences by intensifying research and the exchange of information on drug abuse and on new or increasingly widespread diseases. They will cooperate in particular in combating the spread of AIDS, taking into account the global AIDS strategy of the World Health Organization.

Given the depletion of natural resources, including nonrenewable sources of energy, the participating states will promote cooperation in the rational use of such resources and in the use of alternative sources of energy, including thermonuclear fusion."

On Reuniting Families:

"They will decide upon applications relating to family reunification or marriage between citizens of different states, in normal practice within three months. They will pay immediate attention to applications for travel of an urgent humanitarian nature and deal with them as follows:

They will decide within three working days upon applications relating to visits to a seriously ill or dying family member, travel to attend the funeral of a family member or travel by those who have a proven need of urgent medical treatment or who can be shown to be critically ill;

If in this context an individual's application for travel abroad has been refused for reasons of national security, they will insure that, within strictly warranted time limits, any restriction on that individual's travel is as short as possible and is not applied in an arbitrary manner. They will also insure that the applicant can have the refusal reviewed within six months and, should the need arise, at regular intervals thereafter.

In accordance with the Universal Postal Convention and the International Telecommunication Convention, they will:

Insure the rapid and unhindered delivery of correspondence, including personal mail and parcels.

Respect the privacy and integrity of postal and phone communications.

Insure the conditions necessary for rapid and uninterrupted telephone calls, including the use of international direct dialing systems, where they exist, and their development."

On Freedom of Information:

"They will insure that individuals can freely choose their sources of information. In this context they will:

Insure that radio services operating in accordance with the I.T.U. radio regulations can be directly and normally received in their states;

Allow individuals, institutions and organizations, while respecting intellectual property rights, including copyright, to obtain, possess, reproduce and distribute information material of all kinds.

Recalling that the legitimate pursuit of journalists' professional activity will neither render them liable to expulsion nor otherwise penalize them, they will refrain from taking restrictive measures such as withdrawing a journalist's accreditation or expelling him because of the content of the reporting of the journalist or of his information media.

They will insure that in pursuing this activity, journalists, including those representing media from other participating states, are free to seek access to and maintain contacts with public and private sources of information and that their need for professional confidentiality is respected."

The Agreement is not a legally binding international document, but rather a declaration of intention, signed by 16 members of the NATO and of the Warsaw Pact states.

The New York Times, January 17, 1989.

EAST–WEST CORRIDOR IN EUROPE. A project, discussed in December 1988 of creating a 100 km wide corridor on both sides of the frontier between the GDR and FRG where Warsaw Pact and NATO troops would be stationed, without the support of tanks, artillery and attack helicopters.

R. EARLE, E. RICHARDSON, Now How About an East West Corridor of Safety, in: *International Herald Tribune*, December 9, 1988.

EAST–WEST TRADE. An international term for economic relations between the socialist states and capitalist states. After World War II East–West Trade was the subject of international conflicts examined by the UN and at special conferences in connection with the introduction by the Western Powers 1947–55, of the system of trading, financing and transport restrictions aimed at socialist states (▷ COCOM and CHINCOM). The first conference for East–West trade was held in Moscow in 1955. Liquidation of the Cold War in East–West trade found reflection in the Management Center of Europe in Brussels, which organizes since 1968 annual conferences of scientists and representatives of industry and trade of the CMEA and EEC countries, as well as of Japan and the USA, called the Conference for Co-operation and East-West Trade. A considerable increase of trade in the years 1960–80 took place between the countries of East and West. In Nov., 1974 and in Mar., 1979 under the aegis of the UN Economic Commission for Europe and UNIDO the new initiatives in East–West Trade were discussed at special Conferences in Vienna, with experts from the USA and USSR. In March 1986 an EEC experts session on East–West trade in the 1980's took place in Geneva.

M.L. HOFFMAN, "Problems of East–West trade", in: *International Conciliation*, No. 511, Jan. 1957, pp. 259–308; H. LANGE, *Ost-West Handel für die 70-er Jahre*, Bad Harzburg, 1971; *Directory of Soviet and East European Companies in the West*, Ottawa Carlton University, 1978; M. LAVIGNE, *Les relations économiques Est-Ouest*, Paris, 1979; *Principal International Business*, New York, 1983; *UN Manual on Trading with the Socialist Countries of Eastern Europe*, New York, 1985.

ECA ▷ UN Economic Commission for Africa.

ECCLESIAM SUAM. *Latin* = "Church matter". The first encyclical of Paul VI announced in Aug., 1964 on the subject of dialogue of the Roman Catholic Church with other religions and with persons holding a materialistic world view; the Church sanctioned the dialogue of Catholics with persons of other faiths and with non-believers.

ECE ▷ UN Economic Commission for Europe.

ECLAC ▷ Economic Commission for Latin America and the Caribbean.

ECOLOGICAL WAR. Meteorological war or geographical war. Various forms of artificial ecological disturbances, subject of international negotiations over a treaty to prohibit the waging of wars of this type, recognized by the UN Disarmament Conference in Geneva, Sept. 3, 1976, as catastrophic for the future of mankind and the world. Experts see the possibility of six kinds of catastrophic disturbances: (1) artificial inducement of ocean floods, (2) artificial inducement of earthquakes, (3) expansion of the polar cap which could cause a new ice age in Europe and North America, (4) change in the direction of tropical hurricanes, (5) change in sea currents, (6) destruction over arbitrarily selected countries of part of the ozone layer, causing mass burns and skin cancer.

The Geneva proposal for a treaty of Sept. 3, 1976 was preceded by a joint USA–USSR proposal for a treaty presented to the UN Disarmament Committee in 1975 "on the question of prohibiting the use of techniques to modify the environment for military purposes or any other kinds of hostile aims."

UN Yearbook 1975 and 1976; "The waging of war by Ecological means and destruction of the environment", in: SIPRI, *World Armaments and Disarmament, 1976*, Stockholm–London, 1976, pp. 50–51; A.H. WESTING ed., *Herbicides in War: The Long Term Ecological and Human Consequences*, Stockholm, 1984.

ECOLOGY. An international term for the branch of biology concerned with the mutual relationship between life forms and their respective environments, subject of organized international co-operation, especially developed under UN patronage in

E

the field of human ecology. ▷ Environmental protection. Organizations reg. with the UIA:

Commonwealth Human Ecology Council, f. 1969, London, UK. Publ.: *Law and Human Ecology*.
European Centre for Human Ecology, f. 1972, Geneva, Switzerland.
Inter-American Institute of Ecology, f. 1970, Knoxville, Tn., USA.
International Association for Child Ecology, f. 1985, Seattle, Wa., USA.
International Association for Ecology, f. 1967, Athens, Ga., USA. Publ.: *INTECOL Newsletter*.
International Association for Landscape Ecology, f. 1984, Laersum, Netherlands.
International Centre of Insect Physiology and Ecology, f. 1970, Nairobi, Kenya.
International Committee on Microbial Ecology, f. 1970, Dundee, UK.
International Organization for Human Ecology, f. 1986, Vienna, Austria.
International Society for Chemical Ecology, f. 1983, Lexington, Ky., USA.
International Society for Tropical Ecology, f. 1956, Varanasi, India.
International Statistical Ecology Program, f. 1972, University Park, Pa., USA.
Liason Committee on Statistical Ecology, f. 1972, University Park, Pa., USA.
Nordic Council for Ecology, f. 1965, Lund, Sweden.
Office of the Board of Administration of the Programme for Red Sea Ecology, f. 1984, Tunis, Tunisia.
Pan American Centre for Human Ecology and Health, f. 1975, Mexico, DF., Mexico.

V.S. VASIL'EV, V.D. PISAREV, G.S. CHOZIN: *Ekologija i mezhdunarodnye otnoshenija*, Moskva, 1978; D.W. ORR, M.S. SOROOS, *The Global Predicament. Ecological Perspectives on World Order*, Chapel Hill, 1979; *Yearbook of International Organizations, 1986/87; The Europa Yearbook 1988*. A World Survey, Vol. I, London, 1988; F.D. CASTRO ed., *Ecology in Practice*, 2 Vls, UNESCO, Paris, 1989.

ECONOMETRICS. A science investigating the quantitative regularities taking place in the economy with the aid of mathematical–statistical methods. The name Econometrics was introduced by the Norwegian economist, R. Frish. Econometrics has become the subject of organized continuous international co-operation since Dec. 29, 1930, when the Econometric Society was est. with a seat in New Haven, Conn., USA. It has as its members scholars from *c.* 80 countries. Since 1946 reg. with the UIA; has consultative status with ECOSOC and UNESCO. Publ. a quarterly, *Econometrics*.

R. FRISH, *Sur un problème d'économie pure*, Paris, 1926; L. R. KLEIN, *A Textbook of Econometrics*, New York, 1953; S. VALAVANIS, *Econometrics: an Introduction to Maximum Likelihood Methods*, London, 1959; G. TINTNER, *Handbuch der Oekonometrie*, Berlin, 1960; O. LANGE, *Introducción a la econometria*, México, DF, 1968; *Yearbook of International Organizations*.

ECONOMIC AGGRESSION. An international term for the use in peacetime of economic boycott and economic blockade with regard to another state with a view to causing its socio-economic destabilization.

UN Review, No. 302, 1960.

ECONOMIC AND SOCIAL COMMITTEE. An intergovernmental institution of the European Community, EEC est. in 1958 under arts. 194–198 of the Treaty of Rome. There are 156 members, appointed by the European Commission for a four-year term. The ESC must be consulted in cases specified in the treaties, such as the free movement of workers, freedom of establishment, fredom to supply services, and in all cases where the approximation of provisions laid down by national laws entails amendment of national legislation.

ECONOMIC AND SOCIAL COUNCIL. ▷ ECOSOC.

ECONOMIC AND SOCIAL DEVELOPMENT FUND FOR NON-ALIGNED COUNTRIES. An intergovernmental institution est. by the IV Conference of Heads of State or Government of Non-Aligned Countries, in Algiers, Sept. 5, 1973. ▷ Algiers Economy Action Program of Non-Aligned Countries 1973.

Conference on Economic Co-operation among Developing Countries. Declarations, Resolutions, Recommendations and Decisions, adopted in the UN System, Mexico, DF, 1976, Vol. 3, pp. 505–506.

ECONOMIC AND SOCIAL WORLD DEVELOPMENT. A subject of international co-operation carried out under UN auspices in keeping with the assumptions of the UN Charter, UN Declarations on progress and development and the Decade of Progress. According to UN Secretary-General U Thant, 1962, development should be automatically both economic and social; development is "growth plus change"; change is social and cultural as well as economic, qualitative as well as quantitative. Since 1946 the UN and its specialized agencies have registered, watched and examined the economic–social development of UN member countries and individual regions of the world, the co-ordinating organ being ECOSOC with its regional economic social commissions. A separate organization committed to the study of the Third World is the Centre International du Développement, International Development Center est. in 1964 by the French government with headquarters in Paris. The World bank supplied the following data in 1972:

The poorest nations with national income per capita amounting to less than 200 dollars annually comprised 67% of the Third World population and had a national income growth-rate of less than 4%; countries with national income per capita from 200 to 500 dollars annually made up 20% of Third World population and had a 5.4% national income growth-rate annually; countries with national incomes per capita of 500 dollars annually made up 9% of the Third World population and recorded a 6.2% annual growth-rate of national income; the developing countries, exporting oil on a large scale, inhabited by less than 4% of the world's population, averaged an 8.4% growth-rate of national income annually.

Referring to these data, the President of the World Bank, R. MacNamara, observed that the rate of development of the majority of developing countries was deteriorating and unsatisfactory at the same time, the situation being that the development of these countries failed to ensure their citizens both gratification of basic needs and an equal share in the benefits of economic progress of their own country as well as of the whole world.

According to a UNCTAD analysis from June 1983.

"The world economy is in a state of crisis, the gravest since the Great Depression.

Millions of people are unemployed in countries around the world. The fragile economies of poor countries are burdened by such heavy debts that governments are being forced to cut back on development projects essential for the welfare of their people. The prices of traditional raw material exports of developing countries are at the lowest levels, in real terms, in 45 years, at a time when the prices of manufactured goods climb steadily higher. Monetary instability, declining aid, high interest rates and new discriminatory barriers against trade are stunting economic growth. And to top it all, the affluent countries which have in past decades repeatedly affirmed their support for the processes of development, seem to be withdrawing their co-operation in critical areas, assuming policies that are inward looking and defensive. Of a sample of 103 developing countries for which data are available, one third, most of them least developed countries, which accounted for more than 9 per cent of the population of developing countries in 1978, registered zero or negative growth of GDP per capita during the period 1970–1978. At the other end are the countries that were able to meet the anual per capita growth target of 3.5 per cent for the Second United Nations Development Decade. They accounted for nearly one third of the countries in the sample as well as one third of the population of developing countries. The worsening in the situation of many developing countries in the 1970s is reflected in the frequency distribution of GDP per capita growth rates in the 1960s and 1970s, about one half of the countries recorded per capita growth of less than 2 per cent, whereas the corresponding proportion in the 1960s was one third. It should also be noted that only 12 countries registered a decline in GDP per capita in the 1960s and that about 60 per cent of the countries surpassed the per capita growth target set for the First United Nations development Decade.

The indicators of crisis in the world economy are alarming. In 1981, the GNP of the developing countries taken as a whole grew at a bare 1.5 per cent. In 1982, the growth rate was even lower, Per capita growth has hence been negative. Their total external debt has mounted to over $600 billion. The prices of commodities, on the exports of which many of them still depend, plummeted in real terms to their lowest level in 45 years. In 1981 and 1982 the developing countries other than oil exporters lost $34 billion through the decline in their terms of trade. Both investment and consumption are being curtailed, with consequences for current employment and for future growth. In the developed market-economy countries, growth rates averaged 1 per cent over the last two years, and both investment and employment declined. The unemployed now exceed 30 million in these countries. In the socialist countries of Eastern Europe growth rates declined to less than 2 per cent in 1981 and 1982. But it is not only that countries are in crisis. In the last two years world trade has stagnated and capital flows have contracted. The very systems that sustained international economic relations during the post-war years in the areas of money, finance and trade have been subjected to continuous stresses and strains. In fact, these systems themselves are in crisis.

The crisis has affected virtually every country and given rise to the most adverse economic situation since the 1930s. Yet up to now, national policies have been mostly defensive and inward-looking. In the developed market-economy countries, the primary policy objective has been the dampening of inflationary pressures, with serious consequences for employment and production. In the developing countries – and the socialist countries as well – investment and development activities are being scaled down in order to cope with problems of external payments and indebtedness. The forces of contraction have thus been mutually reinforcing and, as a result, the last two years have seen – almost everywhere – a spiral of declining production, employment and trade."

"The developed market-economy countries are of dominant importance in the world economy. Their fortunes for the remainder of the 1980s and beyond will have, therefore, a major influence on the rest of the world – particularly through the channels of trade and finance. These countries are not, of course, homogeneous and both past experience and future prospects vary from country to country. But if one looks at them as a group, some broad trends and prospects stand out. Already by the end of the 1960s strains were beginning to appear which resulted in a loss of momentum in their rate of growth. A number of factors interacted with each other to bring about this result. In the first place, the period of post-war reconstruction and the impetus given by it to expansion had come to an end. The rising trend of productivitiy during the 1950s and 1960s – also without parallel in earlier history – was beginning to slacken, whilst the growth of the labour force itself was decelerating. Internal changes in economic, social and political power affected the distribution of the national product, introducing new pressures and new rigidities in the structures of prices and costs. The mounting expenditure on armaments and the sharp price increases of imported energy further aggravated tensions.

The developed market-economy countries face a prospect of relatively slow growth in the 1980s. Many projections suggest an average growth performance for these countries at between 2 and 3 per cent annually – in contrast to the roughly 5 per cent growth they experienced during the 1950s and the 1960s. These projections assume a recovery from the present recession. The growth prospects for the socialist countries of Eastern Europe are better. But even there a dampening of the long-term trend of growth is likely because of a slower expansion of the labour force and the reduced scope for the absorption of suplus labour from agriculture and other sectors of low productivity.

In the developing countries the situation is vastly different. In these countries, with their growing workforce and the vast scope that exists for structural and technological transformation, the dynamics for growth are perhaps stronger than ever before. Already one of the major changes that has taken place over the nearly two decades that separate UNCTAD I and UNCTAD VI is the increased 'presence' of the developing countries on the world economic scene. A number of these countries have acquired significant industrial capacities and a growing potential for the export of manufactured goods. A number of oil-exporting developing countries have experiencd a transformation in their economic situation because of dramatic changes in the relative price of petroleum Processes of regional co-operation and integration have gathered momentum in parts of the developing world giving increased strength and cohesion to a number of economies. The results of these developments are reflected in the changing relative shares of these groups of countries in world gross domestic product:"

Growth rates of total and per capita GDP and real income of developing countries (per cent per annum)

	1960–70	1970–80
GDP		
Total developing countries	5.7	5.6
Fast-growing exporters of manufactures	6.4	7.1
Least developed countries	2.6	3.2
Per Capita GDP		
Total developing countries	3.1	3.0
Fast-growing exporters of manufactures	3.6	4.5
Least developed countries	0.0	0.6
Real Income		
Total developing countries	5.0	7.1
Major oil-exporting countries	3.6	14.0
Fast-growing exporters of manufactures	6.3	6.6
Least developed countries	2.6	2.3
Per capita real income		
Total developing countries	2.4	4.5
Major oil-exporting countries	0.9	11.1
Fast-growing exporters of manufactures	3.5	4.0
Least developed countries		−0.3

Shares in world GDP (%)

	USA	EEC	Japan	Socialist countries of Eastern Europe	Developing countries
1950	40	17	2	13	13
1960	36	20	3	15	13
1970	31	20	7	16	12
1980	22	24	9	15	18

Source: UNCTAD, Handbook of International Trade and Development Statistics 1983.

US News and World Report, October 16, 1972; "The world economy in crisis" in: *UN Chronicle*, June, 1983, pp. 37–52.

ECONOMIC ARBITRATION. A system of mediatory institutions in socialist countries. The first were set up in the USSR after World War I and in socialist countries after World War II; they are by law sole mediators in property litigation between collectivized institutions. In the 1970s a uniform system of economic arbitration in trade relations was set up for the CMEA member countries.

ECONOMIC ASSOCIATION TREATY OF GUATEMALA, HONDURAS AND EL SALVADOR, 1960. A treaty signed on Feb. 6, 1960 in Guatemala City by the above states for the purpose of establishing the free flow of persons, goods, and capital between the three countries. It was superseded on Dec. 13, 1960 by the General Treaty on ▷ Central American Economic Integration.

ECONOMIC CHARTER OF THE AMERICAS, 1945. A series of resolutions of the Interamerican Conference on Problems of War and Peace, called ▷ the Chapultepec Conference, passed on March 8, 1945. The Charter proclaimed absolute "economic freedom" throughout the entire Western Hemisphere for the initiatives of private capital, both national as well as foreign, which should be granted "equal and just treatment" with local capital, through the "elimination of all outbreaks of economic nationalism", through "equal rights in access to basic raw materials" and through respect for the private treaties controlling international trade, etc. The Charter ended with the statement that this is "an economic program which will enable the people of the Western Hemisphere and their satellites to attain the highest standard of life."

"Principales, Resoluciones de Indole Económica de la Conferencia Interamericana sobre problemas de la Guerra y de la Paz", *El Trimestre Económico*, México, DF, 1945; A.G. ROBLES, *El Mundo de la Postguerra*, México, DF, 1946, Vol. 2, pp. 398–401.

ECONOMIC COMMUNITY OF THE GREAT LAKES COUNTRIES. Est. 1976 by a Treaty between Burundi, Rwanda and Zaire. Main organs: Conference of Heads of State, Council of Ministers of Foreign Affairs, Secretariat, Commissions and Banque de development des états des Grand Lacs at Goma, Zaire. Publ.: *Grand Lacs*.

Yearbook of International Organizations, 1986/87; The Europa Yearbook 1988, A World Survey, Vol. I. London, 1988.

ECONOMIC COMMUNITY OF WEST AFRICAN STATES, ECOWAS. An intergovernmental organization, est. in 1959 in Ougadougou, as the Customs Union of West Africa by the Ivory Coast (now Côte d'Ivoire), Mali, Mauritania, Niger, Senegal and Upper Volta (now Burkina Faso); changed name to Customs and Economic Union of the States of West Africa following the intergovernmental agreement, signed in Accra, May 4, 1967 by the governments of Benin, Gambia, Guinea, the Ivory Coast, Liberia, Mali, Mauritania, Niger, Senegal, Sierra Leone, Togo and Upper Volta, to promote through the economic co-operation of the member states a coordinated and equitable development of their economies, especially in industry, agriculture, transport and communications, trade and payments, manpower, energy and natural resources, (art. 1a). The Access agreement revised by the Abidjan Treaty, 1973, came into force Jan. 1, 1974. The Economic Community of West African States, ECOWAS was est. in May 1975 in Lagos by a Treaty involving 15 governments of that region: Benin, Cape Verde, Gambia, Ghana, Guinea, Guinea Bissau, the Ivory Coast, Liberia, Mali, Mauritania, Niger, Nigeria, Senegal, Sierra Leone,

Togo and Upper Volta. The Treaty aims at the economic integration of an area of *c.* 5 million sq. km inhabited by *c.* 150 million people, envisaging: the creation of a customs union by 1990; the planned common industrialization and exploitation of natural resources, co-operation in energy, transport, and land, air, and sea communications, telecommunications, a common financial-monetary policy, and co-operation in social and cultural matters.

The 9th and 10th annual summit meetings in June 1986 and on July 1, 1987 took place in Abuja, Nigeria's future capital. The French name of the Community is CEAO: Communauté Economique d'Afrique Occidentale.

UNTS, Vol. 595, p. 288.

ECONOMIC CONFERENCES INTERNATIONAL, 1927–38. The following is a list of international conferences on economic issues which took place in the interwar years:

1927 – First International Economic Conference convened by the LN, held May 2–23, in Geneva, where for the first time the world economic situation was analyzed in the fields of commerce, industry and agriculture. Participants: all member nations of the LN and the USSR.

1930 – Second International Economic Conference summoned by the LN, held in January in Geneva, called Preliminary Conference, debated the memorandum of the Secretary-General of the LN, which suggested the joint elaboration of an economic treaty that would permit free trade between all the states of Europe. In Paris June 30–July 1, the ministers of foreign affairs of Western Europe debated the French plan for the creation of a European Customs Union. No agreement reached.

1932 – Imperial Economic Conference in Ottawa 21 July–20 Aug. Debate on establishing a broad system of British Commonwealth preferential tariffs. No agreement reached.

1933 – World Financial Conference, convened by the LN, held in London June 12–July 27. Taking part were the member states of the LN and the USA; two opposite trends predominated at the conference: one favored the development of international trade on the basis of agreements which would lower tariff barriers and reduce currency restrictions; the other favored the development of economic self-sufficiency. No agreement was reached.

1938 – The governments of Belgium and Great Britain on Jan. 7, began a diplomatic campaign to summon a World Economic Conference, but the German Reich and Italy declined to participate. After World War II economic conferences organized by the UN were transformed into a permanent institution. ▷ UNCTAD.

SdN Rapport définitive de la Conférence Économique Internationale, Genève, 1927 and 1930; *International Conciliation*, No. 311, New York, June 1935, pp. 289–342.

ECONOMIC CO-OPERATION AMONG DEVELOPED COUNTRIES ▷ OECD.

ECONOMIC CO-OPERATION AMONG DEVELOPING COUNTRIES, ECDC. An institution established 1983 by the ▷ Group of 77 as an:

"Integral and essential part of the efforts of the developing countries, to restructure international economic relations with a view to realizing the full potentials of the developing countries to bring about rapid social and economic development and to establishing New International Economic Order."

Report of the ECOSOC, Launching of Global Negotiations on International Economic Co-operation for Development, A/38/494, Oct., 1983.

ECONOMIC DEVELOPMENTS. In accordance with the UN General Assembly Res. 3508/XXX, on Dec. 15, 1975, the regional commissions of the UN have prepared studies on long-term trends in the

E

economic development in the regions of Africa, Asia and the Pacific, Europe and Latin America. A summary of the reports was published on Mar. 17, 1977 by the UN Secretary-General.

UN Doc. E/5937, Mar. 17, 1977.

ECONOMIC INTEGRATION. An international term for a process of gradual unification of national economies of two or more states characterized by the same social and economic system, ultimately resulting in the formation of an economic community allowing for a higher rate of growth in the integrated states. The conditions under which economic integration occurs, particularly the systems of the integrating countries, determine the manner in which profit is shared. The EEC may serve as an example for capitalist states, CMEA for socialist states.

ECONOMIC INTERNATIONAL CO-OPERATION. The subject of international law and world and regional international conferences. Principles of international economic co-operation were not uniform in various regions of the world and in various periods of history. The first attempt to codify these principles and apply them to the contemporary international situation in which there exist three groups of states: capitalist, socialist and the so called developing states of the Third World, was undertaken by the First World Conference on Trade and Development, UNCTAD, which passed in Geneva, 1964, Principles of International Economic Co-operation. The UN General Assembly proclaimed with Res. 2626/XXV the International Development Strategy for the Second UN Development Decade (from Jan. 1, 1971 to Dec. 31, 1980), based on the economic and technical co-operation among developing countries. The Program of Action on the Establishment of a ▷ New Economic International Order adopted by the UN General Assembly with Res. 3202/S-VI, pledge to make full use of the UN system thereby strengthening the role of the UN in the field "of worldwide co-operation for economic and social development."

Conference on Economic Co-operation among Developing Countries. Declarations, Resolutions, Recommendations and Decision adopted in the UN System, 3 Vols., México, DF, 1976; M. BLAUS ed., Who's Who in Economics; A Biographical Dictionary of Major Economists, 1700–1988, Cambridge, Mass., 1986.

ECONOMIC SANCTIONS ▷ Sanctions.

ECONOMIC SECURITY DOCTRINE, 1943. A doctrine proclaimed on Jan. 6, 1943 by US President F.D. Roosevelt:

"We have come to a clear realization of the fact that true individual freedom cannot exist without economic security and independence."

The Public Papers and Addresses of F.D. Roosevelt, 13 Vols., New York, 1938–50.

ECONOMIC, SOCIAL, AND CULTURAL RIGHTS, INTERNATIONAL COVENANT ON, 1966. An intergovernmental convention, one of the ▷ Human Rights Covenants, drafted by the UN Human Rights Commission between 1949 and 1954. It was redrafted by the Third Committee of the UN General Assembly 1955–66 and passed by the UN General Assembly Dec. 16, 1966 with Res. 2200/XXI. For the text ▷ Human Rights International Convention on Economic, Social and Cultural Rights.

ECONOMIC STATISTICS CONVENTION, 1928. An international convention relating to economic statistics, signed on Dec. 14, 1928 in Geneva, amended by the Protocol, signed on Dec. 9, 1948 in Paris. The classes of statistics integrated by the Convention are: external trade, occupations, agriculture, livestock, forestry and fisheries, mining and metallurgy, and industry. States party to the Convention as amended by the Protocol are: Australia, Austria, Canada, Denmark, Egypt, Finland, France, Greece, India, Italy, the Netherlands, Norway, South Africa, Sweden and the UK.

LNTS, Vol. 110, p. 171; UNTS, Vol. 20, p. 229; Vol. 73, p. 39.

ECONOMIC SUMMIT. ▷ Venice Declaration of Industrialized Countries, 1980.

ECONOMIC UNION. An international term for a fusion of a customs union with a currency union in a specific region without any limitations for the free flow of goods and services and with payments to be made in a common currency.

ECONOMIC WAR. An international term for an economic boycott directed against one country or a group of states by another state or group of countries in peacetime. ▷ Customs War.

US Export Control Act of 1949. Public Law no. 703, Washington, DC, 1949.

ECONOMIC WORLD SYSTEMS. An international term for five economic systems in the World in the 1980's:
(1) Centrally planned in countries like China, the Soviet Union, Cuba, etc., that are being restructured since the mid-1980's. Represented in 1986 circa 12% of World trade and circa 24% of World GNP.
(2) Developing countries system, changing with development, representing in 1986 circa 15% of World trade and 14% of World GNP.
(3) Mixed free trade and centrally planned economies like France, Spain, Sweden, etc.
(4) Plan driven economies like Japan representing in 1986 13% of World trade and 10% of World GNP, with private ownership of business and industry as a rule.
(5) Anglo-American free trade model, representing 27% of the World trade and 33% of the World GNP, with private ownership of business and industry as a rule.

Harvard Business Review, January–February, 1988; Economic Impact, No. 2, 1988.

ECONOMIC ZONES. ▷ Fisheries, economic zones.

ECONOMY. A synonym in the UN system of the economic and social problems of development.

J. EARWELL, M. MILGATE, P. NEWMAN, eds., The New Palgrave: A Dictionary of Economics, 4 Vls., London, 1988.

ECOSOC, ECONOMIC AND SOCIAL COUNCIL. ECOSOC, under the authority of the UN General Assembly, is the organ which co-ordinates the economic and social work of the United Nations and the specialized agencies and institutions – known as the "United Nations family" of organizations. The Council makes recommendations and initiates activities relating to development, world trade, industrialization, natural resources, human rights, the status of women, population, social welfare, science and technology, prevention of crime, and many other economic and social questions.
The membership of the Council is 54, with 18 members elected each year by the General Assembly for a three-year term. Retiring members are eligible for immediate re-election. Originally the Council had 18 members. Amendments to the Charter which came into force in 1965 and 1973 enlarged the membership respectively to 27 and 54.
Functions and Powers. The charter sets out the following functions and powers of the Economic and Social Council: to make or initiate studies, reports and recommendations on international economic, social, cultural, educational, health and related matters; to promote respect for, and observance of, human rights and fundamental freedoms for all; to call international conferences and prepare draft conventions for submission to the General Assembly on matters within its competence; to negotiate with the specialized agencies, defining their relationship with the United Nations, and to co-ordinate the activities of the specialized agencies by means of consultation with them and recommendations to them, and by means of recommendations to the General Assembly and members of the United Nations; to perform services, approved by the Assembly, for members of the United Nations and, upon request, for the specialized agencies; and to consult with non-governmental organizations concerned with matters with which the Council deals.
Voting. Voting in the Economic and Social Council is by simple majority; each member has one vote.
Subsidiary bodies. The Economic and Social Council generally holds two regular sessions a year, each one month long, in New York and Geneva. Throughout the year, however, there are meetings of the Council's standing committees, commissions and other subsidiary bodies at headquarters, or in other locations.
There are standing Committees on Non-Governmental Organizations; Negotiations with Intergovernmental Agencies; Programme and Co-ordination; Natural Resources; Review and Appraisal; and Science and Technology for Development. The Commission on Transnational Corporations is also a standing body.
The functional commissions comprise the Statistical Commission; the Population Commission; the Commission for Social Development; the Commission on Human Rights; the Commission on the Status of Women; and the Commission on Narcotic Drugs. The Commission on Human Rights has a Sub-Commission on Prevention of Discrimination and Protection of Minorities. The Commission on Narcotic Drugs has a Sub-Commission on Illicit Drug Traffic and Related Matters in the Near and Middle East.
Also under the Council's authority are the regional commissions, whose aim is to assist in the economic and social development of their respective regions and to strengthen the economic relations of the countries in each region, both among themselves and with other countries. These are the Economic Commission for Africa (with headquarters in Addis Ababa), the Economic and Social Commission for Asia and the Pacific (Bangkok), the Economic Commission for Europe (Geneva), the Economic Commission for Latin America (Santiago) and the Economic Commission for Western Asia (Beirut). The regional commissions study the problems of their regions and recommend courses of action to member governments and specialized agencies. In recent years the work of the commissions has been expanded, and they have been increasingly involved in carrying out development projects.
Related agencies. The intergovernmental agencies are separate, autonomous organizations related to the United Nations by special agreements. They have their own membership, legislative and executive bodies, secretariats and budgets, but they work with the United Nations and with each other through the co-ordinating machinery of the

Economic and Social Council. Fifteen agencies are known as "specialized agencies", a term used in the Charter. They report annually to the Economic and Social Council. The specialized agencies are listed below.

International Labour Organisation (ILO).
Food and Agriculture Organization of the United Nations (FAO).
United Nations Educational, Scientific and Cultural Organization (UNESCO).
World Health Organization (WHO).
International Bank for Reconstruction and Development (World Bank, IBRD).
International Finance Corporation (IFC).
International Development Association (IDA).
International Monetary Fund (Fund, IMF).
International Civil Aviation Organization (ICAO).
Universal Postal Union (UPU).
International Telecommunications Union (ITU).
World Meteorological Organization (WMO).
Inter-Governmental Maritime Consultative Organization (IMCO).
World Intellectual Property Organization (WMO).
Inter-Governmental Maritime Consultative Organization (IMCO).
World Intellectual Property Organization (WIPO).
International Fund for Agricultural Development (IFAD).
The International Atomic Energy Agency (IAEA) and the General Agreement on Tariffs and Trade (GATT), are also listed among the related agencies.

Non-governmental organizations. The Economic and Social Council may consult non-governmental organizations on matters with which they are concerned and which fall within the competence of the Council. The Council recognizes that these organizations should have the opportunity to express their views, and that they often possess special experience or technical knowledge that would be of value to the Council in its work.

Organizations which have been given consultative status may send observers to public meetings of the Council and its subsidiary bodies and may submit written statements relevant to the work of the Council. They may also consult with the United Nations Secretariat on matters of mutual concern. Organizations in consultative status are divided into three categories: those with a basic interest in most of the activities of the Council (Category I); those which have a special competence in, and are concerned specifically with, only a few of the Council's fields of activity (Category II); and those which have a significant contribution to make to the work of the Council which may be placed on a roster for *ad hoc* consultations. In December 1977, 26 organizations were listed in Category I, 102 organizations in Category II, and 501 were on the Roster.

On Dec. 20, 1988, the GA Res 43/432 entitled "Revitalization of the ECOSOC" was adopted without vote. The Annex read as follows:

Recognizing that the process of reforming the economic and social sectors of the United Nations aims at contributing to the full implementation of General Assembly resolution 41/213 and requires continued attention;

Aware that the work of the Economic and Social Council should be enhanced and streamlined in order to make the United Nations system more responsive to the challenges of development, in particular of developing countries, and to the needs of Member States in the coming years;

Fully aware of the urgent need to revitalize the Council in order to enable it, under the authority of the General Assembly, to exercise effectively its functions and powers as set out in the Charter of the United Nations and relevant resolutions of the General Assembly and the Council;

Having heard statements by the President of the Economic and Social Council and by Member States on the revitalization of the Council as the principal organ of the United Nations under Charter in the economic and social fields:

(1) Affirms that the Economic and Social Council should make an important contribution to the major issues and concerns facing the international community, in particular, the economic and social development of developing countries;

(2) Decides to adopt the following measures aimed at revitalizing the Council, improving its functioning and enabling it to exercise effectively its functions and powers as set out in Chapters IX and X of the Charter of the United Nations:

Policy Formulation:

(a) With a view to formulating and elaborating action-oriented recommendations:

(i) The annual general discussion of "international economic and social policy, including regional and sectoral developments" should take place during the first five working days of the second regular session and should allow enough time for a dialogue and an exchange of views between members and executive heads of the organizations of the United Nations system;

(ii) The Council should undertake annually in-depth discussions of previously identified major policy themes, to be selected on the basis of a multi year work programme derived, *inter alia*, from the priorities set out in the medium-term plan of the United Nations and the work programmes of other relevant United Nations bodies;

(iii) The Council shall, as and when necessary, address urgent and emerging issues relating to acute international economic and social problems possibly as one of the themes identified in accordance with subparagraph (ii) above;

(iv) In the context of the above:

(a) The specialized heads of the specialized agencies or their senior representatives should participate actively in the deliberations of the Council;

(b) The specialized agencies should be invited to resume submission of analytical summaries of their annual reports for the consideration of the Council;

Monitoring

(b) The Council shall monitor the implementation of the overall strategies, policies and priorities established by the General Assembly in the economic, social and related fields as set out in relevant resolutions of the Assembly and the Council; it shall also consider all appropriate modalities for carrying out the recommendations of the Assembly on matters falling within the Council's competence; in this regard:

(i) The Secretary-General should circulate each year to Member States and all organizations of the United Nations system, as well as to the Council at its organizational session, a consolidated note on the decisions adopted by the General Assembly in the economic, social and related fields, highlighting matters that require action by them;

(ii) The Council shall obtain information from the specialized agencies on the steps taken to give effect to the recommendations of the General Assembly and the Council on economic, social and related matters that fall within the respective mandates and areas of competence of the agencies; such information is to be included in the analytical summaries of their annual reports;

(c) With a view to submitting appropriate recommendations to the General Assembly on the overall and programme priorities of the United Nations in the economic, social and related fields, the Council shall examine in depth the relevant chapters of the proposed medium-term plan and sections of the proposed programme budget of the United Nations in the light of the recommendations of the Committee for Programme and Co-ordination;

Operational activities:

(d) The Council shall recommend to the General Assembly overall priorities and policy guidelines for operational activities for development undertaken by the United Nations system; for that purpose:

(i) The Council, as part of its co-ordination functions, shall define, as and when necessary, overall priorities and specific activities for the organizations of the United Nations system, within their respective mandates, so that the operational activities for development of the United Nations system are carried out in a coherent and effective manner;

(ii) The Council shall deal, each year, with a limited number of policy co-ordination issues, including those identified in General Assembly resolution 42/196 of 11 December 1987; the executive heads of the organizations concerned should be invited to participate actively in such discussions;

(ii) Once every three years the Council shall conduct a comprehensive policy review of the operational activities for development of the United Nations system, which shall be one of its major policy themes and shall be undertaken in connection with the triennial policy review of operational activities carried out by the General Assembly;

The Council shall monitor the follow-up to its recommendations; organizations of the United Nations system should report to the Council on progress made in the implementation of those recommendations;

Co-ordination:

(e) The Council shall carry out its functions of co-ordinating the activities of the United Nations system in the economic, social and related fields as an integral part of its work; to this effect:

(i) Co-ordination instruments, such as cross-organizational reports, the Joint Meetings of the Committee for Programme and Co-ordination and the Administrative Committee on Co-ordination, and reports of the Administrative Committee on Co-ordination and its subsidiary bodies, should be rationalized in order to enable the Council to carry out its co-ordination functions in an effective manner, based on the measures contained in the present resolution; the Committee for Programme and Co-ordination should assist the Council in this regard and submit specific proposals thereon to the Council at its second regular session of 1989;

(ii) The Administrative Committee on Co-ordination, through its Consultative Committee on Substantive Questions (Operational Activities), and the Joint Consultative Group on Policy should prepare suggestions to assist the Council in fulfilling its central co-ordinating role in the field of operational activities for development and should submit them to the Council at its second regular session of 1989;

(iii) The Council shall consider the activities and programmes of the organs, organizations and bodies of the United Nations system, in order to ensure, through consultation with and recommendations to the agencies, that the activities and programmes of the United Nations and its agencies are compatible and mutually complementary, and shall recommend to the General Assembly relative priorities for the activities of the United Nations system in the economic and social fields; for that purpose, cross-organizational programme analyses shall be discontinued in their present form and be replaced by brief analyses on major issues in the medium-term plan, as referred to in subparagraph (a) (ii) above, to be considered directly by the Council; immediately after the General Assembly adopts the next medium-term plan, the Secretary-General should submit to the Council draft proposals on a multi-year programme for such analyses;

(iv) In considering the question of regional co-operation, the Council shall concentrate on the policy review and co-ordination of activities, particularly with respect to issues of common interest to all regions and matters relating to interregional co-operation;

Working methods and organization of work:

(f) In formulating its biennial programme of work, the Council shall, to the extent possible, consolidate similar or closely related issues under a single agenda item, in order to consider and taking action on them in an integrated manner; the Council shall pay particular attention to bringing the economic and the social activities of the United Nations system closer together; to this effect:

(i) In proposing future calendars of conferences, the Secretary-General should ensure that meetings of the subsidiary bodies of the Council will end at least eight weeks before the session of the Council at which their reports are to be considered; the Committee on Conferences should be requested to act accordingly;

(ii) The Council shall further continue to consider the biennialization of the sessions of its subsidiary bodies and items on its own agenda and programme of work, taking into account the need for a balance between economic and social issues;

(iii) The Secretariat shall prepare for the Council, on the basis of reports submitted by the relevant organs, organizations and bodies of the United Nations system, issue-oriented consolidated reports on economic, social and related questions that the Council will consider under the consolidated agenda items;

(iv) All reports submitted to the Council should be prefaced by an analytical executive summary that highlights the main issues addressed and the recommendations made in the report;

(v) The six-week rule for the circulation of substantive reports of the Secretariat and the eight-week rule for the annotated agenda of the Council should be strictly observed;

(vi) The Council shall report to the General Assembly on the outcome of its work in a manner that will enable the Assembly, in its Main Committees, to consider the recommendations made by the Council in an integrated manner;

(vii) The Council shall review all relevant documentation prepared for the consideration of questions in the economic, social and related fields;

(g) The Secretary-General, in the context of the implementation of General Assembly resolution 41/213, should submit to the Council, at its second regular session of 1989, proposals on the structure and composition of a separate and identifiable secretariat support structure for the Council, which would undertake the substantive functions and technical servicing that will be required to implement subparagraphs (b) (i), (b) (ii), (e) (iii) and (f) (iii) above; (h) To achieve better and more effective co-ordination of the economic, social and related activities of the United Nations system, including operational activities for development, the Office of the Director-General for Development and International Economic Co-operation should be strengthened; in this context, the relevant provisions of General Assembly resolutions 32/197 and 33/202, including those concerning improved policy planning, should be fully implemented;

(i) In the recruitment of staff for the United Nations Secretariat in the economic and social fields, due consideration should be given to the principle of equitable geographical representation;

(j) The Third (Programme and Co-ordination) Committee of the Council shall henceforth focus on:

(i) Operational activities for development of the United Nations system and system-wide co-ordination of those activities;

(ii) Programme questions;

(iii) Co-ordination of the activities of the United Nations and the United Nations system;

(k) The Council shall elect its President and Bureau early in the calendar year, prior to the organizational session of the Council;

(l) Prior to the organizational session, the President, with the co-operation of the other members of the Bureau, should arrange for consultations with members of the Council on the draft programme of work and provisional agenda prepared by the Secretary-General and on the allocation of agenda items and make proposals thereon for consideration by the Council; the duration of the organizational session of the Council could consequently be shortened;

(3) Requests the Secretary-General to submit a report to the Economic and Social Council at its second regular session of 1989 on the feasibility and comparative costs of holding at the United Nations, with the present in-sessional arrangements, one consolidated or two regular sessions of the Council;

(4) Decides to include an item entitled "Revitalization of the Economic and Social Council" in the provisional agenda for its second regular session of 1989 and to consider under that item a report of the Secretary-General on progress in the implementation of the present resolution;

(5) Requests the Secretary-General to report to the Economic and Social Council at its second regular session of 1989 on the progress made in the implementation of the relevant paragraphs of the present resolution and on proposals for incorporating in the biennial programme of work of the Council measures to implement the present resolution;

(6) Also requests the Secretary-General, in order to enable the Council to continue discussions on how its work can be enhanced so as to make it more responsive to the challenge of development in the coming years, to submit to the Council at its second regular session of 1989 a note on:

(a) The functioning of the Council and its subsidiary bodies in relation to the relevant chapters of the medium-term plan, using the following categories: (i) policy formulation, co-ordination and monitoring; (ii) operations and implementation; (iii) technical support;

(b) The mandates of the bodies established to assist the Council in carrying out its functions, listed according to the same three categories."

R. E. ASHER, *The UN and Economic and Social Co-operation*, Washington, DC, 1957; G. J. MANGONE (ed), *UN Administration of Economic and Social Programs*, New York, 1966; M. SEARA VAZQUEZ, *Tratado General de la Organización Internacional*, México, DF, 1974; *Everyone's United Nations*, New York, 1979, pp. 15–17; *UN Resolutions and Decisions adopted by the General Assembly during the First Part of its Forty-Third Session, From 20 September to 22 December 1988*, New York, 1989, pp. 609–613.

ECOWAS. ▷ Economic Community of West African States.

ECS. European Communication Satellite. An acronym accepted for two West European telecommunication satellites, whose construction was started in 1978 by the ▷ European Space Agency.

ECU. ▷ European Currency Unit.

ECUADOR. Member of the UN. República del Ecuador. Republic of Ecuador. State in South America on the Pacific Ocean, bounded by Colombia (frontiers established in 1916) and Peru (frontiers established in 1942). Area: 283,950 sq. km. Pop. 1986 est.: 9,640,000 (census 1974: 6,521,710). Capital city: Quito with 1,110,248 inhabitants 1982. GNP per capita 1986: US $1,160. Official language:

Spanish. Currency: one sucre = 100 centavos. National Day: Aug. 10, anniversary of proclamation of independence, 1809.

Founding member of the League of Nations, formal membership in 1934–39. Founding member of the UN since Oct. 24, 1945 and of all its specialized agencies excluding GATT. Founding member of the OAS, 1948. Member of ALALC and Andine Pact. Member of the ▷ Tlatelolco Treaty, 1967.

International relations: 1563–1809 Spanish colony (*Presidencia de Quito*). Independence proclaimed in Quito on Aug. 10, 1809, confirmed by the Independence Act in Guayaquil on Oct. 9, 1820. In 1822–30 part of Great Colombia. In 1835 the Constitutional Assembly in Quito proclaimed the Republic of Ecuador in the former region of Presidencia de Quito with an area of 1,038,000 sq. km. After separation from Great Colombia, the area of Ecuador shrank to 706,000 sq. km, in 1916 to 472,000 sq. km following cessions to Colombia under the Muñoz-Bernaza Treaty and to 283,000 sq. km in 1942 after cessions to Peru under the Peace, Friendship and Frontiers Protocol called the Rio de Janeiro Protocol, 1942. The Protocol, guaranteed by USA, Brazil, Chile and Argentina, ratified in 1942 by Ecuador and Peru, was declared null and void from the outset by Ecuador's Constitutional Congress of Nov. 23, 1960 because it had been extorted. In response the Peruvian government stated on Nov. 29, 1961 that it would never consent to changes in the Treaty ratified by Ecuador at a time when there was not a single Peruvian soldier on its territory. During World War I, Ecuador was in the Entente. During World War II among the United Nations. On Sept. 8, 1955 accused Peru before the OAS Council of preparing aggression, but the Military Commission of States Guaranteeing the Rio de Janeiro Protocol, 1942 did not find grounds for the accusation. On Mar. 12, 1966 Heads of State of Ecuador and Colombia concluded a treaty on integration of borderlands called the ▷ Rumichaca Act. In 1971–72 acute clashes occurred between Ecuador and USA about the right to fish in Ecuador's territorial waters by US fishing vessels, following the extension by Ecuador of its zone of territorial waters to 200 miles. Arrests of US fishing vessels by Ecuador's warships were dubbed "tuna wars". On a recommendation of Congress the USA applied financial sanctions canceling dollar credits for Ecuador. Nationalization of oil deposits started in 1972 and was carried out gradually. Foreign stocks were taken over by the state enterprise, Corporación Estatal Petrolera Ecuatoriana, CEPE, member of OPEC since Nov. 1973. In Jan. 1981 a border conflict with Peru over the Cordillera del Condor was resolved under the conditions of the Rio Protocol of 1942. New border clashes with Peru occurred in Dec. 1982 and Jan. 1983.

See also ▷ World Heritage UNESCO List.

Bibliografía 1756–1941, Quito 1942; *Dictamen Jurídico acerca del Problema Ecuatoriano-Peruano, dados por ilustres Internacionalistas Americanos*, Quito 1942; J. DONOSO TOBAR, *La Invasión Peruana y el Protocolo del Río*, Quito, 1945; E. BENITEZ VINUEZA, *Ecuador: Drama Paradoja*, México, 1950; L. YOPER, *Síntesis histórica y geográfica del Ecuador*, Madrid, 1951; L. LINKE, *Ecuador, Country of Contrast*, London, 1959; Foreign Area Studies of the American University: *Area Handbook for Ecuador*, Washington, DC, 1966 D.S. ROSS, "The 'Tuna War'", in: *New Republic*, No. 1 of 1972; J.D. MARTZ, *Ecuador: Conflicting Political Culture and the Quest for Progress*, Boston, 1972; F.B. DIKE, *The US and the Andean Republics: Peru, Bolivia, Ecuador*, Cambridge, Mass., 1976; R.J. BROMLEY, *Development Planning in Ecuador*, London, 1977; A. CUEVA, *The Process of Political Domination in Ecuador*, London, 1982; *The Europa Year Book 1984. A World Survey*, Vol. II, pp.

1498–1514, London, 1984; J.D. MARTZ, *Politics and Petroleum in Ecuador*, New Brunswick, N.J., 1987.

ECUMENICAL COUNCILS. An international term for an assemblage of bishops in the Catholic Church in principle under the leadership of the Pope. The Church recognizes the following 21 councils as universal: Nicea I, 325; Constantinople I, 381; Ephesus, 431; Chalcedon, 451; Constantinople II, 553; Constantinople III, 680–681; Nicea II, 787; Constantinople IV, 869–870; Lateran I, 1123; Lateran II, 1139; Lateran III, 1179; Lateran IV, 1215; Lyons I, 1245; Lyons II, 1274; Vienna, 1311–12; Constance, 1414–18, Basel-Ferrara-Florence-Rome, 1431–45; Lateran V, 1512–17; Trent, 1545–63; Vatican I, 1869–70; Vatican II, 1962–65. The majority of councils were convened for the purpose of condemning views or movements regarded as heresies and formulating dogmas. Only in the 20th century did the Roman Catholic Church become conciliatory toward the other Christian churches, which was in response to the modern world Ecumenical movement of the Protestant and Orthodox Churches. This council was called by Pope John XXIII (Angelo Giuseppe Roncalli) in the conviction that the nuclear age required the unification of humanity, that is a dialogue and cooperation among all people and nations, all religions and races, believers and non-believers. Vatican II took place from Oct. 11, 1962 to Dec. 8, 1965. It was opened by John XXIII on Feb. 25, 1959 after the preparatory work of 10 committees from June 5 to Nov. 4, 1960 and the central committee, 1961; it had four sessions: I from Oct. 11 to Dec. 8, 1962; II from Nov. 29, to Dec. 4, 1963; III from Sept. 14 to Sept. 21, 1964; and IV from Sept. 14, to Dec. 8, 1965. On June 3, 1963, during Session I, John XXIII died and his successor became Paul VI (Giovanni Battista Montini). Vatican II initiated the renewal process called ▷ *"aggiornamiento"* of the Roman Catholic Church and unification with other Christian churches as well as a dialogue with non-believers. It was expressed in the following documents:

(1) On Dec. 8, 1965, after centuries of schism, unification took place between the Roman Catholic Church and the Orthodox Church in the form of a common declaration, a public abrogation of the mutual excommunication proclaimed against each other in Rome and Constantinople in 1054.
(2) Generally accepted for the first time was a dialogue with all people of goodwill and all systems without condemning them a priori, with the reminder that discussion is always possible for those who love truth.
(3) On Oct. 28, 1965 the Catholic Church for the first time officially asserted in a declaration on the relation of the Church to non-Christian religions that the Jewish nation cannot be regarded as responsible for the death of Christ.
(4) The Church condemned nuclear weapons.
(5) For the first time the Church stated that Catholics have a moral obligation to fight for peace together with all people of goodwill in the world of whatever race, religion, or ideology.
(6) The Church for the first time gave its full support to the work of the UN.
(7) For the first time the Church recognized the possibility of using force to eliminate social injustice.

Points 2, 4 and 5 were formulated in the pastoral constitution regarding the Church in the contemporary world on Dec. 7, 1965. Point 6 was expressed in the encyclical ▷ *Pacem in Terris*, and then in the development of relations between the Vatican and the UN and its specialized agencies. Point 7 is found in the encyclical ▷ *Populorum progressio*. From Nov. 24 to Dec. 8, 1985 an extraordinary Synod of 165 bishops was held in Rome 20 years after the closure of the Vatican II. The Final Act (Relate) affirmed the results of Vatican II and defined areas of special attention for the future.

HEFELE-LECLERQUE, *Histoire des conciles*, Paris, 1916; C.D. CLERQ, *Histoire des conciles*, Vols. 13, Paris 1907–53; J.D. MANSI, *Sacrorum conciliorum nova et amplissima collectio*, 3 Vol., Paris, 1962–63; H. KÜNG, Y. CONGAR OP, D.O. HANLON, S.J. (eds) *Council Speeches of Vatican II*, 1964; J.H. MILLER C.S.C. (ed), *Vatican II. An Interfaith Unity*, 1966; *Documenti di Vaticano II*, Roma, 1966; *Vaticano II. Enciclopedia Conciliar, Historia. Doctrina. Documentos*, Roma, 1967; R.E. TRACY, *American Bishop at the Vatican Council*, 1967.

ECUMENICAL INSTITUTE IN JERUSALEM. An international institute opened on Sept. 15, 1971, on the initiative of Paul VI and financed by the Catholic Notre Dame University, Indiana. It organizes joint studies for Catholic, Orthodox and Protestant theologians. Besides classrooms and a library, the Institute has a chapel with three altars, before which a common liturgy of the Faith is performed daily, with the Eucharistic Liturgy given separately.

ECUMENICAL MOVEMENT. ▷ World Council of Churches.

EDEN PLAN, 1955. A plan to establish a zone between Central and Eastern Europe controlled by international agencies presented by Anthony Eden, the Prime Minister of Great Britain, on July 18, 1955 at the Summit Conference in Geneva. The essence of the plan was to create a "buffer zone" between the West and the East. The Eden Plan consisted of three documents: (a) a plan to unify Germany under international supervision presented Jan. 29, 1954 in Berlin at a Conference of Ministers of Foreign Affairs; (b) establishment of demilitarized zone proposed at a summit meeting in Geneva, July 1955; (c) being a combination of the above, presented at a Geneva conference of foreign ministers in Oct.–Nov. 1955; the plan implied: (1) conclusion of a security pact by the four powers and a unified Germany; (2) the parties "under conditions specified by themselves" were supposed to declare assistance to a victim of aggression; (3) general reduction of armed forces and armaments in Germany and neighboring countries (buffer zone); (4) establishment of a demilitarized zone. The Eden Plan did not win support of the other Powers: France, the USA and the USSR.

KEESING'S *Contemporary Archive*, 1954 and 1955.

EDITORS ORGANIZATIONS. Associations reg. with the UIA:

European Association of Earth Science Editors, f. 1968, Utrecht. Publ. *Editorra Circular Letters*.
European Association of Editors of Biological Periodicals, f. 1967, Slough, UK. Publ. *Newsletter*.
Federation of European Industrial Editors Associations, f. 1955, Rotterdam, Netherlands.
Latin American Association of Editors in the Earth Sciences, f. 1973, Caracas. Publ. *Boletin Informativo*.

Yearbook of International Organizations.

EDUCATION. A subject of international co-operation since the 19th century. In the UN system from 1946 under the aegis of UNESCO. Subject of international conventions.
The first convention was worked out by the Inter-American Conference for the Consolidation of Peace, 1936, called the Convention on the Pacifist Orientation of Education, signed Dec. 23, 1936 by Argentina, Bolivia, Brazil, Colombia, Cuba, Dominicana, Ecuador, Guatemala, Haiti, Honduras, Mexico, Nicaragua, Panama, Paraguay and Uruguay. The USA refused to sign. The Convention imposed an obligation on its participants to "introduce the teaching of comprehensive principles for the peaceful solution of international disputes and renouncement of the use of force as an instrument of national policy."
The Second Convention of Oct. 4, 1943, on the Inter-American University in Panama, has not entered into force. The next international convention was the Constitution of ▷ UNESCO which is a specialized UN agency dealing with education, science and culture.
In 1960 UNESCO prepared and adopted a Convention and Recommendations on Prevention of Discrimination in Education. The following are regional international organizations: conferences of ministers of education initiated in the Western Hemisphere by the First Inter-American Conference in Panama, 1943; Second – in Lima, 1956; Third – in Bogota, 1963; Fourth – in Washington, 1966; in Europe ▷ EUROCULT; world conferences are held under UNESCO auspices: on adult education, 1960; on the problems of youth, 1964; on suppression of illiteracy, 1965; on social status of teachers, 1966; on higher studies, 1967; on educational planning, 1968, etc. By a decision of the 16th session of the UNESCO General Conference, the International Commission for the Development of Education was founded. Preparation for an unprecedented situation where after centuries of step-by-step evolution education is faced with radical changes was the aim of the Commission. Organizations acting under the auspices of UNESCO, reg. with the UIA:

Catholic International Education Office, f. 1952, Brussels, Consultative status with UNESCO. Publ.: *Bulletin Documentaire*.
Centro de Investigacion y Desarrollo de Educacion, f. 1963, Santiago de Chile.
Comparative Education Society in Europe, f. 1961, London.
Confederation of Latinoamerican Educators, f. 1957, Santiago de Chile.
Conference of Internationally Minded Schools, f. 1951, Berks, UK.
European Association of Teachers, f. 1956, Strasbourg. Consultative status with UNESCO.
European Bureau of Adult Education, f. 1953, Amsterdam. Publ.: *Notes and Studies*.
European Council for Education by Correspondence, f. 1963, Brussels.
International Association of Workers for Maladjusted Children, f. 1951, Paris. Consultative status with UNESCO.
International Bureau of Education, f. 1925, Geneva, intergovernmental organization, since Feb. 23, 1947, in close contact with UNESCO with which it jointly arranges annual International Conferences on Public Education. Publ. together with UNESCO: *International Yearbook of Education*, and since 1971 a quarterly in French, *Documentation et information pédagogique*.
International Federation of "Ecole Moderne" (Movements Frainet), f. 1957, Cannes, France. Consultative status with UNESCO. Publ. *L'Éducateur*.
International Federation of Home Economics, f. 1908, Paris. Consultative status with UNESCO. Publ.: *L'Enseignement Ménager*.
International Federation of Organizations for School Correspondence and Exchange, f. 1929, Paris. Consultative status with UNESCO.
International Federation of Secondary Teachers, f. 1912, London. Publ.: *International Bulletin*.
International Federation of Teachers Associations, f. 1926, Lausanne. Publ.: *Bulletin International*.
International Federation of the Societies of Classical Studies. F. 1948, Paris.
International Federation of Worker Education Associations, f. 1947, London. Consultative status with UNESCO.
International Institute for Educative Planning, f. 1947, Santiago de Chile.
International League of Children and Adult Education, f. 1947, Paris. Consultative status with UNESCO.
International Phonetic Association, f. 1886, London. Publ.: *Le Maitre Phonétique*.
International Reading Association, f. 1955, Newark, Delaware, USA. Publ.: *The Reading Teacher*.

International Association for Educational and Vocational Guidance, f. 1953, Luxembourg. Publ.: *Bulletin bibliographique*.

International Association of Education for World Peace, f. 1969, Huntsville, Alabama, Consultative status with ECOSOC and UNESCO. Publ.: *Peace Education*.

International Society for Business Education, f. 1901, Lausanne.

International Society for Orthopedagogics, f. 1935, Amsterdam. Publ.: *Acta Psychoterapeutica, Psychomatica et Orthopaedogogica*.

International Union for Education through Art, f. 1952, West Berlin. Consultative status with UNESCO.

International Union for the Freedom of Education, f. 1950, Paris, acts in favor of teaching religion in schools.

New Education Fellowship (International), f. 1915, Tunbridge Wells, Kent, UK.

United School International Federation, f. 1961, Delhi, Consultative status with UNESCO.

World Organization for Early Childhood Education, f. 1948, Paris. Consultative status with UNESCO and UNICEF.

World Confederation of Organizations of the Teaching Profession, f. 1952, Washington. Consultative status with UNESCO, ECOSOC, FAO and UNICEF.

World Union of Catholic Teachers, f. 1910, Rome.

The problems of international integration of higher education in Europe are dealt with in ECC countries by a special commission and in CMEA countries by the Conference of Ministers of Education of Socialist Countries. During 1955–72 UNESCO issued five volumes of *L'education dans le monde*, providing information about 149 countries and territories concerning: vol. 1 – schools; vol. 2 – basic education; vol. 3 – secondary education, 1961; vol. 4 – university education, 1966 and vol. 5 – policy, administration and legislation of education, 1972; each volume having about 1000 pages. In 1966 UNESCO issued the first volume of *Guide internationale de la documentation pédagogique*, providing information about education in particular countries during 1955–60, the 2nd volume, 1961–65, was issued in 1971. In 1972 UNESCO published a report on the state of education in the world and on future prospects. The report was based on studies carried out over a period of many years by experts in a majority of countries. In London since 1952 Europa Publ. Ltd publishes a yearbook, a guide to educational, scientific and cultural institutions in all parts of the World, entitled *The World of Learning*.

UNESCO publ.: *Fundamental and Adult Education Bulletin*, (quarterly) in English, French and Spanish.

P. ROSELLO, *Les Précurseurs du Bureau International de l'Éducation*, Genève, 1953; W. GRENTZ, *Educación y Desarrollo en América Latina: Bibliografía Selecta*, Hamburg, 1966; L.H. RAMIREZ, *La influencia de la educación en el desarrollo económico: el caso de México*, México, DF, 1966; S.A. NARTOWSKI, "The UNESCO system of protection of the right to education", in: *Polish Yearbook of International Law*, 1975, pp. 289–310. *UN Chronicle*, November, 1982 p. 42.

EDUCATIONAL FILMS CONVENTION, 1933. A Convention for facilitating international circulation of films of an educational nature, signed on Oct. 11, 1933 in Geneva by the Governments of Albania, Austria, Belgium, Chile, Czechoslovakia, Denmark, Egypt, Finland, France, Great Britain, Greece, Hungary, Italy, Latvia, Nicaragua, Norway, Panama, Poland, Romania, Sweden, Switzerland, the USA and Uruguay.

LNTS, Vol. 155, p. 331.

EDUCATIONAL LEAVE. The subject of an ILO Convention No. 140 June 5, 1974, referring to art. 26 of the Universal Declaration of Human Rights which says: "Everyone has the right to education."

Recognizing the need for continuous education, the Convention also acknowledges that paid educational leave should be granted for a fixed period within working hours, with the guarantee of appropriate financial benefits, and may embrace instruction at all levels, general, social or civilian and along trade union lines.

EDUCATIONAL, SCIENTIFIC AND CULTURAL MATERIALS. A subject of international co-operation and agreement: International Agreement for Facilitating the International Circulation of Visual and Auditory Materials of an Educational, Scientific and Cultural Character, opened for signature in Lake Success, N.Y. on July 15, 1949, and Proces-Verbal, at Lake Success, N.Y. on Sept. 5, 1950.

UNTS, Vol. 197, p. 3.

EDUCATION INTERNATIONAL YEAR, 1970. The UN General Assembly on Dec. 13, 1967, resolved to proclaim 1970 the International Year of Education for the purpose of "mobilizing forces as well as inspiring initiatives in the field of education and professional training throughout the entire world." The organizer of the year was UNESCO.

EDUCATION IN THE UN SYSTEM. In accordance with art. 55 of the UN Charter recommending i.a. support of "international cultural and educational co-operation," the UN in 1946 created a special organization for education, science and culture ▷ UNESCO, one of whose main tasks is to combat illiteracy in the world and to foster education. According to the opinion of the Director General of UNESCO, R. Mathieu, stated on Aug. 6, 1958: "the solution of educational problems should be world-wide .... A radical reform of education in all parts of the world has become a necessity and we cannot lose more time." This opinion was based on a UNESCO study of the state of education in the world and on UN predictions as to the further economic–social and cultural development of the world under the influence of the scientific–technical revolution. The developing countries insisted on a worldwide revision of teaching programs removing from texts material which might be chauvinistic, fascist, or might glorify war as contrary to the UN Charter and introducing mandatory instruction on peace and friendly co-operation among nations. The countries of the Third World have insisted on a basic reform of education with the aim of liberating it from effects of colonialism. ▷ School text-books.

P. LENGRAND, *Life-Long Education*, New York, 1972.

EEC. ▷ European Economic Community.

EFFECTIVENESS DOCTRINE. An international term for a principle in force in international law – the actual existence or non-existence of certain factual situations foreseen by international law *ipso facto* has legal consequences or may be a necessary condition for their coming into existence. However, not every factual situation yields laws. It must be effective.

EFTA. European Free Trade Association. An intergovernmental customs union with headquarters in Geneva; est. on Nov. 20, 1959 in Stockholm by Austria, Denmark, Norway, Portugal, Sweden, Switzerland and the UK; functioning as of May 3, 1960. Finland has been an associate member since June 26, 1961. The aim of EFTA is to achieve in its member countries permanent economic expansion, full employment, financial stabilization, the

development of trade between EFTA members by the reciprocal elimination of customs duties for their products. The latter was realized between 1961 and 1970 with the exception of Portugal, which only reduced them by 50%. The main organ of EFTA is a Ministerial Council together with a Committee and Secretariat. The working language of EFTA is English. It publishes the *EFTA Bulletin* in English, French and German. Treaties were signed in Brussels on July 23, 1972 between the EFTA member states (Austria, Finland, Iceland, Portugal, Sweden and Switzerland) and the EEC on the expansion of the exchange of industrial goods from Jan. 1, 1973. Finland only initialled them. Not signing at all was Norway, whose government joined the EEC; however, this plan was voided by a popular referendum of Oct. 23, 1972, resulting in Norway's remaining in EFTA. Norway signed treaties with the EEC similar to the Brussels ones. On July 1, 1977 duties were eliminated for the majority of industrial articles between the EFTA and the EEC. Finland in Sept. 1985 was a full member of EFTA.

EFTA publ.: *EFTA Bulletin*, quarterly. Convention Establishing the EFTA, Stockholm, 1960. J.S. LABRINDIS, *The Structure, Functions and Law of the Free Trade Area: the EFTA*, London 1965; "Ten years of EFTA, 1960–1970", in: *EFTA Bulletin*, No. 4, 1970; M.CH. BISWANGER, H.M. MAYERZEDT, *Europapolitik der Rest-EFTA Staaten. Perspektiven für die 70-er Jahre*, Zürich, 1972; M. SEARA VAZQUEZ, *Tratado General de la Organización Internacional*, México, 1974, pp. 775–785

EGALITARIANISM. An international term for the equality of states under international law, a principle accepted by the UN Charter.

EGGS. A subject of international conventions on their marking in international trade, signed in Brussels Dec. 11, 1931. The Central Commission on the Marketing of Food Products of the EEC introduced regulations in 1958, updated 1978, controlling the quality of eggs, their packaging, marking, quality control and import.

Organizations reg. with the UIA:

European Union for the Wholesale of Eggs and Poultry Trade, est. 1959, Bilthoven, Holland.
International Eggs Commission, est. 1962, London. Publ.: *Annual Marketing Review*.

LNTS, Vol. 170, p. 251; *Yearbook of International Organizations*.

EGYPT. Member of the UN. Arab Republic of Egypt. State in northeast Africa on the Mediterranean and Red Seas. Borders on Israel, Sudan and Libya. Area: 997,738 sq. km. Pop. 1987 est. 50,954,000 (1960 census: 25,984,000; 1966: 30,083,000 1976 census: 36,626,204). Capital: Cairo with 5,074,016 inhabitants 1976. GNP per capita in 1987: US $710. Official language: Arabic. Currency: one Egyptian pound = 100 piastres. National Day: July 23, Revolution Day, 1952.

Egypt was a member of the League of Nations in 1926–39. Member of the UN since Oct. 24, 1945 (as UAR in 1958–71) and all its specialized agencies. Member of the Arab League the OAU and OAPEC. A signatory of a Preferential Trade Agreement with the EEC since 1973.

International relations: in 16th–19th centuries under control of the Ottoman Empire; from 1882 under that of Great Britain. British protectorate after the 1914 British–Turkish war. Granted independence on Feb. 28, 1922 by Great Britain, whose troops remained in Egypt and Sudan (British–Egyptian condominium since 1899). In 1939 new British–Egyptian treaty signed. During World War II a major British military base. Formally declared war against Germany and Japan on Feb. 26, 1945 and signed the Allied Declaration of 1942. In connection with the economic blockade of Israel ordered by the Arab League, Egypt closed the Suez Canal to Israeli vessels in 1948. In 1951 she renounced the 1936 treaty with Great Britain and the condominium agreement on Sudan. The dethronement of King Farouk by the Military Revolutionary Council on July 26, 1952 was followed by the proclamation of an independent republic on June 18, 1953. On June 18, 1956 British troops withdrew from the Suez Canal Zone and on July 28, 1956 the Canal was nationalized and a subject of a UN Security Council debate. On Oct. 29, 1956 Israel attacked the Sinai Peninsula backed by British and French troops, which landed in the Canal Zone on Nov. 5, 1956. On Nov. 4, 1956 the UN Security Council formed the United Nations Emergency Force, UNEF, which was deployed in Dec. 1956 on the Egyptian–Israeli demarcation line of 1949. British and French troops pulled out in Dec., 1956, and Israel withdrew from the Sinai in Jan., 1957, from Ghaza and Sharm el-sheikh in Mar., 1957. From Feb. 1, 1958 to Sept. 28, 1961 Egypt and Syria formed the ▷ United Arab Republic and on Mar. 8, 1961 with Yemen – the Confederation of United Arab States. In spite of Syria's withdrawal (Sept., 1961) and dissolution of the confederation with Yemen (Dec., 1961), Egypt retained the name UAR. In Sept., 1971 she assumed the name Arab Republic of Egypt. In 1964 a treaty of alliance was concluded with Iraq. After withdrawal of UNEF in June, 1967, Israel captured the entire Sinai Peninsula up to the Suez Canal, an action condemned by the UN Security Council and General Assembly (▷ Israeli UN Resolution, 1967). In Oct., 1973 an Egyptian counteroffensive drove Israeli troops back from the Canal and negotiations started. In 1968–71 Egypt received economic and military aid from the USSR, among others ▷ Aswan High Dam. In 1971 she became member of the ▷ Federation of Arab Republics. On May. 27, 1971 a treaty of friendship and cooperation was concluded with the USSR. In July, 1972 Soviet advisers and instructors were recalled on Egyptian demand. On Aug. 2, 1972 Egypt concluded an agreement on union with Libya; the union due to come into force in Sept., 1973 remained only on paper, however. In July 1978 the Jews who had left Egypt after 1948 were allowed to return. Egyptian–Israeli negotiations resulted in a visit to ▷ Jerusalem of Egyptian President A. Sadat, to further talks at ▷ Camp David, and to the conclusion of the ▷ Egypt–Israeli Peace Treaty, 1979. A political and economic confederation between Egypt and Sudan was initiated by the establishment of a joint Egypt-Sudan Nile Valley Parliament in summer 1982. The first session was held in May 1983.

In Feb., 1984 Egypt urged the USA to open direct talks with the PLO and demanded that Israel withdraw its troops from Lebanon. All Arab League members with the exception of Oman, Somalia and Sudan broke off diplomatic relations with Egypt in March 1979 after it had concluded a peace treaty with Israel. In the week following the Amman summit on the ▷ League of Arab States, Nov. 11, 1987 Bahrain, Iraq, Kuwait, Mauritania, Morocco, North Yemen, Saudi Arabia and the United Arab Emirates re-established diplomatic relations with Egypt.

On Sept. 11–12, 1986 Egypt–Israel summit talks took place in Alexandria.

On Oct. 26, 1986 three economic agreements with Jordan.

See also ▷ World Heritage UNESCO List.

J.A. NEYWORTH-DUMRE, *A Select Bibliography on Modern Egypt*, London, 1952; J. MARLOW, *Anglo-Egyptian Relations 1800–1953*, London, 1954; *Egypt and the UN*, New York, 1958; H. RIAD, *L'Égypte Nasserienne*, Paris, 1964; J. BERQUE, *L'Égypte, Impérialisme et Révolution*, Paris, 1968; N.A. USHAKOVA, *Arabskaia Respublika Eiguptu: sotrudnichestvo so stranami sotsializma i ekonomicheskoye razvitye, 1952–1972*, Moskva, 1974; J.C.B. RICHMOND, *Egypt 1798–1952*, London, 1977; A. RUBINSTEIN, *Red Star on the Nile: The Soviet–Egyptian Relationship since the June War*, Princeton, 1977; R.W. BAKER, *Egypt's Uncertain Revolution Under Nasser and Sadat*, Cambridge, Mass., 1978; M. HEINKAL, *The Sphinx and the Commissar: The Rise and Fall of Soviet Influence in the Middle East*, New York, 1978; J. WATERBURY, *Egypt: Burdens of the Past. Options for the Future*, Indiana Univ. Press, 1979; K. DAWISHA, *Soviet Foreign Policy Towards Egypt*, New York, 1979; P.J. VATIKIOTIS, *The History of Egypt: From Muhammed Ali to Sadat*, London, 1980; A. HIRST, L. BENSON, *Sadat*, London, 1981; D. HOPWOOD, *Egypt Politics and Society 1945–1981*; London, 1982; R.W. VAAGAN, *The USSR and Egypt 1967–1978*, Stockholm, 1982; *The Europa Year Book 1984. A World Survey*, Vol. II, pp. 1512–1533. London, 1984; M.G. WEINBAUM, *Egypt and the Politics of US Economic Aid*, Boulder, Colo., 1986; KEESING'S *Record of World Events*, 1987, No. 6; M.M.EL. HUSSINI, *Soviet Egyptian Relations, 1975–85*, New York, London, 1987; A. McDERMOTT, *Egypt from Nasser to Mubarak: A Flawed Revolution*, London, 1988.

EGYPTIAN–ISRAELI AGREEMENT, 1974. A military truce agreement in pursuance of the Geneva Peace Conference; the Chiefs of Staff of the Egyptian Armed Forces and of the Israeli Defence Forces, signed on Jan. 13, 1974 an agreement on the disengagement of forces. "The area between the Egyptian and Israeli line was called zone of disengagement in which the UN Emergency Force, UNEF, will be stationed" (art. 2). "The area between the Egyptian line and the Suez Canal will be limited in armament and forces" (art. 3). "The area between the Israeli line and the line … which runs along the western base of the mountains where the Gidi and Mitla Passes are located will be limited in armament and forces" (art. 4). Both sides agree that:

"This Agreement is not regarded by Egypt and Israel as a final peace agreement. It constitutes a first step towards a final, just and durable peace according to the provisions of Security Council Res. 338 and within the framework of the Geneva Peace Conference."

UN Monthly Chronicle, February, 1974, pp. 8–9.

EGYPT–ISRAEL PEACE TREATY, 1979. A peace treaty between Egypt and Israel resulting from the commitment made by both states in Camp David, 1978, and signed Sept. 17, 1978 in Camp David (▷ Camp David Agreement 1978). The treaty was signed Mar. 26, 1979 in the White House in Washington in the presence of the President of the USA, Jimmy Carter, by the President of Egypt, A. Sadat, and the Prime Minister of Israel, M. Begin.

The text of the treaty:

"The government of the Arab Republic of Egypt and the government of the State of Israel:

Preamble. Convinced of the urgent necessity of the establishment of a just, comprehensive and lasting peace in the Middle East in accordance with Security Council Resolutions 242 and 338:

Reaffirming their adherence to the 'framework for Peace in the Middle East Agreed at Camp David,' dated Sept. 17, 1978: Noting that the aforementioned framework as appropriate is intended to constitute a basis for peace not only between Egypt and Israel but also between Israel and each of the other Arab neighbors which is prepared to negotiate peace with it on this basis;

Desiring to bring to an end the state of war between them and to establish a peace in which every state in the area can live in security;

Convinced that the conclusion of a treaty of peace between Egypt and Israel is an important step in the search for comprehensive peace in the area and for the attainment of the settlement of the Arab–Israeli conflict in all its aspects;

Inviting the other Arab parties to this dispute to join the peace process with Israel guided by and based on the principles of the aforementioned framework;

Desiring as well to develop friendly relations and cooperation between themselves in accordance with the United Nations Charter and the principles of international law governing international relations in times of peace; Agree to the following provisions in the free exercise of their sovereignty, in order to implement the framework for the conclusion of a peace treaty between Egypt and Israel.

Art. I.(1) The state of war between the parties will be terminated and peace will be established between them upon the exchange of instruments of ratification of this treaty.

(2) Israel will withdraw all its armed forces and civilians from the Sinai behind the international boundary between Egypt and mandated Palestine, as provided in the annexed protocol (Annex I), and Egypt will resume the exercise of its full sovereignty over the Sinai.

(3) Upon completion of the interim withdrawal provided for in Annex I, the parties will establish normal and friendly relations, in accordance with Article III(3).

Art. II. The permanent boundary between Egypt and Israel is the recognized international boundary between Egypt and the former mandated territory of Palestine as shown on the map at Annex II, without prejudice to the issue of the status of the Gaza Strip. The parties recognize this boundary as inviolable. Each will respect the territorial integrity of the other, including their territorial waters and airspace.

Art. III.(1) The parties will apply between them the provisions of the Charter of the United Nations and the principles of international law governing relations among states in times of peace. In particular:

A. They recognize and will respect each other's sovereignty, territorial integrity and political independence.

B. They recognize and will respect each other's right to live in peace within their secure and recognized boundaries.

C. They will refrain from the threat or use of force, directly or indirectly, against each other and will settle all disputes between them by peaceful means.

(2) Each party undertakes to insure that acts or threats of belligerency, hostility or violence do not originate from and are not committed from within its territory, or by any forces subject to its control or by any other forces stationed on its territory, against the population, citizens or property of the other party. Each party also undertakes to refrain from organizing, instigating, inciting, assisting or participating in acts or threats of belligerency, hostility, subversion or violence against the other party, anywhere, and undertakes to insure that perpetrators of such acts are brought to justice.

(3) The parties agree that the normal relationship established between them will include full recognition, diplomatic, economic and cultural relations, termination of economic boycotts and discriminatory barriers to the free movement of people and goods, and will guarantee the mutual enjoyment by citizens of the due process of law. The process by which they undertake to achieve such a relationship parallel to the implementation of other provisions of this treaty is set out in the annexed protocol (Annex III).

Art. IV.(1) In order to provide maximum security for both parties on the basis of reciprocity, agreed security arrangements will be established including limited force zones in Egyptian and Israeli territory, and United Nations forces and observers, described in detail as to nature and timing in Annex I, and other security arrangements the parties may agree upon.

(2) The parties agree to the stationing of United Nations personnel in areas described in Annex I, the parties agree not to request withdrawal of the United Nations personnel and that these personnel will not be removed unless such removal is approved by the Security Council of the United Nations, with the affirmative

vote of the five permanent members, unless the parties otherwise agree.

(3) A joint commission will be established to facilitate the implementation of the treaty, as provided for in Annex I.

(4) the security arrangements provided for in paragraphs 1 and 2 of this article may at the request of either party be reviewed and amended by mutual agreement of the parties.

Art. V.(1) Ships of Israel, and cargoes destined for or coming from Israel, shall enjoy the right of free passage through the Suez Canal and its approaches through the Gulf of Suez and the Mediterranean Sea on the basis of the Constantinople Convention of 1888, applying to all nations. Israeli nationals, vessels and cargoes, as well as persons, vessels and cargoes destined for or coming from Israel, shall be accorded nondiscriminatory treatment in all matters connected with usage of the canal.

(2) The parties consider the Strait of Tiran and the Gulf of Aqaba to be international waterways open to all nations for unimpeded and nonsuspendable freedom of navigation and overflight. The parties will respect each other's right to navigation and overflight for access to either country through the Strait of Tiran and the Gulf of Aqaba.

Art. VI.(1) This treaty does not affect and shall not be interpreted as affecting in any way the rights and obligations of the parties under the Charter of the United Nations.

(2) The parties undertake to fulfill in good faith their obligations under this treaty, without regard to action or inaction of any other party and independently of any instrument external to this treaty.

(3) They further undertake to take all the necessary measures for the application in their relations of the provisions of the multilateral conventions to which they are parties, including the submissions of appropriate notification of the secretary general of the United Nations and other depositories of such conventions.

(4) The parties undertake not to enter into any obligation in conflict with this treaty.

(5) Subject to Article 103 of the United Nations Charter, in the event of a conflict between the obligations of the parties under the present treaty and any of their other obligations, the obligations under this treaty will be binding and implemented.

Art. VII.(1) Dispute arising out of the application or interpretation of this treaty shall be resolved by negotiations.

(2) Any such disputes which cannot be settled by negotiations shall be resolved by conciliation or submitted to arbitration.

Art. VIII. The parties agree to establish a claims commission for the mutual settlement of all financial claims.

Art. IX.(1) This treaty shall enter into force upon exchange of instruments of ratification.

(2) This treaty supersedes the agreement between Egypt and Israel of September 1975.

(3) All protocols, annexes and maps attached to this treaty shall be regarded as an integral part thereof.

(4) The treaty shall be communicated to the secretary general of the United Nations for registration in accordance with the provisions of Article 102 of the Charter of the United Nations. Done at Washington this 26th day of March 1979, in duplicate in the Arabic, English and Hebrew languages, each text being equally authentic. In case of any divergence of interpretation, the English text shall prevail."

Annexes to the Treaty:

Annex I. Protocol Concerning Israeli Withdrawal and Security Arrangements, with Appendix to Annex I: Organization of Movements in the Sinai.

Annex II. Three maps of the Sinai Peninsula.

Annex III. Protocol Concerning Relations of the Parties (Normalization of diplomatic, consular, economic, trade and cultural relations; freedom of movement; good neighborly relations etc.).

Following are the texts of two memorandums of agreement between the US and Israel, one of which provides assurances for Israel in case of Egyptian violations of the Treaty of Peace and the second of which assures Israel of an uninterrupted supply of oil until at least 1990:

Memorandum of Agreement between the US and Israel. Recognizing the significance of the conclusion of the Treaty of Peace between Israel and Egypt and considering the importance of full implementation of the Treaty of Peace to Israel's security interests and the contribution of the conclusion of the Treaty of Peace to the security and development of Israel as well as its significance to peace and stability in the region and to the maintenance of international peace and security; and recognizing that the withdrawal from Sinai imposes additional heavy security, military and economic burdens on Israel; The governments of the United States of America and of the State of Israel, subject to their constitutional processes and applicable law; confirm as follows:

(1) In the light of the role of the United States in achieving the Treaty of Peace and the parties desire that the United States continue its supportive efforts, the United States will take appropriate measures to promote full observance of the Treaty of Peace.

(2) Should it be demonstrated to the satisfaction of the United States that there has been a violation or threat of violation of the Treaty of Peace, the United States will consult with the parties with regard to measures to halt or prevent the violation, ensure observance of the Treaty of Peace, enhance friendly and peaceful relations between the parties and promote peace in the region, and will take such remedial measures as it deems appropriate, which may include diplomatic, economic and military measures as described below.

(3) The United States will provide support it deems appropriate for proper actions taken by Israel in response to such demonstrated violations of the Treaty of Peace. In particular, if a violation of the Treaty of Peace is deemed to threaten the security of Israel, including, inter alia, a blockade of Israel's use of international waterways, a violation of the provisions of the Treaty of Peace concerning limitation of forces or an armed attack against Israel, the United States will be prepared to consider, on an urgent basis, such measures as the strengthening of the United States presence in the area, the providing of emergency supplies to Israel, and the exercise of maritime rights in order to put an end to the violation.

(4) The United States will support the parties' rights to navigation and overflight for access to either country through and over the Strait of Tiran and the Gulf of Aqaba pursuant to the Treaty of Peace.

(5) The United States will oppose and, if necessary, vote against any action or resolution in the United Nations which in its judgement adversely affects the Treaty of Peace.

(6) Subject to congressional authorization and appropriation, the United States will endeavor to take into account and will endeavor to be responsive to military and economic assistance requirements of Israel.

(7) The United States will continue to impose restrictions on weapons supplied by it to any country which prohibit their unauthorized transfer to any third party. The United States will not supply or authorize transfer of such weapons for use in an armed attack against Israel, and will take steps to prevent such unauthorized transfer.

(8) Existing agreements and assurances between the United States and Israel are not terminated or altered by the conclusion of the Treaty of Peace, except for those contained in Articles V, VI, VII, VIII, XI, XII, XV and XVI of the Memorandum of Agreement between the Government of the United States and the Government of Israel (United States-Israeli Assurances) of September 1, 1975.

(9) This Memorandum of Agreement sets forth the full understandings of the United States and Israel with regard to the subject matters covered between them hereby, and shall be carried out in accordance with its terms.

U.S.-Israeli Memorandum of Agreement on Oil.

The oil supply arrangement of September 1, 1975, between the governments of the United States and Israel, annexed hereto, remains in effect. A memorandum of agreement shall be agreed upon and concluded to provide an oil supply arrangement for a total of 15 years, including the 5 years provided in the September 1, 1975, arrangement.

The memorandum of agreement, including the commencement of this arrangement and pricing provisions, will be mutually agreed upon by the parties within 60 days following the entry into force of the Treaty of Peace between Egypt and Israel.

It is the intention of the parties that prices paid by Israel for oil provided by the United States hereunder shall be comparable to world market prices current at the time of transfer, and that in any event the United States will be reimbursed by Israel for the costs incurred by the United States in providing oil to Israel hereunder. Experts provided for in the September 1, 1975, arrangement will meet on request to discuss matters arising under this relationship.

The United States Administration undertakes to seek promptly additional statutory authorization that may be necessary for full implementation of this arrangement.

Moshe Dayan
Cyrus R. Vance

Annex. Israel will make its own independent arrangements for oil supply to meet its requirements through normal procedures. In the event Israel is unable to secure oil this way, the United States Government, upon notification of this fact by the government of Israel, will act as follows for five years, at the end of which period either side can terminate this arrangement on one year's notice.

(a) If the oil Israel needs to meet all its normal requirements for domestic consumption is unavailable for purchase – in circumstances where no quantitative restrictions exist on the ability of the United States to procure oil to meet its normal requirements, the United States government will promptly make oil available for purchase by Israel to meet all of the aforementioned normal requirements of Israel. If Israel is unable to secure the necessary means to transport such oil to Israel, the United States government will make every effort to help Israel secure the necessary means of transport.

(b) If the oil Israel needs to meet all of its normal requirements for domestic consumption is unavailable for purchase in circumstances where quantitative restrictions through embargo or otherwise also prevent the United States from procuring oil to meet its normal requirements, the United States government will promptly make oil available for purchase by Israel in accordance with the International Energy Agency conservation and allocation formula, as applied by the United States government, in order to meet Israel's essential requirements. If Israel is unable to secure the necessary means to transport such oil to Israel, the United States government will make every effort to help Israel secure the necessary means of transport.

Israeli and United States experts will meet annually or more frequently at the request of either party, to review Israel's continuing oil requirement.

Facts on File, Vol. 39, March 30, 1979, pp. 223–227.

EGYPT–SOVIET TREATY, 1971. A treaty signed in Cairo on May 27, 1971, under the title: Treaty on Friendship and Co-operation between the USSR and the UAR; with fifteen years duration; denounced by Egypt on Mar. 15, 1976.

UN Treaty Series, 1971.

EICHMANN CASE. The Nazi war criminal. A. Eichmann, a senior functionary of the Main Security Bureau of the Reich (RSHA), personally responsible for organizing the system of mass destruction of Jewish people in occupied territories, after World War II escaped to Argentina. On May 11, 1960 he was abducted there by Israeli intelligence agents, secretly transported to Israel, placed on trial in the Israeli part of Jerusalem, from Apr. 10 to Dec. 15, 1961; sentenced to death and executed on June 1, 1962, and his ashes, as those of the war criminals sentenced to death in Nuremberg, were scattered in an unknown place (▷ Dachau). Argentina recognized the act of seizure as a violation by Israel of its sovereignty and lodged a protest with the UN Security Council, June 23, 1960. The relevant resolution of the UN Security Council contained a reminder to all UN member states concerning the obligation to extradite war criminals and try them before the proper courts. The diplomatic conflict between Argentina and Israel was settled amicably by a joint declaration of the two states on Aug. 4, 1960.

G. RETTINGER, *The Final Solution*, London, 1953; M. PEARLMAN, *The Capture and Trial of Adolf Eichmann*, New York, 1963; D.B. SCHMORAK, *Der Prozess Eichmann: Dargostellt an Hand der in Nürnberg und Jerusalem vorgelegten Dokumente und der Gerichtsprotokolle*, Vienna, 1964; H. ARENDT, *The Eichmann Trial*, New York, 1965; J. HASEL, *Das Haus in der Garibaldistrasse*, Berlin, 1975; J. PIEKALKIEWICZ, *Israels Langer Arm*, Frankfurt am M., 1975.

EINSTEIN DOCTRINE ON WAR AND PEACE IN ATOMIC AGE, 1948.

An historical address by Albert Einstein (1879–1955) sent to the World Peace Congress of Intellectuals in Wroclaw, Poland, Aug., 1948, but not delivered; the text, first published by the *New York Times*, is as follows:

"We meet today, as intellectuals and scholars of many nationalities, with a deep and historic responsibility placed upon us. We have every reason to be grateful to our French and Polish colleagues whose initiative has assembled us here for momentous objective: to use the influence of wise men in promoting peace and security throughout the world. This is the age-old problem with which Plato, as one of the first, struggled so hard: to apply reason and prudence to the solution of man's problems instead of yielding to atavistic instincts and passions.

By painful experience we have learned that rational thinking does not suffice to solve the problems of our social life. Penetrating research and keen scientific work have often had tragic implications for mankind. On the one hand, they produced inventions which liberated man from exhausting physical labor, making his life easier and richer; but on the other hand, they introduced a grave restlessness into his life, making him a slave to his technological environment, and – most catastrophic of all – creating the means for his own mass destruction. This is indeed a tragedy of overwhelming poignancy.

However poignant the tragedy is, it is perhaps even more tragic that, while mankind has produced many scholars so extremely successful in the field of science and technology, we have been so inefficient in finding adequate solutions to the political conflicts and economic tensions which beset us. No doubt, the antagonism of economic interests within and among nations is largely responsible for the dangerous and threatening situation in the world today. Man has not succeeded in developing political and economic forms of organization which would guarantee the peaceful co-existence of the nations of the world. He has not succeeded in building the kind of system which would eliminate the possibility of war and banish forever the murderous instruments of mass destruction. We scientists, whose tragic destiny it has been to help make the methods of annihilition ever more gruesome and more effective, must consider it our solemn and transcendent duty to do all in our power in preventing these weapons from being used for the brutal purpose for which they were invented. What task could possibly be more important to us? What social aim could be closer to our hearts? That is why this congress has such a vital mission. We are gathered here to take counsel with each other. We must build spiritual and scientific bridges linking the nations of the world. We must overcome the horrible obstacles of national frontiers.

In the smaller units of society man has made some progress toward minimizing sovereignty with its anti-social implications. This is true, for example, of life within cities and, to a certain degree, even of life within individual states. In such communities tradition and education have had a moderating influence and have brought about tolerable relations among the people living within those confines. But in relations among nations complete anarchy still prevails. I do not believe that we have made any real progress in this area during the last few thousand years. All too frequently conflicts among nations are still decided by resort to brute force, by war. The unlimited desire for ever greater power seeks aggressive outlets wherever and whenever a physical possibility offers itself.

Throughout the ages this state of anarchy in international affairs has inflicted indescribable suffering and destruction upon mankind; again and again it has impeded the progress of men, their souls and their well-being. At given times it has almost annihilated whole areas.

However, the desire of nations to be ever prepared for war has still other repercussions upon the lives of men. The power of every state over its citizens has grown steadily during the last few hundred years – no less in countries where the power of the state has been exercised wisely than in those where it has been used for brutal tyranny. The function of the state to maintain peaceful and orderly relations among its citizens has become increasingly complex and extensive largely because of the concentration and centralization of modern industry. In order to protect its citizens from aggression a modern state requires a formidable, expanding military establishment. In addition, the state considers it necessary to educate its citizens for the possibility of war, an 'education' that not only corrupts the soul and spirit of the young, but also adversely affects the mentality of adults. No country can avoid this corruption altogether. It pervades the citizenry even in countries which do not harbor outspoken aggressive tendencies. The state has thus become a modern idol whose suggestive power few men are able to escape.

Education for war, however, is a delusion. The technological developments of the last few years have created a completely new military situation. Horrible weapons have been invented, capable of destroying in a few seconds huge masses of human beings and tremendous areas. Since science has not yet found protection from these weapons, the modern state is no longer in a position to prepare adequately for the safety of its citizens.

How, then, shall we be saved?

Mankind can gain protection against the danger of unimaginable destruction and wanton annihilation only if a supranational organization has alone the authority to produce or possess these weapons. It is unthinkable, however, that, under existing conditions, nations would hand over such authority to a supranational organization, unless the organization had the legal right and duty to solve the kind of conflicts which in the past have led to war. Under such a system the function of individual states would be to concentrate more or less upon internal affairs; and in their relations with one another they would deal only with issues and problems which are in no way conducive to endangering international security. Unfortunately, there are no indications that governments yet realize that the situation in which mankind finds itself makes the adoption of revolutionary measures a compelling necessity. Our situation is not comparable to anything in the past. It is impossible, therefore, to apply methods and measures which, in an earlier age, might have been sufficient. We must revolutionize our thinking, revolutionize our actions and must have the courage to revolutionize relations among the nations of the world. The cliches of yesterday will no longer do today, and will, no doubt, be hopelessly out of date tomorrow. To bring this home to men all over the world is the most important and most fateful social task intellectuals have ever had to shoulder. Will they have enough courage to overcome their own national ties to the extent that is necessary to induce the peoples of the world to change their deep-rooted national traditions in a most radical fashion? A tremendous effort is indispensable. If it fails now, the supranational organization will be built later, but then it will have to be built upon the ruins of a large part of the world. Let us hope that the abolition of the existing international anarchy will not need to be brought about by a self-inflicted world catastrophe, the dimensions of which none of us can possibly imagine. The time is terribly short. We must act now if we are to act at all."

The New York Times, August 29, 1948; O. NATHAN, H. NORDEN (eds), *Einstein on Peace*, Preface by Bertrand Russell, New York, 1968 pp. 491–496; M. BIBROWSKI, "Nieznane Oredzie Einsteina (An Unknown Address of Einstein)", in: *Polityka*, Warsaw, July 5, 1980.

EISENHOWER DOCTRINE, 1957.

A doctrine framed by the US President Dwight Eisenhower (1890–1962) on Jan. 5, 1957 stating that the USA is ready to help all countries of the Middle East that desire to take advantage of the economic and military help furnished by the US armed forces. The doctrine was related to the ▷ Truman Doctrine 1947, which was formally limited to Greece and Turkey. Congress passed the above Eisenhower formula Mar. 5 and Mar. 7, 1957 (in the Senate 72: 19 and in the House 350: 60).

D.D. EISENHOWER, "State of the Union Message", in: *Congressional Record*, 87th Congress, 1st Session, January 5, 1957.

ELBE, LABE.

A river in central Europe, 1165 km long, navigable for 845 km, rises in Czechoslovakia and flows through the German Democratic Republic to the Federal Republic of Germany and into the North Sea at Cuxhaven. The river was the eastern limit of the Romans' advance into Germany and later the frontier of the I Reich; since 1949 it has been part of the state frontier between the FRG and GDR.

The Treaty of Versailles, 1919, placed the Elbe (Labe) under the administration of an International Commission, composed of four representatives from the German States bordering on the river, two from the Czecho-Slovak State, one from the UK, one from France, one from Italy and one from Belgium (art. 340). A convention instituting the Statute of Navigation of the Elbe with Protocol of Signature, signed at Dresden, Feb. 22, 1922, by Germany, Belgium, Great Britain, France, Italy and Czechoslovakia.

"The international system of the Elbe, hereinafter designated by the name of the Elbe, comprises the Elbe from its confluence with the Vltava (Moldau) as far as the open sea and the Vltava from Prague to its confluence with the Elbe ..."

(art. 1). Supplementary Convention to the Statute, signed in Prague, Jan. 27, 1923.

The internationalization of the Elbe from the Vltava River to the North Sea was repudiated by the German III Reich in 1938 after the Munich Pact; reinstalled by the Potsdam Agreement 1945. The Red Army encountered the US Army on May 3, 1945, south of Wirtemberg on the Elbe and the British Army, on May 5, south of Lanenburg.

The delimitation of the Soviet and British occupation zones in June 1945 marked the frontier by the ▷ Thalweg of the Elbe River between Wirtemberg and Lanenburg. From this time the Elbe River is a symbol of the partition of Europe between East and West.

The Elbe is connected by a canal system with the Oder River, with the Rhine River (via the Mittelland Canal) and with the Baltic Sea.

LNTS, Vol. 26, p. 223 and 255.

ELDERLY AND AGED.

A social and demographic problem of the second half of the 20th century, when in developed countries the average life expectancy increased and with it the number of people between the ages 60–80 and over; subject of international research sponsored by the UN. In 1969, in Res. 2599/XXIV, the UN General Assembly took a stand in the matter of the elderly and aged, noting the complexity of social problems and social security. The UN General Assembly on Dec. 14, 1978 decided by Res. 33/52 to organize a World Assembly on the Elderly in 1982. The World Assembly on Aging took place July 26–Aug. 6, 1984 in Vienna. The facts about the ageing world, according to the UN data are as follows:

"The number of people aged 60 and over is the fastest growing section of the population in the world.

While total world population is expected to treble in the 75 years from 1950 to 2025, the United Nations predicts that the population of the over-60s will show a five-fold increase and the over-80s will increase to seven times their present number.

E

This means that one person in every seven will be over 60 years of age in 2025 compared with just one in every 12 in 1950.

In 1950, there were only an estimated 214 million people over the age of 60 in the world. By 2025, that number is expected to reach 1121 million.

The aging of populations will be most dramatic in the developing world where the over-60s are expected to increase nearly seven times between 1950 and 2025, when they will number 800 million.

In 1950, the developing world held only 56 per cent of the over-60s. By 2025, 72 per cent of the over-60s will live there.

The number of over-60s in the developing world will increase fastest between 2000 and 2025, when countries like Bangladesh, Brazil, Mexico and Nigeria will see their over-60s increase by nearly 15 times.

Women:
In almost every country women live longer than men. Most researchers believe this is because of genetic differences. Because they live longer, older women outnumber older men. The difference is especially pronounced in more developed regions where women in their 60s outnumbered men in their 60s by 100 to 74 in 1975. The ratio becomes even more uneven in older age groups – with only 48 men for every 100 women over 80. In developing countries the number of men and women in their 60s is almost equal. But, as development advances, the gap in life expectancy will widen and women over 60 will become a majority.

Health:
The large number of old people in 2025 will be the survivors of the population aged between 15 and 35 today. They owe their survival largely to improvements in health, hygiene and nutrition. The World Health Organization (WHO) has estimated that two thirds of the rise in life expectancy is due to such improvements. The natural process of aging need not be disabling. Healthy people can remain active and vigorous until they die.

Modern research has shown that it is the cumulative effects of actual disease that cause older people to become disabled. In more developed regions WHO has estimated that 75 per cent of over-60s are active and able to care for themselves. Less than five per cent are severely disabled by irreversible brain atrophy.

But the proportion of disabled old is likely to be much larger in the developing world where many people have suffered a lifetime of poor nutrition and disease. One study of over 60s in Costa Rica revealed that 85 per cent had difficulties with their vision and 66 per cent suffered from arthritis.

Throughout the world most disabled old people are cared for at home. Even in more developed regions, estimates reveal that fewer than five per cent of the over-60s are receiving institutional care.

Employment:
The International Labour Organisation (ILO) estimates that only 39 per cent of men and 12 per cent of women over 65 were in employment in 1975. This level of employment is expected to drop so that, by 2000, only 27 per cent of men and ten per cent of women over 65 will be in employment. (Here 'employment' excludes those tasks involved in housework and growing food for domestic consumption.)

Urbanisation:
Migration of younger family members to urban areas in search of employment leaves older people in the countryside. In the expanding cities a higher standard of living will offer the young job-seekers a longer life so that by 2025, the United Nations predicts that the majority of aging people in the developing world will be living in urban areas.

In more developed regions this process of urbanisation has already occurred and the majority of people now live in cities. In 1975, two thirds of the over-60's lived in cities. By 2000, this number is expected to increase by 60 per cent until over three-quarters of the developed world's aged are living in cities.

Pensions:
Most industrialised countries have a fixed retirement age at which people in formal employment stop work and receive a pension from the Government. Retirement age typically ranges from 60 to 65 years for men and 55 to 60 years for women. Nearly all developing countries also have some kind of government pension scheme. But coverage is usually limited to the relatively few people in formal wage employment.

The ILO estimates that only 23 per cent of working men and 6 per cent of working women will be receiving a pension by the year 2000.

Dependence:
People are growing old faster than children are being born to support them in their old age. In 1950, there were 19 people over 60 and 45 children under the age of 15 for every 100 adults aged 15–59. By 2025, there are expected to be 40 over-60s and only 35 children for every 100 active adults.

The ILO predicts that there will be 270 million 'economically inactive' over 55-year olds in industrialized countries by 2020. That will mean 38 older dependents for every 100 workers – twice as many as in 1950.

According to a 1988 WHO prognosis of demographic trends: by 2000, about two-thirds of the world's 600 million persons aged 60 or over – its senior citizens – will be in developing nations compared to half that number in 1960; by 2020, the total population for those nations will increase by 95 per cent, while the numbers of the elderly will jump 240 per cent – or by nearly three and a half times over 1980 totals; by 2020 also, there will be a 'further 270 million elderly citizens' in China and India alone, the two largest developing nations; a rise of 'more than 20 million in both Brazil and Indonesia', and rises of about 10 million in Mexico, Nigeria and Pakistan.

'These developing nations will gradually replace the European nations – where the process of population aging began much earlier – in the ranking of countries with the largest elderly populations', predicts the WHO.

The aging of the population, once a 'privilege of comparatively few' societies 'is now a prospect for more and more people throughout the world'. These are the top 20 greying nations, listed alphabetically: Argentina, Bangladesh, Brazil, Canada, China, the Federal Republic of Germany, France, India, Indonesia, Italy, Japan, Pakistan, Poland, Soviet Union, Spain, Mexico, Nigeria, the United Kingdom, the United States and Vietnam.

The WHO's World Health Assembly established an international research programme in aging, in May 1987, to determine ways and means, in the words of a resolution adopted, of 'adding healthy years to life' of senior citizens.

Among the goals of the programme are an increased understanding of the 'basic process of aging', the prevention and control of 'clinical manifestations of age-related disorders', and the promoting of 'interaction between older people and society".

Organization reg. with the UIA:
European Federation for the Welfare of the Elderly, f. 1962, Graz, Austria.

UN Chronicle, October 1982, pp. 22–23; *UN Chronicle*, No. 9, 1984, p. 22; *UN Chronicle, 1985*, No. 5, pp. XXI–XXIV; *WHO Health Statistics Annual 1987*, Geneva, 1988; *Yearbook of International Organizations, 1986/87*; H. QURESHI, A. WALKER, *The Caring Relationship. The Family Care of Elderly People*, London, 1987; *The Europa Yearbook 1988. A World Survey*. Vol. I, London, 1988.

ELDO. European Launcher Development Organization. An inter-governmental institution est. by a convention of West European states, signed Mar. 31, 1962 in Paris by France, the FRG, Italy and the UK and on Apr. 15, 1962 by Austria, Belgium, and Holland; came in force Feb. 29, 1964. After 10 years of unsuccessful attempts construction of a long-range European rocket was abandoned on May 1, 1973. At the same time the member states decided to disband ELDO, whose agenda was taken over in 1974 by the ▷European Space Agency.

The Europa Year Book 1984. A World Survey, Vol. II, pp. 250–251, London, 1984.

EL DORADO. Spanish = "The Guilded One". An international term coined by the Spanish conquistadors for legendary realms of fabulous riches, held to exist in the New World; mentioned in Milton's *Paradise Lost* and Voltaire's *Candide*.

ELECTION LAW. A subject of international comparative law and organized international studies since the 19th century made under the auspices of the ▷ Inter-parliamentary Union. In countries with parliamentary systems election law as a rule is divided into passive and active (except the Jacobin Constitution in France of June 24, 1793). Age limitations vary from 18 to 25. In a few countries women have still not gained voting rights, or only passive rights. The right to be elected as a deputy is universally limited by age (minimum 21–25 years) and citizenship of the given state; in some countries there are property or educational requirements; more rarely nationality and religious requirements (in Germany up to 1848 and in the III Reich Jews could not be elected; in Great Britain up to the mid-19th century Jews and Catholics, in Spain non-Catholics, in many secular countries – clergymen). After World War I treaties on the protection of national minorities indirectly assured certain rights to minorities to have their deputies in parliament. Several systems for counting votes have been developed authorizing the gaining of a mandate; in many European countries the Belgian system of D'Hondt has been accepted. The first Convention relative to the preparation of projects of Electoral Legislation was adopted by the Conference on Central American Affairs at Washington, DC on Feb. 7, 1923, ratified by Guatemala, Honduras and Nicaragua, entered into force Mar. 15, 1925. After World War II in connection with the establishment of the Western European Parliament in Strasbourg and the tendency to transform it into a parliament elected directly by the citizens of the EEC states, various conceptions of one interstate electoral system were discussed; resolved in 1979 by the first direct election to the ▷ European Parliament.

V. D'HONDT, *Système pratique et raisonné de représentation proportionnelle*, Bruxelles, 1882; *Conference on Central American Affairs*, Washington, DC. 1923.

ELECTORAL LAW, INTERNATIONAL. The first international electoral law was formulated by an Act of the Council of Ministers of the European Communities on Sept. 20, 1976, for the purpose of holding elections to the ▷ European Parliament. The Articles are as follows:

"Art. 1. The representatives in the Assembly of the peoples of the States brought together in the Community shall be elected by direct universal suffrage.
Art. 2. The number of representatives elected in each Member State shall be as follows:

Belgium	24
Denmark	16
Germany	81
France	81
Ireland	15
Italy	81
Luxembourg	6
Netherlands	25
United Kingdom	81

Art. 3.(1) Representatives shall be elected for a term of five years.
(2) This five-year period shall begin at the opening of the first session following each election.
It may be extended or curtailed pursuant to the second sub-paragraph of Article 10 (2).
(3) The term of office of each representative shall begin and end at the same time as the period referred to in paragraph 2.
Art. 4.(1) Representatives shall vote on an individual and personal basis. They shall not be bound by any instructions and shall not receive a binding mandate.

(2) Representatives shall enjoy the privileges and immunities applicable to members of the Assembly by virtue of the Protocol on the privileges and immunities of the European Communities annexed to the Treaty establishing a single Council and a single Commission of the European Communities.

Art. 5. The office of representative in the Assembly shall be compatible with membership of the Parliament of a Member State.

Art. 6.(1) The office of representative in the Assembly shall be incompatible with that of:

member of the Government of a Member State,

member of the Commission of the European Communities,

Judge, Advocate-General or Registrar of the Court of Justice of the European Communities,

member of the Court of Auditors of the European Communities,

member of the Consultative Committee of the European Coal and Steel Community or member of the Economic and Social Committee of the European Economic Community and of the European Atomic Energy Community,

member of committees or other bodies set up pursuant to the treaties establishing the European Coal and Steel Community, the European Economic Community and the European Atomic Energy Community for the purpose of managing the Communities' funds or carrying out permanent direct administrative tasks, member of the Board of Directors, Management Committee or staff of the European Investment Bank,

active official or servant of the institutions of the European Communities or of the specialized bodies attached to them.

(2) In addition, each Member State may, in the circumstances provided for in Article 7 (2), lay down rules at national level relating to incompatibility.

(3) Representatives in the Assembly to whom paragraphs 1 and 2 become applicable in the course of the five-year period referred to in Article 3 shall be replaced in accordance with Article 12.

Art. 7.(1) Pursuant to Article 21 (3) of the Treaty establishing the European Coal and Steel Community, Article 138 (3) of the Treaty establishing the European Economic Community and 108 (3) of the Treaty establishing the European Atomic Energy Community, the Assembly shall draw up a proposal for a uniform electoral procedure.

(2) Pending the entry into force of a uniform electoral procedure and subject to the other provisions of this Act, the electoral procedure shall be governed in each Member State by its national provisions.

Art. 8. No one may vote more than once in any election of representatives to the Assembly.

Art. 9.(1) Elections to the Assembly shall be held on the date fixed by each Member State; for all Member States this date shall fall within the same period starting on a Thursday morning and ending on the following Sunday.

(2) The counting of votes may not begin until after the close of polling in the Member State whose electors are the last to vote within the period referred to in paragraph 1.

(3) If a member State adopts a double ballot system for elections to the Assembly, the first ballot must take place during the period referred to in paragraph 1.

Art. 10.(1) The Council, acting unanimously after consulting the Assembly, shall determine the period referred to in Article 9.(1) for the first elections.

(2) Subsequent elections shall take place in the corresponding period in the last year of the five-year period referred to in Article 3.

Should it prove impossible to hold the elections in the Community during that period, the Council acting unanimously shall after consulting the Assembly, determine another period which shall be not more than one month before or one month after the period fixed pursuant to the preceding subparagraph.

(3) without prejudice to Article 22 of the Treaty establishing the European Coal and Steel Community, Article 139 of the Treaty establishing the European Economic Community and Article 109 of the Treaty establishing the European Atomic Energy Community, the Assembly shall meet, without requiring to be convened, on the first Tuesday after expiry of an interval of one month from the end of the period referred to in Article 9(1).

(4) The powers of the outgoing Assembly shall cease upon the opening of the first sitting of the new Assembly."

In Annex the FRG Government declared:

"The Government of the Federal Republic of Germany declares that the Act concerning the election of the members of the European Parliament by direct universal suffrage shall equally apply to Land Berlin.

In consideration of the rights and responsibilities of France, the United Kingdom of Great Britain and Northern Ireland, and the United States of America, the Berlin House of Deputies will elect representatives to those seats within the quota of the Federal Republic of Germany that fall to Land Berlin."

Official Journal of the European Communities. October 8, 1976; *The Economist*, World Atlas of Elections, 1986.

ELECTRICITY. A subject of international co-operation. Organizations reg. with the UIA:

Commission of Regional Electrical Integration, f. 1964, Montevideo.

European Union of Electrical Wholesalers, f. 1956, Paris.

International Association of Electrical Contractors, f. 1953, Paris.

International Commission on Rules for the Approval of Electrical Equipment, f. 1946, Arnhem.

International Conference on Large High Voltage Electric Systems, f. 1921, Paris. Publ. *Electra* (in English and French).

International Electrical Research Exchange, f. 1969, New York.

International Federation of Industrial Producers of Electricity for Own Consumption, f. 1954, Brussels.

International Union of Producers and Distributors of Electrical Energy, f. 1925, Paris. Publ. *L'Économie électrique* (quarterly).

Latin American Association of Electrical and Electronic Industry, f. 1962, Montevideo.

Maghreb Committee for Electric Energy, f. 1973, Tunis.

Nuclear plants are a new element in the world energy problems of the 1980s. The first country which reached nuclear parity in relation to the old type power plants was France in 1984.

'Oil and Energy. A Special Report', in: *International Herald Tribune*, October 18, 1984; *Yearbook of International Organizations*.

ELECTROCHEMISTRY. Subject of international co-operation. Organization reg. with the UIA:

International Society of Electrochemistry, f. 1949, Vienna, Austria.

Yearbook of International Organizations, 1986/87; The Europa Yearbook 1988. A World Survey, Vol. I, London, 1988.

ELECTRONIC INTELLIGENCE, ELINT. An international military term for information monitored from foreign radio, radar and satellite services, called also Intelligence Signals.

D. ROBERTSON, *Guide to Modern Defense and Strategy*, Detroit, 1988.

ELECTRONICS. International term – subject of international co-operation. Organizations reg. with the UIA:

European Organization for Civil Aviation Electronics, f. 1963, Paris.

European Standards of Nuclear Electronics Committee, f. 1960 Ispra (Italy). In co-operation with CERN and EURATOM.

International Federation of Societies for Electron Microscopy, f. 1951, Berkeley, Calif.

International Federation of Air Traffic Safety Electronic Associations, f. 1972, London. Publ. *Navaire* (quarterly).

Pro Electron, f. 1967, Brussels. Aims: study and define a system of nomenclature for the purpose of identifying and classifying electronic components.

W.E. CLASON, *Elsevier's Dictionary of Electronics and Waveguides*. In English/American (with definitions), French, Spanish, Italian, Dutch and German, Amsterdam, 1966.

ELECTRON MICROSCOPY. A subject of international co-operation: International Center of Academies of Sciences of the Socialist Countries for Raising the Qualifications of Scientific Cadres in Electron Microscopy, f. 1975 in Berlin, GDR, by an Agreement signed at Berlin on Mar. 18, 1975 by the Academies of Sciences of Bulgaria, Czechoslovakia, GDR, Hungary, Poland and the USSR; came into force on May 17, 1975.

Recueil de Documents, Varsovie No. 3, 1975; W.E. BUTLER (ed.), *A Source Book on Socialist International Organizations*, Alphen, 1978, pp. 804–810.

ELECTROTECHNICS. A subject of international co-operation. Organizations reg. with the UIA:

European Committee for Electrotechnical Standardization (CENELEC), f. 1973, Brussels.

International Electrotechnical Commission, f. 1906, London. Consultative status with ECOSOC, ILO, ITU, WHO, IMCO, Publ.: *IEC Standards, Information Bulletin*.

W.E. CLASON, *Elsevier's Electrotechnical Dictionary*. In English/American, French, Spanish, Italian, Dutch and German, Amsterdam, 1979.

ELEVATORS. A subject of international co-operation. Organization reg. with the UIA:

International Union of Elevator Constructors, f. 1901, Philadelphia.

Yearbook of International Organizations.

ELITARISM. An international term for a concept of international law recognizing the greater responsibility for peace of Big Powers, a principle accepted by the UN Charter in the structure of the Security Council, granting veto right to the Great Powers.

EL JEM. A cultural site of Tunisia included in the ▷ World Heritage UNESCO List. The amphitheater was built in the third century A.D. by the citizens of Thysdrus, a city of the Tunisian Sahara, and with its 35,000 seats it is one of the great monuments of Roman architecture. In the vicinity, excavations have brought to light hundreds of mosaic floors from ruined villas.

UNESCO. *A Legacy for All*. Paris, 1984.

ELLIS ISLAND. A small island (10.9 hectares) at the entrance to the port of New York in upper New York Bay, south-west of Manhattan Island. Property of the US government, since 1808; it was long the site of an arsenal and a fort; in the years 1892–1943 an immigration station through which c. 25 million European immigrants passed and where they underwent medical examinations and intelligence tests. Sick persons or those unable to work for other reasons were sent back to their countries of origin. After 1943 Ellis Island remained a place for the deportation of "undesirable foreigners." Now a part of the Statute of Liberty National Monument.

EL SALVADOR. Member of the UN. Republic of El Salvador. República de El Salvador. Central American State on the Pacific Ocean, bordered by Guatemala and Honduras. Area: 21,073 sq. km. Pop. 1985 est. 5,480,000 (1930 census 1,434,000; 1950 1,855,000; 1970 – 3,533,828). Capital: San Salvador with 452,614 inhabitants 1984. GNP per capita 1986 US $820. Currency: one colon = 100 centavos. Official language: Spanish. National Day: Sept. 15, Proclamation of Independence, 1821. Member of the League of Nations 1919–37. Member of the UN

E

since Oct. 24, 1945 and of UN specialized agencies, with the exception of GATT and IMCO. Member of the OAS and the Treaty of Tlatelolco.

International relations: Spanish colony 1542–1821, part of the Capitania General de Guatemala; part of the Central American Federation 1821–39. Formally independent republic as of, Apr. 1, 1841. At war with Guatemala and Honduras 1863, 1876, 1890 and 1906. During World Wars I and II on the side of the Allies. In 1969 fought the "football war" with Honduras. On Aug. 27, 1973 Salvador signed in Teguacigalpa a peace agreement with Honduras, and on June 30, 1976 a demilitarized zone was established between both countries under the observation of representatives of Costa Rica, Guatemala and Nicaragua.

The Salvadorian civil war was internationalized by the involvement of Hondurean troops in border zones. The UN General Assembly Res. 37/185 of Dec. 17, 1982 adopted by 79 votes to 18, with 55 abstentions, expressed its deepest concern at the continued violations of human rights in El Salvador and reaffirmed the right of the Salvadorian people to determine freely their political, economic and social future.

In 1983–84 El Salvador was a subject of ▷ Contadora Group negotiations. On Oct. 15, 1984 the first peace talks between president of El Salvador José Napoleón Duarte and representatives of the Farabundo Martí National Liberation Front and the Democratic Revolutionary Front took place in La Palma near the border with Honduras. The meeting had earlier been proposed by President Duarte in the UN General Assembly. Both sides agreed to continue the talks. In a state of siege 1979–87. New signs of impending civil war 1988. Situation alleviated somewhat in 1989.

M.A. GALLARDO, *Cuatro Constituciones Federales de Centro America y Las Constituciones Politicas de El Salvador*, San Salvador, 1945; W. VOGT, *The Population of Salvador and its Natural Resources*, Washington, DC, 1946; A. MESTAS, *El Salvador, Pais de lagos y volcanes*, Madrid, 1950; CEPAL, *El Desarrollo Económico de El Salvador*, New York, 1960; A. WHITE, *El Salvador*, New York, 1973; J. BEVAN, *El Salvador. Education and Repression*, London, 1981; F.J. DEVIRE, *El Salvador. Embassy under attack*, London, 1981; L. NORTH, *Bitter Grounds: Roots of Revolt in El Salvador*, London, 1981; T.S. MONTGOMERRY, *Revolution in El Salvador. Origins and Evolution*, Boulder, 1982; P. ERDOZAIN, *Archbishop Romero: Martyr of El Salvador*, Guildford, 1982; R. ARMSTRONG, J. SCHENK, *El Salvador: The Race of Revolution*, London, 1982; E.A. BALOYRA, *El Salvador in Transition*, Wilmington, 1982; S.W. SCHMIDT, *El Salvador: America's Next Vietnam*, Salisbury, N.C., 1983; *UN Chronicle*, January, 1984; *The Europa Yearbook 1987. A World Survey*, Vol. I, London, 1987.

ELYSÉE. *French* = Palace Elysée. The Parisian seat of the president of France, metaphorically – a common international term for the policies of the French government. ▷ Downing Street, ▷ Kremlin, ▷ Palazzo Chigi, ▷ White House.

EMANCIPATION PROCLAMATION, 1862. The edict freeing the slaves, in all "rebellious" southern states and since Jan. 1, 1863 in the whole territory of the United States; announced by the US President Abraham Lincoln on Sept. 22, 1862, but did not take effect until 1865, when Congress ratified the so-called 13th amendment to the Constitution. The Proclamation stated:

"... all persons held as slaves within any State or designated part of States, the people whereof shall then be in rebellion against the United States, shall then be, thence forward, and forever free, and the Executive Government of the United States ... will recognize and maintain the freedom of such persons."

J.H. FRANKLIN, *Emancipation Proclamation*, New York, 1963.

EMBARGO. An international term for the economic boycott of a country through partially or wholly prohibiting trade in certain goods; considered a form of economic aggression and against international law if not in the form of self-defense against foreign aggression. The UN Charter in art. 41 permits embargoes in case of military aggression. The term embargo is also used to designate:
(1) A ban on foreign merchant vessels from leaving the ports or territorial waters of a given state. The first US embargo was imposed by US Congress on Dec. 22, 1807, prohibiting the departure of commercial ships carrying specified goods to England and Europe.
(2) A ban on publishing official information or a news bulletin before a certain time (in case of international news before the day and hour agreed upon by the parties).

In 1951 the UN General Assembly adopted a resolution recommending to the UN Member States an embargo on arms and strategic materials shipment to the Chinese People's Republic and North Korea. In the 1960s a multi-nation embargo was organized against Cuba by the OAS and against North Vietnam by the NATO Member States.

On Oct. 4, 1977 the UN Security Council, for the first time in the history of the UN, adopted a mandatory embargo on the supply of arms against a UN member state, the Republic of South Africa. Previously the UN Security Council in 1963 in Res. 181 introduced a voluntary embargo on the supply of arms to South Africa.

C.G. FENWICK, "The Quarantine against Cuba. Legal or Illegal?", in: *American Journal of International Law*, 1963; *UN Chronicle*, November, 1977.

EMBARGO ACT OF 1807 ▷ Embargo.

EMBASSY. A diplomatic institution of the highest degree; organ co-ordinating diplomatic, economic, cultural and other co-operation; office of ambassador; since 1815 subject of international conventions on embassy regulations such as extra-territoriality, the right to use the flag and emblem of the given country on embassy premises.

EMBLEM ▷ Flag, Emblem and Seal of the UN.

EMF. ▷ European Monetary Fund.

EMIGRATION. An international term for people's abandonment of their native lands for the purpose of settling in another region or continent of the world; subject of international conventions and continuous co-operation of international and inter-governmental organizations and UN international statistics. Emigration is most often undertaken for economic or political reasons, more rarely for climatic ones. Up to World War I emigration took place without many formalities, e.g. up to 1917 the USA required neither a passport nor a visa, limitation concerned only health. After World War I many states introduced quota limitations for immigrants from other countries. A Convention on the question of transit cards for emigrants was signed in Geneva, June 14, 1929. ▷ Immigration, ▷ Immigration Act 1965.

L' ONU, *Problèmes de la statistique des migrations*, New York, 1950; L'ONU, *Migrations internationales selon le sexe et l'âge: Statistiques pour les années 1918–1947*, New York, 1953; L'ONU, *Bibliographie analytique des statistiques des migrations internationales pour divers pays, 1925–1950*, New York, 1956; L'ONU, *Migrations internationales selons les caractéristiques*

économiques: statistiques pour certains pays 1918–1954, New York, 1958.

EMISSIONS INTERNATIONAL. An international term for interest-bearing obligations floated on the international market by banks empowered to make issues; emissions quoted on stock markets are a form of international loans.

EMP BOMB. Electro-magnetic-pulse bomb, future arm in a space-war, after explosion some 40 km above the Earth could destroy the entire communications network of an area as large as Europe.

B. JASANI, *Outer Space. A New Dimension of the Arms Race*, Stockholm, SIPRI, 1982.

EMPLOYMENT. Enrollment of a definite number of persons for execution of a job for a salary defined in the employment contract; subject of international statistics research by the ILO and of permanent ECOSOC study; subject of Convention Concerning Employment Policy drawn and adopted at an ILO General Conference, July 9, 1964, art. 1 of which referred to the Universal Declaration of Human Rights, repeating the principle that every person has the right to work and to protection against unemployment, which goal can be attained provided that ILO member states will pursue in their policies: assurance of jobs for all able-bodied people and those who seek work; effectiveness of work; free choice of employment and opportunity for every worker to attain qualifications indispensable for execution of a job; opportunity to take full advantage of workers' skills and talents regardless of race, color, sex, religious denomination, political convictions, nationality, or social background. Such policies were to be reconciled with the stage and level of economic advancement and adapted to the conditions and customs of a given country.

The convention was ratified by Sweden, New Zealand – 1965; Costa Rica, Tunisia, Jordan, Senegal, Norway, Great Britain, Cyprus, Canada – 1966; Poland – 1967. It was anteceded by a Convention Concerning Discrimination in Respect of Employment and Occupation, adopted June 25, 1958, which precluded distinctions or priviliges based on race, color, sex, etc. of workers and called for a non-discriminatory policy.

A CMEA conference was held in Moscow, Mar. 1973, devoted to the problems of employment to be faced by 1990. A World Employment Conference held in Geneva in June 1976, estimated that by the year 2000 some 700 million new jobs have to be created.

An Employment Decade 1971–80 was proclaimed in Sept., 1968 by the ILO, in connection with the demographic explosion of the Third World and the necessity for creating in the decade jobs for *c.* 290 million, including 173 million in Asia, 32 million in Africa, 29 million in Latin America and 56 million in developed regions. The ILO program focuses on creating a system of world employment planning.

BIT, *Programme mondial de l'emploi*, Genève, 1974; V.P. KARAVAYER, *Intiegratsya i inviestitsyi problemy sotrudnichestva stran SEV*, Moskva, 1979; ILO, *Bibliography of Published Research of the World Employment Programme*, Geneva, 1979. ILO, *New Technologies. Their Impact on Employment and the Working Environment*, Geneva, 1982.

EMS. ▷ European Monetary System.

EMS TELEGRAM, THE, 1870. A dispatch sent from the chancellery of the King of Prussia, Wilhelm I, in his summer residence in Bad Ems, July 13, 1870, to Chancellor Otto von Bismarck; it reported that, as a result of contacts between the King and the ambassador of France, Prussia was withdrawing the candidacy of Prince Leopold Hohenzollern to the Spanish throne, which was supposed to resolve the conflict with France over the Spanish succession. Bismarck, who, according to instructions from the King, was to transmit the contents of the telegram, consciously published its text in shortened form in such a way that it became insulting to France. As he noted in his diary: such a text "will act on the Gallic bull like a red flag." The text of the telegram changed by Bismarck became the formal reason for the declaration of war on Prussia by Emperor Napoleon III.

O.F. BISMARCK, *Gedanken und Erinnerungen*, Stuttgart, 1898; R. TESTER, *Die Genesis der Emser Depesche*, Berlin, 1915.

ENCLAVE. An international term for the territory of a state surrounded by the territory of another state, e.g. San Marino; or a territory that is a separate administrative unit located in the territory of another state, e.g. West Berlin.

ENCODED TELEGRAMS. A diplomatic and consular message whose text is unreadable for persons not knowing the code used by the sender; subject of two international conventions: the International Convention on Telecommunications, signed in 1952 in Buenos Aires and the Telegraphic Rules signed in 1949 in Paris.

A MEISNER, *Die Anfänge der modernen diplomatischen Geheimschrift*, Paderborn, 1902; F. PRATT, *Histoire de la Cryptographie*, Paris, 1940; A. GIEYSZTOR, *Zarys dziejów pisma łacińskiego* [Outline of the History of Latin Writing], Warszawa, 1973, pp. 194–199.

ENCOMIENDA. *Spanish*: "order", "commission", in this case the "granting of land by the king." An international term for granting the conquered lands in America along with the Indians living on them to the conquistadors, which from the outset started the process of the feudalization of Latin America and in this way created an economic order called Latifundismo which continues to exist in a large part of the region, as well as the social problem of the pauperization of the Indians. Subject of studies of the UN Economic Commission for Latin America, ECLA.

ENCUENTRO LATINAMERICANO CAMILO TORRES, ELACT. Latin-American Encounter in Memorial to Camilo Torres, with headquarters in Bogota, est. 1966. An international Catholic youth organization professing the ideas of the Colombian scholar and social activist, Father Camilo Torres Restrepo, Professor at the University of Bogota, who as a sign of protest against social injustice on Oct. 18, 1965 joined the revolution of Colombian partisans and fell on Mar. 15, 1966 in an engagement with government armed forces. On the first anniversary of his death, Encuentro published a manifesto in which it came out in support of the ▷ OLAS. See also ▷ Theology of Liberation.

G. GUZMAN, *El Cura Guerrillero*, Bogota, 1968; W.J. BRODERICK, *A Biography of the Priest-Guerrillero Camilo Torres*, Garden City, 1975.

ENCYCLICALS. *Latin*: litterae encyclicae = "apostolic letter". The circular letters of the Pope of the Roman Catholic Church named from their first words; introduced on Dec. 3, 1740 by Benedict XIV in the letter announcing his election, entitled *Epistola enciclica et conmonitaria*. Only some of the papal encyclicals went beyond church problems and became internationally prominent, as Pius IXth's *Quanta Cura*, Dec. 8, 1864 with its attached Syllabus or "list of the most important errors of our times" and the Index of writings condemned by the

Church; Leo XIIIth's *Humanum genus*, Apr. 21, 1884 against freemasonry; *Rerum Novarum*, May 15, 1891 against the Marxist workers' movement; *Pascende dominici gregis*, Sept. 8, 1907 against modernism in art, and others. However, they were always intra-church encyclicals aimed exclusively at the faithful. Exceptions to this rule are the encyclicals of John XXIII ▷ *Pacem in terris*, Paul VI ▷ *Populorum progressio* and John Paul II ▷ *Redemptor hominis*, appealing to all people of good will and transmitted as official documents by the Vatican to the UN and other international institutions. ▷ *Mater et magistra*, ▷ *Gaudium et Spes*, ▷ *Laborem exercens*.

Dictionnaire de la Théologie Catholique, Paris, 1913.

ENCYCLOPEDIA, DIDEROT'S DEFINITION. The highlights of the definition of Encyclopedia by Denis Diderot in "Encyclopédie ou Dictionnaire raisonné des sciences, des arts et des métiers":

"In fact, the purpose of an encyclopedia is to assemble the knowledge scattered over the surface of the earth; to explain its general system to the men with whom we live, and to transmit it to the men who will come after us; in order that the labours of centuries past may not be useless for the centuries to come; that our descendants, by becoming better instructed, may as a consequence be more virtuous and happier, and that we may not die without having deserved well of the human race."

Encyclopaedia Britannica, Vol. 8, Chicago-London, 1973.

ENCYCLOPEDIAS, INTERNATIONAL. Encyclopedic works devoted to regional or global international relations in one or more areas of political, economic, social and cultural life. The first international encyclopedias were published in the 19th century and mainly concerned diplomacy; in the 20th century predominant are encyclopedias devoted to the development of international law, international political and economic relations. The first international encyclopedia in the world devoted to the UN was published in 1975 in Polish, in 1976 in Spanish and in 1985 in English. The Polish and Spanish editions contain a dictionary of international terms and indexes in the four UN working languages: English, French, Russian and Spanish.

E.J. OSMAŃCZYK, *Encyklopedia Spraw Miedzynarodowsch i ONZ*, Warszawa, 1975; E.J. OSMAŃCZYK, *Enciclopedia Mundial de Relaciones Internacionales y Naciones Unidas*, Madrid–Mexico, 1976; K.F. KISTER, *Encyclopedia Buying Guide*, New York and London, 1978; R. DARNTON, *The Business of Enlightenment. A Publishing History of the Encyclopedia*, Harvard, 1979; G.Th. KURIAN, *Encyclopedia of the Third World*, New York, 1978, 1982; E.J. OSMAŃCZYK, *Encyclopedia of the United Nations and International Agreements*, London–Philadelphia, 1985.

ENCYCLOPÉDIE.. The first Encyclopedia with international, political impact in Europe and America, published in French in 28 volumes, 1751–75 with a 5-volume supplement and 2-volume index, 1780, edited by Denis Diderot and Jean d'Alembert, revolutionary by virtue of skepticism and rationalism in the definitions; included 1759 in the general condemnation register of dangerous books; recognized as the intellectual inspiration of the ▷ French Revolution, 1789.

R. COLLISON, *Encyclopaedias: Their History Throughout the Ages*, London, 1964.

ENDLÖSUNG. *German* = "final solution". A cryptonym for a plan developed by the Main Security Office of Germany, RSHA, at the order of A. Hitler and approved on Jan. 20, 1942: the physical liquidation of Jews residing in European territories

then subject to the German III Reich. The RSHA estimated the number of Jews in Europe at that time as 11,292,300 persons. In further RSHA plans a similar "final solution" was foreseen in turn for Poles, by the ▷ German penal law for Poles and Jews, 1941. The "Endlösung" was condemned as crime against Humanity by the ▷ Nuremberg War Criminals Trial 1945–46.

Das Menschenschlachthaus Treblinka, Wien, 1946; "Final solution of the Jewish questions", in: *The Trial of German Major War Criminals. Proceedings of the IMT sitting at Nuremberg, Germany*, 42 Vols., London, 1946–48, Vol. 2, p. 319 and 365; Vol. 10, p. 268; Vol. 11, p. 359; Vol. 12, p. 143; and Vol. 22, p. 494; W. LAQUER, *The Terrible Secret: Suppression of the Truth about Hitler's 'Final Solution'*, Boston–London, 1980; M. GILBERT, *Auschwitz and the Allies. A Devastating Account of How the Allies Responded to the News of Hitler's Mass Murder*, New York, 1981; G. FLEMING, *Hitler and the Final Solution*, Berkeley, 1982; M.N. PENKUWER, *The Jews Were Expendable: Free World Diplomacy and the Holocaust*, Chicago, 1983.

ENEMY STATES UN CHARTER CLAUSE (Art. 107). ▷ Germany and the UN.

ENERGY. The power derived from basic raw materials: coal, petroleum, natural gas, etc. and from the driving force of water; as well as the new source in the 20th century, atomic energy. Subject of international conventions. In the second half of the 20th century the main world source of energy has been coal (c. two-thirds), then petroleum, natural gas, water and atomic energy. In the decade 1961–70 more than half of the world production of energy was consumed by the USA (35%) and the USSR (15.6%). An important consumer of energy was also Western Europe (19.4%). The rest of the world used c. 30%. The main source of energy in that decade, both in the USA and the USSR, was petroleum and gas, pushing coal to second place. American planners have projected that by the year 2000 one-third of electric energy will come from atomic power plants. In 1971 the US Atomic Energy Commission submitted for discussion an international plan for creating a world energy system. The energy crisis became the object of an international conference in 1973 and in Apr., 1974 of a Special Session of the UN General Assembly. The Tenth World Energy Conference in 1977 in Istanbul assumed that if atomic power plants were meeting 4% of the need for electric energy to date, then by the year 2000 this would exceed 50%. The World Energy Conference took place Sept. 18–23, 1983 in New Delhi. The IAEA in 1987 estimates that the nuclear energy production will grow an average of 3.8 to 4.6% per year worldwide from 1987 to 2005; in developing countries, including Eastern Europe, the annual growth could be nearly double that rate.

The OECD publ.: *Energy Policies and Programs of the IAEA Member Countries*, 1977 ff.
Organizations reg. with the UIA:

First World Power Conference, WPC, took place in London in July 1924; from 1926 WPC is a permanent institution; it co-ordinates national committees of the majority of the states of the world; Consultative status with ECOSOC, UNESCO, IAEA, WMO. Publ. information leaflets, *WPC Statistical Yearbook* (from 1936), *WPC Survey of Energy Research*. Connected with WPC is the international Commission on Large Dams of the WPC (ICOLD), est. 1928, Paris; publ. *ICOLD Bulletin* and *Technical Dictionary on Dams*. Solar Energy Society, SES, est. 1954, Melbourne. Publ. quarterly, *Solar Energy*.
Operating within the CMEA system is the Central Bureau for the Control of a Common Energy System of Bulgaria, Czechoslovakia, the GDR, Hungary, Romania, the Ukraine, est. 1962, Prague.

E

International Studies of the Demand for Energy, New York, 1977; R. STOBAUGH, D. YERGIN, *Energy Future, Report of the Energy Project at the Harvard Business School*, New York, 1979; P. BORMET, *Pourquoi l'énergie nucléaire?*, Paris, 1980; *UN Chronicle*, October, 1982, p. 40–41; IAEA, *Energy, Electricity, and Nuclear Power Estimates for the Period up to 2005*, Vienna, 1987.

ENERGY WORLD CRISIS, 1973–80. An international term for disturbances and shortages on the energy market of a lasting character in the 1970s. Chronology of the energy crisis from the beginning in 1973 to 1980:

1973 – In connection with the Arab–Israeli military conflict, which started on Oct. 6, Iraq nationalized the American Exxon and Mobil concessions, the OAPEC countries imposed embargo on oil deliveries to all countries supporting Israel, and on Oct. 16 raised the oil price by 70%; Libya on Oct. 19, increased the oil price to US $8.9 per barrel, Iraq on Oct. 21, nationalized the Royal Dutch/Shell Company, OAPEC countries on Nov. 4 reduced production by 25%, Iran on Dec. 19 raised the price for a barrel of oil to US $17.50.

1974 – An international energy conference held Feb. 11–13, in Washington; highly industrialized countries (except France) on Feb. 26 set up a co-ordination group for energy; the OAPEC countries on Mar. 13 cancelled the embargo towards the USA and on Apr. 8 created the Aid Fund for the Third World; the OPEC sessions, June 15–17 and Sept. 12–13, increased payments collected from foreign oil companies; OECD countries (except France) on Nov. 15 set up the International Energy Agency; OAPEC countries on Dec. 12, froze prices till Sept. 15, 1975.

1975 – In Feb. reduction of oil prices by Abu Dhabi and Libya; the International Energy Agency convenes Feb. 5–7 in Paris; on June 5, opening of the Suez Canal; OPEC countries on June 10 consider going over from dollar clearing to ▷ SDR; the UK on June 11 starts oil drilling in the North Sea, Venezuela on Aug. 29 announces nationalization of the whole oil industry as of Jan. 1, 1976; OPEC session on Sept. 29 raises oil prices by 10%; the North–South Paris conference was held from 16 to 19 Dec.; in the USA on Dec. 22 a bill regulating oil prices was passed.

1976 – on Jan. 30, passing of the co-operation program by member countries of the International Energy Agency; OPEC countries on May 28 freeze oil prices; some OPEC countries on Dec. 17 raise the oil price by 10%, and others by 5%.

1977 – On Apr. 20 President J. Carter announced an energy program for the USA; on June 3 failure of Paris North–South negotiations; the USA on June 20 set in operation the Alaska oil pipeline; on July 13 OPEC session concerning oil prices; member countries of the International Energy Agency establish on Oct. 6, the final limit of oil imports in 1985 from OPEC countries at 26 million barrels daily.

1978 – In March discovery of new oil deposits in Mexico; in June freeze on oil prices by OPEC till the end of the year; in Oct. beginning of the crisis in Iran, strikes in oilfields; on Oct. 15 the Congress of the USA passes the energy program; the OPEC countries on Dec. 26, raise the oil price to US $14.5 for 1979 and suspensions of oil production in Iran.

1979 – On Jan. 16, escape of the Shah from Iran, rise of oil prices and limitation of production in member countries of the OAPEC; on Feb. 14–16 failure of American–Mexican talks at the Carter–Portillo meeting in Mexico; on Mar. 5 resumption of oil exports from Iran; on Mar. 26 OPEC countries raise the oil price and introduce market margins for fixed prices; on Mar. 26, was signed Egypt–Israel peace pact; on Apr. 5, a new energy program of President J. Carter for the USA; in March and May a new rise of oil prices; on May 22, International Energy Agency recommends economizing and searching for new energy sources; on May 24, Algeria increases the price per barrel to over US $20; on June 21 resolutions of the European Council on energy problems; in June session of OECD Council discussed consequences of the oil shock for the 1980s; the UNCTAD session discussed the oil crisis and the OPEC session fixed minimum prices for a barrel at US $18, maximum at US $23.5 and increased the Aid Fund for the Third World to US $1.6 billion (costs of importing oil by those countries increased from US $5.2 billion in 1973 to $40 billion in 1979 and $60 billion in 1980). On Aug. 31, nationalization of the property of the British Petroleum concern in Nigeria; in Sept. a World Oil Congress in Bucharest presented an estimate of proven and potential oil deposits in the world, evaluated at 304 billion tons, with about 3 billion tons of yearly output, under consideration that over half of the resources are located in territories hindering exploitation.

1980 – New price rises for oil (up to US $30 per barrel) and a rapid increase of the gold price (up to US $850 per ounce in January). The petrodollar surpluses deposited at Western banks amounted to about US $175 billion in early 1980. Simultaneously, the debts of the Third World countries exceeded US $300 billion and the debt crises halted energy development projects throughout the Third World. In the same time the West achieved oil security and the demand for OPEC oil fails to rise and a decrease in the price of oil was a universal trend at the end of 1984.

KEESING's *Contemporary Archive 1973–1980*; T. SZULC, *The Energy Crisis*, New York, 1974.

ENEVETAK ATOLL. One of the uninhabited atolls of the Ralik Chain in the Marshall Islands in the Central Pacific; in 1948, 1951, 1952 and 1954 it was the site of US atomic bomb tests. After 30 years the radioactive contamination was still dangerous, particularly from the first hydrogen bomb test on Mar. 1, 1954.

In May, 1985 it was necessary to evacuate 304 inhabitants, one third of which were heavily contaminated from the Rongelup atoll.

National Geographic, June 1986; KEESING's *Record of World Events*, 1986. No. 2.

ENGINEERING. A subject of international co-operation. Organizations reg. with the UIA:

Central American Union of Associations of Engineers and Architects, f. 1958, San José de Costa Rica.
Commonwealth Engineering Conference, f. 1946, London.
Conference of European Engineering Students Association, f. 1965, Wuppertal.
European Federation of National Associations of Engineers, f. 1951, Paris.
European Society for Engineering Education, 1973, Louvain. Publ.: *Newsletter*.
Inter-American Association of Sanitary Engineering, f. 1946, Caracas. Consultative status with ECOSOC.
International Association for Bridge and Structural Engineering, f. 1929. Zurich. Publ.: *Bulletin*.
International Association for Earthquake Engineering, f. 1963, Tokyo.
International Association of Engineering Geology, f. 1964, Paris.
International Commission of Agricultural Engineering, f. 1930, Paris, Consultative status with ECOSOC, FAO, UNESCO.
International Confederation of Technical Agricultural Engineers, f. 1930, Zurich. Publ.: *La technique agricole*.
International Conference of Women Engineers and Scientists, f. 1964, New York.
International Federation for Medical and Biological Engineering, f. 1959, Paris. Consultative status with WHO and ECOSOC. Publ., *Medical and Biological Engineering*.
International Federation of Automobile Techniques Engineers, f. 1947, Paris.
International Federation of Consulting Engineers, f. 1913, The Hague.
International Federation of Doctors in Engineering and Engineers – Doctors of Science, f. 1963, Paris.
International Federation of Municipal Engineers, f. 1960, Vincennes (Seine), France.
International Institute of Biomedical Engineering, f. 1961, Paris. Publ.: *Newsletter*.
Liaison Group for the Engineering Industries, f. 1967, Brussels.
Pacific Asian Federation of Industrial Engineering, f. 1970, New Delhi.
Panamerican Federation of Engineering Societies, f. 1951, Mexico, DF. Consultative status with UNESCO, ECOSOC, OAS. Publ.: *Newsletter* (English and Spanish).
Union of International Engineering Organizations, f. 1951, Paris. Consultative status with UNESCO, ECOSOC.
World Federation of Engineering Organizations, f. 1968, London. Consultative status with UNESCO and UNIDO.

Yearbook of International Organizations.

ENGLAND. Part of the United Kingdom of Great Britain and Northern Ireland; a synonym of Great Britain.

ENGLAND, CHURCH OF. ▷ Anglican Communion.

ENGLISH. One of the official UN languages, dominating in international diplomacy after World War II, subject of organized international propagation (▷ British Council). Contemporary English is a compound of British and American usages. See also ▷ American Language.
Organizations reg. with the UIA:

English Speaking Union, f. 1918, London and New York, organizes World Conferences.
International Association of University Professors of English, f. 1957, Oxford. Publ.: *English Studies Today*.

Yearbook of International Organizations. "Black English", in: *The Concise Columbia Encyclopedia*, New York, 1983; N. MOSS, *The British–American Dictionary*, London, 1984; J.T. SHIPLEY, *The Origins of English Words: A Discursive Dictionary of Indo-European Roots*, Baltimore, 1985; *Financial English*, London, 1986; R. McCRUM, W. ORAN, R. McNEIL, *The Story of English*, London, 1986; A.S. HORNBY, *Oxford Advanced Learner's Dictionary of Current English*, Regularly updated, Oxford; J. SINCLAIR ed., *COLLINS COBUILD English Language Dictionary*, London, 1987.

ENGLISH AMERICA. Common name of ▷ Canada before the mid-19th century.

ENGLISH CHANNEL. *French*: Canal de la Manche. An arm of the Atlantic Ocean, 565 km long, between the coasts of West Europe and Great Britain; 180 km wide at its west entrance, between Lands End, Cornwall, southwest England and Ushant Island, Brittany, France; 33.8 km wide between Dover and Cape Gris Nez. The strait of Dover connects the Channel with the North Sea. Its greatest width, 240 km, is between Lyme Bay and the Gulf of St. Malo. Dover and Dunkirk were the object of international treaties in 1936 between France and Belgium and Great Britain on the opening of permanent communication by ferry, as well as the conflict between France and Great Britain on sovereign rights over a group of islands: Minquiers and Ecreheu submitted by both parties to the International Court of Justice in The Hague in Dec., 1950 (English Channel Case); object of international conventions. In 1970 the number of ships navigating the channel during a one-day period exceeded 300. In 1971 on the initiative of IMCO an international agreement on the principles of navigating the channel was worked out, based on strict adherence to one-way traffic lanes.; international co-operation was undertaken on combatting polution of the waters of the channel. In 1972 the governments of France and Great Britain came to an agreement on the construction of a tunnel under the channel, called ▷ Chunnel. The crossing of the channel claims a number of records: the first to cross the channel in a balloon were J.P. Blanchard and Dr. J. Joffiers in 1785; by plane – L. Blériot, 1909; the first regular ferry for trains on the line Paris–London via Dover and Dunkirk was opened in 1936; an object of a special international swimming competition via Dover-promontory to Gris Nez. The first was an Englishman, Cpt. Matthew Webb on Aug. 24–25, 1875 in the time of 21 hours and 45 minutes; the first woman was Gertrude Ederle, USA, on Aug. 6, 1926 in the time of 14 hours and 3 minutes; the record held by the Egyptian, Hasan Abd el-Rehim, was made Aug. 22, 1950 in the time of 10 hours and 50 minutes.

F.R.G. MENCKE, *The Encyclopedia of Sports*, New York, 1955; E.C.R. HADFIELD, *British Canals*, London, 1969; D.W. BOWETT, "The arbitration between the UK and France concerning the continental shelf boundary in the English Channel", in: *The British Yearbook of International Law*, 1978, Oxford, 1979.

ENGLISH USAGE IN THE UN SYSTEM.
According to the United Nations Editorial Manual, the authors and editors in the UN system should be guided in their choice and use of words by the directives on style given in Fowler's *Dictionary of Modern English Usage* and should bear in mind the special need for discretion, good taste and simplicity in United Nations texts.
Certain words and forms, though given in the *Concise Oxford Dictionary*, are inappropriate in United Nations documents, which are prepared for a multicultural readership. Words marked with an asterisk (*) or parallels (‖), denoting geographical restrictions, should not be used in United Nations documents, neither should "through" in phrases such as "January through June", meaning "from January to June inclusive", and "in back of", meaning "behind". The form "in light of" (for "in the light of") should not be used.
Words designated colloquial, e.g. "liaise", should not be used. As Fowler points out under "Feminine designations" (q.v.), occupational and agent nouns and titles such as "ambassador" are of common gender and are used to designate men or women. The generic word "chairman" should be used in United Nations documents and publications to designate a presiding officer in bodies other than the principal organs and major conferences, in which the term "president" is used. The form "chairperson" should not be used. The form "chairwoman" should not be used to designate a woman presiding officer since its use would, by extension and implication, give rise to the erroneous impression that the word "chairman" referred only to a man and might thereby lead to the false conclusion that it excluded women.
Care should be taken not to use words and terms that do not have an equivalent in other languages and therefore pose a problem for translators and interpreters. The form "Ms." should be used in English texts only if the person concerned has specifically requested that form of address or if the marital status is not known. In French, use "Mme", in Spanish "Sra".
The word "agenda" (neuter plural of the gerundive of the Latin agere, "do"), though a plural form, is treated as a singular noun and used with a verb in the singular. The same form ("agenda", not "agendas") is used with a plural verb to denote two or more lists of agenda items. The words "input" and "output" are acceptable, but the forms "inputs" and "outputs" should be avoided except with regard to computers.
As the designations of the seasons (summer, autumn (fall), winter, spring) relate to different times of the year in the northern and southern hemispheres, they should not be used in reference to the time of a meeting. A phrase such as "a meeting to be held in the spring" is ambiguous.

H.W. FOWLER, *A Dictionary of Modern English Usage*, rev. and ed. by Sir Ernest Gowers, Oxford, 1979; *United Nations Editorial Manual*, New York, 1983, pp. 391–392;

ENIGMA.
An acronym for a German machine cipher, decoded by Polish mathematicians and turned over to France and UK in July 1939 by Polish intelligence. In 1940 a special British ultra-secret intelligence net, called Ultra, utilized the potentialities of Enigma with British, French and Polish cryptoanalytic experts. The Enigma was later passed on to the US.

J. KAHN, *The Codebreakers*, New York, 1967; J. BERTRAND, *Enigma*, Paris, 1973; R. LEWIN, *Ultra Goes to War*, London, 1978; J. GARLINSKI, *Intercept, Secret of the Enigma War*, London, 1980; W. KOZACZUK, *Enigma, How the German Machine Cipher Was Broken and How It Was Read by the Allies in World War II*, Frederick Md., 1983; M.K. DZIEWANOWSKI, *War at Any Price*, Englewood Cliffs, N.J., 1987.

ENMOD CONVENTION, 1977.
An official abbreviation of the Convention on the Prohibition of Military or any other Hostile Use of Environmental Modification Techniques, signed on May 18, 1977 in Geneva; came into force Oct. 5, 1978. Prohibits any deliberate manipulation of natural processes for changing the composition or structure of the Earth including its atmosphere or of outer space. For text ▷ Modification of Environment Convention. The Convention was ratified until Jan. 1, 1987 by 51 countries.

SIPRI, *World Armaments and Disarmament Yearbook*, 1976, pp. 314–323; 1977, pp. 17–18; 1978, pp. 377–382, 392–397; 1980, pp. 448–461; *SIPRI Yearbook 1987*, Oxford, 1988, p. 461.

ENOSIS.
Greek = "Union". A Greek term for the desire of Greeks on Cyprus to form a union between the Republic of Cyprus and Greece. In 1974 the term "dual Enosis" appeared to define the idea of the division of Cyprus into a Greek part, in union with Greece, and a Turkish part in union with Turkey.

ENTEBBE.
Airfield in Uganda, place of the rescue on July 3–4, 1976 by Israeli commandoes of 83 hostages taken by Palestinian terrorists June 27, 1976 aboard an Air France plane flying from Tel Aviv to Paris, The Israeli action was the subject of debate in UN Security Council July 4–12, 1976, justified by Israel and the Western powers as self-defense against international acts of territorial and air piracy. The Arab and socialist states charged Israel with violations of the sovereignty of a foreign state that were "dangerous to world peace." Due to the opposing positions, none of the proposed resolutions were approved by the Council.

UN Yearbook 1976 pp. 315–320.

ENTENTE.
French = "agreement, alliance". The name of a tripartite alliance of France, Great Britain, and Russia before World War I. Particular elements which contributed to the formation of the Entente were: the Franco-Russian alliance, 1893 (obligating both sides in case of aggression by Germany to open an eastern and western front against her); the Franco-British agreement, 1904, the so-called ▷ Entente cordiale; and the British–Russian agreement, 1907, marking out the spheres of influence of Great Britain and Russia in Asia. The Entente was a counterweight to the triple alliance of Germany, Austria-Hungary and Italy created 1879–82. After the outbreak of war, the Entente was joined in 1914 by Serbia, Montenegro, Belgium, Japan; 1915 by Italy (after leaving the triple alliance); 1916 by Portugal and Romania; 1917 by the United States. In addition, the Entente was joined by many other states, mainly from Latin America, which limited themselves to declaring war without taking part militarily. In the London

Declaration, Sept. 4, 1914, France, Great Britain, and Russia obligated themselves not to make a separate peace with Germany and her allies. During World War I, the Entente became generally accepted to mean all of the 25 states of the anti-German coalition. After World War I, three separate systems of alliances appeared using the name Entente to stress their affiliation with France: the ▷ Baltic Entente, the ▷ Balkan Entente, and the ▷ Entente, Little.

B.E. SUNITH, *Triple Alliance and Triple Entente*, London, 1934.

ENTENTE CORDIALE.
French: "friendly agreement". The name first appeared 1832–46 to define the good relations between France and Great Britain, then later as a name for a treaty between France and Great Britain signed Apr. 8, 1904 in London; its aim was the establishment of zones of influence of the signatories in Morocco and Egypt, which settled the basic differences between France and Great Britain and enabled them to develop a common policy against Germany. Subsequently, this treaty became the basis for a Franco-British military convention concluded on July 20, 1911 in Paris, which anticipated, in the event of a conflict, the sending to France of a British expeditionary force of more than 150,000 men with 67,000 horses and nearly 500 cannons through designated ports and places of billeting. The military alliance was strengthened on Nov. 22, 1912 by an exchange of notes between the ministers of foreign affairs, E. Grey and P. Cambon, on joint action at the moment of the outbreak of war. This alliance was implemented in Aug. 1914. The signing of the Entente cordiale was another step on the road to the creation of the triple alliance of France, Russia, and Great Britain. ▷ Entente.

A. TARDIEU, *Questions diplomatiques de l'année 1904*, Paris, 1905; R. GUYOT, *La première entente cordiale*, Paris, 1926; S.M. CARROL, *Germany and the Great Powers 1866–1914*, New York, 1938; P.J. VON ROLO, *The Entente Cordiale*, London, 1969.

ENTENTE, INTERNATIONAL.
An international anti-communist bureau est. in Mar., 1924 with headquarters in Geneva, which collected and distributed materials among delegations of LN member states and waged a campaign "in defense of economic firms against Profintern", "in defense of colonies against bolshevism", and "to liberate the Russian people." It was reg. with the UIA.

ENTENTE, LITTLE.
French = "Petite Entente". Commonly accepted name for a system of alliances made 1920–21 in central Europe and south Europe and supported by France. They included the Allied Conventions: Czechoslovakia with Yugoslavia, signed Aug. 31, 1922 in Belgrade, replaced by a Treaty of Alliance, signed Aug. 31, 1922, extended May. 21, 1929; Czechoslovakia with Romania, signed Apr. 23, 1921 in Bucharest; Yugoslavia with Romania, signed June 7, 1921 in Belgrade. Moreover, a General Act of Conciliation, Arbitration and Legal Proceedings between Czechoslovakia, Romania and Yugoslavia was concluded in Belgrade on May 21, 1929. These alliances had the aim of maintaining the status quo in the Danube basin and in the Balkan peninsula, which was established by peace treaties negotiated after World War I, in Trianon with Hungary and in Neuilly-sur-Seine with Bulgaria which were primarily directed against eventual Hungarian revisionist policies. Concerned by Hitler's rise to power in Germany, the three states in Geneva on Feb. 16, 1933 signed the Little Entente System, "concerned with maintaining the peace under all circumstances" and formed a Permanent Council at the level of minister

of foreign affairs (art. 1) as an organ co-ordinating the policy of the member states, acting on the principle of unanimity, as well as an Economic Council (art. 7) for the purpose of "gradually co-ordinating the economic interests of the three states or in relations between them, or in relations with third states." The Little Entente was one of the basic elements of French policy directed against Germany and the USSR. To further strengthen its influence in those countries France concluded a Treaty of Alliance and Friendship with Czechoslovakia on Jan. 25, 1924 in Paris for an unlimited time, a 10-year Treaty of Friendship with Romania, signed June 10, 1926 in Paris (extended for another 10 years Nov. 8, 1936), as well as a 5-year Friendship Treaty with Yugoslavia, signed on Nov. 1, 1927 in Paris (extended Nov. 10, 1932 and Dec. 2, 1937). None of these treaties was a military alliance, but obligated the parties to consult each other "on questions of foreign policy which could endanger their security and be detrimental to the peace established by the treaties".

Growing tensions in international relations caused by the policies of the III Reich and fascist Italy in the 1930s led to an intensification of differences between the states of the Little Entente, which initially resulted in violations of the provisions of the alliance and then to its liquidation. The first violation of the resolutions of the alliance was the negotiation by Yugoslavia on Jan. 1, 1937 of a Treaty of Eternal Friendship with pro-German and anti-Romanian Bulgaria, followed by the Treaty of Neutrality signed on Mar. 25, 1937 between Yugoslavia and Italy and the consent of the Council of the Little Entente to the militarization of pro-German Hungary. The ▷ Munich Agreement of Sept., 1938 and the annexation of Czechoslovakia which followed finally ended the interwar activity of the Little Entente.

LNTS, Vol. 139, p. 233; A. MOUSSET, *La Petite Entente, ses origines, son histoire, ses connexions, son avenir*, Paris, 1923; R. MACKRAY, *The Little Entente*, London, 1929; E. MALYNSKI, *Les problèmes de l'Est et la Petite Entente*, Paris, 1931; E. BENES, *Le pacte d'organisation de la Petite Entente et l'état actuel de la politique internationale*, Paris, 1933; P.S. WANDYCZ, *France and her Eastern Allies 1919–1925*, London, 1962; J. VOLKOV, *Giermanoyugoslavskie otnosheniya i razval Maloy Antanty*, Moskva, 1966. R. MACHRAY, *The Little Entente*, London, 1969.

"ENTERPRISE". Name of the first atomic aircraft carrier built in the USA in 1962; also the name of the first space shuttle built in the USA.

ENTERPRISES. ▷ Multinational and Transnational Enterprises.

ENTOMOLOGY. ▷ Insects.

ENVIRONMENTAL HYGIENE. An international term introduced by the WHO for a complex of sanitary operations, combatting air pollution, public campaigns, etc. in rural and urban environments aimed at protection of man's environment.

ENVIRONMENTAL PROTECTION. The protection of man's environment is promoted by the UN and UNESCO in connection with the rapid destruction in the second half of the 20th century of flora and fauna by processes of industrial civilization. In 1968 the UN General Assembly Res. No. 2398/XXII, recommended to the UN Secretary-General the collection of data on the condition of man's environment in all regions of the world and suggested protective measures. The so-called U Thant Report, "Man and His Environment",

published on May 26, 1969 stated at the introduction:

"For the first time in the history of humanity a crisis of world-wide scope has come into existence, including both the developed as well as the developing countries – concerning the relation of man to his environment. Threatening signs were visible long ago: the demographic explosion, the inadequate integration of powerful technology with the requirements of the environment, the destruction of cultivated lands, the unplanned development of urban areas, the diminishing of open spaces and the ever growing danger of the extinction of many forms of animal and plant life. There is no doubt that if this process will continue – future life on earth will be threatened."

After reading the U Thant Report, the UN General Assembly requested UNESCO to organize regional symposia – they were held 1969–71 in Asia, Africa, Latin America, the Middle East, and Europe – and to prepare a World Conference on the Protection of Man's Environment, which was preceded by a report published in ten languages and written by more than 100 scholars, entitled "Only One World – *Nous n'avons qu'une Terre*". The Conference was held June 5–14, 1972 in Stockholm with incomplete participation of the European states in view of denying the GDR, which was not yet a member of the UN, the right to participate and the solidarity boycott of the Warsaw Pact states. The Conference worked in three committees: I debated social and cultural needs of planning environmental protection; II on natural resources; III on the international aspects of the struggle against the destruction of man's environment. The plenary session accepted the ▷ Stockholm Declaration 1972. Also passed were around 170 specific recommendations. The Declaration and 26 principles of environmental protection passed by the Stockholm Conference, June 10, 1972, were submitted to all of the states in the world. The Warsaw Pact states on Aug. 17, 1972 submitted to the UN Committee on the peaceful utilization of sea and ocean beds outside the jurisdiction of states a Declaration on the principles for the rational exploitation of the living resources of seas and oceans in the interest of all of the nations of the world. On Dec. 15, 1972 the UN General Assembly approved Res. 2995 and 2997/XXVII concerning co-operation among states in the area of environmental protection. In accordance with a decision of the Conference, a new special organization formed by the UN General Assembly began its work on Jan. 1, 1973 UN Governing Council for Environmental Programs ▷ UNEP. The Council was composed of representatives of 54 states elected by the Assembly for 3 years. The headquarters of the Secretariat is Nairobi. The introductory program of the Council's work included i.a.: the creation of a network of at least 100 stations for measuring the pollution of the atmosphere and the construction of at least 10 stations recording changes in the environment, which have been going on for a long time; introduction of a ban on the dumping of petroleum and gasoline by ships at sea; signing as quickly as possible a convention on the prohibition of disposing of chemical and other industrial wastes in seas and oceans; making up an international list of substances endangering the environment (including figures on the volume of their production and manner of use), including radioactive wastes; organizing international co-operation in the study and control of harmful substances contained in food products; drawing up a world list of rivers so far unpolluted and a list of sewers flowing into rivers and through these to oceans and seas; collecting global information on the negative environmental effects of the exploitation of mines; formulating a world balance sheet of energy resources from the viewpoint of the devastation of the en-

vironment as a consequence of using energy; working out a system of international planning of natural resources; drawing up a world map of regions threatened by the destruction of the natural environment. The USA and USSR in 1972 formed a joint mixed commission on environmental protection which on Sept. 21, 1972 established 30 subjects for joint research. In accordance with a decision of the Heads of State and Government of the nine EEC countries at a conference on Oct. 20, 1972 in Paris, a joint program of environmental protection for western Europe was developed. The CMEA states in 1972 also began joint work on environmental protection. UNESCO initiated two international research programs: Man and the Environment and Man and the Biosphere.

A general European program of environmental protection was initiated by the Conference on Security and Co-operation in Europe (▷ Helsinki Final Act, 1975). In Dec., 1972 American and Soviet veterans of World War II at the so-called Dartmouth conference declared their opposition to disturbing the natural environment for military purposes and called for the drafting of an appropriate international treaty. The US Senate on July 11, 1973 passed a resolution calling on the government to initiate work on an international treaty prohibiting the use of any environmental or geophysical modification activity as a weapon of war or the carrying out of any research or experimentation directed thereto. The existence of many technical possibilities of causing natural catastrophes (earthquakes or seaquakes by underground nuclear explosions or by atomic explosions in the Arctic zone, etc.) became the subject of international consultations on the questions of drafting the appropriate international treaties banning this type of activity. Subject of one of the ▷ American–Soviet Agreements 1957–81. On Dec. 10, 1976 the UN General Assembly by 96 votes in favor, 8 against, and 30 abstentions approved the Convention on the Prohibition of the Use of Environmental Modification Techniques for Military or any other Hostile Purposes called the ▷ ENMOD Convention, signed on May 18, 1977 in Geneva by 33 states. Also in 1977 the ILO drafted and accepted Convention No. 148 concerning the protection of workers against dangers in the work environment caused by air pollution, noise and vibrations. ▷ ILO Conventions.

In Oct., 1977 in Tbilisi (USSR) a UNESCO International Conference was held on the subject of environmental education. The Conference accepted the ▷ Tbilisi Declaration, 1977. The Stockholm institute SIPRI publishes a special periodical in English devoted to environmental protection, entitled *Arubio*.

On Feb. 1, 1980 a Declaration of Environmental Policies and Procedures Relating to Economic Development was signed at UN headquarters by UNEP. A report by UNEP on the state of the world environment was published in May 1983. In April 1984 the first review conference of the ENMOD Convention took place in Geneva, convened by UNEP, UNIDIR and SIPRI, dedicated to the environmental warfare, which in the 1970s in Indochina disrupted the regional environment by plant poisons and the weather patterns by cloud seeding; in the 1980s and 1990s environmental warfare will have the capability of making highly destructive ▷ *tsunamis* or sea waves, awaken quiescent vulcanoes and direct hurricanes to damage the enemy. The World Commission on Environmental Protection and Development, est. 1984 by the General Assembly, published on April 27, 1987 a report titled "Our Common Future", called also "The Brundtlant Report", after the Norwegian Prime Minister Gro Harlem Brundtlant, president of the World Commission. The Commission's report proposed institutional, financial and legal measures to help resolve global, economic and ecological problems through environmental protection and sustainable development. The report was presented to the General Assembly as a draft of a UN Program of Action on Sustainable Development.

M. NICHOLSON, *The Environment Revolution*, London, 1970; M. BALDWIN, K.J. PAGE Jr., *Law and the Environment*, New York, 1970; ECE, *Symposium on Problems Relating Environment*, UN, New York, 1971; J. DORST, *Avant que nature meure*, Paris, 1971; R. DUBOS, B. WARD (eds.), *Only one World – Nous n'avons qu'une Terre*, Paris, 1972; *Protection of Man's Natural Environment*, Warsaw, 1973; J. SYMONIDES, "Protection de l'environment humain au regard du droit international", in: *Polish Yearbook of International Law*, Warsaw, 1975; A.CH. KISS (ed.), *The Protection of the Environment and International Law*, Leiden, 1975; *UN Chronicle*, May, 1983, pp. 33–46; A.H. WESTING (ed.), *Environmental Warfare: A Technical, Legal and Policy Appraisal*, Stockholm, 1984; A.H. WESTING (ed.), *Explosive Remnants of War: Mitigating the Environmental Effects*, Stockholm, 1984; KEESING's *Record of World Events*, 1987; *Our Common Future: Report of World Commission on Environment and Development*, Oxford, 1987; A. MILNE, *Our Drowning World*, New York, 1988.

ENVIRONMENTAL PROTECTION AGENCY. US government agency est. 1970 to control ▷ air, ▷ noise ▷ and water-pollution and ▷ radiation.

ENVIRONMENTAL PROTECTION, UNEP WORLD REPORT, 1983. The text of the UNEP Report on the State of World Environment 1983 is as follows:

"Technological progress has brought enormous numbers of chemicals into everyday life. Five million substances have been identified; about 70,000 of these are marketed, about half of them in quantity. They have brought immense benefits to society – increased food production, improved health care, eradicated deadly diseases, and bestowed longer life expectancy and a better standard of living. But they have also brought new dangers, largely through the wastes generated in their manufacture. Tens of millions of tons of toxic and otherwise hazardous substances enter the environment every year as unwanted wastes. Managing and disposing of these hazardous wastes properly faces mankind with a significant problem. Until recently there were no standards or uniform regulations for disposal even in some industrialized countries. So an alarming number of critical problems built up over the years in places like Love Canal, near Niagara Falls in the United States, where homes were built on an old chemical waste dump and inhabitants were exposed to hazardous substances. Most developed countries have now passed laws controlling the disposal of these wastes. But there is a danger that companies will evade them by moving their processes or exporting their wastes to areas with less strict legislation, particularly developing countries.

Other unwanted wastes, sulphur and nitrogen oxides, are already often exported. They are pushed into the air, carried by the winds and spoil the rain which man has always valued as a prerequisite of life on earth. In many areas of the world the rain must pass through air polluted by these gases, which come from burning fossil fuels in industries, power plants, and cars. As it, and snow, falls, it reacts with the pollutants to produce something new, often a mixture of sulphuric acid, nitric acid and water. It has become acid rain. In Northern Europe, Canada, and the Northeastern United States, the rain is turning rivers, lakes and ponds acidic too, killing fish and decimating other water life. It assaults buildings and water pipes and tanks with corrosion that costs millions of dollars every year. It may even threaten human health, mainly by contaminating drinking water. It is a particularly modern, post-industrial form of ruination, and is as widespread and careless of its victims, and of international boundaries, as the wind that disperses it.

It is partly to avoid such pollution from fossil fuels that much attention has recently been given to developing renewable sources of energy. One of them is already the most important fuel for hundreds of millions of people, especially in developing countries. Trees, crops, aquatic plants and organic wastes of different kinds can all be valuable energy stores, and this "biomass" can be turned into usable energy by a variety of processes. Many countries are now paying special attention to energy farms, areas of land or water exclusively devoted to growing plants for fuel. Any plant which is more valuable for energy than for other uses can be considered as a fuel crop, and there are many promising examples of using them for energy. Large-scale farms running into tens, even hundreds, of thousands of hectares are being considered both on land and at sea. But these could cause pollution and other problems that must be carefully assessed at an early stage to make sure that "green energy" is developed in an appropriate and environmentally-sound way.

Hazardous Waste.

In the last decades there has been a chemical revolution. As industry has expanded, thousands of new chemical substances have been produced and put on the market, and their numbers increase every year. They are used in medicine, in the home, in agriculture and in industry itself and have done much to increase health and living standards. Yet they have also brought new dangers, for they find their way into the environment by many different paths, and can enter food and water supplies. Sometimes the environmental contamination results directly from their use; at other times because they are discharged in wastes.

Fears about their possible environmental effects were raised at the United Nations Conference on the Human Environment, held in Stockholm in 1972. That concern has since been justified, for there has been a succession of incidents where people have been affected by toxic chemicals in food, water and the environment.

One of the most worrying features of the problem is that very little is known about the long-term consequences of exposure to the chemicals. We know a good deal about their short-term effects from experiments on animals, and from the experiences of people who have been exposed to them at work. We know, too, that over longer periods some can cause cancer, delayed nervous damage, malformations in unborn children, and mutagenic changes that could produce disability and disease in future generations. Many other chemicals are likely to have similar effects, but because these take time to show and their causes are hard to pinpoint, we do not yet know which substances are the dangerous ones. The situation is made even more difficult because, once they are in the environment, chemicals spread in a very complex way and may be converted into other substances which have different effects. Some risk from the use of chemicals is, of course, acceptable in return for the benefits they bring, but it is clearly prudent to limit the danger by preventing their release into the environment so far as is practicable. This is particularly important when it comes to disposing of hazardous waste. Yet some of the alarming incidents that have hit world head-lines in the last decades happened because wastes were dumped with almost complete recklessness. Wastes have been considered to be worthless, and so there has been no economic incentive to recover them, and a positive encouragement to getting rid of them as cheaply as possible.

How a waste is handled is all-important. Bad disposal can make a relatively harmless substance troublesome, if not dangerous, while if a hazardous waste is properly treated, as much recent legislation requires, it will probably be safer than many others that are not officially classified as potential dangers.

It has been estimated that over five million chemical substances have been identified; about 70,000 of these are marketed, maybe only half of them in quantity. Several thousand new ones are found every year, and about a tenth of the new discoveries reach the market. Not only are the numbers of substances growing rapidly in the chemical revolution; the quantity produced is increasing just as fast. The total production of synthetic organic chemicals, for example, rose more than 50 per cent in the past decade. It is hard for public health officials, even in developed countries, to keep abreast of the information needed to control their use and disposal.

The United States of America is the biggest manufacturer of chemical substances, generating about 60 million tons of hazardous wastes a year, compared to an estimated 20 to 30 million tons a year in the whole of the European Economic Community. Hazardous waste is about 10 to 20 per cent of the world's manufacturing waste, and only a few per cent of all its solid refuse, which also includes municipal rubbish, agricultural waste, sewage sludge, spoil from mining and ash from power stations.

The term 'hazardous waste' is restricted to wastes from chemical processes and those generated by cleaning or closing chemical factories or contaminated sites. These wastes are extremely varied, and so it is hard to give a simple, brief description of them. Under United States law hazardous wastes are defined generally as those that pose a substantial threat, present or potential, to human health or other life. Laws in other developed countries define them more strictly, specifying the processes giving rise to them, certain poisonous constituents or the results of toxicity tests. They include, to cite only a few of the many possible examples, cyanide and paint residues, wastes from metal refining and finishing, tar from refining and distilling, flue gas sludges, organic solvents, oily wastes, cyanide, asbestos, arsenic, mercury, cadmium, lead, phenols, herbicides and pesticides, acids and alkalis. Many of the damaging incidents that have arisen from bad disposal are related to the production of organic chemicals, which has advanced so spectacularly in recent years. However, the greatest tonnage of chemicals produced are still the common inorganic acids, alkalis, metals and chlorine, and these can also be hazardous.

Undisciplined disposal of these wastes can cause fires, explosions, air, water and land pollution, contamination of food and drinking water, damage to people who get them on their skins or inhale their vapours, and harm to plants and animals. It is an alarming list, and in practice most of the things that could go wrong have indeed occurred, in fact the incidents that have hit the headlines are probably only a few of those that have actually taken place; many more are likely to have gone unreported. Even those incidents which have become internationally famous have not always been critically studied and analysed in a way that might help determine causes of the trouble and bring out other important lessons that developing countries could learn to avoid similar harm as they develop chemical industries.

The Rhine and the Mississippi are classic examples of rivers continually polluted by industrial waste. Both are used for drinking water. The Netherlands draws water from the Rhine, downstream of many industrial waste discharges, and the Mississippi supplies New Orleans. Both rivers are so polluted by organo-chlorine and other compounds that it is doubtful whether they are suitable sources of drinking water. Studies have suggested that their contamination could be linked to the fact that the people who have to use these waters suffer slightly higher cancer rates than expected.

There have been several hundred cases of the contamination of wells by poisons from hazardous wastes – the most common of all the dangers to arise from improper waste disposal. These often occurred because the wastes were put into sand or gravel pits or old mine workings in fractured strata. Places like these attract people disposing of liquid waste and slurry because they are cheap and the liquid disappears quickly, flowing out into the subsoil and into ground water; but this is part of the problem because the soils contain little clay and other absorbent substances. As a result they do not filter the waste, trapping the dangerous chemicals, and so protecting the ground water from contamination. To make things worse, the wells were usually shallow, privately-owned ones and the water received no treatment that could remove the pollution. Among the main poisons that have turned up in such water supplies are arsenic, pesticides, gasoline, phenols, chromate, and chlorinated hydrocarbons.

Other dumping has exposed people to poisonous vapours from organic compounds at concentrations that could not even be permitted in factories (industries necessarily expose their workers under controlled conditions to higher levels than would be tolerated for the general public). The victims have suffered headaches, nausea, dizziness, and discomfort when breathing – and, after prolonged exposure, skin rash, sores, pimples, and numbness of the limbs.

Most developed countries have a heritage of contaminated sites where chemicals have been manufactured or hazardous waste deposited. Some have launched campaigns to find and clean up the sites, financed either with public money or with funds levied from the chemical industry. Others tackle the sites only when they turn up. At any rate, there is now considerable experience both of these problems and of cleaning sites contaminated by spills and accidents.

Laws controlling the disposal of hazardous wastes are now in effect in most developed countries. The immediate need is to make sure that they are enforced in a cost-effective and environmentally sound way. Some developed countries have still to create an effective enforcement system staffed with adequately trained people. Developing countries following the same legislative path may have greater problems in recruiting the right staff. International organizations could consider publishing manuals and providing training facilities, though these should be directed at dealing with the actual wastes generated in developing countries rather than at establishing comprehensive theoretical principles.

The lack of trained staff is only part of the problem. There are so many companies carrying out so many operations with hazardous waste that even well-staffed authorities cannot guarantee full inspection. In the United States, for example, there are about 57,000 firms licensed to generate the waste, 14,000 licensed to transport it, and another 14,000 facilities licensed for disposal. Much, therefore, depends on the integrity and competence of firms – reinforced by the fear that they will lose their licences if they are caught misbehaving. As the controls have tightened in many developed countries, chemical industries have had to pay more for getting rid of their wastes. Some have been tempted to avoid these extra costs by moving their operations or exporting their wastes to countries where the laws are less strict, or less strictly enforced. These countries could well become international dustbins, and end up with the same sort of problems that brought the strict legislation in the first place. There have even been a few cases where companies have shipped waste to another country, ostensibly for storage, and then abandoned it. Waste from the Netherlands ended up in the United Kingdom in this way, and wastes from the United States of America, have been stored in a warehouse in Mexico.

Developing countries would be particularly vulnerable to such pollution exports.

Companies setting up in developing countries often stipulate that their processes must remain secret. If they insist that the composition of their wastes should also be cloaked in secrecy the countries may never know exactly what hazardous substances, in what quantities, have been put into their disposal sites – and will find it almost impossible to control the situation. In fact, so much secrecy can rarely be necessary, and, if companies do insist on it, countries should require them to give assurances about the hazards posed by their wastes, and to accept financial liability for any problems caused.

Action: Taken or Planned.

The major actions are the national laws for controlling the disposal of hazardous waste now in force in the developed countries and international agreements on limiting marine pollution either from disposal at sea (the London Convention) or from discharges from the land (the Paris Convention).

These conventions on pollution of the sea have been supplemented by regional agreements where countries bordering particular seas like the Baltic, the North Sea and the Mediterranean make possible more effective action to solve their local problems. On land, there have also been major clean-up operations on hazardous waste sites in a few developed countries.

The laws have in general laid down that the disposal of hazardous waste should be approved by regulatory authorities, either on a case-by-case basis or through general regulations.

They have brought about a marked improvement, by setting standards where few existed before. Companies have had to pay greater disposal costs, and this has encouraged them to save money by introducing better ways of dealing with wastes. They have increasingly included good waste management in the over-all design of new processes, and chosen ones that generate as little waste as possible.

Countries have drawn up their own statutory definition of what should be regarded as hazardous waste under these laws. There are also different definitions for the international agreements and for EEC directives. The wastes are defined as hazardous because they possess certain characteristics, like flammability, persistence or toxicity; because they are generated by certain listed processes, or because they have certain listed toxic constituents. The laws usually provide that small quantities of hazardous wastes should be exempt from the regulations. This is controversial because it can allow companies to evade controls by breaking larger amounts of wastes down into small packages. Besides, even small amounts of hazardous waste can produce quite serious effects on health when they are disposed of inadequately. In the United States, for example, well over 97 per cent of all the hazardous waste is generated by just five per cent of the factories, which each produce over five tons of it a month. Ninety-one per cent of the factories produce less than a ton a month each. In situations like these, authorities can concentrate on the main waste producers with a relatively small staff, but if they decide to cover all firms, including the smallest producers, they could find themselves having to inspect 10 times as many factories.

Some national laws have set up systems of manifests, papers which ensure that the people who handle the waste as it passes from factory to disposal site acknowledge responsibility for it while it is under their control. These systems are designed to stop irresponsible dumping, but they can be evaded without much difficulty by unscrupulous operators. The United States, the Federal Republic of Germany, and the Netherlands have what are probably more powerful safeguards. They require firms that generate, transport or dispose of the waste to be licensed.

Even these systems are by no means water-tight, however, if only because so many firms are involved that it is impossible to provide very detailed inspection. The United States has developed the most elaborate system of control of all. There, the licensed firms are required to provide financial bonds (promises of money) and vehicles and other equipment to deal with emergencies. They also have to conform to strict conditions laid down in codes of practice for the various means of treating and disposing of waste. These provisions are backed up by a system of inspection which can, for example, demand that incinerators are demonstrated to show they do the job properly. These measures impose a considerable financial burden on both industry and government administration. One result may be that industry moves its operations or exports its wastes to less demanding places – and this could cause more environmental damage in the end.

There are various ways of treating waste so that it is easier or safer to transport or dispose of it. Liquid waste can be put into lagoons or tanks to settle; sludge can be dried out; and waste can be bound into cements, bitumens, polymers or synthetic rocks. It has been said that treatment technology is generally available for most hazardous wastes. Research into better disposal is also proceeding. Among the options for disposal are spreading waste on farms or other land, incinerating it, treating it chemically or biologically, putting it into lined pits, injecting it deep into disused wells and other mineral workings, disposing of it underground, and dumping it at sea. Different options, of course, will be best for different wastes.

Naturally, national laws and codes of practice do not necessarily provide a reliable guide to what actually goes on in a country. That depends on how rigorously the regulations are enforced and on whether codes are merely seen as targets or used as manuals of working practice. It does seem, though, that there are significant differences among the developed countries. This reflects variations in national aims and practices and results in different costs. The United States legislation was aimed, among other things, at outlawing unlined lagoons, and a containment philosophy is now in force. The high water table of the Netherlands has strictly limited disposal in the ground. Disused salt mines in very stable strata in the Federal Republic of Germany make particularly good disposal sites and supplement special local treatment facilities. The United Kingdom and the CMEA member States share a preference for mixing hazardous and other wastes, including household garbage, and disposing of it in the ground in carefully selected sites. This practice protects water supplies by relying on the hazardous wastes being degraded and fixed in the site and undergoing chemical changes in unsaturated and impermeable strata. Developing countries can benefit from the experience of these different approaches when selecting the most economic solution to their particular disposal problems.

The marine conventions and the EEC Directive on Ground Water control disposals on a case-by-case basis. They have black lists of banned substances whose discharge into the sea or ground water is prohibited. Another list comprises substances that can only be discharged with specific permission, while the rest are subject to general authorizations. The specific permissions are given if assessments of how the wastes behave in the environment, and the damage they are likely to do, show that the likely harm is acceptably small if appropriate safety measures are taken. The assessments, however, are necessarily based on models which cannot precisely forecast what will happen and can only make approximate predictions, because we do not yet know enough about the subject. So the permissions are based on probabilities rather than certainties of safety.

The marine conventions, coupled with measures by the International Maritime Organization to restrict pollution from oil spills, have had a positive effect. The dumping of chlorinated hydrocarbons has been reduced, if not eliminated, and partly replaced by incineration at sea. This operation releases acids which fall out into seawater, and was brought under the provisions of the London Convention in 1978.

Recently there have been indications that more waste may be dumped acceptably at sea. The International Atomic Energy Agency has revised the dumping limits for radioactive wastes under the London Convention, and this has already permitted a modest increase. A recent United Nations study concluded that controlled releases of other hazardous wastes to the sea might be increased in the same way, while noting that about 30 compounds or groups of compounds should be studied for their effects on marine pollution. In the United States where severe restrictions were placed on dumping hazardous wastes at sea, attitudes appear to be changing. There has been a recommendation to resume marine disposals which, before being stopped, had been conducted without any demonstrable environmental damage.

Mankind has always reverenced what Tennyson called 'the useful trouble of the rain.' Without the 110,000 cubic kilometres of it that fall each year the continents would be barren, for the land has never been more than an outlying province of the kingdom of life. Long unconquerable by living things, late to be colonized from the waters, the land could still not sustain them if it were not for this constant support from life's home country – the sea.

Yet now the rain in parts of the earth has taken on a new and threatening complexity. It mixes in the air with pollution from burning fossil fuels – particularly from power stations, factories and motor vehicles – and brings down dilute sulphuric and nitric acid. This is killing fish and other water life, and corroding buildings, including some of the world's most important ancient monuments. It may also damage forests and croplands, and possibly pose a substantial threat to health.

Acid rain is not a new phenomenon – the term was first coined by a chemist, Robert Angus Smith, who described pollution in Manchester, England over a century ago. What is new is the realization that it is an international problem. The air of towns like Manchester has been largely cleaned, partly by building tall chimneys at power stations and factories, which push pollution high into the air. These chimneys have made things better locally, by dispersing the pollutants, but aggravated the international difficulties. For the sulphur and nitrogen compounds emitted by burning fossil fuels can be blown thousands of kilometres by the winds, to cause acid rain in countries far from their points of origin.

Acid rain was first raised as an international issue by Sweden at the United Nations Conference on the Human Environment in Stockholm in 1972, and it has now developed into a major international environmental issue. At first the Swedish views were treated with some disbelief, particularly by some of the emitting countries. Over the last decade, however, there has been a great deal of international research into the issue. Ample information was available by the end of 1982 through the activities of the Co-operative Programme for Monitoring and Evaluation of Long-range Transmission of Air Pollutants in Europe (EMEP), under the Convention on Long-range Transboundary Air Pollution 1979, and activities conducted in accordance with the Memorandum of Intent Between the Government of Canada and the Government of the United States of America concerning Transboundary Air Pollution. Furthermore, there was a special conference in Stockholm in 1972 on acidification of the environment, and this reviewed and assessed a large amount of scientific information not previously available. This information has been of great help in preparing this chapter.

The evidence indicates that there is, indeed, an international problem, even though a number of scientific and technical questions are still not resolved. International arrangements – like the Convention and Memorandum of Intent – are now available that could be used to work out a solution.

So far, acid rain has been seen as an essentially regional problem, confined to the industrial areas of the northern hemisphere. But, though the problem was first perceived there, it may become much more widespread – for acid rain is likely to occur wherever fossil fuels are intensively used.

Acidification is an environmental problem, or becoming one, in parts of Europe and North America. Around five to ten million square kilometres of these continents are affected. Similarly polluted areas are likely to exist elsewhere in the world, especially around large urban and industrial conglomerations. We do not yet know where they are, because so far no evidence on them is available.

Industrial regions of the world suffer much more acidic fall-out than they did before the industrial revolution. This is because power plants, some industrial processes, vehicles and homes emit sulphur and nitrogen compounds, mainly from the burning of fossil fuels, and have greatly increased the amount of them in the environment.

Natural processes also put sulphur and nitrogen compounds into the air, besides man-made sources. Nobody knows precisely how much they contribute around the globe. Estimates vary between 78 and 284 million tons of sulphur a year in the form of sulphur oxides, and between 20 and 90 million tons of nitrogen a year in nitrogen oxides.

In comparison, man emits between 75 and 100 million tonnes of sulphur a year. So, despite the differences in estimates of natural sources, it can be concluded that man-made and natural emissions of sulphur are, globally, of the same order of magnitude.

Burning coals provides about 60 per cent of the man-made emissions, burning petroleum products gives rise to another 30 per cent, and various industrial processes account for the remaining 10 per cent. Approximate estimates indicate that burning fuel in electric power stations and industry provides almost three quarters of sulphur emissions in the European Economic Commission countries.

There are indications that sulphur dioxide emissions (the main pollutant in Europe and North America) have not increased during recent years, as they were predicted to do, and are not likely to rise over the coming decades either. This is the result of two factors: better pollution control, and less burning of fossil fuel as a result of energy conservation and, possibly, slower economic growth in the west than had been expected.

Like sulphur oxide pollution, pollution from nitrogen oxides is also of the same order compared to natural sources. Fossil fuel combustion yields about 20 million tons of nitrogen a year, which have already caused environmental problems on a regional and local basis in industrialized countries.

Not all the pollution is acid rain, i.e., sulphuric and nitric acid dissolved in precipitation. Some of it happens when the sulphur and nitrogen oxides themselves fall out on the land, in what is known as 'dry deposition'. In general this tends to be the main form of the pollution near its source, and the longer the gases stay in the air, the more likely they are to go through the complex changes that will turn them into acid rain (or wet deposition), to fall perhaps thousands of kilometres from where they began their journey. Wet deposition rates are fairly well known, but dry deposition is harder to calculate and rates remain more uncertain. Both types of deposition can be intercepted by vegetation canopies. The canopies of evergreen forests, in particular, can be subjected to high deposition rates.

Each country gets part of its acid fall-out from its own pollutants, but receives the rest on the winds from neighbouring countries. EMEP has worked out estimates of how much sulphur is emitted, and how much deposited, in individual European countries. This reveals which of them are 'net importers' and which 'net exporters' of air pollutants. Government agencies and departments in the United States and Canada are monitoring acid deposition under the National Atmospheric Deposition Programme (NADP) and the Canadian Atmospheric Network for Sampling Air Pollutants (CANSAP). These, too, aim at working out deposition rates and identifying which areas export, and which import, the pollution. Co-operation between the two countries was greatly enhanced in 1980 when the Memorandum of Intent Concerning Transboundary Air Pollution was signed by their Governments.

Reductions in emissions might well not benefit everyone equally. Because of the complex changes the pollutants undergo in the air, fall-out might decrease unevenly from place to place. But the experts attending the Stockholm Conference on Acidification of the Environment agreed that total fall-out over a whole continent like Europe or North America would be reduced approximately in direct proportion to cuts in the amounts of sulphur and nitrogen emitted there.

Lakes and rivers were the first victims of acid rain to become evident. Hundreds of lakes in parts of Scandinavia, the north-east United States, south-east Canada and south-west Scotland have turned acid. Parts of these areas are particularly vulnerable because their soil and bedrock offer little protection against acidic rain. They are made up of minerals like granite, gneiss and quartz-rich rocks which contain little lime and do not weather easily, and therefore can do little to neutralize the acid when it falls. In Sweden damage to fisheries attributed to acidification has been observed in 2,500 lakes, and is assumed to have taken place in another 6,500 where signs of the process have been found. Meanwhile, out of 5,000 lakes scattered over 28,000 square kilometres of southern Norway, 1,750 have lost all their fish and 900 others are seriously affected. In Canada, nearly 20 per cent of all the lakes that so far have been examined in Ontario have either been turned acid, or are extremely sensitive to the process. Between 30 and 60 per cent of the lakes in various areas of south-west Quebec are considered to be sensitive or highly sensitive. And in Canada's Atlantic provinces many lakes have been turned 10 to 30 times more acid during the past two decades. Similar situations have been observed in the north-east of the United States.

As the water becomes more acid, the amount of aluminium in it starts to increase rapidly. Concentrations as low as 0.2 milligrams per litre of the metal in acid water kill fish. Large scale kills have been recorded in some Swedish lakes, and these have been attributed to aluminium poisoning rather than to high acidity alone.

At the same time, phosphates, which nourish phytoplankton and other aquatic plants, attach themselves to the aluminium and become less available as a nutrient. So increasing aluminium levels may reduce primary production on which all other water life depends. As the water gets more acid still, other metals, like cadmium, zinc, lead and mercury also become increasingly soluble. Several of them are highly toxic, and some may be taken up by water life through food chains, though little evidence of this is available so far.

Soils are normally much better able to resist acidification than lakes, rivers and streams, and so can take much more acid without noticeable ecological drawbacks. Their vulnerability differs depending on their type, the kind of bedrock they cover, and the use to which man puts them. The most vulnerable lands are those that have bedrocks poor in lime, covered with shallow layers of soil containing low concentrations of protective substances. Large parts of Scandinavia are like this.

The acidification of soils is not merely due to acid deposition; it arises from a natural process as well as the result of biological processes within the soils. Normally the acids thus produced are neutralized during the weathering of mineral soil particles but, depending on the composition of the soils, their capacity to neutralize more than a definite amount of acidity is limited.

Acidification may cause nutrients like potassium, magnesium, calcium and other micro-nutrients to leach more rapidly out of the soil, decreasing soil fertility. Aluminium concentrations would rise, just as they do in water, thus damaging plants and reducing the availability of phosphorus to them. As in water, too, metals like cadmium, zinc, lead, mercury, iron and manganese would spread through the environment more readily with acidification.

Intensive experimental research into the effects of acidification on forest, land and wood production was carried out in the 1970s. It is still going on, but so far the results are inconclusive. Acid fall-out does seem to have a distinct effect on soil microbiology, chemistry and fauna – but the effects on the growth of plants, including trees, are far less clear. Indeed, depositions of nitrogen may even have a fertilizing effect and increase productivity significantly, at least in the short term. Studies on the trends of tree growth in Southern Sweden between 1950 and 1974, for example, failed to reveal any statistically significant pattern.

In the Federal Republic of Germany, on the other hand, 7.7 per cent of the forest area has been reported in 1982 to be damaged (7.5 per cent of the damage being light, 19 per cent medium and 6 per cent heavy) by wasting disease due to the consequences of deposition and accumulation of air pollutants. In addition, trees have suffered more storm damage and experienced regeneration difficulties. These forests receive much more fall-out than Scandinavian ones because they are close to cities and big industrial areas, such as the Ruhr, with many polluting sources.

One reason postulated to explain this damage is the combined effects of surges of naturally produced acid, extreme climatic situations (very high or low rainfall, temperature extremes) and atmospheric acidic deposition. These release aluminium into the soil and make it easier for bacteria to damage the fine roots of the trees. This reduces their vitality, leads eventually to a rotting disease, and may make them more vulnerable to storms. High concentrations of sulphur dioxide in the air may damage leaves, and so cut the trees' productivity. Acid fogs, persisting for several days, may also damage trees in mountain areas.

As well as the health of important ecosystems, human health may also be put at risk by pollution. High concentrations of sulphur dioxide, nitrogen, oxides and dust have long been known to be harmful. This issue is only marginally related to the problem of acid rain, since such concentrations are usually only found close to the sources of pollution, and sulphur oxide levels in many European and North American cities have been decreasing recently. The health effects from such direct pollution have been dealt with extensively under the criteria Programme of the United Nations Environment programme and the World Health Organization, which is now part of the International Programme on Chemical Safety (a joint programme of the United Nations Environment Programme, the International Labour Organisation and the World Health Organization), and they need not be discussed here in detail. Suffice it to say that the minimum concentrations of sulphur dioxide and nitrogen dioxide which the Task Groups considered to cause health damage are: sulphur dioxide, 250 micrograms per cubic metre as a 24-hour average or 100 micrograms per cubic metre as a long-term average; nitrogen dioxide, 190–320 micrograms per cubic metre, as a maximum one hour exposure not to be exceeded more than once a month.

Other, indirect, health hazards are suspected. These would be caused by the metals like lead, copper, zinc, cadmium and mercury released from soils and sediments by increased acidification. They can get into groundwater, rivers, lakes and streams used for drinking water, and be taken up in food chains leading ultimately to man. The releases of cadmium in particular may give rise to a growing problem as acidity increases, as normal levels in human food are already close to the acceptable daily intake. Acid water may also cause galvanized steel and copper water pipes to release metals, and it seems that the risk arises as soon as the acidity of the water rises above normal. Most drinking water in industrialized countries, however, is supplied by public water works which eliminate this problem with proper treatment techniques; but much remains to be done in developing countries. Meanwhile, acid accelerates corrosion in most materials used in the construction of buildings, bridges, dams, industrial equipment, water supply networks, underground storage tanks, hydroelectric turbines, and power and telecommunications cables. It can also severely damage ancient monuments, historic buildings, sculptures, ornaments and other important cultural objects. Some of the world's greatest cultural treasures, including the

Parthenon in Athens and Trajan's column in Rome, are being eaten away by acid fall-out.
Tests have shown that materials corrode between twice and 10 times as fast in polluted urban and industrial atmospheres as they do in the countryside. Carbon steel (both coated and uncoated), zinc and galvanized steel, copper, nickel and nickle-plated steel, sandstone and limestone all corroded faster as the amount of sulphur dioxide in the air increased. On the other hand, materials such as aluminium and stainless steel were only negligibly affected. According to an EEC study the corrosion of painted and galvanized steel structures causes the greatest economic losses to society. The costs average between $2 and $10 each year for every European.

Action: Taken or Planned.

The damage to water can be alleviated by adding lime to lakes, rivers and streams and/or their catchment areas. Many chemicals such as caustic soda, sodium carbonate, slaked lime, limestone, or dolomite can be used to counteract the acidity. Slaked lime and limestone are the most popular. Sweden began a liming programme in the autumn of 1976, and by the summer of 1982 about 1,500 Swedish lakes had been limed at a total cost of about $15 million.
Liming alleviates some of the symptoms of acidification, but it is no real cure, is not practicable for many lakes and running waters, and does not attack the causes of the problem. It should, however, be considered as an interim measure which offers some defence until the emissions of pollutants can be reduced to a satisfactorily low level.
The only lasting solution is to reduce the emissions of the pollutants in the first place. Apart from the effect that strict controls would have in protecting water and forests, they could save millions of dollars by avoiding corrosion. The Organization for Economic Co-operation and Development (OECD) made a first attempt in 1981 to find a way of quantifying corrosion costs. This came up with the estimate that strict emission control measures in 13 European countries could save about $1.2 billion in corrosion costs every year. But the report acknowledges that this is a very approximate figure and more work is being carried out to improve the estimates.
The easiest way to control the pollution is to use fuels that are low in sulphur; but this will not be feasible for long because the world supply of these fuels is believed to be limited. A more permanent solution is to use other sources of energy instead of fossil fuels, and to improve energy conservation.
According to some recent estimates, including ones submitted to the 1982 Stockholm Acidification Conference, taking sulphur out of fuel oils would cost about $20 to $40 for every ton of oil, depending mainly on the type of the oil and the size of the plant, among other factors. This would add about $5–$0 to the cost of every megawatt/hour of energy produced (in 1980 prices), adding about 10 to 20 per cent to the cost of electricity production. Industry, on the other hand, puts the costs at $40 to $85 for every ton of oil.
To look at it another way, the estimated cost of removing each ton of sulphur from oil range from $1,000 to $2,200. Coal contains two kinds of sulphur – pyrite (iron sulphide) and organic sulphur. Washing coal, after first crushing and grinding it, will remove pyrite sulphur. The cost of this mechanical process is estimated to be $1 to $6 per ton of coal. On average it will remove about half of the pyrite, though at best the process can be made to remove up to 90 per cent of it from some coals. The chemical methods are more effective, but also more expensive and have not yet been fully developed. They can remove organic sulphur as well as pyrite. The cost of getting rid of 90 to 95 per cent of the pyrite and half the organic sulphur would be around $20 to $30 per ton of coal. The extra costs for coal washing range from less than $1 to about $3 per megawatt/hour, adding between one and six per cent to electricity costs.
Nitrogen oxide emissions can be reduced by changing the ways of burning fuel, particularly in heat and power stations. One of the main ideas for doing this is to reduce the combustion temperature to below about 1500°C and/or to allow only low intakes of air. Such changes could cut in half the amount of nitrogen oxides emitted.
Removing sulphur from fuel and gases creates waste products – solids and slurries – which have to be disposed of properly to avoid water, groundwater, or soil pollution. Naturally, this problem grows as emission controls are increased.
According to preliminary calculations by OECD, it costs a total of some $800, on average, to stop a ton of sulphur from getting into the air. More recent estimates suggest that the costs may be somewhat higher. If northwestern and southern European countries were to cut their annual sulphur emissions by about half (around 5.9 million tons) within the next 10 to 25 years by controlling the emissions of conventional power stations, it would cost them about 10 per cent of the total cost of producing their electricity.
There are, moreover, other factors that complicate such analyses. One – common to many other instances of damage to shared natural resources – is that the countries which would benefit from the reduced pollution would often be different from those that would have to bear the cost of cutting it back. Another is that all the estimates of benefits assume that the damage caused by acid rain can readily be reversed if enough pollution control is implemented – and in reality this may not be so. It might be a long time before the ecological damage, in particular, began to be reversed. Unfortunately, scientific information on the recovery process is extremely scanty. This is only one of the problem areas in the whole field which, despite considerable progress in research on the subject, still remain unknown or only superficially understood. Research is needed on dry deposition of polluting gases and particles, and their effects on water, soil, young and old foliage, and other recipients of their pollution; on how the pollutants undergo changes in the atmosphere, and how they are transported and deposited; on how bedrocks weather under different acid inputs and release nutrients; on how acid affects the soil, particularly in the long term; and on the possible adverse effects of acid fall-out on forest growth.
In addition to these meteorologically and ecologically orientated research topics, information is needed on the effects on health of the increasing spread of cadmium and other toxic metals as a result of acidification. Among other things, the levels of the metals in food, human tissues and body fluids must continue to be monitored.
So far the acidification of the environment has been seen as a regional problem, restricted to parts of Europe and North America. Other industrialized areas are almost certainly exposed to the same problem, but there is too little information to assess it. Besides, the problem may well spread to new areas as a result of rapid industrialization and the growth of cities in other parts of the world, particularly developing countries. So it is important that areas affected by acid deposition and susceptible to damage from acidification are identified as soon as possible. If they are, the damage could be mitigated, or even avoided, at a minimum cost to society by initiating research, and applying what we already know about pollution control and environmentally appropriate energy production technologies at an early stage. Some areas in the tropics may be highly or moderately susceptible to acidification, and this could cause special problems. We need to work out the nature of these problems. In dry to tropical areas, acid rain itself cannot play a major role owing to scarce precipitation, but the role of dry deposition is unknown. In humid areas the ecosystems, temperature and moisture levels are different from those in the temperate areas where acidification has been studied so far, and quite different problems may arise.
Besides, some soils have too little sulphur in them or are highly alkaline. These could benefit, to a certain extent, from extra sulphur and nitrogen fall-out – or merely from more acidic rain. This could add a significant new factor to calculations of costs and benefits from the pollution, but the issue has not yet been explored.
In the near future the crucial issue is whether countries are ready to take the measures needed to cut back emissions to an acceptable level. The concensus reached by the Ministerial Conference on Acidification of the Environment, held in Stockholm in June 1982, was extremely encouraging about this. Representatives of 21 countries agreed that urgent action should be taken under the Convention on Long-range Transboundary Air Pollution, including:

(a) Establishing and implementing concerted programmes to reduce sulphur and, as soon as possible, nitrogen oxide emissions;
(b) Using the best technology available that is economically feasible to reduce these emissions, taking account of the need to minimize the production of wastes and pollution in other ways;
(c) Supporting research and development of advanced control technologies;
(d) Developing and implementing energy conservation measures further;
(e) Developing the North American monitoring programmes and EMEP further, through better geographical coverage, improved data on emissions, standardizing sampling and measurement techniques, and improved modelling, among other measures.

Environmental Aspects of Energy Farms.

The 1970s brought into focus the general realization that fossil fuel resources, especially oil and natural gas, are finite in nature and that countries should explore the possibilities of using other sources of energy as well, establishing thereby an appropriate energy mix to meet their demands for sustainable development. Recently, much attention has been given to the development of renewable sources of energy. An important social advantage of these sources of energy is their potential for promoting development in rural areas of the developing countries.
One way of exploiting solar power has already been used for thousands of years – and it is still the main source of energy for hundreds of millions of people, especially in developing countries. It is used every time someone cuts down a tree, and burns its wood – for (despite the proverb) energy, and therefore money, does grow on trees. Plants collect energy from the sun by photosynthesis and store it as they grow. Extensive research and development work is under way in many countries to find better ways of using trees, crops, water plants and wastes for fuel. Biomass (Biomass is an ecological term for the total amount of living matter present at any one time in a population or a given area. In an energy context, it is used loosely to mean biologically produced material), as these natural energy stores are known, can be turned into usable energy in several different ways. It can be burned to produce heat, which in turn can be used to raise steam and drive electric turbines. It can be turned into solid or liquid fuels or gas by heating processes, or into methane gas or alcohol by biological ones.
There is an enormous amount of biomass on the globe; every year natural productivity adds enough energy to meet at least 10 times all the world's commercial energy demands, in theory. In practice, of course, it is very unevenly distributed around the world, and in some regions the reserves are being rapidly dissipated because they are being burned faster than they can be replaced by growth. In practice, too, biomass must be economic to harvest and turn into fuel.
Almost any crop produced by farmers anywhere in the world, whether its main use is for food, animal feed, fibre or other products, can technically be turned into some form of energy. But in most cases it would not be economic, practical, or even sensible, to do this.
Many countries are seeking to solve these problems by paying special attention to energy farms – areas of land and water devoted exclusively to growing plants for energy. Fuel crops can be fast growing trees, conventional crops, or water plants – any plants, or mixture of plants, which are more valuable as fuel than as anything else.
Wood has been the primary source of energy for cooking, heating, and other basic needs for almost all man's history since pre-historic times. It remains so in developing countries, in many urban areas as well as in the countryside. Well over two billion people, about half the population of the world, use it for cooking, their most important use of energy.
People in developing countries on average each use between 1.3 and 2.5 cubic metres of it a year. Until recently the sheer weight of fuelwood burned in the world was not realized – and nor was the effect of gathering it on the environment. Uncontrolled and indiscriminate wood collection helps fell forests and turn productive land to desert. Recent estimates suggests that 11 million hectares of tropical forests disappear every year. Between 1976 and 1980 ASEAN countries lost 1.2 million hectares of forest a year, and South Asian countries 339,000 hectares a year. A recent assessment of tropical forest resources shows that Asia is losing 0.61 per cent of its open forest each year, the Americas 0.59 per cent and Africa about 0.48 per cent.

While this shows that the world's tropical rain-forests are not in imminent danger of total destruction, important forests and ecosystems are being lost in many places, and some individual countries face losing all their rain-forests within a few decades. Cutting wood for fuel is one of the major causes of tropical forest destruction. At the same time, the productivity of millions of hectares is being destroyed or impaired annually, because, as trees go, land becomes poorer. The more trees that are cut down the further people have to go to find wood, hacking further into forests, creating ever-widening bare circles round settlements, and making ever longer back-breaking journeys, which undermine their health and take them away from productive work in the fields. When the wood has gone, people collect dung and other wastes to burn, impoverishing the land even more.

By 1980, 96 million people in the countryside of developing countries were acutely short of firewood and could not meet their needs. They lived on the dry land south of the Sahara, in east and south-east Africa, and in mountainous parts of the continent; in the Himalayas and the hills of South Asia; on the Andean Plateau and the arid lands on the Pacific coast of South America. Another 150 million lived in cities surrounded by countryside with not enough firewood.

In 1980, too, another 1,283 million people (about 1,050 million country-dwellers and 231 million urban people) lived in areas where they could still get enough wood, but only by cutting down trees faster than they grow. Seventy million lived in the countryside of North Africa and the Middle East, and 143 million in dry parts of the Latin American countryside; 131 million lived in rural Africa south of the Sahara, mainly in savannah areas in the west, centre and south-east of the continent; and no less than 710 million lived in the countryside and small towns of Asia, mainly in the great plains of the Indus and Ganges rivers and in South-East Asia. As long as this situation continues, the trees will steadily disappear, until the people of these areas become acutely short of firewood around the year 2000. By then, of course, populations will have grown and, in all, about three billion people will be facing acute scarcity or cutting down trees faster than they grow.

The logical, immediate response to this growing crisis is to manage forests better and to plant more trees in energy farms. There are three main types of fuelwood plantations: large-scale forest usually planted on publicly owned land; smaller village woodlots, meeting the needs of rural communities; and even smaller, scattered plantings, including house gardens, fences, and groups of trees to provide shade, protection, fruit or fodder for livestock. In some places, rural communities traditionally grow fuelwood integrated closely with food crops. Even in such crowded areas as Java or the Mekong Delta traditional farming systems set aside between two and five per cent of the agricultural land for tree planting, with great effect.

Many countries have recently been paying a good deal of attention to wood plantations. The Republic of Korea's 'New Community' movement, which began in 1971, planted 40,000 hectares of trees by 1976. An estimated 30 million hectares of land was under plantation in China by 1970. A recent assessment by FAO and UNEP shows that plantations of wood for industry, fuelwood, charcoal, other products and soil protection, cover about 2.7 million hectares in Indonesia, 2.6 million in India, 400,000 in Bangladesh, 300,000 in the Philippines and over 200,000 in Thailand. Plantations were also under way in Sri Lanka, Pakistan, Malaysia, Nepal, Burma and Brunei.

There is a lot more to such silviculture than planting trees. It will not succeed unless the local people are fully involved in making the decisions about how it is to be done. And technical help in choosing the right sites and providing the trees, in supervising planting and harvesting, and for training, is also essential.

In energy farms, specially selected fast-growing trees should be planted in closely spaced rows and harvested every four to seven years. They will need fertilizers, weed and pest controls, and, possibly, irrigation – more intensive cultivation than is normal in forestry. If this is done, yields should be well above those obtained from present forestry practices, which allow trees to grow longer and be harvested less intensively. Productivity will also depend on how well trees suit local conditions. They should be chosen to grow quickly even on poor soil, need as little care as possible, resist pests and diseases, and be able to survive droughts and similar crises. They should also be suitable for coppicing – sprouting anew from their stumps after they have been cut close to the ground, so that they produce crop after crop from the same roots. Their wood should, naturally, have a high heating value. And they should be suitable for as many uses as possible so that their trunks and branches could be exploited for firewood, or charcoal, while their leaves are used for cattle food or fertilizer, or turned into energy in biogas plants.

Some suitable species have already been identified. One important group of them is the tropical legumes, which automatically provide their own fertilizer by 'fixing' nitrogen from the air. As they grow they therefore actually improve the soil. Leucaena leucocephala – the giant 'ipil ipil' is one variety – is the best known member of the family. It is particularly bountiful, for it also produces high protein seeds and foliage, which makes an excellent animal feed supplement and green fertilizer. Other tropical legume trees, such as various Acacia, Calliandra and Sesbania species, also grow fast. So do some trees from other families; Eucalyptus and Casuarina trees are among the most promising.

Fast growing trees like these are enormously productive if they are well-matched to local conditions. Many species will produce more than 20 cubic metres of wood per hectare every year when grown on reasonable good soil. In exceptional cases Leucaena, Eucalyptus and several other species are reported to have produced as much as 50 cubic metres per hectare a year.

Once the wood is harvested it can be used to generate heat, steam or electricity. 'Ipil ipil plantations have already been established in the Philippines to produce electric power. They are intended to fuel several stations with a total capacity of 200 megawatts by 1987 – and by the year 2000, 700,000 hectares of wood plantations and 2,000 megawatts of electricity are planned. In Tamil Nadu, India, 11,500 hectares of Casuarina trees would provide fuel for a power plant generating 100 megawatts.

Alternatively, wood can be turned into charcoal, gas or liquid fuel. None of these uses is new. Charcoal has been produced since the dawn of civilization. Relatively large Eucalyptus energy farms (8,000 hectares), dedicated to charcoal production for steel mills, have been in operation since the early 1950s in Argentina and Brazil. Wood alcohol was used as a liquid fuel for most of the eighteenth and part of the nineteenth centuries. Kerosene and other fuels took its place; but now there is new interest in it, mixing with gasoline for motor fuel. Making gas from wood and charcoal is another old technology that is being revived. Several European countries and Japan had projects for fuelling engines with the gas before the Second World War. By late 1941, 70,000 cars in Sweden alone used it, as did 55 per cent of the trucks and 70 per cent of the buses. Farm equipment also made good use of it. After the war most vehicles switched to gasoline because it was a better and more convenient fuel. Now the gas is coming into its own again in several countries, particularly in the countryside. In the Philippines, for example, the process is used to run fishing boats, water pumps and some public service vehicles, and to produce electricity.

Wood may be the most obvious and widely used form of 'green energy', but it is far from being the only one. Some plants, for example, produce materials like hydro-carbons, some of which are the main constitutents of oil and natural gas. Once again, this has been known for centuries – pre-Columbian civilizations in Latin America systematically cultivated trees which produced liquid that could be made into rubber. Even today the natural rubber tree, Hevea braziliensis, is much the best known of these plants. Its latex is no use for energy farming, since it is made up of hydrocarbons of a very heavy molecular weight; hydrocarbons of lower molecular weight are needed for fuel. Some studies have shown, however, that many species of plants may produce just what is required. Bushes of the Euphorbia group seem to be particularly promising. Experiments with two species (Euphorbia lathyris and Euphorbia tirucalli) have shown that they can yield between 17 and 36 barrels per hectare a year. Better still, many of the 8,000 or so known species in the family will grow on semi-arid land, which means that they can be cultivated where many other plants will not flourish, and can be particularly useful in developing countries that are prone to droughts.

Other plants, including soya beans, sunflowers and groundnuts, also produce oils. Most of them can be used to fuel diesel engines without further processing, either by themselves or blended with diesel fuel. Most of them, too, can grow in a wide range of soils, provided that they get the right amount of water and the right temperature, though their ability to tolerate different climatic conditions varies significantly between species. But such 'peanut power' or 'beanzal' is unlikely to do much to replace diesel, because the oils cost much more and are, of course, wanted for food. Some crops contain sugars and starches that can be turned into fuel by fermentation. Sugar cane and sweet sorghum are the main sugar crops, and both grow fast in good conditions when farmed by modern agricultural methods. Fifty tons of sugar cane will grow each year per hectare in Brazil, and yields may go up to as much as 120 tons per hectare per year as they do in Hawaii. Sweet sorghum will produce an annual crop of about 45 tons per hectare. Both their sugars can be directly fermented to produce ethanol, a form of alcohol. Sugar cane will produce about 3,600 litres of alcohol per hectare and sweet sorghum about 3,500.

Cassava (mandioca) – a subsistence crop in many developing countries – is the primary starch crop of interest. It has many advantages, it tolerates poor soil and adverse weather conditions much better than the sugar crops mentioned above, and unlike them, it does not need high levels of fertilizer or pesticides to give good yields. About 10 to 12 tons of cassava are produced per hectare each year and this can be turned into about 2,160 litres of alcohol.

Other plants, like corn, rice and other cereals can also be turned into ethanol. Corn is indeed used to produce alcohol, particularly in the United States (about 6 tons of corn is produced annually per hectare, yielding about 2,200 litres of alcohol). But of course, these cereals are more valuable for food than for fuel.

Ethanol can either be used as a fuel on its own or blended with gasoline. A motor running on ethanol is 18 per cent more powerful than one using gasoline. Internal combustion engines need some modification if they are to be fuelled entirely by it. No changes at all are needed, however, if up to 20 per cent of ethanol is mixed with gasoline. The alcohol increases the octane rating of the fuel and so eliminates the use of lead additives, which are suspected of causing pollution that lowers the intelligence of young children. Such 'gasohol' or alcogas is now used in Brazil, the United States and the Philippines, among other countries. Brazil has the largest programme for making alcohol from biomass. Its National Alcohol Programme, PROALCOOL, aims to be producing about 10.7 million cubic metres as soon as 1985. Already nearly all the country's cars run on gasohol, and more than 300,000 run on pure alcohol. By 1985, two and a half million cars will have been converted or manufactured to take neat alcohol, and all the rest of Brazil's 12 million strong car fleet will be fuelled by gasohol.

Sometimes even soft, green herbaceous plants may be a viable source of 'green energy'. Some tropical and savannah grasses, ideally adapted to their conditions, grow extremely fast. Elephant grass (Napier grass) is one notable example. Another is Imperata cylindrica, a noxious weed known a lalang in Asia. Very little research has been done to see what yields they could sustain if harvested for fuel – but it is likely that they would need less fertilizer, water and similar requirements than more sensitive crops like sugar cane. So they could well be viable energy sources in countries where land is available which cannot be used effectively for agriculture. They have a high cellulose content, and so (unlike the sugars and starches) are not well suited for conversion into ethanol by current technique. But they could be used effectively to make charcoal and could also provide a feedstock for gas or liquid fuels.

Not only land crops, but water plants as well, can be farmed for energy. In fact energy farming could solve a particularly intractable problem. At present plants like water hyacinth (Eichhornia crassipes) and duckweed (species of the genus Lemna) are a major environmental problem in many countries because they spread and clog up lakes and waterways. So harvesting them for animal feed or energy would be a happy solution. They grow very plentifully in the best conditions, producing about 50 tons of dry matter per hectare a year. Better still, some aquatic plants, including the water hyacinth, have the power to purify water, extracting many organic and inorganic compounds from it. So the same plants could be used simultaneously to clean up pollution and produce energy. Most species can be digested easily by bacteria in airless conditions, as in a biogas plant, and this is the best way of turning them into fuel. A methane-rich gas is produced, and the residue left when the gas is given off is useful as a fertilizer. A single hectare of water hyacinths, grown on sewage, can both purify the waste and yield 0.8 tons of dry material a day, which can be turned into 200 cubic metres of biogas – enough to generate about 250 kilowatts of electricity daily.

Seaweeds can be found too. Large scale seaweed farms are already moored near the Japanese and Chinese coasts, producing the food that has been a delicacy in the Orient for centuries. The open oceans are much the biggest under-used part of the world's surface, and so plans for farming them for energy, as well as food, are receiving considerable attention. Experiments on growing kelp (Macroystis) for fuel have reported yields of as much as 90 tons per hectare a year.

Ocean energy farms would be strange looking structures, enormous offshore platforms with long spokes and ropes sticking out of them. The kelp would grow on these protuberances, fed by nutrient-rich water specially pumped up from great depths. It would then be harvested, and like the freshwater energy crops, turned into methane. The Ocean Farm Project, California, foresees that there will be a vast demonstration sea farm, covering some 40,000 hectares, by the end of the century. Each hectare of cultivated kelp would yield about 10 million kilocalories of food and nearly a hundred million kilocalories of methane energy a year.

All energy production presents practical and environmental problems, and 'green power', for all its attractiveness, is no exception. Conditions have to be right for growing energy crops. When they are, the energy farms could absorb resources needed for food production. Energy crops could impoverish the soil and destroy important wildlife habitats. Some could use up more energy to grow and harvest than they would ever produce, and other could cause pollution and possibly affect the climate.

Many of the problems can be solved or avoided if enough attention is paid to them.

Many countries have recently given proper recognition to the importance of developing renewable sources of energy, and both developed and developing nations are giving special attention to harnessing it from biomass. France, for example, gives 'green energy' a high priority and is concentrating research on energy crops like coppices, Dona reed, sweet sorghum and water hyacinths. It expects to get fuel equal to 4 million tons of oil a year from biomass by 1990. Energy plantations are being intensively researched in Sweden, and special plantations of willow (Salix) and poplar (Populus) trees are expected to produce 20 tons of dry material per hectare a year. Ireland claims to be a world leader in rapid-harvest forestry, and some 400,000 hectares will be planted there by the year 2000. Alcohol is already being produced in the United States, mainly from corn, and extensive research and development work is being done there on energy farms, especially wood plantations and ocean farm systems.

A great deal of activity is also under way in developing countries. Many countries, including China, Kenya, the Philippines, the Republic of Korea, the Sudan and Thailand, have reafforestation programmes aimed at producing new firewood as fast as it is used. The Philippines is also one of the countries giving considerable attention to energy farms using fast-growing species. Cooperation between countries over fuelwood plantations is remarkably strong. Other developing countries have recently embarked on alcohol production programmes similar to the Brazilian sugar cane one. Colombia, Cuba, Kenya and the Philippines are among those that have made a start, though the Brazilian programme remains much the largest.

Several United Nations and intergovernmental bodies have embarked on some activities for harnessing energy from biomass. The main focus of efforts directly related to energy farms are forestry and agroforestry projects, and FAO is the lead agency here, carrying out about 40 national and regional projects concerned with fuelwood production. Meanwhile, the World Bank and UNDP are giving financial and technical help to some developing countries for similar projects. The World Bank is also financing feasibility studies on alcohol production from biomass. FAO and UNEP are planning studies on some of the wider issues raised by 'green energy' – looking at the socio-economic costs and benefits of energy plantations, studing environmental aspects of energy farms, and assessing the effects of using agricultural crops for fuel on the security of the world's food supplies, with particular emphasis on the food needs of the less developed countries.

There is no doubt that biomass is an important renewable source of energy. It has long been used by countless millions of people, particularly in developing countries, to meet their basic energy needs. Recently the subject has gained new and special attention, as Governments and scientists have decided to work out ways of developing 'green energy' and turning it into fuel. Many questions are still largely unanswered. What types of plants are best for energy farming and which can be disregarded, at least for the time being? What are the best sizes of programmes? What fuels should be produced, and how should this be done?

What long-term research and planning is needed, and what should countries be aiming at? Beneath these essentially practical questions lies an even more fundamental one: is large-scale energy farming really feasible economically, socially and environmentally? Economics is critically important because all the costs of growing and harvesting energy crops, and of turning them into fuel, have to be met by selling the end products. Serious social and institutional problems could be caused by conflicts over how much land, water and fertilizer should be given to energy farms, and how much to growing food. And pollution and other environmental problems could result from the large-scale energy farms – running into tens, even hundreds of thousands of hectares – that are being contemplated: they will have to be carefully assessed at an early stage to make sure that 'green energy' is developed in an appropriate and environmentally sound way.

UN Chronicle, No. 5, 1983, pp. 33–46; M. ALLABY, *Dictionary of Environment*, London 1986.

ENVIRONMENTAL UN PERSPECTIVE, 1988.
The following brief summary of the issues, outlooks, goals and actions recommended by the UN for the six main sectors of World environmental problems was published by the *UN Chronicle*, Mar. 1988:

(1) *Population*:
Problem: Population growth – the world may have 6 billion citizens by the year 2000 – continues to overload the capacities of the environment.
Goal: Achieve a balance between population and environmental capacities to make "sustainable development" possible.
Action: Pay special attention to problems of large cities. Anticipate changes in availability and use of natural resources. Design public works projects to simultaneously provide employment and improve the environment.

(2) *Food and Agriculture*:
Problem: Food shortages create insecurity and environmental threats.
Goal: Achieve food security without resource depletion or environmental degradation and restore resource bases where damage has occurred.
Action: Establish relevant governmental policies for agricultural land, forests and water resources. Institute regulatory measures, taxation and price policies and incentives to ensure agricultural productivity. Explore use of alternative crops. Avoid clear-cutting of large forests. Designate protected areas to save wildlife and genetic resources.

(3) *Energy*:
Problem: There are vast disparities in the patterns of energy consumption. There has been little concerted action to balance enviromental imperatives and energy demands.
Goal: Provide sufficient energy at reasonable cost. Increase access to energy in developing countries. Meet current and expanding needs in ways that minimize environmental damage.

Action: Energy plans should systematically encompass environmental requirements. Energy pricing and policies should take account of enviromental costs of all forms of energy.

(4) *Industry*:
Problem: Industrial development often damages the environment.
Goal: Sustained improvements in the levels of living in all countries, especially developing ones, through industrial development which prevents or minimizes environmental damages and risks.
Action: Government policies which assist the transition of economies from wasteful use of natural resources and raw materials to environmentally sound industrial development. Programmes to monitor pollution.

(5) *Health and Human Settlements*
Problem: Inadequacies in shelter and other basic amenities cause widespread disease, death and intolerable living conditions in many areas.
Goal: Provide improved shelter with access to essentials in a clean and secure setting while alleviating serious environmental degradation.
Action: Intensify scientific research to deal with environmental conditions underlying tropical diseases. Promote programmes which integrate improved water supply, sanitation and waste disposal measures.

(6) *International Economic Relations*:
Problem: Inequalities in international economic relations coupled with inappropriate economic policies in many nations, adversely affect sustainable development. Awareness of the environmental aspects of international economic relations is not adequately expressed in policies.
Goal: Establish an equitable system of international economic relations aimed at economic advances for all States.
Action: Increase aid to developing countries. Analyse environmental needs of recipient countries. International trade and commodity agreements should incorporate environmental safeguards.

UN Chronicle, No. 1, 1988.

ENVIRONMENTAL WORLD DAY.
The Stockholm Conference on Human Environment, 1972, designated June 5 of each year as a World Environment Day.

ENVIRONMENT AND DEVELOPMENT.
A United Nations Conference on Environment and Development, according to the GA Res. 43/196 of Dec. 20, 1988, adopted without a vote, will be convened no later than 1992.

UN Resolutions and Decisions adopted by the General Assembly during the First Part of its Forty-Third Session, From 20 Sept. to 22 Dec. 1988, New York, 1989, pp. 291–293.

ENVOY.
The second class chief of a permanent ▷ Diplomatic mission (after an ambassador) both according to the ▷ Vienna Rules of 1815 and the ▷ Vienna Convention on Diplomatic Relations 1961.

EPIDEMIC DISEASES. ▷ Diseases.

EPIDEMIOLOGY.
A subject of international co-operation. Organization reg. with the UIA:

International Epidemiological Association, f. 1954, Baltimore, Officially affiliated with WHO.

WHO publ.: *Weekly Epidemiological Record*, from 1926 in English and French. M. MCCARTHY, *Epidemiology and policies for health planning*, London, 1982; *Yearbook of International Organizations*.

EPILEPSY.
A subject of international co-operation. Organizations reg. with the UIA:

International Bureau for Epilepsy, f. 1961, London. Publ.: *Social Studies in Epilepsy, Handbook of International Epilepsy Centres.*
International League Against Epilepsy, f. 1909. Budapest. Pub.: *Epilepsia* (quarterly).

Yearbook of International Organizations.

EPISCOPAL CURIA. A set of institutions and their functionaries in Christian churches together with the bishop ordinary. The life of the diocese is directed by them under their authority and leadership.

EPISCOPATE. A church term referring to all of the bishops of a given Christian faith in a certain country, e.g. the Episcopate of the American Roman Catholic Church.

EPIZOOTIC. The epidemic of contagious disease in animals: subject of an international convention to combat epizootics, Jan. 25, 1924. The relevant organization is:
Office International d'Epizootie, OIE, f. 1924, Paris, affiliating over 80 countries. Publ.: *Monthly Epizootic Circular, Scientific Technical Bulletin, Statistical Bulletin.* Reg. with UIA.

Yearbook of International Organizations.

E PLURIBUS UNUM. *Latin* = "one out of many." A motto of the United States adopted in 1785 by the Second Continental Congress, replaced by Congress in 1956 by: "In God We Trust."

McDONALD, *E Pluribus Unum: The Formation of the American Republic (1776–1795)*, New York, 1970; G.E. SHANKLE, *State names, Flags, Seals*, London, 1979.

EQUALITY OF RIGHTS. A principle of international law according to which all sovereign states have equal rights. Specific cases of the limitation of equality of rights are known in history in the form of treaty obligations.

EQUALITY OF SEX. A subject of international codification in private international law in reference to marriage, divorce, division of property and relations between parents and children.

EQUALITY OF STATES IN THE UN. The first principle of the UN Charter, stated in Art. 2, para. 1:
"The Organization is based on the principle of the sovereign equality of all its members."
The Principle of the Sovereign Equality of States has been defined in general in the Declaration of the Principles of International Law (VII Principle), adopted by the UN General Assembly on Oct. 24, 1970.

EQUAL PAY FOR MEN AND WOMEN. A subject of intergovernmental declarations and agreements. ▷ Women's rights. The West European Committee for Equality between Women and Men on Feb. 18, 1987 accepted the Third Medium-Term Plan for the years 1987–91.

M. SORENSEN, "The quest for equality", in: *International Conciliation*, No. 507, March, 1956, pp. 291–346; *Council of Europe, Information Sheet*, No. 21, Strasbourg, 1988.

EQUATORIAL GUINEA. Member of the UN. República de Guinea Ecuatorial. Republic of Equatorial Guinea. Central African state on the Atlantic Ocean, bounded by Cameroon and Gabon. Area: including the islands Macias, Nguema and Pigalu: 28,051 sq. km. Pop. 1987 est. 390,000 (1960 census 245,989). Capital: Malabo

(formerly until 1973 named Santa Isabel) with 37,337 inhabitants 1973. GNP per capita in 1980 US $330. Official language: Spanish. Currency: 1 Franc CFA = 100 centimes. National Day: March 5. Independence Day, 1968.
Member of the UN since Nov. 25, 1968 and of the UN specialized agencies save IFC, WMO, WIPO, IAEA and GATT. Member of the OAU. ACP state of the EEC. A signatory of the Lomé Conventions of 1975 and of 1980.
International relations: under Portuguese, British and Spanish control during three centuries; the colonial Congress of Berlin in 1885 awarded the region of Rio Muni and the islands called Spanish Guinea, to Spain. In 1959 one of the overseas provinces of Spain (Provincia del Rio Muni de las Provincias Africanas de Estado de España), not accepted by the UN. In 1963 Spain renamed the province Rio Muni in Equatorial Africa and granted it limited autonomy and on March 5, 1968 full independence. In the 1970s the number of political refugees in Africa from Equatorial Guinea rose to about 100,000. In Aug., 1979 a military coup changed the internal and foreign policy. On Jan. 1, 1985 Equatorial Guinea became the first non-Franco-phone African member of the Franc monetary zone, at an exchange rate of 4 bipkwele = 1 Franc CFA. The Central Bank of Equatorial Guinea became Le Banque des États de l'Afrique Centrale in Yaoundé.

S. BORMAN, *Spanish-Guinea: An Annotated Bibliography*, Washington, DC, 1961; *Los territorios españoles en Africa*, Madrid, 1964; *UN Monthly Chronicle*, October, 1967 and May, 1968; P. PELISSIER, *Étude Hispano-Guinéenne*, Paris, 1969; M. LINIGER-GOUMAZ, *La Guinée équatoriale un pays méconnu*, Paris, 1980; *The Europa Year Book 1984. A World Survey*, Vol. II, pp. 1544–1548, London, 1984; M. LINGER-GOUMAZ, *Small is Not Always Beautiful. The Story of Equatorial Guinea*, London, 1988.

EQUESTRIAN GAMES. Horsemanship. An international sport, since 1920 recognized by International Olympic Committee. Organization reg. with the UIA:
International Equestrian Federation, FEI, f. 1921, Brussels. Publ.: *Official Bulletin.* Members: national federations. Organizes Olympic Games and the Official International Equestrian Competition.

Yearbook of International Organizations.

ERAM. ▷ Mines.

ERAP. *Entreprise des Recherches et d'Activitié Pétrolière.* French state-owned company engaged in oil exploration; provides technical assistance to developing countries within the framework of international co-operation.

ERGONOMY. A subject of international co-operation. Organizations reg. with the UIA:
French Speaking Ergonomic Society, Société d'ergonomie de langue française, f. 1963, Strasbourg, France.
International Ergonomic Association, f. 1961, The Hague, Publ.: *Ergonomics* (quarterly in English).

Yearbook of International Organizations.

ERITREA. A province of northern Ethiopia on the Red Sea; 124,320 sq. km. Pop. 1978 census: 2,295,800. A subject of conflicts and international debates between Ethiopia and Italy. Under Italian occupation 1889–1941; under British occupation 1941–42. In 1948–52 subject of a British–Ethiopian dispute brought before the UN. On Dec. 2, 1950 UN General Assembly recommended the granting of autonomy to Eritrea within the Ethiopian Crown and the withdrawal of British forces, which took

place under UN supervision on Sept. 15, 1952. Autonomy, also organized under UN supervision, was ended with a decision of the Eritrea parliament in Nov. 1962 for unification with Ethiopia. In view of the strong separatist movement, armed conflicts took place. On May 16, 1977 the government of Ethiopia granted Eritrea limited autonomy but in 1980s the Eritrean People's Liberation Front, EPLF and the Tigre People's Liberation Front, TPLF (in the Western Tigre province) started new separatist campaigns.

S.H. LONGRON, *A Short History of Eritrea*, London, 1945; "The Question of Eritrea", *UN Yearbook*, 1951; A.A. SCHILLER, "Eritrea: constitution and federation with Ethiopia", in: *American Journal of Comparative Law*, No. 2, 1953; G.K.N. TREVASKIS, *Eritrea*, London, 1960; *Synopsis of UN Cases*, New York, 1966. *The Europa Year Book, 1984. A World Survey*, Vol. II, p. 1549, London, 1984.

ERMELAND. Polish Warmia. Part of northeast Poland; 1772–1945, part of East Prussia; reverted to Poland after the Potsdam Agreement of 1945.

EROPA. Eastern Regional Organization for Public Administration, f. 1960, Manila. Regional Centers: Training Center in New Delhi. Local Government Center in Tokyo, Organization and Management Center in Seoul.

The Europa Yearbook 1988. A World Survey, Vol. I, London, 1988.

ERP. European Recovery Plan, called the ▷ Marshall Plan.

ESA. ▷ European Space Agency.

ESCALATION. An international term formulated by the American strategist H. Kahn in the 1960s connotating a system of waging war, striking the opponent in stages leading to his total destruction.

A.J. DAY, M.W. DOYLE, eds., *Escalation and Intervention: Multilateral Security and its Alternatives*, London, 1986; D. ROBERTSON, *Guide to Modern Defense and Strategy*, Detroit, 1988.

ESCAP. ▷ UN Economic and Social Commission for Asia and the Pacific.

ESCAPE CLAUSE. A clause in a trade agreement permitting changes in or termination of a tariff concession after a specified period; inserted for the first time in the Reciprocal Trade Agreement of 1934. ▷ Safeguards.

ESCUDO. A monetary unit of Portugal; one escudo = 100 centavos; issued by the Banco do Portugal.

ESKIMOS. A people living in Alaska, Canada and Greenland, and in small groups on the Chukotsk Peninsula and on Wrangel Island, c. 70,000. Their own name is Inuit = "man". In June, 1977 in Fairbank, Alaska, the First Congress of Eskimos from Alaska, Canada and Greenland ratified a resolution submitted to the governments of the USA, Canada and Denmark as well as to the UN Secretary-General demanding the halting of all military activity in the entire area of the Arctic. A permanent secretariat of the Congress was formed.
In June, 1980 a Circumpolar Inuit Conference at Gothaad, Greenland, with an Eskimo delegation from the United States, Canada and Greenland established an International Inuit Association. The Charter of the Association provides an 18-member General Assembly drawn equally from Eskimos in the three countries of the circumpolar region, the Inuit homeland. The Association would promote

Eskimo unity and culture as well as greater self-sufficiency and adequate participation by Eskimos in political, economic and social institutions.

In 1963, WHO supported a genetic study of the polar Eskimos of North Greenland, the most northerly population in the world.

E.M. WEYER, *Eskimos, their Environment and Folkways*, London, 1932; *UN Yearbook*, 1963, p. 618; K. BIRKET-SMITH, *The Eskimos*, London, 1971.

ESPARTO GRASS. *Lygeum spartum*, called also Algerian grass of which clothes, cordage, paper etc. are made, subject of international co-operation:

Maghreb Esparto Bureau, f. 1965, Algiers as a dependent body of the Maghreb Permanent Consultative Committee. Aims: marketing for esparto. Reg. with the UIA.

Yearbook of International Organizations.

ESPERANTO. An unofficial universal language devised 1887 by a Polish physician Dr. L. Zamenhof (1859–1918); subject of international co-operation. Since 1972 an Esperanto Museum exists in Sopot (Poland). Organizations reg. with the UIA:

Centre for Research and Documentation on the World Language Problem, f. 1952, Rotterdam. Publ.; *La Monda Lingvo-Problema.*
Christian Esperanto International Association, f. 1911, Antwerp, Belgium, Publ.: *Dia Regno.*
Esperantist Music League, f. 1963, Harlow, Essex, UK. Publ.: *Mel-Bulteno.*
Esperantist Ornithologists Association, f. 1961, Antwerp, Belgium. Publ.: *La Mevo.*
Esperantist World Peace Movement, f. 1953, Prague. Publ.: *Paco.*
Esperanto Academy, f. 1905, Boulogne, France. Publ.: *Officiala Bulteno.*
International Association of Esperantists Librarians, f. 1971, Rotterdam.
International Esperantist Scientific Association, f. 1906, Belgrade. Publ.: *Scienca Revuo.*
International Esperanto Association of Jurists, f. 1957, Graz, Publ.: *Internacia Jura Revuo.*
International Federation of Esperantist Railwaymen, f. 1948, Frankfurt am M. Publ.: *Internacia Fervojisto.*
International League of Blind Esperantists, f. 1950, Ancona, Publ.: *Esperanto Ligilo.*
International League of Esperantist Amateur Photographers, f. 1961, Skövde.
International League of Esperantists Teachers, f. 1949, Massa. Publ.: *Internacia Pedagogia Revuo.*
International League of Esperantis Radio Amateurs, f. 1970, Vienna. Publ.: *Ilera Bulteno.*
Nationless Worldwide Association, f. 1921, Paris. Publ.: *Semraciea Revuo.*
Philatelic Esperanto League, f. 1964, Soltao, FRG. Publ.: *La Verda Lupo.*
Quaker Esperanto Society, f. 1921, Morecambe, Lane, UK.
Scouts' Esperanto League, f. 1918, London. Publ.: *La Skolta Mundo.*
Universal Esperanto Association, f. 1908, Zurich. Representative at UN. Consultative status with ECOSOC, UNESCO. Publ.: *Esperanto* (monthly).
Universal Medical Esperanto Association, f. 1908, Tiba, Japan. Publ.: *Medicina Internacia Revuo.*
World Association of Esperanto Journalists, f. 1970. Padua. Publ.: *Internacia Journalist.*
World Esperanto Vegetarian Association, f. 1908, Dublin. Publ.: *Buleteno.*
World Organization of Young Esperantists, f. 1938, Uppsala. Publ.: *Kontakto.*

M. BOULTON, *Zamenhof: Creator of Esperanto*, London, 1960; F. FULCHER, B. LONG, *English-Esperanto Dictionary*, London, 1963. *Yearbook of International Organizations.* J. LICHTEN, *Centenary of the Creation of an International Language*, in: New Perspectives, No 1, 1988.

ESPIONAGE. An international term for the acquiring of the secrets of a second state during peace or war; the subject was defined, as far as war es-

pionage is concerned, by art. 29 of the ▷ Hague Rules of 1907.

R.R. BAXTER. "So-called 'unprivileged belligerent': spies, guerrillas and saboteurs", in: *British Yearbook of International Law*, 1951; S. PREVEZER, "Peacetime espionage and the law", in: *Current Legal Problems*, No. 6, 1953; C. COHEN, J.R. KOVAR, "L'espionage en temps de paix", in: *Annuaire Français de Droit International*, No. 6, 1960; J. HINZ, "Spionage", in: *STRUPP-SCHLOCHAUER, Wörterbuch des Völkerrechts*, Berlin, 1962, Vol. 3, pp. 298–300; R. SETH, *Encyclopedia of Espionage*, London, 1975.

ESQUIPULAS DECLARATION, 1986. On May 25, 1986, in the Guatemalian town of Esquipulas, the heads of state of the five Central American countries, after a summit meeting issued a joint Declaration of Esquipulas in which they supported the peace treaty draft of the ▷ Contadora and the idea of establishing a Central American Parliament.

KEESING's *Contemporary Archive*, 1986, No 8.

ESRO. European Space Research Organization, est. by a Convention with Financial Protocols on June 14, 1962 in Paris, by the governments of 12 Western European States (after the name are percentages of financial contributions): Austria (2.99), Belgium (4.21), Denmark (2.10), FRG (21.48), France (18.22), Italy (10.64), Netherlands (4.04), Norway (1.60), Spain (2.53), Sweden (4.92), Switzerland (3.27) and the UK (25). The Convention and Protocols came into force Mar. 20, 1969. Head Office, Paris.

UNTS, Vol. 528, p. 35.

ESTABLISHMENT. An international sociological term for stable, influential groups, dominating in economy, finance, politics and mass media; in the United States one group is known as the Eastern Establishment (East Coast Establishment of the ▷ WASP).

TH. WHITE, *The Making of the President 1964*, New York, 1965; "Eastern Establishment", in: *Safire's Political Dictionary*, New York, 1978, pp. 191–192.

ESTONIA. Eesti Noukogude Sotsialistlik Vabariik. Estonian Soviet Socialist Republic. Federated Republic of the USSR on the Baltic Sea, bounded by Latvia and Russia, SFSR. Area: 45,100 sq. km. Pop. 1983: 1,507,500; 1934 – 92% Estonians, 1959 – 74%; 1987 – 61%. Capital: Tallin with pop. 1983: 454,100. Official Languages: Estonian and Russian. Currency: ruble of the USSR. National Day: Oct. 7, Socialist Revolution Anniversary, 1917.
International relations: part of the Russian Empire since 1721. Following the October Revolution, Soviet government was proclaimed on Nov. 8, 1917. Occupied by German troops Mar.–Nov. 1918 and by British naval forces in May 1919. The Republic of Estonia was proclaimed on May 19, 1919, which on Feb. 2, 1920 signed a Peace Treaty in Dorpat with the Russian Soviet Republic. Member of the League of Nations 1921–39. Member of the Baltic Entente 1934–39. During World War II incorporated within the USSR on Aug. 6, 1940; from June 1941 to Nov. 1944 occupied by the German troops. The Soviet annexation of Estonia was not recognized by the following countries: Australia, Belgium, Canada, Denmark, Finland, France, the FRG, Greece, the Holy See, Ireland, Italy, Luxembourg, Malta, the Netherlands, Norway, Portugal, Spain, Switzerland, Turkey, the UK, Yugoslavia and the USA, which continues to recognize the Estonian Consul General in New York.
On Sept. 11, 1988, the anniversary of the 1939 Hitler–Stalin Pact on the annexation of Estonia, Latvia and Lithuania by the USSR was for the first

time marked by a public demonstration of Estonians in the capital and provincial cities of the republic.
On Nov. 16, 1988 the Estonian Supreme Soviet declared with the overwhelming endorsement of its legislature, "the supremacy of its laws over the laws of the USSR". On Nov. 28, 1988 the Supreme Soviet of the USSR declared the illegality of the decision of the Estonian Supreme Soviet.
The Estonian national flag replaced the Soviet one in Tallin on Feb. 24, 1989, Estonian Independence Day.

J.H. JACKSON, *Estonia*, London, 1948; *Estonia. Basic Facts Geography, History and Economy*, Stockholm, 1948; E. KARCELA, *Estonia in the Soviet Grip*, London, 1949; V. DRUZHININ, *Soviet Estonia*, Moscow, 1953; A. KÜNG, *A Dream of Freedom*, Cardiff, 1980; R.J. MISIURAS, R. TAAGEPERA, *The Baltic States Years of Dependence 1940–80*, Farnborough, 1983.

ESTOPPEL PRINCIPLE. An Anglo-Saxon legal principle allowing for "self-exclusion" from acquiescence during probative proceedings as a result of one's statement used in international jurisdiction in accordance with the rule of ▷ bona fides, in the verdicts of international courts it indicates that a state may not contradict the veracity of statements made previously by an authorized representative or may not contradict the existence of a fact which previously was made public through an oral statement made by a representative or if this representative's behavior undoubtedly evidenced the existence of such a fact.

D.W. BOWETT, "Estoppel before International Tribunals and its Relations to Requiescence", in: *The British Yearbook of International Law*, 1957.

ESTRADA DOCTRINE, 1930. One of the principles of recognizing new governments; formulated in an official communiqué published on Nov. 27, 1930 by the Minister of Foreign Affairs of Mexico, Genaro Estrada (1887–1957). The text is as follows:
"In connection with the change of governments which has taken place in some of the countries of South America, the government of Mexico has once again recognized as necessary the application on its part of the so-called theory of 'recognizing' governments. It is well-known that in recent years Mexico, like few other countries, has experienced the consequences of this doctrine, which leaves to foreign governments the judgement of expressing their opinion as to the legality or illegality of other regimes, thereby creating a situation in which the legal power or national character of governments or authorities seems to depend on the opinion of foreigners. The so-called doctrine of 'recognition' already applied after the Great War, especially to the nations of this continent – for in the case of the known changes of government in Europe they were recognized immediately – became a kind of system and speciality of the Latinoamerican republics. After a careful re-study of the problem, the government of Mexico has sent instructions to the chiefs of its diplomatic missions in countries presently undergoing political crises, instructing them to inform the authorities of those states that Mexico will not give an opinion in the sense of expressing recognition, since it regards this practice as improper, violating the sovereignty of other nations, implying interference in their internal affairs through judgement by foreign governments, irregardless of whether the legalities of foreign governments are profitable or unprofitable. As a consequence, the government of Mexico limits its right to maintaining or recalling, when it deems proper, its diplomats and accreditation, also according to its recognition of foreign diplomats, without judgement, either before of after, of the rights which foreign nations have of accrediting, maintaining, or recalling them by their governments or authorities. Naturally, as concerns the customary forms of accrediting and receiving diplomats and presenting lists signed by Chiefs of states and Ministers of Foreign Affairs

Mexico, as heretofore has applied those which are recognized by International and Diplomatic Law."

On Dec. 1, 1944 an explanation was published by the Minister of Foreign Affairs of Mexico that:

"it is erroneous to interpret the Estrada Doctrine to mean that the government of Mexico is automatically obligated to maintain diplomatic relations with all governments which come into being."

"Declaration of Señor Don Genaro Estrada, Secretary of Foreign Relations of Mexico, published to the Press on Sept. 27, 1930, relating to the express Recognition of Governments", in: *American Journal of International Law*, No. 25, 1931, Supplement; P. JESSUP, "The Estrada Doctrine", in: *American Journal of International Law*, No. 25, 1931; INSTITUTO AMERICANO DE DERECHO Y LEGISLACIÓN COMPARADA. *La Opinión universal sobre la doctrina Estrada expuesta por el Gobierno de México, bajo la presidencia de don Pascual Ortiz Rubio*, México, DF, 1931; *Memorias de la Secretaría de Relaciones Exteriores*, México, 1941, Vol. VI, pp. 111–112; A. GARCIA ROBLES, *El Mundo de la Postguerra*, México, 1946, Vol. II, pp. 324–325.

ÉTAT FANTOCHE. *French* = "puppet state". An international colonial term for make-believe states entirely dependent on a colonial power but represented in international bodies as sovereign countries.

ETHICS. International term related to professional ▷ morality. ▷ Medical Ethics. The Carnegie Council on Ethics and International Affairs publishes in New York, since 1987 a yearbook of Ethics and International Affairs.

J.E. HARE, C.B. JOYNT, *Ethics and International Affairs*, London, 1982.

ETHIOPIA. Member of the UN. People's Democratic Republic of Ethiopia. Formerly Abyssinia. State in East Africa on the Red Sea. Borders Djibouti, Somalia, Kenya and Sudan. Area: 1,223,600 sq. km. Pop. 1982 est.: 32,775,000. Capital city: Addis Ababa with 1,277,159 inhabitants 1980.
GNP per capita 1986: US $120. Official language: Amharic. Currency: one birr = 100 centimes. National Day: Sept. 12, anniversary of revolution, 1974.
Ethiopia is a founding member of the UN since Oct. 24, 1945 and a member of all its specialized agencies except GATT and WIPO. Founding member of the OAU whose headquarters is in Addis Ababa as well as the UN Economic Commission for Africa. International relations: for centuries in conflict with Egypt and Sudan and in the 19th and 20th centuries with the colonial powers. In 1860 lost her coastal territories as a result of the colonial expansion of France, Great Britain and Italy. Under Italian protectorate as provided by the Uccialli treaty of Aug. 2, 1889; protectorate annulled after the Italian defeat at Adua in 1896. In the London Agreement Dec. 13, 1906 the three Big Powers jointly guaranteed independence to Ethiopia, dividing its territory into three zones of influence: British – the springs of the Nile; French – railway line from Eritrea to the port of Djibouti; Italian – from Eritrea to Somalia. The treaty was viewed by the League of Nations Council as an act of aggression threatening the independence of Ethiopia; never came formally into force. In 1928 Ethiopia signed a treaty on co-operation with Italy, which on Dec. 5, 1934 provoked armed incidents on the border of its colony Somaliland with Ethiopia. On Oct. 2, 1935 Italy launched an invasion of Ethiopia. Emperor Haile Selassie personally accused Italy of aggression before the League of Nations Assembly on Jan. 3, 1936. Sanctions against Italy recommended to all members of the League were never applied and,

after total occupation of Ethiopia by Italian armed forces in May 1936, were formally cancelled by the League on July 16, 1936. The occupation of Ethiopia lasted until Apr. 6, 1941. Under a UN General Assembly decision of Dec. 22, 1950 the former Italian colony of ▷ Eritrea in 1952 became an autonomous federated province of Ethiopia and on Nov. 14, 1962 was entirely integrated with Ethiopia. On Sept. 12, 1974 a military coup d'état deposed the Emperor Haile Selassie. In 1977–78 civil war broke out in the region of Eritrea and an armed conflict erupted between Ethiopia and Somalia, which attempted to annex adjacent Ethiopian provinces. In Mar., 1978 upon a request of the Ethiopian government, Cuba sent its military units to aid Ethiopia in the conflict with Somalia. On Nov. 20, 1978 Ethiopia signed in Moscow a 20-year Treaty of Friendship and Co-operation with the USSR. In 1980 Ethiopia concluded an agreement with Sudan.
In Aug., 1981 Ethiopia signed separate Treaties of Friendship and Co-operation with Libya and the People's Democratic Republic of Yemen. In Jan., 1982 the government started an offensive called "Operation Red Star" against the guerillas of the Eritrea People's Liberation Front, supported by Sudan. ▷ Eritrea.
Since 1960 involved in border and military conflicts with ▷ Somalia. Despite negotiations conducted in 1986 and 1987 at the level of Foreign Ministers the problem remains unresolved.
See also ▷ World Heritage UNESCO List.

A.N. MANDELSTAND, *Le Conflit Italo-Éthiopien devant la SdN*, Paris, 1937; Z.J. CIBOT, *L'Éthiopie et la SdN*, Paris, 1939; R. GREENFIELD, *Ethiopia: A New Political History*, New York, 1965; A. ELJANOV, *Etiopia*, Moskva, 1967; R.C. HESS, *Ethiopia the Modernization of Autocracy*, Cornell University Press, 1970; F. HARDIE, *The Abyssinian Crisis*, London, 1975; B. THOMPSON, *Ethiopia. The Country That Cut Off Its Head*, London, 1975; F. HALLIDAY, M. MOLYNEAUX, *The Ethiopian Revolution*, London, 1981; R. KAPUSCINSKI, *The Emperor*, New York, 1983; *The Europa Year Book, 1984. A World Survey*, Vol. II, pp. 1549–1561. London, 1984; D.A. KORN, *Ethiopia, The United States and the Soviet Union*, Carbondale, Ill; London, 1986; J.W. CLAY, B.K. HALCOMB, *Politics and the Ethiopian Famine, 1984–85*, Oxford, 1987; A.J. DAY ed., "*Ethiopia–Somalia*", in: *Border and Territorial Disputes*, London, 1987, pp. 126–132; R. KAPUSCINSKI, *The Emperor: Downfall of an Autocrat*, New York, 1988.

ETHIOPIAN COPTIC CHURCH. One of the Eastern Christian Churches; founded in the 4th century; based on the doctrine of monophysitism; liturgical language Ghiz; certain Judaic practices in the cult (e.g. circumcision and sabbath); from the 4th century to 1959 was formally subject to the Coptic Patriarch in Alexandria; currently autocephalous; national church of Ethiopia.

ETHIOPIAN–SOVIET FRIENDSHIP TREATY, 1978. ▷ Ethiopia.

ETHIOPIA–SOMALIA PEACE AGREEMENT, 1988. A normalization agreement signed on April 3, 1988, restoring diplomatic relations and assuring disengagement of troops deployed in the Ogaden war area since 1977.
KEESING's *Record of World Events*, May 1988.

ETHNOCENTRISM. An international sociological term for a form of nationalism, presented by an ethnic group in relations with other groups, manifested also by xenophobia.

ETHNOCIDE. An international term for the extermination of primitive peoples; term introduced at

the 39th Panamerican Congress on Indians on July 9, 1970 in Lima in a resolution protesting the genocidal destruction of Indian tribes in Brazil in connection with the disclosure of the insidious extermination of tens of thousands of Indians in the state of Mato Grosso. ▷ American Indians. The term "ethnocide" is a synonym for the word ▷ Genocide.

CH. VAHNECKE, "Genocide et ethnocide des indiens d'Amerique Latin", in: *Le Monde*, 26, VIII 1972; R. JAULIN, *La Paix blanche. Introduction à l'ethnocide*, Paris, 1972; *Le Livre Blanc de l'Ethnocide en Amérique*, Paris, 1972; *De l'Ethnocide*, Paris, 1972.

ETHNOLOGY AND FOLKLORE. A subject of international research. Organizations reg. with the UIA:

International Committee of Organizers of Folklore Festivals, COIFF, f. 1975, Charante, France.
International Folk Music Council, f. 1947, London. Publ.: *Journal of IFMC*.
International Society for Ethnology and Folklore, SIEF, f. 1928 as International Commission for Folk Arts and Folklore, present name since 1964. Publ.: *Bulletin d'informations SIEF*.
International Society for Folk Narrative Research, f. 1960, Paris.
International Union of Anthropological and Ethnological Sciences, f. 1948, Berlin.

Yearbook of International Organizations 1986/87; The Europa Yearbook 1988. A World Survey, Vol. I, London, 1988.

EUA. ▷ European Unit of Account.

EUCARPIA ▷ Plant Protection.

EUCHARISTIC INTERNATIONAL CONGRESS. Since 1881, a permanent institution of the Roman Catholic Church: 1881 – Lille (France), 1882 – Avignon (France), 1883 – Liège (Belgium), 1885 – Freiburg (Switzerland), 1886 – Toulouse (France), 1888 – Paris, 1890 – Anvers (France), 1898 – Brussels, 1899 – Lourdes (France), 1901 – Angers (France), 1902 – Namur (Belgium), 1904 – Angoulême (France), 1905 – Rome, 1906 – Turnai (France), 1907 – Metz (Germany), 1908 – London, 1909 – Cologne (Germany), 1910 – Montreal (Canada), 1911 – Madrid, 1912 – Vienna, 1912 – Malta, 1914 – Lourdes (France), 1922 – Rome, 1924 – Amsterdam (Netherlands), 1926 – Chicago (USA), 1928 – Sydney (Australia), 1930 – Cartago (Costa Rica), 1932 – Dublin, 1934 – Buenos Aires, 1936 – Manilla, 1938 – Budapest, 1952 – Barcelona (Spain), 1955 – Rio de Janeiro, 1960 – Munich (FRG), 1964 – Bombay (India), 1968 – Bogota, 1970 – Manila, 1973 – Sydney, 1976 – Philadelphia (USA), 1980 – Fortaleza (Brazil), 1981 – Lourdes, 1985 – Nairobi, 1987 – Warsaw.

EUGENIC RACISM ▷ Genetic Manipulation.

EUHEMERISM. An international philosophical term for the theory of the Greek philosopher and writer Euhemer (*c.* 340–260 BC), a pupil of Theodorus the Atheist of Cyrena, professing that all of the immortal gods were mortal rulers whose cult was created by their successors.
In the 19th century the theory of euhemerism was developed by Marxism and euhemerism became one of the trends in the study of religions. ▷ Atheism.

EUPEN AND MALMEDY. Two regions of the western part of the Belgian province of Liège, subject of a dispute between Germany and Belgium, resolved in favor of Belgium by a plebiscite in 1920 held on the basis of art. 34 of the Versailles Treaty; occupied 1940–44 by Germany; recognized by the

E

FRG as an integral part of Belgium in a border agreement Sept. 24, 1956 and a Protocol of Sept. 6, 1960.

LEAGUE OF NATIONS ARCHIVES, *Eupen and Malmedy*, Geneva, 1921; S. WAMBAUGH, *Plebiscites since the World War, With a Collection of Official Documents*, Washington, DC, 1933.

EUPHRATES. River of SW Asia, ca 2,735 km long, flowing from Turkey through Syria and Iraq into the Persian Gulf; a subject of dispute since the 1960s between Syria, Iraq and Turkey in connection with the Ataturk Dam project, (construction to finish in 1933), which in Syrian and Iraqi opinion would deprive those states of the use of the major part of Euphrates waters. In 1983 Iraq–Syria–Turkey negotiations started in Ankara and Baghdad.

Le Monde, August 29, 1984.

EURAFRICA. An international term for (1) the European and African basin of the Mediterranean Sea taken as a whole; (2) a symbolic name for the inclinations of Anglo-phonic and Franco-phonic states of Africa to align themselves with the EEC.

EURASIA. The largest continent with an area of 53,500,000 sq. km, includes two parts of the world: Asia with an area of 43,400,000 sq. km and Europe with an area of 10,100,000 sq. km. The conventional line of division is drawn from the mouth of the Daidarata River to the Kara Sea along the west tectonic foreland of the Urals, the Emba River, the north shore of the Caspian Sea, the Kumsk–Manitsk Depression, Sea of Azov, Black Sea, the Bosphorus, Marmara Sea, the Dardanelles, and the Aegean Sea.

EURATOM. The European Atomic Energy Commission, f. 1957, Paris. Intergovernmental organization of Austria, Belgium, Denmark, France, the FRG, Ireland, Italy, Luxembourg, the Netherlands. Consultative status with OECD, WHO, ILO, Council of Europe. Publ.: *EURO-Spectra* (quarterly). Reg. with the UIA. ▷ Rome Treaty 1957.

UNTS, Vol. 298, 1958, pp. 176–266.

EUREKA. A name of the European High-Technology Co-operation Program, elaborated at Paris by representatives of the European Community and of Austria, Finland, Norway, Sweden and Switzerland in July 1985 called "The Technological Renaissance of Europe". The Eureka Conference has a permanent secretariat in Brussels, since March 11, 1987.

KEESING'S Record of World Events, 1987, No 6.

EUREX. A computer trading and information system for ▷ Eurobonds, est. by agreement between 69 banks from 14 countries. Signed in Sept. 1973, incorporated as an international consortium named Eurex S.A. in Luxembourg with authorized capital of 100 million Luxembourg francs. Sept. 1977; the IBM system Eurex started operations in Jan. 1979.

Euromoney, London, 1978.

EURO-AFRICAN CO-OPERATION. ▷ Lomé Conventions 1975, 1980, 1985.

EURO-ARAB DIALOGUE. A dialogue initiated by the European Community in May 1974, in Luxembourg at the ambassadorial level, with the aim of establishing a high degree of co-operation between Western Europe and the Arab World. The General Committee of the Euro-Arab Dialogue co-ordinates the work of specialized groups.

EUROBONDS. An international term for bond issues by international banks for the Euro-market, over 60% 1977 in US dollars and over 27% in FRG DM. The leading managers of Eurobonds for 1977 were: Deutsche Bank, Westdeutsche Bank, Credit Suisse, White Weld, Dresdner Bank, Warburg, Union Bank of Switzerland, Morgan Stanley, Commercial Bank, Swiss Bank Corp., Hambros, Orion, Amsterdam-Rotterdam, First Boston, Kidder Peabody and Morgan Grenfell. At first the majority of Eurobond issues were for more than ten years but at the end of the 1970s for no more than seven years. Since Jan., 1979 an automatic trading and information system for Eurobonds has been in operation in Luxembourg, managed by ▷ Eurex S.A.

BANQUE DE BRUXELLES, *The Mechanics of Eurobond Issues*, Brussels, 1967; Y.T. PARKER, *The Eurobond Market*, New York, 1974.

EUROCENTRISM. An international term for recognition of Europe as the main civilizing force of the world; a view of the epoch of colonialism.

EUROCHEMIC. The European Company for Chemical Processing of Irradiated Fuels, an institution created by an international convention signed on Dec. 20, 1967 by Austria, the Benelux countries, Denmark, France, Italy, Norway, Portugal, Sweden, Switzerland and Turkey on the common construction at the atomic center of Mol (Belgium) of a plutonium plant.

EUROCITIZENSHIP. An international term for the 1990's, considering that by 1992 all restrictions on freedom of movement inside the European Community will probably have been removed.

"What it Takes to be European", in: *The Economist*, July 11, 1987.

EUROCOMMUNISM. An international term for a pluralistic trend in the international workers' movement which appeared in 1975, formulated for the first time in the Yugoslav weekly *NIN*, then accepted by the Communist Parties of Western Europe with the exception of the Parties of the FRG and Portugal.

N.M. INNES, *Euro-Communism*, Beverly Hills, Cal., 1976; J. DOUGHERTY, D. PFALTZGRAFF, *Eurocommunism and the Atlantic Alliance*, Cambridge, Mass., 1977; A. DALMA, *Eurokomunismus – Italien, Frankreich, Jugoslavien, Portugal*, Zurich, 1977; F. FONVIEILLE-ALQUIEZ, *L'Eurocommunisme*, Paris, 1977; F. CLAUDIN, *Eurocommunism and Socialism*, New York, 1978; W. LEONARD, *Eurokomunismus: Herausforderung für Ost und West*, München, 1978; H. TIMMERMANN, *Eurokomunismus, Fakten, Analysen, Interview*, Frankfurt am M., 1978; L. SHAPIRO, *The Soviet Union and Eurocommunism*, London, 1978; R.L. TÖKES, *Eurocommunism and Détente*, New York, 1980; K. MIDDLEMAS, *Power and the Party; Changing Facts of Communism in Western Europe*, London, 1980.

EUROCONTROL, EUROPEAN ORGANIZATION FOR THE SAFETY OF AIR NAVIGATION. An intergovernmental institution est. by the International Convention relating to Co-operation for the Safety of Air Navigation, signed on Dec. 13, 1960 by Belgium, France, FRG, Ireland, Luxembourg, the Netherlands and UK, came into force Mar. 1, 1963. Co-operation agreements signed: 1964 by Denmark, Norway, Sweden and US Federal Aviation Administration: 1965 by Switzerland, 1966 by Italy, 1967 by Austria, 1971 by Spain, 1976 by Portugal. Headquarters: Brussels.

UNTS, Vol. 523, pp. 119–149; *Eurocontrol, growth, aims, structure* (English and French), Brussels, 1975.

EUROCRATS. An international term for the civil servants of the EEC, estimated in 1976 to number approximately 14,000.

J. PAXTON, *A Dictionary of the EEC*, London, 1977, pp. 87–91.

EUROCREDITS. An international term for credits on the international market granted in ▷ Eurodollars or other Eurocurrencies, mainly Swiss francs, FRG marks and Dutch guilder. Separate statistical data on non-dollar Eurocredits are published since 1978 by the ▷ Bank of International Settlements in Basel.

EUROCULT. The official name of regional conferences of UNESCO on European culture held periodically with the participation of the ministers of culture of the majority of European states in accordance with the instructions of the World Conference of UNESCO on Culture, which took place in France, 1970. In June 1972 the First Session of EUROCULT took place in Helsinki.

EURODIF S.A. A joint stock company formed within the EEC in 1972 on the initiative of France with the task of constructing common West European plants for the preparation of uranium for atomic power stations by the ultracentrifuge method, different from the diffusion method used by the FRG, Great Britain and other countries. Stockholders are the governments of EEC member states as well as large companies of the power engineering industry. Five states (Belgium, France, Italy, Sweden and Spain) decided on Feb. 8, 1974 to locate the uranium preparation plants in France, in Tricastin near Pierrelette in the Rodan valley.

EURODOLLAR. An international term for the American dollars located in banks outside the USA or loaned abroad through redeposit in other banks. The term was used at a bank conference in Basel in July 1957 in reference to funds designed for short-term credits, comprising 80% of the dollar reserves of West European banks, which soon organized a permanent Eurodollar market. These dollar deposit transactions, often without changing the original place of deposit, were started in 1957 by London banks, which became the major market, and in following years in Paris, Zurich, Frankfurt am Main, Vienna and Milan. Eurodollar credits were initially granted for a period from 7 to 180 days, but later for longer periods, a year or several years. In practice the Eurodollar market was expanded to bank deposits in other convertible currencies (in 1970 this sum reached c. 30%); which still further increased international liquidity. Also taking part in Eurodollar transactions were the overseas branches of US banks, as well as regional banks of integration outside of Western Europe, including the International Bank of Economic Co-operation. Simultaneously, the Eurodollar introduced a speculative element into the non-banking market which, according to the estimate of the Bank of International Settlements, BIS, of June 5, 1971, became very dangerous to the financial policies of the BIS member states, prompting the Council of Governors of the Bank to recommend that the central banks not place any more of their reserves in the Eurodollar market. The situation was complicated when the ▷ OPEC states quadrupled the price of oil by raising it from c. US $20 a ton in 1973 to US $77 dollars one year later, which resulted in an increase on world markets of ▷ Petrodollars, a significant percentage of which was placed in the Eurodollar market.

H.V. PROCHNOV (ed.), *L' Eurodollar*, Paris, 1971; G. BELL, *The Eurodollar Market and the International*

European Coal Organization Agreement, 1946

Financial System, London, 1974; G.W. MACKENZIE, *The Economies of the Eurocurrency System*, London, 1975; J. WALMSLEY, *A Dictionary of International Finance*, London, 1979.

EUROFER. A European steel federation established in 1976 with the task of co-ordinating the policies of steel prices within EEC and common operation against competition on world markets.

EUROFIGHTER–JAGDFLUGZEUG. A product of the European Fighter Aircraft Company, est. 1985 by the FRG, Italy, Spain and the UK.

KEESIGN'S *Contemporary Archive*, July, 1987.

EUROFINA. European Company for the Financing of Railway Equipment, est. by the Convention signed on Oct. 20, 1955 in Berne by the governments of Austria, Belgium, Denmark, France, the FRG, Italy, Luxembourg, the Netherlands, Norway, Portugal, Sweden, Switzerland and Yugoslavia.

UNTS, Vol. 378, p. 159.

EUROFINAS. International organization reg. with the UIA, f. 1959, Brussels; to study the credit financing in Europe. Publ.: Eurofinas Study Report.

Yearbook of International Organizations, 1986/87; The Europa Yearbook 1988. A World Survey, Vol. I, London, 1988.

EUROGROUP. An informal grouping of European NATO countries.

The Europa Yearbook 1988. A World Survey, Vol. I, London, 1988.

EURO-LATIN AMERICAN CO-ORDINATING COMMITTEE. A Committee est. 1971 by the European Community and 22 Latin-American countries to strengthen trade and financial ties.

EUROMEDIC. One of the first international companies which was formed in 1970 in the process of Western European integration, based on the Euro-dollar market; specializes in the manufacture of hospital equipment and in construction of hospital buildings; seat in Luxembourg; main factory: Equipement Hospitalier de France.

EUROMISSILE. An international military term in the 1980's for the sorts of missiles that were the subject of USA–USSR nuclear disarmament negotiations. See also ▷ Double Zero Option; and ▷ Eurostrategic Weapons.

D. ROBERTSON, *Guide to Modern Defense and Strategy*, Detroit, 1988.

EURONET. A West European scientific, technical and socio-economic information network, organized within the EEC in 1978/79 in co-operation with the National Postal and Telecommunication Offices. Intergovernmental enterprise with four computer centers in Frankfurt am Main, London, Paris and Rome, with five information stations in Amsterdam, Brussels, Copenhagen, Dublin and Luxembourg and twenty data centers.

EUROPA ISLAND ▷ Madagascar.

EUROPA NOSTRA. The International Federation of Associations for the Protection of Europe's Cultural and Natural Heritage, f. 1963 in London. Consultative status with the Council of Europe. Reg. with the UIA.

Yearbook of International Organizations.

EUROPE. Region in the Northern Hemisphere forming with Asia the continent of ▷ Eurasia.

Area: 10.1 million sq. km, including 5.6 million sq. km for the European part of the USSR; *c.* 675 million inhabitants in 1980 (1650 – *c.* 100 million, 1750 – *c.* 140; 1800 – *c.* 188; 1850 – *c.* 266; 1900 – *c.* 401; 1950 – *c.* 536; 1960 – 594; 1970 – 645).

The ▷ Stockholm Conference 1984–1986 defined Europe 'as extending from the Atlantic Ocean to the Ural Mountains'.

The UN demographic projection: Europe in 2000 (without the USSR) – 513,110,000 and in 2025 – 520,888,000; the USSR in Europe and Asia in 2000 – 314,818,000; in 2025 – 367,127,000; Eastern Europe – 120,970,000 and 131,159,000.

G.W. HOFFMAN, *A Geography of Europe*, London, 1954; L. CARTON, *Organisations Européennes*, Paris, 1971; *The Major Companies of Europe*, London, 1973; *Who Owns Whom?*, London, 1973; M.Z. BROOCKE, H.L. REMMERS, *The Multinational Company in Europe*, London, 1973; S. POLLIARD, C. HOLMES (eds.), *Documents of European Economic History, The End of the Old Europe 1914–1939*, London, 1973; CH. COOK, J. PAXTON, *European Political Facts 1918–1975*, London, 1975; P.E. ZIMMER, *East-West Relations in Europe*, 1971–1982, Boulder Col., 1983; Ch. COOK, J. PAXTON, *European Political Facts, 1798–1848*, London, 1980; Ch. COOK, J. PAXTON, *European Political Facts, 1848–1918*, London, 1978; J. DEAN, *Watershed in Europe: Dismantling the East-West Military Confrontation*, Lexington, Mass., 1986; J. GUNTHER, *Inside Europe*, New York, 1987; P. LEWIS, *Europe: A Tapestry of Nations*, New York, 1987.

EUROPE 1992. An international term, referring to February 12, 1992, the date for transforming the European Community of Twelve into a totally free market.

EUROPE-AMERICA. Name of an international conference organized periodically by the International European Movement for the purpose of discussing problems of co-operation between Western Europe and North America. Participants: politicians, economists and scientists from both regions. The first meeting took place Mar. 26–28, 1973 in Amsterdam; opened by the Secretary-General of NATO.

EUROPEAN ADVISORY COMMISSION, 1943–45. An intergovernmental institution formed in Dec., 1943 by the Teheran Conference, with the tasks of preparing the unconditional surrender of Germany, developing a system of joint allied control over occupied Germany and formulating a plan for dividing Germany into zones of occupation. The commission began its work on Jan. 14, 1944 in London and was composed of: US ambassador – J. Winant, the representative of Great Britain – W. Strang, the USSR ambassador – F.T. Gusuev. Agreement was quickly reached on unconditional surrender, but not until Oct. 12, 1944, as to the initial plan for the division of Germany (into three zones: American, British and Soviet) and concerning allied control over Germany and an allied Komendantura for Berlin on Nov. 14, 1944. The final agreement, reached just before the beginning of the Yalta Conference, Feb. 1, 1945, became the basis for further international documents: unconditional surrender of Germany and ▷ Germany, Declaration on the Defeat of, on whose basis were created the ▷ Allied Control Council for Germany and ▷ Berlin Allied Komendantura, also including France.

R. OPIE, *Search for Peace Settlements*, London, 1951; W.L. NEMMANN, *After Victory: Churchill, Roosevelt and Stalin and the Making of the Peace*, London, 1967.

EUROPEAN AGRICULTURE FUND. An institution of the ▷ European Communities, est. in 1962, called also by the French acronym FEOGA, as a European Agricultural Guidance and Guarantee Fund, EAGGF, which contributes credits toward the structural reform of agriculture. The Guidance Section expenditures in 1982 were 783 million ▷ ECU's and the Guarantee Section's 12,4 billion.

The Europa Year Book 1984. A World Survey, Vol. I, p. 144, London, 1984.

EUROPEAN ATOMIC ENERGY COMMUNITY. ▷ EURATOM.

EUROPEAN BROADCASTING AREA. The ▷ Stockholm Plan 1952 defined the area as follows:

"on the South: by parallel 30° North;
on the West: by a line extending from the North Pole along meridian 10° West of Greenwich to its intersection with parallel 72° North, thence by great circle arc to the point of inter-section of meridian 50° West and parallel 40° North, and thence by a line leading to the point of intersection of meridian 40° West and parallel 30° North;
on the East: by meridian 40° East of Greenwich, so as to include the western part of the USSR and the territories bordering on the Mediterranean Sea, with the exception of the parts of Arabia and Saudi Arabia which are included in this sector."

ITU, The European Broadcasting Conference, Stockholm Final Acts, Geneva, 1952.

EUROPEAN CLEARING UNION. An institution of the European Organization for Economic Co-operation during the period Sept. 19, 1950–Jan. 1, 1959; settled currency disputes among the member states during the period of currency restrictions. With the introduction of the unrestricted exchange of currencies in EEC member countries on Dec. 31, 1958, it was abolished.

EUROPEAN COAL AND STEEL COMMUNITY, ECSC. An intergovernmental institution of Western Europe with headquarters in Luxembourg, established on the initiative of a French stateman Robert Schuman (1886–1963) on July 25, 1952 by virtue of a treaty, signed Apr. 18, 1951 by the governments of Belgium, France, the FRG, Holland, Italy and Luxembourg; associate members: Switzerland and Great Britain. Organs are: High Authority, main organ of the ECSC, composed of nine members appointed for six years; Council of Ministers, composed of the representatives of the member states at the ministerial level, chairmanship held for three months by each member successively in alphabetical order; Advisory Committee, operating under the High Authority, composed of 51 members: Presiding Committee, Court of Justice, and the ▷ European Parliament, a common organ of ECSC, EEC and EURATOM. (The executives of the ECSC, EUROATOM and EEC merged on July 1, 1967). Main task is to conduct common policy in the coal and steel industries. Co-operates with the UN, GATT and ILO; Publ.: *Noticias de la CECA* (in English, French, German, and Spanish) and *Coal Statistics, Steel Statistics, Annual Report*.

B. VOYENNE, *Petite histoire de l'idée européenne*, Paris, 1954; J. DE SOTO, *La Communauté européenne de charbon et de l'acier*, CECA, Paris, 1965; J. GOORMAGHTIGH, "European Coal and Steel Community", in: *International Conciliation*, No. 503, May, 1955, pp. 343–408; J. PAXTON, *A Dictionary of the EEC*, London, 1978.

EUROPEAN COAL ORGANIZATION AGREEMENT, 1946. An agreement signed by Belgium, Denmark, France, Greece, Luxembourg, the Netherlands, Norway, Turkey, the UK and USA on Jan. 4, 1946 in London; came into force on signature.

UNTS, Vol. 6, pp. 35–43.

EUROPEAN COLLECTIVE SECURITY DRAFT TREATY, 1955. A draft of a General Treaty on Collective Security in Europe submitted to European states by the government of the USSR on July 20, 1955. The basis of the agreement was to include guarantees by all states to refrain from the threat or the use of force against one another and collective defense in case of an aggression launched against any European state. Upon termination of an agreed period after the signing of the treaty, the Warsaw Alliance and the North Atlantic Treaty Organizations were to have been disbanded.

KEESING's *Contemporary Archive*, 1955.

EUROPEAN COLONIES AND POSSESSIONS IN THE AMERICAS. A subject of the Convention on the Provisional Administration of European Colonies and Possessions in the Americas, signed on July 30, 1940 in Havana, at the Second Meeting of Consultation of Ministers of Foreign Affairs by 21 American Republics, not ratified by Bolivia, Chile and Paraguay, came into force on Jan. 8, 1942. The Convention established for the time of war a quasi-protectorate of American Republics over British, Dutch and French colonies and possessions in the Western Hemisphere against claims of the Axis Powers.

International Conferences of American States. First Supplement, 1933–40, Washington, DC, 1940.

EUROPEAN COMMERCIAL ARBITRATION CONVENTION, 1961. The European Convention on International Commercial Arbitration with Annex, was signed on Apr. 21, 1961 in Geneva by 22 European states: Austria, Belgium, Byelorussia, Czechoslovakia, Denmark, Finland, France, the FRG, Hungary, Italy, Luxembourg, the Netherlands, Poland, Romania, Spain, Sweden, Switzerland, Turkey, Ukraine, the USSR and Yugoslavia. The Convention came into force on Jan. 7, 1964.

UNTS, Vol. 484, p. 364.

EUROPEAN COMMISSION OF HUMAN RIGHTS, est. by the ▷ Human Rights European Convention 1950. The Commission examines individual, group, and non-governmental organization applications and decides whether it is possible to reach a friendly settlement or whether it is necessary to present the case to the Committee of Ministers or to the ▷ European Court of Human Rights.

The Europa Yearbook 1987, Vol. I, p. 130, London, 1987.

EUROPEAN COMMON MARKET. Another name for the ▷ European Economic Community, EEC.

J. PAXTON, *A Dictionary of the EEC*, London, 1977.

EUROPEAN COMMUNITIES. The institutional system of Western Europe established 1951–57 by six states: Belgium, France, the FRG, Italy, the Netherlands and Luxembourg, based on the Paris Treaty, signed Apr. 18, 1951, establishing the ▷ European Coal and Steel Community ECSC, and on the Rome Treaties, signed Mar. 25, 1957, establishing the ▷ European Economic Community, EEC and the European Atomic Energy Committee ▷ EURATOM. On Jan. 1, 1973 Great Britain, Denmark and Ireland joined the Community. In 1977 Greece, Portugal and Spain, submitted

formal applications for accession to the European Communities.

Chronicle of the European Communities:

1950, May 9: official French initiative to place Western Europe's coal and steel industries under a common European Authority (▷ Schuman Plan);
1951, Apr. 18: Treaty creating the ECSC signed in Paris;
1952, Aug. 10: est. of the High Authority of the ECSC in Luxembourg;
1955, June 1–2: Foreign Ministers of the Six decide on further economic integration (▷ Messina Conference);
1956, May 29: Foreign Ministers of the Six decide on EEC treaty-drafting conference in Venice;
1957, Mar. 25: Treaties creating the EEC and the Euratom signed in Rome;
1958, Jan. 1: Rome Treaties come into force;
1961, July 9: Association agreement with Greece; Nov. 8: first negotiation on accession of Great Britain (broken off Jan. 29, 1963);
1963, Sept. 12: Association agreement with Turkey;
1964, June 1: Association agreement with 17 African States and Madagascar (First ▷ Yaoundé Convention);
1965, July 1 to Jan. 29, 1966: French boycott of Community's Council of Foreign Ministers; seven-month crisis on financing common agricultural policy;
1967, Feb. 9: First five-year economic program of the Community; May 10: Formal applications of Great Britain, Ireland and Denmark for EC membership;
1968, July 1: EC customs union in force; July 26: Association agreement with Kenya, Tanzania and Uganda (▷ Arusha Convention 1968); July 29; Free movement of blue collar workers in all EC member countries;
1969, Dec. 1–2: summit meeting in The Hague; Dec. 22: agreement on common agricultural policy;
1970, Jan. 1: common foreign trade policy in force; June 9: agreement on monetary and economic union in 1980; June 30: opening in Luxembourg of accession negotiations with Great Britain, Denmark, Ireland and Norway; Second ▷ Yaoundé Convention;
1971, Apr. 1: Association agreement with Malta; July 1: tariff preferences for developing countries in force;
1972, Jan. 22: Great Britain, Denmark, Ireland and Norway, signed Accession Treaty; July 22: EEC free trade agreements with Austria, Iceland, Portugal, Sweden and Switzerland; Sept. 26: Norway accession rejected by Norwegian referendum; Oct. 19–20: summit meeting in Paris; Dec. 19: Association agreement with Cyprus;
1973, Jan. 1: Great Britain, Denmark and Ireland members of the Community; Dec. 14–15: Summit meeting in Copenhagen;
1974, Sept. 14: Summit meeting in Paris; Oct. 11: UN General Assembly approves observer status for Community; Dec. 8–10. Summit meeting in Paris; Dec. 17: Agreement on reducing the dependence of foreign energy to 40–50% of total by 1985;
1975, Feb. 28: Signing of the ▷ Lomé Convention 1975; Mar. 10–11: Summit meeting of the European Council in Dublin; June 12: Greece application; July 11–16: Summit meeting of the European Council in Brussels; Dec. 1–2: Summit meeting of the European Council in Rome consents to election of the ▷ European Parliament by universal suffrage by 1978;
1976, Apr. 25–27: Euro-Maghreb Agreement; July 12–13: Summit meeting of the European Council in Brussels; Nov. 29–30: Summit meeting of the European Council in The Hague;
1977, Jan. 1: extending in the North Sea and North Atlantic fishing limits to 200 miles; July 1: internal tariffs on manufactured goods between the EC and 7 EFTA countries were abolished;
1979, Jan. 1: the EC budget financed by its own resources collected from custom duties, agricultural levies and a uniform assessment of up to one percent of value-added tax;
1980, Lomé Convention II;
1981, Jan. 1: Greece signed Accession Treaty;
1982, Feb.: a referendum of the inhabitants of Greenland voted to end their membership of the Communities;
1983 and 1984: negotiations for the accession of Portugal and Spain to the EEC, foreseen Jan. 1, 1986.
On Feb. 1, 1985 Greenland formally withdrew from the European Community.

Diplomatic Missions accredited to the European Communities in Brussels: Algeria, Argentina, Australia, Austria, Bangladesh, Barbados, Benin, Bolivia, Botswana, Brazil, Burkina Faso /former Upper Volta/, Burma, Burundi, Cameroon, Canada, the Central African Republic, Chad, Chile, China, Cyprus, Columbia, Congo, Costa Rica, the Dominican Republic, Ecuador, Egypt, El Salvador, Ethiopia, Fiji, Finland, Gabon, Gambia, Ghana, Greece, Guatemala, Guyana, Haiti, the Holy See, Honduras, Iceland, India, Indonesia, Iran, Iraq, Israel, the Ivory Coast, Jamaica, Japan, Jordan, Kenya, Lebanon, Lesotho, Liberia, Libya, Madagascar, Malawi, Malaysia, Mali, Malta, Mauritius, Mauritania, Mexico, Morocco, Nepal, New Zealand, Nicaragua, Niger, Nigeria, Norway, Pakistan, Panama, Paraguay, Peru, the Philippines, Portugal, Rwanda, Saudi Arabia, Senegal, Sierra Leone, Singapore, Somalia, South Africa, South Korea, Spain, Sri Lanka, Sudan, Suriname, Switzerland, Swaziland, Sweden, Syria, Tanzania, Thailand, Togo, Tonga, Trinidad and Tobago, Tunisia, Turkey, Uganda, Uruguay, the USA, Venezuela, Yemen, Yugoslavia, Zaïre.

Corps Diplomatique accrédité auprès des Communautés Européennes, Bruxelles, 1977; H. and E. ARBUTHNOTT, *A Common Man's Guide to the Common Market*, London, 1979; J. PAXTON, *A Dictionary to the Common Market*, London, 1982; *European Communities*, The Hague, 1982; *The Europa Year Book 1984. A World Survey*, Vol. I, pp. 135–153, London, 1984; J.L. SAMPEDIO, J.A. PAYNO, *The Enlargement of the European Community. Case Studies of Greece, Portugal and Spain*, London, 1983; F. NICHOLSON, R. EAST, *From the Six to the Twelve. The Enlargement of the European Community*, London, 1987; R. PRYCE, *The Dynamics of European Union*, London, 1987.

EUROPEAN COMMUNITIES COURT OF JUSTICE. The arbitral institution of the European Economic Community, EURATOM and the European Community of Coal and Steel; established by the Rome Treaty of Mar. 25, 1957; headquarters Luxembourg. Publ.: *Recueil de Jurisprudence de la Cour*. The Court's verdicts are binding for the member states of the EEC. In 1981 and 1982 the Court gave four rulings on equal pay for men and women.

EUROPEAN COMMUNITY LAW. The legal system of the European Common Market and of the European Communities.

A.H. ROBERTSON, *The Law of International Institutions in Europe*, New York, 1961; G. PASETTI, A. TRABUCCHI, *Code des Communautés Européennes*, Milano, 1965; R.S. MATHIJSEN, *A Guide to European Community Law*, London, 1972; A. PARRY, S. HARDY, *Encyclopedia of European Community Law*, London, 1973; H.A. ANDRETS, *Supervision on European Community Law*, Amsterdam, 1978.

"EUROPEAN CONCERT". The 19th-century international term for harmonious co-operation of the powers in the anti-Napoleonic alliance – Austria, Prussia, Russia and Great Britain, which by the treaty of Chaumont, Mar. 1, 1814, obligated themselves in art. 1 *dans un parfait concert* to build universal peace in Europe. When France joined the ▷ Holy Alliance at the Congress of Aix-la-Chapelle, Nov. 15, 1818, the Minister of Foreign Affairs of Austria, C. von Metternich, called this document the birth of "a diplomatic concert of five courts" (*concert diplomatique entre les cinque Cours*). Since then commonly used in the language of diplomacy as a formula for the concordant policy of the European powers. "le Concert européen."

C. DUPUIS, *Le Principe d'équilibre et le Concert européen de Westphalie à l'Acte d'Algeciras*, Paris, 1909;

R. LANGHORN, *The Collapse of the Concert of Europe, International Politics 1890–1914*, London, 1981.

EUROPEAN CONFEDERATION. Projects of the 1980's of a confederation of European regions with different sociopolitical systems. Two regional projects are linked to the former ▷ Habsburg Empire or to the German concept of ▷ Mitteleuropa. The third project would integrate Europe from the Atlantic to the Ural Mountains.

G. KONRAD, *Antipolitics*, London, 1984; K. SCHLOGEL, *The Middle Lies Eastwards. The Germans, The Lost East and Mitteleuropa*, London, 1986; M. KUNDERA, *The Tragedy of Central Europe*, London, 1987.

EUROPEAN CONFERENCES, 1947–85. The intergovernmental meetings of the European states, excluding the Four Powers conferences on Germany, in chronological order: May 27–July 1, 1947 and Apr. 11–16, 1948 in Paris, conferences on the ▷ Marshall Plan with the participation of Austria, Belgium, Denmark, France, Greece, Great Britain, Holland, Iceland, Ireland, Italy, Luxembourg, Norway, Portugal, Switzerland, Sweden, Turkey, ending with the signing of the treaty on Organization of European Economic Co-operation, OEEC, also including the western occupied zones of Germany and the region of Trieste. On Mar. 17, 1948 in Brussels, meeting of the ministers of foreign affairs of France, Great Britain and the Benelux states, concluding with the expansion of the French–British Friendship Treaty of 1947 through the Brussels Treaty which took effect on Aug. 25, 1948 for 50 years (After the FRG and Italy became parties to the Treaty on Oct. 23, 1954 it was changed into the Treaty on Western European Unity.) On June 7, 1948 in London a meeting of the ministers of foreign affairs of France, Great Britain, the USA and the Benelux states on the question of Germany, which prepared a monetary reform for the occupied zones of West Germany and the occupied sectors of West Berlin. On June 24, 1948 in Warsaw a meeting of the ministers of foreign affairs of Albania, Bulgaria, Czechoslovakia, Hungary, Poland, Romania, Yugoslavia and the USSR in connection with the introduction on June 18, 1948 of a new currency in the western occupied zones of Germany. On Feb. 25, 1949 in Warsaw an intergovernmental conference of Bulgaria, Czechoslovakia, Hungary, Poland, Romania and the USSR which created CMEA. On May 5, 1949 in London a meeting of the ministers of foreign affairs of Belgium, Denmark, France, Holland, Great Britain, Ireland, Italy, Luxembourg, Norway and Sweden; created the European Council, which the FRG joined on July 13, 1950. On June 18, 1951 in Paris a meeting of the ministers of foreign affairs of Belgium France, the FRG, Holland, Italy and Luxembourg, concluded with the signing of an agreement on the European Coal and Steel Community. On May 26, 1952 signed in Bonn was the General Treaty on the relations between the FRG and the three Western Powers. On Feb. 27, 1953 in London a conference of the creditor states of the German Third Reich (Belgium, Canada, Ceylon, Denmark, France, Greece, Great Britain, Iceland, Liechtenstein, Luxembourg, Norway, Pakistan, the Republic of South Africa, Spain, Sweden, Switzerland, the USA and Yugoslavia) with the FRG, which, considering itself as the legal successor of the Weimar Republic and the III Reich, assumed the obligation of discharging the debts of the German state incurred

since 1919. Concluded with the signing of a treaty which obligated the FRG to pay 14,450 million marks in annual instalments of 567 million marks to 1958; and after this period at the rate of 765 million marks. 1954 Berlin Conference of the Four Powers on the question of Germany. Aug. 19–22, 1954 Brussels Conference of Six (Benelux states, France, the FRG and Italy) on the European Common Market. Sept. 28–Oct. 3, 1954 London Conference of Nine (the Six as well as Canada, Great Britain and the USA) on strengthening military and political co-operation. Jan. 19–23, 1954 Paris Conferences of Nine: First on creating the Western European Union with the participation of the FRG and Italy; Second on the question of admitting the FRG to NATO; Third on ending the state of war with the FRG; Fourth on the issue of the Saar. ▷ Paris Treaties of 1954 on these issues. May 11–14, 1955, First Warsaw Pact Conference. In 1956–71 international conferences within the European Community and NATO as well as CMEA and the Warsaw Pact. Negotiations in 1969–71 were concentrated on the question of a new statute for West Berlin and convening the Conference on Security and Co operation in Europe, CSCE. 1972 in Helsinki, Nov. 21 Dec. 15, introductory meeting on CSCE. 1973 in Helsinki, July 3–7, stage I of CSCE; in Geneva, Sept. 18–Dec. 15, the first part of state II of CSCE. 1974 in Geneva, Jan. 15–July 26, the second part of stage II of CSCE; the third part in Geneva from Sept. 2, followed by the final stage III in Helsinki to Aug. 1, 1975, the date of signing of the ▷ Helsinki Final Act. 1977–78 Conference in Belgrade from Oct. 4 to Dec. 22 of the CSCE states. 1980–81 meeting of the CSCE in Madrid, begun in Nov., 1980 and ended in Feb., 1981. 1984 – meeting of the CSCE in Stockholm.

KEESING'S *Contemporary Archive.*

EUROPEAN CONVENTION FOR THE PROTECTION OF HUMAN RIGHTS AND FUNDAMENTAL FREEDOMS, 1950 ▷ Human Rights European Convention, 1950.

EUROPEAN CONVENTION ON SOCIAL AND MEDICAL ASSISTANCE, 1949. ▷ Medical and Social International Assistance.

EUROPEAN CONVENTION ON THE EQUIVALENCE OF DIPLOMAS, 1953. ▷ Diplomas.

EUROPEAN COURT OF AUDITORS. An institution of the ▷ European Communities, since June 1, 1977; a body responsible for the external audit of the resources managed by the three communities. The ten Members are appointed for six years by unanimous decision of the Council of Ministers, after consultation with the ▷ European Parliament. The Court examines the accounts of all expenditures and revenues of all bodies of the Communities.

European Communities, The Hague, 1982.

EUROPEAN COURT OF HUMAN RIGHTS. est. 1950 by the ▷ Human Rights European Convention. The cases and sentences of the Court of the Committee of Ministers are published by the Council of Europe. See also ▷ European Commission of Human Rights.

The Europa Yearbook. 1987, Vol. 1, London, 1987; R.L. BLEDSOE, B.A. BOCZEK, *The International Law Dictionary*, Oxford, UK, 1987; *Council of Europe. Information Sheet No 21*, Strasbourg, 1988.

EUROPEAN CRIMINAL MATTERS CONVENTION, 1959. The European Convention on Mutual Assistance in Criminal Matters was signed in Strasbourg, Apr. 20, 1959, by the member states of the Council of Europe.

"Assistance may be refused: (a) if the request concerns an offence which the requested Party considers a political offence, an offence connected with a political offence or a fiscal offence; (b) if the request Party considers that execution of the request is likely to prejudice the sovereignty, security, public order or other essential interests of its country" (art. 2).

UNTS, Vol. 472, pp. 186 and 192.

EUROPEAN CULTURAL CENTER. A center est. 1950 in Geneva. Members: national and international cultural institutions associated with the Association of Institutes for European Studies, European Association of Music Festivals and the Center for European Education. Reg. with the UIA.

Yearbook of International Organizations.

EUROPEAN CULTURAL CONVENTION, 1954. An agreement between the members of the Council of Europe, signed on Dec. 19, 1954 in Paris, relating to "the study of the languages, history and civilization of the European States and of the civilization which is common to them all." Each Contracting Party shall take appropriate measures to safeguard and to encourage the development of its national contribution to the common cultural heritage of Europe (art. 1). Came into force on May 5, 1955.

UNTS, Vol. 218, p. 140.

EUROPEAN CULTURAL FUND. An institution f. 1954 in Geneva, under the auspices of the European Cultural Center. Arrangement on coordination of cultural activities with the Council of Europe, 1960. Publ.: *Annual Reports*. Reg. with the UIA.

Yearbook of International Organizations.

EUROPEAN CURRENCY UNIT, ECU. An agreed-upon settlement unit of the European Monetary System, EMS, was introduced by the Western European states on Mar. 13, 1979, by a resolution of the European Council. The foundation of the EMS system is a common monetary unit, ECU, initially retaining the value and make-up of the European Unit of Account, EUA, introduced in settlements of the central banks of the EEC states in June 1974. The value of the ECU is based on a basket of 9 currencies. The number of units of particular currencies in the "basket" and the weight given them are as follows:

	Number	Weight
FRG mark	0.828	27.3%
Pound sterling	0.0895	17.5%
French franc	1.15	19.5%
Italian lire	109.0	14.0%
Dutch guilder	0.286	9.0%
Belgian franc	3.66	7.9%
Luxembourg franc	0.14	0.3%
Danish krona	0.217	3.9%
Irish pound	0.00759	1.5%

The value of the ECU is calculated daily according to the exchange rates of the above currencies. The basic difference between the ECU and EUA is that

E

the EUA is only a unit of account, whereas the ECU, though used as a measuring unit in the exchange rate and credit mechanism and in intervention operations on the foreign exchange market, is simultaneously real money.

On Jan. 12, 1987 a realignment of the EMS currencies took place, following a 3 per cent revaluation of the Deutsch-Mark and the Dutch Guilder and a 2 per cent revaluation of the Belgian and Luxembourg Franc. The rates for each currency against the ECU since Jan. 12, 1987:

FRG mark (DM)	2.05855
English pound (UKL)	0.739615
French frank (FF)	6.90403
Dutch guilder (FL)	2.31943
Belg. Lux. franc (BF)	42.4582
Ital. lira ( )	1.481.58
Dan. krone (DK)	7.85212
Irish punt (IRE)	0.768411

The UNCIFRAL draft Convention on International Bills of Exchange 1987 allows international ▷ bills of exchange and promissory notes to be denominated as payable in monetary units of account such as ECU or SDR's.

J. ASCHAIM, Y.S. PARK, *Artificial Currency Units*, Princenton, 1976; *IMF Survey*, March 19, 1979; *The Europa Yearbook 1984. A World Survey*, Vol. I, pp. 149–151, London, 1984; *UN Chronicle*, November, 1987.

EUROPEAN CUSTOMS UNION.
An international system of free trade between the member countries of the European Community, based on:

"the removal of custom duties and other barriers; the replacement of national tariffs with a single common tariff on imports from non-member countries and the development of a common commercial policy towards them; the harmonization of customs rules and enforcement procedures so that duties will be assessed in the same way."

The founding members of the EC (Belgium, the FRG, France, Italy, Luxembourg and the Netherlands) removed the last quota restriction on trade between them on Dec. 31, 1961 and introduced the common customs tariff on import from non-member countries July 1, 1968. The new members (Britain, Denmark, and Ireland) were assimilated into the European Customs Union in four-, five- and six-stage processes from Jan. 1, 1973 to Dec. 31, 1977.

European Communities Yearbook 1977, pp. 66–68.

EUROPEAN DEFENCE COMMUNITY, EDC, 1952.
An intergovernmental institution created by an agreement signed May 27, 1952 by Belgium, France, the FRG, Italy, Luxembourg and the Netherlands establishing a Western European military organization to serve the integration of Western military forces. The plan suggested by France (so-called ▷ Pleven plan) of Oct. 24, 1950 proposed the creation of a common European army connected with NATO whose make-up would also include FRG military units. This agreement, however, did not take effect in view of the rejection Aug. 30, 1954 by the French parliament of the request of the government for its ratification. However, the plan of bringing the FRG into NATO was shortly realized despite this through the instrumentality of the West European Union.

EUROPEAN DEMOCRATIC UNION, EDU.
A West Euopean political organization, est. in Apr., 1978 in Salzburg on the initiative of the Conservative Party of Great Britain, an association of the Christian Democratic and Conservative Parties of Austria, Denmark, Finland, the FRG, Great Britain, Iceland, Norway, Portugal and Sweden.

EUROPEAN DEVELOPMENT FUND.
An EEC institution with seat in Luxembourg, est. 1959 on the basis of the Rome Treaties of Mar. 25, 1957 as the Development Fund for Associated Overseas Countries and Territories; co-operates with the European Investment Bank.

EUROPEAN ECONOMIC COMMUNITY, EEC.
Communauté économique européenne, CEE; Europäische Wirtschaftsgemeinschaft, EWG; Comunita Economica Europea, CEE, official English, French, German and Italian names of the West-European economic integration organization established under GATT aegis on Jan. 1, 1958, following the decision of the Messina Conference of the governments of Belgium, France, the FRG, Luxembourg, the Netherlands and Italy, six member states of the ▷ European Coal and Steel Community and the ▷ Rome Treaty, signed on Mar. 25, 1957, and ratified by the same six member states between July 5 and Dec. 4, 1957. The Treaty came into force on Jan. 1 1958 and the Foreign Ministers of the six signatory states met on Jan. 6–7, to appoint members of the Commission. In July 1967 the Institutions of the three Communities were merged, a single Commission superseding the High Authority of the ECSC, EEC and EURATOM Councils.

Aims: Promote throughout the Community a harmonious development of economic activities, a continuous and balanced expansion, an increase in stability, an acceleration in the rise of the standard of living and closer relations between its member states, by establishing a customs union over a transitional period of 12 to 15 years (in fact, it was established on July 1, 1968) and progressively approximating the economic policies of member states.

Organization: Decisions in accordance with the Treaty are taken by the Commission and the Council of Ministers, which, following the institutional merger of July, 1967, are common to the three Communities (EEC, ECSC, EURATOM). The Commission and the Council are aided by an Economic and Social Committee composed of representatives of the various categories of economic and social life, in particular representatives of producers, agriculturalists, transport operators, workers, manufacturers, artisans, the liberal professions, and of the general interest.

An internal market without frontiers by 1992 is the main aim of the European Commissions, with all consequences of freedom of movement of capital, common industrial standards, taxation, telecommunications, transportation, agribusiness, banking, customs, insurances and others.

The EEC publ.: *General Report on the Activities of the Community* (annual, from 1958), *Bulletin of the EEC* (monthly), *Bulletin General de Statistique* (monthly), *European Community* (monthly).

J. CALMAN (ed.), *The Rome Treaty, The Common Market Explained*, London, 1967; S.J. WARNECKE (ed.), *The European Community in the 1970s*, New York, 1972; W. HALLSTEIN, *Europe in the Making*, London, 1973; P. COFFEY, *The External Economic Relations of the EEC*, London, 1976; J. PAXTON, *The Developing Common Market*, London, 1976; V. KORAH, *An Introductory Guide to EEC Competition Law and Practice*, Oxford, 1979; C.C. TWITCHETT, *Harmonization in the EEC*, London, 1981; J. PAXTON, *A Dictionary of the European Economic Communities*, London, 1982; H. KAPUR, *China and the EEC*, Dordrecht, 1986; D. LEONARD, *Pocket Guide to the European Community*, London, 1988.

EUROPEAN ECONOMIC CO-OPERATION CONVENTION, 1948.
An intergovernmental agreement initiated by the ▷ Marshall Plan 1947, prepared by the UK and France, signed by all Western European countries which desired to participate in the European Recovery program (with the exception of Spain which was not invited): Austria, Belgium, Denmark, Greece, Iceland, the Irish Republic, Italy, Luxembourg, the Netherlands, Norway, Portugal, Sweden, Switzerland, Turkey and the Anglo-American occupation bizone and the French occupation zone of West-Germany.

Convention for European Economic Co-operation, 16 April, 1948, London, 1948.

EUROPEAN EPISCOPAL COUNCIL.
Italian: Consiglio delle Conferenze Episcopal d'Europa, a Catholic Church institution, f. 1965, Rome.

EUROPEAN ESTABLISHMENT CONVENTION, 1955.
A Western European convention signed on Dec. 13, 1955 in Paris by the member states of the Council of Europe. Came into force Feb. 23, 1965. The text of Six Chapters is as follows:

"The Governments signatory hereto, being Members of the Council of Europe,

Considering that the aim of the Council of Europe is to safeguard and to realise the ideals and principles which are the common heritage of its Members and to facilitate their economic and social progress;

Recognising the special character of the links between the member countries of the Council of Europe as affirmed in conventions and agreements already concluded within the framework of the Council such as the Convention for the Protection of Human Rights and Fundamental Freedoms signed on 4th November, 1950, the Protocol to this Convention signed on 20th March, 1952, the European Convention on Social and Medical Assistance, and the two European Interim Agreements on Social Security signed on 11th December, 1953;

Being convinced that, by the conclusion of a regional convention, the establishment of common rules for the treatment accorded to national of each Member State in the territory of the others may further the achievement of greater unity;

Affirming that the rights and privileges which they grant to each others' nationals are conceded solely by virtue of the close association uniting the member countries of the Council of Europe by means of its Statute;

Noting that the general plan of the Convention, fits into the framework of the organisation of the Council of Europe,

Have agreed as follows:

Chapter I. Entry, Residence and Expulsion.

Art. 1. Each Contracting Party shall facilitate the entry into its territory by nationals of the other Parties for the purpose of temporary visits and shall permit them to travel freely within its territory except when this would be contrary to order public, national security, public health or morality.

Art. 2. Subject to the conditions set out in Article 1 of this Convention, each Contracting Party shall, to the extent permitted by its economic and social conditions, facilitate the prolonged or permanent residence in its territory of nationals of the other Parties.

Art. 3.(1) Nationals of any Contracting Party lawfully residing in the territory of another Party may be expelled only if they endanger national security or offend against public order or morality.

(2) Except where imperative considerations of national security otherwise require, a national of any Contracting Party who has been so lawfully residing for more than two years in the territory of any other Party shall not be expelled without first being allowed to submit reasons against his expulsion and to appeal to, and be represented for the purpose before, a competent authority or a person or persons specially designated by the competent authority.

(3) Nationals of any Contracting Party who have been lawfully residing for more than ten years in the territory of any other Party may only be expelled for reasons of national security or if the other reasons mentioned in paragraph 1 of this Article are of a particularly serious nature.

Chapter II. Exercise of Private Rights.

Art. 4. National of any Contracting Party shall enjoy in the territory of any Party treatment equal to that

enjoyed by nationals of the latter Party in respect of the possession and exercise of private rights, whether personal rights or rights relating to property.
Art. 5. Notwithstanding Article 4 of this Convention, any Contracting Party may, for reasons of national security or defence, reserve the acquisition, possession or use of any categories of property for its own nationals or subject nationals of other Parties to special conditions applicable to aliens in respect of such property.
Art. 6.(1) Apart from cases relating to national security or defence,
(a) Any Contracting Party which has reserved for its nationals or, in the case of aliens including those who are nationals of other Parties, made subject to regulations the acquisition, possession or use of certain categories of property, or has made the acquisition, possession of use of such property conditional upon reciprocity, shall, at the time of the signature of this Convention, transmit a list of these restrictions to the Secretary-General of the Council of Europe indicating which provisions of its municipal law are the basis of such restrictions. The Secretary-General shall forward these lists to the other Signatories;
(b) After this Convention has entered into force in respect of any Contracting Party, that Contracting Party shall not introduce any further restrictions as to the acquisition, possession or use of any categories of property by nationals of the other Parties, unless it finds itself compelled to do so for imperative reasons of an economic or social character or in order to prevent monopolisation of the vital resources of the country. It shall be this event which keeps the Secretary-General fully informed of the measures taken, the relevant provisions of municipal law and the reasons for such measures. The Secretary-General shall communicate this information to the other Parties.
(2) Each Contracting Party shall endeavour to reduce its list of restrictions for the benefit of nationals of the other Parties. It shall notify the Secretary-General of any such changes and he shall communicate them to the other Parties.
Each Party shall also endeavour to grant to nationals of other Parties such exemptions from the general regulations concerning aliens as are provided for in its own legislation.
Chapter III. Judicial and Administrative Guarantees.
Art. 7. Nationals of any Contracting Party shall enjoy in the territory of any other Party, under the same conditions as nationals of the latter Party, full legal and judicial protection of their persons and property and of their rights and interests. In particular, they shall have, in the same manner as the nationals of the latter Party, the right of access to the competent judicial and administrative authorities and the right to obtain the assistance of any person of their choice who is qualified by the laws of the country.
Art. 8.(1) Nationals of any Contracting Party shall be entitled in the territory of any other Party to obtain free legal assistance under the same conditions as nationals of the latter Party.
(2) Indigent nationals of a Contracting Party shall be entitled to have copies of actes de l'etat civil issued to them free of charge in the territory of another Contracting Party in so far as these are so issued to indigent nationals of the latter Contracting Party.
Art. 9.(1) No security or deposit of any kind may be required, by reason of their status as aliens or of lack of domicile or residence in the country, from nationals of any Contracting Party, having their domicile or normal residence in the territory of a Party, who may be plaintiffs or third parties before the Courts of any other Party.
(2) The same rule shall apply to the payment which may be required or plaintiffs of third parties to guarantee legal costs.
(3) Orders to pay the costs and expenses of a trial imposed upon a plaintiff or third party who is exempted from such security, deposit or payment in pursuance either of the preceding paragraphs of this Article or of the law of the country in which the proceedings are taken, shall without charge, upon a request made through the diplomatic channel, be rendered enforceable by the competent authority in the territory of any other Contracting Party.
Chapter IV. Gainful Occupations.
Art. 10. Each Contracting Party shall authorise nationals of the other Parties to engage in its territory in any gainful occupation on an equal footing with its own nationals, unless the said Contracting Party has cogent economic or social reasons for withholding the authorisations. This provision shall apply, but not be limited, to industrial, commercial, financial and agricultural occupations, skilled crafts and the professions, whether the person concerned is self-employed or is in the service of an employer.
Art. 11. Nationals of any Contracting Party who have been allowed by another Party to engage in a gainful occupation for a certain period may not, during that period be subjected to restrictions not provided for at the time the authorisation was granted to them unless such restrictions are equally applicable to nationals of the latter Party in similar circumstances.
Art. 12.(1) Nationals of any Contracting Party lawfully residing in the territory of any other Party shall be authorised, without being made subject to the restrictions referred to in Article 10 of this Convention, to engage in any gainful occupation on an equal footing with nationals of the latter Party, provided they comply with one of the following conditions:
(a) they have been lawfully engaged in a gainful occupation in that territory for an uninterrupted period of five years;
(b) they have lawfully resided in that territory for an uninterrupted period of ten years;
(c) they have been admitted to permanent residence.
Any Contracting Party may, at the time of signature or of deposit of its instrument of ratification of this Convention, declare that it does not accept one or two of the conditions mentioned above.
(2) Such Party may also, in accordance with the same procedure, increase the period laid down in paragraphs 1(a) of this Article to a maximum of ten years, provided that after the first period of five years renewal be conditional upon any change in that occupation. It may also declare that it will not in all cases automatically grant the right to change from a wage-earning occupation to an independent occupation.
Art. 13. Any Contracting Party may reserve for its own nationals the exercise of public functions or of occupations connected with national security or defence, or make the exercise of these occupations by aliens subject to special conditions.
Art. 14.(1) Apart from the functions or occupations mentioned in Article 13 of this Convention.
(a) any Contracting Party which has reserved certain occupations for its own nationals or made the exercise of them by aliens, including nationals of the other Parties, subject to regulations or reciprocity, shall at the time of signature of this Convention transmit a list of these restrictions to the Secretary-General of the Council of Europe, indicating which provisions of its municipal law are the basis of such restrictions. The Secretary-General shall forward these lists to the other Signatories;
(b) after this Convention has entered into force in respect of any Contracting Party, that Party shall not introduce any further restrictions as to the exercise of gainful occupations by the nationals of other Parties unless it finds itself compelled to do so for imperative reasons of an economic or social character. It shall in this event keep the Secretary-General fully informed of the measures taken, the relevant provisions of municipal law and the reasons for such measures. The Secretary-General shall communicate this informations to the other Parties.
(2) Each Contracting Party shall endeavour for the benefit of nationals of the other Parties:
– to reduce the list of occupations which are reserved for its own nationals or the exercise of which by aliens is subject to regulations or reciprocity; it shall notify the Secretary-General of any such changes, and he shall communicate them to the other Parties;
– in so far as its laws permit, to allow individual exemptions from the provisions in force.
Art. 15. The exercise by nationals of one Contracting Party in the territory of another Party of an occupation in respect of which nationals of the latter Party are required to possess professional or technical qualifications or to furnish guarantees shall be made subject to the production of the same guarantees or to the possession of the same qualifications or of others recognised as their equivalent by the competent national authority;
Provided that nationals of the Contracting Parties engaged in the lawful pursuit of their profession in the territory of any Party may be called into the territory of any other Party by one of their colleagues for the purpose of lending assistance in a particular case.
Art. 16. Commercial travellers who are nationals of a Contracting Party and are employed by an undertaking whose principal place of business is situated in the territory of a Contracting Party shall not need any authorisation in order to exercise their occupation in the territory of any other Party, provided that they do not reside therein for more than two months during any half-year.
Art. 17.(1) Nationals of any Contracting Party shall, in the territory of another Party, enjoy treatment no less favourable than nationals of the latter Party in respect of any statutory regulation by a public authority concerning wages and working conditions in general.
(2) The provisions of this Chapter shall not be understood as requiring a Contracting Party to accord in its territory more favourable treatment as regards the exercises of a gainful occupation to the nationals of any other Party than that accorded to its own nationals.
Chapter V. Individual Rights.
Art. 18. No Contracting Party may forbid nationals of another Party who have been lawfully engaged for at least five years in an appropriate occupation in the territory of the former Party from taking part on an equal footing with its own nationals as electors in elections held by bodies or organisations of an economic or professional nature such as Chambers of Commerce or of Agricultural or Trade Associations, subject to the decisions which such bodies or organisations may take in this respect within the limits of their competence.
Art. 19. Nationals of any Contracting Party in the territory of any other Party shall be permitted, without any restrictions other than those applicable to nationals of the latter Party, to act as arbitrators in arbitral proceedings in which the choice of arbitrators is left entirely to the parties concerned.
Art. 20. In so far as access to education is under State control, nationals of school age of any Contracting Party lawfully residing in the territory of any other Party shall be admitted, on an equal footing with the nationals of the latter Party, to institutions for primary and secondary education and technical and vocational training. The application of this provision to the grant of scholarships shall be left to the discretion of individual Parties. School attendance shall be compulsory for nationals of schools age residing in the territory of another Contracting Party if it is compulsory for the nationals of the latter Party.
Chapter VI. Taxation, Compulsory Civilian Services, Expropriation, Nationalisation.
Art. 21.(1) Subject to the provisions concerning double taxation contained in agreements already concluded or to be concluded, nationals of any Contracting Party shall not be liable in the territory of any other Party to duties, charges, taxes or contributions, of any description whatsoever, other, higher or more burdensome than those imposed on nationals of the latter party in similar circumstances; in particular, they shall be entitled to deductions or exemptions from taxes or charges and to all allowances, including allowances for dependents.
(2) A Contracting Party shall not impose on nationals of any other Party any residence charge not required of its own nationals. This provision shall not prevent the imposition in appropriate cases of charges connected with administrative formalities such as the issue of permits and authorisations which aliens are required to have, provided that the amount levied is not more than the expenditure incurred by such formalities.
Art. 22. Nationals of a Contracting Party may in no case be obliged to perform in the territory of another Party any civilian services, whether of a personal nature or relating to property, other or more burdensome than those required of nationals of the latter Party.
Art. 23. Without prejudice to the provisions of Article 1 of the Protocol to the Convention on the Protection of Human Rights and Fundamental Freedoms, nationals of any Contracting Party shall be entitled, in the event of expropriation or nationalisation of their property by any other Party, to be treated at least as favourably as nationals of the latter Party.
Chapter VII. Standing Committee. Chapter VIII. General Provisions. Chapter IX. Field of Application of the Convention. Chapter X. Settlement of Disputes. Chapter XI. Final Provisions."

UNTS, Vol. 529, pp. 142–185.

EUROPEAN FEDERAL UNION, 1930. A French plan of European economic integration. On Sept. 5, 1929 the Prime Minister of France, Aristide Briand, presented to the Tenth Assembly of the UN his plan for an economic European Union. The Assembly accepted that the plan should be discussed one year later. On May 17, 1930, M. Briand addressed to 26 governments of Europe and the USA a Memorandum on the Organization of a Regime of European Federal Union. The text of the Memorandum is as follows:

"(1) In the course of a first meeting held on September 9, 1929, at Geneva, on the request of the Representative of France, the authorized Representatives of the twenty-seven European States, members of the League of Nations, were requested to consider the desirability of an understanding between the Governments concerned with a view to the institution, among European peoples, of a kind of federal bond establishing among them a régime of constant solidarity, and permitting them, in all cases when it might be necessary, to enter into immediate contact for the study, the discussion, and the solution of the problems susceptible of concerning them in common.

Unanimous in recognizing the necessity of an effort in this direction, the Representatives consulted all undertook to recommend to their respective Governments the study of the question which was submitted directly to them by the Representative of France and which the latter had already had occasion, on September 5, to raise before the Tenth Assembly of the League of Nations.

In order better to prove such unanimity which already sanctioned the principle of a European moral union, they believed that they ought to decide, without delay, on the procedure which appeared to them the best adapted to facilitate the study proposed; they entrusted to the Representative of France the task of defining in a memorandum to the Governments concerned the essential points with which their study should deal; of collecting and of registering their opinions; of drawing the conclusions from such broad consultation, and of making it the subject of a report to be submitted to the deliberations of a European Conference which might be held at Geneva at the time of the next Assembly of the League of Nations.

At the moment of discharging the mission which was entrusted to it, the Government of the Republic desires to recall the general preoccupation and the essential reservations which have not ceased to dominate the thought of all the Representatives assembled at Geneva on the 9th of September, last. The proposal taken under consideration by twenty-seven European Governments found its justification in the very definite sentiment of a collective responsibility in the face of the danger which threatens European peace, from the political as well as from the economic and social point of view, because of the lack of coordination which still prevails in the general economy of Europe. The necessity of establishing a permanent régime of conventional solidarity for the rational organization of Europe arises, in fact, from the very conditions of the security and the well-being of the peoples which their geographical situation compels, in this part of the world to participate in de facto solidarity. No one doubts today that the lack of cohesion in the grouping of the material and moral forces of Europe constitutes, practically, the most serious obstacle to the development and deficiency of all political or juridical institutions on which it is the tendency to base the first attempts for a universal organization of peace. This scattering of forces limits, no less seriously, the possibilities of enlargement of the economic market, the attempts to intensify and improve industrial production, and for that very reason all guarantees against labour crises which are sources of political as well as social instability. Now, the danger of such division is still more increased by the circumstance of the extent of the new frontiers (more than 20,000 kilometres of customs barriers) which the treaties of peace had to create in order to do justice, in Europe, to national aspirations. The very action of the League of Nations, the responsibilities of which are the greater because it is universal, might be exposed in Europe to serious obstacles if such breaking up of territory were not offset, as soon as possible, by a bond of solidarity permitting European nations to at last become conscious of European geographical unity and to effect, within the framework of the League, one of those regional understandings which the Covenant formally recommended.

(2) This means that the search for a formula of European cooperation in connection with the League of Nations, far from weakening the authority of this latter must and can tend only to strengthen it, for it is closely connected with its aims.

It is not at all a question of constituting a European group outside of the League of Nations, but on the contrary of harmonizing European interests under the control (contrôle) and in the spirit of the League of Nations by incorporating in its universal system a limited system all the more effective. The realization of a federative organization of Europe would always be attributed to the League of Nations as an element of progress- to its credit from which extra European nations themselves might benefit.

Such a conception can leave no room for doubt, any more than that which gave rise, within still more restricted regional limits, to the collective negotiations of the Locarno Agreements which inaugurated the real policy of European cooperation.

In fact, certain questions concern Europe particularly for which European States may feel the need of an action of their own, more immediate and more direct in the very interest of peace and for which furthermore they enjoy a special competence arising from their ethnical affinities and their community of civilization. The League of Nations itself in the general exercise of its activities, has had more than once to take account of the fact of this geographical unity which Europe presents and which may call for common solutions, the application of which could not be applied to the whole world. Preparing and facilitating the coordination of the strictly European activities of the League of Nations would be precisely one of the tasks of the association contemplated.

Far from constituting a new contentious jurisdiction for the settlement of disputes, the European Association, which could not be called on in such matters to exercise its good offices except in a purely advisory capacity would be without authority to treat thoroughly special problems, the adjustment of which has been entrusted by the Pact or by the Treaties to a special procedure of the League of Nations or to any other procedure expressly defined. But in the very cases in which it might be a question of an essential task reserved to the League of Nations, the federal bond between European States would still play a very useful rôle in preparing a favourable atmosphere for the pacific adjustments of the League or facilitating in practice the execution of its decisions.

Therefore the Representative of France took care from the beginning to avoid any ambiguity when taking the initiative for the first European meeting. He believed that it ought to include only the Representatives of States members of the League of Nations and be held at Geneva itself on the occasion of the first Assembly, that is to say, in the atmosphere and within the framework of the League of Nations.

(3) The European organization contemplated could not oppose any ethnic group, on other continents or in Europe itself, outside of the League of Nations, any more than it could oppose the League of Nations.

The work of European coordination answers to necessities sufficiently immediate and sufficiently vital to seek its end in itself in a labour truly constructive and which it is out of the question to direct or ever to allow to be directed against anyone. Quite on the contrary, this work should be pursued in full friendly confidence and often even in collaboration with all other States or groups of States which are interested with sufficient sincerity in the universal organization of peace to recognize the desirability of a greater homogeneity of Europe, and which understand, furthermore, with sufficient clearness the modern laws of international economics to seek, in the best organization of a simplified Europe, and for that very reason, a Europe removed from the constant menace of conflicts, the condition of stability indispensable to the development of their own economic exchanges.

The policy of European union to which the search for a first bond of solidarity between European Governments ought to tend, implies in fact, a conception absolutely contrary to that which may have determined formerly, in Europe, the formation of customs unions tending to abolish internal customs houses in order to erect on the boundaries of the community a more rigorous barrier, that is to say, to constitute in fact an instrument of struggle against States situated outside of those unions.

Such a conception would be incompatible with the principles of the League of Nations, which is deeply attached to the idea of universality which remains its object and its end even when it pursues or favours partial realizations.

(4) It is important, finally, to place the proposed inquiry under the general conception that in no case and in no degree can the institution of the federal bond sought for between European Governments affect in any manner the sovereign rights of the States, members of such a de facto association.

It is on the basis of absolute sovereignty and of entire political independence that the understanding between European Nations ought to be effected. Furthermore, it would be impossible to imagine the least thought of political domination in an organization deliberately placed under the control (contrôle) of the League of Nations, and two fundamental principles of which are precisely, the sovereignty of States and the equality of rights. And with the rights of sovereignty, it is not the very genius of every nation which can find in its individual cooperation in the collective work the means of affirming itself still more consciously under a régime of federal union fully compatible with the respect of the traditions and characteristics special to each people?

(5) It is under the reservation of these observations and in the light of the general preoccupation recalled at the beginning of this memorandum that the Government of the Republic, in accordance with the procedure decided upon at the first European meeting of September 9, 1929, has the honour to submit to the consideration of the Government concerned a summary of the different points on which they are invited to formulate their opinions.

I. Necessity For a Pact of a General Nature, However Elementary, to Affirm the Principle of the Moral Union of Europe and Solemnly to Sanction the Fact of the Solidarity Established among European States.

In a formula as liberal as possible, but clearly indicating the essential objectives of this association in the service of the collective work of pacific organization of Europe, the signatory Governments would engage to make regular contacts, in periodical or extraordinary meetings, for the examination in common of all questions which might concern primarily the community of European peoples.

(1) The signatory Governments appearing thus committed to the general orientation of a certain common policy, the principle of a European union would henceforth be removed from all discussion and placed above all procedure of daily application: the study of ways and means would be reserved to the European Conference or to the permanent organization which would be called upon to constitute the living bond of solidarity between European nations and thus to incarnate the moral personality of the European union.

(2) This initial and symbolic pact, under which would be pursued in practice the determination, organization, and development of the constituent elements of the European association, should be drawn up in a sufficiently brief form to limit itself to defining the essential rôle of this association. (The possible extension of this pact of principle into the conception of a more definite charter would belong to the future, if it should be favourable to the development of the European union.

(3) The terms of the European pact should, however, take into account the essential reservations indicated in the present memorandum. It would, in fact, be important to define the character of Europe considered as regional entente within the terms of Article 21 of the Covenant of the League of Nations, and exercising its activity within the framework of the League of Nations. (It would particularly be specified that the European Association could not replace the League of Nations in tasks entrusted to that body by the Covenant or by Treaties and that, even in its own domain of the organization of Europe, it should still coordinate its special activity with the general activity of the League of Nations.)

(4) In order better to attest the subordination of the European Association to the League of Nations, the European pact would, at first, be reserved to European States which are members of the League.

II. Necessity of a Mechanism Adapted to Assuring to the European Union the Organs Indispensable to the Accomplishment of its Task.

A. Necessity of a representative and responsible organ, in the form of regularly establishing the 'European Conference', composed of representatives of all the European Governments which are members of the League of Nations and which would be the essential directing organ of the European Union, in liaison with the League of Nations.

The powers of this Conference, the organization of its presidency and of its regular or extraordinary sessions, should be determined at the next meeting of European States, which shall have to deliberate on the conclusions of the report on the inquiry and which, subject to indispensable governmental approvals or parliamentary ratifications, should give assurance that the project of European organization will be perfected.

In order to avoid any predominance in favour of one European State over the others, presidents of the European Conference should be elected annually and function in rotation.

B. Necessity of an executive organ, in the form of a Permanent Political Committee, composed of only a certain number of Members of the European Conference and assuring, in practice, to the European Union its organization for study at the same time as its instrument of action.

The composition and powers of the European Committee, the manner of designation of its members, the organization of its presidency and of its regular or extraordinary sessions, should be determined at the next meeting of European States. As the activity of this Committee, like that of the Conference, is to be exercised within the framework of the League of Nations, its meetings should be held at Geneva itself, where its regular sessions might coincide with those of the Council of the League of Nations.

(1) With a view to protecting the European Committee from any personal predominance, its presidents should function in rotation.

(2) As the Committee can include only a restricted number of representatives of European States which are members of the League of Nations, it should keep the power of inviting the representatives of other European Governments at any time, whether or not they are members of the League of Nations, which might be particularly interested in the study of a question. The power would, further, be formally reserved to it to invite, whenever it should consider it necessary or opportune, a representative of a non-European Power, whether or not a member of the League of Nations, to attend, or even to take part (in an advisory capacity or with the right to vote) in deliberations bearing on a question in which it might be interested.

(3) One of the first tasks of the Committee might include: on the one hand, the general examination of any procedure for the realization and application of the project contemplated, in accordance with essential data from consultation of the Governments and the search, for this purpose, for ways and means tending technically to bring out the constituent elements of the future Federal European Union; on the other, the general itemization of the programme of European cooperation, including:

(e) the study of political, economic, social and other questions of particular interest to the European community and not yet dealt with by the League of Nations;

(b) special action to be taken to stimulate the execution of general decisions of the League of Nations by the European Governments.

(4) The committee, after adopting the general programme of European cooperation, might confide the study of certain chapters to special technical committees, while assuring itself the conditions necessary for always maintaining the work of the experts under the supervision and immediate impetus of the political element, the direct cessation of the Governments, which are jointly responsible for the prosecution of their international enterprise and which alone can assure the success thereof in the political plane on which its higher justification lies. (To this end, the presidency of the technical Committees might be entrusted, in each particular case, to a European statesman selected either within or without the European Political Committee.)

C. Necessity of a secretariat service, however, restricted at the beginning to assure the administrative execution of the instructions of the President of the Conference or of the European Committee, communications between Governments signatory to the European Pact, convocations of the Conference or of the Committee, preparation of their discussions, recording and notification of their resolutions, etc,

(1) In the beginning, the secretariat might be entrusted to the Government charged, in rotation, with the presidency of the European Committee.

(2) When the necessity of a permanent Secretariat is recognized the seat of this Secretariat should be the same as that of the meetings of the Conference and of the Committee, that is, Geneva.

(3) Organization of the secretariat service should always be examined while taking into account that at least partial and temporary utilization of special services of the Secretariat of the League of Nations.

III. Necessity of Deciding in Advance the Essential, Directives Which Must Determine the General Conceptions of the European Committee and Guide It in Its Studies for the Elaboration of the Programme of European Organization. (This third point could be reserved for the consideration of the next European meeting.)

A. General subordination of the Economic Problem to the Political.

All possibility of progress toward economic union being strictly determined by the question of security, and this question being intimately bound up with that of the realizable progress toward political union, it is on the political plane that constructive effort looking to giving Europe its organic structure should first of all be made. It is also on this plane that the economic policy of Europe should afterwards be drawn up, in its broad outlines, as well as the special customs policy of each European State.

The contrary order would not only be useless, it would appear to the weaker nations to be likely to expose them, without guarantees or compensation, to the risks of political domination which might result from an industrial domination of the more strongly organized States.

It is therefore logical and normal that the justification of the economic sacrifices to be made to the whole should be found only in the development of a political situation warranting confidence between peoples and true pacification of minds. And even after the actual accomplishment of such a condition, assured by the establishment of a régime of constant and close peaceful association in peace between the peoples of Europe, there would still be needed, on the political plane, the intervention of a higher feeling of international necessities to impose on the Members of the European community, in favour of the collectivity, the sincere conception and effective prosecution of a truly liberal tariff policy.

B. Conception of European political cooperation as one which ought to tend toward this essential end: a federation built not upon the idea of unity but of union; that is to say, sufficiently flexible to respect the independence and national sovereignty of each of the States, while assuring them all the benefit of collective solidarity for the settlement of political questions involving the fate of the European community or that of one of its Members. (Such a conception might imply, as a consequence, the general development for Europe of a system of arbitration and security, and the progressive extension to the whole European community of the policy of international guarantees inaugurated at Locarno, until such time as special agreements or series of agreements are merged into a more general system.)

C. Conception of the economic organization of Europe as one which ought to tend to this essential end: a rapprochement of the European economic systems effected under the political responsibility of the Governments working in unison.

With this purpose in mind, the Governments might definitively associate themselves in an act of a general nature and of principle which would constitute a simple pact of economic solidarity, the purpose which they intend to set as the ideal end to their tariff policy (establishment of a common market to raise to the maximum the level of human well-being over all the territories of the European community). With the help of such a general orientation, immediate efforts could be undertaken practically for the rational organization of European production and exchanges, by means of the progressive liberation and the methodical simplification of the circulation of goods, capital, and persons, with the single reservation of the needs of national defence in each State. The very principle of this tariff policy having been once sactioned, and definitively sanctioned, on the plane of the general policy of the Governments, the study of the ways and means of its realization could be referred as a whole to the technical examination of a Committee of experts, under the conditions contemplated in title II. B, observation 4.

IV. Advisability of Reserving for Either the Next European Conference or the Future European Committee the Study of All Questions of Application, including the following:

A. Determination in the field of European cooperation, particularly in the following spheres:

(1) General Economy. The effective realization, in Europe, of the Programme drawn up by the last economic conference of the League of Nations; the control of the policy of industrial unions and cartels among various countries; examination and preparation of all future possibilities regarding the progressive lowering of tariffs, etc.

(2) Economic Equipment. Realization of coordination between great public works executed by European States (routes for heavy automobile traffic, canals, etc.).

(3) Communications and Transit. By land, water, and air: Regulation and improvement of inter-European traffic; coordination of the labours of the European waterways commissions; agreements between railways; European régime of posts, telegraphs and telephones; radio-broadcasting rules, etc.

(4) Finances. Encouragement of credit intended for the development of the economically less developed regions of Europe; European market; monetary questions, etc.

(5) Labour. Settlement of certain labour questions peculiar to Europe, such as labour in inland navigation and in glass trades; questions having a continental or regional character, such as the regulation of the social consequences of inter-European emigration (application by one country to another of laws respecting labour accidents, social insurance, workers' pensions, etc.).

(6) Hygiene. General extension of certain methods of hygiene subjects essayed by the health organization of the League of Nations (in particular, reclamation of agricultural regions; application of insurance against illness; regional schools of hygiene; European epidemiology, exchange of information and officials between national health services; scientific and administrative cooperation in the struggle against great social scourges, against occupational diseases and infant mortality, etc.).

(7) Intellectual Cooperation. Cooperation by universities and academies; literary and artistic relations; centralization of scientific research; improvement of the press system in relations between agencies and in transportation of newspapers, etc.

(8) Interparliamentary Relations. Utilization of the organization and labours of the 'Interparliamentary Union' for the development of contacts and exchanges of views between parliamentary circles of the various European countries (in order to prepare the political ground for the accomplishments of the European Union which would necessitate parliamentary approval and, in a general way, to improve the international atmosphere in Europe for the mutual understanding of the interests and sentiments of the peoples).

(9) Administration. Formation of European sections in certain universal international bureaus.

B. Determination of methods of European cooperation in questions which might come before the European Conference or the European Committee.

It might be advisable, according to cases:

either to set up organizations for coordination and study where none exist (for example, for European equipment or for the various European waterways commissions),

or to support the efforts of the League of Nations in questions which are already the subject of methodical studies (especially in preparing, by exchanges of views and friendly negotiations, for the entrance into effect, in the relations of the States of Europe, of conventions drawn up or recommendations formulated by the League of Nations).

or, finally, to stimulate conferences, European or general, of the League of Nations on questions which may be properly dealth with by it, but which have not yet been so dealt with. (Non-European States would be invited to be represented by observers at any European conference and any convention which would be drawn up by a conference convoked at the request of the States of Europe, in so far as its purpose was not strictly continental, would be open to adherence by non-European States.)

C. Determination of all methods of cooperation between the European Union and the countries located outside that union. In requesting the opinion of the twenty-six European Governments by which it was commissioned to make the enquire on the four points set forth above, the Government of the Republic wishes to make the general observation that, for purely practical reasons, it has believed that it should adhere to as elementary a conception as possible of the subject of consultation; not that it is its wish to limit the possibilities of future development of a federal organization of Europe, but because, in the present state of the European world and for the sake of increasing the chances of unanimous consent to the first concrete proposal capable of conciliating all the interests and all the special situations involved, it is of great importance to keep to the initial data of several very simple views. Likewise, the best method is to proceed from the simpler to the more complex, and to trust to time in the task of assuring, with life, by a constant evolution and by a kind of continuous creation, the full expansion of the natural resources which the European Union might contain.

It was a conception of that character which already had guided the Representative of France, when, before the first European meeting convened at Geneva, he limited himself to suggesting, as a starting point, the seeking of a simple federal bond to be set up between the European Governments which were members of the League of Nations to assure their cooperation in practice.

As a matter of fact, it is not a question of setting up completely an ideal structure answering in the abstract all the logical needs of a vast plan of a European federal mechanism but, on the contrary, by avoiding what would be premature, of confining one's self practically to the actual realization of a first means of contact and of constant solidarity between European Governments, for the settlement in common of all problems bearing on the organization of European peace and the rational organization of the vital forces of Europe.

The Government of the Republic would appreciate receiving the reply of the Governments consulted, before July 15, with all the spontaneous observations or suggestions with which they may feel their communications should be accompanied. It expresses the firm hope that such replies, inspired by the deep concern to satisfy the expectation of the peoples and the aspirations of the European conscience, will supply the elements of understanding and conciliation, making possible, with the first embryonic federal organization, the establishment of a lasting framework of this European cooperation, the program of which can be decided on by the next meeting at Geneva.

The time has never been more propitious or more pressing for the inauguration of a constructive work in Europe. The settlement of the main problems, material and moral, incident to the late war, will soon have liberated New Europe from a burden which bore most heavily upon its psychology, as well as on its economic system. It appears henceforward to be ready for a positive effort and one which will fit in with the new order. It is a decisive hour, when watchful Europe may determine her own fate.

Unite to live and prosper: such is the stringent necessity which will henceforth confront the nations of Europe. It seems that the feeling of the peoples has already been made clear on this subject. It behoves the Governments to assume their responsibilities today, under penalty of abandoning to the risk of individual initiatives and disorderly undertakings the grouping of material and moral forces, the collective control of which it is incumbent on them to keep, to the benefit of the European community as well as of humanity."

Memorandum on the Organization of a Federal Régime of European Federal Union, and Replies of Twenty Six Governments of Europe to M. Briand, Memorandum of May 17, 1930, in: *International Conciliation*, Special Bulletin, June 1930, pp. 327–353 and No. 265, December, 1930, pp. 653–769.

EUROPEAN FOUNDATION. Fondation européenne, f. 1982 by the Foreign Ministers of the European Community, Paris.

EUROPEAN FREE TRADE ASSOCIATION. ▷ EFTA.

EUROPEAN HEALTH PROGRAM, 1988. On the occasion of the Meeting of the Social and Health Affairs Committee of the Parliamentary Assembly of the Council of Europe at the WHO Regional Office for Europe in Copenhagen, on May 26 and 27, 1988 a joint declaration was issued. The highlights:

Health and quality of life are intimately linked together. The health of individuals, groups and societies in Europe is increasingly linked to modern lifestyles and to the physical, social, cultural and economic characteristics of the environment in which people live, work and play.

It is necessary for European countries to recognize this much more explicitly in their national policies, and to make health and quality of life an issue not only in the health sector but in other sectors of society as well.

The health services in Europe must continue to benefit from new scientific developments, but more attention needs to be paid to the appropriate use of those new technologies and to the assurance of a human approach to care and to better provision of health services at the local level throughout Europe. The Council of Europe and the World Health Organization share the same preoccupations and concern for improving the health of the people of Europe.

WHO Press, May, 1988.

EUROPEAN HYMN. By a decision of the Strasbourg European Parliament, July 9, 1971, the closing chorus of L. van Beethoven's 9th Symphony has been adopted as the EEC hymn.

EUROPEAN INTEGRATION STUDIES AND RESEARCH INSTITUTES. Third level (for postgraduate students), scientific institutions, specialized in Western European integration. The first institute – Collège d'Europe – was opened in Brugge, Belgium, 1949.

Postgraduate Degrees in European Integration, Enseignement de 3-ème cycle sur l'intégration, Bruxelles, 1976.

EUROPEAN INVESTMENT BANK. An intergovernmental finance institution of the European Economic Community, f. 1957 in Luxembourg. Publ. *Annual Report*.

J.K. WALENSLEY, "The European Investment Bank", in: *Banker's Magazine*, London, Dec., 1977.

EUROPEAN JOURNALISTS' CLUB. A Club est. 1977 in Ohrid (Yugoslavia) by journalists dealing with the problems of peace and co-operation in Europe; seat of the Secretary-General is in Paris.

EUROPEAN LEAGUE. A project to establish organized co-operation of European states, debated in 1804–05 by Russia and Great Britain. Prince Adam Czartoryski (1770–1861), a Polish statesman, was the author of the European League project. Prince Czartoryski believed that the new system of European relations "will inevitably provide for Poland's gradual reconstruction."

M. HANDELSMAN, *Adam Czartoryski*, 3 Vols., Warsaw, 1948–50.

EUROPEAN MONETARY AGREEMENT, EMA, 1955–72. A Western European agreement, concluded Aug. 5, 1955 by the OECD member states. Expired Dec. 31, 1972. Established the European Monetary Agreement Accounting Unit equal to one American dollar and on Dec. 27, 1958 assumed the functions of the ▷ European Clearing Union. The EMA member states cleared all of their transactions through the Bank for International Settlements. The main tasks of the Treaty were: to develop full, comprehensive trade and monetary exchangeability through intergovernmental monetary and central bank co-operation; to establish the basic regulations for currency transactions, combat bilateralism in international payments, assist member states in overcoming temporary payment difficulties. For this last purpose, EMA in the period 1958–72 had at its disposal the European Fund with a capital of 607 million dollars. OECD publishes annual reports of EMA functions. The institution of the new currency guarantees system ratified Oct. 21, 1972 by the OECD states and is called the ▷ European Monetary Co-operation Fund.

R. TRIFFIN, "Monetary Reconstruction in Europe", in: *International Conciliation*, No. 482, June 1952, pp. 263–308; G.L. REES, *Britain and Post-War European Payments Systems*, Cardiff, 1962; B. TEW, *International Monetary Co-operation 1945–70*, London, 1970.

EUROPEAN MONETARY CO-OPERATION FUND, EMCOF. A fund of the European Community for short- and medium-term balance of payment support, est. 1973. Since 1979, under the ▷ European Monetary System, administered also the pooling of the Community's gold and dollar reserves, as a quasi-European Monetary Fund.

J. WALMSLEY, *A Dictionary of International Finance*, London, 1979; J. PAXTON, *A Dictionary of the European Communities*, London, 1982; *European Communities Yearbook 1977*, p. 72.

EUROPEAN MONETARY FUND, EMF. One of the main elements of the ▷ European Monetary System, EMS, managing the common currency reserves of the member countries of the EEC. According to the statutes these countries assign 20% of their reserves of gold and dollars to the Fund and in return receive shares in ▷ European Currency Units, ECU, which fills the role of an element of reserve currencies in certain countries and a means of payment between central banks.

EUROPEAN MONETARY SYSTEM, EMS. The system of stabilizing the currencies of the member states of EEC; in effect from 1979. The basis of the EMS system is the principle that any revaluation or devaluation of whatever currency of the member states of EEC can only take place with the agreement of all EEC members. Thus the currencies of the EEC states became dependent on each other, but independent from fluctuations of the dollar. Control over the exchange rates of the currencies of member states is based on the ▷ European Currency Unit, ECU. The main organ of EMS is the ▷ European Monetary Fund, EMF.

IMF Survey, Mar. 19, 1979; J. WALMSLEY, *A Dictionary of International Finance*, London, 1979; M.T. SUMNER, G. ZIS, *European Monetary Union. Progress and Perspectives*, London, 1982; J.C. KOCUNE, *Le système monétaire européen*, Luxembourg, 1983.

EUROPEAN MOVEMENT. A non-governmental international association, f. 1948 in Paris with the aim of promoting Western European integration. The International Secretariat of the European Movement has its headquarters in Brussels. Reg. with the UIA.

European Social Charter, 1961

Yearbook of International Organizations; The Europa Yearbook 1988. A World Survey, Vol. I, London, 1988.

EUROPEAN NATO. An international term for the NATO group without USA and Canada.

D. ROBERTSON, *Guide to Modern Defense and Strategy*, Detroit, 1988.

EUROPEAN NATURAL HABITATS ▷ European Wildlife and Natural Habitats Convention on the Conservation of.

EUROPEAN ORGANIZATION FOR THE SAFETY OF AIR NAVIGATION. ▷ EUROCONTROL.

EUROPEAN PARLIAMENT. An organ of the European Economic Community, EEC, f. Mar. 19, 1958 to replace the Common Assembly of the European Coal and Steel Community as the representative European Parliamentary Assembly. In the years 1958–79 members were elected by Parliaments of EEC countries, it initially consisted of 142 deputies from 6 countries, later expanded to include 198 deputies from 9 states. Sessions are held twice a year. The Parliament has 13 permanent committees. Headquarters: Centre européen, Plateau de Kirchberg, Luxembourg. Publ.: *Annuaire de Parliament européenne* and *Cahier trimestriel de documentation*. In keeping with art. 138 of the Rome Treaty, elections to the European Parliament are held by direct and universal ballot. Elected June 7, 1979 from Great Britain, Holland and Ireland and on June 10 from other member countries were the following number of deputies: Belgium – 24, Denmark – 16, France – 81, Holland – 25, Ireland – 15, Luxembourg – 6, FRG – 81, Great Britain – 81, Italy – 81, i.e. 410 mandates of which 142 were Socialists and Social Democrats, 106 Christian Democrats, 63 Conservatives, 44 Communists, 40 Liberals and 45 others.
The second election took place in June 1984, in Greece (24 deputies), for 434 mandates of which 132 were won by the Socialists, 109 Christian Democrats, 46 Conservatives, 42 Communists, 32 Liberals, 11 "Greens" and 62 others.
On Jan. 1, 1986 60 Spanish and 24 Portuguese delegates first attended the session of the E.P. The distribution of seats has changed as follows: Socialist Group – 172, European People's Party (Christian Democrats) – 118, European Democratic Group (Conservatives) – 63, Communists and Allies Group – 46, Liberal and Democratic – 34, Rainbow Group – 20, Group of the European Right – 16, Non-attached – 7. A Conference on Parliamentary Democracy was held on Sept. 28–30, 1987 in Strasbourg.

W. PENN, *Plan for Peace of Europe, an essay towards the present and future peace of Europe by the establishment of a European diet, parliament, or estates*, Boston, 1896; H. MANZANARES, *Le Parlament Européen*, Paris, 1964; M. FORSYTH, *The Parliament of the European Communities*, London, 1964; CH. M. DE MOLINES, *L'Europe de Strasbourg*, Paris, 1972; C. HOLLIS, *Parliament and its Sovereignty*, 1973; B. COOKS, *The European Parliament, Structure, Procedure and Practice*, London, 1973; J.L. BURBAN, *Le parlement européen et son élection*, Bruxelles, 1979; D. WOOD, A. WOOD (eds), *The Times Guide to the European Parliament*, London, 1980. J. FITZMAURICE, *European Parliament*, London, 1982; J. LODGE ed. *Direct Elections to the European Parliament, 1984*, London 1986; KEESING'S *Record of World Events*, 1986, No 3; KEESING'S *Contemporary Archive*, 1986.

EUROPEAN PATENT APPLICATIONS CONVENTION, 1973. ▷ Patent European Office.

EUROPEAN PAYMENTS UNION. ▷ European Monetary Agreement.

EUROPEAN POLITICAL COMMUNITY. The political organization also called the European Political Union of Belgium, France, the FRG, Holland, Italy and Luxembourg created by the governments of Western Europe during the period 1952–54. The conferences were held in Paris Sept. 10, 1952 and May 12, 1953, in Baden-Baden Aug. 7–8, 1953, and in The Hague Sept. 22–Oct. 9, 1953 and Nov. 26–28, 1953; it was created as an attempt to aid in the process of Western European integration. The last conference scheduled for Apr. 30, 1954 in Brussels, which was supposed to ratify the Statute of the Community, was not held, since governments were awaiting the ratification of the treaty on the European Defence Community, intended as a counterpart to the European Political Community. In view of the rejection by the French Parliament on the motion of its government to ratify the treaty, the European Political Community plan was automatically voided. However, the concert continued to be developed in the 1960s by the USA and FRG against the opposition of France. In Feb., 1961 the EEC Commission under the chairmanship of the Frenchman C. Fouchet formulated a new plan called European Political Union (cryptonym Fouchet 1). In Jan., 1962 France announced its de Gaulle plan, according to which the main institution was supposed to be a Council of Heads of State or Government, meeting quarterly and making decisions unanimously; its organ was to be a European Political Commission with headquarters in Paris. The FRG, supported by Benelux and Italy, opposed this plan, favoring an institution which would decide by majority vote, not unanimously. After nearly two years of negotiations, the Fouchet Commission was dissolved without reaching any compromise. In Jan., 1963 France signed a bilateral treaty with the FRG on co-operation based on the principles of the de Gaulle plan. The issue was brought up again in Dec., 1969 by The Hague Conference of EEC Heads of State, whose final bulletin in point 4 stated that the participants of the conference "had decided to instruct the ministers of foreign affairs to study the manner which would best ensure the attainment of progress in the area of political unification ...". As a result of this resolution, the so-called Dawignon Commission was formed composed of the representatives of ministers of foreign affairs with the task of holding semi-annual consultations in the field of foreign policy. The first meeting was held in Nov., 1970 in Munich, the Second – in May, 1971 in Paris; the third – in Nov., 1971 in Rome, where in view of the new situation created by Great Britain's joining the EEC (Oct. 28, 1971), it was regarded as necessary to redefine the 1972 foreign policy of the member states toward the USA, Warsaw Pact Europe, the Chinese People's Republic and the Third World. The summit meeting in Oct., 1972 of the expanded EEC again resulted in the clashing of various plans in the preliminary talks and in the West European press, further complicated by the continuing monetary and energy crisis. The fundamental point of dispute within the states of Western Europe was whether Western Europe should be a ▷ Europe of Fatherlands or a United States of Europe.

A.H. ROBERTSON, "The European Political Community", in: *The British Yearbook of International Law*, No. 29, 1952; *Chronique de Politique Étrangère*, No. 3, 1953; W. GENZER, "Die Satzung der Europäischen Gemeinschaft", in: *Europa Archiv*. No. 9, 1953; B. CIALDEO, "La Communauté Politique Européenne. Hier et Demain", in: *Annuaire Européen*, 1955; W.

HALLSTEIN, *United Europe. Challenge and Opportunity*, Cambridge, 1962.

EUROPEAN RECOVERY PROGRAM. The official name of the ▷ Marshall Plan, 1947, started with a Paris Conference of 15 European countries: Austria, Belgium, Denmark, France, Great Britain, Greece, Ireland, Italy, Luxembourg, the Netherlands, Norway, Portugal, Sweden, Switzerland, and Turkey, representing with Western Germany a total population of 270 million.

"The European Recovery Program", in: *International Conciliation*, No. 436, Dec. 1947, pp. 785–880.

EUROPEAN REFUGEES AGREEMENTS. Since Dec. 1, 1980 European Agreement on Transfer of Responsibility for Refugees, signed by Belgium, the FRG, Greece, and Luxembourg in in force. Contracting States: Denmark, Italy, Netherlands, Norway, Portugal, Spain, Sweden, Switzerland and UK.

Council of Europe, *Information Sheet No 21*, Strasbourg, 1988.

EUROPEAN REGIONAL DEVELOPMENT FUND. A Fund est. 1975 to finance investments in areas of the European Community where per capita income is below the Community average.

European Communities Yearbook 1977, p. 73.

EUROPEAN SCHOOLS. The official name of schools for the children of the officials of the European Communities, with six language sections: Danish, Dutch, English, French, German and Italian. The School's Board of Governors consists of the Ministers of Education of the nine member countries. A Statute of the European schools was signed in Luxembourg, Apr. 12, 1957. Came into force on Feb. 22, 1960.

UNTS, Vol. 443, p. 224, Vol. 752, pp. 267–290.

EUROPEAN SCIENCE FOUNDATION. An intergovernmental institution est. 1973, Brussels by the governments of Austria, Belgium, Denmark, France, FRG, Greece, Ireland, Italy, the Netherlands, Norway, Portugal, Spain, Sweden, Switzerland, the UK and Yugoslavia, to promote collaboration among national research programs.

EUROPEAN SENTENCED PERSONS CONVENTION ▷ Prisoners.

EUROPEAN SOCIAL CHARTER, 1961. A Charter, with Annex, signed on Oct. 18, 1961, in Turin, by the member states of the Council of Europe; came into force on Feb. 26, 1965. The text of Part I is as follows:

"The Governments signatory hereto, being Members of the Council of Europe,
Considering that the aim of the Council of Europe is the achievement of greater unity between its Members for the purpose of safeguarding and realising the ideals and principles which are their common heritage and of facilitating their economic and social progress, in particular by the maintenance and further realisation of human rights and fundamental freedoms;
Considering that in the European Convention for the Protection of Human Rights and Fundamental Freedoms signed at Rome on 4th November 1950, and the Protocol thereto signed at Paris on 20th March 1952, the member States of the Council of Europe agreed to secure to their populations the civil and political rights and freedoms therein specified;
Considering that the enjoyment of social rights should be secured without discrimination on grounds of race, colour, sex, religion, political opinion, national extraction or social origin;
Being resolved to make every effort in common to improve the standard of living and to promote the

social well-being of both their urban and rural populations by means of appropriate institutions and action. Here agreed as follows:

PART I. The Contracting Parties accept as the aim of their policy, to be pursued by all appropriate means, both national and international in character, the attainment of conditions in which the following rights and principles may effectively realised;

(1) Everyone shall have the opportunity to earn his living in an occupation freely entered upon.

(2) All workers have the right to just conditions of work.

(3) All workers have the right to safe and healthy working conditions.

(4) All workers have the right to a fair remuneration sufficient for a decent standard of living for themselves and their families.

(5) All workers and employers have the right to freedom of association in national or international organisations for the protection of their economic and social interests.

(6) All workers and employers have the right to bargain collectively.

(7) Children and young persons have the right to a special protection against the physical and moral hazards to which they are exposed.

(8) Employed women, in case of maternity, and other employed women as appropriate, have the right to a special protection in their work.

(9) Everyone has the right to appropriate facilities for vocational guidance with a view to helping him choose an occupation suited to his personal aptitude and interests.

(10) Everyone has the right to appropriate facilities for vocational training.

(11) Everyone has the right to benefit from any measures enabling him to enjoy the highest possible standard of health attainable.

(12) All-workers and their dependents have the right to social security.

(13) Anyone without adequate resources has the right to social and medical assistance.

(14) Everyone has the right to benefit from social welfare services.

(15) Disabled persons have the right to vocational training, rehabilitation and resettlement, whatever the origin and nature of their disability.

(16) The family as a fundamental unit of society has the right to appropriate social, legal and economic protection to ensure its full development.

(17) Mothers and children, irrespective of marital status and family relations, have the right to appropriate social and economic protection.

(18) The nationals of any one of the Contracting Parties have the right to engage in any gainful occupation in the territory of any one of the others on a footing of equality with the nationals of the latter, subject to restrictions based on cogent economic or social reasons.

(19) Migrant workers who are nationals of a Contracting Party and their families have the right to protection and assistance in the territory of any other Contracting Party."

PART II defined the Rights mentioned in Part I.

PART III defined General and Final Provisions (art. 20–38).

On Nov. 19, 1986 a ceremony commemorating the 25th anniversary of the Charter was held in the European Parliamentary Assembly in Strasbourg; a Colloquy marking the anniversary took place in Granada, Spain on Oct. 26–27, 1987.

UNTS, Vol. 529, pp. 90–132; Council of Europe. *Information Sheet No 21*, Strasbourg, 1988.

EUROPEAN SOCIAL FUND. An institution of the ▷ European Communities, est. 1960 by art. 124 of the Rome Treaty, to improve opportunities for employment within the EEC by covering 50% of the expenses incurred by a Member State in retraining or resettling workers or in granting benefits to workers whose employment was temporarily interrupted. The Fund was reorganised in 1972. In 1982 the commitments by the Fund were over 1,5 billion ▷ ECUs, of which 29,7% went to Italy, 29% to the UK, 17,4% to France and 9,5% to Ireland. New

regulations reforming the Fund came into force in 1984 and 1985, concentrating on job promotion for young people.

The Europa Year Book 1984. A World Survey, Vol. I, p. 144, London, 1984; KEESING's *Contemporary Archive*, October, 1985.

EUROPEAN SOCIETY OF CULTURE, SEC. Societe européenne de culture, f. 1950, Venice, Italy. Consultative status with UNESCO and ECOSOC. Publ.: *Comprendre*. Reg. with the UIA.

Yearbook of International Organizations.

EUROPEAN SPACE AGENCY. An intergovernmental agency est. May 31, 1975 in Paris by Belgium, Denmark, France, the FRG, Great Britain, Italy, the Netherlands, Spain, Sweden and Switzerland in place of the dissolved European Space Research Organization, ESRO; headquarters, Paris.

The European participation in the US space station program was decided on Jan. 25, 1985 by an agreement on the conditions of European involvement in the Columbus Venture.

Yearbook of International Organizations. KEESING's *Record of World Events*, No. 9, 1988.

EUROPEAN TRAFFIC ARTERIES. Subject of the Declaration on the Construction of Main International Traffic Arteries, signed in Geneva (with annexes, Sept. 16, 1950).

UNTS, Vol. 92, pp. 91–123.

EUROPEAN UNIT OF ACCOUNT, EUA. A financial unit established in the Common Market by the European Monetary Agreement on Aug. 5, 1955 in the relation of one EUA = one American dollar. The relation to the American dollar was changed in June 1974 for a value resulting from a basket of currencies of EEC member States. The EUA value in whatever currency is equal to the sum of the equivalents in that currency, using daily market exchange rates – of the amount in the following table:

FRG mark	0.828	27.3%
French franc	1.15	19.5%
Pound sterling	0.0885	17.5%
Italian lira	109	14.0%
Dutch guilder	0.286	9.0%
Belgian franc	3.66	7.9%
Danish crown	0.217	3.0%
Irish pound	0.00759	1.5%
Luxembourg franc	0.14	0.3%

Its value varies according to exchange rate fluctuations and is calculated each day on the basis of the exchange rates of the relevant currencies and reflects "the monetary identity of the European Community." Originally, the EUA was defined as 0.88867 of a gram of gold, the equivalent of one US$ until 1970. In 1974 – the value of one Unit of Account was fixed at US $1.20635 equal to the ▷ SDR, but from 1975 the European Community decided to introduce an EUA defined in terms of a "basket." Replaced 1979 by the ▷ European Currency Unit, ECU.

The EUA, Brussels, 1967; *Euromoney*, London, 1976; *European Communities Yearbook 1977.*

EUROPEAN UNIVERSITY. The West European college opened Apr. 19, 1972 in Florence on the basis on a convention of the EEC member states. The city of Florence offered the property Villa Tolomei for the use of the University. Official name: L'Instituto Universitario Europeo. Contains four departments: history and civilization, economics, law, and political and social sciences. Accepted for

two year doctoral studies are citizens of EEC states who have completed university studies.

The World of Learning, London, 1980.

EUROPEAN UN RESOLUTION, 1965. An appeal to European states, adopted by the UN General Assembly, Res. 2129/XX, Dec. 21, 1965. The text is as follows:

"The General Assembly,

Bearing in mind the provisions of the Charter of the United Nations in which Member States have affirmed their resolve to live together in peace with one another as good neighbours and to develop friendly relations among nations in order to strengthen peace.

Recalling its resolutions 1236 (XII) of Dec. 14, 1957 and 1301 (XIII) of Dec. 10, 1958 calling upon States to make every effort to strengthen international peace and to develop friendly and co-operative relations, and to take effective steps towards the implementation of principles of peaceful and neighbourly relations,

Aware of the responsibility which today devolves upon all countries, great and small, to establish an atmosphere of cooperation and security throughout the world, and of the role that the existence and development of bilateral good neighbourly relations and understanding among States can play in achieving that goal,

Noting with satisfaction the increasing concern for the development of reciprocal cooperative relations in many fields among European States having different social and political systems, based on the principles of equal rights, respect and mutual interests,

Convinced that any improvement in relations at the European level, being in the interest of the States of that part of the world, has at the same time a positive effect on international relations as a whole and thus contributes to the creation of an atmosphere conducive to peace and international security and to the settlement of the major problems which have not yet been solved,

(1) Welcomes the growing interest in the development of good neighbourly relations and co-operation among European States having different social and political systems, in the political, economic, technical, scientific, cultural and other fields;

(2) Emphasizes the importance of maintaining and increasing contacts between those States for the purpose of developing peaceful co-operation among the peoples of the European continent, with a view to strengthening peace and security in Europe by all possible means;

(3) Requests the Governments of the European states to intensify their efforts to improve reciprocal relations, with a view to creating an atmosphere of confidence which will be conducive to an effective consideration of the problems which are still hampering the relaxation of tension in Europe and throughout the world;

(4) Decides to continue to give its attention to measures and actions for promoting good neighbourly relations and co-operation in Europe."

UN Yearbook 1965.

EUROPEAN WARS. The main armed conflicts in Europe in the 18th–20th centuries in alphabetical order of the states participating:

Austrian war of succession, 1740–48;
Austrian–Polish war, 1809;
Austrian–Turkish wars, 18th and 19th centuries;
Balkan wars, 1912–13;
Bavarian war of succession ("Kartoffelkrieg"), 1778–79;
Bulgarian–Serbian wars, 19th and 20th centuries;
Crimean war, 1853–56;
Danish–Swedish wars, 1700, 1709–20, 1812–14;
English–Danish war, 1807–14;
English–Dutch wars, 18th and 19th centuries;
English–French wars, 18th and 19th centuries;
English–German wars, 18th and 19th centuries;
English–Spanish wars, 18th and 19th centuries;
English war with the coalition, 1778–83;
English wars during World Wars I and II;
French revolutionary wars, 1792–1802;
French–Spanish wars, 1793–95 and 1803–15;
French–Dutch wars, 1793–95, 1812–15 and 1831–32;
French–German wars, 1805–09, 1813–15, 1870–71;
French wars during World Wars I and II;
German–Yugoslavian war, 1941–45;

German–Belgian wars 1914–1918, 1940–1945;
German–Danish wars, 1848–50 and 1864; 1940–1945;
German–French wars 1914–1918, 1939–1945;
German–Greece war 1941–1945;
German–Norwegian war 1940–1945;
German–Polish war, 1939–45;
German–Soviet war, 1941–45;
German–Russian war, 1914–18;
German wars during World Wars I and II;
Greek–Bulgarian war, 1913;
Greek–Serbian war, 1913;
Greek–Turkish wars, 1821–29, 1897, 1912–13, 1919–22;
Italian–Albanian war 1939–1945;
Italian–Austrian war 1915–1918;
Italian–French war 1940–1944;
Italian Wars during World Wars I and II;
Napoleonic wars, 1803–15;
Polish–Czech conflict, 1918–20;
Polish–German conflicts 1919–1921;
Polish–Lithuanian conflicts, 1918–20;
Polish–Soviet war, 1919–20;
Polish–Ukrainian conflict, 1918–19;
Prussian–Italian–Austrian war, 1866;
Romanian–Bulgarian war, 1912–13;
Romanian–Soviet war, 1941–44;
Russian and Soviet wars during World Wars I and II;
Spanish war with the Quadruple Alliance, 1717–20;
Spanish civil war, 1936–39;
Spanish war of succession, 1701–14;
Spanish–Portuguese wars, 1703–14, 1761–63, 1801, 1807–08;
Turkish–Bulgarian war, 1912–13;
Turkish–Serbian war, 1913;
Turkish–Russian wars of the 19th and 20th centuries;
World Wars: I – 1914–18; II – 1939–45.

EUROPEAN WILDLIFE AND NATURAL HABITATS CONVENTION, 1982, ON THE CONSERVATION OF.

The Berne Convention, entered into force on June 1, 1982. Signed by all European Community members except Iceland and Malta, not ratified by Belgium, Cyprus and France (until May 1987). Two non-members of EC countries, Finland and Senegal signed and ratified the Convention "to co-ordinate their efforts for the protection of the migratory species" (specified in appendices).

KEESING's *Record of World Events*, May, 1987.

EUROPE, CENTRAL, EASTERN, NORTHERN, SOUTHERN AND WESTERN.

International geographical and political terms. The concept of Central Europe accepted by the ▷ MURFAAMCE Conference includes: the Benelux states, Czechoslovakia, the FRG, the GDR and Poland; geographically also Austria.
Eastern Europe geographically integrates the European part of the USSR, politically in the Western press includes all European Warsaw Pact countries;
Northern Europe includes the Scandinavian countries and Finland;
Southern Europe is a synonym of the ▷ Balkan;
Western Europe geographically integrates Italy, Switzerland, France, England, Spain and Portugal, politically also West Germany and the Benelux states.

Z. KNYZIAK, *Economic Development of Eastern Europe*, London, 1968; P.L. HORECKY, *East Central Europe. A Guide to Basic Publications*, Chicago, 1969; I. JOHN (ed.), *EEC Policy Towards Eastern Europe*, Lexington Mass., 1975.

EUROPÊCHE.

The official abbreviation of the Association of National Organizations of Fishing Enterprises of the EEC. From Feb., 1971 the EEC countries have a free access to Community waters and ports, a free market for fish throughout the Community, common control of imports and common market organizations.

J. PAXTON, *A Dictionary of the EEC*, London, 1977.

EUROPE IN THE UN SYSTEM.

Europe is represented in the UN by three groups of states: (1) socialist: Albania, the Byelorussian SSR, Bulgaria, Czechoslovakia, the GDR, Hungary, Poland, the Ukrainian SSR and Yugoslavia; (2) NATO states: Denmark, France, the FRG, Greece, Great Britain, Holland, Iceland, Ireland Italy, Luxembourg, Norway, Portugal and Turkey; (3) the remaining European states in the UN: Austria, Finland, Spain and Sweden. Switzerland and the Vatican State do not belong to the UN, though they have permanent observers in the UN and belong to many specialized UN organizations. On Dec. 21, 1965 the UN General Assembly passed Res. 2129/XX on regional measures for improving neighborly relations between European states with different social and political systems. On Aug. 1, 1975 the Conference on Security and Co-operation in Europe ended with the signing of the ▷ Helsinki Final Act.
A regional UN organization is the ▷ Economic Committee for Europe. Organizations studying the problems of Europe reg. with the UIA:

Association of South-East European States, f. 1963, Bucharest, affiliates institutions of 17 states: Albania, Austria, Bulgaria, Czechoslovakia, the GDR, Great Britain, Greece, the FRG, Hungary, Lebanon, Romania, Turkey, the USA, the USSR and Yugoslavia.
International Association 'Europe 2000', f. 1970, Brussels.
Association of Institutes for European Studies, t. 1951, Geneva. Publ.: *Bibliographie européenne, Annuaire, Bulletin Intérieur* and studies such as e.g. *Formation des cadres européens* (1964).
Association for the Study of European Problems, f. 1958, Paris. Publ.: *Les problèms de l'Europe* (quarterly).

B. MIRKIN-GUTZEVITCH, *Les Constitutions Européennes*, t. 2, Paris, 1961, p. 882; R. PINTO, *Les Organisations Européennes*, Paris, 1965, p. 501; H. BRUGMANS, *L'Idee Européenne 1918–1965*, Burgas, 1966, p. 292; K. GASTEYGER, *Einigung und Spaltung Europas 1942–1965*, Hamburg, 1966; P.L. HORECKY, *East Central Europe. A Guide to Basic Publications*, Chicago, 1969.

EUROPE OF FATHERLANDS.

French: "Europe des patries." The formula of General Charles de Gaulle, 1961, opposing Pan-European integrative ideas (requiring states of the Community to give up their sovereignty to superstate organs), and supporting the idea of an integrated Europe made up of sovereign states. In the opinion of the premier of France, M. Debré: "France in no event intends to dissolve in a collectivity which does not exist and whose prospects are questionable." The West German Christian Democrat, F.J. Strauss, became the main opponent of the French concept, stating that the political unity of Western Europe is a condition "*sine qua non* for the integration of Europe", whereas "*Europe des patries* can only be a group of fatherlands without Europe."

KEESING's *Contemporary Archive* 1961.

EUROPE–THIRD WORLD ASSOCIATION.

A non-profit association, est. 1975 in Brussels, made up of European Community officials who together finance small development projects. Publ.: *Reports on Third World Problems.* Reg. with the UIA.

Yearbook of International Organizations.

EUROPOORT.

Dutch = "Port of Europe". The largest trans-shipping port of Western Europe, servicing vessels of several hundred thousand tons, constructed at the mouth of the Dutch canal Nieuwe Waterwed to the North Sea as the western part of the Port of Rotterdam.

EURO-RIGHT.

A Western European right wing parties organization est. Apr. 20, 1978 in Rome by the neofascist Italian MSI (*Movimiento Social Italiano*), French PFN (*Partie de la Front Nouvelle*) and Spanish NF (*Nueva Fuerza*) for the purpose of combatting Eurocommunism.

EUROSOCIALISM.

An international term promoted from 1976 by the Italian Socialist Party, PSI, as "restoration of closer and more direct relations among European socialist parties and ... giving greater co-ordination to Western European socialism." A controversial term, arose under the influence of ▷ Eurocommunism.

B.E. BROWN (ed.), *Eurocommunism and Eurosocialism: The Left Confronts Modernity*, New York, 1979.

EUROSPACE.

European Industrial Space Study Group. A Western European organization with headquarters in Paris, est. 1961; members are industrial firms of Belgium, Denmark, Finland, France, the FRG, Great Britain, the Netherlands, Norway, Spain, Sweden, Switzerland and USA. Aim: to develop industry related to the production of cosmic probes and telecommunication satellites. In close co-operation with ▷ ELDO and ▷ ESRO.

Consultative Status: UNESCO. Reg. with the UIA.

Yearbook of International Organizations, 1986/87; The Europa Yearbook 1988, Vol. I, London, 1988.

EUROSTRATEGIC WEAPONS.

An international term, defined by SIPRI as "nuclear weapons located in or likely to be used in Europe, and which are capable of hitting targets located a significant distance within the territory of the opponent."

SIPRI, *World Armaments and Disarmament Yearbook 1980*, London, 1980, pp. 175–186; D. ROBERTSON, *Guide to Modern Defense and Strategy*, Detroit, 1988.

EUROTOX.

The official abbreviation of the European Standing Committee for the Protection of Populations against the Long-Term Risks of Chronic Toxicity, f. 1957, Paris. Reg. with the UIA.

Yearbook of International Organizations.

EUROTUNNEL.

A British–French consortium of 15 banks and construction companies, est. 1987 after the ratification on July 30, 1987 of the British–French Agreement on ▷ Chunnel. Boring of the tunnel started Dec. 1, 1987; opening scheduled in 1993.

International Herald Tribune, August 14, 1987; *The Economist*, February 13, 1988.

EUROVISION.

An institution linking the television stations of Western Europe and in association those of Africa, America, Asia and Australasia; administrative seat in Geneva, technical in Brussels; created in 1950 with the task of organizing the exchange of television programs, on a continual basis since 1954; since 1960 also in co-operation with ▷ Intervision. The mother organization is Organisation européenne de radiodiffusion, OER, est. on Feb. 12, 1950 in place of the International Broadcasting Union, f. 1925; OER is a branch of the Brussels Organisation international de radiodiffusion, OIR, presently ▷ OIRT; it has a second official English name: European Broadcasting Union, EBU Eurovision. Publ.: *The EBU Review*, in English and French.

EURO-YEN BONDS.

Bonds also called Samurai Bonds, issued since 1977 by the European Investment Bank.

D.R.W. POTTER, "Samurai-bond market", in: *The Banker*, London, May 1978.

E

EUTHANASIA. An international term for voluntary death (suicide) or murder of persons with incurable diseases or of the mentally retarded. In the Third Reich and in territories occupied by Nazi Germany mass murders took place on the basis of the Nazi Euthanasia Law. Condemned by the Nuremberg Trials as crime against humanity. In 1960 Switzerland became the only country in the world allowing a physician to administer poison under specific conditions at the patient's request. In 1988 the world press started a campaign to introduce voluntary euthanasia, which was condemned by the Catholic Church.

G.E. WILLIAMS, *The Sanctity of Life and the Criminal Law*, London, 1937; *The Trial of German Major War Criminals*, London, 1946–48; "Verschleppt. Der Euthanasie-Mord an behinderten Kindern" in *Nazi-Deutschland*, Essen, 1987; "A Right to Die?", in: *Newsweek*, March 14, 1988; "The Need for Laws on Euthanasia Cannot be Dodged for Much Longer", in: *The Economist*, March 5, 1988.

EVACUATION ▷ Civilian Evacuation.

EVANGELICAL CHURCHES. An international term for churches founded in the wake of the Reformation of Luther and Calvin, professing that the source of faith is "The Gospel broadly conceived", i.e. the Bible. After a long period of fragmentation into national bodies, Evangelical Churches and evangelical societies began to unite in 1846, but not until after World War II, 100 years later, did they begin general international co-operation in the ecumenical movement. Organizations reg. with the UIA:

European Evangelical Alliance, f. 1952, London.
Far Eastern Council of Christian Churches, f. 1951, Manila.
International Council of Christian Churches, f. 1948, Amsterdam. Publ. *The Reformation Review*. Has many subordinate regional organizations, such as:
International Council of Christian Churches European Alliance, f. 1957, De Bilt.
International Fellowship of Evangelical Students (IFES), f. 1947, Lausanne. Publ.: IFES Review.
Latin American Alliance of Christian Churches, f. 1951, Sao Paulo.
Union of Latin American Evangelical Youth, f. 1941, Curitiba.

Yearbook of International Organizations.

EVEREST, MOUNT. CHOMOLUNGMA. The highest elevation in the world, on the border of Tibet and Nepal, in the central Himalayas, 8,848 m high. The Tibetan name Chomolungma was replaced in 1863 in honour of Sir George Everest, English geodesist (1790–1866). In 1921 the first reconnaissance expedition was undertaken and in 1922 the first attempt to scale the peak; the others: 1924, 1933, 1935, 1936, 1951, 1952, were all unsuccessful; on May 28, 1953 Sir Edmund Hillary and Tenzing Norkay, reached the summit; on Feb. 17, 1980 Leszek Cichy and Krzysztof Wielacki of Poland were the first to reach the summit in wintertime. The first women to scale Mount Everest were Chinese (1960), Japanese (1970) and Polish (1978).

E. HILLARY, *High Adventure*, London, 1955.

EVERGLADES. A National Park in Florida, USA, included in the ▷ World Heritage UNESCO List, situated at the southern-most tip of Florida, this "river of grass", a paradise of orchids and a meeting-place of mangroves and oak trees, is the refuge of sixty different species of reptiles, the last retreat of the Florida panther, the manatee, the black bear and of immense colonies of cranes, ibises and herons.

UNESCO. *A Legacy for All*, Paris, 1984.

EVERYMAN'S UNITED NATIONS, EVERYONE'S UNITED NATIONS A handbook *Everyman's United Nations* was published by the UN every 2–3 years since 1948, providing information on the history, structure and activities of the UN as well as its specialized agencies; editions in English as well as French, *L'ONU pour tous*, and Spanish, *Las Naciones Unidas al Alcance de Todos*; from the ninth edition 1979 published under title: *Everyone's United Nations.*

EX AEQUO ET BONO. *Latin* = "equally and well." An international legal term indicating the right of the court to adjudicate according to its own criteria; incorporated into the Statute of the International Court of Justice in art. 38, item 2 as an option: "if the parties agree to it."

R.L. BLEDSOE, B.A. BOCZEK, *The International Law Dictionary*, Oxford, 1987.

EXCHANGE AGREEMENTS. An international term for regulations of the IMF cancelling in 1978 the gold standard of all member states anticipated in its statutes (art. 4) and allowing each country freely to select any exchange rate system and any other standard besides gold.

EXCHANGE OF INFORMATION. An international term promoted by the UNESCO. Exchange of scientific–technological, cultural, press information, subject of bi- and multi-lateral conventions and international meetings under UN auspices. In 1972, General Conference of UNESCO adopted a resolution on the use of satellites for free exchange of information and cultural co-operation.

EXCHANGE OF OFFICIAL DOCUMENTS. Subject of an international convention signed in Brussels on Mar. 15, 1886: (1) on international exchange of official documents and also scientific and literary publications, (2) on the exchange of official gazettes, year books and parliamentary documents. An Inter-American Convention on the exchange of official publications was signed in Buenos Aires on Dec. 23, 1936. A Paris Convention on international exchange of publications was signed on July 5, 1958, and the Paris Convention on international exchange of official publications and governmental documents on Dec. 5, 1958. A separate convention on the exchange of judicial and extrajudicial documents on civil or commercial matters was signed in the Hague on Nov. 15, 1965 and came into force on Feb. 10, 1969.

UNTS, Vol. 658, p. 165; *LNTS*, Vols. 201 and 295.

EXCHANGE RATE. An international banking term for the course of exchange or conversion of one country's currency into that of another.

W.S. JEVONS, *Money and the Mechanism of Exchange*, London, 1933; *IMF, Annual Report on Exchange Restrictions*, 1950 et seq.; S. EDWARDS, L. AHAMED eds., *Economic Adjustment and Exchange Rates in Developing Countries*, Chicago, 1987; R.C. MARSTON, "Exchange Rate Policy Reconsidered", in: *The Economic Impact*, Washington DC, 1988/I.

EXCLUSION. An international term for (1) excluding a certain matter from negotiations; (2) a kind of veto during a conclave, precluding the election of a particular person.

EXCLUSION FROM THE UN. ▷ Expulsion from the United Nations.

EXCLUSIVE ECONOMIC ZONES ▷ Fisheries Economic Zones.

EXCOMMUNICATION. Exclusion from the community. A term of the Catholic Church referring to the punishment of exclusion from the church community; applied in the Middle Ages in the form of a solemn curse, taking away the right to participate in divine services, receive sacraments, or give the excommunicated person a church funeral; in the 20th century applied by Pius XII in The Holy Edict Officium on the excommunication of communists, 1949. The new *Codex iuris canonici*, 1983 has reduced the grounds for excommunication from 42 to 8 cases. ▷ Canon Law.

KEESING's *Contemporary Archive*, 1983.

EXEMPTION FROM TAXATION. An international term for a fiscal privilege granted to diplomats on the basis of reciprocity.

EXEQUATUR. An international term. In consular conventions it indicates consent given by the receiving state to a person nominated to be the consul. The withholding of exequatur is equivalent to voidance of the right to hold consular office. Principles related to exequatur are included in the ▷ Vienna Convention on Consular Relations of Apr. 24, 1963.

R.L. BLEDSOE, B.A. BOCZEK, *The International Law Dictionary*, Oxford, 1987.

EXFOR. International Exchange System for Numerical Nuclear Reaction Data, one of the information systems of the ▷ IAEA.

EXHIBITIONS, WORLD AND INTERNATIONAL. International terms used since the second half of the 19th century for two kinds of exhibitions meeting the conditions determined by a statute of world exhibitions and a separate one of international exhibitions, codified by International Convention on World and International Exhibitions (1912 in Berlin, 1928 and 1948 in Paris); substituted by a new convention signed on Oct. 30, 1972 in Paris by 20 countries; the convention established two types of world and international exhibition: universal, called EXPO with the year and name of place added, and specialized, such as the World Exhibition of Man's Environmental Protection in Spokane, USA, 1974, or World Exhibition of Shipping in Okinawa, 1975.

The first World Exhibition, opened on May 1, 1851 in London, in the Crystal Palace in Hyde Park, was named Great Industrial Exhibition of All Nations and visited by 6 million persons. The first international exhibition was opened July 14, 1853 in New York, named New York World's Fair, visited by 1¼ million persons. The same name was again given to the international exhibition visited by 45 million persons, from Apr. 30, 1939 to Oct. 27, 1940, on the grounds of Flushing Meadow Park, where in 1945 the UN started its activity in the post-fair buildings and remained until the new UN Headquarters were built in Manhattan.

A special place is held by international exhibitions of different fields of fine arts, which have been sponsored by UNESCO since 1946.

On the average, in the decades 1961–80 about 150 international exhibitions were held yearly worldwide. ▷ Inter-American Artistic Exhibition Convention, 1936.

Committee of Collective National Participations in International Fairs. INTER-EXPO, f. 1955, Vienna.
Committee of Organizers of National Participation in International Economic Displays, f. 1955, Vienna.
Federation of Fairs and Exhibitions in BENELUX, f. 1966, Brussels.
International Bureau of Exhibitions, Bureau international des expositions, BIE, f. 1931, Paris. Publ.: *Bulletin de BIE.*

Union of International Exhibitions, Union des Foires, UFI, Paris. Consultative status with ECOSOC. Publ.: *International Stand Magazine*.

UN Review, April, 1958, pp. 31–32; *Que faut-il savoir de la convention internationale sur l'exposition mondiale?*, Paris, 1964; *Yearbook of International Organizations, 1986/87; The Europa Yearbook 1988. A World Survey*, Vol. I, London, 1988.

EXILES. International term for persons forced to leave their country by political repression, economic pressure, domestic war or foreign intervention, or by natural catastrophes. After World War I called ▷ Refugees, after World War II ▷ Displaced persons. In the 1980's the world press preferred the term Exiles.

"The Politics of Exiles", in: *Third World Quarterly*, special issue January, 1987.

EXIMBANK. ▷ Export–Import Bank of the United States.

EX INIURIA LEX NON ORITUR. *Latin* = "no law is born of lawlessness". An international term for the principle of elimination of legislation incompatible with commonly accepted norms, e.g. racist legislation.

EX MORE. *Latin* = "according to custom". An international term used in the UN system.

EX NUNC, EX TUNC. *Latin* international legal terms used in the UN system concerning the moment in which a treaty becomes invalid: (1) only now (nunc) due to special circumstances; (2) from the beginning (tunc), e.g. due to ill-will of signatories.

EXOBIOLOGY. An international term for the search of life on the surface of planets reached by Space Laboratories.

EXODUS. An international term for a mass migration caused by a mortal danger of any kind, from the title of the Second Book of Moses describing the departure of Jews from Egypt.
The GA adopted on Dec. 8, 1988 without a vote Res. 43/154 "Human Rights and Mass Exodus": "Deeply disturbed by the continuing scale and magnitude of exoduses of refugees and displacements of population in many regions of the world and by the human suffering of millions of refugees and displaced persons".

J. COERT RYLAARSDAM, "The Book of Exodus. Introduction and Exegesis", in: *Interpreter's Bible*, 1952.

UN Resolutions and Decisions adopted by the General Assembly during the First Part of its Forty-Third Session, From 20 September to 22 December 1988, New York, 1989, pp. 434–436.

EX OFFICIO. *Latin* = "because of the office held". An international term used in the UN system.

EXPATRIATION. An international term for denationalization of an individual citizen by the state, contrary to international conventions.

R.L. BLEDSOE, B.A. BOCZEK, *The International Law Dictionary*, Oxford, 1987.

EXPEDITION CORPS. An Anglo-American term for troops sent from Great Britain or the USA to Europe or Asia during World Wars I and II.

EXPERTS. ▷ UN Register of Experts.

"EXPLORER". The first American artificial earth satellite launched into orbit on Jan. 31, 1958. Reg. with the UN.

EXPLOSIVE REMNANTS OF WAR. A subject of international studies directed by UNEP in a program on military activities and human environment.

A.H. WESTING ed., *Explosive Remnants of War. Mitigating the Environmental Effects*, SIPRI, London, 1985.

EXPORT. An international term for the transport abroad of agricultural or industrial products, raw materials, services and capital. The majority of the states of the world are not self-sufficient and, in order to import, must develop exports, often raising problems which are among the most important factors of world economic order.

C.M. SCHMITTHOF, *The Export Trade*, London, 1975.

EXPORT CREDIT GUARANTEE DEPARTMENT. The British Government insurance institution which gives guarantees on bank loans.

The Export Credit Financing Systems in OECD Member Countries, OECD, Paris, 1976.

EXPORT–IMPORT BANK OF JAPAN. A bank est. 1950 in Tokyo, under the aegis of the Japanese government, administers government and commercial bank loans to developing countries.

EXPORT–IMPORT BANK OF THE UNITED STATES, EXIMBANK. A state-owned US bank, est. 1934 in Washington, with initial capital of one billion dollars; the task of EXIMBANK is to support the development of foreign trade by the granting of credits or guarantees for financing purchases by foreign countries of goods made in the USA.

EXPORTING COUNTRIES ORGANIZATIONS. The commodities exporting countries under the aegis of UN economic regional commissions or UNCTAD established in the 1960s and 1970s a series of intergovernmental organizations for defense of the producer's interests like ▷ OPEC in 1960. See ▷ Bananas, ▷ Bauxite, ▷ Coffee ▷ Cocoa, ▷ Citrus fruits, ▷ Copper, ▷ Iron ore, ▷ Jute, ▷ Meat, ▷ Mercury, ▷ Oilseeds, ▷ Pepper, ▷ Peanuts, ▷ Phosphorites, ▷ Rubber, ▷ Sugar, ▷ Tea, ▷ Timber.

EXPORT INSTITUTES. A general name for institutes of various kinds, usually state-owned or state-sponsored, founded for the purpose of supporting the development of foreign trade; established after World War II.

EXPORT PRICE. An international term for subsidies granted to exporters by the state to help them to compete in world markets.

EXPROPRIATION. An international term for the compulsory seizure of the property of an individual or institution by the state based on the law of expropriation, resulting in the transfer of property rights to the state or to other persons on conditions defined by the state; it can have the character of necessity created by higher public interest (e.g. for a railroad track, highway, airport, etc.); or a discriminatory character in relation to a given ethnic group, as e.g. paragraphs 13 and following in the legislation of the Prussian Landtag on strengthening the German Way of Life in the Poznan and Western Prussian provinces of Mar. 20,

1908 (*Gesetz betreffend Massnahmen zur Stärkung des Deutschtums in der Provinz Westpreussen und Posen*); or South African legislation concerning ▷ apartheid, which permits the resettlement and expropriation of the black and colored population. Expropriation can be the result of nationalizations. In 1964 the US Congress accepted the so-called Hickenlooper Amendment to the Foreign Assistance Act of 1961 related to the expropriation of American property.

E.D. RE, *Foreign Confiscation in Anglo-American Law*, London, 1951; B.A. WORTLEY, "Observations on the public and private international law relating to expropriation", in: *American Journal of Comparative Law*, No. 5, 1956; B.A. WORTLEY, *Expropriation in Public International Law*, London, 1959; B.A. WORTLEY, "Some early but basic theories of expropriation", in: *German Yearbook of International Law*, 1977, pp. 236–245; R.L. BLEDSOE, B.A. BOCZEK, *The International Law Dictionary*, Oxford, 1987.

EXPULSION. An international term for the sovereign right of every state to removal, either voluntarily or forcibly, of an alien from its territory. Also a forcible dismissal, under guard, of a foreign country's representative in cases where the diplomat is declared ▷ *persona non grata* and has not left the territory of the receiving country at a time determined by the ▷ Vienna Convention on Diplomatic Relations 1961, as "reasonable time." The Convention does not cite expulsion; however, it provides that a *persona non grata* shall be stripped of diplomatic status after the expiration of a "reasonable time." In 1931 the case of the forcible expulsion of the Nuncio of the Holy See from Lithuania gained wide publicity.

G.S. GOODWIN-GILL, "The limits of the power of expulsion in public international law", in: *The British Yearbook of International Law 1974–75*, pp. 55–155.

EXPULSION FROM THE UNITED NATIONS. Art. 6 of the UN Charter states that:
"A member of the United Nations which has persistently violated the Principles contained in the present Charter may be expelled from the Organization by the General Assembly upon the recommendation of the Security Council."

Up to 1985 in only one case – of South Africa – has the Security Council discussed and voted upon a resolution recommending the immediate expulsion from the UN of a member of the Organization. The vote on Oct. 30, 1974 was 10 in favor to 3 against (France, UK and USA), with 2 abstentions (Austria and Costa Rica). The resolution failed because of the negative vote of three permanent members of the Security Council.

UN Monthly Chronicle, November, 1974, pp. 9–40.

EXTENDED DETERRENCE. An international military term for a strategy where one nuclear power tries to safeguard both itself and its allies against attack.

D. ROBERTSON, *Guide to Modern Defense and Strategy*, Detroit, 1988.

EXTERMINATION. An international term used to describe destruction of human groups for the purpose of achieving mass annihilation, a crime against humanity according to the ▷ Nuremberg Principles. ▷ Genocide.

EXTRADITION. An international term for the delivery of a person under allegations of committing a crime or sentenced on such charges by the authorities of one state to the authorities of another state; an institution of international law contained in the uncommonly accepted principle formulated by H. Grotius, *aut punire aut dedere* (either punish or give out, expel from the country). The first of known international agreements on extradition was concluded in 1296 BC between Ramses II, an Egyptian Pharaoh, and Hatusil III, a Hittite Monarch. The First South American Congress on Private International Law at Montevideo, Jan. 23, 1889, elaborated a Treaty on International Penal Law, with Chapters III and IV on Extradition. The Treaty was signed and ratified by Argentina, Bolivia, Paraguay, Peru and Uruguay. Revision of the Treaty was signed on Mar. 19, 1940 in Montevideo at the Second South American Congress on Private International Law by Argentina, Bolivia, Brazil, Colombia, Paraguay, Peru and Uruguay. The first Treaty for the Extradition of Criminals and for Protection Against Anarchism was signed on Jan. 28, 1902 in Mexico City but for lack of a sufficient number of ratifications it never came into force. The second was the Agreement on Extradition, signed on July 19, 1911 in Caracas and ratified by Bolivia, Colombia, Ecuador, Peru and Venezuela. An Agreement interpreting the above Agreement was signed on Aug. 10, 1915 in Quito by Bolivia, Ecuador, Peru and Venezuela.

First attempts to create an international convention on extradition were made by the Oxford Institute of International Law. The first regional Convention on Extradition was prepared and signed in 1907 in Washington, DC by five republics of Central America; also renewed in Washington, DC, on Feb. 7, 1923 and superseded by the Guatemala Convention, 1934. In 1926 the League of Nations initiated studies on extradition but decided that at that time it was impossible to reach an agreement. The Sixth Conference of Pan-American States, held in Havana in Feb. 1928, adopted the so-called ▷ Bustamente Code, which in arts. 344–381 decided the question of extradition and also adopted the principle stating that: "in no case shall the death penalty be pronounced, nor inflicted, for crimes which were the reasons for extradition" (art. 378).

The code was ratified by 15 states of Latin America. In the same year on Aug. 15, 1928, the problem of a universal international convention on extradition was taken up by the International Law Association at its session in Warsaw. The Inter-American Convention on Extradition was signed on Dec. 26, 1933 in Montevideo, together with an Optional Clause that "in no case will the nationality of the criminal be permitted to impede his extradition," by the governments of Argentina, Brazil, Chile, Colombia, Cuba, the Dominican Republic, Ecuador, El Salvador, Guatemala, Haiti, Honduras, Mexico, Nicaragua, Panama, Paraguay, the USA and Uruguay, but was not ratified by Brazil, Haiti, Paraguay, Peru and Uruguay. The Convention came into force Dec. 26, 1934.

The Central American Convention on Extradition signed in Guatemala by the American states adopted the International Convention on Extradition which, however, was not ratified by the majority of signatory states and thus did not enter into force.

After World War II, the UN failed to consider the codification of this issue. Bilateral treaties on mutual extradition of specific crimes were concluded as early as the 19th century, e.g., between the German Reich and Switzerland (1874), Luxembourg (1876), Spain and Norway (1878) and the Netherlands (1896). In countries where the right of asylum is in force with respect to political offenders, the ▷ Belgian Clause is observed to determine cases of extradition of perpetrators of attempts on the life of heads of foreign states.

On June 25, 1985 a revised US–UK extraditions treaty which excluded the prohibition of extradition for offences of a political character and facilitated the extradition of IRA fugitives was signed in Washington DC.

SAINT-AUBIN, *L'extradition et le droit extraditionnel*, Paris, 1913; Carnegie Endowment, *International Legislation*, Vol. 2, Washington, DC, 1924; S. GLASER, *L'uniformation du droit d'extradition*, Varsovie, 1932; W.P. ASPE, *Das Auslieferungsrecht am Ende des Zweiten Welt-Kriegs und seine Fortentwicklung*, Berlin, 1950; HSU CHAO CHING, *Du principle de la spécialité en matière d'extradition*, Paris, 1950; G. GUTZNER, "Auslieferung", in: *STRUPP-SCHLOCHAUER Wörterbuch des Völkerrechts*, Vol. I, Berlin, 1960, pp. 115–123; E. HAMBRO, "Extradition and Asylum". A note in: *Jahrbuch für Internationales Recht*, 1962, pp. 106–113; SATYA DEVA BEDI, *Extradition in International Law and Practice*, Rotterdam, 1966: *Inter-American Treaties and Conventions on Asylum and Extradition*, OAS Treaty Series No. 34, Washington, DC, 1967; OAS, *Inter-American Treaties and Conventions*, Washington, DC, 1971; I.A. SHEARER, *Extradition in International Law*, Manchester, 1971; M.CH. BASSIOUNI, *International Extradition and World Public Order*, Leyden, 1974; R.L. BLEDSOE, B.A. BOCZEK, *The International Law Dictionary*, Oxford, 1987.

EXTRADITION CONVENTION OF AMERICAN STATES, 1933. A Convention adopted by the Seventh International Conference of American States, signed on Dec. 16, 1933 at Montevideo, read as follows:

"Art. 1. Each one of signatory States in harmony with the stipulations of the present Convention assumes the obligation of surrendering to any one of the States which may make the requisition, the persons who may be in their territory and who are accused or under sentence. This right shall be claimed only under the following circumstances:

(a) That the demanding State have the jurisdiction to try and to punish the delinquency which is attributed to the individual whom it desires to extradite.

(b) That the act for which extradition is sought constitutes a crime and is punishable under the laws of the demanding and surrendering States with a minimum penalty of imprisonment for one year.

Art. 2. When the person whose extradition is sought is a citizen of the country to which the requisition is addressed, his delivery may not be made, as the legislation or circumstances of the case may, if in the judgment of the surrendering State it is obliged to bring action against him for the crime with which he is accused, if such crime meets the conditions established in sub-Article (b) of previous Article. The sentence pronounced shall be communicated to the demanding State.

Art. 3. Extradition will not be granted:

(a) When, previous to the arrest of the accused person, the penal action or sentence has expired according to the laws of the surrendering State.

(b) When the accused has served his sentence in the country where the crime was committed or when he may have been pardoned or granted an amnesty.

(c) When the accused has been or is being tried by the State to which the requisition was directed for the act with which he is charged and on which the petition of extradition is based.

(d) When the accused must appear before any extraordinary tribunal or court of the demanding State (tribunal o juzgado de excepcion del Estado requirente). Military courts will not be considered as such tribunals.

(e) When the offense is of a political nature or of a character related thereto. An attempt against the life or person of the Chief of State or members of his family shall not be deemed to be a political offense.

(f) When the offense is purely military or directed against religion.

Art. 4. The determination of whether or not the exceptions referred to in the previous Article are applicable shall belong exclusively to the State to which the request for extradition is addressed.

Art. 5. A request for extradition should be formulated by the respective diplomatic representative. When no such representative is available, consular agents may serve, or the Governments may communicate directly with one another. The following documents, in the language of the country to which the request of extradition is directed, shall accompany every such request:

(a) An authentic copy of the sentence, when the accused has been tried and condemned by the courts of the demanding State.

(b) When the person is only under accusation, an authentic copy of the order of detention issued by the competent judge, with a precise description of the imputed offense, a copy of the penal laws applicable thereto, and a copy of the laws referring to the prescription of the action or the penalty.

(c) In the case of an individual under accusation as also of an individual already condemned, there shall be furnished all possible information of a personal character which may help to identify the individual whose extradition is sought.

Art. 6. When a person whose extradition is sought shall be under trial or shall be already condemned in the State from which it is sought to extradite him, for an offense committed prior to the request for extradition, said extradition shall be granted at once, but the surrender of the accused to the demanding State shall be deferred until his trial ends or his sentence is served.

Art. 7. When the extradition of a person is sought by several States for the same offence, preference will be given to the State in whose territory said offense was committed. If he is sought for several offenses, preference will be given to the State within whose bounds shall have been committed the offense which has the greatest penalty according to the law of the surrendering State.

If the case is one of different acts which the State from which extradition is sought esteems of equal gravity, the preference will be determined by the priority of the request.

Art. 8. The request for extradition shall be determined in accordance with the domestic legislation of the surrendering State and the individual whose extradition is sought shall have the right to use all the remedies and resources authorized by such legislation, either before the judiciary or the administrative authorities as may be provided for by the aforesaid legislation.

Art. 9. Once a request for extradition in the form indicated in Article 5 has been received, the State from which the extradition is sought will exhaust all necessary measures for the capture of the person whose extradition is requested.

Art. 10. The requesting State may ask, by any means of communication, the provisional or preventive detention of a person, if there is, at least, an order by some court for his detention and if the State at the same time offers to request extradition in due course. The State from which the extradition is sought will order the immediate arrest of the accused. If within a maximum period of two months after the requesting State has been notified of the arrest of the person, said State has not formally applied for extradition, the detained person will be set at liberty and his extradition may not again be requested except in the way established by Article 5.

The demanding State is exclusively liable for any damages which might arise from the provisional or preventive detention of a person.

Art. 11. Extradition having been granted and the person requested put at the disposition of the diplomatic agent of the demanding State, then, if within two months from the time when said agent is notified of same, the person has not been sent to his destination, he will be set at liberty, and he cannot again be detained for the same cause.

The period of two months will be reduced to forty days when the countries concerned are conterminous.

Art. 12. Once extradition of a person has been refused, application may not again be made for the same alleged act.

Art. 13. The State requesting the extradition may designate one or more guards for the purpose of taking charge of the person extradited, but said guards will be subject to the orders of the police or other authorities of the State granting the extradition or of the States in transit.

Art. 14. The surrender of the person extradited to the requesting State will be done at the most appropriate point on the frontier or in the most accessible port, if the transfer is to be made by water.

Art. 15. The objects found in the possession of the person extradited, obtained by the perpetration of the illegal act for which extradition is requested, or which might be useful as evidence of same, will be confiscated and handed over to the demanding country, notwithstanding it might not be possible to surrender the accused because of some unusual situation such as his escape or death.

Art. 16. The cost of arrest, custody, maintenance, and transportation of the person, as well as of the objects referred to in the preceding Article, will be borne by the State granting the extradition up to the moment of surrender and from thereon they will be borne by the demanding State.

Art. 17. Once the extradition is granted, the demanding State undertakes:

(a) Not to try nor to punish the person for a common offense which was committed previous to the request for extradition and which has not been included in said request, except only if the interested party expressly consents.

(b) Not to try nor to punish the person for a political offense,

Not to try nor to punish the person for a political offense, or for an offense connected with a political offense, committed previous to the request for extradition.

(c) To apply to the accused the punishment of next lesser degree than death if according to the legislation of the country of refuge the death penalty would not be applicable.

(d) To furnish to the State granting the extradition an authentic copy of the sentence pronounced.

Art. 18. The signatory States undertake to permit the transit through their respective territories of any person whose extradition has been granted by another State in favor of a third requiring only the original or an authentic copy of the agreement by which the country of refuge granted the extradition.

Art. 19. No request for extradition may be based upon the stipulation of this Convention if the offense in question has been committed before the ratification of the Convention is deposited."

LNTS, Vol. 165, 1936, pp. 45–61.

EXTRADITION OF WAR CRIMINALS.

An international term for the obligation to deliver war criminals to the countries where they committed war crimes; a rule of international law reaffirmed during World War II by the UN Declaration on War Criminals and War Crimes. The obligation has never been fully respected, neither after World War I when the ▷ Committee of Responsibilities, established on the basis of the Versailles Treaty, insisted on extradition of former Emperor Wilhelm II and other German war criminals (persons accused of committing acts incompatible with martial law and customs), nor after World War II when many governments made it possible for war criminals to enjoy *de facto* the right of asylum. The question of war criminals was also put on the agenda of the UN Security Council in connection with the so-called ▷ Eichmann case. The duty to extradite war criminals was ultimately reaffirmed by the UN Convention on the Non-Application of Statutory Limitations to War Crimes and Crimes against Humanity on Nov. 26, 1968. No state legislation may restrict the duty of extraditing war criminals.

UN Yearbook 1968.

EXTRATERRITORIALITY. An international term for a diplomatic immunity, exclusion of the territory occupied by a foreign agency from the jurisdiction of the state where the agency is located; a disputable term of international law.

M. HEYKING, *L'extraterritorialité*, Paris, 1926; R.L. BLEDSOE, B.A. BOCZEK, *The International Law Dictionary*, Oxford, 1987.

EXTRATERRITORIAL STATUS OF UN POSSESSIONS. Guaranteed in art. 104 of the UN Charter and the Convention on Immunities and Privileges of the UN of Feb. 13, 1946, art. II, item 3, under which "premises of the Organization are inviolable."

EX USU. *Latin*. international legal term – "in virtue of a custom."

EYE BANK, INTERNATIONAL. A medical institution f. 1964 in Colombo, by the Ceylon Eye Donation Society. A half a million Sri Lankan citizens have signed pledges to ensure that their eyes can be collected after death and distributed to eye surgeons at home and abroad.

"Seeing Through Sri Lanka's Eyes", in: *World Health*, January, 1983, pp. 24–25.

F

FACT-FINDING. A term used in the UN system for settlement of international disputes. The UN Secretariat since 1967 has been keeping a UN Register of Experts for Fact-Finding in accordance with a recommendation of the UN General Assembly Res. 2329/XXII.

By a Res. 2329/XXII of Dec. 18, 1967, the UN General Assembly requested member states to nominate up to five of their nationals for a register of experts in legal and other fields for fact-finding. The Secretary-General published the Register since Aug. 31, 1968.

The first Fact-Finding Commission was established by the United Nations in 1943, in London, registering ▷ war crimes and war criminals.

UN Yearbook 1967, p. 753, and *1968*, p. 852.

FACTORING. A financial term in international banking forms of financing exports by institutes or intermediary groups, which generally also assume service functions such as keeping the accounts of a client. Charges for export factoring are levied at the rate of 1–1.5% of the value of transactions. The first international group was initiated by the First National Bank of Boston in 1963, when 20 financial institutes of Western Europe, the USA, Canada, the Republic of South Africa, Australia and Israel formed the International Factors Group. A second group, also of 20 institutes, was organized by the Chicago firm of Walter and Heller, and a third was formed in Europe in 1968 as Factors Chain International, affiliating 30 institutes of 14 European countries, the USA and Canada.

FADINAP, Information Service on Facilities of Fertilizer Advisory Development Information Network for Asia and Pacific, in the system of information centers of the ▷ UN Economic Commission for Asia.

FAHRENHEIT'S SCALE. A thermometric scale, devised in 1725 by German physicist, G.D. Fahrenheit (1686–1736), in which the freezing point of a solution of salammoniac and ice was marked 0°, freezing point of chemically pure water 32°, and boiling point of water 212°. The Fahrenheit scale remains in use in Anglo-Saxon countries.

AMERICAN INSTITUTE OF PHYSICS. *Temperature, Its Measurement and Control in Science and Industry*, 3 Vols., New York, 1941–1963.

FAIR PLAY. An international term for the adherence to principles established by international law and practice. On the initiative of UNESCO the International Committee for Fair Play was established in Paris in 1960 with the task of publishing the principles of fair play in sports contests. Each year it grants Fair Play Awards to sportsmen or teams which have distinguished themselves in international contests through their adherence to the rules of the game. The 1985 award winners were Egyptian judo champion Mohamed Ali Rashwan, who reduced his own chances for a 1984 Olympic Gold Medal by refusing to take advantage of the situation when his Japanese opponent injured his leg. Polish weightlifter Dariusz Zawadzki, another 1985 winner, drew the attention of judges at a 1984 weightlifting championship in Ligano, Italy, to an error he had committed costing him a victory. Each September, winners receive their trophies in a ceremony at UNESCO headquarters in Paris.

UN Chronicle, 1986, No. 1, p. 84.

FAIR PRICE. A term for the sum of the costs of production and a reasonable profit.

FAIRS, INTERNATIONAL. The joint displays of industrial and agricultural products from various countries held to enhance and facilitate their sales; subject of international conventions. The Union of International Fairs, UFI, at its Congress in Barcelona in 1964 accepted the following definition:

"International Fairs, named after the country in which they are held, are a market organized on a regular basis, always in the same place and fixed time interval and for a limited duration of time set beforehand. The purpose of fairs is to enable all participants to present samples of their production for the purpose of making sales. These commercial events can include several branches of production or they can also specialize in one of several branches."

Organizations reg. with the UIA:

Committee of Organizers of National Participations in International Economic Displays, INTEREXPO, est. 1965, Vienna. Members: governmental bodies of Austria, Finland, Israel, the FRG, Hungary, Italy, the Netherlands, Norway and the UK.
Union of International Fairs–Union de foires internationales, UFI, f. 1925, Paris. Consultative Status with UNESCO. Publ.: *UFI Informations and Vademecum des Foires Internationales.*

Yearbook of International Organizations.

FAIT ACCOMPLI. An international term for an action taken, an accomplished fact which creates for another state the problem of recognizing it in the sense of international law, e.g. *a coup d'état*, an armed rebellion, a revolutionary action. There exist no standardized forms for recognizing or not recognizing *fait accompli*.

FALCON ▷ International Falcon Movement.

FALKLAND ISLANDS–MALVINAS. A double English–Spanish name officially introduced by the UN in 1965 for an archipelago in the southern part of the Atlantic near the coast of Argentina. Area 12,173 sq. km. Pop.: 1,919 inhabitants in 1986, 1,200 of which reside in Stanley the capital on East Falkland Island (The Falkland Islands Dependencies consist of South Georgia and the South Sandwich Islands). Subject of an international dispute between Argentina and Great Britain, which occupied the archipelago in 1833, that is, 10 years after the announcement of the Monroe Doctrine without any protest by the USA. The first colonists were Frenchmen and Spaniards. Argentina claims the Malvinas as a natural part of the Argentine territorial waters. The islands are administered by a Governor of Great Britain, economically by the Falklands Islands Company. Ninety per cent of the inhabitants are British, the remainder are Argentines. The majority of the residents are sheep farmers. On Nov. 15, 1965 Bolivia, Colombia, Costa Rica, Chile, the Dominican Republic, Ecuador, Guatemala, Haiti, Honduras, Nicaragua, Panama, Peru, Salvador, Uruguay and Venezuela supported Argentina when the latter demanded the restoration of her sovereign rights over the Islands receiving the support of the UN General Assembly, Res. 2065/XX on the "question of the Falkland Islands–Malvinas." On Apr. 2, 1982 Argentina occupied the Malvinas militarily. The UN Security Council demanded on Apr. 3, 1982, the withdrawal of Argentinian troops. The UK regained the Islands by force on June 17 1982. Some talks over the dispute between a new civilian Argentinian government and the UK took place in 1984.

In Nov., 1982 the British government reversed a previous decision and agreed to grant the islanders full British citizenship. In Dec., 1983 the new civilian government of Argentina condemned the use of force by the Argentinian military government. On Febr. 1, 1987 the UK unilaterally established a 150 mile fishing zone around the islands.

J. GOEBEL, *The Struggles for the Falkland Islands*, New Haven, 1927; E. SHACKLETON, *Falkland Islands Economic Study 1982*, London, 1982; B. HANRAHAN, R. FOX, *"I counted them all out and I counted them all back"*, London, 1982; *UN Chronicle*, May, June and July 1982; *Falkland Island Review*, HMSO, London, 1983; *The Europa Year Book 1984. A World Survey*, Vol. I, pp. 1245–1247, London, 1984; V. GAMBA, *The Falkland/Malvinas War*, Boston, 1987.

FALLASHAS. ▷ Jews.

FALL-OUT. ▷ An international military term for the radioactive dust particles and water droplets blown into the atmosphere by a nuclear explosion.

D. ROBERTSON, *Guide to Modern Defense and Strategy*, Detroit, 1988.

FAMILIES, REUNIFICATION OF. An international term for humanitarian actions, as a rule carried out by the international Red Cross or national agencies with the aim of achieving the reunification of families separated by war or its effects and residing in different countries. In Europe reunification of families (Action Link) began in 1950 following an agreement reached in Geneva between Czechoslovakia, Poland and the International Red Cross. It concerned persons having close relatives in the British-occupied zone of Germany. Later a similar campaign was carried out by Hungary, Romania, Yugoslavia and other countries. The Polish Red Cross concluded direct agreement with the Red Cross of the FRG in 1955 and 1970. In 1965 the government of Cuba agreed to reunification of families, and a Havana–Miami airbridge was established which by Nov. 30, 1971 had transported c, 24,000 persons to their families in the USA. In Asia a campaign was started for the first time in 1971 by organizations of the Red Cross of the two Koreas, North and South. In the 1980's the problem of family reunification occupied the UN agencies in Africa, Near East, the Indochina region, South and Central America. ▷ Refugees.

W. SZEWCZYK, "Od Akcji Link do laczenia rodzin" (From the Action Link to Reunification of Families), in: *Poglady, Katowice*, No. 16, 1971; A. GRAHL MADEN, *The Status of Refugees in International Law*, 2 Vols. Leiden, 1966–1972.

FAMILY. A basic social group composed of a married or unmarried couple and children, including adopted ones; their rights are subject of international conventions. The UN General Assembly declaration on dissemination among youth of the ideas of peace, mutual respect and understanding between peoples stressed the significance of the role of the family in upbringing of youth. ▷ Youth, UN Declaration on, 1965, and ▷ Child, Declaration of the Rights of, 1959.

P.L. VAN DEN BERGHE, *Human Family Systems*, Amsterdam, 1979.

FAMILY INTERNATIONAL LAW. A part of international private law providing for questions of conflicting laws concerning marriages, personal and property relations in a marriage, annulment of a marriage or divorce, legal relations between parents and children, problems of adaptation, adoption, and care and guardianship; subject of international conventions signed on June 12, 1902 at The Hague. The Convention on the Regulation of Conflicting Legislation with Respect to Marriage introduced, i.a., the first, though incomplete, international norms for marriages contracted by citizens of two different states in a third state before a consul of one of the spouse's states. Numerous states gave a more detailed analysis of these norms in the consular agreements they concluded. On Oct. 22, 1983 Pope John Paul II presented to governments of the UN member states and to the UNESCO and other international organizations interested in social problems of the contemporary world a draft of a Family Rights Charter.
See also ▷ East-West Agreement on the Protection of Human Rights, 1989.

FAMILY OF DIPLOMAT. A subject of the ▷ Vienna Convention on Diplomatic Relations, 1961.

E. DENZA, *Diplomatic Law. Commentary on Vienna Convention*, New York, 1976, pp. 223–325, 248–251, 276–277.

FAMILY PLANNING. An international term introduced after World War II instead of the controversial term birth control. In March, 1976 a study was published, prepared under the aegis of the UN, on abortions in the world in the years 1970–75. The study revealed that in countries representing two-thirds of mankind, abortion was allowed, and that the number of abortions doubled in those five years. The yearly number of abortions was estimated at 40 to 55 million at that time. Family planning is a subject of international co-operation. Organization reg. with the UIA:

International Planned Parenthood Federation, f. 1948, London. Regional bureau: Colombo, Kuala Lumpur, London, Nairobi, New York, Tunis. Consultative status with ECOSOC, WHO, UNICEF, ILO, FAO, UNESCO. Publ. *IPPF Medical Bulletin, IPPF News.*

R. FREEDMAN, *Family Planning, Sterility and Population Growth*, London, 1959; *Population Program Assistance Aid to Developing Countries by the US*, USAID, Washington, DC, 1969; *Yearbook of International Organizations.*

FAMILY RIGHTS. ▷ Family International Law.

FANGATAUFA. A French island in the South Pacific, some 40 km away from ▷ Muroroa, used for underground nuclear testing in 1966 and again in 1988.

KEESING'S *Record of World Events*, May 1988.

FAO. Food and Agriculture Organization of the United Nations; Organisation des Nations Unies pour l'alimentation et l'agriculture; Organizatsya Obyedinionnikh Natsyi po voprosam prodovolstviya i sielskogo khosiaystva; Organización de las Naciones Unidas para la Agricultura y la Alimentación; official English, French, Russian and Spanish name of the specialized agency of the UN, est. Oct. 16, 1945 at a conference in Quebec. Headquarters: Rome. It has Regional Offices in Accra, Ghana and liaison offices in Addis Ababa, Ethiopia, for Africa; Bangkok, Thailand for Asia and the Far East; Santiago de Chile, for Latin America; Cairo, Egypt for the Near East; Washington, DC, for North America. Liaison Office for the UN in New York.

The aims of FAO are: to raise levels of nutrition and standards of living; to secure improvements in the efficiency of production and distribution of all agricultural products; and to better the condition of rural population. To help members achieve these aims, FAO functions in three main ways:
(a) providing an information service, including not only facts and figures relating to nutrition, agriculture, forestry and fisheries, but also appraisals and forecasts of production, distribution and consumption in these industries;
(b) promoting national and international action towards the improvement of all aspects of the production, marketing, processing and distribution of the products of agriculture, including fisheries and forestry; conservation of natural resources; and of policies concerned with credit and with commodity arrangements, and
(c) furnishing, on request and largely through the UN Expanded Program of Technical Assistance, technical assistance to members in any of the above fields of operation.
At the end of 1980 the FAO consisted of 147 member states. The Organization works through a Conference, a Council, and a staff headed by a Director-General.
The Conference formally meeting biennially is the policy-making body, in which each of the member nations has one vote. Between sessions of the Conference, the Council supervises the work of the FAO, reviews the world food and agricultural situation, and makes recommendations to member governments and other international bodies on measures to improve the food and agricultural situation. The Council is composed of representatives of 24 member governments elected by the Conference. The staff, or secretariat, is headed by a Director-General chosen by the Conference. The FAO works through the following Committees: Program Committee, Finance Committee, Committee on Constitutional and Legal Matters, Commodity Problems Committee, Committee on Agriculture, Committee on Fisheries, Committee on Forestry. The last four are open to all FAO member nations.
Its subsidiary bodies include: intergovernmental groups on bananas, on cocoa, on citrus fruit, on grains, on hard fibres, on jute, kenaf and allied fibres, on meat, on oil and fats, on oilseed, on tea, on wine and vine products. Statutory governmental bodies include the council commissions, committees, working parties and panels set up under arts. VI and XIV of the Constitution. The following bodies have been established as a result of conventions and agreements approved by the Conference or Council: International Rice Commission; European Commission for the Control of Foot and Mouth Disease; Regional Animal Production and Health Commission for Asia, the Far East and the South West Pacific; Indo-Pacific Fisheries Council; Commission for Controlling the Desert Locust in the Near East; General Fisheries Council for the Mediterranean; International Poplar Commission; Commission for Controlling the Desert Locust in the Eastern Region of its Distribution Area in South-west Asia; Plant Protection Committee for the South-east Asia and Pacific Region; Commission for Controlling the Desert Locust in northwest Africa.
The following governmental bodies have been established by the Conference or Council to advise on the formulation and implementation of policy (art. VI-1 of the FAO Constitution): European Commission for Agriculture; Joint FAO/WHO Codex Alimentarius Commission; Animal Production and Health Commission in the Near East; Asia-Pacific Forestry Commission (APFC) and subsidiary bodies; African Forestry Commission

(AFC) and subsidiary bodies; Latin American Forestry Commission (LAFC) and subsidiary bodies; Near East Forestry Commission (NEFC); North American Forestry Commission (NAFC) and subsidiary bodies; AFC/EFC/NEFC Committee on Mediterranean Forestry Problems *Silva Mediterranea* (SCM) and subsidiary bodies; Regional Commission on Land and Water Use in the Near East; Regional Commission Farm Management for Asia and the Far East; Joint ECE/FAO Working Party on Mechanization of Agriculture; Joint FAO/WHO/OAU Regional Food and Nutrition Commission for Africa; Regional Food and Nutrition Commission for the Near East; Near East Plant Protection Commission; Caribbean Plant Protection Commission; Technical Working Party on Cocoa Production, Protection and Processing; Commission on Fertilizers; Commission on Horticultural Production in the Near East and North Africa; Regional Fisheries Advisory Commission (EIFAC) and subsidiary bodies; Indian Ocean Fishery Commission, West Central Atlantic Fishery Commission (WECAFC); Near East Commission on Agricultural Planning; African Commission on Agricultural Statistics; Asia and Far East Commission on Agricultural Statistics; Near East Commission on Agricultural Statistics; FAO/ECE Conference of European Statisticians – Study Group on Food and Agricultural Statistics in Europe.
The following bodies, consisting of selected members, have been established by the FAO Conference or Council or by the Director-General on the authority of the Conference or Council to study and report on matters pertaining to the purpose of the Organization (art. VI-2 of the FAO Constitution): FAO Olive Production Committee; Committee on Forest Development in the Tropics; Advisory Committee of Experts on Pulp and Paper; Advisory Committee on Forestry Education; Committee on Wood-Based Panel Products; FAO/Fertilizer Industry Advisory Committee of Experts; Committee on Food and Nutrition Policies; Protein Advisory Group (of the UN System) (PAG); Joint FAO/WHO Committee on Additives; FAO Desert Locust Control Committee and subsidiary bodies, FAO Committee for the Eastern Central Atlantic (CECAF); Advisory Committee of Experts on Marine Resources and Research (ACMRR) and subsidiary bodies; Co-ordinating Working Party on Atlantic Fishery Statistics; Committee for Inland Fisheries of Africa; Sub-Committee of COINS on Agricultural Statistics; IASI/FAO joint machinery on Agricultural Statistics for Latin-American Region; FAO Statistics Advisory Committee of Experts.
The following bodies, consisting of individuals appointed in their personal capacity, have been established by the Director-General to study and advise on specific subject matters withing the scope of the Organization (art. VI-4 of the FAO Constitution): Advisory Panel of Experts on Emergency Control of Livestock Diseases; Panel of Experts on Forest Gene Resources; Panel of Experts on Integrated Pest Control and Resistance Breeding; Panel of Experts on Plant Exploration and Introduction; Panel of Experts on Emergency Action against the Desert Locust; Panel of Experts on the Pest Residues and the Environment; Panel of Experts on Pesticide Specifications, Registration Requirements and Application Standards; Panel of Experts on Pest Resistance to Pesticides and Crop Loss Assessment; FAO/IAEA Panels of Experts on Nuclear Techniques in Soil Moisture and Fertility Studies; Use of Isotopes and Irradiation in Entomology and Related Fields Methods of Production and Use of Mutations in Plant Breeding; Application of Nuclear Techniques to Animal

F

Science; Radiation Preservation of Food; FAO/IAEA/WHO Panel of Experts on IAEA/UN Joint Group of Experts on the Scientific Aspects of Marine Pollution; Panel of Experts for the Facilitation of Tuna Research; FAO/IAEA Panel of Experts of Isotope Aided Studies of Chemical Residues and Pollution; Joint FAO/IOC Panel of Experts on the Aquatic Sciences and Fisheries Information System (ASFIS); Panel of Experts on the International Information System for the Agricultural Sciences and Technology (AGRIS).

The 24-member UN/FAO World Food Programme Intergovernmental Committee, est. 1961, was reorganized, in consequence of Res. XXII of the World Food Conference and by UN General Assembly Res. 3348 (XXIX) and FAO Conference Res. 22/75, into the 30-member Committee on Food Aid Policies and Programmes. A Conference of plenipotentiaries provided in May 1966 for the establishment of an International Commission for the Conservation of Atlantic Tunas.

Relations with intergovernmental and non-governmental organizations (NGOs): as a specialized agency of the UN reports annually to ECOSOC and co-operates closely both with it and its sister agencies. Working relations have also been established with some 55 other NGOs.

The FAO has also entered into formal relations with NGOs that can and do help to promote the purposes of the Organization. As part of the FAO policy concerning relations with NGOs the Conference has adopted principles relating to eligibility, privileges and obligations pertaining to consultative status, specialized consultative status and liaison status. National FAO committees have been established in 60 countries to facilitate liaison between the FAO and the governments and peoples of those countries.

The FAO with the UN sponsors the ▷ World Food Program, and the Freedom from Hunger Action for Development Program ▷ Hunger.

The FAO provides secretarial services for the exchange of information and for co-operative action in its field of concern. One of the first publications the FAO produced was its World Food Survey (1946); the second Survey was published in 1952. From 1947 onwards an annual report on the State of Food and Agriculture has appeared, together with the Director-General's report on The Work of FAO. The Fourth World Food Survey was issued at the beginning of 1978. The *Yearbook of Food and Agriculture Statistics*, the *Yearbook of Forest Products Statistics*, and the *Yearbook of Fishery Statistics* provide details of production, prices and trade. Food and agriculture statistics are kept up to date in the *Monthly Bulletin of Agricultural Economics and Statistics*. Forestry statistics are kept up to date by the quarterly publication of commodity reports in *Unasylva*, FAO's journal of forestry. A series of *Commodity Bulletins* and mimeographed *Commodity Reports* covering all important products are published. FAO produces two technical journals, *World Fisheries Abstracts* and the *Plant Protection Bulletin*. A comprehensive collection of Food and Agriculture Legislation is published quarterly.

The FAO published 1945–80 over 650 non-periodical technical reports. The Catalogue of FAO Publications in English, French or Spanish may be obtained from the FAO Documents Service, Via delle Terme di Caracalla, 00100 Rome.

The FAO Terminology and Reference Service, Translation Service, Publication Division publishes since 1965, the Terminology Bulletin and specialized dictionaries (Dictionary in the Field of Forestry Environment, Multilingual Vocabulary of Soil Science, etc).

FAO information systems: Aglinet Union List of Serials, FAO-AGLINET; Aquatic Sciences and Fisheries Information System, FAO-ASPIS; Current Agricultural Research Information System, FAO-CARIS; International Information System for Agricultural Sciences and Technology, FAO-AGRIS; Food Composition Data Management, FAO-FCDM.

UN, *Everyman's United Nations*, New York, 1979; *Directory of UN Information Systems*, New York, 1980.

FAO CONSTITUTION, 1943. The Constitution of the FAO was adopted by the UN Conference on Food and Agriculture at Hot Springs, Va, on June 13, 1943 and entered into force on Oct. 16, 1945. The text, amended by the Conferences of FAO is as follows:

"Preamble

The Nations accepting this Constitution, being determined to promote the common welfare by furthering separate and collective action on their part for the purpose of:

raising levels of nutrition and standards of living of the peoples under their respective jurisdictions;

securing improvements in the efficiency of the production and distribution of all food and agricultural products;

bettering the condition of rural populations;

and thus contributing toward an expanding world economy and ensuring humanity's freedom from hunger;

hereby establish the Food and Agriculture Organization of the United Nations, hereinafter referred to as the 'Organization', through which the Members will report to one another on the measures taken and the progress achieved in the field of action set forth above.

Art. 1: Functions of the Organization,

(1) The Organization shall collect, analyse, interpret and disseminate information relating to nutrition, food and agriculture. In this Constitution, the term 'agriculture' and its derivatives include fisheries, marine products, forestry and primary forestry products.

(2) The Organization shall promote and, where appropriate, shall recommend national and international action with respect to:

(a) scientific, technological, social and economic research relating to nutrition, food and agriculture;

(b) the improvement of education and administration relating to nutrition, food and agriculture, and the spread of public knowledge of nutritional and agricultural science and practice;

(c) the conservation of natural resources and the adoption of improved methods of agricultural production;

(d) the improvement of the processing, marketing and distribution of food and agricultural products;

(e) the adoption of policies for the provisions of adequate agricultural credit, national and international;

(f) the adoption of international policies with respect to agricultural commodity arrangements.

(3) It shall also be the functions of the Organization:

(a) to furnish such technical assistance as governments may request;

(b) to organize, in co-operation with the governments concerned, such missions as may be needed to assist them to fulfill the obligation arising from their acceptance of the recommendations of the United Nations Conference on Food and Agriculture and of this Constitution; and

(c) generally to take all necessary and appropriate action to implement the purposes of the Organization as set forth in the Preamble.

Art. 2: Membership and Associate Membership,

(1) The original Member Nations of the Organization shall be such of the nations specified in Annex I as accept this Constitution, in accordance with the provisions of Art. 21.

(2) The Conference may by a two-thirds majority of the votes cast, provided that a majority of the Member Nations of the Organization is present, decide to admit as an additional Member of the Organization any nation which has submitted an application for membership and a declaration made in a formal instrument that it will accept the obligations of the Constitution as in force at the time of admission.

(3) The Conference may, under the same conditions regarding the required majority and quorum as prescribed in par. (2), above, decide to admit as an Associate Member of the Organization any territory or group of territories which is not responsible for the conduct of its international relations upon application made in its behalf by the Member Nation or authority having responsibility for its international relations, provided that such Member Nation or authority has submitted a declaration made in a formal instrument that it will accept on behalf of the proposed Associate Member the obligations of the Constitution as in force at the time of admission, and that it will assume responsibility for ensuring the observance of the provisions of Art. 8; par. (1) and (2) of Art. 16 and par. (2) and (3) of Art. 18, of this constitution with regard to the Associate Member.

(4) The nature and extent of the rights and obligations of Associate Members are defined in the relevant provisions of this Constitution and the Rules and Regulations of the Organization.

(5) Membership and Associate Membership shall become effective on the date on which the Conference approves the application.

Art. 3: The Conference

(1) There shall be a Conference of the Organization in which each Member Nation and Associate Member shall be represented by one delegate. Associate Members shall have the right to participate in the deliberations of the Conference but shall not hold office nor have the right to vote.

(2) Each Member Nation and Associate Member may appoint alternates, associates and advisers to its delegate. The Conference may determine the conditions for the participation of alternates, associates and advisers in its proceedings, but any such participation shall be without the right to vote, except in the case of an alternate, associate, or adviser participating in the place of a delegate.

(3) No delegate may represent more than one Member Nation or Associate Member.

(4) Each Member Nation shall have only one vote. A Member Nation which is in arrears in the payment of its financial contributions to the Organization shall have no vote in the Conference if the amount of its arrears equals or exceeds the amount of the contributions due from it for the two preceding calendar years. The Conference may, nevertheless, permit such a Member Nation to vote if it is satisfied that the failure to pay is due to conditions beyond the control of the Member Nation.

(5) The Conference may invite any international organization which has responsibilities related to those of the Organization to be represented at its meetings on the conditions prescribed by the Conference. No representative of such an organization shall have the right to vote.

(6) The Conference shall meet once in every two years in regular session. It may meet in special session:

(a) if at any regular session the Conference decides, by a majority of the votes cast, to meet in the following year;

(b) if the Council so instructs the Director-General, or if at least one third of the Member Nations so request.

(7) The Conference shall elect its own officers.

(8) Except as otherwise expressly provided in this Constitution or by rules made by the Conference, all decisions of the Conference shall be taken by a majority of the votes cast.

Art. 4: Functions of the Conference

(1) The Conference shall determine the policy and approve the budget of the Organization and shall exercise the other powers conferred upon it by this Constitution.

(2) The Conference shall adopt Rules of Procedure and Financial Regulations for the Organization.

(3) The Conference may, by a two-thirds majority of the votes cast, make recommendations to Member Nations and Associate Members concerning questions relating to food and agriculture, for consideration by them with a view to implementation by national action.

(4) The Conference may make recommendations to any international organization regarding any matter pertaining to the purposes of the Organization.

(5) The Conference may review any decision taken by the Council or by any commission or committee of the Conference or Council, or by any subsidiary body of such commissions or committees.

Art. 5: Council of the Organization
(1) A Council of the Organization consisting of forty-two Member Nations shall be elected by the Conference. Each Member Nation on the Council shall have one representative and shall have only one vote. Each Member of the Council may appoint alternates, associates and advisers to its representative. The Council may determine the conditions for the participation of alternates, associates and advisers in its proceedings, but any such participation shall be without the right to vote, except in the case of an alternate, associate or adviser participating in the place of a representative. No representative may represent more than one Member of the Council. The tenure and other conditions of office of the Members of the Council shall be subject to rules made by the Conference.
(2) The Conference shall, in addition, appoint an independent Chairman of the Council.
(3) The Council shall have such powers as the Conference may delegate to it, but the Conference shall not delegate the powers set forth in par. (2) and (3) of Art. 2, Art. 4, par. 1 of Art. 7, Art. 12, par. (4) of Art. 13, par. (1) and (6) of Art. 14 and Art. 20 of this Constitution.
(4) The Council shall appoint its officers other than the Chairman and, subject to any decisions of the Conference, shall adopt its own Rules of Procedure.
(5) Except as otherwise expressly provided in this Constitution or by rules made by the Conference or Council, all decisions of the Council shall be taken by a majority of the votes cast.
(6) To assist the Council in performing its functions, the Council shall appoint a Programme Committee, a Finance Committee, a Committee on Commodity Problems, a Committee on Fisheries and a Committee on Constitutional and Legal Matters. These committees shall report to the Council and their composition and terms of reference shall be governed by rules adopted by the Conference.
Art. 6: Commissions, Committees, Conferences, Working Parties and Consultations
(1) The Conference or Council may establish commissions, the membership of which shall be open to all Member Nations, and Associate Members, or regional commissions open to all Member Nations and Associate Members whose territories are situated wholly or in part in one or more regions, to advise on the formulation and implementation of policy and to co-ordinate the implementation of policy. The Conference or Council may also establish, in conjunction with other intergovernmental organizations, joint commissions open to all Member Nations and Associate Members of the Organization and of the other organizations concerned, or joint regional commissions open to Member Nations and Associate Members of the Organization and of the other organizations concerned, whose territories are situated wholly or in part in the region.
(2) The Conference, the Council, or the Director-General on the authority of the Conference or Council may establish committees and working parties to study and report on matters pertaining to the purpose of the Organization and consisting either of selected Member Nations and Associate members, or of individuals appointed in their personal capacity because of their special competence in technical matters. the Conference, the Council, or the Director-General on the authority of the Conference or Council may, in conjunction with other inter-governmental organizations, also establish joint committees and working parties, consisting either of selected Member Nations and Associated Members of the Organization and of the other organizations concerned, or of individuals appointed in their personal capacity. The selected Member Nations and Associate Members shall, as regards the Organization, be designated either by the Conference or the Council, or by the Director-General if so decided by the Conference or Council. The individuals appointed in their personal capacity shall, as regards the Organization, be designated either by the Conference, the Council, selected Member Nations or Associate Members, or by the Director-General, as decided by the Conference or Council.
(3) The Conference, the Council, or the Director-General on the authority of the Conference or Council, shall determine the terms of reference and reporting procedures, as appropriate of commissions, committees and working parties established by the Conference, the Council, or the Director-General as the case may be. Such commissions and committees may adopt their own rules of procedure and amendments thereto, which shall come into force upon approval by the Director-General subject to confirmation by the Conference or Council, as appropriate. The terms of reference and reporting procedures of joint commissions, committees and working parties established in conjunction with other intergovernmental organizations shall be determined in consultation with the other organizations concerned.
(4) The Director-General may establish, in consultation with Member Nations, Associate Members and National FAO Committees, panels of experts, with a view to developing consultation with leading technicians in the various fields of activity of the Organization. The Director-General may convene meetings of some or all of these experts for consultation on specific subjects.
(5) The Conference, the Council, or the Director-General on the authority of the Conference or Council may convene general, regional, technical or other conferences, or working parties or consultations of Member Nations and Associate Members, laying down their terms of reference and reporting procedures, and may provide for participation in such conferences, working parties and consultations, in such manner as they may determine, of national and international bodies concerned with nutrition, food and agriculture.
(6) When the Director-General is satisfied that urgent action is required, he may establish the committees and working parties and convene the conferences, working parties and consultations provided for in paragraphs 2 and 5 above. Such action shall be notified by the Director-General to Member Nations and Associate Members and reported to the following session of the Council.
(7) Associate Members included in the membership of the commissions, committees or working parties, or attending the conferences, working parties or consultations referred to in par. (1), (2) and (5) above, shall have the right to participate in the deliberations of such commissions, committees, conferences, working parties and consultations, but shall not hold office nor have the right to vote.
Art. 7. The Director-General
(1) There shall be a Director-General of the Organization who shall be appointed by the Conference for a term of six years, after which he shall not be eligible for reappointment.
(2) The appointment of the Director-General under this Article shall be made by such procedures and on such terms as the Conference may determine.
(3) Should the office of Director-General become vacant during the above-mentioned term of office, the Conference shall, either at the next regular session or at a special session convened in accordance with Art. 3, par. (6) of this Constitution, appoint a Director-General in accordance with the provisions of par. (1) and (2) of this Article. However, the duration of the term of office of a Director-General appointed at a special session shall expire at the end of the year of the third regular session of the Conference following the date of his appointment.
(4) Subject to the general supervision of the Conference and the Council, the Director-General shall have full power and authority to direct the work of the Organization.
(5) The Director-General or a representative designated by him shall participate, without the right to vote, in all meetings of the Conference and of the Council and shall formulate for consideration by the Conference and the Council proposals for appropriate action in regard to matters coming before them.
Art. 8: Staff
(1) The staff of the Organization shall be appointed by the Director-General in accordance with such procedure as may be determined by rules made by the Conference.
(2) The staff of the Organization shall be responsible to the Director-General. Their responsibilities shall be exclusively international in character and they shall not seek or receive instructions in regard to the discharge thereof from any authority external to the Organization. The Member Nations and Associate Members undertake fully to respect the international character of the responsibilities of the staff and not to seek to influence any of their nationals in the discharge of such responsibilities.
(3) In appointing the staff, the Director-General shall, subject to the paramount importance of securing the highest standards of efficiency and of technical competence, pay due regard to the importance of selecting personnel recruited on as wide a geographical basis as is possible.
(4) Each Member Nation and Associate Member undertakes, insofar as it may be possible under its constitutional procedure, to accord to the Director-General and senior staff diplomatic privileges and immunities and to accord to other members of the staff all facilities and immunities accorded to non-diplomatic personnel attached to diplomatic missions, or alternatively, to accord to such other members of the staff the immunities and facilities which may hereafter be accorded to equivalent members of the staffs of other public international organizations.
Art. 9: Seat
The Seat of the Organization shall be determined by the Conference.
Art. 10: Regional and Liaison Offices.
(1) There shall be such regional offices and subregional offices as the Director-General, with the approval of the Conference, may decide.
(2) The Director-General may appoint officials for liaison with particular countries or areas, subject to the agreement of the government concerned.
Art. 11: Reports by Member Nations and Associate Members.
(1) Each Member Nation and Associate Member shall communicate periodically to the Organization reports on the progress made toward achieving the purpose of the Organization set forth in the Preamble and on the action taken on the basis of recommendations made and conventions submitted by the Conference.
(2) These reports shall be made at such times and in such forms and shall contain such particulars as the Conference may request.
(3) The Director-General shall submit these reports, together with analyses thereof, to the Conference and shall publish such reports and analyses as may be approved for publication by the Conference, together with any reports relating thereto adopted by the Conference.
(4) The Director-General may request any Member Nation or Associate Member to submit information relating to the purpose of the Organization.
(5) Each Member Nation and Associate Member shall, on request, communicate to the Organization, on publication, all laws and regulations and official reports and statistics concerning nutrition, food and agriculture.
Art. 12: Relations with the United Nations
(1) The Organization shall maintain relations with the United Nations as a specialized agency within the meaning of Art. 57 of the Charter of the United Nations.
(2) Agreements defining the relations between the Organization and the United Nations shall be subject to the approval of the Conference.
Art. 13: Co-operation with Organizations and Persons
(1) In order to provide for close co-operation between the Organization and other international organizations with related responsibilities, the Conference may enter into agreements with the competent authorities of such organizations, defining the distribution of responsibilities and methods of co-operation.
(2) The Director-General may, subject to any decision of the Conference, enter into agreements with other intergovernmental organizations for the maintenance of common services, for common arrangements in regard to recruitment, training, conditions of service and other related matters, and for interchanges of staff.
(3) The Conference may approve arrangements placing other international organizations dealing with questions relating to food and agriculture under the general authority of the Organization on such terms as may be agreed with the competent authorities of the organization concerned.
(4) The Conference shall make rules laying down the procedure to be followed to secure proper consultation with governments in regard to relations between the Organization and national institutions or private persons.
Art. 14: Conventions and Agreements
(1) The Conference may, by a two-thirds majority of the votes cast and in conformity with rules adopted by the Conference, approve and submit to Member

Nations conventions and agreements concerning questions relating to food and agriculture.

(2) The Council, under rules to be adopted by the Conference, may, by a vote concurred in by at least two thirds of the membership of the Council, approve and submit to Member Nations:

(a) agreements concerning questions relating to food and agriculture which are of particular interest to Member Nations of geographical areas specified in such agreements and are designed to apply only to such areas;

(b) supplementary conventions of agreements designed to implement any convention or agreement which has come into force under par. (1) or (2a).

(3) Conventions, agreements, and supplementary conventions and agreements shall:

(a) be submitted to the Conference or Council through the Director-General on behalf of a technical meeting or conference comprising Member Nations, which has assisted in drafting the convention or agreement and has suggested that it be submitted to Member Nations concerned for acceptance;

(b) contain provisions concerning the Member Nations of the Organization, and such nonmember nations as are members of the United Nations, which may become parties thereto and the number of acceptances by Member Nations necessary to bring such convention, agreement, supplementary convention or agreement into force, and thus ensure that it will constitute a real contribution to the achievement of its objectives. In the case of conventions, agreement, supplementary conventions and agreements establishing commissions or committees, participation by nonmember nations of the Organization that are members of the United Nations shall in addition be subject to prior approval by at least two thirds of the membership of such commission or committees;

(c) not entail any financial obligations for Member Nations not parties to it other than their contributions to the Organization provided for in Art. 18, par. (2) of this Constitution.

(4) Any convention, agreement, supplementary convention or agreement approved by the Conference or Council for submission to Member Nations shall come into force for each contracting party as the convention, agreement, supplementary convention or agreement may prescribe.

(5) As regards an Associate Member, conventions, agreements, supplementary conventions and agreements shall be submitted to the authority having responsibility for the international relations of the Associate Member.

(6) The Conference shall make rules laying down the procedure to be followed to secure proper consultation with governments and adequate technical preparations prior to consideration by the Conference or the Council of proposed conventions, agreements, supplementary conventions and agreements.

(7) Two copies in the authentic language or languages of any convention, agreement, supplementary convention or agreement approved by the Conference or the Council shall be certified by the Chairman of the Conference or of the Council respectively and by the Director-General. One of these copies shall be deposited in the archives of the Organization. The other copy shall be transmitted to the Secretary-General of the United Nations for registration once the convention, agreement, supplementary convention or agreement has come into force as a result of action taken under this Article. In addition, the Director-General shall certify copies of those conventions, agreements, supplementary conventions or agreements and transmit one copy to each Member Nation of the Organization and to such nonmember nations as may become parties to the conventions, agreements, supplementary conventions or agreements.

Art. 15: Agreements between the Organization and Member Nations

(1) The Conference may authorize the Director-General to enter into agreements with Member Nations for the establishment of international institutions dealing with questions relating to food and agriculture.

(2) In pursuance of a policy decision taken by the Conference by a two-thirds majority of the votes cast, the Director-General may negotiate and enter into such agreements with Member Nations, subject to the provisions of par. (3) below.

(3) The signature of such agreements by the Director-General shall be subject to the prior approval of the Conference by a two-thirds majority of the votes cast. The Conference may, in a particular case or cases, delegate the authority of approval to the Council, requiring a vote concurred in by at least two thirds of the membership of the Council.

Art. 16: Legal Status

(1) The Organization shall have the capacity of a legal person to perform any legal act appropriate to its purpose which is not beyond the powers granted to it by this Constitution.

(2) Each Member Nation and Associate Member undertakes, insofar as it may be possible under its constitutional procedure, to accord to the Organization all the immunities and facilities which it accords to diplomatic missions, including inviolability of premises and archives, immunity from suit and exemptions from taxation.

(3) The Conference shall make provision for the determination by an administrative tribunal of disputes relating to the conditions and terms of appointment of members of the staff.

Art. 17: Interpretation of the Constitution and Settlement of Legal Questions.

(1) Any question or dispute concerning the interpretation of this Constitution, if not settled by the Conference, shall be referred to the International Court of Justice in conformity with the Statute of the Court or to such other body as the Conference may determine.

(2) Any request by the Organization to the International Court of Justice for an advisory opinion on legal questions arising within the scope of its activities shall be in accordance with any agreement between the organization and the United Nations.

(3) The reference of any question or dispute under this Art., or any request for an advisory opinion, shall be subject to procedures to be prescribed by the Conference.

Art. 18: Budget and Contributions

(1) The Director-General shall submit to each regular session of the Conference the budget of the Organization for approval.

(2) Each Member Nation and Associate Member undertakes to contribute annually to the Organization its share of the budget, as apportioned by the Conference. When determining the contributions to be paid by Member Nations and Associate Members, the Conference shall take into account the difference in status between Member Nations and Associate Members.

(3) Each Member Nation and Associate Member shall, upon approval of its application, pay as its first contribution a proportion, to be determined by the Conference, of the budget for the current financial period.

(4) The financial period of the Organization shall be the two calendar years following the normal date for the regular session of the Conference, unless the Conference should otherwise determine.

(5) Decisions on the level of the budget shall be taken by a two-thirds majority of the votes cast.

Art. 19: Withdrawal

Any Member Nation may give notice of withdrawal from the Organization at any time after the expiration of four years from the date of its acceptance of this Constitution. The notice of withdrawal of an Associate Member shall be given by the Member Nation or authority having responsibility for its international relations. Such notice shall take effect one year after the date of its communication to the Director-General. The financial obligation to the Organization of a Member Nation which has given notice of withdrawal, or of an Associate Member on whose behalf notice of withdrawal has been given, shall include the entire calendar year in which the notice takes effect.

Art. 20: Amendment of Constitution

(1) The Conference may amend this Constitution by a two-thirds majority of the votes cast, provided that such majority is more than one half of the Member Nations of the Organization.

(2) An amendment not involving new obligations for Member Nations or Associate Members shall take effect forthwith, unless the resolution by which it is adopted provides otherwise. Amendments involving new obligations shall take effect for each Member Nation and Associate Member accepting the amendment of acceptance by two thirds of the Member Nations of the Organization and thereafter for each

remaining Member Nation or Associate Member on acceptance by it. As regards an Associate Member, the acceptance of amendments involving new obligations shall be given on its behalf by the Member Nation or authority having responsibility for the international relations of the Associate Member.

(3) Proposals for the amendment of the Constitution may be made either by the Council or by a Member Nation in a communication addressed to the Director-General. The Director-General shall immediately inform all Member Nations and Associate Members of all proposals for amendments.

(4) No proposal for the amendment of the Constitution shall be included in the agenda of any session of the Conference unless notice thereof has been dispatched by the Director-General to Member Nations and Associate Members at least 120 days before the opening of the session."

Art. 21 defines the entry into force of the Constitution and art. 22 states that "the Arabic, English, French and Spanish texts of this Constitution shall be equally authoritative".

Yearbook of the UN, 1946.

FARAKKA. A dam built by India on the River Ganges on the border of Bangladesh. It was the subject of a dispute on the utilization of the waters of the Ganges which was submitted to the UN in 1977 by Bangladesh and considered in bilateral negotiations with India 1977–80.

FAR EAST AND UN. The main UN problems in the Far East were: the Korean war conducted in 1950–53 under UN command and the question of the presence of Taiwan in UN bodies in 1949–72 as representative of China. ▷ UN Economic Commission for Asia and the Far East.

FAR EASTERN COMMISSION, 1946–52. An agreement of the Moscow conference of the ministers of foreign affairs of the USA, Great Britain and the USSR, Dec. 6 to 26, 1945, formed the Far Eastern Commission with representatives from: Australia, Canada, China, France, Great Britain, India, the Netherlands, New Zealand, the Philippines, the USA, and USSR; it had the task of supervising Japan's fulfillment of obligations resulting from her unconditional surrender on Aug. 13, 1945 and the resolutions of the Potsdam Conference, July 17–Aug. 2, 1945, concerning Japan. The organ of the Commission, whose seat was in Washington, was the Allied Council for Japan attached to the American Commander-in-Chief of Occupation Forces in Tokyo, composed of representatives of the USA, China, Great Britain and the USSR. The Chairman of the Council was the US Supreme commander of occupation forces in Japan, or his deputy. The Commission, like the Allied Council, began its activities Apr. 18, 1946, but was suspended Apr. 28, 1952 following the Peace Treaty with Japan signed on Sept. 8, 1951 in San Francisco.

"Three-power conference in Moscow", in: *International Conciliation*, No. 418, Feb., 1946, pp. 103–107.

FAROE ISLANDS. 22 volcanic islands (5 not inhabited) in the North Atlantic between Iceland and the Shetland Islands 1399 sq.km. Pop. 1986 est. 45,728; capital Thorshavn with 14,722 inhabitants. Under Danish rule from 1380. The islands were a Norwegian province 1380–1709. They secured the restoration of their Parliament in 1852 and self-government in 1948. World War II under British protectorate during the German occupation of Denmark. Member of the EFTA 1968–1971, then of the EEC.

Official languages: Danish and Faroese.

K. WILLIAMSON, *The Atlantic Islands: A Study of the Faroe Life and Scene,* London, 1970; J.F. WEST,

Faroe, London, 1973; *The Europa Year Book 1984*. Vol. I, pp. 410–411, London, 1984.

FAS. "Free alongside ship, named port of shipment." One of the formulas of ▷ INCOTERMS, meaning that the price of goods includes the cost of transporting them to shipside in a specified port of landing; the risk passes from the seller to the purchaser from the moment of supplying the goods to shipside in the agreed time-limit.

FASCISM AND NAZISM. Two international terms for two forms of nationalistic totalitarian dictatorship introduced 1922 by Benito Mussolini's Fascist Party in Italy and 1933 by Adolf Hitler's German National Socialist Party ▷ NSDAP in Germany; both barred from functioning 1944/45 by the Allied Powers, condemned by the UN as essentially an anti-human ideology and system of government; which was expressed in the justification of the Nuremberg verdict on war criminals. ▷ Nazi and Fascist postwar activities and the UN.

Mirovoy fashizm. Sbornik statiej, Moskva, 1923; S. MATEOTTI, *The Fascisti Exposed*, London, 1924; C. LANDAUER, H. HONEGGER, *Internationaler Faschismus*, Karlsruhe, 1928; G. DIMITROV, *Nastuplenie fashizma*, Moskva, 1935; D. GUERIN, *Fascisme et Grand Capital*, Paris, 1935; E. FRAENKEL, *The Dual State, A Contribution to the Theory of Dictatorship*, New York, 1941; F.L. NEUMANN, *The Structure and Practice of National Socialism*, New York, 1944; *Nazi Conspiracy and Aggression. A Collection of Documentary Evidence and Guide Materials Prepared by the American and British Prosecuting Staffs for the IMT at Nuremberg*, 2 Vols., Washington, DC, 1946; E. KOGON, *Der SS Staat*, Frankfurt am M, 1946; *The International Fascism, 1920–1945*, New York, 1946; A. BULLOCK, *Hitler. A Study in Tyranny*, London, 1952; A. FRYE, *Nazi-Germany and the American Hemisphere 1933–1941*, New Haven, 1961; A. TASCA, *Nascimiento i avento del fascismo*, Bari, 1965; A. AQUARONE, *L'Organizzazione della Stato totalitario*, Torino, 1965; A.D. GALKIN, *Giermanskij fashizm*, Moskva, 1967; J. WOOLF (ed.), *European Fascism*, London, 1968; M. BROSZAT, *Der Staat Hitlers*, München, 1969; P. TOGLIATI, *Lezzioni sul Fascismo*, Roma, 1970; G. ALLARDYCE (ed.), *The Place of Fascism in European History*, Englewood Cliffs, NJ., 1971; A. HAMILTON, *The Appeal of Fascism. A Study of Intellectuals and Fascism, 1919–1945*, London, 1971; A. ABENDROTH (ed.), *Faschismus und Kapitalismus*, Frankfurt am M., 1972; F. RYSZKA, *Państwo stanu wyjatkowego [The State of Martial Law]*, Wrocław, 1974; R. KÜHEL (ed.), *Texte zur Faschismus*, Hamburg, 1974; J. NOAKS, G. PRIDHAM, *Documents on Nazism 1919–1945*, London, 1974; R. de FELICE, *Intervista sul fascismo*, Bari, 1975; J. BOSCH, A. CASSIGOLI, J. CORTAZAR, "El Fascismo en América", in: *Nueva Politica*, No. 1, México, DF, 1976, pp. 7–281; W. LAQUER (ed.), *Fascism. A Reader's Guide. Analyses, Interpretations, Bibliography*, Berkeley 1976; G. PILICHOWSKI, *Nazi camps in Poland 1939–1945. Encyclopedic Guidebook*, Warsaw, 1979; J. BOREJSZA (ed), *Faszyzmy europejskie 1922–1945 (European Fascism 1922–1945)*, Warszawa, 1979; G.L. MOSSE (ed.), *International Fascism*, London, 1979. *UN Chronicle*, January, 1984, p. 17.

FASHION. An international term for a mode of life, style of living, dress and customs: influenced by the time and certain social trends, in the 20th century especially by industrial manufacturing and the mass media; subject of organized international co-operation through international exhibitions and international organizations. The International Commission for Color Textiles and Ready-Made Clothing, Intercolor, was established in 1972. It was an Association of Industrial Standard Institutes from 18 countries. It decides two years in advance the colors which will dominate in the garment industry. Paris has become the world's leading center of ladies' fashion and design, called *Haute*

couture (literally: High dressing), as London was the leader of men's fashion in the 19th century. A magazine dedicated to fashion, *Mercure galant fashion*, began to appear in Paris in 1672, changing its name to *Mercure de France* in 1820. In the second half of the 20th century television played a significant part in popularizing ready-made clothing, erasing the differences between country and city clothing.

T. UZANNE, *Les Modes de Paris, 1797–1897*, Paris, 1897; R. TURNER WILCOX, *The Mode in Fashion*, New York, 1947; V. STEELE, *Paris Fashion, A Cultural History*, New York, 1988.

FASHODA CRISIS, 1898–1899. A colonial incident in a small Sudanese town Fashoda (present name since 1905 Kodok), occupied by French colonial troops 1898, against British–Egyptian claims, resolved by a British–French agreement on Mar. 21, 1899, establishing a provisional frontier between the French Congo and Sudan along the Nile–Congo Watershed.

R.O. COLLINS, *The Southern Sudan 1833–1898*, London, 1962; D.L. LEVIS, *The Race to Fashoda. European Colonialism and African Resistance in the Scramble for Africa*, New York, 1988.

FASIL GHEBBI. An Ethiopian cultural site included in the ▷ World Heritage UNESCO List, near Gondar where stand the castles of the monarchs of the 17th and 18th centuries. The first is that of Fasilides, a massive square construction, with walls of black stone and four round towers surmounted by another, four-sided, crenelated tower. The other castles, which are smaller in size, display numerous architectural innovations.

UNESCO. *A Legacy for All*, Paris, 1984.

FATS. A subject of international co-operation. Organizations reg. with the UIA:

Association for the Oilseeds, Animal and Vegetable Oils and Fats and Derivates Trade in the EEC, f. 1958, Rotterdam International Society for Fat Research, f. 1959, Göteborg.

Yearbook of International Organizations.

FAUNA AND FLORA PRESERVATION CONVENTION, 1933. A Convention relative to the Preservation of Fauna and Flora in their Natural State, with Annex and Protocol, signed on Nov. 8, 1933 in London, by the governments of Belgium, Egypt, France, Great Britain, Italy, Portugal, Spain, Anglo-Egyptian Sudan and the Union of South Africa.

LNTS, vol. 172, p. 241.

FBI. Federal Bureau of Investigation. The main criminal investigation body of the USA. Established in 1908, headquarters in Washington, DC.

D. WHITEHEAD, *The FBI Story*, New York, 1956; F.L. COLLINS, *The FBI in Peace and War*, New York, 1964; N. OLLESTADT, *Inside the FBI*, New York, 1967.

FBS. Forward Based System. An American military term that refers to American tactical nuclear weapons stationed in Europe, subject of negotiations at the Vienna Disarmament Conference of the NATO states and the Warsaw Pact.

FCDM. Food Composition Data Management, one of the information systems of the ▷ FAO.

FEBRUARY REVOLUTION, 1917. The date of the overthrow of the Russian Tsar Nicholas II, Mar. 15, 1917, and the formation of a provisional government led by Alexander Kerensky, which in

Oct., 1917 was overthrown by the Bolsheviks under the leadership of Vladimir I. Lenin.

E.H. CARR, *The Bolshevik Revolution*, 3 Vols, London, 1950–53; A. KERENSKY, *Memoirs: Russia and History's Turning Point*, Stanford, 1966.

FEDALA CONFERENCE, 1956. A meeting of the governments of Belgium, France, Great Britain, Italy, Morocco, the Netherlands, Portugal, Spain and the USA in the Moroccan city of Fedala (from 1958 renamed Mohammedia) Oct. 8–29, 1956 on the question of the international status of ▷ Tangier.

FEDAYEEN. The Palestinian partisan.

FEDERAL CLAUSES. An international term for special provisions in inter-state agreements stating that the agreement refers to all federated states.

FEDERALISM. An international term for a political movement aiming at integration of a given region in the form of a voluntary union of states; subject of international agreements (e.g. during World War II the governments-in-exile of Belgium, Holland and Luxembourg signed an agreement in London to create ▷ BENELUX after the war; in 1941, also in London, E. Beneš and W. Sikorski signed an agreement obligating the parties to establish a Polish–Czech federation); subject of permanent organized international co-operation. Organizations reg. with the UIA:

Central European Federalist, f. 1948, London.
European Cultural Centre, f. 1950, Geneva.
European Federative Movement, f. 1948, Paris.
European Movement, f. 1947, Brussels.
European Movement of the Left, f. 1947, Paris.
Liberal Movement for United Europe, f. 1952, Brussels.
Movement for the Federation of the Americas, f. 1948, Bogota.
World Association of Federalists, f. 1946, The Hague.
Publ. since 1974 *Transnational Perspectives*.

M. BURGESS, *Federalism and Federation in Western Europe*, London 1986. *Yearbook of International Organizations.*

FEDERAL REPUBLIC OF GERMANY, FRG. The official German name of the FRG is Bundesrepublik Deutschland, but in the English official alphabetical order in the UN as in the Index of the UN Yearbook and other UN documentations only the term: ▷ Germany, Federal Republic of, is in use. The acronym used in the UN is FRG.

FEDERAL RESERVE SYSTEM. A central bank system organized in the USA under a law of Dec. 23, 1913 following a century of fundamental financial disputes between state and federal governments and state and private banks, which had the right to issue their own notes. According to the law, the USA was divided into 12 Federal Reserve Districts in which 12 Federal Reserve Banks were organized: (1) Boston; (2) New York; (3) Philadelphia; (4) Cleveland; (5) Richmond; (6) Atlanta; (7) Chicago; (8) St Louis; (9) Minneapolis; (10) Kansas City; (11) Dallas; (12) San Fransisco. These banks issue two kinds of notes: Federal Reserve Notes, which are obligations of the United States of America, and Federal Reserve Bank Notes, which are obligations of the Reserve Bank that issued them. Publ.: *Federal Reserve Monthly Bulletin*, Washington, DC.

The Federal Reserve System: Purposes and Functions, Washington, DC, 1974.

FEDERAL STATE. ▷ Confederation.

FEDERATE STATE OF MICRONESIA. ▷ Micronesia, Federate State.

F

FEDERATION. A federal state which has its own federal organs; individual federal provinces which give up part of their sovereign rights while retaining their autonomous governments and in some cases retaining the right to make international agreements. Federations with different statutes: Australia, Austria, Brazil, the FRG, India, Malaysia, Mexico, Switzerland, Tanzania, Yugoslavia and the USSR, two of whose federal republics – the Byelorussian SSR and Ukrainian SSR – are together with the Soviet Union members of the UN. ▷ Federal clauses.

FEDERATION OF ARAB REPUBLICS. The union of Egypt, Syria and Libya formed on Apr. 17, 1971 in Benghazi affirmed by a general referendum on Sept. 1, 1971. The name was changed in 1972 to the ▷ United Arab Republic.

FEDERATION OF EUROPE. ▷ European Confederation.

FEDERATION OF MALAYSIA. From Feb. 1, 1948 the name of the Malaysian Union which existed from 1946 under the sovereignty of the UK. On Aug. 31, 1957 it was proclaimed an independent state in the British Commonwealth of Nations and from Oct. 17, 1957 is a member of the UN. On Sept. 16, 1963 it became a part of ▷ Malaysia.

FEDERATION OF RHODESIA AND NYASALAND. A union of African states created in 1953 by Great Britain comprising its colonies of Southern Rhodesia and two protectorates: Northern Rhodesia and Nyasaland. After dissolution of the Federation in 1963, Nyasaland gained independence in 1964 as ▷ Malawi and Northern Rhodesia as ▷ Zambia; Southern Rhodesia took the name Rhodesia, whose independence was unilaterally proclaimed on Nov. 11, 1965 by the government in contravention of a resolution of the UN General Assembly. ▷ Zimbabwe.

FEDERATION OF SOUTH ARABIA 1959–67. A union of seven Arab sheikdoms which remained under the protectorate of Great Britain until the time of the withdrawal of British forces (1967) and the proclamation of the People's Democratic Republic of Yemen. ▷ Yemen, South.

FELLOW TRAVELLERS. An international term for non-party intellectuals who support communist or socialist revolution; appeared in England and the USA at the end of the 1920s and beginning of the 1930s under the influence of the Russian term ▷ Poputchiki.

FEMINISM. A XIX century international term for the idea of women's political and social equality, integrated by the UNESCO Human Rights Declaration 1947. A new international feminist movement started in the 1980's.
See also ▷ Suffragettes; ▷ Women's Rights.
L. DOMINELLI, E. McLEOD, *Feminism and Welfare, Social Action and Social Work*, London 1986.

FENCING. Olympic sport since the first modern Olympic Games in 1896, organized by the International Federation of Fencing, FIE, 1913, which sponsors world championships.
Yearbook of International Organizations.

FERRYBOAT SERVICE. An international term for transport of vehicles, commodities and passengers by ferryboats; known since antiquity in river navigation, developed in the 20th century in maritime navigation on an international scale in connection with the development of railroad and car transportation. The first ferryboats transporting trains from one country to another were introduced for transport of troops in 1917/18 from Richborough to Calais and Dunkirk and from Southampton to Dieppe. Subject of international agreements.

FERTILITY. A subject of international scientific research. Organizations reg. with the UIA:
International Fertility Association, f. 1951, Rio de Janeiro. Official relations with WHO, ECOSOC. Publ.: *International Journal of Fertility*; World Fertility Survey, f. 1972, Voorburg.
Yearbook of International Organizations.

FERTILIZERS. One of the basic products of the chemical industry, subject of international co-operation. Organizations reg. with the UIA:
EEC Special Committee on Fertilizers and Pesticides in Agriculture, f. 1963, Paris.
International Potash Institute, est. 1952, Berlin, Consultative status with FAO. Publ.: *Revue de la Potasse.*
International Superphosphates Manufacturers Associations, f. 1926, London, Publ.: *Bulletin of Documentation*
Union for Fertilizer Trade in the EEC countries, est. 1960, Brussels.
FAO publishes the following yearbooks since 1952: *Fertilizers, A World Report and Statistics of Crop Response to Fertilizers*
V. IGNATIEFF, H.J. PAGE, *The Efficient Use of Fertilizers*, FAO, Rome, 1968; *Fertilizers and Their Use. A Pocket Guide for Extension Officers*, FAO, Rome, 1970; FAO, *Fertilizer Yearbook*, Rome, 1982.

FESTIVALS, INTERNATIONAL. The organized practice of presenting annual festivals of achievements in various areas of the fine arts, theater, film, songs. Many festivals take place under UNESCO sponsorship or that of international organizations reg. with the UIA. ▷ Film Festivals. ▷ Music International Festivals.
World Dictionary of Awards and Prizes, London, 1979.

FIBRE. Subject of international co-operation. Organizations reg. with the UIA:
European Federation of Fibreboard Manufacturers, f. 1950, Giessen, FRG.
Federation of Nordic Fiberboard Industries, f. 1982, Stockholm, Sweden.
Interkhimvolokno, within the framework of CMEA, f. 1974, Bucharest, Romania.
International Association of Users of Yarn of Man-Made Fibres, f. 1954, Gent, Belgium.
International Bureau for the Standardization of Man-Made Fibres, f. 1928, Basel, Switzerland. Publ. Internationally Agreed Methods.
International Mohair Association, f. 1974, London, UK.
International Rayon and Synthetic Fibres Committee, f. 1950, Paris, France.

▷ Multifibre Arrangement, GATT.
Yearbook of International Organizations, 1986/87; The Europa Yearbook 1988; A World Survey, Vol. I, London 1988.

FIDEL CASTRO DOCTRINE, 1975. A thesis advanced at the First Congress of the Cuban Communist Party in Dec., 1975 that "Cuba is a Latino-African country" in view of the African origin of a large part of its population and common cultural traditions. Cuba established diplomatic relations with nearly all of the African states and in 1976 rendered military support to Angola and in 1978 supported Ethiopia in its conflict with Somalia.
Granma, December, 1975.

FIELD HOCKEY. Olympic discipline since 1908, organized internationally since 1907. Since 1971, world championships staged by the Federation internationale de hockey sur gazon, FIHG, Brussels. Reg. with the UIA.
Yearbook of International Organizations.

FIFTH COLUMN. ▷ Quinta Columna.

FIJI. Member of the UN. Independent republic of the Melanesian island group in the South Pacific, comprises *c.* 320 islands, of which one-third are inhabited. Area: 18,376 sq. km. Pop.: 1987 est.: 723,000 (1977 census 601,485, the majority Indians – 300,697, and Fijians – 266,822). The largest island is Viti Levu (area: 10,426 sq. km). The capital: Suva with 68,178 inhabitants, 1981. GNP per capita 1987: US $1510. Official language: English. Currency: one Fiji dollar = 100 cents. National Day: Oct. 10, Independence Day, 1970.
Member of the UN from Oct. 13, 1970 and of all UN specialized agencies. Member of the Commonwealth, the Colombo Plan and is an ACP state of the EEC.
International relations: the islands were discovered in 1643; visited by Capt. J. Cook, 1774; recorded by Capt. Bligh after the mutiny on the *Bounty*, 1789; under British administration from Oct. 10, 1874 until Oct. 10, 1970, when Fiji was proclaimed an independent republic.
G.K. ROTH, *The Fijian way of Life*, London, 1973; R.R. NAYACAKALOU, *Leadership in Fiji*, London, 1976; *The Europa Year Book 1984. A World Survey*, Vol. II, pp. 1562–1567, London, 1984; M. TAYLOR (ed.), *Fiji: Future Imperfect*, Boston, 1987.

FILM. A subject of permanent organized international co-operation since 1927, date of the first international film festival in Paris; subject of international conventions on educational and scientific films. The first was the Geneva Convention on Facilitating the International Circulation of Films of an Educational Nature, signed Oct. 11, 1933; second to the Inter-American Convention concerning Facilities for Educational and Publicity Films, signed on Dec. 23, 1936 in Buenos Aires by 20 American republics, entered into force on Apr. 1, 1938; not signed by the USA; not ratified by Argentina, Bolivia, Paraguay and Uruguay.
Organizations reg. with the UIA:
Arab Film and TV Center, f. 1965, Cairo.
Bureau du Cinema, f. 1959, Rome.
European Film Unions, f. 1962, Brussels.
European Union of Film and TV Workers, f. 1952, Paris.
Film and TV Council, f. 1958, Rome. Advisory status with UNESCO.
International Animated Film Association, f. 1968, Bucharest.
International Committee for the diffusion of Arts and Literature through the Cinema, f. 1930, Paris.
International Committee on Ethnographical and Sociological Films, f. 1966, Paris.
International Council for Education, f. 1950, Paris.
International Experimental and Art Film Theater Confederation, f. 1955, Paris.
International Federation of Art Films, f. 1948, Paris.
International Federation of Film Archives, f. 1938, Brussels, Belgium.
International Federation of Film Producers Association, f. 1933, Paris, France.
International Federation of Film Societies, f. 1947, London.
International Inter-Church Film Centre, f. 1955, Hilversum.
International Liaison Centre for Cinema and Television Schools, f. 1955, Brussels.
International Railway Film Bureau, f. 1961, Paris.
International Scientific Association, f. 1947, Paris.
International Scientific Film Library, f. 1961, Brussels, Belgium.

International Union of Amateur Cine, f. 1937, Paris.
International Union of Technical Cinematograph Association, f. 1957, Paris.
Latin American Institute for Educational Communication, f. 1971, Mexico City.
Union of Cine Exhibitors, 1952, Paris.

LNTS, Vol. 155; *Carnegie Endowment International Conferences of American States, First Supplement 1933–40*, Washington, DC, 1940; W.E. CLASON, *Elsevier's Dictionary of Cinema, Sound and Music*. In English/American (with definitions), French, Spanish, Italian, Dutch and German; Amsterdam, 1956; UNESCO, *Cinematographic Institutions*, Paris, 1973; E. KATZ, *The International Film Encyclopedia*, New York, 1980; *Yearbook of International Organizations, 1986/87; The Europa Yearbook 1988. A World Survey*, Vol. I, London, 1988.

FILM FESTIVALS. The first international film festival was held in Paris in 1927 at the International Exhibition of Fine Arts; first prize was awarded to the Soviet film "Potiomkin", directed by S.M. Eisenstein (1898–1948). Since 1932 international film festivals have been held in France, Germany, the USA and Italy co-ordinated since 1934 by the International Federation of Film Archives in Paris. In Los Angeles the Film Academy grants annual awards, called Oscars. After World War II, besides the renewed film festival in Venice (with the award of the Lion of St Mark's) international film festivals have been held since 1946 in Cannes, since 1948 biennially in Karlovy Vary; since 1948 biennially in Moscow; since 1958 in West Berlin (with the award of the Golden Bear); since 1960 in San Sebastian and elsewhere. Held since 1958 in Mexico City, as well in Acapulco is the Festival of Festivals, in which only films that have received awards in film festivals of the previous year can qualify. It is called *Reseña Mundial de los Festivales Cinematograficos* (with the award of a Golden Aztec Head, *Cabeza de Palenque*). Held annually in Leipzig since 1957 is the International Film Week of Documentary and Short Feature Films for Movies and Television under the traditional slogan of Films of the World in the Struggle for Peace. Several dozen countries take part in this event, as well as the UN, which presents films produced by UN special organizations or at their request. Besides the festival awards, there are many international awards funded by organizations, as e.g. the UNESCO Award or the International Peace Award granted by the World Peace Council. Others: International Festival of Films in Mar del Plata; International Festival of Short Feature Films in Cracow and Oberhausen.

World Dictionary of Awards and Prizes, London, 1979.

FINAL ACT. An international term introduced June 9, 1815 by the Congress of Vienna as the title of a document summarizing the resolutions of the Congress and constituting an international treaty binding on the signatories of the Final Act; since then accepted by international congresses and conferences for international obligations passed by them. Also used in the UN in reference to a summary of the works of commissions which have the task of carrying out tasks entrusted to them by the UN General Assembly. ▷ Helsinki Final Act.

FINAL SOLUTION. ▷ Endlösung.

FINANCIAL CRISIS OF THE UNITED NATIONS 1985-1986. The most severe financial crisis in United Nations history took place, as the Secretary General observed on Sept. 9, 1986, in the budget year 1985/86. The Group High-Level Intergovernmental Experts to Review the Efficiency of the Administration and Financial Functioning of the United Nations has formulated 71 recommendations to streamline the structure of the

Organization, which the experts describe as "too complex, fragmented and top heavy".
See also ▷ Debtors of the UN.

UN Chronicle, No. 1, 1987.

FINANCIAL INTERNATIONAL ORGANIZATIONS. Organizations reg. with the UIA:

Association of African Development Finance Institutions, f. 1975, Abidjan, Ivory Coast.
European Academic Association for Financial Research, f. 1963, Paris.
European Federation of Finance House Associations, f. 1959, Brussels. Publ.: *Newsletter*.
European Federation of Financial Analysts Societies, f. 1962, Paris
International Association of Financial Executive Institutes, f. 1970, Brussels.
International Finance Corporation, IFC, f. 1956, Washington DC.; IFC acts through the World Bank.
International Institute of Public Finance, f. 1937, Paris. Consultative status with ECOSOC and UNESCO.
Latin American Association of Development Financing Institutions, f. 1968, Lima. Consultative status with UNIDO. Publ.: *Boletin Informativo de Instituciones Financieras de Desarrollo*.
Union of the European Economic and Financial Press, f. 1962, Paris.

The IFC publ.: *Government Financial Statistics Yearbook*, and, from June 1964, a quarterly, *Finance and Development*.

F.J. THOMSON, *Elsevier's Dictionary of Financial Terms*. In English, German, Spanish, French, Italian and Dutch, Amsterdam, 1979.

FINANCIAL TERMINOLOGY. The financial terminology used in the UN system. See the list of terms in the Selective Index under "Financial Terminology".

FINANCIAL YEAR OF THE UN. The financial year of the UN comprises the period Jan. 1 to Dec. 31 inclusive.

UN Doc. (ST/SGB) Financial Rules 1/Rev. 1, New York, 1970.

FINANCING OF INTERNATIONAL ORGANIZATIONS. The international organizations are financed from annual membership assessments, donations from members, private institutions, incomes from foundations, and other sources. Ratified annually the UN budget is divided among the membership on the basis of national income from 0.01% to 25%. The scale of assessments is usually revised every three years by the UN General Assembly on the recommendations of the Committee on Contributions. Other international organizations do likewise, but many of them use the ITU system where there are ten lump-sum dues, the level paid by an individual member depending on the lump-sum category in which it has been included; the sum of these determines the size of the budget of the organization.

J.G. STOESSINGER, *Financing the UN System*, Washington, DC, 1964.

FINEFTA. the Finland–EFTA Association, est. June 26, 1961 at Stockholm by an Agreement between Finland and the ▷ EFTA.

EFTA Bulletin, No. 7, 1961.

FINGERPRINTING. An international term since the end of the XIX century, when most European and American countries started to require that all criminals be fingerprinted. In the XX century a controversial custom of obligatory fingerprinting of aliens, political prisoners or dissidents.

C.E. CHAPEL, *Fingerprint*, New York, 1941; *Fingerprinting of Aliens in Japan*, in: KEESING'S *Contemporary Archive*, August 1986.

FINIS BELLI PAX EST. *Latin* = "the War Must End by Peace". A doctrine of the Roman Empire as well of modern international law.

H. KRUGER, "Finis belli pax est", in: *Jahrbuch fur internationales Recht*, 1962, pp. 200–212.

FINLAND. Member of the UN. Suomen Tasavalta – Republiken Finland. Republic of Finland. A state in northern Europe on the Baltic Sea. Borders on the USSR, Norway and Sweden. Area: 304,623 sq. km. Pop. at the 1982 census: 4,841,481 (census 1800 – 832,000;1900 – 4,597,000). Capital: Helsinki with 910,414 inhabitants (metropolitan area 1981). GNP per capita in 1987: US $14,370. Official languages: Finnish (91% of the population) and Swedish (8.6% of the population). Currency: one markka = 100 penni. National Day: Dec. 6, anniversary of the proclamation of independence.

In 1926–40 Finland was a member of the League of Nations. Finland is a member of the UN and all specialized organizations since Dec. 14, 1955. Since 1961 a member of the Nordic Council, OECD and an associated member of the EFTA.

International relations: after centuries of dependence on Sweden and Russia the independent Republic of Finland was proclaimed during World War I on Dec. 6, 1917, after the outbreak of the October Revolution in Russia, and was recognized on Dec. 31, 1917 by the revolutionary government of Russia. On Jan. 27, 1918 a socialist government was formed which on Mar. 1, 1918 concluded a treaty of friendship with the Russian SFSR. Peace with the Russian SFSR was signed on Oct 20, 1920, 1920 in Dorpat, which confirmed the granting to Finland in the treaty of friendship of 1918 of the ice-free port of Petsamo (*Russian*: Pyetchengo) at the mouth of the river of this name on the Barents Sea. In 1920–21 in a dispute with Sweden over the Åland Islands. On Jan. 21, 1932 concluded a non-agression treaty with the Soviet Union (extended in 1934 for 10 years) cancelled by the Soviet–Finnish war in the period from Nov. 30, 1939 to Feb. 12, 1940, when a peace treaty signed in Moscow ceded to the Soviet Union the Carelian Isthmus, the city of Vyborg and the port of Petsamo. At war with the USSR July 1, 1941–Sept. 19, 1944. Frontiers with the USSR were established according to the Moscow treaty of 1940 and the Paris Peace Treaty of Feb. 10, 1947. On Apr. 8, 1948 Finland signed a Treaty of Friendship, Co-operation and Mutual Assistance with the USSR, extended in 1956 and 1970. In 1956 the USSR returned to Finland the naval base in Porkkala, which had been leased in Dec., 1944 for 50 years. On Apr. 20, 1971 Finland signed a ten-year agreement with the USSR on economic, technical and industrial co-operation; on July 22, 1971 Finland initialled the Brussels treaties of the EFTA states on expanding trade with the EEC states. Since 1971 the government of Finland has taken an active part in calling a Conference on Security and Co-operation in Europe by offering Helsinki as the site for initial consultations, which were held in 1972–73, and the conference itself, which was held in 1973–75. Also held in Helsinki from Jan. 26 to Feb. 1, 1973 was the first All-European Parliamentary Conference called by the Inter-parliamentary Union. On May 23, 1973 Finland signed an agreement on co-operation with the CMEA.

W. ROTHOLS, "Finlands Völkerrechtliches Schicksall seit 1917", in: *Archiv für Völkerrecht*, 1948–49; A.G. MAROUX, *Finland between East and West*, New York, 1956; C.L. LUNDIN, *Finland in the Second World War*, Indiana University Press, 1957; E. JUTIK-

F

KALA, K. PIRINEN, *A History of Finland*, New York, 1962; I. ROZDOROZNY, V. FIEDOROV, *Finlandia – Nash Severnyi Sosed* Moskva, 1966; W. HALL, *The Finns and their Country*, New York, 1968; T. JUNILLA, *Finlands Aussenpolitik*, Hamburg, 1972; *Yearbook of Finnish Foreign Policy*, 1973, Helsinki, 1974; W. ULRICH, *Finlands Neutralität*, Hamburg, 1974; "Agreement on Corporation with CMEA": in: *A Source Book on Socialist International Organizations*, Alphen, 1978; *Statistical Yearbook of Finland*, Helsinki, 1980; M. KLINGE, *A Brief History of Finland*, Helsinki, 1981; *The Europa Year Book 1984. A World Survey*, Vol. I, pp. 414–433, London, 1984.

"FINLANDIZATION". An international term of the 1970s referring to the dependence of a small country on a big neighbor in the context of "Finlandization of Western Europe in relations with USSR" brought up in discussions on broader *détente* between East and West. The President of Finland, Urho Kekkonen, speaking on Apr. 4, 1974 in Helsinki, on the occasion of the 25th Anniversary of the Treaty of Friendship, Co-operation and Mutual Assistance between Finland and USSR, declared:

"We do not offer our Treaty with the USSR as a model for other States of the world, but we offer it as a model for its consequences: co-operation based on mutual confidence of two States with different social systems. This is true 'finlandization', and such an interpretation of this term can be applied universally without any discrimination against Finland."

H. ESKELINEN, *Finland*, London, 1974.

FINLAND PEACE TREATY, 1947. A treaty between the Allied and Associated Powers on the one hand, and Finland on the other, concluded on Feb. 10, 1947 in Paris, and came into force on Sept. 15, 1947. The texts of the Preamble and the first articles are as follows:

"The USSR, the UK, Australia, the Byelorussian SSR, Canada, Czechoslovakia, India, New Zealand, the Ukrainian SSR, and the Union of South Africa, as the States which are at war with Finland and actively waged war against the European enemy States with substantial military forces, hereinafter referred to as "the Allied and Associated Powers", on the one part, and Finland, on the other part;
Whereas Finland, having become an ally of Hitlerite Germany and having participated on her side in the war against the USSR, the UK and other United Nations, bears her share of responsibility for this war;
Whereas, however, Finland, on September 4, 1944, entirely ceased military operation against the United Nations, withdrew from the war against the United Nations, broke off relations with Germany and her satellites, and, having concluded on September 19, 1944, an Armistice with the Governments of the USSR and the UK acting on behalf of the United Nations at war with Finland, loyally carried out the Armistice terms; and
Whereas the Allied and Associated Powers and Finland are desirous of concluding a treaty of peace which, conforming to the principles of justice, will settle questions still outstanding as a result of the events hereinbefore recited and will form the basis of friendly relations between them, it by the Soviet–Finnish Peace Treaty of March 12, 1940, and Finland for her part confirms having granted to the Soviet Union on the basis of a fifty years lease at an annual rent payable by the Soviet Union of five million Finnish marks and the use and administration of territory and waters for the establishment of a Soviet naval base in the area of Porkkala-Udd.
(2) Finland confirms having secured to the Soviet Union, in accordance with the Armistice Agreement, the use of the railways, waterways, roads and air routes necessary for the transport of personnel and freight dispatched from the Soviet Union to the naval base at Porkkala-Udd, and also confirms having granted to the Soviet Union the right of unimpeded use of all forms of communication between the Soviet Union and the territory leased in the area of Porkkala-Udd.
Art. 5. The Aalands Islands shall remain demilitarized in accordance with the situation as at present existing.

Art. 6. Finland shall take all measures necessary to secure to all persons under Finnish jurisdiction, without distinction as to race, sex, language or religion, the enjoyment of human rights and of the fundamental freedoms, including freedom of expression, of press and publication, of religious worship, of political opinion and of public meeting.
Art. 7. Finland, which in accordance with the Armistice Agreement has taken measures to set free, irrespective of citizenship and nationality, all persons held in confinement on account of their activities in favour of, or because of the sympathies with, the United Nations or because of their racial origin, and to repeal discriminatory legislation and restrictions imposed thereunder, shall complete these measures and shall in future not take any measures or enact any law which would be incompatible with the purposes set forth in this Article.
Art. 8. Finland, which in accordance with the Armistice Agreement has taken measures for dissolving all organisations of a Fascist type of Finnish territory whether political, military or para-military ..."

UNTS, 1947.

FINNISH–GERMAN PEACE TREATY, 1918. A treaty signed on Mar. 7, 1918 in Berlin. The highlights of the Treaty are:

"The contracting parties declare that no state of war exists between Germany and Finland, and that they are resolved henceforth to live in peace and friendship with one another. Germany will do what she can to bring about the recognition of the independence of Finland by all the Powers. On the other hand, Finland will not cede any part of her possessions to any foreign Power or grant a servitude on her sovereign territory to any such Power without first having come to an understanding with Germany on the matter. The contracting parties are agreed that the fortifications erected on the Aland Islands shall be done away with as soon as possible, and the permanent non-fortification of these islands, and their other management from a military and shipping technical point of view, shall be regulated by a special agreement between Germany, Finland, Russia, and Sweden; other states situated on the Baltic shall also be parties to the agreement if desired by Germany."

International Conciliation, No. 128, July, 1918, pp. 426–428.

FINNISH–SOVIET FRIENDSHIP TREATY, 1948. A treaty signed on Apr. 6, 1948 in Moscow. The highlights of the agreement are: "In the belief that consolidation of the good-neighbourly relations and co-operation between the USSR and Finland is in the interest of the two countries" and "considerate of Finland's aspiration to hold itself aloof of conflicting interests of Big Powers", the governments of the two countries concluded the Treaty of Friendship, Co-operation and Mutual Assistance. Art. 1 specified mutual assistance in case of "aggression by Germany or any other state aligned with it." Under art. 2 both states pledged to consult each other "in case of finding a threat of aggression" and under art. 3 to "participate most earnestly in all ventures aimed to maintain international peace and security in keeping with the aims and principles of the UN." Art. 4 reaffirmed the obligations arising from art. 3 of the Peace Treaty of Feb. 10, 1947, to refrain from partaking in alliances and coalitions against the other Party. Art. 5 postulated development of economic and cultural co-operation. Art. 6 imposed on both sides the obligation of mutual respect of sovereignty and "non-interference in the internal affairs of the other state." Art. 7 determined the validity of the treaty for ten years from the moment of its ratification by both sides, May 31, 1948.
The agreement was prolonged on Sept. 19, 1955; by way of joint statement of Oct. 9, 1968 recognized as "the basis for the development of Finnish–Soviet relations."

C.A. COLLIARD, *Droit international et Histoire diplomatique*, Paris, 1950; KEESING's *Contemporary Archive* 1948/49, 1955 and 1968.

FIRE ARMS. An international term for a weapon propelling a bullet by the force of gun-powder gases, divided into heavy arms (rifle and artillery arms) and short arms (revolvers and pistols). Subject of international conventions:
Convention between Belgium, France, Germany and Italy on Uniform Regulations for the Reciprocal Recognition of Proof Marks on Fire Arms, was signed on July 5, 1914 in Brussels.
Convention (replacing the above-mentioned) for the Reciprocal Recognition of Proof Marks on Small Arms, signed on July 1, 1969 in Brussels; came into force on July 3, 1971 in respect of Austria, Belgium and France; est. a Permanent International Commission for the Proving of Small Arms.

LNTS, Vol. 129, p. 133; *UNTS*, Vol. 795, p. 249; D. ROBERTSON, *Guide to Modern Defense and Strategy*, Detroit, 1988.

FIRE PREVENTION. A subject of international co-operation. Organizations reg. with the UIA:

International Association of Fire Fighters, f. 1945, Washington, DC.
International Fire Service Training Association, f. 1933, Colorado Springs, Col.
International Technical Committee for the Prevention and Extinction of Fire, f. 1900, Paris. Aims: to develop theory and practice of fire prevention and extinction, encourage research into the organization of equipment of fire brigades.

Yearbook of International Organizations.

FIRST OF MAY. An annual international holiday of the working masses since 1890 in accordance with a resolution of the Second International, 1889; it celebrates the anniversary of the workers' strike in Chicago announced by the American Federation of Labor in its fight for an 8-hour work day in May, 1886. The first manifestations and processions of workers took place on May 1, 1890 in Austria–Hungary, Belgium, France, Germany, Great Britain, Spain and Tsarist Russia. In the 20th century it is a state holiday in socialist countries. In other countries celebrated also as a springtime festival. ▷ Work time.

B.L. PIERCE, *A History of Chicago*, 3 Vols., Chicago, 1937–1957.

FIRST USE. ▷ No First use.

FIRST WASHINGTON SECURITIES CORPORATION. A state institution, f. 1970, as the second biggest federal financial institution after the ▷ Export–Import Bank of the United States; its aims include facilitation of international financial operations primarily with Western Europe, Japan and Latin America with a view to extension of international liquidity.

FISCAL INTERNATIONAL ORGANIZATIONS. Organization reg. with the UIA:

International Bureau of Fiscal Documentation, f. 1938, Amsterdam. Publ.: *European Taxation, Bulletin for International Fiscal Documentation*.
International Federation of Legal and Fiscal Consultants, f. 1956, Milano. Publ.: *Chronologie des Congres*.
International Fiscal Association, f. 1938, Rotterdam. Consultative status with ECOSOC.

Yearbook of International Organizations.

FISCAL INTERNATIONAL TREATIES. The treaties registered with the Fiscal Division, UN Department of Economic Affairs which publishes a list in English, French and Spanish. Their legal aspects are discussed in the periodical, *Cahiers de Droit Fiscal International*, publ. by the International Fiscal Association.

FISHERIES, ECONOMIC ZONES.

The zones of exclusive sea fishery extending from 30 to 200 nautical miles, so designated at the first session of the Third Conference on the Law of the Sea, held in Caracas in 1974. They were introduced by means of unilateral acts, providing in general for 200-mile zones by Latin American, African and South Asian states and subsequently by the USSR on Dec. 10, 1976 and the USA on Mar. 1, 1977.

Under claims of domestic jurisdiction a variety of regulations were introduced, such as licenses for fishing in zones, limits on the volume of catch, specification of species of fish to be caught or those partially or totally ruled out, specification of periods and areas of fishing, information and reports on the course of fishing, national systems of control and inspection of alien fishing vessels, means of coercion, taxation of ships corresponding to their tonnage or the worth of catch.

The ▷ Sea Law Convention 1982 (Part V, Arts 55-58) subjected the exclusive economic zones to specific legal regimes.

The main provisions of a common Fisheries policy are as follows: to all 260,000 EEC fishermen (1988) the Community waters are open within a 200 mile limit off the coasts of the Atlantic and North Sea and within narrower limits off the coasts of the Mediterranean and Baltic Seas; the conservation of fish stock, and surveillance measures, marketing, guide prices international relations, etc. are subject of annual directives of the Council of Ministers. The number of fishing zones will be reviewed by 1995.

W.C. EXTAVOUR, *The Exclusive Economic Zone: A Study of the Evolution and Progressive Development of the International Law of the Sea*, Geneva, 1978; *World Oceans and Seas. Maritime Claims by Countries and Categories: 200-nautical miles Exclusive Economic zones*, Washington, DC, 1982; D. LEONARD, *The International Law Dictionary*, Oxford, 1987; R.L. BLEDSOE, B.A. BOCZEK, *Pocket Guide to the European Community*, London 1988.

FISHERY.

An international term for fishing, breeding and ownership of fish and other living resources of the sea, the subject of conventions and international disputes. Deep-sea fishery grew in the 20th century, particularly in its second half, largely owing to technical developments. World fish catches, amounting to 21 million tons in 1950, increased in 1975 to 70 milion tons, 30 million of which were taken in the Pacific and adjacent waters, 26 million tons in the Atlantic Ocean and adjacent waters, 10 million tons in inland waters, and 4 million tons in the Indian Ocean and other seas. According to FAO estimates, with the observation of protective regulations and without disturbing the biological balance, catches can increase to 100 million tons yearly, with the biggest unused reserves in the Indian Ocean. In 1975 the largest fishing nations were: Japan (over 10.5 million tons), the USSR (nearly 10 million tons), and China (nearly 7 million tons). The biggest consumer is Asia (about 32 million tons), Europe (without the USSR) (over 12 million tons), the Americas (almost 11 million tons), and the USSR (almost 10 million tons). Conventions on deep-sea fishery, adopted after 1950, aim to protect living resources through regulation of the mesh size of fishermen's nets, a ban on catching undersize fish, the fixing of fishing seasons, defining closed areas with a concentration of young fish, limiting the size of fishing vessels in some regions, fixing the fishing limit of specified resources because of the possible extinction of single species (such limits were introduced successively for ▷

whales, ▷ seals, ▷ salmon, ▷ halibut, and ▷ herring). Morover, since 1975 cod and silver cod have been overfished in the North Atlantic and in the North Sea, as well as sole, mackerel, flounder and sprat. Deep-sea fishery constitutes a major sector of food economy and according to FAO analyses its development may solve the problem of animal protein shortage in regions of mass hunger. The richest shelf fishing grounds include the North Pacific and Atlantic, the waters of Peru, Chile, Ecuador, Argentina and Uruguay; the waters of Morocco, Mauritania, Senegal, Angola, Namibia and the Republic of South Africa; the waters of the Arabian Gulf, Indonesia, the Philippines, Australia and New Zealand.

The introduction of 200-mile territorial limits in 1972–80 for exclusive fishing in those regions limited access to many fishing grounds, thus mandating the conclusion of bilateral agreements with coastal states.

Since 1954 Congresses on problems of fishing vessels are held under FAO sponsorship. Report of the First Congress was published by the FAO, under the title Modern Fishing Gear of the World, Rome, 1959, as was the report of the Second Congress, 1964. Besides, the FAO also publishes expert studies on fish marketing and fisheries. In Dec. 1950, at the Second FAO Regional Conference in Montevideo, Latin American Training Centres in Deep-Sea Fisheries, Centros Latinoamericanos de Capacitacion Pesquera, were established. The first center for South America (except Colombia) was organized in Valparaiso on Mar. 14, 1952, on the basis of an agreement of the Chilean government with the FAO; the second in the capital of Mexico on Oct. 4, 1954, on the basis of an agreement of the Mexican government with the FAO for states of Central America, the Caribbean, Panama, Colombia and Venezuela. Other regional agreements are: An Agreement on Fishing in the Waters of the Danube River between the governments of Bulgaria, Romania, the USSR and Yugoslavia, signed on Jan. 29, 1958 at Bucharest, came into force on Dec. 20, 1958. The Annex of the Agreement includes the Rules for Fishing on the Danube River. An Agreement between the governments of Bulgaria, Romania, and the USSR on Fishing in the Black Sea, signed on July 7, 1959 in Varna, came into force on Mar. 21, 1960. The Contracting Parties agree to co-operate and to render mutual assistance, in carrying out rational fishing in the Black Sea and in carrying out research in the field of ichthyology and hydrobiology directed toward maintaining and augmenting the stock of fish in the Black Sea. A minimum size of which fish may be taken was established (Beluga 140 cm, Russian Sturgeon 80 cm, Savriuga 75 cm, Turbot 35 cm, Shad 16 cm). A Commission for North East Baltic Fishery was est. in 1963. It encompasses an area greater than the Baltic Sea, extending from the Portuguese Atlantic coast to the Barents Sea and including the waters surrounding Iceland. Members of the Commission are the 17 maritime powers of Europe whose fishing is concentrated in this region. The task of the Commission is to set the norms for the catch and protect the environment.

The USA and Japan exchanged notes at Tokyo, on Dec. 11, 1970, constituting two agreements, one concerning certain fisheries off the coast of the USA and concerning salmon fishing; second regarding king and tanner crab fisheries in the eastern Bering Sea.

The USA and the USSR signed at Washington, on Dec. 11, 1970, three agreements on certain fishery problems on the high sea in the western areas of the Middle Atlantic Ocean; in the northeastern part of the Pacific Ocean; and in the northeastern Pacific Ocean. An agreement relating to fishing for king

and tanner crab, was signed at Washington on Feb. 12, 1971.

Since 1975, an International Commission for Scientific, Technical and Economic Co-operation in the field of Deep-Sea Fisheries has been operating within the CMEA, with Bulgaria, the GDR, Poland, Romania and the USSR participating. These countries participate in a Deep-Sea Fisheries Agreement, signed on July 28, 1962 in Warsaw.

A Common Fisheries Policy Agreement of the EEC countries was accepted on Jan. 25, 1983.

The First World Fisheries Conference took place on June 27–July 6, 1984 in Rome, under the aegis of the FAO with representatives from 147 FAO member states and the USSR. As fish make up for nearly 25 per cent of World consumption of animal protein the conference urged greater use of fishery products in international food aid programs.

The Council of Fishery Ministers in the European Community agreed in December 1987 on the total allowable catches on fish for 1988 and in March 1988 accepted fishing agreement with non-EC countries.

Organizations reg. with the UIA include:

Association of Fish Industries of the EEC, f. 1959, Brussels.

Association of National Organizations of Fishing Enterprises of the EEC, f. 1962, Ostend

Commission for the North-West Atlantic Fisheries, f. 1949, Dartmouth, Canada, Organ of Convention on North-West Atlantic Fisheries. Publ.: *Quarterly Newsletters*.

General Fisheries Council for the Mediterranean, f. 1952, under the aegis of FAO, Rome. Publ.: studies and reviews.

Indo-Pacific Fisheries Council, f. in 1948, under the aegis of FAO, Bangkok. Publ.: *Current Pacific Bulletin*.

Inter-American Tropical Tuna Commission, f. 1949, La Jolla, Calif. An intergovernmental institution of Ecuador, Costa Rica, Mexico, Panama and USA.

International Commission for the Southeast Atlantic Fisheries, f. 1971, Madrid.

International North-Pacific Fisheries Commission, f. 1952, Vancouver. Organ of Convention on North Pacific Fisheries. Publ.: *Research Bulletin*.

International Pacific Halibut Commission, f. 1923, Ottawa and Washington. An intergovernmental institution of Canada and the USA.

Transport, Port and Fishery Workers Trade Union International, f. in 1953, Prague, Member of the World Federation of Trade Unions.

Regional Fisheries Commissions for Europe, West Africa and South-West Atlantic are affiliated with the FAO.

Union of EEC Associations of Fish Meal Producers, f. 1962, Hamburg.

Since July 1971 the FAO publishes a monthly, *Aquatic Sciences*, and *Fisheries Abstracts*; since 1961 it publishes a bimonthly, *World Fisheries Abstracts*; and since 1950, *Annual Yearbook of Fishery Statistics*.

I.N. GRABELSON, F. LAMONTE (eds), *The Fisherman's Encyclopaedia*, New York, 1958; J.O. LAGOREE (ed.) *The Book of Fishes*, London, 1958; *Recueil de Documents*, Varsovie, No. 7, 1959; E.S. HERALD, *Living Fishes of the World*, London, 1961; *UNTS*, Vol. 776, 1971, pp. 197–256; *UNTS*, Vol. 777, 1971, pp. 3–54; *UNTS*, Vol. 781, 1971, pp. 203–221; W.E. BUTLER (ed.), *A Source Book of Socialist International Organizations*, Alphen, 1978, pp. 1104–1113; R.E. STOKES, "Prospects for Foreign Fishing Vessels in US Fisheries Development", in: *Marine Policy*, No. 1, 1980; FAO, *Atlas of the Living Resources of the Seas*, Rome, 1981. FAO, *Yearbook of Fishery Statistics*, Rome, 1982; KEESING'S *Contemporary Archive*, April 1985; *The Europa Yearbook 1988. A World Survey*, Vol I, London 1988.

FIST LAW.

An international term for resolution of international disputes by means of force; contrary to international law.

F

G.I. TUNKIN, *Pravo i sila v mezhdonarodnoy sisteme*, Moskva, 1983.

FIUME. ▷ Rijeka or Fiume.

FLAG. An international symbol in the law of the sea to denote the nationality of a merchant ship or warship and to submission on the high seas to the authority of a state. A subject of international conventions (e.g. the Barcelona Declaration of 1921 and the Second Geneva Convention of 1958 on the Law of the Sea, art. 4–6).

The submission of a ship to the state authority of its flag makes it subject to the control of the warships of the same flag. The use by shipowners of so-called "flags of convenience" creates the problem of merchant ship identification; thus, for instance, a European shipowner may, for taxation reasons, sail his vessels under the flag of Panama, though neither the vessel nor its crew have any connection with that country. The 1958 Geneva Convention on the High Seas pronounced itself against such usage by requiring a "genuine link" between the state and the ship (art. 5). The Convention also pronounced itself against the use of two or more flags by states which do not recognize the state ownership of vessels. In 1976 the US Congress, in connection with the growing pollution of the seas by oil tankers, debated the damages ensuing from the use of flags of convenience. In 1982 the Shipping Committee of UNCTAD initiated a codification of the conditions for registration of ships. According to UNCTAD analysis, 56 countries, representing 45% of the world's deadweight tonnage, insisted on a significant degree of involvement in management and all of those explicitly or implicitly required national participation in the ownership.

The five outright open-registry countries (Liberia, Panama, Cyprus, Bermuda and Bahamas) accounted for 29% of deadweight tonnage. "They appear to apply no conditions at all with regard to participation in equity or management by nationals", the document stated.

A further three countries (the United Kingdom, Greece, Saudi Arabia), accounting for 18%, lay in between with differing requirements as to the nationality of the managers of equity requirements. A Conference of Plenipotentiaries on Febr. 7, 1986 adopted the UN Convention on Conditions for Registration of Ships, Articles 8, 9 and 10 of which provide for participation by nationals of the flag state in the ownership, manning and management of ships, thus establishing key economic links between a ship and the flag state. States have an option between the two mandatory articles on ownership and manning, to take into account the different conditions prevailing in flag states.

Flags are the subject of international co-operation and research. In Winchester, Massachusetts the Flag Research Center f. 1962 publishes The Flag Bulletin and has served as a consultant to the countries established in 1960's and after, on the subject of flags.

Organization reg. with the UIA:

International Federation of Vexillological Associations, f. 1967, Winchester, Mass., USA; to promote the scientific study of the history and symbolism of flags. Publ.: The Flag Bulletin (every 2 months), Archivum Heraldicum (quarterly).

V. BRAJKOVIC, E. POLLUA, *Les conditions dans lesquelles les États accordant aux navires le droit d'aborder le pavillon national*, Bruxelles, 1960; W. SMITH, *Flags Through the Ages and Across the World*, New York, 1976; *UN Chronicle*, June 1982, p. 85; *UN Chronicle*, 1986, No. 3, p.98; R.L. BLEDSOE, B.A. BOCZEK, *The International Law Dictionary*, Oxford, 1987; *The Europa Yearbook 1988. A World Survey*, Vol. I, London 1988.

FLAG, EMBLEM, AND SEAL OF THE UN. The UN General Assembly, Dec. 7, 1946, Res. 92/I approved a design for a UN emblem and simultaneously resolved that this emblem would be "used as the official seal of the Organization", obligating the member states to use legal measures in their countries prohibiting the use of the official emblem, seal, and name United Nations or its abbreviation without the consent of the UN Secretary-General. On Oct. 20, 1947 the UN General Assembly resolved that the UN flag would be a blue banner with an emblem on a white background. On Dec. 11, 1952 the UN Secretary-General published a UN Flag Code.

The emblem may be used in the UN system on all official material used by the Department of Public Information, including publications, pamphlets, booklets, fliers and posters, and on official documents and publications of UN bodies. The UN emblem may be used together with the insignia of individual governments only with the express permission of the Publications Board.

United Nations Editorial Manual, New York, 1983, pp.478-492.

FLAG OF THE LEAGUE OF NATIONS. The League of Nations flag was never officially decided upon, just as the emblem and seal of the LN were never designed. Only in two cases did a LN flag appear in the form of a white rectangle with a blue border, once as a symbol of the Commission of League Observers in the conflict of Peru with Colombia over ▷ Leticia Trapezium (on the flag was the inscription: Leticia Commission League of Nations), and for the second time a similar flag was flown (with the inscription League of Nations) before the LN pavilion at the World's Fair in New York, 1939.

FLAG OF TRUCE OFFICER OR WHITE FLAG. A person who goes to an opposing combatant side with a white flag for the purpose of commencing negotiations and for this reason is entitled to immunity; the term was introduced to international law by the Hague conventions of 1899 and 1907 (Statutes of Laws and Practices of Land War, arts. 32, 33 and 34);

"A flag of truce officer is recognized as a person empowered by one of the combatant sides to commence negotiations with the other and arrives with a white flag. He benefits from the right of immunity just as the accompanying trumpeter or drummer or person carrying the flag and the translator."

"The commander to whom the officer was sent is not obligated to receive him in all circumstances. He can issue all orders to prevent the officer from using his mission to gather information. In the event of abuse he has the right to temporarily detain the officer."

"The officer loses the privilege of neutrality if it is provided concretely and irrefutably that he has used his privileged position to cause of commit a treasonous act."

CARNEGIE ENDOWMENT, Hague Conventions of 1899 and 1907, Washington, DC, 1914.

FLAGS OF THE UN STATES. In accordance with international practice, the flags of all member states are raised and lowered daily on flagpoles before the UN Headquarters in New York in English alphabetical order; and also during UN Conferences in Geneva before the Palace of Nations.

FLEET STREET. An international term, synonymous with the British press. Fleet Street in London is since the beginning of the 18th century dominated by the offices of London daily and periodical newspapers.

B. WEINREB, C. HIBBERT (eds). *The London Encyclopedia*, London, 1983.

FLEMISH, THE. The inhabitants of Flanders (now part of Belgium), who have equal rights under the constitution with the French-speaking population. A small Flemish minority lives in France (300,000 est. 1965) and in Holland (c. 30,000). The disputes between the population who speak Flemish and the Walloons who speak French are regulated by special legislation. In 1962 and 1964 parents of French-speaking children residing in the cities of the Flemish part of Belgium filed a complaint with the European Human Rights Commission concerning the lack of French language instruction in their places of residence. The case was decided by the Court for Human Rights on Feb. 9, 1968 and July 23, 1968 in a verdict which objected to certain provisions of Belgian legislation. In this connection, the Belgian Parliament passed a law whereby six communities on the outskirts of Brussels were incorporated into the Flemish region, while the French minority residing in this region received special cultural privileges. The decisions of the court were the first in this area to establish a precedent for the multi-national states of Western Europe.

J.L. BROECKS, *Flandria nostra*, 5 Vols., Bruxelles, 1957–60.

FLEXIBLE RESPONSE. A strategic US military doctrine formulated during the Kennedy administration (1961–63), also called graduated response; not involving ▷ massive retaliation.

D. ROBERTSON, *Guide to Modern Defense and Strategy*, Detroit 1988.

FLIGHT OF CAPITAL FROM DEVELOPING COUNTRIES. ▷ Development Finances.

FLIGHTS OVER OPEN SEA. The right granted to all planes to fly over non-territorial seas and oceans within the framework of the legal regulations on air navigation in accordance with the Second Geneva Convention on the Open Sea, 1958; the subject of Soviet–American dispute, 1960, when in more than 250 cases US planes circled over ships and vessels of the USSR on the open sea, which the USSR termed a violation of ▷ freedom of the high seas in the sense of freedom of navigation on the open sea, whereas the United States regarded it as an accepted "practice of mutual identification of vessels and planes", in an Exchange of notes July 13–21, 1960.

FLIGHTS WITH NUCLEAR BOMBS, 1961–68. In Jan., 1961 the US Strategic Air Command, SAC, introduced permanent 24 hour flights of US strike over territories bordering the USSR, carried out by 75 bombers with nuclear and thermonuclear bombs aboard; 600 devices of this type were in readiness at airfields in the USA. The USSR lodged a protest in the UN Security Council and General Assembly against such flights so far from the mother country. At the time of these flights SAC bombers lost their nuclear cargoes many times (according to American sources 37 times to 1970); the best-known cases included ▷ Palomares in 1966, where an atomic bomb was lost, as well as Greenland in 1968, where a hydrogen bomb was lost. On Feb. 27, 1968 the US Secretary of Defense announced that the SAC flights on missions of permanent readiness were suspended.

T. SZULC, *The Bombs of Palomares*, New York, 1967.

FLOATING RATE OF EXCHANGE. An international term which appeared after World War I – a rate subject to fluctuations depending on supply and demand without fixed limits, as e.g. the French franc, 1919–26 and July, 1937–May, 1938; the pound sterling and Swedish krona, 1931–39, and the US dollar Apr., 1933–Jan., 1934. After World War II this phenomenon did not appear, since the members of the IMF pegged their currencies to the US dollar in relation to its exchangeability for gold at 35 dollars per ounce of pure gold (unchanged since 1934). All devaluations or revaluations could only take place with the agreement of the IMF (fluctuations on the money market were permissible by the IMF statute in limits of "intervention points", plus and minus 1% in relation to the official rate. Not until the 1971 crisis of the US dollar did the West German mark convert to a floating rate of exchange system in May and Aug. 15, 1971 – the date of the suspension by the USA of the convertibility of the dollar into gold – followed by other "hard currencies" such as the Japanese yen, the currencies of the Benelux states, France and others.

International Currency Experience: Lessons of the Inter-War Period, League of Nations, Geneva, 1944; E. SOHMEN, *Flexible Exchange Rates. Theory and Controversy*, Chicago, 1961; G.N. HALM, *Die Vergrösserung für Devisenkursschwankungen*, Berlin, 1965; M.E. KREININ, "Living with floating rates: a survey of developments 1973–77", in: *Journal of World Trade Law*, Nov.–Dec., 1977.

FLORA. A subject of international protection. Organizations reg. with the UIA:

Association for the Taxonomic Study of Tropical African Flora, f. 1950, Las Palmas, Canary Islands. Publ.: *Bulletin*.
European Federation of Professional Florists Unions, f. 1958, Düsseldorf.
Flora Europaea Organization, f. 1956, Reading, U.K. Publ.: *Flora Europaea, notulae systematicae ad floram Europaea spectantes*.
Interflora, f. 1946, Zurich.
▷ Fauna and Flora Preservation Convention 1933.

Yearbook of International Organizations.

FLORENCE. A city in central Italy on the Arno river which was hit by a natural calamity in 1966, when the river burst its banks. UNESCO waged an international campaign in support of the restoration of the cultural treasures damaged by the flood waters.

KEESING's *Contemporary Archive*, 1966.

FLORIDA AGREEMENT, 1819. An agreement signed on Feb. 22, 1819, in Washington by the USA and Spain and ratified in Feb., 1821. The latter was forced to waive its claims to Florida, an American colony, in exchange for recognition of Spain's rights to Texas. Formal commitment of Florida took place on July 10, 1821.

FLOSSENBURG. Bavarian village, near the Czechoslovakian border, from May, 1938 to Apr., 1945 one of German III Reich concentration camps for prisoners from occupied countries; 73,000 were murdered. Liberated by the US Army Apr. 23, 1945.

The Trial of German Major War Criminals. Proceedings of the IMT Sitting at Nuremberg, 42 Vols., London, 1946–1948, Vol. 2, pp. 367–373; Vol. 11, p. 289; Vol. 22, p. 454.

FLOUNDER. A fish (*Pleuronectes flesus*), a subject of ▷ Baltic Conventions.

FLUVIAL INTERNATIONAL LAW. ▷ Navigation.

FLYING TRAINING CMEA CENTER. The Warsaw Pact countries training center est. 1975 by the governments of Bulgaria, Cuba, Czechoslovakia, the GDR, Hungary, Mongolia, Poland,

Romania and the USSR. The General Agreement on Co-operation in the Creation of a Center for Joint Training of Flying, Technical and Dispatcher Civil Aviation Personnel, signed at Poznan on Dec. 6, 1974, stated that the Center and objects connected therewith shall be the ownership of the USSR.

Recueil de documents, Varsovie, No. 12, 1974; W.E. BUTLER (ed.), *A Source Book on Socialist International Organizations*, Alphen, 1978, pp. 872–875.

FOB. "Free on board ..., named port of shipment", One of the international formulas of ▷ INCOTERMS, 1953. ▷ CIF.

D.M. SASSON, *CIF and FOB Contracts*, London, 1975; INCOTERMS, Paris, 1976.

FODDER. Subject of international co-operation. Organizations reg. with the UIA:

Association of Fodder Seed Producer Houses in the EEC, f. 1969, Brussels, Belgium.
European Union for the Grain, Oilseed and Fodder Trades and Derivatives, f. 1985, Brussels, Belgium.
International Straw, Fodder and Peat Trade Confederation, f. 1967, Paris, France.

Yearbook of International Organizations, 1986/87; The Europa Yearbook 1988, A World Survey, Vol. I, London, 1988.

FOGGY BOTTOM. A term commonly used by the American press for the US Department of State, placed in most foggy part of Washington, DC, as a synonym for US foreign policy. ▷ Foreign Office, ▷ Itamarati, ▷ MID, ▷ Quai d'Orsay, ▷ Wilhelmstrasse.

FOG-M AND POLYAHEM. Two types of fiber-guided missile produced since 1986 by the USA (FOG-M) and France together with the FRG. According to the SIPRI Sweden is developing a mortar projectile with a fibre optic-link. The most revolutionary product of high-technology in the field of ▷ conventional arms in the 1980's.

SIPRI Yearbook 1987, Oxford, 1988, pp. 93–95.

FOLK ART. A subject of international protection by UNESCO. A world program for the development of folk arts and crafts is promoted by the World Crafts Union.

D.F. RUBIN DE LA BORBOLLA, "Supervivencia y Fomento de las Artes Populares Indígenas de América", in: *América Indígena*, Vol. IX, México, DF, 1959; "Resoluciones del Primer Seminario Latino-Americano de Artesanias y Artes Populares", in: *América Indígena*, Vol. XXVI, México, DF, 1966.

FOLLOW ON FORCES ATTACK, FOFA. An international military term for the official NATO doctrine of fighting in a ▷ Central Front Against the Warsaw Pact Forces.

D. ROBERTSON, *Guide to Modern Defense and Strategy*, Detroit, 1988.

FONTAINEBLEAU. An historical site of northern France, south-east of Paris, included in the ▷ World Heritage UNESCO List. The Palace lies at the edge of a vast forest and was first used as a residence by the French royal family in 1137. A tower of the first mediaeval residence still remains. Under François I, new buildings were reconstructed, enlarged and altered. As a result, the palace and its gardens are a real museum of architecture from the 16th to the end of the 18th centuries.

UNESCO, *A Legacy for All*, Paris, 1984.

FONTENAY. A Cistercian abbey in north-central France, included in the ▷ World Heritage UNESCO List, constructed principally in the 12th century by a monastic order which proscribed all

worldy distractions and all unnecessary ornamentation, the Abbey Fontenay is admired nowadays on account of its austerity by all those who seek clarity, orderliness and plainness in architecture.

UNESCO, *A Legacy for All*, Paris, 1980.

FOOD AID. A UN program carried out with the help of contributions for the benefit of developing countries, initiated under the aegis of the FAO with the International Grains Arrangement, 1967 by Argentina, Australia, Belgium, Canada, Denmark, Finland, France, the FRG, Italy, Japan, Luxembourg, the Netherlands, Norway, Sweden, Switzerland, the UK and the USA (42% of all contributions). The World Food Council served as a co-ordinating mechanism in the field of food within the UN system.
A World Food Conference was held in Brussels, on April 7–8, 1988.

UNTS, Vol. 727, p. 198; *UN Chronicle*, October, 1983, p. 39; F.LaMOND TULLIS, W.L. HOLLIST (eds.), *Food, the State and International, Political Economy: Dilemmas of Developing Countries*, Lincoln, Nebraska, 1987; H. SINGER, J. WOOD, T. JENNING, *Food Aid: The Challenge and the Opportunity*, New York, 1987.

FOOD AND ALIMENTATION IN UN SYSTEM. Food production and safeguarding against hunger are two fundamental international problems of the 20th century. The first international organization devoted to the problems of food and agriculture, the International Agricultural Institute was est. 1905 in Rome. In 1929 the LN created a Food Committee to study the food situation in a world of crisis and hunger. A UN Conference on Food and Agriculture was held in 1943 in Hot Springs; ▷ Food Hot Springs Declaration 1943. It suggested the creation of the ▷ FAO, which took place on Oct. 16, 1945. From 1945 to 1948 the International Emergency Food Council, IEFC, operated independently or with the FAO and was connected with the UNRRA and the US government. In 1948 it was absorbed by the FAO, which since that time has become the central world intergovernmental organization for food and agriculture. In addition there are intergovernmental organs dealing with specific raw materials, such as coffee, wheat, petroleum, etc.
In Dec., 1961 the UN General Assembly Res. 1714/XVI approved the establishment of a three-year experimental World Food Program, which the UN put into effect on Jan. 1, 1963. During the initial three-year phase the UN rendered financial, technical and other assistance to 117 development projects in 55 countries and carried out 33 emergency assistance operations in 26 states. This was possible because of voluntary contributions totalling 94.6 million dollars and services offered by 70 states. The program, administered jointly by the UN and the FAO, was extended on a continuing basis in 1965, for as long as food aid was found feasible and desirable. The FAO reviews the world food and agriculture situation and has published every three years (since 1965) a *World Food Survey*; the issue for 1978 indicated that 71 of 128 developing countries remained well below minimum food requirements. On the recommendation of the UN World Food Conference, WFC, held in Rome 1974, the FAO has set up a Committee on world Food Security to monitor world food stocks and develop food security arrangements. The WFC also established a 36-member World Food Council which meets annually at ministerial level; an international Fund for Agricultural Development, now a UN specialized agency funded by pledges of over $1 billion; and adopted a Universal Declaration on the Eradication of Hunger and Malnutrition. The Second World Conference on World Population, 1965,

noted that if the world population were to double from 1965 to 1999 the growth of food production would have to reach 103% by 1980 and 261% by 1999. According to FAO figures for 1970, the inequality of food intake in the world, emphasizing regions of malnutrition and hunger, was as follows: North America 6.7% of the world's food intake; – 22% of the world's food intake; Europe 21.9% – 34.5%; Far East 52.4% – 27.5%; Near East 4.4% – 4.25 per cent; Africa 7.3% – 4.3%; Latin America 6.8% – 6.2%; Oceania 0.5% – 1.3%. Work on an International Food Code, the Codex Alimentaurius Commission jointly sponsored by the FAO and the WHO, has adopted over 130 international food standards and published many safety and quality regulations. The first annual observance of World Food Day was marked by the FAO on Oct. 19, 1981. A Plan for Strengthening World Food Security was approved by a FAO Conference on Nov. 25, 1981. A World Food Conference was held in Brussels, on April 7–8, 1988.

The Third World food deficit by the year 2000, according to international projections could be one third larger than it was in 1980 especially in the ▷ Sahel region and in the ▷ North Africa-Middle Eastern region. Only Asia, including China will probably succeed in turning its 19 million ton deficit into a 51 million ton surplus.

I.D. MORTON, C. MORTON, *Elsevier's Dictionary of Food Science and Technology*. In English, French, Spanish and German, with Index of Latin Names. Amsterdam, 1977; T. MILJAN (ed.), *Food and Agriculture in Global Perspective*, New York, 1979; D.C. KIMMEL, "Food and agriculture: a United Nations view", in: *FAO Agriculture: Toward 2000*, Rome, 1980; *UN Chronicle*, December, 1981 and January, 1982 and March, 1984; J.W. MELLOR, *Food and Development: The Critical Nexus, in: Economic Impact*, Washington DC, No 5, 1987; L.A. PRULINO, *Food in the Third World: Past Trends and Projections to 2000*, Washington DC, 1987.

FOOD AND FERTILIZER TECHNOLOGY CENTER FOR THE ASIAN AND PACIFIC REGION. The Center was est. 1969 in Taipei by an agreement signed in Havana on June 11, 1969 between Australia, the Republic of China, Japan, South Korea, Malaysia, New Zealand, the Philippines, Thailand and Vietnam, as a specialized organization of ASPAC.

UNTS, Vol. 704, p. 18.

FOOD DISEASES. An international term coined by the WHO for all food – or water-borne diseases. The WHO estimated that in 1985 there were some 1000 million cases of acute diarrhoea in children under five years of age in Africa, Asia (excluding China) and Latin America. The WHO started in 1987 a Health Education Programme in Food Safety.

WHO Press Release 19/1987

FOOD HOT SPRINGS DECLARATION 1943. The first UN Conference on Food and Agriculture held at Hot Springs, Virginia, May 18–June 3, 1943, adopted a world program of the Food and Agriculture Organization (▷ FAO). The text of the opening Declaration is as follows:

"This Conference, meeting in the midst of the greatest war ever waged, and in full confidence of victory, has considered the world problems of food and agriculture and declares its belief that the goal of freedom from want of food, suitable and adequate for the health and strength of all peoples, can be achieved.
(1) The first task is to complete the winning of the war and to deliver millions of people from tyranny and from hunger. During the period of critical shortage in the aftermath of war, freedom from hunger can be achieved only by urgent and concerted efforts to economize con-

sumption, to increase supplies and distribute them to the best advantage.
(2) Thereafter we must equally concert our efforts to win and maintain freedom from fear and freedom from want. The one cannot be achieved without the other.
(3) There has never been enough food for the health of all people. This is justified neither by ignorance nor by the harshness of nature. Production of food must be greatly expanded; we now have the knowledge of the means by which this can be done. It requires imagination and firm will on the part of each government and people to make use of that knowledge.
(4) The first cause of hunger and malnutrition is poverty. It is useless to produce more food unless men and nations provide the markets to absorb it. There must be an expansion of the whole world economy to provide the purchasing power sufficient to maintain an adequate diet for all. With full employment in all countries, enlarged industrial production, the absence of exploitation, an increasing flow of trade within and between countries, an orderly management of domestic and international investment and currencies, and sustained internal and international economic equilibrium, the food which is produced can be made available to all people.
(5) The primary responsibility lies with each nation for seeing that its own people have the food needed for life and health; steps to this end are for national determination. But each nation can fully achieve its goal only if all work together.
(6) We commend to our respective governments and authorities the study and adoption of the findings and recommendations of this Conference and urge the early concerted discussion of the related problems falling outside the scope of this Conference.
(7) The first steps toward freedom from want of food must not await the final solution of all other problems. Each advance made in one field will strengthen and quicken advance in all others. Work already begun must be continued. Once the war has been won decisive steps can be taken. We must make ready now."

"UN Conference on Food and Agriculture. Text of the Final Act", in: *International Conciliation*, No. 392, September, 1943.

FOOD INDUSTRIES.. Subject of international co-operation. Organizations reg. with the UIA:

Arab Federation for Food Industries, f. 1977, Baghdad. Publ. Journal.
International Commission for Agricultural and Food Industries, f. 1934, Paris. Publ.: Food and Agricultural Industries.
International Council of Infant Food Industries, f. 1975, Paris. Publ.: Code of Ethics.

The Europa Yearbook, 1988. A World Survey, Vol. I, London, 1988.

FOOD IRRADIATION. An international term, subject of international co-operation under the supervision of IAEA, FAO and WHO, subject of national and regional legislation stipulating requirements for low-dose radiation processing of food. In the USA in 1986 irradiated food requires labels saying "treated with radiation – do not irradiate again".
The food is exposed to a form of energy called ionizing radiation, the same kind of energy used to sterilize medical and hygienic products in order to kill insects, fungi and bacteria.

IAEA Bulletin, Summer, 1986; *Food Irradiation*, WHO Features, December, 1988, no 130.

FOOD RADIATION AGREEMENT 1987. An agreement on acceptable levels of radiation in food, within or for export from the European Community, signed on Dec. 22, 1987 by the Environmental Ministers of the EEC.

KEESING's *Record of World Events*, August, 1988.

FOOT AND MOUTH DISEASE. A contagious animal disease, from 1953 a subject of organized prevention by an intergovernmental European

Commission for Control of Foot and Mouth Disease. The constitution of the Commission was approved by the FAO Conference in Rome, on Dec. 11, 1953.

UNTS, Vol. 191, p. 285.

FOOTBALL. Olympic sport since 1908, organized by the International Federation of Football Associations, Federation Internationale de Football Associations, FIFA, founded in 1904, with headquarters in Paris, sponsors world championships.

Yearbook of International Organizations.

FOOTBALL HOOLIGANISM ▷ Sport Hooliganism.

FOOTBALL WAR OF EL SALVADOR WITH HONDURAS 1969. The commonly accepted name of the five-day military action of the army of El Salvador against Honduras, July 11–18, 1969, touched off by the victory achieved one month earlier, June 16, 1969, of the Honduras team over the El Salvador team in soccer, which decided the entry into the final of the world championships. This prompted the army of the El Salvador military regime to incite an anti-Honduran atmosphere and at a session of the OAS accuse Honduras of committing genocide against landless Salvadorian peasants, who, around 300,000 in number had settled illegally on the territory of Honduras despite laws which permitted only citizens of Honduras to colonize the area in question. During the match itself fights were provoked between fans of both sides, followed by the border incidents which led to the breaking of diplomatic relations between the two states, and finally to the aggression of El Salvador against Honduras, which resulted in the death of some 3000 people. At the demand of the OAS Council, July 18, there was a cease-fire, and the army of El Salvador withdrew from Honduras July 30, 1969, though border incidents continued until 1972.

R. KAPUŚCIŃSKI, *Wojna futbolowa [Football War]*, Warsaw, 1979.

FOR. "f.o.r. free on rail ..., named departure point *franco* wagon." One of the international commercial formulas of ▷ INCOTERMS, 1953.

FORATOM. Forum atomique europeen – European Atomic Forum. West European international organization for atomic energy matters, est. 1960 in Paris; Consultative status with the IAEA. Organizes congresses and symposia; coordinates the national scientific institutions of Austria, Belgium, Denmark, Finland, France, the FRG, Great Britain, Italy, Luxembourg, the Netherlands, Norway, Portugal, Spain, Switzerland and Sweden.

FORCE D'ACTION RAPIDE, FAR. An international military term for the army force of about 40,000 troops organized in the early 1980's by President F. Mitterand of France to serve as a rapid intervention force either in Europe or in Africa or in the Pacific area. A concept of General de Gaulle ▷ Force De Frappe, called also Mitterand Force de Frappe.

D. ROBERTSON, *Guide to Modern Defense and Strategy*, Detroit, 1988.

FORCE DE FRAPPE. *French = "strike force".* The official name of the nuclear arsenal of France which was developed during the presidency of General de Gaulle, independent of NATO; created for the purpose of assuring France the status of a great power by a decree of Jan. 19, 1964; the responsibility for using this force belongs exclusively to the President of the Republic.

D. ROBERTSON, *Guide to Modern Defense and Strategy*, Detroit, 1988.

FORCED LABOR. A subject of international law. A special committee was formed by the ECOSOC and ILO in 1951 to deal with forced labor. It condemned the practice in all its forms as contradictory to the principles of the UN Charter and Universal Declaration of Human Rights and in 1956 drafted a new convention on abolition of forced labor, unanimously approved and signed June 25, 1957 by participants of the ILO General Conference at Geneva. ▷ Labor camps.

FORCE, THREAT AND USE OF. Action recognized in art. 2, p. 4 of the UN Charter as contrary to the aims and principles of the UN; the subject of codification work of the UN Special Committee on Principles of Peaceful Coexistence, SCPPC, which during its session in Mexico City Aug. 24–Oct. 1, 1964 did not reach agreement on a definition of the word "force" (whether this word also includes economic, political and other forms of pressure), but it did reach partial agreement, formulating a general principle prohibiting the use of this kind of threat. The Commission again examined these problems at its Geneva session in July–Aug. 1967; however, there was no agreement, whether the principle prohibiting the use of force and threat of force also applies to war propaganda; whether the principle prohibiting the violation of existing boundaries also includes demarcation lines; whether the prohibition on reprisals includes reprisals without the use of armed force; whether this principle should include the obligation of states to refrain from using force against peoples in dependent territories. An additional difficulty at that time was the lack of a definition of aggression, which hampered all the work of the UN SCPPC concerning the use of force. In Nov., 1972, the UN General Assembly denounced the use and the threat to use force in all its forms, including nuclear weapons, in international relations. In Dec., 1977, the Assembly considered that a declaration on non-interference in the internal affairs of states would be an important contribution to the further elaboration of principles for strengthening friendly relations among states.

UN Monthly Chronicle, November, 1964, pp. 62–64; *UN Yearbook*, 1972 and 1977.

FOREIGN AFFAIRS ASSOCIATION OF JAPAN. A Japanese institution f. 1932, Tokyo. Publ.: *Contemporary Japan* (quarterly) and *Japan Yearbook*.

FOREIGN AFFAIRS COUNCIL. An American institution, f. 1922, New York, dedicated to study world international relations. Publ. *Foreign Affairs*.

FOREIGN AGENTS REGISTRATION ACT, 1938. A law enacted by the US Congress obliging all agents acting in the USA for or on behalf of foreign governments to register with the US Attorney General, with the exception of foreign diplomats and official guests.

FOREIGN AID. An international term commonly used after World War II for economic aid from one government to another or from international organizations to governments. ▷ UNRRA, ▷ Marshall Plan.

J.A. PINCUS, *Economic Aid and International Cost Sharing*, London, 1965; I.M.D. LITTLE, J.M. CLIFFORD, *International Aid*, New York, 1965; J. KAPLAN, *The Challenge of Foreign Aid*, New York, 1967; M.I. GOLDMAN, *Soviet Foreign Aid*, London,

1967; R.C. RIDDEL, *Foreign Aid Reconsidered*, Baltimore, London, 1987; L. YU FAI, *Chinese Foreign Aid*, Bidefad, 1987.

FOREIGN AID OF THE USA. The bilateral and multilateral development programs, financed from the federal budget of the United States, approved by the Congress, as well as international security assistance and military aid.
Major recipients of US economic aid in 1980 were Egypt, Israel, India, Turkey, Indonesia, Bangladesh, Sudan, the Philippines, Pakistan and Jordan; in 1987 – Israel, Egypt, Pakistan, El Salvador, the Philippines, Bangladesh, India, Honduras, Costa Rica and Guatemala

J.W. SEWELL, Ch.E. CONTEE, *Foreign Aid and Gramm-Rudman, in: Foreign Affairs*, Summer 1987.

FOREIGN ASSISTANCE ACT, 1961 ▷ Expropriation.

FOREIGN BALANCE. An international term for financial statement on a given day of all sums due and obligations owed in foreign trade turnover regardless of whether they have already been paid or whether they remain to be settled later.

FOREIGN BONDS ▷ Bonds.

FOREIGN COMMERCE COMMITTEE. An international term for a special parliament committee controlling foreign commerce. In USA the House has an Interstate and Foreign Commerce Committee, the Senate a Commerce Committee.

Interparliamentary Union (ed.), *Parliaments of the World*, London, 1976.

FOREIGN COMPANIES. The subject of a Declaration on the Juridical Personality of Foreign Companies, opened for signature at the Panamerican Union, PAU, in Washington, DC, on June 25, 1936. The text is as follows:
"The Seventh International Conference of American States approved the following resolution (Number XLVIII):
(1) That the Governing Board of the Pan American Union shall appoint a Commission of five experts, to draft a project for simplification and uniformity of powers of attorney, and the juridical personality of foreign companies if such uniformity is possible. If such uniformity is not possible, the Commission shall suggest the most adequate procedure for reducing to a minimum both the number of different systems of legislation on these subjects and the reservations made to the several conventions.
(2) The report should be issued in 1934 and be given to the Governing Board of the Pan American Union in order that it may submit it to the consideration of all the Governments, members of the Pan American Union, for the purposes indicated. In compliance with the foregoing resolution, the Governing Board at its session of Nov. 7, 1934, appointed a Committee of Experts composed of the Ministers of Venezuela, Panama, and Haiti, and Mr. David E. Grant and Dr. E. Gil Borges. This Committee submitted to the Governing Board at the session of Dec. 5, 1934, a report on the juridical personality of foreign companies in the countries of America. The conclusion of the report of the Committee was presented in the form of the following recommendation:
'Companies constituted in accordance with the laws of one of the Contracting States, and which have their seats in its territory, shall be able to exercise in the territories of the other Contracting States, notwithstanding that they do not have a permanent establishment, branch or agency in such territories, any commercial activity which is not contrary to the laws of such States and to enter all appearances in the courts as plaintiffs or defendants, provided they comply with the laws of the country in question.'
The undersigned, being properly authorized by their respective Governments, declare that the principle formulated by the Committee of Experts in the foregoing conclusion to the report mentioned above, is in harmony with the doctrine established in the laws of their respective countries."
The following reservation was made at the time of signing:
"The Representative of Chile, in signing the present Protocol, formulates the principle of the declaration therein contained, on the juridical personality of foreign companies, in the following terms:
'Commercial companies organized according to the laws of one of the signatory States and having their headquarters in its territory that do not have an office, branch, or company representation in another of the signatory States may nevertheless sue or be sued in the territory of such State, subject to the laws of the country, and perform civil and commercial acts that are not contrary to its laws, except that for continued performance of such acts, in such manner that they represent an exercise of the purpose of the company, the commercial company would need special authorization according to the laws of the country in which such acts were to be performed.'
The Representative of the Dominican Republic, in signing the present Protocol, formulates the principle of the declaration therein contained in the following terms:
'Companies organized according to the laws of one of the Contracting States and having their headquarters in its territory that do not have an office, branch, or company representative in another of the Contracting States may nevertheless perform in the territory of such State juridical acts that are not contrary to its laws and sue or be sued, subject to the laws of the country.'"
The Declaration was signed in 1936 by Chile, Ecuador, El Salvador, Nicaragua, Peru and Venezuela and in 1939 by the USA and Dominican Republic. It was ratified in 1939 by Venezuela and in 1941 (with reserve) by the USA.

UNIS, Vol. 161; *CARNEGIE ENDOWMENT, International Conferences of American States*, First Supplement 1933–40, Washington, DC, 1940; PAU, *Conferencias Interamericanas 1889–1948*, Washington, DC, 1953.

FOREIGN CORRESPONDENTS. Press, radio and television journalists sent abroad by their parent organizations. A broader definition of correspondents is found in the Convention on the International Transmission of News and the Right of Correction 1979:
"Correspondent means national of a Contracting State or an individual employed by an information agency of a Contracting State, who in either case is regularly engaged in the collection and the reporting of news material, and who when outside his State is identified as a correspondent by a valid passport or by a similar document internationally acceptable" (art. 1, p.3).

"... the professional responsibility of correspondents and information agencies requires them to report facts without discrimination and in their proper context and thereby to promote respect for human rights and fundamental freedom, to further international understanding and co-operation in international peace and security" (art. 2, p. 1).

In 1951 the ECOSOC issued a memorandum to governments of member states of the UN requesting that they spare no effort to guarantee foreign correspondents the right of the collection and transmission of news. A UNESCO Commission on International News, in 1980 report recommended:

"All countries should take steps to assure admittance of foreign correspondents and facilitate their collection and transmission of news. Free access to news sources by journalists is a indispensable requirement of accurate, faithful and balanced reporting. This necessarily involves access to unofficial, as well as official sources of information, that is access to the entire spectrum of opinion within any country."

F

Operating at UN headquarters in New York is the UN Correspondents Association consisting of correspondents accredited to the UN. ▷ UNCA.

UNTS, Vol. 135, p. 194.

FOREIGN CREDITS. Permission to receive goods, services or money from foreign contractors in exchange for the obligation to return in due time the equivalent value received; short-term credits most often involve raw materials and allow time for the development of the transaction; long-term and medium-term credits usually involve purchase of machinery and industrial plants, rarely services: the former are paid in cash, the latter – often in the form of a share of the production obtained from investments. A separate form of foreign credit is the issuing of bonds to be sold on foreign stock markets.

FOREIGN DEBTS. The financial obligations of national institutions; the subject of international conferences and conventions and a world problem of the developing nations examined in the UN and its special organs. Up to the beginning of the 20th century, foreign debts were often collected by armed force in cases of default. The first convention limiting the use of force in the collection of national foreign debts was signed on Oct. 18, 1907 in The Hague; this was the so-called Drago–Porter Convention (from the names of the Minister of Foreign Affairs of Argentina – Luis M. Drago and the American politician – Gen. Horace Porter) signed on Oct. 18, 1907 and called Convention concernant la limitation de l'emploi de la force pour le recouvrement de dettes contractuelles. In 1938 the Eighth International American Conference in Lima examined the plan for a convention on the principles of diplomatic complaint in cases of disputes over foreign debts. After World War II, the USA signed bilateral treaties with the majority of Latin American states and other regions dependent on the USA, giving a guarantee to those states to repay loans received from the US government as well as from institutions and private US citizens. According to UNCTAD figures, the foreign debt of states of the Third World in 1971 exceeded 70 billion dollars. As a result of this, the payment of the debts plus interest continually lowers the value of credits being received from abroad. At its fourth session the Conference of the Developed Countries, 1976, pledged itself to prompt action to relieve developing countries and least developed countries in particular, suffering from the mounting debt burden and external debt-service difficulty. According to UNCTAD studies, in some developing countries, external debt service alone absorbs over 50% of foreign exchange receipts usually forcing still further borrowing. In Mar., 1978 a ministerial session of UNCTAD in Geneva approved a compromise plan, granting states of the Third World a moratorium on the repayment of debts incurred abroad.

The OAS arranged in Sept., 1983 in Caracas a Latin American Conference on debt. In 1983 the combined foreign debt of Latin American and Carribean countries amounted to US $330 billion with an annual debt service commitment of US $45 billion. The first of the list was Brazil – over US $90 billion; Mexico – over US $88 billion and Argentina over US $40 billion. In Jan., 1984 the debts of African countries reached US $90 billion.

The UNCTAD Report 1984 called for "an urgent examination of how the trade and payments system can be recordered and reconstructed so as to promote better economic performances of national economies." The Third World debts in 1985 reached US $644 billion and the debt service charges rose to US $111 billion and will absorb 33% of Third World export earnings in 1985.

On Nov. 12–14, 1986 in Lima 35 developing countries representing some 70 per cent of Third World indebtedness ($900,000 million) demanded a permanent and global solution.

On March 23, 1987 the debt of developing countries for the first time reached the $1 trillion mark, according to the World Debt Tables 1987. In the opinion of the ▷ Inter Action Council (April 25, 1987) the main industrial powers were all responsible for current difficulties of the Third World financial situation.

"The present unsustainable budget and trade deficits of the United States" and the huge current-account surpluses of Japan and major West European economies create an environment of economic tension and danger". On the other hand the developing countries should not only improve their economic policies, the Council said, but must stop wasting massive sums of money on military spending that is unnecessary for defense.

The World Bank publishes annually in March its World Debt Table of long-term and short term debt and use made of IMF credit, for the 103 developing countries covered by the Bank's Debtor reporting System, DRS.

A.N. POPOV, *Mezhdunarodniye valutniye i kreditniye otnosheniya*, Moskva, 1965; J. MARCHAL, *Monnaie et crédit*, Paris, 1967; *UN Chronicle*, No. 3 and No. 4, 1984; The World Bank, *World Debt Tables: External Debts of Developing Countries, 1984–85*, Washington DC, 1985; The World Bank, *International Debt and Developing Countries*, Washington DC, 1985; Ch.C. CARVOUNIS, *The Foreign Debt National Development Conflict: External Adjustment and Internal Disorder in the Developing Nations*, Westport, Cnt., 1986; Ph.A. WELLONS, *Passing the Buck: Banks, Governments and Third World Debt*, Boston, 1987; *UN Chronicle*, May, 1987, p. 87; KEESING's *Record of World Events*, 1987; B. LOMBARDI, *Debt Trap: Rethinking the Logic of Development*, New York, 1987; KEESING's *Record of World Events*, January, 1987; P. HUNNENKAMP, *The International Debt Crisis of the Third World: Causes and Consequences for the World Economy*, Brighton, 1987.

FOREIGN EXCHANGE. An international term for the system of dealing in and converting the currency of one country into that of another. Means of payment in foreign trade: checks, transfers, bills of exchange, securities and in a broader sense also the paper money of each foreign country. In the 20th century many states introduced exchange restrictions, e.g. a prohibition on the making of contracts which could result in foreign payments without the permission of the state or a prohibition on granting credits and incurring debts abroad. The legal rules governing principles of international foreign currency and foreign exchange turnover as well as turnover of gold, established by each state for its own territory, are differentiated as far as balancing of international foreign exchange accounts is concerned according to bilateral or multilateral agreements.

L.E. WALTON, *Foreign Trade and Foreign Exchange*, London, 1956; S.E. STIEGELER (ed.), *A Dictionary of Economics and Business*, London, 1976.

FOREIGN INVESTMENT. Various investments, state or private, made abroad, subject of bi- and multilateral international agreements.
International organizations reg. with the UIA (investment banks excluded) are:

Investments Federation; f. 1955, headquarters the Hague; World Federation of Investment Clubs, f. 1966, headquarters the Hague; International Association for the Promotion and Protection of Private Foreign Investment, APPI, f. 1958, headquarters Geneva; Consul-

tative status with ECOSOC and UNIDO. Publ.: *APPI Bulletin*.

FOREIGN LAW. According to international custom, recognition and application of foreign law in cases defined by international private law with regard to personal relations is obligatory regardless of whether the states maintain diplomatic relations or recognize each other. Subject of international convention: European Convention on Information on Foreign Law, signed in June, 1968 at London; entered into force on Dec. 17, 1969.

"The Contracting Parties, the member States of the Council of Europe undertake to supply one another with information on their law and procedure in civil and commercial fields as well as on their judicial organizations" (Art. 1).

UNTS, Vol. 720, 1970, pp. 147–164.

FOREIGN LEGION. A multinational unit of mercenary troops formed by France in 1831 (composed mainly of Italians, Germans, Spaniards and Poles) with the task of conquering Algeria. In 1835 sold to Spain, and under French leadership, fought in the Crimean War 1853–56, in the Franco-Italian war against Austria 1859, in the expedition of archduke Maximilian to Mexico, 1864–67. For nearly 100 years they were used in French pacification operations in Africa (i.a. after World War I in Morocco, after World War II in Algeria and Indochina). Finally disbanded in 1962. The reconstructed Foreign Legion of 1946 took part in the "dirty wars" of France in Vietnam and Algeria. The Legion's manpower was then 70% Germans, 10% Frenchmen and 20% other nationalities. Also having Foreign Legions were Switzerland, 1855–61 and Spain (Legion Extranjera), 1835–40 and 1920–40 (used together with the French Legion in Morocco and since 1936 on the side of the anti-republican rebellion of General Franco).

V. REVEN. *Die Fremdenlegion. Eine Sozialpolitische völkerrechtliche und weltpolitische Untersuchung*, Berlin, 1911; CH. POMIZO, *La Legion Etrangère et le Droit International*, Paris, 1913; M. LIVIAN, *Le régime des étrangers en France*, Paris, 1936; G. BLAND, *La Legión Extranjera*, México, 1947; F.B., "L'engagement volontaire dans la Legion Étrangère Française et le Droit International", in: *Revue de Droit International de Sciences Diplomatiques et Politiques*, No. 34, 1956.

FOREIGN MINISTERS MEETINGS, 1945–59. The ten sessions of the Great Powers Foreign Ministers Council, held from 1945 to 1959:

First – London, Sept, 10, 1945; discussed the problem of Peace Treaties with Nazi Germany's satellites. Participants: Wang Ching Wang, J. Byrnes, A. Bidault, R. Bevin and V. Molotov.
Second – Moscow, Dec. 16–27, 1945: discussed the problem of Peace Treaties with Nazi Germany's satellites as well as the issue of Japan and Korea. Participants: J. Byrnes, A. Bidault, R. Bevin and V. Molotov.
Third – Paris, Apr. 25–May 19, 1945 and June 15–July 2, 1946; discussed draft peace treaties and the future of occupied Germany. Participants: J. Byrnes, A. Bidault, R. Bevin and V. Molotov.
Fourth – New York, Dec. 12, 1946; approved the agenda for the forthcoming meeting and received memoranda from South Africa, Australia, Belgium, Byelorussia, Brazil, Canada, Czechoslovakia, China, Denmark, Greece, Holland, India, Luxembourg, Norway, New Zealand, Poland, Ukraine, Yugoslavia, on the future of Germany. Participants: J. Byrnes, A. Bidault, R. Bevin and V. Molotov.
Fifth – Moscow, Mar. 10–Apr. 24, 1947; dedicated to the problem of Germany. On Apr. 23 the meeting approved the decision of the Allied Council for Germany (Mar. 10, 1947) providing for the total liquidation of the State of Prussia. Participants: G.C. Marshall, A. Bidault, R. Bevin and V. Molotov.
Sixth – London, Nov. 25–Dec. 15, 1947; dedicated to the problem of Germany and Austria. Postponed *sine*

die after an intervention by the US representative. Participants: G.C. Marshall, A. Bidault, R. Bevin and V. Molotov.

Seventh – Paris, May 23–June 26, 1949; discussed the Berlin deadlock and the future of Germany and Austria. Participants: D. Acheson, R. Schuman, R. Bevin and A. Vyshinsky.

Eighth – West Berlin, Jan. 18–Feb. 18, 1954; discussed, to no avail, the Peace Treaty with Germany and the Treaty on Collective Security in Europe. Participants: J.F. Dulles, A. Bidault, A. Eden and V. Molotov.

Ninth – Geneva, Oct. 27–Nov. 16, 1955; devoted to guidelines for the Summit Conference of the Heads of State of the USA, France, Great Britain and the USSR.

Tenth – Geneva, May 11–June 20, and July 13–Aug. 5, 1959; dedicated to the problem of the reunification of Germany. Postponed sine die. Participants: Ch. Herter, M. Couve de Murville, S. Lloyd and A. Gromyko.

FOREIGN OFFICE. The ministry of foreign affairs in Great Britain. The term is commonly used as a synonym for British foreign policy. ▷ Foggy Bottom, ▷ Itamarati, ▷ MID, ▷ Quai d'Orsay, ▷ Wilhelmstrasse.

R. BULLEN (ed.), *The Foreign Office, 1782–1982,* Frederick, Md., 1984.

FOREIGN OPERATIONS ADMINISTRATION, FOA, 1953–55. A US state institution for foreign aid, est. in 1953 in place of the ▷ Mutual Security Agency. On July 1, 1955 the State Department took over the functions of the FOA, creating its own administrative unit called the International Co-operation Administration, ICA.

FOREIGN POLICY ASSOCIATION, FPA. An American institution f. 1918, New York, as a non-partisan educational organization to stimulate interest in international relations. Sponsors "Great Decisions" discussion programs. Publ.: *Headline Series, Guide to Key Foreign Policy Issues, Great Decisions.*

FOREIGN SERVICE. The civil, diplomatic and consular service abroad and all kinds of representation of governmental institutions; subject of international conventions.

FOREIGN SERVICE INSTITUTE. A US Department of State institution for training foreign service officers.

FOREIGN TRADE. Exchange of goods between individual countries; financial and credit turnover (also repayment of credit and other types of credits) of a given state and current turnover, apart from the exchange of goods consisting of: freight, broker services and other dues and obligations ensuing from the traffic of persons across borders, pensions, membership fees of international organizations, maintenance of diplomatic and commercial posts abroad, credit interests (received and paid) and the costs of maintenance of fixed assets abroad.

Y.H. JACKSON, *World Trade and the Law of GATT,* New York, 1969; V.V. FOMIN, *OON i Mezdunarodnaya Targovla,* Moskva, 1971; G.P. CASADIO, *Transatlantic Trade: USA – EEC,* Farnborough, 1973.

FOREIGN TRADE CHAMBERS. Institutions of socialist states representing socialized enterprises as well as service institutions of foreign trade, such as banks, insurance, forwarding, shipping, transport. In capitalist countries some of these functions are performed by ▷ Chambers of Commerce.

FOREIGN TRADE COMMISSION OF CMEA. An organization est. May, 1956 in Moscow. Co-operation between socialist countries within the CMEA system is focused on co-ordination of long-term plans for foreign trade.

FOREIGN TRADE FORMULAS. An international term introduced to world commerce by the UK and the USA and codified by the International Chamber of Commerce (▷ INCOTERMS). The British formulas developed through practice, while the American were written in 1919 in code and modified 1954 (Revised American Foreign Trade Definitions); they include the following formulas: (1) ex. . . (point of Origin), Ex Factory, Ex Mill, Ex Plantation Ex Warehouse; (2) fob (Free on Board): (a) (named inland point of departure) (b) Freight Prepaid to (named point of exportation), (c) fob (named inland) carrier at named point of exportation, (e) fob Vessel (named post of shipment, (f) fob (named inland point of country of importation; (3) fas (Free Alongside Ship) Vesel (named port of shipment); (4) c and f (Cost and Freight) (named point of destination; (5) cif (Cost, Insurance, Freight) (named point of destination); (6) ex dock (named port of importation).

FOREIGN TRADE IN THE UN, STATISTICS. The introduction by the UN Statistical Office of unified methods of calculation of international turnover based on comparative statistics. Some of the topics covered include:
(1) exports and imports per capita;
(2) geographic distribution of foreign turnover of CMEA countries;
(3) geographic distribution of foreign turnover of the developed capitalist countries.
(4) distribution of foreign turnover of Third World countries;
(5) growth rate of foreign trade;
(6) foreign trade of EEC, EFTA and CMEA countries.

FOREIGN TRADE MONOPOLY. The absolute state control over goods and finances of imports and exports of raw materials, commodities and services; introduced for the first time in Soviet Russia by a decree of the Council of People's Commissars on Apr. 22, 1918; after World War II in all socialist countries and in some of the developing countries of the Third World.

F. ENDERLEIN, *Aussenhandelsmonopol und ökonomisches System des Sozialismus,* Potsdam, 1968.

FOREIGN TRADE OF AMERICAN STATES. An inter-American system of foreign trade in the Western Hemisphere. The first co-ordinating institution, known as Inter-American Commercial Organization was the ▷ Commercial Bureau of the American Republics, f. Washington, 1892, and renamed the ▷ Pan-American Union. The International Conference for the Strengthening of Peace, in Buenos Aires, Dec., 1936, issued two recommendations regarding equal privileges in foreign trade and restrictions in international trade. The Eighth International American conference in Lima, Dec., 1938, recommended lowering of customs barriers. None of these recommendations ever came into operation, nor did the ▷ Economic Charter of the Americas, adopted in Mexico, 1945, bring any practical effects. The Ninth International American Conference in Bogota, 1948, called a special Latin American conference for economic matters, which did not meet until Aug.–Sept., 1957 on the initiative of the UN Economic Commission for Latin America whose Res. 101/IV of Sept. 15, 1955 set up a standing committee responsible for furthering intensification of inter-Latin-American trade within the framework of the growth of world trade. In Nov., 1956 the Committee initiated a system of multilateral clearings in American trade by establishing a Working Group of Central Banks of those countries and also prepared a draft General

Inter-American Economic Convention with material relating to inter-American trade, technological and shipping co-operation. The OAS Economic Conference, 1957, set up a Group of Experts for Regional Markets to frame LAFTA and to assist in designing Central American economic integration. A serious crisis in 1970 in US–Latin American trade followed the adoption by the US Congress of the ▷ Mills Trade Act, which allowed the US to impose import restrictions. The crisis sharpened in 1971 when nationalization laws in Chile (copper, banks), Peru (oil), Guyana (bauxite) and Venezuela (oil) hit large US concerns and the US Congress considered motions for an economic boycott of Latin American countries (only two countries, Mexico and Venezuela, are among the leading 10 importers from the US market. They follow Canada, Japan, West Germany, Great Britain, Italy, and precede France, Hong Kong, Belgium and Luxembourg). The share of American countries in international trade after World War II declined steadily. In the case of the USA, with a well-developed domestic market and huge direct investments abroad – this was no sign of weakness of the country's growth rate; but rather economic weakness in the case of Latin America, whose losses recorded in 1970 for the preceding decade (CEPAL data) as a result of a drop in raw material prices exceeded US \$20 billion, that is far more than all credits obtained at that time within ▷ Alliance for Progress. Hence the Latin American motto: Not aid but trade. Fair trade the best aid. In 1974 Latin American states supported an Algerian initiative to call a Special UN General Assembly Session to discuss problems of raw materials. ▷ SELA, the Latin-American Economic System, started operations in 1975. In the mid-1980s the ▷ foreign debts of the Latin American countries exceeded US \$330 billion.

FORESTRY. One of the areas of the world economy supported by the FAO, subject of international co-operation and conventions. Seven Regional Forestry Committees are included within the FAO: Asia and the Pacific, Africa, the Near East, North America, Latin America, Europe and the Mediterranean region (Silva Mediterranea). Besides this, the Committee for Forestry Technique and the Training of Foresters works under UN auspices in Geneva. Separate forestry committees exist within regional organizations, e.g. within the CMEA and EEC. The forest extension and restoration recommended by the FAO is one of the forms of protection of man's environment, so-called green belts of woods, many kilometers wide around big industrial centers or conurbations. Model green belt projects in Europe: around Moscow, 50 km wide; Poland's Upper Silesian Industrial Basin, 30 km and London, 10-12 km wide.

Organizations reg. with the FAO:

Central Committee of Forest Ownerships in the EEC, f. 1960, Ougree, Belgium.
Committee of Forestry Nurserymen, f. 1962, Bad Godesberg.
East African Agriculture and Forestry Research Organization, f. 1948, Nairobi.
International Center for Scientific and Technical information in Agriculture and Forestry of CMEA, f. 1964, Prague.
International Union of Forestry Research Organizations, f. 1890 under the name of International Union of Forestry Experimental Stations; under the present name since 1946, Munich; affiliates national forestry institutes of a majority of countries in the world. Consultative status with FAO. Publ.: *Standardization of Symbols in Forest Mensuration, Applications and Research Studies, Aerial Photographs in Forest Inventories* and others.
Standing Committee on Commonwealth Forestry, f. 1929, London.

F

Trade Union International of Agricultural Forestry and Plantation Workers, f. 1949, Prague, member of the World Federation of Trade Unions.

Since 1952, the FAO has organized Forest Congresses and publ.: *Yearbook of Forest Product Statistics*.

The area of forests in the world amounts to 1,826:3 million hectares, among which 425 million are in the USSR, 323.4 million in Asia without the USSR, 312.3 million in North America, 286.1 million in South America, 132.6 million in Europe without the USSR, 43.3 million in Central America, 19.5 million in Australasia and 19.5 million in the Pacific region. Main periodicals: *Unasylva* (FAO), *Revue forestiére française* (France), *Archiv für Forstwesen* (GDR), *Forstarchiv* (FRG), *Sylvan* (Poland), *Forestry Abstracts* (UK), *Journal of Forestry* (USA), *Leshnoyoe khozyaystvo* and *Leshnoy Zhurnal* (USSR). An International Conference on Trees and Forests under the auspices of FAO took place in Paris in February, 1986.

FAO, *Yearbook of Forest Products Statistics*, Rome, 1947, ff. J. WECK, *Dictionary of Forestry*. In German, English, French, Spanish and Russian, Amsterdam, 1966; E.R.C. REYNOLDS, F.B. THOMPSON (eds.), *Forests, Climate and Hydrology, Regional Impacts*, UNU Press, Tokyo 1988.

FORINT. A monetary unit of Hungary; one forint = 100 filler; issued Aug. 1, 1946, replacing the pengoe, by the Magyar Nemzeti Bank (National Bank of Hungary).

FORMOSA. A Portuguese name of the Chinese island Taiwan, since 1590 accepted by European geographical nomenclature; since 1955 replaced by Taiwan. The Formosa Strait, T'ai-wan hai-hsia, arm of the Pacific Ocean, connecting the East and South China Seas, between China mainland and Taiwan island; 193 km wide retained its name. The Strait is since Jan., 1955 under control of the US Seventh Fleet, by a Formosa Resolution passed by the US Congress on Jan. 15, 1955, authorizing the US President to defend the Formosa Strait in connection with the defensive treaty signed on Dec. 2, 1954 by the USA with the Republic of China.

J.W. BALLENTINE, *Formosa*, London, 1952; W.G. GODDARD, *Formosa; A Study in Chinese History*, London, 1966.

FORT ARMSTRONG TREATY, 1832. A peace treaty between the USA and the Confederate Tribes of Sac and Fox Indians, signed at Fort Armstrong, Rock Island, on Sept. 21, 1832.

Major Peace Treaties of Modern History, New York, 1967, Vol. I, pp. 713–717.

FORTEZZA GOLD AGREEMENT, 1947. An agreement between the UK and the US on the one hand and Italy on the other, related to the returning to Italy of gold which was captured at Fortezza by the Allied forces from the German forces. At the time of capture it was in the custody of officials of the Bank of Italy.

UNTS, Vol. 54, pp. 193–196.

FORT GREENVILLE TREATY, 1795. A peace treaty signed in Fort Greenville on Aug. 3, 1795 between the US and the Tribes of Indians: Wyandotts, Delawares, Shawnees, Chippewas, Pottawätomies, Miamis, Eel-river, Weea's, Kickapoos, Piankeshaws and Kaskasias.

Major Peace Treaties of Modern History, New York, 1967, Vol. I, pp. 673–682.

FORT GULICK. A fort in the Panama Canal Zone, location of a military school for officers and non-commissioned officers of the American states (The Military School of the Americas – Escuela Militar de las Americas), which was until 1984 under the command of US officers and specialists in combatting guerilla warfare under tropical jungle conditions; instructors in the school were US officers from units of the Green Berets which have specialized in such actions. In 1984 the school was closed under the terms of the Panama–USA Canal Treaties 1977. ▷ Panama Canal.

M. NIEDERGANG, "Les 'Bérets Verts' de Panama", in: *Le Monde*, Oct. 13–14, 1971.

FORT JACKSON TREATY, 1814. A peace treaty signed in Fort Jackson S.C., on Aug 9, 1814, between the President of the USA and the Chiefs, Deputies and Warriors of the Creek Nation.

Major Peace Treaties of Modern History, New York, 1967, Vol. I, pp. 691–695.

FORTRAN. Formula translating system. The first universal language for the automatic programming of computers; appeared 1957 based on experiments conducted in the years 1951–56; then developed into Fortran II and Fortran IV. Translators of this language were universalized by ▷ IBM. Another language of this type is ▷ ALGOL.

C.P. LECHT, *The Programmer's Fortran II and IV: a Complete Reference*, New York, 1966.

FORUM OF SOUTH PACIFIC. ▷ South Pacific Forum.

FORUM PROROGATUM, PRORROGATED JURISDICTION. A juridical doctrine, linked with some cases brought before the ▷ Permanent Court of International Justice in 1924 (Mavramatis Case) and in 1928 (Rights of Minorities in Polish Upper Silesia Case) and before the ▷ International Court of Justice in 1948 (Corfu Channel Case).

R.L. BLEDSOE, B.A. BOCZEK, *The International Law Dictionary*, Oxford, UK, 1987.

FORWARDING AGENTS ASSOCIATIONS. International Federation of Forwarding Agents, f. 1926, Zurich. Members: national organizations in 125 countries. Activities: railway transport, road transport, seaborne and combined transport, air freight, customs questions, juridical questions, documents and insurance, data processing, representation in other international economic organizations. Reg. with the UIA.

Yearbook of International Organizations.

FOUNDATIONS. Institutions in charge of funds allocated to aims specified by their founders, sometimes of international character (e.g. Nobel Prize, Carnegie Peace Endowment). In 1970 foundations with the greatest amount of money at their disposal were the: Ford Foundation (over 3.6 billion dollars); Rockefeller (c. $890 million); Duke Endowment (c. $629 million); Lily Endowment (c. $579 million); Pew Memorial Trust (C. $437 million); W.K. Kellog (c. $435 million); Charles Stewart Mott (c. $413 million); Nemours (c. $400 million); John A. Hartford (c. $352 million); Carnegie Endowment Corporation of New York (c. $334 million); Andrew P. Sloan (c. $329 million); Andrew W. Mellon (c. $273 million). American analyses of foundation expenditures showed that 41% of the sum total of annual spending is earmarked for education, 14% for science, 12% for international activities, 10% for health, 10% for charity and 13% for other purposes. In 1988 the Backard Foundation was, with over $2 billion at its disposal, second only to the Ford Foundation.

W.A. NIELSEN, *The Big Foundation*, New York, 1972;H.V. HODSON cons. ed., *The International Foundation Directory*, Detroit, 1986; *The Economist*, May 7, 1988.

FOURCHETTE. *French* = fork. An international term for the obligatory limitation of the higher and lower price levels, especially by the agricultural prices in the EEC system.

FOUR FREEDOMS. ▷ Roosevelt's Four Freedoms.

FOUR POWERS. A name adopted during the Versailles Conference in 1919 (▷ Council of Four). After World War II the name was applied to the occupation Powers in Austria and Germany (France, the UK, the USA and the USSR). ▷ Responsibility of the Four Powers.

FRANC. A monetary unit of France; one franc = 100 centimes; issued by the Banque de France.

FRANC BELGIAN. A monetary unit of Belgium; one franc = 100 centimes; issued by the Banque Nationale de Belgique.

FRANC CFA, 1945–60. A colonial monetary unit of the French Colonies in Africa (Colonies Françaises en Afrique), replaced 1960 by the franc CFA of the African Financial Community.

FRANC CFA OF THE AFRICAN FINANCIAL COMMUNITY. The official name of the currency of francophonic African countries used in the African Financial Community, Communauté Financière Africaine, CFA, is closely connected with the French franc, with which it forms a curency zone. The name comes from a currency introduced Dec. 26, 1945 by the French government for its colonies in Africa (Colonies Françaises en Afrique) in the relation one CFA franc = 1.70 French franc or one dollar = 70.058 f. CFA; since Oct. 18, 1948 in the relation one franc CFA = 2 French francs at a gold parity of 3.6 mg of pure gold. After the currency reform in France in 1960 and the creation of a "new franc", the relation changed correspondingly to one franc CFA = 0.02 French francs. As soon as the former French colonies had gained independence and had formed two monetary unions (1) Equatorial Africa and Cameroon (including the Central African Republic, Chad, Gabon Cameroon, and Congo Brazzaville) and (2) Western Africa (including Dahomey, now Benin, Upper Volta, now Burkina Faso, Mali, Mauritania, Algeria, Senegal, Togo and the Ivory Coast), both of these unions on Jan. 1, 1962 accepted the franc CFA as their currency on the understanding that the central bank of Cameroon has its own issue and that for the union the issuing institutions are: Banque de l'Afrique Occidentale et Banque Centrale des États de l'Afrique Equatoriale et du Cameroun. On Nov. 24, 1972 the President of Togo, E. Eyadema, while entertaining the President of France, G. Pompidou, publicly criticised the French banks for not respecting the guarantee of the Bank of France to exchange the franc CFA at the rate of 50 franc CFA = one French franc but at an artificially lowered rate. The President of France defended the French banks by stating that "the CFA franc would collapse tommorrow if it did not have the guarantee of the French State."

F. PICK, *1975 Picks Currency Yearbook*, New York, 1975.

FRANCE. Member of the UN and permanent member of the UN Security Council. République Française. Republic of France. State in Western

Europe. Area: 543,965 sq. km, making it after the USSR the second largest country in Europe, including Corsica in the Mediterranean Sea (incorporated by France in 1768; area: 8700 sq. km) and the coastal islands in the Atlantic Ocean: Ile d'Oleron – 175 sq. km, Belle-Ile – 90 sq. km, Re – 85 sq. km and other, overseas departments: French Guiana, Guadeloupe, Martinque and Reunion; and overseas territories: New Caledonia, French Polynesia, Saint Pierre, Miquelon, Walis and Futuna; territorial community: French Polar Lands; total possessions 157, 100 sq. km (the largest being French Guiana).

Pop. of France: 55,632,000 inhabitants in 1987; The population census: 1821–27,300,000; 1901–38,900,000; 1921–39,209,000; 1946–40,506,000; 1950–41,3000,000; 1970–50,700,000. Capital: Paris with 2,317,000 inhabitants (8,549,000 in the metropolitan area) in 1975. GNP per capita in 1987: US $12,860. Borders with Spain, Andorra, Belgium, Luxembourg, the FRG, Switzerland, Italy and Monaco. Official language: French. Currency: French franc: one franc = 100 centimes. National Day: July 14, anniversary of the storming of the Bastille, 1789.

Founding member of the UN and of all UN specialized organizations. Member of the EEC, NATO, Council of Europe. After the Napoleonic period, France in the years 1815–70 was in a Holy Alliance with the monarchies of Europe. As a result of the defeat at Sedan on Sept. 1, 1870 in the war with Prussia, the monarchy was overthrown. At the turn of the 19th and 20th centuries in alliance with Great Britain and Tsarist Russia (▷ Triple Alliance); during World War I, together with the Allied Powers (▷ Entente), France was victorious over the German Reich and its allies (▷ Versailles Peace Treaty, 1919). In the period 1920–40 a permanent member of the League of Nations Council. Diplomatic relations established with the USSR on Oct. 28, 1924. Under occupation in World War II, from June 1940 to Aug. 1944 France had dual representation: the government of Marshal P. Petain in Vichy, and the Committee for a Free France (since 1943 called the French National Liberation Committee) under the leadership of General Charles de Gaulle in London, formally recognized on Oct. 23, 1944 as the temporary government of France by the USA, Great Britain and the USSR. On Dec. 10, 1944 General de Gaulle signed a Soviet–French alliance in Moscow, abrogated in 1949 after France joined NATO. In 1947–54 in colonial war in Indochina, 1954–62 with Algeria; in 1956 Anglo-French military action against Egypt (▷ Suez Canal). After General de Gaulle's return to power in 1958, the majority of France's colonies were proclaimed independent states within the French Commonwealth. On Mar. 1, 1966, French armed forces were withdrawn from NATO. Since 1949 relations with the FRG and since 1973 normal relations with the GDR. ▷ French-German Reconciliation Treaty 1963. The new president F. Mitterrand reaffirmed the intention of continuing to develop France's independent nuclear deterrent which is based on massive retaliation. In February 1986 President F. Mitterand stated that France would be willing to use tactical nuclear weapons to defend the FRG. The Force Océanique Stratégique since 1986 is equipped with 6,000 km long range submarine missiles of the ▷ MIRV and SLEM types. France did not take part in the ▷ MBFR negotiations.

See also ▷ World Heritage UNESCO List.

Sovetsko-frantsuzskie otnosheniia vo vremia Velikoi Otechestvennoi Voiny 1941–1945 gg. Dokumenty i materialy, Moskva, 1959; P.S. WANDYCZ, *France and Her Eastern Allies 1919–1925*, Mineapolis, 1962; J.W. BORISOW, *Sovetsko-frantsuzskie otnosheniia*

1924–1945 gg, Moskva, 1964; M. LIGOT, *Les Accords des cooperations entre la France et les États Africains et Malgache d'Expression Française. la Documentation française*, Paris, 1966; G. DE CARMCY, *La Politique Étrangère de la France 1944–1966*, Paris, 1967; J. CHAPSAC, R.H. GREARD, J. MEYRIAT, *La France depuis 1945*, Paris, 1967; A. ARMANGAUD, *La population française au XX siècle*, Paris, 1967; *Atlas Historique de la France Contemporaine, 1800–1965*, Paris, 1968; M. MOURIN, *Les relations franco-sovietiques 1917–1967*, Paris, 1968; P. PINCHEMEL, *La France*, Vol. 2, Paris, 1969; L. ORIZET, *Les vins de France*, Paris, 1969; J. CHARDONNET, *L'économie française*, Paris, 1970; P. GAXOTTE, *Histoire des Français jusqu'en 1970*, Paris, 1971; M. FRANÇOIS, *La France et les Français*, Paris, 1973; M. DURVERGER, *La Cinquième République*, Paris, 1974; R. POIDEVIN, J. BAZIETY, *Les relations franco-allemandes 1815–1975*, Paris, 1978; C. DYER, *Population and Society in Twentieth Century France*, London, 1978; F. CARON, *An Economic History of Modern France*, London, 1979; M.C. SMOUTS, *La France à l'ONU*, Paris, 1980; M. CROZIER, *A Strategy for Change. The Future of French Society*, MIT Press, 1982; G.F. KENNAN, *The Fateful Alliance*, New York, 1984; *The Europa Year Book 1984. A World Survey*, Vol. I, pp. 434–474, London, 1984; Ph. PINCHMEL, *France: A Geographical, Social and Economic Survey*, Cambridge, 1987; SIPRI *Yearbook 1987*, Oxford, 1988, pp. 28–33.

FRANC, MALI. A monetary unit of Mali; one franc = 100 centimes; issued by the Banque Centrale du Mali. Linked to the French franc, belongs to the French franc zone.

FRANCO. *Italian* = "free" (from fees). An international term for exemption from charges; introduced 1807 in the postal service in the form of a stamp used by the Napoleonic army for official dispatches; universally accepted in international commerce and mail after the Congress of Vienna, 1815.

FRANCO–AFRICAN SUMMITS. The Conferences of Heads of State on Government of Francophonic African Countries with the President of France, held annually, since 1972, attended by observers from other African states.

KEESING's *Record of World Events*, 1986, No 4.

FRANCOPHONE COMMUNITY ▷ Francophony.

FRANCO D'AVARIE ▷ Average.

FRANCOPHONY = FRANCOPHONIE. An international term created 1960 by the President of Senegal, the poet L. Sedar Senghor, to define a cultural community with France of nations which were under the influence of French language and culture; commonly accepted as a definition of the francophonic African states. The African states of the OCAM in 1969 started to convene Francophonic Conferences. The first took place in Niger on Feb. 17–19, 1969 with the participation of the official representatives of states which fully or partially use the French language: Belgium, Burundi, Cambodia, Cameroon, Canada, Central African Republic, Chad, Dahomey (now Benin), Congo, France, Gabon, Haiti, Ivory Coast (now Côte d'Ivoire), Laos, Lebanon, Luxembourg, Morocco, Mauritius, Niger, Mali, Madagascar, Rwanda, Senegal, Togo, Tunisia and Upper Volta (now Burkina Faso). The Purpose of the Conference was the organization of permanent co-operation among the francophonic states, Communauté Francophone. A Secretariat of the Conference was created with headquarters in Paris. In 1969 the International Association of Francophonic Solidarity, L'Association internationale de solidarité francophone, AISF, was created, whose

aim was to co-ordinate the efforts of similar already existing associations, such as ▷ Alliance Française or Association des ecrivains de langue française, and international ones like the Association internationale des parlementaires de language française and Association des Universités partiellement ou entierement de langue française. According to EEC statistics, in Western Europe knowledge of the English language among adults was estimated in 1970 at c. 28% and that of French at c. 25%. One of the francophonic institutions is the Biennale de la langue française est. in Namur, 1965. A bibliography of French language publishers throughout the world is the quarterly, *Francophonie-Édition* published in Paris since 1973.

A francophone countries conference with delegations from 38 countries, representing 120 million French speaking persons took place in Versailles on Feb. 17–19, 1986. On Sept. 1–4, 1987 a second conference was held in ▷ Quebec. The Canadian Government on this occasion announced the cancelling of 325 million Canadian dollars of debts owed by French-speaking African countries: Cameroon, Congo, Côte d'Ivoire, Gabon, Madagascar, Senegal and Zaïre, and announced aid of one million Canadian dollars to Chad and a similar amount to Lebanon.

The next conference was planned for March 1989 in Dakar. Apart from the Francophone community summits an annual conference of the FAC is held in Africa with the participation of 25 full members of the community and 14 states with observer status. The full members are: Benin, Burundi, Cape Verde, the C.A.R., Chad, the Comoros, Congo, Côte d'Ivoire, Djibouti, France, Gabon, Gambia, Guinea, Guinea-Bissau, Equatorial Guinea, Mali, Morocco, Mauritania, Mauritius, Niger, Rwanda, Senegal, Seychelles, Togo and Zaïre.

Organizations reg. with the UIA:
Agence de cooperation culturelle et technique, f. 1970, Niamey, Niger; to exchange knowledge of the cultures of French speaking countries. Members: 30 francophonic countries. Publ.: Agecoop Liaison (monthly).
Association of French Language Television Services Communauté des television francophone, f. 1964, Geneva.
Club of Dakar, f. 1974, Paris; for discussion on questions of development and co-operation.
Community of French Language Radio Broadcasters, Communauté de radio publiques de langues française, f. 1955, Paris.
Society of African Culture, f. 1956, Paris. Members from 45 countries. Publ.: Presence Africaine.
World Union of French Speakers, Union Mondiale des Voix françaises, f. 1960, paris; cultural exchange in the French language through records, etc. Publ.: Via Vox Contact.

H. DE MONTERA, X. CAMPION (eds.), *Dictionnaire de la Francophonie*, Paris, 1969; *The Europa Yearbook 1988. A World Survey*, Vol. I, London, 1988; KEESING's *Record of World Events*, February, 1988.

FRANC POINCARÉ. Since 1924 an international clearing unit in international post and telecommunication settlements, but also in international trade; a unit consisting of 65.5 milligrams of gold of fineness 900. There is an international rule that, "the date of conversion of the sum awarded into national currencies shall be governed by the Law of the court seized of the case."

F.A. MANN, *The Legal Aspect of Money*, Oxford, 1971.

FRANC SWISS. A monetary unit of Switzerland; one franc = 100 centimes; issued by the Schweizerische Nationalbank.

FRANGLAIS. A French neologism made up of the names of two languages: French and English (Francais + Anglais), universally accepted in France after World War II in reference to English words, mainly in the fields of commerce and industry, used in the French language. In 1963 General de Gaulle came out against the Anglo-Americanization of the French language and formed a commission of linguists with the task of replacing franglais terms with French ones. In Jan., 1973 the *Journal Officiel* published a list of 15,000 *franglais* words with French equivalents, instructing French government offices exclusively to use the latter (e.g. know-how = *savoir-faire*). On the other hand, Americans refer to the use of French words in English, e.g. détente as Frenglish.

FRANKFURT PEACE TREATY, 1871. The definitive treaty of peace (after the preliminary ▷ Versailles Peace Treaty 1871), between France and the German Reich, signed in Frankfurt am Main on May 10, 1871.

Major Peace Treaties of Modern History, New York, 1967, Vol. I, pp. 651–660.

FRATERNIZATION. An international term for the fraternization of soldiers of a victorious army with the population of a defeated nation; introduced at the end of World War II by an order of the commander of allied forces in Western Europe, General Dwight D. Eisenhower, forbidding fraternization; cancelled one year later.

FREE CITIES. A city singled out by a state, having its own international statutes governing its relations with the state within which it forms an enclave and with other states and international organizations; six free cities existed in the German Reich: Augsburg, Bremen, Frankfurt am Main, Hamburg, Lübeck and Nuremberg; on Feb. 25, 1803 they formed the German Conference of German Free Cities in Ratisbon. After World War I, the Allied Powers solved the problem of ▷ Gdansk's (Danzig) affiliation to Poland or to the German Reich by granting it the statute of a Free City under the protectorate of the League of Nations.

Dicctionaire de la terminologie du droit international., Paris, 1960; I.A. MODSHORIAN, "Status Volnogo Goroda", in: *Sovetskoe Gosudarstovo i pravo*, No. 3, 1962.

FREEDOM FIGHTERS IN SOUTHERN AFRICA AND COLONIAL TERRITORIES. A United Nations term introduced officially 1968 into UN nomenclature by Res. 2446/XXIII of the UN General Assembly as a moral–political recognition of the national liberation struggle waged in the colonies.

FREEDOM OF ASSOCIATION OF WORKERS AND EMPLOYERS. A subject of the ILO Convention No. 87 concerning Freedom of Association and Protection of the Right to Organize, adopted on July 10, 1948, in San Francisco; came into force on July 4, 1950. The text is as follows:
"The General Conference of the International Labour Organisation.
Having been convened at San Francisco by the Governing Body of the International Labour Office, and having met in its Thirty-first Session on 17 June 1948;
Having decided to adopt, in the form of a Convention, certain proposals concerning freedom of association and protection of the right to organise, which is the seventh item on the agenda of the session;
Considering that the Preamble to the Consititution of the International Labour Organisation declares 'recognition of the principle of freedom of association' to be a means of improving conditions of labour and of establishing peace;

Considering that the Declaration of Philadelphia reaffirms that 'freedom of expression and of association are essential to sustained progress';
Considering that the International Labour Conference, at its Thirtieth Session, unanimously adopted the principles which should form the basis for international regulation;
Considering that the General Assembly of the United Nations, at its Second Session, endorsed these principles and requested the International Labour Organisation to continue every effort in order that it may be possible to adopt one or several international Conventions;
adopts this ninth day of July of the year one thousand nine hundred and forty-eight the following Convention, which may be cited as the Freedom of Association and Protection of the Right to Organise Convention, 1948:
Part I. Freedom of Association.
Art. 1. Each Member of the International Labour Organisation for which this Convention is in force undertakes to give effect to the following provisions.
Art. 2. Workers and employers, without distinction whatsoever, shall have the right to establish and, subject only to the rules of the organisation concerned, to join organisations of their own choosing without previous authorisation.
Art. 3.(1) Workers' and employers' organisations shall have the right to draw up their constitutions and rules, to elect their representatives in full freedom, to organise their administration and activities and to formulate their programmes.
(2) The public authorities shall refrain from any interference which would restrict this right or impede the lawful exercise thereof.
Art. 4. Workers' and employers' organisations shall not be liable to be dissolved or suspended by administrative authority.
Art. 5. Workers' and employers' organisations shall have right to establish and join federations and confederations and any such organisation, federation or confederation shall have the right to affiliate with international organisations of workers and employers.
Art. 6. The provisions of Articles 2, 3 and 4 hereof apply to federations and confederations of workers' and employers' organisations.
Art. 7. The Acquisition of legal personality by workers' and employers' organisations, federations and confederations shall not be made subject to conditions of such a character as to restrict the application of the provisions of Articles 2, 3 and 4 hereof.
Art. 8.(1) In exercising the rights provided for in this Convention workers and employers and their respective organisations, like other persons or organised collectivities, shall respect the law of the land.
(2). The law of the land shall not be such as to impair, nor shall it be so applied as to impair, the guarantees provided for in this Convention.
Art. 9.(1) The extent to which the guarantees provided for in this Convention shall apply to the armed forces and the police shall be determined by national laws or regulations.
(2) In accordance with the principle set forth in paragraph 8 of article 19 of the Constitution of the International Labour Organisation the ratification of this Convention by any Member shall not be deemed to affect any existing law, award, custom or agreement in virtue of which members of the armed forces or the police enjoy any right guaranteed by this Convention.
Art. 10. In this Convention the term "organisation" means any organisation of workers or of employers for furthering and defending the interests of workers or of employers.
Part. II. Protection of the Right to Organise.
Art. 11. Each Member of the International Labour Organisation for which this Convention is in force undertakes to take all necessary and appropriate measures to ensure that workers and employers may exercise freely the right to organise.
Part III. Miscellaneous Provisions.
Art. 12.(1) In respect of the territories referred to in article 35 of the Constitution of the International Labour Organisation as amended by the Constitution of the International Labour Organisation Instrument of Amendment, 1946, other than the territories referred to in paragraphs 4 and 5 of the said article as so amended, each Member of the Organisation which ratifies this Convention shall communicate to the

Director-General of the International Labour Office with or as soon as possible after its ratification a declaration stating:
(a) the territories in respect of which it undertakes that the provisions of the Convention shall be applied without modification;
(b) the territories in respect of which it undertakes that the provisions of the Convention shall be applied subject to modifications, together with details of the said modifications;
(c) the territories in respect of which the Convention is inapplicable and in such cases the grounds on which it is inapplicable;
(d) the territories in respect of which it reserves its decisions.
(2) The undertakings referred to in subparagraphs (a) and (b) of paragraph 1 of this Article shall be deemed to be an integral part of the ratification and shall have the force of ratification.
(3) Any member may at any time by a subsequent declaration cancel in whole or in part any reservations made in its original declaration in virtue of subparagraph (b), (c) or (d) of paragraph 1 of this Article.
(4) Any Member may, at any time at which this Convention is subject to denunciation in accordance with the provisions of Article 16, communicate to the Director-General a declaration modifying in any other respect the terms of any former declaration and stating the present position in respect of such territories as it may specify.
Art. 13.(1) Where the subject-matter of this Convention is within the self-governing powers of any non-metropolitan territory, the Member responsible for the international relations of that territory may, in agreement with the government of the territory, communicate to the Director-General of the International Labour Office a declaration accepting on behalf of the territory the obligations of this Convention.
(2) A declaration accepting the obligations of this Convention may be communicated to the Director-General of the International Labour Office:
(a) by two or more Members of the Organisation in respect of any territory which is under their joint authority; or
(b) by any international authority responsible for the administration of any territory, in virtue of the Charter of the United Nations or otherwise, in respect of any such territory.
(3) Declarations communicated to the Director-General of the International Labour Office in accordance with the preceding paragraphs of this Article shall indicate whether the provisions of the Convention will be applied in the territory concerned without modification or subject to modifications; when the declaration indicates that the provisions of the Convention will be applied subject to modifications it shall give details of the said modifications.
(4) The Member, Members or international authority concerned may at any time by a subsequent declaration renounce in whole or in part the right to have recourse to any modification indicated in any former declaration.
(5). The Member, Members or international authority concerned may, at any time at which this Convention is subject to denunciation in accordance with the provisions of Article 16, communicate to the Director-General of the International Labour Office a declaration modifying in any other respect the terms of any former declaration and stating the present position in respect of the application of the Convention.
Part IV. Final Provisions.
Art. 14. The formal ratifications of this Convention shall be communicated to the Director-General of the International Labour Office for registration.
Art. 15.(1) This Convention shall be binding only upon those Members of the International Labour Organisation whose ratifications have been registered with the Director-General.
(2) It shall come into force twelve months after the date on which the ratifications of two Members have been registered with the Director-General.
(3) Thereafter, this Convention shall come into force for any Member twelve months after the date on which its ratification has been registered.
Art. 16.(1) A Member which has ratified this Convention may denounce it after the expiration of ten years from the date on which the Convention first comes into force, by an act communicated to the Director-General

of the International Labour Office for registration. Such denunciation shall not take effect until one year after the date on which it is registered.

(2) Each Member which has ratified this Convention and which does not, within the year following the expiration of the period of ten years mentioned in the preceding paragraph, exercise the right of denunciation provided for in this Article, will be bound for another period of ten years and, thereafter, may denounce this Convention at the expiration of each period of ten years under the terms provided for in this Article.

Art. 17.(1) The Director-General of the International Labour Office shall notify all Members of the International Labour Organisation of the registration of all ratifications, declarations and denunciations communicated to him by the Members of the Organisation.

(2) When notifying the Members of the Organisation of the registration of the second ratification communicated to him, the Director-General shall draw the attention of the Members of the Organisation to the date upon which the Convention will come into force.

Art. 18. The Director-General of the International Labour Office shall communicate to the Secretary-General of the United Nations for registration in accordance with Article 102 of the Charter of the United Nations full particulars of all ratifications, declarations and acts of denunciation registered by him in accordance with the provisions of the preceding Articles.

Art. 19. At such times as it may consider necessary the Governing Body of the International Labour Office shall present to the General Conference a report on the working of this Convention and shall examine the desirability of placing on the agenda of the Conference the question of its revision in whole or in part.

Art. 20.(1) Should the Conference adopt a new Convention revising this Convention in whole or in part, then, unless the new Convention otherwise provides,

(a) the ratification by a Member of the new revising Convention shall ipso jure involve the immediate denunciation of this Convention, notwithstanding the provisions of Article 16 above, if and when the new revising Convention shall have come into force;

(b) as from the date when the new revising Convention comes into force, this Convention shall cease to be open to ratification by the Members.

(2) This Convention shall in any case remain in force in its actual form and content for those Members which have ratified it but have not ratified the revising Convention.

Art. 21. The English and French versions of the text of this Convention are equally authoritative."

▷ Right to Organise and to Bargain Collectively.

ILO Conventions, Geneva, 1962, pp. 663–667.

FREEDOM OF INFORMATION. A subject of international conventions, initiated by Latin American countries at the ▷ Chapultepec Conference, Mar. 8, 1945, which adopted a number of recommendations providing that "truth is an enemy of tyranny which cannot exist wherever freedom of information prevails." Therefore the suppression of wartime censorship should immediately be followed by preparations for a convention securing freedom of information. As the UN was founded, the Latin-American states tabled a proposal at the first Session of the UN General Assembly which with Res. 59/I of Dec. 14, 1946, recommended that ECOSOC prepare a relevant convention. A draft proposal by an ECOSOC subcommittee in 1947 laid the groundwork for a UN General Assembly Special Committee and for the UN Conference on Freedom of Information held in Geneva in 1948. The Conference adopted a draft Convention on Freedom of Information, which was revised in 1951 by an ad hoc committee of the UN General Assembly. From 1959 to 1961, the Third Committee approved a preamble and four articles of the draft. In 1968 the General Assembly recommended that all states promote freedom of information and appealed to information media to cooperate in strengthening democratic institutions, promoting economic and social progress and friendly relations among nations. The remaining

articles of the draft Convention have not yet been considered or approved by the UN General Assembly. In the 1980's UNESCO initiated a discussion on a ▷ New International Information Order. See also ▷ East–West Agreement on the Protection of Human Rights, 1989.

A. GARCIA ROBLES: *El Mundo de la Postguerra*, México, 1946, Vol. 2, pp. 393–394, *UN Bulletin*, March 1, 1951; *UN Monthly Chronicle*, No. 2, 1968.

FREEDOM OF MOVEMENT. International term, a subject of regional agreements.

A. DOWTY, *Closed Borders. The Contemporary Assault on Freedom of Movement*, New Haven, 1987.

FREEDOM OF MOVEMENT FOR WORKERS, EEC REGULATION, 1968. The Council of Ministers of the European Community, adopted in Oct. 1968 a Regulation for the conditions relating to free movement of workers, the highlights of which are as follows:

"Any national of a member state, irrespective of his place of permanent residence, shall be entitled to take up and carry on a wage-paid occupation in the territory of another member state in accordance with the provisions governing the employment of nationals in that state imposed by law, regulation or administrative action.

He shall, in particular, receive the same priority with regard to availability of employment in the territory of another member state as nationals of that state."

An Advisory Committee on Freedom of Movement for Workers, was est. in 1961, by the EEC Council of Ministers.

J. PAXTON, *A Dictionary of the EEC*, London, 1977, pp. 110–112.

FREEDOM OF THE HIGH SEAS. A customary norm formulated in the 17th century by H. Grotius in his study Mare librum; a subject of the Second Geneva Convention on the High Seas 1958. Its adoption was preceded by two declarations of substantial international political significance: (1). Point 2 of Wilson's 14 Points which declared freedom of the seas in peace and war as one of the aims of peace; (2). Article 7 of the Atlantic Charter which proclaimed that peace should make the seas free to all.

Attempts to specify the principle of freedom of the sea were made by the London International Law Association, ILA, in Stockholm, 1924 and in Vienna, 1926, as well as by the Parisian International Law Institute, IDI, in Lausanne, 1927. The first full formulation of the principle by the First Geneva Convention is valid since the entry into force of the Convention itself on Sept. 30, 1962, art. 2 reads:

"The high seas are open to all nations, no State may validly purport to subject any part of them to its sovereignty. Freedom of the high seas is exercised under the conditions laid down by these articles and by the other rules of international law. It comprises, inter alia, both for coastal and non-coastal states:

(1) freedom of navigation;
(2) freedom of fishing;
(3) freedom to lay submarine cables and pipelines;
(4) freedom to fly over the high seas."

Art. 4 says that every state, whether coastal or not, has the right to sail ships under its flag on the high seas.

Laws and Regulations on the Regime of the High Sea. UN New York, 1951; C.J. COLOMBOS, *International Law of the Sea*, London, 1959; A. SOBARZO, *Régimen jurídico del Alta Mar*, México, DF, 1970.

FREEDOM OF THE PRESS. The subject of constitutional provisions, defining in different degrees the scope of freedom of printed material. The only

state in the world that has not imposed any limitations on freedom of press for almost 200 years is the United States of America; the first amendment to the Constitution (Bill of Rights of 1791) states that "Congress shall make no law ... abridging the freedom of speech or of the press ...". An attempt to abridge the freedom of press, undertaken by the US President Richard Nixon in a dispute with the *New York Times* and *The Washington Post* on releasing the so-called "Pentagon Papers" on the war in Vietnam, was annulled by a ruling of the Supreme Court of the USA. In 1976-85 the question of the freedom of press became a subject of a major international dispute in UNESCO. ▷ New International Information Order. The Inter-American Court of Human Rights, issued on Nov. 13, 1985 its unanimous advisory opinion that 'the introduction of compulsory state licensing of journalists is incompatible with Art. 13 of the ▷ Human Rights American Convention, 1969.

KEESING's *Contemporary Archive*, 1986.

FREEDOM OF THOUGHT, CONSCIENCE AND RELIGION. A principle of ▷ human rights. Freedom of religion for the first time was proclaimed in art. 10 of the ▷ Rights of Man and of Citizen, Declaration 1789. Freedom of Thought, Conscience and Religion was proclaimed in art. 18 of the ▷ Human Rights Universal Declaration, 1948.

UN Review, March, 1960, pp. 30–31 and 36–38.

FREEDOM OF TRADE. Absolute freedom in exchange of commodities and services within free competition of private enterprises, justified by the doctrine that all limitations of freedom of trade reduce the scope of the international division of labor, and thus the advantages stemming from free international exchange to all partners. The rule of freedom of trade was originated in England by the end of the 18th century, developed in the 19th century by colonial powers and in the first half of the 20th century became a subject of international agreements and conventions which guarantee unlimited freedom of trade to foreign enterprises.

FREEDOM OF TRANSIT, CONVENTION AND STATUTE, 1921. An international agreement, in accord with the purpose of art. 23 of the ▷ League of Nations Covenant, signed at Barcelona, Apr. 20, 1921, by the governments of Albania, Austria, Belgium, Bolivia, Brazil, Bulgaria, Czechoslovakia, Chile, China, Colombia, Costa Rica, Cuba, Denmark, Estonia, Finland, France, Greece, Guatemala, Haiti, Honduras, Italy, Japan, Latvia, Lithuania, Luxembourg, the Netherlands, Norway, Panama, Persia, Poland, Portugal, Romania, the Serb-Croat-Slovene State, Spain, Sweden, Switzerland, the UK, Uruguay and Venezuela.

The Convention proclaimed "the right of free transit ... without prejudice to the rights of sovereignty or authority over routes available for transit." The Status on Freedom of Transit defined (art. 1).

"Persons, baggage and goods, and also vessels, coaching and goods stock, and other means of transport, shall be deemed to be in transit across territory under the sovereignty or authority of one of the Contracting States, when the passage across such territory, with or without transhipment, warehousing, braking bulk, or change in the mode of transport, is only a portion of a complete journey, beginning and terminating beyond the frontier of the State across which the transit takes place."

LNTS, Vol. 7, p. 13 and 27.

FREE EUROPE. Fortnightly Review of International Affairs, ed. by Casimire Smogorzewski in

F

London, from Oct. 1939 to June 1945. See also ▷ Radio Free Europe.

FREE EUROPE, RADIO ▷ Radio Free Europe.

FREE MARKET. An international term for a market not controlled by a state economy.

J. VINER, *Trade Relations between Free Market and Controlled Economies*, LN, Geneva, 1934.

FREEMASONRY. A clandestine international bourgeois association founded in the 18th century, professing a liberal, anticlerical and cosmopolitan outlook; based on traditions of occult associations of the 17th century. In Europe three different formations developed: Anglo-Saxon, French and German. All played a significant role in bourgeois revolutionary movements in the 18th and 19th centuries and national liberation movements of the 20th century. The first to be founded publicly was Bureau International des relations maçonniques, f. 1903, Paris, no data published since 1919. After World War II the only openly operating masonic organizations, reg. with the UIA are on the American Continent:

Federation of Masons of the World, f. 1958, Austin, Tx.
High Twelve International, f. 1921, St Louis, Mass.
Inter-American Masonic Confederation, IMC, f. 1948, Bogota. The Seventh IMC Congress drafted the Bogota Masonic Charter in 1955.
International Masonry Institute, f. 1970, Washington DC.
International Supreme Council of World Masons, f. 1974, Detroit, Mich. USA. Conventions: Jerusalem 1974, Philadelphia 1976, Washington 1977, San Francisco 1978, Montreal 1979, Miami 1980.

Freemasonry was opposed by the Roman Catholic Church (excommunicated by Pope Clement XII in 1738); in the first half of the 20th century, freemasons stopped anti-clerical propoganda and Christian organizations ceased anti-masonic activities. In June 1971 the Jesuit periodical *Civitta Cattolica* suggested lifting the excommunication of freemasons.

A. GUICHARD, "Le Grand Orient de France célèbre son bicentenaire. La Fin de l'anticlericalism", in *Le Monde*, No. 8811, 13–14, V 1973; "Freemasonry", *Encyclopaedia Britannica*, Vol. 9, 1973, pp. 842–847; P. CHEVALIER, *Histoire de la franc-maçonnerie*, 3 Vols., Paris, 1974; *Yearbook of International Organizations*.

FREE MOVEMENT OF CAPITAL. An international term for free transfer of capital from one country to another. The free movement of capital was accepted in Western and Central Europe and in North America in the 19th century. After World War I limited by international monetary instability and by governmental control over capital movements in relation to the balance of payments.

FREE MOVEMENT OF LABOUR. An international term for the free migration of blue- and white-collar workers from one country to another; was accepted in Western and Central Europe and North America before World War I, restricted after World War II, introduced for blue-collar workers 1968 in the European Community, but only for national EC countries, entitling them to equal salaries and wages, working conditions, social security, vocational training and union rights. The free migration of white-collar workers was limited inside the EC because of the disagreement over "diploma equivalence".

FREEPORTS AND FREE TRADE ZONES. Territories excluded from customs borders and areas, as a rule in seaports and less frequently in airports, where foreign firms can keep their commodities duty-free in special warehouses (bonded warehouses, bonded factories) until they are sold. The first freeports were set up in the 15th century: in Livorno 1547, Genoa 1595, Venice 1661, Marseilles and Hamburg 1669. In the 19th century the following were European-owned freeports: Antwerp, Bremen, Copenhagen, Danzig, Emden, Göteborg, Hamburg, Hong Kong, Kiel, London, Marseilles, Malmö, Rotterdam, Stettin, Stockholm; in the Western Hemisphere Punta Arenas in Chile 1847. In the USA the rules for freeports and foreign trade zones are controlled by the Foreign Trade Zones Act 1934/35 for the freeports of Houston, Los Angeles, New Orleans, New York, San Francisco, Seattle and Toledo. In 1970 58 freeports were operating in 21 countries worldwide. Subject of international law, integrated by the Versailles Treaty 1919 (arts. 328–330), recommendations of the Transportation Conference in Barcelona 1921 and by the Peace Treaty with Italy in 1947. In Feb., 1978 the World Export Processing Zone Association, WEPZA, was founded on the initiative of UNIDO in the capital of the Philippines, Manila. The following 31 states which have free trade zones are members of the Association: Bangladesh, Colombia, Egypt, Greece, Honduras, India, Indonesia, Iran, Iceland, Ivory Coast, Jamaica, Japan, South Korea, Lebanon, Liberia, Malaysia, Mauritius, Mexico, Pakistan, Panama, the Philippines, Samoa, Senegal, Somalia, South Yemen, Sri Lanka, Sudan, Syria, Thailand, the USA and the United Arab Emirates. ▷ Duty-free shops.

A.L. LOMAX, *The Foreign-Trade Zone*, London, 1917; R. HAAS, "Régime international des zones franches dans les ports maritimes", in: *Recueil des cours de l'Académie de Droit International*, No. 21, 1928; R. BOZON, *L'affaire franco-suisse de zones franches de la Haute Savoie et du Pays de Gex*, Paris, 1935; *Foreign Trade Zones in the USA*, OEEC, Brussels, 1954; R.S. THOMAN, *Free Ports and Foreign-Trade Zones*, New York, 1956; E.S. ALVAREZ, *Istmo de Tehuantepec*, Mexico, DF, 1967.

FREE SHOPS. ▷ Duty-free shops.

FREETHINKERS MOVEMENT. A libertine movement, originated in the 18th century in connection with the French Revolution. Gained considerable political significance in the 18th and 19th century among national liberation movements in Europe and America, particularly in Latin America. Active in Berlin in 1925–33 was the Internationaler Proletarischer Freidenker Bound. Organization reg. with the UIA:

World Union of Freethinkers, Union mondiale de libres penseurs, f. Brussels, 1880 as La Internationale de Libres Penseurs, present name since 1946, headquarters Paris.

Yearbook of International Organizations.

FREE TIME. Time free from work, the subject of international co-operation on the problem of the use of free time by working people for the benefit of their health and intellectual development. In April, 1976 the First World Congress of Free Time took place in Brussels under the auspices of UNESCO and drafted an International Charter of Free Time.

FREE TRADE. An international term for national and foreign trade not controlled by the State. Organizations reg. with the UIA:

European Free Trade Association, f. 1960, Geneva.
International Union for Land Value Taxation and Free Trade, f. 1926; Publ. *Land and Liberty*.
Latin American Free Trade Association, f. 1961, Montevideo.
There are also two independent organizations:

The International Committee of the International Congress on Free Trade, f. 1908, and the International Committee to Promote Universal Free Trade, f. 1921, both of which suspended their activity during the interwar period.
See also ▷ Economic World Systems.

Yearbook of International Organizations.

FREE TRADE AREA. Area of a group of states which by gradual process of economic integration transform their countries into one territory for duty-free exchange of goods and services; subject of international conventions and treaties, such as the ▷ Montevideo Treaty 1960, establishing a Free Trade Area in Latin America or the ▷ EFTA.

FREE TRADE UNIONS. ▷ Trade Unions.

FREE TRADE ZONES. ▷ Freeports and free trade zones.

FREE WORLD – MUNDO LIBRE. An English–Spanish periodical published 1941–46 by the American Free World Association in New York and Mexico City with the task of propagating the idea of forming the United Nations in place of the League of Nations. The yearbooks of the periodical are a preliminary document to discussions on the subject of the structure of the UN and the UN Charter.

FREIGHT CAR CMEA POOL. An intergovernmental institution est. in 1964 by an Agreement on the creation and joint operation of the Common Freight Car Pool by the member states of the CMEA (Bulgaria, Czechoslovakia, the GDR, Hungary, Poland, Romania and the USSR) at Bucharest on Dec. 21, 1963, with a ruling of the Council of the Common Freight Car Pool, a statute on the Bureau for the operation of the Pool in Prague, and a Protocol on the Character and Forms of Co-operation between the CMEA and the Pool.

Recueil de documents, Varsovie, No. 12, 1963; W.E. BUTLER (ed.), *A Source Book on Socialist International Organizations*, Alphen, 1978, pp. 475–494.

FRENCH. One of the official UN languages; since the 17th century the language of diplomats recognized by most international congresses and conferences until 1945, when at the UN Conference in San Francisco English became the major language; the subject of organized international dissemination. ▷ Alliance Française; and ▷ Francophony). Organizations reg. with the UIA:

Association internationale des études françaises, f. 1949, Paris.
Conseil international de la langue française, f. 1967, Paris. Publ.: *La Banque des Mots*.
Union Mondiale des voix françaises, f. 1960, Paris.

Also registered with the UIA are 30 professional organizations of French-speaking journalists, lawyers, physicians, etc.

Yearbook of International Organizations.

FRENCH AND INDIAN WAR, 1754–1763. A British war in North America against France (Quebec) and Spain (Florida), an extension of Europe's Seven Year War.

FRENCH COMMUNITY. Communauté française. The union of France with her overseas territories and other associated states introduced to the French Constitution proclaimed Oct. 4, 1958 was adopted on the basis of a referendum of Sept. 28, 1958 (on the territory of the ▷ French Union). Only Guinea, which opposed the draft of the new constitution in the referendum, did not accede to the Community and declared its independence on

Oct. 2, 1958. The Community included: (1) metropolitan France; (2) the following overseas departments: Algeria (until 1962), Guadeloupe, French Guiana, Martinique, Reunion and Sahara (until 1962); (3) the following overseas territories: New Caledonia, the Comoros, French Polynesia, Saint Pierre and Miquelon, French Somaliland (since 1967 called French Territory of Afars and Isseas), French South-Polar and Arctic Territory; in 1961 the protectorates of Wallis and Futuna (Pacific islands) became new French overseas territories; other overseas territories including autonomous African republics established in 1958 by the referendum: Chad, Dahomey, Gabon, Upper Volta, Congo (Brazzaville), Madagascar, Mauritania, Niger, Senegal, French Sudan, Ubangi-Shari, the Ivory Coast and two UN trusteeships of Cameroon and Togo. All autonomous republics and trusteeships were granted independence in 1960. Mutual relations among the countries making up the French Community are founded on multi- and bi-lateral agreements; the statute of members of the Community was retained only by those countries which had signed bilateral treaties with France: Chad, Gabon, Congo, the Malagasy Republic, the Central African Republic (formerly Ubangi-Shari) and Senegal.

Documentation Française, 1958–60.

FRENCH CULTURAL UNION, UNION CUL-TURELLE FRANÇAISE. An association f. 1953 in Canada with headquarters in Paris whose task is to facilitate contacts between people and national groups sharing French language and culture; reg. with the UIA; Consultative Status with UNESCO; organizes annual congresses; publ.: *Revue Internationale des Communautés de Langue Française*.

Yearbook of International Organizations.

FRENCH–GERMAN RECONCILIATION TREATY, 1963. The Adenauer–de Gaulle Treaty or the Elysees Treaty, was signed on Jan. 22, 1963 in Paris at the Palais des Elysees by the President of France, General Charles de Gaulle and the FRG Chancellor Konrad Adenauer. The highlights of the Treaty are:

The two governments will consult before any decision on all important questions of foreign policy with a view to reaching as far as possible an analoguous position. These consultations would bear primarily on problems to the European Communities, to European political co-operation and East–West relations, both on the political and economic plans, on NATO, the Council of Europe, WEU, OECD and the UN. The two governments would seek to co-ordinate their programs of aid to less-developed countries.

In the field of strategy and tactics the two countries will endeavor to bring their doctrines closer together. Exchange of personnel between the armies will be increased. These exchanges would include instructors and students of the two countries' general staff colleges and the temporary detachment of entire units. With regard to armaments, the two governments will endeavor to organize work in common from the stage of drawing up appropriate armaments plans and of the preparation of plans for financing them. Joint operation research institutes would be created.

The two countries would stimulate the teaching of each other's languages at every level of schooling; co-ordinate courses of study, examination and university degrees; develop contacts and information exchanges of youth, student, artisan and workers' groups.

The heads of state of France and the FRG were to meet at least twice yearly to determine general policy. Execution of the program as a whole was to be the responsibility of the two foreign ministers who were to meet at least four times yearly, also the two defence ministers and the two countries' chiefs of staff were to consult every two months. The Treaty came in force on ratification by the parliaments of France and the FRG.

Facts on File, 1963, pp. 31–32.

FRENCH GUIANA. Guyane Française. French overseas department. Area: 91,000 sq. km. Pop. 1982 census: 73,022. Capital: Cayenne with 38,901 inhabitants in 1981. French possession was proclaimed in 1604 and reaffirmed by the Congress of Vienna in 1815. It was a penal colony and place of banishment, from 1854 to 1938 with permanent penal camps in Devil's Island for habitual criminals in Cayenne; the last convicts were evacuated to France in 1945. On Mar. 19, 1946, the colonial status was changed to that of an Overseas Department. Space research stations at Kourou from 1967, replaced the French space station in Algerian Sahara.

R. HENRY, *Guyane Française, son histoire 1604–1946*, Cayenne, 1949; A. ABONEE, J. HURRAULT, R. SABAN, *Bibliographie de la Guyane Française*, 2 vols, Paris 1957. J. M. HURRAULT, *Française et Indiens en Guyane 1604–1972*, Paris, 1973; D. MASSE, *La Guyane Française; Histoire, Géographie, Possibilité*, Abbreville, 1979; *The Europa Year Book 1984. A World Survey*, Vol. II, pp. 1568–1570, London, 1984.

FRENCH MINORITIES. Various French-speaking ethnic groups. In mid-April, 1971 the First Conference of French-language ethnic minorities was held in Geneva with the participation of delegates of autonomous Francophile movements of Belgium (*Mouvement de Wallonie Libre* – with a program for setting up a Valois state within the Belgian Federation), Switzerland (*Rassemblement Jurassien*) and Italy (*l'Union de la Valle d'Aoste*); in addition, the conference was attended by delegates from Quebec as observers. The conference established a *Comité permanent des minorités ethniques de langue française*, and convenes biannually.

Documentation Française, 1971; *Le Monde*, No. 8170, April 20, 1971.

FRENCH–POLISH AGREEMENTS, 1921–39. The first such agreement was the military covenant signed on Feb. 19, 1921 in Paris under the name of Political Agreement, composed of 5 articles obliging both sides "to act in agreement in all matters of foreign policy related to the two states" (art. 1); "to economic mutual assistance" (art. 2); "in case of foreign aggression to establish contact for the purpose of their territories' defence" (art. 3). The agreement also provides for "rendering each other effective and quick assistance" in case of German aggression (art. 1); France was obliged to expand military activities on land and sea in case of German assault on Poland and to provide aid in the form of equipment in case of an attack on Poland by Soviet Russia (arts. 2 and 3); Poland was obliged to employ (with the help of French credits totalling 400 million francs) 30 infantry divisions, 9 cavalry brigades as well as special units, and also to introduce 2-year military service (arts. 4 and 5); both sides were to establish close co-operation between their staffs and exchange military missions (arts. 6 and 7). The Treaty of 1921 was supplemented by the so-called Mutual Guarantee Treaty, initialled in Locarno on Oct. 16. 1925 and signed in London on Dec 1, 1925, in case Germany did not live up to the Locarno obligations spelled out in the ▷ Rhine Pact of 1925.

"Art. 1. In the event of Poland or France sufffering from a failure to observe the undertakings arrived at this day between them and Germany with a view to the maintenance of general peace, France, and reciprocally Poland, acting in application of Article 16 of the Covenant of the League of Nations, undertake to lend each other immediately aid and assistance, if such a failure is accompanied by an unprovoked recourse to arms.

In the event of the Council of the League of Nations, when dealing with a question brought before it in accordance with the said undertakings, being unable to succeed in making its report accepted by all members other than the representatives of the parties to the dispute, and in the event of Poland or France being attacked without provocation, France, or reciprocally Poland, acting in application of Article 15, paragraph 7, of the Covenant of the League of Nations, will immediately lend aid and assistance.

Art. 2. Nothing in the present treaty shall affect the rights and obligations of the high contracting parties as members of the League of Nations, or shall be interpreted as restricting the duty of the League to take whatever action may be deemed wise and effectual to safeguard the peace of the world.

Art. 3. The present treaty shall be registered with the League of Nations, in accordance with the Covenant. Art. 4. The present treaty shall be ratified. The ratifications will be deposited at Geneva with the League of Nations at the same time as the ratification of the treaty concluded this day between Germany, Belgium, France, Great Britain and Italy, and the ratification of the treaty concluded at the same time between Germany and Poland.

It will enter into force and remain in force under the same conditions as the said treaties."

The third treaty was the agreement on military supplies and credits, and on the enforcement of the terms of the Locarno Pact on the part of Germany, signed in Paris on Sept. 14, 1926; the fourth agreement was on military supplies and credits, signed on Sept 4, 1939.

LNTS, no. 1297; J. KUKULKA, *Polska i Francja po Traktacie Wersalskim* [Poland and France after the Versailles Treaty], Warsaw, 1970; J. CIALOWICZ, *Polska–Francja šojusz wojskowy* [French–Polish Military Alliance] *1921–1939*, Warsaw, 1970.

FRENCH POLYNESIA. Polynésie française. An overseas territory of France since 1843; until Nov., 1958 *Établissement Français de l'Océanie*, ever since *Territoire d'Outre Mer de la Communauté* Française, consisting of the Windward Islands (Ile du Vent), the Leeward Islands (Iles sous le Vent), the Tuamotu Archipelago, the Austral or Tubuai Islands, the Marquezas Islands, and the uninhabited Clipperton Islands (1 sq. km) off the coast of Mexico. The total area: 3,521 sq km. Population 1983 census 166,753. Capital: Papeete with 78,814 inhabitants 1986. French Polynesia is represented in France in the National Assembly by two deputies, in the Senate by one senator and in the Economic and Social Council by one councillor.

P. O'REILLY, E. REITMAN, *Bibliographie de Tahiti et de la Polynésie française*, Paris, 1967; *The Europa Year Book 1984. A World Survey*, Vol. II, pp. 1579–1581, London, 1984; J. PAXTON ed., *The Statesman's Yearbook 1987–88*, London, 1987.

FRENCH–ROMANIAN TREATY, 1926. A Treaty of friendship, signed Paris, Nov. 8, 1926 on security against aggression and preservation of political status quo of Europe. ▷ Entente Little.

LNTS, 1926; C.A. COLLIARD, *Droit international et Histoire diplomatique*, Paris, 1950.

FRENCH SAHARA. A colonial name of the regions of the Sahara conquered by France in the 19th century. In the middle of the 20th century the French government intended to create the Republic of Sahara, Republique du Sahara, from the Saharan part of Algeria. In the decade 1951–60 this region was divided between *Compagnie Française des Pétroles* (CEP) and two partnerships: *Société Nationale de Recherches et d'Exploitation des Pétroles en Algerie* (REPAL), in which the French government and Algerian government had 40.5% of the shares, and *Compagnie de Recherches et d'Ex-*

F

ploitation de Pétrole au Sahara (CREPS), 65% of whose shares were held by the French government and 35% by Royal Dutch/Shell Group. Concessions were granted for 50 years, and thus to the beginning of the 21st century. In 1961 the French government was forced to abandon its plans to separate the Sahara from Algeria; and in 1971 it was compelled to surrender all of its shares to the Algerian national petroleum company SONATRACH.

Documentation Française, 1961.

FRENCH SOUTHERN AND ANTARCTIC TERRITORIES, Terres Australes et Antarctiques Françaises, TAAF, established Aug. 6, 1955 as part of French Overseas Territories, administered from Paris. The TAAF consists of ▷ Amsterdam Island ▷ Crozet Islands, ▷ Kerguélen Islands, ▷ Terre Adélie and the 1.75 sq. km, uninhabited Saint Paul island. Since 1957, the TAAF *Revue trimestrielle* is published in Paris.

The Europa Year Book 1984. A World Survey, Vol. II, p. 1581, London, 1984.

FRENCH–SOVIET ALLIANCE, 1944. A Treaty signed on Dec. 10, 1944 in Moscow, on the initiative of General Charles de Gaulle.

Arts. 1-2 defined wartime obligations, arts. 3-4 peacetime obligations. In art. 3 the parties undertook to carry out, after the end of war with Germany, all steps necessary to remove any new threat from Germany and prevent new German aggression.

Art. 4 provided that should any party to the treaty be involved in a war with Germany, either as result of an attack by Germany or as a result of the operation of the provisions of the above-mentioned art. 3, the other party would immediately render it all assistance and support.

In art. 5 the parties undertook not to conclude any alliance nor to take part in any coalition which could be directed against any one of them.

In art. 6 the parties resolve to render each other mutual economic assistance after the war to facilitate and accelerate reconstruction of both countries and to contribute to the well-being of the world.

The Alliance was extended on Dec. 29, 1944 by a Trade Agreement, which came into force on Jan. 1, 1945. Denounced by the USSR on May 7, 1955 after the admission of the Bundeswehr to NATO.

C.A. COLLIARD, *Droit international et Histoire Diplomatique*, Paris, 1950.

FRENCH–SOVIET PACT, 1935. A Treaty of mutual assistance between France and the USSR, signed at Paris on May 2, 1935; entered into force on Feb. 27, 1936. The text is as follows:

"The Central Executive Committee of USSR and the President of the French Republic, being desirous of strengthening peace in Europe and of guaranteeing its benefits to their respective countries by securing a fuller and stricter application of those provisions of the Covenant of the League of Nations which are designed to maintain the national security, territorial integrity and political indepenence of states; determined to devote their efforts to the preparation and conclusion of a European agreement for that purpose and in the meantime to promote, as far as lies in their power, the effective application of the provisions of the Covenant of the League of Nations; have resolved to conclude a Treaty to this end ... and have agreed upon the following provisions:

Art. I. In the event of France or USSR being threatened with or in danger of aggression on the part of any European state, USSR and reciprocally France undertake mutually to proceed to an immediate consultation as regards the measures to be taken for the observance of the provisions of Art. X of the Covenant of the League of Nations.

Art. II. Should, in the circumstances specified in Art. XV, par. 7, of the Covenant of the League of Nations, France or USSR be the object, notwithstanding the sincerely peaceful intentions of both countries, of an unprovoked aggression on the part of a European state, USSR and reciprocally France shall immediately come to each other's aid and assistance.

Art. III. In consideration of the fact that under Art. XVI of the Covenant of the League of Nations any member of the League which resorts to war in disregard of its covenants under Arts. XII, XIII or XV of the Covenant is ipso facto deemed to have committed an act of war against all other members of the League, France and reciprocally USSR undertake, in the event of one of them being the object, in these conditions and notwithstanding the sincerely peaceful intentions of both countries, of an unprovoked aggression on the part of a European state, immediately to come to each other's aid and assistance in application of Art. XVI of the Covenant. The same obligation is assumed in the event of France or USSR being the object of an aggression on the part of a European State in the circumstances specified in Art. XVII, par. 1 and 3, of the Covenant of the League of Nations.

Art. IV. The undertakings stipulated above being consonant with the obligations of the High Contracting Parties as members of the League of Nations, nothing in the present Treaty shall be interpreted as restricting the duty of the latter to take any action that may be deemed wise and effectual to safeguard the peace of the world, or as restricting the obligations resulting for the High Contracting Parties from the Covenant of the League of Nations.

Art. V. Ratification to be exchanged as soon as possible. Treaty to remain in force for five years unless denounced by either party giving at least one year's notice; at end of five years the Treaty to continue indefinitely, each party being at liberty to terminate it with one year's notice.

Protocol of Signature.

Upon proceeding to the signature of the Franco-Soviet Treaty of Mutual Assistance of today's date the plenipotentiaries have signed the following Protocol, which shall be included in the exchange of ratifications of the Treaty.

(1). It is agreed that the effect of Art. III is to oblige each Contracting Party immediately to come to the assistance of the other by immediately complying with the recommendations of the Council of the League of Nations as soon as they have been issued in virtue of Art. XVI of the Covenant. It is further agreed that the two Contracting Parties will act in concert to ensure that the Council shall issue the said recommendations with all the speed required by the circumstances, and that should the Council nevertheless, for whatever reason, issue no recommendation or fail to reach a unanimous decision, effect shall nonetheless be given to the obligation to render assistance. It is also agreed that the undertakings to render assistance mentioned in the present Treaty refer only to the case of an aggression committed against either Contracting Party's own territory.

(2). It being the common intention of the two Governments in no way to contradict, by the present Treaty, undertakings previously assumed toward third States by France and by USSR in virtue of published treaties, it is agreed that effect shall not be given to the provisions of the said Treaty in a manner which, being incompatible with treaty obligations assumed by one of the contracting Parties, would expose that party to sanctions of an international character.

(3). The two Governments, deeming it desirable that a regional agreement should be concluded aiming at organizing security between Contracting States, and which might moreover embody or be accompanied by pledges of mutual assistance, recognize their right to become parties by mutual consent, should occasion arise, to similar agreements in any form, direct or indirect, that may seem appropriate, the obligations under these various agreements to take the place of those assumed under the present Treaty.

(4). The two Governments place on record the fact that the negotiations which have resulted in the signature of the present Treaty were originally undertaken with a view to supplementing a security agreement embracing the countries of north-eastern Europe, namely USSR, Germany, Czechoslovakia, Poland and the Baltic States which are neighbours of USSR; in addition to that agreement, there was to have been concluded a treaty of assistance between USSR and France and Germany, by which each of those three states was to have undertaken to come to the assistance of any one of them which might be the object of aggression on the part of any other of those three states. Although circumstances have not hitherto permitted the conclusion of those agreements, which both parties continue to regard as desirable, it is nonetheless the case that the undertakings stipulated in the Franco-Soviet Treaty of Assistance are to be understood as intended to apply only within the limits contemplated in the three-party agreement previously planned. Independently of the obligations assumed under the present Treaty, it is further recalled that, in accordance with the Franco-Soviet Pact of Non-Aggression signed on November 29, 1932, and moreover, without affecting the universal character of the undertakings assumed in the Pact, in the event of either party becoming the object of aggression by one or more third European Powers not referred to in the above-mentioned three-party agreement, the other Contracting Party is bound to abstain, during the period of the conflict, from giving any aid or assistance, either direct or indirect, to the aggressors, each party declaring further that it is not bound by any assistance agreement which would be contrary to this undertaking."

G.F. DE MARTENS: *Nouveau recueil général de traités*, Vol. XXXI, Leipzig, 1937, J.A.S. GRENVILLE; *The Major International Treaties 1914–1973: A History and Guide with Texts*, London, 1974, pp. 152–154.

FRENCH UNION. UNION FRANÇAISE, 1946–58. Name of the state of France along with its overseas colonial and dependent possessions from 1946 to 1958, adopted on the basis of the Constitution of the Republic of France of May 27, 1946. The French Union was composed of four administrative elements:

I – Republic of France including: (1) metropolitan France; (2) overseas departments (Guadeloupe, French Guiana, Martinique, Reunion, Algeria and Sahara); (3) overseas territories: French West Africa (Dahomey, Guinea, the Ivory Coast, Mauritania, Niger, Senegal, French Sudan), French Equatorial Africa (Chad, French Congo, Gabon, Ubangi-Shari, Upper Volta), and the Comoro Islands, Madagascar, New Caledonia, French Polynesia, Saint Pierre and Miquelon, French Somali, French Settlements in India.

II – Autonomous associated states: Cambodia (protectorate since 1863), Laos (protectorate since 1893), Vietnam (protectorate since 1884, including Annam, Tonkin and Cochin-China).

III – Associated territories: Cameroons (LN mandate, then a UN trust territory).

IV – Protectorates: Morocco (protectorate since 1912), Tunisia (protectorate since 1881).

In Place of the French Union the new Constitution of the Republic of France of Oct. 4, 1958, introduced the ▷ French Community.

G. CATROUX, "The French Union," in: *International Conciliation*, No. 495, November, 1953, pp. 195–255.

FRENCH–YUGOSLAVIAN TREATY, 1927. A Treaty of Understanding, signed at Paris on Nov. 11, 1927 and extended on Sept. 10, 1932 and Dec. 2, 1937. ▷ Entente Little.

G.F. MARTENS, *Nouveau Recueil Général des Traités*, Leipzig, 1937, Vol. 21, p.751.

FREQUENCY. An international scientific term applied in frequency technology, which i.a. is the basis of long range telecommunication systems and thus is the subject of international conventions, so-called Frequencies Conventions. The first system was devised at the Berlin Conference, 1903, signed in 1906 in Berlin as the International Radiotelegraphic Convention; slightly modified by the London Convention on 1912, but more thoroughly by the Washington 1927, and Madrid 1932, Conventions. The next significant modifications took place 1947–69, particularly at the Special Geneva Radio Conference, 1963. Proposals for the future, as well as an extensive bibliography, are contained in the work of D.M. Leive. Since 1928 the Berne Bureau of ITU publishes a Frequency List.

D.M LEIVE, *International Telecommunications and International Law*, London, 1970.

FRG ▷ Federal Republic of Germany, ▷ Germany, Federal Republic of Germany.

FRIENDLY ISLANDS. 169 islands and islets in the Pacific Ocean, integrated into the Kingdom of ▷ Tonga.

K.R. BAIN, *The Friendly Islanders*, London, 1967.

FRIENDLY NEUTRALITY. An international term for a formula introduced in the 19th century into treaties of alliance, under which parties pledge to act on the basis of friendly neutrality in case one party becomes involved in a conflict indifferent to the interests of the other party.

P.C. JESSUP, F. DEAKEDS, *A Collection of Neutrality Laws, Regulations and Treaties of Various Countries*, 2 Vols., New York, 1939.

FRIESLAND. A land in northwest Europe, since 1774 divided between the Netherlands (West Friesland) and Prussia (North and East Friesland). The struggle of the Frieslanders against Germanization in the 19th and 20th centuries became a subject of international disputes, i.a. in the LN, where in 1926 the Friesland–Schleswig Union lodged a charge against the Germanization policies of the German state. The Prussian census of 1925 indicated 7389 persons who gave Friesian as their native language and 1133 who gave German and Friesian. The Union published the periodical *Fraschlön*. In the census of May 17, 1939 the German III Reich authorities prohibited the putting down of Friesich as one's nationality, since the Frieslanders in 1938 had been officially included among the Germans as a "primaeval Germanic tribe." After World War II, the Friesian movement revived.

FRIESISCH SCHLESVIGSCHER VEREIN, *Die Unterdrückung der friesischen Minderheit*, Husum, 1926; J. BOGENSEE, J. SKALA, *Die Nationalen Minderheiten in Deutschland*, Berlin, 1929.

FRISIAN ISLANDS. Dutch West Frisian Islands northwest of the Netherlands and German East and North Frisian Islands (Ost-und-Nordfriesische Inseln).

H. KOEHNS, *Die Nordfriesische Inseln*, Schlesvig, 1941; *A Compact Geography of the Netherlands*, Utrecht, 1980.

FRONTIER CONTROL OF GOODS. An International Convention on Frontier Control of Goods, adopted on Oct. 21, 1982 in Geneva by the UN Economic Commission for Europe, ECE.

"The 25-article Convention seeks to facilitate the international movement of goods by reducing the requirements for completing formalities as well as the number and duration of controls. In particular, it deals with national and international co-ordination of controls procedures and of their methods of application. The Convention will apply to all goods being imported or exported or in transit across one or more maritime, air or inland frontiers. It will also apply to all control services of the Contracting Parties, who shall undertake, to the extent possible, to harmonize the intervention of the Customs services and the other control services.
Whenever a common inland frontier is crossed, the Convention states, the Contracting Parties concerned shall endeavour to arrange for the joint control of goods and documents through the provision of shared facilities. In particular, they shall endeavour to ensure that the following correspond: opening hours of frontier posts, the control services operating there, and the categories of goods, the modes of transport and the international customs transit procedures accepted or in use there.
As for documentation, the Contracting Parties shall endeavour to further the use, between themselves and with the United Nations Layout Key. They shall accept documents produced by any appropriate technical process, provided that they comply with official regulations as to their form, authenticity and certification, and that they are legible and understandable. Further, they shall ensure that the necessary documents are prepared and authenticated in strict compliance with the relevant legislation.
The Contracting Parties shall, wherever possible, provide simple and speedy treatment for goods in transit by limiting their inspections to cases where they are warranted by the actual circumstances or risks. Additionally, they shall take into account the situation of land-locked countries. They shall endeavour to provide for extension of the hours and the competence of existing Customs ports available for Customs clearance for goods carried under an international Customs transit procedure. They shall also endeavour to facilitate to the utmost the transit of goods carried in containers or other load units affording adequate security."
On Jan. 1, 1988 the EEC replaced the hitherto required documents for lorries crossing internal EEC borders and into EFTA countries with a Single Administrative Document, SAD. The transport of goods restricted by quota and by licence will end by 1992.

UN Chronicle, December, 1982, p. 104; D. LEONARD, *Pocket Guide to the European Community*, London, 1988.

FRONTIER FREE EUROPEAN COMMUNITY, 1992. The controversial plan to establish a frontier free European Community single market in 1992; rejected formally by the British Prime Minister, Mrs. Margaret Thatcher on Sept. 20, 1988, in a speech at the College of Europe in Bruges, Belgium.

International Herald Tribune, September 21, 1988; KEESING's *Record of World Events*, October, 1988.

FRONTIER LITIGATIONS. In the 20th century the number of border disputes in the world increased in proportion to the increase in the number of independent states, from several dozen at the beginning of the century to well over 100 in the second half. The first continent on which all of the states, up to 1971, had settled their frontier litigations by bilateral or multilateral treaties was Europe, with the exception of the dispute between Ireland and Great Britain on ▷ Ireland, Northern. The ▷ Helsinki Final Act, was signed on Aug. 1, 1975 in which i.a. the principle of the inviolability of frontiers was accepted. Earlier frontier litigation on uninhabited Antarctica had been postponed for 30 years. In Africa there are a number of unsettled frontier litigations resulting from relics of the colonial drawing of boundaries which did not consider the interests of the local population. In Asia the frontier claims of the Chinese People's Republic in relation to India, the USSR and Vietnam became the subject of border incidents. In 1973 in Latin America, Argentina remained in dispute with Chile over the islands in the ▷ Beagle canal; Bolivia with Chile over the Lauca river; Brazil with Paraguay over the Sete Quedas (Guaira) waterfalls; Ecuador with Peru over the territory taken by Peru in 1941; Guatemala made claim to ▷ Belize; Guyana had not settled its frontier litigations with Surinam and Venezuela; Costa Rica with Nicaragua over the frontier through the Fonseca bay and on navigation on the San Juan river.

B. KLIMENKO, *Gosudarstvenniy granitse. Problemy mira*, Moskva, 1964; *Latin America and the Caribbean. A Handbook*, London, 1968, pp. 403–412; C.G. WID-

STRAND, *African Boundary Problems*, Uppsala, 1969; Institute of International Public Law and International Relations. *National and International Boundaries*, Thessaloniki, 1985; A.J. DAY, *Border and Territorial Disputes*, London, 1987.

FRONTIERS, INTERNATIONAL. An international term for a border of a territory with an international status, such as the international city of ▷ Tangier; or between demarcation lines protected by international organs; or territorial borders of another type which do not ensue from sovereignty of a given state but a particular status of a given area, e.g. frontiers of ▷ Jerusalem 1949–67, Alexandretta (now Iskenderun, Turkey) 1920–39, the ▷ Suez Canal 1888–1956. In the 19th and early 20th centuries there were some 50 different types of international frontiers.

H. DUNCAN HALL. "Zones of the international frontier", in: *Geographical Review*, No. 4, 1948, pp. 615–675; J.R.V. PRESCOTT, *Political Frontiers and Boundaries*, London, 1987.

FRONTIERS, INVIOLABILITY OF. A rule of international law contained in the general principle of inviolability of the territorial integrity of states. States-participating in the Conference on Security and Co-operation in Europe recognized in the ▷ Helsinki Final Act 1975, that "all one another's frontiers as well as frontiers of all States of Europe are inviolable." The principle of inviolability of frontiers does not rule out peaceful change of frontiers made in such a manner that the universal international law is not violated and the interests of other states' security are not endangered; however, under art. 62 of the Vienna Convention of 1969 no change of frontiers may be made on the basis of the *rebus sic standibus* clause.

S.B. JOHNES, *Boundary Making. A Handbook for Statesmen, Treaty Editors and Boundary Commissioners*, New York, 1945; A. KLAFKOWSKI, *Inviolability of Frontiers*, Warsaw, 1974; A.J. DAY ed., *Border and Territorial Disputes*, 2nd ed., London, 1988.

FRONTIER WATERS. A subject of international law with respect to countries whose frontiers border the waters of rivers, bays or seas. Since the Peace of Westphalia of 1648, a principle has come into use that the frontier line, as far as rivers are concerned, runs along the main current line (▷ Thalweg) and rarely along the bank as was the case of the river Notec according to the Polish-Prussian Treaty of Sept. 18, 1773. In the case of lakes and bays the principle of the center-line has been adopted, which is not always equivalent to a straight line.

E. NYS, "Rivières et fleuves frontières. La ligne médiane et le Thalweg. Un aperçu historique," in: *Revue de droit international et de législation comparée* No. 33, 1901; B. WINIARSKI, "Principes généraux du droit fluvial", in: *Recueil des Cours de l'Académie Droit International*, No. 43, 1933; K. GLEDISH, "Rivers as international boundaries", in: *Nordisk Fridskrift*, No. 22, 1952.

FRONTIER WORKERS. An international term defined by the Brussels Convention between the Governments of Belgium, France, Luxembourg, the Netherlands and the UK, concerning Frontier Workers, signed on Apr. 17, 1950, came into force on Oct. 10, 1951:

"By Frontier Workers shall be understood nationals of the Contracting Parties who, while continuing to be ordinarily resident in the frontier zone of one of the Parties, to which they return each day, are engaged in paid employment in the adjoining frontier zone of another of the Contracting Parties." (art. 1).
"Frontier Workers shall receive for equivalent work pay equal to that received by nationals of the country of employment for the same occupation in the same locality," (art. 6).

F

UNTS, Vol. 131, pp. 100 and 102.

FRONTIER ZONES. An international term, defined by the Brussels convention 1950, concerning ▷ Frontier Workers, as follows: "... Frontier Zones shall be understood to be zones situated on each side of a frontier and defined by bilateral conventions. In principle these zones are 10 kilometres in depth."

UNTS, Vol, 131, p. 102.

FRONT-LINE STATES. A denomination of Angola, Botswana, Mozambique, Tanzania and Zambia, connected with the armed agression and destabilization carried out in the 1970s by South Africa and Rhodesia. The heads of 95 states or governments, meeting in Havana Conference of Nonaligned Countries in Sept. 1979, agreed:

"that political and diplomatic aid to the Front-Line States should be forthcoming from the UN and all other international forums by openly denouncing the acts of aggression committed against them ... [and also agreed] that military aid to the Front-Line States should be aimed at increasing their defensive capacity ...".

On Dec. 8, 1986 in Res. 41/199 the UN General Assembly urged the UN members "to provide ... the financial, material and technical assistance to ... the front-line states and other bordering states to withstand the effects of economic measures taken by South Africa, or by the international community against South Africa".

Final Declaration of the Sixth Conference of Heads of States or Governments of the Non-Aligned Countries, Havana, 1979; KEESING's *Record of World Events*, 1987.

FRUIT JUICE. A subject of research and promotion by the International Trade Center UNCTAD/GATT, Geneva. See ▷ Citrus Fruits.

ITC. *The World Market for Fruit Juices with Special Reference to Citrus and Tropical Fruit Juices*, Geneva, 1982.

FRUITS AND VEGETABLES. Subjects of international co-operation. Organizations reg. with the UIA:

▷ AGROMASH
EEC Committee for the Fruit and Vegetable Juice Industry, f. 1958, Paris.
European Club of Overseas Fruit and Vegetable Importers, f. 1972, Brussels.
European Organization of Preserves and Tinned Fruit Industries, f. 1959, Brussels.
European Union for the Fruit and Vegetable Wholesale Trade, f. 1958, Brussels.
Fruit and Vegetable Deep-Freeze Industry of the EEC, f. 1962, Brussels.
International Association for Normalization and Commercialization of Fruits and Vegetables, NORCOFEL, f. 1975, Dijon, France.
International Federation of Fruit Juice Producers, f. 1949, Paris. Liaison committee for Tropical Fruits and Off-season Vegetables, f. 1973, Brussels.
Liaison Committee of the EEC Fruit and Vegetable Processing Industries, f. 1963, Brussels.
Specialized Section on Fruit and Vegetables of the EEC, f. 1959, Brussels.

Yearbook of International Organizations.

FST-1. Acronym for Follow-on Soviet Tank. A Soviet battletank with a 135 mm gun and an array of electronic devices, including a laser range finder, an infrared night scope and a counteroptics device called a Lasar.

Newsweek, April 11, 1988.

FUJAIRAH. A sheikdom, one of the former Trucial States, part of the federation of ▷ United Arab Emirates.

"FUKURU MARU." *Japanese* = "happy dragon". The name of a Japanese fishing vessel which happened to be on the open sea at a distance of 136.75 km from Bikini atoll on Aug. 1, 1954 when an atomic bomb was dropped by an American military plane. The crew of the ship (23 persons) had to spend more than a year in a hospital as a result of exposure to radiation, and one of the members of the crew died.

KEESING's *Contemporary Archive*, 1954 and 1955.

FULBRIGHT RESOLUTION, 1943. A US Congress resolution adopted on Sept. 21, 1943 by the US House of Representatives by a vote of 360 to 29, sponsored by Prof. J.W. Fulbright of Arkansas, promoting the participation of the United States in a post-War World Organization of United Nations:

"Resolved by the House of Representatives (the Senate concurring) That the Congress hereby expresses itself as favoring the creation of appropriate international machinery with power adequate to establish and to maintain a just and lasting peace, among the nations of the world, and as favoring participation by the United States therein through its constitutional processes."

On Oct. 31, 1943 the US Secretary of State Cordell Hull signed the ▷ Moscow Declaration on UN General Security recognizing "the necessity of establishing at the earliest possible time a General International Organization."

The US Senate on Nov. 5, 1943 adopted a resolution of its own. The text is as follows:

"That the Senate recognizes the necessity of there being established at the earliest practicable date a general international organization, based on the principle of the sovereign equality of all peace-loving states, and open to membership by all such states, large and small, for the maintenance of international peace and security. That, pursuant to the Constitution of the United States, any treaty made to effect the purposes of this resolution, on behalf of the Government of the United Sates with any other nation or any association of nations, shall be made only by and with the advice and consent of the Senate of the United States, provided two-thirds of the Senators present concur."

Congressional Record (House of Representatives) 28th Congress, 1st session, September, 21, 1943; *p. 7225; Congressional Record (Senate), 78th Congress, 1st session*, November, 5, 1943, p. 9222.

FULBRIGHT SCHOLARSHIP PROGRAM. Name accepted in the USA for an act on international scientific exchange passed in June, 1946 on the motion of the Democratic senator, Prof. J.W. Fulbright, permitting American students to go abroad to study at government expense and inviting foreign students to study in the US. This act, based on scholarships awarded by Congress, has the aim, on the one hand, of spreading knowledge of the United States in other countries and, on the other hand, of allowing American scientists to benefit as fully as possible from foreign scientific achievements. During 25 years of this program 1946–1971 *c.* 30,000 American scientists, scholars, and students visited (usually for one year) foreign schools and scientific research institutions, while about 60,000 foreigners came to the USA.

M. MARTIN, L. GELBER, *Dictionary of American History*, Totowa N.J., 1965.

FUMIGATION. An international term for the application of fumes or smoke to combat insects harmful to plants or their fruits or by using poisons in the form of fumigants, i.e. steam, gases and smoke; subject of international regulations in force with respect to fumigation in the case of food products traded internationally, such as grains, oil-meal, oil cake, cocoa, coffee, sesame, which are all affected by pests.

FUNCTIONARIES, INTERNATIONAL. An international term for those groups of employees of the UN, International Court of Justice and specialized agencies benefiting from diplomatic privileges and immunities in the member states of the UN as defined by the UN Secretary-General in accordance with art 5. of the Convention on UN Privileges and Immunities of Feb. 13, 1946. The first international clerical personnel appeared in 1856 in the European Danube Commission, 1863 in the World Postal Union, 1875 in the International Bureau of Weights and Measures. Up to 1914, 33 of these international organizations with an international clerical personnel were included, while the number of permanent employees was *c.* 100, mostly Swiss citizens. In the interwar period this number grew to *c.* 2000, still predominantly Swiss due to the fact that LN headquarters were in Geneva. A rapid growth in the number of international functionaries occurred after World War II through UN and special organizations as well as more than 110 other intergovernmental organizations. The duties and rights of international functionaries, in 1980 *c.* 40,000, are defined in many legal documents of the UN Secretariat, which serve as a model for the regulations of other intergovernmental institutions.

S. BASDEVANT, *Les Fonctionnaires internationaux*, Paris, 1931; *Rapport sur les normes conduite requises des fonctionnaires internationaux*, UN, New York, 1954; E. KORDT, *Der Europäische Beamte*, Bonn, 1955; A.C. BREYCHA-VAUTIER, *Le fonctionnaire international*, Paris, 1959; E. KERN, "On the establishment of a European Civil Service," in: *Revue internationale des sciences administratives*, No. 25, 1959.

FUND. An international term for governmental or intergovernmental funds, in the UN system development program institutions. ▷ African Development Fund, ▷ European Development Fund, ▷ Pan-American Development Fund.

FUND A. The ▷ Agriculture Fund, est. 1931, by the Bank for International Settlements.

FUNDAMENTALISM. An international term for (1) conservative religious thought (Christian, Moslem etc.). (2) ultra-conservative political movements based on religious doctrines.

W. LIPPMANN, *American Inquisitors*, New York, 1928; G.G. COLE, *History of fundamentalism*, London, 1931; L. CAPLAN, *Studies in Religious Fundamentalism*, London, 1987; I.S. LUSTICK, *For the land and the Lord: Jewish Fundamentalism in Israel*, Dartmouth College, 1988.

FUND B CONVENTION 1931. A Convention between Czechoslovakia, France, Great Britain, Italy, Romania, Switzerland and Yugoslavia, regarding the Constitution of Special Fund called Fund B, signed on Aug. 21, 1931 in Bern, relative to the obligations resulting from the ▷ Hungary Peace Treaty, 1921, and the ▷ Hague Reparations Agreements, 1930.

LNTS, Vol. 121, p. 61 and Vol. 127, p. 95.

FUND OF SPECIAL FISSIONABLE MATERIALS. A Fund created within IAEA 1970 by the UN General Assembly, Res. 2605 and 2664/XXV.

FUNERALS. A subject of international co-operation in problems of transporting coffins from one country to another in accordance with sanitary regulations of the WHO. Organizations reg. with the UIA:

European Funeral Directors Association, f. 1964, Vienna. Publ.: *Handbook of Funeral Directors in Europe*

(in German, English, French, Swedish) and Technical Funeral Directory in 10 languages.
European Thanatological Association, f. 1966, Brussels. Publ.: *International Funeral Directors Annual*.

Yearbook of International Organizations.

FURNITURE. A subject of international co-operation. Organizations reg. with the UIA:

European Furniture Federation, f. 1950, Brussels, Publ.: *Information*.
Federation of International Furniture Removers, f. 1950, Brussels. Publ.: *Journal FIDI*.

International Trade Center UNCTAD/GATT, *Major Import Markets for Wooden Household Furniture*, Geneva, 1982; *Yearbook of International Organizations, 1986/87; The Europa Yearbook 1988. A World Survey*, Vol. I, London, 1988.

FUR TRADE. Subject of international co-operation. Organization reg. with the UIA:

International Fur Trade Federation, f. 1949, London, UK.

Yearbook of International Organizations, 1986/87; The Europa Yearbook 1988. A World Survey, Vol. I, London, 1988.

FUTUROLOGY. A subject of international co-operation. Organizations reg. with the UIA:

▷ Bucharest Club.
Ecoplan International, f. 1975, Paris.
International Association Futuribles, f. 1960, Paris. Publ.: *Futuribles* (quarterly), *Future Information*.
International Conference on Environment Future, f. 1971, Geneva.
World Future Society, f. 1966, Washington DC. Publ.: *The Futurist*.
World Future Studies Federation, f. 1974, Paris, Organizes World Future Research Conferences. Publ.: *News*.

H.S.D. COLE (ed.), *Thinking about the Future*, London, 1973; CH, FREEMAN, M. JAHODA (eds.), *World Futures. The Great Debate*, London, 1978.

G

GAB. General Arrangements to Borrow. A general borrowing agreement negotiated by the IMF in 1961 for the purpose of expanding its credit possiblities with the countries of the ▷ Group of Ten. These countries pledged themselves to lend to the Fund in case of need their own currencies to the total sum of 6 billion dollars – for the use of those among them which would encounter balance of payments problems. However, the use of these means by the IMF requires the approval of the Group of Ten. The extent of the obligations of the countries varies: for the USA 2 billion dollars, for Great Britain and the FRG 1 billion each, France and Italy 550 million each and smaller sums for the remaining countries. Within the GAB scheme the IMF borrowed currencies from those countries several times during periods of monetary difficulties. The GAB was renewed on Nov. 23, 1987 for the five year period from Dec. 26, 1988 to Dec. 25, 1993.

B. STRANGE, *International Monetary Relations 1959–71*, London, 1976.

GABON. Member of the UN. République Gabonaise. Gabon Republic. Central African State on the Atlantic Ocean, bounded by Equatorial Guinea, Cameroon and Congo. Area: 267,667 sq. km. Pop. 1987 est. 1,100,000 (1970 census 950,007). Capital Libreville with 251,000 inhabitants, 1974. GNP per capita 1987 US $2700. Official language: French. Currency: one franc CFA = 100 centimes. National Day: Aug. 17, Independence Day, 1960. Member of the UN since Sept. 20, 1960 and of the UN specialized agencies. Member of the OAU and OPEC: it is an ACP state of the EEC.
International relations: under French control since the late 18th century; from 1910 part of French Equatorial Africa; in 1946 overseas territory of France; which became self-governing in 1958. It became an independent state on Aug. 17, 1960. A signatory of the Yaoundé Convention of 1963 and of 1969 and the Lomé Conventions of 1975 and of 1980. France maintains a marine battalion in Gabon.

R. GELAROZIER, Y. THIERRY, *Carte ethnique du Gabon*, Paris, 1945; G. LASSERRE, *Libreville, la ville et sa région*, Paris, 1958; B. WEINSTEIN, *Gabon, Nation-Building on the Ogooué*, Cambridge, Mass., 1966; M. REMY, *Gabon aujourd'hui*, Paris, 1977; *The Europa Year Book 1984. A World Survey*, Vol. II, pp. 1587–1597, London, 1984.

GADUS CALLARIUS. A salt water fish under the protection of an international convention.

UNTS, Vol. 231, p. 199.

GAITSKELL PLAN, 1958. A scheme for the unification of Germany based on evacuation of French, US and British troops from West Germany and Soviet troops from East Germany, Poland and Hungary and the creation of an atom-free zone on the territory of united Germany, Czechoslovakia, Poland, and Hungary. The Plan was published in Apr., 1958 in London by the then leader of British Labour Party, H. Gaitskell, as a counter-proposal to the ▷ Rapacki Plan.

GAL. A special unit employed in geodesy and geophysics to express the acceleration due to gravity (▷ SI).

GALAPAGOS ISLANDS. Officially called in Ecuador the Archipiélago de Colón. Archipelago of 14 main islands and groups of smaller islands in equatorial Pacific Ocean west of Ecuador, total area 7844 sq. km with 6119 inhabitants, 1982; since 1832 belonging to Ecuador; visited 1835 by Charles Darwin; wildlife sanctuary under the aegis of UNESCO. During World War II to 1946 US naval and air bases on the Seymour Island (Isla Baltra). On the occasion of the centenary of the publication of Darwin's theory of evolution, 1958, the Charles Darwin Research Station was established on the largest island Albermarle (Isla Isabela). The station is directed in agreement with the Ecuador government by the Charles Darwin Foundation for the Galapagos Isles, founded in Brussels. Consultative status with UNESCO. Publ.: *Noticias de Galapagos*. The islands are included in the ▷ World Heritage UNESCO List. On these volcanic islands lying in the Pacific 1000 km off the mainland coast live the giant tortoises, the marine and land iguanas, the birds which revealed to Darwin the principle of natural adaptation to the environment, and large marine mammals – double-coated seals and sea lions. A Charles Darwin Foundation for the Galapagos Islands, was founded in 1959 under the auspices of the UNESCO, Brussels. Publ.: *Noticias de Galapagos*.

C. DARWIN, *Voyage of the "Beagle"*, London, 1839; V.W. HAGEN, *Ecuador and the Galapagos Islands*, Norrian Okla; 1949; UNESCO, *A Legacy for All*, Paris, 1984.

GALLUP INSTITUTE. An American Institute of Public Opinion, est. 1936 by George H. Gallup, originator of the methods of large public opinion polls by means of small representative samples. At the same time Elmo Roper established his survey and Archibald Crossley, the Crossley Poll.

G.H. GALLUP, *A Guide to Public Opinion Polls*, New York, 1948; H.H. REMNERS, *Introduction to Opinion and Attitude Measurement*, New York, 1954.

GALOSH. A NATO code-name for the Soviet Anti-Ballistic Missile, ABM System.

D. ROBERTSON, *Guide to Modern Defense and Strategy*, Detroit, 1988.

GAMBIA, THE. Member of the UN. The Gambia Republic. West African state on the Atlantic Ocean, forming an enclave in Senegal about 48 km wide. Area: 11,295 sq. km. Pop. 1988 est. 788,613 (1973 census 494,279). Capital: Banjul formerly Bathurst with 39,476 inhabitants, 1973. GNP per capita 1986 US $230. Official language: English. Currency: one dalasi = 100 butut. National Day: Feb. 18, Independence Day, 1965.
Member of the UN since Sept. 25, 1965 and of the UN specialized agencies, with the exception of the IAEA and ILO. Member of OAU, the British Commonwealth and is an ACP state of EEC. A signatory of the Lomé Conventions of 1975 and of 1980. International relations: under British control from the 17th century; crown colony 1844–1963; its boundaries were delimited after 1890. It achieved self-government 1963 and independence on Feb. 18, 1965; proclaimed republic within the Commonwealth after a referendum, on Apr. 24, 1970.
In 1980's the economic, military and political integration of Gambia with Senegal began. The Confederation, since Feb. 1, 1982, has been called

▷ Senegambia. On Jan. 1, 1983 the Confederal Parliament hold its inaugural meeting.

The Gambia Independence Order, Bathurst, 1965; H.A. GAILAY, *A History of the Gambia*, New York, 1965; B. RICE, *Enter Gambia. The Birth of an Improbable Nation*, Boston, 1967; *The Gambia since Independence 1965–1980*, Banjul, 1980; *The Europa Year Book 1984. A World Survey*, Vol. II, pp. 1598–1603, London, 1984.

GAMBIA RIVER BASIN DEVELOPMENT ORGANIZATION. f. 1978, Dakar, Senegal. Founders: Senegal and Gambia. Members: Guinea, 1981 and Guinea-Bissau, 1983. Plans include the construction of dams on the Gambia River at Balingho. Reg. with the UIA.

The Europa Yearbook 1988. A World Survey, Vol. I, London, 1988.

GAME THEORY. An international term for the application of mathematical solutions to economic, military and other problems.

J. von NEUMANN, O. MORGENSTERN, *Theory of Games and Economic Behaviours*, Vienna 1940; J. MCDONALD, *Strategy in Poker, Business and War*, London, 1950; D. ROBERTSON, *Guide to Modern Defense and Strategy*, London, 1988.

GANEFO. Games of the New Emerging Forces. The sports games of Third World countries organized Apr. 29, 1963 in the capital of Indonesia, Batavia, intended as an Olympics limited solely to the countries of the Southern Hemisphere, which led to a discriminatory decision by the international Olympic Committee to refuse admission to the XVIII Olympic Games in Tokyo, 1964, to the Chinese People's Republic, Indonesia and North Korea.

GANGES OR GANGA. A river in India and Bangladesh, length 2510 km, river-basin area 1,125,000 sq. km; rising in the Himalayas and flowing through a vast plain to the Bay of Bengal. Sacred river of Hindu India. Subject of a dispute between Bangladesh and India on the division of water at the ▷ Farakka dam.

GARAMBA. The National Park of Zaïre, included in the ▷ World Heritage UNESCO List. The savannahs of the Garamba region extend over 4480 km as far as the Sudan and contain examples of four of the largest mammals on earth: the elephant, the hippopotamus, the giraffe and the white rhinoceros. The latter (which is not in fact white, but dark grey, and is twice the size of the black rhinoceros) is one of the rarest and most endangered animals in Africa.

UNESCO, *A Legacy for all*, Paris, 1984.

GARDUS AEGLEFINUS. Haddock. A fish protected by an international convention.

UNTS, Vol. 231, p. 199.

GAS. A subject of international co-operation and international statistics. Organizations reg. with the UIA:

Economic Research Committee of the Gas Industry, f. 1954, Brussels. Consultative status with ECOSOC. Publ.: *Studies*.
European Gas and Oil Control Manufacturers' Association, f. 1966, Brussels.
European Liquified Petroleum Gas Association, f. 1968, Paris.
International Colloquium on Gas Marketing, f. 1957, Paris.
International European Permanent Commission of Industrial Gases and Calcium Carbide, f. 1923, Paris. Publ.: *Bulletin CPJ*.

International Gas Union, f. 1931, London. Official relations with ITU. Publ.: *International Safety Code for International Transmission of Fuel Gas by Pipelines, Safety Code for Compressors, Regulating and/or Measurement Stations on Gas Transmission System*.
International Group of Importers of Liquified Natural Gas, F. 1975, Paris.

Yearbook of International Organizations; OECD, *Natural Gas*; *Prospects to 2000*, Paris, 1952; L. MEDARD, *Gas Encyclopaedia*, Amsterdam, 1976; J.P. STERN, *Soviet Oil and Gas to the West: Commercial Transaction or Security Threat?*, London, 1986; *The Europa Yearbook 1988. A World Survey*, Vol. I, London, 1988.

GASES ASPHYXIATING OR POISONOUS.

A concern of the law of war, since July 29, 1899, when the 28 participants of the International Peace Conference in The Hague signed the Declaration Concerning Asphyxiating Gases and banned their use in warfare. (▷ Hague Declaration against Poisonous Gases). The Declaration was violated by Germany during World War I by the use of the so-called yperite, mustard-smelling poisonous gas used for the first time on July 12, 1917 near Ypres, Belgium (hence the name); within several hours it may cause fatal poisoning of respiratory organs and burns that heal slowly. The Versailles Treaty, 1919, with Germany, therefore, in art. 171 states:

"The use of asphyxiating, poisonous or other gases and all analogous liquids, materials or devices being prohibited, their manufacture and importation are strictly forbidden for Germany".

Similarly worded are art. 135 of the Treaty of St. Germain, 1919, with Austria, art. 82 of the Treaty of Neuilly 1919, with Bulgaria, and art. 119 of the Treaty of Trianon, 1919, with Hungary. The ban on use of asphyxiating, poisonous and similar gases was again introduced in art. 5 of the Washington Treaty, 1922, relating to use of Submarines and Noxious Gases in Warfare, signed Feb. 6, 1922 by Australia, Canada, Ethiopia, France, Great Britain, India, Japan, New Zealand, South Africa and the USA. The Treaty never came into force because of reservations concerning clauses on submarines; however, its art. 5. formed the basis of the ▷ Geneva Protocol 1925, for the Prohibition of the Use in War of Asphyxiating, Poisonous or Other Gases and of Bacteriological Methods of Warfare. The Central American Limitation Armaments Convention, 1923, in art. 5,

"considers that the use in warfare of asphyxiating gases, poisonous or similar substances, as well as analogous liquids, materials or devices is contrary to humanitarian principles and to international law."

The use of yperite as a chemical warfare agent was banned by the 1925 Geneva Protocol. During World War II Germany violated the Geneva Protocol using for genocidal operations in concentration camps a poisonous gas with the German name ▷ Zyklon B. After World War II, the issue of gases formed part of the larger problem of ▷ Chemical weapons.

International Conciliation, No. 248, New York, Mar. 1929, pp. 125–179; *The Trial of German Major War Criminals. Proceedings of the International Military Tribunal sitting at Nuremberg, Germany*, 42 Vols, London 1946–1948, Vol. 2, pp. 365–410; Vol. 3, pp. 259–320; Vol. 5, p. 209; Vol. 7, pp. 44, 96–112, 116–125; D. SCHINDLER, J. TOMAN, *The Laws of Armed Conflicts*, Leiden–Geneva, 1973, pp. 93–101, 107–119, 657–659.

GAS PIPELINES. ▷ Oil and gas pipelines.

GASTARBEITER. German = "guest-worker".

The name used in Western Europe for the millions of foreign workers employed in agriculture, services and industry; subject of bilateral international agreements and many international legal disputes resulting from conflicts between employees and employers. The total number with their families in EEC states was c. 15 million in 1980.

J. POWER, *Migrant Workers in Western Europe and the US*, Oxford 1979.

GASTROENTEROLOGY.

A subject of international co-operation. Organizations reg. with the UIA:

Asian Association of Gastroenterology, f. 1970, Manila.
Association of National European and Mediterranean Societies of Gastroeterology, f. 1947, Paris.
Bocus International Society of Gastroenterology, f. 1958, Philadelphia, Pa.
European Association for Gastrocamera Diagnosis, f. 1970, Berlin.
Inter-American Association of Gastroenterology, f. 1948, Mexico City.
World Organization of Gastroenterology, f. 1935, Madrid.

Yearbook of International Organizations.

GASTRONOMY.

A subject of international co-operation. Organizations reg. with the UIA:

International Federation of Gastronomical, Vinicultural and Touristic Press, f. 1952, Milano.
International Union of National Associations of Hotel, Restaurant and Café Keepers, f. 1949, Zurich.

Yearbook of International Organizations.

GATT.

The General Agreement on Tariffs and Trade. A multilateral treaty applied by 84 signatory nations and under special arrangements, by an additional 27 countries, together responsible for more than four-fifths of world trade, est. Jan. 1, 1948. The GATT is the only multilateral treaty laying down agreed rules for world trade. It is the major forum for negotiations of tariff reduction and other measures to liberalize trade relations among developed market economy countries and many developing countries. According to *Everyman's United Nations*, the origin and background of the GATT is as follows. In the 1930s, when the world was suffering from a intense economic depression, many governments attempted to shelter behind various kinds of protective trade barriers such as high tariff protection, quota restrictions on imports and exports, and exchange controls. It became evident during World War II that these restrictions might become a permanent fixture in the world unless an attempt was made to re-establish as soon as possible the predepression pattern of multilateral trading between nations. The General Agreements on Tariffs and Trade, GATT, is today the major result of the efforts made in this direction.
The wartime Allies in the Atlantic Charter and in the Lend-Lease Agreements bound themselves to seek together a world trading system based on non-discrimination, and aimed at higher standards of living to be achieved through fair, full and free exchange of goods and services. In pursuit of this aim, long before the end of the war, the United States, the United Kingdom and other important trading countries among the United Nations, discussed the establishment of international organizations to tackle the postwar problems of currency, investment and trade. The International Monetary Fund and the International Bank for Reconstruction and Development were established as a result of the Bretton Woods Conference which was held in July 1944. But for various reasons, including its wide range and its complexity, the Charter for the International Trade Organization, which was intended to be the third agency to operate in a specialized field of economic affairs, was not completed until much later. In 1946, the United Nations Economic and Social Council resolved to convene an International Conference on Trade and Employment, and established a Preparatory Committee to prepare for the consideration of the conference a draft convention for an international trade organization. A draft charter was adopted by the Preparatory Committee in Aug., 1947, and formed the basis for the work of the Coference, held in Havana from Nov. 21, 1947 to Mar. 24, 1948. That conference drew up a Charter for an International Trade Organization (known as the Havana Charter), and established an Interim Commission for the International Trade Organization ICITO. The main task of the Interim Commission was to prepare for the first session of ITO. This task, so far as events could be foreseen, was completed in 1949; but because of the lack of acceptances of the Havana Charter it became evident that the establishment of ITO would be definitely postponed. In 1947, while the Charter for ITO was being prepared at Geneva, the members of the Preparatory Committee decided to proceed forthwith with tariff negotiations among themselves and also drew up the General Agreement on Tariffs and Trade, GATT. The Geneva Tariff Conference was the first of six main tariff conferences which have been held under GATT auspices until 1980. All the countries adhering to the GATT have taken part in these tariff negotiations; in fact, it is a stipulation that a country wishing to join the GATT should undertake to reduce the level of its own customs tariffs through negotiations before it can adhere to the Agreement.
Aims: the GATT is an international treaty, and its terms are set out in a series of articles. First, there are the articles dealing directly with tariffs – art. 1 with the most-favored-nation obligation and art. 2, the basic tariff article, incorporating the schedules of tariff concessions resulting from the tariff conferences. Art. 3 provides agreed rules regarding the application of internal taxes, guaranteeing that foreign goods will be given equal treatment with domestic products. Arts. 4 to 10 – known as the technical articles – are general rules and principles relating to transit trade, anti-dumping duties, customs valuation, customs formalities, and marks of origin. Arts. 11 to 15 deal with quantitative restrictions on imports and exports; art. 11 formally outlaws quantitative restrictions; the remainder of the articles deal with qualifications to this general rule and with state trading, subsidies and assistance for countries in early stages of economic development. Finally, there are provisions for joint discussion and settlement of differences.
Such is the structure of the GATT. In fact, all its provisions are linked to, and stem from, the tariff concessions, because these concessions would be of doubtful value if the parties to the Agreement were to have their hands free in all other fields of commerical policy; given such freedom, it would be possible entirely to nullify the benefits accruing from concessions made in tariff rates. The result has been to create a code of trade-policy rules governing the commercial relations of the countries which adhere to the GATT. One of the most important aspects of the work of the contracting parties in 1957–58 was the consideration of the treaty establishing the European Economic Community, EEC. In 1980 the member states of the GATT represented 85% of world trade. The GATT organization is headed by a Director-General who is appointed by the Contracting Parties. The Director-General appoints the staff of the GATT Secretariat which in 1978 numbered about 200. Languages: English, French, Spanish. Financial contributions by contracting parties; the scale of contributions is assessed for each contracting party in relation to its share in the total trade of the

member countries. Budget for 1978 was 38,585,000 Swiss francs. The GATT Secretariat consists of a number of specialists under the direction of a Director-General. The secretariat offices are in the Centre William Rapparel, 154 rue de Lausanne, Geneva. Publications: *International Trade* (annual) analyses developments in the structure and pattern of international trade. *Basic Instruments and Selected Documents* (annual); four volumes, of which Vol. IV reproduces the current text of the General Agreement, and 21 supplements. *GATT Studies in International Trade* (occasional), *GATT Activities* (annual), etc. All publications can be obtained from GATT, Villa de Bocage, Palais de Nations, 1211 Geneva 10, Switzerland.

Everyman's United Nations, New York, 1970; K.W. DAM, *The GATT Law and International Economic Organization*, Chicago, 1970; P. CASADIO, *Transatlantic Trade USA – EEC. Confrontation in the GATT Negotiations*, Farnborough, 1973; S. GOLT, *The GATT Negotiations 1973–75. A Guide to the Issues*, London, 1974; R.E. HUDEC, *The GATT Legal System and World Trade Diplomacy*, New York, 1975; GATT, *Basic Instruments and Documents*, 4 Vols. and 28 Supplements, Geneva, 1952–82.

GATT GENERAL AGREEMENTS ON TARIFFS AND TRADE, 1947. Final Act adopted at the conclusion of the Session of the Preparatory Committee of the UN Conference on Trade and Development, signed in Geneva on Oct. 30, 1947. The Text is as follows:

"The Governments of the Commonwealth of Australia, the Kingdom of Belgium, the United States of Brazil, Burma, Canada, Ceylon, the Republic of Chile, the Republic of China, the Republic of Cuba, the Czechoslovak Republic, the French Republic, India, Lebanon, the Grand-Duchy of Luxembourg, the Kingdom of the Netherlands, New Zealand, the Kingdom of Norway, Pakistan, Southern Rhodesia, Syria, the Union of South Africa, the United Kingdom of Great Britain and Northern Ireland, and the United States of America:

Recognizing that their relations in the field of trade and economic endeavour should be conducted with a view to raising standards of living, ensuring full employment and a large and steadily growing volume of real income and effective demand, developing the full use of the resources of the world and expanding the production and exchange of goods;

Being desirous of contributing to these objectives by entering into reciprocal and mutually advantageous arrangements directed to the substantial reductions of tariffs and other barriers to trade and to the elimination of discriminatory treatment in international commerce;

Have through their Representatives agreed as follows:

PART I, Art. I. General Most-Favoured-Nation Treatment

(1) With respect to customs duties and charges of any kind imposed on or in connection with importation or exportation or imposed on the international transfer of payments for imports or exports, and with respect to the method of levying such duties and charges, and with respect to all rules and formalities in connection with importation and exportation, and with respect to all matters referred to in paragraphs 1 and 2 of Article III, any advantage, favour, privilege or immunity granted by any contracting party to any product originating in or destined for any other country shall be accorded immediately and unconditionally to the like product originating in or destined for the territories of all other contracting parties.

(2) The provisions of paragraph 1 of this Article shall not require the elimination of any preferences in respect of import duties or charges which do not exceed the levels provided for in paragraph 3 of this Article and which fall within the following descriptions:

(a) preferences in force exclusively between two or more of the territories listed in Annex A, subject to the conditions set forth therein;

(b) preferences in force exclusively between two or more territories which on July 1, 1939, were connected by common sovereignty or relations of protection or suzerainty and which are listed in Annexes B, C and D, subject to the conditions set forth therein;

(c) preferences in force exclusively between the United States of America and the Republic of Cuba;

(d) preferences in force exclusively between neighbouring countries listed in Annexes E and F.

(3) The margin of preference on any project in respect of which a preference is permitted under paragraph 2 of this Article but is not specifically set forth as a maximum margin of preference in the appropriate Schedule annexed to this Agreement shall not exceed:

(a) in respect of duties or charges on any product described in such Schedule, the difference between the most-favoured-nation and preferential rates provided for therein; if no preferential rate is provided for, the preferential rate shall for the purposes of this paragraph be taken to be that in force on April 10, 1947, and, if no most-favoured-nation rate is provided for, the margin shall not exceed the difference between the most-favoured-nation and preferential rates existing on April 10, 1947;

(b) in respect of duties or charges on any product not described in the appropriate Schedule, the difference between the most-favoured-nation and preferential rates existing on April 10, 1947.

In the case of the contracting parties named in Annex G, the date of April 10, 1947, referred to in sub-paragraphs (a) and (b) of this paragraph shall be replaced by the respective dates set forth in that Annex.

Art. 11. Schedules of Concessions.

(1)(a) Each contracting party shall accord to the commerce of the other contracting parties treatment no less favourable than that provided for in the appropriate Part of the appropriate Schedule annexed to this Agreement.

(b) The products described in Part I of the Schedule relating to any contracting party, which are the products of territories of other contracting parties, shall, on their importation into the territory to which the Schedule relates, and subject to the terms, conditions or qualifications set forth in that Schedule, be exempt from ordinary customs duties in excess of those set forth and provided for therein. Such products shall also be exempt from all other duties or charges of any kind imposed on or in connection with importation in excess of those imposed on the date of this Agreement or those directly and mandatorily required to be imposed thereafter by legislation in force in the importing territory on that date.

(c) The products described in Part II of the Schedule relating to any contracting party, which are the products of territories entitled under Article I to receive preferential treatment upon importation into the territory to which the Schedule relates, shall, on their importation into such territory, and subject to the terms, conditions, or qualifications set forth in that Schedule, be exempt from ordinary customs duties in excess of those set forth and provided for in Part II of that Schedule. Such products shall also be exempt from all other duties or charges of any kind imposed on or in connection with importation in excess of those imposed on the date of this Agreement or those directly and mandatorily required to be imposed thereafter by legislation in force in the importing territory on that date. Nothing in this Article shall prevent any contracting party from maintaining its requirements existing on the date of this Agreement as to the eligibility of goods for entry at preferential rates of duty.

(2) Nothing in this Article shall prevent any contracting party from imposing at any time on the importation of any product

(a) a charge equivalent to an internal tax imposed consistently with the provisions of paragraph 1 of Article III in respect of the like domestic product or in respect of an article from which the imported product has been manufactured or produced in whole or in part;

(b) any anti-dumping or countervailing duty applied consistently with the provisions of Article VI;

(c) fees or other charges commensurate with the cost of services rendered.

(3) No contracting party shall alter its method of determining dutiable value or of converting currencies so as to impair the value of any of the concessions provided for in the appropriate Schedule annexed to this Agreement.

(4) If any contracting party establishes, maintains or authorizes, formally or in effect, a monopoly of the importation of any product described in the appropriate Schedule annexed to this Agreement, such monopoly shall not, except as provided for in that Schedule or as otherwise agreed between the parties which initially negotiated the concession, operate so as to afford protection on the average in excess of the amount of protection provided for in that Schedule. The provisions of this paragraph shall not limit the use by contracting parties of any form of assistance to domestic producers permitted by other provisions of this Agreement.

(5) In any contracting party considers that a product is not receiving from another contracting party the treatment which the first contracting party believes to have been contemplated by a concession provided for in the appropriate Schedule annexed to this Agreement, it shall bring the matter directly to the attention of the other contracting party. If the latter agrees that the treatment contemplated was that claimed by the first contracting party, but declares that such treatment cannot be accorded because a court or other proper authority has ruled to the effect that the product involved cannot be classified under the tariff laws of such contracting party so as to permit the treatment contemplated in this Agreement, the two contracting parties, together with any other contracting substantially interested, shall enter promptly into further negotiations with a view to a compensatory adjustment of the matter.

(6)(a) The specific duties and charges included in the Schedule relating to contracting parties members of the International Monetary Fund, and margins of preference in specific duties and charges maintained by such contracting parties, are expressed in the appropriate currency at the par value accepted or provisionally recognized by the Fund at the date of this Agreement. Accordingly, in case this par value is reduced consistently with the Articles of Agreement of the International Monetary Fund by more than twenty per centum, such specific duties and charges and margins of preference may be adjusted to take account of such reduction; Provided that the contracting parties (i.e. the contracting parties acting jointly as provided for in Article XXV) concur that such adjustments will not impair the value of the concessions provided for in the appropriate Schedule or elsewhere in this Agreement, due account being taken of all factors which may influence the need for, or urgency of, such adjustments.

(b) Similar provisions shall apply to any contracting party not a member of the Fund, as from the date on which sub contracting party becomes a member of the Fund or enters into a special exchange agreement in pursuance of Article XV.

(7) The Schedules annexed to this Agreement are hereby made a integral part of Part I of this Agreement.

PART II, Article III, National Treatment on Internal Taxation and Regulations.

(1) The products of the territory of any contracting party imported into the territory of any other contracting party shall be exempt from internal taxes and other internal charges of any kind in excess of those applied directly or indirectly to like products of national origin. Moreover, in cases in which there is no substantial domestic production of like products of national origin, no contracting party shall apply new or increased internal taxes on the products of the territories of other contracting parties for the purpose of affording protection to the production of directly competitive or substitutable products which are not similarly taxed; and existing internal taxes of this kind shall be subject to negotiation for their reduction or elimination.

(2) The products of the territory of any contracting party imported into the territory of any other contracting party shall be accorded treatment no less favourable than that accorded to like products of national origin in respect of all laws, regulations and requirements affecting their internal sale, offering for sale, purchase, transportation, distribution, or use. The provisions of this paragraph shall not prevent the application of differential transportation charges which are based exclusively on the economic operation of the means of transport and not on the nationality of the product.

(3) In applying the principles of paragraph 2 of this Article to internal quantitative regulations relating to the mixture, processing or use of products in specified amounts or proportions, the contracting parties shall observe the following provisions:

(a) no regulations shall be made which, formally or in effect, require that any specified amount or proportion

of the product in respect of which such regulations are applied must be supplied from domestic sources;
(b) no contracting party shall, formally or in effect, restrict the mixing, processing or use of a product of which there is no substantial domestic production with a view to affording protection to the domestic production of a directly competitive or substitutable product.
(4) The provisions of paragraph 3 of this Article shall not apply to:
(a) any measure of internal quantitative control in force in the territory of any contracting party on July 1, 1939 or April 10, 1947, at the option of that contracting party; Provided that any such measure which would be in conflict with the provisions of paragraph 3 of this Article shall not be modified to the detriment of imports and shall be subject to negotiation for its limitation, liberalization or elimination;
(b) any internal quantitative regulation relating to exposed cinematograph films and meeting the requirements of Article IV.
(5) The provisions of this Article shall not apply to the procurement by governmental agencies of products purchased for governmental purposes and not for resale or use in the production of goods for sale, nor shall they prevent the payment to domestic producers only of subsidies provided for under Article XVI, including payments to domestic producers derived from the proceeds of internal taxes or charges and subsidies effected through governmental purchases of domestic products.

Art. IV. Special Provisions Relating to Cinematograph Films

If any contracting party establishes or maintains internal quantitative regulations relating to exposed cinematograph films, such regulations shall take the form of screen quotas which shall conform to the following requirements:
(a) screen quotas may require the exhibition of cinematograph films of national origin during a specified minimum proportion of the total screen time actually utilized, over a specified period of not less than one year, in the commercial exhibition of all films of whatever origin, and shall be computed on the basis of screen time per theatre per year or the equivalent thereof;
(b) with the exception of screen time reserved for films of national origin under a screen quota, screen time including that released by administrative actions from screen time reserved for films of national origin, shall not be allocated formally or in effect among sources of supply;
(c) notwithstanding the provisions of sub-paragraph (b) of this Article any contracting party may maintain screen quotas conforming to the requirements of sub-paragraph (a) of this Article which reserve a minimum proportion of screen time for films of a specified origin other than that of the contracting party imposing such screen quotas; Provided that no such minimum proportion of screen time shall be increased above the level in effect on April 10, 1947;
(d) screen quotas shall be subject to negotiation for their limitation, liberalization or elimination.

Art. V. Freedom of Transit.

(1) Goods (including baggage), and also vessels and other means of transport, shall be deemed to be in transit across the territory of a contracting party when the passage across such territory, with or without trans-shipment, warehousing, breaking bulk, or change in the mode of transport, is only a portion of a complete journey beginning and terminating beyond the frontier of the contracting party across whose territory the traffic passes. Traffic of this nature is termed in this Article "traffic in transit".
(2) There shall be freedom of transit through the territory of each contracting party, via the routes most convenient for international transit, for traffic in transit to or from the territory of other contracting parties. No distinction shall be made which is based on the flag of vessels, the place of origin, departure, entry, exit or destination, or on any circumstances relating to the ownership of goods, of vessels or of other means of transport.
(3) Any contracting party may require that traffic in transit through its territory be entered at the proper custom house, but, except in cases of failure to comply with applicable customs laws and regulations, such traffic coming from or going to the territory of other contracting parties shall not be subject to any unnecessary delays or restrictions and shall be exempt from customs duties and from all transit duties or other charges imposed in respect of transit, except charges for transportation or those commensurate with administrative expenses entailed by transit or with the cost of services rendered.
(4) All charges and regulations imposed by contracting parties on traffic in transit to or from the territories of other contracting parties shall be reasonable, having regard to the conditions of the traffic.
(5) With respect to all charges, regulations and formalities in connection with transit, each contracting party shall accord to traffic in transit to or from the territory of any other contracting party treatment no less favourable than the treatment accorded to traffic in transit to or from any third country.
(6) Each contracting party shall accord to products which have been in transit through the territory of any other contracting party treatment no less favourable than that of which would have been accorded to such products had they been transported from their place of origin to their destination without going through the territory of such other contracting party. Any contracting party shall, however, be free to maintain its requirements of direct consignment existing on the date of this Agreement, in respect of any goods in regard to which such direct consignment is a requisitie condition of eligibility for entry of the goods at preferential rates of duty or has relation to the contracting party's prescribed method of valulation for duty purposes.
(7) The provisions of this Article shall not apply to the operation of aircraft in transit, but shall apply to air transit of goods (including baggage).

Art VI. Anti-Dumping and Countervailing Duties

(1) No anti-dumping duty shall be levied on any product of the territory of any contracting party imported into the territory of any other contracting party in excess of an amount equal to the margin of dumping under which such product is being imported. For the purposes of this Article, the margin of dumping shall be understood to mean the amount by which the price of the product exported from one country to another.
(a) is less than the comparable price, in the ordinary course of trade, for the like product when destined for consumption in the exporting country; or,
(b) in the absence of such domestic price, is less than either
(i) the highest comparable price for the like product for export to any third country in the ordinary course of trade, or
(ii) the cost of production of the product in the country of origin plus a reasonable addition for selling and profit.
Due allowance shall be made in each case for differences in conditions and terms of sale, for differences in taxation, and for other differences affecting price comparability.
(2) No countervailing duty shall be levied on any product of the territory of any contracting party imported into the territory of another contracting party in excess of an amount equal to the estimated bounty or subsidy determined to have been granted, directly or indirectly, on the manufacture, production or export of such product in the country of origin or exportation, including any special subsidy to the transportation of a particular product. The term 'countervailing duty' shall be understood to mean a special duty levied for the purpose of offsetting any bounty or subsidy bestowed, directly or indirectly, upon the manufacture, production or exportation of any merchandise.
(3) No product of the territory of any contracting party imported into the territory of any other contracting party shall be subject to anti-dumping or countervailing duty by reason of the exemption of such product from duties or taxes borne by the like product when destined for consumption in the coutnry of origin or exportation, or by reason of the refund of such duties or taxes.
(4) No product of the territory of any contracting party imported into the territory of any other contracting party shall be subject to both anti-dumping and countervailing duties to compensate for the same situation of dumping or export subsidization.
(5) No contracting party shall levy any anti-dumping or countervailing duty on the importation of any product of the territory of another contracting party unless it determines that the effect of the dumping or subsidization, as the case may be, is such as to cause or threaten material injury to an established domestic industry, or is such as to prevent or materially retard the establishment of a domestic industry. The contracting parties may waive the requirements of this paragraph so as to permit a contracting party to levy an anti-dumping or countervailing duty on the importation of any product for the purpose of offsetting dumping or subsidization which causes or threatens material injury to an industry in the territory of another contracting party exporting the product concerned to the territory of the importing contracting party.
(6) A system for the stabilization of the domestic price or of the return to domestic producers of a primary commodity, independently of the movements of export prices, which results at times in the sale of the product for export at a price lower than the comparable price charged for the like product to buyers in the domestic market, shall be considered not to result in material injury within the meaning of paragraph 5 of this Article, if it is determined by consultation among the contracting parties substantially interested in the product concerned:
(a) that the system has also resulted in the sale of the product for export at a price higher than the comparable price charged for the like product to buyers in the domestic market, and
(b) that the system is so operated, either because of the effective regulation of production or otherwise, as not to stimulate exports unduly or otherwise seriously prejudice the interests of other contracting parties.
(7) No measures other than anti-dumping or countervailing duties shall be applied by any contracting party in respect of any product of the territory of any other contracting party for the purpose of offsetting dumping or subsidization.

Art. VII. Valuation for Customs Purposes.

(1) The contracting parties recognize the validity of the general principles of valuation set forth in the following paragraphs of this Article, and they undertake to give effect to such principles, in respect of all products subject to duties or other charges or restrictions on importation and exportation based upon or regulated in any manner by value at the earliest practicable date. Moreover, they shall, upon a request by another contracting party, review the operation of any of their laws or regulations relating to value for customs purposes in the light of these principles. The contracting parties may request from contracting parties reports on steps taken by them in pursuance of the provisions of this Article.
(2)(a) The value for customs purposes of imported merchandise should be based on the actual value of the imported merchandise on which duty is assessed, or of like merchandise, and should not be based on the value of merchandise of national origin or on arbitrary or fictitious values.
(b) 'Actual value' should be the price at which, at a time and place determined by the legislation of the country of importation, and in the ordinary course of trade, such or like merchandise is sold or offered for sale under fully competitive conditions. To the extent to which the price of such or like merchandise is governed by the quantity in a particular transaction, the price to be considered should uniformly be related to either (i) comparable quantities, or (ii) quantities not less favourable to importers than those in which the greater volume of the merchandise is sold in the trade between the countries of exportation and importation.
(c) When the actual value is not ascertainable in accordance with sub-paragraph (b) of this paragraph, the value for customs purposes should be based on the nearest ascertainable equivalent of such value.
(3) The value for customs purposes of any imported product should not include the amount of any internal tax, applicable within the country of origin or export, from which the imported product has been exempted or has been or will be relieved by means of refund.
(4)(a) Except as otherwise provided for in this paragraph, where it is necessary for the purposes of paragraph 2 of this Article for a contracting party to convert into its own currency a price expressed in the currency of another country, the conversion rate of exchange to be used shall be based on the par values of the currencies involved as established pursuant to the Articles of Agreement of the International Monetary Fund or by special exchange agreements entered into pursuant to Article XV of this Agreement.
(b) Where no such par value has been established, the conversion rate shall reflect effectively the current value of such currency in commercial transactions.

(c) The contracting parties, in agreement with the International Monetary Fund, shall formulate rules governing the conversion by contracting parties of any foreign currency in respect of which multiple rates of exchange are maintained consistently with the Article of Agreement of the International Monetary Fund. Any contracting party may apply such rules in respect of such foreign currencies for the purposes of paragraph 2 of this Article as an alternative to the use of par values. Until such rules are adopted by the contracting parties, any contracting party may employ, in respect of any such foreign currency, rules of conversion for the purposes of paragraph 2 of this Article which are designed to reflect effectively the value of such foreign currency in commercial transactions.
(d) Nothing in this paragraph shall be construed to require any contracting party to alter the method of converting currencies for customs purposes which is applicable in its territory on the date of this Agreement, if such alteration would have the effect of increasing generally the amounts of duty payable.
(5) The bases and methods for determining the value of products subject to duties or other charges or restrictions based upon or regulated in any manner by value should be stable and should be given sufficient publicity to enable traders to estimate, with a reasonable degree of certainty, the value for customs purposes.

Art. VIII. Formalities Connected with Importation and Exportation.
(1) The contracting parties recognise that fees and charges, other than duties, imposed by governmental authorities on or in connection with importation or exportation, should be limited in amount to the approximate coast of services rendered and should not represent an indirect protection to domestic products or a taxation of imports or export for fiscal purposes. The contracting parties also recognize the need for reducing the number and diversity of such fees and charges, for minimizing the incidence and complexity of import and export formalities, and for decreasing and simplifying import and export documentation requirements.
(2) The contracting parties shall take action in accordance with the principles and objectives of paragraph 1 of this Article at the earliest practicable date. Moreover, they shall, upon request by another contracting party, review the operation of any of their laws and regulations in the light of these principles.
(3) No contacting party shall impose substantial penalties for minor breaches of customs regulations or procedural requirements. In particular, no penalty in respect of any omission or mistake in customs documentation which is easily rectifiable and obviously made without fraudulent intent or gross negligence shall be greater than necessary to serve merely as a warning.
(4) The provisions of this Article shall extend to fees, charges, formalities and requirements imposed by governmental authorities in connection with importation and exportation, including those relating to:
(a) consular transactions, such as consular invoices and certificates;
(b) quantitative restrictions;
(c) licensing;
(d) exchange control;
(e) statistical services;
(f) documents, documentation and certification;
(g) analysis and inspection; and
(h) quarantine, sanitation and fumigation.

Art. IX. Marks of Origin
(1) Each contracting party shall accord to the products of the territories of other contracting parties treatment with regard to marking requirements no less favourable than the treatment accorded to like products of any third country.
(2) Whenever it is administratively practicable to do so, contracting parties should permit required marks of origin to be affixed at the time of importation.
(3) The laws and regulations of contracting parties relating to the marking of imported products shall be such as to permit compliance without seriously damaging the products, or materially reducing their value, or unreasonably increasing their cost.
(4) As a general rule no special duty or penalty should be imposed by any contracting party for failure to comply with marking requirements prior to importation unless corrective marking is unreasonably delayed or deceptive marks have been affixed or the required marking has been intentionally omitted.
(5) The Contracting parties shall co-operate with each other with a view to preventing the use of trade names in such manner as to misrepresent the true origin of a product, to the detriment of such distinctive regional or geographical names of products of the territory of a contracting party as are protected by its legislation. Each contracting party shall accord full and sympathetic consideration to such requests or representations as may be made by any other contractng party regarding the application of the undertaking set forth in the preceding sentence to names of products which have been communicated to it by the other contracting party.

Art. X. Publication and Administration of Trade Regulations.
(1) Laws, regulations, judicial decisions and administrative rulings of general application, made effective by any contracting party, pertaining to the classification or the valuation of products for customs purposes, or to rates of duty, taxes or other charges, or to requirements, restrictions or prohibitions on imports or exports or on the transfer of payments therefor, or affecting their sale, distribution, transportation, insurance, warehousing, inspection, exhibition, processing, mixing or other use, shall be published promptly in such a manner as to enable governments and traders to become acquainted with them. Agreements affecting international trade policy which are in force between the government or a governmental agency of any contracting party and the government or governmental agency of any other contracting party shall also be published. The provisions of this paragraph shall not require any contracting party to disclose confidential information which would impede law enforcement or otherwise be contrary to the public interest or would prejudice the legitimate commerical interests of particular enterprises, public or private.
(2) No measure of general application taken by an contracting party effecting an advance in a rate of duty or other charge on imports under an established and uniform practice, or imposing a new or more burdensome requirement, restriction or prohibition on imports, or on the transfer of payments therefor, shall be enforced before such measure has been officially published.
(3)(a) Each contracting party shall administer in a uniform, impartial and reasonable manner all its laws, regulations, decisions and rulings of the kind described in paragraph 1 of this Article.
(b) Each contracting party shall maintain, or institute as soon as practicable, judicial, arbitral or administrative tribunals or procedures for the purpose, inter alia, of the prompt review and correction of administrative action relating to customs matters. Such tribunals or procedures shall be independent of the agencies entrusted with administative enforcement and their decisions shall be implemented by, and shall govern the practice of, such agencies unless an appeal is lodged with a court or tribunal of superior jurisdiction within the time prescribed for appeals to be lodged by importers; Provided that the central administration of such agency may take steps to obtain a review of the matter in another proceeding if there is a good cause to believe that the decision is inconsistent with established principles of law or the actual facts.
(c) The provisions of sub-paragraph (b) of this paragraph shall not require the elimination or substitution of procedures in force in the territory of a contracting party on the date of this Agreement which in fact provide for an objective and impartial review of administrative action even though such procedures are not fully or formally independent of the agencies entrusted with administrative enforcement. Any contracting party employing such procedures shall, upon request, furnish the contracting parties with full information thereon in order that they may determine whether such procedures conform to the requirement of this sub-paragraph.

Art. XI. General Elimination of Quantitative Restrictions.
(1) No prohibitions or restrictions other than duties, taxes or other charges, whether made effective through quotas, import or export licences or other measures, shall be instituted or maintained by any contracting party on the importation of any product of the territory of any other contracting party on the importation of any product of the territory of any other contracting party on the exportation or sale for export of any product destined for the territory of any other contracting party.
(2) The provisions of paragraph 1 of this Article shall not extend to the following:
(a) export prohibitions or restrictions temporarily applied to prevent or relieve critical shortages of foodstuffs or other products essential to the exporting contracting party;
(b) import and export prohibitions or restrictions necessary to the application of standards or regulations for the classification, grading or marketing of commodities in international trade;
(c) import restrictions on any agricultural or fisheries product, imported in any form, necessary to the enforcement of governmental measures which operate:
(i) to restrict the quantities of the like domestic product permitted to be marketed or produced, or, if there is no substantial domestic production of the like product, of a domestic product for which the import product can be directly substituted; or
(ii) to remove a temporary surplus of the like domestic product, or, if there is no substantial domestic production of the like product, of a domestic product for which the imported product can be directly substituted, by making the surplus available to certain groups of domestic consumers free of charge or at prices below the current market level, or
(iii) to restrict the quantities permitted to be produced of any animal product the production of which is directly dependent, wholly or mainly on the imported commodity, if the domestic production of that commodity is relatively negligible.
Any contracting party applying restrictions on the importation of any product pursuant to sub-paragraph (c) of this paragraph shall give public notice of the total quantity or value of the product permitted to be imported during a specified future period and of any change in such quantity or value. Moreover, any restrictions applied under (i) above shall not be such as will reduce the total of imports relative to the total of domestic production, as compared with the proportion which might reasonably be expected to rule between the two in the absence of restrictions. In determining this proportion, the contracting party shall pay due regard to the proportion prevailing during a previous representative period and to any special factors which may have affected or may be affecting the trade in the product concerned.
(3) Throughout Articles XI, XII, XIII and XIV, the terms 'import restrictions' or 'export restrictions' include restrictions made effective through state-trading operations.

Art. XII. Restrictions to Safeguard the Balace of Payments.
(1) Notwithstanding the provisions of paragraph 1 of Article XI, any contracting party, in order to safeguard its external financial position and balance of payments, may restrict the quantity or value of merchandise permitted to be imported, subject to the provisions of the following paragraphs of this Article.
(2) (a) No contracting party shall institute, maintain or intensify import restrictions under this Article except to the extent necessary
(i) to forestall the imminent threat, of, or to stop, a serious decline in its monetary reserves, or
(ii) in the case of a contracting party with very low monetary reserves, to achieve a reasonable rate of increase in its reserves.
Due regard shall be paid in either case to any special factors which may be affecting the contracting party's reserves or need for reserves, including, where special external credits or other resources are available to it, the need to provide for the appropriate use of such credits or resources.
(b) Contracting parties applying restrictions under sub-paragraph (a) of this paragraph shall progressively relax them as such conditions improve, maintaining them only to the extent that the conditions specified in that sub-paragraph still justify their application. They shall eliminate the restrictions when conditions would no longer justify their institution or maintenance under that sub-paragraph.
3(a) The contracting parties recognize that during the next few years all of them will be confronted in varying degrees with problems of economic adjustment resulting from the war. During this period the contracting parties shall, when required to take decisions under this Article or under Article XIV, take full account of the

difficulties of post-war adjustment and of the need which a contracting party may have to use import restrictions as a step towards the restoration of equilibrium in its balance of payments on a sound and lasting basis.

(b) The contracting parties recognize that, as a result of domestic policies directed toward the achievement and maintenance of full and productive employment and large and steadily growing demand or toward the reconstruction or development of industrial and other economic resources and the raising of standards of productivity, such a contracting party may experience a high level of demand for imports. Accordingly,

(i) notwithstanding the provisions of paragraph 2 of this Article, no contracting party shall be required to withdraw or modify restrictions on the ground that a change in the policies referred to above would render unnecessary the restrictions which it is applying under this Article;

(ii) any contracting party applying import restrictions under this Article may determine the incidence of the restrictions on imports of different products or classes of products in such a way as to give priority to the importation of those products which are more essential in the light of such policies.

(c) Contracting parties undertake, in carrying out their domestic policies:

(i) to pay due regard to the need for restoring equilibrium in their balance of payments on a sound and lasting basis and to the desirability of assuring an economic employment of productive resources;

(ii) not to apply restrictions so as to prevent unreasonably the importation of any description of goods in minimum commerical quantities, the exclusion of which would impair regular channels of trade, or restrictions which would prevent the importation of commerical samples, or prevent compliance with patent, trademark, copyright, or similar procedures; and

(iii) to apply restrictions under this Article in such a way as to avoid unnecessary damage to the commerical or economic interests of any other contracting party.

(4)(a) Any contracting party which is not applying restrictions under this Article, but is considering the need to do so, shall, before instituting such restrictions (or, in circumstances in which prior consultation is impracticable, immediately after doing so), consult with the contracting parties as to the nature of its balance-of-payments difficulties, alternative corrective measures which may be available, and the possible effect of such measures on the economies of other contracting parties. No contracting party shall be required in the course of consultations under this sub-paragraph to indicate in advance the choice or timing of any particular measures which it may ultimately determine to adopt.

(b) The contracting parties may at any time invite any contracting party which is applying import restrictions under this Article to enter into such consultations with them, and shall invite any contracting party substantially intensifying such restrictions to consult within thirty days. A contracting party thus invited shall participate in such discussions. The contracting parties may invite any other contracting party to take part in these discussions. Not later than January 1, 1951, the contracting parties shall review all restrictions existing on that day and still applied under this Article at the time of the review.

(c) Any contracting party may consult with the contracting parties with a view to obtaining their prior approval for restrictions which the contracting party proposes, under this Article, to maintain, intensify or institute, or for the maintenance, intensification or institution of restrictions under specified future conditions. As a result of such consultations, the contracting parties may approve in advance the maintenance, intensification or institution of restrictions by the contracting party in question insofar as the general extent, degree of intensity and duration of the restrictions are concerned. To the extent to which such approval has been given, the requirements of sub-paragraph (a) of this paragraph shall be deemed to have been fulfilled, and the action of the contracting party applying the restrictions shall not be open to challenge under sub-paragraph (d) of this paragraph on the ground that such action is inconsistent with the provisions of paragraph 2 of this Article.

(d) Any contracting party which considers that another contracting party is applying restrictions under this Article inconsistently with the provisions of paragraphs 2 or 3 of this Article or with those of Article XIII (subject to the provisions of Article XIV) may bring the matter for discussion to the contracting parties; and the contracting party applying the restrictions shall participate in the discussion. The contracting parties, if they are satisfied that there is a prima facie case that the trade of the contracting parties initiating the procedure is adversely affected, shall submit their views to the parties with the aim of achieving a settlement of the matter in question which is satisfactory to the parties and to the contracting parties. If no such settlement is reached and if the contracting parties determine that the restrictions are being applied inconsistently with the provisions of paragraphs 2 or 3 of this Article or with those of Article XIII (subject to the provisions of Article XIV), they shall recommend the withdrawal or modification of the restrictions. If the restrictions are not withdrawn or modified in accordance with the recommendations of the contracting parties within sixty days, they may release any contracting party from specified obligations under this Agreement towards the contractng party applying the restrictions.

(e) It is recognized that premature disclosure of the prospective application, withdrawal or modification of any restriction under this Article might stimulate speculative trade and financial movements which would tend to defeat the purposes of this Article. Accordingly, the contracting parties shall make provision for the observance of the utmost secrecy in the conduct of any consultation.

(5) If there is a persistent and widespread application of import restrictions under this Article, indicating the existence of a general disequilibrium which is restricting international trade, the contracting parties shall initiate discussions to consider whether other measures might be taken, either by those contracting parties whose balances of payments are under pressure or by those whose balances of payments are tending to be exceptionally favourable, or by any appropriate intergovernmental organization, to remove the underlying causes of the disequilibrium. On the invitation of the contracting parties, contracting parties shall participate in such discussions.

Art. XIII. Non-Discriminatory Administration of Quantitative Restrictions.

(1) No prohibition or restriction shall be applied by any contracting party on the importation of any product of the territory of any other contracting party or on the exportation of any product destined for the territory of any other contracting party, unless the importation of the like product of all third countries or the exportation of the like product to all third countries is similarly prohibited or restricted.

(2) In applying import restrictions to any product, contracting parties shall aim at a distribution of trade in such product approaching as closely as possible to the shares which the various contracting parties might be expected to obtain in the absence of such restrictions, and to this end shall observe the following provisions:

(a) wherever practicable, quotas representing the total amount of permitted imports (whether allocated among supplying countries or not) shall be fixed, and notice given of their amount in accordance with paragraph 3 (b) of this Article;

(b) in cases in which quotas are not practicable, the restrictions may be applied by means of import licences or permits without a quota;

(c) contracting parties shall not; except for purposes of operating quotas allocated in accordance with sub-paragraph (d) of this paragraph, require that import licences or permits be utilized for the importation of the product concerned from a particular country or source;

(d) in cases in which a quota is allocated among supplying countries, the contracting party applying the restrictions may seek agreement with respect to the allocation of shares in the quota with all other contracting parties having a substantial interest in supplying the product concerned. In cases in which this method is not reasonably practicable, the contracting party concerned shall allot to contracting parties having a substantial interest in supplying the product shares based upon the proportions, supplied by such contracting parties during a previous representative period, of the total quantity or value of imports of the product, due account being taken of any special factors which may have affected or may be affecting the trade in the product. No conditions

or formalities shall be imposed which would prevent any contracting party from utilizing fully the shares of any such total quantity or value which has been allotted to it, subject to importation being made within any prescribed period to which the quota may relate.

(3)(a) In cases in which import licences are issued in connection with import restrictions, the contracting party applying the restrictions shall provide, upon the request of any contracting party having an interest in the trade in the product concerned, all relevant information concerning the administration of the restrictions, the import licences granted over a recent period and the distribution of such licences among supplying countries; Provided that there shall be no obligation to supply information as to the names of importing or supplying enterprises.

(b) In the case of import restrictions involving the fixing of quotas, the contracting party applying the restrictions shall give public notice of the total quantity or value of the product or products which will be permitted to be imported during a specified future period and of any change in such quantity or value. Any supplies of the product in question which were en route at the time at which public notice was given shall not be excluded from entry; Provided that they may be counted so far as practicable, against the quantity permitted to be imported in the period in question, and also, where necessary, against the quantities permitted to be imported in the next following period or periods; and provided further that if any contracting party customarily exempts from such restrictions products entered for consumption or withdrawn from warehouse for consumption during a period of thirty days after the day of such public notice, such practice shall be considered full compliance with this sub-paragraph.

(c) In the case of quotas allocated among supplying countries, the contracting parties applying the restrictions shall promptly inform all other contracting parties having an interest in supplying the product concerned of the shares in the quota currently allocated, by quantity or value, to the various supplying countries and shall give public notice thereof.

(4) With regard to restrictions applied in accordance with paragraph 2 (d) of this Article or under paragraph 2 (c) of Article XI, the selection of a representative period for any product and the appraisal of any special factors affecting the trade in the product shall be made initially by the contracting party applying the restrictions; Provided that such contracting party shall upon the request of any other contracting party having a substantial interest in supplying that product or upon the request of the contracting parties, consult promptly with the other contracting party or the contracting parties regarding the need for an adjustment of the proportion determined or of the base period selected, or for the reappraisal of the special factors involved, or for the elimination of conditions, formalities or any other provisions established unilaterally relating to the allocation of an adequate quota or its unrestricted utilization.

(5) The provisions of this Article shall apply to any tariff quota instituted or maintained by any contracting party, and, insofar as applicable, the principles of this Article shall also extend to export restrictions and to any internal regulation or requirement under paragraphs 3 and 4 of Article III.

Art. XIV. Exceptions to the Rule of Non-Discrimination.

(1)(a) The contracting parties recognize that when a substantial and widespread disequilibrium prevails in international trade and payments a contracting party applying restrictions under Article XII may be able to increase its imports from certain sources without unduly depleting its monetary reserves, if permitted to depart from the provisions of Article XIII. The contracting parties also recognize the need for close limitation of such departures so as not to handicap achievement of multilateral international trade.

(b) Accordingly, when a substantial and widespread disequilibrium prevails in international trade and payments, a contracting party applying import restrictions under Article XII may relax such restrictions in a manner which departs from the provisions of Article XIII to the extent necessary to obtain additional imports above the maximum total of import which it could afford in the light of the requirements of paragraph 2 of Article XII if its restrictions were fully

consistent with the provisions of Article XIII, provided that
(i) levels of delivered prices for products so imported are not established substantially higher than those ruling for comparable goods regularly available from other contracting parties, and that any excess of such price levels for products so imported is progressively reduced over a reasonable period;
(ii) the contracting party taking such action does not do so as part of any arrangement by which the gold or convertible currency which the contracting party currently receives directly or indirectly from its exports to other contracting parties not party to the arrangement is appreciably reduced below the level it could otherwise have been reasonably expected to attain;
(iii) such action does not cause unnecessary damage to the commerical or economic interests of any other contracting party.
(c) Any contracting party taking action under this paragraph shall observe the principles of sub-paragraph (b) of this paragraph. A contracting party shall desist from transactions which prove to be inconsistent with that sub-paragraph, but the contracting party shall not be required to satisfy itself, when it is not practicable to do so, that the requirements of that sub-paragraph are fulfilled in respect of individual transactions.
(d) Contracting parties undertake, in framing and carrying out any programme for additional imports under this paragraph, to have due regard to the need to facilitate the termination of any exchange arrangements which deviate from the obligations of Sections 2, 3 and 4 of Article VIII of the Articles of Agreement of the International Monetary Fund and to the need to restore equilibrium in their balances of payments on a sound and lasting basis.
(2) Any contracting party taking action under paragraph 1 of this Article shall keep the contracting parties regularly informed regarding such action and shall provide such available relevant information as they may request.
(3)(a) Not later than March 1, 1952 (five years after the date on which the International Monetary Fund began operations) and in each year thereafter, any contracting party maintaining or proposing to institute action under paragraph 1 of this Article shall seek the approval of the contracting parties which shall thereupon determine whether the circumstances of the contracting party justify the maintenance or institution of action by it under paragraph 1 of this Article. After March 1, 1952 no contracting party shall maintain or institute such action without determination by the contracting parties that the contracting party's circumstances justify the maintenance or institution of such action, as the case may be, and the subsequent maintenance or institution of such action by the contracting party shall be subject to any limitations which the contracting parties may prescribe for the purpose of ensuring compliance with the provisions of paragraph 1 of this Article; Provided that the contracting parties shall not require that prior approval be obtained for individual transactions.
(b) If any time the contracting parties find that import restrictions are being applied by a contracting party in a discriminatory manner inconsistent with the exceptions provided for under paragraph 1 of this Article, the contracting party shall, within sixty days, remove the discrimination or modify it as specified by the contracting parties; Provided that any action under paragraph 1 of this Article, to the extent that it has been approved by the contracting parties under sub-paragraph (a) of this paragraph or to the extent that it has been approved by them at the request of a contracting party under a procedure analogous to that of paragraph 4 (c) of Article XII, shall not be open to challenge under this sub-paragraph or under paragraph 4 (d) of Article XII on the ground that it is inconsistent with the provisions of Article XIII.
(c) Not later than March 1, 1950 and in each year thereafter so long as any contracting parties are taking action under paragraph 1 of this Article, the contracting parties shall report on the action still taken by contracting parties under that paragraph. On or about March 1, 1952, and in each year thereafter so long as any contracting parties are taking action under paragraph 1 of this Article, and at such times thereafter as they may decide, the contracting parties shall review the question whether there then exists such a substantial and widespread disequilibrium in international trade and payments as to justify resort to paragraph 1 of this Article by contracting parties. If it appears at any date prior to March 1, 1952, that that there has been a substantial and gerneral improvement in international trade and payments, the contracting parties may review the situation at that date. If, as a result of any such review, the contracting parties determine that no such disequilibrium exists, the provisions of paragraph 1 of this Article shall be suspended and all actions authorized thereunder shall cease six months after such determination.
(4.) The provisions of Article XIII shall not preclude restrictions in accordance with Article XII which either
(a) are applied against imports from other countries, but not as among themselves, by a group of territories having a common quota in the International Monetary Fund, on condition that such restrictions are in all other respects consistent with the provisions of Article XIII, or
(b) assist, in the period up to December 32, 1951, by measures not involving substantial departure from the provisions of Article XIII, another country whose economy had been disrupted by war.
(5). The provisions of this Agreement shall not preclude:
(a) restrictions with equivalent effect to exchange restrictions authorized under Section 3 (b) of Article VII of the Articles of Agreement of the International Monetary Fund; or
(b) restrictions under the preferential arrangements provided for in Annex A of this Agreement, subject to the conditions set forth therein.
(6)(a) The provisions of Article XIII shall not enter into force in respect of import restrictions applied by any contracting party pursuant to Article XII in order to safeguard its external financial position and balance of payments, and the provisions of paragraph 1 of Article XI and Article XIII shall not enter into force in respect of export restrictions applied by an contracting party for the same reason, until January 1, 1949; Provided that this period may with the concurrence of the contracting parties, be extended for such further periods as they may specify in respect of any contracting party whose supply of convertible currencies is inadequate to enable it to apply the above-mentioned provisions.
(b) If a measure taken by a contracting party in the circumstances refered to in sub-paragraph (a) of this paragraph affects the commerce of another contracting party to such an extent as to cause the latter to consider the need of having recourse to the provisions of Article XII, the contracting party having taken that measure shall, if the affected contracting party so requests, enter into immediate consultation with a view to arrangements enabling the affected contracting party to avoid having such actions, shall temporarily suspend application of the measure for a period of fifteen days.

Art. XV. Exchange Arrangements.

(1) The contracting parties shall seek co-operation, with the International Monetary Fund to the end that the contracting parties and the Fund may pursue a coordinated policy with regard to exchange questions within the jurisdiction of the Fund and questions of quantitative restrictions and other trade measures within the jurisdiction of the contracting parties.
(2) In all cases in which the contracting parties are called upon to consider to deal with problems concerning monetary reserves, balances of payments or foreign exchange arrangements, they shall consult fully with the International Monetary Fund. In such consultation, the contracting parties shall accept all findings of statistical and other facts presented by the Fund relating to foreign exchange, monetary reserves and balances of payments, and shall accept the determination of the Fund as to whether action by a contracting party in exchange matters is in accordance with the Articles of Agreement of the International Monetary Fund, or with the terms of a special exchange agreement between that contracting party and the contracting parties. The contracting parties, in reaching their final decision in cases involving the criteria set forth in paragraph 2 (a) of Article XII, shall accept the determination of the Fund as to what constitutes a serious decline in the contracting party's monetary reserves, a very low level of its monetary reserves or a reasonable rate of increase in its monetary reserves, and as to the financial aspects of other matters covered in consultation in such cases.
(3) The contracting parties shall seek agreement with the Fund regarding procedures for consultation under paragraph 2 of this Article.
(4) Contracting parties shall not, by exchange action, frustrate the intent of the provisions of this Agreement, nor, by trade action, the intent of the provisions of the Articles of Agreement of the International Monetary Fund.
(5) If the contracting parties consider, at any time, that exchange restrictions on payments and transfers in connection with imports are being applied by a contracting party in a manner inconsistent with the exceptions provided for in this Agreement for quantitative restrictions, they shall report thereon to the Fund.
(6) Any contracting party which is not a member of the Fund shall, within a time to be determined by the contracting parties after consultation with the Fund, become a member of the Fund, or, failing that, enter into a special exchange agreement with the contracting parties. A contracting party which ceases to be a member of the Fund shall forthwith enter into a special exchange agreement with the contracting parties. Any special exchange agreement entered into by a contracting party under this paragraph shall thereupon become part of its obligations under this Agreement.
(7)(a) A special exchange agreement between a contracting party and the contracting parties under paragraph 6 of this Article shall provide to the satisfaction of the contracting parties that the objectives of this agreement will not be frustrated as a result of action in exchange matters by the contracting party in question.
(b) The terms of any such agreement shall not impose obligations on the contracting party in exchange matters generally more restrictive than those imposed by the Articles of Agreement of the International Monetary Fund on members of the Fund.
(8) A contracting party which is not a member of the Fund shall furnish such information within the general scope of Section 5 of Article VIII of the Articles of Agreement of the International Monetary Fund as the contracting parties may require in order to carry out their functions under this Agreement.
(9). Subject to the provisions of paragraph 4 of this Article, nothing in this Agreement shall preclude:
(a) the use by a contracting party of exchange controls or exchange restrictions in accordance with the Articles of Agreement of the International Monetary Fund or with that contracting parties special exchange agreement with the contracting parties, or
(b) the use by a contracting party of restrictions or controls on imports or exports, the sole effect of which, additional to the effects permitted under Articles XI, XII, XIII and XIV, is to make effective such exchange controls or exchange restrictions.

Art. XVI. Subsidies.

If any contracting party grants or maintains any subsidy, including any form of income or price support, which operates directly or indirectly to increase exports of any product from, or to reduce imports of any product into, its territory, it shall notify the contracting parties in writing of the extent and nature of the subsidization, of the estimated effect of the subsidization on the quantity of the affected product or products imported into or exported from its territory and of the circumstances making the subsidization necessary. In any case in which it is determined that serious prejudice to the interests of any other contracting party is caused or threatened by any such subsidization, the contracting party granting the subsidy shall, upon request, discuss with the other contracting party or parties concerned, or with the contracting parties, the possiblity of limiting the subsidization.

Art. XVII. Non-Discriminatory Treatment on the Part of State-Trading Enterprises.

1(a) Each contracting party undertakes that if it establishes or maintains a Sate enterprise, wherever located, or grants to any enterprise, formally or in effect, exclusive or special privileges, such enterprise shall, in its purchase or sales involving either imports or export, act in a manner consistent with the general principles of non-discriminatory treatment prescribed in this Agreement for governmental measures affecting imports or export by private traders.
(b) The provisions of sub-paragraph (a) of this paragraph shall be understood to require that such enterprises shall, having due regard to the other provisions of this Agreement, make any such purchases or sales solely in accordance with commercial consid-

erations, including price, quality, availability, marketability, transportation and other conditions of purchase or sale, and shall affore the enterprises of the other contracting parties adequate opportunity, in accordance with customary business practice, to compete for participation in such purchases or sales.
(c) No contracting party shall prevent any enterprise (whether or not an enterprise described in sub-paragraph (a) of this paragraph) under its jurisdiction from acting in accordance with the principles of sub-paragraphs (a) and (b) of this paragraph.
(2) The provisions of paragraph 1 of this Article shall not apply to imports of products for immediate or ultimate consumption in governmental use and not otherwise for re-sale or for use in the production of goods for sale. With respect to such imports, each contracting party shall accord to the trade of the other contracting parties fair and equitable treatment.
Art. XVIII. Adjustments in Connection with Economic Development.
(1) The contracting parties recognize that special governmental assistance may be required to promote the establishment, development or reconstruction of particular industries or particular branches of agriculture, and that in appropriate circumstances the grant of such assistance in the form of protective measures is justified. At the same time they recognize that an unwise use of such measures would impose undue burdens on their own economies and unwarranted restrictions on international trade, and might increase unnecessarily the difficulties of adjustment for the economies of other countries.
(2)(a) If a contracting party, in the interest of its programme of economic development or reconstruction, considers it desirable to adopt any non-discriminatory measure which would conflict with any obligation which it has assumed under Article II, or with any other provision of this Agreement, such applicant contracting party shall so notify the contracting parties and shall transmit to them a written statement of the considerations in support of the adoption of the proposed measure.
(b) The contracting parties shall promptly transmit such statement to all other contracting parties, and any contracting party which considers that its trade would be substantially affected by the proposed measure shall transmit its views to the contracting parties within such period as shall be prescribed by them.
(c) The contracting parties shall then promptly examine the proposed measure to determine whether they concur in it, with or without modification, and shall in their examination have regard to the provisions of this Agreement, to the considerations presented by the applicatnt contracting parties which may be substantially affected, and to the effect which the proposed measure, with or without modification, is likely to have on international trade.
(3)(a) If, as a result of their examination pursuant to paragraph 2 (c) of this Article, the contracting parties concur in principle in any proposed measure, with or without modification, which would be inconsistent with any obligations that the applicant contracting party has assumed under Article II, or which would tend to nullify or impair the benefit to any other contracting party or parties of any such obligation, the contracting parties shall sponsor and assist in negotiations between the applicant contracting party and the other contracting party or parties which would be substantially affected with a view to obtaining substantial agreement. The contracting parties shall establish and communicate to the contracting parties concerned a time schedule for such negotiations.
(b) Contracting parties shall commence the negotiations provided for in sub-paragraph (a) of this paragraph within such period as the contracting parties may prescribe and shall thereafter, unless the contracting parties decide otherwise, proceed continuously with such negotiations with a view to reaching substantial agreement in accordance with the time schedule laid down by the contracting parties.
(c) Upon substantial agreement being reached, the contracting parties may release the applicant contracting party from the obligation referred to in sub-paragraph (a) of this paragraph or from any other relevant obligation under this Agreement, subject to such limitations as may have been agreed upon in the negotiations between the contracting parties concerned.
(4)(a) If, as a result of their examination pursuant to paragraph 2 (c) of this Article, the contracting parties concur in any proposed measure, with or without modification, other than a measure referred to in paragraph 3 (a) of this Article, which would be inconsistent with any provision of this Agreement, the contracting parties may release the applicant contracting party from any obligation under such provision, subject to such limitations as they may impose.
(b) If, having regard to the provisions of paragraph 2 (c) of this Article it is established in the course of such examination that such measure is unlikely to be more restrictive of international trade than any other practicable and reasonable measure permitted under this Agreement which could be imposed without undue difficulty and that it is the one most suitable for the purpose having regard to the economics of the industry or the branch of agriculture concerned and to the current economic condition of the applicant contracting party, the contracting parties shall concur in such measure and grant such release as may be required to enable such measure to be made effective.
(c) If in anticipation of the concurrence of the contracting parties in the adoption of a measure concerning which notice has been given under paragraph 2 of this Article, other than a measure referred to in paragraph 3 (a) of this Article, there should be an increase or threatened increase in the importations of the product or products concerned, including products which can be directly substituted therefor, so substantial as to jeopardize the plans of the applicant contracting party for the establishment, development or reconstruction of the industry or industries or branches of agriculture concerned, and if no preventive measures consistant with this Agreement can be found which seem likely to prove effective, the applicant contracting party may, after informing, and when practicable consulting with, the contracting parties, adopt such other measures as the situation may require pending a determination by the contracting parties, provided that such measures do not reduce imports below the level obtaining in the most recent representative period preceding the date on which the contracting party's original notifications was made under paragraph 2 of this Article.
(5)(a) In the case of measures referred to in paragraph 3 of this Article, the contracting parties shall, at the earliest opportunity but ordinarily within fifteen days after receipt of the statement referred to in paragraph 2 (a) of this Article, adivse the applicant contracting party of the date by which they will notify it whether or not they concur in principle in the proposed measure, with or without modification.
(b) In the case of measures referred to in paragraph 4 of this Article, the contracting parties shall, as in sub-paragraph (a) of this paragraph, advise the applicant contracting party of the date by which they will notify it whether or not it is released from such obligation or obligations as may be relevant; Provided that, if the applicant contracting party does not receive a final reply by the date fixed by the contracting parties, it may, after communicating with the contracting parties, institute the proposed measure upon the expiration of a further thirty days from such date.
(6) Any contracting party may maintain any non-discriminatory measure, in force on September 1, 1947, which has been imposed for the establishment, development or reconstruction of particular industries or particular branches of agriculture and which is not otherwise permitted by this Agreement; Provided that any such contacting party shall have notified the other contracting parties, not later than October 10, 1947, of each product on which any such existing measure is to be maintained and of the nature and purpose of such measure. Any contracting party maintaining any such measure shall, within sixty days of becoming a contracting party, notify the contracting parties of the measure concerned, the considerations in support of its maintenance and the period for which it wishes to maintain the measure. The contracting parties shall, as soon as possible but in any case within twelve months from the day on which such contracting party becomes a contracting party, examine and give a decision concerning the measure as if it had been submitted to the contracting parties for their concurrence under the provisions of the preceeding paragraphs of this Article. The contracting parties, in making a decision under this paragraph specifying a date by which any modification in or withdrawal of the measure is to be made, shall have regard to the possible need of a contracting party for suitable period of time in which to make such modification or withdrawal.
(1)(a) If, as a result of unforeseen developments and of the effect of the obligations incurred by a contracting party under this Agreement, including tariff concessions, any product is being imported into the territory of that contracting party in such increased quantities and under such conditions as to cause or threaten serious injury to domestic producers in that territory of like or directly competitive products, the contracting party shall be free, in respect of such product, and to the extent and for such time as may be necessary to prevent or remedy such injury, to suspend the obligation in whole, or in part or to withdraw or modify the concession.
(b) If any product, which is the subject of a concession with respect to a preference, is being imported into the territory of a contracting party in the circumstances set forth in sub-paragraph (a) of this paragraph, so as to cause or threaten serious injury to domestic producers of like or directly competitive products in the territory of contracting party which receives or received such preference, the importing contracting party shall be free, if that other contracting party so requests, to suspend the relevant obligation in whole or in part or to withdraw or modify the concession in respect of the product, to the extent and for such time as may be necessary to prevent or remedy such injury.
(2) Before any contracting party shall take action pursuant to the provisions of paragraph 1 of this Article, it shall give notice in writing to the contracting parties as far in advance as may be practicable and shall afford the contracting parties and those contracting parties having a substantial interest as exporters of the proposed action. When such notice shall name the contracting party which has requested the action. In critical circumstances, where delay would cause damage which it would be difficult to repair, action under paragraph 1 of this Article may be taken provisionally without prior consultation, on the condition that consultation shall be effected immediately after taking such action.
(3)(a) If agreement among the interested contracting parties with respect to the action is not reached, the contracting party which proposes to take or continue the action shall, nevertheless, be free to do so, and if such action is taken or continued, the affected contracting parties shall then be free, not later than ninety days after such action is taken, to suspend, upon the expiration of thirty days from the day on which written notice of such suspension is received by the contracting parties, the application to the trade of the contracting party taking such action, or, in the case envisaged in paragraph 1 (b) of this Article, to the trade of the contracting party requesting such action, of such substantially equivalent obligations or concessions under this Agreement the suspension of which the contracting parties do not disapprove.
(b) Notwithstanding the provisions of sub-paragraph (a) of this paragraph where action is taken under paragraph 2 of this Article without prior consultation and causes or threatens serious injury in the territory of a contracting party to the domestic producers of products affected by the action, that contracting party shall, where delay would cause damage difficult to repair, be free to suspend, upon the taking of the action and throughout the period of consultation, such obligations or concessions as may be necessary to prevent or remedy the injury.
Art. XX. General Exceptions.
Subject to the requirement that such measures are not applied in a manner which would constitute a means of arbitraty or unjustifiable discrimination between countries where the same conditions prevail, or a disguised restriction on international trade, nothing in this Agreement shall be construed to prevent the adoption or enforcement by any contracting party of measures:
I(a) necessary to protect public morals;
(b) necessary to protect human, animal or plant life or health;
(c) relating to the importation or exportation of gold or silver;
(d) necessary to secure compliance with laws or regulations which are not inconsistent with the provisions of this Agreement, including those relating to customs enforcement, the enforcement of monopolies operated under paragraph 4 of Article II and Article XVII, the

protection of patents, trade marks and copyrights, and the prevention of deceptive practices;

(e) relating to the products of prison labour;

(f) imposed for the protection of national treasures of artistic, historic or archaeological value;

(g) relating to the conservation of exhaustible natural resources if such measures are made effective in conjunction with restrictions on domestic production or consumption;

(h) undertaken in pursuance of obligations under intergovernmental commodity agreements, conforming to the principles approved by the Economic and Social Council of the United Nations in its Resolution of March 28, 1947, establishing an Interim Co-ordinating Committee for International Commodity Arrangements; or

(i) involving restrictions on exports of domestic materials necessary to assure essential quantities of such materials to a domestic processing industry during periods when the domestic price of such materials is held below the world price as part of a governmental stabilization plan; Provided that such restrictions shall not operate to increase the exports of or the protection afforded to such domestic industry, and shall not depart from the provisions of this Agreement relating to non-discrimination;

II(a) essential to the acquisition or distribution of products in general or local short supply; Provided that any such measures shall be consistent with any multilateral arrangements directed to an equitable international distribution of such products or, in the absence of such arrangements, with the principle that all contracting parties are entitled to an equitable share of the international supply of such products;

(b) essential to the control of prices by a contracting party undergoing shortages subsequent to the war; or

(c) essential to the orderly liquidation of temporary surpluses of stocks owned or controlled by the government of any contracting party or of industries developed in the territory of any contracting party owing to the exigencies of the war which it would be uneconomic to maintain in normal conditions; Provided that such measures shall not be instituted by any contracting party except after consultation with other interested contracting parties with a view to appropriate international action. Measures instituted or maintained under part II of this Article which are inconsistent with the other provisions of this Agreement shall be removed as soon as the conditions giving rise to them have ceased, and in any event not later than January 1, 1951; Provided that this period may, with the concurrence of the contracting parties, be extended in respect of the application of any particular product by an particular contacting party for such further periods as the contracting parties may specify.

Art. XXI. Security Exceptions.

Nothing in this Agreement shall be construed

(a) to require any contracting party to furnish any information the disclosure of which it considers contrary to its essential security interests;

(b) to prevent any contracting party from taking any action which it considers necessary for the protection of its essential security interests.

(i) relating to fissionable materials or the materials from which they are derived;

(ii) relating to the traffic in arms, ammunition and implements of war and to such traffic in other goods and materals as is carried on directly for the purpose of supplying a military establishment;

(iii) taken in time of war or other emergency in international relations;

(c) to prevent any contracting party from taking any action in pursuance of its obligations under the United Nations Charter for the maintenance of international peace and security.

Art. XXII. Consultation.

Each of contracting party shall accord sympathetic consideration to, and shall afford adequate opportunity for consultation regarding, such representations as may be made by any other contracting party with respect to the operation of customs regulations and formalities, anti-dumping and countervailing duties, quantitative and exchange regulations, subsidies, state-trading operations, sanitary laws and regulations for the protection of human, animal or plant life or health, and generally all matters affecting the operation of this Agreement.

Art. XXIII. Nullification or Impairment.

If any contracting party should consider that any benefit accruing to it directly of indirectly under this Agreement is being nullified or impaired or that the attainment of any objective of the Agreement is being impeded as the result of (a) the failure of another contracting party to carry out its obligations under this Agreement, or (b) the application by another contracting party of any measure, whether or not it conflicts with the provisions of this Agreement, or (c) the existence of any other situation, the contacting party may, with a view to the satisfactory adjustment of the matter, make written representations or proposals to the other contracting party or parties which it considers to be concerned. Any contracting party thus approached shall give sympathetic consideration to the representations or proposals made to it.

(2). If no satisfactory adjustment is effected between the contracting parties concerned within a reasonable time, or if the difficulty is of the type described in paragraph 1 (c) of this Article, the matter maybe referred to the contracting parties. The contracting parties shall promptly investigate any matter so referred to them and shall make appropriate recommendations to the contracting parties which they consider to be concerned, or give a ruling on the matter, as appropriate. The contracting parties may consult with contracting parties, with Economic and Social Council of the United Nations and with any appropriate intergovernmetal organization in cases where they consider such consultation necessary. If the contracting parties consider that the circumstances are serious enough to justify such action, they may authorize a contracting party or parties to suspend the application to any other contracting party or parties of such obligations or concessions under this Agreement as they determine to be appropriate in the circumstances. If the application to any contracting party of any obligation or concession is in fact suspended, that contracting party shall then be free, not later than sixty days after such action is taken, to advise the Secretary-General of the United Nations in writing of its intention to withdraw from this Agreement and such withdrawal shall take effect upon the expiration of sixty days from the day on which written notice of such withdrawal is received by him.

PART III. Art XXIV. Territorial Application – Frontier Traffic – Customs Unions.

(1) The rights obligations arising under this Agreement shall be deemed to be in force between each and every territory which is a separate customs territory and in respect of which this ageement has been accepted under Article XXVI or is being applied under the Protocol of Provisional Application.

(2) The provisions of this Agreement shall not be construed to prevent:

(a) advantages accorded by any contracting party to adjacent countries in order to facilitate frontier traffic;

(b) the formation of a customs union or the adoption of an interim agreement necessary for the attainment of a customs union; Provided that the duties and other regulations of commerce imposed by, or any margin of preference maintained by, any such union or agreement in respect of trade with other contracting parties shall not on the whole be higher or more stringent than the average level of the duties and regulations of commerce or margins of preference applicable in the constituent territories prior to the formation of such union or the adoption of such agreement; and Provided further that any such interim agreement shall include a definite plan and schedule for the attainment of such a customs union within a reasonable length of time.

(3)(a) Any contracting party proposing to enter into a customs union shall consult with the contracting parties and shall make available to them such information regarding the proposed union as will enable them to make such reports and recommendations to contracting parties as may be deemed appropriate.

(b) No contracting party shall institute or maintain any interim agreement under the provision of paragraph 2 (b) of this Article, if after a study of the plan and schedule proposed in such agreement, the contracting parties find that such agreement is not likely to result in such a customs union within a reasonable length of time.

(c) The plan or schedule shall not be substantially altered without consultation with the contracting parties.

(4) For the purposes of this Article a customs territory shall be understood to mean any territory with respect to which separate tariffs or other regulations of commerce are maintained for a substantial part of the trade of such territory with other territories. A customs union shall be understood to mean the substitution of a single customs territory for two or more customs territories, so that all tariffs and other restrictive regulations of commerce as between the territories of members of the union are substantially eliminated and substantially the same tariffs and other regulations of commerce are applied by each of the members of the union to the trade of territories not included in the union.

(5) Taking into account the exceptional circumstances arising out of the establishment of India and Pakistan as independent States and recognizing the fact that they have long constituted an economic unit, the contracting parties agree that the provision of this Agreement shall not prevent the two countries from entering into special arrangements with respect to the trade between them, pending the establishment of their mutual trade relations on a definitive basis.

(6) Each contracting party shall take such reasonable measures as may be available to it to assure observance of the provisions of this Aggreement by the regional and local governments and authorities within its territory.

Art. XXV. Joint Action by the Contracting Parties.

(1) Representatives of the contracting parties shall meet from time to time for the purpose of giving effect to those provision of this Agreement which involve joint action and, generally, with a view to facilitating the operation and furthering the objectives of this Agreement. Wherever reference is made in this Agreement to the contracting parties acting jointly they are designated as the contracting parties.

(2) The Secretary-General of the United nations is requested to convene the first meeting of the contracting parties which shall take place not later than March 1, 1948.

(3) Each contracting party shall be entitled to have one vote at all meetings of the contracting parties.

(4) Except as otherwise provided for in this Agreement, decisions of the contracting parties shall be taken by a majority of votes cast.

(5) In exceptional circumstances not elsewhere provided for in this Agreement, the contracting parties may waive an obligation imposed upon a contracting party by this Agreement; Provided that any such decision shall be approved by a two thirds majority of the votes cast and that such majority shall comprise more than half of the contracting parties. The contracting parties may also by such a vote

(a) define certain categories of exceptional circumstances to which other voting requirements shall apply for the waiver of obligations, and

(b) prescribe such criteria as may be necessary for the application of this paragraph.

Art. XXVI. Acceptance, Entry into Force and Registration.

(1) The present Agreement shall bear the date of the signature of the Final Act adopted at the conclusion of the Second Session of the Preparatory Committee of the United Nations Conference on Trade and Employment and shall be open to acceptance by an government signatory to the Final Act.

(2) This Agreement, done in a single English original and in a single French original, both texts authentic, shall be deposited with the Secretary-General of the United Nations, who shall furnish certified copies thereof to all interested governments.

(3) Each government accepting this Agreement shall deposit an instrument of acceptance with the Secretary-General of the United Nations, who will inform all interested governments of the date of deposit of each instrument of acceptance and of the day on which this Agreement enters into force under paragraph 5 of this Article.

(4) Each government accepting this Agreement does so in respect of its metropolitan territory and of the other territories for which it has international responsibility; Provided that it may at the time of acceptance declare that any separate customs territory for which it has international responsibility possesses full autonomy in the conduct of its external commercial relations and of the other matters provided for in this Agreement, and that its acceptance does not relate to such territory; and Provided further that if any of the customs territories on behalf of which a contracting party has accepted this Agreement possesses or acquires full autonomy in the

conduct of its external commercial relations and of the other matters provided for in this Agreement, such territory shall, upon sponsorship through a declaration by the responsible contracting party establishing the above-mentioned fact, be deemed to be a contracting party.
(5)(a) This Agreement shall enter into force, as among the governments which have accepted it, on the thirtieth day following the day on which instruments of acceptance have been deposited with the Secretary-General of the United Nations on behalf of governments signatory to the Final Act the territories of which account for eighty-five per centum of the total external trade of the territories of the signatories to the Final Act adopted at the conclusion of the Second Session of the Preparatory Committee of the United nations Conference on Trade and Employment. Such percentage shall be determined in accordance with the table set forth in Annex H. The instrument of acceptance of each other government signatory to the Final Act shall take effect on the thirtieth day following the day on which such instrument is deposited.
(b) Notwithstanding the provisions of sub-pararaph (a) of this paragraph, this Agreement shall not enter into force under this paragraph until any agreement necessary under the provisions of paragraph 2 (a) of Article XXIX had been reached.
(6) The United Nations is authroized to effect registration of this Agreement as soon as it enters into force.
Art. XXVII. Witholding or Withdrawal of Concessions.
Any contracting party shall at any time be free to withold or to withdraw in whole or in part any concession, provided for in the appropriate Schedule annexed to this Agreement, in respect of which such contracting party determines that it was initially negotiated with a government which has not become, or has ceased to be, a contracting party. The contracting party taking such action shall give notice to all other contracting parties and, upon request, consult with the contracting parties which have a substantial interest in the product concerned.
Art. XXVIII. Modification of Schedules.
(1) On or after January 1, 1951, any contracting party may, by negotiation and agreement with any other contracting party with which such treatment was initially negotiated, and subject to consultation with such other contracting party as the contracting parties determine to have a substantial interest in such treatment, modify, or cease to apply, the treatment which it has agreed to accord under Article II to any product described in the appropriate Schedule annexed to this Agreement. In such negotiations and agreement, which may include provision for compensatory adjustment with respect to other products, the contracting parties concerned shall endeavour to maintain a general level of reciprocal and mutually advantageous concessions not less favourable to trade than that provided for in the present Agreement.
(2)(a) If agreement between the contracting parties primarily concerned cannot be reached, the contracting party which proposes to modify or cease to apply such treatment shall, nevertheless, be free to do so, and if such action is taken the contracting party with which such treatment was initially negotiated, and the other contracting parties determined under paragraph 1 of this Article to have a substantial interest, shall then be free, not later than six months after such action is taken, to withdraw, upon the expiration of thirty days from the day on which written notice of such withdrawal is received by the contracting parties, substantially equivalent concessions initially negotiated with the contracting party taking such action.
(b) If agreement between the contracting parties primarily concerned is reached but any other contracting party determined under paragraph 1 of this Article to have a substantial interest is not satisfied, such other contracting party shall be free, not later than six months after action under such agreement is taken, to withdraw, upon the expiration of thirty days from the day on which written notice of such withdrawal is received by the contracting parties, substantially equivalent concessions initially negotiated with a contracting party taking action under such agreement.
Art. XXIX. Relation of this Agreement to the Charter for an International Trade Organization.
(1) The contracting parties, recognizing that the objectives set forth in the preamble of this Agreement can best be attained through the adoption, by the United Nations Conference on Trade and Employment, of a Charter leading to the creation of an International Trade Organization, undertake, pending their acceptance of such a Charter in accordance with their consititutional procedures, to observe to the fullest extent of their executive authority the general principles of the Draft Charter submitted to the Conference by the Preparatory Committee.
(2)(a) On the day on which the Charter of the International Trade Organization enters into force, Article I and Part II of this Agreement shall be suspended and superseded by the corresponding provisions of the Charter; Provided that within sixty days of the closing of the United Nations Conference on Trade and Employment any contracting party may lodge with the other contracting parties an objection to any provision or provisions of this Agreement being suspended and superseded; in such case the contracting parties shall, within sixty days after the final date for the lodging of objections, confer to consider the objection in order to agree whether the provisions of the Charter to which objection has been lodged, or the corresponding provisions of this Agreement in its existing form or any amended form, shall apply.
(b) The contracting parties will also agree concerning the transfer to the International Trade Organization of their functions under Article XXV.
(3) If any contracting party has not accepted the Charter when it has entered into force, the contracting parties shall confer to agree whether, and if so in what way, this Agreement, insofar as it affects relations between the contracting party which has not accepted the Charter and other contracting parties, shall be supplemented or amended.
(4) During the month of January 1949, should the Charter not have entered into force, or at such earlier time as may agreed if it is known that the Charter will not enter into force, or at such later time as may be agreed if the Charter ceases to be in force, the contracting parties shall meet to agree whether this Agreement shall be amended, supplemented or maintained.
(5) The signatories of the Final Act which are not at the time contracting parties shall be informed of any objection lodged by contracting party under the provisions of paragraph 2 of this Article and also of any agreement which may be reached between the contracting parties under paragraph 2, 3 or 4 of this Article.
Art. XXX. Amendments.
(1) Except where provision for modification is made elsewhere in this Agreement, amendments of the provisions of Part I of this Agreement or to the provisions of Article XXIX or of this Article shall become effective upon acceptance by all the contracting parties, and other amendments to this Agreement shall become effective, in respect of those contracting parties which accept them, upon aceptance by two-thirds of the contracting parties and thereafter for each other contracting parties upon acceptance by it.
(2) Any contracting party accepting an amendment to this Agreement shall deposit an instrument of acceptance with the Secretary-General of the United Nations within such period as the contracting parties may specify. The contracting parties may decide that any amendment made effective under this Article is of such a nature that any contracting party which has not accepted it within a period specified by the contracting parties shall be free to withdraw from this Agreement, or to remain a contracting party with the consent of the contracting parties.
Art. XXXI. Withdrawal.
Without prejudice to the provisions of Article XXIII or of paragraph 2 of Article XXX, any contracting party may, on or after January 1, 1951, withdraw from this Agreement, or may separately withdraw on behalf of any of the separate customs territories for which it has international responsibility and which at the time possesses full autonomy in the conduct of its external commercial relations and of the other matters provided for in this Agreement. The withdrawal shall take effect on or after January 1, 1951, upon the expiration of six months from the day on which written notice of withdrawal is received by the Secretary-General of the United Nations.
Art. XXXII. Contracting Parrties.
(1) The contracting parties to this Agreement shall be understood to mean those governments which are applying the provisions of this Agreement under Article XXVI or pursuant to the Protocol of Provisional Application.
(2) At any time after the entry into force of this Agreement pursuant to paragraph 5 of Article XXVI, those contracting parties which have accepted this Agreement pursuant to paragraph 3 of Article XXVI may decide that any contracting party which has not so accpeted it shall cease to be a contracting party.
Art. XXXIII. Accession.
A government not party to this Agreement, or a government acting on behalf of a separate customs territory possessing full autonomy in the conduct of its external commercial relations and of the other matters provided for in this Agreement, may accede to this Agreement, on its own behalf or on behalf of that territory, on terms to be agreed between such government and the contracting parties.
Art. XXXIV. Annexes
The annexes to this Agreement are hereby made an integral part of this Agreement.

UNTS, Vol, 55, pp. 188–316.

GATT ROUNDS. The negotiations held since 1947 under the auspices of the GATT concerning reduction of tariff barriers in international trade. Until 1980 seven rounds were held: the First GATT Round in 1947 in Geneva which dealt with reduction of tariffs on 44% of all commodities then entering international markets; the Second round in 1949 in Annecy concerned only 3%; the Third GATT Round in 1951 in Torquay concerned 9%; the Fourth GATT Round in 1956 in Geneva dealt with 11%; the Fifth GATT Round in 1962 in Geneva, called the Dillon Round, dealt with 15%; the Sixth GATT Round was held in 1967 in Geneva; the Seventh GATT Round started in 1973 in Geneva; moved in 1974 to Tokyo, was ended in 1979. ▷ Nixon Round; ▷ Tokyo Round; ▷ Uruguay Round.

S. GOLT, *The GATT Negotiations 1973–75, A Guide to the Issues*, London, 1974; R.E. HUDEC, *The GATT Legal System and World Trade Diplomacy*, New York, 1975; GATT, *The Tokyo Round of Multilateral Trade Negotiations*, 2 Vols., Geneva, 1979.

GAUCHO. A common Argentina-Brazil monetary unit for bilateral commercial exchange, est. Aug. 17, 1987 by a bilateral agreement called Viedma Agreement signed by the Presidents of both countries in Viedma, Argentina.

KEESING's *Record of World Events, 1987.*

GAUDEAMUS IGITUR, IUVENESDUM SUMUS, *Latin*: "let us rejoice while we are still young". A medieval students' song popularized throughout the entire world at the turn of the 18th and 19th centuries; initiates university festivities. The melody was used by Johannes Brahms in the Academic Festival Overture, 1880.

GAUDIUM ET SPES. *Latin*: "Joy and Hope". A pastoral constitution adopted at the final session of the Second Vatican Council in Dec. 1965, often called a constitution on the Church in the modern world, proclaiming i.a. that the Roman Catholic Church "... by virtue of its task and competence in no way whatsoever identifies itself with a political community or associates itself with any political system."

GAZA AND GAZA STRIP. A Palestinian town and border zone *c.* 40 km long and 11 km wide, area *c.* 250 sq. km. A subject of a dispute between Israel and Egypt. Gaza was granted to Egypt by the cease-fire agreement between Israel and Egypt signed Feb. 24, 1949 on the island of Rhodes. It was in this territory that camps for refugees from Palestine were established under the supervision of the UNRWA. In March 1955 border incidents took place which were the subject of a debate in the

Security Council Jan. 4–Apr. 19, 1955. The Gaza Strip was occupied on Nov. 2, 1956 by the Israeli army, which withdrew on Mar. 7, 1957 in accordance with Res. 997 and 1000/XI of the UN General Assembly, and their place was taken by the UN Emergency Force, UNEF, on the basis of an agreement between the UN and the Egyptian government (Doc. A. 3276).

On March 9, 1962 the Egyptian President, G.A. Nasser, announced a special statute for the Gaza Strip, treating it "as an inseparable part of Palestine, being the property of the Arab nation." Israel indicated before the UN General Assembly that this statute was a hostile act, "changing the Gaza Strip into a symbolic bastion of irredentism of a future Arab State of Palestine, which the Arabs wish to create in the place of Israel."

On May 20, 1967 the government of Egypt requested the Secretary General of the UN, U Thant, to withdraw the UNEF from the Gaza Strip, a request which was immediately executed in accordance with p. 9 Doc. A 3276, that "UNEF may not stay or operate in a given territory without the consent of the government of that region."

On June 5, 1967 Israeli armed forces occupied the Gaza Strip, and the government of Israel asserted that it intended to incorporate it permanently. This incorporation became a subject of Egyptian–Israeli negotiations in 1979–80.

UN Monthly Chronicle, June, 1949, pp. 215–229; *UN Yearbook*, 1956, 1957, 1967; W. HARIS, *Taking Root: Israeli Settlement in the West Bank. The Golan, Gaza and Sinai 1967–1980*, Chichester, 1981.

GAZANKULU. ▷ Bantu Homelands.

GCC ▷ Gulf Co-operation Council.

GDAŃSK. Polish city and chief Baltic port (pop: 1985 est. 468,600. Area of the Gdańsk province: 7,394 sq. km with 1,401,000 inhabitants, 1985), capital of Gdańsk province, northern Poland. History: an old Slavic settlement, first mentioned as *Urbs Gyddany*, part of Poland in 997, conquered by the Teutonic Knights 1308, and named Danzig, passed to Poland 1466; After the first partition of Poland 1772 became a free city; by the second partition, 1793, occupied by Prussia, but restored as a free city 1807, by Napoleon I. In the years 1814–1919 under the name of Danzig, Capital of the Province of West Prussia. The Versailles Treaty proclaimed a Free City of Dantzig in the Polish customs territory, placed under a League of Nations High Commissioner. Annexed to Germany on Sept. 1, 1939, liberated by the Soviet Army in March 1945.

"Constitution of the Free City of Dantzig," in: *Official Journal of the League of Nations*, Special Supplement No. 7, Geneva, 1919; S. ASKENAZY, *Danzig et Pologne*, Paris, 1921; J. MAKOWSKI, *Le caractère de la Ville Libre de Dantzig*, Varsovie, 1933; K.M. SMOGORZEWSKI, *Poland's Access to Sea*, London, 1934; H.L. LEONHARDT, *Nazi Conquest of Danzig*, London, 1942; C.J. BURCKHARDT, *Meine Danziger Mission, 1937–1939*, Zurich, 1960; M.A. SZYPOWSCY, *Gdańsk*, Warsaw, 1979; *The Europa Yearbook. A World Survey, 1987*, London, 1987.

GDAŃSK CHARTER, 1980. The first agreement in a country of a centrally planned economy, between workers and the government, guaranteeing the right to strike, the right to independent but socialist trade unions and the limitation of censorship in all mass media, signed at Gdańsk, Poland, on Aug. 31, 1980, after seventeen days of strike in the Lenin shipyards in Gdańsk and after other Solidarity strikes in Szczecin, Gdynia, Elblag, in the Silesia region and other parts of Poland. Similar agreements between authorities and the striking workers were signed

in Szczecin Shipyard and in Jastrzebie (Silesia) Colliery.

"Gdańsk Charter", in: *Economist*, September 6, 1980, p. 37; *UN Chronicle*, August–September., 1980, pp. 50–51; *The Birth of Solidarity. The Gdańsk Negotiations, 1980*, London, 1984.

GDP. ▷ Gross Domestic Product.

GDR. ▷ German Democratic Republic.

GELATINE. A subject of research and promotion by the International Trade Center UNCTAD/GATT, Geneva, 1983.

An Overview of the Gelatine World Market with Special Reference to the Potential of Developing Countries, Geneva, 1984.

GEMS. Global Environmental Monitoring System. A Part of ▷ UNEP aimed at collecting information by monitoring, observing and interpreting environmental variables. Began operations in 14 countries in 1975, included 42 states in 1978, in co-operation with the WHO and WMO; has scientific stations in Accra, Baghdad, Bangkok, Batavia, Brussels, Cairo, Calcutta, Chicago, Dakar, Iligana in the Philippines, Kuala Lumpur, Lagos, Lahore, Lima, Lisbon, Manila, Nairobi, São Paulo, Santiago, Suva, Sydney, Teheran, Tokyo, Toronto, Warsaw.

GENEALOGISTS INTERNATIONAL ORGANIZATION. Organizations reg. with the UIA:

Balkan and Eastern European American Genealogical and Historical Society, f. 1970, San Francisco.
International Genealogical Friendship, f. 1971, Paris. Publ.: *Information universitaire et culturelle*.

Biography and Genealogy Master Index, 5 Vols., New York, 1981–1986; *Yearbook of International Organizations*; *Biography Almanac*, New York, 1987.

GENERAL ASSEMBLY. ▷ UN General Assembly.

GENERAL ASSEMBLY SPECIAL SESSION, 1990. Convened on the strength of GA Res. 43/443 adopted without a vote with an annex entitled "Common Understanding on the 1990 Special Session of the General Assembly"; a Special Session devoted to International Economic Co-Operation in particular to the Revitalization of Economic Growth and Development in the Developing Countries.

UN Resolutions and Decisions Adopted by the General Assembly during the First Part of its Forty-Third Session, from 20 September to 22 September, 1988, New York, 1989, pp. 616–617.

GENERAL GOUVERNEMENT, 1915–18. A German "General Governorship", name of an administrative unit governed on the model of a British colony by a general-governor; introduced by Germany in World War I in the conquered territories of the East: General Gouvernement Warschau, General Gouvernement Minsk, etc. The forms of governing the occupied areas were contrary to international law, so the Allied Committee of Responsibility, Comité de Responsabilité of the Versailles Conference in 1919, placed the general-governor of Warsaw, H.H. von Beseler (1850–1921), on the list of war criminals.

Das General-Gourvernement Warschau, Oldenburg, 1918.

GENERAL GOUVERNEMENT, 1939–45. A German "General Governship." name of German Administrative unit for central Poland, during World War II, initially as General Gouvernement der polnishen besetzten Gebiete (from Oct. 25, 1939

to July 31, 1940) and then to Jan., 1945 only General Gouvernement. The remaining lands of the Polish Republic were incorporated into Germany 1939–41. The forms of governing the occupied territories were contrary to international law and had the character of organized genocide, and so the UN War Crimes Commission, established 1943 in London, placed on the list of war criminals General-Governor H. Frank (1900–46), who was sentenced by the International Military Tribunal and was hanged in Nuremberg Oct. 16, 1946.

S. PIOTROWSKI (ed.), *Hans Frank's Diary 1939–1945*, Warsaw, 1970.

GENERALIZED SYSTEM OF PREFERENCES. ▷ Preferences.

GENERAL PLAN OST. German: "General Plan East." The official German document on colonization and germanization of the occupied Polish, Byelorussian and Ukrainian territories, prepared by the Security Office of the Reich (▷ Reichssicherheitshauptamt, RSHA) and Reichsministerium für die besetzten Ostgebiete in 1941. The General Plan Ost presented to the Nuremberg Trial 1946, provided for a settlement in these territories of 2,600,000 Gemans from the Reich and of 12,000,000 people of German extraction (▷ Volksdeutsche) from "Germanic counties."

Generalplan Ost. Rechtliche, wirtschaftliche und räumliche Grundlagen des Ostaufbauplanes, vorgeleget von SS-Oberführer Prof. dr. Konrad Meyer, Berlin-Dahlem, June, 1942; Cz. MADAJCZYK, "Generalplan Ost", in: *Polish Western Review*, No. 2, pp. 391–412.

GENERAL STAFF. An international military term dating back to the reform of the Prussian Army during the Napoleonic Wars. The General Staff concept was accepted in the XX century by all modern armies except the US Army. See ▷ Joint Chief of Staff.

W. GÖRLITZ, *Der deutsche Generalstab. Geschichte und Gestalt*, Berlin, 1951; D. ROBERTSON, *Guide to Modern Defense and Strategy*, Detroit, 1988.

GENETIC ENGINEERING. An international term for a group of international research techniques that manipulate the genetic material of cells (▷ DNA). In April 1988 the US Patent and Trademark Office approved a patent for a genetically altered mouse to be used in cancer research and in the medical industry.

M. GLADWELL, "First Patented Animal is a Mouse at Harvard", in: *International Herald Tribune*, April 13, 1988.

GENETIC MANIPULATION. Subject of international ethical debates in the 1980's. Condemned on Feb. 10, 1989 by the Catholic Church – Vatican Declaration on Racism: "There is widespread fear that new and as yet unknown forms of racism might appear. This at times is expressed concerning the use that could be made of 'techniques of artificial procreation' through in vitro fertilization and the possibilities of genetic manipulation. Although such fears are still in part hypothetical, they nonetheless draw the attention of humanity to the new and disquieting dimension of men's power over man and thus to the urgent need for corresponding ethical principles.

It is important that laws determine as soon as possible the limits which must not be surpassed so that such 'techniques' will not fall into the hands of abusive and irresponsible powers who might seek to 'produce' human beings selected according to racial criteria or any other characteristic.

This would give rise to a resurgence of the deadly myth of eugenic racism, the misdeeds of which the world has already experienced. A similar abuse would be to prevent the birth of human beings of one or another social or ethnic category through abortion and sterilization campaigns. Wherever the absolute respect for life and its transmission according to the Creator's intentions disappears, it is to be feared that all moral restraint on a person's power will also disappear, including the power to fashion humanity in the derisive image of these apprentice sorcerers."

The New York Times, Feb. 11, 1989.

GENETICS. A subject of international co-operation. Organizations reg. with the UIA:

European Genetic Counselling Club, f. 1975, Lyon.
International Genetics Federation, f. 1911, Paris.
Scandinavian Association of Genetics, f. 1960, Copenhagen. Pub.: *Hereditas*.

F. BIASS-DUCROUX, *Glossary of Genetics*. In English, French, Spanish, Italian, German and Russian, Amsterdam, 1970; *Yearbook of International Organizations*.

GENEVA, *French*: Genève. A city in southwestern Switzerland. Area of the Geneva canton: 282,2 sq. km; pop. 1986 city 351,545; metropolitan area 840,000; canton 1,283,300. After World War I seat of the LN and ILO; after World War II still the seat of the ILO as well as the European Office of the UN, GATT, ITU, WHO, WMO and several other international organizations reg. with the UIA. Geneva, along with Paris, Brussels, Vienna and London belongs to cities with the largest number of international organizations which from 1929 have their own special organization, Fédération des institutions internationales semiofficielles et privées établies à Genève, Geneva has been the scene of many international conferences, beginning with the conference of the international Red Cross 1864, whose resolutions initiated the Geneva Conventions and Protocols.

Yearbook of International Organizations; The Europa Yearbook. A World Survey, 1987, London, 1987.

GENEVA AIR CONFERENCE. ▷ Air Geneva Convention, 1948.

GENEVA CONFERENCES, 1863–1980. The multilateral conferences and international meetings held in Geneva; in the interwar years under LN auspices, after World War II under the aegis of the UN. In the 19th century the term Geneva Conferences referred to two Conferences of the ▷ Red Cross, the first was held by Swiss welfare workers who, on Oct, 26, 1863, established the International Red Cross; the second, held on Sept. 1–6, 1884, was an international meeting of states which had joined the convention of the Red Cross. The Geneva Conferences of 1906, 1929 and 1949 were associated with Geneva humanitarian conventions. Under the LN auspices two Geneva conferences took place on disarmament: in 1927 a meeting of Japan, Great Britain, and the USA was held on the limitation of cruisers and submarines. The First World Disarmament Conference was held between Feb. 2, 1932 and Nov. 21, 1934, in which the members of the LN and the USA and USSR participated. During the UN years the main Geneva Conferences have been:

Geneva Conference on Korea and Indochina, April 26–July 21, 1954;

Taking part in the Korean deliberations were representatives of both Korean states, Ministers of Foreign Affairs of the five powers (the Chinese People's Republic, France, the UK, USA and USSR) and delegates from the states fighting on the US side against North Korea. Deliberating on the Indochina matter were the Ministers of Foreign Affairs of the five powers

and Cambodia, Laos and North and South Vietnam. The results were the ▷ Indochina Geneva Agreements.
Geneva Conference of the heads of government of France, the UK, USA and USSR of July 18–23, 1955, the first ▷ Summit conferences after World War II. No agreement was reached but the sides expressed the desire to continue negotiations and *détente*.
Geneva Conference of the Ministers of Foreign Affairs of France, the UK, USA, and USSR, Oct 27–Nov. 16, 1955, one of the postwar conferences of Ministers of Foreign Affairs of the four powers concerned with Germany, the security of Europe, and disarmament. No agreement was reached, which implied the de facto consent of the powers to the permanent division of Germany.
Geneva Conference of the UK, USA, and USSR, Oct. 31, 1958–Jan. 18, 1962, on the question of suspending tests of nuclear weapons.
Geneva Conference of the Ministers of Foreign Affairs of France, the UK, USA, and USSR, May 11–June 20 and July 13–Aug. 5, 1959, concerned with East–West relations, the disarmament of Germany (with the participation of representatives of the FRG and GDR), and West Berlin. The only result: the convening of a Disarmament Conference of 10 states (5 socialist and 5 capitalist).
Meetings of the Disarmament Committee in Geneva March 15–June 27, 1960, reached no conclusion and the matter returned to the UN. The Disarmament Committee was then reorganized during the Conference of the Disarmament Committee. Its initial composition was greatly expanded and, since 1961, as a rule it has held its sessions in Geneva.
Geneva Conference on the neutrality of Laos, May 12, 1961–July 23, 1962, with the participation of the five powers (the Chinese People's Republic, France, the UK, USA, USSR and Burma, Cambodia, India, Laos, Poland and North Vietnam, ending with the ▷ Laos Neutrality Declaration.
Geneva Conferences also included the First World Conference on Trade and Development of UNCTAD, Mar. 23–June 6, 1964, convened on the initiative of the UN in the Palace of Nations in Geneva.
The second phase of the Conference on Security and Co-operation in Europe, which started and ended in Helsinki took place in Geneva Sept. 18–Dec. 15, 1973 and Jan. Mar., 1974.
Geneva Conference called Red Cross Conference, 1971. A Conference on the Reaffirmation and Development of International Humanitarian Law Applicable in Armed Conflicts, convoked by the Red Cross to Geneva, under the aegis of the UN.
Geneva Conference on the Arab–Israeli conflict, called the Geneva Peace Conference on the Middle East, opened under UN auspices Dec. 2, 1973 in Geneva under the joint chairmanship of the USA and USSR with the participation of the UN Secretary-General, Israel, Egypt and Jordan, on the basis of the Israeli Res. 338 of the Security Council of Oct. 22, 1973, for the purpose of examining possibilities of peaceful resolution of the Arab–Israeli conflict, a hope not realized in succeeding years, at first as the result of diplomatic complications and then because of direct Egyptian–Israeli negotiations under US sponsorship in ▷ Camp David; remained open to the continual possibility of extending negotiations to all Arab states and Israel under UN sponsorship.
Geneva Conference on Namibia in January 1981.

UN Monthly Chronicle, No. 1, 1971; SIPRI, *World Armaments* and *Disarmament*, 1971, pp. 135–137, 157–163; 1974, pp. 10–11.

GENEVA CONVENTION ON THE STATUS OF REFUGEES, 1951. Signed on July 28, 1951 by the Members of the European Community related to the ▷ Human Rights European Convention. At the end of the 1980's the European Community states introduced permanent consultation to jointly examine the problems caused by the massive arrival of refugees, escaping from political persecutions, civil wars, famine and misery, and at the same time, to establish new rules. See also ▷ Refugees.

Council of Europe, Information Sheet, No. 21, Strasbourg, 1988.

GENEVA GENERAL ACT, 1928. ▷ Pacific Settlement Act, 1928.

GENEVA HUMANITARIAN CONVENTIONS, 1864–1949. The Multinational international agreements concluded in Geneva in 1864, 1906, 1929, 1949. All multilateral Geneva conventions refer to humanitarian rules of warfare,, initiated in 1864 by the Red Cross (hence they are also called Red Cross Conventions).

First Geneva Convention of Aug. 28, 1864 for the Amelioration of the Condition of the Wounded and Sick in Armed Forces in the Field. ▷ Red Cross Convention 1864.
Second Geneva Convention of July 6, 1906 extended the first one in connection with the Hague Conventions, 1899 (▷ Hague International Peace Conferences) and the preparation and extension of the ▷ Hague Rules, 1907. Third Geneva Convention of July 27, 1929 introduced a new provision stating that its terms refer not only to the citizens of states-signatories, but to all people irrespective of their citizenship.
Fourth Geneva Convention of Aug. 12, 1949 on the protection of civilian and military persons in time of war was drawn on the postulates of the International Red Cross to establish strict standards for civilian protection in areas covered by war and on occupied territories as well as after the tragic experience of World War II to ban war offences and war crimes. It embraced four Conventions:
(a) Geneva Convention for the Amelioration of the Condition of the Wounded and Sick and Armed Forces in the Field.
(b) Geneva Convention for the Amelioration of the Condition of Wounded, Sick and Shipwrecked Members of Armed Forces on Sea.
(c) Geneva Convention relating to the Protection of Civilian Persons in Time of War.
(d) Geneva Convention relating to the Treatment of Prisoners of War.
In 1977 two additional Protocols to the 1949 Convention were adopted. See also ▷ Civilian Persons Protection in Time of War.

A. ROLIN, *Le droit moderne de la guerre*, 2 Vols., Bruxelles, 1920–21; P. DE LAPPRADELLA, *La Conférence Diplomatique et les Nouvelles Conventions de Genève*, Paris, 1951; M. BOTHE, K.J. PARTSCH, W.A. SOLF, *New Rules for Victims of Armed Conflicts. A Commentary on the two 1977 Protocols Additional to the Geneva Convention of 1949*, The Hague, 1982.

GENEVA INTERNATIONAL ENCOUNTERS. RENCONTRES INTERNATIONALES DE GENÉVE. Symposia of men and science and art from East and West, organized each autumn since 1956 by the city of Geneva with the participation and assistance of UNESCO.

GENEVA PLAN, 1978. The frequency division among radio stations in the European radiophonic zones, elaborated in 1975 in Geneva by the member states of the European Radiophonic Convention of 1948. The Geneva Plan was enacted on Nov. 23, 1978 and replaced the Copenhagen Plan, 1948.

GENEVA PROTOCOL, 1924. The Protocol concerning the peaceful solution of international disputes, drafted on the initiative of the British Labour Party government with the support of the states of the Little Entente states; it was ratified unanimously Oct. 2, 1924 in Geneva at the Fifth Session of the LN Assembly, but never came into force.
The Protocol acknowledged that "a war of aggression is a violation of solidarity (of the members of the international community) and an international crime", and having in view "the full implementation of the system (of security) stipulated in the Covenant of the League of Nations" and "realization of the reduction of national armaments to a minimum anticipated by art. 8 of the LN Covenant", has enjoyed the pledg-

ing signatory states to avoid recourse to war between themselves in any case or against a state which, taking advantage of the possibility, accepts the obligations resulting from the Protocol – except in the case of repelling acts of aggression or acting with the agreement of the Council or LN Assembly. The Protocol also contained an obligation on the signatories to *ipso facto* recognize the binding jurisdiction of the Permanent Court of International Justice, PCIJ on questions mentioned in art. 26 of the statute of the Court and also obligated the signatories to take the proper measures to effectively fulfill the obligations resulting from art. 15 of the Covenant of the League. The Protocol never took effect, though it was signed by 19 states, since it was rejected by the new British conservative government.

J.T. SHOTWELL, "Protocol for the Pacific Settlement of International Disputes. Text and Analysis", in: *International Conciliation*, No. 205, December, 1924; D.H. MILLER, *The Geneva Protocol*, New York, 1925.

GENEVA PROTOCOL, 1925. The Protocol for the Prohibition of the Use in War of Asphyxiating Poisonous or Other Gases, and of Bacteriological Methods of Warfare, signed in Geneva, June 17, 1925, by the Governments of Austria, Belgium, Brazil, the British Empire, Bulgaria, Canada, Chile, Colombia, Czechoslovakia, Denmark, Egypt, El Salvador, Estonia, Ethiopia, Finland, France, Germany, Greece, Hungary, India, Italy, Ireland, Japan, Latvia, Lithuania, Luxembourg, the Netherlands, Nicaragua, Norway, Panama, Poland, Portugal, Romania, Siam, Spain, Sweden, Switzerland, the Serbo-Croat-Slovene State, Turkey, the USA, Uruguay and Venezuela. Accessions: Liberia (1927), USSR (1929), Persia (1929), China (1929), the Union of South Africa (1930), Australia (1930), New Zealand (1930). The text as follows:

"Protocol on Abolition of Lethal and Other Gases.
The undersigned Plenipotentiaries, in the names of their respective governments:
Whereas the use in war of asphyxiating poisonous or other gases and of all analogous liquids, materials or devices has been justly condemned by the general opinion of the civilized world and –
Whereas the prohibition of such use has been declared in Treaties to which the majority of powers of the world are parties and –
To the end that this prohibition shall be universally accepted as a fact of international law, binding alike the conscience and the practice of nations:
Declare –
That the High Contracting Parties, so far as they are not already Parties to Treaties prohibiting such use, accept this prohibition, agree to extend this prohibition to the use of bacteriological methods of warfare and agree to be bound as between themselves according to the terms of this declaration.
The High Contracting Parties will exert every effort to induce other states to accede to the present Protocol. The present Protocol will come into force for each signatory Power as from the date of deposit of its ratification, and from that moment, each Power will be bound as regards other Powers which have already deposited their ratification."

The Protocol was ratified until Jan. 1, 1987 by 111 countries.

LNTS, Vol. 94, pp. 65–74; *SIPRI, Yearbook 1987*, Oxford, 1988, p. 461.

GENEVA TRACING BUREAU. The Main Tracing Bureau of the International Committee of the Red Cross (formerly Main Bureau for War Prisoners, headquarters in Geneva), provides information on war prisoners. Address: Agence Centrale de Recherches du CICR, Avenue de la Paix CH-1211, Genève, Switzerland.

GENEVA ZONES – LIEUX DE GENÈVE. An international term introduced in 1931 by the International Organization for Protection of Civilian Population during the War for definition of the areas of war operations in which the Red Cross Geneva rules on ▷ civilian persons protection in time of war or in military conflicts are in force.

GENOA ECONOMIC CONFERENCE, 1922. The first International Economic Conference held in Genoa, Apr. 10–16, 1922; it was preceded by a French–British meeting in Cannes, Jan. 6–13, 1922; no resolutions were passed, but the Conference was used by German and USSR delegations for the preparation of the bilateral ▷ Rapallo Treaty, 1922.

GENOCIDE. *Greek*: genos = "clan", "family", *Latin*: occidio = "total extinction", "extermination". A new word, applied in international law after World War II, coined and defined ("Genocide is the crime of destroying national, racial or religious groups") by a Polish lawyer, R. Lemkin (1900–60), who in 1933 called for an international convention, banning mass executions, to be prepared. The first initiative to "recognize extermination of racial, religious or social groups as an offence against the law of nations" (*Delictum ius gentium*) was taken up by the Fifth International Conference on Unification of Penal Law held in Madrid in 1933. For the first time the genocide crimes were officially described in the indictment of major German war criminals at the Nuremberg Trials in 1945 as:

"intended and systematic *genocidio*, that is extermination of racial and national groups of civilian population in certain occupied territories in order to destroy certain races and layers of nations and peoples, racial and religious groups, in particular Jews, Poles, Gypsies and other."

Under Res. 96/I of Dec. 11, 1946, the UN General Assembly initiated work on a draft Convention on the Prevention and Punishment of the Crime of Genocide unanimously approved Dec. 9, 1948. Under Res. 960-B/III of Dec. 9, 1948, the UN General Assembly recommended a study of the possibility of establishing an International Penal Court to try cases of genocide and other crimes against mankind determined under conventions, or a Penal Chamber in the International Court of Justice. On the same day, under Res. 260-C/III, the UN General Assembly ordered the states exercising control over non-self-governing territories to expand as soon as possible the provisions of the Convention on such territories. In reply to the UN General Assembly's Res. 478/V, May 28, 1951, the International Court of Justice issued its opinion concerning the Convention.

R. LEMKIN, *Les actes créant un danger général, considérés comme délits de droit de gens*, Paris, 1933; *Actes de la V Conférence International pour l'Unification du Droit Penal*, Paris, 1935; R. LEMKIN, *Axis Rule in Occupied Europe*, Washington, DC, 1944; R. LEMKIN, "Genocide: A New International Crime 1944", in: *Revue Internationale de Droit Pénal*, Paris, 1946; UN, *The Crime of Genocide. A United Nations Convention*, New York, 1959; N. ROBINSON, *La Convención sobre Genocidio*, Buenos Aires, 1960; TH. HOLTON, *An International Peace Court. Design for a move from State Crime toward World Law*, The Hague, 1970; H. SARON, *Du cannibalisme au genocide*, Paris, 1972; R. JAY LIFTON, *The Nazi Doctors: Medical Killing and the Psychology of Genocide*, New York, 1986.

GENOCIDE CONVENTION, 1948. The Convention on the Prevention and Punishment of the Crime of Genocide adopted unanimously by the UN General Assembly on Dec. 9, 1948 came into force on Jan. 12, 1951. It was ratified by the majority of states, including three Great Powers: France on Oct. 14, 1952, the People's Republic of China on July 19, 1958 and the USSR on May 3, 1954. The Convention was also signed by the USA but not ratified by the US Senate by argument that is poorly drafted and could allow other Governments to intervene in US affairs. On Oct. 16, 1984 the Senate again rejected ratification but in a resolution expressed its support, 87:2, "for the principles embodied in the Convention". The official texts are in Chinese, English, French, Russian and Spanish. The text is as follows:

"The Contracting Parties, having considered the declaration made by the General Assembly of the United Nations in its resolution 96 (I) dated 11 December 1946 that genocide is a crime under international law, contrary to the spirit and aims of the United Nations and condemned by the civilized world;
Recognizing that at all periods of history genocide has inflicted great losses on humanity; and
Being convinced that, in order to liberate mankind from such an odious scourge, international co-operation is required,
Hereby agree as hereinafter provided:
Art. 1. The Contracting Parties confirm that genocide, whether committed in time of peace or in time of war, is a crime under international law which they undertake to prevent and punish.
Art. 2. In the present Convention, genocide means any of the following acts committed with intent to destroy, in whole or in part, a national, ethnical, racial or religious group, as such:
(a) Killing members of the group;
(b) Causing serious bodily or mental harm to members of the group;
(c) Deliberately inflicting on the group conditions of life calculated to bring about its physical destruction in whole or in part;
(d) Imposing measures intended to prevent births within the group;
(e) Forcibly transferring children of the group to another group.
Art. 3. The following acts shall be punishable:
(a) Genocide;
(b) Conspiracy to commit genocide;
(c) Direct and public incitement to commit genocide;
(d) Attempt to commit genocide;
(e) Complicity in genocide.
Art. 4. Persons committing genocide or any of the other acts enumerated in Art. 3 shall be punished, whether they are constitutionally responsible rulers, public officials or private individuals.
Art. 5. The Contracting Parties undertake to enact, in accordance with their respective Constitutions, the necessary legislation to give effect to the provisions of the present Convention and, in particular, to provide effective penalties for persons guilty of genocide or of any of the other acts enumerated in Art. 3.
Art. 6. Persons charged with genocide or any of the other acts enumerated in Art. 3 shall be tried by a competent tribunal of the State in the territory of which the act was committed, or by such international penal tribunal as may have jurisdiction with respect to those Contracting Parties which shall have accepted its jurisdiction.
Art. 7. Genocide and the other acts enumerated in Art. 3 shall not be considered as political crimes for the purpose of extradition.
The contracting Parties pledge themselves in such cases to grant extradition in accordance with their laws and treaties in force.
Art. 8. Any Contracting Party may call upon the competent organs of the United Nations to take such action under the Charter of the United Nations as the consider appropriate for the prevention and suppression of acts of genocide or any of the other acts enumerated in Art. 3.
Art. 9. Disputes between the Contracting Parties relating to the interpretation, application or fulfilment of the present Convention, including those relating to the responsibility of a State for genocide or for any of the other acts enumerated in Art. 3, shall be submitted to the International Court of Justice at the request of any of the parties to the dispute.
Art. 10. The present Convention, of which the Chinese, English, French, Russian and Spanish texts are equally authentic, shall bear the date of 9 December 1948.

Art. 11. The present Convention shall be open until 31 December 1949 for signature on behalf of any Member of United Nations and of any non-member State to which an invitation to sign has been addressed by the General Assembly. The present Convention shall be ratified, and the instruments of ratification shall be deposited with the Secretary-General of the United Nations.

After 1 January 1950 the present Convention may be acceded to on behalf of any Member of the United Nations and of any non-member State which has received an invitation as aforesaid. Instruments of accession shall be deposited with the Secretary-General of the United Nations.

Art. 12. Any Contracting Party may at any time, by notification addressed to the Secretary-General of the United Nations, extend the application of the present Convention to all or any of the territories for the conduct of whose foreign relations that Contracting Party is responsible.

Art. 13. On the day when the first twenty instruments of ratification or accession have been deposited, the Secretary-General shall draw up a procès-verbal and transmit a copy thereof to each Member of the United Nations and to each of the non-member States contemplated in Art. 11.

The present Convention shall come into force on the ninetieth day following the date of deposit of the twentieth instrument of ratification or accession.

Any ratification or accession effected subsequent to the latter day shall become effective on the ninetieth day following the deposit of the instrument of ratification or accession.

Art. 14. The present Convention shall remain in effect for a period of ten years as from the date of its coming into force.

It shall thereafter remain in force for successive periods of five years for such Contracting Parties as have not denounced it at least six months before the expiration of the current period.

Denunciation shall be effected by a written notification addressed to the Secretary-General of the United Nations.

Art. 15. If, as a result of denunciations, the number of Parties to the present Convention should become less than sixteen, the Convention shall cease to be in force as from the date on which the last of these denunciations shall become effective.

Art. 16. A request for the revision of the present Convention may be made at any time by any Contracting Party by means of a notification in writing addressed to the Secretary-General. The General Assembly shall decide upon the steps, if any, to be taken in respect of such request.

Art. 17. The Secretary-General of the United Nations shall notify all Members of the United Nations and the non-member States contemplated in Art. 11 of the following:

(a) Signatures, ratifications and accessions received in accordance with Art. 11;
(b) Notifications received in accordance with Art. 12;
(c) The date upon which the present Convention comes into force in accordance with 13;
(d) Denunciations received in accordance with Art. 14;
(e) The abrogation of the Convention in accordance with Art. 15;
(f) Notifications received in accordance with Art. 16.

Art. 18. The original of the present Convention shall be deposited in the archives of the United Nations.

A certified copy of the Convention shall be transmitted to each Member of the United Nations and to each of the non-member States contemplated in Art. 11.

Art. 19. The present Convention shall be registered by the Secretary-General of the United Nations on the date of its coming into force."

UNTS, Vol. 78, pp. 277–323; W. KORREY, "The Genocide Treaty: Unratified 35 years Embarrassment for the US", in: *New York Times*, June 23, 1984; *International Herald Tribune*, October 17, 1984.

GENTLEMEN'S AGREEMENT. An international term for a specific type of international agreement not made in written form, but orally, yet fully valid legally; a distinction is made between open gentlemen's agreements and secret diplomatic agreements. In the USA in 1890 a prohibition was introduced against gentlemen's agreements in commercial relations between states, since by its nature a secret agreement is not subject to anyone's control.

GEODESY AND GEOPHYSICS. A subject of international co-operation. Organizations reg. with the UIA:

European Association of Exploration Geophysicists, f. 1951, The Hague. Publ.: *Geophysical Prospecting*.

International Union of Geodesy and Geophysics, IUGG, f. 1919, Brussels; recognized by ICAO, special arrangement with WMO and ECOSOC. Members: seven constituent international associations: International Association of Geodesy, f. 1862, Paris; International Association of Geomagnetism and Aeronomy, f. 1919, Tokyo; International Association of Meteorology and Atmospheric Physics, f. 1919, Boulder, USA.; International Association for the Physical Sciences of the Ocean, f. 1919, Victoria, British Columbia; International Association of Hydrological Science, f. 1922, Dublin; International Association of Seismology and Physics of the Earth's Interior, f. 1901, Boston; International Association of Volcanology and Chemistry of the Earth Interior, f. 1919, Leeds;

and 71 adhering countries represented by governments, scientific academies or departments. Publ.: *IUGG Chronicle* (monthly), *IUGG Monographs* (occasional).

Yearbook of International Organizations.

GEOGRAPHICAL NAMES. A subject of international unification since 1967. The First Conference for Unification of Geographical Names was held under the aegis of the UN in Geneva, 1967, with experts from 54 countries participating. It appointed a Permanent Commission of UN Experts for Geographical Names. The Second Conference was held in Geneva in 1970, the Third in 1980.

GEOGRAPHICAL REPRESENTATION. The term adopted by the UN for the subject of a gentlemen's agreement, concluded by the big powers in the UN Preparatory Commission in London in Nov., 1945, to the effect that the non-permanent members of the Security Council shall be elected on the basis of geographical representations; one from Eastern Europe, one from Western Europe, two from the (British) Commonwealth and two from Latin America. The UN General Assembly approved the principle of geographical representation in Res. 153/II of Nov. 15, 1947. This arrangement was broken the following year, when no representative of Eastern Central Europe was elected. In 1959, Czechoslovakia submitted to the UN General Assembly Political Committee a proposal on "the application of the geographical representation principle in electing the President of the UN General Assembly", but on Dec. 10, 1959 the Assembly defeated the proposal by a vote of 40 against, 36 for and 6 abstaining. In 1960, the Third World countries, together with the socialist countries, protested against the non-application of the geographical representation principle in all UN bodies and specialized agencies by Res. 1559/XV of Dec. 18, 1962 and Res. 1928/XVIII of Dec. 11, 1963; these states also requested that the composition of the UN Secretariat be in keeping with the criterion of the geographical representation. In 1964–66 the UN General Assembly increased the number of Security Council members and of ECOSOC, so as to provide for a fuller geographical representation of different regions of the world.

UN Review, No. 1, 1964; *UN Monthly Chronicle*, No. 12, 1966.

GEOGRAPHY. A subject of international co-operation. Organizations reg. with the UIA:

Commonwealth Geographical Bureau f. 1968, London.

International Geographical Union f. 1947, Freiburg in Breisgau. Consultative status with ECOSOC, liaison status with FAO, recognized by ICAO. Commissions on: History of Geographical Thought; International Geographical Terminology; Geographical Education; Geographical Data Sensing and Processing; Environmental Problems; Geomorphological Survey and Mapping; Field Experiments in Geomorphology; International Hydrological Program; Geography of Transport; Population Geography; National Settlement Systems; Agricultural Productivity and World Food Supplies; Rural Development; Coastal Environmental Industrial Systems; Regional Systems and Policies. IGU Working Groups on: Geography of Tourism and Recreation; Desertification in and Around Arid Lands; Market Distribution Systems; Cartography of the Dynamic Environment; Applied Aspects of Geography; Environmental Atlases (jointly with ICA); Geography of Health; Systems Analysis and Mathematical Models; Perception of the Environment; Coordination of Periglacial Research. Members: National Committees. Publ.: *The IGU Bulletin* (twice a year).

International Society of Geographic Ophthalmology, f. 1970, Montreal.

Panamerican Institute of Geography and History, f. 1928, Mexico City.

Yearbook of International Organizations.

GEOLOGY. A subject of international co-operation. The First International Geological Congress took place in Buffalo, 1875. Organizations reg. with the UIA:

African Regional Committee for Geology, f. 1962, Dakar.

Association of African Geological Surveys, f. 1929, Paris, France. Publ.: *Géologie Africaine*.

Association of Geoscientists for International Development, f. 1974, Bangkok, Thailand.

CMEA Geological Commission, f. 1963, Ulan Bator.

Commonwealth Committee on Mineral Resources and Geology, f. 1948, London.

International Association of Engineering Geology, f. 1964, Paris.

International Association of Mathematical Geology, f. 1968, Syracuse.

International Association of Quaternary Research, f. 1928, Brussels.

International Union of Geological Sciences, f. 1961, Haarlem.

Yearbook of International Organizations, 1986/87; The Europa Yearbook 1988. A World Survey, Vol. 1, London, 1988.

GEOPHYSICAL YEAR, INTERNATIONAL, 1957. The International Geophysical Year of 1957 was initiated by the International Union of Scientific Academies; and approved by the UN General Assembly in 1955. For scientific and technical reasons it lasted for more than a year, from 1 July 1957 to 30 June 1959. For the first time international scientific research encompassed the earth's surface, its interior and its atmosphere; 5000 scientists from 48 countries participated. The first International Geophysical Year was organized 1882–3 for exploration of the North Pole; the second 1932–3 for the South Pole.

UN Review, No. 259, pp. 38–42, 1957.

GEOPOLITICS. An international term formulated during World War I by the Swedish Pan-Germanist R. Kjellen, who attempted to show a close relationship between the geographical conditions of a state and its policy; the term was abused by the geopoliticians of the German III Reich to justify the necessity for expanding "living space". ▷ Lebensraum.

K. HAUSHOFER, *Bausteine zur Geopolitik*, München, 1928; G. BAKKER, *Deutsche Geopolitik 1919–1945*, Berlin W., 1968.

G

GEORGIA. Georgian Soviet Socialist Republic. The federative republic of the USSR in western Transcaucasia on the Black Sea, bounded by Turkey, Armenia and Azerbaidzhan. Area: 69,700 sq. km. Pop. 1983 est.: 5,136,600 (1970 census: 4,688,000 of whom 66.8% Georgian, 9.7% Armenian, 8.5% Russians, 4.6% Azeris, 3.2% Ossetinians, 1.9% Greeks and 1.7% Abkhasians). Capital: Tbilisi. Official languages: Georgian and Russian. Currency: ruble of the USSR. National Day: Oct. 7, Socialist Revolution Anniversary, 1917.

International relations: in the 19th century part of the Russian Empire. After the October revolution a Georgian Social Democratic Republic was proclaimed on May 26, 1918. In June, 1918 German troops occupied Georgia; in Dec., 1918 British and 1920/21 also Turkish troops. After the Russian–Turkish peace treaty on Mar. 16, 1921 and the delimitation of the frontier, Georgia, Armenia and Azerbaidzhan formed the Transcaucasian Soviet Federal Socialist Republic, dissolved 1936. On Dec. 5, 1936 the Georgian Soviet Socialist Republic was proclaimed.

Soyuz Sovietskikh Socialisticheskikh Riespublik 1917–1967, Moskva, 1967; *The Europa Year Book 1984. A World Survey*, Vol. I, pp. 917–918, London, 1984.

GEORGETOWN NON-ALIGNED COUNTRIES DECLARATION, 1972.

The Conference of Foreign Ministers of Nonaligned Countries in Georgetown, Guyana, Aug. 8–12, 1972, adopted the Action Programme for Economic Co-operation among Nonaligned countries. The text of the Preamble is as follows:

"The Ministers of Foreign Affairs of the Non-Aligned countries having reviewed the world economic situation in so far as the urgent development needs of the Third World are concerned, particularly in the light of the International Development Strategy of the United Nations Second Development Decade, of the results of UNCTAD III, and of the United Nations Conference on the Human Environment;

Declare that imperialism continues to be the major obstacle in the way of developing countries, and of the Non-Aligned Countries in particular, attaining standards of living consistent with the most elementary norms of human dignity. Imperialism not only opposes the proposals made by the countries of the Third World but assumes a belligerent attitude thereto, and systematically attempts to undermine its social, economic and political structures in order to maintain economic colonialism, dependence, and neo-colonialism. This state of affairs apart from violating sovereignty and independence, takes on the characteristics of an aggression against the economics of the peoples who do not submit to its rules and dictates, going so far as to foster poverty and even wars in large areas of the world. In denouncing these facts to world public opinion, the Non-Aligned Countries rely on the action of developed capitalist and socialist countries that have shown an understanding of the problems of development to induce the community of nations to improve the efficacy of international co-operation and to defeat the purposes of imperialism.

The Non-Aligned Countries believe it is fundamentally important to stress that the full exercise of their sovereignty over natural resources is essential for economic independence, which is closely linked to political independence, and that the latter is consolidated by strengthening the former. The sovereign right of each State to dispose of its natural wealth and resources, including nationalization, is inherent in the principles of self-determination of the peoples and of non-intervention. Any threat and any measure or external pressure constitute an act of aggression and, consequently, a threat to international peace and security.

In analysing the problems of economic development and political independence, the Conference denounced the practices and activities of transnational corporations, some of which violate the sovereignty of developing countries. The Non-Aligned Countries condemn such practices and activities of transnational corporations which invariably impair the principle of non-intervention and self-determination of the peoples, and at the same time issue a call to the end that such activities be systematically denounced to world public opinion. The Ministers analysed in detail the results of UNCTAD III recently held in Santiago, Chile. While these showed once again the crisis international co-operation was experiencing, it was felt essential to continue to press for each of the proposals made by the Group of 77 in the Declaration of Lima. Accordingly it was agreed to encourage every effort to strenghen the unity and co-ordination of the Group of 77 so that it may effectively achieve its purposes. Attainment of the aims and objectives of the International Development Strategy will depend on the concerted and consistent action of that Group evaluation and review of those goals and objectives should be an efficient method of judging the behaviour of international co-operation and, in particular, the extent of the political will of the developed countries to comply with the commitments undertaken in Resolution 2626 (XXV) of the General Assembly. The Stockholm Conference on Human Environment served to show the difference in the environmental problems experienced by the rich and the poor countries. The former were irresponsibly created by the industrialized nations which today try to unload the burden on the international community as a whole. On the other hand, while some of the environmental problems of the Third World are inherent to their under-development, others are a legacy of the practices of imperialism in its manifestations of colonialism and neo-colonialism and, more recently, have been caused by the war waged by imperialism in Indochina, the Middle East and Africa, where chemical and other arms are used for the purpose of destroying the ecology of the territories it hopes to occupy and, in some cases such as that of the Palestinian people, whole populations are displace from their original homes.

The Ministers of Foreign Affairs of the Non-Aligned Countries, in concluding their deliberations on economic problems, have noted that during the period since the Conference of Heads of State and/or Government of Non-Aligned Countries held in Lusaka, the conviction has grown regarding the need for unity among the developing countries in order to attain the aims and objectives they have set themselves. Accordingly, they reaffirm their faith in the principle of self-reliance and co-operation between Non-Aligned Countries, as well as their determination to struggle side by side to mobilize the political will of the international community."

Conference on Economic Co-operation among Developing Countries. Declarations, Resolutions, Recommendations and Decisions adopted in the UN System. México, DF, Vol. 3, pp. 467–485.

GEOS. The name of scientific-explorer satellites constructed by the European Space Agency, ESA, from 1977, put into elliptical earth orbit from Cape Canaveral, USA, controlled by the Space Center ESA in Darmstadt, FRG.

GEOSTATIONARY ORBIT. An international term for a circular orbit above the equator *c.* 35,800 km above the earth, along whose path geostationary satellites have been circling since 1963 in a stable position, since they are subject to the earth's gravitational pull, and encompassing within their range one-third of the earth's surface; subject of an international dispute initiated at a session of the UN General Assembly on Oct. 14, 1975 by Colombia. The equatorial states of Brazil, Colombia, Congo, Ecuador, Indonesia, Kenya, Uganda and Zaire at a special conference Nov. 29–Dec. 3 1976 in Bogota drafted the so-called Bogota Declaration in which they announced their sovereign territorial claims to the geostationary orbit, since "its existence depends exclusively on its connection with gravitational phenomena caused by the Earth, and thus it cannot be regarded as part of outer space". The Bogota Declaration recognized the geostationary orbit as "containing a limited amount of natural resources whose importance and value increases rapidly along with the development of space technology and the growing needs of telecommunication." The claims of the equatorial states were the subject of discussion at the World Conference on Satellite Radiodiffusion in Geneva Jan. 10–Feb. 13, 1977 and at the annual sessions of the UN Legal Subcommittee on the Peaceful Uses of Outer Space. The USA and USSR opposed the claims. In Mar. 1982 the Legal Subcommittee of the Committee on the Peaceful Uses of Outer Space once more discussed the demand of the equatorial countries to establish "a legal régime which would acknowledge the geostationary orbit as a limited natural resource and would recognize the interests of developing countries", currently restricted "by monopolistic utilization of the orbit by the developed countries". The second and third WARC conference on the use of geostationary orbit was held in Geneva in 1985 and 1988. A study (A/AC 105/340) "The Feasibility of Obtaining Closer Spacing of Satellites in the Geostationary Orbit" was prepared in 1986 by a group of experts from Colombia, Czechoslovakia, Italy, Japan, Kenya, Pakistan, Sweden, the UK and the USSR.

Conclusions of the study:

"Closer spacing of satellites in the geostationary orbit is feasible and certain technologies exist to allow greater overall efficiency in the orbit's use. Some technologies and techniques are already in the implementation phase; others could be implemented on a large scale in the next five to 10 years. The efficient use of the orbit is expected to increase noticeably. However, full advantage of the benefits can be achieved only when new techniques are widely used.

The most crowded parts of the orbit are the arcs from 49°E to 90°E (over the Indian Ocean), from 135°W to 87°W (serving North America) and from 1°W to 35°W (over the Atlantic Ocean). For some parts of the orbit, such as over the western Pacific, there would appear to be little prospect of congestion. Since each country or region can only use a portion of the orbit for its communication needs, any competition for positions will be between a certain number of countries and not global. Under present procedures although some countries have had difficulties adapting their proposed satellites to existing assignments, no country has been denied access to the geostationary orbit for any satellite. Technological advances, including those contributing to a reduction in spacing, could help to ensure continuing access.

Given that satellite and Earth station technology will continue to develop and that a growing number of systems using different technologies will be introduced, the potential minimum spacing between satellites will vary with time and with position in the geostationary orbit.

Though the possibility of collisions between satellites and other objects in the geostationary orbit is not yet serious, a systematic study of the problem of collisions may be needed to find ways to avert them.

Advantages offered by communication satellites for telecommunications and broadcasting have influenced planners in developing countries, who want access to space technology. A systematic effort must be made to assist developing countries achieve indigenous capability through transfer of know-how. While it is neither possible nor desirable for all countries to establish independent research and development programmes in the field of satellite communications, every country should be able to participate bilaterally, regionally or internationally in such programmes.

If a country or group of countries has decided to acquire a satellite system or ground system, a key question is the choice between designing and building satellites and Earth stations or buying systems from other countries. A decision to build domestically may have implications for satellite spacing in that a country new to the technology of satellite or Earth station design may have difficulty incorporating the most advanced technology that could maximize communication capacity or minimize spacing.

Nations and organizations with advanced technological capabilities should make a particular effort to provide technical assistance to developing countries in order to provide the greatest possible access to communications to all countries. Such assistance should also include education and training in the planning and design of communication satellite systems and operation and maintenance of ground systems.

UN Doc. A/C. 1/PV. 2052, pp. 43–46; UN Doc. A/C. 1/31/8V.8 pp. 8–18 and 37–38 zl; M.G. MARCOFF, *Traité du droit international public de l'espace*, Fribourg, 1973; A. GORBIEL, "Le statut de l'orbite géostationaire", in: *20-ème Colloque du Droit Spatial International*, Prague, 1977; L. PEREK, "Physics, uses and regulations of the geostationary orbit or ex facto sequitur lex", in: *20th International Space Law Colloquium*, Prague 1977; *UN Chronicle*, May, 1983, p. 60 and April, 1984, p. 35; "Finding a Place in the Geostationary Orbit: Aim is to Ensure Access For All", in: *UN Chronicle*, 1985, No. 2, pp. 21–23.

GERMAN ACADEMIC EXCHANGE SERVICE. (Deutscher Akademischer Austauschdienst, DAAD), f. 1925 by the German Universities with hqs. in Bonn and branches in Cairo, London, Nairobi, New Delhi, New York, Paris, Rio de Janeiro and Tokyo. Publ.: *Study Guides*.

GERMAN-AMERICAN YOUTH EXCHANGE PROGRAM. In 1984, on Oct. 6, the 300th Anniversary of German immigration to North America the parliaments of the FRG and USA established a Youth Exchange Program, organized by Congress-Bundestag Youth Exchange Office.

"German-American Exchange Programs", in: *The New York Times*, Oct. 6, 1987.

GERMAN CONFEDERATION, 1815–1866. Der Deutsche Bund was founded on June 8, 1815 at the Congress of Vienna; associated Austria, Prussia, Bavaria, Württemberg and all other German princedoms and kingdoms until 1866 when the Austro-Prussian conflict, called the Prussian–German war, caused disintegration of the confederation into the north-German Confederation and loose associations of south German states with Prussia and later of Prussia with the ▷ German Reich.

T.S. HAMEROW, *Restoration, Revolution, Reaction* London, 1958.

GERMAN CUSTOMS UNION, 1833. Der Deutsche Zollverein. The first customs union in Europe, formed in Berlin, Mar. 22, 1833 by Prussia, Hesse, Bavaria, Württemberg under a treaty providing for uniform customs tariffs, measurements, weights and monetary systems; entered into force on Jan. 1, 1834; extended on Sept. 7, 1851 to include other German kingdoms and princedoms; linked with the Prussian–Austrian customs treaty on Apr. 4, 1854; dissolved in 1866 as a result of Prussian–Austrian conflict.

W.D. HENDERSON, *The Zollverein*, London, 1939.

GERMAN DEBTS LONDON AGREEMENT 1953. An agreement signed on Aug. 8, 1953, after negotiations initiated by Western Powers. Those Powers on Mar. 6, 1951, stated that full sovereignty for the Federal Republic of Germany, and its entry into the World Bank and the IMF was conditional upon acknowledgement by the Federal Republic of Germany of the obligations and debts incurred by the German Government during the period 1919–45. The Federal Republic of Germany West substantially agreed to this and from Feb. 27 to Aug. 8, 1953, in London, a conference was held between the Federal Republic of Germany and creditor states: Belgium, Canada, Ceylon, Denmark, France, Greece, Ireland, Italy, Liechtenstein, Luxembourg, Norway, Pakistan, Spain, Sweden, Switzerland, the UK, the USA, the Union

of South Africa and Yugoslavia. All debts of the German Reich and those incurred after the war by West Germany in the years 1945–50 were set at 1375 billion Western Marks. The Federal Republic of Germany agreed to pay back the sum in specified installments. On Aug. 8, 1953, the Federal Republic of Germany was admitted to the World Bank and the IMF.

Verträge der Bundesrepublik Deutschland, Serie A, Bd. 3, No. 25: G. ERLER, "Die Rechtsprobleme der deutschen Auslandsschuldenregelung und ihre Behandlung auf der Londoner Schuldenkonferenz", in: *Europa-Archiv*, 1952; J.L. STIMSON, "The Agreement of German External Debts", in *International Law Quarterly*, No. 6, 1957; H. BALLREICH, "Auslandsschulden", in: *STRUPP-SCHLOCHAUER Wörterbuch des Völkerrechts*, Vol. 1, Berlin, 1960, pp. 110–115; H. COING, "Londoner Schuldenabkommen von 1953", in *STRUPP – SCHLOCHAUER Wörterbuch des Völkerrechts*, Vol 2, Berlin, 1961, pp. 425–428.

GERMAN DEMOCRATIC REPUBLIC. Member of the UN. Deutsche Demokratische Republik, DDR. State in Central Europe on the Baltic Sea. Borders with Poland, Czechoslovakia and the FRG. Area: 108,333 sq. km. Pop.: 1987 est.: 16,675,000; Population census of 1939 – 16,745,000; 1946 – 18,847,000; 1960 – 18,790,000; 1970 – 17,068,318. Capital: Berlin (East) with 1,157,600 inhabitants in 1981. GNP per capita in 1980: US $7180. Official language: German. Currency: one GDR Mark = 100 pfennigs. National Day: Oct. 7, anniversary of the proclamation of the GDR, 1949. Member of the UN on Sept. 26, 1973 and of all specialized agencies with the exception of the IMF, FAO, ICAO, IDA, IFAD, IBRD, IFC and GATT. Member of the Warsaw Pact and CMEA.
International relations: East Germany, occupied after the unconditional surrender of the German Reich on May 8, 1945 by the Soviet Army, was subject to the Allied Control Council for Germany until the ending of its activities on Mar. 20, 1948, then exclusively controlled by Soviet occupation forces. On Mar. 19, 1949 the German People's Council formulated and passed the Constitution of the German Democratic Republic, which was ratified on May 30, 1949 by the German People's Congress and entered into force on Oct. 7, 1949, that is, one month after the formation of the FRG. The Soviet Military Administration handed over power to the GDR government 23 days later. The first international treaties concluded by the GDR were: Prague Declaration of June 24, 1950 recognizing the frontier with Czechoslovakia and the Zgorzelec Treaty, signed July 6, 1950, recognizing the frontier with Poland. The frontier with the FRG was delimited on May 27, 1952. The GDR was granted sovereignty in a declaration by the government of the USSR made on Mar. 25, 1954. ▷ German Democratic Republic Sovereignty Act 1954. On Oct. 29, 1950, the GDR was accepted as a full member of the CMEA and in following years became a member of all CMEA specialized institutions. Following the integration of the FRG into NATO on May 9, 1955, the GDR became a signatory of the Warsaw Pact on May 15, 1955. On Sept. 20, 1955 the GDR concluded a 10-year Treaty of Friendship, Co-operation and Mutual Assistance with the USSR and on Dec. 25, 1955 a Treaty of Friendship and Co-operation with the Chinese People's Republic. The GDR on June 12, 1964 renewed the Treaty on Friendship, Co-operation and Mutual Assistance with the USSR and concluded similar treaties with Poland on Mar. 15, 1967, with Czechoslovakia on Mar. 17, 1967, with Hungary on May 18, 1967, with Bulgaria on Sept. 7, 1967 and with Mongolia on Sept. 12, 1968. In 1972 relations with the FRG were normalized. ▷ German Interstate Agreements 1949–74.

The UN General Assembly on Sept. 26, 1973 accepted the GDR as well as the FRG for membership in the UN.
On Oct. 7, 1975 a new Treaty of Friendship, Co-operation and Mutual Assistance between the GDR and the USSR was signed in Moscow (▷ GDR-USSR Treaty, 1975).
The Vatican announced a decision to separate the hierarchy of the GDR Catholic church from that of the FRG Catholic Church on Oct. 26, 1976. On Nov. 1, 1985 all the GDR mines along the frontier with the FRG were removed. Automatic firing devices had been removed on Nov. 1, 1987.
On July 5, 1985 a new credit agreement was signed with the FRG increasing for the years 1986–90 the amount of interest-free "swing"loans from DM 600 million to 850 million.
In Jan. 1988, the Government of the GDR agreed in principle to pay reparations to the Jewish victims of Nazism. The GDR Government first offered in 1976 reparations of US$1 million, but the World Jewish Congress rejected the offer. In Sept. 1987 a willingness to consider reparation to Jews was indicated by GDR officials in unofficial talks at the United Nations.
The GDR Government announced in June 6, 1988 that is willing in principle to pay US$100 million in compensation to individual Jewish victims of Nazism.
See also ▷ Naturalization.

Geschichtliche Zeittafel der DDR 1949–59, Berlin, 1960; *Die Geschichte der Aussenpolitik der DDR*, Bd. 2, Potsdam, 1965; I.N. ARCIBASHEV, *GDR subyekt miezhdunarodnogo prava*, Moskva, 1969; K. SONTHEIMER, W. BLEEK, *Die DDR, Politik, Gesellschaft, Wirtschaft*, Hamburg, 1972; *Beziehungen DDR–UdSSR 1949 bis 1955*, 2 Bd., Berlin, 1974; H.A. JACOBSEN (ed.), *Drei Jahrzehnte Aussenpolitik der DDR*, München, 1979; *The Europa Year Book 1984. A World Survey*, Vol. I, pp. 475–495, London, 1984; G.E. EDWARDS, *GDR Society and Social Institutions, Facts and Figures*, London, 1985; R. WOODS, *Opposition in the GDR Under Honecker, 1971–1985*, New York, 1986; KEESING's *Record of World Events*, No. 9, 1988.

GERMAN DEMOCRATIC REPUBLIC SOVEREIGNTY ACT, 1954. A Declaration of the USSR government concerning the Assumption of Full Sovereignty by the GDR on Mar. 25, 1954, read as follows:

"The Government of the Soviet Union is unswervingly guided by a desire to contribute to a solution of the German problem in accordance with the interests of strengthening peace and securing the national reunification of Germany on a democratic basis.
These aims must be served by practical measures for a rapprochement of Eastern and Western Germany, the holding of free all-Germany elections, and the conclusion of a peace treaty with Germany.
Despite the efforts of the Soviet Union, no steps towards restoring the national unity of Germany and the conclusion of a peace treaty were taken at the recent Berlin Conference of the Foreign Ministers of the Four Powers.
In view of this situation and as a result of negotiations which the Soviet Government has held with the Government of the German Democratic Republic, the Government of the USSR considers it necessary to take at once, even before the unification of Germany and the conclusion of a peace treaty, further steps to meet the interests of the German people, namely:
(1) The Soviet Union establishes the same relations with the German Democratic Republic as with other sovereign States. The German Democratic Republic shall be free to decide on internal and external affairs, including the question of relations with Western Germany, at its discretion.
(2) The Soviet Union will retain in the German Democratic Republic the functions connected with guaranteeing security, and resulting from the obliga-

tions incumbent on the USSR as a result of the Four-Powers Agreement.

The Soviet Government has taken note of the statement of the Government of the German Democratic Republic that it will carry out its obligations arising from the Potsdam Agreement on the development of Germany as a democratic and peace-loving State, as well as the obligations connected with the temporary stationing of Soviet troops on the territory of the German Democratic Republic.

(3) Supervision of the activities of the German Democratic Republic, hitherto carried out by the High Commissioner of the USSR in Germany, will be abolished.

In accordance with this, the functions of the High Commissioner of the USSR in Germany will be limited to questions mentioned above connected with guaranteeing security and maintaining the appropriate liaison with the representatives of the Occupying Authorities of the USA, Great Britain, and France regarding questions of an all-German character and arising from the agreed decisions of the four Powers on Germany.

The Government of the USSR is of the opinion that the existence of the Occupation Statute laid down for Western Germany by the United States of America, Great Britain, and France, is not only incompatible with the principles, of democracy and the national rights of the German people, but constitutes one of the main obstacles on the road to the national reunification of Germany, by impeding the rapprochement between Eastern and Western Germany."

The Allied High Commission of the Western Powers reacted on Apr. 8, 1954 with a Joint Declaration as follows:

"The Allied High Commission desires to clarify the attitude of Governments which it represents toward the statement issued on March 25 by the Soviet Government, purporting to describe a change in its relations with the Government of the so-called German Democratic Republic. This statement appears to have been intended to create the impression that sovereignty has been granted to the German Democratic Republic. It does not alter the actual situation in the Soviet Zone. The Soviet Government still retains effective control there.

The Three Governments represented in the Allied High Commission will continue to regard the Soviet Union as the responsible Power for the Soviet Zone of Germany. These Governments do not recognize the sovereignty of the East German régime which is not based on free elections, and do not intend to deal with it as a Government. They believe that this attitude will be shared by other States, who, like themselves, will continue to recognize the Government of the Federal Republic as the only freely elected and legally constituted Government in Germany. The Allied High Commission also takes this occasion to express the resolve of its Governments that the Soviet action shall not deter them from their determination to work for the reunification of Germany as a free and sovereign nation."

Selected Documents on Germany and the Question of Berlin 1944–1961, HMSO, London, 1961, pp. 186–188.

GERMAN INTERSTATE AGREEMENTS, 1949–74.

The first German interstate agreements include:

The Frankfurt Agreement, signed on Oct. 8, 1949, in Frankfurt am Main by representatives of top economic institutions, also called the Agreement on Interzone Trade.

The Berlin Trade Agreement of Sept. 21, 1951, extolled "trade between German Mark zones" without mentioning either state's name; modified on Aug. 16, 1960, then revised and amended several times. The Berlin Agreement allowed both states to grant each other the most-favored-nation clause in spite of West Germany's duties arising from its participation in the EEC. ▷ Interzonenhandel.

The first political treaty expressing mutual formal recognition of independent statehood was that on West Berlin, signed in 1971, and in 1972 a Treaty on Basis of Relations between the Federal Republic of Germany and the German Democratic Republic,

initiated Nov. 8, 1972 in Bonn; signed Dec. 21, 1972; ratified by the Volkskammer June 13, 1973; by the Bundestag May 18, 1973; effected May 21, 1973. Along with publication of the Agreement's text and the Protocol on Nov. 9, 1972, it was announced that:

(1) Both Governments agreed that in the process of normalization of relations between the German Democratic Republic and the Federal Republic of Germany the states shall consult each other on issues interesting to both Parties, particularly those important to securing peace in Europe.

(2) Both Governments, each in its own right, shall initiate measures to seek membership of the United Nations.

(3) Both Governments agreed on a number of detailed questions, e.g. opening new border crossing points, mutual rights granted to journalists, settlement of problems concerned with reunion of families, etc.

(4) The Government of the German Democratic Republic informed in a note to the Government of the USSR and the Government of the Federal Republic of Germany informed in a note to the Governments of France, USA and Great Britain that both States had initialled the Agreement and under Art. IX had recognized inviolably of ▷ Responsibilities of the Four Powers.

Texts of the Agreement and the Protocol are as follows:

"The high Contracting Parties,
Mindful of their responsibilities for the maintenance of peace; Endeavoring to make a contribution to détente and security in Europe;
Conscious of the inviolability of frontiers and respect for the territorial integrity and sovereignty of all States in Europe within their present frontiers being a fundamental requirement for peace;
Recognizing that the two German States must therefore in their relations refrain from the threat or the use of force;
Proceeding from the historical facts and without prejudice to the differing concepts of the Federal Republic of Germany and the German Democratic Republic on fundamental questions, including the national question;
Guided by the desire to create the preconditions for cooperation between the Federal Republic of Germany and the German Democratic Republic for the benefit of the people in the two German States;
Have agreed as follows:
Art. 1. The Federal Republic of Germany and the German Democratic Republic will develop normal good-neighborly relations with each other on the basis of equality of rights.
Art. 2. The Federal Republic of Germany and the German Democratic Republic will let themselves be guided by the aims and principles which are laid down in the Charter of the United Nations, in particular those of the sovereign equality of all States, respect for independence, sovereignty and territorial integrity, the right of self-determination, the protection of human rights and non-discrimination.
Art. 3. In accordance with the Charter of the United Nations, the Federal Republic of Germany and the German Democratic Republic will solve their differences solely by peaceful means and refrain from the threat of force or the use of force. They affirm the inviolability, now and in the future, of the border existing between them, and pledge themselves to unrestrict respect for each other's territorial integrity.
Art. 4. The Federal Republic of Germany and the German Democratic Republic proceed on the assumption that neither of the two States can represent the other internationally or act in its name.
Art. 5. The Federal Republic of Germany and the German Democratic Republic will promote peaceful relations among the European States and contribute to security and cooperation in Europe. They support the efforts towards a reduction of armed forces and armaments in Europe provided that this does not adversely affect the security of the parties concerned. With a view to achieving general and complete disarmament under effective international control, the German Democratic Republic and the Federal Republic of Germany will support efforts serving international security and designed to bring about arms limitation and disarma-

ment, in particular in the field of nuclear arms and other weapons of mass destruction.
Art. 6. The Federal Republic of Germany and the German Democratic Republic proceed from the principle that the sovereign power of each of the two States is confined to its (own) State territory. They respect the independence and sovereignty of each of the two States in its internal and external affairs.
Art. 7. The Federal Republic of Germany and the German Democratic Republic declare their readiness, in the course of the normalization of their relations, to settle practical and humanitarian questions. They will conclude agreements in order – on the basis of this treaty and for their mutual advantage – to develop and promote cooperation in the economic field, science and technology, transport, juridical relations, posts and telecommunications, public health, culture, sports, the protection of the environment and in other spheres. Details are set out in the Supplementary Protocol.
Art. 8. The Federal Republic of Germany and the German Democratic Republic will exchange permanent representative missions. They will be established at the seat of the respective Governments. Practical questions connected with the establishment of the missions will be settled separately.
Art. 9. The Federal Republic of Germany and the German Democratic Republic are agreed that bilateral and multilateral international treaties and agreements previously concluded by or concerning them are not affected by this treaty.
Art. 10. This treaty is subject to ratification and enters into force on the day after the exchange of the relevant Notes.
The Supplementary Protocol is an integral part of the treaty.
I. Re Art. 3. The Federal Republic of Germany and the German Democratic Republic agree to set up a commission composed of representatives of the Governments of the two States. It will examine and, so far as is necessary, renew or supplement the demarcation of the border existing between the two States, and will also compile the necessary documentation on the line of the border. It will likewise contribute to the settlement of other problems connected of the line of the border – for example water conservation, the supply of energy, and measures to prevent or repair damages.
The commission will take up its work after the signing of the treaty.
II. Re Art. 7 (1) Trade between the Federal Republic of Germany and the German Democratic Republic will be developed on the basis of existing agreements. The Federal Republic of Germany and the German Democratic Republic will conclude long-term agreements with the aim of promoting a continuous development of economic relations, adapting out-dated regulations and improving the structure of trade.
(2) The Federal Republic of Germany and the German Democratic Republic declare their intention of developing cooperation in the fields of science and technology to their mutual advantage, and of concluding the agreements required for this.
(3) Cooperation in the sphere of traffic, begun with the treaty of May 26, 1972, will be expanded and intensified.
(4) The Federal Republic of Germany and the German Democratic Republic declare their readiness, in the interest of those seeking justice, to regulate juridical relations, especially in the fields of civil and criminal law, by agreement as simply and expeditiously as possible.
(5) The Federal Republic of Germany and the German Democratic Republic agree to conclude a postal and telecommunications agreement on the basis of the statutes of the Universal Postal Union and of the International Telecommunication Convention. They will notify the UPU and the ITU of this agreement. Existing agreements and procedures advantageous to both sides will be taken over into this agreement.
(6) The Federal Republic of Germany and the German Democratic Republic declare their interest in cooperation in the field of public health. They agree that the corresponding agreement should also regulate the exchange of medicaments and treatment in special clinics and sanatoria within the framework of existing facilities.
(7) The Federal Republic of Germany and the German Democratic Republic intend to develop cultural cooperation. To this end they will enter into negotia-

tions on the conclusion of inter-governmental agreements.

(8) The Federal Republic of Germany and the German Democratic Republic affirm their readiness, after the signing of the treaty, to support the competent sports organizations in agreements on the promotion of sports relations.

(9) In the field of environmental protection, agreements will be concluded between the Federal Republic of Germany and the German Democratic Republic in order to help avert damage and hazard for either side.

(10) The Federal Republic of Germany and the German Democratic Republic will conduct negotiations with the aim of expanding the reciprocal supply of books, periodicals, and radio and television programmes.

(11) The Federal Republic of Germany and the German Democratic Republic will enter into negotiations, in the interest of the persons concerned, for the regulation and clearing of non-commercial payments. In this connection, they will, in their mutual interest, give priority to the short-term conclusion of arrangements on social considerations."

The Federal Constitutional Court of the Federal Republic of Germany on July 31, 1973 announced its verdict on the Treaty on Basis of Relations between the FRG and the GDR thus starting a bitter controversy between the Court and GDR jurists as the verdict contained controversial theses on the continuity of the German Reich and on German State nationality (▷ dual nationality) as well as a thesis that "the treaty is of a dual character: as to its type it is a treaty compatible with international law, as to its specific content – it is a treaty regulating first of all relations between each other (*inter se*)."

On Mar. 14, 1974 was signed in Bonn the Protocol on Establishing Permanent Representations of the German Democratic Republic in Bonn and of the Federal Republic of Germany in Berlin. Under art. 2 such representations and their heads did not bear names accepted for regular diplomatic relations – "embassy" and "ambassador" – which was objected to by the Federal Republic of Germany to emphasize dissimilarity of the diplomatic relations between the two German states to regular relations, but "Permanent Representations" (*"Ständige Vertretung"*) and "Head of Permanent Representation" (*"Leiter der Ständigen Vertretung"*). Simultaneously, the German Democratic Republic insisted that heads ought to be accredited just as ambassadors of alien states (art. 3) to Heads of State (in the GDR – to the Chairman of the Council of State; in the FRG to the President); whereas in the German Democratic Republic "permanent representatives" of the FRG under art. 6 settled their matters in the Ministry of Foreign Affairs just as representatives of other states; "permanent representatives" of the GDR in the Federal Republic of Germany did so in the Chancellor's Office. In practice the government of the Federal Republic of Germany used the title of "head" for its representative in the GDR and the government of the German Democratic Republic used *ad personam* titles to name its representatives in the FRG, usually "Ambassador Extraordinary and Minister Plenipotentiary". International diplomatic status is assigned to both missions, however, through a compromising formula introduced into art. 4:

"the Vienna Convention of April 18, 1961, with respect to the permanent representations ... respectively is in force."

Art. 6 determines that:

"the permanent representative of the Federal Republic of Germany and the German Democratic Republic will represent in keeping with the Four-Partite Agreement of Sept. 3, 1971, also interests of West Berlin."

UNTS, 1973 and 1974.

GERMANIZATION. An international term for denationalization under economic and political pressure of Slavic ethnic groups in the 19th and 20th century in Prussia. In the III Reich the Germanization of children was carried out according to an SS kidnapping system called ▷ Lebensborn.

Meyers Lexikon, Leipzig, 1926, Vol. 4, pp. 1734–1735; *The Trial of German Major War Criminals. Proceedings of the IMT Sitting at Nuremberg, Germany*, 42 Vols., London 1946–48, Vol. 2, p. 432 and Vol. 5 pp. 342, 349, 370.

GERMAN–JAPANESE ANTI-COMINTERN PACT, 1936. The treaty was signed on Nov. 25, 1936 in Berlin. The text is as follows:

"The German Government and the Japanese Government, recognizing that the aim of the Communist Internationale known as the Comintern is directed at disrupting and violating existing States with all means at its command and convinced that to tolerate the Communist Internationale's interference with the internal affairs of nations not only endangers their internal peace and social well-being but threatens world peace at large, animated by a desire to work in common against Communist disruptive influences, have arrived at the following agreement:

I. The high contracting parties agree to mutually inform each other concerning the activities of the Communist Internationale, to consult with each other concerning measures to combat this activity, and to execute these measures in close cooperation with each other.

II. The two high contracting States will jointly invite third parties whose domestic peace is endangered by the disruptive activities of the Communist Internationale to embark upon measures for warding these off in accordance with the spirit of this agreement or to join in it.

III. For this agreement, both the German and Japanese texts are regarded as original versions. It becomes effective the day of signing and is in force for a period of five years.

The high contracting States will, at the proper time before expiration of this period, arrive at an understanding with each other concerning the form this cooperation is to take."

The *New York Times*, November 26, 1936.

GERMAN-OTTOMAN EMPIRE ALLIANCE, 1914. A secret Treaty of Alliance between the German Reich and the Ottoman Empire, signed Aug. 2, 1914. The highlights of the Treaty:

"Art. 1. The Two Contracting Powers undertake to observe strict neutrality in the present conflict between Austria–Hungary and Serbia.

Art. 2. In the event that Russia should intervene with active military measures and thus should create for Germany a casus foederis with respect to Austria–Hungary, this casus foederis would also come into force for Turkey.

Art. 3. In the event of war, Germany will leave its Military Mission at the disposal of Turkey.

The latter, for its part, assures the said Military Mission effective influence over the general conduct of the army, in conformity with what has been agreed upon directly by His Excellency the Minister of War and His Excellency the Chief of the Military Mission.

Art. 4. Germany obligates itself, by force of arms if need be, to defend Ottoman territory in case it should be threatened.

Art. 5. This Agreement, which has been concluded with a view to protecting the two Empires from the international complications which may result from the present conflict, enters into force at the time of its signing by the above-mentioned plenipotentiaries and shall remain valid, with any analogous mutual agreements, until 31 December 1918."

H. TEMPARLAY, G.P. GOOCH (eds.), *British Documents on the Origin of the War, 1898–1914*, 11 Vols., London, 1928; K. KAUTSKY (ed.), *Die Deutschen Dokumente zum Kriegsausbruch*, Berlin, 1924, Vol. 3, Dok. 723, p. 183; J.C. HUREVITZ, *Diplomacy in the Near and Middle East, A Documentary Record*, Princeton, NJ, 1956, Vol. 2.

GERMAN-OWNED PATENTS AGREEMENT 1946. An intergovernmental accord concerning the treatment of German-owned patents, signed on July 27, 1946 in London; and Protocol Amending the Accord, signed on July 17, 1947 in London.

Art. I decided that all former totally German-owned patents ... shall be donated to the public ... or offered for licensing without royalty to the nationals of all Governments, parties to the Accord.

UNTS, Vol. 90, pp. 229–253.

GERMAN PENAL LAW FOR POLES AND JEWS, 1941. In III Reich, 1933–39, parallel with racist anti-Jewish legislation there appeared German legislation of a racist Pan-German character, *de facto* and *de iure* excluding from many civic rights one and a half million Poles living on the territory of the Reich of that time. The Union of Poles in Germany protested against this legislation in memoranda submitted to the government of the Reich. The incorporation into the Reich in Oct., 1939 of the western lands of the Polish state greatly increased the number of Poles in the Reich, resulting in further sharpening of discriminatory laws, which on Dec. 9, 1941 were codified and published as "German penal law for Poles and Jews", described as follows by the Secretary of State of the Ministry of Justice, R. Freisler, on Dec. 19, 1941:

"This penal law corresponds to the legal position of Poles in the State; it only has application to Poles and Jews and not to any other nationalities."

K.M. POSPIESZALSKI, "Hitlerowskie 'prawo' okupacyjne", in: *Documenta Occupationis*, Vol. 6, Poznań, 1958.

GERMAN–POLISH NON-AGGRESSION PACT, 1934. A bilateral declaration on non-use of coercion, which was preceded by the following events: on Jan. 31, 1933, Hitler's ascent to power as the Reich's Chancellor; on May 2, 1933, Polish envoy to Berlin A. Wysocki held talks with Hitler which initiated negotiations concluded on Jan. 26, 1934 in Berlin by a declaration signed by Polish ambassador J. Lipski and the Reich's foreign minister von Neurath. The text is as follows:

"Polish and German governments consider that the moment has come to begin a new period in Polish–German relations by means of direct communication of one country with the other and agree by the instrument of this declaration to lay foundations for the future shaping of these relations. Both governments believe that the maintenance and consolidation of lasting peace between their countries constitutes a substantial condition of peace in Europe. They are committed to build their mutual relations on the principles stipulated in the Paris Pact [▷ Briand–Kellog Pact] of August 27, 1928 and wish to define more clearly the application of these principles to Polish–German relations. The two governments acknowledge that their other international commitments shall not obstruct peaceful development of their mutual relations, nor are in contradiction with the present declaration or violated by it. The governments agree that the present declaration shall not be applicable to such cases which, in keeping with international law, pertain exclusively to internal affairs of one of the two countries. Both governments declare that their aims is to communicate directly on all matters pertaining to their mutual relations, and that if any controversial matters arise between them which cannot be settled by way of negotiations, both governments will seek to solve each such case through mutual agreements with no infringement of the possibility to use, if necessary, the procedures stipulated in such cases by their other mutually binding agreements. They shall not in any case make recourse to the use of violence to settle such controversial issues. A guarantee of peace founded on the above-mentioned premises shall make easier for both governments the momentous task of looking for political, economic and cultural solutions based on just and right equality of mutual interests. Both governments are convinced that relations between their countries will develop fruitfully and lead to consolidation of good neighbourly coexistence which is to bring beneficial effects not only to their countries but for the remaining peoples of Europe. The declaration will be ratified and ratification documents exchanged as soon as possible in Warsaw. The declaration will remain in force for ten years from the day of the exchange of ratification documents. If none of the governments denounces it six months before the expiry of the ten-year period, its binding force will continue; after which period each government shall be able to denounce any time six months in advance."

On Feb. 27, 1934 the declaration was ratified and on Mar. 7, 1934 Polish foreign minister J. Beck and Reich ambassador H. Moltke signed in Warsaw an Additional Protocol on normalization of economic relations.

Five years later, on Apr. 28, 1939, the German government having failed to obtain Polish consent for incorporation of the Free City of Gdansk into the Reich and for construction of a German motorway across Pomerania connecting Berlin with East Prussia, presented the Polish government with a memorandum on denouncement of the Polish–German treaty, which Hitler thus justified in the Reichstag:

"There can be no doubt that Gdansk will never be Polish. The impudent insinuation by the world press of aggressive designs on the part of Germany has led, March 31, 1939, to British guarantees, well-known to you, Gentlemen, and the Polish government's obligation of mutual assistance. These obligations would force Poland under definite circumstances to an armed assault against Germany."

Polish foreign minister J. Beck thus retorted to the German claim at the Sejm, May 5, 1939:

"Peace is a precious and desirable thing. Our generation drained of blood in wars certainly deserves peace. But peace, like almost all matters of the world, has its price – high but measurable. We, in Poland do not know the notion of peace at all cost. There is only one thing in the life of human beings, nations and states that is priceless. This is honour."

During the Nuremberg Trials, 1945–46, documents were brought to light showing that before denouncing the treaty, Hitler on Nov. 5, 1937 had issued orders to the Reich armed forces chief command to prepare the invasion of Poland, and that on March 25, 1939 he thus specified the goal of aggression:

"Poland should be routed so as to ensure that in the course of the coming decades it is not to be taken into account as a political factor."

Diplomat in Berlin 1933–1939, Papers and Memoirs of Józef Lipski, Ambassador of Poland, New York, 1968.

GERMAN–POLISH NORMALIZATION AGREEMENT, 1970.
The agreement between the FRG and Poland concerning the basis for normalization of their mutual relations was signed on Dec. 7, 1970 in Warsaw; came into force on June 3, 1972. The text is as follows:

"The Polish People's Republic and the Federal Republic of Germany,
Considering that more than 25 years have passed since the end of the Second World War, which claimed Poland as its first victim and brought great suffering to the peoples of Europe,
Mindful of the fact that a new generation has since grown up in the two countries and must be assured a peaceful future,
Desiring to create a lasting basis for peaceful coexistence and the development of normal, good relations between them,
Endeavouring to strengthen peace and security in Europe,
Conscious of the fact that the inviolability of the frontiers of all European States and respect for their territorial integrity and sovereignty within their present frontiers are a basic condition for peace,
Have agreed as follows:

Art. I.(1) The Polish People's Republic and the Federal Republic of Germany agree that the existing frontier line, which, in accordance with chapter IX of the decisions of the Potsdam Conference of 2 August 1945, runs from the Baltic Sea immediately west of Swinoujscie along the Odra (Oder) River to the point of junction with the Nysa Luzycka (Lausitzer Neisse) River and along the Nysa Luzycka (Lausitzer Neisse) River to the frontier with Czechoslovakia, constitutes the western State frontier of the Polish People's Republic.
(2) They confirm the inviolability of their existing frontiers, now and hereafter, and pledge absolute respect for each other's territorial integrity.
(3) They declare that they have no territorial claims against each other and will advance none in the future.
Art. II.(1) The Polish People's Republic and the Federal Republic of Germany shall, in their mutual relations and in matters relating to the safeguarding of security in Europe and throughout the world, be guided by the purposes and principles set out in the Charter of the United Nations.
(2) Accordingly, they shall, in conformity with Articles 1 and 2 of the Charter of the United Nations, settle all disputes between them exclusively by peaceful means and refrain from the threat or use of force in matters affecting European and international security and in their mutual relations.
Art. III.(1) The Polish People's Republic and the Federal Republic of Germany shall take further steps to ensure the complete normalization and comprehensive development of their mutual relations, for which this Agreement shall provide a lasting basis.
(2) They agree that expanded co-operation between them in the matter of economic, scientific, technical, cultural and other relations is in their mutual interest.
Art. IV. This Agreement shall be without prejudice to any bilateral or multilateral international agreements which the Parties have previously concluded or which affect them.
Art. V. This Agreement is subject to ratification and shall enter into force on the date of the exchange of the instruments of ratification, which shall take place at Bonn."

Recueil de Documents, Varsovie, No. 12, 1970.

GERMAN–POLISH ZGORZELEC AGREEMENT, 1950.
The Oder–Neisse Frontier Agreement, 1950, signed at Zgorzelec, Poland, on July 6, 1950, by the heads of the governments of Poland and the German Democratic Republic, J. Cyrankiewicz and O. Grotewohl. Came into force on Nov. 28, 1950. The Treaty concluded between the Republic of Poland and the German Democratic Republic concerning the demarcation of the established and existing Polish–German State Frontier was preceded by a statement by prime minister O. Grotewohl, Oct. 12, 1949, made in the GDR parliament (Volkskammer) concerning recognition of the frontier on Poland by the GDR and June 6, 1950, by the joint declaration of the governments of Poland and the GDR concerning the Polish–German frontier in the following form:

"The Government of the Republic of Poland and the Delegation of the Provisional Government of the German Democratic Republic animated by the desire to consolidate peace and to strengthen the camp of peace struggling under the leadership of the Soviet Union against the plots hatched by imperialist forces, mindful of the accomplishments scored by the German Democratic Republic in consolidating the new democratic order and developing the forces rallied around the National Front of the Democratic Germany have mutually agreed that it is in the interest of further maintenance of peace and the deepening of the good-neighbourly relations and friendship between the Polish and German People to delineate between the two States the determined and existing inviolable frontier of peace and friendship along the Oder and Neisse rivers. Thereby the German Democratic Republic implements the statement made by prime minister Grotewohl of October 12, 1949. In the effecting of the aforementioned both Parties have resolved that by way of agreement they shall delineate within a month the existing state frontier along the Oder and Neisse rivers and settle on

frontier passes, limited cross-frontier traffic and navigation on the frontier zone waters."

The text of the Zgorzelec Treaty reads as follows:

"The President of the Polish Republic and the President of the German Democratic Republic,
Desiring to give expression to their will for the strengthening of universal peace and wishing to make a contribution to the noble cause of harmonious co-operation between peace-loving peoples,
Having regard to the fact that such co-operation between the Polish and German peoples has become possible thanks to the total defeat of German Fascism by the USSR and to the progressive development of the democratic forces in Germany, and
Desirous of establishing, after the tragic experiences of Hitlerism, indestructible foundation upon which the two peoples may live together in peace and as good neighbours, wishing to stabilize and strengthen mutual relations on the basis of the Potsdam Agreement, which established the frontier on the Oder and Western Neisse,
In pursuance of the provisions of the Warsaw Declaration of the Government of the Polish Republic and the Delegation of the Provisional Government of the German Democratic Republic dated 6 June 1950,
Recognizing the established and existing frontier as an inviolable frontier of peace and friendship which does not divide but unites the two peoples,
Have resolved to conclude this Agreement:
Art. 1. The High Contracting Parties concur in confirming that the established and existing frontier, running from the Baltic Sea along a line to the west of the inhabited locality of Swinoujscie and thence along the Oder River to the confluence of the Western Neisse and along the Western Neisse to the Czechoslovak frontier, is the state frontier between Poland and Germany.
Art. 2. The Polish–German State frontier as demarcated in accordance with this Agreement shall also delimit vertically the air space, the sea and the subsoil.
Art. 3. For the purpose of demarcating of the ground the Polish–German State frontier referred to the article 1, the High Contracting Parties shall establish a Mixed Polish–German Commission having its headquarters at Warsaw.
The Commission shall compromise eight members, four of whom shall be appointed by the Government of the Republic of Poland and four by the Provisional Governments of the German Democratic Republic.
Art. 4. The Mixed Polish–German Commission shall meet not later than 31 August 1950 to begin the work referred to in Art. 3.
Art. 5. After the demarcation of the State frontier on the ground, the High Contracting Parties shall draw up an instrument confirming the demarcation of the State frontier between Poland and Germany.
Art. 6. In carrying out the demarcation of the Polish–German State frontier, the High Contracting Parties shall conclude agreements relating to frontier crossing points, local frontier traffic and navigation on frontier waterways. Such agreements shall be concluded within one month after the entry into force of the instrument mentioned in Art. 5 confirming the demarcation of the State frontier between Poland and Germany.
Art. 7. This agreement shall be subject to ratification, which shall take place as soon as possible. The Agreement shall come into force on the exchange of the instruments of ratification, which shall take place at Berlin."

The Instrument Confirming the Demarcation of the State Frontier between Poland and Germany was signed at Frankfurt on the Oder, on Jan. 27, 1951, and read as follows:

"The President of the Republic of Poland and the President of the German Democratic Republic desiring, in accordance with the will of their peoples, to strengthen the inviolable frontier of peace and friendship between the two peoples, have resolved to conclude an instrument confirming the demarcation of the State frontier between Poland and Germany, and for that purpose have appointed as their plenipotentiaries, who, having exchanged their full powers, found in good and due form, have agreed as follows:
Art. 1. In pursuance of Art. 5. of the Agreement between the Republic of Poland and the German Democratic Republic concerning the demarcation of the established and existing Polish–German State fron-

tier, signed at Zgorzelec on 6 July 1950, the two Parties confirm that the State frontier between Poland and Germany referred to in Art. 1 of that Agreement has been demarcated on the ground by the Mixed Polish--German Commission established pursuant to Art. 3 of the Agreement.
Art. 2. The Polish–German State frontier follows a line as indicated in the documents prepared by the Mixed Commission, listed in annex No. 1, and in the map constituting annex No. 2 to this Instrument, the said annexes and documents being an integral part of the Instrument.
The two parties confirm that the documents mentioned in Art. 2 of this Instrument prepared by the Polish--German Mixed Commission for the demarcation of the State frontier and indicating the line followed on the ground by the frontier are as follows:
(1) A descriptive protocol relating to the course followed by the line of the State frontier between Poland and Germany, drawn up on the demarcation of the frontier, in two copies, each consisting of three volumes comprising 646 pages in the Polish language and 548 pages in the German language.
(2) A set of maps of the State frontier between Poland and Germany, in two copies each containing 34 numbered maps comprising 39 pages including the annexes.
(3) A set of sketches of the geodetic grid and measurements of the State frontier line between Poland and Germany, in two copies, each containing 34 sheets comprising 36 pages including the annexes.
(4) A list of the co-ordinates of the frontier marks and geodetic points situated on the State frontier between Poland and Germany, in two copies, containing 143 pages each in Polish and in German.
(5) A set of the protocols relating to frontier marks (Nos. 755 to 923), in two copies, containing 169 pages each in Polish and in German.
(6) Final protocol in two copies, each containing the text in Polish (6 pages) and in German (5 pages).
In accordance with the above-mentioned documents it has been established that the total length of the demarcated Polish–German frontier line is 460.4 kilometres; of this line, the length of the land frontier sector, according to geodetic measurements is 51.1 kilometres; the length of the water sector (rivers and canals), as determined by graphic methods on the basis of the maps of the State frontier (scale – 1 : 25,000) is 389.8 kilometres and the length of the internal sea waters sectors is 19.5 kilometres."

UNTS, Vol. 319, 1959, pp. 93–113; J.A. PROWEIN, "Zur verfassungsrechtlichen Beurteilung des Warschauer Vertrages", in: *Jahrbuch für Internationales Recht*, 1975, pp. 11–61.

GERMAN QUESTION. An international term. After World War II the main issue of contention between West and East in Europe. In the first decade 1945–54 the German question was dominated by the reunification of the divided Germany. Since 1955, after the military integration of the FRG by NATO and of the GDR into the Warsaw Pact, the German question was de facto reduced to FGR-GDR relations and to the problem of ▷ Berlin. The Helsinki Final Act "accepted the partition of Germany and sealed the status quo in Central Europe" (H. Kissinger). In the 1980's the German question was not discussed by the Big Powers.

H. KISSINGER, *Memoirs 1968–1973*, New York, 1979; W.U. FRIEDRICH, "The German Question between West and East" in: *Aussenpolitik*, No. 3, 1987.

GERMAN REICH. *German*: Deutsches Reich. The historical name of the union of German states; applied by historians to the Roman Empire of the German Nation, 962–1806, called the old German Reich or First Reich; to the empire of the Prussian Hohenzollerns, 1871–1918, called the Prussian Reich or Second Reich; also to the Weimar Republic, 1919–33, which had the official name Deutsches Reich. After Hitler's accession to power changed into the fascist III Reich (▷ Germany, 1871–1945). The FRG Federal Constitutional Court on July 31, 1973 in a judgment concerning the German interstate Treaty, 1972, pronounced the opinion that the FRG is identical with the German Reich which thereby continues to exist as a subject of international law. The spokesman for the FRG government recognized this opinion as correct, but it was rejected by the GDR government. Here is an essential fragment of the FRG judgment:

"1. The Basic Law assumes – it is at the same time not only a thesis of the law of nations and a law of the state – that the German Reich survived the collapse of 1945 and did not fall, neither in the moment of surrender nor as a result of the exercise of state power in Germany by the allied occupational powers; this ensues from the introduction, from Art. 16, Art. 23, Art. 116 and Art. 146 of the Basic Law. It is also in accord with the jurisdiction of the Federal Constitutional Court, whose jurisdiction is adhered to by the Senate. The German Reich continues to exist, continues to have legal capacity, though as a common state (Gesamtstaat) it is not able to act due to the lack of organization and special institutional organs. Also contained in the Basic Law is the view on the all-German nation capable of creating a state (gesamtdeutsches Staatsvolk) and an all-German state authority. The responsibility for 'Germany as a whole' is also borne by the Four Powers. With the proclamation of the Federal Republic of Germany, a new West German state was not created, but a part of Germany was organized anew. The Federal Republic of Germany is thus not a 'legal successor' to the German Reich, but as a state is identical with the state of the German Reich – however, in view of its territorial scope it is only partially identical, so that this identicalness does not entail exclusivity. Thus the Federal Republic of Germany, as regards its nation capable of forming a state (Staatsvolk) and its state territory, the whole of Germany, recognizes the united nation as capable of making the state a subject of the international law of Germany (German Reich), to which belong its own population as its inseparable part and the united state territory of the German Reich, which includes its state territory, also as an inseparable part. In the meaning of national law, its authority is limited to the 'region governed by the Basic Law', but it also feels responsible for all of Germany. At the present time, the Federal Republic is composed of the Länder mentioned in Art. 23 of the Basic Law, including Berlin. The Statute of the Land Berlin of the Federal Republic of Germany, however, is limited by the so-called provisions of the governors of the Western Powers. The German Democratic Republic belongs to Germany and cannot be considered as a foreign country in relation to the Federal Republic. For this reason interzonal trade and, correspondingly, present intra-German trade is not foreign trade."

Neues Deutschland, Berlin, August 16, 1973; *Das Parliament*, Bonn, September 1, 1973; C.A. CRAIG, *Germany 1866–1945*, New York, 1978; H.P. SCHWARZ, *Vom Reich zur Bundesrepublik in den Jahren der Besatzungherrschaft 1945–1949*, Stuttgart, 1980.

GERMAN REVOLUTION PROCLAMATIONS, 1918. At the end of World War I a revolutionary movement started in the German Empire with the naval mutiny in Kiel on Nov. 5, 1918; in Munich, Bavaria, on Nov. 7, and in the capital on Nov. 9. One day earlier the socialists had sent an ultimatum to the government demanding the Kaiser's abdication. On Saturday morning at one o'clock, Nov. 9, the Workers' and Soldiers' Council of Berlin decided to call a general strike. The "bloodless revolution" ended with the flight of the Kaiser to Holland, the announcement of his abdication and the handing over of the Chancellorship by the Old Regime to the Socialist Friedrich Ebert (1871–1925). The announcement of the success of the revolution on Nov. 9, 1918, was as follows:

"Workers, Soldiers, Fellow Citizens,
The Free State has come,
Emperor and Crown Prince have abdicated.
Fritz Ebert, the chairman of the Social Democratic party, has become Imperial Chancellor and is forming in the Empire and in Prussia a new government of men who have the confidence of the working population in town and country, of the workers, and of the soldiers. Herewith public power has passed into the hands of the people. A National Assembly to settle the Constitution will meet as quickly as possible.
Workers, soldiers, citizens. The victory of the people has been won; it must not be dishonored by thoughtlessness. Economic life and transport must be maintained at all costs, so that the people's government may be secured under all circumstances.
Obey all the recommendations of the people's government and its representatives. It is acting in the closest union with the workers and soldiers.
Long live the German People's Republic.
The Executive of the Social Democracy of Germany.
The Workers' and Soldiers' Council."

The same day in the evening the new revolutionary government issued a decree as follows:

"Comrades. This day has completed the freeing of the people. The emperor has abdicated, his eldest son has renounced the throne. The Social Democratic party has taken over the government, and has offered entry into the government to the Independent Social Democratic party on the basis of complete equality. The new government will arrange for an election of a Constituent National Assembly, in which all citizens of either sex who are over twenty years of age will take part with absolutely equal rights. After that it will resign its powers into the hands of the new representatives of the people.
Until then its duties are:
To conclude an armistice and to conduct peace negotiations; to assure the feeding of the population.
To secure for the men in the army the quickest possible orderly return to their families and to wage-earning work. For this the democratic administration must begin at once to work smoothly. Only by means of faultless working can the worst disasters be avoided. Let each man, therefore, realize his responsibility to the whole. Human life is sacred. Property is to be protected against illegal interference. Whoever dishonors this glorious movement by vulgar crimes is an enemy of the people and must be treated as such. But whoever cooperates with honest self-sacrifice in our work, on which the whole future depends, may say of himself that at the greatest moment of the world's history he joined in to save the people.
We face enormous tasks. Laboring men and women, in town and country, men in the soldier's uniform and men in the workman's blouse, help, all of you.
Ebert, Scheidemann, Landsberg."

On Nov. 12, 1918, the Wolff Bureau issued a Telegram of the People's Government in Berlin to the High Command (of the Reichswehr), defining the relation of soldiers to officers and regulating military discipline:

"The People's Government is inspired by the wish to see each of our soldiers return to his home as quickly as possible after his unspeakable sufferings and unheard-of deprivations. But this goal can only be reached if the demobilization is carried out according to an orderly plan. If single troops stream back at their own pleasure, they place themselves, their comrades, and their homes in the greatest danger. The consequences would necessarily be chaos, famine, and want. The People's Government expects of you the strictest self-discipline in order to avoid immeasurable calamity. We desire the High Command to inform the army in the field of this declaration of the People's Government, and to issue the following orders:
(1) The relations between officer and rank and file are to be built up on mutual confidence. Prerequisites to this are willing submission of the ranks to the officer, and comradely treatment by the officer of the ranks.
(2) The officer's superiority in rank remains. Unqualified obedience in service is of prime importance for the success of the return home to Germany. Military discipline and army order must, therefore, be maintained under all circumstances.
(3) The Soldier's Councils have an advisory voice in maintaining confidence between officer and rank and file in questions of food, leave, the infliction of disciplinary punishments. Their highest duty is to try to prevent disorder and mutiny.

(4) The same food for officers, officials, and rank and file.
(5) The same bonuses to be added to the pay, and the same allowances for service in the field for officers and rank and file.
(6) Arms are to be used against members of our own people only in cases of self-defense and to prevent robberies. Signed Ebert, Haase, Scheidemann, Landsberg, Barth."

The Government published also the same day a call to the soldiers returning from the front:

"Comrades! The German Republic heartily bids you welcome home! You went forth for a country in which you had no say, in which a handful of men in authority had shared out between themselves power and possession. You were but allowed to be silent and to fight, while hundreds of thousands had to be silent and die before your eyes. Today you return to your own country in which no one in future has anything to say or to decide except the people itself, which is now receiving you once more as members. The revolution has broken the spell: you and we are free, Germany is free. Our Socialist Republic is to enter the League of Nations as the freest of all. And you are not only to find all the political rights of which hitherto you have been deprived; your country is also to become your possession and your inheritance in an economic way, in that no one shall any more, with our consent, exploit you and enslave you.
The Imperial government, which has been created and is being supported by the confidence of your comrades and of the workers, will get you work, protection while you work, and higher wages from your work. The eight-hour day, insurance for unemployment, creation of employment, development of sickness insurance, the solution of the housing question, socialization of those industries which are ready for it: everything is in process, is already partly law!
Come and be welcomed as the men who are to carry on the new Republic and its future. It is true you will find scarcity among us in foodstuffs, in all economic materials; there is distress and deprivation in the country. We can only get help from work in common, from action taken together. Only a Germany which has a government secured and anchored in the workers and soldiers can get from our previous opponents what you have fought for and longed for during four years – peace! Council of the People's Commissaries, Ebert, Haase, Scheidemann, Dittmann, Landsberg, Barth."

The left-wing of the Social-Democratic Party, organized as the Spartacus Group, proclaimed a Manifesto of the Spartacus Group, which read as follows:

"Proletarians! Men and Women of Labor! Comrades! The revolution has made its entry into Germany. The masses of the soldiers who for four years were driven to the slaughter-house for the sake of capitalistic profits, the masses of workers, who for four years were exploited, crushed, and starved, have revolted. That fearful tool of oppression – Prussian militarism, that scourge of humanity – lies broken on the ground. Its most noticeable representatives, and therewith the most noticeable of those guilty of this war, the Kaiser and the Crown Prince, have fled from the country, Workers' and Soldiers' Councils have been formed everywhere. Proletarians of all countries, we do not say that in Germany all the power has really been lodged in the hands of the working people, that the complete triumph of the proletarian revolution has already been attained. There still sit in the government all those Socialists who in August, 1914, abandoned our most precious possession, the International, who for four years betrayed the German working class and at the same time the International. But, proletarians of all countries, now the German proletarian himself is speaking to you. We believe we have the right to appear before your forum in his name. From the first day of this war we endeavored to do our international duty by fighting that criminal government with all our power and branding it as the one really guilty of the war.
Now at this moment we are justified before history, before the International, and before the German Proletariat. The masses agree with us enthusiastically, constantly widening circles of the proletariat share the knowledge that the hour has struck for a settlement with capitalist class rule. But this great task cannot be accomplished by the German proletarian alone; it can only fight and triumph by appealing to the solidarity of the proletarians of the whole world.
Comrades of the belligerent countries, we are aware of your situation. We know very well that your governments, now since they have won the victory, are dazzling the eyes of many strata of the people with the external brilliancy of the triumph. We know that they thus succeed through the success of the murdering in making its causes and aims forgotten. But we also know something else. We know that also in your countries the proletariat made the most fearful sacrifices of flesh and blood, that it is weary of the dreadful butchery, that the proletarian is now returning to his home, and is finding want and misery there, while fortunes amounting to billions are heaped up in the hands of a few capitalists. He has recognized, and will continue to recognize, that your governments, too, have carried on the war for the sake of the big money bags. And he will further perceive that your governments, when they spoke of 'justice and civilization' and of the 'protection of small nations,' meant the profits of capital just as did ours when it talked about the 'defense of the home'; and that the peace of 'justice' and of the 'League of Nations' amounts to the same base brigandage as the peace of Brest-litovsk. Here, as well as there, the same shameless lust for booty, the same desire for oppression, the same determination to exploit to the limit the brutal preponderance of murderous steel.
The imperialism of all countries knows no 'understanding', it knows only one right – capital's profits; it knows only one language – the sword; it knows only one method – violence. And if it is now talking in all countries, in yours as well as ours, about the 'League of Nations', 'disarmament', 'rights of small nations', 'self-determination of the peoples', it is merely using the customary lying phrases of the rulers for the purpose of lulling to sleep the watchfullness of the proletariat.
Proletarians of all countries! This must be the last war! We owe that to the 12,000,000 murdered victims, we owe that to our children, we owe that to humanity.
Europe has been ruined through the infamous international murder. Twelve million bodies cover the gruesome scenes of the imperialistic crime. The flower of youth and the best man power of the peoples have been mowed down. Uncounted productive forces have been annihilated. Humanity is almost ready to bleed to death from the unexampled bloodletting of history. Victors and vanquished stand at the edge of the abyss. Humanity is threatened with the most dreadful famine. A stoppage of the entire mechanism of production, plagues, and degeneration.
The great criminals of this fearful anarchy, of this chaos let loose – the ruling classes – are not able to control their own creation. The beast of capital that conjured up the hell of the world war is not capable of banishing it again, of restoring real order, of insuring bread and work, peace and civilization, justice and liberty, to tortured humanity.
What is being prepared by the ruling classes as peace and justice is only a new work of brutal force from which the hydra of oppression, hatred, and fresh bloody wars raises its thousand heads.
Socialism alone is in a position to complete the great work of permanent peace, to heal the thousand wounds from which humanity is bleeding, to transform the plains of Europe, trampled down by the passage of the apocryphal horseman of war, into blooming gardens, to conjure up ten productive forces for every one destroyed, to awaken all the physical and moral energies of humanity, and to replace hatred and dissension with fraternal solidarity, harmony, and respect for every human being.
If representatives of the proletarians of all countries stretch out their hands to each other under the banner of socialism for the purpose of making peace, then peace will be concluded in a few hours. Then there will be no disputed questions about the left bank of the Rhine, Mesopotamia, Egypt, or colonies. Then there will be only one people: the toiling human beings of all races and tongues. Then there will be only one aim: prosperity and progress for everybody.
Humanity is facing this alternative: dissolution and downfall in capitalist anarchy, or regeneration through the social revolution. The hour for decision has struck. If you believe in socialism, it is now time to show it by deeds. If you are Socialists, now is the time to act. Proletarians of all countries, when we now summon you to a common struggle it is not done for the sake of the German capitalists who, under the label 'German nation', are trying to escape the consequences of their own crimes; it is being done for our sake as well as for yours.
Remember that your victorious capitalists stand ready to suppress in blood our revolution, which they fear as their own. You yourselves have not become any freer through the 'victory', you have only become still more enslaved. If your ruling classes succeed in throttling the proletarian revolution in Germany, as well as in Russia, then they will turn against you with redoubled violence. Your capitalists hope that victory over us and over revolutionary Russia will give them the power to scourge you with a whip of scorpions and to erect the thousand-year empire of exploitation upon the grave of socialism.
Therefore the proletariat of Germany is looking toward you in this hour. Germany is pregnant with the social revolution, but socialism can only be realized by the proletariat of the world.
And therefore we call to you: 'Arise for the struggle! Arise for action! The time for empty manifestoes, platonic resolutions, and high-sounding words has gone by! The hour of action has struck for the International!' We ask you to elect Workers' and Soldiers' Councils everywhere that will seize political power and, together with us, will restore peace.
Not Lloyd George and Poincare, not Sonnino, Wilson, and Erzberger or Scheidemann, must be allowed to make peace. Peace is to be concluded under the waving banner of the socialist world revolution.
Proletarians of all countries! We call upon you to complete the work of socialist liberation, to give a human aspect to the disfigured world, and to make true those words with which we often greeted each other in the old days and which we sang as we parted: 'And the International shall be the human race.'
Klara Zetkin, Rosa Luxemburg, Karl Liebknecht, Franz Mehring."

"The German Revolution", in: *International Conciliation*, No. 137, April 1919.

GERMAN–RUSSIAN TREATIES, 1873–1907. After the rise of the German Reich in 1871, Tsarist Russia concluded the following treaties with Germany:

(1) A military convention signed May 6, 1873, in Petersburg, provided for the rendering of assistance, in the form of a 200,000 man army, or either of the parties in case the other is assailed by any European power.
(2) The Safeguarding Treaty signed on June 18, 1887, in Berlin warranted to both sides the neutrality of the other party in case of a war with another power except for, however, a war between the Reich and France or Russia with Austria (art. 1); the Reich recognized Russian influence on the Balkans (art. 2) and promised to remain neutral if Russia resolves it is necessary to use force in defense of free access to the Black Sea via the Dardanelles (additional protocol) as the key to its Empire (*le clef de son empire*).
(3) A defensive alliance signed on July 25, 1905, in Björko by Wilhelm II and Nicolas II, providing that "if one (of the two Empires) is assailed by any European power the other ally shall render its assistance in Europe with all its land and naval forces."
(4) The Baltic treaty, signed on October 29, 1907, in Petersburg to safeguard the military status quo of the Baltic Sea.

Grosse Politik der Europäischen Kabinette 1871–1914, 40 Vols., Berlin, 1926; *Sbornik Dogovorov Rossyi s drugimi gosudarstvami 1856–1917*, Moskva, 1952.

GERMAN–SOVIET CO-OPERATION AGREEMENT, 1978. The FRG–USSR agreement. The agreement was signed in Bonn on May 6, 1978, on the occasion of the official visit in FRG of L. Brezhnev. It is an agreement on the growth and expansion of long-term co-operation between the USSR and FRG in the areas of economy and industry.

GERMAN–SOVIET FRIENDSHIP TREATY, 1926. A friendship Treaty signed on Apr. 24, 1926 in Berlin, extending the ▷ Rapallo Treaty, 1922.

LNTS, 1926.

GERMAN–SOVIET NON-AGGRESSION PACT, 1939. A Pact signed on Aug. 23, 1939, in Berlin by the Ministers of Foreign Affairs of the USSR and the German III Reich, W.A. Molotov and J. von Ribbentrop; also called the Molotov–Ribbentrop Pact. Included the obligation to refrain from assailing the other party and from participating in an aggression waged by a third party against one of the signatories. Ratified by the USSR on Aug. 31, 1939, included a Secret Protocol concerning spheres of influence in Eastern Europe; acts of ratification exchanged in Berlin, Sept. 24, 1939; terminated by the German aggression on the USSR, June 21, 1941. Not registered in the League of Nations. The text is as follows:

"The Government of the German Reich and the Government of the Union of Soviet Socialist Republics. Desirous of strengthening the cause of peace between Germany and the USSR and proceeding from the fundamental provisions of the Neutrality Agreement concluded in April 1926 between Germany and the USSR, have reached the following Agreement:

Art. I. Both High Contracting Parties obligate themselves to desist from any act of violence, any aggressive action, and any attack on each other, either individually or jointly with other Powers.

Art. II. Should one of the High Contracting Parties become the object of belligerent action by a third Power, the other High Contracting Party shall in no manner lend its support to this third Power.

Art. III. The Governments of the two High Contracting Parties shall in the future maintain continual contact with one another for the purpose of consultation in order to exchange information on problems affecting their common interests.

Art. IV. Neither of the two High Contracting Parties shall participate in any grouping of Powers whatsoever that is directly or indirectly aimed at the other party.

Art. V. Should disputes or conflicts arise between the High Contracting Parties over problems of one kind or another, both parties shall settle these disputes or conflicts exclusively through friendly exchange of opinion or, if necessary, through the establishment of arbitration commissions.

Art. VI. The present Treaty is concluded for a period of ten years, with the proviso that, in so far as one of the High Contracting Parties does not denounce it one year prior to the expiration of this period, the validity of this Treaty shall automatically be extended for another five years.

Art. VII. The present Treaty shall be ratified within the shortest possible time. The ratifications shall be exchanged in Berlin. The Agreement shall enter into force as soon as it is signed."

Secret Additional Protocol:

"On the occasion of the signature of the Non-Aggression Pact between the German Reich and the Union of Socialist Soviet Republics the undersigned plenipotentiaries of each of the two parties discussed in strictly confidential conversations the question of the boundary of their respective spheres of influence in Eastern Europe. These conversations led to the following conclusions:

Art. 1. In the event of a territorial and political rearrangement in the areas belonging to the Baltic States (Finland, Estonia, Latvia, Lithuania), the northern boundary of Lithuania shall represent the boundary of the spheres of influence of Germany and the USSR. In this connection the interests of Lithuania in the Vilna area is recognized by each party.

Art. 2. In the event of a territorial and political rearrangement of the areas belonging to the Polish State the spheres of influence of Germany and the USSR shall be bounded approximately by the line of the rivers Narew, Vistula, and San.

The question of whether the interests of both parties make desirable the maintenance of an independent Polish State and how such a State should be bounded can only be definitely determined in the course of further political developments. In any event both Governments will resolve this question by means of a friendly agreement.

Art. 3. With regard to south-eastern Europe attention is called by the Soviet side to its interests in Bessarabia.

The German side declares its complete political desinterestedness in these areas.

Art. 4. This Protocol shall be treated by both parties as strictly secret."

On Sept. 22, 1939 the Oberkommando der Wehrmacht and the Red Army signed a Demarcation Line Protocol. The line ran along four rivers: Pissa, Narev, Vistula and San (*Deutsches Nachrichten Bureau, Sept. 22, 1939*, Nr. 1381).

On Sept. 28, 1939, at Moscow the Government of the German Reich and the Government of the USSR concluded a Boundary and Friendship Treaty, with a Protocol and Declaration of the German and Soviet Governments on the demarcation of the new frontier between Germany and the Soviet Union (*Reichsgesetzblatt 1940*, Teil 2, Nr. 1, S. 4; *Vedomosti Verchovnogo Sovieta SSSR. Mar. 29, 1940*, Nr. 10, and in English in *The Bulletin of International News*, Vol. XVI, No. 20, p. 11). The exchange of ratification documents took place in Berlin, Dec. 15, 1939. The German-Soviet Demarcation Commission terminated the demarcation on Dec. 12, 1940. After the Soviet integration of Lithuania, Germany and the USSR signed on Jan. 10, 1941, a Treaty on the German-Soviet frontier on the River Igorka to the Baltic Sea (*Izviestia*, No. 9, Jan. 11, 1941. On Aug. 31, 1940 both signatory states of the Frontier Treaty from Sept. 28, 1939, signed an Agreement on the Legal Regulations of the Common Frontier (*Reichsgesetzblatt 1941*, Teil II, Nr. 8).

Izviestia, August 24, 1939; *Reichsgesetzblatt*, No. 38, 1939; L. SHAPIRO (ed.), *Soviet Treaty Series*, Washington, DC, 1955; *Documents on German Foreign Policy 1918–1945*, Series D (1937–45), Vol. VI, London, 1959; *Istoria Velikoi Otchestviennoi Voiny Sovetskogo Soiuza*, Vol. I, Moskva, 1960; W. DASZKIEWICZ, "Geneza paktu o nieagresji z 23.VIII.1939", [Genesis of the Non-Aggression Pact, 1939] in: *Roczniki Historyczne*, Poznań, 1966; J.A.S. GRENVILLE, *The Major International Treaties 1914–1973. A History and Guide with Texts*, London, 1974, pp. 195–196 and 199–200; D.J. DALLIN, *Soviet Russia's Foreign Policy 1939–1942*, New Haven, 1979; A. READ, D. FISHER, *The Deadly Embrace, Hitler, Stalin and the Nazi-Soviet Pact 1939–1941*, New York, 1988.

GERMAN-SOVIET PARTITION OF POLAND, 1939. After Germany's invasion of Poland, which started World War II, on Sept. 1 , 1939, the Red Army acting in accordance with the Secret Additional Protocols to the German-Soviet Non-Aggression Pact signed Aug. 23, 1939, and the German-Soviet Boundary and Friendship Treaty, invaded Poland on Sept. 17, 1939, newly partitioning the Polish state.

On Oct. 31, 1939, during a session of the Supreme Council of the USSR, V.M. Molotov, the Commissioner of Foreign Relations officially proclaimed "Toskutsnoye gosudarstvo, urodilivoye dietishche versalskovo dogovora, Polsha, pierestala sushchestvovat" – "The ragtag State of Poland, grotesque bastard of the Versailles Treaty has ceased to exist".

Official Soviet data on Polish prisoners of war captured in Sept. 1939 was published in "Krasnaya Zvezda" on Sept. 17, 1940, putting the figure at 181,000 men, among whom were 12 generals, 55 colonels, 72 lieutenant colonels and 9,227 officers of lower rank (▷ Katyń). The majority of non-commissioned officers and enlisted men were sent to concentration camps in Siberia, from which over 100,000 did not return.

In a collection of statements made during his visit to Poland in July 1988 published in Moscow in Nov. 1988, M. Gorbachev defended the "inevitability" of the German-Soviet Non-Aggression Pact, adding however, that he considered the Boundary and Friendship Treaty of Sept. 28, 1939 and the relevant

statements by Commissioner of Foreign Affairs, Molotov to be "not only a political error of grave consequences for the USSR and other states, as well as for the whole Communist movement, but also a flagrant deviation from Leninism and a breach of Leninist priniples".

Official Documents Concerning Polish German Relations 1933–1939, London, 1940; R.S. SONNTAG, J.S. BEDDIE, *Nazi-Soviet Relations 1939–41: Documents from the Archives of the German Foreign Office*, Washington DC, 1948; B. KUSNIERZ, *Stalin and the Poles: An Indictment of the Soviet Leaders*, London, 1949; S.L. WEINBERG, *Germany and the Soviet Union 1939–41*, Leiden 1954; A. BERGMAN, *Najlepszy sojusznik Hitlera*, London, 1955; SIKORSKI INSTITUTE, *Documents of Polish-Soviet Relations 1939–45*, Vls. 2, London, 1961–67; S. BORSODY, *The Tragedy of Central Europe. The Nazi and Soviet Conquest of Central Europe*, New York, 1962; J.W. BRUEGEL, *Stalin und Hitler: Pakt gegen Europa*, Vienna, 1973; N. DAVIES, *God's Playground. A History of Poland*, Vol. II, Oxford, 1985; M.K. DZIEWANOWSKI, *War at Any Price, World War II in Europe 1939–1945*, Englewood Cliffs, N.J., 1987.

GERMAN–SOVIET TRADE AGREEMENT, 1939. An agreement concluded on Aug. 29, 1939. Germany granted the USSR a merchandise credit of 200 million Reichsmarks. The Soviet Union bound itself to the delivery of certain raw materials as current business; succeeded by a Commercial Agreement, Feb. 11, 1940.

J.A.S. GRENVILLE, *The Major International Treaties 1914–1973. A History and Guide with Texts*, London, 1974, pp. 194–195, and 200–201.

GERMAN–SOVIET TREATY, 1955. The GDR–USSR Treaty. The Treaty concerning relations between the USSR and the German Democratic Republic was signed on Sept. 20, 1955 at Moscow; came into force on Oct. 6, 1955. The text is as follows:

"The Presidium of the Supreme Soviet of the Union of Soviet Socialist Republics and the President of the German Democratic Republic,

Desirous of promoting close co-operation and further strengthening the friendly relations between the Union of Soviet Socialist Republics and the German Democratic Republic on a basis of equality, respect for each other's sovereignty and non-intervention in each other's domestic affairs,

Mindful of the new situation created by the entry into force of the Paris Agreements of 1954,

Convinced that by combining their efforts towards the maintenance and strengthening of international peace and European security, the reunification of Germany as a peaceful and democratic State, and a settlement by peace treaty with Germany, the Soviet Union and the German Democratic Republic will be serving the interests both of the Soviet and German peoples and of the other peoples of Europe,

Having regard to the obligations of the Soviet Union and of the German Democratic Republic under existing international agreements relating to Germany as a whole,

Have decided to conclude the present Treaty and have appointed as their plenipotentiaries,

Who, having exchanged their full powers, found in good and due form, have agreed as follows:

Art. 1. The Contracting Parties solemnly reaffirm that the relations between them are based on full equality, respect for each other's sovereignty and non-intervention in each other's domestic affairs.

The German Democratic Republic is accordingly free to take decisions on all questions pertaining to its domestic and foreign policy, including its relations with the Federal Republic of Germany and the development of relations with other States.

Art. 2. The Contracting Parties declare their readiness to participate, in a spirit of sincere co-operation, in all international actions designed to ensure peace and security in Europe and throughout the world in conformity with the principles of the United Nations Charter.

To this end they shall consult with each other on all major international questions affecting the interests of the two States and shall adopt all measures within their power to prevent any breach of the peace.

Art. 3. In accordance with the interests of the two countries and guided by the principles of friendship, the Contracting Parties agree to develop and strengthen the existing ties between the Union of Soviet Socialist Republics and the German Democratic Republic in economic, scientific, technical and cultural matters, to extend to each other all possible economic assistance, and to co-operate, wherever necessary, in the economic, scientific and technical fields.

Art. 4. The Soviet forces now stationed in the territory of the German Democratic Republic in accordance with existing international agreements shall temporarily remain in the German Democratic Republic, with the consent of its Government and subject to conditions which shall be defined in a supplementary agreement between the Government of the Soviet Union and the Government of the German Democratic Republic. The Soviet forces temporarily stationed in the territory of the German Democratic Republic shall not intervene in the domestic affairs or the social and political life of the German Democratic Republic.

Art. 5. The Contracting Parties agree that their fundamental aim is to achieve, through appropriate negotiation, a peaceful settlement for the whole of Germany. They will accordingly make the necessary efforts to achieve a settlement by peace treaty and the reunification of Germany on a peaceful and democratic basis.

Art. 6. This Treaty shall remain in force until Germany is reunited as a peaceful and democratic State, or until the Contracting Parties agree that the Treaty should be amended or terminated.

Art. 7. This Treaty shall be ratified and shall enter into force on the date of the exchange of the instruments of ratification, which shall take place at Berlin as soon as possible."

UNTS, Vol. 226, pp. 201–232.

GERMAN STATES UN MEMBERSHIP, 1972.
A Four Power Declaration by the US, Great Britain, France and the USSR on Membership of the FRG and the GDR in the United Nations, released Nov. 9, 1972; read as follows:

"The Governments of the United Kingdom of Great Britain and Northern Ireland, the French Republic, the Union of Soviet Socialist Republics and the United States of America, having been represented by their Ambassadors who held a series of meetings in the building formerly occupied by the Allied Control Council, are in agreement that they will support the applications for membership in the United Nations when submitted by the Federal Republic of Germany and the German Democratic Republic, and affirm in this connection that this membership shall in no way affect the rights and responsibilities of the Four Powers and the corresponding, related quadripartite agreements, decisions and practices."

▷ Germany and the UN

Selected Documents on Germany and the Question of Berlin 1944–1961, HMSO, London, 1961, pp. 134–135.

GERMAN TRIPARTITE AGREEMENTS, 1949.
The Agreements between France, the UK and USA on Germany, signed on Apr. 8, 1949 in Washington, DC:

Agreed Memorandum regarding the principles governing exercise of powers and responsibilities of the USA, UK and French Governments following establishment of the German Federal Republic. Occupation Statute defining the powers to be retained by the Occupation Authorities.

Agreement as to tripartite control.

Agreed minutes respecting Berlin.

Agreed minutes on claims against Germany.

Agreed minutes on Württemberg–Baden plebiscite.

Message to the Military Governors from the Foreign Ministers of the USA, UK and France.

Message to the Bonn Parliamentary Council from the Foreign Minister of the USA, UK and France.

UNTS, Vol. 140, p. 196.

GERMAN–TURKISH TREATY, 1941.
A Non-Aggression Treaty between the German Reich and Turkey concluded on June 18, 1941 at Berlin. The first two arts, read as follows:

"Art. 1. The Turkish Republic and the German Reich undertake to respect mutually the inviolability and integrity of their territories, and to abstain from all action aimed directly or indirectly against one another. Art. 2. The Turkish Republic and the German Reich undertake to enter into friendly contact in the future in regard to all matters involving their mutual interests with a view to reaching an agreement for their solution."

Reichsgesetzblatt 1941, II, p. 261.

GERMANY.
German: Deutschland. An historical term:

(1) A European land inhabited by Germans having various ethnic boundaries during the centuries.

(2) A common name accepted for various unions of German states in various historical periods: German Reich, Weimar Republic, or III Reich.

(3) After World War II an international legal term connected with such documents as art. 107 of the UN Charter, Declaration on the Defeat of Germany, Potsdam Agreement, 1945, Agreement of the Four Powers on West Berlin, and others concerning the "rights and responsibilities in Germany" of the Great Powers resulting from the defeat of the German Reich.

(4) The term "occupied Germany" accepted in the World press after World War II, after the creation of two German states in 1949 changed into two commonly used terms: "Democratic Germany" (GDR) and "Federal Germany" (FRG).

After 1949 the concept "Germany" ceased to be geographically, and politically unequivocal. The First Secretary of the Communist Party of the GDR, Erich Honecker stated in an interview for the *New York Times* on Nov. 23, 1972:

"History has already pronounced its verdict in favor of the existence of two separate German States . . . and this is to the world's benefit."

A. KLAFKOWSKI, *The Legal Effects of World War II and the German Problem*, Warsaw, 1968; M. SCHNITZER, *East and West Germany. A Comparative Economic Analysis*, London, 1972, 470 pp.; E. HONECKER, "On Germany", in: *New York Times*, November 23, 1972; M. WOLFFSOHN, *Deutsch-Israelische Beziehungen*, München, 1986; J. SKIBIŃSKI, *Sprawa Traktatu Pokoju z Niemcami po II wojnie światowej, [The Case of Peace Treaty with Germany after the II World War]*, Warsaw, 1986; E.C. FREY, *Division and Détente: The Germanies and Their Alliances*, New York, 1987; H.A. TURNER Jr., *The Two Germany's since 1945*, New Haven, 1987; W. SCHAUBLE, "Relations Between the Two States in Germany: Problems and Prospects", in: *International Affairs*, London, Spring, 1988.

GERMANY, 1871–1945.
The German state in three formations:

(1) German Reich, Deutsches Reich, restored on Jan. 1, 1871 under the sceptre of the Prussian Hohenzollerns as a constitutional empire (constitution of Apr. 16, 1871). The capital of Prussia, Berlin, also became the capital of the Reich.

The total area of the Reich was 540,800 sq. km and was composed of Prussia (348,700 sq. km), Bavaria (75,800 sq. km), Württemberg (19,000 sq. km), Alsace-Lorraine (14,500 sq. km), Hessen (7600 sq. km), Oldenburg (6400 sq. km), and the smaller territorial duchies of Anhalt, Brunswick, Lippe, Mecklemburg-Strelitz, Neuss, Sachsen-Altenburg, Sachsen-Coburg-Gotha, Sachsen-Meiningen, Sachsen-Weimar, Schwarzburg-Rudolfstadt, Schwarzburg-Sonderhausen and Waldeck, and three small free cities: Bremen, Hamburg and Lübeck.

The pop. of the Reich was 41 million in 1871 (Prussia 25 m); *c*. 56 m, in 1900 (Prussia 34 m.); and *c*. 66.5 m, in 1910 (Prussia 40 m.). In international politics the Reich of the Hohenzollerns belonged to the major European powers along with Russia, Great Britain, France and Austria–Hungary; it was responsible for preparing and initiating World War I, 1914–18, and fell as a result of military defeat and a social revolution. Kaiser Wilhelm II and a number of his high-ranking officials and military leaders were charged with violating international treaties (▷ *Papierfetzen*) and with ▷ War crimes. Due to the opposition of the president of the USA, W. Wilson, and other circumstances, no trial was held. The Kaiser abdicated on Nov. 9, 1918 and went into exile in Holland. Two days later, in the name of the provisional government of the Reich, M. Erzberger, leader of the Catholic Centrum Party, signed the surrender of the Reich to the Powers of the Entente in Compiègne.

(2) A Republic, proclaimed in Berlin on Nov. 9, 1918 by the forces of the revolution, was established on the basis of a constitution ratified by the National Assembly in Weimar on Aug. 11, 1919. Earlier, on June 28, 1919 the Republic signed the ▷ Versailles Peace Treaty, which imposed a number of international obligations on Germany and established new boundaries for the German state. After the establishment of new boundaries with France, Belgium, Denmark, Poland, Lithuania and Czechoslovakia in 1919–24 the area of the Weimar Republic in 1925 was 472,000 sq. km with 62 million inhabitants. The Republic retained the name Deutsches Reich and became a union of "free states", in which the Prussian state continued to be dominant (293,000 sq. km with 38 million inhabitants); the remaining "free states" – Anhalt, Baden, Bavaria, Brunswick, Hessen, Lippe, Mecklemburg-Schwerin, Mecklemburg-Strelitz, Oldenburg, Saxony, Schaumberg-Lippe, Thuringia, Waldeck, Württemberg and the "free cities" which took the name "city republics" (Stadtrepublik): Bremen, Hamburg and Lübeck. In 1926 the Weimar Republic was accepted into the League of Nations. In foreign policy successive, politically diverse governments followed the same line of gradually freeing the Republic from the obligations of the Versailles Treaty and waging a diplomatic and political campaign in support of a "peaceful revision of the eastern boundaries". This excited nationalistic sentiments, primarily anti-Czech and anti-Polish, and facilitated imperialistic propaganda for the "living space in the East" (*Lebensraum*), which had the effect of strengthening the Right, led by the National Socialist German Workers' Party, ▷ NSDAP; the accession to power of A. Hitler, leader of this Party, on Jan. 30, 1933 closed the Weimar period of the German Reich.

(3) The Nazi Reich or the German III Reich played a sinister role in the history of Europe, the world and the German nation. The history of the III Reich belongs to the history of ▷ crimes against humanity and ▷ war crimes and war criminals. It was ended by unconditional surrender, the occupation of Germany by the victorious powers, the liquidation of ▷ Prussia, and the fixing of the eastern ethnic and state boundaries of Germany on the Oder and Lusatian Neisse by the ▷ Potsdam Agreement, 1945. In place of the German Reich, two German states arose: the German Democratic Republic and the Federal Republic of Germany. On the 25th anniversary of the unconditional surrender of the III Reich, the President of the FRG, Gustav Heinemann, stated that:

"In view of the enormous crimes which the National Socialists perpetrated and which brought poverty, suffering and senseless death to many millions of people from many nations, it is useless to lament over what has been lost."

The Chancellor of the FRG, W. Brandt, however, reminded the deputies of the Bundestag that:

"What in those days 25 years ago many Germans, apart from their own personal misfortune, regarded as a national disaster, for other nations was liberation from foreign domination, terror and fear."

"Treaty of Peace with Germany (Versailles)", in: *International Conciliation*, No. 142, September 1919; *Deutsche Geschichte in Daten*, Berlin, 1967; *Die bürgerlichen Parteien in Deutschland 1830–1945*, Handbuch, Bd. 1, Leipzig, 1968, Bd. 2, 1970; M. WOJCIECHOWSKI, *Die polnisch-deutschen Beziehungen 1933–38*, Leiden, 1971; G.F. KENNAN, *The Decline of Bismarck's European Order*, New York, 1979; E. SCHULZ, *Die deutsche Nation in Europa*, Bonn, 1982.

GERMANY AND THE GREAT POWERS. During and after World War I Germany became the main problem of the Allied Powers, which fought against the Reich of the Hohenzollerns and then by the ▷ Versailles Peace Treaty 1919 obligated Germany to demilitarization and repatriations. During World War II the problem of Germany was posed again on Aug. 14, 1941 by Great Britain and the USA in the ▷ Atlantic Charter and on Sept. 24, 1941 by the USSR in a Declaration supporting the wording of the Charter. The next war documents of the Great Powers concerning Germany were the ▷ United Nations Declaration of Jan. 1, 1942; ▷ War Crimes Moscow Declaration of Nov. 1, 1943; Teheran Declaration of Dec. 1, 1943 (Teheran Conference 1943); ▷ Yalta Declaration on Germany of Feb. 11, 1945; and the ▷ Germany, Declaration on the Defeat of, June 5, 1945. This last document was preceded by work of the Consultative Commission of the USA, Great Britain, and the USSR in London, Sept. 12 and Nov. 14, 1944, which drafted the statute for the occupation of Germany and an initial plan for three zones of occupation, expanded on May 1, 1945 with a French zone. After the unconditional surrender of Germany on May 8, 1945, for the first time Germany was left without any political authority, which passed entirely to the military commanders of the Four Powers occupying Germany. On June 5, 1945 they formed the ▷ Allied Control Council for Germany in Berlin and completed the final delimitation of the occupational zones of Germany and the occupational sectors of ▷ Berlin. The Soviet sector comprised five lands: Mecklemburg, Brandenburg, Thuringia, Saxony, and Anhalt Saxony. The American zone comprised Bavaria, North Baden, Hessen-Nassau, North Württemberg and the port of Bremen. The British zone comprised Lower Saxony, Rhineland, Westphalia, Lippe-Detmold, Schleswig-Holstein, Hamburg, Oldenburg, Brunswick and Hannover. The French zone comprised the Bavarian Palatinate. South Rhineland, South Baden, and Württemberg-Hohenzollern. The Allied Control Council resolved that the historical formations (*Länder*) of the German state would be retained in the reconstruction of German administration with the exception of one state, Prussia, which was liquidated completely and for all time by Law No. 46 of the Council, Feb. 25, 1947. This was in accordance with the basic document of the Great Powers, the Potsdam Treaty of Aug. 2, 1945. The common administration of occupied Germany by the Council of the Four Powers lasted from June 5, 1945 to Mar. 20, 1948, when it suspended its activities. Since Jan. 1, 1947 the American and British zones were formed into a so-called Bi-zone and since Jan. 1, 1948 along with the French zone of occupation into a so-called Tri-zone, which on June 18, 1948 received its own monetary system. After this economic separation, a political separation followed with the transformation of the Tri-zone on Sept. 7, 1949 into the Federal Republic of Germany.

The German Democratic Republic was established on Oct. 7, 1949. The existence of two German states did not free the Great Powers from responsibilities accepted in quadrilateral treaties on Germany. The "state of war with Germany" was ended by the Western Powers on July 9, 1951 with a declaration directed exclusively to the government of the FRG. The USSR on Jan. 1, 1955 announced a Declaration on the ending of the war with Germany and began negotiations with the FRG, which on Oct. 13, 1955 led to the exchange of ambassadors and the release by the USSR of the remainder of the German war prisoners. The USSR in the period 1955–72 was the only power which maintained diplomatic relations with both German states. The USSR on Jan. 31, 1959 proposed to the Western Powers, Poland, Czechoslovakia, the FRG and GDR the calling of an International Conference for Drafting a Peace Treaty. The debate on this proposal of the Ministers of Foreign Affairs of the Four Powers in Geneva, May 11–June 20 and July 13–Aug. 5, 1959, failed to reach an understanding. The USSR on June 12, 1964 signed a Treaty of Friendship, Mutual Assistance and Co-operation with the GDR which stated that "three independent political organisms" exist on the territory of Germany: the FRG, the GDR and West Berlin. The Premier of the USSR, A.N. Kosygin, during his official visit to France warned the government of the FRG:

"The Federal Republic of Germany should understand once and for all that the frontiers of the German Democratic Republic are inviolable; the FRG can assist *détente* if it recognizes the realities of the European situation; two German States exist, and there is no power in the world which is able to change this."

As a result of diplomatic negotiations between the powers, from 1968 to 1969 coming to the fore was the conception of normalization of relations in Europe through the recognition of the inviolability of the existing frontiers of sovereign states, the acceptance of both German states into the UN and the formulation of a more precise statute for West Berlin. During the same period the first Christian Democratic and Social Democratic coalition government began to consider a new Eastern policy, which was developed by the next coalition of Social Democrats and Free Democrats, called ▷ Ostpolitik. In 1970 the FRG signed normalization treaties with the USSR and Poland. This in turn enabled the Four Powers to draft treaties on West Berlin. At the end of 1973 and beginning of 1974, all of the powers were in diplomatic contact with the FRG and GDR, which on the recommendation of the Great Powers were accepted into the UN in Sept., 1973. At the same time, in accordance with their interpower treaties the Four Powers retained their rights and responsibilities with respect to Germany in the legal–international sense. This means that any changes whatever of the status quo of the three political organisms – the FRG, GDR and West Berlin – which were formed on the territory of Germany delineated by the Potsdam resolutions require the agreement of all Four Powers.

The chronology of conferences on Germany called by the Four Powers, the Western Powers, or the USSR and its allies:

(1) Conference at the summit of the heads of government of the UK, USA and USSR, July 17–Aug. 2, 1945, in Potsdam, the so-called ▷ Potsdam Conference.

(2) The London Conference of the Ministers of Foreign Affairs of the Four Powers on the question of the permanent demilitarization of Germany, Sept. 10–Oct. 2, 1945.

(3) The Paris Conference of the Four Powers on the question of repatriations, Nov. 9, 1945–Jan. 16, 1946.

(4) The Paris Conference of the Ministers of Foreign Affairs of the Four Powers on the question of the economic and political future of Germany, Apr. 25–July 12, 1946.

(5) The Moscow Conference, Mar. 10–Apr. 24, 1947, and the London Conference, Nov. 25–Dec. 15, 1947, of the Ministers of Foreign Affairs of the Four Powers on the interpretation of the points concerning Germany of the Yalta and Potsdam treaties.

(6) The London Conference of the three Western Powers and Belgium, Holland and Luxembourg, Feb. 23–Mar. 6, 1948, on the question of forming a Western state and including the Tri-zone in the ▷ Marshall Plan.

(7) The Warsaw Conference of the Ministers of Foreign Affairs of the USSR and the European people's democracies, June 23–24, 1948, concerning the development of a dangerous situation in the Western zones of occupied Germany.

(8) The Washington Conference, Apr. 5–8, 1949, of the Western Powers with the German representatives of the Tri-zone on the question of a new statute for occupied Germany, signed on June 20, 1949.

(9) The Paris Conference, May 23–June 20, 1949, of the Ministers of Foreign Affairs of the Four Powers on the question of Germany and Berlin.

(10) The Paris Conference, Nov. 9–11, 1949, of the Ministers of Foreign Affairs of France, Great Britain, the USA and the Benelux states on the question of accepting the FRG into West European organizations.

(11) The London Conference, May 11–13, 1950, of the Ministers of Foreign Affairs of the Western powers of the integration of the FRG into the Atlantic Community.

(12) The New York Conference, Sept. 12–19, 1950, of the Ministers of Foreign Affairs of the Western powers on the question of the international position of the FRG:

"The governments of France, the UK and USA consider the FRG, until the time of the reunification of Germany, as the only free and legally formed State, which, as a consequence, has the right to speak on the international forum as the representative of the German nation in the name of Germany."

This thesis, which was in accord with the so-called ▷ Hallstein doctrine, was confirmed on Oct. 3, 1954 by the London Declaration of the Western powers and on Oct. 23, 1954 in Protocol B p. 2 of the Paris treaties by the remaining NATO members.

(13) The Prague Conference, Oct. 20–21, 1950, of the Ministers of Foreign Affairs of the USSR and the people's democracies on the question of a Peace Treaty with Germany and the formation of a Constitutional Council to be composed of delegates of the FRG and GDR in equal representation for the purpose of establishing a temporary government for Germany. The Proposal was rejected by the Western powers on Dec. 22, 1950.

(14) The Paris Conference, Mar. 5–June 21, 1951, of the Ministers of Foreign Affairs of the Four Powers on the question of the unification of Germany; without results.

(15) The Washington Conference, Sept. 10–14, 1951, of the Ministers of Foreign Affairs of the Western Powers on the integration of the FRG into the Western defense system.

(16) The Berlin Conference, Jan. 25–Feb. 18, 1954, of the Ministers of Foreign Affairs of the Four Powers on the question of a Soviet plan for a Peace Treaty with Germany (submitted in Soviet notes to France, Great Britain and the USA on Mar. 10, 1952, as the first step on the road to the unification of Germany and on the question of the British proposal, so-called ▷ Eden Plan, for the unification of Germany as the first step on the road to conclud-

ing a Peace Treaty with Germany; ended with complete divergence in the positions of the East and West.

(17) The Paris Conference, Oct. 19–23, 1954, of the NATO members on ending the occupational regime in the FRG (Paris Treaties of Oct. 23, 1954) and the integration of the FRG within NATO, from May 9, 1955.

(18) The Moscow Conference, Dec. 2, 1954, of the USSR and the people's democracies on the question of European Security in connection with the remilitarization of the FRG.

(19) The Geneva Conference at the summit of the heads of government of the Four Powers, July 18–23, 1955, on the question of world politics, i.a. on the unification of Germany. The responsibility of the Four Powers for solving German problems was reconfirmed.

(20) The Geneva Conference, Oct. 27–Nov. 14 and Nov. 8–16, 1955, of the Ministers of Foreign Affairs of the Four Powers for the purpose of implementing the recommendations of the conference of heads of government. Without results.

(21) The London UN Conference on disarmament, Mar. 19–May 5, 1956 and Mar. 18–Sept. 6, 1957, i.a. on the question of the demilitarization of Germany. Without results.

(22) The Moscow Conference of the States of the Warsaw Pact, May 20–23, 1958, on the question of a nonaggression treaty between the members of the Warsaw Pact and NATO and a declaration stating that the unification of Germany is not a problem of the Four Powers but exclusively that of the two German states: the FRG and GDR.

(23) The Warsaw Conference, Apr. 27–28, 1959, of the member states of the Warsaw Pact, with the presence of a representative of the People's Republic of China, on the question of a Soviet proposal for a Peace Treaty with Germany, submitted in notes from the government of the USSR on Jan. 10, 1959 and on the question of a counterproposal of the Western powers, submitted Feb. 16, 1959.

(24) The Paris Conference of the Ministers of Foreign Affairs of the Western Powers and the FRG, Apr. 29–30, 1959, on the question of a Peace Treaty with Germany.

(25) The Geneva Conference of the Ministers of Foreign Affairs of the Four Powers in the presence of consultative delegations of the FRG and GDR, May 11–June 20 and July 13–Aug. 5, 1959, on the question of a Peace Treaty with Germany. Without results.

(26) The Washington Conference of the Ministers of Foreign Affairs of the Western powers and the FRG, Sept. 14–15, 1961, on West Berlin as a result of the construction by the GDR of a frontier wall called the Berlin Wall, on Aug. 13, 1961.

(27) The Paris Conference of the Ministers of Foreign Affairs of the Western powers, Dec. 11–12, 1961, on the question of negotiations with the USSR over the solution of German problems.

(28) The Bucharest Conference, Aug. 4–6, 1966, of the states of the Warsaw Pact on the question of the necessity for resolving German problems on the basis of the existence of two German states.

(29) The Paris Conference of the Ministers of Foreign Affairs of the Western powers and the FRG, Dec. 14–16, 1966, on the question of a common policy with respect to the solution of German problems.

(30) The Budapest Conference, Mar. 16–17, 1969, of the member states of the Warsaw Pact on security and co-operation in Europe (▷ Budapest Appeal, 1969).

(31) The Washington Conference in Apr., 1969 and the Brussels Conference in Dec., 1969 of the NATO member states for the purpose of taking a common position on the Budapest proposals of the Warsaw Pact states, especially on the question of the recognition of the inviolability of the existing frontiers and recognizing the existence of two German states.

(32) The Rome Conference, May 26–27, 1970, of the Western powers and the FRG on the question of negotiations of the FRG with the USSR and Poland.

(33) The Moscow Conference of Aug. 20, 1970 of the heads of government of the states of the Warsaw Pact recognizing the conclusion of the treaty between the USSR and FRG on Aug. 12, 1970 on the inviolability of frontiers in Europe, including the frontiers of Poland and the frontier between the FRG and GDR.

(34) The Brussels Conference of the NATO member states, Dec. 3–4, 1970, on the question of the Helsinki Conference on Security and Co-operation in Europe and the question of West Berlin.

(35) Berlin negotiations, Mar. 26, 1970–Aug. 23, 1971, between the Four Powers and the FRG, GDR, and the Senate of West Berlin, ending after 33 sessions with the signing of an agreement on West Berlin on Sept. 3, 1971 in the building of the former Allied Control Council for Germany in Berlin at Potsdammer Strasse.

(36) The Prague Conference, Jan. 25–26, 1972, of the heads of government of the states of the Warsaw Pact drafted a declaration on peace, security and co-operation in Europe, recognizing the situation which arose after the treaties of the FRG with the USSR of Aug. 12, 1970 and with Poland of Dec. 7, 1970 and after the Four-Power understanding of Sept. 3, 1971.

(37) The Bonn Conference of the Ministers of Foreign Affairs of the Western powers and the FRG, May 29, 1972, devoted to German problems after the ratification of treaties with the USSR and Poland.

(38) The Brussels Conference, Dec. 6, 1972, of the Ministers of Foreign Affairs of the Western powers and the FRG on the question of the FRG–GDR treaty ready for signing (ratified on May 11, 1973 by the Bundestag) concerning the diplomatic recognition of the GDR by the Western powers and the acceptance of both German states into the UN in 1973.

(39) The visit of a member of the Presidium of the Supreme Soviet of the USSR, Secretary General of the Central Committee of the Communist Party of the USSR, L.I. Brezhnev, to the FRG, May 18–22, 1973, at the invitation of Chancellor W. Brandt, ending with the statement that both sides regard the treaty of Aug. 12, 1970 as an historic stage in relations between the USSR and the FRG and in the development of the entire situation in Europe.

(40) On the day before the spring session of the Atlantic Council in Copenhagen, June 13, 1971, the traditional conference of the Ministers of Foreign Affairs and the FRG on the question of German problems (the shortest – lasted 20 minutes).

(41) Final Act of the Helsinki Conference on Security and Co-operation in Europe, Aug. 2, 1975, with the participation of the Four Great Powers and Canada and 29 European states, including both German States: the FRG and GDR.

B. MEISSNER, *Russland, die Westmächte und Deutschland. Die sowjetische Deutschlandpolitik 1943–53*, Hamburg, 1954; B. RUHM (ed.), *Documents on Germany under Occupation 1945–1954*, London, 1955; M.E. BATHURST, J.L. SIMPSON, *Germany and the North-Atlantic Community. A Legal Survey*, London, 1956; E. JACKEL, *Die deutsche Frage 1952–56. Notenwechsel und Konferenzdokumente der vier Mächte*, Frankfurt am M., 1957; *The Truth about Western Policy on the German Question*, Moscow–Berlin, 1959; *Documents on Germany 1944–1959*, Washington, DC, 1959; K. JASPERS, *Freiheit und Wiedervereinigung*, München, 1960; H.J. MORGENT-HAU, "The problem of German reunification", in: *The Annals*, Philadelphia 1960; W. CORNIDES, *Die Weltmächte und Deutschland. Geschichte der jüngsten Vergangenheit 1945–55*, Tübingen, 1961; E. DAUER-LEIN, *Die Einheit Deutschlands. Die Erörterungen und Entscheidungen der Kriegs- und Nachkriegskonferenzen 1941–1949. Darstellung und Dokumente*, Frankfurt am M., 1961; H. SIEGLER, *Dokumentation zur Deutschlandfrage von der Atlantik-Charta 1941 bis zur Berlin-Sperre 1961*, Berlin, 1962; F. WERNER, *Reunification and West German–Soviet Relations*, The Hague, 1963; G. MOLTMAN, *Die Entwicklung Deutschlands von 1949 bis zu den Pariser Verträgen 1955*, Hannover, 1963; K. DOEHRING, H. MOSLER, *Die Beendigung der Kriegszustandes mit Deutschland nach dem II Weltkrieg*, Köln, 1963; P.A. NIKOLAEV, *Politika SShA, Anglii i Frantsyi w germanskom voprosie 1945–54*, Moskva, 1964; *Documents on German Foreign Policy 1918–1945*, Washington, DC, 1965; F.H. HARTMAN, *Germany between East and West. The Reunification Problem*, New York, 1965; W.W. SCHÜTZ, *Reform der Deutschlandpolitik*, Köln, 1965; F.J. STRAUSS, *The Grand Design. A European Solution to German Reunification*, New York, 1965; G.W. HEINEMAN, *Verfehlte Deutschlandpolitik*, Frankfurt am M., 1966; P. ROHR, *Faut-il réunifier l'Allemagne?*, Bruxelles, 1966; *Die Spaltung Deutschlands und der Weg zur Wiedervereinigung. Ein dokumentarischer Abriss*, Dresden, 1966; M. SALEWSKI, *Entwaffnung und Militärkontrolle in Deutschland 1919–1927*, München, 1966; A.A. GALKIN, D.J. MELNIKOV, *SSSR, Zapadniye derzhavy i germanski vopros, 1945–1965*, Moskva, 1966; W.W. SCHÜTZ, *Rethinking German Policy. New Approaches to Reunification*, New York, 1967; K.P. TUDYKA, *Das Geteilte Deutschland. Eine Dokumentation der Meinungen*, Stuttgart, 1967; F.A. VALI, *The Quest for a United Germany*, Baltimore, 1967; CH.R. PLANCK, *The Changing Status of German Reunification in Western Diplomacy, 1955–1966*, Baltimore, 1967; F. FISHER, *Germany's Aims in the First World War*, New York, 1967; K. JASPERS, *The Future of Germany*, London, 1967; G. WETTIG, *Entmilitarisierung und Wiederwaffnung in Deutschland 1943–1955*, München, 1967; E. HEIDEMANN, K. WOHLGEMUTH, *Zur Deutschlandpolitik der Anti-Hitler-Koalition (1943–1949)*, Berlin, 1968; A. KLAFKOWSKI, *The Legal Effects of the II World War and the German Problem*, Warsaw, 1968; A. GROSSER, *Germany in our Time, A Political History of the Postwar years*, New York, 1971; F.R. WILLIS, *France, Germany and the New Europe, 1945–1963*, Stanford, Calif., 1972.

GERMANY AND THE UN. Art. 107 of the UN Charter excluded the problems of Germany from the competence of the UN, leaving them to the Great Powers to settle. Nonetheless, problems of Germany were a subject of debate in the UN General Assembly:

(1) The Western powers sponsored a resolution in the UN General Assembly which was adopted on Dec. 20, 1951 by 45 votes in favor and 6 against (the Byelorussian SSR, Czechoslovakia, Israel, Poland, Ukrainian SSR and USSR) with 7 abstentions (Afghanistan, Argentina, Burma, India, Sweden, Yemen, and Yugoslavia), on forming a UN Investigative Commission on elections in Germany, composed of representatives from Brazil, Holland, Iceland, Pakistan, and Poland, with the task of "ascertaining whether the existing situation in Germany permits the carrying out of truly free and secret elections." Poland announced that it would not take part in the Commission, which it considered contrary to art. 107 of the UN Charter. The USSR stated that: "The UN General Assembly does not have the right to intervene in the internal affairs of Germany . . . only the four powers have the right to make such investigations as they commonly regard as proper." In this situation the Commission adjourned on Aug. 5, 1952 *sine die*.

(2) Within the framework of the disarmament proclamation examined by the UN, i.a. the Polish Minister of Foreign Affairs, A. Rapacki, submitted the plan of his government on Oct. 2, 1957 to the

UN General Assembly for the denuclearization of the area of the FRG, GDR, Czechoslovakia, and Poland (▷ Rapacki Plan).

(3) In 1959 the USSR presented to the UN a draft project for demilitarization of Berlin and converting it to a free city under the aegis of the United Nations. The Western Powers rejected the idea.

(4) Since the X Session of the UN General Assembly, 1955, several delegations, including the Warsaw Pact countries, have called attention to the danger to the peace of Europe and the world of the remilitarization and unimpeded rebirth of Nazism and racialism in the FRG. In 1967 the General Assembly condemned neo-Nazism in the FRG. A separate problem in the UN was a law in the FRG on the expiration of war crimes, which ended with the drafting by the UN International Law Commission of a ▷ War Crimes Convention on the Non-applicability of Statutory Limitation to War Crimes and Crimes against Humanity, 1968.

(5) In 1955 a permanent observer at the UN from the FRG was accredited. The GDR observer at the UN was accredited in 1972, after the GDR became, like the FRG before, a member of specialized UN organizations (a UN rule is, since 1955, that the observer status can be accepted only to a country, which is a member of one UN specialized organization).

(6) Debated since 1964 was the question of membership of the FRG and GDR into the UN. The matter was resolved by a Declaration of the Four Powers of Nov. 9, 1972, stating that they would support the applications for UN membership of both the FRG and GDR, stipulating that:

"this membership in no way infringes on the rights and responsibilities of the four powers and competencies concerning four power agreements, decisions, and practices."

The NATO Council on Dec. 8, 1972 stipulated that:

"The Declaration of Nov. 9, 1972 in no way concerns conventions on the questions of relations of the three powers with the FRG and related conventions and documents of May 26, 1952 in the version published on Oct. 23, 1954."

The UN Security Council on June 22, 1973 unanimously recommended to the UN General Assembly the acceptance of the FRG and GDR into the UN, which formally took place on Sept. 26, 1973.

UN Bulletin, January 15 and March 15, 1952; *UN Review*, November, 1962; A. ALBANO MÜLLER, *Der Deutschland-Artikel in der Satzung der Vereinten Nationen*, Stuttgart, 1967; *Die DDR und die Vereinten Nationen*, Dresden, 1968; *UN Monthly Chronicle*, January, 1968; R.L. BLEDSOE, B.A. BOCZEK, *The International Law Dictionary*, Oxford, 1987.

GERMANY, DECLARATION ON THE DEFEAT OF, 1945. A Declaration signed on June 5, 1945, in Berlin on behalf of the USA by Gen. D.D. Eisenhower, the USSR by Marshall G.K. Zhukov, Great Britian by Marshall B.L. Montgomery, France by Gen. J. de Lattre de Tassigny; it announced the total defeat of the German III Reich and the submission of Germany to the supreme authority of the governments of the Four Powers. The Preamble read as follows:

"The German armed forces on land, at sea and in the air have been completely defeated and have surrendered unconditionally, and Germany, which bears responsibility for the war, is no longer capable of resisting the will of the victorious Powers. The unconditional surrender of Germany has thereby been effected, and Germany has become subject to such requirements as may now or hereafter be imposed upon her.
There is no central Government or authority in Germany capable of accepting responsibility for the maintenance of order, the administration of the

country, and compliance with the requirements of the victorious Powers.
It is in these circumstances necessary, without prejudice to any subsequent decisions that may be taken respecting Germany, to make provisions for the cessation of any further hostilities on the part of the German armed forces, for the maintenance of order in Germany and for the administration of the country, and to announce the immediate requirements with which Germany must comply.
The Representatives of the Supreme Commands of the United Kingdom, the United States of America, the Union of Soviet Socialist Republics and the French Republic, hereinafter called the 'Allied Representatives', acting by authority of their respective Governments and in the interests of the United Nations, accordingly make the following Declaration: The Governments of the United Kingdom, the United States of America and the Union of Soviet Socialist Republics, and the Provisional Government of the French Republic, hereby assume supreme authority with respect to Germany, including all the powers possessed by the German Government, the High Command and any state, municipal, or local government or authority. The assumption, for the purposes stated above, of the said authority and powers does not affect the annexation of Germany.
The Governments of the United Kingdom, the United States of America and the Union of Soviet Socialist Republics, and the Provisional Government of the French Republic, will hereafter determine the boundaries of Germany or any part thereof and the status of Germany or of any area at present being part of German territory."

The Declaration provided for "demands resulting from the total defeat and unconditional surrender of Germany" with which Germany had to comply. The demands concerned entire demilitarization and denazification of Germany, Germany's duty to deliver all imprisoned or interned persons to the United Nations, delivery of all war criminals and the obligation to render all necessary assistance to the occupation authorities.
On the same day the governments of the Four Powers made the following supplementary statement to the Declaration on the defeat of Germany:
(1) a declaration on control procedures in Germany which appointed the ▷ Allied Control Council for Germany;
(2) a declaration on supreme authority over Germany, closing with a promise by the Four Powers that "it is our intention to consult the governments of other United Nations in the matter of exercise of this authority;"
(3) a declaration that for the purpose of occupation Germany would be divided into four zones. Each zone would be offered to one of the Four Powers. Furthermore, the Declaration determined that:

"the area of Greater Berlin will be occupied by forces of each of the powers. In order to exercise joint government an Allied Command will be appointed."

Selected Documents on Germany and the Question of Berlin 1944–1961, HMSO, London, December, 1961, p. 38–48.

GERMANY, FEDERAL REPUBLIC OF. Member of the UN. Bundesrepublik Deutschland. State in W. Central Europe on the North and Baltic Sea. Borders with Denmark, the GDR, Czechoslovakia, Austria, Switzerland, France, Luxembourg, Belgium and Holland. Area: 248,690 sq. km. Pop.: 1987 est. 61,082,800 (1981 est. 61,666,000) (census in the same area: 1939 – 40,248,000; 1946 – 43,694,000; 1950 – 47,522,000; 1960 – 56,174,826; 1970 – 60,650,599; Capital: Bonn with 292,200 inhabitants in 1981. GNP per capita in 1987: US $14,460. Official language: German. Currency: one Deutsche Mark = 100 pfennigs. National Day: not established.

Member of the UN from Sept. 26, 1973 and of all UN specialized agencies. Member of the OECD, EEC, NATO and the Council of Europe.
International relations: the western part of Germany was occupied after the unconditional surrender of the Reich on May 8, 1945 by American, British and French forces and divided into three zones of occupation, subject to the Allied Control Council for Germany until the suspension of its activity on Mar. 20, 1948, after which control was exercised exclusively by the military commanders of the American, British and French forces; the state was formed in stages by combining the American and British zones into a so-called Bi-zone on Jan. 1, 1947, then the fusion of three zones by the Marshall Plan on Apr. 16, 1948 and a currency reform (introducing a new currency, the Deutsche Mark) on June 21, 1948; and finally, the economic fusion of the Bi-zone with the French zone (so-called Tri-zone) on Apr. 8, 1949. A Parliamentary Council (Parlamentarischer Rat) was formed for the purpose of drawing up a constitution for the West German state; on Sept. 3, 1948 it began deliberations in Bonn on an "All-German Constitution". On May 10, 1949 the Council resolved that the "temporary capital" of the Federal Republic of Germany would be Bonn; the Constitution (*Grundgesetz*) was ratified on May 23, 1949. The West German Basic Law approved by the Western powers in art. 116 also contained a point whereby West Germany represents "all of Germany" within the frontiers of the Reich of Dec. 31, 1937. The remilitarization of West Germany formally took place on May 9, 1955 with the admission of the FRG to NATO. Up to that time, from Sept. 21, 1949 to May 5, 1955, the Occupation Statute was in effect, modified by the ending of the "state of war with Germany" by Great Britain in July 9, 1951, France on July 13, 1951 and the USA on Oct. 19, 1951; and also by the Bonn Treaty of May 2, 1952, the so-called "General Treaty" (*Generalvertrag*), recognizing the FRG as an independent state "representing the entire German people." This thesis, which denied the existence of the GDR, in accordance with the so-called ▷ Hallstein Doctrine, was repeated in Protocol B, No. 2, to the Paris Treaties, which were signed on Oct. 23, 1954 with a validity to May 5, 1955 following which the Occupation Statute was abolished and the FRG was granted the status of a sovereign state, with the Western powers retaining rights and responsibilities in areas pertaining to Four-Powers agreements; these treaties also defined the role of the FRG in the West European Union and NATO. The normalization treaties with the USSR were signed on Aug. 10, 1970, with Poland on Dec. 7, 1970 (both ratified by the Bundestag on May 17, 1972) and, following an agreement of the Four Powers on the question of Berlin, on Sept. 3, 1971 (signed June 3, 1972), a normalization GDR–FRG Treaty was signed on Dec. 21, 1972 (ratified by the Bundestag on June 18, 1973). With the FRG's recognition of a second German state in this document, the NATO Council on Dec. 8, 1973 resolved that "NATO member states could individually establish bilateral relations with the GDR." Earlier, on Nov. 9, 1972, the Four Great Powers had made a declaration that they would support the applications of the GDR and the FRG for admission to the UN in the Security Council and acted accordingly; thus on Sept. 26, 1973 both the FRG and the GDR became members of the UN. Besides this, the FRG is a member of all UN specialized organizations. Member of NATO, EEC and other agencies of the European community.
On Feb. 9, 1976 a treaty was signed in Bonn by the government of the FRG and NATO Command, establishing the principles according to which Bun-

G

deswehr forces in NATO would be commanded in case of war. On Jan. 6, 1979 Chancellor H. Schmidt participated in the first summit conference of the Western Big Four: France, the FRG, the UK and USA in Guadeloupe. In Dec. 1979 the government of the FRG gave its consent to the location on the territory of the FRG of atomic missiles of Cruise and Pershing II types, effective to 1982, in accordance with a resolution of that same day by the NATO Council, supported by the government of the FRG. On Oct. 26, 1984 the FRG foreign minister, H.D. Genscher, stated in the general debate of the UN General Assembly: "The treaties concluded between my country and our Eastern neighbors in the seventies cleared the way for the CSCE. We stand by every word of these treaties. The Federal Republic of Germany respects the territorial integrity of all States in their present boundaries. It proceeds from the existing situation in Europe. It makes no territorial claims on anyone and will not do so in future either. It considers the borders of all States to be inviolable and will continue to do so." On Mar. 27, 1986 the FRG and the USA signed in Washington an agreement on the participation of non-governmental German firms in ▷ SDI research. The FRG population, according to an official prognosis, will decline from 56,6 million in 1985 to 54,9 million in the year 2000 and 42 million by 2300. The FRG since 1970 has had the lowest birth rate of any country in the world.

See also ▷ World Heritage UNESCO List.

Verträge der Bundesrepublik Deutschland, Berlin, 1955; E. DAUERLEIN, *CDU/CSU 1945–1957,* Köln, 1957; H. KLUTH, *Die KPD in der Bundesrepublik, 1945–1956,* Köln, 1959; H. BERGSTRASSER, *Geschichte der politischen Parteien in Deutschland,* München, 1960; H. GROEGE, F. MUNCH, E. PUTTKAMER, *Die Bundesrepublik Deutschland und die Vereinten Nationen,* München, 1966; M.S. VOSLENSKII, *Vostochnaya politika FRG,* Moskva, 1967; *Auswärtiges Amt der BDR, Die Auswärtige Politik der Bundesrepublik Deutschland,* Köln, 1972; *Volksrepublik Polen – Bundesrepublik Deutschland. Probleme der Normalisierung gegenseitiger Beziehungen. Texte und Documente,* Poznań, 1972; G.K. ROBERTS, *West German Politics,* London, 1972; K. DEUTSCHKRON, *Bonn et Jerusalem,* Paris, 1973; H.P. SCHWARTZ (ed.), *Handbuch der deutschen Aussenpolitik,* Zürich, 1975; SIPRI, *World Armaments and Disarmament Yearbooks 1968–1980;* W.I. KOHL, G. GASEVI, *West Germany. A European and Global Power,* London, 1982; *The Europa Year Book 1984. A World Survey,* Vol. I, pp. 496–537, London, 1984; *Statement by the Minister for Foreign Affairs of the FRG, Hans Dietrich Genscher at the 39th Session of the General Assembly of the UN,* New York, Sept. 26, 1984; D.S. and J.E. DETWILLER, *West Germany,* Oxford, 1987.

GERMANY, OCCUPATION STATUTE OF THE THREE WESTERN ZONES OF GERMANY, 1949 AND THE TERMINATION 1954.

The Western Allied Powers signed in Washington DC, Apr. 8, 1949, a memorandum on the Principles Governing Exercise of Powers and Responsibilities of US–UK–French governments following establishment of the German Federal Republic "the function of the Allies shall be mainly supervisory" and the Occupation Status defining the Powers to be retained by the Occupation Authorities:

"Art. 1. . . . the German people shall enjoy self-government to the maximum possible degree consistent with such occupation."

"Art. 2. . . . The Occupation Authorities specificallly reserved the rights to control the disarmament and demilitarization, the Ruhr, restitution, repatriations, decartelization, foreign affairs, foreign trade and exchange."

The occupation status was announced May 12, with a validity from Sept. 21, 1949. This statute was modified Mar. 6, 1951 and May 26, 1952 and cancelled May 5, 1955, when the FRG was granted sovereign rights, on the basis of a Protocol on Termination of the Occupation Regime in the FRG, signed on Oct, 23, 1954 in Paris as a part of the Paris Treaties, 1954. The text is as follows:

"The United States of America, the United Kingdom of Great Britain and Northern Ireland, the French Republic, and the Federal Republic of Germany agree as follows:

Art. 1. The Convention on Relations between the Three Powers and the Federal Republic of Germany, the Convention on the Rights and Obligations of Foreign Forces and their Members in the Federal Republic of Germany, the Finance Convention, the Convention of the Settlement of Matters arising out of the War and the Occupation, signed at Bonn on 26th May, 1952, the Protocol signed at Bonn on 27th June, 1952, to correct certain textual errors in the aforementioned Conventions, and the Agreement on the Tax Treatment of the Forces and their Members signed at Bonn on 26th May 1952, as amended by the Protocol signed at Bonn on 26th July, 1952, shall be amended in accordance with the five Schedules to the present Protocol and as so amended shall enter into force (together with subsidiary documents agreed by the Signatory States relating to any of the aforementioned instruments) simultaneously with it.

Schedule I. Amendments to the Convention on Relations between the three Powers and the Federal Republic of Germany.

Introductory words. Substitute:

'The United States of America, the United Kingdom of Great Britain and Northern Ireland, the French Republic, and the Federal Republic of Germany have entered into the following Convention setting forth the basis for their new relationship:'

Preamble. Delete.

Art. 1. Substitute:

Art. 1.(1) On the entry into force of the present Convention the United States of America, the United Kingdom of Great Britain and Northern Ireland, and the French Republic (hereinafter and in the related Conventions sometimes referred to as 'the Three Powers') will terminate the Occupation Regime in the Federal Republic, revoke the Occupation Statute and abolish the Allied High Commission and the Offices of the Land Commissioners in the Federal Republic.

(2) The Federal Republic shall have accordingly the full authority of a sovereign State over its internal and external affairs.

Art. 2. Substitute:

Art. 2.(1) In view of the international situation, which has so far prevented the re-unification of Germany and the conclusion of a peace settlement, the Three Powers retain the rights and the responsibilities, heretofore exercised or held by them, relating to Berlin and to Germany as a whole, including the re-unification of Germany and a peace settlement. The rights and responsibilities retained by the Three Powers relating to the stationing of armed forces and the protection of their security are dealt with in Arts. 4 and 5 of the present Convention."

Selected Documents on Germany and the Question of Berlin 1944–1961, HMSO, London, 1961, pp. 208–209.

GERMANY'S EQUALITY, 1932.

Brought up during the Geneva International Conference on Disarmament, which opened Feb. 2, 1932; the German Reich demanded military equality under threat of withdrawing from the Conference; on Dec. 12, 1932, France, Great Britain and Italy made a declaration that the Disarmament Conference was based on the principle that "Germany and the other States disarmed by the Versailles Treaty should be ensured equality in a system which gives security to all nations." This was the first step of the powers made 6 weeks before Hitler's accession to power, on the road to permitting Germany to enter the arms race.

H. RÖNNERFAHRT, *Konferenzen und Verträge,* Vol. 4, Würzburg, 1968.

GERMANY'S UNCONDITIONAL SURRENDER, 1945.

On midnight on May, 8, 1945 empowered by Admiral K. Doenitz, supreme commander of the armed forces of the Reich, Fieldmarshall Keitel, General Stumpf, and Admiral von Friedenburg signed in the district of Karlshorst, Berlin (in the mess-hall of a German officers engineering school building) a document beginning with the statement:

"(1) We the undersigned, acting by authority of the German High Command, hereby surrender unconditionally to the Supreme Commander, Allied Expeditionary Force, and simultaneously to the Supreme High Command of the Red Army all forces on land, at sea, and in the air who are at this date under German control.

(2) The German High Command will at once issue orders to all German military, naval, and air authorities and to all forces under German control to cease active operations at 2301 hours Central European time on 8th May, 1945, to remain in the positions occupied at that time and to disarm completely, handing over their weapons and equipment to the local allied commanders or officers designated by Representatives of the Allied Supreme Commands. No ship, vessel, or aircraft is to be scuttled, or any damage done to their hull, machinery or equipment, and also to machines of all kinds, armament, apparatus, and all technical means of prosecution of war in general.

(3) The German High Command will at once issue to the appropriate commanders and ensure the carrying out of any further orders issued by the Supreme Commander, Allied Expeditionary Force, and by the Supreme High Command of the Red Army.

(4) This act of military surrender is without prejudice to, and will be superseded by any general instrument of surrender imposed by, or on behalf of, the United Nations and applicable to Germany and the German armed forces as a whole.

(5) In the event of the German High Command or any of the forces under their control failing to act in accordance with this Act of Surrender, the Supreme Commander, Allied Expeditionary Force, and the Supreme High Command of the Red Army will take such punitive or other action as they deem appropriate.

(6) This Act is drawn up in the English, Russian, and German languages. The English and Russian are the only authentic texts.

Signed at Berlin on the 8th day of May, 1945."

The document was signed by Keitel, Stumpf, and von Friedenburg in the presence and on behalf of the USSR Red Army of Marshall G.K. Zhukov; on behalf of British Supreme Commander of Allied Expeditionary Force – Marshall A. Tedder; on behalf of US Strategic Air Forces – General C. Spaatz; and on behalf of the First French Army – General J. de Lattre de Tassigny.

Demand for the unconditional surrender of Germany was first publicly made on Jan. 24, 1943 by President of the USA F.D. Roosevelt on the occasion of the meeting with the Prime Minister of Great Britain W.S. Churchill and Gen. C. de Gaulle in Casablanca.

Journal Officiel du Conseil de Contrôle en Allemagne, Berlin, 1945, No. 1, p. 6; A. ARMSTRONG, *Unconditional Surrender. The Impact of the Casablanca Policy upon World War II,* New Brunswick, N.J., 1961; R.L. BLEDSOE, B.A. BOCZEK, *The International Law Dictionary,* Oxford, 1987.

GERONTOLOGY.

A subject of international co-operation. Organizations reg. with the UIA:

European Centre for Gerontological Documentation and Research, f. 1964. Brussels.
International Association for Gerontology, f. 1950, Liège.
International Centre of Social Gerontology, f. 1969, Paris.

Yearbook of International Organizations.

GESAMP. ▷ Water Pollution.

GESTAPO. The German abbreviation for *Geheime Staatspolizei* = Secret State Police of the German III Reich. Appeared simultaneously in two parts of the Reich in the spring of 1933; in April for Bavaria with headquarters in Munich under the leadership of Reichsführer SS, Heinrich Himmler, called Political Police Headquarters (*Politische Polizeikommandatur*) and in May for Prussia with headquarters in Berlin under the leadership of the premier of Prussia, Hermann Goering, called office of the Secret State Police (*Geheimes Staatspolizeiamt – GESTAPA*); Himmler then began to establish similar institutions in all parts of the Reich and on Apr. 20, 1934 the one name, GESTAPO (Geheime Staats Polizei), was accepted for the secret police apparatus, which remained under the formal leadership of H. Goering. On June 17, 1936 H. Himmler as Reichsführer SS und Chef der Deutschen Polizei received full power over all police organs, and in that same year combined the GESTAPO with the Criminal Police (Kriminalpolizei – KRIPO) into one Security Police (Sicherheitspolizei – SIPO); next H. Himmler on Sept. 1, 1939 combined the Main Office of Security Police with the Main Office of Security Service (*Sicherheitsdienst – SD*), the political intelligence service of the NSDAP organized within the SS into the Main Office for the Security of the Reich (*Reichssicherheitshauptamt – RSHA*), in which the GESTAPO was department IV, an organization with the most police power in the Reich and in the occupied territories.

The International Military Tribunal at Nuremberg termed as criminal the operations of Department IV of RSHA and all of the departments associated with it and recommended placing on trial persons belonging to GESTAPO, SD, and SS. In a 1946 judgment of the International Military Tribunal Gestapo was recognized as a criminal organization responsible for genocide and war crimes.

G. CRANKSHAW, *GESTAPO, Instrument of Tyranny*, New York, 1956.

GEURR. Group of Experts on Urban and Regional Research, one of the information centers of the ▷ UN Economic and Social Commission for Asia and Pacific.

GEX. A small region in eastern France in the department of Ain on the Swiss border; a customs-free zone between France and Switzerland. In accordance with the Treaty of Vienna 1815 it belonged to the customs region of Switzerland and was neutralized. The area became the subject of an international dispute when, in accordance with art. 435 of the Versailles Treaty, the resolutions of 1815 were annulled and in Nov., 1923 France moved its customs offices to Gex. The case was heard by the Permanent Court of International Justice, which decided in favor of Switzerland in 1929 and 1932; an understanding between the two sides was reached in 1933.

F. VOSS, *Der Genfer Zonenstreit. Der Streit Zwischen Frankreich und der Schweiz um die zollfrein Zonen Hochsavoyens und die Landschaft Gex*, Zurich, 1933.

GGANTIJA TEMPLES AND HAL SAFLIENI HYPOGEUM. The cultural sites of Malta, included in the ▷ World Heritage UNESCO List. For more than 1000 years (from 3500 to about 2200 BC), the Bronze Age civilization which developed in the Maltese islands inspired the people to build prodigious temples to the memory of their dead and in honor of their gods. One of the earliest of these temples forms part of the site of Ggantija, which stands some 2 km from the sea on a hill on the island of Gozo. At the same period (approximately 2500

BC, according to carbon-14 dating), the same neolithic people honored its divinities – and posterity – with a monument that is every bit as astonishing. From a rock-face, they hollowed out a sanctuary, the hypogeum of Hal Saflieni, near Paola, on the island of Malta. This underground temple is composed of several series of chambers and passage hewn out of the rock on three main levels, the deepest of which is 10.60 m below the present ground level.

J. D. EVANS, *The Prehistoric Antiquities of Malta*, London, 1970; UNESCO. *A Legacy for All*, Paris, 1984.

GHANA. Member of the UN. Republic of Ghana. West African state on the Gulf of Guinea. Area: 238,537 sq. km. Pop. 1987 est. 13,599,000 (1970 census 8,559,313). Capital: Accra with 636,067 inhabitants 1970. GNP per capita 1987 US $390. Official language: English. Currency: one cedi = 100 pesevas. National Day: Mar. 7, Independence Day, 1957.

Member of the UN since Sept. 29, 1957 and of all UN specialized agencies. Member of the OAU, ECOWAS: ACP state of the EEC.

International relations: a powerful monarchy from the 4th to the 13th century; since 1901 British crown colony with the name Gold Coast; other part of the territory was the Togoland. The independent state of Ghana was proclaimed on Mar. 6, 1957, after the union of the Gold Coast with Togoland on July 1, 1960 declared a republic within the Commonwealth. A signatory of the Lomé Conventions of 1975 and 1980. In 1983 Nigeria expelled one million Ghanian illegal immigrants. Involved in border disputes with Togo, 1957–62, 1974–78 and in the 1980's over the area inhabited by the Eve tribe, divided by the frontier between Togo and Ghana, with the presence of pro-Togolese secessionists in Ghana

Along the coast of Ghana is an astonishing series of forts and castles of all sizes, constructed from the end of the 15th century up to the 18th century to protect the trading stations of the competing Portuguese, Dutch, British, Danes, Germans, Swedes, etc. These forts and castles are included in the ▷ World Heritage UNESCO List. ▷ Ashanti.

G.E. METCALFE, *Great Britain and Ghana. Documents of Ghana History 1807–1957*; London, 1964; E. ALEKSANDROVSKAIA, *Gana*, Moskva, 1965; I.I. POTIECHIN, *Stanovlenie Novoi Gana*, Moskva, 1965; W. BIRMINGHAM (ed.), *A Study of Contemporary Ghana*, Evanston, 1966; W. CLAUSEN, *Die Staatwerdung Ghana*, Kiel, 1966, p. 196; B. FITSCH, M. OPPENHEIMER, *Ghana: End of an Illusion*, New York, 1966; G. KAY (ed.), *The Political Economy of Colonialism in Ghana. Collection of Documents and Statistics 1900–1960*, London, 1972; T. JONES, *Ghana's First Republic 1960–1966*, London, 1975; C.L.R. JAMES, *Nkrumah and the Ghana Revolution*, London, 1977; *The Europa Year Book 1984. A World Survey*, Vol. II, pp. 1605–1617, London, 1984; "Ghana-Togo", in: A.J. DAY ed., *Border and Territorial Disputes*, London, 1987, pp. 138–144.

GHENT PEACE TREATY 1814. A peace treaty concluded in the Belgian city of Ghent on Dec. 24, 1814 between Great Britain and the USA, which put an end to the 1812–14 war, called the "second American independence war"; it established the border between the USA and Canada, but not completely; after repeated consultations the border was agreed upon as a result of three separate treaties, the so-called Rush–Bagot Convention of Apr. 27, 1817, Webster–Ashburton of Aug. 9, 1842, and "Utica solution" of June 18, 1882. The Ghent Peace Treaty put both sides under obligation to discontinue slave trade and persecution of Indians.

Major Peace Treaties of Modern History, New York, 1967, Vol. I, pp. 697–712.

GHETTO. *Italian*: "glass works". An international term for an area of a city inhabited by a social, religious, racial, or ethnic group which has been isolated or has isolated itself. The historical term ghetto appeared in Venice in 1516, where the Jewish population had been confined in an area called Ghetto. In 1555 Pope Paul IV in the bull *Cum nimis absurdum* used the term *ghetto* in reference to areas established by him in Rome exclusively for Jews, which was a return to the ancient and medieval isolation of Jews, whose areas in Western Europe then were called *Judeca, Juderia, Juiverie*, in North Africa, *Mellah, Hara, Ca'at al Yahud*. In the 19th century the name ghetto was also applied to districts of other minority groups, primarily immigrants. In the 20th century during World War II in states under German occupation special closed ghettos were established for Jews where hunger, illness and Gestapo terror decimated the population, which en masse was transported to extermination camps. A tragic rebellion was the ▷ Warsaw Ghetto Uprising 1943. The Ordinance on Residence Restrictions in the General-Government, issued on Oct. 15, 1941 proclaimed "that Jews who leave the Jewish quarter without permission are subject to the penalty of death". The Polish population was warned by an announcement concerning Jews in hiding, that "in accordance with this Ordinance, persons who offer the said Jews shelter, food, or sell provisions to them, will also be punished by death". This announcement of German occupation forces was published only in Eastern Europe.

L. WIRTH, *The Ghetto*, London, 1928; R. C. WEAVER, *The Negro Ghetto*, New York, 1948; T. BERENSTEIN (ed.), *Faschismus, Getto. Massenmord, Dokumentation uber Aussrottung und Wiederstand der Juden in Polen Während des Zweiten Weltkrieges*, Berlin, 1961; B. GOLDSTEIN, *Cinq années dans le ghetto de Varsovie*, Bruxelles, 1965; L. DOBROSZYCKI, *The Chronicle of the Lódź Ghetto 1941–1944*, Yale University Press, 1984; J. BAUMA, *Winter in the Morning. Young Girl's Life in the Warsaw Ghetto and Beyond 1939–1945*, London, 1986. R. CALIMANI, *The Ghetto of Venice*, New York, 1987.

GIBRALTAR. A British naval base on the southern tip of a rocky Spanish peninsula of the same name (Penon de Gibraltar). Area: 5,5 sq. km. Pop.: est. 29,692 inhabitants in 1987; at the censuses: 1931 – 17,600, 1961 – 24,500, 1970 – 26,800, 1981 – 28,719. The territory has been a subject of dispute between Spain and Great Britain since 1779; Gibraltar was acquired by the British in the war of the Spanish succession, 1704, and granted to Great Britain by the Treaty of Utrecht, 1714. The cession was confirmed by the treaty of Great Britain with France on Morocco, 1904, to which Spain acceded, and by the 1907 treaty on freedom of navigation and demilitarization of the Gibraltar Strait. A British colony 1714–1964; and then a British unit with its own constitution, administered by a governor with the assistance of a Council of Ministers elected by the residents of Gibraltar. Since 1779, Spain has laid claim to Gibraltar. In 1963 it submitted the case to the UN; and in 1964 it began a partial blockade of Gibraltar, expanded 1968. On Sept. 22, 1964 the UN Committee on decolonization began its examination of the positions of both states. In May 1966 Spain proposed to Great Britain that she retain her naval base but hand the territory of Gibraltar over to Spanish administration. Great Britain refused and on Sept. 10, 1968 held a plebiscite in which 12,310 permanent residents, "night population", voted for Great Britain and only 44 for Spain. The UN Committee recognized the referendum as contrary to the provisos of the UN General Assembly Res. 2231/XXI, of Dec. 20, 1966, which clearly excluded self-determination as a means of decolonization in the case of Gibraltar.

G

Condemnation of the plebiscite was expressed by the UN General Assembly Res. 2353/XXII, of Dec. 17, 1967, by 72 votes for, 10 against and 27 abstentions. The resolution called upon both governments to recommence negotiations for the purpose of ending the colonial situation existing in Gibraltar. The UN General Assembly Res. 2429/XXIII of Dec. 18, 1968 called upon Great Britain to end the colonial status of Gibraltar by Oct. 1, 1969. On May 30, 1969 Great Britain announced a new constitution for Gibraltar creating autonomy for the British residents. The Spanish government protested and on June 6, 1969 closed the border and cut off telephone communications; it informed the UN Secretary-General of these actions on June 17, 1969. Meetings between the ministers of foreign affairs of Spain and Great Britain were held in 1971 in New York and 1972 in Madrid. On Jan. 1, 1973 Gibraltar together with the UK was accepted as a member of the EEC; Gibraltar is not included in the customs area of the EEC. On Dec. 20, 1979. Morocco and the UK signed an agreement on construction of a bridge between Ceuta and Gibraltar. In 1980 Great Britain and Spain resumed negotiations. On Dec. 15, 1982 the border between Spain and Gibraltar was reopened. Talks continued in 1983–1986. On Nov. 27, 1984 Spain and the UK signed in Brussels a Declaration on Gibraltar and in Feb. 1985 the governments decided to resolve the problem in all its aspects including that of sovereignty through negotiations. On Jan. 13–14, 1987 negotiations on the future of Gibraltar were held in London between the British Government and the Spanish Foreign Minister. An agreement on co-operation over the airport in Gibraltar and a ferry service between Gibraltar and Algeciras and of traffic across the Spanish-Gibraltar border was signed in Madrid on Dec. 2, 1987 by Spain and the UK. GA Res. 43/411 adopted without a vote on Nov. 22, 1988, recalling GA decision 42/418 of Dec. 4, 1987, and quoting the Brussels declaration of Nov. 27, 1984, of the Governments of Spain and the United Kingdom of Great Britain and Northern Ireland, states the following:

"The establishment of a negotiating process aimed at overcoming all the differences between them over Gibraltar and promoting co-operation on a mutually beneficial basis on economic, cultural, touristic, aviation, military and environmental matters. Both sides accept that the issues of sovereignty will be discussed in that process. The British Government will fully maintain its commitment to honour the wishes of the people of Gibraltar as set out in the preamble of the 1969 Constitution;
The General Assembly takes note that, as part of this process, the Ministers for Foreign Affairs met in Madrid on Dec. 5 and 6, 1985, in London on Jan. 13 and 14, 1987, in Madrid on Nov. 27 and 28, 1987 and in London on Dec. 2, 1987, on the last of which occasions they reached agreement on arrangements for co-operation over the use of Gibraltar airport, resumption of the ferry service between Gibraltar and Algeciras and improving the flow of surface traffic between Spain and Gibraltar; regrets that the same measures have not yet been brought into effect; and urges both Governments to continue their negotiations with the object of reaching a definite solution to the problem of Gibraltar, in the light of relevant resolutions of the General Assembly and in the spirit of the Charter of the United Nations"

J. ABBOT, *An introduction to the documents relating to the international status of Gibraltar, 1704–1934*, London, 1935; R. DE LUNA, *Historia de Gibraltar*, Madrid, 1944; H.W. HOVES, *The Story of Gibraltar*, London, 1946; J. PLA, *El Alma en Pena de Gibraltar*, Madrid, 1953; J. PLA, *Gibraltar*, London, 1955; *Documents sur Gibraltar présentées aux Cortes Espagnoles par le Ministre des Affaires étrangères*, Madrid, 1955; *Gibraltar, Talks with Spain*, May–Oct., 1966, London, 1966; *UN Monthly Chronicle*, No. 9, 1973; G. HILLS, *Rock of Contention: A History of Gibraltar*, London,

1974; M.M. GREEN, *A Gibraltar Bibliography*, London, 1980 – Supplement, London, 1982. *The Europa Year Book 1984. A World Survey*, Vol. 1, pp. 538–542, London, 1984; Spain–UK (Gibraltar) in: A.J. DAY, ed., *Border and Territorial Disputes*, London, 1987; KEESING's *Record of World Events*, April, 1987; *UN Resolutions and Decisions adopted by the General Assembly during the First Part of its Forty-Third Session, from 20 September to 22 December*, New York 1989, p. 624.

GILBERT AND ELLICE ISLANDS. A former British colony in the Central and South Pacific. ▷ Kiribati and ▷ Tuvalu.

GISCARD D'ESTAING DOCTRINE, 1974. An international term for a principle of French foreign policy expressed in two words by the President of France Giscard d'Estaing, "*mondialisme et conciliation*" – "globalism and reconciliation," on December 20, 1974, meaning that the foreign policy of France includes the whole world and that France as "a friend of the entire world desires to be a factor of reconciliation in every case where this is possible and in every case where the independence of our position gives us the opportunity." This policy meant a departure from "the civilization of the group towards world civilization."

Le Monde, December 21, 1974.

GLACIARES. ▷ Los Glaciares.

GLASNOST. Russian "openness", a Soviet political slogan, coined by the General Secretary of the CPSU, Michail Gorbachev, 1985/6 suggesting that the activities of the state and communist organizations should be opened to the public via the mass media, open public discussions and criticism, as the main way for democratization of the socialist system."
See also ▷ Perestroika; ▷ Socialist democracy.

N. GROSS, Glasnost: Roots and Practice, in: *Problems of Communism*, November–December, 1987; KEESING's *Record of World Events*, April, 1988.

GLASS. A subject of international co-operation. Organizations reg. with the UIA:

Congress of the European Glass Federations, f. 1968, Vienna.
European Glass Container Manufacturers Committee, f. 1951, London.
European Union for the Scientific Study of Glass, f. 1950, Charleroi.
Glass in Building, f. 1970, Brussels.
Glass Industry Club of the Common Market, f. 1958, Brussels.
International Association for the History of Glass, f. 1958, Musee du verre, Liège.
International Commission on Glass Status, f. 1933, Sheffield.
Standing Committee of Glass Industries of the EEC, f. 1964, Paris.

W.B. HONEY, *Glass: a Handbook and a Guide*, London, 1946; F.W. TOOLEY (ed.), *A Handbook of Glass Manufacture*, London, Vol. 1, 1953, Vol. 2, 1960; M.K. BERLYE, *The Encyclopaedia of Working with Glass*, London, 1968; F.J. TERENCE MALONEY, *Glass in the Modern World*, London, 1968.

GLASSBORO. A town in New Jersey, USA, where on June 23–25, 1967 a summit meeting took place between the Heads of Governments of the USA and USSR: President L.B. Johnson and Premier A.N. Kosygin on the Arab–Israeli war; for reasons of prestige a place was selected halfway between the residence of the President of the USA in Washington and New York, where the USSR Prime Minister was attending a Special Session of the UN.

GLAVKOSMOS. A Soviet civilian space agency for scientific research, remote sensing applications and for joint space programs with other countries, est. in Oct. 1985 as the Main Administration for the Creation and Use of Space Technology for the Economy and for Scientific Research. Space photos of Earth are offered by the Soviet agency *Soyuzkarta*.
See also ▷ Landsats; and ▷ SPOT.

KEESING's *Contemporary Archive*, 1986.

GLEBAE ADSCRIPTI. *Latin* = "attached to the land." An international term for peasants without the right to leave the land on which they work. A historical formula of the Roman Empire, where since the 4th century peasants were hereditarily attached to the land and could be sold along with it. In the Middle Ages a formula describing the status of villein peasants, who were unable to move to other villages or cities without the permission of the owner of the land. In the 20th century one of the forms of ▷ slavery, condemned by the UN.

GLEICHSCHALTUNG. *German* = "equalization." An official German III Reich term, 1933, for the subordination of all state institutions and organizations and associations to the total power of the Nazi party, ▷ NSDAP; begun with the Law on equalization of the German lands, *Gesetz zur Gleichschaltung der deutschen Länder*, May 31, 1933.

Reichsgesetzblatt, Berlin, 1933.

GLIDING. One of the areas of 20th century international sports competition, initially, from 1905, developed under the initiatives of the International Air Federation, FAI, organizer of sport flying; from 1948 within its own International Technical and Scientific Organization for Soaring Flight – Organization Scientifique et Technique Internationale du Vol a Voile, OSTIV under the patronage of FAI. It organizes international gliding competitions and establishes their rules; it carries on research at the International Gliding Research Institute, and arranges annual congresses.

Yearbook of International Organizations.

GLOBAL DIPLOMATIC OFFENSIVE. An international term of the 1980's related to the globalism in the military strategy of the superpowers (▷ Global Strategy), evidenced in the United Nations in ▷ Global Negotiations and in ▷ Global Actions of the UN specialized agencies.

GLOBAL ENVIRONMENTAL MONITORING SYSTEM. ▷ GEMS.

GLOBALISME. An international term coined by the French President Valery Giscard d'Estaing, 1980 for the impact of global, economic, financial, military and political problems.

GLOBAL NEGOTIATIONS. An international term of the UN system, introduced in 1980 by UNCTAD for negotiations on the economic situation of the Third World, involving all United Nations members with the aim of speeding progress toward the ▷ New International Economic Order. The foreign ministers of the Group of 77 in a meeting in the UN headquarters in Oct., 1983, accepted a Declaration on Global Negotiation on international economic co-operation for development. A special plenary session of the UN General Assembly dedicated only to the Global Negotiations took place on June 26, 1983.

UN Chronicle, July 1980, November, 1981, October, 1982 and November, 1983.

GLOBAL STRATEGY. An international term for a US military doctrine formulated in 1963 by President L.B. Johnson, professing the maintenance by the USA of military forces that could permit military action anywhere in the entire globe; also called the ▷ Johnson–Mann doctrine of two and a half wars.

GLORIENSY ISLAND ▷ Madagascar.

GLUCOSE. A subject of international co-operation. Organizations reg. with the UIA:

Association of EEC Glucose Manufacturers, f. 1960, Paris.
International Federation of Glucose Industries, f. 1976, Brussels.

Yearbook of International Organizations.

GMT. Greenwich Meridian Time. An international term for European zonal time established by ▷ Greenwich Observatory.

GNILYI ZAPAD. *Russian* = "The rotten West". A conservative expression coined in 1841 by a professor at Moscow University S.P. Shevyriov (1806–64), in the periodical *Moskvichanin*, stating that the West is like a rotting corpse.

GNOMES OF ZURICH. An international term coined in 1964 by British Foreign Minister George Brown (1914–66) denoting bankers who, like gnomes, are guarding the gold deposits.

GNP. ▷ Gross National Product.

GOA, DAMAN AND DIU. A federal territory of India (area: 3800 sq. km with *c.* 700,000 inhabitants in 1962). Former Portuguese colony in India (1510–1962); subject of Portuguese Indian dispute on the right of transit for goods and civilian and military personnel through India to Goa, Daman and Diu filed by Portugal Dec. 22, 1955 with the ICJ, settled by the judgment of Nov. 26, 1957 (ICJ Reports, 1957). India intervened 1962 in Goa, Daman and Diu with the consent of an absolute majority of the UN member states. In succeeding years the majority of Portuguese were repatriated. On Dec. 4, 1974 the government of Portugal formally recognized the right of India to the former Portuguese enclave and resumed diplomatic relations with India which had been broken off in 1961. On Feb. 4, 1987 an official language bill replaced English with Goanian, Konkani, Portuguese and Marathi languages. On May 30, 1987 Goa became the 25th State of India and Daman and Diu a separate territory.

K.M. MENON, *Portuguese Pockets in India*, London, 1953; K. NARAYAN, "The problem of Goa", in: *The Indian Yearbook of International Affairs*, 1956; KEESING's *Record of World Events*, 1987, No. 3; KEESING's *Record of World Events*, 1987, No. 6; P.D. GAITONDE, *The Liberation of Goa: A Participant's View of History*, London 1987.

GOBI. One of the largest deserts in the world, located in Mongolia, crossed by the trans-Mongolian railroad Ulan-Bator–Peking. Subject of international archeological research (dinosaurs and fossilized mammals).

GOITRE. Enlargement of the thyroid gland, endemic illness in certain regions of Africa, Asia and Latin America, caused by a lack of iodine in the body. The WHO estimates that 200 million people suffer from goitre. The WHO has popularized a simple effective way of dealing with goitre: adding iodine to salt, which does not change its color or taste.

GOLAN HEIGHTS. A Syrian territory occupied during the Six Day War of June 1967 by Israel, a subject of dispute in the UN Security Council. On Dec. 14, 1981, Israel imposed in the Golan Heights area its laws, jurisdiction and administration. The UN Security Council on Dec. 17, 1981 decided unanimously that the Israeli decision was "null and void and without international legal effects," but the UN Security Council has not adopted proposals for sanctions against Israel for Golan Heights seizure. The vote on the draft resolution on Jan. 20, 1981, was nine in favor (China, Ghana, Jordan, Poland, Spain, Togo, Uganda, USSR and Zaïre), to one against (USA) with five abstentions (France, Israel, Japan, Panama and the UK). On Feb. 5, 1982, the UN General Assembly, Res. ES.91, adopted a roll-call vote of 86 in favor to 21 against, with 34 abstentions, and declared the Israeli decision of Dec. 14, 1981 "an act of aggression" under the United Nations Charter and called for sanctions against Israel.

W. HARRIS, *Taking Root, Israeli Settlements in the West Bank. The Golan and Gaza Strip 1968–1980*, Chichester, 1981; *UN Chronicle*, February, March, April, 1982.

GOLD. Subject of international co-operation and agreements. In the period 1945–76 played a special role in international currency systems of the IMF. Major producers: the Republic of South Africa, the USSR, Canada, Australia, Ghana, Zimbabwe, the Philippines, Mexico, Colombia. Pure gold is extracted from gold ore, usually containing silver impurities and, upon assay made by official institutions, is assigned hallmarks printed on gold ingot and jewelry. Fineness of gold is measured by the carat system in which the highest standard is 24 carat gold, actually no more than 23.6 carat or 986 g of pure gold in 1000 g (34.7801 oz in 35.27399 oz). The second standard is 18 carat gold or 750 g (26.4554 oz) and the third standard is 14 carat gold or 583 g (20.5647 oz). The value of gold in proportion to silver was set in ancient times at 12:1, in the early 19th century at 16:1 and in the late 19th century at 22:1.

As a metallic currency, gold became superior to ▷ silver only at the end of the 19th century, serving thereafter as a basis for international currency systems. By 1913, in 44 countries, banknotes could be easily exchanged for gold and, in 15 other countries, notes could be exchanged with small restrictions. The gold standard depended on the immediate convertibility of bank notes into gold bullion by banks who paid in gold coins of a specified weight and standard (e.g. one pound sterling in paper was equivalent to a 7.32 g, 23 carat gold coin). The years 1900–14 were called "the Golden Age of the Gold Standard." World War I destroyed the ubiquity of the system of gold standard in Europe. The revival began in 1919 when the USA revalued gold parity of the dollar to equal that of the dollar before the war – 1.50463 g per $1; in turn, in 1920, gold parity was established by Cuba, Dominica, Honduras, Panama, Salvador, Uruguay and Venezuela. In 1922, the Conference of Genoa recommended the restoration of gold parity, which was then done by Costa Rica and Latvia in 1922; Austria and Colombia in 1923; Germany, Guatemala, Lithuania, Poland and Sweden in 1924; Albania, Australia, Egypt, Finland, the Free Town of Gdansk, Great Britain, Hungary, the Netherlands, New Zealand, Switzerland and the Union of South Africa in 1925; Belgium, Bolivia, Canada, Chile and Mexico in 1926; Argentina, Denmark, Ecuador, India, Paraguay, Poland, Portugal and Italy in 1927; Brazil, Bulgaria, Estonia, France, Greece, Norway in 1928; Czechoslovakia, Japan and Romania in 1929; Peru in 1930 and in 1931 –

Portugal and Yugoslavia. It should be noted that in 1925 Poland waived gold parity only to return to it in 1927; Great Britain returned to gold parity in 1925 limiting, however, convertibility of bank notes into gold ingot (▷ Gold Bullion Standard) and not into gold coins. That system was soon adopted by all other states, except the USA, with some states, however, still retaining limited convertibility into coins.

The great world crisis that began on Black Friday, Oct. 25, 1929, in the USA, made Argentina, Brazil, Paraguay and Uruguay immediately waive gold parity, and in 1930 Venezuela followed suit. The biggest bank in Austria, Credit-Anstalt, went bankrupt in 1931 and sparked off an international panic. In the same year, waivers of convertibility into gold, or severe restrictions concerning currency exchange, were instituted by as many as 22 countries: Austria, Bolivia, Canada, Colombia, Czechoslovakia, Denmark, Egypt, Estonia, Finland, Germany, Great Britain, India, Japan, Hungary, Latvia, Mexico, New Zealand, Norway, Portugal, Salvador, Sweden and Yugoslavia; in 1932, by Chile, Costa Rica, Ecuador, Peru, Romania, the Union of South Africa; in Mar., 1933, by Cuba, Dominican Republic, Honduras, Panama, the USA, Belgium; in 1934 by Italy; in 1935, by Belgium, the Free Town of Gdansk, Lithuania; in 1936, by France, the Netherlands and Poland. The embargo imposed on Mar. 6, 1933, by President Roosevelt on the export of gold by the USA brought the old currency system based on gold to an end. A new system, introduced in the USA on Jan. 30, 1934, under the Gold Reserve Act, determined the price of an ounce of gold at not less than 34.45 dollars. However, in keeping with the Act, it was the US President who was to determine the value of paper dollars and who, on Jan. 31, 1934, set the price of an ounce of gold at 35 dollars so that $1 = 0.888671 g. Simultaneously, all gold currency in the USA was "nationalized", i.e. gold ingot was sold to the State Treasury and deposited in Fort Knox, Kentucky. A ban on minting gold coins was issued and those then existing were recast in the form of gold ingot. Gold export, import, transport and trade were prohibited with respect to all kinds of metallic gold currency in the USA. This policy was to remain in force until 1975. Owners of gold coin collections retained the right to possess or exchange them only under permission from the relevant authorities and only within US frontiers. At the Brussels Conference of the "gold bloc" states, held on Oct. 20, 1934, the decision was taken to retain gold parity, reaffirming an agreement among France, Great Britain and the USA signed on Sept. 26, 1936, concerning the establishment of a monetary bloc adhering to the system of stable gold prices. That system generated an enormous flow of gold into the USA (see Table) as a result of an exodus of capital from Europe and southern Asia.

Gold reserves in the USA during 1929–45.

Year	Gold reserves ($ million)	Year	Gold reserves ($ million)
1929	3,997	1938	14,512
1930	4,306	1939	17,644
1931	4,173	1940	21,995
1932	4,226	1941	22,737
1933	4,036	1942	22,739
1934	8,238	1943	21,981
1935	10,125	1944	20,631
1936	11,258	1945	20,083
1937	12,760		

Source: *Banking and Monetary Statistics*, Washington, DC, 1946.

Gold parity was not strictly adhered to during the war period. Gold became an item of black market

G

speculation and contraband both in Europe occupied by Germany and in southern Asia, the Middle East, Great Britain, the Scandinavian states and Turkey.

London is accepted as the world center of the gold trade. The USSR handles its gold operations through the Moscow Narodny Bank Limited in London. The second-biggest gold center is Switzerland with its exchanges in Zurich, Geneva and Lausanne. Following the temporary closing of the London gold exchange, Zurich became the major gold market in 1968 followed by Paris. Gold exchanges are also located in Amsterdam, Brussels, Hamburg, Istanbul, Milan and Vienna; in the Middle East – Dubai, Beirut; in Asia – Bombay, Dacca, Karachi, Madras, Hong Kong, Macao, Vientiane, Saigon, Bangkok, Djakarta, Manila, Seoul, Singapore, Taipei, Tokyo; in Africa – Alexandria, Dakar, Djibouti, Casablanca, Cairo, Tripoli, Kinshasa; in the Western Hemisphere – Buenos Aires, Mexico City, Montevideo, Panama, Rio de Janeiro; and in the USA – Detroit, Buffalo, New York City and San Francisco. In international exchange, in the 19th and early 20th centuries, gold was a generally recognized instrument of payment while paper notes were immediately convertible to metal. The system broke down during World War I and received a *coup de grace* from the world economic crisis of the midwar period. Along with the establishment of the International Monetary Fund, IMF, the USA initiated, in 1946, together with France and Great Britain, the Tripartite Commission for the Restitution of Monetary Gold on the basis of the Treaty on Reparations, signed on Jan. 14, 1946. The Commission had its headquarters in Brussels. Each of the three powers had its own currency zone but maintained co-operation among themselves. In the decade after World War II, economic reconstruction in the leading capitalist states was aided by the American system of gold parity. However, under the impact of inflation, the scale of transfer was split in two: official gold and paper currency.

The official price was kept stable in relation to US currency: $1 = 0.888671 g of pure gold, thus – 1 oz = 31.1035 g: 0.888671 g = 35 US dollars. At the same time, the price of paper money fluctuated considerably. The trouble began in 1955 when the expansion of capitalist states in world trade proved to be much more rapid, and higher than, international fluctuation. The USA was endangered by the "hemorrhage of the dollar" as it was dramatically described by President J.F. Kennedy in 1960, when world gold exchanges paid $40–50 for 1 oz of pure gold while the USA was still maintaining the 1934 price of $35 per oz. Restitution of the 1934 price in world exchanges was achieved through a co-ordinated action taken up by the Council of the Seven Central Banks of France, the Netherlands, the Federal Republic of Germany, Switzerland, Sweden, Great Britain and the USA. The Council, called the Gold Consortium, was transformed, in 1961, into a permanent international institution and in 1963 was joined by Japan, Canada and Italy. It was called the Group of Ten and established its headquarters in London. Those states represented over four-fifths of the gold reserves in the possession of all IMF member-states. The Consortium organized the International Gold Pool, IGP, and the Exchange Stabilization Fund, ESF, to sustain the 1934 price of gold.

In 1966, France recognized that the joint monetary policy was overly beneficial to the USA and withdrew from the gold pool. In 1967–68 the world was caught by "gold fever." On Nov. 18, 1967, the pound sterling started to lose value and, as a result, the currencies of 22 British Commonwealth countries were devalued. On Dec. 3, 1967, the USA

granted a credit to the amount of $475 million to the IGP and ESF. At the IGP session in Basel, Dec. 10, 1967, a US representative gave assurances tht "the United States is absolutely resolute to keep up the gold value of the US dollar and the London gold exchange will be kept open." The USA, on Dec. 28, 1967, transferred to the account of the EFC an additional $450 million. A new IGP session, held on Mar. 11, 1968, resolved to maintain the status quo. On Mar. 11, 1968, the United States transferred a third credit to EFC totaling $450 million. The sums proved to be insufficient. The "gold fever" in Western Europe reached its apex on Mar. 14, 1968: $44 were paid for an ounce of gold. On that night the US Senate issued an act by which the 25% gold coverage of dollar bills in circulation, which had been in effect since Jan. 1, 1934 was rescinded. The US government simultaneously raised the discount rate from 4.5% to 5% and requested the British government to close the London gold exchange. All gold exchanges in the world, apart from that in Paris, stopped selling gold ingot and bullion on Mar. 15, 1968. On Mar. 16–17, 1968, in the absence of a French representative, the Gold Consortium decided to divide the gold market into: the Central Bank market, retaining the price of $35 per ounce, and the free exchange market, governed by supply and demand. According to data supplied by the IMF, in 1967, world gold reserves (besides the reserves in the possession of socialist states) were worth $40,9 billion; and USA had $13,4 billion, France – $5,2 billion, the Federal Republic of Germany – $4,3 billion, Benelux – $3,3 billion, Switzerland – $2,8 billion, Italy – $2,1 billion, Great Britain – $2 billion, Canada – 1 billion, Latin America – $983 million with the rest in the remaining IMF member states. The USA, which in 1945 possessed 63% of gold reserves, in 1950 as much as 68%, in 1960 had only 47%, in 1965 – 34%, in 1967 – 32% and in 1968 as little as 25%. In 1971, gold reserves dropped below $10 billion, i.e. to the level of 1938. On Aug. 15, 1971, President Nixon totally suspended the dollar's convertibility to gold, which resulted in international repercussions and was twice a cause of the devaluation of the US dollar on Apr. 3, 1972, and Feb. 13, 1973, as well as elimination of the dual gold market on Nov. 14, 1973. In May of 1972, on the free market, the price of an ounce of gold exceeded $50; in Jan., 1973 – $65. In Feb., 1973, following an official devaluation of the US dollar to $42.22 per ounce on the free market, the price exceeded $102 in the London exchange, $101 in Frankfurt and $106 in Paris. The dual gold market was cancelled on Nov. 14, 1973, except in the USA, Belgium, the Netherlands, the Federal Republic of Germany, Switzerland, Great Britain and Italy. The official price continued to be $42.22 per ounce, the free market price – over $100. It marked, in fact, the end of gold as a common denominator of world currencies. This was formally recognized by the IMF in Jan. 8, 1976. Thus the fixing of the price of gold in gold exchanges, historically speaking, has gone through three phases: (1) from 1814, when France introduced a gold-based currency (in 1816 – Great Britain, 1850 – Switzerland, 1872 – Scandinavian states, 1873 – the USA, 1876 – Germany, 1883 – Italy, 1889 – Russia), until World War I, when paper money was almost generally convertible to gold ingot or bullion; (2) from 1914 to 1971, when periodical or permanent inconvertibility of paper money into gold was a result of the general decrease in international gold turnover due to state control and the general recognition of official and free market gold prices in settlement of accounts; (3) from 1971, when it became impossible to exchange paper currency for gold, official gold prices were eliminated. This was an effect of the processes triggered by the currency crisis. No longer would gold

be the basis of the international currency system. The demonetarization of gold has become a generally recognized fact.

In the decade 1971–80, world gold reserves in banks rose to $55 billion, while those in private possession were estimated at $22 billion; traditionally the French remain the greatest hoarders (nearly $5 billion) with southern Asians close behind (over $4 billion). A low level of hoarding in the Western Hemisphere is a result of the USA being excluded from gold traffic from Jan. 31, 1934, until 1975. In the United States, for 41 years, possession of gold, apart from jewelry, was only allowed in the form of gold coins and only those minted before 1933. The traffic in them was restricted to exchange among coin collectors. Since July 20, 1962, import of gold coins has been prohibited; export has been banned since 1934. Similar rulings restricting possession of gold are in force in Afghanistan, Algeria, the Dutch Antilles, Bolivia, Chile, Colombia, Dominican Republic, Ethiopa, Iran, Libya, Malawi, Spain, the Republic of South Africa and Yugoslavia. The following are the countries in which the ban on possession of gold in ingot and bullion is upheld: Albania, Australia, Bulgaria, the Chinese People's Republic, Cyprus, Czechoslovakia, Canada, Costa Rica, Cuba, Great Britain, Guinea, Hungary, India, the German Democratic Republic, Malaysia, Nigeria, Zimbabwe, Romania, El Salvador, Sri Lanka, Tunisia, Zambia and the USSR. In the remaining states, gold may be possessed in the form of ingot or bullion. However, free gold traffic is prohibited in some states, while in others, free import and export of gold is permitted including: Belgium, Luxembourg, Cambodia, Ecuador, Finland, Lebanon, the Federal Republic of Germany, Macao, Paraguay and Sweden. The only states in which export is allowed but import is prohibited are Uruguay and Venezuela. States which allow only import are: Argentina, Chile (gold coins only), Indonesia, Ireland, Israel (gold coins only), Poland, and the Republic of South Africa (gold coins only). In 1978, the price of gold exceeded US $200 and in 1979 – US $500, in Jan. 1980 – US $700 and in Oct. 1984 – US $350. A senior French economist, Jacques Rueff, advocated the return of gold to its previous significance.

In 1980's the world's largest gold producer was still South Africa whose output was steadily declining however to 18,5m ounces in 1988. The USA production has risen from 1,4m ounces in 1987 to 5,9m ounces in 1988 as a result of implementing new technology in the Carlin area in North-central Nevada discovered in the 1970's.

The weakness of the dollar in Dec. 87 pushed the gold price to a high approaching $500 an ounce for the first time since January 1983.

R.H. BRAND, "Gold: A World Economic Problem", in: *International Conciliation*, No. 333, New York, October 1937, pp. 661–667; R. TRIFFIN, *L'or et le crise du dollar*, Paris, 1971; T. GREEN, *The World of Gold Today*, London, 1974; *The Economist*, April 30, 1988; R.N. COOPER, Gold as Basis for the Monetary System? in: *Economic Impact*, Washington DC, 1988/I.

GOLD BLOCKADE. The boycott of Soviet gold by the Western powers on the money markets of the world 1920–29. The boycott, in fact, had already begun on Nov. 24, 1917 when the USA suspended supplies to Russia and, in 1918–19, when the Western powers attempted military intervention and economic blockade. The gold blockade was first applied in 1920 by Great Britain when that country issued a ban on the import and export of Soviet gold throughout the British empire. Also in 1920 the USA and many other countries issued a ban on supplying the Soviet state with any trade credits whatsoever. At the turn of 1921/22 Great

Britain signed the first trade agreement with the USSR. Poland began trade negotiations with the USSR on Mar. 6, 1922; the Germans on May 21, 1922 signed the Rapallo Treaty; on June 6, 1922 the Italians signed a trade agreement with the USSR. However, the gold blockade was maintained by the USA and several other countries which in 1924 came to a "gentleman's agreement" in Berne that they would continue the gold blockade against the USSR until it paid the debts of tsarist Russia.

N. RUBINSHTEYN, *Sovietskaya Rossiya i kapitalisticheskiye gosudarstva v gody pierekhoda od woyni do mira, 1921–1924*, Moskva, 1945.

GOLD BULLION. An international term for pure gold in bars. Great Britain in 1925 introduced Gold Bullion Standard, a system for the exchangeability of banknotes issued by the Bank of England exclusively for a bar of gold of certain purity; in contrast to the system before World War I which allowed the exchange of coins for gold. The system was accepted in the majority of states whose currencies were based on ▷ gold parity.

GOLD CLAUSE. A 19th-century international term for a reservation in international commercial agreements that the basis for settlements is the current value of gold or a certain currency struck in gold coins. The Brussels Sea Conventions, i.e. before World War I and in the interwar period, established that the financial obligations of charterers, shipowners and sea transporters should be settled not in paper pound sterling, but in pounds struck in gold. In practice, after World War II there was an almost universal departure from the gold clause in international maritime commerce with the exception of a few states.

F.A. MANN, *The Legal Aspect of Money*, Oxford, 1971.

GOLD COINS. The names of gold coins from the 19th and 20th century offered in the international market (in alphabetical order):
Azteca, the Mexican 20 peso gold coin (15 grams fine gold);
Centenario, the Mexican 50 peso gold coin (37.5 grams fine gold);
Chervonets, the Russian 10 ruble gold coin (7.742 grams fine gold);
Double Eagle, the US $20 gold coin (30.09 grams fine gold);
Gold-Reichsmark, the Imperial German 20-Reichsmarks, gold coin (7.168 grams fine gold);
Hildago, the Mexican 10 peso gold coin (7.5 grams fine gold);
King Faud, the Egyptian gold coin of 20 piastres (1.53 grams fine gold), 50-piastres (3.72 grams fine gold), 100-piastres (7.44 grams fine gold) and 500-piastres (37.19 grams fine gold);
Korona, the Hungarian gold coin of 100 korona (30.49 grams fine gold);
Korone, the Austrian gold coin of 20 krones (6.10 grams fine gold) and 100 krones (31.49 grams fine gold);
Krugerrand, the South African gold coin (31.103 grams fine gold);
Napoleon, the French 20 franc gold coin (5.806 grams fine gold);
Pahlevi, the Iranian gold coin (7.29 grams fine gold);
Sovereign, the British pound sterling gold coin (7.32 grams fine gold);
Union Latin, the ▷ Latin Monetary Union gold coin (5.806 grams fine gold);
Vreneli, the Swiss 20 franc gold coin (5.806 grams fine gold).

GOLD EXCHANGE STANDARD. A system in which the national currency is not directly exchangeable for gold, but for foreign currencies based on gold, while simultaneously having a constant value relationship to gold (▷ gold parity). States using the gold exchange standard usually retained a reserve of gold, foreign currencies and securities, but only covered part of the banknotes in circulation. In the USA the law of Jan. 31, 1934, rescinded Mar. 16, 1968, required 25% coverage. The gold exchange standard ceased to be binding for the IMF member states on Mar. 16, 1973.

B. TEW, *International Monetary Co-operation, 1945–70*, London, 1970; "Gold Exchange standard n'existe plus", *Le Monde*, December 25, 1973; J. GOLD, *SDR's, Gold and Currencies*, IMF, Washington, DC, 1979.

GOLD FEVER. An international term for greed and excitement caused by a gold rush – quest for gold in California 1849, in Australia 1851, in the Klondike 1896, in Nevada 1903, etc.; the term also referred to flight into gold (rush for gold), i.e. purchase of gold from banks as a result of falling confidence in paper currency and debentures, as was the case on ▷ Black Friday, 1929. ▷ Klondike.

GOLD FIELDS OF SOUTH AFRICA, LTD. A company f. 1887 by Cecil John Rhodes, in Witwatersrand, the largest gold-field in the world, presently called the Consolidated Gold Fields of South Africa Ltd., with an associated company, New Consolidated Gold Fields.

GOLD, GLORY AND GOSPEL. A slogan of the early colonialism.

GOLD PARITY. An international term for the content of pure gold in a monetary unit; fixed in an act of legislation or in force on the basis of another normative document, e.g. resolutions of the government or agreements; was generally applied under the system of gold currency and abandoned after the suspension of the convertibility of the dollar in 1971. ▷ Gold.

GOLD POINTS. An international term for limits within which the exchange rate of currency fluctuates under conditions where banknotes were exchangeable for gold and gold was freely transported abroad; the allowed fluctuation of rates for foreign currency above or below ▷ gold parity.

GOLD POOL INTERNATIONAL. An agreement of the central banks of France, the FRG, Great Britain, Italy, the Netherlands, Sweden, Switzerland and the USA made in 1961 on the maintenance of the 1934 price of gold in the international monetary system; revised in the middle of Mar., 1968 with the introduction of a two-tiered price system for gold, i.e. an official one of 1934 and a free market price; in force until 1971. ▷ Gold, ▷ Gold parity.

GOLD RESERVE ACT, 1934. The American law, passed 1934 when the US treasury took title to all gold reserves in United States.

GOLD STANDARD. A monetary system, national or international, in which the standard unit is a fixed weight of gold or a paper money is freely convertible into gold at a fixed price.

W.A. BROWN Jr., *The International Gold Standard Reinterpreted 1914–1934*, London, 1940; R.G. HAWTREY, *The Gold Standard in Theory and Practice*, London, 1948.

GOLF. A subject of international co-operation. Organizations reg. with the UIA:

Continental Tournaments Players Association, f. 1975, Paris.
Professional Golfers' Association, f. 1901, London.
World Amateur Gold Council, f. 1958, Far Hills, NJ Publ.: *Record Book* (every 2 years).
Yearbook of International Organizations.

GOMULKA PLAN, 1963. A scheme for the freezing of atomic armaments in Central Europe formulated on Dec. 28, 1963 by Polish United Workers' Party First Secretary Wladyslaw Gomulka in his address at Plock, Poland. On Feb. 29, 1964, the Polish government sent notes with the Gomulka Plan to all European governments and to Canada and the US.

Recueil de Documents, Varsovie, No. 12, 1963; SIPRI, *World Armament Yearbook*, 1969, pp. 408–409.

GONCOURT LITERARY SOCIETY. Société Littéraire des Goncourt-Academie Goncourt, f. 1896, Paris. The Academy has 10 French Members and six foreign ones (Belgium, Canada, Mexico, Senegal, Switzerland and the USSR).

GONDRA DOCTRINE, 1923. A theory on preventing conflicts between American states formulated by Paraguayan author, statesman and president (1910–11 and 1920–21) M. Gondra (1872–1927) at the Fifth Inter American Conference in Santiago, Chile, 1923, in a draft of a Treaty on Terms of Conciliation of Conflicting Parties, based on The Hague Conventions, 1899 and 1907, but with the obligation of immediate renouncement of force when one of the parties petitions for setting up an investigating commission. The ▷ Inter-American Treaty to Avoid or Prevent Conflicts Between the American States was called the Gondra Treaty, and included the Gondra Doctrine. It was signed May 3, 1923 and ratified by all Latin American states with the exception of Argentina.

Conferencias Internacionales Americanas, 1889–1936, Washington, DC, 1938, pp. 222–226; J.M. SIERRA, *Derecho Internacional Público*, México, DF, 1963, pp. 435–438.

GOOD NEIGHBOR DOCTRINE, 1933. A trend of US foreign policy in relation to Latin America during the presidency of F.D. Roosevelt. This policy was preceded 1920–32 by introductory gestures of goodwill by President Herbert Hoover, who from Nov., 1928 to Feb., 1929 sailed on the ship *Maryland* to El Salvador, Honduras, Nicaragua, Costa Rica, Ecuador, Peru, Chile, Argentina, Uruguay, and Brazil declaring that:

"The United States desires not only friendly relations with the governments of Latin America, but also the relations of a good neighbor."

In 1930 H. Hoover published the so-called Clark Memorandum, which was directed against President T.R. ▷ Roosevelt's Corollary to the Monroe Doctrine 1904; in 1932 he did not oppose the initiative of Argentina to prepare the Anti-War Treaty of Non-Aggression and Conciliation, containing the principle of ▷ non-intervention. F.D. Roosevelt stated his opinion on the subject of the relationship of the USA to Latin America for the first time in 1928 in the quarterly *Foreign Affairs*:

"The use by us of unilateral intervention in the internal affairs of other nations on the American continent should be relinquished."

F.D. Roosevelt declared the good neighbor doctrine in his inauguration speech, on Mar. 4, 1933:

"In the field of world affairs dedicate this nation to the policy of the good neighbor – the neighbor who resolutely respects himself and because he does so, respects the rights of others – the neighbor who respects his obligations and respects the sanctity of his agreements in and with a world of neighbors."

During World War II the Third Council of Ministers of Foreign Affairs of the American Republics in Rio de Janeiro, Jan. 15–28, 1942 passed the Good Neighbor Declaration, announcing that:

"the principle that international behavior should stem from the policy of the good neighbor is a norm of international law for the American continent."

F.D. ROOSEVELT, Address to the Congress on Mar. 4, 1933; *Congressional Record*, Washington, DC, 1933; *Conferencias Internacionales Americanas, Primer Suplemento*, Washington, DC 1943, pp. 202–203; O.E. GUERRANT, *Roosevelt's Good Neighbor Policy*, Albuquerque, 1950; A. De CONDE, *Hoover's Latin-american Policy*, Stanford, 1951; F. CUEVAS CANCICO, *Roosevelt y la Buena Vecindad*, México, DF, 1954; J.L. MECHAM, *The US and Interamerican Security 1889–1960*, Austin, 1967.

GOOD-NEIGHBOURLINESS. A subject of a UN study. In 1980 the UN Secretary-General initiated a study on development and strengthening of good-neighborliness between states. In Dec., 1983 the views and suggestion of 21 countries (Belgium, China, Cuba, Cyprus, France, the FRG, Greece, Hungary, Indonesia, Morocco, Oman, Peru, Portugal, Singapore, Sudan, Syria, Uganda, the USA, Vietnam and Zambia) were presented by the UN Secretary-General as a part of a process of elaborating, at an appropriate time, a suitable international document on this subject.

On Dec. 9, 1988 the GA Res. 43/171 A entitled "Development and Strengthening of Good Neighbourliness between States" was adopted by 67 votes to 9 (Bulgaria, Cameroon, Laos, Madagascar, Mongolia, the Philippines, Romania, Sudan, Vietnam) and 65 abstentions and GA Res. 43/171B by 124 votes to 8 (Belgium, France, the FRG, Luxembourg, Netherlands, Portugal, the UK, the USA) with 22 abstentions, stating that:

"Considering that the great changes of a political, economic and social nature, as well as the scientific and technological advances that have taken place in the world and led to unprecedented interdependence of nations, have given new dimensions to good-neighbourliness in the conduct of States and increased the need to develop and strengthen it . . ."

Reaffirms that good-neighbourliness fully conforms with the purposes of the United Nations and shall be founded upon the strict observance of the principles of the United Nations as embodied in the Charter and in the Declaration of Principles of International Law concerning Friendly Relations and Co-operation among States in accordance with the Charter of the United Nations and so presupposes the rejection of any acts seeking to establish zones of influence or domination . . .

Calls once again upon States, in the interest of the maintenance of international peace and security, to develop good neighbourly relations, acting on the basis of these principles."

UN Chronicle, January, 1984, p. 70; *UN Resolutions and Decisions adopted by the General Assembly during the First Part of its Forty-Third Session, from 20 September to 22 December, 1988.*, New York, 1989, pp. 580-582.

GOOD OFFICES. Broadly understood arbitration (mediation) in disputes between two states or groups of states, offered by another state or competent international intergovernmental organization (Good Offices of the UN); subject of international conventions starting from 1898 (the date of the First Hague Convention) and obligations undertaken by American republics in the Treaty on Obligatory Arbitration of 1902; Inter-American Good Services and Mediation Treaty of 1936; and in the American Treaty on Peaceful Settlement of Disputes of 1948, also called the Bogota Pact. In the UN system one of the competences of the United

Nations provided for in the UN Charter in Chapter IV on peaceful settlement of disputes, offering the UN members good offices through the General Assembly or the Security Council in the case of "any dispute, the continuance of which is likely to endanger the maintenance of international peace and security."

According to the definition supplied by L. Erlich differentiating "the form of good offices in its broader sense" from mediation:

"Good offices in its stricter sense may consist in communicating to one party the statements of the other, if the two parties do not maintain diplomatic relations with each other; good offices may also consist in inviting the two states in dispute to a conference for the resolution of the dispute or for undertaking other steps facilitating the two parties to arrive at an agreement."

L. ERLICH, *Prawo Miedzynarodowe* [International Law], Warszawa, 1969; R.L. BLEDSOE, B.A. BOCZEK, *The International Law Dictionary*, Oxford, 1987.

GOODS DELIVERY IN THE CMEA SYSTEM. The Council for Mutual Economic Assistance elaborated and adopted the following international instruments on delivery of goods between the foreign trade organizations of the CMEA countries (Bulgaria, Czechoslovakia, the GDR, Hungary, Mongolia, Poland, Romania, the USSR):

(1) General Conditions of Assembly and Provision of Other Technical Services in Connection with Reciprocal Deliveries and Equipment, called CMEA General Conditions of Assembly, 1962; came into force on June 1, 1962. The Preamble is as follows:

"All assembly and specialized assembly work, adjustment and start-up of equipment and machinery and other technical services (inspection, supervision, etc.) in connexion with reciprocal deliveries of machinery and equipment between foreign trade organizations of member countries of CMEA, hereinafter called assembly work, carried out by specialist personnel of the supplier in the country of the client shall be performed on the basis of these General Conditions of Assembly. All contracts for assembly work shall be concluded on the basis of the General Conditions of Assembly. If, when concluding a contract, the parties reach the conclusion that the assembly work to be carried out is of a special nature and that a departure from particular provisions of these General Conditions of Assembly is accordingly required, they may so agree in the contract."

(2) General Conditions for the Technical Servicing of Machinery. Equipment and Other Items, called General Conditions of Technical Servicing, 1962; came into force on Nov. 1, 1962. The preamble is as follows:

"Technical servicing of articles delivered by foreign trade organizations of member countries of CMEA shall be conducted on the basis of the present General Conditions, hereinafter referred to as the General Conditions of Technical Servicing. All the contracts for technical servicing shall be concluded on the basis of the General Conditions of Technical Servicing. If, when concluding a contract for the performance of technical servicing, the parties reach the conclusion that the articles for which the contract for technical servicing is being concluded are of a specific nature and/or that the special characteristics of the technical servicing require a departure from particular provisions of these General Conditions of Technical Servicing, they may so agree in the contract."

(3) General Conditions of Delivery of Goods, called General Conditions of Delivery, 1968; came into force on Jan. 1, 1969. The Preamble is as follows:

"All deliveries of goods between organizations of the member-countries of the Council for Mutual Economic Assistance, authorized to engage in foreign trade operations, shall be made on the basis of the following General Conditions of Delivery. In those instances

when the parties in making a contract come to the conclusion that because of the specific nature of the goods and/or special characteristics of its delivery a departure from particular provisions of the present General Conditions of Delivery is required, they may so agree in the contract."

(4) General Conditions for Assembly and Rendering Other Technical Services Connected with Deliveries of Machines and Equipment between CMEA Member Countries (General Conditions of Assembly 1973).

(5) General Conditions for Technical Servicing of Machines, Equipment and Other Articles Delivered between Organizations of CMEA Member Countries Empowered to Perform Foreign Trade Operations (General Conditions of Assembly, 1973).

(6) General Principles for Providing Spare Parts for Machines and Equipment Delivered in Mutual Trade between CMEA Member Countries and Yugoslavia with Supplementary Conditions entered into force on Jan. 1, 1974.

(7) General Conditions and Procedure for the Mutual Allocation of Maritime Tonnage and Foreign Trade Cargoes of CMEA Member Countries.

Register of Texts of Conventions and other Instruments Concerning International Trade Law, UN, New York, 1973, Vol. I, pp. 17, 31 and 72; W.E. BUTLER (ed.), *A Source Book on Socialist International Organizations*, Alphen, 1978, pp. 923–1026.

GOODS FRONTIER CONTROL CONVENTION, 1984. The ten member States of the ▷ European Economic Community and the Council of European Communities signed on Feb. 1, 1984 in Geneva the International Convention on Frontier Control of Goods. Hungary and Switzerland also signed the Convention, which seeks to facilitate the international movement of goods by reducing the requirements for completing formalities as well as the number and duration of controls. The Convention applies to all goods being imported or exported or in transit across one or more maritime, air or inland frontiers.

UN Chronicle, No. 3, 1984, p. 34.

GORBACHEV ASIA PLAN 1988 ▷ Asia Gorbachev Plan.

GORBACHEV DOCTRINE ON WARSAW PACT COUNTRIES, 1987. A doctrine presented by the Secretary General of the CPSU, Mikhail S. Gorbachev, Nov. 2, 1987 in Moscow:

"Today the socialist world appears before us in all its national and social variety. This is good and useful. We have satisfied ourselves that unity does not mean identity and uniformity. We have also become convinced of there being no 'model' of socialism to be emulated by everyone".

M.S. Gorbachev outlined five principles to guide relations between the Soviet Union and other Communist countries.

". . . unconditional and full equality, the ruling party's responsibility for the state of affairs in the country, concern for the common cause of socialism, respect for one another, including voluntary and diverse cooperation, and a strict observance of the principles of peaceful co-existence by all".

The New York Times, November 3, 1987.

GORBACHEV PLAN 1986. A nuclear disarmament proposal of the Soviet leader M. Gorbachev in Jan. 1986 to the Great Powers "that we enter the third millenium without nuclear weapons".

Newsweek, January 27, 1986.

GORDON BENNET CUP. The international balloon competitions, founded in 1887 by James Gordon Bennet Jr. (1841–1918), editor of the *New York Herald.* The first race started from Paris in 1906 and the 26th in 1938 from Brussels. In 1979 on the initiative of the *International Herald Tribune* the 27th race took place in California, and in 1980 the 28th also in the USA.

D.C. SIETZ, *The James Gordon Bennets,* New York, 1928; H.S. VILLARD. *Blue Ribbon of the Air. The Gordon Bennett Race,* Washington DC, 1988.

GOREE. A small volcanic island near Cape Verde belonging to Senegal; area 88 acres (35 ha) with *c.* 900 inhabitants; center of the slave trade in the 18th century. A group of buildings dating from that period, Maison des Esclaves, have been preserved; in 1978 the island was included together with ▷ Auschwitz on the UNESCO list of Human Heritage in accordance with the Convention on the Protection of World Heritage, 1972.

UNESCO, *A Legacy for All,* Paris, 1984. UNESCO, Gorée, *Island of Memories,* Paris 1986.

GOSBANK SSSR. Gosudarstvyenniy Bank SSSR, the central bank of issue of the USSR, est. 1921 as Gosbank FSRR, from 1923 under its present name; headquarters in Moscow.

GOSPELS. *Latin*: evangelia. A subject of international co-operation. Organizations reg. with the UIA:
Gospel Literature International, f. 1961, Glendale, Calif.
World Gospel Crusades, f. 1949, Upland, Calif.
World Gospel Mission, f. 1910, St Marion, Ind.
▷ Bible.

Yearbook of International Organizations; V. TAYLOR, *The Formation of the Gospel Tradition,* London, 1953.

"GOULASH COMMUNISM". An international ironic term, coined by the Western press in 1985/86 for the economic reform in Hungary, which mixes Eastern planning economy with Western management.

GOURDE. Monetary unit of the Haiti Republic; one gourde = 100 centimes; issued by the Banque Nationale de la République d'Haïti. Linked with the US dollar from 1934, belongs to the US dollar zone.

GOVERNING COUNCIL FOR UNEP. ▷ UNEP.

GOVERNMENT IN EXILE. An international term defining, in principle, the superior authorities of an occupied state, who find shelter abroad; also authorities which, in view of revolutionary or counterrevolutionary changes within their state, take shelter on the territory of a friendly state. Subject of legal, international, but not uniform customs depending on political situations and legal rules governing the state of refuge. In spring 1939 the republican government of Spain became a government in exile and found refuge in Mexico. During World War II a number of governments of this type existed, among others, in Paris until May, 1940 – of Poland: in London from May, 1940 – of Belgium, Czechoslovakia, Holland, Yugoslavia, Greece, Norway and Poland, as well as Committees of Free Frenchmen (on June 28, 1940 the government of Great Britain acknowledged General Charles de Gaulle as Chairman of the Committee of Free France). Those governments did not have an identical status, except for benefiting from the law on diplomatic privileges; each government in exile concluded a separate bilateral agreement with the government of Great Britain. After World War II many states, which repudiated revolutionary changes in Eastern Europe, acknowledged governments in exile for quite some time.

P.E. OPPENHEIMER, "Governments and authorities in exile", in: *American Journal of International Law,* No. 36, 1942; M. FLORY, *Le statut international des gouvernements réfugiés et le cas de la France Libre,* Paris, 1952; G. SPERDUTI, "Governi in exilice comitati nazionali all'estero", in *La communita internazionale,* No. 7, 1952; G. KACEWICZ, *Great Britain, The Soviet Union and the Polish Government in Exile, 1939–1945,* The Hague, 1979; R.L. BLEDSOE, B.A. BOCZEK, *The International Law Dictionary,* Oxford, 1987.

GOVERNMENT, LOCAL. A subject of international co-operation. Organization reg. with the UIA:
International Union of Local Authorities, f. 1913, The Hague. Consultative statute with the ECOSOC, UNESCO, UNICEF, WHO and Council of Europe. Publ.: IULA Newsletters, and Studies in Comparative Local Government.

Yearbook of International Organizations.

GRAIN. A subject of international co-operation. A Special Protocol on Basic Grains was signed on Oct. 28, 1965 in Limon, Costa Rica. Organizations reg. with the UIA:
European Union for the Grain, Oilseed and Fodder Trades and Derivates, f. 1953, Paris.
Grain and Food Trade Committee of the EEC, f. 1958, Brussels.
Group for Assistance on Storage of Grains in Africa, f. 1972, Paris.

UNTS, Vol. 781, p. 47: *Yearbook of International Organizations;* N. BUTLER, *The International Grain Trade,* New York, 1986.

GRAM. An international mass and weight unit one gram = approx. 0.35 ounce.

GRAMM-RUDMAN LAW, formally the Balanced Budget and Emergency Control Act of 1985 of the US Congress, adopted on December 12, 1985, limited military spending and foreign military aid. Excluded from the military budget cuts was the Strategic Defence Initiative, SDI.

KEESING's *Record of World Events,* April, 1986.

GRAN CHACO. The Central South American lowland plain, 647,000 sq. km, divided among Paraguay, Bolivia and Argentina, called Chaco Boreal, Chaco Central and Chaco Austral; subject of disputes between Argentina and Bolivia in the 19th century, which were ended in 1878 with Bolivia's granting to Argentina the part located between the Pilcomayo and Verde rivers; and between Bolivia and Paraguay ▷ Chaco War, 1932–33.

GRAND CANYON. A natural site of USA, included in the ▷ World Heritage UNESCO List. The Grand Canyon walls give us a complete view of a geological evolution extending over a period of two billion years.

UNESCO, *A Legacy for All,* Paris, 1984.

GRAND CAYMAN ▷ Cayman Island.

GRAND DESIGN. Under this name the President of the USA John F. Kennedy on July 4, 1962 announced a plan for US military and economic ties with Western Europe which would take the form of a suprastate, Atlantic Commonwealth Organization, in which one group would comprise the USA and Canada, the second, the collective European states of the EEC and EFTA. In the speech of Secretary of State C.A. Herter of Jan., 1963 the Commonwealth was called "Atlantica" and had four aims: (1) to maintain close political ties between the countries of Western Europe and North America; (2) to solidify economic and military ties; (3) to foster the political affiliation of all free nations; (4) to form a common front against communist aggression. This conception was sharply opposed by the French head of state General Charles de Gaulle in a speech of Jan. 14, 1963, which made its implementation impossible.

J. KRAFT, *The Grand Design. From the Common Market to Atlantic Partnership,* New York, 1962; C.A. HERTER, "Atlantica", in: *Foreign Affairs,* January 1963.

"GRANMA". A yacht of the Cuban guerillas, which under the command of Fidel Castro on Dec. 1, 1956 sailed from the Mexican port of Tuxpan and landed in Cuba at the foot of the Sierra Maestra to begin a 25 month armed struggle against the dictatorship of Fulgencio Batista. This date is observed in Cuba as the anniversary of the armed rebellion. The name "Granma" was given to the town established at the place of landing and to a government newspaper. From the fall of 1976 the yacht is in the Museum of the Revolution in Havana.

H.L. MATHEWS, *The Cuban Story,* New York, 1960.

GRANT DOCTRINE, 1870. A doctrine enunciated by the US president Ulysses S. Grant (1822–85) as an expansion of the ▷ Monroe doctrine, stating that the European powers do not have a right to territory in the Western Hemisphere even if the population of those territories should so desire. This doctrine had the purpose of excluding rights resulting from ties between the European monarchies and the states of Latin America of the kind declared by Maximilian of Habsburg, who in 1863 proclaimed himself Emperor of Mexico.

La doctrina Monroe y el fracaso de una Conferencia Panamericana. Investigación y Prologo por Genaro Estrada, Mexico, DF, 1959, pp. 111–112.

GRAPHIC ART. A subject of international co-operation. Organizations reg. with the UIA:
Alliance Graphique Internationale, f. 1949, Zürich, Switzerland.
European Graphic Circle, f. 1954, Amsterdam.
International Association of Art Painting, Sculpture, Graphic Art. f. 1954, Paris. Consultative status with UNESCO and ECOSOC. Publ.: *Art.*
International Association of Research Institutes for the Graphic Arts Industry, f. 1965, Leatherhead, Sussex.
International Council of Graphic Design Associations, f. 1963, London. Publ.: *Icographic* (twice a year).
International Graphic Arts Education Association, f. 1923, Tempe, Ariz.
International Graphic Arts Society, f. 1951, New York.

Yearbook of International Organizations 1986/87; The Europa Yearbook 1988, Vol. 1, A World Survey, London 1988.

GRASSHOPPER. ▷ Locust and Grasshopper Infestation.

GRASSLAND. Subject of international co-operation. Organization reg. with the UIA:
European Grassland Federation, f. 1963, Haren, Netherlands; maintains liason between European grassland organizations.

The Europa Yearbook, 1988. A World Survey, Vol. I, London, 1988.

GRAVE OF THE UNKNOWN SOLDIER. The first monument to fallen soldiers with the ashes of an unknown soldier was erected after World War I in Paris near the Arc of Triumph and became a place for paying homage to the war dead and demonstrations for peace. Similar monuments are located i.a. in Brussels, Belgrade, Berlin, Moscow, Rio de Janeiro, Warsaw and Washington.

GRAVES OF PRISONERS OF WAR. A subject of international agreements. The ▷ Versailles Peace Treaty, 1919, in art. 226 stated:

"The graves of prisoners of war and interned civilians who are nationals of the different belligerent States and have died in captivity shall be properly maintained in accordance with Article 225 of the present Treaty. The Allied and associated governments on the one part and the German government on the other part reciprocally undertake also to furnish each other:

(1) A complete list of those who have died, together with all information useful for identification;
(2) All information as to the number and position of the graves of all those who have been buried without identification."

LNTS, 1920.

GREAT BARRIER REEF. The Australian north coast natural site, included in the ▷ World Heritage UNESCO List. The largest coral reefs in the world. They contain 400 different species of coral, 1500 different species of fish, 4000 of molluscs, 242 of birds, the dugong and turtles which are seriously threatened by extinction elsewhere. It is a paradise for scientific research.

UNESCO, *A Legacy for All*, Paris, 1984.

GREAT BRITAIN. A geographical term, describing the main island of the British isles, but in international relations former synonym of the British Empire.

GREAT BRITAIN AND NORTHERN IRELAND. ▷ United Kingdom.

GREAT CRASH. ▷ World Economic Crisis 1929–1939.

GREAT DEPRESSION ▷ World Economic Crisis 1929–1939.

"GREAT EASTERN". The largest metal ocean-going vessel of the 19th century, in service 1856–88, laid the first undersea cable connecting Europe with America.

GREAT POWERS. An international term for (1) in the 19th century: Austria, France, Germany, Great Britain and Russia; (2) after World War I: France, Great Britain, Italy, Japan, and the USA; after World War II: China, France, Great Britain, the USA and the USSR. ▷ Big Powers or Great Powers in the UN.

K. SKUBISZEWSKI, "The Great Powers and the settlement in Central Europe", in: *Jahrbuch für Internationales Recht*, 1975, pp. 92–126; P. KENNEDY, *The Rise and Fall of the Great Powers: Economic Change and Military Conflict from 1500 to 2000*, New York, 1988; D.P. CALLEO, *Beyond American Hegemony: The Future of the Western Alliance*, London, 1988.

GREAT WAR, THE. Up to 1939 the commonly accepted name for World War I, 1914–18.

GREECE. Member of the UN. Elliniki Dimokratia. Republic of Greece. State in southern Europe in the Balkan Peninsula and surrounding islands (Crete, Euboea, Cyclades, Sporades, Dodekanese, Ionian and in Asia Minor: Lesbos, Chios, etc.) in the Mediterranean. Bordering on Albania, Yugoslavia, Bulgaria and the European part of Turkey. Area: 131,990 sq. km. Pop. 1987 est.: 10,007,000 (1961 census: 8,387,000; 1970: 8,768,000). Capital city: Athens with 4,667,489 inhabitants in 1970.

Official language: Greek. GNP per capita 1981: US $4,350. Currency: one drachma = 100 lepta. National Day: March 25, anniversary of proclamation of independence, 1821.

A founding member of the UN. Oct. 24, 1945; member of all UN specialized agencies. Member of the EEC, the Council of Europe and the political wing of NATO.

International relations: 1453–1821 under Ottoman rule; 1821–29 fought a victorious war of independence; on Feb. 3, 1830 under the London Protocol France, Great Britain and Russia guaranteed independence to the Greek Kingdom. In World War I Greece fought alongside the Allies. Founding member of the League of Nations 1920–29. The attempted Greek intervention in Asia Minor failed in 1922. ▷ Greek Refugees Declaration 1923. In 1924 dispute with Italy over ▷ Corfu, examined by the League of Nations Council and Conference of Ambassadors. In Oct. 1925 Greece was accused by Bulgaria before the League of Nations Council of armed intervention and had to pay US $215,000 remuneration to Bulgaria. During World War II Greece was occupied by the German III Reich 1941–44. The monarchy had been maintained since 1821, apart from the periods 1924–35 and 1941–44 and was restored 1945–46 with armed help from Great Britain. In Jan., 1946 the USSR made a protest to the UN Security Council against British intervention. On Dec. 3, 1946 Greece accused Albania, Bulgaria and Yugoslavia of supporting guerillas in northern Greece, this prompted the Council to convene a special commission on Dec. 19, 1946 that remained in session from Jan. 29 to Sept., 1947. On Sept. 2, 1947 the UN General Assembly appointed by Res. 109/II a Special Committee in the Balkans, UNSCOB, composed of Austria, Brazil, China, France, Mexico, the Netherlands, Pakistan, Poland, the UK, USA, USSR. Poland and the USSR refused to participate. The Committee was formally dissolved on Dec. 7, 1951 when the UN General Assembly Res. 508/VI established a sub-committee for observance of peace which was effective until Apr. 28, 1954 when the "Greek question" was concluded at the UN. In 1976 Greek--Turkish issue of ▷ Cyprus was brought before the UN. The Republic was proclaimed on May 30, 1973. On Oct. 22, 1980 Greece returned to NATO after five years absence in relation to the Cyprus Crisis. Special assistance of the EEC under the 1985–1991 Integrated Plan for the Mediterranean Region. After 45 years Greece announced on August 23, 1985, the end of state of war with Albania. In 1986/87 increased tension with Turkey over the ▷ Aegean Sea.

See also ▷ World Heritage UNESCO List.

UN Bulletin, October 15, 1945; December 1, 1949; December 15, 1950; UN Commission of Investigation Concerning Greek Frontier Incidents, New York, 1949, p. 31; *The Subsidiary Group of the UN Commission of Investigation Concerning Greek Frontier Incidents*, New York, 1949; S. CALOGEROPOULOS-STRATIS, *La Grece et les Nations Unies*, N New York, 1957; S. ZYDIS, *Greece and the Great Powers: Prelude to the Truman Doctrine*, Thessaloniki, 1963; D.S. CONSTANTOPOULOS (ed.), *The Integration of Europe and Greece. The Congress of Thessaloniki*, Thessaloniki, 1965; S. ROSSEAS, *The Death of a Democracy: Greece and the American Conscience*, New York, 1968; J. ASKINAS, O. DOBROVOLSKIJ, *Nepokorionnaia Eliada*, Moskva, 1971; C.M. WOODHOUSE, *The Struggle for Greece, 1941–1949*; London, 1976; N.P. MONZELIS, *Modern Greece*, London, 1978; L. TSOUKALIS, *Greece and the European Community*, London, 1979; R. and M.J. CLOGG, *Greece. A Bibliography*, Oxford, 1980; *The Europa Year Book 1984. A World Survey*, Vol. I, pp. 543–559, London, 1984; KEESING's *Record of World Events*, March 1986.

GREECE–USA MILITARY AGREEMENTS, 1953 AND 1956. The Kingdom of Greece and the USA entered into a Military Facilities Agreement on Oct. 12, 1953 and having become parties to the Agreement of June 19, 1951 between the parties to the North Atlantic Treaty regarding the status of their forces, signed Sept. 7, 1956 in Athens the following agreement regarding the status of US forces in Greece.

"Art. 1(1) Paragraph 1. Article 3 of the Agreement between the Government of the United States of America and the Kingdom of Greece concerning Military Facilities, dated October 12, 1953, is abrogated except insofar as it refers to the Memorandum of Understanding dated February 4, 1953, which shall continue in effect.

(2) Agreement between the Parties of the North Atlantic Treaty Regarding the Status of Their Forces, dated June 19, 1951 shall govern the status of the forces of the United States in Greece as well as members of these forces, members of the civilian component, and their dependents, who are in Greece and who are serving in that country in furtherance of objectives of the North Atlantic Treaty Oganization, or who are temporarily present in Greece.

Art. 2(1) The Greek authorities recognizing that it is the primary responsibility of the United States authorities to maintain good order and discipline where persons subject to United States military law are concerned, will, upon the request of the United States authorities, waive their primary right to exercise jurisdiction under Art. 7, paragraph 3 (C) of that Agreement, except when they determine that it is of particular importance that jurisdiction be exercised by the Greek authorities.

(2) In those cases where, in accordance with the foregoing paragraph, there is waiver of jurisdiction by the Greek authorities, the competent United States authorities shall inform the Greek Government of the disposition of each such case.

Art. 3(1) In such cases where the Government of Greece may exercise criminal jurisdiction as provided for in Art. 2 above, the United States authorities shall take custody of the accused pending completion of trial proceeding. Custody of the accused will be maintained in Greece. During the trial and pretrial proceedings the accused shall be entitled to have a representative of the United States Government present. The trial shall be public unless otherwise agreed.

Art. 4(1) In civil matters, including damages arising from automobile accidents. Greek courts will exercise jurisdiction as provided in Art. 8 of NATO Status of Forces Agreement.

Art. 5 This agreement will come into force from the date on which it is signed.

Done at Athens in duplicate, in the English and Greek languages, the two texts having equal authenticity, this 7th day of September, 1956."

US Department of State Bulletin, September 10, 1956.

GREEK CATHOLIC CHURCH. Commonly called the Uniate Church, united with the Roman Catholic Church under the authority of the Pope, but retaining the Greek service (▷ Uniates).

GREEK EASTERN CHURCHES. The name used for Churches which broke away from Rome and formed the "orthodox, universal and apostolic Church of the East"; however, they do not comprise an indivisible unit such as the Roman Catholic Church, but are divided into several ▷ Autocephalia, called Orthodox Churches.

GREEK REFUGEES, 1923. A Declaration of the governments by Great Britain, France and Italy relating to the settlement of refugees from Turkey in Greece and the creation for this purpose of a Refugees Settlement Commission, Geneva, Sept. 29, 1923; Additional Declaration, Geneva, Sept. 25, 1924.

LNTS, Vol. 20, p. 41 and Vol. 30, p. 422; *League of Nations, Greek Refugee Settlement*, Geneva, 1926.

GREEK-TURKISH WAR of 1921–1922. A war which broke out after the ▷ Sèvres Peace Treaty 1920 was not accepted by the Turkish government; won by Turkey; ended with the ▷ Lausanne Peace Treaty 1923, which restored the Maritsi River in Thrace as the border between Greece and Turkey.

L. MONZELIS, *Modern Greece*, London 1978.

GREEN BERETS. The accepted name for the US Special Forces, which have the task of combatting partisans, especially in Latin America. According to a Bulletin of the Pentagon of Sept. 23, 1967:

"The group of Special Forces is subordinate to the North American Supreme International Command with headquarters in Panama. At the request of 17 governments of Latin America with which we exchange military missions on the continent, small mobile training groups were sent to these countries with the task of assisting in various types of schooling, including police functions."

1969 News Dictionary. An Encyclopedic Summary of Contemporary History, New York, 1970.

GREEN INTERNATIONAL. An international term used after World War I for solidarity movement of European agricultural producers aimed against US producers dictating world prices. After World War II, this term covered a political peasant movement in Western Europe that organized integrational congresses. In the EEC, it became customary to call the integration of agriculture, Green Europe – Europe verte.

"GREEN" INTERNATIONAL. An international ecological movement, initiated by the "green" political parties in West European Parliaments in the 1980's.

GREENLAND. *Danish*: Grønland. The largest island in the world, located in the Atlantic east of North America. A Danish territory with its own self-government since June 5, 1953 and with internal autonomy since May 1, 1979. Area: 2,175,600 sq. km. Pop. est. 1983: 51,903. Capital: Godthåb with 10,335 inhabitants 1983. A subject of a longstanding dispute between Norway and Denmark, the latter proclaimed sovereign rights over Greenland in 1921 and in 1924 announced Greenland a colony. Norway filed a complaint with the Permanent Court of International Justice; which decided Apr. 5, 1953: "Denmark had valid claims to sovereignty over Greenland."
On Apr. 9, 1941 in Washington, Denmark and the USA signed a treaty permitting the USA to establish military bases, which was extended in 1945. Denmark and the USA signed on Apr. 27, 1951 in Copenhagen an Agreement pursuant to the North Atlantic Treaty, concerning the defense of Greenland. From 1945 to 1953 Greenland was included by the UN among the dependent territories, and each year Denmark submitted information to the appropriate UN body. On June 5, 1953 the population of Greenland, at that time numbering *c*. 35,000 inhabitants, in a plebiscite voted for complete integration with Denmark, which was accepted by the UN Committee Sept. 13, 1953. In a plebiscite held by the Danish government Oct. 2, 1972 for or against joining the EEC Greenland voted against, while Denmark voted for, which created a conflict between the self-government of Greenland and the Danish government. On May 1, 1979 the internal autonomy of Greenland within the Danish kingdom was proclaimed. In a plebiscite 1984 the population of Greenland rejected integration into the EEC as an autonomous part of Denmark. On February 1, 1985, Greenland formally withdrew from the European Community.

L. PREUSS, "The dispute between Denmark and Norway over the sovereignty of East Greenland", in: *American Journal of International Law*, No. 26, 1932; *UN Review*, No. 10, 1954; J. DUASON, *Die Koloniale Stellung Grönlands*, Göttingen, 1960; K. HERTLING (ed.), *Greenland Past and Present*, Copenhagen, 1972; F. GAD, *A History of Greenland*, 2 Vols, London, 1973; *The Europa Year Book*, *1984. A World Survey*, Vol. I, pp. 412–413, London, 1984.

GREENLAND – ICELAND – UK GAP, GIUK. An international geopolitical term for the only viable sea-way from the USSR into the Atlantic Ocean. A NATO strategic problem.

D. ROBERTSON, *Guide to Modern Defense and Strategy*, Detroit, 1988.

GREEN MONEY. The currency used in the Common Agricultural Policy of the EEC.

GREEN PARTIES. The so called "Green Parties" from 20 countries organize every year, since 1985, the International Green Conference characterized by an anti-militaristic program, rejection of male-dominated hierarchies and rejection of capitalist and socialist models, and a belief in decentralization.

KEESING's *Record of World Events*, No. 9, 1988.

"GREENPEACE". A West European ecological movement founded in 1972. Its campaigns are directed primarily against nuclear testing. In July 1987 Greenpeace launched its International Nuclear Free Sea Campaign.

J. DYSON, *Sink the Rainbow: An Enquiry Into the Greenpeace Affair*, London, 1987; KEESING's *Contemporary Archive*, 1986, No. 8.

GREEN REVOLUTION. An international term for the process of rapid increase of agricultural production, due to new varieties of crops grown in the decade of 1960s in two institutions working under the aegis of the FAO: International Center for Improvement of Maize and Wheat in Mexico, which developed several varieties of wheat including the so-called Mexican variety, reaching extraordinary yields of up to 60 quintals per hectare; and the International Rice Institute in Los Banos in the Philippines which turned over to farmers of South Asia the varieties of rice named IR, yielding from 40 to 80 quintals per hectare. In Mexico the application of the International Center program allowed average increases of wheat yields of 8 to 28 quintals per hectare in the years 1950–70, with an eight-fold increase of fertilizer use. In Pakistan the application of that program gave 8.6 million tons in 1970, compared with 4.6 million tons in 1965. In 1971, India discontinued imports of wheat, as Ceylon stopped rice imports; the Philippines, which formerly imported about one million tons of rice yearly, became a rice exporter. Nevertheless, people in many countries of the Third World, which benefited from the green revolution, were still starving, and food was more expensive than before because of an outdated social structure and the need for agrarian reforms. UN Secretary-General U Thant in a report of Jan., 1971, warned those countries that if they did not rapidly implement agrarian reform, the green revolution, instead of being a cornucopia, might prove to be a Pandora's box.

International Maize and Wheat Improvement Centre: Strategies for Increasing Agricultural Production on Small Holdings, Mexico DF, 1970; *UN Monthly Chronicle*, Feb., 1971; L. NULTY, *The Green Revolution in West Pakistan. Implications of Technological Change*, New York, 1971; Z.M. AHMAD, "Les conséquences sociales et économiques de la révolution verte en Asie", in: *Revue internationale du travail*, No. 1, 1972, pp. 9–38; M. CEPEDE, "Révolution verte et emploie", in: *Revue internationale du travail*, No. 1, 1972, pp. 1–8; W. THIESENHAUSEN, "The 'Green Revolution' in Latin America", in: *Monthly Labour Review*, March, 1972; K. GRIFFIN, *The Green Revolution. An Economic Analysis*, Geneva, 1972.

GREENWICH OBSERVATORY. An astronomical observatory in South London, est. 1875. In 1884 the meridian which passes through Greenwich was accepted as the zero meridian, and the zonal time of this meridian was called universal or Greenwich time. European zonal time in abbreviation is called GMT. Since 1953 these names have become imprecise inasmuch as the Observatory itself, because of atmospheric disturbances over London (smog) at that time, was moved to Herstmonceaux Castle in the county of Sussex. A maritime museum is now located in the former building. Nonetheless, the name Greenwich has been universally retained.

B. PLATTS, *A History of Greenwich*, London, 1973; B. WEINREB, B.C. HIBBERT eds. *The London Encyclopedia*, 1983.

GRENADA. Member of the UN. State of Grenada. West Indies State in the Windward Islands. Area: 344 sq. km. Pop. 1987 est. 100,000 (1970 census: 93,858). Capital: St George's with 7,500 inhabitants, 1980. GNP per capita 1987 US $1,340. Official language: English. Currency: one East Caribbean dollar = 100 cents. National Day. Feb. 7, Independence Day, 1974.
Member of the UN and of UN specialized agencies save WMO, IMO, WIPO, IAEA and GATT. Member of the OAS, CARICOM, the Commonwealth and is an ACP state of the EEC. A signatory of the Lomé Conventions of 1975 and 1980.
International relations: British possession since 1783. Associated state under the West Indies Act 1967–74. Complete independence achieved on Feb. 7, 1974. On Mar. 13, 1979 a military junta took power. On Oct. 21, 1983 the Prime Minister Maurice Bishop was shot. On October. 25, 1983 an armed intervention took place in Grenada by troops of the US. Jamaica, Barbados and members of the Organization of Eastern Caribbean States, OECS, which had determined that a "dangerous vacuum of authority in Grenada constituted an unprecedented threat to the peace and security of the region." The US intervention in Grenada was a subject of a dispute in the UN Security Council Oct. 25–28, 1983. The majority of the 62 speakers, according to the *UN Chronicle*, found unacceptable the justification given for the action.
Restoration of normalcy in Grenada was the universal goal of participants in the debate. Respect for the sovereignty, independence and territorial integrity of Grenada was stressed, along with the right to self-determination of its people. In September 1985 the US and Caribbean military forces were withdrawn from Grenada. A 550-member police force and paramilitary unit, trained by UK and US officers assumed control over the island.
On October 31, 1985, Queen Elizabeth II, and on February 20, 1986, President R. Reagan visited Grenada.

C. SEARLE, D. ROJAS (eds.), *To Construct from Morning*, Grenada, 1982; P. WHEATON, C. SUNSHINE, *Grenada. The Peaceful Revolution*, Washington, DC, 1982; *UN Chronicle*, January, 1984, pp. 4–8; *The Europa Year Book 1984. A World Survey*, Vol. II, pp. 1618–1621, London, 1984; G.K. LEWIS, *Grenada: The Jewel Despoiled*, Baltimore Md., 1987; S. DAVIDSON, *Grenada: A Study in Politics and the Limits of International Law*, Aldershot, 1987.

GRENADINES. Archipelago in the Windward Islands in the Carribean Sea. The southern part belongs to ▷ Grenada, the northern to ▷ Saint Vincent and the Grenadines.

UN Chronicle, April, 1980, p. 17.

G

GRESHAM'S LAW. A term commonly adopted in Anglo-Saxon countries equivalent to ▷ Copernicus' Principle of 1526 stating that "bad money drives out good." The law was made public in 1560 in England in a proclamation by Queen Elizabeth I prepared by the Royal Treasurer T. Gresham (1519–79).

F.R. SALTER, *Sir Thomas Gresham. A Biography*, London, 1925.

GROCERS ASSOCIATION. International organizations reg. with the UIA:

International Federation of Grocers Associations, f. 1927, Bern. Publ.: *Information Bulletin.*
International Federation of Importers and Wholesale Grocers Associations, f. 1927, Brussels. Publ.: *Bulletin.*

Yearbook of International Organizations, 1986/87; The Europa Yearbook 1988. A World Survey, Vol. 1, London 1988.

GROMYKO PLAN, 1946. A Soviet plan for the international control of atomic energy, presented by Andrei Gromyko on June 19, 1946 at the second session of the UN Atomic Energy Commission, after the presentation of the US ▷ Baruch Plan 1946. The highlights of the statement.

"I will place before the Commission for consideration two concrete proposals which, in the opinion of the Soviet Government, may constitute a basis for the adoption by the commission of recommendations to the Security Council and play an important role in the strengthening of peace. These proposals are as follows: (1) concerning the conclusion of an international convention prohibiting the production and employment of weapons based on the use of atomic energy for the purpose of mass destruction; (2) concerning the organization of the work of the Atomic Energy Commission."

The preamble and the first and second article of the proposed draft convention were as follows:

"Being profoundly aware of the vast significance of the great scientific discoveries connected with the splitting of the atom and the obtaining and use of atomic energy for the purpose of promoting the welfare and raising the standard of living of the peoples of the world, as well as for the development of culture and science for the benefit of mankind;
animated by the desire to promote in every way the fullest possible utilization by all peoples of scientific discoveries in the sphere of atomic energy for the purpose of improving the conditions of life of the peoples of the world and promoting their welfare and the further progress of human culture;
fully realizing that the great scientific discoveries in the sphere of atomic energy carry with them a great danger, above all, for peaceful towns and the civilian population in the event of these discoveries being used in the form of atomic weapons for the purpose of mass destruction;
recognizing the great significance of the fact that international agreements have already prohibited the use in warfare of asphyxiating, poisonous and other similar gases, as well as similar liquids, substances and processes, and likewise bacteriological means, rightly condemned by the public opinion of the civilized world, and considering that the international prohibition of the use of atomic weapons for the mass destruction of human beings corresponds in still greater measure to the aspirations and the conscience of the peoples of the whole world;
being firmly resolved to avert the danger of these scientific discoveries being used to the detriment and against the interests of mankind;
resolved to conclude a convention to prohibit the production and the employment of weapons based on the use of atomic energy, and for this purpose appoints as their plenipotentiaries, who, after presenting their credentials found to be in good and due form, agreed as follows:
Art. 1. The high contracting parties solemnly declare that they are unanimously resolved to prohibit the production and employment of weapons based on the

use of atomic energy, and for this purpose assume the following obligations:
(a) not to use atomic weapons in any circumstances whatsoever;
(b) to prohibit the production and storing of weapons based on the use of atomic energy;
(c) to destroy, within a period of three months from the day of the entry into force of the present convention, all stocks of atomic energy weapons whether in a finished or unfinished condition.
Art. 2. The high contracting parties declare that any violation of Article I of the present convention is a most serious international crime against humanity."

UN Atomic Energy Commission, *Official Record*, June 19, 1946; *UN Yearbook 1945/46.*

GROSS DOMESTIC PRODUCT, GDP. An international term in the UN system for the total value, at current price, of a nation's goods and services during a given period of time, usually a year.

UN Chronicle, October, 1982, p. 47.

GROSS NATIONAL PRODUCT, GNP. An international term in the US system for an internationally used index of economic growth. This is ▷ Gross Domestic Product minus or plus a country's foreign payments or receipts of factor income (interest, dividend etc.). Such payments by developing countries usually exceed their receipts, so their GNP is usually lower than their GDP. The reverse is true for most developed countries. UN regional economic committees' investigations of GNP and national income per capita showed the level of growth as well as annual stagnation in individual countries, territories, or regions. For example, surveys carried out by CEPAL/ECLA in Latin America showed an absolute fall in GNP per capita throughout the continent in the 1950–64 period. In 1950–55 annual GNP increase was 2.2%, national income per capita was growing by 1.9%, whereas the figures for 1962–64 were below 1% and 0.8% respectively.

El Financiamento Externo de America Latina, CEPAL, New York, 1964.

GROSS ROSEN. A German concentration camp in Lower Silesia, between the Oder and Neisse, est. 1940 as branch of ▷ Sachsenhausen, since 1941 an autonomous concentration camp for Jews, Poles and Soviet soldiers. About 125,000 prisoners passed through it and about 40,000 were murdered. Liberated by the Soviet Army Feb. 13, 1945.

The Trial of German Major War Criminals. Proceedings of the International Military Tribunal Sitting at Nuremberg, Germany, 42 Vols., London 1946–1948, Vol. 3, p. 204; Vol. 5, pp. 235–237; Vol. 22, p. 452; J. GUTTO, *Gross Rosen*, Warsaw, 1970; C.Z. PILICHOWSKI (ed.), *Obozy hitlerowskie na ziemiach polskich 1939–1945. Informator Encyklopedyczny* [Nazi camps on Polish territory 1939–1945, Encyclopedic Guide], Warsaw, 1979, pp. 425–433.

GROTIUS FOUNDATION. The international Grotius Foundation for the Propaganda of the Law of Nations, f. 1947, Munich, FRG. Consultative status with UNESCO. Publ.: *The Grotius Letters.* Reg. with the UIA.

C.H. ALEKSANDROWICZ, *Grotius Society Papers 1972: Studies in the History of the Law of Nations*, The Hague, 1972; *Yearbook of International Organizations.*

GROUP OF EIGHTEEN. The official name of a consultative body of GATT, set up Aug., 1975 with the aim of analyzing regional and world markets and noting any types of discrimination in foreign trade. Members: Australia, Argentina, Brazil, Canada, Egypt, Spain, the USA, France, India, Japan, Malaysia, Nigeria, Pakistan, Peru, Poland, Great Britain, Zaïre and the EEC representative.

GROUP OF FIVE. A group of finance ministers and central bankers of France, the FRG, Japan, the UK and the USA in permanent financial co-operation with the major industrialized countries of the Western community. In 1986 replaced by the ▷ Group of Seven.

KEESING's *Record of World Events*, January, 1987.

GROUP OF SEVEN, established by the ▷ Tokyo summit 1986, including the ▷ Group of Five, Canada and Italy, and requesting the seven finance ministers and central bankers "to review their individual economic objectives and forecasts collectively at least once a year".

KEESING's *Contemporary Archive*, September 1985; KEESING's *Contemporary Archive*, 1986; KEESING's *Record of World Events*, 1987.

GROUP OF 77. An international term in the UN system for 77 states of the Third World which at the First UNCTAD Conference in Geneva, 1964, formed a solid front. Before the Second UNCTAD Conference, 1968 in Delhi, the Group of 77 now numbering 83 states, met in Algiers Oct. 10–25, 1967 and formulated a common position (▷ Algiers Group of 77 Charter, 1967). Also before the Third UNCTAD Conference, 1972, in Santiago de Chile the Group of 77, in Oct. 1971, held a meeting in Lima for the purpose of drafting a platform for common action. The number of states had grown to 95; Africa – 41, Asia – 29, Latin America – 24, and from Europe traditionally Yugoslavia. The meeting in Lima lasted from Oct. 25, to Nov. 6, 1971. For the first time Cuba participated in the work of the Group of 77. Cuba had not taken part in the previous sessions of the Group due to a boycott by the Latin American states demanded by the OAS. The ▷ Lima Declaration 1971 reiterated the main thesis of the Algiers Charter of 1967, since, as speakers stated, the situation had not improved in the preceding years.
At a conference in Manila, Feb. 2–10, 1976 the Group of 77, now with 106 states participating, prepared a common platform (▷ Manila Group of 77 Declaration, 1976) for the Fourth UNCTAD Conference in Nairobi in May 1977. A Conference of the Group of 77 was held in Mexico, Sept. 13–20, 1976, on the question of the ▷ New International Economic Order and economic co-operation among the developing countries.
A Conference held in Buenos Aires, Mar. 28–Apr. 9, 1983 declared that 125 states are in the deepest economic crisis. The Twentieth Anniversary of the establishment of the Group 77 was commemorated on June 15, 1984. From the 162 member States of UNCTAD in 1984 the absolute majority participated in the Group of 77 Conferences.

The Europa Year Book 1984. A World Survey, Vol. I, p. 41, London, 1984.

GROUP OF SUPPORT. A group of 4 countries: Argentina, Brazil, Peru and Uruguay, supporting since September 1985 the ▷ Contadora Group.

KEESING's *Contemporary Archive*, September 1985.

GROUP OF TEN. The name universally accepted for meetings of the finance ministers of ten states: Belgium, Canada, France, the FRG, Great Britain, Italy, Japan, the Netherlands, Sweden and the USA, which Dec. 13, 1961 in Paris ratified a general agreement on the granting of loans by the International Monetary Fund, IMF, to stimulate international liquidity, in short called ▷ GAB; the Group of Ten *de facto* became a superior authority over

IMF executives and has been institutionalized since Nov. 1966, when Group of Ten and IMF executives began periodic meetings (2–3 times a year) alternatively in Washington or London. Taking part in these meetings, besides the finance ministers of the ten states, are the chief executives of central banks as well as the president of the Bank for International Settlements. In 1963 Switzerland joined the Group of Ten as an observer.

IMF Report, 1966.

GROUP OF THIRTY. A Consultative Group on International Economic and Monetary Affairs Incorporated, f. 1978. Members: 30 central and private bankers, economists, meeting twice a year with secretariats in London and New York.

The Economist, December 28, 1987.

GROUP OF TWENTY. The officially accepted IMF name for a body composed of the financial representatives of twenty states charged with working out a reform of the international monetary system created by the XXVII Session of the IMF on Oct. 20, 1972 in Washington. Members of the Group of Twenty are the ten states of ▷ Group of Ten and Argentina, Australia, Brazil, India, Indonesia, Iraq, Morocco, Mexico, Switzerland and Zaïre.

IMF Report, 1972.

GROUP SANTO DOMINGO. The nine states of the Caribbean region (Barbados, Colombia, Dominican Republic, Guyana, Haiti, Jamaica, Mexico, Trinidad and Tobago, and Venezuela), which in 1972 at a conference in the capital of the Dominican Republic formally declared a 12-mile limit for territorial waters, but in fact recognized the 200-mile limit as a patrimonial sea, subject to the jurisdiction of the coastal states, whose advocate was the ▷ Montevideo Group. In 1973 they agreed on a common position at the UN Conference on Law of the Sea.

GROUPS OF PRESSURE. ▷ Pressure Groups.

GSP. ▷ Preferences.

GUADALAJARA AIR CONVENTION. ▷ Air Guadalajara Convention, 1961.

GUADALUPE HIDALGO TREATY, 1848. A peace treaty between Mexico and the US, signed on Feb. 2, 1848 in Guadalupe Hidalgo. The treaty established a new boundary line between the two Republics in the middle of the Rio Grande, otherwise called Rio Bravo del Norte. This frontier was partly changed by the Gadsden Treaty, 1853.

Major Peace Treaties of Modern History, New York, 1967. Vol. II, pp. 733–751.

GUADELOUPE. Two islands in the Lesser Antilles, separated by the Salee River, called Guadeloupe proper and Grand Terre, total area 1434 sq. km, with dependencies 1779 sq. km. Pop. 1985 est.: 332,000. Capital: Basse-Terre with 13,656 inhabitants. French possession since 1635. Overseas department of France since Mar. 19, 1946; in 1973 an administrative region.

G. LASSERE, *La Guadeloupe*, 2 Vols., Bordeaux, 1961; *The Europa Year Book 1984. A World Survey*, Vol. II, pp. 1570–1572, London, 1984.

GUAM. The largest island of the Marianas archipelago, located in the Pacific, a US possession, area 541 sq. km. with 116,000 inhabitants in 1983; Spanish in the 17–19th centuries first as Ladrones, then Mariana Island; by the Treaty of Paris, Dec.

10, 1898 ceded by Spain to the United States; occupied by Japan from Dec. 10, 1941 to Aug. 10, 1944; after World War II Guam was the major US submarine base in that area of the Pacific. On Aug. 1, 1950 the inhabitants of Guam became US citizens, but without the right to vote in presidential elections; the administration of the island was transferred from the Department of the Navy to the Department of the Interior. The fate of the local population, whose language is Chamorro (Micronesian), was the subject of studies by the UN Committee on Decolonization. In Nov. 1970 the inhabitants for the first time elected a governor, who until then had been appointed by the President of the USA; in 1976 Guam elected delegates to the House of Representatives. On Sept. 4, 1982 a political status referendum had been organized. In it 75% of the participants had voted for Commonwealth status in association with the US. The UN Special Committee on Sept. 14, 1983 reaffirmed its strong conviction that the US administration must ensure that military installations on Guam did not hinder the population from exercising its right to self-determination and independence.

C. BEARDSLEY, *Guam Past and Present*, Rutland, Vt, 1964; P. CARANO, P.C. SANCHEZ, *Complete History of Guam*, Rutland, Vt, 1964; *The Europa Year Book 1984. A World Survey*, Vol. II, pp. 2629–2630, London, 1984.

GUANTANAMO. A US military base in Cuba with about 2,100 American troops, located in the Oriente province on the Gulf of Guantanamo, 64 km east of the city of Santiago de Cuba. The first European who sailed into the Gulf of Guantanamo, Apr. 30, 1494, and appreciated its advantages was Columbus, then successively Spaniards, Englishmen and Frenchmen; after the Spanish–American war, which resulted in the liberation of Cuba, the USA, on the basis of the so-called Platt Amendment, later attached to the treaty with Cuba, May 22, 1903, compelled Cuba i.a. to lease Guantanamo for 99 years as a condition for recognizing its independence. The Cuban–American Treaty of 1934 reaffirmed the proviso on Guantanamo. When the revolutionary government of Cuba appealed to the USA 1960 and then to the UN to nullify the treaty of 1934, the US government declared that: "The Treaty cannot be nullified without the agreement of both sides," and furthermore "Guantanamo is important to the security of the USA and the Western Hemisphere." In 1962, during the American–Soviet crisis, the base was reinforced by several thousand marines and additional equipment. In 1964 the Cuban government cut off the flow of drinking water to Guantanamo from the Oriente waterworks, and since that time the sources of drinking water for the base are desalinization plants.

F.A. TOBIO, "La base naval de Guantanamo y el derecho internacional", in: *Cuba Socialista*, No. 11, 1962; *The US Naval Base in Guantanamo*, La Habana, 1966; *The Europa Yearbook*, A World Survey 1987, London 1987.

GUARANI. A monetary unit of Paraguay; one guarani = 100 centimos; issued by the Banco Central del Paraguay.

GUARANI INDIANS. An indigenous people of Paraguay, southern Argentine and northern Brazil: to this day speaking Guarani. The system of Indian settlements organized in Paraguay by the Jesuits at the beginning of the 17th century was called Doctrinas de Guaranis. In the second half of the 20th century the Guarani Indian tribes in Paraguay and Brazil became the object of genocidal policies connected with the discovery of oil fields in territories inhabited by the Indians. ▷ American Indians.

A.N. LOCKWOOD, *Indians of the Andes*, New York, 1956; A. ARMANI, *Ciudad de Dios y Ciudad de Sol. El "Estado" Jesuita de los Guaranies (1609–1768)*, México, DF, 1983.

GUARANTEE CHAIN, INTERNATIONAL. An international term for customs conventions guarantee of payment of customs duty by the appropriate institutions designated by states participating in the convention in a case where goods brought in for a temporary period without customs duty are not taken out within a definite period.

GUARANTEE OF QUALITY. An international term for a clause accepted in foreign trade allowing the recipient to refuse to accept a product not meeting the quality specified in the contract. The period of the guarantee ranges from 6 to 15 months.

GUARANTEES FOR FOREIGN INVESTMENTS. An international term, appeared after World War II for two kinds of guarantees: state and interstate for private foreign investors in countries of the Third World, ensuring full compensation in case of the nationalization of factories constructed abroad. The state system of guarantees for foreign investments ensuring the coverage of losses through political risks, was introduced for private investors in 1955 by the USA, Japan and the FRG for the purpose of encouraging foreign investment.

GUARANTEES IN INTERNATIONAL TRADE. An international term for bank guarantees commonly used in foreign transactions (by a guaranteed bill of exchange, called naval, or by a guaranteed bank letter) or insurance (policies insuring against business and political risks). In highly developed countries there are special institutions for guarantees in international trade, such as e.g. UK Export Credit Guaranty Department, ECGD; Compagnie Française d'Assurance pour le Commerce Exterieur, COFACE and Foreign Credit Insurance Association in the USA, est. 1962 as a partnership association of the states of the Export–Import Bank with 72 private American insurances companies.

P.C. JESSUP, *International Security*, New York, 1936; W. KAGI, "Garantie", in: *STRUPP-SCHLOCHAUER Wörterbuch des Völkerrechts*, Berlin, 1960.

GUATEMALA. Member of the UN. República de Guatemala. Republic of Guatemala. State in Central America on the Pacific Ocean and the Caribbean. Bounded by Belize, Honduras, El Salvador. Area: 108,889 sq. km. Pop. 1987 est. 8,434,339 (1880 census: 1,224,000; 1893: 1,264,000; 1921: 1,743,000; 1940: 2,300,000; 1950: 2,790,000; 1970: 5,650,000). Capital city: Guatemala City with 749,784 inhabitants 1981. GNP per capita 1987: US $950. Official language: Spanish. Currency: one quetzal = 100 centavos. National Day: Sept. 15, anniversary of proclamation of independence, 1821.

Member of the League of Nations 1919–36; Original member of the UN since Oct. 24, 1945 and all its specialized agencies except the GATT; member of the OAS and Central American Common Market. International relations: 1523 conquered by Spain; 1543–1821 Spanish colony called Capitania General de Guatemala. Independent since Sept. 15, 1821. In federation of Central America 1839; border disputes with Mexico and British Honduras over ▷ Belize, to which it had claims and with Honduras, borders delimited under treaty of July 16, 1930 pursuant to arbitration settlement of Jan. 23, 1930. In World War I on the Allied side. In World War II

G

with the United Nations. The question of Guatemala was considered on June 25, 1954 by the UN Security Council in connection with US armed intervention in Guatemala. In the 1970s and in the beginning of the 1980s the situation of human rights was a subject of the UN investigations. The UN General Assembly Res. 37/184 of Dec. 17, 1982 expressed its deep concern at the serious violations of human rights in Guatemala, particularly the widespread repressions, killings and displacement of rural and indigenous population. In Nov. 1983 Guatemala supported the British presence in ▷ Belize. After the resumption of full diplomatic relations with the UK on December 29, 1986 (broken off in 1963), the first direct talks with the government of Belize were held on April 29, 1988 in Miami. See also ▷ World Heritage UNESCO List.

F.C. FISHER, "The arbitration of the Guatemala–Honduras boundary", in: *American Journal of International Law*, No. 27, 1933; *Guatemala White Book of the Belize Question*. Ciudad de Guatemala, 1938; M. MONTEFORTE TOLEDO, *Guatemala. Monografia Sociológica*, México, DF. 1965; R. PLANT, *Guatemala, Unnatural Disaster*, London, 1978; W.B. FRANKLIN, *Guatemala. Bibliography*, Oxford, 1981; S. SCHLESINGER, S. KINZER, *Bitter Front. The Untold Story of The American Coup in Guatemala*, New York, 1982; *The Europa Year Book 1984. A World Survey*, Vol. II, pp. 1622–1634, London, 1984; KEESING's *Record of World Events*, No. 6, 1988.

GUERILLA. *Spanish* = "little war". The Ibero-American term for partisan warfare. A historical name accepted on the Iberian subcontinent in the years 1809–13 during the anti-Napoleonic partisan war waged by irregular units of guerrilleros. The term is currently accepted in the Anglo-Saxon world.

L. NURICH, R. BARRET, "Legality of guerrilla forces under laws of war", in: *American Journal of International Law*, 1946; A. CAMBELL, *Guerrillas, A History and Analysis*, London, 1967; R. GOTT, *Guerrilla Movements in Latin America*, London, 1970; L. CANN, *Guerrillas in History*, Stanford, 1971; R.B. ASPREY, *War in the Shadow: The Guerilla in History*, Garden City, 1975; W. LAQUER, *Guerrilla: A Historical and Critical Study*, Boston, 1976; UN Chronicle, January, 1984, pp. 52–53; D. ROBERTSON, *Guide to Modern Defense and Strategy*, Detroit, 1988.

GUERNICA. Guernica y Luno, city in northern Spain in the Basque province of Viscaya (1970 pop. 9997); during the Spanish Civil War on Apr. 26, 1937 totally destroyed by bombing raids of the Nazi Condor Legion; the ruins of Guernica became a symbol for the war barbarity of the fascists, which was highlighted by the famous painting "Guernica", 1937, by P. Picasso. In answer to soundings by Great Britain to convene an international commission to investigate the unrestricted bombing of an open city only the Soviet Union and France replied. The League of Nations did not react at all.

KEESING's *Contemporary Archive*, 1937, pp. 3038, 3048 and 3109.

GUILDER. A monetary unit of Netherlands Antilles; one guilder = 100 cents; issued by the Bank van de Nederlandse Antillen. Linked to the Netherlands guilder, belongs to the Dutch monetary zone.

GUILDER. A monetary unit of Suriname; one guilder = 100 cents; issued by the Centrale Bank van Suriname. Linked to the Netherlands guilder, belongs to the Dutch monetary zone.

GUILDER OR FLORIN. A monetary unit of the Netherlands; one guilder = 100 cents; issued by De Nederlandsche Bank.

GUINEA. Member of the UN. République de Guinée. Republic of Guinea. West African state on the Atlantic Ocean, bordered by Guinea-Bissau, Senegal, Mali, Côte d'Ivoire, Liberia and Sierra Leone. Area: 245,857 sq. km. Pop. 1988 est. 6,530,000 (1955 census: 2,570,219; 1972 census: 4,143,284). Capital: Conakry with 525,671 inhabitants. 1972. GNP per capita 1985 US $370. Official language: French. Currency: Guinea franc = 100 centimes. National Day: Oct. 2, Independence Day, 1958.

Member of the UN since Sept. 25, 1959 and of the UN specialized agencies with the exception of the IAEA, and GATT. Member of the OAU. ACP state of the EEC. A signatory of the Lomé Conventions of 1975 and 1980.

International relations: Guinea was under French control since the late 18th century; French protectorate in 1864; French colony in 1893; in 1904 part of French West Africa; since 1946 with autonomous status in the French Union; on Sept. 28, 1958 voted in a referendum against the French Community and opted for complete independence, which was granted on Oct. 2, 1958. Treaty of co-operation with France signed on May 22, 1963 in Paris. In 1967 in disputes with the Ivory Coast (now Côte d'Ivoire), and in 1970 with Portugal. After the death of President Sekou Touré Guinea started a new internal and foreign policy 1982.

SEKOU TOURÉ, *La Révolution guinéenien et le progrès social,* Conacry, 1963; B. AMEILLON, *La Guinée*, Paris, 1964; A.A. FIRSOW, *Ekonomicheskye problemy Gvineiskoy Respubliki*, Moskva, 1965; L. ADAMOLEKUM, SEKOU TOURÉ, *Guinea*, London, 1976; S. CAMARA, *La Guinée sans France*, Paris, 1976; C. ROVIERE, *Guinea*, Cornell University Press, 1977; *The Europa Year Book 1984. A World Survey*, Vol. II, pp. 1635–1642, London, 1984.

GUINEA-BISSAU. Member of the UN. West African state on the Atlantic Ocean, bordered by Senegal,and Guinea. Area including the adjacent archipelago Bijagot with the island of Bolamo: 36,125 sq. km. Pop. 1988 est. 932,000 (1979 census: 777,214). Capital: Bissau City with 109,486 inhabitants 1979. GNP per capita 1986 US $170. Official language: Portuguese. Currency: one peso = 100 centavos. National Day: September 24, Independence Day 1973.

Member of the UN since Sept. 25, 1973 and of all its specialized agencies save IAEA and GATT. Member of the OAU and is an ACP state of the EEC. A signatory of the Lomé Conventions of 1975 and 1980.

International relations: formally Portuguese Guinea, a separate colony since 1879. The boundary with Senegal and Guinea fixed by a French–Portuguese Treaty of May 12, 1886. A guerrilla war against colonial rule 1963–73. Independence proclaimed on Sept. 24, 1973, formally recognized by the UN Sept. 25, 1973, by Portugal Sept. 10, 1974.

A. CABRAL, *Revolution in Guinea*, London, 1969; R. RUDEBECK, *Guinea-Bissau. A Study of Political Mobilization*, Uppsala, 1974; O. GJERSTAD, C. SARRAZIN, *Saving the First Harvest: National Reconstruction in Guinea-Bissau*, Oakland, 1978; *The Europa Year Book 1984: A World Survey*, Vol. II, pp. 1643–1646, London, 1984.

GUINEA PIGS. An international term applied in the 19th century for animals used in laboratories for tests and experiments (▷ Laboratory Animals) in most of which guinea pigs were used. After World War II used in world press to denote persons, chiefly women, subjected to medical experiments in Nazi concentration camps. In 1965, Norman Cousins, American publisher of *Saturday Review*, launched an international campaign on behalf of the sur-

vivors of these criminal experiments. In the 1980's research testing on animals whose biological characteristics resemble those of humans is mainly performed on: cats, dogs, monkeys, rabbits, rats and sheep.

Les expériences médicales au camp de concentration de Ravensbruck. Les expériences pratiques sur les "cabayes", Poznań, 1960; N. COUSINS, *The Celebration of Life*, New York, 1967; Office of Technological Assessment, *Alternative to Animal Use in Research, Testing and Education*, February, 1986.

GULAG. ▷ Labor camps.

GULF CO-OPERATION COUNCIL, GCC. An intergovernmental institution, officially called Co-operation Council for the Arab States of the Gulf, est. on May 25, 1981, by six Arab states: Bahrain, Kuwait, Oman, Qatar, Saudi Arabia and the United Arab Emirates. Headquarters. Riyadh. Organs: the Supreme Council of the heads of member states, the Ministerial Council consisting of the foreign ministers and the Secretariat General. The aims of the GCC are to realize co-ordination, integration and co-operation in all economic, social, cultural and defence affairs. In Nov., 1984 the GCC member states reached an agreement on the creation of a joint ▷ rapid deployment force. In 1985–87 the main problem of the GCC was the negative impact of the Iraq-Iran war.

The Europa Year Book 1984. A World Survey, Vol. I, p. 125, London, 1984; KEESING's *Record of World Events*, 1986, No. 3; H.T. AZZAM, *The Gulf Economies in Transition*, London, 1988.

GULF OF ADEN. ▷ Aden, Gulf of.

GULF OF PERSIA. ▷ Persian Gulf.

GULFS AND BAYS. A subject of international disputes related to international waters and territorial seas. Such disputes occurred between the USA and Great Britain and between Great Britain and Chile in the Western Hemisphere in the 19th century; in the 20th century – between El Salvador, Costa Rica and Nicaragua on the Fonseca Bay. In the latter case the Central American Court of Justice rendered a verdict that the Fonseca Bay "forms a part of the territory of the three states laying on it," so Nicaragua cannot build an inter-oceanic canal without the consent of the two other states exercising territorial jurisdiction over that bay.

J. MOCHOT, *La régime des baies et do golfes en droit international*, Paris, 1933; M.P. STROHL, *The International Law of Bays*, The Hague, 1963; L.J. BOUCHEZ, *The Regimes of Bays in International Law*, Leiden, 1964.

GULF STREAM. A warm ocean current of the North Atlantic, flows from the Gulf of Mexico in the direction of northwestern Europe; subject of international research.

H. STOMMEL, *The Gulf Stream*, London, 1965.

GUNBOAT DIPLOMACY. An international term for the interventionist policy of colonial powers in the 19th century, executed by naval forces.

J. CABLE, *Gunboat Diplomacy 1919–1979*, London 1981.

GURKHA. Name of soldiers from Nepal in the British Army, and in the Indian Army.

GUTENBERG GESELLSCHAFT. The Gutenberg International Association for Past and Present History of the Art of Printing, f. 1901, Gutenberg Museum Mainz. Publ.: *Gutenberg Jahrbuch*. Reg. with the UIA.

Yearbook of International Organizations.

GUYANA. Member of the UN. The Co-operative Republic of Guyana. State in South America on the Atlantic Ocean, bordered by Suriname, Brazil and Venezuela. Area: 214,969 sq. km. Pop.1987 est. 812,000 (census 1970: 701,885). Capital: Georgetown with 183,000 inhabitants in the metropolitan area est. 1978. GNP per capita 1986: US $500. Official language: English. Currency one Guyana dollar = 100 cents. National Day: Feb. 23, Proclamation of Republic, 1970.

Member of the UN from Oct. 2, 1966 and of all UN specialized agencies, with exception of the IAEA and WIPO. Member of the Commonwealth, the CARICOM and is an ACP state of the EEC. A signatory of the Lomé Conventions of 1975 and 1980.

International relations: 1621–1814 eastern part of the Dutch Guiana (three settlements of the Dutch West India Company: Berbice, Demerara and Essequibo), ceded to Great Britain by the Congress of Vienna 1815; unified as British Guiana with colonial status in 1831. Autonomy was achieved in 1928, self-government in 1953; independence within the Commonwealth on May 26, 1966. Guyana became the world's first independent co-operative republic on Feb. 23, 1970. In frontier disputes with Brazil, Suriname and Venezuela. The US Government relinquished its claims to Timehriarca, formerly Atkinson US military base on the Demerara river during World War II. The border disputes with Suriname was resolved in Apr. 1970, with Venezuela in June 1970 by the Port of Spain Protocol, which put the issue in abeyance until 1982 (Venezuelan claims to two thirds of Guyana's territory are based on the ▷ Tordesillas Treaty, 1493). The negotiations in 1982 failed, Venezuela rejected Guyana's suggestion to accept an international arbitration. Guyana in March 1983 presented the dispute to the UN. In. 1982 Guyana established diplomatic relations with Nicaragua. A reform of the ▷ Charter of OAS by the Protocol of Cartagena, 1985, opened to Guyana the possibility of OAS membership after 1990. In November 1986 signed with Venezuela an agreement on scientific and technical co-operation.

T. SMITH, *British Guyana*, London, 1964. CH. JACON, *The West on Trial: My Fight for Guyana Freedom*, London, 1966; L.H. DALY, *From Revolution to Republic*, Georgetown, 1970; L.A. DESPRES, *Cultural Pluralism and Nationalism. Politics in British Guyana*, Chicago, 1967. T.V. DALY, *A Short History of the Guyanese People*, London, 1975; K.R. HOPE, *Development Policy in Guyana*, London, 1979; H.A. LUTCHMAN, *From Colonialism to Co-operative Republic: Aspects of Political Development in Guyana*, Puerto Rico, 1979; *The Europa Year Book 1984. A World Survey*, Vol. II, pp. 1647–1654, London, 1984. C. BABER, H.B. JEFFREY, *Guyana: Politics. Economic and Society*, London 1986.

GWADAR. A seaport on the Baluchistan coast of the Arabian Sea, 459 km west of Karachi with *c.* 10,000 inhabitants 1975; part of Sultanate of Muscat 1797–1958, then transferred to Pakistan.

GYMNASTICS. A subject of international co-operation. Organization reg. with the UIA:

International Gymnastic Federation, f. 1881, Liège; recognized by International Olympic Committee, 1936. Publ.: *Bulletin.*

Yearbook of International Organizations.

GYNECOLOGY. A subject of international co-operation. Organizations reg. with the UIA:

Federation of French-Language Gynecologists and Obstetricians, f. 1920. Paris. Publ.: *Journal de gynecologie.*
International Federation of Gynecology and Obstetrics, f. 1954, Geneva. Official relations with WHO and ECOSOC. Publ.: *Journal.*
International Union of Professional Gynaecologists and Obstetricians, f. 1954, Paris.
Scandinavian Society of Obstetricians and Gynaecologists, f. 1953, Stockholm.

Yearbook of International Organizations.

GYPSIES. Roma, or Rom (*Sanskrit*: roma – "wandering caste"). A nomadic people whose original homeland was India; they live in Western Asia, Africa, America, Australia, and Europe (main concentrations: Romania, Slovakia and Hungary). The International Military Tribunal in Nuremberg asserted that as a result of the genocidal policies of the German III Reich during World War II more than 20,000 Gypsies died in concentration camps. The extermination policy in relation to Gypsies was initiated in the German III Reich by a direction of Reichsführer SS, Heinrich Himmler, of 1936 including Gypsies among "asocial elements"; on Dec. 8, 1938 a directive was issued on "settlement of the Gypsies problem for racial reasons". In Apr., 1940 the forced resettlement of Gypsies to German-occupied Poland was undertaken; in Oct., 1942 the arrest of Gypsies and internment in Auschwitz concentration camp Auschwitz was begun; in total *c.* 20,000 were interned, most of whom perished in 1943; in 1944 those who remained alive were murdered in gas chambers. The First Congress of Gypsies took place in London in 1971, the Second in Geneva in Apr., 1978, which sent a request to the UN on granting to the Permanent Secretary of the Congress a consultative status with the UN Conferences on Human Rights and the status of a national minority and not an ethnic group. The Congress set the number of Gypsies in the world at 10–12 million, among whom only one-third lead a nomadic life. In 1980 the Gypsy Patriotic Organization of Romistan prepared a program of an independent Romistan state. In Switzerland the charity organization Pro-Juvennile has apologized to the 30,000 strong Gypsy community for its program in the years 1922–1973 to integrate into Swiss society more than 600 Gypsy children removed from their families with federal support.

H.J. DÖRING, *Die Zigeuner in NS-Staat*, Hamburg, 1964; D. HENVICK, G. PUXON, *Destin gitans*, Paris, 1973; G. VON SOEST, *Zigeuner zwischen Verfolgung und Integration*, Basel, 1979; G. SCHWAB, E. WUEPPER, *Zigeuner, Porträt einer Randgruppe*, Frankfurt am Main, 1979. Gypsies Autonomous Regions Considered by Racial Discrimination Committee, in: *UN Chronicle*, 1985, No 7, pp. 26–29; *GUARDIAN*, July 8, 1986; KEESING's *Record of World Events*, 1986, No 2.

H

HABEAS CORPUS ACT. *Latin* = "may you have the body." The historical name of the British Parliamentary bill of 1679 that prohibited detention of persons without a court warrant and guaranteed that each case would be heard in an appropriate court. The act broadened principles of civil rights protection contained in Magna Carta (1215) and the Petition of Right (1628). Since it did not apply to British colonies in North America, it was one of main reasons for the American Revolution and was integrated in the Constitution of the USA; it remains in force today in all Anglo-Saxon countries.

HABITAT. An international term used by town-planners to designate the architectural environment. It was coined in 1952 by the Congrès International d'Architecture Moderne, CIAM. A multi-storey building composed of prefabricated concrete villas called "Habitat" was displayed at EXPO '67 in Montreal. An international conference on human settlements, Habitat, was convened by the UN General Assembly on May 31–June 11, 1976 in Vancouver, following regional meetings of town-planners and architects (June 1975 – Asian, Teheran, and African, Cairo; June–July 1975 – Latin American, Caracas; and May 1976 – American and European, Warsaw). It adopted the Declaration of Principles, called the ▷ Habitat Vancouver Declaration, 1976. The UN General Assembly adopted on Dec. 19, 1977, Res. 32/162 on Institutional Arrangements for International Co-operation in the Field of Human Settlements, deciding that: "a small and effective secretariat shall be established in the UN to service the Commission on Human Settlements to be named Habitat, Centre for Human Settlements."

T. CROSBY, "The character of habitat", in: *Architectural Design*, No. 8, 1955; *Habitat, UN Conference on Human Settlement, Report of the Secretary General*, A.G. A/10234, October 13, 1975; *Conferencia Regional Preparatoria para la América Latina sobre los Asentamientos Humanos: Habitat, Caracas 30 VI–4 VII 1975, Informe del Relator*, St/CEPAL/CONF 55/L.5, 21 VIII 1975; A. CIBOROWSKI, *Settlement planning*, New York, 1975; *UN Chronicle*, January 1978, pp. 131–133.

HABITAT-DOC. Habitat Library and Documentation Centre, one of the information systems of the ▷ UNHCR (▷ Refugees).

HABITAT VANCOUVER DECLARATION, 1976. A Declaration adopted by the UN Conference on Human Settlements (Habitat), at Vancouver on June 11, 1976.
The text is as follows:

"Habitat: United Nations Conference on Human Settlements,
Aware that the Conference was convened following recommendation of the United Nations Conference on the Human Environment and subsequent resolutions of the General Assembly, particularly resolution 3128 (XXVIII) by which the nations of the world expressed

their concern over the extremely serious condition of human settlements, particularly that which prevails in developing countries,
Recognizing that international cooperation, based on the principles of the United Nations Charter, has to be developed and strengthened in order to provide solutions for world problems and to create an international community based on equity, justice and solidarity,
Recalling the decisions of the United Nations Conference on the Human Environment, as well as the recommendations of the World Population Conference, the United Nations World Food Conference, the Second General Conference of the United Nations Industrial Development Organization, the World Conference of the International Women's Year, the Declaration and Programme of Action adopted by the sixth special session of the General Assembly of the United Nations and the Charter of Economic Rights and Duties of States that establish the basis of the New International Economic Order,
Noting that the condition of human settlements largely determines the quality of life, the improvement of which is a prerequisite for the full satisfaction of basic needs, such as employment, housing, health services, education and recreation,
Recognizing that the problems of human settlements are not isolated from the social and economic development of countries and that they cannot be set apart from existing unjust international economic relations,
Being deeply concerned with the increasing difficulties facing the world in satisfying the basic needs and aspirations of peoples consistent with principles of human dignity,
Recognizing that the circumstances of life for vast numbers of people in human settlements are unacceptable, particularly in developing countries, and that, unless positive and concrete action is taken at national and international levels to find and implement solutions, these conditions are likely to be further aggravated as a result of:
Inequitable economic growth, reflected in the wide disparities in wealth which now exist between countries and between human beings and which condemn millions of people to a life of poverty, without satisfying the basic requirements for food, education, health services, shelter, environmental hygiene, water and energy;
Social, economic, ecological and environmental deterioration which is exemplified at the national and international levels by inequalities in living conditions, social segregation, racial discrimination, acute unemployment, illiteracy, disease and poverty, the breakdown of social relationships and traditional cultural values and the increasing degradation of life-supporting resources of air, water and land;
World population growth trends which indicate that numbers of mankind in the next 25 years would double, thereby more than doubling the need for food, shelter and all other requirements for life and human dignity which are at the present inadequately met;
Uncontrolled urbanization and consequent conditions of overcrowding, pollution, deterioration and psychological tensions in metropolitan regions;
Rural backwardness which compels a large majority of mankind to live at the lowest standards of living and contribute to uncontrolled urban growth;
Rural dispersion exemplified by small scattered settlements and isolated homesteads which inhibit the provision of infrastructure and services, particularly those relating to water, health and education;
Involuntary migration, politically, racially and economically motivated, re-location and expulsion of people from their national homeland,
Recognizing also that the establishment of a just and equitable world economic order through necessary changes in the areas of international trade, monetary systems, industrialization, transfer of resources, transfer of technology, and the consumption of world resources, is essential for socio-economic development and improvement of human settlement, particularly in developing countries,
Recognizing further that these problems pose a formidable challenge to human understanding, imagination, ingenuity and resolve, and that new priorities to promote the qualitative dimensions to economic development, as well as a new political commitment to find solutions resulting in the practical implementation

of the New International Economic Order, became imperative:
I. Opportunities and Solutions
(1) Mankind must not be daunted by the scale of the task ahead.
There is need for awareness of and responsibility for increased activity of the national Governments and international community, aimed at mobilization of economic resources, institutional changes and international solidarity by:
(a) Adopting bold, meaningful and effective human settlement policies and spatial planning strategies realistically adapted to local conditions;
(b) Creating more livable, attractive and efficient settlements which recognize human scale, the heritage and culture of people and the special needs of disadvantaged groups especially children, women and the infirm in order to ensure the provision of health, services, education, food and employment within a framework of social justice;
(c) Creating possibilities for effective participation by all people in the planning, building and management of their human settlements;
(d) Developing innovative approaches in formulating and implementing settlement programmes through more appropriate use of science and technology and adequate national and international financing;
(e) Utilizing the most effective means of communications for the exchange of knowledge and experience in the field of human settlements;
(f) Strengthening bonds of international co-operation both regionally and globally;
(g) Creating economic opportunities conducive to full employment where, under healthy, safe conditions, women and men will be fairly compensated for their labour in monetary, health and other personal benefits.
(2) In meeting this challenge, human settlements must be seen as an instrument and object of development. The goals of settlement policies are inseparable from the goals of every sector of social and economic life. The solutions to the problems of human settlements must therefore be conceived as an integral part of the development process of individual nations and the world community.
(3) With these opportunities and considerations in mind, and being agreed on the necessity of finding common principles that will guide Governments and the world community in solving the problems of human settlements the Conference proclaims the following general principles and guidelines for action.
II. General Principles
(1) The improvement of the quality of life of human beings is the first and most important objective of every human settlement policy. These policies must facilitate the rapid and continuous improvement in the quality of life of all people, beginning with the satisfaction of the basic needs of food, shelter, clean water, employment, health, education, training, social security without any discrimination as to race, colour, sex, language, religion, ideology, national or social origin or other cause, in a frame of freedom, dignity and social justice.
(2) In striving to achieve this objective, priority must be given to the needs of the most disadvantaged people.
(3) Economic development should lead to the satisfaction of human needs and is a necessary means towards achieving a better quality of life, provided that it contributes to a more equitable distribution of its benefits among people and nations. In this context particular attention should be paid to the accelerated transition in developing countries from primary development to secondary development activities, and particularly to industrial development.
(4) Human dignity and the exercise of free choice consistent with overall public welfare are basic rights which must be assured in every society. It is therefore the duty of all people and Governments to join the struggle against any form of colonialism, foreign aggression and occupation, domination, apartheid and all forms of racism and racial discrimination referred to in the resolutions as adopted by the General Assembly of the United Nations.
(5) The establishment of settlements in territories occupied by force is illegal. It is condemned by the international community. However, action still remains to be taken against the establishment of such settlements.
(6) The right of free movement and the right of each individual to choose the place of settlement within the

domain of his own country should be recognized and safeguarded.

(7) Every State has a sovereign and inalienable right to choose its economic system, as well as its political, social and cultural system, in accordance with the will of its people, without interference, coercion or external threat of any kind.

(8) Every State has the right to exercise full and permanent sovereignty over its wealth, natural resources and economic activities, adopting the necessary measures for the planning and management of its resources, providing for the protection, preservation and enhancement of the environment.

(9) Every country should have the right to be a sovereign inheritor of its own cultural values created throughout its history, and has the duty to preserve them as an integral part of the cultural heritage of mankind.

(10) Land is one of the fundamental elements in human settlements. Every State has the right to take the necessary steps to maintain under public control the use, possession, disposal and reservation of land. Every State has the right to plan and regulate use of land, which is one of its most important resources, in such a way that the growth of population centres both urban and rural are based on a comprehensive land use plan. Such measures must assure the attainment of basic goals of social and economic reform for every country, in conformity with its national and land tenure system and legislation.

(11) The nations must avoid the pollution of the biosphere and the oceans and should join in the effort to end irrational exploitation of all environmental resources, whether non-renewable or renewable in the long term. The environment is the common heritage of mankind and is protection is the responsibility of the whole international community. All acts by nations and people should therefore be inspired by a deep respect for the protection of the environmental resources upon which life itself depends.

(12) The waste and misuse of resources in war and armaments should be prevented. All countries should make a firm commitment to promote general and complete disarmament under strict and effective international control, in particular in the field of nuclear disarmament. Part of the resources thus released should be utilized so as to achieve a better quality of life for humanity and particularly the peoples of developing countries.

(13) All persons have the right and the duty to participate, individually and collectively in the elaboration and implementation of policies and programmes of their human settlements.

(14) To achieve universal progress in the quality of life, a fair and balanced structure of the economic relations between States has to be promoted. It is therefore essential to implement urgently the New International Economic Order, based on the Declaration and Programme of Action approved by the General Assembly in its sixth special session, and on the Charter of Economic Rights and Duties of States.

(15) The highest priority should be placed on the rehabilitation of expelled and homeless people who have been displaced by natural or man-made catastrophes, and specially by the act of foreign aggression. In the latter case, all countries have the duty to fully co-operate in order to guarantee that the parties involved allow the return of displaced persons to their homes and to give them the right to possess and enjoy their properties and belongings without interference.

(16) Historical settlements, monuments and other items of national heritage, including religious heritage should be safeguarded against any acts of aggression or abuse by the occupying Power.

(17) Every State has the sovereign right to rule and exercise effective control over foreign investments, including the transnational corporations – within its national jurisdiction, which affect directly or indirectly the human settlements programmes.

(18) All countries, particularly developing countries, must create conditions which make possible the full integration of women and youth in political, economic and social activities particularly in the planning and implementation of human settlement proposals and in all the associated activities, on the basis of equal rights, in order to achieve an efficient and full utilization of available human resources, bearing in mind that women constitute half of the world population.

(19) International co-operation is an objective and a common duty of all States, and necessary efforts must therefore be made to accelerate the social and economic development of developing countries, within the framework of favourable external conditions, which are compatible with their needs and aspirations and which contain the due respect for the sovereign equality of all States.

III. Guidelines for Action

(1) It is recommended that Governments and international organizations should make every effort to take urgent action as set out in the following guidelines:

(2) It is the responsibility of Governments to prepare spatial strategy plans and adopt human settlement policies to guide the socio-economic development efforts. Such policies must be an essential component of an over-all development strategy, linking and harmonizing them with policies on industrialization, agriculture, social welfare, and environmental and cultural preservation or that each supports the other in a progressive improvement in the well-being of all mankind.

(3) A human settlement policy must seek harmonious integration or co-ordination of a wide variety of components, including, for example, population growth and distribution, employment, shelter, land use, infrastructure and services. Governments must create mechanisms and institutions to develop and implement such a policy.

(4) It is of paramount importance that national and international efforts give priority to improving the rural habitat. In this context, efforts should be made towards the reduction of disparities between rural and urban areas, as needed between regions and within urban areas themselves, for a harmonious development of human settlements.

(5) The demographic, natural and economic characteristics of many countries, require policies on growth and distribution of population, land tenure and localization of productive activities to ensure orderly processes of urbanization and arrange for rational occupation of rural space.

(6) Human settlement policies and programmes should define and strive for progressive minimum standards for an acceptable quality of life. These standards will vary within and between countries, as well as over periods of time, and therefore must be subject to change in accordance with conditions and possibilities. Some standards are most appropriately defined in quantitative terms, thus providing precisely defined targets at the local and national levels. Others must be qualitative, with their achievement subject to felt need. At the same time, social justice and a fair sharing of resources demand the discouragement of excessive consumption.

(7) Attention must also be drawn to the detrimental effects of transposing standards and criteria that can only be adopted by minorities and could heighten inequalities, the misuse of resources and the social, cultural and ecological deterioration of the developing countries.

(8) Adequate shelter and services are a basic human right which places an obligation on Governments to ensure their attainment by all people, beginning with direct assistance to the least advantaged through guided programmes of self-help and community action. Governments should endeavour to remove all impediments hindering attainments of these goals. Of special importance is the elimination of social and racial segregation, inter alia, through the creation of better balanced communities, which blend different social groups, occupation, housing and amenities.

(9) Health is an essential element in the development of the individual and one of the goals of human settlement policies should be to improve environmental health conditions and basic health services.

(10) Basic human dignity is the right of people, individually and collectively, to participate directly in shaping the policies and programmes affecting their lives. The process of choosing and carrying out a given course of action for human settlement improvement should be designed expressly to fulfil that right. Effective human settlement policies require a continuous co-operative relationship between a Government and its people at all levels. It is recommended that national Governments promote programmes that will encourage and assist local authorities to participate to a greater extent in national development.

(11) Since a genuine human settlement policy requires the effective participation of the entire population, recourse must therefore be made at all times to technical arrangements permitting the use of all human resources, both skilled and unskilled. The equal participation of women must be guaranteed. These goals must be associated with a global training programme to facilitate the introduction and use of technologies that maximize productive employment.

(12) International and national institutions should promote and institute education programmes and courses in the subject of 'human settlements',

(13) Land is an essential element in development of both urban and rural settlements. The use and tenure of land should be subject to public control because of its limited supply through appropriate measures and legislation including agrarian reform policies – as an essential basis for integrated rural development – that will facilitate the transfer of economic resources to the agricultural sector and the promotion of the agro-industrial effort, so as to improve the integration and organization of human settlements, in accordance with national development plans and programmes. The increase in the value of land as a result of public decision and investment should be recaptured for the benefit of society as a whole. Governments should also ensure that prime agricultural land is destined to its most vital use.

(14) Human settlements are characterized by significant disparities in living standards and opportunities. Harmonious development of human settlements requires the reduction of disparities between rural and urban areas, between regions and within regions themselves. Governments should adopt policies which aim at decreasing the differences between living standards and opportunities in urban and non-urban areas. Such policies at the national levels should be supplemented by policies designed to reduce disparities between countries within the framework of the New International Economic Order.

(15) In achieving the socio-economic and environmental objectives of the development of human settlements, high priority should be given to the actual design and physical planning processes which have as their main tasks the synthesis of various planning approaches and the transformation of broad and general goals into specific design solutions. The sensitive and comprehensive design methodologies related to the particular circumstances of time and space, and based on consideration of the human scale should be pursued and encouraged.

(16) The design of human settlements should aim at providing a living environment in which identities of individuals, families and societies are preserved and adequate means for maintaining privacy, the possibility of face-to-face interactions and public participation in the decision-making process are provided.

(17) A human settlement is more than a grouping of people, shelter and work places. Diversity in the characteristics of human settlements reflecting cultural and aesthetic values must be respected and encouraged and areas of historical, religious or archaeological importance and nature areas of special interest preserved for posterity. Places of worship, especially in areas of expanding human settlements, should be provided and recognized in order to satisfy the spiritual and religious needs of different groups in accordance with freedom of religious expression.

(18) Governments and the international community should facilitate the transfer of relevant technology and experience and should encourage and assist the creation of endogenous technology better suited to the socio-cultural characteristics and patterns of population by means of bilateral or multilateral agreements having regard to the sovereignty and interest of the participating States. The knowledge and experience accumulated on the subject of human settlements should be available to all countries. Research and academic institutions should contribute more fully to this effort by giving greater attention to human settlements problems.

(19) Access should be granted, on more favourable terms, to modern technology, which should be adapted, as necessary, to the specific economic, social and ecological conditions and to the different stages of development of the developing countries. Efforts must be made to ensure that the commercial practices governing the transfer of technology are adapted to the

needs of the developing countries and to ensure that buyers' rights are not abused.

(20) International, technical and financial co-operation by the developed countries with the developing countries must be conducted on the basis of respect for national sovereignty and national development plans and programmes and designed to solve problems relating to projects under human settlement programmes, aimed at enhancing the quality of life of the inhabitants.

(21) Due attention should be given to implementation of conservation and recycling technologies.

(22) In the planning and management of human settlements, Governments should take into consideration all pertinent recommendations on human settlements planning which have emerged from earlier conferences dealing with the quality of life and development problems which affect it, starting with the high global priority represented by the transformation of the economic order at the national levels (sixth and seventh special sessions), the environmental impact of human settlements (Stockholm Conference on the Human Environment), the housing and sanitary ramifications of population growth (World Population Conference, Bucharest), rural development and the need to increase food supply (World Food Conference, Rome) and the effect on women of housing and urban development (International Women's Conference, Mexico City).

(23) While planning new human settlements of restructuring existing ones, a high priority should be given to the promotion of optimal and creative conditions for human coexistence. This implies the creation of a well-structured urban space on a human scale, the close interconnexion of the different urban functions, the relief of urban man from intolerable psychological tensions due to overcrowding and chaos, the creation of chances of human encounters and the elimination of urban concepts leading to human isolation.

(24) Guided by the foregoing principles, the international community must exercise its responsibility to support national efforts to meet the human settlements challenges facing them. Since resources of Government are inadequate to meet all needs, the international community should provide the necessary financial and technical assistance, evolve appropriate institutional arrangements and seek new effective ways to promote them. In the meantime, assistance to developing countries must at least reach the percentage targets set in the International Development Strategy for the Second United Nations Development Decade."

UN Chronicle, July 1976, pp. 51–52; *Report of Habitat, UN Conference on Human Settlements*, New York, 1978.

HABSBURG EMPIRE or HAPSBURG EMPIRE or AUSTRIA HOUSE EMPIRE.
Historical terms for the European feudal condominium of the Habsburg family since the XIII century until the end of the World War I. The ▷ Versailles Treaty 1919 and the ▷ Austria State Treaty, 1955 forbade the Habsburg family's return as royalty to Austria and Austria's integration with Germany (▷ Anschluss).

Encylopaedia Britannica, Vol. 10, Chicago – London, 1973.

HAGUE ARBITRATION CODE, 1899.
The Code of International Arbitration proposed on July 5, 1899 to The Hague Peace Conference by the Third Commission, stated in Art. 10:

"Arbitration will be obligatory between the high contracting Parties in the following cases, so far as they do not concern the vital interests or national honor of the States in dispute:

I. In case of disputes concerning the interpretation or application of the conventions mentioned below:

(1) Conventions relating to posts, telegraphs and telephones.

(2) Conventions concerning the protection of submarine cables.

(3) Conventions concerning railroads.

(4) Conventions and regulations concerning the methods of preventing collisions of vessels at sea.

(5) Conventions concerning the protection of literary and artistic works.

(6) Conventions concerning the protection of industrial property (patents, trade-marks and trade names).

(7) Conventions concerning the system of weights and measures.

(8) Conventions concerning reciprocal free assistance to the indigent sick.

(9) Conventions relating to sanitation, conventions concerning epizooty, phylloxera and other similar scourges.

(10) Conventions concerning civil procedure.

(11) Conventions of extradition.

(12) Conventions for settling boundaries so far as they concern purely technical and non-political questions.

II. In case of disputes concerning pecuniary claims for damages when the principle of indemnity is recognized by the parties."

The Proceedings of the Hague Peace Conferences, The Conference of 1899, New York, 1920, pp. 837–849.

HAGUE BALLOONS DECLARATION, 1907.
The Declaration Prohibiting the Discharge of Projectiles and Explosives from Balloons, signed at The Hague, on Oct. 18, 1907, stating as follows:

"The Contracting Powers agree, for a period extending to the close of the Third Peace Conference, to forbid the discharge of projectiles and explosives from balloons or by other new methods of a similar nature.

The present Declaration is only binding on the contracting Powers in case of war between two or more of them.

It shall cease to be binding from the time when, in a war between the contracting Powers, one of the belligerents is joined by a non-contracting Power."

The Proceedings of the Hague Peace Conferences, New York, 1920, Vol. 1, p. 678.

HAGUE CLUB, THE.
A Club of the chief executive officers of international European foundations, f. 1975 in The Hague. Reg. with the UIA.

Yearbook of International Organizations.

HAGUE CONFERENCES ON PRIVATE INTERNATIONAL LAW, 1893–1980.
Conferences initiated by the Queen of the Netherlands with a view to starting work on the codification of private international law attended by Austria, Hungary, Belgium, Denmark, France, Italy, Germany, Luxembourg, the Netherlands, Norway, Portugal, Russia, Romania, Spain, Sweden and Switzerland. The same participants met at subsequent conferences in 1894, 1900, 1905 (also attended by Japan) and 1908. Six conventions were adopted: three on June 12, 1902 on conflicting legislation regarding marriages, on conflicting legislation regarding development and specialization, and on care for the under aged; and three on July 17, 1905 on interdiction, on conflicting legislation regarding the effects of marriage and on civic trials. In the interwar period the following conferences were held: in 1925 and 1928; they introduced amendments to the abovementioned conventions. Since World War II conferences have been held in 1956, 1960 and in 1964, in which period a further 14 conventions were adopted: and in 1968, 1972, 1976 and 1980. The Hague Conference on Private International Law is a permanent institution based at The Hague and operating in keeping with the statute of July 15, 1955, which provides procedures for its sessions and for the work of its permanent office.

"Conférences de la Hague sur le droit international privé", in: *Recueil de législation et de jurisprudence.*

HAGUE CONVENTION ON NEUTRAL POWERS, 1907.
The Convention respecting the Rights and Duties of Neutral Powers and Persons in Case of War on Land, signed at The Hague on Dec. 18, 1907. The highlights of the Convention:

"With a view to laying down more clearly the rights and duties of neutral Powers in case of war on land and regulating the position of the belligerents who have taken refuge in neutral Territory;

Being likewise desirous of defining the meaning of the term 'neutral', pending the possibility of settling, in its entirety, the position of neutral individuals in their relations with the belligerents.

Chapter I – The rights and duties of neutral powers.

Art. 1. The territory of neutral Powers is inviolable.

Art. 2. Belligerents are forbidden to move troops or convoys of either munitions of war or supplies across territory of a neutral Power.

Art. 3. Belligerents are likewise forbidden:

(a) To erect on the territory of a neutral Power a wireless telegraphy station or any apparatus for the purpose of communicating with belligerent forces on land or sea;

(b) To use any installation of this kind established by them before the war on the territory of a neutral Power for purely military purposes, and which has not been opened for the service of public messages.

Art. 4. Corps of combatants cannot be formed nor recruiting agencies opened on the territory of a neutral Power to assist the belligerents.

Art. 5. A neutral Power must not allow any of the acts referred to in Art. 2 to 4 to occur on its territory.

It is not called upon to punish acts in violation of neutrality unless the said acts have been committed on its own territory.

Art. 6. The responsibility of a neutral Power is not engaged by the fact of persons crossing the frontier separately to offer their services to one of the belligerents.

Art. 7. A neutral Power is not called upon to prevent the export or transport, on behalf of one or other of the belligerents, of arms, munitions of war, or, in general, of anything which can be of use to an army or a fleet.

Art. 8. A neutral Power is not called upon to forbid or restrict the use on behalf of the belligerents of telegraph or telephone cables or of wireless telegraphy apparatus belonging to it or to companies or private individuals.

Art. 9. Every measure of restriction or prohibition taken by a neutral Power in regard to the matters referred to in Art. 7 and 8 must be impartially applied by it to both belligerents.

A neutral Power must see to the same obligation being observed by companies or private individuals owning telegraph or telephone cables or wireless telegraphy apparatus.

Art. 10. The fact of a neutral Power resisting, even by force, attempts to violate its neutrality cannot be regarded as a hostile act."

▷ Hague Conventions on Naval War.

The Proceedings of The Hague Conferences, New York, 1920, Vol. 1, pp. 632–636.

HAGUE CONVENTION ON THE OPENING OF HOSTILITIES, 1907.
The Convention relative to the Opening of Hostilities, signed at The Hague on Dec. 18, 1907. The text of the Preamble and the first three Articles read as follows:

"Considering that it is important, in order to ensure the maintenance of pacific relations that hostilities should not commence without previous warning;

That it is equally important that the existence of a state of war should be notified without delay to neutral Powers;

Being desirous of concluding a Convention to this effect, have appointed the following as their plenipotentiaries.

Who, after depositing their full powers, found in good and due form, have agreed upon the following provisions:

Art. 1. The contracting Powers recognize that hostilities between themselves must not commence without a previous and explicit warning, in the form either of a reasoned declaration of war or of ultimatum with conditional declaration of war.

Art. 2. The existence of a state of war must be notified to the neutral Powers without delay, and shall not take effect in regard to them until after the receipt of a notification, which may, however, be given by telegraph. Neutral Powers, nevertheless, cannot rely on the absence of notification if it is clearly established that they were in fact aware of the existence of a state of war.

Art. 3. Art. 1 of the present Convention shall take effect in case of war between two or more of the contracting Powers.
Art. 2. is binding as between a belligerent Power which is a party to the Convention and neutral Powers which are also parties to the Convention."

The Proceedings of the Hague Peace Conferences, New York, 1920, Vol. 1, pp. 618–619.

HAGUE CONVENTIONS ON NAVAL WAR, 1907.
The Hague Peace Conference has adopted on Oct. 18, 1907 the following Conventions related to Naval War:
Convention VI relative to the Status of Enemy Marchant Ships at the Outbreak of Hostilities, stating in the first two Articles:

"Art. 1. When a merchant ship belonging to one of the belligerent Powers is at the commencement of hostilities in an enemy port, it is desirable that it should be allowed to depart freely, either immediately, or after a reasonable number of days of grace, and to proceed, after being furnished with a pass, direct to its port of destination or any other port indicated.
The same rule should apply in the case of a ship which has left its last port of departure before the commencement of the war and entered a port belonging to the enemy while still ignorant that hostilities had broken out.
Art. 2. A merchant ship unable, owing to circumstances of force majeure, to leave the enemy port within the period contemplated in the above art., or which was not allowed to leave, cannot be confiscated.
The belligerent may only detain it, without payment of compensation, but subject to the obligation of restoring it after the war, or requisition it on payment of compensation."

Convention VII relating to the Convention of Merchant Ships into War-Ships, stating in the first two Articles:

"Art. 1. A merchant ship converted into a war-ship cannot have the rights and duties accruing to such vessels unless it is placed under the direct authority, immediate control, and responsibility of the Power whose flag it flies.
Art. 2. Merchant ships converted into war-ships must bear the external marks which distinguish the war-ships of their nationality."

Convention VIII relative to Laying of Automatic Submarine Contact Mines, stating in the first two Articles:

Art. 1. It is forbidden:
(1) To lay unanchored automatic contact mines, except when they are so constructed as to become harmless one hour at most after the person who laid them ceases to control them;
(2) To lay anchored automatic contact mines which do not become harmless as soon as they have broken loose from their moorings;
(3) To use torpedoes which do not become harmless when they have missed their mark.
Art. 2. It is forbidden to lay automatic contact mines off the coasts and ports of the enemy, with the sole object of intercepting commercial shipping."

Convention IX concerning Bombardment by Naval Forces in Time of War stating in the first four Articles:

"Art. 1. It is forbidden to bombard by naval forces undefended ports, towns, villages, dwellings or buildings.
A place cannot be bombarded solely because automatic submarine contact mines are anchored off the harbor.
Art. 2. Military works, military or naval establishment, depots of arms or war material, workshops or plant which could be utilized for the needs of the hostile fleet or army, and the ships of war in the harbor, are not, however, included in this prohibition. The commander of a naval force may destroy them with artillery, after a summons followed by a reasonable time of waiting, if all other means are impossible, and when the local authorities have not themselves destroyed them within the time fixed.

He incurs no responsibility for any unavoidable damage which may be caused by a bombardment under such circumstances. If for military reasons immediate action is necessary, and no delay can be allowed the enemy, it is understood that the prohibition to bombard the undefended town holds good, as in the case given in paragraph 1, and that the commander shall take all due measures in order that the town may suffer as little harm as possible.
Art. 3. After due notice has been given, the bombardment of undefended ports, towns, villages, dwellings, or buildings may be commenced, if the local authorities, after a formal summons has been made to them, decline to comply with requisitions for provisions or supplies necessary for the immediate use of the naval force before the place in question. These requisitions shall be in proportion to the resources of the place. They shall only be demanded in the name of the commander of the said naval force, and they shall, as far as possible, be paid for in cash; if not, they shall be evidenced by receipts.
Art. 4. The bombardment of undefended ports, towns, villages, dwellings, or buildings for non-payment of money contributions is forbidden."

Convention X for the Adaptation to Maritime Warfare of the Principles of the Geneva Convention 1906 relative to the Hospital Ships, stating in the first three Articles:

Art. 1. Military hospital ships, that is to say, ships constructed or assigned by States specially and solely with a view to assist the wounded, sick, and shipwrecked, the names of which have been communicated to the belligerent Powers at the commencement or during the course of hostilities, and in any case before they are employed, shall be respected, and cannot be captured while hostilities last.
These ships, moreover, are not on the same footing as men-of-war as regards their stay in a neutral port.
Art. 2. Hospital ships, equipped wholly or in part at the expense of private individuals or officially recognized relief societies, shall likewise be respected and exempt from capture, if the belligerent Power to which they belong has given them an official commission and has notified their names to the hostile Power at the commencement of or during hostilities, and in any case before they are employed.

Convention XI relative to certain Restrictions with regard to the Exercise in Naval War, relative to the postal correspondence, ("The postal correspondence of neutral or belligerents, whatever its official or private character may be, found on the high seas on board a neutral or enemy ship, is inviolable. If the ship is detained, the correspondence is forwarded by the captor with the least possible delay"); to the exception from Capture of certain vessels.
("Vessels used exclusively for fishing along the coast or small boats employed in local trade are exempt from capture, as well as their appliances, rigging, tackle and cargo. They cease to be exempt as soon as they take any part whatever in hostilities.");
to the Regulations regarding the crews of enemy merchant ships captured by belligerent
("When an enemy merchant ship is captured by a belligerent, such of its crew as are nationals of a neutral State are not made prisoners of war.
The same rule applies in the case of the captain and officers, likewise nationals of neutral State, if they promise formally in writing not to serve on an enemy ship while the war lasts. The captain, officers, and members of the crew, when nationals of the enemy State, are not made prisoners of war, on condition that they make a formal promise in writing, not to undertake, while hostilities last, any service connected with the operations of the war.")
Convention XII relative to the creation of an International Prize Court (▷ Prizes Law).
Convention XIII concerning the Rights and Duties of Neutral Powers in Naval War, stating in the first ten Articles (of 33) as follows:

"Art. 1. Belligerents are bound to respect the sovereign rights of neutral Powers and to abstain, in neutral territ-

ory or neutral waters, from any act which would, if knowingly permitted by any Power, constitute a violation of neutrality.
Art. 2. Any act of hostility, including capture and the exercise of the right of search, committed by belligerent war-ships in the territorial waters of a neutral Power, constitutes a violation of neutrality and is strictly forbidden.
Art. 3. When a ship has been captured in the territorial waters of a neutral Power, this Power must employ, if the prize is still within its jurisdiction, the means at its disposal to release the prize with its officers and crew, and to intern the prize crew.
If the prize is not in the jurisdiction of the neutral Power, the captor Government, on the demand of that Power, must liberate the prize with its officers and crew.
Art. 4. A prize court cannot be set up by a belligerent on neutral territory or on a vessel in neutral waters.
Art. 5. Belligerents are forbidden to use neutral ports and waters as a base of naval operations against their adversaries, and in particular to erect wireless telegraphy stations or any apparatus for the purpose of communicating with belligerent forces on land or sea.
Art. 6. The supply, in any manner, directly, by a neutral Power to a belligerent Power, of war-ships, ammunition, or war material of any kind whatever, is forbidden.
Art. 7. A neutral Power is not bound to prevent the export or transit, for the use of either belligerent, of arms, ammunition, or, in general, of anything which could be of use to an army or fleet.
Art. 8. A neutral Government is bound to employ the means at its disposal to prevent the fitting out or arming within its jurisdiction of any vessel which it has reason to believe is intended to cruise, or engage in hostile operations, against a Power with which that Government is in peace. It is also bound to display the same vigilance to prevent the departure from its jurisdiction of any vessel intended to cruise, or engage in hostile operations, which had been adapted entirely or partly within the said jurisdiction for use in war.
Art. 9. A neutral Power must apply impartially to the two belligerents the conditions, restrictions, or prohibitions made by it in regard to the admission into its ports, roadsteads, or territorial waters, of belligerent war-ships or of their prizes.
Nevertheless, a neutral Power may forbid a belligerent vessel which has failed to conform to the orders and regulations made by it, or which has violated neutrality, to enter its ports or roadsteads.
Art. 10. The neutrality of Power is affected by the mere passage through its territorial waters of war-ships or prizes belonging to belligerents."

The Proceedings of the Hague Peace Conferences, New York, 1920, Vol. 1, pp. 672–677.

HAGUE DEBTS CONVENTION, 1907.
The Convention respecting the Limitation of the Employment of Force for the Recovery of Contract Debts, signed on Oct. 18, 1907 at The Hague, stating in Art. 1:

"The contracting Powers agree not to have recourse to armed force for the recovery of contract debts claimed from the Government of one country by the Government of another country as being due to its nationals. This undertaking is, however, not applicable when the debtor State refuses or neglects to reply to an offer of arbitration, or, after accepting the offer, prevents any compromise from being agreed on, or, after the arbitration, fails to submit to the award."

The Proceedings of the Hague Peace Conferences, New York, 1920, Vol. 1, pp. 616–617.

HAGUE DECLARATION AGAINST POISONOUS GASES, 1899.
The text of the Declaration IV concerning Asphyxiating Gases, of the Hague First Peace Conference on July 29, 1899, is as follows:

"Inspired by the sentiments which found expression in the declaration of St. Petersburg of November 29 (December 11) 1868, declare that: The contracting powers agree to abstain from the use of projectiles, the sole object of which is the diffusion of asphyxiating or deleterious gases. The present declaration is only binding on the contracting powers in the case of war between two or more of them. It shall cease to be binding from the time when in a war between the contracting powers, one of the belligerents shall be joined by a non-contracting power."

This convention was ratified by Austria-Hungary, Belgium, Bulgaria, China, Denmark, France, Germany, Greece, Italy, Japan, Luxembourg, Mexico, Montenegro, The Netherlands, Norway, Persia, Portugal, Romania, Russia, Serbia, Spain, Sweden, Switzerland and Turkey.

The Hague Rules, regarding the rights and customs of land warfare, annexed to the Convention IV of Oct. 18, 1907, in art. 23 states: "in addition ... it is especially forbidden: to employ poison or poisonous weapons."

D. SCHINDLER, J. TOMAN, *The Laws of Armed Conflicts*, Leiden-Geneva, 1973, pp. 99–101.

HAGUE FIRST CONVENTION, 1899. The First Convention for the Pacific Settlement of International Disputes, called Hague Convention I. Signed on July 29, 1899 in The Hague by the representatives of Austria–Hungary, Belgium, China, Denmark, Spain and the USA and with reservations by France, Greece, Italy, Japan, Luxembourg, Mexico, Montenegro, the Netherlands, Norway, Persia, Portugal, Romania, Russia, Serbia, Siam, Sweden, Switzerland and Turkey. The first 24 articles are as follows:

"I. *On the Maintenance of the General Peace.* Art. 1, with a view to obviating, as far as possible, recourse to force in the relations between States, the Signatory Powers agree to use their best efforts to insure the pacific settlement of international differences.

II. *On the Good Offices and Mediation.*

Art. II. In case of serious disagreement or conflict, before an appeal to arms, the Signatory Powers agree to have recourse, as far as circumstances allow, to the good offices or mediation of one or more friendly Powers.

Art. III. Independently of this recourse, the Signatory Powers recommend that one or more Powers, strangers to the dispute, should, on their own initiative, and as far as circumstances may allow, offer their good offices for mediation to the States at variance.

Powers, strangers to the dispute, have the right to offer good offices for mediation, even during the course of hostilities.

The exercise of this right can never be regarded by one or the other of the parties in conflict as an unfriendly act.

Art. IV. The part of the mediator consists in reconciling the opposing claims and appeasing the feelings of resentment which may have arisen between the States at variance.

Art. V. The functions of the mediator are at an end when once it is declared, either by one of the parties to the dispute, or by the mediator himself, that the means of reconciliation proposed by him are not accepted.

Art. VI. Good offices and mediation, either at the request of the parties at variance, or on the initiative of Powers strangers to the dispute, have exclusively the character of advice and never have binding force.

Art. VII. The acceptance of mediation can not, unless there be an agreement to the contrary, have the effect of interrupting delaying, or hindering mobilization or other measures of preparation for war.

If mediation occurs after the commencement of hostilities it causes no interruption to the military operations in progress, unless there be an agreement to the contrary.

Art. VIII. The Signatory Powers are agreed in recommending the application, when circumstances allow, of special mediation in the following form:

In case of a serious difference endangering the peace, the States at variance choose respectively a Power, to whom they entrust the mission of entering into direct communication with the Power chosen on the other side, with the object of preventing the rupture of pacific relations.

For the period of this mandate, the term of which, unless otherwise stipulated, cannot exceed thirty days, the States in conflict cease from all direct communication on the subjects of the dispute, which is regarded as referred exclusively to the mediating Powers, who must use their best efforts to settle it.

In case of a definite rupture of pacific relations, these Powers are charged with the joint task of taking advantage of any opportunity to restore peace.

III. *On International Commissions of Inquiry.*

Art. IX. In differences of an international nature involving neither honour nor vital interests, and arising from a difference of opinion on points of fact, the Signatory Powers recommend that the parties, who have not been able to come to an agreement by means of diplomacy, should as far as circumstances allow, institute an International Commission of Inquiry to facilitate a solution of these differences by elucidating the facts by means of an impartial and conscientious investigation.

Art. X. The International Commissions of Inquiry are constituted by special agreement between the parties in conflict. The Convention for an inquiry defines the facts to be examined and the extent of the Commissioners' powers.

It settles the procedure.

On the inquiry both sides must be heard.

The form and the periods to be observed, if not stated in the inquiry Convention, are decided by the Commission itself.

Art. XI. The International Commissions of Inquiry are formed, unless otherwise stipulated, in the manner fixed by Article XXXII of the present convention.

Art. XII. The powers in dispute engage to supply the International Commission of Inquiry, as fully as they may think possible, with all means and facilities necessary to enable it to be completely acquainted with and to accurately understand the facts in question.

Art. XIII. The International Commission of Inquiry communicates its Report to the conflicting Powers, signed by all the members of the Commission.

Art. XIV. The report of the International Commission of Inquiry is limited to a statement of facts, and has in no way the character of an Arbitral Award. It leaves the conflicting Powers entire freedom as to the effect to be given to this statement.

IV. *On International Arbitration.* Chapter I. – On the System of Arbitration.

Art. XV. International arbitration has for its object the settlement of differences between States by judges of their own choice, and on the basis of respect for law.

Art. XVI. In questions of a legal nature, and especially in the interpretation or application of International Conventions, arbitration is recognized by the Signatory Powers as the most effective, and at the same time the most equitable, means of settling disputes which diplomacy has failed to settle.

Art. XVII. The Arbitration Convention is concluded for questions already existing or for questions which may arise eventually.

It may embrace any dispute or only disputes of a certain category.

Art. XVIII. The Arbitration Convention implies the engagement to submit loyally to the Award.

Art. XIX. Independently of general or private Treaties expressly stipulating recourse to arbitration as obligatory on the Signatory Powers, these Powers reserve to themselves the right of concluding, either before the ratification of the present Act or later, new Agreements, general or private, with a view to extending obligatory arbitration to all cases which they may consider it possible to submit it.

Chapter II. – On the Permanent Court of Arbitration.

Art. XX. With the object of facilitating an immediate recourse to arbitration for international differences, which it has not been possible to settle by diplomacy, the Signatory Powers undertake to organize a permanent Court of Arbitration, accessible at all times and operating, unless otherwise stipulated by the parties, in accordance with the Rules of Procedure inserted in the present Convention.

Art. XXI. The Permanent Court shall be competent for all arbitration cases, unless the parties agree to institute a special Tribunal.

Art. XXII. An International Bureau, established at The Hague, serves as record office for the Court.

This Bureau is the channel for communications relative to the meetings of the Court.

It has the custody of the archives and conducts all the administrative business.

The Signatory Powers undertake to communicate to the International Bureau at The Hague a duly certified copy of any conditions of arbitration arrived at between them, and of any award concerning them delivered by special Tribunals.

They undertake also to communicate to the Bureau the Laws, Regulations, and documents eventually showing the execution of the awards given by the Court.

Art. XXIII. Within the three months following its ratification of the present Act, each Signatory Power shall select four persons at the most, of known competency in questions of international law, of the highest moral reputation, and disposed to accept the duties of Arbitrators.

The persons thus selected shall be inscribed as members of the Court, in a list which shall be notified by the Bureau to all the Signatory Powers.

Any alteration in the list of Arbitrators is brought by the Bureau to the knowledge of the Signatory Powers.

Two or more Powers may agree on the selection in common of one or more Members.

The same person can be selected by different Powers.

The Members of the Court are appointed for a term of six years. Their appointments can be renewed.

In case of the death or retirement of a member of the Court, his place shall be filled in accordance with the method of his appointment.

Art. XXIV. When the Signatory Powers desire to have recourse to the Permanent Court for the settlement of a difference that has arisen between them, the Arbitrators called upon to form the competent Tribunal to decide this difference, must be chosen from the general list of members of the Court.

Failing the direct agreement of the parties on the composition of the Arbitration Tribunal, the following course shall be pursued:

Each party appoints two Arbitrators, and these together choose an Umpire.

If the votes are equal, the choice of the Umpire is entrusted to a third Power, selected by the parties by common accord.

If an agreement is not arrived at on this subject, each party selects a different Power, and the choice of the Umpire is made in concert by the Powers thus selected.

The Tribunal being thus composed, the parties notify to the Bureau their determination to have recourse to the Court and the names of the Arbitrators.

The Tribunal of Arbitration assembles on the date fixed by the parties.

The Members of the Court, in the discharge of their duties and out of their own country, enjoy diplomatic privileges and immunities.

Art. XXV. The Tribunal of Arbitration has its ordinary seat at The Hague. Except in cases of necessity, the place of session can only be altered by the Tribunal with the assent of the parties."

The Articles XXVI–XXIX are concerned with the Permanent Court of Arbitration. Chapter III (arts. XXX–LXI), on Arbitral Procedure.

CARNEGIE ENDOWMENT, Signatures, Ratifications, Adhesions and Reservations to the Conventions and Declarations of the First and Second Hague Conference, Washington, DC, 1914.

HAGUE INTERNATIONAL PEACE CONFERENCES, 1899 AND 1907. Two first international meetings devoted to problems of peace: the First Hague Conference held at Maison du Pois; in the suburbs of The Hague, May 18–July 19, 1899, convened by the Queen of the Netherlands, proposed by Russia, attended by 26, mostly European, states; the USA and Mexico from the Americas; China, Japan and Persia from Asia; Africa was not represented because of the inconclusive British–Dutch dispute regarding the representation of Transvaal. The conference adopted a number of conventions and founded the Permanent Court of Arbitration popularly called The Hague Tribunal and, in its Final Act, recommended that the participating states consider the possibility of a reduction of armaments to be discussed further at the Second Hague Conference. The text of the Final Act read as follows:

"The International Peace Conference, convoked in the best interests of humanity by His Majesty the Emperor of All the Russias, assembled, on the invitation of the

Government of her Majesty the Queen of the Netherlands, in the Royal House in the Wood at The Hague on the 18th May, 1899.

In a series of meetings, between the 18th May and the 29th July, 1899, in which the constant desire of the delegates above-mentioned has been to realize, in the fullest manner possible, the generous views of the august initiator of the Conference and the intentions of their Governments, the Conference has agreed, for submission for signature by the plenipotentiaries, on the text of the Conventions and Declarations enumerated below and annexed to the present Act:

I. Convention for the peaceful adjustment of international differences.

II. Convention regarding the laws and customs of war on land.

III. Convention for the adaptation to maritime warfare of the principles of the Geneva Convention of the 22nd August, 1864.

IV. Three Declarations:

(1) To prohibit the launching of projectiles and explosives from balloons or by other similar new methods.

(2) To prohibit the use of projectiles, the only object of which is the diffusion of asphyxiating or deleterious gases.

(3) To prohibit the use of bullets which expand or flatten easily in the human body, such as bullets with a hard envelope, of which the envelope does not entirely cover the core or is pierced with incisions.

These Conventions and Declarations shall form so many separate Acts. These Acts shall be dated this day, and may be signed up to the 31st December, 1899, by the plenipotentiaries of the Powers represented at the International Peace Conference at The Hague.

Guided by the same sentiments, the Conference has adopted unanimously the following Resolution:

The Conference is of opinion that the restriction of military charges, which are at present a heavy burden on the world, is extremely desirable for the increase of the material and moral welfare of mankind.

It has besides formulated the following views:

(1) The Conference taking into consideration the preliminary step taken by the Swiss Federal Government for the revision of the Geneva Convention, expresses the wish that steps may be shortly taken for the assembly of a special Conference having for its object the revision of that Convention. This wish was voted unanimously.

(2) The Conference expresses the wish that the questions of the rights and duties of neutrals may be inserted in the program of a Conference in the near future.

(3) The Conference expresses the wish that the questions with regard to rifles and naval guns, as considered by it, may be studied by the Governments with the object of coming to an agreement respecting the employment of new types and calibres.

(4) The Conference expresses the wish that the Governments, taking into consideration the proposals made at the Conference, may examine the possibility of an agreement as to the limitation of armed forces by land and sea, and of war budgets.

(5) The Conference expresses the wish that the proposal, which contemplates the declaration of the inviolability of private property in naval warfare, may be referred to a subsequent Conference for consideration.

(6) The Conference expresses the wish that the proposal to settle the question of the bombardment of ports, towns, and villages by a naval force may be referred to a subsequent Conference of consideration. The last five wishes were voted unanimously, saving some abstentions.

In faith of which, the plenipotentiaries have signed the present Act, and have affixed their seals thereto.

Done at The Hague, 29th July, 1899, in one copy only, which shall be deposited in the Ministry for Foreign Affairs, and of which copies, duly certified, shall be delivered to all the Powers represented at the Conference."

The second Hague Conference met May 15–Oct. 18, 1907 at Binnenhof Palace, Ridderzaal, in the city center, on the initiative of Russian Tsar and US President, attended by 44 States including, besides USA and Russia, 16 Latin American republics, China, Japan, Persia, Siam and Liberia; 13 conventions and one declaration were adopted. The most

substantial achievement of the Hague Peace Conferences was that they extended international law with a view to reducing the necessity of reverting to war, the so-called ▷ Kriegsräson, and were the first to attempt, though unsuccessfully, to examine the issue of disarmament as the major problem for achieving global peace and security.

The text of the Final Act of the Second Hague Conference read as follows:

"The Second International Peace Conference, proposed in the first instance by the President of the United States of America, having been convoked, on the invitation of His Majesty The Emperor of All the Russias, by Her Majesty the Queen of Netherlands, assembled on the 15th June, 1907, at The Hague in the Hall of the Knights, for the purpose of giving a fresh development to the humanitarian principles which served as a basis for the work of the First Conference of 1899.

The following Powers took part in the Conference, and appointed the delegates named below . . .

At a series of meetings, held from the 15th June to the 18th October, 1907, in which the above delegates were throughout animated by the desire to realize, in the fullest possible measure, the generous views of the august initiator of the Conference and the intentions of the Government, the Conference drew up, for submission for signature by the plenipotentiaries, the text of the Conventions and of the Declaration enumerated below and annexed to the present Act:

I. Convention for the pacific settlement of international disputes.

II. Convention respecting the limitation of the employment of the force for the recovery of contract debts.

III. Convention relative to the opening of hostilities.

IV. Convention respecting the laws and customs of war on land.

V. Convention respecting the rights and duties of neutral powers and persons in case of war on land.

VI. Convention relative to the status of enemy merchant ships at the outbreak of hostilities.

VII. Convention relative to the conversion of merchant ships into warships.

VIII. Convention relative to the laying of automatic submarine contact mines.

IX. Convention respecting bombardment by naval forces in time of war.

X. Convention for the adaptation to naval war of the principles of the Geneva Convention.

XI. Convention relative to certain restrictions with regard to the exercise of the right of capture in naval war.

XII. Convention relative to the creation of an International Prize Court.

XIII. Convention concerning the rights and duties of neutral Powers in naval war.

XIV. Declaration prohibiting the discharge of projectiles and explosives from balloons.

These Conventions and Declaration shall form so many separate Acts. These Acts shall be dated this day, and may be signed up to the 30th June, 1908, at The Hague, by the plenipotentiaries of the Powers represented at the Second Peace Conference

The Conference, actuated by the spirit of mutual agreement and concession characterizing its deliberations, has agreed upon the following Declaration, which, while reserving to each of the Powers represented full liberty of action as regards voting, enables them to affirm the principles which they regard as unanimously admitted:

It is unanimous:

(1) In admitting the principle of compulsory arbitration.

(2) In declaring that certain disputes, in particular those relating to the interpretation and application of the provisions of international agreements, may be submitted to compulsory arbitration without any restriction.

Finally, it is unanimous in proclaiming that, although it has not yet been found feasible to conclude a Convention in this sense, nevertheless the divergences of opinion which have come to light have not exceeded the bounds of judicial controversy, and that, by working together here during the past four months, the collected Powers not only have learnt to understand one another and to draw closer together, but have succeeded in the

course of this long collaboration in evolving a very lofty conception of the common welfare of humanity.

The Conference has further unanimously adopted the following Resolution:

The Second Peace Conference confirms the Resolution adopted by the Conference of 1899 in regard to the limitation of military expenditure; and inasmuch as military expenditure has considerably increased in almost every country since that time, the Conference declares that it is eminently desirable that the Government should resume the serious examination of this question. It has besides expressed the following views:

(1) The Conference recommends to the signatory Powers the adoption of the annexed draft Convention for the creation of a Judicial Arbitration Court, and the bringing it into force as soon as an agreement has been reached respecting the selection of the judges and the constitution of the Court.

(2) The Conference expresses the opinion that, in case of war, the responsible authorities, civil as well as military, should make it their special duty to ensure and safeguard the maintenance of pacific relations, more especially of the commercial and industrial relations between the inhabitants of the belligerent States and neutral countries.

(3) The Conference expresses the opinion that the Powers should regulate, by special treaties, the position, as regards military charges, of foreigners residing within their territories.

(4) The Conference expresses the opinion that the preparation of regulations relative to the laws and customs of naval war should figure in the program of the next Conference, on that in any case the Powers may apply, as far as possible, to war by sea the principle of the Convention relative to the laws and customs of war on land.

Finally, the Conference recommends to the Powers the assembly of a Third Peace Conference, which might be held within a period corresponding to that which has elapsed since the preceding Conference, at a date to be fixed by common agreement between the Powers, and it calls their attention to the necessity of preparing the program of this Third Conference a sufficient time in advance to ensure its deliberations being conducted with the necessary authority and expedition. In order to attain this object the Conference considers that it would be very desirable that, some two years before the probable date of the meeting, a preparatory committee should be charged by the Governments with the task of collecting the various proposals to be submitted to the Conference, of embodiment in an international regulation, and of preparing a program which the Governments should decide upon in sufficient time to enable it to be carefully examined by the countries interested. This committee should further be entrusted with the task of proposing a system of organization and procedure for the Conference itself.

In faith whereof the Plenipotentiaries have signed the present Act and have affixed their seals thereto.

Done at The Hague, the 18th October, 1907, in a single copy, which shall remain deposited in the archives of the Netherland Government, and duly certified copies of which shall be sent to all the Powers represented at the Conference."

J.H. CHOATE, *The Two Hague Conferences*, Princeton, 1913; *The Proceedings of the Hague Peace Conferences*, New York, 1920.

HAGUE REPARATION AGREEMENTS, 1930.

A Reparation Agreement with 11 Annexes, signed on Jan. 20, 1930 at The Hague by Germany and Belgium, Czechoslovakia, France, Great Britain, Greece, Italy, Japan, Poland, Portugal, Romania and Yugoslavia. ▷ Fund B Convention 1931 and ▷ Reparations.

Reichsgesetzblatt 1930, II, p. 83.

HAGUE RULES, 1907.
The Convention respecting the Laws and Customs of War on Land, signed at The Hague, on Oct. 18, 1907 with Annex: Regulations respecting the Laws and Customs of War on Land, called the Hague Rules of 1907. The Convention reads as follows:

Considering that, while seeking means to preserve peace and prevent armed conflicts between nations, it is likewise necessary to bear in mind the case where an appeal to arms may be brought about by events which their solicitude could not avert.

Animated by the desire to serve, even in this extreme case, the interests of humanity and the ever progressive needs of civilization;

Thinking it important, with this object, to revise the general laws and customs of war, either with the view of defining them with greater precision, or of confining them with such limits as would mitigate their severity as far as possible.

Have deemed it necessary to complete and render more precise in certain particulars the work of the First Peace Conference, which, following on the Brussels Conference of 1874, and inspired by the ideas dictated by a wise and generous forethought, adopted provisions intended to define and govern the usages of war on land. According to views of the high contracting parties, these provisions, the wording of which has been inspired by the desire to diminish the evils of war so far as military requirements permit, are intended to serve as a general rule of conduct for the belligerents in their mutual relations and in their relations with the inhabitants.

It has not, however, been found possible at present to concert regulations covering all the circumstances which arise in practice;

On the other hand, the high contracting parties clearly do not intend that unforeseen cases should, in the absence of a written undertaking, be left to the arbitrary judgement of military commanders.

Until a more complete code of the laws of war has been issued, the high contracting parties deem it expedient to declare that, in cases not included in the Regulations adopted by them, the inhabitants and the belligerents remain under the protection and the rule of the principles of the law of nations, as they result from the usages established among civilized peoples, from the laws of humanity, and from the dictates of the public conscience.

They declare that it is in this sense especially that Arts. 1 and 2 of the Regulations adopted must be understood. Section I. – On Belligerents, Chapter I. – *The qualifications of belligerents.*

Art. 1. The laws, rights, and duties of war apply not only to armies, but also to militia and volunteer corps fulfilling the following conditions:

(1) That they be commanded by a person responsible for his subordinates;

(2) That they have a fixed distinctive emblem recognizable at a distance;

(3) That they carry arms openly; and

(4) That they conduct their operations in accordance with the laws and customs of war.

In countries where militia or volunteer corps constitute the army or form part of it, they are included under the denomination 'army'.

Art. 2. The population of a territory which has not been occupied who, on the approach of the enemy, spontaneously take up arms to resist the invading troops without having had time to organize themselves in accordance with Art. 1, shall be regarded as belligerents if they carry arms openly and if they respect the laws and customs of war.

Art. 3. The armed forces of the belligerent parties may consist of combatants and non-combatants. In case of capture by the enemy both have a right to be treated as prisoners of war.

Chapter II. – *Prisoners of war*

Art. 4. Prisoners of war are in the power of the hostile Government, but not in that of the individuals or corps who captured them.

They must be humanely treated.

All their personal belongings, except arms, horses, and military papers, remain their property.

Art. 5. Prisoners of war may be interned in a town, fortress, camp or other place, under obligation not to go beyond certain fixed limits; but they can only be placed in confinement as indispensable measure of safety, and only while the circumstances which necessitate the measure continue to exist.

Art. 6. The State may utilize the labor of prisoners of war according to their rank and aptitude, officers excepted. The tasks shall not be excessive and shall have no connection with the operations of the war.

Prisoners may be authorized to work for the public service, for private persons, or on their own account.

Work done for the State is paid for at the rates in force for work of a similar kind done by soldiers of the national army, or, if there are none in force, at a rate according to the work executed.

When the work is for other branches of the public service or for private persons, the conditions are settled in agreement with the military authorities.

The wages of the prisoners shall go towards improving their position, and the balance shall be paid them at the time of their release, after deducting the cost of their maintenance.

Art. 7. The government into whose hands prisoners of war have fallen is charged with their maintenance.

In the absence of a special agreement between the belligerents, prisoners of war shall be treated as regards food, quarters and clothing, on the same footing as the troops of the Government which has captured them.

Art. 8. Prisoners of war shall be subject to the laws, regulations, and orders in force in the army of the State in whose power they are. Any act of insubordination justifies the adoption towards them of such measures of severity as may be necessary. Escaped prisoners who are retaken before being able to rejoin their army or before leaving the territory occupied by the army that captured them are liable to disciplinary punishment. Prisoners who, after succeeding in escaping, are again taken prisoners, are not liable to any punishment for the previous flight.

Art. 9. Every prisoner of war is bound to give, if questioned on the subject, his true name and rank, and if he infringes this rule, he is liable to a curtailment of the advantages accorded to the prisoners of war of his class.

Art. 10. Prisoners of war may be set at liberty on parole if the laws of their country allow it, and, in such cases, they are bound, on their personal honor, scrupulously to fulfill both towards their own Government and the Government by which they were made prisoners, the engagements they have contracted.

In such cases their own Government is bound neither to require of nor accept from them any service incompatible with the parole given.

Art. 11. A prisoner of war cannot be compelled to accept his liberty on parole; similarly the hostile Government is not obliged to accede to the request of the prisoner to be set at liberty on parole.

Art. 12. Any prisoner of war liberated on parole and retaken bearing arms against the Government to which he had pledged his honor, or against the allies of that Government, forfeits his right to be treated as a prisoner of war, and can be brought before the courts.

Art. 13. Individuals who follow an army without directly belonging to it, such as newspaper correspondents and reporters, sutlers and contractors, who fall into the enemy's hands, and whom the latter thinks fit to detain, are entitled to be treated as prisoners of war, provided they are in possession of a certificate from the military authorities of the army they were accompanying.

Art. 14. An information bureau relative to prisoners of war is instituted, on the commencement of hostilities, in each of the belligerent States, and when necessary, in neutral countries which have received belligerents in their territory. The function of this bureau is to reply to all inquiries about the prisoners, receive from the various services concerned all the information respecting internments and transfers, releases on parole, exchanges, escapes, admissions into hospital, deaths, as well as other information necessary to enable it to make out and keep up to date an individual return for each prisoner of war. The bureau must state in this return the regimental number, name and surname, age, place of origin, rank, unit, wounds, date and place of capture, internment wounding, and death, as well as any observations of a special character. The individual return shall be sent to the Government of the other belligerent after the conclusion of peace.

It is likewise the function of the information bureau to receive and collect all objects of personal use, valuables, letters, etc., found on the field of battle or left by prisoners who have been released on parole, or exchanged, or who have escaped or died in hospitals or ambulances, and to forward them to those concerned.

Art. 15. Relief societies for prisoners of war, which are properly constituted in accordance with the laws of their country and with the object of serving as the channel for charitable effort, shall receive from the belligerents, for themselves and their duly accredited agents, every facility for the efficient performance of their humane task within the bounds by military

necessities and administrative regulations. Agents of these societies may be admitted to the places of internment for the purpose of distributing relief, as also to the halting-places of repatriated prisoners, if furnished with a personal permit by the military authorities, and on giving an undertaking in writing to comply with all measures of order and police which the latter may issue.

Art. 16. Information bureaus enjoy the privilege of free postage. Letters, money orders, and valuables, as well as parcels by post, intended for prisoners of war, or dispatched by them, shall be exempt from all postal duties in the countries or origin and destination, as well as in the countries they pass through.

Presents and relief in kind for prisoners of war shall be admitted free of all import or other duties, as well as of payments for carriage by State railways.

Art. 17. Officers taken prisoners shall receive the same rate of pay as officers of corresponding rank in the country where they are detained, the amount to be refunded by their Government.

Art. 18. Prisoners of war shall enjoy complete liberty in the exercise of their religion, including attendance at the services of whatever church they may belong to, on the sole condition that they comply with the measures of order and police issued by the military authorities.

Art. 19. The wills of prisoners of war are received or drawn up in the same way as for soldiers of the national army. The same rules shall be observed regarding death certificates as well as for the burial of prisoners of war, due regard being paid to their grade and rank.

Art. 20. After the conclusion of peace, the repatriation of prisoners of war shall be carried out as quickly as possible.

Chapter III. – *The sick and wounded*

Art. 21. The obligations of belligerents with regard to the sick and wounded are governed by the Geneva Convention.

Section II. – On Hostilities

Chapter I. – Means of injuring the enemy, sieges, and bombardments.

Art. 22. The right of belligerents to adopt means of injuring the enemy is not unlimited.

Art. 23. In addition to the prohibitions provided by special Conventions, it is especially forbidden:

(a) To employ poison or poisoned weapons;

(b) To kill or wound treacherously individuals belonging to the hostile nation or army;

(c) To kill or wound an enemy who, having laid down his arms, or having no longer means of defense, has surrendered at discretion;

(d) To declare that no quarter will be given;

(e) To employ arms, projectiles, or material calculated to cause unnecessary suffering;

(f) To make improper use of a flag of truce, of the national flag or of the military insignia and uniform of the enemy, as well as the distinctive badges of the Geneva Convention;

(g) To destroy or seize the enemy's property, unless such destruction or seizure be imperatively demanded by the necessities of war;

(h) To declare abolished, suspended or inadmissible in a court of law the rights and actions of the nationals of the hostile party.

It is likewise forbidden for a belligerent to force the nationals of the hostile party to take part in the operations of war directed against their country, even if they were in its service before the commencement of the war.

Art. 24. Ruses of war and the employment of measures necessary for obtaining information about the enemy and the country are considered permissible.

Art. 25. It is forbidden to attack or bombard, by any means whatever, towns, villages, dwellings or buildings that are not defended.

Art. 26. The officer in command of an attacking force must, before commencing a bombardment, except in cases of assault, do all in his power to warn the authorities.

Art. 27. In sieges and bombardments all necessary steps must be taken to spare, as far as possible, buildings dedicated to religion, art, science, or charitable purposes, historic monuments hospitals, and places where the sick and wounded are collected, provided they are not being used at the time for military purposes.

It is the duty of the besieged to indicate the presence of such buildings or places by distinctive and visible signs, which shall be notified to the enemy beforehand.

Art. 28. It is forbidden to give over to pillage a town or place even when taken by storm.

Chapter II. – *Spies*

Art. 29. A person can only be considered a spy when, acting clandestinely or on false pretenses, he obtains or endeavors to obtain information in the zone of operations of a belligerent, with the intention of communicating it to the hostile party.

Thus, soldiers not wearing a disguise who have penetrated into the zone of operations of the hostile army, for the purpose of obtaining information, are not considered spies. Similarly, the following are not considered spies: Soldiers and civilians, carrying out their mission openly, entrusted with the delivery of dispatches intended either for their own army or for the enemy's army. To this class belong likewise persons sent in balloons for the purpose of carrying dispatches and, generally, of maintaining communications between the different parts of an army or a territory.

Art. 30. A spy taken in the act shall not be punished without previous trial.

Art. 31. A spy who, after rejoining the army to which he belongs, is subsequently captured by the enemy, is treated as a prisoner of war, incurs no responsibility for his previous acts of espionage.

Chapter III. – *Parlementaires*

Art. 32. A person is regarded as a parlementaire who has been authorized by one of the belligerents to enter into communication with the other, and who advances bearing a white flag. He has a right to inviolability, as well as the trumpeter, bugler or drummer, the flag-bearer and the interpreter who may accompany him.

Art. 33. The commander to whom a parlementaire is sent is not in all cases obliged to receive him.

He may take all necessary steps in order to prevent the parlementaire taking advantage of his mission to obtain information. In case of abuse, he has the right to detain the parlementaire temporarily.

Art. 34. The parlementaire loses his rights of inviolability if it is proved in a clear and incontestable manner that he has taken advantage of his privileged position to provoke or commit an act of treason.

Chapter IV. – *Capitulations*

Art. 35. Capitulations agreed upon between the contracting parties must take into account the rules of military honor. Once settled, they must be scrupulously observed by both parties.

Chapter V. – *Armistices*

Art. 36. An armistice suspends military operations by mutual agreement between the belligerent parties. If its duration is not defined, the belligerent parties may resume operations at any time, provided always that the enemy is warned within the time agreed upon, in accordance with the terms of the armistice.

Art. 37. An armistice may be general or local. The first suspends the military operations of the belligerent States everywhere; the second only between certain fractions of the belligerent armies and within a fixed radius.

Art. 38. An armistice must be notified officially and in good time to the competent authorities and to the troops. Hostilities are suspended immediately after the notification, or on the date fixed.

Art. 39. It rests with the contracting parties to settle, in the terms of the armistice, what communications may be held in the theater of war with the populations and between them.

Art. 40. Any serious violation of the armistice by one of the parties gives the other party the right of denouncing it, and even, in cases of urgency, of recommending hostilities immediately.

Art. 41. A violation of the terms of the armistice by private persons acting on their own initiative only entitles the injured party to demand the punishment of the offenders and, if necessary compensation for the losses sustained.

Section III. – On Military Authority over the Territory of the Hostile State.

Art. 42. Territory is considered occupied when it is actually placed under the authority of the hostile army.

The occupation extends only to the territory where such authority has been established and can be exercised.

Art. 43. The authority of the legitimate power having in fact passed into the hands of the occupant, the latter shall take all the measures in his power to restore and ensure, as far as possible, public order and safety, while respecting, unless absolutely prevented, the laws in force in the country.

Art. 44. It is forbidden a belligerent to force the population of occupied territory to furnish information about the army of the other belligerent, or about its means of defense.

Art. 45. It is forbidden to compel the population of occupied territory to swear allegiance to the hostile Power.

Art. 46. Family honor and rights, the lives of persons, and private property, as well as religious convictions and practice, must be respected.

Private property cannot be confiscated.

Art. 47. Pillage is formally forbidden.

Art. 48. If, in the territory occupied, the occupant collects the taxes, dues, and tolls imposed for the benefit of the State, he shall do so, as far as possible, in accordance with the rules of assessment and incidence in force, and shall in consequence be bound to defray the expenses of the administration of the occupied territory to the same extent as the legitimate Government was so bound.

Art. 49. If, in addition to the taxes mentioned in the above art., the occupant levies other money contributions in the occupied territory, this shall only be for the needs of the army or of the administration of the territory in question.

Art. 50. No general penalty, pecuniary or otherwise, shall be inflicted upon the population on account of the acts of individuals for which they cannot be regarded as jointly and severally responsible.

Art. 51. No contribution shall be collected except under a written order, and on the responsibility of a commander in chief. The collection of the said contribution shall only be effected as far as possible in accordance with the rules of assessment and incidence of the taxes in force. For every contribution a receipt shall be given to the contributors.

Art. 52. Requisitions in kind and services shall not be demanded from municipalities or inhabitants except for the needs of the army of occupation. They shall be in proportion to the resources of the country, and of such a nature as not to involve the population in the obligation of taking part in the operations of the war against their country.

Such requisitions and services shall only be demanded on the authority of the commander in the locality occupied. Contributions in kind shall, as far as possible, be paid for in cash; if not, a receipt shall be given and the payment of the amount due shall be made as soon as possible.

Art. 53. An army of occupation can only take possession of cash, funds, and realizable securities which are strictly the property of the State, depots of arms, means of transport, stores and supplies, and, generally, all movable property belonging to the State which may be used for the operations of the war.

All appliances, whether on land, at sea, or in the air, adapted for the transmission of news, or for the transport of persons or things, exclusive of cases governed by naval law, depots of arms and, generally, all kinds of munitions of war, may be seized, even if they belong to private individuals, but must be restored and compensation fixed when peace is made.

Art. 54. Submarine cables connecting an occupied territory with a neutral territory shall not be seized or destroyed except in the case of absolute necessity. They must likewise be restored and compensation fixed when peace is made.

Art. 55. The occupying State shall be regarded only as administrator and usufructuary of public buildings, real estate, forests, and agricultural estates belonging to the hostile State, and situated in the occupied country. It must safeguard the capital of these properties, and administer them in accordance with the rules of usufruct.

Art. 56. The property of municipalities, that of institutions dedicated to religion, charity, and education, the arts and sciences, even when State property, shall be treated as private property.

All seizure or destruction of, or wilful damage to, institutions of this character, historic monuments, works of art and science, is forbidden, and should be made the subject of legal proceedings."

A number of provisions of the Hague Rules have been expanded in the Geneva Conventions of 1949 (▷ Geneva Humanitarian Conventions 1864–1949).

The Proceedings of the Hague Peace Conferences. Translation of the Official Texts. The Conference of 1907, New York, 1920, Vol. 1, pp. 620–631.

HAGUE RULES, 1924. The official name of a convention on the unification of the principles related to ▷ Bills of lading, elaborated at the Hague Conference of 1921 and adopted at the Brussels Conference on Aug. 25, 1924.

HAGUE SECOND CONVENTION, 1907. The Convention for the Pacific Settlement of International Disputes, called Hague Convention II, concluded on Oct. 18, 1907 at The Hague; signed by the Heads of States of Austria–Hungary, Belgium, Bolivia, Brazil, Bulgaria, Chile, China, Colombia, Cuba, Denmark, the Dominican Republic, Ecuador, El Salvador, France, Germany, Greece, Guatemala, Haiti, Italy, Japan, Luxembourg, Mexico, Montenegro, the Netherlands, Norway, Panama, Paraguay, Peru, Persia, Portugal, Romania, Serbia, Siam, Spain, Sweden, Switzerland, Turkey, UK, Uruguay, USA and Venezuela. The highlights of the Convention are as follows:

"Animated by the sincere desire to work for the maintenance of general peace;
Resolved to promote by all the efforts in their power the friendly settlement of international disputes;
Recognizing the solidarity uniting the members of the society of civilized nations;
Desirous of extending the empire of law and of strengthening the appreciation of international justice;
Convinced that the permanent institution of a Tribunal of Arbitration accessible to all, in the midst of independent Powers, will contribute effectively to this result;
Having regard to the advantages attending the general and regular organization of the procedure of arbitration;
Sharing the opinion of the august initiator of the International Peace Conference that it is expedient to record in an International Agreement the principles of equity and right on which are based the security of States and the welfare of peoples;
Being desirous, with this object, of insuring the better working in practice of Commissions of Inquiry and Tribunals of Arbitration, and of facilitating recourse to arbitration in cases which allow of a summary procedure;
Have deemed it necessary to revise in certain particulars and to complete the work of the First Peace Conference for the pacific settlement of international disputes;
The High Contracting Parties have resolved to conclude a new Convention for this purpose:
I. *The Maintenance of General Peace.*
Art. I. With a view to obviating as far as possible recourse to force in the relations between States, the Contracting Powers agree to use their best efforts to ensure the pacific settlement of international differences.
II. *Good Offices and Mediation.*
Art. II. In case of serious disagreement or dispute, before an appeal to arms, the Contracting Powers agree to have recourse, as far as circumstances allow, to the good offices or mediation of one or more friendly Powers.
Art. III. Independently of this recourse, the Contracting Powers deem it expedient and desirable that one or more Powers, strangers to the dispute, should, on their own initiative and as far as circumstances may allow, offer their good offices or mediation to the States at variance. Powers strangers to the dispute have the right to offer good offices or mediation even during the course of hostilities.
The exercise of this right can never be regarded by either of the parties in dispute as an unfriendly act.
Art. IV. The part of the mediator consists in reconciling the opposing claims and appeasing the feelings of resentment which may have arisen between the States at variance.
Art. V. The functions of the mediator are at an end when once it is declared, either by one of the parties to the dispute or by the mediator himself, that the means of reconciliation proposed by him are not accepted.
Art. VI. Good offices and mediation undertaken either at the request of the parties in dispute or on the initiative of Powers strangers to the dispute have exclusively the character of advice, and never have binding force.

Art. VII. The acceptance of mediation cannot, unless there be an agreement to the contrary, have the effect of interrupting, delaying or hindering mobilization or other measures of preparation for war.

If it takes place after the commencement of hostilities, the military operations in progress are not interrupted in the absence of an agreement to the contrary.

Art. VIII. The Contracting Powers are agreed in recommending the application, when circumstances allow, of special mediation in the following form:

In case of a serious difference endangering peace, the States at variance choose respectively a Power, to which they intrust the mission of entering into direct communication with the Power chosen on the other side, with the object of preventing the rupture of pacific relations. For the period of this mandate, the term of which, unless otherwise stipulated, cannot exceed thirty days, the States in dispute cease from all direct communication on the subject of the dispute, which is regarded as referred exclusively to the mediating Powers, which must use their best efforts to settle it.

In case of a definite rupture of pacific relations, these Powers are charged with the joint task of taking advantage of any opportunity to restore peace.

III. *International Commissions of Inquiry.*

Art. IX. In disputes of an international nature involving neither honor nor vital interests, and arising from a difference of opinion on points of fact, the Contracting Powers deem it expedient and desirable that the parties who have not been able to come to an agreement by means of diplomacy, should as far as circumstances allow, institute an International Commission of Inquiry, to facilitate a solution of these disputes by elucidating the facts by means of an impartial and conscientious investigation.

Art. X. International Commissions of Inquiry are constituted by special agreement between the parties in dispute.

The Inquiry Convention defines the facts to be examined; it determines the mode and time in which the Commission is to be formed and the extent of the powers of the Commissioners. It also determines, if there is need, where the Commission is to sit, and whether it may remove to another place, the language the Commission shall use and the languages the use of which shall be authorized before it, as well as the date on which each party must deposit its statement of facts, and, generally speaking, all the conditions upon which the parties have agreed.

If the parties consider it necessary to appoint Assessors, the Convention of Inquiry shall determine the mode of their selection and the extent of their powers.

Art. XI. If the Inquiry Convention has not determined where the Commission is to sit, it will sit at The Hague. The place of meeting, once fixed, cannot be altered by the Commission except with the assent of the parties.

If the Inquiry Convention has not determined what languages are to be employed, the question shall be decided by the Commission.

IV. *International Arbitration.* Chapter I. – The System of Arbitration.

Art. XXXVII. International arbitration has for its object the settlement of disputes between States by Judges of their own choice and on the basis of respect for law.

Recourse to arbitration implies an engagement to submit in good faith to the Award.

Art. XXXVIII. In questions of a legal nature, and especially in the interpretation or application of International Conventions, arbitration is recognized by the Contracting Powers as the most effective, and, at the same time, the most equitable means of settling disputes which diplomacy has failed to settle.

Consequently, it would be desirable that, in disputes about the above-mentioned questions, the Contracting Powers should, if the case arose, have recourse to arbitration, in so far as circumstances permit.

Art. XXXIX. The Arbitration Convention is concluded for questions already existing or for questions which may arise eventually.

It may embrace any dispute or only disputes of a certain category.

Art. XL. Independently of general or private Treaties expressly stipulating recourse to arbitration as obligatory on the Contracting Powers, the said Powers reserve to themselves the right of concluding new Agreements, general or particular, with a view to extending compulsory arbitration to all cases in which they may consider it possible to submit to it.

Chapter II. – The Permanent Court of Arbitration.

Art. XLI. With the object of facilitating an immediate recourse to arbitration for international differences, which it has not been possible to settle by diplomacy, the Contracting Powers undertake to maintain the Permanent Court of Arbitration, as established by the First Peace Conference, accessible at all times, and operating, unless otherwise stipulated by the parties, in accordance with the rules of procedure inserted in the present Convention.

Art. XLII. The Permanent Court is competent for all arbitration cases, unless the parties agree to institute a special Tribunal.

Art. XLIII. The Permanent Court sits at The Hague.

An International Bureau serves as registry for the Court. It is the channel for communications relative to the meetings of the Court; it has charge of the archives and conducts all the administrative business.

The Contracting Powers undertake to communicate to the Bureau, as soon as possible, a certified copy of any conditions of arbitration arrived at between them and of any Award concerning them delivered by a special Tribunal.

They likewise undertake to communicate to the Bureau the laws, regulations, and documents eventually showing the execution of the Awards given by the Court.

Art. XLIV. Each Contracting Power selects four persons at the most, of known competence in questions of international law, of the highest moral reputation, and disposed to accept the duties of Arbitrator.

The persons thus selected are inscribed, as members of the Court, in a list which shall be notified to all the Contracting Powers by the Bureau.

Any alteration in the list of Arbitrators is brought by the Bureau to the knowledge of the Contracting Powers.

Two or more Powers may agree on the selection in common of one or more members.

The same person can be selected by different Powers. The members of the Court are appointed for a term of six years.

These appointments are renewable.

Should a member of the Court die or resign, the same procedure is followed for filling the vacancy as was followed for appointing him. In this case the appointment is made for a fresh period of six years.

Chapter III – Arbitration Procedure.

Art. LI. With a view to encouraging the development of arbitration, the Contracting Powers have agreed on the following rules, which are applicable to arbitration procedure, unless other rules have been agreed on by the parties.

Art. LII. The Powers which have recourse to arbitration sign a 'Compromis', in which the subject of the dispute is clearly defined, the time allowed for appointing Arbitrators, the form, order, and time in which the communication referred to in Article LXIII must be made, and the amount of the sum which each party must deposit in advance to defray the expenses.

The 'Compromis' likewise defines, if there is occasion, the manner of appointing Arbitrators, any special powers which may eventually belong to the Tribunal, where it shall meet, the language it shall use, and the languages the employment of which shall be authorized before it, and, generally speaking, all the conditions on which the parties are agreed.

Art. LIII. The Permanent Court is competent to settle the 'Compromis', if the parties are agreed to have recourse to it for the purpose.

It is similarly competent, even if the request is only made by none of the parties, when all attempts to reach an understanding through the diplomatic channel have failed, in the case of:

(1) A dispute covered by a general Treaty of Arbitration concluded or renewed after the present Convention has come into force, and providing for a 'Compromis' in all disputes and not either explicitly or implicitly excluding the settlement of the 'Compromis' from the competence of the Court. Recourse cannot, however, be had to the court if the other party declares that in its opinion the dispute does not belong to the category of disputes which can be submitted to compulsory arbitration, unless the Treaty of Arbitration confers upon the Arbitration Tribunal the power of deciding this preliminary question.

(2) A dispute arising from contract debts claimed from one Power by another Power as due to its nationals, and for the settlement of which the offer of arbitration has been accepted. This arrangement is not applicable if acceptance is subject to the condition that the 'Compromis' should be settled in some other way.

Art. LIV. In the cases contemplated in the preceding Article, the 'Compromis' shall be settled by a Commission consisting of five members selected in the manner arranged for in Art. XLV, paragraphs 3 to 6. The fifth member is President of the Commission ex officio.

Art. LV. The duties of Arbitrator may be conferred on one Arbitrator alone or on several Arbitrators selected by the parties as they please, or chosen by them from the members of the Permanent Court of Arbitration established by the present Convention.

Failing the constitution of the Tribunal by direct agreement between the parties, the course referred to in art. XLV, paragraphs 3 to 6, is followed.

Art. LVI. When a Sovereign or the Chief of a State is chosen as Arbitrator, the arbitration procedure is settled by him.

Art. LVII. The Umpire is President of the Tribunal ex officio.

When the Tribunal does not include an Umpire, it appoints its own President.

Art. LVIII. When the 'Compromis' is settled by a Commission, as contemplated in Article LIV, and in the absence of an agreement to the contrary, the Commission itself shall form the Arbitration Tribunal.

Art. LIX. Should one of the Arbitrators either die, retire, or be unable for any reason whatever to discharge his functions, the same procedure is followed for filling the vacancy as was followed for appointing him.

Art. LX. The Tribunal sits at The Hague, unless some other place is selected by the parties.

The Tribunal can only sit in the territory of a third Power with the latter's consent.

The place of meeting once fixed cannot be altered by the Tribunal, except with the consent of the parties.

Chapter IV. – Arbitration by Summary Procedure.

Art. LXXXVI. With a view to facilitating the working of the system of arbitration in disputes admitting of a summary procedure, the Contracting Powers adopt the following rules, which shall be observed in the absence of other arrangements and subject to the reservation that the provisions of Chapter III apply so far as may be.

Art. LXXXVII. Each of the parties in dispute appoints an Arbitrator. The two Arbitrators thus selected choose an Umpire. If they do not agree on this point, each of them proposes two candidates taken from the general list of the members of the Permanent Court exclusive of the members appointed by either of the parties and not being nationals of either of them; which of the candidates thus proposed shall be the Umpire is determined by lot.

The Umpire presides over the Tribunal, which gives its decisions by a majority of votes.

Art. LXXXVIII. In the absence of any previous agreement the Tribunal, as soon as it is formed, settles the time which the two parties must submit their respective cases to it.

Art. LXXXIX. Each party is represented before the Tribunal by an agent, who serves as intermediary between the Tribunal and the Government who appointed him.

Art. XC. The proceedings are conducted exclusively in writing. Each party, however, is entitled to ask that witnesses and experts should be called. The Tribunal has, for its part, the right to demand oral explanations from the agents of the two parties, as well as from the experts and witnesses whose appearance in Court it may consider useful.

V. *Final Provisions.*

Art. XCI. The present Convention, duly ratified, shall replace, as between the Contracting Powers, the Convention for the Pacific Settlement of International Disputes of the 29th July, 1899."

CARNEGIE ENDOWMENT, Signatures, Ratifications, Adhesions and Reservations to the Conventions and Declarations of the First and Second Hague Conference, Washington D.C., 1914.

HAGUE, THE. The seat of the government of the Kingdom of Netherlands, capital of South Holland province, city population, 1986 estimate, 674,548. Since the First Hague Peace Conference 1899, a center for international arbitration (▷ International Court of Justice). International Institute of Statistics and about 40 international organizations reg. with the UIA: in 1913 the Carnegie Foundation erected the Palace of Peace (▷ Carnegie Endowment for International Peace).

Yearbook of International Organizations. J. PAXTON ed., *The Statesman's Yearbook 1987–88*, London 1987.

HAIL. One of the natural calamities; a subject of organized international co-operation. Organization reg. with the UIA:

International Association of Hail Insurers, f. 1951, Zurich.

Yearbook of International Organizations.

HAIRDRESSING TRADE. A subject of international co-operation. Organizations reg. with the UIA:

International Confederation of the Hairdressing Trade, f. 1948, Paris.
Journeyman Barbers, Hairdressers, Cosmetologists and Proprietors International Union of America, f. 1887, Indianapolis, Ind.

Yearbook of International Organizations.

HAITI. Member of the UN. République d'Haïti. Republic of Haiti. Caribbean state in the western part of the island of Hispaniola, bounded in the eastern part by the Dominican Republic. Area: 27,750 sq. km. Pop. 1982 census: 5,053,792 (1975 census: 4,329,991). Capital: Port au Prince with 862,900 inhabitants in 1982. GNP per capita 1986 US $370. Currency: one gourde = 100 centimes. Official language: French. National Day: Jan. 1. Independence Day, 1804.
Original member of the UN since Oct. 24, 1945 and of UN specialized agencies. Member of the OAS. International relations: French colony 1697–1801. After three guerrilla wars, Haiti gained complete independence on Jan. 1, 1804. Under occupation of US Marines 1915–34 and under US fiscal control until 1947. Treaty of Friendship with the United States signed on Nov. 3, 1933 in Washington, DC. Member of the League of Nations 1920–39. In dispute with the Dominican Republic in Oct. 1937, in 1949, 1963 and 1967. In World War II on the side of the Allies. In Nov. 1982 CARICOM granted to Haiti a limited observer status. In Mar., 1983 the Pope visited Haiti. On Febr. 7, 1986, the President Jean–Claude Duvalier ("Baby-Doc") after 15 years of dictatorial rule fled to France.
See also ▷ World Heritage UNESCO List.

A.C. MILLISPANGH, *Haiti under American Control 1915–1930*, Boston, 1931; L.L. MONTAGUE, *Haiti and the US 1714–1938*, Durham, 1940; R.C. GERARD, *La economia haitiana y su via de desarrollo*, Mexico, DF, 1966; B. DIEDERICH, A.L. BURT, *Papa Doc. The Truth about Haiti Today*, New York, 1969; C.K. CLAQUE, R.S. ROTBERG, *Haiti*, Boston, 1971; S. RODMAN, *Haiti, The Black Republic*, New York, 1973; M.S. LAGUERRE, *The Complete Haitiana. Bibliography*, London, 1982; *The Europa Year Book 1984. A World Survey*, Vol. II, pp. 1655–1663, London, 1984.

HAKE. *Merluccius merluccius.* A fish of the Mediterranean and the Atlantic coast of Europe; under international protection, subject of an international convention.

UNTS, Vol. 231, p. 199.

HALIBUT. *Reinhardtius hippoglossoiden.* A marine fish from the flounder family, native to the Atlantic

and Pacific, subject of an international convention imposing limits on catches.

UNTS, Vol. 231, p. 199.

HALLEY'S COMET. Subject of international research in March 1986, when Halley's comet reached the nearest point to the Earth in its 76-year cycle. The USA took measurements of the comet from the International Cometary Explorer, the USSR from the Spacecrafts Vega I and Vega II, Japan from Sakigaki and Suisei and the European Space Agency, ESA, from Giotto Satellite which approached the comet to a nearest distance of less than 600 km. The preliminary result of all encounters was published in the British Science Magazine "Nature".

"Nature", May, 1986; KEESING's *Contemporary Archive, 1986.*

HALLSTEIN DOCTRINE, 1955. An international term for a principle of the foreign policy of the FRG of not maintaining diplomatic relations with states recognizing the GDR, formulated on Dec. 1, 1955 in Bonn at a Conference of ambassadors of FRG by the under-secretary of state in the ministry of foreign affairs (1951–58), Walter Hallstein. He acknowledged that the consequence of the thesis of Chancellor Konrad Adenauer, stated in the Bundestag that the "FRG is the sole representative of the German nation in international affairs", was the principle that foreign states which established and maintained diplomatic relations with the GDR could not maintain relations with the FRG and vice-versa. This theory, approved by the Bundestag and the FRG government, called the Hallstein Doctrine, had its political consequences in the breaking by the FRG of diplomatic relations with Yugoslavia in 1957 and with Cuba in 1963, as well as in diplomatic and economic pressures on states of the Third World for the purpose of politically isolating the GDR; several times criticized in the UN General Assembly as contrary to the principles of the UN Charter. The use of the Hallstein Doctrine was *de facto* halted from 1970 by the government of Chancellor Willy Brandt. This was manifested in the resumption of diplomatic relations with Yugoslavia in 1970, the non-severance of diplomatic relations with Chile after the government of President Salvadore Allende had also established diplomatic relations with GDR, 1971. In 1972 the Hallstein Doctrine was autonomously cancelled in connection with the signing of inter-state FRG–GDR treaties.

R. BIERZANEK. "Doktryna Hallsteina", in: *Sprawy Miedzynarodowe*, Warsaw, 1962; R. ZIVIER, *Die Nichtannerkennung in Modernem Völkerrecht*, Berlin, 1967.

HALLUCINOGENS. A chemically diverse group of drugs of abuse, which produce mental changes such as hallucinations, paranoid reactions, depressions.
See also ▷ LSD-25 and ▷ Mescaline.

UN Chronicle, May 1987.

HAMBURG RULES, 1978. The official name of a Convention on the Carriage of Goods by Sea prepared by the working Group on International Shipping Legislation of UNCTAD and presented to the UN General Assembly, which decided to convene the UN Conference on the Carriage of Goods by Sea. This Conference, Mar. 31, 1978 in Hamburg approved the Convention on the Carriage of Goods by Sea. ▷ Bills of Lading.

UN Yearbook, 1972, p. 822; *UN Chronicle*, January, 1978; p. 80.

HAMMARSKJÖLD DAG LIBRARY. The main UN library, New York. Received this name on Oct. 16, 1961 by a decision of the UN General Assembly in honor of the memory of the UN Secretary-General, the Swede Dag Hammarskjöld (1905–61) killed in action in the service of the UN. A Dag Hammarskjöld Memorial Scholarship fund was established in 1969.

DAG HAMMARSKJÖLD. *A Selection of the Speeches and the Statements of Secretary General of the UN, 1953–1961*, New York, 1962.

HANDBALL. Olympic sport since 1936, organized in International Handball Federation, IHF, founded in 1928, sponsoring world championships held every three years since 1954. Reg. with the UIA.

HANDICAPPED. Subject of international co-operation. Organizations reg. with the UIA:

Council of World Organizations Interested in the Handicapped, f. 1953, New York, NY, USA.
International Federation of Disabled Workers and Civilian Handicapped, f. 1953, Bonn, FRG.

Yearbook of International Organizations, 1986/87; The Europa Yearbook 1988. A World Survey, Vol. I, London 1988.

HANOI. The capital of Viet-Nam. Area 597 sq km. Pop. 1983 estimated: 2,674,400. Capital of French Indochina 1874–1940. Occupied by the Japanese 1940–1945. Seat of the Vietnam government 1945 and scene of heavy fighting between French and Viet Minh forces 1946–1954. The capital of North Vietnam and, since 1976, of Viet-Nam.

The Europa Yearbook. A World Survey, 1987. London, 1987.

HANSARD SOCIETY FOR PARLIAMENTARY GOVERNMENT, f. 1944, London. Publ.: Parliamentary Affairs. A Journal of Comparative Politics (quarterly).

The Europa Yearbook 1988. A World Survey, Vol. I, London 1988.

HAPI, Hispanic American Periodicals Index. The HAPI lists annually by subject and author articles, reviews, documents in nearly two hundred and fifty journals published throughout the world which regularly treat of Latin America and the Caribbean area or Latin American Groups in the United States. Publ. since 1980 by the UCLA Latin American Center Publications University of California, Los Angeles.

B.G. WALK ed, *HAPI 1985*, Los Angeles, 1987. *Yearbook of International Organizations.*

HARARE. An African city formerly Salisbury, since Apr. 20, 1980 capital of Zimbabwe.

HARARE DECLARATION. ▷ Nonaligned Countries Declaration, 1986.

HARBIN. ▷ Manchuria.

HARD CURRENCIES. An international term for exchangeable currencies recognized as such by the International Monetary Fund, IMF. Economists differentiate hard currencies on the basis of their real strength, the monies of highly developed countries are called ▷ Key currencies.

HARMEL PLAN, 1967. A resolution adopted unanimously by the NATO Council of Ministers on Dec. 14, 1967 as proposed by the Belgian Foreign Minister, P.Ch. Harmel. The proposer recommended that member states should use every opportun-

H

ity to improve relations with the USSR and other Warsaw Pact states, taking the view that the participation of the USSR and the USA was necessary for the solution of Europe's political problems.

KEESING's *Contemporary Archive*, 1967.

HARMON DOCTRINE, 1895. An international term for the legal opinion of the Attorney General of the US, H. Harmon, announced 1895 concerning the dispute between the USA and Mexico on the use of the waters of the Rio Grande. According to Harmon, the sovereignty and jurisdiction of a state over all of its territory – in this case over half of a border river – is exclusive and absolute. As a consequence, there was no obligation to limit the use of water which flows through the territory of states, even if this should harm the interests of a neighboring state. The government of Mexico strongly opposed the Harmon Doctrine but only after the ▷ Good neighbor doctrine had gone into effect in 1933. The matter of using the waters of the Rio Grande was settled with respect to the interests of both sides, by the Treaty on Waters, 1944, and the Harmon Doctrine annulled.

R. CRUZ MIRAMONTES, "La Doctrina Harmon, el Tratado de Agnus de 1944 y algunos problemas derivados de su aplicacion", in: *Foro Internacional*, No. 21, Mexico, DF, 1961, pp. 39–121.

HARVARD CONSULAR RESEARCH 1932. The Harvard studies on the codification of consular law, published by the Harvard Law School in 1928 and entitled: *The Legal Position and Function of Consuls.*

HARVARD INTERNATIONAL RESEARCH, 1935–39. The scientific work conducted at Harvard University in Cambridge, Mass. between 1935 and 1939 by a group of scientists called also the Harvard Group, on codification of international law with respect to such areas as: territorial waters, competence of international courts, legal turnover in civil cases, rights and obligations of a state in case of aggression, rights and obligations of a neutral state in case of sea and air wars, law of extradition, diplomatic immunities and privileges, functions of consuls, nationality, piracy and liability of states for damages suffered by foreigners or their property on their territories. Codification drafts have been published in supplements to the *American Journal of International Law*, 1935–39.

Ch.G. FENWICK, *The International Law*, New York, 1959.

HASHISH. Any of narcotic preparations made from Indian hemp, smoked in pipes, popular in Moslem countries. In many countries listed among prohibited narcotic drugs.

HATAY. A littoral province in Turkey. It was the subject of an international dispute involving Turkey, to which it belonged between 1516 and 1918, and France, which occupied it and later, under the terms of the Franklin–Bouillon Agreement, 1921, incorporated it into Syria as an autonomous district, the Sarnjak of Alexandretta. Turkey renounced its claims after the Lausanne Peace Treaty, 1923, but turned to the League of Nations for a re-examination of the case, in view of the Turkish population of the district when Syria was due to emerge as an independent state. The council decision and the French–Turkish agreement of Nov. 28, 1937 produced an autonomous republic of Hatay independent of Syria. Under the terms of another French–Turkish treaty, agreed on June 23, 1939, the republic was abolished and re-integrated with Turkey as Hatay province with the port town of Iskenderun (formerly Alexandretta).

P. DU VEOU, *Le désastre d'Alexandrette 1934–38*, Paris, 1938; S. NAVA, *La questione del Hatay (Alexandrette) et la sua soluzione*, Florence, 1939.

HATTUSILIS AND RAMSES II TREATY, 1269 BC. The oldest known peace treaty in the world, concluded in 1269 BC between the King of the Hittites and the King of Egypt. The treaty was written in both the Accadian cuneiform and the Egyptian hieroglyphic script. A clay tablet with the text was recovered in 1906 from the site of the Hittite Capital Hattusas, in Bogazkoy, central Turkey,
The hieroglyphic version was found in Egypt on the walls of the temple of Amon at Karnak, the cuneiform version accepted as the original, Accadian being the diplomatic language of the region, is now at the Archeological Museum in Istanbul, Turkey. The treaty which comprises eternal friendship, lasting peace, territorial integrity, non-aggression, extradition and mutual help, is of unique significance in the history of international relations. A copper reproduction of the Accadian clay tablet was given to the UN by Turkey in 1970.

G. BOUTHOVL, *Huit mille Traités de Paix*, Paris, 1948.

HAUSSE. An international term for a rise in prices of stocks and bonds or prices of goods on stock exchanges. ▷ Baisse.

HAVANA. *Spanish*: Habana. The capital city of Cuba; and of La Habana province. Area: 740 sq. km. Population 1984 estimate: 1,992,620. Site of the Sixth International Conference of American States, 1928; Second Council of Foreign Ministers of American Republics, 1945; First and Second Conferences of Three Continents, 1966 and 1967; Third Conference of Non aligned states, 1979; the seat of a UNESCO Regional Office.

Yearbook of International Organizations.

HAVANA CHARTER, 1948. The constitution of the International Trade Organization, ▷ ITO. Its Charter was prepared by the UN Conference on International Trade held Nov. 21, 1947–Mar. 24, 1948 in Havana and signed on Mar. 24, 1948, by Afghanistan, Australia, Belgium, Bolivia, Brazil, Burma, Canada, Ceylon, Chile, China, Costa Rica, Cuba, Czechoslovakia, Denmark, the Dominican Republic, Ecuador, El Salvador, France, Greece, Guatemala, Haiti, India, Indonesia, Iraq, Iran, Italy, Liberia, Luxembourg, Mexico, the Netherlands, New Zealand, Nicaragua, Norway, Pakistan, Panama, Peru, the Philippines, Portugal, South Africa, Syria, Sweden, Switzerland, Transjordan, the UK, Uruguay, the USA and Venezuela.
Argentina, Poland and Turkey did not sign the Charter and the Byelorussian SSR, Bulgaria, Finland, Romania, Hungary, Ukraine, the USSR and Yugoslavia did not participate.
The purpose of the Charter was to promote the expansion of international trade by establishing a code of fair dealing that would preclude economic warfare, and by encouraging countries to reduce artificial trade barriers thus establishing a multilateral, non-discriminatory trading system. The Charter covers: tariffs, quotas, export subsidies, exchange matters, customs formalities, cartels, commodity agreements, state-trading, the international aspects of foreign investments and of employment and economic development, and a procedure for the settlement of trade disputes.
In its first chapter, the Charter sets out the purpose and objectives as follows:

"(1) To assure a large and steadily growing volume of real income and effective demand, to increase the production, consumption and exchange of goods, and thus to contribute to a balanced and expanding world economy.
(2) To foster and assist industrial and general economic development, particularly of those countries which are still in the early stages of industrial development, and to encourage the international flow of capital for productive investment.
(3) To further the enjoyment by all countries, on equal terms, of access to the markets, products and productive facilities which are needed for their economic prosperity and development.
(4) To promote on a reciprocal and mutually advantageous basis the reduction of tariffs and other barriers to trade and the elimination of discriminatory treatment in international commerce.
(5) To enable countries, by increasing the opportunities for their trade and economic development, to abstain from measures which would disrupt world commerce, reduce productive employment or retard economic progress.
(6) To facilitate through the promotion of mutual understanding, consultation and co-operation the solution of problems relating to international trade in the fields of employment, economic development, commercial policy, business practices and commodity policy."

The remaining eight chapters of the Charter deal with:

(1) maintaining high levels of employment and economic activity;
(2) promoting economic development, especially in economically backward countries, and reconstructing war-devastated countries;
(3) commercial policy as affecting tariffs and other barriers to trade, and the numerous aspects of commercial relations between countries;
(4) restrictive business practices, such as some practices of international cartels;
(5) inter-governmental commodity agreements;
(6) the structure and functions of ITO;
(7) the procedures for settlement of differences between ITO members;
(8) general provisions affecting ITO members, such as their trading relations with non-members and security exceptions.

The Havana Charter was not ratified by a majority of signatories and thus did not enter into force. The major ideas were adopted by the General Agreement on Tariffs and Trade ▷ GATT.

UN Yearbook 1949, pp. 1106–1108; C. WILCOX, *A Charter for World Trade*, New York, 1949.

HAVANA CULTURAL CONGRESS, 1968. A Solidarity Congress of Intellectuals of Three Continents held Jan. 4–12, 1968 in the capital of Cuba and passed the Havana Appeal. Here are its main theses:

"1. One should quickly cast aside the false opinion that the responsibility of the intellectual in underdeveloped countries is different from that of the intellectual in highly developed capitalist countries ... (2) The Eurocentrist view of the world has entered a state of crisis in the last decade. Asia, Latin America and Africa in one way or another have begun to shape the history of the world ... (3) One should ask whether the measure ultimately fixing the responsibility of the European intellectual toward the Third World remains the same as that which measures the responsibility of this intellectual in relation to European history and culture, which in reality is the history of a class as far as the history of colonialism and neo-colonialism are concerned ... (4) What we have said about the European intellectual also relates to the responsibility of the intellectual of the underdeveloped countries, which means that ... in the end it is dependent on the political class and its basic function; either revolutionary or reformistic ... (5) With the Cuban revolution, the posing of the problem of culture in Latin America has radically changed, whose consequences are – and for a long time will remain completely open. In effect a radicalization of concepts has taken place in the Latin

American intellectual on a continental scale ... both in relation to imperialism and the dominant local classes as well as to the rest of the capitalist and socialist world ..."

"El Congreso Internacional de Intelectuales Tricontinental", in: *Tricontinental*, La Habana, February, 1968.

HAVANA DEBT CONFERENCE, 1985. Conference on alternative approaches to the debt problem with 1000 participants from Latin America. The Conference agreed that both creditors and debtors should share the costs of adjustment and demanded a solution on the basis of ▷ New Economic International Order. Fidel Castro called for cancelation of illegitimate debt, because it was due to high rates of interest.

KEESING's *Record of World Events*, 1987, No. 2.

HAVANA DECLARATION , 1940. A Declaration on Reciprocal Assistance and Co-operation adopted on July 30, 1940 at Havana by the Second Consultative Meeting of the Foreign Ministers of American Republics.

CARNEGIE ENDOWMENT. International Conferences of American States, First Supplement 1933–40, Washington, DC, 1941; E.J. OSMAŃCZYK, *Enciclopedia Mundial de Relaciones Internacionales y Naciones Unidas*, Mexico, DF, 1976, p. 398.

HAVANA DECLARATION, 1966. The General Declaration of the First Conference of Tricontinental Solidarity of Africa, Asia and Latin America held in Jan. 3–14, 1966.

Granma, January 15, 1966; E.J. OSMAŃCZYK, *Enciclopedia Mundial de Relaciones Internacionales y Naciones Unidas*, Mexico, DF, 1976, pp. 398–399.

HAVANA DECLARATION, 1975. The final act of the Conference of the Communist Parties of Latin America and the Caribbean held at Havana in June 1975, signed by the Communist Parties of Argentina, Bolivia, Brazil, Colombia, Costa Rica, Cuba, Chile, the Dominican Republic, Ecuador, El Salvador, Guadeloupe, Guatemala, Guyana, Haiti, Honduras, Martinique, Mexico, Panama, Paraguay, Peru, Puerto Rico, Uruguay and Venezuela. The Declaration gave analysis of the situation in Latin American Countries and proclaimed a plan of action for national independence, democracy, peace and socialism.

Granma, June 14, 1975; E.J. OSMAŃCZYK, *Enciclopedia Mundial de Relaciones Internacionales y Naciones Unidas*, Mexico, DF, 1976, pp. 399–404.

HAVANA NON-ALIGNED COUNTRIES CONFERENCE, 1979. The Sixth Conference of Heads of State or Govenment of the Non-Aligned Countries was held in the capital of Cuba, Sept. 3–9, 1979. The following countries, which are full members of the movement, took part in it: Afghanistan, Algeria, Angola, Argentina, Bahrain, Bangladesh, Benin, Bhutan, Bolivia, Botswana, Burma, Burundi, Cape Verde, the Central African Empire, Comoros, Congo, Cuba, Cyprus, the Democratic People's Republic of Korea, Democratic Yemen, Djibouti, Egypt, Equatorial Guinea, Ethiopia, Gabon, Gambia, Ghana, Grenada, Guinea, Guinea-Bissau, Guyana, India, Indonesia, Iran, Iraq, the Ivory Coast, Jamaica, Jordan, Kenya, Kuwait, the Laos People's Democratic Republic, Lebanon, Lesotho, Liberia, the Socialist People's Libyan Arab Jamahiriya, Madagascar, Malawi, Malaysia, the Maldives, Mali, Malta, Mauritania, Mauritius, Morocco, Mozambique, Nepal, Nicaragua, Niger, Nigeria, Oman, Pakistan, the Palestine Liberation Organization, Panama, the Patriotic Front of Zim-

babwe, Peru, Qatar, Rwanda, Sao Tome and Principe, Senegal, the Seychelles, Sierra Leone, Singapore, Somalia, the South West Africa People's Organization, Sri Lanka, Sudan, Suriname, Swaziland, the Syrian Arab Republic, Togo, Trinidad and Tobago, Tunisia, Uganda, the United Arab Emirates, the United Republic of Cameroon, the United Republic of Tanzania, Upper Volta (now Burkina Faso), Viet Nam, the Yemen Arab Republic, Yugoslavia, Zaïre, Zambia. The Conference granted Belize special status, including the right to speak. The following countries and organizations and national liberation movements attended as observers: Barbados, Brazil, Colombia, Costa Rica, Dominica, Ecuador, El Salvador, Mexico, the Philippines, St Lucia, Uruguay, Venezuela, African National Congress (South Africa), Afro-Asian People's Solidarity Association, Arab League, Islamic Conference, Organization of African Unity, Pan-Africanist Congress of Azania, Socialist Party of Puerto Rico, United Nations Organization. As guests were also present: Austria, Finland, Portugal, Romania, San Marino, Spain, Sweden, Switzerland, the ECLA, FAO, OLADE, SELA, UNCTAD, UNESCO, UNIDO, United Nations Council for Namibia, Special Committee Against Apartheid, Committee on the Exercise of the Inalienable Rights of the Palestinian People.

Granma, September 4, 1979.

HAVES AND HAVE-NOTS. An international term, coined by the Spanish author M. Cervantes in *Don Quixote* (1605–15): "There are in the world two families only, the Haves and the Have-Nots." This phrase was paraphrased in 20th century in the "Have and Have-Not Nations."

HAWAII. An archipelago in Pacific Ocean, since 1959 a non-contiguous state of the United States. Area: 16,759 sq. km. Pop. 1986 census: 1,005,000. Capital: Honolulu on Oahu island with 805,266 inhabitants (without armed forces). The largest island is Hawaii (10,455 sq. km), the most populous (761,964) Oahu; the others: Manui, Kanai, Molokai, Lauai, Niihau, Kahoolave. The Hawaiian islands, named the Sandwich Islands by Capt. James Cook in Aug. 1778, formed an independent Polynesian Kingdom; in 1884 a Republic was proclaimed and on Aug. 12, 1898 formally annexed by the US, with a US Territory of Hawaii statute from June 14, 1900 until Mar. 18, 1959 when admitted to the Union as the 50th state. Since the surprise Japanese air attack on ▷ Pearl Harbor, Dec. 7, 1941, the Hawaiian Islands as the major Pacific naval base were under martial law until Mar. 1943. In 1961 the University of Hawaii opened the Center for Cultural and Technical Interchange between East and West.

R.S. KUYKENDAL, A.J. DAY, *Hawaii. A History*, New Jersey, 1961; J.R. MORGAN, *Hawaii*, Boulder, 1982; R.J. BELL, *Last Among Equals: Hawaian Statehood and American Politics*, Honolulu, 1984; J. PAXTON ed., *The Statesman's Yearbook 1987–88*, London, 1987.

HAWLEY–SMOOT TARIFF ACT, 1930. A US Law No. 361, adopted by the US Congress, July 13, 1930, and signed by President H. Hoover, July 17, 1930, establishing the highest customs tariff for imported goods in the history of USA, deepening the economic crisis in Latin America and Europe. The authors: the congressmen J.P. Hawley and Senator Reed Smoot.

F.A. MAGNEDER, *American Government 1935*, New York, 1936; pp. 165–168.

HAY–PAUNCEFOTE TREATY, 1901. A Treaty to Facilitate the Construction of a Ship-Canal on the Isthmus of Panama concluded on Nov. 18, 1901; it was signed by the US Secretary of State, J. Hay and the UK ambassador J. Pauncefote and superseded the ▷ Clayton–Bulver Treaty, 1850. It introduced the principles of international law on neutrality and freedom of navigation established for the Suez Canal as binding for the future Panama Canal and was ratified in Dec., 1901; it came into force on Feb. 22, 1902.

C.A. COLLIARD, *Droit international et histoire diplomatique*, Paris, 1950.

HAY–VARILLA TREATY, 1903. A treaty concluded on Nov. 18, 1903 in Washington, DC, between the USA and the Republic of Panama. It was signed by the Secretary of State J. Hay and the private banker Bunau Varilla, a shareholder of the Panama Canal Construction Company, who was recognized by the USA as a plenipotentiary of the seven-man governing group. That group, under the protection of US cruisers, had announced an anti-Colombian separatist document on Nov. 4, 1903, proclaiming the independence of the Republic of Panama. The Hay–Varilla Treaty, officially the Convention for the Construction of a Ship-Canal, was ratified in Panama on Dec. 2, 1903 and in Washington, DC, on Feb. 25, 1904, Art. 1 guarantees the independence of the Republic of Panama. Art. 2 defines the width of the Panama Canal Zone granted in perpetuity to the USA; in art. 3 Panama renounced all of its sovereign rights to this zone; and art. 4 warns that "no change of government or laws or treaties" can infringe on the rights of the USA. The renouncement by the USA of art. 3 was announced by the Panama and the USA governments on Feb. 7, 1974, ▷ Panama Canal.

C.A. COLLIARD, *Droit international et histoire diplomatique*, Paris, 1950, p. 112.

HD–MAC ▷ Television.

HEAD SMASHED IN BISON COMPLEX. A Canadian natural site, included in the ▷ World Heritage UNESCO List. On account of its topography and the remains of settlement which it contains, this site, covering 40 sq. km to the south of Calgary, shows how over a period of thousands of years the first inhabitants of the North American plains made use of the immense herds of bison which inhabited these regions.

UNESCO, *A Legacy for All*, Paris, 1984.

HEALTH. Health was defined by the ▷ WHO Constitution as "a state of complete physical, mental and social well-being and not merely the absence of disease or infection." A subject of international health protection conventions and of permanent organized international and intergovernmental co-operation through the World Health Organization, WHO, and of non-governmental co-operation through over 150 international associations and institutes, reg. with the UIA, among which the co-ordinating role is performed by the UNESCO Council for International Organizations of Medical Sciences. The First WHO International Conference on Primary Health Care took place on Sept. 1978 at Alma-Ata. ▷ Alma-Ata Health Declaration 1978 and ▷ Health International Regulations 1969.

A Conference of the Council for International Organizations of Medical Sciences (CIOMS), took place in November 1984 in Athens, and was dedicated to the health policy, ethics and human value of the WHO program "Health for All by the Year 2000". An international conference jointly organized in Ottawa by the WHO and the Canadian Health Organization in Nov., 1986 with participants from 38 countries drew up a Charter of action for health promotion to achieve health for all by the year 2000. On May 5–7, 1988, during the 41st World Health Assembly a technical discussion on Leadership Development for Health for All took place, to mobilize greater social and political commitment to the Health-for-All movement. The WHO publ. from 1948 in English: *International Digest on Health Legislation.*

Yearbook of International Organizations; N.J.I. DEBLOCK, *Elsevier's Dictionary of Public Health.* In English, French, Spanish, Italian, Dutch and German, Amsterdam, 1976; *UN Chronicle*, June, 1978, p. 43, April, 1980, p. 43, and February, 1982, p. 60; A. GRIFFITHS, M. MILLS, *Money for Health: A Manual for Surveys in Developing Countries*, Geneva, 1982; *ILO Encyclopaedia of Occupational Health and Safety*, 2 Vols., Geneva, 1983; *World Health*, May, 1987.

HEALTH AS AN INTEGRAL PART OF DEVELOPMENT.
The UN General Assembly Res. 34/58, adopted on Nov. 29, 1979 during an examination of long-term trends in economic development and the working out of a New International Economic Order. The text of the Resolution under the title Health as an Integral Part of Development is as follows:

"The General Assembly recalling its resolutions 3201 (S–VI) and 3202 (S–VI) of 1 May 1974 containing the Declaration and the Programme of Action on the Establishment of a New International Economic Order, 3281 (XXIX) of 21 December 1974 containing the Charter of Economic Rights and Duties of States, and 3362 (S–VII) of 16 September 1975 on development and international economic co-operation,

Recalling also the United Nations conferences held during recent years on major issues relating to economic and social development and the establishment of the new international economic order, particularly the 1978 Conference on Primary Health Care, jointly sponsored by the World Health Organization and the United Nations Children's Fund at Alma Ata in the Soviet Union,

Noting that a substantial portion of the population in many countries, developing as well as developed, lacks access to basic health services, and that people lacking adequate health cannot fully participate in or contribute to the economic and social development of their nation,

Welcoming the important efforts of the World Health Organization, the United Nations Children's Fund and the other agencies of the United Nations system associated with the effort to attain the goal of 'health for all by the year 2000', as expressed in World Health Assembly resolutions WHA20.43 (1977) and WHA32.30 (1979),

Considering that peace and security are important for the preservation and improvement of the health of all people and that co-operation among nations in vital health issues can contribute importantly to peace,

Cognizant of the vital role that health and health care play in the development of countries, particularly that of developing countries,

(1) Endorses the Alma-Ata Declaration and in particular its view that primary health care, aimed at the solution of the major world health problems through a combination of promotive, preventive, curative and rehabilitative measures, constitutes the key to the ultimate achievement of a healthful society, especially when primary health care is incorporated into the development process, particularly that of developing countries;

(2) Notes with approval the World Health Assembly decision contained in resolution WHA32.30 that the development of the World Health Organization's programmes and the allocation of its resources at the global, regional and country levels should reflect the commitment of that organization to the priority of the achievement of health for all by the year 2000;

(3) Calls upon the relevant bodies of the United Nations system to co-ordinate with and support the

efforts of the World Health Organization by appropriate actions within their respective spheres of competence;

(4) Appeals to Member States to carry out the actions called for in the Alma-Ata Declaration;

(5) Reiterates the appeal contained in paragraph 10 of the World Health Assembly resolution WHA32.30 to the international community 'to give full support to the formulation and implementation of national, regional and global strategies for achieving an acceptable level of health for all'.

(6) Welcomes the decision of the World Health Assembly to ensure that the global strategy is to be reflected in the World Health Organization's contribution to the preparation of the new international development strategy of the United Nations and calls upon the Preparatory Committee for the New International Development Strategy to give full and careful attention to the World Health Organization's contribution;

(7) Calls upon Member States, both developed and developing to co-operate with each other and with the World Health Organization in the exchange of technological information and expertise in order to facilitate the achievement of the primary health care goals;

(8) Requests the Director-General of the World Health Organization, following the Sixty-seventh session of the World Health Organization Executive Board and the Thirty-fourth session of the World Health Assembly, to submit a report to the appropriate session of the Economic and Social Council in 1981 on the progress achieved in the formulation of the global health strategy and, in turn, calls upon the Council to submit recommendations for further action by the General Assembly at its thirty-sixth session."

UN Yearbook 1979.

HEALTH DAY.
A World Health Day since 1950 is observed on the anniversary of the entry into force of the WHO Constitution on April 7, 1948. The theme for 1950 was: "Know Your Own Health Service"; for 1980: "Smoking or Health: The Choice is Yours."

WHO Chronicle, February, 1980.

HEALTH HAZARD ALERT ILO SYSTEM.
A system installed by the ILO in Geneva after a five year experimental period, in June 1982 under the name International Occupational Safety and Health Hazard Alert System of the ILO which transmits warnings or requests for information concerning newly discovered or suspected occupational hazards to a world-wide network. The system was proposed to the ILO by the US Department of Labor in 1976 and formally adopted as a work item by the ILO in 1977. Under the new tripartite mechanism all alerts received by the ILO will be sent to the Secretariats of the Employers' and Workers' Groups of the Governing Body and also to the three designated bodies belonging to the System.

UN Chronicle, September., 1983, p. 83.

HEALTH INTERNATIONAL CHRONOLOGY.
1851–First International Sanitary Conference in Paris.
1902–International Sanitary Bureau.
1923–Health Organization of the League of Nations.
1946–International Commission of the World Health Organization.
1948–Constitution of the WHO.
1977–WHO Program: Health for All by the Year 2000.
1978–Alma Ata Declaration on Primary Health Care.
1979–Global eradication of smallpox.
1988–WHO's 40th anniversary slogan: Health for all–all for health.

World Health, Jan–Feb, 1988.

HEALTH INTERNATIONAL CONFERENCE, 1946.
A Conference convened by ECOSOC, met in New York from June 19 to July 22, 1946. The UN member States governments signed the ▷ WHO Constitution and Protocol concerning the *Office international d'hygiène publique* (A League of Nations institution).

UNTS, Vol. 9, pp. 3–7.

HEALTH INTERNATIONAL REGULATIONS, 1969.
The International Health Regulations, adopted by the World Health Assembly on July 25, 1969 in Boston; came into force Jan., 1, 1971 in respect of all WHO Member states. These regulations replace all ▷ Sanitary International Conventions, 1903–1965. The highlights of the IHR:

"Part I. Definitions. (Art. 1)
Part. II. Notifications and Epidemiological Information (Arts. 2–13):
Art. 2. For the application of these Regulations, each State recognizes the right of the Organization to communicate directly with the health administration of its territory or territories. Any notification or information sent by the Organization to the health administration shall be considered as having been sent to the State, and any notification or information sent by the health administration to the Organization shall be considered as having been sent by the State.
Art. 3.(1) Each health administration shall notify the Organization by telegram or telex within twenty-four hours of its being informed that the first case of a disease subject to the Regulations, that is neither an imported case nor a transferred case, has occurred in its territory, and, within the subsequent twenty-four hours, notify the infected area.
(2) In addition each health administration shall notify the Organization by telegram or telex within twenty-four hours of its being informed:
(a) that one or more cases of a disease subject to the Regulations has been imported or transferred into a non-infected area – the notification to include all information available on the origin of infection;
(b) that a ship or aircraft has arrived with one or more cases of a disease subject to the Regulations on board – the notification to include the name of the ship or the flight number of the aircraft, its previous and subsequent ports of call, and the health measures, if any, taken with respect to the ship or aircraft.
(3) The existence of the disease so notified on the establishment of a reasonable certain clinical diagnosis shall be confirmed as soon as possible by laboratory methods, as far as resources permit, and the results shall be sent immediately to the Organization by telegram or telex.
Art. 4.(1) Each health administration shall notify the Organization immediately of evidence of the presence of the virus of yellow fever, including the virus found in mosquitoes or vertebrates other than man, or the plague bacillus, in any part of its territory, and shall report the extent of the area involved.
(2) Health administration, when making a notification of rodent plague, shall distinguish wild rodent plague from domestic rodent plague, in the case of the former, describe the epidemiological circumstances and the area involved.
Art. 5. Any notification required under par. 1 of Art. 3 shall be promptly supplemented by information as to the source and type of the disease, the number of cases and deaths, the conditions affecting the spread of the disease and the prophylactic measures taken.
Art. 6.(1) During an epidemic the notifications and information required under Art. 3 and Art. 5 shall be followed by subsequent communications sent at regular intervals to the Organization.
(2) These communications shall be as frequent and as detailed as possible. The number of cases and deaths shall be communicated at least once a week. The precautions taken to prevent the spread of the disease, in particular the measures which are being applied to prevent the spread of the disease to other territories by ships, aircraft, trains, road vehicles, other means of transport, and containers leaving the infected area, shall be stated. In the case of plague, the measures taken against rodents shall be specified. In the case of the diseases subject to the Regulations which are trans-

mitted by insect vectors, the measures taken against such vectors shall also be specified.

Art. 7.(1) The health administration for a territory in which an infected area has been defined and notified shall notify the Organization when that area is free from infection.

(2) An infected area may be considered as free from infection when all measures of prophylaxis have been taken and maintained to prevent the recurrence of the disease or its spread to other areas, and when:

(a) in the case of plague, cholera or smallpox, a period of time equal to at least twice the incubation period of the disease, as hereinafter provided, has elapsed since the last case identified has died, recovered or been isolated, and there is no epidemiological evidence of spread of that disease to any contiguous area;

(b) (i) in the case of yellow fever not transmitted by Aedes aegypti, three months have elapsed without evidence of activity of the yellow-fever virus;

(ii) in the case of yellow fever transmitted by Aedes aegypti, three months have elapsed since the occurrence of the last human case, or one month since that occurrence if the Aedes aegypti index has been continuously maintained below one per cent;

(c) (i) in the case of plague in domestic rodents, one month has elapsed since the last infected animal was found or trapped;

(ii) in the case of plague in wild rodents, three months have elapsed without evidence of the disease in sufficient proximity to ports and airports to be a threat to international traffic.

Art. 8 (1) Each health administration shall notify the Organization of:

(a) the measures which it has decided to apply to arrivals from an infected area and the withdrawal of any such measures, indicating the date of application or withdrawal;

(b) any change in its requirements as to vaccination for any international voyage.

(2) Any such notification shall be sent by telegram or telex, and whenever possible in advance of any such change or of the application or withdrawal of any such measure.

(3) Each health administration shall send to the Organization once a year, at a date to be fixed by the Organization, a recapitulation of its requirements as to vaccination for any international voyage.

(4) Each health administration shall take steps to inform prospective travellers, through the co-operation of, as appropriate, travel agencies, shipping firms, aircraft operators or by other means, of its requirements and of any modifications thereto.

Art. 9. In addition to the notifications and information required under Arts. 3 to 8 inclusive, each health administration shall send to the Organization weekly:

(a) a report by telegram or telex of the number of cases of the diseases subject to the Regulations and deaths therefrom during the previous week in each of its towns and cities adjacent to a port or an airport including any imported or transferred cases;

(b) a report by airmail of the absence of such cases during the period referred to in sub-pars. (a), (b) and (c) or par. 2 of Art. 7.

Art. 10. Any notification and information required under Arts. 3 to 9 inclusive shall also be sent by the health administration, on request, to any diplomatic mission or consulate established in the territory for which it is responsible.

Art. 11.(1) The Organization shall send to all health administrations, as soon as possible and by the means appropriate to the circumstances, all epidemiological and other information which it has received under Arts. 3 to 8 inclusive and par. (a) of Art. 9 as well as information as to the absence of any returns required by Art. 9. Communications of an urgent nature shall be sent by telegram, telex or telephone.

(2) Any additional epidemiological data and other information available to the Organization through its surveillance programme shall be made available, when appropriate, to all health administrations.

(3) The Organization may, with the consent of the government concerned, investigate an outbreak of a disease subject to the Regulations which constitutes a serious threat to neighbouring countries or to international health. Such investigation shall be directed to assist governments to organize appropriate control measures and may include on-the-spot studies by a team.

Art. 12. Any telegram or telex sent, or telephone call made, for the purposes of Arts. 3 to 8 inclusive and Art. 11 shall be given the priority appropriate to the circumstances; in any case of exceptional urgency, where there is a risk of the spread of a disease subject to the Regulations, the priority shall be the highest available under international telecommunication agreements.

Art. 13.(1) Each State shall forward annually to the Organization, in accordance with Art. 62 of the Constitution of the Organization, information concerning the occurrence of any case of a disease subject to the Regulations due to or carried by international traffic, as well as on the action taken under these Regulations or bearing upon their application.

(2) The Organization shall, on the basis of the information required by par. 1 of this Art., of the notifications and reports required by these Regulations, and of any official information, prepare an annual report on the functioning of these Regulations and on their effect on international traffic.

(3) The Organization shall review the epidemiological trends of the diseases subject to the Regulations, and shall publish such data, not less than once a year, illustrated with maps showing infected and free areas of the world, and any other relevant information obtained from the surveillance programme of the Organization.

Part III. Health Organization (Arts. 14–23):

Art. 14.(1) Each health administration shall ensure that ports and airports in its territory shall have at their disposal an organization and equipment adequate for the application of the measures provided for in these Regulations.

(2) Every port and airport shall be provided with pure drinking water and wholesome food supplied from sources approved by the health administration for public use and consumption on the premises or on board ships or aircraft. The drinking water and food shall be stored and handled in such manner as to ensure its protection against contamination. The health authority shall conduct periodic inspections of equipment, installations and premises, and shall collect samples of water and food for laboratory examinations to verify the observance of this Art. For this purpose and for other sanitary measures, the principles and recommendations set forth in the guides on these subjects published by the Organization shall be applied as far as practicable in fulfilling the requirements of these Regulations.

(3) Every port and airport shall also be provided with an effective system for removal and safe disposal of excrement, refuse, waste water, condemned food, and other matter dangerous to health.

Art. 15. There shall be available to as many of the ports and airports in a territory as practicable an organized medical and health service with adequate staff, equipment and premises, and in particular facilities for the prompt isolation and care of infected persons, for disinfection, disinsecting and deratting, for bacteriological investigation, and for the collection and examination of rodents for plague infection, for collection of water and food samples and for their dispatch to a laboratory for examination, and for other appropriate measures provided for by these Regulations.

Art. 16. The health authority for each port and airport shall:

(a) take all practicable measures to keep port and airport installations free of rodents;

(b) make every effort to extend rat-proofing to the port and airport installations.

Art. 19.(1) Depending upon the volume of its international traffic, each health administration shall designate as sanitary airports a number of the airports in its territory, provided they meet the conditions laid down in par. 2, of this Art., and the provisions of Art. 14.

(2) Every sanitary airport shall have at its disposal:

(a) an organized medical service with adequate staff, equipment and premises;

(b) facilities for the transport, isolation, and care of infected persons or suspects;

(c) facilities for efficient disinfection and disinsecting, for the control of vectors and rodents, and for any other appropriate measure provided for by these Regulations;

(d) a bacteriological laboratory, or facilities for dispatching suspected material to such a laboratory;

(e) facilities within the airport for vaccination against smallpox, and facilities within the airport or available to it for vaccination against cholera and yellow fever.

Art. 20.(1) Every port and the area within the perimeter of every airport shall be kept free from Aedes aegypti in its immature and adult stages, and the mosquito vectors of malaria and other diseases of epidemiological significance in international traffic. For this purpose active anti-mosquito measures shall be maintained within a protective area extending for a distance of at least 400 metres around the perimeter.

Part IV. Health Measures and Procedure (Arts. 24–50):

Art. 24. The health measures permitted by these Regulations are the maximum measures applicable to international traffic, which a State may require for the protection of its territory against the diseases subject to the Regulations.

Art. 25. Health measures shall be initiated forthwith, completed without delay, and applied without discrimination.

Art. 26.(1) Disinfection, disinsecting, deratting, and other sanitary operations shall be carried out so as:

(a) not to cause undue discomfort to any person, or injury to his health;

(b) not to produce any deleterious effect on the structure of a ship, an aircraft, or a vehicle, or on its operating equipment;

(c) to avoid all risk of fire.

(2) In carrying out such operations on cargo goods, baggage, containers and other articles, every precaution shall be taken to avoid any damage.

(3) Where there are procedures or methods recommended by the Organization they should be employed.

Art. 27.(1) A health authority shall, when so requested, issue free of charge to the carrier a certificate specifying the measures applied to a ship, or an aircraft or a train, road vehicle, other means of transport or container, the parts therof treated, the methods employed, and the reasons why the measures have been applied. In the case of an aircraft this information shall, on request, be entered instead in the Health Part of the Aircraft General Declaration.

(2) Similarly, a health authority shall, when so requested, issue free of charge:

(a) to any traveller a certificate specifying the date of his arrival or departure and measures applied to him and his baggage;

(b) to the consignor, the consignee, and the carrier, or their respective agents, a certificate specifying the measures applied to any goods.

Art. 28.(1) A person under surveillance shall not be isolated and shall be permitted to move about freely. The health authority may require him to report to it, if necessary, at specified intervals during the period of surveillance. Except as limited by the provisions of Art. 71, the health authority may also subject such a person to medical investigation and make any inquiries which are necessary for ascertaining his state of health.

(2) When a person under surveillance departs for another place, within or without the same territory, he shall inform the health authority, which shall immediately notify the health authority for the place to which the person is proceeding. On arrival the person shall report to that health authority which may apply the measure provided for in par. 1 of this Art.

Art. 29. Except in case of an emergency constituting a grave danger to public health, a ship or an aircraft, which is not infected or suspected of being infected with a disease subject to the Regulations, shall not on account of any other epidemic disease be refused free pratique by the health authority for a port or an airport; in particular it shall not be prevented from discharging or loading cargo or stores, or taking on fuel or water.

Art. 30. A health authority may take all practicable measures to control the discharge from any ship of sewage and refuse which might contaminate the waters of a port, river or canal.

Part V. Special Provisions relating to Each of the Diseases subject to the Regulations (Arts. 51–61 relating to ▷ Plague; Arts. 62–71 relating to ▷ Cholera; Arts. 72–88 relating to ▷ Yellow Fever.)

Part. VI. Health Documents (arts. 89–94).

Part. VII. Charges (Art. 95):

Art. 95.(1) No charge shall be made by a health authority for:

(a) any medical examination provided for in these Regulations, or any supplementary examination, bacteriological or otherwise, which may be required to ascertain the state of health of the person examined;

(b) any vaccination of a person on arrival and any certificate thereof.

(2) Where charges are made for applying the measures provided for in these Regulations, other than the measures referred to in par. 1 of this Art., there shall be in each territory only the tariff for such charges and every charge shall:

(a) conform with this tariff;

(b) be moderate and not exceed the actual cost of the service rendered;

(c) be levied without distinction as to the nationality, domicile, or residence of the person concerned, or as to the nationality, flag, registry or ownership of the ship, aircraft, train, road vehicle or other means of transport and containers. In particular, there shall be no distinction made between national and foreign persons, ships, aircraft, trains, road vehicles or other means of transport and containers.

(3) The levying of charge for the transmission of a message relating to provisions of these Regulations by radio, may not exceed the normal charge for radio messages.

(4) The tariff, and any amendment thereto, shall be published at least ten days in advance of any levy thereunder and notified immediately to the Organization.

Part. VIII. Various Provisions (arts. 96–98):

Art. 97.(1) Migrants, nomads, seasonal workers or persons taking part in periodic mass congregations, and any ship, in particular small boats for international coastal traffic, aircraft, train, road vehicle or other means of transport carrying them, may be subjected to additional health measures conforming with the laws and regulations of each State concerned, and with any agreement concluded between any such States.

(2) Each State shall notify the Organization of the provisions of any such laws and regulations or agreement.

(3) The standards of hygiene on ships and aircraft carrying persons taking part in periodic mass congregations shall not be inferior to those recommended by the Organization.

Part IX. Final Provisions (Arts. 99–107).

UNTS, Vol. 764, 1971, pp. 3–105.

HEART. ▷ Cardio-Vascular Diseases.

HEAT AND MASS TRANSFER. A subject of international co-operation. Organization reg. with the UIA:

International Center of Academy of Sciences of the Socialist Countries for Raising the Qualifications of Scientific Cadres for the Problem of Heat and Mass Transfer, f. 1973, in Minsk. An international scientific research organization established by an Agreement signed on Nov. 21, 1973 at Minsk, between the Academies of Sciences of the Byelorussian SSR, Bulgaria, Czechoslovakia, the GDR, Hungary, Mongolia and Poland.

W.E. BUTLER (ed.), *A Source Book on Socialist International Organizations*, Alphen, 1978, pp. 797–803.

HECTARE. An international area unit = 10,000 square meters or approx. 2.47 acres.

HECTOGRAM. An international mass and weight unit = 100 grams, or approx. 3.527 ounces.

HECTOLITER. An international capacity unit = 100 liters, or approx. 3.53 cubic feet, or 2.84 bushels (dry).

HECTOMETER. An international length unit = 100 meters, or approx. 109.36 yards.

HEGEMONISM. Subject of a UN resolution 1979. The term "hegemonism" was introduced by Yugoslav press in 1967 during the Czechoslovak crisis; used for the first time in international documentation on July 13, 1974 in a Yugoslav–Romanian communiqué on the occasion of President J.B. Tito's visit to Bucharest in the formula that

nonaligned policy is an important part of the struggle "against imperialism and hegemonism." The People's Republic of China adopted this term in 1977 as "superpower hegemonism." An anti-hegemonism clause was included in ▷ China–Japan Peace Treaty 1978. In Sept., 1979 the USSR initated a UN resolution against hegemonism. A Resolution on Inadmissibility of the Policy of Hegemonism in International Relations was adopted by the UN General Assembly on Dec. 14, 1979, by 111 votes in favor, 4 against (Australia, Canada, Israel and the USA) 2 not participating in the voting (Albania and Brazil) and 26 abstaining (Austria, Belgium, Chile, Denmark, Fiji, Finland, France, the FRG, Guatemala, Iceland, Ireland, Italy, Japan, Luxembourg, the Netherlands, New Zealand, Norway, Paraguay, Portugal, Samoa, Spain, Sweden, Turkey, the UK, Uruguay, Venezuela).

UN Yearbook 1979; *UN Chronicle*, March., 1980, p. 51

HEILONGJIANG. ▷ Manchuria.

HELGOLAND. An island of the FRG, on the North Sea. Area: 60.8 hectares. Pop. 2,377 in 1970. The island was Danish from 1714 to 1807; ceded to England on Jan. 14, 1814, then a British fortress given away to the German Reich under the terms of the Helgoland–Zanzibar agreement, July 1, 1890, in return for the Reich's renouncement of claims in Equatorial Africa, Zanzibar among others. On the strength of Art. 115 of the Versailles Treaty, Helgoland and the Island of Dunes were demilitarized and construction of military facilities was banned; refortified by the German Third Reich in 1936. In 1945 occupied by the British and after evacuation of population in 1947, used by British airforce as a bomber range until 1949, when it was returned to West Germany.

B. SCHWERTFEGER, *Dokumentarium zum Vorgeschichte des Weltkrieges, 1871 bis 1914*, Berlin 1928; H.P. IPSEN, "Helgoland", in: *STRUPP-SCHLOCHAUER Wörterbuch des Völkerrechts*, Berlin, 1980, Vol. 1, pp. 783–785.

HELICOPTERS. Civil and military aircraft, capable of moving in any direction and remaining stationary in the air, subject of international co-operation. The heavy attack helicopter was first produced in 1972, by the USSR, and in 1982 by the USA.

SIPRI, *World Armaments and Disarmament Yearbook*, 1968, pp. 135–139, 276–279.

HELMSTEDT. A city in Lower Saxony, FRG. Frontier railway and highway station at the GDR border, closed during the Berlin Blockade, 1948.

HELSINKI. The capital city of Finland since 1918. Pop. 1985 est. 486,098; metropolitan area: 953,020. The site of American–Soviet SALT negotiations 1969–72; Conference on Security and Co-operation in Europe 1972–75; Interparliamentary European Conference 1973; Diplomatic Conference for the Baltic 1974; First Session of International Commission of Inquiry into the Crimes of Chilean Junta, 1974. The seat of World Peace Council and ten Scandinavian regional organizations reg. with the UIA.

Yearbook of International Organizations; J. PAXTON, ed., *The Statesman's Yearbook 1987–88*, London, 1987.

HELSINKI CONFERENCE, 1973–75. The Conference on Security and Co-operation in Europe, which opened at Helsinki on July 3, 1973 and continued at Geneva from Sept. 18, 1973 to July 21, 1975 and was concluded at Helsinki on Aug. 1, 1975

by the representatives of Austria, Belgium, Bulgaria, Canada, Cyprus, Czechoslovakia, Denmark, Finland, France, the FRG, the GDR, Greece, The Holy See, Hungary, Iceland, Ireland, Italy, Liechtenstein, Luxembourg, Malta, Monaco, the Netherlands, Norway, Poland, Portugal, Romania, San Marino, Spain Sweden, Switzerland, Turkey, the UK, the USSR, the USA and Yugoslavia.

During the opening and closing stages of the Conference, the participants were addressed by the Secretary-General of the United Nations, their guest of honor.

The Conference was the first in the history of Europe with the participation of all European countries, with the exception of Albania. Preceded by long years of negotiations the Conference has opened new negotiations as a prolongation of the Helsinki accord. ▷ Madrid CSCE Meeting 1980–83 and ▷ Stockholm Conference 1984–85. An anniversary meeting on the level of Foreign Ministers was held on July 30–Aug. 1, 1985.

J. RUPEREZ, *Europa en la Conferencia de Helsinki*, Madrid 1976; KEESING's *Contemporary Archive*, 1986, No 12.

HELSINKI FINAL ACT, 1975. The Final Act of the Helsinki Conference on Security and Co-operation in Europe signed Aug. 2, 1975. The text is as follows:

"Motivated by the political will, in the interest of peoples, to improve and intensify their relations and to contribute in Europe to peace, security, justice and co-operation as well as to rapprochement among themselves and with the other States of the world,

Determined, in consequence, to give full effect to the results of the Conference and to assure, among their States and throughout Europe, the benefits deriving from those results and thus to broaden, deepen and make continuing and lasting the process of détente,

The High Representatives of the participating States have solemnly adopted the following:

Questions relating to Security in Europe:

The States participating in the Conference on Security and Co-operation in Europe,

Reaffirming their objective of promoting better relations among themselves and ensuring conditions in which their people can live in true and lasting peace free from any threat to or attempt against their security;

Convinced of the need to exert efforts to make détente both a continuing and an increasingly viable and comprehensive process, universal in scope, and that the implementation of the results of the Conference on Security and Co-operation in Europe will be a major contribution to this process;

Considering that solidarity among peoples, as well as the common purpose of the participating States in achieving the aims as set forth by the Conference on Security and Co-operation in Europe, should lead to the development of better and closer relations among them in all fields and thus to overcoming the confrontation stemming from the character of their past relations, and to better mutual understanding;

Mindful of their common history and recognizing that the existence of elements common to their traditions and values can assist them in developing their relations, and desiring to search, fully taking into account the individuality and diversity of their positions and views, for possibilities of joining their efforts with a view to overcoming distrust and increasing confidence, solving the problems that separate them and co-operating in the interest of mankind;

Recognizing the indivisibility of security in Europe as well as their common interest in the development of co-operation throughout Europe and among themselves and expressing their intention to pursue efforts accordingly;

Recognizing the close link between peace and security in Europe and in the world as a whole and conscious of the need for each of them to make its contribution to the strengthening of world peace and security and to the promotion of fundamental rights, economic and social progress and well-being for all peoples;

Have adopted the following:

1.(a) *Declaration on Principles Guiding Relations between Participating States*:
The participating States, reaffirming their commitment to peace, security and justice and the continuing development of friendly relations and co-operation;
Recognizing that this commitment, which reflects the interest and aspirations of peoples, constitutes for each participating State a present and future responsibility, heightened by experience of the past;
Reaffirming, in conformity with their membership in the United Nations and in accordance with the purposes and principles of the United Nations, their full and active support for the United Nations and for the enhancement of its role and effectiveness in strengthening international peace, security and justice, and in promoting the solution of international problems, as well as the development of friendly relations and co-operation among States;
Expressing their common adherence to the principles which are set forth below and are in conformity with the Charter of the United Nations, as well as their common will to act, in the application of these principles, in conformity with the purposes and principles of the Charter of the United Nations;
Declare their determination to respect and put into practice, each of them in its relations with all other participating States, irrespective of their political, economic or social systems as well as of their size, geographical location or level of economic development, the following principles, which all are of primary significance, guiding their mutual relations:
I. Sovereign equality, respect for the rights inherent in sovereignty
The participating States will respect each other's sovereign equality and individuality as well as all the rights inherent in and encompassed by its sovereignty, including in particular the right of every State to juridical equality, to territorial integrity and to freedom and political independence. They will also respect each other's right freely to choose and develop its political, social, economic and cultural systems as well as its right to determine its laws and regulations. Within the framework of international law, all the participating States have equal rights and duties. They will respect each other's right to define and conduct as it wishes its relations with other States in accordance with international law and in the spirit of the present Declaration. They consider that their frontiers can be changed, in accordance with international law, by peaceful means and by agreement. They also have the right to belong or not to belong to international organizations, to be or not to be a party to bilateral or multilateral treaties including the right to be or not to be a party to treaties of alliance; they also have the right to nuetrality.
II. Refraining from the threat or use of force.
The participating States will refrain in their mutual relations, as well as in their international relations in general, from the threat or use of force against the territorial integrity or political independence of any State, or in any other manner inconsistent with the purposes of the United Nations and with the present Declaration. No consideration may be invoked to serve to warrant resort to the threat or use of force in contravention of this principle.
Accordingly, the participating States will refrain from any acts constituting a threat of force or direct or indirect use of force against another participating State. Likewise they will refrain from any manifestation of force for the purpose of inducing another participating State to renounce the full exercise of its sovereign rights. Likewise they will also refrain in their mutual relations from any act of reprisal by force.
No such threat or use of force will be employed as a means of settling disputes, or questions likely to give rise to disputes, between them.
III. Inviolability of frontiers.
The participating States regard as inviolable all one another's frontiers as well as the frontiers of all States in Europe and therefore they will refrain now and in the future from assaulting these frontiers.
Accordingly, they will also refrain from any demand for, or act of, seizure and usurpation of part or all of the territory of any participating State.
IV. Territorial integrity of States.
The participating States will respect the territorial integrity of each of the participating States.
Accordingly, they will refrain from any action inconsistent with the purposes and principles of the Charter of the United Nations against the territorial integrity, political independence or the unity of any participating State, and in particular from any such action constituting a threat or use of force. The participating States will likewise refrain from making each other's territory the object of military occupation or other direct or indirect measures of force in contravention of international law, or the object of acquisition by means of such measures or the threat of them. No such occupation or acquisition will be recognized as legal.
V. Peaceful settlement of disputes
The participating States will settle disputes among them by peaceful means in such a manner as not to endanger international peace and security, and justice.
They will endeavour in good faith and a spirit of co-operation to reach a rapid and equitable solution on the basis of international law.
For this purpose they will use such means as negotiation, enquiry, mediation, conciliation, arbitration, judicial settlement or other peaceful means of their own choice including any settlement procedure agreed to in advance of disputes to which they are parties.
In the event of failure to reach a solution by any of the above peaceful means, the parties to a dispute will continue to seek a mutually agreed way to settle the dispute peacefully. Participating States, parties to a dispute among them, as well as other participating States, will refrain from any action which might aggravate the situation to such a degree as to endanger the maintenance of international peace and security and thereby make a peaceful settlement of the dispute more difficult.
VI. Non–intervention in internal affairs
The participating States will refrain from any intervention, direct or indirect, individual or collective, in the internal or external affairs falling within the domestic jurisdiction of another participating State, regardless of their mutual relations.
They will accordingly refrain from any form of armed intervention or threat of such intervention against another participating State.
They will likewise in all circumstances refrain from any other act of military, or of political, economic or other coercion designed to subordinate to their own interest the exercise by another participating State of the rights inherent in its sovereignty and thus to secure advantages of any kind.
Accordingly, they will, inter alia, refrain from direct or indirect assistance to terrorist activities, or to subversive or other activities directed towards the violent overthrow of the regime of another participating State.
VII. Respect for human rights and fundamental freedoms, including the freedom of thought, conscience, religion or belief
The participating States will respect human rights and fundamental freedoms, including the freedom of thought, conscience, religion or belief, for all without distinction as to race, sex, language or religion.
They will promote and encourage the effective exercise of civil, political, economic, social, cultural and other rights and freedoms all of which derive from the inherent dignity of the human person and are essential for his free and full development.
Within this framework the participating States will recognize and respect the freedom of the individual to profess and practise, alone or in community with others, religion or belief acting in accordance with the dictates of his own conscience.
The participating States on whose territory national minorities exist will respect the right of persons belonging to such minorities to equality before the law, will afford them the full opportunity for the actual employment of human rights and fundamental freedoms and will, in this manner, protect their legitimate interests in this sphere.
The participating States recognize the universal significance of human rights and fundamental freedoms, respect for which is an essential factor for the peace, justice and well-being necessary to ensure the development of friendly relations and co-operation among themselves as among all States.
They will constantly respect these rights and freedoms in their mutual relations and will endeavour jointly and separately, including in co-operation with the United Nations, to promote universal and effective respect for them.
They confirm the right of the individual to know and act upon his rights and duties in this field.
In the field of human rights and fundamental freedoms, the participating States will act in conformity with the purposes and principles of the Charter of the United Nations and with the Universal Declaration of Human Rights. They will also fulfil their obligations as set forth in the international declarations and agreements in this field, including inter alia the International Covenants on Human Rights, by which they may be bound.
VIII. Equal rights and self-determination of peoples
The participating States will respect the equal rights of peoples and their right to self-determination, acting at all times in conformity with the purposes and principles of the Charter of the United Nations and with the relevant norms of international law, including those relating to territorial integrity of States.
By virtue of the principle of equal rights and self-determination of peoples, all peoples always have the right, in full freedom, to determine, when and as they wish, their internal and external political status, without external interference, and to pursue as they wish their political, economic, social and cultural development.
The participating States reaffirm the universal significance of respect for and effective exercise of equal rights and self-determination of peoples for the development of friendly relations among themselves as among all States; they also recall the importance of the elimination of any form of violation of this principle.
IX. Co-operation among States
The participating States will develop their co-operation with one another and with all States in all fields in accordance with the purposes and principles of the Charter of the United Nations. In developing their co-operation the participating States will place special emphasis on the fields as set forth within the framework of the Conference on Security and Co-operation in Europe, with each of them making its contribution in conditions of full equality.
They will endeavour, in developing their co-operation as equals, to promote mutual understanding and confidence, friendly and good-neighbourly relations among themselves, international peace, security and justice. They will equally endeavour, in developing their co-operation, to improve the well-being of peoples and contribute to the fulfilment of their aspirations through, inter alia, the benefits resulting from increased mutual knowledge and from progress and achievement in the economic, scientific, technological, social, cultural and humanitarian fields. They will take steps to promote conditions favourable to making these benefits available to all; they will take into account the interest of all in the narrowing of differences in the levels of economic development, and in particular the interest of developing countries throughout the world.
They confirm that governments, institutions and persons have a relevant and positive role to play in contributing toward the achievement of these aims of their co-operation.
They will strive, in increasing their co-operation as set forth above, to develop closer relations among themselves on an improved and more enduring basis for the benefit of peoples.
X. Fulfilment in good faith of obligations under international law
The participating States will fulfil in good faith their obligations under international law, both those obligations arising from the generally recognized principles and rules of international law and those obligations arising from treaties or other agreements, in conformity with international law, to which they are parties.
In exercising their sovereign rights, including the right to determine their laws and regulations, they will conform with their legal obligations under international law; they will furthermore pay due regard to and implement the provisions in the Final Act of the Conference on Security and Co-operation in Europe.
The participating States confirm that in the event of a conflict between the obligations of the members of the United Nations under the Charter of the United Nations and their obligations under any treaty of other international agreement, their obligations under the Charter will prevail, in accordance with Article 103 of the Charter of the United Nations.
All the principles set forth above are of primary significance and, accordingly, they will be equally and unreservedly applied, each of them being interpreted taking into account the others. The participating States express their determination fully to respect and apply these principles, as set forth in the present Declaration,

in all aspects, to their mutual relations and co-operation in order to ensure to each participating State the benefits resulting from the respect and application of these principles by all.

The participating States, paying due regard to the principles above and, in particular, to the first sentence of the tenth principle. 'Fulfilment in good faith of obligations under international law', note that the present Declaration does not affect their rights and obligations, nor the corresponding treaties and other agreements and arrangements.

The participating States express the conviction that respect for these principles will encourage the development of normal and friendly relations and the progress of co-operation among them in all fields. They also express the conviction that respect for these principles will encourage the development of political contacts among them which in turn would contribute to better mutual understanding of their positions and views. The participating States declare their intention to conduct their relations with all other States in the spirit of the principles contained in the present Declaration.

(b) Matters related to giving effect to certain of the above Principles

(i) The participating States, reaffirming that they will respect and give effect to refraining from the threat or use of force and convinced of the necessity to make it an effective norm of international life,

Declare that they are resolved to respect and carry out, in their relations with one another, inter alia, the following provisions which are in conformity with the Declaration on Principles Guiding Relations between Participating States:

To give effect and expression, by all the ways and forms which they consider appropriate, to the duty to refrain from the threat or use of force in their relations with one another.

To refrain from any use of armed forces inconsistent with the purposes and principles of the Charter of the United Nations and the provisions of the Declaration on Principles Guiding Relations between Participating States, against another participating State, in particular from invasion of or attack on its territory.

To refrain from any manifestation of force for the purpose of inducing another participating State to renounce the full exercise of its sovereign rights.

To refrain from any act of economic coercion designed to subordinate to their own interest the exercise by another participating State of the rights inherent in its sovereignty and thus to secure advantages of any kind.

To take effective measures which by their scope and by their nature constitute steps towards the ultimate achievement of general and complete disarmament under strict and effective international control.

To promote, by all means which each of them considers appropriate, a climate of confidence and respect among peoples consonant with their duty to refrain from propaganda for wars of aggression or for any threat or use of force inconsistent with the purposes of the United Nations and with the Declaration on Principles Guiding Relations between Participating States, against another participating State.

To make every effort to settle exclusively by peaceful means any dispute between them, the continuance of which is likely to endanger the maintenance of international peace and security in Europe, and to seek, first of all, a solution through the peaceful means set forth in Article 33 of the United Nations Charter.

To refrain from any action which could hinder the peaceful settlement of disputes between the participating States.

(ii) The Participating States, reaffirming their determination to settle their disputes as set forth in the Principle of Peaceful Settlement of Disputes;

Convinced that the peaceful settlement of disputes is a complement to refraining from the threat or use of force, both being essential though not exclusive factors for the maintenance and consolidation of peace and security;

Desiring to reinforce and to improve the methods at their disposal for the peaceful settlement of disputes;

(1) Are resolved to pursue the examination and elaboration of a generally acceptable method for the peaceful settlement of disputes aimed at complementing existing methods, and to continue to this end to work upon 'Draft Convention on a European System for the Peaceful Settlement of Disputes' submitted by Switzerland during the second stage of the Conference on Security and Co-operation in Europe, as well as other proposals relating to it and directed towards the elaboration of such a method.

(2) Decide that, on the invitation of Switzerland, a meeting of experts of all the participating States will be convoked in order to fulfil the mandate described in paragraph 1 above within the framework and under the procedures of the follow-up to the Conference laid down in the chapter 'Follow-up to the Conference'.

(3) The meeting of experts will take place after the meeting of the representatives appointed by the Ministers of Foreign Affairs of the participating States, scheduled according to the chapter 'Follow-up to the Conference' for 1977; the results of the work of this meeting of experts will be submitted to Governments.

2. Document on confidence-building measures and certain aspects of security and disarmament

The participating States, desirous of eliminating the causes of tension that may exist among them and thus of contributing to the strengthening of peace and security in the world; Determined to strengthen confidence among them and thus to contribute to increasing stability and security in Europe; Determined further to refrain in their mutual relations, as well as in their international relations in general, from the threat or use of force against the territorial integrity or political independence of any State, or in any other manner inconsistent with the purposes of the United Nations and with the Declaration on Principles Guiding Relations between Participating States as adopted in this Final Act;

Recognizing the need to contribute to reducing the dangers of armed conflict and of misunderstanding or miscalculation of military activities which could give rise to apprehension, particularly in a situation where the participating States lack clear and timely information about the nature of such activities;

Taking into account considerations relevant to efforts aimed at lessening tension and promoting disarmament;

Recognizing that the exchange of observers by invitation at military manoeuvers will help to promote contacts and mutual understanding;

Having studied the question of prior notification of major military movements in the context of confidence-building;

Recognizing that there are other ways in which individual States can contribute further to their common objectives;

Convinced of the political importance of prior notification of major military manoeuvres for the promotion of mutual understanding and the strengthening of confidence, stability and security;

Accepting the responsibilty of each of them to promote these objectives and to implement this measure, in accordance with the accepted criteria and modalities, as essentials for the realization of these objectives;

Recognizing that this measure deriving from political decision rests upon a voluntary basis;

Have adopted the following:

I   Prior notification of major military manoeuvres

They will notify their major military manoeuvres to all other participating States through usual diplomatic channels in accordance with the following provisions: Notification will be given of major military manoeuvres exceeding a total of 25,000 troops, independently or combined with any possible air or naval components (in this context the word 'troops' includes amphibious and airborne troops).

In the case of independent manoeuvres of amphibious or air-borne troops, or of combined manoeuvres involving them, these troops will be included in this total. Furthermore, in the case of combined manoeuvres which do not reach the above total but which involve land forces together with significant numbers of either amphibious or airborne troops, or both, notification can also be given.

Notification will be given of major military manoeuvres which take place on the territory, in Europe, of any participating State as well as, if applicable, in the adjoining sea area and air space.

In the case of a participating State whose territory extends beyond Europe, prior notification need be given only of manoeuvres which take place in an area within 250 kilometres from its frontier facing or shared with any other European participating State, the participating State need not, however, give notification in cases in which that area is also contiguous to the participating State's frontier facing or shared with a non-European non-participating State.

Notification will be given 21 days or more in advance of the start of the manoeuvre or in the case of a manoeuvre arranged at shorter notice at the earliest possible opportunity prior to its starting date.

Notification will contain information of the designation, if any, the general purpose of and the States involved in the manoeuvre, the type or types and numerical strength of the forces engaged, the area and estimated time-frame of its conduct. The participating States will also, if possible, provide additional relevant information, particularly that related to the components of the forces engaged and the period of involvement of these forces.

Prior notification of other military manoeuvres

The participating States recognize that they can contribute further to strengthening confidence and increasing security and stability, and to this end may also notify smaller-scale military manoeuvres to other participating States, with special regard for those near the area of such manoeuvres.

To the same end, the participating States also recognize that they may notify other military manoeuvres conducted by them.

Exchange of observers

The participating States will invite other participating States, voluntarily and on a bilateral basis, in a spirit of reciprocity and goodwill towards all participating States, to send observers to attend military manoeuvres.

The inviting State will determine in each case the number of observers, the procedures and conditions of their participation, and give other information which it may consider useful. It will provide appropriate facilities and hospitality.

The invitation will be given as far ahead as is conveniently possible through usual diplomatic channels.

Prior notification of major military movements

In accordance with the Final Recommendations of the Helsinki Consultations the participating States studied the question of prior notification of major military movements as a measure to strengthen confidence.

Accordingly, the participating States recognize that they may, at their own discretion and with a view to contributing to confidence-building, notify their major military movements.

In the same spirit, further consideration will be given by the States participating in the Conference on Security and Co-operation in Europe to the question of prior notification of major military movements, bearing in mind, in particular, the experience gained by the implementation of the measures which are set forth in this document.

Other confidence-building measures

The participating States recognize that there are other means by which their common objectives can be promoted.

In particular, they will, with due regard to reciprocity and with a view to better mutual understanding, promote exchanges by invitation among their military personnel, including visits by military delegations.

In order to make a fuller contribution to their common objective of confidence-building, the participating States, when conducting their military activities in the area covered by the provisions for the prior notification of major military manoeuvres, will duly take into account and respect this objective.

They also recognize that the experience gained by the implementation of the provisions set forth above, together with further efforts, could lead to developing and enlarging measures aimed at strengthening confidence.

II. Questions relating to disarmament

The participating States recognize the interest of all of them in efforts aimed at lessening military confrontation and promoting disarmament which are designed to complement political détente in Europe and to strengthen their security. They are convinced of the necessity to take effective measures in these fields which by their scope and by their nature constitute steps towards the ultimate achievement of general and complete disarmament under strict and effective international control, and which should result in strengthening peace and security throughout the world.

III. General considerations

Having considered the views expressed on various subjects related to the strengthening of security in

Europe through joint efforts aimed at promoting détente and disarmament, the participating States, when engaged in such efforts, will, in this context, proceed, in particular, from the following essential considerations:

The complementary nature of the political and military aspects of security;

The interrelation between the security of each participating State and security in Europe as a whole and the relationship which exists, in the broader context of world security, between security in Europe and security in the Mediterranean area;

Respect for the security interests of all States participating in the Conference on Security and Co-operation in Europe inherent in their sovereign equality;

The importance that participants in negotiating foresee to it that information about relevant developments, progress and results is provided on an appropriate basis to other States participating in the Conference on Security and Co-operation in Europe and, in return, the justified interest of any of those States in having their views considered.

Co-operation in the Field of Economics, of Science and Technology and of the Environment

The participating States, convinced that their efforts to develop co-operation in the fields of trade, industry, science and technology, the environment and other areas of economic activity contribute to the reinforcement of peace and security in Europe and in the world as a whole.

Recognizing that co-operation in these fields would promote economic and social progress and the improvement of the conditions of life,

Aware of the diversity of their economic and social systems,

Reaffirming their will to intensify such co-operation between one another, irrespective of their systems,

Recognizing that such co-operation, with due regard for the different levels of economic development, can be developed, on the basis of equality and mutual satisfaction of the partners, and of reciprocity permitting, as a whole, an equitable distribution of advantages and obligations of comparable scale, with respect for bilateral and multilateral agreements.

Taking into account the interests of the developing countries throughout the world, including those among the participating countries as long as they are developing from the economic point of view; reaffirming their will to co-operate for the achievement of the aims and objectives established by the appropriate bodies of the United Nations in the pertinent documents concerning development, it being understood that each participating State maintains the positions it has taken on them; giving special attention to the least developed countries.

Convinced that the growing world-wide economic interdependence calls for increasing common and effective efforts towards the solution of major world economic problems such as food, energy, commodities, monetary and financial problems, and therefore emphasizes the need for promoting stable and equitable international economic relations, thus contributing to the continuous and diversified economic development of all countries.

Having taken into account the work already undertaken by relevant international organizations and wishing to take advantage of the possibilities offered by these organizations, in particular by the United Nations Economic Commission for Europe, for giving effect to the provisions of the final documents of the Conference,

Considering that the guidelines and concrete recommendations contained in the following texts are aimed at promoting further development of their mutual economic relations, and convinced that their co-operation in this field should take place in full respect for the principles guiding relations among participating States as set forth in the relevant document.

Have adopted the following:

1. Commercial Exchanges. General provisions:

The participating States, conscious of the growing role of international trade as one of the most important factors in economic growth and social progress,

Recognizing that trade represents an essential sector of their co-operation, and bearing in mind that the provisions contained in the above preamble apply in particular to this sector,

Considering that the volume and structure of trade among the participating States do not in all cases correspond to the possibilities created by the current level of their economic, scientific and technological development,

are resolved to promote, on the basis of the modalities of their economic co-operation, the expansion of their mutual trade in goods and services, and to ensure conditions favourable to such developments;

recognize the beneficial affects which can result for the development of trade from the application of most favoured nation treatment;

will encourage the expansion of trade on as broad a multilateral basis as possible, thereby endeavouring to utilize the various economic and commercial possibilities;

recognize the importance of bilateral and multilateral inter-governmental and other agreements for the long-term development of trade;

note the importance of monetary and financial questions for the development of international trade, and will endeavour to deal with them with a view to contributing to the continuous expansion of trade;

will endeavour to reduce or progressively eliminate all kinds of obstacles to the development of trade;

will foster a steady growth of trade while avoiding as far as possible abrupt fluctuations in their trade;

consider that their trade in various products should be conducted in such a way as not to cause or threaten to cause serious injury – and should the situation arise, market disruption – in domestic markets for these products and in particular to the detriment of domestic producers of like or directly competitive products; as regards the concept of market disruption, it is understood that it should not be invoked in a way inconsistent with the relevant provisions of their international agreements;

if they resort to safeguard measures, they will do so in conformity with their commitments in this field arising from international agreements to which they are parties and will take account of the interests of the parties directly concerned;

will give due attention to measures for the promotion of trade and the diversification of its structure;

note that the growth and diversification of trade would contribute to widening the possibilities of choice of products; consider it appropriate to create favourable conditions for the participation of firms, organizations and enterprises in the development of trade.

Business contacts and facilities:

The participating States, conscious of the importance of the contribution which an improvement of business contacts, and the accompanying growth of confidence in business relationships, could make to the development of commercial and economic relations,

will take measures further to improve conditions for the expansion of contacts between representatives of official bodies, of the different organizations, enterprises, firms and banks concerned with foreign trade, in particular, where useful, between sellers and users of products and services, for the purpose of studying commercial possibilities, concluding contracts, ensuring their implementation and providing after-sales services; will encourage organizations, enterprises and firms concerned with foreign trade to take measures to accelerate the conduct of business negotiations;

will further take measures aimed at improving working conditions of representatives of foreign organizations, enterprises, firms and banks concerned with external trade, particularly as follows:

by providing the necessary information, including information on legislation and procedures relating to the establishment and operation of permanent representation by the above mentioned bodies;

by examining as favourably as possible requests for the establishment of permanent representation and of offices for this purpose, including, where appropriate, the opening of joint offices by two or more firms;

by encouraging the provision, on conditions as favourable as possible and equal for all representatives of the above-mentioned bodies, of hotel accommodation, means of communication, and of other facilities normally required by them, as well as of suitable business and residential premises for purposes of permanent representation;

recognize the importance of such measures to encourage greater participation by small and medium sized firms in trade between participating States.

Economic and commercial information:

The participating States, conscious of the growing role of economic and commercial information in the development of international trade,

Considering that economic information should be of such a nature as to allow adequate market analysis and to permit the preparation of medium and long term forecasts, thus contributing to the establishment of a continuing flow of trade and a better utilization of commercial possibilities,

Expressing their readiness to improve the quality and increase the quantity and supply of economic and relevant administrative information,

Considering that the value of statistical information on the international level depends to a considerable extent on the possibility of its comparability,

will promote the publication and dissemination of economic and commercial information at regular intervals and as quickly as possible, in particular:

statistics concerning production, national income, budget, consumption and productivity;

foreign trade statistics drawn up on the basis of comparable classification including breakdown by product with indication by volume and value, as well as country of origin or destination;

laws and regulations concerning foreign trade;

information allowing forecasts of development of the economy to assist in trade promotion, for example, information on the general orientation of national economic plans and programmes;

other information to help businessmen in commercial contacts, for example, periodic directories, lists, and where possible, organizational charts of firms and organizations concerned with foreign trade;

will in addition to the above encourage the development of the exchange of economic and commercial information through, where appropriate, joint commissions for economic, scientific and technical co-operation, national and joint chambers of commerce, and other suitable bodies;

will support a study, in the framework of the United Nations Economic Commission for Europe, of the possibilities of creating a multilateral system of notification of laws and regulations concerning foreign trade and changes therein;

will encourage international work on the harmonization of statistical nomenclatures, notable in the United Nations Economic Commission of Europe.

Marketing:

The participating States, recognizing the importance of adapting production to the requirements of foreign markets in order to ensure the expansion of international trade,

Conscious of the need of exporters to be as fully familiar as possible with and take account of the requirements of potential users,

will encourage organizations, enterprises and firms concerned with foreign trade to develop further the knowledge and techniques required for effective marketing;

will encourage the improvement of conditions for the implementation of measures to promote trade and to satisfy the needs of users in respect of imported products, in particular through market research and advertising measures as well as, where useful, the establishment of supply facilities, the furnishing of spare parts, the functioning of after sales services, and the training of the necessary local technical personnel;

will encourage international co-operation in the field of trade promotion, including marketing, and the work undertaken on these subjects within the international bodies, in particular the United Nations Economic Commission for Europe.

2. Industrial co-operation and projects of common interest.

Industrial co-operation:

The participating States, considering that industrial co-operation, being motivated by economic considerations, can create lasting ties thus strengthening long-term overall economic co-operation,

contribute to economic growth as well as to the expansion and diversification of international trade and to a wider utilization of modern technology,

lead to the mutually advantageous utilization of economic complementaries through better use of all factors of production, and accelerate the industrial development of all those who take part in such co-operation, propose to encourage the development of industrial co-operation between the competent organizations, enterprises and firms of their countries;

consider that industrial co-operation may be facilitated by means of inter-governmental and other bilateral and multilateral agreements between the interested parties;

note that in promoting industrial co-operation they should bear in mind the economic structures and the development levels of their countries;

note that industrial co-operation is implemented by means of contracts concluded between competent organizations, enterprises and firms on the basis of economic considerations;

express their willingness to promote measures designed to create favourable conditions for industrial co-operation;

recognize that industrial co-operation covers a number of forms of economic relations going beyond the framework of conventional trade, and that in concluding contracts on industrial co-operation the partners will determine jointly the appropriate forms and conditions of co-operation, taking into account their mutual interests and capabilities;

recognize further that, if it is in their mutual interest, concrete forms such as the following may be useful for the development of industrial co-operation: joint production and sale, specialization in production and sale, construction, adaptation and modernization of industrial plants, co-operation for the setting up of complete industrial installations with a view to thus obtaining part of the resultant products, mixed companies, exchanges of 'know how', of technical information, of patents and of licences, and joint industrial research within the framework of specific co-operation projects;

recognize that new forms of industrial co-operation can be applied with a view to meeting specific needs;

note the importance of economic, commercial, technical and administrative information such as to ensure the development of industrial co-operation;

Consider it desirable:

to improve the quality and the quantity of information relevant to industrial co-operation, in particular the laws and regulations, including those relating to foreign exchange, general orientation of national economic plans and programmes as well as programme priorities and economic conditions of the market;

and

to disseminate as quickly as possible published documentation thereon;

will encourage all forms of exchange of information and communication of experience relevant to industrial co-operation, including through contacts between potential partners and, where appropriate, through joint commissions for economic, industrial, scientific and technical co-operation, national and joint chambers of commerce, and other suitable bodies; consider it desirable, with a view to expanding industrial co-operation, to encourage the exploration of co-operation possibilities and the implementation of co-operation projects and will take measures to this end, inter alia, by facilitating and increasing all forms of business contacts between competent organizations, enterprises and firms and between their respective qualified personnel;

note that the provisions adopted by the Conference relating to business contacts in the economic and commercial fields also apply to foreign organizations, enterprises and firms engaged in industrial co-operation, taking into account the specific conditions of this co-operation, and will endeavour to ensure, in particular, the existence of appropriate working conditions for personnel engaged in the implementation of co-operation projects;

consider it desirable that proposals for industrial co-operation projects should be sufficiently specific and should contain the necessary economic and technical data, in particular preliminary estimates of the cost of the project, information on the form of co-operation envisaged, and market possibilities, to enable potential partners to proceed with initial studies and to arrive at decisions in the shortest possible time; will encourage the parties concerned with industrial co-operation to take measures to accelerate the conduct of negotiations for the conclusion of co-operation contracts;

recommend further the continued examination – for example within the framework of the United Nations Economic Commission for Europe – of means of improving the provision of information to those concerned on general conditions of industrial co-operation and guidance on the preparation of contracts in this field; consider it desirable to further improve conditions for the implementation of industrial co-operation projects, in particular with respect to:

the protection of the interests of the partners in industrial co-operation projects, including the legal protection of the various kinds of property involved;

the consideration, in ways that are compatible with their economic systems, of the needs and possibilities of industrial co-operation within the framework of economic policy and particularly in national economic plans and programmes;

consider it desirable that the partners, when concluding industrial co-operation contracts, should devote due attention to provisions concerning the extension of the necessary mutual assistance and the provision of the necessary information during the implementation of these contracts, in particular with a view to attaining the required technical level and quality of the products resulting from such co-operation;

recognize the usefulness of an increased participation of small and medium sized firms in industrial co-operation projects.

Projects of common interest:

The participating States, considering that their economic potential and their natural resources permit, through common efforts, long-term co-operation in the implementation, including at the regional or sub-regional level, of major projects of common interest, and that these may contribute to the speeding-up of the economic development of the countries participating therein,

Considering it desirable that the competent organizations, enterprises and firms of all countries should be given the possibility of indicating their interest in participating in such projects, and, in case of agreement, of taking part in their implementation,

Noting that the provisions adopted by the Conference relating to industrial co-operation are also applicable to projects of common interest,

regard it as necessary to encourage, where appropriate, the investigation by competent and interested organization, enterprises and firms of the possibilities for the carrying out of projects of common interest in the fields of energy resources and of the exploitation of raw materials, as well as of transport and communications;

regard it as desirable that organizations, enterprises and firms exploring the possibilities of taking part in projects of common interest exchange with their potential partners, through the appropriate channels, the requisite economic, legal, financial and technical information pertaining to these projects;

consider that the fields of energy resources, in particular, petroleum, natural gas and coal, and the extraction and processing of mineral raw materials, in particular, iron ore and bauxite, are suitable ones for strengthening long-term economic co-operation and for the development of trade which could result;

consider that possibilities for projects of common interest with a view to long-term economic co-operation also exist in the following fields:

exchanges of electrical energy within Europe with a view to utilizing the capacity of the electrical power stations as rationally as possible;

co-operation in research for new sources of energy and, in particular, in the field of nuclear energy;

development of road networks and co-operation aimed at establishing a coherent navigable network in Europe;

co-operation in research and the perfecting of equipment for multimodal transport operations and for the handling of containers;

recommend that the States interested in projects of common interest should consider under what conditions it would be possible to establish them, and if they so desire, create the necessary conditions for their actual implementation.

3. Provisions concerning trade and industrial co-operation.

Harmonization of standards:

The participating States, recognizing the development of international harmonization of standards and technical regulations and of international co-operation in the field of certification as an important means of eliminating technical obstacles to international trade and industrial co-operation, thereby facilitating their development and increasing productivity,

reaffirm their interest to achieve the widest possible international harmonization of standards and technical regulations;

express their readiness to promote international agreements and other appropriate arrangements on acceptance of certificates of conformity with standards and technical regulations;

consider it desirable to increase international co-operation on standardization, in particular by supporting the activities of intergovernmental and other appropriate organizations in this field.

Arbitration:

The participating States, considering that the prompt and equitable settlement of disputes which may arise from commercial transactions relating to goods and services and contracts for industrial co-operation would contribute to expanding and facilitating trade and co-operation,

Considering that arbitration is an appropriate means of settling such disputes,

recommend, where appropriate, to organizations, enterprises and firms in their countries, to include arbitration clauses in commercial contracts and industrial co-operation contracts, or in special agreements;

recommend that the provisions on arbitration should provide for arbitration under a mutually acceptable set of arbitration rules, and permit arbitration in a third country, taking into account existing intergovernmental and other agreements in this field.

Specific bilateral arrangements:

The participating States, conscious of the need to facilitate trade and to promote the application of new forms of industrial co-operation,

will consider favourably the conclusion, in appropriate cases, of specific bilateral agreements concerning various problems of mutual interest in the fields of commercial exchanges and industrial co-operation, in particular with a view to avoiding double taxation and to facilitating the transfer of profits and the return of the value of the assests invested.

4. Science and technology:

The participating States, convinced that scientific and technological co-operation constitutes an important contribution to the strengthening of security and co-operation among them, in that it assists the effective solution of problems of common interest and the improvement of the conditions of human life,

Considering that in developing such co-operation, it is important to promote the sharing of information and experience, facilitating the study and transfer of scientific and technological achievements, as well as the access to such achievements on a mutually advantageous basis and in fields of co-operation agreed between interested parties,

Considering that it is for the potential partners, i.e. the competent organizations, institutions, enterprises, scientists and technologists of the participating States to determine the opportunities for mutually beneficial co-operation and to develop its details,

Affirming that such co-operation can be developed and implemented bilaterally and multilaterally at the governmental and non-governmental levels, for example, through intergovernmental and other agreements, international programmes, co-operative projects and commercial channels, while utilizing also various forms of contacts, including direct and individual contacts,

Aware of the need to take measures further to improve scientific and technological co-operation between them.

Possibilities for improving co-operation:

Recognize that possibilities exist for further improving scientific and technological co-operation, and to this end, express their intention to remove obstacles to such co-operation, in particular through:

the improvement of opportunities for the exchange and dissemination of scientific and technological information among the parties interested in scientific and technological research and co-operation including information related to the organization and implementation of such co-operation;

the expeditious implementation and improvement in organization, including programmes, of international visits of scientists and specialists in connexion with exchanges, conferences and co-operation;

the wider use of commercial channels and activities for applied scientific and technological research and for the transfer of achievements obtained in this field while providing information on and protection of intellectual and industrial property rights;

Fields of co-operation:

Consider that possibilities to expand co-operation exist within the areas given below as examples, noting that it is for potential partners in the participating countries to identify and develop projects and arrangements of mutual interest and benefit;

Agriculture:

Research into new methods and technologies for increasing the productivity of crop cultivation and animal husbandry; the application of chemistry to agriculture; the design, construction and utilization of agricultural machinery; technologies of irrigation and other agricultural land improvement works;

Energy:

New technologies of production, transport and distribution of energy aimed at improving the use of existing fuels and sources of hydroenergy, as well as research in the field of new energy;

New technologies, rational use of resources:

Research on new technologies and equipment designed in particular to reduce energy consumption and to minimize or eliminate waste;

Transport technology:

Research on the means of transport and the technology applied to the development and operation of international, national and urban transport networks including container transport as well as transport safety;

Physics:

Study of problems in high energy physics and plasma physics; research in the field of theoretical and experimental nuclear physics;

Chemistry

Research on problems in electrochemistry and the chemistry of polymers, of natural products, and of metals and alloys, as well as the development of improved chemical technology, especially materials processing; practical application of the latest achievements of chemistry to industry, construction and other sectors of the economy;

Meteorology and hydrology:

Meteorological and hydrological research, including methods of collection, evaluation and transmission of data and their utilization for weather forecasting and hydrology forecasting;

Oceanography:

Oceanographic research, including the study of air/sea inter-actions:

Seismological research:

Study and forecasting of earthquakes and associated geological changes; development and research of technology of seismo-resisting constructions;

Research on glaciology, permafrost and problems of life under conditions of cold:

Research on glaciology and permafrost; transportation and construction technologies; human adaptation to climatic extremes and changes in the living conditions of indigenous populations;

Computer, communication and information technologies:

Development of computers as well as of telecommunications and information systems; technology associated with computers and telecommunications, including their use for management systems, for production processes, for automation, for the study of economic problems, in scientific research and for the collection, processing and dissemination of information;

Space research:

Space exploration and the study of the earth's natural resources and the natural environment by remote sensing in particular with the assistance of satellites and rocket-probes;

Medicine and public health:

Research on cardiovascular, tumour and virus diseases, molecular biology, neurophysiology; development and testing of new drugs; study of contemporary problems of pediatrics, gerontology and the organization and techniques of medical services;

Environmental research

Research on specific scientific and technological problems related to human environment.

Forms and methods of co-operation:

Express their view that scientific and technological co-operation should, in particular, employ the following forms and methods:

exchange and circulation of books, periodicals and other scientific and technological publications and papers among interested organizations, scientific and technological institutions, enterprises and scientists and technologists, as well as participation in international programmes for the abstracting and indexing of publications;

exchanges and visits as well as other direct contacts and communications among scientists and technologists, on the basis of mutual agreement and other arrangements, for such purposes as consultations, lecturing and conducting research, including the use of laboratories, scientific libraries, and other documentation centres in connexion therewith;

holding of international and national conferences, symposia, seminars, courses and other meetings of a scientific and technological character, which would include the participation of foreign scientists and technologists; joint preparation and implementation of programmes and projects of mutual interest on the basis of consultation and agreement among all parties concerned, including, where possible and appropriate, exchanges of experience and research results, and correlation of research programmes, between scientific and technological research institutions and organizations;

use of commercial channels and methods for identifying and transferring technological and scientific developments, including the conclusions of mutually beneficial co-operation arrangements between firms and enterprises in fields agreed upon between them and for carrying out, where appropriate, joint research and development programmes and projects;

consider it desirable that periodic exchanges of views and information take place on scientific policy, in particular on general problems of orientation and administration of research and the question of a better use of large-scale scientific and experimental equipment on a co-operative basis;

recommend that, in developing co-operation in the field of science and technology, full use be made of existing practices of bilateral and multilateral co-operation, including that of a regional or sub-regional character, together with the forms and methods of co-operation in this document;

recommend further that more effective utilization be made of the possibilities and capabilities of existing international organizations, intergovernmental and non-governmental, concerned with science and technology, for improving exchanges of information and experience, as well as for developing other forms of co-operation in fields of common interest, for example; in the United Nations Economic Commission for Europe, study of possibilities for expanding multilateral co-operation, taking into account models for projects and research used in various international organizations; and for sponsoring conferences, symposia, and study and working groups such as those which would bring together younger scientists and technologists with eminent specialists in their field;

through their participation in particular international scientific and technological co-operation programmes, including those of UNESCO and other international organizations, pursuit of continuing progress towards the objectives of such programmes, notably those of UNISIST with particular respect to information policy guidance, technical advice, information contributions and data processing.

5. Environment:

The participant States, affirming that the protection and improvement of the environment, as well as the protection of nature and the rational utilization of its resources in the interests of present and future generations, is one of the tasks of major importance to the well-being of peoples and the economic development of all countries and that many environmental problems, particularly in Europe, can be solved effectively only through close international co-operation,

Acknowledging that each of the participating States, in accordance with the principles of international law, ought to ensure, in a spirit of co-operation, that activities carried out on its territory do not cause degradation of the environment in another State or in areas lying beyond the limits of national jurisdiction,

Considering that the success of any environmental policy pre-supposes that all population groups and social forces, aware of their responsibilities, help to protect and improve the environment, which

necessitates continued and thorough educative action, particularly with regard to youth,

Affirming that experience has shown that economic development and technological progress must be compatible with the protection of the environment and the preservation of historical and cultural values; that damage to the environment is best avoided by preventive measures; and that the ecological balance must be preserved in the exploitation and management of natural resources.

Aims of co-operation:

Agree to the following aims of co-operation, in particular: to study, with a view to their solution, those environmental problems which, by their nature, are of a multilateral, bilateral, regional or sub-regional dimension; as well as to encourage the development of an interdisciplinary approach to environmental problems;

to increase the effectiveness of national and international measures for the protection of the environment, by the comparison and, if appropriate, the harmonization of methods of gathering and analyzing facts, by improving the knowledge of pollution phenomena and rational utilization of natural resources, by the exchange of information, by the harmonization of definitions and the adoption, as far as possible, of a common terminology in the field of the environment;

to take the necessary measures to bring environmental policies closer together and, where appropriate and possible, to harmonize them;

to encourage, where possible and appropriate, national and international efforts by their interested organizations, enterprises and firms in the development, production and improvement of equipment designed for monitoring, protecting and enhancing the environment.

Fields of co-operation:

To attain these aims, the participating States will make use of every suitable opportunity to co-operate in the field of environment and, in particular, within the areas described below as examples;

Control of air pollution:

Desulphurization of fossil fuels and exhaust gases; pollution control of heavy metals, particles, aerosols, nitrogen oxides, in particular those emitted by transport, power stations, and other industrial plants; systems and methods of observation and control of air pollution and its effects, including long-range transport of air pollutants:

Water pollution control and fresh water utilization:

Prevention and control of water pollution, in particular of transboundary rivers and international lakes; techniques for the improvement of the quality of water and further development of ways and means for industrial and municipal sewage effluent purification; methods of assessment of fresh water resources and the improvement of their utilization, in particular by developing methods of production which are less polluting and lead to less consumption of fresh water;

Protection of the marine environment: Protection of the marine environment of participating States, and especially the Mediterranean Sea, from pollutants emenating from land-based sources and those from ships and other vessels, notably the harmful substances listed in Annexes I and II to the London Convention on the Prevention of Marine Pollution by the Dumping of Wastes and Other Matters; problems of maintaining marine ecological balances and food chains, in particular such problems as may arise from the exploration and exploitation of biological and mineral resources of the seas and the sea-bed;

Land utilization and soils:

Problems associated with more effective use of lands, including land amelioration, reclamation and recultivation; control of soil pollution, water and air erosion, as well as other forms of soil degradation; maintaining and increasing the productivity of soils with due regard for the possible negative effects of the application of chemical fertilizers and pesticides;

Nature conservation and nature reserves:

Protection of nature and nature reserves; conservation and maintenance of existing genetic resources, especially rare animal and plant species; conservation of natural ecological systems; establishment of nature reserves and other protected landscapes and areas, including their use for research, tourism, recreation and other purposes;

Improvement of environmental conditions in areas of human settlement:
Environmental conditions associated with transport, housing, working areas, urban development and planning, water supply and sewage disposal systems; assessment of harmful effects of noise, and noise control methods; collection, treatment and utilization of wastes, including the recovery and re-cycling of materials; research on substitutes for non-biodegradable substances;
Fundamental research, monitoring, forecasting and assessment of environmental changes:
Study of changes in climate, landscapes and ecological balances under the impact of both natural factors and human activities; forecasting of possible genetic changes in flora and fauna as a result of environmental pollution; harmonization of statistical data, development of scientific concepts and systems of monitoring networks, standardized methods of observation, measurement and assessment of changes in the biosphere; assessment of the effects of environmental pollution levels and degradation of the environment upon human health; study and development of criteria and standards for various environmental pollutants and regulations regarding production and use of various products;
Legal and administrative measures:
Legal and administrative measures for the protection of the environment including procedures for establishing environmental impact assessments.
Forms and methods of co-operation:
The participating States declare that problems relating to the protection and improvement of the environment will be solved on both a bilateral and a multilateral, including regional and sub-regional, basis, making full use of existing patterns and forms of co-operation. They will develop co-operation in the field of the environment in particular by taking into consideration the Stockholm Declaration on the Human Environment, relevant resolutions of the United Nations General Assembly and the United Nations Economic Commission for Europe, Prague symposium on environmental problems.
The participating States are resolved that co-operation in the field of the environment will be implemented in particular through:
exchanges of scientific and technical information, documentation and research results, including information of the means of determining the possible effects on the environment of technical and economic activities;
organization of conferences, symposia and meetings of experts;
exchanges of scientists, specialists and trainees;
joint preparation and implementation of programmes and projects for the study and solution of various problems of environmental protection;
harmonization, where appropriate and necessary, of environmental protection standards and norms, in particular with the object of avoiding possible difficulties in trade which may arise from efforts to resolve ecological problems of production processes and which relate to the achievement of certain environmental qualities in manufactured products;
consultations on various aspects of environmental protection, as agreed upon among countries concerned, especially in connexion with problems which could have international consequences.
The participating States will further develop such co-operation by:
promoting the progressive development, codification and implementation of international law as one means of preserving and enhancing the human environment, including principles and practices as accepted by them, relating to pollution and other environmental damage caused by activities within the jurisdiction or control of their States affecting other countries and regions;
supporting and promoting the implementation of relevant international Coventions to which they are parties, in particular those designed to prevent and combat marine and fresh water pollution, recommending States to ratify Conventions which have already been signed, as well as considering possibilities of accepting other appropriate Conventions to which they are not parties at present;
advocating the inclusion, where appropriate and possible, of the various areas of co-operation into the programmes of work of the United Nations Economic Commission for Europe, supporting such co-operation within the framework of the Commission and of the United Nations Environment Programme, and taking into account the work of other competent international organizations of which they are members;
making wider use, in all types of co-operation, of information already available from national and international sources, including internationally agreed criteria, and utilizing the possibilities and capabilities of various competent international organizations.
The participating States agree on the following recommendations on specific measures: to develop through international co-operation an extensive programme for the monitoring and evaluation of the long-range transport of air pollutants, starting with sulphur dioxide and with possible extension to other pollutants, and to this end to take into account basic elements of a co-operation programme which were identified by the experts who met in Oslo in December 1974 at the invitation of the Norwegian Institute of Air Research;
to advocate that within the framework of the United Nations Economic Commission for Europe a study be carried out of procedures and relevant experience relating to the activities of Governments in developing the capabilities of their countries to predict adequately environmental consequences of economic activities and technological development.
6. Co-operation in other areas. Development of transport:
The Participating States, considering that the improvement of the conditions of transport constitutes one of the factors essential to the development of co-operation among them.
Considering that it is necessary to encourage the development of transport and the solution of existing problems by employing appropriate mational and international means,
Taking into account the work being carried out on these subjects by existing international organizations, especially by the Inland Transport Committee of the United Nations Economic Commission for Europe,
note that the speed of technical progress in the various fields of transport makes desirable a development of co-operation and an increase in exchanges of information among them;
declare themselves in favour of a simplification and a harmonization of administrative formalities in the field of international transport, in particular at frontiers;
consider it desirable to promote, while allowing for their particular national circumstances in this sector, the harmonization of administrative and technical provisions concerning safety in road, rail, river, air and sea transport;
express their intention to encourage the development of international inland transport of passengers and goods as well as the possibilities of adequate participation in such transport on the basis of reciprocal advantage;
declare themselves in favour, with due respect for their rights and international commitments, of the elimination of disparities arising from the legal provisions applied to traffic on inland waterways which are subject to international conventions and, in particular, of the disparity in the application of those provisions; and to this end invite the member States of the Central Commission for the Navigation of the Rhine, of the Danube Commission and of other bodies to develop the work and studies now being carried out, in particular within the United Nations Economic Commission for Europe;
express their willingness with a view to improving international rail transport and with due respect for their rights and international commitments, to work towards the elimination of difficulties arising from disparities in existing international legal provisions governing the reciprocal railway transport of passengers and goods between their territories;
express the desire for intensification of the work being carried out by existing international organizations in the field of transport, especially that of the Inland Transport Committee of the United Nations Economic Commission for Europe, and express their intention to contribute thereto by their efforts; consider that examination by the participating States of the possibility of their accession to the different conventions or to membership of international organizations specializing in transport matters, as well as their efforts to implement conventions when ratified, could contribute to the strengthening of their co-operation in this field.
Promotion of tourism:
The participating States, aware of the contribution made by international tourism to the development of mutual understanding among peoples, to increased knowledge of other countries' achievements in various fields, as well as to economic, social and cultural progress,
Recognizing the interrelationship between the development of tourism and measures taken in other areas of economic activity, express their intention to encourage increased tourism on both an individual and group basis in particular by:
encouraging the improvement of the tourist infrastructure and co-operation in this field;
encouraging the carrying out of joint tourist projects including technical co-operation, particularly where this is suggested by territorial proximity and the convergence of tourist interests;
encouraging the exchange of information, including relevant laws and regulations, studies, data and documentation relating to tourism, and by improving statistics with a view to facilitating their comparability;
dealing in a positive spirit with questions connected with the allocation of financial means for tourist travel abroad, having regard to their economic possibilities, as well as with those connected with the formalities required for such travel, taking into account other provisions on tourism adopted by the Conference;
facilitating the activities of foreign travel agencies and passenger transport companies in the promotion of international tourism;
encouraging tourism outside the high season;
examining the possibilities of exchanging specialists and students in the field of tourism, with a view to improving their qualifications;
promoting conferences and symposia on the planning and development of tourism;
consider it desirable to carry out in the appropriate international framework, and with the co-operation of the relevant national bodies, detailed studies on tourism, in particular: a comparative study on the status and activities of travel agencies as well as on ways and means of achieving better co-operation among them;
a study of the problems raised by the seasonal concentration of vacations, with the ultimate objective of encouraging tourism outside peak periods;
studies of the problems arising in areas where tourism has injured the environment;
consider also that interested parties might wish to study the following questions:
uniformity of hotel classification; and
tourist routes comprising two or more countries;
will endeavour, where possible, to ensure that the development of tourism does not injure the environment and the artistic, historic and cultural heritage in their respective countries; will pursue their co-operation in the field of tourism bilaterally and multilaterally with a view to attaining the above objectives.
Economic and social aspects of migrant labour:
The participating States, considering that the movements of migrant workers in Europe have reached substantial proportions, and that they constitute an important economic, social and human factor for host countries as well as for countries of origin,
Recognizing that workers' migrations have also given rise to a number of economic, social, human and other problems in both the receiving countries and the countries of origin,
Taking due account of the activities of the competent international organizations, more particularly the International Labour Organisation, in this area,
are of the opinion that the problems arising bilaterally from the migration of workers in Europe as well as between the participating States should be dealt with by the parties directly concerned, in order to resolve these problems in their mutual interest, in the light of the concern of each State involved to take due account of the requirements resulting from its socio-economic situation, having regard to the obligation of each State to comply with the bilateral and multilateral agreements to which it is party, and with the following aims in view:
to encourage the efforts of the countries of origin directed towards increasing the possibilities of employment for their nationals in their own territories, in particular by developing economic co-operation appropriate for this purpose and suitable for the host countries and the countries of origin concerned;

to ensure, through collaboration between the host country and the country of origin, the conditions under which the orderly movement of workers might take place, while at the same time protecting their personal and social welfare and, if appropriate, to organize the recruitment of migrant workers and the provision of elementary language and vocational training;

to ensure equality of rights between migrant workers and nationals of the host countries with regard to conditions of employment and work and to social security, and to endeavour to ensure that migrant workers may enjoy satisfactory living conditions, especially housing conditions;

to endeavour to ensure, as far as possible, that migrant workers may enjoy the same opportunities as nationals of the host countries of finding other suitable employment in the event of unemployment;

to regard with favour the provision of vocational training to migrant workers and, as far as possible, free instruction in the language of the host country, in the framework of their employment;

to confirm the right of migrant workers to receive, as far as possible, regular information in their own language, covering both their country of origin and the host country;

to ensure that the children of migrant workers established in the host country have access to the education usually given there, under the same conditions as the children of that country and, furthermore, to permit them to receive supplementary education in their own language, national culture, history and geography;

to bear in mind that migrant workers, particularly those who have acquired qualifications, can by returning to their countries after a certain period of time help to remedy any deficiency of skilled labour in their country of origin;

to facilitate, as far as possible, the reuniting of migrant workers with their families;

to regard with favour the efforts of the countries of origin to attract the savings of migrant workers, with a view to increasing, within the framework of their economic development, appropriate opportunities for employment, thereby facilitating the reintegration of these workers on their return home.

Training of personnel;

The participating States, conscious of the importance of the training and advanced training of professional staff and technicians for the economic development of every country,

declare themselves willing to encourage co-operation in this field notably by promoting exchange of information on the subject of institutions, programmes and methods of training and advanced training open to professional staff and technicians in the various sectors of economic activity and especially in those of management, public planning, agriculture and commercial and banking techniques;

consider that it is desirable to develop, under mutually acceptable conditions, exchanges of professional staff and technicians, particularly through training activities, of which it would be left to the competent and interested bodies in the participating States to discuss the modalities – duration, financing, education and qualification levels of potential participants;

declare themselves in favour of examining, through appropriate channels, the possibilities of co-operating on the organization and carrying out of vocational training on the job, more particularly in professions involving modern techniques.

Co-operation in Humanitarian and Other Fields

The participating States, desiring to contribute to the strengthening of peace and understanding among peoples and to the spiritual enrichment of the human personality without distinction as to race, sex, language or religion,

Conscious that increased cultural and educational exchanges, broader dissemination of information, contacts between people, and the solution of humanitarian problems will contribute to the attainment of these aims,

Determined therefore to co-operate among themselves, irrespective of their political, economic and social systems, in order to create better conditions in the above fields, to develop and strengthen existing forms of co-operation and to work out new ways and means appropriate to these aims,

Convinced that this co-operation should take place in full respect for the principles guiding relations among participating States as set forth in the relevant document,

Have adopted the following:

1. Human Contacts:

The participating States, considering the development of contacts to be an important element in the strengthening of friendly relations and trust among peoples,

Affirming, in relation to their present effort to improve conditions in this area, the importance they attach to humanitarian considerations,

Desiring in this spirit to develop, with the continuance of détente, further efforts to achieve continuing progress in this field

And conscious that the questions relevant hereto must be settled by the States concerned under mutually acceptable conditions,

Make it their aim to facilitate freer movement and contacts, individually and collectively, whether privately or officially, among persons, institutions and organizations of the participating States, and to contribute to the solution of the humanitarian problems that arise in that connexion,

Declare their readiness to these ends to take measures which they consider appropriate and to conclude agreements or arrangements among themselves, as may be needed, and

Express their intention now to proceed to the implementation of the following:

(a) Contacts and Regular Meetings on the Basis of Family Ties:

In order to promote further development of contacts on the basis of family ties the participating States will favourably consider applications for travel with the purpose of allowing persons to enter or leave their territory temporarily, and on a regular basis if desired, in order to visit members of their families. Applications for temporary visits to meet members of their families will be dealt with without distinction as to the country of origin or destination: existing requirements for travel documents and visas will be applied in this spirit. The preparation and issue of such documents and visas will be effected within reasonable time limits; cases of urgent necessity – such as serious illness or death – will be given priority treatment. They will take such steps as may be necessary to ensure that the fees for official travel documents and visas are acceptable. They confirm that the presentation of an application concerning contacts on the basis of family ties will not modify the rights and obligations of the applicant or of members of his family.

(b) Reunification of Families:

The participating States will deal in a positive and humanitarian spirit with the applications of persons who wish to be reunited with members of their family, with special attention being given to requests of an urgent character – such as requests submitted by persons who are ill or old.

They will deal with applications in this field as expeditiously as possible.

They will lower where necessary the fees charged in connexion with these applications to ensure that they are at a moderate level.

Applications for the purpose of family reunification which are not granted may be renewed at the appropriate level and will be considered at reasonably short intervals by the authorities of the country of residence or destination, whichever is concerned; under such circumstances fees will be charged only when applications are granted.

Persons whose applications for family reunification are granted may bring with them or ship their household and personal effects; to this end the participating States will use all possibilities provided by existing regulations.

Until members of the same family are reunited meetings and contacts between them may take place in accordance with the modalities for contacts on the basis of family ties.

The participating States will support the efforts of Red Cross and Red Crescent Societies concerned with the problems of family reunification.

They confirm that the presentation of an application concerning family reunification will not modify the rights and obligations of the applicant or of members of his family.

The receiving participating State will take appropriate care with regard to employment for persons from other participating States who take up permanent residence in that State in connexion with family reunification with its citizens and see that they are afforded opportunities equal to those enjoyed by its own citizens for education, medical assistance and social security.

(c) Marriage between Citizens of Different States:

The participating States will examine favourably and on the basis of humanitarian considerations requests for exit or entry permits from persons who have decided to marry a citizen from another participating State.

The processing and issuing of the documents required for the above purposes and for the marriage will be in accordance with the provisions accepted for family reunification.

In dealing with requests from couples from different participating States, once married, to enable them and the minor children of their marriage to transfer their permanent residence to a State in which either one is normally a resident, the participating States will also apply the provisions accepted for family reunification.

(d) Travel for Personal or Professional Reasons:

The participating States intend to facilitate wider travel by their citizens for personal or professional reasons and to this end they intend in particular:

– gradually to simplify and to administer flexibly the procedures for exit and entry;

– to ease regulations concerning movement of citizens from the other participating States in their territory, with due regard to security requirements.

They will endeavour gradually to lower, where necessary, the fees for visas and official travel documents.

They intend to consider, as necessary, means – including, in so far as appropriate, the conclusion of multilateral or bilateral consular conventions or other relevant agreements or understandings – for the improvement of arrangements to provide consular services, including legal and consular assistance.

They confirm that religious faiths, institutions and organizations, practising within the constitutional framework of the participating States, and their representatives can, in the field of their activities, have contacts and meetings among themselves and exchange information.

(e) Improvement of Conditions for Tourism on an Individual or Collective Basis:

The participating States consider that tourism contributes to a fuller knowledge of the life, culture and history of other countries, to the growth of understanding among peoples, to the improvement of contacts and to the broader use of leisure. They intend to promote the development of tourism, on an individual or collective basis, and, in particular, they intend:

– to promote visits to their respective countries by encouraging the provision of appropriate facilities and the simplification and expediting of necessary formalities relating to such visits;

– to increase, on the basis of appropriate agreements or arrangements where necessary, co-operation in the development of tourism, in particular by considering bilaterally possible ways to increase information relating to travel to other countries and to the reception and service of tourists, and other related questions of mutual interest.

(f) Meetings among Young People:

The participating States intend to further the development of contacts and exchanges among young people by encouraging:

– increased exchanges and contacts on a short or long term basis among young people working, training or undergoing education through bilateral or multilateral agreements or regular programmes in all cases where it is possible;

– study by their youth organizations of the question of possible agreements relating to frameworks of multilateral youth co-operation;

– agreements or regular programmes relating to the organizations of exchanges of students, of international youth seminars, of courses of professional training and foreign language study;

– the further development of youth tourism and the provision to this end of appropriate facilities;

– the development, where possible, of exchanges, contacts and co-operation on a bilateral or multilateral basis between their organizations which represent wide circles of young people working, training or undergoing education;

– awareness among youth of the importance of developing mutual understanding and of strengthening friendly relations and confidence among peoples.
(g) Sport:
In order to expand existing links and co-operation in the field of sport the participating States will encourage contacts and exchanges of this kind, including sports meetings and competitions of all sorts, on the basis of the established international rules, regulations and practice.
(h) Expansion of Contacts:
By way of further developing contacts among governmental institutions and non-governmental organizations and associations, including women's organizations, the participating States will facilitate the convening of meetings as well as travel by delegations, groups and individuals.
2. Information:
The participating States, conscious of the need for an ever wider knowledge and understanding of the various aspects of life in other participating States,
Acknowledging the contribution of this process to the growth of confidence between peoples,
Desiring, with the development of mutual understanding between the participating States and with the further improvement of their relations, to continue further efforts towards progress in this field,
Recognizing the importance of the dissemination of information from the other participating States and of a better acquaintance with such information,
Emphasizing therefore the essential and influential role of the press, radio, television, cinema and news agencies and of the journalists working in these fields,
Make it their aim to facilitate the freer and wider dissemination of information of all kinds, to encourage co-operation in the field of information and the exchange of information with other countries, and to improve the conditions under which journalists from one participating State exercise their profession in another participating State, and
Express their intention in particular:
(a) Improvement of the Circulation of, Access to, and Exchange of Information:
(i) Oral Information; to facilitate the dissemination of oral information through the encouragement of lectures and lecture tours by personalities and specialists from the other participating States, as well as exchanges of opinions at round table meetings, seminars, symposia, summer schools, congresses and other bilateral and multilateral meetings.
(ii) Printed Information: to facilitate the improvement of the dissemination, on their territory, of newspapers and printed publications, periodical and non-periodical, from the other participating States. For this purpose:
they will encourage their competent firms and organizations to conclude agreements and contracts designed gradually to increase the quantities and the number of titles of newspapers and publications imported from the other participating States. These agreements and contracts should in particular mention the speediest conditions of delivery and the use of the normal channels existing in each country for the distribution of its own publications and newspapers, as well as forms and means of payment agreed between the parties making it possible to achieve the objectives aimed at by these agreements and contracts;
where necessary, they will take appropriate measures to achieve the above objectives and to implement the provisions contained in the agreements and contracts.
To contribute to the improvement of access by the public to periodical and non-periodical printed publications imported on the bases indicated above. In particular:
They will encourage an increase in the number of places where these publications are on sale;
they will facilitate the availability of these periodical publications during congresses, conferences, official visits and other international events and to tourists during the season;
they will develop the possibilities for taking out subscriptions according to the modalities particular to each country; they will improve the opportunities for reading and borrowing these publications in large public libraries and their reading rooms as well as in university libraries.
They intend to improve the possibilities for acquaintance with bulletins of official information issued by diplomatic missions and distributed by those missions on the basis of arrangements acceptable to the interested parties.
(iii) Filmed and Broadcast Information: to promote the improvement of the dissemination of filmed and broadcast information. To this end:
they will encourage the wider showing and broadcasting of a greater variety of recorded and filmed information from the other participating States, illustrating the various aspects of life in their countries and received on the basis of such agreements or arrangements as may be necessary between the organizations and firms directly concerned;
they will facilitate the import by competent organizations and firms of recorded audio-visual material from the other participating States.
The participating States note the expansion in the dissemination of information broadcast by radio, and express the hope for the continuation of this process, so as to meet the interest of mutual understanding among peoples and the aims set forth by this Conference.
(b) Co-operation in the Field of Information:
– To encourage co-operation in the field of information on the basis of short or long term agreements or arrangements. In particular:
they will favour increased co-operation among mass media organizations, including press agencies, as well as among publishing houses and organizations;
they will favour co-operation among public or private, national or international radio and television organizations, in particular through the exchange of both live and recorded radio and television programmes, and through the joint production and the broadcasting and distribution of such programmes;
they will encourage meetings and contacts both between journalists' organizations and between journalists from the participating States;
they will view favourably the possibilities of arrangements between periodical publications as well as between newspapers from the participating States, for the purpose of exchanging and publishing articles;
they will encourage the exchange of technical information as well as the organization of joint research and meetings devoted to the exchange of experience and views between experts in the field of the press, radio and television.
(c) Improvement of Working Conditions for Journalists:
The participating States, desiring to improve the conditions under which journalists from one participating State exercise their profession in another participating State, intend in particular to:
examine in a favourable spirit and within a suitable and reasonable time scale requests from journalists for visas,
grant to permanently accredited journalists of the participating States, on the basis of arrangements, multiple entry and exit visas for specified periods;
facilitate the issue to accredited journalists of the participating States of permits for stay in their country of temporary residence and, if and when these are necessary, of other official papers which it is appropriate for them to have;
ease, on a basis of reciprocity, procedures for arranging travel by journalists of the participating States in the country where they are exercising their profession, and to provide progressively greater opportunities for such travel, subject to the observance of regulations relating to the existence of areas closed for security reasons;
ensure that requests by such journalists for such travel receive, in so far as possible, an expeditious response, taking into account the time scale of the request;
increase the opportunities for journalists of the participating States to communicate personally with their sources, including organizations and official institutions;
grant to journalists of the participating States the right to import, subject only to its being taken out again, the technical equipment (photographic, cinematographic, tape recorder, radio and television) necessary for the exercise of their profession; enable journalists of the other participating States, whether permanently or temporarily accredited, to transmit completely, normally and rapidly by means recognized by the participating States to the information organs which they represent, the results of their professional activity, including tape recordings and undeveloped film, for the purpose of publication or of broadcasting on the radio or television.
The participating States reaffirm that the legitimate pursuit of their professional activity will neither render journalists liable to expulsion nor otherwise penalize them. If an accredited journalist is expelled, he will be informed of the reasons for this act and may submit an application for re-examination of this case.
While recognizing that appropriate local personnel are employed by foreign journalists in many instances, the participating States note that the above provisions would be applied, subject to the observance of the appropriate rules, to persons from the other participating States, who are regularly and professionally engaged as technicians, photographers or cameramen of the press, radio, television or cinema.
3. Co-operation and Exchanges in the Field of Culture:
The participating States, considering that cultural exchanges and co-operation contribute to a better comprehension among people and among peoples, and thus promote a lasting understanding among States,
Confirming the conclusions already formulated in this field at the multilateral level, particularly at the Intergovernmental Conference on Cultural Policies in Europe, organized by UNESCO in Helsinki in June 1972, where interest was manifested in the active participation of the broadcast possible social groups in an increasingly diversified cultural life,
Desiring, with the development of mutual confidence and the further improvement of relations between the participating States, to continue further efforts toward progress in this field,
Disposed in this spirit to increase substantially their cultural exchanges, with regard both to persons and to cultural works, and to develop among them an active co-operation, both at the bilateral and the multilateral level, in all the fields of culture,
Convinced that such a development of their mutual relations will contribute to the enrichment of the respective cultures, while respecting the originality of each, as well as to the reinforcement among them of a consciousness of common values, while continuing to develop cultural co-operation with other countries of the world,
Declare that they jointly set themselves the following objectives:
(a) to develop the mutual exchange of information with a view to a better knowledge of respective cultural achievements,
(b) to improve the facilities for the exchange and for the dissemination of cultural property,
(c) to promote access by all to respective cultural achievements,
(d) to develop contacts and co-operation among persons active in the field of culture,
(e) to seek new fields and forms of cultural co-operation, Thus give expression to their common will to take progressive, coherent and long-term action in order to achieve the objectives of the present declaration; and
Express their intention now to proceed to the implementation of the following:
Extension of Relations:
To expand and improve at the various levels co-operation and links in the field of culture, in particular by:
– concluding, where appropriate, agreements on a bilateral or multilateral basis, providing for the extension of relations among competent State institutions and non-governmental organizations in the field of culture, as well as among people engaged in cultural activities, taking into account the need both for flexibility and the fullest possible use of existing agreements, and bearing in mind that agreements and also other arrangements constitute important means of developing cultural co-operation and exchanges;
– contributing to the development of direct communication and co-operation among relevant State institutions and non-governmental organizations, including, where necessary, such communication and co-operation carried out on the basis of special agreements and arrangements;
– encouraging direct contacts and communications among persons engaged in cultural activities, including, where necessary, such contacts and communications carried out on the basis of special agreements and arrangements.
Mutual Knowledge:
Within their competence to adopt, on a bilateral and multilateral level, appropriate measures which would

give their peoples a more comprehensive and complete mutual knowledge of their achievements in the various fields of culture, and among them:

to examine jointly, if necessary with the assistance of appropriate international organizations, the possible creation in Europe and the structure of a bank of cultural data, which would collect information from the participating countries and make it available to its correspondence on their request, and to convene for this purpose a meeting of experts from interested States;

to consider, if necessary in conjunction with appropriate international organizations, ways of compiling in Europe an inventory of documentary films of a cultural or scientific nature from the participating States;

to encourage more frequent book exhibitions and to examine the possibility of organizing periodically in Europe a large-scale exhibition of books from the participating States; to promote the systematic exchange, between the institutions concerned and publishing houses, of catalogues of available books as well as of pre-publication material which will include, as far as possible, all forthcoming publications; and also to promote the exchange of material between firms publishing encyclopaedias, with a view to improving the presentation of each country;

to examine jointly questions of expanding and improving exchanges of information in the various fields of culture, such as theatre, music, library work as well as the conservation and restoration of cultural property.

Exchanges and Dissemination:

To contribute to the improvement of facilities for exchanges and the dissemination of cultural property, by appropriate means, in particular by:

studying the possibilities for harmonizing and reducing the charges relating to international commercial exchanges of books and other cultural materials, and also for new means of insuring works of art in foreign exhibitions and for reducing the risks of damage or loss to which these works are exposed by their movement;

facilitating the formalities of customs clearance, in good time for programmes of artistic events, of the works of art, materials and accessories appearing on lists agreed upon by the organizers of these events;

encouraging meetings among representatives of competent organizations and relevant firms to examine measures within their field of activity – such as the simplification of orders, time limits for sending supplies and modalities of payment – which might facilitate international commercial exchanges of books;

promoting the loan and exchange of films among their film institutes and film libraries;

encouraging the exchange of information among interested parties concerning events of a cultural character foreseen in the participating States, in fields where this is most appropriate, such as music, theatre and the plastic and graphic arts, with a view to contributing to the compilation and publication of a calendar of such events, with the assistance, where necessary, of the appropriate international organizations;

encouraging a study of the impact which the foreseeable development, and a possible harmonization among interested parties, of the technical means used for this dissemination of culture might have on the development of cultural co-operation and exchanges, while keeping in view the preservation of the diversity and originality of their respective cultures;

encouraging, in the way they deem appropriate, within their cultural policies, the further development of interest in the cultural heritage of the other participating States, conscious of the merits and the value of each culture;

endeavouring to ensure the full and effective application of the international agreements and conventions on copyrights and on circulation of cultural property to which they are party or to which they may decide in the future to become party.

Access:

To promote fuller mutual access by all to the achievements – works, experiences and performing arts – in the various fields of culture of their countries, and to that end to make the best possible efforts, in accordance with their competence, more particularly:

to promote wider dissemination of books and artistic works, in particular by such means as:

facilitating, while taking full account of the international copyright conventions to which they are party,

international contacts and communications between authors and publishing houses as well as other cultural institutions, with a view to a more complete mutual access to cultural achievements;

recommending that, in determining the size of editions, publishing houses take into account also the demand from the other participating States, and that rights of sale in other participating States be granted, where possible, to several sales organizations of the importing countries, by agreement between interested partners;

encouraging competent organizations and relevant firms to conclude agreements and contracts and contributing, by this means, to a gradual increase in the number and diversity of works by authors from the other participating States available in the original and in translation in their libraries and bookshops; promoting, where deemed appropriate, an increase in the number of sales outlets where books by authors from the other participating States, imported in the original on the basis of agreements and contracts, and in translation, are for sale; promoting, on a wider scale, the translation of works in the sphere of literature and other fields of cultural activity, produced in the languages of the other participating States, especially from the less widely-spoken languages, and the publication and dissemination of the translated works by such measures as: encouraging more regular contacts between interested publishing houses; developing their efforts in the basic and advanced training of translators; encouraging, by appropriate means, the publishing houses of their countries to publish translation; facilitating the exchange between publishers and interested institutions of lists of books which might be translated; promoting between their countries the professional activity and co-operation of translators; carrying out joint studies on ways of further promoting translations and their dissemination; improving and expanding exchanges of books, bibliographies and catalogue cards between libraries;

to envisage other appropriate measures which would permit, where necessary by mutual agreement among interested parties, the facilitation of access to their respective cultural achievements, in particular in the field of books;

to contribute by appropriate means to the wider use of the mass media in order to improve mutual acquaintance with the cultural life of each; to seek to develop the necessary conditions for migrant workers and their families to preserve their links with their national culture, and also to adapt themselves to their new cultural environment;

to encourage the competent bodies and enterprises to make a wider choice and effect wider distribution of full-length and documentary films from the other participating States, and to promote more frequent non-commercial showings, such as premières, film weeks and festivals, giving due consideration to films from countries whose cinematographic works are less well known;

to promote, by appropriate means, the extension of opportunities for specialists from the other participating States to works with materials of a cultural character from film and audio-visual archives, within the framework of the existing rules for work on such archival materials;

to encourage a joint study by interested bodies, where appropriate with the assistance of the competent international organizations, of the expediency and the conditions for the establishment of a repertory of their recorded television programmes of a cultural nature, as well as of the means of viewing them rapidly in order to facilitate their selection and possible acquisition.

Contacts and Co-operation:

To contribute, by appropriate means, to the development of contacts and co-operation in the various fields of culture, especially among creative artists and people engaged in cultural activities, in particular by making efforts to:

promote for persons active in the field of culture, travel and meetings including, where necessary, those carried out on the basis of agreements, contracts or other special arrangements and which are relevant to their cultural co-operation;

encourage in this way contacts among creative and performing artists and artistic groups with a view to their working together, making known their works in other participating States or exchanging views on topics relevant to their common activity; encourage, where

necessary through appropriate arrangements, exchanges of trainees and specialists and the granting of scholarships for basic and advanced training in various fields of culture such as the arts and architecture, museums and libraries, literary studies and translation, and contribute to the creation of favourable conditions of reception in their respective institutions;

encourage the exchange of experience in the training of organizers of cultural activities as well as of teachers and specialists in fields such as theatre, opera, ballet, music and fine arts;

continue to encourage the organization of international meetings among creative artists, especially young creative artist, on current questions of artistic and literary creation which are of interest for joint study;

study other possibilities for developing exchanges, and co-operation among persons active in the field of culture, with a view to a better mutual knowledge of the cultural life of the participating States.

Fields and Forms of Co-operation:

To encourage the search for new fields and forms of cultural co-operation, to these ends contributing to the conclusion among interested parties, where necessary, of appropriate agreements and arrangements, and in this context to promote:

joint studies regarding cultural policies, in particular in their social aspects, and as they relate to planning, town-planning, educational and environmental policies, and the cultural aspects of tourism;

the exchange of knowledge in the realm of cultural diversity, with a view to contributing thus to a better understanding by interested parties of such diversity where it occurs;

the exchange of information, and as may be appropriate, meetings of experts, the elaboration and the execution of research programmes and projects, as well as their joint evaluation, and the dissemination of the results, on the subjects indicated above;

such forms of cultural co-operation and the development of such joint projects as:

international events in the fields of the plastic and graphic arts, cinema, theatre, ballet, music, folklore, etc.; book fairs and exhibitions, joint performances of operatic and dramatic works, as well as performances given by soloists, instrumental ensembles, orchestras, choirs and other artistic groups, including those composed of amateurs, paying due attention to the organization of international cultural youth and the exchange of young artists;

the inclusion of works by writers and composers from the other participating States in the repertoires of soloists and artistic ensembles;

the preparation, translation and publication of articles, studies and monographs, as well as of low-cost books and of artistic and literary collections, suited to making better known respective cultural achievements, envisaging for this purpose meetings among experts and representatives of publishing houses;

the co-production and the exchange of films and of radio and television programmes, by promoting in particular, meetings among producers, technicians and representatives of the public authorities with a view to working out favourable conditions for the execution of specific joint projects and by encouraging, in the field of co-production, the establishment of international filming teams;

the organization of competitions for architects and town-planners, bearing in mind the possible implementation of the best projects and the formation, where possible, of international teams;

the implementation of joint projects for conserving, restoring and showing to advantage works of art, historical and archaeological monuments and sites of cultural interest, with the help, in appropriate cases, of international organizations of a governmental and nongovernmental character as well as of private institutions – competent and active in these fields – envisaging for this purpose:

periodic meetings of experts of the interested parties to elaborate the necessary proposals, while bearing in mind the need to consider these questions in a wider social and economic context;

the publication in appropriate periodicals of articles designed to make known and to compare, among the participating States, the most significant achievements and innovations;

a joint study with a view to the improvement and possible harmonization of the different systems used to in-

ventory and catalogue the historical monuments and places of cultural interest in their countries;
the study of the possibilities for organizing international courses for the training of specialists in different disciplines relating to restoration.
National minorities or regional cultures:
The participating States, recognizing the contribution that national minorities or regional cultures can make to co-operation among them in various fields of culture, intend, when such minorities or cultures exist within their territory, to facilitate this contribution, taking into account the legitimate interests of their members.
4. Co-operation and Exchanges in the Field of Education:
The participating States, conscious that the development of relations of an international character in the fields of education and science contributes to a better mutual understanding and is to the advantage of all peoples as well as to the benefit of future generations,
Prepared to facilitate, between organizations, institutions and persons engaged in education and science, the further development of exchanges of knowledge and experience as well as of contacts, on the basis of special arrangements where these are necessary,
Desiring to strengthen the links among educational and scientific establishments and also to encourage their co-operation in sectors of common interest, particularly where the levels of knowledge and resources require efforts to be concerted internationally, and
Convinced that progress in these fields should be accompanied and supported by a wider knowledge of foreign languages.
Express to these ends their intention in particular:
(a) Extension of Relations:
To expand and improve at the various levels co-operation and links in the fields of education and science, in particular by:
– concluding, where appropriate, bilateral or multilateral agreements providing for co-operation and exchanges among State institutions, non-governmental bodies and persons engaged in activities in education and science, bearing in mind the need both for flexibility and the fuller use of existing agreements and arrangements;
promoting the conclusion of direct arrangements between universities and other institutions of higher education and research, in the framework of agreements between governments where appropriate;
encouraging among persons engaged in education and science direct contacts and communications, including those based on special agreements or arrangements where these are appropriate.
(b) Access and Exchanges:
To improve access, under mutually acceptable conditions, for students, teachers and scholars of the participating States to each other's educational, cultural and scientific institutions, and to intensify exchanges among these institutions in all areas of common interest, in particular by:
increasing the exchange of information on facilities for study and courses open to foreign participants, as well as on the conditions under which they will be admitted and received;
facilitating travel between the participating States by scholars, teachers and students for purposes of study, teaching and research as well as for improving knowledge of each other's educational, cultural and scientific achievements;
encouraging the award of scholarships for study, teaching and research in their countries to scholars, teachers and students of other participating States;
establishing, developing or encouraging programmes providing for the broader exchange of scholars, teachers and students, including the organizations of symposia, seminars and collaborative projects, and the exchanges of educational and scholarly information such as university publications and materials from libraries;
– promoting the efficient implementation of such arrangements and programmes by providing scholars, teachers and students in good time with more detailed information about their placing in universities and institutes and the programmes envisaged for them; by granting them the opportunity to use relevant scholarly, scientific and open archival materials; and by facilitating their travel within the receiving State for the purpose of study or research as well as in the form of vacation tours on the basis of the usual procedures;

– promoting a more exact assessment of the problems of comparison and equivalence of academic degrees and diplomas by fostering the exchange of information on the organization, duration and content of studies, the comparison of methods of assessing levels of knowledge and academic qualifications, and, where feasible, arriving at the mutual recognition of academic degrees and diplomas either through governmental agreements, where necessary, or direct arrangements between universities and other institutions of higher learning and research;
– recommending, moreover, to the appropriate international organizations that they should intensify their efforts to reach a generally acceptable solution to the problems of comparison and equivalence between academic degrees and diplomas.
(c) Science:
Within their competence to broaden and improve co-operation and exchanges in the field of science, in particular:
To increase, on a bilateral or multilateral basis, the exchange and dissemination of scientific information and documentation by such means as:
– making this information more widely available to scientists and research workers of the other participating States through, for instance, participation in international information-sharing programmes or through other appropriate arrangements;
– broadening and facilitating the exchange of samples and other scientific materials used particularly for fundamental research in the fields of natural sciences and medicine;
– inviting scientific institutions and universities to keep each other more fully and regularly informed about their current and contemplated research work in fields of common interest. To facilitate the extension of communications and direct contacts between universities, scientific institutions and associations as well as among scientists and research workers, including those based where necessary on special agreements or arrangements, by such means as:
– further developing exchanges of scientists and research workers and encouraging the organizations of preparatory meetings or working groups on research topics of common interest;
– encouraging the creation of joint teams of scientists to pursue research projects under arrangements made by the scientific institutions of several countries;
– assisting the organization and successful functioning of international conferences and seminars and participation in them by their scientists and research workers;
– furthermore envisaging, in the near future, a 'Scientific Forum' in the form of a meeting of leading personalities in science from the participating States to discuss interrelated problems of common interest concerning current and future developments in science, and to promote the expansion of contacts, communications and the exchange of information between scientific institutions and among scientists;
– foreseeing, at an early date, a meeting of experts representing the participating States and their national scientific institutions, in order to prepare such a 'Scientific Forum' in consultation with appropriate international organizations, such as UNESCO and the ECE;
– considering in due course what further steps might be taken with respect to the 'Scientific Forum'.
To develop in the field of scientific research, on a bilateral or multilateral basis, the co-ordination of programmes carried out in the participating States and the organization of joint programmes, especially in the areas mentioned below, which may involve the combined efforts of scientists and in certain cases the use of costly or unique equipment. The list of subjects in these areas is illustrative; and specific projects would have to be determined subsequently by the potential partners in the participating States, taking account of the contribution which could be made by appropriate international organizations and scientific institutions:
exact and natural sciences, in particular fundamental research in such fields as mathematics, physics, theoretical physics, geophysics, chemistry, biology, ecology and astronomy;
medicine, in particular basic research into cancer and cardiovascular diseases, studies on the diseases endemic in the developing countries, as well as medico-social research with special emphasis on occupational

diseases, the rehabilitation of the handicapped and the care of mothers, children and the elderly;
the humanities and social sciences, such as history, geography, philosophy, psychology, pedagogical research, linguistics, the legal, political and economic sciences; comparative studies on social, socio-economic and cultural phenomena which are of common interest to the participating States, especially the problems of human environment and urban development; and scientific studies on the methods of conserving and restoring monuments and works of art.
(d) Foreign Languages and Civilizations:
To encourage the study of foreign languages and civilizations as an important means of expanding communication among peoples for their better acquaintance with the culture of each country, as well as for the strengthening of international co-operation; to this end to stimulate, within their competence, the further development and improvement of foreign language teaching and the diversification of choice of languages taught at various levels, paying due attention to less widely-spread or studied languages, and in particular:
to intensify co-operation aimed at improving the teaching of foreign languages through exchanges of information and experience concerning the development and application of effective modern teaching methods and technical aids, adapted to the needs of different categories of students, including methods of accelerated teaching; and to consider the possibility of conducting, on a bilateral or multilateral basis, studies of new methods of foreign language teaching;
to encourage co-operation between institutions concerned, on a bilateral or multilateral basis, aimed at exploiting more fully the resources of modern educational technology in language teaching, for example, through comparative studies by their specialists and, where agreed, through exchanges or transfers of audio-visual materials, of materials used for preparing textbooks, as well as of information about new types of technical equipment used for teaching languages;
to promote the exchange of information on the experience acquired in the training of language teachers and to intensify exchanges on a bilateral basis of language teachers and students as well as to facilitate their participation in summer courses in languages and civilizations, wherever these are organized;
to encourage co-operation among experts in the field of lexicography with the aim of defining the necessary terminological equivalents, particularly in the scientific and technical disciplines, in order to facilitate relations among scientific institutions and specialists;
to promote the wider spread of foreign language study among the different types of secondary education establishments and greater possibilities of choice between an increased number of European languages; and in this context to consider, wherever appropriate, the possibilities for developing the recruitment and training of teachers as well as the organization of the student groups required;
to favour, in higher education, a wider choice in the languages offered to language students and greater opportunities for other students to study various foreign languages; also to facilitate, where desirable, the organization of courses in languages and civilizations, on the basis of special arrangements as necessary, to be given by foreign lecturers, particularly from European countries having less widely-spread or studied languages;
to promote, within the framework of adult education, the further development of specialized programmes, adapted to various needs and interests, for teaching foreign languages to their own inhabitants and the languages of host countries to interested adults from other countries; in this context to encourage interested institutions to co-operate, for example, in the elaboration of programmes for teaching by radio and television and by accelerated methods, and also, where desirable, in the definition of study objectives for such programmes, with a view to arriving at comparable levels of language proficiency;
to encourage the association, where appropriate, of the teaching of foreign languages with the study of the corresponding civilizations and also to make further efforts to stimulate interest in the study of foreign languages, including relevant out-of-class activities.
(e) Teaching Methods:
To promote the exchange of experience, on a bilateral or multilateral basis, in reaching methods at all levels of

education, including those used in permanent and adult education, as well as the exchange of teaching materials, in particular by:

further developing various forms of contacts and co-operation in the different fields of pedagogical science, for example through comparative or joint studies carried out by interested institutions or through exchanges of information on the results of teaching experiments;

intensifying exchanges of information on teaching methods used in various educational systems and on results of research into the processes by which pupils and students acquire knowledge, taking account of relevant experience in different types of specialized education;

facilitating exchanges of experience concerning the organization and functioning of education intended for adults and recurrent education, the relationships between these and other forms and levels of education, as well as concerning the means of adapting education, including vocational and technical training, to the needs of economic and social development in their countries;

encouraging exchanges of experience in the education of youth and adults in international understanding, with particular reference to those major problems of mankind whose solution calls for a common approach and wider international co-operation;

encouraging exchanges of teaching materials – including school textbooks, having in mind the possibility of promoting mutual knowledge and facilitating the presentation of each country in such books – as well as exchanges of information on technical innovations in the field of education.

National minorities or regional cultures:

The participating States, recognizing the contribution that national minorities or regional cultures can make to co-operation among them in various fields of education, intend, when such minorities or cultures exist within their territory, to facilitate this contribution, taking into account the legitimate interests of their members.

Follow-up to the Conference

The participating States, having considered and evaluated the progress made at the Conference on Security and Co-operation in Europe,

Considering further that, within the broader context of the world, the Conference is an important part of the process of improving security and developing co-operation in Europe and that its results will contribute significantly to this process,

Intending to implement the provisions of the Final Act of the Conference in order to give full effect to its results and thus to further the process of improving security and co-operation in Europe,

Convinced that, in order to achieve the aims sought by the Conference, they should make further unilateral, bilateral and multilateral efforts and continue, in the appropriate forms set forth below, the multilateral process initiated by the Conference:

(1) Declare their resolve, in the period following the Conference, to pay due regard to and implement the provisions of the Final Act of the Conference:

(a) unilaterally, in all cases which lend themselves to such action;

(b) bilaterally, by negotiations with other participating States;

(c) multilaterally, by meetings of experts of the participating States, and also within the framework of existing international organizations, such as the United Nations Economic Commission for Europe and UNESCO, with regard to educational, scientific and cultural co-operation;

(2) Declare furthermore their resolve to continue the multilateral process initiated by the Conference:

(a) by proceeding to a thorough exchange of views both on the implementation of the provisions of the Final Act and of the tasks defined by the Conference, as well as, in the context of the questions dealt with by the latter, on the deepening of their mutual relations, the improvement of security and the development of co-operation in Europe, and the development of the process of détente in the future;

(b) by organizing to these ends meetings among their representatives, beginning with a meeting at the level of representatives appointed by the Ministers of Foreign Affairs. This meeting will define the appropriate modalities for the holding of other meetings which could include further similar meetings and the possibility of a new Conference;

(3) The first of the meetings indicated above will be held at Belgrade in 1977. A preparatory meeting to organize this meeting will be held at Belgrade on 15 June 1977. The preparatory meeting will decide on the date, duration, agenda and other modalities of the meeting of representatives appointed by the Ministers of Foreign Affairs;

(4) The rules of procedure, the working methods and the scale of distribution for the expenses of the Conference will, mutaris mutandis, be applied to the meetings envisaged in paragraphs 1(c), 2 and 3 above. All the above-mentioned meetings will be held in the participating States in rotation. The services of a technical secretariat will be provided by the host country.

The original of the Final Act, drawn up in English, French, German, Italian, Russian and Spanish, will be transmitted to the Government of the Republic of Finland, which will retain it in its archives. Each of the participating States will receive from the Government of the Republic of Finland a true copy of this Final Act. The text of this Final Act will be published in each participating State, which will disseminate it and make it known as widely as possible.

Done at Helsinki on 1st August 1975 in the name of: The Federal Republic of Germany, The German Democratic Republic, The United States of America, The Republic of Austria, The Kingdom of Belgium, The People's Republic of Bulgaria, Canada, The Republic of Cyprus, Denmark, Spain, The Republic of Finland, The French Republic, The United Kingdom of Great Britian, The Hellenic Republic, The Hungarian People's Republic, Ireland, Iceland, The Italian Republic, The Principality of Liechtenstein, The Grand Duchy of Luxembourg, The Republic of Malta, The Principality of Monaco, Norway, The Kingdom of the Netherlands, Polish People's Republic, Portugal, The Socialist Republic of Romania, San Marino, The Holy See, Sweden, The Swiss Confederation, The Czechoslovak Socialist Republic, The Republic of Turkey, The Union of Soviet Socialist Republics, The Socialist Federal Republic of Yugoslavia."

Conference on Security and Co-operation in Europe. Final Act, Helsinki, 1975.

HELSINKI RULES, 1966. A legal regulation concerning use of water for domestic and industrial purposes from international rivers, elaborated by the Helsinki Conference in Aug., 1966 of the Association of International Law.

International Rivers and Lakes. Official Documents, Washington, DC, 1967, pp. 609–621.

HEMATOLOGY. A subject of international co-operation. Organizations reg. with the UIA:

International Society of Hematology, f. 1946, Caracas. Official Relations with WHO.
International Society on Thrombosis and Haemostatis, f. 1969, Bethesda, Md. Research concerning blood coagulation. Publ.: *Thrombosis et Diathesis Hemorrhagica* (journal).
Society of Haematology and Blood Transfusion of African and Near Eastern Countries, f. 1965. Tunis.

Yearbook of International Organizations; M.M. WINTROBE, *Clinical Hematology*, London, 1967; W. RUDOWSKI (ed), *Disorder in Hemostatis in Surgery*, University Press of England, 1977.

HEMOPHILIA. A subject of international co-operation. Organizations reg. with the UIA:

Asian Hemophiliaes Rescue Association, f. 1975, Osaka.
World Federation of Hemophilia, f. 1963, Montreal. Official relations with WHO. Publ.: *Bulletin*.
Under the auspices of WFH a World Hemophilia AIDS Center, was established 1985 in Los Angeles, Calif., USA.

Yearbook of International Organizations, 1986/87.

HERALDRY. A subject of international co-operation. Organizations reg. with the UIA:

International Academy of Heraldry, f. 1949, Paris. Publ.: *Archivum heraldicum.*
International Society of Heraldry and Family Trees, f. 1976, Washington, DC.

Yearbook of International Organizations.

HERBICIDES. Plant-killing substances; one of the types of chemical weapons whose purpose is to destroy plants, shrubs and trees; the object of the Geneva Protocol prohibiting Chemical Weapons, 1925. Herbicides were discovered toward the end of the 19th century in weed-killing substances. These are arbocides which cause trees to dry out; defoliants which destroy leaves by depriving them of chlorophyll; desectants which dry out plants, and herbicides which have a lethal effect on a series of plants, and if ingested by consuming plants or drinking water infected by herbicides malformations in the foetus may result. The production of herbicides became an international problem due to use of herbicides in Vietnam. The US stated that it signed but did not ratify the Geneva Protocol of 1925. In May 1974 the American Academy of Science in Washington, DC, published a report on the effects of using herbicides in Viet Nam. The SIPRI findings include the following:

The intentional military destruction of vegetation in enemy territory, particularly the destruction of crops and forests, has been a continuing act of warfare for millennia – for example, references are found in the Bible and Roman history to the use of salt to destroy the fertility of fields, and the British used herbicides for counterinsurgency purposes in Malaya during the 1950s.

Herbicidal operations in Indochina were carried out between 1961 and 1971, with the peak years being 1967–69. South Viet Nam was the prime target with 10 per cent of its total area sprayed one or more times, but parts of Kampuchea, Laos and possibly North Viet Nam were also affected. The dense inland tropical rain forests and coastal mangrove swamps, habitats of a rich variety of flora and fauna with an innate and, in some cases, commercial value, were the targets of 86 per cent of the missions using mostly the compunds known as Agents Orange and White; attacks on crops accounted for 14 per cent of the missions using mostly Agent Blue.

G.C. HICKEY, *Effects of Herbicides in South Vietnam*, Washington, DC, 1974; A.H. WESTING, M. LUMSDEN, *Threat of Modern Warfare to Man and his Environment. An Annotated Bibliography*, UNESCO, Paris, 1979; A.H. WESTING, *Herbicides in War. The Long-Term Ecological and Human Consequences*, SIPRI, London, Philadelphia, 1984.

HEREROS AND HOTTENTOTS. A people of south and south-west Africa from a Bantu-speaking group, most of them killed in the course of German genocidal operation in Deutsche West Africa, now Namibia, during a rising 1904–07 against the colonial regime. Emperor Wilhelm II gave the notorious order in 1904 of complete extermination of Hereros and Hottentots (*Ausrottenbefehl*). In 1909 only several hundred survivors were reported. The name Herero or Ovaherero is vernacular, while Hottentot is Dutch to denote "stammerer", in vernacular it was Khoi-Khoin – "primaeval people". In 1970 the estimated population of Hereros was 55,000 Hottentots 80,000.

I. SHAPERA, *Khoisan Peoples of South Africa*, London, 1952; M. WILSON, L. THOMPSON, *The Oxford History of South Africa*, Vol. I, Oxford, 1969.

HERITAGE. ▷ UNESCO Heritage Protection.

HERITAGE WORLD COMMITTEE. The official shortened name for the Intergovernmental Committee for the Protection of Cultural and Natural

Heritage of Exceptional Universal Value, created by UNESCO by a Convention on the protection of the world cultural and natural heritage, 1972. The task of the Committee is to organize co-operation and international assistance for identifying and preserving this heritage. One of the initial tasks is to catalogue the list of objects of "world cultural and natural heritage" whose preservation is an obligation of mankind and also a list of monuments of this type threatened with destruction, for the purpose of undertaking rescue operations under the aegis of UNESCO. Up to 1984 140 items in *c.* 70 countries were on the list. The precursor of the World Committee is the International Federation of Associations for the Protection of Europe's Cultural and Natural Heritage, est. 1963, seat in London, reg. with the UIA.

UNESCO, *Patrimoine Culturel de l'Humanité*, Paris, 1983; *Yearbook of International Organizations.*

HERM. ▷ Bailiwick of Guernsey.

HEROIN. Diacetyl ▷ morphine, having the chemical formula $C_{21}H_{23}NO_5$. A subject of international ▷ Opium Conventions 1912 and 1925. The WHO has recommended replacing heroin as a pain reliever by less dangerous synthetic analgesics. In the 1980's most countries followed the WHO recommendation on both the manufacture and use of heroin.

UN Chronicle, March, 1978, p. 25; *UN Chronicle*, May 1987; N. DORN, N. SOUTH, *A Land Fit for Heroin--Drugs Policies in the 1980's*, London, 1987.

HERRERA REPORT, 1976. A study conducted 1970–75 within the Argentinian Bariloche Foundation by a team of Latin American scholars headed by A.O. Herrera, of a model of world progress called, *Catastrophe of New Society?* The report proposed an alternative to global catastrophe, similar to the Third Report of the ▷ Club of Rome, involving nationalization of world natural resources and a universal democratic system; it also claimed that mankind had, in principle, the features of a socialist society and should be based on equality and full participation of all people in decisions of significance to their fate.

A.O. HERRERA, *Catastrophe or New Society? A Latin American World Model*, Ottawa, 1976.

HERRING. *Clupes harengus.* An ocean fish, lives in the northern Pacific and Atlantic and in adjacent seas. In the decade of the 1970s there was a sudden fall in herring stocks, leading in 1977 to the first international convention on the limitation of herring catches.

HIBERNATION. A scientific international term first used in early 20th century in connection with the application of artificial hibernation (the state of artificially lowered intensity of processes in organisms). Subject of international scientific co-operation since the First International Meeting for Hibernation in Massachusetts which in 1960 established the Hibernation Information Exchange; headquarters Chicago; Publ.: *HIE Information Sheet*. Org. reg. with the UIA.

International Hibernation Society, f. 1960, Rockville Md., USA. Publ.: *Newsletter.*

Yearbook of International Organizations 1986/87 The Europa Yearbook 1988. A World Survey, Vol. I, London 1988.

HICKENLOOPER AMENDMENT, 1964. ▷ Expropriation.

HIDES AND SKINS. The subject of international co-operation and conventions, especially of the International Agreement between the Governments of Austria, Belgium, Bulgaria, Czechoslovakia, Denmark, Finland, France, Germany, Hungary, Italy, Luxembourg, the Netherlands, Norway, Poland, Romania, Sweden, Switzerland, Turkey and the UK, relating to the Exportation of Hides and Skins. It was signed on July 11, 1928 in Geneva and a Protocol was signed on Sept. 11, 1929. Art. 1 states that "the exportation of raw or prepared hides and skins shall not be subject to any prohibition or restrictions."

LNTS, Vol. 45, p. 357.

HIGH SEAS CONVENTION, 1958. A convention elaborated and adopted by the UN Conference on the Law of Sea, held in Geneva, from Feb. 24 to Apr. 27, 1958, and signed in Geneva, Apr. 29, 1958 by the governments of Afghanistan, Argentina, Australia, Austria, Bolivia, Bulgaria, Byelorussia, Canada, Ceylon, China, Colombia, Costa Rica, Cuba, Czechoslovakia, Denmark, the Dominican Republic, Finland, France, the FRG, Ghana, Guatemala, Haiti, the Holy See, Hungary, Iceland, Indonesia, Iran, Ireland, Israel, Lebanon, Liberia, Nepal, the Netherlands, New Zealand, Pakistan, Panama, Poland, Portugal, Romania, Switzerland, Thailand, Tunisia, Ukraine, the UK, Uruguay, the USA, the USSR, Venezuela and Yugoslavia. Came into force on Sept. 30, 1962. The text of the Convention is as follows:

"The States Parties to this Convention, Desiring to codify the rules of international law relating to the high seas, recognizing that the United Nations Conference on the Law of Sea, held at Geneva from 24 February to 27 April 1958, adopted the following provisions as generally declaratory of established principles of international law, Have agreed as follows:

Art. 1. The term 'high seas' means all parts of the sea that are not included in the territorial sea or in the internal waters of a State.

Art. 2. The high seas being open to all nations, no State may validly purport to subject any part of them to its sovereignty. Freedom of the high seas is exercised under the conditions laid down by these articles and by the other rules of international law. It comprises, inter alia, both for coastal and non-coastal States:

(1) Freedom of navigation;
(2) Freedom of fishing;
(3) Freedom to lay submarine cables and pipelines;
(4) Freedom to fly over the high seas.

These freedoms, and others which are recognized by the general principles of international law, shall be exercised by all States with reasonable regard to the interests of other States in their exercise of the freedom of the high seas.

Art. 3.(1) In order to enjoy the freedom of the seas on equal terms with coastal States, States having no sea-coast should have free access to the sea. To this end States situated between the sea and a State having no sea-coast shall by common agreement with the latter, and in conformity with existing international conventions, accord:

(a) To the State having no sea-coast, on the basis of reciprocity, free transit through their territory; and

(b) To ships flying the flag of that State treatment equal to that accorded to their own ships, or to the ships of any other States, as regards access to sea-ports.

(2) States situated between the sea and a State having no sea-coast shall settle, by mutual agreement with the latter, and taking into account the rights of the coastal State or State of transit and the special conditions of the State having no sea-coast, all matters relating to freedom of transit and equal treatment in ports, in case such States are not already parties to existing international conventions.

Art. 4. Every State, whether coastal or not, has the right to sail ships under its flag on the high seas.

Art. 5.(1) Each State shall fix the conditions for the grant of its nationality to ships, for the registration of ships in its territory, and for the right to fly its flag. Ships have nationality of the State whose flag they are entitled

to fly. There must exist a genuine link between the State and the ship; in particular, the State must effectively exercise its jurisdiction and control in administrative, technical and social matters over ships flying its flag.

(2) Each State shall issue to ships to which it has granted the right to fly its flag documents to that effect.

Art. 6.(1) Ships shall sail under the flag of one State only and, save in exceptional cases expressly provided for in international treaties or in these articles, shall be subject to its exclusive jurisdiction on the high seas. A ship may not change its flag during a voyage or while in a port of call, save in the case of a real transfer of ownership or change of registry.

(2) A ship which sails under the flags of two or more States, using them according to convenience, may not claim any of the nationalities in question with respect to any other State, and may be assimilated to a ship without nationality.

Art. 7. The provisions of the preceding articles do not prejudice the question of ships employed on the official service of an inter-governmental organization flying the flag of the organization.

Art. 8.(1) Warships on the high seas have complete immunity from the jurisdiction of any State other than the flag State.

(2) For the purposes of these articles, the term 'warship' means a ship belonging to the naval forces of a State and bearing the external marks distinguishing warships of its nationality, under the command of an officer duly commissioned by the government and whose name appears in the Navy List, and manned by a crew who are under regular naval discipline.

Art. 9. Ships owned or operated by a State and used only on government non-commercial service shall, on the high seas, have complete immunity from the jurisdiction of any State other than the flag State.

Art. 10.(1) Every State shall take such measures for ships under its flag as are necessary to ensure safety at sea with regard inter alia to:

(a) The use of signals, the maintenance of communications and prevention of collisions;

(b) The manning of ships and labour conditions for crews taking into account the applicable international labour instruments;

(c) The construction, equipment and seaworthiness of ships.

(2) In taking such measures each State is required to conform to generally accepted international standards and to take any steps which may be necessary to ensure their observance.

Art. 11(1) In the event of a collision or of any other incident of navigation concerning a ship on the high seas, involving the penal or disciplinary responsibility of the master or of any other person in the service of the ship, no penal or disciplinary proceedings may be instituted against such persons except before the judicial or administrative authorities either of the flag State or of the State of which such person is a national.

(2) In disciplinary matters, the State which has issued a master's certificate or a certificate of competence or licence shall alone be competent, after due legal process, to pronounce the withdrawal of such certificates, even if the holder is not a national of the State which issued them.

(3) No arrest or detention of the ship, even as a measure of investigation, shall be ordered by authorities other than those of the flag State.

Art. 12.(1) Every State shall require the master of a ship sailing under its flag in so far as he can do without serious danger to the ship, the crew or the passengers,

(a) To render assistance to any person found at sea in danger of being lost;

(b) To proceed with all possible speed to the rescue of persons in distress if informed of their need of assistance, in so far as such action may reasonably be expected of him;

(c) After a collision, to render assistance to the other ship, her crew and her passengers and, where possible, to inform the other ship of the name of his own ship, her port of registry and the nearest port at which she will call.

(2) Every coastal State shall promote the establishment and maintenance of an adequate and effective search and rescue service regarding safety on and over sea and – where circumstances so require – by way of mutual regional arrangements co-operate with neighbouring States for this purpose.

Art. 13. Every State shall adopt effective measures to prevent and punish the transport of slaves in ships authorized to fly its flag, and to prevent the unlawful use of its flag for that purpose. Any slave taking refuge on board any ship, whatever its flag, shall ipso facto be free.

Art. 14. All States shall co-operate to the fullest possible extent in the repression of piracy on the high seas or in any other place outside the jurisdiction of any State.

Art. 15. Piracy consists of any of the following acts:

(1) Any illegal acts of violence, detention or any act of depredation, committed for private ends by the crew or the passengers of a private ship or a private aircraft, and directed:

(a) On the high seas, against another ship or aircraft, or against persons or property on board such ship or aircraft;

(b) Against a ship, aircraft, persons of property in a place outside the jurisdiction of any State;

(2) Any act of voluntary participation in the operation of a ship or of an aircraft with knowledge of facts making it a pirate ship or aircraft;

(3) Any act of inciting or intentionally facilitating an act described in sub-paragraph 1 or sub-paragraph 2 of this art.

Art. 16. The acts of piracy, as defined in Art. 15, committed by a warship, government ship or government aircraft whose crew has mutinied and taken control of the ship or aircraft are assimilated to acts committed by a private ship.

Art. 17. A ship or aircraft is considered a pirate ship or aircraft if it is intended by the persons in dominant control to be used for the purpose of committing one of the acts referred to in Art. 15. The same applies if the ship or aircraft has been used to commit any such act, so long as it remains under the control of the persons guilty of that act.

Art. 18. A ship or aircraft may retain its nationality although it has become a pirate ship or aircraft. The retention or loss of nationality is determined by the law of the State from which such nationality was derived.

Art. 19. On the high seas, or in any other place outside the jurisdiction of any State, every State may seize a pirate ship or aircraft, or a ship taken by piracy and under the control of pirates, and arrest the persons and seize the property on board. The courts of the State which carried out the seizure may decide upon the penalties to be imposed and may also determine the action to be taken with regard to the ships, aircraft or property, subject to the rights of third parties acting in good faith.

Art. 20. Where the seizure of a ship or aircraft on suspicion of piracy has been effected without adequate grounds, the State making the seizure shall be liable to the State the nationality of which is possessed by the ship or aircraft, for any loss or damage caused by the seizure.

Art. 21. A seizure on account of piracy may only be carried out by warships or military aircraft, or other ships or aircraft on government service authorized to the effect.

Art. 22.(1) Except where acts of interference derive from powers conferred by treaty, a warship which encounters a foreign merchant ship on the high seas is not justified in boarding her unless there is reasonable ground for suspecting:

(a) That the ship is engaged in piracy; or

(b) That the ship is engaged in the slave trade; or

(c) That though flying a foreign flag or refusing to show its flag, the ship is, in reality, of the same nationality as the warship.

(2) In the cases provided for in sub-paragraphs (a), (b), and (c) above, the warship may proceed to verify the ship's right to fly its flag. To this end, it may send a boat under the command of an officer to the suspected ship. If suspicion remains after the documents have been checked, it may proceed to a further examination on board the ship, which must be carried out with all possible consideration.

(3) If the suspicions prove to be unfounded, and provided that the ship boarded has not committed any act justifying them, it shall be compensated for any loss or damage that may have been sustained.

Art. 23.(1) The hot pursuit of a foreign ship may be undertaken when the competent authorities of the coastal State have good reason to believe that the ship has violated the laws and regulations of that State. Such pursuit must be commenced when the foreign ship or one of its boats is within the internal waters or the territorial sea of the contiguous zone of the pursuing State, and may only be continued outside the territorial sea or the contiguous zone if the pursuit has not been interrupted. It is not necessary that, at the time when the foreign ship within the territorial sea or the contiguous zone receives the order to stop, the ship giving the order should likewise be within the territorial sea or the contiguous zone. If the foreign ship is within a contiguous zone, as defined in art. 24 of the Convention on the Territorial Sea and the Contiguous Zone, the pursuit may only be undertaken if there has been a violation of the rights for the protection of which the zone was established.

(2) The right of hot pursuit ceases as the ship pursued enters the territorial sea of its own country or of a third State.

(3) Hot pursuit is not deemed to have begun unless the pursuing ship has satisfied by such practicable means as may be available that the ship pursued or one of its boats or other craft working as a team and using the ship pursued as a mother ship are within the limits of the territorial sea, or as the case may be within the contiguous zone. The pursuit may only be commenced after a visual or auditory signal to stop has been given at a distance which enables it to be seen or heard by the foreign ship.

(4) The right of hot pursuit may be exercised only by warships or military aircraft, or other ships or aircraft on government service specially authorized to that effect.

(5) Where hot pursuit is effected by an aircraft:

(a) The provisions of paragraph 1 to 3 of this art. shall apply mutatis mutandis;

(b) The aircraft giving the order to stop must itself actively pursue the ship until a ship or aircraft of the coastal State, summoned by the aircraft, arrives to take over the pursuit, unless the aircraft is itself able to arrest the ship. It does not suffice to justify an arrest on the high seas that the ship was merely sighted by the aircraft as an offender or suspected offender, if it was not both ordered to stop and pursued by the aircraft itself or other aircraft or ships which continue the pursuit without interruption.

(6) The release of a ship arrested within the jurisdiction of a state and escorted to a port of that State for the purposes of an enquiry before the competent authorities may not be claimed solely on the ground that the ship, in the course of its voyage, was escorted across a portion of the high seas, if the circumstances rendered this necessary.

(7) Where a ship has been stopped or arrested on the high seas in circumstances which do not justify the exercise of the right of hot pursuit, it shall be compensated for any loss or damage that may have been thereby sustained.

Art. 24. Every State shall draw up regulations to prevent pollution of the seas by the discharge of oil from ships or pipelines or resulting from the exploitation and exploration of the seabed and its subsoil, taking account of existing treaty provisions on the subject.

Art. 25.(1) Every State shall take measures to prevent pollution of the seas from the dumping of radio-active waste, taking into account any standards and regulations which may be formulated by the competent international organizations.

(2) All States shall co-operate with the competent international organizations in taking measures for the prevention of pollution of the seas or air space above, resulting from any activities with radio-active materials or other harmful agents.

Art. 26.(1) All States shall be entitled to lay submarine cables and pipelines on the bed of the high seas.

(2) Subject to its right to take reasonable measure for the exploration of the continental shelf and the exploitation of its natural resources, the coastal State may not impede the laying or maintenance of such cables or pipelines.

(3) When laying such cables or pipelines the State in question shall pay due regard to cables or pipelines already in position on the seabed. In particular, possibilities of repairing existing cables or pipelines shall not be prejudiced.

Art. 27. Every State shall take the necessary legislative measures to provide that the breaking or injury by flying its flag or by a person subject to its jurisdiction of a submarine cable beneath the high seas done wilfully or through culpable negligence, in such a manner as to be liable to interrupt or obstruct telegraphic or telephonic communications, and similarly the breaking or injury of a submarine pipeline or high-voltage power cable shall be a punishable offence. This provision shall not apply to any break or injury caused by persons who acted merely with the legitimate object of saving their lives or ships, after having taken all necessary precautions to avoid such break or injury.

Art. 28. Every State shall take the necessary legislative measures to provide that, if persons subject to its jurisdiction who are the owners of a cable or pipeline beneath the high seas, in laying or repairing that cable or pipeline, cause a break in or injury to another cable or pipeline, they shall bear the cost of the repairs.

Art. 29. Every State shall take the necessary legislative measures to ensure that the owners of ships who can prove that they have sacrificed an anchor, a net or any other fishing gear, in order to avoid injuring a submarine cable or pipeline, shall be indemnified by the owner of the cable or pipeline, provided that the owner of the ship has taken all reasonable precautionary measures beforehand.

Art. 30. The provisions of this Convention shall not affect conventions or other international agreements already in force, as between States Parties to them.

Art. 31. This Convention shall, until 31 October 1958, be open for signature by all States Members of the United Nations or of any of specialized agencies, and by any other State invited by the General Assembly of the United Nations to become a Party to the Convention.

Art. 32. This Convention is subject to ratification. The instruments of ratification shall be deposited with the Secretary-General of the United Nations.

Art. 33. This Convention shall be open for accession by any States belonging to any of the categories mentioned in art. 31. The instruments of accession shall be deposited with the Secretary-General of the United Nations.

Art. 34.(1) This Convention shall come into force on the thirtieth day following the date of deposit of the twenty-second instrument of ratification or accession with the Secretary-General of the United Nations.

(2) For each State ratifying or acceding to the Convention after the deposit of the twenty-second instrument of ratification or accession, the Convention shall enter into force on the thirtieth day after deposit by such State of its instrument of ratification or accession.

Art. 35.(1) After the expiration of a period of five years from the date on which this Convention shall enter into force, a request for the revision of this Convention may be made at any time by any Contracting Party by means of notification in writing addressed to the Secretary-General of the United Nations.

(2) The General Assembly of the United Nations shall decide upon the steps, if any, to be taken in respect of such request.

Art. 36. The Secretary-General of the United Nations shall inform all States Members of the United Nations and the other States referred to in art. 31:

(a) Of signatures to this Convention and of the deposit of instruments of ratification or accession, in accordance with ars. 31, 32 and 33;

(b) Of the date on which this Convention will come into force, in accordance with art. 34;

(c) Of request for revision in accordance with art. 35.

Art. 37. The original of this Convention, of which the Chinese, English, French, Russian and Spanish texts are equally authentic, shall be deposited with the Secretary-General of the United Nations, who shall send certified copies thereof to all States referred to in art. 31.

UNTS, Vol. 450, pp. 82–102 and 169.

HIGH VOLTAGE CMEA LABORATORIES. CMEA institution est. 1973, by an Agreement on Co-operation of Large Capacity and High Voltage Experimental Laboratories, signed on Oct. 18, 1973 at Brno by Bulgaria, Czechoslovakia, the GDR, Hungary, Poland, Romania, the USSR and Yugoslavia. The agreement created the International Organization for Co-operation in Large Capacity and High Voltage Experimental Laboratories under the name "Interelekrotest".

Recueil de Documents, Varsovie, No. 10, 1973; W.E. BUTLER (ed.), *A Source Book on Socialist International Organizations*, Alphen, 1978, pp. 864–871.

HIGHWAYS. The automobile roads; first constructed by Italy 1922–24 on the route Milan–Varese; subject of international agreements, statistics and organizations (▷ Roads, International and Intercontinental).

HIJACKING. ▷ Air piracy. ▷ Cuba – USA Understanding on Hijacking, 1973.

HILLSBOROUGH ACCORD, 1985. An Anglo-Irish Agreement, signed on Nov. 15, 1985 by the Prime Ministers of the UK and of Ireland, at Hillsborough Castle (former residence of British governors in Northern Ireland).
Article 1 of the Accord reads as follows:
"The two governments (a) affirm that any change in the status of Northern Ireland would only come about with the consent of a majority of the people of Northern Ireland; (b) recognize that the present wish of the majority of the people of Northern Ireland is for no change in the status of Northern Ireland; (c) declare that, if in the future a majority of the people of Northern Ireland clearly wish for and formally consent to the establishment of a united Ireland, they will introduce and support in the respective parliaments legislation to give effect to that wish".
Article 2, after providing for the establishment of the Inter-Government Conference, continued:
"The UK government accept that the Irish government will put forward views and proposals on matters relating to Northern Ireland within the field of activity of the Conference in so far as those matters are not the responsibility of a developed administration in Northern Ireland ... The Conference will be mainly concerned with Northern Ireland, but some of the matters under consideration will involve co-operative action in both parts of the island of Ireland, and possibly also in Great Britain. Some of the proposals considered in respect of Northern Ireland may also be found to have application by the Irish government. There is no derogation from the sovereignty of either the UK government or the Irish government and each retains responsibility for the decisions and administration of government within its own jurisdiction".
The accord was approved by the Irish parliament (Dáil) on Nov. 21, 1985 by 88 votes to 75 and by the Irish senate on Nov. 28, 1985 by 37 votes to 16; the House of Lords on Nov. 26, 1985 approved the Accord, and House of Commons voted 473 in favour, and 47 against, on Nov. 27, 1985.
The meetings of the States Governmental Conference established under the 1985 Accord are held at regular intervals since 1986 in Belfast, in London or in Dublin.

"The Northern Ireland Question", in: A.J. DAY, ed., *The Border and Territorial Disputes*, London, 1987.

HIMALAYAS, THE. The world's highest mountain range, in South Asia separating China from Pakistan, India, Nepal, Bhutan and Bangladesh. The highest summit Mt. Everest (8848 m) conquered in 1953 by New Zealander E. Hillary and Sherpa T. Norkay; the first woman to reach the peak – W. Rutkiewicz, Poland, 1978.

HINDUISM. According to B. Walker's definition: hinduism is the religious beliefs and social observances of the Hindus who form the bulk of the population of India, excluding the Muslim, Buddhist, Zoroastrian, Jewish and Christian minorities.

A.C. BOUQUET, *Hinduism*, London, 1948; S.C. CHATTERJEE, *The Fundamentals of Hinduism*, Calcutta, 1950; K.M. SON, *Hinduism*, London, 1961; B. WALKER, *Hindu World. An Encyclopaedic Survey of Hinduism*, 2 Vols, London, 1968.

HIPPOCRATIC OATH. A medical ethical code promoted by the WHO, formulated by Greek physician Hippocrates (*c.* 400 BC), "father of medicine" and accepted throughout the ages up to today by many schools of medicine, especially in Europe and America as medical oaths sworn by doctors during the graduation ceremony. The text is as follows:
"I will look upon him who shall have taught me this Art even as one of my parents. I will share my substance with him, and I will supply his necessities, if he be in need. I will regard his offspring even as my own brethren and I will teach them this Art, if they would learn it, without fee or covenant. I will impart this Art by precept, by lecture and by every mode of teaching not only to my own sons but to the sons of him who has taught me, and to disciples bound by covenant and oath, according to the Law of Medicine. The regimen I adopt shall be for the benefit of my patients according to my ability and judgment and not for their hurt or for any wrong. I will give no deadly drug to any, though it be asked of me, nor will I counsel such, and especially I will not aid a woman to procure abortion. Whatsoever house I enter, there will I go for the benefit of the sick, refraining from all wrongdoing or corruption, and especially from any act of seduction, of male or female, of bond or free. Whatsoever things I see or hear concerning the life of men in my attendance on the sick or even apart therefrom, which ought not to be to noised abroad, I will keep silence thereon, counting such things to be as sacred secrets."

Handbook of Resolutions and Decisions of the WHO, 1948–1972, Geneva, 1973.

HIROSHIMA AND NAGASAKI. The first (Pop. 1985 census: 1,044,000) – capital of Hiroshima prefecture, SW Honshu, Japan, on Hiroshima Bay; the second: city and port (Pop, 1985 census: 449,000) – capital of Nagasaki prefecture, west Kyushu, Japan; on Nagasaki Bay; two cities in Japan where on Aug. 6 and 9, 1945, at the order of US President H.S. Truman, US military aircraft dropped two atomic bombs. According to the *White Book of Japan* about the consequences of the two explosions submitted to UN on June 25, 1961, the bombs caused the death of over 200,000 people in Hiroshima and about 100,000 in Nagasaki, whereas the official US government data referred to 70,000–80,000 victims and the same number of wounded in Hiroshima and 40,000 dead and 25,000 injured in Nagasaki. A gutted area in Hiroshima, the 'Peace City' remains unreconstructed as a memorial. At the end of the 1980's the destructive power of a modern nuclear missile is 60–70 times larger that that of the bomb dropped on Hiroshima.

J. HERSHEY, *Hiroshima*, New York, 1946; H. STIMSON, "The decision to use the atomic bomb", in: *Harper's Magazine*, Feb. 20, 1947; G. ALPEROVITZ, *Atomic Diplomacy: Hiroshima and Potsdam. The Use of the Atomic Bomb and the American Confrontation with Soviet Power*, New York, 1955; L. GIOVATETTIX, F. FREED, *The Decision to Drop the Bomb*, New York, 1965; R.J. LIFTON, *Death in Life: Survivors of Hiroshima*, New York, 1967; R. LEGER SILVARD, *World Military and Social Expenditures 1987–88*, Washington DC, 1987.

HISPANIC POPULATION IN THE USA. An international term for the US population of Hispanic extraction. According to a Census Bureau report, Sept. 10, 1987, the 18.8 million Hispanic Americans (1980–14.5 million) have a relatively high birth rate and their number is increasing due to legal and illegal immigration. The majority are of Mexican origin–11.8 million; from Puerto Rico–2.3 million and from Central and South America–2.1 million.

R. PEAR, "US Records Rapid Growth in Hispanic Population Since 1980", in: *International Herald Tribune*, Sept. 12-13, 1987.

HISPANIDAD. A term denoting supra-national and supra-governmental spiritual and cultural community with the Spanish motherland of former colonial territories remaining within the sphere of influence of Spanish culture in Latin America, Africa and the Philippines. The Consejo de Hispanidad operating in Madrid since 1946, has the aim of fostering communications between Spain and countries of the aforementioned regions, one of the forms being bilateral agreements on double citizenship.

M. ARTAJO, *Hacia la Comunidad Hispánica de Naciones*, Madrid, 1956.

HISPANIOLA. An island of the West Indies in the Caribbean Sea between Cuba and Puerto Rico; occupied in western part by the Haiti Republic, the remainder by the Dominican Republic. Area: 76,482 sq. km.

HISPANISTS ASSOCIATION. Organization reg. with the UIA:
International Association of Hispanists, f. 1962, Oxford. Publ.: *Actas* (triennial).
Yearbook of International Organizations.

HISTORICAL COMPROMISE DOCTRINE. COMPROMESSO STORICO. An Italian term, adopted internationally, coined in 1975 by the Italian Communist Party as a political program of co-operation of all political groups in Italy from left to the right with the exception of fascist groups.

HISTORIC SITES DAY. An International Monuments and Historic Sites Day was proclaimed by UNESCO, Apr. 18, 1984.

HISTORIC VALUE PROPERTY PROTECTION. A subject of a Treaty on Protection of Movable Property of Historic Value, signed by the member states of the Pan American Union on Apr. 15, 1935, ratified by Chile (1936), El Salvador (1936), Guatemala (1936), Mexico (1939) and Nicaragua (1935). It entered into force on May 1, 1936. The Preamble and Art. 1 are as follows:
"The High Contracting Parties, desirous of securing, by means of cooperation, for all the Signatory States the knowledge, protection, and preservation of movable monuments of the pre-Columbian and Colonial periods and of the epoch of emancipation and the republic, which exist in each of them have resolved to celebrate a convention, and to this end have agreed on the following articles:
Art. 1. For the purpose of this Treaty, the following shall be considered as movable monuments:
(a) Of the pre-Columbian period: arms and war and implements of labor, pottery, woven fabrics, jewels and amulets, engravings, drawings and codices, guipure, costumes, adornments, of all sorts, and in general all movable objects which by their nature or origin show that they are separated from some immovable monument which belongs authentically to that period of history.
(b) Of the Colonial period: arms of war and implements of labor, costumes, medals, coins, amulets and jewels, drawings, paintings, plans and geographical charts, codices, and rare books, objects of gold and silver, porcelain, ivory, tortoise-shell, and lace, and, in general association articles having historic or artistic value.
(c) Of the period of emancipation and the republic: objects included in the above paragraph which belong to this period.
(d) Of all periods: (1) Official and institutional libraries, private libraries valuable as a whole, national archives and collections of manuscripts, both official and private, having a high historic significance: (2) as natural movable wealth, zoological specimens of beautiful and rare species threatened with extermin-

ation or natural extinction and whose preservation may be necessary to the study of the fauna."

Treaty on the Protection of Historic Value Property. OAS Treaty Series, No. 28, Washington, DC, 1962.

HISTORY. A subject of international co-operation. Organizations reg. with the UIA:

European Association for Contemporary History, f. 1968, Strasbourg.
International Association for the History of Religion, f. 1950, Marburg, FRG.
International Commission for the Teaching of History, f. 1956, Brussels.
International Committee for Historical Science, f. 1926, Paris. Publ.: *Bibliographic international des sciences historiques (1926–1939, 1946–1969), Bulletin d'Information.*
International Committee on the History of Art, f. 1900, Strasbourg, Publ.: *Repetoire d'art.*
International Committee for the Publication of Documentation History, f. 1968, Paris.
International Institute of Social History, f. 1935, Amsterdam.
International Society for the History of Ideas, f. 1960, New York. Publ.: *Journal of the History of Ideas.*
International Union of Prehistoric and Protohistoric Sciences, f. 1931, Ghent, Belgium.
Pan-American Institute of Geography and History, f. 1928, Mexico, DF.

Yearbook of International Organizations, 1986/87; The Europa Yearbook 1988. A World Survey, Vol. I, London, 1988; *The Harper Atlas of History*, New York, 1987.

HISTORY OF WORLD WAR II. A subject of international research by the Comité international d'histoire de la 2-ème guerre mondiale, International Committee for History of World War II, f. 1951, Paris. Publ.: *La Revue d'histoire de la 2-ème guerre mondiale.*

Yearbook of International Organizations.

HISTORY, TEACHING OF. A subject of international conventions and disputes. The Seventh International Conference of American States approved on Dec. 26, 1933 at Montevideo a Convention on the Teaching of History, signed by 18 Latin American Republics, which came into force on July 17, 1936; ratified by Brazil, Colombia, the Dominican Republic, Ecuador, Guatemala, Honduras, Mexico and Panama.
A Declaration regarding the Teaching of History was signed under the aegis of the League of Nations on Oct. 20, 1937 in Geneva; undersigned by Afghanistan, the Union of South Africa, Argentina, Belgium, Chile, Colombia, the Dominican Republic, Egypt, Estonia, Greece, Iran, Norway, the Netherlands, and Sweden; entered into force on Nov. 24, 1937. ▷ School Textbooks.

LNTS, Vol. 182, p. 263; *CARNEGIE ENDOWMENT, International Conferences of American States.* First Supplement 1933–1940, Washington, DC, 1940.

HI-TECH, HIGH TECHNOLOGY. An international term of the 1980's. See ▷ Scientific and Technological Revolution.

H. PATRICK ed., *Japan's High Technology Industries: Lessons and Limitations of Industrial Policy*, Seattle, 1986; T.W. RUSHING, C. GANZ eds., *National Policies for Developing High Technology Industries: International Comparisons*, Boulder, Col., 1986.

HIV. Acronym of Human Immunodeficiency Virus which causes ▷ AIDS.

HOA. The Chinese name for a Chinese living permanently outside China, meaning "residing in a foreign country."

HO CHI MINH CITY. Formerly ▷ Saigon. A city in South Vietnam; the new name was proclaimed together with the unification of North and South Vietnam into the Socialistic Republic of Vietnam on July 2, 1976. Area 1845 sq. km. Pop. 1986 est. 4 million.

J. PAXTON ed., *The Statesman's Yearbook 1987/88*, London, 1987.

HOCKEY. A subject of international co-operation. Organizations reg. with the UIA:

Federation of Women's Hockey Associations, f. 1927, London.
International Hockey Federation, f. 1924, Paris; recognized by International Olympic Committee, 1924; Publ.: *Bulletin.*
International Ice Hockey Federation, f. 1908, Antwerp; recognized by International Olympic Committee, 1924.

Yearbook of International Organizations.

HOLDING. An international term for the exercise of control by one firm (or by a bank) over another through the purchase of part or all of its shares; the controlling firm is called the Holding Company. The main center of European holding societies is Luxembourg, where the International Holding societies in Luxembourg operate. From July 31, 1929 a law has been in force there (modified Sept. 9, 1965) which guarantees foreign capital free movement without state control on the basis of anonymous holding companies. The amendments of 1965 expanded the privileges of the companies.

HOLIDAYS. A subject of international research. Since 1980 the Morgan Guaranty Trust Company in New York published annually a *World Calendar of Holidays*, formerly issued as *Bank and Public Holidays Throughout the World*. The same kind of information is published monthly in the *ABC World Airways Guide.*

HOLOCAUST, THE. *Greek*: "holokauston" = burnt whole. An international term for burnt sacrifices or destruction by fire. After World War II synonymous with the crime of genocide against six million Jews murdered by the Nazis 1939–45. The term was introduced in literature and press in the 1960s but popularized world wide in 1979 by an American film "The Holocaust". In Washington DC a US Holocaust Memorial Museum was built in the late 1980's. A review of secret ▷ Red Cross files from World War II concluded in February 1989 that "the Red Cross shared the same blindness as the Allies on this (Holocaust) question".

G. REITLINGER, *The Final solution*, London, 1953; L. POLIAKOV, *Harvest of Hate*, London, 1954; R. HILBERG, *The Destruction of the European Jews*, New York, 1961; W. BARTOSZEWSKI, Z. LEWIN, *The Samaritans, Heroes of the Holocaust*, New York, 1970; A. HILLGRUBER, "War in the East and the Extermination of the Jews", in: *Yad Vashem Studies*, 1987; B. WYTWYCKY, *The Other Holocaust: Many of Circles of Hell*, Washington DC, 1980; R.C. LUKAS, *The Forgotten Holocaust: the Poles under German Occupation 1939–1944*, Lexington Ky., 1986; M.R. MARRUS, *The Holocaust in History*, University Press of New England, 1987; S. ZUCCOTTI, *The Italians and the Holocaust*, New York, 1987; J.C. FAVEZ, *Une Mission impossible?* Geneve 1989; E. CODY, "Study says Red Cross Did Too Little to Help Jews in World War II", in: *The Washington Post*, Feb. 17, 1989.

HOLY ALLIANCE. A term suggested by Tsar Alexander to name the alliance of Austria, Prussia and Russia, signed on Sept. 26, 1815 in Paris, by Francis I of Austria, Frederick William III of Prussia and Alexander I of Russia. The Act of Holy Alliance was written in French and expressed the absolute solidarity of the three conservative monarchs

(Catholic, Protestant and Orthodox) in the face of rising revolutionary movements in Europe.
The Russian-language version published in Russia was first edited by Alexander I and disapproved of by Francis I and Frederick William III. The text of the French version in English translation is as follows:

"In the Name of the Most Holy and Indivisible Trinity Holy Alliance of Sovereigns of Austria, Prussia, and Russia. Their Majesties the Emperor of Austria, the King of Prussia, and the Emperor of Russia, having, in consequence of the great events which have marked the course of the three last years in Europe, and especially of the blessings which it has pleased Divine Providence to shower down upon those States which place their confidence and their hope on it alone, acquired the intimate conviction of the necessity of settling the steps to be observed by the Powers, in their reciprocal relations, upon the sublime truths which the Holy Religion of our Saviour teaches;
Government and Political Relations
They solemnly declare that the present Act has no other object than to publish, in the face of the whole world, their fixed resolution, both in the administration of their respective States, and in their political relations with every other Government, to take for their sole guide the precepts of that Holy Religion, namely, the precepts of Justice, Christian Charity, and Peace, which, far from being applicable only to private concerns, must have an immediate influence on the councils of Princes, and guide all their steps, as being the only means of consolidating human institutions and remedying their imperfections. In consequence, their Majesties have agreed on the following Articles:
Principles of the Christian Religion.
Art. I. Conformably to the words of the Holy Scriptures, which command all men to consider each other as brethren, the Three contracting Monarchs will remain united by the bonds of a true and indissoluble fraternity, and considering each other as fellow countrymen, they will, on all occasions and in all places, lend each other aid and assistance; and regarding themselves towards their subjects and armies as fathers of families, they will lead them, in the same spirit of fraternity with which they are animated, to protect Religion, Peace, and Justice.
Fraternity and Affection
Art. II. In consequence, the sole principle of force, whether between the said Governments or between their Subjects, shall be that of doing each other reciprocal service, and of testifying by unalterable good will the mutual affection with which they ought to be animated, to consider themselves all as members of one and the same Christian nation; the three allied Princes looking on themselves as merely delegated by Providence to govern three branches of the One family, namely, Austria, Prussia and Russia, thus confessing that the Christian world, of which they and their people form a part, has in reality no other Sovereign than Him to whom alone power really belongs, because in Him alone are found all the treasures of love, science, and infinite wisdom, that is to say, God, our Divine Saviour, the Word of the Most High, the Word of Life. Their Majesties consequently recommend to their people, with the most tender solicitude, as the sole means of enjoying that Peace which arises from a good conscience, and which alone is durable, to strengthen themselves every day more and more in the principles and exercise of the duties which the Divine Saviour has taught to mankind.
Accession of Foreign Powers
Art. III. All the Powers who shall choose solemnly to avow the sacred principles which have dictated the present Acts, and shall acknowledge how important it is for the happiness of nations, too long agitated, that these truths should henceforth exercise over the destinies of mankind all the influence which belongs to them, will be received with equal ardour and affection into this Holy Alliance.
Done in triplicate, and signed at Paris, the year of Grace 1815, 14/26th September."
(L.S.) Francis.
(L.S.) Frederick William.
(L.S.) Alexander.

E. HERTSLET, *The Map of Europe by Treaty*, London, 1908, Vol. 3, p. 317; *British and Foreign State*

H

Papers, Vol. 3, p. 211; A.W. PHILLIPS, *The Confederation of Europe; A Study of the European Alliance 1813–1823*, London, 1914.

HOLY LAND. Name given by Christians to the country where Jesus Christ lived and taught: the Canaan valley (▷ Palestine). A Catholic order of the Minor Brothers, f. 1217 is dedicated only to the spiritual custody of the Holy Land (*La Custodia di Terra Santa Dei Frati Minori*).

HOLY LEAGUE. A term coined by the Roman Catholic Church to describe allied states defending the interests of Christianity. The first League, established by the Pope in 1511, was a coalition of Spain, Venice, Austria and England, and forced France to withdraw from northern Italy. The second Holy League was composed of the Italian states and Spain, directed against Turkey, 1571–73. The third Holy League was formed in Linz, on Mar. 5, 1684, by Emperor of Austria Leopold I, King of Poland Jan III and Doge of Venice Marco Antonium Giustianini; documents ratified at the end of March the same year by all parties; concluded under the patronage of the Pope to consolidate the victory over Turkey at Vienna on Sept. 12, 1683; aimed exclusively against Turks; open for accession for all Christian monarchs, particularly to the tsar of Moscow, who joined the League in 1686. The war of the Holy League with Turkey ended in the latter's defeat and in a peace treaty concluded in Karlowice in 1699.

J. DUMONT, *Nouveau Recueil des Traités*, Amsterdam, 1970, Vol. 1.

HOLY SEE. Roman Catholic term for the seat of the pontiff and the Roman Curia, called officially ▷ Apostolic See. See also ▷ World Heritage UNESCO List.

HOLY YEAR. An international term introduced by the Roman Catholic Church for a year connected with the anniversary of the birth or death of Christ in which Catholics make mass pilgrimages to Rome, receiving special dispensations. Modelled on the jubilee (sabbatical) year in Biblical tradition, celebrated every 50 years on the model of the Roman jubilee holidays (*festa saecularia*) at the beginning of each century. In the Catholic Church based on this tradition, Pope Boniface VIII, for the purpose of strengthening papal authority, announced the first jubilee year in 1300 in the bull of Feb. 22, 1299; it was supposed to be celebrated in the first year of every century, but in 1349 Clement VI fixed the celebration of the holy year every 50 years, Urban VI – every 33 years (the number of years in the life of Christ), finally Paul II in 1470 established the celebration of the holy year every 25 years. Besides these ordinary holy years, the Pope sometimes announces extraordinary holy years associated with some important anniversary (e.g. the Holy year in 1933 on the 1900th anniversary of the Salvation). This is always a year of pilgrimages to Rome for the purpose of taking part in special services, visiting the main basilicas, and receiving so-called jubilee dispensations.

HOMELAND. An international term introduced by the British Foreign Minister A.J. Balfour on Nov. 2, 1917 (▷ Balfour Declaration) to denote an unspecified locality in Palestine for reconstruction of the state of Israel. The word Fatherland was deliberately avoided because Palestine was the native land of both Palestinians and Jews. In March, 1977 US President Jimmy Carter referred to a Homeland for Palestinian refugees which meant in principle US endorsement of the settlement of the problem of native land also for Palestinian refugees.

In the world press this idea is known as ▷ Carter's Near East Doctrine 1978. In the South African Republic the term is used with reference to ▷ Bantustans.

HOMELESS. ▷ International Year of Shelter for the Homeless, 1987.

HOMEOPATHY. A subject of international co-operation. Organization reg. with the UIA:

International Homeopathic League, f. 1925, Paris. Publ.: *Congress Acta*.

Yearbook of International Organizations.

HONDURAS. Member of the UN. República de Honduras. Republic of Honduras. State in Central America on the Caribbean Sea. Borders on Nicaragua, El Salvador and Guatemala. Area: 112,088 sq. km. Pop.: 4,300,000 estimated in 1986 (1950 census: 1,884,000; 1974 – 2,656,948). Capital: Tegucigalpa with 533,626 inhabitants 1982. GNP per capita in 1986: US $740. Currency: one lempira (also called a peso) = 100 centavos. Official language: Spanish. National Day: Sept. 15, anniversary of the proclamation of independence, 1821.

In 1919–32 Honduras was a member of the League of Nations and is an original member of the UN and of all specialized organizations with the exception of the IAEA and GATT. Member of the OAS and ODECA.

International relations: from 1539 to 1821 Honduras was a Spanish colony. It has been independent since Sept. 15, 1821. From 1821 to 1823 in federation with Mexico, and from Nov. 5, 1838 in the Federation of Central America. There have been border disputes with Guatemala, 1871, and with Nicaragua, 1894 and 1907. From the beginning of the 20th century it has been economically dependent on American Citibank, which controls the issuing of lempiras. The border disputes with Guatemala were resolved by the treaty of July 16, 1930 according to an arbitration decision by the US Secretary of State, C.E. Hughes, of Jan. 23, 1931; and the disputes with Nicaragua over the regions of the Coco and Bodega rivers were the subject of arbitration by the King of Spain in 1906, partially unresolved because of the partial non-recognition of the arbitration by Nicaragua. In 1937 Honduras and Nicaragua carried on a "postage stamp war", printing postage stamps with different delimitations of frontiers. In World War I Honduras was on the side of the Allies; and in World War II of the United Nations. Tegucigalpa is the headquarters of the Central American Bank for Economic Integration. In Apr., 1957 Honduras charged Nicaragua before the OAS Council with aggression in the region of the Coco and Bodego rivers. Treaty on Migration with El Salvador signed at San Salvador on Dec. 21, 1965, came into force on Jan. 25, 1967. In 1970 in a ▷ "football war" with Salvador, ended with the signing of the Treaty on Friendship and Peaceful Co-operation on Aug. 27, 1973. On July 30, 1976 a demilitarized zone was established with Salvador, Guatemala, Costa Rica and Nicaragua as observers. On Aug. 8, 1983 American military advisers came to Honduras. In 1982 Honduras started a border war with the guerillas of El Salvador supported by US troops and special units with a training base at Puerto Castillo (May 1983). A refugee camp for Misquito Indians from Nicaragua was used as an anti-Sandinista training base. See also ▷ World Heritage UNESCO List.

R. DE LA BORBOLLA, P. RIVAS, *Honduras: Monumentos Históricos y Arqueológicos*, Mexico, DF, 1953; V. CECCHI (ed.), *Honduras. A Problem in Económic Development*, New York, 1959; W.D. HARRIS, H.A. HOSSE, *La vivienda en Honduras*, Washington, DC, 1964; *El Desarrollo Económico de*

Honduras, CEPAL Santiago, 1966; *Boletín Informativo de ODECA*, No. 41, 1967; *UN Chronicle*, July 1981, p. 36 and April 1984, p. 4; *Europa Year Book 1984. A World Survey*, Vol. II, pp. 1664–1675, London, 1984; B.B. ROSENBERG, Th.I. SHEPHERD, eds., *Honduras Confronts its Future*, Boulder Colo., 1986.

HONEY. A subject of international co-operation. Organization reg. with the UIA:

European Federation of Importers of Dried Fruits, Preserves, Spices and Honey, FRUCOM, f. 1960, Rotterdam.

Yearbook of International Organizations.

HONG KONG. An island 2 miles east of the mouth of Pearl River on the estuary of the Canton River; it is separated from the Chinese mainland by a natural harbor. Total area: 1,068.61 sq. km (38% country park), comprising the Hong Kong island (75 sq. km), the Kowloon peninsula (9 sq. km) and the New Territories in Chinese mainland (979 sq. km). Pop., 1986 census: 5,431,200 (1945 about 600,000; in 1950 estimated 2,240,000; 1981 census 4,956,560). 50% of the population born in Hong Kong. Capital officially named Victoria but commonly called Hong Kong free port 1976 census: 501,680. GNP per capita 1987: US $8,260. National currency: one Hong Kong dollar = 100 cents. Official Language: English and Chinese.

International relations: Hong Kong was ceded by China to Great Britain in Jan., 1841, confirmed by the Nanking Treaty in Aug., 1842 and Apr. 5, 1843 and since then has been a Crown Colony. It was occupied by the Japanese from Dec. 25, 1941 to Aug. 30, 1945. Hong Kong has had special relations with the Chinese People's Republic since 1949, and with the EEC as part of the UK. The negotiations between China and UK about the transfer of the New Territories in 1997 started in 1983 at diplomatic level. On Sept. 26, 1984 a British-Chinese Declaration on Hong Kong was signed in Peiping stating that from July 1, 1997 Hong Kong will become a "special administrative region" of the People's Republic of China, enjoying an extraordinary degree of local, economic and social autonomy for at least another 50 years, in accordance with the ▷ 'one country, two systems' doctrine. Hong Kong until 2047 will have the international status of a free port with its own customs rules and its own international banking system. On April 23, 1986 Hong Kong became the 91st contracting party to the GATT, after 38 years of application; its interest had been represented during this time by the UK delegation.

The June 4 massacre of students in Peking, caused great uneasiness in Hong Kong, in relation to its 1997 transfer to China. Hong Kong citizens holding British passports demanded that Great Britain guarantee them the right of abode, which could result in the exodus of some three million people to the UK. The issue remains unsettled, as does the problem caused by the continuing influx of Vietnamese boat people, subject to forced repatriation by a British act of Parliament.

Hong Kong Bibliography, Hong Kong, 1965; G.B. ENDACOFT, *A History of Hong Kong*, New York, 1965; YU CHING JAO, *Banking and Currency in Hong Kong*, London, 1974; N. MINERS, *The Government and Politics of Hong Kong*, London, 1976; W.F. BEARER, *The Commercial Future of Hong Kong*, New York, 1978; *Europa Year Book 1984. A World Survey*, Vol. II, pp. 1248–1260, London, 1984; B. BUENO, D. NEWMAN, A. RABUSHKA, *Forecasting Political Events: The Future of Hong Kong*, London, 1985; KEESING's *Contemporary Archive*, 1986, No. 8; H. CHIU, Y.C. YAO, Y.L. WU, eds., *The Future of Hong Kong: Toward 1997 and Beyond*, Westport Ct., 1987; J.V.S. CHENG, "Hong Kong: the pressure to converge", in *International Affairs*, Nr 2, 1987; J. PAXTON, ed., *The Statesman's Yearbook 1987–88*,

London, 1987. KEESING'S Record of World Events Oct–Dec 1989.

HONG PING TAEL. The Chinese unit of weight for gold and other precious metals = 1.203 troy ounces.

HOOVER INSTITUTION ON WAR, REVOLUTION AND PEACE. Established 1919 by Herbert Hoover at Palo Alto, Calif., as the Hoover War Library of Stanford University. One of the greatest collections in the world of source material on World War I and II, the ▷ October Revolution and the Chinese ▷ Long March.

HOP. A subject of international co-operation. Organizations reg. with the UIA:

Committee of Hop Planters of the Common Market, f. 1961, Strasbourg.
European Union for the Hop Trade, f. 1976, Nurmberg, FRG.
Hop Trade Group of the Common Market, f. 1960, Nurmberg, FRG.
International Hop Growers Convention, f. 1950, Strasbourg. Publ.: *Hopfen Rundschau*.

Yearbook of International Organizations.

HORMUZ, STRAIT OF. A strait in Asia, 150 km long, connecting the Persian gulf with the Gulf of Oman. A subject of international dispute. ▷ Iranian Iraqi Dispute on the Strait of Hormuz, 1971–75.

HORN OF AFRICA. An international term for Ethiopia, Djibouti, Somalia and Keyna. A region of American-Soviet political competition for influence since the 1950's.

S.M. MANKIDD, *Superpower Diplomacy in the Horn of Africa*, London, 1987; J. MARKAKIS, *National and Class Conflict in the Horn of Africa* , Cambridge, UK, 1987.

HORSEMANSHIP. ▷ Equestrian Games.

HORSEMEAT. A subject of research and promotion by the International Trade Center UNCTAD/GATT, Geneva.

ITC, The World Market for Horsemeat, Geneva, 1983.

HORSES. A subject of international co-operation. Organizations reg. with the UIA:

European Organization for the Promotion of Horse-Riding Tourism, f. 1971, Brussels.
Harness Horsemen International, f. 1964, Windsor, Conn.
International Arabian Horse Association, f. 1950, Burbank, Calif.
International Federation of Associations for Horse-Riding Tourism, f. 1974, Paris.
International League for the Protection of Horses, f. 1976, London.
World Arabian Horse Organization, f. 1972, Burbank, Calif. Members: national committees of Australia, Belgium, Bulgaria, Canada, Czechoslovakia, Denmark, Egypt, the FRG, France, Hungary, Israel, New Zealand, Poland, Portugal, Romania, Spain, South Africa, Sweden, the UK, the USA, the USSR.

Yearbook of International Organizations.

HORTICULTURE. A subject of international co-operation. Organizations reg. with the UIA:

Commonwealth Bureau of Horticulture and Nutrition Crops, f. 1927, Kent. Publ.: *Horticultural Abstracts*.
EEC Committee for Non-Edible Horticultural Products, f. 1956, Brussels.
European Community of Young Horticulturists, f. 1965, Paris.
International Association of Horticultural Producers, f. 1948, Zurich.

International Society for Horticultural Science, f. 1959, The Hague.
World Federation of Rose Societies, f. 1976, London.
ELSEVIER's *Dictionary of Horticulture*. In English, French, Dutch, German, Danish, Swedish, Spanish, Italian and Latin, Amsterdam, 1970; *Yearbook of International Organizations, The Europa Yearbook 1988. A World Survey*, Vol I, London, 1988.

HOSPITALS. Subject of international co-operation, initiated in the 19th century by an exchange of experiences between the leading hospitals of Europe (Hotel Dieu in Paris, est. 1905; Charité in Berlin, est. 1710; Dzieciatka Jezus in Warsaw, est. 1757; All-gemeines Krankenhaus in Vienna, est. 1784; and Royal Hospital in London, est. 1826); in the 20th century (1923–40) by the International Hospital Association. They were the subject of the Tenth Hague Convention, Oct. 18, 1907, which in art. 5 concerns the protection of hospitals during wartime, stating that they must be marked as such by a red cross on the roof. The same law is in effect for hospital ships during naval war. The organization reg. with UIA:

International Hospital Federation, est. 1947. London; bureau attached to the UN in New York and a branch attached to the Pan-American Health Organization in Washington; advisory status with ECOSOC; in permanent affiliation with WHO and UNICEF. Publ.: (quarterly) *World Hospitals*. Maintains the International Bureau of Information on all kinds of hospital services. Organizes the visitation of foreign hospitals by hospital workers; biennial Congresses and International Research Committees.

Yearbook of International Organizations.

HOSTAGES. The persons seized by force and held against ransom or political concession by an individual or a group of persons, in peace time. A subject of the ▷ Hostages Convention 1979. A separate category are war hostages.

UN Chronicle, March, 1978, p. 232; March, 1979, p. 37; January, 1980, p. 85; Lord WRIGHT, "The Killing of Hostages as a War Crime", in: *British Yearbook of International Law*, 1948.

HOSTAGES CONVENTION, 1979. An International Convention against the Taking of Hostages, adopted by the UN General Assembly on Dec. 17, 1979 by consensus. The text is as follows:

"The States Party to this Convention,
Having in mind the purposes and principles of the Charter of the United Nations concerning the maintenance of international peace and security and the promotion of friendly relations and co-operation among States.
Recognizing in particular that everyone has the right to life, liberty and security of person, as set out in the Universal Declaration of Human Rights and the International Covenant on Civil and Political Rights,
Reaffirming the principle of equal rights and self-determination of peoples as enshrined in the Charter of the United Nations and the Declaration on Principles of International Law concerning Friendly Relations and Co-operation among States in accordance with the Charter of the United Nations, as well as in other relevant resolutions of the General Assembly,
Considering that the taking of hostages is an offence of grave concern to the international community and that, in accordance with the provisions of this Convention, any person committing an act of hostage-taking shall be either prosecuted or extradited,
Being convinced that it is urgently necessary to develop international co-operation between States in devising and adopting effective measures for the prevention, prosecution and punishment of all acts of taking of hostages as manifestations of international terrorism,
Have agreed as follows:
Art. 1.(1) Any person who seizes or detains and threatens to kill, to injure or to continue to detain another person (hereinafter referred to as the 'hostage') in order to compel a third party, namely, a State, an

international intergovernmental organization, a natural or juridical person, or a group of persons, to do or abstain from doing any act as an explicit or implicit condition for the release of the hostage commits the offence of taking of hostages ('hostage-taking') within the meaning of this Convention.
(2) Any person who:
(a) attempts to commit an act of hostage-taking, or
(b) participates as an accomplice of anyone who commits or attempts to commit an act of hostage-taking likewise commits an offence for the purposes of this Convention.
Art. 2. Each State Party shall make the offences set forth in article 1 punishable by appropriate penalties which take into account the grave nature of those offences.
Art. 3.(1) The State Party in the territory of which the hostage is held by the offender shall take all measures it considers appropriate to ease the situation of the hostage, in particular, to secure his release and, after his release, to facilitate, when relevant, his departure.
(2) If any object which the offender has obtained as a result of the taking of hostages comes into the custody of a State Party, that State Party shall return it as soon as possible to the hostage or the third party referred to in article 1, as the case may be, or to the appropriate authorities thereof.
Art. 4. States Parties shall co-operate in the prevention of the offences set forth in article 1, particularly by:
(a) taking all practicable measures to prevent preparations in their respective territories for the commission of those offences within or outside their territories, including measures to prohibit in their territories illegal activities of persons, groups and organizations that encourage, instigate, organize or engage in the perpetration of acts of taking of hostages;
(b) exchanging information and co-ordinating the taking of administrative and other measures as appropriate to prevent the commission of those offences.
Art. 5.(1) Each State Party shall take such measures as may be necessary to establish its jurisdiction over any of the offences set forth in article 1 which are committed:
(a) in its territory or on board a ship or aircraft registered in that State;
(b) by any of its nationals or, if that State considers it appropriate, by those stateless persons who have their habitual residence in its territory;
(c) in order to compel that State to do or abstain from doing any act; or
(d) with respect to a hostage who is a national of that State, if that State considers it appropriate.
(2) Each State Party shall likewise take such measures as may be necessary to establish its jurisdiction over the offences set forth in article 1 in cases where the alleged offender is present in its territory and it does not extradite him to any of the States mentioned in paragraph 1 of this article.
(3) This Convention does not exclude any criminal jurisdiction exercised in accordance with internal law.
Art. 6.(1) Upon being satisfied that the circumstances so warrant, any State Party in the territory of which the alleged offender is present shall, in accordance with its laws, take him into custody or take other measures to ensure his presence for such time as is necessary to enable any criminal or extradition proceedings to be instituted. That State Party shall immediately make a preliminary inquiry into the facts.
(2) The custody or other measures referred to in paragraph 1 of this article shall be notified without delay directly or through the Secretary-General of the United Nations to:
(a) the State where the offence was committed;
(b) the State against which compulsion has been directed or attempted;
(c) the State of which the natural or juridical person against whom compulsion has been directed or attempted is a national;
(d) the State of which the hostage is a national or in the territory of which he has his habitual residence;
(e) the State of which the alleged offender is a national or, if he is a stateless person, in the territory of which he has his habitual residence;
(f) the international intergovernmental organization against which compulsion has been directed or attempted;
(g) all other States concerned.

(3) Any person regarding whom the measures referred to in paragraph 1 of this article are being taken shall be entitled:
(a) to communicate without delay with the nearest appropriate representative of the State of which he is a national or which is otherwise entitled to establish such communication or, if he is a stateless person, the State in the territory of which he has his habitual residence;
(b) to be visited by a representative of that State.
(4) The rights referred to in paragraph 3 of this article shall be exercised in conformity with the laws and regulations of the State in the territory of which the alleged offender is present, subject to the proviso, however, that the said laws and regulations must enable full effect to be given to the purposes for which the rights accorded under paragraph 3 of this article are intended.
(5) The provisions of paragraphs 3 and 4 of this article shall be without prejudice to the right of any State Party having a claim to jurisdiction in accordance with paragraph 1(b) of article 5 to invite the International Committee of the Red Cross to communicate with and visit the alleged offender;
(6) The State which makes the preliminary inquiry contemplated in paragraph 1 of this article shall promptly report its findings to the States or organization referred to in paragraph 2 of this article and indicate whether it intends to exercise jurisdiction.
Art. 7. The State Party where the alleged offender is prosecuted shall in accordance with its laws communicate the final outcome of the proceedings to the Secretary-General of the United Nations, who shall transmit the information to the other States concerned and the international intergovernmental organizations concerned.
Art. 8.(1) The State Party in the territory of which the alleged offender is found shall, if it does not extradite him, be obliged, without exception whatsoever and whether or not the offence was committed in its territory, to submit the case to its competent authorities for the purpose of prosecution, through proceedings in accordance with the laws of that State. Those authorities shall take their decision in the same manner as in the case of any ordinary offence of a grave nature under the law of that State.
(2) Any person regarding whom proceedings are being carried out in connexion with any of the offences set forth in article 1 shall be guaranteed fair treatment at all stages of the proceedings, including enjoyment of all the rights and guarantees provided by the law of the State in the territory of which he is present.
Art. 9(1) A request for the extradition of an alleged offender, pursuant to this Convention, shall not be granted if the requested State Party has substantial grounds for believing:
(a) that the request for extradition for an offence set forth in article 1 has been made for the purpose of prosecuting or punishing a person on account of his race, religion, nationality, ethnic origin or political opinion; or
(b) that the person's position may be prejudiced:
(i) for any of the reasons mentioned in subparagraph (a) of this paragraph, or
(ii) for the reason that communication with him by the appropriate authorities of the State entitled to exercise rights of protection cannot be effected.
(2) With respect to the offences as defined in this Convention, the provisions of all extradition treaties and arrangements applicable between States Parties are modified as between States Parties to the extent that they are incompatible with this Convention.
Art. 10.(1) The offences set forth in article 1 shall be deemed to be included as extraditable offences in any extradition treaty existing between States Parties. States Parties undertake to include such offences as extraditable offences in every extradition treaty to be concluded between them.
(2) If a State Party which makes extradition conditional on the existence of a treaty receives a request for extradition from another State Party with which it has no extradition treaty, the requested State may at its option consider this Convention as the legal basis for extradition in respect of the offences set forth in art. 1. Extradition shall be subject to the other conditions provided by the law of the requested State.
(3) States Parties which do not make extradition conditional on the existence of a treaty shall recognize the offences set forth in art. 1 as extradible offences between themselves, subject to the conditions provided by the law of the requested State.
(4) The offences set forth in article 1 shall be treated, for the purpose of extradition between States Parties, as if they shall had been committed not only in the place in which they occurred but also in the territories on the States required to establish their jurisdiction in accordance with paragraph 1 of article 5.
Art. 11.(1) States Parties shall afford one another the greatest measure of assistance in connexion with criminal proceedings brought in respect of the offences set forth in article 1, including the supply of all evidence at their disposal necessary for the proceedings.
(2) The provisions of paragraph 1 of this article shall not affect obligations concerning mutual judicial assistance embodied in any other treaty.
Art. 12. In so far as the Geneva Convention of 1949 for the protection of war victims or the Additional Protocols to those Conventions are applicable to a particular act of hostage-taking, and in so far as States Parties to this Convention are bound under those Conventions to prosecute or hand over the hostage-taker, the present Convention shall not apply to an act of hostage-taking committed in the course of armed conflicts as defined in the Geneva Conventions of 1949 and the Protocols thereto, including armed conflicts mentioned in article 1, paragraph 4, of Additional Protocol I of 1977, in which peoples are fighting against colonial domination and alien occupation and against racist regimes in the exercise of their right of self-determination, as enshrined in the Charter of the United Nations and the Declaration of Principles of International Law concerning Friendly Relations and Co-operation among States in accordance with the Charter of the United Nations.
Art. 13. This Convention shall not apply where the offence is committed within a single State, the hostage and the alleged offender are nationals of that State and the alleged offender is found in the territory of that State.
Art. 14. Nothing in this Convention shall be construed as justifying the violation of the territorial integrity or political independence of a State in contravention of the Charter of the United Nations.
Art. 15. The provisions of this Convention shall not affect the application of the Treaties on Asylum, in force at the date of the adoption of this Convention, as between the States which are parties to those Treaties; but a State Party to this Convention may not invoke those Treaties with respect to another State Party to this Convention which is not a party to those Treaties.
Art. 16.(1) Any dispute between two or more States Parties concerning the interpretation or application of this Convention which is not settled by negotiation shall, at the request of one of them, be submitted to arbitration. If within six months from the date of the request for arbitration the parties are unable to agree on the organization of the arbitration, any one of those parties may refer the dispute to the International Court of Justice by request in conformity with the Statute of the Court.
(2) Each State may at the time of signature or ratification of this Convention or accession thereto declare that it does not consider itself bound by paragraph 1 of this article. The other States Parties shall not be bound by paragraph 1 of this article with respect to any State Party which has made such a reservation.
(3) Any State Party which has made a reservation in accordance with paragraph 2 of this article may at any time withdraw that reservation by notification to the Secretary-General of the United Nations.
Art. 17.(1) This Convention is open for signature by all States until 31 December 1980 at United Nations Headquarters in New York.
(2) This Convention is subject to ratification. The instruments of ratification shall be deposited with the Secretary-General of the United Nations.
(3) This Convention is open for accession by any State. The instruments of accession shall be deposited with the Secretary-General of the United Nations.
Art. 18.(1) This Convention shall enter into force on the thirtieth day following the date of deposit of the twenty-second instrument of ratification or accession with the Secretary-General of the United Nations.
(2) For each State ratifying or acceding to the Convention after the deposit of the twenty-second instrument of ratification of accession, the Convention shall enter into force on the thirtieth day after deposits by such State of its instrument of ratification or accession.
Art. 19.(1) Any State Party may denounce this Convention by written notification to the Secretary-General of the United Nations.
(2) Denunciation shall take effect one year following the date on which notification is received by the Secretary-General of the United Nations.
Art. 20. The original of this Convention, of which the Arabic, Chinese, English, French, Russian and Spanish texts are equally authentic, shall be deposited with the Secretary-General of the United Nations, who shall send certified copies thereof to all States."

The UN Convention to prevent the taking of hostages, 1979 signed by 34 countries was signed May 1987 by the USSR.

UN Yearbook 1979, pp. 1144–1146, New York, 1982.

HOSTAGE IRAN–USA INCIDENT, 1979. ▷ Iran; ▷ Sanctions.

HOST COUNTRY RELATIONS BODY. The Committee on Relations with the Host Country of the UN Headquarters in New York, established by the 1947 Agreement between the UN and the USA regarding the Headquarters of the UN. The Committee considers security of missions and the safety of their personnel, implementation of the Headquarters Agreement between the UN and the US, entry visas issued by the host country, exemption from taxes etc. ▷ United Nations Headquarters. The Committee composed of Bulgaria, Canada, China, Costa Rica, Cyprus, France, Honduras, Iraq, Ivory Coast, Mali, Senegal, Spain, the UK, the USA and the USSR, heard statements both by its members and observers. On Dec. 2, 1988, the General Assembly adopted a Res. 43/49 by 154 votes to 2 (Israel and US) with 1 abstaining (UK) demanding the US to reconsider and reverse its decision to deny the visa requested for Mr Yasser Arafat, Chairman of the ▷ PLO.

UN Chronicle, April, 1978, p. 71; and June 1983, pp. 66–70; January 1984, pp. 68–69; *UN Resolutions and Decisions adopted by the General Assembly during the First Part of its Forty-Third Session, from 20 September to 22 December 1988*, New York, 1989.

HOSTES HUMANI GENERIS. *Latin* = "enemies of mankind". An international term; the ancient name for sea pirates.

HOSTESSES. ▷ Air Hostesses.

HOTELS, HOSTELS, MOTELS. The subjects of international co-operation. Organizations reg. with the UIA:

Arabs Hotels Union, f. 1967, Cairo.
Caribbean Hotel Association, f. 1959, Puerto Rico. Publ.: *Caribbean Reporter*.
European Association of Hotel School Directors, f. 1955, Lausanne.
European Motel Federation, f. 1956. Maarsbergen.
Hotel Company for the Development of Tourism in Africa, f. 1970, Abidjan.
Inter-American Hotel Association, f. 1941, California.
International Hotel and Motel Educational Exposition, f. 1915, New York.
International Hotel Association, f. 1946, Paris. Consultative status with ECOSOC, ILO, Council of Europe and OAS. Publ.: *International Hotel Review* (quarterly), *International Hotel Guide* (yearly), *Directory of Travel Agencies* (yearly).
International Union of National Associations of Hotel, Restaurant and Cafe Keepers, f. 1949, Paris.
International Youth Hostel Federation, f. 1932, Amsterdam.
Liaison Committee of the Hotel Association of the European Community, f. 1963, Paris.
Trade Union International of Food, Tobacco, Hotel and Allied Industries Workers, f. 1949, Sofia. Publ.: *Bulletin*.

World Federation of Workers in Food, Tobacco and Hotel Industries, f. 1948, Brussels. Consultative status with ILO and FAO. Publ.: *Contact*.

Yearbook of International Organizations.

HOT LINE. A system of direct line telecommunications between governments of big powers. It was initiated on Aug. 30, 1963 by the US and USSR Heads of State – after the Cuban missiles crisis – to reduce the danger of a chance nuclear war and provide immediate communication in any emergency when immediate consultations are required because of a risk to world security and peace. The system was extended in 1971, to include satellite communications through ▷ Molniya and ▷ Intelsat systems. Agreements of Apr. 20, 1963 and Sept. 30, 1971 went into operation upon signing. Similar hot lines were installed between other powers. In June, 1977 home secretaries of EEC countries concluded an agreement on the use of hot lines for the suppression of terrorism, allowing security services of one country to establish immediate and direct contacts with their counterparts in other EEC countries. In 1988 the telex hot line was replaced by fax.

UNTS, 1971; D. ROBERTSON, *Guide to Modern Defense and Strategy*, Detroit, 1988.

HOT MONEY. An international term for speculative money placed at short term interest in other countries with the guarantee of rapid withdrawal, related to the rapid change of exchange rates.

HOTOL. ▷ Spaceplane.

HOT PURSUIT DOCTRINE. An international term for a customary rule of international law allowing pursuit of a foreign ship out of the territorial waters; first mentioned in *Casaregis Discursos Legales de Comercio*, Florence, 1719, defined in art. 23 of the Geneva Convention on the High Seas, 1958, as follows:

"The hot pursuit of a foreign ship may be undertaken when the competent authorities of the coastal State have good reason to believe that the ship has violated the laws and regulations of that State. Such pursuit must be commenced when the foreign ship or one of its boats is within the internal waters or the territorial sea or the contiguous zone of the pursuing State, and may only be continued outside the territorial sea or the contiguous zone if the pursuit has not been interrupted."

S. MAIDMENT, "Historical aspects of the doctrine hot pursuit", in: *British Year Book of International Law 1972–1973*, Oxford, 1975, pp. 365–381; R.L. BLEDSOE, B.A. BOCZEK, *The International Law Dictionary*, Oxford, 1987.

HOT SPRINGS. A holiday resort in USA (Arkansas) where on Apr. 4–June 3, 1943 the first UN Conference on Food and Agriculture, also known as the Hot Springs Conference, was held attended by 45 states, which issued the Hot Springs Declaration of Principles. The first postulated aim of the UN was to achieve victory in the war and liberation of millions of people from the tyranny of famine; the Hot Springs Agreement, Feb. 28, 1945, provided for the establishment of the Food and Agriculture Organization ▷ FAO, f. Oct. 16, 1945 in Quebec (after ratification of the Agreement, Feb. 28, 1945).

UN Yearbook, 1945.

HOTTENTOTS. ▷ Hereros and Hottentots.

HOUSEHOLDS. An international term introduced by the UN Statistical Committee, 1950 for unification of methods for counting households and their living conditions recognized as indices of the standard of living in various countries; used in world population censuses. Organization reg. with the UIA:

International Federation for Household Maintenance Products, f. 1967, Brussels, Belgium.

UN Chronicle, November, 1982, pp. 36 and 43; *Yearbook of International Organizations, 1986/87*; *The Europa Yearbook 1988. A World Survey*, Vol. I, London 1988.

HOUSING AND PLANNING. Subject of international co-operation. Organizations reg. with the UIA:

Action SELA Committee on Housing and Social Construction, f. 1977, Caracas, Venezuela.
Association for Planning and Housing, ASEAN, f. 1979, Manilla, Philippines.
Eastern Regional Organization for Planning and Housing, f. 1958, New Delhi, India.
European Federation of Building Societies, f. 1962, Dublin, Ireland.
Inter-African Committee on Building Materials and Housing, f. 1983, Lagos, Nigeria.
Inter-American Rural Housing Association, f. 1980, Caracas, Venezeula.
Intergovernmental Documentation Centre on Housing and Environment for the Countries of UN Economic Commission for Europe, f. 1982, Paris, France.
International Association for Housing Science, f. 1972, Coral Gable, Fla, USA. Publ.: *Housing Science*.
International Comparative Housing Development Association, f. 1966, Coalville, UK.
International Federation of Housing and Planning, fl. 1913, The Hague, Netherlands. Publ: *News Sheet*.
Organization of Nordic Cooperative and Municipal Housing Enterprises, f. 1950, Stockholm, Sweden.
United Nations Regional Housing Centre, f. 1985, Bandung, Indonesia.

Yearbook of International Organizations, 1986/87; *The Europa Yearbook 1988. A World Survey*, Vol. I, London 1988.

HOUSING, WORLD PROBLEMS. A subject of permanent, organized, international co-operation under the aegis of the UN. In Dec., 1946 the UN General Assembly stated the necessity of permanent exchange of technical experiences of different countries and world regions in solving housing problems. The task was assigned to ECOSOC. In 1949 the Social Department of the UN Secretariat began publication of a periodical entitled *Housing and Country Planning* (in 1959 the title was changed to *Housing and Community Development*, and since 1963, *Housing, Building and Planning*). The long-term program of UN assistance in solving world housing problems, prepared by ECOSOC in 1950, was not approved by the UN General Assembly. The issue was resumed in 1959 and 1962, when a new Committee for Housing, Building and Planning Problems was appointed within ECOSOC. In 1962 ECOSOC established by Res. 903-C/XXXIV the Center for Housing, Building and Planning, CHBP, in the Social and Economic Department of the UN Secretariat, to carry out world studies and render assistance to countries where acute housing crises occur, mainly as a result of rapid urbanization in the second half of the 20th century and establishment of urban slums for millions of people.

In 1969 the General Assembly called for a report by the Secretary-General on the problems and priorities confronting member states in housing, building and planning and, in particular, on trends in building and financing costs and the need for low-income housing, rural housing, community facilities and environmental improvements. The report, issued in 1970, contained recommendations for international action, which included planning a strategy for developing human settlements within the context of national development.

Taking note of the report, the UN General Assembly later the same year recommended that member states should formulate definite and long-term housing, building and planning policies and programs for the improvement of human settlements. The Assembly invited developed countries and the international organizations concerned to provide increased technical and financial assistance to developing countries to ameliorate conditions in housing and human settlements. It also recommended strengthening the catalytic role of the United Nations in programs and projects relating to housing and human settlements. In 1972 the UN General Assembly proposed that, in establishing criteria for eligibility for loans under more favorable terms, the International Bank for Reconstruction and Development IBRD, should also take into account such critical factors as levels of unemployment, rates of urban growth, population density and the general condition of the housing stock in the developing country concerned.

A 1975 report by the UN Secretary-General analyzed the needs and possibilities for international financing and recommended a number of changes to the criteria then being used. For example, it proposed that greater attention should be paid to the probable distribution of benefits among various income groups, with priority to be given to programs that would benefit a large number of low-income families. The report also recommended that the levels of per capita income, set for various degrees of concessionality, should allow for the balance-of-payments difficulties of countries with small or isolated economies. During its existence, the Center for Housing, Building and Planning collected, evaluated and disseminated information on problems and trends in human settlements, conducted research and development work, participated in technical co-operation projects, and organized seminars and meetings of experts. The Center's projects were concerned with such questions as the financing of housing, rent-control practices, housing policy guidelines for developing countries, rural housing, design of low-cost housing, and the effects of development and population growth on human settlements. Work continued on the improvement of slums and squatter settlements and the amelioration of conditions of the lowest-income groups and those particularly vulnerable, such as children, women and youth.

A major contribution by the Center was the publication of the first United Nations World Housing Survey, 1974, which aims to alert people to the urgency and scale of the world's housing problems, and to assist governments in dealing with them. This review of housing will be updated every five years.

The convening of ▷ Habitat: UN Conference on Human Settlements in Vancouver, Canada, from May 31, to June 11, 1976 highlighted a decade of activity to improve the living places of people. ▷ (Habitat Vancouver Declaration, 1976.) In Dec., 1977 the Assembly acted on the question of new international machinery for human settlements as recommended by the Vancouver Conference. As directed by the UN General Assembly, the ECOSOC transformed the 27-member Committee on Housing, Building and Planning into a 58-member Commission on Human Settlements. The assembly set up a small secretariat named Habitat, Center for Human Settlements, replacing the Center for Housing, Building and Planning, to service the Commission and function as a focal point for human settlements action. In view of its close links with the United Nations Environment

Program, UNEP, whose headquarters are in Nairobi, Kenya, the new Center is located there. Among the functions of the Commission will be supervision of the operations of the UN Habitat and Human Settlements Foundation, established by the UN General Assembly in 1974 to help developing countries strengthen their national human settlements programs through the provision of seed capital and the extension of financial and technical assistance.

Everyone's United Nations, New York, 1979, pp. 171–174.

HOVERING ACTS. An international maritime term for action taken against vessels suspected of carrying contraband to prevent them from entering territorial waters.

HUDSON INSTITUTE. Name of an American scientific institute; its headquarters until 1984 was in Croton-on-Hudson in the state of New York; makes studies of the total development of societies and works out economic predictions on the social development of humanity.

HUMANAE VITAE. *Latin* = "human life". The name of the encyclical of Paul VI on July 25, 1968 directed against birth control by artificial means, which occasioned the declaration of differing views of the World Council of Christian Churches and the director-general of the FAO. Organization reg. with the UIA:

International Centrum *Humanae Vitae*, f. 1968, Paris. Publ.: *Report*.

Yearbook of International Organizations.

HUMAN BIOLOGY. A subject of international research and co-operation. Organizations reg. with the UIA:

Council for Biology in Human Affairs, f. 1970, San Diego, Calif.
International Association of Human Biologists, f. 1967, Porto Alegre.
International Committee for Standardization in Human Biology, f. 1958, Brussels. Publ.: *International Journal of Human Biology*.

Yearbook of International Organizations.

HUMAN DIGNITY PROTECTION. An international term for legal norms of domestic laws protecting nationals from libel and insult; international problems related to techniques of wiretapping and long-distance photography used for monitoring ▷ private life to obtain information about persons and publish it for slanderous reasons.

HUMAN ENVIRONMENTAL PROTECTION. ▷ Environmental Protection.

HUMANISM. An international term which appeared in the 19th century to define an intellectual trend at the turning point of the Middle Ages and the Renaissance; not an unambiguous term due to the various philosophical meanings attributed to it; subject of permanent organized international co-operation. Organizations reg. with the UIA:

International Council for Philosophy and Humanistic Studies, f. 1949, Paris. Publ.: *Diogenes* (quarterly).
International Humanism and Ethical Union, f. 1952, Utrecht. Consultative status with ECOSOC. Publ.: *International Humanism* (quarterly).

Yearbook of International Organizations.

HUMANITARIAN INTERNATIONAL LAW APPLIED IN ARMED CONFLICTS. An international term introduced in 1970 by the UN General Assembly in Res. 2677/XXV for norms in force for armed conflicts.

UN Yearbook 1970, pp. 533–534, New York, 1972.

HUMAN RELATIONS. An international term for one of the humanitarian aspects included in ▷ Helsinki Final Act 1975, aimed at facilitation of family contacts, family reunions, mixed marriages and foreign trips for private or business purposes as well as improvement of conditions for tourism, sports exchange, or social meetings.

HUMAN RIGHTS. An international term which is not defined in any act of international law; introduced by US Declaration of Independence, 1776, and the Declaration of the Rights of Man and Citizen, 1789, of the French Revolution. It was adopted by the US Constitution and extended by the 16th constitutional amendment, 1913 and is the subject of international declarations, the first being the Declaration of Human Rights and Duties worked out in 1929 by the New York Institute of International Law and submitted to Inter-American Legal Committees. In art. 1 it proclaimed that it is a duty of every state to recognize equal rights of an individual to life, freedom, and property and to fully grant and protect these rights on its entire territory regardless of nationality, sex, race, language or religion; and in art. 2, that it is a duty of every state to recognize equal rights of an individual to the free execution, whether in public or in private, of any faith, religion or worship, the practice of which is not in violation of public order and good manners. This declaration, together with the resolution of Inter-American Conference in Chapultepec, Mar. 8, 1945 on the need to establish international protection of human rights, laid the foundations for a draft of the Universal Declaration of Human Rights submitted to the UN Human Rights Commission. Earlier, the UN Charter introduced an unspecified term, "fundamental human rights", of international character and set up a special UN Commission for its promotion of human rights. The obligation of protecting human rights was introduced into peace treaties concluded Feb. 10, 1947 with Bulgaria (arts. 2, 3, 4), Finland (arts. 6, 7, 8), Romania (arts. 3, 4, 5), Hungary (arts. 2 and 4) and Italy (art. 15) as well as on May 15, 1955 with Austria (arts. 6, 7, 8). Work on the Universal Declaration of Human Rights went on in the years 1946–48 concurrently in the UN Human Rights Commission and the International Legal Commission which, in Mar. 1948, won approval of the 9th Inter-American Conference in Bogota for the Declaration of American Human Rights and Duties (specifying 28 rights and 10 duties) and served as a basis for an Inter-American convention (the convention consisting of 88 articles was debated internationally in the years 1950, 1953, 1954 and 1959 as well as elaborated on for many years by the Human Rights Commission set up by the OAS). The UN Human Rights Commission prepared Dec. 10, 1948 the ▷ Human Rights, Universal Declaration of, which enumerates human rights alone and only mentions (art. 29) human duties "to the community in which alone the free and full development of his personality is possible." Though not an international treaty but a UN General Assembly resolution, the Declaration bears significantly on the shaping of modern norms of International Law which found two-fold reflection in international agreements concluded outside the UN and referring to the Declaration (e.g. the 1951 Peace Treaty with Japan); in the international conventions concluded with a view to protecting particular human rights, as well as in pacts and declarations, presented here in chronological order:

The Convention on prevention and prosecution of the crime of Genocide, 1948.
The European Convention on protection of human rights and the fundamental freedoms adopted by members of European Council Nov. 5, 1950.
The Convention on the status of refugees 1951.
The Convention on international right for rectification 1952.
The Convention on political rights of women, 1952.
The Protocol on the modification of the 1926 convention on slavery, 1953.
The Convention on the status of stateless persons, 1954
The supplementary Convention on elimination of slavery, 1956.
The Convention on citizenship of the married woman, 1957.
The Convention on reduction of the number of apatridos (stateless persons), 1961.
The Convention on marriage (terms, minimum age, registry), 1962.
The Convention on elimination of all forms of racial discrimination, 1965.
The International Pacts of Human Rights: Civil and Political Rights and Economic, Social and Cultural Rights, 1966.
The Protocol on the status of refugees, 1966.
Added to these acts is the UN General Assembly resolution of Nov. 20, 1959 called "Declaration of the Rights of the Child", stipulating for legal protection the rights of the child, as well as the resolution of Nov. 20, 1963 called "Declaration on elimination of all forms of racial discrimination," the fruit of which was an International Convention to this effect, of Dec. 22, 1965.
In keeping with UN General Assembly Res. 2081/XX of Dec. 20, 1965, the year 1968 was declared the International Year of Human Rights. An International Conference of Human Rights was held in Teheran Apr. 22–May 13, 1968 and concluded with the adoption of 28 resolutions and (unanimously) the so-called ▷ Human Rights Teheran Proclamation. The International Covenant of Economic, Social and Political Rights introduced (arts. 16, 22) a monitoring system for human rights based on reports submitted by states parties to the Covenant. An 18-nation Human Rights Committee considered the reports, including communications alleging human rights violations. The Committee held its first and second sessions in 1977.
The position of the Warsaw Pact countries is stated in the Declaration of Consultative Political Committee signed on Nov. 23, 1978 at Moscow whose provisions concerning human rights were as follows:

"The UN Charter obliges all countries to contribute to the respect and effectuation of freedoms for all regardless of race, sex, language, or religion. Accordingly, the socialist countries, showing initiative and consistent efforts, have added considerably to the preparation and adoption of the most important international agreements and treaties in this respect: human rights pacts, conventions on prevention of genocide, liquidation of all forms of racial discrimination and many others; they implement in practice all the provisions of these treaties and agreements."

The US Department of State in Jan., 1978 has released an official US Government definition of human rights:

"Freedom from arbitrary arrest and imprisonment, torture, unfair trial, cruel and unusual punishment, and invasion of privacy. Rights to food, shelter, health care, and education; and Freedom of thought, speech, assembly, religion, press, movement, and participation in government."

Organizations reg. with the UIA:

Institut International des Droits de l'Homme, f. 1959, Strasbourg; studying development of the protection of human rights in the world.

International Federation for the Rights of Man, f. 1922 by the League for the Rights of Man; assembles national organizations. Consultative status with ECOSOC, headquarters Paris.

International League for the Rights of Man, f. 1941 in New York. Consultative status with ECOSOC and UNESCO. Publ.: *Annual Report*.

Union for the Protection of the Human Person by International Social and Economic Cooperation, f. 1938, New York.

The Johns Hopkins University Press in Baltimore publishes an internationally oriented Human Rights Quarterly.

A. GARCIA ROBLES, *El Mundo de la Postguerra*, Mexico, DF, 1946; H. LANTERPACHT, *International Law and Human Rights*, New York, 1950, 475 pp.; *Actas y Documentos de la IX Conferencia Internacional Americana*, Bogota, 1953, Vol. 8; R. CHAHRAVARTI, *Human Rights and the UN*, Calcutta, 1958; *Derechos Humanos en los Estados Americanos*, PAU, Washington, DC, Jun 1960; J.F. GREEN, *The UN and Human Rights*, Washington, DC, 1967; *Les droits de l'Homme en droit interne et en droit international*, Bruxelles, 1969; *Respect for Human Rights in Armed Conflicts*. Report of the Secretary-General, A/77, 20 Nov., 1969, UN General Assembly; A.P. SCHREIBER, *The Inter-American Commission on Human Rights*, Leyden, 1970; I. BROWNILOE, *Basic Documents on Human Rights*, Oxford, 1971; A.H. ROBERTSON, *Human Rights in the World*, London, 1972; *Human Rights Commission Report*, UN, New York, 1973; *US Department of State on Human Rights*, Washington, DC, January, 1978; J.A. JOYCE, *Human Rights: International Documents*, 3 Vols., Alphen aan den Rijn, 1978; D.P. KOMMERS, G.D. LOESCHER (eds.), *Human Rights and American Foreign Policy*, London, 1979; *UN Chronicle*, January, 1979, p. 62; *Human Rights. Collection of International Instruments*, UN New York, 1983; J.R. FRIEDMAN, M.I. SHERMAN eds., *Human Rights. An International Comparative Law Bibliography*, London, 1985; UNESCO *Violation of Human Rights: Possible Rights of Recourse and Forms of Resistance*, Paris, 1985; THE ECONOMIST, *World Human Rights Guide*, London, 1986; C. HUMANA, *World Human Rights Guide*, London, 1986; D.D. NEWSOM, *The Diplomacy of Human Rights*, Lanham Md., 1986; Th. MERON, *Human Rights Law-Making in the UN: A Critique of Instruments and Processes*, Oxford, 1986; "Individuals, Human Rights and International Organizations", in *International Law Dictionary*, Oxford, 1987; *Sollicitudo Rei Socialis*. Encyclical letter of the Supreme Pontiff John Paul II for the Twentieth Anniversary of Populorum Progressio, London 1988, p.43–44 and 61.

HUMAN RIGHTS AFRICAN CHARTER. ▷ African Charter on Human and People's Rights, 1986.

HUMAN RIGHTS AMERICAN CONVENTION, 1969. A Convention called also the Pact of San José 1969, was signed by the OAS member states on Nov. 22, 1969 in San José. The text of the Preamble and the first six Chapters is as follows:

"The American states signatory to the present Convention, reaffirming their intention to consolidate in this hemisphere, within the framework of democratic institutions, a system of personal liberty and social justice based on respect for the essential rights of man;

Recognizing that the essential rights of man are not derived from one's being a national of a certain state, but are based upon attributes of the human personality, and that they therefore justify international protection in the form of a convention reinforcing or complementing the protection provided by the domestic law of the American states;

Considering that these principles have been set forth in the Charter of the Organization of American States, in the American Declaration of the Rights and Duties of Man, and in the Universal Declaration of Human Rights, and that they have been reaffirmed and refined in other international instruments, worldwide as well as regional in scope;

Reiterating that, in accordance with the Universal Declaration of Human Rights, the ideal of free men enjoying freedom from fear and want can be achieved only if conditions are created whereby everyone may enjoy his economic, social and cultural rights, as well as his civil and political rights; and

Considering that the Third Special Inter-American Conference (Buenos Aires, 1967) approved the incorporation into the Charter of the Organization itself of broader standards with respect to economic, social, and educational rights and resolved that an inter-American convention on human rights should determine the structure, competence, and procedure of the organs responsible for these matters,

Have agreed upon the following:

Part I – State Obligations and Rights Protected.

Chapter I – General Obligations.

Art. 1. Obligation to Respect Rights.

(1) The States Parties to this Convention undertake to respect the rights and freedoms recognized herein and to ensure to all persons subject to their jurisdiction the free and full exercise of those rights and freedoms, without any discrimination for reasons of race, color, sex, language, religion, political or other opinion, national or social origin, economic status, birth, or any other social condition.

(2) For the purpose of this Convention 'person' means every human being.

Art. 2. Domestic Legal Effects.

Where the exercise of any of the rights or freedoms referred to in Art. 1 is not already ensured by legislative or other provisions, the States Parties undertake to adopt, in accordance with their constitutional processes and the provisions of this Convention, such legislative or other measures as may be necessary to give effect to those rights or freedoms.

Chapter II – Civil and Political Rights.

Art. 3. Right to Juridical Personality.

Every person has the right to recognition as a person before the law.

Art. 4. Right to Life.

(1) Every person has the right to have his life respected. This right shall be protected by law and, in general, from the moment of conception. No one shall be arbitrarily deprived of his life.

(2) In countries that have not abolished the death penalty, it may be imposed only for the most serious crimes and pursuant to a final judgment rendered by a competent court and in accordance with a law establishing such punishment, enacted prior to the commission of the crime. The application of such punishment shall not be extended to crimes to which it does not presently apply.

(3) The death penalty shall not be reestablished in states that have abolished it.

(4) In no case shall capital punishment be inflicted for political offenses or related common crimes.

(5) Capital punishment shall not be imposed upon persons who, at the time the crime was committed, were under 18 years of age; or over 70 years of age; nor shall it be applied to pregnant women.

(6) Every person condemned to death shall have the right to apply for amnesty, pardon, or commutation of sentence, which may be granted in all cases. Capital punishment shall not be imposed while such a petition is pending decision by the competent authority.

Art. 5. Right to Humane Treatment.

(1) Every person has the right to have his physical, mental, and moral integrity respected.

(2) No one shall be subjected to torture or to cruel, inhuman, or degrading punishment or treatment. All persons deprived of their liberty shall be treated with respect for the inherent dignity of the human person.

(3) Punishment shall not be extended to any person other than the criminal.

(4) Accused persons shall, save in exceptional circumstances, be segregated from convicted persons and shall be subject to separate treatment appropriate to their status as unconvicted.

(5) Minors while subject to criminal proceedings shall be separated from adults and brought before specialized tribunals, as speedily as possible, so that they may be treated in accordance with their status as minors.

(6) Punishments consisting of deprivation of liberty shall have as an essential aim the reform and social readaptation of the prisoners.

Art. 6. Freedom from Slavery.

(1) No one shall be subject to slavery or to involuntary servitude, which are prohibited in all their forms, as are the slave trade and traffic in women.

(2) No one shall be required to perform forced or compulsory labor. This provision shall not be interpreted to mean that, in those countries in which the penalty established for certain crimes is deprivation of liberty at forced labor, the carrying out of such a sentence imposed by a competent court is prohibited. Forced labor shall not adversely affect the dignity or the physical or intellectual capacity of the prisoner.

(3) For the purposes of this article, the following do not constitute forced or compulsory labor:

(a) work or service normally required of a person imprisoned in execution of a sentence or formal decision passed by the competent judicial authority. Such work or service shall be carried out under the supervision and control of public authorities, and any persons performing such work or service shall not be placed at the disposal of any private party, company, or juridical person;

(b) Military service and, in countries in which conscientious objectors are recognized, national service that the law may provide for in lieu of military service;

(c) service exacted in time of danger or calamity that threatens the existence or the well-being of the community; or

(d) work or service that forms part of normal civic obligations.

Art. 7. Right to Personal Liberty.

(1) Every person has the right to personal liberty and security.

(2) No one shall be deprived of his physical liberty except for the reasons and under the conditions established beforehand by the constitution of the State Party concerned or by a law established pursuant thereto.

(3) No one shall be subject to arbitrary arrest or imprisonment.

(4) Anyone who is detained shall be informed of the reasons for his detention and shall be promptly notified of the charge or charges against him.

(5) Any person detained shall be brought promptly before a judge or other officer authorized by law to exercise judicial power and shall be entitled to trial within a reasonable time or to be released without prejudice to the continuation of the proceedings. His release may be subject to guarantee to assure his appearance for trial.

(6) Anyone who is deprived of his liberty shall be entitled to recourse to a competent court, in order that the court may decide without delay on the lawfulness of his arrest or detention and order his release if the arrest or detention is unlawful. In States Parties whose laws provide that anyone who believes himself to be threatened with deprivation of his liberty is entitled to recourse to a competent court in order that it may decide on the lawfulness of such threat, this remedy may not be restricted or abolished. The interested party or another person on his behalf is entitled to seek these remedies.

(7) No one shall be detained for debt. This principle shall not limit the orders of a competent judicial authority issued for nonfulfillment of duties of support.

Art. 8. Right to a Fair Trial.

(1) Every person has the right to a hearing, with due guarantees and within a reasonable time, by a competent, independent, and impartial tribunal, previously established by law, in the substantiation of any accusation of a criminal nature made against him or for the determination of his rights and obligations of a civil, labor, fiscal, or any other nature.

(2) Every person accused of a criminal offense has the right to be presumed innocent so long as his guilt has not been proven according to law. During the proceedings, every person is entitled, with full equality, to the following minimum guarantees:

(a) the right of the accused to be assisted without charge by a translator or interpreter, if he does not understand or does not speak the language of the tribunal or court;

(b) prior notification in detail to the accused of the charges against him;

(c) adequate time and means for the preparation of his defense;
(d) the right of the accused to defend himself personally or to be assisted by legal counsel of his own choosing, and to communicate freely and privately with his counsel;
(e) the inalienable right to be assisted by counsel provided by the state, paid or not as the domestic law provides, if the accused does not defend himself personally or engage his own counsel within the time period established by law;
(f) the right of the defense to examine witnesses present in the court and to obtain the appearance, as witnesses, of experts or other persons who may throw light on the facts;
(g) the right not to be compelled to be a witness against himself or to plead guilty; and
(h) the right to appeal the judgment to a higher court.
(3) A confession of guilt by the accused shall be valid only if it is made without coercion of any kind.
(4) An accused person acquitted by a nonappealable judgment shall not be subjected to a new trial for the same cause.
(5) Criminal proceedings shall be public, except insofar as may be necessary to protect the interests of justice.
Art. 9. Freedom from Ex Post Facto Laws,
No one shall be convicted of any act or omission that did not constitute a criminal offense, under the applicable law, at the time it was committed. A heavier penalty shall not be imposed than the one that was applicable at the time the criminal offense was committed. If subsequent to the commission of the offense the law provides for the imposition of a lighter punishment, the guilty person shall benefit therefrom.
Art. 10. Right to Compensation.
Every person has the right to be compensated in accordance with the law in the event he has been sentenced by a final judgment through a miscarriage of justice.
Art. 11. Right to Privacy.
(1) Everyone has the right to have his honor respected and his dignity recognized.
(2) No one may be the object of arbitrary or abusive interference with his private life, his family, his home, or his correspondence, or of unlawful attacks on his honor or reputation.
(3) Everyone has the right to the protection of the law against such interference or attacks.
Art. 12. Freedom of Conscience and Religion.
(1) Everyone has the right to freedom of conscience and of religion. This right includes freedom to maintain or to change one's religion or beliefs, and freedom to profess or disseminate one's religion or beliefs, either individually or together with others, in public or in private.
(2) No one shall be subject to restrictions that might impair his freedom to maintain or to change his religion or beliefs.
(3) Freedom to manifest one's religion and beliefs may be subject only to the limitations prescribed by law that are necessary to protect public safety, order, health, or morals, or the rights or freedoms of others.
(4) Parents or guardians, as the case may be, have the right to provide for the religious and moral education of their children or wards that is in accord with their own convictions.
Art. 13. Freedom of Thought and Expression.
(1) Everyone has the right to freedom of thought and expression. This right includes freedom to seek, receive, and impart information and ideas of all kinds, regardless of frontiers, either orally, in writing, in print, in the form of art, or through any other medium of one's choice.
(2) The exercise of the right provided for in the foregoing paragraph shall not be subject to prior censorship but shall be subject to subsequent imposition of liability, which shall be expressly established by law to the extent necessary to ensure;
(a) respect for the rights or reputations of others; or
(b) the protection of national security, public order, or public health or morals.
(3) The right of expression may not be restricted by indirect methods or means, such as the abuse of government or private controls over newsprint, radio broadcasting frequencies, or equipment used in the dissemination of information, or by any other means tending to impede the communication and circulation of ideas and opinions.
(4) Notwithstanding the provisions of paragraph 2 above, public entertainments may be subject by law to prior censorship for the sole purpose of regulating access to them for the moral protection of childhood and adolescence.
(5) Any propaganda for war and any advocacy of national, racial, or religious hatred that constitute incitements to lawless violence or to any other similar illegal action against any person or group of persons on any grounds including those of race, color, religion, language, or national origin shall be considered as offenses punishable by law.
Art. 14. Right of Reply.
(1) Anyone injured by inaccurate or offensive statements or ideas disseminated to the public in general by a legally regulated medium of communication has the right to reply or to make a correction using the same communications outlet, under such conditions as the law may establish.
(2) The correction or reply shall not in any case remit other legal liabilities that may have been incurred.
(3) For the effective protection of honor and reputation, every published, and every newspaper, motion picture, radio, and television company, shall have a person responsible who is not protected by immunities or special privileges.
Art. 15. Right to Assembly.
The right of peaceful assembly, without arms, is recognized. No restrictions may be placed on the exercise of this right other than those imposed in conformity with the law and necessary in a democratic society to the interest of national security, public safety or public order, or to protect public health or morals or the rights or freedoms of others.
Art. 16. Freedom of Association.
(1) Everyone has the right to associate freely for ideological, religious, political, economic, labor, social, cultural, sports, or other purposes.
(2) The exercise of this right shall be subject only to such restrictions established by law as may be necessary in a democratic society, in the interest of national security, public safety or public order, or to protect public health or morals or the rights and freedoms of others.
(3) The provisions of this article do not bar the imposition of legal restrictions, including even deprivation of the exercise of the right of association, on members of the armed forces and the police.
Art. 17. Rights of the Family.
(1) The family is the natural and fundamental group unit of society and is entitled to protection by society and the state.
(2) The right of men and women of marriageable age to marry and to raise a family shall be recognized, if they meet the conditions required by domestic laws, insofar as such conditions do not affect the principle of nondiscrimination established in this Convention.
(3) No marriage shall be entered into without the free and full consent of the intending spouses.
(4) The States Parties shall take appropriate steps to ensure the quality of rights and the adequate balancing of responsibilities of the spouses as to marriage, during marriage, and in the event of the dissolution. In case of dissolution, provision shall be made for the necessary protection of any children solely on the basis of their own best interests.
(5) The law shall recognize equal rights for children born out of wedlock and those born in wedlock.
Art. 18. Right to a Name.
Every person has the right to a given name and to the surnames of his parents or that of one of them. The law shall regulate the manner in which this right shall be ensured for all, by the use of assumed names if necessary.
Art. 19. Rights of the Child.
Every minor child has the right to the measures of protection required by his condition as a minor on the part of his family, society, and the state.
Art. 20. Right to Nationality.
(1) Every person has the right to a nationality.
(2) Every person has the right to the nationality of the state in whose territory he was born if he does not have the right to any other nationality.
(3) No one shall be arbitrarily deprived of his nationality or of the right to change it.
Art. 21. Right to Property.
(1) Everyone has the right to the use and enjoyment of his property. The law may subordinate such use and enjoyment to the interest of society.
(2) No one shall be deprived of his property except upon payment of just compensation, for reasons of public utility or social interest, and in the cases and according to the forms established by law.
(3) Usury and any other form of exploitation of man by man shall be prohibited by law.
Art. 22. Freedom of Movement and Residence.
(1) Every person lawfully in the territory of a State Party has the right to move about in it, and to reside in it subject to the provisions of the law.
(2) Every person has the right to leave any country freely, including his own.
(3) The exercise of the foregoing rights may be restricted only pursuant to a law to the extent necessary in a democratic society to prevent crime or to protect national security, public safety, public order, public morals, public health, or the rights or freedoms of others.
(4) The exercise of the rights recognized in paragraph 1 may also be restricted by law in designated zones for reasons of public interest.
(5) No one can be expelled from the territory of the state of which he is a national or be deprived of the right to enter it.
(6) An alien lawfully in the territory of a State Party to this Convention may be expelled from it only pursuant to a decision reached in accordance with law.
(7) Every person has the right to seek and be granted asylum in a foreign territory, in accordance with the legislation of the state and international conventions, in the event he is being pursued for political offenses or related common crimes.
(8) In no case may an alien be deported or returned to a country, regardless of whether or not it is his country of origin, if in that country his right to life or personal freedom is in danger of being violated because of his race, nationality, religion, social status, or political opinions.
(9) The collective expulsion of aliens is prohibited.
Art. 23. Right to Participate in Government.
(1) Every citizen shall enjoy the following rights and opportunities:
(a) to take part in the conduct of public affairs, directly or through freely chosen representatives;
(b) to vote and to be elected in genuine periodic elections, which shall be by universal and equal suffrage and by secret ballot that guarantees the free expression of the will of the voters; and
(c) to have access, under general conditions of equality, to the public service of his country.
(2) The law may regulate the exercise of the rights and opportunities referred to in the preceding paragraph only on the basis of age, nationality, residence, language, education, civil and mental capacity, or sentencing by a competent court in criminal proceedings.
Art. 24. Right to Equal Protection.
All persons are equal before the law. Consequently, they are entitled, without discrimination, to equal protection of the law.
Art. 25. Right to Judicial Protection.
(1) Everyone has the right to simple and prompt recourse, or any other effective recourse, to a competent court or tribunal for protection against acts that violate his fundamental rights recognized by the constitution or laws of the state concerned or by this Convention, even though such violation may have been committed by persons acting in the course of their official duties.
(2) The States Parties undertake:
(a) to ensure that any person claiming such remedy shall have his rights determined by the competent authority provided for by the legal system of the state;
(b) to develop the possibilities of judicial remedy; and
(c) to ensure that the competent authorities shall enforce such remedies when granted.
Chapter III – Economic, Social, and Cultural Rights.
Art. 26. Progressive Development.
The States Parties undertake to adopt measures, both internally and through international cooperation, especially those of an economic and technical nature, with a view to achieving progressively, by legislation or other appropriate means, the full realization of the rights implicit in the economic, social, educational, scientific, and cultural standards set forth in the Charter of the Organization of American States as amended by the Protocol of Buenos Aires.
Chapter IV – Suspension of Guarantees, Interpretation, and Application.
Art. 27. Suspension of Guarantees.

(1) In time of war, public danger, or other emergency that threatens the independence or security of a State Party, it may take measures derogating from its obligations under the present Convention to the extent and for the period of time strictly required by the exigencies of the situation, provided that such measures are not inconsistent with its other obligations under international law and do not involve discrimination on the ground of race, color, sex, language, religion, or social origin.
(2) The foregoing provision does not authorize any suspension of the following articles: Art. 3 (Right to Juridical Personality); Art. 4 (Right to Life), Art. 5 (Right to Humane Treatment); Art. 6 (Freedom from Slavery), Art. 9 (Freedom from Ex Post Facto Laws), Art. 12 (Freedom of Conscience and Religion); Art. 17 (Rights of the Family), Art. 18 (Right to a Name), Art. 19 (Rights of the Child), Art. 20 (Right to Nationality), and Art. 23 (Right to Participate in Government), or of the judicial guarantees essential for the protection of such rights.
(3) Any State Party availing itself of the right of suspension shall immediately inform the other States Parties, through the Secretary-General of the Organization of American States, of the provisions the application of which it has suspended, the reasons that gave rise to the suspension, and the date set for the termination of such suspension.
Art. 28. Federal Clause.
(1) Where a State Party is constituted as a federal state, the national government of such State Party shall implement all the provisions of the Convention over whose subject matter it exercises legislative and judicial jurisdiction.
(2) With respect to the provisions over whose subject matter the constituent units of the federal state have jurisdiction, the national government shall immediately take suitable measures, in accordance with its constitution and its laws, to the end that the competent authorities of the constituent units may adopt appropriate provisions for the fulfillment of this Convention.
(3) Whenever two or more States Parties agree to form a federation or other type of association, they shall take care that the resulting federal or other compact contains the provisions necessary for continuing and rendering effective the standards of this Convention in the new state that is organized.
Art. 29. Restrictions Regarding Interpretation.
No provision of this Convention shall be interpreted as:
(a) permitting any State Party, group, or person to suppress the enjoyment or exercise of the rights and freedoms recognized in this Convention or to restrict them to a greater extent than is provided for herein;
(b) restricting the enjoyment or exercise of any right or freedom recognized by virtue of the laws of any State Party or by virtue of another convention to which one of the said states is a party;
(c) precluding other rights or guarantees that are inherent in the human personality or derived from representative democracy as a form of government; or
(d) excluding or limiting the effect that the American Declaration of the Rights and Duties of Man and other international acts of the same nature may have.
Art. 30. Scope of Restrictions.
The restrictions that, pursuant to this Convention, may be placed on the enjoyment or exercise of the rights or freedoms recognized herein may not be applied except in accordance with laws enacted for reasons of general interest and in accordance with the purpose for which such restrictions have been established.
Art. 31. Recognition of Other Rights.
Other rights and freedoms recognized in accordance with the procedures established in Art. 76 and 77 may be included in the system of protection of this Convention.
Chapter V – Personal Responsibilities.
Art. 32. Relationship between Duties and Rights.
(1) Every person has responsibilities to his family, his community, and mankind.
(2) The rights of each person are limited by the rights of others, by the security of all, and by the just demands of the general welfare, in a democratic society.
Part II – Means of Protection.
Chapter VI – Competent Organs.
Art. 33. The following organs shall have competence with respect to matters relating to the fulfillment of the commitments made by the States Parties to this Convention:
(a) the Inter-American Commission on Human Rights, referred to as the Commission and
(b) the Inter-American Court of Human Rights, referred to as The Court."

Chapter VII defined the Inter-American Commission of Human Rights; Chapter VIII the Inter-American Court of Human Rights; Chapter IX Common Provisions; Chapter X Signature, Ratification, Reservations, Amendments, Protocols and Denunciation; Chapter XI Transitory Provisions. Annex: Statements and Reservations.

The Convention was prepared by the Inter-American Conference on Human Rights, Nov. 7–22, 1969 in San José de Costa Rica but signed only by 12 American States: Chile Colombia, Costa Rica, Ecuador, El Salvador, Guatemala, Honduras, Nicaragua, Panama, Paraguay, Uruguay, and Venezuela. According to art. 74, it will enter into force as soon as eleven states have deposited instruments of ratification or adherence (until 1981 ratified only by Colombia and Costa Rica). Competent organs of the Convention (Part. II, arts. 33 to 73): Inter-American Commission on Human Rights and Inter-American Court on Human Rights. In 1988 there were 20 State Parties to the Convention of which 10 have recognized the Court of Human Rights Jurisdiction.

American Convention on Human Rights – Pact of San José, Costa Rica; OAS Treaty Series 36, Washington, DC, 1970; R.L. BLEDSOE, B.A. BOCZEK, *The International Law Dictionary*, Oxford, 1987; *Council of Europe. Human Rights Information Sheet*, No 20 and No 21, Strasbourg, 1988.

HUMAN AND PEOPLE'S RIGHTS IN THE ARAB WORLD, CHARTER ON, 1986. Prepared by the League of Arab States and accepted as draft by the Conference in Syracuse, Sicily, Italy, on Dec. 5–12, 1986. The text is as follows:

Preamble.
Whereas recognition of the inherent dignity and of the equal and inalienable rights of all members of the human family is the foundation of freedom, justice and peace in the world, Considering the indissoluble national ties of shared values, heritage, history, civilization and common interests uniting citizens of all regions of the Arab Nation whose land God has blessed by making it the cradle of revealed religions, Having regard for the shared aspirations of Arabs to resume their contribution in building and advancing human civilization, Whereas the disregard for the collective rights of the Arab Nation and for human rights in its land has led to countless disasters beginning with the occupation of Palestine and the setting up of an alien, racist entity therein and the uprooting of its people and ending with the violation of the territorial integrity of all Arab lands, squandering their human and material resources and tying up of their future and destiny to external forces, thus impeding their ability to cope with the tasks of development, independence and the realization of their legitimate aspirations,
Whereas transcending this tragic reality can only be achieved through a common understanding of those rights and the necessary means for their protection under the rule of law if the Arab Nation is not to be compelled to have recourse, as a last resort, to rebellion against tyranny and oppression.
Reaffirming their faith in the principles in the Charter of the United Nations and the International Bill of Human Rights, a number of Arab jurists and intellectuals committed to the Arab cause and Arab future, having met in Siracusa, Italy, at the invitation of the International Institute of Higher Studies in Criminal Sciences,
Declare the following Draft Charter on Human and People's Rights in the Arab World, and appeal to citizens of all regions of the Arab Nation to adopt it as a common ideal to achieve and a first step in a general scheme to transcend the Arab predicament and initiate the national renaissance;
Appeal to all Arab countries, individually and collectively, and to their common bodies, particularly the League of Arab States, to consider this Draft Charter with a view to adopting and implementing it.
Part I–Rights and Fundamental Freedoms.
Art. 1. Everyone has the right to recognition everywhere as a person before the law.
Art. 2.
1. The right to life is inviolable and protected by law.
2. The death penalty may be imposed only for the most serious crimes. A death sentence may not be imposed for a political crime unless it is accompanied by murder or attempted murder.
3. A death sentence may only be imposed by a competent court. Anyone sentenced to death has the right to appeal to a higher court and has the right to seek pardon or commutation of the sentence.
Art. 3.
1. Everyone has the right to the integrity of person.
2. No one shall be subjected to torture, bodily or mental harm, to inhuman, cruel or degrading treatment or punishment. Such acts or complicity therein shall be considered a criminal offense punishable by law and not covered by statutory limitations.
3. No one shall be subjected without his free consent to medical or scientific experimentation or experimental treatment.
Art. 4.
1. Everyone has the right to liberty and security of person and the pursuit of happiness. This right may not be infringed upon except on such grounds and in accordance with such procedures as are established by law.
2. No one shall be arbitrarily arrested or detained. Anyone who is so deprived of his liberty shall be entitled to be assisted by a lawyer and shall be brought promptly before a competent judicial authority.
3. Anyone who has been the victim of unlawful arrest or detention shall have the right to compensation.
Art. 5.
1. There shall be no criminal offense or penalty unless stipulated by law. No one shall be punished for an act which did not constitute a criminal offense under the law at the time when it was committed.
2. A defendent is presumed innocent until proved guilty pursuant to a judgment rendered by a competent court.
3. A defendant shall be entitled to the necessary guarantees to defend himself in person or through the assistance of a lawyer of his own choosing in a public trial. The court shall provide him with a lawyer to defend him without payment by him in case he does not have sufficient means to pay for his defense.
Art. 6.
1. All persons deprived of their liberty shall be treated with humanity and with respect for their dignity.
2. In carrying out sentences, due consideration shall be given to the Standard Minimum Rules for the Treatment of Prisoners as adopted by the United Nations.
3. In deciding and carrying out sentences on juvenile offenders, due consideration shall be given to their reformation, education and rehabilitation.
Art. 7. No one shall be imprisoned merely on the ground of his inability to fulfil a civil obligation.
Art. 8.
1. Everyone has the right to liberty of movement within his country and freedom to choose his residence.
2. Everyone who is a citizen of an Arab country or of Arab origin has the right to leave his country and return to it and to enter any other Arab country.
3. No citizen shall be expelled from his country.
Art. 9.
1. Everyone has the right to freedom of belief and thought.
2. Everyone has the right to manifest his religion or belief in observance, worship and teaching either individually or in community with others without prejudice to the rights and freedoms of others. Restrictions on the enjoyment of this right shall be minimal and may only be imposed as prescribed by law.
Art. 10.
1. Everyone has the right to freedom of opinion and expression. This right shall include freedom to seek, receive, impart and disseminate information and ideas in all media, regardless of frontiers.
2. Restrictions on the exercise of this right shall be minimal and only as prescribed by law and where

necessary for the respect of the rights and freedoms of others.

Art. 11.

1. All persons are equal before the law without discrimination on the basis of race, color, sex, birth, national origin, language, religion or opinion.

2. All persons are equal before the courts. The State shall guarantee the independence and impartiality of the judiciary.

3. The State shall guarantee the independence of the legal profession.

Art. 12. The privacy of the individual is inviolable. Privacy shall include the private affairs of the family, the home and correspondence, and other means of private communication. Such privacy may be impinged upon only as prescribed by law.

Art. 13. The family is the fundamental unit of society and is entitled to care and protection by the State.

Art. 14. Everyone has the right to found a family. Marriage shall be entered into with the free will and full consent of the intending spouses.

Art. 15. The State shall provide care and protection to mothers and infants.

Art. 16. The State shall care for the physical and mental health of minors and protect them from social and economic exploitation.

Art. 17. Everyone has the right to social and health care, both physical and mental, as guaranteed by the State within its capabilities. The State shall provide citizens with the necessary protection against epidemic, endemic and occupational diseases.

Art. 18. Everyone has the right to live in an adequate, pollution-free environment.

Art. 19. The State shall, by all available means, provide youth with possibilities for their physical and intellectual development.

Art. 20. The State shall provide care for the aged and secure a decent life for them.

Art. 21. The State shall provide special care for the handicapped according to their needs and their physical and mental abilities.

Art. 22. Everyone has the right to social security, including the right of victims to compensation in cases where offenders are indigent.

Art. 23. Everyone has the right to an adequate standard of living to meet the basic needs of himself and his family, especially in respect of food, clothing and housing.

Art. 24. The State shall guarantee an equitable distribution of the national income among its citizens.

Art. 25. Every citizen has the right to work where he freely chooses in his own country or in any other Arab country.

Art. 26. Everyone has the right to the enjoyment of just and discrimination-free conditions of work which ensure him fair wages and a favorable, safe and healthy work environment with reasonable limitations on working hours, periodic holidays, and opportunities for promotion to higher positions.

Art. 27. Citizens have the right to form and to freely join trade and professional unions to protect their social and economic rights and to defend their common interests. Such unions have the right to establish pan-Arab federations.

Art. 28. Unions and federations have the right to function and exercise their legitimate activities freely, subject to no limitations other than those necessary for the protection of public order (ordre publique) and the rights and freedoms of others, and as required by the nature of the union's own organization.

Art. 29. The State shall ensure the right to strike in accordance with the provisions of law.

Art. 30. The State shall protect private property. No one shall be deprived of this right arbitrarily or without fair compensation.

Art. 31. Everyone has the right to education. Primary education shall be compulsory. The State shall make education at the higher levels including technical and vocational education, accessible to all.

Art. 32. Education shall be free at all levels in government schools, institutes and universities.

Art. 33. Everyone has the right to live in a free intellectual environment, to take part in cultural life, to develop his intellectual and creative talents and to enjoy the benefits of scientific and artistic progress. Everyone has the right to benefit from the protection of the moral and material interests resulting from any scientific, artistic or literary production of which he is the author.

Art. 34. Education and culture shall aim at developing the human personality, consolidating faith in Arab unity, stressing spiritual and religious values and strengthening respect for human rights and the fundamental freedoms of individuals and groups.

Art. 35. National communities whose members feel bound together by an ethnic or cultural heritage have the right to preserve and enjoy their own culture and use their own language.

Art. 36. Every citizen has the right to a nationality. He has the right to change it and to keep it together with any other Arab nationality. He has the right to pass nationality to his children without discrimination in this regard between men and women.

Art. 37. Everyone has the right to peaceful assembly and meeting. No restrictions may be placed on the exercise of this right other than those imposed in conformity with the law and which are necessary in a democratic society to protect and guarantee the rights and freedoms provided from in this Charter.

Art. 38. Every citizen has the right to freedom of association with others including the right to form and join political parties and trade unions for the protection of common interests. Such organizations shall have the right to exercise their activities freely in all Arab countries.

(2) No restrictions may be placed on the exercise of this right other than those which are prescribed by law and which are necesary in a democratic society to protect and guarantee the rights and freedoms provided for in this Charter.

Art. 39. Every citizen is entitled to enjoy the following rights:

(1) To take part in the conduct of public affairs, directly or through freely chosen representatives;

(2) To vote and to be elected at genuine periodic elections, which shall be held under universal and equal suffrage and by secret ballot, guaranteeing the free expression of the will of the electorate;

(3) To have access, on general term of equality, to public service in his country.

Art. 40.(1) Every citizen who is subjected to persecution on political grounds has the right to seek and obtain asylum in any Arab country in accordance with the law and the provisions of this Charter.

(2) No person enjoying asylum or seeking it shall be expelled to an Arab or foreign country where his life would be in danger or where he may be prosecuted.

Art. 41. Mass expulsion of citizens of any Arab country shall be prohibited.

Art. 42.(1) Any country in case of actual war, imminent danger or any crisis threatening its independence and security may declare a state of emergency and may take measures derogating from its obligations under the present Charter to the extent strictly required by the exigencies of the situation.

(2) No derogation may be permitted under the preceding provision from respect for the right to life, security of person, recognition as a person before the law, the right to a nationality, the principle of supremacy of law or the right to freedom of religion and thought.

(3) Any Arab country availing itself of the right of derogation shall immediately inform the other Arab parties to the present Charter of those provisions it has derogated, the reasons for its action and the date on which it will terminate such derogation.

Art. 43. Orders from superiors or from a higher authority shall not be an admissible defense against violations of the rights stipulated in the present Charter.

Part II — Collective Rights of the Arab People

Art. 44.(1) The Arab people has the right to self determination, and by virtue of this right it freely determines its political status and pursues its comprehensive economic, social and cultural development in the light of its national interests while preserving its national heritage.

(2) The Arab people has the right to eliminate all forms of foreign economic exploitation, especially the practices of monopolies and international cartels, and to end all forms of economic dependence.

(3) The Arab people has all rights to its natural wealth and resources. It has the right to freely dispose of its natural wealth and resources in a manner conductive to the furtherance of its own national interests without prejudice to any obligation arising out of the exigencies of international economic cooperation, based upon the principles of mutual benefit and international law.

(4) The Arab people has the right to an adequate standard of living and to ensure its food security.

Art. 45. The Arab people, in all its countries, has a natural right to unity and to work towards achieving it by all legitimate means.

Art. 46. The Arab people has the right to resist the occupation of any part of its homeland by all legitimate means including armed struggle, and to participate in the defense thereof in case of foreign aggression.

Art. 47. Disputes among Arab Countries shall not be settled by the use of force, Arab citizens shall have the right, for reasons of conscience or nationalism, to refuse to take part in fighting against any Arab country.

Art. 48. Arab citizens shall have the right to volunteer in favour of and assist, by all legitimate means, peoples subjected to colonialism, occupation or racial discrimination.

Art. 49. The Arab people shall have the right to peace and security in accordance with the principles of solidarity and friendly relations as enshrined in the Charter of the United Nations and other international instruments.

Part III — Measures for Safeguarding Human Rights
Section I — The Arab Commission on Human Rights
Art. 50. An Arab Commission on Human Rights, hereinafter called "the Commission", shall be established in accordance with the following principles:

(1) The Commission shall perform the functions stipulated in the present Charter and shall consist of eleven experts known for their high moral character and recognized competence in the field of human rights. They shall serve in their personal capacity.

(2) Each party may nominate two persons possessing the qualifications specified in the previous paragraph. One of those persons so nominated shall not be a national of the party making the nomination. The bar association in each party shall nominate a third person for the same purpose.

(3) Representatives of parties shall elect the members of the Commission by secret ballot at a meeting to be held for that purpose from a list of all the names of the persons nominated in accordance with the previous paragraph. The Commission may not include more than one national of the same party.

Art. 51.(1) The members of the Commission shall be elected for a term of four years, which may be renewed. However, the term of five members elected at the first election shall expire at the end of two years. These five members shall be chosen by lot.

(2) Every member of the commission shall, before taking up his duties, make a solemn declaration, in an open session, that he will perform his functions impartially and conscientiously.

Art. 52.(1) The Commission shall elect its officers for a term of two years. They may be re-elected.

(2) The Commission shall establish its own rules of procedure.

Art. 53. The Commission shall:

(1) Work for the promotion of Arab human and people's rights and the strengthening of public awareness thereof through the compilation and dissemination of documents, studies and research papers, the organization of seminars and conferences, publicizing them in all media as well as encouraging national organizations operating in the same field and the co-operation with international and regional organizations to achieve their goals.

(2) Consider periodic reports submitted by the parties on measures taken by the parties to give effect to the provisions of the present Charter.

(3) Consider communications submitted by any party claiming that another party is not fulfilling its obligations under the present Charter.

(4) Consider communications submitted by individuals or jurisdicial persons from any Arab party or persons under its jurisdiction regarding violations by any party of their rights as provided by the present Charter. The Commission shall not consider any such communication unless it has ascertained that the petitioner has failed to obtain satisfaction, either because domestic remedies have been exhausted or did not exist, or was unable to gain access to them or due to unreasonable delay in settling the matter.

(5) Consider any gross violations of human rights on the part of any party upon the request of at least two of its members.

(6) Publish an annual report on its activities.

Art. 54. The Commission shall submit, in connection with matters considered under the preceding paragraph, any such comments and recommendations as it may consider appropriate to the parties concerned, and shall publish them without the delay as prescribed in its rules of procedures.

Section Two — The Arab Court of Human Rights

Art. 55. There shall be established under the provisions of the present Charter a Court to be named "The Arab Court of Human Rights", hereinafter called "the Court", which shall carry out its functions in accordance with the provisions of the present Charter, its statute, and the rules of procedure established thereunder.

Art. 56.(1) The Court shall be composed of seven judges to be elected by representatives of the parties to the present Charter from a list of persons nominated for that purpose.

(2) Each party shall nominate two persons for membership in the Court, and the bar association therein shall nominate a third person. All nominees shall be prominent legal experts.

(3) Representatives of the parties shall elect members of the Court by secret ballot at a meeting to be held for that purpose. The Court may not include more than one national of the same party.

Art. 57. Members of the Court shall be elected for a term of six years which may be renewed. However, the term of three members elected at the first election shall expire at the end of three years. These three members shall be chosen by lot.

Art. 58. The jurisdiction of the Court shall comprise:

(1) Cases brought before it by one party against another party following the failure of the Commission to reach a solution satisfactory to that party during the time allowed in the rules of procedures for settling the matter after submission of the petition to the Commission.

(2) Individual communications referred to it by the Commission because of the Commission's inability to reach a solution. Each party may appoint a representative before the Court.

(3) Interpretation of the Charter and determination of the obligations of parties requested by such parties and organizations permitted to do so in the rules of procedure.

(4) Publication of an annual report on its activities.

Art. 59. Decisions of the Court shall be as binding as the final decisions handed down by the national courts of the states in which the parties reside.

Art. 60. The Court shall meet in open sessions unless it decides otherwise in accordance with its rules of procedure.

Art. 61. The Court's rules of procedure shall set out its system of work.

Part IV — Final Provisions

Art. 62.(1) The parties to the present Charter undertake to respect and to ensure to all individuals within their territory and subject to their jurisdiction the rights recognized in the present Charter, without regard to race, color, sex, language, religion, political or other opinions, national or social origin, property, birth or other status.

(2) Where not already provided for by existing legislative or other measures, the parties to the present Charter further undertake to develop the necessary steps, in accordance with their constitutional procedures and with the provisions of the present Charter, to adopt such legislative or other measures as may be necessary to give effect to the rights recognized in the present Charter.

(3) The parties to the present Charter undertake to develop steps, individually and through mutual assistance and co-operation, especially economic and technical, to the maximum of their available resources, to achieve the full realization of the rights recognized in the present Charter.

(4) The parties to the present Charter undertake to ensure that any person whose rights or freedoms as herein recognized are violated shall have an effective remedy, notwithstanding that the violation has been committed by persons acting in an official capacity. They further undertake to ensure that any person claiming such a remedy shall have his right thereto determined by competent judicial, administrative or legislative authorities and to develop the possibilities of judicial remedy. The parties also undertake to ensure that the competent authorities shall enforce such remedies when granted.

Art. 63.(1) The present Charter is open for signature by all Arab countries. Each Arab country as well as inter-Arab Governmental bodies, especially the League of Arab States, may take the initiative to call a meeting of all Arab countries to discuss and sign this Charter.

(2) The present Charter shall enter into force three months after the date of the deposit of the third instrument of ratification or of accession with the depositary organization. For each country ratifying the present Charter or acceding to it, the present Charter shall enter into force three months after the date of the deposit of its own instrument of ratification or (instrument) of accession. As for the establishment of the Commission and the Court, the present Charter shall enter into force three months after the date of the deposit of the eleventh instrument of ratification or instrument of accession.

Art. 64. The parties to the present Charter shall lay down the statute of the Court and shall take the necessary measures for setting up the Court and the Commission in accordance with the provisions of the present Charter.

Art. 65. The parties to the present Charter shall determine the budget for both the Commission and the Court and the administrative and technical services necessary for their appropriate smooth operation as well as emoluments for members of their bodies.

Council of Europe, Human Rights, *Information Sheet No 21*, Strasbourg, 1988, pp. 243–261.

HUMAN RIGHTS CHARTER OF THE OAU, 1986. ▷ OAU.

HUMAN RIGHTS COMMISSION. An ECOSOC Commission which prepared the ▷ Human Rights, Universal Declaration of, 1948, and the ▷ Human Rights Convention, 1966.

HUMAN RIGHTS COVENANTS, 1966. The official name shared by two international conventions unanimously adopted by the UN General Assembly Res. 2200/XXI, Dec. 16, 1966, extending the Universal Declaration of Human Rights, 1948 (collection of principles without legal force): the ▷ Human Rights International Convention on Economic, Social and Cultural Rights and the ▷ Human Rights International Convention on Civil and Political Rights. The two Covenants came into force in 1976.

UN Yearbook, 1966, pp. 406–488.

HUMAN RIGHTS DAY. The World Human Rights Day is celebrated each Dec. 10 since 1950 on the anniversary of the proclamation of the ▷ Human Rights, Universal Declaration of, 1948. The UN General Assembly adopted a number of resolutions on the solemn celebration of Human Rights Day. The year 1968 was declared Human Rights Year.

HUMAN RIGHTS EUROPEAN CONVENTION, 1950. A Convention for the Protection of Human Rights and Fundamental Freedom, signed in Rome, Nov. 4, 1950, by the Governments of Belgium, Denmark, France, the GDR, Iceland, Ireland, Italy, Luxembourg, Netherlands, Norway, Turkey and the UK. Institution of the Convention: European Commission of Human Rights and European Court of Human Rights. Came into force Nov. 3, 1953. The text of the main 19 Articles is as follows:

"The Governments signatory hereto, being Members of the Council of Europe,

Considering the Universal Declaration of Human Rights proclaimed by the General Assembly of the United Nations on 10th December 1948;

Considering that this Declaration aims at securing the universal and effective recognition and observance of the Rights therein declared;

Considering that the aim of the Council of Europe is the achievement of greater unity between its Members and that one of the methods by which that aim is to be pursued is the maintenance and further realisation of Human Rights and Fundamental Freedoms;

Reaffirming their profound belief in those Fundamental Freedoms which are the foundation of justice and peace in the world and are best maintained on the one hand by an effective political democracy and on the other by a common understanding and observance of the Human Rights upon which they depend;

Being resolved, as the Governments of European countries which are like-minded and have a common heritage of political traditions, ideals, freedom and the rule of law, to take the first steps for the collective enforcement of certain of the Rights stated in the Universal Declaration;

Have agreed as follows:

Art. 1. The High Contracting Parties shall secure to everyone within their jurisdiction the rights and freedoms defined in Section I of this Convention.

Art. 2.(1) Everyone's right to life shall be protected by law. No one shall be deprived of his life intentionally save in the execution of a sentence of a court following his conviction of a crime for which this penalty is provided by law.

(2) Deprivation of life shall not be regarded as inflicted in contravention of this Article when it results from the use of force which is no more than absolutely necessary:

(a) in defence of any person from unlawful violence;

(b) in order to effect a lawful arrest or to prevent the escape of a person lawfully detained;

(c) in action lawfully taken for the purpose of quelling a riot or insurrection.

Art. 3. No one shall be subjected to torture or to inhuman or degrading treatment or punishment.

Art. 4.(1) No one shall be held in slavery or servitude.

(2) No one shall be required to perform forced or compulsory labour.

(3) For the purpose of this Article the term 'forced or compulsory labour' shall not include:

(a) any work required to be done in the ordinary course of detention imposed according to the provisions of Article 5 of this Convention or during conditional release from such detention;

(b) any service of a military character or, in case of conscientious objectors in countries where they are recognised, service exacted instead of compulsory military service;

(c) any service exacted in case of an emergency or calamity threatening the life or well-being of the community;

(d) any work or service which forms part of normal civic obligations.

Art. 5.(1) Everyone has the right to liberty and security of person.

No one shall be deprived of his liberty save in the following cases and in accordance with a procedure prescribed by law:

(a) the lawful detention of a person after conviction by a competent court;

(b) the lawful arrest or detention of a person for non-compliance with the lawful order of a court or in order to secure the fulfilment of any obligation prescribed by law;

(c) the lawful arrest or detention of a person effected for the purpose of bringing him before the competent legal authority on reasonable suspicion of having committed an offence or when it is reasonably considered necessary to prevent his committing an offence or fleeing after having done so;

(d) the detention of a minor by lawful order for the purpose of educational supervision or his lawful detention for the purpose of bringing him before the competent legal authority;

(e) the lawful detention of persons for the prevention of the spreading of infectious diseases, of persons of unsound mind, alcoholics or drug addicts or vagrants;

(f) the lawful arrest or detention of a person to prevent his effecting an unauthorised entry into the country or of a person against whom action is being taken with a view to deportation or extradition.

(2) Everyone who is arrested shall be informed promptly, in a language which he understands, of the reasons for his arrest and of any charge against him.

(3) Everyone arrested or detained in accordance with the provisions of paragraph 1(c) of this Article shall be brought promptly before a judge or other officer authorised by law to exercise judicial power and shall be entitled to trial within a reasonable time or to release

pending trial. Release may be conditioned by guarantees to appear to trial.

(4) Everyone who is deprived of his liberty by arrest or detention shall be entitled to take proceedings by which the lawfulness of his detention shall be decided speedily by a court and his release ordered if the detention is not lawful.

(5) Everyone who has been the victim of arrest or detention in contravention of the provision of this Article shall have an enforceable right to compensation. Art. 6.(1) In the determination of his civil rights and obligations or of any criminal charge against him, everyone is entitled to a fair and public hearing within a reasonable time by an independent and impartial tribunal established by law. Judgment shall be pronounced publicly but the press and public may be excluded from all or part of the trial in the interests of morals, public order or national security in a democratic society, where the interests of juveniles or the protection of the private life of the parties so require, or to the extent strictly necessary in the opinion of the court in special circumstances where publicity would prejudice the interests of justice.

(2) Everyone charged with a criminal offence shall be presumed innocent until proved guilty according to law.

(3) Everyone charged with a criminal offence has the following minimum rights:

(a) to be informed promptly, in a language which he understands and in detail, of the nature and cause of the accusation against him;

(b) to have adequate time and facilities for the preparation of his defence;

(c) to defend himself in person or through legal assistance of his own choosing, or, if he has not sufficient means to pay for legal assistance, to be given it free when the interests of justice so require;

(d) to examine or have examined witnesses against him and to obtain the attendance and examination of witnesses on his behalf under the same conditions as witnesses against him;

(e) to have the free assistance of an interpreter if he cannot understand or speak the language used in court. Art. 7.(1) No one shall be held guilty of any criminal offence on account of any act or omission which did not constitute a criminal offence under national or international law at the time when it was committed. Nor shall a heavier penalty be imposed than the one that was applicable at the time the criminal offence was committed.

(2) This Article shall not prejudice the trial and punishment of any person for any act or omission which, at the time when it was committed, was criminal according to the general principles of law recognised by civilised nations. Art. 8.(1) Everyone has the right to respect for his private and family life, his home and his correspondence.

(2) There shall be no interference by a public authority with the exercise of this right except such as is in accordance with the law and is necessary in a democratic society in the interests of national security, public safety or the economic well-being of the country, for the prevention of disorder or cime, for the protection of health or morals, or for the protection of the rights and freedoms of others. Art. 9.(1) Everyone has the right to freedom of thought, conscience and religion; this right includes freedom to change his religion or belief and freedom, either alone or in community with others and in public or private, to manifest his religion or belief, in worship, teaching, practice and observance.

(2) Freedom to manifest one's religion or beliefs shall be subject only to such limitations as are prescribed by law and are necessary in a democratic society in the interests of public safety, for the protection of public order, health or morals, or for the protection of the rights and freedoms of others. Art. 10.(1) Everyone has the right to freedom of expression. This right shall include freedom to hold opinions and to receive and impart information and ideas without interference by public authority and regardless of frontiers. This Article shall not prevent States from requiring the licensing of broadcasting, television or cinema enterprises.

(2) The exercise of these freedoms, since it carries with it duties and responsibilities, may be subject to such formalities, conditions, restrictions or penalities as are prescribed by law and are necessary in a democratic society, in the interests of national security, territorial integrity or public safety, for the prevention of disorder or crime, for the protection of health or morals, for the protection of the reputation or rights of others, for preventing the disclosure of information received in confidence, or for maintaining the authority and impartiality of the judiciary. Art. 11.(1) Everyone has the right to freedom of peaceful assembly and to freedom of association with others, including the right to form and to join trade unions for the protection of his interests.

(2) No restrictions shall be placed on the exercise of these rights other than such as are prescribed by law and are necessary in a democratic society in the interests of national security or public safety, for the prevention of disorder or crime, for the protection of health or morals or for the protection of the rights and freedoms of others. This Article shall not prevent the imposition of lawful restrictions on the exercise of these rights by members of the armed forces, of the police or of the administration of the State. Art. 12. Men and women of marriageable age have the right to marry and to found a family, according to the national laws governing the exercise of this right. Art. 13. Everyone whose rights and freedoms as set forth in this Convention are violated shall have an effective remedy before a national authority notwithstanding that the violation has been committed by persons acting in an official capacity. Art. 14. The enjoyment of rights and freedoms set forth in this Convention shall be secured without discrimination on any ground such as sex, race, colour, language, religion, political or other opinion, national or social origin, association with a national minority, property, birth or other status. Art. 15.(1) In time of war or other public emergency threatening the life of the nation any High Contracting Party may take measures derogating from its obligations under this Convention to the extent strictly required by the exigencies of the situation, provided that such measures are not inconsistent with its other obligations under international law.

(2) No derogation from Article 2, except in respect of deaths resulting from lawful acts of war, or from Articles 3, 4 (paragraph 1) and 7 shall be made under this provision.

(3) Any High Contracting Party availing itself of this right of derogation shall keep the Secretary-General of the Council of Europe fully informed of the measures which it has taken and the reasons therefor. It shall also inform the Secretary-General of the Council of Europe when such measures have ceased to operate and the provisions of the Convention are again being fully executed. Art. 16. Nothing in Articles 10, 11 and 14 shall be regarded as preventing the High Contracting Parties from imposing restrictions on the political activity of aliens. Art. 17. Nothing in this Convention may be interpreted as implying for any State, group or person any right to engage in any activity or perform any act aimed at the destruction of any of the rights and freedoms set forth herein or at their limitation to a greater extent than is provided for in the Convention. Art. 18. The restrictions permitted under this Convention to the said rights and freedoms shall not be applied for any purpose other than those for which they have been prescribed. Art. 19. To ensure the observance of the engagements undertaken by the High Contracting Parties in the present Convention, there shall be set up:

(1) A European Commission of Human Rights hereinafter referred to as 'the Commission';

(2) A European Court of Human Rights, hereinafter referred to as 'the Court'."

A Protocol to the Convention signed at Paris on Mar. 20, 1952 stated:

"Art. 1. Every natural or legal person is entitled to the peaceful enjoyment of his possessions. No one shall be deprived of his possessions except in the public interest and subject to the conditions provided for by law and by the general principles of international law.

The preceding provisions shall not, however, in any way impair the right of a State to enforce such laws as it deems necessary to control the use of property in accordance with the general interest or to secure the payment of taxes or other contributions or penalties.

Art. 2. No person shall be denied the right to education. In the exercise of any functions which it assumes in relation to education and to teaching, the State shall respect the right of parents to ensure such education and teaching in conformity with their own religious and philosophical convictions.

Art. 3. The High Contracting Parties undertake to hold free elections at reasonable intervals by secret ballot, under conditions which will ensure the free expression of the opinion of the people in the choice of the legislature."

Came into force on May 18, 1954. On March 19–20, 1985, in Vienna, a conference of 21 Justice and Foreign Ministers reviewed the 1950 Convention and signed Protocol Eight designed to speed up procedures before the ▷ European Commission of Human Rights and the ▷ European Court of Human Rights.

The substantive provisions of the Convention 1950 were incorporated, until 1988, into the domestic law of all 15 member states of the Council of Europe.

UNTS, Vol. 213, pp. 222–261 and pp. 262–269. KEESING's *Contemporary Archive*, September 1985; R.L. BLEDSOE, B.A. BOCZEK, *The International Law Dictionary*, Oxford 1987. Council of Europe, Human Rights Information Sheet No. 21, November 1986–October 1987, Strasbourg, 1988.

HUMAN RIGHTS, EUROPEAN COURT ▷ European Court of Human Rights.

HUMAN RIGHTS, INTERNATIONAL CONVENTION ON CIVIL AND POLITICAL RIGHTS, 1966. One of two ▷ Human Rights Covenants, 1966, unanimously adopted by the UN General Assembly Res. 2200/XXI on Dec. 16, 1966; entered into force in 1976. The text is as follows:

"Preamble. The States Parties to the present Covenant, Considering that, in accordance with the principles proclaimed in the Charter of the United Nations, recognition of the inherent dignity and of the equal and inalienable rights of all members of the human family is the foundation of freedom, justice and peace in the world,

Recognizing that these rights derive from the inherent dignity of the human person,

Recognizing that, in accordance with the Universal Declaration of Human Rights, the ideal of free human beings enjoying civil and political freedom and freedom from fear and want can only be achieved if conditions are created whereby everyone may enjoy his civil and political rights, as well as his economic, social and cultural rights,

Considering the obligations of States under the Charter of the United Nations to promote universal respect for, and observance of, human rights and freedoms,

Realizing that the individual, having duties to other individuals and to the community to which he belongs, is under a responsibility to strive for the promotion and observance of the rights recognized in the present Covenant,

Agree upon the following articles:

Part I Art. 1.(1) All peoples have the right of self-determination. By virtue of that right they freely determine their political status and freely pursue their economic, social and cultural development.

(2) All peoples may, for their own ends, freely dispose of their natural wealth, and resources without prejudice to any obligations arising out of international economic co-operation, based upon the principle of mutual benefit, and international law. In no case may a people be deprived of its own means of subsistence.

(3) The States Parties to the present Covenant including those having responsibility for the administration of Non-Self-Governing and Trust Territories, shall promote the realization of the right of self-determination, and shall respect that right, in conformity with the provisions of the Charter of the United Nations.

Part II Art. 2.(1) Each State Party to the present Covenant undertakes to respect and to ensure to all individuals within its territory and subject to its jurisdiction the rights recognized in the present Covenant, without distinction of any kind, such as race, colour, sex, language, religion political or other opinion, national or social origin, property, birth or other status.

(2) Where not already provided for by existing legislative or other measures, each State Party to the present Covenant undertakes to take the necessary steps, in accordance with its constitutional processes and with the provisions of the present Covenant, to adopt such legislative or other measures as may be necessary to give effect to the rights recognized in the present Covenant.

(3) Each State Party to the present Covenant undertakes:

(a) To ensure that any person whose rights or freedoms as herein recognized are violated shall have an effective remedy, notwithstanding that the violation has been committed by persons acting in an official capacity;

(b) To ensure that any person claiming such a remedy shall have his right thereto determined by competent judicial, administrative or legislative authorities, or by any other competent authority provided for by legal system of the State, and to develop the possibilities of judicial remedy;

(c) To ensure that the competent authorities shall enforce such remedies when granted.

Art. 3. The States Parties to the present Covenant undertake to ensure the equal right of men and women to the enjoyment of all civil and political rights set forth in the present Covenant.

Art. 4.(1) In time of public emergency which threatens the life of the nation and the existence of which is officially proclaimed, the States Parties to the present Covenant may take measures derogating from their obligations under the present Covenant to the extent strictly required by the exigencies of the situation, provided that such measures are not inconsistent with their other obligations under international law and do not involve discrimination solely on the ground of race, colour, sex, language, religion, or social origin.

(2) No derogation from articles 6, 7, 8 (paragraphs 1 and 2), 11, 15, 16 and 18 may be made under this provision.

(3) Any State Party to the present Covenant availing itself of the right of derogation shall immediately inform the other States Parties to the present Covenant, through the intermediary of the Secretary-General of the United Nations, of the provisions from which it has derogated and of the reasons by which it was actuated. A further communication shall be made, through the same intermediary, on the date on which it terminates such derogation.

Art. 5.(1) Nothing in the present Covenant may be interpreted as implying for any State, group or person any right to engage in any activity or perform any act aimed at the destruction of any of the rights and freedoms recognized herein or at their limitation to a greater extent than is provided for in the present Covenant.

(2) There shall be no restriction upon or derogation from any of the fundamental human rights recognized or existing in any State Party to the present Covenant pursuant to law, conventions, regulations or custom on the pretext that the present Covenant does not recognize such rights or that it recognizes them to a lesser extent.

Part III Art. 6.(1) Every Human being has the inherent right to life. That right shall be protected by law. No one shall be arbitrarily deprived of his life.

(2) In countries which have not abolished the death penalty, sentence of death may be imposed only for the most serious crimes in accordance with the law in force at the time of the commission of the crime and not contrary to the provisions of the present Covenant and to the Convention on the Prevention and Punishment of the Crime of Genocide. This penalty can only be carried out pursuant to a final judgment rendered by a competent court.

(3) When deprivation of life constitutes the crime of genocide, it is understood that nothing in this article shall authorize any State Party to the present Covenant to derogate in any way from any obligation assumed under the provisions of the Convention on the Prevention and Punishment of the Crime of Genocide.

(4) Anyone sentenced to death shall have the right to seek pardon or commutation of the sentence. Amnesty, pardon or commutation of the sentence of death may be granted in all cases.

(5) Sentence of death shall not be imposed for crimes committed by persons below eighteen years of age and shall not be carried out on pregnant women.

(6) Nothing in this article shall be invoked to delay or to prevent the abolition of special punishment by any States Party to the present Covenant.

Art. 7. No one shall be subjected to torture or to cruel inhuman or degrading treatment or punishment. In particular, no one shall be subjected without his free consent to medical or scientific experimentation.

Art. 8.(1) No one shall be held in slavery; slavery and the slave-trade in all their forms shall be prohibited.

(2) No one shall be held in servitude.

(3)(a) No one shall be required to perform forced or compulsory labour;

(b) Paragraph 3 (a) shall not be held to preclude, in countries where imprisonment with hard labour may be imposed as a punishment for a crime, the performance of hard labour in pursuance of a sentence to such punishment by a competent court;

(c) For the purpose of this paragraph the term 'forced or compulsory labour' shall not include:

(i) Any work or service, not referred to in subparagraph (b), normally required of a person who is under detention in consequence of a lawful order of a court, or of a person during conditional release from such detention;

(ii) Any service of a military character and, in countries where conscientious objection is recognized, any national service required by law of conscientious objectors;

(iii) Any service exacted in cases of emergency or calamity threatening the life or well-being of the community;

(iv) Any work or service which forms part of normal civil obligations.

Art. 9.(1) Everyone has the right to liberty and security of person. No one shall be subjected to arbitrary arrest or detention. No one shall be deprived of his liberty except on such grounds and in accordance with such procedure as are established by law.

(2) Anyone who is arrested shall be informed, at the time of arrest, of the reasons for his arrest and shall be promptly informed of any charges against him.

(3) Anyone arrested or detained on a criminal charge shall be brought promptly before a judge or other officer authorized by law to exercise judicial power and shall be entitled to trial within a reasonable time or to release. It shall not be the general rule that persons awaiting trial shall be detained in custody, but release may be subject to guarantees to appear for trial, at any other stage of the judicial proceedings, and, should occasion arise, for execution of the judgment.

(4) Anyone who is deprived of his liberty by arrest or detention shall be entitled to take proceedings before a court, in order that that court may decide without delay on the lawfulness of his detention and order his release if the detention is not lawful.

(5) Anyone who has been the victim of unlawful arrest or detention shall have an enforceable right to compensation.

Art. 10.(1) All persons deprived of their liberty shall be treated with humanity and with respect for the inherent dignity of the human person.

(2)(a) Accused persons shall, save in exceptional circumstances, be segregated from convicted persons and shall be subject to separate treatment appropriate to their status as unconvicted persons;

(b) Accused juvenile persons shall be separated from adults and brought as speedily as possible for adjudication.

(3) The penitentiary system shall comprise treatment of prisoners the essential aim of which shall be their reformation and social rehabilitation. Juvenile offenders shall be segregated from adults and be accorded treatment appropriate to their age and legal status.

Art. 11. No one shall be imprisoned merely on the ground of inability to fulfil a contractual obligation.

Art. 12.(1) Everyone lawfully within the territory of a State shall, within that territory, have the right to liberty of movement and freedom to choose his residence.

(2) Everyone shall be free to leave any country including his own.

(3) The above-mentioned rights shall not be subject to any restrictions except those which are provided by law, are necessary to protect national security, public order (ordre public), public health or morals or the rights and freedoms of others, and are consistent with the other rights recognized in the present Covenant.

(4) No one shall be arbitrarily deprived of the right to enter his own country.

Art. 13. An alien lawfully in the territory of a State Party to the present Covenant may be expelled therefrom only in pursuance of a decision reached in accordance with law and shall, except where compelling reasons of national security otherwise require, be allowed to submit the reasons against his expulsion and to have his case reviewed by, and be represented for the purpose before, the competent authority or a person or persons especially designated by the competent authority.

Art. 14.(1) All persons shall be equal before the courts and tribunals. In the determination of any criminal charge against him, or of his rights and obligations in a suit at law, everyone shall be entitled to a fair and public hearing by a competent, independent and impartial tribunal established by law. The Press and the public may be excluded from all or part of a trial for reasons of morals, public order (ordre public) or national security in a democratic society, or when the interest of the private lives of the parties so requires, or to the extent strictly necessary in the opinion of the court in special circumstances where publicity would prejudice the interests of justice; but any judgment rendered in a criminal case or in a suit at law shall be made public except where the interest of juvenile persons otherwise requires or the proceedings concern matrimonial disputes or the guardianship of children.

(2) Everyone charged with a criminal offence shall have the right to be presumed innocent until proved guilty according to law.

(3) In the determination of any criminal charge against him, everyone shall be entitled to the following minimum guarantees, in full equality:

(a) To be informed promptly and in detail in a language which he understands of the nature and cause of the charge against him;

(b) To have adequate time and facilities for the preparation of his defence and to communicate with counsel of his own choosing;

(c) To be tried without undue delay;

(d) To be tried in his presence, and to defend himself in person or through legal assistance of his own choosing; to be informed, if he does not have legal assistance, of this right; and to have legal assistance assigned to him, in any case where the interests of justice so require, and without payment by him in any such case if he does not have sufficient means to pay for it;

(e) to examine, or have examined, the witnesses against him and to obtain the attendance and examination of witnesses on his behalf under the same conditions as the witnesses against him;

(f) To have the free assistance of an interpreter if he cannot understand or speak the language used in court;

(g) Not to be compelled to testify against himself or to confess guilt.

(4) In the case of juvenile persons the procedure shall be such as will take account of their age and the desirability of promoting their rehabilitation.

(5) Everyone convicted of a crime shall have the right to his conviction and sentence being reviewed by a higher tribunal according to law.

(6) When a person has by a final decision been convicted of a criminal offence and when subsequently his conviction has been reversed or he has been pardoned on the ground that a new or newly discovered fact shows conclusively that there has been a miscarriage of justice, the person who has suffered punishment as a result of such conviction shall be compensated according to law, unless it is proved that the non-disclosure of the unknown fact in time is wholly or partly attributable to him.

(7) No one shall be liable to be tried or punished again for an offence for which he has already been finally convicted or acquitted in accordance with the law and penal procedure of each country.

Art. 15.(1) No one shall be held guilty of any criminal offence on account of any act or omission which did not constitute a criminal offence, under national or international law, at the time when it was committed. Nor shall a heavier penalty be imposed than the one that was applicable at the time when the criminal offence was committed. If, subsequent to the commission of the offence, provision is made by law for the imposition of a lighter penalty, the offender shall benefit thereby.

(2) Nothing in this article shall prejudice the trial and punishment of any person for any act or omission which, at the time when it was committed, was criminal

according to the general principles of law recognized by the community of nations.

Art. 16. Everyone shall have the right to recognition everywhere as a person before the law.

Art. 17.(1) No one shall be subjected to arbitrary or unlawful interference with his privacy, family, home or correspondence, nor to unlawful attack on his honour and reputation.

(2) Everyone has the right to the protection of the law against such interference or attacks.

Art. 18.(1) Everyone shall have the right to freedom of thought, conscience and religion. This right shall include freedom to have or to adopt a religion or belief of his choice, and freedom, either individually or in community with others, and in public or private, to manifest his religion or belief in worship, observance, practice and teaching.

(2) No one shall be subject to coercion which would impair his freedom to have or to adopt a religion or belief of his choice.

(3) Freedom to manifest one's religion or beliefs may be subject only to such limitations as are prescribed by law and are necessary to protect public safety, order, health, or morals or the fundamental rights and freedoms of others.

(4) The States Parties to the present Covenant undertake to have respect for the liberty of parents and, when applicable, legal guardians to ensure the religious and moral education of their children in conformity with their own convictions.

Art. 19.(1) Everyone shall have the right to hold opinions without interference.

(2) Everyone shall have the right to freedom of expression; this right shall include freedom to seek, receive and impart information and ideas of all kinds, regardless of frontiers, either orally, in writing or in print, in the form of art, or through any other media of his choice.

(3) The exercise of the rights provided for in paragraph 2 of this article carries with it special duties and responsibilities. It may therefore be subject to certain restrictions, but these shall only be such as are provided by law and are necessary;

(a) For respect of the rights or reputations of others;

(b) For the protection of national security or of public order (ordre public), or of public health or morals.

Art. 20.(1) Any propaganda for war shall be prohibited by law.

(2) Any advocacy of national, racial or religious hatred that constitutes incitement to discrimination, hostility or violence shall be prohibited by law.

Art. 21. The right of peaceful assembly shall be recognized. No restrictions may be placed on the exercise of this right other than those imposed in conformity with the law and which are necessary in a democratic society in the interests of national security or public safety, public order (ordre public), the protection of public health or morals or the protection of the rights and freedoms of others.

Art. 22.(1) Everyone shall have the right to freedom of association with others, including the right to form and join trade unions for the protection of his interests.

(2) No restrictions may be placed on the exercise of these rights other than those which are prescribed by law and which are necessary in a democratic society in the interests of national security or public safety, public order (ordre public), the protection of public health or morals or the protection of the rights and freedoms of others. This article shall not prevent the imposition of lawful restrictions on members of the armed forces and of the police in their exercise of this right.

(3) Nothing in this article shall authorize States Parties to the International Labour Organisation Convention of 1948 concerning Freedom of Association and Protection of the Right to Organize to take legislative measures which would prejudice, or to apply the law in such a manner as to prejudice, the guarantees provided for in that Convention.

Art. 23.(1) The family is the natural and fundamental group unit of society and is entitled to protection by society and the State.

(2) The right of men and women of marriageable age to marry and to found a family shall be recognized.

(3) No Marriage shall be entered into without the free and full consent of the intending spouses.

(4) States Parties to the present Covenant shall take appropriate steps to ensure equality of rights and responsibilites of spouses as to marriage, during marriage

and at its dissolution. In the case of dissolution, provisions shall be made for the necessary protection of any children.

Art. 24.(1) Every child shall have, without any discrimination as to race, colour, sex, language, religion, national or social origin, property or birth, the right to such measures of protection as are required by his status as a minor, on the part of his family, society and the State.

(2) Every child shall be registered immediately after birth and shall have a name.

(3) Every child has the right to acquire a nationality.

Art. 25. Every citizen shall have the right and the opportunity, without any of the distinctions mentioned in article 2 and without unreasonable restrictions;

(a) To take part in the conduct of public affairs, directly or through freely chosen representatives;

(b) To vote and to be elected at genuine periodic elections which shall be by universal and equal suffrage and shall be held by secret ballot, guaranteeing the free expression of the will of the electors;

(c) To have access, on general terms of equality, to public service in his country.

Art. 26. All persons are equal before the law and are entitled without any discrimination to the equal protection of the law. In this respect, the law shall prohibit any discrimination and guarantee to all persons on any ground such as race, colour, sex, language, religion, political or other opinion, national or social origin, property, birth or other status.

Art. 27. In those States in which ethnic, religious or linguistic minorities exist, persons belonging to such minorities shall not be denied the right, in community with the other members of their group, to enjoy their own culture, to profess and practice their own religion, or to use their own language.

Part IV Art. 28(1) There shall be established a Human Rights Committee (hereafter referred to in the present Covenant as the Committee). It shall consist of eighteen members and shall carry out the functions hereinafter provided.

(2) The Committee shall be composed of nationals of the States Parties to the present Covenant who shall be persons of high moral character and recognized competence in the field of human rights, consideration being given to the usefulness of the participation of some persons having legal experience.

(3) The members of the Committee shall be elected and shall serve in their personal capacity.

Art. 29.(1) The members of the Committee shall be elected by secret ballot from a list of persons possessing the qualifications prescribed in article 28 and nominated for the purpose by the States Parties to the present Covenant.

(2) Each State Party to the present Covenant may nominate not more than two persons. These persons shall be nationals of the nominating State.

(3) A person shall be eligible for renomination.

Art. 30.(1) The initial election shall be held no later than six months after the date of entry into force of the present Covenant.

(2) At least four months before the date of each election to the Committee, other than an election to fill a vacancy declared in accordance with article 34, the Secretary-General of the United Nations shall address a written invitation to the States Parties to the present Covenant to submit their nominations for membership of the Committee within three months.

(3) The Secretary-General of the United Nations shall prepare a list in alphabetical order of all the persons thus nominated, with an indication of the States Parties which have nominated them, and shall submit it to the States Parties to the present Covenant no later than one month before the date of each election.

(4) Elections of the members of the Committee shall be held at a meeting of the States Parties to the present Covenant convened by the Secretary-General of the United Nations at the Headquarters of the United Nations. At that meeting, for which two thirds of the States Parties to the present Covenant shall constitute a quorum, the persons elected to the Committee shall be those nominees who obtain the largest number of votes and an absolute majority of the votes of the representatives of States Parties present and voting.

Art. 31.(1) The Committee may not include more than one national of the same State.

(2) In the election of the Committee, considerations shall be given to equitable geographical distribution of

membership and to the representation of the different forms of civilization and of the principal legal system.

Art. 32.(1) The members of the Committee shall be elected for a term of four years. They shall be eligible for re-election if renominated. However, the terms of nine of the members at the first election shall expire at the end of two years; immediately after the first election, the names of these nine members shall be chosen by lot by the Chairman of the meeting referred to in article 30, paragraph 4.

(2) Elections at the expiry of office shall be held in accordance with the preceding articles of this part of the present Covenant.

Art. 33.(1) If, in the unanimous opinion of the other members, a member of the Committee has ceased to carry out his functions for any cause other than absence of a temporary character, the Chairman of the Committee shall notify the Secretary-General of the United Nations, who shall then declare the seat of that member to be vacant.

(2) In the event of the death or the resignation of a member of the Committee, the Chairman shall immediately notify the Secretary-General of the United Nations, who shall declare the seat vacant from the date of death or the date on which the resignation takes effect.

Art. 34.(1) When a vacancy is declared in accordance with article 33 and if the term of office of the member to be replaced does not expire within six months of the declaration of the vacancy, the Secretary-General of the United Nations shall notify each of the States Parties to the present Covenant, which may within two months submit nominations in accordance with article 29 for the purpose of filling the vacancy.

(2) The Secretary-General of the United Nations shall prepare a list in alphabetical order of the persons thus nominated and shall submit it to the States Parties to the present Covenant. The election to fill the vacancy shall then take place in accordance with the relevant provisions of this part of the present Covenant.

(3) A member of the Committee elected to fill a vacancy declared in accordance with article 33 shall hold office for the remainder of the term of the member who vacated the seat on the Committee under the provisions of that article.

Art. 35. The members of the Committee shall, with the approval of the General Assembly of the United Nations, receive emoluments from United Nations resources on such terms and conditions as the General Assembly may decide, having regard to the importance of the Committee's responsibilities.

Art. 36. The Secretary-General of the United Nations shall provide the necessary staff and facilities for the effective performance of the functions of the Committee under the present Covenant.

Art. 37.(1) The Secretary-General of the United Nations shall convene the initial meeting of the Committee at the Headquarters of the United Nations.

(2) After its initial meeting, the Committee shall meet at such times as shall be provided in its rules of procedure.

(3) The Committee shall normally meet at the Headquarters of the United Nations or at the United Nations Office at Geneva.

Art. 38. Every member of the Committee shall, before taking up his duties, make a solemn declaration in open committee that he will perform his functions impartially and conscientiously.

Art. 39.(1) The Committee shall elect its officers for a term of two years. They may be re-elected.

(2) The committee shall establish its own rules of procedure, but these rules shall provide, inter alia, that:

(a) Twelve members shall constitute a quorum;

(b) Decisions of the Committee shall be made by a majority vote of the members present.

Art. 40.(1) The States Parties to the present Covenant undertake to submit reports on the measures they have adopted which give effect to the rights recognized herein and on the progress made in the enjoyment of those rights:

(a) Within one year of the entry into force of the present Covenant for the States Parties concerned;

(b) Thereafter whenever the Committee so requests.

(2) All reports shall be submitted to the Secretary-General of the United Nations, who shall transmit them to the Committee for consideration. Reports shall indicate the factors and difficulties, if any, affecting the implementation of the present Covenant.

(3) The Secretary-General of the United Nations may, after consultation with the Committee, transmit to the specialized agencies concerned copies of such parts of the reports as may fall within their field of competence.
(4) The Committee shall study the reports submitted by the States Parties to the present Covenant. It shall transmit its reports, and such general comments as it may consider appropriate, to the States Parties. The Committee may also transmit to the Economic and Social Council these comments along with the copies of the reports it has received from States Parties to the present Covenant.
(5) The States Parties to the present Covenant may submit to the Committee observations on any comments that may be made in accordance with paragraph 4 of this article.
Art. 41.(1) A State Party to the present Covenant may at any time declare under this article that it recognizes the competence of the Committee to receive and consider communications to the effect that a State Party claims that another State Party is not fulfilling its obligations under the present Covenant. Communications under this article may be received and considered only if submitted by a State Party which has made a declaration recognizing in regard to itself the competence of the Committee. No communication shall be received by the Committee if it concerns a State Party which has not made such a declaration. Communications received under this article shall be dealt with in accordance with the following procedure:
(a) If a State Party to the present Covenant considers that another State Party is not giving effect to the provisions of the present Covenant, it may, by written communication, bring the matter to the attention of that State Party. Within three months after the receipt of the communication, the receiving State shall afford the State which sent the communication an explanation or any other statement in writing clarifying the matter, which should include, to the extent possible and pertinent, reference to domestic procedures and remedies taken, pending, or available in the matter.
(b) If the matter is not adjusted to the satisfaction of both States Parties concerned within six months after the receipt by the receiving State of the initial communication, either State shall have the right to refer the matter to the Committee, by notice given to the committee and to the other State.
(c) The Committee shall deal with a matter referred to it only after it has ascertained that all available domestic remedies have been invoked and exhausted in the matter, in conformity with the generally recognized principles of international law. This shall not be the rule where the application of the remedies is unreasonably prolonged.
(d) The Committee shall hold closed meetings when examining communications under this article.
(e) Subject to the provisions of sub-paragraph (c), the Committee shall make available its good offices to the States Parties concerned with a view to a friendly solution of the matter on the basis of respect for human rights and fundamental freedoms as recognized in the present Covenant.
(f) In any matter referred to it, the Committee may call upon the States Parties concerned, referred to in sub-paragraph (b), to supply any relevant information.
(g) The States Parties concerned, referred to in sub-paragraph (b), shall have the right to be represented when the matter is being considered in the Committee and to make submissions orally and/or in writing.
(h) The Committee shall, within twelve months after the date of receipt of notice under sub-paragraph (b), submit a report:
(i) If a solution within the terms of sub-paragraph (e) is reached, the committee shall confine its report to a brief statement of the facts and of the solution reached;
(ii) If a solution within the terms of sub-paragraph (e) is not reached, the Committee shall confine its report to a brief statement of the facts; the written submissions and record of the oral submissions made by the States Parties concerned shall be attached to the report.
In every matter, the report shall be communicated to the States Parties concerned.
(2) The provisions of this article shall come into force when ten States Parties to the present Covenant have made declarations under paragraph 1 of this article. Such declarations shall be deposited by the States Parties with the Secretary-General of the United Nations, who shall transmit copies thereof to the other

States Parties. A declaration may be withdrawn at any time by notification to the Secretary-General. Such a withdrawal shall not prejudice the consideration of any matter which is the subject of a communication already transmitted under this article:; no further communication by any State Party shall be received after the notification of withdrawal of the declaration has been received by the Secretary-General, unless the State Party concerned has made a new declaration.
Art. 42.(1)(a) If a matter referred to the Committee in accordance with article 41 is not resolved to the satisfaction of the States Parties concerned, the Committee may, with the prior consent of the States Parties concerned, appoint an ad hoc Conciliation Commission (hereinafter referred to as the Commission). The good offices of the Commission shall be made available to the States Parties concerned with a view to an amicable solution of the matter on the basis of respect for the present Covenant;
(b) The Commission shall consist of five persons acceptable to the States Parties concerned. If the States Parties concerned fail to reach agreement within three months on all or part of the composition of the Commission, the members of the Commission concerning whom no agreement has been reached shall be elected by secret ballot by a two-thirds majority vote of the Committee from among its members.
(2) The members of the Commission shall serve in their personal capacity. They shall not be nationals of the States Parties concerned, or of a State not party to the present Covenant, or of a State Party which has not made a declaration under article 41.
(3) The Commission shall elect its own Chairman and adopt its own rules of procedure.
(4) The meetings of the Commission shall normally be held at the Headquarters of the United Nations or at the United Nations Office at Geneva. However, they may be held at such other convenient places as the Commission may determine in consultation with the Secretary-General of the United Nations and the States Parties concerned.
(5) The secretariat provided in accordance with article 36 shall also service the commissions appointed under this article.
(6) The information received and collated by the Committee shall be made available to the Commission and the Commission may call upon the States Parties concerned to supply any other relevant information.
(7) When the Commission has fully considered the matter, but in any event not later than twelve months after having been seized of the matter, it shall submit to the Chairman of the Committee a report for communication to the States Parties concerned:
(a) If the Commission is unable to complete its consideration of the matter within twelve months, it shall confine its report to a brief statement of the status of its consideration of the matter;
(b) If an amicable solution to the matter on the basis of respect for human rights as recognized in the present Covenant is reached, the Commission shall confine its report to a brief statement of the facts and of the solution reached;
(c) If a solution within the terms of sub-paragraph (b) is not reached, the Commission's report shall embody its findings on all questions of fact relevant to the issues between the States Parties concerned, and its views on the possibilities of an amicable solution of the matter. This report shall also contain the written submissions and a record of the oral submissions made by the States Parties concerned;
(d) If the Commission's report is submitted under sub-paragraph (c), the States Parties concerned shall, within three months of the receipt of the report, notify the Chairman of the Committee whether or not they accept the contents of the report of the Commission.
(8) The provisions of this article are without prejudice to the responsibilities of the Committee under article 41.
(9) The States Parties concerned shall share equally all the expenses of the members of the Commission in accordance with paragraph 9 of this article.
Art. 43. The members of the Committee, and of the ad hoc conciliation commissions which may be appointed under article 42, shall be entitled to the facilities, privileges and immunities of experts on missions for the United Nations as laid down in the relevant sections of the Convention on the Privileges and Immunities of the United Nations.

Art. 44. The provisions for the implementation of the present Covenant shall apply without prejudice to the procedures prescribed in the field of human rights by or under the constituent instruments and the conventions of the United Nations and of the specialized agencies and shall not prevent the States parties to the present Covenant from having recourse to other procedures for settling a dispute in accordance with general or special international agreements in force between them.
Art. 45. The Committee shall submit to the General Assembly of the United Nations, through the Economic and Social Council, an annual report on its activities.
Part V. Art. 46. Nothing in the present Covenant shall be interpreted as impairing the provisions of the Charter of the United Nations, and of the constitutions of the specialized agencies which define the respective responsibilities of the various organs of the United Nations and of the specialized agencies in regard to the matters dealt with in the present Covenant.
Art. 47. Nothing in the present Covenant shall be interpreted as impairing the inherent right of all peoples to enjoy and utilize fully and freely their natural wealth and resources.
Part VI. Art. 48.(1) The present Covenant is open for signature by any State Member of the United Nations or member of any of its specialized agencies, by any State Party to the Statute of the International Court of Justice, and by any other State which has been invited by the General Assembly of the United Nations to become a party to the present Covenant.
(2) The present Covenant is subject to ratification. Instruments of ratification shall be deposited with the Secretary-General of the United Nations.
(3) The present Covenant shall be open to accession by any State referred to in paragraph 1 of this article.
(4) Accession shall be effected by the deposit of an instrument of accession with the Secretary-General of the United Nations.
(5) The Secretary-General of the United Nations shall inform all States which have signed this Covenant or acceded to it of the deposit of each instrument of ratification or accession.
Art. 49.(1) The present Covenant shall enter into force three months after the date of the deposit with the Secretary-General of the United Nations of the thirty-fifth instrument of ratification or instrument of accession.
(2) For each State ratifying the present Covenant or acceding to it after the deposit of the thirty-fifth instrument of ratification or instrument of accession, the present Covenant shall enter into force three months after the date of the deposit of its own instrument of ratification or instrument of accession.
Art. 50. The provisions of the present Covenant shall extend to all parts of federal States without any limitations or exceptions.
Art. 51.(1) Any State Party to the present Covenant may propose an amendment and file it with the Secretary-General of the United Nations. The Secretary-General of the United Nations shall thereupon communicate any proposed amendments to the States Parties to the present Covenant with a request that they notify him whether they favour a conference of States Parties for the purpose of considering and voting upon the proposals. In the event that at least one third of the States Parties favours such a conference the Secretary-General shall convene the conference under the auspices of the United Nations, any amendment adopted by a majority of the States Parties present and voting at the conference shall be submitted to the General Assembly of the United Nations for approval.
(2) Amendments shall come into force when they have been approved by the General Assembly of the United Nations and accepted by a two-thirds majority of the States Parties to the Present Covenant in accordance with their respective constitutional processes.
(3) When amendments come into force, they shall be binding on those States Parties which have accepted them, other States Parties still being bound by the provisions of the present Covenant and any earlier amendment which they have accepted.
Art. 52. Irrespective of the notification made under article 48, paragraph 5, the Secretary-General of the United Nations shall inform all States referred to in paragraph 1 of the same article of the following particulars:

(a) Signatures, ratifications and accessions under Art. 48.

(b) The date of the entry into force of the present Covenant under article 49 and the date of the entry into force of any amendments under article 51.

Art. 53.(1) The present Covenant, of which the Chinese, English, French, Russian and Spanish texts are equally authentic, shall be deposited in the archives of the UN.

(2) The Secretary-General of the United Nations shall transmit certified copies of the present Covenant to all States".

On Dec. 16, 1966 the UN General Assembly adopted the Optional Protocol to the Covenant on Civil and Political Rights.

UN Yearbook, 1966, pp. 423–433.

HUMAN RIGHTS, INTERNATIONAL CONVENTION ON ECONOMIC, SOCIAL AND CULTURAL RIGHTS, 1966.

One of two ▷ Human Rights Covenants, unanimously adopted by the UN General Assembly Res. 2200/XXI, on Dec. 16, 1966; entered into force in 1976. The text is as follows:

"The States Parties to the present Covenant,
Considering that, in accordance with the principles proclaimed in the Charter of the United Nations, recognition of the inherent dignity and of the equal and inalienable rights of all members of the human family is the foundation of freedom, justice and peace in the world,
Recognizing that these rights derive from the inherent dignity of the human person,
Recognizing that, in accordance with the Universal Declaration of Human Rights, the ideal of free human beings enjoying freedom from fear and want can only be achieved if conditions are created whereby everyone may enjoy his economic, social and cultural rights, as well as his civil and political rights,
Considering the obligation of States under the Charter of the United Nations to promote universal respect for, and observance of, human rights and freedoms,
Realizing that the individual, having duties to other individuals and to the community to which he belongs, is under a responsibility to strive for the promotion and observance of the rights recognized in the present Covenant,
Agree upon the following articles:
Part I. Art. 1.(1) All peoples have the right of self-determination. By virtue of that right they freely determine their political status and freely pursue their economic, social and cultural development.
(2) All peoples may, for their own ends, freely dispose of their natural wealth and resources without prejudice to any obligations arising out of international economic co-operation, based upon the principle of mutual benefit, and international law. In no case may a people be deprived of its own means of subsistence.
(3) The States Parties to the present Covenant, including those having responsibility for the administration of Non-Self-Governing and Trust Territories, shall promote the realization of the right of self-determination, and shall respect that right, in conformity with the provisions of the Charter of the United Nations.
Part II. Art. 2.(1) Each State Party to the present Covenant undertakes to take steps, individually and through international assistance and co-operation, especially economic and technical, to the maximum of its available resources, with a view to achieving progressively the full realization of the rights recognized in the present Covenant by all appropriate means, including particularly the adoption of legislative measures.
(2) The States Parites to the present Covenant, undertake to guarantee that the rights enunciated in the present Covenant will be exercised without discrimination of any kind as to race, colour, sex, language, religion, political or other opinion, national or social origin, property, birth or other status.
(3) Developing countries, with due regard to human rights and their national economy, may determine to what extent they would recognize the economic rights recognized in the present Covenant to non-nationals.
Art. 3. The States Parties to the present Covenant undertake to ensure the equal right of men and women to the enjoyment of all economic, social and cultural rights set forth on the present Covenant.
Art. 4. The States Parties to the present Covenant recognize that, in the enjoyment of those rights provided by the State in conformity with the present Covenant, the State may subject such rights only to such limitations as are determined by law only in so far as this may be compatible with the nature of these rights and solely for the purpose of promoting the general welfare in a democratic society.
Art. 5.(1) Nothing in the present Covenant may be interpreted as implying for any State, group or person any right to engage in any activity or to perform any act aimed at the destruction of any of the rights or freedoms recognized herein, or at their limitation or to a greater extent than is provided for in the present Covenant.
(2) No restriction upon or derogation from any of the fundamental human rights recognized or existing in any country in virtue of law, conventions, regulations or custom shall be admitted on the pretext that the present Covenant does not recognize such rights or that it recognizes them to a lesser extent.
Part III. Art. 6.(1) The States Parties to the present Covenant recognize the right to work, which includes the right of everyone to the opportunity to gain his living by work which he freely chooses or accepts, and will take appropriate steps to safeguard this right.
(2) The steps to be taken by a State Party to the present Covenant to achieve the full realization of this right shall include technical and vocational guidance and training programmes, policies and techniques to achieve steady economic, social and cultural development and full and productive employment under conditions safeguarding fundamental political and economic freedoms to the individual.
Art. 7. The States Parties to the present Covenant recognize the right of everyone to the enjoyment of just and favourable conditions of work which ensure, in particular:
(a) Renumeration which provides all workers, as a minimum, with:
(i) Fair wages and equal remuneration for work of equal value without distinction of any kind, in particular women being guaranteed conditions of work not inferior to those enjoyed by men, with equal pay for equal work;
(ii) A decent living for themselves and their families in accordance with the provisions of the present Covenant;
(b) Safe and healthy working conditions;
(c) Equal opportunity for everyone to be promoted in his employment to an appropriate higher level, subject to no consideration other than those of seniority and competence;
(d) Rest, leisure and reasonable limitation of working hours and periodic holidays with pay, as well as remuneration for public holidays.
Art. 8. The States Parties to the present Covenant undertake to ensure:
(a) The right of everyone, to form trade unions and join the trade union of his choice, subject only to the rules of the organization concerned, for the promotion and protection of his economic and social interests. No restrictions may be placed on the exercise of this right other than those prescribed by law and which are necessary in a democratic society in the interests of national security or public order or for the protection of the rights and freedoms of others;
(b) The right of trade unions to establish national federations or confederations and the right of the latter to form or join international trade-union organizations;
(c) The right of trade unions to function freely subject to no limitations other than those prescribed by law and which are necessary in a democratic society in the interests of national security or public order or for the protection of the rights and freedoms of others;
(d) The right to strike, provided that it is exercised in conformity with the laws of the particular country.
(2) This article shall not prevent the imposition of lawful restrictions on the exercise of these rights by members of the armed forces or of the police or of the administration of the State.
(3) Nothing in this article shall authorize States Parties to the International Labour Organization Convention of 1948 concerning Freedom of Association and Protection of the Right to Organize to take legislative measures which would prejudice, or apply the law in such a manner as would prejudice, the guarantees provided for in that Convention.
Art. 9. The States Parties to the present Convention recognize the right of everyone to social security, including social insurance.
Art. 10. The States Parties to the present Covenant recognize that:
(1) The widest possible protection and assistance should be accorded to the family, which is the natural and fundamental group unit of society, particularly for its establishment and while it is responsible for the care and education of dependent children. Marriage must be entered into with the free consent of the intending spouses.
(2) Special protection should be accorded to mothers during a reasonable period before and after child-birth. During such period working mothers should be accorded paid leave or leave with adequate social security benefits.
(3) Special measures of protection and assistance should be taken on behalf of all children and young persons without any discrimination for reasons of parentage or other conditions. Children and young persons should be protected from economic and social exploitation. Their employment in work harmful to their morals or health or dangerous to life or likely to hamper their normal development should be punishable by law. States should also set age limits below which the paid employment of child labour should be prohibited and punishable by law.
Art. 11.(1) The States Parties to the present Covenant recognize the right of everyone to an adequate standard of living for himself and his family, including adequate food, clothing and housing, and to the continuous improvement of living conditions. The States Parties will take appropriate steps to ensure the realization of this right, recognizing to this effect the essential importance of international co-operation based on free consent.
(2) The States Parties to the present Covenant, recognizing the fundamental right of everyone to be free from hunger, shall take, individually and through international co-operation, the measures, including specific programmes, which are needed:
(a) To improve methods of production, conservation and distribution of food by making full use of technical and scientific knowledge, by disseminating knowledge of the principles of nutrition and by developing or reforming agrarian systems in such a way as to achieve the most efficient development and utilization of natural resources;
(b) Taking into account the problem of both food-importing and food-exporting countries, to ensure an equitable distribution of world food supplies in relation to need.
Art. 12.(1) The States Parties to the present Covenant recognize the right of everyone to the enjoyment of the highest attainable standard of physical and mental health.
(2) The steps to be taken by the States Parties to the present Covenant to achieve the full realization of this right shall include those necessary for:
(a) The provision for the reduction of the still-birth-rate and of infant mortality and for the healthy development of the child;
(b) The improvement of all aspects of environmental and industrial hygiene;
(c) The prevention, treatment and control of epidemic, endemic, occupational and other diseases;
(d) The creation of conditions which would assure to all medical service and medical attention in the event of sickness.
Art. 13.(1) The States Parties to the present Covenant recognize the right of everyone to education. They agree that education shall be directed to the full development of the human personality and the sense of its dignity, and shall strengthen the respect for human rights and fundamental freedoms. They further agree that education shall enable all persons to participate effectively in a free society, promote understanding, tolerance and friendship among all nations and all racial, ethnic or religious groups, and further the activities of the United Nations for the maintenance of peace.
(2) The States Parties to the present Covenant recognize that, with a view to achieving the full realization of this right:
(a) Primary education shall be compulsory and available free to all;

(b) Secondary education in its different forms, including technical and vocational secondary education, shall be made generally available and accessible to all by every appropriate means, and in particular by the progressive introduction of free education;
(c) Higher education shall be made equally accessible to all, on the basis of capacity, by every appropriate means, and in particular by the progressive introduction of free education;
(d) Fundamental education shall be encouraged or intensified as far as possible for those persons who have not received or completed the whole period of their primary education;
(e) The development of a system of schools at all levels shall be actively pursued, an adequate fellowship system shall be established, and the material conditions of teaching staff shall be continuously improved.
(3) The States Parties for the present Covenant undertake to have respect for the liberty of parents and, when applicable, legal guardians to choose for their children schools, other than those established by the public authorities, which conform to such minimum educational standards as may be laid down or approved by the State and to ensure the religious and moral education of their children in conformity with their own convictions.
(4) No part of this article shall be construed so as to interfere with the liberty of individuals and bodies to establish and direct educational institutions, subject always to the observance of the principles set forth in paragraph 1 of this article and to the requirement that the education given in such institutions shall conform to such minimum standards as may be laid down by the State.
Art. 14. Each State Party to the present Covenant which, at the time of becoming a Party, has not been able to secure in its metropolitan territory or other territories under its jurisdiction compulsory primary education, free of charge, undertakes, within two years, to work out and adopt a detailed plan of action for the progressive implementation, within a reasonable number of years, to be fixed in the plan, of the principle of compulsory education free of charge for all.
Art. 15. The States Parties to the present Covenant recognize the right of everyone:
(a) To take part in cultural life;
(b) To enjoy the benefits of scientific progress and its applications;
(c) To benefit from the protection of the moral and material interests resulting from any scientific, literary or artistic production of which he is the author.
(2) The steps to be taken by the States Parties to the present Covenant to achieve the full realization of this right shall include those necessary for the conservation, the development and the diffusion of science and culture.
(3) The States Parties to the present Covenant undertake to respect the freedom indispensable for scientific research and creative activity.
(4) The States Parties to the present Covenant recognize the benefits to be derived from the encouragement and development of international contacts and co-operation in the scientific and cultural fields.
Part IV. Art. 16.(1) The States Parties to the present Covenant undertake to submit in conformity with this part of the Covenant reports on the measures which they have adopted and the progress made in achieving the observance of the rights recognized herein.
(2)(a) All reports shall be submitted to the Secretary-General of the United Nations, who shall transmit copies to the Economic and Social Council for consideration in accordance with the provisions of the present Covenant;
(b) The Secretary-General of the United Nations shall also transmit to the specialized agencies copies of the reports, or any relevant parts therefrom, from States Parties to the present Covenant which are also members of these specialized agencies in so far as these reports, or parts therefrom, relate to any matters which fall within the responsibilities of the said agencies in accordance with their constitutional instruments.
Art. 17.(1) The States Parties to the present Covenant shall furnish their reports in stages, in accordance with a programme to be established by the Economic and Social Council within one year of the entry into force of the present Covenant after consultation with the States Parties and the specialized agencies concerned.

(2) Reports may indicate factors and difficulties affecting the degree of fulfillment of obligations under the present Covenant.
(3) Where relevant information has previously been furnished to the United Nations or to any specialized agency by any State Party to the present Covenant, it will not be necessary to reproduce that information, but a precise reference to the information so furnished will suffice.
Art. 18. Pursuant to its responsibilities under the Charter of the United Nations in the field of human rights and fundamental freedoms, the Economic and Social Council may make arrangements with the specialized agencies in respect of their reporting to it on the progress made in achieving the observance of the provisions of the present Covenant falling within the scope of their activities. These reports may include particulars of decisions and recommendations on such implementation adopted by their competent organs.
Art. 19. The Economic and Social Council may transmit to the Commission on Human Rights for study and general recommendation or, as appropriate, for information the reports concerning human rights submitted by States in accordance with articles 16 and 17, and those concerning human rights submitted by the specialized agencies in accordance with article 18.
Art. 20. The States Parties to the present Covenant and the specialized agencies concerned may submit comments to the Economic and Social Council on any general recommendation under article 19 or reference to such general recommendation in any report of the Commission on Human Rights or any documentation referred to therein.
Art. 21. The Economic and Social Council may submit from time to time to the General Assembly reports with recommendations of a general nature and a summary of the information received from the States Parties to the present Covenant and the specialized agencies on the measures taken and the progress made in achieving general observance of the rights recognized in the present Covenant.
Art. 22. The Economic and Social Council may bring to the attention of other organs of the United Nations, their subsidiary organs and specialized agencies concerned with furnishing technical assistance any matters arising out of the reports referred to in this part of the present Covenant, which may assist such bodies in deciding, each within its field of competence, on the advisability of international measures likely to contribute to the effective progressive implementation of the present Covenant.
Art. 23. The States Parties to the present Covenant agree that international action for the achievement of the rights recognized in the present Covenant includes such methods as the conclusion of conventions, the adoption of recommendations, the furnishing of technical assistance and the holding of regional meetings for the purpose of consultation and study organized in conjunction with the Governments concerned.
Art. 24. Nothing in the present Covenant shall be interpreted as impairing the provisions of the Charter of the United Nations and of the constitutions of the specialized agencies which define the respective responsibilities of the various organs of the United Nations and of the specialized agencies in regard to the matters dealt with in the present Covenant.
Art. 25. Nothing in the present Covenant shall be interpreted as impairing the inherent right of all peoples to enjoy and utilize fully and freely their natural wealth and resources.
Part V. Art. 26.(1) The present Covenant is open for signature by any State Member of the United Nations or member of any of its specialized agencies, by any State Party to the Statute of the International Court of Justice, and by any other State which has been invited by the General Assembly of the United Nations to become a party to the present Covenant.
(2) The present Covenant is subject to ratification. Instruments of ratification shall be deposited with the Secretary-General of the United Nations.
(3) The present Covenant shall be open to accession by any State referred to in Paragraph 1 of this article.
(4) Accession shall be effected by the deposit of an instrument of accession with the Secretary-General of the United Nations.
(5) The Secretary-General of the United Nations shall inform all States which have signed the present Covenant or acceded to it of the deposit of each instrument of ratification or instrument of accession.
Art. 27.(1) The present Covenant shall enter into force three months after the date of the deposit with the Secretary-General of the United Nations of the thirty-fifth instrument of ratification or instrument of accession.
(2) For each State ratifying the present Covenant or acceding to it after the deposit of the thirty-fifth instrument of ratification or instrument of accession, the present Covenant shall enter into force three months after the date of the deposit of its own instrument of ratification or instrument of accession.
Art. 28. The provisions of the present Covenant shall extend to all parts of federal States without any limitations or exceptions.
Art. 29.(1) Any State Party to the present Covenant may propose an amendment and file it with the Secretary-General of the United Nations. The Secretary-General shall thereupon communicate any proposed amendments to the States Parties to the present Covenant with a request that they notify him whether they favour a conference of States Parties for the purpose of considering and voting upon the proposals. In the event that at least one third of the States Parties favours such a conference, the Secretary-General shall convene the conference under the auspices of the United Nations. Any amendment adopted by a majority of the States Parties present and voting at the conference shall be submitted to the General Assembly of the United Nations for approval.
(2) Amendments shall come into force when they have been approved by the General Assembly of the United Nations and accepted by a two-thirds majority of the States Parties to the present Covenant in accordance with their respective constitutional processes.
(3) When amendments come into force they shall be binding on those States Parties which have accepted them, other States Parties still being bound by the provisions of the present Covenant and any earlier amendment which they have accepted.
Art. 30. Irrespective of the notifications made under article 26, paragraph 5, the Secretary-General of the United Nations shall inform all States referred to in paragraph 1 of the same article of the following particulars:
(a) Signatures, ratifications and accessions under article 26;
(b) The date of the entry into force of the present Covenant under article 27 and the date of entry into force of any amendments under article 29.
Art. 31.(1) The present Covenant, of which the Chinese, English, French, Russian and Spanish texts are equally authentic, shall be deposited in the archives of the United Nations.
(2) The Secretary-General of the United Nations shall transmit certified copies of the present Covenant to all States referred to in article 26."

UN Yearbook, 1966, pp. 419–423.

HUMAN RIGHTS INTERNATIONAL YEAR. On the 20th anniversary of the adoption of the ▷ Human Rights, Universal Declaration of, 1948, the UN General Assembly declared 1968 the International Year for Human Rights, and Res. 2081/XX of Dec. 20, 1965 set up a Commission with the task of preparing an International Conference of Human Rights which should evaluate the effectiveness of UN methods of fighting first of all discrimination and the policy of apartheid, as well as elaborate a program of additional measures to be applied after 1968. The Conference was held in Teheran on Apr. 22–May 13, 1968 and unanimously adopted the ▷ Human Rights Teheran Proclamation which condemned colonialism, racial and religious discrimination, aggression and acknowledged apartheid as a crime against humanity. It urged all peoples and governments to dedicate themselves to the principles of the Declaration on Human Rights and to redouble their efforts "to provide for all human beings a life consonant with freedom and dignity . . .". The Conference adopted 29 other resolutions dealing with various aspects of human rights and proposals for action by other UN bodies.

HUMAN RIGHTS LEAGUE.
An organization active in the years 1898–1922, headquarters in Paris, founded in connection with the Dreyfus case, one of most active French organizations of the time to speak in defense of human rights and peace; inspired the foundation of analogous institutions under the name in other countries, fused into one International Federation in 1922. Organizations reg. with the UIA:

International Federation for the Rights of Man, f. 1922, Paris. Consultative status with ECOSOC.
International League for the Rights of Man, f. 1941, New York. Consultative status with ECOSOC and UNESCO.

Yearbook of International Organizations.

HUMAN RIGHTS NATIONAL COMMISSIONS.
Commissions postulated by the UN General Assembly Res. 2200C/XXI, Dec. 16, 1966 as appropriate institutions to perform certain functions pertaining to the observance of the ▷ Human Rights Covenants, 1966.

UN Yearbook, 1966, p. 433.

HUMAN RIGHTS OTTAWA MEETING ▷
Ottawa CSCE Meeting, 1985.

HUMAN RIGHTS TEHERAN PROCLAMATION, 1968.
The official name of a declaration adopted unanimously on May 13, 1968, by the International UN Conference on Human Rights held in Teheran from Apr. 22 to May 13, 1968 in keeping with Res. 2081/XX of the UN General Assembly. The proclamation called on all peoples and governments to intensify efforts in pursuit of ensuring all people the possibility of physical, spiritual, intellectual and social development in conditions of freedom and respect for human dignity and in the spirit of the principles of the Universal Declaration of Human Rights adopted 20 years earlier.

UN Yearbook, 1968.

HUMAN RIGHTS, UNIVERSAL DECLARATION OF, 1948.
The name of a UN document adopted Dec. 10, 1948 by the UN General Assembly by 48 votes in favor and eight members abstaining: Saudi Arabia, Czechoslovakia, Yugoslavia, Poland, the Republic of South Africa, Ukrainian SSR and the USSR. The socialist States abstained because the majority deleted amendments proposed by those states which postulated: equality not only of all people, but of all nations; (2) abolition of capital punishment in peacetime; (3) a ban on fascist propaganda, as well as militarist and racist propaganda as anti-human. The Republic of South Africa and Saudi Arabia abstained because they considered the Declaration too progressive.

The text of the Declaration reads:

"Whereas recognition of the inherent dignity and of the equal and inalienable rights of all members of the human family is the foundation of freedom, justice and peace in the world, whereas disregard and contempt for human rights have resulted in barbarous acts which have outraged the conscience of mankind, and the advent of a world in which human beings shall enjoy freedom of speech and belief and freedom from fear and want has been proclaimed as the highest aspiration of the common people,
whereas it is essential, if man is not to be compelled to have recourse, as a last resort, to rebellion against tyranny and oppression, that human rights should be protected by the rule of law,
whereas it is essential to promote the development of friendly relations between nations,
whereas the peoples of the United Nations have in the Charter reaffirmed their faith in fundamental human rights, in the dignity and worth of the human person and in the equal rights of men and women and have determined to promote social progress and better standards of life in larger freedom,
whereas Member-States have pledged themselves to achieve, in cooperation with the United Nations, the promotion of universal respect for and observance of human rights and fundamental freedoms,
whereas a common understanding of these rights and freedoms is of the greatest importance for the full realization of this pledge. Now, therefore, the General Assembly proclaims this Universal Declaration of Human Rights as a common standard of achievement for all peoples and all nations, to the end that every individual and every organ of society, keeping this Declaration constantly in mind, shall strive by teaching and education to promote respect for these rights and freedoms and by progressive measures, national and international, to secure their universal and effective recognition and observance, both among the peoples of Member-States themselves and among the peoples of territories under their jurisdiction.
Art. 1. All human beings are born free and equal in dignity and rights. They are endowed with reason and conscience and should act towards one another in a spirit of brotherhood.
Art. 2. Everyone is entitled to all the rights and freedoms set forth in this Declaration, without distinction of any kind, such as race, color, sex, language, religion, political or other opinion, national or social origin, property, birth or other status.
Furthermore, no distinction shall be made on the basis of the political, jurisdictional or international status of the country or territory to which a person belongs, whether it be independent, trust, non-self-governing or under any other limitation of sovereignty.
Art. 3. Everyone has the right to life, liberty and security of person.
Art. 4. No one shall be held in slavery or servitude; slavery and the slave trade shall be prohibited in all their forms.
Art. 5. No one shall be subjected to torture or to cruel, inhuman or degrading treatment or punishment.
Art. 6. Everyone has the right to recognition everywhere as a person before the law.
Art. 7. All are equal before the law and are entitled without any discrimination to equal protection of the law. All are entitled to equal protection against any discrimination in violation of the Declaration and against any incitement to such discrimination.
Art. 8. Everyone has the right to an effective remedy by the competent national tribunals for acts violating the fundamental rights granted him by the constitution or by law.
Art. 9. No one shall be subjected to arbitrary arrest, detention or exile.
Art. 10. Everyone is entitled in full equality to a fair and public hearing by an independent and impartial tribunal, in the determination of his rights and obligations and of any criminal charge against him.
Art. 11.(I) Everyone charged with a penal offence has the right to be presumed innocent until proved guilty according to law in a public trial at which he has had all the guarantees necessary for his defence.
(II) No one shall be held guilty of any penal offence on account of any act of omission which did not constitute a penal offence, under national or international law, at the time it was committed. Nor shall a heavier penalty be imposed than the one that was applicable at the time the penal offence was committed.
Art. 12. No one shall be subjected to arbitrary interference with his privacy, family, home or correspondence, nor to attacks upon his honor and reputation. Everyone has the right to the protection of the law against such interference or attacks.
Art. 13(I) Everyone has the right to freedom of movement and residence within the borders of each state.
(II) Everyone has the right to leave any country, including his own, and to return to his country.
Art. 14.(I) Everyone has the right to seek and to enjoy in other countries asylum from persecution.
(II) This right may not be invoked in the case of prosecutions genuinely arising from non-political crimes or from acts contrary to the purposes and principles of the United Nations.
Art. 15.(I) Everyone has the right to a nationality.
(II) No one shall be arbitrarily deprived of his nationality nor denied the right to change his nationality.
Art. 16.(I) Men and women of full age, without any limitation due to race, nationality or religion, have the right to marry and to found a family. They are entitled to equal rights as to marriages, during marriage and at its dissolution.
(II) Marriage shall be entered into only with the free and full consent of the intending spouses.
(III) The family is the natural and fundamental group unit of society and is entitled to protection by society and the state.
Art. 17.(I) Everyone has the right to own property as well as in association with others.
(II) No one shall be arbitrarily deprived of his property.
Art. 18. Everyone has the right to freedom of thought, conscience and religion; the right includes freedom to change his religion or belief, and freedom, either alone or in community with others and in public or private, to manifest his religion or belief in teaching, practice, worship and observance.
Art. 19. Everyone has the right to freedom of opinion and expression; this right includes the right to freedom to hold opinions without interference and to seek, receive and impart information and ideas through any media and regardless of frontiers.
Art. 20.(I) Everyone has the right to freedom of peaceful assembly and association.
(II) No one may be compelled to an association.
Art. 21.(I) Everyone has the right to take part in the government of his country, directly or through freely chosen representatives.
(II) Everyone has the right of equal access to public service in his country.
(III) The will of the people shall be the basis of the authority of the government; this will shall be expressed in periodic and genuine elections which shall be by universal and equal suffrage and shall be held by secret vote or by equivalent free voting procedures.
Art. 22. Everyone, as a member of society, has the right to social security and is entitled to realization, through national effort and international cooperation and in accordance with the organization and resources of each State, of the economic, social and cultural rights indispensable for his dignity and the free development of his personality.
Art. 23.(I) Everyone has the right to work, to free choice of employment, to just and favorable conditions of work and to protection against unemployment.
(II) Everyone, without any discrimination, has the right to equal pay for equal work.
(III) Everyone who works has the right to just and favorable remuneration ensuring for himself and his family an existence worthy of human dignity, and supplemented if necessary, by other means of social protection.
(IV) Everyone has the right to form and to join trade unions for the protection of his interests.
Art. 24. Everyone has the right to rest and leisure, including reasonable limitation of working hours and periodic holidays with pay.
Art. 25.(I) Everyone has the right to a standard of living adequate for the health and well-being of himself and of his family, including food, clothing, housing and medical care and necessary social services, and the right to security in the event of unemployment, sickness, disability, widowhood, old age or other lack of livelihood in circumstances beyond his control.
(II) Motherhood and childhood are entitled to special care and assistance. All children, whether born in or out of wedlock, shall enjoy the same social protection.
Art. 26.(I) Everyone has the right to education. Education shall be free, at least in the elementary and fundamental stages. Elementary education shall be compulsory. Technical and profession education shall be made generally available and higher education shall be equally accessible to all on the basis of merit.
(II) Education shall be directed to the full development of the human personality and to the strengthening of respect for human rights and friendship among all nations, racial or religious groups and shall further the activities of the United Nations for the maintenance of peace.
(III) Parents have a prior right to choose the kind of education that shall be given to their children.
Art. 27.(I) Everyone has the right freely to participate in the cultural life of the community, to enjoy the arts and to share in scientific advancement and its benefits.
(II) Everyone has the right to the protection of the moral and material interest resulting from any scientif-

ic, literary or artistic production of which he is the author.

Art. 28. Everyone is entitled to a social and international order in which the rights and freedoms set forth in this Declaration can be fully realized.

Art. 29.(I) Everyone has duties to the community in which alone the free and full development of his personality is possible.

(II) In the exercise of his rights and freedoms, everyone shall subject only to such limitations as are determined by law solely for the purposes of securing due recognition and respect for the rights and freedoms of others and of meeting the just requirements of mortality, public order and the general welfare in a democratic society.

(III) These rights and freedoms may in no case be exercised contrary to the purposes and principles of the United Nations.

Art. 30. Nothing in this Declaration may be interpreted as implying for any State, group or person any right to engage in any activity or to perform any act aimed at the destruction of any of the rights and freedoms set forth herein."

The Secretary-General of the UN, Javier Perez de Cuellar concluded his speech at the celebration of the fortieth anniversary of the Universal Declaration as follows:

I should like to say that the rights recognized by the Declaration exist truly only in so far as they are exercised by those who possess them. One learns to be free. One can also renounce freedom. The best and most scrupulously applied laws mean nothing if people prefer assistance and dependence. Freedoms can die if they are insufficiently used, insufficiently valued, or insufficiently cherished. Whatever view one takes of the revolutionaries whose memory you will soon be evoking, they cannot be denied one essential virtue: they loved freedom. May we, like the authors of the Universal Declaration and the innumerable defenders of human rights share their enthusiasm, we who know by experience that world peace, progress and civilization are at stake and that henceforth it is our hopes that hang in the balance.

UN Yearbook, 1948; *UN Bulletin*, 1948 and 1949; R. CASSIN, *La Déclaration Universelle de Droit de l'Homme et sa mise en oeuvre*, Paris, 1956; *The UN and the Human Rights*, New York, 1968.

HUMAN SETTLEMENTS. ▷ UN Center for Human Settlements.

HUNDRED FLOWERS DOCTRINE. A Chinese doctrine on development of art in socialistic system, formulated by Mao Tse-tung, May 2, 1956:

"Let one hundred flowers bloom, let one hundred schools compete with one another."

In China People's Republic the doctrine was ten years later discarded and combatted by the Cultural Revolution, 1966. In the fifth volume of Mao's writings, covering the years 1951–69, published in Peking in 1977, the text of the speech of May 2, 1956 was omitted.

R. MAC FARQUHAR (ed.), *The Hundred Flowers*, London, 1960.

HUNGARY. Member of the UN. Magyar Nepköztarsasag. People's Republic of Hungary. State in the south-eastern part of Central Europe. Borders with the USSR, Romania, Yugoslavia, Austria and Czechoslovakia. Area: 93,036 sq. km. Population 1988 census: 10,700,000 (1960 census – 9,961,000; 1971 – 10,347,000). Capital: Budapest with 2,064,000 inhabitants in 1983. GNP per capita in 1987: US $2,270. Currency: one forint = 100 filler. National day: Apr. 4, Independence Day, 1945. Official language: Hungarian.

Member of the League of Nations from Mar., 1921 to Apr., 1939. Member of the UN from Dec. 14, 1955 and specialised organisations with the exception of the IFAD. Member of the Warsaw Pact. Member of the CMEA.

International relations: an independent state from the 10th century; in the 16th and 17th centuries under the domination of the Ottoman Empire, then of Austria. In a monarchic union with Austria, 1867–1918. The boundaries of Hungary were established after World War I by the Peace Treaty of Trianon. Joined the ▷ Anticomintern Pact in 1939 and on Nov. 20, 1940 adhered to the German-Italian-Japanese ▷ Tripartite pact. On June 27, 1941 Hungary declared war on the USSR and on Dec. 12, 1941 on the USA. On Mar. 19, 1944 occupied by German troops; liberated by Soviet troops from Jan. to Apr. 4, 1945. In 1946 Hungary signed a Treaty of Peace in Paris. On Feb. 18, 1948 signed with the USSR a Treaty of Friendship and Mutual Co-operation.

On Oct. 27, 1956 the USSR withdrew its troops from Budapest, but on Nov. 4 entered again to Budapest. In the period Oct. 1956–Dec. 1962 the "Hungarian question" was debated in the UN Security Council.

A separate matter between Hungary and the Vatican was the refuge of Cardinal J. Mindszenty in the US Embassy from Nov. 1956, which ended with an agreement with the Vatican and the Cardinal's permanent departure for Italy on Sept. 28, 1971. Signatory of the Helsinki Final Act, 1975. In 1978 the USA returned to Hungary after 33 years, the crown of St. Stephen. In Oct., 1984 Hungarian leader J. Kadar visited France.

See also ▷ World Heritage UNESCO List.

UNTS, Vol. 41, p. 135; *Monumenta Hungariae Historica*, Budapest, 1868–1917, 112 Vols., *La Hongrie et la Conférence de Paris*, Budapest, 1947, 2 Vols.; M.J. LASKY (ed), *The Hungarian Revolution*, London, 1957; *UN Yearbooks*, 1952–62; *Sovetsko-venguerskie otnoshenie 1945–48*, Moskva, 1969; O. GADO, *The Economic Mechanism of Hungary*, Leiden, 1976; A. HEGEDUS, *The Structure of Socialist Society*, London, 1977; Z. HALASZ, *Hungary: A Guide with a Difference*, Budapest, 1979; F. DONATH, *Reform and Revolution. Transformation of Hungary's Agriculture 1945–1970*, Budapest, 1980; T. KABDEBO, *Hungary. Bibliography*, Oxford, 1980; G. NEMETH (ed.), *Hungary. A Comprehensive Guide*, Budapest, 1980; P.G. HARE (ed.), *Hungary. A Decade of Economic Reform*, London, 1981; *The Europa Year Book 1984. A World Survey*, vol. I, pp. 560–577 London, 1984. KEESING's *Border and Territorial Disputes*, London, 1987. Ch. GATI, *Hungary and the Soviet Bloc*, Durham N.C., 1986. M. MOLNAR, *De Bela Kun a Janos Kadar: Soixante-dix ans de communisme hongrois*, Paris, 1987.

HUNGARY PEACE TREATY, 1920. A Treaty between the Principal Allied Powers: France, Great Britain, Italy, Japan and the US; and Associated Powers: Belgium, China, Cuba, Czechoslovakia, Greece, Nicaragua, Panama, Poland, Portugal, Romania, the Serbo-Croat-Slovene State and Siam, on the one hand, and Hungary on the other; signed on July 26, 1920 in Petit Trianon. The highlights of the Treaty are as follows:

Part I. The Covenant of the League of Nations (art. 1 to 26 and Annex),
Part II. Frontiers of Hungary (art. 27 to 35).
Part III. Political Clauses for Europe (art. 36 to 78):
"The independence of Hungary is inalienable otherwise than with the consent of the Council of the League of Nations. Consequently, Hungary undertakes in the absence of the consent of the said Council to abstain from any act which might directly or indirectly or by any means whatever compromise her independence, particularly, and until her admission to membership of the League of Nations, by participation in the affairs of another Power" (art. 73).

"Hungary hereby recognises and accepts the frontiers of Austria, Bulgaria, Greece, Poland, Roumania, the Serbo-Croat-Slovene State and the Czecho-Slovak State as these frontiers may be determined by the Principal Allied and Associated Powers. Hungary undertakes to recognise the full force of the Treaties of peace and additional conventions which have been or may be concluded by the Allied and Associated Powers with the Powers who fought on the side of the former Austro-Hungarian Monarchy, and to recognise whatever dispositions have been or may be made concerning the territories of the former German Empire, of Austria, of the Kingdom of Bulgaria and of the Ottoman Empire, and to recognise the new States within their frontiers as there laid down" (art. 74).

"Hungary renounces, so far as she is concerned, in favour of the Principal Allied and Associated Powers all rights and title over the territories which previously belonged to the former Austro-Hungarian Monarchy and which, being situated outside the new frontiers of Hungary as described in Article 27, Part II (Frontiers of Hungary), have not at present been otherwise disposed of. Hungary undertakes to accept the settlement made by the Principal Allied and Associated Powers in regard to these territories, particularly in so far as concerns the nationality of the inhabitants" (art. 75).

"No inhabitant of the territories of the former Austro-Hungarian Monarchy shall be disturbed or molested on account either of his political attitude between July 28, 1914, and the definitive settlement of the sovereignty over these territories, or of the determination of his nationality effected by the present Treaty" (art. 76).

"Hungary will hand over without delay to the Allied and Associated Governments concerned archives, registers, plans, title-deeds and documents of every kind belonging to the civil, military, financial, judicial or other forms of administration in the ceded territories. If any one of these documents, archives, registers, title-deeds or plans is missing, it shall be restored by Hungary upon the demand of the Allied or Associated Government concerned. In case the archives, registers, plans, title-deeds or documents referred to in the preceding paragraph, exclusive of those of a military character, concern equally the administrations in Hungary, and cannot therefore be handed over without inconvenience to such administrations, Hungary undertakes, subject to reciprocity, to give access thereto to the Allied and Associated Governments concerned" (art. 77).

"Separate conventions between Hungary and each of the States to which territory of the former Kingdom of Hungary is transferred, and each of the States arising from the dismemberment of the former Austro-Hungarian Monarchy, will provide for the interests of the inhabitants, especially in connection with their civil rights, their commerce and the exercise of their professions" (art. 78).

Major Peace Treaties of Modern History, New York, 1977, pp. 1862–2053.

HUNGARY PEACE TREATY, 1947. A Treaty signed on Feb. 10, 1947 in Paris, between the Allied and Associated Powers on the one hand and Hungary on the other. The texts of the Preamble and of the first 2 Articles are as follows:

"The USSR, the UK, the USA, Australia, the Byelorussian SSR, Canada, Czechoslovakia, India, New Zealand, the Ukrainian SSR, the Union of South Africa, and Yugoslavia, as the States which are at war with Hungary and actively waged war against the European enemy States with substantial military forces, hereinafter referred to as the Allied and Associated Powers, of the one part,
and Hungary, of the other part;
Whereas Hungary, having become an ally of Hitlerite Germany and having participated on her side in the war against the USSR, the UK, the USA, and other United Nations, bears her share of responsibility for this war;
Whereas, however, Hungary on December 28, 1944, broke off relations with Germany, declared war on Germany and on January 20, 1945, concluded an Armistice with the Governments of the USSR, the UK and the USA, acting on behalf of all the United Nations which were at war with Hungary; and
Whereas the Allied and Associated Powers and Hungary are desirous of concluding a treaty of peace, which, conforming to the principles of justice, will settle questions still outstanding as a result of the events hereinbefore recited and form the basis of friendly relations between them, thereby enabling the Allied and

Associated Powers to support Hungary's application to become a member of the United Nations and also to adhere to any Convention concluded under the auspices of the United Nations;

Have therefore agreed to declare the cessation of the state of war and for this purpose to conclude the present Treaty of Peace, and have accordingly appointed the undersigned Plenipotentiaries who, after presentation of their full powers, found in good and due form, have agreed on the following provisions:

Art. 1.(1) The frontiers of Hungary with Austria and with Yugoslavia shall remain those which existed on January 1, 1938.

(2) The Decisions of the Vienna Award of August 30, 1940, are declared null and void. The frontier between Hungary and Roumania as it existed on January 1, 1938, is hereby restored.

(3) The frontier between Hungary and the Union of Soviet Socialist Republics, from the point common to the frontier of those two States and Roumania to the point common to the frontier of those two States and Czechoslovakia, is fixed along the former frontier between Hungary and Czechoslovakia as it existed on January 1, 1938.

(4)(a) the decisions of the Vienna Ward of November 2, 1938, are declared null and void.

(b) the frontier between Hungary and Czechoslovakia from the point common to the frontier of those two States and Austria to the point common to those two States and the Union of Soviet Socialist Republics is hereby restored as it existed on January 1, 1938, with the exception of the change resulting from the stipulations of the following sub-paragraph.

(c) Hungary shall cede to Czechoslovakia the villages of Horvathjarfalu, Oroszvar and Dunacsun, together with their cadastral territory as indicated on Map No. 1A annexed to the present Treaty. Accordingly, the Czechoslovak frontier on this sector shall be fixed as follows: from the point common to the frontiers of Austria, Hungary and Czechoslovakia, as they existed on January 1, 1938, the present Hungarian-Austrian frontier shall become the frontier between Austria and Czechoslovakia as far as a point roughly 500 meters south of hill 134 (3.5 kilometers northwest of the church of Rajka), this point now becoming common to the frontiers of the three named States; thence the new frontier between Czechoslovakia and Hungary shall go eastwards along the northern cadastral boundary of the village of Rajka to the right bank of the Danube at a point approximately 2 kilometers north of hill 128 (3.5 kilometers east of the church of Rajka), where the new frontier will, in the principal channel of navigation of the Danube, join the Czechoslovak-Hungarian frontier as it existed on January 1, 1938; the dam and spillway within the village limits of Rajka will remain on Hungarian territory.

(d) The exact line of the new frontier between Hungary and Czechoslovakia laid down in the preceding sub-paragraph shall be determined on the spot by a boundary Commission composed of the representatives of the two Governments concerned. The Commission shall complete its work within two months from the coming into force of the present Treaty.

(e) In the event of a bilateral agreement not being concluded between Hungary and Czechoslovakia concerning the transfer to Hungary of the population of the ceded area, Czechoslovakia guarantees them full human and civic rights. All the guarantees and prerogatives stipulated in the Czechoslovak-Hungarian Agreement of February 27, 1946, on the exchange of populations will be applicable to those who voluntarily leave the area ceded to Czechoslovakia.

(5) The frontiers described above are shown on Maps I and IA in Annex I of the present Treaty.

Art. 2.(1) Hungary shall take all measures necessary to secure to all persons under Hungarian jurisdiction, without distinction as to race, sex, language or religion, the enjoyment of human rights and of the fundamental freedoms, including freedom of expression, of press and publication, of religious worship, of political opinion and of public meeting."

Came into force on Sept. 15, 1947 upon the deposit with the Government of the USSR of the instruments of ratification by the USSR, the UK and the USA, in accordance with article 42.

UNTS, Vol. 41, pp. 135–262.

HUNGER. The major international problem in past centuries and into the 20th century; subject of organized international co-operation on combating the causes of hunger on a world scale since May 1943, date of the First UN Conference on Food and Agriculture in Hot Springs, USA, which formed the FAO. In its First Declaration, the Conference analyzed the causes of hungers in the World, a report which is still of immediate interest:

"The cause of hunger is diet and poverty. The increase of food production is futile if people and nations cannot obtain it. An expansion of the entire world economy is necessary if we wish to acquire the purchasing power needed for everyone to feed himself properly. Plans must be accepted which will enable all nations to continually expand their industrial production, eliminate human exploitation, develop internal and international trade, make investments, stabilize currencies and achieve national and international economic balance."

The slowing of industrial growth in countries of the Third World after World War II retarded the struggle against hunger. In 1947–48 the UN stated that there were only seven countries in the world completely free from hunger: Australia, Canada, Denmark, New Zealand, Norway, Sweden and the USA. The political division of the world and the Cold War following in its wake also slowed down the world struggle with hunger.

In 1957, on the initiative of the Brazilian scholar, José de Castro, author of the celebrated *Geography of Hunger*, the World Association for the Struggle against Hunger was established in Paris – Association Mondiale de Lutte contre la Faim, ASCOFAM, reg. with UN and with special status to the FAO.

In July 1960 the FAO initiated a five-year world campaign against hunger extended ad infinitum in 1965; national committees were formed in the majority of states of the world. The World FAO Congress on Food was held June 4–18, 1963 in Washington. The Congress stated that every day thousands of people in the world continued to die from hunger, the majority of them children; that "half of the population of the world is badly nourished" and "a billion people can be included – in various degrees – among the permanently undernourished." In the opinion of the Congress, this state of affairs was incompatible with modern civilization, which had the means to completely eliminate hunger on the condition that the "tremendous sums invested in the production of destructive weapons" were used for this purpose. The 1350 participants of the Congress, who represented more than 100 States, resolved that "the matter of eliminating hunger and undernourishment had become the major problem of the present generation." the FAO, as part of the Freedom from Hunger Campaign, had recommended that member states increase food production by a minimum of 3% annually and make use of new highly fertile varieties of rice and wheat, which initiated the "green revolution." Simultaneously, UN Regional Economic Commissions started work on development plans for industry and agriculture and on the organization of UN technical assistance for countries undertaking agricultural reforms. According to calculations made by FAO the number of hungry people grew by 15 million a year in the 1970s reaching a high of 475 million in 1980. In the 1980s the annual rate of increase dropped to 8 million. The FAO estimates that 40,000 children die of hunger related causes every day.

In the years 1984, 1985 and 1986 three international actions under the name: 'Band Aid', 'Live Aid' and 'Sport Aid' started with worldwide publicity to raise funds for famine and drought relief. The first two actions raised around $90 million in two years;

On April 7–8, 1988 the European Parliament organized in Brussels a World Food Conference to discuss the global imbalance in food and Third-World hunger.
▷ Drought.

A. GARCIA ROBLES, *El Mundo de la Postguerra*, Mexico, DF, 1944, Vol. 2, p. 24; J. DE CASTRO, *Geography of Hunger*, London, 1954; *Man and Hunger*, FAO, Rome, 1962; E.G. STACKMAN, *Campaign against Hunger*, Cambridge, 1967; G. BERGSTRÖM, *The Hungry Planet*, London, 1968; A. SAUVY, *La fin des riches*, Paris, 1975; *UN Chronicle*, July, 1981, p. 36 and December, 1982, p. 95; KEESING's *Contemporary Archive*, 1986. K. GRIFFIN, *World Hunger and the World Economy*, London, 1987; J.W. WARNOCK, *The Politics of Hunger: The Global Food System*, London, 1987; M.H. GLANTZ ed., *Drought and Hunger in Africa*, Cambridge, 1987.

HUNGER, WORLD ZONE. An international term for overpopulated regions without a sufficient amount of food, partly afflicted by droughts, located in the zone between 30° latitude north and 30° latitude south. These regions, depending on the degree of scarcity of food, are defined in the UN as being at the starvation level (Chad, Ethiopia, Mali, Mauritania, Niger, Senegal, afflicted by a many years' drought, and Upper Volta); on the verge of starvation (Bolivia, Gambia, Kenya, Syria, Tanzania and Yemen), potential hunger (Bangladesh, Cameroon, India, and South Yemen) and chronically undernourished (Algeria, Angola, the Central African Republic, Ecuador, Haiti, Indonesia, Iraq, Iran, El Salvador, Saudi Arabia). In the second half of the 20th century some 55% of the total world inhabitants lived in the World Hunger Zone. ▷ Drought.

UN Chronicle, March, 1984, pp. 1–28.

HUNTER KILLER SUBMARINE. An international military term for modern submarines designed to destroy ships and other submarines. See also ▷ Submarines.

D. ROBERTSON, *Guide to Modern Defense and Strategy*, Detroit, 1988.

HUNTING. A subject of international co-operation. Organizations reg. with the UIA:

East African Professional Hunters Association, f. 1976, Nairobi.
European Committee for Big Game Hunting, 1976, Nice, France.
International Hunting and Shooting Council, f. 1930, Paris. Publ.: *Yearbook of National Hunting*.
International Professional Hunters Association, f. 1976, Nairobi.

Yearbook of International Organizations.

HUNTING LAW. An international term for civil law regulations related to game hunting; integrated in international private law with regard to the principles of international protection of some species of hunting game.

HUSSEIN PLAN, 1972. A scheme announced Mar. 15, 1972 by King Hussein of Jordan to form a federated state called the United Arab Kingdom composed of Jordan and Palestine, integrating Israeli-occupied territories on the Western Bank of the River Jordan, the Gaza Strip, and the Arab part of Jerusalem; dismissed by Arab states and Israel.

KEESING's *Contemporary Archive*, 1972.

HYDERABAD. The capital city of the Indian state of Andhra Pradesh. In 1948–50 the city and surrounding area were subject of a dispute between Pakistan and India; investigated by the UN Security

Council and General Assembly, Aug. 21, 1948–July 17, 1949; in Jan. 1950 integrated by India.

India White Paper on Hyderabad, New Delhi, 1948.

HYDROGEN BOMB OR THERMONUCLEAR BOMB. An international military term for a bomb which, unlike the fission based ▷ atomic bomb, relies on the rapid joining of light atomic nuclei in high temperatures for its energy. It was first tested by the USSR in 1953.

D. ROBERTSON, *Guide to Modern Defense and Strategy*, Detroit, 1988.

HYDROLOGY AND HYDRAULIC POWER. A subject of international co-operation and convention. The International Convention relating to the Development of Hydraulic Power affecting more than one state, was signed in Geneva on Dec. 9, 1923, by the governments of Austria, Belgium, the British Empire, Bulgaria, Chile, Denmark, France, Greece, Hungary, Italy, Lithuania, Poland, the Serbo-Croat-Slovene State, Siam and Uruguay promoting international investigation on the exploitation of hydraulic power. In Vienna from March 30 to April 3, 1987 an international symposium of 160 scientists from 45 countries, sponsored by IAEA/UNESCO reviewed the use of stable and radio-isotopes as research tools at aquifers, lakes, reservoirs, rivers and estuaries to describe water properties and characteristics and to assess prospects of supplies under different climatic and geographical conditions.

International organizations reg. with the UIA:

Inter-African Committee for Hydraulic Studies, f. 1960, Ougadougou, Burkina Faso, Publ.: *Bulletin*.
International Association of Hydrogeologists, f. 1956, Paris. Publ.: *Information Bulletin*.
International Association of Hydrological Sciences, f. 1922, Paris. Publ.: *Hydrological Bibliography*.
International Hydrographic Organization, est. 1922, Monte Carlo as the International Hydrographic Bureau. On Sept. 22, 1970 the Convention on the International Hydrographic Organizations, signed by 48 governments, came into force. Publ.: *International Hydrographic Review* (2 a year) and *IHO Bulletin* (monthly).

International Society for Hydrothermal Techniques, f. 1970, Paris.
International Society of Ichtiology and Hydrobiology, f. 1970, Singapore.
International Society of Medical Hydrology and Climatology, f. 1921, Rome. Publ.: *Archives of Medical Hydrology*.
North Sea Hydrographic Commissions, f. 1963, The Hague.

LNTS, Vol. 36, p. 76; E. VOLLMER, *Encyclopaedia of Hydraulics, Soil and Foundation Engineering*, Amsterdam, 1967; H.O. PFANNKUCH, Elsevier's *Dictionary of Hydrogeology*. In English, French and German, Amsterdam, 1969. *Yearbook of International Organizations*, 1986/87; *The Europa Yearbook 1988, A World Survey, Vol. I*, London 1988.

HYGIENE. The science of health protection, subject of international conventions and organized international co-operation, especially in the fields of social hygiene, sometimes called social medicine, and mental hygiene. In Europe the first international organizations on hygiene were: the Permanent Committee of the International Congress on School Hygiene, est. 1903 in London and operating until 1914; Comité permanent international des congrès internationaux d'hygiène et de démographie, est. 1903 in Paris and operating to 1913. The first world-wide organization on hygiene was established in 1919 by the LN, called Bureau International of Hygiene, BIH, with headquarters in Geneva and a branch in Singapore. Besides promoting hygiene it carried out research on methods for the protection of the health of infants, fighting cancer, tuberculosis, smallpox, sleeping sickness, malaria, cholera, trade in narcotics, etc. It established the first international system for preventive vaccinations. In 1946 the functions of BIH were taken over by WHO. As far as work hygiene is concerned, a crucial role was played by conventions and recommendations made since 1920 by ILO, which in 1959 in Geneva established Centre international d'information de sécurité et d'hygiène du travail, CIS, with several dozen branches in ILO member countries.

Organizations reg. with UIA:

International Federation for Hygiene, Preventive Medicine and Social Medicine, f. 1952, Paris.

World Association of Veterinary Food Hygienists, f. 1955, Bilthoven.

Major periodicals devoted to hygiene: *Revue d'Hygiène et de Médecine Sociale* (France), *British Journal of Preventive and Social Medicine* (UK), *American Journal of Public Health and Nations Health* (US), *Zdrowie Publiczne* (Poland), and *Gigiyena i sanitariya* (USSR).

Yearbook of International Organizations.

HYPERTENSION INTERNATIONAL RESEARCH. A WHO Expert Committee on Hypertension Research, stated in Oct. 1979, that about 40–50 million people in Europe (out of a total population of 800 million) are reported to have blood pressure in the hypertension range, and approximately 500 million are in the age group at risk of arterial hypertension. About 3 million deaths occur in Europe each year from strokes as a direct consequence of hypertension or from myocardial infunction of which high blood pressure is one of the most important causes.

International organization reg. with the UIA:

European High Blood Pressure Research Group, f. 1962, Umea, Sweden.

F.H. GROSS, J.I. ROBERTSON (eds.), *Arterial Hypertension, A WHO Expert Committee Report*, Tunbridge Wells, 1979. Ten rules for the drug treatment of hypertension, in: *WHO Chronicle*, 1985, No 5, p. 175; F. GROSS ed., *Management of Arterial Hypertension, WHO*, Geneva, 1985.

HYPNOSIS. A subject of international co-operation. Organizations reg. with the UIA:

International Center of Medical and Psychological Hypnosis, f. 1976, Milan.
International Society for Clinical and Experimental Hypnosis, f. 1958, Uppsala.

Yearbook of International Organizations.

HYTHE CONFERENCE, 1920. A French–British meeting in the English resort of Hythe, May 15–16, 1920 on the issue of the general settlement of ▷ Repatriations. Decided to convene the ▷ Spa Conference.

I

IAEA. International Atomic Energy Agency, Agence internationale de l'énergie atomique, Mezhdunarodnoye agientstvo po atomnoy energyi, Agencia Internacional de la Energía Atómica, official English, French, Russian and Spanish names of an inter-governmental autonomous organization, est. in Oct., 1957 in Vienna; related to the UN by the terms of an Agreement, approved by the UN General Assembly on Nov. 14, 1957, which recognizes it as "the agency under the aegis of the United Nations responsible for international activities concerned with the peaceful uses of atomic energy."

In view of the fact that its work is relevant to international security, the IAEA has direct reporting links with the UN General Assembly and Security Council. It also reports to the UN Economic and Social Council, ECOSOC, on questions of interest to that body. The IAEA works closely with sister agencies like the FAO with which it has a Joint Division. Common program interests have led to close co-operation with other organizations, such as the WHO (radiation protection), and UNESCO (theoretical physics). The IAEA also co-operates with regional organizations that deal with atomic energy, like the European Nuclear Energy Agency of the OECD and Euratom (the nuclear branch of the European Community) and the Joint Institute for Nuclear Research at Dubna near Moscow.

Aims: The International Atomic Energy Agency, in the words of its Statute,

"shall seek to accelerate and enlarge the contribution of atomic energy to peace, health and prosperity throughout the world. It shall ensure, so far as it is able, that assistance provided by it or at its request or under its supervision or control is not used in such a way as to further any military purposes."

To achieve this aim, the Agency is authorized to undertake a number of tasks, of which the most important are the following:

(a) to assist research on, and practical application of, atomic energy for peaceful purposes, including the production of electric power, with special consideration being given to underdeveloped areas;

(b) to act as an intermediary for the purposes of securing the performance of services or the supplying of materials, equipment or facilities by one member of the Agency for another;

(c) to foster the exchange of scientific and technical information on peaceful uses of atomic energy;

(d) to encourage the exchange and training of scientists and experts in the field of peaceful uses of atomic energy;

(e) to establish and administer safeguards to ensure that fissionable and other materials, services, equipment, facilities and information made available by or through the Agency are not used for the furtherance of any military purposes; and

(f) to establish, in consultation or in collaboration with the competent organs of the United Nations family concerned, standards of safety for protection of health and minimization of dangers to life and property, and to provide for the application of these standards.

Organization: The three main organs of the Agency are:

The General Conference in which all member states of the IAEA meet once a year to review the work of the IAEA, to give guidance on the future program, and to approve the annual budget.

The Board of Governors, the executive organ of the Agency in which 25 government representatives usually meet four times a year. The Board approves the program, submits the budget to the General Conference, approves all important agreements and decisions and generally carries out the functions of the IAEA subject to its responsibilities to the General Conference.

The Secretariat, headed by the Director-General, which carries out the IAEA's approved program and draws up program and budgets for the future. The Secretariat is organized into five departments, four headed each by a Deputy Director General, and, in the case of Safeguards and Inspection, by the Inspector General. The Secretariat makes great use of scientific and technical advice given by leading experts from member states. About 40 advisory groups on specific problems meet each year. The Agency's Scientific Advisory Committee, composed of ten eminent scientists, gives advice on the Agency's program in general.

Nuclear information exchange is a major IAEA activity. To put the exchange on a continuing computerized basis, the IAEA has set up the International Nuclear Information System, INIS; and to ensure the exchange and compilation of neutron data, the International Nuclear Data Committee. The International Centre for Theoretical Physics in Trieste, as well as the IAEA laboratories in Monaco and in Seibersdorf (Austria), are operated jointly by UNESCO and IAEA. The Agency provides advice and assistance to member states on technical feasibility, design, technology and economics of power reactor systems. One of the Agency's major functions is the establishment and administration of safeguards to ensure that nuclear materials intended for peaceful purposes are not diverted to military purposes. The implementation of the Treaty on the Non-Proliferation of Nuclear Weapons entails a growth of the Agency's safeguards activities and a shift from the application of safeguards to nuclear material in individual facilities to nuclear material in entire fuel cycles.

According to the IAEA 1982 *Nuclear Safety Review* by the end of 1982 almost 300 nuclear power plants, with more than 2800 reactor years of accumulated experience, were in operation in 25 countries.

The IAEA safeguards system is designed to verify that no diversion of safeguarded nuclear material is taking place and that safeguarded nuclear plants are not used for military purposes. Safeguarded plants are visited regularly by Agency inspectors, who audit the records and verify the presence of nuclear material through sampling and chemical analysis, non-destructive measuring instruments or other security methods.

At the end of 1982, the IAEA report states, there were 440 facilities under safeguards or containing safeguarded nuclear material, not counting five selected for inspection under voluntary-offer agreements with nuclear-weapon states. The total amount of nuclear material under Agency safeguards, excluding that covered by the voluntary-offer agreements, was 6 tons of separated plutonium, 10 tons of highly enriched uranium, 83 tons of plutonium contained in irradiated fuel and almost 42,000 tons of low-enriched uranium and source material (natural or depleted uranium and thorium). The IAEA safety evaluation and information program exchange since the early 1980's services plant operations and advises on radiological protection in response to the needs of Member

States and international developments. These impartial reviews are not an international regulatory inspection; they can complement, but never replace, the activities of national regulatory bodies and the responsibility of governments for nuclear safety. In 1983 the Agency established an incident reporting system ▷ IRS. After the ▷ Chernobyl accident the IAEA convened in Vienna on Aug. 25–29, 1986 a symposium to discuss the findings of the official Soviet report.

The IAEA services:
ASSET–Assessment of Safety Significant Events Team; INSARR–Integrated Safety Assessment of Research Reactors; IRS–Incident Reporting System; OSART–Operational Safety Review Team; OSIP–Operational Safety Indicators Programme; RAPAT–Radiation Protection Advisory Team.

IAEA information systems:
Collection of Nuclear Data Libraries, IAEA–CONDL; International Exchange System for Numerical Nuclear Reaction Data, IAEA–EXFOR; International Nuclear Information System, IAEA–INIS; World Request List for Nuclear Data, IAEA–WRENDA.

Publications: *IAEA Bulletin* (monthly), *Meetings on Atomic Energy* (quarterly), IAEA Publications on *Life Sciences*, on *Nuclear Safety and Environmental Protection*, on *Physics, Chemistry, Geology and Raw Materials*, on *Reactors and Nuclear Power* and *Miscellaneous* All publications can be obtained from the Publishing Section IAEA, PO Box 590, A-1011, Vienna, Austria.

See also ▷ EXFOR.
See also ▷ Nuclear Power Performance and Safety Conference.

W. GROSSE, *Internationale Kernenergie Organisationen*, Wien, 1957; *Aspect du Droit de l'Énergie Atomique*, Paris, 1965.
UN, *Everyone's United Nations, Directory of UN Information Systems, Vol. 2*, New York, 1980; UIA *Yearbook of International Organizations*; IAEA, *Nuclear Safety Review*, 1982; *UN Chronicle*, September, 1983, pp. 81–82; D. FISCHER, *The Safeguard System of IAEA*, SIPRI, London, 1984; J.A. HALL, "The IAEA. Origin and the Early Years", in: *IAEA Bulletin*, 1987, No. 2; L. SCHEINMAN, *The IAEA and World Nuclear Order*, Washington DC, 1987; *IAEA News Features*, April 15, 1988.

IAEA–OSART. International Atomic Energy Operational Service Teams, a service to Member States since 1982.

IAEA Newsbriefs No. 14, 1987.

IAEA SAFEGUARDS. ▷ Safeguards IAEA System.

IATA, INTERNATIONAL AIR TRANSPORT ASSOCIATION. The voluntary organization of airline companies whose membership is composed of scheduled airlines flying flags of the majority of countries, f. April 1945 in Havana, in accordance with the agreement of the International Civil Aviation Conference, Chicago, 1944, as successor of the International Air Traffic Association, f. 1919 at The Hague. Aims: promote safe, regular and economical air transport for the benefit of the peoples of the world, foster air commerce and study problems connected therewith; provide means for collaboration among air transport enterprises engaged directly or indirectly in international air transport service, co-operate with the ▷ ICAO and other international organizations. General Office: Geneva, Regional Technical Offices: Bangkok, Nairobi, London, Rio de Janeiro. Traffic Service Offices: Montreal, New York, Singapore. Consultative status with

ECOSOC, IAEA, ICAO, ITU and WHO. Publ. *IATA Bulletin* (annual), *IATA Review* (monthly).

R.Y. CHUANG, The IATA. *A Case Study of a Quasi-Governmental Organization*, The Hague, 1972; *UN Chronicle*, September, 1983, p. 82.

IBE–NETWORK. IBE World-Wide Network for Education Information, one of the information systems of ▷ UNESCO.

IBERIC PACT, 1939. The official name of a Treaty of Friendship and Non-Aggression, between the two states of the Iberian Peninsula, Spain and Portugal, signed on Mar. 18, 1939 in Lisbon; replaced by the Spanish–Portuguese Treaty of Friendship and Co-operation, signed on Nov. 23, 1977 in Madrid.

KEESING's *Contemporary Archive*, 1939 and 1977.

IBERLANT. An official abbreviation of the High Command of Ibero-Atlantic Forces, term which appeared in Dec. 1966 by a decision of the NATO Council to establish within the Atlantic Pact a separate naval unit to patrol and defend the region of the Atlantic Ocean from the Tropic of Cancer to the Straits of Gibraltar and to Portugal (about 1.5 million sq. km); under the direct command of ▷ SACLANT; independent of ▷ SACEUR.

IBM. International Business Machines World Trade Corporation. The world's largest computer company, f. 1924, Armonk N.Y., USA; produced and introduced the first universal computer language ▷ FORTRAN.

IBRD/WORLD BANK. The Bretton Woods Conference 1944 conceived the International Bank for Reconstruction and Development, which was established by an Agreement of 28 nations on Dec. 27, 1945 at Washington under the official abbreviated name IBRD/World Bank, but in the following years the name World Bank dominated in the UN system. ▷ World Bank.

B.A.de VRIES, *Remaking the World Bank*, Washington DC, 1988.

ICA. International Communication Agency. The central US office for foreign information and international relations in the field of culture, learning, science and information, founded on Apr. 1, 1978. The Agency took over all institutions and tasks of ▷ USIA and also incorporated the State Department's division of culture.

ICAO. International Civil Aviation Organization, Organisation de l'aviation civile internationale, Mezhdunarodnaya Organizatsya grazhdanskoy aviatsyi, Organización de la Aviación Civil Internacional, official English, French, Russian and Spanish names of a specialized agency of the UN, est. by a Convention on International Civil Aviation, signed on Dec. 7, 1944 at Chicago; came into being on Apr. 14, 1947 (pending ratifications of the Convention by 26 states, the Provisional ICAO was established and functioned from June 6, 1945 to Apr. 4, 1947).

Headquarters: Montreal, Canada. Regional Offices: Mexico, DF, for North America and the Caribbean, Bangkok for the Far East and Pacific; Neuilly-sur-Seine, France for Europe; Cairo, for the Middle East and Eastern Africa; Dakar for Africa; Lima for South America.

Aims: The aims and objective of ICAO are to develop the principles and techniques of international air navigation, and to foster the planning and development of international air transport so as to:

(a) ensure the safe and orderly growth of international civil aviation throughout the world;
(b) encourage the arts of aircraft design and operation for peaceful purposes;
(c) encourage the development of airways, airports and air navigation facilities for international civil aviation;
(d) meet the needs of the peoples of the world for safe, regular, efficient and economical air transport;
(e) prevent economic waste caused by unreasonable competition;
(f) ensure that the rights of contracting states are fully respected and that every contracting state has a fair opportunity to operate international airlines;
(g) avoid discrimination between contracting states;
(h) promote safety of flight in international air navigation;
(i) promote generally the development of all aspects of international civic aeronautics.

Organization: ICAO operates through an Assembly, a Council, a President of the Council, a Secretary-General and a Secretariat. ICAO also works through its Air Navigation Commission (restricted to 15 members), Air Transport Committee, Joint Support Committee, Finance Committee, Legal Committee.

Languages: English, French, Russian and Spanish. The Assembly consists of all of the member states of ICAO, each of which has one vote. It is convened by the Council twice in a three-year period. The Assembly decides on ICAO policy, votes on the budget and deals with any question not specifically referred to the Council. The Council, composed of twenty-one states elected by the Assembly, meets in virtually continuous session and carries out the directives of the Assembly. It elects its Presidents, appoints the Secretary-General, and administers the finances of the organization. It creates standards for international air navigation and collects, examines and publishes information concerning air navigation. It may also act, if so requested by the countries concerned, as a tribunal for the settlement of any dispute arising among member states relating to international civil aviation. The Secretary-General of ICAO appoints the staff of the secretariat.

ICAO Standards: To ensure the highest practicable degree of uniformity in international civil aviation regulations, the ICAO Council has adopted fifteen sets of standards and recommended practices. The standards and recommended practices are constantly revised, and amendments are made when necessary. All fifteen sets of standards and recommended practices are in effect, as annexes to the ICAO Convention, in all territories of ICAO's member states. Standards were established for:

(1) personnel licensing – indicating the technical requirements and experience necessary for pilots and aircrews flying on international routes;
(2) aeronautical maps and charts – providing specifications for the production of all maps and charts required in international flying;
(3) rules of air – including general flight rules, instrument flight rules, and right-of-way rules;
(4) dimensional practices – providing progressive measures to improve air–ground communications;
(5) meteorological codes – which specify the various systems used for the transmission of meteorological information;
(6) operation of aircraft in scheduled international air services – governing flight preparations, aircraft equipment and maintenance, and, in general, the manner in which aircraft must be operated to achieve the desired level of safety on any kind of route;
(7) aircraft nationality and registration marks;
(8) airworthiness of aircraft;

(9) facilitation of international air transport – to simplify customs, immigration and health inspection regulations at border airports;
(10) aeronautical telecommunications – dealing with the standardization of communications systems and radio air navigation aids;
(11) air traffic services – dealing with the establishment and operation of air traffic control, flight information and alerting services;
(12) search and rescue – dealing with the organization to be established by states for the integration of facilities and services necessary for search and rescue;
(13) aircraft accident enquiry – dealing with the promotion of uniformity in the notification, investigation of and reporting on aircraft accidents;
(14) aerodromes – dealing with the physical requirements, lighting and marking of international aerodromes; and
(15) aeronautical information services – dealing with the uniformity in methods of collection and dissemination of aeronautical information.

If a state is unable to put a standard into effect in its territory, it must notify ICAO of the differences between its own practices and those established by the international standard. The Council must, in turn, notify all other members of ICAO of these differences. Notification of non-compliance with recommended practices is, however unnecessary.

ICAO principal achievements are international air law conventions. ▷ Air Law International.

Agreements and contracts concluded by member states or by airlines in those states are registered with ICAO, and national aviation laws and regulations are filed by ICAO. ICAO had also assembled an extensive collection of texts of national laws and regulations on aviation.

Publications: ICAO continually collects, analyzes and publishes statistical information relating to international aviation services. It issues a wide range of technical publications, including operational standards, regional manuals, and multi-language glossaries, and it publishes the *ICAO Bulletin*, which contains a review of ICAO's current activities. A detailed report on the aims and work of ICAO is contained in the *Memorandum on ICAO*; this publication can be obtained free in English, French and Spanish versions, from the Public Information Office of ICAO, International Aviation Building, Montreal, Canada.

On May 10, 1984 an amendment to the Chicago Convention 1944 was unanimously adopted by the ICAO Assembly, stating that every State "must refrain from resorting to the use of weapons against civil aircraft in flight and . . . in cases of interception, the lives of persons on board and the safety of aircraft must not be endangered." The amendment must be ratified by 102 or two-thirds of ICAO Contracting States before it comes into force.

ICAO information system: Communication on Frequency and Facility Information System, ICAO–COFFI.

J. SHENKMAN, *ICAO*, Geneva, 1958; *The Convention of ICAO*, Montreal, 1963; J. ERLER, *Die Rechtsfragen der ICAO*, Köln, 1967; UN, *Everyone's United Nations*, New York, 1979; *Yearbook of International Organizations; UN Chronicle*, March 1984, p. 34, and April 1984, p. 54.

ICAO ALPHABET. A unified system for designating letters introduced by ICAO, used in international phonic communication by civil airplanes and airport traffic service. The signs are chosen in such a way that misunderstanding is minimal even during interferences in reception: A – Alpha, B – Bravo, C – Charlie, D – Delta, E – Echo, F – Foxtrot, G – Golf, H – Hotel, I – India, J – Juliet, K – Kilo, L – Lima, M – Mike, N – November, O – Oscar, P –

Papa, Q – Quebec, R – Romeo, S – Sierra, T – Tango, U – Uniform, V – Victor, W – Whisky, X – X-Ray, Y – Yankee, Z – Zulu.

ICAO NEW LANDING SYSTEM, 1978. On Apr. 21, 1978 in Montreal the ICAO All-Weather Operations Divisional Meeting adopted the US–Australian TRSR/INTERSCAN microwave non-visual precision approach landing and guidance system (MLS) that could replace the Instrument Landing System (ILS) which the ICAO had selected for world-wide use in 1946. In the light of technical, operational and economic considerations the ILS system could remain in use at least until 1995.

UN Chronicle, June, 1978, pp. 110–111.

ICARA. ▷ Refugees.

ICBM. Inter-Continental-Ballistic Missiles, defined by SALT agreements as follows:

"Intercontinental Ballistic Missiles, ICBM, are landbased launches of ballistic missiles capable of a range in excess of the shortest distance between the northeastern border of the continental part of the territory of the United States of America and the northwestern border of the continental part of the territory of the Union of Soviet Socialist Republics, that is, a range in excess of 5,500 kilometres." ▷ SALT II Documents, 1979.

Under the SALT agreement the test ranges where ICBMs are tested are located: for the USA near Santa Maria, Calif., and at Cape Canaveral, Florida; and for the USSR in the areas of Tynra, Tam and Plesetskaya. The first ICBM was produced in 1957 by the USSR, and in 1958 by the USA.

M.B. DONLEY, *The SALT Handbook*, Washington, DC, 1979; D. ROBERTSON, *Guide to Modern Defense and Strategy*, Detroit, 1988.

ICEBERGS. A subject of international observation and agreements. In Washington, DC, the member governments of the International Convention for Safety at Sea on Jan. 14, 1956 signed the Treaty on Financing the Observation of Icebergs in the North Atlantic carried on by the US North Atlantic Ice Patrol. The Treaty took effect on July 5, 1956.

UNTS, Vol. 164, p. 113 and Vol. 256, p. 172.

ICEBREAKERS. A subject of international bilateral and regional agreements. On Dec. 20, 1961 in Helsinki, Denmark, Finland, Norway and Sweden signed the Agreement on Common Use of Icebreakers.

UNTS, Vol. 419, p. 79.

ICE CREAM INDUSTRY. A subject of international co-operation. Organizations reg. with the UIA:

Association of the Ice Cream Industry of the EEC (Euro-glaces), f. 1976, Paris.
International Association of Ice Cream Manufacturers, f. 1900, Washington, DC.

Yearbook of International Organizations.

ICE HOCKEY. Olympic discipline since 1928. International Ice Hockey Federation, IIHF, f. 1908, since 1942 organizes world championships, held since 1962 exclusively indoors; headquarters – Antwerp (Belgium).

Yearbook of International Organizations.

ICELAND. Member of the UN. Lyoveldio Island. Republic of Iceland. A large island in the North Atlantic Ocean near the Arctic Circle. Area: 103,000 sq. km. Pop.: 1987 est.: 247,300 (1960 census: 175,680; 1970 census: 204,930; 1976 census:

220,918). Capital: Reykjavik with 86,092 inhabitants, 1982. GNP per capita 1986: US $15,483. Official language: Icelandic. Currency: one Icelandic krona = 100 aurars. National Day: June 17, Proclamation of Republic, 1944.

Member of the UN since Nov. 19, 1946 and of the UN specialized agencies save IFAD and UNIDO. Member of NATO, OECD, EFTA, the Nordic Council and the Council of Europe.

International relations: a feudal state under the rule of the kings of Norway 1263–1381, later under the Danish kings, since Dec. 1, 1918 as a sovereign state in personal union with Denmark. Complete independence came with the proclamation of the republic on June 17, 1944. Involved in the ▷ Cod Fish War with Great Britain in 1958 and in 1972–73. In July, 1975 Iceland extended its fishery limits from 50 to 200 miles. In Oct., 1981 Iceland signed with Norway an Agreement on Jan Mayen Continental shelf rights.

D.H.N. JOHNSON, "Icelandic fishery limits", in: *International Law Quarterly*, No. 1, 1952; *The Iceland Fishery Question*, Reykjavik, 1958; H.W. HANSEN, *Island, von der Vikingerzeit bis zur Gegenwart*, Frankfurt am M., 1965; J. NORDAL, V. KRISTINSSON eds., *Iceland 1874–1974*, Reykjavik, 1975; S.A. MAGNUSSON, *Northern Sphinx: Iceland and the Icelanders from the Settlement to the Present*, London, 1977; *The Europa Year Book 1984. A World Survey*, Vol. I, p. 578–589. London, 1984.

ICHKEUL. A National Park of Tunisia, included in the ▷ World Heritage UNESCO List. This park contains a wooded mountainous massif, marshes and a lake covering 100 sq. km, which communicates with the lagoon of Bizerte. It is one of the major stopping places for birds migrating between Europe and Africa, and in the winter some 300,000 go there to feed. In July, the salt waters attract pink flamingoes and in September – white storks.

UNESCO, *A Legacy for All*, Paris, 1984.

ICJ. ▷ International Court of Justice.

ICRP. The International Commission on Radiological Protection. Est. 1960 in London. Its recommendations for protection against natural and artificial sources of radiation are used by the IAEA in developing its guidelines and safety standards; also used by governments in setting their regulations. Member of the UIA.

IAEA News Features, May 20, 1988.

ICSID. International Centre for Settlement of Investment Disputes. An intergovernmental institution, est. on Oct. 14, 1966, in Washington, by the Convention on the Settlement of Investment Disputes between States and Nationals of Other States, formulated by the World Bank. Aims: Encourage the growth of private foreign investment for economic development by creating the possibility, subject to the consent of both parties, for a contracting state and a foreign investor who is a national of another contracting state to settle any legal dispute that might arise out of such an investment by conciliation and/or arbitration before an impartial international forum. Members: member states of the World Bank or by invitation other parties to the Statute of the International Court of Justice. Publ.: *Annual Report*.

Regulations and Rules of ICSID, Washington, DC, 1967; *Legal History of ICSID Convention*, Washington, DC, 1970: A. BROCHES, "The ICSID convention", in: *Recueil des Cours de l'Académie du Droit International de La Haye*, 1972, Vol. 36, pp. 342–348; J. CHARIAN, *Investments Contracts and Arbitration. The World Bank Convention*, London, 1975.

IDA. International Development Association. A specialized agency of the UN, est. in Sept., 1960 in Washington, DC; its European office is in Paris. The IDA is an intergovernmental organization which promotes economic development in the poorest member countries by providing finance on terms more flexible, and bearing less heavily on the balance of payments of the recipient countries, than those conventional loans, thereby supplementing the World Bank's activities.

Though legally and financially distinct from the World Bank, the IDA is administered by the same officers and staff and membership is open only to members of the World Bank. The IDA's assistance concentrates on countries with an annual GNP per capita in 1975 of less than US $520. More than 50 countries are eligible under this criterion. Its objectives are to promote economic development, increase productivity and thus raise standards of living by providing its membership finance to meet important development requirements. Nearly all IDA "credits", as distinct from World Bank loans, have been, for a period of 50 years, without interest, except for a small charge to cover administrative costs. Repayment of principal does not begin until after a 10-year period of grace. The bulk of IDA resources comes from three sources: transfers from the World Bank's net earnings; capital subscribed in convertible currencies by the members; and contributions from the IDA's richer members.

IBRD, *Articles of Agreement of the IDA*, New York, 1960; M. SEARA VAZQUES, *Tratado General de la Organización Internacional*, Mexico, DF, 1964, pp. 591–596; *Everyone's United Nations*, UN, New York, 1979, pp. 365–366.

IDEOLOGIES. International term for regional and global political or religious trends of thought..

IEPG. ▷ Independent European Program Group.

IERS. International Education Reporting Service, one of the information systems of ▷ UNESCO.

IFAD. International Fund for Agricultural Development. The agency in the UN system which began its operation in Dec., 1977, subsequent to the entry into force of the Agreement establishing it on Nov. 30, 1977. The main objective of the International Fund for Agricultural Development is to mobilize additional resources to be made available on concessional terms for agricultural development in developing member states. The IFAD provides financing primarily for projects and programs specifically designed to introduce, expand or improve food production systems and to strengthen related policies and institutions within the framework of national priorities and strategies. In setting priorities for allocating resources, the Fund is guided by the need to increase food production and to improve the nutritional level of the poorest populations in the poorest food-deficit countries as well as the potential for increasing food production in other developing countries. Within the framework of these priorities, eligibility for assistance is on the basis of objective economic and social criteria. The Fund places special emphasis on the needs of the low-income countries and their potential for increasing food production and on the need to expand the incomes and employment of the poorest people. The highest directing body of IFAD is the Governing Council, on which all member countries are represented. The Secretariat is headed by a President elected by the Council and responsible for the management of the Fund. The members of the Fund, totalling 139 governments, in Oct. 1984, during the annual session in Paris, were informed, that during the 7 years of Fund activities US $

2 billion were distributed, but for the future years only US $ 760 million are promised by the main donors: the OECD, OPEC and the USA.

UN Yearbook 1977; *Directory of UN Information System*, New York, 1980, p. 435; *UN Chronicle*, January, 1978 and October, 1983 and November, 1984.

IFC. International Finance Corporation. A Corporation affiliated with the World Bank, est. on July 24, 1956 in Washington, DC by agreement among the majority of member countries of the World Bank, to assist its less developed member states by promoting the growth of the private sector of their economies, help develop local capital markets and seek to stimulate the international flow of private capital. The IFC draws on the World Bank for administrative and other services, but has its own operating and legal staff. While closely associated with the World Bank, the IFC is a separate legal entity and its staff and funds are distinct from those of the Bank. The Bank does provide, however, a wide range of administrative and other services for the IFC. Membership is open to all governments that are members of the Bank.

The principal objectives of the IFC are to provide risk capital for productive private enterprise in association with private investors and managements, to encourage the development of local capital markets and to stimulate the international flow of private capital. The Corporation makes investments in the form of share subscriptions and long-term loans. It carries out stand-by and underwriting arrangements, and it provides financial and technical assistance to privately controlled development finance companies. It neither requires nor accepts guarantees by governments in its operations. Generally the IFC investments are either in the form of a loan, a share subscription or a combination of both, with other investors, local and foreign, providing the bulk of the funds required for any given project. In the years 1957–1983 the IFC had approved investments of US $ 4,547 million in 77 countries.

R.I. GARNER, *The IFC*, London, 1956; F. ELBIALY, *La SFJ et le développement capitaliste des pays sous-développées*, Genève, 1963; F.A. MANS, "The interpretation of the constitution of IFC", in: *The British Yearbook of International Law*, 1968–69; *IFC. What it is. What it does. How it does it*, Washington, DC, 1979; *Everyone's United Nations*, UN, New York, 1979; *Yearbook of International Organizations*.

IFNI. A Moroccan province on the northwest African coast. Area: 1502 sq. km. Ifni was under Spanish administration, as stipulated by the Tetuan Treaty, 1860, and the Madrid Convention, 1912, until June 30, 1969, when a plebiscite under the aegis of the UN decided that Ifni should be returned to Morocco.

R. PELISSIER, *Les territoires espagnoles d'Afrique*. Paris, 1963.

IGAT. Iranian Gas Trunkline, Iranian–Soviet firm which constructed and controls a pipeline, approximately 1300 km, opened on Oct. 28, 1970 in the Iranian locality of Astara, linking gas fields of South Iran – Agha Dhari, Kara Faris, Marun and others – with Baku in the USSR; current passage force: c. 1650 million cubic feet per day.

The Middle East and North Africa, 1972–73. A Survey and Reference Book, London, 1972.

I.G. FARBEN TRIAL, 1947. War crime trial of the largest German chemical cartel, 1925–1945, the *Interessen-Germeinschaft Farbenindustrie*, called *I.G. Farben*, integrating the main German chemical factories: *Badische Anilin und Sodafabrik (BASF)*, *Farbenfabriken Bayer AG*, *Farbwerke Hoechst, AG*

für Anilinfabrikation (AGFA) and other. The cartel was accused of producing poisonous gases and of employment during World War II of slave labor from occupied countries and of medical experiments with concentration camp prisoners (▷ Guinea Pigs). In 1945 Allied occupation authorities ordered confiscation of property, and directors responsible for war crimes were brought before the International Military Tribunal, 1947. The I.G. Farben headquarters in Frankfurt am M. was in 1945–1946 Gen. D. Eisenhower's Supreme Headquarters of Allied European Forces.

I.G. Farben Prozess 1947. IG Farben Auschwitz Experimente, Berlin, 1965.

IGNORANTIA IURIS NOCET. *Latin* = "ignorance of law is harmful" or Ignorantia legis excusat neminem = "ignorance of law is no excuse". A commonly accepted principle of penal law stating that ignorance of legal norms does not free one from the responsibility for acts inconsistent with the law; also observed by military courts martial.

IKEBANA. The Japanese art of composing artistic bouquets from flowers and other parts of flora. A subject of organized international co-operation. Organization reg. with the UIA:

Ikebana International, f. 1956, Tokyo; unites ikebanists from five continents. Publ.: monthly *Newsletter*, a bimonthly *Hana Kagami*, and the semi-annual *International Ikebana Magazine*.

Yearbook of International Organizations.

ILLITERACY. A subject of international programs carried out under UN auspices. The largest percentage of illiterates is recorded in African countries. 73.3% (Arab countries included), followed by South Asian: 46.8% and Latin-American: 23.6%. According to UN data, there were 780 million illiterates in the world in 1970 (i.e. some 100 million more than in 1950 in absolute figures) though the percentage dropped markedly from 50% in 1950 (adults) through 40% in 1960 to 34% in 1970.

OEA/OAS. *Perspectivas de Desarrollo de Educación en América Latina*, Washington, DC, 1963; UNESCO, *Statistical Yearbook*, 1973; *Courrier de l'UNESCO*, November, 1974.

ILLUMINATION. A subject of international co-operation. Organization reg. with the UIA;

International Commission on Illumination, f. 1900, Paris. Publ. *International Vocabulary of Illumination* in 9 languages.

Yearbook of International Organizations.

ILO. International Labour Organization, Organisation internationale du travail, Mezhdunarodnaya Organizatsya truda, Organización Internacional del Trabajo, official English, French, Russian and Spanish names of a UN specialized agency, est. on June 28, 1919 by Part XIII (Labour) of the Treaty of Versailles, taking over the activities of the International Labour Office as an autonomous body associated with the League of Nations. The Constitution became operative on Apr. 11, 1919. It was recognized by the UN in 1946 as a specialized agency under the terms of an agreement which recognized the responsibility of the ILO in its own field of competence. The International Labour Conference, 1944 in Philadelphia, adopted a Declaration redefining its aims and purposes. Amendments in the original Constitution were adopted by the Conference in 1945, 1946, 1953, 1962 and 1972, and came into effect respectively in 1946, 1948, 1954, 1963 and 1975. The ILO head-

quarters was established at Geneva in 1920 but between 1940 and 1948 its activities were directed from a working center in Montreal. Was awarded the Nobel Peace Prize in 1969.

The ILO aims to contribute to the establishment of universal and lasting peace through the promotion of social justice.

Its tripartite structure is unique among the United Nations system. Representatives of workers, employers and governments join in determining ILO policies and supervising its activities.

The aims and objectives of the ILO are indicated in its Constitution, which was drawn up in 1919. Among the questions to which the ILO devotes itself are:

(a) hours of work, including a maximum working day and week;

(b) the regulation of the labor supply and the prevention of unemployment;

(c) the provision of an adequate living wage;

(d) the protection of the worker against sickness, disease and injury arising out of his employment;

(e) the protection of the interests of workers when employed in countries other than their own;

(f) recognition of the principle of equal remuneration for work of equal value;

(g) recognition of the principle of freedom of association; and

(h) technical assistance to underdeveloped countries.

The Philadelphia Declaration, adopted by the International Labour Conference in 1944 and later annexed to the ILO Constitution, reaffirms the principles on which the ILO is based, and maintains that

"all human beings, irrespective of race, creed, or sex, have the right to pursue both their material well-being and their spiritual development in conditions of freedom and dignity, of economic security, and equal opportunity."

Organization: the ILO works through an International Labour Conference, a Governing Body, and an International Labour Office headed by a Director-General.

The Conference is the policy-making body of the ILO and meets at least once a year. It is composed of national delegations comprising two government delegates and two delegates representing respectively employers and workers. Each delegate has one vote in the Conference.

The principal function of the Conference is to establish international social standards in the form of international labor conventions and recommendations. (An ILO convention is binding on governments that ratify it; an ILO recommendation sets up targets but is not subject to ratification.) In addition, the Conference designates the members of the Governing Body, adopts the annual budget, examines the application of conventions and recommendations, and expresses itself on questions submitted to it by the Governing Body or raised by the delegates.

The Governing Body is the executive council of the ILO. It is composed of forty members: ten representing employers, ten representing labor, and twenty representing government. Each of these three groups at the Conference elects its own representatives to the Governing Body – with the exception of ten government representatives from the countries which hold permanent seats as states of chief industrial importance, and do not participate in the election of the other ten government representatives. Elections take place every three years.

The Governing Body elects the Director-General and supervises the work of the International Labour Office and of the various committees and commissions of ILO. It determines policy and work programs; establishes the agenda for the Conference in so far as it is not fixed by the Conference itself; and prepares the annual budget. The Governing Body names its own committees to deal with particular problems.

The International Labour Office, located at Geneva, Switzerland, is the permanent secretariat of the ILO. The Office provides the staff for the Conference, for the Governing Body, and for other meetings or conferences. It prepares the documents for these meetings; publishes periodicals, studies and reports on social and economic questions, and collects and distributes information on all subjects within the ILO's competence. It undertakes enquiries and programs of works as directed by the Governing Body or the Conference. Major programs in recent years have included technological change and social policy, labor-management relations, development of skills, productivity, labor administration (including vocational training), social security, and human rights. Since its establishment the ILO has played a leading role in raising living standards throughout the world. It works toward this goal – with the help of governments, employers and workers – in three basic ways: by setting international labor and social standards; by aiding countries to make their own social gains through technical assistance; and by gathering and distributing information of social and economic interest.

In 1983 the main ILO problem was the violation of the ILO's Conventions on Freedom of Association and the Right to Organize, involving 46 countries in all regions of the world. On May 31, 1985 Vietnam withdrew from the ILO. In 1984 and 1985 the ILO published 2 Vls of its World Labour Report.

Publications: international studies, surveys, works of practical guidance or reference on questions of social policy manpower, industrial relations, working conditions, social security, training, management development, etc. (English, French, Spanish unless otherwise stated). *International Labour Review* (monthly): special articles, notes on current developments and bibliography. *Official Bulletin* (quarterly): information and documents relating to ILO activities. Legislative series (bi-monthly): selected labor and social security laws and regulations. *Bulletin of Labour Statistics* (quarterly). *Year Book of Labour Statistics. CIRF Abstracts* (in English and French) a service providing digests of articles, laws, reports dealing with vocational training (annual subscription). CIRF monographs, reports for the annual sessions of the International Labour Conference (English, French, German, Russian, Spanish). Minutes of the Governing Body of the ILO, *ILO-Information* (6 a year) a bulletin issued in Arabic, Danish, English, Finnish, French, German, Hindi, Italian, Japanese, Norwegian, Russian, Spanish, Swedish and Urdu. All publications can be obtained from International Labour Office, Geneva, Switzerland.

ILO information system: International Occupational Safety and Health Information Centre, ILO–CIS.

L. JONHAUX, *L'Organisation Internationale du Travail*, Paris, 1921; H. GUERREAU, *Une Nouvelle Institution du Droit des Gens: l'Organisation Permanente du Travail*, Paris, 1923; G.N. BANNEY, *History of the International Labour Office*, London, 1926; C. ARGENTIER, *Les resultats acquis par l'Organisation Permanente du Travail de 1919 à 1929*. Paris, 1930; J.T. SHOTWELL, *The Origins of the ILO, History, Documents*, 2 Vols., New York 1934; G. FISHER, *Les rapports entre l'OIT et la CPJI*, Paris, 1946; *L'OIT. Trente Ans du Combat pour la Justice Sociale, 1919-1949*, Genève, 1950; L TROCLET, *Législation Sociale Internationale*, Brussels, 1952; *Bibliographie de l'OIT*, Genève, 1959; C.W. JENGS,

Human Rights and International Labour Standards, London, 1960; *ILO Conventions and Recommendations, 1919-1966*, Geneva, 1966; *Everyman's United Nations*, 1975; *UN Chronicle*, January, 1984, p. 95; *ILO, Structural Adjustment: By Whom, for Whom?*, New Delhi, 1987.

ILO ADMINISTRATIVE TRIBUNAL. An institution of the International Labour Organization founded in Geneva in 1924. Its purpose is to settle disputes between ILO employees and the ILO. The Statute of the Tribunal allowed other international organizations, as well as non-governmental organizations, to make use of its provisions, thereby in effect it became a major institution of arbitration, after the Administrative Tribunal of the League of Nations and later of the UNO, to settle problems between staff and the administration.

F. WOLF, "Le Tribunal Administratif de l'OIT", in: *La vue générale du droit public*, No. 58, 1954: G. BENAR, *Le Tribunal Administratif de l'OIT. Les juridictions internationales*, Brussels, 1958.

ILO CONVENTIONS, 1919-1980. The Labour Conventions adopted by the International Labour Organization General Conferences: 1919 at Washington; 1920 at Geneva; 1921-39 at Geneva; 1946 at Seattle and Montreal; 1947 at Geneva, 1948 at San Francisco and from 1949 at Geneva. The list of 153 Conventions adopted before Dec. 31, 1980 reads as follows:

 1. Hours of Work (Industry) Convention, 1919
 2. Unemployment Convention, 1919
 3. Maternity Protection Convention, 1919
 4. Night Work (Women) Convention, 1919
 5. Minimum Age (Industry) Convention, 1919
 6. Night Work of Young Persons (Industry) Convention, 1919
 7. Minimum Age (Sea) Convention, 1920
 8. Unemployment Indemnity (Shipwreck) Convention, 1920
 9. Placing of Seamen Convention, 1920
10. Minimum Age (Agriculture) Convention, 1921
11. Right of Association (Agriculture) Convention, 1921
12. Workmen's Compensation (Agriculture) Convention, 1921
13. White Lead (Painting) Convention, 1921
14. Weekly Rest (Industry) Convention, 1921
15. Minimum Age (Trimmers and Stokers) Convention, 1921
16. Medical Examination of Young Persons (Sea) Convention, 1921
17. Workmen's Compensation (Accidents) Convention, 1925
18. Workmen's Compensation (Occupational Diseases) Convention, 1925
19. Equality of Treatment (Accident Compensation) Convention, 1925
20. Night Work (Bakeries) Convention, 1925
21. Inspection of Emigrants Convention, 1926
22. Seamen's Articles of Agreement Convention, 1926
23. Repatriation of Seamen Convention, 1926
24. Sickness Insurance (Industry) Convention, 1927
25. Sickness Insurance (Agriculture) Convention, 1927
26. Minimum Wage-Fixing Machinery Convention, 1927
27. Marking of Weight (Packages Transported by Vessels) Convention, 1929
28. Protection against Accidents (Dockers) Convention, 1929
29. Forced Labour Convention, 1930
30. Hours of Work (Commerce and Offices) Convention, 1930
31. Hours of Work (Coal Mines) Convention, 1931
32. Protection against Accidents (Dockers) Convention (Revised), 1932
33. Minimum Age (Non-Industrial Employment) Convention, 1932
34. Fee-Charging Employment Agencies Convention, 1933
35. Old-Age Insurance (Industry, etc.) Convention, 1933
36. Old-Age Insurance (Agriculture) Convention, 1933
37. Invalidity Insurance (Industry, etc.) Convention, 1933
38. Invalidity Insurance (Agriculture) Convention, 1933
39. Survivor's Insurance (Industry, etc.) Convention, 1933
40. Survivors' Insurance (Agriculture) Convention, 1933
41. Night Work (Women) Convention (Revised), 1934
42. Workmen's Compensation (Occupational Diseases) Convention (Revised), 1934
43. Sheet-Glass Works Convention, 1934
44. Unemployment Provision Convention, 1934
45. Underground Work (Women) Convention, 1935
46. Hours of Work (Coal Mines) Convention (Revised), 1935
47. Forty-Hour Week Convention, 1935
48. Maintenance of Migrants' Pension Rights Convention, 1935
49. Reduction of Hours of Work (Glass-Bottle Works) Convention, 1935
50. Recruiting of Indigenous Workers Convention, 1936
51. Reduction of Hours of Work (Public Works) Convention, 1936
52. Holidays with Pay Convention, 1936
53. Officers' Competency Certificates Convention, 1936
54. Holidays with Pay (Sea) Convention, 1936
55. Shipowners' Liability (Sick and Injured Seamen) Convention, 1936
56. Sickness Insurance (Sea) Convention, 1936
57. Hours of Work and Manning (Sea) Convention, 1936
58. Minimum Age (Sea) Convention (Revised), 1936
59. Minimum Age (Industry) Convention (Revised), 1937
60. Minimum Age (Non-Industrial Employment) Convention (Revised), 1937
61. Reduction of Hours of Work (Textiles) Convention, 1937
62. Safety Provisions (Building) Convention, 1937
63. Convention concerning Statistics of Wages and Hours of Work, 1938
64. Contracts of Employment (Indigenous Workers) Convention, 1939
65. Penal Sanctions (Indigenous Workers) Convention, 1939
66. Migration for Employment Convention, 1939
67. Hours of Work and Rest Periods (Road Transport) Convention, 1939
68. Food and Catering (Ships' Crews) Convention, 1946
69. Certification of Ships' Cooks Convention, 1946
70. Social Security (Seafarers) Convention, 1946
71. Seafarers' Pensions Convention, 1946
72. Paid Vacations (Seafarers) Convention, 1946
73. Medical Examination (Seafarers) Convention, 1946
74. Certification of Able Seamen Convention, 1946

75. Accommodation of Crews Convention, 1946
76. Wages, Hours of Work and Manning (Sea) Convention, 1946
77. Medical Examination of Young Persons (Industry) Convention, 1946
78. Medical Examination of Young Persons (Non-Industrial Occupations) Convention, 1946
79. Night Work for Young Persons (Non-Industrial Occupations) Convention, 1946
80. Final Articles Revision Convention, 1946
81. Labour Inspection Convention, 1947
82. Social Policy (Non-Metropolitan Territories) Convention, 1947
83. Labour Standards (Non-Metropolitan Territories) Convention, 1947
84. Rights of Association (Non-Metropolitan Territories) Convention, 1947
85. Labour Inspectorates (Non-Metropolitan Territories) Convention, 1947
86. Contracts of Employment (Indigenous Workers) Convention, 1947
87. Freedom of Association and Protection of the Right to Organize Convention, 1948
88. Employment Service Convention, 1948
89. Night Work (Women) Convention (Revised), 1948
90. Night Work of Young Persons (Industry) Convention (Revised), 1948
    Labour Standards (Non-Metropolitan Territories) Convention Instrument of Amendment, 1948
91. Paid Vacations (Seafarers) Convention (Revised), 1949
92. Accommodation of Crews Convention (Revised), 1949
93. Wages, Hours of Work and Manning (Sea) Convention (Revised), 1949
94. Labour Clauses (Public Contracts) Convention, 1949
95. Protection of Wages Convention, 1949
96. Fee-Charging Employment Agencies Convention (Revised), 1949
97. Migration for Employment Convention (Revised), 1949
98. Right to Organize and Collective Bargaining Convention, 1949
99. Minimum Wage Fixing Machinery (Agriculture) Convention, 1951
100. Equal Remuneration Convention, 1951
101. Holidays with Pay (Agriculture) Convention, 1952
102. Social Security (Minimum Standards) Convention, 1952
103. Maternity Protection Convention (Revised), 1952
104. Abolition of Penal Sanctions (Indigenous Workers) Convention, 1955
105. Abolition of Forced Labour Convention, 1957
106. Weekly Rest (Commerce and Offices) Convention, 1957
107. Indigenous and Tribal Populations Convention, 1957
108. Seafarers' Identity Documents Convention, 1958
109. Wages, Hours of Work and Manning (Sea) Convention (Revised), 1958
110. Plantations Convention, 1958
111. Discrimination (Employment and Occupation) Convention, 1958
112. Minimum Age (Fishermen) Convention, 1959
113. Medical Examination (Fishermen) Convention, 1959
114. Fishermen's Articles of Agreement Convention, 1959
115. Radiation Protection Convention, 1960
116. Final Articles Revision Convention, 1961

117. Social Policy (Basic Aims and Standards) Convention, 1962
118. Equality of Treatment (Social Security) Convention, 1962
119. Guarding of Machinery Convention, 1963
120. Hygiene (Commerce and Offices) Convention, 1964
121. Employment Injury Benefits Convention, 1964
122. Employment Policy Convention, 1964
123. Minimum Age (Underground Work) Convention, 1965
124. Medical Examination of Young Persons (Underground Work) Convention, 1965
125. Fishermen's Competency Certificates Convention, 1966
126. Accommodation of Crews (Fishermen) Convention, 1966
127. Maximum Permissible Weight to be Carried by One Worker Convention, 1967
128. Invalidity, Old Age and Survivors Benefits Convention, 1967
129. Labour Concerning Labour Inspection in Agriculture Convention, 1969
130. Medical Care and Sickness Benefits Convention, 1969
131. Minimum Wage Fixing Convention, 1970
132. Annual Holidays Pay Convention (Revised), 1970
133. Crew Accommodation Board Ship Convention (Supplementary Provisions), 1970
134. Prevention of Occupational Accidents to Seafarers Convention, 1970
135. Protection and Facilities to be Afforded to Workers Representatives in the Undertaking Convention, 1971
136. Protection Against Hazards of Poisoning Arising From Benzene Convention, 1971
137. Social Repercussions of New Methods of Cargo Handling in Docks Convention, 1973
138. Minimum Age for Admission to Employment Convention, 1973
139. Prevention and Control of Occupational Hazards Caused by Carcinogenic Substances and Agents Convention, 1974
140. Paid Educational Leave Convention, 1974
141. Organizations of Rural Workers and Their Role in Economic and Social Development Convention, 1975
142. Vocational Guidance and Vocational Training in the Development of Human Resources Convention, 1975
143. Migrations in Abusive Conditions and the Promotion of Equality of Opportunity and Treatment of Migrant Workers Convention, 1975
144. Tripartite Consultation to Promote the Implementation of International Labour Standards Convention, 1976
145. Continuity of Employment of Seafarers Convention, 1976
146. Annual Leave for Seafarers Convention, 1976
147. Minimum Standard in Merchandise Ships Convention, 1976
148. The Protection of Work Against Occupational Hazards in the Work Environment Due to Air Pollution, Noise and Vibration Convention, 1977
149. Employment and Condition of Work and Life of Nursing Personal Convention, 1977
150. Labour Administration Role, Function and Organisation Convention, 1978
151. Protection of the Rights to Organize and Procedures for Determining Conditions of Employment in the Public Service Convention, 1978
152. Occupational Safety and Health in Dockwork Convention, 1979

153. Hours of Work and Rest Period in Road Transport Convention, 1979.

ILO, *Conventions and Recommendations, 1919–1966*, Geneva, 1966; ILO, *International Conventions and Recommendations 1919–1981*, Geneva, 1982.

ILO INTERNATIONAL OCCUPATIONAL SAFETY AND HEALTH HAZARD ALERT SYSTEM. ▷ Health Hazard Alert ILO System.

ILO RECOMMENDATIONS, 1919–1980.
Recommendations adopted by the International Labour Organization General Conferences in: 1919 at Washington, 1920 at Geneva, 1921–39 at Geneva, 1944 at Philadelphia, 1945 at Paris, 1946 at Seattle and Montreal, 1947 at Geneva, 1948 at San Francisco and from 1949 at Geneva. The list of 155 Recommendations adopted before Dec. 31, 1980 reads as follows:

1. Unemployment Recommendation, 1919
2. Reciprocity of Treatment Recommendation, 1919
3. Anthrax Prevention Recommendation, 1919
4. Lead Poisoning (Women and Children) Recommendation, 1919
5. Labour Inspection (Health Services) Recommendation, 1919
6. White Phosphorus Recommendation, 1919
7. Hours of Work (Fishing) Recommendation, 1920
8. Hours of Work (Inland Navigation) recommendation, 1920
9. National Seamen's Codes Recommendation, 1920
10. Unemployment Insurance (Seamen) Recommendation, 1920
11. Unemployment (Agriculture) Recommendation, 1921
12. Maternity Protection (Agriculture) Recommendation, 1921
13. Night Work of Women (Agriculture) Recommendation, 1921
14. Night Work of Children and Young Persons (Agriculture) Recommendation, 1921
15. Vocational Education (Agriculture) Recommendation, 1921
16. Living-in Conditions (Agriculture) Recommendation, 1921
17. Social Insurance (Agriculture) Recommendation, 1921
18. Weekly Rest (Commerce) Recommendation, 1921
19. Migration Statistics Recommendation, 1922
20. Labour Inspection Recommendation, 1923
21. Utilisation of Spare Time Recommendation, 1924
22. Workmen's Compensation (Minimum Scale) Recommendation, 1925
23. Workmen's Compensation (Jurisdiction) Recommendation, 1925
24. Workmen's Compensation (Occupational Diseases) Recommendation, 1925
25. Equality of Treatment (Accident Compensation) Recommendation, 1925
26. Migration (Protection of Females at Sea) Recommendation, 1926
27. Repatriation (Ship Masters and Apprentices) Recommendation, 1926
28. Labour Inspection (Seamen) Recommendation, 1926
29. Sickness Insurance Recommendation, 1927
30. Minimum Wage-Fixing Machinery Recommendation, 1928
31. Prevention of Industrial Accidents Recommendation, 1929
32. Power-driven Machinery Recommendation, 1929

150. Vocational Guidance and Vocational Training in the Development of Human Resources Recommendation, 1975
151. Migrant Workers Recommendation, 1975
152. Tripartite Consultations to Promote the Implementation of International Labour Standards and National Action Relating to the Activities of the ILO Recommendation, 1976
153. Protection of Young Seafarers Recommendation, 1976
154. Continuity of Employment of Seafarers Recommendation, 1976
155. Protection of the Right to Organize and Procedures for Determining Conditions of Employment in the Public Service Recommendation, 1978

ILO, *Conventions and Recommendations, 1919–1981*, Geneva, 1982

IMCO, 1958–1982. Inter-Governmental Maritime Consultative Organization, Organisation intergouvernementale consultative de la navigation maritime, Mezhpravitielstviennaya morskaya konsultativnaya organizatsya, Organización Consultiva Marítima Intergubernamental, official English, French, Russian and Spanish names of a specialized agency of the UN, est. Feb.19–Mar. 6, 1948 in Geneva during the Maritime Conference of the UN, on the drawing up of a convention which came into force on Mar. 17, 1958 after ratification by 21 states (seven having a minimum shipping of 1 million gross tons). Since 1982 under the name International Maritime Organization, ▷ IMO.

The relationship of the IMCO to the United Nations as a specialized agency was approved by the UN General Assembly on Nov. 18, 1948, and by the IMCO Assembly on Jan. 13, 1959. Headquarters was in London.

Aims: As defined at its first Assembly, the functions of the IMCO, which acts in a consultative and advisory capacity, are:

(a) to provide machinery for co-operation among governments in the field of governmental regulation and practices relating to technical matters, including those concerning safety at sea;
(b) to consider any matters concerning shipping that might be referred to it by any organ or specialized agency of the United Nations;
(c) to provide for the exchange of information among governments on matters under consideration by the organization; and
(d) to provide for the drafting of conventions and agreements to recommend these to governments and to intergovernmental organizations, and to convene such conferences as may be necessary.

Organization: an Assembly of all members, a Council of sixteen members (elected for two year terms), a Maritime Safety Committee of fourteen members, and a secretariat headed by a Secretary-General.

In view of a disagreement over the interpretation of Article 28 of the IMCO Convention relating to the "eight largest shipowning nations" – for membership in the Maritime Safety Committee – the first Assembly decided to refer this matter to the International Court of Justice: the Court was asked to give an advisory opinion on the following question: "Is the Maritime Safety Committee of IMCO, which was elected on January 15, 1959, constituted in accordance with the Convention for the establishment of the organization?"

A number of countries, including the United States, Liberia and Panama, had contested the validity of these elections in view of the failure of Liberia and Panama to obtain seats on the Committee. Both Liberia and Panama have gross registered tonnage in Lloyd's Register which, under one interpretation

of Article 28 of the IMCO Convention, would entitle them to be considered among the "eight largest shipowning nations." Other countries, however, including the United Kingdom and the USSR, had argued that neither Liberia nor Panama could be considered among the "eight largest shipowning nations" since there was doubt regarding the existence of a genuine link between these states and the ships flying their flags. It was also stated that neither Liberia nor Panama could make a major contribution at this time to the work of the Maritime Safety Committee.

The First IMCO Assembly elected the following governments as the first eight members of the Committee (listed in the order of election): the United States, the United Kingdom, Norway, Italy, the Netherlands, Japan, France and the Federal Republic of Germany. For the remaining six seats the Assembly elected Argentina, Canada, Greece, Pakistan, the United Arab Republic and the USSR.

Convention on IMCO, London, 1961; *IMCO. What it is. What it does*, London, 1962; *IMCO and its Archives*, London, 1979.

IMF. International Monetary Fund, Fond monétaire international, Mezhdunarodniy valutniy fond, Fondo Monetario Internacional, official English, French, Russian and Spanish names of a UN specialized agency, est. on Dec. 27, 1945 in Washington, DC, when 29 governments, representing 80% of the original quotas, signed the Articles of Agreement that had been prepared at the UN Monetary and Financial Conference, Bretton Woods, on July 1–22, 1944. An inaugural, organizational meeting of the Board of Governors was convened at Savannah, Georgia, on Mar. 8, 1946. On Dec. 18, 1946 the IMF announced its agreement to the establishment of par values in gold and US dollars for the currencies of 32 of its members, and on Mar. 1, 1947 announced its readiness to commence exchange transactions. An agreement of relationship concluded with the UN outlines a program of mutual assistance between the UN and the Fund, as an independent international organization and UN Specialized agency. The IMF co-operates particularly in the work of the UN secretariat, the ECOSOC, UNCTAD, Economic Commissions for Europe, Africa, Asia and the Far East, and Latin America, through participation at their meetings and through joint working parties, missions and study groups. Co-ordination with the GATT is continuous. It also has close ties with the World Bank. The two were established as complementary institutions, and Executive Directors and Alternative Directors of the IMF in some cases also serve on the Executive Board of the World Bank, and the same is true of some Governors.

Aims: The IMF was established to promote international monetary co-operation through a permanent institution which provides the machinery for consultation and collaboration on international monetary problems. Its purposes are mainly:

(a) to facilitate the expansion and balanced growth of international trade, and to contribute thereby to the promotion and maintenance of high levels of employment and real income, and to the development of the productive resources of all members as primary objectives of economic policy;
(b) to promote exchange stability, to maintain orderly exchange arrangements among members, and to avoid competitive exchange depreciation; and
(c) to give confidence to members by making the IMF's resources available to them under adequate safeguards.

Organizations: The IMF works through a Board of Governors, Executive Directors, a Managing Director, and a staff.

All powers of the IMF are vested in the Board of Governors, consisting of one Governor and one alternative appointed by each member. The voting power of the Governors is approximately in proportion to the size of the quota of the members which they represent.

The Executive Directors are responsible for the conduct of the general operations of the IMF; they exercise the powers delegated to them by the Board of Governors. Five of the Executive Directors are appointed by members having the largest quotas, and the twelve others are elected by the Governors representing the remaining members. Each appointed Director casts all the votes of the country which appointed him, and each elected Director casts as a unit all the votes of the countries which elected him.

The Executive Directors elect a Managing Director, who must not be a Governor or an Executive Director. He is the Chairman of the Executive Directors and chief of the operating staff. Under the direction of the Executive Directors, he conducts the ordinary business of the IMF.

The IMF also operates a Compensatory Financing Facility to support members, particularly those producing primary products, suffering from fluctuations in receipts from exports. Other IMF activities include a Buffer Stock Financing Facility to assist members in financing contributions to buffer stock arrangements, and an Extended Facility under which the Fund may aid members in meeting balance-of-payments deficits for longer periods and in amounts larger in relation to quotas than has been the practice under normal credit tranche policies.

A Subsidy Account was established in Aug., 1975 to reduce for the most seriously affected members the burden of interest payable under the temporary oil facility. Created in 1974 and renewed through Feb., 1976, the facility helped 55 members meet the impact of the increased costs of imported petroleum and petroleum products. In May, 1976 the Executive Board established a Trust Fund, financed by the profits from the sale of the IMF's gold, by voluntary contributions and by loans, to provide developing countries with special balance-of-payments assistance. The first amendment to the IMF's Articles of Agreement, establishing a new facility based on Special Drawing Rights (▷ SDR), entered into force on July 28, 1969. The SDR allows a country to purchase currency – sterling, dollars, francs, etc. – with which it can transact its business. The value of an SDR is based on the average of a basket of 16 currencies, weighted according to their importance in world trade. The mixing of currencies represented in the SDR cushions the effect of fluctuations in exchange rates of national currencies, so that the SDR remains relatively stable. With the advent of the SDRs, the IMF has been able to supplement the existing reserve assets of participating members. A total of 9300 million SDRs were allocated between 1970 and 1972. As of 31 Dec., 1977, the SDR was equivalent to about $1.21.

Four years of efforts in the IMF and elsewhere directed towards international monetary reform culminated in a second amendment. This was approved by the Board of Governors on Apr. 30, 1976 and entered into force on Apr. 1, 1978. The amendment introduced new and more flexible provisions dealing with exchange arrangements, a gradual reduction in the role of gold in the international monetary system, and changes in the characteristics and expansion of the uses of the SDR which are intended to enhance its status as an international reserve asset. Other provisions include: simplification and expansion of the IMF's financial operations and transactions, the possible establishment of a permanent Council to be composed of

Governors of the IMF, ministers or persons of comparable rank, and improvements in a number of organizational aspects of the IMF.

The IMF also provides technical assistance in various forms to its member countries. In addition, regular consultations with members are an important part of the IMF's work and provide a major instrument for effective surveillance of members' policies. The IMF also provides technical assistance in various forms to its member countries. In addition, regular consultations with members are an important part of the IMF's work and provide a major instrument for effective surveillance of members' policies. The IMF also issues a broad range of studies, reports and publications on its activities and related economic subjects.

Total cumulative drawings on the IMF, as of Feb. 22, 1977, amounted to SDR 43,170,9 million, comprising SDR 32,470 million of tranche drawings, SDR 3,570,0 million drawn under the Extended Facility and SDR 30 million of Buffer Stock drawings. On March 27, 1986, the IMF established a $3 billion pool of economic adjustment loans for the World's poorest countries (60) with interest payments of 0.5% and repayment in 6–10 years administered by the IMF and the World Bank.

Publications: *Annual Report; International Financial Statistics; Direction of Trade, IMF Survey; Balance of Payments Yearbook; Staff Papers; Annual Report on Exchange Restrictions; Summary Proceedings of the Annual Meeting; Finance and Development*, quarterly review of the IMF and IBRD; quarterly financial statements. Public statements by the IMF's officials, explanatory materials, reports of operations. All publications can be obtained from IMF, Washington, DC 20431, USA.

H. AUFRECHT, *The IMF. Legal Bases, Structure, Functions*, New York, 1964; M. FLEMING, *The IMF. Its Forms and Functions*, IMF, Washington, DC, 1964; J. GOLD, *Membership and Non-membership in the IMF. A Study in International Law and Organization*, Washington, DC, 1974; M.G. de VRIES, *The IMF, 1966–1971*, Washington, DC, 1976; W. BRANDT, "International Monetary Reform is Crucial", in: *Newsweek*, November 12, 1984; *IMF Glossary*. English-French–Spanish, Washington DC, 1979; S. DELL ed., *The IMF and its Reform*, 3 Vls, Amsterdam, 1987; S.R. SIDELL, *The IMF and Third World Political Instability*, London 1987.

IMF STAND-BY CREDIT. International Monetary Fund credit assurance arrangement for a fixed period of time.

J. GOLD, *The Stand-by Arrangements of the IMF*, Washington, DC, 1970.

IMMIGRATION. An international term for settlement outside of the country of birth of a person or a group of persons who for any reason left their homeland; in international analyses immigration is considered jointly with ▷ emigration; subject of international agreements, most often bilateral, aimed at protecting interests of newcomers in an alien country. Both emigration and immigration (jointly called ▷ migration) are the subject of permanent co-operation between international intergovernmental and non-governmental organizations. In Australia and in South Africa since the 19th century the immigration restrictions excluded "aboriginal natives of Asia", as well as Chinese, Japanese and Indians. The UN has published in 1953 in English, French and Spanish a *Handbook for the Migrants*.

A.H. CHARTERIS, "Australian immigration policy", in: *International Conciliation*, No. 235, December, 1927; *Manuel des mesures internationales destinées à protéger les migrants et conditions générales à observer pour l'établissement des migrants*, UN, New York, 1953; T.C. HARTLEY, *EEC Immigration Law*, Amsterdam,

1978; *Passenger and Immigrations List Index*, A 3 Vols set indexing nearly 500,000 immigrants arriving in the United States and Canada over a century, furnishing details as to date, post of arrival and names of accompanying relatives, New York, 1981. Supplement, New York, 1982–85; A.H. RICHMOND, *Immigration and Ethnic Conflict*, London, 1987.

IMMIGRATION ACTS, 1965, 1984, 1986. The US law passed by the US Congress and signed on Oct. 3, 1965, by President L.B. Johnson providing for rules for permitting immigrants from outside the US to become permanent residents, thereby voiding the Act of 1924 which introduced the so-called "national quota" to encourage immigration from north and west Europe and discriminate against immigrants from south and east Europe, and Africa and Asia (National Origins Quota Systems). The new Act allows for permanent settlement of relatives of US nationals irrespective of their place of origin or persons well educated or talented who may contribute to the growth of the US. The Act was criticized by Third World countries as enhancing ▷ Brain-drain. A new Immigration Act, the Aliens Bill was passed by the US Congress on June 26, 1984. On Oct. 15 and 17, 1986 the US Congress approved a comprehensive Immigration Act, that prohibits the hiring of illegal aliens, offers legal status to those who had entered the USA before Jan. 1, 1982 and allows foreign farm laborers who could prove they had worked in the US for at least 90 days for each of the last 3 years to gain legal status and eventually citizenship.

R. MENDOR, *International Migration Law*, The Hague, 1972.

IMMUNITIES AND PRIVILEGES. An institution of international law determining rights and privileges granted to diplomats on the basis of reciprocity. In the light of international law these are granted not to particular persons but to states and organizations on behalf of which such persons act in foreign countries. Immunities and privileges are granted to "provide persons enjoying them with best possible conditions for executing their tasks." Immunities and privileges are subject to international treaties concluded at the Congress of Vienna in 1815 and the ▷ Vienna Convention on Diplomatic Relations of 1961. These documents use the term "diplomatic privileges" instead of "immunities" and in keeping with the Convention of 1961, comprise: the personal inviolability of diplomatic officers, inviolability of premises of diplomatic missions, their means of transportation, liaison, archives and documents, revenue privileges including exemption, in principle, from all kinds of taxation, except under precisely defined circumstances, jurisdictional privileges (penal and civil privileges) and customs privileges. The violation of diplomatic immunities is considered an international dereliction which may result in the liability of the state concerned. Due to a growing number of terrorist assaults, also against diplomatic and consular staff, the UN General Assembly adopted the Convention on Prevention and Punishment of Offences Committed on Persons Granted International Protection, also on Diplomats, Dec. 14, 1973.

On Dec. 15, 1980 the UN General Assembly Res. 35/167 called the States concerned to accord to the delegations of the national liberation movement recognized by the Organization of African Unity and/or the League of Arab States and which were accorded observer status by international organizations, the facilities privileges and immunities necessary for the performance of their functions in accordance with provisions of the Vienna Convention in the Representation of States in Their Relations with International Organizations of Universal

Character (▷ Privileges and Immunities of the UN). The Res. was adopted by 97 votes in favor to 10 against with 29 abstentions.

The definition of the term discussed but not adopted during the 232nd session of the International Law Commission May 5–July 25, 1980 read as follows:

" 'Immunity' means the privilege of exemption from, or suspension of, or non-amenability to, the exercise of jurisdiction by the competent authorities of a territorial State."

UN Yearbook, 1973; *Report of the ILO*, UN, New York, 1980, pp. 316–391; "Immunities for representatives of liberation movements urged", in: *UN Chronicle*, March, 1981, pp. 60–61; J. DUFFAR, *Contribution à l'étude des privilèges et immunités des organisations internationales*, Paris, 1982; G. MOURSI BADR, *State Immunity*, The Hague, 1984.

IMMUNITIES OF THE UN. ▷ Privileges and Immunities of the UN.

IMMUNITY. An international term for a privilege of being exempt from charges, particularly from national or other taxation levied, conferred on diplomatic representatives on the basis of appropriate laws or customs; subject to international conventions. ▷ Immunities and privileges.

R.L. BLEDSOE, B.A. BOCZEK, *The International Law Dictionary*, Oxford, 1987.

IMMUNITY OF STATE SHIPS. A specific right of certain ships laid down in the international conventions on the unification of certain principles relating to the immunity of state ships signed on Apr. 10, 1926 in Brussels. Under arts. 1 and 2 of the Convention, state ships are subject to "the same rules of responsibility and the same duties as private ships." However, under art. 3 "the provisions contained in the two preceding articles shall not apply to warships, state yachts, guard, hospital, auxiliary and supply vessels as well as other ships used only by governments". ▷ merchant ships.

Laws Concerning the Nationality of Ships, New York, 1955.

IMMUNIZATION. According to the WHO immunization services remain tragically under utilized in the world today. In developing countries 0.5% of all newborns can be expected to become crippled from poliomyelitis and 1% can be expected to die from neonatal tetanus, 2% from pertussis and 3% from measles. In all, some 5 million children die of these illnesses each year. Yet all these diseases can be prevented inexpensively and with a high degree of efficacy. One challenge facing many of the developing countries is to ensure that their Expanded Program on Immunization, EPI, can rely on a continuous supply of good-quality low-cost vaccine. To this end the Pan-American Health Organization, PAHO, has established the EPI Revolving Fund for the procurement of vaccines. The Revolving Fund, authorized by the PAHO Directing Council in 1977 and operational since Jan., 1979, essentially provides countries in the Americas with a reimbursement mechanism for the purchase of vaccines, syringes, needles, and cold-chain equipment. Vaccine orders are consolidated and vaccines are procured on a group basis by PAHO with money drawn from the Fund – capitalized in US dollars – and each country then reimburses the Fund, normally in its local currency. Orders for syringes, needles, and cold-chain equipment are made on an individual basis. The example of PAHO's Revolving Fund has given rise to smaller-scale efforts in the common procurement and centralized distribution of vaccines, notably in the Western Pacific Region, and may well serve as a model for future regional-level schemes for the purchase of other essential drugs. According to the WHO statistics in 1988 over 50% of the world's children are now being immunized with BCG, diptheria, pertussis, tetanus, poliomyelitis and measles vaccines: ten years ago the figure was below 5%. The WHO Expanded Programme on Immunization (EPI) is now preventing more than one million deaths from measles, neonatal tetanus and pertussis and over 175,000 cases of polio are being prevented in the developing world. On Oct. 25, 1985 a Declaration affirming commitment to immunization of all children by 1990, was signed at UN Headquarters.

WHO Chronicle, No. 37, 1983; *WHO Weekly Epidemiological Record*, No. 13, Aug. 14, 1987; *UN Chronicle*, 1985, No. 10–11, p. 107.

IMMUNOLOGY. A subject of international co-operation. Organizations reg. with the UIA:
European Academy of Allergology and Clinical Immunology, f. 1952, Brussels.
International Co-ordination Committee for Immunology of Reproduction, f. 1975, Paris.
International Union of Immunological Societies, f. 1966, Berne.
World Association of Veterinary Microbiologists, Immunologists and Specialists in Infectious Diseases, f. 1968, Paris.

H. GOODMAN, "WHO First Research Unit: Immunology", in: *World Health*, December, 1983; P.H. LAMBERT, J. LOUIS, "The WHO immunology programme for developing countries", in: *World Health*, November, 1983; *Yearbook of International Organizations*; F. ROSEN, *Dictionary of Immunology*, London 1986.

IMO. International Maritime Organization, formerly ▷ IMCO, Intergovernmental Maritime Consultative Organization, redesignated on May 22, 1982. A specialized agency of the UN to facilitate co-operation among governments on technical matters affecting international shipping. Its main functions are the achievement of safe and efficient navigation and the control of pollution caused by ships and craft operating in the marine environment. Members: 125 UN member States. Organization: Assembly, consisting of delegates from all member States; Council of 24 members elected by the Assembly for a term of two years; Committees: Legal, Facilitation, on Technical Co-operation, The Maritime Safety and Marine Environment Protection; Secretariat with headquarters in London. ▷ World Maritime University. Publ. IMO News. The IMO is the depository of the following conventions: International Convention for Safety at Sea, 1948 (administration taken over from the UK).
International Convention for Safety of Life at Sea, 1960, and Collision Regulations, 1960, effective from 1965.
International Convention for the Prevention of Pollution of the Sea by Oil, 1954 (taken over from the UK).
Convention on Facilitation of International Maritime Traffic, 1965. Came into force in March 1967.
International convention on Load Lines, 1966. Came into force in July 1968.
International Convention on Tonnage Measurement of Ships, 1969. Convention embodies a universal system for measuring ships' tonnage. Came into force in 1982.
International Convention relating to Intervention on the High Seas in Cases of Oil Pollution casualties, 1969. Came into force in May 1975. Drawn up at a conference called by IMO in Brussels in 1969.
International Convention on Civil Liability for Oil Pollution Damage, 1969. Came into force in June 1975.

International Convention on the Establishment of an International Fund for Compensation for Oil Pollution Damage, 1971. Came into force in October 1978.
Convention on the International Regulations for Preventing Collisions at Sea, 1972. Came into force in July 1977.
International Convention for Safe Containers, 1972. Came into force in September 1977.
International Convention on the Prevention of Pollution from Ships, 1973 /as modified by the Protocol of 1978/. Came into force in October 1983.
International Convention for Safety of Life at Sea, 1974. Came into force in May 1980. A Protocol drawn up in 1978 came into force in May 1981.
Athens Convention relating to the Carriage of Passengers and their Luggage by Sea, 1974.
Convention on the International Maritime Satellite Organization, 1976. Came into force in July 1979.
Convention on Limitation of Liability for Maritime Claims, 1976.
International Convention for the Safety of Fishing Vessels, 1977.
International Convention on Standards of Training, Certification and Watchkeeping for Seafarers, 1978. Came into force in 1984.
International Convention on Maritime Search and Rescue, 1979.
The Rome IMO Conference on Mar. 10, 1988, adopted by consensus a Convention for the Supression of Unlawful Acts Against the Safety of Maritime Navigation and a supplementary Protocol for the suppression of Unlawful Acts Against the Safety of Fixed Platforms Located on the Continental Shelf.

United Nations. Basic Facts, New York, 1983; *Yearbook of the United Nations, 1982*, New York, 1984; KEESING's *Record of World Events*, June, 1988.

IMO. ▷ International Meteorological Organization, 1878–1947.

IMPEACHMENT. A term for formal charge by a parliament or similar body against a public official, head of state or member of government; used by the British Parliament, since the 19th century also by the US Congress, certain Latin American and European parliaments. The first case of impeachment took place during the English parliament of 1376. The US Constitution of 1787 provides in Art. ii sec. 4 that "the President, Vicepresident and all civil officers shall be removed from office on impeachment for, and conviction of treason, bribery or other crimes and misdemeanors."
In Great Britain the parliament decision could include fines and imprisonment, but the US Constitution limits the judgment to removal and disqualification from office. In 1868 the US President Andrew Johnson was acquitted by the margin of one vote. In 1973–74 US Congress Commissions examined ▷ Watergate affair; on July 28, 1974 the Impeachment Committee of the House of Representatives found President Richard Nixon guilty of violating the principle of law and order and motioned the House of Representatives for the President to be removed from office. In view of unfavourable balance of forces in Congress, Richard Nixon resigned as President on Aug. 9, 1974.

C. CANNON, *Cannon's Precedents of the House of Representatives of the US*, New York, 1935; T.F.T.V. PLUCKERT, "The Origin of Impeachment", in: *Transactions of the Royal Historical Society*, 1942. Bar Association of the City of New York, *The Law of Presidential Impeachment*, New York, 1973.

IMPERIALISM. An international term with a double meaning: (1) in the traditional meaning – foreign policy consisting of colonial conquests,

militarism, the aspiration to subordinate other countries to the homeland; (2) in Lenin's interpretation, the highest, final stage of capitalism, characterized by the concentration of production and capital and the replacement of free competition by the domination of monopolies; appeared as a result of changes in capitalism at the end of the 19th century.
According to nonaligned countries "imperialism continues to be the major obstacle in the way of developing countries, and of the nonaligned countries in particular" (▷ Georgetown Non-Aligned Countries Declaration, 1972).

J.I. RAGATZ, *The Literature of European Imperialism, 1815–1932*, London, 1942; A.P. THORNTON, *The Imperial Idea and its Enemies*, London, 1959; J.A. SCHUMPETER, *Imperialism and Social Classes*, London, 1960; J.A. HOBSON, *Imperialism*, London, 1965; Ph. DARBY, *Three Faces of Imperialism. British and American Approaches to Asia and Africa, 1870–1970*, New Haven, 1987.

IMPERIUM. An international term for a great power. Historically three states used the name officially: (1) the ancient Roman state from the 1st century A.D. (Imperium Romanum); (2) the Russian state (Rossiyskoy Imperial) since the adoption by Peter I of the title imperator, 1721, to the abdication of Emperor Nicholas II, 1917; (3) The United Kingdom (British Empire) until 1931.

IMPORT. An international term for the act of bringing in agricultural produce, industrial goods, raw materials, capital or services from a foreign country.

IMPORT–EXPORT. The acts, respectively, of bringing in and taking out goods; a subject of international bilateral and multilateral contracts. The first convention lifting barriers and bans imposed on exports and imports was the Convention for the Abolition of Import and Export Prohibitions and Restrictions with Protocol and Annexed Declaration, signed on Nov. 8, 1927 in Geneva. The Supplementary Agreement with Protocol and Declaration Annexed was signed on July 11, 1928, in Geneva; and Protocol concerning the entry into force of the Convention and Agreement was signed on Dec. 20, 1929 in Paris.

LNTS, Vol. 97, p. 391.

IMPRIMATUR. *Latin* = "let it be printed". An international term for ecclesiastic permission for printing an article in the press or a book in a publishing house. On Apr. 7, 1975 Pope Paul VI signed a new decree on imprimatur, prohibiting priests and all Roman Catholics alike from publishing articles critical of the Church in the press.

IMPRISONMENT AND DETECTION. ▷ Protection of All Persons under any Form of Detention or Imprisonment, Principles, 1988.

IMPROVED ACCESS TO MARKET. An economic term in the UN system for the removal of tariff and non-tariff barriers to allow goods from developing countries freer access to the markets of the rich nations.

UN Chronicle, October, 1983, p. 47.

INAKODUMCY. ▷ Dissidents.

INCB. International Narcotics Control Board. An intergovernmental institution established in 1961 under UN auspices with headquarters in Geneva as an organ of the Convention on Narcotic Drugs, ratified as of Dec. 1, 1971 by 81 states. Works in close co-operation with the UN Secretariat, the

ECOSOC, Commission on Narcotic Drugs and the WHO. ▷ Narcotics.

INCENDIARY WEAPONS.

An international term for all incendiary arms including ▷ napalm and phosphorus arms used against personnel, the human habitat and natural resources, regarded generally as inhumane which in the opinion of UN experts should be recognized as illegal.

F.B. FISHER, *Incendiary Warfare*, New York, 1946; R.T. HOLZMANN, *Chemical Rockets and Flame and Explosives Technology*, London, 1969; *Napalm and other Incendiary Weapons and all Aspects of their Possible Use*, UN, New York, 1973; M. LUMSDEN, *Incendiary Weapons*, SIPRI, London, 1975.

INCH.

A medieval unit for the measure of length, retained after the second half of the 20th century in Anglo-Saxon countries, universally replaced by the metric system. In relation to the latter the inch differs insignificantly depending on the country: in Spain = 23.22 mm, in Poland = 24.8 mm, in Great Britain = 25.39 mm, in USA, as in Tsarist Russia = 25.40 mm, and in France = 27.07 mm.

INCITEMENT TO MURDER.

An international diplomatic and ethical affair began on Feb. 14, 1989 when Ayatollah Khomeini of Iran put a price on the head of British author Salman Rushdie for having written a novel, "The Satanic Verses", that is blasphemous from the Muslim point of view. On Feb. 20, 1989, the Foreign Ministers of the European Community unanimously accepted the following declaration:

"The Ministers of Foreign Affairs of the 12 member states of European Community, meeting in Brussels on February 20, discussed the Iranian threats and incitement to murder against novelist Salman Rushdie and his publishers, now repeated despite the apology made by the author on 18 February.
The Foreign Ministers view those threats with the gravest concern. They condemn this incitement to murder as an unacceptable violation of the most elementary principles and obligations that govern relations among sovereign states. They underline that such behavior is contrary to the Charter of the United Nations.
They believe that fundamental principles are at stake. They reaffirm that the 12 have the fullest respect for the religious feelings of all peoples. They remain fully committed to the principles of freedom of thought and expression within their territories. They will insure the protection of the life and properties of their citizens. In no case will they accept attempts to violate these basic rights.
The 12 express their continuing interest in developing normal constructive relations with the Islamic Republic of Iran, but if Iran shares this desire, it has to declare its respect for international obligations and renounce the use or threatened use of violence.
Meanwhile, the Foreign Ministers of the 12 decided to simultaneously recall their Heads of Mission in Teheran for consultations and to suspend exchanges of high-level official visits.
The Iranian authorities will be informed of the above in the hope that the universal values of tolerance, freedom and respect for international law will prevail. They look to the Iranian authorities to protect the life and safety of all Community citizens in their country."

On Feb. 22, 1989 US president Bush declared that he strongly supported the EC–12 Declaration in response to Iranian threats against Rushdie, saying "However offensive that book may be, inciting the murder and offering rewards for its perpetration are deeply offensive to the norms of civilized behaviour. Our position on terrorism is well known. In the light of Iran's incitement should any action be taken against American interests, the Government of Iran can expect to be held accountable."

The New York Times, Feb. 21 and 22, 1989.

INCOGNITO.

Italian "unknown". An international term for common diplomatic practice, applied by e.g. a Head of State who travels abroad for personal reasons under an assumed name to avoid protocol procedure due to his position.

INCOME AND WEALTH.

A subject of international research. Organization reg. with the UIA:

International Association for Research in Income and Wealth, f. 1947, Washington, DC. Research in the definition and measurement of national income and wealth. Consultative Status with ECOSOC. Publ.: *The Review of Income and Wealth* (quarterly), *International Bibliography on Income and Wealth*.

Yearbook of International Organizations.

INCOTERMS.

International Commercial Terms. The uniform trade terms, formulated and published 1936 by the International Chamber of Commerce, ICC, in Paris after preparatory conferences in Warsaw 1928 and Oxford 1932; they were codified by ICC 1953 and published as International Rules for the Interrelation of Trade Terms, Incoterms 1953, including the following terms:

1. Ex Works (ex factory, ex mill, ex plantation, ex warehouse, etc.)
A. Seller must:
(1) Supply the goods in conformity with the contract of sale, together with such evidence of conformity as may be required by the contract.
(2) Place the goods at the disposal of the buyer at the time provided in the contract, at the point of delivery named or which is usual for the delivery of such goods and for their loading on the conveyance to be provided by the buyer.
(3) Provide at his own expense the packing, if any, that is necessary to enable the buyer to take delivery of the goods.
(4) Give the buyer reasonable notice as to when the goods will be at his disposal.
(5) Bear the cost of checking operations (such as checking quality, measuring, weighing, counting) which are necessary for the purpose of placing the goods at the disposal of the buyer.
(6) Bear all risks and expense of the goods until they have been placed at the disposal of the buyer at the time as provided in the contract, provided that the goods have been duly appropriated to the contract, that is to say, clearly set aside or otherwise identified as the contract goods.
(7) Render the buyer, at the latter's request, risk and expense, every assistance in obtaining any documents which are issued in the country of delivery and/or of origin and which the buyer may require for the purposes of exportation and/or importation (and, where necessary, for their passage in transit through another country).
B. Buyer must:
(1) Take delivery of the goods as soon as they are placed at his disposal at the place and at the time, as provided in the contract, and pay the price as provided in the contract.
(2) Bear all charges and risks of the goods from the time when they have been so placed at his disposal, provided that the goods have been duly appropriated to the contract, that is to say, clearly set aside or otherwise identified as the contract goods.
(3) Bear any customs duties and taxes that may be levied by reason of exportation.
(4) Where he shall have reserved to himself a period within which to take delivery of the goods and/or the right to choose the place of delivery, and should he fail to give instruction in time, bear the additional costs thereby incurred and risks of the goods from the date of the expiration of the period fixed, provided that the goods shall have been duly appropriated to the contract, that is to say, clearly set aside or otherwise identified as the contract goods.
(5) Pay all costs and charges incurred in obtaining the documents mentioned in art. A.7, including the costs of certificates of origin, export licence and consular fees.
2. For-Fot: free on rail ... (named departure point); free on track ... (named departure point).
A. Seller must:

(1) Supply the goods in conformity with the contract of sale, together with such evidence of conformity as may be required by the contract.
(2) In the case of goods constituting either a wagon-load (car-load, truck-load) or a sufficient weight to obtain quantity rates for wagon loading, order in the due time a wagon (car, truck) of suitable type and dimensions, equipped, where necessary, with tarpaulins, and load it at his own expense at the date or within the period fixed, the ordering of the wagon (car, truck) and the loading being carried out in accordance with the regulations of the dispatching station.
(3) In the case of a load less than either a wagon-load (car-load, truck-load) or a sufficient weight to obtain quantity rates for wagon loading, deliver the goods into the custody of the railway either at the dispatching station or, where such facilities are included in the rate of freight, into a vehicle provided by the railway, at the date or within the period fixed, unless the regulations of the dispatching station shall require the seller to load the goods on the wagon (car, truck).
Nevertheless, it shall be understood that if there are several stations at the point of departure, the seller may select the station which best suits his purpose, provided it customarily accepts goods for the destination nominated by the buyer, unless the buyer shall have reserved to himself the right to choose the dispatching station.
(4) Subject to provisions of art. B.5 below, bear all costs and risks of the goods until such time as the wagon (car, truck) on which they are loaded shall have been delivered into the custody of the railway or, in the case provided for in art. A.3, until such time as the goods shall have been delivered into the custody of the railway.
(5) Provide at his own expense the customary packing of the goods, unless it is the custom of the trade to dispatch the goods unpacked.
(6) Pay the costs of any checking operations (such as checking quality, measuring, weighing, counting) which shall be necessary for the purpose of loading the goods or of delivering them into the custody of the railway.
(7) Give notice, without delay, to the buyer that the goods have been loaded or delivered into the custody of the railway.
(8) At his own expense, provide the buyer, if customary, with the usual transport document.
(9) Provide the buyer, at the latter's request and expense (see art B.6), with the certificate of origin.
(10) Render the buyer, at the latter's request, risk and expense, every assistance in obtaining the documents issued in the country of dispatch and/or of origin which the buyer may require for purposes of exportation and/or importation (and, where necessary, for their passage in transit through another country).
B. Buyer must:
(1) Give the seller in time the necessary instructions for dispatch.
(2) Take delivery of the goods from the time when they have been delivered into the custody of the railway and pay the price as provided in the contract.
(3) Bear all costs and risks of the goods (including the cost, if any, of hiring tarpaulins) from the time when the wagon (car, truck) on which the goods are loaded shall have been delivered into the custody of the railway or, in the case provided for in art. A.2, from the time when the goods shall have been delivered into the custody of the railway.
(4) Bear any customs duties and taxes that may be levied by reason of exportation.
(5) Where he shall have reserved to himself a period within which to give the seller instructions for dispatch and/or the right to choose the place of loading, and should he fail to give instructions in time, bear the additional costs thereby incurred and all risks of the goods from the time of expiration of the period fixed, provided, however, that the goods shall have been duly appropriated to the contract, that is to say, clearly set aside or otherwise indentified as the contract goods.
(6) Pay all costs and charges incurred in obtaining the documents mentioned in arts. A.9 and 10 above, including the cost of certificates of origin and consular fees.
(3) Fas; free alongside ship ... (named port of shipment)
A. Seller must:

(1) Supply the goods in conformity with the contract of sale, together with such evidence of conformity as may be required by the contract.

(2) Deliver the goods alongside the vessel at the loading berth named by the buyer, at the named port of shipment, in the manner customary at the port, at the date or within the period stipulated, and notify the buyer, without delay, that the goods have been delivered alongside the vessel.

(3) Render the buyer at the latter's request, risk and expense, every assistance in obtaining any export licence, or other governmental authorization necessary for the export of the goods.

(4) Subject to the provisions of arts. B.3 and B.4 below, bear all costs and risks of the goods until such time as they shall have been effectively delivered alongside the vessel at the named port of shipment, including the costs of any formalities which he shall have to fulfil in order to deliver the goods alongside the vessel.

(5) Provide at his own expense the customary packing of the goods, unless it is the custom of the trade to ship the goods unpacked.

(6) Pay the costs of any checking operations (such as checking quality, measuring, weighing, counting) which shall be necessary for the purpose of delivering the goods alongside the vessel.

(7) Provide at his own expense the customary clean document in proof of delivery of the goods alongside the named vessel.

(8) Provide the buyer, at the latter's request and expense (see art. B.5), with the certificate of origin.

(9) Render the buyer, at the latter's request, risk and expense, every assistance in obtaining any documents, other than that mentioned in art. A.8, issued in the country of shipment and/or of origin (excluding a bill of lading and/or consular documents) and which the buyer may require for the importation of the goods into the country of destination (and, where necessary, for their passage in transit through another country).

B. Buyer must:

(1) Give the seller due notice of the name, loading berth of and delivery dates to the vessel.

(2) Bear all the charges and risks of the goods from the time when they shall have been effectively delivered alongside the vessel at the named port of shipment, at the date or within the period stipulated, and pay the price as provided in the contract.

(3) Bear any additional costs incurred because the vessel named by him shall have failed to arrive on time, or shall be unable to take the goods, or shall close for cargo earlier than the stipulated date, and all the risks of the goods from the time when the seller shall have placed them at the buyer's disposal, provided, however, that the goods shall have been duly appropriated to the contract, that is to say, clearly set aside or otherwise identified as the contract goods.

(4) Should he fail to name the vessel in time or, if he shall have reserved to himself a period within which to take delivery of the goods and/or the right to choose the port of shipment. Should he fail to give detailed instructions in time, bear any additional costs incurred because of such failure and all the risks of the goods from the date of expiration of the period stipulated for delivery, provided, however, that the goods shall have been duly appropriated to the contract, that is to say, clearly set aside or otherwise identified as the contract goods.

(5) Pay all costs and charges incurred in obtaining the documents mentioned in arts. A.3, A.8 and A.9 above.

4. Fob; free on board ... (named port of shipment)

A. Seller must:

(1) Supply the goods in conformity with the contract of sale, together with such evidence of conformity as may be required by the contract.

(2) Deliver the goods on board the vessel named by the buyer, at the named port of shipment, in the manner customary at the port, at the date or within the period stipulated, and notify the buyer, without delay, that the goods have been delivered on board the vessel.

(3) At his own risk and expense obtain any export licence or other governmental authorization necessary for the export of the goods.

(4) Subject to the provisions of arts. B.3 and B.4 below, bear all costs and risks of the goods until such time as they shall have effectively passed the ship's rail at the named port of shipment, including any taxes, fees or charges levied because of exportation, as well as the costs of any formalities which he shall have to fulfil in order to load the goods on board.

(5) Provide at his own expense the customary packing of the goods, unless it is the custom of the trade to ship the goods unpacked.

(6) Pay the costs of any checking operations (such as checking quality, measuring, weighing, counting) which shall be necessary for the purpose of delivering the goods.

(7) Provide at his own expense the customary clean document in proof of delivery of the goods on board the named vessel.

(8) Provide the buyer, at the latter's request and expense (see art. B.6), with the certificate of origin.

(9) Render the buyer, at the latter's request, risk and expense, every assistance in obtaining a bill of lading and any documents, other than that mentioned in the previous article, issued in the country of shipment and/or of origin and which the buyer may require for the importation of the goods into the country of destination (and, where necessary, for their passage in transit through another country).

B. Buyer must:

(1) At his own expense, charter a vessel or reserve the necessary space on board a vessel and give the seller due notice of the name, loading berth of and delivery dates to the vessel.

(2) Bear all costs and risks of the goods from the time when they shall have effectively passed the ship's rail at the named port of shipment, and pay the price as provided in the contract.

(3) Bear any additional costs incurred because the vessel named by him shall have failed to arrive on the stipulated date or by the end of the period specified, or shall be unable to take the goods or shall close for cargo earlier than the stipulated date or the end of the period specified and all the risks of the goods from the date of expiration of the period stipulated, provided, however, that the goods shall have been duly appropriated to the contract, that is to say, clearly set aside or otherwise identified as the contract goods.

(4) Should he fail to name the vessel in time or, if he shall have reserved to himself a period within which to take delivery of the goods and/or the right to choose the port of shipment, should he fail to give detailed instructions in time, bear any additional costs incurred because of such failure, and all the risks of the goods from the date of expiration of the period stipulated for delivery, provided, however, that the goods shall have been duly appropriated to the contract, that is to say, clearly set aside or otherwise identified as the contract goods.

(5) Pay any costs and charges for obtaining a bill of lading if incurred under art. A.9 above.

(6) Pay all costs and charges incurred in obtaining the documents mentioned in arts. A.8 and A.9 above, including the costs of certificates of origin and consular documents.

5. C and F cost and freight ... (named port of destination)

A. Seller must:

(1) Supply the goods in conformity with the contract of sale, together with such evidence of conformity as may be required by the contract.

(2) Contract on usual terms at his own expense for the carriage of the goods to the agreed port of destination by the usual route, in a seagoing vessel (not being a sailing vessel) of the type normally used for the transport of goods of the contract description, and pay freight charges and any charges for unloading at the port of discharge which may be levied by regular shipping lines at the time and port of shipment.

(3) At his own risk and expense obtain any export licence or other governmental authorization necessary for the export of the goods.

(4) Load the goods at his own expense on board the vessel at the port of shipment and at the date or within the period fixed or, if neither date nor time have been stipulated, within a reasonable time, and notify the buyer, without delay, that the goods have been loaded on board the vessel.

(5) Subject to the provisions of art. B.4 below, bear all risks of the goods until such time as they have effectively passed the ship's rail at the port of shipment.

(6) At his own expense furnish to the buyer without delay a clean negotiable bill of lading for the agreed port of destination, as well as the invoice of the goods shipped. The bill of lading must cover the contract goods, be dated within the period agreed for shipment, and provide by endorsement or otherwise for delivery to the order of the buyer or buyer's agreed representative. Such bill of lading must be a full set of "on board" or "shipped" bills of lading, or a "received for shipment" bill of lading duly endorsed by the shipping company to the effect that the goods are on board, such endorsement to be dated within the period agreed for shipment. If the bill of lading contains a reference to the charter-party, the seller must also provide a copy of this latter document.

Note: A clean bill of lading is one which bears no superimposed clauses expressly declaring a defective condition of the goods or packaging.

The following clauses do not convert a clean into an unclean bill of lading: (a) clauses which do not expressly state that the goods or packaging are unsatisfactory, e.g. "second-hand cases", "used drums", etc.; (b) clauses which emphasize carrier's non-liability for risks arising through the nature of the goods or the packaging; (c) clauses which disclaim on the part of the carrier knowledge of contents; weight, measurement, quality, or technical specification of the goods.

(7) Provide at his own expense the customary packaging of the goods, unless it is the custom of the trade to ship the goods unpacked.

(8) Pay the costs of any checking operations (such as checking quality, measuring, weighing, counting) which shall be necessary for the purpose of loading the goods.

(9) Pay any dues and taxes incurred in respect of the goods up to the time of their loading, including any taxes, fees or charges levied because of exportation, as well as the costs of any formalities which he shall have to fulfil in order to load the goods on board.

(10) Provide the buyer, at the latter's request and expense (see art. B.5), with the certificate of origin and the consular invoice.

(11) Render the buyer, at the latter's request, risk and expense, every assistance in obtaining any documents, other than those mentioned in the previous article, issued in the country of shipment and/or of origin and which the buyer may require for the importation of the goods into the country of destination (and, where necessary, for their passage in transit through another country).

B. Buyer must:

(1) Accept the documents when tendered by the seller, if they are in conformity with the contract of sale, and pay the price as provided in the contract.

(2) Receive the goods at the agreed port of destination and bear with the exception of the freight, all costs and charges incurred in respect of the goods in the course of their transit by sea until their arrival at the port of destination, as well as unloading costs, including lighterage and wharfage charges, unless such costs and charges shall have been included in the freight or collected by the steamship company at the time freight was paid.

Note: If the goods are sold "C and F landed", unloading costs, including lighterage and wharfage charges, are borne by the seller.

(3) Bear all risks of the goods from the time when they shall have effectively passed the ship's rail at the port of shipment.

(4) In case he may have reserved to himself a period within which to have the goods shipped and/or the right to choose the port of destination, and he fails to give instructions in time, bear the additional costs thereby incurred of the period fixed for shipment, provided always that the goods shall have been duly appropriated to the contract, that is to say, clearly set aside or otherwise identified as the contract goods.

(5) Pay the costs and charges incurred in obtaining the certificate of origin and consular documents.

(6) Pay all costs and charges incurred in obtaining the documents mentioned in art. A.11 above.

(7) Pay all customs duties as well as any other duties and taxes payable at the time of or by reason of the importation.

(8) Procure and provide at his own risk and expense any import licence or permit or the like which he may require for the importation of the goods at destination.

6. CIF, cost, insurance, freight ... (named port of destination)

A. Seller must:

(1) Supply the goods in conformity with the contract of sale, together with such evidence of conformity as may be required by the contract.

(2) Contract on usual terms at his own expense for the carriage of the goods to the agreed port of destination

by the usual route, in a seagoing vessel (not being a sailing vessel) of the type normally used for the transport of goods of the contract description, and pay freight charges and any charges for unloading at the port of discharge which may be levied by regular shipping lines at the time and port of shipment.
(3) At his own risk and expense obtain any export licence or other governmental authorization necessary for the export of the goods.
(4) Load the goods at his own expense on board the vessel at the port of shipment and the date or within the period fixed or, if neither date nor time have been stipulated, within a reasonable time, and notify the buyer, without delay, that the goods have been loaded on board the vessel.
(5) Procure at his own cost and in a transferable form, a policy of marine insurance against the risks of the carriage involved in the contract. The insurance shall be contracted with underwriters or insurance companies of good repute on FPA terms as listed in the Appendix and shall cover the CIF price plus 10%. The insurance shall be provided in the currency of the contract, if procurable. Unless otherwise agreed, the risks of carriage shall not include special risks that are covered in specific trades or against which the buyer may wish individual protection. Among the special risks that should be considered and agreed upon between seller and buyer are theft, pilferage, leakage, chipping, sweat, contact with other cargoes and others peculiar to any particular trade.
When required by the buyer, the seller shall provide, at the buyer's expense, war risk insurance in the currency of the contract, if procurable.
(6) Subject to the provisions of art. B.4 below, bear all risks of the goods until such time as they shall have effectively passed the ship's rail at the port of shipment.
(7) At his own expense furnish to the buyer without delay a clean negotiable bill of lading for the agreed port of destination, as well as the invoice of the goods shipped and the insurance policy or, should the insurance policy not be available at the time the documents are tendered, a certificate of insurance issued under the authority of the underwriters and conveying to the bearer the same rights as if he were in possession of the policy and reproducing the essential provision thereof. The bill of lading must cover the contract goods, be dated within the period agreed for shipment, and provide by endorsement or otherwise for delivery to the order of the buyer or buyer's agreed representative. Such bill of lading must be a full set of "on board" or "shipped" bills of lading, or a "received for shipment" bill of lading duly endorsed by the shipping company to the effect that the goods are on board, such endorsement to be dated within the period agreed for shipment. If the bill of lading contains a reference to the charter party, the seller must also provide a copy of this latter document.
Note: A clean bill of lading is one which bears no superimposed clauses expressly declaring a defective condition of the goods or packaging.
The following clauses do not convert a clean into an unclean bill of lading: (a) clauses which do not expressly state that the goods or packaging are unsatisfactory, e.g. "second-hand cases", "used drums", etc.; (b) clauses which emphasize the carrier's non-liability for risks arising through the nature of the goods or the packaging; (c) clauses which disclaim on the part of the carrier knowledge of contents, weight, measurement, quality, or technical specification of the goods.
(8) Provide at his own expense the customary packing of the goods, unless it is the custom of the trade to ship the goods unpacked.
(9) Pay the costs of any checking operations (such as checking quality, measuring, weighing, counting) which shall be necessary for the purpose of loading the goods.
(10) Pay any dues and taxes incurred in respect of the goods up to the time of their loading, including any taxes, fees or charges levied because of exportation, as well as the costs of any formalities which he shall have to fulfil in order to load the goods on board.
(11) Provide the buyer, at the latter's request and expense (see art. B.5), with the certificate of origin and the consular invoice.
(12) Render the buyer, at the latter's request, risk and expense, every assistance in obtaining any documents, other than those mentioned in the previous article, issued in the country of shipment and/or of origin and which the buyer may require for the importation of the goods into the country of destination (and, where necessary, for their passage in transit through another country).
B. Buyer must:
(1) Accept the documents when tendered by the seller, if they are in conformity with the contract of sale, and pay the price as provided in the contract.
(2) Receive the goods at the agreed port of destination and bear, with the exception of the freight and marine insurance, all costs and charges incurred in respect of the goods in the course of their transit by sea until their arrival at the port of destination, as well as unloading costs, including lighterage and wharfage charges, unless such costs and charges shall have been included in the freight or collected by the steamship company at the time freight was paid.
If war insurance is provided, it shall be at the expense of the buyer (see art. A.5).
Note: If the goods are sold "CIF landed", unloading costs, including lighterage and wharfage charges, are borne by the seller.
(3) Bear all risks of the goods from the time when they shall have effectively passed the ship's rail at the port of shipment.
(4) In case he may have reserved to himself a period within which to have the goods shipped and/or the right to choose the port of destination, and he fails to give instructions in time, bear the additional costs thereby incurred and all risks of the goods from the date of the expiration of the period fixed for shipment, provided always that the goods shall have been duly appropriated to the contract, that is to say, clearly set aside or otherwise identified as the contract goods.
(5) Pay the costs and charges incurred in obtaining the certificate of origin and consular documents.
(6) Pay all costs and charges incurred in obtaining the documents mentioned in art. A.12 above.
(7) Pay all customs duties as well as any other duties and taxes payable at the time of or by reason of the importation.
(8) Procure and provide at his own risk and expense any import licence or permit or the like which he may require for the importation of the goods at destination.
7. Freight or carriage paid to ... (named point of destination) (Inland transport only)
A. Seller must:
(1) Supply the goods in conformity with the contract of sale, together with such evidence of conformity as may be required by the contract.
(2) Forward the goods at his own expense, at the date or within the period fixed, to the agreed delivery point at the place of destination. If the delivery point is not agreed or is not determined by custom, the seller may select the delivery point at the place of destination which best suits his purpose.
(3) Subject to the provisions of art. B.3 below, bear all risks of the goods until they shall have been delivered into the custody of the first carrier, at the time as provided in the contract.
(4) Give notice, without delay, to the buyer that the goods have been delivered into the custody of the first carrier.
(5) Provide at his own expense the customary packing of the goods, unless it is the custom of the trade to dispatch the goods unpacked.
(6) Pay the costs of any checking operations (such as checking quality, measuring, weighing, counting) which shall be necessary for the purpose of loading the goods or of delivering them into the custody of the first carrier.
(7) At his own expense, provide the buyer, if customary, with the usual transport document.
(8) At his own risk and expense obtain any export licence or other governmental authorization necessary for the export of the goods, and pay any dues and taxes incurred in respect of the goods in the country of dispatch, including any export duties, as well as the costs of any formalities he shall have to fulfil in order to load the goods.
(9) Provide the buyer, at the latter's request and expense (see art. B.4), with the certificate of origin and consular invoice.
(10) Render the buyer, at the latter's request, risk and expense, every assistance in obtaining any documents, other than those mentioned in the previous article, issued in the country of loading and/or of origin and which the buyer may require for the importation of the goods into the country of destination (and, where necessary, for their passage in transit through another country).
B. Buyer must:
(1) Take delivery of the goods at the delivery point at the place of destination and pay the price as provided in the contract, and bear all charges from the time of the arrival of the goods at the delivery point.
(2) Bear all risks of the goods from the time when they shall have been delivered into the custody of the first carrier in accordance with art. A.3.
(3) Where he shall have reserved to himself a period within which to have the goods forwarded to him and/or the right to choose the point of destination, and should he fail to give instructions in time, bear the additional costs thereby incurred and all risks of the goods from the date of expiration of the period fixed, provided always that the goods shall have been duly appropriated to the contract, that is to say, clearly set aside or otherwise identified as the contract goods.
(4) Pay all costs and charges incurred in obtaining the documents mentioned in arts. A.9 and A.10 above, including the cost of certificates of origin and consular fees.
(5) Pay all customs duties as well as any other duties and taxes payable at the time of or by reason of the importation.
8. Ex Ship ... (named port of destination)
A. Seller must:
(1) Supply the goods in conformity with the contract of sale, together with such evidence of conformity as may be required by the contract.
(2) Place the goods effectively at the disposal of the buyer, at the time as provided in the contract, on board the vessel at the usual unloading point in the named port, in such a way as to enable them to be removed from the vessel by unloading equipment appropriate to the nature of the goods.
(3) Bear all risks and expense of the goods until such time as they shall have been effectively placed at the disposal of the buyer in accordance with art. A.2, provided, however, that they have been duly appropriated to the contract, that is to say, clearly set aside or otherwise identified as the contract goods.
(4) Provide at his own expense the customary packing of the goods, unless it is the custom of the trade to ship the goods unpacked.
(5) Pay the costs of any checking operations (such as checking quality, measuring, weighing, counting) which shall be necessary for the purpose of placing the goods at the disposal of the buyer in accordance with art. A.2.
(6) At his own expense, notify the buyer, without delay, of the expected date of arrival of the named vessel, and provide him in due time with the bill of lading or delivery order and/or any other documents which may be necessary to enable the buyer to take delivery of the goods.
(7) Provide the buyer, at the latter's request and expense (see art. B.3), with the certificate of origin and the consular invoice.
(8) Render the buyer, at the latter's request, risk and expense, every assistance in obtaining any documents, other than those mentioned in the previous articles, issued in the country of shipment and/or of origin and which the buyer may require for the importation of the goods into the country of destination (and where necessary, for their passage in transit through another country).
B. Buyer must:
(1) Take delivery of the goods as soon as they have been placed at his disposal in accordance with the provisions of art. A.2, and pay the price as provided in the contract.
(2) Bear all risks and expense of the goods from the time when they shall have been effectively placed at his disposal in accordance with art. A.2, provided always that they have been duly appropriated to the contract, that is to say, clearly set aside or otherwise identified as the contract goods.
(3) Bear all expenses and charges incurred by the seller in obtaining any of the documents referred to in arts. A.7 and A.8.
(4) At his own risk and expense, procure all licences or similar documents which may be required for the purpose of unloading and/or importing the goods.
(5) Bear all expenses and charges of customs duties and clearance, and all other duties and taxes payable at the

time or by reason of the unloading and/or importing of the goods.

9. Ex Quay (duty paid) . . . (named port)

A. Seller must:

(1) Supply the goods in conformity with the contract of sale, together with such evidence of conformity as may be required by the contract. (There are two "Ex Quay" contracts in use, namely Ex Quay (duty paid) which has been defined above and Ex Quay (duties on buyer's account) in which the liabilities specified in art. A.3 above are to be met by the buyer instead of the seller.) Parties are recommended always to use the full descriptions of these terms, namely Ex Quay (duty paid) or Ex Quay (duties on buyer's account).

(2) Place the goods at the disposal of the buyer on the wharf or quay at the agreed port and at the same time, as provided in the contract.

(3) At his own risk and expense, provide the import licence and bear the cost of any import duties or taxes, including the costs of customs clearance, as well as any other taxes, fees or charges payable at the time or by reason of importation of the goods and their delivery to the buyer.

(4) At his own expense, provide for customary conditioning and packing of the goods, regard being had to their nature and to their delivery from the quay.

(5) Pay the costs of any checking operation (such as checking quality, measuring, weighing, counting) which shall be necessary for the purpose of placing the goods at the disposal of the buyer in accordance with art. A.2.

(6) Bear all risks and expense of the goods until such time as they shall have been effectively placed at the disposal of the buyer in accordance with art. A.2, provided, however, that they have been duly appropriated to the contract, that is to say, clearly set aside or otherwise identified as the contract goods.

(7) At his own expense, provide the delivery order and/or any other documents which the buyer may require in order to take delivery of the goods and to remove them from the quay.

B. Buyer must:

(1) Take delivery of the goods as soon as they have been placed at his disposal in accordance with art. A.2, and pay the price as provided in the contract.

(2) Bear all expense and risks of the goods from the time when they shall have been effectively placed at his disposal in accordance with art. A.2, provided always that they have been duly appropriated to the contract, that is to say, clearly set aside or otherwise identified as the contract goods.

INCOTERMS, London, 1953.

INDEPENDENCE DAYS. ▷ **National Days.**

INDEPENDENCE DECLARATION, 1776. ▷ United States Declaration of Independence, 1776.

INDEPENDENCE TO COLONIAL COUNTRIES, UN DECLARATION 1960. A Declaration on the Granting of Independence to Colonial Countries and Peoples adopted by the UN General Assembly Res. 1514/XV, Dec. 14, 1960, by 89 votes for and 9 abstentions (Australia, Belgium, Denmark, France, Portugal, South Africa, Spain, the UK and the USA). The text is as follows:

"The General Assembly,

Mindful of the determination proclaimed by the peoples of the world in the Charter of the United Nations to reaffirm faith in fundamental human rights, in the dignity and worth of the human person, in the equal rights of men and women and of nations large and small and to promote social progress and better standards of life in larger freedom.

Conscious of the need for the creation of conditions of stability and well-being and peaceful and friendly relations based on respect for the principles of equal rights and self-determination of all peoples, and of universal respect for, and observance of, human rights and fundamental freedoms for all without distinction as to race, sex, language or religion.

Recognizing the passionate yearning for freedom in all dependent peoples and the decisive role of such peoples in the attainment of their independence.

Aware of the increasing conflicts resulting from the denial of or impediments in the way of the freedom of such peoples, which constitute a serious threat to world peace,

Considering the important role of the United Nations in assisting the movement for independence in Trust and Non-Self-Governing Territories.

Recognizing that the peoples of the world ardently desire the end of colonialism in all its manifestations.

Convinced that the continued existence of colonialism prevents the development of international economic co-operation, impedes the social, cultural and economic development of dependent peoples and militates against the United Nations ideal of universal peace.

Affirming that peoples may, for their own ends, freely dispose of their natural wealth and resources, without prejudice to any obligations arising out of international economic co-operation, based upon the principle of mutual benefit, and international law.

Believing that the process of liberation is irresistible and irreversible and that, in order to avoid serious crises, an end must be put to colonialism and all practices of segregation and discrimination associated therewith.

Welcoming the emergence in recent years of a large number of dependent territories into freedom and independence, and recognizing the increasingly powerful trends towards freedom in such territories which have not yet attained independence.

Convinced that all peoples have an inalienable right to complete freedom, the exercise of their sovereignty and the integrity of their national territory.

Solemnly proclaims the necessity of bringing to a speedy and unconditional end colonialism in all its forms and manifestations;

And to this end

Declares that:

(1) The subjection of peoples to alien subjugation, domination and exploitation constitutes a denial of fundamental human rights, is contrary to the Charter of the United Nations and is an impediment to the promotion of world peace and co-operation.

(2) All peoples have the right to self-determination; by virtue of that right they freely determine their political status and freely pursue their economic, social and cultural development.

(3) Inadequacy of political, economic, social or educational preparedness should never serve as a pretext for delaying independence.

(4) All armed action or repressive measures of all kinds directed against dependent peoples shall cease in order to enable them to exercise peacefully and freely their right to complete independence, and the integrity of their national territory shall be respected.

(5) Immediate steps shall be taken, in Trust and Non-Self-Governing Territories or all other territories which have not yet attained independence, to transfer all powers to the peoples of those territories, without any conditions or reservations, in accordance with their freely expressed will and desire, without any distinction as to race, creed or colour, in order to enable them to enjoy complete independence and freedom.

(6) Any attempt aimed at the partial or total disruption of the national unity and the territorial integrity of a country is incompatible with the purposes and principles of the Charter of the United Nations.

(7) All States shall observe faithfully and strictly the provisions of the Charter of the United Nations, the Universal Declaration of Human Rights and the present Declaration on the basis of equality, non-interference in the internal affairs of all States, and respect for the sovereign rights of all peoples and their territorial integrity."

On Nov. 27, 1961, Dec. 17, 1962, Oct. 14, 1970 and on Nov. 11, 1980 the UN General Assembly adopted Res. 1654/XVI, 1810/XVII, 2708/XXV and 35/29 with regard to the implementation of the Declaration of 1960. The 1980 resolution was adopted by record vote of 141 to 0, with 8 abstentions (Belgium, Canada, France, the FRG, Israel, Luxembourg, the UK and the USA).

UN Yearbook, 1960, 1961, 1962, 1970.

INDEPENDENT EUROPEAN PROGRAM GROUP, IEPG. A West European commission of experts on armaments, established on the initiative of the NATO Eurogroup in Dec., 1975 on the basis of an understanding with France which in 1966 had withdrawn from the Military Committee of NATO's North Atlantic Council. Belonging to the IEPG are France, as the largest producer and exporter of arms in West Europe and the 10 member states of the NATO Eurogroup (Belgium, the FRG, Greece, Italy, Luxembourg, the Netherlands, Norway, Turkey and the UK) and two observers: Spain and Sweden. The task of the IEPG is to coordinate the problems of armaments of the Eurogroup with France, which aims toward an armaments partnership of Europe with the USA. The first session in Rome on Feb. 2, 1976 resulted in acceptance of a principle for co-ordinating armament plans and negotiating co-production agreements in order to avoid duplication of efforts. In France the IEPG is called Groupe Européen d'armaments independent, European independent armaments group.

KEESING's *Contemporary Archive*, 1975 and 1976; D. ROBERTSON, *Guide to Modern Defense and Strategy*, Detroit, 1988.

INDEPENDENT STATE. A state subject to international law. ▷ Rights and Duties of States; ▷ Rights and Obligations of American States. In the 20th century the number of independent states exceeds 160, of which over 100 gained independence during that century and the majority of those during the century's second half.

H. KELSEN, "The draft Declaration on Rights and Duties of States. Critical Remarks", in: *American Journal of International Law*, No. 44, 1950.

INDEX. An international term for an alphabetical list of names of all kinds, i.e. surnames, concepts or alphabetical lists of objects, a subject of constant organized international co-operation. Since 1950 two bibliographical indexes are published by UNESCO (*Index Bibliographicus* and *Index Translationum*).

Organization reg. with the UIA:

Society of Indexers, f. 1957, London, with the task of introducing a world-wide unification of indexes in scientific works. Publ.: *The Indexer*.

Yearbook of International Organizations.

INDEXATION. An international term for a system proposed in the UN by the developing countries to link the prices of their exports to the prices of manufactured goods imported from developing countries. Under indexation, the prices of their exports, primarily commodities, would be keyed to the prices of their imports, primarily manufactured goods.

UN Chronicle, October, 1982, p. 47.

INDEX LIBRORUM PROHIBITORUM. *Latin* = "index of prohibited books", compiled from 1559 by the Catholic Church. From 1616 till 1802 included Nicolaus Copernicus' *De revolutionibus orbis coelestium*. In the case of books of which only short passages were prohibited for the Catholics the Church published *Index Expurgatorum* of quotations recommended for removal so that the book could be read by the international Catholic community. The last index of 1960 embraced some 5000 titles.

A. BRUDINHON. *La Nouvelle Législation de l'Index*, Paris, 1925.

INDEX MEDICUS LATINO-AMERICANO. A bibliographical guide to bio-medical journals published every year in Latin America. It has been prepared and published since 1979 by the Pan American Health Organization Regional Medical Library in Sao Paulo, Brazil, in Portuguese and Spanish.

INDIA. Member of the UN. Bharat Ganatantra. Republic of India. State in South Asia on the Indian Ocean in the central part of the Indian Peninsula. Borders on Pakistan, the People's Republic of China, Nepal, Bhutan, Burma, Bangladesh. Area: 3,166,829 sq. km. Pop. 1981 census: 683,810,051 Capital: New Delhi with 273,086 inhabitants, 1981. GNP per capita 1986: US $270. Currency: 1 Indian rupee = 100 paisa. Official language: Hindi, and English as auxiliary official language plus 12 regional dialects. National Day: Jan. 26, anniversary of proclamation of the republic, 1950 and Aug. 15. anniversary of establishment of independence, 1947.

India is an original member of the UN and of the UN specialized agencies of the Commonwealth and the Colombo Plan.

International relations: British colony since 1858 with limited self-rule 1912; new administrative status since Aug. 20, 1935 with Council of State and Legislative Assembly. On Apr. 11, 1942 granted autonomy by Great Britain, not acknowledged by Indian leaders. Independent state since Aug. 15, 1947 within British Commonwealth. On Jan. 6, 1950 proclamation of republic within British Commonwealth. In Oct., 1954 with French approval assumed control over French enclaves on Indian territory: Pondicherry, Karikal, Mahe and in Dec., 1961 by unilateral action the Portuguese enclaves: Goa, Daman and Diu. From Oct., 1947 in border conflict with Pakistan over Kashmir and Jammu; in July, 1949 the UN sent a UN Military Observers Group for India and Pakistan, UNMOGIP, against whose activity India protested in May, 1954; conflict with Pakistan intensified following armed incidents in Apr., 1965 in the region of Rann of Cutch and in the fall of 1965 in Kashmir; resorted to Soviet arbitration in Jan., 1966 (▷ Tashkent Declaration); after Indian–Pakistani armed clashes in Nov. and Dec., 1971 in the region of Kashmir related to West Pakistani defeat in civil war 1971–72, i.e. proclamation of Bangladesh Republic in East Pakistan millions of refugees came to India from Bangladesh. The UN General Assembly Res. of Dec. 8, 1971 considered the conflict and direct Indo-Pakistani negotiations concluded with the signing on July 3, 1972 in Simla of an agreement on renouncement of the use of force. The Indo-Chinese dispute over the Himalayan border led to armed incidents Oct. 20–Nov. 21, 1962 preceded by the signing on June 3, 1962 of Sino-Pakistani agreement on delimitation of frontiers between Kashmir and Sintiang-Uigur (on Sept. 28, 1968 India protested against China and Pakistan's decision to open a road connection between Gilgit and Sintiang-Uigur). India is one of the chief initiators and advocates of the policy of nonalignment. In Aug., 1971 in Delhi was signed the Treaty of Peace, Friendship and Co-operation with the USSR for 20 years. Since 1952 India receives UN assistance in solving demographic problems (birth control promotion campaign in connection with high birth rate which increased the country's population in 1961–71 by 24.6%) and UNESCO aid in fighting illiteracy (reduced by 5%

to 70.6%, mostly in Kerala province where it was brought down to 39.8%. In Apr., 1974 Indian government took over 74% of shares of oil concessions of the American company, EXXON on the territory of India. On May 18, 1974 the first Indian underground nuclear explosion took place which according to India did not violate the treaty on partial ban on tests with nuclear weapons 1963. India is not a member of the 1968 Treaty on Non-Proliferation of Nuclear Weapons. India was in dispute with Ceylon, over territorial waters in the Palk Strait, settled by agreement of June 28, 1974. The disputes with Pakistan were settled on May 14, 1976. In the 1980s India every year repeated a call for the denuclearization of the ▷ Indian Ocean. In July, 1982 the USA agreed to deliver nuclear fuel for India's Tarapur atomic reactor. On Nov. 2, 1984 the UN General Assembly commemorated the tragic death of Indira Gandhi (1917–1984). In 1985/86 two conferences on the longstanding China–India border dispute took place: in New Delhi (Nov. 1985) and Beijing (July 1986). On Nov. 28, 1986 during the official visit of the General Secretary of the CPSU a Delhi Declaration was signed by M. Gorbachev and R. Gandhi.

See also ▷ World Heritage UNESCO List.

The Times of India Directory and Yearbook; R. PLATT, *India: A Compendium*, New York, 1962; A. LAMB, *The China–India Border: The Origins of the Disputed Boundaries*, New York, 1964; B.M. SHANNA, *The Republic of India. Constitution and Government*. New York, 1966; D.W. WAINHOUSE, *International Peace Observation*, Baltimore, 1966, pp. 357–372; O.T.THIEU, *India and South-East Asia 1947–1960*, Geneva, 1967; N.R. GUSEVA, *India: Tysiacheletiia i sovremennostzt*, Moskva, 1971; A. DATAR, *India's Economic Relations with the USSR and Eastern Europe 1953–1969*, Cambridge, 1973; S. HASAN, *Struktur des Bankwesens in India*, Frankfurt a. M., 1973; S. ETIENNE, *Les chances de l'Inde, Paris, 1973, India, 1974*, New Delhi, 1975; S.G. RUADIKER, *Banking in India*, New Delhi, 1975; *India: The Speeches and Reminiscences of Indira Gandhi*, New Delhi, 1975; R.K. PACHUARI, *Energy and Economic Development in India*, New York, 1977; W.M. JONES, *Politics Mainly Indian*, New Delhi, 1979; D. MOREAU, *Miss Gandhi*, London, 1980; A. HALL, *The Emergence of Modern India*, New York, 1981; R.C. BORN, *Soviet–Indian Relations*, New York, 1982; *The Europa Yearbook 1984. A World Survey*, Vol. II, pp. 1676–1709 London, 1984.

INDIAN COUNCIL OF WORLD AFFAIRS. A non-governmental institution for the study of Indian and international questions f. 1943 in New Delhi. Publ.: *India Quarterly, Foreign Affairs Reports* (monthly).

INDIAN–NEPAL PEACE TREATY, 1950. A Treaty of Peace and Friendship signed on July 31, 1950 at Kathmandu by India and Nepal. The highlights of the Treaty are:

"Art 1. There shall be everlasting peace and friendship between the Government of India and the Government of Nepal. The two Governments agree mutually to acknowledge and respect the complete sovereignty, territorial integrity and independence of each other.
Art. 2. The two Governments hereby undertake to inform each other of any serious friction or misunderstanding with any neighbouring State likely to cause any breach in the friendly relations subsisting between the two Governments.
Art. 5. The Government of Nepal shall be free to import, from or through the territory of India, arms, ammunition or warlike material and equipment necessary for the security of Nepal. The procedure for giving effect to this arrangement shall be worked out by the two Governments acting in consultation.
Art. 6. Each Government undertakes, in token of the neighbourly friendship between India and Nepal, to give to the nationals of the other, in its territory, national treatment with regard to participation in industrial

and economic development of such territory and to the grant of concessions and contracts relating to such development.
Art. 7. The Governments of India and Nepal agree to grant, on a reciprocal basis, to the nationals of one country in the territories of the other the same privileges in the matter of residence, ownership of property, participation in trade and commerce, movement and other privileges of a similar nature.
Art. 8. So far as matters dealt with herein are concerned, this Treaty cancels all previous Treaties, agreements, and engagements entered into on behalf of India between the British Government and the Government of Nepal."

Came into force on July 31, 1950.

UNTS, Vol. 94, 1951, pp. 4–8.

INDIAN OCEAN. The smallest of the three main oceans with chief arms: the ▷ Arabian Sea, the ▷ Bengal Bay, and ▷ Andaman Sea. 6,440 km wide at the equator; area: 73,426,500 sq. km; connected with the ▷ Pacific Ocean by the Malay Archipelago passage and a passage between Australia and Antarctica; connected with ▷ the Atlantic Ocean by the passage between Africa and Antarctica and by the Suez Canal. The greatest depth 7,730 m. south of Java. It was the subject of international peaceful co-operation under the patronage of the UN and its specialized agencies.

In 1971 the General Assembly, by its Res. 2832(XXVI), declared the Indian Ocean a zone of peace "with limits to be determined, together with the airspace above and the ocean floor subjacent thereto." It also called on the Great Powers to enter into immediate consultatiis with the littoral states regarding limiting military activity in the area, and called on littoral and hinterland states, permanent members of the Security Council and other major maritime users to enter into consultations with a view to implementing the Declaration to ensure the restriction and elimination of military activity in the area.

The Ad Hoc Committee was created in 1972 to implement the General Assembly's 1971 Declaration of the Indian Ocean as a Zone of Peace. Its initial membership was 15 states of the Indian Ocean region, but that was gradually enlarged to 46. Members now include Security Council members and other major maritime users of the ocean, as well as nations of the region.

The Fourth Conference of Nonaligned States came out in favor of implementing the resolutions of the UN General Assembly in the Algiers ▷ Non-Aligned Countries Declaration of 1973. The UN General Assembly Political Committee, on Nov. 25, 1973, requested the UN Secretary-General to prepare a report on the military presence of the Great Powers in the Indian Ocean. In Feb., 1974 the USA concluded an agreement with the UK on the establishment of a US naval base for ships patroling the Indian Ocean on the UK island Diego Garcia; this brought protests from the government of India on the basis of the 1971 Res. of the UN General Assembly. In Mar., 1974 the US atomic-powered aircraft carrier *Kitty Hawk* began patroling the Indian Ocean. In May that year a UN report, *Problems of Peace in the Indian Ocean*, was published. In 1974 the Assembly first called for convening of an international conference to implement provisions of the 1971 Declaration.

Talks between the United States and Soviet Union on limiting military activities in the region were begun in 1977 and suspended in Feb., 1978. The General Assembly has urged a resumption of those negotiations.

A Meeting of Littoral (coastal) and Hinterland States (those situated directly behind coastal states) of the Indian Ocean was held in 1979 as part of the preparatory process.

The Final Document of the Meeting sets out seven principles of agreement for implementing the 1971 Declaration. They deal with limits of the ocean as a zone of peace; eliminating the military presence of the Great Powers in the ocean; eliminating military bases and other installations of Great Powers; denuclearization of the ocean; non-use of force and peaceful settlement of disputes; regional and other co-operation; and free and unimpeded use of the ocean by vessels of all nations.

Later in 1979, by Res. 34/80 B, the General Assembly decided the Conference would be convened during 1981 at Colombo, Sri Lanka.

In 1981 the Assembly regretted that consensus on finalization of dates for the Conference had not been reached and stressed the need for its convening as a necessary step in implementing the 1971 Declaration.

In 1982, by Res. 37/96, it asked the Committee "to make every effort to accomplish the necessary preparatory work, including consideration of its convening not later than the first half of 1984."

In 1983 a formulation proposed by Australia, Canada, the Federal Republic of Germany, Italy, Japan, the Netherlands, Norway, the United Kingdom and the United States – put foward a set of principles regarding the concept of the Indian Ocean as a zone of peace, divided into three categories: political, security and economic.

Political principles would include respect of national sovereignty; peaceful settlement of disputes; ensuring equal rights and self-determination of peoples; non-use of force; respect of right to be free from military occupation resulting from use of force; co-operation in solution of refugee problems; and promotion of and respect for human rights

Security principles would include respect of the right of individual and collective self-defense, and right of freedom of navigation and overflight; recognition of the need for undiminished security for all states and adequate verification under arms control or disarmament agreements; a declaration that the strengthening of security and peace in the region depends on a climate of confidence and trust at global and regional levels; prevention of the spread of nuclear weapons; creation of appropriate nuclear-free zones in the area; withdrawal of foreign occupying forces from states of the region; and refraining from any manifestation or use of force for the purpose of inducing a state of the region to renounce the full exercise of its sovereign rights.

Economic principles would include encouragement of expansion of mutual trade; recognition of benefits of co-operation in trade, industry, science and technology, transport, health, environment and other related activities; promotion of application of new technologies to industrial, scientific and environmental activities in region; and encouragement of protection of right of migrant laborers in both receiving states and states of origin.

The 46 members of the Ad Hoc Committee are: Australia, Bangladesh, Bulgaria, Canada, China, Democratic Yemen, Djibouti, Egypt, Ethiopia, France, the German Democratic Republic, the Federal Republic of Germany, Greece, India, Indonesia, Iran, Iraq, Italy, Japan, Kenya, Liberia, Madagascar, Malaysia, the Maldives, Mauritius, Mozambique, the Netherlands, Norway, Oman, Pakistan, Panama, Poland, Romania, Seychelles, Singapore, Somalia, Sri Lanka, Sudan, Thailand, the USSR, the United Kingdom, the United Republic of Tanzania, the United States, Yemen, Yugoslavia and Zambia.

The Ad Hoc Committee on the Indian Ocean, est. 1971 by the Res. 2832/XXVI, in 1983 and 1984 continued its efforts to convene an International Conference on the Indian Ocean in 1985. On June 21, 1985 in Nairobi the Comoros, France (on the part

of ▷ Réunion), Kenya, Madagascar, Mauritius, Mozambique, the Seychelles, Somalia, and Tanzania signed a Convention on Controlling Pollution of the Indian Ocean. The UN Ad Hoc Committee on the Indian Ocean concluded its first session in March, 1987 in New York. The GA Res. 41/87 of Dec. 16, 1985 decided to convene the conference on the Indian Ocean at Colombo, 1990. The GA Res. 43/79 of Dec. 7, 1988 on Implementation of the Declaration of the Indian Ocean as a Zone of Peace, requested the Committee on the Indian Ocean to complete the preparatory work for the Colombo Conference in 1990.

Organization reg. with the UIA:

Indian Ocean Commission, f. 1982, Paris. Members: France, the Comoros, Madagascar, Mauritius, the Seychelles.

M. REZA DJALILI: *L'Océan indien*, Paris, 1978; *UN Chronicle*, April, 1983, p. 21; *UN Chronicle*, May 1987, p. 53; *The Europa Yearbook 1988. A World Survey*, Vol. I, London, 1988; *UN Resolutions and Decisions adopted by the General Assembly during the first part of its Forty-Third Session, from Sept. 20 to Dec. 22 1988*, New York 1989, p. 197.

INDIAN OCEAN ANTI-POLLUTION CONVENTION. The Convention on Controlling Pollution in the Indian Ocean, signed on Jan. 21, 1985 in Nairobi, by the Comoros, France (on the part of the French overseas department of Réunion), Kenya, Madagascar, Mauritius, Mozambique, Seychelles, Somalia and Tanzania.

KEESING's *Contemporary Archive*, 1986.

INDIAN WAR 1865–1880. The fifteen years war against Indians in the Middle and Western regions of the US, financed by the US Government, culminated in extermination of the absolute majority of the Indian tribes and in uncompensated seizure of Indian lands.

W.E. DRIVER, *Indians of North America*, New York, 1961.

INDIA OFFICE LIBRARY AND RECORDS IN LONDON. f. 1867. One of the greatest oriental libraries and archive collections in the world entitled to a copy of every work published in India and Burma; since 1948 also collecting works from Pakistan in English and oriental languages.

B. WEIRREB, C. HIBBERT eds., *The London Encyclopedia*, London 1983.

INDICATION OF SOURCE ON GOODS, MADRID AGREEMENT, 1891. An agreement for the repression of false or deceptive indications of source on goods, signed on Apr. 14, 1891 in Madrid, revised on June 2, 1911 in Washington; on Nov. 6, 1925 in The Hague; on June 2, 1934 in London and on Oct. 31, 1958 in Lisbon, came into force on June 1, 1963; Additional Act of Stockholm of July 14, 1964, came into force on Apr. 26, 1970. It was agreed that

"all goods bearing a false or deceptive indication by which one of the countries to which this Agreement applies, or a place situated therein is directly or indirectly indicated as being the country or place of origin, shall be seized on importation into any of the said countries."

UNTS, Vol. 828, p. 165.

INDIGENOUS AND TRIBAL POPULATION. Subject of the ILO Convention No. 107 of 1957. In Sept. 1986 an ILO meeting of experts came to the following conclusions:

"1. The Convention's integrationist approach is inadequate and no longer reflects current thinking.

2. Indigenous and tribal peoples should enjoy as much control as possible over their own economic, social and cultural development.

3. The right of these peoples to interact with the national society on an equal footing through their own institutions should be recognised.

4. The Meeting concluded that the traditional land rights of these peoples should be recognised and effectively protected, and noted that the indigenous and tribal representatives present unanimously considered that these lands should be inalienable.

5. The Meeting agreed that, in order to make these rights effective, ratifying States should take measures to determine the lands to which these peoples have rights, by demarcation or delimitation where this has not already been done.

6. The authority of States to appropriate indigenous or tribal lands, or to remove these peoples from their lands, should be limited to exceptional circumstances, and should take place only with their informed consent. If this consent cannot be obtained, such authority should be exercised only after appropriate procedures designed to meet the exceptional circumstances for such taking and which guarantee to these peoples the opportunity to be effectively represented.

7. In cases where the appropriation or removals referred to in the previous paragraph proves necessary after these procedures, these groups should receive compensation including lands of at least equal extent, quality and legal status which allow the continuation of their traditional lifestyles and which are suitable to provide for their present needs and future development.

8. In all activities proposed to be taken by the ILO or by ratifying States affecting indigenous and tribal peoples these peoples should be integrally involved at every level of the process.

9. The Meeting noted that the indigenous and tribal representatives present unanimously stressed the importance of self-determination in economic, social and cultural affairs as a right and as a basic principle for the development of new standards within the ILO".

Organizations reg. with the UIA:

International Work Group for Indigenous Affairs, f. 1968, Copenhagen.

World Congress for Indigenous Peoples, f. 1975, Ottawa.

▷ American Indians.

Yearbook of International Organizations; *International Commission of Jurists Newsletter*, No. 32, Jan/Mar. 1987, pp. 21–22.

INDIS. Industrial Information System, one of the information centers of the ▷ UNIDO.

INDOCHINA. The common name for the former colonies and protectorates of France on the Indochina peninsula (now the territory of Viet Nam, Laos and Kampuchea) under the direct or indirect rule of France from 1884 to 1954. ▷ Indochina Geneva Agreements 1954.

R. LEVY *L'Indochine et ses traités*, Paris, 1948; R.S. ROSS, *The Indochina Tangle: China's Vietnam Policy, 1975–1979*, New York, 1988.

INDOCHINA DEFENCE ASSISTANCE AGREEMENT, 1950. An agreement between the USA and Cambodia, France, Laos and South Vietnam for mutual defence assistance in Inodochina (with Annexes), signed on Dec. 23, 1950 in Saigon.

UNTS, Vol. 185, p. 4.

INDOCHINA GENEVA CONFERENCE AND AGREEMENTS, 1954. A Conference on the problem of restoring peace in Indochina. The first world conference held in Geneva after World War II in which delegations from the Five Great Powers participated. Ministers of foreign affairs of China, France, the UK, USA and the USSR, held negotiations with the representatives of the Democratic Republic of Vietnam, the State of Vietnam and delegates from Cambodia and Laos. The defeat of

French colonial forces at Dien Bien Phu and the decision of US President D.D. Eisenhower forbidding the sending of atomic weapons to Vietnam led the French government to sign a cease-fire with the Democratic Republic of Vietnam on July 24, 1954 and simultaneously treaties with both Vietnamese states and with Laos and Cambodia on the complete withdrawal of French forces from all of Indochina. The list of the agreements and declarations read as follows:

(1) on cessation of war operations in Vietnam;
(2) on cessation of war operations in Laos;
(3) on cessation of war operations in Cambodia;
(4) Laotian government declaration on the rights of the population and the elections;
(5) Laotian government declaration on military alliances, foreign military bases and military assistance;
(6) Cambodian government declaration on the rights of the population and the elections;
(7) Cambodian government declaration on military alliances, foreign military bases and military assistance;
(8) French government declaration on pulling out of its troops from the territories of the three Indochina States;
(9) French declaration of observance of independence and sovereignty of the three Indochina States;
(10) Declaration of a US representative including US government stance regarding Geneva Agreements;
(11) Geneva Conference Final Declaration on restoration of peace in Indochina, attended by representatives of Cambodia, Laos, Democratic People's Republic of Vietnam, South Vietnam, China, France, USA, Great Britain, and USSR. The declaration had the legal force of an international treaty integrating truce resolutions and unilateral statements;
(12) Agreement on economic and cultural relations between Democratic Vietnam and France concluded in the form of the exchange of notes between Deputy Premier Pham Van Dong and Premier Mendes-France;

The above treaties put an end to hostilities in Cambodia, Laos and Vietnam. The United States tabled reservations regarding the multilateral agreement; President Eisenhower observed that since USA had not taken part in the decision-making, it was not bound by them.

Three international commissions were formed to supervise compliance with the terms of the treaties, International Commission for Supervision and Control, comprising: IOC Vietnam, IOC Cambodia and IOC Laos. Chairmen of the Conference were *ex aequo* the ministers of foreign affairs of the UK and the USSR. ▷ Indochina Geneva Declaration 1954.

Conférence de Genève sur l'Indochine. Documentation française, Paris, 1954; KEESING's *Contemporary Archive*, 1954; M. LACHS, *Uklady Indochińskie* (Indochina Agreements), Warszawa, 1955; *Konferenzen und Verträge. Vertrags-Plötz*, Würzburg, 1968; J.N. MOORE, *Law and the Indo-China War*, London, 1973.

INDOCHINA GENEVA DECLARATION 1954. The Final Declaration of the Geneva Conference on the problem of restoring peace in Indochina, dated July 21, 1954, in which the representatives of Cambodia, the Democratic Republic of Vietnam, France, Laos, the People's Republic of China, the State of Vietnam, the USSR, the UK and the USA took part. The text read as follows:

"(1) The Conference takes note of the agreements ending hostilities in Cambodia, Laos and Viet-Nam and organizing international control and the supervision of the execution of the provisions of these agreements.
(2) The Conference expresses satisfaction at the ending of hostilities in Cambodia, Laos and Viet-Nam; the Conference expresses its conviction that the execution of the provisions set out in the present declaration and in the agreements on the cessation of hostilities will permit Cambodia, Laos and Viet-Nam henceforth to play their part, in full independence and sovereignty, in the peaceful community of nations.
(3) The Conference takes note of the declarations made by the Governments of Cambodia and of Laos of their intention to adopt measures permitting all citizens to take their place in the national community, in particular by participating in the next general elections, which, in conformity with the constitution of each of these countries, shall take place in the course of the year 1955, by secret ballot an in conditions of respect for fundamental freedoms.
(4) The Conference takes note of the clauses in the agreement on the cessation of hostilities in Viet-Nam prohibiting the introduction into Viet-Nam of foreign troops and military personnel as well as of all kinds of arms and munitions. The Conference also takes note of the declarations made by the Governments of Cambodia and Laos of their resolution not to request foreign aid, whether in war material, in personnel or in instructors except for the purpose of the effective defence of their territory and, in the case of Laos, to the extent defined by the agreements on the cessation of hostilities in Laos.
(5) The Conference takes note of the clauses in the agreement on the cessation of hostilities in Viet-Nam to the effect that no military base under the control of a foreign State may be established in the regrouping zones of the two parties, the latter having the obligation to see that the zones alloted to them shall not constitute part of any military alliance and shall not be utilized for the resumption of hostilities or in the service of an aggressive policy. The Conference also takes note of the declarations of the Governments of Cambodia and Laos to the effect that they will not join in any agreement with other States if this agreement includes the obligation to participate in a military alliance not in conformity with the principles of the Charter of the United Nations or, in the case of Laos, with the principles of the agreement on the cessation of hostilities in Laos or, so long as their security is not threatened, the obligation to establish bases on Cambodian or Laotian territory for the military forces of foreign Powers.
(6) The Conference recognizes that the essential purpose of the agreement relating to Viet-Nam is to settle military questions with a view to ending hostilities and that the military demarcation line is provisional and should not in any way be interpreted as constituting a political or territorial boundary. The Conference expresses its conviction that the execution of the provisions set out in the present declaration and in the agreement on the cessation of hostilities creates the necessary basis for the achievement in the near future of a political settlement in Viet-Nam.
(7) The Conference declares that, so far as Viet-Nam is concerned, the settlement of political problems, effected on the basis of respect for the principles of independence, unity and territorial integrity, shall permit the Viet-Namese people to enjoy the fundamental freedoms, guaranteed by democratic institutions established as a result of free general elections by secret ballot. In order to ensure that sufficient progress in the restoration of peace has been made, and that all the necessary conditions obtained for free expression of the national will, general elections shall be held in July 1956, under the supervision of an international commission composed of representatives of the Member States of the International Supervisory Commission, referred to in the agreement on the cessation of hostilities. Consultations will be held on this subject between the competent representative authorities of the two zones from 20 July, 1955 onwards.
(8) The provisions of the agreements on the cessation of hostilities intended to ensure the protection of individuals and of property must be most strictly applied and must, in particular, allow everyone in Viet-Nam to decide freely in which zone he wishes to live.
(9) The competent representative authorities of the Northern and Southern zones of Viet-Nam, as well as the authorities of Laos and Cambodia, must not permit any individual or collective reprisals against persons who have collaborated in any way with one of the parties during the war, or against members of such persons' families.
(10) The Conference takes note of the declaration of the Government of the French Republic to the effect that it is ready to withdraw its troops from the territory of Cambodia, Laos and Viet-Nam, at the request of the governments concerned and within periods which shall be fixed by agreement between the parties except in the cases where, by agreement between the two parties, a certain number of French troops shall remain at specified points and for a specified time.
(11) The Conference takes note of the declaration of the French Government to the effect that for the settlement of all the problems connected with the re-establishment and consolidation of peace in Cambodia, Laos, and Viet-Nam, the French Government will proceed from the principle of respect for the independence and sovereignty, unity and territorial integrity of Cambodia, Laos and Viet-Nam.
(12) In their relations with Cambodia, Laos and Viet-Nam, each member of the Geneva Conference undertakes to respect the sovereignty, the independence, the unity and the territorial integrity of the above-mentioned states, and to refrain from any interference in their internal affairs.
(13) The members of the Conference agree to consult one another on any question which may be referred to them by the International Supervisory Commission, in order to study such measures as may prove necessary to ensure that the agreements on the cessation of hostilities in Cambodia, Laos and Viet-Nam are respected."

Declarations related to the Final Declaration:

"Declaration by the Royal Government of Cambodia
(Reference: art. 3 of the Final Declaration)
The Royal Government of Cambodia,
In the desire to ensure harmony and agreement among the peoples of the Kingdom.
Declares itself resolved to take the necessary measures to integrate all citizens, without discrimination, into the national community and to guarantee them the enjoyment of the rights and freedoms for which the Constitution of the Kingdom provides;
Affirms that all Cambodian citizens may freely participate as electors or candidates in general elections by secret ballot.
Declaration by the Royal Government of Cambodia
(Reference: Arts. 4 and 5 of the Final Declaration)
The Royal Government of Cambodia is resolved never to take part in an aggressive policy and never to permit the territory of Cambodia to be utilised in the service of such a policy.
The Royal Government of Cambodia will not join in any agreement with other states, if this agreement carries for Cambodia the obligation to enter into a military alliance not in conformity with the principles of the Charter of the United Nations, or, as long as its security is not threatened, the obligation to establish bases on Cambodian territory for the military forces of foreign powers.
The Royal Government of Cambodia is resolved to settle its international disputes by peaceful means, in such a manner as not to endanger peace, international security and justice. During the period which will elapse between the date of the cessation of hostilities in Viet-Nam and that of the final settlement of political problems in this country, the Royal Government of Cambodia will not solicit foreign aid in war material, personnel or instructors except for the purpose of the effective defence of the territory.
Declaration by the Representative of the United States of America.
The Government of the United States being resolved to devote its efforts to the strengthening of peace in accordance with the principles and purposes of the United Nations.
Takes Note of the Agreements concluded at Geneva on July 20 and 21, 1954 between the (a) Franco-Laotian Command and the Command of the Peoples Army of Viet-Nam; (b) The Royal Khmer Army Command and the Command of the Peoples Army of Viet-Nam; (c) Franco-Vietnamese Command and the Command of the Peoples Army of Viet-Nam
and of paragraphs 1 to 12 inclusive of the Declaration presented to the Geneva Conference on July 21, 1954
Declares with regard to the aforesaid Agreements and paragraphs that (i) it will refrain from the threat or the use of force to disturb them, in accordance with Art. 2(4) of the Charter of the United Nations dealing with the obligation of Members to refrain in their international relations from the threat or use of force; and (ii) it would view any renewal of the aggression in violation of the aforesaid agreements with grave concern and as seriously threatening international peace and security.

Declaration by the Government of the French Republic (Reference art. 10 of the Final Declaration)
The Government of the French Republic declares that it is ready to withdraw its troops from the territory of Cambodia, Laos and Viet-Nam, at the request of the Governments concerned and within a period which shall be fixed by agreement between the parties, except in the cases where, by agreement between the two parties, a certain number of French troops shall remain at specified points and for a specified time.
Declaration by the Government of the French Republic (Reference: art. 11 of the Final Declaration)
For the settlement of all the problems connected with the re-establishment and consolidation of peace in Cambodia, Laos and Viet-Nam, the French Government will proceed from the principle of respect for the independence and sovereignty, the unity and territorial integrity of Cambodia, Laos and Viet-Nam.
Declaration by the Royal Government of Laos (Reference: art. 3 of the Final Declaration)
The Royal Government of Laos,
In the desire to ensure harmony and agreement among the peoples of the Kingdom,
Declares itself resolved to take the necessary measures to integrate all citizens, without discrimination, into the national community and to guarantee them the enjoyment of the rights and freedoms for which the Constitution of the Kingdom provides;
Affirms that all Laotian citizens may freely participate as electors or candidates in general elections by secret ballot;
Announces, furthermore, that it will promulgate measures to provide for special representation in the Royal Administration of the provinces of Phang Saly and Samnenuea during the interval between the cessation of hostilities and the general elections of the interests of Laotian nationals who did not support the Royal forces during hostilities.
Declaration of the Royal Government of Laos (art. 4 and 5 of the Final Declaration).
The Royal Government of Laos is resolved never to pursue a policy of aggression and will never permit the territory of Laos to be used in furtherance of such a policy.
The Royal Government of Laos will never join in any agreement with other States if this agreement includes the obligation for the Royal Government of Laos to participate in a military alliance not in conformity with the principles of the Charter of the United Nations or with the principles of the agreement on the cessation of hostilities or, unless its security is threatened, the obligation to establish bases on Laotian territory for military forces of foreign powers. The Royal Government of Laos is resolved to settle its international disputes by peaceful means so that international peace and security and justice are not endangered. During the period between the cessation of hostilities in Viet-Nam and the final settlement of that country's political problems, the Royal Government of Laos will not request foreign aid, whether in war material, in personnel or in instructors, except for the purpose of its effective territorial defence and to extent defined by the agreement on the cessation of the hostilities.
Proposal for Insertion in the Final Act, Submitted by the Delegation of the State of Viet-Nam.
The Conference takes note of the declaration of the Government of the State of Viet-Nam to the effect that it undertakes:
– To make and to support every effort for the restoration of peace in Viet-Nam;
– Not to use force to oppose the agreed procedure for execution of the cease-fire, despite the objections and reservations it has expressed, in particular in its final statement."
UNTS, Vol. 935, 1974, pp. 95–105.

INDOCHINA TREATIES OF 19TH CENTURY.
The international agreements concluded by France relating to its colonial possessions in Indochina:
(1) Saigon treaty of June 5, 1862 by which Annam ceded its three eastern provinces of Cochin-China;
(2) 1864, Siam acknowledged the French protectorate over Cambodia;
(3) Second Saigon agreement with Annam, Feb. 15, 1874, by which France obtained protectorate over Tongking;

(4) After its occupation of Hanoi in 1882, France spread its protectorate over all Annam and Tongking by the treaty of Hue, Aug. 25, 1883;
(5) China, which opposed the French occupation of Annam, was forced by French military action including occupation of Taiwan, to recognize it under terms the Treaty of Tientsin, on June 9, 1885;
(6) Treaty with Siam, signed on May 3, 1893 in Bangkok, following French armed intervention which incorporated Laos and several other border districts of Siam into an administrative unit called Indochina; the French protectorate was established in 1887. In the years 1904, 1907, 1936, 1941 and 1946 there were French–Siamese conflicts, which were settled finally in Geneva by the Indo-china Treaties, 1954.
G.F. MARTENS, *Nouveau Recueil Général*, 2 S. Vol. 20, pp. 172 and 175.

INDOCHINA UNION. UNION DE L'INDOCHINE.
French colonial territory 1887–1941 in the eastern part of Indochinese Peninsula, embracing Laos, Cambodia and Vietnam; occupied by Japan, 1941; liberated by national liberation forces, 1945.

INDOCTRINATION.
An international term for systematic implantation of certain social, political or religious ideas for the purpose of permanently influencing the attitudes of those indoctrinated. Various methods of indoctrination are used in radio diversion, psychological warfare and in operations called ▷ Brain-wash.

INDONESIA.
Member of the UN. Republik Indonesia. Republic of Indonesia. State in southeast Asia covering some 3000 islands in the Malay Archipelago in the Pacific, and western part of New Guinea. Area: 1,904,569 sq. km. Pop. 1987 est. 171,400,000 (1961 census: 96,318,000; 1971: 122,864,000; 1980 census: 146,936,000). Capital: Djakarta with 6,503,000 inhabitants, 1980. GNP per capita 1987 US $ 450. Currency: one Indonesian rupee = 100 sens. Official language: Indonesian. National Day: Aug. 17, anniversary of proclamation of independence, 1945. Member of the UN since Sept.28, 1950 and of all UN specialized agencies and the ASEAN.
International relations: Colony of the Dutch East India Company 1607–1798 and of the Kingdom of the Netherlands since 1816. In World War II 1942–45 occupied by Japan. The Indonesian People's Movement proclaimed an independent republic on Aug. 17, 1945, which was not recognized by Great Britain and the Netherlands, whose troops occupied Indonesia after the capitulation of Japan. The Treaty signed on Nov. 15, 1946 between the Netherlands and Indonesia (▷ Linggaldjiati Agreement) on the formation of Dutch–Indonesian Union as two sovereign states under rule of the Dutch Queen was abrogated by the Netherlands as was the next treaty of Mar. 25, 1947 which restored its colonial rule. The UN Security Council considered the Indonesian question on July 21, 1947 and on Aug. 25 established an Information Commission composed of the consuls of Australia, Belgium, China, France and the USA accredited in Djakarta and Good Offices Committee (GOC) composed of representatives of Australia, Belgium and the USA which on Jan. 19, 1948 brought to effect the Renville Agreement, shortly thereafter rejected by The Netherlands. By UN Security Council decision of Jan. 28, 1949, the GOC was renamed the UN Commission for Indonesia, UNCI, which succeeded in obtaining Dutch recognition of sovereignty of the United States of Indonesia on Nov. 21, 1949 on the entire Indonesian

territory except for West Irian and with the maintenance of economic union between Indonesia and Holland; affairs of the Union examined at joint conference in The Hague, Aug. 29, 1954; dissolved finally on Feb. 15, 1956. UN mediation on West Irian started in Aug. 1954, ended with the Dutch–Indonesian agreement of Aug. 1962 providing for withdrawal of Dutch colonial troops from West Irian, which was brought under the UN Temporary Authority, UNTEA, and was transferred to Indonesia on May 1, 1963. Conflict with Malaysia 1964–66 concluded with the peace treaty of June 1, 1966 and establishment of diplomatic relations on Aug. 11, 1966. Indonesia refused to contribute to UN activities between Jan. 20, 1965 and Sept. 20, 1966 because of the admission of Malaysia to the UN. Since 1967 receives military assistance from the USA. The East ▷ Timor island, administered *de facto* by Indonesia, is not recognized by the UN as Indonesian property. Since 1988 the 13,000 islands of the Indonesian archipelago are linked by a satellite communication system named Palapa ('unity') launched for the Indonesian government by an American spacecraft.

The UN Security Council Committee of Good Offices on the Indonesian Question, New York, 1949; *UN Peaceful Settlement in Indonesia*, New York. 1951; A.A. SCHILLER, *The Formation of Federal Indonesia 1945–49*, The Hague, 1955; A.M. TAYLOR, *Indonesian Independence and the United Nations*, New York, 1960; A.B. BELENSKIY, *Natsionalnoye probushdenie Indonezyi*, Moskva, 1965; D.E. WEDTHERBEE, *Ideology in Indonesia: Sukarno's Indonesian Revolution*, Detroit, 1966; T. ALISJAHBANA, *Indonesia Social, Cultural Revolution*, New York, 1967; V.I. ANTONOV, *Indoneziya*, Moskva, 1967; W.J. ARCHIPOV, *Ekonomika i ekonomicheskaiya politika Indonezyi, 1945–1968*, Moskva, 1971; U. MONTIEL, *Indonesie*, Paris, 1972; J.D. LEGGE, *Sukarno, A Political Biography*, London, 1972; W.T. NAIL, *Twentieth Century Indonesia*, New York, 1973; F.B. WEINSTEIN, *Indonesian Foreign Policy and the Dilemma of Dependence*, Cornell University Press, 1977; H. MCDONALD, *Suharto's Indonesia*, University Press of Hawaii, 1981; *The Europa Yearbook 1984. A World Survey*, Vol. II, pp. 1710–1727, London, 1984.

INDO-PACIFIC COUNCIL.
An inter-governmental organization f. 1948 in Bangkok by the governments of Australia, Bangladesh, Burma, France, India, Indonesia, Japan, Kampuchea, South Korea, Malaysia, New Zealand, Pakistan, the Philippines, Sri Lanka, Thailand the UK the USA and Vietnam. Publ.: *Regional Studies* Reg. with the UIA.

Yearbook of International Organizations.

INDULT.
A term of medieval law, adopted to denote the privilege granted by an authority to a person or institution; maintained in canon law as a form of permissions granted by the Pope for the departure in special cases from the regulations of the Roman Catholic Church.

INDUS.
A river, 3060 km long, rising in the Tibet region of China, flowing across the Jamun and Kashmir region of India and then through Pakistan to the Arabian Sea. A subject of disputes between India and Pakistan, resolved by the Indus Water Treaty, signed on Sept. 19, 1960 in Karachi by the governments of India and Pakistan and the World Bank; on the basis of an Agreement between the World Bank and Australia, Canada, the FRG, India, New Zealand, Pakistan, the UK and the USA signed on Sept. 19, 1960 in Karachi, which was related to the Indus Water Treaty of 1960 and provided i.a. for the sharing between India and Pakistan of the use of the waters of the Indus Basin. The World Bank Agreement came into force on Jan. 12, 1961, the date of entry into force of the

Indus Water Treaty, with retroactive effect as from Apr. 1, 1960.

UNTS, Vol. 419, p. 125; Vol. 444, p. 260; *International Rivers and Lakes*, Washington, DC, 1967.

INDUSTRIAL DESIGNS OR MODELS.
A subject of international agreements. The first agreement concerned the International Registration of Industrial Designs or Models was signed on Nov. 6, 1925 in The Hague with due regard to Art. 15 of the Union Convention of 1883 (▷ Industrial Property Protection); after World War II an agreement establishing International Classification for Industrial Designs (with Annex) was signed on Oct. 8, 1968 in Locarno; came into force on Apr. 27, 1971.
Organizations reg. with the UIA:
International Council of Societies of Industrial Design, f. 1957, Brussels, Belgium. Publ. *ICSID News* (bi-monthly).

LNTS, Vol. 74, p. 341; *UNTS*, Vol. 828, p. 435; *Yearbook of International Organizations, 1986/87*; *The Europa Yearbook 1988. A World Survey*, Vol. I, London, 1988.

INDUSTRIAL DOCUMENTATION.
The blueprints for industrial buildings and installations and descriptions of technological processes; a subject of international exchange against payment (▷ licence) or along the lines of reciprocity within bi- or multilateral agreements.

CIINTE, *Bibliographic Bulletin of the Clearinghouse*, 1980.

INDUSTRIAL INTERNATIONAL ORGANIZATIONS.
Organizations reg. with the UIA (with exception of ▷ UNIDO):
African and Malagasy Industrial Property Office, f. 1962, Yaoundé.
Arab States Industrial Development Centre, f. 1968, Cairo.
Asian Industrial Development Council, f. 1966, Bangkok.
Business and Industry Advisory Committee, f. 1962, Paris. Recognized by OECD.
Caribbean Association of Industry and Commerce, f. 1919, Kingston.
Central American Research Institute for Industry, f. 1956, Guatemala City.
Commonwealth Industries Association, f. 1926, London.
East African Industrial Licensing Council, f. 1976, Nairobi.
East African Industrial Research Organization, f. 1976, Nairobi.
European Centre for Overseas Industrial Equipment and Development, f. 1957, Paris.
European Federation of Associations of Industrial Safety and Medical Officers, f. 1952, Brussels. Consultative status with ILO Special List.
European Industrial Research Management Association, f. 1966, Paris.
European Industrial Space Study Group, f. 1961, Paris.
Federation of European Industrial Editors Associations, f. 1955, Rotterdam.
Inter-American Association of Industrial Property, f. 1963, Buenos Aires.
International Association for Industrial Studies, f. 1971, Brussels.
International Association for the Protection of Industrial Property, f. 1897, Zurich. Consultative status with ECOSOC, UNIDO and Council of Europe. Publ.: *Yearbook*.
International Council of Societies of Industrial Design, f. 1957, Brussels. Consultative status with UNESCO and UNIDO.
International Industrial Relations Association, f. 1966, Geneva.
International Union for the Protection of Industrial Property, f. 1883, Geneva.
Organization for Industrial, Spiritual and Cultural Advancement International, f. 1961, Tokyo.

Pacific–Asian Federation of Industrial Engineering, f. 1970, New Delhi.
Union of the Industries of the European Community, f. 1952, Brussels.
World Federation of Industrial Workers Union, f. 1920, Brussels.

Yearbook of International Organizations.

INDUSTRIALIZATION.
The subject of organized international co-operation, international conventions, and UN resolutions and studies since 1952, when the issue of industrialization was first discussed at the UN General Assembly, as a key problem of growth for Third World countries. In 1960 the UN General Assembly recommended setting up the Committee for Industrial Development under the ECOSOC, and called for development of international exchange of industrial experience. On the recommendation of the Committee for Industrial Development, the UN General Assembly in 1961 requested that the UN Centre for Industrial Development, est. in July 1961, should begin its work with special attention to financing industrial development.
The first International Symposium for Industrial Development called by the UNIDO was held in Athens, between Nov. and Dec., 1967 and attended by 42 delegates from Third World countries, 30 from industrialized countries and representatives of 54 international organizations concerned with problems of industrialization. Earlier, in 1963, a UN conference on the planning of industrialization was held in São Paulo, and in 1963 the first Regional Conference of Latin American States was held in Lima on industrial planning and development, it set up the ALALC Advisory Commission for Industrial Development. In 1964 the first agreements on complementary co-operation in industry concluded within the ALALC. In Mar., 1968 the first Industrial Congress for Latin America was organized in Mexico City by the Latin American Industrial Association. In 1975–78 problems of industrialization formed a significant part of work on the New International Economic Order. The UN General Assembly Special Session, 1974, in Res. 3202/S-VI adopted a Program of Action on the Establishment of a New International Economic Order. The third chapter was dedicated to the problem of industrialization of developing countries. The text read as follows:

"All efforts should be made by the international community to take measures to encourage the industrialization of the developing countries, and to this end:
(a) The developed countries should respond favourably, within the framework of their official aid as well as international financial institutions, to the requests of developing countries for the financing of industrial projects;
(b) The developed countries should encourage investors to finance industrial production projects, particularly export-oriented production, in developing countries, in agreement with the latter and within the context of their laws and regulations;
(c) With a view to bringing about a new international economic structure which should increase the share of the developing countries in world industrial production, the developed countries and the agencies of the United Nations system in co-operation with the developing countries, should contribute to setting up new industrial capacities including raw materials and commodity-transforming facilities as a matter of priority in the developing countries that produce those raw materials and commodities;
(d) The international community should continue and expand, with the aid of the developed countries and the international institutions, the operational and instruction-oriented technical assistance programmes, including vocational training and management development of national personnel of the developing countries, in the light of their special development requirements."

▷ Lima UNIDO Declaration, 1975.

Acta Final de la Conferencia Interamericana sobre Problemas de la Guerra y de la Paz, llamada Conferencia de Chapultepec, Mexico, DF, 1945; G. WYTHE, *La Industria Latinoamericana*, Mexico, DF, 1947; *Patterns of Industrial Growth, 1938–1958*, UN, New York, 1959; W.G. HOFFMAN, *The Growth of Industrial Economies*, Manchester, 1958; ONU: *Estudio Economico Mundial*, New York, 1961, *The Growth of World Industry 1938–1961, National Tables*, UN, New York, 1963; P.C.M. TEICHERT, *Revolución Económica e Industrialización en América Latina*, Mexico, DF, 1963; J.A. KAHL, *La industrialización en América Latina*, Mexico, DF, 1965; *El Proceso de Industrialización en América Latina*, CEPAL, Santiago de Chile, 1965; *Industrial Development in Asia and the Far East*, UN, New York, 1966; *Industrial Development in Arab Countries*, UN, New York, 1966; A. DORFMAN, *La industrialización de la América Latina y las políticas de fomento*, Mexico, DF, 1967; *Estudio sobre Desarrollo Industrial*, UN, New York, 1967; A.F. EWING, *Industry in Africa*, New York, 1968; *Conference on Economic Co-operation among Developing Countries. Declarations, Resolutions, Recommendations and Decisions adopted in the UN System*, Mexico, DF, 1976, Vol. 1, pp. 56–57; M. POOLE, *Industrial Relations: Origins and Patterns of National Diversity*, Boston, 1987.

INDUSTRIALIZED COUNTRIES.
▷ Venice Declaration of Industrialized Countries, 1980.

INDUSTRIAL PROPERTY PROTECTION.
A subject of international agreements. Art. I, p. 3 of the Paris Convention, 1883 defines industrial property as follows:

"Industrial property shall be understood in the broadest sense and shall apply not only to industry and commerce proper, but likewise to agricultural and extractive industries and to all manufactured or natural products, for example, wines, grain, tobacco leaf, fruit, cattle, minerals, mineral waters, beer, flowers and flour."

The protection of industrial property has as its object patents, utility models, industrial designs, trade marks, service marks, trade names, indications of sources or appellations of origin, and the repression of unfair competition. This Convention for the Protection of Industrial Property was signed on Mar. 20, 1883 in Paris, revised in Brussels, Dec. 14, 1900; Washington, June 2, 1911; The Hague, Nov. 6, 1925; London, June 2, 1934; Lisbon Oct. 31, 1958; Stockholm, July 14, 1967; came into force Apr. 26 or May 19, 1970. The countries to which the convention applied constituted a Union for the Protection of Industrial Property. The Convention of 1970 established the World Intellectual Property Organization ▷ WIPO.

UNTS, Vol. 828, p. 307.

INDUSTRY.
A subject of international co-operation; an international measure of progress and economic development of regions and countries of the world.

Organizations reg. with the UIA:
European Confederation of Iron and Steel Industries, f. 1976, Brussels, Belgium.
European Confederation of Woodworking Industries, f. 1952, Brussels, Belgium.
European Federation of Handling Industries, f. 1953, Zurich, Switzerland.
European Federation of Plywood Industry, f. 1958, Giessen, FRG.
Gulf Organization for Industrial Consulting, f. 1976, Qatar.
International Organization of the Flavour Industry, f. 1969, Geneva, Switzerland.
Liason Organization of the European Engineering Industries, f. 1954, Brussels, Belgium.
Union of Industries of the European Community, f. 1976, Brussels, Belgium. Publ.: *Monthly Report*.

See ▷ Microenterprises.

Yearbook of International Organizations, 1986/87; The Europa Yearbook 1988. A World Survey, Vol. I, London, 1988.

INF. ▷ Intermediate Nuclear Forces.

INFANT MORTALITY AND LIFE EXPECTANCY. A subject of international statistics kept by the WHO; index of economic and social conditions in given countries. According to a 1973 WHO report, the lowest infant mortality was achieved in Sweden – 13.1 per 1000; in the two decades, 1950–69, the following countries significantly lowered their infant mortality: Yugoslavia from 118.6 to 58.6, Poland from 108 to 34.3, France from 51 to 19.6, and Switzerland from 31.2 to 15.4 per 1000. The highest infant mortality rates were noted in Pakistan – 130, Guatemala – 92, Chile – 91.6. Life expectancy in industrialized countries has risen during the two decades, 1950–70, from 64 to 70, and in developing countries from 42 to 50 years of age.

In 1980 the lowest mortality was achieved again by Sweden – 6,7 (Switzerland – 8,5; France – 10,0; Poland – 21,2; Yugoslavia – 32,8). The highest rates were noted in Africa and Asia. In the USA the expectation of life at birth has risen in 1978 for males to 69,5 and for females to 77,2.

World Health, April, 1973; *UN Demographic Yearbook 1980*, New York, 1982.

INFANTS. A subject of international protection and of the Convention concerning the Powers of Authorities and the Law Applicable in Respect of the Protection of Infants, opened for signature in The Hague, Oct. 5, 1961, came into force on Feb. 4, 1969.

UNTS, Vol. 658, p. 143.

INFLATION. An international term for a phenomenon of too much money in circulation, lowering its purchasing power, manifesting itself in a rise in prices; supposedly used for the first time in 1864 by the American economist A. Delmer. The phenomenon of the unproportional growth of the amount of money in the market to the production of goods and services appeared much earlier. From the standpoint of its international repercussions, the most well-known was the affair of John Law, who received a royal charter to open a private bank of issue, 1716, which in financing, both the state as well as private overseas trade companies, issued such an amount of money and shares that after five years the bank crashed. A similar phenomenon of inflation was experienced by the United States during the civil war, when in 1861 the first paper dollars (greenbacks) were issued in such numbers that their convertibility to gold was suspended by the Gold Act of 1864, which resulted in an immediate 40% drop in their value. Even more violent inflation appeared in Germany after World War I. In international terminology a distinction is made between creeping inflation, where prices rise rather slowly, i.e. a few percentage points annually; and galloping inflation, when the growth of prices exceeds a dozen or so percentage points annually, and hyperinflation, when the growth of prices may even be several hundred percent daily, as occurred in some European states in the 1920s. (Hyperinflation starts when the rise of prices exceeds 50% monthly and remains at that rate for at least one year.) Hyperinflation in the years 1921–85: Austria 1921, USSR 1922, Germany and Poland 1923, Greece 1944, Hungary 1946, China 1949, Bolivia 1985.

The problem of inflation in the majority of states in the world became one of the most discussed subjects in the UN in connection with the formulation of the principles of a program for a ▷ New International Economic Order.

H. SCHACHT, *Die Stabilisierung der Mark*, Berlin, 1926; P. CAGAN, "The Monetary Dynamics of Hyperinflation", in: *Studies on the Quantity Theory of Money*, Chicago, 1956; A. SMITHIES, *La inflación en America Latina*, Buenos Aires, 1963; J. RUEFF, *Inflation et Ordre Monétaire International*, Genève, 1967; M. FRIEDMAN, *Inflation et systèmes monetaires*, Paris, 1971; C.H. LEVINSON, *L'inflation mondiale et les firmes multinationales*, Paris, 1973; T. LIESNER, M. KING, *Indexing for Inflation*, London, 1975; J. DENIZET, *La grande inflation*, Paris, 1978; R.E. HALL, *Inflation: Causes and Effects*, Chicago, 1982; A.J. BROWN, *World Inflation Since 1950: An International Comparative Study*, London, 1985; Th.J. SARGENT, *Rational Expectation and Inflation*, New York, 1987.

INFLUENZA. A contagious virus disease dangerous for humans, animals and birds, also called flu. It was the subject of international campaigns to fight epidemics. A particularly widespread epidemic occurred in Europe in 1881–91; in the years 1918–20 an influenza epidemic took the lives of more than 20 million people. After World War II, because of increased regional mobility and the growth of inter-continental air transport, epidemics of influenza have assumed global dimensions. The WHO World Influenza Programme was initiated in 1947; in 1972 in addition to a WHO World Influenza Centre in Rome, there were two international and 92 national centres. The discovery in 1953 of the influenza A virus (the incidence of B and C type viruses occurs mainly in animals and birds) after World War II led to the use of vaccines, but in 1980 their effectiveness was shown to be below 80%; dissemination of the vaccines failed due to high production costs. After World War II epidemics were recorded by the WHO in 1947, 1957 (called Singapore flu), 1968 (Hong Kong flu), and 1974–75 (Port Chalmers flu). The WHO publishes in the *Weekly Epidemiological Record* each February the world data collection of influenza and recommendations on vaccine compositions for the forthcoming two years. The recommendations may be also obtained directly through Virus Diseases, WHO, 1211, Geneva 27, Switzerland.

W.C. COCBUM, "Influenza in Man and Animals", in: *WHO Chronicle*, May 1973, pp. 185–191; Y. SHENDON, "Influenza is Preventable", in: *World Health Organization*, July, 1988; "Influenza", in: *WHO, In Point of Fact*, No. 52, 1988.

INFORMATICS. Subject of international cooperation. Organizations reg. with the UIA:

African Institute of Informatics, f. 1972, Libreville, Gabon.
Association des informaticiens de langue française, f. 1981, Vincennes, France.
Association internationale d'histoire des télécommunications et de l'informatique, f. 1982, Paris, France.
European Association for Shipping Informatics, f. 1980, Brussels, Belgium.
European Cooperation for Informatics, f. 1977, Karlsruhe, FRG.
European Federation for Medical Informatics, f. 1976, Brussels, Belgium. Publ: *Medical Informatics*.
European Informatics Network, f. 1973, Brussels, Belgium. Members: Governments: France, Portugal, Sweden, Switzerland, UK.
Informatics and Biosphere, f. 1971, Paris, France.
Informatics for the Third World, f. 1979, Paris, France.
Intergovernmental Bureau for Informatics, f. 1969, Rome, Italy. Publ.: *Agora* (quarterly), *IBI Newsletter* (bi-monthly).
International Medical Informatics, Association, f. 1979, Brentwood, Essex, England. Publ.: *IMIA Newsletter*.
Latin-American Centre for Studies in Informatics, f. 1979, Valparaiso, Chile.

World Information System on Informatics, f. 1983, Paris, France.

Yearbook of International Organizations, 1986/87; The Europa Yearbook 1988. A World Survey, Vol. I, London, 1988.

INFORMATION. A subject of a Convention on the International Transmission of Information and the Right to Make Corrections. Art. 1 defines "informational materials" as applying to all kinds of written, recorded or filmed news intended for publication; and the term "dispatch of information" as applying to all kinds of transmission of information by telecommunications to the place where it will be published. The Conference on Security and Co-operation in Europe in its ▷ Helsinki Final Act, 1975, devoted a whole chapter to the problems of information and international co-operation to improve it. In Nov., 1976 an international symposium was held in Venice, devoted to the circulation of information in the light of the Helsinki Act. In 1976 the nonaligned states formed an Intergovernmental Council on the Co-ordination of Information composed of countries from Africa (Ghana, Mozambique, Somalia, Togo, Tunisia and Zaïre), from Latin America (Guyana, Cuba and Peru), from Asia (India, Indonesia, Iraq, Jordan and Vietnam) and from Europe (Yugoslavia). In Nov., 1978 a general session of UNESCO ratified by consensus a declaration on the question of information. Subsequently, the UN General Assembly, on Dec. 18, 1978, unanimously approved a proposal by countries of the Third World on the matter of establishing "a new, more just and more effective world system of information and communication"; and established a 41-Nation Committee to review information policy. ▷ New International Information Order.

UN Chronicle, January, 1979, pp. 34–35; A. SMITH: *The Geo-politics of Information*, London, 1980; A.V. STOKES, *Concise Encyclopedia of Information Technology*; Hants, England, 1982; R.R. BEHER, *Information Industry Market Place*, New York, 1983.

INFORMATION AGENCY. An international term, defined in the Convention on the International Right of Correction, 1953, as follows:

"Information Agency means a press, broadcasting, film, television or facsimile organization, public or private, regularly engaged in the collection and dissemination of news material, created and organized under the laws and regulations of the Contracting State in which the central organization is domiciled and which in each Contracting State where it operates, functions under the laws and regulations of that State."

UNTS, Vol. 435, p. 194.

INFORMATION PROCESSING OR DATA PROCESSING. Subject of international co-operation. Organizations reg. with the UIA:

African Data Processing Institute, f. 1971, Yaoundé.
Committee on Data for Science and Technology, CODATA, f. 1968, Paris. Consultative status with IAEA and UNESCO.
Intergovernmental Council for Automatic Data Processing, f. 1968, Edinburgh. Publ.: *ICADP Information*.
International Federation for Information Processing, f. 1959, Geneva, Publ.: *IFIP Information Bulletin*.
International Federation of Data Processing Associations, f. 1970, Vienna.
International Group of Users of Information Systems, f. 1980, Almelo-Stad, Netherlands.
International Society for the Abolition of Data Processing Machines, f. 1965, Essex, UK.

A. WITTMAN, J. KLOS (eds), *Dictionary of Data Processing. Including Applications in Industry Administration and Business*. In English, German, and French, on an English Alphabetical Basis, Amsterdam, 1977; *Yearbook of International Organizations, 1986/*

87; *The Europa Yearbook 1988. A World Survey*, Vol. I, London, 1988.

INFORMATION UN SYSTEM. An internal body of the United Nations concerned with the co-ordination and harmonization of information systems and services within the UN family was convoked in the 1970s by the ECOSOC in Palais des Nations in Geneva as the Inter-Organization Board for Information Systems, IOB. The data elements for description of systems have been defined in co-operation with the Commission of European Communities and the International Federation of Documentation. The IOB is financed by the UN, UNDP, ILO, FAO, UNESCO, WHO, UPU, IFU, WMO, IMCO and WIPO.

The IOB has published in 1980 the following list of country codes with corresponding country name in English:

AFG	Democratic Republic of Afghanistan (Afghanistan)
AGO	People's Republic of Angola (Angola)
ALB	People's Socialist Republic of Albania (Albania)
ANT	Netherlands Antilles
ARE	United Arab Emirates
ARG	Argentine Republic (Argentina)
AUS	Commonwealth of Australia (Australia)
AUT	Republic of Austria (Austria)
BDI	Republic of Burundi (Burundi)
BEL	Kingdom of Belgium (Belgium)
BEN	People's Republic of Benin (Benin)
BGD	People's Republic of Bangladesh (Bangladesh)
BGR	People's Republic of Bulgaria (Bulgaria)
BHR	State of Bahrain (Bahrain)
BHS	Commonwealth of the Bahamas (Bahamas)
BLZ	Belize
BOL	Republic of Bolivia (Bolivia)
BRA	Federative Republic of Brazil (Brazil)
BRB	Barbados
BRN	Brunei
BTN	Kingdom of Bhutan (Bhutan)
BUR	Socialist Republic of the Union of Burma (Burma)
BWA	Republic of Botswana (Botswana)
BYS	Byelorussian Soviet Socialist Republic (Byelorussian SSR)
CAF	Central African Republic
CAN	Canada
CHE	Swiss Confederation (Switzerland)
CHL	Republic of Chile (Chile)
CHN	People's Republic of China (China)
CIV	Republic of the Ivory Coast (Ivory Coast)
CMR	United Republic of Cameroon
COG	People's Republic of the Congo (Congo)
COK	Cook Islands
COL	Republic of Colombia (Colombia)
COM	Federal and Islamic Republic of the Comoros (Comoros)
CPV	Republic of Cape Verde (Cape Verde)
CRI	Republic of Costa Rica (Costa Rica)
CSK	Czechoslovak Socialist Republic (Czechoslovakia)
CUB	Republic of Cuba (Cuba)
CYP	Republic of Cyprus (Cyprus)
DDR	German Democratic Republic
DEU	Federal Republic of Germany (Germany, Federal Republic of)
DJI	Republic of Djibouti (Djibouti)
DNK	Kingdom of Denmark (Denmark)
DOM	Dominican Republic
DZA	People's Democratic Republic of Algeria (Algeria)
ECU	Republic of Ecuador (Ecuador)
EGY	Arab Republic of Egypt (Egypt)
ESP	Spanish State (Spain)
ETH	Ethiopia
FIN	Republic of Finland (Finland)
FJI	Fiji
FRA	French Republic (France)

GAB	Gabonese Republic (Gabon)
GBR	United Kingom of Great Britain and Northern Ireland (United Kingdom)
GEL	Gilbert Islands
GHA	Republic of Ghana (Ghana)
GIN	Revolutionary People's Republic of Guinea (Guinea)
GMB	Republic of the Gambia (Gambia)
GNB	Republic of Guinea-Bissau (Guinea-Bissau)
GNQ	Republic of Equatorial Guinea (Equatorial Guinea)
GRC	Hellenic Republic (Greece)
GRD	Grenada
GTM	Republic of Guatemala (Guatemala)
GUY	Republic of Guyana (Guyana)
HKG	Hong Kong
HND	Republic of Honduras (Honduras)
HTI	Republic of Haiti (Haiti)
HUN	Hungarian People's Republic (Hungary)
HVO	Republic of the Upper Volta (Upper Volta)
IDN	Republic of Indonesia (Indonesia)
IND	Republic of India (India)
IRL	Ireland
IRN	Islamic Republic of Iran (Iran)
IRQ	Republic of Iraq (Iraq)
ISL	Republic of Iceland (Iceland)
ISR	State of Israel (Israel)
ITA	Italian Republic (Italy)
JAM	Jamaica
JOR	Hashemite Kingdom of Jordan (Jordan)
JPN	Japan
KEN	Republic of Kenya (Kenya)
KHM	Democratic Kampuchea
KOR	Republic of Korea
KWT	State of Kuwait (Kuwait)
LAO	Lao People's Democratic Republic (Laos)
LBN	Lebanese Republic (Lebanon)
LBR	Republic of Liberia (Liberia)
LBY	Socialist People's Libyan Arab Jamahiriya (Libyan Arab Jamahiriya)
LKA	Democratic Socialist Republic of Sri Lanka (Sri Lanka)
LSO	Kingdom of Lesotho (Lesotho)
LUX	Grand Duchy of Luxembourg (Luxembourg)
MAR	Kingdom of Morocco (Morocco)
MCO	Principality of Monaco (Monaco)
MDG	Democratic Republic of Madagascar (Madagascar)
MDV	Republic of Maldives (Maldives)
MEX	United Mexican States (Mexico)
MLI	Republic of Mali (Mali)
MLT	Republic of Malta (Malta)
MNG	Mongolian People's Republic (Mongolia)
MOZ	People's Democratic Republic of Mozambique (Mozambique)
MRT	Islamic Republic of Mauritania (Mauritania)
MSR	Montserrat
MUS	Mauritius
MWI	Republic of Malawi (Malawi)
MYS	Malaysia
NAM	Namibia
NER	Republic of the Niger (Niger)
NGA	Federal Republic of Nigeria (Nigeria)
NIC	Republic of Nicaragua (Nicaragua)
NIU	Niue
NLD	Kingdom of the Netherlands (Netherlands)
NOR	Kingdom of Norway (Norway)
NPL	Kingdom of Nepal (Nepal)
NZL	New Zealand
OMN	Sultanate of Oman (Oman)
PAK	Islamic Republic of Pakistan (Pakistan)
PAN	Republic of Panama (Panama)
PER	Republic of Peru (Peru)
PHL	Republic of the Philippines (Philippines)
PNG	Papua New Guinea
POL	Polish People's Republic (Poland)
PRK	Democratic People's Republic of Korea
PRT	Portuguese Republic (Portugal)
PRY	Republic of Paraguay (Paraguay)

QAT	State of Qatar (Qatar)
RHO	Zimbabwe
ROM	Socialist Republic of Romania (Romania)
RWA	Rwandese Republic (Rwanda)
SAU	Kingdom of Saudi Arabia (Saudi Arabia)
SDN	Democratic Republic of the Sudan (Sudan)
SEN	Republic of Senegal (Senegal)
SGP	Republic of Singapore (Singapore)
SLB	Solomon Islands
SLE	Republic of Sierra Leone (Sierra Leone)
SLV	Republic of El Salvador (El Salvador)
SOM	Somali Democratic Republic (Somalia)
STP	Democratic Republic of Sao Tome and Principe (Sao Tome and Principe)
SUN	Union of Soviet Socialist Republics (USSR)
SUR	Republic of Suriname (Suriname)
SWE	Kingdom of Sweden (Sweden)
SWZ	Kingdom of Swaziland (Swaziland)
SYC	Republic of Seychelles (Seychelles)
SYR	Syrian Arab Republic
TCD	Republic of Chad (Chad)
TGO	Togolese Republic (Togo)
THA	Kingdom of Thailand (Thailand)
TON	Kindom of Tonga (Tonga)
TTO	Republic of Trinidad and Tobago (Trinidad and Tobago)
TUN	Republic of Tunisia (Tunisia)
TUR	Republic of Turkey (Turkey)
TZA	United Republic of Tanzania
UGA	Republic of Uganda (Uganda)
UKR	Ukranian Soviet Socialist Republic (Ukranian SSR)
URY	Eastern Republic of Uruguay (Uruguay)
USA	United States of America (United States)
VAT	Holy See
VCT	St. Vincent
VEN	Republic of Venezuala (Venezuala)
VNM	Socialist Republic of Viet Nam (Viet Nam)
WSM	Independent State of Western Samoa (Samoa)
YEM	Yemen Arab Republic (Yemen)
YMD	People's Democratic Republic of Yemen (Democratic Yemen)
YUG	Socialist Federal Republic of Yugoslavia (Yugoslavia)
ZAF	Republic of South Africa (South Africa)
ZAR	Republic of Zaire (Zaire)
ZMB	Republic of Zambia (Zambia)

Directory of United Nations Information Systems, 2 Vols., Geneva 1980; *Directory of United Nations Information Systems, Vol. 1. Information Systems and Data Bases*, New York, 1980 (trilingual: English, French, Spanish).

INFORMBIURO. Informatsyonnoye Biuro Kommunisticheskih y Rabochih Partyi, Information Bureau of Communist and Workers' Parties, f. Sept. 29, 1947 in Szklarska Poręba (Poland) by seven European communist parties, which agreed: "that the absence of contacts among the Communist and Workers Parties participating at this Conference was a serious shortcoming in the present situation" in which "the struggle between two diametrically opposed camps – the imperialist camp and the anti-imperialist camp is taking place". In view of this, the participants in the Conference agreed on the following:

"(1) To set up an Information Bureau consisting of representatives of the Communist Party of Yugoslavia, the Bulgarian Workers' Party, the Communist Party of Romania, the Hungarian Communist Party, the Polish Workers' Party, the Communist Party of the Soviet Union (Bolsheviks), the Communist Party of France, the Communist Party of Czechoslovakia and the Communist Party of Italy.
(2) To charge the Information Bureau with the organization on interchange of experience, and if need be, coordination of the activities of the Communist Parties on the basis of mutual agreement.

(3) The Information Bureau is to consist of two representatives from each Central Committee, the delegations of the Central Committees to be appointed and replaced by the Central Committees.
(4) The Information Bureau is to have a printed organ – a fortnightly and subsequently, a weekly. The organ is to be published in French and Russian, and when possible, in other languages as well.
(5) The Information Bureau is to be located in the city of Belgrad."

Yugoslavia withdrew from the Informbiuro 1948, and the headquarters moved from Belgrad to Prague. Published a periodical *For Lasting Peace and People's Democracy* in several language versions. Known in the world press and referred to as Kominform. See ▷ Komintern. The Kominform was dissolved in Feb., 1956.

KEESING's *Contemporary Archive*, 1947 and 1956; E. REALE, *Nascito del Cominformo*, Milano, 1958; A. DEL ROSAL, *Los Congresos Obreros Internacionales en el Siglo XX*, Mexico, DF, 1963, pp. 231–234.

INFORSTRADA. An international term introduced by ITU for channels of telecommunications for teletransmission lines which ensure international automatic communication.

INFOTERM. International Information Centre for Terminology. The name of an institution f. by UNESCO (1971), headquarters Vienna (Austrian Standard Institute) with the aim of co-ordinating and initiating projects for the establishment of precise multi-linguistic terminology in different fields of international co-operation. Publ. *News Bulletin*.

UNESCO, *Report on the Meeting of the UNISIST Steering Committee for the Evaluation of the INFOTERM*, Paris, Aug. 13, 1976.

INFOTERRA. International Referral System for Sources of Environmental Information, one of the information systems of the ▷ UNEP.

INFRASTRUCTURE. An international term for a set of facilities and installations such as roads, bridges, energy and telecommunications networks. Economic infrastructures are all economic facilities and economic–financial institutions contributing to the operation of a country's or region's economy; social infrastructures are all social amenities and institutions rendering services in education, health protection, social security. In the UN system subject of regional international research under UN auspices, by the ECOSOC and the UN regional economic commission.

INGWAVUMA. ▷ Bantu Homelands.

INIIALANTS. An international term for a kind of ▷ drugs of abuse, not under international control. The sniffing of chemical inhalants such as aerosol, butyl nitrates, gasoline, some glues and solvents is dangerous considering the possibility of death of respiratory collapse or heart failure.

UN Chronicle, May, 1987.

INHERITANCE. An international term for inheriting by request, by legal right of succession or by a will of a person who died, subject of international private law where the prevalent principle is that of the so-called single statute, that is, a single law regulating inheritance (ensuing from ▷ Domicile) used by the USSR, GDR, FRG, Czechoslovakia, Poland, Scandinavian and other countries. Anglo-Saxon countries, Austria, Belgium, France, Romania and Hungary apply the principle of duality of inheritance (dual statute – separate ones for chattels and realty). Inheritance law is the subject of conventions framed by the Hague International Conferences for International Private Law 1925–28 and 1961.

M. RHEINSTEIN, *The Law of Decedent's Estates*, London, 1955; J.N. HAZARD, I. SHAPIRO, *The Soviet Legal System*, London, 1962.

INHUMANE WEAPONS. A subject of the Convention on Prohibition or Restriction on the Use of Certain Conventional Weapons which May be Deemed to be Excessively Injurious or to have Indiscriminate Effects, signed on Apr. 10, 1981 in the UN headquarters in New York by Afghanistan, Austria, Bulgaria, the Byelorussian SSR, Canada, Cuba, Czechoslovakia, Denmark, Egypt, Finland, France, the German Democratic Republic, the Federal Republic of Germany, Greece, Hungary, Iceland, Ireland, Italy, Luxembourg, Mexico, Mongolia, Morocco, the Netherlands, New Zealand, Norway, Poland, Portugal, Spain, Sudan, Sweden, the Ukrainian SSR, the USSR, the United Kingdom and Viet Nam. Any other state signing the Convention would be considered among the original signatories. Belgium became the thirty-fifth signatory when it signed the convention later the same day.

Three Protocols annexed to the Convention, which are not subject to signature, deal with weapons designed to injure by fragments that escape X ray detection in the human body (Protocol I); mines, booby-traps and other devices (Protocol II); and incendiary weapons (Protocol III). Expression of consent to be bound by the three Protocols is optional for each state, provided that at the time they deposit their instruments of ratification, accession or approval, they consent to be bound by any two or more of the Protocols. The Convention entered into force on Dec. 2, 1983, and was ratified until Jan 1, 1987 by 25 countries.

"New Convention Banning Inhumane Weapons Signed", in: *UN Chronicle*, June, 1981, p. 23; *SIPRI Yearbook 1987*, Oxford, 1988, p. 461.

INIS. International Nuclear Information System. A system est. in 1970 by the IAEA, to put the international exchange of information on a continuing computerized basis. Participating nations and organizations scan all nuclear literature published in their country or area for which they are responsible They feed in to the Agency, once a month, descriptions of this material, i.e. the name of the author, the title of the article, the name of the journal, together with a set of well-chosen words from a specialized dictionary (thesaurus) which define the content of the article, as well as an abstract of the text.

The IAEA merges this input into a master computer tape which is distributed to all participating nations and to other information services. The IAEA also distributes a print-out from the computer tape (the INIS Atomindex) in English and Russian. The IAEA makes available, on request, full texts of "non-conventional literature", i.e. technical reports, conference pre-prints, patents, university theses, and other material which is difficult to obtain. These texts are made available on microfiches.

INIS covers: Reactors and Reactor Materials, Uranium Production and Fuel Cycles, Nuclear Techniques in Food and Agriculture, Health, Safety and Waste Management, Isotope Production, Industrial Application and Radiation, Peaceful Nuclear Explosions, Safeguards, Legal and Economic Questions. The IAEA publishes a semimonthly in English and Russian and, since May 1970, a computer-assembled bibliography, *INIS Atom-index*.

IAEA Bulletin, 1970; A.F. FILIPPOV, "INIS: Nuclear Information for Development", in: *IAEA Bulletin*, Winter, 1986; "INIS Covering the World's Nuclear Literature", in: *IAEA Bulletin*, No. 3, 1987.

INITIALESE INTERNATIONAL. ▷ Acronyms and abbreviations.

INJURIOUS CONVENTIONAL WEAPONS. ▷ Weapons Injurious.

INMARSAT. International Maritime Satellite Organization. An intergovernmental institution est. Sept. 8, 1976 in London. It was established on the basis of the Treaty on the Principles Governing the Activity of States in the Exploration and Utilization of Outer Space Including the Moon and Other Heavenly Bodies, 1967, for the purpose of: "improving conditions for offering aid and safety at sea and intership communication and between ships and their owners, between crews or passengers on board and persons on land by utilizing satellites." The system of Maritime Satellites, launched in 1976 was extended in 1987 to determine via satellite the position of ships at sea.

Publ.: *Ocean Voice* (quarterly) and *Aeronautical Satellite News* (quarterly).

UN Yearbook, 1976; *Yearbook of International Organizations*, 1986/87; *The Europa Yearbook*, 1988, A World Survey, Vol. I, London, 1988.

INNOCENT PASSAGE. An international term for the right of foreign ships to passage through territorial or internal waters "that is not prejudicial to the peace, good order or security of the coastal state".

See also ▷ Sea Law Convention, 1982 (Art. 17–21, 45).

R.L. BLEDSOE, B.A. BOCZEK, *The International Law Dictionary*, Oxford, UK, 1987.

INPUT–OUTPUT. An international economic term introduced by the American scholar W. Leontief, for the analysis of outlays and results of production.

W. LEONTIEF, "Quantitative Input and Output in the Economic System of the United States", in: *The Review of Economics and Statistics*, 1966.

INQUIRY AND CONCILIATION. The international terms introduced by the Hague Conventions 1899 and 1907 for the "impartial and conscientious" research of international commissions into the causes of conflicts, with the aim of facilitating a solution of those conflicts. The League of Nations assigned the Permanent Court of International Justice to carry out international inquiries and the UN the International Court of Justice. International inquiry is also a term for information investigations or polls of opinion on international problems, carried out by the UN Secretary-General or other inter-governmental institutions. The organ of inquiry and conciliation in the League of Nations was the LN Council or the LN Assembly, in the UN the Security Council and the UN General Assembly. Multipartite treaties providing for inquiry and conciliation include the Central American States and the US Treaty, Feb. 7, 1923; the Gondra Treaty, May 3, 1923, revised Jan. 5, 1929; the Baltic States Co-operation Treaty, Jan. 17, 1925 and the Geneva General Act, 1928.

N.L. HILL, "International Commission of Inquiry and Counciliation", in: *International Conciliation*, No. 278, New York, March, 1932, pp. 87–134; R.L. BLEDSOE, B.A. BOCZEK, *The International Law Dictionary*, Oxford, 1987.

INQUISITION. An institution of the Roman Catholic Church, called *Inquisitio Haereticae Pravitatis Sanctum Officium*; centralized in 1229 and entrusted to the Dominicans by Pope Gregory IX; its purpose was to investigate heresy and try heretics; initiated by Pope Lucius III (1181–85). During the investigations tortures were applied, and those admitting their guilt were handed over to secular courts, which as a rule from 1231 burned heretics at the stake. From Europe the Inquisition was brought to Latin America in 1561. The first victims of the *auto da fe* were Indians from the settlements of Maui on Yucatan (now a southern province of Mexico). The Inquisition for Hispanic America was formally abolished by the Cortes of Feb. 22, 1813. In Europe the last countries to liquidate the Inquisition were: Portugal (1820), Spain (1835) and Italy (1859).

H.C. LEA, *A History of the Inquisition in the Middle Ages*, 3 Vols., London, 1887–1889; J.T. MEDINA, *Historia de la Inquisición en Chile*, Santiago, 1890; J. GUIRARD, *Histoire de l'inquisition au Moyen Age*, 2 Vols., Paris, 1935–1938; W.T. WALSH, *Characteristic of the Inquisition*, New York, 1940; B. LLORCA, *La Inquisición en España*, Madrid, 1946.

INRA. ▷ Institute for Natural Resources in Africa.

INSAS. International Nuclear Safety Advisory Group ▷ Nuclear Safety Standards.

INSEAD. Institut Europeen d'Administration des Affaires, international business school in Fontainebleau, near Paris, f. 1958. English, French and German is obligatory.

INSECTS. A subject of international control. The International Health Rules, est. 1969 by the WHO ordered obligatory desinsectisation of international railways, ports and airports. The Joint IAEA/FAO Division for Food and Agricultural Development initiated Integrated Pest Management (IPM) to reduce overdependence on insecticides. The Joint Division Insect and Pest Control Section has been involved in the use of isotopes and radiation in insect control since 1964. In Nov. 1987 the IAEA/FAO sponsored the International Symposium on Modern Insect Control: Nuclear Techniques and Biotechnology in Vienna. Organizations reg. with the UIA:

Council for the International Congresses of Entomology, f. 1910, London, UK; to promote biological study of insects. Publ.: *Congress Proceedings* (after each Congress).
International Union for the Study of Social Insects, f. 1952, Paris. Organizes Entomological Congresses. Publ.: *Insectes sociaux* (quarterly).

D.A. LINDQUIST, "Insects, Isotopes and Radiation", in: *IAEA Bulletin 1987*, No. 2; *Yearbook of International Organizations, 1986/87*; *The Europa Yearbook 1988. A World Survey*, Vol. I, London, 1988.

INSPECTION INTERNATIONAL. An intergovernmental institution introduced in art. 87 of the UN Charter which provided for "periodic visits (by UN representatives) to the respective trust territories at times agreed upon with the administering authorities." In international relations it was the first agreement on the right to international inspections by an international organization, a fact which had a positive effect in the process of decolonization of the trust territories.

R.B. CORY, "International Inspection From Proposals to Realization", in: *International Organization*, No. 13, 1959.

INSPECTION. ▷ Arms Inspection.

INSPECTION OF ATOMIC POWER PLANTS. ▷ Nuclear Reactors Inspection.

INSTITUTE FOR EAST-WEST. Est. in 1981 in New York as permanent center of "dialogue, study and research on security issues which affect countries of the NATO and Warsaw Treaty Organization alliances". Publ.: *East-West Monograph Series, Occasional Paper Series, Meeting Reports, Annual Reports.*

INSTITUTE FOR EDUCATIONAL PLANNING, INTERNATIONAL. World centre for advanced training and research in education planning f. 1963 in Paris. Publ. *Bulletin* (quarterly). Reg. with the UIA.

Yearbook of International Organizations.

INSTITUTE FOR EUROPEAN–LATIN AMERICAN RELATIONS, IRELA. f. 1984 in Madrid by the European and Latin American Parliaments, financed by the European Community. Aims to intensify dialogue between Western Europe and Latin America, promote specific research, collect and systematize information on relations between the two regions. Publ.: *Reports, Guides*, and *IRELA*.

IRELA, Handbook for Europan–Latin American Relations. European Institutions and Organizations and their Relations with Latin America and the Caribbean. In English and Spanish, Madrid, 1987.

INSTITUTE FOR LATIN AMERICAN INTEGRATION. ▷ Latin American Institute for Integration.

INSTITUTE FOR NATURAL RESOURCES IN AFRICA, INRA. A scientific institute of the United Nations University, UNU, est. 1987.

INSTITUTE FOR TRAINING AND RESEARCH. ▷ UNITAR.

INSTITUTE OF AIR TRANSPORT. F. 1944, Paris. International organization for the study of economic, technical and policy aspects of air transport. Members: 82 national bodies.

Yearbook of International Organizations.

INSTITUTE OF DIFFERING CIVILIZATION, INTERNATIONAL, INCIDI. F. 1894, Brussels (formerly International Colonial Institute, present name since 1946). Consultative status with UNESCO. Publ.: *Civilizations*. Reg. with the UIA.

Yearbook of International Organizations; INCIDI, *International Guide to Study Centres on Civilization and their Publications*, Brussels. 1973.

INSTITUTE OF ECONOMIC PROBLEMS OF THE SOCIALIST WORLD SYSTEM, INTERNATIONAL. Mezhdunarodniy Institut Ekonomicheskikh Problemov Mirovoy Sotsyalisticheskoy Sistiemy. An intergovernmental institute est. on July 24, 1970 in Moscow by the CMEA member states. The Statute of the Institute convoked an Academic Council which determines the basic orientation of scientific research, considers the draftwork plans, and evaluates the scientific research.

W.E. BUTLER, *A Source Book on Socialist International Organizations*, Alphen, 1978, pp. 264–268.

INSTITUTE OF INTELLECTUAL CO-OPERATION, INTERNATIONAL. Institut international de la coopération intellectuelle. A French government institution est. in Paris and ceded in 1925 to the LN as an organ of the League of Nations

International Commission for Intellectual Co-operation (Commission internationale de coopération intellectuelle, f. 1922). Membership of the Institute and the Commission was composed of 12 and then 17 distinguished scholars from member-states of the LN (including Maria Sklodowska-Curie, Albert Einstein and Robert A. Millikan). Both organizations extended patronage to other institutions connected directly or indirectly with the LN, e.g., the International Institute for the Unification of Private Law, headquarters Rome; International Union of Academies, headquarters Brussels; International Institute of Educational Films, headquarters Rome; Graduate Institute of International Studies, headquarters Geneva; International Research Council, headquarters Brussels. The Institute's major contributions include the publication of international bibliographies, e.g. *Index Bibliographicus*, the development of legal protection of literary and artistic creation and the initiation of international scientific research on folk art by a special congress organized under the aegis of the LN at Prague in 1928. Publ.: *Bulletin des relations universitaires*. Organizationally the Institute was divided into departments of general problems; international co-operation of universities, scientific bibliography and documentation, legal problems, international intellectual exchange, intellectual co-operation of artists, information and administrative services. Active up to 1940, formally until 1946 when its functions, rights, duties and property were taken over by UNESCO.

H. AUFRECHT. *Guide to League of Nations. Publications: A Bibliographical Survey of the Work of the League 1920–1947*, New York, 1951.

INSTITUTE OF INTERNATIONAL LAW. INSTITUT DU DROIT INTERNATIONAL, IDI. An institute f. 1873 in Ghent. It was awarded the Nobel Peace Prize 1904. The IDI promotes the progress of international law by giving assistance to all genuine attempts at gradual and progressive codification of international law. Its membership is made up of individuals from 39 countries. Publ.: *Annuaire*. Reg. with the UIA.

Tableau général des résolutions de l'IDI, 1873–1856, Bruxelles. 1937; *Yearbook of International Organizations.*

INSTITUTE OF LATIN AMERICAN ECONOMIC AND SOCIAL PLANNING. Instituto Latinoamericano de Planificación Económica y Social. An institute est. 1962 in Santiago de Chile by the UN Economic Commission for Latin America, ECLA. At the request of the governments concerned it provides training and advisory services to the countries and areas within the geographical scope of the ECLA. Reg. with the UIA.

Yearbook of International Organizations.

INSTITUTE OF LATIN AMERICAN RESEARCH. Institut des Hautes Études d'Amérique Latine, f. 1950, Paris University.

INSTITUTE OF LONDON UNDERWRITERS CLAUSES. A set of rules which defined the insurance conditions for sea vessels and goods transported by sea. The Institute of London Underwriters, est. 1884, publ. annually since 1939. *Reference Book of Marine Insurance Clauses*, which is a supplement to and modernization of the so-called ▷ Lloyd's policies of 1779. After World War II they were recognized in international insurance by the names of the main clauses; Institute Total Loss and Excess Liabilities Clauses, ITLC; Institute War and Strikes Clauses, IWSC; Institute Fishing Vessel Clauses, IFVC.

INSTITUTE OF MANAGEMENT SCIENCES (THE), TIMS. Est. 1953, New York, aims: identify, extend and unify scientific knowledge of management. Publ. *Management Science* (monthly), *Interfaces, Mathematics of Operations Research*.

Yearbook of International Organizations.

INSTITUTE OF MARITIME CULTURE, INTERNATIONAL. An institute on intercultural relations, f. 1968 in Fribourg. Reg. with the UIA.

Yearbook of International Organizations.

INSTITUTE OF PACIFIC RELATIONS. An institute, f. July 14, 1925 by national committees of Australia, Great Britain, Canada, China, Japan, New Zealand and the USA, dissolved July 1, 1961. The Constitution, adopted July 29, 1928 stated that its object was "to study the conditions of the Pacific peoples with a view to improvement of their mutual relations." Organized conferences with representatives of all countries from the Pacific region. The permanent secretariat was located at Honolulu, Hawaii, with American office at San Francisco. The first Conference was held in Honolulu in July, 1925, the second in July, 1928, the third in Kyoto, Japan, in Oct.–Nov., 1929.

"The Kyoto Conference of the Institute of Pacific Relations", in: *International Conciliation*, No. 260, New York, May, 1930.

INSTITUTE OF PUBLIC ADMINISTRATION OF CENTRAL AMERICA. ▷ Central American Institute of Public Administration.

INSTITUTE OF WORLD AFFAIRS. An American institute, f. 1924, Salisbury, Conn., USA. Summer seminar for advanced students interested in international affairs. Publ.: *Studies*.

Yearbook of International Organizations.

INSTITUTES, INTERNATIONAL. International term for national, regional or global research bodies.

INSTITUTES OF INTERNATIONAL AFFAIRS. During the interwar period, and especially after World War II, in a majority of the states of the world at least one institution was formed, usually connected with the ministry of foreign affairs of foreign policy bodies, devoted to the study of world or regional international relations. In the Five Great Powers the leading i.a.i. are: in China – The Chinese People's Institute of Foreign Affairs, Peiping; in France – Centre des Études de Politique Étrangère, Paris; in Great Britain – The Royal Institute of International Affairs, London; in the USA – Council of Foreign Relations, New York; in the USSR – Mezhdunarodniy institut, Moscow.

CARNEGIE ENDOWMENT, *Institutes of International Affairs*, New York, 1953.

INSTITUT UNIVERSITAIRE DES HAUTES ÉTUDES INTERNATIONALES. Graduate Institute of International Studies, f. 1927, Geneva, associated with the Université de Genève. A research and teaching institution studying international questions from the juridical, political and economic viewpoints. Maintains a library which owns the printed documents of the League of Nations and serves as a depository of the publications of the UN System.

UNESCO, *World of Learning*, Paris, 1983.

INSTRAW. ▷ International Research and Training Institute for the Advancement of Women.

INSURANCE. An international term for protection against all kinds of material losses through the conclusion of agreements with domestic or foreign insurance companies; subject of international conventions and interstate agreements. First insurance on life was introduced in England in 1583, and after the great fire in London in 1666 – insurances against fire; since 1779 – marine insurances. These three kinds of insurances became popular in Europe and America in the 19th century, also in the second half of the 20th century. As international investments grew, international companies insuring credits were established; in the 20th century aviation insurance, motor vehicle insurance and social insurance were established. The development of communications and technology brought about an increase in casualty insurance. Accidents at work are also included in ▷ social security. The oldest form of formally institutionalized insurance in England was the Life Assurance Act in 1774. A century later American life insurance companies introduced insurance covering in principle all states of the world, and in 1875 they started to popularize life insurance among industrial workers who, in 1890, paid 400 million dollars in fees. In total life insurance fees collected by American companies in 1920 exceeded 100 billion dollars, in 1960 – 500 billion dollars, and in 1970 – 1200 billion dollars.

The motor vehicles insurance, covering cars, drivers, passengers and damages done to third persons was initiated in 1898 in England; in the 20th century applied worldwide, in a majority of countries unified under international rules established in keeping with conventions on international transit and transport by motor vehicles. Insurance characteristic for the second half of 20th century is unemployment insurance, initiated during 1911–20 in Great Britain; during 1932–1937 in the USA and broadly applied after World War II in other parts of the world. On the basis of agreements, between trade unions and employers, deductions from wages and salaries are assigned to unemployment funds and thus make workers eligible for unemployment allowances at a rate corresponding to the period of work and family situation for a specified number of weeks (from eight weeks up to 104 weeks in various countries). In many countries included in social insurance.

H.F. GLASS, *International Insurance*, New York, 1960; W.A. RUYSCH, *Elsevier's Multilingual Dictionary on Insurance Terminology*. In English, Dutch, French, German, Spanish and Italian, Amsterdam, 1978.

INSURANCE INTERNATIONAL LAW. A part of international private law, subject of regional codification of insurance provisions and of organized international co-operation. Such codification took place on the Amerian continent and in Western Europe after World War I.
Organization reg. with the UIA:
International Association for Insurance Law, AIDA, est. 1960, Rome. Unites national committees of 46 states, develops and unifies international insurance law and organizes International Congresses every four years; the first Congress took place in Rome in 1962.

Yearbook of International Organizations.

INSURANCE POLICY. International term for a certificate of insurance contract usually in the form accepted in international turnover (▷ Lloyd's policy).

INSURED LETTERS AND BOXES. A subject of international co-operation and convention: the UPU Agreement concerning Insured Letters and Boxes, July 11, 1952, in art. 1, p. 1 defined the subject of the agreements: "letters containing paper valuables or documents of value and boxes containing jewelry or other valuable articles ... with insurance of the contents for the value declared by the sender."

UNTS, Vol. 170, p. 11.

INSURRECTIONS. An international term for armed national-liberation uprisings, subject of international legal disputes in the 19th and 20th centuries, in connection with not applying rules of war to insurgents. Not until after World War II was the norm of international law relating to prisoners and wounded extended to cover the participants of uprisings and national liberation struggles.

J. CIECHANOWSKI, *The Warsaw Rising of 1944*, New York, 1974.

INTECOL. International Association for Ecology, f. 1967, Athens, Greece. Reg. with the UIA.

INTEGRATION. An international term for an economic or political process involving combination into an integral whole of economies or policies of a number of states. Processes of economic integration on a considerable scale took place after World War II in Europe, Africa, Latin America and South Asia.

International Organization and Integration. Annotated Basic Documents and Descriptive Directory of International Organizations and Arrangements, 2 Vols., The Hague, 1981; W. LIPGENS ed., *Documents on the History of European Integration*, Vol. 1, Florence, 1986.

INTEGRATION OF EUROPE. The idea of economic and political consolidation of the European continent which appeared after World War I (▷ Pan-Europe). After World War II the concepts of integration of countries with planned economies were realized within the framework of the ▷ CMEA and of Western European countries of the ▷ EEC.

J. PAXTON, *A Dictionary of the European Economic Community*, London, 1977; J.W. POPOV, L.I. LUKIN, *Riealizatsya Kompleksovey Programmy Sotsyalisticheskoy Ekonomicheskoy Intiegratsyi Stran-Chlenov SEV*, Moskva, 1983.

INTEGRATION OF GREATER COLOMBIA. The concept of economic consolidation of Colombia, Ecuador and Venezuela which at the beginning of the 19th century formed one state – Greater Colombia. Three subsequent meetings, in 1958, 1959 and 1960 of government experts of the states concerned were held in Bogota, Caracas and Quito to work out the main lines of the IBC. The name was abandoned when the concept was extended to embrace a number of Andean states and negotiations began with Chile, Bolivia, and Peru within the ▷ Andean Group.

Multilateral Economic Corporation in Latin America, UN, New York, 1962, pp. 152–163.

INTEGRATION OF SOUTH ASIA. An economic integration initiated with the establishment of a Free Trade Zone by the Philippines, Indonesia and Thailand in 1963, and the Treaty on Economic Co-operation signed by the governments of the Philippines, Indonesia, Singapore, Malaysia, and Thailand, 1967.

INTELLECTUAL CO-OPERATION INTERNATIONAL ACT, 1938. An intergovernmental document signed on Dec. 3, 1938 in Paris, by the governments of Albania, Argentina, Belgium, Brazil, Chile, China, Colombia, Costa Rica, Czechoslovakia, Denmark, the Dominican Republic, Ecuador, Egypt, Estonia, Finland, France, Greece, Guatemala, Haiti, Iraq, Iran,

Ireland, Latvia, Lithuania, Luxembourg, Mexico, Monaco, the Netherlands, Norway, Panama, Paraguay, Peru, Poland, Portugal, Romania, Siam, Spain, Sweden, Switzerland, South Africa, Turkey, Uruguay, Venezuela and Yugoslavia.
Art. 1 stated that:

". . . the work of intellectual co-operation is independent of politics and based entirely on the principle of universality."
Art. 2: "National committees on Intellectual Co-operation, established in each of the States Parties to the present Act, shall act as centres for the development of this work on both the national and international planes."
Art. 3. "The International Institute of Intellectual Co-operation shall by its effective collaboration assist the National Committee."

LNTS, Vol. 200, p. 261.

INTELLECTUAL PROPERTY PROTECTION. An international term, defined in the Stockholm Convention, signed July 14, 1967 (effected Apr. 26, 1970), which established the World Intellectual Property Organization ▷ WIPO. In May 1973 the WIPO convened the Diplomatic Conference on the Protection of Intellectual Property in Vienna. In 1974 acquired the status of a specialized UN agency.
The definition of the field of interest of the convention has the following form:

"Art. 1. The countries to which this Convention applies constitute a Union for the protection of the rights of authors in their literary artistic works.
Art. 2.(1) the expression "literary and artistic works" shall include every production in the literature, scientific and artistic domain, whatever may be the mode or form of its expression, such as books, pamphlets or other writings; lectures, addresses, sermons and other works of the same nature; dramatic or dramatico-musical works; choreographic works and entertainments in dumb show; musical compositions with or without words; cinematographical works to which are assimilated works expressed by a process analogous to cinematography; works of drawing, painting, architecture, sculpture, engraving and lithography; photographic works to which are assimilated works expressed by a process analogous to photography; works of applied art; illustrations, maps, plans, sketches and three-dimensional works relative to geography, topography, architecture or science."

In the 1980's the protection of intellectual property rights has become a contentious issue in international trade. This is a result of a definite relationship between protection of intellectual property and incentives for industrial innovations. In 1986 in Puenta del Este, the Uruguay Round of GATT on further trade liberalization decided to discuss the trade related aspects of intellectual property including trade in counterfeit goods. The issue is scheduled to be resolved by 1990. The international system of ▷ Copyright is based on the ▷ Berne Convention 1886, on the ▷ WIPO Convention 1967, and the ▷ Copyright Universal Convention 1952, updated in 1971. See also ▷ Industrial Property Protection; ▷ Patent Co-operation Treaty 1978.
▷ Trade related aspects of intellectual property.

H. DEBOIS, "L'organisation de la propriété intellectuelle", in: *Revue internationale du droit d'auteur*, Numéro spécial 1967/68, pp. 573–662 and 769–931; T. ABU-GHAZALEZ, "The GATT and Intellectual Property", in: *Economic Impact*, Washington DC, 1988/3; R.P. ROZEK, "Intellectual Property and Economic Growth", in: *Economic Impact*, Washington DC, 1988/I; E. MANSFIELD, "Intellectual Property, Technology and Economic Growth", in: *Economic Impact*, 1988/3.

INTELLIGENCE SERVICE. An international term and historical name of the intelligence and counter-intelligence service in Great Britain and after World War II also in the USA. The intelligence office charged with collecting intelligence information, exercising respective advisory functions towards the government as well as co-ordinating the work of other intelligence institutions. In Great Britain the organization of the Intelligence Service was called Joint Intelligence Bureau up to 1964, when the War Office and Admiralty and Air Ministry created the Ministry of Defence and the Intelligence Service received the name Defence Intelligence Staff, DIS. In the US-CIA. In tsarist Russia the political police Okhrana organized the intelligence service; in the Soviet Union since 1960 under the directive of the State Security Committee are working the chief intelligence directorate of the Soviet Army and the intelligence unit within the Secretariat of the Communist Party of the Soviet Union. Former formations of the Soviet political police: Cheka, GPU, NKVD; KGB The International Journal of Intelligence and Counterintelligence is published since 1985 in the USA.

R. BOUCARD, *The Secret Service in Europe*, New York, 1940; S. KENT, *Strategic Intelligence for American World Policy*, New York, 1949; R. STORRY, *The Case of Richard Sorge*, London 1966; V.E. MARCHETTI, J. MARKS, *The CIA and the Cult of Intelligence*, New York, 1974; C. FITZGIBON, *Secret Intelligence in the XXth Century*, London, 1976; R. JEFFREY-JONES, *American Espionage*, New York, 1977; D. KAHN, *Hitler's Spies*, London, 1978; F.H. HINSLEY, *British Intelligence in the Second World War*, 2 Vls, London, 1979; D. LEITCH, P. KNIGHTLEY, *The Philby Conspiracy*, New York, 1981; J. BLOCH, P. FITZGERALD, *British Intelligence and Covert Action: Africa, Middle East and Europe since 1945*, London, 1983; J.J. DZIAK, *Chekisty. The KGB in Soviet History*, Lexington, 1987; G. GLESS, *The Secrets of the Service, A Story of Soviet Subversion of Western Intelligence*, New York, 1987; J. TRICHELSON, *Foreign Intelligence Organizations*, New York, 1988; R. GODSON, *Comparing Foreign Intelligence. The USA, The USSR, the UK and the Third World*, Oxford, 1988.

INTELLIGENZAKTION. *German* = "action intelligentsia". A code-name for German extermination of the leading strata of Polish intelligentsia launched in the first year of Nazi occupation of Poland 1939–40. Lists of Polish academists and leading political, social and cultural activists prepared long before the outbreak of World War II by German research Ostinstitut allowed Gestapo to launch arrests and executions among the Polish intelligentsia, especially in Pomerania, Silesia and Great Poland. In Central Poland extermination of the Polish intelligentsia started in Nov., 1939 with the arrest and detention in KZ Sachsenhausen of 183 renowned scientists of the Jagellonian University and other Cracow institutions of higher learning (Sonderaktion Krakau).

W. GAWEDA, *Uniwersytet Jagielloński 1939–45* (The Jagiellonian University during the Nazi Occupation 1939–45), Warsaw 1978; M. WALCZAK, *Szkolnictwo wyższe i nauka polska w latach wojny i okupacji 1939–45* (Polish Institutions of Higher Learning and Research during the War and Occupation 1939–45), Wroclaw, 1979; W. KONOPCZYŃSKI, *Sonderaktion Krakau*, Warsaw, 1982.

INTELSAT. International Telecommunications Satellite Organization. A Western agency est. 1964, in Washington, DC, by the Washington convention with the task of constructing and launching into orbit artificial Earth satellites and utilizing them for global satellites communication systems. Members: 106 governments. The first satellites were launched 1965–70: Intelsat I, called Early Bird – 1965; Intelsat II – 1966; Intelsat III – 1968; Intelsat III F3 and III R4 – 1969; Intelsat III F7 – 1970. On Sept. 30, 1971 the USA and USSR in Washington signed an agreement on improving lines of direct communication with an appendix on the conditions for the mutual use of the Intelsat system, ▷ Molniya. ▷ Hot Line. In 1984 eleven INTELSAT satellites in synchronous orbit provided a global communications service with 206 earth stations antennae carrying international commercial traffic.

Organización Program de Intelsat, Mexico, DF, 1967; *The Europa Year Book 1984. A World Survey*, London, 1984, p. 246.

INTERACTION COUNCIL OF FORMER HEADS OF GOVERNMENT. An independent international organization, f. in Vienna, March 1983; chairman Kurt Waldheim, former UN Secretary General. Members: former Heads of Government from developed and developing countries from East and West. Organs: The Policy Board, The Communication Committee, The Interaction Network, Secretariat in Vienna. Headquarters – New York. Aims: promote action on a limited number of key international problems eg the promotion of peace and disarmament, the revitalization of the world economy, the strengthening of co-operation for development.
The members of the council intend to use their experience, their ideas and their high level contacts for effective action, through a variety of channels, including missions to selected countries and sustained efforts to generate widespread public interest and support. The Interaction Council's first plenary session took place in Nov., 1983 in Vienna, the second in May, 1984 in Brioni, Yugoslavia. Since 1986 under the leadership of Helmut Schmidt, former Chancellor of the Federal Republic of Germany.

INTER-ALLIED COMMISSION FOR THE GOVERNMENT AND PLEBISCITE IN UPPER SILESIA. An intergovernmental institution, established on Nov. 3, 1919 for the plebiscite region of Upper Silesia by the Council of the LN in accordance with art. 88 of the Versailles Treaty. It operated from Nov. 11, 1920 to June 30, 1922 under the chairmanship of French General Le Rond.

S. WAMBAUGH, *Plebiscites since the World War*, 2 Vols., London, 1933.

INTER-ALLIED MILITARY COMMITTEE. A commanding organ of Allied armies to co-ordinate their operations, f. Jan. 1918 in Paris. Headed by French General F. Foch.

INTER-ALLIED REPARATION AGENCY, IARA, 1945–49. An institution established on the basis of the Potsdam Agreement of Aug. 2, 1945 by the Paris Reparations Conference of Sept. 9–Dec. 21, 1945. 18 states participated: Albania, Australia, Belgium, Czechoslovakia, Canada, Denmark, Egypt, France, Greece, Holland, India, Luxembourg, New Zealand, Norway, South Africa, UK, the USA and Yugoslavia. The task of the Agency was to divide reparations from Germany among the 18 entitled states and to divide German property intended for reparations into two categories. Category A included German bank accounts, gold, real estate and securities, including those located in neutral, allied or belligerent countries; category B – industrial fittings and sea and river merchant vessels which were to be taken out of Germany. In accordance with the Potsdam resolutions, the Soviet Union and Poland received reparations separately and thus did not belong to the IARA. Nonetheless, according to these resolutions they were supposed to receive 25% of the total reparations taken out of Germany. The operations of IARA, which had its headquarters in Brussels, were suspended *sine die* in Dec., 1949.

R. CASTILLON, *Les réparations allemandes. Deux experiences: 1919–1922 et 1945–1952*, Paris, 1953.

INTER-AMERICAN ACADEMY. A scientific institution, f. 1959, Washington, DC. Publ. *Journal of Inter-American Studies*.

INTER-AMERICAN AFFAIRS OFFICE. An institution of the US government between 1940 and 1946; had the task of developing inter-American trade for the purpose of guaranteeing important strategic raw materials and developing press, radio and film centers from the point of view of propagating US War interests; liquidated after World War II; its functions were assumed by the under-secretary of state for Latin America in the Department of State.

Anuario Panamericano 1925, pp. 25–26.

INTER-AMERICAN ANTI-WAR TREATY, 1933. A Nonaggression and Conciliation Treaty between Argentine, Brazil, Chile, Mexico, Paraguay and Uruguay, signed on Oct. 10, 1933 in Rio de Janeiro. Art. 1 reads:

"The High Contracting Parties solemnly declare that they condemn wars of aggression in their mutual relations or against other states and that the settlement of disputes and controversies shall be effected only through the peaceful means established by International Law."

UNTS, Vol. 163, p. 405.

INTER-AMERICAN ARBITRATION GENERAL TREATY, 1929. A General Inter-American Treaty of Arbitration and Protocol of Progressive Arbitration signed on Jan. 5, 1929 in Washington by the American Republics of Bolivia, Brazil, Chile, Colombia, Costa Rica, Cuba, the Dominican Republic, Ecuador, El Salvador, Guatemala, Haiti, Honduras, Mexico, Nicaragua, Panama, Paraguay, Peru, Uruguay, the USA and Venezuela. It entered into force on Oct. 28, 1929 but was superseded by the American Treaty on Peaceful Settlement (▷ Bogota Pact 1948).

LNTS, Vol. 130, pp. 140–144; OAS, *Inter-American Treaties and Conventions*, Washington, DC, 1971, p. 58–59.

INTER-AMERICAN ARTISTIC EXHIBITIONS CONVENTION, 1936. A Convention Concerning Facilities for Artistic Exhibition, adopted by the Inter-American Conference for the Maintenance of Peace, signed on Dec. 23, 1936 at Buenos Aires by all American Republics Art. 1 of the Convention read as follows:

"Each of the High Contracting Parties agree to grant, so far as its legislation may permit, all possible facilities for the holding within its territory of artistic exhibitions of each of the other Parties."

LNTS, Vol. 188, 1938, pp. 152–161; OAS, *Inter-American Treaties and Conventions*, Washington, DC, 1971, p. 76.

INTER-AMERICAN ASSOCIATION FOR DEMOCRACY AND FREEDOM. Asociación Interamericana pro Democracia y Libertad, f. 1950, New York. Member of International League for the Rights of Man. Publ. *Hemispherica*. Reg. with the UIA.

Yearbook of International Organizations.

INTER-AMERICAN ASSOCIATION OF BROADCASTERS. Asociación Interamericana de Radiodifusión, f. 1946, Montevideo. Consultative Status with the ECOSOC, ITU, UNESCO and OAS. Reg. with the UIA.

Yearbook of International Organizations.

INTER-AMERICAN ASSOCIATION OF INDUSTRIAL PROPERTY. Asociación Interamericana de la Propiedad Industrial, f. 1963, Buenos Aires. Reg. with the UIA.

Yearbook of International Organizations.

INTER-AMERICAN ASYLUM CONVENTIONS, 1928–54. The first Convention on Asylum was signed on Feb. 20, 1928 in Havana by Argentina, Bolivia, Brazil (ratified 1929), Chile, Colombia (r. 1937), Costa Rica (r. 1933), Cuba (r. 1931), the Dominican Republic (r. 1932; denounced Oct. 6, 1954), Ecuador (r. 1936), El Salvador (r. 1937), Guatemala (r. 1931), Haiti (r. 1952; denounced 1961), Honduras (r. 1956), Mexico (r. 1929), Nicaragua (r. 1930) Panama (r. 1929), Paraguay (r. 1948), Peru (r. 1945), USA (no r.), Uruguay (r. 1933), Venezuela (no r.). It entered into force on May 21, 1929. The text reads as follows:

"Art. 1. It is not permissible for States to grant asylum in legations, warships, military camps or military aircraft, to persons accused or condemned for common crimes, or to deserters from the army or navy.

Persons accused of or condemned for common crimes taking refuge in any of the places mentioned in the preceding paragraph, shall be surrendered upon request of the local government.

Should said persons take refuge in foreign territory surrender shall be brought about through extradition, but only in such cases and in the form established by the respective treaties and conventions or by the constitution and laws of the country of refuge.

Art. 2, Asylum granted to political offenders in legations, warships, military camps or military aircraft, shall be respected to the extent in which allowed, as a right or through humanitarian toleration, by the usages, the conventions or the laws of the country in which granted and in accordance with the following provisions:

First: Asylum may not be granted except in urgent cases and for the period of time strictly indispensable for the person who has sought asylum to ensure in some other way his safety.

Second: Immediately upon granting asylum, the diplomatic agent, commander of a warship, or military camp or aircraft, shall report the fact to the Minister for Foreign Relations of the State of the person who has secured asylum, or to the local administrative authority, if the act occurred outside the capital.

Third: The Government of the State may require that the refugee be sent out of the national territory within the shortest time possible: and the diplomatic agent of the country who has granted asylum may in turn require the guaranties necessary for the departure of the refugee with due regard to the inviolability of his person, from the country

Fourth: Refugees shall not be landed in any point of the national territory nor in any place too near thereto.

Fifth: While enjoying asylum, refugees shall not be allowed to perform acts contrary to the public peace.

Sixth: States are under no obligation to defray expenses incurred by one granting asylum.

Art. 3. The present Convention does not affect obligations previously undertaken by the contracting parties through international agreements."

The second Convention on Political Asylum was signed on Dec. 26, 1933 in Montevideo by Argentina, Brazil (ratified 1937), Chile (r. 1936), Colombia (r. 1936), Costa Rica (r. 1951), the Dominican Rep. (r. 1934; denounced Oct. 6, 1954), Ecuador (r. 1955), El Salvador (r. 1937), Guatemala (r. 1935), Haiti (r. 1952; denounced Aug. 1, 1967; denunciation revoked 1974), Honduras (r. 1936), Mexico (r. 1936), Panama (r. 1938), Paraguay (r. 1948), Peru (r. 1960), Uruguay (r. 1935). It entered into force on March 22, 1935. A Treaty on Political Asylum and Refugees was signed on Aug. 4, 1939 in Montevideo by Argentina, Bolivia, Chile, Paraguay (r. 1939), Peru, and Uruguay (r. 1939).

A ▷ Diplomatic Asylum Convention was signed on Mar. 28, 1954 at Caracas by Argentina, Bolivia, Brazil (ratified 1957), Chile, Colombia, Costa Rica (r. 1955), Cuba, the Dominican Rep. (r. 1961), Ecuador (r. 1955), El Salvador (r. 1954), Guatemala, Haiti (r. 1955; denounced 1967; denunciation revoked 1974), Honduras, Mexico (r. 1957), Nicaragua, Panama (r. 1958), Paraguay (r. 1957), Peru (r. 1962), Uruguay (1967), and Venezuela (r. 1954). It entered into force on Dec. 29, 1954.

A Convention on Territorial Asylum was signed on Mar. 22, 1954 in Caracas by the same 20 states, but was ratified only by Brazil (1965), Colombia (1968), Costa Rica (1955), Ecuador (1955), El Salvador (1954), Haiti (1955; denounced 1967; denunciation revoked 1974), Panama (1958), Paraguay (1957), Uruguay (1967) and Venezuela (1954). The text read as follows:

"The governments of the Member States of the Organization of American States, desirous of concluding a Convention regarding Territorial Asylum, have agreed to the following articles:

Art. 1. Every State has the right, in the excercise of its sovereignty, to admit into its territory such persons as it deems advisable, without, through the exercise of this right, giving rise to complaint by any other State.

Art. 2. The respect which, according to international law, is due the jurisdicional right of each State over the inhabitants in its territory, is equally due, without any restriction whatsoever, to that which it has over persons who enter it proceeding from a State in which they are persecuted for their beliefs, opinions, or political affiliations, or for acts which may be considered as political offenses.

Any violation of sovereignty that consists of acts committed by a government or its agents in another State against the life of security of an individual, carried out on the territory of another State, may not be considered attenuated because the persecution began outside its boundaries or is due to political considerations or reasons of state.

Art. 3. No State is under the obligation to surrender to another State, or to expel from its own territory, persons persecuted for political reasons or offenses.

Art. 4. The right of extradition is not applicable in connection with persons who, in accordance with the qualifications of the solicited State, are sought for politial offenses, or for common offenses committed for political ends, or when extradition is solicited for predominantly political motives.

Art. 5. The fact that a person has entered into the territorial jurisdiction of a State surreptitiously or irregularly does not affect the provisions of this Convention.

Art. 6. Without prejudice to the provisions of the following articles, no State is under the obligation to establish any distinction in its legislation, or in its regulations or administrative acts applicable to aliens, solely because of the fact that they are political asylees or refugees.

Art 7. Freedom of expression of thought, recognized by domestic law for all inhabitants of a State, may not be ground of complaint by a third State on the basis of opinions expressed publicly against it or the government by asylees or refugees, except when these concepts constitute systematic propaganda through which they incite to the use of force or violence against the government of the complaining State.

Art. 8. No State has the right to request that another State restrict for the political asylees or refugees the freeom of assembly or association which the latter States's internal legislation grants to all aliens within its territory, unless such assembly or association has as its purpose fomenting the use of force or violence against the government of the soliciting State.

Art. 9. At the request of the interesting State, the State that has granted refuge or asylum shall take steps to keep watch over or to intern at a reasonable distance from its border, those political refugees or asylees who are notorious leaders of a subversive movement, as well as those against whom there is evidence that they are disposed to join it.

Determination of the reasonable distance from the border, for the purpose of internment, shall depend upon the judgment of the authorities of the State of refuge.

All expenses incurred as a result of the internment of political asylees and refugees shall be chargeable to the State that makes the request.

Art. 10. The political internees referred to in the preceding article shall advise the government of the host State whenever they wish to leave its territory. Departure therefrom will be granted, under the condition that they are not to go to the country from which they came and the interested government is to be notified.

Art. 11. In all cases in which a complaint or request is permissible in accordance with this Convention, the admissibility of evidence presented by the demanding State shall depend on the judgment of the solicited State.

Art. 12. This Convention remains open to the signature of the Member States of the Organization of American States, and shall be ratified by the signatory States in accordance with their respective constitutional procedures.

Art. 13. The original instrument, whose texts in the English, French, Portuguese, and Spanish languages are equally authentic, shall be deposited in the Pan American Union, which shall send certified copies to the governments for the purpose of ratification The instruments of ratification shall be deposited in the Pan American Union; this organization shall notify the signatory governments of said deposit.

Art. 14. This Convention shall take effect among the States that ratify it in the order in which their respective ratifications are deposited.

Art. 15. The Convention shall remain effective indefinitely, but may be denounced by any of the signatory States by giving advance notice of one year, at the end of which period it shall cease to have effect for the denouncing State, remaining, however, in force among the remaining signatory States. The denunciation shall be forwarded to the Pan American Union which shall notify the other signatory States thereof."

The Convention came into force on Dec. 29, 1954; ratified by Brazil, Colombia, Costa Rica, Ecuador, El Salvador, Haiti, Panama, Paraguay, Uruguay and Venezuela.

International Conferences of American States. Second Supplement 1942–1954, Washington, DC, 1958; OAS, *Inter-American Treaties and Conventions*, Washington, DC, 1967.

INTER-AMERICAN AVIATION CONVENTIONS, 1928.
A Convention signed on Feb. 20, 1928 in Havana by governments of 21 American republics. It recognized the full and exclusive sovereignty of each state in the air over its territory and territorial waters, guaranteed freedom in the time of peace for the innocent passage of private aircraft of the signatories. It came into force on May 4, 1929; but was superseded by the Chicago Convention, 1944.

LNTS, Vol. 129, pp. 227–229; OAS, *Law and Treaty Series*, Washington, DC, 1929.

INTER-AMERICAN BANK.
A project initiated by an Inter-American Convention for the Establishment of an Inter-American Bank, signed on May 10, 1940 in Washington, DC, by Bolivia, Brazil, Colombia, the Dominican Republic, Ecuador, Mexico, Nicaragua, Paraguay, the United States. Did not enter into force; superseded by the Agreement establishing the ▷ Inter-American Development Bank, 1959.

OAS, *Inter-American Treaties and Conventions*, Washington, DC, 1971, p. 95.

INTER-AMERICAN BAR ASSOCIATION.
Federación Interamericana de Abogados, f. 1940, Washington, DC. Publ. *Newsletter*. Reg. with the UIA.

Yearbook of International Organizations.

INTER-AMERICAN CENTER OF EXPORT PROMOTION.
A center est. 1968 under the auspices of the ECOSOC, in Washington. It has the task of "developing the expansion of the export of non-traditional products of Latin America, above all finished and semi-finished goods."

Yearbook of International Organizations.

INTER-AMERICAN CHARTER OF SOCIAL GUARANTIES, 1948.
A Charter adopted by the Ninth International American Conference held on May 2, 1948 in Bogota. It embraced some basic social rights; equality of men and women, universal right to employment contract, to minimum wage, to eight-hour workday and a 48 week work year. It forbade child labor and upheld the right of workers to unionize, to strike, and to welfare securities. Art. 38 provided that farm employees have the right to better living conditions. Art. 39 granted State care to Indians. The Charter was not signed by the USA and was not ratified by a majority of American republics and therefore never entered into force, remaining a document of intent.

The text read as follows:

"The American States,

Desirous of making effective the constant and generous aspiration of the Inter-American Conferences that on the Continent there be standards providing ample protection to workers;

Inspired by the aim of furthering the rehabilitation of the life, economy and ethical and social standards of the American peoples, strengthening them as an element of humanity, increasing their ability to work, adding to their productive value and raising their purchasing power in order that they may enjoy a better standard of living:

Convinced that the State attains its goals not only by recognizing the rights of citizens alone, but also by concerning itself with the fortunes of men and women, considered not only as citizens but also as human beings;

Agreed, therefore, that the present stage of juridicial evolution demands that democratic systems guarantee respect for political and spiritual freedoms, together with the realization of the postulates of social justice;

Encouraged by the fact that the countries of America fervently desire to achieve this social justice;

United in the belief that one of the principal objectives of the present international organization is to bring about the cooperation of the various States for the solution of labor problems, and that it is to the public interest, from the international point of view, to enact the most comprehensive social legislation possible, to give workers guarantees and rights on a scale not lower than that fixed in the Conventions and recommendations of the International Labor Organization;

Agreed that economic cooperation, of such great importance for the American Republics, cannot be truly effective unless measures are taken to ensure the rights of workers and unless living and working conditions are improved as much as possible;

Unanimous in realizing that the aggravation of social problems is an obvious factor of international unrest, with international repercussions that endanger the maintenance of peace;

Conscious that Christian principles teach the duty of contributing to the material well-being of men and women and to their spiritual welfare by according to them a decent way of life that will provide for their liberty, dignity and security, and conscious that those principles successfully reconcile individual initiative with the undeniable worth that human labor has acquired in modern societies; and

Desirous of giving effect to Resolution LVIII of the Inter-American Conference on Problems of War and Peace, which provides for the preparation of a "Charter of Social Guarantees";

Adopt the following Inter-American Charter of Social Guarantees as the declaration of the social rights of workers:

General Principles

Art. 1. It is the aim of the present Charter of Social Guarantees to proclaim the fundamental principles that must protect workers of all kinds, and it sets forth the minimum rights they must enjoy in the American States, without prejudice to the fact that the laws of each State may extend such rights or recognize others that are more favorable.

This Charter of Social Guarantees gives equal protection to men and women.

It is recognized that the supremacy of these rights and the progressive raising of the standard of living of the community in general depend to a large degree upon the development of economic activities, upon increased productivity, and upon cooperation between workers and employers, expressed in harmonious relations and in mutual respect for and fulfilment of their rights and duties.

Art. 2. The following principles are considered to be fundamental in the social legislation of the American countries:

(a) Labor is a social function; it enjoys the special protection of the State and must not be considered as a commodity.

(b) Every worker must have the opportunity for a decent existence and the right to fair working conditions.

(c) Intellectual, as well as technical and manual labor, must enjoy the guarantees established in labor laws, with the distinctions arising from the application of the law under the different circumstances.

(d) There should be equal compensation for equal work, regardless of the sex, race, creed or nationality of the worker.

(e) The rights established in favor of workers may not be renounced, and the laws that recognize such rights are binding on and benefit all the inhabitants of the territory, whether nationals or aliens.

Art. 3. Every worker has the right to engage in his occupation and to devote himself to whatever activity suits him. He is likewise free to change employment.

Art. 4. Every worker has the right to receive vocational and technical training in order to perfect his skills and knowledge, obtain a greater income from his work, and contribute effectively to the advancement of production. To this end, the State shall organize adult education and the apprenticeship of young people, in such a way as to assure effective training in a given trade or work, at the same time that it provides for their cultural, moral and civic development.

Art. 5. Workers have the right to share in the equitable distribution of the national well-being, by obtaining the necessary food, clothing and housing at reasonable prices.

To achieve these purposes, the State must sponsor the establishment and operation of popular farms and restaurants and of consumer and credit cooperatives, and should organize institutions to promote and finance such farms and establishments, as well as to supply low-cost, comfortable, hygienic housing for laborers, salaried employees and rural workers.

Individual Labor Contracts. Art. 6. The law shall regulate individual labor contracts, for the purpose of guaranteeing the rights of workers.

Collective Labor Contracts and Agreements. Art. 7. The law shall recognize and regulate collective labor contracts and agreements. In the enterprises that are governed by these contracts and agreements, the provisions shall apply not only to the workers affiliated with the trade association that signed them, but also to the other workers who are or shall be employed in those enterprises. The law shall establish the procedure for extending collective contracts and agreements to all the activities in respect to which they were made and for widening the geographical sphere of their application.

Wages. Art. 8. Every worker has the right to earn a minimum wage, fixed periodically with the participation of the State and of workers and employers, which shall be sufficient to cover his normal home needs, material, moral and cultural, taking into account the characteristics of each type of work, the special conditions of each region and each job, the cost of living, the worker's relative aptitude, and the wage systems prevalent in the enterprises.

A minimum occupational wage shall also be set up for those activities in which this matter is not regulated by a collective contract or agreement.

Art. 9. Workers have the right to an annual bonus, in proportion to the number of days worked during the year.

Art. 10. Wages and social benefits, in the amount fixed by law, are not subject to attachment, with the excep-

tion of payments for support that the worker has been ordered by a court to pay. Wages should be paid in cash in legal tender. The value of wages and social benefits constitutes a privileged claim in the case of the bankruptcy of the employer, or a meeting of his creditors.
Art. 11. Workers have the right to a fair share in the profits of the enterprises in which they work, in the form and amount and under the conditions that the law provides.
Work Periods, Rest and Vacations. Art. 12. The ordinary effective work period should not exceed eight hours a day or 48 hours a week. The maximum duration of the work period in agricultural, livestock or forestry work, shall not exceed nine hours a day or 54 hours a week. The daily limits may be extended up to one hour in each case, provided that the work period of one or more days during the week is shorter than the indicated limit, without prejudice to the provisions with respect to a weekly rest period. The period for night work, and that for dangerous or unhealthful work, shall be less than the daytime work period.
The work period limitation shall not apply in cases of force majeure.
Overtime work shall not exceed a daily and weekly maximum.
In work that is by nature hazardous or unhealthful, the limit of the work period may not be exceeded by means of overtime work.
The laws of each country shall determine both the length of the intervals that are to interrupt the work periods when for reasons of health the nature of the tasks demands it, and the intervals that should come between two work periods.
Workers may not exceed the limit of the work period, whether working for the same or for another employer.
Night and overtime work shall give the right to extra pay.
Art. 13. Every worker has a right to a weekly paid rest period in the form established by the law of each country.
Workers who do not enjoy the rest period referred to in the foregoing paragraph shall be entitled to special pay for the services rendered on those days and to a compensatory rest period.
Art. 14. Workers shall also have the right to a paid rest period on the civil and religious holidays established by law, with the exceptions that the law itself may determine, for the same reasons that justify work on the weekly days of rest. Those who do not enjoy the rest period on these days have a right to extra pay.
Art. 15. Every worker who has to his credit a minimum of service rendered during a given period shall be entitled to paid annual vacations, on work days, the length of such vacations to be in proportion to the number of years of service. Monetary compensation may not be given in lieu of vacations, and the obligation of the worker to take them shall follow from the obligation of the employer to grant them.
Child Labor. Art. 16. Persons less than 14 years of age, and those who, having reached that age, are still subject to the compulsory education laws of the country, may not be employed in any type of work. The authorities responsible for supervising the work of such minors may authorize their employment when it is essential for their own maintenance, or that of their parents or brothers and sisters, provided that the minimum compulsory education requirements are met. The work period for those under 16 years of age may not be greater than six hours daily or 36 hours weekly in any type of work.
Art. 17. Night work and work hazardous or injurious to health is forbidden for persons under 18 years of age; exceptions concerning weekly rest set forth in the laws of the respective countries may not be applied to such workers.
The Work of Women. Art. 18. In general, night work is forbidden for women in industrial establishments, whether public or private, and in the work that is hazardous or injurious to health, except in cases where only the members of the same family are employed, in cases of force majeure that render it necessary, in cases where women perform administrative or responsible duties not normally requiring manual labor, and in other cases expressly provided for by law.
By industrial establishments and by work that is hazardous or injurious to health, are understood those so defined by law or by international labor conventions. Exceptions concerning weekly rest set forth in the laws of the respective countries may not be applied to women.
Tenure. Art. 19. The law shall guarantee stability of employment, due consideration being given to the nature of the respective industries and occupations and justifiable causes for dismissal. In case of unjustified discharge, the worker shall have the right to indemnification.
Apprenticeship Contracts. Art. 20. Apprenticeship contracts shall be regulated by law, to assure to the apprentice instruction in his trade or occupation, just treatment, fair pay and the benefits of social security and welfare.
Work at Home. Art. 21. Work at home is subject to social legislation. Home workers have the right to an officially determined minimum wage, to compensation for time lost because of the employer's delay in ordering or receiving the work, or for arbitrary or unjustified suspension of the supply of work. Home workers shall be entitled to a legal status similar to that of other workers, due consideration being given to the special nature of their work.
Domestic Work. Art. 22. Domestic workers have a right to the protection of the law with respect to wages, work periods, rest periods, vacations, dismissal pay and social benefits in general; the extent and nature of this protection shall be determined with due regard to the conditions and special nature of their work. Those who render services of a domestic nature in industrial, commercial, social and similar establishments should be considered as manual workers, and granted the rights to which workers are entitled.
Work in the Merchant Marine and Aviation. Art. 23. The law shall regulate the contracts of those serving in the merchant marine and in aviation, in accordance with the special character of their work.
Public Employees. Art. 24. Public employees have the right to be protected in their administrative careers by being guaranteed, so long as they perform their duties satisfactorily, permanent employment, the right to promotion and the benefits of social security. Such employees also have the right to be protected by a special court of administrative contentious jurisdiction and, in case penalties are imposed, the right to defend themselves in the respective proceedings.
Intellectual Workers. Art. 25. Independent intellectual workers and the product of their activity should be the subject of protective legislation.
The Right of Association. Art. 26. Workers and employers, without distincition as to sex, race, creed or political ideas, have the right freely to form associations for the protection of their respective interests, by forming trade associations or unions, which in turn may form federations among themselves. These organizations have the right to enjoy juridical personality and to be duly protected in the exercise of their rights. Their suspension or dissolution may not be ordered save by due process of law.
Conditions of substance and of form that must be met for the constitution and functioning of trade and union organizations should not go so far as to restrict freedom of association. The organization, functioning and dissolution of federations and confederations shall be subject to the same formalities as those prescribed for unions.
Members of boards of directors of trade unions, in the number established by the respective law and during their term of office, may not be discharged, transferred or given less satisfactory working conditions, without just cause, previously determined by competent authority.
The Right to Strike. Art. 27. Workers have the right to strike. The law shall regulate the conditions and exercise of that right.
Social Security and Welfare. Art. 28. It is the duty of the State to provide measures of social security and welfare for the benefit of workers.
Art. 29. States should promote and provide for recreational and welfare centers that can be freely utilized by workers.
Art. 30. The State should take adequate measures to ensure healthful, safe and moral conditions at places of work.
Art. 31. Workers, including agricultural workers; home workers; domestic workers; public servants, apprentices, even when not receiving wages; and independent workers, when it is possible to include them, have the right to a sytem of compulsory social security designed to realize the following objectives:
(a) To provide for the elimination of hazards that might deprive workers of their wage-earning ability and means of support;
(b) To reestablish as quickly and as completely as possible the wage-earning ability lost or reduced as a result of illness or accident;
(c) To supply means of support in case of the termination or interruption of occupational activity as a result of illness or accident, maternity, temporary or permanent disability, unemployment, old age, or premature death of the head of the family.
Compulsory social security should provide for protection of the members of the worker's family and should establish additional benefits for those of the insured who have large families.
Art. 32. In countries where a social security system does not yet exist, or in those in which one does exist but does not cover all occupational and social hazards, employers shall be responsible for providing adequate welfare and assistance benefits.
Art. 33. Every working woman shall be entitled to have leave with pay for a period of not less than six weeks before and six weeks after childbirth, to keep her job, and to receive medical attention for herself and the child and financial assistance during the nursing period. The law shall make it obligatory for employers to install and maintain nurseries and playrooms for the children of workers.
Art. 34. Independent workers have a right to the cooperation of the State in joining associations of social protection organized to give them benefits equal to those of wage earners. Persons who practice the liberal professions and are not employed by third parties have a similar right.
Supervision of Labor Conditions. Art. 35. Workers have a right to have the State maintain a service of trained inspectors, to ensure faithful compliance with legal provisions in regard to labor and social security, assistance and welfare; to study the results of such provisions; and to suggest the indicated improvements.
Labor Courts. Art. 36. Each State shall have a special system of labor courts and an adequate procedure for the prompt settlement of disputes.
Conciliation and Arbitration. Art. 37. It is the duty of the State to promote conciliation and arbitration as a means of obtaining peaceful solutions for collective labor disputes.
Rural Work. Art. 38. Rural or farm workers have the right to be guaranteed an improvement in their present standard of living, to be furnished proper hygienic conditions and to have effective social assistance organized for them and their families.
The State shall carry on planned and systematic activity directed toward putting agricultural development on a rational basis, organizing and distributing credit, improving rural living conditions, and achieving the progressive economic and social emancipation of the rural population.
The law shall establish the technical and other conditions, consistent with the national interest of each State, under which effect shall be given to the exercise of the right which the State recognizes on behalf of associations of rural workers, and on behalf of individuals suited to agricultural work who lack land or do not possess it in sufficient quantity, to be granted land and the means necessary to make it productive.
Art. 39. In countries where the problem of an indigenous population exists, the necessary measures shall be adopted to give protection and assistance to the Indians, safeguarding their life, liberty and property, preventing their extermination, shielding them from oppression and exploitation, protecting them from want and furnishing them an adequate education.
The State shall exercise its guardianship in order to preserve, maintain and develop the patrimony of the Indians or their tribes; and it shall foster the exploitation of the natural, industrial or extractive resources or any other sources of income proceeding from or related to the aforesaid patrimony, in order to ensure in due time the economic emancipation of the indigenous groups.
Institutions or agencies shall be created for the protection of Indians, particularly in order to ensure respect for their lands, to legalize their possession thereof and to prevent encroachment upon such lands by outsiders.
Reservation of the Delegation of the United States.

I

In view of the negative vote of the United States and of the reasons for which it was given, the United States, although firmly adhering to the principle of appropriate international action in the interests of labor, does not regard itself as bound by the specific terms of this Inter-American Charter of Social Guarantees."

Novena Conferencia Internacional Americana, Actas y Documentos, Vol. 6, Bogota 1953, pp. 239–246; *International Conferences of American States, Second Supplement, 1942–1954*, Washington DC, 1958.

INTER-AMERICAN CHARTER OF WOMEN'S AND CHILDREN'S RIGHTS, 1945. A Charter adopted on Mar. 7, 1945, by the Inter-American Conference on War and Peace (▷ Chapultepec Conference). The Charter proclaimed the full rights of women and children and also stated that a majority of American republics had not ratified, nor observed, the principles of the Declaration of the Rights of Women adopted in Lima, 1938, the General Declaration on the Rights of Women of 1939, the ILO convention and recommendations, the Pan-American Charter of the Child. The Charter recommended that States "ratify and effect the above mentioned declarations and conventions in the shortest possible time."

The History of Recognition of the Political Rights of American Women, Washington, DC, 1965.

INTER-AMERICAN CHILDREN's INSTITUTE. Instituto Interamericano del Niño, f. 1919, Montevideo. A specialized organization of OAS. Publ.: *Boletin*. Reg. with the UIA.

Yearbook of International Organizations.

INTER-AMERICAN COMMERCIAL ARBITRATION COMMISSION. An arbitration institution, f. 1939, Rio de Janeiro. Its membership is made up of national committees, commercial firms and individuals of all American Republics and it aims to establish an inter-American system of arbitration for the settlement of commercial disputes by creating branch organizations in each American Republic; to authorize the establishment of commercial arbitration tribunals; to arrange for the conduct of arbitrations and to recommend arbitration laws. Publ.: *Rules of Procedure*. Reg. with the UIA.

Yearbook of International Organizations.

INTER-AMERICAN COMMISSION OF WOMEN. Comisión Interamericana de Mujeres, f. 1928, Washington, DC. A specialized organization of the OAS. Publ.: *Noticiero – News Bulletin*. Reg. with the UIA.

Yearbook of International Organizations.

INTER-AMERICAN COMMISSION ON HUMAN RIGHTS. Est. by the OAS, 1960 on the basis of the ▷ American Declaration of the Rights and Duties of Man, 1948 in Washington DC.

R.L. BLEDSOE, B.A. BOCZEK, *The International Law Dictionary*, Oxford, UK, 1987.

INTER-AMERICAN COMMISSIONS AND COMMITTEES. The OAS or intergovernmental bodies, regional institutions in the UN system:
Ad Hoc Committee for Co-operation of OAS-IBRD-ECLA, Comité ad Hoc de Cooperación OEA-BIRD-CEPAL, f. in Dec. 1960 with the task of providing technical. assistance to the member governments of Latin American Free Trade Association, LAFTA.
Ad Hoc Committee of the Representatives of the Presidents of American States, Comité ad Hoc de Representantes de los Presidentes de Estados Americanos, created July 22, 1956 in Panama City

during a meeting of the Presidents of the American Republics on the initiative of the US President D.D. Eisenhower with the task of studying the work of the OAS for the purpose of making it "a more effective instrument of inter-American co-operation"; the Committee drafted a memorial, May 8, 1957. In 1967 the Committee prepared a meeting of the Presidents of the American Republics in Punta del Este.
Caribbean Commission, f. Oct. 30, 1946 in Washington by the governments of the USA, France, Great Britain and The Netherlands as a successor to the Anglo-American Caribbean Commission, which existed during World War II; has the task of co-ordinating economic and administrative policies on the non-autonomous territories in the Caribbean region.
Central American Commercial Commission, Comisión Centroamericana de Comercio, f. June 10, 1958 by the Treaty on Free Trade and Economic Integration of Central America and by the Convention on principles of import, Sept. 1, 1959, with the task of co-ordinating the customs integration introduced by the member states (Costa Rica, Guatemala, Honduras, Nicaragua, El Salvador). The Commission, together with the Permanent Secretariat, is a part of ODECA.
Committee on Central American Economical Co-operation, Comité de Cooperación Económica de Centroamérica, f. in Aug. 1952 as an organ of the UN Economic Commission for Latin America, ECLA; composed of the finance ministers of Guatemala, Costa Rica, Honduras, Nicaragua and El Salvador; Panama is an observer; the Committee initiated the integration of Central America.
Inter-American Demographic Committee, Comité Demográfico Interamericano, f. in Nov. 1943, headquarters Mexico City, by the governments of Argentina, Brazil, Colombia, the Dominican Republic, Peru and the USA.
Inter-American Emergency Advisory Committee for Political Defense IAEACPO, Comité Consultivo Interamericano de Emergencia para Defensa Política, f. Jan. 28, 1942 by the III Council of ministers of foreign affairs in Rio de Janeiro; members; Argentina, Brazil, Chile, Mexico, Uruguay, the USA and Venezuela; had the task of waging a common struggle against Nazi diversion; headquarters was Montevideo; dissolved in 1948.
Inter-American Committee for Agricultural Development, Comité Interamericano de Desarrollo Agrícola, f. in Aug. 1961, headquarters in Washington; since then is an organ co-ordinating work in the OAS, the UN Economic Commission for Latin America, International Bank for Development, and regional OAS bureaus.
Inter-American Juridical Committee, Comité Jurídico Interamericano, was formed in Jan. 1942 from the Inter-American Neutrality Committee with headquarters in Rio de Janeiro; in 1948 in accordance with arts. 68–71 of the OAS Charter, the Committee became a permanent organ of the Inter-American Legal Council. It is composed of nine jurists appointed for one year by the Inter-American Conference and deliberates for three months each year.
Inter-American Neutrality Committee, Comité Interamericano de Neutralidad, f. Sept. 23, 1939, headquarters Rio de Janeiro, by the I Council of ministers of foreign affairs in Panama as an organ of the General Declaration on Neutrality of the American Republics; changed its name in Jan., 1942 to the Inter-American Juridical Committee.
Special Co-ordination Committee for Latin America, Comisión Especial de Coordinación de América Latina, CECLA, f. Dec. 9, 1964 in Lima by the signatory states of the ▷ Alta Gracia Charter, Feb., 1964, as an autonomous organ of the Inter-

American Socio-Economic Council, CIES, with the task of formulating common positions in UNCTAD; as a rule plenary sessions of CECLA are held in the presence of the Secretary-General of UNCTAD.

Informe Annual del Secretario General de la OEA/OAS, Washington, DC, 1948–1984.

INTER-AMERICAN CONCILIATION GENERAL CONVENTION, 1929. A Convention signed on Jan. 5, 1929 in Washington by the governments of Bolivia, Brazil, Chile, Colombia, Costa Rica, Cuba, the Dominican Republic, Ecuador, El Salvador, Guatemala, Haiti, Honduras, Mexico, Nicaragua, Panama, Paraguay, Peru, the USA, Uruguay and Venezuela represented at the Conference on Conciliation and Arbitration, "desiring to demonstrate that the condemnation of war as an instrument of national policy in their mutual relations ... constitutes one of the fundamental bases of inter-American relations". The Convention is supplementary to the Treaty to Avoid or Prevent Conflicts between the American States, 1923. Art 1 states that,
"the High Contracting Parties agree to submit the procedure of conciliation established by this convention all controversies of any kind which have arisen or may arise between them for any reason and which it may not have been possible to settle through diplomatic channels."

It was not ratified by Bolivia and Costa Rica. The Convention came into force on Nov. 15, 1929 and was superseded by the ▷ Bogotá Pact 1948.

LNTS, Vol. 100, p. 399 and p. 404.

INTER-AMERICAN CONFERENCE FOR THE MAINTENANCE OF PEACE, 1936. Assembled Dec. 1–23, 1936 at Buenos Aires, with representatives of 21 American Republics; called on the initiative of the US President F.D. Roosevelt, on Jan. 30, 1936. The Conference discussed methods for the prevention and peaceful settlement of inter-American disputes; rules regarding the rights and duties of neutrals and belligerents; limitation of armaments, economic and juridical problems, and intellectual co-operation. President F.D. Roosevelt addressed the opening session of the Conference. The Conference adopted the ▷ Inter-American Peace Maintenance Convention, the ▷ Inter-American Convention on Co-ordination of Treaties; the ▷ Inter-American Treaty on Good Offices and Mediation, the ▷ Inter-American Treaty on the Prevention of Controversies, the ▷ Inter-American Cultural Convention, the Convention on the ▷ Pan-American Highway; the ▷ Inter-American Convention concerning Artistic Exhibitions and the Inter-American Convention on Interchange of Official Publications and Documents ▷ Inter-American Conventions on Interchange of Publications, 1902–1936.

"The Inter-American Conference for the Maintenance of Peace. Text of Addresses, Treaties, Acts and Resolutions", in: *International Conciliation*, No. 328, New York, March, 1937, pp. 195–289.

INTER-AMERICAN CONFERENCE ON WAR AND PEACE, 1945. ▷ Chapultepec Conference, 1945.

INTER-AMERICAN CONSULAR AGENTS CONVENTION, 1928. ▷ Consular Havana Convention, 1928.

INTER-AMERICAN CONSULTATIVE MEETINGS OF THE MINISTERS OF FOREIGN AFFAIRS. The meetings of government representatives of all American republics during World War

II. The supreme inter-American organ but since 1948 they are subordinated to the meetings of heads of government in the hierarchy of the OAS. The following were held:

1939–Panama City, Sept. 23–Oct. 3, 1939. It passed a common declaration on continental solidarity; a declaration on carrying out international activities in the spirit of Christian morality; the Panama declaration on neutrality of American states in the European conflict; a resolution on territories subjected to non-American states in Western Hemisphere; a resolution on economic co-operation and on organization of a consultative inter-American committee for economy and finances.

1940 – Havana, July 21–30, 1940. It passed a declaration on mutual assistance and defensive co-operation of American nations; a resolution on consultation procedure; the Havana Charter on the temporary administration of colonies and European property in America, and a convention on their temporary administration; and a resolution on economic and financial co-operation.

1942 – Rio de Janeiro, Jan. 15–28, 1942. It adopted a recommendation to break diplomatic, trade and financial relations with Japan, Germany and Italy; a resolution on economic consolidation of American states; a declaration on good-neighbor policy; a resolution on postwar problems; a resolution requiring the closing down of penal colonies of non-colonial states on American territory; a resolution on the rules of Consultative Meetings of the Ministers of Foreign Affairs; a resolution on the treatment of non-participants in the war; a resolution on subversive activity; a resolution on the Inter-American Law Committee; and recommendations on the Inter-American Defense Council.

The three war debates concluded with the ▷ Chapultepec Conference in 1945 and the Ninth American International Conference in 1948, which prepared an inter-American peace system, institutionalizing the meetings as an organ of the OAS.

1951 – Washington, Mar.–Apr. 17, 1951. Devoted to consolidation of "anti-communist solidarity of American states". Also, in Washington, at the invitation of the USA government, on Sept. 23/24, 1958, the First Special Conference of Ministers of Foreign Affairs of 21 American states was held, devoted to the evaluation of the world situation and to OAS problems.

1959 – Santiago de Chile, Aug. 12–18, 1959. It passed the Santiago de Chile Declaration and 17 resolutions.

1960 – San José de Costa Rica, Aug. 16–26, 1960. It considered accusations of the Venezuelan government against the Dominican Republic on acts of aggression.

1960 – San José de Costa Rica, Sept. 22–29, 1960. Called on the initiative of Peru and devoted to the defense of "American democratic principles against the endangering of peace from the outside by continental forces appearing in Cuba."

1962 – Punta del Este, Uruguay, Jan. 22–31, 1962. Devoted solely to the exclusion of the Revolutionary Government of Cuba from membership in the OAS. Moreover, in Washington DC, on Oct. 2/3, 1960, at the invitation of the US government, the Second Special Conference took place for discussion of the issue of nuclear rockets in Cuba.

1964 – Washington, DC, July 21–26, 1964. Called on the initiative of Venezuela. Most of the delegations resolved not to maintain any relations with Cuba to introduce economic sanctions, and to suspend all trade and transport communication with Cuba.

1965 – Washington, DC, May 6, 1965. The Third Special Conference took place, devoted to US armed interference in the Dominican Republic.

1967 – Montevideo, Jan. 1967. Devoted to ▷ representative democracy and to the preparations for the Fourth American Special Conference.

1967 – Buenos Aires, Jan. 24 to Feb. 1 and Feb. 26, 1967, devoted to preparations for the American Summit Conference in Punta del Este in April 1967; a matter of a prestige was solved as to whether a member state of the OAS, not maintaining diplomatic relations with another member state, could participate in an OAS ministers' conference held in the capital of the latter state. It was agreed that "the multilateral character of the conference . . . is independent of bilateral relations of any member state with the state playing host to the conference."

1967 – Washington, Sept. 22–24, 1967. Called on the initiative of Venezuela, which demanded sanctions against Cuba; the anti-Cuban resolution was passed with abstentions on the most controversial item of the resolution by Chile, Ecuador, Colombia, Mexico and Uruguay. For the first time no minister attended the conference but only permanent ambassadors to Washington (actual suspension of conferences of Ministers of Foreign Affairs was the effect of an internal OAS crisis and the breaking by many member countries with the anti-communist solidarity of American states, proclaimed at the Fourth Special Conference in 1951).

1973 – Bogota, Nov. 1973. A Conference of Ministers of Foreign Affairs of American states was held without US participation. It passed resolutions concerning Latin America only, and outlined problems for discussion with the USA. The scheduled meeting with the Secretary of State, H. Kissinger, took place on Feb. 23–24, 1974 in Mexico City, at the ▷ Tlatelolco Conference and brought the assurance given by the US Secretary of State that "in the future, the USA will not impose their political wishes on anyone or interfere in the internal problems of the continent."

1974 – the Inter-American Consultative Meeting of the Foreign Ministers took place in Atlanta.

1976 – the Consultative Meeting in San José, Costa Rica, agreed that the OAS member States could normalize relations with Cuba.

1981 – the Ministers of Foreign Affairs called on Ecuador and Peru to stop military operations in their border area.

1982 – the Ministers of Foreign Affairs called on Argentina and the UK to cease hostilities over the Falkland Islands/Malvinas.

1984 – Brasilia, Nov., 1984. A Conference of Ministers of Foreign Affairs of the OAS member States discussed the political situation in Central America and Latin America's huge foreign debts.

Pan-American Union Documentation of all Inter-American Consultative Conferences was printed in Washington, DC, 1939, 1940, 1942, 1955, 1959, 1960, 1961, 1962, 1964, 1967, 1973, 1974, 1976, 1984.

INTER-AMERICAN CONVENTION AGAINST THE ACTS OF TERRORISM, 1971.

The Convention to Prevent and Punish the Acts of Terrorism Taking the Form of Crimes Against Persons and Related Extortion that are of International Significance, signed on Feb. 2, 1971 at Washington, DC by Colombia, Costa Rica, the Dominican Republic, El Salvador, Honduras, Jamaica, Mexico, Nicaragua, Panama, Trinidad and Tobago, the USA, Uruguay, Venezuela; ratified by Costa Rica, the Dominican Republic, Mexico, Nicaragua and Venezuela. The main points of the Convention are as follows:

"Art. 1. The contracting states undertake to cooperate among themselves by taking all the measures that they may consider effective, under their own laws, and especially those established in this convention, to prevent and punish acts of terrorism, especially kidnapping, murder, and other assaults against the life or physical integrity of those persons to whom the state has the duty according to international law to give special protection, as well as extortion in connection with those crimes.

Art. 2. For the purposes of this convention, kidnapping, murder, and other assaults against the life or personal integrity of those persons to whom the state has the duty to give special protection according to international law, as well as extortion in connection with those crimes, shall be considered common crimes of international significance, regardless of motive.

Art. 3. Persons who have been charged or convicted for any of the crimes referred to in Art. 2 of this convention shall be subject to extradition under the provisions of the extradition treaties in force between the parties or, in the case of states that do not make extradition dependent on the existence of a treaty, in accordance with their own laws. In any case, it is the exclusive responsibility of the state under whose jurisdiction or protection such persons are located to determine the nature of the acts and decide whether the standards of this convention are applicable.

Art. 4. Any person deprived of his freedom through the application of this convention shall enjoy the legal guarantees of due process.

Art. 5. When extradition requested for one of the crimes specified in Art. 2 is not in order because the person sought is a national of the requested state, or because of some other legal or constitutional impediment, that state is obliged to submit the case to its competent authorities for prosecution, as if the act had been committed in its territory. The decision of these authorities shall be communicated to the state that requested extradition. In such proceedings, the obligation established in Art. 4 shall be respected.

Art. 6. None of the provisions of this convention shall be interpreted so as to impair the right of asylum.

International Legal Materials, Washington, DC, Vol. X, March 1971.

INTER-AMERICAN CONVENTION CONCERNING ARTISTIC EXHIBITIONS, 1936.

A Convention signed on Dec. 23, 1936 in Buenos Aires by all American Republics. It entered into force on Dec. 7, 1937.

OAS. *Inter-American Treaties and Conventions*, Washington, DC, 1971, p. 76.

INTER-AMERICAN CONVENTION CONCERNING THE DUTIES AND RIGHTS OF STATES IN THE EVENT OF CIVIL STRIFE, 1928.

A convention adopted by the Sixth International Conference of American States and signed on Feb. 20, 1928 at Havana. It reads as follows:

"Art. 1. The contracting States bind themselves to observe the following rules with regard to civil strife in another one of them:

First: To use all means at their disposal to prevent the inhabitants of their territory, nationals or aliens, from participating in, gathering elements, crossing the boundary or sailing from their territory for the purpose of starting or promoting civil strife.

Second: To disarm and intern every rebel force crossing their boundaries, the expenses of internment to be borne by the State where public order may have been disturbed. The arms found in the hands of the rebels may be seized and withdrawn by the Government of the country granting asylum, to be returned, once the struggle has ended, to the State in civil strife.

Third: To forbid the traffic in arms and war material, except when intended for the Government, while the belligerency of the rebels has not been recognised, in which latter case the rules of neutrality shall be applied.

Fourth: To prevent that within their jurisdiction there be equipped, armed or adapted for warlike purposes any vessel intended to operate in favour of the rebellion.

Art. 2. The declaration of piracy against vessels which have risen in arms, emanating from a Government, is not binding upon the other States.

The State that may be injured by depredations originating from insurgent vessels is entitled to adopt the following punitive measures against them: Should the authors of the damages be warships, it may capture and return them to the Government of the State, to which they belong, for their trial; should the damage originate with merchantmen, the injured State may capture and subject them to the appropriate penal laws.

The insurgent vessel, whether a warship or a merchant-man, which flies the flag of a foreign country to shield its actions, may also be captured and tried by the State of said flag.

Art. 3. The insurgent vessel, whether a warship or a merchantman, equipped by the rebels, which arrived at a foreign country or seeks refuge therein, shall be delivered by the Government of the latter to the con-stituted Government of the State in civil strife, and the members of the crew shall be considered as political refugees.

Art. 4. The present Convention does not affect obliga-tions previously undertaken by the contracting parties through international agreements."

LNTS, Vol. 134, 1932, pp. 45–63.

INTER-AMERICAN CONVENTION ON CO-ORDINATION OF TREATIES, 1936.

A Conven-tion adopted by the Inter-American Conference for the Maintenance of Peace in Dec., 1936 in Buenos Aires. The Convention to Co-ordinate, Extend, Assure and Unify Fulfilment of Existing Treaties between the American States was signed by 21 American Republics and came into force on Nov. 24, 1938. It was not ratified by Argentina, Bolivia, Costa Rica, Paraguay, Peru, Uruguay and Venezuela, and superseded by the ▷ Bogota Pact, 1948.

LNTS, Vol. 195, p. 229.

INTER-AMERICAN CONVENTION ON HUMAN RIGHTS, 1969.
▷ Human Rights American Convention, 1969.

INTER-AMERICAN CONVENTION ON RIGHTS AND DUTIES OF STATES, 1933.
A Convention adopted by the Seventh International Conference of American States, signed on Dec. 26, 1933 at Montevideo. It reads as follows:

"Art. 1. The State as a person of international law should possess the following qualifications: (a) a per-manent population; (b) a defined territory; (c) govern-ment; and (d) capacity to enter into relations with the other States.

Art. 2. The Federal State shall constitute a sole person in the eyes of international law.

Art. 3. The political existence of the State is indepen-dent of recognition by the other States. Even before recognition the State has the right to defend its integrity and independence, to provide for its conservation and prosperity, and consequently to organize itself as it sees fit, to legislate upon its interests, administer its service, and to define the jurisdiction and competence of its courts.

The exercise of these rights has not other limitation than the exercise of the rights of other States according to international law.

Art. 4. States are juridically equal, enjoy the same rights, and have equal capacity in their exercise. The rights of each one do not depend upon the power which it possesses to assure its exercise, but upon the simple fact of its existence as a person under international law.

Art. 5. The fundamental rights of States are not suscept-ible of being affected in any manner whatsoever.

Art. 6. The recognition of a State merely signifies that the State which recognizes it accepts the personality of the other with all the rights and duties determined by international law. Recognition is unconditional and ir-revocable.

Art. 7. The recognition of a State may be express or tacit. The latter results from any act which implies the intention of recognizing the new State.

Art. 8. No State has the right to intervene in the internal or external affairs of another.

Art. 9. The jurisdiction of States within the limits of national territory applies to all the inhabitants. Nation-als and foreigners are under the same protection of the law and national authorities and the foreigners may not claim rights other or more extensive than the nation-als.

Art. 10. The primary interest of States is the conserva-tion of peace. Differences of any nature which arise between them should be recognized pacific methods.

Art. 11. The contracting States definitely establish as the rule of their conduct the precise obligation not to recognize territorial acquisitions or special advantages which have been obtained by force whether this consists in the employment of arms, in threatening diplomatic representations, or in any other effective coercive measure. The territory of a State in inviolable and may not be the object of military occupation nor of other measures of force imposed by another State directly or indirectly for any motive whatever even temporarily.

Art. 12. The present Convention shall not affect obliga-tions previously entered into by the High Contracting Parties by virtue of international agreements.

Art. 13. The present Convention shall be ratified by the High Contracting Parties in conformity with their res-pective constitutional procedures. The Minister of Foreign Affairs of the Republic of Uruguay shall trans-mit authentic certified copies to the Governments for the aforementioned purpose of ratification. The instru-ment of ratification shall be deposited in archives of the Pan-American Union in Washington, which shall notify the signatory Governments of said deposit. Such notification shall be considered as an exchange of ratif-ications.

Art. 14. The present Convention will enter into force between the High Contracting Parties in the order in which they deposit their respective ratifications.

Art. 15. The present Convention shall remain in force indefinitely but may be denounced by means of one year's notice given to the Pan-American Union, which shall transmit it to the other signatory Governments. After the expiration of this period the Convention shall cease in its effects as regards the Party which denounces but shall remain in effect for the remaining High Contracting Parties.

Art. 16. The present Convention shall be open for the adherence and accession of the States which are not signatories. The corresponding instruments shall be deposited in the archives of the Pan-American Union which shall communicate them to the other High Contracting Parties."

LNTS, Vol. 165, 1936, pp. 19–43.

INTER-AMERICAN CONVENTION ON STATUS OF ALIENS, 1928.
A Convention regarding the Status of Aliens in the respective Ter-ritories of the Contracting Parties signed on Feb. 20, 1928 at Havana. It was adopted by the Sixth International Conference of American States. It reads as follows:

"Art. 1. States have the right to establish by means of laws the conditions under which foreigners may enter and reside in their territory.

Art. 2. Foreigners are subject as are nationals to local jurisdiction and laws, due consideration being given to the limitations expressed in conventions and treaties.

Art. 3. Foreigners may not be obliged to perform milit-ary service; but those foreigners who are domiciled, unless they prefer to leave the country, may be com-pelled, under the same conditions as nationals, to perform police, fire-protection, or militia duty for the protection of the place of their domicile against natural catastrophes or dangers not resulting from war.

Art. 4. Foreigners are obliged to make ordinary or extraordinary contributions, as well as forced loans always provided that such measures apply to the population generally.

Art. 5. States should extend to foreigners, domiciled or in transit through their territory all individual guaran-tees extended to their own nationals, and the enjoyment of essential civil rights without detriment, as regards foreigners, to legal provisions governing the scope of and usages for the exercise of said rights and guaranties.

Art. 6. For reasons of public order or safety, States may expel foreigners domiciled, resident, or merely in transit through their territory.

States are required to receive their nationals expelled from foreign soil who seek to enter their territory.

Art. 7. Foreigners must not mix in political activities, which are the exclusive province of citizens of the country in which they happen to be; in cases of such interference, they shall be liable to the penalties established by local law.

Art. 8. The present Convention does not affect obliga-tions previously undertaken by the contracting parties through international agreements."

UST, No. 815, 1930; *LNTS*, Vol. 132, 1932, pp. 303–311.

INTER-AMERICAN CONVENTIONS ON INTERCHANGE OF PUBLICATIONS, 1902–36.
Three conventions: The Convention relative to the Exchange of Official, Scientific, Literary and Industrial Publications, signed on Jan. 27, 1902 in Mexico City by 22 American Republics. It came into force on Aug. 5, 1902. It was not ratified by Argentina, Bolivia, Chile, Haiti, Paraguay, Peru, Uruguay. The Agreement on Publication of Unpublished Documents, signed on July 22, 1911 at Caracas, by Bolivia, Colombia, Ecuador, Peru and Venezuela. It came into force on Aug. 22, 1915. It was not ratified by Colombia.

Convention on Interchange of Official Publications and Documents, signed on Dec. 23, 1936 at Buenos Aires, by 21 American Republics. It came into force on Apr. 1, 1938. It was not ratified by Argentina, Bolivia, Chile, Cuba, Ecuador, Mexico, Peru and Uruguay.

LNTS, Vol. 201, p. 295; *OAS Inter-American Treaties and Conventions*, Washington, DC, 1971.

INTER-AMERICAN COPYRIGHT CONVEN-TIONS.
The following Inter-American Copyright Conventions have been formulated:

The first Convention on Literary and Artistic Property prepared the First South American Congress on Private International Law, in Mon-tevideo, 1888–89. It was ratified by Argentina, Bolivia, Paraguay, Peru and Uruguay.

The Convention on Literary and Artistic Copyrights, was signed on Jan. 27, 1902 in Mexico City by 17 American Republics but ratified only by Costa Rica, the Dominican Republic, El Salvador, Guatemala, Honduras, Nicaragua and the United States. It is known as the Mexico Copyright Con-vention 1902.

The Convention on Patents of Invention, Drawings and Industrial Models, Trade Marks and Literary and Artistic Property was signed on Aug. 23, 1906 in Rio de Janeiro by 19 American Republics but ratified only by Brazil, Chile, Costa Rica, Ecuador, El Salvador, Guatemala, Honduras, Nicaragua and Panama.

The Convention on the Protection of Literary and Artistic Copyrights was signed on Aug. 11, 1910 in Buenos Aires by the governments of the 21 American Republics, Members of the Pan-American Union. It was not ratified by Cuba, El Salvador and Venezuela. It is known as the Buenos Aires Copyright Convention 1910; revised by the Sixth International Conference of American States signed on Feb. 18, 1928 at Havana, which changed the arts. 2, 3, 5, 6 and 13bis as follows:

"Art. 2. In the expression 'literary and artistic works' are included books, writings, pamphlets of all kinds, whatever may be the subject they deal with and what-ever the number of their pages; dramatic or dramatico-musical works; choreographic and musical com-positions, with or without words; drawings, paintings, sculpture, engravings, lithographic, photographic and cinematographic works, or reproductions by means of mechanical instruments designed for the reproduction of sounds; astronomical or geographical globes; plans, sketches or plastic works relating to geography, geology, or topography, architecture or any other science as well as the arts applied to any human activity whatever; and, finally, all productions that can be published by any means of impression or reproduc-tion."

"Art. 3. The acknowledgement of a copyright obtained in one State, in conformity with its laws, shall produce its effects of full right in all the other States, without the necessity of complying with any other formality, provided always there shall appear in the work a statement that indicates the reservation of the property right, and the name of the person in whose favour the reservation is registered. Likewise the country of origin, the country in which the first publication was made, or those in which simultaneous publications were made, as well as the year of the first publication, must be indicated."

"Art. 5. The authors of literary and musical works have the exclusive right to authorize: (1) The adaption of said works to instruments that serve to reproduce them mechanically; (2) The public rendering of the same works by means of said instruments."

"Art. 6. The duration of the protection granted by this convention embraces the life of the author and fifty years after his death.

However, in case this duration period shall not be adopted by all the signatory States in a uniform manner, the period shall be regulated by the law of the country where the protection is requested and may not exceed the period of duration fixed by the country of origin of the work. Therefore, the signatory countries shall not be obliged to apply the provision of the preceding paragraph except in so far as their internal laws permit."

"Art. 13bis. The authors of literary or artistic works on disposing of them pursuant to their copyrights do not cede the right of enjoyment and of reproduction. They shall hold upon said works a moral right or inalienable control which will permit them to oppose any public reproduction of exhibition of their altered, mutilated or revised works."

The revision was ratified only by Costa Rica, Ecuador, Guatemala, Nicaragua and Panama.

An Agreement on Literary and Artistic Property was signed on July 17, 1911 in Caracas at the Bolivarian Congress by Bolivia, Colombia, Ecuador, Peru and Venezuela.

The Treaty on Intellectual Property was prepared by the Second South American congress on Private International Law, in Montevideo, 1939–40, ratified only by Paraguay and Uruguay.

The Inter-American Convention on the Rights of the Author in Literary, Scientific and Artistic Works was prepared by the Inter-American Conference of Experts on Copyright, in June 1946 and signed on June 22, 1946 at Washington, DC. It came into force on April 14, 1947. It was not ratified by Panama, Peru, the USA, Uruguay and Venezuela.

LNTS, Vol. 132, 1932, pp. 281–284; OAS, *Inter-American Treaties and Conventions*, Washington, DC, 1971.

INTER-AMERICAN COUNCIL OF COMMERCE AND PRODUCTION. An institution f. 1941 in Bogota. Consultative status with the ECOSOC and OAS. Organizes Hemispheric Insurance and Stock Exchanges Conferences. Publ. *Boletin Informativo* (monthly), *Libre Empresa* (bimonthly), *Informes y Documentos*. Reg. with the UIA.

Yearbook of International Organizations.

INTER-AMERICAN COURT OF HUMAN RIGHTS. Est. by the OAS, 1978 on the basis of the ▷ American Declaration of the Rights and Duties of Man, 1948, in San José de Costa Rica.

R.L. BLEDSOE, B.A. BOCZEK, *The International Law Dictionary*, Oxford, 1987.

INTER-AMERICAN CULTURAL CONVENTION, 1936. A Convention for the Promotion of Inter-American Cultural Relations, adopted by the Inter-American Conference for the Maintenance of Peace. It was signed on Dec. 23, 1936 at Buenos Aires by all American Republics and reads as follows:

"The Governments represented at the Inter-American Conference for the Maintenance of Peace, Considering that the purpose for which the Conference was called would be advanced by greater mutual knowledge and understanding of the people and institutions of the countries represented and a more consistent educational solidarity on the American continent; and That such results would be appreciably promoted by an exchange of professors, teachers and students among the American countries, as well as by the encouragement of a closer relationship between unofficial organizations which exert an influence on the formation of public opinion,

Have resolved to conclude a Convention for that purpose:

Art. 1. Every year each Government shall award to each of two graduate students or teachers of each other country selected in accordance with the procedure established in Art. 2 hereof, a fellowship for the ensuing scholastic year. The awards shall be made after an exchange between the two Governments concerned of the panels referred to in Art. 2 hereof. Each fellowship shall provide tuition and subsidiary expenses and maintenance at an institution of higher learning to be designated by the country awarding the fellowship, through such agency as may seem to it appropriate, in co-operation with the recipient so far as may be practicable. Travelling expenses to and from the designated institution and other incidental expenses shall be met by the recipient or the nominating Government. Furthermore, each Government agrees to encourage, by appropriate means, the interchange of students and teachers of institutions within its territory and those of the other contracting countries, during the usual vacation periods.

Art. 2. Each Government shall have the privilege of nominating and presenting to each other Government on or before the date fixed at the close of this Article a panel of the names of five graduate students or teachers together with such information concerning them as the Government awarding the fellowship shall deem necessary, from which panel the latter Government shall select the names of two persons. The same students shall not be nominated for more than two successive years; and, except under unusual circumstances, for more than one year. There shall be no obligation for any country to give consideration to the panel of any other country not nominated and presented on or before the date fixed at the close of this Article, and fellowships for which no panel of names is presented on or before the date specified may be awarded to applicants nominated on the panels of any other country but not receiving fellowships.

Unless otherwise agreed upon between the countries concerned, the following dates shall prevail:

Countries of South America, November 30th.

All other countries, March 31st.

Art. 3. If for any reason it becomes necessary that a student be repatriated the Government awarding the fellowship may effect the repatriation, at the expense of the nominating Government.

Art. 4. Each High Contracting Party shall communicate to each of the other High Contracting Parties through diplomatic channels, on the first of January of every alternate year, a complete list of the full professors available for exchange service from the outstanding universities, scientific institutions and technical schools of each country. From this list each one of the other High Contracting Parties shall arrange to select a visiting professor who shall either give lectures in various centers, or conduct regular courses of instruction, or pursue special research in some designated institution and who shall in other appropriate ways promote better understanding between the parties co-operating, it being understood, however, that preference shall be given to teaching rather than to research work. The sending Government shall provide the expenses for travel to and from the capital where the exchange professor resides and the maintenance and local travel expenses while carrying out the duties for which the professor was selected. Salaries of the professors shall be paid by the sending country.

Art. 5. The High Contracting Parties agree that each Government shall designate or create an appropriate agency or appoint a special officer charged with the responsibility of carrying out in the most efficient manner possible the obligations assumed by such Government in this Convention.

Art. 6. Nothing in this Convention shall be construed by the High Contracting Parties as obligating any one of them to interfere with the independence of its institutions of learning or with the freedom of academic teaching and administration therein.

Art. 7. Regulations concerning details for which it shall appear advisable to provide, shall be framed, in each of the contracting countries, by such agency as may seem appropriate to its Government, and copies of such regulations shall be promptly furnished, through the diplomatic channel, to the Governments of the other High Contracting Parties.

Art. 8. The present Convention shall not affect obligations previously entered into by the High Contracting Parties by virtue of international agreements."

LNTS. Vol. 188, 1938, pp. 125–149.

INTER-AMERICAN DEFENCE BOARD. An intergovernmental organization set up in 1942 in Washington as "a committee composed of army and navy technicians appointed by each state government of the American Republics with the task of performing studies and suggesting necessary means for the defence of the continent." On Mar. 8, 1945 the Inter-American Conference on War and Peace (▷ Chapultepec Conference) stated that the Board "proved to be a valuable organ", and decided that it should carry on its work as the "Inter-American defence body until the establishment of a permanent organ set up by representatives from the General Staffs of the armies of member states." Such a reorganization was prepared by the International American Conference on Mar. 30–May 2, 1948 in Bogota (Resolutions VI, VII and XXXIV) and entered into force in 1949. The OAS Consultative Committee on Defence of the OAS shares a common Secretariat with the Board. In 1951, the Fourth Consultative Conference of Foreign Ministers modified the Constitution of the Board, expanding its duties. As a rule it is headed by a high-ranking US officer. Apart from the Board, there is a Joint General Staff with the task of preparing general military plans for defending the military Inter-American sea communication lines and principles for uniform military services. The Board published a dictionary of military terms, *Diccionario de Términos Militares*, in Spanish, English and Portuguese, and also elaborated the standards on safeguarding information.

A. GARCIA-ROBLES, *El Mundo de la Postguerra*, Mexico, DF, 1946, Vol. II, pp. 385–390. *Novenas Conferencias Internacionales Americanas Actas y Documentos*, Bogota, 1953, Vol. VI, pp. 223 and 227; *La OEA 1954–1959*, Washington, DC, 1959, pp. 252–255.

INTER-AMERICAN DEVELOPMENT BANK, IDB. The intergovernmental financial institution est. on Apr. 8, 1959 in Washington, DC by an Agreement between all American Republics with "the purpose of contributing to the acceleration of the process of economic development of the Member Countries, individually and collectively." The Bank has the following functions: "to promote the investment of public and private capital for development purposes, to utilize its own capital, to encourage private investments, to co-operate with the Member Countries to orient their development policies toward a better utilization of their resources, to provide technical assistance."

The Agreement went into force on Dec. 30, 1959. Membership was expanded in 1972 and 1976 to include countries in other world regions.

In the Board are represented the Governmental finance institution of 24 regional countries: Argentina, Barbados, Bolivia, Brazil, Canada, Chile, Colombia, Costa Rica, the Dominican Republic, Ecuador, El Salvador, Guatemala, Haiti, Honduras, Jamaica, Mexico, Nicaragua, Panama, Paraguay, Peru, Trinidad–Tobago, the USA, Uruguay, Venezuela; and 16 non-regional states: Austria, Belgium, Denmark, Finland, France, the FRG, Israel, Italy, Japan, the Netherlands, Portugal, Spain, Sweden, Switzerland, the UK, and Yugoslavia. Publ.: *Annual Report.* ▷ Inter-American Bank. Total lending during the years 1960–1982 amounted to US $ 22,500 million; the loans for 1983–1986 were projected at US $ 13,000 million.

J. WHITE, *Regional Development Banks*, New York, 1972; *The Europa Year Book 1984. A World Survey*, Vol. I, p. 156–157, London, 1984.

INTER-AMERICAN DIPLOMATIC OFFICERS CONVENTION, 1928. A Convention adopted by the Sixth International American Conference, signed on Feb. 20, 1928 in Havana. It came into force on May 21, 1929. The main points read as follows:

"Art. 1. States have the right of being represented before each other through diplomatic officers."
"Art. 3. Except as concerns precedence and etiquette, diplomatic officers, whatever their category, have the same rights, prerogatives and immunities."
"Art. 12. Foreign diplomatic officers may not participate in the domestic or foreign politics of the State in which they exercise their functions."

LNTS, Vol. 155, pp. 265 and 267.

INTER-AMERICAN ECONOMIC AND SOCIAL COUNCIL, IA-ECOSOC. The Council was est. 1945 in Washington to supersede the Inter-American Financial and Economic Advisory Committee; since 1948 an organ of the OAS, composed of one representative from each member country, usually of cabinet rank, meets annually in different countries and promotes economic and social development.
A Permanent Executive Committee of the IA-ECOSOC was est. on Nov. 1963. A Secretariat service is provided by the OAS, Washington, DC. Members: all member states of the OAS. Belgium, Canada, France, the FRG, Guyana, Israel, Italy, Japan, the Netherlands, Portugal and Spain are observers.
In 1965 the IA-ECOSOC est. the Special Development Assistance Fund and in 1969 the Inter-American Export Promotion Center. Reg. with the UIA.

Yearbook of International Organizations.

INTER-AMERICAN ECONOMIC FUND. During the meeting of presidents of American republics in Panama, July 1956, the President of Venezuela made a proposal to set up an Inter-American economic fund to be made up of contributions equalling a percentage of the national budgets of every country on the continent. The OAS Council discussed the proposal on Sept. 13, 1956 and Sept. 19, 1957, but since no unanimous agreement was reached (US veto) the proceedings were suspended.

PAU, *La Organización de los Estados Americanos 1954–59*, Washington, DC, 1959.

INTER-AMERICAN ECONOMIC MEETINGS. Inter-American or Latin-American Economic Conferences, they include the following:
1939 – Inter-American Economic Conference took place in Nov. 1939 in Guatemala City with Ministers of Economy participating; it established bank and foreign currency policy for war-time and considered the Mexican proposal to call into being a Pan-American financial institution.
1945 – Inter-American Economic–Technical Conference in Washington, DC, called on the initiative of Mexico, according to the Economic Charter of the Americas 1945. In view of US opposition it did not take place.
1948 – The Ninth American International Conference resolved that "it is necessary to call without

delay the Inter-American Economic Meeting in order to study urgent economic problems of American States." It did not take place either.
During 1948 only regional economic conferences were held in Colombia, Ecuador, Panama and Venezuela, concluded with the signing of the ▷ Quito Charter.
1951 – The Economic Conference of Government Heads of Central American States concluded with passing of the ▷ San Salvador Charter, 1951.
1954 – An Inter-American Conference of Economic Ministers of the OAS on ports of Latin America.
1957 – The OAS Economic Conference, Aug. 15–Sept. 4, in Buenos Aires, called on the initiative of the ECLA, which provided the documents and technical service. Participants: all OAS member states took part, and as observers: Belgium, Canada, Czechoslovakia, Denmark, Finland, France, the FRG, Greece, India, Japan, the Netherlands, Norway, Poland, Portugal, Spain, Switzerland, Sweden, the UK and Yugoslavia, as well as representatives of international organizations. The Conferences debated a General Inter-American Economic Convention (which was not subsequently resolved), and problems of Inter-American trade and co-operation in the field of technology and transport. Some 44 resolutions and recommendations were adopted together with the Buenos Aires Economic Declaration.
1961 – Conference of Economic Ministers of the OAS in connection with the Alliance for Progress program. Proposed by the President of the USA. It concluded with the passing of the ▷ Punta del Este Charter.
1964 – A preparatory conference of economic ministers of Latin American states for the first UNCTAD session. It concluded with the ▷ Alta Gracia Charter.
1965 – The Second Inter-American Extraordinary OAS Conference at which the ▷ Rio de Janeiro Declaration was adopted.
1967 – A preparatory conference of economic ministers of Latin American states for the Second UNCTAD session, concluded with the passing of the ▷ Tequendama Charter.
1969 – Debate of the Special Commission for Latin American Co-ordination. It concluded with the adoption of an extensive economic and social program for Latin American states, called the ▷ Viña del Mar Charter.
Apart from the above, there were conferences for Latin American integration and routine economic and socio-economic conferences convened by the ECLA. In Mar. 1973 a Special ECLA Conference was held in Quito, at which a new development strategy for the development of Latin American states was elaborated.
1976 – The ▷ OAS General Assembly adopted resolutions concerning the US Trade Act of 1976 and transnational enterprises.
1977 – The OAS General Assembly adopted in Grenada resolutions on financial problems, energy crisis and foreign trade.
1984 – Jan. 13, the ECLA Conference in Quito adopted unanimously a common declaration of the 24 member States related to the ▷ foreign debts of Latin America.
In June 22–23, 1984 in Cartagena (Colombia) a meeting of foreign ministers and finance ministers of Argentina, Bolivia, Brazil, Chile, Colombia, the Dominican Republic, Ecuador, Mexico, Peru, Uruguay and Venezuela, representing 90% of foreign debts of Latin America, adopted a common appeal to the Western countries and to the World Bank, related to the critical economic and financial situation of Latin America.
On Sept. 13, 1984 in Mar del Plata a Conference of eleven finance ministers of the Cartagena Group.

Final Act of the OAS Economic Conference, Washington, DC, 1957; J.M. SIERRA, *Derecho Internacional Público*, Mexico, DF, 1963, pp. 89–90; G. GORDON-SMITH, *The Interamerican System*, London, 1966. 'Consensus in Cartagena', in: *Newsweek*, August 2, 1984; *The Europa Year Book 1984. A World Survey*, Vol. I, p. 191, London, 1984.

INTER-AMERICAN EXTRAORDINARY OAS CONFERENCES. The official name of meetings of OAS member states as provided for in Art. 33 of the OAS Charter. Between 1948 and 1984 three such conferences were held:
1964 – Washington, DC, Dec. 16–18, 1964. Formulated admission procedures. Participants: governments of Jamaica, Trinidad and Tobago attended as observers; Guyana and Belize were denied the status of observers as a result of opposition by Venezuela or Guatemala which claimed these territories; the conference adopted a resolution called "The Act of Washington, 1964", providing that any independent American states wishing to become members of the OAS should send a note to the General Secretary declaring willingness to sign and ratify the OAS Charter and abide by all commitments ensuing from OAS membership. The OAS Council decisions are made by two-thirds majority vote.
1965 – Rio de Janeiro, Nov. 17–30, 1965. Considered problems of significance to consolidation of the Inter-American System. Participants: Ministers of Foreign Affairs of 19 states and observers: Canada, Jamaica, Trinidad and Tobago. Among problems considered were: functioning of the international system of economic and social development on the continent; improvement of methods and instruments of pacific settlement of disputes; protection of human rights; strengthening of ▷ representative democracy on the continent; utilization of agriculture, industry and commerce, international rivers and lakes; activities of the Inter-American Peace Committee; adopted 30 resolutions, the major one (Res. No. 1.) called the Act of Rio de Janeiro 1965 acknowledged a need for change of the functional structure of OAS as defined in OAS Charter and Res. No. 2, called "Economic–Social Act of Rio de Janeiro 1965" determining priority of socio-economic issues in the Inter-American System;
1967 – Buenos Aires, Feb. 15–27, 1967, to prepare and adopt final text of amended OAS Charter; attended by 21 foreign ministers of member states who signed, Feb. 27, 1967, the reformed text known as the Protocol of Buenos Aires, 1967.

Annual Report of the General Secretary of the OAS, Washington, DC, 1965, pp. 7–8, and 1966, pp. 1–2 and 19–29; *La Crónica de la OEA*, No. 5, 1967, pp. 23–53.

INTER-AMERICAN FINANCIAL AND ECONOMIC COMMISSION. ▷ Inter-American Economic and Social Council, IA-ECOSOC.

INTER-AMERICAN FOOD FUND. A project, conceived by the Mexican government, published in 1965, suggesting that the spirit of solidarity among members of the OAS should manifest itself through voluntary contributions of food, medicines and other goods or services indispensable for a country threatened by earthquakes, floods, droughts, other calamities or conflicts of social character. The idea was formulated by Mexican President Gustavo Díaz Ordaz in his statement at the Congress on Sept. 1, 1965.

INTER-AMERICAN FORCES OF PEACE, IAFP. A multi-national interventional army planned by the OAS, empowered to take immediate action in case of a threat in whatever country of

Latin America "to the security of the interests of the continent" by aggression from outside or inside by international communism. The project was presented for the first time in Jan. 1962 at a conference of Ministers of Foreign Affairs of the OAS in Punta del Este by the Secretary of State of the USA, D. Rusk, but was rejected by the majority of states; it was then presented with the same result at subsequent conferences of the OAS. In 1965, on the initiative of the government of the USA, the Congress introduced an amendment to the law on US foreign aid, giving it the following interpretation: "Part of the funds can be used in each budget year for aid for the region of Latin America within the framework of the plan of regional defense. 25 million dollars can be used for Inter-American Forces of Peace, controlled by OAS."
In Oct., 1968 the Chief of US Forces Staff General W.L. Westmoreland, presented the project of Inter-American Forces of Peace in Rio de Janeiro during the Eighth Conference of American Military Forces, but the majority of states rejected it again.

Annual Report of the General Secretary of the OAS, Washington, DC, 1968.

INTER-AMERICAN HIGH COMMISSION. A financial institution created by the First Pan-American Financial Conference on May 29, 1919. It was in operation between 1915 and 1933 when it studied economic and financial problems of American states, it resumed activities on Nov. 15, 1939 as the Inter-American Financial and Economic Advisory Commission and on Mar. 8, 1945 became the Inter-American Economic and Social Council, IA-ECOSOC.

G. CONNELL-SMITH, *The Inter-American System*, New York, 1966.

INTER-AMERICAN INDIAN INSTITUTE. Instituto Indigenista Interamericano, f. 1940, in Patzcuaro, Mexico, by a resolution of the Fist Inter-American Congress on Indian Life. This resolution was incorporated into an intergovernmental convention for the Inter-American Indian Institute and signed by 19 American Republics. It was not ratified by Argentina, Costa Rica, Cuba and Venezuela. It came into force on Dec. 13, 1941. It has special agreements with the UN, UNESCO and the OAS. Organizes congresses: Patzcuaro 1940, Cuzco 1949, La Paz 1954, San Salvador 1955, Guatemala City 1959, Mexico City 1968, Caracas 1977. Publ.: *América Indígena* (quarterly in English, Portuguese and Spanish) and *Annuario Indigenista*. Reg. with UIA.

TIAS, Washington, DC, 1940; A.J. PEASLE (ed.), *International Intergovernmental Organizations*, 2 Vols., The Hague, 1961.

INTER-AMERICAN INSTITUTE OF AGRICULTURAL SCIENCES OF THE OAS. Instituto Interamericano de Ciencias Agrícolas. It was established by a Convention signed on Jan. 15, 1944 in San José de Costa Rica by 21 American Republics. It came into force on Nov. 30, 1944. An intergovernmental organization of all American republics, specialized agency of the OAS. Publ. *Turrialba* (quarterly), *Cacao* (quarterly), *Desarrollo Rural en Las Americas* (3 a year), *Boletín Bibliográfico Agrícola* (quarterly). Reg. with the UIA.

UNTS, Vol. 161, no. 489, *OAS, Inter-American Treaties and Conventions*, Washington, DC. 1971; *Yearbook of International Organizations*.

INTER-AMERICANISM. An international term denoting a US doctrine of the late 19th century calling for an Inter-American system as a new form of ▷ Pan-Americanism; opposite of Pan-Latin-Americanism.

INTER-AMERICAN MONETARY UNION. A Pan-American financial integration system designed by the USA and debated at the First International American Conference held in Washington in 1889/90. The Union's purpose was to "establish an international currency for all of the American Countries."

International Conferences of American Republics 1889–1926, Washington, DC, 1951, p. 32.

INTER-AMERICAN MUNICIPAL ORGANIZATION. An institution, f. 1938 in New Orleans by the First Pan-American Congress of Municipalities. Official relations with the OAS. Publ.: *A Municipal Review*. Reg. with the UIA.

Yearbook of International Organizations.

INTER-AMERICAN MUSIC COUNCIL. Consejo Interamericano de Música, est. 1956, under the aegis of the OAS. Members of the Council are: Argentina, Bolivia, Brazil, Canada, Chile, Colombia, the Dominican Republic, Guatemala, Jamaica, Mexico, Paraguay, the USA and Venezuela. Reg. with the UIA.

Yearbook of International Organizations.

INTER-AMERICAN NUCLEAR ENERGY COMMISSION, IANEC. An intergovernmental institution, est. 1959 by the OAS in Washington. It has the task of assisting member states in the peaceful use of nuclear energy. A meeting of representatives of member states takes place every two years.

Yearbook of International Organizations

INTER-AMERICAN PATENTS AGREEMENTS. The following agreements have been formulated:The First South American Congress on Private International Law, in 1888–89 in Montevideo, prepared the first Convention on Patents of Invention. It was ratified by Argentina, Bolivia, Paraguay, Peru and Uruguay.
The first Treaty on Patents of Invention, Industrial Drawings and Models and Trade-Marks, was signed on Jan. 27, 1902 at Mexico City by 17 American Republics and ratified by Chile, Costa Rica, Cuba, the Dominican Republic, Ecuador, El Salvador, Guatemala, Honduras and Nicaragua. It came into force on Aug. 6, 1902. A Convention on Patents of Invention, Drawings and Industrial Models, Trade-Marks and Literary and Artistic Property was signed on Aug. 23, 1906, at Rio de Janeiro by 19 American Republics. It was ratified by Brazil, Chile, Costa Rica, Ecuador, El Salvador, Guatemala, Honduras, Nicaragua and Panama. The Convention on Inventions, Patents, Design and Industrial Models was signed on Aug. 20, 1910, at Buenos Aires by 21 American Republics. It came into force on July 31, 1912. It was not ratified by Argentina, Chile, Colombia, El Salvador, Mexico, Peru and Venezuela.
The Agreement on Patents and Privileges on Invention was signed and ratified on July 18, 1911 in Caracas, at the Bolivarian Congress by Bolivia, Colombia, Ecuador, Peru and Venezuela.

OAS Inter-American Treaties and Conventions, Washington, DC, 1971.

INTER-AMERICAN PEACE COMMITTEE. An intergovernmental institution est. Dec. 4, 1940 in Washington, DC, by the Pan-American Union as The Inter-American Committee on Methods for the Peaceful Solution of Conflicts; under the present name from June 7, 1949 with new statutes ratified by the OAS Council, 1956. From 1967, in accordance with the revised OAS Charter, it is one of the permanent organs of the OAS in Washington, DC.

Inter-American Juridical Yearbook, 1949, 1956 and 1967; L. QUINTANILLA, "La Comisión Interamericana de Metodos para la Solución Pacífica de Conflictos", in: *Inter-American Juridical Yearbook*, 1948; Ch.G. FENWICK, "The Inter-American Peace Committee", in: *Americal Journal of International Law*, No. 43, 1949.

INTER-AMERICAN PEACE MAINTENANCE CONVENTION, 1936. A Convention for the Maintenance, Preservation and Re-establishment of Peace, adopted by the Inter-American Conference for the Maintenance of Peace and signed on Dec. 23, 1936, at Buenos Aires. It reads as follows:
"The Governments represented at the Inter-American Conference for the Maintenance of Peace,
Considering:
That, according to the statement of Franklin D. Roosevelt, the President of the United States, to whose lofty ideals the meeting of this Conference is due, the measures to be adopted by it "would advance the cause of world peace, inasmuch as the agreements which might be reached would supplement and reinforce the efforts of the League of Nations and of all other existing or future peace agencies in seeking to prevent war';
That every war or threat of war affects directly or indirectly all civilized peoples and endangers the great principles of liberty and justice which constitute the American ideal and the standard of American International policy;
That the Treaty of Paris of 1928 (Kellog–Briand Pact) has been accepted by almost all the civilized states, whether or not members of other peace organizations, and that the Treaty of Non-Aggression and Conciliation of 1933 (Saavedra Lamas Pact) signed at Rio de Janeiro) has the approval of the twenty-one American Republics represented in this Conference; Have resolved to give contractual form to these purposes by concluding the present Convention:
Art. 1. In the event that the peace of the American Republics is menaced, and in order to coordinate efforts to prevent war, any of the Governments of the American Republics signatory to the Treaty of Paris of 1928 or to the Treaty of Non-Aggression and Conciliation of 1933, or to both, whether or not a member of other peace organizations, shall consult with the other Governments of the American Republics, which, in such event, shall consult together for the purpose of finding and adopting methods of peaceful cooperation.
Art. 2. In the event of war, or a virtual state of war between American States, the Governments of the American Republics represented at this Conference shall undertake without delay the necessary mutual consultations, in order to exchange views and to seek, within the obligations resulting from the pacts above mentioned and from the standards of international morality, a method of peaceful collaboration; and, in the event of an international war outside America which might menace the peace of the American Republics, such consultation shall also take place to determine the proper time and manner in which the signatory States, if they so desire, may eventually cooperate in some action tending to preserve the peace of the American Continent.
Art. 3. It is agreed that any question regarding the interpretation of the present Convention, which it has not been possible to settle through diplomatic channels, shall be submitted to the procedure of conciliation provided by existing agreements, or to arbitration or to judicial settlement.
Art. 4. The present Convention shall be ratified by the High Contracting Parties in conformity with their respective constitutional procedures. The original Convention shall be deposited in the Ministry of Foreign Affairs of the Argentine Republic, which shall communicate the ratifications to the other signatories. The Convention shall come into effect between the High Contracting Parties in the order in which they have deposited their ratifications.
Art. 5. The present Convention shall remain in effect indefinitely but may be denounced by means of one year's notice, after the expiration of which period the Convention shall cease in its effects as regards the party which denounces it but shall remain in effect for the

remaining signatory States. Denunciations shall be addressed to the Government of the Argentine Republic, which shall transmit them to the other contracting States."

The additional Protocol relative to Non-intervention, read as follows:

"The Governments represented at the Inter-American Conference for the Maintenance of Peace,
Desiring to assure the benefits of peace in their mutual relations and in their relations with all the nations of the earth, and to abolish the practice of intervention; and
Taking into account that the Convention on Rights and Duties of States, signed at the Seventh International Conference of American States, December 26th, 1933, solemnly affirmed the fundamental principle that 'no State has the right to intervene in the internal or external affairs of another',
Have resolved to reaffirm this principle through the negotiation of the following Additional Protocol:
Art. 1. The High Contracting Parties declare inadmissible the intervention of any one of them, directly or indirectly, and for whatever reason, in the internal or external affairs of any other of the Parties.
The violation of the provisions of this Article shall give rise to mutual consultation, with the object of exchanging views and seeking methods of peaceful adjustment.
Art. 2. It is agreed that every question concerning the interpretation of the present Additional Protocol which it has not been possible to settle through diplomatic channels, shall be submitted to the procedure of conciliation provided for in the agreements in force, or to arbitration, or to judicial settlement.
Art. 3. The present Additional Protocol shall be ratified by the High Contracting Parties in conformity with their respective constitutional procedures. The original instrument and the instruments of ratification shall be deposited in the Ministry of Foreign Affairs of the Argentine Republic, which shall communicate the ratifications to the other signatories.
The Additional Protocol shall come into effect between the High Contracting Parties in the order in which they shall have deposited their ratifications.
Art. 4. The present Additional Protocol shall remain in effect indefinitely but may be denounced by means of one year's notice, after the expiration of which period the Protocol shall cease in its effects as regards the Party which denounces it but shall remain in effect for the remaining signatory States. Denunciations shall be addressed to the Government of the Argentine Republic which shall notify them to the other contracting States."

LNTS, Vol. 188, pp. 14 and 16, *International Conciliation*, No. 328, New York, March, 1937, pp. 221–222.

INTER-AMERICAN PLANNING SOCIETY.
Sociedad Interamericana de Planificación, f. 1956, Mexico DF. Consultative Status with ECOSOC. Agreement with the OAS. Publ.: *Journal*. Reg. with the UIA.

Yearbook of International Organizations.

INTER-AMERICAN POLICE CONVENTION, 1920.
A Convention signed on Feb. 29, 1920 at Buenos Aires by the Governments of Argentina, Bolivia, Brazil, Chile, Paraguay and Uruguay. It reads as follows:

"Art. 1. The Contracting countries permanently undertake to send one another particulars of:
(a) Attempts to commit or the committing of anarchical or similar acts, whether collective or individual, designed to overthrow the social order, and any other movements whatsoever which could be regarded as subversive or may affect the said social order;
(b) Newspapers, periodicals, pamphlets, pictures, prints, or handbills, or any other kind of publication connected with propaganda of the character referred to above, which may concern one of the Contracting Parties. The publications in question shall be forwarded with the information communicated;
(c) Legal or administrative measures connected with the prevention and suppression of the above-mentioned movements;
(d) Conspiracies to commit or the committing of offences against the ordinary law likely to concern the other Contracting Parties, the notification being accompanied by all data and information necessary for forming an opinion on the case;
(e) Individuals who are dangerous to society;
(f) Respectable persons who make a request to that effect; and
(g) Corpses of unknown persons, such information to be accompanied by finger-prints.
Art. 2. For the purpose of paragraph (e) of the previous Article, the following shall be regarded as dangerous persons:
(a) Any individual who has been proved to have participated more than once, as the offender or as an accessory before or after the fact, in offences against property or other offences of a similar character, and any person who has no legitimate means of support and lives with habitual offenders, or makes use of instruments or articles notoriously designed for committing offences against property;
(b) Any person who has been implicated on one occasion, as the offender or as an accessory before or after the fact, in a case of coining or forging securities or scrip;
(c) Any person who has been guilty of serious personal violence on more than one occasion;
(d) Any alien, or any national who has been abroad, participating in any offence against property or persons, should the manner in which the offence is committed, the motive or other circumstances, give reason to presume that the said person's past in the country from which he comes has been unsatisfactory;
(e) Persons who habitually and for purposes of gain engage in the traffic in women;
(f) Persons who habitually incite others to overthrow the social order by means of offences against property or persons or against the authorities;
(g) Persons who are habitual agitators or incite persons by coercion, violence, or force, to interfere with freedom of labour or to attack property or institutions.
Art. 3. The information referred to under (e), (f), and (g) of Article 1 shall, when the case requires, include: finger-prints taken in accordance with the Vucetich classification; parentage or personal particulars; a morphological description according to the "Province of Buenos Aires" system; information as to previous convictions and conduct; and a photograph. The finger-prints shall be reproduced on a card or slip of 20 × 9 cm., and the other information shall be supplied on sheets attached; on all of them the name and register number of the person to whom they refer shall be mentioned.
(a) The personal particulars shall include: surname and Christian names and aliases; nicknames; surnames and Christian names of parents whenever possible; nationality; province or department and place of birth; date of birth; civil status; profession, education, and duration of residence.
(b) The morphological description shall include special marks and scars, preferably those visible in ordinary life.
(c) Information as to previous convictions shall include proceedings taken against the person and sentences, and the category in which the individual is placed in criminal slang.
(d) Two photographs shall be taken of the face, one full-face and the other in profile, on 9 × 13 plates with a reduction to one-seventh of natural size according to the Bertillon system.
Art. 4. The exchange of information referred to in the preceding Articles shall take place whenever any Contracting Party has reason to suppose that the information might for any reason be useful to any other Contracting Party. Nevertheless, for the purpose of gradually compiling an International Information Register, a duplicate of the information shall always be sent to the Argentine Government, even when it does not concern the latter.
Art. 5. Information as to acts or persons connected with political offences and lawful labour movements involved in the struggle between capital and labour shall not be included in the said exchange of information.
Art. 6. The Contracting Parties shall acknowledge receipt of the information and in their turn supply information, if any exist at the receiving Office, with regard to the acts or persons in question; they shall always mention the register number of the said information.
Art. 7. The Contracting Parties shall inform each other as soon as possible of the departure or expulsion of the dangerous individuals referred to in this Convention, irrespective of their country of destination.
Art. 8. The Contracting Parties shall supply facilities and give their co-operation to the officials or agents of the police who have to watch or search for an offender or to carry out criminal investigations or other activities in connection with their official duties outside their country. The said facilities and co-operation shall consist in the fact that the police of the country to which application is made shall carry out all formalities and take all action which, within their legal and administrative powers, should or could be carried out if the offence or act in respect of which application is made had taken place within the territory; and with regard to the prosecution of offenders, the police shall take the necessary action to ensure that the person concerned is available until the request for extradition concerning that person has been made, so that it may be possible to detain or apprehend him.
Art. 9. In order to be able to apply for facilities and co-operation, the police officials or agents mentioned in the preceding Article must prove their identity and the duty with which they are entrusted by one of the following means:(a) A certificate or note from the Chief of Police of the capital of the Republic which makes the application;
(b) A similar document from any other official of the same service outside the capital whose signature is legalised or certified by the consul of the nation to which application is made;
(c) Failing such documents, any other document which, in the judgment of the authorities of the country to which application is made, is provisionally sufficient pending the obtaining of the necessary documents to attest the authenticity of the credentials presented or the identity of the person and the nature of the duties of the official making the application.
Art. 10. The Contracting Parties shall take steps to ensure that every respectable person shall be provided with an identity card or certificate made out in accordance with the dactyloscopic system; besides protecting its holder from possible annoyance, this document will be a useful source of personal information in many circumstances.
Art. 11. The absolutely confidential treatment of the information forwarded or exchanged is an essential condition of the present Convention, and its use shall be strictly limited to the police purposes defined in No. V of the Act of the Second Session of the Inter-Police Conference of 1905.
Art. 12. This Convention is of an administrative character, and the information and data to be exchanged in compliance with it, and all other obligations involved thereby, shall be restricted to those which are allowed by the laws and regulations of each country.
Art. 13. The minutes of he meetings held by the delegates shall be regarded as forming an integral part of the present Convention, and may be used to elucidate the intention and scope of its provisions. Similarly, and for the same purpose, the minutes of the Inter-Police Conference held at Buenos Aires in October 1905 shall also be incorporated in the present Convention.
Art. 14. The Governments of other countries not parties to the present Convention may accede to it by notifying any of the contracting Governments, which in its turn shall inform the other signatories.
Such accession shall not be prevented by the fact that the country acceding has adopted systems of personal description or identification different from those contemplated by the present Convention. In such case the provisions of Article 12 shall apply.
Art. 15. This Convention shall enter into force as the various Governments ratify it and communicate their ratification to the Contracting Parties.
Art. 16. The obligations laid down in the present Convention as between the Contracting Parties shall be carried out by the Chief of Police of the capital of each of them, who shall communicate direct with the Chiefs of Police of the other countries for all purposes mentioned in the present Convention."

LNTS, Vol. 127, 1931, pp. 444–453.

INTER-AMERICAN PRESS ASSOCIATION.
Sociedad Interamericana de Prensa, f. 1942, Miami,

Inter-American Telecommunications Agreements

USA. Consultative status with ECOSOC. Publ. *News*. Reg. with the UIA.

Yearbook of International Organizations.

INTER-AMERICAN RESEARCH AND DOCU-MENTATION CENTRE ON VOCATIONAL TRAINING. Centro Interamericano de Investigación y Documentación sobre Formatión Profesional CINTEFOR, est. Sept. 17, 1967 in Montevideo under the aegis of the ILO by an intergovernmental agreement of Argentina, Brazil, Chile, Costa Rica, Guatemala, Mexico, Panama, Peru, Trinidad and Tobago and Venezuela. Publ. *CINTEFOR Legislación y Documentación*. Reg. with the UIA.

Yearbook of International Organizations.

INTER-AMERICAN SPECIAL MEETINGS. Specialized institutions within the Inter-American system as envisaged in arts. 32, 83, 93 and 94 of the OAS Charter, 1954. They were the subject of Inter-American Conferences Commission, f. on June 20, 1962, by the OAS Council. Documents, archives and instruments of ratification are kept by the Pan American Union. The meetings held so far include in alphabetical order:

General Assembly of Pan-American Institute of Geography and History, f. in 1928 by Inter-American Conference.

Inter-American Conference on Agriculture, f. at Inter-American Conference 1928; sessions: Washington, DC, 1928; Mexico City, 1942; Caracas, 1945; Montevideo, 1950; Mexico City, 1960.

Inter-American Congress on Hygiene, f. in 1950 by American Sanitary Conference; first session held in Havana, 1952.

Inter-American Congress on Tourism, f. in 1938 by Inter-American Conference; sessions: San Francisco, 1939; Mexico City, 1941; San Carlos de Beriloche, 1949; Lima, 1952; Panama, 1954; San José de Costa Rica, 1956; Montevideo, 1958; Guadalajara, 1962; Bogota, 1965; Mexico City, 1969.

Inter-American Congress for Indian Life, f. in 1938 by Inter-American Conference; sessions: Patzcuaro, 1940; Cuzco, 1949; La Paz, 1954; Guatemala, 1959; Quito, 1964; Patzcuaro, 1968; Brasilia, 1972.

Inter-American Conference of Labor Ministers, f. in 1963 by OAS Council with the aim of promoting the program of the Alliance for Progress; held only one session in Bogota, May, 1963.

Inter-American Conference on Ports, f. in 1954 by Council of Ministers for Economy; session held in San José de Costa Rica, 1956 and in Mar del Plata, 1963.

Inter-American Conference for Preservation of Natural Resources, f. in 1954 by Inter-American Conference; first session held in San Domingo, 1956.

Inter-American Conference on Statistics, f. in 1947 by Inter-American Statistical Institute, but since Oct. 27, 1955 it has been associated with the OAS; sessions: Washington, DC, 1947; Bogota, 1950; Petropolis, 1955; Washington, DC, 1967.

Meeting of Copyright Experts, f. in 1951, first session in Washington, DC, 1952.

Meeting of Education Ministers, f. in 1943 on the initiative of Pan-American Union; sessions: Panama, 1943; Lima, 1956; Bogota, 1963; Buenos Aires, 1966.

OAS Economic Conference, f. at Inter-American Conference 1948. First and only session was held in 1957.

Pan-American Congress on the Child, f. in 1913; sessions: Buenos Aires, 1916; Montevideo, 1919;

Rio de Janeiro, 1922; Santiago de Chile, 1924; Havana, 1927; Lima, 1930; Mexico City, 1935; Washington, DC, 1942; Caracas, 1948; Panama, 1955; Bogota, 1959; Santiago 1964; Quito, 1968.

Pan-American Highway Congress, f. in 1923 by Inter-American Conference, sessions: Buenos Aires, 1925; Rio de Janeiro, 1929; Santiago de Chile, 1939; Mexico City, 1941; Lima 1951; extraordinary session in Mexico City, 1952; Caracas, Panama, 1957; Bogota, 1960; Washington DC, 1963; Rio de Janeiro, 1968.

Pan-American Sanitary Conference, f. in 1902 by Inter-American Conference; sessions: Washington, DC, 1902 and 1905, Mexico City, 1907; San José de Costa Rica, 1909/10; Santiago de Chile, 1911; Montevideo, 1920; Havana, 1924; Lima, 1927; Buenos Aires, 1934; Bogota, 1939; Rio de Janeiro, 1942; Caracas, 1948; Santo Domingo, 1950; Santiago de Chile, 1954; San Juan, 1958; Minneapolis, 1962; Washington, DC, 1966; Mexico City, 1970.

UPA, *Compilación de Datas: Conferencias Especializadas Interamericanas*, Washington, DC, 1963.

INTER-AMERICAN STATISTICAL INSTITUTE. An OAS institution, f. 1940, Washington, DC. Consultative Status with the ECOSOC and OAS. Publ.: *Estadistica* (monthly), *América en Cifras* (biennial), *Boletín Estadístico* (monthly). Reg. with the UIA.

Yearbook of International Organizations.

INTER-AMERICAN STATISTICS. A subject of research under the aegis of the OAS of the Inter-American Statistical Institute and of Inter-American Statistics Conferences, since 1952.

Estado actual de las estadisticas de cuentas nacionales en los Paises Latino-Americanos y sus problemas principales, CEPAL, Santiago de Chile, 1965

INTER-AMERICAN SUMMIT MEETINGS. Deliberations of the heads of government of the American states.

1956 – Panama City, July 21–22, 1956. A meeting on the occasion of the 130th anniversary of the Panama Congress, convened 1826 by Simon Bolivar. On the initiative of the President of the USA, D.D. Eisenhower, the chiefs of state resolved to create the Inter-American Ad Hoc Committee of Presidential Representation.

1963 – San José de Costa Rica, Mar. 18–20, 1963. A meeting of the President of the USA, J.F. Kennedy, with the heads of government of El Salvador, Guatemala, Honduras, Costa Rica, Nicaragua and Panama held to demonstrate the solidarity of the states of the Isthmus with the USA against Cuba.

1967 – Punta del Este, Uruguay, Apr. 12–14, 1967. A meeting of the heads of government of the 21 OAS member states (the President of Haiti was represented by a special ambassador); they approved the giving of priority to socio-economic problems in Latin America, and adopted a program of action in the area of economic integration of Latin America, which was announced in the ▷ Punta del Este Declaration, 1967.

PAU, *The OAS 1954–59*, Washington, DC, 1960; *Reunión de los Presidentes en San José de Costa Rica*, Washington, DC, 1963; *Reunión de Jefes de Estado Americanos, Punta del Este, Uruguay*, Washington, DC, 1967.

INTER-AMERICAN SYSTEM. Legal relations established for North, South and Central American states in the 19th and early 20th century. The institutionalization of the inter-American system began on Apr. 14, 1890, along with the establishment of the international Union of American Republics whose permanent office was the Trade

Office of American Republics in Washington, DC. renamed in 1910, the Pan-American Union. After World War I, the American states concluded a number of multilateral treaties relating to the inter-American system: the Gondra Treaty of 1923, the General Convention on Inter-American Conciliation of 1929, the Convention on the Rights and Obligations of the State of 1933, the Anti-War Treaty of 1933, the Declaration of the Principles of American Solidarity, called the Lima Declaration of 1938, the Declaration of American Principles of 1938, the Joint Declaration of Continental Solidarity of 1939, the declaration on the Preservation of International Activities within Christian Morality of 1939, the Declaration on Mutual Assistance and Defense among the Peoples of the Americas of 1941, and the Declaration on Good-Neighborly Relations Policy of 1942.

In Mexico City in 1945, the Chapultepec Act called for joint action in repelling aggression against American states and established machinery to enforce peace in the Western Hemisphere; it was later formalized by the Inter-American Treaty of Reciprocal Assistance. Co-operation also advanced in commercial and financial matters (e.g. the Inter-American Bank began operations in 1960), and the Ninth International American Conference of 1948 in Bogota established the Organization of American States, the OAS to promote hemispheric unity. Since 1960, a continuing problem for the Inter-American system was the establishment of a revolutionary government in Cuba, which led in Punta del Este to Cuba's expulsion from the OAS, with six states abstaining in the vote: Argentina, Bolivia, Brazil, Chile, Ecuador and Mexico. With the introduction in 1961 of the Alliance for Progress, a long-term plan for USA economic assistance to Latin America was attempted. The Declaration of the Presidents of America was signed, in 1967, in Punta del Este, Uruguay, expressing commitment to the creation of two common markets, the Central American Common Market CACM and Latin American Free Trade Association, LAFTA.

R.N. BURR, D. HUSSEY, *Documents on Inter-American Co-operation*, Vol. 1, 1810–1881, Vol. 2, 1881–1948, Philadelphia, 1955; *El Sistema Inter-Americano*, Madrid, 1966; G. CONNELL-SMITH, *The Inter-American System*, New York, 1966; B.J. GVOZDARER, *Evolutsya i Krizis Mezhamerikanskoy Sistemy*, Moskva, 1966.

INTER-AMERICAN TELECOMMUNICA-TIONS AGREEMENTS. At the Bolivarian Congress on July 17, 1911 in Caracas, Bolivia, Colombia, Ecuador, Peru and Venezuela signed the first Agreement on Telegraphs. The first Inter-American Conference on Electrical Communication, approved on July 21, 1924 at Mexico City the Inter-American Convention on Electrical Communications, signed by 15 Latin-American Republics, but ratified only by the Dominican Republic, Mexico, Panama and Paraguay. It came into force on July 1, 1926. The Inter-American Telecommunications Convention, signed on Sept. 27, 1945 in Rio de Janeiro by 21 American Republics, but ratified only by Brazil, Canada and Mexico did not enter into force.

The five Central American Republics, Costa Rica, El Salvador, Guatemala, Honduras, and Nicaragua signed on Apr. 26, 1966 at Managua the Treaty on Telecommunications; entered into force in Nov. 1966.

▷ Radio American Conventions.

CARNEGIE ENDOWMENT, International Legislation, Vol. 2, Washington, DC, 1924; *Tratados Públicos y Acuerdos Internacionales de Venezuela*,

441

I

Vol. 2, 1900–1920, Caracas, 1925; *Boletin Informativo de ODECA*, No. 37, Apr.–June, 1966.

INTER-AMERICAN TRADE MARK CONVENTIONS. The following conventions have been formulated:

The first Convention on Trade Marks prepared by the First South American Congress on Private International Law at Montevideo 1888–89, signed and ratified by Argentina, Bolivia, Paraguay, Peru and Uruguay.

The Treaty on Patents of Invention, Industrial Drawings and Models and Trade Marks was prepared by the Second International Conference of American States and signed on Jan. 27, 1902 at Mexico City. It came into force on Aug. 6, 1902.

The Convention on Patents of Intention, Drawings and Industrial Models, Trade Marks and Literary and Artistic Property was signed on Aug. 23, 1906 at Rio de Janeiro by 19 American Republics and ratified by Brazil, Chile, Costa Rica, Ecuador, El Salvador, Guatemala, Honduras, Nicaragua and Panama.

The Convention on the Protection of Trade Marks was signed on Aug. 20, 1910 at Buenos Aires by 21 American Republics. It came into force on July 31, 1912. It was not ratified by Argentina, Chile, Colombia, El Salvador, Mexico and Venezuela.

The Convention for the Protection of Commercial, Industrial and Agricultural Trade Marks and Commercial Names was signed on Apr. 28, 1929, at Santiago de Chile by 18 American Republics and ratified by Brazil, Cuba, Dominicana, Haiti, Paraguay, the USA and Uruguay. It came into force on Sept. 19, 1926; superseded together with the Buenos Aires Convention 1910 by the Washington Convention 1929.

The Washington General Convention for Trade Mark and Commercial Protection, with Protocol on the Inter-American Registration of Trade Marks, and Final Act of the Pan American Trade Mark Conference, was signed on Feb. 20, 1929 in Washington by 19 American Republics, and ratified by Colombia, Cuba, Guatemala, Haiti, Honduras, Nicaragua, Panama, Paraguay, Peru and the USA. It came into force on Apr. 2, 1930. The Convention established the Inter-American Trade Mark Bureau (Chapter II), and encompasses the Protection of Commercial Names (Chapter III), Repression of Unfair Competition (Chapter IV), and Repression of False Indications of Geographical Origin or Source (Chapter V).

LNTS, Vol. 124, p. 375; OAS, *Inter-American Treaties and Conventions*, Washington, DC, 1971.

INTER-AMERICAN TRAVEL CONGRESS. Congreso Interamericano de Turismo, f. 1939, Washington DC. A specialized organization of the OAS. Reg. with the UIA.

Yearbook of International Organizations.

INTER-AMERICAN TREATIES CODIFICATION. The subject of the Convention on Co-ordination, Expansion and Assurance of Implementation of Treaties concluded by American States, signed on Dec. 23, 1936 in Buenos Aires by the participating governments at the Conference on the Consolidation of Peace, whose objective was:

"to codify treaties denouncing wars and creating means of settlement of conflicts in a peaceful manner; particularly the Gondra Treaty of 1923, the Briand–Kellog Pact of 1928, the General Convention on Interamerican Conciliation of 1929, the General Interamerican Treaty on Arbitration of 1929, the Saavedra–Lomas Treaty of 1933, the Convention on maintenance, assurance and establishment of peace of 1936."

The Convention was signed with reservations by Argentina, Colombia, Paraguay and El Salvador;

ratified by: Brazil (Jan. 10, 1939), Colombia (Mar. 10, 1938) (with reservations), Cuba (Mar. 25, 1938), Chile (Aug. 18, 1938), Ecuador (Sept. 10, 1937), Salvador (Apr. 12, 1938) (with reservations), the USA (Aug. 25, 1937) (with reservations), Guatemala (Aug. 4, 1938), Haiti (Aug. 20, 1938), Honduras (Aug. 16, 1938) (with reservations), Mexico (Dec. 15, 1937), Nicaragua (Nov. 24, 1938), Panama (Dec. 7, 1938) and the Dominican Republic (July 1, 1937). Argentina, Costa Rica, Paraguay, Peru, Uruguay and Venezuela did not ratify the treaty. It came into force on Nov. 24, 1938 and it is still binding on the states that have not ratified the American Treaty on Peaceful Solutions; ▷ Bogota Pact, 1948.

A.S. DE BUSTAMANTE, *The Progress of Codification under the Pan-American Union*, Washington, DC, 1926; J.M. JEPES, *La Codificación del Derecho Inter-Americano y la Conferencia de Rio de Janeiro*, Buenos Aires, 1927; F.J. URRUTIA, *Le continent américain et le droit international*, Paris, 1928; *Tratados y Convenciones Interamericanos de Paz*, Washington, DC, 1961, pp. 52–58.

INTER-AMERICAN TREATIES CONVENTIONS. The first treaties convention was signed on Feb. 20, 1928 at Havana by 21 American Republics and ratified by Brazil, the Dominican Republic, Ecuador, Haiti, Honduras, Nicaragua, Panama and Peru. It came into force on Aug. 29, 1929.

The second was the Inter-American Convention to Co-ordinate, Extend and Assure the Fulfillment of the Existing Treaties, between the American States, adopted by the Inter-American Conference for the Maintenance of Peace, signed on Dec. 23, 1936 in Buenos Aires by 21 American Republics. It came into force on Nov. 24, 1938. It was not ratified by Argentina, Bolivia, Costa Rica, Paraguay, Peru, Uruguay and Venezuela; superseded by the ▷ Bogota Pact, 1948.

LNTS, Vol. 195, p. 229.

INTER-AMERICAN TREATY OF RECIPROCAL ASSISTANCE, 1947. A Treaty called also the Rio de Janeiro Treaty, with Final Act of the Inter-American Conference for the Maintenance of Continental Peace and Security, signed and ratified on Sept. 2, 1947 in Rio de Janeiro by all member states of the Pan-American Union. It came into force on Dec. 3, 1948. The text is as follows:

"In the name of their Peoples, the Governments represented at the Inter-American Conference for the Maintenance of Continental Peace and Security, desirous of consolidating and strengthening their relations of friendship and good neighborliness, and Considering:

That Resolution VIII of the Inter-American Conference on Problems of War and Peace, which met in Mexico City, recommended the conclusion of a treaty to prevent and repel threats and acts of aggression against any of the countries of America;

That the High Contracting Parties reiterate their will to remain united in an inter-American system consistent with the purposes and principles of the United Nations, and reaffirm the existence of the agreement which they have concluded concerning those matters relating to the maintenance of international peace and security which are appropriate for regional action;

That The High Contracting Parties reaffirm their adherence to the principles of inter-American solidarity and cooperation, and especially to those set forth in the preamble and declarations of the Act of Chapultepec, all of which should be understood to be accepted as standards of their mutual relations and as the juridical basis of the Inter-American System;

That the American States propose, in order to improve the procedures for the pacific settlement of their controversies, to conclude the treaty concerning the 'Inter-American Peace System' envisaged in Resolutions IX and XXXIX of the Inter-American Conference on Problems of War and Peace,

That the obligation of mutual assistance and common defense of the American Republics is essentially related to their democratic ideals and to their will to cooperate permanently in the fulfillment of the principles and purposes of a policy of peace;

That the American regional community affirms as a manifest truth that juridical organization is a necessary pre-requisite of security and peace, and that peace is founded on justice and moral order and, consequently, on the international recognition and protection of human rights and freedoms, on the indispensable well-being of the people, and on the effectiveness of democracy for the international realization of justice and security,

Have resolved, in conformity with the objectives stated above, to conclude the following Treaty, in order to assure peace, through adequate means, to provide for effective reciprocal assistance to meet armed attacks against any American States, and in order to deal with threats of aggression against any of them:

Art. 1. The High Contracting Parties formally condemn war and undertake in their international relations not to resort to the threat or the use of force in any manner inconsistent with the provisions of the Charter of the United Nations or of this Treaty.

Art. 2. As a consequence of the principle set forth in the preceding Article, the High Contracting Parties undertake to submit every controversy which may arise between them to methods of peaceful settlement and to endeavor to settle any such controversy among themselves by means of the procedures in force in the Inter-American System before referring it to the General Assembly or the Security Council of the United Nations.

Art. 3.(1) The High Contracting Parties agree that an armed attack by any State against an American State shall be considered as an attack against all the American States and, consequently, each one of the said Contracting Parties undertakes to assist in meeting the attack in the exercise of the inherent right of individual or collective self-defense recognized by Art. 51 of the Charter of the United Nations.

(2) On the request of the State or States directly attacked and until the decision of the Organ of Consultation of the Inter-American System, each one of the Contracting Parties may determine the immediate measures which it may individually take in fulfillment of the obligation contained in the preceding paragraph and in accordance with the principle of continental solidarity. The Organ of Consultation shall meet without delay for the purpose of examining those measures and agreeing upon the measures of a collective character that should be taken.

(3) The provisions of this Article shall be applied in case of any armed attack which takes place within the region described in Art. 4 or within the territory of an American State. When the attack takes place outside of the said areas, the provisions of Art. 6 shall be applied.

(4) Measures of self-defense provided for under this Article may be taken until the Security Council of the United Nations has taken the measures necessary to maintain international peace and security.

Art. 4. The region to which this Treaty refers is bounded as follows: beginning at the North Pole; thence due south to a point 74 degrees north latitude, 10 degrees west longitude; thence by a rhumb line to a point 47 degrees 30 minutes north latitude, 50 degrees west longitude; thence by a rhumb line to a point 35 degrees north latitude, 60 degrees west longitude; then due south to a point in 20 degrees north latitude; thence by a rhumb line to a point 5 degrees north latitude, 24 degrees west longitude; thence due south to the South Pole; thence due north to a point 30 degrees south latitude, 90 degrees west longitude; thence by a rhumb line to a point on the Equator at 97 degrees west longitude; thence by a rhumb line to a point 15 degrees north latitude, 120 degrees west longitude; thence by a rhumb line to a point 50 degrees north latitude, 170 degrees east longitude; thence due north to a point 54 degrees north latitude; thence by a rhumb line to a point 65 degrees 30 minutes north latitude, 168 degrees 58 minutes 5 seconds west longitude; thence due north the North Pole.

Art. 5. The High Contracting Parties shall immediately send to the Security Council of the United Nations, in conformity with Art. 51 and 54 of the Charter of The United Nations, complete information concerning the activities undertaken or in contemplation in the exercise of the right of self-defense or for the purpose of maintaining inter-American peace and security.

Art. 6. If the inviolability or the integrity of the territory or the sovereignty or political independence of any American State should be affected by an agression which is not an armed attack or by an extracontinental or intracontinental conflict, or by any other fact or situation that might endanger the peace of America, the Organ of Consultation shall meet immediately in order to agree on the measures which must be taken in case of aggression to assist the victim of the aggression or, in any case, the measures which should be taken for the common defense and for the maintenance of the peace and security of the Continent.

Art. 7. In the case of a conflict between two or more American States, without prejudice to the right of self-defense in conformity with Art. 51 of the Charter of the United Nations, the High Contracting Parties, meeting in consultation shall call upon the contending States to suspend hostilities and restore matters to the status quo ante bellum, and shall take in addition all other necessary measures to reestablish or maintain inter-American peace and security and for the solution of the conflict by peaceful means. The rejection of the pacifying action will be considered in the determination of the aggressor and in the application of the measures which the consultative meeting may agree upon.

Art. 8. For the purposes of this Treaty, the measures on which the Organ of Consultation may agree will comprise one or more of the following: recall of chiefs of diplomatic missions; breaking of diplomatic relations; breaking of consular relations; partial or complete interruption of economic relations or of rail, sea, air, postal, telegraphic, telephonic, and radiotelephonic or radiotelegraphic communications, and use of armed force.

Art. 9. In addition to other acts which the Organ of Consultation may characterize as aggression, the following shall be considered as such:
(a) Unprovoked armed attack by a State against the territory, the people, or the land, sea or air forces of another State;
(b) Invasion, by the armed forces of a State, of the territory of an American State, through the trespassing of boundaries demarcated in accordance with a treaty, judicial decision, or arbitral award, or, in the absence of frontiers thus demarcated, invasion affecting a region which is under the effective jurisdiction of another State.

Art. 10. None of the provisions of this Treaty shall be construed as impairing the rights and obligations of the High Contracting Parties under the Charter of the United Nations.

Art. 11. The consultations to which this Treaty refers shall be carried out by means of the Meetings of Ministers of Foreign Affairs, of the American Republics which have ratified the Treaty, or in the manner or by the organ which in the future may be agreed upon.

Art. 12. The Governing Board of the Pan-American Union may act provisionally as an organ of consultation until the meeting of the Organ of Consultation referred to in the preceding Article takes place.

Art. 13. The consultations shall be initiated at the request addressed to the Governing Board of the Pan-American Union by any of the Signatory States which has ratified the Treaty.

Art. 14. In the voting referred to in this Treaty only the representatives of the Signatory States which have ratified the Treaty may take part.

Art. 15. The Governing Board of the Pan-American Union shall act in all matters concerning this Treaty as an organ of liaison among the Signatory States which have ratified this Treaty and between these States and the United Nations.

Art. 16. The decisions of the Governing Board of the Pan-American Union referred to in Arts. 13 and 15 above shall be taken by an absolute majority of the Members entitled to vote.

Art. 17. The Organ of Consultation shall take its decisions by a vote of two-thirds of the Signatory States which have ratified the Treaty.

Art. 18. In the case of a situation or dispute between American States, the parties directly interested shall be excluded from the voting referred to in the two preceding Articles.

Art. 19. To constitute a quorum in all the meetings referred to in the previous Articles, it shall be necessary that the number of States represented shall be at least equal to the number of votes necessary for the taking of the decision.

Art. 20. Decisions which require the application of the measures specified in Art. 8 shall be binding upon all the Signatory States which have ratified this Treaty, with the sole exception that no State shall be required to use armed force without its consent.

Art. 21. The measures agreed upon by the Organ of Consultation shall be executed through the procedures and agencies now existing or those which may in the future be established.

Art. 22. This Treaty shall come into effect between the States which ratify it as soon as the ratifications of two-thirds of the Signatory States have been deposited.

Art. 23. This Treaty is open for signature by the American States at the City of Rio de Janeiro, and shall be ratified by the Signatory States as soon as possible in accordance with their respective constitutional processes. The ratifications shall be deposited with the Pan-American Union, which shall notify the Signatory States of each deposit. Such notification shall be considered as an exchange of ratifications.

Art. 24. The present Treaty shall be registered with the Secretariat of the United Nations through the Pan-American Union, when two-thirds of the Signatory States have deposited their ratifications.

Art. 25. This Treaty shall remain in force indefinitely, but may be denounced by any High Contracting Party by a notification in writing to the Pan-American Union, which shall inform all the Other High Contracting Parties of each notification of denunciation received. After the expiration of two years from the date of the receipt by the Pan-American Union of a notification, of denunciation by any High Contracting Party, the present Treaty shall cease to be in force with respect to such State, but shall remain in full force and effect with respect to all the other High Contracting Parties.

Art. 26. The principles and fundamental provisions of this Treaty shall be incorporated in the Organic Pact of the Inter-American System.

Reservation of Honduras:
The Delegation of Honduras, in signing the present Treaty and in connection with Article 9, section (b), does so with the reservation that the boundary between Honduras and Nicaragua is definitively demarcated by the Joint Boundary Commission of nineteen hundred and nineteen hundred and one, starting from a point in the Gulf of Fonseca, in the Pacific Ocean, to Portillo de Teotecacinte and, from this point to the Atlantic, by the line that His Majesty the King of Spain's arbitral award established on the twenty-Third of December of nineteen hundred and six."

Interpretation of the Pact was subject to a fundamental controversy between the USA and Latin American states raised by a statement made by the US State Department of Aug. 18, 1967, concerning American obligations arising from bilateral and multilateral defensive treaties concluded after World War II with 42 states:

"... In case of any of our bilateral treaties, rendering assistance to rebuff an armed attack is an individual matter and thus does not require verification and collective decision. As to the Treaty signed in 1947 in Rio de Janeiro, in keeping with its provisions each of the Parties renders assistance in face of attack."

The interpretation was defined by Mexico, Aug. 21, 1967, in a statement:

"... Consistently with the explicit text of the Rio de Janeiro Treaty no state may claim the right to defense by forces of another American state, unless it was called for."

The government of Ecuador said Aug. 22, 1967, that the US interpretation was

"extremely dangerous as in the XX century no state in the western hemisphere has been assailed from outside of the Continent, however, many of them have been victims of armed interventions made by the USA."

President O. Arosemena added:

"Latin American states are free, independent and sovereign and as such should solve their domestic problems by their own means."

LNTS, vol. 21, p. 71; *International Organization*, Vol. 2, 1947, p. 202; *El Día*, August 22 and 23, Mexico, DF, 1967.

INTER-AMERICAN TREATY ON COMMERCIAL TERRESTIAL LAW, 1940.
A Treaty prepared by the Second South American Congress on Private International Law, 1939–40 in Montevideo, and adopted and ratified by Argentina, Brazil, Colombia, Paraguay and Uruguay, and signed but not ratified by Bolivia and Peru.

M.A. VIEIRA, *Tratados de Montevideo 1939–1940*, Montevideo, 1959.

INTER-AMERICAN TREATY ON GOOD OFFICES AND MEDIATION, 1936.
A Treaty adopted by the Inter-American Conference for the Maintenance of Peace; signed by the governments of all American Republics Dec. 23, 1936 in Buenos Aires. It came into force on July 29, 1937. It was not ratified by Argentina, Bolivia, Paraguay, Peru, Uruguay and Venezuela; superseded by the Bogota Pact 1948. The Treaty established a system of election of mediators, chosen from among eminent citizens, whose job was to facilitate reference to a peaceful method of resolving a dispute.

LNTS, Vol. 188, p. 80; *CARNEGIE ENDOWMENT, International Conferences of American States, Supplement 1933–1940*; Washington, DC, 1940.

INTER-AMERICAN TREATY ON INTERNATIONAL COMMERCIAL LAW, 1889.
A Treaty prepared by the First South-American Congress on Private International Law, in 1888–89 in Montevideo. It was adopted and ratified by Argentina, Bolivia, Paraguay, Peru and Uruguay; and signed but not ratified by Brazil and Chile.

M.A. VIEIRA, *Tratados de Montevideo 1888–1889*, Montevideo, 1959.

INTER-AMERICAN TREATY ON THE LAW OF INTERNATIONAL COMMERCIAL NAVIGATION, 1940.
A Treaty prepared by the Second South American Congress on Private International Law, 1939–40, in Montevideo. It was adopted and ratified by Argentina, Bolivia, Paraguay and Uruguay and signed but not ratified by Brazil, Chile, Colombia and Peru.

M.A. VIEIRA, *Tratados de Montevideo 1939–1940*, Montevideo, 1959.

INTER-AMERICAN TREATY ON THE PREVENTION OF CONTROVERSIES, 1936.
A Treaty adopted by the Inter-American Conference for the Maintenance of Peace, signed by the governments of all American Republics on Dec. 23, 1936 in Buenos Aires. It came into force in July 1937. It was not ratified by Argentina, Bolivia, Brazil, Paraguay, Peru, Uruguay and Venezuela; superseded by the ▷ Bogota Pact 1948.

LNTS, Vol. 188, p. 58; *CARNEGIE ENDOWMENT, International Conferences of American States, First Supplement 1933–40*, Washington, DC, 1940; PAU, *Conferencias Interamericanas 1889–1948*, Washington, DC, 1953.

INTER-AMERICAN TREATY ON THE PROTECTION OF ARTISTIC AND SCIENTIFIC INSTITUTIONS AND HISTORIC MONUMENTS, 1935.
A Treaty also called the Roerich Pact was signed on April 15, 1935 at Washington and reads as follows:

"The High Contracting Parties, animated by the purpose of giving conventional form to the postulates of the resolution approved on December 16th, 1933, by all the States represented at the Seventh International Conference of American States, held at Montevideo, which recommended to 'the Governments of America which have not yet done so that they sign the "Roerich Pact" initiated by the "Roerich Museum" in the United States, and which has as its object the universal adoption of a flag, already designed and generally known, in order thereby to preserve in any time of danger all nationally and privately owned immovable monuments which form the cultural treasure of peoples', have resolved to conclude a Treaty with that end in view, and to the effect that the treasures of culture be respected and protected in time of war and in peace, have agreed upon the following Articles:

Art. 1. The historic monuments, museums, scientific, artistic, educational and cultural institutions shall be considered as neutral and as such respected and protected by belligerents. The same respect and protection shall be due to the personnel of the institutions mentioned above. The same respect and protection shall be accorded to the historic monuments, museums, scientific, artistic, educational and cultural institutions in time of peace as well as in war.

Art. 2. The neutrality of, and protection and respect due to, the monuments and institutions mentioned in the preceding Article shall be recognized in the entire expanse of territories subject to the sovereignty of each of the signatory and acceding States, without any discrimination as to the State allegiance of said monuments and institutions. The respective Governments agree to adopt the measures of internal legislation necessary to insure said protection and respect.

Art. 3. In order to identify the monuments and institutions mentioned in Article 1, use may be made of a distinctive flag (red circle with a triple red sphere in the circle on a white background) in accordance with the model attached to this Treaty.

Art. 4. The signatory Governments and those which accede to this Treaty shall send to the Pan-American Union, at the time of signature or accession, or at any time thereafter, a list of the monuments and institutions for which they desire the protection agreed to in this Treaty.

The Pan-American Union, when notifying the Governments of signatures or accessions, shall also send the list of monuments and institutions mentioned in this Article, and shall inform the other Governments of any changes in said list.

Art. 5. The monuments and institutions mentioned in Article 1 shall cease to enjoy the privileges recognized in the present Treaty in case they are made use of for military purposes.

Art. 6. The States which do not sign the present Treaty on the date it is opened for signature may sign or adhere to it any any time.

Art. 7. The instruments of accession, as well as those of ratification and denunciation of the present Treaty, shall be deposited with the Pan-American Union, which shall communicate notice of the act of deposit to the other signatory or acceding States."

▷ Roerich Pact.

LNTS, Vol. 168, 1936, pp. 290–295.

INTER-AMERICAN TREATY TO AVOID OR PREVENT CONFLICTS BETWEEN THE AMERICAN STATES, 1923. The Treaty, also known as the Gondra Treaty, was signed by 21 American Republics on May 3, 1923 in Santiago de Chile at the Fifth International American Conference, in the presence of president of Paraguay, M. Gondra, the initiator of diplomatic action, started in 1922, against the arms race with regard to land and sea forces on the American continent, and the author of the draft Treaty, entered into force on Oct. 8, 1924. The Gondra Treaty condemned "armed peace, which requires more land and naval forces than is needed for the internal security and sovereignty and independence of states"; it postulated that all conflicts and disputes which cannot be settled in a diplomatic way shall be submitted to special Standing Committees, seated in Washington and Montevideo, the detailed constitution of which was not defined until 1929, at the General Inter-American Convention on Conciliation. Most of the American Republics signed the Treaty in Santiago on May 3, 1923, only Brazil, Costa Rica, Peru, Salvador and Uruguay chose to wait. The treaty was,

however, ratified by all of them, with the exception of Argentina, between 1924 and 1931 (the first to ratify was the United States of America, the last Nicaragua). The Treaty has been suspended by the ▷ Bogota Pact 1948.

LNTS, Vol. 33, p. 36; *International Conferences of American States 1889–1928*, Washington, DC, 1931; PAU, *Tratados y Convenciones Interamericanos de la Paz*, Washington, DC, 1961, pp. 5–9.

INTER-AMERICAN UNIVERSITY. A subject of a Convention, signed on Oct. 4, 1943 in Panama City, at the First Conference of Ministers and Directors of Education of the American Republics, by all 21 American Republics, but ratified only by Venezuela, 1945.

CARNEGIE ENDOWMENT, *International Legislation 1922–1945*, 9 Vols., Washington, DC, 1947.

INTER-AMERICAN UNIVERSITY OF PUERTO RICO. A University f. 1912 in San German de Puerto Rico. Languages of instruction: Spanish and English. Publ. *Polygraph.*

UNESCO, *The World of Learning*, 1980.

INTER-AMERICAN WASHINGTON DECLARATION, 1973. A Declaration on the Principles Governing Relations among American states, adopted by the OAS General Assembly on Apr. 15, 1973, at Washington, DC. The text is as follows:

"Whereas:

At its third regular session the General Assembly has considered topics 9 and 10 of the agenda, which refer to the purpose and mission of the Organization of American States and to revision of the system of inter-American cooperation for development, with a view to improving it, thereby strengthening the action of regional solidarity in this field, among other ways by preventing acts or measures that serve unilateral positions or interests prejudicial to the objectives of cooperation;

The member states of the Organization are always prepared to respect and to enforce respect for the underlying principles of the regional system, among which are the prohibition of direct or indirect intervention by a state or group of states in the internal or external affairs of any other state, the self-determination of peoples, and juridical equality among states;

At its second regular session the General Assembly adopted Resolution AG(RES. 78(II–O)72) on 'Strengthening of the principles of non-intervention and the self-determination of peoples and measures to guarantee their observance', which solemnly reiterates 'the need for the member states of the Organization to observe strictly the principles of non-intervention and self-determination of peoples as a means of ensuring peaceful coexistences among them and to refrain from committing any direct or indirect act that might constitute a violation of those principles';

As laid down in Art. 34 of the Charter, 'The Member States should make every effort to avoid policies, actions, or measures that have serious adverse effects on the economic or social development of another Member State';

The Declaration on Principles of International Law Concerning Friendly Relations and Co-operation among States in accordance with the Charter of the United Nations, Res. 2625/XXV of the UN General Assembly, included the principles of non-intervention, self-determination, equality of rights among states, abstention from the use of force, and other intended to foster co-operation among states;

In recent years profound changes have taken place in international relations, in the direction of full cooperation among states for the sake of peace, and these relations should be strengthened within the context of international law;

It is desirable that the Organization of American States manifest the principles upon which relations among the member states should be conducted; and

It is therefore timely to make a declaration to that end, but subject to the standards and obligations of the Charter and the special treaties enumerated therein.

The General Assembly declares

(1) That in accordance with the principles of the Charter of the Organization, and especially with those of mutual respect for sovereignty, the self-determination of peoples, and the juridical equality of respect the principles of non-intervention and self-determination of peoples and the right to demand compliance with those principles by the other states.

(2) That, under the Charter, plurality of ideologies is a pre-supposition of regional solidarity, which is based on the concept of cooperation freely accepted by sovereign states, to achieve common objectives of maintenance of peace and understanding among them for the sake of their vigorous and dynamic development in the economic and social fields and in those of education, science, and culture.

(3) That plurality of ideologies in relations among the member states implies the duty of each state to respect the principles of non-intervention and self-determination of peoples and the right to demand compliance with those principles by the other states.

(4) That this declaration is made without prejudice to the standards and obligations of the Charter of the Organization, the special treaties mentioned therein, and Res. 78 of the second regular session of the General Assembly."

The Department of State Bulletin, No. 1770, May 22, 1973.

INTERAMPOL. Inter-American Police. An Inter-American police force proposed since 1961 by the US government which under US supervision was to carry out "co-ordinated actions against international communism." The plan was submitted for the first time at the Eighth Conference of the Ministers of Foreign Affairs of the American Republics held in Jan., 1962 in Punta del Este but was rejected by a majority of states; resubmitted on various occasions, it was partially realized through the subordination of the political police of military dictatorships. In subsequent years, the Interampol idea was linked with the project of ▷ Inter-American Forces of Peace. On Feb. 15, 1967 the minister of foreign affairs of Chile, G. Valdes, stated that:

"the states of Latin America do not believe it is proper for the nations of America to form one police or military force. We are against the idea of creating any organ whatsoever which would exert military pressure."

The US Under-Secretary of State for Inter-American affairs, C. Oliver, was of a different opinion, stating Mar. 6, 1968 in the Senate that the USA "aims at the strengthening of police forces and the intelligence services in Latin America", and in this connection the Inter-American Police Academy was established in Washington. The first integration of the political police took place in Central America, then in 1969/70 in Argentina, Brazil, Uruguay and Paraguay with financial, technical and instructional assistance from the USA.

Resumen de la VIII Reunión de los Ministros de los Relaciones Exteriores, Montevideo, 1962.

INTERATOMENERGO. International Economic Association for the Organization of Co-operation in Production, Deliveries of Equipment and Rendering Technical Assistance in Building Nuclear Power Stations, set up on Dec. 13, 1973 by the governments of Bulgaria, Czechoslovakia, Hungary, Poland, Romania, and the USSR. It came into force on Mar. 1, 1974.

W.E. BUTLER (ed.), *A Source Book on Socialist International Organizations*, Alphen, 1978, pp. 705–734.

INTERATOMINSTRUMENT. International Economic Association for Nuclear Instrument-Building established at the initiative of the CMEA Department for Peaceful Utilization of Nuclear Energy, on which an agreement was signed on Feb.

22, 1972 in Warsaw by Czechoslovakia, Bulgaria, the GDR, Hungary, Poland, and the USSR. The aim is to meet the demands of the signatories for equipment and installations of high-quality nuclear technologies corresponding to world standards. The association is an open organization with seat in Warsaw.

W.E. BUTLER (ed.), *A Source Book on Socialist International Organizations*, Alphen, 1978, pp. 656–679.

INTERBRAS. A joint name of state foreign trade companies in Brazil, founded 1976 to represent abroad the state oil company, Petrobras, and several hundred private producers of both raw material (coffee) as well as industrial manufactures.

INTERCHIM. International Branch Organization for Co-operation in Small-Tonnage Chemical Products set up within the CMEA by an agreement of the governments of Bulgaria, Czechoslovakia, the GDR, Poland, Hungary, and the USSR signed and the Statute adopted on July 17, 1969 in Moscow. The depository of the agreement is the GDR.

W.E. BUTLER (ed.), *A Source Book on Socialist International Organizations*, Alphen, 1978, pp. 408–426.

INTERCHIMVOLOKNO. International Economic Association for Chemical Fibers. A CMEA institution for branch co-operation in artificial fibers, est. on June 21, 1974 in Sofia.

W.E. BUTLER (ed.), *A Source Book on Socialist International Organizations*, Alphen, 1978, pp. 735–762.

INTERCONTAINER. An international agreement concluded in 1968 between shipyards of 12 countries on adoption of standardized sizes of 20-ton steel cases ▷ containers, admitted in international transport.

INTERCONTINENT. The name adopted by the world press to denote intercontinental areas which make up an integrated whole in terms of specific military or economic systems, eg. Euro-America of NATO or Euro-Asia of the Warsaw Treaty.

INTERCONTINENTAL BALLISTIC MISSILES. ▷ ICBM.

INTERCONTINENTAL WEAPONS. An international term since 1948 for the first US intercontinental bomber (USSR–1955) and for intercontinental ballistic missiles ▷ ICBM.

R. LEGER SIVARD, *World Military and Social Expenditures 1987–88*, Washington DC, 1987.

INTERCOSMOS. The name of a program of international exploration of space by the socialist states of the Warsaw Pact, institutionalized 1963. Its main organ is a Council which initiates the joint construction of exploratory artificial Earth satellites called Intercosmos and co-ordinates ground research. Intercosmos I was launched on Oct. 14, 1969 and investigated the short-wave ultraviolet and X-ray radiation of the sun and outer layers of the earth's atmosphere. Intercosmos II was launched on Dec. 25, 1969 and for 50 days and nights carried out experiments in the ionosphere. Intercosmos III was launched on Dec. 7, 1970 with the aim of studying the outer ionosphere. The research apparatus of the sputniks is the result of the co-operation of the industries of several socialist states, especially the USSR, GDR, Czechoslovakia and Poland. In 1978/79 cosmonauts from Czecho-

slovakia, Poland, the GDR and Bulgaria took part in Soviet space expeditions. In honor of the 500th anniversary of the birth of the great Polish astronomer, Nicholaus Copernicus on Apr. 19, 1973 in accordance with the program of co-operation of socialist countries in the field of exploring and utilizing outer space for peaceful purposes an artificial earth satellite, Intercosmos-Copernicus 500 was launched. The scientific apparatus mounted aboard was designed to investigate the radio waves of the sun.

W.E. BUTLER (ed.), *A Source Book on Socialist International Organizations*, Alphen, 1978.

INTERDEPENDENCE. An international term for reciprocal dependency between states or regions; in the atomic era global interdependence of all nations is a prerequisite for peace. In the last decade of the 20th century, the absolute majority of countries are economically interdependent. The USA for example was self-sufficient in the 1950's; in the 1960's foreign trade already accounted for more than 10% of its GNP, while in the 1980's that figure has risen to more than 20%; 40% of US farm products are exported and 70% of US industry is forced to compete with foreign industry.

The Final Act of the UNCTAD VII session in Geneva, July 9–Aug. 3, 1987 calls attention to the important factors of interdependence:

In view of the substantial and increasing interdependence in the world economy, both among countries and across the trade, money, finance and commodity sectors, national economic policies, through their interaction with the international economic environment, have become important factors influencing the development process. The more significant the country in terms of its economic weight, the greater is the effect of its policies on other countries. The structural characteristics of most developing economies leave them especially vulnerable to the impact of structural change and external shocks.

Interdependence among countries has been increasing as the growth of world trade has outpaced that of world output.

Furthermore, there has been a closer integration of the various sectors of the world economy . With the rapid diffusion of new technologies, the secondary and tertiary sectors have become more tightly integrated, as in the merger of many service activities with production processes.

In the financial sector, a number of recent developments have accentuated the dependence of many countries upon their trade sectors. These have included the progressive dismantling of controls over international capital movements, the increasingly close connections between domestic and international financial markets, facilitated by the revolution in information and communications technology, the rise in the importance of the procyclical movement of international lending, the decline in net financial flows, and the scale of debt-servicing burdens compared with domestic savings capacities.

The policies and measures delineated by the Conference in the different areas of its agenda, being interrelated, should be pursued in such a manner as to make their effects mutually reinforcing. The appropriate international forums should keep under review the interrelationships among these policies and measures, together with their implementation and the need to adopt and strengthen them in the light of changing circumstances. As a universal forum with a focus on trade and development, which also encompasses the interlinkages of a wide range of issues, UNCTAD can make a significant contribution to this process.

The constructive dialogue which took place at UNCTAD VII has been an important step in heightening awareness and sharpening perceptions of problems arising from the complex interactions among national policies adopted by governments, internationally accepted rules and disciplines, and the operation of markets. This dialogue should be continued in the intergovernmental machinery of UNCTAD so as to enhance these perceptions and thus assist in providing fresh impetus to policy formulation and to multilateral

cooperation for development. With this in mind, the Trade and Development Board should consider how best to strengthen its regular review of the interdependence of economic issues.

Many UNCTAD members despite opposition from some countries, proposed an international conference on money and finance for development with universal participation, with the aim of evolving a stable, effective and equitable monetary system.

UNCTAD VII Final Act, Geneva, 1987; *OECD, Interdependence and Co-operation in Tomorrow's World*, Washington DC, 1987; *Sollicitudo Reo Socialis*. Encyclical letter of the Supreme Pontiff John Paul II for the Twentieth Anniversary of Populorum Progressio, London, 1988, p. 77.

INTERDEPENDENT WORLD. An international term since the 1980's propagated by the International Commission of Jurists, ICJ.

S.S. RAMPHAL, "Justice World-Wide: The Rule of Law in an Interdependent World", in: *IC Newsletter*, No. 34, 1987.

INTERDICTION. An international term for depriving a person of his legal capacities due to minor age or, if mature, due to mental illness or mental retardation. Subject of international convention of July 1905, the date of signing at the first Hague International Conference on Private Law of the Convention on Interdiction and Other Patronage Decisions. The Convention rules that in court proceedings on the interdiction of a foreigner, his homeland laws should be applied parallel to the laws in force in the place of his stay (Art. 69).

INTERELEKTRO. International Organization for Economic and Scientific–Technical Co-operation in the Electrical Engineering Industry, set up Sept. 13, 1973 in Moscow by Bulgaria, Czechoslovakia, the GDR, Poland, Romania, Hungary and the USSR with the aim of co-ordinating joint forecasting of development, demand, production and sales, production plans, joint planning of particular kinds of products; long-range and current co-ordination of investment, streamlining of scientific –technological co-operation, unification and normalization projects; headquarters Moscow.

W.E. BUTLER (ed.), *A Source Book on Socialist International Organizations*, Alphen, 1978, pp. 427–441.

INTERELEKTROTEST. International Organization for Co-operation in Large Capacity and High Voltage Experimental Laboratories set up by an Agreement on Co-operation of Large Capacity and High Voltage Experimental Laboratories, signed on Oct. 18, 1973 at Brno by Bulgaria, Czechoslovakia, the GDR, Hungary, Poland, Romania, the USSR and Yugoslavia.

W.E. BUTLER (ed.), *A Source Book on Socialist International Organizations*, Alphen, 1978, pp. 864–871.

INTEREST GROUPS. ▷ Pressure Groups.

INTEREST RATE. An international term for charge for the use of money; object of religious (interest charge, usury) condemnations and administrative limitations (legal low interest rates, illegal usury rates). In the 1980's an international problem in relation to ▷ foreign debts. In May 1986 the ▷ Group of Five Finance Ministers and Central Bankers have helped to change the pattern of exchange rates and to lower interest rates on an 'orderly and non-inflationary basis'.

See also ▷ Group of Seven.

J. FISHER, *Interest Rate*, London, 1930; J.M. KEYNES, *General Theory of Employment, Interest, and*

Money, London 1936; KEESING's *Record of World Events*, 1987, No. 1.

INTERFLORA. An international organization, reg. with the UIA, f. 1946 in Zurich, represents retail florists and enables them to send flowers anywhere in the world through three regional bodies: Fleurop (Europe), Interflora (UK) and Transworld Delivery Association. ▷ Flora.

Yearbook of International Organizations.

INTERGOVERNMENTAL AGENCIES. ▷ Specialized agencies within the UN system.

INTERGU. International Copyright Society, Sociètè Internationale pour la droit d'auteur, f. 1954 in West Berlin. The acronym from German: Internationale Gesellschaft für Urheberrecht. A non-governmental organization concerned with the scope and adequate protection of the rights of authors, composers and other copyrights owners and with the introduction or adaption of modern copyright legislation around the world. Consultative Status: ECOSOC, UNESCO, WIPO. Publ.: *INTERGU Jahrbuch*

INTERIOR SEA. A sea area belonging to one or more states, e.g. the Caspian Sea. A controversial issue raised by an English lawyer of the 17th century, J. Seldon, the author of a treatise *Mare clausum seu de dominio maris.* (The closed sea or Of superiority at sea) opposing the doctrine of H. Grotius on the freedom of seas. The doctrine of Grotius prevailed in issues relating to the international law of the sea.

R. LAPIDITH. *Les détroits en droit international,* Paris, 1972, pp. 64–65.

INTERLAINE. The official abbreviation of the Committee for the Wool Industries of the EEC.

INTERLIGHTER. An international interland shipping enterprise, est. in May 1978 by the governments of Bulgaria, Czechoslovakia, Hungary, and the USSR, seat in Budapest. The first common organization of transport on the Danube by the socialist states, open for other countries and foreign firms.

Recueil de documents, Warsaw, May, 1978.

INTERLINGUE. One of the artificial international languages; also called *Latina sine flexione* (Latin without inflection), developed by the Italian mathematician G. Peano, used i.a. in international astronomical publications; subject of organized international co-operation.

Organization reg. with the UIA:

Interlingue Institute, est. 1928, Cheseaux, Switzerland.

Yearbook of International Organizations.

INTERMEDIATE NUCLEAR FORCES, INF. An international military term for missiles with a range from 1000 to 5500 km defined in the USA–USSR arms control negotiations of the mid 1980's, called also Theatre Nuclear Forces, TNF or Long-Range or Short-Range Intermediate Nuclear Forces, LRINF or SRINF (▷ Double Zero Option).

M.R. GORDON, "Dateline Washington: INF: A Hollow Victory", in: *Foreign Policy*, Fall, 1987; D. ROBERTSON, *Guide to Modern Defense and Strategy*, Detroit, 1988.

INTERMEDIATE-RANGE BALLISTIC MISSILE, IRBM. An international military term for a ballistic missile of the ▷ ICBM type but with a shorter range of about 1,000 km.

D. ROBERTSON, *Guide to Modern Defense and Strategy*, Detroit, 1988.

INTERMETAL. A CMEA-intergovernmental organization of Bulgaria, Czechoslovakia, GDR, Hungary, Poland and the USSR for the purpose of co-ordinating production, development and co-operation in the iron and steel industry, est. by an agreement (with annexed Charter of the Organization), signed on July 15, 1964 in Moscow. It came into force on Nov. 2, 1964. Headquarters Budapest.

UNTS, Vol. 610, op. 152 and 162; W.E. BUTLER (ed.), *A Source Book on Socialist International Organizations*, Alphen, 1978, pp. 387–407.

INTERNAL CURRENCY. A currency performing monetary functions only within the confines of the state in which it was issued, officially unexchangeable and not quoted on foreign money markets. In exchange with foreign countries it is only a means of accounting in non-currency settlement of accounts.

INTERNAL EXPORT. An international term for sale at home of imported goods and domestic goods from export production at export prices for convertible currencies flowing from abroad and foreign currency existing at home; employed mainly in Warsaw Pact countries and some other countries with foreign exchange control.

INTERNAL WATERS. An international term for the waters on the landward side of the ▷ territorial sea.

See also ▷ Sea Law Convention, 1982 (Art. 8)

R.L. BLEDSOE, B.A. BOCZEK, *The International Law Dictionary*, Oxford, 1987.

INTERNATIONAL. The International, commonly adopted name by the international workers' movement for any of a succession of international socialist and communist organizations of the 19th and 20th century; inspired by the ▷ Communist Manifesto of 1848; institutionalized by the ▷ International Working Men's Association, founded in London, on Sept. 28th, 1864, called the First International.

The Second International became in 1889 the ▷ Socialist International, and in 1919 the Third International called ▷ Komintern. It was dissolved in 1943. The traditions of the Third International were continued in the years 1947–56, the ▷ Informbiuro, called Kominform. The "Two and Half" International was called in 1921 the International Community of Socialist Parties, an association of 13 European Social Democratic Parties which left the Socialist International and did not join the Communist Third International. In 1923 the "Two and Half" International joined the Socialist International.

The Fourth International was organized in 1938 by the followers of the views of L.D. Trotsky and other communist activists expelled in the years 1928–38 from the Komintern.

A hymn of the world proletariat was written 1871 by the French poet Eugene Pottier (1816–1887) with music by the French composer Adolf de Geyter (1827–1888) with the title *L'internationale*. It was translated into the majority of the world's languages. In the years 1921–44 it was the official national anthem of the USSR; it is sung during demonstrations and workers' congresses and at international meetings of both communist and socialist workers' parties.

ARDEL ROSAL, *Los Congresos Obreros Internacionales*, 2 Vols., Mexico, DF, 1958–64; J. DEGRAS (ed.), *The Communist International 1919–1943*, 3 Vols, London, 1956–1965; W.S. SWORAKOWSKI, *The*

Communist International and Its Front Organizations, Stanford, 1965.

INTERNATIONAL ACADEMY OF POLITICAL SCIENCE AND CONSTITUTIONAL HISTORY. Académie internationale de science politique et d'histoire constitutionnelle, f. 1936 in Paris as one of the institutes of the Sorbonne (Université de Paris). The present name was adopted in 1949 with the status of an independent academy whose members are political scientists of different nationality. Membership limited to 100. Publ.: *Revue d'histoire Politique et Constitutionnelle, Revue Internationale des Doctrines et Institutions.* Reg. with the UIA.

Yearbook of International Organizations.

INTERNATIONAL AGREEMENT. An international law term defined by Polish scientist A. Klafkowski: any interstate understanding which comes under and is regulated by international law is called an international agreement. This distinguishes international agreements from agreements concluded by states under law of one of the parties concerned, or from agreements in which the parties state the terms of internal legislation decisive for the character of the particular agreement. International agreements are the main source for international law, both bilateral and multilateral agreements. International agreements are limited to the extent they do not impose obligations on or vest rights in third parties (*pacta tertiis nec nocent prosunt*).

A. KLAFKOWSKI, *Prawo miedzynarodowe publiczne* (Public International Law), Warszawa, 1972; G.W. BAER (ed.), *International Agreements, 1918–1945.* A guide to research and research material. Wilmington, Del., 1981.

INTERNATIONAL AMERICAN ACADEMY OF COMPARATIVE AND INTERNATIONAL LAW. The Academy was f. in 1938 in Havana by the Inter-American Bar Association, with the purpose of promoting research, particularly in the interest of the American countries.

INTERNATIONAL BANK FOR ECONOMIC CO-OPERATION, IBEC. The CMEA Bank est. on Jan. 1, 1964 in Moscow. Intergovernmental finance institution of Bulgaria, Cuba, Czechoslovakia, the GDR, Hungary, Mongolia, Poland, Romania, the USSR, members of CMEA. The Statute of the Bank constitutes an integral part of the intergovernmental agreement, signed on Oct. 22, 1963 in Moscow. Publ.: *Economic Bulletin and Annual Report.*

J.S. EARLAND, *Financing Foreign Trade in Eastern Europe*, New York, 1977; G. GARVEY, *Money, Financial Flows and Credit in the Soviet Union*, Cambridge, Mass., 1977; W.E. BUTLER (ed.), *A Source Book on Socialist International Organizations.* Alphen, 1978.

INTERNATIONAL BRIGADES. The anti-fascist volunteer units from 54 countries which fought in the Spanish civil war, 1936–39, on the side of the Republican People's Army against the armies of General Franco and German and Italian units. There were the following brigades: German –Austrian (XI), Italian (XII), Polish (XIII), French (XIV), Anglo–American (XV), and Balkan–Czechoslovak (129).

L. LONGO, *Le Brigate internazionali*, Roma, 1972.

INTERNATIONAL BUREAU OF AMERICAN REPUBLICS. An intergovernmental institution existed 1902–20 as a successor of the Commercial Bureau of the American Republics and a precursor of the ▷ Pan-American Union.

INTERNATIONAL BUREAU OF EDUCATION. Bureau international d'éducation, BIE, est. 1925 in Geneva as a non-governmental organization; in July, 1929 changed to an intergovernmental organization; in Jan., 1949 incorporated by UNESCO. The main organ is a Council composed of the representatives of 21 states, who are selected every two years by a general conference of UNESCO. Functions: organizes international conferences on public education; organizes Permanent International Education Exhibitions, in Geneva manages the International Library of Education, which has more than 70,000 volumes and receives *c.* 700 periodicals. Headquarters Palais Wilson, Geneva. Publ.: *International Yearbook of Education* and the quarterlies, *Education* and *Educational Documentation and Information.* In addition it is the publisher of the UNESCO periodicals: *Bulletin for Libraries, Copyright Bulletin, Impact of Science on Society, International Social Science Journal, Museum, Prospect in Education, UNESCO Chronicle* and *UNESCO Courier.*

Yearbook of International Organizations.

INTERNATIONAL CENTRE OF SCIENTIFIC–TECHNICAL INFORMATION. A Center est. in 1970 in Moscow on the basis of an agreement of the CMEA states signed Feb. 27, 1969.

UNTS, Vol. 789, p. 284.

INTERNATIONAL COMMISSION ON RADIOLOGICAL PROTECTION. ▷ ICRP.

INTERNATIONAL COMMISSIONS FOR CONTROL AND SUPERVISION, ICCS. An international institution created by governments participating in a cease-fire for the purpose of control and supervision of cease-fire conditions by the parties to the cease-fire agreement. After World War II many commissions were created, i.a. by the Korean cease-fire agreement, 1953; three commissions by the Indochina Conference in Geneva, 1954: ICC for Vietnam, ICC for Cambodia, and ICC for Laos; and by the Geneva Conference on Vietnam in Jan. 1973.

INTERNATIONAL COMMITTEE FOR SECURITY AND CO-OPERATION IN EUROPE. Comité international pour la securité et la coopération européenne, CISCE, est. 1969 in Vienna by committees of eastern and western European countries. Headquarters in Brussels.

Yearbook of International Organizations.

INTERNATIONAL COMPARATIVE LAW. The civil and commercial law, a subject of international research and analyses.

K. ZWEIGERT (ed.), *International Encyclopedia of Comparative Law,* 17 Vols, The Hague, 1984 ff.

INTERNATIONAL CONCILIATION. An American periodical publication, appearing monthly in New York, was founded by the American Association for International Conciliation in 1907. Since July, 1924, when the Association was dissolved and its activities taken over by the Carnegie Endowment, published by the Carnegie Endowment.

INTERNATIONAL CONFEDERATION OF FREE TRADE UNIONS, ICFTU. A trade union organization f. 1949 in Brussels. Consultative status with ECOSOC. Reg. with the UIA. ▷ Trade Unions.

Yearbook of International Organizations.

INTERNATIONAL CO-OPERATION ADMINISTRATION. ▷ Mutual Security Agency.

INTERNATIONAL COUNCIL OF SCIENTIFIC UNIONS, ICSU. The Council was f. in 1919 in Brussels. Co-ordinates and facilitates activities in the field of exact and natural sciences on an international basis. Established the following committees and commissions: Scientific Committee on Oceanic Research; Scientific Committee on Antarctic Research; Committee on Space Research; Special Committee for the International Biological Programme; Committee on Teaching of Science; Committee on Water Research; Committee on Science and Technology in Developing Countries; Committee on Data for Science and Technology; Committee on Solar–Terrestrial Physics; Committee on Genetic Experimentation; Scientific Committee on Problems of the Environment, Joint Committee with WMO for the Global Atmospheric Research Programme. Established the following Inter-Union Commissions: Frequency Allocations for Radio Astronomy and Space Science; Geodynamics; Radio-meteorology; Spectroscopy. Established the following Permanent Services: Federation of Astronomical and Geophysical Services; ICSU Abstracting Board. Responsible for organization of the International Geophysical Year, International Years of the Quiet Sun, International Biological Programme. Consultative status with UNESCO, ECOSOC, FAO, IAEA, WMO, ITU and WHO. Publ.: *ICSU Bulletin* (quarterly), *ICSU Yearbook.* Reg. with the UIA.

Yearbook of International Organizations.

INTERNATIONAL COURT OF JUSTICE ICJ. Cour internationale de Justice, CIJ. The main judicial body of the United Nations, set up in 1945 by the UN Conference in San Francisco, which prepared and adopted the Charter of the United Nations and the statute of the ICJ forming an integral part of the Charter. All state members of the UN are *eo ipso* parties to the Statute of the Court. The Court is open to certain states which are not members of the United Nations; such a state may become a party to the Statute on conditions to be determined in each case by the General Assembly upon the recommendation of the Security Council (Charter, Art. 93, para. 2). At the request of Switzerland – the first such government to ask to become a party to the Statute – the Assembly adopted a resolution defining these conditions as follows: (a) acceptance of the provisions of the Statute; (b) acceptance of the obligations of a member of the United Nations under Art. 94 of the Charter; (c) an undertaking to contribute to the expenses of the Court such equitable amount as may be assessed by the Assembly. Switzerland became a party to the Statute in July, 1948. Identical conditions were approved by the General Assembly in the case of Liechtenstein and San Marino, which subsequently became parties to the Statute. The Court is also open to states which are not parties to its Statute, on conditions laid down by the Security Council in a resolution of 15 October 1946. Such states must file with the Registrar of the Court a declaration by which they accept the Court's jurisdiction in accordance with the United Nations Charter and the Statute and Rules of the Court, and undertake to comply in good faith with the decision or decisions of the Court and to accept all the obligations of a member of the United Nations under Art. 94 of the Charter. Such a declaration may be either particular or general. A particular declaration is one accepting the Court's jurisdiction in respect of a particular dispute or disputes which have already arisen. A general declaration is one accepting the jurisdiction in respect of all disputes, or of a particular class or classes of dispute, which have already arisen or which may arise in the future. Such declarations were filed in the past by several states which have since become members of the United Nations.

The Court is therefore not open to private individuals. It has always refused to entertain the petitions and requests which have often been addressed to it by individuals. However, this does not prevent interests from being the subject of proceedings before the Court, for it is always open to a state to take up the complaint of one of its nationals against another state, and to bring a case before the Court if it is entitled to do so. But what is then involved is a dispute between states.

The fact that the Court is open to a state does not mean that the state is obliged to have its disputes with other states decided by the Court. The Court's jurisdiction to try contentious cases depends upon the consent of states, since international justice, in contrast to national justice, is still optional.

The consent of states may be expressed in many ways. First two states which are in disagreement regarding a certain question may agree to refer it to the Court (Statute, Art. 36, para. 1). In such cases, the matter is brought before the Court by the notification of a special agreement concluded for that putpose by the two states. But a state may also accept the jurisdiction of the Court with regard to disputes which have not yet arisen: this is an undertaking to appear before the Court if a dispute should arise. In such cases, the matter is brought before the Court by one state's unilateral application against another. There is a large number of treaties and conventions under which states bind themselves in advance to accept the jurisdiction of the Court: bilateral treaties relating to all disputes that may arise between two states or to certain categories of dispute, multilateral conventions relating to one or more categories of dispute, etc. (Statute, Arts. 36, para. 1, and 37). Likewise, states which are parties to the Statute may give a very broad undertaking in accordance with Article 36, paragraph 2: they may at any time declare that they recognize as compulsory, in relation to any other state accepting the same obligation, the jurisdiction of the Court in all legal disputes concerning: (a) the interpretation of a treaty; (b) any question of international law; (c) the existence of any fact which, if established, would constitute a breach of an international obligation; and (d) the nature or extent of the reparation to be made for the breach of an international obligation. Such declarations are generally accompanied by conditions: limited duration, nature of the dispute, etc. The following is a list of the 47 states which accept the compulsory jurisdiction of the Court; this list, which represents the situation on Jan. 1, 1983, includes states whose declarations accepting the compulsory jurisdiction of the Permanent Court of International Justice have not lapsed or been withdrawn and are therefore applicable to the present Court (Statute, Art. 36, para. 5):

Australia, Austria, Barbados, Belgium, Botswana, Canada, Colombia, Costa Rica, Democratic Kampuchea, Denmark, the Dominican Republic, Egypt, El Salvador, Finland, Gambia, Haiti, Honduras, India, Israel, Japan, Kenya, Liberia, Liechtenstein, Luxembourg, Malawi, Malta, Mauritius, Mexico, the Netherlands, New Zealand, Nicaragua, Nigeria, Norway, Pakistan, Panama, Philippines, Portugal, Somalia, Sudan, Swaziland, Sweden, Switzerland, Togo, Uganda, the United Kingdom of Great Britain and Northern Ireland, the United States of America, Uruguay. In the event of a dispute as to whether the Court has jurisdiction in a given case, the Court decides the matter.

The seat of the International Court of Justice is at The Hague, Netherlands. A special agreement concluded between the United Nations and the Carnegie Foundation governs the terms on which the Court occupies premises in the Peace Palace. The Court may, however, sit and discharge its duties elsewhere should it consider it advisable to do so. The official languages of the Court are French and English, but the Court may authorize a party to use another language. The ICJ is composed of 15 Judges who are elected by the UN General Assembly and the Security Council. They are chosen from a list of persons nominated by the national groups in the Permanent Court of Arbitration; or, in the case of members of the UN not represented in the Permanent Court of Arbitration, by national groups appointed for this purpose by their governments under the same conditions as those prescribed for members of that Permanent Court. The UN General Assembly and the Security Council hold separate elections independently of each other. They must be satisfied not only that the persons to be elected individually possess the qualifications required in their respective countries for appointment to the highest judicial offices or are jurisconsults of recognized competence in international law, but also that, in the main body as a whole, the main forms of civilization and the principal legal systems of the world are represented. In order to be elected, a candidate must obtain a majority of votes, both in the Assembly and in the Council. Not more than one candidate of the same nationality may be elected. The members of the International Court of Justice are, as of Jan. 1, 1983, in order of precedence: Taslim Olawale Elias (Nigeria), President: Jose Settle Camara (Brazil), Vice President; Judges Manfred Lachs (Poland), Platon Dmitrievich Morozov (USSR), Nagendra Singh (India), Jose Maria Ruda (Argentina), Hermann Mosler (Federal Republic of Germany), Shigeru Oda (Japan), Roberto Ago (Italy), Abdallah Fikri El-Khani (Syrian Arab Republic), Stephen M. Schwebel (United States), Sir Robert Jennings (United Kingdom), Guy Ladreit de Lacharriere (France), Keba Mbaye (Senegal) and Mohammed Bedjaoui (Algeria). The Registrar of the Court is Santiago Torres Bernardez.

On Nov. 7, 1984 the UN General Assembly elected for the years 1985–94 new members (one-third every three years) of the ICJ: Taslim Olawale Elias, Nigeria (for the second term), Jens Evensen, Norway (for the first term), Manfred Lachs, Poland (for the third term), Ni Zhengyu, China (for the first term) and Shigeru Oda, Japan (for the second term). Cases may be brought before the International Court of Justice either by notification to the Registry of a special agreement under which the parties agree to refer a dispute to the Court, or by an application by one of the parties founded on a clause providing for compulsory jurisdiction. These documents have to specify the subject of the dispute and the parties. The Registrar forthwith communicates the special agreement of application to all concerned and also to members of the United Nations and to any other states entitled to appear before the court.

The various stages of the proceedings are laid down in the Rules of the Court adopted in 1946, amended in 1972 and completely revised in 1978. The parties are represented by agents and may be assisted by counsel and advocates. The proceedings consist of two parts: written and oral. The written part usually consists of the presentation by each of the parties of pleadings which are filed within time-limits fixed by Orders. The oral part consists of the hearing by the Court, at public sittings, of the agents, counsel, advocates, witnesses and experts.

Intervention is another incidental question that may arise. A third state may ask to intervene in a case, if it considers that it has an interest of a legal nature which may be affected by the decision. It is for the Court to decide upon a request of this kind. Furthermore, if the dispute between the parties relates to the application of a treaty which has also been signed by other states, those states are entitled to intervene and take part in the proceedings, in which case the Judgment's construction of the treaty will be binding upon them.

A Judgment of the Court is final and without appeal. After the Court has given a Judgment, the only procedure available to a party is a request for an interpretation of the Judgment (in the event of dispute as to its meaning or scope) or an application for its revision if some new fact is discovered which, when the Judgment was given was unknown to the Court and to the party claiming revision.

Unless otherwise decided by the Court, each party bears its own costs.

Apart from its jurisdiction to deal with contentious cases, the International Court of Justice also has the power to give advisory opinions – that is, its views on any legal question – at the request of the General Assembly of the United Nations, the Security Council, or other bodies so authorized. An opinion given by the Court is in principle purely advisory, but the requesting body will be bound by it if – as is sometimes the case – a provision in that sense is inseparable from its authorization to submit the question to the Court.

The following organizations are at present authorized to request advisory opinions of the Court:

United Nations: General Assembly, Security Council, Economic and Social Council, Trusteeship Council, Interim Committee of the General Assembly, Committee on Applications for Review of Administrative Tribunal Judgment.
International Labour Organization (ILO).
Food and Agriculture Organization of the United Nations (FAO).
United Nations Educational, Scientific and Cultural Organization (UNESCO).
World Health Organization (WHO).
International Bank for Reconstruction and Development (World Bank).
International Finance Corporation (IFC).
International Development Association (IDA).
International Monetary Fund (IMF).
International Civil Aviation Organization (ICAO).
International Telecommunication Union (ITU).
World Meteorological Organization (WMO).
World Intellectual Property Organization (WIPO).
International Fund for Agricultural Development (IFAD).
International Atomic Energy Agency (IAEA).
Each year the ICJ publishes *ICJ Yearbook*, in which until 1964 Chapter IX was devoted to bibliography of the work done and documents related to the ICJ during the last year. Starting with 1966, an annual *ICJ Bibliography* (the first volume covering the period between July 16, 1946 and Dec. 31, 1966) has been published.

On Jan. 10, 1974 France informed the Secretariat of the UN that it refused to recognize the jurisdiction of the ICJ any longer, since the Court in The Hague had neglected the statement of the French government that the ICJ is not competent to give verdicts in matters regarding the defense of France (the ICJ in 1973 examined the complaint filed by Australia and New Zealand against France related to French nuclear tests in the Pacific; recognizing the Australian and New Zealand concerns as justified, the Court appealed to France to stop further tests of nuclear arms).

In 1984 the USA refused to recognize the jurisdiction of the ICJ in the Nicaragua v. USA case.
On Mar. 8, 1989 the Soviet representative in the UN Human Rights Commission announced that the USSR recognizes ICJ jurisdiction over interpretation and application of the 1948 convention on ▷ genocide, the 1949 convention banning ▷ trafficking in prostitutes, the 1952 convention on ▷ women's rights, the 1965 convention against ▷ racism and the 1984 convention outlawing ▷ torture.

H. LAUTERPACHT, *The Development of International Law by the International Court*, London, 1938; P.L. ZOLLIKOFER, *Les relations prévues entre les institutions spécialisées des Nations Unies et la Cour international de Justice*, Paris, 1955; H.J. SCHLOCHAUER, "Internationaler Gerichtshof", in: *STRUPP-SCHLOCHAUER Wörterbuch des Völkerrechts*, Berlin, 1960, Bd. II, pp. 96–117; M. SORENSEN, "The ICJ: its role in Contemporary International Relations", in: *International Organizations*, 14/1960; K. HERNDL, "Rechtsgutachten des Internationalen Gerichtshofes", in: *STRUPP-SCHLOCHAUER Wörterbuch des Völkerrechts*, Berlin, 1962, Bd. III, pp. 12–37; S.H. ROSENNE, *The Law and Practice on the ICJ*, Leiden, 1965; J. DOUMA, *Bibliography of the International Court, Including the Permanent Court, 1918–1964*, Leiden, 1965; A. BASAK, *Decisions of the UN Organs in the Judgments and Opinions of the ICJ*, Wroclaw, 1969; F.I. KOZHEVNIKOV, G.V. SHARNANSHVILI, *Meshdunarodnii Sud OON*, Moskva, 1971; K.J. KEITH, *The extent of the advisory jurisdiction of the ICJ*, Leiden 1971; *UN Chronicle*, November, 1983, pp. 41–47.

INTERNATIONAL COURT OF JUSTICE, THE CASES DEALT WITH BY THE COURT SINCE 1946.

Between 1946 and 1984 the ICJ dealt with 49 contentious cases and 17 requests for advisory opinions, delivering 42 judgments and 18 opinions. The UN Chronicle chronological description of the 42 cases and 48 advisory opinions read as follows:

(1) *Corfu Channel (United Kingdom v. Albania)*
This dispute, which gave rise to three Judgments by the Court, arose out of the explosions of mines by which some British warships suffered damage while passing through the Corfu Channel in 1946, in a part of the Albanian waters which had been previously swept. The ships were severely damaged and members of the crew were killed. The United Kingdom accused Albania of having laid or allowed a third party to lay the mines after mine-clearing operations had been carried out by the Allied naval authorities. The case was brought before the United Nations and, in consequence of a recommendation by the Security Council, was referred to the court. In a first Judgment (25 Mar., 1948), the Court dealt with the question of its jurisdiction, which Albania had challenged. A second Judgment (9 April 1949) related to the merits of the case. The Court found that Albania was responsible under international law for the explosions that had taken place in Albanian waters and for the damage and loss of life which had ensued. It did not accept the view that Albania had itself laid the mines. On the other hand, it held that the mines could not have been laid without the knowledge of the Albanian Government. Albania, for its part, had submitted a counter-claim against the United Kingdom. It accused the latter of having violated Albanian sovereignty by sending warships into Albanian territorial waters and of carrying out mine-sweeping operations in Albanian waters after the explosions. The Court did not accept the first of these complaints but found that the United Kingdom had exercised the right of innocent passage through international straits. On the other hand, it found that the mine-sweeping had violated Albanian sovereignty, because it had been carried out against the will of the Albanian Government. In a third Judgment (15 December 1949), the Court assessed the amount of reparation owed to the United Kingdom and ordered Albania to pay £844,000 (see also No. 12 below).

(2) *Fisheries (United Kingdom v. Norway)*
The Judgment delivered by the Court in this case ended a long controversy between the United Kingdom and Norway which had aroused considerable interest in other maritime states. In 1935 Norway enacted a decree

by which it reserved certain fishing grounds situated off its northern coast for the exclusive use of its own fishermen. The question at issue was whether this decree, which laid down a method for drawing the baselines from which the width of the Norwegian territorial waters had to be calculated, was valid international law. This question was rendered particularly delicate by the intricacies of the Norwegian coastal zone, with its many fjords, bays, islands, islets and reefs. In its Judgment of Dec. 18, 1951, the Court found that, contrary to the submissions of the United Kingdom, neither the method nor the actual baselines stipulated by the 1935 decree were contrary to international law.

(3) *Protection of French Nationals and Protected Persons in Egypt (France v. Egypt)*
As a consequence of certain measures adopted by the Egyptian government against the property and persons of various French nationals and protected persons in Egypt, France instituted proceedings in which it invoked the Montreux Convention of 1935, concerning the abrogation of the capitulations in Egypt. However, the case was not proceeded with, as the Egyptian government desisted from the measures in question. By agreement between the parties, the case was removed from the Court's List (Order of Mar. 29, 1950).

(4–5) *Asylum (Colombia/Peru)*
The granting of asylum in the Colombian Embassy at Lima, on Jan. 3, 1949, to a Peruvian national, Victor Raul Haya de la Torre, a political leader accused of having instigated a military rebellion, was the subject of a dispute between Peru and Colombia which the parties agreed to submit to the Court. The Pan-American Havana Convention on Asylum (1928) laid down that, subject to certain conditions, asylum could be granted in a foreign embassy to a political offender who was a national of the territorial state. The question in dispute was whether Colombia, as the state granting the asylum, was entitled unilaterally to "qualify" the offence committed by the refugee in a manner binding on the territorial state – that is, to decide whether it was a political offence or a common crime. Furthermore, the Court was asked to decide whether the territorial state was bound to afford the necessary guarantees to enable the refugee to leave the country in safety. In its Judgment of Nov. 20, 1950, the Court answered both these questions in the negative, but at the same time it specified that Peru had not proved that Mr. Haya de la Torre was a common criminal. Lastly, it found in favor of a counter-claim submitted by Peru that Mr. Haya de la Torre had been granted asylum in violation of the Havana Convention. On the day on which the Court delivered this Judgment, Colombia filed a request for interpretation, seeking a reply to the question whether the Judgment implied an obligation to surrender the refugee to the Peruvian authorities. In a Judgment delivered on Nov. 27, 1950, the Court declared the request inadmissible.

(6) *Haya de la Torre (Colombia v. Peru)*
This case, a sequel to the earlier proceedings (see Nos. 4–5 above), was instituted by Colombia by means of a fresh application. Immediately after the Judgment of Nov. 20, 1950, Peru had called upon Colombia to surrender Mr. Haya de la Torre. Colombia refused to do so, maintaining that neither the applicable legal provisions nor the Court's Judgment placed it under an obligation to surrender the refugee to the Peruvian authorities. The Court confirmed this view in its Judgment of June 13, 1951. It declared that the question was a new one, and that although the Havana Convention expressly prescribed the surrender of common criminals to the local authorities, no obligation of the kind existed in regard to political offenders. While confirming that asylum had been irregularly granted and that on this ground Peru was entitled to demand its termination, the Court declared that Colombia was not bound to surrender the refugee; these two conclusions, it stated, were not contradictory because there were other ways in which the asylum could be terminated besides the surrender of the refugee.

(7) *Rights of Nationals of the United States of America in Morocco (France v. United States)*
By a decree of Dec. 30, 1948, the French authorities in the Moroccan Protectorate imposed a system of licence control in respect of imports not involving an official allocation of currency, and limited these imports to a number of products indispensable to the Moroccan economy. The United States maintained that this measure affected its rights under treaties with Morocco and contended that, in accordance with these treaties and with the General Act of Algeciras of 1906, no Moroccan law or regulation could be applied to its nationals in Morocco without its previous consent. In its Judgment of Aug. 27, 1952, the Court held that the import controls were contrary to the Treaty between the United States and Morocco of 1836 and the General Act of Algeciras since they involved discrimination in favour of France against the United States. The Court considered the extent of the consular jurisdiction of the United States in Morocco and held that the United States was entitled to exercise such jurisdiction in the French Zone in all disputes, civil or criminal, between United States citizens or persons protected by the United States. It was also entitled to exercise such jurisdiction to the extent required by the relevant provisions of the General Act of Algeciras. The Court rejected the contention of the United States that its consular jurisdiction included cases in which only the defendant was a citizen or protege of the United States. It also rejected the claim by the United States that the application to United States citizens of laws and regulations in the French Zone of Morocco required the assent of the United States government. Such assent was required only in so far as the intervention of the consular courts of the United States was necessary for the effective enforcement of such laws or regulations as against United States citizens. The Court rejected a counter-claim by the United States that its nationals in Morocco were entitled to immunity from taxation. It also dealt with the question of the valuation of imports by the Moroccan customs authorities.

(8) *Ambatielos (Greece v. United Kingdom)*
In 1919, Nicolas Ambatielos, a Greek shipowner, entered into a contract for the purchase of ships with the Government of the United Kingdom. He claimed he had suffered damage through the failure of that Government to carry out the terms of the contract and as a result of certain judgments given against him by the English courts in circumstances said to involve the violation of international law. The Greek government took up the case of its national and claimed that the United Kingdom was under a duty to submit the dispute to arbitration in accordance with Treaties between the United Kingdom and Greece of 1886 and 1926. The United Kingdom objected to the Court's jurisdiction. In a Judgment of July 1, 1952, the Court held that it had jurisdiction to decide whether the United Kingdom was under a duty to submit the dispute to arbitration but, on the other hand, that it had no jurisdiction to deal with the merits of the Ambatielos claim. In a further Judgment of May 19, 1953, the Court decided that the dispute was one which the United Kingdom was under a duty to submit to arbitration in accordance with the Treaties of 1886 and 1926.

(9) *Anglo-Iranian Oil Company (United Kingdom v. Iran)*
In 1933 an agreement was concluded between the government of Iran and the Anglo-Iranian Oil Company. In 1951, laws were passed in Iran for the nationalization of the oil industry. These laws resulted in a dispute between Iran and the company. The United Kingdom took up the company's case and instituted proceedings before the Court. Iran disputed the Court's jurisdiction. In its Judgment of July 22, 1952, the Court decided that it had no jurisdiction to deal with the dispute. Its jurisdiction depended on the declarations by Iran and the United Kingdom accepting the Court's compulsory jurisdiction under Article 36, paragraph 2, of the Court's Statute. The Court held that the declaration by Iran, which was ratified in 1932, covered only disputes based on treaties concluded by Iran after that date, whereas the claim of the United Kingdom was directly or indirectly based on treaties concluded prior to 1932. The Court also rejected the view that the agreement of 1933 was both a concessionary contract between Iran and the company and an international treaty between Iran and the United Kingdom, since the United Kingdom was not a party to the contract. The position was not altered by the fact that the concessionary contract was negotiated through the good offices of the Council of the League of Nations. By an Order of July 5, 1951, the Court had indicated interim measures of protection, that is, provisional measures for protecting the rights alleged by either party, in proceedings already instituted, until a final Judgment was given. In its Judgment, the Court declared that the Order had ceased to be operative.

(10) *Miniquiers and Ecrehos (France/United Kingdom)*
The Miniquiers and Ecrehos are two groups of islets situated between the British island of Jersey and the coast of France. Under a special agreement between France and the United Kingdom, the Court was asked to determine which of the parties had produced a more convincing proof of title to these groups of islets. After the conquest of England by William, Duke of Normandy, in 1066, the islands formed part of the Union between England and Normandy which lasted until 1204, when Philip Augustus of France conquered Normandy but failed to occupy the islands. The United Kingdom submitted that the islands then remained united with England and that this situation was placed on a legal basis by subsequent treaties between the two countries. France contended that the Miniquiers and Ecrehos were held by France after 1204, and referred to the same medieval treaties as those relied on by the United Kingdom. In its Judgment of Nov. 17, 1953, the Court considered that none of those Treaties stated specifically which islands were held by the King of England or by the King of France. Moreover, what was of decisive importance was not indirect presumptions based on matters in the Middle Ages, but direct evidence of possession and the actual exercise of sovereignty. After considering this evidence, the Court arrived at the sovereignty over the Miniquiers and Ecrehos belonged to the United Kingdom.

(11) *Nottebohm (Liechtenstein v. Guatemala)*
In this case, Liechtenstein claimed restitution and compensation from the government of Guatemala on the ground that the latter had acted towards Friedrich Nottebohm, a citizen of Liechtenstein, in a manner contrary to international law. Guatemala objected to the Court's jurisdiction but the Court overruled this objection in a Judgment of Nov. 18, 1953. In a second Judgment, of Apr. 6, 1955, the Court held that Liechtenstein's claim was inadmissible on grounds relating to Mr. Nottebohm's nationality. It was the bond of nationality between a state and an individual which alone conferred upon the state the right to put forward an international claim on his behalf. Mr. Nottebohm, who was then a German national, had settled in Guatemala in 1905 and continued to reside there. In October 1939 – after the beginning of World War II – while on a visit to Europe, he obtained Liechtenstein nationality and returned to Guatemala in 1940, where he resumed his former business activities until his removal as a result of war measures in 1943. On the international plane, the grant of nationality was entitled to recognition by other states only if it represented a genuine connection between the individual and the state granting its nationality. Mr. Notteborm's nationality, however, was not based on any genuine prior link with Liechtenstein and the object of his naturalization was to enable him to acquire the status of a neutral national in time of war. For these reasons, Liechtenstein was not entitled to take up his case and put forward an international claim on his behalf against Guatemala.

(12) *Monetary Gold Removed from Rome in 1943 (Italy v. France, United Kingdom and United States).*
A certain quantity of monetary gold was removed by the Germans from Rome in 1943. It was later recovered in Germany and found to belong to Albania. The 1946 agreement on reparation from Germany provided that monetary gold found in Germany should be pooled for distribution among the countries entitled to receive a share of it. The United Kingdom claimed that the gold should be delivered to it in partial satisfaction of the Court's Judgment of 1949 in the Corfu Channel case (see No. 1 above). Italy claimed that the gold should be delivered to it in partial satisfaction for the damage which it alleged it had suffered as a result of an Albanian law of Jan. 13, 1945. In the Washington statement of Apr. 25, 1951, the governments of France, the United Kingdom and the United States, to whom the implementation of the reparations agreement had been entrusted, decided that the gold should be delivered to the United Kingdom unless, within a certain time limit, Italy or Albania applied to the Court requesting it to adjudicate on their respective rights. Albania took no action, but Italy made an application to the Court. Later, however, Italy raised the preliminary question as to whether the Court had jurisdiction to adjudicate upon the validity of the Italian claim against Albania. In its Judgment of June 15, 1954, the Court found that, without the consent of Albania, it could not deal with a

dispute between that country and Italy and that it was therefore unable to decide the questions submitted.

(13) *Electricité de Beyrouth Company (France v. Lebanon)*

This case arose out of certain measures taken by the Lebanese government which a French company regarded as contrary to undertakings that the government had given in 1948 as part of an agreement with France. The French government referred the dispute to the Court, but the Lebanese government and the company entered into an agreement for the settlement of the dispute and the case was removed from the Court's List by an Order of July 29, 1954.

(14–15) *Treatment in Hungary of Aircraft and Crew of the United States of America (United States v. Hungary; United States v. USSR)*

(16) *Aerial Incident of Mar. 10, 1953 (United States v. Czechoslovakia)*

(17) *Aerial Incident of Oct. 7, 1952 (United States v. USSR)*

(18) *Aerial Incident of Sept. 4, 1954 (United States v. USSR)*

(19) *Aerial Incident of Nov. 7, 1954 (United States v. USSR)*

In these six cases the United States did not claim that the States against which the applications were made had given any consent to jurisdiction, but relied on art. 36, para. 1, of the Court's Statute, which provides that the jurisdiction of the Court comprises all cases which the parties refer to it. The United States stated that it submitted to the Court's jurisdiction for the purpose of the above-mentioned cases and indicated that it was open to the other governments concerned to do likewise. These governments having stated in each case that they were unable to submit to the Court's jurisdiction in the matter, the Court found that it did not have jurisdiction to deal with the cases and removed them from its List by Orders dated July 12, 1954 (Nos. 14–15), Mar. 14, 1956 (Nos. 16 and 17), Dec. 9, 1958 (No. 18) and Oct. 7, 1959 (No. 19).

(20–21) *Antarctica (United Kingdom v. Argentina; United Kingdom v. Chile)*

On May 4 1955, the United Kingdom instituted proceedings before the Court against Argentina and Chile concerning disputes as to the sovereignty over certain lands and islands in the Antarctic. In its applications to the Court, the United Kingdom stated that it submitted to the Court's jurisdiction for the purposes of the case, and although, as far as it was aware, Argentina and Chile had not yet accepted the Court's jurisdiction, they were legally qualified to do so. Moreover, the United Kingdom relieved on art. 36, para. 1, of the Court's Statute. In a letter of July 15, 1955, Chile informed the Court that in its view the application was unfounded and that it was not open to the Court to exercise jurisdiction. In a note of Aug. 1, 1955, Argentina informed the Court of its refusal to accept the Court's jurisdiction to deal with the case. In these circumstances the Court found that neither Chile nor Argentina had accepted its jurisdiction to deal with the cases, and, on Mar. 16, 1956, Orders were made removing them from its List.

(22) *Certain Norwegian Loans (France v. Norway)*

Certain Norwegian loans had been floated in France between 1885 and 1909. The bonds securing them stated the amount of the obligation in gold, or in currency convertible into gold as well as in various national currencies. From the time when Norway suspended the convertibility of its currency into gold, the loans had been serviced in Norwegian kroner. The French government, espousing the cause of the French bondholders, filed an application requesting the Court to declare that the debt should be discharged by payment of the gold value of the coupons of the bonds on the date of payment and of the gold value of the redeemed bonds on the date of repayment. The Norwegian government raised a number of preliminary objections to the jurisdiction of the Court and, in the Judgment it delivered on July 6, 1957, the Court found that it was without jurisdiction to adjudicate on the dispute. Indeed, the Court held that, since its jurisdiction depended upon the two unilateral declarations made by the parties, jurisdiction was conferred upon the Court only to the extent to which those declarations coincided in conferring it. The Norwegian government was therefore entitled, by virtue of the condition of reciprocity, to invoke in its own favor the reservation contained in the French declaration which excluded from the jurisdiction of the Court differences relating to matters which were essentially within the national jurisdiction as understood by the government of the French Republic.

(23) *Right of Passage over Indian Territory (Portugal v. India)*

The Portuguese possessions in India included the two enclaves of Dadra and Nagar-Aveli which, in mid-1954, passed under an autonomous local administration. Portugal claimed that it had a right of passage to those enclaves and between one enclave and the other to the extent necessary for the exercise of its sovereignty and subject to the regulation and control of India; it also claimed that, in July, 1954, contrary to the practice previously followed, India had prevented it from exercising that right and that that situation should be redressed. A first Judgment, delivered on Nov. 26, 1957, related to the jurisdiction of the Court, which had been challenged by India. The Court rejected four of the preliminary objections raised by India and joined the other two to the merits of the case. In a second Judgment, delivered on Apr. 12, 1960, after rejecting the two remaining preliminary objections the Court gave its decision on the claims of Portugal, which India maintained were unfounded. The Court found that Portugal had in 1954 the right of passage claimed by it but that such right did not extend to armed forces, armed police, arms and ammunition, and that India had not acted contrary to the obligations imposed on it by the existence of that right.

(24) *Application of the Convention of 1902 Governing the Guardianship of Infants (Netherlands v. Sweden)*

The Swedish authorities had placed an infant of Netherlands nationality residing in Sweden under the regime of protective upbringing instituted by Swedish law for the protection of children and young persons. The father of the child, jointly with the deputy-guardian appointed by a Netherlands court, appealed against the action of the Swedish authorities, but the measure of protective upbringing was maintained. The Netherlands claimed that the decisions which instituted and maintained the protective upbringing were not in conformity with Sweden's obligations under the Hague Convention of 1902 governing the guardianship of infants, the provisions of which were based on the principle that the national law of the infant was applicable. In its Judgment of Nov. 28, 1958, the Court held that the 1902 Convention did not include within its scope the matter of the protection of children as understood by the Swedish law on the protection of children and young persons and that the Convention could not have given rise to obligations in a field outside the matter with which it was concerned. Accordingly, the Court did not, in this case, find any failure to observe the Convention on the part of Sweden.

(25) *Interhandel (Switzerland v. United States)*

In 1942 the government of the United States vested almost all the shares of the General Aniline and Film Corporation (GAF), a company incorporated in the United States, on the ground that those shares, which were owned by Interhandel, a company registered in Basel, belonged in reality to I.G. Farbenindustrie of Frankfurt, or that GAF was in one way or another controlled by the German company. On Oct. 1, 1957, Switzerland applied to the Court for a declaration that the United States was under an obligation to restore the vested assets to Interhandel or, alternatively, that the dispute on the matter between Switzerland and the United States was one fit for submission for judicial settlement, arbitration or conciliation. Two days later Switzerland asked the Court to indicate, as an interim measure of protection, that the United States should not part with the assets in question so long as proceedings were pending before the Court. On Oct. 24, 1957, the Court made an Order noting that, in the light of the information furnished, there appeared to be no need to indicate interim measures. The United States raised preliminary objections to the Court's jurisdiction, and in a Judgment delivered on Mar. 21, 1959 the Court found the Swiss application inadmissible because Interhandel had not exhausted the remedies available to it in the United States courts.

(26) *Aerial Incident of 27 July 1955 (Israel v. Bulgaria)*

This case arose out of the destruction by Bulgarian anti-aircraft defense forces of an aircraft belonging to an Israeli airline. Israel instituted proceedings before the Court by means of an application in Oct. 1957. Bulgaria having challenged the Court's jurisdiction to deal with the claim, Israel contended that, since Bulgaria had in 1921 accepted the compulsory jurisdiction of the Permanent Court of International Justice for an unlimited period, that acceptance became applicable, when Bulgaria was admitted to the United Nations in 1955, to the jurisdiction of the International Court of Justice by virtue of art. 36, para. 5, of the present Court's Statute, which provides that declarations made under the Statute of the former Court and which are still in force shall be deemed, as between the parties to the present Court's Statute, to be acceptances applicable to the International Court of Justice for the period which they still have to run and in accordance with their terms. In its Judgment on the preliminary objections, delivered on May 26, 1959, the Court found that it was without jurisdiction on the ground that art. 36, para. 5, was intended to preserve only declarations in force as between states signatories of the United Nations Charter, and not subsequently to revive undertakings which had lapsed on the dissolution of the Permanent Court.

(27) *Aerial Incident of July 27, 1955 (United States v. Bulgaria)*

This case arose out of the incident which was the subject of the proceedings mentioned above (see No. 26). The aircraft destroyed by Bulgarian anti-aircraft defense forces was carrying several United States nationals, who all lost their lives. Their government asked the Court to find Bulgaria liable for the losses thereby caused and to award damages. Bulgaria filed preliminary objections to the Court's jurisdiction, but, before hearings were due to open, the United States informed the Court of its decision, after further consideration, not to proceed with its application. Accordingly, the case was removed from the List by an Order of 30 May 1960.

(28) *Aerial Incident of 27 July 1955 (United Kingdom v. Bulgaria)*

This arose out of the same incident as that mentioned above (see Nos. 26 and 27). The aircraft destroyed by Bulgarian anti-aircraft defense forces was carrying several nationals of the United Kingdom and Colonies, who all lost their lives. The United Kingdom asked the Court to find Bulgaria liable for the losses thereby caused and to award damages. After filing a Memorial, however, the United Kingdom informed the Court that it wished to discontinue to proceedings in view of the decision of 26 May 1959 whereby the Court found that it lacked jurisdiction in the case brought by Israel. Accordingly, the case was removed from the List by an Order of 3 August 1959.

(29) *Sovereignty over Certain Frontier Land (Belgium/Netherlands)*

The Court was asked to settle a dispute as to sovereignty over two plots of land situated in an area where the Belgo-Dutch frontier presented certain unusual features, as there had long been a number of enclaves formed by the Belgian commune of Baerle-Duc and the Netherlands commune of Baarle-Nassau. A Communal Minute drawn up between 1836 and 1841 attributed the plots to Baarle-Nassau, whereas a Descriptive Minute and map annexed to the Boundary Convention of 1843 attributed them to Baerle-Duc. The Netherlands maintained that the Boundary Convention recognized the existence of the status quo as determined by the Communal Minute, that the provision by which the two plots were attributed to Belgium was vitiated by a mistake, and that Netherlands sovereignty over the disputed plots had been established by the exercise of various acts of sovereignty since 1843. After considering the evidence produced, the Court, in a Judgment delivered on June 20, 1959, found that sovereignty over the two disputed plots belonged to Belgium.

(30) *Arbitral Award Made by the King of Spain on Dec. 23, 1906 (Honduras v. Nicaragua)*

On Oct. 7, 1894, Honduras and Nicaragua signed a Convention for the demarcation of the limits between the two countries, one of the articles of which provided that, in certain circumstances, any points of the boundary-line which were left unsettled should be submitted to the decision of the Government of Spain. In Oct., 1904, the King of Spain was asked to determine that part of the frontier-line on which the Mixed Boundary Commission appointed by the two countries had been unable to reach agreement. The King gave his arbitral award on Dec. 23, 1906. Nicaragua contested the validity of the award and, in accordance with a resolution of the Organization of American States, the two countries agreed in July, 1957 on the procedure to be followed for submitting the dispute on this matter to the Court. In the application by which the case was brought before the Court on July 1, 1958, Honduras claimed that failure by Nicaragua to give effect to the arbitral award constituted a breach of an international obligation and asked the Court to declare the Nicaragua was under an obligation to give effect to the award. After considering the evidence produced, the Court found that Nicaragua had in fact freely accepted the designation of the King of Spain as arbitrator, had fully participated in the arbitral proceedings, and had thereafter accepted the award. Consequently the Court found in its Judgment delivered on Nov. 18, 1960 that the award was binding and that Nicaragua was under an obligation to give effect to it.

(31) *Barcelona Traction, Light and Power Company, Limited (Belgium v. Spain)*
On Sept. 23, 1958, Belgium instituted proceedings against Spain in connection with the adjudication in bankruptcy in Spain, in 1948, of the above-named company, formed in Toronto in 1911. The application stated that the company's share capital belonged largely to Belgian nationals and claimed that the acts of organs of the Spanish state whereby the company had been declared bankrupt and liquidated were contrary to international law and that Spain, as responsible for the resultant damage, was under an obligation either to restore or to pay compensation for the liquidated assets. In May, 1960, Spain filed preliminary objections to the jurisdiction of the Court, but before the time-limit fixed for its observations and submissions thereon, Belgium informed the Court that it did not intend to go on with the proceedings. Accordingly, the case was removed from the List by an Order of Apr. 10, 1961.

(32) *Barcelona Traction, Light and Power Company, Limited (New Application: 1962) (Belgium v. Spain)*
Belgium had ceased pursuing the case summarized above (see No. 31) on account of efforts to negotiate a friendly settlement. The negotiations broke down, however, and Belgium filed a new application on June 19, 1962. The following March, Spain filed four preliminary objections to the Court's jurisdiction, and on July 24, 1964 the Court delivered a Judgment dismissing the first two but joining the others to the merits of the case. After the filing, within the time limits requested by the parties, of the pleadings on the merits and on the objections joined thereto, hearings were held from Apr. 15, to July 22, 1969. Belgium sought compensation for the damage claimed to have been caused to its nationals, shareholders in the Barcelona Traction, Light and Power Company, Ltd, as the result of acts contrary to international law said to have been committed by organs of the Spanish State. Spain, on the other hand, submitted that the Belgian claim should be declared inadmissible or unfounded. In a Judgment delivered on Feb. 5, 1970, the Court found that Belgium had no legal standing to exercise diplomatic protection of shareholders in a Canadian company in respect of measures taken against that Company in Spain. The Court accordingly rejected Belgium's claim.

(33) *Compagnie du Port, des Quais et des Entrepots de Beyrouth and Société Radio-Orient (France v. Lebanon)*
This case arose out of certain measures adopted by the Lebanese Government with regard to two French companies. France instituted proceedings against Lebanon because it considered these measures contrary to certain undertakings embodied in a Franco-Lebanese agreement of 1948. Lebanon raised preliminary objections to the Court's jurisdiction, but before hearings could be held the parties informed the Court that satisfactory arrangements had been concluded. Accordingly, the case was removed from the List by an Order of 31 August 1960.

(34) *Temple of Preah Vihear (Cambodia v. Thailand)*
Cambodia complained that Thailand occupied a piece of its territory surrounding the ruins of the Temple of Preah Vihear, a place of pilgrimage and worship for Cambodians, and asked the Court to declare that territorial sovereignty over the Temple belonged to it and that Thailand was under an obligation to withdraw the armed detachment stationed there since 1954. Thailand filed preliminary objections to the Court's jurisdiction, which were rejected in a Judgment given on May 26, 1961. In its Judgment on the merits, rendered on June 15, 1962, the Court found that the Temple was situated on Cambodian territory. It also held that Thailand was under an obligation to withdraw any military or police force stationed there and to restore any objects removed from the ruins since 1954.

(35–36) *South West Africa (Ethiopia; South Africa; Liberia v. South Africa)*
On Nov. 4, 1960, Ethiopia and Liberia instituted separate proceedings against South Africa in a case concerning the continued existence of the mandate for South West Africa and the duties and performance of South Africa as mandatory Power. The Court was requested to make declarations to the effect that South West Africa remained a Territory under a mandate, that South Africa had been in breach of its obligations under that mandate, and that the mandate and hence the mandatory authority were subject to the supervision of the United Nations. On May 20, 1961, the Court made an Order finding Ethiopia and Liberia to be in the same interest and joining the proceedings each had instituted. South Africa filed four preliminary objections to the Court's jurisdiction. In a Judgment of Dec. 21, 1962, the Court rejected these and upheld its jurisdiction. After pleadings on the merits had been filed within the time limits requested by the parties, the Court held public sittings from Mar. 15 to Nov. 29, 1965 in order to hear oral arguments and testimony, and Judgment in the second phase was given on July 18, 1966. By the casting vote of the President – the votes having been equally divided (7–7) – the Court found that Ethiopia and Liberia could not be considered to have established any legal right or interest appertaining to them in the subject matter of their claims, and accordingly decided to reject those claims.

(37) *Northern Cameroons (Cameroons v. United Kingdom)*
The Republic of Cameroon claimed that the United Kingdom had violated the Trusteeship Agreement for the Territory of the Cameroons under British administration by creating such conditions that the Trusteeship had led to the attachment of the Northern Cameroons to Nigeria instead of to the Republic of Cameroon. The United Kingdom raised preliminary objections to the Court's jurisdiction. The Court found that to adjudicate on the merits would be devoid of purpose since, as the Republic of Cameroon had recognized, its judgment thereon could not affect the decision of the General Assembly providing for the attachment of the Northern Cameroons to Nigeria in accordance with the results of a plebiscite supervised by the United Nations. Accordingly, by a Judgment of Dec. 2, 1963, the Court found that it could not adjudicate upon the merits of the claim.

(38–39) *North Sea Continental Shelf (Federal Republic of Germany/Denmark; Federal Republic of Germany/Netherlands)*
These cases concerned the delimitation of the continental shelf of the North Sea as between Denmark and the Federal Republic of Germany, and as between the Netherlands and the Federal Republic, and were submitted to the Court by special agreement. The parties asked the Court to state the principles and rules of international law applicable, and undertook thereafter to carry out the delimitations on that basis. By an Order of Apr. 26, 1968 the Court, having found Denmark and the Netherlands to be in the same interest, joined the proceedings in the two cases. In its Judgment, delivered on Feb. 20, 1969, the Court found that the boundary lines in question were to be drawn by agreement between the parties and in accordance with equitable principles in such a way as to leave to each party those areas of the continental shelf which constituted the natural prolongation of its land territory under the sea, and it indicated certain factors to be taken into consideration for that purpose. The Court rejected the contention that the delimitations in question had to be carried out in accordance with the principle of equidistance as defined in the 1958 Geneva Convention on the Continental Shelf. The Court took account of the fact that the Federal Republic had not ratified that Convention, and held that the equidistance principle was not inherent in the basic concept of continental shelf rights, and that this principle was not a rule of customary international law.

(40) *Appeal Relating to the Jurisdiction of the ICAO Council (India v. Pakistan)*
In Feb., 1971, following an incident involving the diversion to Pakistan of an Indian aircraft, India suspended flights over its territory by Pakistan civil aircraft, Pakistan took the view that this action was in breach of the 1944 Convention on International Civil Aviation and the International Air Services Transit Agreement and complained to the Council of the International Civil Aviation Organization. India raised preliminary objections to the jurisdiction of the Council, but these were rejected and India appealed to the Court. During the ensuing written and oral proceedings before the Court, Pakistan contended, i.a., that the Court was not competent to hear the appeal. In its Judgment of Aug. 18, 1972, the Court found that it was competent to hear the appeal and that the Council had jurisdiction to deal with Pakistan's case.

(41) *Trial of Pakistani Prisoners of War (Pakistan v. India)*
In May, 1973, Pakistan instituted proceedings against India concerning 195 Pakistani prisoners of war whom, according to Pakistan, India proposed to hand over to Bangladesh, which was said to intend trying them for acts of genocide and crimes against humanity. India stated that there was no legal basis for the Court's jurisdiction in the matter and that Pakistan's application was without legal effect. Pakistan having also filed a request for the indication of interim measures of protection, the Court held public sittings to hear observations on this subject; India was not represented at the hearings. In July, 1973, Pakistan asked the Court to postpone further consideration of its request in order to facilitate negotiations. Before any written pleadings had been filed, Pakistan informed the Court that negotiations had taken place, and requested the Court to record discontinuance of the proceedings. Accordingly, the case was removed from the List by an Order of Dec. 15, 1973.

(42–43) *Fisheries Jurisdiction (United Kingdom v. Iceland; Federal Republic of Germany v. Iceland)*
On Apr. 14 and June 5, 1972, respectively, the United Kingdom and the Federal Republic of Germany instituted proceedings against Iceland, as from Sept. 1, 1972, of the limits of its exclusive fisheries jurisdiction from a distance of 12 to a distance of 50 nautical miles. Iceland declared that the Court lacked jurisdiction, and declined to be represented in the proceedings or file pleadings. At the request of the United Kingdom and the Federal Republic, the Court in 1972 indicated, and in 1973 confirmed, interim measures of protection to the effect that Iceland should refrain from implementing, with respect to their vessels, the new Regulations for the extension of the fishery zone, and that the annual catch of those vessels in the disputed area should be limited to certain maxima. In Judgments given on Feb. 2, 1973, the Court found that it possessed jurisdiction; and in Judgments of July 25, 1974, it found that the Icelandic Regulations constituting a unilateral extension of exclusive fishing rights to a limit of 50 nautical miles were not opposable to either the United Kingdom or the Federal Republic, that Iceland was not entitled unilaterally to exclude their fishing vessels from the disputed area, and that the parties were under mutual obligations to undertake negotiations in good faith for the equitable solution of their differences.

(44–45) *Nuclear Tests (Australia v. France; New Zealand v. France)*
On May 9, 1973, Australia and New Zealand each instituted proceedings against France concerning tests of nuclear weapons which France proposed to carry out in the atmosphere in the South Pacific region. France stated that it considered the Court manifestly to lack jurisdiction and refrained from appearing at the public hearings or filing any pleadings. By two Orders of June 22, 1973, the Court, at the request of Australia and New Zealand, indicated interim measures of protection to the effect, i.a., that pending judgment France should avoid nuclear tests causing radioactive fallout on Australian or New Zealand territory. By two Judgments delivered on Dec. 20, 1974, the Court found that the applications of Australia and New Zealand no longer had any object, and that it was therefore not called upon to give any decision thereon. Herein the Court based itself on the conclusion that the objective of Australia and New Zealand had been achieved inasmuch as France, in various public statements, had announced its intention of carrying out no further atmospheric nuclear tests on the completion of the 1974 series.

(46) *Aegian Sea Continental Shelf (Greece v. Turkey)*
On Aug. 10, 1976, Greece instituted proceedings against Turkey in a dispute over the Aegean Sea continental shelf. It asked the Court in particular to declare

that the Greek islands in the area were entitled to their lawful portion of continental shelf and to delimit the respective parts of that shelf appertaining to Greece and Turkey. At the same time, it requested interim measures of protection indicating that, pending the Court's judgment, neither state should without the other's consent engage in exploration or research with respect to the shelf in question. On Sept. 11, 1976, the Court found that the indication of such measures was not required and, as Turkey had denied that the Court was competent, ordered that the proceedings should first concern the question of jurisdiction. In a Judgment delivered on Dec. 19, 1978, the Court found that jurisdiction to deal with the case was not conferred upon it by either of the two instruments relied upon by Greece: the application of the General Act of Geneva, 1928, whether or not the Act was in force, was excluded by the effect of a reservation made by Greece upon accession, while the Greco-Turkish press communiqué of May 31, 1975 did not contain an agreement binding upon either state to accept the unilateral referral of the dispute to the Court.

(47) *Continental Shelf (Tunisia/Libyan Arab Jamahiriya)*

The Court was requested in 1978 to determine what principles and rules of international law were applicable to the delimitation as between Tunisia and the Libyan Arab Jamahiriya of the respective areas of continental shelf appertaining to each. After considering arguments as well as evidence based on geology, physiography and bathymetry on the basis of which each party sought to claim particular areas of the sea bed as the natural prolongation of its land territory, the Court concluded in a Judgment of Feb. 24, 1982, that the two countries abutted on a common continental shelf and that physical criteria were therefore of no assistance for the purpose of delimitation. Hence it had to be guided by "equitable principles" (as to which it emphasized that this term cannot be interpreted in the abstract, but only as referring to the principles and rules which may be appropriate in order to achieve an equitable result) and by certain factors such as the necessity of ensuring a reasonable degree of proportionality between the areas allotted and the lengths of the coastlines concerned; but the application of the equidistance method could not, in the particular circumstances of the case, lead to an equitable result. With respect to the course to be taken by the delimitation line, the Court distinguished two sectors: near the shore, it considered, having taken note of some evidence of historical agreement as to the maritime boundary, that the delimitation should run in a north-easterly direction at an angle of 26°; further seawards, it considered that the line of delimitation should veer eastwards at a bearing of 52° to take into account the change of direction of the Tunisian coast and the existence of the Kerkennah Islands.

During the course of the proceedings, Malta requested permission to intervene, claiming an interest of a legal nature under art. 62 of the Court's Statute. In view of the very character of the intervention for which permission was sought, the Court considered that the interest of a legal nature which Malta had invoked could not be affected by the decision in the case and that the request was not one to which, under art. 62, the Court might accede. It therefore rejected it.

(48) *United States Diplomatic and Consular Staff in Tehran (United States v. Iran)*

The case was brought before the Court by application by the United States following the occupation of its Embassy in Tehran by Iranian militants on Nov. 4, 1979, and the capture and holding as hostages of its diplomatic and consular staff. On a request by the United States for the indication of provisional measures, the Court held that there was no more fundamental prerequisite for relations between states than the inviolability of diplomatic envoys and embassies, and it indicated provisional measures for ensuring the immediate restoration to the United States of the Embassy premises and the release of the hostages. In its decision on the merits of the case, at a time when the situation complained of still persisted, the Court in its Judgment of May, 24, 1980, found that Iran had violated and was still violating obligations owed by it to the United States under conventions in force between the two countries and rules of general international law, that the violation of these obligations engaged its responsibility, and that the Iranian government was bound to secure the immediate release of the hostages, to restore the Embassy premises, and to make reparation for the injury caused to the United States government. The Court reaffirmed the cardinal importance of the principles of international law governing diplomatic and consular relations. The Court gave judgment, notwithstanding the absence of the Iranian government and after rejecting the reasons put forward by Iran in two communications addressed to the Court for its assertion that the Court could not and should not entertain the case. The Court was not called upon to deliver a further judgment on the reparation for the injury caused to the United States government since, by Order of 12 May 1981, the case was removed from the List following discontinuance.

(49) *Nicaragua v. United States.*

On May 10, 1984 the ICJ in an Order of provisional measures has ruled that Nicaragua's right to sovereignty and political independence should not be jeopardized by any military or para-military activities, and that the United States should cease restricting access to and from Nicaragua's ports, particularly through the laying of mines. A request by the USA that the case be dismissed on jurisdictional grounds was unanimously rejected by the Court. The US Secretary of State informed the ICJ that the USA will not accept any ICJ judgment in Central American cases during the next two years.

Advisory opinions:

(1) *Conditions of Admission of a state to membership in the United Nations (Article 4 of the Charter).*

Prior to this case, from the creation of the United Nations some 12 states had unsuccessfully applied for admission. Their applications were rejected by the Security Council in consequence of a veto imposed by one or other of the states which are permanent members of the Council. A proposal was then made for the admission of all the candidates at the same time. The General Assembly referred the question to the Court. In the interpretation it gave of art. 4 of the Charter of the United Nations, in its Advisory Opinion of May 28, 1948, the Court declared that the conditions laid down for the admission of states were exhaustive and that if these conditions were fulfilled by a state which was a candidate, the Security Council ought to make the recommendation which would enable the General Assembly to decide upon the admission.

(2) *Competence of the General Assembly for the Admission of a state to the United Nations.*

The preceding Advisory Opinion (No. 1 above) given by the Court did not lead to a settlement of the problem in the Security Council. A member of the United Nations then proposed that the word "recommendation" in art. 4 of the Charter should be construed as not necessarily signifying a favorable recommendation. In other words, a state might be admitted by the General Assembly even in the absence of a recommendation – this being interpreted as an unfavorable recommendation – thus making it possible, it was suggested, to escape the effects of the veto. In the Advisory Opinion which it delivered on Mar. 3, 1950, the Court pointed out that the Charter laid down two conditions for the admission of new Members: a recommendation by the Security Council and a decision by the General Assembly. If the latter body had power to decide without a recommendation by the Council, the Council would be deprived of an important function assigned to it by the Charter. The absence of a recommendation by the Council, as the result of a veto, could not be interpreted as an unfavorable recommendation, since the Council itself had interpreted its own decision as meaning that no recommendation had been made.

(3) *Reparation for Injuries Suffered in the Service of the United Nations.*

As a consequence of the assassination in Sept., 1948 in Jerusalem of Count Folke Bernadotte, the United Nations Mediator in Palestine, and other members of the United Nations Mission to Palestine, the General Assembly asked the Court whether the United Nations had the capacity to bring an international claim against the state responsible with a view to obtaining reparation for damage caused to the Organization and to the victim. If this question were answered in the affirmative, it was further asked in what manner the action taken by the United Nations could be reconciled with such rights as might be possessed by the state of which the victim was a national. In its Advisory Opinion of Apr. 11, 1949, the Court held that the Organization was intended to exercise functions and rights which could only be explained on the basis of the possession of a large measure of international personality and the capacity to operate upon the international plane. It followed that the Organization had the capacity to bring a claim and to give it the character of an international action for reparation for the damage that had been caused to it. The Court further declared that the Organization can claim reparation not only in respect of damage caused to itself, but also in respect of damage suffered by the victim or persons entitled through him. Although, according to the traditional rule, diplomatic protection had to be exercised by the national state, the Organization should be regarded in international law as possessing the powers which, even if they are not expressly stated in the Charter, are conferred upon the Organization as being essential to the discharge of its functions. The Organization may require to entrust its agents with important missions in disturbed parts of the world. In such cases it is necessary that the agents should receive suitable support and protection. The Court therefore found that the Organization has the capacity to claim appropriate reparation, including also reparation for damage suffered by the victim or by persons entitled through him. The risk of possible competition between the Organization and the victim's national state could be eliminated either by means of a general convention or by a particular agreement in any individual case.

(4–5) *Interpretation of Peace Treaties with Bulgaria, Hungary and Romania.*

This case concerned the procedure to be adopted in regard to the settlement of disputes between the states signatories of the peace Treaties of 1947 (Bulgaria, Hungary, Romania, on the one hand, and the Allied states, on the other). In the first Advisory Opinion (Mar. 30, 1950), the Court stated that the countries, which had signed a Treaty providing an arbitral procedure for the settlement of disputes relating to the interpretation or application of the Treaty, were under an obligation to appoint their representatives to the arbitration commissions prescribed by the Treaty. Notwithstanding this Advisory Opinion the three states, which had declined to appoint their representatives on the arbitration commissions, failed to modify their attitude. A time limit was given to them within which to comply with the obligation laid down in the Treaties as they had been interpreted by the Court. After the expiry of the time limit, the Court was requested to say whether the Secretary-General, who, by the terms of the Treaties, was authorized to appoint the third member of the arbitration commission in the absence of agreement between the parties in respect of this appointment, could proceed to make this appointment, even if one of the parties had failed to appoint its representative. In a further Advisory Opinion of July 18, 1950, the Court replied that this method could not be adopted since it would result in creating a commission of two members, whereas the Treaty provided for a commission of three members, reaching its decision by a majority.

(6) *International Status of South West Africa.*

This Advisory Opinion, given on July 11, 1950, at the request of the General Assembly, was concerned with the determination of the legal status of the Territory, the administration of which had been placed by the League of Nations after World War I under the mandate of the Union of South Africa. The League had disappeared, and with it the machinery for the supervision of the mandates. Moreover, the Charter of the United Nations did not provide that the former mandated Territories should automatically come under trusteeship. The Court held that the dissolution of the League of Nations and its supervisory machinery had not entailed the lapse of the mandate, and that the mandatory Power was still under an obligation to give an account of its administration to the United Nations, which was legally qualified to discharge the supervisory functions formerly exercised by the League of Nations. The degree of supervision to be exercised by the General Assembly should not, however, exceed that which applied under the mandates system and should conform as far as possible to the procedure followed in this respect by the Council of the League of Nations. On the other hand, the mandatory Power was not under an obligation to place the Territory under trusteeship, although it might have certain political and moral duties in this connection. Finally it had no competence to modify the international status of South West Africa unilaterally.

(7) *Voting Procedure on Questions relating to Reports and Petitions concerning the Territory of South West Africa.*
Following the preceding Advisory Opinion (No. 6 above), the General Assembly, on Oct. 11, 1954, adopted a special Rule F on voting procedure to be followed by the Assembly in taking decisions on questions relating to reports and petitions concerning the Territory of South West Africa. According to this Rule, such decisions were to be regarded as important questions within the meaning of art. 18, para. 2, of the United Nations Charter and would therefore require a two-thirds majority of Members of the United Nations present and voting. In its Advisory Opinion of June 7, 1955, the Court considered that Rule F was a correct application of its earlier Advisory Opinion. It related only to procedure, and procedural matters were not material to the degree of supervision exercised by the General Assembly. Moreover, the Assembly was entitled to apply its own voting procedure and Rule F was in accord with the requirement that the supervision exercised by the Assembly should conform as far as possible to the procedure followed by the Council of the League of Nations.

(8) *Admissibility of Hearings of Petitioners by the Committee on South West Africa.*
In this Advisory Opinion, of June 1, 1956, the Court considered that it would be in accordance with its Advisory Opinion of 1950 on the international status of South West Africa (see No. 6 above) for the Committee on South West Africa, established by the General Assembly, to grant oral hearings to petitioners on matters relating to the Territory of South West Africa if such a course was necessary for the maintenance of effective international supervision of the mandated Territory. The General Assembly was legally qualified to carry out an effective and adequate supervision of the administration of the mandated Territory. Under the League of Nations, the Council would have been competent to authorize such hearings. Although the degree of supervision to be exercised by the Assembly should not exceed that which applied under the mandates sustem, the grant of hearings would not involve such an excess in the degree of supervision. Under the circumstances then existing, the hearing of petitioners by the Committee on South West Africa might be in the interest of the proper working of the mandates system.

(9) *Legal Consequences for States of the Continued Presence of South Africa in Namibia (South West Africa) notwithstanding Security Council Resolution 276 (1970).*
On Oct. 27, 1966, the General Assembly decided that the mandate for South West Africa (see Advisory Cases, Nos. 6–8 above, and Contentious Cases, Nos. 35–36) was terminated and that South Africa had no other right to administer the Territory. In 1969 the Security Council called upon South Africa to withdraw its administration from the Territory, and on Jan. 30, 1970 it declared that the continued presence there of the South African authorities was illegal and that all acts taken by the South African Government on behalf of or concerning Namibia after the termination of the mandate were illegal and invalid; it further called upon all states to refrain from any dealings with the South African government that were incompatible with that declaration. On July 29, 1970, the Security Council decided to request of the Court an advisory opinion on the legal consequences for states of the continued presence of South Africa in Namibia. In its Advisory Opinion of June 21, 1971, the Court found that the continued presence of South Africa in Namibia was illegal and that South Africa was under an obligation to withdraw its administration immediately. The Court was further of the opinion that states members of the United Nations were under an obligation to recognize the illegality of South Africa's presence in Namibia and the invalidity of its acts on behalf of or concerning Namibia, and to refrain from any acts implying recognition of the legality of, or lending support or assistance to, such presence and administration. Finally, it was of the opinion that it was incumbent upon states which were not members of the United Nations to give assistance in the action which had been taken by the United Nations with regard to Namibia.

(10) *Reservations to the Convention on the Prevention and Punishment of the Crime of Genocide.*
In November, 1950, the General Assembly asked the Court a series of questions as to the position of a state which attached reservations to its signature of the multilateral Convention on genocide if other states, signatories of the same Convention, objected to these reservations. The Court considered, in its Advisory Opinion of May 28, 1951, that, even if a convention contained no article on the subject of reservations, it did not follow that they were prohibited. The character of the convention, its purposes and its provisions must be taken into account. It was the compatibility of the reservation with the purpose of the convention which must furnish the criterion of the attitude of the state making the reservation, and of the state which objected thereto. The Court did not consider that it was possible to give an absolute answer to the abstract question put to it. As regards the effects of the reservation in relations between states, the Court considered that a state could not be bound by a reservation to which it had not consented. Every state was therefore free to decide for itself whether the state which formulated the reservation was or was not a party to the convention. The situation presented real disadvantages, but they could only be remedied by the insertion in the convention of an article on the use of reservations. A third question referred to the effects of an objection by a state which was not yet a party to the convention, either because it had not signed it or because it had signed but not ratified it. The Court was of the opinion that, as regards the first case, it would be inconceivable that a state which had not signed the convention should be able to exclude another state from it. In the second case, the situation was different: the objection was valid, but it would not produce an immediate legal effect; it would merely express and proclaim the attitude which a signatory state would assume when it had become a party to the convention. In all the foregoing, the Court adjudicated only on the specific case referred to it, namely the genocide Convention.

(11) *Effect of Awards of Compensation Made by the United Nations Administrative Tribunal.*
The United Nations Administrative Tribunal was established by the General Assembly to hear applications alleging non-observance of contracts of employment of staff members of the United Nations Secretariat or of the terms of appointment of such staff members. In its Advisory Opinion of July 13, 1954, the Court considered that the Assembly was not entitled on any grounds to refuse to give effect to an award of compensation made by the Administrative Tribunal in favor of a staff member of the United Nations whose contract of service had been terminated without his assent. The Tribunal was an independent and truly judicial body pronouncing final judgments without appeal within the limited field of its functions and not merely an advisory or subordinate organ. Its judgments were therefore binding on the United Nations Organization and thus also on the General Assembly.

(12) *Judgments of the Administrative Tribunal of the ILO upon Complaints Made against UNESCO*
The Statute of the Administrative Tribunal of the International Labour Organization (ILO) (the jurisdiction of which had been accepted by the United Nations Educational, Scientific and Cultural Organization (UNESCO) for the purpose of settling certain disputes which might arise between the organization and its staff members) provides that the Tribunal's judgments shall be final and without appeal, subject to the right of the organization to challenge them. It further provides that in the event of such a challenge, the question of the validity of the decision shall be referred to the Court for an advisory opinion, which will be binding. When four UNESCO staff members holding fixed-term appointments complained of the Director-General's refusal to renew their contracts on expiry, the Tribunal gave judgment in their favor. UNESCO challenged these judgments, contending that the staff members concerned had no legal right to such renewal and that the Tribunal was competent only to hear complaints alleging non-observance of terms of appointment or staff regulations. Consequently, UNESCO maintained, the Tribunal lacked the requisite jurisdiction. In its Advisory Opinion of Oct. 23, 1956, the Court said that an administrative memorandum which had announced that all holders of fixed-term contracts would, subject to certain conditions, be offered renewals might reasonably be regarded as binding on the organization and that it was sufficient to establish the jurisdiction of the Tribunal, that the complaints

should appear to have a substantial and not merely artificial connection with the terms and provisions invoked. It was therefore the Court's opinion that the Administrative Tribunal had been competent to hear the complaints in question.

(13) *Constitution of the Maritime Safety Committee of the Inter-Governmental Maritime Consultative Organization.*
The Inter-Governmental Maritime Consultative Organization (IMCO) (now the International Maritime Organization) comprises, among other organs, an Assembly and a Maritime Safety Committee. Under the terms of article 28(a) of the Convention for the establishment of the organization, this Committee consists of 14 members elected by the Assembly from the members of the organization having an important interest in maritime safety, "of which not less than eight shall be the largest ship-owning nations". When, on Jan. 15, 1959, the IMCO Assembly, for the first time, proceeded to elect the members of the Committee, it elected neither Liberia nor Panama, although those two states were among the eight members of the organization which possessed the largest registered tonnage. Subsequently, the Assembly decided to ask the Court whether the Maritime Safety Committee was constituted in accordance with the Convention for the establishment of the organization. In its Advisory Opinion of June 8, 1960, the Court replied to this question in the negative.

(14) *Certain Expenses of the United Nations*
Art. 17, para. 2, of the Charter of the United Nations provides that "The expenses of the Organization shall be borne by the Members as apportioned by the General Assembly." On Dec. 20, 1961, the General Assembly adopted a resolution requesting an advisory opinion on whether the expenditures authorized by it relating to United Nations operations in the Congo and to the operations of the United Nations Emergency Force in the Middle East constituted "expenses of the Organization" within the meaning of this Article and paragraph of the Charter. The Court, in its Advisory Opinion of July 20, 1962, replied in the affirmative that these expenditures were expenses of the United Nations. The Court pointed out that under art. 17, para. 2, of the Charter, the "expenses of the Organization" are the amounts paid out to defray the costs of carrying out the purposes of the Organization. After examining the resolutions authorizing the expenditures in question, the Court concluded that they were so incurred. The Court also analyzed the principal arguments which had been advanced against the conclusion that these expenditures should be considered as "expenses of the Organization" and found these arguments to be unfounded.

(15) *Application for Review of Judgment No. 158 of the United Nations Administrative Tribunal.*
On April 28, 1972, the United Nations Administrative Tribunal gave, in Judgment No. 158, its ruling on a complaint by a former United Nations staff member concerning the non-renewal of his fixed-term contract. The staff member applied for the review of this ruling to the Committee on Applications for Review of Administrative Tribunal Judgments, which decided that there was a substantial basis for the application and requested the Court to give an advisory opinion on two questions arising from the applicant's contentions. In its Advisory Opinion of July 12, 1973, the Court decided to comply with the Committee's request and expressed the opinion that, contrary to those contentions, the Tribunal had not failed to exercise the jurisdiction vested in it and had not committed a fundamental error in procedure having occasioned a failure of justice.

(16) *Western Sahara.*
On Dec. 13, 1974, the General Assembly requested an advisory opinion on the following questions: "I. Was Western Sahara (Rio de Oro and Sakiet El Hamra) at the time of colonization by Spain a territory belonging to no one (terra nullius)?" If the answer to the first question is in the negative, "II. What were the legal ties between this territory and the Kingdom of Morocco and the Mauritanian entity?" In its Advisory Opinion, delivered on Oct. 16, 1975, the Court replied to Question I in the negative. In reply to Question II, it expressed the opinion that the materials and information presented to it showed the existence, at the time of the Spanish colonization, of legal ties of allegiance between the Sultan of Morocco and some of the tribes living in

the territory of Western Sahara. They equally showed the existence of rights, including some rights relating to the land, which constituted legal ties between the Mauritanian entity, as understood by the Court, and the territory of Western Sahara. On the other hand, the Court's conclusion was that the materials and information presented to it did not establish any tie of territorial sovereignty between the territory of Western Sahara and the Kingdom of Morocco or the Mauritanian entity. Thus the Court did not find any legal ties of such a nature as might affect the application of the General Assembly's 1960 resolution 1514 (XV) – containing the Declaration on the Granting of Independence to Colonial Countries and Peoples – in the decolonization of Western Sahara and, in particular, of the principle of self-determination through the free and genuine expression of the will of the peoples of the territory.

(17) *Interpretation of the Agreement of Mar. 25, 1951 between the WHO and Egypt.*

Having regard to a possible transfer from Alexandria of the World Health Organization's Regional Office for the Eastern Mediterranean Region, the World Health Assembly in May 1980 submitted a request to the Court for an advisory opinion on the following questions: "I. Are the negotiation and notice provisions of Section 37 of the Agreement of 25 March 1951 between the World Health Organization and Egypt applicable in the event that either Party to the Agreement wishes to have the regional office transferred from the territory of Egypt? 2. If so, what would be the legal responsibilities of the World Health Organization and Egypt, with regard to the regional office in Alexandria, during the two-year period between notice and termination of the Agreement?" The Court expressed the opinion that in the event of a transfer of the seat of the Regional Office to another country, the WHO and Egypt were under mutual obligations to consult together in good faith as to the conditions and modalities of the transfer, and to negotiate the various arrangements needed to effect the transfer with a minimum of prejudice to the work of the organization and to the interests of Egypt. The party wishing to effect the transfer had a duty, despite the specific period of notice indicated in the 1951 Agreement, to give a reasonable period of notice to the other party, and during this period the legal responsibilities of the WHO and of Egypt would be to fulfill in good faith their mutual obligations as set out above.

(18) *Application for Review of Judgment No. 273 of the United Nations Administrative Tribunal.*

A former staff member of the United Nations Secretariat had challenged the Secretary-General's refusal to pay him a repatriation grant unless he produced evidence of having relocated upon retirement. By a Judgment of May 15, 1981, the United Nations Administrative Tribunal had found that the staff member was entitled to receive the grant and, therefore, to compensation for the injury sustained through its non-payment. The injury had been assessed at the amount of the repatriation grant of which payment was refused. The United States government addressed an application for review of this Judgment to the Committee on Applications for Review of Administrative Tribunal Judgments, and the Committee decided to request an Advisory Opinion of the Court on the correctness of the decision in question. In its Advisory Opinion of July 20, 1982, the Court, after pointing out that a number of procedural and substantive irregularities had been committed, decided nevertheless to comply with the Committee's request, whose wording it interpreted as really seeking a determination as to whether the Administrative Tribunal had erred on a question of law relating to the provisions of the United Nations Charter, or had exceeded its jurisdiction or competence. As to the first point, the Court said that its proper role was not to retry the case already dealt with by the Tribunal, and that it need not involve itself in the question of the proper interpretation of United Nations Staff Regulations and Rules further than was strictly necessary in order to judge whether the interpretation adopted by the Tribunal had been in contradiction with the provisions of the Charter. Having noted that the Tribunal had only applied what it had found to be the relevant Staff Regulations and Staff Rules made under the authority of the General Assembly, the Court found that the Tribunal had not erred on question of law relating to the provisions of the Charter. As to the second point, the Court considered that the Tribunal's jurisdiction included the scope of Staff Regulations and Rules and that it had not exceeded its jurisdiction or competence.

UN Chronicle, December, 1983, pp. 47–56; T.O. ELIAS, *The ICJ and Some Contemporary Problems*, The Hague, 1983; S. ROSENANE, *Procedure in the International Court*, The Hague, 1983; J.B. ELKIND, *Non-Appearance before the ICJ*, The Hague, 1984; I. HUSSAIN, *Dissenting and Separate Opinions at the World Court*, The Hague, 1984.

INTERNATIONAL COURT OF JUSTICE, THE 1978 RULES OF. The Court having regard to chapter XIV of the Charter of the UN, having regard to the Statute of Court, acting in pursuance of art. 30 of the Statute, adopted the amendments of the Rules of Court 1946, approved on May 10, 1972. The amended Rules came into force on Sept. 1, 1972. The Court revised completely the amended Rules in 1978. The text was published in the *ICJ Acts and Documents*, No. 4, 1978.

UN Yearbook, 1978.

INTERNATIONAL COURT OF JUSTICE, THE 1945 STATUTE OF. An integral part of the ▷ United Nations Charter, entered into force on Oct. 24, 1945. The text is as follows:

"Art. 1. The International Court of Justice established by the Charter of the United Nations as the principal judicial organ of the United Nations shall be constituted and shall function in accordance with the provisions of the present Statute.

Chapter I. Organization of the Court.

Art. 2. The Court shall be composed of a body of independent judges, elected regardless of their nationality from among persons of high moral character, who possess the qualifications required in their respective countries for appointment to the highest judicial offices, or are jurisconsults of recognized competence in international law.

Art. 3.(1) The Court shall consist of fifteen members, no two of whom may be nationals of the same state.

(2) A person who for the purposes of membership in the Court be regarded as a national of more than one state shall be deemed to be a national of the one in which he ordinarily excercises civil and political rights.

Art. 4.(1) The members of the Court shall be elected by the General Assembly and by the Security Council from a list of persons nominated by the national groups in the Permanent Court of Arbitration, in accordance with the following provisions.

(2) In the case of Members of the United Nations not represented in the Permanent Court of Arbitration, candidates shall be nominated by national groups appointed for this purpose by their governments under the same conditions as those prescribed for members of the Permanent Court of Arbitration by Article 44 of the Convention of The Hague of 1907 for the pacific settlement of international disputes.

(3) The conditions under which a state is a party to the present Statute but is not a Member of the United Nations may participate in electing the members of the Court shall, in the absence of a special agreement, be laid down by the General Assembly upon recommendation of the Security Council.

Art. 5.(1) At least three months before the date of the election, the Secretary-General of the United Nations shall address a written request to the members of the Permanent Court of Arbitration belonging to the states which are parties to the present Statute, and to the members of the national groups appointed under Article 4, paragraph 2, inviting them to undertake, within a given time, by national groups, the nomination of persons in a position to accept the duties of a member of the Court.

(2) No group may nominate more than four persons, not more than two of whom shall be of their own nationality. In no case may the number of candidates nominated by a group be more than double the number of seats to be filled.

Art. 6. Before making these nominations, each national group is recommended to consult its highest court of justice, its legal faculties and schools of law, and its national academies and national sections of international academies devoted to the study of law.

Art. 7.(1) The Secretary-General shall prepare a list in alphabetical order of all the persons thus nominated. Save as provided in Article 12, paragraph 2, these shall be the only persons eligible.

(2) The Secretary-General shall submit this list to the General Assembly and to the Security Council.

Art. 8. The General Assembly and the Security Council shall proceed independently of one another to elect the members of the Court.

Art. 9. At every election, the electors shall bear in mind not only that the person to be elected should individually possess the qualifications required, but also that in the body as a whole the representation of the main forms of civilization and of the principal legal systems of the world should be assured.

Art. 10(1) Those candidates who obtain an absolute majority of votes in the General Assembly and in the Security Council shall be considered as elected.

(2) Any vote of the Security Council, whether for the election of judges or for the appointment of members of the conference envisaged in Article 12, shall be taken without any distinction between permanent and non-permanent members of the Security Council.

(3) In the event of more than one national of the same state obtaining an absolute majority of the votes both of the General Assembly and of the Security Council, the eldest of these only shall be considered as elected.

Art. 11. If, after the first meeting held for the purpose of the election, one or more seats remain to be filled, a second and, if necessary, a third meeting shall take place.

Art. 12.(1) If, after the third meeting, one or more seats still remain unfilled, a joint conference consisting of six members, three appointed by the General Assembly and three by the Security Council, may be formed at any time at the request of either the General Assembly or the Security Council, for the purpose of choosing by the vote of an absolute majority one name for each seat still vacant, to submit to the General Assembly and the Security Council for their respective acceptance.

(2) If the joint conference is unanimously agreed upon any person who fulfils the required conditions, he may be included in its list, even though he was not included in the list of nominations referred to in Article 7.

(3) If the joint conference is satisfied that it will not be successful in procuring an election, those members of the Court who have already been elected shall, within a period to be fixed by the Security Council, proceed to fill the vacant seats by selection from among those candidates who have obtained votes either in the General Assembly or in the Security Council.

(4) In the event of an equality of votes among the judges, the eldest judge shall have a casting vote.

Art. 13.(1) The members of the Court shall be elected for nine years and may be re-elected; provided, however, that of the judges elected at the first election, the terms of judges shall expire at the end of thee years and the terms of five more judges shall expire at the end of six years.

(2) The judges whose terms are to expire at the end of the above-mentioned initial periods of three and six years shall be chosen by lot to be drawn by the Secretary-General immediately after the first election has been completed.

(3) The members of the Court shall continue to discharge their duties until their places have been filled. Though replaced, they shall finish any cases which they may have begun.

(4) In the case of the resignation of a member of the Court, the resignation shall be addressed to the President of the Court for transmission to the Secretary-General. This last notification makes the place vacant.

Art. 14. Vacancies shall be filled by the same method as that laid down for the first election, subject to the following provision: the Secretary-General shall, within one month of the occurrence of the vacancy, proceed to issue the invitations provided for in Article 5, and the date of the election shall be fixed by the Security Council.

Art. 15. A member of the Court elected to replace a member whose term of office has not expired shall hold office for the remainder of his predecessor's term.

Art. 16.(1) No member of the Court may exercise any political or administrative function, or engage in any other occupation of a professional nature.

(2) Any doubt on this point shall be settled by the decision of the Court.

Art. 17.(1) No member of the Court may act as agent, counsel, or advocate in any case.

(2) No member may participate in the decision of any case in which he has previously taken part as agent, counsel, or advocate for one of the parties, or as a member of a national or international court, or of a commission of enquiry, or in any other capacity.

(3) Any doubt on this point shall be settled by the decision of the Court.

Art. 18.(1) No member of the Court can be dismissed unless, in the unanimous opinion of the other members, he has ceased to fulfil the required conditions.

(2) Formal notification thereof shall be made to the Secretary-General by the Registrar.

(3) This notification makes the place vacant.

Art. 19. The members of the Court, when engaged in the business of the Court, shall enjoy diplomatic privileges and immunities.

Art. 20. Every member of the Court shall, before taking up his duties, make a solemn declaration in open court that he will exercise his powers impartially and conscientiously.

Art. 21.(1) The Court shall elect its President and Vice-President for three years; they may be re-elected.

(2) The Court shall appoint its Registrar and may provide for the appointment of such other officers as may be necessary.

Art. 22.(1) The seat of the Court shall be established at The Hague. This, however, shall not prevent the Court from sitting and exercising its functions elsewhere whenever the Court considers it desirable.

(2) The President and the Registrar shall reside at the seat of the Court.

Art. 23.(1) The Court shall remain permanently in session, except during the judicial vacations, the dates and duration of which shall be fixed by the Court.

(2) Members of the Court are entitled to periodic leave, the dates and duration of which shall be fixed by the Court, having in mind the distance between The Hague and the home of each judge.

(3) Members of the Court shall be bound, unless they are on leave or prevented from attending by illness or other serious reasons duly explained to the President, to hold themselves permanently at the disposal of the Court.

Art. 24.(1) If, for some special reason, a member of the Court considers that he should not take part in the decision of a particular case, he shall so inform the President.

(2) If the President considers that for some special reason one of the members of the Court should not sit in a particular case, he shall give him notice accordingly.

(3) If in any such case the member of the Court and the President disagree, the matter shall be settled by the decision of the Court.

Art. 25.(1) The full Court shall sit except when it is expressly provided otherwise in the present Statute.

(2) Subject to the condition that the number of judges available to constitute the Court is not thereby reduced below eleven, the Rules of the Court may provide for allowing one or more judges, according to circumstances and in rotation, to be dispensed from sitting.

(3) A quorum of nine judges shall suffice to constitute the Court.

Art. 26.(1) The Court may from time to time form one or more chambers, composed of three or more judges as the Court may determine, for dealing with particular categories of cases; for example, labour cases and cases relating to transit and communications.

(2) The Court may at any time form a chamber for dealing with a particular case. The number of judges to constitute such a chamber shall be determined by the Court with the approval of the parties.

(3) Cases shall be heard and determined by the chambers provided for in this Article if the parties so request.

Art. 27. A judgment given by any of the chambers provided for in Articles 26 and 29 shall be considered as rendered by the Court.

Art. 28. The chambers provided for in Articles 26 and 29 may, with the consent of the parties, sit and exercise their functions elsewhere than at The Hague.

Art. 29. With a view to the speedy dispatch of business, the Court shall form annually a chamber composed of five judges which, at the request of the parties, may hear and determine cases by summary procedure. In addition, two judges shall be selected for the purpose of replacing judges who find it impossible to sit.

Art. 30.(1) The Court shall frame rules for carrying out its functions. In particular, it shall lay down rules of procedure.

(2) The Rules of the Court may provide for assessors to sit with the Court or with any of its chambers, without the right to vote.

Art. 31.(1) Judges of the nationality of each of the parties shall retain their right to sit in the case before the Court.

(2) If the Court includes upon the Bench a judge of the nationality of one of the parties, any other party may choose a person to sit as judge. Such person shall be chosen preferably from among those persons who have been nominated as candidates as provided in Articles 4 and 5.

(3) If the Court includes upon the Bench no judge of the nationality of the parties, each of these parties may proceed to choose a judge as provided in paragraph 2 of this Article.

(4) The provisions of this Article shall apply to the case of Article 26 and 29. In such cases, the President shall request one or, if necessary, two of the members of the Court forming the chamber to give place to the member of the Court of the nationality of the parties concerned, and, failing such, or if they are unable to be present, to the judges specially chosen by the parties.

(5) Should there be several parties in the same interest, they shall, for the purpose of the preceding provisions, be reckoned as one party only. Any doubt upon this point shall be settled by the decision of the Court.

(6) Judges chosen as laid down in paragraphs 2, 3, and 4 of this Article shall fulfil the conditions required by Articles 2, 17 (paragraph 2), 20, and 24 of the present Statute. They shall take part in the decision on terms of complete equality with their colleagues.

Art. 32.(1) Each member of the court shall receive an annual salary.

(2) The President shall receive a special annual allowance.

(3) The Vice-President shall receive a special allowance for every day on which he acts as President.

(4) The judges chosen under Article 31, other than members of the Court, shall receive compensation for each day on which they exercise their functions.

(5) These salaries, allowances, and compensation shall be fixed by the general Assembly. They may not be decreased during the term of office.

(6) The salary of the Registrar shall be fixed by the General Assembly on the proposal of the Court.

(7) Regulations made by the General Assembly shall fix the conditions under which retirement pensions may be given to members of the Court and to the Registrar and the conditions under which members of the Court and the Registrar shall have their travelling expenses refunded.

(8) The above salaries, allowances, and compensation shall be free of all taxation.

Art. 33. The expenses of the Court shall be borne by the United Nations in such a manner as shall be decided by the General Assembly.

Chapter II. Competence of the Court.

Art. 34.(1) Only states may be parties in cases before the Court.

(2) The Court, subject to and in conformity with its Rules, may request of public international organizations information relevant to cases before it, and shall receive such information presented by such organizations on their own initiative.

(3) Whenever the construction of the constituent instrument of a public international organization or of an international convention adopted thereunder is in question in a case before the Court, the Registrar shall so notify the public international organization concerned and shall communicate to it copies of all the written proceedings.

Art. 35.(1) The Court shall be open to the states parties to the present Statute.

(2) The conditions under which the Court shall be open to other states shall, subject to the special provisions contained in treaties in force, be laid down by the Security Council, but in no case shall such conditions place the parties in position of inequality before the Court.

(3) When a state which is not a Member of the United Nations is a party to a case, the Court shall fix the amount which the party is to contribute towards the expenses of the Court. This provision shall not apply if such state is bearing a share of the expenses of the Court.

Art. 36.(1) The jurisdiction of the Court comprises all cases which the parties refer to it and all matters specially provided for in the Charter of the United Nations or in treaties and conventions in force.

(2) The states parties to the present Statute may at any time declare that they recognize as compulsory ipso facto and without special agreement, in relation to any other state accepting the same obligation, the jurisdiction of the Court in all legal disputes concerning:

(a) the interpretation of a treaty;

(b) any question of international law;

(c) the existence of any fact which, if established, would constitute a breach of an international obligation;

(d) the nature of extent of the reparation to be made for the breach of an international obligation.

(3) The declarations referred to above may be made unconditionally or on condition of reciprocity on the part of several or certain states, or for a certain time.

(4) Such declarations shall be deposited with the Secretary-General of the United Nations, who shall transmit copies thereof to the parties to the Statute and to the Registrar of the Court.

(5) Declarations made under Article 36 of the Statute of the Permanent Court of International Justice and which are still in force shall be deemed, as between the parties to the present Statute, to be acceptances of the compulsory jurisdiction of the International Court of Justice for the period which they still have to run and in accordance with their terms.

(6) In the event of a dispute as to whether the Court has jurisdiction, the matter shall be settled by the decision of the Court.

Art. 37. Whenever a treaty or convention in force provides for reference of a matter to a tribunal to have been instituted by the League of Nations, or to the Permanent Court of International Justice, the matter shall, as between the parties to the present Statute, be referred to the International Court of Justice.

Art. 38.(1) The Court, whose function is to decide in accordance with international law such disputes as are submitted to it, shall apply:

(a) international conventions, whether general or particular, establishing rules expressly recognized by the contesting states;

(b) international custom, as evidence of a general practice accepted as law;

(c) the general principles of law recognized by civilized nations;

(d) subject to the provisions of Article 59, judicial decisions and the teachings of the most highly qualified publicists of the various nations, as subsidiary means for the determination of rules of law.

(2) This provision shall not prejudice the power of the Court to decide a case ex aequo et bono, if the parties agree thereto.

Chapter III. Procedure. Art. 39.(1) The official languages of the Court shall be French and English. If the parties agree that the case shall be conducted in French, the judgment shall be delivered in French. If the parties agree that the case shall be conducted in English, the judgment shall be delivered in English

(2) In the absence of an agreement as to which language shall be employed, each party may, in the pleadings, use the language which it prefers; the decision of the Court shall be given in French and English. In this case the Court shall at the same time determine which of the two texts shall be considered as authoritative.

(3) The Court shall, at the request of any party, authorize a language other than French or English to be used by that party.

Art. 40.(1) Cases are brought before the Court, as the case may be, either by the notification of the special agreement or by a written application addressed to the Registrar. In either case the subject of the dispute and the parties shall be indicated.

(2) The Registrar shall forthwith communicate the application to all concerned.

(3) He shall also notify the Members of the United Nations through the Secretary-General, and also any other states entitled to appear before the Court.

Art. 41.(1) The Court shall have the power to indicate, if it considers that circumstances so require, any provisional measures which ought to be taken to preserve the respective rights of either party.

(2) Pending the final decision, notice of the measures suggested shall forthwith be given to the parties and to the Security Council.

Art. 42.(1) The parties shall be represented by agents.

(2) They may have the assistance of counsel or advocates before the Court.

(3) The agents, counsel, and advocates of parties before the Court shall enjoy the privileges and immunities necessary to the independent exercise of their duties.

Art. 43.(1) The procedure shall consist of two parts: written and oral.

(2) The written proceedings shall consist of the communication to the Court and to the parties of memorials, counter-memorials and, if necessary, replies; also all papers and documents in support.

(3) These communications shall be made through the Registrar, in the order and within the time fixed by the Court.

(4) A certified copy of every document produced by one party shall be communicated to the other party.

(5) The oral proceedings shall consist of the learning by the Court of witnesses, experts, agents, counsel, and advocates.

Art. 44.(1) For the service of all notices upon persons other than the agents, counsel, and advocates, the Court shall apply direct to the government of the state upon whose territory the notice has to be served.

(2) The same provision shall apply whenever steps are to be taken to procure evidence on the spot.

Art. 45. The hearing shall be under the control of the President or, if he is unable to preside, of the Vice-President; if neither is able to preside, the senior judge present shall preside.

Art. 46. The hearing in Court shall be public, unless the Court shall decide otherwise, or unless the parties demand that the public be not admitted.

Art. 47(1) Minutes shall be made at each hearing and signed by the Registrar and the President.

(2) The minutes alone shall be authentic.

Art. 48. The Court shall make orders for the conduct of the case, shall decide the form and time in which each party must conclude its arguments, and make all arrangements connected with the taking of evidence.

Art. 49. The Court may, even before the hearing begins, call upon the agents to produce any document or to supply any explanations. Formal note shall be taken of any refusal.

Art. 50. The Court may, at any time, entrust any individual, body, bureau, commission, or other organization that it may select, with the task of carrying out an enquiry or giving an expert opinion.

Art. 51. During the hearing any relevant questions are to be put to the witnesses and experts under the conditions laid down by the Court in the rules of procedure referred to in Article 30.

Art. 52. After the Court has received the proofs and ecidence within the time specified for the purpose, it may refuse to accept any further oral or written evidence that one party may desire to present unless the other side consents.

Art. 53.(1) Whenever one of the parties does not appear before the Court, or fails to defend its case, the other party may call upon the Court to decide in favour of its claim.

(2) The Court must, before doing so, satisfy itself, not only that it has jurisdiction in accordance with Articles 36 and 37, but also that the claim is well founded in fact and law.

Art. 54.(1) When, subject to the control of the Court, the agents, counsel advocates have completed their presentation of the case, the President shall declare the hearing closed.

(2) The Court shall withdraw to consider the judgment.

(3) The deliberations of the court shall take place in private and remain secret.

Art. 55.(1) All questions shall be decided by a majority of the judges present.

(2) In the event of an equality of votes, the President or the judge who acts in his place shall have a casting vote.

Art. 56.(1) The judgment shall state the reasons on which it is based.

(2) It shall contain the names of the judges who have taken part in the decision.

Art. 57. If the judgment does not represent in whole or in part the unanimous opinion of the judges, any judge shall be entitled to deliver a separate opinion.

Art. 58. The Judgment shall be signed by the President and by the Registrar. It shall be read in open court, due notice having been given to the agents.

Art. 59. The decision of the Court has no binding force except between the parties and in respect of that particular case.

Art. 60. The judgment is final and without appeal. In the event of dispute as to the meaning or scope of the judgment, the Court shall construe it upon the request of any party.

Art. 61.(1) An application for revision of a judgment may be made only when it is based upon the discovery of some fact of such a nature as to be a decisive factor, which fact was, when the judgment was given, unknown to the Court and also to the party claiming revision, always provided that such ignorance was not due to negligence.

(2) The proceedings for revision shall be opened by a judgment of the Court expressly recording the existence of the new fact, recognizing that it has such a character as to lay the case open to revision, and declaring the application admissible on this ground.

(3) The Court may require previous compliance with the terms of the judgment before it admits proceedings in revision.

(4) The application for revision must be made at latest within six months of the discovery of the new fact.

(5) No application for revision may be made after the lapse of ten years from the date of the judgment.

Art. 62.(1) Should a state consider that it has an interest of a legal nature which may be affected by the decision in the case, it may submit a request to the Court to be permitted to intervene.

(2) It shall be for the Court to decide upon this request.

Art. 63.(1) Whenever the construction of a convention to which states other than those concerned in the case are parties is in question, the Registrar shall notify all such states forthwith.

(2) Every state so notified has the right to intervene in the proceedings; but if it uses this right, the construction given by the judgment will be equally binding upon it.

Art. 64. Unless otherwise decided by the Court, each party shall bear its own costs.

Chapter IV. Advisory opinions. Art. 65.(1) The Court may give an advisory opinion on any legal question at the request of whatever body may be authorized by or in accordance with the Charter of the United Nations to make such a request.

(2) Questions upon which the advisory opinion of the Court is asked shall be laid before the Court by means of a written request containing an exact statement of the question upon which an opinion is required, and accompanied by all documents likely to throw light upon the question.

Art. 66.(1) The Registrar shall forthwith give notice of the request for an advisory opinion to all states entitled to appear before the Court.

(2) The Registrar shall also, by means of a special and direct communication, notify any state entitled to appear before the Court or international organization considered by the Court, or, should it not be sitting, by the President, as likely to be able to furnish information on the question, that the Court will be prepared to receive, within a time limit to be fixed by the President, written statements, or to hear, at a public sitting to be held for the purpose, oral statements relating to the question.

Art. 67. The Court shall deliver its advisory opinions in open court, notice having been given to the Secretary-General and to the representatives of Members of the United Nations, of other states and of international organizations immediately concerned.

Art. 68. In the exercise of its advisory functions the Court shall further be guided by the provisions of the present Statute which apply in contentious cases to the extent to which it recognizes them to be applicable.

Chapter V. Amendment. Art. 69. Amendments to the present Statute shall be effected by the same procedure as is provided by the Charter of the United Nations for amendments to that Charter, subject however to any provisions which the General Assembly upon recommendation which the Security Council may adopt concerning the participation of states which are parties to the present Statute but are not Members of the United Nations.

Art. 70. The Court shall have power to propose such amendments to the present Statute as it may deem necessary, through written communications to the Secretary-General, for consideration in conformity with the provisions of Article 69.

The Charter of the United Nations and the Statute of the International Court of Justice, New York, 1975.

INTERNATIONAL DAY AGAINST DRUG ABUSE. ▷ Drug Abuse.

INTERNATIONAL DEMOCRATIC UNION. A union of the conservative and democratic parties of Western Europe, Japan and the USA, f. 1938, in London.

INTERNATIONAL DEVELOPMENT ASSOCIATION. ▷ IDA.

INTERNATIONAL DEVELOPMENT STRATEGY, IDS. In the UN system the agreed measures among governments to reach economic and social development targets. ▷ Development international strategy for the 1980s.

UN Chronicle, Oct. 1982, p. 97.

INTERNATIONAL ECONOMIC CO-OPERATION. A subject of international law and world and regional international conferences. Principles of international economic co-operation were not uniform in various regions of the world and in various periods of history. The first attempt to codify these principles and apply them to the contemporary international situation was undertaken by the First World Conference on Trade and Development, UNCTAD in Geneva in 1964, where a resolution Principles of International Economic Co-operation was adopted.

INTERNATIONAL FALCON MOVEMENT–SOCIALIST EDUCATIONAL INTERNATIONAL, f. 1924, Brussels. Consultative Status with ECOSOC, UNESCO and Council of Europe. Publ.: IFM-SEI Documents.

Yearbook of International Organizations 1986/87; The Europa Yearbook 1988, A World Survey, Vol. I, London, 1988.

INTERNATIONAL FAMILY LAW. ▷ Family International Law

INTERNATIONAL FINANCE CORPORATION. ▷ IFC.

INTERNATIONAL FINANCES. An international term for monetary transactions of both interstate and international financial institutions playing the most important role in international economic relations. International finances also comprise the ▷ loans, international. The problem of modern policies in the field of international finances arose after World War I in connection with the efforts of the LN to rebuild the international monetary system based on a universal restoration of the gold standard. The great economic crisis of 1929–39 almost completely paralyzed international financial policies, and only one American–British–French convention, 1936, went into force. On the initiative of the USA two plans for a new system of international finances were developed during the period of World War II:

The Keynes plan for creating an International Compensation Union announced in April, 1943 by the English economist G.M. Keynes (1883–1946).

The White Plan for establishing a Stabilization Fund announced in April 1943 by the American economist H.D. White (1903–48), an advisor to the US Treasury Department.

Both plans were fundamental documents at the UN Conference in Bretton Woods, 1944, which decided

International Law

in favor of the White Plan and created the ▷ IMF (Bretton Woods Conference and Agreements 1944).

B. HANSEN, *Foreign and Exchange Reserves. A Contribution to the Theory of International Capital Movements*, Amsterdam, 1961; E. BURTRAND, *Économie financière internationale*, Paris, 1971; C. CARLSON, *International Financial Decisions, A Study in the Theory of International Business Finance*, London, 1976.

INTERNATIONAL INSTITUTE FOR PEACE, f. 1957, Vienna; studies the possibilities of peaceful co-existence and co-operation between the two social world systems. Publ.: Peace and the Sciences.

Yearbook of International Organizations, 1986/87.

INTERNATIONAL INSTITUTE FOR STRATEGIC STUDIES. F. 1955, London as Institute for Strategic Studies. International center in Europe for continuous study, discussion and research on the problems of international security, defense and arms control in the nuclear age. Publ. *Studies in International Security, Adelphi Papers, Military Balance, Strategic Survey*. Members: ordinary and associate in 57 countries.

Yearbook of International Organizations. D. ROBERTSON, *Guide to Modern Defense and Strategy*, Detroit, 1988.

INTERNATIONAL INVESTMENTS BANK, IIB, Mezhdunarodniy Bank Inviestitsiy, f. Jan. 1, 1970 in Moscow. Intergovernmental finance institution of the CMEA countries: Bulgaria, Cuba, Czechoslovakia, the GDR, Hungary, Mongolia, Poland, Romania and the USSR. The Statute of the Bank constitutes an integral part of the intergovernmental agreement signed on July 10, 1970 in Moscow. Consultative status with UNCTAD. Publ.: *Information Bulletin*.
The text of art. 2 of the Agreement concerning the establishment of the Bank reads as follows:

"The Basic function of the Bank shall be the provision of long-term and medium-term credits primarily for the implementation of measures relating to the international socialist division of labor, specialization and co-operation in production, expenditure for the broadening of the raw materials and fuels base in the common interest and the building of projects in other branches of the economy which are in the common interest with a view to the development of the economy of the countries members of the Bank, and for the building of projects to further the development of the national economies of those countries and for other purposes established by the Council of the Bank and compatible with its functions.
In its activities the Bank shall be guided by the necessity of ensuring the effective utilization of its resources, guaranteeing solvency with respect to its liabilities and strict responsibility for the repayment of credits which it provides.
Projects financed by credits from the Bank must meet the highest scientific and technical standards and be capable of producing high-quality goods at lowest possible cost to sell at prices consistent with the world market.
The Bank shall provide credits for the implementation of measures and the building of projects of interest to some of the member countries, subject to the conclusion of long-term agreements or other understandings concerning the implementation of the measures, the building of the projects and the sale of their output in the common interest of the member countries, recommendations concerning the co-ordination of the national economic plans of the countries members of the Bank also being taken into account.
The bank's activities shall be organically linked with the system of measures for further developing socialist economic co-operation and reducing the difference between and gradually equalizing the levels of economic development of member countries, subject to observance of the principle of optimal effectiveness in the utilization of credits. By agreement with the Council for Mutual Economic Assistance the Bank shall join with the appropriate organs of the Council for Mutual Economic Assistance in considering questions relating to the co-ordination of the national economic plans of member countries in the field of capital investments which are in the common interest."

UNTS, Vol. 801, 1971, pp. 319–388; W.E. BUTLER (ed.), *A Source Book on Socialist International Organizationns*, Alphen, 1978, pp. 319–358.

INTERNATIONALISM. An international term for a working class solidarity movement, initiated by the ▷ International Working Men's Association, 1864. ▷ Religious internationalism.

T. RUYSSEN, *Les sources doctrinales de l'internationalisme*, 2 Vols., Paris, 1957; Ch.L. LANGE, A. SCHON, *Histoire de l'internationalisme*, 3 Vols., Oslo, 1963; F. HALLIDAY, *Three Concepts of Internationalism, in: International Affairs*, London, Spring, 1988.

INTERNATIONALIST. An international term of dual meaning for: a person whose world view is described as internationalism and for a scholar, expert in international law and international relations. The former concept was created in the 19th century and referred to international workers' movements, the latter was introduced in the UN system by Latin American States.

INTERNATIONALIZATION. An international term for multilateral protection of land or sea zones, rivers, canals or straits; subject of international agreements.

INTERNATIONALIZED SEAT. A territory, over which the state does not exercise full sovereignty, having transferred it to an intergovernmental organization. In 1968, the OAS legal advisers agreed to apply a legal fiction in relation to the Western Hemisphere cities serving as seats of intergovernmental conferences, with the aim of avoiding prestige absences from such conferences by those states that did not maintain diplomatic relations or were in conflict with the host state. Owing to the legal fiction that a city is throughout a conference an internationalized seat (adopted by the XI Consultative Meeting of Ministers of Foreign Affairs of American Republics in 1968), the protracted internal crisis of the OAS, preventing the attendance at OAS meetings of all member states, because one or more was always in conflict with the host state, came to an end.

PAU, *The Final Act of the XI Consultative Meeting of Ministers of Foreign Relation of American Republics*, Washington, DC, 1967.

INTERNATIONAL LAW. A system of principles and provisions regulating relations among states; earlier a Latin term: ius gentium, "law of nations", was in general use; appeared in English and French at the end of 18th century. The term "law of nations" is still preserved in German as Völkerrecht. The first principles of international law were formulated in antiquity: in the East, in Greece and Rome. The oldest and so far most important source of international law are bilateral and multilateral treaties. One of the oldest treaties is the one between Eannatum, ruler of Lagash in Mesopotamia, and Umma, also a city-state in Mesopotamia (3100 B.C.); one of the most important is the treaty of friendship and alliance between Ramses II and the King of the Hittites, Hattusilis III (1269) B.C., carved in stone); its replica, a gift of the Turkish government, is on display at the UN headquarters (▷ Hattusilis and Ramses II Treaty, 1269 B.C.). In the 20th century the number of bi- and multilateral treaties registered in the League of Nations and in the United Nations exceeded 10,000. Of different importance are the verdicts and opinions pronounced by the Permanent Court of Justice founded by the League of Nations and by the International Court of Justice established by the United Nations. International law has been developing since late medieval times under the dominating influence of European states. Development of international law in Europe was stimulated by the first discoveries and beginnings of colonization. Numerous advocates of restricting the rule *ius ad bellum* included the Dominican Francisco de Vitoria (1482–1546), whose views were similar to those of Andrzej Frycz-Modrzewski (1503–72), a Polish scholar, as well as the Spaniard Francisco Suarez (1548–1617) and the Italian Alberto Gentilus (1552–1608). In the 17th century, a Dutch lawyer Stuing de Groot (1583–1645), also known as Hugo Grotius, became famous for three books entitled, *De Iure Belli ac Pacis*, publ. in Amsterdam in 1625. In the 18th century a significant contribution to the development of international law was made by Charles de Secondat Montesquieu (1689–1755), author of *Esprit des Lois*, in which he formulated the principles of the sovereignty of states and the doctrine ▷ *Pacta sunt servanda*; and Immanuel Kant (1724–1804), author of *Zum ewigen Frieden*. Also in the 18th century, a number of ideas on international law from the Enlightenment found their expression in the Declaration of Independence of the United States of America of July 4, 1775 and in the Constitution of the United States of Sept. 17, 1787; and then in the ideas of the ▷ Rights of Man and of Citizen, Declaration of, 1789, annexed to the Constitution of the Republic of France of June 24, 1793. A great contribution to the development of modern international law was made by the provisions of the Vienna Congress of 1815 and the conventions restricting the rule *Ius in bello* of 1864, 1874, 1899 and 1907.
The ban on war as a method for resolving international disputes and the call for non-intervention and peaceful international co-operation were developed in the 19th century by the young Latin American Republics in the spirit of Simon Bolivar (1783–1830). The development of the international law in the 20th century began after World War I under the aegis of the League of Nations, and after World War II, of the United Nations. On Dec. 20, 1965 the UN General Assembly Res. 2099/XX established the UN Program of Assistance in the Teaching Study, Dissemination and wider Appreciation of International Law.
Major inter-governmental and extra-governmental organizations working in the area of codification and development of the international law:
Institut de Droit International, f. 1873, in Brussels, with the task of developing and codifying international law and composed of 120 prominent scholars elected from various countries. Publ.: *Annuaire*, and specific papers.
Hispano-Luso-American Institute of International Law, Instituto Hispano-Luso Americano de Derecho Internacional, est. 1951 in Madrid, in order to develop international law in the spirit of the Spanish school, with scholars from Latin America, Spain, Philippines and Portugal. Publ.: *Annuario*.
Inter-American Research Institute of International Law, f. 1964, in Washington, DC, with the task of conducting legal research on the international system and unifying the science of international law on the American continent. Publ.: various studies and papers.
International Federation for European Law, f. 1961, in Brussels, with the task of unifying laws binding in the member states of the European Economic Community. Unites national associations of the EEC.

International Institute of Space-Law, Institut International du Droit Spatial, f. 1960 in Paris, by the International Astronautical Federation, with scholars from various countries.

International Maritime Committee, IMC, f. 1897, Antwerp, Belgium, with the task of unifying international law. Affiliates national associations. Publ.: *Bulletin of IMC*.

International Law Association, ILA, f. 1873 in Brussels, under the name: Association for the Reform and Codification of the Law of Nations; its constitution was modified in 1895, 1950 and 1958; headquarters London. Members from several dozen countries. Consultative status with ECOSOC and UNESCO. One of the first to begin codification of international law. Structure: Conference every two years. Executive Council and Commissions. Between Aug. 30 and Sept. 1, 1973 in Brussels, a session of the ILA was held on the occasion of the hundredth anniversary of that organization. Publ.: *ILA Reports* and studies.

A separate and important chapter in the development of international law has been played by national associations of legal sciences, which initiate developmental and codification work in co-operation with international and other legal associations, both national and international.

The Max Planck Institute for Comparative Public Law and International Law, publ.: *Public International Law*, a current bibliography of articles in English, French, German and Spanish.

The sources of International Law include the customs, general principles conventions, treaties, judicial decisions, doctrines, the United Nations Charter and other general acts of the UN system recognized by the majority of nations.

A. BELLO, *Principios de Derecho Internacional*, Santiago, 1844; H. WHEATON, *A History of the Law of Nations*, London, 1855; C. CALVO, *Dictionnaire du Droit International Public et Privé*, Paris, 1885; J.B. MOORE, *A Digest of International Law*, London, 1906; L. OPPENHEIM, *International Law*, London, 1906; A. ALVAREZ, *La Codification du Droit International*, Paris, 1912; K. STRUPP, *Wörterbuch des Völkerrechts und Diplomatie*, Berlin, 1924–1929; H. LAUTERPACHT, *Annual Digest and Reports of Public International Law Cases (1919–1950)*, 23 Vols., London 1929–60; M.O. HUDSON, *International Legislation. A Collection of the Texts of Multilateral International Instruments of General Interest (1919–1945)*, 9 Vols., Washington, DC, 1931–50; H. LAUTERPACHT, *The Functions of Law in the International Community*, London, 1933; J. SPIROPOULUS, *Traité Théorique et Pratique du Droit International Public*, Paris, 1933; *Recueil des Cours, 1936*; IV, pp. 475–692; A. ALVAREZ, *Exposé des motifs et declarations des grands principes du droit international*, Paris, 1938; R. MORENO, *Derecho Internacional Público*, Buenos Aires, 1940; A. DE BUSTAMANTE, *Manual de Derecho Internacional Público*, La Habana, 1943; G.H. HACKWORT, *Digest of International Law*, 8 Vols., Washington, DC, 1940–44; L.A. PODESTA COSTA, *Manual de Diritto Internazional Publico*, Roma, 1943; C.C. HYDE, *International Law Chiefly as Interpreted and Applied by the United States*. Boston, 1945; W.N. DURDIENEVSKI, S.B. KRILOV, *Mezhdunarodnoye Pravo*, Moskva, 1947; L. EHRLICH, *Prawo Narodów*, Cracow, 1947; P.C. JESSUP, *A Modern Law of Nations*, New York, 1948; J. BRIERLY, *The Law of Nations*, Oxford, 1949; M. SIBERT, *Traité du Droit International Public*, Paris, 1951; M.J. SIERRA, *Tratado de Derecho Internacional Público*, Mexico, DF, 1951; A.M. PAREDES, *Manual de Derecho Internacional Público*, Buenos Aires, 1951; H. KELSEN, *Principles of International Law*, New York, 1952; C. BAEZ, *Derecho Internacional Público Europeo y Americano*, Asunción, 1952; W.I. LISOV-SKI, *Mezhdunarodnoye pravo*, Moskva, 1957; W.L. GOULD, *An Introduction to International Law*, New York, 1957; D.B. LEVIN, *Osnovnie problemy sovremennogo sovdunarodnogo prava*, Moskva, 1958; L.A. MODZHORIAN, *Subiekty mezhdunarodnogo prava*, Moskva, 1958; M. LACHS, *Umowy wielostronne*, Warszawa, 1958; C. SEPULVEDA, *Curso de Derecho Internacional Publico*, Mexico, DF, 1960; *Dictionnaire de la Terminologie du Droit International*, Paris, 1960; K. STRUPP, H.J. SCHLOCHAUER, *Wörterbuch des Völkerrechts*, Berlin, 1960–62; A. KLAFKOWSKI, *Prawo Miedzynarodowe Publiczne*, Warszawa, 1964; W.K. SOBAKIN, *Sovremmennoye Mezhdunarodnoye Pravo*, Moskva, 1964; F.I. KOZHEVNIKOV, *Kurs Mezhdunarodnogo Prava*, Moskva, 1966; M. SORENSEN, *Manual of Public International Law*, London, 1968; J.H.W. VERZIJL, *International Law in Historical Perspective*, 7 Vols., Leiden, 1968–73; R. LOPEZ JIMINEZ, *Tratado de Derecho Internacional Público*, San Salvador, 1970; W.M. CHJIKVADZE, *Kurs Mezhdunarodnogo prava*, 6 Vols., Moskva, 1967–71; H. BOKOR-SZEGO, *New States and International Law*, Budapest, 1970; P.E. CORBETT, *The Growth of World Law*, Princeton, N.Y., 1971; R.P. ANADHI (ed.), *Asian States and the Development of Universal International Law*, Delhi, 1972; M. AKEHURST, "The Hierarchy of the Sources of International Law", in: *The British Year Book of International Law 1974–1975*; Ch.N. OKEKE, *Controversial Subjects of Contemporary International Law*, The Hague, 1974; A. FAVRE, *Principe du droit des gens*, Fribourg, 1974; J.A. COHEN, H. CHIN, *People's China and International Law. A Documentary Study*, Princeton, 1974; A. VERDROSS, B. SIMMA, *Universelles Völkerrecht. Theorie und Praxis*, Berlin, 1976; *Encyclopedia of Public International Law*, Amsterdam, 1981; M. AKEHURST, *A Modern Introduction to International Law*, Winchester, 1982; BIN CHANG (ed.), *International Law Teaching and Practice*, London, 1982; B.B. FERENCZ, *Enforcing International Law. A Way to World Peace. A Documentary History and Analysis*, 2 Vols., Dobbs Ferry, N.Y., 1983; R.St.J. MACDONALD, *The Structure and Process of International Law*, The Hague, 1983. *UN Chronicle*, January, 1984, p. 69; C. PARRY, J.P. GRANT, A. PARRY, A.D. WATTS, *Encyclopedic Dictionary of International Law*, New York, 1986; B. URQUHART, *The United Nations and International Law*, Cambridge, 1986; I. DETTER DE LUPIS, *The Concepts of International Law*, Stockholm, 1987; R.L. BLEDSOE, R.L. BOCZEK, *The International Law Dictionary*, Oxford, 1987.

INTERNATIONAL LAW AND NATIONAL LAW.

A subject of dispute on the relation of the one to the other between the advocates of an essential separation of the two (dualism) and the advocates of their essential unity (monism). The first view held by A. Anzilotti, H. Lauterbach, and L. Ehrlich among others, stemmed from the conclusion that different sources of international law and national law (also called internal law) determined their different legal relations; hence international law could be binding for a given state if it was integrated by the state's constitution or by a legal act. The second monistic view, represented by, i.a., H. Helsen and A. Verdross, holds that all legal norms form a unity, the higher stage of which is international law, or in a controversy between the provisions of international law and national law, the former is superior to the latter. The monistic view is opposed by antagonists of supranational institutions, in whose opinion it reduces the sovereignty of states.

H. LAUTERPACHT, *The Function of Law in the International Community*, London, 1933; H. KELSEN, *Principles of International Law*, New York, 1952.

INTERNATIONAL LAW AND THE LEAGUE OF NATIONS AND THE UNITED NATIONS.

The 20th century marked a hundred years of codification and development of international public law. An initiative to this end was taken by the League of Nations, which on Sept. 22, 1927, established a Committee of Experts for the Progressive Codification of International Law. In 1927 the League of Nations convened Conferences for Codification of law in the areas of citizenship, shipping law, and certain fields of responsibilities of states. In turn, between Mar. 13 and Apr. 12, 1930, in The Hague, the Second Conference on Codification of International Law was held, with the participation of 42 states: Argentina, Australia, Austria, Belgium, Brazil, Bulgaria, Canada, Chile, China, Colombia, Cuba, Czechoslovakia, Denmark, Egypt, El Salvador, Estonia, Finland, France, Germany, Greece, Hungary, India, Ireland, Japan, Luxembourg, Latvia, Lithuania, Mexico, Monaco, the Netherlands, Nicaragua, Norway, Peru, Persia, Poland, Romania, South Africa, Sweden, Switzerland, Turkey, the USSR and Yugoslavia. The Conference adopted the Convention on Citizenship and recommendations regarding the territorial sea. In Geneva, codification by the League of Nations was presented in the Report of the Committee of Experts of the League of Nations of Nov. 25, 1941. In the spring of 1945, the United Nations Charter recommended that the UN General Assembly promote the progressive development of international law and its codification. The Assembly in accordance with this recommendation, by Res. 94/I of Dec. 11, 1946 established a Commission for the Progressive Development of International Law and its Codification, which after 30 meetings between May 12 and June 17, 1948 recommended the establishment of a Commission on International Law and prepared its constitution, which was approved by the UN General Assembly Res. 174/II, Nov. 21, 1947. Under UN auspices numerous important areas of international law have been codified. The greatest contribution to this end has been made by the UN Commission on International Law, whose work covered: part of the law of the sea, diplomatic and consular law, the legal situation of international organizations, the law of treaties; and also drafting the Nuremberg Principles and the verdict of the Nuremberg Court, the declarations of the rights and duties of states, codification of principles on the responsibility and succession of states and international rules for waterways.

Other agencies of the United Nations began codification of international trade law (Commission of the United Nations for the International Trade Law, UNCITRAL, established in 1966) and the law of outer space (UN Commission for Peaceful Utilization of Outer Space, established in 1959). In 1962 the Legal Sub-Committee began work on the declaration of Principles of International Law and in 1966 on the law of treaties, followed by international law governing environmental protection. The codification of aeronautical law is being done by the ICAO, of maritime law by the IMCO, war-time law by the International Committee of the Red Cross, labor law by the ILO. UN efforts have given international law a universal character, recognizing the equality of all states. The war crimes against humanity have played an important role in preparation and adoption of such significant treaties for international law as the Convention on genocide of 1948, Convention on the prohibition of racial discrimination of 1965, the Covenants on human rights of 1966. The UN General Assembly also adopted conventions and treaties concerning the limitation of armaments, the Treaty on the Antarctic of 1959, the treaties on the prohibition of nuclear tests in the air, outer space and under water of 1963, non-proliferation of nuclear arms of 1968 and many others. A great achievement of the UN was the fact that the UN General Assembly in the execution of its Resolutions: 1815/XVII of Dec. 18, 1962, 1966/XVIII of Dec. 16, 1963, 2103/XX of Dec. 20, 1965, 2181/XXI of Dec. 12, 1966, 2327/XXII of Dec. 18, 1967, 2463/XXIII of Dec. 20, 1968, and 2533/XXIV of Dec. 8, 1969 on the necessity for developing and modifying the principles of international law concerning friendly relations and co-operation among states, on Oct. 24, 1972 adopted Res. 2625/XXVII, prepared by the Special Committee in Geneva, Mar. 30–May 1, 1970, Declaration on the Principles of International Law concerning friendly relations and co-operation among states, in accordance with the UN Charter.

Recently, both regional and universal international organizations are growing in importance due to the fact that they have acquired numerous rights, which previously were vested only in states (e.g. the right to conclude international agreements).

Regional codification of international law forms a separate chapter in the development of international law in the second half of the 20th century, connected with processes of integration in Europe, Africa and Latin America, where the traditions of legal congresses held in 1877, 1883, 1888 are still vital and the treaties and conventions adopted by the International American Conferences between 1889 and 1948. The United Nations in its numerous publications keeps detailed documentation of the growth of international law, such as *UN Legislative Series, UN Treaty Series, Yearbook of International Law Commission, Reports of International Arbitral Awards* and others. An auxiliary publication is the *Cumulative Index of the UN Series*. These publications help to promote the dissemination of international law, a task entrusted to the Special Committee on Technical Assistance to Promote the Teaching, Study, Dissemination and Wider Appreciation of International Law, established in 1968 by UN Res. 1968/XVIII. At the same time, the UN General Assembly requested the Committee to keep a world register of experts and lectures in international law.

Q. WRIGHT, *International Law and the UN*, New York, 1960; J. ROBINSON, *International Law and Organization*, Leiden, 1967; U. THANT, "International Law and the UN", in *Monthly Chronicle*, August 1968; K. WOLFKE, *Rozwój i kodyfikacja prawa międzynarodowego. Wybrane zagadnienia z polityki ONZ*, Wrocław, 1972; H. BOKOR-SZEGO, *The Role of the UN in International Legislation*, Amsterdam, 1978.

INTERNATIONAL LAW COMMISSION. A UN Commission established Dec. 11, 1946, initiated its activity on June 17, 1948. The International Law Commission is an expert group involved in the progressive development of international law and its codification. The Commission seeks to make international law a more effective means of implementing the purposes and principles set forth in the Charter of the United Nations. Most of its work consists of drafting articles on various aspects of international law which could ultimately be included in international conventions of other legal instruments. The 34 members of the Commission serve five-year terms, which will expire on 31 Dec. 1986. The membership is as follows:

Richard Osuolale A. Akinjide (Nigeria), Riyadh Mahmoud Sami Al-Qaysi (Iraq), Balanda Mikuin Leliel Balanda (Zaïre), Julio Barboxa (Argentina), Boutros Boutros-Ghali (Egypt), Carlos Calero Rodrigues (Brazil), Jorge Castañeda (Mexico), Leonardo Diaz Gonzalez (Venezuela), Khalafalla El Rasheed Mohamed-Ahmed (Sudan), Jens Evensen (Norway), Constantin Flitan (Romania), Laurel B. Francis (Jamaica), Jorge E. Illueca (Panama), Andreas J. Jacovides (Cyprus), S.P. Jagota (India), Abdul G. Goroma (Sierra Leone), Jose Manuel Lacleta-Muñoz (Spain), Ahmed Mahiou (Algeria), Chafic Malek (Lebanon), Stephen C. McCaffrey (United States), Zhengyu Ni (China), Frank X Njenga (Kenya), Motoo Ogiso (Japan), Syed Sharifuddin Pirzada (Pakistan), Robert Quentin-Baxter (New Zealand), Edilbert Razafindralambo (Madagascar), Paul Reuter

(France), Willem Riphagen (Netherlands), Sir Ian Sinclair (United Kingdom), Constantin A. Stravropoulos (Greece), Sompong Sucharitkul (Thailand), Doudou Thiam (Senegal), Nikolai A. Ushakov (Soviet Union) and Alexander Yankov (Bulgaria). Since 1949 the ILC issues annually the Yearbook of the International Law Commission, in two volumes, containing summary records of sessions and documents; also Annual Report of the ILC to the General Assembly.

"Commission Continues Broad Effort at Developing International Law", in: *UN Chronicle*, October, 1983, pp. 23–26.

INTERNATIONAL LAW PRINCIPLES POSTULATED IN 1944. Early in 1942 a number of American and Canadian internationalists in a series of exploratory meetings in United States and Canada prepared Postulates, Principles and Proposals to aid in revitalizing and strengthening international law after World War II. The text of the Principles served as a basis for the American draft of the UN Charter. The text is as follows:

"Principle 1. Each State has a legal duty to carry out in full good faith its obligations under international law, and it may not invoke limitations contained in its own constitution or laws as an excuse for a failure to perform this duty.

Principle 2. Each State has a legal duty to see that conditions prevailing within its own territory do not menace international peace and order, and to this end it must treat its own population in a way which will not violate the dictates of humanity and justice or shock the conscience of mankind.

Principle 3. Each State has a legal duty to refrain from intervention in the internal affairs of any other State.

Principle 4. Each State has a legal duty to prevent the organization within its territory of activities calculated to foment civil strife in the territory of any other State.

Principle 5. Each State has a legal duty to cooperate with other States in establishing and maintaining agencies of the Community of States for dealing with matters of concern to the Community, and to collaborate in the work of such agencies.

Principle 6. Each State has a legal duty to employ pacific means and none but pacific means in seeking to settle its disputes with other States, and failing settlement by other pacific means to accept the settlement of its disputes by the competent agency of the Community of States.

Principle 7. Each State has a legal duty to refrain from any use of force and from any threat to use force in its relations with another State, except as authorized by the competent agency of the Community of States; but subject to immediate reference to and approval by the competent agency of the Community of States, a State may oppose by force an unauthorized use of force made against it by another State.

Principle 8. Each State has a legal duty to take, in co-operation with other States, such measures as may be prescribed by the competent agency of the Community of States for preventing or suppressing a use of force by any State in its relations with another State.

Principle 9. Each State has a legal duty to conform to the limitations prescribed by the competent agency of the Community of States and to submit to the supervision and control of such agency, with respect to the size and type of its armaments.

Principle 10. Each State has a legal duty to refrain from entering into any agreement with another State, the performance of which would be inconsistent with the discharge of its duties under general international law."

The text of the Postulates is as follows:

"Postulate 1. The States of the world form a community, and the protection and advancement of the common interests of their peoples require effective organization of the Community of States.

Postulate 2. The law of the Community of States is international law. The development of an adequate system of international law depends upon continuous collaboration by States to promote the common welfare of all peoples and to maintain just and peaceful relations between States.

Postulate 3. The conduct of each State in its relations with other States and with the Community of States is subject to international law, and the sovereignty of a State subject to the limitations of international law.

Postulate 4. Any failure by a State to carry out its obligations under international law is a matter of concern to the Community of States.

Postulate 5. Any use of force or any threat to use force by a State in its relations with another State is a matter of concern to the Community of States.

Postulate 6. The maintenance of just and peaceful relations between States requires orderly procedures by which international situations can be readjusted as need arises."

"The International Law of the Future. A Statement of a Community of Views by North America", in: *International Conciliation*, No. 399, April, 1944, pp. 251–373.

INTERNATIONAL LAW PRINCIPLES, UN DECLARATION, 1970. Declaration on Principles of International Law concerning Friendly Relations and Co-operation among States, adopted unanimously by the UN General Assembly, Res. 2625/XXV, on Oct. 24, 1970. The text is as follows:

"The General Assembly,
Recalling its resolutions 1815 (XVII) of 18 December 1962, 1966 (XVIII) of 16 December 1963, 2103 (XX) of 20 December 1965, 2181 (XXI) of 12 December 1966, 2327 (XXII) of 18 December 1967, 2463 (XXIII) of 20 December 1968 and 2533 (XXIV) of 8 December 1969, in which it affirmed the importance of the progressive development and codification of the principles of international law concerning friendly relations and co-operation among States.

Having considered the report of the Special Committee on Principles of International Law concerning Friendly Relations and Co-operation among States which met in Geneva from 31 March to 1 May, 1970.

Emphasizing the paramount importance of the Charter of the United Nations for the maintenance of international peace and security and for the development of friendly relations and co-operation among States,

Deeply convinced that the adoption of the Declaration on Principles of International Law concerning Friendly Relations and Co-operation among States in accordance with the Charter of the United Nations on the occasion of the twenty-fifth anniversary of the United Nations would contribute to the strengthening of world peace and constitute a landmark in the development of international law and of relations among States, in promoting the rule of law among nations and particularly the universal application of the principles embodied in the Charter,

Considering the desirability of the wide dissemination of the text of the Declaration,

(1) Approves the Declaration on Principles of International Law concerning Friendly Relations and Co-operation among States in accordance with the Charter of the United Nations, the text of which is annexed to the present resolution;

(2) Expresses its appreciation to the Special Committee on Principles of International Law concerning Friendly Relations and Co-operation among States for its work resulting in the elaboration of the Declaration;

(3) Recommends that all efforts be made so that the Declaration becomes generally known.

Declaration on Principles of International Law concerning Friendly Relations and Co-operation among States in accordance with the Charter of the United Nations.

Preamble
The General Assembly,
Reaffirming in the terms of the Charter of the United Nations that the maintenance of international peace and security and the development of friendly relations and co-operation between nations are among the fundamental purposes of the United Nations, Recalling that the peoples of the United Nations are determined to practise tolerance and live together in peace with one another as good neighbours,

Bearing in mind the importance of maintaining and strengthening international peace founded upon freedom, equality, justice and respect for fundamental human rights and of developing friendly relations among nations irrespective of their political, economic and social systems of the levels of their development,

Bearing in mind also the paramount importance of the Charter of the United Nations in the promotion of the rule of law among nations,
Considering that the faithful observance of the principles of international law concerning friendly relations and co-operation among States and the fulfilment in good faith of the obligations assumed by States, in accordance with the Charter, is of the greatest importance for the maintenance of international peace and security and for the implementation of the other purposes of the United Nations,
Noting that the great political, economic and social changes in scientific progress which have taken place in the world since the adoption of the Charter give increased importance to these principles and to the need for their more effective application in the conduct of States wherever carried on,
Recalling the established principle that outer space, including the Moon and other celestial bodies, is not subject to national appropriation by claim of sovereignty, by means of use of occupation, or by any other means, and mindful of the fact that consideration is being given in the United Nations to the question of establishing other appropriate provisions similarly inspired,
Convinced that the strict observance by States of the obligation not to intervene in the affairs of any other State is an essential condition to ensure that nations live together in peace with one another, since the practice of any form of intervention not only violates the spirit and letter of the Charter, but also leads to the creation of situations which threaten international peace and security,
Recalling the duty of States to refrain in their international relations from military, political, economic or any other form of coercion aimed against the political independence or territorial integrity of any State.
Considering it essential that all States shall refrain in their international relations from the threat or use of force against the territorial integtity or political independence of any State, or in any other manner inconsistent with the purposes of the United Nations,
Considering it equally essential that all States shall settle their international disputes by peaceful means in accordance with the Charter,
Reaffirming, in accordance with the Charter, the basic importance of sovereign equality and stressing that the purposes of the United Nations can be implemented only if States enjoy sovereign equality and comply fully with the requirements of this principle in their international relations,
Convinced that the subjection of peoples to alien subjugation, domination and exploitation constitutes a major obstacle to the promotion of international peace and security,
Convinced that the principle of equal rights and self-determination of peoples constitutes a significant contribution to contemporary international law, and that its effective application is of paramount importance for the promotion of friendly relations among States, based on respect for the principle of sovereign equality,
Convinced in consequence that any attempt aimed at the partial or total disruption of the national unity and territorial integrity of a State or country or at its political independence is incompatible with the purposes and principles of the Charter,
Considering the provisions of the Charter as a whole and taking into account the role of relevant resolutions adopted by the competent organs of the United Nations relating to the content of the principles,
Considering that the progressive development and codification of the following principles:
(a) The principle that States shall refrain in their international relations from the threat or use of force against the territorial integrity or political independence of any State, or in any other manner inconsistent with the purposes of the United Nations,
(b) The principle that States shall settle their international disputes by peaceful means in such a manner that international peace and security and justice are not endangered,
(c) The duty not to intervene in mattters within the domestic jurisdiction of any State, in accordance with the Charter,
(d) The duty of States to co-operate with one another in accordance with the Charter,
(e) The principle of equal rights and self-determination of peoples,
(f) The principle of sovereign equality of States,
(g) The principle that States shall fulfill in good faith the obligations assumed by them in accordance with the Charter so as to secure their more effective application within the international community, would promote the realization of the purposes of the United Nations,
Having considered the principles of international law relating to friendly relations and co-operation among States,
1. Solemnly proclaims the following principles:
The principle that States shall refrain in their international relations from the threat or use of force against the territorial integrity or political independence of any State, or in any other manner inconsistent with the purposes of the United Nations,
Every State has the duty to refrain in its international relations from the threat or use of force against the territorial integrity or political independence of any State or in any other manner inconsistent with the purposes of the United Nations. Such a threat or use of force constitutes a violation of international law and the Charter of the United Nations and shall never be employed as a means of settling international issues.
A war of aggression constitutes a crime against the peace, for which there is responsibility under international law. In accordance with the purposes and principles of the United Nations, States have the duty to refrain from propaganda for wars of aggression.
Every State has the duty to refrain from the threat or use of force to violate the existing international boundaries of another State or as a means of solving international disputes, including territorial disputes and problems concerning frontiers of States,
Every State likewise has the duty to refrain from the threat or use of force to violate international lines of demarcation, such as armistice lines, established by or pursuant to an international agreement to which it is a party or which it is otherwise bound to respect. Nothing in the foregoing shall be construed as prejudicing the positions of the parties concerned with regard to the status and effects of such lines under their special regimes or as affecting their temporary character.
States have a duty to refrain from acts of reprisal involving the use of force.
Every State has the duty to refrain from any forcible action which deprives peoples referred to in the elaboration of the principle of equal rights and self-determination of their right to self-determination and freedom and independence.
Every State has the duty to refrain from organizing or encouraging the organization of irregular forces of armed bands, including mercenaries, for incursion into the territory of another State.
Every State has the duty to refrain from organizing, instigating, assisting or participating in acts of civil strife or terrorist acts in another State or acquiescing in organized activities within its territory directed towards the commission of such acts, when the acts referred to in the present paragraph involve a threat or use of force.
The territory of a State shall not be the object of military occupation resulting from the use of force in contravention of the provisions of the Charter. The territory of a State shall not be the object of acquisition by another State resulting from the threat or use of force. No territorial acquisition resulting from the threat or use of force shall be recognized as legal.
Nothing in the foregoing shall be construed as affecting:
(a) Provisions of the Charter or any international agreement prior to the Charter regime and valid under international law; or
(b) The powers of the Security Council under the Charter. All States shall pursue in good faith negotiations for the early conclusion of a universal treaty on general and complete disarmament under effective international control and strive to adopt appropriate measures to reduce international tensions and strengthen confidence among States.
All States shall comply in good faith with their obligations under the generally recognized principles and rules of international law with respect to the maintenance of international peace and security, and shall endeavour to make the United Nations security system based on the Charter more effective. Nothing in the foregoing paragraphs shall be construed as enlarging or diminishing in any way the scope of the provisions of the Charter concerning cases in which the use of force is lawful.
The principle that States shall settle their international disputes by peaceful means in such a manner that international peace and security and justice are not endangered.
Every State shall settle its international disputes with other States by peaceful means, in such a manner that international peace and security and justice are not endangered.
States shall accordingly seek early and just settlement of their international disputes by negotiation, inquiry, mediation, conciliation, arbitration, judicial settlement, resort to regional agencies or arrangements or other peaceful means of their choice. In seeking such a settlement the parties shall agree upon such peaceful means as may be appropriate to the circumstances and nature of the dispute.
The parties to a dispute have the duty, in the event of failure to reach a solution by any one of the above peaceful means, to continue to seek a settlement of the dispute by other peaceful means agreed upon by them.
States parties to an international dispute, as well as other States, shall refrain from any action which may aggravate the situation so as to endanger the maintenance of international peace and security, and shall act in accordance with the purposes and principles of the United Nations.
International disputes shall be settled on the basis of the sovereign equality of States and in accordance with the principle of free choice of means. Recourse to, or acceptance of a settlement procedure freely agreed to by States with regard to existing or future disputes to which they are parties shall not be regarded as incompatible with sovereign equality.
Nothing in the foregoing paragraphs prejudices or derogates from the applicable provisions of the Charter, in particular those relating to the pacific settlement of international disputes.
The principle concerning the duty not to intervene in matters within the domestic jurisdiction of any State, in accordance with the Charter.
No State or group of States has the right to intervene, directly or indirectly, for any reason whatever, in the internal or external affairs of any other State. Consequently, armed intervention and all other forms of interference or attempted threats against the personality of the State or against its political, economic and cultural elements, are in violation of international law.
No State may use or encourage the use of economic, political or any other type of measures to coerce another State in order to obtain from it the subordination of the exercise of its sovereign rights and to secure from it advantages of any kind. Also, no State shall organize, assist, foment, finance, incite or tolerate subversive, terrorist or armed activities directed towards the violent overthrow of the regime of another State, or interfere in civil strife in another State.
The use of force to deprive peoples of their national identity constitutes a violation of their inalienable rights and of the principle of non-intervention.
Every State has an inalienable right to choose its political, economic, social and cultural systems, without interference in any form by another State.
Nothing in the foregoing paragraph shall be construed as affecting the relevant provisions of the Charter relating to the maintenance of international peace and security.
The duty of States to co-operate with one another in accordance with the Charter.
States have the duty to co-operate with one another, irrespective of the differences in their political, economic and social systems, in the various spheres of international relations, in order to maintain international peace and security and to promote international economic stability and progress, the general welfare of nations and international co-operation free from discrimination based on such differences.
To this end:
(a) States shall co-operate with other States in the maintenance of international peace and security;
(b) States shall co-operate in the promotion of universal respect for, and observance of, human rights and fundamental freedoms for all, and in the elimination of all forms of racial discrimination and all forms of religious intolerance;

(c) States shall conduct their international relations in the economic, social, cultural, technical and trade fields in accordance with the principles of sovereign equality and non-intervention

(d) States Members of the United Nations have the duty to take joint and separate action in co-operation with the United Nations in accordance with the relevant provisions of the Charter.

States should co-operate in the economic, social and cultural fields as well as in the field of science and technology and for the promotion of international cultural and educational progress. States should co-operate in the promotion of economic growth throughout the world, especially that of the developing countries.

The principles of equal rights and self-determination of peoples.

By virtue of the principle of equal rights and self-determination of peoples enshrined in the Charter of the United Nations, all peoples have the right freely to determine, without external interference, their political status and to pursue their economic, social and cultural development, and every State has the duty to respect this right in accordance with the provisions of the Charter.

Every State has the duty to promote, through joint and separate action, realization of the principle of equal rights and self-determination of peoples, in accordance with the provisions of the Charter, and to render assistance to the United Nations in carrying out the responsibilities entrusted to it by the Charter regarding the implementation of the principle, in order:

(a) To promote friendly relations and co-operation among States; and

(b) To bring a speedy end to colonialism, having due regard to the freely expressed will of the peoples concerned;

and bearing in mind that subjection of peoples to alien subjugation, domination and exploitation constitutes a violation of the principle, as well as a denial of fundamental human rights, and is contrary to the Charter.

Every State has the duty to promote through joint and separate action universal respect for an observance of human rights and fundamental freedoms in accordance with the Charter.

The establishment of a sovereign and independent State, the free association or integration with an independent State or the emergence into any other political status freely determined by a people constitute modes of implementing the rights of self-determination by that people.

Every State has the duty to refrain from any forcible action which deprives peoples referred to above in the elaboration of the present principle of their right to self-determination and freedom and independence. In their actions against, and resistance to, such forcible action in pursuit to the exercise of their right to self-determination, such peoples are entitled to seek and to receive support in accordance with the purposes and principles of the Charter. The territory of a colony or other Non-Self-Governing Territory has, under the Charter, a status separate and distinct from the territory of the State administering it; and such separate and distinct status under the Charter shall exist until the people of the colony or Non-Self-Governing Territory have exercised their right of self-determination in accordance with the Charter, and particularly its purposes and principles. Nothing in the foregoing paragraphs shall be construed as authorizing or encouraging any action which would dismember or impair, totally or in part, the territorial integrity or political unity of sovereign and independent States conducting themselves in compliance with the principle of equal rights and self-determination of peoples as described above and thus possessed of a government representing the whole people belonging to the territory without distinction as to race, creed or colour.

Every State shall refrain from any action aimed at the partial or total disruption of the national unity and territorial integrity of any other State or country.

The principle of sovereign equality of States

All States enjoy sovereign equality. They have equal rights and duties and are equal members of the international community, notwithstanding differences of an economic, social, political or other nature.

in particular, sovereign equality includes the following elements:

(a) States are juridically equal;

(b) Each State enjoys the rights inherent in full sovereignty;

(c) Each State has the duty to respect the personality of other States;

(d) The territorial integrity and political independence of the State are inviolable;

(e) Each State has the right freely to choose and develop its political, social, economic and cultural systems;

(f) Each State has the duty to comply fully and in good faith with its international obligations and to live in peace with other States.

The principle that States shall fulfil in good faith the obligations assumed by them in accordance with the Charter.

Every State has the duty to fulfil in good faith the obligations assumed by it in accordance with the Charter of the United Nations.

Every State has the duty to fulfil in good faith its obligations under the generally recognized principles and rules of international law

Every State has the duty to fulfil in good faith its obligations under international agreements valid under the generally recognized principles and rules of international law.

Where obligations arising under international agreements are in conflict with the obligations of Members of United Nations under the Charter of the United Nations, the obligations under the Charter shall prevail.

General Part

2. Declares that:

In their interpretation and application the above principles are interrelated and each principle should be construed in the context of the other principles.

Nothing in this declaration shall be construed as prejudicing in any manner the provisions of the Charter or the rights and duties of Member States under the Charter or the rights of peoples under the Charter, taking into account the elaboration of these rights in this Declaration.

3. Declares further that:

The principles of the Charter which are embodied in this Declaration constitute basic principles of international law, and consequently appeals to all States to be guided by these principles in their international conduct and to develop their mutual relations on the basis of the strict observance of these principles."

UN Yearbook 1970; *UN Monthly Chronicle*, November, 1970.

INTERNATIONAL MARITIME ORGANIZATION. ▷ IMO.

INTERNATIONAL MARITIME SATELLITE ORGANIZATION. ▷ INMARSAT.

INTERNATIONAL METEOROLOGICAL ORGANIZATION, IMO, 1878–1947. One of the oldest intergovernmental organizations; its successor is the ▷ WMO. The acronym ▷ IMO in the UN system, since 1982 means International Maritime Organization.

INTERNATIONAL MILITARY TRIBUNAL. ▷ Military Tribunal, International, IMT, for Germany, 1945–46.

INTERNATIONAL MILITARY TRIBUNAL CHARTER. ▷ Charter of International Military Tribunal, IMT, 1945.

INTERNATIONAL MILITARY TRIBUNAL FOR FAR EAST. ▷ Military Tribunal, International for Far East, 1946–48.

INTERNATIONAL MONETARY FUND. ▷ IMF.

INTERNATIONAL ORGANIZATION. ▷ Organizations International.

INTERNATIONAL PEACE BUREAU. Bureau international de la paix. Internationales Friedensbureau, f. 1892 in Rome, with headquarters in Berne until 1919, afterwards in Geneva. Nobel Peace Prize 1910. Promotes consultation and co-operative action among international and national peace organizations. Members: national committees in Austria, France, the FRG, Japan, Norway, Switzerland and the UK.

A.H. FRIED, *Handbücher der Friedensbewegung*, 2 Vols., Berne, 1911–1913; *Yearbook of International Organizations*.

INTERNATIONAL RED CROSS AND RED CRESCENT MOVEMENT. ▷ Red Cross.

INTERNATIONAL RESEARCH AND TRAINING INSTITUTE FOR THE ADVANCEMENT OF WOMEN, INSTRAW. A UN institute est. 1976, Teheran, by the ECOSOC as an autonomous body under the auspices of the UN. The Institute will give special attention to the needs of developing countries.

Yearbook of International Organizations.

INTERNATIONAL TRADE ORGANIZATION. ▷ ITO.

INTERNATIONAL TRIBUNAL FOR THE LAW OF THE SEA. The Tribunal was est. on Dec. 10, 1982, by the Sea Law Convention, 1982. Art. 1 of the Statute of the ITLS read as follows:

"1. The International Tribunal for the Law of the Sea is constituted and shall function in accordance with the provision of this Convention and Statute.

2. The seat of the Tribunal shall be in the Free and Hanseatic City of Hamburg in the Federal Republic of Germany.

3. The Tribunal may sit and exercise its functions elsewhere whenever it considers this desirable.

4. A reference of a dispute to the Tribunal shall be governed by the provisions of Parts XI and XV."

UN. *The Law of the Sea, United Nations Convention on the Law of the Sea*, New York, 1983, pp. 140–152.

INTERNATIONAL WATERS. ▷ Waters, International.

INTERNATIONAL WORKING MEN'S ASSOCIATION, 1864. The first international organization *sensu stricto*, est. Sept. 28, 1864 in London during a meeting of solidarity with the uprising in Poland by representatives of the revolutionary movements of England, France, Italy, Germany, Poland and Switzerland; beginning of a workers' movement organized on a world wide scale; commonly known as the ▷ International. For 8 years the headquarters were in London, then from 1872 to 1876 in New York. The Association was dissolved by a motion of Marx and Engels at a conference held in Philadelphia in Sept., 1876.

La première Internationale, Recueil de documents publiés sous la direction de J. Freymond, 2 Vols., Genève, 1962.

INTERNATIONAL YEAR OF PEACE, 1985/1986. The UN General Assembly adopted on Dec. 7, 1983 Res. 38/56 proclaiming on the fortieth anniversary of the UN on Oct. 24, 1985 the International Year of Peace. One of the main objectives of the Year would be to stimulate effective action to promote peace on the part of the UN system and its member States, disarmament and the prevention of the nuclear catastrophe. The Year would also encourage reflection on peace as a pre-condition for security, national independence, justice, human rights, development and social progress.

UN Chronicle, March, 1984, p. 28; The International Year of Peace of the United Nations: *Reports, Statements and Resolutions*, UN, New York, 1987.

INTERNATIONAL YEAR OF SHELTER FOR THE HOMELESS, 1987. The United Nations declared 1987 the I.Y. of Shelter for the Homeless and 135 countries designed national local points to co-ordinate domestic shelter programs, to set in motion policies and strategies that will see the world's population adequately housed by the year 2000. By then, 13 out of the largest cities in the world will be in developing countries, and for the first time in history, more people will be living in urban areas than in rural areas. The provision of adequate shelter and services to such a phenomenal population and the management of these burgeoning cities is one of the greatest challenges facing the world. In the UN opinion "shelter is a global issue. Although the problem of poor living conditions is most marked in developing countries, there are also many millions of people without adequate shelter or living conditions in what we call the developing world. The shelter issue is not simply one of poverty. Urbanisation, economic development and social policies all have direct effects on shelter conditions and must be addressed bearing this in mind".

United Nations Review, January-February, 1987.

INTERNEFT PRODUCT. Governmental body of the CMEA countries: Bulgaria, Czechoslovakia, Hungary, Poland, the USSR, f. 1978, Burgas, Bulgaria.

INTERNMENT. Forced settlement of alien citizens in camps or strictly defined regions of a country; subject of international conventions. The 1907 Hague Conventions V and XIV obliged neutral states to intern alien troops, vessels and military aircraft on their territories in ports and at airstrips. The principles of treatment of internees are specified by Geneva Conference of Aug. 12, 1949 on prisoners of war and protection of civilians during war operations and were developed by the International Red Cross Conference in 1958 in New Delhi.

F. LAFITTE, *The Internment of Aliens*, London, 1940; E.J. COHN, 'Legal Aspects of Internment', in: *Modern Law Review*, No. 4, 1941; R.M.W. KEMPNER. 'The Enemy Alien Problem in the Present War', in: *American Journal of International Law*, No. 37, 1943; R.R. WILSON, 'Recent Development in the Treatment of Civilian Alien Enemies', in: *American Journal of International Law*, No. 38, 1944; L. DE LA PRADELLE, *La Conférence diplomatique et les nouvelles Conventions de Genève du 12 août 1949*, Paris, 1950; *XIX Conférence internationale de la Croix Rouge. Actes concernant le Projet de règles limitant les risques courus par la population civile en temps de guerre*, Genève, 1958.

INTEROCEANMETAL. A CMEA intergovernmental organization of Bulgaria, Cuba, Czechoslovakia, the GDR, Poland, the USSR and Vietnam, for the purpose of co-ordinating exploration of polymetallic concretion on the seabed of the Atlantic Ocean, est. April 27, 1987; in co-operation with the UN International Sea-Bed Organization. Hq. Szczecin, Poland.

INTER-ORGANIZATION INFORMATION BOARD, IOB. One of the agencies of the United Nations system, est. 1983 by ECOSOC. ▷ Information UN System.

INTER-PARLIAMENTARY UNION, IPU. The IPU was f. on July 30, 1889 in Paris by the parliaments of Belgium, Denmark, France, Great Britain, Hungary, Italy, Liberia and the USA with the task of developing interparliamentary co-operation in support of world peace. The statute was modified 1920 at a session in Vienna and 1960 in Tokyo. The IPU was the initiator of the first two Conferences on Peace, 1889 and 1907 in The Hague. Almost all states from different parliamentary systems are members. The statute of the Union was ratified by the Vienna Conference, 1922, supplemented by Conferences in Copenhagen, 1923, Berne, 1924, Berlin, 1928, Bucharest, 1931, Cairo, 1947, Helsinki, 1955, Bangkok, 1956, Warsaw, 1959, Tokyo, 1960, Teheran, 1966 and Paris, 1971.

In Sept., 1983 the 70th Conference of the Interparliamentary Union in Seoul was boycotted by the Warsaw Pact countries and Algeria, South Yemen and eleven African parliaments.

Encyclopaedia of Parliament, London, 1961; V.L. SHVETSOV, *Mezhduparlamenskoy Soyuz*, Moskva, 1964; I. HOUPANIENI, *Parliaments and European raprochement*, Leiden, 1973; V. HERMAN, F. MENDEL (eds.), *Parliaments of the World. A Reference Compendium of the Inter-Parliamentary Union*, London, 1976.

INTERPERSONAL LAW. An international term for various sets of civil law provisions in force in one state, used with regard to different communities living in that state depending on their religion. Interpersonal law was introduced by colonial powers in the 19th century in Africa and Southern Asia, still preserved in the Arab states, India and Pakistan.

INTERPOL. International Criminal Police Organization. An intergovernmental organization f. 1923 in Paris. Members: official police bodies in 122 countries. Ensure and promote widest possible mutual assistance between all criminal police authorities within the limits of laws existing in different countries and in the spirit of the Universal Declaration of Human Rights. Special arrangement with ECOSOC. Permanent contact with the WHO and the UN Commission on Narcotic Drugs Controls and documentation pertaining to suppression of international crime. In May 1984 China joined Interpol, the first state ruled by a Communist Party to do so. Publ.: *International Counterfeits and Forgery*. Reg. with the UIA.

Yearbook of International Organizations.

INTERPORT. An economic institution for the integration of ports of Poland and the GDR, est. on Jan 1, 1974 with a view to the fullest possible utilization of handling capacities of the ports of Rostock, Stralsund, Wismar and Szczecin, Gdynia, and Gdansk. Members: Polish Association of Sea Ports and German Seeverkehr und Hafenwirtschaft industrial combine.

INTERPRETATION. An international term for commentaries on treaties or declarations serving as an explanation of what was the true intention guiding the parties to conclude the agreement or "statement of genuine good will".

R.L. BLEDSOE, B.A. BOCZEK, *The International Law Dictionary*, Oxford, 1987.

INTERREGNUM. An international term for vacancy on the throne; a period when, due to the death of abdication of a ruler, preparations are undertaken for the nomination, election or enthronment of a successor.

INTERREX. In ancient Rome a senator ruling the state after the death of an emperor until the coronation of a new ruler. The function existed in Poland from 1573 until the partition of Poland.

INTERROBOT. A CMEA institution to develop robotics facilities, est. Dec. 18, 1985 in Moscow.

INTERSHIPNIK. An organization for co-operation of bearings industries, f. Mar. 25, 1964 by intergovernmental agreement between Bulgaria, Czechoslovakia, the GDR, Poland and Hungary; the USSR joined in 1965 and Romania in 1971.

W.E. BUTLER (ed.), *A Source Book on Socialist International Organizations*, Alphen, 1978.

INTERSPUTNIK. International System and Organization for Space Communications. A CMEA institution established on Nov. 15, 1971 in Moscow by a convention signed by Bulgaria, Cuba, Czechoslovakia, the GDR, Hungary, Mongolia, Poland, Romania and the USSR with the task of assuring member states international telephone, telegraph and phototelegraph communication and an exchange of TV and TVC programs by satellites and developing mutual co-operation in these areas as well as co-operation with other systems of space communication. The Intersputnik System includes:
(1) a space complex composed of communications satellites and ground steering elements (the elements of this complex are either the property of the organization or are loaned from the states which make it up);
(2) earth stations which maintain contact through satellites, constructed by individual member states on their territories with their own funds according to standardized technical norms.
The Intersputnik Organisation is also open to other countries. ▷ Molniya.

UNTS, Vol. 862, p. 5; W.E. BUTLER (ed.), *A Source Book on Socialist International Organizations*, Alphen, 1978, pp. 532–542.

INTERSTATE LAW. An international term for private law regulating the principles for solving problems arising from colliding legal systems in force in federated states; provisions of interstate law are used with respect to colliding interstate legal systems in the USA, Great Britain, Mexico, and to a lesser degree in the USSR and Switzerland.

INTERSTATE ORGANIZATIONS. An international term for institutions created by two states through bilateral treaties as instruments of co-operation in a certain field. International organizations formed by three or more states are called Intergovernmental organizations.

INTERSTENO. International Federation of Shorthand and Typewriting, f. 1954 in Berne. Members: national groups totalling 200,000 members in 21 countries. Reg. with the UIA.

Yearbook of International Organizations.

INTERTEXTILMASH. International Economic Association for the Production of Technological Equipment for the Textile Industry, established within the CMEA on Dec. 13, 1973 by an agreement of the governments of Bulgaria, Czechoslovakia, Hungary, the GDR, Poland, Romania and the USSR. In Dec., 1975 the Yugoslav Association Textil Mashina concluded a co-operation agreement with Intertextilmash.

W.E. BUTLER (ed.), *A Source Book on Socialist International Organizations*, Alphen, 1978, pp. 680–704.

INTERVENTION. An international term for various forms of interference by one or several states into affairs which are within the jurisdiction of another state in pursuance of their own interest. The ban on intervention is defined in the UN

Charter (art. 2, item 7) and is a generally accepted rule of international law. Individual or collective self-defense provided for under UN Charter is not considered intervention; states taking measures to effect their right to self-defense are obliged to notify the UN Security Council to this effect. Intervention was widely used as an instrument of foreign policy in ancient times, particularly by the Roman Empire. In the Middle Ages intervention was used in the context of the competing imperial and papal rules. In the 19th century, international law adopted the principle of intervention as a Pan-European principle, which was expressed by the Holy Alliance; it was to be used against revolutionary governments of Europe in defense of legitimate governments and systems *"pour conserver ce qui est légalement établi"* (the Ljubliana note of Austria, Prussia and Russia of May 12, 1821). On the basis of this principle interventions were undertaken, e.g. by Austria in Naples (1821), by France in Spain (1823), by the Western Powers during the Turkish–Russian war (1853–56) and by France in support of the Pope (1867). Stipulations were included in treaties concerning "the right to intervene", such as the Berlin Treaty of 1878 allowing European powers to interfere into internal affairs of Turkey and Africa. In the late 19th century, under the influence of Latin American states endangered by intervention not only on the part of European powers but also by the USA, there was a departure from the principle of intervention in favor of non-intervention. Nevertheless, there were still numerous cases of intervention, e.g., the provisions of treaties between the USA and Cuba and between the USA and Panama of 1903 authorizing US intervention.

Intervention was undertaken by the Entente in Soviet Russia during 1919–20.

After World War II the Truman Doctrine confirmed the principle of intervention, which intensified the struggle within the UN in favor of non-intervention and non-interference into internal affairs of states. After World War II in both East and West various forms of intervention have been recorded: military intervention consisting of attempts at or actual occupation of a part or whole territory of an alien state, diplomatic intervention which may take the form of direct diplomatic pressure through diplomatic channels or diplomatic conspiracy to exert pressure by a group of states; economic intervention which may take the form of a boycott, customs barriers or waging customs wars, refusing to implement contractual provisions, economic embargo, economic blockade; and intervention "on humanitarian grounds" consisting of diplomatic pressure or threats of economic intervention to induce a country to abandon a policy of discrimination – racial, religious or political – against a group of its citizens (e.g., the Republic of South Africa in the context of its policy of apartheid). In the 1980's the UN General Assembly and the UN Security Council discussed the case of ▷ Afghanistan 1980 and the case of ▷ Grenada 1983 as problems of intervention.

E.C. STOWELL, *Intervention in International Law*, Washington, DC, 1921; P.H. WIENFIELD, "The History of Interventions", in: *The British Yearbook of International Law 1922–1923*; Ch.G. FENWICK, "Intervention", in: *American Journal of International Law*, No. 39, 1945; T. KOMARNICKI, "La intervention en droit international moderne", in: *Revue général du droit international public*, No. 55, 1955; A. VAN WYNEN, A.J. THOMAS, *La No-Intervención*, Buenos Aires, 1959; *UN Chronicle*, March, 1980, pp. 5–17 and January, 1984, pp. 4–8.

INTERVENTION, UN DECLARATION ON THE INADMISSIBILITY OF, 1965. The UN Declaration on the Inadmissibility of Intervention in Internal Affairs of States and on the Protection of their Independence and Sovereignty, was adopted on Dec. 21, 1965 by the UN General Assembly. Res. 2131/XX and reads as follows:

"The General Assembly, deeply concerned at the gravity of the international situation and the increasing threat soaring over universal peace due to armed intervention and other direct or indirect forms of interference threatening the sovereign personality and the political independence of States,

Considering that the United Nations, according to their aim to eliminate war, threats to the peace and acts of aggression, created an Organization, based on the sovereign equality of States, whose friendly relations would be based on respect for the principle of equal rights and self-determination of peoples and on the obligation of its Members to refrain from the threat or use of force against the territorial integrity or political independence of any State.

Recognizing that, in fulfilment of the principle of self-determination, the General Assembly, by the Declaration on the Granting of Independence to Colonial Countries and Peoples contained in Res. 1514(XV) of 14 December 1960, stated its conviction that all peoples have an inalienable right to complete freedom, the exercise of their sovereignty and the integrity of their national territory and that, by virtue of that right, they freely determine their political status and freely pursue their economic, social and cultural development,

Recalling that in the Universal Declaration of Human Rights the Assembly proclaimed that recognition of the inherent dignity and of the equal and inalienable rights of all members of the human family is the foundation of freedom, justice and peace in the world, without distinction of any kind,

Reaffirming the principle of non-intervention, proclaimed in the charters of the Organization of American States, the League of Arab States and of the Organization of African Unity and affirmed in the Conferences of Montevideo, Buenos Aires, Chapultepec and Bogota, as well as in the decisions of the Afro-Asian Conference in Bandung, the Conference of Non-Aligned Countries in Belgrade, in the 'Programme for Peace and International Co-operation' adopted at the end of the Cairo Conference of Non-Aligned Countries, and in the Declaration on subversion adopted in Accra by the Heads of State or Government of the African States,

Recognizing that full observance of the principle of the non-intervention of States in the internal and external affairs of other States is essential to the fulfilment of the purposes and principles of the United Nations,

Considering that armed intervention is synonymous with aggression, and as such is contrary to the basic principles on which peaceful international co-operation between States should be built,

Considering further that direct intervention, subversion, as well as all forms of indirect intervention are contrary to these principles and, consequently, a violation of the Charter of the United Nations,

Mindful that violation of the principle of non-intervention poses a threat to the independence and freedom and normal political, economic, social and cultural development of countries, particularly those which have freed themselves from colonialism, and can pose a serious threat to the maintenance of peace,

Fully aware of the imperative need to create appropriate conditions which would enable all States, and in particular the developing countries, to choose without duress or coercion their own political, economic and social institutions,

In the light of the foregoing considerations, the General Assembly of the United Nations solemnly declares:

(1) No state has the right to intervene, directly or indirectly, for any reason whatever, in the internal or external affairs of any other State. Consequently armed intervention as well as all other forms of interference or attempted threats against the personality of the States or against its political, economic and cultural elements, are condemned;

(2) No State may use or encourage the use of economic, political or any other type of measures to coerce another State in order to obtain from it the subordination of the exercise of its sovereign rights or to secure from it advantages of any kind. Also, no State shall organize, assist, foment, finance, incite or tolerate subversive, terrorist or armed activities directed to the violent overthrow of the regime of another State, or interfere in civil strife in another State;

(3) The use of force to deprive peoples of their national identity constitutes a violation of their inalienable rights and of the principle of non-intervention;

(4) The strict observance of these obligations is an essential condition to ensure that the nations live together in peace with one another, since the practice of any form of intervention not only violates the spirit and letter of the Charter but also leads to the creation of situations which threaten international peace and security;

(5) Every State has an inalienable right to choose its political, economic, social and cultural systems, without interference in any form by another State;

(6) All States shall respect the right of self-determination and independence of peoples and nations, to be freely exercised without any foreign pressure, and with absolute respect for human rights and fundamental freedoms. Consequently, all States shall contribute to the complete elimination of racial discrimination and colonialism in all its forms and manifestations;

(7) For the purpose of this Declaration, the term 'State' covers both individual States and groups of States;

(8) Nothing in this Declaration shall be construed as affecting in any manner the relevant provisions of the Charter of the United Nations relating to the maintenance of international peace and security, in particular those contained in Chapters VI, VII and VIII."

On Dec. 19, 1966 the UN General Assembly Res. 2225/XXI adopted an appeal to all states to respect unconditionally the UN Declaration on Inadmissibility of Intervention by 114 votes to 0, with 2 abstentions.

The text is as follows:

"The General Assembly,

Deeply concerned at the evidence of unceasing armed intervention by certain States in the domestic affairs of other States in different parts of the world and at other forms of direct or indirect interference committed against the sovereign personality and political independence of States, resulting in increased international tension,

Reaffirming all the principles and rules embodied in the Declaration on the Inadmissibility of Intervention in the Domestic Affairs of States and the Protection of Their Independence and Sovereignty, contained in its Res. 2131/XX of Dec. 21, 1965,

Deems it to be its bounden duty:

(a) To urge the immediate cessation of intervention, in any form whatever, in the domestic or external affairs of States;

(b) To condemn all forms of intervention in the domestic or external affairs of States as a basic source of danger to the cause of world peace;

(c) To call upon all States to carry out faithfully their obligations under the Charter of the United Nations and the provisions of the Declaration on the Inadmissibility of Intervention in the Domestic Affairs of States and the Protection of Their Independence and Sovereignty and to urge them to refrain from armed intervention or the promotion or organization of subversion, terrorism or other indirect forms of intervention for the purpose of changing by violence the existing system in another State or interfering in civil strife in another State."

UN Yearbook, 1965 and 1966.

INTERVISION. Intergovernmental organization of Bulgaria, Czechoslovakia, Finland, the GDR, Hungary, Poland, Romania and the USSR set up by the OIRT on Jan. 28, 1960 in Budapest to organize exchange of TV programs between member countries and ▷ Eurovision and other continents by means of telecommunications satellites.

Yearbook of International Organizations.

INTERVODOCHISTKA. A specialized CMEA agency, f. Feb. 8, 1978 in Sofia by intergovernmental agreement to organize co-operation of member states in the field of rational utilization and protection of water resources.

W.E. BUTLER (ed), *A Source Book on Socialist International Organizations*, Alphen, 1978.

INTERZONENHANDEL, *German* = "interzone trade". A term accepted officially after World War II for trade between the occupied zones of Germany; up to 1948 included all four zones of occupation; after the creation of the ▷ Bi-Zone, and then the ▷ Tri-Zone, only between West and East Germany. After the formation of two German states in 1949, despite the fact that the FRG belonged to the EEC and the GDR to the CMEA, FRG–GDR trade takes place under special conditions without regard to the customs barriers imposed by the EEC on the other Warsaw Pact States. In the foreign trade of the GDR exchange with the FRG accounted for *c.* 10 per cent of the GDR's total foreign trade turnover. The special conditions of the "internal trade" between the GDR and the FRG were officially recognized by the EEC states by a special protocol appended 1958 to the EEC Rome Treaties, 1957. ▷ Interzonenhandel Rome Protocol, 1957. The validity of this protocol remained in force despite the signing of an interstate GDR–FRG treaty Dec. 21, 1972.

E. HOFMAN, *Die Zerstörung der deutschen Wirtschaftseinheit. Interzonenhandel und Wiedervereinigung*, Hamburg, 1964; H. LAMBRECHT, *Die Entwicklung des Interzonenhandels von seinen Anfängen bis zur Gegenwart*, Berlin, 1965; *Deutsch–Deutsche Beziehungen*, Opladen, 1978.

INTERZONENHANDEL ROME PROTOCOL, 1957. The signatory states of the ▷ Rome Treaty 1957 (Belgium, France, the FRG, Italy, Luxembourg and the Netherlands) annexed to the Rome Treaty and signed at Rome, Mar. 25, 1957 a Protocol related to German International Trade and Connecting Problems. The text is as follows:

"The High Contracting Parties,
Considering the conditions at present existing by reason of the division of Germany,
Have agreed upon the following provisions which shall be annexed to this Treaty:
(1) Since exchanges between the German territories subject to the Basic Law for the Federal Republic of Germany and the German territories in which the Basic Law does not apply are part of the German internal trade, the application of this Treaty requires no amendment of the existing system of such trade within Germany.
(2) Each Member State shall inform the other Member States and the Commission of any agreements affecting exchanges with the German territories in which the Basic Law for the Federal Republic of Germany does not apply, as well as of the provisions for their implementation. Each Member State shall ensure that such implementation shall not conflict with the principles of the Common Market and shall, in particular, take appropriate measures to avoid any prejudice which might be caused to the economies of the other Member States.
(3) Each Member State may take suitable measures to prevent any difficulties which might arise for it from trade between another Member State and the German territories in which the Basic Law for the Federal Republic of Germany does not apply."

UNTS, Vol. 298, 1958, pp. 131–132.

INTIB. Industrial and Technological Information Bank, one of the information centers of the ▷ UNIDO.

INTIFADA, Arabic = Uprising. An international term for the Palestinian insurrection against Israeli troops in the Gaza Strip, the West Bank and Jerusalem since December 1987. Discussed in March 1988 by the UN Commission of Human Rights.
The GA Res. 43/176 adopted by 138 votes to 2 with 2 abstentions on Dec. 15, 1988 "aware of the ongoing uprising (intifadah) of the Palestinian people since 9 December 1987, aimed at ending Israeli occupation of Palestinian territory occupied since 1967.
(1) Affirms the urgent need to achieve a just and comprehensive settlement of the Arab-Israeli conflict, the core of which is the question of Palestine;
(2) Calls for the convening of the International Peace Conference on the Middle East, under the auspices of the United Nations, with the participation of all parties to the conflict, including the Palestine Liberation Organization, on an equal footing, and five permanent members of the Security Council, based on Security Council resolutions 242 (1967) of 22 November 1967 and 338 (1973) of 22 October 1973 and the legitimate national rights of the Palestinian people, primarily the right to self-determination;
(3) Affirms the following principles for the achievement of comprehensive peace:
(a) The withdrawal of Israel from Palestinian territory occupied since 1967, including Jerusalem, and from the other occupied Arab territories;
(b) Guaranteeing arrangements for security of all States in the region, including those named in resolution 181 (II) of 29 November 1947, within secure and internationally recognized boundaries;
(c) Resolving the problem of the Palestine refugees in conformity with General Assembly resolution 194 (III) of 11 December 1948, and subsequent relevant resolutions;
(d) Dismantling the Israeli settlements in the territories occupied since 1967;
(e) Guaranteeing freedom of access to Holy Places, religious buildings and sites;
(4) Notes the expressed desire and endeavours to place the Palestinian territory occupied since 1967, including Jerusalem, under the supervision of the United Nations for a limited period, as part of the peace process.

D. PERETZ, *Intifadah. The Palestinian Uprising, in: Foreign Affairs*, Summer, 1988; *ICJ Newsletter*, January, March, 1988, pp. 26–28; J. LEDERMAN, *Dateline West Bank: Interpreting the Intifada, in: Foreign Policy*, Fall, 1988; UN, *Resolutions and Decisions adopted by the General Assembly during the first part of its forty-third Session, from 20 September to 22 December, 1988*, New York, 1989, p. 111.

INVASION. An international term for armed attack on the territory of another state and the waging of an aggressive war, usually without declaring it; one of the forms of ▷ Aggression.

INVENTORS AND INVENTIONS. The first European convention was introduced in 1883 ▷ Industrial Property Protection (▷ Patents); and in the Western Hemisphere the Inter-American Convention regarding protection of patents, inventions, samples and industrial models, was signed Aug. 20, 1910 in Buenos Aires. After World War I the Paris Convention Nov. 13, 1920 (modified by the Stockholm Act July 14, 1967) established a central patent bureau for inventions and formulated a rule that inventions registered at home patent offices and then submitted to the Brussels bureau would be subject to international protection in all member countries of the convention. With the advanced rate of engineering development UNESCO came out in favor of concentrating on inventions essential for the progress and evolution of humanity. Its study on the role of science and technology in economic development (1971) drew attention to the accelerating rate of introducing inventions into production. The 19th century invention of photography took 100 years to be applied on a wide scale, radar – 15 years, and integrated circuits in micro-electronics – 2 years. In the USA the average period from the time of invention to its introduction was as follows: 1885–1919 *c.* 37 years, 1920–44 *c.* 24 years, whereas in the years 1945–64 only 14 years. Inventors are a subject of organized international co-operation since 1900, when the first international organization, called Union international des associations d'inventeurs et d'artistes industrielles, was established, with seat in Paris, active until 1939. After World War II, each year in March the International Show of Inventions (Salon international des inventeurs) is held in Brussels. Organizations reg. with the UIA:

International Federation of Inventors Associations, est. 1968, London; associating home committees of Scandinavian countries, the FRG, Switzerland and Great Britain; Publ.: *IFIA Bulletin*.
The Scandinavian Union of Inventors, est. 1967, Stockholm.

LNTS, Vol. 155, p. 179; *Yearbook of International Organizations*.

INVESTIGATION OF INTERNATIONAL INCIDENTS. An international term for establishing the causes of an international incident by a commission consisting of persons designated by governments or the proper international organization; subject of international conventions. In the UN only the Security Council is authorized to convene investigation commissions, according to art. 34 and 39 of the UN Charter.

INVESTIGATIVE INTERNATIONAL COMMISSION. An international term for a committee of experts formed by the governments concerned for the purpose of clarifying some international incident; subject of international conventions ratified at the Hague Conference 1899 and 1907. The Convention of 1899 was the foundation for convening the first Investigative International Commission, composed of five admirals (Austria, France, Great Britain, Russia, the USA) to investigate and pass judgment on an accident in the North Sea, when an English fishing fleet was fired on during the night of Oct. 22/23, 1904 by the Russian Baltic fleet. The Convention of 1907 widened the powers of the Commission. The convening of Investigative International Commissions was also anticipated in other, later treaties and agreements (Taft Treaties, 1911, Bryan Treaties, 1913–14 and 1928/29; Gondra Treaty, 1922, and many bilateral agreements). After World War I the LN formed its own Investigative Commission, and after World War II, the UN.

INVESTMENT DISPUTES SETTLEMENT. A juridical voluntary pacific settlement of investment disputes, subject of the Convention on the Settlement of Investment Disputes between States and Nationals of Other States signed on Mar. 18, 1965 at Washington DC, formulated under the aegis of the World Bank. It came into force on Oct. 14, 1966: ratified by: Afghanistan, Austria, Belgium, Botswana, Burundi, Cameroon, the Central African Republic, Ceylon, Chad, Congo, Dahomey (now Benin), Denmark, Egypt, the FRG, Finland, France, Gabon, Ghana, Greece, Guinea, Guyana, Iceland, Indonesia, Italy, the Ivory Coast, Jamaica, Japan, Kenya, Lesotho, Liberia, Luxembourg, Madagascar, Malawi, Malaysia, Mauritania, Mauritius, Morocco, Nepal, the Netherlands, Niger, Nigeria, Norway, Pakistan, the Republic of China, the Republic of Korea, Senegal, Sierra Leone, Singapore, Somalia, Swaziland, Sweden, Switzerland, Togo, Trinidad and Tobago, Tunisia, Uganda, the UK, Upper Volta (now Burkina Faso), the USA, Yugoslavia, Zaïre and Zambia. The Convention was also signed but not ratified by Ethiopia, Ireland, New Zealand and Sudan,
The Preamble and the first 3 Articles reads as follows:

"The Contracting States, Considering the need for international co-operation for economic development, and the role of private international investment therein;

Bearing in mind the possibility that from time to time disputes may arise in connection with such investment between Contracting States and nationals of other Contracting States;

Recognizing that while such disputes would usually be subject to national legal processes, international methods of settlement may be appropriate in certain cases;

Attaching particular importance to the availability of facilities for international conciliation or arbitration to which Contracting States and nationals of other Contracting States may submit such disputes if they so desire;

Desiring to establish such facilities under the auspices of the International Bank for Reconstruction and Development;

Recognizing that mutual consent by the parties to submit such disputes to conciliation or to arbitration through such facilities constitutes a binding agreement which requires in particular that due consideration be given to any recommendation of conciliators, and that any arbitral award be complied with;

and Declaring that no Contracting State shall by the mere fact of its ratification acceptance or approval of this Convention and without its consent be deemed to be under any obligation to submit any particular dispute to conciliation or arbitration;

Have agreed as follows:

Art. I. There is hereby established the International Centre for Settlement of Investment Disputes (hereinafter called the Centre), ICSID.

The purpose of the Centre shall be to provide facilities for conciliation and arbitration of investment disputes between Contracting States and nationals of other Contracting States in accordance with the provisions of their Conventions.

Art. II. The seat of the Centre shall be at the principal office of the International Bank for Reconstruction and Development (hereinafter called the Bank). The seat may be moved to another place by decision of the Administrative Council adopted by a majority of two-thirds of its members.

Art. III. The Centre shall have an Administrative Council and a Secretariat and shall maintain a Panel of Conciliators and a Panel of Arbitrators."

▷ ICSID.

UNTS, Vol. 575, p. 160; *Regulations and Rules of ICSID*, Washington, DC, 1967; *Legal History of SID Convention*, Washington, DC, 1970: A. BROCHES, "The SID Convention", in: *Recueil des Cours de l'Académie du Droit International de La Haye*, 1972, Vol. 36, pp. 342–348; J. CHARIAN, *Investments Contracts and Arbitration. The World Bank Convention*, London, 1975.

INVESTMENT GUARANTY AGENCY. ▷ Multilateral Investment Guarantee Agency, MIGA.

INVESTMENT GUARANTY AGREEMENTS. The governmental guaranties to encourage the flow of private foreign investments to the Third World Countries. The US in the 1960s promoted a policy of investment guaranties issued by the Country of the investor. An Investment Guaranty Agreement between the Government of the USA and the Government of Brazil, signed on Feb. 6, 1965 in Washington, DC, and came into force on Sept. 17, 1965, read as follows:

"Art. 1. When nationals of one Signatory Government propose to make investments, guaranteed pursuant to this Agreement, in a project or activity within the territorial jurisdiction of the other Signatory Government, the two Governments shall, upon the request of either, consult respecting the project or activity and its contribution to economic and social development.

Art. 2. The provisions of this Agreement shall be applicable only with respect to guaranteed investments in projects or activities approved for guaranty purposes by the Government in whose territory the project or activity will take place (hereafter referred to as 'the Government of the Recipient Country'). The Government issuing guaranties pursuant to this Agreement (hereafter referred to as 'the Guaranteeing Government') shall keep the Government of the Recipient

Country currently informed on the types of investment guaranties it is prepared to issue, on the criteria it employs in determining whether to issue guaranties, as well as on the types and amounts of guaranties issued for projects or activities approved by the Government of the Recipient Country.

Art. 3.(1) If the Guaranteeing Government makes payment in its national currency to any investor under a guaranty issued pursuant to the present Agreement, the Government of the Recipient Country shall, subject to the provisions of the following paragraph, recognize the transfer to the Guaranteeing Government of any currency, credits, assets, or investment on account of which such payment is made, as well as the succession of the Guaranteeing Government to any right, title, claim, privilege, or cause of action existing, of which may arise, in connection therewith.

(2) To the extent that the laws of the Recipient Country partially or wholly prevent the acquisition of any interests in any property within its national territory by the Guaranteeing Government, the Government of the Recipient Country shall permit such investor and the Guaranteeing Government to make appropriate arrangements pursuant to which such interests are transferred to an entity permitted to own such interests under the laws of the Recipient Country.

Art. 4.(1) Amounts in the lawful currency of the Recipient Country and credits thereof acquired by the Guaranteeing Governments, as subergee in accordance with the provisions of the preceding Article, shall be accorded treatment neither less nor more favorable than that accorded to funds of nationals of the Guaranteeing Government deriving from investment like those of the subrogating investor, and such amounts and credits shall be freely available to the Guaranteeing Government to meet its expenditures in the Recipient Country.

(2) Whenever economic circumstances indicate the advisability of holding the surplus over expenditures referred to in the preceding paragraph of such currency and credits in a mutually agreed financial institution, the two Governments will consult concerning appropriate actions to be taken.

Art. 5. Nothing in this Agreement shall grant to the Guaranteeing Government other rights than those available to the subrogating investor with respect to any petition or claim or right to which the Guaranteeing Government may be subrogated.

Art. 6.(1) Differences between the two Governments concerning the interpretation of the provisions of this Agreement shall be settled, insofar as possible, through negotiations between them. If such a difference cannot be resolved within a period of six months following the request for such negotiations, it shall be submitted, at the request of either Government, to arbitration in accordance with paragraph 4 of this Article.

(2) Any claim against either Government concerning an investment guaranteed in accordance with this Agreement which may constitute a matter involving public international law, shall, at the request of the Government presenting the claim, be submitted to negotiations. If at the end of six months following the request for negotiations the two Governments have not resolved the claim by mutual agreement, the claim, including the question of whether it constitutes a matter involving public international law, shall be submitted to arbitration in accordance with paragraph 4 of this Article.

(3) There shall be excluded from the negotiations and the arbitral procedures herein contemplated matters which remain exclusively within the internal jurisdiction of a sovereign state. It is accordingly understood that claims arising out of the expropriation of property of private foreign investors do not present questions of public international law unless and until the judicial process of the Recipient Country has been exhausted, and there exists a denial of justice, as those terms are defined in public international law. The monetary amount of any claim submitted for negotiation or arbitration in accordance with the provisions of this Agreement shall not exceed the amount of compensation paid under guaranties issued in accordance with this Agreement with respect to the investment involved in the claim.

(4) Matters arising under paragraphs 1, 2 and 3 of this Article shall be submitted at the request of either Government to an arbitral tribunal which shall be guided by the principles of public international law

recognized in Articles 1 and 2 of the General Inter-American Arbitration Treaty signed in Washington on January 5, 1929. Only the respective governments may request the arbitral procedure and participate in it. The selection of arbiters and the method of their proceeding shall be in accordance with Articles 3, 4, 5 and 6 of the General Treaty of 1929; the finality of the technique for interpreting awards of the arbitral tribunal shall be in accordance with Article 7 of the General Treaty of 1929.

Art. 7. This Agreement shall enter into force on the date of the receipt of the note which the Government of the United States of Brazil communicates to the Government of the United States of America that the Agreement has been approved in conformity with Brazil's constitutional procedures.

Art. 8. When either of the Signatories to the present Agreement considers that multilateral arrangements in which both Governments may come to participate provide a framework for the operation of a program of investment guaranties similar to that herein contained, it may seek the concurrence of the other Government for the termination of the present Agreement. Such termination will become effective on the date of the receipt of the note expressing that concurrence, unless otherwise agreed.

Art. 9. Unless terminated in accordance with Article VIII, this Agreement shall continue in force until six months from the date of receipt of a note by which one Government informs the other of an intent no longer to be a party to the Agreement. In such event, the provisions of the Agreement with respect to guaranties issued while the Agreement was in force shall remain in force for the duration of those guaranties, in no case longer than twenty years after the denunciation of the Agreement."

UNTS, Vol. 719, 1970, pp. 4–21.

INVISIBLE COMMERCE. An international term introduced in Great Britain in the late 19th century for those current commercial transactions which do not involve trade in goods, e.g. payments for services, such as banking, insurance, freightage, tourist, foreign investment and other services. After World War II the significance of invisible commerce in balance of payments increased. In the 1980s this type of turnover amounted to one-third of overall value of world foreign turnover. Largest profits: the USA, Great Britain, France, Italy, Switzerland.

World Trade in Invisibles, London, 1978; *UN Chronicle*, October, 1982, p. 47.

IOAMRINA AGREEMENT. ▷ Albania–Greece Border Dispute.

IOB. ▷ Inter-Organization Information Board.

IOC-MEDI. Marine Environmental Data and Information Referral System, one of the information systems of the ▷ UNESCO.

IPDC. International Program for the Development of Communication. Created in 1980 by the General Conference of UNESCO, IPDC is intended to help developing countries build up capacities for communications, for preparing and producing their own news and radio and TV programs.

UN Chronicle, March, 1980, p. 53.

IPL. Information Processing Language. One of the computer language systems.

IR. ▷ Green Revolution.

IRA. Irish Republican Army. Mustered in 1919 as an underground military organization of Irish nationalists demanding incorporation of Northern Ireland (Ulster) to the Free Irish State, est. in 1921. See also ▷ extradition.

P. COOGAN, *The IRA*, London, 1970; S. WINCHESTER, *Northern Ireland in Crisis: Reporting the Ulster*

Troubles, New York, 1975; J. BOYER BELL, *The Secret Army: The IRA 1916–1979*, London, 1980.

IRAN. Member of the UN. Islamic Republic of Iran. Country in southwest Asia bounded by the Caspian Sea, the Persian Gulf and the Gulf of Oman, also bordering on the USSR, Afghanistan, Pakistan, Iraq, Turkey. Area: 1,648,000 sq. km. Pop. 1986 census: 49,857,384 (1956 census: 18,954,000; 1966: 25,788,000; 1976: 33,708,000). Capital Teheran with 5,443,000 inhabitants, 1980. GNP per capita (1980): US $2160. Currency: one Iranian Rial: = 100 dinars. Official language: Persian. National Day: Feb. 11, Proclamation of Islamic Republic, 1979.

Original member of the UN and all its specialized agencies except the GATT and WIPO. Member of Colombo Plan and OPEC.

International relations: history reaching back to ancient times; in the late 19th century semi-colonial status with European countries; 1907 partitioned by Russia and Great Britain into two influence zones. In World War I alongside the Allies. Member of the League of Nations 1919–39. In 1935 changed the historical name of Persia into Iran. In World War II, Emperor Raza Shah Pahlavi, though formally neutral, collaborated with the Third Reich which caused the entry into Iran of Soviet and British troops, abdication of the Emperor and the takeover of his power by his son Muhammad Raza Pahlavi (Sept. 18, 1941, crowned Emperor on Oct. 26, 1967). In Sept., 1943 Iran declared war against Germany and concluded an agreement with the main Allies on their use of Iranian territory. At the ▷ Teheran Conference (Nov. 28–Dec. 1, 1943) heads of US, British, and Soviet governments recognized the Iranian contribution to the war and declared willingness to guarantee its independence, sovereignty and territorial integrity. British and Soviet troops withdrew 1945–46 after the UN Security Council recommendation. In 1951, nationalization of Anglo-Iranian Oil Co. Ltd., debated by the UN Security Council in Sept.–Oct., 1951 (▷ Anglo-Iranian Oil Company Case 1951). On Oct. 24, 1968 Iran and Saudi Arabia signed an agreement on division of the continental shelf in the Persian Gulf. In 1969 Iran initiated talks with Iraq on border controversy. In 1971 a dispute with the United Arab Emirates over three oil-rich islands in the Strait of Ormuz: Abu Musa, Great and Small Tumb; settled under a treaty providing for a fifty–fifty division of profits from Abu Musa oil-fields between Iran and Shardha Sheikhanate. Following the nationalization, Western oil companies in Teheran on May 24, 1973 signed an agreement under which all oil facilities, including the world's largest oil refinery and the world's biggest tanker port – became Iranian state property. At the same time, Iran took over management of its oil industry from the consortium, 101 years after granting the British the first oil concession. After the overthrow and flight of the Shah on Jan. 17, 1979, a new Iranian Constitution founded an Islamic Republic of Iran. On Nov. 4, 1979 Iranian students took over the US Embassy in Teheran taking hostage fifty-two American diplomats; they were to be released on the condition that the USA extradite the deposed Shah, who was receiving medical treatment in New York. On Nov. 5, 1979 Iran canceled two articles of the Iran–Soviet Friendship Treaty, 1921, that in case of aggression on Iran gave the Soviet Union the right to intervene militarily in Iran; and Iran canceled also that Iran–USA Friendship Treaty, 1959. The Treaty says that:

"In case of aggression, the government of the US will take up such appropriate action, including the use of armed forces, as may be mutually agreed upon and as it envisaged in the joint resolution to promote peace and stability in the Middle East."

The issue of extradition of the Shah and the release of hostages was subject of the UN Security Council and General Assembly sessions at the turn of 1980 that condemned in principle the violation of diplomatic immunity. The Shah left the USA and settled on a Panamanian island; Iran applied to Panama for his extradition in Jan., 1980;, the Shah moved to Egypt where he died July 30, 1980. On April 24–25, 1980 the US airforce launched an abortive attempt to free the hostages. The US government, members of NATO and Japan imposed an economic boycott on Iran from Jan., 1980, which aggravated the crisis between Iran and the USA and its allies. On Jan. 20, 1981 the hostages returned home after an American–Iranian Agreement was signed the previous day in Algiers. Since Sept. 20, 1980 a military conflict with Iraq. The War with Iraq dominated in the 1980s over internal and foreign policy.

On June 10, 1984 Iran and Iraq agreed under the terms of a first limited cease-fire, proposed by UN Secretary-General Javier Perez de Cuellar to stop shelling each other's cities. Since Aug. 20, 1988 a UN-arranged cease-fire is in effect.

See also ▷ World Heritage UNESCO List.

J. MARLOVE, *Iran. A Short Political Guide*, New York, 1963; R.K. RAMZANI, *The Foreign Policy of Iran 1500–1941. A Developing Nation in World Affairs*, New York, 1966; F. KAZEMZADEH, *Russia and Britain in Persia 1864–1914*, New Haven, 1967; G. HANDLEY-TAYLOR, *Bibliography of Iran*, London, 1968; S.L. AGAEV, *Iran, Vneshniaya politika i problemy nezavisimosti 1925–1941*, Moskva, 1971; *The Cambridge History of Iran*, 8 Vols, Cambridge 1968–73; R.K. RAMZANI, *Iran's Foreign policy 1941–1973*, Charlottesville, 1975; H.L. KASTER, *Iran Heute*, Wien, 1974, "Ayatollah Khomeini Defines His Stance in Respect to Embassy Occupation", in: *New York Times*, Nov. 18, 1979; A. SAIKAL, *The Rise and Fall of the Shah*, Princeton, 1980; "Council Call on Iran to Release Detained US Personnel", in: *UN Chronicle*, January, 1980, pp. 5–13; H. KATOUZIAN, *The Political Economy of Iran*, London, 1981; N. KEDDIE, *Roots of Revolution*, Yale University Press, 1981; W.H. SULLIVAN, *Mission to Iran*, New York, 1981; M. HEIKAL, *Iran, The Untold Story*, New York, 1982; S. ZABIGH, *Mossadegh Era. Roots of the Iranian Revolution*, Chicago, 1982; *The Europa Year Book 1984. A World Survey*, Vol. II, pp. 1728–1741, London, 1984; G. SICK, *All Fall Down: America's Tragic Encounter with Iran*, New York, 1985; N.R. KEDDIE, E. HOOGLUND eds., *The Iranian Revolution and the Islamic Republic*, Syracuse, N.Y., 1986; G. SICK, *Iran's Quest for Superpower Status*, in: *Foreign Affairs*, Spring, 1987; A. BILL, *The Eagle and the Lion: The Tragedy of American-Iranian Relations*, New Haven, 1988.

IRAN-GATE OR IRAN-CONTRAS AFFAIR. A USA international affair compared to the ▷ Watergate scandal, initiated on Nov. 3, 1986 by news, printed in the Lebanese Magazine Al Shirah that a secret mission to Teheran of President Reagan's former adviser was linked to a transfer of military spare parts. On Nov. 25, 1986 the US Attorney General announced that Iran paid a sum of between US$ 10 million to 30 million for the supplied arms to Swiss bank accounts for the use of Nicaraguan anti-government contras, with the knowledge of Admiral Pointdexter and Lt. Col. Oliver L. North of the National Security Council, but without the knowledge of President Ronald Reagan. The affair was investigated by a select committee of the House and the Senate in 1987.

K.E. SHARPE, *The Real Cause of Irangate: in Foreign Policy*, Fall, 1987; KEESING's *Record of World Events*, April, 1988.

IRANIAN–IRAQI DISPUTE ON THE STRAIT OF HORMUZ, 1971–75. The Strait of Hormuz connecting the Persian Gulf with the Gulf of Oman, a crude oil rich region, was a subject of international dispute between Iran and Iraq due to the occupation of the Abu Musa Island and two smaller islands by Iranian troops Nov. 30, 1971 in agreement with Great Britain. On that day the British left these islands after holding them for 80 years. Iraq addressed a protest to the UN, demanding immediate UN intervention, in which it was supported by Syria. Abu Musa Island belongs to the Shardha Sheikhanate (Federation of United Arab Emirates), which concluded an agreement with Iran about substituting British armed forces by Iranian units. Two islets (the Big and the Small Tumb) belong to the Ra's al-Chaima Sheikhanate, which lodged a protest against the occupation of the islands and compulsory evacuation of its 100 inhabitants. In Jan. of 1975, Iran and Oman concluded an agreement regarding joint control over the Strait, promoting exclusivity for Iranian navy and air force patrols. ▷ Hormuz, Strait of.

Le Monde, December 1, 1971; KEESING's *Contemporary Archive*, 1975.

IRANIAN–IRAQI WAR, 1980. A war that started in September 1980 with a drive of Iraqi troops and air forces carrying 50 miles into Iran in the first six days. The first limited cease-fire to stop shelling each others cities proposed by UN Secretary General Javier Perez de Cuellar was agreed upon on June 10, 1984. Since Aug. 20, 1988 a UN-arranged cease fire is in effect.

UN Chronicle, September, 1983, pp. 11–16; *Medical expert reports use of chemical weapons in Iran-Iraq war*, in: *UN Chronicle*, 1985, No. 5, pp. 24–26; E. KARSH, *A Case Study in Military Planning: The Gulf War. Military Power and Foreign Policy Goals: The Iran-Iraq War Revisited*, in: *International Affairs*, Winter, 1987/88; S. CHUBIN, Ch. TRIPP, *Iran and Iraq at War*, London, 1988.

IRANIAN-SOVIET TREATY, 1921. The Treaty was called at the time of signing the Persian–Soviet Russia Peace Treaty. Signed on Feb. 26, 1921 in Moscow. The Soviet Union renounced all concessions granted Tsarist Russia in Persia and withdrew its troops from Iran concurrently with withdrawal of British troops, with the reservation (art. 5) that should any third party wish to use Persian territory as a basis for operations directed against Russia or threaten its borders or should the Persian government be unable, in response to Russian demand, to remove such threat, the Russian government has the right to send its troops to Persian territory to defend Russian interests, The troops, however, are to be withdrawn when the threat disappears. Art. 16 provided the basis for the entry into Iran of the Red Army (concurrently with the British army) in Sept., 1941, where they were stationed until 1945–46 (as were British troops). The treaty has not been denounced and its validity was automatically extended.

G.F. MARTENS, *Nouveau Recueil Général*, 3 s., Vol. 13, p. 173; M. REZUM, *The Soviet Union and Iran*, Leiden, 1981.

IRAQ. Member of the UN. Iraqi Republic. Country in Western Asia on the Persian Gulf, bordering on Turkey, Iran, Kuwait, Saudi Arabia, Jordan, Syria. Area: 438,317 sq. km. Pop. 1987 census: 16,278,316 (1957 census: 6,336,000; 1965: 8,047,000; 1977: 12,000,497). Capital: Baghdad with 3,236,000 inhabitants 1977. GNP per capita 1980: US $3020. Currency: one Iraqi Dinar = 1000 fils. Official language: Arabic and in Iraqi Kurdes-

tan Kurdish and Arabic. National Day: July 14, anniversary of proclamation of republic, 1958. Founding member of the UN, and all its specialized agencies with the exception of the GATT. Member of the Arab League since 1945 and of the ▷ Baghdad Pact, 1955–58 which it left in 1959 after proclamation of the republic (July 14, 1958). International relations: From the early 16th century until 1917 under Turkish rule; during and after World War I under British occupation; from 1920 League of Nations mandate under British administration which proclaimed an Iraqi Kingdom in 1921; 1924–25 border dispute with Turkey over ▷ Mosul, subject of League of Nations debate. In 1932–58 formally independent monarchy in alliance with Great Britain (military bases and other privileges). Member of the League of Nations 1932–39. In World War II occupied by British troops 1941–45. Iraqi–Jordanian Federation founded Feb. 14, 1958, abolished in July of the same year due to a republican coup in Iraq. Egyptian Union (United Arab Republic) with Iraq existed from May 25, 1964 until July 1968. On Mar. 20, 1973 armed clashes between Iraqi troops and Kuwait border-guards in the Persian Gulf. Iraq claims from Kuwait a coastal strip adjacent to Umm Kasr and the islands of Bubiyan and Warb. The Northern part of Iraq inhabited by c. 2 million Kurds (Iraqi Kurdestan) was granted autonomy on Mar. 11, 1974. In 1975, Iraq concluded a treaty on co-operation with the CMEA. In Apr. 1976 joined the Arab Monetary Fund. Frontier disputes with Iran in 1974 and a military conflict since Sept. 20, 1980. On June 7, 1981 Israeli bombs destroyed Iraq's French-built nuclear reactor 'Osira' southeast of Baghdad. The war with Iran dominated in the 1980's over internal and foreign policy. On June 10, 1984 Iran and Iraq agreed under the terms of a first limited cease-fire proposed by UN Secretary-General Javier Perez de Cuellar to stop shelling each other's cities. In the years 1985-86 Iraq was accused of using chemical weapons against Iranian forces. Since Aug. 20, 1988 a UN-arranged cease-fire is in effect.
See also ▷ World Heritage UNESCO List.

K.M. LANGLEY, *The Industrialization of Iraq*, Boston, 1961; E. WIRTH, *Agrogéographie d'Irak*, Hamburg, 1962; B. VERNIER, *L'Irak d'aujourd'hui*, Paris, 1963; *Sovremenniy Irak*, Moskva, 1966; H. ARFA, *The Kurds*, London, 1966; M. KHADDURI, *Socialist Iraq. A Study of Iraq Politics since 1968*. Oxford, 1978; E. GHAREEB, *The Kurdish Question in Iraq*, Syracuse, 1981; *The Europa Yearbook 1984. A World Survey*, Vol. II, pp. 1742–1755, London, 1984; M. FAROUK-SLUGLETT, P. SLUGLETT, *Iraq since 1958: from Revolution to Dictatorship*, London, 1987.

IRAQ PETROLEUM COMPANY, IPC. The oldest petroleum company on the Arabian peninsula, f. 1925 as successor to the Turkish Petroleum Company, which was est. in 1912 and which had operated in the region of the Persian Gulf and on Cyprus; in 1931, 1932 and 1938 it received concessions from the government of Iraq extending to the year 2000 and including the whole of Iraq. This ensured the IPC a production monopoly as well as a transport monopoly through the ownership of two pipelines through Syria to the ports of Banijas and Lebanese Tripoli on the Mediterranean Sea and by a pipeline to Al-Fau on the Persian Gulf. The Revolutionary Council of Iraq nationalized the IPC by a directive of June 1, 1972, stating that the "recovery of natural resources is for the purpose of attaining genuine national independence." Simultaneously, the government of Syria nationalized IPC property in its country. The directive of the Revolutionary Council of Iraq was preceded by the formation in 1967 of the national petro-

leum association INOC, which was granted the right to exploit 89% of the deposits discovered by the IPC; the limitation of the region of exploitation of the IPC and its subsidiary the Basra and Mosul Petroleum Company to 1902 sq. km. and finally by the negotiations of the government of Iraq with IPC shareholders British Petroleum, Royal Dutch Shell Group and Compagnie Francaise des Petroles 23.75% each; Standard Oil of New Jersey and Socony Mobil Oil shares of 11.875%; and Gulbenkian Group shares of 5%; on the settlement of back taxes to the sum of 240 million dollars and increase in the production of petroleum which had been significantly retarded since 1967 and the transfer of IPC headquarters from London to Baghdad. In the face of the IPC's refusal, the Directive of June 1, 1972 ordered the take-over of IPC operations by the INOC as well as all extractive, drilling and transportation equipment and pipelines. According to Art. 3 of the directive:

"The state of Iraq agrees to guarantee compensation to IPC. It will be covered after the settlement by the company of taxes due to the state of Iraq, debts, etc."

In view of the "positive attitude of France toward the Arab question" the government of Iraq held separate talks with the Compagnie Française des Pétroles, which by an agreement signed June 17, 1972 in Paris retained rights to 23.75% of the production for another 20 years. On June 19, 1972 OPEC published a resolution at its Conference supporting the decision of Iraq in all its phases as a "legal act of sovereignty and defense of its just interests."

The Middle East and North Africa 1972–73, London, 1972.

IRA, THE PROVISIONAL. A faction of the IRA as of 1969; active in the 1970's and 1980's in military underground actions in Northern Ireland against the British.

H. ARENDT, *The Origin of Totalitarianism*, New York, 1951; P. BISHOP, E. MAILIE, *The Provisional IRA*, London, 1987.

IRBM. ▷ Intermediate-Range Ballistic Missile.

IRELAND. Member of the UN. Republic of Ireland. Country in northwest Europe on the Irish Island on the Atlantic bordering on Northern Ireland, a division of the United Kingdom. Area: 70,283 sq. km. Pop. 1988 est.: 3,540,000 (1841 census: 6,528,000; 1901: 3,221,000; 1936: 2,955,000; 1960: 2,818,000; 1971: 2,978,000). Capital city: Dublin with 427,000 inhabitants (1981). GNP per capita 1986: US $5080. Currency: one Irish Pound = 100 pennies. Official languages: Gaelic and English. National Day: Mar. 17, St Patrick's Day (patron saint of Ireland).
Ireland was a member of the League of Nations in 1926–39; member of the UN since Dec. 14, 1955 and all its specialized agencies; member of the EEC, OECD and the Council of Europe.
International relations: 1542–1916 under British rule. In 1914 granted autonomy by the British Parliament but suspended until the end of World War I. The liberation movement organized an uprising in Dublin, Apr. 24, 1916. In public elections to the House of Commons 1918 advocates of an independent Irish republic won the majority of votes and est. the republic on Jan. 21, 1919 with capital in Dublin. In armed conflict with Great Britain until May, 1921; truce signed in July, 1921. Irish Free State (Saorstat Eireann) founded on Dec. 6, 1921; granted dominion status within the British Commonwealth. Pursuant to a

treaty signed on the same day and ratified by Irish and English parliaments on Dec. 6, 1922 – the Irish Free State did not include Northern Ireland (area: 14,147 sq. km with 1,601,000 inhabitants 1977). This caused a rift in the Irish independence movement whose radical wing carried out political and periodic armed struggle; its underground body is the ▷ IRA (Irish Republican Army). Ireland was neutral during World War II. The country, renamed The Republic of Ireland, left the Commonwealth on Dec. 21, 1949, on the strength of a new constitution. The Northern Ireland controversy remains unsettled. In 1979 Ireland broke its alignment with the sterling zone and joined the ▷ European Monetary System. The ▷ Hillsborough accord came into force on Nov. 29, 1985. The first meeting of the established Intergovernmental Conference was held in Belfast on Dec. 11, 1985, the second on March 11, 1986.

E. NORMAN, *A History of Modern Ireland*, London, 1971; F.S.L. LYONS, *Ireland since the Famine*, London, 1971; C. BOURNIQUEL, *Irlande*, Paris, 1972; *The Gall History of Ireland*, 11 vols., Dublin, 1975; P. HARBISSON, *Guide to the National Monuments of Ireland*, Dublin, 1975; P. KEATINGE, *A Place Among the Nations. Issues of Irish Foreign Policy*. Dublin, 1978; THOM's *Directory of Ireland*, 2 Vols., Dublin, 1979–80; *Facts about Ireland*, Dublin, 1980; A.R. EAGER, *A Guide to Irish Bibliographical Material*, London, 1980; D.J. HICKEY, J. DOHERTY, *A Dictionary of Irish History since 1800*, Dublin, 1980; H. AKENCON, *The US and Ireland*, Cambridge, Mass., 1980; A. BROWN, *Ireland. A Social and Cultural History 1922–1979*, London, 1981; *The Europa Year Book 1984. A World Survey*, Vol. I, pp. 590–607, London, 1984; R.F. FOSTER, *Modern Ireland 1600–1972*, London, 1988.

IRELAND, NORTHERN. A division of the United Kingdom of Great Britain and Northern Ireland, embracing six counties in northeast Ireland, most of historical Ulster province; bordering on Ireland (Eire). Area: 14,147 sq.km. Pop. 1981 census: 1,490,228 (1971 census: 1,536,000; 1966: 1,484,000). The counties of what is now Northern Ireland voted for separation from the Irish Free State founded on Dec. 6, 1921 and a year later, on Dec. 6, 1922, were incorporated into Great Britain as an autonomous province with its own parliament, Stormont, and a capital in Belfast. Subject of dispute between Great Britain and Ireland over social and religious discrimination against the Catholic minority; riots and demonstrations at Londonderry and Belfast in 1968 and again in Apr., 1970. In Aug., 1970 British troops moved in to which the ▷IRA reacted with armed resistance carried on into the 1980s. Since 1971 Northern Ireland is the scene of a regular civil war between armed groups of Catholics and Protestants accompanied by intensified military activity of British troops. On Mar. 30, 1973 the British cabinet assumed formal direct control over Northern Ireland. On Nov. 15, 1985 the prime ministers of the UK and Ireland signed an Anglo-Irish Agreement, called the ▷ Hillsborough Accord, concerning the future of Northern Ireland. On Sept. 18, 1986 on the basis of the 1985 Agreement the British and Irish Governments established an International Aid Fund of £35 million to promote economic and social development in the border area.

T. PAT COOGAN, *The IRA*, London, 1971; J. DE BAILLY, *Héroïque et ténébreuse IRA*, Paris, 1972; *Ulster by the Sunday Times Team*, London, 1972; K. HESKIN, *Northern Ireland. A Psychological Analysis*, Dublin, 1980; D. WATT (ed), *The Constitution of Northern Ireland*, London, 1981; F.W. BOAL, J.N.H. DOUGLAS, *Integration and Division*, London, 1982; *The Northern Ireland Question in*: A.J. DAY ed., *Border and Territorial Disputes*, London, 1987; J. DARBY,

Intimidation and the Control of Conflict in Northern Ireland, Syracuse, N.Y., 1987.

IRI. *Instituto per la Riconstruzione Industriali.* The Institute for Industrial Reconstruction, an Italian nationalized holding company of heavy and light industry, including the steel, machinery and shipyard, telecommunications, agricultural and food products, construction, highway construction industries, and chartering companies, the airlines Alitalia and ATI, and the state radio and television network RAI.

IRIAN BARAT OR IRIAN WEST. Indonesian province. Area: 419,580 sq. km. Pop. (1970 est.): 957,000. Subject of Indonesian–Dutch dispute in 1954–69; a Dutch colony since the 18th century (Netherlands New Guinea or Dutch New Guinea) till 1942; occupied by Japan until 1945; by Holland till 1962.

After withdrawal of Dutch troops the territory was administered by the UN Temporary Executive Authority from Aug. 15, 1962 (Dutch–Indonesian Treaty approved by the UN General Assembly) until May 1, 1963; designed to fall under Indonesian administration or become independent if so voted by the population. The UN assigned official observers of the plebiscite. In the plebiscite (July 14–Aug. 5, 1969) which had two stages, the absolute majority gave votes for integration with Indonesia. An agreement on delimitation of borderline between West Irian and Papua–New Guinea was signed by the Australian and Indonesian governments on Feb. 12, 1973.

R.L. BONE, *The Dynamics of the Western New Guinea (Irian Barat) Problems,* Ithaca, 1958; *the UN in West Guinea. An Unprecedented Story,* UN, New York, 1963; D.W. WAINHOUSE, *International Peace Observation,* Baltimore, 1966; *UN Monthly Chronicle,* April, 1968; KEESING's *Contemporary Archive,* 1969 and 1973.

IRINF. ▷ Intermediate Nuclear Forces.

IRISH PEACE TREATY, 1921. A Treaty between Great Britain and the Irish Free State, signed on Dec. 6, 1921 in London. It came into force on Mar. 31, 1922. The text is as follows:

"I. Ireland shall have the same constitutional status in the Community of Nations known as the British Empire as the Dominion of Canada, the Commonwealth of Australia, the Dominion of New Zealand, and the Union of South Africa, with a Parliament having powers to make laws for the peace, order and good government of Ireland and an Executive responsible to that Parliament, and shall be styled and known as the Irish Free State.

II. Subject to the provisions hereinafter set out, the position of the Irish Free State in relation to the Imperial Parliament and Government and otherwise shall be that of the Dominion of Canada, and the law, practice and constitutional usage governing the relationship of the Crown or the representative of the Crown and of the Imperial Parliament to the Dominion of Canada shall govern their relationship to the Irish Free State.

III. The representative of the Crown in Ireland shall be appointed in like manner as the Governor-General of Canada, and in accordance with the practice observed in the making of such appointments.

IV. The oath to be taken by Members of the Parliament of the Irish Free State shall be in the following form: I ... do solemnly swear true faith and allegiance to the Constitution of the Irish Free State as by law established and that I will be faithful to H.M. King George V, his heirs and successors by law, in virtue of the common citizenship of Ireland with Great Britain and her adherence to and membership of the group of nations forming the British Commonwealth of Nations.

V. The Irish Free State shall assume liability for the service of the Public Debt of the United Kingdom as existing at the date hereof and towards the payment of war pensions as existing at that date in such proportion as may be fair and equitable, having regard to any just claims on the part of Ireland by way of set-off or counter-claim, the amount of such sums being determined in default of agreement by the arbitration of one or more independent persons being citizens of the British Empire.

VI. Until an arrangement has been made between the British and Irish Governments whereby the Irish Free State undertakes her own coastal defence, the defence by sea of Great Britain and Ireland shall be undertaken by His Majesty's Imperial Forces. But this shall not prevent the construction or maintenance by the Government of the Irish Free State of such vessels as are necessary for the protection of the Revenue or the Fisheries.

The foregoing provisions of this article shall be reviewed at a Conference of Representatives of the British and Irish Governments to be held at the expiration of five years from the date hereof with a view to the undertaking by Ireland of a share in her own coastal defence.

VII. The Government of the Irish Free State shall afford His Majesty's Imperial Forces:

(a) In time of peace such harbour and other facilities as are indicated in the Annex hereto, or such other facilities as may from time to time be agreed between the British Government and the Government of the Irish Free State; and

(b) In time of war or of strained relations with a Foreign Power such harbour and other facilities as the British Government may require for the purposes of such defence as aforesaid.

VIII. With a view to securing the observance of the principle of international limitation of armaments, if the Government of the Irish Free State establishes and maintains a military defence force, the establishments thereof shall not exceed in size such proportion of the military establishments maintained in Great Britain as that which the population of Ireland bears to the population of Great Britain.

IX. The ports of Great Britain and the Irish Free State shall be freely open to the ships of the other country on payment of the customary port and other dues.

X. The Government of the Irish Free State agrees to pay fair compensation on terms not less favorable than those accorded by the Act of 1920 to judges, officials, members of Police Forces and other Public Servants who are discharged by it or who retire in consequence of the change of government effected in pursuance hereof. Provided that this agreement shall not apply to members of the Auxiliary Police Force or to persons recruited in Great Britain for the Royal Irish Constabulary during the two years next preceding the date hereof. The British Government will assume responsibility for such compensation or pensions as may be payable to any of these excepted persons.

XI. Until the expiration of one month from the passing of the Act of Parliament for the ratification of this instrument, the powers of the Parliament and the Government of the Irish Free State shall not be exercisable as respects Northern Ireland and the provisions of the Government of Ireland Act, 1920, shall, so far as they relate to Northern Ireland, remain of full force and effect, and no election shall be held for the return of members to serve in the Parliament of the Irish Free State for constituencies in Northern Ireland, unless a resolution is passed by both Houses of the Parliament of Northern Ireland in favour of the holding of such elections before the end of the said month.

XII. If, before the expiration of the said month, an address is presented to His Majesty by both Houses of the Parliament of Northern Ireland to that effect, the powers of the Parliament and Government of the Irish Free State shall no longer extend to Northern Ireland, and the provisions of the Government of Ireland Act, 1920 (including those relating to the Council of Ireland), shall, so far as they relate to Northern Ireland, continue to be of full force and effect, and this instrument shall have effect subject to the necessary modifications.

Provided that if such an address is so presented a commission consisting of three persons, one to be appointed by the Government of the Irish Free State, one to be appointed by the Government of Northern Ireland and one, who shall be Chairman, to be appointed by the British Government, shall determine in accordance with the wishes of the inhabitants, so far as may be compatible with economic and geographic conditions, the boundaries between Northern Ireland and the rest of Ireland, and for the purposes of the Government of Ireland, Act, 1920, and of this instrument, the boundary of Northern Ireland shall be sucy as may be determined by such Commission.

XIII. For the purpose of the last foregoing article, the powers of the Parliament of Southern Ireland under the Government of Ireland Act, 1920, to elect members of the Council of Ireland shall after the Parliament of the Irish Free State is constituted be exercised by that Parliament.

XIV. After the expiration of the said month, if no such address as is mentioned in Article XII hereof is presented, the Parliament and Government of Northern Ireland shall continue to exercise as respects Northern Ireland the powers conferred on them by the Government of Ireland Act, 1920, but the Parliament and Government of the Irish Free State shall in Northern Ireland have in relation to matters in respect of which the Parliament of Northern Ireland has not power to make laws under that Act (including matters which under the said Act are within the jurisdiction of the Council of Ireland) the same powers as in the rest of Ireland) subject to such other provisions as may be agreed in manner hereinafter appearing.

XV. At any time after the date hereof the Government of Northern Ireland and the provisional Government of Southern Ireland hereinafter constituted may meet for the purpose of discussing the provisions subject to which the last foregoing article is to operate in the event of no such address as is therein mentioned being presented and those provisions may include:

(a) Safeguards with regard to patronage in Northern Ireland;

(b) Safeguards with regard to the collection of revenue in Northern Ireland;

(c) Safeguards with regard to import and export duties affecting the trade or industry of Northern Ireland;

(d) The settlement of the financial relations between Northern Ireland and the Irish Free State;

(f) The establishment and powers of a local militia in Northern Ireland and the relation of the Defence Forces of the Irish Free State and of Northern Ireland respectively; and if at any such meeting provisions are agreed to, the same shall have effect as if they were included amongst the provisions subject to which the powers of the Parliament and Government of the Irish Free State are to be exercisable in Northern Ireland under Article XIV hereof.

XVI. Neither the Parliament of the Irish Free State nor the Parliament of Northern Ireland shall make any law so as either directly or indirectly to endow any religion or prohibit or restrict the free exercise thereof or give any preference or impose any disability on account of religious belief or religious status or affect prejudicially the right of any child to attend a school receiving public money without attending the religious instruction at the school or make any discimination as respects State aid between schools under the management of different religious denominations or divert from any religious denomination or any educational institution any of its property except for public utility purposes and on payment of compensation.

XVII. By way of provisional agreement for the administration of Southern Ireland during the interval which must elapse between the date hereof and the constitution of a Parliament and Government of the Irish Free State in accordance therewith, steps shall be taken forthwith for summoning a meeting of members of Parliament elected for constituencies in Southern Ireland since the passing of the Government of Ireland Act, 1920, and for constituting a provisional Government, and the British Government shall take the steps necessary to transfer to such provisional Government the powers and machinery requisite for the discharge of its duties, provided that every member of such provisional Government shall have signified in writing his or her acceptance of this instrument. But this arrangement shall not continue in force beyond the expiration of twelve months from the date hereof."

UNTS, Vol. 26, 1924, pp. 9–20; *Major Peace Treaties of Modern History,* New York, 1967, pp. 2269–2276.

IRON. A subject of international co-operation. Organizations reg. with the UIA:

Arab Iron and Steel Union, f. 1972, Cairo. Publ.: *Arab Steel Review.*

International Federation of Ironmongers and Iron Merchants Associations, f. 1909, Zurich. Publ.: *Documentation and Press Service* (quarterly).

International Iron and Steel Insitute, f. 1967, Brussels. Insitute of Western European Producers of Iron Alloys, f. 1970, Oslo.

Latin American Iron and Steel Institute, f. 1959, Santiago. Consultative status with ECOSOC, UNIDO and UNCTAD. Publ.: *Siderurgia Latinoamericana*.

South East Asia Iron and Steel Institute, f. 1970, Singapore.

In the EEC system the ▷ STABEX includes iron ore in the APC countries.

Yearbook of International Organizations.

IRON CURTAIN. An international term coined by Winston L.S. Churchill (1874–1965) at Westminster College, Fulton, Missouri, Mar. 5, 1946:

"From Stettin in the Baltic to Trieste in the Adriatic an iron curtain has descended across the Continent. Behind that line lie all capitals of the ancient states of central and eastern Europe: Warsaw, Berlin, Prague, Vienna, Budapest, Belgrade, Bucharest and Sofia, all these famous cities and the population around them lie in what I must call the Soviet sphere, and all are subject in one form or another, not only to Soviet influence but to a very high and in many cases increasing measure of control from Moscow."

New York Times, Mar. 6, 1946; W.L.S. CHURCHILL, *Sinews of Peace, Post War Speeches*, Cassell, 1948; F.B. CZARNOMSKI (ed.), *The Wisdom of W. Churchill*, London, 1956; F.J. HARBUTT, *The Iron Curtain: Churchill, America and the Origin of the Cold War*, New York, 1986.

IRON GATE. *Serbo-Croatian*: Djerdapska Klisura. *Romanian*: Portile de Fier. A gorge of the Danube River on the Romanian–Yugoslav border, 3.2 km long and 170 m wide, between the Carpathian and the East-Serbian Mountains. Since 1860 the Iron Gate is clear of rock obstructions and since 1896 is a ship canal; subject of Romanian–Yugoslav co-operation based on an agreement of Oct. 30, 1963 on mutual construction of a water dam and a hydro power station worth over $400 million. The construction, concluded in the Spring of 1972, made the Danube available for sea-going ships up to 5000 tons and enabled the building of super-highway and railway sections on the dam connecting both countries. The opening of the biggest hydroenergetic and communication system on the Danube took place May 16, 1972 in the presence of President J. Broz Tito and Chairman of the State Council N. Ceaucescu.

KEESING's *Contemporary Archive*, 1972.

IRON LETTER. ▷ Safe conduct.

IRON-ORE. A subject of intergovernmental agreement, signed Apr. 3, 1975 in Geneva by the governments of Algeria, Brazil, Australia, Chile, India, Mauritania, Peru, Sierra Leone, Sweden, Tunisia, Venezuela. It came into force Oct. 12, 1975. Permanent body of the agreement: Association for Iron-Ore Exporting Countries with a Secretariat in London. Every 2 years ministerial meeting. Activities limited to a purely consultative role, without powers for concerted governmental action, such as price fixing. The Association members represented about 42% of world production and about 57% of export. Reg. with the UIA.

Yearbook of International Organizations.

IRPTC. International Register of Potentially Toxic Chemicals, one of the information systems of the ▷ UNEP.

IRREDENTA. *Italian* = "unredeemed". An international term for desire to join the country of

origin by a population living outside its frontiers; the term derived from the Italian unification movement Italia irredenta, 1878.

A. VIVENTE, *Irredentismo adriatico*, Rome, 1912; A. SANDOVA, *L'irredentismo selle lotte politiche e nello contese diplomatiche italo-austriache*, 3 Vols, Rome, 1932–38.

IRRIGATION. A subject of organized international co-operation in connection with the desertization of many regions of the world. Organization reg. with the UIA:

International Commission on Irrigation and Drainage, ICID, est. 1950, Delhi; unites national committees, co-operates with FAO; publ.: *ICID Bulletin, Bibliography on Irrigation, Drainage Flood Control and River Training*, multilingual *Technical Dictionary on Irrigation and Drainage*.

The only country in the world whose cultivated land is 100% watered by artificial means is Egypt, China – 67%, Taiwan – 61%, Guyana and Japan – 55%, Iraq – 49%, Albania – 45%, Pakistan – 42%, Peru – 41%, Iran 40%, Israel 38%, Indonesia – 28%.

Yearbook of International Organizations; A. TAMAKI, I. HATATE, N. IMAMURA eds., *Irrigation in Development, The Social Structure of Water Utilization in Japan*, Tokyo, 1984.

IRS. ▷ Incident Reporting System, est. 1983 by the IAEA, called IAEA–IRS.

V.G. TOLSKYKH, IAEA–IRS. *New directions in Co-operative Network for Nuclear Safety*, in: *IAEA Bulletin*, Winter, 1986.

ISBN. International Standard Book Number. A bibliographic computer system introduced first in Anglo-Saxon countries, then in other countries. Each new book title is given its own number (ISBN). The first part of the number gives the country of publication (e.g. 84 – Spain), the second part – the publishing house (e.g. 375 – Ediciones Fondo de Cultura Economica, Espana SA), the third part – the subject matter (e.g. 0079 – encyclopaedia), the fourth part – the code symbol (e.g. 6). Thus the *Enciclopedia Mundial de Relaciones Internacionales y Naciones Unidas*, published in Madrid, has the number: ISBN 84–375–0079–6. The International Standard Book Number Agency, ISBNA, with headquarters in Berlin, registers member countries, e.g. 0 Great Britain, the US and other English-speaking countries; 2 France, 3 German-speaking countries, 83 Poland, 84 Spain, 87 Denmark, 90 the Netherlands, 91 Sweden, 92 UNESCO, 951 Finland, 963 Hungary. Each member country has a national ISBN Agency.

ISDS. International Serials Data System, one of the information systems of the ▷ UNESCO.

ISKENDERUN. Formerly Alexandretta, city and port in the province ▷ Hatay, southern Turkey, on the Gulf of Alexandretta. Greek city 333 B.C.–A.D. 1515 then annexed by the Ottoman Empire, occupied by the French 1919–39 under League of Nations Mandate. Returned by France to Turkey in June 1939.

ISLAM. Mohammedanism. *Arabic*: aslama = "surrender to the will of Allah". One of the three great religions of the world besides Buddhism and Christianity, arose in the 7th century from the teachings of Mohammed (Muhammad ibn Abd Allah) contained in the Koran. Followers of Islam in Arabia are called muslimun, hence Moslems. Contemporary Islam has a unique role as a bond for the Arab states in their conflict with Israel. A Moslem World Congress, Mutamar al-Arab al-

Islami, was called for the first time in Mecca, 1926; created as a permanent organization, 1951 in Karachi, unites Moslem organizations from 42 countries, consultative status with ECOSOC and a Permanent Representation with the UN in New York. Publ.: *World Muslim Gazetteer*. In Leiden (Holland) a quarterly is published in English, French and German, *The World of Islam, Le Monde d'Islam, Die Welt des Islam*. The Index Islamicus 1906–1955, was published in London; the Quarterly Index Islamicus, 1976/80, Index Islamicus Supplement in 1956–1960 and the Index Islamicus 1961–1965, 1966 1970, 1971 1976, 1976/1980 were also published in London.

The Encyclopaedia of Islam, 4 Vols, Leiden–London, 1954; G.H. JANSEN, *Militant Islam*, London, 1979; "The Explosion in the Moslem World: A Roundtable on Islam", in: *The New York Times*, Dec. 15–16, 1979; W.R. POLK, *The US and the Arab World*, Cambridge, Mass., 1980; *Yearbook of International Organizations*; UNESCO, *ISLAM*, Paris 1982, also in Arabic, French and Spanish; J.P. PISCATORI, *Islam in a World of Nation-States*, London, 1986; A. BENNIGSEN, S.E. WIMBUSH, *Muslims of the Soviet Empire. A Guide*, London, 1987; S. ARJOMAND, *From Nationalism to Revolutionary Islam*, New York, 1987; R. MOTTAHEDEH, *The Mantle of the Prophet*, New York, 1987; M. MOMEN, *An Introduction to Shiite Islam*, Princeton, 1987; A.S. AHMED, *Discovering Islam*, London, 1988.

ISLAMIC CAIRO. A historic site of the capital of Egypt, included in the ▷ World Heritage UNESCO List. Several foundations along the Nile contributed to the establishment of Cairo as a business center, a cultural and theological center, the seat of powerful political and religious dynasties and the largest Islamic city in the Middle Ages. It now contains 600 extremely important historical monuments, including mosques, colleges, churches and convents, military buildings, palaces and markets.

UNESCO, *A Legacy for All*, Paris, 1984.

ISLAMIC CONFERENCES. ▷ Islamic states.

ISLAMIC DEVELOPMENT BANK. An intergovernmental financial institution, f. 1974 in Jedda, Saudi Arabia, by the governments of Afghanistan, Algeria, Bahrain, Bangladesh, Cameroon, Egypt, Guinea, Indonesia, Jordan, Kuwait, Libya, Malaysia, Mauritania, Morocco, Niger, Oman, Pakistan, Qatar, Saudi Arabia, Senegal, Somalia, Sudan, Syria, Tunisia, Turkey, the United Arab Emirates and the Republic of Yemen.

Arab Development Funds and Banks, OECD, Paris, 1978.

ISLAMIC REPUBLICS. International term for states of mostly Moslem population which declared themselves Islamic Republics in the second half of the 20th century, combining religious and state legislation, e.g. Iran, 1979.

ISLAMIC STATES. In the UN system the term is used with respect to 30 states of Africa, the Middle East and South Asia, the population of which is mostly Moslem. In the second half of the 20th century conferences were convened by the Islamic states that aimed at transforming religious unity into political unity, with permanent political institutions and economic organizations (Conference of Foreign Ministers). In Sept., 1969 in Rabat (Morocco) a summit meeting of 25 heads of Islamic states initiated the Organization of Islamic Conferences as a standing institution; since May, 1971 it has a permanent Islamic Secretariat with its seat in

Jedda, Saudi Arabia, an organ of which is the International Islamic News Agency, IINA), since Aug., 1972 publishing the *Weekly News Bulletin*. On Nov. 9, 1981 the UN General Assembly adopted Res. 36/23 on co-operation between United Nations and Organization of Islamic Conference, which represented 42 Islamic states (Algeria, Bahrain, Bangladesh, Burkina Faso, Cameroon, Chad, Comoros, Gabon, Gambia, Guinea, Guinea-Bissau, Indonesia, Iraq, Iran, Jordan, Kuwait, Lebanon, Libya, Mali, Maldives, Malaysia, Mauritania, Morocco, Niger, Oman, Pakistan, the Palestinian Liberation Organization, Qatar, Saudi Arabia, Senegal, Somalia, Sudan, Syria, Tunisia, Uganda, the United Arab Emirates, North Yemen, South Yemen (not invited were Afghanistan and Egypt). The conference's official languages are Arabic, English and French. The second summit meeting of the Islamic heads of state was held in Lahore (Pakistan) in Feb., 1974 with the participation of 37 states, including 18 Arab states (Algeria, Saudi Arabia, Bahrain, Egypt, Iraq as observer, Yemen, South Yemen as observer, Jordan, Qatar, Kuwait, Libya, Lebanon as observer, Morocco, Oman, Sudan, Syria, Tunisia, the United Arab Emirates); 12 African states (Chad, Gabon, Guinea-Bissau, Mali, Mauritania, Niger, Senegal, Sierra Leone, Somalia, Uganda); and 7 Asian states (Afghanistan, Bangladesh, Indonesia, Iran, Malaysia, Pakistan, Turkey). After the recognition of Bangladesh – on the opening day of the conference by the host government – the government of Pakistan sent an invitation to Bangladesh, the representatives of which arrived at the conference on the last day of the session. The conference was attended also by the Mufti of Jerusalem and by the head of the Palestine Liberation Organization, Mr. Y. Arafat, who was given the status of a head of state and the sole representative of the people of Palestine. The conference ended with the adoption of the Lahore Declaration of 1974, which included two postulates:

"The Arab cause is the cause of all countries which oppose aggression and shall not tolerate the use of force to be awarded with territorial or any other gains. The Arab countries should be rendered full and effective assistance for regaining their occupied lands by any accessive means whatsoever."

The Third Summit took place in 1980 in Islamabad and the Fourth in 1984 in Casablanca, which accepted the invitation of Egypt (32 for, 9 abstentions). The foreign ministers' meetings in the framework of the Organization of Islamic Conference are held every year since 1969. The Conference decided to establish a common credit institution called the ▷ Islamic Development Bank, and a joint credit agency. Participating in these institutions are both the states in which Islam is the state-approved religion, as well as lay-states (Algeria, Indonesia, Lebanon, Turkey). A summit meeting of the Islamic Conference Organization was held in Casablanca from Jan. 16 to 19, 1984.

UN Chronicle, Jan. 1982, pp. 20–21; J. PISCATORI, *Islam in a World of Nation–States*, New York, 1986.

ISLANDS. A subject of the ▷ Sea Law Convention, 1982 (Art. 121).

R.L. BLEDSOE, B.A. BOCZEK, *The International Law Dictionary*, Oxford, UK, 1987.

ISLANDS, ARTIFICIAL. A subject of international co-operation and disputes.

N. PAPADOKIS, *The International Legal Regime of Artificial Islands*, Leiden, 1977.

ISMAILIA. City (1986 population census 145,978) in north-eastern Egypt, f. 1863, by Ferdinand de Lesseps (1865–94) during the construction of the Suez Canal; place of first visit on Egyptian soil, on Dec. 26, 1977, of Israeli Prime Minister Menahem Begin, to meet Egyptian President Anwar Sadat.

ISMUN. The International Student Movement for the United Nations, founded in 1948 by the World Federation of United Nations Associations (WFUNA) with headquarters in Geneva; associations in 42 countries. Consultative status ECOSOC, ILO. Publ.: the quarterly *ISMUN Bulletin*. Reg. with the UN.

Yearbook of International Organizations.

ISOLATIONISM. An international term applying mainly to a policy of the USA to separate itself from world politics in the 19th and early 20th century by avoiding involvement in international conflicts in accordance with the ▷ Non-Entangling Alliances Doctrine, 1796 and the ▷ Monroe Doctrine 1873. On March 19, 1920 the US Senate in a dramatic expression of American isolationism refused to ratify the League of Nations Covenant drawn up on the initiative and with the participation of President W. Wilson. In 1935, 1936, 1937 and 1939 to prevent the country's involvement in conflicts brewing up in Europe and Asia the US Congress adopted four ▷ Neutrality Acts.

D. WECTER, *The Age of the Great Depression, 1929–1941*, New York, 1948; F.L. PAXTON, *American Democracy and the World War*, 3 Vols., New York, 1948; G.F. KENNAN, *American Diplomacy 1900–1950*, New York, 1951; D. ROBERTSON, *Guide to Modern Defense and Strategy*, Detroit, 1988.

ISORIO. International Information Systems on Research inform Documentation, one of the information systems of the ▷ UNESCO.

ISOTOPE PRODUCTS. Subject of international agreements and co-operation. The research institutions of Czechoslovakia, the GDR, Hungary, Poland, Romania and the USSR signed at Moscow, Jan. 10, 1974, an Agreement on Multilateral International Specialization and Co-operation in Production of Isotope Products.

Recueil de Documents, Varsovie, No. 1, 1974; W.E. BUTLER (ed.), *A Source Book on Socialist International Organizations*, Alphen, 1978, pp. 908–918.

ISOTOPES. Subject of international scientific co-operation, sponsored by the IAEA, in ▷ agriculture, ▷ hydrology, ▷ environment, ▷ insect, ▷ soil studies, etc.

R. GONFIANTINI, G. HUT, *Water and Earth Sciences: Isotopes in the Field: in IAEA Bulletin 1987*, No. 2; P.D. KLEIN, E.R. KLEIN, *Stable Isotope Usage in Developing Countries: Safe Tracer Tools to Measure Human Nutritional Status, in: IAEA Bulletin*, No. 4, 1987.

ISRAEL. Member of the UN. State of Israel. State in southwestern Asia on the Mediterranean Sea. Area: 21,946 sq. km. Pop. (including occupied territories) 1987 est.: 4,449,000 (1961 census: 2,183,000; 1971: 3,200,000). Capital until 1950, Tel Aviv, with 334,900 inhabitants in 1981. Since Jan, 23, 1950 ▷ Jerusalem with 407,000 inhabitants in 1981. Israel borders with Lebanon, Syria, Jordan and Egypt. GNP per capita in 1987: US $6810. Official languages: Hebrew and Arabic. Currency: one Israeli shekel = 100 agorot. National Day: variable (April or May), Independence Day, 1948. Since 1948 member of the UN and of all UN specialized organizations.

International relations: the idea of rebuilding a "cradle of the Jewish nation" as the state of Israel on the historical territory of ▷ Palestine was announced in 1897 by the First Zionist Congress in Basel, Switzerland; this idea was officially supported on Nov. 2, 1918 in the so-called ▷ Balfour Declaration by the government of Great Britain, to whom the Supreme Allied Council in 1920 granted a mandate over Palestine; confirmed on July 24, 1922 by the League of Nations; Great Britain in 1921 formed the emirate of ▷ Transjordan from the western part of Palestine. The influx of Jewish immigrants from the whole world to Palestine aroused the opposition of the Arab population, which turned into an armed conflict in 1936–39. After World War II the UN Special Commission on Palestine, UNISCOP, drew up a plan for the division of Palestine into two states: Arab and Jewish, in economic union, and with Jerusalem having the status of an internationalized territory distinct from both states. This plan envisaged giving the Jews nearly half of Palestine (c. 14,000 sq. km) and was approved by the UN General Assembly on Nov. 29, 1947 over the opposition of the Arab states. Great Britain gave up its mandate and on May 14, 1948 withdrew its forces and administration. On the same day the State of Israel was proclaimed in Tel Aviv. Immediately after the UN resolution of Nov. 29, 1947, the armed intervention of the Arab states began (Egypt, Iraq, Lebanon, Syria, Transjordan and Saudi Arabia), ending though UN mediation with a cease-fire in 1949; with Egypt on Feb. 24, with Lebanon on Mar. 23, with Transjordan on Apr. 3, with Syria on July 20 (Iraq and Saudi Arabia did not enter into negotiations with Israel). The demarcation lines which were drawn extended Israel's territory to 20,7000 sq. km. No peace treaty was signed. Israel also occupied part of Jerusalem (New City) and on Jan. 23, 1950, in spite of the resolutions of the UN on the internationalization of the Holy City, announced it as the capital of the country. On Oct. 22, 1956 Israel signed a secret treaty with France and Great Britain in Sèvres near Paris on the taking of joint military action against Egypt in connection with the nationalization of the Suez Canal. Military action was commenced on Oct. 29, 1956 by Israeli forces, which occupied the Gaza Strip and the Sinai peninsula. In face of a Soviet ultimatum, the negative position of the USA and resolutions of the UN General Assembly, military operations were halted on Nov. 6, and Israeli forces withdrew to the demarcation line of 1949; the inviolability of this line was supervised by the United Nations Emergency Force, UNEF, to the beginning of June, 1967, when they were withdrawn at the request of Egypt. On June 5, 1967 Israel began new military operations against Egypt, Jordan and Syria, resulting after the Six Day War in the occupation of the ▷ Gaza Strip and of Egyptian Sinai peninsula up to the Suez Canal, Jordanian territory to the river Jordan and Syrian, the so-called Golan region and all of Jerusalem. The Security Council, Res. 242, accepted the so-called ▷ Israeli UN Resolution 1967, confirmed by votes in the UN General Assembly in Dec. 1971 and 1972. A mediation mission on behalf of the UN was carried out in 1970–72 by the Swedish ambassador in Moscow, G. Jarring, who submitted a memorandum to the governments of Egypt and Israel on Feb. 8, 1971, to which only Egypt replied positively. In 1973 the UN mediation mission was renewed. In Oct., 1973 Egypt and Syria began military operations against Israel. They lasted from Oct. 6 to 23 (called in Israel the "Yom Kippur War" and in the Arab states the "Ramadan

War"), ending with the partial dislodgement of Israeli forces from the Suez Canal. At the call of the UN Security Council and joint action by the USA and USSR, a cease-fire was put into effect on Oct. 22–24, 1973, and a Conference on the Middle East was convened. To safeguard the cease-fire with Egypt, again the UNEF was called to complete the separation of opposing forces in the Sinai peninsula on Mar. 3, 1974, moving Israeli forces back 20 km east of the Suez Canal. At the Conference on the Middle East in Geneva on Jan. 13, 1974 a Treaty on the separation of armed forces by the UNEF was signed. (▷ Israeli-Syrian Agreement on Disengagement, 1974). Efforts to solve the Arab–Israeli conflict by calling a special Geneva Conference under the sponsorship of the Great Powers were unsuccessful.

Egypt recognized the State of Israel in Nov. 1977 during a visit of President Sadat in Israel. The Israeli-Egypt negotiations supported by the USA (see ▷ Camp David) ended with a peace treaty, signed in Washington DC on Mar. 26, 1979. In June, 1982 Israel started "Operation Peace for Gallilea" against the ▷ PLO bases in Lebanon. On Nov. 25, 1983, in Damascus an agreement was signed on cease-fire and withdrawal of PLO troops from Lebanon.

The Israel-USSR negotiations started in the UN in Sept. 1984 (Shamir-Gromyko) and after semi-official low level contacts in 1985 and 1986 official negotiations started in July 1987. In July 1986 the Israel Aircraft Industries launched the first fighter aircraft (Lavi) developed and built in Israel and successfully tested its first anti-missile.

On the basis of the revelation by a technician employed at the Dimona nuclear research plant in the Nagov Desert, that Israel is able to manufacture nuclear warheads for its Jericho medium-range rockets, the UN General Assembly with the Res. 42/44 on Nov. 30, 1987 condemned Israel for its failure to sign the Non-Proliferation Treaty and called on the IAEA to suspend any scientific cooperation with Israel that could contribute to its nuclear capability.

The IAEA General Conference in Vienna, on Sept. 23, 1988 demanded that Israel 'place all its nuclear facilities under IAEA safeguards'.

The government of Israel from 1948/49 published *Israel Yearbook*, from 1949/50 *Statistical Abstract of Israel*.

See also ▷ Muslim Religious Courts in Israel.
▷ Luxembourg Treaty FRG-Israel, 1952.

M. BURNSTEIN, *Self-Government of the Jews in Palestine Since 1900*, Tel Aviv, 1934; *Great Britain and Palestine 1915–1945*, London, 1946; W. ZANDER, *Soviet-Jewry, Palestine and the West*, London, 1947; *General Report of the UN Special Committee on Palestine*, Lake Success, 1947; C. WEIZMANN, *Trial and Error*, London, 1949; A.M. HYAMSON, *Palestine under the Mandate 1920–1948*, London, 1950; R. FRYE (ed.), *The Near East and the Great Powers*, Cambridge, Mass., 1951; H. SACHER, *Israel. The Establishment of a State*, New York, 1952; J. PARKES, *End of an Exile: Israel, the Jews and the Gentile World*, New York, 1954; *Israel and the United Nations. Report of a Study Group set up by the Hebrew University of Jerusalem*, Jerusalem, 1956. L.F. RUSBROOK, *The State of Israel*, London, 1957; R. CROSMAN, *Nation Reborn*, London, 1960; D.R. ELSTON, *Israel: The Making of a Nation*, New York, 1963; BEN GURION, *The Jews in Their Land*, London, 1966; M.A. LILIENTHAL, *The Other Side of Coin. An American Perspective of the Arab–Israeli Conflict*, New York, 1966; R.W. CHURCHILL, *The Six Day War*, London, 1967; S.N. EISENSTADT, *Israeli Society*, London, 1969; M. LANDAU, *The Arabs in Israel*, London, 1969; W. LAQUER (ed.), *The Israel–Arab Reader*, London, 1970; E.S. LIKHOVSKI, *Israel's Parliament:*

The Law of Knesset, Oxford, 1971; N. LUCAS, *A Modern History of Israel*, London, 1975; N. SAFRAN, *Israel: The Embattled Ally*, Harvard, 1976; *Who's Who in Israel*, Tel Aviv, 1978; D. PERETZ, *The Government and Politics of Israel*, Folkestone, 1979; *Facts about Israel*, Jerusalem, 1979; W. FRANKEL, *Israel Observed*, London, 1980; M. DAYAN, *Breakthrough*, New York, 1981; W. HARIS, *Taking Root. Israeli Settlements in the West Bank. The Golan and Gaza Strip 1967–1980*, Chichester, 1981; *The Europa Year Book 1984. A World Survey*, Vol. II, pp. 1756–1774, London, 1984; B. BAHBAH, *Israel and Latin America: The Military Connection*, New York, 1986; E.M. SNYDER, ed.: *Israel, World Bibliographical Series*, Vol. 58, Oxford, UK, Santa Barbara, Calif., 1985; KEESING's *Contemporary Archive*, 1986, No. 11; Y. BAR-SIMAN-TOV, *Israel, the Superpowers, and the War in the Middle-East*, New York, 1987; G.B. ENDOR, D.B. DEVITT eds., *Conflict Management in the Middle East*, Lexington, 1987; G. ARONSON, *Creating Facts: Israel, Palestinians and the West Bank*, Washington DC, 1987; H.M. SACHAR, *A History of Israel*, 2 Vls., New York, 1977 and 1987; KEESING's *Record of World Events*, April, 1988; D. NEFF, *Warriors against Israel*, Bratleboro, 1988; KEESING's *Record of World Events*, May, 1988; S. HILLEL, *Operation Babylon: Jewish Clandestine Activity in the Middle East 1946–51*, New York, 1988; G. GROSSMAN, *The Yellow Wind*, New York, 1988; S. GREEN, *Living by Swords*, London, 1988.

ISRAELI–SYRIAN AGREEMENT ON DISENGAGEMENT, 1974. An agreement signed on May 13, 1974 in Geneva, negotiated in implementation of Security Council Res. 338/1973/ dated Oct. 22, 1973.

The highlights of the agreement:

"A. Israel and Syria will scrupulously observe the cease-fire on land, sea and air, will refrain all military actions against each other."

"H. This Agreement is not a Peace Agreement. It is a step towards a just and durable peace on the basis of Security Council Res. 338/1973."

In a Protocol concerning the UN Disengagement Observer Force, ▷ UNDOF, Israel and Syria agree that the UNDOF will supervise the Agreement.

UN Monthly Chronicle, June 1974, pp. 19–28.

ISRAEL-UNITED STATES AGREEMENTS, 1979. A Memorandum of Agreement Between the US and Israel, which provides assurance for Israel in case of Egyptian violation of the Peace Treaty, signed on Mar. 26, 1979, and US–Israel Memorandum of Agreement on Oil, which assures Israel of an uninterrupted supply of oil until at least 1990. ▷ Egypt–Israel Peace Treaty 1979.

ISRAEL UN RESOLUTION, 1967. The UN Security Council Res. No. 242 unanimously adopted on Nov. 22, 1967 on withdrawal of Israeli armed forces from Arab territories occupied in June, 1967. The Resolution is of significance for the development of international law since the Big Powers as well as other members of Security Council unanimously confirmed the principle of "inadmissibility of the acquisition of territory by war." Here is the full text of the resolution:

"The Security Council,
Expressing its continuing concern with the grave situation in the Middle East, emphasizing the inadmissibility of the acquisition of territory by war and the need to work for a just and lasting peace in which every State in the area can live in security, emphasizing further that all Member States in their acceptance of the Charter of the United Nations have undertaken a commitment to act in accordance with Article 2 of the Charter.
(1) Affirms that the fulfilment of Charter principles requires the establishment of a just and lasting peace in the Middle East which should include the application of both the following principles:

(i) Withdrawal of Israeli armed forces from territories occupied in the recent conflict;
(ii) Termination of all claims of states of belligerency and respect for and acknowledgement of the sovereignty, territorial integrity and political independence of every State in the area and their right to live in peace within secure and recognized boundaries free from threats or acts of force.
(2) Affirm further the necessity:
(a) For guaranteeing freedom of navigation through international waterways in the area;
(b) For achieving a just settlement of the refugee problem;
(c) For guaranteeing the territorial inviolability and political independence of every State in the area, through measures including the establishment of demilitarized zones.
(3) Requests the Secretary-General to designate a Special Representative to proceed to the Middle East to establish and maintain contacts with the States concerned in order to promote agreement annd assist efforts to achieve a peaceful and accepted settlement in accordance with the provisions and principles of this Resolution.
(4) Requests the Secretary-General to report to the Security Council on the progress of the efforts of the Special Representative as soon as possible."

The importance of the Israel Resolution was fully affirmed by the UN General Assembly in a Res. on the Middle East adopted Dec. 8, 1972 and by the ▷ Israeli–Syrian Agreement on Disengagement, 1974.

UN Yearbook, 1967.

ISTRIA. *Serbo-Croatian*: Istra. A peninsula on the Adriatic Sea on the border of Yugoslavia and Italy, subject of a dispute between Yugoslavia and Italy. Italy in the war with Austria occupied Istria on Nov. 4, 1918 and claimed successional rights after Austria to the entire province of Istria including the cities of Trieste, Riyeka (Italian Fiume), Pula, Koper and Opatiya. The Italian–Yugoslavian treaty concluded on Nov. 12, 1920 in Rapallo ceded Istria to Italy, but made Riyeka a Free City. On Jan. 27, 1924, under a treaty signed in Rome, Yugoslavia also agreed to the annexation of Riyeka by Italy. Yugoslavian partisan forces liberated Istria in Apr. 1945; Trieste and Pula on May 2 and 3 of that year. Istria, with the exception of Trieste, which received the status of a Free City was granted to Yugoslavia in arts. 11 and 12 of the Peace Treaty with Italy, signed on Feb. 10, 1947 in Paris. In the Spring of 1974, new Italian claims created tensions in Italian–Yugoslavian relations.

M. ROJNIC, *Nacionalno pitanje v Istrii, 1848–1919*, Zagreb, 1949; F. CULINOVIC, *Rijecka drzava od Londonskog paktu o Danundijade de Rapallo i aneksije Italiji*, Zagreb, 1953.

ITAIPÚ. *Indian* = singing stone. A locality in the state of Parana, Brazil, on the River Parana bordering on Paraguay, 20 km from the Argentine frontier. In 1970, the Brazilian government commissioned blueprints for construction in Itaipú by 1980 of the world's largest dam with a 12,600 million-kilowatt capacity, which stirred an international controversy between Brazil and Argentina, the latter objecting against the use without its permission of the waters of a multinational, Brazilian–Paraguayan–Argentine river. In Oct., 1972 Argentine and Brazilian governments signed an agreement on mutual exchange of information about all projects related to the River Parana. The foreign ministries of Brazil and Paraguay signed on Apr. 26, 1973 at Brasilia the Itaipú Treaty on the construction within 8–10 years of a 170-metre-high dam. On Oct. 19, 1979, Argentina, Brazil and Paraguay signed a treaty by which the waters of Parana are to be shared between the Itaipú dam and the ▷ Corpus dam built by Argentina (4400 million-kilowatt capacity). In Nov., 1984 the first transmission line between Itaipú – São Paulo was opened, with 1,5 million-kilowatt capacity. On Jan. 9, 1987 President Sarney of Brazil and Gen. Stroessner of Paraguay inaugurated two further hydroelectric turbines at the Itaipú dam. The full capacity is scheduled to be attained by 1990.

KEESING's *Contemporary Archive*, 1973; *Le Monde*, June 3, 1973; 'Itaipú: the singing stone', in: *Newsweek*, November 12, 1984.

ITALIAN GOLD. Gold held by Italian banks, which was taken away from Rome in 1944 by the German armed forces, captured in 1944 by allied troops in the town of Fortezza, Italy, and returned to the Italians in 1947 by virtue of the agreement on gold concluded by the USA and Great Britain with Italy.

UNTS, *Vol. 54, pp. 193–196.*

ITALIAN LATIN AMERICAN INSTITUTE. Instituto Italo-Latino-Americano, f. June 1, 1966; Rome, on signature of an intergovernmental convention of 20 Latin American states and Italy. Promotion of economic, technical, scientific and cultural co-operation. Publ. *Bulletin*. Reg. with the UIA.

Yearbook of International Organizations.

ITALY. Member of the UN. Republica Italiana. Republic of Italy. State in southern Europe on the Apennine peninsula (and the islands: Sicily and Sardinia). Borders with France, Switzerland, Austria, Yugoslavia and San Marino. Area: 301,278 sq.km. Pop. 1987 est.: 57,317,000 (1871 census: 27,577,000; 1901 – 33,370,000; 1951 – 47,158,000; 1971 – 54,136,000). Capital: Rome with 2,834,094 inhabitants in 1982. Official language: Italian. GNP 1987 US $10,420. Currency: one lire = 100 centesimi. National Day: June 2, anniversary of the Proclamation of the Republic, 1946.
Member of the UN since Dec. 14, 1955 and of all UN specialized organizations. Member of NATO, the EEC and OECD.
International relations: unified in the second half of the 19th century after centuries of fragmentation. The Italian Kingdom in 1870–1914 followed a policy of Triple Alliance with Germany and Austria, signed May 20, 1882, and colonial expansion in North Africa (in Ethiopia, Eritrea, Libya and Somalia). During World War I Italy was neutral at first, but after the London agreement of Apr, 26, 1915 she broke away from the Triple Alliance and declared war on Austria–Hungary on May 23, 1915 and on Aug. 25, 1916 on the German Reich. By the Treaty of Saint Germain-en-Laye in 1919 Italy acquired Alto Adige (South Tirol) and by the Rapallo Treaty in 1921 Venezia Giulia. In conflict with Yugoslavia 1919–24 over Rijeka. The coup d'etat of Benito Mussolini on Oct. 28, 1922 gave the Kingdom of Italy the character of a fascist state. Treaties between the wars: with Albania a Pact of Friendship and Security on Nov. 27, 1926, a Treaty of Defensive Alliance on Nov. 22, 1927 and after the invasion a treaty of personal union of Albania with Italy on Apr. 16, 1939; with Hungary Apr. 5, 1927 a Treaty of Friendship, Conciliation and Arbitration and Mutual Judicial Assistance; with Turkey May 30, 1928 a Treaty of Neutrality, Conciliation and Mutual Judicial Assistance, prolonged Apr. 29, 1934; with the Apostolic See Feb. 11, 1929 a Treaty on settling the "Roman question", the so-called Lateran Treaty and a concordat of that same date; with Austria and Hungary Mar. 17, 1934 consultative protocols; with France Jan. 7, 1935 an agreement settling disputed issues, mainly

concerning Africa, repudiated by Italy Dec. 17, 1938; with Great Britain Jan. 2, 1937 a Declaration signed in Rome on the Mediterranean Sea, recognizing "freedom of entry and exit and passage through the Mediterranean Sea" as well as renouncing "all desire to affect changes or allowing changes in the status quo with respect to national territorial sovereignty in the area of the Mediterranean"; confirmed April 16, 1938 by a British–Italian Treaty signed in Rome extending British–Italian co-operation to seven other problems connected with the colonial interests of both sides in Africa (i.a. establishing the boundaries between British and Italian colonies in Africa and freedom of navigation through the Suez Canal). A supplement to this treaty signed on the same day was a Good Neighbor Treaty between Italy, Great Britain and Egypt. With Yugoslavia, Mar. 28, 1937 a treaty on mutual relations. When A. Hitler came to power in Germany in 1933, B. Mussolini came out with a proposal for a ▷ Pact of Four (France, Germany, Great Britain and Italy) as the dominant powers in Europe. In 1935 Italy started a war with Ethiopia and then participated in the civil war in Spain. She signed an agreement with the German III Reich on Oct. 25, 1936, the so-called Rome–Berlin Axis; on Nov. 6, 1937 she joined the ▷ Anti-comintern pact; she withdrew from the League of Nations on Dec. 11, 1937; on Mar. 13, 1938 she recognized the ▷ Anschluss of Austria with the German III Reich; on May 10, 1939 a military alliance with the III Reich, the so-called Pact of steel; in Apr., 1939 she launched an attack on Albania. In the first months of World War II Italy was neutral, entering the war with an attack on France June 10, 1940 and signing on Sept. 27, 1940 the Berlin Pact of Three with Germany and Japan. The fascist government fell July 25, 1943 after the landing of allied forces in Sicily; B. Mussolini was liberated from his place of detention on Sept. 12, 1943 by Nazi paratroopers; he was executed by Italian partisans Apr. 27, 1945. German forces occupying Italy from Sept., 1943 were pushed north and surrendered on May 2, 1945. The allied powers: the USA, the UK and the USSR in the Moscow Declaration of Oct. 30, 1943 pronounced the complete liquidation of fascism in Italy and the future establishment of a democratic system. A popular referendum on June 2, 1946 made Italy a republic. The peace treaty with Italy signed Feb. 10, 1947 in Paris drew new boundaries for Italy, granting Yugoslavia Rijeka, Istria, part of Venezia Giulia, and to Greece, the Dodecanese; in art. XXIII Italy also abandoned all claims to Eritrea, Libya and Somalia. In 1947–54 in a dispute with Yugoslavia over Trieste. In 1983 the government of Italy gave its consent to the NATO Council to place on her territory as well as in the FRG and Great Britain missiles of the Cruise and Pershing II types with thermonuclear warheads.
The Institute of International Affairs, Instituto Affari Internazionali, f. 1966, Rome. Publ.: The International Spectator (English/quarterly), and a yearbook: L'Italia della politica internazionale. See also ▷ World Heritage UNESCO List.

G. VEDOVATO, *Il trattato di pace con Italia*, Roma, 1948; N. KOGAN, *Italy and the Allies*, London, 1956; *Italy and the United Nations*, New York, 1959; S. MANUNARELLA, *Italy after Fascism*, Montreal, 1964; H.S. HUGHES, *The Fall and Rise of Modern Italy*, New York, 1968; BANCO DI ROMA, *The Italian Banking System*, Rome, 1969; E. WISKEMAN, *Italy since 1945*, London, 1971; S.J. WOOLFEED, *The Rebirth of Italy 1943–50*; New York, 1972; J. GODICHOT, *Histoire de l'Italie Moderne 1770–1870*, Paris, 1973; M. VAUSSARD, *Histoire de l'Italie Moderne 1870–1970*, Paris, 1973; C. GHISALBERTI,

Storia Constituzionale d'Italia 1849–1948, Rome, 1973; C.J. LOVE, F. MARZARI, *Italian Foreign Policy 1870–1940*, Boston, 1975; P. NICHOLS, *Italia*, London, 1975; P. LARGE, S. TARROW (eds.), *Italy in Transition. Conflict and Consensus*, London, 1980; H.S. HUGHES, *The US and Italy*, Cambridge, Mass, 1981; *The Europa Year Book 1984. A World Survey*, Vol. I, pp. 608–640, London, 1984; J.E. MILLER, *The United States and Italy 1940–1950*, London, 1986; M.F. FINLEY, D. MACK SMITH, Ch. DUSSAN, *A History of Sicily*, New York, 1987.

ITALY–MOSCOW DECLARATION, 1943. A Declaration published on Oct. 31, 1943 in Moscow in the name of the Three Big Powers, read as follows:

"The Foreign Secretaries of the United States, United Kingdom and Soviet Union have established that their three Governments are in complete agreement that allied policy towards Italy must be based upon the fundamental principle that Fascism and all its evil influence and emanations shall be utterly destroyed, and that the Italian people shall be given every opportunity to establish governmental and other institutions based upon democratic principles.
The Foreign Secretaries of the United States and United Kingdom declare that the action of their Governments from the inception of the invasion of Italian territory, in so far as paramount military requirements have permitted, has been upon this policy. In furtherance of this policy in the future the Foreign Secretaries of the three Governments are agreed that the following measures are important and should be put into effect:
(1) It is essential that the Italian Government should be made more democratic by the introduction of representatives of those sections of the Italian people who have always opposed Fascism.
(2) Freedom of speech, of religious worship, of political belief, of Press, and of public meeting shall be restored in full measure to the Italian people, who shall also be entitled to form anti-Fascist political groups.
(3) All institutions and organizations created by the Fascist regime shall be suppressed.
(4) All Fascist or pro-Fascist elements shall be removed from administration and from institutions and organizations of a public character.
(5) All political prisoners of the Fascist regime shall be released and accorded a full amnesty.
(6) Democratic organs of local government shall be created.
(7) Fascist chiefs and army generals known or suspected to be war criminals shall be arrested and handed over to justice.
In making this declaration the three Foreign Secretaries recognize that so long as active military operations continue in Italy the time at which it is possible to give full effect to the principles set out above will be determined by the Commander-in-Chief on the basis of instructions received through the combined Chiefs of Staff. The three Governments parties to this declaration will at the request of any one of them consult on this matter. It is further understood that nothing in this resolution is to operate against the right of the Italian people ultimately to choose their own form of government."

The New York Times, Nov. 2, 1943; *A Decade of American Foreign Policy. Basic Documents 1941–1949*, Washington, DC, 1950.

ITALY–ROMANIA TREATY, 1927. A Treaty signed at Rome on July 18, 1927. The highlights of the Treaty:

"Art. 1 – The High Contracting Parties undertake reciprocally to lend each other their mutual support and cordial co-operation for the maintenance of international order and to ensure respect for, and the execution of, the undertakings contained in the treaties to which they are signatories.
Art. 2 – In the event of international complications and if they are agreed that their common interests are or may be endangered, the High Contracting Parties undertake to confer with one another as to joint measures to be taken to safeguard those interests."

LNTS, Vol. 156.

ITALY–YUGOSLAVIA TREATY, 1924. A Treaty signed on Feb. 22, 1924 in Rome between Italy and the Kingdom of Serbs, Croats and Slovenes, on cordial co-operation, benevolent neutrality, diplomatic support and mutual consultation.

LNTS, No. 596 and 637.

ITAMARATI. The common name of the Brazilian Ministry of Foreign Affairs, located (1881–1970) in Rio de Janeiro in the Palace of Itamarati. After the transfer of capital from Rio de Janeiro to Brasilia the same name is used to refer to the foreign ministry office. ▷ Foggy Bottom, ▷ Foreign Office, ▷ MID, ▷ Quai d'Orsay, ▷ Wilhelmstrasse.

D. DE CARVALHO, *Historia diplomática do Brasil*, São Paulo, 1959.

ITO. International Trade Organization. Proposed by the Havana UN Conference on Trade and Employment, Nov. 21, 1947–Mar. 24, 1948, International Trade Organization as a specialized agency of the UN to administer and implement a code of principles or rules of fair dealing in international trade. This code is contained in the ▷ Havana Charter, 1948. The world trade organization was never actually founded due to major differences in interpretation between Charter signatories. Part of its functions were taken over by the General Agreement on Tariffs and Trade ▷ GATT, prepared by the ITO Interim Commission during 1949. In Feb., 1975 the Dakar Conference of Developing Countries on Raw Materials postulated in Res. 10 the creation of an International Trade Organization, "considering that special importance will have to be given to the vital problem of remodelling the structure of the UN system." The functions of the ITO to a large extent were assumed by the ▷ UNCTAD.

The ITO. An Appraisal of the Havana Charter in relation to US Foreign Policy, with a Definitive Study of Its Provisions. Committee on Foreign Affairs, House of Representatives, 80th Congress, 2nd Session, Washington, DC, 1948; "The US and the ITO", in: *International Conciliation*, No. 449, Mar. 1949, pp. 185–238; W. DIEBOLD Jr., "The End of the ITO", in: *Princeton Essays in International Finance*, No. 16, Oct. 1952.

ITU. International Telecommunication Union, Union internationale de télécommunication, Mezhdunarodniy soyuz elektroviazi, Unión Internacional de Telecomunicación, official English, French, Russian and Spanish names of a UN specialized agency, est. May 17, 1865, Paris, as Union Télégraphique Internationale by the plenipotentiaries of twenty founding states: Austria, Baden, Bavaria, Belgium, Denmark, France, Greece, Hanover, Italy, the Netherlands, Norway, Portugal, Prussia, Russia, Saxony, Spain, Sweden, Switzerland, Turkey and Würtemberg. In 1885, at Berlin, the first regulations relating to international telephone services were inserted in the Telegraph Regulations annexed to this Convention.

At the first International Radiotelegraph Conference, held at Berlin, 27 states signed the International Radio-telegraph Convention of Nov. 3, 1906, establishing the principle of compulsory intercommunication between vessels at sea and the mainland.

In 1932, the International Telegraph Convention and the International Radiotelegraph Convention were merged to form the International Telecommunication Convention, which was signed on Dec. 9, 1932 at Madrid. Under this Convention, which came into force on Jan. 1, 1934, the International Telecommunication Union, ITU, replaced the International Telegraph Union.

The ITU was governed from Jan. 1949 until Dec. 1953 by the International Telecommunication Convention adopted on Oct. 2, 1947 by the Atlantic City Plenipotentiary Conference. A revised Convention, adopted by the Buenos Aires Plenipotentiary Conference, Oct. 3–Dec. 22, 1952, entered into force on Jan. 1, 1954. ITU has been a UN specialized agency since Nov. 15, 1947. Legal status is based on Radio Regulations and Additional Radio Regulations, signed on Dec. 21, 1959 in Geneva; Telegraph Regulations and Telephone Regulations signed on Nov. 29, 1958 in Geneva and the International Telecommunication Convention signed on Nov. 12, 1965 at Montreux and came into force Jan. 1, 1967 replaced by a Convention signed on Oct. 25, 1973 in Malaga-Torremolinos, and came into force Jan. 1, 1975. Aims: The ITU has three main purposes:
(a) to maintain and extend international co-operation for the improvement and rational use of telecommunication;
(b) to promote the development and most efficient operation of technical facilities in order to increase their usefulness, and, as far as possible, to make them generally available to the public; and
(c) to harmonize the actions of nations in the attainment of these common ends.

The ITU has six main functions:
(a) it allocates the radio-frequency spectrum and registers radio-frequency assignments to avoid harmful interference between radio stations of different countries;
(b) it co-ordinates efforts to eliminate harmful interference between radio stations;
(c) it seeks to establish the lowest rates possible, consistent with efficient service and taking into account the necessity for keeping the independent financial administration of telecommunication on a sound basis;
(d) it fosters the creation and development of telecommunications in newly independent and developing countries;
(e) it promotes the adoption of measures for ensuring the safety of life through telecommunication; and
(f) it makes studies and recommendations, and collects and publishes information for the benefit of its members.

Organization: The organization of the ITU consists of a Plenipotentiary Conference, which is the supreme organ; Administrative Conferences; an Administrative Council; a General Secretariat; an International Frequency Registration Board; an International Telegraph and Telephone Consultative Committee; and an International Radio Consultative Committee. The Plenipotentiary Conference, at which each member has the right to be represented, normally meets once every five years, at a place and date fixed by the preceding Conference. Each member has one vote in the Conference. It considers the report of the Administrative Council of the activities of ITU; approves the accounts, and establishes the general basis for the ITU's budget for the next five years; enters into and revises formal agreements with other international organizations; and deals with such other telecommunication questions as may be necessary.

The Administrative Conferences of all members are, so far as practicable, held at the same time and place as the Plenipotentiary Conference. The Administrative Telegraph and Telephone Conference revises the Telegraph Regulations and the Telephone Regulations. The Administrative Radio Conference revises the Radio Regulations and the Additional Radio Regulations. It also elects the members of the International Frequency Registration Board and reviews its activities.

The Administrative Council, which is composed of eighteen members of ITU elected by the Plenipotentiary Conference, supervises ITU's administrative functions between sessions of the Plenipotentiary Conference, reviews and approves the annual budget, appoints the Secretary-General and the two Assistant Secretaries-General, and co-ordinates the work of ITU with other international organizations. It meets annually at the headquarters of ITU. The General Secretariat, headed by the Secretary-General succeeds the Bureau of ITU, which had been located at Berne since 1868.

The International Frequency Registration Board records all frequency assignments, and furnishes advice to members of ITU with a view to the operation of the maximum practicable number of radio channels in those portions of the spectrum where harmful interference may occur.

The Board consists of eleven independent members elected, as explained above, by the Administrative Radio Conference, serving not as representatives of any country or region, but as custodians of an international public trust. The Board has the assistance of a specialized secretariat. The International Telegraph and Telephone Consultative Committee (CCITT) on Jan. 1, 1957, replaced the former International Telegraph Consultative Committee and the former International Telephone Consultative Committee. It studies and issues recommendations on technical questions connected with radio, and on operational matters, the solution of which largely depends on considerations bound up with radio technique. Each Consultative Committee is composed of all members of ITU and any recognized private operating agencies interested in participating. Each Committee works through a Plenary Assembly which normally meets every three years, study groups set up by the Plenary Assembly, and a Director appointed by the Plenary Assembly. The Radio Committee have a Vice-Director specialized in broadcasting, and the Telegraph and Telephone Committee, a telephone laboratory. Each Consultative Committee is serviced by specialized secretariat.

The headquarters of ITU are in Geneva. Publ. *Journal Telegraphique*, 1869–1933; *Telecommunication Journal* (monthly since 1948) in English, French and Spanish; Documents of the international conferences, Conventions and Regulations relating to telecommunications. Tables of telegraphic rates. Charts of telegraph channels and radio channels. European telephone cables, circuits adapted for the transmission of music, coastal stations open to public correspondence. Official lists of telegraph offices open to the international service, radiocommunication channels between fixed points, fixed stations, broadcasting, coastal and ship radiolocation stations carrying out special services. Radio Frequency List. List of Call Signs, Maps, Charts, Statistics.
International Convention on Telecommunication, Malaga, 1973; UN, *Everyone's United Nations*; *Yearbook of International Organizations*.

IUNCTIM
Latin = "together", "jointly". An international term for dependence of the solution or consideration of one question on the solution of another.

IVANOVO ROCK-HEWN CHURCHES. A Bulgarian cultural site included in the ▷ World Heritage UNESCO List. The rock caves near this village, in the northeast of the country, were converted into churches by monks who first arrived at the end of the 12th century. They are decorated with wall paintings, the most remarkable of which date from the 14th century.

UNESCO, *A Legacy for All*, Paris, 1984.

IVORY COAST. Since 1960 until 1985 one of official names in the UN system of the ▷ Côte d'Ivoire. The others: Costa de Marfil and Chinese and Russian denominations. The use of different language versions had led to variable seating positions for the country's delegates at the UN system forum and to other semantic problems. The government of Côte d'Ivoire asked in November 1985 the UN Secretary General to avoid other language versions than the official French name of the francophonic country. Since Jan. 1, 1986 the only official name in the UN system of this African country is Côte d'Ivoire.

KEESING's *Record of World Events*, 1986, No. 6.

IYSH. ▷ **International Year of Shelter for the Homeless.**

IZMIR. A major Turkish seaport, population 1980 census 757,854, West Turkey, called Smyrna before 1923; subject of international dispute 1918–23 between Turkey and the Allies who under a secret treaty undertook to assign the port to Italy for its participation in World War I, while at the same time granting it to Greece because 45% of the total (1,057,000 in 1914) population of Smyrna was of Greek origin and because in Nov., 1918 the Greek army had seized the port. In 1922 Kemal Pasha launched a successful Turkish counter-offensive which entailed the emigration of the Greek population, Smyrna becoming predominantly Turkish. The Treaty of Lausanne of June 24, 1923 restored Izmir to Turkey.

J. CADOUX, *Ancient Smyrna*, Paris, 1938; P. LEMERLE, *L'Émirat d'Aydin*, Paris, 1957.

J

JACKSON AMENDMENT, 1975.
An amendment to the US Trade Law, accepted by the US Congress in 1975, denying most-favored-nation status to all countries that do not permit free emigration. The initiator of the amendment was Sen. H. Jackson.

US Congressional Record, 1975.

JACOBITE CHURCH.
One of Christian Oriental churches also known as the Syrian-Jacobite Church, formed in the 5th century; its doctrine is founded on monophysitism; liturgical idioms: ancient Syrian and Persian; headed by a patriarch seated in the Convent of San Marco in Jerusalem (previously in the Convent of Zafran, near Baghdad); in the early 17th century some disciples joined Rome; national church of Syria.

J.D. ATTAWATER, *The Christian Churches of the East*, London, 1948.

JAGDFLUGZEUG.
▷ Eurofighter.

JAGIELLONIAN UNIVERSITY.
One of the oldest universities of Europe, est. 1364 in Cracow, at this time capital of Poland (from 1380 to 1772 capital of Poland and Lithuania). During the Nazi-German occupation Sept. 1939–Jan. 1945 closed, and the majority of professors deported to Sachsenhausen concentration camp.

K. LEPSZY, *Guide Book to the 600th Jubilee of Jagiellonian University in Cracow*, Cracow, 1964; E. RYBKA, *Four Hundred Years of Copernican Heritage*, Cracow, 1964; *Homenaje a la Universidad de Cracovia en su Sexto Centenario*, UNAM, Mexico, DF, 1964; J. DUZYK, *Cracow and its University*, Cracow, 1966; S. GAWĘDA, *Uniwersytet Jagielloński w okresie okupacji hitlerowskiej 1939–1945* (The Jagiellonian University during the Nazi occupation 1939–1945), Kraków, 1980.

JAKARTA.
▷ Djakarta.

JAMAICA.
Member of the UN. Republic of Jamaica. Caribbean state on the Island of Jamaica in the Caribbean Sea, South of Cuba and West of Haiti. Area: 11,425 sq. km. Pop. 1987 est. 2,300,000 (1970 census 1,848,512). Capital: Kingston with 634,000 inhabitants, 1977. Official language: English. GNP per capita 1987 US $1,070. Currency: one Jamaica dollar = 100 cents. National Day: Aug. 6, Independence Day, 1962.
Member of the UN since Sept. 18, 1962 and of the UN specialized agencies with the exception of the IDA. Member of the Commonwealth, the OAS and the Tlatelolco Treaty. ACP state of the EEC.
International relations: the island was a Spanish colony from 1509 to 1655 and later a British colony 1670–1958 self-governing since 1944. A member of the Federation of West Indies 1958–61. Independent on Aug. 6, 1962 by the London Treaty with Great Britain signed on Feb. 2, 1962. In Oct. 1983 Jamaican troops participated in the US-led invasion of Grenada and took part in the training of the new Grenadian police force.

Bibliography of Jamaica 1900–1963, Kingston, 1963; M.M. CARLEY, *Jamaica*, London, 1963; R. DELATTRE, *A Guide to Jamaica. Reference Material*, Kingston, 1965; C.V. BLACK, *History of Jamaica*, London, 1965; S.J. HURASITZ, *Jamaica. A Historical Portrait*, London, 1972; O. JEFFERSON, *The Postwar Economic Development of Jamaica*, Kingston, 1972; A. KUPER, *Changing Jamaica*, London, 1975; B. FLOYD, *Jamaica. An Island Microcosm*, London, 1974; *UN Chronicle*, July 1979, p. 271; C. STONE, *Democracy and Clientalism in Jamaica*, London, 1981; G. BACKFORD, M. WITTER, *Small Garden Bitter Weed. The Political Struggle and Change in Jamaica*, London, 1982; *The Europa Year Book 1984. A World Survey*, Vol. II, pp. 1787–1798, London, 1984; A.J. MAYNE, *Politics in Jamaica*, London, 1988.

JAMBOREE.
An international term for international rallies organized since 1913 by ▷ Scouting.

JAMMU AND KASHMIR.
A territory in the north-west of India, bounded by China, Tibet, Himachal Pradesh, Punjab and Pakistan. Area: 222,236 sq. km. Pop. 1981 census: 5,987,000 (1971 census: 4,616,000). Capital: Srinagar with 520,000 inhabitants 1981. Jammu and Kashmir was the subject of international disputes and armed conflicts between Pakistan and India, after the decision by the maharajah of Kashmir on Oct. 28, 1947 to incorporate it into India. Pakistan refused to acknowledge the annexation of Kashmir, but on Nov. 9, 1947 India assumed administrative control over the area now called Jammu and Kashmir. After the Pakistani invasion of Kashmir, India brought the case before the UN Security Council on Jan. 1, 1948 and on Jan. 20, 1948 the Security Council appointed the UN Commission for India and Pakistan, UNCIP, composed of representatives from Czechoslovakia, Argentina and the USA appointed by India, Pakistan and the Chairman of the Security Council respectively, joined later by Belgium and Colombia. On Apr. 21, 1948 the Security Council ordered the withdrawal of Pakistani troops from India; the reduction of troops; and the holding of a plebiscite. A cease-fire was achieved on Jan. 1, 1949 and a cease-fire line demarcated on July 27, 1949. At a meeting on July 14–24, 1949 the Indian and Pakistani prime ministers failed to agree on an exact date for the plebiscite. A demilitarized zone was established on Mar. 30, 1950 with the participation of a UN Military Observer Group for India and Pakistan, UNMOGIP, and in 1955 fighting ended. In 1956 the Indian part was proclaimed without plebiscite, the state of Jammu and Kashmir. In 1959 China occupied part of the district of ▷ Ladakh. In Aug.-Sep., 1965 a second military conflict between India and Pakistan terminated after mediation of the USSR on Jan. 10, 1966 with a joint declaration of the Heads of States of India and Pakistan on a peaceful settlement of the Kashmir problem (▷ Tashkent Declaration, 1966). In Dec., 1971 new military incidents terminated by an agreement signed on July 3, 1972 in Simla and a delimitation of the frontier accepted on Dec. 11, 1972.

Kashmir Meetings and Correspondence between the Prime Ministers of India and Pakistan, July 1953–October 1954, New Delhi, 1955; *Negotiations between the Prime Minister of Pakistan and India regarding the Kashmir Dispute, June 1953–September 1954*, Karachi, 1954; P.N. BAZAN, *The History of Struggle for Freedom in Kashmir*, Delhi, 1954; S. LOURIE, "The UNMOGIP", in: *International Organizations*, No. 9, 1955; LORD BIRDWOOD, *Two Nations and Kashmir*, London, 1956; J.B. DAS GUFTER, *Indo-Pakistan Relations 1947–1955*, Amsterdam, 1958; B.L. SHARMA, *The Kashmir Story*, New York, 1954; P.B. GAYENDRAGATKAR, *Kashmir Retrospect and Prospect*, Bombay, 1967; S. GUPTA, *Kashmir. A Study in India–Pakistan Relations*, London, 1967; *The Europa Year Book 1984. A World Survey*, Vol. II, p. 1697-London, 1984.

JAPAN.
Member of the UN. State occupying an archipelago off the coast of East Asia between the East China Sea, the Sea of Japan and the Pacific Ocean. The main islands: Hokkaido, Honshu, Shikoku and Kyushu. Area: 337,748 sq. km. Pop. 1987 est: 122,129,000, with a density of 316 per sq. km. (1975 census: 111,939,000). Capital: Tokyo with 8,336,000 inhabitants in 1982. Official language: Japanese. Currency: one yen = 100 sen. GNP per capita in 1987: US $15,770.
Member of the UN since Feb. 18, 1956 and of all international organizations, the Colombo Plan and the OECD.
International relations: from the 16th century in commercial relations with Europe, then in the 17th and 18th centuries in self-imposed isolation; in the second half of the 19th century the USA, France, Great Britain, Russia and the Netherlands forced Japanese ports to be opened to foreign ships and vessels (▷ Open door policy). In 1904/5 at war with tsarist Russia, ending in a Japanese victory; by the Treaty of Portsmouth, Sept. 5, 1905, Japan acquired part of the Manchurian railway, the southern part of Sakhalin and rights of possession in the Kuangtung region in China and the right to maintain a protectorate over Korea. During World War I Japan was an ally of the Entente; and in the interwar period one of the Great Powers. Japan was a founding member of the League of Nations, 1919, from which she withdrew in 1933. In 1931 Japan occupied Manchuria and in 1937 attacked China. Japan concluded an ▷ Anti-Comintern Pact with the German Third Reich and with Italy (Rome–Berlin–Tokyo Axis) in 1936, and then on Sept. 27, 1940 signed a military alliance with the same powers. In Jan., 1941 Japanese forces, with the consent of the Vichy government, entered French Indochina; a nonaggression pact was signed with the USSR Apr. 13, 1941. Attacking Pearl Harbor in Hawaii on Dec. 7, 1941 started a war with the USA. From Aug. 9, 1945 was at war with the USSR. Japan's unconditional surrender to the Allied Powers was signed on Sept. 2, 1945, following the explosions in Aug., 1945 of American atomic bombs on ▷ Hiroshima and Nagasaki. In a radio speech to the Japanese nation on Jan. 1, 1946, the Emperor stated that he was not a "divine being" and that the Japanese were not a "chosen nation". Japanese military and political war criminals were brought before the International Military Tribunal for the Far East; some of them were hung, the majority amnestied in 1948. The USA and her allies on Sept. 8, 1951 signed the Japan Peace Treaty in San Francisco, which was not recognized by the Chinese People's Republic, India and the USSR. The treaty came into force on Apr. 28, 1952. In the Treaty Japan abandoned rights to southern Sakhalin and the ▷ Kurile islands, but without stating that these territories had been ceded by Japan in 1946 to the USSR. One of the results of the absence of this declaration was that the USSR did not sign the treaty and then 20 years later Japan laid claim to the Kurile islands, proposing to the USSR that talks be held on the signing of a Japanese–Soviet peace treaty. Japan is not a member of any military pact, but US military bases are located on her territory: US land, sea and air bases with thermonuclear weapons in accordance with the Japan–USA Treaty of Mutual Co-operation and Security of Jan. 19, 1960. Japan's military potential is formally limited by art. 9 (written, according to official American sources by the Commander in Chief of US armed forces, General D. MacArthur) of the Japanese Constitution of 1946 which states

"The Japanese nation in its sincere desire for international peace based on justice and order forever abandons war as a sovereign right of the nation as well as the use of force in the solution of international problems. In order to fulfill the above assumptions it will never maintain land, sea or air forces nor any other war potential. The right to wage war by the state will not be recognized."

In Feb., 1970 Japan signed a Treaty on the Non-proliferation of Nuclear Weapons and ratified it on May 14, 1967. The heads of government of the USA and Japan met for the first time from Aug. 31 to Sept. 1, 1972 in Hawaii (President Nixon and Prime Minister Tanaka). In 1968 the USA returned the Bonin islands (Ogasawara Guntō) to Japan; in May 1972 the Ryukyu Islands (▷ Okinawa), while retaining the right to maintain military bases. On Sept. 29, 1972 during a visit by Chou En-lai to Tokyo, a document was signed on normalization of relations between China and Japan.

In the general debate at the XVII and XVIII Sessions of the UN General Assembly the USA came out in favor of granting Japan a permanent seat in the Security Council. Japan signed a Treaty of Friendship and Co-operation with Australia on June 15, 1976. In 1976/77 at the request of the EEC Japan began negotiations on the limitation of Japanese exports to Western Europe. On Aug. 12, 1978 the Chinese–Japanese Treaty was signed. In 1982 the new school textbooks in Japan caused a controversy with China and South Korea. In 1986 the trade surplus reached nearly $90 billion.

The Japan Foundation, f. 1972, Tokyo, for international cultural exchange, to encourage friendship and good-will among people of the World; operates internationally by offering fellowships to overseas scholars. The Japanese Government publ. *Japanese Annual of International Law.*

T. MIYAOKA, "The Japanese Law of Nationality and the Rights of Foreigners in Land under the Laws of Japan", in: *International Conciliation,* No. 206, January, 1925; "Diplomatic Relations between the US and Japan 1908–1924", in: *International Conciliation,* No. 211, June 1925; M. RAMMING, *Japan Handbuch, Nachschlagwerk der Japankunde,* Berlin, 1941; *Conference for the Conclusion and Signature of the Treaty of Peace with Japan,* Washington, DC, 1951; E.J. LEWE VON ADUARD, *Japan. From Surrender to Peace,* London, 1953; F.C. JONES, *Japan's New Order in East Asia: Its Rise and Fall 1937–45,* New York, 1954; I. KIJOSI, *Istoriia sovremiennoy Iaponyii,* Moskva, 1955; F.W. IKLE, *German–Japanese Relations 1936–1940,* New York, 1956; J.W. MORLAY, *The Japanese thrust into Siberia 1918,* New York, 1957; *Guide to Japanese Reference Books,* Chicago, 1966; H. KAHN, *The Emerging Japanese Superstate,* New York, 1971; J.H. BOYLE, *China and Japan at War 1937–45,* London, 1972; R. GUILLAIN, *Japon,* Paris, 1972; TH. TERSCHNER, *Japanese Foreign Trade,* Lexington, 1974; J.E. ENDICOTT, *Japan's Nuclear Option,* New York, 1975; J. HIRSHMEIER, Y. TSUNEHIKO, *The Development of Japanese Business 1600–1973,* London, 1976; H. KAHN, TH. PEPPER, *The Japanese Challenge,* New York, 1979; S. IENAGA, *Japan's Last War: World War II and the Japanese, 1931–1945,* London, 1979; E.F. VOGEL, *Japan as Number One,* Harvard, 1979; SIPRI, *World Armaments and Disarmament 1968–1985;* M. KAJIMA, *The Diplomacy of Japan 1894–1922,* Tokyo, 1980; W.J. BARNDS, *Japan and the United States,* New York, 1980; K. MURATA, *An Industrial Geography of Japan,* London, 1980; U.A. JOHNSON (ed), *The Common Security Interests of Japan, the USA and NATO,* Cambridge, 1981; E.O. REISCHAUER, *The US and Japan,* Cambridge Mass., 1982; L. TSOUCALIS, M. WHITE, *Japan and Western Europe. Conflict and Co-operation,* London, 1982; M.L. KRUPIANKO, *Sovietsko-Yaponskiye ekonomicheskiye otnosheniya,* Moskva, 1982; J.P. LEHMANN, *The Roots of Modern Japan,* London, 1982; R.C. CHRISTOPHER, *The Japanese Mind: the Goliath Explained,* New York, 1983; K. YABUKIED, *Japan Bibliographic Annual,* 2 Vols., Tokyo, annual; KODANSHA *Japanese Encyclopedia of Japan,* 9 Vls., Tokyo, 1983; J.E. HUNTER, *Concise Dictionary of Modern Japan's History,* Berkeley, 1984; *The Europa Year Book 1984. A World Survey,* Vol. II, pp. 1798–1828, London, 1984; T.

GIBNEY, *Japan: Japan the Fragile Superpower,* New York, 1985; R. BUCKLEY, *Japan Today,* Cambridge, 1985; S.D. COHEN, *Uneasy Partnership: Competition and Conflict in US–Japan Trade Relations,* Cambridge, 1985; T.K. McCRAW, ed., *America versus Japan: A Comparative Study,* Cambridge, 1986; R. MOVER, Y. SUGIMOTO, *Images of Japanese Society,* London, 1986; H. PATRICK, L. MEISSNER eds., *Japan's High Technology Industries: Lessons and Limitations of Industrial Policy,* Seattle, 1987; A.M. ANDERSON, *Science and Technology in Japan,* London, 1987; M. WHITE, *The Japanese Educational Challenge: A Commitment to Children,* New York, 1987; E.O. REISCHAUER, *The Japanese Today. Change and Continuity,* Cambridge, Mass.; London 1988.

JAPAN–CAIRO DECLARATION, 1943.

A declaration of the President of the USA, F.D. Roosevelt, the President of China, Chiang Kai-shek, and the Prime Minister of the UK, W.S. Churchill on Nov. 26, 1943, after the summit meeting in Cairo; published on Dec. 1, 1943 as follows:

"The Three Great Allies are fighting this war to restrain and punish the aggression of Japan. They covet no gain for themselves and have no thought of territorial expansion. It is their purpose that Japan shall be stripped of all the islands in the Pacific which she has seized or occupied since the beginning of the first World War in 1914, and that all the territories Japan has stolen from the Chinese, such as Manchuria, Formosa and the Pescadores, shall be restored to the Republic of China. Japan will also be expelled from all other territories which she has taken by violence and greed. The aforesaid three great powers, mindful of the enslavement of the people of Korea, are determined that in due course Korea shall become free and independent."

US Department of State Bulletin, Dec. 1, 1943; *Postwar Foreign Policy Preparation 1939–1945,* Washington, DC, 1949, pp. 201–202.

JAPANESE DOCTRINE OF EQUAL DISTANCE.

A foreign policy doctrine of neutrality, proclaiming that Japan should maintain "equal distance" in relations with the USSR as well as with the Chinese People's Republic, abandoned by Japan Aug. 12, 1978 with the signing of the ▷ China–Japan Peace Treaty.

JAPANESE–RUSSIAN TREATIES, 1858–1916.

Concluded up to World War I were as following:

(1) On the establishing of diplomatic relations, Aug. 10, 1858;

(2) On common interests in Korea, June 9, 1896;

(3) On the recognition of Japan's domination in Korea, Apr. 25, 1898;

(4) Peace concluded in Portsmouth after the Japanese–Russian war over Manchuria, begun with an unexpected attack Feb. 8, 1904 of Japanese torpedo boats on the Russian fleet at Port Arthur, ended June 7, 1905 (after the defeat of the Russian fleet at Tsushima, May 27–29, 1905) with an armistice, followed by a peace treaty Sept. 5, 1905. ▷ Portsmouth Japan-Russia Peace Treaty, 1905.

(5) Convention Aug. 30, 1907, supplementing the Peace Treaty of Portsmouth with reference to Manchuria;

(6) Charbin Treaty June 28, 1910, supplemented by a secret convention (signed July 4, 1910 in Petersburg), meaning abandonment of the ▷ open door policy; establishing a Japanese–Russian alliance defending Manchuria's sovereignty against influence of other powers, in connection with American neutralization projects for the Manchurian railway, by entrusting it to an International Consortium;

(7) finally the ▷ Sasanov–Motono Treaty, 1916, closing the list of treaties between tsarist Russia and the Empire of Japan.

G.F. MARTENS, *Nouveau Recueil Général,* 1 s., Vol. 17; 2 s., Vol. 33, 3 s., Vol. 1.

JAPANESE–RUSSIAN WAR 1904–1905. ▷
Japanese–Russian Treaties.

JAPAN PEACE TREATY, 1951.

A Treaty of Peace with Japan, signed Sept. 8, 1951 in San Francisco by Argentina, Australia, Belgium, Bolivia, Brazil, Cambodia, Canada, Ceylon, Chile, Colombia, Costa Rica, Cuba, the Dominican Republic, Ecuador, Egypt, El Salvador, Ethiopia, France, Greece, Guatemala, Haiti, Honduras, Indonesia, Iran, Iraq, Laos, Lebanon, Liberia, Luxembourg, Mexico, the Netherlands, New Zealand, Nicaragua, Norway, Pakistan, Panama, Paraguay, Peru, Philippines, Saudi Arabia, Syria, Turkey, Union of South Africa, the UK, the USA, Uruguay, Venezuela, Vietnam Rep. and Japan. The main first articles are as follows:

"Whereas the Allied Powers and Japan are resolved that henceforth their relations shall be those of nations which, as sovereign equals, cooperate in friendly association to promote their common welfare and to maintain international peace and security, and are therefore desirous of concluding a Treaty of Peace which will settle questions still outstanding as a result of the existence of a state of war between them; Whereas Japan for its part declares its intention to apply for membership in the United Nations and in all circumstances to conform to the principles of the Charter of the United Nations; to strive to realize the objectives of the Universal Declaration of Human Rights; to seek to create within Japan conditions of stability and well-being as defined in arts. 55 and 56 of the Charter of the United Nations and already initiated by post-surrender Japanese legislation; and in public and private trade and commerce to conform to internationally accepted fair practices;

Whereas the Allied Powers welcome the intentions of Japan set out in the foregoing paragraph;

The Allied Powers and Japan have therefore determined to conclude the present Treaty of Peace, and have accordingly appointed the undersigned Plenipotentiaries, who, after presentation of their full powers, found in good and due form, have agreed on the following provisions:

Chapter I. Peace

Art. 1.(a) The state of war between Japan and each of the Allied Powers is terminated as from the date on which the present Treaty comes into force between Japan and the Allied Power concerned as provided for in article 23.

(b) The Allied Powers recognize the full sovereignty of the Japanese people over Japan and its territorial waters.

Chapter II. Territory

Art 2.(a) Japan, recognizing the independence of Korea, renounces all right, title and claim to Korea, including the islands of Quelpart, Port Hamilton and Dagelet.

(b) Japan renounces all right, title and claim to Formosa and the Pescadores.

(c) Japan renounces all right, title and claim to the Kurile Islands, and to that portion of Sakhalin and the islands adjacent to it over which Japan acquired sovereignty as a consequence of the Treaty of Portsmouth of September 5, 1905.

(d) Japan renounces all right, title and claim in connection with the League of Nations Mandate System, and accepts the action of the United Nations Security Council of April 2, 1947, extending the trusteeship system to the Pacific Islands formerly under mandate to Japan.

(e) Japan renounces all claim to any right or title to or interest in connection with any part of the Antarctic area, whether deriving from the activities of Japanese nationals or otherwise.

(f) Japan renounces all right, title and claim to the Spratly Islands and to the Paracel Islands.

Art. 3. Japan will concur in any proposal of the United States to the United Nations to place under its trusteeship system, with the United States as the sole administering authority, Nansei Shoto south of 29° north latitude (including the Ryukyu Islands and the Daito

Islands), Nanpo Shoto south of Sofu Gan (including the Bonin Islands, Rosario Island and the Volcano Islands) and Parece Vela and Marcus Island. Pending the making of such a proposal and affirmative action thereon, the United States will have the right to exercise all and any powers of administration, legislation and jurisdiction over the territory and inhabitants of these islands, including their territorial waters.

Art. 4.(a) Subject to the provisions of paragraph (b) of this article, the disposition of property of Japan and of its nationals in the areas referred to in article 2, and their claims, including debts, against the authorities presently administering such areas and the residents (including juridical persons) thereof, and the disposition in Japan of property of such authorities and residents, and of claims, including debts, of such authorities and residents against Japan and its nationals, shall be the subject of special arrangements between Japan and such authorities. The property of any of the Allied Powers or of its nationals in the areas referred to in art. 2 shall, in so far as this has not already been done, be returned by the administering authority in the condition in which it now exists. (The term nationals whenever used in the present Treaty includes juridical persons.)

(b) Japan recognizes the validity of dispositions of property of Japan and Japanese nationals made by or pursuant to directives of the United States Military Government in any of the areas referred to in arts 2 and 3.

(c) Japanese-owned submarine cables connecting Japan with territory removed from Japanese control pursuant to the present Treaty shall be equally divided, Japan retaining the Japanese terminal and adjoining half of the cable, and the detached territory the remainder of the cable and connecting terminal facilities.

Chapter III. Security.

Art. 5.(a) Japan accepts the obligations set forth in article 2 of the Charter of the United Nations, and in particular the obligations

(i) to settle its international disputes by peaceful means in such a manner that international peace and security, and justice, are not endangered;

(ii) to refrain in its international relations from the threat or use of force against the territorial integrity or political independence of any State or in any other manner inconsistent with the Purposes of the United Nations;

(iii) to give the United Nations every assistance in any action it takes in accordance with the Charter and to refrain from giving assistance to any State against which the United Nations may take preventive or enforcement action.

(b) The Allied Powers confirm that they will be guided by the principles of art. 2 of the Charter of the United Nations in their relations with Japan.

(c) The Allied Powers for their part recognize that Japan as a sovereign nation possesses the inherent right of individual or collective self-defense referred to in art. 51 of the Charter of the United Nations and that Japan may voluntarily enter into collective security arrangements.

Art. 6.(a) All occupation forces of the Allied Powers shall be withdrawn from Japan as soon as possible after the coming into force of the present Treaty, and in any case not later than 90 days thereafter. Nothing in this provision shall, however, prevent the stationing or retention of foreign armed forces in Japanese territory under or in consequence of any bilateral or multilateral agreements which have been or may be made between one or more of the Allied Powers, on the one hand, and Japan on the other.

(b) The provisions of article 9 of the Potsdam Proclamation of July 26, 1945, dealing with the return of Japanese military forces to their homes, to the extent not already completed, will be carried out.

(c) All Japanese property for which compensation has not already been paid, which was supplied for the use of the occupation forces and which remains in the possession of those forces at the time of the coming into force of the present Treaty, shall be returned to the Japanese Government within the same 90 days unless other arrangements are made by mutual agreement.

Chapter IV. Political and Economic Clauses

Art. 7(a) Each of the Allied Powers, within one year after the present Treaty has come into force between it and Japan, will notify Japan which of its prewar bilateral treaties or conventions with Japan it wishes to continue in force or revive, and any treaties or conventions so notified shall continue in force or be revived subject only to such amendments as may be necessary to ensure conformity with the present Treaty. The treaties and conventions so notified shall be considered as having been continued in force or revived three months after the date of notification and shall be registered with the Secretariat of the United Nations. All such treaties and conventions as to which Japan is not so notified shall be regarded as abrogated.

(b) Any notification made under paragraph (a) of this Article may except from the operation or revival of a treaty or convention any terrority for the international relations of which the notifying Power is responsible, until three months after the date on which notice is given to Japan that such exception shall cease to apply.

Art. 8(a) Japan will recognize the full force of all treaties now or hereafter concluded by the Allied Powers for terminating the state of war initiated on September 1, 1939, as well as any other arrangements by the Allied Powers for or in connection with the restoration of peace. Japan also accepts the arrangements made for terminating the former League of Nations and Permanent Court of International Justice.

(b) Japan renounces all such rights and interests as it may derive from being a signatory power of the Conventions of St. Germain-en-Laye of September 10, 1919, and the Straits Agreement of Montreux of July 20, 1936, and from article 16 of the Treaty of Peace with Turkey signed at Lausanne on July 24, 1923.

(c) Japan renounces all rights titles and interests acquired under, and is discharged from all obligations resulting from the Agreement between Germany and the Creditor Powers of January 20, 1930, and its annexes, including the Trust Agreement dated May 17, 1930; the Convention of January 20, 1930, respecting the Bank for International Settlements; and the Statutes of the Bank for International Settlements. Japan will notify to the Ministry of Foreign Affairs in Paris within six months of the first coming into force of the present Treaty its renunciation of the rights, title and interests referred to in this paragraph.

Art. 9. Japan will enter promptly into negotiations with the Allied Powers so desiring for the conclusion of bilateral and multilateral agreements providing for the regulation or limitation of fishing and the conservation and development of fisheries on the high seas.

Art. 10. Japan renounces all special rights and interests in China, including all benefits and privileges resulting from the provisions of the Final Protocol signed at Peking on September 7, 1901, and all annexes, notes and documents supplementary thereto, and agrees to the abrogation in respect to Japan of the said protocol, annexes, notes and documents.

Art. 11. Japan accepts the judgments of the International Military Tribunal for the Far East and of other Allied War Crimes Courts both within and outside Japan, and will carry out the sentences imposed thereby upon Japanese nationals imprisoned in Japan. The power to grant clemency, to reduce sentences and to parole with respect to such prisoners may not be exercised except on the decision of the Government or Governments which imposed the sentence in each instance, and on the recommendation of Japan. In the case of persons sentenced by the International Military Tribunal for the Far East, such power may not be exercised except on the decision of a majority of the Governments represented on the Tribunal, and on the recommendation of Japan.

Art. 12.(a) Japan declares its readiness promptly to enter into negotiations for the conclusion with each of the Allied Powers of treaties or agreements to take place their trading, maritime and other commercial relations on a stable and friendly basis.

(b) Pending the conclusion of the relevant treaty or agreement, Japan will, during a period of four years from the first coming into force of the present Treaty

(1) accord to each of the allied Powers, its nationals, products and vessels

(i) most-favored-nation treatment with respect to customs duties, charges, restrictions and other regulations on or in connection with the importation and exportation of goods;

(ii) national treatment with respect to shipping, navigation and imported goods, and with respect to natural and juridical persons and their interests – such treatment to include all matters pertaining to the levying and collection of taxes, access to the courts, the making and performance of contracts, rights to property (tangible and intangible), participation in juridical entities constituted under Japanese law, and generally the conduct of all kinds of business and professional activities;

(2) ensure that external purchases and sales of Japanese state trading enterprises shall be based solely on commercial considerations.

(c) In respect to any matter, however, Japan shall be obliged to accord to an Allied Power national treatment, or most-favored-nation treatment, only to the extent that the Allied Power concerned accords Japan national treatment or most-favored-nation treatment, as the case may be, in respect of the same matter. The reciprocity envisaged in the foregoing sentence shall be determined, in the case of products, vessels and juridical entities of, and persons domiciled in, any non-metropolitan territory of an Allied Power, and in the case of juridical entities of, and persons domiciled in, any state or province of an Allied Power having a federal government, by reference to the treatment accorded to Japan in such territory, state or province.

(d) In the application of this article, a discriminatory measure shall not be considered to derogate from the grant of national or most-favored-nation treatment, as the case may be, if such measure is based on an exception customarily provided for in the commercial treaties of the party applying it, or on the need to safeguard that party's external financial position or balance of payments (except in respect to shipping and navigation), or on the need to maintain its essential security interests, and provided such measure is proportionate to the circumstances and not applied in an arbitrary or unreasonable manner.

(e) Japan's obligations under this article shall not be affected by the exercise of any Allied rights under article 14 of the present Treaty; nor shall the provisions of this Article be understood as limiting the undertakings assumed by Japan by virtue of art. 15 of the Treaty.

Art. 13.(a) Japan will enter into negotiations with any of the Allied Powers, promptly upon the request of such Power or Powers, for the conclusion of bilateral or multilateral agreements relating to international civil air transport.

(b) Pending the conclusion of such agreement or arrangements, Japan will, during a period of four years from the first coming into force of the present Treaty, extend to such Powers treatment not less favorable with respect to air-traffic rights and privileges than those exercised by any such Powers at the date of such coming into force, and will accord complete equality of opportunity in respect to the operation and development of air services.

(c) Pending its becoming a party to the Convention on International Civil Aviation in accordance with Article 93 thereof, Japan will give effect to the provisions of that Convention applicable to the international navigation of aircraft, and will give effect to the standards, practices and procedures adopted as annexes to the Convention in accordance with the terms of the Convention."

Chapter V Claims and Property (arts. 14–21) recognizes that Japan "should pay reparations to the Allied Powers for the damage and suffering caused by it during the war."

Chapter VI defined Settlement of Disputes (art. 22); chapter VII Final Clauses (arts. 23–27).

The Contracting Parties later appended:

(a) Protocol relating provisions for regulating the question of contracts, periods of prescription and negotiable instruments, and the questions of contracts of insurance upon the restoration of peace with Japan, opened for signature in San Francisco Sept. 8, 1951, came into force during 1952;

(b) Agreement for the settlement of disputes arising under art. 15(a) of the Treaty of Peace with Japan, signed in Washington, DC, June 12, 1952, came into force during 1952.

UNTS, Vol. 136, and 138.

JAPAN SECURITY TREATY WITH THE USA, 1951. The Security Treaty between the USA and Japan was signed at San Francisco on Sept. 8, 1951.

It came into force on April 28, 1952, and reads as follows:

"Japan has this day signed a Treaty of Peace with the Allied Powers. On the coming into force of that Treaty, Japan will not have the effective means to exercise its inherent right of self-defense because it has been disarmed.

There is danger to Japan in this situation because irresponsible militarism has not yet been driven from the world. Therefore Japan desires a Security Treaty with the United States of America to come into force simultaneously with the Treaty of Peace between the United States of America and Japan.

The Treaty of Peace recognizes that Japan as a sovereign nation has the right to enter into collective security arrangements, and further, the Charter of the United Nations recognizes that all nations possess an inherent right of individual and collective self-defense. In exercise of these rights, Japan desires, as a provisional arrangement for its defense, that the United States of America should maintain armed forces of its own in and about Japan so as to deter armed attack upon Japan.

The United States of America, in the interest of peace and security, is presently willing to maintain certain of its armed forces in and about Japan, in the expectation, however, that Japan will itself increasingly assume responsibility for its own defense against direct and indirect aggression, always avoiding any armament which could be an offensive threat or serve other than to promote peace and security in accordance with the purposes and principles of the United Nations Charter.

Accordingly, the two countries have agreed as follows:

Art. I. Japan grants, and the United States of America accepts, the right, upon the coming into force of the Treaty of Peace and of this Treaty, to dispose United States land, air and sea forces in and about Japan. Such forces may be utilized to contribute to the maintenance of international peace and security in the Far East and to the security of Japan against armed attack from without, including assistance given at the express request of the Japanese Government to put down large-scale internal riots and disturbances in Japan, caused through instigation or intervention by an outside power or powers.

Art. II. During the exercise of the right referred to in article I, Japan will not grant, without the prior consent of the United States of America, any bases or any rights, powers or authority whatsoever, in or relating to bases or the right of garrison or of maneuver, or transit of ground, air or naval forces to any third power.

Art. III. The conditions which shall govern the disposition of armed forces of the United States of America in and about Japan shall be determined by administrative agreements between the two Governments.

Art. IV. This Treaty shall expire whenever in the opinion of the Governments of the United States of America and Japan there shall have come into force such United Nations arrangements or such alternative individual or collective security dispositions as will satisfactorily provide for the maintenance by the United Nations or otherwise of international peace and security in the Japan Area."

UNTS, Vol. 136, pp. 215–219.

JAPAN–SOVIET NEUTRALITY TREATY, 1925. A Treaty signed on Jan. 20, 1925 at Peking. A Peace and Neutrality Treaty. The Japanese troops has previously withdrawn from Siberia and northern Sakhalin.

American Journal of International Law, 1925, Vol. 19, Doc. p. 78; G.F. DE MARTENS, *Nouveau Recueil Général*, 3 s., Vol. 15, p. 323.

JAPAN–SOVIET NEUTRALITY TREATY, 1941. A Treaty signed on Jan. 13, 1941 in Moscow. In art. 1 respected mutual "territorial integrity and inviolability of each of the Parties," and in art. 2 included a provision that in case either of the Parties should become engaged in war, the other "shall preserve neutrality for the whole period of the conflict." The Pact is annexed with a solemn declaration that "the USSR shall take the obligation to respect the integrity and territorial inviolability of Manchukuo and Japan assumes the obligation to respect the same with regard to the Republic of Mongolia." This Pact was the first Japan–Soviet treaty after the USSR was officially recognized by Japan in the Peiping Treaty of Jan. 20, 1925.

"The Japan–Soviet Neutrality Pact, 1941", in: *American Journal of International Law*, Vol. 35, Doc. p. 171.

JAPAN'S ULTIMATUM TO CHINA, 1915. After the outbreak of World War I, Japan occupied the German Chaochow concession on Nov. 7, 1915 (leased by the German Reich from China 1898 for 99 years). China demanded its return; Japan refused, pretending its rights to Chaochow were motivated by blood shed in engagements with German troops; at the same time, Japan submitted to China an ultimatum, called the 21 Demands. China was forced to accept most of them May 5, 1915, among others: the lease of southern Manchuria to Japan for a period of 99 years; the recognition of Japan's influence in eastern Mongolia, Chantung and in the Yangtze valley; Japan's control over China's armament and mining industries. China committed herself not to lease concessions on her sea coast to any other third power. The 21 Demands were the guiding lines of Japan's policy towards China in the decades following World War I.

G. F. DE MARTENS, *Nouveau Recueil Général*, 3 s., Vol. 9, p. 334; MAC MURRAY, *Treaties and Agreements with and concerning China 1894–1919*, New York, 1921, Vol. 2, p. 1220.

JAPAN'S UNCONDITIONAL SURRENDER, 1945. The instrument of surrender, signed on Sept. 2, 1945 at Tokyo Bay read as follows:

"We, acting by command of and on behalf of the Emperor of Japan, the Japanese Government and the Japanese Imperial General Headquarters, hereby accept the provisions set forth in the declaration issued by the heads of the Governments of the United States, China and Great Britain on 26 July 1945, at Potsdam and subsequently adhered to by the Union of Soviet Socialist Republics, which four powers are hereafter referred to as the Allied Powers.

We hereby proclaim the unconditional surrender to the Allied Powers of the Japanese Imperial General Headquarters and of all Japanese armed forces and all armed forces under Japanese control wherever situated.

We hereby command all Japanese forces wherever situated and the Japanese people to cease hostilities forthwith, to preserve and save from damage all ships, aircraft, and military and civil property and to comply with all requirements which may be imposed by the Supreme Commander for the Allied Powers or by agencies of the Japanese Government at his direction. We hereby command the Japanese Imperial General Headquarters to issue at once orders to the Commanders of all Japanese forces and all forces under Japanese control wherever situated to surrender unconditionally themselves and all forces under their control.

We hereby command all civil, military and naval officials to obey and enforce all proclamations, orders and directives deemed by the Supreme Commander for the Allied Powers to be proper to effectuate this surrender and issued by him or under his authority and we direct all such officials to remain at their posts and to continue to perform their noncombatant duties unless specifically relieved by him or under his authority.

We hereby undertake for the Emperor, the Japanese Government and their successors to carry out the provisions of the Potsdam Declaration in good faith, and to issue whatever orders and take whatever action may be required by the Supreme Commander for the Allied Powers or by any other designated representative of the purpose of giving effect to that Declaration.

We hereby command the Japanese Imperial Government and the Japanese Imperial General Headquarters at once to liberate all allied prisoners of war and civilian internees now under Japanese control and to provide for their protection, care, maintenance and immediate transportation to places as directed.

The authority of the Emperor and the Japanese Government to rule the state shall be subject to the Supreme Commander for the Allied Powers who will take such steps as he deems proper to effectuate these terms of surrender.

Mamoru Shigemitsu, Yoshijiro Umezu, Mac Arthur."

A Decade of American Foreign Policy, Basic Documents 1941–1949, Washington, DC, 1950, Doc. 109, p. 625; R.L. BLEDSOE, B.A. BOCZEK, *The International Law Dictionary*, Oxford, 1987.

JAPAN–TAIWAN TREATY, 1952. Officially named the Peace Treaty between the Republic of China and Japan, signed on Apr. 28, 1952 in Taipei; denounced by Japan on Aug. 12, 1978 on signing in Peiping a Treaty of Peace and Friendship with the People's Republic of China.

UNTS, Vol. 138, pp. 38–42.

JAPAN–USA AGREEMENTS, 1908–1922. The agreements were as follows:

A Convention on Arbitration, signed on May 5, 1908 at Washington DC. It came into force on Sept. 1, 1908.

Treaty of Commerce and Navigation, signed on Feb. 21, 1911 at Washington, DC. It came into force on April 5, 1911. Art. I reads as follows:

"The citizens or subjects of each of the High Contracting Parties shall have liberty to enter, travel and reside in the territories of the other to carry on trade, wholesale and retail, to own or lease and occupy houses, manufactories, warehouses and shops, to employ agents of their choice, to lease land for residential and commercial purposes, and generally to do anything incident to or necessary for trade upon the same terms as native citizens or subjects, submitting themselves to the laws and regulations there established. They shall not be compelled, under any pretext whatever, to pay any charges or taxes other or higher than those that are or may be paid by native citizens or subjects. The citizens or subjects of each of the High Contracting Parties shall receive, in the territories of the other, the most constant protection and security for their persons and property, and shall enjoy in this respect the same rights and privileges as are or may be granted to native citizens or subjects, on their submitting themselves to the conditions imposed upon the native citizens or subjects.

They shall, however, be exempt in the territories of the other from compulsory military service either on land or sea, in the regular forces, or in the national guard, or in the militia; from all contributions imposed in lieu of personal service, and from all forced loans or military exactions or contributions."

Agreement effected by exchange of notes between the US and Japan declaring their Policy in the Far East, signed Nov. 30, 1908. The main points of the agreement:

"(1) It is the wish of the two Governments to encourage the free and peaceful development of their commerce on the Pacific Ocean.

(2) The policy of both Governments, uninfluenced by any aggressive tendencies, is directed to the maintenance of the existing status quo in the region above mentioned and to the defense of the principle of equal opportunity for commerce and industry in China.

(3) They are accordingly firmly resolved reciprocally to respect the territorial possessions belonging to each other in said region.

(4) They are also determined to preserve the common interest of all powers in China by supporting by all pacific means at their disposal the independence and integrity of China and the principle of equal opportunity for commerce and industry of all nations in that Empire."

Gentlemen's Agreement embodied in a series of diplomatic correspondence in 1907 and 1908 that "a policy of discouraging emigration of Japan's subjects of the laboring classes to continental

United States should be continued." ▷ Lodge Anti-Japanese Doctrine, 1924.

Treaty between the US and Japan regarding Rights of the Two Governments and Their Respective Nations in Former German Islands in the Pacific Ocean North of the Equator, and in Particular the Island of Yap, signed on Feb. 11, 1922, at Washington DC. It came into force on July 13, 1922.

International Conciliation, No. 211, June 1925, pp. 163–223.

JAPAN–UNITED STATES AGREEMENTS 1985–1990.
The growing economic and financial American-Japanese interdependence observed at the beginning of the 1980's, has led to formal co-operation on a number of economic and financial issues of mutual concern. On Sept. 22, 1985 Japan agreed for the US dollar to be lowered against the yen as against the UK pound, German mark, and French franc. On October 13, 1986 an agreement was reached that the United States will continue a steady reduction of the US budget deficit on the basis of Balanced Budget and Emergency Deficit Control Act of 1985 (▷ Gramm-Rudman Law). On July 21, 1987 the USA and Japan signed a framework agreement for the participation of Japanese companies in ▷ SDI research.

KEESING'S *Record of World Events*, August and October 1987.

JARUZELSKI PLAN.
One of the Polish initiatives for European Security, presented on May 8, 1987, by General Wojciech Jaruzelski, Head of the Polish State Council.

The text is as follows:

"We have always favoured the idea of tackling complex problems on a regional basis, thus opening up the way for contributing to the common European cause. Proceeding from this premise, the Polish People's Republic has come up with a new plan for arms reductions and confidence-building measures in Central Europe through gradually thinning out the nuclear and conventional forces in the region where the confronting military-political groupings are in contact.

Our proposal, aimed at lowering the level of military confrontation, is related to the territories of nine states, including the German Democratic Republic, Czechoslovakia, Hungary, and Poland, and also the Federal Republic of Germany, Belgium, the Netherlands, Luxembourg and Denmark. Eventually, it could be extended to the whole of Europe from the Atlantic to the Urals.

The draft plan calls for:
– first, the phased withdrawal and reduction of shorter-range nuclear weapons of agreed types; we believe that talks to this effect should cover every type of these weapons;
– second, the phased withdrawal and reduction of conventional weapons of agreed types, primarily the more powerful and accurate ones which could be used in a surprise attack;
– third, revision of military doctrines so that the parties involved should view each other's doctrines as exclusively defensive;
– fourth, a continuous search for accords on ever new means of strengthening security and building trust, and also strict verification measures.

It may prove far from easy to carry out this plan: it is bound to call for extensive consultations and the unity of political will and action. Our relevant proposals will be communicated to all the CSCE states through diplomatic channels.

We view our plan as part and parcel of the European process initiated in Helsinki and a follow-up on the other disarmament initiatives of the Warsaw Treaty member-states. The concept of the plan, we are convinced, meets the expectations of those numerous political forces and governments which are seeking in a constructive spirit practical solutions to build trust and remove the sources of the existing danger without detracting from any CSCE states' sense of security."

See also ▷ Gomulka Plan, ▷ Rapacki Plan.

Peace and Socialism. Information Bulletin, Prague, 1987, No. 14; *Trybuna Ludu*, May 9, 1987.

JAVORZYNA.
A locality in Czechoslovakia in Spisz along the northern side of the High Tatras at the mouth of the Javorzyna Valley; subject of a dispute between Poland and Czechoslovakia, 1920–24, in connection with the delimitation of Spisz in accordance with a decision of the Conference of Ambassadors, July 28, 1920 (▷ Teschen, Spisz and Orava Conference of Ambassadors, 1920). The Javorzyna question was submitted to the Permanent Court of International Justice. On the basis of its decision, the LN Council on Mar. 12, 1924, marked out the final border, leaving Javorzyna within Czechoslovakia, recognized by both sides in a Protocol signed on May 6, 1924 in Cracow, and approved by the Conference of Ambassadors, Sept. 5, 1924. A revision made on Sept. 30, 1938 in favor of Poland by a New Protocol of Delimitation, signed in Zakopane, was annulled after World War II.

Recueil des documents diplomatiques, concernant la Question de Javorzina, Décembre 1918–Août 1924, Varsovie, 1925.

JAY'S TREATY, 1794.
An American–British agreement concerning an amicable settlement of controversial problems, elaborated by the US representative, John Jay and Lord Grenville, signed on Nov. 19, 1794 in London, enforced Oct. 28, 1795.

F. BEMBIS, *Jay's Treaty: a Study in Commerce and Diplomacy*, New York, 1923; A DECONDE, *Entangling Alliance: Politics and Diplomacy Under George Washington*, New York, 1958.

JAZZ.
A term first used in Chicago in 1916 by the Jazz Band of Bert Kelly, in the 1920s in America and Europe symbol of popular music of the Jazz Age, subject of international festivals. Organization reg. with the UIA.

International Association of Jazz Record Collectors, f. 1964, Syracuse, N.Y.
International Jazz Federation, f. 1969, London.

Yearbook of International Organizations 1986/87; The Europa Yearbook 1988. A World Survey, Vol. I, London, 1988.

JEDDA RED SEA CONVENTION 1982. ▷ Red Sea Jedda Convention.

JEHOVAH'S WITNESSES.
A millennialist religious group, f. 1872 as the International Bible Students Association, incorporated 1884 as Zion's Watch Tower Tract Society; since 1896 under the name Watch Tower Bible and Tract Society; organized under laws of Pennsylvania, USA and Brooklyn, New York, USA. The name Jehovah's Witnesses was adopted in 1931, as a concept of "primitive Christian, recognizing and teaching the Bible as God's Word of Truth, believing in following its commandments which accounts for their constant neutrality toward any political interests." They act in complete separation from secular governments, regarding all political powers as allies of Satan; they refuse military service, political elections and to salute flags of any nation; they also are against the ecumenical movement in Christian Churches. The Society acts as servant of and legal worldwide governing agency for that body of Christian persons known as Jehovah's Witnesses; to preach the Gospel of God's Kingdom under Christ Jesus to all nations as a witness to the name, word and supremacy of Almighty God Jehovah; to print and distribute the Bible, and disseminate Bible truths in various languages; to establish and maintain gratuitous private Bible schools and classes;

teach, train, prepare and equip men and women as ministers, missionaries, evangelists, preachers, teachers and lecturers. Members (1975): 96 branches directing 2,179,256 active workers in 210 countries. Publ.: *Jehovah's Witness in the Divine Purpose; The Watch Tower*, in 32 languages. Bibles in over 185 languages. Reg. with the UIA.

M. COLE, *Jehovah's Witnesses: the New World Society*, New York, 1955; R.D. QUIDAM, *The Doctrine of Jehovah's Witnesses*, New York, 1959; W.J. WHALEN, *Armageddon Around the Corner*, New York, 1962; *Yearbook of International Organizations*.

JERICHO-2.
According to press information in 1987, an Israeli missile tested to a range of some 850–1700 km.

The Economist, August 1, 1987.

JERUSALEM.
Hebrew = Jerushalaim, *Arabic* = Al-Kuds. The historic capital of Palestine and the Holy City for Christians, Jews and Moslems. On Jan. 23, 1950 the Israeli parliament proclaimed Jerusalem capital of the Israeli State. The City is situated west of the Dead Sea and the Jordan River. 1985 census 557,000 inhabitants. In 1850 the pop. numbered only 15,490 of whom 8000 were Jews, 4000 Moslems, the rest Christians, On Dec. 31, 1946 the population census showed 99,320 Jews, 33,680 Moslems, 31,330 Christians, 110 of other faiths. From 1517 to 1917 under the rule of the Ottoman Empire; in 1917 it was occupied by Great Britain, to whom the LN granted a mandate over Jerusalem in 1920 and in 1922 over all of Palestine. Jerusalem became the mandate center of British authorities in Palestine. After 1948, when the UK gave up its mandate to the UN in accordance with a recommendation of the UN General Assembly of Nov. 29, 1947, in Apr., 1949 the UN Trusteeship Council drew up a plan for an International Statute for Jerusalem under the administration of the UN, guaranteeing the followers of the three religions access to the religious sites. On Dec. 9, 1949 the UN General Assembly restated its intention that Jerusalem should be placed under a permanent international regime with appropriate safeguards for the Holy Places, but Israel and Jordan would only accept a provisional division resulting from their cease-fire treaties. The statute, which anticipated that Jerusalem would be neutral and inviolable, could not be implemented due to the Israeli–Arab conflict, which also encompassed Jerusalem, and the cease-fire line of the front divided Jerusalem between Jordan and Israel. UN efforts established a demilitarized zone, Apr. 4, 1950, which allowed the free movement of pilgrims. Debate in the UN General Assembly in Dec., 1950 failed to resolve the problem and in 1951 Israel announced against Arab protests that Tel Aviv would be the seat of government, and Jerusalem the capital of Israel. In June, 1967 the Israeli army occupied all of Jerusalem and the matter returned to the UN. At a Special Commission the UN General Assembly on July 4, 1967 by 99 votes in favor (including France, Great Britain, and the USSR), none against, and 20 abstentions (including the USA) adopted a resolution stating "the invalidity of the means used by Israel for the purpose of changing the Statute of Jerusalem." On July 5, 1967 the Assembly voted to recognize the annexation of Jerusalem by Israel as invalid and declared itself in favor of "the internationalization of Holy Places." Israel did not participate in either vote, based on the justification that in the opinion of the government of Israel the problem of Jerusalem is "outside the legal competency of the UN General Assembly." On that same day the Vatican, as the representative of Catholic interests, announced that it did not recognize the annexation and declared itself in favor

J

of the internationalization of Jerusalem. On May 21, 1968 the UN Security Council by 13 votes in favor, with two abstentions (USA and Canada), addressed a demand to Israel to cancel all dispositions violating the international status of Jerusalem. This demand was repeated in resolutions of the UN General Assembly concerning the Israeli conflict in succeeding years. In Jan., 1973 premier Golda Meir visited Pope Paul VI to initiate the first official talks between Israel and the Vatican on Jerusalem. The Second Summit Conference of Moslem States in Lahore in Feb., 1974 made a declaration on the question of Jerusalem, called in Arabic Al-Kuds.

"Al-Kuds is the only symbol of its kind of the fusion of Islam with the sacred divine religions. For more than 1300 years Jerusalem was under Moslem trusteeship, open to all who revered it. Only Moslems can be its loving and impartial guardians for the simple reason that only Moslems believe in all three of the prophets of the religions rooted in Jerusalem. No agreement, protocol or adjustment stipulating the continuation of Israeli occupation in the holy city of Jerusalem or its transfer to whatsoever sovereign non-Arab authority, or also making the question of Jerusalem the subject of adjudication or concessions will be possible for the Moslem countries to accept. The withdrawal of Israel from Jerusalem is the most important and unalterable preliminary condition for the establishment of permanent peace in the Near East."

In 1985 Jerusalem was still the seat of the Abyssinian Abbot, Armenian Catholic Patriarchal Vicar, Armenian Patriarch, Coptic Bishop, Father Custos of the Holy Land, Greek Catholic Patriarchal Vicar, Latin Patriarch, Maronite Patriarchal Vicar, Moderator of the Church of Scotland and Anglican Bishop in Jerusalem, Orthodox Patriarch, Syrian Catholic Patriarchal Vicar, Syrian Orthodox Bishop. Pope John Paul II pronounced himself in July, 1980 in favor of the internationalization of Holy Places in Jerusalem. On July 30, 1980 the Israeli parliament passed (69 : 15) a basic law declaring unified Jerusalem, including predominantly Arab East Jerusalem occupied by Israel during the 1967 war, as the capital of the Jewish state. The majority of UN member states declared this act illegal.

The Old City of Jerusalem and its walls are included in the ▷ World Heritage UNESCO List. Lying within its 16th-century walls, the Holy City, medieval in appearance, contains 226 historical monuments, nearly all of which are religious, e.g. churches, mosques, tombs, theological schools. They include three buildings of particular importance for the whole world, either as places of pilgrimage or as outstanding works of art in their own right. These are the Church of the Holy Sepulchre containing the rotunda of the Resurrection dating from the 4th century, and the mosques known as the "Dome of the Rock" and "Al-Aqsa", which were built at the end of the 7th century. See also ▷ Mufti of Jerusalem.

H. KENDALL, *Jerusalem City Plan. Preservation and Development 1914–1918*, HMSO, Jerusalem, 1948; P. MOHN, "Jerusalem and the UN", in: *International Conciliation*, No. 464, Oct. 1950, pp. 421–471; J. DE REYNIER, *A Jérusalem un Drapeau Flottait sur la Ligne de Feu*, Neuchâtel, 1950; *Jerusalem before UN*, UN, New York, 1950; G. FOLKE BERNADOTTE, *To Jerusalem*, London, 1951; R. FALAISE, "Le Statut de Jérusalem", in: *Revue générale de droit international public*, No. 62, 1958; H.E. BOVIS, *Jerusalem Question 1917–1968*, Stanford, Calif., 1971; R. SEGAL, *Whose Jerusalem? The Conflict of Israel*, London, 1973; UNESCO, *A Legacy for All*, Paris, 1984; D. NEFF, *Warriors for Jerusalem*, New York 1985. A. RABINOWICH *Jerusalem on Earth. People, Passions and Politics in Holy City*, New York, 1988.

JERUSALEM MEETING, 1977. The first meeting between the Egyptian President Anwar Sadat and Israeli Prime Minister Menahem Begin, on Dec. 6, 1977 in Jerusalem.

JESUITS. Member of the order called The Society of Jesus (SJ), *Latin = Societas Jesu* (SJ); one of the most active international Catholic orders, est. 1534 by I. Loyola in Paris; ratified by the bull *Regimini militantis* of Paul III on Sept. 27, 1540; dissolved July 21, 1773 by the bull *Dominus ac Redemptor* of Clement XIV; revised on Aug. 7, 1814 by the bull *Sollicitudo omnium Eclesiarum* of Pius VII. In the modern age members of the Jesuits included P. Teilhard de Chardin (1881–1955), whose ideas played an important role in adapting the Church to the new age. Through their scientific centres, mainly in the USA and Italy, Jesuits take an active part in international scientific organizations connected with UNESCO. In 1946 SJ est. in Brussels the International Centre for Studies in Religious Education, Centre international d'études de la formation religieuse. Member of the Vatican Conference of International Catholic Organizations. Publ.: *Lumen Vitae*. Reg. with the UIA. There were 25,175 Jesuits in the World in Sept. 1987.

Yearbook of International Organizations.

JETHOU. ▷ Bailiwick of Guernsey.

JET INTERNATIONAL FLIGHTS. The first jet aircraft, a De Havilland Comet IV, took off on Oct. 4, 1958 from London Airport and less than seven hours later arrived in New York. The ICAO incorporated in the ▷ Chicago Conventions new standards for runways, landings and take offs obligatorily monitored by radar. The 'second jet generation' started by 1963 with the Boeing 727.

UN Chronicle, September 1958.

JEWISH AUTONOMOUS REGION IN THE USSR. An administrative region, est. in 1928 in Habarovsk Territory as the Jewish National District. It became an autonomous region on May 7, 1934. Area: 36,000 sq. km. Pop. 1980: 193,400 (Russians 84%, Ukrainians 6.3% and 5.4% of Jews). Capital: Birobidjan with 67,000 inhabitants, 1980. Official languages: Russian and Yiddish.

J. PAXTON (ed.), *The Statesman's Yearbook 1983–84*, London, 1984.

JEWISH HISTORICAL INSTITUTE IN POLAND. A Jewish scientific institution est. 1947 in Warsaw. Publ. a Yiddish language *Bletter far Geshikhte* and in Polish a *Biuletyn Instytutu Żydowskiego w Polsce*.

M. HORN, *The Jewish Historical Institute in Poland*, in: R. WASITA ed., *In the Land We Shared*, Warsaw, 1988.

JEWISH–POLISH STUDIES INSTITUTE. The Institute for Polish–Jewish Studies at Oxford, UK, and its US wing the American Foundation for Polish Jewish Studies in Boston, Chicago, New York and Miami, which emerged out of the International Conference on Polish–Jewish Studies held at Oxford in September 1984, were established to: preserve the unique heritage of Polish Jewry, and to promote research on an interdisciplinary international basis. Publ.: A Journal of Polish–Jewish Studies (annually) since 1986 Patrons Nobel Laureates: Joseph Brodsky, Czeslaw Milosz, Isaac B. Singer, Elie Wiesel.

G. LERSKI, H. LERSKI, *Jewish–Polish Coexistence 1772–1939. A Topical Bibliography*, Greenwood Press, 1986; E. GIERAT, *A Polish Vademecum. A Handbook on Poles and Other Soviet Dominated European Nations in the Free World*, Bethleem, Ct., USA, 1988, p. 44.

JEWISH WORLD CONGRESS. ▷ Jews.

JEWS. *Hebrew*: Yehūdhī = "Judea'n.' A people inhabiting Palestine until AD 135, when they were expelled for rebelling against the Roman Empire; since then living in the "great dispersal" (*diaspora*). The number of Jews in the world was estimated Jan. 1, 1964 at *c.* 13,200,000 and Jan. 1, 1974 at 14,370,000 – according to *American Jewish Yearbook* – of which in the USA – 5,510,000, in Israel – 2,723,000, in the USSR – 2,687,000 (this figure is over-estimated in relation to official USSR statistics, which for 1970 gave 2,157,000), (Jewish emigration from the Soviet Union 1968–1985 total: 265,657) in France – 550,000, in Argentina – 500,000, in Great Britain – 410,000, in Canada – 305,000, in Brazil – 305,000. According to this source, 51% of the Jews live in North and South America, 28% in Europe, 19% in Israel, 1.5% in Africa and 0.5% in the remaining regions of the world. According to the *1983 Encyclopaedia Britannica Book of the Year* the number of Jews in the world was estim. 16,820,850 (in N. America 7,266,900, in S. America 699,950, in Europe 4,470,800, in Asia 4,096,870, in Africa 213,530 and in Oceania 72,800). The Jewish people are divided into three major groups: ▷ Ashkenazim, ▷ Oriental Jews and ▷ Sephardim. The first group was estimated in the 1980's to number 12 million, the majority in the USA and in USSR; the second group numbered about 1,600,000 and the third about 600,000. There are also minor Jewish communities: the Italian-speaking and Greek speaking; the Black Jews of Ethiopia (Fallashas) and the Black Jews of India (Bene-Israel). In the 19th century Jews were strongly influenced by Zionism, to rebuild their own state in Palestine. At the First Zionist Congress 1897, the World Zionist Organization was founded. The Committee of Jewish Delegations f. 1918 (succeeded by the Jewish World Congress, f. 1936) played an important role at the Paris Peace Conference (1919) and under the patronage of the LN created a system for the protection of minorities in Central and Eastern Europe, but not in Germany. In executing the ▷ Balfour Declaration 1917, in 1929 the British government entrusted to the World Zionist Organization the functions of an agency representing all Jewish groupings, including non-Zionist ones, interested in recreating the national Jewish homeland in Palestine. The parliamentary victory of Hitler's NSDAP party in Germany, Jan. 30, 1933, initiated the holocaust for all European Jews. During World War II the Jews, suffered the greatest losses from Nazi genocidial actions. On Jan. 20, 1942, the ▷ Gestapo ordered the ▷ 'Endlösung' (in *German*: "final solution") a cryptonym for a plan developed by the Main Security Office of the Reich, RSHA, at the order of A. Hitler, providing for the physical liquidation of Jews residing in European territories then subject to the German III Reich. RSHA estimated the number of Jews in Europe at that time as 11,292,300 persons. The total number of Jews put to death has been computed at about 5,700,000–6,100,000. Due to genocide perpetrated against the Jewish people and the birth of the state of Israel in 1949, new Catholic–Jewish relations took shape in the international arena, the first concrete expression of which was the Vatican II Declaration on the Relations of the Church to Non-Christian Religions Oct. 28, 1965. This stated that the Jewish nation could not be held responsible for the death of Christ, as had been believed in past centuries, and thus set the stage for a Catholic–Jewish dialogue. Paul VI on Jan. 10, 1975 and John Paul II on Mar. 12, 1979 granted audiences to representatives of the Jewish Agency as well as the International Committee on Catholic–Jewish Contacts, est. 1970. The Vatican II Declaration in art. 4, *Nostra Aetate*, recalled "the bond by which the people of the New Testament is spiritually linked to the tribe Abraham," for "through the mediation of this people, with which God in His Ineffable mercy decided to conclude the Old Testament, he received The Revelation of the Old Testament." In 1974 a Vatican Committee for Religious Relations with Judaism began work on the main policy lines and directions for implementing the terms of *Nostra Aetate*. The policy lines condemned "all forms of antisemitism and discrimination as clearly contrary to the very spirit of Christianity," especially since "human dignity alone would be sufficient to condemn them." The history of the Jews has resulted in their being the only nationality with a significant number of international organizations; those registered with the UIA include:

Agudath Israel World Organizations, AIWO, f. 1912, in Katowice. Headquarters London and New York, Consultative status with ECOSOC, UNESCO, Publ.: *Hamodia* (Israel daily) and weeklies in Antwerp, Buenos Aires, London, New York, Tel Aviv and Zürich.
Alliance Israélite Universelle, f. 1860, Paris. Publ.: *Cahier de l'AIU*.
B'nai B'rith International Council, f. 1959, Washington, DC. Consultative status with UNESCO, ECOSOC.
Conference of European Rabbis and Associated Religious Organizations, f. 1961, Geneva. Consultative status with ECOSOC, UNESCO, UNICEF, UNHCR, WHO, FAO.
Consultative Council of Jewish Organizations, f. 1946, New York, Consultative status with ECOSOC, UNESCO, UNICEF, ILO.
Co-ordination Board of Jewish Organizations, f. 1947, Washington. Consultative status with UNICEF, European Council.
Council for Jews from Germany, f. 1945, London.
European Council of Jewish Community Services, f. 1964, Paris.
International Association of Jewish Lawyers, Tel Aviv.
International Association of Libraries of Judaica and Hebraics in Europe, f. 1955, Copenhagen; affiliates libraries in Austria, Denmark, France, Great Britain, Holland, Italy, Poland, Spain, Switzerland and Yugoslavia.
International Consultative Committee of Organizations for Christian–Jewish Co-operation, f. 1955, London.
International Council of Jewish Women, f. 1912, London. Consultative status with ECOSOC, UNESCO, UNICEF. Publ.: *Newsletter*.
International Council on Jewish Social and Welfare Services, f. 1961, Geneva. Consultative status with ECOSOC, UNESCO, UNICEF, WHO and FAO.
International Hebrew Christian Alliance, f. 1925, London, Publ · *The Hebrew Christian* and *Der Zeuge*.
International Jewish Committee on Interreligious Consultation, New York, Geneva.
International Jewish Labor Bund, f. 1947, New York. Publ.: *Unser Tsait*.
International League for the Repatriation of Russian Jews, f. 1968, New York, Jerusalem, Paris, London, New York, Geneva.
Jewish Agency for Israel World Zionist Organization, f. 1897 at the First Zionist Congress as World Zionist Organization, to which the government of Great Britain, in executing of the so-called ▷ Balfour Declaration 1917, in 1929 entrusted the functions of an agency representing all of the Jewish groupings, also non-Zionist ones, interested in rebuilding "the national Jewish homeland in Palestine," a function it performed until the creation of the state of Israel, after which it received a special statute in Israel as the representative of the Zionist federations of 49 countries. Headquarters: Jerusalem, international secretariats: Geneva, London, New York and Paris. Publ. weekly: *Israel Digest*; monthly: *Israel Youth Horizon, Economic Horizons* and *Folk and Zion*.

World Federation of Polish Jews, f. 1960, Tel Aviv, New York.
World Federation of UMHA and Jewish Community Centers, f. 1947, New York.
World ORT Union, f. 1880 in Petersburg as a Jewish artisan organization in Russia; in 1921 transferred to Geneva as an organization promoting the teaching of crafts and agriculture in the Jewish diaspora. Consultative status with UNESCO and ILO. Publ.: *Technical and Pedagogical Bulletin*.
World OSE Union, World Wide Organization for Child Care, Health and Hygiene among Jews, f. 1912 as an organization of Jews in Russia: in 1921 transferred to Berlin, since 1933 in Paris. Consultative status with WHO and UNICEF. Publ.: *Bulletin de l'OSE*.
World Sephardi Federation, f. 1925, London.
World Union for Progressive Judaism, f. 1926, New York; a religious organization which in Paris conducts the International Institute of Hebraic Studies, Institute d'études hébraiques, which trains teachers for progressive Judaism. Consultative status with ECOSOC, UNESCO and UNICEF. Publ.: *Information Service*.
World Union of Jewish Students, f. 1924, Paris.

H. GRAETZ, *History of the Jews*, 6 Vols., London, 1891–1926; D. PHILIPSON, *Old European Jewries*, Philadelphia, 1894; J. MARCUS, *The Jews in the Medieval World*, Cincinnati, 1939; F.R. BIENENFELD, *The Germans and the Jews*, New York, 1939; J.W. PARKES, *The Conflict of the Church and the Synagogue*, London, 1939; C. ROTH, *A History of the Jews in England*, London, 1941; O. JANOWSKI (ed.), *The American Jews*, New York, 1942; A.A. NEWMAN, *The Jews in Spain*, 2 Vols., New York, 1942; N. LÖVENTHAL, *The Jews of Germany*, Philadelphia, 1944; R. ANCHEL, *Les Juifs en France*, Paris, 1946; S.M. DUBNOW, *A History of the Jews in Russia and Poland*, 3 Vols., Philadelphia, 1946; *Das Menschenschlachthaus Treblinka*, Wien, 1946; *The Trial of German Major War Criminals. Proceedings of the International Military Tribunal Sitting at Nuremberg, Germany*, 42 Vols., London 1946–48, Vols. 2, 10, 11, 12 and 22; *Universal Jewish Encyclopaedia*, New York, 1948; M.U. SCHAPPES, *A Documentary History of the Jews in the United States 1654–1875*, New York, 1950; S.M. SCHWARTZ, *The Jews in the Soviet Union*, Syracuse, 1951; E. KOHN, *American Jewry*, New York, 1955; G. REITLINGER, *The Final Solution: the Attempt to Exterminate the Jews of Europe, 1939–1945*, London, 1952; L. POLIAKOV, *Harvest of Hate*, Syracuse, N.Y., 1954; L. FINKELSTEIN, *The Jews. Their History, Culture and Religion*, 2 Vols., London, 1956; H.M. SACHAR, *The Course of Modern Jewish History*, New York, 1958; *Documentae Occupationis*, Vol. 6, Poznań, 1958; A. EISENBACH, "Operation Reinhard. Mass Extermination of the Jewish Population," in: *Western Polish Review*, No. 1, 1962, pp. 80–124; T. BERENSTEIN, A. RUTKOWSKI, *Assistance to the Jews in Poland*, Warsaw, 1963; H. ARENDT, *Eichmann in Jerusalem: A Report on the Banality of Evil*, New York, 1964; J.S. CONWAY, 'The Silence of Pope Pius XII', in: *Review of Politics*, 1965; C.B. SHERMAN, *The Jews within American Society*, New York, 1965; N. LEVIN, *The Holocaust: the Destruction of European Jewry, 1933–1945*, New York, 1968; W. BARTOSZEWSKI, Z. LEWIN, *Righteous Among Nations, How Poles Helped the Jews 1939–1944*, London, 1970; B.D. WEINRYB, *The Jews of Poland*, Philadelphia, 1973; A. RHODES, *The Vatican in the Age of the Dictators*, London, 1973; S. FRIEDMAN, *No Haven for the Oppressed: United States Policy Towards Jewish Refugees, 1932–1945*, Detroit, 1973; R. AINSZTEIN, *Jewish Resistance in Nazi-Occupied Eastern Europe*, New York, 1974; F. LITTEL, G.H. LOCKE, *The German Church. Struggle and the Holocaust*, Detroit, 1974; R. REUTHER, *Faith and Fratricide: the Theological Route of Anti-Semitism*, New York, 1974; L. DAWIDOWICZ, *The War Against the Jews, 1933–1945*, New York, 1975; F. LITTEL, *The Crucifixion of the Jews: the Failure of Christians to Understand the Jewish Experience*, New York, 1975; U. TAL, *Christians and Jews in Germany: Religion, Politics and Ideology in the Second Reich 1870–1914*, Ithaca, N.Y., 1975; R. GUTTERIDGE, *Open the Mouth for the Dumb: the German Evangelical Church and the Jews, 1879–1950*, Oxford, 1976; Ch.R. BROWNING, *The Final Solution and the German Foreign Office*, New York, 1978; I. ABELLA, H.

TROPER, "The Line Must be Drawn Somewhere: Canada and Jewish Refugees, 1933–1939", in: *Canadian Historical Review*, 1979; B. WASSERSTEIN, *Britain and the Jews in Europe 1939–1945*, Oxford, 1979; 'Reflections on the Holocaust', in: *The Annuals of the American Academy of Political and Social Science*, July 1980; A. BONIECKI, "O dialogu katolicko-żydowskim. Wywiad z dr. J. Lichtenem" (Catholic-Jewish Dialogue. Interview with Dr. J. Lichten), in: *Tygodnik Powszechny*, Kraków, August 10, 1980; W.W. HEGEN, *Germans, Poles and Jews. The Nationality Conflict in the Prussian East, 1772–1914*, Chicago, 1980; E. KOGON (ed), *National-sozialistische Massentötung durch Giftgas. Eine Dokumentation*, Frankfurt am M., 1983; E. BLACK, *The Transfer Agreement. The Untold Story of the Secret Agreement Between the Third Reich and Jewish Palestine*, London, 1984; R.O. FREEDMAN, *Soviet Jewry in Decisive Decade, 1971–80*, Durham, N.C., 1984; R.B. CULLEN, *Soviet Jewry*, in: *Foreign Affairs*, Winter, 1986/87; J. LEWIN, *The Jewish Community in Poland, Historical Essays*, New York, 1985; E. WIESEL, *The Jews of Silence*, New York, 1987; P. JOHNSON, *A History of the Jews*, New York, 1987; E. TIVNAN, *The Lobby, Jewish Political Power and American Foreign Policy*, New York, 1987; I. GUTMAN, S. KRAKOWSKI, *The Unequal Victims, Poles and Jews During World War II*, Oxford, 1987; H. RAUTKALLIO, *Finland and the Holocaust*, Oxford, 1987; S. ABRAMSEN, *The Holocaust in Norway*, Oxford, 1987; A.A. POWIŃSKI, *Życie i śmierć Zygelbojma (The Life and Death of Zygelbojm)*, Warsaw, 1988; A. EISENBACH, *Emancypacja ludności żydowskiej na ziemiach polskich 1780–1870 (Emancipation of the Jewish Population on Polish Lands 1780–1870)*, Warsaw, 1988.

JIM CROW. A North-American term, derived from Jim Crow Rice (Thomas Dartmouth, 1808–1860), regarded as the father of the American minstrel show, who caught the public fancy with his impersonations of Negroes; this stereotype was later applied to customs and laws discriminating against Negroes, e.g. in 1840 when the Boston Railroad established cars for Negroes only, called "Jim Crow cars."

JOHN BULL. A colloquial jocular international term for the British, adopted in the 18th century after John Bull, the leading character in an allegory by a Scottish mathematician and physicist, John Arbuthnot (1667–1735).

L.M. BEATTIE, *John Arbuthnot, Mathematician and Satirist*, London, 1935.

JOHNSON–MANN DOCTRINE, 1963. A principle of US foreign policy in Latin America formulated in Dec., 1963 by the US President L.B. Johnson, and imparted to US ambassadors in that region by the Under-Secretary of State for Latin American affairs, T.C. Mann, to the effect that the ▷ Kennedy doctrine of support solely for representative governments in Latin America formed through general elections would be cancelled and in its place the US government would support any Latin American government whose interests are compatible with those of the United States.

M.A. URIBE, *Le Livre Noire de l'intervention américaine au Chili*, Paris, 1974.

JOINERY. Subject of international co-operation. Organization reg. with the UIA:

European Federation of Unions of Joinery Manufacturers, f. 1957, Frankfurt n/M, FRG.

Yearbook of International Organizations, 1986/87; The Europa Yearbook 1988. A World Survey, Vol. I, London, 1988.

JOINT CHIEFS OF STAFF, JCS. A United States military term for a committee consisting of the Chief of Naval Operations, the Commandant of the US Marine Corps, the Chiefs of Staff of the Army and the Air-Force and the Chairman of the Joint Chiefs appointed by the President. The Secretary of Defense and the senior civil servants in the Office of the Secretary of Defense participate in the JCS sessions.

D. ROBERTSON, *Guide to Modern Defense and Strategy*, Detroit, 1988.

JOINT COMMISSIONS. An international term with dual meaning: one for inter-governmental bi- or multilateral commissions of states interested in direct solution of problems that arise between them in definite fields, or composed of representatives of states elected by parties in conflict, sometimes having a neutral chairman, with a view to registering, describing and estimating matters of dispute or incidents on a given territory; second for international joint commissions set up for evaluation by international bodies; subject of bi- and multilateral international agreements. After World War II they gained popularity in connection with the processes of economic integration and were appointed for co-ordination and planning of the development of co-operation in specific fields. The institutional form of joint commissions was employed in international economic co-operation between East and West aimed at facilitation of collaboration of the two different economic systems.

JOINT INSTITUTE FOR NUCLEAR RESEARCH. ▷ Nuclear Research Dubna Joint Institute.

JOINT VENTURES. An international term for joint industrial or capital undertakings conducted by institutions or companies of different countries. Subject of UNIDO studies. Term adopted by socialist countries for co-operation of states with different social systems. In the 1980's some Comecon countries permitted joint ventures (Hungary 1983).
On Jan. 13, 1987 the Soviet Government accepted the procedure for setting up joint ventures in the Soviet Union with the participation of firms from foreign countries.

FRIEDMANN–KALMANOFF, *Joint International Business Venture*, New York, 1961; K. BIVENS, E. LOWELL, *Joint Ventures with Foreign Partners*, New York, 1966; *UNIDO Manual on the Establishment of Industrial Joint Ventures agreements in Developing Countries*, New York, 1968; KEESING's *Record of World Events*, 1987, No. 3; OECD, *Competition Policy and Joint Ventures*, Washington DC, 1987; ECE, *Economic, Business, Financial and Legal Aspects of East–West Joint Ventures*, Geneva, 1988.

JORDAN. Member of the UN; The Hashemite Kingdom Jordan. State of south-west Asia, bordering on Israel, Syria, Iraq and Saudi Arabia. Area: 97,740 sq. km. Pop. 1987 est. 3,804,000 of which *c.* two-thirds live on the East Bank and *c.* one-third on the West Bank (1961 census 1,706,202; 1979 census of East Bank: 2,147,594). Capital: Amman with 1,712,000 inhabitants, 1980. GNP per capita 1987 US $1,540. Currency: one Jordanian dinar = 1,000 fils. National Day: Nov. 14, birthday of King Hussein, 1935.
Jordan has been a member of the UN since Dec. 14, 1955 and of UN specialized agencies, with the exception of the GATT. Member of the Arab League. International relations: part of the Ottoman Empire 1516–1919, with the name Transjordan; since 1920 part of the League of Nations mandate of Palestine under British administration, but not regarded as a part of a Jewish homeland (▷ Balfour Declaration 1917). In 1928 a constitutional monarchy; recognized by Great Britain as a sovereign independent kingdom by a treaty signed on Mar. 22, 1946 in

London. On June 17, 1946 the name Transjordan was changed to The Hashemite Kingdom of Jordan. In 1948 Jordan started a war against Israel and annexed the West Bank; in Dec., 1949 concluded an armistice with Israel. During the Seven-Day Arab–Israeli War of Nov., 1967, Jordan lost the West Bank. In 1974 Jordan recognized the Palestine Liberation Organization and formally ceded to PLO all claims to the West Bank. A signatory of a Co-operation Agreement with the EEC, 1978. In 1982–1984 King Hussein participated in international talks on a plan for peace in the Middle East. On Oct. 24, 1984 Jordan resumed diplomatic relations with Egypt, severed 1979. Relations with Syria strained since 1980 reconciliated in Dec. 1985 (visit of King Hussein in Damascus).
On Oct. 26, 1986 three economic agreements with Syria.
See also ▷ World Heritage UNESCO List.

C.R.W. SETTON, *Legislation of Transjordania 1918–1930*, London, 1931; *The Constitution of the Hashemite Kingdom of Jordan*, Amman, 1952; J. MORRIS, *The Hashemite Kings*, London, 1959; *Sovremiennaya Yordania*, Moskva, 1964; A.H. HASAN ABIOLI, *Jordan: A Political Study, 1948–1957*, New York, 1965; N.H. ARURI, *Jordan: A Study in Political Development (1921–1965)*, The Hague, 1972; S. MOUSA, Y.T. TONI, *Jordan: Land and People*, Amman, 1973; J. HAAS, *Husseins Königreich: Jordanian Stellung in Nahen Osten*, Munich, 1975; P. SUBSER, *Jordan*, Boulder, 1982; *The Europa Year Book 1984. A World Survey*, Vol. II, pp. 1829–1838, London, 1984; M.C. WILSON, *King Abdullah, Britain and the Making of Jordan*, Cambridge, UK, 1987.

JORDAN RIVER. A river in the Middle East, most of its total length of 320 km flows through Jordan and Israel, then through the Sea of Galilee to the Dead Sea; subject of dispute between the two countries since 1948 over proportional utilization of its waters and tributaries. In 1953, the US proposed a 60% share for Jordan and 40% for Israel. The proposal was rejected by both sides. In 1974 King Hussein renounced all Jordanian claims to the West Bank of the Jordan recognizing the claims of the Palestine Liberation Organization.

S.G. STEVENS, "The Jordan River Valley", in: *International Conciliation*, No. 506, January, 1956, pp. 227–283.

JOURNALISM. A subject of international co-operation and international agreements. In 1971 on the initiative of the UN General Assembly a UN expert committee worked out a convention on the rights and duties of journalists ▷ War correspondents. The status of journalists in international relations was mentioned in the ▷ Helsinki Final Act 1975 in the chapter entitled Information. ▷ Press and the UN.

UN Chronicle, November, 1981, p. 27; G. BOHERE. *Profession: Journalist. A Study on Employment and Conditions of Work of Journalists*, ILO, Geneva, 1983.

JOURNALIST, COMPULSORY LICENSING. The ▷ Inter-American Court of Human Rights issued on Nov. 13, 1985 a unanimous advisory opinion that the introduction of compulsory state licensing of journalists is incompatible with Art. 13 of the ▷ Human Rights American Convention.
See also ▷ Freedom of the Press.

New York Times, Nov. 29, 1985; KEESING's *Record of World Events*, 1986, No. 1.

JOURNALIST'S INTERNATIONAL ETHICS CODE. The Code approved by the Subcommission on Freedom of Information and Press of the UN Human Rights Commission, Mar. 13, 1953, with 7

votes in favor and 3 abstentions (the UK, the US, and the USSR). The text is as follows:
"Preamble. Freedom of information and of the press is a fundamental human right and is the touchstone of all the freedoms consecrated in the Charter of the United Nations and proclaimed in the Universal Declaration of Human Rights; it is essential to the promotion and to the preservation of peace.
That freedom will be the better safeguarded when the personnel of the press and of all other media of information constantly and voluntarily strive to maintain the highest sense of responsibility, being deeply imbued with the moral obligation to be truthful and to search for the truth in reporting, in explaining and in interpreting facts. This International Code of Ethics is therefore proclaimed as a standard of professional conduct for all engaged in gathering, transmitting, disseminating and commenting on news and information and in describing contemporary events by the written word, by word of mouth or by any other means of expression.
Art. 1. The personnel of the press and information should do all in their power to ensure that the information the public receives is factually accurate. They should check all items of information to the best of their ability. No fact should be willfully distorted and no essential fact should be deliberately suppressed.
Art. 2. A high standard of professional conduct requires devotion to the public interest. The seeking of personal advantage and the promotion of any private interest contrary to the general welfare, for whatever reason, is not compatible with such professional conduct.
Willful calumny, slander, libel and unfounded accusations are serious professional offences; so also is plagiarism.
Good faith with the public is the foundation of good journalism. Any published information which is found to be harmfully inaccurate should be spontaneously and immediately rectified. Rumor and unconfirmed news should be identified and treated as such.
Art. 3. Only such tasks as are compatible with the integrity and dignity of the profession should be assigned or accepted by personnel of the press and information, as also by those participating in the economic and commercial activities of information enterprises. Those who make public any information or comment should assume full responsibility for what is published unless such responsibility is explicitly disclaimed at the time.
The reputation of individuals should be respected and information and comment on their private lives likely to harm their reputation should not be published unless it serves the public interest, as distinguished from public curiosity. If charges against reputation or moral character are made, opportunity should be given for reply. Discretion should be observed concerning sources of information. Professional secrecy should be observed in matters revealed in confidence; and this privilege may always be invoked to the furthest limits of law.
Art. 4. It is the duty of those who describe and comment upon events relating to a foreign country to acquire the necessary knowledge of such country which will enable them to report and comment accurately and fairly thereon.
Art. 5. This Code is based on the principle that the responsibility for ensuring the faithful observance of professional ethics rests upon those who are engaged in the profession, and not upon any government. Nothing herein may therefore be interpreted as implying any justification for intervention by a government in any manner whatsoever to enforce observance of the moral obligations set forth in this Code."

UN Bulletin, April 1, 1952, pp. 345–349.

JOURNAL OF THE UNITED NATIONS. The Journal presents information of the program of meetings and the agenda of UN organs in session. A separate Journal is issued throughout each session of the General Assembly and also elsewhere on the occasion of special UN conferences.

United Nations Editorial Manual, New York, 1983, p. 9.

JUAN DE NOVA. ▷ Madagascar.

JUAREZ BENITO DOCTRINE, 1865. A fundamental principle of peace between nations formulated by the President of Mexico, Benito Juarez:

"Between nations as between people: respect for the rights of others makes for peace" (Entre los pueblos como entre los hombres: el respecto al derecho ajeno es la paz).

R. ROEDES, *Benito Juárez and his Mexico*, New York, 1947; D.C. VILLEGAS, *Historia Moderna de México*, 5 Vols., México, 1955–60; E. MORENO, *Juárez jurista*, Mexico, DF, 1972.

JUAREZ BENITO PRIZE. A prize est. by Mexico in 1967, annual artistic and scientific award for Latin Americans; first prize winners were: Ecuadorian writer B. Carion, Brazilian architect O. Niemeyer, and Argentinian biochemist L. Leboir.

JUDAISM. A religion also called Mosaism, professed by the Jews, arose in the 2nd millennium BC on the legal and doctrinal foundation of the Five Books of Moses and the Talmud, with no hierarchical organization except communities, whose administrator was a Rabbi. In the 20th century the religious bond of Judaism became an element uniting Jews politically in support of creating and then strengthening the state of Israel. Nearly all the Jewish international organizations registered with the UIA stress their ties with both Judaism and Israel.

M. KAPLAN, *Judaism as a Civilization*, London, 1934; M. WAXMAN, *Tradition and Change: the Development of Conservative Judaism*, New York, 1958; 'Judaism', in: *Encyclopaedia Britannica*, Vol. 13, pp. 103–116, London, 1973.

JUDICIAL AND EXTRAJUDICIAL DOCUMENTS. A subject of international co-operation and agreements: Convention on the Service Abroad of Judicial or Extrajudicial Documents in Civil or Commercial Matters (with Annex), opened for signature on Nov. 15, 1965 in The Hague. It came into force on Feb. 10, 1969. Art. 1. states that:

"The Convention shall apply in all cases, in civil or commercial matters, where there is occasion to transmit a judicial or extrajudicial document for service abroad. The Convention shall not apply where the address of the person to be served with the document is not known."

UNTS, Vol. 658, p. 165.

JUDICIARY. A subject of international co-operation. Organizations reg. with the UIA:

International Union of Judges, f. 1953, Rome. Publ.: *Bulletin*.
World Association of Judges, f. 162, Geneva. Members: Supreme and High Court justices eligible on individual basis. Other judges eligible in appropriate categories.

Yearbook of International Organizations.

JUDO. An Olympic sport since 1964, organized in 1951 in the International Judo Federation, IJF, Paris.

Yearbook of International Organizations.

JUMP COMPLEX. A cultural site of Canada, included in the ▷ World Heritage UNESCO List.

UNESCO, *A Legacy for All*, Paris, 1984.

JUNTA MILITAR. Spanish "military council." An Hispano–American term which appeared at the beginning of the 19th century. Representative government established by military conspiracies in the states of Latin America liberating themselves from the rule of the Spanish monarchy; in the 20th century an international term for the dictatorial rule of the commander of the armed forces.

JUPITER. The largest of the ▷ planets. A subject of international space research.

B.M. PEAK, *The Planet Jupiter*, London, 1958.

JURIDICAL INTERSTATE ASSISTANCE. An international term for legal contestations carried out on the territory of one state by its judicature at the request of another state when certain circumstances of the case in question can be established only on the territory of the former (e.g. registry of documents, examination of witnesses). No multilateral convention exists to regulate standard norms accordingly, but most states are bound by bilateral agreements referring mainly to civil questions as well as including in their legal codes appropriate provisions for such assistance.

H. LEROY JONES, 'International judical assistance: procedural chaos and a program for reform', in: *Yale Law Journal*, No. 62, 1952/53.

JURISDICTION. *Latin*: iurisdiction = "administration of the law." An international term for various formal rights of authority or legal power to hear a case; in international law synonymous with competence of various authorities such as international jurisdiction (arbitration jurisdiction), consular jurisdiction (the Vienna Consular Convention, 1963) and others.

M. AKEHURST, "Jurisdiction in International Law", in: *British Year Book of International Law 1972–1973*, Oxford, 1975, pp. 145–258; M.S. RAJAN, *The expanding jurisdiction of the UN*, Bombay, 1982; *Jurisdiction and Jurisdictional Immunities, in:* R.L. BLEDSOE, B.A. BOCZEK, *The International Law Dictionary*, Oxford, 1987.

JURISDICTIONAL IMMUNITY. An international term for freedom from penal, civil or administrative jurisdiction of the receiving state conferred on members of foreign diplomatic and consular agencies and their families duly accredited; does not apply if they are nationals or permanent residents of the country. The principle of jurisdictional immunity is not commonly applied, particularly with respect to consular officers.

H. LAUTERPACHT, "The Problem of Jurisdictional Immunities of Foreign States", in: *British Year Book*, No. 28, 1951; W.W. BISHOP Jr., "New US Policy Limiting Sovereign Immunity", in: *American Journal of International Law*, No. 47, 1953; J.F. LALIVE, 'L'immunité de juridiction des états et des organisations internationales', in: *Recueil des Cours de l'Académie de Droit International*, No. 84, 1953; C.M. SCHMITT-HOFF, 'Sovereign Immunity in International Trade', in: *International Law Quarterly*, No. 7, 1958.

JURISDICTION, INTERNATIONAL. An international term for conciliatory jurisdiction arbitration of investigative commissions of international organizations, institutions established to render good services, international courts (International Court of Justice, International Military Court and others).
See also ▷ Forum Prorogatum.

K. HAMMARSKJÖLD, *Juridiction International*, The Hague, 1939; H.J. SCHLOCHAUER, 'Internationale Gerichtsbarkeit', in: *Strupp-Schlochauer Wörterbuch des Völkerrechts*, Vol. 2, pp. 56–64, Berlin, 1961.

JURISPRUDENCE. An international term for the science or philosophy of law or a system of laws, including such fields as logic, forensic medicine, forensic psychology, etc.; subject of organized international co-operation.

A. DE LA PRADELLE, *Jurisprudence internationale*, Paris, 1936; C. MORRIS (ed), *The Great Legal Philosophers: Selected Readings in Jurisprudence*, London, 1959.

JUS AD BELLUM. *Latin* = "the right to declare and wage wars". Until World War I a generally acceptable principle for solving disputes between states by use of force in a way controlled by customary rules and to a limited extent by first international conventions of 1856–1907. The right to war was denounced for the first time in principle by the ▷ Decree on Peace 1917. In the Preamble of the League of Nations to the Treaty of Versailles States signatories pledged "non-recourse to war". The first formal international treaty denouncing "recourse to war to settle international disputes" and renouncing war as an "instrument of national policy in mutual relations" was the ▷ Briand--Kellogg Treaty signed in Paris, Aug. 17, 1928. After World War II such principles found their expression in the UN Charter which made it an objective "to save succeeding generations from the scourge of war" and imposed on all UN members the obligation to refrain from the Threat or use of force in any manner inconsistent with the Purposes of the United Nations. Called also Just War Theory.

S. KALEGOROPOULOS-STRATIS, *Ius ad bellum*, Athens, 1950, (in French); D. ROBERTSON, *Guide to Modern Defense and Strategy*, Detroit, 1988.

JUS AVOCANDI. *Latin* = "the right to appeal". An international term for a principle stating that the victim has the right to appeal to higher (also international) instances; observed in case of persons referred to in the Minority Treaties of the League of Nations (▷ Minorities, Protection of) or in the case of inhabitants of ▷ Trusteeship Territories.

JUS BANDERAE. *Latin* = "the right of flag". An international term for a norm determining that it is the colors under which a ship sails, not the nationality of its owner, that decides the ship's nationality. Polish legislation allows only Polish ships to fly Polish colors; contary to that of Panama and other Latin American countries that permit the use of their colors for payment by alien ships. ▷ Flag.

JUS CADUCUM. *Latin* = "the right to derelict property". An international term with dual meaning: (1) for a concept in Roman law concerning heirless and non-bequeathed property; a synonym for lawlessness; (2) for appropriation of derelict property.

JUS CIRCA SACRA. *Latin* = "the law is greater than religion". A principle of supremacy of state law over ecclesiastic law granting to the state a number of rights restricting ecclesiastic rule in favor of the state advocated by Luther's reformation movement and further by government of many contemporary states, thus becoming a cause for international conflicts. After the separation of the church and state in many countries, some elements of *jus circa sacra* were preserved. Eight detailed laws arose from *jus circa sacra*:
jus domini in bona ecclesiastica or the possibility to control and secularize church estates;
jus cavendi or a ban on ecclesiastic activities inconsistent with the interests of the states;
jus inspicionis, or the right to keep under surveillance not only the activities exercised by church hierarchy, but also its relations with the Holy See;
jus placeti regii, or the need to obtain permission of the government to publish or read at the pulpit any papal writs;
jus exclusive, or the right to disagree to accept nominees to bishoprics;
jus appelationis tamquam ab abusu, or the right to appeal to civil authorities enjoyed by each citizen if he disagrees with verdicts passed by ecclesiastic authorities;

jus advocatiae, or the right to defend the church by the state acting in the capacity of a patron;

jus reformandi, or the right to recognize other denominations and to influence reforms in the church system.

JUS CIVILE. Latin = 'civil law'. An international term for the oldest of national legal systems in Europe based on civil law applied in ancient Rome only to Roman citizens as opposed to ▷ ius gentium to non-Roman citizens of the Empire.

R.L. BLEDSOE, B.A. BOCZEK, *The International Law Dictionary,* Oxford, UK, 1987.

JUS COGENS. *Latin* = "invariable law". A principle stating that there exist basic legal rules in international law which are to be applied unconditionally and may not be altered or waived by particular states, e.g., the ban on homicide. The UN International Law Commission facing many controversial opinions abandoned its attempt to register rules related to *jus cogens*. The 1969 Vienna Convention on the Law of Treaties determined in art. 59 that the formula of *jus cogens* was adopted and recognized by the international community of states as a rule which did not permit any deviation and modification could be made only through another rule of universal international law having the same character. In international law *jus cogens* is the opposite of ▷ *jus dispositivum*.

R.L. BLEDSOE, B.A. BOCZEK, *The International Law Dictionary,* Oxford, 1987.

JUS CONTRA BELLUM. *Latin* = "anti-war law". An international term for norms of international law banning aggressive wars and warmongering.

JUS DENEGATA. *Latin* = "a refusal to provide legal protection". An international term for failing to grant or refusing to grant legal protection to which nationals of alien states are entitled, commonly in cases of civil or criminal wrongdoings.

JUS DISPOSITIVUM. *Latin* = "law of disposition". An international term for relatively binding law applied until the parties have settled the question according to their will. Contrary to ▷ *jus cogens*.

JUS GENTIUM. = "law of peoples". An international term for the oldest form of international public law.

R.L. BLEDSOE, B.A. BOCZEK, *The International Law Dictionary,* Oxford, 1987.

JUS IN BELLO. *Latin* = "martial legal rules". An international term describing laws, customary and those contained in international conventions (foremost of which are the Geneva and The Hague conventions), as well as legal acts determining relations among states: neutral and belligerent. *Jus in bello* has developed since the 16th century mainly through bilateral treaties between warring parties; since Aug. 22, 1864, the date of the First Geneva Conference, through multilateral conventions, of which of particular importance were the legal acts

passed by the UN during World War II and UN Conventions.

JUS LEGATIONIS. *Latin* = "the right of legation". An international term for rights vested in an envoy to an alien country.

JUS NATURALE. *Latin* = "natural law". A Roman legal concept based on reason and the adaptability of people to live together.

R.L. BLEDSOE, B.A. BOCZEK, *The International Law Dictionary,* Oxford, 1987.

JUS PRIMI OCCUPANTIS. *Latin* = "the right of first occupation". An international term used in colonial times for granting the right to annex overseas territories to their European discoverers.

JUS PROTECTIONIS. *Latin* = "the right to protection". An international term for norms ensuring legal protection.

JUS PUBLICUM EUROPAEUM. *Latin* = "European public law". An international term promoted mostly by German lawyers in the 19th century; a Eurocentric term for an imperialist concept recognizing superiority of state law over international law.

JUS RESISTENDI. *Latin* = "the right of resistance". An international term for resistance against injustice. ▷ Theology of liberation.

JUS SANGUINIS. Latin = 'the right of blood'. An international term for a norm applied in the European countries when granting nationality on the basis of parental citizenship. In the UK and the USA the norm is ▷ *jus soli*.

R.L. BLEDSOE, B.A. BOCZEK, *The International Law Dictionary,* Oxford, 1987.

JUS SOLI. *Latin* = "the right of land". An international term for a norm applied in various countries under which nationality is granted respectively of the place of birth.

R.L. BLEDSOE, B.A. BOCZEK, *The International Law Dictionary,* Oxford, 1987.

JUS TALIONIS. *Latin* = "the right to retaliation". An international medieval term for a customary law sanctioning retaliation (e.g. shooting hostages or burning of open cities and villages); considered contradictory to the provisions of international law.

A.K. KUHN, 'The Execution of Hostages', in: *American Journal of International Law,* No. 36, 1942.

JUSTITIA ET PAX. A shortened name of the Papal Commission for Justice and Peace.

JUSTICE. An international term for basic rules for fair settlement in relations between individuals and states; subject of the law of nations, the interpreter of which is the International Court of Justice in The Hague; double ethical norm: for interhuman relations, *iustitia commutativa,* and in relation to society, divided by rights and duties of citizens, ius titia distributiva. In law – *iustitia legalis* – criteria of

justice serve the administration of justice. The French Revolution, which was the first to establish the office of Minister of Justice (ministre de la Justice) on May 27, 1771, was also the first to introduce the term social justice (justice sociale), later developed by various philosophical trends and ideological movements. Struggle for social justice became the chief motivating power for the international workers' movement. In Oct., 1971 the World Bishops' Synod of the Catholic Church devoted its debates primarily to the problem of social justice, considered to be "the widest, the most important and the most urgent in the world of our time," requiring from the Church a "courageous return to basic recommendations of the Gospel in this respect."

G. DEL VECCHIO, *La Giustizia,* Roma, 1946.

JUSTICIALISMO. A Latin-American term for a program of social justice formulated Feb. 24, 1947 by the President of Argentina General J. Peron in the so-called Declaration on Workers' Rights and then propagated without success in other Latin American countries as a Pan-American idea.

Declaración de los Derechos de Trabajadores, Buenos Aires, 1947; J. PERÓN, *El Concepto Justicialista,* Madrid, 1968,

JUSTITZMORD. *German* = "judicial murder." An international term for a death sentence handed down on an innocent person by a court on the basis of circumstantial evidence, false testimony, or non-admission by the court of proof of innocence. The term appeared in 1777 in France: *Meurtre juridique,* but in 1788 became widespread in German.

JUST AND UNJUST WAR. ▷ Belum justum et iniustum.

JUST WAR THEORY. ▷ Ius ad Bellum.

JUTE. A subject of international co-operation. Organizations reg. with the UIA:

Association of European Jute Industry, f. 1954, Paris. Publ.: *Jute Statistical Yearbook.*
Common Market Jute Industrial Committees, f. 1958, Paris.
European Association for the Trade in Jute Products, f. 1970, The Hague, Consultative status with UNCTAD, FAO.
Organization of Jute Exporting Countries, est. 1976, New Delhi, by the governments of Bangladesh, India, Nepal and Thailand representing *c.* 65% of world production and *c.* 93% of export.

In June 1984 the International Jute Council of the International Jute Organization est. 1976 sponsored by UNCTAD was convened.
On Jan. 9, 1986 the first International Jute Agreement valid until 1991 came into force.

UN Chronicle, February 1978, p. 31; *Yearbook of International Organizations;* KEESING's *Record of World Events,* 1986, No. 7.

JUVENILE DELINQUENCY. A subject of international research under the aegis of UNESCO. In Rome 1968 a Social Defence Research Institute of the UN was founded.

UN Yearbook, 1963, pp. 311.

K

KA'BA OR KA'BAH. A shrine of worship in the courtyard of the Great Mosque at Mecca, Saudi Arabia, location of a cult and pilgrimages of believers in Islam, who come there each year.

KABUL. Capital of Afghanistan since 1773, in south central Asia; on the Kabul River; pop. 1,036,000 in 1982. Occupied by British troops 1839, 1842 and 1879. Soviet troops 1979–1989. ▷ Afghanistan.

The Europa Yearbook 1987. A World Survey, Vol. I, London, 1987.

KAGERA. A river 400 km long in central Africa, subject of a border treaty between Uganda and Rwanda on the joint management of the navigable part of the Kagera, signed in Apr., 1971.
Organization reg. with the UIA:

Organization for the Management and Development of the Kagera River, f. 1978, Kigali, Rwanda. Members: Mali, Mauritania, Senegal.

The Europa Yearbook 1988. A World Survey, Vol. I, London, 1988.

KAHUZI BIEGA. National Park of Zaïre, included in the ▷ World Heritage UNESCO List. In the spectacular landscapes of two extinct volcanoes, Mounts Kahuzi and Biega, are to be found numerous characteristic species, viz.: chimpanzees, baboons, forest elephants, giant forest hogs, hyraxes, etc. At a height of between 2100 and 2400 meters is a sizeable population of mountain gorillas. On account of the protection which they receive, this park is a sanctuary of outstanding importance.

UNESCO, *A Legacy for All,* Paris, 1984.

KAIROS DOCUMENT 1985. A Christian South African declaration of 150 theologues and laymen, signed in Sept. 1985 in the Johannesburg Institute of Contextual Theology.
The highlights:

"The minority regime elected (in South Africa) by one small section of the population is given an explicit mandate to govern in the interests of and for the benefit of the white community. It became an enemy of the people, a tyrant".

The Document, called Kairos ("Moment of truth") demanded the replacing of a such regime by a democratically elected government adding that, the Christian churches should offer resistance, participate in civil disobedience and regard violence with understanding in the spirit of the ▷ Theology of Liberation.

KEESING's *Contemporary Archive,* No. 11, 1986.

KAKADU NATIONAL PARK. Australian natural site, included in the ▷ World Heritage UNESCO List, situated in the Alligator River basin. It covers an area of over 6000 sq. km and extends from the sea to the sandstone plateaux. It provides protection for the rarest animals in the continent. The first inhabitants of Australia landed here 50,000 years ago. Several groups of aborigines live inside the park and the oldest examples of their cave art are to be found here.

UNESCO, *A Legacy for All,* Paris, 1984.

KALININGRAD. Formerly German; Königsberg, Polish: Królewiec, city and sea port and capital of Kaliningrad oblast of the Russian SSR in western European USSR, on the Pregolya River and the Gulf of Kaliningrad on the Baltic Sea. Pop. Jan. 1, 1986 city 389,000. Founded 1255 by the Teutonic Knights, from 1340 a member of the Hanseatic League. In 1457 residence of the grand master of the order of Teutonic Knights; in feudal dependence on the King of Poland until 1701, the coronation in Königsberg of the King of Prussia. Immanuel Kant (1724–1804), author of *Zum Ewigen Frieden* (To Perpetual Peace) was a teacher at the University f. 1599. On Aug. 2, 1945 ceded to the USSR under the Potsdam Agreement. Naval base of the USSR on the Baltic and a commercial port open in winter. Headquarters of the Baltic Research Institute of Marine Fisheries. In 1984 the *Kaliningrad-Nieftiegazprom* initiated the oil drilling in the Baltic seabed in Gulf of Kaliningrad, near the Taran peninsula.

KAMIKAZE. *Japanese:* divine wind. The pilot of a Japanese combat aircraft filled with explosives directed suicidally at an enemy target. The first kamikaze flights took place Oct. 25, 1944, the last at the beginning of Aug., 1945. A total of *c.* 500 Japanese pilots were lost in kamikaze flights. The initiator of "Action Kamikaze" was Vice-Admiral Oniski, who committed harakiri on Aug. 15, 1945.

KAMPALA. The capital of Uganda since 1962; seat of the East African Development Bank, intergovernmental institution of Kenya, Tanzania and Uganda.

KAMPUCHEA. Member of the UN. Formerly Cambodia. Democratic Kampuchea. Country in south-east Asia on the Indochina Peninsula. Borders on Thailand, Laos and Vietnam. Area: 181,035 sq. km. Pop. 1986 est.: 7,492,000; 1981 census: 6,682,000 (1962 census: 5,729,000; 1971 – 7,700,000). Capital: Phnom Penh with *c.* 600,000 inhabitants 1983 (in 1971 *c.* 2,500,000). Official language: Khmer. Currency: one Riel = 100 sens. National Day: January 7, Liberation Day. Member of the UN since Dec. 14, 1955 and all its specialized agencies save the IFC, WIPO, IFAD, UNIDO and GATT. International relations: sovereign Cambodian monarchy under formal French protectorate 1863–1942; 1943–45 under Japanese occupation; since 1945 in the Federation of Indochina. On May 6, 1947 proclaimed constitutional monarchy and French dependency as member of the French Union: Since 1949 affiliated country of the French Union. Independence guaranteed by the Geneva Conference for Indochina July 22, 1954 which set up an International Control Commission composed of representatives of Canada, Poland and India. After complete withdrawal of French troops, the Cambodian Assembly on Sept. 25, 1955 announced its withdrawal from the French Union and changes in the country's constitution. Cambodia participated in the Indochina Geneva Conference May 16, 1961–July 21, 1962. In June, 1962 the International Court of Justice ruled in favor of Cambodia in its dispute with Thailand over ▷ Preah Vihear temple. In the southern part of Cambodia the Front Unie National du Kampuchea FUNK was founded under Prince Sihanouk on May 3, 1970 and assumed political control over the Liberation Army. On Apr. 17, 1975 the Liberation Army captured Phnom Penh. On Jan. 5, 1976 a new constitution entered into force, changing the name of the Khmer Republic into Kampuchea. The Red Khmer regime under Pol Pot was accused in 1978 by the People's Revolutionary Council of having killed millions during three years. On Dec. 2, 1978 the United Front of National Salvation of Cambodia was founded. Border frictions with Vietnam were subject of disputes and negotiations in: 1960, 1964, 1966, 1967, 1977, 1978. On Jan. 7, 1979 the Salvation Front together with Vietnamese troops seized Phnom Penh. On Jan. 11–12, 1979 the UN Security Council considered the new situation in Kampuchea; the majority (13:2) accused Vietnam of armed intervention into the internal affairs of Kampuchea. The resolution was vetoed by the USSR. On Nov. 14, 1979 the majority of the UN General Assembly (91:21 with 29 abstentions) have not accepted the replacement of the Pol Pot delegation by the Salvation Front representation, and called upon Vietnam to withdraw its forces from Kampuchea. A similar resolution was adopted in Nov., 1980 by the UN General Assembly. An International Conference on Kampuchea called for by the 1980 UN General Assembly decision was held in July, 1981 in New York. A Declaration on Kampuchea was adopted reaffirming the elements of political settlement. In 1982 the UN General Assembly in Res. 37/S deplored continued foreign armed intervention and occupation in Kampuchea, reaffirmed its 1981 decision to reconvene the International Conference at an appropriate time and reiterated appeals for the cessation of hostilities and continued humanitarian relief.
On July 23, 1982, Kampuchea proclaimed that Kampuchea's territorial waters extended 12 nautical miles, as determined by the French–Siamese Treaty of 1907, but the contiguous zone extended for a further 72 nautical miles and the exclusive economic zone and the continental shelf extended 200 nautical miles from the coast. In July 1982, Kampuchea and Vietnam signed an agreement on the delimitation of the territorial waters of the two countries, and on July 20, 1983 an agreement on the delimitation of the border.
During sessions of the UN General Assembly the majority in 1983 (105 to 23 with 19 abstentions) and in 1984 (110 to 22 with 18 abstentions) accepted similar resolutions as in 1979–82.
In Kampuchea a 'Day of Hatred' for the genocidal Pol Pot-Ieng Sary regime to remember, condemn and whip up more vigorously and broadly hatred against the Red Khmer and GATT is celebrated annually on May 20.

L.P. BRIGS, *The Ancient Khmer Empire,* Philadelphia, 1951; M.F. HERZ, *A Short History of Cambodia from the days of Angkor to the Present,* London, 1958; T. FITZSIMONIS (ed.), *Cambodia, its People, its Society, its Culture,* New Haven, Conn., 1959; R. MIGOT, *Les Khmers,* Paris, 1960; R.M. SOUNTH, *Cambodia's Foreign Policy,* Ithaca, N.Y., 1965; D.W. WAINHOUSE, *International Peace Observation,* Baltimore, 1966, pp. 512–525; F. DEBRÉ, *La Révolution de la Forêt,* Paris, 1976; J. BARRON, A. PAUL, *Murder of a Gentle Land,* New York, 1977; F. PONCHAUD, *Cambodia, Year Zero* 1978; W. SHAWCROSS, *The Sides: Nixon, Kissinger and the Destruction of Cambodia,* London, 1979; *Yearbook of the UN 1979,* pp. 306–307, New York, 1982; *UN Chronicle,* December, 1983, pp. 27–33. W. SHAWCROSS, *The Quality of Mercy: Cambodia Holocaust and Modern Conscience,* New York, 1984; *The Europa Year Book 1984. A World Survey,* Vol. I, p. London, 1984; M. VICKERY, *Kampuchea, Politics, Economics and Society,* London, 1986; KEESING's *Record of World Events,* No. 6, 1988.

KANAGAWA TREATY, 1854. An unequal peace and trade treaty between the USA and the empire of Japan, signed on Mar. 31, 1854 in Kanagawa (Japanese port from 1858 joined to Yokohama),

K

initiating an "open door" policy in the Far East; establishing in art. 2 that:

"the port of Shimoda in the duchy of Idzu, as well as the port of Hakodate in the duchy of Matsati, are recognized by Japan as open ports for American ships where they will be able to supply themselves with available food, water, stores, coal and other articles as needed."

W.M. MALLOY, *Treaties, Conventions*, Washington, DC, 1910, Vol. 1, p. 96; *Major Peace Treaties of Modern History*, New York, 1967, Vol. II, pp. 759–762.

KANAKY. ▷ New Caledonia.

KANGWANE. ▷ Bantu Homelands.

KANONENFUTTER. *German* = "cannon fodder." An international term, coined during World War I in Germany after the blood bath of young soldiers sent to the western front.

KANONEN STATT BUTTER. *German* = "Guns before butter." A German austerity slogan during World War I and since 1936 in the German III Reich.

KARACHI. A former capital of Pakistan, population 1981 census: 5,103,000, 1949–59; seat of the World Federation of Islamic Missions and of the World Muslim Congress.

Yearbook of International Organizations; J. PAXTON ed., *The Statesman's Yearbook 1987–88*, London, 1987.

KARAFUTO. ▷ Pacific Ocean Washington Treaty, 1921.

KARAIMI OR KARAITES. An ethnic group of Turkish origin and Karaist creed (▷ Karaism) from the 14th century found in Poland, Lithuania, Crimea and the Ukraine, as well as Turkey, Egypt, France and USA, an offshoot of Judaism. The Karaim community in Israel near Ramla totals about 12,000 people, the majority being immigrants from Egypt.

A. ZAJACZKOWSKI, *Karaims in Poland, History, Language, Folklore, Science*, Warsaw, 1961.

KARAISM OR QARAIS. A Jewish religious sect originating in Persia in the 8th century, which rejected the Talmud and accepted only the Bible.

Z. ANKORI, *Karaites in Byzantium: the Formative Years, 970–1100*, London, 1959; *Encyclopaedia Judaica*, Vol. 9, pp. 923–945.

KARAT OR CARAT. A small measure of mass used for weighing jewelry, international term of dual meaning: (1) the content of gold in alloy metal; three categories of fineness exist: 29, 18 and 14 carat gold. (2) a jewelers unit for the mass of a precious stone, unified 1907 by the International Bureau of Weights and Measures in the metric system as 0.2 grams; in Great Britain up to 1971 –0.205 grams.

KARELIA. Northwest European region of the USSR bordering Finland in the west and the White Sea in the east and from the Kola Peninsula in the north to Lakes Ladoga and Onega in the south. Subject of disputes between Russia and Sweden (Treaty of Nystad 1721); in the 20th century object of military conflicts between the Soviet Union and Finland (Peace Treaties 1940, 1944). In 1918 the northern part of Karelia with the city of Vyborg fell to Finland, while the south became on July 25, 1923 the Karelian SSR. On the strength of the peace treaty ending the Finno-Soviet War, Mar. 12, 1940, the Soviet Union gained exclusive possession of the Karelo–Finnish SSR, as it was then called. Since Jul. 16, 1955 the Karelian Autonomous SSR. Area 172,400 sq. km. Population Jan. 1, 1985 official

778,000. According to the 1979 census: 11.1% are of Karelian nationality, 71.3% Russians, 8.1% Byelorussian, 3.2% Ukranians and 2.7% Finns. Capital Petrozavodsk with 259,000 inhabitants on Jan. 1, 1986.

LIVRE ROUGE. *Document russo-finlandais concernant la Carelie Orientale*, Moscow, 1922; TH. KALIYARVI, "The Question of East Carelia", in: *American Journal of International Law*, No. 18, 1924; H. FORTUNI, *La question carelienne*, Paris, 1925; *East Carelia. A Survey of the Country and its Population and a Review of the Carelian Question*, Helsinki, 1932; P.E. LYDOLPH, *Geography of the USSR*, New York, 1970; *The Europa Year Book. A World Survey 1984*, Vol. 1, pp. 414 and 871, London, 1984; J. PAXTON ed., *The Statesman's Yearbook 1987–88*, London, 1987.

KARELIAN ISTHMUS. An isthmus between the Gulf of Finland and Ladoga Lake (north-west European USSR), 144.8 km long and from 40.2 to 112.6 km wide. Russian under the Treaty of Nystad 1721 with Sweden; Finnish 1917–44; since the 1944 Soviet Peace Treaty with Finland, part of the Karelian Autonomous Soviet Socialist Republic.

KARLOVE VARY DECLARATION, 1967. The final act of the Conference of the European Communist and Workers Parties at Karlove Vary, Czechoslovakia, in Apr., 1967. Participants from Austria, Belgium, Bulgaria, Czechoslovakia, Cyprus, Denmark, Finland, France, the FRG, the GDR, Great Britain, Greece, Hungary, Italy, Luxembourg, Poland, Spain, Sweden, Switzerland, and the USSR.

KARLOVICI OR KARLOWITZ TREATY, 1699. A peace treaty between Austria, Poland and Venice on one hand and the Ottoman Empire on the other, signed Jan. 26, 1699 in Karlovici Sremski, north Serbia; called also Karlovitz Treaty.

Major Peace Treaties of Modern History, New York, 1967, Vol. II, pp. 869–882.

KARNTEN. ▷ Carinthia.

KASHMIR. The former princely state in northwest India, northeast Pakistan and southwest China, with a 228,800 sq. km area; territory divided since 1956 into two parts: the Indian state Jammu and Kashmir, with capital city Srinagar, and the Pakistani part Azad-Kashmir, with capital Muzzafarabad. ▷ Jammu and Kashmir.

LORD BIRDWOOD, *Two Nations and Kashmir*, London, 1956; S. SANGULI, *The Origins of War in South Asia: Indo-Pakistan Conflicts Since 1947*, Boulder, Colo., 1986.

"KASHMIR PRINCESS". An Air India plane chartered by the government of Chinese People's Republic in Apr., 1955 for the purpose of transporting the Chinese delegation to the Bandung Conference in Indonesia. After stopping in Hong Kong, this plane blew up over Indonesian territorial waters. In 1971 the results of the investigation were made public: the cause of the catastrophe was a time-bomb placed on board at Hong Kong airport by a technician who was bribed by Taiwan intelligence. The plotters of the outrage fled to Taiwan, where the authorities refused their extradition.

KEESING's *Contemporary Archive*, 1955.

KATANGA. ▷ Shaba.

KATMANDU. The capital of Nepal since 1768, seat of a UN Information Center.

KATMANDU VALLEY. A natural site of Nepal, included in the ▷ World Heritage UNESCO List. Seven groups of buildings make up the heritage of the valley. These are the royal squares in the three large cities of Kathmandu, Patan and Bhaktapur, and the sacred enclosures of Swagambhu, Bodnath, Pashupati and Changy Narayan. A total of 132 monuments have been safeguarded.

UNESCO, *A Legacy for All*, Paris, 1984.

KATYŃ CASE, 1943. Katyń, a village in west central European USSR, west of Smolensk, occupied by the Germans during World War II, from Aug., 1941 to Sept., 1943. On Apr. 13, 1943 the Germans announced the discovery in the Katyń Forest of mass graves of about 10,000 Polish officers and accused the Soviets of having massacred them. Two days later the Soviet government published a communiqué to the effect that Polish prisoners of war who were engaged in construction work west of Smolensk had been captured and executed by German units, 1941. On Apr. 17, 1943 the Polish government in exile in London asked the International Committee of the Red Cross to examine the situation on the spot but under the pressure from their allies withdrew their proposal of an investigation and issued a following communiqué: "The Polish government condemns all crimes performed on Polish citizens and denies the right to anyone to exploit them in political games. Whoever is guilty of this atrocities against the Polish nation should be punished." According to Polish sources there were 9361 Polish officers and 181,223 soldiers of lower rank interned in the USSR in Sept., 1939. The officers were confined in three camps, at Kozielsk, Starobielsk and Ostaszków. On Apr. 26 1943 the Soviet government severed diplomatic relations with the Polish government. The Katyń case against the German units was presented by the Soviet Prosecutor during the Nuremberg Trial, 1946, but the case was not mentioned in the verdict of the International Military Trial. The postwar investigations, never again supported by the Soviet Union, led to the conclusion that the Polish officers had been killed before the Soviet evacuation of the Katyń region.

In April 1987 the USSR and Poland established a Polish–Soviet Commission charged with clearing up the 'blank spots' in the history of the two countries relations since 1918, including 'the circumstances of the Katyń tragedy'. In March 1988, as the subject of Katyń has remained untouched by the Commission, 59 Polish intellectuals appealed to Soviet intellectuals to speak out about the 'most sensitive issues in Polish–Soviet history'.
The letter says:

"The truth must be told. That word is demanded from us by the debt of memory to those murdered and by the conviction that this is an essential condition for radical change to the relations between our two nations . . . The time has come for a public dialogue, a dialogue of free and independent people unrestricted by official visits and diplomatic agreements. We want relations from which servility, lies and the danger of repression are eliminated".

On February 8, 1989 the Polish officials in the joint Polish–Soviet Commission investigating the Katyń massacre published a secret wartime report of the Polish Red Cross setting the date of the murders between March and May of 1940, one year before Germany invaded the Soviet Union. On February 20, 1989, the inscription on the Katyn Cross erected by the Polish Government in 1985: "To the Victims of the Nazis 1941" was changed to: "To the Victims of the Soviet NKVD 1940".

KEESING's *Contemporary Archive*, Apr. 24, 1943; *The Trial of German Major War Criminals. Proceedings of the International Military Tribunal Sitting at Nurem-*

berg, Germany, 42 Vols., London, 1946–48, Vol. 7, p. 16; Vol, 8, p. 226; Vol. 12, pp, 19 and 329; Vol. 15, pp. 279–282, 348 and 361; Vol. 17, pp. 324, 328–335, 341–362; Vol. 18, pp. 2–3, 11–22, 29–30, 131–132; J. MACKIEWICZ, *Katyń Wood Murders,* London, 1951; L. FITZGIBBON, *Katyn. A Crime Without Parallel,* London, 1971; J.K. ZAWODNY, *Death in the Forest,* University of Notre Dame Press, 1972. A. MOSZYN-SKI (ed.), *Lista Katyńska. Jeńcy obozów Kozielsk, Ostaszków, Starobielsk, zaginieni w Rosji Sowieckiej* (A Katyń List. The Prisoners of war of the Koselsk, Starobelsk and Ostashkov Camps). London, 1977; *The Katyn Crime,* London, 1977: W. SWIANIEWICZ, *W cieniu Katynia* (In Katyn Shadow), Paris, 1978; *Zbrodnia Katyńska w świetle dokumentow. Z przedmową Władysława Andersa,* London, 1982 (10th edition); L. JERZEWSKI, *Dzieje Sprawy Katynia,* New York, 1983; H. de MONTFORT, *Le Massacre de Katyń, crime russe ou crime allemand?,* Paris, 1986; *Polish Resistance Movement in Poland and Abroad 1939–1945,* Warszawa, 1987.

KEKKONEN PLANS, 1963 AND 1978. Two disengagement proposals debated by the Scandinavian states. A proposal for Scandinavian denuclearization presented by the President of Finland, Urho Kekkonen to Denmark, Norway and Sweden on May 28, 1963, rejected by the Nordic Council in Feb., 1965; and on May 8, 1978 a plan concerning the drafting of a treaty between Denmark, Finland, Norway, and Sweden on the mutual control of armaments, submitted to Scandinavian states also by President U. Kekkonen. ▷ Denuclearized Zones; ▷ Rapacki Plan, 1957; ▷ Tito Plan, 1958.

KEESING's *Contemporary Archive,* 1963 and 1968.

KELVIN. Symbol: K. An international unit of thermodynamic temperature, defined by the General Conference of Weights and Measures (CGPM), 1967, as follows: "The kelvin, unit of thermodynamic temperature, is the fraction 1/273.16 of the thermodynamic temperature of the triple point of water." Since 1960 one of base units of the International System of Units (▷ SI).

KELVIN SCALE. The so-called absolute thermometric scale worked out by the English physicist, Lord Kelvin, alias William Thomson (1824–1907), who in 1848 as the point of zero took the temperature of absolute zero = − 273.15°C, the temperature of freezing water is + 273.15°K, boiling water + 373.15°K.

KEMALISM. An international term for political doctrine proclaimed May 13, 1935 in Ankara to the Congress of Republican People's Party of Turkey by President Kemal Atatürk (1880–1938).

T. ALP, *Le Kemalisme,* Paris, 1937.

KEMBS CANAL AGREEMENT, 1922. An agreement concerning the scheme for the Kembs lateral canal, with *procès-verbal* signed May 10, 1922 in Strasbourg, by the governments of Germany, France and Switzerland, in application of art. 358 of the Versailles Treaty and in relation to the recommendations of the Central Rhine Navigation Commission.

LNTS, Vol. 26, p. 267.

KENNAN DOCTRINE. ▷ Containment Doctrine, 1947.

KENNAN PLAN, 1957. A plan presented by the American diplomat, George Kennan, Nov., 1957, concerning the uniting of Germany on the following terms: withdrawal of armed forces from West Europe by Western powers and of Soviet arms from East Europe; armament limitation of united Germany and prohibition of its participating in any

military bloc. None of the governments supported the Kennan Plan.

KEESING's *Contemporary Archive,* 1957.

KENNEDY DOCTRINE, 1961. A principle of US foreign policy in Latin America formulated July 5, 1961 by President John F. Kennedy (1917–63) in a speech to the Conference of the Alliance for Progress in Punta del Este, that the US government would give economic and military assistance only to those countries of the region which have democratic representative governments established through general elections.

L.F. SIMONS, *The Kennedy Doctrine,* New York, 1974.

KENNEDY ROUND. The sixth (since 1947) round of GATT negotiations concerning tariffs, held in 1962–67 and initiated by the US President J.F. Kennedy through the passage of the Trade Expansion Act which allowed the US government to gradually lower tariffs by 50% within a five-year period and on the condition of reciprocity. After protracted talks within the GATT, a trade agreement was signed on June 30, 1967, the eve of the expiration of the American Trade Act, by Austria, Australia, Belgium, Canada, Ceylon, Chile, Czechoslovakia, Denmark, the Dominican Republic, Egypt, Finland, France, the FRG, Greece, Iceland, India, Indonesia, Israel, Jamaica, Japan, Malawi, the Netherlands, New Zealand, Nicaragua, Nigeria, Norway, Pakistan, Peru, Poland, Portugal, Sierra Leone, South Korea, Spain, Sweden, Switzerland, Trinidad and Tobago, Turkey, Uruguay, the UK, the USA, Yugoslavia. It provided for a 35% reduction in tariffs on most industrial articles not manufactured, or manufactured in small quantities by the developing countries; no agreement was reached regarding tropical products. According to the UNCTAD, only US $1 billion out of US $40 billion expected from concessions went to the developing countries. The Chairman of the GATT Executive Council observed that the Kennedy Round brought few tangible results to the developing countries. In his report of Sept. 7, 1967, R. Prebisch, then Secretary General of the UNCTAD, accused the rich countries and the Kennedy Round of having impaired the developing countries' share in world trade. In 1968–72, the West European signatories of the Kennedy Round agreements, as well as the USA, Israel and Japan, gradually brought down tariffs for certain products through a pre-planned reduction on Jan. 1 of each year. Total reduction was accomplished by Jan. 1, 1972.

The Foreign Policy Aspects of the Kennedy Round. Hearings before the Subcommittee on Foreign Affairs, Washington, DC, 1967; J. EVANS, "The Kennedy Round", in: *American Trade Policy,* London, 1972; A. SHONFIELD (ed.), *International Economic Relations of the Western World 1959–71,* Oxford, 1976.

KENNEL CLUBS. ▷ Dogs.

KENYA. Member of the UN. Republic of Kenya. State in East Africa on the Indian Ocean, bounded by Ethiopia, Somalia, Tanzania, Uganda and Sudan. Area: 580,367 sq. km. Pop. 1989 est. 23,727,000 (1969 census: 10,942,000; 1979: 15,327,000). Capital city: Nairobi with 835,000 inhabitants (1981). Official languages: English and Swahili; since 1973 exclusively Swahili. Currency: one Kenyan Shilling = 100 cents. GNP per capita 1987: US $330. National Day: Dec. 12, proclamation of independence, 1963.
Member of the UN since Dec. 17, 1963 and all its specialized agencies; member of the Commonwealth, OAU and is an ACP state of the EEC.

International relations: 1895–1920 British protectorate (East Africa Protectorate) and British colony until 1963. In 1952 a national liberation uprising broke out, led by the clandestine Mau-Mau organization under the leadership of Jomo Kenyatta. Independence proclaimed Dec. 12, 1963. Economic agreements with Tanzania and Uganda, 1983.

The Economic Development of Kenya, IBRD Baltimore, 1963; J. KENYATTA, *Haramble! The Prime Minister of Kenya, Speeches 1963–1964,* New York, 1964; R. COX, *Kenyatta's Country,* New York, 1966; A.M. MACPHEE, *Kenya,* New York, 1968; CENTRAL BANK OF KENYA, *Money and Banking in Kenya,* Nairobi, 1973; K. BOLTO, *Haramble Country: A guide of Kenya,* London, 1974; G. ARNOLD, *Kenyatta and the Politics of Kenya,* London, 1974; C. LEYS, *Underdevelopment in Kenya,* London, 1975; J.B. HOVELL, *Kenya: subject guide to official publications,* Washington, 1978; P. MUTALIK-DESAI, *Economic and Political Development in Kenya,* Bombay, 1979; A. HARLEWOOD, *The Economy of Kenya. The Kenyatta Era,* Oxford, 1980; S.W. LANDON, *Multinational Corporations in the Political Economy of Kenya,* London, 1981; R.J. COLLISON, *Kenya. Bibliography,* London, 1982; *Who's Who in Kenya 1982–83,* London, 1983; *The Europa Year Book 1984. A World Survey,* Vol. II, pp. 1847–1861 London, 1984.

KERGUÉLEN ISLANDS. One large and 300 small volcanic subantarctic islands, area: 7,125 sq km, with about 100 people working at research stations in 1987, in the South Indian Ocean, occupied by France in 1949; a scientific research station Port-aux-Français (92 members); part of the French Antarctic Territories.

Expéditions Polaires Français. Études et Rapports, Paris, 1949–59; J. PAXTON ed., *The Statesman's Yearbook 1987–88,* London, 1987.

KEY CURRENCIES. An international term for currencies which predominate in international monetary systems, thus in the capitalist system mainly American dollar, French franc, Japanese yen, FRG mark as well as other "hard currencies" of the remaining states in the Group of Ten. In the socialist system USSR rouble.

KGB. ▷ Intelligence Service.

KHALISTAN. On April 29, 1986, in the Golden Temple in ▷ Amritsar, India, a group of Sikhs called the Panthic Committee announced the establishment of a separate Sikh State Khalistan which was to seek formal recognition by India and Pakistan and a seat in the UN.

KEESING's *Contemporary Archive,* 1986, No. 8.

KIDNAPPER, KIDNAPPING. An international term for a criminal or a crime usually involving the abduction of a child or an adult for the purpose of gaining ransom or other benefits, e.g. the exchange of an abducted person for a person or persons imprisoned by a certain state; subject of inter-governmental agreements on mutual assistance in combatting kidnappers. In 1972 the USA proposed drafting an international convention on kidnapping as part of combatting international ▷ terrorism.

R. CLUTTERBUCK, *Kidnap, Hijack and Extortion. The Response,* London, 1987.

KIDNAPPING OF DIPLOMATS. A form of political action contrary to international law, known in various epochs. In the second half of the 20th century it appeared as a reaction to counter-revolutionary terror in some states of Latin America; for the first time Sept. 4, 1969 in Rio de Janeiro when the US ambassador to Brazil, B. Elbrick, was kidnapped and two days later was exchanged for 15 political prisoners from leftist un-

K

derground organizations (flown to Mexico by the government of Brazil); 1970 ten kidnappings of diplomats took place in Latin America; Mar. 4 an American diplomat in Guatemala, exchanged for 3 prisoners; March 11 in Sao Paulo, the consul general of Japan for 5 prisoners; March 24 in Buenos Aires, the Paraguayan consul, released after 4 days; March 24 in Santo Domingo the American air attaché, exchanged for 25 prisoners; Mar. 31 in Guatemala the ambassador of the FRG, C. von Spretti, whose corpse was found Apr. 5 (the government of Guatemala refused his exchange for prisoners); Mar. 31 in Porto Alegre (Brazil) an unsuccessful attempt to kidnap the US consul; June 30 in Rio de Janeiro, the ambassador of the FRG, E. von Helleben, exchanged for a group of prisoners; July 31 in Montevideo an agent of the CIA, an advisor to the Uruguay police, D. Mitrione, was killed, and the Brazilian consul, D. Gomide and a US agronomist, C. Fly, whose fate, in view of the refusal of the government of Uruguay to make an exchange for prisoners, remains unknown; Dec. 7 in Rio de Janeiro the Swiss ambassador, exchanged for 70 prisoners who were transported to Chile. Also, in 1970 three politicians were kidnapped in their own countries; in Guatemala the minister of foreign affairs T. Mohra, in Ecuador, the commander of the air force, General C. Rohn, and in Argentina General P. Aramburu (was put to death). In 1971 on Jan. 8 in Montevideo the British amabassdor, G. Jackson, was kidnapped. Similar in character were the actions of the Palestine organization "Black September" (1972–73). A separate case constituted the taking as hostages the American diplomatic personnel in Teheran in Nov., 1978, ▷ Iran; ▷ Hostages. Kidnapping is a violation of diplomatic privileges and immunities. On Oct. 28, 1972 a law took effect in the USA on the protection of foreign diplomats, introducing the principle that an attack on a representative of a foreign country is a federal crime, and not as hitherto a state crime. Demonstrations can take place no closer than 30 meters from an agency or residence of foreign diplomats. The UN General Assembly on Dec. 14, 1973, ratified the Convention on the Prevention and Punishment of Crimes Against Persons under International Protection, Among them Diplomats.

International Terrorism. A Select Bibliography, UN st/lib. 38, Sept. 21, 1973; P. WILKINSON, *Political Terrorism*, New York, 1975.

KIEL CANAL. A canal in Schleswig-Holstein, FRG, 98.1 km long, connecting the North Sea and the Baltic Sea; one of the main international artificial waterways in Europe; constructed 1887–95, it is the shortest water route between the mouth of the Elbe to the North Sea and the Kiel Gulf of the Baltic Sea; until 1918 closed to international navigation, internationalized by the Kiel proviso of the Versailles Treaty of July 28, 1919 in arts. 380–386. Art. 380 determined that:

"The Kiel Canal and its approaches shall be maintained free and open to vessels of commerce and of war of all nations."

Further articles defined the conditions of passage, the obligations of the German administrators of Kiel Canal as well as the jurisdiction of the League of Nations in debated issues. The first case in the name of the League was heard on Apr. 17, 1923 by the Permanent Court of International Justice in the dispute between Great Britain and the German Reich, the so-called Wimbledon Case. Kiel Canal was occupied by the French and English military forces from Nov., 1918 to Dec., 1925. On Nov. 16, 1936 the German III Reich refused to comply to arts. 380–386 of the Versailles Treaty. International

navigation was suspended until May 8, 1945, when it was again reinstated.

H.W.V. TEMPERLEY, *A History of the Peace Conference of Paris*, 6 Vols., London, 1920–24, Vol. 3, p. 242; KEESING's *Archiv der Gegenwart 1936*, pp. 2811–2812; W. BÖHNERT, "Zur völkerrechtlichen Lage des Kieler Kanals", in: *Recht und Diplomatie*, 1958.

KILLED IN THE SERVICE OF THE UNITED NATIONS. An official recognition given to those persons who lost their lives in the fulfillment of peaceful UN functions in regions of armed conflict.

UN Bulletin, February 15, 1953, p. 755.

KILOGRAM. Symbol: kg. An international unit of mass which was an integral part of the ▷ metric system, introduced Dec. 10, 1799 by the General Assembly of the French Republic; recognized by the International Metric Convention on May 20, 1875. The General Conference of Weights and Measures CGPM, 1889, legalized the international prototype made from an alloy of platinum and iridium and preserved in the International Bureau of Weights and Measures in the Breteuil pavilion in Sèvres near Paris. In 1901 the CGPM declared:

"(1) The kilogram is the unit of mass; it is equal to the mass of the international prototype of the kilogram; (2) The word weight denotes a quantity of the same nature as a force; the weight of a body is the product of its mass and the acceleration due to gravity; in particular, the standard weight of a body is the product of its mass and the standard acceleration due to gravity; (3) The value adopted in the International Service of Weights and Measures for the standard acceleration due to gravity is 980.665 cm/s², value already stated in the laws of some countries."

In 1960 the kilogram was integrated by the international ▷ SI system.

KILOLITER. An international capacity unit = 1000 liters, or approx. 1.31 cubic yards.

KILOMETER. An international length unit = 1000 meters, or approx. 0.62 miles. Square kilometer = 1,000,000 square meters, or approx. 0.3861 square miles.

KILOTON. International measure of the explosive yield of a nuclear weapon: 1,000 metric tons of Tri-Nitro-Toluene high explosive. The bomb detonated at Hiroshima in World War II had a yield of about 12-15 kilotons. ▷ Megaton.

J. GOLDBLAT, *Arms Control Agreements. A Handbook*, New York, 1983.

KILWA KISIWANI AND SONGO MANARI. Historical sites of Tanzania, included in the ▷ World Heritage UNESCO List. On these small islands, 230 kilometers to the south of Dar-es-Salaam, are a fort, several mosques and large houses built of coral. They recall the kingdom which, from the 13th century to the end of the Middle Ages, controlled a large part of the trade in the Indian Ocean.

UNESCO, *A Legacy for All*, Paris, 1984.

KINSHASA. The capital of Zaïre, population Dec. 31, 1986, including the common of Maluku, 2,778,281, since 1960; the present national name since 1966 (former colonial name Leopoldville). Seat of the UN Information Center.

The Europa Yearbook 1987. A World Survey, Vol. II, London, 1987.

KIP. A monetary unit of Laos; one kip = 100 at; issued by the Banque Nationale du Laos.

KIRIBATI. The Republic of Kiribati. Member of the Commonwealth. Coral atolls and volcanic islands of the Central Pacific; it comprises Banaba or Ocean Island, and groups of the Gilbert Islands, Phoenix Islands and Line Islands. A total land area 717 sq. km. Pop. 1987 est.: 66,250, almost all Micronesian. Capital: Tarawa with 22,148 inhabitants 1980. Official language: English. GNP per capita 1985 US $390. Currency: one Australian dollar = 100 cents. National Day: Nov. 1, Independence Day, 1979.
An ACP state with the EEC. Member of ICAO, WHO, IBRD, IFC, IDA, IMF and ITU.
International relations: the Gilbert and Ellice Islands were annexed by the British, 1892. A British colony, 1915–75. On Oct. 1, 1975 the Ellice Islands achieved independence as ▷ Tuvalu. The Gilbert Islands obtained self-government on Nov. 1, 1976 and independence on Nov. 1, 1979 as the Kiribati Republic.
A Treaty of Friendship with the USA signed 1979, was ratified by the USA on June 21, 1983.
The two year agreement from August 1986 with the USSR permitting it to fish within the 200 mile exclusive economic zone, has not been renewed in 1988.

Kiribati. Aspects of History, University of South Pacific, 1979; *UN Yearbook 1979*, pp. 1040–1041; *The Europa Year Book 1984. A World Survey*, Vol. II, pp. 1862–1865, London, 1984; KEESING's *Record of World Events*, June, 1987; KEESING's *Record of World Events*, May, 1988.

KISSINGER COMMISSION ON CENTRAL AMERICA, 1983–84. The US President R. Reagan convoked in Fall of 1983 a National Bi-Partisan Commission to investigate the political and social crisis of Central American states. The Commission under the chairmanship of Henry Kissinger, published on Jan. 10, 1984 report, supporting the policy of President R. Reagan in Central America and recommending US $8 billion economic assistance to the Central American region over five years and substantial military aid in the same time. The Commission also recommended a Literacy Corps for teaching people to read. The Kissinger report raised controversy among the Central American countries, and was not supported by the ▷ Contadora Group.

"More Money and More Guns", in: *Newsweek*, January 23, 1984.

KISSINGER–SONNENFELDT DOCTRINE, 1975. A doctrine made public in Apr., 1976 by the US Department of State in statements of the Secretary of State, Henry Kissinger, and his deputy, Helmut Sonnenfeldt, formulated in London at a meeting in Dec., 1975 with the US ambassadors in Europe, stating that the foreign policy of the US should support the socialist countries' aspirations for a more autonomous existence within the context of a strong Soviet geopolitical influence. The second part of the doctrine declared that, should communist parties come to power in Western Europe, the US would become an island and "the United States could be forced to manipulate various communist centers of power against each other."

'Text of Summary of Sonnenfeldt's Remarks on Eastern Europe and Kissinger's on Managing Emergence of Russia as Superpower', in: *International Herald Tribune*, April 12, 1976.

KIWANIS, INTERNATIONAL. An international club, f. 1915, Chicago. Clubs in America, Australia and Western Europe to "promote the adoption and application of higher social, business and professional standards." Publ. *The Kiwanis Magazine*. Reg. with the UIA.

Yearbook of International Organizations.

KLAYPEDA. A city in the Lithunian SSR with 196,000 inhabitants 1976. Between 1919 and 1939 subject of a dispute between Germany and Lithuania. The city located on the Kuron Gulf, includes the port of Klaypeda and the adjoining region with a total area of 2656 sq. km, inhabited at that time by a Lithuanian and German pop.; subject of a decision of the Great Powers, which in art. 99 of the Versailles Treaty included it within the boundaries of German East Prussia; initially under French military administration. On Nov. 11, 1921 the Lithuanian Constitution incorporated Klaypeda *de iure*; this took place *de facto* on Jan. 10, 1923 after the entry of the Lithuanian army and the acceptance of this situation by the Conference of Ambassadors with a stipulation, included in the convention on Klaypeda signed May 8, 1924 in Paris, that Klaypeda "will be an entity under the sovereignty of Lithuania benefiting from legislative, administrative and fiscal autonomy," whose limits were defined by the Lithuanian Republic in an appendix to the Convention. According to the Statute, Klaypeda was ruled by a governor appointed by the President of Lithuania and an autonomous Parliament and Directorate of Klaypeda. The German government, on Mar. 20, 1938, issued an ultimatum to the government of Lithuania in which it laid claim to Klaypeda and threatened the use of force. On Mar. 22, 1938 a Treaty was signed in Berlin on the incorporation of Klaypeda–Memel into the German III Reich. The Treaty was annulled by the liberation of Klaypeda Jan. 28, 1945 by the Soviet Army, its return to Lithuania, and by the Potsdam Treaty which set new boundaries for Germany.

Reichsgesetzblatt 1919, No. 140; *LNTS*, Vol. 29, pp. 85–115; *League of Nations Monthly Summary*, No. 12, 1923; A. GAIGALATÉ, *Klaipédos Krasto uzgrobimas 1939 metais*, Vilnius, 1959.

KLONDIKE. A region of Yukon Territory, northwestern Canada, on the Alaska border. The discovery of rich gold deposits in Bonnanza Creek, a tributary of the Klondike River, on Aug. 16, 1896, initiated a gold rush of over 100,000 persons from USA and Canada and provoked a diplomatic ▷ Alaska boundary controversy between Canada and the USA, resolved 1903.

D.F. PUTRAM (ed.), *The Canadian Northland*, London, 1956.

KLUANE NATIONAL PARK: WRANGEL ST. ELLIS NATIONAL MONUMENT. A common natural site of Canada and the USA, included in the ▷ World Heritage UNESCO List. This is the largest natural reservation in the world and lies on either side of the frontier separating Alaska from the Canadian Yukon. It consists of a huge chain of glaciers, most of which are expanding, lying within a mountain system which contains twelve peaks over 4500 meters high.

UNESCO, *A Legacy for All*, Paris, 1984.

KNITTING. A subject of international co-operation. Organizations reg. with the UIA:

Committee of the Knitting and Hosiery Industries of the EEC, f. 1958, Brussels.
International Federation of Knitting Technologists, f. 1955, Frauenfeld, FRG.

Yearbook of International Organizations.

KNOT. A special unit employed for marine navigation with value in SI units: 1 nautical mile per hour = (1852/3600) m/s. ▷ SI.

KNOW-HOW. An international term in the UN system for technical and technological knowledge, subject of international trade and transfer of technologies. Under Res. 2821/XXVI Dec. 16, 1971, the UN General Assembly declared itself in favor of propagating technology transfer, including know-how and licences.

KOH-I-NOOR. *Persian*: koh-i-nur = "mountain of light". A synonym for precious things, deriving from the name of a diamond acquired in the Punjab 1849 by the English, ever since the greatest treasure in the collection of British crown jewels; initially weighing 191 carats but after it was cut, 1852, its weight equals 108.93 carats.

UN Monthly Chronicle, January 1972.

KOLKHOZ. Abbreviation of Russian "kolektiv-noye hozyastvo" = co-operative farms. In the USSR farms administered by farmers' co-operatives. ▷ Sovkhoz.

KOMINFORM OR COMINFORM. The name commonly used for the Information Bureau of the Communist and Workers' Parties, ▷ Informbiuro.

KOMINTERN. Russian and German official abbreviation of Komunisticheski Internatsional and Kommunistische Internationale; English abbreviation Comintern. The Third International was founded in Moscow, Mar., 1919, by the First International Congress of Communist Parties as their main body. The First Congress witnessed the proclamation by V.I. Lenin of the principles of communism: the Second Congress established organizational forms; the Third Congress called for a worldwide mobilization to the struggle for victory of the proletarian majority. The 4th Congress of 1922 elaborated a program of a uniform working class front. Communist parties were members of the Communist International, forming its sections. The Congress elected a permanent body of the Komintern called the Executive Committee of the Communist International. After the outbreak of World War II the Executive Committee on May 15, 1943 adopted the decision on the dissolution of the Communist International. In 1939 communist parties in Komintern had 1,750,000 members in capitalist countries and 2,652,000 members in the USSR.

A. DEL ROSAL, *Los Congresos Obreros Internacionales en el Siglo XX*, México, DF, 1963; pp. 195–228; J. DEGRAS (ed.), *The Communist International 1919–1943. Documents*, 3 Vols. London–New York, 1956–65; T. PIRKER, *Komintern und Fashismus 1920–1940*, Stuttgart, 1966; W.S. SWORAKOWSKI, *The Communist International and Its Front Organizations: a research guide and checklist of holdings in American and European Libraries*, Stanford, 1967; *Komunisticheski International, Kratki istoricheski ocherk*, Moskva, 1969; F. FIRSOV, "Komintern", in: *Voprosy istorii KPSS*, No. 6, 1973; M. CABALLERO, *Latin America and the Comintern 1919–1943*, Cambridge, 1986.

KONKANI LANGUAGE. ▷ Goa, Daman and Diu.

KORAN OR QUR'AN. The sacred book of ▷ Islam, written in the Arabic language in the early 650s AD, composed of 114 suras (chapters); translated first into Persian, Turkish, Latin, Greek and Hebrew; in the 14th century in Spanish, in French 1648, in English 1649, in Russian 1716; first printed in Europe 1530. A modern Arabic official edition was printed in Cairo 1919.

R. BLACHERE, *Le Coran*, Paris, 1976.

KORCZAK JANUSZ, INTERNATIONAL LITERARY AWARD. An international award founded in 1978 on the initiative of Poland by the International Board on Books for Young People, to commemorate the well-known writer and educator, Janusz Korczak (Henryk Goldszmit), born in 1878, killed 1942 by the Nazis in a gas chamber in Treblinka together with children from the Orphanage at Krochmalna Street in Warsaw, who were his pupils. The first award winners were Astrid Lindgren (Sweden) and Bohumil Riha (Czechoslovakia). The award is granted every second year by the Polish section of the Board. Also Korczak Medals are granted.

J. KORCZAK, *Ghetto Diary*, New York, 1978; E. GIERAT, *A Polish Vademecum. A Handbook on Poles and other Soviet Dominated European Nations in the Free World*, Bethleem, Ct., USA, 1988, p. 45; B.J. LIPTON, *The King of Children. A Bibliography of Janusz Korczak*, New York, 1988.

KOREA. A land located in East Asia on the Sea of Japan, Yellow Sea and Korean Strait. Area: 220,277 sq. km. Population: *c.* 55,000,000 inhabitants in 1980. Borders with the People's Republic of China and USSR. From Sept. 2, 1945 divided into two administrations along the 38th parallel: South Korea, officially ▷ Korea Republic of, and North Korea, officially ▷ Korea Democratic People's Republic of.

International relations: in isolation from other countries to 1876, when Japan forced Korea to conclude a treaty on the establishment of diplomatic relations, in 1882 with the USA, in 1886 with interested European states. By the Shimonoseki Treaty of Apr. 17, 1895 China, at the demand of Japan, recognized Korea's full independence. Korea's growing dependence on Japan was followed by occupation and integration into the Japanese empire, 1910–45. The contemporary history of Korea was initiated by a joint declaration on Korea by the US President F.D. Roosevelt, President Chiang Kai-shek of China and the Prime Minister of the UK, W. Churchill, on Nov. 26, 1943 in Cairo:

"The three above-mentioned powers have not forgotten about the enslavement of the Korean nation and are determined to act in such a manner that this nation in due course will regain its freedom and independence."

As a result of an agreement between the USA and the USSR on Sept. 2, 1945, the Japanese occupation forces in Korea to the north of the 38th parallel surrendered to the Red Army, while those to the south of this parallel surrendered to the US Army. On Dec. 27, 1945, in Moscow, the Council of Ministers of Foreign Affairs of the Great Powers convened a mixed commission composed of the military commanders of US and USSR forces stationed in Korea with the task "of reconstructing an independent Korean state" by forming a temporary Korean government representing "Korean democratic parties and social organization." The commission debated from Mar. 20 to May 8, 1945, when it suspended its sessions *sine die*, since it was unable to agree on which 'democratic parties and social organizations" should be represented. On Sept. 17, 1947 the USA submitted the Korean question to the UN General Assembly, which in Res. 112/II, Feb. 14, 1947 stated that the Korean question "is primarily a matter for the Korean people itself and concerns its freedom and independence", and formed a Temporary Commission for establishing a national Korean government and overseeing the withdrawal of US and Soviet forces. The Commission was composed of representatives of Australia, Canada, China, India, Philippines, Salvador, Syria and the Ukrainian SSR. The latter refused to participate on the basis of arts. 106 and 107 of the UN Charter.

The *Everyman's United Nations. A Basic History of the Organization 1945 to 1963* informs about the crucial period for Korean history 1948–1953:

"Because the Commission was unable to enter North Korea and fulfill its task of observing Korea-wide elections, it consulted the Assembly's Interim Committee and was directed by the latter to implement the Assembly's program in such parts of Korea as were accessible to it. The Commission on May 10, 1948, observed elections only in South Korea, which led to the establishment of a government in South Korea on August 15, 1948. In September a separate government came into being in North Korea. having considered the Commission's report, the General Assembly declared that the Government of the Republic of Korea had been established as a lawful government in South Korea, based on elections which expressed the free will of the electorate of that part of Korea, and that this was the only such government in Korea. The Assembly recommended the withdrawal of the occupying forces, and, since the unification of all Korea had not been attained, it established a United Nations Commission on Korea of seven member states to lend its good offices to that end.

On July 28, 1949, the Commission reported that it had not been able to make any progress toward unification. It had observed the withdrawal, in June 1949, of the United States forces but not the reported withdrawal of those of the Soviet Union in December 1948. on October 21, 1949, the United Nations Commission on Korea was assigned the additional task of observing and reporting developments which might lead to military conflict in Korea.

On June 25, 1950, the Secretary-General was informed by the United States and the United Nations Commission on Korea that North Korean forces had invaded Korea that morning. On the same day the Security Council determined by 9 votes to none, with 1 abstention (Yugoslavia, and 1 member absent (USSR), that the armed attack was a breach of peace, called for withdrawal of North Korean forces to the thirty-eighth parallel, and the assistance of members in carrying out the resolution. (The USSR had not participated in the Council's work since January 13,1950, explaining that it did not recognize as legal any decision of the Council until "the representative of the Kuomintang Group had been removed". It resumed, however, attendance at the meetings on August 1, 1950, when the Presidency of the Council again devolved upon it under the system of monthly rotation).

On June 27, 1950 the Council adopted a United States draft resolution noting that the authorities in North Korea had neither ceased hostilities nor withdrawn their armed forces, and recommending that members furnish such asistance to the Repubic of Korea as might be necessary to repel the armed attack and restore international peace and security in the area. The vote was 7 to 1 (Yugoslavia), with 1 member absent (USSR), and with Egypt and India not voting but later indicating their positions as abstention from and acceptance of the resolution, respectively.

Also on June 27, 1950 the United States announced that it had ordered its air and sea forces to give cover and support to the troops of the Korean Government. On June 30 it informed the Council that it had ordered a naval blockade of the Korean coast and authorized the use of ground forces as a further response to the June 27 resolution.

Fifty-one member states expressed support for the stand taken by the Council, while five, including USSR, together with the People's Republic of China and the Democratic People's Republic of Korea, shared the view that the June 27, resolution was illegal because it had been adopted in the absence of two permanent members of the Council, The People's Republic of China and the Soviet Union also declared that the events in Korea were the result of an unprovoked attack by South Korean troops and demanded the cessation of United State intervention.

On July 7 the Council, by 7 votes to none, with 3 abstentions (Egypt, India, Yugoslavia) and 1 member absent (USSR), requested all member states providing military forces in pursuance of the Council's resolutions to make them available to a unified command under the United States. The next day General Douglas MacArthur, of the United States, was designated Commanding General. Subsequently, combatant units were provided by the following sixteen member states: Australia, Belgium, Canada, Colombia, Ethiopia, France, Greece, Luxembourg, the Netherlands, New Zealand, the Philippines, Thailand, Turkey, the Union of South Africa, the United Kingdom, and the United States. In addition, five nations – Denmark, India, Italy, Norway and Sweden – supplied medical units. The Republic of Korea also placed all its military forces under the Unified Command.

Korea's capital, Seoul, fell on June 28, 1950, and in August the United Nations forces were confined within a small area in southeast Korea. By mid-October, however, following an amphibious landing at Inchon, they had regained almost all the territory of the Republic of Korea and were advancing far into North Korea. Meanwhile, on October 7, 1950 the General Assembly adopted a resolution which recommended that "all appropriate steps be taken to ensure conditions of stability throughout Korea"; established the United Nations Commission for the Unification and Rehabilitation of Korea (UNCURK).

On November 6, 1950, a special report of the United Nations Command informed the Security Council that United Nations forces were in contact in North Korea with military units of the People's Republic of China. A representative of the People's Republic of China participated in the Council's subsequent combined discussion of complaints of aggression upon the Republic of Korea and of armed invasion of Taiwan (Formosa). On November 30, because of the negative vote of a permanent member (USSR), the Council did not adopt a resolution calling, among other things, on all states and authorities to refrain from assisting the North Korean authorities, and affirming that it was United Nations policy to hold inviolate the Chinese frontier with Korea. The Council rejected by a vote of 1 (USSR) to 9, with India not participating, a draft resolution condemning the United States for armed aggression against Chinese territory and armed intervention in Korea, and demanding withdrawal of United States forces. The Security Council, which had been unable to agree on a solution, decided unanimously, on January 31, 1951, to remove the item "Complaint of aggression upon the Republic of Korea" from its agenda.

On December 6, 1950, the General Assembly included the item "Intervention of the Central People's Government of the People's Republic of China in Korea" in its agenda. On December 14, it established a three-man Cease-Fire Group – the President of the Assembly, Canada, and India – to recommend satisfactory cease-fire arrangements in Korea. The Group program, aimed at achieving a cease-fire by successive stages, was transmitted to the People's Republic of China on January 13, 1951.

Armistice negotiations between the military commanders of the opposing sides began in Korea on July 10, 1951.

The Armistice Agreement was signed on July 27, 1953, by the Commanders of the United Nations Command, the Korean People's Army, and the Chinese People's Volunteers, and hostilities ceased. The Agreement established a demarcation line and demilitarized zone; provided that no reinforcing personnel or combat equipment be introduced except on a replacement basis, set up a Military Armistice Commission of representatives from the two sides to supervise and settle any violations of the Agreement; set up a Neutral Nations Supervisory Commission of four – Sweden and Switzerland appointed by the United Nations Command, and Czechoslovakia and Poland by the other side – to observe and investigate troop withdrawals and weapons replacement".'

The conference on peace in Korea was held in Geneva from Apr. 26 to June 15, 1954 with the participation of the Five Powers and states which had participated in the war; it reached no result. The "Korean question" remained a separate agenda of the UN General Assembly. On the other hand, NNSC in Panmunjom continued to supervise the armistice. The UN Secretariat, in a press release of Jan. 7, 1966, stated that from 1953 no UN organ had received any report from the UN United Command in Korea, which had been formed on June 27, 1950. Both territories remained completely isolated from each other until Sept. 21, 1970, when both sides agreed to hold talks; these began in 1971 in Pyongyang and Seoul and continued in 1972. Their result, announced July 4, 1972, was the Joint Declaration of North and South, On Aug. 18, 1972 the telephone connection between Seoul and Pyongyang was reopened after 27 years.

On Aug. 30, 1972 the first plenary sessions were held in Pyongyang of representatives of the Red Cross of both Korean states on the question of reuniting families separated by the war of 1950–53. In Nov., 1972 the Red Cross Committee for the normalization of relations between North and South reached agreement concerning the joint cessation of radio propaganda against the other side by a system of loudspeakers placed along the demarcation line.

On Nov. 28, 1973 the UN General Assembly unanimously decided to dissolve the UN Commission on Korea, UNCURK, without vote and with no protest. On Aug. 19, 1974 30 members of the UN, including China, Cuba and the USSR, placed on the agenda of the UN General Assembly the "question of the withdrawal of all foreign forces stationed in South Korea under the UN flag." The UN General Assembly, Res. 3333/XXIX on Dec. 17, 1974 "recalling the Joint Declaration at Seoul and Pyongyang on July 1972 and the declared intention of both the South and North of Korea to continue the dialogue between them ..." expressed the hope that the Security Council would continue its efforts for a peaceful solution of the "Korean question, including the dissolution of the UN Command."

During the next decade, until 1985 the Security Council had not reached the aims of the 1974 Resolution.

On Sept. 13, 1984 South Korea accepted an offer from North Korea to provide assistance to victims of a flood "to pave the way for genuine, mutual and humanitarian assistance between fellow Koreans and to improve inter-Korean relations."

UN GENERAL ASSEMBLY INTERIM COMMITTEE, *Problem of the Independence of Korea. List of Documents*, Lake Success, 1948; UN TEMPORARY COMMISSION ON KOREA, *Report to the General Assembly*, 3 Vols., Lake Success, 1948; P. C. JESSUP, *The Question of Korea in the UN*, Washington, DC, 1948; US DEPARTMENT OF STATE, *Korea 1945 to 1948*, Washington, DC, 1948; *Yearbook of the UN 1947–48*, pp. 81–88, 282–284, 302–304, 321, 548, 814; *Korea: An annotated Bibliography*, Washington, DC, 1950; *Mezhdunarodnoye otnoshenia na Dalnem Vostoke, 1870–1943*, Moskva, 1951; J. ROSINGER, *The States of Asia. A Contemporary Survey*, New York, 1951; M. LACHS, *Rozejm w Korei* (The Armistice in Korea), Warsaw, 1953; M.H. PAK, *Istoriia Korei*, Moskva, 1960; TAE-HO YOO, *The Korean War and the UN. A Legal and Diplomatic Historical Study*, Louvain, 1965; SIPRI, *World Armaments and Disarmament Yearbook*, 1971, pp. 144–148; *The Far East and Australasia 1972*, London, 1972, pp. 895–938; H. SICHROVSKY, *Korea report. Vom Bruderkrieg zur Wiedervereinigung?*, Vienna, 1973; SUNG YOO HAN, *The Failure of Democracy in South Korea*, Berkeley, 1974; *UN Monthly Chronicle*, No. 1, 1975, pp. 48–50; KIM IL SUNG, "Let us Achieve the independent, peaceful reunification of the Country," in: *New York Times*, October 24, 1975, p. 13; G. McCORMACK, M. SELDEN (eds), *Korea North and South. The Deepening Crisis*, New York, 1978; M.F. LABOUZ, *L'ONU et la Corée*, Paris, 1981; *Yearbook of the UN 1980*, New York, 1982, p.342; *The Europa Year Book 1984. A World Survey*, Vol. II, pp. 1866 and 1876, London, 1984, *International Herald Tribune*, September 15–16, 1984; P. LOWE, *The origins of the Korean War*, Lexington, 1986; W.H. GLEYSTEEN, A.D. ROMBERG, *Korea: Asian Paradox, in: Foreign Affairs*, Summer, 1987; M. HASTINGS, *The Korean War*, New York, 1987; D. ROBERTSON, *Guide to Modern Defense and Strategy*, Detroit, 1988; R. SPURR, *Enter the Dragon. China's Undeclared War Against the US in Korea 1950–1951*, New York, 1988.

KOREA, DEMOCRATIC PEOPLE'S REPUBLIC OF /NORTH KOREA/. Chosun Min-chu-chui Inmin Konghwa-guk. Not a member of the UN. Has observer status in the UN. The northern part of ▷ Korea, located north of the 38th parallel. Area: 120,538 sq. km. Pop. 1986 est.: 20,883,000 (1960 est. 10,799,000; 1970 est. 17,892,000). Capital: Pyongyang with 1,950,000 inhabitants in 1980. Official language: Korean. Currency: one won = 100 chon. GNP per capita in 1978: US$1,000. National Day: Sept. 9, anniversary of the Proclamation of the Korean Democratic People's Republic, 1948.

International relations: created three months after the proclamation of the Korean Republic in the southern part of the country through elections held Aug. 25, 1948 and the proclamation of the Korean Democratic People's Republic by the Supreme People's Assembly on Sept. 9, 1948. In armed conflict with South Korea from June 25, 1950 to July 27, 1953. ▷ Korea. North Korea's application of Feb., 1949, for admission to the UN was rejected because of a US veto, just as South Korea was not admitted because of a Soviet veto. In 1972 entered into introductory talks with South Korea. In 1973 North Korea was admitted to the first UN specialized organization, the WHO, and on this legal basis in 1973 opened a North Korean observer office at the European headquarters of the UN in Geneva. In the spring of 1973 North Korea became a member of the Interparliamentary Union. On June 30, 1973 she received the status of a permanent observer at the UN and on Aug. 26, 1975 was accepted as a member of the nonaligned states movement. Member of FAO, UNESCO, ICAO, WHO, UPU, ITU, WMO, IMO, IFAD, UNIDO, WIPO and IAEA. Japan imposed sanctions on North Korea from Oct., 1983 to Nov., 1984 in relation to the killing by a bomb explosion of 20 South Koreans on official visit in Rangoon. ▷ Burma.

On Dec. 29, 1986 President Kim Ir Sen proposed "the Founding of a Confederal State (of North and South Korea) which would make neither side the conqueror or the conquered".

Communist North Korea: A Bibliographic Survey, Washington, 1971; *Sovershennaya Koreia. Spravochnoye izdanie*, Moscow, 1971; J. SURET-CANAL, J.E. VIDAL, *La Corée populaire vers les matins calmes*, Paris, 1973; I.J. KIM, *Communist Policies in North Korea*, New York, 1975; E. BRUN, J. HERSH, *Socialist Korea, A Case Study in the Strategy of Economic 35 Development*, New York, 1976; W.S. KIYOSAKI, *North Korea's Foreign Relations*, New York, 1976; G. McCORMACK, M. SELDENS (eds), *Korea North and South: The Deepening Crisis*, New York, 1978; C.S. LEE, *The Korean Workers' Party. A Short History*, Stanford, 1978; KIM HAN GIL, *Modern History of Korea*, Pyongyang, 1979; Y.S. KINZ (ed.), *The Economy of the Korean Democratic People's Republic*, Kiel, 1979; *The Europa Year Book 1984. A World Survey*, Vol. II, pp. 1866–1875, London, 1984, KEESING's *Record of World Events*, 1987, No. 2.

KOREA, JAPANESE–RUSSIAN TREATIES. ▷ Japanese–Russian Treaties, 1858–1916.

KOREA, REPUBLIC OF (SOUTH KOREA). Han Kook. Not a member of the UN. Has observer status at the UN. The southern part of ▷ Korea, located south of the 38th parallel. Area: 98,966 sq. km. Pop. 1987 est.: 42 m (1970 census: 31,460,000). Capital: Seoul with 8,346,000 inhabitants in 1980. Official language: Korean. Currency: 1 won = 100 chon. GNP per capita in 1988: US $3,450. National Day: Aug. 15, anniversary of liberation from Japanese occupation, 1945.

International relations: created on May 10, 1948; on Jan. 26, 1950 signed a military treaty with the USA. In armed conflict with North Korea from June 25, 1950 to July 27, 1953. Signed a Treaty on Mutual Defense with the USA on July 27, 1953, granting US armed forces the right to maintain land, sea and air bases on Korean territory. A Treaty on Normalization of Relations was signed with Japan in Tokyo on June 23, 1965. South Korea's application of Jan. 1, 1949 for admission to the UN was rejected by the Security Council because of a Soviet veto, as was the motion of North Korea of Feb. 19, 1949, by a US veto. Since 1953 has the status of a permanent observer at the UN; is a member of all specialized UN organizations with the exception of the ILO. The destruction of Korean Air Lines passenger plane, flight 007, on Sept. 1, 1983 by a Soviet military aircraft was a subject of a UN Security Council debate and of an ICAO declaration that "such use of armed force is a great threat to safety of international civil aviation." ▷ ICAO.

On March 9, 1986 Roman-Catholic Primate, Cardinal Stephen Kim Son Hwan called on President Chun to introduce a direct presidential election.

UNESCO, *Korean Survey*, Seoul, 1960; *Korea Major Economic Indicators, 1958–69*, Seoul, 1970; P.M. BARTZ, *South Korea*, London, 1972; E.R. WRIGHT, *Korean Politics in Transitions*, Washington, 1976; *A Handbook of Korea*, Seoul, 1982; *UN Chronicle*, March 1984, p. 54; *The Europa Year Book 1984. A World Survey*, Vol. II, pp. 1876–1891, London, 1984; S. WINCHESTER, *Korea: A Walk Through the Land of Miracles*, Englewood, Cliffs, N.J., 1988.

KOREA, REPUBLIC OF–UNITED STATES OF AMERICA TREATY OF FRIENDSHIP, COMMERCE AND NAVIGATION, 1956. Signed at Seoul on Nov. 28, 1956; came into force on Nov. 7, 1957, read as follows:

"The United States of America and the Republic of Korea, desirous of strengthening the bonds of peace and friendship traditionally existing between them and of encouraging closer economic and cultural relations between their peoples, and being cognizant of the contributions which may be made toward these ends by arrangements encouraging mutually beneficial investments, promoting mutually advantageous commercial intercourse and otherwise establishing mutual rights and privileges, have resolved to conclude a Treaty of Friendship, Commerce and Navigation, based in general upon the principles of national and of most-favored-nation treatment unconditionally accorded ... have agreed upon the following articles:

Art. I. Each Party shall at all times accord equitable treatment to the persons, property, enterprises and other interests of nationals and companies of the other Party.

Art. II.(1) Nationals of either Party shall be permitted to enter the territories of the other Party and to remain therein:

(a) for the purpose of carrying on trade between the territories of the two Parties and engaging in related commercial activities; (b) for the purpose of developing and directing the operations of an enterprise in which they have invested, or in which they are actively in the process of investing, a substantial amount of capital; and (c) for other purposes subject to the laws relating to the entry and sojourn of aliens.

(2) Nationals of either Party, within the territories of the other Party, shall be permitted: (a) to travel therein freely, and to reside at places of their choice; (b) to enjoy liberty of conscience; (c) to hold both private and public religious services; (d) to gather and to transmit material for dissemination to the public abroad; (e) to communicate with other persons inside and outside such territories by mail, telegraph and other means open to general public use.

(3) The provisions of the present article shall be subject to the right of either Party to apply measures that are necessary to maintain public order and protect the public health, morals and safety.

Art. III.(1) Nationals of either Party within the territories of the other Party shall be free from molestations of every kind, and shall receive the most constant protection and security, in no case less than that required by international law.

(2) If, within the territories of either Party, a national of the other Party is taken into custody, the nearest consular representative of his country shall on the demand of such national be immediately notified and shall have the right to visit and communicate with such national. Such national shall: (a) receive reasonable and humane treatment; (b) be formally and immediately informed of the accusations against him; (c) be brought to trial as promptly as is consistent with the proper preparation of his defense; and (d) enjoy all means reasonably necessary to his defense, including the services of competent counsel of his choice.

Art. IV.(1) Nationals of either Party shall be accorded national treatment in the application of laws and regulations within the territories of the other Party that establish a pecuniary compensation or other benefit or service, on account of disease, injury or death arising out of and in the course of employment or due to the nature of employment.

(2) In addition to the rights and privileges provided in paragraph 1 of the present article, nationals of either Party within the territories of the other Party shall be accorded national treatment in the application of laws and regulations establishing compulsory systems of social security, under which benefits are paid without an individual test of financial need: (a) against loss of wages or earnings due old age, unemployment, sickness or disability, or (b) against loss of financial support due to the death of father, husband or other person on whom such support had depended.

Art. V.(1) Nationals and companies of either Party shall be accorded national treatment and most-favored-nation treatment with respect to access to the courts of justice and to administrative tribunals and agencies within the territories of the other Party, in all degrees of jurisdiction, both in pursuit and in defense of their rights. It is understood that companies of either Party not engaged in activities within the territories of the other Party shall enjoy such access therein without any requirement of registration or domestication.

(2) Contracts entered into between nationals and companies of either Party and nationals and companies of the other Party, that provide for the settlement by arbitration of controversies, shall not be deemed unenforceable within the territories of such other Party merely on the grounds that the place designated for the arbitration proceedings is outside such territories or that the nationality of one or more of the arbitrators is not that of such other Party. No award duly rendered pursuant to any such contract, and final and enforceable under the laws of the place where rendered, shall be deemed invalid or denied effective means of enforcement within the territories of either Party merely on the grounds that the place where such award was rendered is outside such territories or that the nationality of one or more of the arbitrators is not that of such Party.

Art. VI.(1) Property of nationals and companies of either Party shall receive the most constant protection and security within the territories of the other Party.

(2) The dwellings, offices, warehouses, factories and other premises of nationals and companies of either Party located within the territories of the other Party shall not be subject to molestation or to entry without just cause. Official searches and examinations of such premises and their contents, when necessary, shall be made only according to law and with careful regard for the convenience of the occupants and the conduct of business.

(3) Neither Party shall take unreasonable or discriminatory measures that would impair the legally acquired rights or interests within its territories of nationals and companies of the other Party in the enterprises which they have established, in their capital, or in the skills, arts or technology which they have supplied.

(4) Property of nationals and companies of either Party shall not be taken within the territories of the other Party except for a public purpose, nor shall it be taken without the prompt payment of just compensation. Such compensation shall be in an effectively realizable form and shall represent the full equivalent of the property taken; and adequate provision shall have been made at or prior to the time of taking for the determination and payment thereof.

(5) Nationals and companies of either Party shall in no case be accorded, within the territories of the other Party, less than national treatment and most-favored-nation treatment with respect to the matters set forth in paragraphs 2 and 4 of the present article. Moreover, enterprises in which nationals and companies of either Party have a substantial interest shall be accorded, within the territories of the other Party, not less than

national treatment and most-favored-nation treatment in all matters relating to the taking of privately owned enterprises into public ownership and to the placing of such enterprises under public control.

Art. VII.(1) Nationals and companies of either Party shall be accorded national treatment with respect to engaging in all types of commercial, industrial, financial and other activities for gain (business activities) within the territories of the other Party, whether directly or by agent or through the medium of any form of lawful juridical entity. Accordingly, such nationals and companies shall be permitted within such territories: (a) to establish and maintain branches, agencies, offices, factories and other establishments appropriate to the conduct of their business; (b) to organize companies under the general company laws of such other Party, and to acquire majority interests in companies of such other Party; and (c) to control and manage enterprises which they have established or acquired. Moreover, enterprises which they control, whether in the form of individual proprietorships, companies or otherwise, shall in all that relates to the conduct of the activities thereof, be accorded treatment no less favorable than that accorded like enterprises controlled by nationals and companies of such other Party.

(2) Each Party reserves the right to limit the extent to which aliens may establish, acquire interests in, or carry on enterprises engaged within its territories in transport, communications, public utilities, banking involving depository or fiduciary functions, or the exploitation of land or other natural resources. However, new limitations imposed by either Party upon the extent to which aliens are accorded national treatment, with respect to carrying on such activities within its territories, shall not be applied as against enterprises which are engaged in such activities therein at the time such new limitations are adopted and which are owned or controlled by nationals and companies of the other Party. Moreover, neither Party shall deny to transportation, communications and banking companies of the other Party the right to maintain branches and agencies to perform functions necessary for essential international operations in which they are permitted to engage.

(3) The provisions of paragraph 1 of the present article shall not prevent either Party from prescribing special formalities in connection with the establishment of alien-controlled enterprises within its territories; but such formalities may not impair the substance of the rights set forth in said paragraph.

(4) Nationals and companies of either Party, as well as enterprises controlled by such nationals and companies, shall in any event be accorded most-favored-nation treatment with reference to the matters treated in the present article.

Art. VIII.(1) Nationals and companies of either Party shall be permitted to engage, within the territories of the other Party, accountants and other technical experts, executive personnel, attorneys, agents and other specialists of their choice. Moreover, such nationals and companies shall be permitted to engage accountants and other technical experts regardless of the extent to which they may have qualified for the practice of a profession within the territories of such other Party, for the particular purpose of making examinations, audits and technical investigations for, and rendering reports to, such nationals and companies in connection with the planning and operation of their enterprises in which they have a financial interest, within such territories.

(2) Nationals and companies of either Party shall be accorded national treatment and most-favored-nation treatment with respect to engaging in scientific, educational, religious and philanthropic activities within the territories of the other Party, and shall be accorded the right to form associations for that purpose under the laws of such other Party. Nothing in the present Treaty shall be deemed to grant or imply any right to engage in political activities.

Art. IX.(1) Nationals and companies of either Party shall be accorded, within the territories of the Party: (a) national treatment with respect to leasing land, buildings and other immovable property appropriate to the conduct of activities in which they are permitted to engage pursuant to articles VII and VIII and for residential purposes, and with respect to occupying and using such property; and (b) other rights in immovable property permitted by the applicable laws of the other Party.

(2) Nationals and companies of either Party shall be accorded within the territories of the other Party national treatment and most-favored-nation treatment with respect to acquiring, by purchase, lease, or otherwise, and with respect to owning and possessing, movable property of all kinds, both tangible and intangible. However, either Party may impose restrictions on alien ownership of materials dangerous from the standpoint of public safety and alien ownership of interests in enterprises carrying on particular types of activity, but only to the extent that this can be done without impairing the rights and privileges secured by article VII or by other provisions of the present Treaty.

(3) National and companies of either Party shall be accorded national treatment within the territories of the other Party with respect to acquiring property of all kinds by testate or intestate succession or through judicial process. Should they because of their alienage be ineligible to continue to own any such property, they shall be allowed a period of at least five years in which to dispose of it.

(4) Nationals and companies of either Party shall be accorded within the territories of the other Party national treatment and most-favored-nation treatment with respect to disposing of property of all kinds.

Art. X.(1) Nationals and companies of either Party shall be accorded, within the territories of the other Party, national treatment and most-favored-nation treatment with respect to obtaining and maintaining patents of invention, and with respect to rights in trade marks, trade names, trade labels and industrial property of every kind.

(2) The Parties undertake to co-operate in furthering the interchange and use of scientific and technical knowledge, particularly in the interests of increasing productivity and improving standards of living within their respective territories.

Art. XI.(1) Nationals of either Party residing within the territories of the other Party, and nationals and companies of either Party engaged in trade or other gainful pursuit or in scientific, educational, religious or philanthropic activities within the territories of the other Party, shall not be subject to the payment of taxes, fees or charges imposed upon or applied to income, capital, transactions, activities or any other object, or to requirements with respect to the levy and collection thereof, within the territories of such other Party, more burdensome than those borne by nationals and companies of such other Party.

(2) With respect to nationals of either Party who are neither resident nor engaged in trade or other gainful pursuit within the territories of the other Party, and with respect to companies of either Party which are not engaged in trade or other gainful pursuit within the territories of the other Party, it shall be the aim of such other Party to apply in general the principle set forth in paragraph 1 of the present article.

(3) Nationals and companies of either Party shall in no case be subject, within the territories of the other Party, to the payment of taxes, fees or charges imposed upon or applied to income, capital, transactions, activities or any other object, or to requirements with respect to the levy and collection thereof, more burdensome than those borne by nationals, residents and companies of any third country.

(4) In the case of companies of either Party engaged in trade or other gainful pursuit within the territories of the other Party, and in the case of nationals of either Party engaged in trade or other gainful pursuit within the territories of the other Party but not resident therein, such other Party shall not impose or apply any tax, fee or charge upon any income, capital or other basis in excess of that reasonably allocable or apportionable to its territories, nor grant deductions and exemptions less than those reasonably allocable or apportionable to its territories. A comparable rule shall apply also in the case of companies organized and operated exclusively for scientific, educational, religious or philanthropic purposes.

(5) Each Party reserves the right to: (a) extend specific tax advantages on the basis of reciprocity; (b) accord special tax advantages by virtue of agreements for the avoidance of double taxation or the mutual protection of revenue; and (c) apply special provisions in allowing, to non-residents, exemptions of a personal nature in connection with income and inheritance taxes.

Art. XIII(1) Nationals and companies of either Party shall be accorded by the other Party national treatment and most-favored-nation treatment with respect to payments, remittances and transfers of funds or financial instruments between the territories of the two Parties as well as between the territories of such other Party and of any third country.

(2) Neither Party shall impose exchange restrictions as defined in paragraph 5 of the present article except to the extent necessary to prevent its monetary reserves from falling to a very low level or to effect a moderate increase in very low monetary reserves. It is understood that the provisions of the present article do not alter the obligations either Party may have to the International Monetary Fund or preclude imposition of particular restrictions whenever the Fund specifically authorizes or requests a Party to impose such particular restrictions.

(3) If either Party imposes exchange restrictions in accordance with paragraph 2 of the present article, it shall, after making whatever provision may be necessary to assure the availability of foreign exchange for goods and services essential to the health and welfare of its people and necessary to the avoidance of serious economic instability, make reasonable provision for the withdrawal, in foreign exchange in the currency of the other Party, of (a) the compensation referred to in article VI, paragraph 4, (b) earnings, whether in the form of salaries, interest, dividends, commissions, royalties, payments for technical services, or otherwise, and (c) amounts for amortization of loans, depreciation of direct investments, and capital transfers, giving consideration to special needs for other transactions. If more than one rate of exchange is in force, the rate applicable to such withdrawals shall be a rate which is specifically approved by the International Monetary Fund for such transactions or, in the absence of a rate so approved, an effective rate which, inclusive of any taxes or surcharges on exchange transfers, is just and reasonable.

(4) Exchange restrictions shall not be imposed by either Party in a manner unnecessarily detrimental or arbitrarily discriminatory to the claims, investments, transport, trade, and other interests of the nationals and companies of the other Party, nor to the competitive position thereof.

(5) The term "exchange restrictions" as used in the present article includes all restrictions, regulations, charges, taxes, or other requirements imposed by either Party which burden or interfere with payments, remittances, or transfers of funds or of financial instruments between the territories of the two Parties.

(6) Each Party shall afford the other Party adequate opportunity for consultation at any time regarding application of the present article.

Art. XIII. Commercial travelers representing nationals and companies of either Party engaged in business within the territories thereof shall, upon their entry into and departure from the territories of the other Party and during their sojourn therein, be accorded most-favored-nation treatment in respect of the customs and other matters, including, subject to the exceptions in paragraph 5 of article XI, taxes and charges applicable to them, their samples and the taking of orders, and regulations governing the exercise of their functions,

Art. XIV.(1) Each Party shall accord most-favored-nation treatment to products of the other Party, from whatever place and by whatever type of carrier arriving, and to product destined for exportation to the territories of such other Party, by whatever route and by whatever type of carrier, with respect to customs duties and charges of any kind imposed on or in connection with importation or exportation or imposed on the international transfer of payments for imports or exports, and with respect to the method of levying such duties and charges, and with respect to all rules and formalities in connection with importation and exportation.

(2) Neither Party shall impose restrictions or prohibitions on the importation of any product of the other Party, or on the exportation of any product to the territories of the other Party, unless the importation of the like product of, or the exportation of the like product to, all third countries is similarly restricted or prohibited.

(3) If either Party imposes quantitative restrictions on the importation or exportation of any product in which the other Party has an important interest: (a) It shall as

a general rule give prior public notice of the total amount of the product, by quantity or value, that may be imported or exported during a specified period, and of any change in such amount or period; and (b) If it makes allotments to any third country, it shall afford such other Party a share proportionate to the amount of the product, by quantity or value, supplied by or to it during a previous representative period, due consideration being given to any special factors affecting the trade in such products.

(4) Either Party may impose prohibitions or restrictions on the importation or exportation of any product on sanitary or other customary grounds of a noncommercial nature, or in the interest of preventing deceptive or unfair practices, provided such prohibitions or restrictions do not arbitrarily discriminate against the commerce of the other Party.

(5) Nationals and companies of either Party shall be accorded national treatment and most-favored-nation treatment by the other Party with respect to all matters relating to importation and exportation.

(6) The provisions of the present article shall not apply to advantages accorded by either Party; (a) to products of its national fisheries; (b) to adjacent countries in order to facilitate frontier traffic; or (c) by virtue of a customs union or free-trade area of which it may become a member, so long as it informs the other Party of its plans and affords such other Party adequate opportunity for consultation.

(7) Notwithstanding the provisions of paragraphs 2 and 3(b) of the present article, a Party may apply restrictions or controls of importation and exportation of goods that have effect equivalent to, or which are necessary to make effective exchange restrictions applied pursuant to article XII. However, such restrictions or controls shall not depart further than necessary from the above paragraphs and shall be conformable to a policy designed to promote the maximum development of nondiscriminatory foreign trade and to expedite the attainment both of a balance-of-payments position and of monetary reserves which will obviate the necessity of such restrictions.

Art. XV.(1) Each Party shall promptly publish laws, regulations and administrative rulings of general application pertaining to rates of duty, taxes or other charges, to the classification of articles for customs purposes, and to requirements or restrictions on imports and exports or the transfer of payments therefor, or affecting their sale, distribution or use; and shall administer such laws, regulations and rulings in a uniform, impartial and reasonable manner. As a general practice, new administrative requirements or restrictions affecting imports, with the exception of those imposed on sanitary grounds or for reasons of public safety, shall not go into effect before the expiration of 30 days after publication, or alternatively, shall not apply to products en route at time of publication.

(2) Each Party shall provide an appeals procedure under which nationals and companies of the other Party, and importers of products of each other Party, shall be able to obtain prompt and impartial review, and correction when warranted, of administrative action relating to customs matters, including the imposition of fines and penalties, confiscations, and rulings on questions of customs classification and valuation by the administrative authorities. Penalties imposed for infractions of the customs and shipping laws and regulations concerning documentation shall, in cases resulting from clerical errors or when good faith can be demonstrated, be no greater than necessary to serve merely as a warning.

(3) Neither Party shall impose any measure of a discriminatory nature that hinders or prevents the importer or exporter of products of either country from obtaining marine insurance or such products in companies of either Party. The present paragraph is subject to the provisions of article XII.

Art. XVI.(1) Products of either Party shall be accorded, within the territories of the other Party, national treatment and most-favored-nation treatment in all matters affecting internal taxation, sale, distribution, storage and use.

(2) Articles produced by nationals and companies of either Party within the territories of the other Party, or by companies of the latter Party controlled by such nationals and companies, shall be accorded therein treatment no less favorable than that accorded to like articles of national origin by whatever person or company produced, in all matters affecting exportation, taxation, sale, distribution, storage and use.

Art. XVII.(1) Each Party undertakes (a) that enterprises owned or controlled by its Government, and that monopolies or agencies granted exclusive or special privileges within its territories, shall make their purchases and sales involving either imports or exports affecting the commerce of the other Party solely in accordance with commercial considerations, including price, quality, availability, marketability, transportation and other conditions of purchase or sale; and (b) that the nationals, companies and commerce of such other Party shall be afforded adequate opportunity, in accordance with customary business practice, to compete for participation in such purchases and sales.

(2) Each Party shall accord to the nationals, companies and commerce of the other Party fair and equitable treatment, as compared with that accorded to the nationals, companies and commerce of any third country, with respect to: (a) the governmental purchase of supplies, (b) the awarding of concessions and other government contracts, and (c) the sale of any service sold by the Government or by any monopoly or agency granted exclusive or special privileges.

Art. XVIII.(1) The two Parties agree that business practices which restrain competition, limit access to markets or foster monopolistic control, and which are engaged in or made effective by one or more private or public commercial enterprises or by combination, agreement or other arrangement among such enterprises, may have harmful effects upon commerce between their respective territories. Accordingly, each Party agrees upon the request of the other Party to consult with respect to any such practices and to take such measures as it deems appropriate with a view to eliminating such harmful effects.

(2) No enterprise of either Party, including corporations, associations, and government agencies and instrumentalities, which is publicly owned or controlled shall, if it engages in commercial, industrial, shipping or other business activities within the territories of the other Party, claim or enjoy, either for itself or for its property, immunity therein from taxation, suit, execution of judgment or other liability to which privately owned and controlled enterprises are subject therein.

Art. XIX.(1) Between the territories of the two Parties there shall be freedom of commerce and navigation.

(2) Vessels under the flag of either Party, and carrying the papers required by its law in proof of nationality, shall be deemed to be vessels of that Party both on the high seas and within the ports, places and waters of the other Party.

(3) Vessels of either Party shall have liberty, on equal terms with vessels of any third country, to come with their cargoes to all ports, places and waters of such other Party open to foreign commerce and navigation. Such vessels and cargoes shall in all respects be accorded national treatment and most-favored-nation treatment within the ports, places and waters of such other Party; but each Party may reserve exclusive rights and privileges to its own vessels with respect to the coasting trade, inland navigation and national fisheries.

(4) Vessels of either Party shall be accorded national treatment and most-favored-nation treatment by the other Party with respect to the right to carry all products that may be carried by vessel to or from the territories of such other Party; and such products shall be accorded treatment no less favorable than that accorded like products carried in vessels of such other Party, with respect to: (a) duties and charges of all kinds, (b) the administration of the customs, and (c) bounties, drawbacks and other privileges of this nature.

(5) Vessels of either Party that are in distress shall be permitted to take refuge in the nearest port or haven of the other Party, and shall receive friendly treatment and assistance.

(6) The term "vessels", as used herein, means all types of vessels, whether privately owned or operated, or publicly owned or operated; but this term does not, except with reference to paragraphs 2 and 5 of the present article, include fishing vessels or vessels of war.

Art. XX. There shall be freedom of transit through the territories of each Party by the routes most convenient for international transit: (a) for nationals of the other Party, together with their baggage; (b) for other persons, together with their baggage, en route to or from the territories of such other Party; and (c) for products of any origin en route to or from the territories of such other Party.

Such persons and things in transit shall be exempt from customs duties, from duties imposed by reason of transit, and from unreasonable charges and requirements; and shall be free from unnecessary delays and restrictions. They shall, however, be subject to measures referred to in paragraph 3 of article II, and to nondiscriminatory regulations necessary to prevent abuse of the transit privilege.

Art. XXI.(1) The present Treaty shall not preclude the application of measures: (a) regulating the importation or exportation of gold or silver; (b) relating to fissionable materials, to radioactive byproducts of the utilization of processing thereof, or to materials that are the source of fissionable materials; (c) regulating the production of or traffic in arms, ammunition and implements of war, or traffic in other materials carried on directly or indirectly for the purpose of supplying a military establishment; (d) necessary to fulfill the obligations of a Party for the maintenance or restoration of international peace and security or necessary to protect its essential security interests; and (e) denying to any company in the ownership or direction of which nationals of any third country or countries have directly or indirectly the controlling interest, the advantages of the present Treaty, except with respect to recognition of juridical status and with respect to access to courts.

(2) The most-favored-nation provisions of the present Treaty relating to the treatment of goods shall not apply to advantages accorded by the United States of America or its Territories and possessions to one another, to the Republic of Cuba, to the Republic of the Philippines, to the Trust Territory of the Pacific Islands or to the Panama Canal Zone.

(3) The provision of the present Treaty relating to the treatment of goods shall not preclude action by either Party which is required or specifically permitted by the General Agreement on Tariffs and Trade during such time as such Party is a contracting party to the General Agreement. Similarly, the most-favored-nation provisions of the present Treaty shall not apply to special advantages accorded by virtue of the aforesaid Agreement.

(4) Nationals of either Party admitted into the territories of the other Party for limited purposes shall not enjoy rights to engage in gainful occupations in contravention of limitations expressly imposed, according to law, as a condition of their admittance.

Art. XXII.(1) The term "national treatment" means treatment accorded within the territories of a Party upon terms no less favorable than the treatment accorded therein, in like situations, to nationals, companies, products, vessels or other objects, as the case may be, of such Party.

(2) The term "most-favored-nation treatment" means treatment accorded within the territories of a Party upon terms no less favorable than the treatment accorded therein, in like situations, to nationals, companies, products, vessels or other objects, as the case may be, of any third country.

(3) As used in the present Treaty, the term "companies" means corporations, partnerships, companies and other associations, whether or not with limited liability and whether or not for pecuniary profit. Companies constituted under the applicable laws and regulations within the territories of either Party shall be deemed companies thereof and shall have their juridical status recognized within the territories of the other Party.

(4) National treatment accorded under the provisions of the present Treaty to companies of the Republic of Korea shall, in any State, Territory or possession of the United States of America, be the treatment accorded therein to companies created or organized in other states, territories, and possessions of the United States of America.

Art. XXIII. The territories to which the present Treaty extends shall comprise all areas of land and water under the sovereignty or authority of each Party, other than the Panama Canal Zone and the Trust Territory of the Pacific Islands.

Art. XXIV.(1) Each Party shall accord sympathetic consideration to, and shall afford adequate opportunity for consultation regarding, such representations as the other Party may make with respect to any matter affecting the operation of the present Treaty.

(2) Any dispute between the Parties as to the interpretation or application of the present Treaty, not

satisfactorily adjusted by diplomacy, shall be submitted to the International Court of Justice, unless the Parties agree to settlement by some other pacific means.

UNTS, Vol. 302, pp. 304–334.

KOREA RESOLUTIONS, 1950. Three resolutions adopted by the Security Council in June and July 1950 (the USSR delegate was absent in the Security Council since Jan. 1950):
(1) Resolution relative to the outbreak of the hostilities in Korea, adopted 9:0 with Yugoslavia abstaining on June 25, 1950:

"The Security Council
Recalling the finding of the General Assembly in its resolution of 21 October 1949 that the Government of the Republic of Korea is a lawfully established government "having effective control and jurisdiction over that part of Korea where the United Nations Temporary Commission on Korea was able to observe and consult and in which the great majority of the people of Korea reside; and that this Government is based on elections which were a valid expression of the free will of the electorate of that part of Korea and which were observed by the Temporary Commission; and that this is the only such Government in Korea;
Mindful of the concern expressed by the General Assembly in its resolutions of 12 December 1948 and 21 October 1949 of the consequences which might follow unless Member States refrained from acts derogatory to the results sought to be achieved by the United Nations in bringing about the complete independence and unity of Korea; and the concern expressed that the situation described by the United Nations Commission on Korea in its report menaces the safety and well being of the Republic of Korea and of the people of Korea and might lead to open military conflict there;
Noting with grave concern armed attack upon the Republic of Korea by forces from North Korea,
Determines that this action constitutes a breach of the peace,
I. Calls for the immediate cessation of hostilities; and calls upon the authorities of North Korea to withdraw forthwith their armed forces to the thirty-eighth parallel;
II. Requests the United Nations Commission on Korea
(a) To communicate its fully considered recommendations on the situation with the least possible delay;
(b) To observe the withdrawal of the North Korean forces to the thirty-eighth parallel; and
(c) To keep the Security Council informed on the execution of this resolution;
III. Calls upon all Members to render every assistance to the United Nations in the execution of this resolution and to refrain from giving assistance to the North Korean authorities."

(2) Resolution relative to hostilities in Korea, adopted 7:0, with Egypt, India and Yugoslavia abstaining, on June 27, 1950:

"The Security Council,
Having determined that the armed attack upon the Republic of Korea by forces from North Korea constitutes a breach of the peace, having called for an immediate cessation of hostilities, and having called upon the authorities of North Korea to withdraw forthwith their armed forces to the 38th parallel, and having noted from the report of the United Nations Commission for Korea that the authorities in North Korea have neither ceased hostilities nor withdrawn their armed forces to the 38th parallel and that urgent military measures are required to restore internaional peace and security, and having noted the appeal from the Republic of Korea to the United Nations for immediate and effective steps to secure peace and security,
Recommends that the Members of the United Nations furnish such assistance to the Republic of Korea as may be necessary to repel the armed attack and to restore international peace and security in the area."

(3) Resolution authorizing the UN Unified Command, adopted 7:0, with Egypt, India, Yugoslavia abstaining, on July 7, 1950:

"The Security Council,
Having determined that the armed attack upon the Republic of Korea by forces from North Korea constitutes a breach of the peace,
Having recommended that the members of the United Nations furnish such assistance to the Republic of Korea as may be necessary to repel armed attack and to restore international peace and security in the area,
(1) Welcomes the prompt and vigorous support which Governments and peoples of the United Nations have given to its resolutions of 25 and 27 June 1950 to assist the Republic of Korea in defending itself against armed attack and thus to restore international peace and security in the area;
(2) Notes that members of the United Nations have transmitted to the United Nations offers of assistance for the Republic of Korea;
(3) Recommends that all members providing military forces and other assistance pursuant to the aforesaid Security Council resolutions make such forces and other assistance available to a unified command under the United States;
(4) Requests the United States to designate the commander of such forces;
(5) Authorizes the unified command at its discretion to use the United Nations flag in the course of operations against North Korean forces concurrently with the flags of the various nations participating;
(6) Requests the United States to provide the Security Council with reports as appropriate on the course of action taken under the unified command."

UN Security Council Official Record, 1950, No. 15, p. 18; No. 16, p. 4; No. 18 p. 8.

KOREA WAR, 1950–53. ▷ Korea.

KORUNA. Czechoslovak (Kc) monetary unit of Czechosolovakia, 1 koruna = 100 haleru; issued by the Statni Banka Československa.

KOŚCIUSZKO FOUNDATION. The leading cultural–scientific organization of Polish–Americans, established 1925 by its first president, S. Mierzwa for the purpose of granting financial aid to deserving Polish students desiring to study at higher educational institutions in the USA and to American students wishing to study in Poland; the cultivating of close intellectual and cultural relations between Poland and the USA; and encouraging and rendering help in the exchange of professors, scientists and lecturers. The Foundation collaborates with the ▷ Jagiellonian University of Cracow.

B. BIERZANEK, "What Led to the Establishing of the Kościuszko Foundation", in: *Culture and Society*, No. 4, Warsaw, 1972, pp. 223–227.

KOSOVO. A province of ▷ Montenegro with an Albanian minority, since 1981 place of nationalist riots, resulting in emigration of thousands of Serbs and Montenegrians from Kosovo to Serbia.

The Europa Yearbook 1987, Vol. II, p. 3149–51; KEESING's *Contemporary Archive*, 1987, 1988; KEESING's *Record of World Events*, March, 1988.

KOSOVO QUESTION. ▷ Albania–Yugoslavia Border Dispute.

KOTOR. A natural site in Montenegro, Yugoslavia, included in the ▷ World Heritage UNESCO List. On the shores of a gulf lying between the steep hills of Montenegro are several small towns which are important on account of their architecture and history. The former prosperity of the most famous of them, Kotor, was due in part to the abundance of marine fauna, which still includes today some very rare species.

UNESCO, *A Legacy for All*, Paris, 1984.

KOZIELSK. ▷ Katyń Case, 1943.

KRACH. ▷ Black Friday.

KRA CHANNEL. A channel cutting across the Isthmus of Kra and connecting the Gulf of Siam with the Andaman Sea; 115 km long, 120 m wide; under construction 1972–80. Shortens the route for big tankers plying between South China Sea and the Indian Ocean by about 1000 nautical miles; the project was to be completed before World War II with the help of Japan but was delayed because of objections by Great Britain.

Le Monde, No. 8555, July, 18, 1972.

KRASNOYARSK. A Soviet city, capital of Krasnoyarski Kray, West Siberia, on the Yenisei River. The site of a 30 story radar tower subject of US–USSR controversy in 1988. The ABM Treaty obliged both sides to use new phased arrays radars only for warning, not for co-ordinating missile defense, and require them to be sited on a country's periphery.

KREISKY PLAN, 1984. The former Chancellor of Austria, B. Kreisky's proposal made in Vienna on Nov. 30, 1984 of a European denuclearized zone from Nord Kap in Norway to Turkey. The control of the nuclear-weapon-free zone (▷ denuclearized zones) according to Kreisky could be like control of a "Four Power Jeep" as was the case in Vienna in the years 1945–1955.

KEESING's *Archiv der Gegenwart*, 1984.

KREMLIN, THE. A historic hill in Moscow, seat of the Soviet Council of Ministers; metaphorically a common international term for the policies of the Soviet Communist Party and the Soviet Government. ▷ Downing Street, ▷ Elysée, ▷ Palazzo Chigi, ▷ White House.

KRIEGSRASON. *German* = "reason of war." An international term introduced in the 19th century by Germany. A doctrine interposing, against the principles of international law, the priority of war reasons over military custom (*Kriegsräson geht vor Kriegsmanier* or *Kriegsnotwendigkeit geht vor Kriegsrecht*). The Prussian General Staff, opposed to Prussia's and the Reich's participation in codification work concerning martial law, fostered this doctrine by linking law idealism with war realism. An identical attitude by Great Britain led to the fiasco at the Brussels Conference 1874, which considered a proposal for the first international convention on customs and martial laws, a question not resolved until 1899 in The Hague (although the Reich's delegate demanded acceptance of a clause that in particular cases the necessity of war might be a priority). The doctrine was in force in the armed forces of the German I Reich, the Weimar Republic and the German III Reich. In trials of war criminals after World War II, Nazi leaders repeatedly referred to military necessity; the International Military Tribunal in Nuremberg twice rejected it as an inadmissible justification, and contrary to the norms of martial laws.

H. LATERNSER, "Der Zweite Weltkrieg und das Recht", in: *Bilanz des Zweiten Weltkrieges*, Oldenburg–Hamburg, 1953.

KRIEGSSCHULDFRAGE, 1914. *German* = "Question of Responsibility for the 1914 War". A German name of a special inquiry committee of the Reichstag for clearing the matter of responsibility for the outbreak of the war (Reichstaguntersuchungausschuss für die Kriegsschuldfrage), f. Aug. 1923. The Committee asked Prof. Herman Kantorowicz to prepare an expert opinion. The expertise presented to the Reichstag 1927 was in absolute contradiction with the official opinion of the German government and the absolute majority of the Reichstag, as it blamed Germany and Austria for the outbreak of the war in 1914. In consequence, Prof. H. Kantorowicz emigrated 1933 to Great Britain and his report was published after his death, in 1967.

H. KANTOROWICZ, *Gutachten zur Kriegsschuldfrage 1914*, mit Vorwort von G. Heinemann, Frankfurt a.M., 1967.

KRIESTINTERN. The International Peasants Council. *Russian* = "Kriestianski International". An international organization established under the auspices of Communist International (▷ Komintern) with the aim of co-ordinating on a world scale the revolutionary struggle of peasantry in alliance with the working class. Active between the wars.

W.S. SWORAKOWSKI, *The Communist International and Its Front Organizations*, Stanford, 1965, pp. 453–455; G.D. JACKSON Jr., *Comintern and Peasants in East Europe 1919–1930*, New York, 1966; W.S. SWORAKOWSKI, *World Communism. A Handbook 1918–1965*, Stanford, 1973, pp. 219–220.

KRILL. A species of marine crustacean, subject of international conventions on fishing and protection of marine environment, also of international scientific research in the region of Antarctica.

KRISHNA MOVEMENT. A religious international movement. Organization reg. with the UIA: International Society for Krishna Consciousness, f. 1966, Los Angeles, Calif. to: "promote a worldwide awakening to the ecstatic experience of Krishna consciousness which involves a process of self purification." Publ.: *Back to Godhead* (monthly).

Yearbook of International Organizations.

KRISTALLNACHT *German* = "crystal night." The night of Nov. 9–10, 1938 in Germany when Jewish synagogues, cemeteries and public institutions, shops and residences were set on fire and devastated by the ruling NSDAP party. It was the beginning of an extermination campaign of that part of the German population whom the ▷ Nuremberg Anti-Semic Laws of 1935 had defined as racially alien because they were of Jewish descent. The *pogrom* was called "crystal" because of the thick crystal glass which scattered the streets from the broken windows of Jewish stores. Its immediate cause was the assassination on Nov. 7, 1938 in Paris by a Pole, H.S. Grynszpan, of a German ambassadorial adviser, von Rath, who died from wounds on Nov. 9. On Nov. 12, the III Reich government banned any Jewish participation in German economic life and imposed a fine of one billion DM on the Jewish population.

KEESING's *Archiv der Gegenwart*, 1938, p. 3806; F.R. BIENENFELD, *The Germans and the Jews*, New York, 1939; W. LOWENTHAL, *The Jews in Germany*, Philadelphia, 1944.

KRONA. Icelandic krona. A monetary unit of Iceland; one króna = 100 aurar; issued by the Sedlabanki Islands.

KRONA. Swedish krona. A monetary unit of Sweden; one krona = 100 öre; issued by the Sveriges Riksbank.

KRONE. Danish krone. A monetary unit of Denmark; one krone = 100 ore; issued by the Denmark Nationalbank.

KRONE. Norwegian krone. A monetary unit of Norway; one krone = 100 öre; issued by the Norges Bank.

KRUPP CONCERN. One of the largest concerns of the steel and machine industries of the FRG, est. 1811 in Essen by Friedrich Krupp (1787–1826), taken over by his son Alfred Krupp (1812–87). In the years 1870–1945 became the armaments concern of the Reich. Its last owner, Alfried Krupp von Bohlen und Halbach (1907–67) was tried as a war criminal before the American Military Tribunal in Nuremberg and sentenced in August 1947 to 12 years imprisonment and the confiscation of his property. Released Jan. 31, 1951 by the US High Commissioner in the FRG, J. McCloy, he regained his property, which in the sixties was transformed into a joint-stock company administered by a Foundation established by Alfried Krupp. In 1967 the government of Iran purchased 25% of the shares. The concern changed its character from armaments to industrial production, involved mainly in the production of industrial equipment and steel products and also in the mining of iron ore in Brazil and Burma as well as phosphates in the southern Sahara.

B. MENNE, *Blood and Steel: the Rise of the House of Krupp*, London, 1938; *Der Krupp Prozess Stenographisches Bericht*, Frankfurt am M., 1947; G. von KLASS, *Krupp, the Story of an Industrial Empire*, London, 1954.

KUALA LUMPUR. The capital of the Federation of Malaysia, population 1980 census: 937,875, since 1896 (Federated Malaysia States). Seat of the Asian Regional Medical Student Association and of the Asian Regional Office of International Planned Parenthood Federation.

Yearbook of International Organizations; The Europa Yearbook 1987. A World Survey, Vol. II, London, 1987.

KU KLUX KLAN. An American organization active 1865–71, in the southern states of the USA, established Dec. 1865 in Pulaski, Tennessee, fighting against equal rights for Negroes, using ▷ lynching, forbidden by Congress of the USA 1870. A Ku Klux Klan Act passed by Congress in 1871, authorizing the President to suppress Ku Klux Klan disturbance by military force as well as to suspend the right of ▷ Habeas Corpus. The Ku Klux Klan operating from 1915 throughout the USA as a racist organization, is prohibited in northern states, but legally still exists in many southern states, with seat in Tuscaloosa, Alabama.

J.M. MECKLIN, *The Ku Klux Klan*, New York 1924; F. HORN, *Invisible Empire: The Story of the Ku Klux Klan 1866–1871*, New York 1939; D.M. CHALMERS, *Hooded Americanism 1865–1965*, Baltimore, 1965; A.W. TORGEE, *The Invisible Empire*, New York, 1968.

KULTURKAMPF. *German* = "struggle in civilization." A struggle between the Roman Catholic Church and Prussia over the clerical control of education forbidden by Prussian Landstag in May 1873, promoted by Adalbert Falk, the Prussian Minister of Education and Otto von Bismarck, chancellor of German Reich. Terminated by a compromise agreement 1887.

A. GOLDSCHMIDT, *Das Reich und Preussen im Kampf um die Führung: von Bismarck bis 1918*, Berlin, 1931; J. KRASUCKI, *Kulturkampf*, Poznań, 1962.

KULTURWEHR. A monthly organ of Union of National Minorities in Germany published in Berlin 1925–38 (first yearbook entitled, *Kulturwille*) which played a significant part in fighting Germany's subversive policy towards European minorities and in formulation of principles of co-existence in state–minorities relations. Chief theoreticians: Jan Kaczmarek (1895–1978), head of

Union of Poles in Germany, and the Serbo-Lusatian Jan Skala (1889–1945), editor of *Kulturwehr*.

JAN KACZMAREK, *Paz belifera*, Santiago de Chile, 1944.

KURDISTAN. The land of Kurds, southwestern Asian region, 191,600 sq. km, divided between eastern Turkey (est. 3,200,000 Kurds, 1970) northeastern Iraq (est. 1,550,000), northwestern Iran (est. 1,800,000), northeastern Syria (est. 320,000) and southern Soviet Armenia (est. 80,000) with a total of about 7,000,000 Kurds in 1970; subject of international disputes in the 17th and 19th centuries between Turkey and Persia. After World War I, under the Treaty of Sèvres 1920, the leading powers decided to separate Kurdistan from Turkey and to form an autonomous Kurdistan under a British Mandate of the League of Nations. The treaty never came into force and the future of Kurdistan was the subject of a Conference in Lausanne, 1922–23, and of resolutions of the League's Council, 1924–25. On the basis of these, Great Britain concluded, 1925, a treaty with Iraq and Turkey dividing Kurdistan into a larger Turkish part and a smaller Iraqi part which was rich in crude oil; another part of Kurdistan belonged to Persia. The struggle for unification and independence grew stronger after World War II when in Iranian Kurdistan the Kurdish Republic was proclaimed, 1947; liquidated by the central government, insurrections took place in Iraq and riots in Turkey. The President of Iraq proclaimed on Mar. 11, 1947, autonomy for Iraqi Kurdistan. In view of the Iranian–Iraq agreement of 1975, Kurdish partisans in Iraq gave up the fight; later accepted an amnesty. New controversial problems arose 1979–80 in connection with the existence of the Islamic Republic of Iran and the Iraqi–Iran war.

H. ARFA, *The Kurds*, London, 1966; E. O'BALLANCE, *The Kurdis Revolt, 1961–1970*, London, 1971.

KURILE ISLANDS. Russian: Kurilskiye Ostrova. A USSR archipelago in the Pacific; subject of international dispute between tsarist Russia and Japan in 19th century: Russian–Japanese agreement 1875 gave the Japanese possession in return for Sakhalin. Under the ▷ Yalta Declaration, of 1945 the Great Powers conceded the islands to the USSR after the end of war with Japan. Pursuant to the Peace Treaty with Japan, signed on Sept. 8, 1951 in San Francisco, Japan renounced all rights and claims to the Kuriles but as the Soviet Union was not among signatories, Japan renewed its claims and proposed a bilateral peace agreement with the USSR on the proviso that four islands are returned: Habomai, Etorofu, Kunashirii and Shikotan. The USSR expressed readiness to grant Japan Habomai and Shikotan, but the latter maintained its claims to all four islands. In Dec., 1978 the Soviet ambassador to Japan stated that his country "would never yield a single stone" to Japan; this hardened Soviet line was related to the ▷ China–Japan Peace Treaty, 1978. The People's Republic of China supported the Japanese claims publicly since 1976, and officially on Aug. 11, 1984, on the occasion of accreditation of a new Japanese ambassador.

The Japanese claims to the "Northern Territories" of the Kurile Islands are based on the Treaty of Commerce, Navigation and Delimitation, called the Shimeda Treaty, signed with Russia in 1855 and the Russo–Japanese Treaty in 1875 when ▷ Sakhalin was ceded to Tsarist Russia in exchange for the Kuriles, but the Russo-Japanese War 1905 nullified both agreements. In the Japanese opinion the "Northern Territories" (the islands of Kunashir, Etorofu, Shiashkotan and the Hotoman group) are distinct from the Kurile Islands. The

K

Japanese claims were also repeated in 1986 and 1987.

J.J. STEPHEN, *The Kurile Islands: Russo–Japanese Frontier in the Pacific*, New York, 1975; KEESING's *Record of World Events*, March, 1986.

KUROPATY. Name of a park area near the capital of Byelorussia ▷ Minsk, where in June 1988 mass graves of Byelorussian peasants murdered on the order of J.V. Stalin at the time of forced collectivization in 1937 were found. The first report on the excavation was published in Minsk with the comment: 'we note that there is no pardon for genocide'.

W. BYKAU, *Kuropaty, in: Literatura i Mastustva*, Minsk, June 5, 1987; *Unearthing Stalin's Crimes, in: The Economist*, August 27, 1988.

KUROSHIO. *Japanese* = "black stream". A warm ocean current, called also the Japan Current, similar to the Gulf Stream, flowing from the Philippines towards the south of Japan and continuing into the North Pacific; subject of international research.

KUWAIT. Member of the UN. Dowlat al Kuwait. State of Kuwait. Independent sheikdom on the Arabian peninsula at the head of the Persian Gulf, bounded by Saudi Arabia and Iraq. Area: 17,818 sq. km. Pop. 1982 census: 1,565,121 (1975 census: 984,837). Capital: Kuwait City with 60,525 inhabitants, 1980 GNP per capita 1980 US $22,840. Official language: Arabic. Currency: one Kuwaitti dinar = 10 dirhams = 1000 fils. National Day: Feb. 25, Independence Day, 1961.

Member of the UN since May 14, 1963 and of UN specialized agencies. Member of the Arab League, OAU, OAPEC, OPEC, and Gulf Co-operation Council /GCC/.
International relations: British protectorate 1897–1961. The Independence of Kuwait on Feb. 25, 1961 was protested by Iraq which claimed sovereignty over Kuwait. Recognized by Iraq in 1963. In 1974 nationalized 60% of oil production; the state-owned Kuwait Petroleum, Gas and Energy Company controls all oil and gas exploration. Since 1983 Kuwait co-operated with other member States of the GCC on a military defence system, independent of any super power. ▷ Neutral Arabic Zone. A tragic 15 day hijacking of a Kuwaiti airliner took place on April 5, 1988.
See also ▷ Air Piracy.

The Economic Development of Kuwait, Baltimore, 1965; *Synopses of UN Cases*, New York, 1966; *The Oil of Kuwait, Facts and Figures*, Kuwait 1970; H.V. WINSTONE, Z. FREETH, *Kuwait, Prospects and Reality*, London, 1972; *UN Review*, June, 1972; M.W. KHOUJA, P.G. SADLER, *The Economy of Kuwait*, London, 1979; *The Europa Year Book 1984. A World Survey*, Vol. II, pp. 1892–1902, London, 1984.

KWACHA. Malawi kwacha. A monetary unit of Malawi: one kwacha = 100 tambala; issued since Feb. 15, 1971 (replacing the Malawi pound) by the Reserve Bank of Malawi.

KWACHA. Zambia kwacha. A monetary unit of Zambia; one kwacha = 100 ngwee: issued (replac-

ing the Zambian pound Jan. 16, 1968) by the Bank of Zambia.

KWANDEBELE. ▷ Bantu Homelands.

KWANZA. A monetary unit of Angola, one kwanza = 100 lwei, issued since 1978 by the Banco Central de Angola.

KWAZULU BANTUSTAN. Since 1959 official name of ▷ Zululand in the South African Republic. Area: 31,442 sq. km. The area is not coterminous with the historic region of Zululand, and only half of the Zulu live in Kwazulu.

KWAZULU. ▷ Bantu Homelands.

KWIC. Key Word in Context. A bibliographical index based on key words or phrases in a text: opposite ▷ KWOC.

KWOC. Key Word out of Context. A bibliographical index based on key words or phrases not used in the context; opposite ▷ KWIC.

UNBIS *Thesaurus*, New York, 1985, p. IX.

KYAT. A monetary unit of Burma: one kyat = 100 pyas; issued by the Union of Burma Bank. The Bank withdrew from the pound sterling area on Oct. 17, 1966.

KYOTO PRINCIPLES ON MENTALLY ILL PERSONS. ▷ Mentally Ill Persons.

L

LABOR. ▷ Labour.

LABORATORY ANIMALS. The animals on which scientists experiment for medical purposes; subject of organized international scientific co-operation. Organizations reg. with the UIA:

International Committee of Laboratory Animals, ICLA, f. 1956 Oslo, under the sponsorship of UNESCO, financed by WHO. Publ. *ICLA Bulletin* and *Recommended Definitions for Current Terms Employed in the Care, Maintenance and Use of Laboratory Animals.*
Society for Laboratory Animal Science, f. 1968, Frankfurt am Main.

Yearbook of International Organizations.

LABORATORY FOR STRONG MAGNETIC FIELDS AND LOW TEMPERATURE, INTERNATIONAL. An international scientific research organization, f. 1968, in Wroclaw, Poland by an Agreement signed at Warsaw in May, 1968 by the academies of sciences of Bulgaria, the GDR, Poland and the USSR to carry on theoretical and experimental research in the realm of strong stationary magnetic fields with special reference to the Charter of the International Laboratory, which entered into force on Nov. 29, 1968.

W.E. BUTLER (ed.), *A Source Book on Socialist International Organizations*, Alphen, 1978, pp. 775–783.

LABOREM EXERCENS. *Latin* (literally): Engaging in work. The encyclical of Pope John Paul II "On Human Work" dated Sept. 15, 1981, transmitted as an official document by the Vatican to the ILO.

LABOUR. The subject of international law, international co-operation and international conventions. The attitude toward labour, which plays diverse roles in religious and philosophical systems, as well as in social, economic and political doctrines, was the main cause of the international workers' movement which began with the publication of the ▷ Communist Manifesto, 1848. This movement after 1864 in France forced the passing of the first Strike Law; in 1866 it began to agitate for the right to work and for an equitable work time; and in following years for syndicate rights. The International Labour Organization, ILO, created in 1919, and since 1924 the International Congress for the Scientific Organization of Labour have contributed to the development of labour law. The problems of employment and unemployment have been the subject of regional studies by ECOSOC and the ILO. In 1960, Africa represented a potential working force of the order of 112 million people; Latin America – 71m.; North America – 77m.; Asia - 728m.; Europe – 191m.; Oceania – 6m.; and the world as a whole – 1296m. Those employed in agriculture accounted for: Africa – 78%, Asia – 69%, Latin America – 46%, USSR – 42%, Europe (without the USSR) – 26%, Oceania and North America – 20%. In 1960, the developed countries, representing one-third of the world's population, employed 62% of the global work force. According to studies made in 1971 by the subcommittee on science of the US Congress, labour costs in the highly developed countries were quite varied. In relation to American labour costs, the cost is lower in all other countries. In 1970 in Canada it was 83%, in the FRG 54%, in France 39%, in Great Britain 37%, and in Japan only 26% of US costs. The ILO World Labour Report, 1985, noted a general deterioration in the global labour situation. A world-wide worsening was observed in working conditions and fatality rates. Organizations reg. with UIA besides the ILO:

Caribbean Congress of Labour, 1960, Port of Spain.
European Work Study Federation, est. 1961, The Hague.
International Association for Social Progress, est. 1925, Paris. Advisory status with ECOSOC. Publ.: *AIPS Bulletin d'Information.*
International Labour Film Institute, est. 1953, Brussels.
International Society for Labour Law and Social Legislation, est. 1958, Geneva.

Yearbook of International Organizations; OIT, *Annuaire de statistiques du travail 1971*, Genève, 1971, p. 799; ILO. *World Labour Report with Statistical Annex*, Geneva, 1984; ILO, *World Labour Report*, Geneva 1985.

LABOUR CAMPS. State institutions of ▷ forced labour, organized in colonial empires and in different social systems in the 19th and 20th century. On the basis of the Soviet Penal Code a system of labour camps for "socialistic reeducation" (*Gulags*) was built since 1924 in the USSR by J.V. Stalin. During the XXth Congress of the Communist Party of the Soviet Union in 1956 the existence of labour camps was criticized by N.S. Khrushchev. In Nazi Germany, 1933–1945 a system of forced labour camps was built by ▷ Gestapo as a part of ▷ concentration camp structure, called in German: *Arbeitslager-Aussenlager der KZ*.
A Convention on abolition of forced labour was adopted by the ILO on June 27, 1957. In communist countries the labor camps are called re-education camps. The criminal code of e.g. Vietnam designates forced labour as the punishment for "crimes against the people".

R. LEMKIN, *Axis Rule in Occupied Europe*, London, 1944; H. BÜLCK, *Die Zwangsarbeit im Friedensvölkerrecht*, Stuttgart, 1953; G.C. GUINS, *Soviet Law and Soviet Society*, The Hague, 1954; J. ROSSI, *The Gulag Handbook. The Encyclopedic Dictionary of Soviet Penitentiary Institutions and Terms Related to Forced Labour Camps*, London, 1987; KEESING's *Record of World Events*, May 1988.

LABOUR, COST OF. In industrialized countries a measure of wages by the hour, subject of international comparative statistics.

LABOUR DAY. A holiday of the working class since 1890, is celebrated in the majority of European countries on May 1 (in the USSR and in socialist countries official holiday); in the United States on the first Monday in September.

LABOUR, DIVISION OF, INTERNATIONAL. The adjustment of the economy of individual countries to the specific production of certain goods, in relation to other countries. A consequence of selective production in countries forming a common market. Its aim is to obtain an increased growth rate through a broadened market with a reduction in production costs. Before World War II division of labour was designed to develop the production of raw materials. After the war the modern forms of division of labour began in the EEC through agreements and the formation of international concerns; and in the CMEA they began through co-ordination of the economic plans of member countries. In June, 1962, a meeting of communist and working parties of CMEA members adopted a document entitled Basic Principles of International Socialist Division of Labour, where the co-ordination of plans of national economies was ascertained to be a fundamental factor of socialist economies. The World Conference for Employment, Division of Income, Social Progress and International Division of Labour was held in Geneva from June 4 to 17, 1976, under auspices of ILO.

Recueil de document, Varsovie, 1962; *UN Yearbook 1976*, p. 942. W.E. BUTLER (ed.), *A Source Book on Socialist International Organizations*, Alphen, 1978, pp. 13–120.

LABOUR INSPECTION. A subject of an ILO international convention on the principles of organization of labour inspection aimed at occupational safety and hygiene.

LABOUR-INTENSIVE. An economic term describing production methods which use more labour than capital per unit produced.

LABOUR LAW. A subject of international co-operation and international conventions, including the Berlin Convention of 1890 and the Berne Conventions of 1905, 1906 and 1913. Since 1921, all work in this area has been concentrated in the committees and conferences of the ILO. The ILO adopted, in the years 1919–85, over 120 conventions and an equal number of separate recommendations; two-thirds have come into force and are called collectively the Code of International Labour and Social Legislation. Since 1955, under ILO auspices, International Congresses of Labour Law and Social Security have been convened by three associations: the Geneva Association of the Labour Law, the Paris International Association of Social Progress and the Geneva International Association of Industrial Relations (the first Congress was held in Trieste in 1955). ILO publications on the subject are the *Legislative Series* and the *Labour Review*. ▷ Right to Work.
Organizations reg. with the UIA:

International Society for Labour Law and Social Legislation, f. 1958, Geneva, in result of a fusion of the International Society for Social Law (1950) and the International Congress of Labour Law (1951) with the task of developing internal and international labour law and social security. The organization maintains contact with the ILO, its congresses are held every three years, the first in 1951. Seat. Geneva.

L. TROCLET, *Legislation Sociale Internationale*, Bruxelle, 1952; C.W. JENGS, *Human Rights and International Labour Standards*, London, 1960; *Conventions and recommendations adopted by the International Labour Conference 1919–1966*, ILO Geneva, 1966; *Conventions et Recommendations 1919–1966*, OIT/ILO Genève, 1966; P. EHUAN (ed.), *International Labour Law Reports*, Alphen, 1978; O. KAHN-FREUND, B.A. HEPPLE (eds) *International Encyclopedia of Comparative Law, Vol. XV, Labour Law*, The Hague, 1985.

LABOUR STUDIES INTERNATIONAL INSTITUTE. Institut international d'études sociales. An ILO institute est. 1960, Geneva, as an international center for advanced education and research in the field of labour. Publ.: *Labour and Society* (English and French). Reg. with the UIA.

Yearbook of International Organizations.

LABRADOR. ▷ Newfoundland.

L

LADAKH. A frontier district in ▷ Kashmir state. Area: 118,524 sq. km. Pop.: 105,001 (1971) bordering China and Pakistan. In the 16th centuries dependency of Tibet; since the mid-19th century integrated by Kashmir. In 1959 Chinese troops occupied the southeast part of Ladakh and constructed a road connecting China with Pakistan, 1962. A new demarcation of the Chinese–Pakistan border was signed on 1963, giving to Pakistan the Oprang valley (1880 sq. km). China rejected the protests of India, and Chinese–Indian border demarcation negotiations, begun in Geneva 1963 did not produce results.

The International Geographic Encyclopedia and Atlas, London, 1979.

LAGOS. The capital of Nigeria since 1960; seat of organizations reg. with the UIA: Cocoa Producers Alliance and African Ground-nut Council. A World Conference for Action against Apartheid was held at Lagos Aug. 22–26, 1977.

LAGOS PLAN, 1980. African Plan of Action, adopted on Apr. 29, 1980 by the heads of state and government of the OAU as a follow-up to the Monrovia Declaration of July 1979, which set the goal for Africa of attaining self-reliant and self-sustaining development and economic growth.
The African leaders agreed on certain broad principles to guide their policies on those subjects. Those principles indicated that:

– Africa's huge resources must be applied principally to meet the needs of its people;
– the region's almost total reliance on exports of raw materials must change;
– Africa must mobilize its entire human and natural resources for its development;
– Africa must cultivate the virtue of self-reliance;
– efforts put into and benefits derived from the development must be equally shared; and
– efforts towards African economic integration must be pursued with renewed determination.
Agriculture had undergone drastic deterioration, and per capita food production and consumption had fallen below national requirements. To cope with that problem, the Plan called for an immediate improvement in the food situation and for laying the foundation for self-sufficiency in cereals, livestock and fish products. Investment required in agriculture and related activities for the period 1980–85 was estimated at \$21.4 billion (at 1979 prices). The desirability of financing at least 50% of investments from domestic resources was indicated.
In the industrial sector, the article further stated, the Plan set three concrete objectives for the expansion of industrial production between 1981 and the end of the century. Firstly, by 1985, output of member states was expected to reach 1% of total world industrial output, 1.4% by 1990, and 2% by the year 2000.
In the final chapter of the Plan, dealing with development planning, statistics and population, the article stated, developing countries in Africa were projected to grow by an average of 7% a year in the 1980s, with oil-exporting countries growing by about 8% and non-oil-exporting countries at about 6% annually. Projected agricultural growth was estimated at 4%, while the growth rate in manufacturing was to attain 9.5% a year in the 1980s. Exports were expected to expand by 7% a year, while imports would have to maintain a growth rate of less than 8.2% annually. The Plan ultimately stressed the urgency of strengthening the statistical bases for effective policy-making and for integrating the population variable into planning, bearing in mind the expected doubling of the African population between 1975 and 2000. Under the Final Act of Lagos, the heads of state and government confirmed their adherence to the Lagos Plan of Action and to the setting up of regional structures and to the strengthening of existing ones as a first step towards the creation of an African Economic Community by the year 2000.

The UN General Assembly on Dec. 5, 1980 adopted Res. 35/64 without vote, which "takes note with satisfaction of the Lagos Plan of Action for the Implementation of the Monrovia Strategy for the Development of Africa".

Yearbook of the UN, 1980, pp. 557–558, New York, 1982; *UN Chronicle*, March, 1984.

LAHORE. A city in Pakistan, capital of Punjab. The Fort and Shalamar Gardens of Lahore are included in the ▷ World Heritage UNESCO List. The Fort of Lahore owes its charm and poetry to the 16th century Emperor Akbar. The fort is surrounded by ramparts strengthened by bastions and contains pavilions, mosques, audience halls and royal apartments. A hundred years later, one of Akbar's descendants, Shah Jehan, had the park of Shalamar ("Abode of Joy") laid out to the northeast of the city. These gardens cover more than 16 hectares and are spread out over three terraces. They contain pavilions and summer houses in *"piedra dura"*, red sandstone and marble. The whole scene is given additional charm by the waterfalls and fountains.

UNESCO, *A Legacy for All*, Paris, 1984.

LAIBACH CONGRESS, 1821. A meeting in Laibach, Austria (now Ljubljana in Yugoslavia) between the Austrian Emperor, Russian Tsar, and the King of Naples and diplomats from these countries as well as from Prussia and France, and observers from Great Britain; a follow-up to the ▷ Troppau Congress, 1820, in connection with revolutionary upheavals in the Balkans, Italy, Latin America, Austria, Prussia and Russia; it endorsed the principle of intervention to put an end to the unrest which threatened peace. This principle was opposed by Great Britain which recognized the newly formed Latin-American republics and announced its adherence to the principle of non-intervention, Jan. 28, 1823.

G.F. DE MARTENS, *Nouveau Recueil des Traités depuis 1808 jusqu'à présent*, Vol. 5, Göttingen, 1839.

LAICAL APOSTOLATE. *Latin = Apostolato laici.* The name used by the Catholic Church for the disseminating of Church doctrines by laical persons and organizations. The Laical Apostolate was initiated by Pope Leon XIII, organized by Pius XI who made the Catholic Action organization (appearing also under other names, such as the Catholic League, the Catholic Union etc.) the main laical political instrument of the Church. The Laical Apostolate was reformed by John XXIII who united scores of Catholic international organizations within the hierarchy, but without giving priority to any one of these.

LAICIZATION. An international term for the domination of secular world-views in place of religious ones, above all in science and education; a process which became almost universal in the 19th and 20th centuries, initiated by the liberal ideas of the French Revolution. Laicization appeared simultaneously with ▷ Separation of church and state.

LAIKA. *Russian* = Laika Kudryavka. Name of a dog from the group of Siberian hunting Spitzes, so called Laikas, which after special training was placed in a Soviet artificial Earth satellite, Sputnik II, launched Nov. 3, 1957 into earth orbit and was the first live specimen for studying the reaction of an organism during space flight. Perished during flight.

KEESING's *Contemporary Archive*, 1957.

LAISSEZ-PASSER. *French* = "let pass". An international term for a travel document, issued presently to employees of the UN and of its specialized agencies according to the Convention on Immunities and Privileges of the UN, which states (art. VII):

"Section 24. The United Nations may issue United Nations laissez-passer to its officials. These laissez-passer shall be recognized and accepted as valid travel documents by the authorities of Members, taking into account the provision of Section 25.
Section 25. Applications for visas (where required) from the holders of United Nations laissez-passer, when accompanied by a certificate that they are travelling on the business of the United Nations, shall be dealt with as speedily as possible. In addition, such persons shall be granted facilities for speedy travel.
Section 26. Similar facilities to those specified in Section 25 shall be accorded to experts and other persons who, though not the holders of United Nations laissez-passer, have a certificate that they are travelling on the business of the United Nations.
Section 27. The Secretary-General, Assistant Secretaries-General and Directors travelling on United Nations laissez-passer on the business of the United Nations shall be granted the same facilities as are accorded to diplomatic envoys.
Section 28. The provision of this article may be applied to the comparable officials of specialized agencies if the agreements for relationship made under article 63 of the Charter so provide."

UN Convention on the Privileges and Immunities of the UN, New York, 1946; UNTS, Vol. 1, p. 162.

LAKE SUCCESS. A city on Long Island in the state of New York; the first temporary headquarters of the UN in the years 1946–47.

LALIBELA. An Ethiopian cultural site, included in the ▷ World Heritage UNESCO List. Around the beginning of the 13th century, skilful Ethiopian craftsmen constructed rock-hewn churches by completely excavating blocks of tuff, hollowing them out and then decorating them inside and out. The most famous are the eleven churches of Lalibela, a holy city. Each church is different in plan and style and presents different bas-relief and wall paintings.

I. BIDDAR, *Lalibela, the Monolithic Churches of Ethiopia*, London, 1959; UNESCO, *A Legacy for All*, Paris, 1984.

LAMAISM. A religious system introduced in the 7th century. Tibetan form of ▷ Buddhism, derived from the Tibetan name of a Buddhist priest (Lama), prevalent in Tibet and in the Diaspora. The ▷ Dalai Lama escaped in 1959 to India.

G. SCHULEMANN, *Die Geschichte der Dalai Lamas*, Berlin, 1911.

LAMBETH CONFERENCE OF ANGLICAN BISHOPS. Established 1867 by the Archbishop of Canterbury in his London residence named Lambeth House, held approximately every ten years. Publ. *Lambeth Quadrilateral*.

S.F. BOYNE, *Mutual Responsibility and Interdependence in the Body of Christ*, London 1963.

LANCE. A missile with a set of rockets with different warheads. The Lance missile with a neutron payload is called the Lance Enhanced Radiation Warhead. ▷ Neutron bomb.

LAND. A subject of international co-operation. Organizations reg. with the UIA:

Commonwealth Association of Surveying and Land Economy, f. 1969, London.
International Institute for Land Reclamation and Improvement, f. 1955, Wageningen, Netherlands.
International Union for Land Value Taxation and Free Trade, f. 1926, London. Publ.: *Land and Liberty*.
International Union of Landed Property Owners, f. 1923, Paris. Publ.: *Bulletin*.

Yearbook of International Organizations.

LAND LOCKED STATE. An international term, defined 1965 in the Convention on Transit Trade of Land Locked States as "any State which has no sea coast"; generally countries among the poorest developing nations, with special and overriding transportation difficulties because of lack of access to the sea. The IV Conference of Heads of States or Government of Nonaligned Countries, in Algiers, Sept. 5–9, 1973, adopted a Resolution on Special Measures Related to the Particular Needs of the Land Locked Countries. The UN General Assembly, 1975, established with the Res. 3504/XXX a Special Fund for Land-Locked Countries; and on Dec. 19, 1979 the Res. 34/209 requested the UNDP and the UNCTAD to pursue activity in favour of land locked developing countries. ▷ New International Economic Order.

UNTS, Vol. 597, p. 46; *UN Chronicle*, March, 1980, pp. 58–59; R.L. BLEDSOE, B.A. BOCZEK, *The International Law Dictionary*, Oxford, 1987.

LAND MILE. A heterogeneous unit of length. In antiquity it was equal to 1000 paces = 1481 m; in Anglo-Saxon countries 1760 yards = 1609.44 m; in Austria – 7585.6 m; in Poland – 8534.31 m; in Prussia – 7532.8 m.

LANDSAT. The US civilian space industry which offers space photos of Earth in the world market.

LAND WAR. A military action carried out on land; the law and customs obligating sides engaged in land war were codified in the Hague Conventions of 1899 and 1907 as well as the Geneva Conventions of 1929 and 1949.

LANGUAGES. A subject of international co-operation. The growth of international organizations in the 20th century, increasing number of international bi- and multilateral agreements, conferences, congresses and multilateral meetings as well as growing international tourist traffic caused great demand for knowledge of foreign languages and training of professional interpreters. Schools were opened where knowledge of two or three foreign languages is required for admission. In the ▷ Helsinki Final Act the chapter on education contains the sub-heading Languages and Civilization and recommends the fostering of translation of literature of less widely spread and less studied languages.
See also ▷ Computer Languages, and ▷ Programming Languages.

C.F. VOEGELIN, F.M. VOEGELIN, *Classification and Index of the World's Languages*, 3 Vols., Amsterdam, 1978; UNESCO, *Language, Identity and Communication*, Paris, 1986.

LANGUAGES, OFFICIAL. An international term for a language or languages operative in international organizations or at international conferences. In uninational countries the official language is identical with the national language; in multinational ones, two or more official languages may be used in domestic offices and international relations; furthermore languages spoken by ethnic minorities in a given region may be temporarily granted official status and are sometimes called "second official languages". Official languages are specified in constitutions of states, statutes of organizations, regulations of international conferences and, in particular cases, peace treaties or bilateral agreements, e.g. the Treaty of Versailles, June 28, 1919.

V. DURDIENIEVSKI, *Ravnopravniye iazykov w sovietskom stroie*, Moskva, 1927.

LANGUAGES OF THE UN. Under the UN Charter the official languages of all the institutions in the UN System are Chinese, English, French, Russian and Spanish. Arabic has been added as an official language of the UN General Assembly, the Security Council and the ECOSOC, 1977. On Jan. 17 1974 it was ruled that "speeches made in any of the five languages of the Security Council should be interpreted into the other languages" and (Rule 44) "any representative may make a speech in a language other than the languages of the Security Council. In this case, he shall himself provide for interpretation into one of those languages. Interpretation into the other (official) languages of the Security Council by the interpreters of the Secretariat may be based on the interpretation given in the first such language". The same Rules are observed by the UN General Assembly. The German speaking countries organized in 1970 a pool translating and printing UN documents in German at their own cost but terminated the co-operation in 1982.

Provisional Rules of Procedure of the Security Council, UN, New York 1974; *UN Bulletin*, No. 1 and No. 11, 1949; *Everyone's United Nations*, New York, 1979, p. 11; Lexique Géneral Anglais–Français avec Suplément Espagnol–Français et Russe–Français, Nations Unies, New York, 1980.

LANGUAGES, UNIVERSAL. The first attempts to create universal languages appeared in antiquity in the form of ideographic languages, but introductory phonetic elaborations did not appear until the 17th century (Characteristic Universalis, 1696). The most popular universal language is ▷ Esperanto (1887), which is promoted by 27 international organizations reg. with the UIA. Other universal languages: Volapuk, 1879; Interlingua (*Latino sine flexione*), 1905; Ido, 1907; Occidental, 1922. In 1960 UNESCO initiated work on international ideographic writing that would be universally understandable.

J. COUTOURA, L. LEAN, *Histoire de la langue universelle*, Paris, 1903; J. BAUDOUIN DE COURTENAY, *Zur Kritik der Künstlichen Weltsprachen*, Berlin, 1907.

LANOUX. A lake in the French Pyrenees, close to the Spanish border. Subject of international dispute provoked by Spanish protest against French plans to harness its waters for industrial purposes with a consequent lowering of the water level of the Legre River on the Spanish side. Spain considered the French project to be in violation of the Spanish--French treaties signed in Bayonne on May 26, 1866. In accordance with the French–Spanish arbitration agreement of July 10, 1929 an International Arbitration Tribunal was set up on Nov. 19, 1956, in Geneva, which ruled on Oct. 16, 1957, that it found no violation of the Bayonne treaties.

F. DULERY, "L'affaire du Lac Lanoux", in: *Revue général de droit international 1958*; W.L. GRIFFIN, "The use of Waters of International Drainage Basins", in: *American Journal of International Law*, No. 53, 1959; M.H. GOTZ, "Lac Lanoux-Fall", in: *STRUPP-SCHLOCHAUER Wörterbuch des Völkerrechts*, Berlin, 1961, pp. 394–396.

L'ANSE AUX MEDOWS. A Canadian National Historic Park, included in the ▷ World Heritage UNESCO List. On this site, in the north of Newfoundland, are the remains of eight buildings and stone, bone, copper and bronze objects all of Scandinavian origin. They are proof of the landing in America of Europeans from Iceland, 400 years before Christopher Columbus.

UNESCO, *A Legacy for All*, Paris, 1984.

LANSING-ISHII AGREEMENT, 1917. An American–Japanese agreement, signed at Washington, Nov. 2, 1917 by the US Secretary of State Robert Lansing (1864–1928) and the Japanese Foreign Minister Kikujiro Ishii (1866–1945). It recognized Japan's "special interests in China", but not in Manchuria; it was abrogated by an exchange of notes on Mar. 30, 1923.

MAC MURRAY, *Treaties and Agreements with and concerning China, 1894–1919*, New York, 1921; W.M. MALLOYS, *Treaties, Conventions between the USA and other Powers*, Washington, 1923.

LAOS. Member of the UN. Lao People's Democratic Republic. State in south-east Asia, north-west Indochina. Borders on the People's Republic of China, Democratic Republic of Vietnam, Kampuchea, Thailand and Burma. Area: 236,800 sq. km. Population 1985 census: 3,584,000. Capital: Vientiane with 176,000 inhabitants, 1981. Official language: Laotian. Currency: one kip = 100 att. GNP per capita 1987: US $220. National Day: Dec. 2, proclamation of the republic, 1975.
Member of the UN since Sept. 17, 1955 and of all its specialized agencies with the exception of the IAEA, IFC, IMO, WIPO and GATT.
International relations: 1893 to 1949 kingdom called Lanxang under French protectorate; Laos was an independent state within the French Union in 1949–54. Following the Indochina treaties signed in Geneva July 22, 1954, French troops were withdrawn in Sept., 1954. The International Commission for Control and Supervision in Laos composed of representatives of India, Canada and Poland was in operation from 1954 to 1958. In 1962 the International Conference on Laos, Geneva 1961/62, drafted and adopted the Laos Neutrality Declaration of July 21, 1962. Internal conflicts grew into a civil war. In Oct. 1972 negotiations between belligerents (Vientiane and Pathet Lao) started, wound up Feb. 20, 1973 with the signature of a Treaty on the Restoration of Peace and the Assuring of National Agreement in Laos. Another agreement concluded on Feb. 21, 1973 was supplemented with an extensive Protocol Sept. 14, 1973 which obliged all foreign troops to withdraw from the country, and conditions were provided for the work of the International Commission for Control and Supervision. On Dec. 2, 1975 the Republic was proclaimed. A treaty with Vietnam on mutual assistance and co-operation in all areas of the economy and defense was concluded on July 18, 1977. From 1982 a partial normalization of the border relations with Thailand.

P.L. BOULANGER, *Histoire du Laos Français*, Paris, 1931; *UNTS*, Vol. 956, p. 1964; S. MODELSKI, *International Conference on the Settlement of the Laotian Question 1961–62*, Vancouver, 1963; J.M. HALPERN, *Government, Politics and Social Structure in Laos*, Detroit, 1964; W.P. KOZHEVNIKOV, R.A. POPOVKINA, *Sovremennyi Laos*, Moskva, 1966; D.W. WAINHOUSE, *International Peace Observation*, Baltimore, 1966, pp. 503–512; *Accord sur le rétablissement de la paix et la réalisation de la concorde nationale au Laos-Vientiane, le 21 février 1973*, Paris, 1973; J.J. ZASLOFF, *The Pathet Lao: Leadership and Organization*, London, 1973; The Europa Year Book 1984. A World Survey, Vol. II, pp. 1903–1910, London, 1984; M. STUART-FOX, *Laos: Politics, Economics and Society*, London 1986.

LAOS NEUTRALITY DECLARATION, 1962. A Declaration on the Neutrality of Laos, signed on July 23, 1962 in Geneva; it came into force upon signature. The text is as follows:

"The Governments of the Union of Burma, the Kingdom of Cambodia, Canada, the People's Republic of China, the Democratic Republic of Viet-Nam, the Republic of France, the Republic of India, the Polish People's Republic, the Republic of Viet-Nam, the Kingdom of Thailand, the Union of Soviet Socialist

Republics, the United Kingdom of Great Britain and Northern Ireland and the United States of America, whose representatives took part in the International Conference on the Settlement of the Laotian Question, 1961–1962;

Welcoming the presentation of the statement of neutrality by the Royal Government of Laos of July 9, 1962,and taking note of this statement, which is, with the concurrence of the Royal Government of Laos, incorporated in the present Declaration as an integral part thereof, and the text of which is as follows:

The Royal Government of Laos,

Being resolved to follow the path of peace and neutrality in conformity with the interests and aspirations of the Laotian people, as well as the principles of the Joint Communiqué of Zurich dated June 22, 1961, and of the Geneva Agreements of 1954, in order to build a peaceful, neutral, independent, democratic, unified and prosperous Laos,

Solemnly declares that:

(1) It will resolutely apply the five principles of peaceful co-existence in foreign relations, and will develop friendly relations and establish diplomatic relations with all countries, the neighbouring countries first and foremost, on the basis of equality and of respect for the independence and sovereignty of Laos;

(2) It is the will of the Laotian people to protect and ensure respect for the sovereignty, independence, neutrality, unity, and territorial integrity of Laos;

(3) It will not resort to the use or threat of force in any way which might impair the peace of other countries, and will not interfere in the internal affairs of other countries;

(4) It will not enter into any military alliance or into any agreement, whether military or otherwise, which is inconsistent with the neutrality of the Kingdom of Laos; it will not allow the establishment of any foreign military base on Laotian territory, nor allow any country to use Laotian territory for military purposes or for the purposes of interference in the internal affairs of other countries, nor recognise the protection of any alliance or military coalition, including SEATO;

(5) It will not allow any foreign interference in the internal affairs of the Kingdom of Laos in any form whatsoever;

(6) Subject to the provisions of Article 5 of the Protocol, it will require the withdrawal from Laos of all foreign troops or military personnel to be introduced into Laos;

(7) It will accept direct and unconditional aid from all countries that wish to help the Kingdom of Laos build up an independent and autonomous national economy on the basis of respect for the sovereignty of Laos;

(8) It will respect the treaties and agreements signed in conformity with the interests of the Laotian people and of the policy of peace and neutrality of the Kingdom, in particular the Geneva Agreements of 1962, and will abrogate all treaties and agreements which are contrary to those principles. This statement of neutrality by the Royal Government of Laos shall be promulgated constitutionally and shall have the force of law.

The Kingdom of Laos appeals to all the States participating in the International Conference on the Settlement of the Laotian Question, and to all other States, to recognise the sovereignty, independence, neutrality, unity and territorial integrity of Laos, to conform to these principles in all respects, and to refrain from any action inconsistent therewith.

Conforming the principles of respect for the sovereignty, independence, unity and territorial integrity of the Kingdom of Laos and non-interference in its internal affairs which are embodied in the Geneva Agreements of 1954;

Emphasising the principle of respect for the neutrality of the Kingdom of Laos;

Agreeing that the above-mentioned principles constitute a basis for the peaceful settlement of the Laotian question; Profoundly convinced that the independence and neutrality of the Kingdom of Laos will assist the peaceful democratic development of the Kingdom of Laos and the achievement of national accord and unity in that country, as well as the strengthening of peace and security in South-East Asia;

(1) Solemnly declare, in accordance with the will of the Government and people of the Kingdom of Laos, as expressed in the statement of neutrality by the Royal Government of Laos of July 9, 1962, that they recognise and will respect and observe in every way the sovereign-

ty, independence, neutrality, unity and territorial integrity of the Kingdom of Laos.

(2) Undertake, in particular, that

(a) they will not commit or participate in any way in any act which might directly or indirectly impair the sovereignty, independence, neutrality, unity or territorial integrity of the Kingdom of Laos;

(b) they will not resort to the use or threat of force or any other measure which might impair the peace of the Kingdom of Laos;

(c) they will refrain from all direct or indirect interference in the internal affairs of the Kingdom of Laos;

(d) they will not attach conditions of a political nature to any assistance which they may offer or which the Kingdom of Laos may seek;

(e) they will not bring the Kingdom of Laos in any way into any military alliance or any other agreement, whether military or otherwise, which is inconsistent with her neutrality, nor invite or encourage her to enter into any such alliance or to conclude any such agreement;

(f) they will respect the wish of the Kingdom of Laos not to recognise the protection of any alliance or military coalition, including SEATO;

(g) they will not introduce into the Kingdom of Laos foreign troops or military personnel in any form whatsoever, nor will they in any way facilitate or connive at the introduction of any foreign troops or military personnel;

(h) they will not establish nor will they in any way facilitate or connive at the establishment in the Kingdom of Laos of any foreign military base, foreign strong point or other foreign military installation of any kind;

(i) they will not use the territory of the Kingdom of Laos for interference in the internal affairs of other countries;

(j) they will not use the territory of any country, including their own for interference in the internal affairs of the Kingdom of Laos.

(3) Appeal to all other States to recognise, respect and observe in every way the sovereignty, independence and neutrality, and also the unity and territorial integrity, of the Kingdom of Laos and to refrain from any action inconsistent with these principles or with other provisions of the present Declaration.

(4) Undertake, in the event of a violation or threat of violation of the sovereignty, independence, neutrality, unity or territorial integrity of the Kingdom of Laos, to consult jointly with the Royal Government of Laos and among themselves in order to consider measures which might prove to be necessary to ensure the observance of these principles and the other provisions of the present Declaration.

(5) The present Declaration shall enter into force on signature and together with the statement of neutrality by the Royal Government of Laos of July 9, 1962, shall be regarded as constituting an international agreement. The present Declaration shall be deposited in the archives of the Governments of the United Kingdom and the Union of Soviet Socialist Republics, which shall furnish certified copies thereof to the other signatory States and to all the other States of the world."

Came into force on July 23, 1962, upon signature, in accordance with the provisions of par. 5.

UNTS, Vol. 456, pp. 302–305.

LAOTIAN CONFERENCE IN GENEVA, 1961–62. A Geneva Conference in connection with the civil war in Laos, which started 1960 and ended with an armistice May 14, 1961; an international conference with the participation of five Great Powers: the Chinese People's Republic, France, Great Britain, the USA and the USSR as well as Burma, Cambodia, Canada, India, Laos, Poland, Siam, the Democratic Republic of Vietnam, and South Vietnam. The Conference ended with the signing of the ▷ Laos Neutrality Declaration, 1962.

Declaration and Protocol on the Neutrality of Laos, HMSO, London, l963; G. MODELSKI, *International Conference on the Settlement of the Laotian Question, 1961–62*, Vancouver, 1963.

LA PAZ. The administrative capital of Bolivia since 1898 (the legislative is Sucre); Population 1982

estim. 881,401. The highest located capital city in the world (3,660 m); seat of a UN Information Centre.

LAPPEENRANTA – VYBORG CANAL. ▷ Saimaa.

LARCEF. ▷ Bolivia.

LARRETA DOCTRINE, 1945. A thesis formulated on Nov. 21, 1945 by the foreign minister of Uruguay E.R. Larreta, in a note to the ambassadors of the Latin American republics in Montevideo, professing that to safeguard peace the American states should obligate themselves to collective military defense, and to collective intervention for the protection of democracy. A negative reply was sent by l3 states; in favor of the Larreta doctrine were: Guatemala, Honduras, Costa Rica, Nicaragua, Panama and Uruguay.

A. GARCIA ROBLES, *El Mundo de la Postguerra*, Mexico, DF, l946, Vol. l. pp. 245–247; VAN WYNEN, A.F. THOMAS, *La Non-Intervención*, Buenos Aires, 1959, pp. 449–450.

LASER. Light Amplification by Stimulated Emission of Radiation. An international term for a device of quantum electronics, the source of electromagnetic waves, subject of international scientific co-operation, especially in telecommunications and medicine. Intensive research is also under way concerning the use of lasers for military purposes.

SIPRI, *World Armaments and Disarmaments Yearbook l970*, pp. 9–10; 1972, pp. 349–50; 1977, pp. 259–261.

LA SERENA. ▷ Observatories.

LASER WEAPONS. An international military term for 'devices that produce tightly-focused beams of very high energy electromagnetic radiation'. The ▷ SDI would rely heavily on laser weapons i.a. as a means of destroying enemy satellites.

D. ROBERTSON, *Guide to Modern Defense and Strategy*, Detroit, 1988.

LASO. ▷ OLAS.

LATERAN TREATIES, 1929. Two treaties which the Apostolic See and Italy signed on Feb. 11, 1929 in the Lateran Palace in Rome. Relations between the parties were normalized following a controversy which had started in 1870 over Church authority. The Roman Catholic religion as the only state religion of Italy was recognized and a concordat was concluded; The extraterritoriality and sovereign status of the Vatican City was acknowledged.

A. PIOLA, *Trattato e Concordati fra Italia e Santa Sede, Nota di critica giuridica*, Roma, 1935.

LATIFUNDISMO. An international term for an archaic extensive agricultural structure still present in Latin America; according to the UN Economic Committee for Latin America, ECLA, it has been a major contributing factor to the poverty of the rural areas of the majority of states of that region. In Mexico, Chile, and Peru the liquidation of latifundia took place through agricultural reforms.

LATIN AMERICA. The 20th century denomination of all Latin American countries, replacing the 19th century Ibero-America. Latin America includes the Spanish, French and Portuguese-speaking countries of North America, Central America and South America as well as the Caribbean

Islands. The main periodical journals dedicated to Latin American problems:

América Latina, ed. by the Latin American Centre of Social Sciences in Rio de Janeiro.
Americas, ed. by the Panamerican Union, Washington, DC.
CEPAL, Notas sobre economía y el desarrollo de América Latina, ed. by the UN Economic Commission for Latin America, Santiago de Chile.
Cuadernos Latinoamericanos de Economía Humana, ed. by the Latin American Centre for Political Economy, Montevideo.
Desarrollo Económico, ed. by the Economic Institute, Buenos Aires.
Estudios Americanos, ed. by the Escuela de Estudios Hispano Americanos in Sevilla, Spain.
Hispanic American Historical Review, ed. by the Johns Hopkins University, Baltimore.
Inter-American Economic Affairs, ed. by the American University, Washington, DC.
Journal of Interamerican Study, ed. by the University of Florida, Miami, Fla., USA.
Latinskaya Amerika, ed. since 1969 by the Latin American Institute, Moscow.
Revista de Historia de América, ed. by the Panamerican Institute of Geography and History, Mexico, DF.
Revista Interamericana de Ciencias Sociales, ed. by the Panamerican Union, Washington, DC.
Südamerika, Deutsche Zeitschrift in Argentinien, ed. in Buenos Aires.
El Trimestre Económico, ed. by the UNAM, Mexico, DF.

The international annuals:

Guide to the Sources for the History of Latin America, ed. since 1967 by the Consejo International de Archivos, Paris.
Handbook of Latin American Studies, ed. since 1935 by the University of Florida in Gainsville.
Ibero-Amerika. Ein Handbuch, ed. by the Ibero-Amerika Verein in Hamburg.
Jahrbuch fur Geschichte von Staat, Wirtschaft und Gesellschaft Lateinamerikas, ed. by the University of Cologne in Köln-Lindenthal, FRG.
South-American Handbook, South America, Central America, Cuba, Mexico, ed. since 1924 in London.

Encyclopedia of Latin America, New York, 1918; L.A. SANCHES, *Existe América Latina?* México, DF, 1945; G. PLAZA, "Latin America's Contribution to the UNO", in: *International Conciliation, Documents for the year 1946*, New York, 1946, pp. 150–158; *Diccionario enciclopédico de las Americas*, Buenos Aires, 1947; *Encyclopédie de l'Amérique latine*, Paris, 1954; M.R. MARTIN, G.H. LOVETT, *An Encyclopaedia of Latin American History*, New York, 1956; S.A. GONIONSKIY, *Latinskaja Amierika y SShA 1939–1959, Ocherki istorii diplomaticheskiy otnosheni*, Moscow, 1960; E.M. ESTRADA, *Diferencias y Semejanzas entre los Paises de America Latina*, Mexico, DF, 1962; *Mezhdunarodnoye pravo i Latinskaya Amieryka*, Moscow, 1962; P. CHAUNU, *L'Amérique et les Amériques*, Paris, 1964; L.A. SHUR, *Rossiya i Latinskaya Amierika*, Moscow, 1964; J.A. HOUSTON, *Latin America in the UN*, New York, 1965; T. SZULC, *Latin America*, New York, 1966; G. DE PRAT GAY, *Política exterior del Grupo Latinoamericano*, Buenos Aires, 1967; N.N. RAZUMOWICH, *Kto y kak pravit w Latinskoy Amierikye?* Moscow, 1967; M.I. LAZAREV, *Dvortsovye perevoroty v strankh Latinskoy Ameriky*, Moscow, 1967; J. LAMBERT, *Amérique Latine, Structures Sociales et Institutions Publiques*, Paris, 1967; *SSSR y Latinskaya Amerika 1917–1967*, Moscow, 1967; M. NIEDERGANG, *Les 20 Amériques Latines*, Paris, 1967; B. WOOD, *The US and Latin American Wars 1922–1942*, New York, 1967; *Latin America and the Caribbean. A Handbook*, New York, 1968; V. ALBA, *The Latin Americans*, New York, 1969; J.P. POLE, *Latin America*, London, 1970; C. FURTADO, *Economic Development of Latin America*, London, 1970; O. SUNKEL, P. PAZ, *El subdesarrollo latinoamericano y la teoria del desarrollo*, México, DF, 1970; E. LEDERMAN, *Los recursos humanos en el desarrollo de América Latina*, Santiago de Chile, 1971; G. PLAZA, *Latin America today and tomorrow*, Washington, DC, 1971; T. HALPERIN DONGHI, *Histoire contemporaine de l'Amérique Latine*, Paris, 1972; T. LEPKOWSKI, *Sociétés et nations latino-*

Latin America's Population 1950–1978 (in thousands)

Country	1950	1960	1970	1975	1976	1977	1978
Argentina	17,150	20,611	23,748	25,384	25,718	26,056	26,395
Barbados	211	233	239	245	246	248	249
Bolivia	2703	3325	4282	4888	5018	5150	5285
Brazil	52,901	71,539	95,204	109,730	112,893	116,142	119,447
Columbia	11,597	15,753	21,261	23,838	24,411	25,003	25,614
Costa Rica	858	1236	1732	1965	2013	2062	2111
Cuba	5858	7029	8572	9332	9467	9594	9718
Chile	6091	7585	9368	10,196	10,371	10,550	10,732
Dominican Republic	2313	3160	4343	5118	5292	5472	5658
Ecuador	3307	4422	5958	6891	7101	7318	7543
El Salvador	1940	2574	3582	4143	4226	4393	4524
Guatemala	2962	3966	5353	6243	6437	6635	6839
Guyana	423	560	709	791	809	827	846
Haití	3097	3723	4605	5157	5279	5405	5534
Honduras	1401	1943	2639	3093	3202	3318	3439
Jamaica	1403	1629	1882	2029	2058	2086	2115
México	26,606	36,369	50,313	59,204	61,203	63,274	65,421
Nicaragua	1109	1472	1970	2318	2396	2476	2559
Panamá	809	1083	1458	1676	1724	1772	1823
Paraguay	1371	1774	2301	2647	2725	2805	2888
Perú	7832	10,162	13,504	15,485	15,918	16,364	16,821
Trinidad and Tobago	632	843	955	1009	1020	1030	1041
Uruguay	2194	2531	2824	2842	2854	2869	2886
Venezuela	5145	7632	10,709	12,666	13,095	13,536	13,989
Total	**159,913**	**211,154**	**277,511**	**316,890**	**325,516**	**334,385**	**343,507**

Source: CEPAL, *Notas sobre la economia y el desarrollo de América Latina*, No. 300, Santiago de Chile, Agosto 1979.

américaines, Warsaw, 1972; R.J. ALEXANDER, *Latin American Political Parties*, New York, 1973; *Latein Amerika. Kontinent in der Krise*, Hamburg, 1973; CEPAL, *Plan de acción regional para la aplicación de la ciencia y la tecnología al desarrollo de América Latina*, México, DF, 1973; *Latin America and the US*, Stanford, 1974; H. DELPAR, *Encyclopedia of Latin America*, New York, 1974; E.J. OSMAŃCZYK, *Encyclopedia Mundial de Relaciones Internacionales y de Naciones Unidas*, Madrid–México, 1976; F. PARKINSON, *Latin America, the Cold War and the World Powers 1945–1973*, London, 1980; "La Integración en América Latina", in: *CEPAL Notas*, No. 319, June, 1980; R. WESSON, *US Influence in Latin America in the 1980s*, New York, 1982; *UN Five Studies on the Situation of Women in Latin America*, New York, 1982; Declaration and Action Plan for Latin American Economic Recovery, in: *UN Chronicle*, March, 1983; T.O. ENDER, R.P. MATTIONE, *Latin America. The Crisis of Debt and Growth*, Washington, DC, 1984; *Latin American Politics, A Historical Bibliography*, Santa Barbara, 1984; UNESCO, *America Latina en sus lenguas indigenas*, Paris, 1984; UNESCO, Cultural Identity in Latin-America, Paris, 1986; R.L. SCHEINA, *Latin America. A Naval History, 1810–1987*, Annapolis, 1987; Handbook of Latin American Studies. *A Selective and Annotated Guide to Recent Publications in Anthropology, Economics, Education, Geography, Government and Politics, International Relations and Sociology*. Hispanic Division, Library of Congress, Washington DC, 20540. Published since 1934; No 47 in 1987; UNESCO, *America Latina en sus ideas*, Paris, 1987; A.F. LOWENTHAL, *Partners in Conflict. The United States and Latin America*, Baltimore, Md., 1987; E.P. ARCHETTI, P. CAMMACK, B. ROBERTS, *Latin America*, London 1987.

LATIN AMERICAN ASSOCIATION OF FINANCIAL INSTITUTIONS FOR DEVELOPMENT. Asociación Latinoamericana de Instituciones Financieras de Desarrollo), ALIDE f. 1968, Lima. Publ.: *Directorio Latinoamericano de Instituciones Financieras de Desarrollo*. Reg. with the UIA.

Yearbook of International Organizations.

LATIN AMERICAN BANKING FEDERATION. Federación Latinoamericana de Bancos. FELABAN, f. 1965, Bogota. Members: banking associations of Argentina, Bolivia, Brazil, Chile, Colombia, Costa Rica, the Dominican Republic, Ecuador, El Salvador, Guatemala, Honduras, Mexico, Nicaragua, Panama, Paraguay, Peru, Uruguay and Venezuela. Reg. with the UIA.

Yearbook of International Organizations.

LATIN AMERICAN COMMON MARKET. A regional common market proposed in 1957–59, by the Economic Commission for Latin America, ECLA. Part of the draft was effected in 1959 within the program of Pan-American Operation; partly through the program of the Alliance for Progress; partly through ALALC and the Central American Common Market. In Apr., 1967 government heads of OAS states met at Punta del Este and decided to establish, during the period 1970–85, a free market to span both South and Central America; in Nov. of 1967, the Mixed Coordinating Commission for ALALC and the South American Common Market started their operations. ▷ Latin American Free Trade Association, 1960–1980; ▷ Latin American Integration Association, ALADI; ▷ Latin American Integration.

CEPAL, *El Mercado Común Latinoamericano*, México, DF, 1959; A.M. CALDERON, *De la ALALC al Mercado Común Latinoamericano*, México, DF, 1966; S. DELL, *A Latin-American Common Market?* New York, 1966; J.E. NAVARETTE, "La Reunión de los Presidentes de América: Antecedentes, Debates y Resoluciones", in: *Foro Internacional*, México, DF, January–March, 1967, pp. 179–209; *The Europe Year Book*, Vol. 2, London, 1984.

LATIN AMERICAN CONFERENCE OF POLITICAL PARTIES. Conferencia de los Partidos Politicos de América Latina, est. Oct. 19, 1979 in Oaxaca, Mexico by 23 social-democratic, socialist and revolutionary parties from 15 Latin American countries. The headquarters are in Mexico City under the aegis of the Mexican governing party PRI (Partido Revolucionario Institucional).

El Dio, October 20, 1979.

LATIN AMERICAN CULTURAL COMMUNITY. A Latin American solidarity institution

L

of artists, set up after the fashion of the ▷ Writers European Community COMES; initiated by a group of leading Chilean, Mexican and Venezuelan writers, who announced 1965 in Switzerland the so-called Geneva Declaration concerning the need for Latin American cultural integrity as protection against the flood of mass cultural-entertainment production. The First Congress of Latin American Writers was held from Jan. 29 to Feb. 6, 1966 in Arica, Chile and the Second Congress was held from Mar. 15 to 24, 1967, in Guanajuato and Guadalajara. Seat of secretariat: Mexico City.

LATIN AMERICA DISARMAMENT ACTIONS.
The states of Latin America were the first in the world to limit their armaments beginning in the year 1829. Here is a chronicle of disarmament actions in this region:

In 1829, Peru and Colombia were the first to decide to limit the number of their frontier garrisons.

In 1881, Argentina and Chile resolved to neutralize and demilitarize the Strait of Magellan.

In 1902, Argentina and Chile limited their naval armaments.

In 1923, Guatemala, Honduras, Costa Rica, and Salvador signed a treaty that forbade the purchase of warships, not including coastal gunboats, and limited each signatory to 10 military planes. Due to US intervention in Nicaragua this treaty was not adhered to in practice; it was formally renounced in 1953 by Honduras.

In 1923, the Fifth International American Conference held in Santiago (Chile), recommended that the American states "consider the possibility of reducing and limiting expenditures for the army and navy on a suitable and practical basis".

In 1936, the Interamerican Conference on the Strengthening of Peace held in Buenos Aires, resolved to "recommend to governments the negotiation of treaties . . . for the purpose of limiting armaments to the barest possible minimum".

In the Spring of 1945, the Interamerican Conference on Problems of War and Peace recommended the introduction of armaments control.

In 1947, the Interamerican Conference on the Maintenance of Peace and Security of the Continent, held in Rio de Janeiro, supplemented the text of the Treaty on Mutual Assistance of the American States with the statement:

"In none of its resolutions does this Treaty obligate states to excessive armaments beyond what is required for common defence in the interest of peace and security".

From the time of this resolution up to 1967, no organization or interamerican Conference took up the question of the limitation of armaments or disarmament in Latin America. The only document on this question, rejected by the OPA Council, was a memorandum of Costa Rica in 1958 (the only country of Latin America which completely disarmed itself in 1946), abolishing its army and navy, entrusting the protection of its frontiers to the police, stating:

"The system of interamerican collective security has, in practice, achieved the following: that war between the nations of this continent has become impossible, and extracontinental aggression extremely difficult; that none of the nations of Latin America possesses nuclear weapons or has expressed the desire to possess and manufacture them; that the maintenance of armed forces with conventional weapons consumes significant resources of the Latin American states [In view of the fact that] Latin American armies have ceased to be a protection against the danger of an interamerican war, if such a war were to happen, or as a defence against a world war, if such a war should break out, and would be practically helpless [they should be transformed into] a supplementary force for the realization of programs of economic development and into training centers

preparing the Latin American masses for the battle for production".

The OPA Council tabled the plan of Costa Rica ad acta. In 1965 OPA recommended the formation of sapper brigades designed mainly to assist the civilian population; they wear an insignia with the inscription Accion Civica Militar (▷ Civil Military Action).

The idea of the denuclearization of Latin America was considered by Mexico in March, 1963 (after the USA–USSR atomic crisis over Cuba in Oct., 1962) and was accomplished with the signing of the ▷ Tlatelolco Treaty in 1967 and the creation of ▷ OPANAL in 1969. In Apr., 1967, the president of the American Republics, at a summit meeting in Punta del Este, Uruguay, accepted a resolution on the need for arms limitation, but without any collective obligations. Simultaneously, it was revealed that work in the US State Dept. (1966/67) on a plan for a Latin American states treaty on arms limitation had been suspended. In the decade 1970–80, expenditures of the Latin American states on armaments continued to increase despite tendencies toward détente in the world.

V. ALBA, *El Militarismo*, México, DF, 1959, pp. 192–289; *Síntesis Informativa Iberoamericana 1974*, Madrid, 1975.

LATIN AMERICAN DOCTRINE, 1890.
The "principle of equivalent treatment" expressed in a document passed by the International American Conference, 1889/90 in Washington, by the votes of all the republics of Latin America, while the USA voted against. It stated that:

"(1) Aliens have the right to make use of all the civic rights possessed by natives and are entitled to all of the benefits resulting from those rights, in form as well as in content, and due legal measures should be guaranteed them in the same way as to natives. (2) The state does not recognize other obligations and responsibilities in favor of foreigners besides those which are established for the benefit of natives by the Constitution and laws".

The Convention on the Rights and Obligations of States drafted and signed at the Seventh International American Conference in Montevideo, 1933, stated in art. 9, that "foreigners cannot demand other laws or more extensive rights than those possessed by citizens of the state". It was not approved by the USA. ▷ Aliens' Rights.

International American Conferences, 1889–1936, Washington, DC, 1938.

LATIN AMERICAN ECONOMIC CONFERENCE, 1984. ▷ Quito Declaration, 1984.

LATIN AMERICAN EPISCOPAL COUNCIL.
Consejo Episcopal Latinoamericano, CELAM. ▷ Council of the Episcopate of Latin America.

LATIN AMERICAN FACULTY OF SOCIAL SCIENCES, FLACSO.
The autonomous regional organization of higher education for teaching and research in the field of social science in Santiago de Chile. It was established by the Latin American and the Caribbean states under the auspices of the government of Chile, on the basis of an agreement signed in Paris, June 18, 1971 by the governments of Chile, Cuba and Panama; came into force on June 19, 1972; liquidated by the Military Junta in Oct., 1973.

UNTS, Vol. 839, p. 171.

LATIN AMERICAN FEATURE AGENCY. ▷ Communication.

LATIN AMERICAN FOREST RESEARCH AND TRAINING INSTITUTE.
An intergovernmental institute, est. Nov. 18, 1959 under the auspices of the FAO in Merida, Venezuela. It conducts research into conservation, utilization and development of Latin American forest resources; and holds training courses for forestry technicians.

Yearbook of International Organizations.

LATIN AMERICAN FORUM.
An institution f. 1974, Buenos Aires, under the aegis of the Institute for Latin American Integration, INTAL, as a non-official independent organization representing all schools of Latin American thought. Reg. with the UIA.

Yearbook of International Organizations.

LATIN AMERICAN FREE TRADE ASSOCIATION, LAFTA, 1960–1980.
Asociación Latinoamericana de Libre Comercio, ALALC. The Association constituted by the ▷ Montevideo Treaty, 1960, which was signed on Feb. 18, 1960 by Argentina, Brazil, Chile, Mexico, Paraguay, Peru and Uruguay; it came into force on May 2, 1961. The following states also acceded to the Treaty: Colombia, Sept. 30, 1961; Ecuador, Nov. 3, 1961; Bolivia and Venezuela, Dec. 12, 1966. The Protocol was amended in 1973, in Caracas. The ▷ Andean Group was established as a subregional bloc under LAFTA aegis in 1969. The LAFTA had special relations with the UN Economic Commission for Latin America, the Inter-American Development Bank and the OAS. The ▷ Montevideo Treaty, 1960 provided for the reduction of tariffs and other trade barriers for the gradual establishment of a free trade area during 20 years, but in 1980 only 14% of annual trade among member States were integrated by LAFTA agreements. Replaced on Aug. 13, 1980 by the ▷ Latin American Integration Association, ALADI.

La Cooperación Económica Multilateral en la América Latina, Estudio de las NU, México, DF, 1961, pp. 96–122; E.S. MILENKY, *The Politics of Regional Organization in Latin America. The LAFTA*, New York, 1973; *Instruments of Economic Integration in Latin America and the Caribbean*, New York, 1975.

LATIN AMERICAN INSTITUTE FOR ECONOMIC AND SOCIAL PLANNING.
Instituto Latinoamericano de Planificación Económica y Social, ILPES, est. 1962 in Santiago de Chile under the aegis of the UN Economic Commission for Latin America, ECLA; since Jan., 1974 a permanent institution within the ECLA. Publ.: Cuadernos. Reg. with the UIA.

Yearbook of International Organizations.

LATIN AMERICAN INSTITUTE FOR EDUCATIONAL COMMUNICATION.
Instituto Latinoamericano de la Comunicación Educativa, ILCE, est. 1956 in Mexico, DF, under aegis of UNESCO. Members: governments of all Latin American countries. Publ.: *Sintesis*. Reg. with the UIA.

Yearbook of International Organizations.

LATIN AMERICAN INSTITUTE FOR INTEGRATION.
Instituto para la Integración de América Latina, INTAL, est. 1965 in Buenos Aires by the Interamerican Development Bank, conducts research concerning the process of integration in legal, social, economic and political aspects. Publ.: *Integración Latinoamericana* (monthly), *Boletín de Información Legal* (monthly), *El proceso de integración en América Latina* (annual report), *Derecho de la Integración* (3 a year). Reg. with the UIA.

Yearbook of International Organizations.

Latin American Trade Unions

LATIN AMERICAN INTEGRATION. The first integration was attempted by a Convention on lifting import and export bans and restrictions, 1927, which failed to come into force because of the lack of required number of ratifications. From 1929 the economic depression raised customs barriers; repeated appeals by Inter-American Conferences, 1933, 1936 and 1938 for joint trade and customs policy remained on paper. First programmatic elaboration of Latin American integration was published by the UN Economic Commission for Latin America, ECLA, 1949, followed in 1951 under its auspices, by the process of Central American Integration. In 1955 the ECLA set up the Committee for Trade with the aim of working out: (1) multilateral clearing system for trade dealings; (2) measures to facilitate trade between Latin American states; (3) customs conveniences; in Aug., 1958 in Mexico the ECLA Experts Committee started work on the principles of gradual formation of a Latin American Common Market; the Committee called for establishing a Free Trade Zone in keeping with the GATT; approved by the ECLA Conference in Panama, May, 1959, which prepared a draft treaty on inception of the Associación Latino Americana de Libre Comercio, ALALC, Latin American Free Trade Association, LAFTA, adopted and signed, Montevideo, Feb. 18, 1960 by Argentina, Brazil, Chile, Mexico, Paraguay, Peru and Uruguay; in 1961 by Colombia; 1962 by Ecuador; in 1966 by Bolivia and Venezuela. Growth of integration through LAFTA was soon impeded despite an initial 25% reduction of customs tariffs on less substantial goods and services, followed in 1964/65 by a discussion on future reductions of relevance to free trade. A new body, the LAFTA Council of Ministers, was appointed, which on Dec. 12, 1966 recommended establishment of an ad hoc mechanism for the settlement of disputes between LAFTA members. In Apr., 1967 in Punta del Este a summit conference of heads of OAS states resolved to set up a Latin American Common Market for 1970–85 but no decisions were taken concerning LAFTA development difficulties. Since then no significant changes have occurred in the impeded process of integration of all of Latin America though in various ways and at various places three subregional integrations have evolved: ▷ Andean Group, La Plata Group (▷ Plata, Rio de la), ▷ Central American Economic Integration. Propagation of the ideas of Latin American Integration or scientific research into its problems are carried out by: Instituto para la Integración de América Latina, INTAL, Institute for Latin American Integration, in Buenos Aires; Comite de Acción para la Integración de América Latina, Committee of Action for Latin American Integration, in Buenos Aires; and a number of regional specialized non-governmental bodies for various economic problems: eg: Asociación Latinoamericana de Armadores, ALAMAR, Latin American Shipowners Association, or Latin American Association of Wine Growers, etc. On Aug. 13, 1980 the LAFTA was replaced by the ▷ Latin American Integration Association, ALADI. ▷ Montevideo Treaty, 1960. ▷ Montevideo Treaty, 1980.

La Cooperación Económica Multilateral en América Latina, UN, México, DF, 1961, Vol. 1, p. 234; La Integración Económica Latinoamericana, México, DF, 1964; Tratado de Montevideo de Divulgación, México, DF, 1964; J.A. MAYOBRE, F. HERERA, C. SANZ DE SANTAMARIA, R. PREBISCH, Hacia la Integración Acelerada de América Latina. Proposiciones a los Presidentes Latinoamericanos con un Estudio Técnico de CEPAL, México, DF, 1965; M.S. WIONCZEK, Integración de la América Latina, México, DF, 1964; P. GARCIA REYNOSO, Integración Latinoamericana. Primera Etapa 1960–1964, México, DF, 1965; La Integración Latinoamericana: Situación y Perspectivas, INTAL, Buenos Aires, 1965; A.M. CALDERON, De la ALALC al Mercado Común Latinoamericano, México, DF, 1966; INSTITUTO IA DE ESTUDIOS JURIDICOS, Problemática Jurídica e Institucional de la Integración de América Latina. Ensayo de Sistematización, Washington, DC, 1967; G. CEVALLO, La integración de la América Latina, México, DF, 1971.

LATIN AMERICAN INTEGRATION ASSOCIATION, ALADI. Asociación Latinoamericana de Integración, est. on Aug. 13, 1980 at Montevideo by Argentina, Bolivia, Brazil, Chile, Colombia, Ecuador, Mexico, Paraguay, Peru, Uruguay and Venezuela as successor of the Latin American Free Trade Association, LAFTA, est. 1960. Members are divided into three categories, most developed: Argentina, Brazil, Mexico; intermediate: Chile, Colombia, Peru, Uruguay and Venezuela; and least developed: Bolivia, Ecuador and Paraguay. Organs: a Council of Ministers of Foreign Affairs, an Evaluation and Convergence Conference, a Committee of Permanent Representatives, the General Secretariat. The dissolution of LAFTA took place by a Treaty of Montevideo, signed on Aug. 13, 1980, which came into force in March 1981 and was fully ratified in March 1982. ▷ Latin American Integration. ▷ Latin American Free Trade Association, LAFTA. The new ▷ Montevideo Treaty, 1980, differing from the previous one, 1960, founded a more flexible organization without a definite timetable for establishment of a Latin American free trade area. In August 1983 the transition from LAFTA to ALADI was completed with renegotiations of tariffs cuts granted in the years 1962–1980 (only 14% of annual trade among LAFTA members) Two LAFTA agreements were retained by the ALADI: the Accord for the Attenuation of Transitory Deficiencies in Liquidity signed in 1969, 1981, and the Accord on Reciprocal Payments and Credits signed in 1965 and modified in 1981. The total value of exports within ALADI accounted for 10.3% of member countries exports in 1987 (1970 – 11.2%, 1975 – 10.6%, 1980 – 12%). In June 1986 Cuba was granted observer status in ALADI.

The Europa Year Book 1984. A World Survey, Vol. I, p. 170, London, 1984.

LATIN AMERICAN IRON AND STEEL INSTITUTE. Instituto Latinoamericano del Hierro y el Acero, ILAFA, f. 1959, Santiago de Chile. Consultative status with ECOSOC, UNIDO and UNCTAD, Publ.: *Siderurgía Latinoamericana* (monthly). Reg. with the UIA.

Yearbook of International Organizations.

LATIN-AMERICANISM. ▷ Pan-Americanism and Pan-Latin-Americanism.

LATIN AMERICAN PARLIAMENT. Parlamento Latinoamericano. The parliament of Latin America, f. Dec. 7, 1964 in Lima by parliamentary delegates from Argentina, Brazil, Chile, Costa Rica, El Salvador, Guatemala, Nicaragua, Panama, Paraguay, Peru, Uruguay, and Venezuela, in the presence of two observers from the Mexican Congress. On June 1985 the Parliament accepted the admission of delegates from Cuba.

Documentación Iberoamericana, Madrid, 1964–67; Síntesis Informativa Iberoamericana, Madrid, 1971.

LATIN AMERICAN PHYSICS CENTRE. The Centre was est. 1962 under the aegis of UNESCO, with headquarters in Rio de Janeiro. An Agreement was signed on Mar. 26, 1962, in Rio de Janeiro by the governments of Argentina, Bolivia, Brazil, Colombia, Cuba, Chile, Ecuador, Haiti, Honduras, Mexico, Nicaragua, Panama, Paraguay, Peru, Uruguay and Venezuela; it came into force on June 10, 1965. The main function of the Centre is to conduct scientific research and organize specialized instruction in the physical sciences.

UNTS, Vol. 539, p. 93.

LATIN AMERICAN RAILWAYS ASSOCIATION. Asociación Latinoamericano de Ferrocarriles, ALAF, f. 1964, Buenos Aires. Official relations with the ECLA. Members: national railways of Argentina, Bolivia, Brazil, Chile, Colombia, Ecuador, Mexico, Paraguay, Peru, Uruguay and Venezuela. Reg. with the UIA.

Yearbook of International Organizations.

LATIN AMERICAN REGIONAL CENTER FOR PEACE, DISARMAMENT AND DEVELOPMENT. est. by GA Res. 42/39 K of Nov. 1987 (name changed on Dec. 7, 1988 to Regional Centre of the UN for Peace, Disarmament and Development in Latin America and the Caribbean.) "to explore new avenues for concerted political action among the countries of the region and to strengthen further the intra-Latin American and Caribbean links in a framework of harmony solidarity and co-operation that will enable Latin America and the Caribbean to become an effective area for peace."

UN Resolutions and Decisions adopted by the General Assembly during the First Part of its Forty-Third Session, from 20 September to 22 December 1988, New York 1989, p. 176.

LATIN AMERICAN SHIPOWNERS ASSOCIATION. Asociación Latinoamericana de Armadores, ALAMAR. An international organization, reg. with the UIA, f. July 13, 1963 in Viña del Mar, with headquarters in Montevideo. Members: national associations in 10 countries: Argentina, Brazil, Chile, Colombia, Ecuador, Mexico, Paraguay, Peru, Uruguay and Venezuela. Aims: Promote the development of the merchant marine in the countries of the LAFTA (since 1980 ALADI), co-operate in attaining the objectives of the Treaty of Montevideo as regards zonal integration. Consultative status with UNCTAD, ECOSOC and IMCO. Publ.: *ALAMAR Documentos.*

Yearbook of International Organizations.

LATIN AMERICAN SOLIDARITY ORGANIZATION. Organización Latinoamericana de Solidaridad. ▷ OLAS.

LATIN AMERICAN TRADE UNIONS. The I Conference of Latin American Trade Unions was held in Dec., 1927 at Montevideo, headquarters of the Permanent Secretariat of Latin American Trade Unions linked with the International Trade Union in Moscow; published 1928–33 *El Trabajador Latinoamericano.* In 1938 the "red" Unions of Argentina, Brazil, Cuba, Chile, El Salvador, Guatemala, Mexico and Peru formed the Latin American Worker's Confederation, Confederación de Trabajadores de America Latina. In 1951 on the AFL-CIO initiative was founded the Inter-American Regional Organization of Workers of the ICFTU.

Organizations reg. with the UIA:

Agrupación de Trabajadores Latinoamericanos Sindicalistas, ATLAS, f. 1952, Montevideo; dissolved 1956.
Caribbean Congress of Labour, f. 1960, Bridgetown, Barbados. Publ.: *Caribbean Labour.*
Confederación Sindical de los Trabajadores de América Latina, CSTAL, Trade Union Confederation of Latin American Workers, f. 1962, Santiago de Chile; 1973 Havana.

L

Inter-American Regional Organizations of Workers of the International Confederation of Free Trade Unions, CFTU, f. 1951, Mexico City. Official relation with OAS. Publ.: *Noticiero Obrero Interamericano* (monthly), *Unido de Trabajo Libre* (bi-monthly).
Permanent Congress of Trade Union Unity of Latin American Workers, f. 1964, Brazil.
Trade Union Council of Andean Workers, Consejo Sindical de Trabajadores, CSTA, f. 1973, Lima.

A. DEL ROSAL, *Los Congresos Obreros Interamericanos en el Sigle XX*, México, DF, 1963; Vol. 2, pp. 379–400; V. ALBA, *Historia del Movimiento obrero en América Latina*, México, DF, 1964; *Profsoyuzi Sieviernoy Amieriki*, Moskva, 1965; J. DAVIES, *The Trade Unions*, Harmondsworth, 1965.

LATIN AMERICAN UNIVERSITY OF WORKERS. Universidad de los Trabajadores de América Latina UTAL, f. 1970, Caracas, Venezuela. Reg. with the UIA.

Yearbook of International Organizations.

LATIN AMERICAN WORKERS PERMANENT CONGRESS. Congreso Permanento de Unidad Sindical de Trabajadores de América Latina, CPUSTAL, founded on Jan. 28, 1964 in Brasilia by delegates representing workers' organizations of 18 Latin American countries. The seat of the CPUSTAL Executive Secretariat, 1964–73, was Santiago de Chile; moved to Havana following the military coup in Chile. On Jan. 11, 1977 the CPUSTAL signed in Havana a common declaration with the World Federation of Trade Unions, FSM, on co-operation and mutual assistance.

Yearbook of International Organization.

LATIN AMERICA QUITO DECLARATION, 1984. ▷ Quito Declaration, 1984.

LATIN FORMULAS. International terms, accepted in international law and in the UN system. (e.g. ▷ Pacta Sunt Servanda).

LATIN LANGUAGES. All languages belonging to the Romance family: classical and modern Latin, French, Spanish, Portuguese, Romanian, Italian, Catalan, Provençal, Rhaeto-Romanic, Sardinian; a subject of international co-operation. Attempts made between the wars and after World War II to promote an international movement for restoration to Latin of its role as an international language as in the Middle Ages. By decision of Vatican Council II concerning the replacement of Latin by national languages in the liturgy of the Catholic Church further limited the use of classical Latin as a mass medium.
Organizations reg. with the UIA:

International Alliance of Journalists and Writers in the Latin Languages, f. 1955, Rome. Publ.: *Il Corriere Lettarario Latino.*
International Association for Latin Epigraphy, Association international d'epigraphie latine, AIEL, f. 1963, Paris, gathering academics from Bulgaria, Czechoslovakia, France, FRG, GDR, Poland, Switzerland, the UK and Yugoslavia.
International Bureau for the Study of the Problems Relating to the teaching of Greek and Latin, f. 1960, Ghent.

Yearbook of International Organizations.

LATIN MONETARY UNION. The Union Monetaria Latina, UML, concluded on Dec. 23, 1865 by virtue of a treaty between France, Belgium, Italy, and Switzerland (Greece joined in 1869), and based on the principles of ▷ Bimetalism; the value ratio of silver to gold was fixed at 15.5 : 1. The treaty also permitted the free circulation in the member countries of their gold coins as well as some Austrian, Spanish, and Russian gold coins. The

Conventions of 1878, 1885, and 1908 set temporary upper limits on the minting of gold coins by the UML member states. The Union de facto ceased to exist during World War I. Switzerland formally withdrew in 1920, Belgium in 1925, and France, Greece, and Italy in 1927.

H.P. WILLIS, *A History of the Latin Monetary Union*, London, 1901; H. FOURTIN, *La fin de l'Union Monétaire Latine*, Paris, 1930; J. ROUMET, *Dictionnaire des Sciences Economiques*, Vol. 2, Paris, 1958, pp. 1125–1126.

LATINOAMERICANISM. A designation for a 19th-century idea for an ethnic–cultural bond between the Metise and Creole populations of Latin America, speaking either Spanish, Portuguese or French.

J.M. TORRES CALCEDO, *Union Latino-Americana, Acusamiento de Bolivar para formar una Liga Americana*, Paris, 1865.

LATIN UNION, 1957. Union Latina. An intergovernmental institution initiated 1948 by national committees, and formally est. May 15, 1951 at the First International Congress of the Latin Union in Rio de Janeiro. Its aim is to foster intellectual co-operation between countries of Latin culture. The statute of the Union was framed at the Second Congress held in Madrid in the form of an international convention whose signatories were France, Italy, the Philippines, Portugal, Spain and all Latin American countries excluding Mexico and Guatemala.

Yearbook of International Organizations.

LATITUDE. International geographical term for the angular distance from the Equator of any point on the Earth's surface, subject of international research. Organizations reg. with the UIA:

International Latitude Observatory, f. 1969, Mizusava, Japan, replacing the International Latitude Service. Publ.: Monthly Notes.
International Latitude Service, 1899–1969.
International Polar Motion Service.
See also▷ Longitude.

Yearbook of International Organizations, 1986/87; The Europa Yearbook 1988. A World Survey, Vol. I, London 1988.

LATRINES. A subject of the WHO world sanitation action for construction of simple, clean and appropriate latrines.

World Health, April, 1984.

LATVIA. Latvijas Padomuj Socialistiska Republika. Latvian Soviet Socialist Republic. Federal Republic of the USSR on the Baltic Sea, bounded by Lithuania, Byelorussia and Russia. Area: 63,700 sq. km. Pop. 1983 est. 2,568,000 of whom 57% are Letts, 30% Russians, 4% Byelorussians, 2.7% Poles, 1.7% Jews, 1.6% Lithuanians, 1.3% Ukrainians, 2.1% others. Capital: Riga with 867,000 inhabitants 1983. Official languages: Latvian and Russian. Currency: rouble of the USSR. National Day: Oct. 7, Socialist Revolution Anniversary, 1917.
International relations: in 19th century part of the Russian Empire; independent republic 1919–40; member of the ▷ Baltic Entente 1934–40; member of the League of Nations 1920–39. On Oct. 5, 1939 signed a Pact with the USSR. During World War II, incorporated into the USSR on Aug. 5, 1940; occupied by German troops July, 1941–July, 1944. The Soviet annexation of Latvia was not recognized by the following countries: Australia, Belgium, Canada, Denmark, Finland, France, the FRG, Greece, the Holy See, Ireland, Italy, Luxembourg, Malta, the Netherlands, Norway, Portugal, Spain,

Switzerland, Turkey, the UK, the USA, and Yugoslavia. The US government continues to recognize the Latvian Chargé d'Affaires in Washington DC. See also▷ Russian Language.

A. BILMANIS, *A History of Latvia*, Princeton, 1951; A. SPEKKE, *History of Latvia*, Stockholm, 1951; *Istoria Latviyskoy SSR*, Riga, 1952–58; *Soyuz Sovietskikh Socialistichekskikh Riespublik 1917–1967*, Moskva, 1967; *The Europa Year Book 1984. A World Survey*, Vol. I, pp. 923–924, London, 1984.

LATVIA–SOVIET RUSSIA PEACE TREATY, 1920. The Peace Treaty between the Republic of Latvia and the Russian SFSR, signed on Aug. 11, 1920 in Riga.

LNTS, Vol. 2, No. 67, p. 215.

LAUCA. A river flowing through two states: Chile *c.* 100 km and Bolivia *c.* 250 km. It has been the subject of a dispute between the two countries since 1939, when Chile began to use the waters of the Lauca to irrigate the Azapa region in the province of Tarapaca. In 1949, both countries established the Mixed Technical Commission on the Lauca on the basis of art. 8 of the Declaration of the Inter-American Convention of 1933 concerning the industrial and agriculture use of international rivers. The many years' deliberations of the Commission did not solve the dispute, and on Apr. 14, 1962 Bolivia accused Chile, before the OAS Council, of violating her sovereign rights over the waters of the Lauca; simultaneously Bolivia broke off diplomatic relations with Chile. The case was the subject of a debate by the OAS Council on Apr. 18, 1962 and of a resolution adopted by the Council on May 24, 1963. That resolution recommended reconciliation between the two sides and the re-establishment of diplomatic relations; Bolivia reacted by a boycott of the OAS Council from May 25, 1963 to Jan. 21, 1965.

Aplicaciones del Tratado Latino Americano sobre la Asistencia Reciproca, 1960–1964, Washington, DC, 1963, pp. 80–100; *Informe Sobre el Rio Lauca, presentado por el Concilier J. Fellman Velarde ante la Comisión Legislativa*, La Paz, 1962; MINISTERIO DE RELACIONES EXTERISES, *La Cuestión de Rio Lauca*, Santiago, 1963; J. EYZAGUIRRE, *Chile y Bolivia, Erquema de un Processo Diplomático*, Santiago, 1963; R.D. TOMASEK, "The Chile–Bolivia Lauca River Dispute", in: *Journal of American Studies*, 1967; M.J. GLASSPER, "The Rio Lauca Dispute and International Rivers", in: *Geographical Review*, No. 2, 1970.

LAUNDRY INDUSTRY. A subject of international co-operation. Organizations reg. with the UIA:

European Laundry and Dry Cleaning Machinery Manufacturers Organization, f. 1959, The Hague.
International Committee for Dyeing and Dry Cleaning, f. 1950, Paris.
International Laundry Association, f. 1950, London.

Yearbook of International Organizations.

LAUSANNE. A city in Switzerland, site of the Peace Conference and subsequent peace treaties signed on Oct. 18, 1912 between Italy and Turkey (since it was concluded in the Lausanne suburb of Ouchy, also known as the Ouchy Treaty); signed on July 24, 1923 between Greece and Turkey; and the ▷ Lausanne Peace Treaty, 1923, signed on the same date, between France, Greece, Japan, Yugoslavia, Romania, Great Britain, Italy and Turkey.

LNTS, 1923.

LAUSANNE PEACE TREATY, 1923. A peace treaty between the Allied Powers (British Empire, France, Italy, Japan, Greece, Romania and the Serb–Croat–Slovene State) and Turkey, signed on

504

July 24, 1923 in Lausanne. The main points of Part I of the Treaty were as follows:

Part I. Political Clause (art. 1 to 45):
"... the state of peace will be definitely re-established between the Contracting Powers ... Official relations will be resumed on both sides ..." (art. 1).
"The frontiers (with Bulgaria, Greece, Iraq and Syria) described by the present Treaty are traced on the one-in-a-million maps attached to the present Treaty ..." (art. 4).
"Turkey hereby recognizes the annexation of Cyprus proclaimed by the present Treaty are traced on Nov. 5, 1914" (art. 20).
"Turkish nationals belonging to non-Moslem minorities will enjoy the same civil and political rights as Moslems ..." (art. 39).
Part II. Financial Clause (arts. 46 to 63).
Part III. Economic Clauses (arts. 64 to 100).
Part IV. Communications and Sanitary Questions (arts. 101 to 118).
Part V. Miscellaneous Provisions (arts. 119 to 143).
Major Peace Treaties of Modern History, New York, 1967, pp. 2305–2368.

LAW. The subject of international codification. ▷ Inter-American Treaties Codification.

R. LANSKY, *Basic Literature on Law* (English, French, German, Spanish). München, 1978; R. DWORKIN, *Taking Rights Seriously*, London 1978; R. DWORKIN, *Law's Empire*, London 1986; R.G. LOGAN, L.L.B.FLA, *Information Sources in Law*, London – Boston, 1986.

LAW, ABUSE OF. An international term used both in domestic and international law; misfeasance, in ill faith, of legal norms or international conventions to the detriment of the other party; subject of international disputes which, in some cases, are settled by arbitration courts.

LAW GENERAL PROVISIONS. An international term for "general provisions of the law recognized by the civilized nations" which under art. 38 of the Statute of the ▷ International Court of Justice, apart from conventions and international customs, constitute one of the three major sources of international law.

LAWN TENNIS. A subject of international co-operation. Organization reg. with the UIA:
International Lawn Tennis Federation, f. 1912, London; ensures application of the international lawn tennis code. Members: national associations in 68 countries.
Yearbook of International Organizations.

LAW OF CHECKS. Conventions on checks. Checks and bills of exchange are subjects of private international law; rules concerning checks have been codified since the First Hague Conference on Letters of Lien, Bills of Exchange and Checks held in 1920. At the Second Hague Conference. July 23, 1912, an agreement was signed on the unification of the law of checks. It delineated principles, which were adopted by European states after World War I for commercial reasons.
On Mar. 19, 1931, on the initiative of the League of Nations the International Conference on the Law of Currencies and Checks was held in Geneva. The Conference adopted three international conventions on checks: on the unified laws, on the elimination of conflicting legislation and on stamp fees. The first convention art. 3 determined that the laws of the country in which a check is to be remitted can specify to whom it can be made out. Participants were the Netherlands Antilles, Austria, Belgium, Denmark, Finland, France, Germany, Greece, Hungary, India, Italy, Japan, Monaco, the Netherlands, Nicaragua, Norway, Poland, Portugal, Surinam, Sweden, Switzerland. These states incor-

porated the provisions of the convention into their domestic legislation. The Anglo-Saxon states retain separate legislation. Work on the codification of the law of checks in the Anglo-Saxon and European states was initiated by the International Congress of Private Law, Rome, 1950.

LNTS, 1931; *Comptes rendus de la Conférence internationale pour l'unification du droit en matière de lettres de change, billets à ordre et cheques à Genève du 25 février au 19 mars 1931*, Genève, 1931: *Actes du Congrès international du droit privé tenu à Rome en julliet 1950*, 2 Vols. L'Unidroit, Paris, 1951.

LAW OF CONCLUSION OF INTERNATIONAL AGREEMENTS. A part of the law of treaties, specifying which subjects of international law have the right to conclude international agreements, and which bodies of these subjects are established for this purpose. In the 19th century, in principle, the states were subjects of international law and in the case of federal states, the countries (states) belonging to the federation, but in a restricted sense, dependent states were subjects of international law only with the consent of their protector. In the 20th century treaty competence is enjoyed by inter-governmental international organizations (jus tractuum), and also by the Holy See and insurgents accorded limited recognition. The ▷ Vienna Convention on the Law of International Treaties of 1969, prepared by the Commission on International Law of the UN, is limited to regulating the treaty competence of states, leaving the competences "of other subjects of international law" unspecified in greater detail. The Convention in art. 7 states which state bodies are competent to conclude agreements.

H. CHIN, *The Capacity of International Organizations to Conclude Treaties and the Special Legal Aspect of the Treaties so Concluded*, The Hague, 1966.

LAW OF DISCOVERY. The colonial European law permitting from the end of 15th century Portugal and Spain, and in following centuries all colonial powers, to occupy any territory discovered outside of Europe, in the Western or Eastern Hemisphere, reaffirmed by the ▷ Berlin Congress 1885.

J.N.L. BAKER, *History of Geographical Discovery and Exploration*, London, 1933; R. HENNING *Terrae incognitae*, 4 Vols., Leiden, 1936–39.

LAW OF INTERNATIONAL ORGANIZATIONS. A branch of international law unified by the UN and relating exclusively to public international organizations. The law of international organizations is a set of legal norms relating to public international organizations, organs of an international organization or its officials.

E.G. SCHERMERS, *International Institutional Law*, Leiden, 1972.

LAW OF NATIONS. ▷ International Law.

LAW OF NATIONS, GRÉGOIRE'S PRINCIPLES, 1795. The French draft declaration on the right of nations occupies a special place in the history of international law. The draft perpared by Jansenist Bishop H. Grégoire, representing the Nancy clergy in the revolutionary National Convent of France includes the first attempt to codify the principles of international law. It was presented to the Convention May 23, 1795 on behalf of the Nancy clergy. The text is as follows:

"Idea and General Principles of the Law of Nations.
(1) Nations co-exist in the state of nature; they are bound by common morality.
(2) Nations are independent and sovereign in their relations irrespective of their population and territorial area they occupy. This sovereignty is inalienable.

(3) Nations should behave in their relations with other nations in the same way they wish the latter to behave toward them.
(4) Individual interest of a nation is subjected to the common interest of mankind.
(5) Nations should render each other all possible service in peacetime, and in time of war – possibly less evil.
(6) Each nation has the right to organize and change its form of government.
(7) A nation has no right to interfere into the government of other nations.
(8) Only governments based on equality and freedom are consistent with the right of nations.
(9) All that is inexhaustible or indestructible, as the sea, shall be a common property and shall not belong to any individual nation.
(10) Each state is the master of its own territory.
(11) Being in the possession from time immemorial creates among nations the right of prescription.
(12) A nation has the right to refuse entry to its territory and to expel aliens, when its security requires such measures.
(13) Aliens are amenable to nation's internal laws and regulations and are liable to statutory penalties.
(14) Exile for criminal offences is an indirect violation of alien territory.
(15) Conspiracy against the freedom of a country constitutes an assault against all nations.
(16) Alliances aimed at aggressive war, treaties or covenants that may become harmful to the interests of a nation are an assault against all humanity.
(17) A nation may wage war for the defence of its sovereignty, its freedom, its property.
(18) Nations at war should allow for the possibility of negotiations aimed at reaching peace.
(19) Diplomatic agents sent by one nation to another shall not be amenable to the laws and regulations of the country to which they have been sent with regard to that which is related to their mission.
(20) There is no precedent among diplomatic agents from different states.
(21) Treaties between nations shall be sacred and inviolable."

L. MAGGIOLO, *La vie et l'oeuvre de l'abbé Grégoire*, Paris, 1884. C. DOSNIT, H. MOUNIER, R. BONNARD, *Les Constitutions et les principales lois politiques de la France depuis 1789, précédées des notices historiques, Paris*, 1945; R. GRUENBAUM BALLIN, *Henri Grégoire, l'ami des hommes de toutes les couleurs*, Paris, 1948.

LAW OF NATIONS, VATTEL'S PRINCIPLES, 1758. The classic work of the Swiss jurist Emerich de Vattel (1714–67) published in 1758. The text of the Introduction is as follows:

Introduction: Idea and General Principles of the Law of Nations.
"(1) *What is meant by the term nation or state.*
Nations or states are political bodies, societies of men who have united together and combined their forces, in order to procure their mutual welfare and security.
(2) *It is a moral person.*
Such a society has its own affairs and interests; it deliberates and takes resolutions in common, and it thus becomes a moral person having an understanding and a will peculiar to itself, and susceptible at once of obligations and of rights.
(3) *Definition of the law of nations.*
The object of this work is to establish on a firm basis the obligations and the rights of Nations. The Law of Nations is the science of the rights which exist between Nations or states, and of the obligations corresponding to these rights. It will be seen from this treatise how states, as such, ought to regulate their actions. We shall examine the obligations of a Nation towards itself as well as towards other Nations, and in this way we shall determine the rights resulting from those obligations; for since a right is nothing else but the power of doing what is morally possible, that is to say, what is good in itself and conformable to duty, it is clear that right is derived from duty, or passive obligation, from the obligation of acting in this or that manner. A Nation must therefore understand the nature of its obligations, not only to avoid acting contrary to its duty, but also to

obtain therefrom a clear knowledge of its rights, of what it can lawfully exact from other Nations.

(4) *How nations or states are to be regarded.*

Since Nations are composed of men who are by nature free and independent, and who before the establishment of civil society lived together in the state of nature, such Nations or sovereign states must be regarded as so many free persons living together in the state of nature. Proof can be had from works on the natural law that liberty and independencc belong to man by his very nature, and that they can not be taken from him without his consent. Citizens of a state, having yielded them in part to the sovereign, do not enjoy them to their full and absolute extent. But the whole body of the Nation, the state, so long as it has not voluntarily submitted to other men of other Nations, remains absolutely free and independent.

(5) *To what laws nations are subject.*

As men are subject to the laws of nature, and as their union in civil society can not exempt them from the obligation of observing those laws, since in that union they remain none the less men, the whole Nation, whose common will is but the outcome of the united wills of the citizens, remains subject to the laws of nature and is bound to respect them in all its undertakings. And since right is derived from obligation, as we have just remarked, a Nation has the same rights that nature gives to men for the fulfillment of their duties.

(6) *The law of nations in origin.*

We must therefore apply to nations the rules of the natural law to discover what are their obligations and their rights; hence the Law of Nations is in its origin merely the Law of Nature applied to Nations. Now the just and reasonable application of a rule requires that the application be made in a manner suited to the nature of the subject; but we must not conclude that the Law of Nations is everywhere and at all points the same as the natural law, except for a difference of subjects, so that no other change need be made than to substitute Nations for individuals. A civil society, or a state, is a very different subject from an individual person, and therefore, by virtue of the natural law, very different obligations and rights belong to it in most cases. The same general rule, when applied to two different subjects, can not result in similar principles, nor can a particular rule, however just for one subject, be applicable to a second of a totally different nature. Hence there are many cases in which the natural law does not regulate the relations of states as it would those of individuals. We must know how to apply it conformably to its subjects; and the art of so applying it, with a precision founded upon right reason, constitutes of the Law of Nations a distinct science.

(7) *Definition of the necessary law of nations.*

We use the term necessary Law of Nations for that law which results from applying the natural law to Nations. It is necessary, because Nations are absolutely bound to observe it. It contains those precepts which the natural law dictates to states, and it is no less binding upon them than it is upon individuals. For states are composed of men, their policies are determined by men, and these men are subject to the natural law under whatever capacity they act. This same law is called by Grotius and his followers the internal Law of Nations, inasmuch as it is binding upon the conscience of Nations. Several writers call it the natural Law of Nations.

(8) *It is not subject to change.*

Since, therefore, the necessary Law of Nations consists in applying the natural law to states, and since the natural law is not subject to change, being founded on the nature of things and particularly upon the nature of man, it follows that the necessary Law of Nations is not subject to change.

(9) *Nations can not change it nor release themselves from its obligations.*

Since this law is not subject to change and the obligations which it imposes are necessary and indispensable, Nations can not alter it by agreement, nor individually or mutually release themselves from it.

It is by the application of this principle that a distinction can be made between lawful and unlawful treaties or convention and between customs which are innocent and reasonable and those which are unjust and deserving of condemnation. Things which are just in themselves and permitted by the necessary Law of Nations may form the subject of an agreement by Nations or may be given sacredness and force through practice and custom. Indifferent affairs may be settled either by treaty, if Nations so please, or by the introduction of some suitable custom or usage. But all treaties and customs contrary to the dictates of the necessary Law of Nations are unlawful. We shall see, however, that they are not always conformable to the inner law of conscience, and yet, for reasons to be given in their proper place, such conventionsand treaties are often valid by the external law. Owing to the freedom and independence of Nations, the conduct of one Nation may be unlawful and censurable according to the laws of conscience, and yet other Nations must put up with it so long as it does not infringe upon their perfect rights. The liberty of a Nation would not remain complete if other Nations presumed to inspect and control its conduct; a presumption which would be contrary to the natural law, which declares every Nation free and independent of all other Nations.

(10) *The society established by nature among all men.*

Such is man's nature that he is not sufficient unto himself and necessarily stands in need of the assistance and intercourse of his fellows, whether to preserve his life or to perfect himself and live as befits a rational animal. Experience shows this clearly enough. We know of men brought up among bears, having neither the use of speech nor of reason, and limited like beasts to the use of the sensitive faculties. We observe, moreover, that nature has denied man the strength and the natural weapons with which it has provided other animals, and has given him instead to the use of speech and of reason, or at least the ability to acquire them by intercourse with other men. Language is a means of communication, of mutual assistance, and of perfecting man's reason and knowledge; and, having thus become intelligent, he finds a thousand means of caring for his life and its wants. Moreover, every man realizes that he could not live happily or improve his condition without the help of intercourse with other men. Therefore, since nature has constituted men thus, it is a clear proof that it means them to live together and mutually to aid and assist one another.

From this source we deduce a natural society existing among all men. The general law of this society is that each member should assist the others in all their needs, as far as he can do so without neglecting his duties to himself – a law which all men must obey if they are to live conformably to their nature and to the designs of their common Creator; a law which our own welfare, our happiness, and our best interests should render sacred to each one of us. Such is the general obligation we are under of performing our duties; let us fulfill them with care if we would work wisely for our greatest good. It is easy to see how happy the world would be if all men were willing to follow the rule we have just laid down. On the other hand, if each man thinks of himself first and foremost, if he does nothing for others, all will be alike miserable. Let us labor for the good of all men; they in turn will labor for ours, and we shall build our happiness upon the firmest foundations.

(11) *And among nations.*

Since the universal society of the human race is an institution of nature itself, that is, a necessary result of man's nature, all men of whatever condition are bound to advance its interests and to fulfill its duties. No convention or special agreement can release them from the obligation. When, therefore, men unite in civil society and form a separate state or Nation they may, indeed, make particular agreement with other of the same state, but their duties towards the rest of the human race remain unchanged; but with this difference, that when men have agreed to act in common, and have given up their rights and submitted their will to the whole body as far as concerns their common good, it devolves thenceforth upon that body, the state, and upon its rulers, to fulfill the duties of humanity towards outsiders in all matters in which individuals are no longer at liberty to act, and it peculiarly rests with the state to fulfill these duties towards other states. We have already seen (5) that men, when united in society, remain subject to the obligations of the Law of Nature. This society may be regarded as a moral person, since it has an understanding, a will, and a power peculiar to itself; and it is therefore obliged to live with other societies or states according to the laws of the natural society of the human race, just as individual men before the establishment of civil society lived according to them; with such exceptions, however, as are due to the difference of the subjects.

(12) *The end of this society of nations.*

The end of the natural society established among men in general is that they should mutually assist one another to advance their own perfection and that of their condition; and Nations, too, since they may be regarded as so many free persons living together in a state of nature, are bound mutually to advance this human society. Hence the end of the great society established by nature among all nations is likewise that of mutual assistance in order to perfect themselves and their condition.

(13) *The general obligation which it imposes.*

The first general law, which is to be found in the very end of the society of Nations, is that each Nation should contribute as far as it can to the happiness and advancement of other Nations.

(14) *Explanation of this obligation.*

But as its duties towards itself clearly prevail over its duties towards others, a Nation owes to itself, as a prime consideration, whatever it can do for its own happiness and advancement. (I say whatever it can do, not meaning physically only, but morally also, what it can do, lawfully, justly, and honestly). When, therefore, a Nation can not contribute to the welfare of another without doing an essential wrong to itself, its obligation ceases in this particular instance, and the Nation is regarded as lying under a disability to perform the duty.

(15) *Liberty and independence of nations; second law.*

Since Nations are free and independent of one another as men are by nature, the second general law of their society is that each Nation should be left to the peaceable enjoyment of that liberty which belongs to it by nature. The natural society of nations can not continue unless the rights which belong to each by nature are respected. No Nation is willing to give up its liberty; it will rather choose to break off all intercourse with those who attempt to encroach upon it.

(16) *Effect of this liberty.*

In consequence of liberty and independence it follows that it is for each Nation to decide what its conscience demands of it, what it can or can not do; what it thinks well or does not think well to do; and therefore it is for each Nation to consider and determine what duties it can fulfill towards others without failing in its duty towards itself. Hence in all cases in which it belongs to a Nation to judge of the extent of its duty, no other Nation may force it to act one way or another. Any attempt to do so would be an encroachment upon the liberty of Nations. We may not use force against a free person, except in cases where this person is under obligation to us in a definite matter and for a definite reason not depending upon his judgment; briefly, in cases in which we have a perfect right against him.

(17) *Distinction of obligations and rights as internal and external, perfect and imperfect.*

To understand this properly we must note that obligations and the corresponding rights produced by them are distinguished into internal and external. Obligations are internal in so far as they bind the conscience and are deduced from the rules of our duty; they are external when considered relatively to other men as producing some right on their part. Internal obligations are always the same in nature, though they may vary in degree; external obligations, however, are divided into perfect and imperfect, and the rights they give rise to are likewise perfect and imperfect. Perfect rights are those which carry with them the right of compelling the fulfillment of the corresponding obligations; imperfect rights can not so compel. Perfect obligations are those which give rise to the right of enforcing them; imperfect obligations give but the right to request.

It will now be easily understood why a right is always imperfect when the corresponding obigation depends upon the judgment of him who owes it; for if he could be constrained in such a case he would cease to have the right of deciding what are his obligations according to the law of conscience. Our obligations to others are always imperfect when the decision as to how we are to act rests with us, as it does in all matters where we ought to be free.

(18) *Equality of nations.*

Since men are by nature equal, and their individual rights and obligations the same, as coming equally from nature, Nations, which are composed of men and may be regarded as so many free persons living together in a state of nature, are by nature equal and hold from nature the same obligations and the same rights. Strength or weakness, in this case, counts for nothing. A dwarf is as much a man as a giant is; a small Republic is no less a sovereign state than the most powerful Kingdom.

(19) *Effect of this equality.*
From this equality it necessarily follows that what is lawful or unlawful for one Nation is equally lawful or unlawful for every other Nation.

(20) *Each is free to act as it pleases so far as its acts do not affect the perfect rights of others.*
A Nation is therefore free to act as it pleases, so far as its acts do not affect the perfect rights of another Nation, and so far as the Nation is under merely internal obligations without any perfect external obligation. If it abuses its liberty it acts wrongfully; but other Nations can not complain, since they have no right to dictate to it.

(21) *Foundation of the voluntary law of nations.*
Since Nations are free, independent, and equal, and since each has the right to decide in its conscience what it must do to fulfill its duties, the effect of this is to produce, before the world at least, a perfect equality of rights among Nations in the conduct of their affairs and in the pursuit of their policies. The intrinsic justice of their conduct is another matter which it is not for others to pass upon finally; so that what one may do another may do, and they must be regarded in the society of mankind as having equal rights.
When differences arise each Nation in fact claims to have justice on its side, and neither of the interested parties nor other Nations may decide the question. The one who is actually in the wrong sins against its conscience; but as it may possibly be in the right, it can not be accused of violating the laws of the society of Nations.
It must happen, then, on many occasions that Nations put up with certain things although in themselves unjust and worthy of condemnation, because they can not oppose them by force without transgresssing the liberty of individual Nations and thus destroying the foundations of their natural society. And since they are bound to advance that society, we rightly presume that they have agreed to the principle just established. The rules resulting from it form what Wolf calls the voluntary Law of Nations; and there is no reason why we should not use the same expression, although we have thought it our duty to differ from that learned man as to how the foundation of that law should be established.

(22) *Rights of nations against those who violate the law of nations.*
The laws of the natural society of Nations are so important to the welfare of every state that if the habit should prevail of treading them under foot no Nation could hope to protect its existence or its domestic peace, whatever wise and just and temperate measures it might take. Now all men and all states have a perfect right to whatever is essential to their existence, since this right corresponds to an indispensable obligation. Hence all Nations may put down by force the open violation of the laws of the society which nature has established among them, or any direct attacks upon its welfare.

(23) *Rule of these rights.*
But care must be taken not to extend these rights so as to prejudice the liberty of Nations. They are all free and independent, though they are so far bound to observe the laws of nature that if one violates them the others may restrain it; hence the Nations as a body have no rights over the conduct of a single Nation, further than the natural society finds itself concerned therein. The general and common rights of Nations over the conduct of a sovereign state should be in keeping with the end of the society which exists among them.

(24) *Conventional law of nations, or law of treaties.*
The various agreements which Nations may enter into give rise to a new division of the Law of Nations which is called conventional, or the law of treaties. As it is clear that a treaty binds only the contracting parties the conventional Law of Nations is not universal, but restricted in character. All that can be said upon this subject in a treatise on the Law of Nations must be limited to a statement of the general rules which Nations must observe with respect to their treaties. The details of the various agreements between certain Nations, and of the resulting rights and obligations, are questions of fact to be treated of in historical works.

(25) *Customary law of nations.*
Certain rules and customs, consecrated by long usage and observed by Nations as a sort of law, constitute the customary Law of Nations, or international custom. This law is founded upon a tacit consent, or rather upon

a tacit agreement of the Nations which observe it. Hence it evidently binds only those Nations which have adopted it and is no more universal than the conventional law. Hence we must also say of this customary law that its details do not come within a systematic treatise on the Law of Nations, and we must limit ourselves to stating the general theory of it, that is to say, the rules to be observed in it, both as regards its effects and its substance. In this latter point these rules will serve to distinguish lawful and innocent customs from unlawful and unjust ones.

(26) *General rule of this law.*
When a custom of usage has become generally established either between all the civilized countries of the world or only between those of a given continent, Europe for example, or those which have more frequent intercourse with one another, if this custom be indifferent in nature, much more so if it be useful and reasonable, it becomes binding upon all those Nations which are regarded as having given their consent to it. They are bound to observe it towards one another so long as they have not expressly declared their unwillingness to follow it any longer. But if there be anything unjust or unlawful in such a custom it is of no force, and indeed every Nation is bound to abandon it, since there can be neither obligation nor authorization to violate the Law of Nature.

(27) *Positive law of nations.*
These three divisions of the Law of Nations, the voluntary, the conventional, and the customary law, form together the positive Law of Nations, for they all proceed from the agreement of Nations; the voluntary law from their presumed consent; the conventional law from their express consent; and the customary law from their tacit consent. And since there are no other modes of deducing a law from the agreement of Nations, there are but these three divisions of the positive Law of Nations.
We shall be careful to distinguish them from the natural or necessary Law of Nations, without, however, treating them separately. But after having established on each point what the necessary law prescribes, we shall then explain how and why these precepts must be modified by the voluntary law; or, to put it in another way, we shall show how, by reason of the liberty of nations and the rules of their natural society, the external law which they must observe towards one another differs on certain points from the principles of the internal law, which, however, are always binding upon the conscience. As for rights introduced by treaties or by custom, we need not fear that anyone will confuse them with the natural Law of Nations. They form that division of the Law of Nations which writers term the arbitrary law.

(28) *General rule for the application of the necessary and the voluntary law.*
In order from the start to lay down broad lines for the distinction between the necessary law and the voluntary law we must note that since the necessary law is at all times obligatory upon the conscience, a Nation must never lose sight of it when deliberating upon the course it must pursue to fulfill its duty; but when there is question of what it can demand from other states, it must consult the voluntary law, whose rules are devoted to the welfare and advancement of the universal society."

The text of the two first paragraphs of Chapter 1: Peace and the Obligation to Cultivate it, are as follows:

"(1) *What peace is.*
Peace is the reverse of war; it is that desirable state in which every man lives in the peaceful enjoyment of his rights, or subjects them, in case of controversy, to friendly discussion and argument. Hobbes has dared to assert that war is the natural state of man. But if by the 'natural state' of man we mean (as reason requires we should) that state to which he is destined and called by his nature, we must rather say that peace is his natural state. For it is the part of rational being to decide differences by submitting them to reason; whereas it is characteristic of the brute to settle them by force. Nam cum sint duo genera decertandi, unum per disceptationem, alterum per vim; cumque illud proprium sit hominis, hoc belluarum: confugiendum est ad posterius, si uti non licet superiore. Cicero, De Officiis, Lib. I, Cap. II. Man, as we have already observed (Introd., 10), when alone and destitute of help, can not but be wretched; he needs the intercourse and assistance of his

fellows if he is to enjoy the pleasures of life and develop his faculties and live in a manner suited to his nature, all of which is only possible in a time of peace. It is in time of peace that men respect one another, mutually assist one another, and live on friendly terms. They would never give up the happiness of a life of peace if they were not carried away by their passions and blinded by the base illusions of self-love. The little that we have said of the effects of war is sufficient to make clear how disastrous a measure it is. It is unfortunate for the human race that the injustice of the wicked renders war so often unavoidable.

(2) *The obligation to cultivate it.*
Nations which are influenced by humane sentiments, which are seriously intent upon the performance of their duties, and which have an enlightened sense of their true and permanent interests, will never seek their own gain at the expense of another; though solicitous for their own happiness, they will manage to combine it with that of others and bring it in accord with justice and equity. If this be their attitude they will never fail to cultivate peace. How can they fulfill the sacred duties which nature has imposed upon them if they do not live together in peace? And the state of peace is no less necessary to their happiness than it is to the fulfillment of their duties. Accordingly, the natural law obliges them in every way to seek and to promote peace. That divine law has no other end than the happiness of the human race; to that object are directed all its rules and all its precepts; they can all be deduced from this principle, that men should seek their own happiness; morality is nothing else than the science of attaining happiness, As this is true of individuals, it is no less true of Nations – a conclusion which will readily appear to any one who will but reflect upon what we have said of the common and mutual duties of Nations, in the first chapter of Book II."

E. DE VATTEL, *Le Droit des gens*, Neuchâtel, 1758; Ch.S. FENWICK, "The Authority of Vattel", in:*American Political Science Review*, No. 7, 1913 and No. 8, 1914; E. DE VATTEL, *The Law of Nations and the Principles of Natural Law*, Washington, DC, 1916.

LAW OF NON-NAVIGATIONAL USE OF INTERNATIONAL WATERCOURSES. A subject of codification by the International Law Commission, ILC.

Report of the ILC on the Work of Its 32nd Session, 5 May–25 July, 1980, UN, New York, 1980, pp. 237–315.

LAW OF OUTER SPACE. An international term coined in the second half of the 20th century, also called the interplanetary law. A new branch of international public law, extending beyond the globe and its atmosphere, originated on Oct. 4, 1957, the date of the launching of the first artificial earth satellite Sputnik I. On Mar. 15, 1958 the USSR submitted to the UN General Assembly a proposal for a new international convention on the use of outer space under the supervision of the United Nations exclusively for peaceful purposes and on the prohibition of establishing military bases in outer space. The Law of Outer Space stems from the conclusion that the sovereign rights of states to their air space are not extended to include outer space, "where the principle *res communis omnis universi* (a thing common to all humanity) is in force". ▷ Outer Space.
The International Telecommunications Union, ITU, took up the question of the legal aspects of ▷ satellite telecommunication and satellite ▷ television. Separate preparatory work for the development of outer space law has been started by three international non-governmental organizations: Institute of International Law in Brussels, London Society of International Law and in the International Institute of Space Law, f. 1960, Paris. *The Yearbook of Space Law – Annuaire de Droit Aérienne et Spatial* is published in Montreal.

J.E. FAWCETT, *International Law and the Uses of Outer Space*, London, 1968; M. LACHS, *The Law of*

L

Outer Space: An Experience in Contemporary Law-Making, Leiden, 1972; J. KISH, *The Law of International Space*, Leiden, 1973.

LAW OF SPORT IN INTERNATIONAL RELATIONS. A subject of continuous internationally organized co-operation in the form of codification of legal regulations connected with international celebration of Olympic Games and other international competitions. The First International Congress of Sports Law was held in Mexico City on June 26, 1968 on the initiative of the International Olympic Committee, IOC. The Congress recognized the need for: an international legal basis for the international organization of sport and for relations with national organizations; a clear-cut definition of the legal relationship between the IOC and the national committees organizing subsequent Olympic Games; an international convention on protection of the flag, emblems and IOC names and codification of laws for the protection of health in sport. The prolonged controversy has continued within the IOC on the definition of amateur and professional sport. American jurists have put forward the question of international legal protection of professional sportsmen. The congress appealed to the ILO to study the present working conditions of such sportsmen, with a view to preparing an international convention that would secure the basic interests of this labor group, a convention which would recognize professional sportsmen as a category of workers with the right to all welfare and other securities provided for by laws recognized by the ILO. ▷ Sport.

I Congreso Internacional del Derecho Deportivo. Materiales y Documentos, México, DF, June, 1968.

LAW OF THE SEA. ▷ Sea Law International.

LAW OF TREATIES. An international term for law on international agreements between states, between states and international organizations, or between two or more international organizations. An international common law, regulates questions on the conclusion, application and interpretations as well as the termination and invalidity of international bi- and multilateral agreements; subject of the Havana Convention of Feb. 20, 1928, and of codification work undertaken by the International Law Commission of the UN in the years 1952–66, in pursuance of the request of the UN General Assembly of 1949, Res. 1765/XVII of Nov. 20, 1962, and Res. 2166/XXI of Dec. 5, 1966. The draft convention prepared by the International Law Commission of the UN was discussed at two sessions of the UN Conference on the Law of Treaties held in Vienna on Mar. 26, 1968 and between Apr. 9 and May 31, 1969. In the first session 103 states participated while in the second session 110 states took part. On May 23, 1969 the Conference adopted the ▷ Vienna Convention on the Law of International Treaties.

UN Systematic Survey of Treaties 1928–1948, New York, 1949; *Laws and Practices Concerning the Conclusions of Treaties*, UN, New York, 1953; B.KASME: *La Capacité de l'ONU de conclure des traités*, Paris, 1960; M. LACHS, *Evolución y Funciones de los Tratados Multilaterales*, México, DF, 1962; T.I.H. DETTER, *Law Making by International Organizations*, Stockholm, 1965; H. CHIN, *The Capacity of International Organizations to Conclude Treaties, and the Special Legal Aspects of the Treaties so Concluded*, The Hague, 1966; *A Selected Bibliography of the Law of Treaties*, UN A/Conf. 39/4, Vienna Feb. 1, 1968; *UN Monthly Chronicle*, No. 6, 1969, pp. 54–56; S. ROSENNE, *The Law of Treaties. A Guide to the Legislative History of the Vienna Convention*, Amsterdam, 1970; Y. RENOUX, *Glossary of International Treaties*, The Hague, 1970; M. FRANKOWSKA, "The Vienna Convention on the Law of Treaties", in: *The Polish Yearbook of International Law*, 1970, pp. 227–256; K. ZEMANEK (ed.), *Agreements of International Organizations and the Vienna Convention on the Law of Treaties*, Vienna, 1971; G. HARASZTI, *Some Fundamental Problems of the Law of Treaties*, Budapest, 1973; P. REUTER, *Introduction au droit des traités*, Paris, 1973.

LAW OF WAR. All conventions and international practices binding hostile sides and neutral states in an armed conflict; a subject of international law and of humanitarian development which was initiated by the Red Cross, 1864. The first international agreement, introducing four principles on the law of the sea during war, was the so-called Paris Declaration of the Law of the Sea, 1856, followed by: the Geneva Convention, 1864 on prisoners and wounded, expanded 1906 and 1949; Petersburg Declaration, 1868, defining banned arms; Hague Conventions and Declarations, 1889, expanded by 13 Hague Conventions, 1907; Geneva Protocol, 1925 on the prohibition of the use in war of poisonous gases; London Treaty, 1930 on the protection of cultural treasures. Since 1969 frequently a subject on the agenda of the UN General Assembly relating to problems of "respecting human rights during armed conflicts", which forecasts the further development of the law of war pertaining to the protection of man and his environment. At the Conference on Human Rights in Geneva, Feb. 20–Mar. 29, 1974, the Third World as well as the socialist countries passed by a majority vote of 77 in favor, 22 against, 12 abstentions, and 31 absent a supplement to the Geneva Conventions of 1949 in the form of a resolution that included among international armed conflicts "wars against foreign domination, colonialism and racism, and self-determination", which means i.a. the granting of the same rights to the participants in such struggles as those enjoyed by combatants in other armed conflicts.

A. ROLIN, *Le droit moderne de la guerre*, Paris, 1920; P. DE LA PRADELLE, *Utopie en calcul, négligera-t-on longtemps encore l'étude des lois de la guerre?* Paris, 1933; P. DE LA PRADELLE, *La reconstruction du droit de la guerre*, Paris, 1936; J.L. KUNZ, "The Chaotic Status of the Laws of War", in: *American Journal of International Law*, No. 45, 1951; H. LAUTERPACHT, "The Problem of the Revision of the Laws of War", in: *The British Yearbook of International Law*, 1952; Q. WRIGHT, "The Outlawry of War and the Laws of War", in: *American Journal of International Law*, No. 47, 1953; E. CASTREN, *The Present Law of War and Neutrality*, Helsinki, 1954; M. GREENSPAN, *The modern Law of Land Warfare*, New York, 1959; V. DEDIJER, *On Military Conventions*, Lund, 1961; D. BINDSCHEDLER, *Reconsidération du droit des conflits armés*, Genève, 1969; CARNEGIE ENDOWMENT, *Report of the Conference on contemporary problems of the law of armed conflicts, Geneva, Sept. 15–20, 1969*, New York, 1971; T.J. FARER, *International Armed Conflicts. The International Character of Conflict*, Bruxelles, 1971; T.J. FARER "The Laws of War 25 Years after Nuremberg", in: *International Conciliation*, May, 1971; D. SCHINDLER (ed.), *The Laws of Armed Conflicts*, Leiden, 1973; F. KALSHOVEN, *The Law of Warfare. A Summary of Its Recent History and Trends Development*, Leiden, 1973; *CBW and the Law of War*, SIPRI, Stockholm, 1973; J.E. BOND, *The Rules of Riot. International Conflict and the Law of War*, Princetown, 1974; S. DĄBROWA, "A mi-chemin de la codification du droit international des conflits armés", in: *Polish Yearbook of International Law 1972–73*, Wroclaw, 1974; J. GOLDBLAT, *Arms Control Agreements. A Handbook*, New York, 1983.

LAWYERS ▷ Bar Lawyers.

LDC ▷ Least Developed Countries.

LEAD AND ZINC. Subjects of international co-operation and agreements (1935 and 1958). The first UN Conference on Lead and Zinc was held in 1948. Organizations reg. with the UIA:

International Lead and Zinc Research Organization, Inc., f. 1958, New York. Publ.: *Research Digest*. (2 a year).
International Lead and Zinc Study Group, f. 1959, New York. Publ.: *Lead and Zinc Statistics* (monthly).
Lead Development Association, f. 1954, London.
Scandinavian Lead and Zinc Development Association, f. 1961, Stockholm.
Zinc and Lead Development Association, f. 1961, London.

UN Review, June 1958; *The Yearbook of International Organizations*, 1986/87; *The Europa Yearbook 1988. A World Survey*, Vol. I, London 1988.

LEAD POLLUTION. The UNEP experts reported in January 1984 that the contamination with lead of the Mediterranean Sea was ten times higher than that of the open sea, and could cause brain damage to persons eating its fish and shellfish.
In February 1989 the British Government decreed that as of 1990, all new cars must be able to run on unleaded fuel.

KEESING's *Record of World Events*, July 1986.

LEAGUE OF AMERICAN NATIONS. At the suggestion of Uruguay's President B. Brumm in Apr. 1920, when the US boycott of the League of Nations became apparent a project of a League of American Nations was considered by the Fifth International American Conference in Santiago de Chile, 1923. At the 1936 and 1938 Conferences in Buenos Aires and Lima, the Dominican Republic, Guatemala and Colombia put the project forward for consideration, suggesting the name League of American Republics – Sociedad de las Republicas Americanas.

Conferencias Internacionales Americanas 1889–1936, Washington, DC, 1938.

LEAGUE OF ARAB STATES OR ARAB LEAGUE. A regional organization of Arab states recognized by the UN. The League was est. by a Pact of the League of Arab states, signed Mar. 22, 1945 in Cairo by the heads of the governments of Egypt, Iraq, Lebanon, Saudi Arabia, Syria, Transjordan (presently Jordan), and Yemen; Libya joined in 1953; 1955 – Sudan; 1958 – Morocco and Tunisia; 1962 – Algeria; 1964 – Kuwait; 1967 – South Yemen; 1971 – Bahrain, Qatar, Oman; 1972 – the United Arab Emirates; 1973 – Mauritania; 1974 – Somalia; 1975 – Djibouti; 1976 – the Palestine Liberation Organization. The supreme organ is the Council composed, depending on the need, of heads of state, heads of government, or ministers of foreign affairs. Unanimity is required in all basic matters (art. 7 of the Statute), and only in some, such as budget, nomination of functionaries of the League, etc., does a simple majority suffice (art. 16). A "delegate of Palestine" had the right to participate as an observer in the meetings of the Council "until the time of the creation of a Palestinian State". Since Sept. 9, 1976 by a unanimous decision of the Council the ▷ Palestine Liberation Organization became a full member of the League.

The chronicle of treaties integrating the member states of the League: Mar. 22, 1945 signed the Pact of the Arab League; Nov. 27, 1945, Treaty on Cultural Cooperation; June 18, 1950, Treaty on Joint Defence and Economic Co-operation and creation of Arab League Economic Council; Apr. 9, 1953, Convention on the establishment of the Arab Telecommunications Union, Convention of privileges and immunities of the League, and Treaty on inter-Arab trade; July 7, 1954, Convention on formation of the Arab Postal Union; in June, 1957, Convention of the creation of the Arab Develop-

ment Bank; May 16, 1959 the First Arab Petroleum Conference was held; in Mar., 1960 Arab League headquarters was opened in Cairo; also in Mar., 1960, Treaty on the co-ordination of oil policies (▷ OAPEC); in June, 1961, Treaty on the establishment of the International Arab Airline; June 6, 1962, Treaty on the Economic Community of Egypt, Jordan, Kuwait, Morocco, and Syria, later joined by Yemen, Iraq, and Sudan; in Dec., 1963, Treaty on the formation of the Arab Navigation Company and the Treaty on the creation of the Arab Organization on Social Defense against Crime; in Jan., 1964, formation of the Arab Board for the Diversion of the Jordan River; in Aug., 1964, treaty on the creation of the Arab Common Market as of Jan. 1, 1965; in June, 1965, Treaty on Arab co-operation in the Peaceful Uses of Atomic Energy; 1966, Treaty on the establishment of the Arab League Administrative Court; in Dec., 1967, creation of the Civil Aviation Council for Arab States and the Arab Tanker Company; in Sept., 1968, establishment of the Arab Fund for Economic and Social Development Center for the Arab States; in Jan., 1970, formation of the Arab Organization for Agricultural Development and the Arab Educational, Cultural and Scientific Organization. In 1976 the Arab League together with the EEC formed the Great Arab–European Commission, which meets twice each year (alternatively in one of the Arab and European states) and sets guidelines for economic co-operation. In 1978/79 Egyptian–Israeli negotiations caused a serious crisis in the Arab League; the signing of the ▷ Egypt–Israel Peace Treaty, 1979, led to a transfer of the headquarters of the League from Cairo to Tunis and the exclusion of the Egyptian government from participation in the work of the League. In Nov., 1980 the Summit Conference in Amman adopted a Strategy for Joint Arab Economic Action up to the year 2000. In Nov., 1981 the Summit Conference in Fez, Morocco, was suspended after the majority disagreed over a Saudi Arabian proposal called Fahd's Plan, suggesting de facto recognition of Israel, but the reconvened Summit in Sept., 1982 adopted a ▷ League of Arab States Peace Plan, 1982 similar to the Fahd Plan
In 1984 the Arab League members were: Algeria, Bahrain, Djibouti, Egypt (suspended in March, 1979), Iraq, Jordan, Kuwait, Lebanon, Libya, Mauritania, Morocco, Oman, Palestine Liberation Organization (since 1976), Qatar, Saudi Arabia, Somalia, Sudan, Syria, Tunisia, United Arab Emirates, Yemen Arab Republic and Yemen People's Democratic Republic. On Aug. 7–9, 1985 in Casablanca a summit meeting adopted a Plan of Action, compatible with the Fez Peace Plan of 1982, to implement the Arab peace plan … guaranteeing the withdrawal of Israeli occupation forces from all occupied Arab territories.
An extraordinary summit meeting was held in Amman, on Nov. 8–11 1987 to establish a unified Arab stand towards Iran. The summit unanimously condemned Iran's occupation of part of Iraq's territory and its procrastination in accepting UN Security Res. 598. In the Palestine question the summit members agreed that "peace in the Middle East could only be achieved by regaining all the Arab and Palestinian territories including Jerusalem". As for the Egyptian Issue it was decided that the re-establishment of diplomatic relations with Egypt is a sovereign matter of each Arab League Member State. An extraordinary summit meeting of the 21 member states was held in Algiers on June 7–9, 1988.
Structure: The permanent General Secretariat organizes the work of sixteen committees attached to the Council: political, cultural, economic, communications, social, legal, arab oil experts, information, health, human rights, for administrative and financial affairs, for meteorology, of arab experts on co-operation, arab women's, organization of youth welfare and conference of liaison officers.
In the sphere of defence and economic co-operation there are four institutions, est. under the Treaty of Joint Defence and Economic Co-operation, concluded in 1950 to complement the Charter of the League:
Arab Unified Military Command, f. 1964 to co-ordinate military policies for the liberation of Palestine.
Economic Council to compare and co-ordinate the economic policies of the member states. The first meeting in 1953.

Joint Defence Council supervises implementation of those aspects of the treaty concerned with common defence.
Permanent Military Commission, f. 1950 to draw up plans of joint defence for submission to the Joint Defence Council.
Arab Deterrent Force set up in June 1976 by the Arab League Council to supervise successive attempts to cease hostilities in Lebanon, and afterward to maintain the peace. The mandate of the Force has been successively renewed.
Other institutions of the Council:
Academy of Arab Music, HQ's Baghdad.
Administrative Tribunal of the Arab League, f. 1964.
Special Bureau of Boycotting Israel, HQ's Damascus.
Specialized agencies:
Arab Academy of Maritime Transport, f. 1975, HQ's Sharjah, UAE.
Arab Centre for the Study of Arid Zones and Dry Lands, f. 1968, HQ's Damascus.
Arab Civil Aviation Council, f. 1965, HQ's Rabat.
Arab Industrial Development Organization, f. 1968, HQ's Baghdad.
Arab Institute of Petroleum Research, f. 1966.
Arab League Educational, Cultural and Scientific Organization, ALECSO, f. 1964, HQ's Tunis. There are four institutions within its framework: Institute of Arab Research and Studies, f. 1953, HQ's Cairo; Arab Literacy and Adult Education Organization, f. 1966, HQ's Baghdad. Arab Manuscript Institute. f. 1946, HQ's Kuwait, and Permanent Bureau for Arabization, HQ's Rabat. Arab Labour Organization, f. 1965, HQ's Baghdad. Arab Organization of Administrative Sciences, f. 1961, HQ's Amman.
Arab Organization for Agriculture Development, f. 1969, HQ's Khartoum.
Arab Organization for Mineral Resources, f. 1979, HQ's Rabat.
Arab Organization for Social Defence Against Crime, f. 1960, HQ's Rabat. The organization consists of three bureaux: Arab Bureau for Narcotics, HQ's Amman; Arab Bureau for Prevention of Crime, HQ's Baghdad; and Arab Bureau of Criminal Police, HQ's Damascus.
Arab Organization for Standardization and Meteorology, f. 1968, HQ's Amman.
Arab Postal Union, f. 1954, HQ's Dubai.
Arab Satellite Communications Organization, ASCO, f. 1969, HQ's Riyadh.
Arab States Broadcasting Union, ASBU, f. 1969, HQ's Tunis.
Arab Telecommunications Union, f. 1953, HQ's Baghdad. The Arab League has information bureaus in Addis Ababa, Bonn, Brussels, Buenos Aires, Chicago, Dakar, Dallas, Geneva, London, Madrid, Nairobi, New Delhi, New York, Ottawa, Paris, Rio de Janeiro, Rome, Tokyo, San Francisco, and Washington. In Tunis publ.: Journal of Arab Affairs and Information Bulletin, in Bonn Arabische Korrespondenz, in Buenos Aires Revista Arabe, in Geneva Le Monde Arabe and Nouvelles du Monde Arabe, in London The Arab, in Delhi Al Arab, in Ottawa The Arab Case, in Rio de Janeiro Oriente Arabe, and in Rome Ressegna del Mondo Arabe.

M. LAISSY, Du Panarabisme à la Ligue Arabe, Paris, 1948; B. BOUTROSGHALI, "The Arab League, 1945–1955", in: International Conciliation, No. 498, May 1954, pp. 387–448; T.R. LITTLE, "The Arab League. A Reassessment", in: The Middle East Journal, No. 10, 1956; M. KHALI, The Arab States, and the Arab League. A Documentary Record, Vol. 1, Constitutional Development, Vol. II, International Affairs, Beirut, 1962; G.J. MIRSKI, Arabskie narody prodolzhayut bor'bu, Moskva, 1965; R.W. MACDONALD, The League of Arab States. A study in Dynamics of Regional Organizations, Princeton, 1965; A.M. EL HADI, The Arabs and the United Nations, Oxford, 1965; G. VALABTRAGA, La Rivoluzione Araba, Milano, 1967; J. HOARE, G. TAYAR, The Arabs. A Handbook on the Politics and Economics of the Contemporary Arab World, London, 1970; A.M. GOMMAA, The Foundation of the League of Arab States, London, 1977; Arab Maritime Data 1979–80, London, 1979; The Europa Year Book 1984. A World Survey, Vol. I, pp. 171–175, London, 1984; KEESING's Record of World Events, February, 1988.

LEAGUE OF ARAB STATES AND THE OAU CONFERENCE, 1977.
The first conference at the summit of the heads of government of the members of the League of Arab States and the Organization of African Unity, was held Mar. 7–9, 1977 in Cairo; accepted two declarations: Political Declaration and a Declaration on African–Arabian Economic and Financial Co-operation.

KEESING's Contemporary Archive, 1977.

LEAGUE OF ARAB STATES PACT, 1945.
Signed Mar., 22, 1945 in Cairo by Egypt, Iraq, Lebanon, Saudi Arabia, Syria, Transjordan and Yemen. Came into force on May 10, 1945 (ratified by Egypt, Iraq, Saudi Arabia and Transjordan, in Apr. 1944, by Lebanon and Syria in May 1945 and by Yemen in Febr., 1946). The text is as follows:
"With a view to strengthening the close relations and numerous ties which bind the Arab States,
And out of concern for the cementing and reinforcing of these bonds on the basis of respect for the independence and sovereignty of these states,
And in order to direct their efforts toward the goal of the welfare of all the Arab States, their common wealth, the guarantee of their future and the realization of their aspirations,
And in response to Arab public opinion in all the Arab countries,
Have agreed to conclude a pact to this effect and have delegated as their plenipotentiaries those whose names are given below …
Art. 1. The League of Arab States shall be composed of the independent Arab States that have signed this Pact. Every Independent Arab State shall have the right to adhere to the League. Should it desire to adhere, it shall present an application to this effect which shall be filed with the permanent Secretariat-General and submitted to the Council at its first meeting following the presentation of the application.
Art. 2. The purpose of the League is to draw closer the relations between member states and co-ordinate their political activities with the aim of realizing a close collaboration between them, to safeguard their independence and sovereignty, and to consider in a general way the affairs and interests of the Arab countries.
It also has among its purposes a close co-operation of the member states with due regard to the structure of each of these states and the conditions prevailing therein, in the following matters:
(a) Economic and financial matters, including trade, customs, currency, agriculture and industry.
(b) Communications, including railways, roads, aviation, navigation, and posts and telegraphs.
(c) Cultural matters.
(d) Matters connected with nationality, passports, visas, execution of judgments and extradition.
(e) Social welfare matters.
(f) Health matters.
Art. 3. The League shall have a Council composed of the representatives of the member states. Each state shall have one vote, regardless of the number of its representatives. The Council shall be entrusted with the function of realizing the purposes of the League and of supervising the execution of the agreements concluded between the member states on matters referred to in the preceding article or on other matters.
It shall also have the function of determining the means whereby the League will collaborate with the international organizations which may be created in the future to guarantee peace and security and organize economic and social relations.
Art. 4. A special Committee shall be formed for each of the categories enumerated in article 2, on which the member states shall be represented. These Committees shall be entrusted with establishing the basis and scope of co-operation in the form of draft agreements which shall be submitted to the Council for its consideration preparatory to their being submitted to the states referred to.
Delegates representing the other Arab countries may participate in these Committees as members. The Council shall determine the circumstances in which the participation of these representatives shall be allowed as well as the basis of the representation.

Art. 5. The recourse to force for the settlement of disputes between two or more member states shall not be allowed. Should there arise among them a dispute that does not involve the independence of a state, its sovereignty or its territorial integrity, and should the two contending parties apply to the Council for the settlement of this dispute, the decision of the Council shall then be effective and obligatory.

In this case, the states among whom the dispute has arisen shall not participate in the deliberations and decisions of the Council.

The Council shall mediate in a dispute which may lead to war between two member states or between a member state and another state in order to conciliate them.

The decisions relating to arbitration and mediation shall be taken by a majority vote.

Art. 6. In case of aggression or threat of aggression by a state against a member state, the attacked or threatened with attack may request an immediate meeting of the Council. The Council shall determine the necessary measures to repel this aggression. Its decision shall be taken unanimously. If the aggression is committed by a member state the vote of that state will not be counted in determining unanimity. If the aggression is committed in such a way as to render the Government of the state attacked unable to communicate with the Council, the representative of the state in the Council may request the Council to convene for the purpose set forth in the preceding paragraph. If the representative is unable to communicate with the Council, it shall be the right of any member state to request a meeting of the Council.

Art. 7. The decisions of the Council taken by a unanimous vote shall be binding on all the member states of the League; those that are reached by a majority vote shall bind only those that accept them.

In both cases the decisions of the Council shall be executed in each state in accordance with the fundamental structure of that state.

Art. 8. Every member state of the League shall respect the form of government obtaining in the other states of the League, and shall recognize the form of government obtaining as one of the rights of those states, and shall pledge itself not to take any action tending to change that form.

Art. 9. The states of the Arab League that are desirous of establishing among themselves closer collaboration and stronger bonds than those provided for in the present Pact, may conclude among themselves whatever agreements they wish for this purpose.

The treaties and agreements already concluded or that may be concluded in the future between a member state and any other states, shall not be binding on the other members.

Art. 10. The permanent seat of the League of Arab States shall be Cairo. The Council of the League may meet at any other place it designates.

Art. 11. The Council of the League shall meet in ordinary session twice a year, during the months of March and October. It shall meet in extraordinary session at the request of two member states whenever the need arises.

Art. 12. The League shall have a permanent Secretariat-General, composed of a Secretary-General, Assistant Secretaries and an adequate number of officials.

The Secretary-General shall be appointed by the Council upon the vote of two-thirds of the states of the League.

The Assistant Secretaries and the principal officials shall be appointed by the Secretary-General with the approval of the Council.

The Council shall establish an internal organization for the Secretariat-General as well as the conditions of service of the officials.

The Secretary-General shall have the rank of Ambassador; and the Assistant Secretaries the rank of Ministers Plenipotentiary.

The first Secretary-General of the League is designated in an annex to the present Pact.

Art. 13. The Secretary-General shall prepare the draft of the budget of the League and submit it for approval to the Council before the beginning of each fiscal year.

The Council shall determine the share of each of the states of the League in the expenses. It shall be allowed to revise the share if necessary.

Art. 14 The members of the Council of the League, the members of its Committees and such of its officials as shall be designated in the internal organization, shall enjoy, in the exercise of their duties, diplomatic privileges and immunities.

The premises occupied by the institutions of the League shall be inviolable.

Art. 15. The Council shall meet the first time at the invitation of the Head of the Egyptian Government. Later meetings shall be convoked by the Secretary-General.

In each ordinary session the representatives of the states of the League shall assume the chairmanship of the Council in rotation.

Art. 16. Except for the cases provided for in the present Pact, a majority shall suffice for decisions by the Council effective in the following matters:
(a) Matters concerning the officials.
(b) The approval of the budget of the League.
(c) The internal organization of the Council, the Committees and the Secretariat-General.
(d) The termination of the sessions.

Art. 17. The member states of the League shall file with the Secretariat-General copies of all treaties and agreements which they have concluded or will conclude with any other state, whether a member of the League or otherwise.

Art. 18. If one of the member states intends to withdraw from the League, the Council shall be informed of its intention one year before the withdrawal takes effect. The Council of the League may consider any state that is not fulfilling the obligations resulting from this Pact as excluded from the League, by a decision taken by a unanimous vote of all the states except the state referred to.

Art. 19. The present Pact may be amended with the approval of two-thirds of the members of the League in particular for the purpose of strengthening the ties between them, of creating an Arab Court of Justice, and of regulating the relations of the League with the international organizations that may be created in the future to guarantee security and peace.

No decisions shall be taken as regards an amendment except in the session following that in which it is proposed.

Any state that does not approve an amendment may withdraw from the League when the amendment becomes effective, without being bound by the provisions of the preceding article."

UNTS, Vol. 70, 1950, pp. 248–262.

LEAGUE OF ARAB STATES PEACE PLAN, 1982.

A peace plan for the Arab-Israeli conflict, adopted by the Twelfth Summit Conference of the Arab League in Feb. 1982 in Fez, Morocco. The plan presented in name of the League by King Hussein of Jordan in Moscow, Paris, Peking and Washington, demanded Israel's withdrawal from Arab territories occupied since 1967, UN temporary supervision for the West Bank and Gaza Strip, the right of the Palestinian people led by the PLO to self-determination and to creation of an independent Palestinian State with Jerusalem as its capital. The plan was rejected by Israel.

KEESING's *Contemporary Archive*, 1982.

LEAGUE OF ARAB STATES SATELLITE, ARABSAT.

The Arab Satellite Communication Organization (ASCO) f. 1969 by the Arab League elaborated a project of a satellite with name ARABSAT for the improvement of telephone, telex, data transmission and radio and television in Arab Countries, launched in 1985.

LEAGUE OF ARAB STATES TREATY OF JOINT DEFENCE AND ECONOMIC CO-OPERATION, 1950.

The treaty was signed on June 18, 1950 in Cairo. The text is as follows:

"In view of the desire of the above mentioned Governments to consolidate the relations between the states of the Arab League to maintain their independence and their mutual heritage and corresponding with the desire of their peoples to rally in order to realize mutual defense and maintain security and peace according to the principles of both the Arab League Pact and the UN Charter, together with the aims of the said Pact, to consolidate stability and security and provide means of welfare and construction in their countries.

Art. 1. In an effort to maintain and stabilize peace and security the contracting states hereby confirm their desire to settle their internationaldisputes by peaceful means, whether such disputes concern their own relations or those with other Powers.

Art. 2. The contracting states consider any act of armed aggression made against any one or more of them or against their forces to be directed against them all, and therefore in accordance with the right of legal defence, individually and collectively, they undertake to hasten to the aid of the state or states against whom such an aggression is made, and to take immediately, individually and collectively, all means available including the use of armed force to repel the aggression and restore security and peace. And, in conformity with art. 6 of the Arab League Pact and art. 51 of the UN Charter, the Arab League Council and UN Security Council should be notified of such act of aggression and the means and procedure taken to check it.

Art. 3. At the invitation of any of the signatories of this Treaty, the contracting states should hold consultations whenever there are reasonable grounds for the belief that the territorial integrity, the independence or security of any of the parties is threatened. In the event of the risk of war or the existence of an international emergency, the contracting states should immediately proceed to unify their plans and defensive measures as the situation may demand.

Art. 4. Desiring to implement the above obligations fully, and effectively carry them out, the contracting states will co-operate in consolidating and co-ordinating their armed forces and participating according to their resources and needs in preparing the individual and collective means of defence to repulse the armed aggression.

Art. 5. A Permanent Military Commission composed of representatives of the General Staffs of the forces of the contracting states is to be formed to co-ordinate the plans of joint defence and their implementation. The powers of the Permanent Military Commission are set forth in an annex attached to this Treaty, include drafting of necessary reports, containing the method of co-operation and participation mentioned in art. 4. The Permanent Military Commission will submit to the mutual Joint Defence Council, provided hereunder in art. 6, reports dealing with questions within its province.

Art. 6. Under the control of the Arab League Council shall be formed a Joint Defence Council to deal with all matters concerning the implementation of the provisions of arts. 2, 3, 4, 5, of this Treaty. It shall be assisted in the performance of its task by the Permanent Military Commission referred to in art. 5. The Joint Defence Council shall consist of the Foreign Ministers and the Defence Ministers of the contracting states, or their representatives. Decisions taken by a majority of two-thirds shall be binding on all the contracting states.

Art. 7. In order to fulfill the aims of the Treaty and to bring about security and prosperity in Arab countries and in an effort to raise the standard of life in them, the contracting states undertake to collaborate for the development of their economic conditions, the exploitation of their natural resources, the exchange of their respective agricultural and industrial products, and generally to organize and co-ordinate their economic activities and by concluding the necessary inter-Arab agreement to realize such aims.

Art. 8. An Economic Council consisting of the Ministers in charge of economic affairs, or their representatives if necessary, is to be formed from the contracting states to submit recommendations for the realization of all such aims as are set forth in the previous article. This Council can, in the performance of its duties, seek the co-operation of the Committee for Financial and Economic Affairs referred to in art. 4 of the Arab League Pact.

Art. 9. The annex to this treaty shall be considered as an integral and indivisible part of it.

Art. 10. The contracting states undertake to conclude no international agreements which may be contradictory to the provisions of this treaty, nor to act in their international relations in a way which may be contrary to the aims of this Treaty.

Art. 11. No provisions of this Treaty shall in any way affect nor is intended to so affect any of the rights or

League of Nations

obligations accruing to the contracting states from the UN Charter or the responsibilities borne by the UN Security Council for the maintenance of International Peace and Security.

Art. 12. After the lapse of 10 years from the date of the ratification of this Treaty, any one of the contracting states may withdraw from it providing 12 months' notice is previously given to the Secretariat-General of the Arab League. The League Secretariat-General shall inform the other contracting states of such notice."

M. KAHALIL, *The Arab States and the Arab League: A Documentary Record*, 2 Vols., Beirut, 1962.

LEAGUE OF FREE NATIONS ASSOCIATION. An American organization f. Nov. 27, 1918 in New York by a group of about fifty editors to promote the establishment of League of Nations.

International Conciliation, No 134, January, 1919, pp. 34–37.

LEAGUE OF HUMAN RIGHTS. ▷ Human Rights League.

LEAGUE OF NATIONS. The first world organization for maintaining peace and for development of international peaceful co-operation. The LN was est. after World War I on the initiative of the US President T. Woodrow Wilson (1856–1924) in accordance with the Recommendations of Havana prepared by the American Institute of International Law 1917 in Havana. At the Versailles Conference a special Committee, headed by T.W. Wilson, prepared from Jan. 16 –Feb. 13, 1919, the LN Covenant which was accepted as an "integral part of the General Peace Treaty" (▷ Versailles Peace Treaty), signed June 28, 1919. The Covenant came into force on Jan. 10, 1920. It was an autonomous document and in compliance with art. 26 open to changes. Other peace treaties signed after World War I, such as the Saint-Germain Treaty of Sept 10, 1918, the Manila Treaty of Nov. 22, 1919, the Trianon Treaty of June 4, 1920, turned part of their jurisdiction over to the League of Nations, thus making it a guardian of the order created by these treaties. Any state, dominion or even self-governing colony could become a member of the League under the conditions that it give a warranty accepting LN commitments and that two-thirds of the League's Assembly voted in favor of admission. The conditions did not pertain to the original members of the League, i.e. the 32 victorious states which signed the Versailles Treaty, and the 13 neutral states invited to join the League which could "join the Covenant with no reservations". These countries were listed in an annex to the Covenant in the following order: United States, Belgium, Bolivia, Brazil, Great Britain, Canada, Australia, Union of South Africa, New Zealand, India, China, Cuba, Ecuador, France, Greece, Guatemala, Haiti, Al Hejaz (now Saudi Arabia), Honduras, Italy, Japan, Liberia, Nicaragua, Panama, Peru, Poland, Portugal, Romania, Kingdom of Serbs, Croats and Slovenes (now Yugoslavia), Siam (now Thailand), Czechoslovakia, Uruguay and countries "invited to join the Covenant": Argentina, Chile, Colombia, Denmark, El Salvador, the Netherlands, Norway, Paraguay, Persia (now Iran), Spain, Sweden, Switzerland and Venezuela. At the request of the US one of the countries, Mexico, was eliminated from the list of countries invited and because of this Mexico joined the League on Sept. 19, 1931, after it was unanimously invited by the Assembly to become a member. Three signatory states – USA, Ecuador and Al-Hejaz – did not ratify the Versailles Treaty and thus did not become "original members of the League of Nations". The number of League members varied: at the beginning of 1920 there were 42 states, later the number increased by 12 – including three states that were on the side of the League; in 1937 – 58 states (the greatest number); in 1940 – 43 states; in 1943 – 10 states. There were no legal or formal differences between the original members accepted on the strength of the Assembly's resolutions. The rights and obligations of all members were equal. Each state was allowed three delegates and only one vote in adopting resolutions, elections, etc. The LN Assembly and the Council were the supreme organs of the League; both had equal power and could pass resolutions only unanimously, which often presented problems. The first Assembly session was held in Hôtel National in Geneva from Nov. 15 to Dec. 18, 1920. The Assembly was composed of all League members, as were its commissions: I – legal; II – technological and intellectual organizations; III – reduction of armaments; IV – budgetary; V – social; VI – political, mandates and slavery. Within the scope of the Assembly were all matters of League activities or matters relating to world peace. All decisions required unanimity among those League members who voted except for decisions strictly specified by the Covenant (procedure, election to the Council) which could be passed by ordinary or qualified majority vote. The offices of the Secretariat were situated in a building named in 1924 the *Palais Wilson* after the death of the League's initiator. The LN Assembly met in its headquarters in Geneva once a year in September in regular sessions, special sessions could be convened if necessary. The Assembly's rights included the adoption of resolutions, making recommendations, electing non-permanent members of the Council and increasing their number, establishing the budget and the contributions of the Council's members. Only the Assembly had the right to accept new members and introduce changes in the Covenant as well as revise treaties which no longer applied. Actual work of the Assembly was carried out by committees elected after the opening of the session. In accordance with art. 4 of the League's Covenant, the Council consisted of permanent (Chief Allied and Associated Powers) and non-permanent (Belgium, Brazil, Greece, and Spain were the first) members. Thus the USA, France, Japan, Great Britain and Italy were to be the permanent members, but since the US had not ratified the Versailles Treaty, it did not join the Council. Contrary to what art. 5 stated, it was not the US president but the French prime minister who summoned the first session of the Council, which was held in Paris, Jan. 18, 1920, with the participation of 18 member states. Germany was co-opted as a permanent member of the Council Sept. 10, 1926 and left the League 1933 (Japan left the same year, Italy four years later). The Soviet Union acted as a permanent member of the Council 1934–39. Great Britain and France were the last permanent members and Belgium, Bolivia, China, the Dominican Republic, Egypt, Finland, Greece, Iran, Peru, the Union of South Africa and Yugoslavia were the last non-permanent members. The Council convened as often as circumstances required (in fact several times a year), at first in Paris, then in London, Rome, San Sebastian (Spain), Brussels, and more often in Geneva.

The number of non-permanent members of the League's Council gradually increased: 1922–6, 1926–9, 1933–10, 1936–11. The Council held the exclusive right to dismiss members of the League (this was used only in relation to the USSR, Dec. 14, 1939) and to distribute colonial mandates of the League. In 1921 the Council created the Commission of Enquiry of the League of Nations, which investigated international disputes and conflicts. The Convention to Improve the Means of Preventing War, Sept. 1931, was one of the results of the Commission's proceedings. The Council, like the Assembly, could consider any matter relating to the maintenance of peace. The division of power between the two bodies was not clearly outlined, a fact which was in the interest of the allied powers. Nevertheless the Covenant assigned to the Council the task of preparing a project for disarmament and the control of League mandates; on the strength of the peace treaties, the Council was also given the exclusive right to intervene in matters dealing with defense of national minorities, and to appoint committee members who were to govern the Saar region; the Council appointed the High Commissioner in Danzig and settled disputes between Danzig and Poland. In addition, the Council appointed the Secretary-General and was empowered to undertake mediatory efforts in order to maintain peace; it also established ▷ sanctions (e.g. dismissal of member) in the case of non-compliance with the League's resolutions. The Secretariat of the League was the only permanently active body; it consisted of the Secretary-General, two deputies, three under-secretaries and office staff, which numbered about 600 persons; it was divided into the following sections: political, legal, disarmament, minorities, economic, financial and others. In 1922 separate bureaus for Latin America were created to facilitate and improve relations between Latin America and the Secretariat. Senior officers of the Secretariat were granted diplomatic privileges and immunities. The duties of the Secretary-General were carried out by: 1920–32 Sir James Eric Drummond from Great Britain, 1933–40 Joseph Avenol from France, 1940–46 Sean Lester from Ireland. The Secretariat publ. *Journal Officiel* in English and French.

The Recommendations of Havana concerning International Organization adopted by the American Institute of International Law at Havana, January 23, 1917; New York, 1917; "Criticism of the draft plan for the League of Nations", in: *International Conciliation*, Special Bulletin, April, 1919, pp. 627–717; "The US and the LN Rejected Resolutions of ratification, November 19, 1919 and March 19, 1920", in: *International Conciliation*, No. 152, July, 1920; *League of Nations Official Journal 1920–1939; The League from Year to Year*, Geneva, 1926–39; M.O. HUDSON *American Co-operation with Other Nations through the League of Nations, 1919–1926*, Boston, 1926; W. KULSKI, *Le problème de la securité depuis le Pacte de la Société des Nations*, Paris, 1927; *La Société des Nations et la Coopération Intellectuelle*, Genève, 1927; C.H. ROUSSEAU, *La compétence de la SdN dans les règlements des conflits internationaux*, Paris, 1927; *La Société des Nations et la protection de minorités de race, de langue et de religion*, Genève, 1928; S. SWEELSER, 'The First Ten Years of the League of Nations', in: *International Conciliation*, No. 256, New York, January, 1930; "The Co-operation of the US with the League of Nations and with the ILO, 1919–1931" in: *International Conciliation*, No. 274, New York, November, 1931; C.K. WEBSTER, *The League of Nations in Theory and Practice*, London, 1933; G.T. ELES, *Le principe de l'unanimité dans la SdN et les exceptions à ce principe*, Paris, 1935; M. PREVOST, *Les Commissions de l'Assemblée de la Société des Nations*, Paris 1936; *Publications issued by the League of Nations 1920–1935*, Geneva, 1939; *First Supplement to General Catalogue 1920–1935*, Geneva, 1939; A.E. ZIMMERN, *The League of Nations and the Rule of Law 1918–1935*, 2 Vols., London–1939; M.J. YEPPES, *Commentaire théorique et pratique du Pacte de la SdN et des Status de l'Union Panaméricaine*, 3 Vols., Paris, 1934–39; *Monthly Summary of the League of Nations*, Geneva, 1921–40; *The Committees of the League of Nations Classified List and Essential Facts*, Geneva, 1944; *Compétences attribuées à Société des Nations par les traités internationaux*, Genève, 1944; R.E. DELL, *The Geneva Racket 1920–1939*, London, 1945; *Reports on the Work of League of Nations*, Geneva 1921–45; *Second Supplement to General Catalogue 1936–1945*, Geneva, 1946; E. GIRAUD, *La Nullité de la politique internationale des Grandes Democraties, 1919–1939*,

511

L'Echec de la Société des Nations. La Guerre, Paris, 1946; H. AUFRICHT, *Guide to League of Nations Publications. A Bibliographical Survey of the World of the League 1920–1947*, New York, 1951; F.P. WALTERS, *A History of the League of Nations*, London, 2 Vols., 1952, Vol. 1–2; B. DEXTER, *The Years of Opportunity; The League of Nations 1920–1926*, New York, 1967; W. BALCERZAK, *Dzieje Ligi Narodów*, Warsaw, 1969; G. SCOTT, *The Rise and Fall of the League of Nations*, London, 1974.

LEAGUE OF NATIONS ADMINISTRATIVE TRIBUNAL. A Tribunal with headquarters in Geneva est. in 1923, for the purpose of settling disputes involving the League of Nations and its personnel. It was dissolved in 1946.

LEAGUE OF NATIONS AND THE AMERICAN STATES. The concept of the League of Nations was originated in the US and supported by the majority of American states, but rejected by the US Senate Nov. 19, 1919 during the first voting for the ratification of the Covenant with 55 votes against and 39 for; and during the second voting (requiring a two-thirds majority) with 49 votes for and 35 against. Ecuador was another American state which did not ratify the Pact, the remaining majority of states having ratified it. From 1920 to 1928 the United States did not maintain relations with the League of Nations. The first official US support for the League of Nations' position was on Sept. 22, 1919, in a dispute with Japan, and in Sept. 1931 during the international crisis caused by the aggression of Japan in Manchuria. In 1932 the USA took part in the League's preliminary work for the Conference on Disarmament; The US Secretary of State H.L. Stimpson attended the League's Council meetings during the conference, discussed disarmament problems, as well as presented his government's view on the Far East crisis. Other American states were active League of Nations members but were limited in their rights by art. 2 of the Covenant which had been edited by the US President. When the inter-American arbitration system, based on the Monroe doctrine, failed, the League could offer services only in the disputes over the ▷ Gran Chaco and the ▷ Leticia Trapezium.

H. CABOT LODGE, *The US Senate and the League of Nations*, New York, 1925; W. H. KELCHNER, *Latin-american Relations with the League of Nations 1918–1920*, New York, 1932; M.P. GUERRERO, *Les Relations des États de l'Amérique Latine avec la SdN*, Paris, 1936; J.R. SIERRA, *La SdN. Su Valor y sus Ventajas para Iberoamerica*, México, DF, 1938; S.P. SUAREZ, *La SdN y el Tratado de Versalles. Una Institución Inutil y Peligrosa para Iberoamerica*, Barcelona, 1938; D. PERKINS, *Hands off! A History of the Monroe Doctrine*, Boston, 1941; Ch.G. FENWICK, *The Organization of American States. The Inter American Regional System*, Washington, DC, 1962.

LEAGUE OF NATIONS AND THE UNITED NATIONS. During World War II the United Nations in 1942 came to the conclusion that after the war the League of Nations could no longer function as the universal organization dealing with collective security. On Feb. 2, 1946, after the establishment of the new Universal Organization the UN General Assembly set up the Negotiating Committee of the UN for League of Nations Assets (members: Chile, China, France, Great Britain, Poland, the US, the Union of South Africa and the USSR) and requested the Secretary General to formally take over some of the functions, activities, obligations and property of the League of Nations. The Committee and the Secretary General had their representatives at the last, 21st session of the LN, Apr. 8–18, 1946. The Committee, in co-operation with the Board of League of Nations Liquidation carried out the tasks assigned to them, as stated in UN General Assembly Res. 54/I of Nov. 19, 1946 and Res. 79/I of Dec. 1, 1946. Many international agreements which came into being under the League remained valid. At present the UN Secretary General acts as their depository. The UN General Assembly has frequently confirmed the validity of these resolutions (e.g. Res. 1903/XVIII of 1963 and Res. 2021/XX of 1965). The UN Secretariat regularly publishes a collection of international agreements whose depository is the Secretary General. The list includes several dozen agreements signed at the initiative of the League of Nations.

The former League of Nations headquarters, the Geneva Palace of Nations, is now occupied by the UN European Office.

F.P. WALTERS, *History of the League of Nations*, London, 1952; *UN Status of Multilateral Conventions*, New York, 1965.

LEAGUE OF NATIONS COVENANT, 1919. PACTE DE LA SOCIÉTÉ DES NATIONS, 1919. Part I of the ▷ Versailles Peace Treaty, 1919. The text is as follows:

"Part I. *The Covenant of the League of Nations*
The High Contracting Parties,
In order to promote international co-operation and to achieve international peace and security
by the acceptance of obligations not to resort to war, by the prescription of open, just and honourable relations between nations,
by the firm establishment of the understanding of international law as the actual rule of conduct among Governments,
and by the maintenance of justice and a scrupulous respect for all treaty obligations in the dealings of organized peoples with one another,
Agree to this Covenant of the League of Nations.
Art. 1. The Original Members of the League of Nations shall be those of the Signatories which are named in the Annex to this Covenant and also such of those other states named in the Annex as shall accede without reservation to this Covenant. Such accession shall be effected by a Declaration deposited with the Secretariat within two months of the coming into force of the Covenant. Notice thereof shall be sent to all other members of the League.
Any fully self-governing state, Dominion, or Colony not named in the Annex may become a Member of the League if its admission is agreed to by two-thirds of the Assembly, provided that it shall give effective guarantees of its sincere intention to observe its international obligations, and shall accept such regulations as may be prescribed by the League in regard to its military, naval, and air forces and armaments.
Any Member of the League may, after two years' notice of its intention so to do, withdraw from the League, provided that all its international obligations and all its obligations under this Covenant shall have been fulfilled at the time of its withdrawal.
Art. 2. The action of the League under this Covenant shall be effected through the instrumentality of an Assembly and of a Council, with a permanent Secretariat,
Art. 3. The Assembly shall consist of Representatives of the Members of the League.
The Assembly shall meet at stated intervals and from time to time as occasion may require at the Seat of the League or at such other place as may be decided upon.
The Assembly may deal at its meetings with any matter within the sphere of action of the League or affecting the peace of the world.
At meetings of the Assembly each Member of the League shall have one vote, and may not have more than three Representatives.
Art. 4. The Council shall consist of Representatives of the Principal Allied and Associated Powers, together with Representatives of four other Members of the League. These four Members of the League shall be selected by the Assembly from time to time in its discretion. Until the appointment of the Representatives of the four Members of the League first selected by the Assembly, Representatives of Belgium, Brazil, Spain, and Greece shall be members of the Council.

With the approval of the majority of the Assembly, the Council may name additional Members of the League whose Representatives shall always be members of the Council; the Council with like approval may increase the number of Members of the League to be selected by the Assembly for representation on the Council.
The Council shall meet from time to time as occasion may require, and at least once a year, at the Seat of the League, or at such other place as may be decided upon. The Council may deal at its meetings with any matter within the sphere of action of the League or affecting the peace of the world.
Any Member of the League not represented on the Council shall be invited to send a Representative to sit as a member at any meeting of the Council during the consideration of matters specially affecting the interests of that Member of the League.
At meetings of the Council, each Member of the League represented on the Council shall have one vote, and may have not more than one Representative.
Art. 5. Except where otherwise expressly provided in this Covenant or by the terms of the present Treaty, decisions at any meeting of the Assembly or of the Council shall require the agreement of all the Members of the League represented at the meeting.
All matters of procedure at meetings of the Assembly or of the Council, including the appointment of Committees to investigate particular matters, shall be regulated by the Assembly or by the Council and may be decided by a majority of the Members of the League represented at the meeting.
The first meeting of the Assembly and the first meeting of the Council shall be summoned by the President of the United States of America.
Art. 6. The permanent Secretariat shall be established at the Seat of the League. The Secretariat shall comprise a Secretary General and such secretaries and staff as may be required.
The first Secretary General shall be the person named in the Annex; thereafter the Secretary General shall be appointed by the Council with the approval of the majority of the Assembly. The secretaries and staff of the Secretariat shall be appointed by the Secretary General with the approval of the Council.
The Secretary General shall act in that capacity at all meetings of the Assembly and of the Council.
The expenses of the Secretariat shall be borne by the Members of the League in accordance with the apportionment of the expenses of the International Bureau of the Universal Postal Union.
Art. 7. The Seat of the League is established at Geneva. The Council may at any time decide that the Seat of the League shall be established elsewhere.
All positions under or in connection with the League, including the Secretariat, shall be open equally to men and women. Representatives of the Members of the League and officials of the League when engaged on the business of the League shall enjoy diplomatic privileges and immunities.
The buildings and other property occupied by the League or its officials or by Representatives attending its meetings shall be inviolable.
Art. 8. The Members of the League recognise that the maintenance of peace requires the reduction of national armaments to the lowest point consistent with national safety and the enforcement by common action of international obligations.
The Council, taking account of the geographical situation and circumstances of each state, shall formulate plans for such reduction for the consideration and action of the several Governments.
Such plans shall be subject to reconsideration and revision at least every ten years.
After these plans shall have been adopted by the several Governments, the limits of armaments therein fixed shall not be exceeded without the concurrence of the Council.
The Members of the League agree that the manufacture by private enterprise of munitions and implements of war is open to grave objections. The Council shall advise how the evil effects attendant upon such manufacture can be prevented, due regard being had to the necessities of those Members of the League which are not able to manufacture the munitions and implements of war necessary for their safety.
The Members of the League undertake to interchange full and frank information as to the scale of their armaments, their military, naval, and air programmes and

Members and non-members of the League of Nations and other international instruments, 1919–39

State	Member of Postal Union	Member of Telecommunications Union	Sometime Party to the Covenant of LN	Sometime Party to ILO Constitution	Party to Court Statute	Party to 1928 Paris Treaty	Party to an Opium Treaty
1. Afghanistan	x	x	x	x	x	x	x
2. Albania	x	x	x	x	x	x	x
3. Argentina	x	x	x	x			x
4. Australia	x	x	x	x	x	x	x
5. Austria	x	x	x	x	x	x	x
6. Belgium	x	x	x	x	x	x	x
7. Bolivia	x	x	x	x	x		x
8. Brazil	x	x	x	x	x	x	x
9. Bulgaria	x	x	x	x	x	x	x
10. Canada	x	x	x	x	x	x	x
11. Chile	x	x	x	x	x	x	x
12. China	x	x	x	x	x	x	x
13. Colombia	x	x	x	x	x	x	x
14. Costa Rica	x	x	x	x		x	x
15. Cuba	x	x	x	x	x	x	x
16. Czechoslovakia	x	x	x	x	x	x	x
17. Danzig	x	x				x	x
18. Denmark	x	x	x	x	x	x	x
19. Dominican Rep	x	x	x	x	x	x	x
20. Ecuador	x	x	x	x		x	x
21. Egypt	x	x	x	x		x	x
22. Estonia	x	x	x	x	x	x	
23. Ethiopia	x	x	x	x	x	x	
24. Finland	x	x	x	x	x	x	x
25. France	x	x	x	x	x	x	x
26. Germany	x	x	x	x	x	x	x
27. Great Britain	x	x	x	x	x	x	x
28. Greece	x	x	x	x	x	x	x
29. Guatemala	x	x	x	x		x	x
30. Haiti	x	x	x	x	x	x	x
31. Honduras	x	x	x	x		x	x
32. Hungary	x	x	x	x	x	x	x
33. Iceland	x	x				x	
34. India	x	x	x	x	x	x	x
35. Iran	x	x	x	x	x	x	x
36. Iraq	x	x	x	x		x	x
37. Ireland	x	x	x	x	x	x	x
38. Italy	x	x	x	x	x	x	x
39. Japan	x	x	x	x	x	x	x
40. Latvia	x	x	x	x	x	x	x
41. Liberia	x	x	x	x		x	x
42. Liechtenstein	(x)				(x)		x
43. Lithuania	x	x	x	x	x	x	x
44. Luxembourg	x	x	x	x	x	x	x
45. Mexico	x	x	x	x		x	x
46. Monaco	(x)				(x)		
47. Nepal							
48. Netherlands	x	x	x	x	x	x	x
49. New Zealand	x	x	x	x	x	x	x
50. Nicaragua	x	x	x	x	x	x	x
51. Norway	x	x	x	x	x	x	x
52. Panama	x	x	x	x	x	x	x
53. Paraguay	x	x	x	x	x	x	x
54. Peru	x	x	x	x	x	x	x
55. Poland	x	x	x	x	x	x	x
56. Portugal	x	x	x	x	x	x	x
57. Romania	x	x	x	x	x	x	x
58. El Salvador	x	x	x	x	x		x
59. San Marino	x						x
60. Saudi Arabia	x					x	x
61. South Africa	x	x	x	x		x	x
62. Soviet Union	x	x	x	x		x	x
63. Spain	x	x	x	x	x	x	x
64. Sweden	x	x	x	x	x	x	x
65. Switzerland	x	x	x	x	x	x	x
66. Thailand	x	x	x	x	x	x	x
67. Turkey	x	x	x	x	x	x	x
68. United States of America	x	x		x		x	x
69. Uruguay	x	x	x	x	x		x
70. Vatican City	x	x					
71. Venezuela	x	x	x	x	x	x	x
72. Yemen	x	x					
73. Yugoslavia	x	x	x	x	x	x	x
Total	**72**	**68**	**63**	**64**	**53**	**63**	**68**

Source: *International Conciliation*, No. 399, Apr. 1944, pp. 377–379.

the condition of such of their industries as are adaptable to war-like purposes.

Art. 9. A permanent Commission shall be constituted to advise the Council on the execution of the provisions of article 1 and 8 and on military, naval, and air questions generally.

Art. 10. The Members of the League undertake to respect and preserve as against external aggression the territorial integrity and existing political independence of all Members of the League. In case of any such aggression or in case of any threat or danger of such aggression the Council shall advise upon the means by which this obligation shall be fulfilled.

Art. 11. Any war or threat of war, whether immediately affecting any of the Members of the League or not, is hereby declared a matter of concern to the whole League, and the League shall take any action that may be deemed wise and effectual to safeguard the peace of nations. In case any such emergency should arise the Secretary General shall on the request of any Member of the League forthwith summon a meeting of the Council.

It is also declared to be the friendly right of each Member of the League to bring to the attention of the Assembly or of the Council any circumstance whatever affecting international relations which threatens to disturb international peace or the good understanding between nations upon which peace depends.

Art. 12. The Members of the League agree that if there should arise between them any dispute likely to lead to a rupture, they will submit that matter either to arbitration or to inquiry by the Council, and they agree in no case to resort to war until three months after the award by the arbitrators or the report by the Council.

In any case under this article the award of the arbitrators shall be made within a reasonable time, and the report of the Council shall be made within six months after the submission of the dispute.

Art. 13. The Members of the League agree that whenever any dispute shall arise between them which they recognise to be suitable for submission to arbitration and which cannot be satisfactorily settled by diplomacy, they will submit the whole subject-matter to arbitration.

Disputes as to the interpretation of a treaty, as to any question of international law, as to the existence of any fact which if established would constitute a breach of any international obligation, or as to the extent and nature of the reparation to be made for any such breach, are declared to be among those which are generally suitable for submission to arbitration.

For the consideration of any such dispute the court of arbitration to which the case is referred shall be the Court agreed on by the parties to the dispute or stipulated in any convention existing between them.

The Members of the League agree that they will carry out in full good faith any award that may be rendered, and that they will not resort to war against a Member of the League which complies therewith. In the event of any failure to carry out such an award, the Council shall propose what steps should be taken to give effect thereto.

Art. 14. The Council shall formulate and submit to the Members of the League for adoption plans for the establishment of a Permanent Court of International Justice. The Court shall be competent to hear and determine any dispute of an international character which the parties thereto submit to it. The Court may also give an advisory opinion upon any dispute or question referred to it by the Council or by the Assembly.

Art. 15. If there should arise between Members of the League any dispute likely to lead to a rupture, which is not submitted to arbitration in accordance with article 13, the Members of the League agree that they will submit the matter to the Council.

Any party to the dispute may effect such submission by giving notice of the existence of the dispute to the Secretary General, who will make all necessary arrangements for a full investigation and consideration thereof.

For this purpose the parties to the dispute will communicate to the Secretary General, as promptly as possible, statements of their case with all the relevant facts and papers, and the Council may forthwith direct the publication thereof.

The Council shall endeavour to effect a settlement of the dispute, and if such efforts are successful, a statement shall be made public giving such facts and explanations regarding the dispute and the terms of settlement thereof as the Council may deem appropriate.

If the dispute is not thus settled, the Council either unanimously or by a majority vote shall make and publish a report containing a statement of the facts of the dispute and the recommendations which are deemed just and proper in regard thereto. Any Member of the League represented on the Council may make public a statement of the facts of the dispute and of its conclusions regarding the same.

If a report by the Council is unanimously agreed to by the members thereof other than the Representatives of one or more of the parties to the dispute, the Members of the League agree that they will not go to war with any party to the dispute which complies with the recommendations of the report.

If the Council fails to reach a report which is unanimously agreed to by the members thereof, other than the Representatives of one or more of the parties to the dispute, the Members of the League reserve to themselves the right to take such action as they shall consider necessary for the maintenance of right and justice.

If the dispute between the parties is claimed by one of them, and is found by the Council, to arise out of a matter which by international law is solely within the domestic jurisdiction of that party, the Council shall so report, and shall make no recommendation as to its settlement.

The Council may in any case under this article refer the dispute to the Assembly. The dispute shall be so referred at the request of either party to the dispute, provided that such request be made within fourteen days after the submission of the dispute to the Council.

In any case referred to the Assembly, all the provisions of this article and of article 12 relating to the action and powers of the Council shall apply to the action and powers of the Assembly, provided that a report made by the Assembly, if concurred in by the Representatives of those Members of the League represented on the Council and of a majority of the other Members of the League, exclusive in each case of the Representatives of the parties to the dispute, shall have the same force as a report by the Council concurred in by all the members thereof other than the Representatives of one or more of the parties to the dispute.

Art. 16. Should any Member of the League resort to war in disregard of its covenants under articles 12, 13, or 15, it shall ipso facto be deemed to have committed an act of war against all other Members of the League, which hereby undertake immediately to subject it to the severance of all trade or financial relations, the prohibition of all intercourse between their nations and the nationals of the covenant-breaking state, and the prevention of all financial, commercial, or personal intercourse between the nationals of the covenant-breaking state and the nationals of any other state, whether a Member of the League or not.

It shall be the duty of the Council in such case to recommend to the several Governments concerned what effective military naval, or air force the Members of the League shall severally contribute to the armed forces to be used to protect the covenants of the League.

The Members of the League agree, further, that they will mutually support one another in the financial and economic measures which are taken under this article, in order to minimise the loss and inconvenience resulting from the above measures, and that they will mutually support one another in resisting any special measures aimed at one of their number by the covenant-breaking state, and that they will take the necessary steps to afford passage through their territory to the forces of any of the Members of the League which are co-operating to protect the covenants of the League.

Any Member of the League which has violated any covenant of the League may be declared to be no longer a Member of the League by a vote of the Council concurred in by the Representatives of all the other Members of the League represented thereon.

Art. 17. In the event of a dispute between a Member of the League and a state which is not a Member of the League, or between states not Members of the League, the state or states, not Members of the League shall be invited to accept the obligations of membership in the League for the purposes of such dispute, upon such conditions as the Council may deem just. If such invitation is accepted, the provisions of articles 12 to 16 inclusive shall be applied with such modifications as may be deemed necessary by the Council.

Upon such invitation being given the Council shall immediately institute an inquiry into the circumstances of the dispute and recommend such action as may seem best and most effectual in the circumstances.

If a state so invited shall refuse to accept the obligations of membership in the League for the purposes of such dispute, and shall resort to war against a Member of the League, the provisions of article 16 shall be applicable as against the state taking such action.

If both parties to the dispute when so invited refuse to accept the obligations of membership in the League for the purpose of such dispute, the Council may take such measures and make such recommendations as will prevent hostilities and will result in the settlement of the dispute.

Art. 18. Every treaty or international engagement entered into hereafter by any Member of the League shall be forthwith registered with the Secretariat and shall as soon as possible be published by it. No such treaty or international engagement shall binding until so registered.

Art. 19. The Assembly may from time to time advise the reconsideration by Members of the League of treaties which have become inapplicable and the consideration of international conditions whose continuance might endanger the peace of the world.

Art. 20. The Members of the League severally agree that this Covenant is accepted as abrogating all obligations or understandings inter se which are inconsistent with the terms thereof, and solemnly undertake that they will not hereafter enter into any engagements inconsistent with the terms thereof. In case any Member of the League shall, before becoming a Member of the League, have undertaken any obligations inconsistent with the terms of this Covenant, it shall be the duty of such Member to take immediate steps to procure its release from such obligations.

Art. 21. Nothing in this Covenant shall be deemed to affect the validity of international engagements, such as treaties of arbitration or regional understandings like the Monroe doctrine, for securing the maintenance of peace.

Art. 22. To those colonies and territories which as a consequence of the late war have ceased to be under the sovereignty of the states which formerly governed them and which are inhabited by peoples not yet able to stand by themselves under strenuous conditions of the modern world, there should be applied the principle that the well-being and development of such peoples form a sacred trust of civilisation and that securities for the performance of this trust should be embodied in this Covenant.

The best method of giving practical effect to this principle is that the tutelage of such peoples should be entrusted to advanced nations who by reason of their resources, their experience or their geographical position can best undertake this responsibility, and who are willing to accept it, and that this tutelage should be exercised by them as Mandatories on behalf of the League.

The character of the mandate must differ according to the stage of the development of the people, the geographical situation of the territory, its economic conditions, and other similar circumstances.

Certain communities formerly belonging to the Turkish Empire have reached a stage of development where their existence as independent nations can be provisionally recognized subject to the rendering of administrative advice and assistance by a Mandatory until such time as they are able to stand alone. The wishes of these communities must be a principal consideration in the selection of the Mandatory.

Other peoples, especially those of Central Africa, are at such a stage that the Mandatory must be responsible for the administration of the territory under conditions which will guarantee freedom of conscience and religion, subject only to the maintenance of public order and morals, the prohibition of abuses such as the slave trade, the arms traffic, and the liquor traffic, and the prevention of the establishment of fortifications or military and naval bases and of military training of the natives for other than police purposes and the defence of territory, and will also secure equal opportunities for the trade and commerce of other Members of the League.

There are territories, such as South-West Africa and certain of the South Pacific Islands, which, owing to the sparseness of their population, or their small size, or their remoteness from the centres of civilisation, or their geographical contiguity to the territory of the Mandatory, and other circumstances, can be best administered under the laws of the Mandatory as integral portions of its territory, subject to the safeguards above mentioned in the interests of the indigenous population.
In every case of mandate, the Mandatory shall render to the Council an annual report in reference to the territory committed to its charge.
The degree of authority, control, or administration to be exercised by the Mandatory shall, if not previously agreed upon by the Members of the League, be explicitly defined,in each case by the Council.
A permanent Commission shall be constituted to receive and examine the annual reports of the Mandatories and to advise the Council on all matters relating to the observance of the mandates.
Art. 23. Subject to and in accordance with the provisions of international conventions existing or hereafter to be agreed upon, the Members of the League:
(a) will endeavour to secure and maintain fair and humane conditions of labour for men, women, and children, both in their own countries and in all countries to which their commercial and industrial relations extend, and for that purpose will establish and maintain the necessary international organisations;
(b) undertake to secure just treatment of the native inhabitants of territories under their control;
(c) will entrust the League with the general supervision over the execution of agreements with regard to the traffic in women and children, and the traffic in opium and other dangerous drugs;
(d) will entrust the League with the general supervision of the trade in arms and ammunition with the countries in which the control of this traffic is necessary in the common interest;
(e) will make provision to secure and maintain freedom of communications and of transit and equitable treatment for the commerce of all Members of the League. In this connection, the special necessities of the regions devastated during the war of 1914–1918 shall be borne in mind;
(f) will endeavour to take steps in matters of international concern for the prevention and control of disease.
Art. 24. There shall be placed under the direction of the League all international bureaux already established by general treaties if the parties to such treaties consent. All such international bureaux and all commissions for the regulation of matters of international interest hereafter constituted shall be placed under the direction of the League. In all matters of international interest which are regulated by general conventions but which are not placed under the control of international bureaux or commissions, the Secretariat of the League shall, subject to the consent of the Council and if desired by the parties, collect and distribute all relevant information and shall render any other assistance which may be necessary or desirable. The Council may include as part of the expenses of the Secretariat the expenses of any bureau of commission which is placed under the direction of the League.
Art. 25. The Members of the League agree to encourage and promote the establishment and co-operation of duly authorised voluntary national Red Cross organizations having as purposes the improvement of health, the prevention of disease, and the mitigation of suffering throughout the world.
Art. 26. Amendments to this Covenant will take effect when ratified by the Members of the League whose representatives compose the Council and by a majority of the Members of the League whose Representatives compose the Assembly.
No such amendment shall bind any Member of the League which signifies its dissent therefrom, but in that case it shall cease to be a Member of the League.
Annex. I. Original members of the League of Nations signatories of the Treaty of Peace: United States of America, Belgium, Bolivia, Brazil, British Empire, Canada, Australia, South Africa, New Zealand, India, China, Cuba, Ecuador, France, Greece, Guatemala, Haiti, Hedjaz, Honduras, Italy, Japan, Liberia, Nicaragua, Panama, Peru, Poland, Portugal, Romania, Serb-Croat-Slovene State, Siam, Czecho-Slovakia.
States invited to accede to the Covenant:
Argentine Republic, Chile, Colombia, Denmark, The Netherlands, Norway, Paraguay, Persia, Salvador, Spain, Sweden, Switzerland, Venezuela.
II. First Secretary General of the League of Nations. The Honourable Sir James Eric Drummond, KCMG, CB."

LNTS, Vol. 1, Geneva, 1920.

LEAGUE OF NATIONS GENEVA HEADQUARTERS. The signatories of the Covenant following the invitation of the Swiss government, 1919, unanimously decided that the LN headquarters should be situated at Geneva. Buildings and land occupied by the League as well as its offices, enjoyed special immunities, and the delegates to the LN and its officials enjoyed diplomatic privileges and immunities. For the LN headquarters a Geneva park district was chosen, called Parc de l'Ariana, and there the Palace of Nations, Palais des Nations, was erected. The design of the Palace was worked out between 1926 and 1929 by a team of architects of various nationalities. The foundation stone of the Palace was laid on Sept. 7, 1929 and by Feb., 1936 construction work was sufficiently advanced for the Secretariat to move from its temporary headquarters. The Council Chamber was completed in Oct., 1936 and the Assembly Hall one year later. Many nations contributed to the decorations, furniture and works of art representing artistic skills from five continents. Especially famous is the series of gold and sapia murals executed for the Council Chamber by the Spanish artist José Maria Sert. The Library, with over 600,000 volumes, is one of the richest collections of official documents and works relating to international affairs. Until the Palace was completed, the League staff was housed in a former lakeside hotel – Hôtel National. Following the death of one of the League's founding fathers, the US President Woodrow Wilson, the hotel was renamed *Palais Wilson*. The XXI Session LN Assembly, Apr. 19, 1946, which dissolved the Organization, transferred all its assets to the UN. The UN Secretary-General, on June 11, 1946, concluded with the Swiss Government the Ariana Agreement, which embodied the Swiss consent to the transfer of LN rights to the Ariana site to the UN. The Palace of Nations became the UN European headquarters.

UNTS, Vol. 1. 1946, pp. 153–154; *The Cultural Legacy of the Palais des Nations*, UN Geneva, 1985.

LEAGUE OF NATIONS J.C. SMUTS SUGGESTION, 1918. The South African statesman Lieut.-Gen. J.C. Smuts member of the War Cabinet of Great Britain (1917–18) was co-author of the League of Nations Covenant 1919, as well of the UN Charter 1945. The text of final 21 recommendations reads as follows:

"(1) That in the vast multiplicity of territorial, economic and other problems with which the conference will find itself confronted it should look upon the setting up of a league of nations as its primary and basic task, and as supplying the necessary organ by means of which most of those problems can find their only stable solution. Indeed, the conference should regard itself as the first or preliminary meeting of the league, intended to work out its organization, functions, and programme.
(2) That, so far at any rate as the peoples and territories formerly belonging to Russia, Austria-Hungary, and Turkey are concerned, the league of nations should be considered as the reversionary in the most general sense and as clothed with the right of ultimate disposal in accordance with certain fundamental principles. Reversion to the league of nations should be substituted for any policy of national annexation.
(3) That there shall be no annexation of any of these territories to any of the victorious Powers, and secondly, that in the future government of these territories and peoples the rule of self-determination, or the consent of the governed to their form of government, shall be fairly and reasonably applied.
(4) That any authority, control, or administration which may be necessary in respect of these territories and peoples, other than their own self-determined autonomy, shall be the exclusive function of and shall be vested in the league of nations and exercised by or on behalf of it.
(5) That it shall be lawful for the league of nations to delegate its authority, control, or administration in respect of any people or territory to some other state whom it may appoint as its agent or mandatary, but that wherever possible the agent or mandatory so appointed shall be nominated or approved by the autonomous people or territory.
(6) That the degree of authority, control, or administration exercised by the mandatory state shall in each case be laid down by the league in a special act or charter, which shall reserve to it complete power to ultimate control and supervision, as well as the right of appeal to it from the territory or people affected against any gross breach of the mandate by the mandatory state.
(7) That the mandatory state shall in each case be bound to maintain the policy of the open door, or equal economic opportunity for all, and shall form no military forces beyond the standard laid down by the league for purposes of internal police.
(8) That no new state arising from the old empires be recognized or admitted into the league unless on condition that its military forces and armaments shall conform to a standard laid down by the league in respect of it from time to time.
(9) That, as the successor to the empires, the league of nations will directly and without power of delegation watch over the relations inter se of the new independent states arising from the break-up of those empires, and will regard as a very special task the duty of conciliating and composing differences between them with a view to the maintenance of good order and general peace.
(10) The constitution of the league will be that of a permanent conference between the Governments of the constituent states for the purpose of joint international action in certain defined respects, and will not derogate from the independence of those states. It will consist of a general conference, a council and courts of arbitration and conciliation.
(11) The general conference, in which all constituent states will have equal voting power, will meet periodically to discuss matters submitted to it by the council. These matters will be general measures of international law or arrangements or general proposals for limitation of armaments for securing world peace, or any other general resolutions, the discussion of which by the conference is desired by the council before they are forwarded for the approval of the constituent Governments. Any resolutions passed by the conference will have the effect of recommendations to the national Governments and Parliaments.
(12) The council will be the executive committee of the league, and will consist of the Prime Ministers or Foreign Secretaries or other authoritative representatives of the Great Powers, together with the representatives drawn in rotation from two panels of the middle Powers and minor states respectively, in such a way that the Great Powers have a bare majority. A minority of three or more can veto any action or resolution of the council.
(13) The council will meet periodically, and will, in addition, hold an annual meeting of Prime Ministers or Foreign Secretaries for a general interchange of views, and for a review of the general policies of the league. It will appoint a permanent secretariat and staff, and will appoint joint committees for the study and coordination of the international questions with which the council deals, or questions likely to lead to international disputes. It will also take the necessary steps for keeping up proper liaison, not only with the Foreign Offices of the constituent Governments, but also with the authorities acting on behalf of the league in various parts of the world.
(14) Its functions will be:
(a) To take executive action or control in regard to the matters set forth in Section A or under any international arrangements or conventions;

(b) To administer and control any property of an international character, such as international waterways, rivers, straits, railways, fortifications, air stations, etc.;

(c) To formulate for the approval of the Governments general measures of international law, or arrangements for limitation of armaments or promotion of world peace.

[Its remaining functions in regard to world peace are dealt with in the following Section C.]

(15) That all the states represented at the peace conference shall agree to abolition of conscription or compulsory military service; and that their future defence forces shall consist of militia or volunteers, whose numbers and training shall, after expert inquiry, be fixed by the council of the league.

(16) That while the limitation of armaments in the general sense is impracticable, the council of the league shall determine what direct military equipment and armament is fair and reasonable in respect of the scale of forces laid down under paragraph 15, and that the limits fixed by the council shall not be exceeded without its permission.

(17) That all factories for the manufacture of direct weapons of war shall be nationalized and their production shall be subject to the inspection of the officers of the council; and that the council shall be furnished periodically with returns of imports and exports of munitions of war into or from the territories of its members and as far as possible into or from other countries.

(18) That the peace treaty shall provide that the members of the league bind themselves jointly and severally not to go to war with one another –

(a) without previously submitting the matter in dispute to arbitration, or to inquiry by the council of the league; and

(b) until there has been an award, or a report by the council; and

(c) not even then, as against a member which complies with the award, or with the recommendation (if any) made by the council in its report.

(19) That the peace treaty shall provide that if any member of the league breaks its covenant under paragraph 18, it shall ipso facto become at war with all the other members of the league which shall subject it to complete economic and financial boycott, including the Severance of all trade and financial relations and the prohibition of all intercourse between their subjects and the subjects of the covenant-breaking state and the prevention, as far as possible, of the subjects of the covenant-breaking state from having any commercial or financial intercourse with the subjects of any other state whether a member of the league or not.

While all members of the league are obliged to take the above measures, it is left to the council to recommend what effective naval or military force the members shall contribute and, if advisable, to absolve the smaller members of the league from making such contribution. The covenant-breaking state shall after the restoration of peace be subject to perpetual disarmament and to the peaceful regime established for new states under paragraph 8.

(20) That the peace treaty shall further provide that if a dispute should arise between any members of the league as to the interpretation of a treaty, or as to any question of international law, or as to any fact which if established would constitute a breach of any international obligation, or as to any damage alleged and the nature and measure of the reparation to be made thereof, and if such dispute cannot be settled by negotiation, the members bind themselves to submit the dispute to arbitration and to carry out any award or decision which may be rendered.

(21) That if on any ground it proves impracticable to refer such dispute to arbitration, either party to the dispute may apply to the council to take the matter of the dispute into consideration. The council shall give notice of the application to the other party, and make the necessary arrangements for the hearing of the dispute. The council shall ascertain the facts with regard to the dispute and make recommendations based on the merits, and calculated to secure a just and lasting settlement. Other members of the league shall place at the disposal of the council all information in their possession which bears on the dispute. The council shall do its utmost by mediation and conciliation to induce the disputants to agree to a peaceful settlement.

The recommendations shall be addressed to the disputants and shall not have the force of decisions. If either party threatens to go to war in spite of the recommendations, the council shall publish its recommendations. If the council fails to arrive at recommendations, both the majority and minority on the council may publish statements of the respective recommendations they favor, and such publication shall not be regarded as an unfriendly act by either of the disputants."

J.C. SMUTS, *The League of Nations: A Practical Suggestion*, London, 1918.

LEAGUE OF NATIONS SECRETARY-GENERAL. ▷ League of Nations.

LEAGUE OF NATIONS SOCIETY. English organization, f. 1916, London; promoted the project of a League of Nations; published 42 pamphlets on the subject in the years 1916–18.

Th. MARBURG, *League of Nations*, 2 Vols., London, New York 1917–18.

LEAGUE OF PEACE. The first American project of a League of Nations, presented Sept. 28, 1914 in the New York daily *The Independent*, by its editor Hamilton Holt. The highlights of the project:

"Let the League of Peace be formed on the following five principles:

First. The nations of the League shall mutually agree to respect the territory and sovereignty of each other.

Second. All questions that cannot be settled by diplomacy shall be arbitrated.

Third. The nations of the League shall provide a periodical Assembly to make all rules to become law unless vetoed by a nation within a stated period.

Fourth. The nations shall disarm to the point where the combined forces of the League shall be a certain per cent higher than those of the most heavily armed nation or alliance outside the League. Detailed rules for this pro rata disarmament shall be formulated by the Assembly.

Fifth. Any member of the League shall have the right to withdraw on due notice, or may be expelled by the unanimous vote of the others.

It would seem to the manifest destiny of the United States to lead in the establishment of such a league. The United States is the world in miniature. The United States is the greatest league of peace known to history. The United States is a demonstration to the world that all the races and peoples of the earth can live in peace under one form of government, and its chief value to civilization is a demonstration of what this form of government is.

When the Great War is over and the United States is called upon to lead the nations in reconstructing a new order of civilization, why might not Woodrow Wilson do on a world scale something similar to what George Washington did on a continental scale?

Stranger things than this have happened in history. Let us add to the Declaration of Independence a Declaration of Interdependence."

The project was later publicized by the American League to Enforce Peace, 1915, in New York, whose inaugural platform on Apr. 9, 1915 was as follows:

"League of Peace

It is desirable for the United States to join a League of great nations binding the signatories to the following:

First, all justiciable questions arising between the signatory powers not settled by negotiation, shall be submitted to a judicial tribunal for hearing and judgment both upon the merits and upon any issue as to its jurisdiction of the question.

Second, all non-justiciable questions arising between the signatories and not settled by negotiations, shall be submitted to a Council of Conciliation for hearing, consideration and recommendation.

Third, the signatory powers shall jointly use their military forces to prevent any one of their number from going to war or committing acts of hostility against another of the signatories before any question arising shall be submitted as provided in the foregoing.

Fourth, that conferences between signatory powers shall be held from time to time to formulate and codify rules of international law which, unless some signatory shall signify its dissent within a stated period, shall thereafter govern in the decisions of the Judicial Tribunal mentioned in article one."

J.H. LATANE (ed.), *Development of the League of Nations Idea: Documents and Correspondence of Theodore Marburg*, 2 Vols., New York, 1932.

LEAGUE OF WOMEN VOTERS. ▷ Suffragettes.

LEASE OF TERRITORY. The subject of international agreements under which one state agrees to place at the disposal of another state or group of states, for a specified period of time and on the terms of reimbursement a territory for the purpose of transportation, military or other purposes, retaining, however, sovereignty over the territory. In the 19th century such agreements were usually concluded under pressure from colonial states.

LEASING. An Anglo-Saxon term accepted in international trade. A system for the renting of machines and equipment by a company of one country to firms of a second for a precisely defined period of time, for payment and a banking or customs guarantee; subject of international agreements; the system is widely used in capitalist economies, and in the 1970s was introduced in the socialist economies. Historically, the term "leasing" first appeared in the USA when in 1877 the Bell Telephone Company introduced not only the sales, but also the leasing, of telephones.

T.M. CLARK, *Leasing*, London, 1978.

LEAST DEVELOPED COUNTRIES, LDC. An international term, introduced in the 1980's by the UNCTAD. An LDC list of the countries identified by the UN as being the world's poorest and most economically backward named forty countries in 1987:

Afghanistan, Bangladesh, Benin, Bhutan, Botswana, Burundi, Cape Verde, Central African Republic, Chad, Comoros, Democratic Yemen, Djibouti, Equatorial Guinea, Ethiopia, Gambia, Guinea, Guinea-Bissau, Haiti, Kiribati, Lao People's Democratic Republic, Lesotho, Malawi, Maldives, Mali, Mauritania, Nepal, Niger, Rwanda, Samoa, Sao Tome and Principe, Sierra Leone, Somalia, Sudan, Togo, Tuvalu, Uganda, United Republic of Tanzania, Upper Volta, Vanuatu, Yemen.

The UNCTAD review of the official development assistance (ODA) to the LDC's took place in Geneva, Sept. 30–Oct. 12, 1985, the next review is due in 1990.

See also ▷ Preferences.

UN *The Least Developed Countries. Introduction to the LDC's and to the Substantial New Programme of Action for Them*, New York, 1985; *UN Chronicle*, 1985, No. 10–11, pp. 92–94; KEESING's *Record of World Events*, March, 1987.

LEBANON. Member of UN. Al-Dhimhuria al-Lubnania. Lebanese Republic. Country of southwest Asia on the Mediterranean. Enclosed by Syria and Israel. Area: 10,400 sq. km. Pop. 1984 est. 3,400,000 (1965 census: 2,200,000; 1973 census – 2,260,000). *c*. 1,500,000 Lebanese are living abroad, including *c*. 600,000 in Brazil, 500,000 in USA, 200,000 in Argentina, 200,000 in other countries. Capital: Beirut with 702,000 inhabitants 1980. Official language: Arabic. Currency: one Lebanese Pound = 100 piastres. GNP per capita 1974: US $1070. National Day: Nov. 22, anniversary of declaration of independence 1943.

Original member of UN and all its specialized agencies excluding the GATT. Founding member of the Arab League.

International relations: from 1517 to 1918 under Ottoman control (in 1861 granted autonomy within the Turkish Empire); during World War I occupied by British and French armies; 1922–41 under French administration as League of Nations' mandate territory. After declaration of independence Nov. 26, 1941 by the leadership of Free France following the support given to General Charles de Gaulle by French troops stationed in Lebanon, the country was formally recognized as sovereign in 1943 and French troops were withdrawn in 1944–46 on the basis of a UN Security Council decision. In May 1955 Lebanon and Jordan accused Egypt of subversive action in which the intervention of the Arab League failed to help. On June 1, 1958 the UN Security Council appointed a UN Observer Group in Lebanon, UNOGIL which started operation in Beirut on June 16, 1958. The USA considered UNOGIL action insufficient and sent its Navy to Lebanon on July 15, 1958. The Lebanese crisis prompted an extraordinary session of the UN General Assembly which recommended that the USA pull out its troops from Lebanon; they were withdrawn on Oct. 25, 1958. The UNOGIL mission ended on Dec. 19, 1958. In June 1967 Lebanon sided with Arab countries against Israel, admitted Palestinian refugees and in the following years concluded several agreements with the Palestine Liberation Organization. In Dec., 1968 Israel bombed the civilian airport in Beirut in retaliation for Palestinian military actions and invaded Lebanese border regions on several occasions in 1969–80 about which Lebanon lodged complaints at the UN Security Council. Civil war 1976–80. An Israeli–Lebanon Agreement was signed on May 17, 1983, rejected by the majority of Arab States, dissolved in Mar., 1984.

The headquarters of the PLO was, since 1964, the capital of Lebanon, until 1982 when it was moved to Tunisia. The involvement of Lebanon in the Arab conflict with Israel complicated the internal and foreign situation of Lebanon in the 1970s and 1980s. The Arab Deterrent Force under the aegis of Arab League arrived in Lebanon in 1976 and later the UN Security Council set up a UN Interim Force in Lebanon, UNIFIL. The Arab Deterrent Force was dissolved in Dec., 1982–Apr., 1983, after the PLO removal to Tunisia. In Oct.–Nov., 1983 a National Reconciliation Conference started in Geneva. On Feb. 29, 1984 a French proposal to establish a UN Force in Beirut was vetoed by the USSR in the UN Security Council.

See also ▷ World Heritage UNESCO List.

J. DAGHAR, *Bibliographie en Liban*, Beyrouth, 1945; *UN Review*, June, 1958 and January, 1959; K.S. SALIER, *The History of Lebanon*, New York, 1965; M.S. AGWAN, *The Lebanese Crisis 1958. A Documentary Study*, New York, 1965; Ch. RIZK, *Le régime politique Libanais*, Paris, 1966; L. BINDER, *Politics in Lebanon*, New York 1966; P.K. HITTI, *Lebanon in History*, London, 1967; J. SALEM, *Le peuple Libanais*, Beyrouth, 1968; P. DEVOLVE, *L'administration Libanaise*, Paris, 1971; G.A. MURRAY, *Lebanon. The New Future*, London, 1974. S. KHAIRALLAH, *Lebanon. Bibliography*, Oxford, 1979. K.S. SALIBI, *Crossroad to Civil War. Lebanon 1958–1976*, New York, 1979; M. DEEB, *The Lebanese Civil War*, New York, 1980; J. TIMERMAN, *The Longest War: Israel in Lebanon*, New York, 1982; G. CORM, "La question libanaise", in: *Esprit*, No. 1, 1984, pp. 129–150; G. NACCACHE, *Un rêve libanais*, Paris, 1984; J. RANDAL, *La guerre de mille ans*, Paris, 1984; *The Europa Year Book 1984. A World Survey*, Vol. II, pp. 1911–1925, London, 1984; *UN Chronicle*, March, 1984, pp. 18–25.

LEBANON AGREEMENT, 1976. A treaty concluded by the government of Egypt, Saudi Arabia, and Syria to restore peace in Lebanon. It was prepared in Riyadh and approved in Cairo on Oct. 26, 1976, by all Arab states except Iraq and Libya.

LEBENSBORN. *German* = "source of life". Name of a Gestapo organization, established in Dec., 1935 by H. Himmler to encourage the propagation of large "racially pure" German families as well as to take care of illegitimate children who were of "pure Arian blood". During World War II, the Lebensborn organization became one of the most maleficent instruments of the German III Reich's policy. It was applied to segregate children of Non-German parents imprisoned in camps. Racially unacceptable children were directed to extermination camps, whereas children fit for Germanization were taken to special Lebensborn centers. In 1972 a TV film was produced by the FRG entitled: "A secret Affair of the Third Reich: Children Camps".

R. HRABAR, *Lebensborn*, Katowice, 1972; M. HILLEL, M. HENRY, *Au nom de la race*, Paris, 1975.

LEBENSRAUM. *German* = "living space". The term of imperialist Germany, formulated for the first time in 1897 by Friedrich Ratzel, then by Karl Haushofer, since 1924 publisher of *Zeitschrift für Geopolitik*; it became the main concept of genocidal, anti-Slav plans of the German III Reich designed to increase the "living space of the German nation".

F. RATZEL, *Politische Geographie*, Berlin, 1897; K HAUSHOFER, *Geopolitik*, München, 1924.

LEBOWA. ▷ Bantu Homelands.

LEDO ROAD. ▷ Burma Road.

LEEWARD ISLANDS. A group of islands to the north of the Windward group, and south-east of Puerto Rico in the Caribbean Sea; a part of the Lesser Antilles archipelago; subject of French–British wars in the 17th and 18th centuries. Together with the Windward Islands they comprise the West Indies. The Leeward Islands group consist of Antigua (with Barbuda and Redonda) and St. Christopher-Nevis, Anguilla and the British Virgin Islands.

LEGALIZATION OF DOCUMENTS. An international term defined by the European Convention on the abolition of legalization of documents executed by diplomatic agents and consular officers, June 7, 1968, as follows:

"… legalization means only the formality used to certify the authenticity of the signature on a document, the capacity in which the person signing such document has acted and, where appropriate, the identity of the seal or stamp which such document bears."

The Convention was preceded by the European Convention on the repeal of the obligation to legalize alien states' documents; signed on Oct. 5, 1961 in The Hague. The Convention did not refer to documents issued by embassies and consulates.

UNTS, Vol. 788, p. 172 and Vol. 527, p. 191.

"LEGION CONDOR". German air-force intervention troops operating on the side of General Franco in Spain during the 1936–39 civil war, in part as instructors, mainly as pilots in transport and bomber squadrons. They caused grave devastation of Bilbao, Madrid and ▷ Guernica. The Condor Legion was comprised of 5500 men; casualties – 420.

K.H. VÖLKER, *Die deutsche Luftwaffe 1933–1939*, Hamburg, 1968.

LEIPZIGER PROZESS OR REICHSTAGS-BRANDPROZESS, 1933. Names of trial stages of the Reich's Tribunal in Leipzig, from Sept. 20 to Dec. 23, 1933 against the three Bulgarian communists G. Dimitrov, B. Popov, V. Tanev, German communist E. Torgler and the young Dutch communist M. van der Lubbe, accused of setting fire to Berlin's Reichstag. The intention of the German III Reich government was to prove the complicity of the international communist movement in the fire and thus to justify the ▷ NSDAP terrorist actions against their political opponents. The trial failed to prove the guilt of either the Bulgarian Communist or E. Torgler; M. van der Lubbe in a state of stupor confessed to having personally started the fire in protest against Hitler's take-over and was sentenced to death. The chief defendant at the trial was G. Dimitrov who took advantage of the hearing to protest against dictatorship in Germany. The accused Bulgarians were deported from Germany and E. Torgler sent to a concentration camp (he was released in 1936 after publicly renouncing communism); M. van der Lubbe was executed. In the course of the trial a Brown Book appeared in London which accused H. Goering, Reichstag chairman and Prime Minister of Prussia, of planning the fire.

F. TOBIAS, *Der Reichstagbrand, Legende und Wirklichkeit*, Rastadt, 1962; A. BULLOCK, *Hitler*, London, 1962.

LEIPZIG PROCESSES, 1920–22. The trials in Leipzig before the Reich's Court of German war criminals during World War I, in accordance with arts. 227–230 of the Treaty of Versailles.

G.G. BATTLE, "The Trial Before the Leipzig Supreme Court of Germans Accused of War Crimes", in: *Virginia Law Review*, No. 8, 1926.

LEND-LEASE ACT. The act, passed by the US Congress on Mar. 11, 1941 (60 : 31 in the Senate, 317 : 71 in the House of Representatives), authorizing the US President "to lend, lease or grant any military equipment to any country … whose defense the President will recognize as vital interest to the defense of the US". At first assistance was given only to the UK (the first convoy sailed on Apr. 16, 1941) and to China. From Feb. 24, 1942, the remaining UN countries were covered by the Act. On Oct. 30, 1941 the US government granted the USSR credit in the amount of $1 billion and on Apr. 11, 1942 both governments signed the Master Lend-Lease Agreement; the USA undertook to supply the USSR with military equipment and services; the USSR undertook not to pass them on to a third party without consent, and to return unused materials as soon as the state of emergency was over. Supplies were shipped to Archangel, Vladivostok and through the Persian Gulf and Iran. The Lend-Lease Act expired on Mar. 21, 1945. The value of all loans, leases and grants amounted to $50.6 billion, of which $31 billion was given to the UK, $11 billion to the USSR and the remaining $8.6 billion were divided between the remaining 32 countries of the UN. The Lend-Lease Act's special conditions for the USSR were the subject of American–Soviet negotiations in 1953–54, and in Jan.–Feb., 1960. The USA demanded repayment, but without reaching an agreement. Talks were renewed in Washington in early 1972 and an agreement was concluded on Oct. 18, 1972. Of the $921 million owed for civil supplies, USSR had repaid $199 million and undertook to pay the remaining $722 million in instalments of $24 million, within the period 1972–2001. The rest of the debt for military supplies had been cancelled earlier.

Q. WRIGHT, "The Lend-Lease Bill and the International Law", in: *American Journal of International Law, No. 55, 1941*; E.R. STETTINIUS, *Lend-Lease Weapon for Victory*, Washington, DC, 1949; US STATE DEPARTMENT, *Foreign Aid of the US*

Government 1940–1951, Washington, DC, 1955; N. JAKOVLEV, Historia Contemporanea de Estados Unidos, Buenos Aires, 1965, Vol. 2, pp. 33–40.

LENIN INTERNATIONAL AWARD. The highest international award of the USSR prior to 1956 called the Stalin International Award, granted "for establishment of peace among nations" (Za ukriepleniye mira mezhdu narodamy), annually to social and political activists, scientists and artists. Prize-winners of the Stalin Award granted from 1950 to 1955 were included in 1956 among Lenin Award winners. A Committee of the Lenin International Award with the seat in Moscow was appointed by the Decree of the Presidium of the USSR Supreme Council on Sept. 6, 1956.

LEONTIEF REPORT. A UN study of the future of the world's economy, prepared by an expert group (Anne P. Carter, Richard Drost, Peter Petri, Ira Cohn, Joseph J. Stern) under the direction of Vassily Leontief, published 1977. The findings of this study were summarized by the authors as follows:

"(a) Target rates of growth of gross product in the developing regions, set by the International Development Strategy for the Second United Nations Development Decade, are not sufficient to start closing the income gap between the developing and the developed countries. Higher growth rates in developing countries in the 1980s and 1990s, coupled with slightly lower rates in the developed countries (as compared to their long-term trends), would reduce, at least by half, the average income gap by 2000;
(b) The principal limits to sustained economic growth and accelerated development are political, social and institutional in character rather than physical. No insurmountable physical barriers exist within the twentieth century to the accelerated development of the developing regions;
(c) The most pressing problem of feeding the rapidly increasing population of the developing regions can be solved by bringing under cultivation large areas of currently unexploited arable land and by doubling and trebling land productivity. Both tasks are technically feasible but are contingent on drastic measures of public policy favourable to such development and on social and institutional changes in the developing countries;
(d) The problem of the supply of mineral resources for accelerated development is not a problem of absolute scarcity in the present century but, at worst, a problem of exploiting less productive and more costly deposits of minerals and of intensive exploration of new deposits, especially in the regions which are not currently known to be richly endowed with vast mineral resources, so as to reduce the unevenness in the distribution of such reserves between the various regions of the world;
(e) With current commercially available abatement technology, pollution is not an unmanageable problem. It is technically possible to keep net emissions of pollution in the developed regions at their current levels. Full application of relatively strict abatement standards would be less of a general problem in most of the developing regions in this century and would be largely limited to abatement activities in certain industrial areas and to urban solid-waste disposal. However, even if relatively strict abatement standards were gradually applied in the developing regions, the over-all economic cost of pollution abatement is not estimated to exceed 1.5–2 per cent of gross product – that is, it does not present an insurmountable barrier for economic development of these regions;
(f) Accelerated development in developing regions is possible only under the condition that from 30 to 35 per cent, and in some cases up to 40 per cent, of their gross product is used for capital investment. A steady increase in the investment ratio to these levels may necessitate drastic measures of economic policy in the field of taxation and credit, increasing the role of public investment and the public sector in production and the infrastructure. Measures leading to a more equitable income distribution are needed to increase the effectiveness of such policies. Significant social and institutional

changes would have to accompany these policies. Investment resources coming from abroad would be important but are secondary as compared to the internal sources;
(g) Accelerated development points to the necessity of a faster growth, on the average, of heavy industry, as compared to the overall rates of expansion for the manufacturing industry. This is certainly true on the broad regional if not on a small country basis, increasing the possibilities of industrial co-operation between the developing countries. In many regions, however, light industry would remain a leading manufacturing sector for a long time, providing, among other things, a basis for a significant increase in the exports of manufactured products from the developing countries;
(h) Accelerated development would lead to a continuous significant increase in the share of the developing regions in world gross product and industrial production, as compared to the relative stagnation of these shares in recent decades. Because of the high income elasticity of the demand for imports this would certainly entail a significant increase in the share of these regions in world imports to support internal development. However, the increase in their share of world exports is expected to be slower, owing to severe supply constraints in the developing regions and the relatively slower pace at which the competitive strength of their manufacturing industries would be built up. For those reasons accelerated development poses the danger of large potential trade and payments deficits in most of the developing regions;
(i) There are two ways out of the balance-of-payments dilemma. One is to reduce the rates of development in accordance with the balance of payments constraint. Another way is to close the potential payments gap by introducing changes into the economic relations between developing and developed countries, as perceived by the Declaration on the Establishment of the New International Economic Order – namely, by stabilizing commodity markets, stimulating exports of manufactures from the developing countries, increasing financial transfers and so on;
(j) A relatively stable increase in the prices of minerals and agricultural goods exported by the developing countries, as compared to prices of manufactured goods, is one way of increasing the export earnings of these countries and closing their potential payments deficit. Higher mineral and agricultural prices are also called for, owing to technological requirements and the relative scarcity of natural resources, which makes them relatively more costly as time goes by. However, because of the uneven way in which mineral resources are currently distributed between various developing regions, these price changes would be of advantage to some regions, while placing an additional economic and financial burden on the others. Special schemes, providing for financial compensation to the net importing developing regions would be a possible way to reduce these imbalances;
(k) For developing regions which are not large net exporters of minerals or agricultural goods, the main way to reduce the potential trade imbalance is to significantly decrease their import dependence on manufactured products in the course of industrialization, while at the same time increasing their share of world exports of some manufactured products, particularly those emanating from light industry. Building up the competitive strength of such products in the world market is an important prerequisite, combined with the reduction of tariffs and other barriers imposed on the exports of the developing regions to the developed regions. An increase in the flow of aid to the developing regions; measures to create a more favourable climate for and a better mix of capital investment flows to these regions; a reduction in the financial burden arising from foreign investment in these regions are important but are secondary measures as compared to the necessary changes in the commodity markets and trade in manufactured products;
(l) To ensure accelerated development two general conditions are necessary: first, far-reaching internal changes of a social, political and institutional character in the developing countries, and second, significant changes in the world economic order. Accelerated development leading to a substantial reduction of the income gap between the developing and the developed countries can only be achieved through a combination of both these conditions. Clearly, each of them taken

separately is insufficient, but when developed hand in hand, they will be able to produce the desired outcome."

The Future of the World Economy. A UN Study by Vassily Leontief et al., New York, 1977.

LEPROSY. The subject of international research and anti-leprosy co-operation. Organizations reg. with the UIA:

Association of French Language Leprologists, f. 1973, Strasbourg.
East African Leprosy Centre, f. 1967, Alupe-Busia, Kenya.
International Federation of Anti-Leprosy Association ILEP, f. 1966, Paris. Publ.: ILEP Flash.
International Leprosy Association, f. 1931, Manila. Official Relations with FAO. Publ.: International Journal of Leprosy and other Mycobacterial Diseases (quarterly in English, French and Spanish).

WHO. A Guide to Leprosy Control, Geneva, 1980: Yearbook of International Organizations; J. MAURICE, Leprosy: Light at the End of the Tunnel, in: World Health Organization, July, 1988.

LERV. ▷ Neutron Bomb.

LESOTHO. Member of the UN. Kingdom of Lesotho. South African enclave within the Republic of South Africa. Area: 30,355 sq. km. Pop. 1988 est.: 1,570,000 (1976 census = 1,216,815). Capital: Maseru with 292,200 inhabitants, 1981. GNP per capita 1987: US $360. Official language: English and Sotho. Currency: Loti. National Day: Oct. 4, Independence Day, 1966.
Member of the UN since Oct. 14, 1966 and of the UN specialized agencies: FAO, UNESCO, WHO, ILO, ICAO, GATT, WMO, WIPO, IFAD, IBRD, IMF, IFC, IDA, UPU and ITU. Member of the OAU. ACP state of the EEC.
International relations: British colony from 1868 to 1965 named Basutoland; became an independent and sovereign member of the Commonwealth on Oct. 4, 1966 as the Kingdom of Lesotho. In customs union with the Republic of South Africa. On Dec. 9, 1982 South Africa launched a surprise attack on Maseru, the capital of Lesotho. The UN Security Council on Dec. 15, 1982 unanimously condemned South Africa and demanded "full and adequate payment for the damage to life and property resulting from this aggressive act". In 1983 Lesotho severed diplomatic relations with Taiwan and S. Korea, while establishing relations with the People's Republic of China, N. Korea and the USSR. In 1984 Lesotho started talks with South Africa. On April 30, 1987 Lesotho and South Africa signed an agreement for the mutual establishment of trade missions in Johannesburg and Maseru.

J. HALPERN, South Africa's Hostages: Basutoland, Bechuanaland and Swaziland, Baltimore, 1965; Implementation of the Declaration on the Granting of Independence to Colonial Countries and Peoples: Basutoland, Bechuanaland, Swaziland, HMSO, London, 1965; R.P. STEVENS, Lesotho, Botswana and Swaziland, The Former High Commission Territories in Southern Africa, New York, 1967; B.M. KHAKETLA, Lesotho 1970, London, 1971; A. AMBROSE, The Guide to Lesotho, Johannesburg, 1976; D. JONES, Aid on Development in Southern Africa, London, 1977; C. STEVENS, Food, Aid and the Developing World, London, 1979; UN Chronicle, February and September, 1983; The Europa Year Book 1984. A World Survey, Vol. II, pp. 1926–1934 London, 1984.

LETICIA TRAPEZIUM. A region on the border between Peru and Colombia which Peru ceded to Colombia as the latter's only access to the Amazon under terms of the Salomon–Lozano Treaty signed in Lima on Mar. 24, 1922 and ratified by Colombia in Oct., 1925 and by Peru in Dec., 1927. The delimitation was completed in Mar., 1930. The territory was the cause of a conflict between Colombia and Peru. On Sept. 1, 1932, Peruvian troops under Colonel L.M. Sanchez Cerro seized Leticia. Conciliatory efforts by Brazil failed and the matter was sent by Colombia to the League of Nations Council. A commission to govern the territory on behalf of the LN was appointed (Administrative Committee for Leticia Trapezium) which operated from June, 1933 until June, 1934. The death of Peruvian President Colonel L.M. Sanchez Carro on Apr. 30, 1934 ended the conflict. His successor General O. Benavide restored the Treaty of 1922, and a new Colombian–Peruvian agreement was signed on May 21, 1934 in Rio de Janeiro; ratified in Sept., 1935. The capital of the region is Leticia, with *c.* 5000 inhabitants, 1975.

J.M. YEPPES, *L'Affaire de Leticia devant le Droit International*, Paris, 1932; *Monthly Summary, League of Nations Official Journal*, 1933, pp. 533, 944 and 1107; 1934, p. 933; "L'Affaire de Leticia Documents", in: *Revue de droit international*, No. 11, 1933; M.O. HUDSON, *The Verdict of the League: Colombia and Peru at Leticia, The Official Documents*, Boston, 1933; G. IRELAND, *Boundaries, Possessions and Conflict in South America*, Cambridge, 1938, pp. 188–198; J.C. CAREY, *Peru and the US 1900–1962*, Notre Dame, 1963, pp. 94–98.

LETTER OF CREDENCE. Lettre de créance. The international term in English and French for a formal document presented to the head of state by the new ambassador of a foreign country.
See also ▷ Accreditation to the UN ▷ Accreditation.
R.L. BLEDSOE, B.A. BOCZEK, *The International Law Dictionary*, Oxford, UK, 1987.

LETTER OF CREDIT. An international banking term for a document authorizing use of credit or transferable letter of credit, called Documentary Credit.

INTERNATIONAL CHAMBER OF COMMERCE, *Uniform Customs and Practice for Documentary Credits*, Paris, 1975. BARCLAYS BANK INTERNATIONAL, *Documentary Letters of Credit*, London, 1976.

LETTER OF INTENT. An international term used in the UN system. Official information on readiness to conclude a specified agreement (i.e. IMF standby agreement).

LETTERS ROGATORY, INTER-AMERICAN CONVENTION ON, 1975. The Inter-American Convention on the Taking of Evidence Abroad was signed on Jan. 30, 1975 in Panama at the Inter-American Specialized Conference on Private International Law by the following OAS members: Brazil, Colombia, Costa Rica, Chile, Ecuador, El Salvador, Guatemala, Honduras, Nicaragua, Panama, Peru, Uruguay and Venezuela. The essential articles read as follows:

"Art. 2. Letters rogatory issued in conjunction with proceedings in civil or commercial matters for the purpose of taking evidence or obtaining information abroad and addressed by a judicial authority of one of the States Parties to this Convention to the competent authority of another, shall be executed in accordance with the terms specified therein, provided:
(1) The procedure requested is not contrary to legal provisions in the State of destination that expressly prohibit it;
(2) The interested party places at the disposal of the authority of the State of destination the financial and other means necessary to secure compliance with the request.
Art. 3. The authority of the State of destination shall have jurisdiction over disputes arising in connection with the execution of the measure requested.
Should the authority of the State of destination find that it lacks jurisdiction to execute the letter rogatory

but consider that another authority of the same State has jurisdiction, it shall ex officio forward to it, through the appropriate channels, the documents and antecedents of the case. In the execution of letters rogatory, the authority of the State of destination may apply the measures of compulsion provided for in its law.
Art. 4. Letters rogatory requesting the taking of evidence or the obtaining of information abroad shall specify the following information needed for fulfilling the request:
(1) A clear and precise statement of the purpose of the evidence requested;
(2) Copies of the documents and decisions that serve as the basis and justification of the letter rogatory, as well as such interrogatories and documents as may be needed for its execution;
(3) Names and addresses of the parties to the proceedings, as well as of witnesses, expert witnesses, and other persons involved and all information needed for the taking of the evidence;
(4) A summary report on the proceeding and the facts giving rise to it, if needed for the taking of the evidence;
(5) A clear and precise statement of such special requirements or procedures as may be requested by the authority of the State of origin for the taking of the evidence, except as provided in Article 2.1 and Article 6.
Art. 5. Letters rogatory concerning the taking of evidence shall be executed in accordance with the laws and procedural rules of the State of destination.
Art. 6. At the request of the authority issuing the letter rogatory, the authority of the State of destination may accept the observance of additional formalities or special procedures in performing the act requested, unless the observance of those procedures or of those formalities is contrary to the laws of the State of destination or impossible of performance.
Art. 7. The costs and other expenses involved in the processing and execution of letters rogatory shall be borne by the interested parties.
The State of destination may, in its discretion, execute a letter rogatory that does not indicate the person to be held responsible for costs and other expenses when incurred.
The identity of the person empowered to represent the applicant for legal purposes may be indicated in the letter rogatory or in the documents relating to its execution.
The effects of a declaration in forma pauperis shall be regulated by the law of the State of destination.
Art. 8. Execution of letters rogatory shall not imply ultimate recognition of the jurisdiction of the authority issuing the letter rogatory or a commitment to recognize the validity of the judgment it may render or to execute it.
Art. 9. Pursuant to Article 2.1, the authority of the State of destination may refuse execution of a letter rogatory whose purpose is the taking of evidence prior to judicial proceedings or 'pretrial discovery of documents' as the procedure is known in Common Law countries."

Inter-American Convention on Letter Rogatory, OAS Treaty Series No 43, Washington, DC, 1975; R.L. BLEDSOE, B.A. BOCZEK, *The International Law Dictionary*, Oxford, 1987.

LETTRE D'INTRODUCTION. ▷ Accreditation.

LEU. A monetary unit of Romania; one leu = 100 bani; issued by the Banca Nationala a Republicii Socialiste Romania.

LEV. A monetary unit of Bulgaria; one lev = 100 stotinki; issued by the Banque Nationale de Bulgarie.

LEX ABROGATA. *Latin* = "a law repealed". An international term for the law that has already expired.

LEX DILATIONES EXHORRET. An international legal doctrine to the effect that "the law tolerates no delay".

LEXICOGRAPHY. A subject of international co-operation. The standardization of terminologies and norms in various branches of science and tech-

nology is of great importance for 50 to 60 thousand scientific journals all over the world as well as the transposition of scientific terminology into Arabic, Chinese, Greek, Hebrew, Latin, Russian and other alphabets.

Organizations reg. with the UIA:
Committee for Unification of Terminological Neologisms, f. 1981, Warsaw. Publ. *Neoterm*.
International Association of Terminology (TERMIA), f. 1979, Luxembourg.
International Center for the Terminology of the Social Science (INTERCENTRE), f. 1966, Vienna. Publ. *Systematic Glossary*.
International Information Centre for Terminology (INFOTERM), f. 1971 under UNESCO sponsorship, Vienna.

J. GOETSCHALCKX, L. ROLLING (eds.), *Lexicography in the Electronic Age*, Amsterdam, 1982; Z. STOBERSKI, "The Worldwide Process of Internationalization of Scientific Terminology", in: *Neoterm*, No. 1, 1984; *Yearbook of International Organizations*.

LEX NON SCRIPTA. *Latin* = "an unwritten law". An international term for customary law.

LEX PATRIAE. *Latin* = "the native law". An international term for the criterion of nationality in international private law indicating that person-to-person relations should be ruled by the law of the state of which the persons are nationals; contrary to Lex Domicilii under which the law of the persons' state of residence is decisive (▷ Domicile).

LEX POSTERIOR DEROGAT PRIORI. A Latin international legal doctrine that "a later law supplants an earlier one".

R.L. BLEDSOE, B.A. BOCZEK, *The International Law Dictionary*, Oxford, 1987.

LEX RETRO NON AGIT. An international legal term, stating that "the law may not be retroactive".

LEX SPECIALIS DEROGAT LEGI GENERALI. *Latin* = "a specific law supersedes a general law". An international term for a principle for resolving conflicts in legislation in favor of a specific law.

LEX TALIONIS. ▷ *jus talionis*.

LHASSA. Capital of Tibet. Population 1982, est. 105,000. Until 1959 seat of the ▷ Dalai Lama and center of Tibetan Buddhism, known as the Forbidden City inaccessible to foreigners. Integrated 1950 to the People's Republic of China, since 1965 became the capital of the Xizang (Tibet) Autonomous Region. In Spring 1988 religious riots in Lhassa were crushed by Chinese Communist forces.

KEESING's *Record of World Events*, 1988.

LIABILITY NUCLEAR SHIPS CONVENTIONS, 1962. ▷ Maritime Law Conventions, 1882–1978.

LIAONING. ▷ Manchuria.

LIBERAL INTERNATIONAL – WORLD LIBERAL UNION. An organization reg. with the UIA, f. 1947, London. Promotes the spread of liberal ideals throughout the nations of the world. Consultative status with UNESCO. Publ.: *Spires of Liberty*.

Yearbook of International Organizations; N.P. BARRY, *On Classical Liberalism and Liberalianism*, London, 1987.

L

LIBERATION DOCTRINE, 1952. A program of US foreign policy announced after the outbreak of the Korean War by the democratic and republican conventions, 1952, in their election platforms as an expression of the anti-communist solidarity of both parties; supported by the FRG government, whose undersecretary of state, W. Hallstein, in a lecture at Georgetown University in Washington on Mar. 13, 1952 declared that in Europe this doctrine should result in the "liberation on nations enslaved by communism up to the Urals".

J. BURNHAM, *Containment or Liberation*, New York, 1951.

LIBERATION MOVEMENTS. In the UN system the national liberation movements recognized by the OAU or the League of Arab States have the right to representation in international conferences and organizations, as well as to the facilities, privileges and immunities necessary to function according to the provisions of the 1975 Vienna Convention on the Representation of States in their Relations with International Organizations of a Universal Character. The Res. 37/104 was adopted by a recorded vote of 110 to 10, with 17 abstentions.

UN Chronicle, February, 1983, pp. 117 and 120.

LIBERATION THEOLOGY. ▷ Theology of Liberation.

LIBERATION WAR. An anti-colonial war, justified by international law.

N. RONZITTI, *La guerra di liberazione e il diritto internazionale*, Pisa, 1974.

LIBERIA. Member of the UN. Republic of Liberia. State in West Africa, bordered by Sierra Leone, Guinea, the Côte d'Ivoire and the Atlantic Ocean. Area: 111,370 sq. km. Population (census 1984): 2,200,000 (1974 census: 1,503,368; 1978: 1,715,973). Capital: Monrovia with 306,460 inhabitants 1981. GNP per capita 1987: US $440. Currency: the US dollar which since Nov. 3, 1942 is in circulation and a Liberian coinage of dollar in silver and copper called the Liberian dollar = 100 cents. National Day: Aug. 22, Independence Day, 1847.
Member of the UN since Oct. 24, 1945 and of all specialized agencies with exception of the GATT, UNIDO and WIPO. Member of the OAU, ECOWAS and is an ACP state of the EEC.
International relations: founded 1821 by the American Colonization Society as a place for the resettlement of groups of freed American Negro slaves. The Free and Independent Republic of Liberia was constituted on July 26, 1847. The immigration of American Negroes ended with the American Civil War. In Aug. 1983 Liberia as the first Black African state re-established after 10 years diplomatic relations with Israel, and signed a co-operation agreement.

F.J. FRENKEL, *SSha i Liberia. Negritianskaia problema v SSha i obrazovanie respubliki Liberii*, Moskva, 1964; I.A. MARINELLI, *The New Liberia*, New York, 1964; L.W. GLOWER, *Growth without Development. An Economic Survey of Liberia*, Evaston, 1966; C.M. WILSON, *Liberia: Black Africa in Microcosmos*, New York, 1971; D.E. DUNN, *The Foreign Policy of Liberia during the Tubman Era, 1944–71*, London, 1979; *The Europa Year Book 1984. A World Survey*, Vol. II, pp. 1935–1944 London, 1984; J. GUS, *Liberia: The Quest for Democracy*, Bloomington, Ind., 1987.

LIBERTÉ, EGALITÉ, FRATERNITÉ. *French =* liberty, equality, brotherhood. The motto of the French Revolution, declared on June 30, 1793.

LIBERTY OF ASSOCIATION CONVENTION, 1947. The official name of a convention whose principles were adopted unanimously by the International Labour Conference convened by the ILO in July 1947 in Geneva. It was approved Nov., 1947 by the UN General Assembly and submitted to the Human Rights Commission for framing a draft convention.

LIBERTY, STATUE OF. Statue of Liberty Enlightening the World, National Monument. A monument, gift of the French nation to the American nation, erected at the entrance to the port of New York on Oct. 28, 1886, according to the design of the French sculptor F.A. Bartholdi; construction by the French engineer A.G. Eiffel. Rising 93m high the statue depicts a striding woman with a lamp in her right hand (height of the figure 45m). At the feet of the statue are broken chains and in her left hand a tablet with the date of the US Independence Day, July 4, 1776. The statue is forged in copper plate covering a green steel construction. In the crown adorning the head of the statue is an observation platform, which is reached by a spiral staircase within the interior of the figure. Since 1960 the island on which the statue is located bears the official name Liberty Island, and since that year the American Immigration Museum has been located on Liberty Island.
On July 3, 1986 in New York the Presidents Ronald Reagan and François Mitterand presided over the 100th Birthday ceremonies of the Statue of Liberty and the 210th Anniversary of American Independence.

"Liberty Statue" in: *The British Encyclopaedia*, Vol. 13, p. 1030, Chicago, London, 1973; *The World Almanac and Book of Facts*, New York, 1988.

LIBERUM VETO. *Latin =* "a free objection". The historical right to break up Seyms (parliaments) in Poland (1652–1791) by the vote of one deputy pronouncing his *Liberum Veto*; in common language the maximum freedom of action of the individual, even against the will of, and with harm to, the entire society.

LIBOR. London Inter-Bank Offered Rate, international interest rate in the London Inter-Bank Eurocurrency Market (Dec., 1977–6%; Dec., 1979–13%; Spring 1980–19.5%).

LIBRARIANS. Organizations reg. with the UIA:

Inter-American Association of Agricultural Librarians and Documentalists, f. 1953, Turialba, Costa Rica. Publ.: Boletín Informativo.
International Association of Agricultural Librarians and Documentalists, f. 1955, Thorpe Bay, Essex, UK. Publ.: Quarterly Bulletin.

The Europa Yearbook 1988. A World Survey, Vol I, 1988, London.

LIBRARIES. The subject of permanent organized international co-operation, co-ordinated by UNESCO since 1948. Libraries have been subject to international law since the Brussels Convention of 1866, which concerned the exchange of public documents and publications of scientific and literary societies, and was the first international library agreement. From 1905 to 1933 the International Bibliographic Institute in Brussels worked out and supplemented the universally accepted ▷ decimal universal classification. In 1936 the International Library Committee adopted rules for international book lending; new rules were elaborated in 1954. The First International Libraries and Similar Institutions Conference, sponsored by UNESCO, was held in Paris in Nov., 1948. Organizations reg. with the UIA:

Asiatic Federation of Libraries Associations, f. 1957, Tokyo.
Association of International Libraries, f. 1963, Geneva.
Inter-American Bibliographical and Libraries Association, f. 1930, North Miami Beach, Fla.
International Association for Development of Libraries, 1957, Dakar.
International Association of Law Libraries, f. 1959, Marburg.
International Association of Metropolitan City Libraries, f. 1967, The Hague, Netherlands.
International Association of Technological University Libraries, f. 1955, Oxford, England.
International Federation of Libraries Associations, f. 1929, London.
A Public Affairs Information Service PAIS a non-profit association of libraries was founded in 1914 in New York. Publishes PAIS Bulletin dealing with material in English, and PAIS Foreign Language Index concerning publications in French, German, Italian, Portuguese and Spanish (monthly).

UNESCO publ., *UNESCO Bulletin for Libraries*, monthly in English, French and Spanish; W.E. CLASON, *Elsevier's Dictionary of Library Science, Information and Documentation. In English/American, French, Spanish, Italian, Dutch and German*, Amsterdam, 1976; *Yearbook of International Organizations, 1986/87*; A. KENT, H. LANCOUR eds. *Encyclopedia of Library and Information Science*, Vol. 1–33, New York, 1968–1983. *Supplement* Vol. 1–7, New York, 1983–1987; *Encyclopedia of Library and Information Science, World Guide to Libraries*, Muenchen–New York–London–Paris, 1987; *The Europa Yearbook 1988. A World Survey*, Vol. I, London, 1988; *American Library Directory 1988–89*, New York–London, 1989.

LIBRARY OF CONGRESS. The world's greatest library collecting works in all languages, founded by president Thomas Jefferson, advocate of universal education as an international library. Three quarters of the approximately 20 million books are in languages other than English. Since 1976 the Library of Congress collects recordings of radio and television broadcasts. Publ. Quarterly Journal of the Library of Congress.

Ch. A. GOODRUM, *Treasury of the Library of Congress*, New York, 1980.

LIBRARIES, MAJOR WORLD INTERNATIONAL LIBRARIES. The greatest collections of world international literature are:

Ambrosian Library, Milan. f. 1605.
Biblioteca Apostolica in the Vatican, f. 15th century.
Biblioteca Nacional in Madrid, f. 1712.
Biblioteca Nazionale Centrale in Florence, f. 1747.
Bibliotecca Nazionale Centrale in Rome, f. 1876.
Bibliotheque Nationale in Paris, f. 1480.
Bodleian Library at Oxford University, f. 1602.
Boston Public Library, Boston, Mass., f. 1852.
British Museum Library, London, f. 1753.
Dag Hammarskjöld Library, United Nations ▷ Hammarskjöld Dag Library.
Det Kongalike Bibliotek in Copenhagen, f. 1657.
Deutsche Bibliothek in Frankfurt/M, f. 1946.
Deutsche Staatsbibliothek in Berlin, f. 1661.
Harvard University Library, f. 1638 in Cambridge, Mass.
Hoover War Library, est. 1919 (▷ Hoover Institution).
Jagiellonian Library of the Jagiellonian University, f. 1364, in Cracow.
Klementinum State Library in Prague, f. 1348.
Kunrgliga Bibliotekat in Stockholm, f. in XVII century.
Lenin Library in Moscow, est. 1917–1925, replacing the Imperial Library St. Petersburg.
Library of Congress in Washington DC, f. 1800. q.v.
National Diet Library in Tokyo, f. 1948.
New York Public Library, f. 1895 in New York.
Schweizerische Landerbibliothek in Berne, f. 1895.
Universitets Biblioteket in Oslo, f. 1811.

LIBREVILLE. The capital of Gabon, since 1960, population 1986 estimate: 370,000. Seat of the intergovernmental Interafrican Organization for Forestry Economy and Marketing of Timber.

Yearbook of International Organizations.

LIBYA. Member of the UN. Libyan Arab People's Socialist Republic. North African state on the Mediterranean, bounded by Tunisia, Algeria, Niger, Chad, Sudan, Egypt. Area: 1,775,500 sq. km. Pop. 1988 est.: 4,080,000 (1973 census: 2,249,237). Capital: Tripoli with 481,295 inhabitants 1973. GNP per capita 1988: US $5,100. Official language: Arabic. Currency: one Libyan dinar = 1000 dirhems. National Day: Sept. 1, Revolution Day, 1969.

UN member since Dec. 14, 1955 and member of all UN specialized agencies excluding the GATT. Member of the Arab League and OAU.

International relations: from 1835 to 1912 a province of the Ottoman Empire; from 1912 to 1942 Italian colony Tripolitania and Cyrenaica; 1943–45 under control of French and British armies; 1945–51 under UN trusteeship. UN General Assembly Res. 289/IV, Nov. 21, 1949, provided that the trusteeship known as Tripolitania Cyrenaica and Fazzan as of Dec. 24, 1951 should become a sovereign, independent country under the historical name of Libya. Turned under British influence into a constitutional monarchy governed by the venerable emir of Cyrenaica (appointed king at the age of 79) Muhammad Idris as-Sanusi (Idris I), who granted military bases to the UK and the USA and guaranteed oil concessions to foreign companies (crude oil accounts for 99% of the value of Libyan exports) The parliament which enacted liquidation of foreign military bases in 1964 was dissolved. Armed forces carried out a revolutionary coup on Sept. 1, 1969 and declared a republic headed by the Revolutionary Council under Colonel Muammar Gaddafi. Islam was declared the established religion determining the principles of nationalist domestic and foreign policy. In Dec., 1971 British petroleum enterprises were nationalized. On Sept. 3, 1973 the Libyan government nationalized 51% of all foreign oil companies on its territory (California Asiatic Oil Co., ESSO Standard Libya, Libyo-American Petroleum Co., Shell, Socal, Texaco).

The Heads of State of Egypt, Libya and Syria signed in Benghazi on Apr. 17, 1971 an agreement on the establishment of the Federation of Arab Republics whose draft constitution was adopted at Damascus on Aug. 20, 1971. On Aug. 2, 1972 Egypt and Libya merged under uniform political leadership but a plebiscite Sept. 1 failed due to substantial differences of opinion between M. Gaddafi and Egyptian President A. Sadat; on Jan. 12, 1972 leader of the Libyan Revolutionary Council, M. Gaddafi and Tunisian President Habib Bourgiba signed a proclamation on the union of Libya and Tunisia as one state, called Islamic Arab Republic. The plebiscite scheduled for Jan. 8 was postponed *sine die*. On Mar. 8, 1977 Libya became a People's Socialist Republic. In 1980s in controversy with Chad, Sudan and the USA. The US Oil Company EXXON closed down its Libyan operation in Nov., 1981. In 1983–1984 Libyan troops remained in the northern part of Chad, and French troops in the southern part. On Nov. 15, 1984 the Head of State F. Mitterrand and M. Gaddafi signed an agreement on simultaneous withdrawal of all French and Libyan troops from Chad.

On April 15, 1986 the USA conducted 5 air raids on Tripoli and Benghasi in retaliation for the bombing, organized in US opinion by Libya, of an American discotheque in West Berlin, that left one US soldier dead and 200 people wounded. The number of civilian victims of the American raids was estimated at 130. The UN Secretary General Javier Perez de Cuellar condemned both the Libyan support for the West Berlin attack, and the US air strikes.

On Oct. 3, 1988 Libya formally ended war with Chad over the Aouzou Strip.

A Law on Arab Nationality, adopted in Sept. 1980 states that: citizens of Libya are Arab nationals (Art 1) but those who abandon Islam forfeit Arab Nationality (Art 3).

See also ▷ World Heritage UNESCO List.

O. PICHON, *La question de Libye dans le règlement de la paix*, Paris, 1945; *Libya: The Road to Independence through the UN*, New York, 1952. A. NELMS LOCK-WOOD, "Libya. Building a Desert Economy", in: *International Conciliation*, No. 512, Mar., 1957, pp. 313–377; IBRD, *The Economic Development of Libya*, Washington, DC, 1960; M. KHADDURI, *Modern Libya: A Study in Political Development*, Baltimore, 1963; J. WRIGHT, *Libya*, London, 1969; M. BIANCO, *Gaddafi: Voice from the Desert*, London, 1975; J.A. ALLEN, *Libya, The Experience of Oil*, London, 1981; J. WRIGHT, *Libya. A Modern History*, London, 1982; *The Europa Year Book 1984. A World Survey*, Vol. II, pp. 1945–1954 London, 1984; *UN Chronicle*, April, 1984; UNESCO, *Libya Antiqua*, Paris, 1986; KEESING's, *Record of World Events*, June, 1986; Chad–Libya, in: A.J. DAY ed., *Border and Territorial Disputes*, London, 1987, pp. 113–117; R. BRUCE ST JOHN, *Quadaffis World Design: Libyan Foreign Policy, 1969–1987*, London, 1987; D. BLUNDY, A. LYCETT, *Qadaffi and Libyan Revolution*, London, 1987.

LICENSE. An international trade term for: (1) a permit of state authorities for import, export or transit of goods whose turnover in a given country is limited for some reason; or (2) a permit to use foreign technological processes. In the 1950s the NATO, CENTO and SEATO states introduced an anti-license system whose bodies were the Committees of ▷ COCOM and CHINCOM. Highly developed states assign 90% of their expenses for their own research and only a small percentage for foreign purchases, while the reverse is true for developing countries. It was estimated that in the early 1970s there were more than 40,000 significant license agreements in the world. All countries participated in them but only the USA and Switzerland showed a surplus in license turnover. Car industry licenses are the most widely accepted in the world.

LICENSING, COMPULSORY OF JOURNAL-ISTS. ▷ **Journalist, Compulsory Licensing.**

LIDICE. A small village in Western Czechoslovakia, west of Prague, with about 450 inhabitants before World War II, burnt to the ground on June 10, 1942 by German units as a reprisal for helping patriots who May 27, 1942 had made an attempt on the life of R. Heydrich, deputy governor-general of the occupied Czechoslovakian provinces: Bohemia and Moravia. All men over 15 were executed, women were deported to concentration camps, children were given over to the Gestapo germanization institution ▷ Lebensborn. The massacre in Lidice has become an international symbol of barbarity, as Oradour is in France and Warsaw in Poland. An international rose garden was established, after the war, in Lidice.

H.G. STEARS, "Lidice", in: *Encyclopaedia Britannica*, Vol. 13, pp. 1073–1074.

LIEBER'S CODE. A Code of Martial Law announced by President A. Lincoln (1809–65) during the Civil War on Apr. 24, 1863, in General Instruction No. 200, issued by the War Department. The Code included instructions for the Government Army concerning its conduct during the war. It was prepared by the American philosopher F. Lieber (1800–72). Lieber's Code is believed to be the cornerstone of martial law and was also the foundation of the First Hague Conventions of 1899 and 1907.

LIECHTENSTEIN. The Principality of Liechtenstein. Non-Member of the UN. Situated between Austria and Switzerland. Area: 160 sq. km. Pop. 1982 census: 26,380 (1980 census: 25,215, including 9,276 resident aliens). Capital: Vaduz with 4,904 inhabitants 1982. GNP 1974 per capita: US $8000. Currency: the Swiss franc. Official language: German. National Day: Aug. 16, Birthday of the Prince, 1926.

Non-member of the UN but member of the IAEA, WIPO, ITU and UPU. Member of the EFTA, the ICJ and the Council of Europe.

International relations: independent since May 3, 1342, since 1434 in present boundaries, since 1712 in the possession of the house of Liechtenstein, up to 1919 in customs union with Austria; since 1921 in financial, and since 1924 in customs union with Switzerland. Switzerland which administers the post and telecommunication system represents Liechtenstein diplomatically since 1919. Liechtenstein, a unique European country with absolute bank secrecy and the lowest taxes is one of the world ▷ tax havens, and more than 25,000 foreign companies and holding corporations have nominal headquarters there. In Apr., 1980 a new law introduced control over the register and activities of foreign firms. On Feb. 2, 1986 women voted for the first time in parliamentary elections.

G. FEGER, *Fürstentum Liechtenstein*, Vaduz, 1947; B. GREENE, *Valley of Peace: the Story of Liechtenstein*, London, 1948; E.H. BATLINER, *Das Geld und Kreditwesen des Fürstentums Liechtenstein*, Vaduz, 1967; B. STEGER, *A Survey of Liechtenstein History*, Vaduz, 1970; S. MALICZ, *Kunstführer Liechtenstein*, Berlin, 1977; *The Europa Year Book 1984. A World Survey*, Vol. I, pp. 641–646, London, 1984.

LIENS AND MORTGAGE CONVENTION, 1926 AND 1967. ▷ Maritime Law Conventions, 1882–1978.

LIFE AND PEACE. ▷ Christian World Peace Conference, 1983.

LIFEBOATS. A subject of organized international co-operation to ensure the rescue of persons shipwrecked at sea, i.e. the unification of lifeboat equipment and co-ordination of sea rescue rules. Organization reg. with the UIA:

International Life Boat Conference, f. 1924, London. *Yearbook of International Organizations*.

LIFE EXPECTANCY IN THE WORLD. A subject of UN research and analysis. The Development Research and Policy Analysis Department of the International Economic and Social Affairs Council of the UN Secretariat put the estimated life expectancy at birth 1975–80 in the world at 57.5 years; but in developed countries – 71.9 and in developing regions – 55.1 years. The highest life expectancy was in Japan (75.6), North America (73.5), Western Europe and Australia–New Zealand (73.0); the lowest in Central Africa (44.6), Western Africa (46.3), Eastern Africa (46.8) and Central Southern Asia (49.2).

According to WHO statistics in the 1980's Japan still leads the world in life expectancy at birth, with 75.5 years for males and 81.6 years for females; Iceland for males 75.1 years; Switzerland for females: 80.6 years; France 80.1 for females. Sweden and Switzerland are third highest in male life expectancy with 73.8 years.

Life expectancy for females is over 75 years for all developed countries, including the German Democratic Republic and Poland but excluding other Eastern European countries. Among others: Canada 80; Sweden 79.9; Iceland 79.4; Australia

78.7; the Federal Republic of Germany, along with the United States 78.5; Portugal 77.1; Israel 77; the German Democratic Republic 75.4; and Poland 75.1.

Life expectancy for males is over 70 years for all developed countries except those in Eastern Europe. Among others: Holland 73.1; Canada 73.0; Australia 72.2; England and Wales along with the Federal Republic of Germany 71.9; France 71.8; Italy and the United States 71.3; and Hungary 65.3. "Not only is the aged population increasing", the WHO says, "but the elderly population is itself getting older as more people survive to the higher ages". Added to increased longevity is the fact in a number of developing countries, notably Brazil, "declines in fertility are accelerating".

UN Chronicle, November, 1982, p. 40; WHO *Health Statistics Annual 1987,* Geneva, 1988.

LIFE IN PEACE, UN DECLARATION. ▷ Peace, UN Declaration on Preparation of Societies for Life in Peace, 1978.

LIFELONG EDUCATION. An educational doctrine introduced by UNESCO recommending lifelong education for the purpose of ensuring the individual full participation in a rapidly developing world. In Dec., 1972 the UNESCO Institute of Pedagogy held an international seminar in Hamburg on the subject of the consequences of lifelong education for the development of the content of education in the area of international education.

G. WILLIAMS, *Towards Lifelong Education. A New Role for Higher Education Institution,* UNESCO, Paris, 1978.

LIFE SAVING. A subject of international co-operation. Organizations reg. with the UIA:

International Association for Life Saving and First Aid to the Injured, f. 1926, Hellerup, Denmark.
International Life Boat Conference, f. 1924, Dorset.

Yearbook of International Organizations.

LIGHTHOUSES. A subject of international conventions and organizations. First international agreement was concluded on May 31, 1865 in Morocco between Austria, Belgium, France, Great Britain, The Netherlands, Norway, Portugal, Sweden, and the USA on maintenance of an international lighthouse at Cap Spartel, near Tangier, off the strait of Gibraltar. The second agreement was concluded in 1866 between Great Britain and Japan, providing for the erection of lighthouses in the ports of the latter (▷ Open door policy). The Netherlands and German Reich concluded, Oct. 16, 1896, an agreement on shared maintenance of lighthouses on the island of Borkum and at the mouth of the River Ems. Great Britain and the USA concluded an agreement on lighthouses at Taganak Island, the Philippines, Jan. 2, 1930. In 1929 the First International Conference on Lighthouses and other Aids to Navigation drafted and adopted an international convention on internationalization of lighthouses in the Black Sea, signed in 1930 (never came into force). The Second Conference was held in Paris, 1933; the Third in Berlin, 1937; the Fourth in Paris, 1950; the Fifth in Shaveningen, 1957, which set up an international institution assembling 60 states; reg. with the UIA:

International Association of Lighthouse Authorities (IALA), Association international de signalisation maritime, AISM, f. 1957, Paris. Consultative status with IMCO. Publ.: *AISM-IALA Bulletin.*

Lighthouses were also the subject of arbitration proceedings: the Permanent Court of Justice at The Hague considered the French–Greek dispute on lighthouses, Mar. 17, 1934 (PCIJ series A/B No 62) and Oct. 8, 1937 (PCIJ series A/B No 71) reconsidered by the Court of Arbitration on July 24, 1956. A UN International Law Commission debate on lighthouses was held on July 4, 1956 and the Conference on the Law of the Sea in 1958.

G.W. STUART, "The International Lighthouse at Cap Spartel", in: *American Journal of International Law,* No. 24, 1930; G. MARCHEGIANO, "The Juristic Character of the International Commission of Cape Spartel Lighthouse", in: *American Journal of International Law,* No. 25, 1931; V.A. SANTOS, Ch. D.T. LENNHOFF, "The Taganak Island. Lighthouse Dispute", in: *American Journal of International Law,* No. 45, 1951; Ch. ROUSSEAU, "L'Affaire franco-hellenique des phares, et la sentence arbitrale du 24 juillet 1956", in: *Revue Générale de Droit International Public,* No. 63, 1959.

LIGHTSHIPS AGREEMENT, 1930. An agreement concerning Manned Lightships not on their Stations, was signed on Oct. 23, 1930 in Lisbon by the governments of Belgium, China, Cuba, Denmark, Estonia, Finland, France, Germany, Great Britain, Greece, Monaco, Morocco, the Netherlands, Poland (with Danzig), Portugal, Romania, Sweden, the USSR and Yugoslavia.

LNTS, Vol. 112, p. 21.

LIGURIAN STUDIES. Subject of international co-operation. Organization reg. with the UIA:

International Institute for Ligurian Studies, f. 1947, Bordighera, Italy; to conduct research on ancient monuments of the Mediterranean. Library of 55,000 volumes.
Yearbook of International Organizations 1986/87; The Europa Yearbook 1988. A World Survey, Vol. I, London, 1988.

LIHOU. ▷ Bailiwick of Guernsey.

LILIENTHAL REPORT, 1946. An American program on the international control of atomic energy, elaborated by a Board of Consultants of the Department of State. The chairman of the Tennessee Valley Authority, David E. Lilienthal, who acted as chairman of the consulting board, presented the report on Mar. 16, 1946. The main proposal of the report was that an International Atomic Development Authority be established to own all uranium and thorium in the world as well as to organize a global control over their radioactivity. ▷ Baruch Plan, 1946.

US Department of State Publication 2498, Washington, DC, 1946.

LIMA. The capital of Peru. Population 1985 estimate 5,005,400. Occupied by Chile 1881–1883 during the War of the Pacific. Its port is Callao. Seat of the UN Information Office, Inter-American Institute of Agricultural Sciences, Latin American Federation of Christian Trade Unionists.

The International Geographic Encyclopedia and Atlas, London, 1979; *The Europa Yearbook 1987. A World Survey,* London, 1987.

LIMA AMERICAN PRINCIPLES DECLARATION, 1938. The Eighth International American Conference at Lima, on Dec. 27, 1938, approved the American Principles Declaration, called the Lima Declaration 1938.

Conferencias Internacionales Americanas. Primer Suplemento, 1938–42, Washington, DC, 1938, pp. 97–98 and 367; "Declaracion de Principios Americanos 1938", in: E.J. OSMAŃCZYK, *Enciclopedia Mundial de Relaciones Internacionales y Naciones Unidas,* Mexico, DF, 1976, pp. 417–418.

LIMA CONVENTION FOR THE PROTECTION OF SOUTH PACIFIC. ▷ South Pacific Lima Convention.

LIMA DECLARATION, 1975. ▷ Nonaligned Countries Declaration, 1975.

LIMA DECLARATION 1985. A Declaration made in Lima on July 28, 1985 by Latin American leaders on flexible and realistic criteria on the level of debt repayment.

KEESING's *Record of World Events,* 1986, No. 2.

LIMA GROUP OF 77 DECLARATION 1971. A Declaration adopted by the Ministerial Meeting of the Group of 77 on Nov. 7, 1971 in Lima. The main points of the Declaration:

"Deem it their duty: to invite the attention of the international community and the peoples and the Governments of the developed countries to the following:
(a) The standard of living of the hundreds of millions of people of the developing countries is extremely low and the raising of their standard of living to a level consistent with human dignity constitutes a real challenge for international co-operation and contributes to the creation of conditions of stability and well-being for all humanity.
(b) In spite of an over-all improvement in international trade and the world economy, as a whole, the relative position of the developing countries continues to deteriorate:
(i) While during the 1960s the per capita income in developed countries increased by over $650, that in developing countries increased only by about $40;
(ii) Their share of world trade in exports declined from 21.3 per cent in 1960 to 17.6 per cent in 1970;
(iii) Their external debt burden is growing at such an alarming rate that it stood at about $60 billion at the end of 1969;
(iv) The financial flows from developed to developing countries are declining in terms of the percentage of the gross national product of the former along with their component of official development assistance;
(v) The technological gap between the developed and developing countries is steadily widening.
(c) The present international monetary crisis and the intensification of protectionism by developed countries jeopardize vital trade and development interests of the developing countries and threaten the very basis of international economic co-operation at the very outset of the Second United Nations Development Decade.
(d) The gap in the standard of living between the developed and the developing countries has widened as a result of all these unfavourable trends; since their meeting in Algiers in 1967, the poor countries have become relatively poorer and the rich countries richer."

Conference on Economic Co-operation among Developing Countries. Declarations, Resolutions, Recommendations and Decisions adopted in the UN System. México, DF, 1976, Vol. II, pp. 253–368.

LIMA PROGRAM FOR MUTUAL ASSISTANCE AND SOLIDARITY, 1975. A Program adopted by the Conference of Ministers for Foreign Affairs of the Nonaligned Countries, on Aug. 30, 1975, in Lima. The main points of the Economic Declaration and Plan of Action for strengthening co-operation, solidarity and action capacity of nonaligned and other developing countries and for achieving the establishment of the ▷ New International Economic Order, are as follows: – to oppose division of the world into blocs in order to attenuate contradictions in international life;
– to eliminate force and pressure in international relations;
– to found relations between nations on the equality of states, respect for their territorial integrity, national sovereignty, and the right of every country to choose freely its political regime;
– to spread and respect the right of every nation to self-determination and freedom,

– the nonaligned countries are anti-imperialist, anti-colonialist and anti-racist.

UN Chronicle, April 1975, pp. 28–30 and May 1975, pp. 39–49.

LIMA THIRD WORLD INDEBTEDNESS CONFERENCE 1986. The Conference held in the capital of Peru, Nov. 12–14, 1986, at which 35 developing countries representing some 70 per cent of Third World indebtedness (about $900 billion) demanded a global permanent solution and political dialogue between debtors, creditors, financial institutions and commercial banks.

KESSING's *Record of World Events*, 1987, No. 2.

LIMA UNIDO DECLARATION, 1975. Declaration and Plan of Action on Industrial Development and Co-operation, adopted on Mar. 27, 1975 in Lima by the II Unido General Conference with 82 votes for, 1 against (USA) and 7 absentions (Belgium, Canada, the FRG, Israel, Italy, Japan and the UK). The text of the Declaration is as follows:

"(1) The Second General Conference of the United Nations Industrial Development Organization, convened by General Assembly resolution 3087 (XXVIII) of 6 December 1973, entrusted with establishing the main principles of industrialization and defining the means by which the international community as a whole might take action of a broad nature in the field of industrial development within the framework of new forms of international co-operation, with a view to the establishment of a new international economic order, adopts the Lima Declaration on Industrial Development and Co-operation.

(2) Having examined the situation with respect to industrialization in the developing countries during the past decade,

(3)(a) Recalling General Assembly resolution 3176 (XXVIII), of 17 December 1973, which judged that in terms of international action the cause of development has lost momentum since 1970;

(b) Recalling General Assembly resolutions 2952 (XXVII), of 11 December 1972, and 3087 (XXVIII), of 6 December 1973;

(4) Bearing in mind resolutions 3201 (S-VI) and 3202 (S-VI), of 1 May 1974, adopted at the sixth special session of the General Assembly on the Declaration and Programme of Action on the Establishment of a New International Economic Order, according to which every effort should be made by the international community to take measures to encourage the industrialization of the developing countries with a view to increasing their share in world industrial production, as envisaged in the International Development Strategy,

(5) Recognizing the urgent need to bring about the establishment of a new international economic order based on equity, sovereign equality, interdependence and co-operation, as has been expressed in the Declaration and Programme of Action on the Establishment of a New International Economic Order, in order to transform the present structure of economic relations,

(6) Noting resolutions 62 (III) of 19 May 1972, adopted by the United Nations Conference on Trade and Development at its third session, concerning measures in aid of the least developed countries, and resolution 1797 (LV) of 11 July 1973 (aid to the Sudano-Sahelian population threatened with famine), on assistance to the drought-stricken areas of Africa, adopted by the Economic and Social Council at its fifty-fifth session,

(7) Recalling the Charter of Economic Rights and Duties of States adopted at the twenty-ninth session of the General Assembly as an instrument designed to bring about new international economic relations and to contribute to the establishment of a new international economic order,

(8) Convinced that peace and justice encompass an economic dimension helping the solution of the world economic problems, the liquidation of under-development, offering a lasting and definitive solution to the industrialization problem for all peoples and guaranteeing to all countries the right to implement freely and effectively their development programmes. To this effect, it is necessary to eliminate threats and resort to force and to promote peaceful co-operation between States to the fullest extent possible, to apply the principles of non-interference in each others internal affairs, full equality of rights, respect of national independence and sovereignty as well as to encourage the peaceful co-operation between all States, irrespective of their political, social and economic systems. The further improvement of international relations will create better conditions for international co-operation in all fields which should make possible large financial and material resources to be used, inter alia, for developing of industrial production.

(9) Considering further that the remaining vestiges of alien and colonial domination, foreign occupation, racial discrimination, and the practice of apartheid, and neo-colonialism in all its forms continue to be among the greatest obstacles to the full emancipation and progress of the developing countries and their populations,

(10) Bearing in mind that the situation in the developing countries has become aggravated by the persistent and marked tensions to which the present international economic situation is subjected and that to these must be added as well as the unacceptable practices of those transnational corporations that infringe the principle of sovereignty of developing countries, the effects of the inflationary increase in the import costs of developing countries, the pressures exerted upon their balance of payments particularly by such factors as heavy foreign debt servicing, the aggravation of the international monetary crisis, and the transfers resulting from private investment and that this situation is not conducive to the spirit of the new international economic order,

(11) Recognizing that problems of industrial development in developing countries at their present stage of development do not lie entirely in those countries but also arise from the policies of most of the developed countries, and that without meaningful changes in the economic policies of the developed countries, the achievement of the objectives of a new international order would be in serious jeopardy,

(12) Recognizing that the developing countries constitute 70 per cent of the world population and generate less than 7 per cent of industrial production, that the gap between the developed and developing countries has been widened owing, inter alia, to the persistence of obstacles in the way of the establishment of a new international economic order based on equity and justice,

(13) Taking into account the fact that industrial progress has not displayed significant advances in the developing countries as a whole, in spite of serious efforts on their part, and that, in many cases, the dependence of their economies on the export of primary goods and the measures taken in the majority of the developed countries have not made it possible to achieve a profound dynamic effect which would be capable of transforming internal socio-economic structures and laying the basis for real development,

(14) Bearing in mind that any real process of industrialization worthy of the name must conform to the broad objectives of self-sustaining and integrated socio-economic development and that all countries have the sovereign right to make the necessary changes to ensure the just and effective participation of their peoples in industry and share in the benefits deriving therefrom,

(15) Noting with anxiety that the present international crisis has aggravated the industrialization problems of the developing countries, resulting, inter alia, in the under-utilization of resources, constraints in the planning and execution of industrial projects and increasing costs of industrial inputs, equipment and freight charges,

(16) Aware that some of the obstacles which are inhibiting industrial expansion in the developing countries are of an internal structural nature, and that there also continue to exist numerous impediments arising from colonial and neo-colonial policies or new forms of dependency,

(17) Considering the present general trend of industrialized to reduce the technical and financial assistance needed to promote the economic and social development of developing countries in general and their industrial development in particular, as well as the unsatisfactory terms of the assistance given,

(18) Considering also that development assistance is a legitimate need and that neither in its present volume nor form is it sufficient, particularly taking into account the worsening of the terms of trade of the developing countries and the drainage of their resources,

(19) Observing with concern the grave consequences with which the present international crisis confronts the developing countries as a result of growing inflation and economic instability, aware of the need to establish a just and equitable relationship between the prices of raw materials, primary commodities, manufactured and semi-manufactured goods exported by the developing countries and the prices of raw materials, primary commodities, foodstuffs, manufactured and semi-manufactured goods exported by the developing countries and the prices of raw materials, primary commodities, foodstuffs, manufactured and semi-manufactured goods and capital equipment imported by them, and to work for a link between the prices of exports of developing countries and the prices of their imports from developed countries.

(20) Convinced that the establishment of a new and just international economic order based on the common interests and co-operation of all States can only be achieved through the equitable participation of the developing countries in the production and exchange of goods and services, in order to achieve just and equitable international economic relations,

(21) Persuaded that, since not all developing countries have socio-economic structures which permit them through industrialization, to attain the objectives pursued by the establishment of a new international economic order, it is essential to adopt more favourable treatment for the least developed, land-locked and island developing countries o render possible harmonious and balanced development,

(22) Having decided to adopt a common position and line of action, solemnly declare

(23) Their firm conviction of the role of industry as a dynamic instrument of growth essential to the rapid economic and social development of the developing countries, in particular of the least developed countries;

(24) Their firm intention to promote industrial development through concerted measures at the national, subregional, regional, interregional and international levels with a view to modernizing the economies of the developing countries, and in particular those of the least developed countries, and eliminating all forms of foreign political domination and socio-economic exploitation wherever they might exist;

(25) Their resolve to ensure the speedy and effective implementation of the principles of industrialization laid down in the International Development Strategy for the 1970s which is being adapted to the Programme of Action on the Establishment of a New International Economic Order;

(26) That in order to facilitate the establishment of a new international economic order and the achievement of the targets set forth in the Declaration on that subject, a system of consultations be established in the United Nations Industrial Development Organization and other appropriate international bodies between developed and developing countries;

(27) That countries, particularly developed countries, should undertake an objective and critical examination of their present policies and make appropriate changes in such policies so as to facilitate the expansion and diversification of imports from developing countries and thereby make possible international economic relations on a rational, just and equitable basis;

(28) That, in view of the low percentage share of the developing countries in total world industrial production, recalling General Assembly Res. 3306/XXIX of Dec. 14, 1974, and taking into account the policy guidelines and qualitative recommendations made in the present Declaration, their share should be increased to the maximum possible extent and as far as possible to at least 25 per cent of total world industrial production by the year 2000, while making every endeavour to ensure that the industrial growth so achieved is distributed among the developing countries as evenly as possible. This implies that the developing countries should increase their industrial growth at a rate considerably higher than the 8 per cent recommended in the International Development Strategy for the Second United Nations Development Decade;

(29) That the Governments of the developing countries should adopt, in order to accelerate industrialization, all measures which would ensure the exercise of their national sovereignty over their natural resources and the full utilization of these resources and of human and material potential at their disposal, not only at the national level but also within the framework of systems of economic co-operation;
(30) That in order to render really effective the full utilization their available human resources, conditions should be created by the developing countries which make possible the full integration of women in social and economic activities and, in particular, in the industrialization process, on the basis of equal rights;
(31) That, in order to carry out their national development plans, and, in particular, those involving industrialization, the developing countries should raise the general cultural standard of their peoples, in order to have available a qualified work force not only for the production of goods and services but also for management skills, thus making possible the assimilation of modern technologies;
(32) That every State has the inalienable right to exercise freely its sovereignty and permanent control over its natural resources, both terrestrial and marine, and over all economic activity for the exploitation of these resources in the manner appropriate to its circumstances, including nationalization in accordance with its laws as an expression of this right, and that no State shall be subjected to any forms of economic, political or other coercion which impedes the full and free exercise of that inalienable right;
(33) That the principles set out in the Charter of the Economic Rights and Duties of States must be fully implemented. Consequently, it is the right and duty of all States, individually and collectively, to eliminate colonialism, apartheid, racial discrimination, neo-colonialism, occupation and all forms of foreign aggression, and domination and the economic and social consequences thereof, as a prerequisite for development. States which practise such policies are responsible to the countries, territories and peoples affected for restitution and full compensation for the exploitation and depletion of, and damage to, the natural and other resources of these countries, territories and peoples. It is, in addition, the duty of all States to extend assistance to these countries, territories and peoples;
(34) That effective control over natural resources and the harmonization of policies for their exploitation, conservation, transformation and marketing constitute for developing countries an indispensable condition for economic and social progress;
(35) That special attention should be given to the least developed countries, which should enjoy a net transfer of resources from the developed countries in the form of technical and financial resources as well as capital goods, to enable the least developed countries in conformity with the policies and plans for development, to accelerate their industrialization;
(36) That developing countries with sufficient means at their disposal should give careful consideration to the possibility of ensuring a net transfer for financial and technical resources to the least developed countries;
(37) That special emphasis should be laid on the need of the least developed countries for the establishment of production facilities involving a maximum utilization of local human resources, the output of which meets identified material and social requirements, thus assuring a convergence between local resource use and needs as well as offering adequate employment opportunities;
(38) That in view of the needs to conserve non-renewable resources, all countries, particularly developed countries, should avoid wasteful consumption and, in that context, the developing countries possessing such resources should formulate a policy of economic diversification with a view to acquiring other means of financing which are not based on intensive exploitation of those resources;
(39) That the international community, and especially the developed countries, must mobilize human and material resources in order to cope with problems which threaten the environment. In this connexion, the developed countries should intensify their efforts to prevent environmental pollution and should refrain from actions which according to scientific knowledge would create pollution problems or cause upheavals in developing countries;
(40) That the countries concerned should:
(a) Fully discharge their obligations under the International Development Strategy;
(b) In the context of the review and appraisal mechanism of the International Development Strategy:
(i) Consider withdrawing the reservations they expressed at the time of the adoption thereof, and
(ii) Consider entering into new commitments thereunder; and
(c) Consider withdrawing the reservations they expressed at the time of the adoption of the Declaration and Programme of Action on the Establishment of a New International Economic Order with a view to its full implementation. These countries should also, together with the developing countries, consider formulating, adopting and implementing codes of conduct and other instruments designed to assist in the establishment of a new international economic order;
(41) That the developed countries should adhere strictly to the principle that the Generalized System of Preferences must not be used as an instrument for economic and political pressure to hamper the activities of those developing countries which produce raw materials;
(42) That the unrestricted play of market forces is not the most suitable means of promoting industrialization on a world scale nor of achieving effective international co-operation in the field of industry and that the activities of transnational corporations should be subject to regulation and supervision in order to ensure that these activities are compatible with the development plans and policies of the host countries, taking into account relevant international codes of conduct and other instruments;
(43) That the developing countries should fully and effectively participate in the international decision-making process on international monetary questions in accordance with the existing and evolving rules of the competent bodies and share equitably in the benefits resulting therefrom;
(44) That urgent discussion should be continued in competent bodies for the establishment of a reformed international monetary system, in the direction and operation of which the developing countries should fully participate. This universal system should inter alia be designed to achieve stability in flows and conditions of development financing and to meet the specific needs of developing countries;
(45) That steps should be taken to strengthen and restructure UNIDO, thereby making it more responsive to the needs of developing countries and especially the least developed countries in the promotion of industrialization and in the establishment of a new international economic order;
(46) That in the strengthened and restructured UNIDO, developing countries, including the least developed countries, should be given greater participation at all levels in the policy-making and management activities of the Organization and that their membership be substantially increased on the Industrial Development Board;
(47) That it is urgently necessary that the developing countries change their traditional method of negotiation with the developed countries. To bring this about, they must undertake joint action in order to strengthen their negotiating position vis-a-vis the developed countries. For this purpose, the developing countries must consider all possible means of strengthening the action of producers' associations already established, encourage the creation of other associations for the principal commodities exported by them, and establish a mechanism for consultation and co-operation among the various producers' associations for the purpose of the co-ordination of their activities and for their mutual support, in particular as a precaution against any economic or other form of aggression;
(48) That developing countries should use effective means of strengthening their bargaining power individually and collectively to obtain favourable terms for the acquisition of technology, expertise, licences and equipment, fair and remunerative prices for their primary commodities and improved and substantially liberalized access to the developed countries for their manufactures;
(49) That developing countries should place a premium on self-reliance in their development effort for the realization of their full potential in terms of both human and natural resources and, to that end, adopt meaningful and concerted policies and pursue action directed towards greater technical and economic co-operation among themselves;
(50) That developing countries should lend support to the concept of an integrated and multisectoral approach to industrial development whereby the technological and the socio-economic implications of the process are fully taken into account at both the planning and implementation stages;
(51) That, in view of the basic complementarity between industry and agriculture, every attempt should be made to promote agro-based or agro-related industries which besides arresting rural exodus and stimulating food production activities, provide an incentive for the establishment of further natural resource-based industries;
(52) That developing countries should devote particular attention to the development of basic industries such as steel, chemicals, petro-chemicals and engineering, thereby consolidating their economic independence while at the same time assuring an effective form of import-substitution and a greater share of world trade;
(53) That the educational system be adapted in order to give young people an appreciation of industrial work and that policies and programmes should be adopted to train the qualified personnel needed for new sources of employment created in the developing countries, at the regional and sub-regional levels. The training activities linked with the industrial development must be conceived in such a way that they make possible the processing of natural resources and other raw materials in the country of origin and the establishment of permanent structures for specialized, rapid, large-scale and high-quality training of national labour at all levels and for all professional specializations, whether technical or managerial without discrimination with regard to sex;
(54) That co-ordinated programmes of literacy and workers' training must be conceived to ensure professional promotion and development of local expertise at all levels of employment;
(55) That appropriate measures should be taken by developing countries to organize research institutions and establish training programmes to cover the needs of their industrial development and make possible progressive mastery of the different production and management techniques and of industrial development, thus facilitating the establishment of structures to absorb modern technologies.
(56) That intensive efforts should be made by the competent bodies to formulate an international code of conduct for transfer of technology corresponding to needs and conditions prevalent in developing countries by defining terms and conditions to such transactions to take place under the most advantageous conditions for those countries;
(57) That in view of the foregoing, the Conference adopts the various measures set in the Plan of Action."

UN Monthly Chronicle, No. 4, 1975, pp. 30–31; *Conference on Economic Co-operation among Developing Countries. Declarations, Resolutions, Recommendations, and Decisions adopted in the UN System*. México, DF, 1976, Vol. I, pp. 164–204.

LIMITATION OF SHIPOWNERS LIABILITY CONVENTION, 1924 AND 1957. ▷ Maritime Law Conventions, 1882–1978.

LIMITED SOVEREIGNTY DOCTRINE. ▷ Brezhnev Doctrine, 1970; ▷ Truman Doctrine, 1947.

LINE-FISHING. One of the oldest sports; since 1912 world records in line fishing are recorded by the International Game Fish Association.

LINEN AND HEMP. The subjects of international co-operation. Organizations reg. with the UIA:

Common Market Committee on the International Linen and Hemp Confederation, f. 1959, Paris.
International Linen and Hemp Confederation, f. 1950, Paris.

Yearbook of International Organizations.

LINER CONFERENCES CODE. The Convention on a Code of Conduct for Liner Conferences, discussed within UNCTAD in the late 1960s and adopted on Apr. 6, 1974.

The Convention was due to come into force six months after the date on which at least 24 nations with combined shipping equal to 25% of world tonnage had become contracting parties. That requirement was met on Apr. 6, 1983, and at present, there are 59 contracting parties with 29.68% of world liner tonnage.

The following countries have become contracting parties: Bangladesh, Barbados, Benin, Bulgaria, Cape Verde, the Central African Republic, Chile, China, Congo, Costa Rica, Cuba, Czechoslovakia, Egypt, Ethiopia, Gabon, Gambia, the German Democratic Republic, the Federal Republic of Germany, Ghana, Guatemala, Guinea, Guyana, Honduras, India, Indonesia, Iraq, the Ivory Coast, Jamaica, Jordan, Kenya, Lebanon, Madagascar, Malaysia, Mali, Mauritius, Mexico, Morocco, the Netherlands, Niger, Nigeria, Pakistan, Peru, the Philippines, the Republic of Korea, Romania, Senegal, Sierra Leone, Sri Lanka, Sudan, Togo, Tunisia, the USSR, the United Republic of Cameroon, the United Republic of Tanzania, Trinidad and Tobago, Uruguay, Venezuela, Yugoslavia, Zaïre.

One of the most innovative provisions of the Code of Conduct calls for sharing of cargo – on what has become known as the 40–40–20 principle – among the fleets of the country of origin, of the country receiving the cargo and of third parties (cross traders). In other words, if a country in West Africa has a national shipping line (or lines), it would be entitled to carry 40% of its trade with, for example, the United Kingdom. The United Kingdom would have another 40% and the rest could be shared by shipping lines not based in either of the two countries. The entry into force of the Code of Conduct represents the culmination of several years of determined efforts on the part of many member states of the UNCTAD to redress inequities in the international liner conference system and to promote an equitable balance of interests between shippers and shipowners and between traditional shipowners situated in developed market-economy countries and new shipowners in developing countries.

In the years immediately following the adoption of the Convention, the Code received increasingly widespread support among developing countries so that by the fifth session of the UNCTAD, held at Manila in 1979, the minimum required number of 24 contracting states had long since been achieved. However, owing to the limited size of the merchant fleets in existence in developing countries, it had not been possible to meet the tonnage requirement.

Nevertheless, at the Manila session, as well as in subsequent meetings of the UNCTAD Committee on Shipping, a sufficient number of developed and socialist countries indicated their intention to become contracting parties to ensure the coming into force of the Convention.

Gamani Corea, Secretary-General of the UNCTAD, described the entry into force as "a major step forward to provide a rational framework for the orderly and equitable development of world liner shipping". He said:

"The fact that the Code is now finally entering into force, a decade after its adoption in 1974, demonstrates that although international action may at times appear to be a relatively slow process, it nevertheless can result in concrete results for the benefit of the international community".

▷ Latin American Shipowners Association, ▷ Shipping Law.

UN Chronicle, December, 1983, p. 83.

LINE SHIPPING, COASTING TRADE, TRAMP NAVIGATION. The carriage of passengers or cargo by sea-going vessels: (1) on fixed regular inland and coastal water routes; (2) between ports of one country; (3) on temporary routes chiefly for bulk cargo shipment. Subjects of international conventions and bilateral agreements. The IMCO Conference on safety of navigation, held in London, 1972, drew up an Annex to the UN Maritime Convention regarding the application of new safety measures by supertankers with a view to reducing the risk of damaging local ships on congested routes.

LINGGADJATI AGREEMENT, 1947. The text of the Agreement between Indonesia and The Netherlands, signed on Mar. 25, 1947 in Linggadjati (Cheribon), read as follows:

"Preamble: The Netherlands Government, represented by the Commission-General for the Netherlands Indies, and the Government of the Republic of Indonesia, represented by the Indonesian delegation, moved by a sincere desire to insure good relations between the peoples of The Netherlands and Indonesia in new forms of voluntary co-operation which offer the best guarantee for sound and strong development of both countries in the future and which make it possible to give a new foundation to the relationship between the two peoples; agree as follows and will submit this agreement at the shortest possible notice for the approval of the respective parliaments:
Article I: The Netherlands Government recognizes the Government of the Republic of Indonesia as exercising de facto authority over Java, Madura and Sumatra. The areas occupied by Allied or Netherlands forces shall be included gradually, through mutual co-operation, in Republican territory. To this end, the necessary measures shall at once be taken in order that this inclusion shall be completed at the latest on the date mentioned in Article XII.
Article II: The Netherlands Government and the Government of the Republic shall co-operate in the rapid formation of a sovereign democratic state on a federal basis to be called the United States of Indonesia.
Article III: The United States of Indonesia shall comprise the entire territory of the Netherlands Indies with the provision, however, that in case the population of any territory, after due consultation with the other territories, should decide by democratic process that they are not, or not yet, willing to join the United States of Indonesia, they can establish a special relationship for such a territory to the United States of Indonesia and to the Kingdom of the Netherlands."

A.M. TAYLOR, *Indonesian Independence and the United Nations*, Cornell University Press, 1960.

LINGUA FRANCA. Latin = language of the Franks. An international term for an auxiliary language in multinational communication; the term originated in the Middle Ages when Arabs engaged in Mediterranean commerce called all European 'Franks'. The language of Mediterranean ports was based on French, Arabic, Greek, Italian, Spanish and Dutch, and was also called Sabir. This type of jargon, also developed in other multinational commercial posts, such as the Caribbean, South Asia, Oceania, ▷ Pidgin, has nothing in common with the lingua franca of diplomacy: Latin in the Middle Ages, French in the XVII–XIX century, British English in the League of Nations and American English in the United Nations.

WEBSTER's *New World Dictionary of the American Language*, New York, 1970.

LINGUISTICS. Subject of international co-operation. Organization reg. with the UIA:

International Association of Applied Linguistics, f. 1964, Bloomington, Ind., USA. Publ. IAAL Review (annually).

Permanent International Committee of Linguists, f. 1928, Voorhut, Netherlands. Publ. Linguistic Bibliography, Dictionaries of Linguistic Terminology.

Yearbook of International Organizations 1986/87; The Europa Yearbook 1988. A World Survey, Vol. I, London, 1988.

LINKAGE. An international term for the objective dependence of one question on another or the dependence of both questions on each other with the purpose of compelling a nation to approve both questions at the same time.

L'INTERNATIONALE. ▷ International, The.

LIPTAKO-GOURMA INTEGRATED DEVELOPMENT AUTHORITY. f. 1972, N'Gourma, Burkina Faso; to promote regional development in transport and water resources. Members: Burkina Faso, Mali, Niger.

The Europa Yearbook 1988. A World Survey, Vol. I, London, 1988.

LIQUIDATION OF WAR EFFECTS. A legal process definitively regulating the results of an armed conflict. The 1919 Peace Conference after World War I aimed at liquidation once and for all of the effects of war; in fact it failed to protect Europe and the world against World War II. Terms of Liquidation of the effects of World War II were determined by the Great Powers in the ▷ Potsdam Agreement 1945.

A. KLAFKOWSKI, *Les conséquences juridiques de la Seconde Guerre Mondiale et le problème allemand*, Varsovie, 1968.

LIQUIDITY INTERNATIONAL. The possibility of financing foreign trade payments through international reserve funds of exchangeable currencies and gold; an object of international councils in the interwar period on the initiative of J.M. Keynes; after World War II it became the object of continual analyses by the International Monetary Fund, IMF, because of the increasing gap in the size of payments in world trade and international reserves. According to these analyses this ratio varied greatly between 1958 and 1967, since world turnover doubled, while reserves only grew by 27%. In 1968 the IMF modified its statute increasing international liquidity by introducing Special Drawing Rights, the ▷ SDR.

LIQUOR TRAFFIC IN AFRICA, CONVENTION RELATING TO, 1919. An agreement between the USA, Belgium, the British Empire, France, Italy, Japan and Portugal, signed on Sept. 10, 1919 in Saint-Germain-en-Laye, prohibiting the importation of distilled beverages to the whole of the continent of Africa, with the exception of Algeria, Tunis, Morocco, Libya, Egypt and the Union of South Africa. It was agreed that (art. 2):

"The importation, distribution, sale and possession of trade spirits of every kind, and of beverages mixed with this spirit, are prohibited in this area."

Also forbidden were (art. 3): distilled beverages containing essential oils or chemical products, which are recognized as injurious to health, such as thujone, staranise, benzoic aldehyde, salicylic esters, hyssop and absinthe.

LNTS, Vol. 8, p. 17.

LIRA. A monetary unit of Italy; one lira = 100 centesimi; issued by the Banca d'Italia.

LIRA. A monetary unit of Turkey; one lira = 100 kusus = 4000 paras; issued by the Türkiye Cumhusiyet Merkez Bankasi – Banque Centrale de la République de Turquie.

L

LISBON. The capital of Portugal, since 1260, population 1981 census: 807,937. Seat of the International Federation of Landscape Architects.

Yearbook of International Organizations.

LISBON TREATY, 1887. ▷ Macau.

LITBIEL. ▷ Lithuania.

LITER. An international capacity unit = 1 liter, or approx. 61.02 cubic inches, or 0.908 quart (dry) or 1.057 quarts (liquid).

LITERACY YEAR INTERNATIONAL, 1990. Proclaimed by the UN General Assembly on December 7, 1987 authorising the UNESCO to organize the project.

LITERARY AND ARTISTIC WORKS. An international term, defined by the Berne Convention 1881 (revised 1908) as follows (art. 2):

"The expression 'literary and artistic works' shall include any production in the literary, scientific or artistic domain, whatever may be the mode or form of its reproduction, such as books, pamphlets, and other writings; dramatic or dramatico-musical works, choreographic works and entertainments in dumb show, the acting form of which is fixed in writing or otherwise; musical compositions with or without words; works of drawing, painting, architecture, sculpture, engraving and lithography; illustrations, geographical charts, plans, sketches and plastic works relative to geography, topography, architecture or science. Translations, adaptations, arrangements of music and other reproductions in an altered form of a literary or artistic work, as well as collections of different works, shall be protected as original works without prejudice to the rights of the author of original works."

LNTS, Vol. 1, pp. 221–222.

LITERARY AND ARTISTIC WORKS PROTECTION, BERNE CONVENTION, 1886. International Convention signed on Sept. 9, 1886 in Berne, revised on Nov. 13, 1908 at Berlin, and on June 27, 1928 in Rome.

LNTS, Vol 123, p. 233.

LITERATURE. A subject of international research and co-operation. Organizations reg. with the UIA:

Association for Commonwealth Literature and Language Studies, f. 1965, Mysore. Publ.: *Bulletin.*
East African Literature Bureau, f. 1976, Nairobi.
International Association of Literary Critics, f. 1969, Paris. Consultative status with UNESCO. Publ.: *Bulletin.*
International Committee for the Diffusion of Arts and Literature through the Cinema, f. 1930, Rome. Publ.: *Cinéma éducatif et culturel.*
International Comparative Literature Association, f. 1954, Paris. Publ.: *Comparative History of Literature.*
International Federation of Modern Languages and Literature, f. 1928, Cambridge. Publ.: *Répertoire chronologique des literatures modernes.*
International Institute for Children's Literature and Reading Research, f. 1965, Vienna. Consultative status with UNESCO. Publ.: *Bookbird* (quarterly).
International Institute of Iberoamerican Literature, f. 1938, Mexico, DF. Publ.: *Revista Iberoamericana.*
International Literary and Artistic Association, f. 1878, Paris. Consultative status with UNESCO, ECOSOC, Council of Europe. Publ.: *Bulletin.*
International Union for the Protection of Literary and Artistic Works, f. 1886, Geneva. Publ.: *Le Droit d'Auteur.*
▷ Copyright ▷ Intellectual property.

Yearbook of International Organizations.

LITHOGRAPHY. A subject of international co-operation. Organization reg. with the UIA:

The International Federation of Lithographers, Lithographic Printers and Similar Professions. f. 1896, Paris.

W. WEBER, *History of Lithography*, London, 1966.

LITHUANIA. Lietuvos Tarybu Socialistine Respublika. Lithuanian Soviet Socialist Republic. Federative republic of the USSR on the Baltic Sea, bounded by Byelorussia, Poland and the Kaliningrad area of the RSFSR. Area: 65,200 sq. km. Pop. 1983 est. 3,504,000 (1970 census 3,129,000, of whom 80.1% Lithuanians, 8.6% Russians, 7.7% Poles, 1.5% Byelorussians, 0.8% Ukrainians, and 0.3% others). Capital: Vilna with 525,000 inhabitants 1983. Official languages: Lithuanian and Russian. Currency: rouble of the USSR. National Day: Oct. 7, Socialist Revolution Anniversary, 1917.
International relations: in union with Poland 1569 until the partitions of Poland (1772, 1793, 1795), then part of the Russian Empire until 1914. Occupied by German troops 1914–18. Soviet power proclaimed on Dec. 8, 1918 and on Feb. 20, 1919 the Socialist Republic of Lithuania and Byelorussia, called *Litbiel*. In conflict with Poland 1919–21 (▷ Vilna). Independent republic 1919–39. Member of the League of Nations 1920–39. Incorporated into the USSR on Aug. 3, 1940. Occupied by German troops 1941–44. On June 15–22, 1941 over 30,000 Lithuanians were deported to Siberia. In the years of Nazi occupation about 170,000 of Lithuania's 200,000 Jews were murdered. In July 1944 after the Red Army re-entered Lithuania some 60,000 Lithuanian refugees reached Western Europe. In August–September 1945 60,000 Lithuanians were deported to Siberia, and in February 1946–40,000, in May 1948–70,000 and in March–August 1949–80,000.
The Soviet annexation of Lithuania was not recognized by the following countries: Australia, Belgium, Canada, Denmark, Finland, France, the FRG, Greece, the Holy See, Ireland, Italy, Luxembourg, Malta, the Netherlands, Norway, Portugal, Spain, Switzerland, Turkey, the UK, Yugoslavia and the USA, which continues to recognize the Lithuanian Chargé d'Affaires in Washington DC. About 1 million Lithuanians live in 16 countries: 800,000–USA, 50,000–Brazil, 40,000–Canada, 40,000–Argentina, 11,000–Great Britain, 10,000–Australia. A free general election on Feb. 24, 1990 gave the majority to the Sajudis national movement. Secession of the republic from the Soviet Union by the end of 1990 is not unlikely.

"Documents concerning the Dispute between Poland and Lithuania", *League of Nations Official Journal*, Special suppl. No. 4, Dec., 1929; *Recueil des traités conclus par Lituanie avec Pays Étrangers (1919–1929)*, Kaunas, 1929; *Documents diplomatiques: Relations Polono–Lituaniens*, Varsovie, 1929; J. MAKOWSKI, *Kwestia litewska, Studium Prawne*, Warszawa, 1929; *Questions raised by the Council in connection with Freedom and Communications and Transit when considering the Relations between Poland and Lithuania*, League of Nations, Geneva, 1930; X. GORZU-CHOWSKI, *Les rapports politiques de la Pologne et de la Lituanie*, Paris, 1930; L. NATKEVICIUS, *Aspect politique et juridique du différend polono–lithuanien*, Paris, 1930; H. CHAMBROS, *La Lithuanie moderne*, Paris, 1933; *Lietuvos TSR istoriyos saltinias*, 4 Vols., Vilnius, 1961; S. VARDYSED, *Lithuania under the Soviets. Portrait of a Nation 1940–45*, New York, 1965; C.R. JURGELA, *History of the Lithuanian Nations*, New York, 1968; F. KANTANTAS, *A Lithuanian Bibliography*, University of Alberta Press, 1975; P.P. GRISKOVICIUS, *Land on the Nemnas*, Moscow, 1977; S. SUZIEDLIS ed., *Encyclopedia Lithuanica*, Boston, 1970–78; *The Europa Year Book 1984. A World Survey*, Vol. I, pp. 925–926, London, 1984; E. GIERAT, *A Polish Vademecum. A Handbook on Poles and Other Soviet Dominated European Nations in the Free World*, Bethleem, Ct., USA, 1988, p. 15.

LITHUANIA–SOVIET RUSSIA PEACE TREATY, 1920. The Peace Treaty between the Republic of Lithuania and the Russian SFSR signed on July 12, 1920 in Moscow, with Protocol. Art. 5 read as follows:

"In the event of international recognition of the permanent neutrality of Lithuania, Russia on its part undertakes to conform to such neutrality and to participate in the guarantees for the maintenance of the same."

LNTS, Vol. 3, No. 94, pp. 126–127.

LITTLE ARKANSAS TREATY, 1865. A peace treaty between USA and the Cheyenne and Arapaho tribes of Indians, signed in the camp on the Little Arkansas River, in the State of Kansas, Oct. 14, 1865.

Major Peace Treaties of Modern History, New York, 1967, pp. 791–801.

LITTLE BAELT OR LITTLE BELT. ▷ Danish Straits.

LITTLE CAYMAN. ▷ Cayman Islands.

LITTLE ENTENTE. ▷ Entente, Little.

LITURGY. A subject of international scientific studies. Organization reg. with the UIA:

Societas Liturgica. International Society for Liturgical Study and Renewal, f. 1967, Trier. Publ.: *Societas Liturgica Documents.*

Yearbook of International Organizations.

LITVINOV DOCTRINE OF INDIVISIBLE PEACE, 1936. A principle formulated by the USSR delegate M. Litvinov, at the XVI Session of the Assembly of the League of Nations on July 1, 1936 to the effect that "world peace is indivisible".

The League from year to year, Geneva, 1936.

LITVINOV PROTOCOL, 1929. The agreement between the USSR and its neighbours, also known as the Moscow Protocol, regarding immediate entry into force of the ▷ Briand–Kellog Pact, signed by the USSR on Feb. 9, 1929 with Estonia, Latvia, Poland, Romania; and on Feb. 28, 1929 with Turkey; on Apr. 4, 1929 with Persia; and on Apr. 5, 1929 with Lithuania. The main points of the Protocol were as follows:

"The Government of the ... and the Central Executive Committee of the Union of Socialist Soviet Republics, Animated by the desire to contribute to the maintenance of the peace existing between their countries and to this end to put forthwith into force between the peoples of these countries, the treaty of renunciation of war as an instrument of national policy, signed at Paris, on August 27, 1928.
Have decided to realize these intentions through the effect of the present protocol:
Art. 1. The treaty of renunciation of war was an instrument of national policy, signed at Paris on August 27, 1928, a copy of which is attached to the present protocol as an integral part thereof, shall take effect between the Contracting Parties after the ratification of the said Treaty of Paris of 1928 by the competent legislative organisms of the respective Contracting States.
Art. 5. The present protocol is open to adhesion by the governments of all countries."

International Conciliation, No. 243, New York, Oct., 1928; A.N. MANDELSTEIN, *L'interprétation du pacte Briand–Kellog par les gouvernements et les parlaments des états signataires*, Paris, 1929.

LIVE AID. ▷ Hunger.

LIVESTOCK. A subject of FAO studies on various aspects of animal production in different regions of the world.

Organizations reg. with the UIA:

International Livestock Centre for Africa, f. 1974, Addis Ababa. Publ.; ILCA Bulletin.
World Association for Animal Production, f. 1965, Rome. Publ.: News Items.

The Europa Yearbook 1988. A World Survey, Vol. I, London, 1988.

LLOYD'S, CORPORATION OF LLOYD'S. The Lloyd's Register of Shipping, an English amalgamated insurance classification association of international scope. The first printing of Lloyd's Shipping List by Edward Lloyd, owner of a well-known London coffee house, took place in 1696. In 1760 the firm began the classification of ships. In 1796 Lloyd's introduced the insurance policy for sea-going vessels and goods transported by sea, recognized up until today as an authoritative model in international insurance transactions, though modernized by the so-called London insurance clauses. After the merger with a competitive company, in 1834, it took the name Lloyd's Register of British and Foreign Shipping; up to the end of the 19th century it handled solely the insurance of sea transport and the registration of the quality of ships, but it now provides all kinds of insurance, except life and fire.

V. DOVER, *A Handbook of Marine Insurance,* London, 1975, *Lloyd's Calendar,* annually.

LNTS. League of Nations Treaty Series. A publication of the LN from 1920 to 1946 in Geneva. ▷ Registration and Publication of International Agreements.

LOAD LINE. The limit of loading merchant ships in international traffic fixed for the purpose of ensuring safety of the crew and cargo at sea. A subject of the International Convention on Load Line signed in London, Apr. 5, 1966, specifying uniform rules of setting load lines and introducing the principle that the ship to which this convention applies may not leave harbor until it is examined, marked and provided with the international Plimsoll Line or a clearance exempting from it in cases foreseen by the Convention. The first Load Lines International Convention with Final Protocol and Annexes, was signed in London, July 5, 1930, by the Governments of Australia, Belgium, Canada, Chile, Cuba, Czechoslovakia, Denmark, Finland, France, Germany, Great Britain, Greece, India, Iceland, Ireland, Italy, Japan, Latvia, the Netherlands, Mexico, New Zealand, Norway, Paraguay, Peru, Poland, Portugal, Spain, Sweden, the USSR and USA. Exchange of Notes relating thereto, London 1933. After World War II on April 5, 1966 in London the IMCO International Convention on Load Lines was signed; came into force July 21, 1968, establishing:

"uniform principles and rules with respect to the limits to which ships on international voyages may be loaded having regard to the need for safeguarding life and property at sea."
The Convention decided (art. 16 p. 1 and 2) that "an International Load Line Certificate (1966) shall be issued to every ship which has been surveyed and marked in accordance with the present convention" (p. 1) and "an International Load Line Exemption Certificate shall be issued to any ship, to which an exemption has been granted ..." (p. 2).

LNTS, Vol. 135, pp. 135 and 301; *UNTS,* Vol. 340, pp. 134 and 146.

LOANS, INTERNATIONAL. The loans made by states or financial institutions to other states for reconstruction after wars or natural calamities, expansion of economic exchange or currency stabilization, in the form of obligations offered on foreign capital markets. The international loans with the consent of the loaning party or the owner of the obligation may be subject to conversion, i.e. changes in terms of interest or time of repayment; moreover, they may be subject to consolidation, that is including all of the international loans of one state in one obligation. In accordance with their international statute they supplement international credits furnished for investments, services or as aid in foreign trade transactions. There are three financial corporations whose task is to protect the interests of private capital located abroad in the form of international loans: The British Corporation of Foreign Bondholders; L'association nationale des porteurs francais de valeurs mobilières; and the Foreign Bondholders Protective Council Inc. New York.

V.P. KOMISSAROV, A.N. POPOV, *Mezhdunarodne valutne i kreditne otnoshenia,* Moskva, 1965; J. MARCHAL, *Monnaie et credit,* Paris, 1967; S. RĄCZKOWSKI, *Międzynarodowe stosunki finansowe* (International Financial Relations), Warsaw, 1972; M.J. TREBILCOCK et al., *Debtor and Creditor: Cases, Notes and Materials,* Toronto, 1979.

LOBBY. ▷ Pressure groups.

LOBSTER. *Homarus vulgaris* and *Nephrops norwegius.* Crustaceans, subject of international protection, among others by the Scandinavian Treaty on Fishing, 1952.

LOBSTER WAR. The ironic name for the Brazilian–French international dispute over lobsters in the years 1966–70, when Brazil refused to allow French fishing vessels to catch lobsters in the South Atlantic waters near Brazil, arguing that "lobsters walk along the bottom of the continental shelf" belonging to Brazil, whereas France asserted that "lobsters swim in the ocean". The dispute was resolved unilaterally by Brazil through the extension of its territorial waters to a 200-mile zone, which took in the disputed lobster beds. The Brazilian lobster catch in 1970 exceeded 20 million dollars in value.

LOCARNO. A city in southern Switzerland, on Lake Maggiore, seat of Locarno Conference in 1925, at which the Locarno Agreements were signed.

LOCARNO CONFERENCE AND TREATY, 1925. A Conference in Locarno convened on the initiative of France as the first peaceful meeting since World War I of the neighbours of Germany with the German Reich, from Oct. 5 to 16, 1925. The Conference was attended by Belgium, Czechoslovakia, France, Great Britain, Italy, Germany and Poland. The text of the Final Protocol of the Locarno Conference is as follows:

"The representatives of the German, Belgian, British, French, Italian, Polish and Czechoslovak Governments, who have met at Locarno from the 5th to 16th October, 1925, in order to seek by common agreement means for preserving their respective nations from the scourge of war and for providing for the peaceful settlement of disputes of every nature which might eventually arise between them,
Have given their approval to the draft treaties and conventions which respectively affect them and which, framed in the course of the present conference, are mutually interdependent:
Treaty between Germany, Belgium, France, Great Britain and Italy
Arbitration Convention between Germany and Belgium,
Arbitration Convention between Germany and France,
Arbitration Treaty between Germany and Poland,
Arbitration Treaty between Germany and Czechoslovakia

These instruments, hereby initialled ne varietur, will bear today's date, the representatives of the interested parties agreeing to meet in London on the 1st December next, to proceed during the course of a single meeting to the formality of the signature of the instruments which affect them. The Minister for Foreign Affairs of France states that as a result of the draft arbitration treaties mentioned above, France, Poland and Czechoslovakia have also concluded at Locarno draft agreements in order reciprocally to assure to themselves the benefit of the said treaties. These agreements will be duly deposited at the League of Nations, but M. Briand holds copies forthwith at the disposal of the Powers represented here.
The Secretary of State for Foreign Affairs of Great Britain proposes that, in reply to certain requests for explanations concerning art. 16 of the Covenant of the League of Nations presented by the Chancellor and the Minister for Foreign Affairs of Germany, a letter of which the draft is similarly attached should be addressed to them at the same time as the formality of signature of the above-mentioned instruments takes place. This proposal is agreed to.
The representatives of the Governments represented here declare their firm conviction that the entry into force of these treaties and conventions will contribute greatly to bring about a morale relaxation of the tension between nations, that it will help powerfully towards the solution of many political or economic problems in accordance with the interests and sentiments of peoples, and that, in strengthening peace and security in Europe, it will hasten on effectively the disarmament provided for in art. 8 of the Covenant of the League of Nations. They undertake to give their sincere co-operation to the work relating to disarmament already undertaken by the League of Nations and to seek the realization thereof in a general agreement."
The major aim of the conference was to guarantee the borders of Germany's western neighbours and was reached under Treaty of Mutual Guarantee between Germany, Belgium, France, Great Britain and Italy on Oct. 16, 1925 at Locarno. The Locarno Treaty called also Rhine Pact because it related to Belgian and French borders with German Rhineland; the parties guaranteed territorial status quo ensuing from common boundaries of Belgium, France and Germany and inviolability of these boundaries as fixed by the Treaty of Versailles June 28, 1919 as well as to observe the provisions of arts 42 and 43 of the said Treaty relating to the Rhineland demilitarized zone (art. 1); arts 2–4 specified terms of peaceful settlement of disputes and self-defence in case of violation of provisions of art. 1. The Pact entered into force Sept. 30, 1926 and was denounced by Third Reich Mar. 7, 1936, in the moment of re-militarization of ▷ Rhineland.
The text of the Treaty is as follows:
"The President of the German Reich, His Majesty the King of the Belgians, the President of the French Republic, and His Majesty the King of the United Kingdom of Great Britain and Ireland and of the British Dominions beyond the Seas, Emperor of India, his Majesty the King of Italy;
Anxious to satisfy the desire for security and protection which animates the peoples upon whom fell the scourge of the war 1914–18;
Taking note of the abrogation of the treaties for the neutralisation of Belgium, and conscious of the necessity of ensuring peace in the area which has so frequently been the scene of European conflicts;
Animated also with the sincere desire of giving to all the signatory Powers concerned supplementary guarantees within the framework of the Covenant of the League of Nations and the treaties in force between them;
Have determined to conclude a treaty with these objects, and have appointed as their plenipotentiaries:
Who, having communicated their full powers, found in good and due form, have agreed as follows:
Art. 1. The high contracting parties collectively and severally guarantee, in the manner provided in the following articles, the maintenance of the territorial status quo resulting from the frontiers between Germany and Belgium and between Germany and France and the inviolability of the said frontiers as fixed by or in pursuance of the Treaty of Peace signed at Versailles on the 28th June, 1919, and also the observance of the stipulations of articles 42 and 43 of the said treaty concerning the demilitarized zone.

Art. 2. Germany and Belgium, and also Germany and France, mutually undertake that they will in no case attack or invade each other or resort to war against each other. This stipulation shall not, however, apply in the case of
(1) The exercise of the right of legitimate defence, that is to say, resistance to a violation of the undertaking contained in the previous paragraph or to a flagrant breach of articles 42 or 43 of the said Treaty of Versailles, if such breach constitutes an unprovoked act of aggression and by reason of the assembly of armed forces in the demilitarised zone immediate action is necessary.
(2) Action in pursuance of article 16 of the Covenant of the League of Nations.
(3) Action as the result of a decision taken by the Assembly or by the Council of the League of Nations or in pursuance of article 15, paragraph 7, of the Covenant of the League of Nations, provided that in this last event the action is directed against a state which was the first to attack.
Art. 3. In view of the undertakings entered into in article 2 of the present treaty, Germany and Belgium and Germany and France undertake to settle by peaceful means and in the manner laid down herein all questions of every kind which may arise between them and which it may not be possible to settle by the normal methods of diplomacy:
Any question with regard to which the parties are in conflict as to their respective rights shall be submitted to judicial decision, and the parties undertake to comply with such decision.
All other questions shall be submitted to a conciliation commission. If the proposals of this commission are not accepted by the two parties, the question shall be brought before the Council of the League of Nations, which will deal with it in accordance with article 15 of the Covenant of the League. The detailed arrangements for effecting such peaceful settlement are the subject of special agreements signed this day.
Art. 4. (1) If one of the high contracting parties alleges that a violation of article 2 of the present treaty or a breach of articles 42 or 43 of the Treaty of Versailles has been or is being committed, it shall bring the question at once before the Council of the League of Nations.
(2) As soon as the Council of the League of Nations is satisfied that such violation or breach has been committed, it will notify its finding without delay to the Powers signatory of the present treaty, who severally agree that in such case they will each of them come immediately to the assistance of the Power against whom the act complained of is directed.
(3) In case of a flagrant violation of article 2 of the present treaty or of a flagrant breach of articles 42 or 43 of the Treaty of Versailles by one of the high contracting parties, each of the other contracting parties hereby undertakes immediately to come to the help of the party against whom such a violation or breach has been directed as soon as the said Power has been able to satisfy itself that this violation constitutes an unprovoked act of aggression and that by reason either of the Assembly of armed forces in the demilitarized zone immediate action is necessary. Nevertheless, the Council of the League of Nations, which will be seized of the question in accordance with the first paragraph of this article, will issue its findings, and the high contracting parties undertake to act in accordance with the recommendations of the Council provided that they are concurred in by all the members other than the representatives of the parties which have engaged in hostilities.
Art. 5. The provisions of article 3 of the present treaty are placed under the guarantee of the high contracting parties as provided by the following stipulations:
If one of the Powers referred to in article 3 refuses to submit a dispute to a peaceful settlement or to comply with an arbitral or judicial decision and commits a violation of article 2 of the present treaty or a breach of articles 42 or 43 of the Treaty of Versailles, the provisions of article 4 shall apply.
Where one of the Powers referred to in article 3 without committing a violation of article 2 of the present treaty or a breach of articles 42 or 43 of the Treaty of Versailles, refuses to submit a dispute to peaceful settlement or to comply with an arbitral or judicial decision, the other party shall bring the matter before the Council of the League of Nations, and the Council shall propose what steps shall be taken; the high contracting parties shall comply with these proposals.
Art. 6. The provisions of the present treaty do not affect the rights and obligations of the high contracting parties under the Treaty of Versailles or under arrangements supplementary thereto, including the agreements signed in London on the 30th August, 1924.
Art. 7. The present treaty, which is designed to ensure the maintenance of peace, and is in conformity with the Covenant of the League of Nations, shall not be interpreted as restricting the duty of the League to take whatever action may be deemed wise and effectual to safeguard the peace of the world.
Art. 8. The present treaty shall be registered at the League of Nations in accordance with the Covenant of the League. It shall remain in force until the Council, acting on a request of one or other of the high contracting parties notified to the other signatory Powers three month in advance, and voting at least by a two-thirds' majority, decides that the League of Nations ensures sufficient protection to the high contracting parties; the treaty shall cease to have effect on the expiration of a period of one year from such decision.
Art. 9. The present treaty shall impose no obligation upon any of the British dominions, or upon India, unless the Government of such dominion, or of India, signifies its acceptance thereof.
Art. 10. The present treaty shall be ratified and the ratifications shall be deposited at Geneva in the archives of the League of Nations as soon as possible."
On Nov. 3, 1925 German Foreign Minister, Gustav Stresemann made a statement in the press that the absence in the Locarno Treaty of the international guarantee for the German–Polish frontier had been dictated by the necessity of its revision; earlier, on Mar. 25, 1925, Lloyd George, one of the architects of the Treaty of Versailles, spoke in the same vein at the House of Commons.

LNTS, Vol. 54, pp. 293–300; *International Conciliation*, No. 216, January, 1926; and No. 319, April, 1936.

LOCK AND FITTING INDUSTRIES. A subject of international co-operation. Organization reg. with the UIA:

Community of European Lock and Fitting industries, f. 1959, The Hague.

Yearbook of International Organizations.

LOCK OUT. An international term for a break of strike by new workers or dismissal and prevention of reemployment of striking workers.

LOCOMOTIVES. A subject of international co-operation. Organization reg. with the UIA:

European Builders of Internal Combustion Engines and Electric Locomotives, f. 1953, Paris, France.

Yearbook of International Organizations, 1986/87; The Europa Yearbook 1988. A World Survey, Vol. I, London, 1988.

LOCUST. An insect of the superfamily *Acridoidea* (grasshoppers), subject of international co-operation. In Aug. 1986 the FAO established an Emergency Center for Locust Operation ECLO, in Rome with $35 million from donor countries and multinational organizations.
The fight against locust and grasshopper infestation is organized by the ▷ OAU in co-operation with the ▷ FAO. The GA Res. 43/203 of Dec. 20, 1988:

"Aware that, in the course of the current infestation, swarms of locusts and grasshoppers have affected or may invade the great majority of African countries and other countries in Asia, Latin America, the Caribbean and Europe, and concerned at the disastrous consequences that may result for food production and agriculture in the world...
Aware that current campaigns for locust and grasshopper control have so far been unable to put an end to the infestation, in particular because of the limited financial resources of the affected countries and convinced that the fight against the plague, which, by virtue of its recurrent nature and geographical extent, is international in scope, requires increased and co-ordinated mobilization of appropriate human, scientific, technical material and financial resources;
Expresses its deep concern at the worsening locust and grasshopper infestations, especially in Africa, which may adversely affect food production and result in renewed famine, and reaffirms the need to accord the highest priority to locust and grasshopper control and eradication;
Calls upon the international scientific community to develop co-ordinated research programmes to identify new and more effective methods of control, with a view to establishing a reliable forecasting system that would permit a better understanding of the relationship between climatic phenomena and the bio-ecology of the desert locust;
Urges the multilateral financial and development institutions, including the United Nations Development Programme, to give the high priority, within the framework of their activities, to the fight against locust and grasshopper infestation and to grant financial and technical assistance to the affected countries, particularly those which have issued appeals for international assistance or have declared a state of emergency".
Organizations reg. with the UIA:

Desert Locust Control Organization for Eastern Africa, f. 1962, Addis Ababa. Agreement with FAO. Intergovernmental institution of Ethiopia, France, Kenya, Somalia, Tanzania and Uganda. Publ.: *Desert Locust Situation Reports* (monthly).
International African Migratory Locust Organization, f. 1951, Bamako, Mali. Intergovernmental institution of Cameroon, Central African Rep., Chad, Congo, Gambia, Ghana, Ivory Coast, Mali, Mauritania, Niger, Nigeria, Senegal, Sierra Leone, Togo, Uganda, Upper Volta, Zaïre. Publ.: *Locusta Migratoria* (monthly).
International Red Locust Control Organization for Southern Africa, f. 1970, Mbala, Zambia. Intergovernmental institution of Botswana, Burundi, Kenya, Lesotho, Malawi, Swaziland, Rwanda, Tanzania, Uganda, Zaïre, Zambia. Publ.: *Red Locust* (*Locustana pardalina*) Annual Report.
Joint Anti-Locust and Anti-Avarian Organization, f. 1965, Dakar. Intergovernmental institution of Benin, Cameroon, Chad, Ivory Coast, Mali, Mauritania, Niger, Senegal, Upper Volta. Publ.: *Bulletin de signalisation mensuel pour le criquet pelerin.*

P.B. UVAROU, *Locust Research and Control 1925–50*, London, 1951; *Desert Locust Project*, FAO Rome, 1968; S. BARON, *The Desert Locust*, London, 1971; *Yearbook of International Organizations*; UN *Resolutions and Decisions adopted by the General Assembly during the First Part of its Forty-Third Session, From 20 September to 20 December 1988*, New York, 1989, pp. 305–307.

LODGE ANTI-JAPANESE DOCTRINE, 1924. A principle of selective immigration; anti-Japanese regulations passed 1924 by the US Congress on the initiative of Senator Henry Cabot Lodge (1850–1924) for the purpose of protecting the then thinly-settled west coast of the North American continent against the mass settlement by Japanese organized by the government of Japan. The doctrine contained in the law does not mention the Japanese; it stated that on the coasts of America all commercial, settlement rights, etc. belong to the American states and their citizens, corporations and private companies.

Selective Immigration Act of 1924, House Report, No. 350, 68 Congress, I Session, Washington, DC, 1924.

LODGE RESERVATIONS TO THE VERSAILLES TREATY, 1919. The reservations to the Treaty of Versailles with the Covenant of the League of Nations, presented in 14 points to the Senate by the Chairman of the Senate Foreign Relations Committee, Senator Henry Cabot Lodge of Massachusetts. The reservations influenced the second voting for the ratification of the Treaty on Mar. 19, 1920. 49 votes were in favor and 35 against, 7 votes less than the two-thirds required.
The text is as follows:

"Resolved (two-thirds of the Senators present concurring therein). That the Senate advise and consent to the

ratification of the treaty of peace with Germany concluded at Versailles on the 28th day of June, 1919, subject to the following reservations and understandings, which are hereby made a part and condition of this resolution of ratification, which ratification is not to take effect or bind the United States until the said reservations and understandings adopted by the Senate have been accepted by an exchange of notes as a part and a condition of this resolution of ratification by at least three of the four principal allied and associated powers, to wit, Great Britain, France, Italy, and Japan:
(1) The United States so understands and construes article 1 that in case of notice of withdrawal from the League of Nations, as provided in said article, the United States shall be the sole judge as to whether all its international obligations and all its obligations under the said covenant have been fulfilled, and notice of withdrawal by the United States may be given by a concurrent resolution of the Congress of the United States.
(2) The United States assumes no obligation to preserve the territorial integrity or political independence of any other country or to interfere in controversies between nations, whether members of the League or not, under the provisions of art. 10, or to employ the military or naval forces of the United States under any article of the treaty for any purpose, unless in any particular case the Congress, which, under the Constitution, has the sole power to declare war or authorize the employment of the military or naval forces of the United States, shall by act or joint resolution so provide.
(3) No mandate shall be accepted by the United States under art. 22, part I, or any other provision of the treaty of peace with Germany, except by action of the Congress of the United States.
(4) The United States reserves to itself exclusively the right to decide what questions are within its domestic jurisdiction and declares that all domestic and political questions relating wholly or in part to its internal affairs, including immigration, labor, coastwise traffic, the tariff, commerce, the suppression of traffic in women and children, and in opium and other dangerous drugs, and all other domestic questions, are solely within the jurisdiction of the United States and are not under this treaty to be submitted in any way either to arbitration or to the consideration of the Council or of the Assembly of the League of Nations, or any agency thereof, or to the decision or recommendation of any other power.
(5) The United States will not submit to arbitration or to inquiry by the Assembly or by the Council of the League of Nations, provided for in said treaty of peace, any questions which in the judgment of the United States depend upon or relate to its long-established policy, commonly known as the Monroe doctrine, the said doctrine is to be interpreted by the United States alone and is hereby declared to be wholly outside the jurisdiction of said League of Nations and entirely unaffected by any provision contained in the said treaty of peace with Germany.
(6) The United States withholds its assent to articles 156, 157, and 158, and reserves full liberty of action with respect to any controversy which may arise under said articles between the Republic of China and the Empire of Japan.
(7) The Congress of the United States will provide by law for the appointment of the representatives of the United States in the Assembly and the Council of the League of Nations, and may in its discretion provide for the participation of the United States in any commission, committee, tribunal, court, council, or conference, or in the selection of any members thereof and for the appointment of members of said commissions, committees, tribunals, courts, councils, or conferences or any other representatives under the treaty of peace, or in carrying out its provisions, and until such participation and appointment have been so provided for and the powers and duties of such representatives have been defined by law, no person shall represent the United States under either said League of Nations or the treaty of peace with Germany or be authorized to perform any act for or on behalf of the United States thereunder, and no citizen of the United States shall be selected or appointed as a member of said commissions, committees, tribunals, courts, councils, or conferences except with the approval of the Senate of the United States.
(8) The United States understands that the reparation commission will regulate or interfere with exports from the United States to Germany, or from Germany to the United States, only when the United States by act or joint resolution of Congress approves such regulation or interference.
(9) The United States shall not be obligated to contribute to any expenses of the League of Nations, or of the secretariat, or of any commission, or committee, or conference, or other agency organized under the League of Nations or under the treaty of for the purpose of carrying out the treaty provisions, unless and until an appropriation of funds available for such expenses shall have been made by the Congress of the United States.
(10) If the United States shall at any time adopt any plan for the limitation of armaments proposed by the Council of the League of Nations under the provisions of art. 8, it reserves the right to increase such armaments without the consent of the council whenever the United States is threatened with invasion or engaged in war.
(11) The United States reserves the right to permit, in its discretion, the nationals of a covenant-breaking state, as defined in art. 16 of the Covenant of the League of Nations, residing within he United States or in countries other than that violating said article 16, to continue their commercial, financial, and personal relations with the nationals of the United States.
(12) Noting in arts 296, 297, or in any of the annexes thereto or in any other article, section, or annex of the treaty of peace with Germany shall, as against citizens of the United States, be taken to mean any confirmation, ratification, or approval of any act otherwise illegal or in contravention of the rights of citizens of the United States.
(13) The United States withholds its assent to Part XIII (arts. 387 to 427, inclusive) unless Congress by act or joint resolution shall hereafter make provision for representation in the organization established by said Part XIII, and in such event the participation of the United States will be governed and conditioned by the provisions of such act or joint resolution.
(14) The United States assumes no obligation to be bound by any election, decision, report, or finding of the Council or Assembly in which any member of the League and its self-governing dominions, colonies, or parts of empire, in the aggregate have cast more than one vote, and assumes no obligation to be bound by any decision, report, or finding of the Council or Assembly arising out of any dispute between the United States and any member of the League if such member, or any self-governing dominion, colony, empire, or part of empire united with it politically has voted."

Congressional Record (Senate), 66th Congress, 1st session, November 19, 1919, p. 8773 and March 19, 1920, p. 4599.

LOG BOOKS. An international term for the records kept on board vessels and aircraft, obligatory in international traffic, such as journey log, signal log, engine log, etc. Specific requirements are provided in maritime and aviation conventions on civil international traffic of ships and aircraft.

LOGISTICS. A military term used for the first time in the work of the French strategist, A.H. Jomini, entitled Precis de l'art de la guerre, 1836, then in the USA 1917; introduced in the USA, 1944, for the administrative aspect of the art of war dealing with the organization of the entire home front; the concept was accepted and developed by strategic doctrines as a term for three sets of military tasks: (1) researching the potential for the possibility of waging war by the state and planning tasks during wartime; (2) organization of billeting, stockpiling, supplies, transport, investments, telecommunications technology, etc. of the armed forces during military operations; (3) theoretical studies of the above areas supplementing strategic and tactical analyses.

G.C. THORPE, *Pure Logistics*, New York, 1917; A. HUSTON, *The Sinews of War: Army Logistics 1775–1953*, London, 1966; D. ROBERTSON, *Guide to Modern Defense and Strategy*, Detroit, 1988.

LOGOPEDICS AND PHONIATRICS. The subjects of international co-operation. Organization reg. with the UIA:

International Association of Logopedic and Phoniatrics, f. 1924, Vienna. Consultative status with UNESCO, WHO, UNICEF and ECOSOC. Publ.: *Folia Phoniatrica* (bi-monthly).

LOK SABHA. The Parliament of India.

LOMBARD STREET. A street in London, where in the 19th century main banks were located, a synonym of British financial circles, like the American Wall Street. At present the seat of headquarters of Barclays Bank and Lloyds Bank.

LOMÉ. The capital of Togo since 1897, population 1983 census: 366,467. Seat of the West African Development Bank of Benin, Côte d'Ivoire, Niger, Senegal, Togo and Upper Volta (now Burkina Faso). ▷ Lomé Conventions, 1975, 1980, 1985.

Yearbook of International Organizations.

LOMÉ CONVENTIONS, 1975, 1980 AND 1985. A common name of association-conventions between the European Economic Council and ▷ ACP countries, called also Treaty of Lomé, one of the most relevant agreements for developing countries, related to agricultural products (duty-free entry except for: rice, maize, beef, fresh oranges with reduced duties; special arrangements for beef, rum, sugar and bananas) and to industrial products (duty-free entry, no quota). The Lomé Conventions replaced the ▷ Yaoundé Convention, 1965 and 1970, and the ▷ Arusha Convention, 1968. The first Lomé Convention was signed on Feb. 28, 1975 in Lomé, the second Nov. 20, 1979 in Brussels the third Dec. 8, 1984 in Lomé. The First Convention was valid for five years (1975–80). It was managed by Ministerial and Ambassadorial Councils, with equal representation of the 9 EEC and the 49 ACP countries. Also, on the basis of parity, there was a Consultative Assembly of Parliamentarians from both sides. An Industrial Co-operation Committee and an Industrial Development Centre promote the exchange of industrial know-how. The Convention has established new terms of trade:

(a) All ACP manufactured exports and 96% by value of ACP agricultural exports enter the European Community free of import duties and quotas (the remaining 4% get preferential treatment).
(b) The nine EEC members receive from the 49 APC countries not "reverse preferences" but the most-favoured-nation treatment.
(2) The Convention has established new instruments of financial stabilization:
(a) export earnings stabilization plan STABEX, to protect the ACP countries against price and production level fluctuations of certain agriculture and raw materials items (bananas, cocoa, coconuts, coffee, cotton, hides and skins, iron ore kernels, palm nut, tea, timber products and raw sisal),
(b) a special Export-Stabilization Fund for compensation when the receipts from exports drop by a certain percentage. The poorest countries do not reimburse the Fund.
(3) The Convention has established a large credit system for regional programs, for the development of small and medium enterprises and special measures for the poorest countries.
(4) The Convention guaranteed purchase and supply of fixed quantities of sugar (12% of ACP agriculture exports or maximum total of 1,400,000 tons). The price was related to the price guaranteed to the European Community's own sugar-producer.

The main points of the Second Lomé Convention 1980 are as follows:

"Title I. Trade co-operation. Art. 1. In the field of trade co-operation, the object of this Convention is to promote trade between the ACP States and the Community, taking account of their respective levels of development, and also between the ACP States themselves.

In the pursuit of this objective, particular regard will be had to the need to secure effective additional benefits for the trade of the ACP States with the Community, in order to accelerate the growth of their trade and in particular of the flow of their exports to the Community and in order to improve the conditions of access for their products to the market of the Community, so as to ensure a better balance in the trade of the Contracting Parties.

Chapter 1. Trade arrangements. Art. 2.1. Products originating in the ACP States shall be imported into the Community free of customs duties and charges having equivalent effect.

Art. 3.1. The Community shall not apply to imports of products originating in the ACP States any quantitative restrictions or measures having equivalent effect.

Art. 5.1. The provisions of article 3 shall not preclude prohibitions or restrictions on imports, exports or goods in transit justified on grounds of public morality, public policy or public security; the protection of health and life of humans, animals and plants; the protection of national treasures possessing artistic, historic or archaeological value or the protection of industrial and commercial property.

Art. 6. The treatment applied to imports of products originating in the ACP States may not be more favourable than that applied to trade among the Member States.

Art. 7. Where new measures or measures stipulated in programmes adopted by the Community for the approximation of laws and regulations in order to facilitate the movement of goods are likely to affect the interests of one or more ACP States the Community shall, prior to adopting such measures, inform the ACP States thereof through the Council of Ministers.

In order to enable the Community to take into consideration the interests of the ACP States concerned, consultations shall be held at the request of the latter with a view to reaching a satisfactory solution.

Art. 8.(1) Where existing rules or regulations of the Community adopted in order to facilitate the movement of goods affect the interests of one or more ACP States or where these interests are affected by the interpretation, application or administration of such rules or regulations, consultations shall be held at the request of the ACP States concerned with a view to reaching a satisfactory solution.

(2) With a view to finding a satisfactory solution, the ACP States may also bring up within the Council of Ministers any other problems relating to the movement of goods which might result from measures taken or envisaged by the Member States.

(3) The competent institutions of the Community shall to the greatest possible extent inform the Council of Ministers of such measures.

Art. 9.(1) In view of their present development needs, the ACP States shall not be required for the duration of this Convention to assume in respect of imports or products originating in the Community, obligations corresponding to the commitments entered into by the Community in respect of imports of the products originating in the ACP States, under this Chapter.

(2)(a) In their trade with the Community, the ACP States shall not discriminate among the Member States, and shall grant to the Community treatment no less favourable than the most-favoured-nation treatment.

(b) The most-favoured-nation treatment referred to in sub-paragraph (a) shall not apply in respect of trade or economic relations between ACP States or between one or more ACP States and other developing countries.

Art. 10. Unless it has already done so under the terms of the ACP-EEC Lomé Convention, each Contracting Party shall communicate its customs tariff to the Council of Ministers within a period of three months following the entry into force of this Convention. Each Contracting Party shall also communicate any subsequent amendments to its tariff as and when they come into force.

Chapter 3. Trade Promotion. Art. 20. With a view to attaining the objectives set in article 1, the Contracting Parties shall implement trade promotion measures from the production stage to the final stage of distribution. The object is to ensure that the ACP States derive maximum benefit from the provisions of this Convention in the fields of trade, agricultural and industrial co-operation and can participate under the most favourable conditions in the Community, domestic, regional and international markets by diversifying the range and increasing the value and volume of ACP exports.

Art. 21. The trade promotion measures provided for in article 20 shall include the provision of technical and financial assistance for achieving the following objectives:

(a) the establishment and/or improvement of the structure of organizations, centres or firms involved in the development of the trade of ACP States and the assessment of their staffing requirements, financial management and working methods.

(b) basic training, management training, and vocational training of technicians in fields related to the development and promotion of national and international trade;

(c) product policy inclusive of research, processing, quality guarantee and control, packaging and presentation;

(d) development of supportive infrastructure, including transport and storage facilities, in order to facilitate the flow of exports from ACP States;

(e) advertising;

(f) establishing promoting and improving co-operation among economic operators in ACP States and between such operators and those in the Member States of the Community and in third countries and introducing appropriate measures to promote such co-operation;

(g) carrying out and making use of market research and marketing studies;

(h) collecting, analysing and disseminating quantitative and quantitative trade information and facilitating free access to existing or future information systems or bodies in the Community and in the ACP States;

(i) participation by the ACP States in fairs, exhibitions and, in particular, specialized international shows, the list of which shall be drawn up in consultation with the ACP States, and the organization of trade events.

(j) special assistance to small- and medium-sized undertakings for product identification and development, market outlets and joint marketing ventures;

(k) the participation of the least developed ACP States in the various trade promotion activities envisaged shall be encouraged by special provisions, inter alia the payment of travel expenses of personnel and costs of transporting articles and goods that are to be exhibited, on the occasion of their participation in fairs and exhibitions.

Title II. Export earnings from commodities. Chapter 1. Stabilization of export earnings. Art. 23.(1) With the aim of remedying the harmful effects of the instability of export earnings and to help the ACP States overcome one of the main obstacles to the stability, profitability and sustained growth of their economies, to support their development efforts and to enable them in this way to ensure economic and social progress for their peoples by helping to safe-guard their purchasing power, a system shall be operated to guarantee the stabilization of earnings derived from the ACP States' exports to the Community of products on which their economies are dependent and which are affected by fluctuations in price or quantity or both these factors.

(2) In order to attain these objectives, transfers must be devoted to maintaining financial flows in the sector in question or, for the purpose of promoting diversification, directed towards other appropriate sectors and used for economic and social development.

Art. 24. Export earnings to which the stabilization system applies shall be those accruing from the export by each ACP State to the Community of each of the products on the following list, in the drawing up of which account has been taken of factors such as employment, deterioration of the terms of trade between the Community and the ACP State concerned and the level of development of that ACP State.

Art. 25. The following products shall be covered:

1. Groundnuts, shelled or not
2. Groundnut oil
3. Cocoa beans
4. Cocoa paste
5. Cocoa butter
6. Raw or roasted coffee
7. Extracts, essences or concentrates of coffee
8. Cotton, not carded or combed
9. Cotton linters
10. Coconuts
11. Copra
12. Coconut oil
13. Palm oil
14. Palm nut and kernel oil
15. Palm nuts and kernels
16. Raw hides and skins
17. Bovine cattle leather
18. Sheep and lamb skin leather
19. Goat and kid skin leather
20. Wood in the rough
21. Wood roughly squared or half-squared, but not further manufactured
22. Wood sawn lengthwise, but not further prepared
23. Fresh bananas
24. Tea
25. Raw sisal
26. Vanilla
27. Cloves – whole fruit, cloves and stems
28. Sheep's or lambs' wool, not carded or combed
29. Fine animal hair of Angora goats – mohair
30. Gum arabic
31. Pyrethrum – flowers, leaves, stems, peel and roots; saps and extracts from pyrethrum
32. Essential oils, not terpeneless, of cloves, of niaouli and of ylang-ylang
33. Sesame seed
34. Cashew nuts and kernels
35. Pepper
36. Shrimps and prawns
37. Squid
38. Cotton seeds
39. Oil-cake
40. Rubber
41. Peas
42. Beans
43. Lentils
44. Iron ore (ores, concentrates, and roasted iron pyrites).

Title V. Industrial co-operation. Art. 65. The Community and the ACP States, acknowledging the pressing need to promote the industrial development of the ACP States, agree to take all measures necessary to bring about effective industrial co-operation.

Art. 66. Industrial co-operation between the Community and the ACP States shall have the following objectives:

(a) to promote new relations of dynamic complementarity in the industrial field between the Community and the ACP States, notably by establishing new industrial and trade links between the industries of the Community and those of the ACP States;

(b) to promote development and diversification of all types of industry in the ACP States and to foster in this respect co-operation at both regional and interregional levels;

(c) to promote the establishment of integral industries capable of creating links between various industrial sectors in the ACP States in order to provide those States with the basis on which the build-up of their technology will principally rely;

(d) to encourage the complementarity between industry and other sectors of the economy, in particular agriculture, by developing agro-allied industries in order to slow down the rural exodus, stimulate food and other production activities as well as to promote the establishment of further natural resource-based industries;

(e) to facilitate the transfer of technology and to promote the adaptation of such technology to the specific conditions and needs of the ACP States, and to help the ACP States to identify, evaluate and select technologies required for their development and to develop their efforts to increase their capacity in applied research for adaptation of technology, and for training in industrial skills at all levels;

(f) to foster the participation of nationals of ACP States in all the types of industry that are being developed in their countries;

(g) to contribute as far as possible to the creation of jobs for nationals of the ACP States, to the supply of national and external markets and to procurement of foreign exchange earnings for those States;

(h) to facilitate the overall industrial development of the ACP States, in particular their production of manufactured goods, by taking due account of their specific needs in the formulation of policies designed to

adjust the industrial structures of the Community to changes occurring at the world level;
(i) to encourage the establishment in the ACP States of joint ACP-EEC industrial ventures;
(j) to encourage and promote the establishment and reinforcement of industrial, business and trade associations in the ACP States which would contribute to the full utilization of the internal resources of those States with a view to developing their national industries;
(k) to assist in the establishment and operation of institutions in ACP States for the provision of regulatory and advisory services to industry;
(l) to strengthen the existing financial institutions and bring about conditions favourable to capital borrowing for the stimulation of the growth and development of industries in ACP States, including the promotion of the basic rural small- and medium-scale and labour-intensive industries.
Art. 67. In order to attain the objectives set out in article 66 the Community shall help to carry out, by all the means provided for in the Convention, programmes, projects and schemes submitted to it on the initiative or with the agreement of the ACP States in the fields of industrial training, small- and medium-sized industries, local processing of ACP raw materials, technology co-operation, industrial infrastructures, trade promotion, energy co-operation and industrial information and promotion.
Title IV. Agricultural co-operation. Art. 83. 1. The basic objective of agricultural co-operation between the Community and the ACP States must be to assist the latter in their efforts to resolve problems relating to rural development and the improvement and expansion of agricultural production for domestic consumption and export and problems they may encounter with regard to security of food supplies for their populations.
(2) Accordingly, co-operation in rural development shall contribute in particular, within the general objectives of financial and technical co-operation:
(a) to a higher standard of living for the rural population, in particular by raising incomes and creating jobs, by means of increasing agricultural production generally;
(b) to reinforcing the security of the food supplies of the ACP States and to satisfying their nutritional requirements, particularly by improving the quantity and quality of food production;
(c) to improving the productivity of and diversifying rural activities, in particular through the transfer of appropriate technology and rational use of crop and livestock resources while protecting the environment;
(d) to local exploitation of agricultural produce, in particular through the processing of crops and livestock products in the countries concerned;
(e) to the social and cultural development of the rural community, in particular through integrated health and educational schemes;
(f) to increasing the populations' capacity for self-development, notably through greater control over their technical and economic environment.
Art. 84. In order to help attain the objectives referred to in article 83, co-operation schemes in the field of rural development shall take the form inter alia of:
(a) integrated rural development projects involving in particular peasant family holdings and co-operatives and also fostering craft and trading activities in rural areas;
(b) different kinds of hydro-agricultural improvement schemes using available water resources; village water-engineering micro-projects, stabilization of water courses and land development involving partial or total water control;
(c) projects for crop protection, preservation and storage and for marketing agricultural products designed to bring about conditions giving farmers an incentive to produce;
(d) the establishment of agro-industrial units combining primary agricultural production, processing, and the preparation, packaging and marketing of the finished product;
(e) stock-farming projects; protection, exploitation and improvement of livestock and the development of livestock products;
(f) fishery and fish farming projects: exploitation of natural resources and development of new products; preservation and marketing of products;
(g) exploitation and development of forestry resources for production or environmental protection purposes;
(h) the implementation of measures to raise the standard of living in rural areas, for example by improving the social infrastructure, drinking water supply and communications networks;
(i) such applied agronomic and livestock research projects as prove necessary prior to or in the course of the implementation of agricultural co-operation schemes;
(j) training schemes at all levels for national supervisory staff who will have to take over responsibility for the planning, execution and management of rural development operations and applied agronomic and livestock research projects.
Title VII. Financial and technical co-operation. Chapter 1. General Provisions. Art. 91. (1). The objective of financial and technical co-operation shall be to promote the economic and social development of the ACP States on the basis of the priorities laid down by those States and in the mutual interest of the parties.
(2) This co-operation shall complement the efforts of the ACP States and shall be in keeping with them. It shall relate to the preparation, financing and implementation of projects and programmes that contribute to the economic and social development of the ACP States and whose nature is adapted to the needs and characteristics of each of those States.
(3) It should help the least developed, landlocked and island ACP States to overcome the specific obstacles which hamper their development efforts.
(4) It should encourage the regional co-operation of the ACP States.
Chapter 2. Financial resources and methods of financing.
Art. 95. For the duration of the Convention, the overall amount of the Community's financial assistance shall be 5227 million EUA.
Art. 101.(1) Projects or programmes may be financed by grant, or by special loan, or by risk capital, or by loans from the Bank from its own resources, or jointly by two or more of these means of financing.
(2) The financing of productive investment projects in industry, agro-industry, tourism, mining and energy production linked with investment in those sectors shall be borne in the first place by loans from the Bank from its own resources and by risk capital.
(3) For resources of the Fund which are managed by the Commission the means of financing shall be fixed jointly in accordance with the level of development and the geographical, economic and financial situation of the ACP State or States concerned, so as to ensure the best use of available resources. Account may also be taken of their economic and social impact.
(4) For resources managed by the Bank, the means of financing shall be fixed in accordance with the nature of the project, the prospects for its economic and financial return and the stage of development and economic and financial situation of the ACP State or States concerned. Account shall be taken in addition of factors guaranteeing the servicing of repayable aid.
Art. 102. Special loans shall be made for a duration of 40 years, with a grace period of 10 years. They shall bear interest at the rate of 1% per annum.
Art. 103.(1) Grants or special loans may be accorded to an ACP State or may be channelled by that State to a final recipient.
(2) In the latter case, the terms on which the money may be made available by the ACP State to the final recipient shall be laid down in the financing agreement.
(3) Any profit accruing to the ACP State because it receives either a grant or a loan for which the interest rate or the repayment period is more favourable than that of the final loan shall be used by the ACP State for development purposes on the conditions laid down in the financing agreement.
(4) Taking account of a request of the ACP State concerned, the Bank may, in accordance with article 101, grant finance which it shall administer either directly to the final recipient, via a development bank, or via the ACP State concerned.
Chapter 3. ACP and EEC responsibilities. Art. 108.(1) Operations financed by the Community shall be implemented by the ACP States and the Community in close co-operation, the concept of equality between the partners being recognized.
(2) The ACP States shall be responsible for:
(a) defining the objectives and priorities on which the indicative programmes drawn up by them shall be based;
(b) choosing the projects and programmes which they decide to put forward for Community financing;
(c) preparing and presenting to the Community the dossiers of projects and programmes;
(d) preparing, negotiating and concluding contracts;
(e) implementing projects and programmes financed by the Community;
(f) managing and maintaining operations carried out in the context of financial and technical co-operation.
(3) If requested by the ACP States, the Community may provide them with technical assistance in performing the tasks referred to in paragraph 2. It shall examine in particular specific measures for alleviating the particular difficulties encountered by the least developed, landlocked and island ACP States in the implementation of their projects and programmes.
(4) The ACP States and the Community shall bear joint responsibility for:
(a) defining, within the joint institutions, the general policy and guidelines of financial and technical co-operation;
(b) adopting the indicative programmes of Community aid;
(c) appraising projects and programmes, and examining the extent to which they fit the objectives and priorities and comply with the provisions of the Convention;
(d) taking the necessary implementing measures to ensure equality of conditions for participation in invitations to tender and contracts;
(e) evaluating the effects and results of projects and programmes completed or under way;
(f) ensuring that the projects and programmes financed by the Community are executed in accordance with the arrangements decided upon and with the provisions of the Convention.
(5) The Community shall be responsible for preparing and taking financing decisions on projects and programmes.
Title X. Institutions. Art. 163. The institutions of this Convention are the Council of Ministers, the Committee of Ambassadors, and the Consultative Assembly.
Art. 164.(1) The Council of Ministers shall be composed, on the one hand, of the members of the Council of the European Communities and of members of the Commission of the European Communities and, on the other hand, of a member of the Government of each of the ACP States.
Art. 170. The Committee of Ambassadors shall be composed, on the one hand, of one representative of each Member State and one representative of the Commission and, on the other, of one representative of each ACP State.
Art. 188. 1. This Convention shall expire after a period of five years from the first day of March 1980, namely the 28th day of February 1985."

The Lomé III negotiations started in May, 1984 in Suva, Fiji. On Dec. 8, 1984 a new five-year convention was signed in Lomé, entered into force on March, 1, 1985. The signatories are 10 EEC countries and 64 developing ACP countries.

G. SCHIFLER, "Das Abkommen von Lomé", in: *Jahrbuch für Internationales Recht 1975*, pp. 320–339; F.A. ALTUNG (ed.), *The Lomé Convention and New International Economic Order*, Leiden, 1977; R. BORDMAN, *Europe, Africa and Lomé*, Washington DC, 1985.

LONDON. The capital of Great Britain, metropolis of the Commonwealth of Nations, south-east England, on the Thames River. Area: 1605 sq. km; pop. 1980 est. 8,000,000. The City of London as part of the County of Greater London with some independent powers, had in 1985 an estimated resident population of 5,100,000. During World War II partly destroyed by German air raids. Headquarters of about 400 intergovernmental and non-governmental organizations.

Yearbook of International Organizations; B. WEINREB, Ch. HIBBERT, *The London Encyclopedia*, London, 1983; J. PAXTON ed., *The Statesman's Yearbook 1987–88*, London, 1987.

L

LONDON CLUB OF NUCLEAR SUPPLIERS.
The conference of 15 exporter states of nuclear materials, in session from 1975 under the auspices of the IAEA, acting in accordance with the recommendations of the ▷ Non-Proliferation Treaty, 1968. Members of the Club agreed that they would export only to countries which signed an agreement with the IAEA on safe-guarding fissile materials as well as obligating themselves not to use them for the production of explosive devices of any kind for any purposes whatsoever.

Belonging to the Club are: Belgium, Canada, Czechoslovakia, France, the FRG, Great Britain, the GDR, Italy, Japan, the Netherlands, Poland, Sweden, Switzerland, the USA and USSR. The agreed resolutions concerning the export of materials, technology, and atomic devices include atomic reactors and their components, devices for enriched uranium, heavy water, graphite and other materials which are on the list of so-called sensitive materials.

SIPRI, *World Armaments and Disarmament Yearbook* 1974, pp. 374–375; 1975, pp. 20–23, 360–361; 1976, pp. 35–42; 1977, pp. 320–321; "Guidelines for Nuclear Transfers adopted by the State-Members of the so-called Club of London, Vienna, January 11, 1978", in: *Recueil de Documents*, Varsovie No. 1–2, 1978.

LONDON CONFERENCE, 1921. The Conference held in London from Feb. 21 to Mar. 14, 1921, attended by States of the Entente: Britain, Belgium, France, Greece, Japan, Italy, with representatives from Germany and Turkey; concerning German reparations payments and the Turkish question; the former matter was brought up because the German delegate refused to recognize the decisions of the Paris Conference, 1921, on the payment by Germany of damages of 226 billion DM in gold, regarding as sufficient the sum of 50 billion DM, of which, he claimed, 20 billion DM were already paid. No agreement was reached. In view of German opposition, the countries of the Entente issued a London Ultimatum May 5, 1921, notifying the German Reich government of the preparation for the occupation of the Rhine Basin and demanding immediate demilitarization of the Reich, prosecution of war criminals and a 12 billion DM reparations payment. Settled in Wiesbaden, Oct. 7, 1921, was the German–French agreement on payment of part of the reparations in goods. Negotiations on the revision of the Peace Treaty of Sèvres (1920) and the cessation of war operations between Greece and Turkey failed to bring results.

J. HOCHFELD, *Deutsche Reichsgeschichte in Dokumenten, 1849–1934*, Berlin, 1935, Vol. 4.

LONDON CONFERENCES, 1930, 1935 AND 1936. ▷ London Naval Treaties, 1930, 1935 and 1936.

LONDON DECLARATION, 1909. The conclusion of the London Naval Conference attended by representatives of 10 maritime states. The Declaration codified principles of naval war, concerning rules of protection of vessels of neutral states, in case of War Blockade; nine chapters, 71 articles. Not ratified and never entered into force.

LONDON DECLARATION, 1941. The Resolution of the Governments Engaged in the Fight against Aggression, adopted at London on June 12, 1941. The text is as follows:

"The Governments of the United Kingdom of Great Britain and Northern Ireland, Canada, Australia, New Zealand and South Africa, the Government of Belgium, the Provisional Czecho-Slovak Government, the Governments of Greece, Luxembourg, The Netherlands, Norway, Poland, and Yugoslavia, and the

representatives of General de Gaulle, leader of Free Frenchmen,

Engaged together in the fight against aggression,

Are resolved:

(1) That they will continue the struggle against German or Italian aggression until victory is won, and will mutually assist each other in this struggle to the utmost of their respective capacities;

(2) That there can be no settled peace and prosperity so long as free peoples are coerced by violence into submission to domination by Germany or her associates, or live under the threat of such coercion;

(3) That the only true basis of enduring peace is the willing co-operation of free peoples in a world in which, relieved of the menace of aggression, all may enjoy economic and social security; and that it is their intention to work together, and with other free peoples, both in war and peace to this end."

Documents on American Foreign Relations, New York, 1941, Vol. 3, p. 444.

LONDON DECLARATION OF INDUSTRIALIZED NATIONS, 1977. The Joint Declaration issued at the conclusion of the International Economic Summit Conference of Industrialized Nations, at London, on May 8, 1977. Participants: President of the US Jimmy Carter, President of France Valery Giscard d'Estaing, Prime Minister of Canada Pierre Trudeau, Chancellor of the FRG Helmut Schmidt, Prime Minister of Italy Giulio Andreotti, Prime Minister of Japan Takeo Fukuda and Prime Minister of the UK James Callaghan. The main points of the Declaration are as follows:

"The message of the Downing Street Summit is thus one of confidence:

– in the continuing strength of our societies and the proved democratic principles that give them vitality;
– that we are undertaking the measures needed to overcome problems and achieve a more prosperous future.
World Economic Prospects
Since 1975 the world economic situation has been improving gradually. Serious problems still persist in all of our countries. Our most urgent task is to create jobs while continuing to reduce inflation. Inflation is not a remedy to unemployment but one of major causes. Progress in the fight against inflation has been uneven. The needs for adjustment between surplus and deficit countries remain large. The world has not yet fully adjusted to the depressive effects of the 1974 oil price rise. We commit our governments to targets for growth and stabilization which vary from country to country but which, taken as a whole, should provide a basis for sustained non-inflationary growth worldwide.
Some of our countries have adopted reasonably expansionist growth targets for 1977. The governments of these countries will keep their policies under review, and commit themselves to adopt further policies, if needed to achieve their stated target rates and to contribute to the adjustment of payments imbalances. Others are pursuing stabilization policies designed to provide a basis for sustained growth without increasing inflationary expectations. The governments of these countries will continue to pursue those goals.
These two sets of policies are interrelated. Those of the first group of countries should help to create an environment conducive to expansion in the others without adding to inflation. Only if growth rates can be maintained in the first group and increased in the second, and inflation tackled successfully in both, can unemployment be reduced.
We are particularly concerned about the problem of unemployment among young people. Therefore we shall promote the training of young people in order to build a skilled and flexible labor force so that they can be ready to take advantage of the upturn in economic activity as it develops. All of our governments, individually or collectively, are taking appropriate measures to this end. We must learn as much as possible from each other and agree to exchange experiences and ideas. Success in managing our domestic economies will not only strengthen world economic growth but also contribute to success in four other main economic fields to which we now turn – balance of payments financing, trade, energy and North–South relations. Progress in

these fields will in turn contribute to world economic recovery.
Energy
We welcome the measures taken by a number of governments to increase energy conservation. The increase in demand for energy and oil imports continues at a rate which places excessive pressure on the world's depleting hydrocarbon resources. We agree therefore on the need to do everything possible to strengthen our efforts still further.
We are committed to national and joint efforts to limit energy demand and to increase and diversify supplies. There will need to be greater exchanges of technology and joint research and development aimed at more efficient energy use, improved recovery and use of coal and other conventional resources, and the development of new energy sources.
North–South Relations
The world economy can only grow on a sustained and equitable basis if developing countries share in that growth. Progress has been made. The industrial countries have maintained an open market system despite a deep recession. They have increased aid flows, especially to poorer nations. Some $8 billion will be available from the IDA for these nations over the next three years, as we join others in fulfilling pledges to its Fifth Replenishment. The IMF has made available to developing countries, under its conpensatory financing facility nearly an additional $2 billion last year.
An International Fund for Agricultural Development has been created, based on common efforts by the developed OPEC, and other developing nations. The progress and the spirit of co-operation that have emerged can serve as an excellent base for further steps. The next step will be the successful conclusion of the Conference on International Economic Co-operation and we agreed to do all in our power to achieve this. We shall work:
(i) to increase the flow of aid and other real resources from the industrial to developing countries, particularly to the 800 million people who now live in absolute poverty; and to improve the effectiveness of aid;
(ii) to facilitate developing countries' access to sources of international finance;
(iii) to support such multilateral lending institutions as the World Bank, whose lending capacity we believe will have to be increased in the years ahead to permit its lending to increase in real terms and widen in scope;
(iv) to promote the secure investment needed to foster world economic development;
(v) to secure productive results from negotiations about the stabilization of commodity prices and the creation of a Common Fund for individual buffer stock agreements and to consider problems of the stabilization of export earnings of developing countries; and
(vi) to continue to improve access in a non-disruptive way to the markets of industrial countries for the products of developing nations."

Presidential Documents, No. 20, May 16, 1977.

LONDON DUMPING CONVENTION, 1972. ▷ Radioactivity of the Deep Sea.

LONDON MARITIME CODE DECLARATION, 1909. ▷ London Declaration 1909.

LONDON MARITIME CONVENTIONS. Four conventions on safety at sea signed in London; the first was concluded at the *Titanic* Conference held in London, 1913 to investigate circumstances of the disaster of the largest British White Star liner (Cunard Line) ▷ *Titanic*. The cause of so many casualties was an insufficient number and poor handling of lifeboats; the convention known as the First International Convention on Safety of Life at Sea was signed on Jan. 20, 1914 but never entered into force because of the outbreak of World War I. In a modified form the Second Convention was signed on May 31, 1929 (remained in force until Nov. 19, 1952); the Third Convention was signed on Apr. 10, 1948 (in force from Nov. 19, 1952 till May 26, 1965); the Fourth Convention on June 17, 1960 (in force since May 26, 1965).

The English acronym SOLAS stands for Safety of Life at Sea. The first three London Conventions were convened by the British government, the Fourth by the IMCO.

IMCO, Maritime Conventions, Geneva, 1970.

LONDON METAL EXCHANGE. World Centre of Metals Trading. A trade centre like ▷ COMEX in New York.

WOLFF's *Guide to London Metal Exchange*, London, 1976; R. GIBSON-JARVIE, *The London Metal Exchange*, Woodhead-Faulkner, UK, 1976.

LONDON NAVAL TREATIES, 1930, 1935 AND 1936. Three international agreements on limitation of naval armaments:
(1) The International Treaty for the Limitation and Reduction of Naval Armaments, signed on Apr. 22, 1930 in London by the governments of the US, France, Great Britain, Italy and Japan, with Proces-Verbal of Deposit of Ratifications, signed on Oct. 27, 1930 in London and Exchange of Notes regarding the Interpretation of art. 19 of the Treaty signed on May 21 and 24, 1930 in Tokyo and on June 5, 1930 in London. The Treaty was not ratified by France and Italy and remained binding only for the remaining powers. It set up the following ratios for their navies: Britain – 100, USA – 102.4, Japan – 63.6. Reduction of vessels was to be completed by Dec. 31, 1931. Tonnage ceilings for warships and ships guns were specified.
(2) A British–German Treaty, concluded on June 8, 1935 in London, in the form of an exchange of notes relating to tonnages of navies; their ratio was established at 100:35 and 100:100 for submarines with a reservation that the 100:35 proportion in overall tonnage is not to be exceeded; extended by additional agreements of Oct. 12, 1936 and July 17, 1937 and the London Protocol of June 30, 1938. The Naval Treaty was denounced by Germany on Apr. 28, 1939.
(3) A Treaty for the Limitation of Naval Armaments, with Protocol of Signature and Additional Protocol, signed on Mar. 25, 1936 in London, by the governments of the USA, France, Great Britain and Canada, Australia, New Zealand and India; ratified on July 29, 1936; reduced the size of various types of warships on the condition that Japan sign the agreement. That never occurred. Annulled by signatories on Apr. 1, 1938.

British and Foreign State Papers, London, 1936.

LONDON PROTOCOL, 1839. An agreement signed on Apr. 19, 1839 by the Austrian Emperor Ferdinand I, Tsar Nikolai I of Russia, King Louis Philippe of France, King William I of the Netherlands, Frederic William III King of Prussia and a representative of the King of Belgium to establish the separation of Belgium and the Netherlands. The neutrality of Belgium was guaranteed in keeping with the provisions of the London Conference of July 26, 1831 (art. 7); the port of Antwerp was to become a commercial port (art. 14); Belgium acquired the larger part of Luxembourg (art. 6). The Protocol came into force on June 8, 1839 and was replaced by the Joint Agreement of May 22, 1926.

G.F. DE MARTENS, *Nouveau Recueil*, Vol. 16, p. 770.

LONDON SECRET TREATY WITH ITALY, 1915. The Treaty concluded secretly on Apr. 26, 1915 between the Triple Alliance of France, Russia, Great Britain and Italy. For joining the war as their ally Italy was promised the Trentino-Alto Adige, Trieste, the Istrian peninsula with a number of islands on the Adriatic, Dalmatia, Libya and the Dodecanese, as well as a 50 million pound sterling loan from England.

G.F. DE MARTENS, *Nouveau Recueil Général*, 3 s, Vol. 9, p. 72b.

LONDON TRAVEL PERMIT. A travel document issued 1939–44 by the London Office of the Intergovernmental Committee for Refugees, IGCR, on the pattern of ▷ Nansen Passport.

LONDON WAR ALLIANCE TREATY, 1914. The Treaty signed on Sept. 4, 1914 in London within the framework of the war alliance. It obligated the three principal allied powers, France, Great Britain and Russia not to conclude any separate peace, or propose peace conditions with Central States without earlier joint consultations. Joined by Japan on Oct. 15, 1915 and Italy on Nov. 30, 1915.

G.F. DE MARTENS, *Nouveau Recueil Général*, 3 s, Vol. 10, p. 324.

LONGITUDE. International geographical term for the angular distance measured East or West along the Equator of points on the Earth's surface from the Prime or ▷ Greenwich Meridian. Subject of international research. See also ▷ Latitude.

LONG MARCH, 1934–36. The march of the 100,000 members of the Chinese People's Army under the leadership of the Chairman of the Chinese Communist Party, Mao Tse Tung (1894–1976) from Kiangsi to the areas of China not controlled by Chiang Kai Shek's (1887–1977) Kuomintang Party (Vhenshi, Kansu and Yenan). The long march covered, during 16 months, from Nov. 1934 to Mar. 1936, more than 10,000 km and only 2000 soldiers survived.

R.C. THORNTON, *A Political History of China, 1917–1980*, Boulder, 1982; B. HOOK, *The Cambridge Encyclopaedia*, Cambridge, 1982; P. CHENG, *China. Bibliography*, Oxford, 1982; H.E. SALISBURY, *The Long March. The Untold Story*, London, 1985.

LONG TON. A non-metric unit of the Anglo-Saxon countries = 1016 kg.

LORAN. Long Range Navigation. An international term for the radio-navigational system for great distances in maritime and air navigation.

LORD HOVE ISLAND GROUP. Australian natural site, included in the ▷ World Heritage UNESCO List.

LORO SAE. The name of an Indonesian province since July 17, 1976. Formerly Timor Oriental. ▷ Timor Island.

LOS ALAMOS. An American town in central New Mexico (1978 est. population 16,800), the site of the first atomic bomb laboratory built 1942, called the Los Alamos Scientific Laboratory which succeeded in its work 1945 (▷ Alamogordo); at present a national historic landmark.
See also ▷ Manhattan Project.

D. ROBERTSON, *Guide to Modern Defense and Strategy*, Detroit, 1988.

LOS GLACIARES. Argentinian National Park, included in the ▷ World Heritage UNESCO List; with an area of 600,000 hectares into which glaciers have advanced and melted to form immense lakes of perfectly clear water; these are the habitat of thousands of birds such as geese, ducks, black-necked swans and Chilean flamingos. Overhead one can see Andean condors flying and on the banks are American ostriches.

UNESCO, *A Legacy for All*, Paris, 1984.

LOST GENERATION. An international term for the young generation which survived World War I; the term was coined in France and publicized by a group of young American writers in Paris (among them, M. Cowley, J. dos Passos, E. Hemingway, F. Scott-Fitzgerald).

LOUISIANA PURCHASE TREATY, 1803. A treaty of cession, signed on April 30, 1803 by France and the USA ratified Oct 20–21 1803, after Napoleon offered to sell all of the Louisiana region to the United States for $15 million. The territory extended from the Mississippi River to the Rocky Mts., and from the Gulf of Mexico to British North America, and included the Spanish region of Louisiana, secretly ceded to France by Spain in 1800. The whole region c. 2,144,520 sq km doubled the area of the United States.

R. HITCHCOCK, *The Louisiana Purchase and the Exploration. Early History and Building of the West, 1903; The British Encyclopedia*, Vol. II, Chicago–London, 1973.

LOUVRE ACCORD, 1987. Official name of an agreement of the central bank governors and finance ministers of the major industrialized countries (France, the FRG, Japan, the UK and the USA) on currency rate stabilization, signed in Paris on Feb. 22, 1987, replacing the ▷ Plaza Accord, 1985.

KEESING's *Record of World Events*, 1987; C.F. BERGSTEN, *Louvre Lesson. The World Needs a New Monetary System, in: Economic Impact*, No. 2, 1988.

LOW ARMAMENT ZONES. ▷ Asymmetry.

LRTNF. Long-Range Theater Nuclear Force. The intermediate-range nuclear weapons, a subject of American–Soviet negotiations in the framework of SALT II.

J. GOLDBLAT, *Arms Control Agreements. A Handbook*, New York, 1983.

LSD-25. Lysergic Acid Diethylamide. A drug obtained from ergot causing hallucinations and distortions of the senses; produced in 1938 by two Swedish chemists, A. Hoffmann and A. Stoll, in the laboratory of the firm Sandoz in Basel, marked with the number – 25 as the twenty-fifth derivative of synthesized compounds in the Sandoz laboratory. Subject of organized international co-operation under the WHO protectorate in the struggle against growing drug abuse among young people, mainly in the USA and Western Europe.

"UN Current Terminology 1971", *Terminology Bulletin*, No. 267.

LUCERNE CONFERENCE, 1973. A Conference of government experts at Lucerne, Switzerland in June 1973 on weapons which may cause unnecessary suffering or have indiscriminate effects.

SIPRI, *World Armaments and Disarmament Yearbook 1973*, pp. 48–59.

LUGGAGE CONVENTION, 1967. ▷ Maritime Law Conventions, 1882–1978.

LUMBER. In the EEC system ▷ STABEX includes lumber in the ACP States.

LUMUMBA PATRICE UNIVERSITY. The name of an international higher educational institution in Moscow, named after P. Lumumba (1925–61) by a decision of the Soviet government to honor the African leader of the Congolese National Movement for Independence, murdered by political opponents in 1961.

LÜNEBURG PRINCIPLES, THE. ICJ term, for the Principles on the Implementation of the International Covenant on Economic, Social and Cultural Rights, adopted by a meeting of experts in international law, convened by the ICJ, the faculty of law of the University of Lüneburg and the Urban Morgan Institute for Human Rights, held in Maastricht, the Netherlands, from June 2 to 6, 1986.

Human Rights Quarterly, Vol. 9, No. 2, May, 1987.

LUNNIK. also called Myechta, *Russian:* "dream", name of artificial earth satellites produced by the USSR, whose model L-2 was the first to reach the ▷ Moon on Sept. 12, 1959.

KEESING's *Contemporary Archive,* 1959.

LUNOHOD. A Russian name for a wheeled vehicle capable of moving on the surface of the Moon. L-1 was transported to the Moon Nov. 17, 1970 on the spaceship Luna 17, from which it descended down the accommodation-ladder remotely controlled from Earth to the surface of the Moon and began to penetrate the surroundings. The experiments made by L-1 showed the possibility of exploring space with the aid of robots controlled from Earth. The self-acting automatic device L-2, which was placed on the Moon by the automatic station Luna 21 on Jan. 16, 1973, carried out a program of exploration of the surface of the Moon, and the brightness of the lunar sky until May 30, 1973. The device covered 37 km and transmitted 86,000 photos to Earth.

KEESING's *Contemporary Archive,* 1970 and 1972.

LUSAKA. The capital of Zambia (population 1980 census: 535,830) since 1935, of the Zambian republic since 1964. Seat of an ILO Regional Office and of the International University Exchange Fund.

Yearbook of International Organizations.

LUSAKA DECLARATION, 1970. ▷ Nonaligned Countries Declaration, 1970.

LUSAKA DECLARATION ON NAMIBIA, 1978. The UN Council for Namibia on Mar. 23, 1978 in Lusaka adopted a Declaration reaffirming the territorial integrity of Namibia and condemned any so-called internal settlements in Namibia and supported the ▷ SWAPO "as the vanguard of the struggle of the Namibian people".

UN Chronicle, April 1978, pp. 42–46.

LUSATIA. *German* = Lausitz, *Lusatian* = Łużyce. A region of the GDR between the Lusatian Neisse and Elbe. Its first inhabitants were Lusatian Serbs, subjects of centuries of German–Polish and German–Czech disputes and conflicts; 1002–31 unified with Poland, 1355–1815 unified with the Czech Crown; by a decision of the Congress of Vienna in 1815, it was divided between Prussia (Lower Lusatia and the northern part of Upper) and Saxony (Upper Lusatia with Budzishin – capital of the national movement of Lusatian Serbs). The end of World War I brought hope of liberation and Lusatian unification. Just before the capitulation of the German Reich, two delegates to the Landtag of Saxony, A. Bart and M. Kohl, on Nov. 4, 1918 presented a demand for cultural autonomy for the Lusatians, based on the resolutions of 1848 and 1873. After the pronouncement of the Reich as a republic, the Union of Lower and Upper Lusatian Serbs at a congress in Chroshtitse on Nov. 20, 1918 passed a proclamation, asserting i.a.:

"We Lusatian Serbs, on the basis of the right of nations to self-determination recognized by the entire world, demand the unification of Upper and Lower Lusatia. ... We therefore create the Serbian National Committee (*Serbski Narodny Vubyerk, SNV*) ... and demand that it be present at the forthcoming peace conference as a representative of the Serbian nation."

The demand for an autonomous organism of states within the framework of the German Republic was supported by the Czech Committee in Paris, but was unable to gain the support of the Main Allied and Associated Powers. On Nov. 24, 1919 the minister of internal affairs of the Reich, asserted that the Serbo–Lusatian population is assured of all rights under art. 113 of the Constitution of the Weimar Republic. At the I Congress of National Minorities in Geneva, 1925, held under the sponsorship of the LN, a Special International Committee stated that the Prussian census of 1925 had deliberately reduced the number of the Slavic population speaking "*wendisch*" to 65,000, while in reality the population speaking Serbo–Lusatian was 160,000.

Serbo–Lusatians took an active part in the work of the Union of National Minorities in Germany. In 1937 a Nazi directive recognized the Serbo–Lusatians as a "new German tribe" (*Neudeutscher Stamm*), speaking the "*wendisch*" language. The political organization *Domovina*, est. 1912, firmly rejected the scheme for a fascist statute in which the Lusatians were designated as a "new German tribe". As a result of this, *Domovina* was banned in 1937. After this ban, the Serbo–Lusatian cultural organizations were abolished, a ban was imposed on the press and literature and the use of the Serbo–Lusatian language in schools and public places. In April, 1945 Lusatia was liberated by the Soviet Army and by a decision of the Great Powers became part of the Soviet zone of occupied Germany. In 1948 the National Parliament (Landtag) of Saxony unanimously passed a Law:

"(1) The Lusatian population benefits from the legal protection and assistance of the state in its cultural and linguistic development. (2) Elementary and secondary schools should be established for Lusatian children with the language of instruction in Serbo–Lusatian and teaching of the German language. (3) In offices and in public administration on the Lusatian–German territory the Serbo–Lusatian language should be introduced alongside German. (4) On the Lusatian–German territory in a democratic public administration Lusatians should be employed in a number proportional to the percentage of the Lusatian population. (5) To direct and assist Lusatian cultural life a cultural-educational bureau shall be established with headquarters in Budzishyn under the Minister of Education. The staff of the bureau will be appointed by the Minister on the recommendation of recognized anti-fascist Serbian organizations. The costs of rebuilding and further development of cultural life of the Lusatians will be borne by the state. (6) Public authorities and administration of linguistically mixed territories in each case have the obligation to assist Lusatian cultural needs. (7) Executive orders will be issued by the Ministry of Internal Affairs and the Ministry of Education."

The law entered into force on the day of its announcement, Mar. 23, 1948. After the formation of the GDR, Oct. 7, 1949, art. 11 of the GDR constitution sanctioned legally the cultivation of the Serbo–Lusatian language and culture. In the GDR Constitution of 1968, besides the individual rights of each citizen, the national rights of the Serbo–Lusatian population were recognized and guaranteed in art. 40 as follows:

"Citizens of GDR have the right to cultivate their native language and culture. The exercise of these rights will be supported by the State."

Serbo–Lusatians take an active part in the national life of GDR. Four Lusatians sit in the Volkskammer (People's Chamber), 33 are deputies to the municipal governments of the districts of Kotzebow and Dresden, more than 2000 serve on town and village councils. The Serbo–Lusatian language is used as a native language in Lusatia in schools, in local administration and in law. The training of teachers and university staff takes place in the Serbo–Lusatian Teacher Education Institute in Budzishin and in the Serbo–Lusatian Institute of the Karl Marx University in Leipzig. Since 1948 Serbo–Lusatian literature is published by the *Domovina* Publishing House, which during 25 years has printed 1445 books and brochures. Within the German Academy of Sciences, a Serbian Ethnography Institute was formed in 1951 called *Institut za Serbski Ludozpyt*. In 1975 *Domovina* published in Lusatian and German a 4-volume *History of the Serbs*.

H. ZWAHR, *Sorbische Volksbewegung 1872–1918*, Bautzen, 1968; B. CZYZ, *Die DDR und die Sorben*, Bautzen, 1969; *60 let Domovina*, Budisin, 1972; *Geschichte der Sorben*, 4 Vols., Bautzen, 1975.

"LUSITANIA". The British passenger steamship of the Cunard Line, sunk on May 7, 1915 on its voyage home from the USA by a German submarine in Icelandic waters; about 1200 passengers and crew members perished, including 128 citizens of the then neutral USA; subject of a diplomatic argument between the USA and the German Reich which, in a note of Dec. 4, 1916, expressed consent to pay indemnity to families of drowned USA citizens. The sinking of the *Lusitania* as well as of other passenger ships (▷ *Ancona*) aroused public indignation in the USA and contributed to the abandoning by the USA of its traditional policy of ▷ isolationism.

J. PERRINJAQUED, "La Guerre Commerciale Sous-Marine. Les torpillages du *Lusitania*, de l'*Arabie*, de l'*Ancona* et du *Persia*. Les protestations des États Unis et concessions de l'Allemagne", in: *Revue générale du droit internationale public*, No. 13, 1916; "The *Lusitania*", in: *International Conciliation*, No. 132, November, 1918, pp. 605–647.

LUSOPHONE AFRICAN CONFERENCES. The annual summits of the Portuguese speaking African States (Angola, Cape Verde, Guinea-Bissau, Mozambique and Sao Tomé and Principe) since 1978. See also ▷ African Intergovernmental Conferences.

KEESING's *Contemporary Archive, Record of World Events,* April, 1985.

LU-TA. Formerly ▷ Port Arthur. A Chinese city and seaport on the Liaotung peninsula; 1977 population 4,200,000.

LUTHERAN CHURCHES. One of the Christian Protestant religious groups also called the Augsburg-Evangelical Church, professing the theological–moral doctrines of Martin Luther; since 1923 united under one organization, initially called the Lutheran World Convention, since 1947 called Lutheran World Federation, headquarters in Geneva. Consultative status with ECOSOC; takes an active part in the ecumenical movement; affiliates 84 autonomous churches of 51 countries. Publ.: *Lutheran World* and *Lutheran.*

C.E. LUNDQUIST (ed.), *The Lutheran Church of the World*, Geneva, 1957; *Yearbook of International Organizations.*

LUTHERANISM. An international term for one of the main doctrines of ▷ Protestantism (besides ▷ Calvinism and ▷ Zwinglianism), which was formulated in 1529 in the Great Catechism and in 1530 in the Augusburg Confession of Faith by the German reformer Martin Luther (1483–1546), proclaiming that the source of salvation is faith alone and the source of faith, the Bible.

W. ELERT, *Morphologie des Luthertums*, 2 Vols., Berlin, 1931–32 (English edition 1961); A. ROSS-WENTZ, *A Basic History of Lutheranism in America*, New York, 1955.

LUXEMBOURG. Member of the UN. Grand-Duché de Luxembourg, Grossherzogtum Luxemburg. Grand Duchy of Luxembourg. State in Western Europe. Area: 2586 sq. km. Pop.: 1987 est.: 366,000 (census of 1977: 360,200). Capital: Luxembourg-Ville with 78,900 inhabitants 1981. Borders with Belgium, France and the FRG. Official language: French and Luxembourgian (a Mosel–Franconian dialect). GNP per capita in 1987: US $15,860. Currency: one Luxembourg franc and one Belgium Franc = 100 centimes with an identical value within the currency union. National day: June 23, birthday of the reigning Grand Duke, 1921.
Founding member of the League of Nations, 1919–39, and the UN on Oct. 24, 1945 and all its specialized organizations with the exception of the IMO. Member of the BENELUX, the EEC, OECD, NATO, WEU and the Council of Europe. International relations: a vassal duchy since 1354; a Grand Duchy in the Kingdom of Holland since the Congress of Vienna, 1815; independent since 1830, with the exception of a period of subordination to Prussia, 1842–67. Returned to independence by the London Treaty of 1867, with neutrality guaranteed by the Great Powers; violated by Germany in Aug. 1914; restored by the Versailles Treaty of 1919. In customs union with Belgium since May 1922 (on the Brussels Treaty, signed on July 25, 1921, ratified on Mar. 5, 1922; the Union was dissolved by German occupation in 1940, but re-established on May 1, 1945). During World War II Luxembourg was occupied and incorporated into the German Reich on May 10, 1940; liberated by the American–British armies on Sept. 10, 1944. Neutrality was not restored and formally abolished in 1948/49 when Luxembourg became economically, politically and militarily integrated with Belgium and Holland (▷ Benelux) and became a member of the West European Union and NATO.
Luxembourg on Apr. 17, 1946 signed a railroad Convention with Belgium and France and a supplementary treaty on June 26, 1946. Since 1945 the government of Luxembourg publ. *Bulletin de Documentation*. The representative of Luxembourg, former Premier Minister, Gaston Thorn, became President of the Commission of the European Economic Community, 1981.

UNTS, Vol. 27, 1946, p. 103; *Le Luxembourg. Livre du Centenaire*, Luxembourg, 1948; P. LECOEUR, *Histoire économique, monétaire et financiére contemporaine du Grand-Duché de Luxembourg*, Luxembourg, 1950; J. PETIT, *Luxembourg, plate-forme internationale*, Luxembourg, 1960; K.C. EDWARDS, *Historical Geography of the Luxembourg Iron and Steel Industry*, London, 1961; *Tausend Jahre Luxemburg 963–1963*, Luxembourg, 1963; G. TAUSCH, *Le Luxembourg indépendant*, Luxembourg, 1975; C. CALMES, *Au Fil de l'Histoire*, Luxembourg, 1977; C. HURY, J. CHRISTOPHERY, *Luxembourg. Bibliography*, Oxford, 1981; *The Europa Year Book 1984. A World Survey*, Vol. I, pp. 645–654, London, 1984.

LUXEMBOURG AGREEMENT, 1946. The Convention concerning the Luxembourg railways, with Additional Protocol signed by the Governments of Luxembourg, Belgium and France in Luxembourg on Apr. 17, 1946, and a Supplementary Agreement modifying the said Convention, signed on June 26, 1946 in Luxembourg.

UNTS, Vol. 27, pp. 103–115.

LUXEMBOURG AGREEMENT, 1971. The Agreement concluded in Luxembourg on June 23, 1971 between the EEC and the UK, specifying the terms of the UK's accession to the EEC on Jan. 1, 1973. Negotiations between the European states and the UK started on May 9, 1950 with an address by the French Foreign Minister Robert Schuman, calling for the UK to join the European Coal and Steel Community. The UK refused. Further negotiations 1955–56, also failed. Following the entry into force of the Rome Treaties 1957 on the EEC and Euratom in 1960 the UK formed a free market with Austria, Denmark, Norway, Portugal, Switzerland and Sweden (▷ EFTA). In Nov. 1961, the British Prime Minister Harold Macmillan initiated another round of talks with a delegation headed by Edward Heath. The talks ended in Jan., 1963 because of France's opposition, expounded by General Charles de Gaulle at a press conference on Jan. 14, 1963. In May, 1967 the Prime Minister Harold Wilson undertook further negotiations which were also thwarted by France, at a conference in Brussels in Nov. 1967. After de Gaulle's resignation from the French Presidency, 1968, and the establishment of a Conservative Cabinet under Edward Heath in July 1970, the final agreement was reached in Luxembourg in July 1971. Under its terms:
(1) The UK undertook to adjust itself to the common agricultural market within a 5-year transition period 1973–78 through regulation of prices for farm produce to reconcile them with those of the EEC countries;
(2) accession to the common industrial market was to proceed in five stages within 4.5 years, by Jan. 1, 1977;
(3) during the period of transition, the export to Great Britain of butter and cheese from New Zealand on favourable conditions was upheld;
(4) a separate agreement was to regulate the issues of developing commonwealth countries;
(5) the UK undertook to adopt the VAT system in Apr. 1973;
(6) accession to the European Coal and Steel Community was to be accomplished within a 5-year period;
(7) the UK was granted the same privileges as the FRG, France, and Italy in the institutions of the extended Community;
(8) the UK withdrew the pound sterling from the position of an international reserve currency and started reduction of sterling rate; the operation was to be executed gradually as the European economic union transformed into a union of currency;
(9) the UK became member of Euratom and the European Investment Bank;
(10) British contribution to the common budget grew gradually during the 5-year transition period

from 8.64% in the first year (1973) to 18.92% in the fifth (1977).

J. PAXTON, *A Dictionary of the European Economic Community*, London, 1978.

LUXEMBOURG TREATY FRG-ISRAEL, 1952. An agreement signed on Sept. 10, 1952 in Luxembourg between the Federal Republic of Germany on the one hand and on the other hand the State of Israel and the Conference on Jewish Material Claims Against Germany, representing the Jewish organizations in the world, on reparation for the State of Israel and indemnification of Jewish victims, residing outside Israel. The "global compensation" accepted by the FRG was a sum of US $1,241 million, of which the FRG paid Israel and the Jewish individuals two-thirds, stating that one-third should be paid by the German Democratic Republic, which refused to accept any claims from Israel.

KEESING's *Contemporary Archive*, 1952.

LYNCH, LYNCHING. An international term for the execution, generally by hanging, of someone by a mob taking the law into its own hands; the name is alleged to derive from the American C. Lynch (1736–96), who as justice of the peace in the town of Bedford, Virginia, applied in 1780 mob law against a group of anti-republican conspirators, called since Lynch-Law. The first Anti-Lynch bill passed in the House in 1922, but was rejected by the Senate, as were 59 others presented in Congress till 1937, opposed on State's Rights grounds. In the second half of the 19th century the use of lynching against Negroes was introduced by the racist organization Ku Klux Klan. These terrible cases of mob law were continued in the 20th century. After World War II, a trial was held in 1947 in Greenville, North Carolina, of 26 white citizens accused of lynching a Negro, but it was discontinued due to the absence of state anti-lynching legislation, which existed only in the Northern states. In 1882–1944 a total of 4715 persons were lynched, among them 3423 Negroes and 1292 whites. In 1945–59 the total was 20 persons, including one white in 1948. Since 1959, when one Negro was lynched, no cases of lynching have been recorded in the USA and since 1965 lynching statistics have vanished from American information yearbooks.

The World Almanac and Book of Facts 1962, New York, 1962, p. 310.

LYTTON'S REPORT, 1932. A report signed on Nov. 4, 1932 by a special Commission called into existence by the Council of the League of Nations on Jan. 14, 1932, including representatives from France, Germany, Italy, the UK and the USA, headed by Lord Lytton to investigate the Chinese–Japanese conflict deriving from Japan's occupation of Manchuria. Its eight chapters gave an appraisal of the situation; the last two stated principles and made suggestions for an amicable settlement. The Report was not accepted by Japan.

LEAGUE OF NATIONS, *Lord Lytton Report*, Geneva, October 1, 1932.

M

M. In the international Maritime Signal Code, the letter M in whichever form transmitted: signifies "Stopped my ship and am not moving on water."

MAB. ▷ Man and Biosphere.

MACAU. (*Chinese* = Aomen; *Portuguese* = Macao.) A Portuguese possession in southeast China on the Macau peninsula including two islands, Taipa and Colôane (Cionao), near the estuary of the Sikiang river opposite Hong Kong. Area: 15,5 sq. km. Pop. 1987 est. 450,000 (1970 census: 248,636). Official language: Portuguese. GNP per capita 1987 US $5250. Currency: one pataca = 100 avos. The area was leased to the Portuguese as a site for a trade factory in 1557. On Dec. 1, 1887 it was integrated into Portugal under the Lisbon treaty that granted it the status of a colony; from 1951 it was an overseas territory of Portugal (*provincia ultramarina*). In 1966 the first pamphlets calling for unification with China appeared in Macau. On Feb. 17, 1976, under the decolonization program of the Portuguese government Macau was granted the new autonomous status of "a Chinese territory under Portuguese administration." The People's Republic of China establishing diplomatic relations with Portugal in Feb., 1979 announced that Macau would remain under Portuguese administration and confirmed this again in June, 1981. In Nov., 1984 the Chinese foreign minister Wu Xueqian said in Lisbon that the Chinese–British agreement on ▷ Hong Kong could serve as an example for the solution of the problem of Macau's future.

On Jan. 6, 1987 Portugal agreed that Macau should be transferred to China before the year 2000.

The China–Portugal agreement on the transfer (Dec. 20, 1999) of Macau signed on April 13, 1987 in Bejing was based upon the "one country two systems doctrine Macao–China" and for the 50 year period – until 2037 guaranteed Macau the right to regulate its own autonomy in matters other than foreign policy and defence.

E. BRAZAO, *Macau*, Lisboa, 1957; *Estatuto Administrativo do Macau*, Lisboa, 1976; *The Europa Year Book 1984. A World Survey*, Vol. II, pp. 1955-1958, London, 1984.

MACEDONIA. A region on the Balkan Peninsula in southeast Europe, divided in 19th century between Bulgaria, Greece and Serbia. ("Macedonian Question.") After World War II, the Serbian part of Macedonia was proclaimed on Nov. 29, 1945 one of six federal republics of Yugoslavia. A new Macedonian dispute between Bulgaria and Yugoslavia started in the 1960's. In December 1969 a visit to Belgrade by the Bulgarian Foreign Minister for discussion of the Macedonian question ended without a concluding communiqué. The escalation of disputes in the 1970's has continued into the 1980's.

S. BAZHDAROV, *The Macedonian Question*, London, 1926; C. BASKER, *Macedonia. Its Place in Balkan Power Politics*, London, 1950; MACEDONICUS, *Stalin and the Macedonian Question*, London, 1950; The Macedonian Question, in: A.J. DAY ed., *The Border and Territorial Disputes*, London, 1987.

MACHIAVELLIAN DIPLOMACY. An international term for the diplomatic tactics guided by the idea that the end justifies or even sanctifies the means, as described by the Florentine diplomat Niccolo Machiavelli (1469–1529) in his book, *Il Principe (The Prince)*, published posthumously, 1532.

A. NORSA, *Il principio della forza nel pensiero politico di Machiavelli*, Roma, 1936; H. BUTTERFIELD, *The Statecraft of Machiavelli*, London, 1955.

MACHINERY. A subject of international co-operation. Organizations reg. with the UIA:

European Committee for Co-operation of the Machine Tool Industries, f. 1950, Brussels.
European Committee of Associations of Agricultural Machinery, f. 1959, Paris.
European Committee of Machinery Manufacturers for the Plastic and Rubber Industries, f. 1964, Paris.
European Committee of Woodworking Machinery Manufacturers, f. 1960, Neuilly-sur-Seine.
European Laundry and Dry Cleaning Machinery Manufacturers Organization, f. 1959, Milan.
International Liaison Centre for Agricultural Machinery Distributors and Maintenance, f. 1953, The Hague.

Yearbook of International Organizations.

MACHINE TOOLS. A subject of international co-operation and statistics. Organization reg. with the UIA:

European Committee for Co-operation of the Machine Tool Industries, f. 1950, Brussels. Since 1959 European Machine Tool Exhibition held annually, and since 1975 World Machine Tool Exhibition held every two years. Publ.: *Studies and Statistics*.

Yearbook of International Organizations.

MACHT GEHT VOR RECHT. *German* = "force before law." A political doctrine stating that not the law but violence determines the rule of nations and people, attributed in 19th century to the Prussian statesman Otto von Bismarck (1815–98); known since the Middle Ages as a German proverb, used by Martin Luther (1483–1546) in his translation of the Bible (*Habakuk* 1, 3) and by J.W. Goethe (1749–1832) in *Faust* (II, act 5, 1.11184).

MACHU PICHU. Stronghold and purported last capital of the Incas in Peru, near Cuzco, 610 m above the Vilcamota river between two mountain peaks, discovered 1911 by the American explorer Hiram Bingham. A unique monument of Inca architecture (temples, palaces, towers, fountains, terraces and staircases) and city planning (area *c.* 13 sq. km not counting the farming terraces constructed for the maintenance of the community). On the ▷ World Heritage Unesco List.

H. BINGHAM, *Machu Pichu. A Citadel of the Incas*, New Haven, 1930; UNESCO, *A Legacy for All*, Paris, 1984.

MACHU PICHU, CHARTER OF, 1978. Carta de Machu Pichu, 1978. A manifesto proclaimed by city planners elaborating on the ideas of the Charter of Athens, 1933, signed by world's prominent architects and city planners. ▷ Urbanization.

Architektura, Warsaw, No. 9–10, 1978 (also English text).

MACIAS NGUEMA. Formerly Fernando Po; island in the Gulf of Guinea. Territory of Equatorial Guinea (2,034 sq. km) together with Pagalu Island (17 sq. km), formerly Annobon.

MACROTHESAURUS. A Dag Hammarskjöld Library Macrothesaurus for information processing in the field of economic and social development.

UNBIS *Thesaurus, English Edition*, New York, 1985.

MAD. Mutual Assured Destruction. An international term, introduced in the USA during the 1960s atomic stalemate.
See also ▷ Mutual Strategic Security, MSS.

D. ROBERTSON, *Guide to Modern Defense and Strategy*, Detroit, 1988.

MADAGASCAR. Member of the UN. République Democratique de Madagascar or Republique Malgache. Democratic Republic of Madagascar or Malagasy Republic. Island in the Indian Ocean, separated from East Africa by the Mozambique Channel. Area: 587,044 sq. km. Pop. 1987 est.: 10,894,000 (1965 census 6,335,000; 1975 census: 7,603,790). Capital: Antananarivo (formerly Tananarive) with 551,000 inhabitants 1982. GNP per capita 1980 US $350. Official language: French and Malagasy. Currency: one Malagasy franc = 100 centimes. National Day: June 26, Independence Day, 1960.

Member of the UN since Sept. 20, 1960 and of the UN specialized agencies except WIPO. Member of the OAU, and is an ACP state of the EEC.

International relations: independent kingdom until 1883. French protectorate May 1895; French colony since Aug. 6, 1896 until Oct. 14, 1958; autonomous state within the French Community 1958–60, became fully independent on June 26, 1960. A signatory of the Yaounde Conventions of 1963 and 1969, and of the Lomé Conventions of 1975 and of 1980.

A letter of Nov. 12, 1979 of the Representative of Madagascar to the UN Secretary General demanded the reintegration of four islands in the Indian Ocean between Madagascar and Mozambique. The Memorandum stated that the islands were arbitrarily separated by France from Madagascar and placed under the authority of the French Minister for Overseas Departments and Overseas Territories but the islands were natural dependencies of Madagascar and international law provided that geographical proximity gave a neighboring state a natural right of sovereignty. On Dec. 12, 1979 the UN General Assembly Res. 31/91 adopted by a vote of 93 in favor to 7 against (Belgium, France, Italy, Luxembourg, Senegal, the UK and USA) with 36 abstentions, invited the Government of France to initiate negotiations with the Government of Madagascar. France categorically rejected the resolution saying that the Assembly had no right to distribute territories, the islands were, without doubt, French, and the resolution constituted an infringement of France's national sovereignty. The islands in question are: the archipelago of Gloriensy (10 sq. km), Juan de Nova (10 sq. km), Europa Island (30 sq. km) and Bassas da India (4 sq. km). On Dec. 11, 1980 the UN General Assembly adopted Res. 35/129 inviting France to initiate negotiations with Madagascar by recorded vote of 81 to 13 with 37 abstentions. France repeated that she did not recognize the Assembly's competence in this matter.

In January 1986 Madagascar decreed the extension of its exclusive economic zone to 200 nautical miles from the shore and in accordance with the ▷ Sea Law Convention 1982, a reduction in its territorial waters limit from 56 to 12 miles.

G. GRANDIDIER, *Bibliographie de Madagascar, 1500 1933–1955*, 3 vols. Paris, 1905, 1935, 1958; A. and G.GRANDIDIER, *Histoire de Madagascar*, 30 vols., Paris 1873–1958; P. BOTTEAU, *Contribution à une histoire de la nation malgache*, Paris, 1958; S. THIERRY, *Madagascar*, Paris, 1961; R.

GENOLARME, *L'économie malgache*, Paris, 1963; Ch. ROBEQUIN, *Madagascar et les bases dispersées de l'Union française*, Paris, 1965; R. ADOLFF, V. THOMPSON, *The Malgasy Republic: Madagascar Today*, Stanford, 1965; R. PASCAL, *La République Malgache*, Paris, 1965; R. RAJEMISA-RAOLISON, *Dictionnaire géographique et historique de Madagascar*, Flanarantsoa, 1966; R. BATTISTINI, *L'Afrique australé et Madagascar*, Paris, 1967; Ch. CADAOUX, *La République malgache. Encyclopédie politique et constitutionelle*, Paris, 1969; A. SPACENSKY, *Madagascar, cinquante ans de vie politique*, Paris, 1970; R. BATTISTINI, P. LE BOURDIAC, *Atlas De Madagascar*, Tananarive, 1971; N. HESELTINE, *Madagascar*, London, 1971; M. BROWN, *Madagascar Rediscovered*, London, 1978; *Yearbook of the UN 1980*, pp. 261–263, New York, 1982; *The Europa Year Book 1984. A World Survey*, Vol. II, pp. 1959–1969, London, 1984; France–Madagascar, in: A.J. DAY ed., *Border and Territorial Disputes*, London, 1987, pp. 132–136.

MADEIRA ISLANDS. The Portuguese archipelago in the Atlantic Ocean, 565 km off Morocco. Total area: 797 sq. km. Population, 1985 estimate: 267,400. A Portuguese possession since 1419; occupied by the British 1801 and 1807–14. Capital: Funchal with 44,111 inhabitants, 1981 census. Funchal is also the name of the administrative district that integrates the whole archipelago. Since Sept., 1976 home rule.

F. ROGERS, *Atlantic Islanders of the Azores and Madeiras*, North Quincy, 1979.

MADRID. The capital of Spain since 1561, in New Castile, on the Manzanares River. Population 1981 census: 3,188,297. Seat of 22 international organizations reg. with the UIA, e.g. the Hispano-Luso-American Institute of International Law, Ibero-American Bureau of Education, Ibero-American Institute of Space Law and Commercial Aviation, Ibero-American Municipal Secretariat, Ibero-American Social Security Organization, Ibero-American Society for Numismatic Research.

Yearbook of International Organizations.

MADRID CSCE MEETING, 1980–83. The representatives of the participating States of the Conference on Security and Co-operation in Europe, CSCE, met in Madrid from Nov. 11, 1980 to Sept. 9, 1983 on the basis of the provisions of the ▷ Helsinki Final Act 1975. The full text of the Concluding Document, adopted on Sept. 6, 1983, is as follows:

"(1) The representatives of the participating States of the Conference on Security and Co-operation in Europe met in Madrid from 11 November 1980 to 9 September 1983 in accordance with the provisions of the Final Act relating to the Follow-up to the Conference, as well as on the basis of the other relevant documents adopted during the process of the CSCE.

(2) The participants addressed on 12 November 1980 by the Spanish Prime Minister.

(3) Opening statements were made by all Heads of Delegations among whom were Ministers and Deputy Ministers of Foreign Affairs of a number of participating States. Some Ministers of Foreign Affairs addressed the Meeting also at later stages.

(4) Contributions were made by representatives of the United Nations Economic Commission for Europe (ECE) and UNESCO. Contributions were also made by the following non-participating Mediterranean States: Algeria, Egypt, Israel, Morocco and Tunisia.

(5) The representatives of the participating States stressed the high political significance of the Conference on Security and Co-operation in Europe and of the process initiated by it as well as of the ways and means it provides for States to further their efforts of increase security, develop co-operation and enhance mutual understanding in Europe. They therefore reaffirmed their commitment to the process of the CSCE and emphasized the importance of the implementation of all the provisions and the respect for all the principles of the Final Act by each of them as being essential for the development of this process. Furthermore, they stressed the importance they attach to security and genuine detente, while deploring the deterioration of the international situation since the Belgrade Meeting 1977.

Accordingly, the participating States agreed that renewed efforts should be made to give full effect to the Final Act through concrete action, unilateral, bilateral and multilateral, in order to restore trust and confidence between the participating States which would permit substantial improvement in their mutual relations. They considered that the future of the CSCE process required balanced progress in all sections of the Final Act.

(6) In accordance with the mandate provided for in the Final Act and the Agenda of the Madrid Meeting, the representatives of the participating States held a thorough exchange of views on the implementation of the provisions of the Final Act and of the tasks defined by the Conference, as well as, in the context of the questions dealt with by the latter, on the deepening of their mutual relations, the improvement of security and the development of the process of detente in the future.

(7) It was confirmed that the thorough exchange of views constitutes in itself a valuable contribution towards the achievement of the aims set by the CSCE. In this context, it was agreed that these aims can be attained by continuous implementation, unilaterally, bilaterally and multilaterally, of all the provisions and by respect for all the principles of the Final Act.

(8) During this exchange of views, different and at times contradictory opinions were expressed as to the degree of implementation of the Final Act reached so far by participating States. While certain progress was noted, concern was expressed at the serious deficiencies in the implementation of this document.

(9) Critical assessments from different viewpoints were given as to the application of and respect for the principles of the Final Act. Serious violations of a number of these principles were deplored during these assessments.

Therefore, the participating States, at times represented at a higher level, considered it necessary to state, at various stages of the Meeting, that strict application of and respect for these principles, in all their aspects, are essential for the improvement of mutual relations between the participating States.

The necessity was also stressed that the relations of the participating States with all other States should be conducted in the spirit of these principles.

(10) Concern was expressed about the continued lack of confidence among participating States.

Concern was also expressed as to the spread of terrorism.

(11) The implementation of the provisions of the Final Act concerning Confidence-Building Measures, Co-operation in the field of Economics, of Science and Technology and of Environment, as well as Co-operation in Humanitarian and other fields was thoroughly discussed. It was considered that the numerous possibilities offered by the Final Act had not been sufficiently utilized. Questions relating to Security and Co-operation in the Mediterranean were also discussed.

(12) The participating States reaffirmed their commitment to the continuation of the CSCE process as agreed to in the chapter on the Follow-up to the Conference contained in the Final Act.

(13) The representatives of the participating States took note of the reports of the meetings of experts and of the 'Scientific Forum', and in the course of their deliberations took the results of these meetings into account.

(14) The representatives of the participating States examined all the proposals submitted concerning the above questions and agreed on the following:

Questions Relating to Security in Europe

The participating States express their determination

– to exert new efforts to make detente an effective, as well as continuing, increasingly viable and comprehensive process, universal in scope, as undertaken under the Final Act;

– to seek solutions to outstanding problems through peaceful means;

– to fulfil consistently all the provisions under the Final Act and, in particular, strictly and unreservedly to respect and put into practice all the ten principles contained in the Declaration of Principles Guiding Relations between Participating States, irrespective of their political, economic or social systems, as well as of their size, geographical location or level of economic development, including their commitment to conduct their relations with all other States in the spirit of these principles;

– to develop relations of mutual co-operation, friendship and confidence, refraining from any action which, being contrary to the Final Act, might impair such relations;

– to encourage genuine efforts to implement the Final Act;

– to exert genuine efforts towards containing an increasing arms build-up as well as towards strengthening confidence and security and promoting disarmament.

Principles

(1) They reaffirm their determination fully to respect and apply these principles and accordingly, to promote by all means, both in law and practice, their increased effectiveness. They consider that one such means could be to give legislation expression – in forms appropriate to practices and procedures specific to each country – to the ten principles set forth in the Final Act.

(2) They recognize it as important that treaties and agreements concluded by participating States reflect and be consonant with the relevant principles and, where appropriate, refer to them.

(3) The participating States reaffirm the need that refraining from the threat or use of force as a norm of international life, should be strictly and effectively observed. To this end they stress their duty, under the relevant provisions of the Final Act, to act accordingly.

(4) The participating States condemn terrorism, including terrorism in international relations, as endangering or taking innocent human lives or otherwise jeopardizing human rights and fundamental freedoms, and emphasize the necessity to take resolute measures to combat it. They express their determination to take effective measures for the prevention and suppression of acts of terrorism, both at the national level and through international co-operation including appropriate bilateral and multilateral agreements, and accordingly to broaden and reinforce mutual co-operation to combat such acts. They agree to do so in conformity with the Charter of the United Nations, the United Nations Declaration on Principles of International Law concerning Friendly Relations and Co-operation among States and the Helsinki Final Act.

(5) In the context of the combat against acts of terrorism, they will take all appropriate measures in preventing their respective territories from being used for the preparation, organization or commission of terrorist activities, including those directed against other participating States and their citizens. This also includes measures to prohibit on their territories illegal activities of persons, groups and organizations that instigate, organize or engage in the perpetration of acts of terrorism.

(6) The participating States confirm that they will refrain direct or indirect assistance to terrorist activities or to subversive or other activities directed towards the violent overthrow of the regime of another participating State. Accordingly, they will refrain, inter alia, from financing, encouraging, fomenting or tolerating any such activities.

(7) They express their determination to do their utmost to assure necessary security to all official representatives and persons who participate on their territories in activities within the scope of diplomatic, consular or other official relations.

(8) They emphasize that all the participating States recognize in the Final Act the universal significance of human rights and fundamental freedoms, respect for which is an essential factor for the peace, justice and well-being necessary to ensure the development of friendly relations and co-operation among themselves, as among all States.

(9) The participating States stress their determination to promote and encourage the effective exercise of human rights and fundamental freedoms, all of which derive from the inherent dignity of the human person and are essential for his free and full development, and to assure constant and tangible progress in accordance with the Final Act, aiming at further and steady development in this field in all participating States, irrespective of their political, economic and social systems.

They similarly stress their determination to develop their laws and regulations in the field of civil, political, economic, social, cultural and other human rights and fundamental freedoms; they also emphasize their determination to ensure the effective exercise of these rights and freedoms.

They recall the right of the individual to know and act upon his rights and duties in the field of human rights and fundamental freedoms, as embodied in the Final Act, and will take the necessary action in their respective countries to effectively ensure this right.

(10) The participating States reaffirm that they will recognize, respect and furthermore agree to take the action necessary to ensure the freedom of the individual to profess and practise, alone or in community with others' religion or belief acting in accordance with the dictates of his own conscience.

In this context, they will consult, whenever necessary, the religious faiths, institutions and organizations, which act within the constitutional framework of their respective countries.

They will favourably consider applications by religious communities of believers practising or prepared to practise their faith within the constitutional framework of their States, to be granted the status provided for in their respective countries for religious faiths, institutions and organizations.

(11) They stress also the importance of constant progress in ensuring the respect for and actual enjoyment of the rights of persons belonging to national minorities as well as protecting their legitimate interests as provided for in the Final Act.

(12) They stress the importance of ensuring equal rights of men and women; accordingly, they agree to take all actions necessary to promote equally effective participation of men and women in political, economic, social and culture life.

(13) The participating States will ensure the right of workers freely to establish and join trade unions, the right of trade unions freely to exercise their activities and other rights as laid down in relevant international instruments. They note that these rights will be exercised in compliance with the law of the State and in conformity with the State's obligations under international law. They will encourage, as appropriate, direct contacts and communication among such trade unions and their representatives.

(14) They reaffirm that governments, institutions, organizations and persons have a relevant and positive role to play in contributing toward the achievement of the above-mentioned aims of their co-operation.

(15) They reaffirm the particular significance of the Universal Declaration of Human Rights, the International Covenants on Human Rights and other relevant international instruments of their joint and separate efforts to stimulate and develop universal respect for human rights and fundamental freedoms; they call on all participating States to act in conformity with those international instruments and on those participating States, which have not yet done so, to consider the possibility of acceding to the covenants.

(16) They agree to give favourable consideration to the use of bilateral round-table meetings, held on a voluntary basis, between delegations composed by each participating State to discuss issues of human rights and fundamental freedoms in accordance with an agreed agenda in a spirit of mutual respect with a view to achieving greater understanding and co-operation based on the provisions of the Final Act.

(17) They decide to convene a meeting of experts of the participating States on questions concerning respect, in their States, for human rights and fundamental freedoms; in all their aspects, as embodied in the Final Act.

Upon invitation of the Government of Canada, the meeting of experts will be held in Ottawa, beginning on 7 May 1985. It will draw up conclusions and recommendations to be submitted to the governments of all participating States. The meeting will be preceded by a preparatory meeting which will be held in Ottawa upon the invitation of the Government of Canada, starting on 23 April 1985.

(18) In conformity with the recommendation contained in the Report of the Montreux Meeting of Experts, another meeting of experts of the participating States will be convened, at the invitation of the Government of Greece. It will take place in Athens and will commence on 21 March 1984, with the purpose of pursuing, on the basis of the Final Act, the examination of a generally acceptable method for the peaceful settlement of disputes aimed at complementing existing methods. The meeting will take into account the common approach set forth in the above-mentioned report.

(19) Recalling the right of any participating State to belong or not to belong to international organizations, to be or not to be a party to bilateral or multilateral treaties including the right to be or not to be a party to treaties of alliance, and also the right to neutrality, the participating States take note of the declaration of the Government of the Republic of Malta in which it stated that, as an effective contribution to detente, peace and security in the Mediterranean region, the Republic of Malta is a neutral State adhering to a policy of non-alignment. They call upon all States to respect that declaration.

Conference on Confidence- and Security-building Measures and Disarmament in Europe.

The participating States

Recalling the provisions of the Final Act according to which they recognize the interest of all of them in efforts aimed at lessening military confrontation and promoting disarmament.

Have agreed to convene a Conference on Confidence- and Security-building Measures and Disarmament in Europe.

(1) The aim of the Conference is, as a substantial and integral part of the multilateral process initiated by the Conference on Security and Co-operation in Europe, with the participation of all the States signatories of the Final Act, to undertake, in stages, new, effective and concrete actions designed to make progress in strengthening confidence and security and in achieving disarmament, so as to give effect and expression to the duty of States to refrain from the threat or use of force in their mutual relations.

(2) Thus the Conference will begin a process of which the first stage will be devoted to the negotiation and adoption of a set of mutually complementary confidence- and security-building measures designed to reduce the risk of military confrontation in Europe.

(3) The first stage of the Conference will be held in Stockholm commencing on 17 January 1984.

(4) On the basis of equality of rights, balance and reciprocity, equal respect for the security interests of all CSCE participating States, and of their respective obligations concerning confidence- and security-building measures and disarmament in Europe, these confidence- and security-building measures will cover the whole of Europe as well as the adjoining sea area and air space. They will be of military significance and politically binding and will be provided with adequate forms of verification which correspond to their content.

As far as the adjoining sea area and air space is concerned, the measures will be applicable to the military activities of all the participating States taking place there whenever these activities affect security in Europe as well as constitute a part of activities taking place within the whole of Europe as referred to above, which they will agree to notify. Necessary specifications will be made through the negotiations on the confidence- and security-building measures at the Conference.

Nothing in the definition of the zone given above will diminish obligations already undertaken under the Final Act.

The confidence- and security-building measures to be agreed upon at the Conference will also be applicable in all areas covered by any of the provisions in the Final Act relating to confidence-building measures and certain aspects of security and disarmament.

The provisions established by the negotiators will come into force in the forms and according to the procedure to be agreed upon by the Conference.

(5) Taking into account the above-mentioned aim of the Conference, the next follow-up meeting of the participating States of the CSCE, to be held in Vienna, commencing on 4 November 1986, will assess the progress achieved during the first stage of the Conference.

(6) Taking into account the relevant provisions of the Final Act, and having reviewed the results achieved by the first stage of the Conference, and also in the light of other relevant negotiations on security and disarmament affecting Europe, a future CSCE follow-up meeting will consider ways and appropriate means for the participating States to continue their efforts for security and disarmament in Europe, including the question of supplementing the present mandate for the next stage of the Conference on Confidence- and Security-building Measures and Disarmament in Europe.

(7) A preparatory meeting, charged with establishing the agenda, time-table and other organizational modalities for the first stage of the Conference, will be held in Helsinki, commencing on 25 October 1983. Its duration shall not exceed three weeks.

(8) The rules of procedure, the working methods and the scale of distribution for the expenses valid for the CSCE will, mutatis mutandis, be applied to the Conference and to the preparatory meeting referred to in the preceding paragraph. The services of a technical secretariat will be provided by the host country.

Co-operation in the Field of Economics, of Science and Technology and of the Environment.

(1) The participating States consider that the implementation of all provisions of the Final Act and full respect for the principles guiding relations among them set out therein are an essential basis for the development of co-operation among them in the field of economics, of science and technology and of the environment. At the same time they reaffirm their conviction that co-operation in these fields contributes to the reinforcement of peace and security in Europe and in the world as a whole. In this spirit they reiterate their resolve to pursue and intensify such co-operation between one another, irrespective of their economic and social systems.

(2) The participating States confirm their interest in promoting adequate, favourable conditions in order further to develop trade and industrial co-operation among them, in particular by fully implementing all provisions of the second chapter of the Final Act, so as to make greater use of the possibilities created by their economic, scientific and technical potential. In this context and taking into consideration, the efforts already made unilaterally, bilaterally and multilaterally in order to overcome all kinds of obstacles to trade, they reaffirm their intention to make further efforts aimed at reducing or progressively eliminating all kinds of obstacles to the development of trade.

Taking account of the activities of the United Nations Economic Commission for Europe (ECE) already carried out in the field of all kinds of obstacles to trade, they recommend that further work on this subject be directed in particular towards identifying these obstacles and examining them with a view to finding means for their reduction or progressive elimination, in order to contribute to harmonious development of their economic relations.

(3) On the basis of the provisions of the Final Act concerning business contacts and facilities the participating States declare their intention to make efforts to enable business negotiations and activities to be carried out more efficiently and expeditiously and further to create conditions facilitating closer contacts between representatives and experts of seller firms on the one hand and buyer as well as user firms on the other at all stages of transaction. They will also further other forms of operational contacts between sellers and users such as the holding of technical symposia and demonstrations and after-sales training or requalification courses for technical staff of user firms and organizations.

They also agree to take measures further to develop and improve facilities and working conditions for representatives of foreign firms and organizations on their territory, including telecommunications facilities for representatives of such firms and organizations, as well as to develop these and other amenities for temporarily resident staff including particularly site personnel. They will endeavour further to take measures to speed up as far as possible procedures to the registration of foreign firms' representations and offices as well as for granting entry visas to business representatives.

(4) The participating States declare their intention to ensure the regular publication and dissemination, as rapidly as possible, of economic and commercial information compiled in such a way as to facilitate the appreciation of market opportunities and thus to contribute effectively to the process of developing international trade and industrial co-operation.

To this end in order to make further progress in achieving the aims laid down in the relevant provisions of the Final Act they intend to intensify their efforts to improve the comparability, comprehensiveness and clarity of their economic and commercial statistics, in particular by adopting where necessary the following measures: by accompanying their economic and trade statistics by adequately defined summary indices based wherever possible on constant values; by publishing their interim statistics whenever technically possible at least on a quarterly basis; by publishing their statistical compilations in sufficient detail to achieve the aims referred to above, in particular by using for their foreign trade statistics a product breakdown permitting the identification of particular products for purposes of market analysis; by striving to have their economic and trade statistics no less comprehensive than those previously published by the state concerned.

They further express their willingness to co-operate towards the early completion of work in the appropriate United Nations bodies on the harmonization and alignment of statistical nomenclatures.

The participating States further recognize the usefulness of making economic and commercial information existing in other participating States readily available to enterprises and firms in their countries through appropriate channels.

(5) The participating States, conscious of the need further to improve the conditions conducive to a more efficient functioning of institutions and firms acting in the field of marketing, will promote a more active exchange of knowledge and techniques required for effective marketing, and will encourage more intensive relations among such institutions and firms. They agree to make full use of the possibilities offered by the ECE to further their co-operation in this field.

(6) The participating States note the increasing frequency in their economic relations of compensation transactions in all their forms. They recognize that a useful role can be played by such transactions, concluded on a mutually acceptable basis. At the same time they recognize that problems can be created by the linkage in such transactions between purchases and sales.

Taking account of the studies of the ECE already carried out in this field, they recommend that further work on this subject be directed in particular towards identifying such problems and examining ways of solving them in order to contribute to a harmonious development of their economic relations.

(7) The participating States recognize that the expansion of industrial co-operation, on the basis of their mutual interest and motivated by economic considerations, can contribute to the further development and diversification of their economic relations and to a wider utilization of modern technology.

They note the useful role bilateral agreements on economic, industrial and technical co-operation, including where appropriate, those of a long-term nature can play. They also express their willingness to promote favourable conditions for the development of industrial co-operation among competent organizations, enterprises and firms. To this end and with a view to facilitating the identification of new possibilities for industrial co-operation projects they recognize the desirability of further developing and improving the conditions for business activities and the exchange of economic and commercial information among competent organizations, enterprises and firms including small and medium-sized enterprises.

They also note that, if it is in the mutual interest of potential partners, new forms of industrial co-operation can be envisaged, including those with organizations, institutions and firms of third countries.

They recommend that the ECE pursue and continue to pay particular attention to its activities in the field of industrial co-operation, inter alia by further directing its efforts towards examining ways of promoting favourable conditions for the development of co-operation in this field, including the organization of symposia and seminars.

(8) The participating States declare their readiness to continue their efforts aiming at a wider participation by small and medium-sized enterprises in trade and industrial co-operation. Aware of the problems particularly affecting such enterprises, the participating States will endeavour further to improve the conditions dealt with in the preceding paragraphs in order to facilitate the operations of these enterprises in the above-mentioned fields. The participating States further recommend that the ECE develop its special studies pertaining to these problems.

(9) The participating States recognize the increasing importance of co-operation in the field of energy, inter alia that of a long-term nature, on both a bilateral and multilateral basis. Welcoming the results so far achieved through such endeavours and in particular the work carried out by the ECE they express their support for continuing the co-operation pursued by the Senior Advisors to ECE Governments on Energy aiming at the fulfilment of all parts of their mandate.

(10) The participating States reaffirm their interest in reducing and preventing technical barriers to trade and welcome the increased co-operation in this field, inter alia the work of the Government Officials Responsible for Standardization Policies in the ECE. They will encourage the conclusion of international certification arrangements covering where appropriate the mutual acceptance of certification systems providing mutually satisfactory guarantees.

(11) The participating States recommend that appropriate action be taken in order to facilitate the use and enlarge the scope of arbitration as an instrument for settling disputes in international trade and industrial co-operation. They recommend in particular the application of the provisions of the United Nations Convention on Recognition and Enforcement of Foreign Arbitral Awards of 1958 as well as a wider recourse to the arbitration rules elaborated by the United Nations Commission on International Trade Law. They also advocate that parties should, on the basis of the provisions of the Final Act, be allowed freedom in the choice of arbitrators and the place of arbitration, including the choice of arbitrators and the place of arbitration in a third country.

(12) The participating States recognize the important role of scientific and technical progress in the economic and social development of all countries in particular those which are developing from an economic point of view. Taking into account the objectives which countries or institutions concerned pursue in their bilateral and multilateral relations they underline the importance of further developing, on the basis of reciprocal advantage and on the basis of mutual agreement and other arrangements, for the forms and methods of co-operation in the field of science and technology provided for in the Final Act, for instance international programmes and co-operative projects, while utilizing also various forms of contacts, including direct and individual contacts among scientists and specialists as well as contacts and communications among interested organizations, scientific and technological institutions and enterprises. In this context they recognize the value of an improved exchange and dissemination of information concerning scientific and technical developments as a means of facilitating, on the basis of mutual advantage, the study and the transfer of, as well as access to scientific and technical achievements in fields of co-operation agreed between interested parties.

The participating States recommend that in the field of science and technology the ECE should give due attention, through appropriate ways and means, to the elaboration of studies and practical projects for the development of co-operation among member countries.

Furthermore, the participating States, aware of the relevant part of the Report of the "Scientific Forum", agree to encourage the development of scientific co-operation in the field of agriculture at bilateral, multilateral and sub-regional levels, with the aim, inter alia, of improving livestock and plant breeding and ensuring optimum use and conservation of water resources. To this end, they will promote further co-operation among research institutions and centres in their countries through the exchange of information, the joint implementation of research programmes, the organization of meetings among scientists and specialists, and other methods.

The participating States invite the ECE and other competent international organizations to support the implementation of these activities and to examine the possibilities of providing a wider exchange of scientific and technological information in the field of agriculture.

(13) The participating States welcome with satisfaction the important steps taken to strengthen co-operation within the framework of the ECE in the field of the environment, including the High-Level Meeting on the Protection of the Environment (13–16 November 1979). Taking due account of work undertaken or envisaged in other competent international organizations, they recommend the continuation of efforts in this field, including, inter alia,

– giving priority to the effective implementation of the provisions of the Resolution on Long-Range Transboundary Air Pollution adopted at the High-Level Meeting,

– the early ratification of the Convention of Long-Range Transboundary Air Pollution signed at the High-Level Meeting,

– implementation of the Recommendations contained in the Declaration on Low and Non-Waste Technology and Reutilization and Recycling of Wastes,

– implementation of Decisions B and C of the thirty-fifth session of the ECE concerning the Declaration of Policy on Prevention and Control of Water Pollution, including transboundary pollution,

– support in carrying out the programme of work of the ECE concerning the protection of the environment, including, inter alia, the work under way in the field of the protection of flora and fauna.

(14) In the context of the provisions of the Final Act concerning migrant labour in Europe, the participating States note that recent developments in the world economy have affected the situation of migrant workers, In this connection, the participating States express their wish that host countries and countries of origin, guided by a spirit of mutual interest and co-operation, intensify their contacts with a view to improving further the general situation of migrant workers and their families, inter alia the protection of their human rights including their economic, social and cultural rights while taking particularly into account the special problems of second generation migrants. They will also endeavour to provide or promote, where reasonable demand exist, adequate teaching of the language and culture of the countries of origin.

The participating States recommend that, among other measures for facilitating the social and economic reintegration of returning migrant labour, the payment of pensions as acquired or established under the social security system to which such workers have been admitted in the host country should be ensured by appropriate legislative means or reciprocal agreements.

(15) The participating States further recognize the importance for their economic development of promoting the exchange of information and experience on training for management staff. To this end they recommend the organization, in an appropriate existing framework and with the help of interested organizations such as, for example, the ECE and the International Labour Organization, of a symposium of persons responsible for services and institutions specializing in management training for administrations and enterprises with a view to exchanging information on training problems and methods, comparing experiences and encouraging the development of relations among the centres concerned.

(16) The participating States welcome the valuable contribution made by the ECE to the multilateral implementation of the provisions of the Final Act pertaining to co-operation in the fields of economics, of science and technology and of the environment. Aware of the potential of the ECE for intensifying co-operation in these fields, they recommend the fullest use of the existing mechanisms and resources in order to continue and consolidate the inplementation of the relevant provisions of the Final Act in the interest of its member countries, including those within the ECE region which are developing from an economic point of view.

(17) The participating States, bearing in mind their will expressed in the provisions of the Final Act, reiterate the determination of each of them to promote stable and equitable international economic relations in the mutual interest of all States and, in this spirit, to participate equitably in promoting and strengthening economic co-operation with the developing countries in particular the least developed among them. They also note the usefulness, inter alia, of identifying and executing, in co-operation, with developing countries, concrete projects, with a view to contributing to economic development in these countries. They also declare their readiness to contribute to common efforts towards the establishment of a new international economic order and the implementation of the Strategy for the Third United Nations Development Decade, as adopted. They recognize the importance of the launching of mutually beneficial and adequately prepared global negotiations relating to international economic co-operation for development.

Questions Relating to Security and Co-operation in the Mediterranean

(1) The participating States, bearing in mind that security in Europe, considered in the broader context of world security, is closely linked to security in the Mediterranean area as a whole, reaffirm their intention to contribute to peace, security and justice in the Mediterranean region.

(2) They further express their will
– to take positive steps towards lessening tensions and strengthening stability, security and peace in the Mediterranean and, to this end, to intensify efforts towards finding just, viable and lasting solutions, through peaceful means, to outstanding crucial problems, without resort to force or other means incompatible with the Principles of the Final Act, so as to promote confidence and security and make peace prevail in the region;
– to take measures designed to increase confidence and security;
– to develop good neighbourly relations with all States in the region, with due regard to reciprocity, and in the spirit of the principles contained in the Declaration on Principles Guiding Relations between Participating States of the Final Act;
– to study further the possibility of ad hoc meetings of Mediterranean States aimed at strengthening security and intensifying co-operation in the Mediterranean.

(3) In addition the participating States will, within the framework of the implementation of the Valletta report, consider the possibilities offered by new transport infra-structure developments to facilitate new commercial and industrial exchanges, as well as by the improvement of existing transport networks, and by a wider co-ordination of transport investments between interested parties. In this context they recommend that a study be undertaken, within the framework of the ECE, in order to establish the current and potential transport flows in the Mediterranean involving the participating States and other States of this region taking account of the current work in this field. They will further consider the question of introducing or extending, in accordance with the existing IMO regulations, the use of suitable techniques for aids to maritime navigation, principally in straits.

(4) They further note with satisfaction the results of the Meeting of Experts held in Valletta on the subject of economic, scientific and cultural co-operation within the framework of the Mediterranean Chapter of the Final Act. They reaffirm the conclusions and recommendations of the report of this Meeting and agree that they will be guided accordingly. They also take note of efforts under way aiming at implementing them as appropriate. To this end, the participating States agree to convene from 16 to 26 October 1984 a seminar to be held at Venice at the invitation of the Government of Italy, to review the initiatives already undertaken, or envisaged, in all the sectors outlined in the report of the Valletta Meeting and stimulate, where necessary, broader developments in these sectors. Representatives of the competent international organizations and representatives of the non-participating Mediterranean States will be invited to this Seminar in accordance with the rules and practices adopted at the Valletta Meeting.

Co-operation in Humanitarian and Other Fields

The participating States,

Recalling the introductory sections of the Chapter on Co-operation in Humanitarian and other Fields of the Final Act including those concerning the development of mutual understanding between them and detente and those concerning progress in cultural and educational exchanges, broader dissemination of information, contacts between people and the solution of humanitarian problems,

Resolving to pursue and expand co-operation in these fields and to achieve a fuller utilization of the possibilities offered by the Final Act,

Agree now to implement the following:

Human Contacts

(1) The participating States will favourably deal with applications relating to contacts and regular meetings on the basis of family ties, reunification of families and marriage between citizens of different States and will decide upon them in the same spirit.

(2) They will decide upon these applications in emergency cases for family meetings as expeditiously as possible, for family reunification and for marriage between citizens of different States in normal practice within six months and for other family meetings within gradually decreasing time limits.

(3) They confirm that the presentation or renewal of applications in these cases will not modify the rights and obligations of the applicants or of members of their families concerning inter alia employment, housing, residence status, family support, access to social, economic or educational benefits, as well as any other rights and obligations flowing from the laws and regulations of the respective participating State.

(4) The participating States will provide the necessary information on the procedures to be followed by the applicants in these cases and on the regulations to be observed, as well as, upon the applicant's request, provide the relevant forms.

(5) They will, where necessary, gradually reduce fees charged in connection with these applications, including those for visas and passports, in order to bring them to a moderate level in relation to the average monthly income in the respective participating State.

(6) Applicants will be informed as expeditiously as possible of the decision that has been reached. In case of refusal applicant will also be informed of their right to renew applications after reasonably short intervals.

(7) The participating States reaffirm their commitment fully to implement the provisions regarding diplomatic and other official missions and consular posts of other participating States contained in relevant multilateral or bilateral conventions, and to facilitate the normal functioning of those missions. Access by visitors to these missions will be assured with due regard to the necessary requirements of security of these missions.

(8) They also reaffirm their willingness to take, within their competence, reasonable steps, including necessary security measures, when appropriate, to ensure satisfactory conditions for activities within the framework of mutual co-operation on their territory, such as sporting and cultural events, in which citizens of other participating States take part.

(9) The participating States will endeavour, where appropriate, to improve the conditions relating to legal, consular and medical assistance for citizens of other participating States temporarily on their territory for personal or professional reasons, taking due account of relevant multilateral or bilateral conventions or agreements.

(10) They will further implement the relevant provisions of the Final Act, so that religious faiths, institutions, organizations and their representatives can, in the field of their activity, develop contacts and meetings among themselves and exchange information.

(11) The participating States will encourage contacts and exchanges among young people and foster the broadening of co-operation among their youth organizations. They will favour the ridding among young people and youthorganizations of educational, cultural and other comparable events and activities. They will also favour the study of problems relating to the younger generation. The participating States will further the development of individual or collective youth tourism, when necessary on the basis of arrangements, inter alia by encouraging the granting of suitable facilities by the transport authorities and tourist organizations of the participating States or such facilities as those offered by the railway authorities participating in the "Inter-Rail" system.

Information

(1) The participating States will further encourage the freer and wider dissemination of printed matter, periodical and non-periodical, imported from other participating States, as well as an increase in the number of places where these publications are on public sale. These publications will also be accessible in reading rooms in large public libraries and similar institutions.

(2) In particular, to facilitate the improvement of dissemination of printed information, the participating States will encourage contacts and negotiations between their competent firms and organizations with a view to concluding long-term agreements and contracts designed to increase the quantities and number of titles of newspapers and other publications imported from other participating States. They consider it desirable that the retail prices of foreign publications are not excessive in relation to prices in their country of origin.

(3) They confirm their intention, according to the relevant provisions of the Final Act, to further extend the possibilities for the public to take out subscriptions.

(4) They will favour the further expansion of co-operation among mass media and their representatives, especially between the editorial staffs of press agencies, newspapers, radio and television organizations as well as film companies. They will encourage a more regular exchange of news, articles, supplements and broadcasts as well as the exchange of editorial staff for better knowledge of respective practices. On the basis of reciprocity, they will improve the material and technical facilities provided for permanently or temporarily accredited television and radio-reporters. Moreover, they will facilitate direct contacts among journalists as well as contacts within the framework of professional organizations.

(5) They will decide without undue delay upon visa applications from journalists and re-examine within a reasonable time frame applications which have been refused. Moreover, journalists wishing to travel for personal reasons and not for the purpose of reporting shall enjoy the same treatment as other visitors from their country of origin.

(6) They will grant permanent correspondents and members of their families living with them multiple entry and exit visas valid for one year.

(7) The participating States will examine the possibility of granting, where necessary on the basis of bilateral arrangements, accreditation and related facilities to journalists from other participating States who are permanently accredited in third countries.

(8) They will facilitate travel by journalists from other participating States within their territories, inter alia by taking concrete measures where necessary, to afford them opportunities to travel more extensively, with the exception of areas closed for security reasons. They will inform journalists in advance, whenever possible, if new areas are closed for security reasons.

(9) They will further increase the possibilities and, when necessary, improve the conditions for journalists from other participating States to establish and maintain personal contacts and communication with their sources.

(10) They will, as a rule, authorize radio and television journalists, at their request, to be accompanied by their own sound and film technicians and to use their own equipment.

Similarly, journalists may carry with them reference material, including personal notes and files, to be used strictly for their professional purposes.

(11) The participating States will, where necessary, facilitate the establishment and operation, in their capitals, of press centres or institutions performing the same functions, open to the national and foreign press with suitable working facilities for the latter.

They will also consider further ways and means to assist journalists from other participating States and thus to enable them to resolve practical problems they may encounter.

Co-operation and Exchanges in the Field of Culture

(1) They will endeavour, by taking appropriate steps, to make the relevant information concerning possibilities offered by bilateral cultural agreements and programmes available to interested persons, institutions and non-governmental organizations, thus facilitating their effective implementation.

(2) The participating States will further encourage wider dissemination of and access to books, films and other forms and means of cultural expression from other participating States, to this end improving by appropriate means, on bilateral and multilateral bases, the conditions for international commercial and non-commercial exchange of their cultural goods, inter alia by gradually lowering customs duties on these items.

(3) The participating States will endeavour to encourage the translation, publication and dissemination of works in the sphere of literature and other fields of cultural activity from other participating States, especially those produced in less widely spoken languages, by facilitating co-operation between publishing houses, in particular through the exchange of lists of books which might be translated as well as of other relevant information.

(4) They will contribute to the development of contacts, co-operation and joint projects among the participating States regarding the protection, preservation and recording of historical heritage and monuments and the relationship between man, environment and this heritage; they express their interest in the possibility of convening an inter-governmental con-

ference on these matters within the framework of UNESCO.

(5) The participating States will encourage their radio and television organizations to continue developing the presentation of the cultural and artistic achievements of other participating States on the basis of bilateral and multilateral arrangements between these organizations, providing inter alia for exchanges of information on productions, for the broadcasting of shows and programmes from other participating States, for co-productions, for the invitation of guest conductors and directors, as well as for the provision of mutual assistance to cultural film teams.

(6) At the invitation of the Government of Hungary a 'Cultural Forum' will take place in Budapest, commencing on 15 October 1985. It will be attended by leading personalities in the field of culture from the participating States. The 'Forum' will discuss interrelated problems concerning creation, dissemination and co-operation, including the promotion and expansion of contacts and exchanges in the different fields of culture. A representative of UNESCO will be invited to present to the 'Forum' the views of that organization. The 'Forum' will be prepared by a meeting of experts, the duration of which will not exceed two weeks and which will be held upon the invitation of the Government of Hungary in Budapest, commencing 21 November 1984.

Co-operation and Exchanges in the Field of Education

(1) The participating States will promote the establishment of governmental and non-governmental arrangements and agreements in education and science, to be carried out with the participation of educational or other competent institutions.

(2) The participating States will contribute to the further improvement of exchanges of students, teachers and scholars and their access to each other's educational, cultural and scientific institutions, and also their access to open information material in accordance with the laws and regulations prevailing in each country. In this context, they will facilitate travel by scholars, teachers and students within the receiving State, the establishment by them of contacts with their colleagues, and will also encourage libraries, higher education establishments and similar institutions in their territories to make catalogues and lists of open archival material available to scholars, teachers and students from other participating States.

(3) They will encourage a more regular exchange of information about scientific training programmes, courses and seminars for young scientists and facilitate a wider participation in these activities of young scientists from different participating States. They will call upon the appropriate national and international organizations and institutions to give support, where appropriate, to the realization of these training activities.

(4) The representatives of the participating States noted the usefulness of the work done during the 'Scientific Forum' held in Hamburg, Federal Republic of Germany, from 18 February to 3 March 1980. Taking into account the results of the 'Scientific Forum', the participating States invited international organizations as well as the scientific organizations and scientists of the participating States to give due consideration to its conclusions and recommendations.

(5) The participating States will favour widening the possibilities of teaching and studying less widely spread or studied European languages. They will, to this end, stimulate, within their competence, the organization of and attendance at summer university and other courses, the granting of scholarships for translators and the reinforcement of linguistic faculties including, in case of need, the provisions of new facilities for studying these languages.

(6) The participating States express their readiness to intensify the exchange, among them and within competent international organizations, of teaching materials, school textbooks, maps, bibliographies and other educational material, in order to promote better mutual knowledge and facilitate a fuller presentation of their respective countries.

Follow-up to the Conference

(1) In conformity with the relevant provisions of the Final Act and with their resolve and commitment to continue the multilateral process initiated by the CSCE, the participating States will hold further meetings regularly among their representatives.

The third of these meetings will be held in Vienna commencing on 4 November 1986.

(2) The agenda, working programme and modalities of the main Madrid Meeting will be applied mutatis mutandis to the main Vienna Meeting, unless other decisions on these questions are taken by the preparatory meeting mentioned below.

For the purpose of making the adjustments to the agenda, working programme and modalities of the main Madrid Meeting, a preparatory meeting will be held in Vienna commencing on 23 September 1986. It is understood that in this context adjustments concern those items requiring change as a result of the change in date and place, the drawing of lots, and the mention of the other meetings held in conformity with the decisions of the Madrid Meeting 1980. The duration of the preparatory meeting shall not exceed two weeks.

(3) The participating States further decide that in 1985, the tenth Anniversary of the signature of the Final Act of the CSCE will be duly commemorated in Helsinki.

(4) The duration of the meetings mentioned in this document, unless otherwise agreed, should not exceed six weeks. The results of these meetings will be taken into account, as appropriate, at the Vienna Follow-up Meeting.

(5) All the above-mentioned meetings will be held in conformity with Paragraph 4 of the Chapter on 'Follow-up to the Conference' of the Final Act.

(6) The Government of Spain is requested to transmit the present document to the Secretary-General of the United Nations, to the Director-General of UNESCO and to the Executive Secretary of the United Nations Economic Commission for Europe. The Government of Spain is also requested to transmit the present document to the Governments of the non-participating Mediterranean States.

(7) The text of this document will be published in each participating State, which will disseminate it and make it known as widely as possible.

(8) The representatives of the participating States express their profound gratitude to the people and Government of Spain for the excellent organization of the Madrid Meeting and warm hospitality extended to the delegations which participated in the Meeting.

Annex I

Chairman's Statement

Venice Seminar on Economic, Scientific and Cultural Co-operation in the Mediterranean within the Framework of the Results of the Valletta Meeting of Experts

(1) The Seminar will open on Tuesday, 16 October 1984 at 10 a.m. in Venice, Italy. It will close on Friday, 26 October 1984.

(2) The work of the Seminar, guided by a Co-ordinating Committee composed of the delegations of the participating States, will be divided to Economics, Science and Culture respectively.

(3) The first three days of the Seminar will be devoted to six sessions of the Committee.

(4) The first session of the Committee will be public and will be devoted to the opening of the Seminar, to be followed by an address by a representative of the host country.

(5) The second session of the Committee will decide whether to hold further sessions of the participating States to guide the work of the Study Groups and to take any other decisions necessary for the Seminar.

(6) The following four sessions of the Committee will be public and will be devoted to introductory statements by the representatives of the participating States which so desire (in an order selected by lot in advance) and to introductory statements by the representatives of the non-participating Mediterranean States and the international organizations invited. The statements should not exceed 10 minutes per delegation.

(7) Beginning on the fourth day and for the following three and a half working days, simultaneous meetings of the three Study Groups will be held.

(8) The last one and a half days will be devoted to three sessions of the Committee. Two sessions will decide upon the most appropriate use for the documentation presented in the course of the work concerning the specific sectors indicated in the Valletta Report, such as publication of the introductory statements and distribution of the studies to the relevant international organizations, and will take any other necessary decisions.

The final session of the Committee will be public and will be devoted to the official closing of the Seminar with an address by a representative of the host country.

(9) The Chair at the opening and closing session of both the Committee and the Study Groups will be taken by a representative from the delegation of the host country. Selection of the successive chairmen by lot will then ensure daily rotation of the Chair, in French alphabetical order, among the representatives of the participating States.

(10) Participation in the work of the Seminar by the non-participating Mediterranean States (Algeria, Egypt, Israel, Lebanon, Libya, Morocco, Syria and Tunisia) and the international organizations (UNESCO, ECE, UNEP, WHO, ITU) invited will follow the rules and practices adopted at Valletta. This means, inter alia, that they will take part in the work of the three Study Groups and of the four sessions of the Committee on the second and third day as well as its opening and closing sessions.

(11) Contributions, on the subjects for consideration in one or more of the working languages of the CSCE, may be sent through the proper channels – preferably not later than three months before the opening of the Seminar – to the Executive Secretary, who will circulate them to the other participating States, and to the non-participating Mediterranean States and to the international organizations which have notified their intention of taking part.

(12) The Italian Government will designate the Executive Secretary of the Seminar. This designation should be agreed to by the participating States. The services of a technical secretariat will be provided by the host country.

(13) Other rules of procedure, working methods and the scale of distribution for the expenses of the CSCE will, mutatis mutandis, be applied to the Seminar.

(14) The arrangements outlined above will not constitute a precedent for any other CSCE forum.

Annex II

Chairman's Statement

Bern Meeting of Experts on Human Contacts

The Chairman notes the absence of objection to the declaration made by the representative of Switzerland on 15 July 1983 extending an invitation by the Swiss Government to hold a meeting of experts on human contact. Consequently, the Chairman notes that there is agreement to convene such a meeting to discuss the development of contacts among persons, institutions and organizations, with due account for the introductory part of the Chapter of the Final Act entitled Co-operation in Humanitarian and Other Fields and for the introductory part of section one (Human Contacts) of that Chapter, which reads inter alia as follows:

'The participating States,

Considering the development of contacts to be an important element in the strengthening of friendly relations and trust among peoples,

Affirming, in relation to their present effort to improve conditions in their area, the importance they attach to humanitarian considerations,

Desiring in this spirit to develop, with the continuance of detente, further efforts to achieve continuing progress in this field; . . .'

The meeting will be convened in Bern, on 15 April 1986. Its duration will not exceed six weeks. The meeting will be preceded by preparatory consultations, which will be held in Bern commencing on 2 April 1986. The results of the meeting will be taken into account, as appropriate, at the Vienna Follow-up Meeting.

The Swiss Government will designate the Executive Secretary of the meeting. This designation should be agreed to by the participating States. The services of a technical secretariat will be provided by the host country. Other rules of procedure, working methods and the scale of distribution for the expenses of the CSCE will be applied mutatis mutandis to the Bern meeting.

The Chairman notes further that this statement will be an annex to the concluding document of the Madrid Meeting and will be published with it."

A.D. ROTFELD (ed.), *From Helsinki to Madrid. CSCE Documents*, Warsaw, 1984, pp. 274–312.

MADRID DECLARATION OF THE COMMUNIST PARTIES OF FRANCE, ITALY, AND SPAIN, 1977. A Declaration signed on Mar. 3, 1977

M

in the capital of Spain. A common declaration of the secretaries general of the CP of France, G. Marchais, CP of Spain, S. Carrillo and CP of Italy, E. Berlinguer.

It stated, *inter alia*, the following:

"Our three countries are presently experiencing a crisis which is simultaneously economic, political, social and moral. This crisis brings into relief the demand for new solutions in the development of society. Apart from different conditions existing in each of these three countries, Italian, French and Spanish communists affirm the necessity for reaching the broadest understanding of political and social forces ready to contribute to a policy of progress and renewal. Such a policy requires the presence of working people and their party in centers of political decision-making; at the same time, communists recommend the carrying out of far-reaching democratic reforms ... More than ever before, the crisis of the capitalist system requires the development of democracy and the advance towards socialism. The communists of France, Italy, and Spain intend to work on behalf of creating a new society on the principle of pluralism of social and political forces, respecting, guaranteeing and developing all collective and individual freedoms: freedom of thought and of the press, association and assembly, demonstration, unrestrained movement of persons in their own country and abroad, the right to unionize, the independence of union organizations and the right to strike, the inviolability of private life, observance of general elections and the possibility of making changes by the majority carried out in a democratic manner, freedom of religion, freedom of culture, freedom to profess various philosophical, cultural and artistic views and trends. This desire to create socialism in conditions of democracy and freedom is a leading theme of the concepts worked out independently by each of the three parties.

In the future the three parties also intend to develop international solidarity and friendship on the basis of the independence of each party, equal rights, non-interference, respect for the free choice of their own party and solutions in forming socialist societies suitable to the conditions of each country. This meeting in Madrid is also an opportunity for French, Italian and Spanish communists to affirm the great significance which they attach to new steps forward on the road to detente and peaceful co-existence, to real progress in the reduction of armaments, to a full realization by all countries of all of the resolutions of the Helsinki Final Act and to a positive outcome of the meeting in Belgrade, to action in support of liquidating the division of Europe into opposing military blocks, to the establishment of new relations between the developed and developing countries, and to a new international economic order. In this way the three parties see the prospect for a democratic and independent Europe without military bases and an armaments race and the prospect for a Mediterranean Sea of peace and co-operation between the countries of this region."

Press Release, March 3, 1977.

MAFIA. The Italian name of a clandestine organization set up in Sicily in the 18th century, and operating in 19th and 20th centuries throughout Italy and in exile (in the USA) resorting to different forms of violence and blackmail to maintain its influences and economic profits; in international terminology the name used for secret political unions applying criminal fighting methods.

See also ▷ Cosa Nostra.

F. SONDERN Jr., *Brotherhood of Evil: the Mafia*, New York, 1959.

MAGALHAES DOCTRINE, 1966. A thesis of the foreign minister of Brazil, General J. Magalhaes, announced on Feb. 20, 1966 in Rio de Janeiro that the sovereignty of states was an anachronistic concept which could no longer be maintained, since it no longer had any connections with the realities of the contemporary world, which inexorably was moving toward ever wider regional integration.

Jornal do Brasil, Feb. 21, 1966.

MAGELLAN STRAIT. A natural channel connecting the Atlantic Ocean with the Pacific Ocean in the region of Patagonia and the Tierra del Fuego, discovered Nov. 28, 1520 by F. Magellan. The strait was neutralized by Argentina and Chile in a treaty of 1881, when they abandoned the fortification of its shores. In 1952 Chile signed an agreement with the USA on mutual assistance, committing itself to the military defense of this natural channel of the Western Hemisphere, in the event of the destruction of the Panama Canal.

VISCONDA DE LAEGOS, *Fernão de Magalhais: A Sua e a Sua Viagem*, 2 Vols., Lisboa, 1938; *UST*, 1952.

MAGHREB. *Arabian* = "al-maghrib" = "West." Three international terms:
(1) the name of Arab North-West Africa derived from the Middle Ages and indicating the community of language, religion and culture of the population living today in Mauritania, Morocco, Algeria, Tunisia and Libya;
(2) in the 1930s the name of a nationalist Arab movement for unification of the countries of the Maghreb;
(3) an intergovernmental organization of ministers of economy of Algeria, Morocco and Tunisia (in the first year also of Libya) called Comité permanent consultatif du Maghreb, Permanent Consultative Committee for the Maghreb, CPCM, established on Oct. 1, 1964, seated in Tunis; it aims to expand economic co-operation and form a customs union of member states. The supreme organ is the conference of ministers; permanent institutions are commissions: for trade relations, communications, post and telecommunications, employment, insurances and securities, standardization, tourism and the center for industrial research. Official languages: Arab and French. In permanent contact with the ILO, FAO, UNDP and UNIDO. Publ.: *Statistique commerciale*. The railroad connecting Morocco, Algeria and Tunisia, constructed during 1973–75, was named *Transmaghreb*. Apr. 27, 1976 the EEC states signed a treaty on economic, financial, technical co-operation with the countries of Maghreb: Algeria, Morocco and Tunisia.

On June 27, 1986 King Hassan II of Morocco called for a Maghrebian Union of Algeria, Morocco and Tunisia with a Joint Consultative Assembly.

The first summit of the heads of state of the five countries took place in Algiers on June 10–28, 1988, at which the first common Declaration of intent was accepted.

A. TIANO. *Le Maghreb entre les Mythes*, Paris, 1967; B. ETIENNE, *Les problèmes juridiques des minorités européennes en Maghreb*, Paris, 1968; C. GASTEYER, *Europe and the Maghreb. A series of Papers*, Paris, 1972; "L'Unité Maghrébine. Dimensions et Perspectives," in: *Annuaire de l'Afrique du Nord 1972*, Paris, 1972; CRESM, *La formation des élites politiques maghrébines*, Paris, 1973; CRESM, *Élites pouvoir et legitimité au Maghreb*, Paris, 1974; CRESM, *Indépendance et interdépendance au Maghreb*, Paris, 1975; CRESM, *Annuaire de l'Afrique du Nord*, Paris, 1975. J. PAXTON, *A Dictionary of the EEC*, London, 1977; *Yearbook of International Organizations*; KEESING's *Contemporary Archive*, 1986, and 1988.

MAGHREB FRATERNITY AND CO-OPERATION TREATY, 1983. An agreement between the Maghreb countries, signed first in March, 1983 by Algeria and Tunisia, and in Dec., 1983 by Mauritania.

MAGHREB TRADE AND COOPERATION AGREEMENTS. Signed since 1976 between the EEC and Maghreb countries on tariff concessions from 40% to 80% for about 80% of all agricultural

products exports subject to duties; and duty-free entry, no quota, for industrial products.

MAGIC ARTS. A subject of international co-operation. Organizations reg. with the UIA:

International Brotherhood of Magicians, f. 1920, Detroit, USA.
International Federation of Magical Societies, f. 1943, Amsterdam. Congress held every three years.
International Magic Dealers Association, f. 1945, Baltimore, MD.

Yearbook of International Organizations.

MAGINOT LINE. A fortification system which was intended to safeguard France against German aggression, constructed (on the initiative of the minister of defense A. Maginot) (1929–40) along the French–German border from Thionville to Basel. The fortifications did not cover northern France and the German army, attacking through Belgium, by-passed them from the north.

W.L. SHIRER, *The Nightmare Years 1930–1940*, Boston, 1984, pp. 498–502; A. KEMP, *The Maginot Line: Myth and Reality*, New York, 1988; Maginot Neutrality, in: D. ROBERTSON, *Guide to Modern Defense and Strategy*, Detroit, 1988.

MAGNA CHARTA LIBERTATUM. *Latin* = "the great charter of freedoms." The act passed in England on June 15, 1215, by King John Lackland which limited royal rule relating to taxes and jurisdiction in favor of king's vassals, thus starting a succession of acts restricting royal power and broadening civil rights. ▷ Petition of Right, 1628.

F. THOMPSON, *Magna Carta. Its Role in the Making of English Constitution, 1300–1629*, London, 1948; J.C. TOLT, *Magna Charta*, Cambridge, 1969.

MAISONS DE L'EUROPE. An organization reg. with the UIA, dedicated to the promotion of European unity: Federation internationale des Maisons de l'Europe, FIME, International Federation of Europe Houses, f. 1962, London, Europe House Club.

Yearbook of International Organizations.

MAIZE. A subject of international research and co-operation. Organizations reg. with the UIA:

The International Maize and Wheat Improvement Centre, Centre Internacional de Mejoramiento de Maiz y Trigo, CIMMYT, f. 1966 by the Government of Mexico and the Rockefeller Foundation in Mexico. Publ. *CIMMYT Research Highlights*.
Maize Industry Association Group of the EEC, f. 1959, Paris.
Maize-Starch Industries Association of the EEC, f. 1959, Brussels.

Yearbook of International Organizations.

MAJDANEK. A suburb of the city of Lublin in Poland, in 1941–44 site of a German concentration camp, second to ▷ Auschwitz-Birkenau in size; about 500,000 people, citizens of 26 countries, passed through it, and about 360,000 perished, killed in mass executions or in seven gas chambers with ▷ Zyklon B. At first the camp was named Kriegsgefangenenlager Lublin, and since Feb., 1943 Konzentrationslager der Waffen SS Majdanek. It was liberated on July 24, 1944 by the Soviet Army.

Die Hölle von Majdanek, Singen, 1945; *The Trial of German Major War Criminals. Proceedings of the International Military Tribunal Sitting at Nuremberg, Germany*, 42 Vols., London, 1946–48, Vol. 10, p. 289; Vol. 12, pp. 122–144; E. GRYN, Z. MURAWSKA, *Das Konzentrationslager Majdanek*, Lublin, 1966; E. ROSIAK, "Bibliografia Majdanka" (Majdanek Bibliography), in: *Zeszyty Majdanka*, Lublin, 1969–73; J. MARSZAŁEK, *Majdanek. The Concentration Camp in Lublin*, Warsaw, 1986; St. KANIA, *proces zbrodniarzy z Majdanka*, Warszawa, 1987.

MAJORCA. The Spanish island in the Mediterranean, largest of the ▷ Balearic Islands; area: 3,639 sq. km. Pop. 1980 census: 460,030. Independent kingdom 1276–1343. Part of the Baleares province of the Spanish State.

L. VILLALONGA, *Mallona*, Barcelona, 1962.

MALACCA, STRAIT OF. A channel between Sumatra and the Malay Peninsula, 805 km long and from *c.* 50 to 320 km wide; linking the Indian Ocean with the South China Sea; subject of an international dispute since 1972, when Malaysia, Singapore and Indonesia questioned the international character of the waters of Malacca Strait at the narrowest point of passage and opposed international control and plans to clean and deepen the passage by international bodies. The government of Indonesia demanded that the huge 200–300,000-ton tankers transporting crude oil from the Near East to the Far East avoid Malacca Strait and take the longer, more costly route through the straits of Lombok and Makasar. The USSR, Japan and the USA supported the maintenance of the international character of the waters of Malacca.
On Feb. 11, 1981 a Memorandum of Understanding for the Prevention of Pollution in the Malacca Strait was signed in Djakarta by Indonesia, Malaysia and Singapore. A contribution of three quarters of the money required for a special anti-pollution fund was offered by Japan.

KEESING's *Contemporary Archive*, 1986, No. 7.

MALA FIDES. *Latin* = "bad faith." An international term designating bad faith in interstate relations; the opposite of ▷ Bona fides. Also a concept commonly applied in penal law, when the determination of *mula fide* is a basis for sentencing.

MALARIA. A disease, called marsh fever or ague, caused by protozoan parasites transmitted by mosquitoes. Since 1900, the date when it was discovered, the control of malaria has been the subject of international co-operation. The First International Congress for Malaria took place in London 1913. The fight against malaria on a worldwide scale was undertaken by the WHO after World War II. According to WHO data (1978), cases of malaria doubled within the previous five years due to immunization of germs to applied medicines, particularly in southeastern Asia. A disease that is more and more often reported among travellers. In the 1980's malaria still causes 90 per cent of infant mortality in Congo. The WHO initiated in 1987 a new method to limit the malaria mortality. Adults learn the alphabet using letters printed on packets of an antimalarial drug. Radio broadcasts teach writing and, at the same time, the proper treatment of water and inform why latrines are necessary.
Organization reg. with the UIA:

International Congress on Tropical Medicine and Malaria, f. 1939, Rio de Janeiro.

M.F. BOYDED, *Malariology: A Comprehensive Survey of All Aspects of this Group of Diseases from a Global Standpoint*, 3 Vols., London, 1949; 'Information on Malaria Risk for International Travellers', in: *WHO Weekly Epidemiological Record*, No. 3, 1973; *UN Chronicle*, March, 1988, p. 90.

MALAWI. Member of the UN. Republic of Malawi. State in southern Africa. Area: 118,484 sq. km. Pop. 1985 est.: 7,100,000 (1966 census: 4,039,583; 1977 census: 5,547,460). Capital: Lilongwe with 102,924 inhabitants, 1977. Official languages: English and Chichewa. Currency: one kwacha = 100 tambala. GNP per capita in 1986:

US $160. National Day: July 6, Independence Day, 1964.
Member of the UN since Dec. 1, 1964 and all specialized UN organizations with the exception of the IAEA and IMO. Member of the OAU and is an ACP state of the EEC.
International relations: 1891 to 1953 a British Protectorate, from 1891 to 1907 a Protectorate of British Central Africa, since 1907 known as Nyasaland; from 1953 to 1964 it was part of the Federation of Rhodesia and Nyasa within the British Commonwealth. After the dissolution of the Federation on Jan. 1, 1964, Nyasa received independence on July 6, 1964; it remained a member of the Commonwealth but changed its name to the Republic of Malawi. In 1971 the government of Malawi came out in favor of a dialogue to improve relations with the Republic of South Africa and in Aug.–Sept., 1971 the lifelong president, Dr Banda, made a visit there. A signatory of the Lomé Conventions of 1975 and of 1980.
On April 25, 1986 Malawi signed an agreement with Tanzania on greater access to the port of Dar-es-Salaam. On May 9, 1986 Malawi signed with Zimbabwe an agreement on trade, air service and general co-operation.
April 1987 a mutual co-operation and military assistance agreement signed with Mozambique.
In 1987 some 200,000 Mozambican refugees entered Malawi.
See also ▷ World Heritage UNESCO List.

G. JONES, *Britain and Nyasaland*, London, 1964; J.G. PIKE, G.T. REMINGTON, *Malawi, A Geographical Study*, Oxford, 1965; E.M. KONOWALOW, J.G. LIPIEC. *Malawi*, Moskva, 1966; J.G. PIKE, *Malawi, A Political History*, London, 1967; C. McMASTER, *Malawi: Foreign Policy and Development*, London, 1974; T.D. WILLIAMS, *Malawi. The Politics of Despair*, Cornell University Press, 1979; R.B. BOEDAR, *Malawi, Bibliography*, Oxford, 1981, *The Europa Year Book 1984. A World Survey*, Vol. II, pp. 1970–1980, London, 1984.

MALAYSIA. Member of the UN. Federation of Malaysia. State in southeast Asia. Total area: 329,750 sq. km. Pop. 1986 est.: 16,108,700 (1970 census: 10,439,430; 1976 census: 12,608,095 of which 10,614,469 lived in peninsular Malaysia, 1,131,234 in Sarawak and 862,392 in Sabah; 1980 census: 13,435,588). Pop. by races: 52% Malaysians, 38% Chinese, and about 10% Indians. Capital: Kuala Lumpur with 987,875 inhabitants in 1980. Official languages: Malay and English. Currency: 1 Malay dollar = 100 cents. GNP per capita in 1987: US $1,800. National Day: Aug. 31, day of independence, 1957.
Member of the UN since Sept. 17, 1957 and UN specialized agencies with the exception of the IFAD. Member of the Commonwealth, Colombo Plan, ASPAC (1966–73) and ASEAN, ACP State of the EEC.
International relations: from 1795 to 1942 a British colony on the Malaysian Peninsula known as Malaya with the administrative center in Kuala Lumpur and a military base at Singapore and the island provinces of Borneo, Sabah, Sarawak and ▷ Brunei. Japan occupied the country from 1942 to 1945. On Aug. 31, 1947 Malaya was granted autonomy within the British Commonwealth and on Aug. 31, 1957 independence. In military alliance with Great Britain Malaya in 1961 began an operation to unite with Singapore and British Borneo, which was opposed by Indonesia. The Federation of Malaysia was formed on Sept. 16, 1963, uniting Malaya, Singapore and British Borneo without Brunei. In Sept., 1965 Singapore withdrew and proclaimed itself an independent republic. Indonesia, which in the autumn of 1963 had imposed an economic

blockade on Malaysia, lifted it after the treaty signed in Aug., 1966 in Bangkok and established diplomatic relations in Aug., 1967. In May, 1969 a conflict occurred between the Malaysians and Chinese in Kuala Lumpur which led to the imposition of a state of emergency lasting until Sept., 1970. Agreement with the UK signed on July 9, 1963 in London. As a result of the UK's withdrawal of the British fleet from the region of south Asia, Malaysia and Singapore began military consultations with Australia, New Zealand and the UK leading to the signing on Nov. 1, 1971 of a Treaty of Defence and the establishment of the Consultative Council of the above-mentioned states for the defense of Malaysia and Singapore. In Kuala Lumpur in July, 1972 the Council of Asia and the Pacific, ASPAC at a session examined a proposal by Malaysia to create a "zone of peace, freedom and neutrality" in south Asia. After declaring its support for a policy of neutrality, Malaysia on Mar. 12, 1973 withdrew from the Pact and ASPAC. In dispute with the UK over commercial relations from Oct., 1981 until Apr., 1983.

Malaysia: Agreement Concluded Between the United Kingdom, the Federation of Malaya, North Borneo, Sarawak and Singapore, London, 1963; J.M. GULLICK, *Malaya*, London, 1963; I. WANG, *Malaysia. A Survey*, London, 1965; K.G. TREGONNING, *Malaysia and Singapore*, Melbourne, 1966; H. MILLER, *A Short History of Malaysia*, New York, 1966, R.S. MILNE, *Government and Politics in Malaysia*, Boston, 1967; V. KANAPATHY, *The Malaysian Economy*, Singapore, 1970; UNTS, Vol. 750, 1970, pp. 1–487; S. LEE, *The Monetary and Banking Development of Malaysia and Singapore*, Singapore, 1974; R.S. MILNE, K.J. RATMAN, *Malaysia, New States in a New Nation. Political Development of Saravak and Sabah in Malaysia*, London, 1974; J.W. GOULD, *The US and Malaysia*, Cambridge, Mass., 1980; D.R. SNODGRASS, *Inequality and Economic Development in Malaysia*, Oxford, 1982; L. HUK TEE, J.W. SOOK, *Malaysia, Bibliography*, Oxford, 1983; *The Europa Year Book 1984. A World Survey*, Vol. II, pp. 1981–2001, London, 1984.

MALAYSIA-SINGAPORE TREATY OF DEFENCE, 1971. ▷ Malaysia.

MALDA RIDER. A Bulgarian cultural monument included in the ▷ World Heritage UNESCO List. This recalls the first Bulgarian tribes who came from the eastern steppes. It is carved on a rock face, 20 metres above ground level, and represents a horseman, followed by his dog, with his horse trampling a lion underfoot. This bas relief, unique in Europe, dates from the 8th century.

UNESCO. *A Legacy for All*, Paris, 1984.

MALDIVES. Member of the UN. Republic of Maldives. State on the coral islands of the Indian Ocean. Area: 298 sq. km. Pop. 1988 est.: 200,000 (1970 census: 142,832). Capital: Malé with 29,522 inhabitants 1977. Official language: Maldive (Divehi). GNP per capita 1986 US $310. Currency: one Maldive rupee = 100 laria. National Day: July 26, day of independence, 1965.
Member of the UN since Nov. 29, 1965 and of all its specialized agencies with the exception of IAEA, ILO and WIPO. Member of the Colombo Plan. Special member of the Commonwealth.
International relations: from 1887 to 1965 a sultanate under British protection, confirmed by the treaties of 1948 and 1960; gained independence on July 26, 1965, with Great Britain's retaining property rights acquired by the treaty of 1960 to the atoll of Addu, where until 1976 a British military base, Gan, was located. In 1977 the Government rejected an offer of the USSR to lease Gan for military purposes and in 1981 an international business

M

complex was projected in Gan. An attempted coup in November 1988 was put down by Indian forces.

H.C.P. BELL, *History, Archaeology and Epigraphy of the Maldives Islands*, Colombo, 1940; F. BERUINI, G. CORBIN, *Maldive*, Turin, 1973; *The Europa Year Book 1984. A World Survey*, Vol. II, pp. 2002–2005.

MALI. Member of the UN. République du Mali. Republic of Mali. State in western Africa. Borders with Guinea, Senegal, Mauritania, Algeria, Niger, Burkina Faso and the Côte d'Ivoire. Area: 1,240,142 sq. km. Population: 1987 census 7,620,225 (1965 census: 4,575,000; 1976: 6,524,650). Capital: Bamako with 404,022 inhabitants 1976. Official language: French. Currency: one CFA franc = 100 centimes. GNP per capita in 1987: US $210. National Day: Sept. 22, Independence Day, 1960.
Member of the UN since Sept. 28, 1960 and specialized agencies with the exception of the IMO and GATT. Member of the OUA. ACP state of the EEC.
International relations: from 1896 to 1946 a French colony known as the French Sudan; from 1946 to 1958 a French overseas territory within French West Africa; in 1959 two provinces West Sudan and Senegal, separated themselves and formed the Federation of Mali, which on June 19, 1960 withdrew from the French Commonwealth; then on Sept. 22, 1960, following Senegal's separation in Aug., 1960, West Sudan announced its complete independence and took the name Republic of Mali. A signatory of the Yaoundé Conventions of 1963 and of 1969; of the Lomé Conventions of 1975, 1980 and 1985. The border disputes with Algeria ended with agreement signed in May, 1983; disputes with Upper Volta (now Burkina Faso) were submitted to the ICJ in 1983; disputes with Nigeria were the subject of negotiations 1984.
On Dec. 22, 1986 the International Court of Justice decided a border dispute between Mali and Burkina Faso. Under the verdict the disputed area (2,252 sq km) was divided into approximately equal parts.

F.G. SNYDER, *One-Party Government in Mali: Transition Toward Control*, New Haven, 1965; W.S. MERZLIAKOV, *Stanovlenie Natsional' noi Gosudarstvennosti Republiki Mali*, Moskva, 1970; J. SURET, *Afrique Noire occidental et centrale*, Paris, 1973; W.S. HOPKINS, *Popular Government in an African Town*, Chicago, 1973; W. JONES, *Planning and Economic Policy: Socialist Mali and Her Neighbours*, New York, 1974; *The Europa Year Book 1984. A World Survey*, Vol. II, pp. 2006–2014, London, 1984.

MALTA. Member of the UN. Republic of Malta. State on three islands (Malta, Gozo and Comino) in the central area of the Mediterranean Sea. Area: 246 sq. km. Pop. 1987 census: 345,636 (1967 census: 314,216). Capital: La Valletta with 13,950 inhabitants 1982. Official languages: Maltese and English. GNP per capita 1986: US $3,470. Currency: one Maltese lira = 100 cents. National Day: Sept. 8, anniversary of the repulsion of the Turkish siege, 1565 and March 31, Independence Day, 1979.
Member of the UN since Dec. 1, 1964. Member of the UN specialized agencies with the exception of the IAEA, IDA, IFC and IPCJ. Member of the Commonwealth and the Council of Europe.
International relations: from 1530 to 1798 a feudal possession of the Order of Malta; 1798–99 occupied by France, then by Great Britain, which did not recognize the Treaty of Amiens, 1802, which returned Malta to the Order, and continued to occupy the islands, giving Malta in 1841 the status of a British colony.
From Jan. 30 to Feb. 30, 1945 in Malta took place an Anglo-American Conference, shortly before the Yalta Conference. After World War II, Malta

enjoyed limited autonomy from 1947 to 1964 and on Sept. 21, 1964 was granted independence within the Commonwealth, with Britain retaining a naval base on Malta, which was given up on Mar. 31, 1979. Established in 1976 on Malta was the Regional Center for Preventing Oil Pollution of the Mediterranean Sea. 1980–1982 in dispute with Libya over oil drilling rights in the Mediterranean Sea. In 1981 neutrality agreements with Algeria, France, Italy and the USSR. In 1981 an agreement with the USSR permitting the Soviet fleet in the Mediterranean oil storage in Malta. In Oct., 1983 an expropriation bill of 75 percent of church property was brought before court by the Archbishop of Malta.
In 1980 Malta declared a status of neutrality "based on non-alignment". On Jan. 27, 1987 the parliament unanimously accepted a constitutional amendment reaffirming the island's neutral and non-aligned status.
See also ▷ World Heritage UNESCO List.

E.W. SCHERMERHORN. *Malta of the Knights*, London, 1929; H. SMITH, *Britain in Malta*, London, 1953; T. ZAMMIT, *Malta: the Maltese Islands and their History*, London, 1954; US Department of State, *The Conference at Malta and Yalta 1945*, 2 Vols., Washington, DC, 1955; H. BOVEN-JONES, *Malta Background for Development*, London, 1961; B. BLONET, *The Story of Malta*, London, 1967; E. DOBIE, *Malta's Road to Independence*, London, 1968; E. GERADA, C. ZUBER, *Malta. An Island Republic*, Paris, 1979; *Malta Handbook 1981*; *The Europa Year Book 1984. A World Survey*, Vol. I, pp. 655–664, London, 1984.

MALTESE RED CROSS. An international sea rescue badge: a red Maltese Cross, the emblem of the Knights of Malta, on a white background in a red circle placed on starboard of special rescue units. The practice of international ships and vessels is to salute ships of the Maltese Red Cross at sea.

MALTHUSIANISM. An international term for a population theory formulated by a British economist T.R. Malthus (1766–1834), stating that a continuous disproportion existed between the birthrate and the growth of the food supply, since the former expands at a geometric rate, the latter arithmetically. This disproportion was the main cause of poverty and disease. In 1927, on the initiative of M. Sanger, an American supporter of the theory of Malthus and founder of the League of Birth Control, the First World Population Conference was held in London.

M. SANGER, *Proceedings of World Population Conference*, London, 1927; P. JAMES, *Population Malthus. His Life and Times*, London, 1979. *Yearbook of International Organizations*.

MALVINAS. ▷ Falkland Islands-Malvinas.

MAMMOTH CAVE. A natural site of the USA, included in the ▷ World Heritage UNESCO List. Over a period of six million years, the Green River and its underground tributaries have carved out of the Kentucky limestone immense caves, lakes and galleries at five different levels and vertical wells with a depth of 40 meters. Up to the present, 306 kilometers have been explored. They are inhabited by cave-dwelling animals which are not found elsewhere. On account of the atmosphere in the caves, prehistoric remains left there by pre-Columbian peoples have been preserved intact.

UNESCO. *A Legacy for All*, Paris, 1984.

MANAGEMENT. A subject of international research and co-operation. Organizations reg. with the UIA:

African Association for Public Administration and Management, f. 1971, Nairobi.
Asian Association of Personnel Management, f. 1968, Calcutta.
Association for Systems Management, f. 1947, Cleveland, Ohio. Publ.: *Journal of Systems Management*.
European Association for Personnel Management, f. 1962, Paris. ILO Special List.
European Federation of Management Consultants Associations, f. 1960, Paris.
European Federation of Young Managers, f. 1958, Paris. Publ.: *Bulletin*.
European Foundation for Management Development, f. 1971, Brussels. Publ.: *Management*.
European Industrial Research Management Association, f. 1966, Paris.
European Institute for Advanced Studies in Management, f. 1971, Brussels.
European Management Forum, f. 1971, Geneva. Publ.: *EMF Synopsis*.
Institute of Management Sciences, The, f. 1953, Providence, RI. Publ.: *Management Science*.
International Academy of Management, f. 1958, Geneva.
International Centre for the Management of Publicly Owned Firms, f. 1974, Ljubljana.
International Committee of Scientific Management in Agriculture, f. 1950, Paris.
International Management Association, f. 1956, New York.
International Management Council, f. 1944, New York.
International Research Center on Management Aptitude, f. 1972, Paris.
Nordic Management Board, f. 1972, Stockholm.
North European Management Institute, f. 1975, Oslo.
World Council of Management, f. 1962, Geneva. Consultative status with ECOSOC, UNESCO, UNIDO.

P. FERNANDEZ, *Managing Relations Between Government and Public Enterprises. A Handbook for Administration and Managers*, ILO, Geneva, 1986; *Yearbook of International Organizations, 1986/87; The Europa Yearbook 1988. A World Survey*, Vol. I, London, 1988.

MANAGEMENT AND OPERATIONS RESEARCH OF THE CMEA. The subject of international co-operation of the Warsaw Pact Countries. An Agreement on Scientific Co-operation in Organized Management, Cybernetics and Operations Research between Bulgaria, Czechoslovakia, the GDR, Hungary, Poland, Romania and the USSR, was signed on Apr. 29, 1970 in Moscow. International collectives of scholars were created by the interested parties to carry on joint scientific research in selected problems of topics agreed among them. In accordance with this Agreement the signatories have signed the same day a Treaty on the Creation of the International Collective of Scholars attached to the Institute of Management Problems (Automation and Remote Control) in Moscow.

Recueil de Documents, Varsovie, No. 4, 1970; W.E. BUTLER (ed.), *A Source Book on Socialist International Organizations*, Alphen, 1978, pp. 851–863.

MANAGEMENT CONSULTANCY INTERNATIONAL. An international term for the service, which expanded rapidly after World War I in the USA and Western Europe and worldwide in the 1970's.

A Survey of Management Consultancy, in: *The Economist*, February 13, 1988.

MAN AND BIOSPHERE. The UNESCO Program of ▷ Environmental Protection.

MANCHURIA. The northeast part of China, roughly identical with the three provinces: Liaoning, Kilin and Heilungkiang. Area: 1,950,000 sq. km. Population, 1985 estimate: 81,640,000.

Capitals of the 3 provinces: Shenyang in Liaoning, Changchun in Kilin, and Harbin in Heilungkiang. A subject of controversies and international conflicts between China and Russia in the 19th century, Russia and Japan (1904–05) and Japan and China (1931–45). Japanese occupation of Manchuria, resulted in Japan being accused of aggression in the League of Nations, Sept. 21, 1931. On Mar. 21, 1931 Japan installed a puppet regime in Manchuoko (Manchutikuo). On Feb. 19, 1933, the League of Nations recognized formally China's rights to Manchuria and Japan on Mar. 27, 1933 withdrew from the LN. On the basis of the Soviet–Chinese Friendship and Alliance Treaty on Aug. 14, 1945, Manchuria was returned to China, except for Port Arthur which was taken over by China ten years later in 1955.

B.A. ROMANOW, *Rossiya w Manchuryi 1892–1906*, Leningrad, 1928; M.O. HUDSON (ed.), *The Verdict of the League: China and Japan in Manchuria, The Official Documents*, Boston, 1933; F.C. JONES, *Manchuria since 1931*, London, 1949; S.R. SMITH, *The Manchurian Crisis 1931–1932*, New York, 1949; H. HERRFAHRDT, "Mandschurei", in: STRUPP-SCHLOCHAUER *Wörterbuch des Völkerrechts*, Vol. 2, Berlin, 1961; J. PAXTON ed., *The Statesman's Yearbook, 1987–88*, London, 1987.

MANCHURIAN RAILWAY. The Eastern Chinese railroad line constructed 1887–1903 by an inter-governmental Sino-Russian company, connecting Transbaikalia across northern Manchuria with Vladivostok, its southern arm from Changerum to Port Arthur under many different administrations: Japanese 1905–19, British–French 1919–21, Sino-Soviet 1924–34, Japanese 1935–45, Sino-Soviet 1945–50; finally, transferred under terms of the Sino-Soviet treaty of Feb. 14, 1950 to the Chinese as the Chang Tsuk railway.

O. LATTIMORE, *Manchuria Cradle of Conflict*, London, 1935.

MANDATES, INTERNATIONAL. An international institution established 1919 by the League of Nations Covenant (art. 22). This authorized colonial powers victorious in World War I, to administer prewar overseas possessions of Germany and Arab territories separated from Ottoman Turkey; the system advanced by Marshal J.C. Smuts, a delegate of the Union of South Africa was meant as a sanction for former colonial powers adopted by the Versailles Conference, Jan. 30, 1919. Under the terms of art. 119 of the Versailles Treaty Germany renounced its claims to the advantage of the principal allied and associated powers. The colonies were distributed among the Entente by the Supreme Council May 7, 1919. The former Ottoman Empire was partitioned from Apr. 19 to 26, 1920. Under art. 22 of the LN Covenant the mandates were to be framed so as to alleviate the colonial system in the name of "sacred trust of civilization" in colonies and territories inhabited by "peoples not yet able to stand by themselves." It did not cover all dependent territories but only those which belonged to the defeated powers and among them only some, called emancipation mandates, were supposed to lead to an independent statehood. The mandates were executed on behalf of the LN through the Permanent Mandates Commission which examined the annual reports of mandatories regarding administration of the territories they were in charge of. The colonies of the defeated powers were divided into three groups of mandates – A, B, and C classified according to: the degree of ability of the indigenous population to stand alone, and to the country's geographical situation and economic conditions. The widest range of independence was granted to class A (emancipation) mandates, the least to class C which were practically entirely dependent on the mandatory. Class B mandates were open for trade to all LN members and the USA, although not a member of the LN. The mandatories were: Australia, Belgium, France, Great Britain, Japan, New Zealand and the Union of South Africa. Class A mandates included former Ottoman possessions: Lebanon and Syria assigned to France; Iraq, Palestine and Transjordan assigned to Great Britain (mandate for ▷ Palestine, confirmed by the League of Nations Council under changed terms, July 24, 1922). Class B mandates comprising former German colonies: Tanganyika – to Great Britain; Togoland and Cameroon divided between Great Britain and France; Rwanda-Urundi to Belgium. Class C mandates comprising former German possessions: South-West Africa (now Namibia) to the Union of South Africa; the Pacific islands north of the equator (Caroline, Marshall, Mariana Islands) to Japan; the island of Nauru to Australia; West Samoa to New Zealand. The USA was granted the privilege of an "open door" to all LN class A and C mandates.

W.R. BATSELL, "The US and the System of Mandates," in: *International Conciliation*, No. 213, October 1925; J. STOYANOWSKY, *La Theorie Générale des Mandats Internationaux*, Paris, 1925; D.F.W. VAN REES, *Les mandats internationaux*, Vol. 2, Paris, 1927–28; N. BENTWICH, *The Mandates System*, London, 1930; Q. WRIGHT, *Mandates under the League of Nations*, London, 1930; LEAGUE OF NATIONS. *The Mandates System, Origin, Principles, Application*, Geneva, 1945; *UN Terms of the League of Nations Mandates*, New York, 1946; H.D. HALL, *Mandates, Dependencies and Trusteeship*, Washington, DC, 1948; R.N. CHOWDBURY, *International Mandates and Trusteeship*, The Hague, 1955; E. MENZEL, "Mandate,"in: STRUPP-SCHLOCHAUER *Wörterbuch des Völkerrechts*, Bd. 2, Berlin, 1961, pp. 460–468.

MANGANESE. A subject of international research. Organization reg. with the UIA:

Manganese Centre, f. 1975, Neuilly-sur-Seine. Promote the use of manganese, its alloys and compound by supporting research programs. Publ.: *Manganese in Ferrous Metallurgy, Literature Revue*.

Yearbook of International Organizations.

MANHATTAN ISLAND. A central borough of New York City, N.Y., 57 sq. km, the site of the United Nations headquarters. The island was sold in 1626 by the Manhathan Indians to the Dutch West India Company, and under the name of New Amsterdam was capital of the New Netherlands Colony. In 1664 the English occupied Manhattan and renamed it New York; since 1898 one of the five boroughs established by the Greater New York Charter.

L.S. MITCHEL, C. LAMBERT, *Manhattan, Now and Long Ago*, New York, 1934.

MANHATTAN PROJECT. A code name of the program to build the first atomic bomb, named after the Manhattan District of Tennessee, where a chemical plant for enriching uranium was located at Oak Ridge. The other development laboratories were in ▷ Los Alamos and ▷ Alamogordo, New Mexico.

D. ROBERTSON, *Guide to Modern Defense and Strategy*, Detroit, 1988.

MANIFEST DESTINY. The American 19th-century doctrine to the effect that it was the destiny of the United States to absorb all of North America, extending the US boundaries to the Pacific Ocean. The phrase "our manifest destiny (is) to overspread the continent," was printed first time in July 1845 in *The US Magazine and Democratic Review*, published in New York by John L. O'Sullivan.

F. MERK, *Manifest Destiny and Mission in American History: A Reinterpretation*, New York, 1963.

MANILA. The capital of the Philippines since 1901, population, 1980 census: 1,630,485, city, and 5,925,884 Metropolitan area, (seat of the government), southwest Luzon on Manila Bay. Seat of international organizations reg. with the UIA, e.g. the Asian Development Bank, Asian Development Committee, Asian Oceanic Postal Union, International Rice Research Institute, ILO Regional Office, UN Information Centre, WHO Regional Office.

Yearbook of International Organizations.

MANILA DECLARATION ON THE PEACEFUL SETTLEMENT OF INTERNATIONAL DISPUTES, 1982. A Declaration negotiated by the Special Committee on the Charter of the UN and Strengthening of the Role of the Organization over a two year period, beginning its work in Manila in 1980 and accepting the draft at a meeting in Geneva in 1981; adopted on Oct. 27, 1982 with the consensus of the UN General Assembly. ▷ Peaceful Settlement of International Disputes. The text of the Manila Declaration is as follows:

"The General Assembly,
Reaffirming the principle of the Charter of the United Nations that all States shall settle their international disputes by peaceful means in such a manner that international peace and security, and justice, are not endangered. Conscious that the Charter of the United Nations embodies the means and an essential framework for the peaceful settlement of international disputes, the continuance of which is likely to endanger the maintenance of international peace and security,
Recognizing the important role of the United Nations and the need to enhance its effectiveness in the peaceful settlement of international disputes and the maintenance of international peace and security, in accordance with the principles of justice and international law, in conformity with the Charter of the United Nations,
Reaffirming the principle of the Charter of the United Nations that all States shall refrain in their international relations from the threat or use of force against the territorial integrity or political independence of any State or in any other manner inconsistent with the purposes of the United Nations,
Reiterating that no State or group of States has the right to intervene, directly or indirectly, for any reason whatsoever, in the internal or external affairs of any other State. Reaffirming the Declaration on Principles of International Law concerning Friendly Relations and Co-operation among States in accordance with the Charter of the United Nations. Bearing in mind the importance of maintaining and strengthening international peace and security and the development of friendly relations among States irrespective of their political, economic and social systems or levels of economic development,
Reaffirming the principle of equal rights and self-determination of peoples as enshrined in the Charter of the United Nations and referred to in the Declaration on Principles of International Law concerning Friendly Relations and Co-operation among States in accordance with the Charter of the United Nations and in other relevant resolutions of the General Assembly,
Stressing the need for all States to desist from any forcible action which deprives peoples, particularly peoples under colonial and racist régimes or other forms of alien domination, of their inalienable right to self-determination, freedom and independence, as referred to in the Declaration on Principles of International Law concerning Friendly Relations and Co-operation among States in accordance with the Charter of the United Nations,
Mindful of existing international instruments as well as respective principles and rules concerning the peaceful settlement of international disputes, including the exhaustion of local remedies whenever applicable,
Determined to promote international co-operation in the political field and to encourage the progressive development of international law and its codification,

particularly in relation to the peaceful settlement of international disputes, Solemnly declares:

I. (1) All States shall act in good faith and in conformity with the purposes and principles enshrined in the Charter of the United Nations with a view to avoiding disputes among themselves likely to affect friendly relations among States, thus contributing to the maintenance of international peace and security. They shall live together in peace with one another as good neighbours and strivc for the adoption of meaningful measures for strengthening international peace and security.

(2) Every State shall settle its international disputes exclusively by peaceful means in such a manner that international peace and security, and justice, are not endangered.

(3) International disputes shall be settled on the basis of the sovereign equality of States and in accordance with the principle of free choice of means in conformity with obligations under the Charter of the United Nations and with the principles of justice and international law. Recourse to, or acceptance of, a settlement procedure freely agreed to by States with regard to existing or future disputes to which they are parties shall not be regarded as incompatible with the sovereign equality of States.

(4) States parties to a dispute shall continue to observe in their mutual relations their obligations under the fundamental principles of international law concerning the sovereignty, independence and territorial integrity of States, as well as other generally recognized principles and rules of contemporary international law.

(5) States shall seek in good faith and in a spirit of co-operation an early and equitable settlement of their international disputes by any of the following means: negotiation, inquiry, mediation, conciliation, arbitration, judicial settlement, resort to regional agencies or arrangements, or other peaceful means of their own choice, including good offices. In seeking such a settlement, the parties shall agree on such peaceful means as may be appropriate to the circumstances and the nature of their dispute.

(6) States parties to regional arrangements or agencies shall make every effort to achieve pacific settlement of their local disputes through such regional arrangements or agencies before referring them to the Security Council. This does not preclude States from bringing any dispute to the attention of the Security Council or of the General Assembly in accordance with the Charter of the United Nations.

(7) In the event of failure of the parties to a dispute to reach an early solution by any of the above means of settlement, they shall continue to seek a peaceful solution and shall consult forthwith on mutually agreed means to settle the dispute peacefully. Should the parties fail to settle by any of the above means a dispute the continuance of which is likely to endanger the maintenance of international peace and security, they shall refer it to the Security Council in accordance with the Charter of the United Nations and without prejudice to the functions and powers of the Security Council set forth in the relevant provisions of Chapter VI of the Charter of the United Nations.

(8) States parties to an international dispute, as well as other States shall refrain from any action whatsoever which may aggravate the situation so as to endanger the maintenance of international peace and security and make more difficult or impede the peaceful settlement of the dispute, and shall act in this respect in accordance with the purposes and principles of the United Nations.

(9) States should consider concluding agreements for the peaceful settlement of disputes among them. They should also include in bilateral agreements and multilateral conventions to be concluded, as appropriate, effective provisions for the peaceful settlement of disputes arising from the interpretation or application thereof.

(10) States should, without prejudice to the right of free choice of means, bear in mind that direct negotiations are a flexible and effective means of peaceful settlement of their disputes. When they choose to resort to direct negotiations, States should negotiate meaningfully, in order to arrive at an early settlement acceptable to the parties. States should be equally prepared to seek the settlement of their disputes by the other means mentioned in the present Declaration.

(11) States shall in accordance with international law implement in good faith all the provisions of agreements concluded by them for the settlement of their disputes.

(12) In order to facilitate the exercise by the peoples concerned of the right to self-determination as referred to in the Declaration on Principles of International Law concerning Friendly Relations and Co-operation among States in accordance with the Charter of the United Nations, the parties to a dispute may have the possibility, if they agree to do so and as appropriate, to have recourse to relevant procedures mentioned in the present Declaration, for the peaceful settlement of the dispute.

(13) Neither the existence of a dispute nor the failure of a procedure of peaceful settlement of disputes shall permit the use of force or threat of force by any of the States parties to the dispute.

II. (1) Member States should make full use of the provisions of the Charter of the United Nations, including the procedures and means provided for therein, particularly Chapter VI, concerning peaceful settlement of disputes.

(2) Member States shall fulfil in good faith the obligations assumed by them in accordance with the Charter of the United Nations. They should, in accordance with the Charter, as appropriate, duly take into account the recommendations of the Security Council relating to the peaceful settlement of disputes. They should also, in accordance with the Charter, as appropriate, duly take into account the recommendations adopted by the General Assembly, subject to Articles 11 and 12 of the Charter in the field of peaceful settlement of disputes.

(3) Member States reaffirm the important role conferred on the General Assembly by the Charter of the United Nations in the field of peaceful settlement of disputes and stress the need for it to discharge effectively its responsibilities. Accordingly, they should:

(a) Bear in mind that the General Assembly may discuss any situation, regardless of origin, which it deems likely to impair the general welfare or friendly relations among nations and, subject to article 12 of the Charter, recommend measures for its peaceful adjustment;

(b) Consider making use, when they deem it appropriate, of the possibility of bringing to the attention of the General Assembly any dispute or any situation which might lead to international friction or give rise to a dispute;

(c) Consider utilizing, for the peaceful settlement of their disputes, the subsidiary organs established by the General Assembly in the performance of its functions under the Charter;

(d) Consider, when they are parties to a dispute brought to the attention of the General Assembly, making use of consultations within the framework of the General Assembly, with the view to facilitating an early settlement of their dispute.

(4) Member States should strengthen the primary role of the Security Council so that it may fully and effectively discharge its responsibilities, in accordance with the Charter of the United Nations, in the area of the settlement of disputes or of any situation the continuance of which is likely to endanger the maintenance of international peace and security. To this end they should:

(a) Be fully aware of their obligation to refer to the Security Council such a dispute to which they are parties if they fail to settle it by the means indicated in Article 33 of the Charter;

(b) Make greater use of the possibility of bringing to the attention of the Security Council any dispute or any situation which might lead to international friction or give rise to a dispute;

(c) Encourage the Security Council to make wider use of the opportunities provided for by the Charter in order to review disputes or situations the continuance of which is likely to endanger international peace and security;

(d) Consider making greater use of the fact-finding capacity of the Security Council in accordance with the Charter;

(e) Encourage the Security Council to make wide use, as a means to promote peaceful settlement of disputes, of the subsidiary organs established by it in the performance of its functions under the Charter;

(f) Bear in mind that the Security Council may, at any stage of a dispute of the nature referred to in Article 33 of the Charter or of a situation of like nature, recommend appropriate procedures of methods of adjustment;

(g) Encourage the Security Council to act without delay, in accordance with its functions and powers, particularly in cases where international disputes develop into armed conflicts.

(5) States should be fully aware of the role of the International Court of Justice which is the principal judicial organ of the United Nations. Their attention is drawn to the facilities offered by the International Court of Justice for the settlement of legal disputes especially since the revision of the Rules of the Court. States may entrust the solution of their differences to other tribunals by virtue of agreements already in existence or which may be concluded in the future.

States should bear in mind:

(a) That legal disputes should as a general rule be referred by the parties to the International Court of Justice, in accordance with the provisions of the Statute of the Court;

(b) That it is desirable that they:

(i) Consider the possibility of inserting in treaties, whenever appropriate, clauses providing for the submission to the International Court of Justice of disputes which may arise from the interpretation of application of such treaties;

(ii) Study the possibility of choosing, in the free exercise of their sovereignty, to recognize as compulsory the jurisdiction of the International Court of Justice in accordance with Article 36 of its Statute;

(iii) Review the possibility of identifying cases in which use may be made of the International Court of Justice.

The organs of the United Nations and the specialized agencies should study the advisability of making use of the possibility of requesting advisory opinions of the International Court of Justice on legal questions arising within the scope of their activities, provided that they are duly authorized to do so.

Recourse to judicial settlement of legal disputes, particularly referral to the International Court of Justice, should not be considered an unfriendly act between States.

(6) The Secretary-General should make full use of the provisions of the Charter of the United Nations concerning the responsibilities entrusted to him. The Secretary-General may bring to the attention of the Security Council any matter which in his opinion may threaten the maintenance of international peace and security. He shall perform such other functions as are entrusted to him by the Security Council or by the General Assembly. Reports in this connexion shall be made whenever requested to the Security Council or the General Assembly.

Urges all States to observe and promote in good faith the provisions of the present Declaration in the peaceful settlement of their international disputes,

Declares that nothing in the present Declaration shall be constructed as prejudicing in any manner the relevant provisions of the Charter or the rights and duties of States, or the scope of the functions and powers of the United Nations organs under the Charter, in particular those relating to the peaceful settlement of disputes,

Declares that nothing in the present Declaration could in any way prejudice the right to self-determination, freedom and independence, as derived from the Charter, of peoples forcibly deprived of that right and referred to in the Declaration on Principles of International Law concerning Friendly Relations and Co-operation among States in accordance with the Charter of the United Nations, particularly peoples under colonial and racist regimes or other forms of alien domination; nor the right of these peoples to struggle to that end and to seek and receive support, in accordance with the principles of the Charter and in conformity with the above-mentioned Declaration,

Stresses the need, in accordance with the Charter of the United Nations, to continue efforts to strengthen the process of the peaceful settlement of disputes through progressive development and codification of international law, as appropriate, and through enhancing the effectiveness of the United Nations in this field."

UN Chronicle, Dec., 1982, pp. 80–81.

MANILA GROUP OF 77 DECLARATION, 1976. The Third Ministerial Meeting of the Group of 77, Jan. 26–Feb. 7, 1976, in Manila, adopted the

Manila Declaration and Programme of Action. The text of the Declaration is as follows:

"The Ministers of the Group of 77 at their Third Meeting held at Manila

Having examined in depth the economic situation of the developing countries and having reviewed the policies pursued and the results obtained since the adoption of the International Development Strategy and the third session of UNCTAD in the field of trade, international economic relations and development in the light of the Declaration and Programme of Action on the Establishment of a New International Economic Order and the Charter of Economic Rights and Duties of States, Inspired by the Charter of Algiers and the Lima Declaration of the Group of 77,

Bearing in mind the Declaration and Programme of Action adopted at the Fourth Conference of Heads of State or Government of Non-Aligned Countries,

Noting with deep disappointment that very few concrete results have been obtained in those fields, that the developed countries have generally not implemented the policy measures and fulfilled the commitments undertaken designed to improve the situation of the developing countries, and that the relative position of the developing countries in the world economy – especially the position of the least developed, land-locked and island developing countries and the most seriously affected developing countries – has worsened during this period,

Declare that international economic conditions – particularly world inflation, monetary disorders, recession in the highly industrialized regions, the appearance of new forms of economic discrimination and coercion, certain forms of action by transnational corporations and the revival of protectionist trends in the developed countries – have seriously affected the economies of all developing countries,

Recognize that, in view of this situation, some developing countries have made and continue to make major efforts to provide other developing countries with financial and other assistance to help them overcome their economic difficulties, including their food and energy problems, and hope that such initiatives will encourage further assistance in these fields by those countries which are in a position to do so.

Deplore the application by the developed countries of unjust and discriminatory trade regulations, and the obstacles which they impose on developing countries in regard to access to modern technology;

Affirm their conviction that it is necessary and urgent to bring about radical changes in economic relations in order to establish new relations based on justice and equity which will eliminate the inequitable economic structures imposed on the developing countries, principally through the exploitation and marketing of their natural resources and wealth;

Emphasize the close solidarity of all the developing countries which has made it possible for them to evolve a unified position, as well as the importance of harmonizing positions which help to enhance the irreversible process they have created in international economic relations and to consolidate and strengthen their unity and solidarity through joint concerted action, thus laying the foundation for the new international economic order and for the adoption of the Charter of Economic Rights and Duties of States;

Affirm that the current situation presents a favourable opportunity for the international community to take steps and reach agreements at the fourth session of the United Nations Conference on Trade and Development aimed at solving the economic and financial problems of the developing countries and achieving the objectives of the new international economic order;

Decide to promote the urgent implementation, on the basis of a programme of concerted action, of the new international economic order within the framework of the Declaration and the Programme of Action on the Establishment of a New International Economic Order, the Charter of Economic Rights and Duties of States and the decisions and recommendations adopted by the General Assembly at its seventh special session;

Reaffirm their conviction that the implementation of the new international economic order is essential for the promotion of justice and the maintenance of peace and international co-existence, owing to the ever-increasing interdependence of nations and peoples;

Reaffirm further their conviction that responsibility for achieving economic development and ensuring social justice lies in the first instance with countries themselves and that the achievement of national, regional and international objectives depends on the efforts of each individual country. As a necessary corollary to those national efforts and in accordance with the principle of collective self-reliance, they urge the need for closer and more effective co-operation among the developing countries, including the harmonization and co-ordination of their respective economic policies;

Declare once again that international economic relations should be based on full respect for the principles of equality among States, and non-intervention in internal affairs, on respect for different economic and social systems and on the right of each State to exercise full and permanent sovereignty over its natural resources and all its economic activities;

Resolve that the developing countries should be assured wider and increasing participation in the process of adoption and in the adoption of decisions in all areas concerning the future of international economic relations and in the benefits derived from the development of the world economy;

Reiterate the need and urgency for the principle of differential and preferential treatment in favour of developing countries to be applied in accordance with specific and effective formulae in all fields of their economic relations with developed countries;

Reaffirm the importance of international co-operation for the establishment of the new international economic order;

Accordingly, declare their firm conviction to make full use of the bargaining power of the developing countries, through joint and united action in the formulation of unified and clearly defined positions, with a view to achieving, inter alia, the following objectives in the various fields of international economic co-operation:

(1) Restructuring international trade in commodities so that it offers a viable solution to the problems concerning commodities, to raise and maintain the value of the exports and the export earnings of the developing countries, increasing processing and improving the terms of trade of those countries. Bearing these fundamental objectives in mind, the fourth session of UNCTAD should take concrete and operational decisions concerning the integrated programme and all its elements and the implementation of each of its objectives and each necessary international measure, including the negotiating plan;

(2) Reshaping of the structure of world industrial production and trade to ensure a substantial increase in the share of the developing countries in world exports of manufactures and semi-manufactures, in accordance with the goals set forth, inter alia, in the Lima Declaration and Plan of Action on Industrial Development and Co-operation. To this end, suitable internal and external conditions, including new forms and areas of industrial co-operation, must be created for accelerated industrial development and for promoting the export of manufactures and semi-manufactures from developing countries, without giving rise to restrictions on their access to the markets of developed countries;

(3) Expanding the total export capacity of the developing countries, in terms both of volume and of the diversification of their products, and thus promoting the increasing participation of those countries in world trade;

(4) Achieving substantive results for the developing countries in the multilateral trade negotiations and additional benefits through the adoption of differential measures and special procedures for them in all areas of the negotiations. Pending the completion of those negotiations, ensuring that the developed countries strictly observe the standstill with regard to their imports from the developing countries. In this context, substantial improvements should be made in the existing GSP schemes to help developing countries to achieve the agreed objectives of the GSP;

(5) Condemning and rejecting all forms of discrimination, threats of coercive economic policies and practices, either direct or indirect, against individual or groups of developing countries by developed countries, which are contrary to fundamental principles of international economic relations;

(6) Urgently achieving a reform of the international monetary system which will meet the interests and needs of the developing countries, with the full and effective participation of those countries in the decision-making process involved in that reform;

(7) Securing short-term and long-term financing in sufficient volume and on favourable terms and accelerating the flow of bilateral and multilateral financial assistance from the developed to all the developing countries, and in particular to the least developed, land-locked and island developing countries and the most seriously affected countries, on a more continuous, assured and stable basis, in order that the target for official development assistance is reached without delay; moreover, access of developing countries to the capital markets of developed countries should be substantially increased;

(8) Taking immediate steps by developed countries and international organizations to alleviate the increasing debt problems of developing countries and to expand and improve short-term financing facilities to mitigate their balance-of-payments difficulties;

(9) Promoting national technological progress through the acquisition, development, adaptation and dissemination of technology in accordance with the needs, interests and priorities of the developing countries, and ensuring the transfer of technology on international conditions consistent with those objectives, with a view to strengthening the technological capabilities of developing countries and thus reducing their dependency in this field, through appropriate institutional arrangements, the adoption of a multilaterally binding code of conduct on the transfer of technology and the review and revision of international conventions on patents and trademarks;

(10) Ensuring that the activities of transnational corporations operating in territories of developing countries are compatible with their objectives of national development, through the free exercise of the right to regulate the operations of those corporations, and promoting international co-operation as an effective instrument for achieving that objective;

(11) Promoting and fostering a programme of economic co-operation among developing countries through suitable permanent machinery for strengthening their mutual co-operation and making possible the adoption of concrete measures in the various fields of their economic relations, in order to promote the individual and collective self-reliance, interdependence and progress of the developing countries;

(12) Devoting efforts towards urgent action for the expansion of trade between the developing countries and developed countries with centrally planned economies, including suitable institutional arrangements for dealing with this issue, with a view to increasing the economic benefits accruing to developing countries from such trade and economic co-operation;

(13) Establishing more effective and realistic measures and policies through suitable mechanisms in favour of the least developed, land-locked and island developing countries and implementing them as speedily as possible, so that their results may help to alleviate or diminish the specific and long-existing problems affecting those countries.

(14) Implementing without delay effective measures in favour of the most seriously affected developing countries to enable them to overcome their special problems, in accordance with General Assembly resolutions 3201 (S-VI) and 3202 (S-VI);

(15) Furthering co-operation in the solution of major and urgent international economic problems affecting a large number of developing countries;

(16) Continuing and intensifying their efforts to effect the changes urgently needed in the structure of world food production and taking appropriate steps, particularly in the field of trade, to ensure an increase in agricultural production, especially of foodstuffs) and in the real income which the developing countries obtain from exports of these products. Developed countries and developing countries in a position to do so should provide food grains and financial assistance on most favourable terms to the most seriously affected countries, to enable them to meet their food and agricultural development requirements;

(17) Strengthening the negotiation function of UNCTAD so that it could evolve into an effective negotiating arm of the United Nations in the fields of trade and development capable of translating principles and policy guidelines, particularly those enunciated by the General Assembly, into concrete agreements and

thus directly contribute to the establishment of the New International Economic Order."

Conference on Economic Co-operation among Developing Countries. Declarations, Resolutions, Recommendations and Decisions adopted in the UN System, Mexico, DF, 1976, Vol. 2, pp. 369–466.

MANILA PACT, 1954. The ▷ SEATO Treaty signed on Sept. 8, 1954, in Manila, together with the ▷ Pacific Charter 1954 proclaimed on the same day.

MANILA SUMMIT, 1966. The official name of a conference of the heads of state of Australia, Philippines, New Zealand, Thailand and South Vietnam with the President of the USA, L.B. Johnson. The main discussed problem was the Vietnam war.

KEESING's *Contemporary Archive*, 1966.

MANILA UNCTAD CONFERENCE, 1979. The fifth session of the UNCTAD held in Manila from May 7 to June 3; adopted a comprehensive new Program of Action for the Least Developed Countries and called for the provision of much larger flows of assistance to such countries.

UN Chronicle, July, 1979, pp. 44–53.

MAN, ISLE OF. A British island in the Irish Sea; area: 588 sq. km. Population, 1986, census: 64,282; the principal town: Douglas with 20,368 inhabitants. The island was purchased in the 18th century from feudal lords. It is not part of the United Kingdom but is a largely self-governing dependency of the British Crown. Special relations with the EEC under the Accession Treaty, 1972. Every external company conducting trade on the island, is registered at a flat tax rate of $250 free of capital gains tax; there is also no inheritance tax.

M. SOLLY, *The Isle of Man. A Low Tax Area*, London, 1984; E.H. STENNING, *Portrait of the Isle of Man*, London, 1984; J. PAXTON ed., *The Statesman's Year-Book 1987–88*, London, 1987.

MANKIND 2000. An international organization f. 1965, Brussels, reg. with the UIA, promoting all aspects of human development. Publ.: *Yearbook of World Problems and Human Potential.*

Yearbook of International Organizations.

MANNERHEIM LINE. The Finnish defense fortifications on the Karelian isthmus, constructed 1929–33 and named after the Marshal of Finland, E. von Mannerheim (1867–1951); breached by the Soviet Army Feb., 1940 and June, 1944.

Memoirs of Marshal Mannerheim, London, 1954.

MANO RIVER UNION. A customs union between Sierra Leone and Liberia, est. Oct. 3, 1973, with HQ in Freetown. The Mano is the border river between the two countries. The Union is open to other West African States.

The Europa Yearbook 1988. A World Survey, Vol. I, London, 1988.

MANSHOLT PLAN, 1969. A project of comprehensive development of agriculture in 10 member-states of the EEC for the decade 1971–80, elaborated by the Netherlands Minister of agriculture Sine L. Mansholt in 1969 (before the Norwegian refusal to join the EEC), anticipating an increase in the profits of farmers to the level existing in other branches of economy through rapid modernization of agriculture and integration of farm lands left behind as a result of youth migration to towns (60% of EEC farmers were more than 60 years old in 1980, and 73% of them indicated they had no one to work the farms in the case of their death).

J. PAXTON, *Dictionary of the EEC*, London, 1978, pp. 160–161.

MANUFACTURED PRODUCTS. A subject of international co-operation. An international problem of the Third World countries in connection with the growing postwar disproportion of prices for manufactured products and for basic raw materials. In 1950 the production of developing countries compared with that of the industrial world was less than 10%, and in 1970 less than 15%.

MAOISM. An international term for the ideas of Mao Tse-tung, chairman of the Chinese Communist Party, spread by the Chinese People's Republic within the international workers' movement and also reflected in Chinese foreign policy, *inter alia*, in the UN, where the Chinese PR delegation in 1973–74 advanced the thesis that, according to the thoughts of Mao Tse-tung, the world regardless of predominant socio-political orders, was divided into three zones (1) the socialist countries, i.e. the Chinese PR and Albania; (2) the imperialist and social-imperialist powers; (3) the remaining countries of the "middle zone."

S.S. KIM, *China, the United Nations and World Order*, Princeton, 1979.

MAP OF THE WORLD. A subject of international co-operation, since 1891 called the International Map of the World on the Millionth Scale. In 1891 the International Geographical Congress started basic work on a map on the millionth scale, which means that each sq. cm represents 10 sq. km of the surface of the globe. Only such a scale makes it possible to show such important topographical features as communication lines or scattered populations. In 1913 in Southampton the Central Office for the International Map on the Millionth Scale was created, which, up to 1939, had published *c*. 350 maps of the 1,000 planned. In 1953, ECOSOC, on the recommendation of the UN General Assembly, took over the tasks of the Central Office and moved the center from Southampton to UN Headquarters in New York. Since 1955, ECOSOC publishes an annual report on the work of the center, controlled by a UN Technical Conference on the International Map of the World, IMW.

UN Yearbook 1963, pp. 407–408; *UN Technical Conference on the International Map of the World*, New York, 1963; *International Map of the World on the Millionth Scale*, UN New York, 1969; *Supplement*, 1972.

MAPS AND SIGNS AERONAUTICAL. The Paris Air Convention, 1919, introduced general maps, Cartes generales aeronatiques internationales, detailed maps, Cartes normales aeronautiques internationales, and a universal system of signs binding all international air traffic. These rules are subject to modification in accordance with technical progress. In force now are the ICAO rules which include navigational maps on the scale of 1 : 1 million or 1 : 500,000, and situational, topographic and magnetic maps.

Code international de l aviation, Paris, 1939 (in French and English); W.W. RISTOW, *Aviation Cartography. A Historico-Bibliographic Study of Aeronautical Charts*, 1956; *ICAO Bulletin*, 1973.

MAPS, INTERNATIONAL. An international term for all kinds of regional and world maps, geographical, political, sea, air, thematic (e.g. climatic geobotanic, demographic, geologic, soil, etc.). Subject of international co-operation, in the last decades of the 20th century with the aid of satellite measurements under the sponsorship of the UN as well as of regional organizations.

Bibliographie cartographique internationale, publ. since 1949.

MAPS OF SEA AND OCEAN BEDS. These were drawn up and published on the initiative of the International Oceanographic Commission, IOC, f. 1960 with Headquarters in the UNESCO building in Paris. Based on data from scientific expeditions of the IOC member States. The first publications concerned the Mediterranean Sea and the north part of the Indian Ocean. The IOC publ. *Deep Sea Research and Oceanographic Abstracts.*

UNESCO, *International Oceanographic Tables*, Paris, 1966.

MAPUTO DECLARATION ON ZIMBABWE AND NAMIBIA, 1977. The Declaration of the Namibia Conference in Support of the Peoples of Zimbabwe and the Namibia and the Program of Action for the Liberation of Zimbabwe and Namibia, adopted on May 19, 1977 in Maputo.

UN Chronicle, Mar., 1983, pp. 19–20.

MAQUIS. The *nom de guerre* of the French resistance movement fighting in partisan actions during World War II, which besides Frenchmen also included other nationalities. The word *maquis* refers to the bush in Corsica: *macchia*.

H. MICHEL, *Histoire de la Résistance*, Paris, 1965; M.K. DZIEWANOWSKI, *War at any Price, World War II in Europe 1939–45*, Englewood Cliffs, 1987.

MARATHI LANGUAGE. ▷ Goa, Daman and Diu.

MARATHON. A Greek village, site of a victory of Greek infantry over Persian cavalry in Sept. 490 B.C. To commemorate the legend that a Greek soldier ran 40 km after the battle to Athens with news of victory, a Marathon Race is one of the official Olympic Games competitions since the first modern Olympic Games in Athens, 1896.

MARATHON RACE. A branch of sport recognized by the International Olympic Committee since the first modern ▷ Olympic Games, 1896, named for ▷ Marathon, Greece. Since 1924 the Olympic Marathon distance is standardized at 42.2 km (26 miles 385 yards). At the 1952 Olympic Games, the Czech Emil Zatopek set an Olympic record of 2 hr. 23 min. 3.2 sec., broken in 1960 and 1964 by Abebe Bikila: 2 hr. 15 min. 16.2 sec. and 2 hr. 12 min. 11 sec.
International Marathon races are also organized by the Boston Athletic Association since 1897, and the New York City Marathon Committee.

J.A. CUDDON, *Dictionary of Sport and Games*, London, 1980; S. TREADWELL, *The World of Marathons*, New York, 1987.

MARCELLI-SIEBERG SCALE. A scale developed by the Italian G. Marcelli (1850–1914) and the German A. Sieberg (1875–1945), an international scale for measuring earthquakes according to their felt effects, from 0 to 12 degrees: (1) unfelt by people; (2) very light; (3) light; (4) moderate (shaking of walls); (5) stronger (swaying of objects); (6) strong (falling objects); (7) very strong (falling plaster); (8) destructive; (9) devasting; (10) annihilating; (11) and (12) catastrophic.

A. SIEBERG, *Geologische, physikalische und angewandte Erdbenkunde*, Berlin, 1923.

MAR DEL PLATA. A port city in Argentina (population, 1980, census: 414,694), site of the first World Conference on Water matters in 1977, which passed an international plan of operation to secure drinking water for all people, ▷ Mar del Plata Plan of Action, 1977.

The Europa Yearbook 1987. A World Survey, London, 1987.

MAR DEL PLATA CONVENTION, 1963. The Inter-American Convention on Facilitation of International Waterborne Transportation, signed on June 7, 1963 at the Second Inter-American Port and Harbor Conference in Mar del Plata, by Argentina, Bolivia, Chile, Colombia, Costa Rica, the Dominican Republic, Haiti, Honduras, Mexico, Panama, Paraguay, Peru, Uruguay and the USA.

Acta Final de la Segunda Conferencia Portuaria Interamericana, Documentos Oficiales, Mar del Plata, 7 de junio de 1963; *OAS Treaty Series,* Washington, DC, 1963.

MAR DEL PLATA, PLAN OF ACTION OF, 1977. The recommendations adopted Mar. 25, 1977 in Mar del Plata by the First World Water Conference 1977. The Plan, prepared by experts and governments together emphasized special action plans on the provision of water for home use and agricultural purposes, calling for the commitment by national governments, to do at least 85% of the work. The highlights of the Action Plan relating to the regional and international co-operation are as follows:

"(84) In the case of shared water resources, co-operative action should be taken to generate appropriate data on which future management can be based and to devise appropriate institutions and understandings for co-ordinated development.

(85) Countries sharing water resources, with appropriate assistance from international agencies and other supporting bodies, on the request of the countries concerned, should review existing and available techniques for managing shared water resources and co-operate in the establishing of programmes, machinery and institutions necessary for the co-ordinated development of such resources. Areas of co-operation may with agreement of the parties concerned include planning, development, regulation, management, environmental protection, use and conservation, forecasting, etc. Such co-operation should be a basic element in an effort to overcome major constraints such as the lack of capital and trained manpower as well as the exigencies of natural resources development.

(86) To this end it is recommended that countries sharing a water resource should:
(a) Sponsor studies, if necessary with the help of international agencies and other bodies as appropriate, to compare and analyse existing institutions for managing shared water resources and to report on their results;
(b) Establish joint committees, as appropriate with agreement of the parties concerned, so as to provide for co-operation in areas such as the collection, standardization and exchange of data, the management of shared water resources, the prevention and control of water pollution, the prevention of water associated diseases, mitigation of drought, flood control, river improvement activities and flood warning systems;
(c) Encourage joint education and training schemes that provide economies of scale in the training of professional and sub-professional officers to be employed in the basin;
(d) Encourage exchanges between interested countries and meetings between representatives of existing international or interstate river commissions to share experiences. Representatives from countries which share resources but yet have no developed institutions to manage them could be included in such meetings;
(e) Strengthen if necessary existing governmental and inter-governmental institutions, in consultation with interested Governments, through the provision of equipment, funds and personnel;

(f) Institute action for undertaking surveys of shared water resources and monitoring their quality;
(g) In the absence of an agreement on the manner in which shared water resources should be utilized, countries which share these resources should exchange relevant information on which their future management can be based in order to avoid foreseeable damages;
(h) Assist in the active co-operation of interested countries in controlling water pollution in shared water resources. This co-operation could be established through bilateral, subregional or regional conventions or by other means agreed upon by the interested countries sharing the resources.
(87) The regional water organizations, taking into account existing and proposed studies as well as the hydrological, political, economic and geographical distinctiveness of shared water resources of various drainage basins should seek ways of increasing their capabilities of promoting co-operation in the field of shared water resources and, for this purpose, draw upon the experience of other regional water organizations.
(88) The Conference took note of all the specific regional recommendations emanating from the regional commissions in Africa, Asia and the Pacific, Europe, Latin America and Western Asia and referred them to the regional commissions concerned for appropriate action in the light of the other relevant recommendations approved by the Conference. These recommendations are reproduced in the annex to this section of the present chapter.
(89) The Conference also took note of the valuable contributions provided by the regional commissions. These formed part of the material on which the consolidated action recommendations had been based.
(90) It is necessary for States to co-operate in the case of shared water resources in recognition of the growing economic, environmental and physical interdependencies across international frontiers. Such co-operation, in accordance with the Charter of the United Nations and principles of international law, must be exercised on the basis of the equality, sovereignty and territorial integrity of all States, and taking due account of the principle expressed, inter alia, in principle 21 of the Declaration of the United Nations Conference on the Human Environment.
(91) In relation to the use, management and development of shared water resources, national policies should take into consideration the right of each state sharing the resources to equitably utilize such resources as the means to promote bonds of solidarity and co-operation.
(92) A concreted and sustained effort is required to strengthen international water law as a means of placing co-operation among states on a firmer basis. The need for progressive development and codification of the rules of international law regulating the development and use of shared water resources has been the growing concern of many governments.
(93) To this end it is recommended that:
(a) The work of the International Law Commission in its contribution to the progressive development of international law and its codification in respect of the law of the non-navigational uses of international watercourses should be given a higher priority in the working programme of the Commission and be co-ordinated with activities of other international bodies dealing with the development of international law of waters with a view to the early conclusion of an international convention;
(b) In the absence of bilateral or multilateral agreements, Member States continue to apply generally accepted principles of international law in the use, development and management of shared water resources;
(c) The Intergovernmental Working Group of Experts on Natural Resources Shared by Two or More States of the United Nations Environment Programme be urged to expedite its work on draft principles of conduct in the field of the environment for the guidance of States in the conservation and harmonious exploitation of natural resources shared by two or more States;
(d) Member States take note of the recommendations of the Panel of Experts on Legal and Institutional Aspects of International Water Resources Development set up under Economic and Social Council resolution 1033 (XXXVI) of August 14, 1964 as well as

the recommendations of the United Nations Inter-regional Seminar on River Basin and Inter-basin Development Budapest, 1975.
(e) Member States also take note of the useful work of non-governmental and other expert bodies on international water law;
(f) Representatives of existing international commissions on shared water resources are urged to meet as soon as possible with a view to sharing and disseminating the results of their experience and to encourage institutional and legal approaches to this question;
(g) The United Nations system should be fully utilized in reviewing, collecting, disseminating and facilitating exchange of information and experiences on this question. The system should accordingly be organized to provide concreted and meaningful assistance to States and basin commissions requesting such assistance."

UN Chronicle, April 1977, pp. 36–37.

MARE APERTUM. *Latin* = "open sea'.' In international maritime law a sea open to the ships of all countries. ▷ High Seas Convention, 1958.

"MARECHAL-JOFFRE" CLAIMS AGREEMENT, 1948. An agreement between the US, France and Australia in respect of cargo claims arising out of the requisitioning of the SS *Marechal-Joffre* (with memorandum of understanding), signed on Oct. 19, 1948 in Washington.

UNTS, Vol. 84, pp. 201–205.

MARE CLAUSUM. *Latin* = "closed sea." In international maritime law the internal sea of some states, inaccessible to foreign ships.

MARGARINE. A subject of international co-operation research and agreements.

J.H. Van STUYVENSBERG, ed., *Margarine: An Economic, Social and Scientific History 1869–1969,* Liverpool, 1969. *Yearbook of International Organizations.*

MARIANAS ISLANDS. Group of 15 islands in the west Pacific east of the Philippines and south of Japan; a part of the ▷ Pacific Islands Trust Territory. Total area: *c.* 1000 sq. km; 1984 population estimate: 19,635. Discovered 1521, named Thieves Islands (Ladrones), renamed by Spanish Jesuits 1668, Spanish possession until 1898, when Guam was ceded to the USA and other islands to the German Reich. They were occupied (with the exception of Guam) by Japan 1914 and 1920 mandated by the LN to Japan; occupied by the US 1944, trusteed by the UN to the US 1947. On June 17, 1975 the majority of the population voted to become a Commonwealth of the USA (like Puerto Rico). The US Congress approved the new status on July 21, 1975 and on Jan. 9, 1978 the Commonwealth of the Northern Marianas was associated with the United States, but without formal dissolution of the UN trusteeship agreement. On Oct. 13, 1983 the UN Special (Decolonization) Committee, reaffirmed its strong conviction that the Administrative Authority must ensure that military bases and installations and military activities did not hinder the population from exercise of its right to self-determination and independence.

UN Chronicle, January, 1984, p. 63; J. PAXTON ed., *The Statesman's Year-Book 1987–88,* London, 1987.

MARIJUANA. A hemp plant, called in Asia ▷ Hashish, smoked by itself or mixed with tobacco, one of the ▷ drugs of abuse.

UN Chronicle, May, 1987.

MARINE CORPS. The specially trained autonomous military forces within the US Department of Navy, est. in 1776, used in special missions abroad to guard US embassies or US bases.

M

R.D. HEINL JR., *Soldiers of the Sea: the US Marine Corps, 1775–1962*, Washington, DC, 1962.

MARINE FISHING AGREEMENT, 1962. The Agreement between the governments of the GDR, Poland and USSR on Co-operation in Marine Fishing, signed on July 28, 1962 in Warsaw; came into force Feb. 22, 1963. The Contracting Parties agreed to co-operate in the development of marine fishing, of commercial technology, on scientific research into the state of stocks of living resources of the sea and also exchange experience in fishing technology and the production of fish products, their transportation and storage.

Recueil de Documents, Varsovie, No. 7, 1962; W.E. BUTLER (ed.), *A Source Book on Socialist International Organizations*, Alphen, 1978, pp. 1114–1116.

MARINE INSURANCE. The insurance covering sea vessels, passengers, crew and cargo in sea shipments. Most often used in international trade are: the London insurance clauses (▷ Institute of London Underwriters Clauses).
Organization reg. with the UIA:

International Union of Marine Insurance, f. 1873, Zürich, Switzerland.

Yearbook of International Organizations, 1986/87; The Europa Yearbook 1988. A World Survey, Vol. I, London, 1988.

MARINE LIVING RESOURCES. A subject of international conventions to protect the marine living resources. See ▷ Antarctica.

MARINE POLLUTION. A subject of the International Convention for the Prevention of Pollution of the Sea by Oil and of the UN General Assembly Res. 34/83 of Dec. 18, 1979 on Marine Pollution, adopted without a vote. By its terms the Assembly urged that the competent international institutions and organizations, and in particular the IMCO, expedite and intensify their activities relating to the prevention of pollution. It called upon states parties to the 1979 Convention to discharge fully their obligations under the Convention.
In the 1980's the marine pollution control was carried out world-wide under the aegis of the UNEP, on the basis of regional conventions (▷ Baltic Helsinki Conventions, Barcelona Convention on ▷ Mediterranean Pollution Control, Agreement on Antipollution Action in the ▷ North Sea, ▷ Indian Ocean Pollution Convention, ▷ South Pacific Lima Convention, ▷ Red Sea Jeddah Convention and others.

UN Chronicle, March, 1980, p. 56; R.L. BLEDSOE, B.A. BOCZEK, *The International Law Dictionary*, Oxford, 1987.

MARINER. An unmanned American space vehicle. See also ▷ Mars; ▷ Mercury.

MARINE RESOURCES. A subject of international co-operation and conventions.

F.E. FIRTH, *An Encyclopaedia of Marine Resources*, New York, 1969.

MARIONETTES. ▷ Puppetry.

MARISAT. ▷ INMARSAT.

MARITIME ARBITRATION. The oldest form of non-political arbitration, a part of commercial arbitration organized by ▷ Lloyd's and operated in conformity with English Law which is accepted in the majority of the maritime traffic documents by subscribing to a relevant clause. In the Warsaw Pact states there are national maritime arbitration courts, such as the Maritime Arbitration Com-

mission (Morskaya Arbitralnaya Komisya) set up in 1930 at the All-Union Commercial Chamber of the USSR, or the Council of Arbitrators established in 1949 at the Polish Chamber of Foreign Trade; there is also an International Arbitration Court for Maritime and Inland Navigation in Gdynia, which was set up in the pursuance of the agreement between the Polish, Czechoslovakian and GDR Chambers of Commerce exercising in turn the chairmanship of the Court for a term of one year. The rules of the International Court at Gdynia are described the following general provisions:

"Art. 1.(1) The Court of Arbitration for Marine and Inland Navigation decides upon issues that may arise from all affairs of marine and inland navigation.
(2) These are, in particular, issues arising from:
– Charter parties and bills of lading,
– Contract on handling goods,
– Broker and forwarding contracts,
– Insurance policies,
– Collisions of ships and assistance, inasmuch as a sea-going or inland vessel is involved,
– Salvage,
– Damages of port accomodations and equipment,
– General average.
(3) The court of Arbitration is not competent for labour issues.
Art. 2. The competency of the Court is justified:
(a) if the parties have agreed so in writing, or
(b) if the demandant in his statement of claim has submitted to the competency of the Court and the defendant, upon interrogation of the Court of Arbitration, has agreed to its competency in writing, or
(c) if the competency is provided by international agreement.
Art. 3.(1) The residence of the Court of Arbitration is Gdynia.
(2) The venue is, as a rule, Gdynia.
(3) The parties may agree that the venue be Berlin, Prague, or Warsaw. Upon request of one of the parties and upon hearing the other parties, the president may dispose that the proceedings take place and the decision be made in another place.
Art. 4. The Court of Arbitration comprises: the president, the council, the arbitration commission and the secretary."

See also ▷ Shipping Law and International Legislation and ▷ York-Antwerp Rules.

UN *Register of Text of Conventions and Other Instruments concerning International Trade Law*, New York.

MARITIME BOUNDARIES. A subject of international agreements and delimitations. During the years 1952–1982 a total of 94 maritime agreements were concluded and the potential number of boundaries of continental shelves and economic zones under negotiation was estimated in 1987 to be between 353 and 373.

G. BLAKE ed., *Maritime Boundaries and Ocean Resources*, London, 1987.

MARITIME BRUSSELS CONVENTIONS, 1910–62. The conventions concluded in the years 1910–62 by Diplomatic Conferences on Maritime Law in Brussels:

"(1) on unification of certain rules relating to collisions of sea-going vessels, signed Sept. 23, 1910, ratified by 37 states;
(2) on unification of certain rules relating to assistance and salvage at sea, signed Sept. 23, 1910, ratified by 38 states;
(3) on unification of certain principles relating to limitation of liability of shipowners of sea-going vessels, signed Aug. 25, 1924, ratified by 10 states;
(4) on unification of certain principles relating to bills of lading, signed Aug. 25, 1924, ratified by 32 states;
(5) on unification of certain principles relating to maritime lines and mortgages, signed Apr. 10, 1926, ratified by 17 states;
(6) on unification of certain principles relating to immunities for state vessels, signed Apr. 10, 1926, ratified by 18 states;
(7) on unification of certain principles relating to penal

competence in matters resulting from collisions of vessels and other accidents in navigation, signed May 10, 1952, ratified by 15 states;
(8) on unification of certain principles relating to civil competence in cases resulting from collision of vessels, signed May 10, 1952, ratified by 17 states;
(9) on unification of certain principles relating to detention of sea-going vessels, signed May 10, 1952, ratified by 13 states;
(10) on reduction of liability of shipowners of sea-going vessels, signed Oct. 10, 1957, ratified by 12 states;
(11) on illegal passengers (stowaways travelling without tickets), signed Oct. 10, 1957, ratified by 7 states (▷ Stowaways);
(12) on unification of certain principles relating to carriage of passengers by sea, signed Apr. 29, 1961, ratified by 6 states;
(13) on liability of persons operating vessels equipped with nuclear reactors, signed May 25, 1962;
(14) In 1969 a conference convened by IMCO concluded three conventions:
(a) international convention on tonnage measurement of vessels, which introduced the first universal system of tonnage measurement,
(b) international convention relating to intervention on the high seas in case of pollution by oil;
(c) international convention on civil liability for damage caused by pollution by oil prompted by an increasing number of tankers and cases of contamination of seas (marine pollution). Preparatory works for further diplomatic conferences of Maritime Law and Brussels Maritime Conventions carried out from 1897 by the International Maritime Committee, since 1948 on recommendation of the IMCO. Headquarters Brussels. The Brussels Conventions are of great significance for the uniformization of the civil maritime law."
▷ Maritime Law Conventions, 1882–1978.

IMC *Maritime Conventions*, Geneva, 1970.

MARITIME CARGO. The maritime cargo was defined in the Convention on Facilitation of International Maritime Traffic, 1965 (Annex, Section 1A):

"Any goods, wares, merchandise, and articles of every kind whatsoever carried on ship, other than mail, ship's spare parts, ship's equipment, crew's effects and passengers' accompanied baggage."

UNTS, Vol. 591, p. 298.

MARITIME CHAMBER. An institution investigating accidents at sea which result in damage or loss of the ship or cargo, death, or bodily injury, as well as each collision, running aground, or fire on a vessel (arts. 92 and 93 P of the Maritime Code). Collisions between ships of various flags, after determination of the circumstances of the collision by national maritime chambers, are either the subject of agreement between shipowners or international arbitration on the basis of international principles on questions of insurance, accepted in 1910, 1960 and 1972.

MARITIME COMMISSION OF THE FOUR POWERS. The Commission was called into being by the Paris Protocol signed Feb. 10, 1947 by France, the UK, USA and USSR. The task of the commission was to divide up the Italian fleet in accordance with the Peace Treaty with Italy 1947 as well as the return by the USSR of ships loaned from the USA – one cruiser, and from Great Britain – one battleship, seven destroyers, and three submarines.

UNTS, Vol. 140, p. 111.

MARITIME ECONOMIC ZONE. The 200-mile zone reserved by a coastal state for its own exclusive fishing rights created at the UN Conference on Law of the Sea. It is the subject of international disputes since some 95% of the stock of fish is located within the maritime economic zones, thereby penalizing more than 50 states with unfavorable geographical position. On Aug. 26, 1976 at the Third Conference on Law of the Sea, these states announced a plan for a new definition of the maritime economic zone; this was not accepted by the more privileged coastal states.

MARITIME ILO CONVENTIONS. 16 maritime ILO conventions listed below in chronological order:

1920 – International ILO Convention (No. 7) specifying the lowest age of admission of children to work on board ship, draft adopted on July 3, 1920 in Genoa; International ILO Convention (No. 8) on compensation payment in case of unemployment caused by shipwreck, adopted in draft on July 9, 1920 in Genoa; International ILO Convention (No. 9) on employment agencies for seamen, adopted as draft on July 10, 1920 in Genoa;
1921 – Declaration on recognition of the right of states with no seacoast to fly the flag, signed on Apr. 20, 1921 in Barcelona;
International ILO Convention (No. 15) specifying the lowest age admission of underaged persons to work underdeck and in the heat rooms, adopted as draft on Nov. 11, 1921 in Geneva;
International ILO Convention (No. 16) on compulsory medical examination of children and underaged persons employed on board ship, adopted as draft on Nov. 11, 1920 in Geneva;
ILO Agreement on facilitation of treatment of venereal diseases for commercial seamen, signed on Dec. 1, 1924 in Brussels;
ILO Convention (No. 22) regarding hire contract for seamen, signed on July 26, 1926 in Geneva;
ILO Convention (No. 23) relating to repatriation of seamen, signed on July 26, 1926 in Geneva;
1929 – ILO Convention (No. 27) relating to weight markings on heavy consignments carried on board, signed on Aug. 15, 1929 in Geneva;
ILO Convention (No. 68) relating to supply of food and catering services for crews of ships, adopted on June 27, 1946 in Seattle;
ILO Convention (No. 69) relating to certificate of competence for ship cooks, adopted on June 27, 1946 in Seattle;
ILO Convention (No. 70) relating to seamen's social security, adopted on June 28, 1946 in Seattle;
ILO Convention (No. 73) relating to medical examination of seamen, adopted on June 29, 1946 in Seattle;
ILO Convention (No. 74) relating to certificate of competence for able seamen, adopted on June 29, 1946 in Seattle;
1949 – ILO Convention (No. 91) relating to paid leaves for seamen (revised 1949), adopted June 18, 1949 in Geneva;
ILO Convention (No. 92) relating to crew accommodation on board (revised 1949), adopted on June 18, 1949 in Geneva;
IMCO, *Maritime Conventions*, Geneva, 1970.

MARITIME INTER-AMERICAN NEUTRALITY CONVENTION, 1928, adopted by the Sixth International Conference of American States and signed at Havana, Feb. 20, 1928. The Convention on Maritime Neutrality defined the rules of freedom of commerce in time of war; entered into force on Jan. 12, 1931; ratified by Bolivia, Colombia, the Dominican Republic, Ecuador, Haiti, Nicaragua, Panama, the USA (with reservation).

LNTS, Vol. 135, p. 187; *CARNEGIE ENDOWMENT, International Conferences of American States, 1889–1928*, Washington, DC, 1931.

MARITIME LAW CONVENTIONS 1882–1978. Inter-governmental organizations monitoring maritime conventions are the ▷ IMO (formerly ▷ IMCO) and the International Diplomatic Conference of Maritime Law; the non-governmental body which associates national maritime organizations of individual countries and initiates codification of maritime law is, since 1897, the International Maritime Committee, IMC, Headquarters, Antwerp; Publ.: *IMC Bulletin and collections of maritime conventions*. A chronological list of international conventions on Maritime Law:

International agreement relating to police regulation of fisheries on the North Sea beyond the coastal belt, signed on May 6, 1882 in The Hague;
International Convention on protection of submarine cables, signed on Mar. 4, 1884 in Paris;
Convention relating to hospital ships, signed on Dec. 21, 1904 in The Hague;
Convention on refurnishing of commercial vessels into warships, signed on Oct. 18, 1907 in The Hague;
Convention on certain restrictions in execution of the right of prize during warfare at sea, signed on Oct. 18, 1907 in The Hague;
Convention on bombardment by navy during war, signed on Oct. 18, 1907 in The Hague;
Convention on adjustment to sea war of the provisions of Geneva Convention, signed on Oct. 18, 1907 in The Hague;
Convention on handling commercial vessels of the enemy at the beginning of war operations, signed on Oct. 18, 1907 in The Hague;
International Convention for the unification of certain rules of law with respect to collision between vessels and Protocol, signed on Sept. 23, 1910, in Brussels, called Collision Convention, 1910.
Convention for the unification of certain rules of law relating to assistance and salvage at sea and Protocol, signed on Sept. 23, 1910 in Brussels and Protocol to amend the Convention, May 27, 1967, called Assistance and Salvage Convention, 1910/1967.
International Convention for the unification of certain rules relating to the limitation of the liability of owners of sea-going vessels and Protocol, signed on Aug. 25, 1924 in Brussels, called Limitation of Shipowners' Liability Convention, 1924.
International Convention for the unification of certain rules of law relating to bills of lading and Protocol, signed on Aug. 25, 1924 in Brussels, and Protocol to amend the Convention, Feb. 23, 1968, called Bills of Lading Convention, 1924/1968.
International Convention for the unification of certain rules relating to maritime liens and mortgages and Protocol, signed on Apr. 10, 1926 in Brussels, called Liens and Mortgages Convention, 1926.
International Convention for the unification of certain rules concerning the immunity of state-owned ships, signed on Apr. 10, 1926 in Brussels, and Additional Protocol, Brussels, May 24, 1934, called Immunity State-Owned Ships Convention, 1926/1934.
International Convention on load-lines, signed on July 5, 1930 in London;
Agreement on Signals: the Regulation concerning warning of storms expected to affect the locality, tide and depth signals, signals concerning the movements of vessels at the entrances to harbors or important channels; and Regulations concerning certain Description of Maritime Signals, signed on Oct. 23, 1930 in Lisbon;
Agreement on light vessels which are not at their usual accommodation berth, signed on Oct. 23, 1930 in Lisbon;
International Convention on certain rules concerning civil jurisdiction in matters of collision, signed on May 10, 1952 in Brussels, called Collision/Civil Jurisdiction Convention, 1952.
International Convention for the unification of certain rules relating to penal jurisdiction in matters of collision or other incidents of navigation, signed on May 10, 1952 in Brussels, called Collision/Penal Jurisdiction Convention, 1952.
International Convention for the unification of certain rules relating to the arrest of sea-going ships, signed on May 10, 1952 in Brussels, called Arrest Convention, 1952.
International Convention on prevention of pollution of the sea by oil, signed on May 12, 1954 in London.
International Convention relating to the limitation of the liability of owners of sea-going ships and Protocol, signed on Oct. 10, 1957 in Brussels, called Limitation of Shipowners' Liability (revised) Convention, 1957.
International Convention relating to stowaways, signed on Oct. 10, 1957 in Brussels, called Stowaways Convention, 1957.
International Convention for the unification of certain rules relating to the carriage of passengers by sea and

Protocol, signed on Apr. 29, 1961 in Brussels, called Carriage of Passengers Convention, 1961.
Convention on liability of operators of nuclear ships and Additional Protocol, signed on May 25, 1962 in Brussels, called Liability/Nuclear Ships Convention, 1962.
Convention on load-lines, signed on Apr. 5, 1966 in London.
International Convention for the unification of certain rules relating to carriage of passenger luggage by sea, signed on May 27, 1967 in Brussels, called Luggage Convention, 1967.
International Convention relating to registration of rights in respect of vessels under construction, signed on May 27, 1967 in Brussels, called Vessels under Construction Convention, 1967.
International Convention for the unification of certain rules relating to maritime liens and mortgages, signed on May 27, 1967 in Brussels, called Liens and Mortgages (revised) Convention, 1967.
International Convention on Civil Liability for Oil Pollution Damage, signed on Nov. 29, 1969 in Brussels, called Pollution Civil Liability Convention, 1969.
Convention relating to civil liability in the field of maritime carriage of nuclear material, signed on Dec. 17, 1971 in Brussels, called Carriage/Nuclear Material Convention, 1971.
International Convention on the establishment of an international fund for compensation for oil pollution damage, signed on Dec. 18, 1971 in Brussels, called Pollution/Fund Convention, 1971.
Athens Convention relating to the carriage of passengers and their luggage by sea, signed on Dec. 13, 1974 in Athens, called Carriage of Passengers Convention, 1974.
Convention on limitation of liability for maritime claims, signed on Nov. 19, 1976 in London, called Limitation of Shipowners' Liability Convention, 1976.
International Convention on the Carriage of Goods by Sea, signed on March 31, 1978 in Hamburg, called Hamburg Rules.
A Comprehensive Index to Marine Law and Policy Literature is published as a yearbook since 1980 by the Dalhousie Law School, Halifax, Canada.

Register of Texts of Conventions and Other Instruments Concerning International Trade Law, UN New York, 1973, Vol. 1; *UN Chronicle*, April 1978, p. 69.

MARITIME LIENS AND MORTGAGES. The subject of international conventions (▷ Maritime Law Conventions, 1882–1978). The Brussels Conventions 1926 and 1967 stated that:

"Mortgages, hypothecations, and other similar charges upon vessels, duly effected in accordance with the law of the contracting State to which the vessel belongs, and registered in a public register either at the port of the vessel's registry or at a central office, shall be regarded as valid and respected in all the other contracting countries."

and

"the following give rise to maritime liens on a vessel, on the freight for voyage during which the claim giving rise to the lien arises, and on the accessories of the vessel and freight accrued since the commencement of the voyage:
(1) Law costs due to the State, and expenses incurred in the common interest of the creditors in order to preserve the vessel or to procure its sale and the distribution of the proceeds of sale ...
(2) Claims arising out of the contract of engagement of the master, crew, and other persons hired on board;
(3) Renumeration for assistance and salvage, and the contribution of the vessel in general average;
(4) Indemnities for collision or other accident of navigation, ...
(5) Claims resulting from contracts entered into or acts done by the master."

The Anglo-Saxon states did not participate in the Conventions. In the UK there is in force the Merchant Shipping Act the arts. 31–46 of which provide for the principles of taking the vessel in possession by the creditor if the debt is not paid.

IMC, *Maritime Conventions*, 1970.

M

MARITIME PERPETUAL TRUCE, 1853. The Treaty of Maritime Peace in Perpetuity, between Great Britain and the sheikhs of the Pirate Coast on the Arab Peninsula (today the territory of the United Arab Emirates), signed in May, 1853.

S. MORRISON, "A Collection of Piracy Laws of Various Countries", in: *American Journal of International Law*, 1932.

MARITIME PILOTS ASSOCIATION. An international organization, reg. with the UIA:

International Maritime Pilots Association, f. 1970, London.
Publ.: *Pilot International*.

Yearbook of International Organizations.

MARITIME PORTS CONVENTION AND STATUTE, 1923. The Convention and Statute on the International Regime of Maritime Ports, signed on Dec. 9, 1923 in Geneva, by the governments of Belgium, Brazil, the British Empire, Bulgaria, Chile, Czechoslovakia, Denmark, El Salvador, Estonia, Germany, Hungary, Italy, Japan, Lithuania, Netherlands, Norway, the Serbo-Croat-Slovene State, Siam, Spain, Sweden, Switzerland and Uruguay. The art. 1 stated:

All ports which are normally frequented by sea-going vessels and used for foreign trade shall be deemed to be maritime ports within the meaning of the present Statute.

LNTS, Vol. 58, p. 301.

MARITIME PROTEST. International term for a statement given before a consul, court or other competent authority by a master of a ship in the presence of one of his officers and one of his crew members on the possibility that the cargo might suffer damage due to a storm at sea or any other anomalies during the journey. Such protest, together with notes done in the ship's logbook, serve in courts as a reason for examining why a cargo has not been transported to its destination as specified by a relevant contract.

MARITIME RADIO. The subject of international co-operation. Organization reg. with the UIA:

International Maritime Radio Association, CIRM, f. 1928, Brussels.
It is the international body for advancing maritime telecommunications services to enhance safety of life at sea and the speedy and safe voyage of ships. Official relations with ITU, ICAO, WMO and IMCO. Publ.: *Introduction to CIRM*.

Yearbook of International Organizations.

MARITIME SEARCH AND RESCUE CONVENTION. Adopted in 1979 under the auspices of the IMO to facilitate co-operation between search and rescue organizations and between those participating in search and rescue (SAR) operations at sea by establishing legal and technical bases for an international SAR plan, entered into force on June 22, 1985.

UN Chronicle, 1985, No. 6, p. 59.

MARITIME TRADE. ▷ Carriage of Goods by Sea.

MARITIME TRANSPORT. The subject of international conventions and disputes in connection with the dominance by twelve highly developed states of 85% of world maritime transport. Thus in the foreign trade of Africa and Latin America for example 80% of the cargo is transported under a foreign flag. According to the opinion of ALAMAR: "At 35 conferences of the merchant fleets which have their headquarters in the great

seaports – London, New York, Rotterdam, Hamburg, Tokyo, etc. – not one directed the least amount of attention to the interests of the developing states." The fees of the fleets reflect the conditions of the developed States and have a discriminatory and restrictive character in relation to the developing states. The countries of the Third World have thus called for a basic revision of international conventions on maritime transport, arguing that "conventions on practices and customs of maritime trade were established in epochs in which the interests of the developing countries had little importance" (▷ Tequendama Charter, 1967). The developing countries also request the "right to participate in all conferences of merchant fleets as an equal partner of the shipowners of the developed countries" (▷ Algiers Group of 77 Charter, 1967). The states of the so-called Group of 77 presented these problems at the First and Second Conferences of UNCTAD, 1965 and 1968, which established the Maritime Transport Committee, based in Geneva, as a permanent intermediary institution on the question of charges for maritime cargoes between users and shipowners and also with the task of studying possibilities of building maritime fleets and ports in the developing countries. The small share of developing countries in maritime transport (▷ Namucar) led to the following assumption being included in the Program of Action for Introducing the New International Economic Order, adopted May 1, 1974 by the Sixth Special Session of the UN General Assembly:

"All efforts should be made:
(a) to support an increasing and just share of the developing countries in world shipping tonnage;
(b) to halt and reduce the continually increasing cargo charges with the aim of reducing costs of importing to the developing countries and export from those countries;
(c) to minimize the costs of insurance and reinsurance borne by the developing countries and to grant aid to develop insurance and reinsurance markets in the developing countries and to establish for this purpose, where it is feasible, suitable institutions in those countries on a regional level;
(d) to insure the rapid implementation of the code of behaviour in shipping conferences;
(e) to take urgent measures for the purpose of increasing the import and export capabilities of the least developed countries and for recompensating disadvantages connected with the unfavourable geographical position of States without access to the sea, especially in relation to the costs of transport and transit incurred by them, and also to increase the commercial capabilities of island countries;
(f) so that the developed countries would refrain from undertaking measures or applying policies with the aim of not permitting the import of goods from the developing countries at fair prices and that they refrain from counteracting the introduction by the developing countries of just measures and policies with the aim of raising prices and stimulating the export of these goods."

Consultation in Shipping, UN New York, 1968; H. MEYERS, *The Nationality of Ships*, The Hague, 1970; H.W. DEGENHARDT, *Maritime Affairs – A World Handbook*, London, 1986.

MARITIME UNIVERSITY. ▷ World Maritime University.

MARKETING. An international term for the process of the distribution and sale of products and services; according to the definition of the American Marketing Association it is the management of economic activity directed toward and relating to the flow of goods and services from the producer to the consumer or user. Organizations reg. with the UIA:

Europanel, f. 1975, Geneva.

European Association for Marketing Research, f. 1965, London.
European Council for Industrial Marketing, f. 1968, Winterthur.
European Financial Marketing Association, f. 1971, Paris.
European Marketing Association, f. 1965, Nuneaton Warwickshire. Publ.: *Journal of International Marketing and Marketing Research*.
European Marketing Council, f. 1967, Amsterdam.
European Society for Opinion and Marketing Research, ESOMAR, f. 1948, Amsterdam. Publ.: *ESOMAR Handbook*.
International Marketing Federation, f. 1961, Copenhagen. Publ.: *News Bulletin*.
International Marketing Public Relations and Advertising Consultants, f. 1975, London.
Marketing Communications Executives International, f. 1964, Philadelphia, USA.
World Marketing Contact Group, f. 1975, Copenhagen.

M. J. BAKE, *Dictionary of Marketing*, London 1986.

MARKET, INTERNATIONAL. Areas of the world which come within the scope of international bilateral and multilateral trade agreements as well as regional or universal regulations concerning the legal organization of the international market.

MARKETS, IMPROVED ACCESS TO MARKETS. An international term, used in the UN for the removal of tariff and non-tariff barriers to allow goods from developing countries free access to the markets of the rich nations.

UN Chronicle, Oct., 1983, p. 47.

MARKKA. A monetary unit of Finland; one markka = 100 pennis; issued by the Suomen Pankki-Bank of Finland.

MARK OF FRG. A currency unit of the Federal Republic of Germany; one Deutsche Mark = 100 pfennigs; issued from June, 1948 to Aug., 1957 by the Bank Deutscher Länder; and since by the Deutsche Bundesbank.

MARK OF GDR. A monetary unit of the German Democratic Republic; one Mark = 100 pfennigs; issued from 1949 to 1967 by the Deutsche Notenbank with the name: Mark der Deutschen Notenbank, and from Dec. 1, 1967 by the Staatsbank der DDR.

MARONITES. Al-Mawarinah, the orthodox Christian sect in union with Rome, since the 15th century called Roman Catholics of Syro-Antiochene rite, est. in the 4th century by the Syrian anchorite, St. Maron, recognizing as its immediate spiritual head, after the Pope, the patriarch of Antioch, residing in Bkirki near Beirut. About 400,000 live in Lebanon and *c.* 15,000 in Egypt, Israel and Jordan.

R. JANIN, *Les Églises orientales et les rites orientaux*, Paris, 1955.

MARRIAGE. The subject of international conventions since June 12, 1902, when the First International Conference on Private Law signed the Convention relating to Conflict of Law concerning ▷ Divorces and Separations. The Fourth Conference on Private International Law concluded a Convention relating to the Conflicts of Laws with regard to the Effects of Marriage, on July 17, 1905. A Protocol concerning the Adhesion of States not represented at the Fourth Conference was signed on Nov. 28, 1923 in The Hague. The issue of marriage was also integrated in international conventions on ▷ nationality. In the 19th century a number of European states introduced legislations on mixed marriages (Great Britain Foreign Marriage Act, 1892). On Feb. 6, 1931 in Stockholm, Denmark, Iceland, Norway and Sweden signed the Convention on Marriages, Adoption and Tutelage; this was amended by the Treaty signed on Mar. 23, 1953 in Stockholm.

DE MARTENS, *Nouveau Recueil Général de Traités*, 3° série, tome IV, p. 480; *LNTS*, Vol. 51, p. 233; *UNTS*, Vol. 202, p. 241; R. HAW, *The State of Matrimony in England after the Reformation*, London, 1953; L. PALSON, *Marriage and Divorce in Comparative Conflict Law*, Vol. 2, Leiden, 1974.

MARS. The fourth closest planet to the Sun; distance from Earth: 55.5 million km to 400 million km. The first unmanned spacecraft expedition to Mars was initiated by the USA on Nov. 28, 1964. The vehicle from a distance of about 87,000 km from Mars, relayed 22 photographs. On Nov. 13, 1971 the American spaceprobe Mariner-9 began three months orbit around the planet, its shortest distance from the surface of Mars averaging 1200 km, the greatest: 17,000 km. On Aug. 20, 1976 the unmanned American spacecraft Viking landed on Mars. During the USA–USSR summit 1987 an agreement on space providing for the exchange of scientific data obtained from unmanned space vehicles missions to Mars and ▷ Venus was signed in Washington DC.

L.A. SOBEL (ed.), *Space from Sputnik to Gemini*, New York, 1965; S. GLADSTONE, *The Book of Mars*, NASA, Washington, D.C., 1968; R.A. WELLS, *Geophysics of Mars*, Amsterdam, 1979; KEESING's *Record of World Events*, March, 1988.

MARSAT. The name of international radiocommunication satellite system used by the world merchant marine from 1976 to 1979, before coming into force of the Convention on International Maritime Satellite Organization ▷ INMARSAT

MARSHALL ISLANDS. One of the Micronesian archipelagos in the Central Pacific; area: 181 sq. km; 1970 pop. census: 22,888. A part of the US Trust Territory of the Pacific Islands. On Mar. 1, 1979 the people of the Islands adopted a new constitution through a referendum, with the presence of UN Trusteeship Council observers. The islands were discovered by the Spaniards in 1526 and were a German protectorate from 1885 to 1914; when they were occupied by Japan; In 1920 mandated by the LN to Japan; seized 1943–44 by the US Forces, since 1947 included in the US Trust Territory of the Pacific Islands. Two Marshall atolls of the Ralik Chain: ▷ Bikini and ▷ Enevetak have been the site of US atomic and hydrogen bomb tests. On Oct. 13, 1983, the UN Special (Decolonization) Committee reaffirmed its strong conviction that the Administering Authority must ensure that military bases and installations and military activities did not hinder the population from exercising its right to self-determination and independence.

UN Chronicle, Jan., 1984, p. 63.

MARSHALL PLAN, 1947. The European Recovery Plan, ERP, a plan for economic reconstruction of Europe after World War II, formulated June 5, 1947 at Harvard by General G.C. Marshall, Secretary of State in the Truman administration read as follows:

"It is already evident that, before the United States Government can proceed much further in its efforts to alleviate the situation and help start the European world on its way to recovery, there must be some agreement among the countries of Europe as to the requirements of the situation and the part those countries themselves will take in order to give proper effect to whatever action might be undertaken by this Government. It would be neither fitting or efficacious for this

Government to undertake to draw up unilaterally a program designed to place Europe on its feet economically. This is the business of the Europeans. The initiative, I think, must come from Europe. The role of this country should consist of friendly aid in the drafting of a European program and of later support of such a program so far as it may be practical for us to do so. The program should be a joint one, agreed to by a number, if not all European nations."

The Western European countries formed, 1948, the Organization for European Economic Co-operation, OEEC. A broad program of American supplies of goods and credits for European countries under the terms of the Foreign Assistance Act was adopted by Congress Apr. 3, 1948. The distribution of goods and credits was vested in the Economic Co-operation Administration, ECA, headed by American financier P.G. Hoffman. During the first two years, from Apr. 4, 1948 to Apr. 4, 1950, the total value of goods and credits surpassed 8.7 billion dollars which were earmarked as follows: Great Britain – 2.4 billion, France – 1.8 billion, Italy – 974 million, FRG – 840 million, Holland – 808 million, Belgium and Luxembourg – 472 million, Austria – 404 million, Greece –301 million, Denmark – 181 million, Norway – 172 million, Ireland – 117 million, Sweden – 84 million, Turkey – 82 million, Trieste – 24 million, Portugal – 13 million, Iceland – 11 million. In the next two years the total sum also exceeded 8 billion dollars. During the Korea war the ECA was transformed into the Mutual Security Administration, MSA, which included also South Asian countries and in June, 1953 it was re-organized into the Foreign Operations Administration, FOA. Two years later on June 30, 1955, it became the International Co-operation Administration, ICA, as part of the Department of State to cover all US contracts for goods and credits both civil and military with all countries of the world with whom the USA entered into agreements in the 1948–55 period.

Formally the Marshall Plan expired together with ECA on Oct. 31, 1951 but the phrase "within the Marshall Plan" lingered on in Europe until 1955 to denote the whole complex of economic-military relations of OEEC countries with the USA.

The European Recovery Program Basic, Documents and Background Information, US Senate Documents, No. 111, 80th Congress, 1st Session; Washington, DC, 1948; A. WITKOWSKI, *Schrifttum zum Marshallplan und zur wirtschaftlichen Integration Europas*, Hamburg, 1953; H.B. PRICE, *The Marshall Plan and its Meaning*, New York, 1955; *UN Chronicle*, July 1979, pp. 96–97; R. von WEIZSÄCKER, *A Trans-Atlantic Task: To complete the Marshall Plan, in: Los Angeles Times,* June 12, 1987; M.J. HOGAN, *The Marshall Plan: America, Britain and the Reconstruction of Western Europe 1947–1952*, New York, 1987.

MARSHALL'S PROGRAM FOR THE UN, 1947. The United States proposals, presented to the UN General Assembly on Sept. 17, 1947, by the US Secretary of State General G.C. Marshall, a "Program for a More Effective United Nations," read as follows:

"The effective operation of the United Nations Security Council is one of the crucial conditions for the maintenance of international security. The exercise of the veto power in the Security Council has the closest bearing on the success and the vitality of the United Nations.

In the past the United States has been reluctant to encourage proposals for changes in the system of voting in the Security Council. Having accepted the Charter provisions on this subject and having joined with other permanent members at San Francisco in a statement of general attitude toward the question of permanent member unanimity, we wished to permit full opportunity for practical testing. We were always fully aware that the successful operation of the rule of unanimity would require the exercise of restraint by the permanent

members, and we so expressed ourselves at San Francisco. It is our hope that, despite our experience to date, such restraint will be practiced in the future by the permanent members. The abuse of the right of unanimity has prevented the Security Council from fulfilling its true functions. That has been especially true in cases arising under chapter VI and in the admission of new members. The Government of the United States has come to the conclusion that the only practicable method for improving this situation is a liberalization of the voting procedure in the Council. The United States would be willing to accept, by whatever means may be appropriate, the elimination of the unanimity requirement with respect to matters arising under chapter VI of the Charter and such matters as applications for membership. We recognize that this is a matter of significance and complexity for the United Nations. We consider that the problem of how to achieve the objective of liberalization of the Security Council voting procedure deserves careful study. Consequently, we shall propose that this matter be referred to a special committee for study and report to the next session of the Assembly. Measures should be pressed concurrently in the Security Council to bring about improvements within the existing provisions of the Charter, through amendments to the rules of procedure or other feasible means.

The scope and complexity of the problems on the agenda of this Assembly have given rise to the question whether the General Assembly can adequately discharge its responsibilities in its regular annual sessions. There is a limit to the number of items to which it can give through consideration during the few weeks in which this body meets. There would seem to be a definite need for constant attention to the work of the Assembly in order to deal with continuing problems. Occasional special sessions are not enough. The General Assembly has a definite and continuing responsibility, under articles 11 and 14 of the Charter, in the broad field of political security and the preservation of friendly relations among nations. In our fast-moving world an annual review of developments in this field is not sufficient. The facilities of the General Assembly must be developed to meet this need. I am therefore proposing, today, that this Assembly proceed at this session to create a standing committee of the General Assembly, which might be known as the Interim Committee on Peace and Security, to serve until the beginning of its third regular session next September. The Committee would not, of course, impinge on matters which are the primary responsibility of the Security Council or of special commissions, but, subject to that, it might consider situations and disputes impairing friendly relations brought to its attention by member states or by the Security Council pursuant to articles 11 and 14 of the Charter and report to the Assembly or to the Security Council thereon; recommend to the members the calling of special sessions of the General Assembly when necessary; and might report at the next regular session on the desirability of establishing such a committee on a permanent basis.

In our opinion, every member of the United Nations should be seated on this body.

The creation of the Interim Committee will make the facilities of the General Assembly continually available during this next year to all its members. It will strengthen the machinery for peaceful settlement and place the responsibility for such settlement broadly upon all the members of the United Nations. Without infringing on the jurisdiction of the Security Council, it will provide an unsurpassed opportunity for continuing study, after the adjournment of this Assembly, of the problems with which the United Nations must contend if it is to succeed.

The attitude of the United States toward the whole range of problems before the United Nations is founded on a very genuine desire to perfect the Organization so as to safeguard the security of states and the well-being of their peoples. These aims can be accomplished only if the untapped resources of the United Nations are brought to bear with full effect through the General Assembly and in other organs. The Assembly cannot dodge its responsibilities; it must organize itself effectively, not as an agency of intermittent action but on a continuous basis. It is for us, the members of the Assembly, to construct a record of achievement in dealing with crucial problems which will buttress the

M

M

authority of the Organization and enable it to fulfil its promise to all peoples.

The Great Powers bear special responsibilities because of their strength and resources. While these responsibilities bring with them special advantages, the Great Powers must recognize that restraint is an essential companion of power and privilege. The United Nations will never endure if there is insistence on privilege to the point of frustration of the collective will. In this spirit we have indicated our own willingness to accept a modification of our special voting rights in the Security Council. In the same spirit we appeal to the other permanent members of the Security Council, in this and in all matters, to use their privileged position to promote the attainment of the purposes of the Organization.

The Government of the United States believes that the surest foundation for permanent peace lies in the extension of the benefits and the restraints of the rule of law to all peoples and to all governments. This is the heart of the Charter and of the structure of the United Nations. It is the best hope of mankind."

UN General Assembly Official Records, 2nd Session, Vol. 1, pp. 19–35.

MARTENS CLAUSE. An international term in international law contained in the Sixth Hague Convention on Rules and Customs of Land Warfare (▷ Hague Rules, 1907), prepared by F.F. Martens (1845–1907), a professor of international law at Petersburg University. It provided, among other issues, that:

"Until a more comprehensive code of rules of war is prepared, the High Contracting Parties wish to state that when the rules in force adopted by them do not apply to a case, the people and belligerent parties are under the protection of principles of the law of nations stemming from the customs adopted by the civilized peoples, from the rights of humanity and public conscience."

F.F. MARTENS, *O prawie chastnoi sobstviennosti vo vremia voini*, Petersburg, 1869.

MARTIAL LAW. An international term for (1) rule by domestic military forces over a province or whole country, called also state of siege, when the army authorities take over the administration and judicial functions and civil rights are suspended; (2) the military command in occupied territory, called also military government, applied to all persons, civil and military. ▷ Lieber's code.

C. FAIRMAN, *Law of Martial Rule*, Washington, DC, 1943.

MARTINIQUE. One of the Windward Islands, West Indies, and an overseas department of France. Area: 1100 sq. km; pop. 1980 est.: 363,000; capital Fort-de-France. A French colony was established on the island in 1635, and, apart from brief periods of British occupation, it has remained under French control. During World War II, 1940, on the side of the Vichy régime, 1943 a US Naval blockade forced the island administration over to the United Nations. It became an overseas department of France on Mar. 19, 1946.

MARV. Maneuvering Reentry Vehicle. A missile with a warhead that contains a navigational system; subject of SALT negotiations (▷ SALT II Documents, 1979).

D. ROBERTSON, *Guide to Modern Defense and Strategy*, Detroit, 1988.

MAS. ▷ NATO. [New abbreviation]

MASHRAQ COUNTRIES. The Arabic States: Egypt, Jordan, Lebanon and Syria, signatories of the Trade and Co-operative Agreements with the EEC in Jan. and Feb. 1977, called Mashraq Agreements.

MASHRAQ TRADE AND COOPERATION AGREEMENTS. Signed since 1977 between the EEC and Mashraq countries, on tariff concessions (from 20% to 100%) for about 80–90% of all agricultural products, of all exports subject to duties and duty free entry for industrial products with a quota for textiles.

MASS COMMUNICATION. A subject of international co-operation and research. Organizations reg. with the UIA:

Asian Mass Communication Research and Information Centre, f. 1971, Singapore. Sponsored by the Singapore Government and the Friedrich Ebert Foundation, FRG. Recognized as the UNESCO regional Mass Communication Centre for Asia.

International Association for Mass Communication Research, f. 1956, Strasbourg. Aims: facilitate contact between research institutions and individuals concerned with mass communication. Consultative status with UNESCO.

International Centre of Advanced Studies on Mass Communication for Latin America. Centro Internacional de Estudios Superiores de Comunicación para América Latina, CIESPAL, f. 1959, Quito. Grants from the Government of Ecuador, UNESCO, OAS, Ford Foundation and Friedrich Ebert Foundation, FRG.

Yearbook of International Organizations; K. WARD, *Mass Communication in the Modern World*, London, 1986.

MASS EXODUS. An international term in the UN System for mass flows of refugees; a subject of special actions of the UN relief agencies.

UN Secretary-General Report on Human Rights and Mass Exodus (UN Doc. A/38/538), 1983; *UN Chronicle*, Jan., 1984, pp. 58–59.

MASSIVE RETALIATION. The American strategic military doctrine defined by US Secretary of State, J.F. Dulles at New York on Jan. 12, 1954:

Local defence must be reinforced by the further deterrent of massive retaliatory power.

B.F. FINKE, *John Foster Dulles, Master of Brinkmanship and Diplomacy*, New York, 1965; D. ROBERTSON, *Guide to Modern Defense and Strategy*, Detroit, 1988.

MASS MEDIA. The mass communications media, an international term, originated in the USA in the mid-20th century for overall definition of all instruments for reaching readers, listeners and spectators, such as: press, radio, film, television, sound and visual recordings.

M. ALVARADO, R. GUTCH, T. WOLLEN, *Learning the Media. An Introduction to Media Teaching*, London, 1987.

MASS MEDIA UNESCO DECLARATION, 1978. A Declaration adopted by acclamation by the General Conference of the UNESCO, Oct. 24–Nov. 28, 1978 in Paris.

The Declaration of Fundamental Principles concerning the contribution of the mass media to the strengthening of peace and international understanding, the promotion of human rights and the countering of racialism, apartheid and incitement to war contains 11 articles which read as follows:

"Art. I. The strengthening of peace and international understanding, the promotion of human rights and the countering of racialism, apartheid and incitement to war demand a free flow and a wider and better balanced dissemination of information. To that end, the mass media have a leading contribution to make. That contribution will be more effective to the extent that the information reflects the different aspects of the subject dealt with.

Art. II.(1) The exercise of freedom of opinion, expression and information, recognized as an integral part of human rights and fundamental freedoms, is a vital factor in the strengthening of peace and international understanding.

(2) Access by the public to information should be guaranteed by the diversity of the sources and means of information available to it, thus enabling each individual to check the accuracy of facts and to appraise events objectively. To that end, journalists must have freedom to report and the fullest possible facilities of access to information. Similarly, it is important that the mass media be responsive to concerns of peoples and individuals, thus promoting the participation of the public in the elaboration of information.

(3) With a view to the strengthening of peace and international understanding, to promoting human rights and to countering racism, apartheid and incitement to war, the mass media throughout the world, by reason of their role, contribute effectively to promoting human rights, in particular by giving expression to oppressed peoples who struggle against colonialism, neocolonialism, foreign occupation and all forms of racial discrimination and oppression and who are unable to make their voices heard within their own territories.

(4) If the mass media are to be in a position to promote the principles of this Declaration in their activities, it is essential that journalists and other agents of the mass media, in their own country or abroad, be assured of protection guaranteeing them the best conditions for the exercise of their profession.

Art. III.(1) The mass media have an important contribution to make to the strengthening of peace and international understanding and in countering racism, apartheid and incitement to war.

(2) In countering aggressive war, racism, apartheid and other violations of human rights which are inter alia spawned by prejudice and ignorance, the mass media, by disseminating information on the aims, aspirations, cultures and needs of all people, contribute to eliminate ignorance and misunderstanding between peoples, to make nationals of a country sensitive to the needs and desires of others, to ensure the respect of the rights and dignity of all nations, all peoples and all individuals without distinction of race, sex, language, religion or nationality and to draw attention to the great evils which afflict humanity, such as poverty, malnutrition, and diseases, thereby promoting the formulation by states of policies best able to promote the reduction of international tension and the peaceful and the equitable settlement of international disputes.

Art. IV. The mass media have an essential part to play in the education of young people in a spirit of peace, justice, freedom, mutual respect and understanding, in order to promote human rights, equality of rights as between all human beings and all nations, and economic and social progress. Equally they have an important role to play in making known the views and aspirations of the younger generation.

Art. V. In order to respect freedom of opinion, expression and information and in order that information may reflect all points of view, it is important that the points of view presented by those who consider that the information published or disseminated about them has seriously prejudiced their effort to strengthen peace and international understanding, to promote human rights or to counter racism, apartheid and incitement to war be disseminated.

Art. VI. For the establishment of a new equilibrium and greater reciprocity in the flow of information, which will be conducive to the institution of a just and lasting peace and to the economic and political independence of the developing countries, it is necessary to correct the inequalities in the flow of information to and from developing countries, and between those countries. To that end, it is essential that their mass media should have conditions and resources enabling them to gain strength and expand, and to co-operate both among themselves and with the mass media in developed countries.

Art. VII. By disseminating more widely all of the information concerning the objectives and principles universally accepted which are the bases of the resolutions adopted by the different organs of the United Nations, the mass media contribute effectively to the strengthening of peace and international understanding, to the promotion of human rights, as well as to the establishment of a more just and equitable international economic order.

Art. VIII. Professional organizations, and people who participate in the professional training of journalists and other agents of the mass media and who assist them in performing their functions in a responsible manner should attach special importance to the principles of this Declaration when drawing up and ensuring application of their codes of ethics.
Art. IX. In the spirit of this Declaration it is for the international community to contribute to the creation of the conditions for a free flow and wider and more balanced dissemination of information, and the conditions for the protection, in the exercise of their functions, of journalists and other agents of the mass media. UNESCO is well placed to make a valuable contribution in this respect.
Art. X.(1) With due respect for constitutional provisions designed to guarantee freedom of information and for the applicable international instruments and agreements, it is indispensable to create and maintain throughout the world the conditions which make it possible for the organizations and persons professionally involved in the dissemination of information to achieve the objectives of this Declaration.
(2) It is important that free flow and wider and better balanced dissemination of information be encouraged.
(3) To that end, it is necessary that states should facilitate the procurement, by the mass media in the developing countries, of adequate conditions and resources enabling them to gain strength and expand, and that they should support co-operation by the latter both among themselves and with the mass media in developed countries.
(4) Similarly, on a basis of equality of rights, mutual advantage, and respect for the diversity of cultures which go to make up the common heritage of mankind, it is essential that bilateral and multilateral exchanges of information among all states, and in particular between those which have different economic and social systems be encouraged and developed.
Art. XI. For this Declaration to be fully effective it is necessary, with due respect for the legislative and administrative provisions and the other obligations of member states, to guarantee the existence of favourable conditions for the operation of the mass media, in conformity with the provisions of the Universal Declaration of Human Rights and with the corresponding principles proclaimed in the International Covenant on Civil and Political Rights adopted by the General Assembly of the United Nations in 1966."

UN Chronicle, December, 1978, pp. 54–55.

MASURIA. Historical region in northeast Poland, named Mazury; Germanized partly by the Teutonic Knights passed to Prussia but returned to Poland by the Potsdam Agreement 1945.

Warmia i Mazury, 2 Vols., Poznań, 1953.

MATER ET MAGISTRA. *Latin:* Mother and Teacher. The encyclical of pope John XXIII dated May 15, 1961, on social questions. ▷ Catholic social doctrines.

KEESING's *Contemporary Archive*, 1961; E.E. HADLES, *Pope John and His Revolution*, New York, 1965.

MATERIAL LAW. International term – civil law rules on the institution of ownership and on the right to administer, integrated by international private law.

MATERNITY. The subject of an ILO convention determining conditions of work and rest for expectant mothers and maternity leave. The Scandinavian Convention on Maternity was signed by Denmark, Finland, Iceland, Norway and Sweden on July 20, 1952 in Reykjavik.

UNTS, Vol. 228, p. 3.

MATHEMATICS. A subject of international research and co-operation. Organizations reg. with the UIA:

Balkan Mathematical Union, f. 1973, Belgrade.

Banach Stefan International Mathematical Centre for Raising Research Qualifications, f. 1972, Warsaw. Publ.: *Research Papers*.
Bernoulli Society for Mathematical Statistics and Probability, f. 1961, Voorburg. Publ.: *Reports*.
Commonwealth Association of Science and Mathematics Educators, f. 1974, London.
Institute of Mathematical Statistics, f. 1935, Hayward, Calif. Publ.: *Annals of Statistics*.
International Association for Mathematical Geology, f. 1968, Syracuse, N.Y. Publ.: *Journal of Mathematical Geology*.
International Mathematical Union, f. 1950, Paris, Publ.: *IMU Bulletin and World Directory of Mathematicians*.
International Society of Mathematical Biology, f. 1962, Paris. Publ.: *Biomathematics*.
International Study Group for Mathematical Learning, f. 1961, London.
Latin Language Mathematicians Group, f. 1955, Bucharest.
Mathematical Programming Society, f. 1971, Voorburg.

Yearbook of International Organizations.

MATSU. Island in the East China Sea, 160 km from Taiwan, annexed by Taiwan after the proclamation of People's Republic of China 1949; bombarded several times by China in the 1950's together with the ▷ Quemoy Islands.

KEESING's *Contemporary Archive*, 1955.

MAU-MAU. The National Liberation Army of Kenya, organized mainly by the Kikiyu tribe in 1946. First military operations of the army in 1948–49 transformed in 1952 into a military uprising against British colonial authorities. Although in 1957 the uprising was quelled, it contributed to initiation by Great Britain of a policy of concession towards the liberation movement, and to granting Kenya independence on Dec. 12, 1963.

R. BUIJTENHNIJ, *Le Mouvement "Mau-Mau"*, The Hague, 1971.

"MAURETANIA". The first passenger ship driven by steam turbine, constructed in 1906, winner of the Atlantic Blue Ribbon in 1907–28, owned by the British Cunard Line, sailed until 1935. Its sister ship ▷ *Lusitania* was sunk by a German submarine in 1915.

MAURITANIA. Member of the UN. République Islamique de Mauritanie. The Republic of Mauritania. State in northwestern Africa on the Atlantic Ocean. Borders with Senegal, Mali, Algeria and Western Sahara. Area: 1,030,700 sq. km. Pop. 1987 est.: 1,858,000 (1976 census: 1,407,939). Capital: Nouakchott with 134,986 inhabitants in 1976. GNP per capita in 1987: US $400. Official languages: Arabic and French. Currency: one ouguiya = 5 khoums. National Day: Nov. 28, Independence Day, 1960.
Member of the UN since Oct. 27, 1961. Member of all UN specialized organizations with the exception of the IAEA. Member of the OAU and the League of Arab States, ACP state of the EEC.
International relations: from the 15th century Mauritania was under Portuguese influence and then in following centuries under that of Great Britain and France. In 1898 the coast was annexed by France and progressively occupied until 1903 when it became a French protectorate. In 1920 it was made a colony within French West Africa; from 1946 it was a French overseas territory. In 1958 the population was granted wide autonomy and in a plebiscite voted in favor of remaining within the French Community; on Nov. 28, 1960 Mauritania was granted independence within the Community with the protest of Morocco, which had historical claims to the entire territory. The dispute ended

when Morocco abandoned her claims in 1969; diplomatic relations between the two countries were established in 1971. Mauritania signed on Aug. 5, 1979 in Algier a Treaty with Polisario on Western Sahara and in Feb., 1984 recognized the Sahrawi Arab Democratic Republic of Western Sahara. In Dec., 1983 Mauritania signed the ▷ Maghreb Fraternity and Co-operation Treaty.

MOKHTAR OULD HAMIDOUN, *Precis sur la Mauritanie*, Paris, 1952; G. DESIRE VUELLEMIN, *Contribution à l'histoire de la Mauritanie de 1900 a 1934*, Paris, 1962; J. GUJOS, *Croissance économique et impulsion extérieure: étude sur l'economie mauritienne*, Paris, 1964; C.C. STEWART, E.K. STEWART, *Islam and Social Order in Mauritania*, New York, 1970; B.M. WESTEBBE, *The Economy of Mauritania*, New York, 1971; *Study on the Monetary and Financial System of the Islamic Republic of Mauritania*, Nouakchott, 1975; *The Europa Year Book 1984. A World Survey*, Vol. II, pp. 2015–2023, London, 1984.

MAURITIUS. Member of the UN. State on a volcanic island in the Indian Ocean, situated about 800 km east of Madagascar. Area: 2,040 sq. km. Pop. 1988 est.: 1,042,000 (1972 census: 851,334). Capital: Port Louis with 147,599 inhabitants in 1981. GNP per capita in 1987: US $1,470. Official language: English and Creole derived from French, the *lingua franca*. The greatest language groups are Hindi (38,8%), Creole (32,9%), Urdu (8,7%), Tamil (6,9%) and French (4,4%). Currency: one Mauritius rupee = 100 cents. National Day Mar. 12, day of the declaration of independence, 1968. Member of the UN since Apr. 24, 1968. Member of all UN specialized organizations. Member of the OCAM and OAU. ACP state of the EEC.
International relations: a Dutch colony in the 17th century under the name Mauritius. In 1715–1810 a French colony under the name Île de France; 1810–1964 a British colony under its former name; granted autonomy in 1964 and independence within the British Commonwealth on Mar. 12, 1968. Involved in a border dispute over ▷ Tromelin Island with France, since 1976; negotiated since 1983 without final solution. On Jan. 3, 1988 the Prime Minister Ancerood Jugnauth stated: "we maintain our claim over ▷ Diego Garcia Island".

P.J. BARMWELL, A. TOUSSAINT, *A Short History of Mauritius*, London, 1949; A. TOUSSAINT, *Bibliography of Mauritius*, Port Louis, 1956; B. BURTON, *Indians in a Plural Society: A Report on Mauritius*, London, 1961; H. TONGERE, *A Survey of the Fisheries of Mauritius*, Port Louis, 1964; A. TOUSSAINT, *History of Mauritius*, London, 1978; *The Europa Year Book. A World Survey*, Vol. II, pp. 2024–2034, London, 1984; France–Mauritius (Tromelin Island), in: A.J. DAY ed., *Border and Territorial Disputes*, London, 1987, pp. 136–137.

MAUTHAUSEN. The German concentration camp est. Aug. 8, 1938 in Austria in quarries near Linz for Austrian political prisoners; since 1940 also for other nationalities. About 335,000 people passed through it and about 122,000 were murdered. Liberated by the US Army on May 5, 1945. Organization reg. with the UIA:

International Mauthausen Committee, f. 1953, Luxembourg.

The Trial of German Major War Criminals. Proceedings of The International Military Tribunal, Sitting at Nuremberg, Germany, Vols. 42, London 1946–48, Vol. 2 pp. 369, 374–377; Vol. 3 pp. 205, 236, 298–299; Vol. 5 pp. 169, 171, 203, 205, 218–219, 222, 226–227, 229, 231; Vol. 11 pp. 251, 259, 265–266, 276, 296–298, 302, 303, 352–353, 357; and Vol. 16 p. 394; V. e L. PAPALETTERA, *Il passarai per il Camino. Vita e morte a Mauthausen*, Murcia, 1966; H. MARSALEK, *Priester in KZ Mauthausen*, Wien, 1971; C. BERNADAC, *Mauthausen*, 2 Vols., Paris, 1975; *Yearbook of International Organizations, 1986/87; The Europa Yearbook 1988. A World Survey*, Vol. I, London, 1988.

M

"MAYAGUEZ". US commercial vessel, a subject of conflict between the USA and Cambodia in May, 1975. The vessel was confiscated by Cambodia in her territorial waters; on May 15 the USA reacted with an armed intervention by US marines from an American base in Thailand; governments of Cambodia and Thailand made protests; at the UN the use of force in a dispute between UN members was condemned.

"US Marines Land on Cambodian Island", in: *International Herald Tribune*, May 16, 1975; *Seizure of "Mayaguez". Hearings, House, May 14–15, 1975*, Washington, DC, 1975.

"MAYFLOWER". A merchant ship for wine transportation (34m long, 8m wide), which on Aug. 15, 1620 left the port of Southampton in England, chartered by a London group of 102 persons, most of them religiously persecuted Puritans later called the Pilgrim Fathers, to undertake "a Voyage to plant the first colony in the northern part of Virginia" and on Nov. 21, 1620 reached the coast of America at Cape Cod, now Provincetown, Massachusetts. The Pilgrim Fathers started the Anglo-Saxon colonization of America.

S.E. MORRISON, "The 66-Day Saga of 'Mayflower'", in: *New York Times Magazine*, April 14, 1957.

MAYOTTE. An island in Mozambique Channel, Indian Ocean, part of the ▷ Comoros Islands; area: 373 sq. km; pop. 1978 census: 47,246. After the proclamation of independence by the Comoros Islands remained under French jurisdiction. This status was not accepted by the UN. On Nov. 21, 1983 the UN General Assembly reaffirmed the sovereignty of the Comoros over Mayotte and invited France to open negotiations to ensuring the effective and prompt return of the island Mayotte to the Comoros, by Res. 38/13 by a recorded vote of 115 to 1 (France) with 24 abstentions. On Oct. 11, 1986 the French Prime Minister, Jacques Chirac, visiting Mayotte reaffirmed the status of Mayotte as a French overseas department. On Dec. 9, 1985 the General Assembly reaffirmed Comorian Sovereignty over island of Mayotte.

UN Chronicle, March, 1980, p. 45 and January, 1984, pp. 21–22; *UN Chronicle 1986*, No. 2, pp. 52–53; Comoros (Mayotte)–France, in: A.J. DAY ed., *Border and Territorial Disputes*, London, 1987, pp. 117–125.

MAZDAISM. Zoroastrianism, Parseeism, a dualistic religion of ancient Iran in which God, the Creator Ahura Mazda (Ormuzd), struggles with the spirit of evil, Ariman; survived in India and at the turn of the 19th century became the source of a new wave of the teaching of Zoroaster. Also developing on the basis of Mazdaism in Germany and in the Anglo-Saxon countries at the beginning of the 20th century, there developed a trend in medicine for treating illnesses by a system of dieting and breathing exercises prescribed for the followers of Mazdaism called the Mazdaian System. Organization reg. with the UIA:

Mazdaznan Movement, est. 1908, Frankfurt am Main, which has under its protection the International Mazdaian Youth Movement and the Federation of Mazdaian Women, est. 1951, Ravensburg. Publ.: *Mazdaznan Bulletin*.

Yearbook of International Organizations.

MBFR. Mutual and Balanced Forces Reduction. The official formula for disarmament negotiations in Europe adopted at the session of the NATO Ministerial Council on May 27, 1970 in Rome and reaffirmed on June 4, 1971 in Lisbon. This position was justified as follows: such a reduction must be in keeping with the vital defense requirements of the interested parties and must take into account "differences resulting from geographical and other factors"; it must be based on mutuality, take place in phases, and be precisely fixed both as to its scope and timetable; it must include native and foreign forces and be subject to verification and control. The states of the Warsaw Pact opposed the formula MBFR as a conception of non-proportional reduction (more in the East, less in the West) and made a counter-proposal for "reduction without detriment to security." ▷ MURFAAMCE. The MBFR negotiations have failed in 15 years to produce any agreements. On January 17, 1989 the Vienna Conference on Security and Cooperation in Europe agreed to start new East–West talks: the ▷ Conventional Stability Talks.
See also ▷ SALT; and ▷ START.

Recueil de Documents, No. 5, 1970, No. 6, 1971; D. ROBERTSON, *Guide to Modern Defense and Strategy*, Detroit, 1988.

McCARRAN – WOOD ACT, McCARRAN – WALTER ACT, 1952. Two anti-communist acts of the US Congress obligating organizations named in a list compiled by the Department of Justice and which in 1950 included the Communist Party of the USA, to present to authorities a roster of their members, reveal the sources of their finances and register as "subversive organizations." According to the law, in case of the danger of war those belonging to this type of organization could be confined without trial. The more rigid law of 1953, which Congress passed over a veto of President Harry Truman, introduced the right to take away the citizenship and deport to the country of their birth not only those then belonging to "subversive organizations" but also those who had belonged in the past and also those who by a determination by the FBI were considered "subversive." Opposing this law were the Communist Party of the USA and the American Civil Liberties Union, ACLU. The names of the laws derived from their movers in Congress, senator P.A. McCarran, an ally of senator J. McCarthy, and Congressmen F.E. Wood and J.H. Walter. Recognized as expired in July, 1974. ▷ McCarthyism.

McCARTHYISM. An international term for system for investigating citizens under the charge of disloyalty to their country. The name appeared in the USA, 1950–54, when in the House of Representatives the House Un-American Activities Investigation Committee, HUAC, and in the Senate the Internal Security Subcommittee carried on investigations of this kind on the initiative of the Republican Senator J. McCarthy (1909–1957). An international aspect appeared in the fall of 1952, when Senator J. McCarthy demanded and then carried out an investigation of US citizens employed in the UN Secretariat. Senator McCarthy charged with pro-Soviet bias among others two ex-Secretaries of State General George Marshall and Dean Acheson. The chief consultant to Senator J. McCarthy was Roy Cohn, a young prosecutor in the 1951 trial of Julius and Ethel (mother of two young children) Rosenberg on charges of passing America's atomic secrets to the Soviet Union. The Rosenbergs were condemned to death and were, as the first civilians in US history, executed for espionage, in 1953, in an atmosphere of fanatical anticommunism. The Senate on Dec. 2, 1954 approved a resolution condemning by a vote 67–22 certain acts by McCarthy, which "tended to bring the Senate into dishonor and disrepute, to obstruct the constitutional process of the Senate."

W.F. BUCKLAY Jr., L. BRENT BOWELL, *McCarthy and His Enemies*, New York, 1954; R.H. ROVERS, *Senator Joe McCarthy*, London, 1959; V.

GOODMAN, *The Committee: The Extraordinary Career of the House Committee on Un-American Activities*, New York, 1968; H. von HOFFMAN, *Citizen Cohn*, London, 1988; S. ZION, *The Autobiography of Roy Cohn*, New York, 1988.

McCLOY-ZORIN PRINCIPLES, 1961. ▷ Disarmament Negotiations Principles, 1961.

McMAHON LINE. A plan for the eastern frontier between Tibet and British India, proposed 1914 by the representative of Great Britain, H. McMahon, during a conference in Simla with the participation, besides Britain of China and Tibet (where a Chinese army was present); the proposed frontier ran along the top of the Himalayas (between Bhutan and Burma); despite approval by Tibetan lords, the McMahon Line was rejected by China, which demanded a frontier running along the southern slopes of the mountains. Chinese military border crossing in Aug., 1959 and Oct., 1962; withdrawal to the McMahon Line.

The British Encyclopaedia, Vol. 16, p. 621, Chicago, London, 1973.

McNAMARA DOCTRINE, 1964. The nuclear defence of Western Europe has the same priority in the US strategy as the defence of North American territory. A statement of the US Secretary of Defence, R. McNamara on Dec. 16, 1964 during a NATO session in Paris.

L. BEATON, "The Western Alliance and the McNamara Doctrine", in: *Adelphi Papers*, No. 11, 1964.

McNAMARA LAW. Robert McNamara, American statesman, Secretary of Defence (1961–1968), formulated the doctrine: that

"It is impossible to predict with a high degree of confidence what the effects of the use of military force will be because of the risks of accident, mis-calculation, mis-perception and inadvertence".

Foreign Affairs, Fall, 1987, p. 186; D. ROBERTSON, *Guide to Modern Defense and Strategy*, Detroit, 1988.

M.D. The French abbreviation: "m'aider" – "help me." An international radio-telephone signal used as a distress call.

MEASLES. ▷ Immunization.

MEAT. A subject of international trade and of International Meat Committees in such regional organizations as the EEC and COMECON. Since 1968 the FAO organises periodical World Meat Conferences. According to FAO estimates, world meat production does not meet the needs of developing countries. The developed countries account for 75% of world meat consumption. Organizations reg. with the UIA:

Cattle and Meat Economic Committee of the CEBV, est. 1970, Ougadougou, by the governments of Benin, Ivory Coast, Niger and Upper Volta (now Burkina Faso).
European Cattle and Meat Trade Union, f. 1952, Strasbourg.
European Union of Export Abattoirs, the Cattle and Meat Trade, f. 1965, Bonn.
European Wholesale Meat Trade Association, f. 1958, Paris.
International Federation of Meat Traders' Associations, f. 1977, Zurich.
Latin American Association of Meat Exporting Countries, est. 1974, Buenos Aires, by the governments of Argentina, Colombia, Paraguay and Uruguay.
Specialized EEC Cattle and Meat Committee, f. 1960, Brussels.

See ▷ Bovine Meat.

Yearbook of International Organizations.

MECANOGRAPHY. A subject of international co-operation. Organization reg. with the UIA:

International Association of Studies on Mecanography and Informatics, f. 1964, Rome. Study and research on the application of mecanography and informatics to the mechanization of planning in development and technological progress.

Yearbook of International Organizations.

MECCA. Arabic Makkah, the birthplace of Mohammed, the sacred city of Islam, capital of the Hedjaz (province of Saudi Arabia), place of annual pilgrimage of Muslims. On Aug. 31, 1987 over 400 Muslims were killed inside and around the Grand Mosque. Saudi Arabia blamed Iranian pilgrims for the massacres, but Iran maintained that the Saudi police had opened fire on Iranian pilgrims.

KEESING's *Record of World Events, 1987*, January, 1988.

MECHANICS. A subject of international co-operation. Organizations reg. with the UIA:

European Association of Industries and Precision Mechanics and Optics, f. 1960, Milan.
European Mechanics Colloquia, EUROMECH, f. 1964, Munich.
International Center for Mechanical Sciences, f. 1968, Udine.
International Union of Theoretical and Applied Mechanics, f. 1946, Paris.

Yearbook of International Organizations.

MEDALS. An international term for decorations mainly made from metal by casting, coining or plaque-hammering techniques, as works of art, to commemorate events, distinguished merits and awards; a separate category comprises medals awarded as state decorations. Production of medals, called medaling, is the subject of permanent organized international co-operation. Organization reg. with the UIA:

International Medal Federation, Federation internationale de medaille, FIDEM, f. 1937, Paris. Publ.: *Medailles.*

Yearbook of International Organizations.

MEDDIA. An international Slidebank on Tropical Diseases, established by the Royal Tropical Institute in Amsterdam. The Meddia system is intended for the training of students and intermediate level health workers. Its aim is to make more widely available the valuable photographic collections existing in schools and institutes.

World Health, March, 1984, p. 25.

MEDIACULT. International Institute for Audio-Visual Communication and Cultural Development, f. 1978, Vienna. Publ. *Media-cult Newsletter.*

MEDIATION. The activity consisting in facilitating the reaching of an agreement between conflicting parties through a third party's attempts to prepare grounds for the accord. The part of a third state may be played by an authorized international organization, such as the UN (arts. 11 and 33–38 of the UN Charter). One of the means for the peaceful settlement of international disputes is the institution of international law. Mediation was provided for by the Paris Treaty of 1856 under which the Crimean War was terminated and it was determined that in case of a new conflict, prior to the use of force the parties should seek mediation of other powers; the legal grounding of mediation is contained in conventions signed during the Hague Peace Conference in 1899 and 1907 which were the first to lay down rules of good services and mediation. After World War I the Covenant of the League

of Nations in arts. 11 and 15 determined mediation as being one of the most important instruments of peacekeeping and granted conciliatory and mediatory rights to the Council. In 1933 the International Conference of American States, held in Montevideo, stated that:

"it shall never be conceived as a hostile act if one or several states should offer good services and mediation."

The Bogota Pact defined mediation in art. 11:

"Parties to a dispute expressing consent to mediate, may elect another state, international organization or natural person to act as an intermediary. Mediation is strictly of an advisory character and ceases when the means suggested are not accepted by the parties."

F. MEYNOND, R. SCHROEDER, *La médiation. Tendance de la recherche et bibliographie, 1945–1965*, Amsterdam, 1965; R.L. BLEDSOE, B.A. BOCZEK, *The International Law Dictionary*, Oxford, 1987.

MEDICAL AND SOCIAL INTERNATIONAL ASSISTANCE. The subject of international agreements, establishing the principle of equal treatment for the nationals of each contracting party in the application of legislation providing for social and medical assistance. A Convention between Belgium, France, Luxembourg, the Netherlands and the UK on social and medical assistance, was signed on Nov. 7, 1949 in Paris, and a Supplementary Agreement (with Annexes) to give effect to the above-mentioned Convention, was signed on Apr. 17, 1950 in Brussels.

UNTS, Vol. 131, p. 4.

MEDICAL ETHICS. The subject of the following documents formulated by the World Medical Association, 1947–75, in spirit of the ▷ Hippocratic Oath:

(1) *The Geneva Declaration, 1948:*
"I solemnly pledge myself to consecrate my life to the service of humanity;
I will give to my teachers the respect and gratitude which is their due;
I will practice my profession with conscience and dignity;
The health of my patient will be my first consideration;
I will respect the secrets which are confided in me, even after the patient has died;
I will maintain by all means in my power the honour and the noble traditions of the medical profession;
My colleagues will be my brothers;
I will not permit considerations of religion, nationality, race, party politics or social standing to intervene between my duty and my patient;
I will maintain the utmost respect for human life from the time of conception; even under threat, I will not use my medical knowledge contrary to the laws of humanity.
I make these promises solemnly, freely and upon my honour."

(2) *The International Code of Medical Ethics, 1949:*
"Duties of Doctors in General:
A Doctor must always maintain the highest standards of professional conduct.
A doctor must practice his profession uninfluenced by motives of profit.
The following practices are deemed unethical:
(a) Any self-advertisement except such as is expressly authorized by the national code of medical ethics.
(b) Collaboration in any form of medical service in which the doctor does not have professional independence.
(c) Receiving any money in connection with services rendered to a patient other than a proper professional fee, even with the knowledge of the patient.
Any act or advice which could weaken physical or mental resistance of a human being may be used only in his interest.
A doctor is advised to use great caution in divulging discoveries or new techniques of treatment.
A doctor should certify or testify only to that which he has personally verified.

Duties of doctors to the sick:
A doctor must always bear in mind the obligation of preserving human life.
A doctor owes to his patient complete loyalty and all the resources of his science. Whenever an examination or treatment is beyond his capacity he should summon another doctor who has the necessary ability.
A doctor shall preserve absolute secrecy on all he knows about his patient because of the confidence entrusted in him.
A doctor must give emergency care as a humanitarian duty unless he is assured that others are willing and able to give such care.
Duties of doctors to each other:
A doctor ought to behave to his colleagues as he would have them behave to him.
A doctor must not entice patients from his colleagues.
A doctor must observe the principles of The Declaration of Geneva approved by the World Medical Association."

(3) *The Helsinki Declaration 1964*, which formulated the recommendations for doctors who have to use human subjects for research, whether of a therapeutic nature or not.

(4) *The Sydney Declaration 1968* on determination by doctors of the precise moment of death (problem of euthanasia or of maintaining life artificially in case of irreversibly damaged brain; and problem in case of organ transplants relating to the need of the doctor to be absolutely certain that a heart or kidney donor is truly dead).

(5) *The Oslo Declaration 1970* on the problem of abortion

(6) *The Tokyo Declaration 1975* with guidelines for doctors regarding torture and other cruel, inhuman or degrading treatment or punishment in relation to detention and imprisonment. (Problems of intensive interrogation methods and biomedical experiments on prisoner, castration of recidivist sexual offenders, psychosurgery, electroconvulsion therapy, corporal punishment, restricted diets, solitary confinement, drug-dependent persons, mentally disordered offenders etcetera.)

(7) On Dec. 18, 1982 the UN General Assembly formally adopted the *UN Principles of Medical Ethics* relevant to the role of health personnel, particularly physicians, in the protection of prisoners against torture. In the resolution to which the Principles are annexed, the General Assembly calls upon all Governments to give both the resolution and the Principles "the widest possible distribution, in particular among medical and paramedical associations and institutions of detention or imprisonment in an official language of the state" and invites intergovernmental and non-governmental organizations, in particular WHO, to bring the Principles "to the attention of the widest possible group of individuals, especially those active in the medical and paramedical field".
WHO's Director-General transmitted the resolution to the Organization's Member States on Apr. 13, 1983.
Principles of Medical Ethics relevant to the role of health personnel, particularly physicians, in the protection of prisoners and detainees against torture and other cruel, inhuman or degrading treatment or punishment.

Principle I. Health Personnel, particularly physicians, charged with the medical care of prisoners and detainees have a duty to provide them with protection of their physical and mental health and treatment of disease of the same quality and standard as is afforded to those who are not imprisoned or detained.
Principle 2. It is a gross contravention of medical ethics, as well as offence under applicable international instruments, for health personnel, particularly physicians, to engage, actively or passively, in acts which constitute participation in, complicity in, incitement to or attempts to commit torture or other cruel, inhuman or degrading treatment or punishment.
Principle 3. It is a contravention of medical ethics for health personnel, particularly physicians, to be involved in any professional relationship with prisoners or detainees the purpose of which is not solely to evaluate, protect or improve their physical and mental health.
Principle 4. It is a contravention of medical ethics for health personnel, particularly physicians:
(a) To apply their knowledge and skills in order to assist in the interrogation of prisoners and detainees in a manner that may adversely affect the physical or

mental health or condition of such prisoners or detainees and which is not in accordance with the relevant international instruments;

(b) To certify, or to participate in the certification of, the fitness of prisoners or detainees for any form of treatment or punishment that may adversely affect their physical or mental health and which is not in accordance with the relevant international instruments, or to participate in any way in the infliction of any such treatment or punishment which is not in accordance with the relevant international instruments.

Principle 5. It is a contravention of medical ethics for health personnel, particularly physicians, to participate in any procedure for restraining a prisoner or detainee unless such a procedure is determined in accordance with purely medical criteria as being necessary for the protection of the physical or mental health or the safety of the prisoner or detainee himself, of his fellow prisoners or detainees, or of his guardians, and presents no hazard to his physical or mental health.

Principle 6. There may be no derogation from the foregoing principles on any ground whatsoever, including public emergency."

F.K. KAUL, *Arzte in Auschwitz*, Berlin, 1968; *Health aspects of avoidable maltreatment of prisoners and detainees*, WHO Report, Geneva, 1975; J.S. NEKI, "Medical Ethics: a View Point from the Developing World", in: *World Health*, July, 1979; E. VIEDMA, "I swear Apollo", in: *World Health*, July, 1979; *UN Chronicle*, February 1982, p. 48, and February 1983, p. 103.

MEDICAL HELP FOR TRAVELLERS. The

subject of international agreements. In Europe medical help for travellers was first organized by the Scandinavian countries for all citizens of those countries travelling in Scandinavia. The CMEA and EEC countries have similar arrangements.

J. PAXTON, *A Dictionary of the EEC*, London, 1978, p. 163.

MEDICAL RESEARCH OF THE WHO. The

medical international research efforts of the World Health Organization started in Apr., 1950 with the calling of an Expert Committee on Rabies for an assessment of anti-rabies vaccination and rabies prophylaxis. The committee designed a series of collaborative efforts between laboratories in France, Iran, Israel, Spain, the USA and the USSR. In 1958 the WHO set up an Advisory Committee on Medical Research, ACMR, in Geneva. This Committee during its first 25 years until 1984 has built its activity on the basis of co-operation of scientific investigators in 430 institutions in 77 countries. The ACMR established on a global scale a Special Program for Research and Training in Tropical Diseases, with co-sponsorship of the UNDP and the World Bank, other Special Programs of Research covered Development and Research Training in Human Reproduction.

World Health, December, 1983.

MEDICINAL PLANTS. The subject of interna-

tional co-operation. Organizations reg. with the UIA:

Association of Producers and Collectors of Medicinal and Aromatic Plants of the EEC, f. 1959, Paris.
European Confederation of Distributors, Producers and Importers of Medical Plants, f. 1962, Paris.

R. BOISSON, "Medicinal Plants", in: *WHO World Health*, No. 9, 1973.

MEDICINE. The subject of international research

and co-operation. Organizations registered with the UIA:

Aerospace Medical Association, f. 1929, Washington, DC. Recognized by ICAO.
Aid for International Medicine, Wilmington, Del.
American College of Chest Physicians, f. 1935, Park Ridge, Ill.

Asian Pacific League of Physical Medicine and Rehabilitation, f. 1968, Melbourne.
Asian Regional Medical Student Association.
Association of Medical Schools in Africa, f. 1972, Khartoum.
Balkan Medical Union, f. 1964, Bucharest. Publ.: *Archives*.
Christian Medical Commission, f. 1967, Geneva. Publ.: *Contact*.
Common Market Medical Students Liaison Committee, f. 1968, Dublin.
Commonwealth Medical Association, f. 1962, London. Publ.: *CMEA Bulletin*.
Council for International Organizations of Medical Sciences, f. 1949, Geneva. Consultative Status WHO, ECOSOC, UNESCO. Publ.: *International Nomenclature of Diseases*.
East Africa Medical Research Council, f. 1967, Arusha.
European Association of International Medicine, f. 1969, Strasbourg.
European Association of Perinatal Medicine, f. 1968, Uppsala. Publ.: *Congress Proceedings*.
European Association of Social Medicine, f. 1955, Turin.
European College for the Study and Evaluation of Bodily Damage, f. 1973, Neuilly-sur-Seine.
European Federation for Physical Medicine and Rehabilitation, f. 1963, Brussels.
European Nuclear Medicine Society, f. 1976, Vienna.
European Proprietary Medicines Association, f. 1964, Paris.
European Underseas Bio-Medical Society, f. 1971. Alverstoke, Hants, UK.
European Union of Medical Specialists, f. 1958, Brussels.
Federation of African Medical Student Associations, f. 1968, Lagos.
Group of European Medical Research Councils, f. 1971, Bad Godesborg.
International Academy of Aviation and Space Medicine, f. 1959, Paris.
International Academy of Legal Medicine and of Social Medicine, f. 1938, Rome. Consultative status with ECOSOC, WHO. Publ.: *Acta Medicinae Legalis et Socialis* (quarterly).
International Academy of Preventive Medicine, f. 1971, Houston, Texas.
International Academy of the History of Medicine, f. 1962, London. Publ.: *Clio Medica* (quarterly). *Analacta Medico-Historica* (biannual).
International Association for Accident and Traffic Medicine, f. 1960, Stockholm. Publ.: *Journal of Traffic Medicine* (quarterly).
International Association for Aquatic Medicine, f. 1969, Suffern, N.Y.
International Association for Medical Assistance to Travellers, f. 1976, New York.
International Association for Medical Research and Cultural Exchange, f. 1965, Paris. Publ.: *Medicine d'Afrique Noire* (monthly).
International Association for Medicine and Biology of Environment, f. 1971, Paris.
International Association of Agricultural Medicine, f. 1961, Tours.
International Association of Medical Laboratory Technologists, f. 1954, Zurich, Switzerland. Consultative status with WHO, Council of Europe. Publ.: *Newsletter*.
International Association of Medical Oceanography, f. 1975, Nice.
International Bronchoesophagological Society, f. 1951, Philadelphia, Pens. Publ.: *Transactions*.
International Cardiovascular Society, f. 1950, Boston, Mass., USA. Publ.: *The Journal of Cardiovascular Surgery*.
International College of Pomology, f. 1958, Paris.
International College of Psychosomatic Medicine, f. 1971, Buenos Aires. Publ.: *Congress Proceedings*.
International College of Surgeons, f. 1935, Geneva. Publ.: *International Surgery*.
International Committee for Life Assurance Medicine, f. 1932, Zurich. Publ.: *Congress Proceedings*.
International Committee of Military Medicine and Pharmacy, f. 1921, Liege. Special agreement with WHO. Publ.: *International Review of the Army, Navy and Air Force Medical Services*.
International Committee on the Neutrality of Medicine, f. 1959, Paris. Publ.: *Congress reports*.

International Conference on Social Science and Medicine, f. 1968, Brighton, UK.
International Congress on Tropical Medicine and Malaria, f. 1913, London. Publ.: *Congress proceedings*.
International Council of Botanic Medicine, f. 1938, Los Angeles, Calif., USA.Publ.: *Journal of Natural Therapeutics* (quarterly), *Health from Herbs* (monthly), *The Herbal Practitioner* (quarterly).
International Federation for Hygiene Preventive Medicine and Social Medicine, f. 1952, Rome. Publ.: *Journal*.
International Federation for Medical and Biological Engineering, f. 1979, Utrecht, Netherlands. Consultative status with ECOSOC, WHO. Publ.: *Medical and Biological Engineering*.
International Federation of Manual Medicine, f. 1965, London.
International Federation of Medical Students Association, f. 1951, Helsinki. Publ.: *IFMSA News*.
International Federation of Physical Medicine and Rehabilitation, f. 1950. London. Consultative status with WHO.
International Federation of Sportive Medicine, f. 1928, St Moritz, Switzerland. Consultative status with ECOSOC, WHO. Publ.: *Journal of Sports Medicine and Physical Fitness*.
International Medical Association for the Study of Living Conditions and Health, f. 1951, Bologna, Italy. Consultative status with ECOSOC, FAO. Publ.: *Living Conditions and Health*.
International Medical Exchange, f. 1971, Hilsboro, Ill., USA.
International Medical Sports Federation for Aid to Cancer Research, f. 1970, Beziers, France.
International Medical Society for Endoscopy and Radiocinematography, f. 1955, Reims, France. Publ.: *Acta Endoscopia et Radiocinematographica*.
International Organization for Medical Physics, f. 1963, Stockholm.
International Reference Organization in Forensic Medicine and Sciences, f. 1966, Wichita, Kansas.
International Rehabilitation Medicine Association, f. 1969, Guaynabo, Puerto Rico. Publ.: *News Views*.
International Society for Aerosols in Medicine, f. 1974, Berlin, GDR.
International Society for Ski Traumatology and Medicine of Winter Sport, f. 1956, Arosa. Publ.: *Congress Reports*.
International Society for Interdisciplinary Medical Check-Up, f. 1974, Brussels.
International Society of Internal Medicine, f. 1948, Lausanne. Publ.: *Congress reports*.
International Society of General Medical Practice, f. 1959, Klagenfurt.
International Society of Medical Hydrology and Climatology, f. 1921, Rome. Publ.: *Archives of Medical Hydrology*.
International Study Group on Systematic Examinations in Preventive Medicine and in Medicine, f. 1973, Paris.
International Union of Railway Medical Services, f. 1949, Brussels.
International Union of School and University Health and Medicine, f. 1959, Paris. Consultative status with WHO, UNESCO, Publ.: *Review*.
International Union of the Medical Press, f. 1952, Paris. Publ.: *Congress Reports*.
Latin American Association of National Academies of Medicine, f. 1970, Bogota.
Latin American Association of Societies of Nuclear Biology and Medicine, f. 1961, Rio de Janeiro, Publ.: *Revista de la ALASBIMN*.
Latin American Society of Pathology, f. 1955, México, DF.
Medic-Alert Foundation International, f. 1956, Turlock, Calif.
Medical Press Committee of the European Committee, f. 1961, Paris.
Medical Women's International Association, f. 1919, Vienna. Consultative status with ECOSOC, WHO, UNICEF. Publ.: *Congress Reports*.
Medicus Mundi International – International Organization for Medical Co-operation, f. 1964, Köln, FRG. Publ.: *Concepts*.
Nordic Federation for Medical Education, f. 1966, Risskov, Denmark.
Panamerican Federation of Associations of Medical Schools, f. 1962, Bogota. Publ.: *Boletin*.

Panamerican Federation of Pharmacy and Biochemistry, f. 1966, San Juan, Puerto Rico.

Panamerican Medical Association, f. 1952, New York.

Pan-American Medical Women's Alliance Inc., f. 1947, Kansas, USA.

Scandinavian Association for Social Medicine, f. 1977, Uppsala, Sweden.

Scandinavian Society of Forensic Medicine, f. 1961, Lund, Sweden.

Society of Haematology and Blood Transfusion of African and Near Eastern Countries, f. 1965, Tunis.

Transplantation Society, f. 1966, Dallas, Tex., USA. Publ.: *Transplantation Proceedings*.

World Federation for Ultrasound in Medicine and Biology, f. 1976, Oklahoma City, Okl., USA.

World Medical Association, f. 1947, Paris. Official Relations with WHO, ECOSOC, ILO Special List. Publ.: *World Medical Journal* (bi monthly).

World Medical Law Association, f. 1967, Ghent, Belgium.

World Medical Relief, f. 1953, Detroit.

A. SLIOSBERG, *ELSEVIER'S, Medical Dictionary. In English/American, French, Italian, Spanish and German*, Amsterdam, 1975; *World directory of medical schools*. Fifth edition. Geneva, 1979; *Yearbook of International Organizations, 1986/87; The Europa Yearbook 1988. A World Survey*, Vol. I, London, 1988.

MEDINA OF FEZ. A historic city in Morocco, included in the ▷ World Heritage UNESCO List. Founded at the beginning of the 9th century (year 192 of the Hegira), by the 12th century Fez had become a large and flourishing city, famous for its religious monuments (e.g. the Mosque of the Andalusians, Qarawiyin). It is now attempting to preserve and renovate its colleges, souks, workshops and palaces.

UNESCO. *A Legacy fo All*, Paris, 1984.

MEDINA OF TUNIS. A historical site of Tunisia, included in the ▷ World Heritage UNESCO List. A remarkably well-preserved ancient city lying in the heart of a modern capital of Tunisia. Around the ancient mosque of Az Zaytunah (11th century) are religious buildings and the mansions of the rich which, for the most part, are as full of life as the shopping streets given over to the guilds since the 13th century.

UNESCO. *A Legacy for All*, Paris, 1984.

MEDITERCONGRESS. The International Association of the Organizations and Congress Cities of the States Interested in the Mediterranean, f. 1967, Madrid. Reg. with the UIA.

Yearbook of International Organizations.

MEDITERRANEAN ACTION PLAN, 1975. The Plan was elaborated and accepted by an intergovernmental meeting of Mediterranean Coastal States, in Barcelona, 1975. The meeting was convened by the UN Environment Program, UNEP and the plan gave priority to the protection of soil, management of water resources, marine living resources, management of fisheries and agriculture.

MEDITERRANEAN CONFERENCE, 1979. In accordance with the Final Helsinki Accords of 1975 the First Conference of Mediterranean States was convened in Feb., 1979.

MEDITERRANEAN CONVENTION, 1976. A Convention to Protect the Mediterranean Sea (with two Protocols) was signed on Feb. 16, 1976 in Barcelona. The Regional Centre for the Prevention of Oil Pollution was established in Malta. In 1984 all 17 signatory countries established a network of monitoring and research centers in 84 laboratories. See also ▷ Lead pollution.

UN Chronicle. March, 1976, p. 27.

MEDITERRANEAN POLLUTION CONTROL. Under the auspices of UNEP the signatories of the 1976 Barcelona Convention on Pollution Control in the Mediterranean, the European Community and 17 other countries have established a network of monitoring or research centers in 84 laboratories in the whole area.

KEESING's *Contemporary Archive*, 1986.

MEDITERRANEAN SEA. The largest inland sea, 2,499,350 sq. km, surrounded by Europe, Asia and Africa; 3860 km long and 1610 km maximum width; connecting the Atlantic Ocean with the Black Sea, the Sea of Marmara and the Red Sea (through the Suez Canal); has four main divisions: The Tyrrhenian, Adriatic, Ionian and Aegean Seas. Subject of international co-operation. Organizations reg. with the UIA:

General Fisheries Council for the Mediterranean, est. 1952 under aegis of the FAO in Rome by the governments of 19 Mediterranean countries (Algeria, Bulgaria, Cyprus, Egypt, France, Greece, Israel, Italy, Lebanon, Libya, Malta, Monaco, Morocco, Romania, Spain, Syria, Tunisia, Turkey and Yugoslavia). Publ.: *Studies*.

International Commission for the Scientific Exploration of the Mediterranean Sea, est. 1919 by the governments of Mediterranean countries. HQs. Monaco. Publ.: *Bulletin de liaison des laboratoires*.

Mediterranean Association for Marine Biology and Oceanology, f. 1964 in Malta, under aegis of UNESCO.

Yearbook of International Organizations.

MEDITERRANEAN STATES. All African and European states in the Mediterranean Basin. Questions relating to security and co-operation in the Mediterranean were discussed during the Helsinki Conference 1973–75 in which the African Mediterranean States did not participate. The text of the Helsinki resolution is as follows:

"The participating States, conscious of the geographical, historical, cultural, economic and political aspects of their relationship with the non-participating Mediterranean States,

Convinced that security in Europe is to be considered in the broader context of world security and is closely linked with security in the Mediterranean area as a whole, and that accordingly the process of improving security should not be confined to Europe but should extend to other parts of the world, and in particular to the Mediterranean area,

Believing that the strengthening of security and the intensification of co-operation in Europe would stimulate positive processes in the Mediterranean region, and expressing their intention to contribute towards peace, security and justice in the region, in which ends the participating States and the non-participating Mediterranean States have a common interest,

Recognizing the importance of their mutual economic relations with the non-participating Mediterranean States, and conscious of their common interest in the further development of co-operation,

Noting with appreciation the interest expressed by the non-participating Mediterranean States in the Conference since its inception, and having duly taken their contributions into account,

Declare their intention:

to promote the development of good-neighbourly relations with the non-participating Mediterranean States in conformity with the purposes and principles of the Charter of the United Nations, on which their relations are based, and with the United Nations Declaration on Principles of International Law concerning Friendly Relations and Co-operation among States and accordingly, in this context, to conduct their relations with the non-participating Mediterranean States in the spirit of the principles set forth in the Declaration on Principles Guiding Relations between Participating States;

to seek, by further improving their relations with the non-participating Mediterranean States, to increase

mutual confidence, so as to promote security and stability in the Mediterranean area as a whole;

to encourage with the non-participating Mediterranean States the development of mutually beneficial co-operation in the various fields of economic activity, especially by expanding commercial exchanges, on the basis of a common awareness of the necessity for stability and progress in trade relations, of their mutual economic interests, and of differences in the levels of economic development, thereby promoting their economic advancement and well-being;

to contribute to a diversified development of the economies of the non-participating Mediterranean countries, whilst taking due account of their national development objectives, and to co-operate with them, especially in the sectors of industry, science and technology, in their efforts to achieve a better utilization of their resources, thus promoting a more harmonious development of economic relations;

to intensify their efforts and their co-operation on a bilateral and multilateral basis with the non-participating Mediterranean States directed towards the improvement of the environment of the Mediterranean, especially the safeguarding of the biological resources and ecological balance of the sea, by appropriate measures including the prevention and control of pollution; to the end, and in view of the present situation, to co-operate through competent international organizations and in particular within the United Nations Environment Programme, UNEP;

to promote further contacts and co-operation with the non-participating Mediterranean States in other relevant fields.

In order to advance the objectives set forth above, the participating States also declare their intention of maintaining and amplifying the contacts and dialogue as initiated by the CSCE with the non-participating Mediterranean States to include all the States of the Mediterranean, with the purpose of contributing to peace, reducing armed forces in the region, strengthening security, lessening tensions in the region, and widening the scope of co-operation, ends in which all share a common interest, as well as with the purpose of defining further common objectives.

The participating States would seek, in the framework of their multilateral efforts, to encourage progress and appropriate initiatives and to proceed to an exchange of views on the attainment of the above purposes."

The first meeting of experts representing States of CSCE was held from Feb. 13 to Mar. 26, 1979, in Valetta, Malta, to consider within the frame of the Mediterranean Chapter of the ▷ Helsinki Final Act.

GA Res. 43/84 on the Strengthening of Security and Cooperation in the Mediterranean Region was adopted without a vote on Dec. 7, 1988.

G.G. ROSENTHAL, *The Mediterranean Basin. Its Political Economy and Changing International Relations*, Boston, 1982; A.D. ROTFELD (ed.), *From Helsinki to Madrid. Documents*, Warsaw, 1984, pp. 222–230; *UN Resolutions and Decisions adopted by the General Assembly during the First Part of its Forty-Third Session, from 20 September to 22 December 1988*, New York, 1989, pp. 203–206.

MEDITERRANEAN VENICE MEETING. ▷ Venice CSCE meeting.

MEETING OF EXPERTS IN PUBLIC ADMINISTRATION. ▷ UN Public Administration Programme.

MEETINGS OF COMMONWEALTH PRIME MINISTERS. Since 1937 the official name of the Conferences of the (British) Commonwealth. Meetings of Prime Ministers are informal conferences.

MEETINGS PLANNING. A subject of international co-operation. Organizations reg. with the UIA:

Meeting Planners International, f. 1972, Chicago.

World Meeting Planners Congress and Exposition, f. 1971, Chicago.

Yearbook of International Organizations.

MEGADEATH. The metric unit of a million deaths. An international term referring to the capacity of certain genocidal weapons of mass destruction in the conventional unit "one million killed."

MEGATON. International measure of the explosion yield of a nuclear weapon: one million metric tons of Tri-Nitro-Toluene, high explosive. ▷ Kiloton.

J. GOLDBLAT, *Arms Control Agreements. A Handbook*, New York, 1983; D. ROBERTSON, *Guide to Modern Defense and Strategy*, Detroit, 1988.

MEIDAN-E SHAH, ISFAHAN. A cultural site of Iran, included in the ▷ World Heritage UNESCO List. This is the Royal Square in Isfahan created by Shah Abbas I (1587–1629), the Safavid. It is surrounded by two-storyed buildings with arched recesses, forming an immense rectangle previously used for processions and polo games. Four buildings decorated with paintings and ceramics give on to square: three mosques and a palace, together with a portico.

UNESCO. *A Legacy for All*, Paris, 1984.

MEKONG. The river in China and on the Indochina Peninsula, 4185 km long, internationalized 1811, border river between Laos and Thailand and between Laos and Burma, sailable for ocean-going ships up to Phnom Penh, Cambodia. The Mekong Delta is 194,250 sq. km in area. In 1956 the UN Economic Commission for Asia and the Far East, ECAFE, began development of the Mekong basin and its mouth. The program, aided by international help, included embankment of the river in regions of repeated flood disaster and the deepening of its bed to increase navigability to serve as a waterway for Cambodia, Laos, Thailand and Vietnam. A Coordinating Committee for the lower Mekong Basin was established 1957 in Bangkok as an international organization of Cambodia, Laos, Vietnam and Thailand within the ECAFE. Countries co-operating with the Committee: Australia, Austria, Belgium, Canada, Denmark, Finland, France, the FRG, Hong Kong, India, Indonesia, Iran. Israel, Japan, the Netherlands, New Zealand, Norway, Pakistan, the Philippines, Sweden, Switzerland, the UK and USA; co-operating organizations: UNDP, IAEA, IBRD, ILO, ITU, UNESCO, UNOID, WHO, the Asiatic Bank of Development, the Foundation of Asia, the Ford Foundation and the Rockefeller Foundation. It publishes: *The Mekong Monthly Bulletin.*

MELANESIA. The Oceanian Islands in the southwest Pacific: Solomon Islands, New Hebrides, New Caledonia, the Bismarck Archipelago, Admiralty and Fiji Islands.

R.H. CODRINGTON, *The Melanesians*, London, 1891; C.S. BELSHAW, *Changing Melanesia*, London, 1954.

MELLILA. ▷ Ceuta and Mellila.

MELTING POT. An international term derived from a drama The Melting Pot (1914 by English author Israel Zeangwill (1864–1926). The term is in common use for the result of the multinational migrations from Europe to the United States, which had become a place where the mixing of various ethnic groups had occurred and an American nation had come into being with a dominant

"White Anglo-Saxon Protestant culture" (▷ WASP). In the second half of the 20th century reverse tendencies appeared in the USA and in other world regions, a renewed separation of ethnic groups and their solidarity in defense of their rights and own cultural values. This process in the US was revealed in ethnic studies by the US Census Bureau published 1973 (and 1983), which showed that the majority of Americans still identified themselves with one of ten ethnic groups.

Ethnic Groups in the USA in 1980:

British[1]	61,311,000
German	49,224,000
Irish	40,165,000
Afro-American	20,964,000
Spanish	13,699,000
French	12,892,000
Italian	12,183,000
Polish	8,228,000
American Indian	6,715,000
Russian	2,781,000

[1]English, Scottish and Welsh.

Other US Census Bureau statistics stated that in 1980 the number of foreign born US residents was as follows:

Mexico	2,199,221
Germany	849,384
Canada	842,859
Italy	831,922
UK	669,149
Cuba	607,814
Philippines	501,440
Poland	418,128
USSR	406,022
Korea	289,885
China	286,120
Vietnam	231,120
Japan	221,794
Portugal	211,614
Greece	210,998
India	206,087
Ireland	197,817
Jamaica	196,811
Dominican Rep.	169,147
Yugoslavia	152,967
Austria	145,607
Hungary	144,368
Colombia	143,508
Iran	121,505
France	120,215
Czechoslovakia	112,707
Netherlands	103,136
El Salvador	94,447
Haiti	92,395
Ecuador	86,128
Hong Kong	80,380
Sweden	77,157
Taiwan	75,353
Spain	73,735
Argentina	68,887
Romania	66,994
Israel	66,961
Trinidad and Tobago	65,907
Norway	63,368
Guatemala	63,073
Panama	60,740
Peru	55,496
Laos	54,881
Thailand	54,803
Lebanon	52,674
Turkey	51,915
Guyana	48,608
Lithuania	48,194
Nicaragua	44,166
Egypt	43,424

Source; US Department of Commerce, US Census Bureau, April 1983.

N. GLASER, D.P. MOYNIHAN, *Beyond the Melting Pot. The Negroa, Puerto Ricans, Jews*, New York, 1964; A. PORTES, *La etnicidad indisoluble: recuenta de susj causas e evolucion reciente en Estados Unidos*, in: *Foro International*, Abril–Junio, 1987.

MEMBERS OF THE UN. ▷ UN Members.

MEMEL CONVENTION AND STATUTE, 1924. An agreement concerning the territory of Memel, signed on May 8, 1924 in Paris, between the Principal Allied and Associated Powers to the Treaty of Peace of Versailles, 1919, on the one part and Lithuania, on the other part, transferring to Lithuania all the rights and titles ceded to them by Germany in virtue of art. 99 of the Treaty of Versailles over the Memel territory. The art. 2 stated:

The Memel Territory shall constitute, under the sovereignty of Lithuania, a unit enjoying legislative, judicial, administrative and financial autonomy within the limits prescribed by the Statute set out in Annex I.

LNTS, Vol. 29, pp. 85–115.

MEMORANDA AND NOTES IN THE UN SYSTEM. Documents bearing the designation "memorandum" are normally issued for the purpose of placing facts on record or sketching in the background of the Subject; "notes" are, as a rule short documents transmitting information or comments; both should have subtitles indicating authorship.

United Nations Editorial Manual, New York, 1983, pp. 48–49.

MEMPHIS. A historic site of Egypt, included in the ▷ World Heritage UNESCO list, existed in the earliest days of the oldest state in history. Its best-preserved monuments are those which were built for its dead, viz. the pyramids of the kings Cheops, Chehren and Mycerinus at Giza, the sun temples at Abu Ghurab and Abu Sir; at Saqqara, the pyramids of ten other kings and the magnificently decorated tombs of important officials; at Dahsbur, the monuments of Snofru and the tombs that are like jewel boxes.

UNESCO. *A Legacy for All*, Paris, 1984.

MENNONITES. The name derived from the Dutch religious reformer Menno Simons (1496–1561), leader of the Anabaptists in Holland. In 1683 the Mennonites started to emigrate to North America, escaping persecution in Europe, and organized the first permanent settlement in Germantown, Pennsylvania, famous for the first anti-slavery manifesto, voiced by Americans called the Germantown Mennonites Protest against Slavery 1688:

"... Now, though they are black, we cannot conceive there is more liberty to have them slaves, as it is to have other white ones. There is a saying, that we should do to all men like as we will be done ourselves; making no difference of what generation, descent, or colour they are. And those who steal or rob men, and those who buy or purchase them, are they not all alike? ... And we who profess that it is not lawful to steal, must, likewise, avoid to purchase such things as are stolen, but rather help to stop this robbing and stealing, if possible ..."

In the 20th century the majority of Mennonites live in the USA and Canada, the rest in Europe and South America. They are unified by the Mennonite World Conference. The (Old) Mennonite Church headquarters is at Scottdale, Pa., USA. Publ.: *Mennonite Yearbook.*

H.S. BENDER, C.H. SMITH, *The Mennonite Encyclopaedia*, 4 Vols., Scottdale, Pa., 1955–59.

MENTAL HEALTH. The subject of international research. Organizations reg. with the UIA:

Apex Foundation for Research into Mental Retardation, f. 1967, Melbourne.
Caribbean Federation for Mental Health, f. 1975, Port of Spain, Trinidad.
European League for Mental Hygiene, f. 1951, Paris.
Ibero-Latin American Group for Scientific Study of Mental Deficiency, f. 1968, Mexico DF.

Metallurgy

International Association for the Scientific Study of Mental Deficiency, f. 1964, Larbert, Scotland. Publ.: *Newsletter*.

International Committee Against Mental Illness, f. 1958, New York.

International Committee on Occupational Mental Health, f. 1966, Stockholm. Publ.: *Bulletin*.

International League of Societies for the Mentally Handicapped, f. 1922, Bentweld, the Netherlands.

International Union of Societies for Mental Health, f. 1972, Clermont-Ferrand.

Joint Commission on International Aspects of Mental Retardation, f. 1970, Brussels.

Neurotics Anonymous International Liason Inc., f. 1964, Washington, DC. Publ.: *Journal of Mental Health* (monthly).

Working Group on the Internment of Dissenters in Mental Hospitals, f. 1971, London.

World Federation for Mental Health, f. 1948, London. Consultative status with ECOSOC, UNESCO, WHO and UNICEF.

Special list of ILO. Publ.: *World Mental Health Bulletin*.

Yearbook of International Organizations.

MENTALLY ILL PERSONS. A subject of UN study. On Dec. 11, 1980 the UN General Assembly Res. 35/130 B, adopted by 78 in favor to none against with 62 abstentions, requested the Commission on Human Rights and the ECOSOC to consider the draft guidelines related to procedures for determining whether adequate grounds existed for detaining mentally ill persons on the grounds of ill-health and the draft principles for the protection of persons suffering from mental disorder.

In January 1987 an International Forum on Mental Health reform took place in Kyoto, Japan, sponsored by the WHO Collaborating Center on Health Legislation at the Harvard Law School of Public Health. The Forum adopted unanimously the following declaration known as the Kyoto principles:

(1) Mentally ill persons should receive human, dignified and professional treatment;
(2) Mentally ill persons should not be discriminated against by reason of their mental illness;
(3) Voluntary admission should be encouraged whenever hospital treatment is necessary;
(4) There should be impartial and informal hearing before an independent tribunal to decide, within a reasonable time of admission, whether an involuntary patient needs continued hospital care;
(5) Hospital patients should enjoy as free an environment as possible, and should be able to communicate with other persons.

UN Chronicle. March, 1981, pp. 40–41; *ICJ Newsletter*, April/June, 1988, p. 33.

MERCENARIES. An international term for military troops formed from volunteers, usually multinational, who enlist for money to fight, most often in colonial interventions or for subversive purposes. H. Grotius was opposed to the idea of mercenaries, saying that no way of living is more dishonest than hiring oneself to fight for money, whatever the reason for the war, and considered the use of a mercenary army as unjust. In the 19th century France organized mercenaries into the ▷ Foreign Legion, composed mostly of adventurers or people with a criminal past. During World War II, the Third Reich formed mercenary brigades within SS troops. After the war mercenaries were enlisted by the Netherlands in Indonesia (until 1949); by France in Indochina (1946–54); by Great Britain in India and Pakistan (until the 1950s); by USA in Guatemala (1954) and Cuba (1961); by Belgium in Katanga (1960–62); by Portugal in Angola and other colonies; by the South African Republic in Namibia. The core of mercenary military units formed after World War II consisted of former SS soldiers, members of former fascist organizations of

different nationalities, self-styled "*les affreux*," they showed particularly outrageous cruelty and terror. Mercenary recruitment agencies operated in 1960–70 in Johannesburg, Salisbury, port towns in Mozambique, Belgium, Spain, West Germany and Portugal. Basic monthly pay was up to US $375 for ground troops, US $2000 for pilots; in case of death the family was paid a US $20,000 compensation. In June and July, 1976 at Luanda, the capital of Angola, English and American mercenaries were placed on trial for war crimes: four of them (three English and one American) were sentenced to death and executed by a firing squad in spite of telegrams from the Queen of England and President Carter asking for pardon on their behalf. Angolan President Aghostino Neto stated that justice had been dispensed not only on behalf of the people of Angola, but also for the benefit of friendly nations of Namibia, Zimbabwe and other peoples of the world which are bound to face new aggression by mercenaries.

On Dec. 14, 1979 the UN General Assembly Res. 34/140 decided to consider the drafting of an international convention to outlaw the activities of mercenaries. An Ad Hoc Committee was established on Dec. 4, 1980 by the UN General Assembly Res. 35/48, on the drafting of an International Convention against the Recruitment, Use, Financing and Training of Mercenaries. The Ad Hoc Committee continued its work in the following years and had not finished the draft by 1987.

On Dec. 8, 1988, the GA Res. 43/147 condemned the use of mercenaries as a means to violate human rights and to impede the exercise of the right of peoples to self-termination.

V. MARCHETTI, J.D. MARKS, *The CIA and the Cult of Intelligence*, New York, 1975, pp. 137–145; W. BURCHETT, D. ROEBUCK, *The Whores of War: Mercenaries Today*, New York, 1978: *UN Chronicle*, March, 1980, p. 52; April, 1981, pp. 12–13 and 40; October, 1982, p. 22; December, 1983, p. 72; *UN Chronicle*, May, 1987, p. 85; *Resolutions and Decisions adopted by the General Assembly during the First part of its Forty-Third Session from 20 September to 22 December*, New York, 1989, pp. 357–359.

MERCHANDISE CLASSIFICATION, AMERICAN CONVENTION, 1923. An agreement between the American States on Uniformity of Nomenclature for the Classification of Merchandise, signed on May 3, 1923 in Santiago de Chile.

LNTS, Vol. 33, p. 93.

MERCHANT SHIPS. Vessels of all types for the transport of cargo by sea or river, subject to international maritime law. Up to the middle of the 20th century the commercial shipping lines of private companies under the flags of the colonial powers were dominant. In 1926 in connection with the appearance on the seas of the first state merchant ships fleet of the USSR, the colonial powers formulated the so-called Brussels Convention on Privileges for State Vessels, subjecting them to foreign jurisdiction (▷ Cargo vessels). A tonnage Measurement of Merchant Ships Convention was signed on Apr. 16, 1934 in Warsaw, by the Governments of Great Britain, Australia, Canada, India, New Zealand and Poland.

LNTS, Vol. 163, p. 185; W. SINGH, *International Convention of Merchant Shipping*, London, 1973.

MERCHANTS OF DEATH. An international term for sellers of armaments; in the United States also sellers of firearms by mail.

H.C. ENGELBRECHT, F.C. HANIGHAN, *The Merchants of Death*, New York, 1925.

MERCURY. The smallest of the major ▷ Planets. The nearest planet to the Sun. A subject of international space research. The American unmanned space vehicle Mariner 10 made three encounters with Mercury in 1974–75.

MERCURY OR QUICKSILVER, METALLIC ELEMENT. A subject of international co-operation. In May, 1974, the governments of Algeria, Canada, Spain, Italy, Mexico, Turkey, Yugoslavia (about 78% of World production and about 95% of exports) signed a convention on an Organization of Mercury Producers. Headquarters: Algiers.

Yearbook of International Organizations; New York Academy of Science, *Mercury and its Compounds*, New York, 1957.

MERCY KILLING. ▷ Euthanasia.

MESA VERDE. A natural site in Colorado, USA, included in the ▷ World Heritage UNESCO List. On this "green table" in southwestern Colorado, are the remains of the villages, reservoirs and temples built or hewn in the rock by the Anasazi people between the 7th and the 13th centuries. They have been deserted ever since the Anasazi abandoned them for unknown reasons and emigrated towards the south where their descendants still live today.

UNESCO. *A Legacy for All*, Paris, 1984.

MESCALINE. A hallucinogen used during religious ceremonies practised by Indians in Mexico, extracted from the peyote cactus (loporophora williamsis); one of the ▷ drugs of abuse, a subject of international control.

UN Chronicle, May, 1987.

MESO-AMERICA. An international term introduced by American anthropologists for areas of southern Mexico and western Central America.

MESSINA CONFERENCE, 1955. A meeting of the Foreign Ministers of Belgium, France, the FRG, Italy, Luxembourg and the Netherlands, member-states of European Coal and Steel Community, on June 2–4, 1955 at Messina, Italy. The ministers agreed

that the moment has arrived to initiate a new phase on the path of constructing Europe, that the aim of this course in the field of economic policy is the creation of an European Market free from all customs barriers and quantitative restriction.

J. PAXTON, *A Dictionary of the EEC*, London, 1978, pp. 164–167.

MESTIZOS. An international term for persons descended from mixed parentage, called in French "*meti's*" = "half breed." ▷ Creole and ▷ Mulatto. Organization to protect mestizos against discrimination, reg. with the UIA:

International Union of Individuals of Mixed Parentage, Union internationale des métis, f. 1957, Dakar, Senegal. Publ.: *L'Eurafricaine*.

Yearbook of International Organizations.

METAL EXCHANGE. The international trade centers, like ▷ COMEX and ▷ London Metal Exchange.

METALLURGY. A subject of international co-operation. Organizations reg. with the UIA:

Benelux Society of Metallurgy, f. 1975, Brussels.
CMEA Commission for Iron and Steel Metallurgy, f. 1956, Moscow.
CMEA Commission for the Metallurgy of Non-ferrous Metals, f. 1956, Budapest.

M

Council of Commonwealth Mining and Metallurgical Institutions, f. 1924, London.

European Association for the Exchange of Technical Literature in the Field of Ferrous Metallurgy, f. 1959, Luxembourg.

Institution of Mining and Metallurgy, f. 1892, London.

Organization for Co-operation in the Field of Heavy Metallurgy, INTERMETAL, f. 1964, Budapest.

E.F. TYRKIEL, *Dictionary of Physical Metallurgy. In English, German, French, Polish and Russian*, Amsterdam, 1977; W.E. CLASON (ed.), *Elsevier's Dictionary of Metallurgy and Metal Working. In English/American, French, Spanish, Italian, Dutch and German*, Amsterdam, 1978. *Yearbook of International Organizations*.

METAPHYSICS. A subject of international research. Organizations reg. with the UIA:

International New Thought Alliance, f. 1914, Los Angeles, Calif.

International Society of Metaphysics, f. 1973, Varna, Bulgaria.

Society of Metaphysicians, f. 1944, London.

Yearbook of International Organizations.

METEOROLOGICAL AND ECOLOGICAL WARFARE. A subject of international negotiations on a treaty banning this kind of warfare, recognized by the UN Disarmament Conference in Geneva Sept. 3, 1976 as catastrophic for the future of mankind and the world. Experts saw possibilities of six types of meteorological and ecological warfare: (1) artificially created sea tides, (2) artificially created earthquakes, (3) the expansion of the polar cap, which could lead to a new ice age in Europe and North America, (4) the changing of the direction of tropical hurricanes, (5) the changing of sea currents, (6) the partial destruction of the ozone layer over chosen countries, causing widespread burns and cancer of the skin. The Geneva consideration of the subject was preceded by a joint US–USSR draft of a Convention on the Prohibition of Military or any other Hostile Use of Environmental Modification Techniques, signed on May 18, 1977 at Geneva; came into force on Oct. 5 1978. ▷ Modification of environment convention, 1977.

J. GOLDBLAT, *Arms Control Agreements, A Handbook*, New York, 1983, pp. 194–197.

METEOROLOGICAL SATELLITES. The first meteorological satellites were launched into orbit around the earth under the name 1959 Alpha in the USA, 1959.

METEOROLOGY. The physics of the atmosphere, a subject of organized international co-operation since 1878, the date of the First Meteorological Congress in Rome and the founding of the International Meteorological Organization, IMO. In 1919, by the Paris Air Convention, the 33 signatory states obliged themselves to collect and mutually transmit meteorological information daily at specified hours. To simplify the transmission, communications are made with the help of meteorological symbols of letters or a number code (Annex 9 to the above Convention). On Oct. 11, 1947 in Washington, DC, a Convention was signed on creating the World Meteorological Organization ▷ WMO in place of the IMO, also with headquarters in Geneva, for the purpose of "co-ordinating, harmonizing and improving meteorological operations in the world and for the purpose of adequately supporting the exchange of meteorological information between countries." The Convention entered into force Mar. 23, 1950, and since 1961 that day is celebrated as World Meteorological Day. The WMO began its operations Apr. 4, 1951 (up to that day the IMO continued its work), and since then all international problems concerning meteo-

rology have been under the management of the WMO, one of the specialized agencies of the UN. Norway, Sweden and the UK signed a treaty on Feb. 28, 1949 in Oslo on joint meteorological stations in the North Atlantic.

UNTS, Vol. 28, p. 54; *WMO Basic Documents*, Geneva, 1952.

METER. An international length unit. One meter = 100 centimeters, or approx. 39.37 inches.

METHODISTS. A Protestant religious group, formed 1729 in Oxford on the basis of the Anglican Church as a "free church" of a missionary character. In 1784 the Methodist Episcopal Church was organized in the USA, at the beginning of the 19th century in German-speaking countries as Deutsche Bischöfliche Methodistenkirche, then in Africa and Black America the segregationist Methodist churches, called Colored Episcopal Methodist Churches. In 1881 the first world Methodist organization was formed: Ecumenical Methodist Conference, meeting every year; after World War II transformed into a permanent body, The World Methodist Council. Organizations reg. with the UIA:

Council of the Methodist Central Conferences in Europe, f. 1966, Bad Bramstedt, FRG.

United Methodist Committee on Relief, f. 1940, New York. Publ.: *Inasmuch*.

World Association of Methodist Radio Amateurs and Clubs, WAMRAC, f. 1957, Melton Mowbray, Leics, UK. Publ.: *World Methodist Register of Church Radio Amateurs and Clubs and Short Wave Radio Listeners*.

World Federation of Methodist Women, f. 1939, St. Paul, Minn., USA. In affiliation with WMC.

World Methodist Council, WMC, f. 1951, London, unites Methodist religious communities of 78 countries; takes an active part in the ecumenical movement. Publ.: *World Parish*.

World Methodist Historical Society, f. 1967, Cambridge, Mass., USA.

Yearbook of International Organizations, 1986/87; The Europa Yearbook 1988. A World Survey, Vol. I, London, 1988.

METICAL. A monetary unit since 1980 of Mozambique: one metical = 100 centavos, issued by the Central Bank of Mozambique, replacing the escudo of colonial times.

METRIC SYSTEM. A system of weights and measures based on the norms of the meter and the kilogram, introduced by a resolution of the General Assembly of the French Republic on Apr. 7, 1795, confirmed by the law of Dec. 10, 1799 on a "universal metric system." This system was introduced in 1803 by Italy, 1821 by Holland and Belgium, 1836 by Spain and Latin America, 1872 by the German Reich. The first International Metric Convention was adopted May 20, 1875 in Paris, with a view to dissemination of a unified metric system of weights and measures, by the governments of Argentina, Austria–Hungary, Belgium, Brazil, Denmark, France, Germany, Italy, Norway, Peru, Portugal, Russia, Spain, Switzerland, Turkey, the USA, and Venezuela. Many other states joined in the course of the following two decades which implied no obligation to the exclusive use of the metric system but allowed the use of etalons (standards) worked out and kept by the Convention's supreme body, the International Bureau of Weights and Measures in Sèvres near Paris, as well as the application of scientific achievements of General Conferences for Weights and Measures and the International Measurements Committee. The second metric convention was drafted and signed on Sept. 6, 1921 at Sèvres. In the second half of the 20th century the unification of weights and measures became univer-

sal. In 1960 the International System of Measurement Units ▷ SI, was introduced, which integrated the meter and the metric system. In the years 1966–76 the UK and other states of the Commonwealth introduced the metric system in all fields of economy and finances; in 1966 the USA introduced the metric system as obligatory in the armament industry; in 1980 in all fields.

Organizations reg. with the UIA:

Arab Organization for Standardization and Metrology, est. 1950 in Cairo as a specialized agency within the League of Arab States. Publ.: *Standardization and Metrology* (arabic).

International Organization of Legal Metrology, est. on Oct. 12, 1955 in Paris, by intergovernmental convention (came into force May 28, 1958), with the purpose of setting up a documentation and information centre, to translate and edit the texts of legal requirements for measuring instruments and their use in force in the different states, to determine the general principles of legal metrology. Publ.: *International Recommendations*.

A *Metric Conversion Chart* for approximate measures to find:

(1) Length:
inches when you know millimeters multiply millimeters by 0.04.
inches when you know centimeters multiply centimeters by 0.4.
feet when you know meters multiply meters by 3.3.
yards when you know meters multiply meters by 1.1.
miles when you know kilometers multiply kilometers by 0.6.
centimeters when you know inches multiply inches by 2.5.
centimeters when you know feet multiply feet by 30.
meters when you know yards multiply yards by 0.9.
kilometers when you know miles multiply miles by 1.6.

(2) Area:
square inches when you know square centimeters multiply square centimeters by 0.16.
square yards when you know square meters multiply square meters by 1.2.
square miles when you know square kilometers multiply square kilometers by 0.4.
acres when you know hectares (10,000 m²) multiply hectares by 2.5.
square centimeters when you know square inches multiply square inches by 6.5.
square meters when you know square feet multiply square feet by 0.09.
square meters when you know square yards multiply square yards by 0.8.
square kilometers when you know square miles multiply square miles by 2.6.
hectares when you know acres multiply acres by 0.4.

(3) Mass and Weight:
ounce when you know grams multiply grams by 0.035.
pounds when you know kilograms multiply kilograms by 2.2.
short tons when you know tons (100 kg) multiply tons by 1.1.
grams when you know ounces multiply ounces by 28.
kilograms when you know pounds multiply pounds by 0.45.
tons when you know short tons (2000 lb) multiply short tons by 0.9.

(4) Volume:
fluid ounces when you know milliliters multiply milliliters by 0.03.
pints when you know liters multiply liters by 2.1.
quarts when you know liters multiply liters by 1.06.
gallons when you know liters multiply liters by 0.26.
cubic feet when you know cubic meters multiply cubic meters by 35.
cubic yards when you know cubic meters multiply cubic meters by 1.3.
milliliters when you know fluid ounces multiply fluid ounces by 30.
liters when you know pints multiply pints by 0.47.
liters when you know quarts multiply quarts by 0.95.
liters when you know gallons multiply gallons by 3.8.
cubic meters when you know cubic feet multiply cubic feet by 0.03.
cubic meters when you know cubic yards multiply cubic yards by 0.76.

Ch. E. GUILLAUME, *La Convention du Mètre et le Bureau International des Poids et Mesures*, Paris, 1902; V. TALLENT, *Histoire du Système Métrique*, Paris, 1911; *UNTS*, Vol. 560, p. 79; *Yearbook of International Organizations*; THE ECONOMIST, *World Measurement Guide*, London, 1980.

METRIC TON. The international mass and weight unit = 1,000,000 grams, or approx. 1.1 US tons.

MEUSE RIVER. *Flemish*: Maas. A river in France, Belgium and the Netherlands; length 925 km, basin surface 48,600 sq. km; connected by canals with the Seine, Rhine and Escaut Rivers; subject of international dispute 1937 before the Permanent Court of International Justice between Holland and Belgium over excessive exploitation of the Meuse waters, a Dutch–Belgian disagreement which dates back to May 12, 1863 concerning the means of supplying canals with water from the Meuse River; settled on June 28, 1937. ▷ International Court of Justice.

ICJ Series A/B, No. 70.

MEXAMERICA. An international term for the community of US citizens of Mexican descent (▷ Chicanos), bilingual, bicultural and binational, living in permanent touch with both Mexico and the USA.

MEXICAN CESSION. An interamerican term for the Mexican territory ceded to the United States by the ▷ Guadalupe Hidalgo Treaty, 1848.

"MEXICAN SOLUTION". An international term for a first step toward a pluralistic system in one-party states permitting, as in Mexico in the 1960's, a fragmented opposition to be represented in the parliament.

J.G. CASTAÑEDA, *Nicaragua: A 'Mexican Solution' for the Sandinistas*, in: *International Herald Tribune*, April 12, 1988.

MEXICAN WAR. A North American term for the war between the US and Mexico, Apr., 1846–Sept., 1847, terminated by the ▷Guadalupe Hidalgo Treaty, 1848.

MEXICO. Member of the UN. Estados Unidos Mexicanos. United States of Mexico. State in northern and central America in the west on the Pacific Ocean and in the east on the Gulf of Mexico. Borders with the USA, Belize and Guatemala. Area: 1,958,201 sq. km. Pop. 1988 est.: 82,700,000; at the censuses: 1900 – 13,607,000; 1910 – 15,160,000; 1921 – 14,334,000; 1940 – 19,653,000; 1950 – 24,791,000; 1970 – 48,225,000; 1980 – 67,382,581. Capital: Mexico City with 13,993,866 inhabitants in 1980. Official language: Spanish. GNP per capita in 1986: US $1,850. Currency: one Mexican peso = 100 centavos. National Day: Sept 16, Independence Day, 1810.
Founding member of the UN, and member of all specialized UN agencies. Member of the OAS and ALIDE (formerly LAFTA), of the Tlatelolco Treaty, and since 1972 in co-operation with the Andes Group.
International relations: a Spanish colony, from 1533 to 1810. A war of independence was waged from Sept. 16, 1810 (call to arms of Fr. M. Hidalgo in the town of Dolores-Grito de Dolores de Miguel Hidalgo) to Oct. 4, 1824, when Constitution of the Federal Republic was passed by the Constitutional Assembly. At war with the USA in 1835–47, ended by a treaty signed on Feb. 2, 1848 in Guadelupe Hidalgo, which recognized the annexation by the USA of the northern provinces of Mexico: Texas, New Mexico, Upper California. In 1853 Mexico sold to the USA the territory of Mesilla for 10

million dollars. The French invasion in 1862–67 ended with a Mexican victory under the leadership of Benito Juarez on May 15, 1867 in Queretaro and the execution of Emperor Maximillian on June 19, 1967. In 1877–1910 the dictatorship of P. Diaz, was supported by the USA, as were the counter-revolutionary forces after the outbreak of revolution on Nov. 20, 1910. The armed intervention of the USA on Apr. 21, 1914 in Veracruz and the hostile attitude of the US President T. Woodrow Wilson to the Mexican revolution influenced the decision of Mexico not to enter World War I. President T.W. Wilson then acted to exclude Mexico from the Versailles Conference in 1919 and blocked her acceptance into the League of Nations. Not until 1930, when all of the member states of the League had unanimously invited Mexico, did she join the League. In 1924 Mexico was the first country in the Western Hemisphere to establish diplomatic relations with the USSR. In Oct., 1932 the papal legate was expelled. In 1933 Mexico supported the US President Franklin Delano Roosevelt's ▷ good neighbor doctrine. In 1938 Mexico was the first country in the Western Hemisphere to nationalize its oil industry.

During World War II on the side of the allies; entered the war against Germany in 1942. At the beginning of 1945 the palace of Chapultepec in Mexico City was the site of the Conference on War and Peace, the so-called Chapultepec Conference. A dispute with the USA going on since 1961 on pollution of the border river, Rio Colorado, was ended on Aug. 30, 1973 with the signing of an appropriate agreement. In 1973 President Luis Echeverria postulated the ▷ Charter of Economic Rights and Duties of States, 1974. Mexico expanded her territorial waters to 200 miles in 1975. A signatory of the five-year Non-Preferential Treaty Agreements with the EDC of 1975 and of 1980. In 1979 vast new oil reserves were discovered. In Jan., 1981 Mexico terminated unilaterally all its fisheries agreements with the USA.
In 1980s a new problem for Mexico was the influx of refugees from Guatemala and El Salvador. Mexico is one of the leading forces in the ▷ Contadora Group. In May, 1983 and in June, 1984 Mexico took part in Conferences on Latin American Countries' debt.
See also ▷ World Heritage UNESCO List.

"Mexican Expropriation: The Mexican Oil Problem", in: *International Conciliation. Documents for the Year 1938*, pp. 489–558. J. CASTAÑEDA, *Mexico and the UN*, New York, 1958; H.F. CLINE, *Mexico. Revolution to Evolution, 1940–60*, New York, 1962; *México 50 Años de Revolución. La Economia. La Vida Social. La Política. La Cultura*, México, DF, 1963; *50 Años de Revolución Mexicana en Cifras*, México, DF, 1963; F. TENA RAMIREZ, *Leyes Fundamentales de México 1808–1964*, México, DF, 1964; L.G. ZORRILLA, *Historia de las Relaciones entre México y Estados Unidos de América 1800–1958*, 2 Vols., México, DF, 1965–66; D. COSTO VILLEGAS, *Cuestiones Internacionales de México. Una Bibliografía*, México, DF, 1966; *Bibliografía Histórica Mexicana*, México, DF, 1967; R.M. FERNANDEZ ESQUIVIL, *Las Publicaciones Oficiales de México: Guia de Publicaciones Periodicas 1937–67*, México, DF, 1967; E. LIEUVEN, *Mexican Militarism: The Political Rise and Fall of the Revolutionary Army 1910–1940*, Albuquerque, 1968; *Diccionario Porrua de História, Biografía y Geografía de México*, 2 Vols., México, DF, 1970–71; A. GARCIA ROBLES, *México en las NU*, 2 Vols., México, DF, 1970; *Constituciones vigentes en la República Mexicana, con las Leyes Organicas de los Territorios Federales y del Departamento del Distrito Federal*, 2 Vols., México, DF, 1972; *Tratados Bilaterales de los EU Mexicanos*, Tlatelolco, DF, 1973; L. CARDENAS, *Las relaciones mexicano-soviéticas, Antecedentes y primeros contactos diplomaticos 1789–1927*, México, DF, 1974; J. BAZANT, *A Concise History of Mexico*, Oxford, 1977; K.F. JACKSON,

Mexican Democracy. A Critical View, New York, 1978; S. KAUFMAN, *The Politics of Mexican Oil*, Pittsburgh, 1981; S. KAUFMAN, *Mexico-United States Relations*, New York, 1981; F. CARRADA BRAVO, *Oil. Money and the Mexican Economy*, Boulder, 1982; J.I. DOMINGUEZ (ed.), *Mexico's Political Economy: Challenges at Home and Abroad*, London, 1982; 'Will Mexico make it? The IMF sees an Economic Turnaround,' in: *Business Week*, October 1, 1984; *The European Year Book 1984. A World Survey*, Vol. II, pp. 2035–2057, London, 1984; J. PADUA, *Educación, Industrialización y Progreso, Técnico en México*, UNESCO, Paris, 1985; J.R. ALVAREZ ed., *Enciclopedia de Mexico*, Mexico DF, 1987 (3 Vols A–C); R.A. PASTOR, J.G. CASTANEDA, *Limits to Friendship: The United States and Mexico*, New York, 1988; AL SANTOLI, *New Americans, An Oral History: Immigrants and Refugees in the US Today*, New York, 1988; J. KANDELL, *The Biography of Mexico City*, New York, 1988.

MEXICO CITY. Capital of Mexico, most populated of the world's capitals in the 1980's. Population of the metropolitan area of the Federal Districts (Mexico DF): 12,932,116; in 1988 estimated at about 20 million. During the ▷ Mexican War captured by US troops, 1847; occupied by French soldiers 1864–1867. Site of the ▷ Chapultepec Conference 1948, the ▷ Tlatelolco Conference 1967 and 1974 and of the ▷ Olympic Games 1968. In 1957 and 1986 earthquakes caused extensive damage.

Mexico Ciudad de, in: *Dictionario Porrua*, México DF., 1971.

MEXICO DECLARATION, 1978. ▷ World Food Council Mexico Declaration, 1978.

MEXICO GROUP OF SIX DECLARATION 1986. A call for an agreement on ending all testing of nuclear weapons, signed in Mexico City on Aug. 9, 1986 by the President of Mexico, de la Madrid; the President of Argentina, Alfonsin; former President Nyerere of Tanzania; the Prime Minister of Greece, Andreas Papandreou; Swedish Prime Minister, Olof Palme and the Prime Minister of India, Rajiv Gandhi; presented to the UN.

MEXICO–US TREATY, 1853. A Treaty also called the Gadsden Treaty from the name of an American diplomat James Gadsden (1788–1858), signed on Dec. 30, 1853 in Mexico, amending and substituting the ▷ Guadalupe Hidalgo Treaty of 1848, granting the United States the Mesilla Valley (77,700 sq. km) near Rio Grande in South Arizona, for the price of 10 million dollars.

W. McMALLOY, *Treaties, Conventions*, Washington, DC, 1910, Vol. 1, p. 1121; P.N. GARBER, *The Gadsden Treaty*, New York, 1923; *The Major Peace Treaties of Modern History*, New York, 1967.

MEXICO–US TREATY ON RETURN OF STOLEN ART OBJECTS, 1970. The Treaty of Co-operation providing for the Recovery and Return of Stolen Archaeological, Historical and Cultural Properties, signed on July 17, 1970 at Mexico City; came into force on Mar. 24, 1971 by the exchange of the instruments of ratification. The text reads as follows:

"The United States of America and the United Mexican States, in a spirit of close co-operation and with the mutual desire to encourage the protection, study and appreciation of properties of archaeological, historical and cultural importance, and to provide for the recovery and return of such properties when stolen, have agreed as follows:
Art. I.(1) For the purposes of this Treaty, "archaeological, historical and cultural properties" are defined as
(a) art object and artifacts of the pre-Columbian cultures of the United States of America and the United

M

Mexican States of outstanding importance to the national patrimony, including stelae and architectural features such as relief and wall art;

(b) art objects and religious artifacts of the colonial periods of the United States of America and the United Mexican States of outstanding importance to the national patrimony;

(c) documents from official archives for the period up to 1920 that are of outstanding historical importance; that are property of federal, state, or municipal governments of their instrumentalities, including portions or fragments of such objects, artifacts, and archives.

(2) The application of the foregoing definitions to a particular item shall be determined by agreement of the two governments, or failing agreement, by a panel of qualified experts whose appointment and procedures shall be prescribed by the two governments. The determinations of the two governments, or of the panel, shall be final.

Art. II.(1) The Parties undertake individually and, as appropriate, jointly

(a) to encourage the discovery, excavation, preservation, and study of archaeological sites and materials by qualified scientists and scholars of both countries;

(b) to deter illicit excavations of archaeological, historical, or cultural properties;

(c) to facilitate the circulation and exhibition in both countries of archaeological, historical and cultural properties in order to enhance the mutual understanding and appreciation of the artistic and cultural heritage of the two countries; and

(d) consistent with the laws and regulations assuring the conservation of national archaeological, historical and cultural properties, to permit legitimate international commerce in art objects.

(2) Representatives of the two countries, including qualified scientists and scholars, shall meet from time to time to consider matters relating to the implementation of these undertakings.

Art. III.(1) Each Party agrees, at the request of the other Party, to employ the legal means at its disposal to recover and return from its territory stolen archaeological, historical and cultural properties that are removed after the date of entry into force of this Treaty from the territory of the requesting Party.

(2) Requests for the recovery and return of designated archaeological, historical and cultural properties shall be made through diplomatic offices. The requesting Party shall furnish, at its expense, documentation and other evidence necessary to establish its claim to the archaeological, historical or cultural property.

(3) If the requested Party cannot otherwise effect the recovery and return of a stolen archaeological, historical or cultural property located in its territory, the appropriate authority of the requested Party shall institute judicial proceedings to this end. For this purpose, the Attorney General of the United States of America is authorized to institute a civil action in the appropriate district court of the United States of America, and the Attorney General of the United Mexican States is authorized to institute proceedings in the appropriate district court of the United Mexican States. Nothing in this Treaty shall be deemed to alter the domestic law of the Parties otherwise applicable to such proceedings.

Art. IV. As soon as the requested Party obtains the necessary legal authorization to do so, it shall return the requested archaeological, historical, or cultural property to the persons designated by the requesting Party. All expenses incident to the return and delivery of an archaeological, historical or cultural property shall be borne by the requesting Party. No person or Party shall have any right to claim compensation from the returning Party for damage or loss to the archaeological, historical or cultural property in connection with the performance by the returning Party of its obligations under this Treaty.

Art. V. Notwithstanding any statutory requirements inconsistent with this Treaty for the disposition of merchandise seized for violation of laws of the requested Party relating to the importation of merchandise, stolen archaeological, historical or cultural property which is the subject matter of this Treaty and has been seized, or seized and forfeited to the requested Party, shall be returned to the requesting Party in accordance with the provisions of this Treaty. The Parties shall not impose upon archaeological, historical or cultural property returned pursuant to this Treaty any charges

or penalties arising from the application of their laws relating to the importation of merchandise.

Art. VI.(1) The Parties shall ratify this Treaty in accordance with the provisions of their respective constitutions, and instruments of ratification shall be exchanged at Washington as soon as possible.

(2) This Treaty shall enter into force on the day of exchange of the instruments of ratification, and shall remain in force for two years from that date and thereafter until thirty days either Party gives written notice to the other Party of its intention to terminate it.

UNTS, Vol. 791, pp. 314–321.

MFN. ▷ Most Favoured Nation, IMF Clause.

MHV. Miniature Homing Vehicle. ▷ Space War.

MICROBIOLOGY. A subject of international co-operation. Within the WHO Special Programme on Safety Measures in Microbiology special emphasis has been placed on the development of Standards of Laboratory Safety to protect the health of laboratory workers, the public and the environment from hazards associated with accidental exposure to microorganisms and experimental biological materials. These minimum standards were formulated by the WHO Working Group on Laboratory Safety Elements, August, 1979.

WHO. *Weekly Epidemiological Record*, No. 44, 1979.

MICROCHIP PACT, 1986. An agreement between Japan and US to maintain high prices for its exports of Microchips, signed in Washington DC, 1986. The European Commission charged in April, 1968, that the agreement broke GATT rules because keeping Japanese export prices high improved the competition position of US microchip exporters and raised the cost for EEC users of such products.

MICROELECTRONIC REVOLUTION. An international term introduced 1982 by the ▷ Club of Rome, for a new scientific and industrial revolution, similar to the two technological revolutions of 19th and 20th centuries.

Club of Rome, *Microelectronics and Society. For Better or for Worse*, Tokyo, 1982; A. SCHAFF. *The Social Consequences of the Microelectronic Revolution*, Tokyo, 1982.

MICROENTERPRISES. An international term in the 1980's for a growing number of small-scale enterprises in all parts of the World with fewer than 50 workers, in the majority with fewer than 10 employees. The US Agency of International Development since 1988 has a Micro-Enterprise Development Programm.

ILO, *Rural Small-Scale Industries and Employment in Africa and Asia*, Geneva, 1984; C. LEIDHOLM, D. MEAD, Small-Scale Enterprises. A Profile, in: *Economic Impact*, No. 2, 1988.

MICROGRAPHY. A subject of international co-operation. Organization reg. with the UIA:

International Micrographic Congress, f. 1963, San Francisco. Publ.: *Newsletter*.

Yearbook of International Organizations.

MICRONESIA. The Oceanian Islands in the west Pacific: Caroline Islands, Marshall Islands, Mariana Islands, Gilbert Islands and Nauru Island; Trust Territory of the Pacific Islands; On July 12, 1978 a constitutional referendum was held with the UN Trusteeship Council as observer.

In Palau, one of the four administrative entities of Micronesia, a referendum was held in 1986. Separate plebiscites held in off-island Palauan communities – Northern Mariana Islands, Guam, the Federate States of Micronesia and the Marshall

Islands – also on Nov. 29, and in communities in Hawaii and the continental United States on Dec. 7. The UN observers reported that two thirds of the people of Palau approved the revised Compact of Free Association with the United States.

R.W. ROBSON (ed.), *Pacific Islands Year Book*, London, 1959; *UN Chronicle*, July, 1979, pp. 95–96; *Trusteeship Council Calls Termination of Micronesia Agreement "Appropriate"*, in: *UN Chronicle*, August, 1986, p. 67.

MICRO-STATES. An international term for states not surpassing several hundred sq. km. in area such as Andorra, Liechtenstein, Monaco, San Marino; subject of international conventions.

MICUM. Mission Interalliée de Controle des Usines et des Mines, Inter-Allied Control Mission for Factories and Mines. The name of interallied institutions supervising the economy of the Ruhr Basin after World War I. Six agreements concluded by MICUM with German concerns in 1923–24 formed the basis for normalization of relations between France and Germany.

MID. The Russian abbreviation for Ministierstwo Innostrannykh Diel, USSR Ministry of Foreign Affairs. ▷ Foggy Bottom, ▷ Foreign Office, ▷ Jtamarati, ▷ Quai d'Orsay, ▷ Wilhelmstrasse.

MIDDLE AMERICA. An international term introduced by American geographers for the area of Central America, Mexico, Panama and the West Indies.

MIDDLE EAST. An international geographical term applied to the countries of south-west Asia and northeast Africa: the Asian part of Turkey, Syria, Israel, Jordan, Iraq, Iran, Lebanon, Bahrain, Kuwait, Qatar, United Arab Emirates, Oman, Yemen, Southern Yemen and Saudi Arabia; in the cultural sense also to Afghanistan and Pakistan.

In Sept., 1984 the Soviet foreign minister A. Gromyko in diplomatic talks in the UN Hqs. presented a proposal for an international Middle East peace conference, "to be attended by the parties to the conflict in the Middle East, including the PLO and the permanent members of the UN Security Council." The proposal rejected by the USA and Israel was welcomed by Jordan. The UK did not support "the convening of an international conference at present, but attached the highest importance to the irreplacable role of the UN in promoting peace in the Middle East".

The item "the situation in the Middle East" is discussed every year since 1981 by the General Assembly "gravely concerned that the Palestinian territory occupied since 1967 including Jerusalem, and the other occupied Arab territories still remain under Israeli occupation". (Res. 43/54, adopted on Dec. 2, 1986, by 143 votes, to 2, with 7 abstentions).

G. KIRK, *The Middle East in the War, 1939–1946*, London, 1952; J.C. HUREWITZ, *The Middle East and North Africa, in World Politics. A Documentary Record*, (Vol. 1 European Expansions 1535–1914, Vol. 2 British–French Supremacy, 1914–1945) New Haven, 1975–1979; *The Middle East in Conflict. A Historical Bibliography*, Santa Barbara, Ca., Oxford, UK, 1985; H. CARADON, "Proposal: Time for a Middle East Peace Conference", in: *International Herald Tribune*, October 19, 1984; R.O. FREEDMAN ed., *The Middle East After the Israeli Invasion of Lebanon*, Syracuse, N.Y., 1986; T.Y. ISMAEL, *International Relations of the Contemporary Middle East*, Syracuse, N.Y., 1986; *The Papacy and the Middle East*; G.E. IRANI, *The Role of the Holy See in the Arab–Israeli Conflict, 1962–1984*, Notre Dame, Ind., 1986; SHEIKH R. ALI, *Oil and Power: Political Dynamics in the Middle East*, London, 1987; *UN Resolutions and Decisions adopted by the General Assembly during the First Part of its*

Forty-Third Session, from 22 September to 22 December 1988, New York, 1989, p. 97; D. PIPES, *The Long Shadow. Culture and Politics in the Middle East*, New Brunswick, N.J., 1989.

MIDDLE EAST INSTITUTE. An American institute f. 1946 in Washington, DC. The Institute holds annual conferences on Middle East problems. Publ.: *Middle East Journal* (quarterly).

MIDDLE EAST REGIONAL CO-OPERATION FOR DEVELOPMENT, RCD. Intergovernmental organization reg. with the UIA, est. July 21, 1964, Istanbul, by an agreement concluded between Iran, Pakistan and Turkey. Its aims: encourage and plan regional economic and cultural collaboration; harmonize national development plans of the member states. The RCD initiated a joint international airline, joint shipping company, joint petroleum organization, regional cultural institute, joint insurance and reinsurance centers. Publ.: *The RCD Magazine* (quarterly) and *RCD Newsletter* (monthly).

C. LEGUM (ed.), *Middle East Contemporary Survey*, New York, 1979.

MIDGETMAN. Name of a projected system of ▷ SICBM to be built by the USA in the 1980's.

D. ROBERTSON, *Guide to Modern Defense and Strategy*, Detroit, 1988.

MIDSETMAN. An American project, 1986, for a single-warhead missile, less vulnerable to attack than the ▷ MX.

MIDWAY. An island group in the central Pacific. Area: 5.2 sq. km. Annexed by the United States in 1867, since 1941 US naval base. The Battle of Midway between the US and Japanese Navy, June 3–6, 1942, ended with an American victory and was the turning point of World War II in the Pacific. After the war, under administration of US Department of Interior.

M. FUJIDA, M. OKUMIYA, *Midway: The Battle That Doomed Japan*, New York, 1969.

MIG-29. A Soviet military aircraft that entered into service with the Soviet Air Force in 1984, since 1985 delivered to foreign customers (India, Iraq, Syria, Yugoslavia) presented as an air superiority fighter at the airshow in Farnborough, England, in September 1988.

K.B. TIMMERMAN, Soviet Push MIG-29 Marketing, in: *International Herald Tribune*, September 5, 1988.

MIGA. ▷ Multilateral Investment Guarantee Agency.

MIGRATION. A subject of international conventions, studies, statistics, charity actions. On Oct. 2, 1951, in Naples an international conference of West European states on displaced persons established the Intergovernmental Committee for European Migration, in The Hague. It publishes *International Migration* (quarterly). On Dec. 17, 1979 the UN General Assembly Res. 34/172 decided to create a working group to elaborate an International Convention on the Protection of the Rights of All Migrant Workers and their Families.
Since the 1980's the problem of migrants has taken on a new dimension, especially in Western Europe but also in North America and South East Asia. Highlights of an analysis of the Council of Europe 1988:

"There is scarcely any more immigration at the present time; the flow of foreign workers has practically stopped. Nevertheless there is a continuous flow (although on a smaller scale) of members of established immigrants, families and a large flow (although impossible to measure) of clandestine migrants or applicants for asylum (Political refugees or 'economic refugees'). In spite of very strict immigration rules, a number of inhabitants from third world countries are exerting considerable pressure to gain entrance to Europe. A comparison of population trends alone shows clearly that the pressure exerted by the Third World will intensify. Because of the enormous economic imbalance between 'North' and 'South', a number of people from the Third World are ready to pay the price of a precarious or illegal situation in order to live and work in Europe. The main victims of this phenomenon are the immigrants who have entered the territory legally and are exposed to unfair competition on the part of the illegal immigrants as far as employment is concerned".
The Council of Europe created in March 1987 The European Committee on Migration and in May 1987 the first Conference on European Ministers responsible for Migration Affairs took place in Oporto, Portugal.
▷ Gastarbeiter; and ▷ Mass exodus.

A Handbook for International Measures for the Protection of Migrants, and General Conditions to be Observed in their Settlement, Geneva, 1950; R. PLENDER, *International Migration Law*, Leiden, 1972; *UN Chronicle*, March, 1980, p. 77. T.E. SMITH, *Commonwealth Migration. Flows and Policies*, London, 1981; Migrant Workers: Recent Trends, in: *UN Chronicle*, 1985, No. 2, p. 12; Council of Europe, *Information Sheet No. 21*, Strasbourg, 1988, p. 101 and 100 183.

MIGRATORY BIRDS. A subject of international protection, defined by the International American Convention on Nature Protection, 1940, as follows:
Birds of those species, all or some of whose individual members may at any season cross any of the boundaries between the American countries. Some of the species of the following families are examples of birds characterized as migratory: Charadriidae, Scolopacidae, Caprimulgidae, Hirundinidae.

OAS Treaty Series, No. 31, Washington, DC, 1964.

MILAN. A city in north Italy. The Church and Dominican Convent of Santa Maria delle Grazie, with The Last Supper by Leonardo da Vinci, is included in the ▷ World Heritage UNESCO List. This Dominican convent in Milan was completed at the end of the 16th century by Bramante, who constructed a splendid dome for the church and built for the monks a cloister and refectory. There, Leonardo da Vinci painted "the Last Supper" which, with the possible exception of the Mona Lisa, is his most famous work.

UNESCO. *A Legacy for All*, Paris, 1984.

MILE. An unstandardized measure of length accepted in Europe and America: the English mile consists of 1760 yards = 1609.3 m; the Australian mile = 7586 m; the geographical mile = 7421.6 m or one one-fifteenth of a degree of an arc at the equator; German mile = 5500 m; Polish long mile = 7400 m; Prussian mile = 7532.48 m: Roman mile = 1479 m or 1000 pairs of steps. A separate measure is the ▷ Nautical mile, international.

MILITARIA. An international term for the collections of weapons, insignia, medals and military publications, subject of organized international cooperation through the ICOM sections of military museums. Two international exhibitions and fairs of militaria organized by antique dealers are held periodically under the accepted name Militaria Exchange (in Stuttgart, FRG – *Waffenbörse*; in Neuchâtel, Switzerland – *Bourse aux armes*).
The International Association of Museums of Arms and Military History, f. 1957, London, affiliates under the aegis of ICOM, 231 museums in 47 countries. Reg. with the UIA.

Yearbook of International Organizations; T. HARTMAN, J. MITCHELL, *A World Atlas of Military History, 1945–1984*, New York, 1987.

MILITARISM. An international term of double meaning: for a form of government expressed by the army exercising decisive influence on state policy; for state activity covering both preparation for and waging of invasive wars and the defense of class rule inside the state; a classical example of that kind of state activity was the Prussian militarism in Europe.
▷ Potsdam Agreement 1945.

G.A. CRAIG, *The Policy of the Prussian Army 1640–1945*, London, 1955.

MILITARY ASSISTANCE PROGRAM. The official name of USA military assistance to more than 40 states under the terms of bilateral military treaties; voted on annually by the US Congress since 1950; is one of the main components of the ▷ Mutual Security Program.

MILITARY BASES. The stationing of military forces and equipment on foreign territory, usually by virtue of international agreements, which as a rule limit the territorial sovereignty of the state where they are maintained. Military bases may include special centers or regions, strategically or politically important, equipped with airports, harbors, barracks, magazines, hospitals, repair workshops, etc., supplied with all kind of equipment and means, and with a permanent garrison; also used for temporary stationing and supplying of various military units and as a point of departure for military operations. Internationally, treated by the UN as a remnant of colonial rule, under which various states maintained their military bases on foreign territories to secure and defend their local interests. The maintenance of military bases in former colonial areas or in their vicinity may constitute an instrument of foreign intervention which, at the same time, can lead to the conversion of tactical weapons into strategic ones. A different problem which, under art. 53 of the UN Charter is referred to as regional arrangement, was posed by the existence, after the World War II, of the Four Powers military bases in Europe and the Far East (in 1955, France, Great Britain, the USA and the USSR withdrew from Austria, and in 1947–49, the USSR withdrew from the Korea and Manchuria, as well as from Bulgaria, Czechoslovakia, and Romania). Since then with regard to Europe, the Western Powers in accordance with international agreements maintain permanent military bases in the FRG, West Berlin and, within the framework of the NATO, also in several member states of this organization, whereas the USSR maintains such bases in the GDR and, within the framework of bilateral agreements and the Warsaw Pact, in Czechoslovakia (since 1968), Poland and Hungary (since 1945). France subsequently withdrew from Indochina and Algeria, but kept its bases in a few overseas departments in the Western Hemisphere; Great Britain liquidated its bases in Asia, Africa and the Middle East; Belgium, the Netherlands and Portugal liquidated all their bases. In 1965 the UN General Assembly, in Res. 2105/XX demanded that the colonial Powers liquidate their military bases in the colonies and countries of the Third World. The Res. 2165/XXI of Dec. 5, 1966 called for the elimination of foreign military bases in the countries of Asia, Africa and Latin America. In the following years, the question of military bases was discussed several times in the UN and demands were put forward for liquidation of all military bases throughout the world. Among others, China put forward in 1978, as a precondition for its participation in the Disarmament Conference, the demand

M

that all atomic Powers undertake the obligation not to use nuclear weapons and to liquidate all their military bases on foreign territories.

G. FIORAVANZO, *Basi Navali nel Mondo*, Roma, 1936; H.W. WEIGER, "US Strategic Bases and Collective Security", in: *Foreign Affairs*, No. 25, 1947; J.W. VILLACRES MOSCOSO, *El Problema del Control Internacional de las Bases Estratégicas y las Naciones Unidas*, Guayaquil, 1951; A. QUINTANA RIPOLLES, "Soberanía, Jurisdicción Territorial y Bases Militares", in: *Revista Española de Derecho Internacional*, No. 8, 1955; M. FONDY, "Les bases militaires à l'étranger", in: *Annuaire Française de Droit International, 1955*; G. STAMBUK, *American Military Forces Abroad. Their Impact on the Western State System*, Columbus, Ohio, 1963; M. LAZARIEV, *Voyenne bazy SShA v Latinskoy Amerike*, Moscow, 1970; S. DUKE, *US Defence Bases in the United Kingdom. A Matter of Joint Decision*, London, 1987.

MILITARY BLOCS. An international term created after World War II, to define the defensive alliances of free market countries set up in the years 1949–55 (NATO, ANZUS, SEATO and CENTO); and the military alliance of planned economy countries (Warsaw Pact) created in 1955.

T. HARTMAN, J. MITCHELL, *A World Atlas of Military History, 1945–1984*, New York, 1987.

MILITARY BUDGETS OR MILITARY EXPENDITURE. A subject of international agreements. On Dec. 7, 1973 the UN General Assembly Res. 3903 B (XXVII) established a Special Committee on Reduction of Military Budgets, consisting of the permanent members of the Security Council; three countries each from the regional groups of Africa, Asia and Latin America, and two countries from the regional groups of Eastern Europe and Western Europe and other states. Over the years the UN had called upon states to limit expenditures on armaments and to allocate the resources thus freed for economic and social development. In Dec., 1973, the UN General Assembly Res. 3903 A (XXVII) recommended that the five permanent members of the Security Council, as well as other states with a major economic and military potential, reduce their military budgets by 10% from the 1973 level and appealed to them to allot 10% of the funds thus released for assistance to the developing countries. The ▷ SIPRI published a statistical study of world military expenditures in the 1980s.

According to SIPRI the military ▷ Research and Development Expenditure is concentrated in the USA and the USSR and in Japan, the FRG, France, the UK and China, but "it is not possible to be precise about total world military R and D expenditures because of the lack of hard information about many countries".

UN Monthly Chronicle, January, 1974, pp. 23–30; *SIPRI World Armaments and Disarmament Yearbook*, Stockholm, 1983–84; R. LEGER SIVARD, *World Military and Social Expenditures 1987–88*, Washington DC, 1987; *SIPRI Yearbook 1987*, Oxford, 1988, pp. 119–179.

MILITARY CHAPLAINS. The clerics who perform priestly functions within the military forces, included in the Geneva Conventions on treatment of war prisoners. Chaplains exist in all American and West European as well as Polish military forces.

MILITARY COMPULSORY SERVICE CONSCIENTIOUS OBJECTION TO. The Council of Europe on April 9, 1987 adopted a Recommendation No. 2 (87) 8 for the Member States, as follows:

The Committee of Ministers, under the terms of Article 15(b) of the Statute of the Council of Europe.

Considering that the aim of the Council of Europe is to achieve a greater unity between its members;
Recalling that respect for human rights and fundamental freedoms is the common heritage of member states of the Council of Europe, as is borne out, in particular, by the European Convention on Human Rights;
Considering that it is desirable to take common action for the further realisation of human rights and fundamental freedoms;
Noting that in the majority of member states of the Council of Europe military service is a basic obligation of citizens;
Considering the problems raised by conscientious objection to compulsory military service;
Wishing that conscientious objection to compulsory military service be recognised in all the member states of the Council of Europe and governed by common principles;
Noting that, in some member states where conscientious objection to compulsory military service is not yet recognised, specific measures have been taken with a view to improving the situation of the individuals concerned;
Recommends that the governments of member states, insofar as they have not already done so, bring their national law and practice into line with the following principles and rules
(A) Basic principle
(1) Anyone liable to conscription for military service who, for compelling reasons of conscience, refuses to be involved in the use of arms, shall have the right to be released from the obligation to perform such service, on the conditions set out hereafter. Such persons may be liable to perform alternative service.
(B) Procedure
(2) States may lay down a suitable procedure for the examination of application for conscientious objector status or accept a declaration giving reasons by the person concerned;
(3) With a view to the effective application of the principles and rules of this recommendation, persons liable to conscription shall be informed in advance of their rights. For this purpose, the state shall provide them with all relevant information directly or allow private organisations concerned to furnish that information;
(4) Applications for conscientious objector status shall be made in ways and within time-limits to be determined having due regard to the requirement that the procedure for the examination of an application should, as a rule, be completed before the individual concerned is actually enlisted in the forces;
(5) The examination of applications shall include all the necessary guarantees for a fair procedure;
(6) An applicant shall have the right to appeal against the decision at first instance;
(7) The appeal authority shall be separate from the military administration and composed so as to ensure its independence;
(8) The law may also provide for the possibility of applying for and obtaining conscientious objector status in cases where the requisite conditions for conscientious objection appear during military service or periods of military training after initial service;
(C) Alternative service
(9) Alternative service, if any, shall be in principle civilian and in the public interest. Nevertheless, in addition to civilian service, the state may also provide for unarmed military service, assigning to it only those conscientious objectors whose objections are restricted to the personal use of arms;
(10) Alternative service shall not be of a punitive nature. Its duration shall, in comparison to that of military service, remain within reasonable limits;
(11) Conscientious objectors performing alternative service shall not have less social and financial rights than persons performing military service. Legislative provisions or regulations which relate to the taking into account of military service for employment, career or pension purposes shall apply to alternative service.

In the Warsaw Pact States the Polish Seym adopted on July 26, 1988 the first regulation of compulsory military service law.

Council of Europe. Human Rights. *Information Sheet No. 21*, pp. 16, 160–161 and 170.

MILITARY DOCTRINES. An international term for strategic military planning concepts. See also ▷ Blitzkrieg; ▷ Conventional Arms Ogarkov Doctrine; ▷ Clausewitz Doctrine; ▷ Collective Defence; ▷ Escalation; ▷ Flexible Response Doctrine; ▷ Massive Retaliation; ▷ NATO Strategic Doctrine; ▷ No First Use; ▷ On the 132Brink of the War; ▷ Pacification; ▷ Retortion; ▷ Repulsion Doctrine; ▷ Rollback ▷ Soviet Military Defence Doctrine.

S. TROFIMENKO, *The US Military Doctrine*, Moscow, 1986; T.N. DUPUY, C. JOHNSON, G.P. HAYES eds. *Dictionary of Military Terms. A Guide to the Language of Warfare and Military Institutions*, New York, 1986; D. YAZOV, *Soviet Defence*, Moscow, 1987.

MILITARY INDUSTRIAL COMPLEX. An international term for co-operation of the military establishment with industry. The US President General Dwight D. Eisenhower in his farewell address in Jan., 1961 warned that "only an alert and knowledgeable citizenry can compel the proper meshing of the huge industrial and military machinery of defense with our peaceful methods and goals, so that security and liberty may prosper together."

MILITARY LAW. A system of rules of government applying only to persons in military service, distinguished from ▷ Martial law, applied also to civilians.

H.J. BERMAN, M. KERNER, *Soviet Military Law and Administration*, London, 1955; *Manual of Military Law*, HMSO, London, 1965; S. LAZAROFF, *Status of Military Forces under Current International Law*, Leiden, 1971.

MILITARY MANEUVERS. The periodic exercises of the army of one country, or jointly the allied armies of several states, subject of international agreements. The ▷ Helsinki Final Act in the Document on Confidence-Building Measures and Certain Aspects of Security and Disarmament adopted provisions on prior notification of major military maneuvers, exceeding a total of 25,000 troops, independently or combined with any possible air or naval components. In 1976 the above provisions were realized for the first time. The SIPRI World Armaments and Disarmament Yearbook published a chronicle of the notifications of military maneuvres in compliance with the Helsinki Final Act.

Conference on Security and Co-operation in Europe. Final Act, Helsinki, 1975, pp. 84–86.

MILITARY MISSIONS. The military units dispatched by one state at the invitation of a second state to carry out strictly defined tasks: advisory, assistance, or by order of intergovernmental resolutions to perform control or mediatory functions. ▷ Allied Military Missions in Berlin.

MILITARY SECURITY FORCE IN WEST GERMANY. A military unit created on Jan. 17, 1949 in Coblenz by the three Western powers for the Western zones of occupied Germany and West Berlin; abolished May 8, 1955 after the acceptance of the FRG into NATO.

MILITARY SERVICE. An international term for compulsory or volunteer service in military forces; subject of bilateral and multilateral agreements in Latin-America and Europe. On Mar. 3, 1956 in Oslo, Denmark, Norway, and Sweden signed the so-called Scandinavian Treaty on the Recognition of Military Service performed in any one of these countries.

According to a special report, March 1985, of the Sub-Committee on Prevention of Discrimination and Protection of Minorities, conscientious objectors should be exempted from the obligation to perform military service. The report stated the view that states should recognize by law the right of release from military service for persons who refuse to perform armed service for reasons of conscience or profound conviction arising from religious, ethical, moral, humanitarian or similar motives. The other recommendations in the report were:

States should, as minimum, extend the right of objection to persons whose conscience forbids them to take part in armed service under any circumstances (the pacifist position);
States should recognize by law the right to be released from service in armed forces which the objector considers likely to be used to enforce *apartheid*, in action amounting to or approaching genocide, and for illegal occupation of foreign territory;
States should recognize the right of persons to be released from service in armed forces which the objector holds to be engaged in, or likely to be engaged in, gross violations of human rights; and
States should recognize the right of persons to be released from the obligation to perform service in armed forces which the objector considers likely to resort to the use of weapons of mass destruction or weapons which have been specifically outlawed by international law, or to use means and methods which cause unnecessary suffering.
On the question of *procedural aspects,* the report stated that States should maintain or establish independent decision-making bodies to determine whether a conscientious objection was valid under national law in any specific case. There should always be a right of appeal to an independent, civilian judicial body. Applicants should be granted a hearing and be entitled to be represented by legal counsel and to call witnesses. States should disseminate information about the right of objection, and allow non-governmental organizations to do likewise.
As to *alternative service,* the Rapporteurs said States should provide alternative service for the objector, which should be at least as long as the military service, but not excessively long so that it became in effect a punishment. States should, to the extent possible, seek to give the alternative service a meaningful content, including social work or work for peace, development and international understanding.
About *trial and penalties where the objection is not found valid,* the report observed that even when States had given effect to the above recommendations, there would be some cases where the objection was not found valid, and where penalties would be imposed on persons who persisted in their objection. Imposition of such penalties should be decided upon by impartial civilian court applying the normal criteria of fair trial. Penalties should not be excessively severe, and should take due account, as mitigating factors, of the conscience or conviction of the person concerned.
On the question of *asylum,* the report stated that, taking into account the existence of rules of international law, under which an individual retained the right and the duty to refuse illegal orders under national law, and the provisions of General Assembly resolution 33/165, as well as basic right to freedom of conscience, international standards should be established which would ensure a favourable attitude towards conscientious objectors requesting asylum in conformity with obligations under international law. (It appeared to be the practice of many countries not to refuse asylum to conscientious objectors to military service. International legislation on that practice might clarify an area of human rights in which there were international and individual obligations.)
The report said there were some "fundamental dilemmas" on the subject of conscientious objection to military service. One was between the "assertion of national community and the search for a global community". Another was between the "assertion of national authority and the respect for those who dissent on grounds of conscience". Those dilemmas reflected some "basic contradictions" – on the one hand, the need felt by almost every State for some degree of military strength, and on the other, the "dual vocation" of the United Nations to advance peace and international understanding as well as respect for the human being.
The United Nations and the specialized agencies, such as the United Nations Educational, Scientific and Cultural Organization, had provided young people everywhere with the vision of a world based on solidarity, justice and human dignity, the report observed. Activities of the United Nations in support of peace, disarmament, respect for human rights and fundamental freedom influenced the thinking of young people, and some respect should be shown for their dedication to such ideals.
State practice regarding the extent to which military service was voluntary or enforced, the report pointed out, varied widely.
Sixty-six States had no conscription or compulsory military service. The problem of conscientious objection was of less significance in such cases.
Five countries had conscription in law, but did not enforce it, and there were 15 States which enforced conscription but which recognized conscientious objection, at least on some grounds.
Then there were 12 countries which enforced compulsory service and did not recognize the right of objectors to be exempted from military service, but which did allow objectors, in certain circumstances, to be given non-combatant roles in the armed forces, either by provisions of law or on an *ad hoc* basis.
Finally, there was a group of 39 States with conscription which did not recognize conscientious objection in law, and where there had been no indication that objectors had been allowed, by administrative decision, to perform unarmed services within the armed forces. It was possible that in some of these countries nobody had actually objected to military service.

UNTS, Vol. 243, p. 169.

MILITARY SERVICE OF NON-NATIONALS. A subject of alien's rights regulated by internal law of the state on the territory in which an alien is staying, and by international law and inter-state bilateral agreements. There are no uniform rules concerning military service of non-nationals; they depend on state legislature, that is, whether it exacts military service not only from its nationals, but also from its residents, e.g. Denmark since Nov. 8, 1912; the United States since May 18, 1917, under a law amended on July 9, 1918, Sept. 16, 1940, June 24, 1948, and June 19, 1951. In France, since Apr. 12, 1939 and Nov. 4, 1953 every person of military age residing in France longer than a year is liable to military service. In the FRG, since July 21, 1956, non-nationals are liable to military service on a reciprocal basis, and stateless persons according to an order of the FRG authorities. The attempt of the LN Conference in 1929 to work out a uniform convention on the treatment of aliens ended in failure (*LN Doc. C 36 M 21, 1929, II*). The Pan-American Convention on the Status of Aliens, adopted on Feb. 20, 1928, prohibited under art. 3 the conscription of aliens, but permitted calling them to manual labour in the event of natural calamity. The USA ratified this Convention with a substantial reservation concerning art. 3. After World War II, the EEC states attempted to establish a uniform rule concerning military service of nationals encompassing a convention on aliens, but eventually gave up, and the Convention on Nationality was signed on Dec. 13, 1955 without mentioning the military service of non-nationals (*European Treaty Series, No. 19*).

C. PARRY, "International Law and Conscription of Non-Nationals", in: *The British Yearbook of International Law*, 1954; K. DOEHRING, "Wehrpflicht von Ausländern", in: STRUPP-SCHLOCHAUER *Wörterbuch des Völkerrechts*, Vol. 3, Berlin, 1962, pp. 811–816.

MILITARY SPECIAL FORCES. called also secret armies. An international term for special military units highly trained in sabotage, antiterrorist-actions, reconnaissance, training of foreign guerrilla forces and various other covert military actions. Not to be confused with ▷ Foreign Legions or ▷ Mercenaries.

J. ADAMS, *Secret Armies: Inside the American, Soviet and European Special Forces*, New York, 1988.

MILITARY TESTAMENT. An international term for certain legal rules which permit military personnel or civilians employed by the military, who during wartime are on the verge of death due to wounds or illness, to pass on their last will and testament either to a military judge or to two witnesses without adhering to the regulations of the Civil Code.

MILITARY TRIBUNAL INTERNATIONAL FOR FAR EAST, 1946–48. The Tribunal came into being on Jan. 19, 1946 in Tokyo on the basis of a proclamation of the supreme commander of the allied military forces in the Far East, General D. MacArthur in compliance with the prior understanding of China, France, Great Britain, the USA and USSR as well as Australia, Canada, the Netherlands, New Zealand (India and the Philippines later acceded to the understanding) on crimes against peace and humanity as well as war crimes. The Tokyo Tribunal based itself on the Nuremberg principles. ▷ Tokyo Military Trial, 1946–48.

Trial of Japanese War Criminals, Washington, DC, 1948; S. HOROWITZ, "The Tokyo Trial", in: *International Conciliation*, No. 465, 1950; *The Tokyo Trial: A Functional Index to the Proceedings of the IMT for the Far East*, Ann Arbor, 1957; H. MINEAR, *Victor Justice. The Tokyo War Crimes Trial*, London, 1971.

MILITARY TRIBUNAL INTERNATIONAL, IMT, FOR GERMANY, 1945–46. The intergovernmental institution formed on the basis of an understanding between France, the UK, USA, and USSR for the purpose of prosecuting and punishing the major war criminals of the German Third Reich, signed on Aug. 8, 1945 in London. Also party to the agreement were: Australia, Belgium, Czechoslovakia, Ethiopia, Greece, Haiti, Honduras, India, Luxembourg, the Netherlands, Norway, New Zealand, Panama, Paraguay, Poland, Uruguay, Venezuela, Yugoslavia. The co-author of this Agreement, US Supreme Court of Justice, Robert H. Jackson, said at the signing:

"For the first time four of our powers have agreed not only on the principle of punishing war crimes and crimes of persecution, but also on the principle of individual responsibility for the crime of attack against international peace. If we could develop the idea in the world that the aggressive waging of war is the road to prison walls rather than to honors, we would have already done something in the direction of securing peace."

The Agreement which based itself on the ▷ War Crimes Moscow Declaration, 1943 includes a preamble and 7 arts. as well as the ▷ Charter of International Military Tribunal, IMT, 1945. The text of the London Agreement read as follows:

"Agreement by the Government of the United States of America, the Provisional Government of the French Republic, the Government of the United Kingdom of Great Britain and Northern Ireland and the Government of the Union of Soviet Socialist Republics for the prosecution and punishment of the major war criminals of the European Axis.
Whereas the United Nations have from time to time made declarations of their intention that war criminals shall be brought to justice;
And whereas the Moscow Declaration of the 30th October 1943 on German atrocities in occupied Europe stated that those German officers and men and members of the Nazi party who have been responsible for or have taken a consenting part in atrocities and crimes will be sent back to the countries in which their abominable deeds were done in order that they may be judged and punished according to the laws of those

M

liberated countries and of the free governments that will be created therein;

And whereas this declaration was stated to be without prejudice to the case of major criminals whose offenses have no particular geographic location and who will be punished by the joint decision of the Governments of the Allies;

Now, therefore, the Government of the United States of America, the Provisional Government of the French Republic, the Government of the United Kingdom of Great Britain and Northern Ireland, and the Government of the Union of Soviet Socialist Republics (hereinafter called "the signatories") acting in the interests of all the United Nations and by their representatives duly authorized thereto have concluded this agreement.

Art. 1. There shall be established, after consultation with the Control Council for Germany, an International Military Tribunal for the trial of war criminals whose offenses have no particular geographical location, whether they be accused individually or in their capacity as members of organizations or groups or in both capacities.

Art. 2. The constitution, jurisdiction, and functions of the International Military Tribunal shall be those set out in the charter annexed to this agreement, which Charter shall form an integral part of this agreement.

Art. 3. Each of the signatories shall take the necessary steps to make available for the investigation of the charges and trial the major war criminals detained by them who are to be tried by the International Military Tribunal. The signatories shall also use their best endeavors to make available for investigation of the charges against, and the trial before the International Military Tribunal, such of the major war criminals as are not in the territories of any of the signatories.

Art. 4. Nothing in this agreement shall prejudice the provisions established by the Moscow Declaration concerning the return of war criminals to the countries where they committed their crimes.

Art. 5. Any Government of the United Nations may adhere to this agreement by notice given through the diplomatic channel to the Government of the United Kingdom, who shall inform the other signatory and adhering Governments of each such adherence.

Art. 6. Nothing in this agreement shall prejudice the jurisdiction or the powers of any national or occupation court established or to be established in any Allied territory or in Germany for the trial of war criminals.

Art. 7. This agreement shall come into force on the day of signature and shall remain in force for the period of one year and shall continue thereafter, subject to the right of any signatory to give, through the diplomatic channel, one month's notice of intention to terminate it. Such termination shall not prejudice any proceedings already taken or any findings already made in pursuance of this agreement."

The London Agreement initiated the ▷ Nuremberg War Criminals Trial 1945–46, and the ▷ Tokyo Military Trial, 1946–48. See also the ▷ Nuremberg Principles.

The Department of State Bulletin, No. 320, 1945, pp. 222–226; *The Trial of German Major War Criminals. Proceedings of the International Military Tribunal Sitting at Nuremberg, Germany*, 42 Vols., London, 1946–48; *Trial of Japanese War Criminals*, Washington, DC, 1948; *History of the UN War Crimes Commission and the Development of the Laws of War*, London, 1948; UNWCC, *Law Reports of Trials of War Criminals*, London, 1948; J.A. APPLEMAN, *Military Tribunals and International Crimes*, New York, 1954; B.F. SMITH, *The Road to Nuremberg*, New York, 1981.

MILITIA. In the USSR and in the socialist countries the police forces; in the US the federal armed forces, called also the National Guard.

MILK. Subject of international co-operation. Organizations reg. with the UIA:

Association of Powdered Milk Manufacturers of the EEC, f. 1959, Paris.
Dairy Society International, f. 1946, Chambersburg, Pa., USA; Organizer of the World Congress for Milk Utilization. Publ.: Dairy Situation Review.

European Milk Trade Union, f. 1959, Bonn, FRG.
European Union for Milk and Milk-Product Commerce, f. 1959, Paris.
International Association of Milk, Food and Environmental Sanitarians, f. 1911, Shelbyville, Ind.
International Committee for Recording the Productivity of Milk Animals, f. 1951, Rome.
International Dairy Federation, f. 1903, Brussels. Publ.; Annual Bulletin.
Milk Industry Association of the EEC, f. 1959, Paris.
Special Section of Milk and Milk Products in the EEC, f. 1959, Brussels.

In the EEC Countries in April 1968 a common price policy for milk was established.

In 1984 the world milk production exceeded 500 million tons.

J. PAXTON, *A Dictionary of the European Economic Community*, 1977, pp. 63–64; *Yearbook of International Organizations*; *The Europa Yearbook 1988. A World Survey*, Vol. I, London, 1988.

MILLER-TYDINGS ACT, 1937. ▷ Anti-Trust Act, 1890.

MILLIGRAM. An international mass and weight unit = 0.001 gram, or approx. 0.015 grain.

MILLILITER. An international capacity unit = 0.001 liter, or approx. 0.06 cubic inch, or 0.27 fluid dram.

MILLIMETER. An international length unit = 0.001 meter, or approx. 0.04 inch.

MILLS TRADE ACT, 1970. A legislative act passed by the US House of Representatives on Nov. 19, 1970, which introduced protectionist norms limiting imports of oil and its by-products as well as textiles, footwear and other goods. It authorized the President of the USA to extend these norms to other sectors of agricultural and industrial production; it primarily affected exports of Latin American countries to the USA, which brought about a protest by Latin American countries in the OAS Council. The bill was drafted by the Chairman of the Tax Commission of The House of Representatives, W.L. Mills.

MIMES AND PANTOMIMISTS. The international artistic organization, reg. with the UIA:

International Mimes and Pantomimists, f. 1973, New York.

Yearbook of International Organizations.

MINDERHEIT IST WER WILL. *German* = "who so wishes belongs to a minority." The Germanization doctrine proclaiming that nationality is not determined by descent and mother tongue but by the subjective will to belong to this or that nation. The Union of National Minorities in Germany opposed to this doctrine represented by German minorities at European Minority Congresses in the inter-war period. ▷ Quinta Columna.

J. BOGENSEE, J. SKALA, *Die Nationalen Minderheiten im Deutschen Reich und ihre rechtliche Situation*, Berlin, 1929.

MINERALOGY. A subject of international co-operation. Organizations reg. with the UIA:

Arab Mineral Resources Exploitation Corporation, f. 1975, Cairo.
Committee for Co-ordination of Joint Prospecting for Mineral Resources in Asian Offshore Areas, f. 1966, Bangkok, under the aegis of the UN Economic Commission for Asia. Publ.: *Bulletin.*
Commonwealth Committee on Mineral Resources and Geology, f. 1948, London. Publ.: *Newsletter.*
International Mineralogical Association, f. 1958, Washington, DC.

C.K. LEITH, "The Political Control of Mineral Resources", in: *Foreign Affairs*, July, 1925; "Minerals and International Relations", in: *International Conciliation*, No. 266, New York, January, 1931, pp. 5–47; R.J. ROZENBERG, J. GUIZERIX, *Nuclear Techniques in Mineral Exploration, Extraction and Processing, in: IAEA Bulletin 1987*, No. 2.

MINERAL WATER. A subject of international co-operation. Organization reg. with the UIA:

European Union of Natural Mineral Water Sources of the Common Market, f. 1959, Paris.

Yearbook of International Organizations.

MINES. One of the ▷ Conventional Arms, known since the 16th century, developed into minefields systems, during the I and II World War; placed both on land and sea. In the second part of the 1980's modernized by a high-technology Extended Range Antiarmour Mine, ERAM.

SIPRI Yearbook, 1987, Oxford 1988, pp 91-92.

MINESPOL. Ministres responsables de la politique scientifique. A French abbreviation, used for conferences of ministers responsible for scientific policy in the region of Europe and North America, organized under the aegis of UNESCO. Conference MINESPOL I was held in 1970, MINESPOL II in 1978.

MINIATURE HOMING VEHICLE. MHV. ▷ Space War.

MINIMUM AGE. An international term introduced by the ILO for the admissible juvenile age in specific occupations, subject of 12 international ILO conventions.

MINING. A subject of international co-operation. Organizations reg. with the UIA:

Council of Commonwealth Mining and Metallurgical Institutions, f. 1924, London.
Institution of Mining and Metallurgy, f. 1892, London.
World Mining Congress, f. 1958, with International Organizing Committee as permanent organs in Warsaw, Poland. In Oct., 1971 the Committee convened the International Bureau of Rock Mechanics in Gliwice, Poland. Members: National Committees of 34 countries. Publ.: *Congress Reports.*

G.C. AMSTUTZ, *Glossary of Mining Geology, in English, Spanish, French and German*, Amsterdam, 1971.

MINISTER. The second-ranking official at a permanent diplomatic mission (after an ambassador) both according to ▷ Vienna Rules, 1815, and ▷ Vienna Convention on Diplomatic Relations, 1961.

MINISTRY OF FOREIGN AFFAIRS. The institution developed into its present-day form during the 19th century following the Vienna Congress, where the rule of diplomatic ceremony institutionalized interstate relations. The head of the Ministry of Foreign Affairs is the Minister of Foreign Affairs or Secretary of State (in the USA and in Vatican City) or Federal Councillor (Bundesrat) in Switzerland. In the USSR he was titled People's Commissar for Foreign Affairs (1921–46).

MINORITIES, PROTECTION OF. The international agreements supporting ethnic and religious minorities' rights to cultural development. The first international treaties on the protection of minorities and prevention of discrimination were: the Oliva Peace, concluded on May 3, 1660 in Oliva between Poland and Sweden and including a clause on protection of the Catholic minority in Protestant Sweden; and the Paris Peace Treaty, Feb. 10, 1763, between France and Great Britain guaranteeing religious rights to the French Catholic minority in Canada. In the 19th century the rights of minorities were guaranteed by the Vienna Congress (1814–15) to Poles living under Austrian, Prussian and Russian occupation; the Paris Peace Treaty between European Powers and Turkey, Mar. 30, 1856, provided for freedom to Moslems living in Ottoman Empire, and the Berlin Treaty of July 13, 1878, obliged Bulgaria, Serbia and Turkey to guarantee religious freedom to their nationals. After World War I, the Allied and Associated Powers forced Austria, Bulgaria, Czechoslovakia, Greece, Poland, Romania, Hungary and Yugoslavia to sign unilateral treaties on the protection of minorities. In practice of the League of Nations, a system of petitions was applied. Such petitions were submitted to the LN directly by members of national minorities; a similar practice was applied after World War II with respect to the UNO.

The Treaty between the Main Allied and Associated Powers and Poland, signed June 28, 1919, in Versailles, (Annex No. 3 to the Treaty of Versailles, called "Little Treaty of Versailles") was a typical example of a treaty on the protection of minorities. In keeping with art. 39 of the Treaty of Versailles, it imposed on Austria, Bulgaria, Czechoslovakia, Greece, Poland, Romania, Hungary and Yugoslavia obligations "to protect interests of people distinct from others by race, language or religion." On the basis of the treaty with Poland as a cession state an obligation was assumed to recognize "... as Polish nationals of the same rights of itself and without formal requirements those German, Austrian, Hungarian or Russian nationals who, at the time of this Treaty's entry into force, permanently resided (domiciled) in the territory that has been recognized or will be recognized as an integral part of Poland ..." (art. 3), whereas "all Polish nationals irrespective of their race, language or religion shall be equals before the law and enjoy the same civic and political rights ..." (art. 7) and "Polish nationals who originate from ethnic, religious or linguistic minorities shall be treated equally and enjoy the same statutory and actual guarantees as other Polish nationals ..." (art. 8) which in effect imposed on Poland the obligation to open minority schools (arts. 8, 9 and 10).

In addition, special provisions concerned the Jews who were not to be forced "... to perform any jobs in violation of the Sabbath ...", excepting "... obligations imposed on all Polish nationals due to mandatory military service, national defense or keeping public order ..." (art. 11). The state sovereignty was limited under art. 12:

"Poland recognizes that the provisions of the aforementioned articles, provided that they concern racial, religious or language minorities, be obligations of international character and admits control over them by the League of Nations. They shall not be changed without the consent of a majority in the League of Nations. The United States of America, the British Empire, France, Italy and Japan pledge not to refuse their consent to any change in the aforementioned articles that could be made by agreement of a majority in the Council of the League of Nations expressed in due form. Poland recognizes that each member of the Council of the League of Nations enjoys the right to draw attention of the Council to acts of trespassing or danger thereof with respect to any of these obligations, and that the Council may act and instruct in a way it regards advisable and effective under relevant circumstances. Poland further recognizes that in case of different opinions concerning legal or actual questions relevant to this article expressed to the Government of Poland and any of the Main Allied and Associated Powers or any Power being a member of the Council of the League of Nations, the difference of opinions be considered a dispute of international character in keeping with article 14 of the Covenant of the League of Nations.

The government of Poland agrees that all disputes of this kind upon request of the other side be transmitted to the Permanent Court of Justice. Decisions made by the Court shall be binding unconditionally and shall be of the same force and significance as those made on the basis of article 13 of the Covenant."

The protection of minorities was also guaranteed in the form of special clauses to peace treaties (by Austria, Bulgaria, Turkey and Hungary) or in the form of declarations made while joining the League of Nations, e.g. by the Baltic states. Germany, however, was not covered by the obligation to protect minorities, thereby posing a serious problem before ethnic minorities in Germany (1919–39) in spite of three large national groups within the Reich, namely: Polish, numbering over 1.5 million, Jewish – 640,000, Lusatian – 160,000, and four smaller groups of a few thousand persons each (Czech in the South and Berlin, Lithuanian in East Prussia, Danish in Schleswig and Frisian in Friesland). The Union of National Minorities in Germany, founded in Berlin in 1924, submitted evidence of the existence of national minorities in Germany and of their discrimination by the authorities of the Weimar Republic at the Geneva Congress of National Minorities Union in Europe, called under the auspices of the League of Nations in 1926. In 1933 all non-Fascist minority groups, among them all Jewish minority organizations, withdrew from the Union of National Minorities in Europe. In consequence of the openly anti-Semitic program of German groups, the European Union, though it continued to hold its Congresses (1937 in London and 1938 in Stockholm), did not play any role in the League of Nations. The problem of national minorities in Europe was aggravated in 1939–45 when the government of the Third Reich implemented compulsory mass deportations, often of a genocidal character. ▷ Endlosung.

In 1946 the UN Human Rights Commission established a Sub-commission on Prevention of Discrimination and Protection of Minorities. The Sub-commission prepared studies on the rights of persons belonging to national, ethnic, religious and linguistic minorities, as well as the right to self-determination. The second study, 1977, systematized, codified and updated all the various decisions relating to the right of peoples under colonial and allied domination to self-determination. The Sub-commission consists of 26 members elected by the Commission on Human Rights from candidates nominated by member states of the UN in accordance with a scheme to ensure geographical distribution. Members serve in their individual capacities as experts, rather than as governmental representatives, each for a 3-year term.

LNTS, Vol. 28, pp. 254–256; J. FOUGES-DUPARC, *La Protection des Minorités de race, de langue et de religion*, Paris, 1922; J. BOGENSEE, J. SKALA, *Die Nationalen Minderheiten im Deutschen Reich und ihre rechtliche Situation*, Berlin, 1929; *Protection des Minorités de langue, de race, de religion par la SdN*, Genève, 1929; F. BRANCHU, *Le problème des minorités en droit international depuis la seconde guerre mondiale*, Paris, 1952; I.L. CLAUDE, *National Minorities. An International Problem*, London, 1955; *UN Yearbook 1946, 1951, 1952, 1970, 1978, 1980*; S.J. PAPROCKI, S. HORAK, *Poland and her Minorities, 1919–1939*, New York, 1961.

MINORITY RIGHTS GROUP.
An international specialized research and information unit, f. 1960, London, maintains a continual survey of current events throughout the world to monitor development in ethnic, religious and cultural minorities situation. Consultative status with ECOSOC. Publ.: *World Minorities* and specialized MRG Reports. Reg. with the UIA.

Yearbook of International Organizations.

MINORS.
The persons below the age of 14, subject of international conventions providing for mandatory care over minors. The first convention was signed on June 12, 1902 in The Hague, amended by the protocol of Nov. 28, 1923. The League of Nations and later the UN assigned to the ILO the task of protecting minors in the field of labour; the ILO prepared a number of conventions on the lowest age of children and youth allowed to work in industries (1919), the navy (1920), farming (1921), (modified in 1946) and mining (1965). In addition minors are the concern of conventions on ▷ adoption, ▷ alimony, and ▷ marriage.

LNTS, Vol. 51, p. 221.

MINUTEMAN.
American long-range ballistic missile, "ground-to-ground," constructed with a nuclear warhead.

J. GOLDBLAT, *Arms Control Agreements. A Handbook*, New York, 1983; D. ROBERTSON, *Guide to Modern Defense and Strategy*, Detroit, 1988.

MIR.
Russian = 'Peace. The first Soviet permanently manned space vehicle, launched on Feb. 20, 1986 from the Baikonur Cosmodrome in Kazakhstan. On March 13, 1986 two Soviet cosmonauts boarded the Mir station from the spaceship Soyuz T15.

KEESING's *Record of World Events*, May, 1986.

MIRAGE.
A French military airplane.

MIRV.
Multiple Independent Reentry Vehicles. A long-range ballistic missile which permits one booster to carry several warheads, each of which can be directed to separate target; subject of the SALT negotiations. (▷ SALT II Documents, 1979). First launched by the USA in 1970 and by the USSR in 1975.

World Armaments and Disarmament SIPRI Yearbooks, 1968–1984; D. ROBERTSON, *Guide to Modern Defense and Strategy*, Detroit, 1988.

MIRZA.
Arab by-name vested in persons descending on the distaff side from the Mohammedan line.

MISSILES.
An international term for rockets developed with ever-greater thrust; in the 19th century with a range of 2–4 km; in the second half of the 20th century with an intercontinental range. The development of missiles of various types (land–land, land–air, land–sea, sea–sea, sea–air, air–air) has influenced the adoption of new strategic doctrines and new disarmament problems. The first computer guided missile was produced in 1960 by the USA and in 1966 by the USSR; the first TV guided missile in 1972 by the USA and in 1987 by the USSR.

SIPRI World Armaments and Disarmament Yearbook 1968–1984; R. LEGER SILVARD, *World Military and Social Expenditures 1987–88*, Washington DC, 1957.

MISSIONARIES.
The clerics of various religions who proceed to countries which have no or very little knowledge of a given faith for the purpose of proselytizing it; the object of international conflicts when the work of missionaries collides with the ruling interests of the country, which is seen in the missionary history of Buddhism, Islam, the Catholic Church and other Christian churches. The Catholic Church in 1622 created the Congregation for the Propagation of the Faith to co-ordinate all of its missionary activities. It played an important role in the colonization of Latin-America and other areas acquired by the Catholic European colonial

states. A similar role for the Protestant colonial states was played by Christian missionaries, who along with the Catholic missionaries represented in the eyes of the colored people a Christian faith that was identified with the colonial oppression by the white man. After World War II both Protestant and Catholic missionaries began to renounce colonial systems and educate a greater percentage of clergy from the local population. In the Catholic Church the departure from colonial Eurocentrism is contained in papal encyclicals: *Maximum allud*, 1919, *Rerum Ecclesiae*, 1926, and *Evangelii praecones*, 1951, put into practice during the pontificate of John XXIII, whose new principles for the work of missionaries were formulated in the encyclical *Princeps pastorum*, 1959, developed by the Vatican Council II, 1964 in the directive concerning the missionary activity of the Church *Ad Gentes Divinitus* of Dec. 7, 1965. In 1967 The Congregation for the Propagation of the Faith was changed into The Congregation for the Evangelization of Nations. The general principles which should guide Catholic missionaries were formulated by Paul VI in an apostolic adhortation *Evangelii muntiandi*, 1976. The Catholic order of White Fathers in 1970 departed from Mozambique, admitting that leaving missions there would cause the Church to be regarded as an institution associated with racism, an unjust socio-political structure, and with the occupation of the country by the Portuguese army. An echo of this decision was the resolution of the Commission for Missions and Evangelism of the World Council of Churches, charging its evangelical missionaries to act similarly in Mozambique and in other countries where crises of this type could occur. It was also decided to consider a suggestion made by the Congress of Anthropologists in Barbados, 1971, that churches suspend all missionary activity among the Indians, since these missions *de facto* patronize the Indian tribes through inhuman exploitation, which was applied for centuries by the descendants of the conquistadors.

The World Council of Churches publishes an *International Missionary Bibliography*.

K. SCOTT LATOURETTE, *A History of the Expansion of Christianity*, 7 Vols., New York, 1937–45; M. SCHLUNK, *Religions- und Missionskarte der Erde*, Münster, 1951; *World Christian Handbook*, New York, 1952; S. DELACROIX, *Histoire universelle des Missions catholiques*, 4 Vols., Paris, 1956–58.

MITBESTIMMUNG. German 'codecision'. International term for worker co-management as a form of industrial democracy in capitalist states, coined in the 1950's in West Germany.

Gesetz über die Mitbestimmung der Arbeitsnehmer in den Aufsichtsräten in Vorständen der Unternehmen des Blergbaus und der Eisen und Stahlerzeugenden Industrie vom 21 Mai 1951, Bonn, 1951.

MITTELAFRIKA. *German* = Central Africa. A German colony planned by A. Hitler in 1940, to be set up after the victory of the German Third Reich in World War II; it was to cover black Africa, south of the Arab countries.

MITTELEUROPA. *German* = Central Europe. A German term for the concept of Wilhelm II during World War I aimed at setting up a federation of central European states under the leadership of the Prussian Reich.

J. PAJEWSKI, "Germany, Poland and Mitteleuropa", in: *Polish Western Affairs*, No. 2, 1961, pp. 215–234.

MIXED COMMISSIONS. An international term for (1) intergovernmental commissions of two or more states interested in solving problems which have arisen between them or composed of representatives selected by states in conflict or dispute, often with a neutral chairman, with the task of recording, describing, and evaluating disputed issues or incidents; (2) international mixed commissions formed by an international body to investigate a specific problem and eventually hand down a judgment of arbitration; subject of bilateral or multilateral international agreements. After World War II, they became widespread in connection with processes of economic integration.

MLF. Multilateral Force or Multilateral Fleet. An international term for multilateral nuclear forces proposed by the USA 1960–65 as multinational NATO naval units equipped with nuclear weapons. These forces were to be composed of 25 submarines, each carrying Polaris missiles and manned by international crews. Realization of this plan made possible the use of nuclear weapons by the FRG. The Soviet government protested in notes to the Western powers against the consequences of extending nuclear weapons to the FRG, a state which was then demanding official changes of the status quo in Europe and a revision of borders. Besides, France (during President Charles de Gaulle's term) lodged a veto in NATO on this matter, which was also criticized by some other members of this pact. After withdrawal of US support for the idea of MLF by the Kennedy administration in 1963, the Johnson administration returned to it in 1964, but in the face of new protests by the USSR and France finally abandoned the scheme in 1965.

C.L. SULZBERGER, "The MLF", in: *New York Times*, November, 1964; S.H. LOORY, "Moscow MLF Equal Proliferation", in: *New York Herald Tribune*, August 1, 1965; D. ROBERTSON, *Guide to Modern Defense and Strategy*, Detroit, 1988.

MODELS. ▷ Industrial Designs and models.

MODIFICATION OF ENVIRONMENT CONVENTION ON THE PROHIBITION OF MILITARY OR ANY OTHER HOSTILE USE OF ENVIRONMENTAL MODIFICATION TECHNIQUES, 1977. A convention drafted by the US and USSR, signed on May 18, 1977 in Geneva, *inter alia* by the US, USSR and UK, but not by China and France, with Annex and Understandings relating to the Convention, called the ENMOD Convention; came into force on Oct. 5, 1978. The texts are as follows:

"The States Parties to this Convention,
Guided by the interest of consolidating peace, and wishing to contribute to the cause of halting the arms race, and of bringing about general and complete disarmament under strict and effective international control, and of saving mankind from the danger of using new means of warfare,
Determined to continue negotiations with a view to achieving effective progress towards further measures in the field of disarmament,
Recognizing that scientific and technical advances may open new possibilities with respect to modification of the environment,
Recalling the Declaration of the United Nations Conference on the Human Environment, adopted at Stockholm on 16 June 1972,
Realizing that the use of environmental modification techniques or peaceful purposes could improve the interrelationship of man and nature and contribute to the preservation and improvement of the environment for the benefit of present and future generations,
Recognizing, however, that military or any other hostile use of such techniques could have effects extremely harmful to human welfare,
Desiring to prohibit effectively military or any other hostile use of environmental modification techniques in order to eliminate the dangers to mankind from such use, and affirming their willingness to work towards the achievement of this objective,

Desiring also to contribute to the strengthening of trust among nations and to the further improvement of the international situation in accordance with the purposes and principles of the Charter of the United Nations,
Have agreed as follows:
Art. I.(1) Each State Party to this Convention undertakes not to engage in military or any other hostile use of environmental modification techniques having widespread, long-lasting or severe effects as the means of destruction, damage or injury to any other State Party.
(2) Each State Party to this Convention undertakes not to assist, encourage or induce any State, group of States or international organization to engage in activities contrary to the provisions of paragraph 1 of this article.
Art. II. As used in article I, the term "environmental modification techniques" for changing – through deliberate manipulation of natural processes – the dynamics, composition or structure of the earth, including its biota, lithosphere, hydrosphere and atmosphere, or of outer space.
Art. III.(1) The provisions of this Convention shall not hinder the use of environmental modification techniques for peaceful purposes and shall be without prejudice to the generally recognized principles and applicable rules of international law concerning such use.
(2) The States Parties to this Convention undertake to facilitate, and have the right to participate in, the fullest possible exchange of scientific and technological information on the use of environmental modification techniques for peaceful purposes. States Parties in a position to do so shall contribute, alone or together with other States or international organizations, to international economic and scientific co-operation in the preservation, improvement and peaceful utilization of the environment, with due consideration for the needs of the developing areas of the world.
Art. IV. Each State Party to this Convention undertakes to take any measures it considers necessary in accordance with its constitutional processes to prohibit and prevent any activity in violation of the provisions of the Convention anywhere under its jurisdiction or control.
Art. V.(1) The States Parties to this Convention undertake to consult one another and to co-operate in solving any problems which may arise in relation to the objectives of, or in the application of the provisions of, the Convention. Consultation and co-operation pursuant to this article may also be undertaken through appropriate international procedures within the framework of the United Nations and in accordance with its Charter. These international procedures may include the services of appropriate international organizations, as well as of a Consultative Committee of Experts as provided for in paragraph 2 of this article.
(2) For the purpose set forth in paragraph 1 of this article, the Depositary shall, within one month of the receipt of a request from any State Party to this Convention, convene a Consultative Committee of Experts. Any State Party may appoint an expert to the Committee whose functions and rules of procedure are set out in the annex, which constitutes an integral part of this Convention. The Committee shall transmit to the Depositary a summary of its findings of fact, incorporating all views and information presented to the Committee during its proceedings. The Depositary shall distribute the summary to all States Parties.
(3) Any State Party to this Convention which has reason to believe that any other State Party is acting in breach of obligations deriving from the provisions of the Convention may lodge a complaint with the Security Council of the United Nations. Such a complaint should include all relevant information as well as possible evidence supporting its validity.
(4) Each State Party to this Convention undertakes to co-operate in carrying out any investigation which the Security Council may initiate, in accordance with the provisions of the Charter of the United Nations, on the basis of the complaint received by the Council. The Security Council shall inform the States Parties of the results of the investigation.
(5) Each State Party to this Convention undertakes to provide or support assistance, in accordance with the provisions of the Charter of the United Nations, to any State Party which so requests, if the Security Council decides that such Party has been harmed or is likely to be harmed as a result of violation of the Convention.

Art. VI.(1) Any State Party to this Convention may propose amendments to the Convention. The text of any proposed amendment shall be submitted to the Depositary, who shall prompty circulate it to all States Parties.

(2) An amendment shall enter into force for all States Parties to this Convention which have accepted it, upon the deposit with the Depositary of instruments of acceptance by a majority of States Parties. Thereafter it shall enter into force for any remaining State Party on the date of deposit of its instrument of acceptance.

Art. VII. This Convention shall be of unlimited duration.

Art. VIII.(1) Five years after the entry into force of this Convention, a conference of the States Parties to the Convention shall be convened by the Depositary at Geneva, Switzerland. The conference shall review the operation of the Convention with a view to ensuring that its purposes and provisions are being realized, and shall in particular examine the effectiveness of the provisions of paragraph 1 of article I in eliminating the dangers of military or any other hostile use of environmental modification techniques.

(2) At intervals of not less than five years thereafter, a majority of the States Parties to this Convention may obtain, by submitting a proposal to this effect to the Depositary, the convening of a conference with the same objectives.

(3) If no conference has been convened pursuant to paragraph 2 of this article within ten years following the conclusion of a previous conference, the Depositary shall solicit the views of all States Parties to this Convention, concerning the convening of such a conference. If one third or ten of the States Parties, whichever number is less, respond affirmatively, the Depositary shall take immediate steps to convene the conference.

Art. IX.(1) This Convention shall be open to all States for signature. Any State which does not sign the Convention before its entry into force in accordance with paragraph 3 of this article may accede to it at any time.

(2) This Convention shall be subject to ratification by signatory States. Instruments of ratification or accession shall be deposited with the Secretary-General of the United Nations.

(3) This Convention shall enter into force upon the deposit of instruments of ratification by twenty Governments in accordance with paragraph 2 of this article.

(4) For those States whose instruments of ratification or accession are deposited after the entry into force of this Convention, it shall enter into force on the date of the deposit of their instruments of ratification or accession.

(5) The Depositary shall promptly inform all signatory and acceding States of the date of each signature, the date of deposit of each instrument of ratification or accession and the date of the entry into force of this Convention and of any amendments thereto, as well as of the receipt of other notices.

(6) This Convention shall be registered by the Depositary in accordance with article 102 of the Charter of the United Nations.

Art. X. This Convention, of which the English, Arabic, Chinese, French, Russian and Spanish texts are equally authentic, shall be deposited with the Secretary-General of the United Nations, who shall send duly certified copies thereof to the Governments of the signatory and acceding States.

In witness whereof, the undersigned, being duly authorized thereto by their respective Governments, have signed this Convention, opened for signature at Geneva on the eighteenth day of May, one thousand nine hundred and seventy-seven.

Annex. Consultative Committee of Experts

(1) The Consultative Committee of Experts shall undertake to make appropriate findings of fact and provide expert views relevant to any problem raised pursuant to paragraph 1 of article V of this Convention by the State Party requesting the convening of the Committee.

(2) The work of the Consultative Committee of Experts shall be organized in such a way as to permit it to perform the functions set forth in paragraph 1 of this annex. The Committee shall decide procedural questions relative to the organization of its work, where possible by consensus, but otherwise by a majority of those present and voting. There shall be no voting on matters of substance.

(3) The Depositary or his representative shall serve as the Chairman of the Committee.

(4) Each expert may be assisted at meetings by one or more advisers.

(5) Each expert shall have the right, through the Chairman, to request from States, and from international organizations, such information and assistance as the expert considers desirable for the accomplishment of the Committee's work.

Understanding relating to art. I

It is the understanding of the Committee that, for the purposes of this Convention, the terms "widespread", "long-lasting" and "severe" shall be interpreted as follows:

(a) "widespread": encompassing an area on the scale of several hundred square kilometers;

(b) "long-lasting": lasting for a period of months, or approximately a season;

(c) "severe": involving serious or significant disruption or harm to human life, natural and economic resources or other assets.

It is further understood that the interpretation set forth above is intended exclusively for this Convention and is not intended to prejudice the interpretation of the same or similar terms if used in connection with any other international agreement.

Understanding relating to art. II

It is the understanding of the Committee that the following examples are illustrative of phenomena that could be caused by the use of environmental modification techniques as defined in art. II of the Convention: earth-quakes; tsunamis; an upset in the ecological balance of a region; changes in weather patterns (clouds, precipitation, cyclones of various types and tornadic storms); changes in climate patterns; changes in ocean currents; changes in the state of the ozone layer; and changes in the state of the ionosphere.

It is further understood that all the phenomena listed above, when produced by military or any other hostile use of environmental modification techniques, would result, or could reasonably be expected to result in widespread, long-lasting or severe destruction, damage or injury. Thus, military or any other hostile use of environmental modification techniques as defined in art. II, so as to cause those phenomena as a means of destruction, damage or injury to another State Party, would be prohibited.

It is recognized, moreover, that the list of examples set out above is not exhaustive. Other phenomena which could result from the use of environmental modification techniques as defined in art. II could also be appropriately included. The absence of such phenomena from the list does not in any way imply that the undertaking contained in art. I would not be applicable to those phenomena, provided the criteria set out in that article were met.

Understanding relating to art. III

It is the understanding of the Committee that this Convention does not deal with the question whether or not a given use of environmental modification techniques for peaceful purposes is in accordance with generally recognized principles and applicable rules of international law.

Understanding relating to art. VIII

It is the understanding of the Committee that a proposal to amend the Convention may also be considered at any Conference of Parties held pursuant to art. VIII. It is further understood that any proposed amendment that is intended for such consideration should, if possible, be submitted to the Depositary no less than 90 days before the commencement of the Conference."

J. GOLDBLAT, *Arms Control Agreement, A Handbook*, New York, 1983, pp. 194–197.

MODUS VIVENDI. Latin, international term for a temporary manner of co-existing before the sides resolve the dispute dividing them.

MOEN-JODARO OR MOHENJO-DARO. A historical site of Pakistan, included in the ▷ World Heritage UNESCO List. This immense city, built entirely of bricks, is the most representative, bronze-age site in the Indus Valley. It is astonishing on account of its systematic layout and highly developed drainage system. The objects excavated, such as jewels, seals, and terracotta figurines, recall the artistic vitality of a civilization which disappeared 3500 years ago.

J. MARSHALL, *Mohenjo-Daro and the Indus Civilization*, London, 1931; UNESCO. *A Legacy for All*, Paris, 1984.

MOGADISHU. The capital of the Somali Republic on the Indian Ocean, city and seaport. Regional office of the World Muslim Congress.

Yearbook of International Organizations.

MOHAIR. ▷ Fibre.

MOHENJO-DARO. ▷ Moen-Jodaro.

MOLDAVIA. The Moldavian Soviet Socialist Republic, federal republic of the USSR, bounded in the east and south by the Ukraine, on the west by Romania. Area: 33,700 sq. km. Pop. 1983 census: 4,052,800, of whom 63.9% are Moldavians, 14.2% Ukrainians, 12.8% Russians, 3.5% Gaguazi, 2% Jews and 2% Bulgarians. Capital: Kishinev with 580,000 inhabitants 1983. The Moldavian Autonomic Soviet Socialist Republic set up on Oct. 12, 1924, integrated ▷ Bessarabia, ceded by Romania on June 28, 1940. According to the new constitution promulgated in April 1978 the two official languages of the Republic are: Russian and 'Moldavian'.

In early 1989 the Moldavian Communist Party declared the official "Moldavian" language to be identical with Romanian and decreed that all publications should be in the Latin alphabet, which had been replaced by the Cyryllic after the Soviet annexation of Moldavia in 1940. The concept of Moldavian nationality has been called "most artificial" by The Cambridge Encyclopedia of Russia and the Soviet Union.

V. KOTELNIKOV, Y. ZLATOVA, *Across Moldavia*, Moscow, 1959; *Istoriya Moldavskoi SSR*, 2 Vols., Kishinev, 1965–68; *The Europa Year Book 1984. A World Survey*, Vol. I, pp. 927–928, London, 1984; *Romania–Soviet Union, in:* A.J. DAY ed., *Border and Territorial Disputes*, London, 1987; B. KELLER, *Confession in Moldavia: They Speak Romanian. The New York Times*, February 25, 1989.

MOLE. Symbol: mol. An international unit of molecular weight of a substance, one of the base units of the International System of Units (▷ SI); definition adopted by the General Conference of Weights and Measures (CGPM), 1969, as follows:

"1. The mole is the amount of substance of a system which contains as many elementary entities as there are atoms in 0.012 kilogram of carbon 12.

2. When the mole is used, the elementary entities must be specified and may be atoms, molecules, ions, electrons, other particles, or specified groups of such particles."

MOLECULAR BIOLOGY. A subject of international co-operation. Organization reg. with the UIA:

European Molecular Biology Organization, EMBO, organ of the Agreement establishing the European Molecular Biology Conference, signed on Feb. 13, 1969 at Geneva, by Austria, Denmark, France, the FRG, the Netherlands, Sweden, Switzerland and the UK; came into force on Apr. 2, 1970.

UNTS, Vol. 727, 1970, pp. 309–342; *Yearbook of International Organizations, 1986/87; The Europa Yearbook 1988. A World Survey*, Vol. I, London, 1988.

MOLNIYA. *Russian:* "lightening." The name of Soviet artificial telecommunication satellites; in use since 1965; from Apr., 1967 satellites of this type have been serving the telecommunication system ▷ Intersputnik. On Nov. 24, 1971 Molniya-2 was

M

launched in the USSR into a high elliptical communication orbit with retransmitting equipment on board that makes possible long-distance telephone-telegraph communication in the USSR, the transmission of central television programs to points of the "Orbit" net, as well as international co-operation, as specified in the annex to the agreement on measures to improve direct radio communication between the USSR and USA, signed on Sept. 20, 1971 in Washington. (▷ Hot Line). The Soviet side made available a satellite communication channel through the Molniya system, the American side through the system ▷ Intelsat.

World Armaments and Disarmament SIPRI Yearbook 1977, pp. 125–127, London, 1977.

MOLUCCAS. A group of islands called also the Spice Islands in the Malayan Archipelago, between Celebes and New Guinea; area 83,660 sq. km, pop. 1971 census: 2,012,385; former Dutch colony, since 1949 part of Indonesia. A group of Molucca inhabitants declared in 1950 a separatist South Moluccas Republic under leadership of Andi Azisa. After the rebellion was suppressed by the Indonesian government, Azisa moved to The Hague and established a Permanent Information Bureau of the South Moluccas Republic in New York. In 1970 Moluccan separatists controlled for 24 hours the Indonesian Embassy (killing one person of Dutch nationality) to manifest their protest against the official visit of Indonesia's President, General Suharto, to The Hague.

G. DECKE, *Republik Malaku Selatan*, Göttingen, 1957.

MONACO. Principauté de Monaco. Principality of Monaco. An enclave state on the Mediterranean coast of France. Area: 195 hectares. Pop. 1982 census: 27,063. Capital: Monaco-Ville. Official language: French. Currency: French franc. National Day: May 31, birthday of the reigning prince, 1923. Monaco is not a member of the UN, but of its specialized organizations, the IAEA, ICAO, ITU, UNESCO, UPU, WHO and WIPO.
International relations: An independent Principality since 1297; 1524–1641 under the protectorate of Spain, then of France; 1793–1814 integrated by France; 1815–60 by a decision of the Congress of Vienna under the protectorate of the Kingdom of Sardinia, then again of France, with a new delimitation of the frontier on Feb. 2, 1861, which reduced its area to the present size by detaching Mentony and Roquebrune. Monaco on Nov. 9, 1865 formed a customs union with France, expanded on Apr. 10, 1912, modified May 18, 1963. The formation of the customs union of 1865 induced the citizens of Nice to appeal to the French Senate in 1871 to close the gambling casino established in Monaco in 1863, since from 1836 there existed a ban on running gaming houses in France. The Nice campaign which was carried on for many years ended in 1891 with a declaration by the government of France that "The Principality of Monaco is completely independent." Monaco became a constitutional Principality on Jan. 7, 1911; the constitution was modified on Nov. 18, 1917, amended Dec. 17, 1962. By virtue of the Treaty of July 17, 1918, France had the right to station its forces on the territory of Monaco and the right to accept or reject all Monacan international agreements. In 1951 a treaty was concluded with France on administrative assistance, superseded by a series of new conventions of May 18, 1963, i.a. one on finances which introduced the obligation on persons and firms on Monacan territory doing business abroad to pay taxes to France. Monaco is the seat of the International Hydrographic Bureau. Since 1961 Monaco is the seat of the International

Laboratory of Marine Radioactivity, governed by the IAEA, the Government of the Principality and the Foundation Albert I Oceanographic Institute in Paris, which owns the Musée Océanographique in Monaco.
In 1982 Monaco was visited by 216,110 tourists.

G. HANDLEY-TAYLOR, *Bibliography of Monaco*, London, 1968; P.M. DE LA GORCE, *Monaco*, Lausanne, 1969; *The Europa Year Book 1984. A World Survey*, Vol. I, pp. 665–667, London, 1984.

MONETARY AREAS (ZONES). An int. term for regions of the world which, in monetary turnover, are subject to domination by one of the key currencies. Monetary zones came into being between the two world wars as a result of the financial crisis of 1929–32 and the introduction of limitations in exchange of paper money for gold and currency restrictions, which became universal about 1940, with the exception of the USA, Canada and Latin American countries linked with the dollar zone. The capitalist monetary zones, with the exception of the dollar zone, emerged from the dependence of colonial territories. Thus, there were the monetary zones of the pound sterling, of the Belgium franc, of the French franc and of the Dutch gulden. The European Payments Union was a different form of a monetary zone. The beginning of the Sterling Zone marked the retreat in 1931 of Great Britain and the Commonwealth countries, as well as of numerous Middle East countries, from the gold parity and creation of a Sterling block, establishing a relationship between the currencies of the Commonwealth countries and the pound sterling and the retention by those countries of a considerable part of their reserves in pounds sterling. With the outbreak of World War II, Great Britain and the Commonwealth countries (except for Canada) and the aforementioned Arab countries introduced restrictions with regard to the rest of the world, thus becoming the formal monetary zone of the pound sterling. This zone included 38 countries in 1970, i.e. the countries of the British Commonwealth (apart from Canada) and Bahrain, Ireland, Jordan, Kuwait, Libya, Qatar, Oman and the Republic of South Africa. The system of payments in world trade based on the pound sterling made up for one-third of the international turnover (up to 40%). In the decades after World War II a strong link between the Sterling Zone and the Dollar Zone occurred. The Sterling Zone twice took advantage of considerable credit facilities designed for stabilizing the pound sterling: in Dec., 1964 – to the amount of 1000 million dollars and in Sept., 1968 – after the devaluation of the pound from 2.80 to 2.40 dollars per pound that took place in Nov. 1967, to the amount of 2000 million dollars in non-pound currencies, granted between 1969 and 1971, and serviceable between 1979 and 1981; in return, Great Britain guaranteed a part of the official reserves of the area's members in US dollars. Both credits were granted within the framework of the ▷ GAB. In 1975–76 the majority of member-countries of the Sterling Zone broke with the monetary system of Great Britain, due to the constant decrease in the value of the pound. In the spring of 1985, only Gibraltar together with Great Britain formed the Sterling Zone.
The Dollar Zone includes almost the whole Western Hemisphere and Liberia; its characteristic feature was the lack of currency restrictions, although a few Latin American countries introduced such restrictions.
The third main capitalist monetary zone is the French franc, *La Zone Franc (ZF)*, which was formally established in its present state on May 24, 1951, formed by Comité Monétaire de ZF, a French government agency. After granting independence to former French colonies in Africa a separate body was formed: ▷ African Financial Community, *Communauté Finan-*

cière Africain (CFA), which linked the same countries as the ZF: i.e. France with her overseas departments and territories, and the Central African Republic, Chad, Dahomey, Cameroon, Congo, Malgasy Republic, Mauritania, Niger, Senegal, Togo and the Ivory Coast, as well as Algeria, Morocco and Tunisia. Since 1963 all CFA countries and the Malagasy Republic have been associated members of the EEC. Starting in July, 1967, all ZF currencies became transferable. In 1971/72, Algeria, Morocco and Tunisia left the ZF, and in autumn 1972 Congo, Malgasy Republic, Niger, Togo and Mauritania requested revision of the monetary accords of 1961 with France. The crisis became more severe when the remainder of the countries of former French Africa also requested revision of the 1961 monetary agreement and reorganization of the Central Bank of the West African States or of the Bank of Central African States, which occurred in 1973.
The monetary zone of the Dutch gulden, which covered Holland and her colonies, now includes only Holland and her territories in the Western Hemisphere.
The monetary zone of the Portuguese Escudo, until mid-1974, included Portugal and her colonies, strongly linked with the Sterling Zone.
The CMEA states established a different form of financial co-operation, sometimes called "The Eastern ruble zone." A distinctive feature of the monetary area of CMEA states is the existence of a state monetary monopoly, tightly connected with the planned economy. The CMEA countries, in bilateral payments among themselves, use ▷ roubles, transferable or each own clearing currencies with a stated gold parity (e.g. Polish Transferable Zloty). In payments to capitalist states, the CMEA states at first used transfers in the Sterling Zone; later they almost completely turned to dollar payments or in currencies convertible into dollars. As regards payments within the CMEA community, the question of the correct relationship of national currencies to the transferable ruble and to the third countries' currencies was the subject of debates and agreements elaborated by central banks. This problem was partially solved by mid-1971 through new accords on the relation of national currencies to the transferable ruble, in particular payment turnover betwen members of CMEA. For other types of turnover further accords were prepared in 1972/73. Details on perfecting the monetary-financial relations were published in the comprehensive program of CMEA in 1972, in which the principle was adopted to the effect that the monetary zone of CMEA states should undergo modifications toward multilateral clearing and one common and stable payment currency that would also be a yardstick of the national currencies' values, in pace with the growth of trade among these countries. This plan was not implemented before 1980.
The Economic Council of the Arab League in Dec., 1973 recommended that its crude oil exporting member states gradually withdraw their monetary deposits from Western banks and create a common Arab bank with the right to issue one Arab currency ("Arab dinar"). This would mean creation of a new monetary zone, eventually with the Arab Monetary Fund within the framework of the International Monetary Fund.

MONETARY CONVENTION, 1885. An agreement between the governments of Belgium, France, Greece, Italy and Switzerland, of Nov. 6, 1885, concerning small silver currency, revised by the Supplementary Convention, signed at Paris Mar. 25, 1920.

LNTS, Vol. 1, p. 45; A.R. CONAN, *The Sterling Area*, London, 1952.

MONETARY CRISIS, 1971–80. The unsettling of the monetary system created after World War II within the framework of the IMF. The crisis occurred after a unilateral decision by the US government on Aug. 15, 1971 to suspend the convertibility of the dollar into gold as a consequence of the worsening of the US balance of payments in 1970, when the deficit reached 10 billion dollars and continued in succeeding years. The beginning of the global crisis was the unsettling of the market for gold, which had been stabilized since 1934, when

Great Britain on Nov. 18, 1967 announced a 14.3% devaluation of the pound sterling. Four months later, Mar. 18, 1968, the central banks of the IMF members introduced a dual market for gold. Then on Aug. 8, 1969 the French franc was devalued by 12.5% and on Sept. 28, 1969 the FRG introduced a floating rate for the mark and on Oct. 24, 1969 its revaluation by 9.3%. On Apr. 31, 1970 Canada introduced a floating rate for its currency. In the critical year of 1971, the massive inflow of dollars to the FRG resulted in the closing of most exchanges from May 5 to 9, 1971, the revaluation of the Swiss franc by 7.1%, the Austrian schilling by 5.05% and new floating rates for the FRG mark, Dutch guilder. Three months later, Aug. 15, 1971, the outflow of dollars from the USA and the growing balance of payments deficit forced President Richard Nixon to suspend the convertibility of the dollar into gold and impose a 10% surtax, which immediately resulted in a week-long closing of most currency markets, introduction of a floating rate for the Belgian franc, and a dual currency market in France; on Dec. 18, 1972 the US government introduced new currency rates, the dollar was devalued by 7.89% in relation to gold, in the FRG and Japan revaluation of the mark and gold; the USA abolished the 10% surcharge on imports. The years 1972 and 1973 were characterized by a significant increase in the price of gold and ever greater fluctuations in the rates of "hard currencies." The EEC states on Apr. 24, 1972 decided to tighten the margin of fluctuations of their currencies. The IMF Administrative Council on Sept. 6, 1972 published a report of experts on the question of the reform of the international monetary system, revealing significant differences in views between US experts and others, especially concerning the role of gold and the settlement of payments deficits and surpluses.

The chiefs of state and the governments of the 9 EEC member countries at a session in Paris on Oct. 21, 1972 resolved to undertake joint action to reform the international monetary system with the goal of creating a new "just and lasting system." Such a system would be entirely compatible with the realization of an economic and monetary union (such as the chiefs of state and governments at this session resolved to create in the period Jan. 1, 1974–Dec. 31, 1980). Besides this the Fund for European Monetary Co-operation was formed. Earlier, at a General Assembly of the IMF in place of the Group of Ten the Group of Twenty was created with the task of formulating a program for reform. In Jan., 1973 Switzerland introduced a floating rate for the Swiss franc, Belgium and Italy a dual currency market. A further decline in the exchange rate of the dollar was noted on European exchanges; Feb. 2, 1973 the FRG introduced control of capital movements and on Feb. 8, 1973 purchased 1.4 billion dollars; on Feb. 9–11, 1973 a meeting was held in Paris of the Ministers of Foreign Affairs of France, FRG, Italy, the UK, with the US Secretary of State, with most of the markets reacting by closing. On Feb. 13, 1973 there was another official devaluation of the dollar by 10%, floating rates for the Japanese yen and Italian lire, and devaluations of the currencies of Argentina, Israel, Nigeria, Spain, Turkey, and Yugoslavia and revaluation in Finland, Iceland, and Sweden. At the end of Feb., 1973 the value of an ounce of gold reached 100 dollars; on March 4, 1973 a special session of the finance ministers of the EEC states was held; March 9–16, 1973 a session of the Group of Ten in Paris; on March 12, 1973 the EEC states decided on a joint float of their currencies against the American dollar, while simultaneously the FRG revalued the mark by 3% and Austria the schilling by 2.25%. The resolutions adopted by the Group of Ten for the common safeguarding of the system of

exchange rates by elastic pragmatic actions clearly did not solve the crisis. In the opinion of IMF experts, until the USA brings its balance of trade into equilibrium, which is a difficult and long-range task, the monetary crisis in the capitalist world will be of a permanent nature. In such conditions the dollar can no longer be the main privileged currency and should be reduced to the role of one of the IMF hard currencies. The background of the crisis was the deposit in foreign banks outside the USA of c. 80 billion dollars, reflecting the fact that the USA was spending much more abroad than it took in. The committee on customs duties of the US Senate on Feb. 13, 1973 called attention to the role of multinational corporations, which controled such large financial resources that they could easily hasten or cause an international financial crisis, or in making a transfer of a minor part of their financial resources from one country to another would easily bring about the collapse of any given currency. These corporations and private financial institutions had at their disposal financial power that could paralyze even the monetary operations of central banks. In Dec., 1971 multinational corporations and private institutions had deposits valued at 268 billion dollars. This was a sum twice as large as the financial reserves of all of the central banks and international financial institutions. It was obvious – in the opinion of the US Senate committee – that it would be sufficient to transfer only a small part of the financial reserves of multinational corporations in order to cause a monetary crisis in a given country. Taking into consideration the impossibility of eliminating multinational corporations from economic life, the report of the committee suggested that the US government, the countries of the Common Market, Japan and Canada pass legislation which would permit: (1) multinational corporations to act only for the purpose of protecting their assets, or (2) would obligate multinational corporations to take a passive posture, not touching their own assets in a situation when the signs of monetary disturbances appear on the world market. One of the signs of the crisis was the provisionally agreed upon and unilaterally broken exchange relationships (4.5% band of fluctuation of the ▷ Currency snake); then the absence of a common policy of West European central banks in relation to the market of inconvertible dollars (some increased their reserves of dollars by making interventionary purchases in order to prevent the rate of the dollar from falling, others did the opposite); finally, the absence of a common policy toward the huge mass of dollar liabilities (80 billion American dollars); discussed was their transfer to the IMF or conversion into long-term US obligations or using them to buy out the large American companies in Europe.

A new element was the energy crisis, which at the beginning of 1974 influenced both the exchange rate of the dollar and the price of raw materials. In the West some began to discuss the idea that a new "world monetary system" would not arise without the participation of the CMEA states, which in these years began work on improving their monetary–financial relations for the purpose of "factually ensuring exchangeability and the reality of their currency rates." In the opinion of the French politician, former premier E. Faure: "A New Bretton Woods should include monetary co-operation with the countries of the East, which after several years should result in an exchangeable ruble being included among the world's currency reserves." (Le Monde, Nov. 23, 1971.)

The IMF Council since July 1, 1974 introduced a new system for the ▷ SDR and simultaneously abandoned a fixed price for gold in transactions of Central Banks. It was considered expanding the

SDR system and making it, after gold, the second standard of a world monetary system, called a gold-currency standard, or making a third system based on commodities. Its characteristic feature would be a departure from the principle that monetary obligations perform the function of an international currency reserve and acceptance of the principle that this function is created by material values. The states of the Third World, disturbed by the world monetary crisis, in 1975–80 developed a program for a ▷ New International Economic Order, both in the forum of the UN General Assembly and at sessions of UNCTAD. The EEC states formed a new ▷ european currency unit, ECU.

The new situation in the international monetary system at the end of the decade 1971–80 was summarized by S. Rączkowski, a Polish expert in the UN, in the following points:

1. Gold has ceased to be the basis of the international monetary system and has ceased to perform the function of world money;

2. There is no longer any uniform system for all countries for determining the rates of currencies. Former parities in gold have ceased to be binding; the IMF has departed from art. IV of its statute on parities, introducing new concepts of exchange rules (Exchange Agreements) and the freedom of each member country in using a floating rate of any other standard besides gold. Some of the IMF member countries use the Floating Rate of Exchange or one managed by central banks (Managed Floating). Some 25 capitalist countries, including the Western powers, use such an individualized floating rate for their currencies. The FRG, Benelux, Denmark and Norway use their own system. The majority of the IMF members (65) set the central rate of their currency in relation to the currency of the country with which they have the most extensive economic relations. Thus 42 states, including most of Latin America, have tied the rates of their currencies to the American dollar, 14 African countries with the French franc, 5 with the pound sterling. A separate group is made up of 15 states which have tied their currency rates to the SDR. According to a 1982 UN analysis "shocks affecting the major currencies thus create shock waves spreading throughout the world." The floating rate being far less structured than the previous system and therefore less easy to control or operate, the floating rate system has shown advantages because of its flexibility, but also disadvantages because of its volatility. The world is still in search of a monetary system with more stability than the current one and less rigidity than that of Bretton Woods. This search has been seriously complicated by the rise of inflationary pressures affecting the prices of manufactured goods and the large swings in balance-of-payments movements due to the shifts in the price of energy. In a period of stagnating trade and high unemployment, the world monetary system also has to contend with an unprecedented burden of debt and increasingly protectionist sentiments in major developed countries. The result has been an imperfect system operating in very difficult conditions.

Under pressure of circumstances there have been changes in the policies and practices of the IMF. Faced with the growing trade deficits of developing countries which commercial banks are reluctant to fund, the IMF has been playing a bigger credit role. Its lendable resources have been increased and some of its repayment conditions have been eased in recent years. However these changes cannot deal with the structural problems of trade and monetary imbalances in the world economy.

A matter of high priority in the monetary field is the crushing burden of international debt borne by developing countries. Over the past decade they have borrowed heavily to keep their economies going and their total outstanding debt has grown from about $114 billion in 1973 to about $400 billion 1982. A number of countries are so deeply in debt that the yearly interest and service charges account for up to 50% of their annual export earnings. The monetary world crisis also in the 1980s is still a reflection of the fact that the monetary system is essentially one that is used for payments in world trade. Big trading countries have strong voices in monetary affairs and their currencies are "hard," capable of use without restrictions in world trade. Conversely, developing countries with small shares in world trade and weak agricultural economies have "soft" currencies which cannot be used to pay for their imports. Their trade is limited by the amount of "hard" currencies they can earn at any given time by their exports. Not surprisingly, most developing countries have little credit in the world's market place.

F.A. MANN, *Legal Aspects of Money*, Oxford, 1971; M.R. SHUSTER, *The Public International Law of Money*, Oxford, 1973; J.K. GALBRAITH, *Money*, Boston, 1975; H. BOURGINAT, S. RĄCZKOWSKI, *The International Payments Crisis*, Brussels, 1977; D. SMITH, *The Rise and Fall of Monetarism: The Theory and Politics of an Economic Experiment*, London, 1987.

MONETARY INTERNATIONAL SYSTEM AND FINANCING OF THE DEVELOPMENT OF DEVELOPING COUNTRIES.

A subject of a Program of Action on the Establishment of the ▷ New International Economic Order, adopted 1974 by the UN General Assembly Special Session Res. 3202/S-VI. The text of the chapter on the international monetary system is as follows:

"(1) Objectives. All efforts should be made to reform the international monetary system with, inter alia, the following objectives:

(a) Measures to check the inflation already experienced by the developed countries, to prevent it from being transferred to developing countries and to study and devise possible arrangements within the International Monetary Fund to mitigate the effects of inflation in developed countries on the economies of developing countries;

(b) Measures to eliminate the instability of the international monetary system, in particular the uncertainty of the exchange rates, especially as it affects adversely the trade in commodities;

(c) Maintenance of the real value of the currency reserves of the developing countries by preventing their erosion from inflation and exchange rate depreciation of reserve currencies;

(d) Full and effective participation of developing countries in all phases of decision-making for the formulation of an equitable and durable monetary system and adequate participation of developing countries in all bodies entrusted with this reform and, particularly, in the proposed Council of Governors of the International Monetary Fund;

(e) Adequate and orderly creation of additional liquidity with particular regard to the needs of the developing countries through the additional allocation of special drawing rights based on the concept of world liquidity needs to be appropriately revised in the light of the new international environment; any creation of international liquidity should be made through international multilateral mechanisms;

(f) Early establishment of a link between special drawing rights and additional development financing in the interest of developing countries consistent with the monetary characteristics of special drawing rights;

(g) Review by the International Monetary Fund of the relevant provisions in order to ensure effective participation by developing countries in the decision-making process;

(h) Arrangements to promote an increasing net transfer of real resources from the developed to the developing countries;

(i) Review of the methods of operation of the International Monetary Fund, in particular the terms for both credit repayments and "stand-by" arrangements, the system of compensatory financing, and the terms of the financing of commodity buffer stocks so as to enable the developing countries to make more effective use of them.

(2) Measures. All efforts should be made to take the following urgent measures to finance the development of developing countries and to meet the balance-of-payment crises in the developing world:

(a) Implementation at an accelerated pace by the developed countries of the time-bound programme, as already laid down in the International Development Strategy for the Second United Nations Development Decade, for the net amount of financial resource transfers to developing countries; increase in the official component of the net amount of financial resource transfers to developing countries so as to meet and even to exceed the target of the Strategy;

(b) International financing institutions should effectively play their role as development financing banks without discrimination on account of the political or economic system of any member country, assistance being untied;

(c) More effective participation by developing countries, whether recipients or contributors, in the decision-making process in the competent organs of the International Bank for Reconstruction and Development and the International Development Association, through the establishment of a more equitable pattern of voting rights;

(d) Exemption, wherever possible, of the developing countries from all import and capital outflow controls imposed by the developed countries;

(e) Promotion of foreign investment, both public and private, from developed to developing countries in accordance with the needs and requirements in sectors of their economies as determined by the recipient countries;

(f) Appropriate urgent measures, including international action, should be taken to mitigate adverse consequences for the current and future development of developing countries arising from the burden of external debt contracted on hard terms;

(g) Debt renegotiation on a case-by-case basis with a view to concluding agreements on debt cancellation, moratorium, rescheduling or interest subsidization;

(h) International financial institutions should take into account the special situation of each developing country in reorientating their lending policies to suit these urgent needs; there is also need for improvement in practices of international financial institutions in regard to, inter alia, development financing and international monetary problems;

(i) Appropriate steps should be taken to give priority to the least-developed, land-locked and island developing countries and to the countries most seriously affected by economic crises and natural calamities, in the availability of loans for development purposes which should include more favourable terms and conditions."

M.J. WASSERMAN, *International Money Management*, New York, 1973; B. TEW, *The Evolution of the International Monetary System*, London, 1977; *Conference on Economic Cooperation among Developing Countries. Declarations, Resolutions, Recommendation and Decisions adopted in the US System*, México, DF, 1976; Vol. 1, pp. 52–56. S.I. DAVIS, *The Euro-Bank*, London, 1976; G. DUFEY, I.H. GUIDY, *The International Money Market*, Prentice Hall, 1978; J. WALMSLEY, *A Dictionary of International Finance*, London, 1979; R. FRASER, *The World Financial System 1944–86. A Comprehensive Reference Guide*, London, 1987; R.N. COOPER, *The International Monetary System*, Cambridge, Mass, 1987.

MONETARY UNION.

A common multi- or one-currency system of several or more than ten countries. The first monetary unions were formed in the 19th century: the Inter-American Monetary Union, the Bolivar Latin Monetary Union and the Swedish–Scandinavian Monetary Union. After World War II specific post-colonial conditions created the Monetary Union of Equatorial Africa, the Monetary Union of West Africa and the Monetary Union of East Africa and also the Monetary Union of Central America. The difference between a single- and multi-currency system is that in the latter the currencies of the individual states, follow-ing their entrance into the Union, have a stable and unchanging relationship not only among themselves, but also to gold or to some other measure of value. In Luxembourg on Jan. 9, 1970 the leaders of the governments and states of the member nations of the EEC resolved to form an economic and monetary union for the period up to Dec. 31, 1980. An important stage in the creation of the union was the initiation on Mar. 13, 1979 of the ▷ European Monetary System.

A. NIELSEN, "Monetary Union", in: *Encyclopedia of Social Sciences*, Vol. 10, 1949.

MONETARY UNION OF CENTRAL AMERICA. ▷ Central American Monetary Union.

MONETARY UNION OF EAST AFRICA.

The Union was est. 1919 in London as the East African Currency Board for the British colonies: Kenya, Tanganyika and Uganda, since 1936 also Zanzibar; reorganized and renamed 1946; dissolved 1966.

Yearbook of International Organizations.

MONETARY UNION OF EQUATORIAL AFRICA.

Union monétaire de l'Afrique Equatoriale, est. June 22, 1959 on signature of financial convention by the governments of Chad, Gabon, the Central African Republic, Congo, under aegis of Banque de France. Monetary unit ▷ Franc CFA.

Yearbook of International Organizations.

MONETARY UNION OF WEST AFRICA.

Union monétaire ouest africaine, UMOA. The Union was est. May 12, 1962 on signature of a financial convention by the governments of Dahomey (now Benin), Ivory Coast (now Côte d'Ivoire), Mali, Mauritania, Niger, Senegal, Upper Volta (now Burkina Faso), and (1963) Togo. The convention was replaced on Nov. 14, 1974 by a new Treaty signed by Benin, the Ivory Coast, Niger, Senegal, Togo and Upper Volta. Monetary unit Franc CFA, issued by Banque Central des Etats de l'Afrique de l'Ouest in Paris, under aegis of Banque de France, in accord with Intergovernmental Agreement of the UMOA Members with France, signed on Dec. 12, 1973 in Dakar. In relations with the African Centre for Monetary Studies, f. 1978, Dakar. Reg. with the UIA. Publ.: *Annual Report*.

Yearbook of International Organizations, 1986/87; The Europa Yearbook 1988. A World Survey, Vol. I, London, 1988.

MONEY.

A measure of value, means of payment, equivalent for goods and services, subject of international conventions and systems.

F.A. MANN, *Legal Aspects of Money*, Oxford, 1971; M.R. SHUSTER, *The Public International Law of Money*, Oxford, 1973; *UN Chronicle*, October, 1982, pp. 43–44.

MONEY BOXES.

A subject of international co-operation. Organization reg. with the UIA:

International Society of Money Box Collectors. The Argyrotheocologysts Club, f. 1957, Barneveld, The Netherlands.

Yearbook of International Organizations.

MONEY EXCHANGE.

A subject of international conventions. The Convention on International Monetary Fund, names among the Fund's purposes the establishment of a multilateral system of exchanges and stability in types of exchange. See also ▷ Convertibility principle.

D. CARREAN, *Souveraineté et coopération monétaire international*, Paris, 1970.

MONEY, GLOBAL SYSTEM. An international term of the 1980's related to the external debt crisis and to the idea of a new ▷ Bretton Woods Conference.

I.S. FRIEDMAN, *Toward World Prosperity. Reshaping the Global Money System,* Lexington, Mass, 1987; R.Z. ALIBER ed., *The Reconstruction of International Monetary Arrangements,* London, 1987.

MONEY, INTERNATIONAL. A monetary unit created by international financial institutions for the purpose of increasing international monetary liquidity, facilitating settlement of international accounts as well as creating basic reserves in international monetary systems. The first international money in history was the unit based on the special drawing right (▷ SDR) created in 1970 by the IMF, which serves the function of a measure of value, means of payment, and an integral part of monetary reserves. A similar function is planned for the ECU which is the monetary unit of the EEC; the monetary unit of the CMEA, functioning on a more limited scale is the Transfer Rouble.

J.K. GALBRAITH, *Money, Whence it came? Where it went?* Boston, 1975; H. BOURGINAT, S. RACZKOWSKI, *The International Payments Crisis,* Brussels, 1977.

MONEY INTERNATIONAL LAW. A subject of codification work of UN monetary institutions and intergovernmental bi and multilateral agreements, mainly within the IMF system.

R.M. SHUSTER, *The Public International Law of Money,* Oxford, 1973.

MONGOLIA. Member of the UN. Mongolian People's Republic. State in Central Asia. Area: 1,565,000 sq. km. Pop. 1983 census: 1,773,000 (1,018,000 at the census of 1963; 1973 census: 1,594,800). Capital: Ulan Bator with 457,000 inhabitants in 1977. Borders with the USSR and the Chinese People's Republic. Official language: Mongolian. GNP per capita in 1980: US $940. Currency: one tughrik = 100 mongo. National Day: July 11, anniversary of the people's revolution in 1921 and Nov. 26, day of the proclamation of the Republic, 1924.

Member of the UN since Dec. 15, 1961 and a member of ten specialized UN organizations: the ILO, UNESCO, WHO, UPU, ITU, UNIDO, IAEA, FAO, WIPO and WMO.

International relations: unified in the 12th century by the founder of the Mongolian empire, Ghengis Khan. Mongolia through the centuries passed from periods of independence to dependency (as a result of the breakdown of the feudal system); in the 17th century the Manchus occupied southern Mongolia, known since then as Inner Mongolia; in the 18th century also northern Mongolia became part of the Manchu empire as Outer Mongolia. A rebellion in 1911 upset the authorities of the Manchu dynasty and on Dec. 1, 1911 an independent feudal-theocratic state was proclaimed. During World War I, tsarist Russia in May 1915 recognized the autonomy of Outer Mongolia. After the October Revolution in Russia, Mongolia became the theater of operations of Chinese and Japanese counter-revolutionary forces, and in 1920 the White Russian units of Ungern von Sternberg took refuge in Mongolia. The struggle for the liberation of Mongolia was taken up by the Mongolian People's Revolutionary Party which at the beginning of 1921 expelled Chinese forces and then together with the Red Army defeated the forces of Ungern; on July 11, 1921 a revolution broke out in Urdza (now Ulan Bator). The independent Mongolian People's Republic was proclaimed on Nov. 26, 1924; in 1936 a treaty on mutual assistance was signed with the USSR. After having occupied Manchuria, Japan attacked Mongolia in May, 1939. During World War II, Mongolia was on the side of the USSR; on Aug. 10, 1945 Mongolia declared war on Japan and Mongolian forces participated in the fighting along with Soviet forces. With the aim of accelerating development, raising the effectiveness of the economy, science and technology of Mongolia a special CMEA program was developed. Has treaties of friendship and co-operation with the USSR and the socialist countries as well as treaties and agreements on economic issues and technical assistance. In addition, Mongolia concluded an inter-state agreement on cultural co-operation with 30 countries. In 1963 she signed a general treaty with UN specialized agencies. A partial withdrawal of Soviet troops took place between April and June 1987 (around 65,000 men or some 20 per cent). Soviet troops are stationed in Mongolia in accordance with the 1966 Treaty of Friendship, Co-operation and Mutual Assistance extended to 1996 in January 1986. China called again for the withdrawal of all Soviet troops from Mongolia.

The disputed border issues between China and Mongolia started to be negotiated in Ulan Bator 1986–87. On Aug. 9, 1986 Mongolia est. consular relations with the Peoples Republic of China (diplomatic relations 1949). On Jan. 27, 1987 in Washington DC. Mongolia and the USA signed a memorandum of understanding establishing diplomatic relations. On Nov. 28, 1988 Mongolia signed in Peking with the Peoples Republic of China the first frontier agreement. Negotiations had taken place in 1950–1956 and 1982–1988.

R. GROUSSET, *L'empire des steppes,* Paris, 1941; O. LATTIMORE, *Nationalism and Revolution in Mongolia,* London, 1955; *Mongolskaia Narodnaia Respublika 1921–61,* Moscow, 1961; *Sovetsko-Mongolskie otnosheniia. Sbornik dokumentov 1921–66,* Moscow, 1966; *Istoriya Mongolskoi Narodnoi Respubliki,* Moscow, 1967; Y. TSEDENBAL, *Mongolian People's Republic on the Road to Socialism,* Ulan Bator, 1967; J.E. VIDAL, *La Mongolie,* Paris, 1971; V.P. PETROV, *Mongolia. A profile,* London, 1971; E.M. ZHUKOV (ed.), *History of the Mongolian People's Republic,* Moscow, 1973; E.P. BAVRIAN, *Mongolskaia Narodnaia Respublika: Spravochnik,* Moscow, 1976; B. SHIRENDOR, M. SANJDORJ (eds.), *History of the Mongolian People's Republic,* 3 Vols., Harvard, 1976; R.A. RUPEN, *How Mongolia is Really Ruled: A Political History of the Mongolian People's Republic 1900–1978,* Stanford, 1979; *The Socialist Mongolia,* Ulan Bator, 1981; L. CHAISANDAI, *Mongolskaia Narodnaia Respublika 1955–1980,* Ulan Bator, 1982; *The Europa Year Book 1984. A World Survey,* Vol. II, pp. 2058–2062, London, 1984; KEESING's *Contemporary Archive,* 1986, No. 10; A.J.K. SANDERS, *Mongolia: Politics, Economics and Society,* London, 1987; KEESING's *Record of World Events,* April, 1988.

MONOMETALISM. A monetary system based on only one precious metal (silver or gold); the opposite of ▷ bimetalism. Gold monometalism was introduced by Great Britain in 1816, Australia, Canada, and Germany – 1873. Silver monometalism existed in colonial Mexico, and 1910–40 in China and India.

MONOPOLY. An international term with a double meaning: (1) the right of exclusive production or trade granted by the state in a certain field to itself or to a private or collective legal person; (2) a national or international association dominant in a certain area of the economy and dictating the prices for its products on the national or international market. In the socialist countries there exists a monopoly in foreign trade, introduced for the first time in Soviet Russia, Apr. 22, 1918.

P. ENDERLEIN, *Aussenhandels-monopol und ökonomisches System des Sozialismus,* Potsdam, 1968.

MONOPOLY PRICES. An international term for the price of goods set by large international monopolies controlling the majority of production and sales in a certain branch of the economy.

MONOPSONY. An international term for the only "monopolistic purchaser" who sets the price for the purchase of an article by virtue of having exclusive possession, just as a monopolist sells his products at the price set by him. ▷ Monopoly.

MONROE DOCTRINE, 1823. A principle of the US foreign policy of not permitting the intervention of European powers in the internal affairs of the states of the Western Hemisphere; formulated by the President of the USA, J. Monroe (1758–1831), in a speech to Congress on Dec. 2, 1823. The text is as follows:

"... At the proposal of the Russian Imperial Government, made through the minister of the Emperor residing here, full power and instructions have been transmitted to the minister of the United States at St. Petersburg to arrange by amicable negotiations the respective rights and interests of the two nations on the north-west coast of this continent. A similar proposal has been made by His Majesty to the Government of Great Britain, which has likewise been acceded to. The Government of the United States has been desirous by this friendly proceeding of manifesting the great value which they have invariably attached to the friendship of the Emperor and their solicitude to cultivate the best understanding with his Government. In the discussions to which this interest has given rise and in the arrangements by which they may terminate the occasion has been judged proper for asserting, as a principle in which the rights and interests of the United States are involved, that the American continents, by the free and independent condition which they have assumed and maintain, are henceforth not to be considered as subjects for future colonization by any European powers ...

It was stated at the commencement of the last session that a great effort was then making in Spain and Portugal to improve the condition of the people of those countries, and that it appeared to be conducted with extraordinary moderation. It need scarcely be remarked that the result has been so far very different from what was then anticipated. Of events in that quarter of the globe, with which we have so much intercourse and from which we derive our origin, we have always been anxious and interested spectators. The citizens of the United States cherish sentiments the most friendly in favor of the liberty and happiness of their fellow-men on that side of the Atlantic. In the wars of the European powers in matters relating to themselves we have never taken any part, nor does it comport with our policy so to do. It is only when our rights are invaded or seriously menaced that we resent injuries or make preparation for our defense. With the movements in this hemisphere we are of necessity more immediately connected, and by causes which must be obvious to all enlightened and impartial observers. The political system of the allied powers is essentially different in this respect from that of America. This difference proceeds from that which exists in their respective Governments, and to the defense of our own, which has been achieved by the loss of so much blood and treasure, and matured by the wisdom of their most enlightened citizens, and under which we have enjoyed unexampled felicity, this whole nation is devoted. We owe it, therefore, to candor and to the amicable relations existing between the United States and those powers to declare that we should consider any attempt on their part to extend their system to any portion of this hemisphere as dangerous to our peace and safety. With the existing colonies or dependencies of any European power we have not interfered and shall not interfere. But with the Governments who have declared their independence and maintained it, and whose independence we have, on great consideration and on just principles, acknowledged, we could not view any interposition for the purpose of oppressing them, or controlling in any other manner their destiny, by any European power in any other light than as the manifestation of an unfriendly disposition toward the United States. In the war between those new Governments and Spain we declared our neutrality at the time of their recognition, and to this we have adhered, and shall continue to adhere, provided no change shall occur which, in the judgment of the competent authorities of this Government, shall make a corresponding change on the part of the United States indispensable to their security.

The late events in Spain and Portugal show that Europe is still unsettled. Of this important fact no stronger proof can be adduced than that the allied powers should have thought it proper, on any principle satisfactory to themselves, to have interposed by force in the internal concerns of Spain. To what extent such interposition may be carried on the same principle, is a question in which all independent powers whose governments differ from theirs are interested, even those most remote, and surely none more so than the United States. Our policy in regard to Europe, which was adopted at an early stage of the wars which have so long agitated that quarter of the globe, nevertheless remains the same, which is, not to interfere in the internal concerns of any of its powers; to consider the government de facto as the legitimate government for us; to cultivate friendly relations with it, and to preserve those relations by a frank, firm, and manly policy, meeting in all instances the just claims of every power, submitting to injuries from none. But in regard to those continents circumstances are eminently and conspicuously different. It is impossible that the allied powers should extend their political system to any portion of either continent without endangering our peace and happiness; nor can anyone believe that our southern brethren, if left to themselves, would adopt it of their own accord. It is equally impossible, therefore, that we should behold such interposition in any form with indifference. If we look to the comparative strength and resources of Spain and those new Governments, and their distance from each other, it must be obvious that she can never subdue them. It is still the true policy of the United States to leave the parties to themselves, in the hope that other powers will pursue the same course ...''

In the opinion of the Mexican scholar, I. Fabeli, the Monroe doctrine "was justified in its time against the manifest intentions of the Holy Alliance to regain their possessions in America," but toward the end of the 19th century it began to change from an instrument against European intervention into an instrument of US intervention in Latin America and already in such a character was included in art. 21 of the League of Nations Covenant, 1919, by a unilateral decision of the US President Woodrow Wilson, which resulted in the exclusion from this institution of a number of Latin American republics less dependent on the USA. The Mexican General Louis Cardenas then stated:

"The Monroe doctrine is an arbitrary protectorate over nations which have neither asked for it nor, even less, needed it. The Monroe doctrine is not based on mutuality and thereby is unjust. One can cite examples in which the application of the Monroe doctrine had unfavourable consequences for the Hispano–American republics."

The same Mexican statesman, now as the President of Mexico stated on Jan. 12, 1940:

"The Monroe doctrine never was and never could be recognized by Mexico or any other Hispano–American nation; thus it was only an expression of the one-sided policy which the States imposed, having a two-fold aim in view: to exclude the European states from this continent and to defend its interests in America. The doctrine poorly interpreted and applied moved away from its original content and was repeatedly transformed into a pretext for intervention."

On Sept. 23, 1988 Senator Dan Quayle, before being elected vice president asserted that the American people and Soviet leaders should be reminded that 'the Monroe Doctrine is alive and well'.

A. ALVARES. *The Monroe Doctrine. Its importance in the International Life of the New World*, New York, 1922; D. PERKINS, *The Monroe Doctrine 1823–26*, Boston, 1932; *Hands Off. A History of the Monroe Doctrine*, Boston, 1945; I. FABELA, *Las Doctrinas Monroe y Drago*, México, DF, 1957; G. ESTRADA, *La Doctrina Monroe y el fracasso de una conferencia Panamericana en México*, México, DF, 1959; D. MARQUANT (ed.), *The Monroe Doctrine. Its Modern Significance*, Santa Barbara, 1965; *International Herald Tribune*, Sept. 24–25, 1988.

MONROE PLAN, 1958. A proposal of US senator H.J. Monroe of Feb. 24, 1958 for establishing, as part of the World Bank, a special financial institution which would make it possible for developing countries without "hard currencies" to receive credits in those currencies for large investments through multilateral treaties which would not only include the dollar, but also other currencies, including those of the developing countries. The US government submitted the Monroe Plan to the Council of the World Bank which established the International Development Association ▷ IDA with a statute taking into consideration the provisions of the Monroe Plan.

IBRD Annual Report, 1958.

MONROVIA. The capital of Liberia at the mouth of the St. Paul River, city and sea port. Headquarters of the West Africa Rice Development Association.

Yearbook of International Organizations.

MONROVIA GROUP. The African states which joined neither ▷ Brazzaville Group nor ▷ Casablanca Group: Ethiopia, Libya, Nigeria, Sierra Leone, Somalia, Togo and Tunisia, whose heads of government met May 10–14, 1961 in Monrovia. In their declaration they opposed Pan-African ideas of forming a suprastate organization. As a basis for unity they recognized broad inter-African co-operation in all fields based on mutual respect of sovereignty and territorial integrity.

MONROVIA STRATEGY FOR DEVELOPMENT OF AFRICA. ▷ Lagos Plan, 1980.

MONTEBELLO DECISION. An international term for the agreement of NATO defense ministers during a meeting in Montebello, Canada in October 1983, to reduce the amount of nuclear warheads in Western Europe and to modernize retained stocks.

KEESING's *Contemporary Archive*, 1983; D. ROBERTSON, *Guide to Modern Defense and Strategy*, Detroit, 1988.

MONTENEGRO. Crna Gora = Black Mountain. Constituent republic of Yugoslavia; area: 13,810 sq. km, pop. 1980 est.: 580,000. From the end of the 15th century under Turkish sovereignty; in the 17th century autonomous, from the 18th century independent; constitutional duchy from 1905, occupied 1916–18 by the Austro-Hungarian army. On Dec. 1, 1918 Montenegro became part of the Kingdom of Serbs, Croats, and Slovenes, which in 1929 took the name Yugoslavia. In Apr. 1941 occupied by the Italian army and during the course of the liquidation of Yugoslavia by Germany and Italy announced as a so-called independent state under the Italian name Montenegro. This state was never organized due to an uprising of the population on July 13, 1941 and the years' long partisan struggles. Liberated toward the end of 1944. On Nov. 29, 1945 Montenegro once again became part of Yugoslavia as one of six federal republics.

Bibliografia Montenegro, Belgrade, 1948; M. DJILAS, *Land Without Justice*, London, 1958.

MONTENEROS. The South American underground organization originating from the Peron movement, operating in the 1970s in Argentina, connected with ▷ Tupamaros in Uruguay.

MONTEVIDEO. The capital of Uruguay on the Rio de la Plata, city and port. Headquarters of the Inter-American Institute of Agricultural Science, Inter-American Broadcasting Association, Latin American Integration Association, ALADI (formerly LAFTA), Latin American Shipowners' Association, Mutual Assistance of Latin American Government Oil Companies and others.

Yearbook of International Organizations.

MONTEVIDEO CONVENTION, 1933. The official name of the ▷ Inter-American Convention on Rights and Duties of States, 1933 adopted in Montevideo by Seventh International American Conference.

MONTEVIDEO GROUP. Nine Latin American states (Argentina, Brazil, Chile, Ecuador, El Salvador, Nicaragua, Panama, Peru and Uruguay), which in 1971 at the session of the Latin American Free Trade Association, LAFTA, in Montevideo came out in favor of the 200-mile limit for territorial waters, taking a more radical stance than the ▷ Santo Domingo Group. In 1973 both groups agreed on a common platform at the UN Conference on Law of the Sea.

MONTEVIDEO TREATIES, 1888–1940. Treaties prepared by the First and Second South American Congress on Private International Law at Montevideo.
Treaties adopted by the First Congress 1888–89:
Treaty on International Civil Law.
Treaty on International Commercial Law.
Treaty on International Procedural Law.
Treaty on International Penal Law.
Convention on Literary and Artistic Property.
Convention on Patents of Invention.
Convention on Trademarks.
Convention on the Practice of Learned Professions with Additional Protocol.
Treaties adopted by the Second Congress 1939–40:
Treaty on Asylum and Political Refugees.
Treaty on Intellectual Property.
Treaty on the Law of Commercial Navigation.
Treaty on International Procedure.
Treaty on International Penal Law.
Treaty on International Commercial Terrestrial Law.

M.A. VIEIRA (ed.), *Tratados de Montevideo 1888–1889 y 1939–1940*, Montevideo, 1959.

MONTEVIDEO TREATY, 1960. The official name of the Treaty establishing a Free Trade Zone and the ▷ Latin American Free Trade Association, the LAFTA; originally concluded by Argentina, Brazil, Chile, Mexico, Paraguay, Peru, Uruguay on Feb. 18, 1960 at Montevideo. Entered into force after the governments' signatories deposited with the Government of Uruguay ratification instruments. Suspended by the ▷ Latin American Integration Association, ALADI, 1980.

Documents on International Affairs 1960, Oxford, 1964; *Instruments relating to Economic Integration of Latin America*, Washington, DC, 1964.

MONTEVIDEO TREATY, 1980. A Latin American integration treaty, elaborated in Santiago on March 12, 1980 and adopted by the LAFTA member States Aug. 13, 1980 in Montevideo, replacing the ▷ Montevideo Treaty, 1960. On the base of the new treaty, the ▷ Latin American Free

Trade Association (LAFTA) was replaced by the ▷ Latin American Integration Association (ALADI), with no definite timetable for the establishment of a Latin American common market, and with a more flexible organization of regional and partial scope agreements related to the different stages of development of the member States.

The Europa Year Book 1984. A World Survey, Vol. I, p. 170, London, 1984.

MONTREUX. A city in western Switzerland where two international conferences were held: June 22–July 21, 1936, at which the convention on the Turkish straits was approved, and Apr. 12–May 18, 1937 on Egypt; the so-called ▷ Montreux Conventions 1936–37.

MONTREUX CONFERENCE, 1978. The meeting from Oct. 31 to Dec. 10, 1978 at Montreux of experts representing the participant states of the Conference on Security and Co-operation in Europe, foreseen by the ▷ Helsinki Final Act of the CSCE, 1975, in order to pursue the examination and elaboration of a generally accepted method for ▷ peaceful settlement of international disputes. The experts discussed a draft Convention on an European System for the Peaceful Settlement of Disputes. ▷ Madrid CSCE meeting 1980–83.

A.D. ROTFELD, *From Helsinki to Madrid. Documents*, Warsaw, 1984, pp. 218–221.

MONTREUX CONVENTIONS, 1936 AND 1937. Two multilateral agreements framed and signed in Montreux: (1) A Convention on the use of the Dardanelles, signed on July 2, 1936 by Bulgaria, Greece, Japan, Romania, Turkey, the USSR, and Yugoslavia.

The first article reads as follows:

"In time of Peace merchant vessels shall enjoy complete freedom of transit and navigation in the Straits, by day and by night, under any flag and with any kind of cargo without any formalities except as provided in art. 3 below.

(Art. 3. All ships entering the Straits by the Aegean Sea or by the Black Sea shall stop at sanitary station near the entrance to the Straits.)"

(2) A Convention on the status of foreigners in Egypt, signed on May 8, 1937 by Austria, Belgium, Czechoslovakia, Egypt, Denmark, France, Germany, Great Britain, Greece, Hungary, Italy, the Netherlands, Norway, Poland, Portugal, Romania, Spain, Sweden, Switzerland, the USA, Yugoslavia.

LNTS, Vol. 173, p. 213.

MONTSERRAT. An island in the Caribbean Sea. Discovered by Columbus in 1493 and settled by the Irish in 1632. A British crown colony. Area: 102 sq. km. Pop. 1982 census 11,675 (1980 census: 12,073). Capital: Plymouth with 3200 inhabitants, 1980. GNP per capita 1985: US $3,127. Currency East Caribbean dollar. The UN Special (Decolonization) Committee on Aug. 12, 1983 reaffirmed that it was ultimately for the people of Montserrat to determine their future political status, and reiterated its call upon the UK to inform the people of the options available to them in the exercise of their right to self-determination and independence.

UN Chronicle, January, 1984, p. 63; *The Europa Year Book 1984. A World Survey*, Vol. I, pp. 1261–1262, London, 1984.

MONT ST. MICHEL. A historical site of northwest France, in the Gulf of St. Malô, included in the ▷ World Heritage UNESCO List. This small island lies in a shallow bay and was a Celtic place of worship until the 8th century, when an oratory

dedicated to the archangel Michael was built there. Because of the steady stream of pilgrims, the monks were constantly forced to build upwards and on an ever larger scale. The monastery as a whole, called *la Merveille*, was built in the 13th century. It consists of five large rooms superimposed on two levels, and above them a cloister, which seems to hang between sky and sea.

UNESCO. *A Legacy for All*, Paris, 1984.

MONUMENTS PROTECTION. Subject of international conventions on protection of cultural values, and of a special UNESCO Committee on Monuments, Artistic and Historical Sites, and Archaeological Excavations. The Committee initiated Conferences for Monuments Protection (First in Paris in 1957, Second in Venice in 1964), the organ of which became the International Council of Monuments and Sites, ICOMOS, founded on June 21, 1965 in Warsaw, with headquarters in Paris; publ.: *Monumentum*. In 1972 the International Centre of Documentation of Monuments was founded in Paris under the aegis of UNESCO and ICOMOS. ▷ UNESCO.

Yearbook of International Organizations.

MOON, THE. Satellite of the Earth, the object of international co-operative exploration in connection with the expeditions of space-craft initiated 1959 by the USSR with Lunnik II, which landed on the Moon Sept. 13, 1959 and Lunnik III, which on Oct. 7, 1959 transmitted the first photographs of the other side of the Moon. On Jan. 21, 1967 the Agreement on the Principles Governing the Activities of States in the Exploration and Utilization of Outer Space including the Moon and other Heavenly Bodies was signed in London, Moscow and Washington. The expeditions organized by the USA from July 31, 1964 (landing of Ranger) were capped on July 20, 1969 by the arrival on the Moon of the first human crew on the ship ▷ Apollo. The flight, in which N. Armstrong, E. Aldrin and M. Collins took part, lasted from July 16 to July 20, 1969. The first to stand on the surface of the Moon was N. Armstrong, who made the historic statement: "This is a small step for a man, but a great step for humanity."

On July 24, 1969 Apollo II returned to Earth, bringing the first mineral samples from the Moon. On Sept. 20, 1970 the Soviet automatic space device Luna 16 landed on the Moon, and its special drilling probe collected a core sample of Moon surface, after which it started back and arrived at Kazakhstan on Sept. 24, 1970. Next, on Nov. 17, 1970 at the XXVIth Session of the UN General Assembly the USSR introduced a proposal (submitted to the UN Committee on the Peaceful Uses of Outer Space) for the drafting of an International Treaty on the Moon containing clauses for the complete demilitarization of both the surface of the Moon as well as the space around it; the complete internationalization of the surface and natural wealth of the Moon; international supervision, control, and government of the territory of the Moon as well as a legal statute on lunar settlements of states, which may be constructed on the Moon in connection with scientific expeditions. In Sept. 1972 the UN Outer Space Committee began debate on the draft on an International Treaty on the Moon prepared by its subcommittee. Among the 21 articles governing various aspects of human activity on the Moon are those stating that the Moon and other celestial bodies shall be used exclusively for peaceful purposes; that explorations in space shall be for the benefit of all peoples; and that steps be taken to avoid disturbing the environmental balance on the Moon and other celestial bodies. Outstanding issues involve the

scope of the Treaty and the status of the natural resources to be covered by it.

An Agreement Governing the Activities of States on the Moon and Other Celestial Bodies was approved by the UN General Assembly Res. 34/68 on Dec. 5, 1979, and the Assembly recommended that the Second UN Conference on the Exploration and Peaceful Uses of Outer Space should be held 1982.

L.A. SOBEL (ed.), *From Sputnik to Gemini*, New York, 1965; *UN Monthly Chronicle*, No. 4, 1975, p. 19; P. LEONARDI, *Volcanoes and Impact Craters on the Moon and Mars*, Amsterdam, 1976; *UN Chronicle*, May, 1978, p. 25 and March, 1980, p. 43.

MOORS. A subject of organized international co-operation. Organization reg. with the UIA:

International Society for Research on Moors, f. 1955, Vaduz, Liechtenstein.

Yearbook of International Organizations.

MOPR. ▷ Red Secours or MOPR.

MORAL DISARMAMENT COMMITTEE. One of the *ad hoc* committees of the League of Nations, operated 1932–33 and worked out a plan for a Convention on Moral Disarmament, carrying the obligation to educate youth in the spirit of peace and for the press, radio and cinema to work in this spirit, and to develop cultural co-operation.

MORALITY INTERNATIONAL. The ethical principles which are to rule international relations, such as pacta sunt servanda principle or basic principles of the UN Charter aimed at consolidation of peace, development of human rights and universal international co-operation.

K KIPNIS, D.T. MEYERS, *Political Realism and International Morality: Ethics in the Nuclear Age*, London, 1987.

MORAL REARMAMENT MOVEMENT. An anti-communist movement, f. 1938, in London, under the name World Assembly for Moral Rearmament; since 1950 Headquarters Caux, Switzerland. Publ.: *Tribune de Caux*. Reg. with the UIA.

Yearbook of International Organizations.

MORATORIUM. *Latin* = "delay." An international term for unilateral or contractual postponement of payment of international obligations, due to exceptional circumstances such as wars, natural disasters, epidemics or economic crises. An example of contractual Moratorium was US President Hoover's moratorium of July 26, 1931, with the consent of the Allies, to postpone war reparations payments by Germany.

A. MAYAR, "Zur Geschichte und Theorie des Moratoriums," in *Schmollers Jahrbuch*, No. 39, 1915; A. NUSBAUM, *Money in the Law. National and International*, London, 1950.

MORBIDITY STATISTICS. As early as the 17th century, attempts had been made to classify diseases and causes of death, and in 1853 the first International Statistical Congress, meeting in Brussels, decided to create "une nomenclature uniforme des causes de décès applicable à tous les pays." This was one of the first examples of international co-operation in the field of health. From that date until 1948, the international nomenclature was periodically revised and updated, but continued to be restricted to causes of death. In 1948, the Conference for the sixth revision, the first to be held under the auspices of the WHO modified the nomenclature so that it could be used also for the classification of morbidity data. Since then, the international classification has

M

been amplified to keep pace with progress in statistics and, above all, in medicine. In 1980 the ninth revision of the International Classification of Diseases and several other volumes have been established in order to facilitate the collection of data and to improve comparability between data from different sources. Thus WHO, at the request of a number of countries, has prepared a classification of procedures in medicine; it includes procedures used in medical diagnosis, laboratories, prophylaxis, surgery and radiology (both diagnostic and therapeutic), as well as drugs, medicaments and biological agents (vaccines, etc.). In addition, three adaptations of the international classification have been created for use by specialists; the first deals with oncology and allows tumors to be classified by their topography, morphology and behavior; the second concerns dentistry and stomatology and the third is an extended classification of eye diseases. Similar adaptations are proposed in fields such as ear, nose and throat diseases, dermatology and childhood disorders. Finally, a classification of impairments, disabilities and handicaps has been prepared.

WHO Chronicle, 1980.

MORE MONEY AND MORE GUNS. ▷ Kissinger Commission on Central America, 1983–84.

MORESNET. A small frontier territory of Belgium (5.5 sq. km) in the province of Liège; from 1816 to 1841 administered in common by Belgium and Prussia on the basis of the Napoleonic Code. Later acknowledged by both sides as independent and neutral, it was governed by mayors until Aug. 1, 1914, when it was occupied by the German Reich. According to arts. 32 and 33 of the Versailles Treaty of June 28, 1919, Germany acknowledged "total sovereignty of Belgium over the whole controversial Moresnet area" and renounced in favor of Belgium all rights and claims "to the territory of Prussian Moresnet situated westward of the road from Liège to Aix-la-Chapelle/ Aachen." It was occupied again by the Third Reich in 1940–45, and recovered by Belgium after World War II.

L. HOCH, *Un territoire oublié au centre de l'Europe,* Bruxelles, 1881; M. LEICHSENRING, *Neutral Moresnet,* Erlangen, 1911.

MORGENTHAU PLAN, 1944. The plan for the complete dismantling of industry in Western Germany "in order to put an end to the military and economic potential of the Ruhr and Saar Basins and to transform Germany into a primarily agricultural country," elaborated in summer 1944 by the US Treasury Secretary Henry Morgenthau. The Morgenthau Plan was approved on Sept. 15, 1944 by the President Franklin Delano Roosevelt and Prime Minister Winston C. Churchill at the conference in Quebec; however, they completely rejected the plan a month later.

H. MORGENTHAU, *Germany is Our Problem,* New York, 1945; F. SMITH, "The Rise and Fall of the Morgenthau Plan", in: *The United Nations World,* March, 1947; J. CHASE, "The Development of the Morgenthau Plan Through the Quebec Conference", in: *The Journal of Politics,* May, 1954.

MORMONS. Members of the Church of Jesus Christ of Latter-Day Saints. A religious community founded in the USA by Joseph Smith (1805–44), who in 1830 published The Book of Mormons containing revelations conveyed by the prophet Mormon. The denominational organization of Mormons was set up in 1836 in the State of Missouri (the date of consecration of the first church), moved to the State of Utah after the death of Smith in 1845, with the seat in Salt Lake City; in 1970 the

congregation numbered over 2,500,000. In 1852 a religious group was set up in Detroit, Michigan, named Reorganized Church of Jesus Christ of Latter-Day Saints, which rejected polygamy, allegedly allowed to Mormons by J. Smith.

J. WIDT SOE, *Eine Vernunftgemässe Theologie,* Basel, 1945; F.M. BACONS, *No Man Know my History. The Life of Joseph Smith,* New York, 1946.

MOROCCO. Member of the UN. Kingdom of Morocco. State in northwest Africa on the Atlantic Ocean and Mediterranean Sea. Borders with Algeria and partly integrates ▷ Western Sahara. Area: 458,730 sq. km. Pop. 1987 est.: 23,000,000 (1960 census – 11,625,000; 1980 – 20,464,000). Capital: Rabat with 941,000 inhabitants in 1981. GNP per capita in 1986: US $590. Currency: one dirham = 100 centimes. Official language: Arabic. National Day: Mar. 3, anniversary of king Hassan II's succession to the throne, 1961.
Member of the UN since Nov. 12, 1956 and of all UN specialized organizations. Member of the Arab League, of OAU and of the Consultative Committee of the Maghreb States.
International relations: in the 19th century divided into a French and Spanish protectorate; in conflict with Germany 1905 and 1911, which wished to establish a naval base in Morocco (the so-called Moroccan crisis). In 1923 France, Spain and Great Britain established an international zone in ▷ Tangier and a special zone in ▷ Ceuta and Melilla. During World War II, Morocco in 1940–42 was under the administration of the French Vichy government; in 1942–45 a sallyport for allied UN forces against German and Italian units in Africa and Europe. Morocco gained independence with the Paris Protocol signed Mar. 2, 1956. On Apr. 7, 1956 she integrated the special zone without the ports of Ceuta and Melilla; on Oct. 29, 1956 the international status of the Tangier Zone was abolished. In 1963 Morocco laid claim to part of the Algerian Sahara (from Colombo-Bechar to the border of Spanish Sahara); in Oct., 1963 a three-week armed conflict broke out which was suspended through the arbitration of the USA in Jan., 1964. King Hassan II in 1966 appealed to the UN and in 1967 to Spain for the return of ▷ Ifni and Spanish Sahara. In 1968 Morocco integrated Ifni. The frontier treaty with Algeria was signed on June 25, 1972. In 1976–84 in a dispute over Western Sahara with Algeria. ▷ Polisario.
A signatory of a Preferential Trade Agreement with the EEC, 1976.
On Nov. 13, 1984 Morocco and Zaïre left the OAU summit conference in Addis Ababa to protest the presence of the Polisario Front.
In Nov., 1984 Morocco broke off diplomatic relations with Yugoslavia after Belgrade recognized the Sahrawi Arab Democratic Republic (▷ Western Sahara). See also ▷ World Heritage UNESCO List.

H. TERASSE, *Histoire du Maroc,* 2 Vols., Casablanca, 1949–50; A. AYACHE, *Le Maroc: bilans d'une colonisation,* Paris, 1956; S. BERNARD, *Le Conflit Franco-Marocain 1943–56,* 3 Vols., Bruxelles, 1963; V. MONTEIL, *Maroc,* Paris, 1963; L. CARYCH, *Européens et Marocains 1930–56, Sociologie d'une décolonisation,* Bruges, 1964; J.M. GOLOVIN, *Marokko,* Moscow, 1964; Ch.F. STEWART, *The Economy of Morocco 1912–62,* Cambridge, 1964; S. BERNARD, M. COHEN, L. HAHN, *Morocco. Old Land. New Nation,* London, 1966; *The Economic Development of Morocco,* IBRD, Washington, DC, 1966; N.R. BENNET, *A Study Guide for Morocco,* Boston, 1970; J. WATERBURG, *The commander of the Faithful. The Moroccan Political Elite,* London, 1970; *La situation économique de Maroc en 1970,* Rabat, 1971; L.J. HALL, *The USA and Morocco 1776–1956,* Metuchen NJ, 1971; LORD KINROSS, D. HALES-

GARY, *Morocco,* London, 1971; *The Middle East and North-Africa 1972–73,* London, 1972, pp. 547–578; C. PALAZZOLI, *Le Maroc politique,* Paris, 1975; F. NATAF, *L'Indépendance du Maroc,* Paris, 1976; Ch.T. GALLAGHER, *The US and North Africa: Morocco, Algeria and Tunisia,* Cambridge Mass., 1982; *The Europa Year Book 1984. A World Survey,* Vol. II, pp. 2068–2081, London, 1984.

MORPHINE. The principal alkaloid of opium, having the chemical formula $C_{17}H_{19}NO_3$; subject of International ▷ Opium Conventions 1912 and 1925. See also ▷ opium.

UN Chronicle, may, 1987.

MORSE CODE. International telegraphic code, invented 1837 by S.F.B. Morse (1791–1872), a US artist; first used in communication between Washington, DC and Baltimore, Md, 1844. Morse was founder of the first electric telegraph company in the USA in 1845.

F.C. MABEL, *Samuel Finley Breese Morse,* New York, 1943.

MORTMAIN LAW. *Latin: manus mortua.* An international term dating back to medieval times when the Catholic Church expanded its real estate by way of succession granted in a last will written at a person's deathbed. Such property, in the light of canon law, was inalienable, i.e. excluded from further sale: *res extra commercium.* European parliaments issued ▷ amortizations law to prevent this practice. In 1279 in England the first Statute of Mortmain was issued, followed by others of 1290, 1390, 1392 and 1531. Further Mortmain and Charitable Uses Acts were issued in 1888 and 1891. Voided in 1960 by Charities Act.

MOSCOW. The capital of the USSR and of the Russian SFSR, on the Moscow River. Area: 58 sq. km. The seat of the General Staff of Warsaw Pact and of the CMEA.

A. KOVALYEV, *Moscow. A Short Guide to Moscow,* 1957.

MOSCOW AGREEMENT, 1945. ▷ Moscow Declaration 1945.

UNTS, Vol. 20, pp. 259–293.

MOSCOW APPEAL, 1960. An appeal to the people of the world on the problems of world peace drawn up and approved by the Second International Meeting of Communist and Workers' Parties, Moscow, Nov. 10, 1960.

MOSCOW COMMUNIQUÉ, 1972. The Joint Communiqué by the USA and USSR, published in Moscow, May 29, 1972 after the official visit to the USSR by President R. Nixon, May 22–30, 1972:

"The discussions covered a wide range of questions of mutual interest and were frank and thorough.
I. *Bilateral relations*
As a result of progress made in negotiations which preceded the summit meeting, and in the course of the meeting itself, a number of significant agreements were reached.
Limitation of strategic armaments
The two sides gave primary attention to the problem of reducing the danger of nuclear war.
The two sides attach great importance to the treaty on the limitation of anti-ballistic systems and the interim agreement on certain measures with respect to the limitation of strategic offensive arms concluded between them. These agreements, which were concluded as a result of the negotiations in Moscow, constitute a major step towards curbing and ultimately ending the arms race.
The two sides intended to continue active negotiations for the limitation of strategic offensive arms and to conduct them in a spirit of goodwill, respect for each

other's legitimate interests and observance of the principle of equal security.

Commercial and economic relations

Both sides agreed on measures designed to establish more favourable conditions for developing commercial and other economic ties between the USA and the USSR.

Maritime matters: Incidents at sea

The two sides agreed to continue the negotiations aimed at reaching an agreement on maritime and related matters. An agreement was concluded between the two sides on measures to prevent incidents at sea and in air space over it between vessels and aircraft of the United States and Soviet navies. By providing agreed procedures for ships and aircraft of the two navies operating in close proximity, this agreement will diminish the chances of dangerous accidents.

Co-operation in science and technology

The two sides signed an agreement for co-operation in the fields of science and technology. A United States–Soviet Joint Commission on Scientific and Technical Co-operation will be created for identifying and establishing co-operation programmes.

Co-operation in Space

The two sides agreed to make suitable arrangements to permit the docking of American and Soviet spacecraft and stations. The first joint docking experiment of the two countries' piloted spacecraft, with visits by astronauts and cosmonauts to each other's spacecraft, is contemplated for 1975.

Co-operation in the field of health

The two sides concluded an agreement on health co-operation which marks a fruitful beginning of sharing knowledge about, and collaborative attacks on, the common enemies, disease and disability.

Environment co-operation

The two sides agreed to initiate a programme of co-operation in the protection and enhancement of man's environment.

Exchanges in the field of science, technology, education and culture

The two sides have agreed to expand the areas of co-operation, as reflected in new agreements concerning space, health, the environment and science and technology.

II. International issues

Europe

In the course of the discussions on the international situation, both sides took note of favourable developments in the relaxation of tensions in Europe.

Recognizing the importance to world peace of developments in Europe ... the USA and the USSR, intend to make further efforts to ensure a peaceful future for Europe, free of tensions, crises and conflicts. They agree that the territorial integrity of all States in Europe should be respected.

Both sides view the September 3, 1971, quadripartite agreement relating to the Western sectors of Berlin as a good example of fruitful co-operation between the States concerned, including the USA and the USSR. Both sides welcomed the treaty between the USSR and the Federal Republic of Germany signed on August 12, 1970. The USA and the USSR are in accord that multilateral consultations looking towards a conference on security and co-operation in Europe could begin after the signature of the final quadripartite protocol of the agreement of September 3, 1971.

The two Governments agree that the conference should be carefully prepared in order that it may concretely consider specific problems of security and co-operation and thus contribute to the progressive reduction of the underlying causes of tension in Europe. This conference should be convened at a time to be agreed by the countries concerned, but without undue delay.

Both sides believe that the goal of ensuring stability and security in Europe would be served by a reciprocal reduction of armed forces and armaments, first of all in Central Europe.

The Middle East

The two sides ... reaffirm their support for a peaceful settlement in the Middle East in accordance with Security Council Resolution 242.

Noting the significance of constructive co-operation of the parties concerned with the special representative of the United Nations Secretary-General, Ambassador Jarring, the USA and the USSR confirm their desire to contribute to his mission's success and also declare their readiness to play their part in bringing about a peaceful settlement in the Middle East.

Indo-China

Each side set forth its respective standpoint with regard to the continuing war in Vietnam and the situation in the area of Indo-China as a whole.

The United States side emphasizes the need to bring an end to the military conflict as soon as possible and reaffirmed its commitment to the principle that the political future of South Vietnam should be left for the South Vietnamese people to decide for themselves, free from outside interference.

The United States reiterated its willingness to enter into serious negotiations with the North Vietnamese side to settle the war in Indo-China on a basis just to all. The Soviet side stressed its solidarity with the just struggle of the peoples of Vietnam, Laos and Cambodia for their freedom, independence and social progress.

Disarmament issues

The two sides note that in recent years their joint and parallel actions have facilitated the working out and conclusion of treaties which curb the arms race or ban some of the most dangerous types of weapons.

Both sides regard the convention on the prohibition of the development and stockpiling of bacteriological (biological) and toxic weapons, and on their destruction as an essential disarmament measure.

Along with Great Britain, they are the depositories for the convention which was recently opened for signature by all States. The USA and the USSR will continue their efforts to reach an international agreement regarding chemical weapons.

The USA and the USSR, will actively participate in negotiations aimed at working out new measures designed to curb and end the arms race. The ultimate purpose is general and complete disarmament, including nuclear disarmament, under strict international control. A world disarmament conference could play a role in this process at an appropriate time.

Strengthening the United Nations

Both sides will strive to strengthen the effectiveness of the United Nations on the basis of strict observance of the United Nations Charter.

Both sides emphasized that agreements and understandings reached in the negotiations in Moscow, as well as the contents and nature of these negotiations, are not in any way directed against any other country. Both sides believe that positive results were accomplished in the course of the talks at the highest level. Both sides expressed the desire to continue close contact on a number of issues that were under discussion. They agreed that regular consultations on questions of mutual interest, including meetings at the highest level, would be useful.

In expressing his appreciation for the hospitality accorded him in the Soviet Union, President Nixon invited General Secretary L.I. Brezhnev, Chairman N.V. Podgorny, and Chairman A.N. Kosygin to visit the United States at a mutually convenient time. This invitation was accepted."

UST 1972; Recueil de Documents, No. 5, 1972.

MOSCOW CONFERENCE, 1943. The conference of American, British and Soviet foreign ministers, from Oct. 19 to 30, 1943 in Moscow, adopted four Moscow Declarations (concerning universal security; Italy; Austria; and the responsibility of Germany for war crimes). Also discussed was stepping up action to defeat Germany and its allies in Europe. The US and British foreign ministers declined to assume the obligation to form a second front in northern France by Spring 1944 as demanded by the Soviet delegation. The timing for this was finally settled at the ▷ Teheran Conference, 1943. The Moscow Conference recognized as indispensable the establishment of a European Advisory Commission to ensure closer co-operation between the three allies on European matters emerging in the course of war operations.

Diplomaticheski Slovar, Moskva, 1971, Vol. 2.

MOSCOW DECLARATION, 1945. A declaration by Foreign Ministers of the UK, USA, and USSR, published after a Three-Power Conference from Dec. 16 to 26, 1945 in Moscow referring to agreements on preparation of peace treaties with Bulgaria, Finland, Hungary, Italy and Romania (▷ Paris Peace Conference, 1946); the setting up of the ▷ Far Eastern Commission with the Allied Council for Japan; the re-establishment of Korea as an independent state and the establishment by the UN of a Commission for the Control of Nuclear Energy.

"Three-Power Conference at Moscow", in: *International Conciliation*, No. 418, February, 1946, pp. 101–112; UNTS, Vol. 20, pp. 259–293.

MOSCOW DECLARATION ON A GENERAL INTERNATIONAL ORGANIZATION, 1943. The Declaration issued on Oct. 30, 1943 after the Conference in Moscow of the Foreign Ministers of UK, US and USSR and the Chinese Ambassador, affirming that they recognize "the necessity of establishing at the earliest practicable date a General International Organization." The first document initiating the foundation of the UN, read as follows:

"The Governments of the United States of America, the United Kingdom, the Soviet Union and China:
United in their determination, in accordance with the Declaration by the United Nations of January 1, 1942, and subsequent declarations, to continue hostilities against those Axis powers with which they respectively are at war until such powers have laid down their arms on the basis of unconditional surrender;
conscious of their responsibility to secure the liberation of themselves and the peoples allied with them from the menace of aggression;
recognizing the necessity of ensuring a rapid and orderly transition from war to peace and of establishing and maintaining international peace and security with the least diversion of the world's human and economic resources for armaments;
jointly declare:
(1) That their united action, pledged for the prosecution of the war against their respective enemies, will be continued for the organization and maintenance of peace and security.
(2) That those of them at war with a common enemy will act together in all matters relating to the surrender and disarmament of that enemy.
(3) That they will take all measures deemed by them to be necessary to provide against any violation of the terms imposed upon the enemy.
(4) That they recognize the necessity of establishing at the earliest practicable date a general international organization, based on the principle of the sovereign equality of all peace-loving states, and open to membership by all such states, large and small, for the maintenance of international peace and security.
(5) That for the purpose of maintaining international peace and security pending the re-establishment of law and order and the inauguration of a system of general security, they will consult with one another and as occasion requires with other members of the United Nations with a view to join action on behalf of the community of nations.
(6) That after the termination of hostilities they will not employ their military forces within the territories of other states except for the purposes envisaged in this declaration and after joint consultation.
(7) That they will confer and cooperate with one another and with other members of the United Nations to bring about a practicable general agreement with respect to the regulation of armaments in the post-war period."

US Department of State Bulletin, November 6, 1943, p. 308; Yearbook of the UN, 1946–47, p. 3.

MOSCOW DECLARATION ON GERMANY, 1954. Declaration by the Governments of Albania, Bulgaria, China, Czechoslovakia, the GDR, Hungary, Poland, Romania and the USSR, signed at Moscow on Dec. 2, 1954. The text is as follows:

"Representatives of the Union of Soviet Socialist Republics, the Polish People's Republic, the Czechoslovak Republic, the German Democratic Republic, the Hungarian People's Republic, the Romanian People's

Republic, the People's Republic of Bulgaria and the People's Republic of Albania, with an observer from the People's Republic of China, have met at a conference in Moscow in order to examine the situation that has come about in Europe in connexion with the decisions of the London and Paris Conferences of certain Western States.

The Governments of the States participating in this Conference regret that not all European countries have found it possible to take part in the discussion of the situation which has arisen. The sponsors of the London and Paris Agreements – the United States of America, France and the United Kingdom – have likewise refrained from participating. Their reply of 29 November indicates that they are determined to ensure, at all costs, that the Paris Agreements are ratified.

Agreements concerning West Germany were signed at a conference in Paris on 23 October 1954 after a conference of nine countries – United States of America, United Kingdom, France, West Germany, Italy, Belgium, Netherlands, Luxembourg and Canada – had been held in London. These agreements provide for the remilitarization of West Germany and its inclusion in military groups – the North Atlantic bloc and the so-called "Western European Union" which is in process of formation.

Attempts were made very recently to revive German militarism through the remilitarization of West Germany under the flag of the notorious "European Defence Community." In the face of the natural opposition of the European peoples, and above all the French people, those attempts failed. Now an attempt is being made to revive German militarism under a different flag, and every effort is being made to expedite the ratification of the Paris Agreements to this end.

In these circumstances the Governments of the States participating in this Conference consider it necessary to draw the attention of all European States to the fact that application of the Paris Agreements will cause a serious deterioration of the international situation in Europe. It will not only create new and even greater obstacles to the settlement of the German question and the reunification of Germany as a peace-loving and democratic State; it will also pit one part of Germany against the other and convert West Germany into a dangerous breeding-ground for a new war in Europe. Instead of facilitating a peaceful settlement of the German question, these agreements give a free hand to the militarist and revanchist elements in West Germany, thereby increasing the threat to the security of the European peoples.

The Paris Agreements run directly counter to the possibilities for a further relaxation of international tension which have recently become apparent. Thanks to the efforts of peace-loving States, the Korean war was brought to an end in the middle of last year. The Geneva Conference of this year helped to bring the eight-year-old war in Indochina to an end and to regularize the situation in that area to some extent. It must further be noted that some progress has been made in the negotiations in the United Nations on the general reduction of armaments and the prohibition of atomic weapons. All this has been achieved despite the attitude of aggressive elements in certain States which seek to render the international situation more acute. Yet precisely at this juncture, when conditions have become more favourable for the solution of pressing international problems, the ruling circles in certain States parties to the London and Paris Agreements have adopted the dangerous course of reviving German militarism in utter disregard of the consequences.

The Paris Agreements provide for the creation of a West German army of half a million men. The strength of these West German armed forces is five times that of the army formerly allowed to the whole of Germany under the Versailles Treaty of Peace, although it is known that the German Reichswehr of 100,000 men established at that time served as foundation for the formation of a Hitlerite army many millions strong. Even now the German militarists do not conceal their intention to expand the West German army further and enlarge it from twelve to thirty, and later to sixty, divisions. The establishment of a West German army will, in fact, mean that that army will preponderate over those of the other members of the Western European Union and, inevitably, that the armed forces at the disposal of the West German militarists will hold a dominant position in Western Europe.

The danger implicit in the creation of a West German army is sufficiently evident from the fact that it will be commanded by generals of the former Hitlerite army, who only recently were the organizers of and accomplices in fascist aggression against the peoples of both Eastern and Western Europe.

In defiance of international agreements for the elimination of German war potential, industry for war production is being openly rebuilt in West Germany. To an ever-increasing degree, heavy industry in the Ruhr is switching to the production of armaments. It should not be forgotten that it is this same Ruhr which has repeatedly been the main arsenal where weapons for the German militarists' aggressive wars have been forged. Furthermore the Paris Agreements make provision for atomic research, which will make possible the production of atomic and hydrogen weapons in West Germany, and also for the supply of atomic weapons to West Germany by other States. Under these agreements West Germany will be able to include atomic weapons in its armoury.

This means that atomic weapons will fall into the hands of the very men who only recently, in implanting Hitler's bloodthirsty "new order," were sowing death and destruction in Europe and planning to wipe out entire peoples; the very men who, in their death camps, slaughtered millions of civilians – Poles, Russians, Jews, Ukrainians, Byelorussians, Frenchmen, Serbs, Czechs, Slovaks, Belgians, Norwegians and others. It means that atomic weapons will be at the disposal of the very men who even now announce their plans for revenge in Europe. The application of these agreements will greatly increase the danger of a destructive atomic war, with all its disastrous consequences for the peoples, especially those of the most densely populated parts of Europe.

The peoples of Europe view with justifiable scepticism the expectation that the inclusion of a remilitarized West Germany in a Western European military alliance will make it possible to set some sort of limits to the growth of German militarism. Such attempts have been made before, but have always ended in fiasco. Peace in Europe cannot be secured by opening the way for a rebirth of German militarism and lulling oneself by devising safeguards against it which are quite obviously ineffective. If peace in Europe is to be secured, the rebirth of German militarism must be made an impossibility.

Remilitarization of West Germany means that the weight and influence of militarist and revanchist elements in that country will grow ever greater, with the inevitable result that democratic freedoms in West Germany will be further curtailed and the country converted into a militarist State. It is characteristic that there was no room in the Paris Agreements for provisions to secure the democratic rights of the West German population, whereas they do contain a provision placing the West German authorities under an obligation to enact legislation concerning a 'state of emergency,' which is obviously directed against the democratic rights and freedoms of the population.

By reviving German militarism and giving the militarists virtual authority and emergency powers, the Paris Agreements pave the way for the establishment of a military dictatorship in West Germany. Not only are these Agreements foreign to the interests of the German people; they are aimed directly against the German working class and are intended to stifle the democratic forces in West Germany. The conditions which the Paris Agreements propose to establish in West Germany are in many respects reminiscent of the situation which existed in Germany shortly before the Hitlerites came to power. It is no secret that the powers possessed by Hindenburg, the then President of Germany, to proclaim a 'state of emergency' were used by the German militarists to destroy democratic rights and freedoms, suppress labour organizations and establish a fascist dictatorship in Germany. The Paris Agreements speak of 'the termination of the occupation regime' and the conferment of so-called 'sovereignty' on West Germany. But in reality the West German 'sovereignty' to which the Paris Agreements refer merely means the grant to the West German militarists and revanchists of the right to form an army which the sponsors of the Paris Agreements propose to use as cannon-fodder to further their own ends.

Furthermore the Paris Agreements force on West Germany the extension until 1998 of the occupation of

its territory by United States, United Kingdom and French forces, and thus propose to make West Germany the main bridgehead for the furtherance of United States aggressive designs in Europe. In these circumstances it is not difficult to gauge the true value of the references to so-called West German 'sovereignty', especially when it is remembered that the Paris Agreements leave intact all the basic provisions of the one-sided Bonn Convention.

Despite the assertions of certain Western statesmen, the Paris Agreements can only be regarded as a virtual refusal to solve the German problem, a refusal to reunify Germany on peaceful and democratic lines for a long time to come. The plans to remilitarize West Germany and include it in military groups are now the chief obstacle to the national reunification of Germany. Hence the removal of that obstacle would make it possible for the four Powers to reach agreement on the restoration of the unity and sovereignty of Germany and, to that end, the holding of free elections throughout Germany with due regard to the interests of the German people.

It is estimated in political quarters in Bonn that to form and arm a West German army half a million strong will cost some 100,000 million marks, the whole burden of which will fall upon the working people of West Germany and primarily upon the working class, inevitably causing a sharp decline in their level of living. The remilitarization of West Germany promises to benefit only the great West German monopolies and the vast United States, United Kingdom and French monopolies closely associated with them, which are already anticipating enormous profits from the supply of arms for the projected West German army. These armament dealers have more than once battened on wars which have brought the peoples of Europe only limitless sacrifice and privation.

What is happening now is a repetition of events before the Second World War, when German concerns forged weapons for Hitlerite aggression with the support and direct participation of foreign, especially United States, monopolies. Today United States Government agencies are coming increasingly under the influence of the capitalist monopolies which once helped to engineer and unleash the Second World War.

The Paris Agreements are evidence that once again the ruling circles of certain Powers, and first and foremost the United States of America, are banking on the resurgence of German militarism and are seeking support in the accomplishment of their imperialist designs in the remilitarization of West Germany. These agreements create a military block linking aggressive elements in the United States, the United Kingdom and France with German militarism. They represent a deal transacted behind the back of the German people and the peoples of other European States who, it is common knowledge, were not consulted by anyone when these agreements were drafted.

Such an aggressive bloc cannot serve the interests of peace and security in Europe. Its creation renders the whole situation in Europe more acute, and greatly increases the threat of a new world war.

The formation of the new military bloc runs counter to the Franco–Soviet Treaty of Alliance and Mutual Assistance of 1944 and the Anglo–Soviet Treaty of 1942 concerning Collaboration and Mutual Assistance after the War, which provide for the adoption by France, the United Kingdom and the Soviet Union of joint measures to render impossible new aggression by German militarism. It also runs counter to international agreements concluded by the States participating in this Conference and by other States, with the object of guaranteeing peace and security for all European States. The remilitarization of West Germany and its inclusion in military groups are likewise incompatible with the international obligation not to permit a resurgence of German militarism which was assumed by the United States of America and the United Kingdom, and later by France, under the Potsdam Agreement. This violation of the obligations assumed by the United States, France and the United Kingdom under these treaties and agreements undermines confidence in relations between States and is utterly irreconcilable with the security of the peoples of Europe.

The formation of this new military group is defended on the ground that it is essential to the security of its member States, although in reality these States are threatened by no one. An attempt is made to justify the remilitarization of West Germany and its inclusion in military groups embracing certain Western countries by the argument that relations with the Soviet Union and the people's democracies should be based on 'a position of strength'. It is claimed that such a policy will help to create more favourable conditions for negotiation and the settlement of outstanding international problems. The advocates of this policy, which is already substantially discredited, do not conceal their desire to impose on other States decisions advantageous to the imperialist elements of certain Western Powers. In reality the policy reflects the ambition of these elements to dominate the world. However, the eventual outcome of similar attempts by past aspirants to world domination should not be forgotten. Military alignments of certain European States directed against other European States have, of course, existed in the past. On the eve of the Second World War, Hitlerite Germany and fascist Italy formed an aggressive military group which was later joined by militarist Japan. The organizers of this group, known as the 'Anti-Comintern Pact', endeavoured to justify its formation on 'ideological' grounds. In reality, however, this was merely a screen behind which they tried to conceal the true aggressive character of this military bloc, whose aim was to achieve world supremacy. It is a known fact that the organizers of this military group were chiefly responsible for the outbreak of the Second World War.

Something of a similar nature is taking place today, when the organizers of the new military groups seek to justify their formation by referring to differences in the social structure of States. But there is no more truth in their assertions than there was in those made by the founders of the 'Anti-Comintern Pact', who used that pact to engineer and unleash the late World War.

It is clear from the foregoing that, no matter what arguments are advanced in their support, military groups composed of certain Western States and a remilitarized West Germany, far from being able to serve the cause of peace and security in Europe, merely introduce serious complications into the situation in Europe and will inevitably intensify the armaments race, with all its dangerous consequences not only for all European States but for other States too.

If these military groups in Europe should enlarge their armies, air forces and other armed services and go to the length of reviving aggressive German militarism, the other European States will inevitably be compelled to take effective measures to defend themselves and guard against attack.

Accordingly, all States concerned to safeguard peace and security in Europe must endeavour to prevent the revival of German militarism, avert the possibility of an intensification of the armaments race, and assist in uniting the efforts of all European States in order to safeguard security in Europe.

Recognizing that settlement of the German question is the major task in the consolidation of peace in Europe, the Governments of the USSR, the Polish People's Republic, the Czechoslovak Republic, the German Democratic Republic, the Hungarian People's Republic, the Romanian People's Republic, the People's Republic of Bulgaria and the People's Republic of Albania consider that the solution of the German question requires first and foremost:

Renunciation of plans for the remilitarization of West Germany and its inclusion in military groups; this will remove the main obstacle to the reunification of Germany on peaceful and democratic lines;

Attainment of agreement on the holding of free elections throughout Germany in 1955 and the formation, on the basis of those elections, of an all-German Government for a unified, democratic and peace-loving Germany.

Then at last it will be possible to conclude a peace treaty with Germany, which is essential for the establishment of a lasting peace in Europe.

It must be recognized that the withdrawal of occupation forces from East and West Germany, as proposed by the Soviet Union, would do much to effect a rapprochement between the two parts of Germany and to solve the problem of German reunification.

It is essential for the security of Europe that the Powers concerned should reach agreement on the question of German unification, which would serve the interests of all the peace-loving peoples of Europe and of the German people themselves. The course of remilitarizing West Germany and including it in military groups

which has been adopted by the United States of America, France and the United Kingdom makes it impossible to reach such agreement. Far from contributing to European security, that course is regarded by all peace-loving peoples as reflecting a policy which imperils the preservation of peace in Europe. Genuine security in Europe can be assured only if, instead of closed military groups being formed among certain European States and directed against other European States, a system of collective security is established in Europe. Such a system of security, based on the participation of all European States irrespective of their social and political systems, would make it possible for the European States to unite their efforts for the protection of peace in Europe. It stands to reason that the German people must be allowed to join in solving this general European problem on an equal footing with other peoples. The United States of America and other States bearing responsibility for the settlement of the German question, which is of decisive importance for the peace of Europe, would also be able to participate in this collective security system.

The general European system of collective security should provide for the assumption by all its participant States of an obligation to settle all disputes that may arise among them, in accordance with the provisions of the United Nations Charter, in such a manner that peace and security in Europe are not endangered. It should provide for consultation whenever any of the participant States considers that a threat of armed attack has arisen in Europe, so that effective measures may be taken to remove that threat. To be effective, this system must provide that an attack on one or more States in Europe shall be regarded as an attack on all the parties to the relevant general European treaty, and that each party shall afford the State so attacked assistance by all the means at its disposal, including the use of armed force, in order to restore and maintain peace and security in Europe. The establishment of such an all-European system of collective security would wholly meet the need to strengthen international co-operation in accordance with the principles of respect for the independence and sovereignty of States large and small and of non-intervention in their domestic affairs. It would also greatly increase the possibility of a solution of the German problem in that it would preclude the conversion of West Germany into a militarist State and would create favourable conditions for the reunification of Germany.

The organization of collective security in Europe and the unification of Germany on peaceful and democratic lines constitute the course of action which will ensure Germany's development as one of the great Powers. In contrast to the militaristic course taken by Germany's development in the past, which has repeatedly had the direst consequences for the German nation, the reunification of Germany within a framework of collective security in Europe will offer ample prospects for the growth of Germany's peace economy, industry and agriculture and for the development of extensive economic ties between Germany and other countries, especially the Eastern European countries and the countries of Asia, with their huge populations and inexhaustible resources. The development of Germany in the enjoyment of peaceful conditions and extensive economic ties with other States would provide its industries with vast markets, assure employment for its population and promote the improvement of its level of living. Germany's destiny as a great Power thus depends closely on whether it takes the course of peaceful development and co-operation with all other European States or the course of preparing a new war. The course of peaceful development and international co-operation followed by the German Democratic Republic leads to regeneration and prosperity for Germany. The other course, into which the German militarists are seeking to direct West Germany, leads to a new war and, hence, to the conversion of West Germany into a region of fire and destruction.

All this goes to prove that the true national interests of the German people are inseparable from the interests of peace and the establishment of an effective system of collective security in Europe.

The States participating in this Conference fully endorse the principles formulated in the draft 'General European Treaty concerning Collective Security in Europe' proposed by the Government of the USSR, and call upon all European States jointly to examine

these proposals, which fulfil the requirements for the establishment of a lasting peace in Europe. They also state that they are prepared to examine any other proposals made on this subject with a view to the preparation of a draft treaty concerning European collective security acceptable to all States concerned.

The States participating in this Conference are profoundly convinced that security in Europe based upon the principles set forth above and fortified by friendly relations among European States would make it possible to put an end to a situation in which Europe is periodically visited by devastating wars and limitless sacrifice is exacted from the European peoples.

The question of ratifying the Paris Agreements will shortly be under discussion in the parliaments of certain Western States. Official circles in certain States are exerting ever-increasing pressure on the parliaments and the public in order to force through the ratification of these agreements. In these circumstances the Governments of the USSR, the Polish People's Republic, the Czechoslovak Republic, the German Democratic Republic, the Hungarian People's Republic, the Romanian People's Republic, the People's Republic of Bulgaria and the People's Republic of Albania consider it their duty to draw the attention of all European States, and especially of the States parties to the Paris Agreements, to the fact that ratification of these agreements will be an act directed against the preservation of peace and towards the preparation of a new war in Europe. Such ratification will greatly complicate the whole situation in Europe and undermine the possibility of settling outstanding European problems, and first and foremost the German problem.

The ratification and application of these agreements, by increasing the danger of war, will represent a threat to the national security of the peace-loving States of Europe, especially those States which are Germany's neighbours. This threat arises from the fact that the States parties to the Paris Agreements are constantly increasing the scope of their military and economic measures against the peace-loving States of Europe. They have now gone to the length of entering into a military bloc with German militarism, they are proceeding to remilitarize West Germany with their own hands and are threatening the future peaceful existence of the States which are not members of their military groups. The armed forces of the States parties to the Paris Agreements are now to include a West German army, headed by Hitlerite generals. This means that for the future the policy of operating from 'a position of strength' will be pursued with the direct support of resurgent German militarism, which brings the danger of a new war in Europe much closer. The situation which has arisen makes it necessary for the States represented at this Conference to consider ways and means of joining forces to safeguard their security. The peace-loving States are compelled to adopt urgent measures in order to confront the aggressive forces of this military bloc of Western Powers with their combined might, in order to protect their security.

The States parties to this Conference declare that they have decided that, if the Paris Agreements are ratified, they will take concerted action relating to the organization and command of their armed forces and such other action as may be necessary to reinforce their defensive strength, in order to defend the peaceful labour of their peoples, guarantee the inviolability of their frontiers and territories and afford protection against possible aggression.

All such measures are in accordance with the inherent right of States to self-defence, with the Charter of the United Nations, and with the treaties and agreements previously concluded for the purpose of preventing the resurgence of German militarism and the renewal of aggression in Europe.

The States participating in this Conference have agreed that, if the Paris Agreements are ratified, they will re-examine the situation with a view to taking the necessary steps to safeguard their security and to promote the maintenance of peace in Europe.

The States participating in this Conference are resolved to continue to press for the creation of a system of collective security in Europe, in the conviction that only the concerted efforts of the European States can provide the basis for a stable and lasting peace in Europe. To this end they remain prepared to co-operate with such other European States as may express their desire to adopt this course.

M

The Governments of the States participating in the Moscow Conference of European Countries on the safeguarding of peace and security in Europe are profoundly convinced that their policy, which is designed to strengthen peace and general security, and the measures outlined at this Conference accord with the interests of our peoples and of all other peace-loving peoples.The peoples of the Soviet Union, Poland, Czechoslovakia, Hungary, Romania, Bulgaria, Albania and the German Democratic Republic are engaged in peaceful, constructive labours. Their efforts are directed towards further economic and cultural progress and the steady improvement of the level of living of the workers and, at the same time, towards ensuring the firm defence of their great socialist achievements. There is no power on earth that can turn back the wheel of history and impede the building of socialism in our countries.
The peoples of our States recognize that the Paris Agreements have considerably increased the threat of a new war; but they will not allow the course of events to take them by surprise.
Our peoples have confidence in their strength and their inexhaustible resources. The forces of peace and socialism are strong and united as never before. Any attempt to attack, to unleash war and to disrupt the peaceful life of our peoples will meet with an overwhelming rebuff; and then our peoples, sustained by the sympathy and support of other peoples, will spare no effort to destroy the forces of aggression and to secure the triumph of our just and righteous cause.
Our peoples desire to live in peace and to enjoy friendly relations with all other peoples. For this very reason, while continuing in every way to uphold the interests of peace and general security, they will do everything essential to ensure their further peaceful development and the necessary security of their States."

UNTS, Vol. 226, 1956, pp. 153–186.

MOSCOW NARODNY BANK LTD. The Soviet merchant international bank, est. on Oct. 18, 1919 in London commonly known as The Bank for East–West Trade, with branches in Beirut (from 1963) and Singapore (1971) and with representative office in Moscow. Correspondent in London for banks throughout the world, including in particular the State Bank of the USSR (▷ Gosbank SSSR), Bank for Foreign Trade of the USSR, International Bank for Economic Co-operation and the International Investment Bank.

MOSCOW OPTION OR MOSCOW CRITERION. An international military term for the NATO strategic project dating from the mid-1960's to damage the ▷ GALOSH anti ballistic missile defence screen around Moscow and destroy Moscow in retaliation for a nuclear attack on the United Kingdom. This 'unofficial but widely accepted plan' was a subject of disputes inside NATO.

D. ROBERTSON, *Guide to Modern Defense and Strategy*, Detroit, 1988.

MOSCOW PEACE TREATY FINLAND–USSR, 1940. The peace treaty signed on Mar. 12, 1940 in Moscow, ending the armed conflict between the USSR and Finland which began on Nov. 30, 1939; the treaty outlined new state frontiers which were more advantageous to the USSR from the strategic point of view (art. 2); lease of Hango island by Finland for a duration of 30 years for 8 million Finnish Marks annually (art. 4); in keeping with the Dorpat Peace of Oct. 14, 1920, a ban against the presence of Finnish warships in the Arctic Sea (art. 5); the right of transit to Sweden for the USSR (art. 7); annulled on June 26, 1941.

C.A. COLLIARD, *Droit international et Histoire Diplomatique*, Paris, 1950.

MOSCOW RED SQUARE. A historical place in the center of the capital of Russia, adjacent to the Kremlin. In 1987, a 21 year old German civil pilot Mathias Rust from Hanover, coming from Helsinki; without any intervention of the Soviet air defense landed a small Cessna type plane in the Red Square. He was sentenced in Sept. 4, 1987 by a Moscow court to 4 years in a Soviet Labor Camp, for hooliganism, breaking flight rules and entering the USSR illegally.

MOSCOW TREATY 1963. ▷ Outer Space Moscow Treaty 1963.

MOSELLE RIVER. *French*: Moselle, *German*: Mosel. The left bank tributary of Rhine, 545 km long, it rises in France in the Vosges, confluence with the Rhine at Coblentz. Subject of an agreement, 1956, between France, the FRG and Luxembourg on a Moselle canal from Metz to Coblentz, open in 1964 for 13,000–15,000 ton ships.

MOSER DOCTRINE. An international term accepted in international law for the thesis of the German jurist, Johann Jacob Moser (1701–85), elaborated in a work entitled, *Basis for Legal Principles During War*, publ. 1752 in Stuttgart, stating that captured soldiers who have broken laws and practices of war during military actions should be treated as ordinary criminals. This was the first doctrine relating to the punishment of war criminals.

J.J. MOSER, *Versuch des neuesten europäischen Völkerrechts*, 10 Vols., 1777–80.

MOSLEM. ▷ Muslim.

MOSS NEGOTIATIONS. Market-Oriented Sector Specific talks between the USA and Japan, started 1986, ended on Jan. 8, 1987 having achieved great progress in the area of telecommunication and a joint agreement of the Governments to continue negotiations on new sectors.

MOST FAVOURED NATION, IMF CLAUSE. An economic term in the UN system for the principle under which the most favorable terms of trade extended by one country to another are automatically extended to all other trading partners who have MFN status, e.g. the GATT member states.
An Agreement on the Application of the Most Favoured-Nation Clause was opened for signature at the Pan-American Union in Washington, DC, on July 15, 1934 and signed by Belgium, Luxembourg, Colombia, Cuba, Greece, Guatemala, Nicaragua, Panama and the USA, and ratified by Cuba and the USA in 1935 and by Greece in 1938.
The GA Res. 43/429 adopted without a Vote on Dec. 9, 1988.

"(a) Took note of the complexity of codification of progressive development of the international law on most-favoured-nation-clauses;
(b) Considered that additional time should be given to Governments for thorough study of draft articles and for determining their respective positions on the most appropriate procedure work, including the forum for further discussion;
(c) Decided to include in the provisional agenda of its forty-sixth session the item entitled "Consideration on the draft articles on most-favoured-nation clauses".
CARNEGIE ENDOWMENT, International Legislation, 9 Vols., Washington, DC, 1939; *UN Chronicle*, October, 1982, p. 48; December, 1983, p. 76; *UN Resolutions and Decisions adopted by the General Assembly during the first part of its Forty-Third Session*, from 20 September to 22 December, 1988.

MOST SERIOUSLY AFFECTED COUNTRIES, MSAC. An international term in the UN system for countries suffering severe balance-of-payment deficits as a result of global inflation.

UN Chronicle, October, 1982, p. 47.

MOSUL. The Mosul Province in Iraq, with a town of the same name, subject of international dispute between 1916 and 1926, touched off by the confidential treaty between France and Great Britain (Sykes–Picot Treaty 1916), guaranteeing Mosul to France after conquering Turkey, which occurred on Oct. 30, 1918, after the latter's capitulation at Mudros. During the Versailles Conference of 1919, France renounced control over Mosul in favour of Great Britain, which became the Mandatory power under the League of Nations for the whole Iraqi territory. British troops entered Mosul in accordance with the decision of the Entente Conference in San Remo of Apr. 26, 1920 and the Treaty of Sèvres, concluded with the sultanate of Turkey on Aug. 10, 1920 which, however, was not recognized by the revolutionary government of Kemal Pasha. The dispute was considered at the Peace Conference in Lausanne between Nov. 20, 1922 and July 24, 1923, but its final settlement at the League of Nations on Mar. 1, 1925 gave Mosul to Iraq, a fact that was accepted by Turkey in the Treaty signed in Ankara on Apr. 5, 1926 with Great Britain and Iraq. The Treaty on the Delimitation and Good-neighbourly Relations between Iraq and Turkey, regulated the question of oil-fields in Mosul in keeping with the Iraqi–British accords of Oct. 10, 1922 and Jan. 1, 1926 and with the decisions taken by the League of Nations on Oct. 29, 1924 on the delimitation of the frontier between Iraq and Turkey. Turkey as compensation for the lost oil-fields in Mosul, received from Iraq a share amounting to 10% of profits from the exploitation of these fields for a period of 25 years.

G.F. DE MARTENS, *Nouveau Recueil Général*, 3 s., Vol. 18, p. 332.

MOTHERS WORLD MOVEMENT. MOUVEMENT MONDIAL DES MÈRES, MMM. International organization reg. with the UIA, f. 1947, Paris. Consultative status with ECOSOC, UNESCO, UNICEF, FAO. Publ.: *MMM Nouvelles et documents*.

Yearbook of International Organizations.

MOTORCYCLES. Subject of international co-operation. Organizations reg. with the UIA:

International Motorcycle Federation, f. 1904, Chambesy, Switzerland. Publ.: *Annuaire international*.
International Union of Cycle and Motor-Cycle Trade and Repairs, f. 1958, Bielefeld, FRG.
Motor Cycle Industry Liaison Committee for the EEC Countries, f. 1962, Paris.
Permanent International Bureau of Motor Cycle Manufacturers, f. 1948, Paris. Consultative status with ECOSOC.

Yearbook of International Organizations.

MOTOR MANUFACTURERS. Organization reg. with the UIA:

International Organization of Motor Manufacturers, f. 1919, Paris, France. Publ.: *Répertoire international de l'industrie automobile*.

Yearbook of International Organizations 1986/87; The Europa Yearbook 1988. A World Survey, Vol. I, London, 1988.

MOTOR TRAFFIC CONVENTION, 1926. An international convention relative to automobile traffic, signed on Apr. 24, 1926, in Paris.

MOTOR VEHICLE CONVENTION, 1970. The European Convention on Compulsory Insurance Against Civil Liability in respect of Motor Vehicles, signed on Apr. 20, 1959 at Strasbourg.

UNTS, Vol. 720, 1970, pp. 119–146.

Multinational Corporations

MOUNT NIMBA STRICT NATURE RESERVE.
A natural site of Guinea included in the ▷ World Heritage UNESCO List. The slopes of Mt. Nimba, with their dense forests lying beneath alpine pasture lands, possess particularly valuable flora and fauna. Two hundred animal species are found only in this reserve, and these include the viviparous toad and chimpanzees which use stones as tools.

UNESCO. *A Legacy for All*, Paris, 1984.

MOURIR POUR DANTZIG? *French* = "Die for Danzig?" A slogan protesting against French involvement in the Polish–German conflict over Danzig, formulated in the spring of 1939 by the French politician Marcel Déat (1894–1955), spokesman for French collaboration with the German Third Reich.

MOUTH OF RIVERS. ▷ Base line of the territorial sea.

MOVEMENT OF PERSONS, INTERNATIONAL. Individual or group travel in peacetime outside one's homeland or place of permanent residence for the purpose of temporarily residing abroad; subject of international studies under UN auspices in connection with the massive geographical mobility of persons which occurred in the second half of the 20th century under the influence of improvements in transportation and international tourism; subject of bilateral and multi-lateral migrational agreements, and treaties on tourism.

G.S. GOODWIN-GILL, *International Law and the Movement of Persons between States*, Oxford, 1978.

MOZAMBIQUE. Member of the UN People's Republic of Mozambique. An African state, bounded by the Indian Ocean, South Africa, Swaziland, Zimbabwe, Zambia, Malawi and Tanzania. Area: 799,380 sq. km. Pop. 1987 est.: 14,591,000 (1980 census: 12,130,000). Capital: Maputo with 354,684 inhabitants census 1970. GNP per capita 1987: US $150. Currency: one metical = 100 centavos. Official language: Portuguese. National Day: June 25, Independence Day, 1975. Member of all UN specialized agencies except WIPO and OAU.
International relations: discovered by Vasco da Gama 1498; occupied by the Portuguese in 16th century as part of Portuguese India, Portuguese colony from 1752 to 1951, until 1974 an Overseas Province of Portugal. The liberation struggle was directed by Frenta de Libertacao de Mozambique, FRELIMO. On June 25, 1975 independent by a Treaty with Portugal. On Mar. 16, 1984 on the frontier River Nhomati the Heads of Government of Mozambique and South Africa signed a Treaty of Non-Aggression and Good-neighbourhood Pact. ▷ South Africa. April 1987, a mutual co-operation and military assistance agreement was signed with Malawi. On Dec. 20, 1988 the GA Res. 43/431 included Mozambique in the list of the least developed countries.

F. ANSPRENGER (ed.), *Eine Dokumentation zum Krieg in Mozambique*, München, 1974; S. HOUSER, H. SHORE, *Mozambique. Dream the Size of Freedom*, New York, 1975; T.H. HENRIKSEN, *Mozambique, A History*, London, 1978; A. ISAACMAN, *La Luta Continua, Building a New Society in Mozambique*, New York, 1978; *The Europa Year Book 1984. A World Survey*, Vol. II, pp. 2082–2092, London, 1984; C. DARCH, *Mozambique*, Oxford, 1987; *UN Resolutions and Decisions adopted by the General Assembly during the First Part of its Forty-Third Session*, from 20 September to 22 December, 1988, New York, 1989, p. 609.

MRV, MULTIPLE RE-ENTRY VEHICLE. An international military term for two or more warheads carried by a single missile. First US multiple warhead missile 1960; USSR – 1968. Subject of USA–USSR negotiations in the 1980's.

D. ROBERTSON, *Guide to Modern Defense and Strategy*, Detroit, 1988.

MUFTI. The authoratative interpreter of the law in Islamic states, acting on the request of a judge or private individual. In the Ottoman empire the Mufti of Istanbul was the highest legal authority. The institution of Mufti was abolished by the Turkish revolution in 1924, but the British administration in Palestine revived the office, nominating the ▷ Mufti of Jerusalem.

Encyclopedia of Islam, London, 1927.

MUFTI OF JERUSALEM. The Muslim population of Israel according to the 1983 census numbered 526,639. The Islamic canon lawyer (▷ Mufti) has his office in Jerusalem since 1921 and his role during the II World War was a subject of political controversy. In Israel the authoritative interpreter of the Koran for the Islamic community.

G. KIRK, *The Middle East in the War*, London, 1953.

MUJAHEDDIN. ▷ Afghanistan.

MULATTO. An international term for persons descended from mixed parentage: Negro and White. ▷ Creole, ▷ Mestizos.

MULTI-CULTURAL SOCIETIES. An international term since the 1980's related to migratory movements, continuing after the II World War, especially in Western Europe, the USA and Canada, Australia, South-East Asia, related also the enormous economic imbalance between ▷ North–South. In the opinion of the Council of Europe the evident North–South interdependence requires North–South solidarity.

Council of Europe, *Information Sheet No. 21*, Strasbourg, 1988, pp. 102–104.

MULTI-FIBRE AGREEMENTS. The agreements concerning ▷ textiles and textile products, signed since the 1970's on the basis of tariff ▷ preferences, established by UNCTAD which do not facilitate the trade, but through auto-limitation agreements a number of developing countries do not export more than a fixed quantity to the EEC countries.

MULTIFIBRE ARRANGEMENT, MFA. GATT arrangement regarding international trade in textiles concluded in Dec. 1973, effective Jan. 1, 1974, extended in Dec. 1977 and Dec. 1981, July 1986 and valid until July 31, 1991; accepted by 43 signatories (1986).
See also ▷ Textiles. International Trade.

MULTILATERAL FORCE. ▷ MLF.

MULTILATERAL INVESTMENT GUARANTY AGENCY, MIGA. Est. 1985 by the World Bank to promote international investment in developing countries through a system of long-term guarantees against commercial risk. The MIGA Convention was signed in June–Sept. 1986 by 11 capital exporting and 34 importing countries. The initial subscriptions provided 457 out of a projected 1000 million ▷ SDR.

KEESING's *Record of World Events*, January, 1987.

MULTINATIONAL CORPORATIONS. According to the UN definition the term "multinational" means that a company or corporation includes more than one nation. The following English and French terms are also used in the UN system:
Cosmocorp (World Corporation) – Cosmosociété (Société à vocation mondiale);
Global Corporation – Société Mondiale;
International Corporation – Société transnationale;
Multinational Company – Société multinationale;
Transnational Corporation – Société transnationale.
The term was introduced in the second half of the 20th century by the large international concerns, mainly American, which had expanded their network of foreign branches and were employing local labor. But despite the multinational personnel, as a rule the essential decisions were made in one-nation headquarters, which in the majority of cases were guided by the interests of their country. According to the opinion of the official representative of the government of Canada at a Symposium of the American Management Association on Feb. 15, 1972 in New York,

the international corporations treat foreign countries as extended colonial bridge-heads of the head office. And so to prevent this, governments should draft an international convention establishing rules of international law for the operations of multinational corporations, whose rapid and unrestricted growth is characteristic of the contemporary world.

In Western Europe American corporations gained such great influence that J. Servan-Schreiber in his book, *The American Challenge*, states that since 1982 the third economic power of the world, besides the USA and USSR, are American corporations in Europe.
At the Third UNCTAD Session in Santiago de Chile, Apr. 25, 1972, the delegate of the Vatican, Bishop Ramon Torrella Cascante, stated that:

Multinational corporations are large private empires, escaping the control of state authorities and international organizations, which results in the fact that in practice they are outside of any control subordinated to the common good of humanity. If we realize the role of these companies, then why should we not carefully study their operations, and then establish limits for them which would take into consideration the common good? Should an international treaty not be negotiated on this matter?

In the USA it is assumed that an international company is a company with sales of more than 100 million dollars, which operates in at least two countries, with its foreign branches accounting for at least 20% of its assets. In 1972 *c*. 4000 companies met these criteria, accounting for 15% of the total world gross national product. The major companies at this time were: General Motors, Exxon, Ford, IBM, General Electric, Chrysler and Texaco.
The European multinational corporations, called from Latin, *Societas Europea*, in abbreviation SE, have the right to operate throughout all of integrated Western Europe on the basis of a special supranational European statute prepared by the EEC and registered by the EEC Court of Justice in Luxembourg. According to the statute, the shares of the corporations can be traded on the stock markets of the member states; these corporations, besides their own board of directors, must have a multinational supervisory council, one-third of whose members are elected by the employees; each member state, taxes the profits earned in that state.
According to sales volume, among the first 20 European multinational companies are i.a.: Royal Dutch/Shell Group, UNILEVER, Philips Gloeilampenfabrieken, Volkswagenwerk GmbH, British Petroleum Company, Imperial Chemical Industries Ltd., British Steel, Montecatini Edison, Siemens, British Leyland Motors, Daimler-Benz AG, Fiat, Thyssen, Farbwerke Hoechst AG, BASF, Renault, General Electric and English

583

M

Electric, Nestle Alimentana Co., Bayer, and Rhône-Poulenc.

In 1971 it was estimated that 75% of the capital of the entire Western world belonged to less than 3% of all industrial and commercial companies; with further concentration by 1985 c. 300 multinational companies will dominate international commerce. In July, 1972 at the motion of the government of Chile ECOSOC resolved that the UN should investigate the operations of multinational companies. In the middle of Sept., 1973 the UN Secretary-General formed a 20-member group of experts which began its work in New York. In a report, published Aug. 12, 1973, on the role of the large international corporations, the UN group of experts stated that in 1971 the aggregate production of the 10 largest corporations (8 of which are based in the USA) amounted to c. 500 billion dollars, which was one-fifth of the gross national product of the entire non-socialist world. As far as the role of the corporations is concerned, the report stated i.a. that in view of the means at their disposal they can successfully violate the national sovereignty of individual states. The report made the suggestion that a "group of outstanding personalities" should recommend i.a. the co-ordinated action of countries on whose territories the multinationals operate and the creation in those countries of a mechanism for investigating the operations of these corporations independent of those organs whose task is to enforce tax and anti-trust legislation. For the developing countries, it was suggested that an international organ be formed which would provide information on dangers stemming from the operations of corporations. The group of experts was transformed by ECOSOC into the UN Committee for Multinational Corporations; the first session was held Mar. 1–12, 1976 in Lima, Peru.

World Directory of Multinational Enterprises, Detroit, 1982. *UN Chronicle*, July, 1983, p. 104; K. ACQUAAH, *International Regulation and Transnational Corporations: The New Reality*, New York, 1986 Ch. PEARSON, *Multinational Corporations, Environment and The Third World*, London, 1987.

MULTINATIONAL OR TRANSNATIONAL ENTERPRISES.
A synonym of ▷ multinational corporations in international usage, also without clear definition in UN studies.

UN Multinational Corporations in World Development, New York, 1973; B. KLAUS, A. SANGHREN, *Transnational Corporation Terminology*, in: *International Associations*, 1978, pp. 577–578.

MUNICH.
German: München. The capital of Bavaria, southwest Germany, on the Isar River. Headquarters of the European Union of Public Accountants, International Basketball Federation, International Catholic Association of Radio and TV, International Copyright Society and others.

Yearbook of International Organizations.

MUNICH AGREEMENT, 1938.
The Agreement or Pact signed on Sept. 29, 1938 in Munich, by heads of government of the German Reich – A. Hitler, and Italy – B. Mussolini and Prime Minister of France – E. Daladier and Great Britain – N. Chamberlain. Entered into force with the signature. The text is as follows:

"Germany, the United Kingdom, France, and Italy, taking into consideration the agreement which has already been reached in principle for cession to Germany of the Sudeten German territory, have agreed on the following terms and conditions governing the said cession and the measures consequent thereon and by this agreement they each hold themselves responsible for the steps necessary to secure its fulfilment:

I. The evacuation will begin on October 1.

II. The United Kingdom, France and Italy agree that the evacuation of the territory shall be completed by October 10 without any existing installations having been destroyed and that the Czechoslovak Government will be held responsible for carrying out the evacuation without damage to the said installations.

III. The conditions governing the evacuation will be laid down in detail by an international commission composed of representatives of Germany, the United Kingdom, France, Italy, and Czechoslovakia.

Occupation by stages of the predominantly German territories by German troops will begin on October 1. The four territories marked on the attached map will be occupied by German troops in the following order:

Territory marked No. 1 on the 1st and 2nd of October; territory marked No. 2 on the 2nd and 3rd of October; territory marked No. 3 on the 3rd, 4th and 5th of October; territory marked No. 4 on the 6th and 7th October.

The remaining territory of preponderantly German character will be ascertained by the aforesaid international commission forthwith and be occupied by German troops by the tenth of October.

The international commission referred to in Paragraph III will determine the territories in which a plebiscite is to be held. These territories will be occupied by international bodies until the plebiscite has been completed. The same commission will fix the conditions in which the plebiscite is to be held, taking as a basis the conditions of the Saar plebiscite. The Commission will also fix a date, not later than the end of November, on which the plebiscite will be held.

There will be a right of option into and out of the transferred territories, the option to be exercised within six months from the date of this agreement.

A German–Czechoslovak commission shall determine details of the option, consider ways for facilitating the transfer of population and settle questions of principle arising out of the said transfer.

The final determination of the frontiers will be carried out by the international commission. This commission will also be entitled to recommend to the four Powers, Germany, the United Kingdom, France and Italy, in certain exceptional cases minor modifications in strictly ethnographical determination of the zones which are to be transferred without plebiscite. The Czechoslovak Government will within a period of four weeks from the date of this agreement release from their military and police forces any Sudeten Germans who may wish to be released and the Czechoslovak Government will within the same period release Sudeten German prisoners who are serving terms of imprisonment for political offenses.

Annex to the Agreement:

His Majesty's Government in the United Kingdom and the French Government in the United Kingdom and the French Government have entered into the above agreement on the basis that they stand by the offer contained in Paragraph IV of the Anglo–French proposals of September 19 relating to an international guarantee of the new boundaries of the Czechoslovak State against unprovoked aggression. When the question of the Polish and Hungarian minorities in Czechoslovakia has been settled, Germany and Italy, for their part, will give a guarantee to Czechoslovakia. The heads of the Governments of the four Powers declare that the problems of the Polish and Hungarian minorities in Czechoslovakia if not settled within three months by agreements between the respective Governments shall form the subject of another meeting of the heads of Governments of the four Powers here present.

Supplementary Declaration:

All questions which may arise out of the transfer of territory shall be considered as coming within the terms of reference to the international commission."

The Munich pact is an exception among interwar treaties as it was not subjected to mandatory registration and publication by the League of Nations in keeping with art. 18 of the Covenant of the League of Nations providing that: "no treaty . . . shall be binding until it is registered." The fact that the German Third Reich and Italy were not members of the League of Nations was of no importance as France and Great Britain were in the League and were bound by the League's Covenant. In 1945 the allied powers recognized the immorality and illegal character of the pact and thereby re-turned to the Czechoslovak frontiers of 1938. The government of the German Democratic Republic reaffirmed in the treaty of friendship and mutual assistance signed with Czechoslovakia in 1967 that "the Munich Agreement is considered invalid from the very beginning with all the consequences arising from this." The government of the Federal Republic of Germany refused to recognize the invalidity of the agreement *ex tunc* (from the very beginning) and took a stance that the agreement was invalid *ex nunc* (only later). Finally, the treaty on normalization of relations signed by heads of the governments of Czechoslovakia and the FRG on Dec. 21, 1973 in Prague, in art. 1 provides that "the Socialist Republic of Czechoslovakia and the Federal Republic of Germany in recognition of mutual relations between them, in keeping with the present treaty consider the Munich Agreement of September 29, 1938, invalid." ▷ Czechoslovakia–FRG Agreement 1973.

Documents on British Foreign Policy 1919–1939, Third Series, Vols. 1–3, London, 1940–50; *Akten zur Deutschen Auswärtigen Politik 1918–1945*, Serie D (1937–1945), Vols. 2 und 4, 1950–51; *International Conciliation. Documents for the Year 1938*, pp. 399–488; H. BATOWSKI, "Munich 1938, the Realization of Pangermans Plans of 1918/19", in: *Polish Western Affairs, Poznań*, No. 2, 1968, pp. 204–224; J.W. WHEELER-BENNET, *Munich: Prologue to Tragedy*, London, 1968; G.L. WENBERG, *Munich After 50 Years*, in: *Foreign Affairs*, Fall., 1988.

MUNICH BRITISH–GERMAN COMMUNIQUÉ, 1938.
A Joint Communiqué issued on Sept. 30, 1938 at Munich by Neville Chamberlain and Adolph Hitler:

"We, the German Führer and Chancellor and the British Prime Minister, have had a further meeting today and are agreed in recognizing the question of Anglo–German relations as of the first importance for the two countries and for Europe. We regard the agreement signed last night and the Anglo–German naval agreement as symbolic of the desire of our two peoples never to go to war with one another again. We are resolved that the method of consultation shall be the method adopted to deal with any other questions that may concern our two countries, and we are determined to continue our efforts to remove probable sources of difference and thus contribute to assure the peace of Europe."

The New York Times, Oct. 1, 1938; E.L. WOODWARD, R. BUTLER (eds.), *Documents on British Foreign Policy 1919–1939*, London, 1974, Vol. 2, p. 640.

MUNICIPAL CO-OPERATION IN THE UN SYSTEM.
The co-operation organized by regional institutions operating under UN auspices such as the co-operation of United Towns (▷ United Towns Organization) and UN campaigns since 1950 in support of Community Development, primarily backward communities or districts, mainly rural. UN activity aims at improving the economic, social, and cultural conditions of such communities, whose integration in the life of the country would enable them to participate fully in national progress. There are two essential elements within this set of processes: the efforts of the population itself to improve its standard of living and technical or other assistance granted by international centers as a result of the initiatives of the population. In 1951 UNESCO created the first regional center of basic education for municipal development in Latin America, CREFAL, and in 1962, a similar one for Asia, AARRO. A separate operation is targeted at Indian villages in the Andes, called Andes Action, Acción Andina.

Organizations reg. with the UIA:

Afro–Asian Rural Reconstruction Organization (AARRO), f. 1962, Delhi.

Council of European Municipalities, f. 1951, Luxembourg. Publ.: *Communes d'Europe, Finances communales*, and others.

Ibero–American Secretariat for Municipal Affairs, Secretariado Ibero–Americano de Municipios, SIAMU, f. 1955, Madrid.

Inter-American Municipal Organization, IMO, f. 1938, New Orleans, USA. Publ.: *Inter-American Municipal Review*.

International Union of Local Authorities, f. 1913, The Hague; advisory status with ECOSOC, UNESCO and UNICEF. Publ.: *Local Government throughout the World*, and studies.

Regional Center for Basic Education for Community Development, Centro Regional de Educacion Fundamental para el Desarrollo de la Comunidad en América Latina, CREFAL; an intergovernmental institution created in 1951 in Patzcuaro (Mexico) on the basis of an agreement by UNESCO with the government of Mexico, in affiliation with FAO, ILO, WHO and OAS, with the task of training cadres which can organize literacy campaigns, elementary education, health services, the construction of housing, etc. in the local economy. In 1951–65 more than 800 persons from all States of the region completed studies in CREFAL. Since 1965 publ.: *Boletin Trimestral del CREFAL*.

Yearbook of International Organizations.

MUOTKAVAARA-KROKFJELLET. The meeting point of the frontiers of Norway, Finland and the USSR, subject of a Protocol signed on Feb. 7, 1953 in Helsinki by these three Governments regarding the maintenance of the frontier mark erected at Muot kavaara-Krokfjellet.

UNTS, Vol. 173, p. 154.

MURFAAMCE. Mutual Reduction of Forces and Armaments and Associated Measures in Central Europe. A term for the tasks of a disarmament conference of 17 states of Eastern and Western Europe and Canada and the USA, which began in Vienna on Oct. 30, 1973, suspended Dec. 15, 1983. A subject of the dispute was ▷ MBFR.

J. GOLDBLAT, *Arms Control Agreements. A Handbook*, New York, 1983.

MUROROA ATOLI. An inhabited atoll in ▷ French Polynesia, site of French ▷ nuclear tests in the 1970's and 1980's. International opposition against the tests was expressed in resolutions of the Asian and Pacific Commonwealth summit meeting and by the ▷ South Pacific Forum in August 1985, as also by the South Pacific Permanent Commission and the European Parliament.

In March 1988 the French government decided to transfer its South Pacific underground nuclear test site from Muroroa Atoll to the island of Fangataufa some 40 km away.

KEESING's *Contemporary Archive*, September, 1985; KEESING's *Record of World Events*, May, 1988.

MUSCAT. The capital of Oman, main market for East African slaves in the 18th and early 19th century until the General Peace Treaty concluded by the Sultan of Muscat and Oman with Great Britain in 1882.

MUSCAT AND OMAN. The historical name of the Sultanate ▷ Oman, until 1970.

I. SHEET, *Muscat and Oman. The End of an Era*, London, 1974.

MUSEUMS. A subject of international co-operation.

Organizations reg. with the UIA:

African Museums Association, f. 1977, Lusaka.
Association of European Open Air Museums, f. 1966, Kommern, FRG.
Commonwealth Association of Museums, f. 1974, London.

International Association of Agricultural Museums, f. 1968, Reading, UK.
International Association of Museums of Arms and Military History, f. 1957, London. Publ.: *Glossarium Armorum*.
International Association of Transport Museums, f. 1968, Cologne, FRG.
International Council of Museums, f. 1946, Paris. Under aegis of UNESCO. Consultative status with UNESCO and ECOSOC. Publ.: *ICOM News*.
International Council of the Museums of Modern Art, f. 1953, New York.
International Society for Performing Arts Libraries and Museums, f. 1954, Paris. Publ.: *Spectacles*.
Latin-American Museological Association, f. 1972, Mexico, DF.
Museums Association of Tropical Africa, f. 1975, Accra, Ghana.
Scandinavian Union of Museums, f. 1975, Copenhagen.
World Federation of Friends of Museums, f. 1976, Brussels.

UNESCO, *Museum* (quarterly); K. HUDSON, *Museums for the 1980: A Survey of World Trends*, Paris, 1977; *Yearbook of International Organizations*.

MUSHROOMS. A subject of international research and co-operation. Organization reg. with the UIA:

International Commission on Mushroom Science, f. 1968, Braunschweig. Organizes international congresses. Publ.: *Mushrooms Science*.

Yearbook of International Organizations.

MUSIC. A subject of international co-operation. Organizations reg. with the UIA:

Afro-American Music Opportunities Association, f. 1969, Minneapolis.
Esperantists Music League, f. 1963, Harlow, Essex.
European Association of Music Conservatories, Academies and High Schools, f. 1953, Geneva.
European Association of Music Festivals, f. 1951, Geneva. Publ.: *Season* (annual), *Festivals* (annual).
European Union of National Music Competitions, f. 1970, Brussels.
Federation of International Music Competitions, f. 1956, Geneva.
Inter-American Music Council, f. 1956, Washington, DC.
International Association of Music Libraries, f. 1951, Stockholm. Publ.: *Fontes artis musicae* (quarterly).
International Cello Centre, f. 1953, Duns, Scotland. Publ.: Diary of Events.
International Confederation of Authors and Composers, f. 1926, Paris.
International Conference of Symphony and Opera Musicians, f. 1960, Belleville, Ill.
International Council for Traditional Music, f. 1947, New York, N.Y., USA.
International Federation of Jeunesses Musicales, f. 1945, Brussels. Publ.: *Bulletin de Presse International*.
International Federation of Musicians, f. 1948, Zurich. Consultative status with UNESCO and Council of Europe.
International Folk Music Council, f. 1947, Kingston, Ont. Publ.: *Journal*.
International Heinrich Schutz Society, f. 1930, Kiel, dedicated to old and new sacred music. Publ.: *Acta Sagitariana*.
International Institute for Comparative Music Studies and Documentation, f. 1963, Berlin W. Publ.: for UNESCO anthologies of recorded music.
International Institute for Music, Dance and Theatre in the Audio-Visual Media, f. 1969, Vienna. Publ.: *Newsletters*.
International Jazz Federation, f. 1969, London.
International Music Centre, f. 1961, Vienna. Publ.: *IMC Bulletin* (monthly).
International Music Council, f. 1949, Paris. Under aegis of UNESCO. Consultative status with ECOSOC, UNESCO. Publ.: *The World of Music* (quarterly in English, French and German).
International Musicological Society, f. 1927, Basel. Publ.: *Acta Musicologica* (quarterly).
International Rock and Roll Music Association, IRMA, f. 1968, Miami, Flo., USA.
International Society for Contemporary Music, f. 1922, W Berlin.

Nordic Musicians Union, f. 1916, Stockholm.

Yearbook of International Organizations 1986/87; The Europa Yearbook 1988. A World Survey, Vol. I, London, 1988.

MUSIC INTERNATIONAL FESTIVALS. A 20th century institution, initiated by the Salzburg Mozart Festival (1877) which became an international event in 1945. Other festivals:

Aspen Music Festival in Aspen, Colorado, 1949; Berliner Festage in W. Berlin, 1957; Festival de due Mondi, in Spoleti, 1958, Festival International de Musique in Aix-en-Provence, 1948; Llangollen International Musical Eisteddfod at Llangollen, N. Wales, 1947; Montreux International Jazz Festival in Montreux Casino, Switzerland, 1967; Newport Jazz Festival, started in Newport, N.J., 1954 since 1971 in New York City; Prazska Iaro in Prague, 1946; Warsaw Autumn in Warsaw, 1956. New music festivals are listed in the Britannica Book of the Year.

MUSIC TERMINOLOGY. The international directions for performers of music scores generally adopted in Italian (e.g. *adagio* – slowly, *alegretto* – fast, *allegro* – joyfully, *andante* – moderately slow, *capriccioso* – jocosely, *forte* – strongly, *impetuoso* – violently, *de capo al segno* – from the beginning to the mark, *staccato* – separating sounds, *veloce* – fast, *vivace* – lively).

MUSLIM BROTHERHOOD. An orthodox Arabic group established 1929 in Egypt, by believers of the orthodox Islam–Sunni sect, considering themselves as the only orthodox Muslims; main centers: Saudi Arabia, Egypt, Sudan and Syria. The Brotherhood and congenial organizations have been charged with organizing international terrorism in both Egypt and Syria (massacre of cadets in Aleppo, June 16, 1979).

MUSLIM ORGANIZATIONS. The Muslim organizations registered with the UIA:

Muslim World League, f. 1962, Mecca. Promotes translations of the Koran, establishment of Islamic centers, supports international peace. Publ.: *Majalla Rabetat al-Alam al-Islami* (monthly in Arabic). *The Journal* (monthly in English).
Union musulmane internationale, f. 1968, Grand Mosquee de Paris. Aims: to protect the Muslim community and culture.
World Muslim Congress, f. 1926. Headquarters Karachi. Consultative status with ECOSOC. Regional Offices: Beirut, Kaolack (Senegal), Manila, Mogadishu, Selangor (Malaysia). UN Liaison Office in New York. Publ.: *World Muslim Gazetteer*.

Yearbook of International Organizations.

MUSLIM RELIGIOUS COURTS IN ISRAEL. In the Israeli system of religious courts the Muslim Courts have exclusive jurisdiction in matters of marriage and divorce and other matters of personal status of Muslims who are Israeli citizens or residents.

The Europa Yearbook 1987. A World Survey, London, 1987.

MUSLIM WORLD CONGRESS. ▷ Islam.

MUSTANGS. A subject of international protection. Organization reg. with the UIA:

International Society for the Protection of Mustangs and Burros, f. 1965, Reno, Nevada.

Yearbook of International Organizations.

MUSTARD. A subject of international co-operation. Organization reg. with the UIA:

EEC Committee for the Mustard Industries, f. 1960, Brussels.

Yearbook of International Organizations.

M

MUTUAL AND BALANCED FORCE REDUCTIONS. ▷ MBFR.

MUTUAL ASSISTANCE ACT, 1950. The US Congress legislation which permitted the US to negotiate bilateral treaties within NATO, signed by the US on Jan. 27, 1950 in Washington with Belgium, Denmark, France, Italy, Luxembourg, the Netherlands, Norway and the UK. The treaties were of identical content, but the annexes defined in detail the elements resulting from the separate nature of the relations of a given country with the USA. Art. 1 stated that the parties will render each other all possible military assistance in accordance with the specific protocols to the treaty negotiated periodically. Art. 2 contained a prohibition against transmitting the received aid to third parties.

KEESING'S Contemporary Archive, 1958.

MUTUAL LEGAL ASSISTANCE TREATIES. ▷ Bank Drug Money Accounts.

MUTUAL SECURITY AGENCY, MSA, 1952–1953. A US government institution for foreign aid, established by a law of Congress of Oct. 10, 1951 in place of the Economic Co-operation Administration, ECA, whose functions it assumed on Jan. 1, 1952 and carried out until Aug. 1, 1953, when in turn it was replaced by the ▷ Foreign Operations Administration, FOA. While the ECA was an independent institution at the cabinet level, the MSA and FOA were subordinate to the State Department, which on July 1, 1955 took over the functions of the FOA, creating its own administrative unit called the International Co-operation Administration, ICA.

MUTUAL SECURITY PROGRAM. The official name since 1957 for a system of US economic and military assistance for states linked with the US through bilateral agreements; implemented by US government agencies: International Co-operation Administration, ICA, US Department of Defense, Department of Agriculture, Development Loan Fund, and The President's Fund for Asian Economic Development. Co-ordination of the Program is the responsibility of the Department of State, which each year in January, publishes its Report to Congress on the Mutual Security Program.

MUTUAL STRATEGIC SECURITY, MSS. An international military doctrine defined by Zb. Brzeziński:

'MSS means that each side is strategically secure – that it knows that a disarming first strike against its opponent would be militarily futile and that it is confident that a first strike by its opponent would be suicidal. In effect the goal of MSS incorporates the essentials of the doctrine ▷ MAD – for the ultimate sanction remains the same'.

Zb. BRZEZIŃSKI, *Game Plan. How to Conduct the US–Soviet Contest,* Boston, 1987.

MX. An American rocket project to replace the rocket ▷ Minuteman. It differs from the latest model of those rockets (Minuteman 3) above all in a larger number of warheads (a dozen or more) and a greater striking precision. MX missile production started in 1984. In Feb. 1985 the first MX missiles were installed in the USA.

H. SCOVILLE JR., *MX. Prescription for Disaster,* Cambridge, 1981; *World Armaments and Disarmaments SIPRI Yearbook 1983,* London, New York, 1983, p. 664; D. ROBERTSON, *Guide to Modern Defense and Strategy,* Detroit, 1988.

MYANMA. Member of the UN. Since Jun. 18, 1989 official name of Burma Myanma Naingngan, Union of Myanma. South East Asian State bordered by Bangladesh, India, the Bay of Bengal, China, Laos, Thailand and the Andaman Sea. Area: 678,030 sq. km. Pop.: 1987 est. 39,300,000 (1969 census 26,980,000). Capital: Rangoon with 3,662,312 inhabitants, 1973. GNP per capita 1979 US $160. Currency: one kyat = 100 pia. Official language: Burmese. National Day: Jan. 1, Independence Day, 1948.

Member of the UN since June 19, 1948 and of all UN specialized agencies except WIPO, IFAD and UNIDO. Member of the Colombo Plan.

International relations: independent feudal state until 1824, when Great Britain started the first Anglo-Burmese war. Ended with the Treaty of Yandabo in 1826 and the loss of the Arakan Tenasserim coast to British India. In the second war, 1852 Burma lost the Irravady delta. After the third war in 1885 the remainder of Burma was incorporated by India. In 1935 Burma was separated from India and became an autonomous state within the British Commonwealth. Occupied by Japan 1941–45. On Jan 1, 1948 Burma became an independent republic outside the Commonwealth by the London Treaty of Oct. 17, 1947.

A Burmanian Statesman U Thant was UN Secretary General, 1961–1971. During an official visit to Rangoon, in Oct. 1983, two Korean terrorists killed 20 members of the Korean Republic delegation. Korea then broke diplomatic relations with Burma. On Dec. 23, 1986 a maritime boundary agreement with India was signed in Rangoon, delineating the Andaman Sea, Coca Channel and the Bay of Bengal. Student demonstrations starting in Sept. 1987 brought about the imposition of military rule in Aug. 1988, which in turn led to the abolition of the one-party system in Sept. 1988. General election scheduled for May 1990.

UN Yearbook 1953 and 1954; D. WOODMAN, *The Making of Burma,* London, 1962; *Everyman's United Nations,* New York, 1964, pp. 22–123; F.N. TRAGER, *Burma: from Kingdom to Republic,* London, 1966; J. SILVERSTEIN, *Burmese Politics: The Dilemma of National Unity,* Rutgers University Press, 1980; D.I. STEINBERG, *Burma,* Boulder, 1982; *The Europa Year Book 1984. A World Survey,* Vol.I, pp. 1273–1283, London, 1984; KEESING's *Record of World Events,* March 1987; KEESING's *Record of World Events,* July–Aug. 1989.

MYASISHCHEV. A heavy Soviet bomber, counterpart to the American B.1, included in the SALT II Treaty. ▷ SALT II Documents, 1979.

J. GOLDBLAT, *Arms Control Agreements. A Handbook,* New York, 1983.

MYCOLOGY. A branch of botany dealing with fungi, a subject of international co-operation. Organizations reg. with the UIA:

Commonwealth Mycological Institute, f. 1930, Ken, Surrey.
International Commission for the European Mycological Congresses, f. 1953, Paris.
International Society for Human and Animal Mycology, f. 1954, Basel. Official relations with WHO. Publ.: *Sabouraudia.*

Yearbook of International Organizations.

MY LAI. The village in South Vietnam whose population was massacred on Mar. 16, 1968 by a US army unit. During a trial held at Fort Benning, Georgia, from Nov. 16, 1970 to Mar. 15, 1971 William Laws Calley, Jr. was charged with the killing of 102 defenseless old men, women and children, and sentenced to life imprisonment. Not indicted were Generals S. Koster and G. Young, who were responsible for issuing the "order of pacification," and the Commander-in-Chief of the US expeditionary force in Vietnam, General W. Westmoreland despite the fact that according to the opinion of Professor M. Telford Taylor, former US deputy prosecutor at the Nuremberg Trial (1945–46), these generals, according to the Nuremberg principles, bore full responsibility (General Westmoreland at the suggestion of General Koster on Mar. 17, 1968 sent congratulations to the company which carried out the massacre). Since Calley's sentence caused protests among part of American public opinion, President R. Nixon ordered that the prisoner be removed from prison and placed under house arrest and, in Apr., 1974, pardoned him completely. In Sept., 1971 a US court martial exonerated Captain E. Medina, Calley's immediate superior.

Newsweek, March 29, 1971; US Congress, *House of Representatives, Investigation of the My Lai Incident,* Washington DC., GPO, 1970; M. GERSHEN, *Destroy or Die: The True Story of My Lai,* New Rochelle, N.Y., 1971; KEESING's *Contemporary Archive,* 1974; J. GOLDSTEIN, B. MARSHALL, F. SCHWARTZ, *The My Lai Massacre and Its Cover-up: Beyond the Reach of the Law?* New York, 1976.

MYOPIA. Nearsightedness. A subject of international research. Organization reg. with the UIA:

Myopia International Research Foundation, f. 1963, New York.

Yearbook of International Organizations.

MYRIAMETER. The international length unit = 10,000 metres, or approx. = 6.2 miles.

M'ZAB VALLEY. An Algerian natural site, included in the ▷ World Heritage UNESCO List. Seven oases in the South of Algiers, with the holy town of Beni–Isguen built in the 11th century and other historical towns with a unique system of dams and water distribution and immense palm parks.

UNESCO. *A Legacy for All,* Paris, 1984.

N

NAC. An acronym of the North Atlantic Council the ▷ NATO meetings on the level of foreign ministers.

NACA. ▷ NASA.

NACISO. ▷ NATO.

NADEFCOL. ▷ NATO.

NAGASAKI. ▷ Hiroshima and Nagasaki

NAGORNO-KARABAKH AUTONOMOUS REGION OF THE USSR. A part of ▷ Azerbaidzhan. Population Jan 1, 1985 official 174,000 (75% Armenians, 23% Azeris). In February 1988 witnessed ▷ pogroms of Armenians by Azeris and protest actions in Armenia, demanding integration of the region with the Armenian Republic. Virtual Civil War since Sept. 1989; intensified Jan. 1990.

KEESING's *Record of World Events*, 1988.

NAHANNI. A Canadian National Park, included in the ▷ World Heritage UNESCO List. It contains meanders of the Flat River, a 290 km long canyon cut into the Cordillera by the south Nahanni River, ice pockets, chimney dolines, 100 m. high waterfalls, granite peaks, hot springs, underground rivers ... peregrine falcons and golden eagles, caribou, wolves and grizzly bears.

UNESCO, *A Legacy for All*, Paris, 1984.

NAIRA. The monetary unit of Nigeria; one naira = 100 kobo; issued (replacing the Nigerian pound) from Jan. 1, 1973 by the Central Bank of Nigeria.

NAIROBI. The capital of Kenya, 1963, population, 1985, estimate 827,000, in the East African highlands, bordering with Nairobi National Park. Seat of the Secretariat of the UN Commission on Human Settlements named Habitat, Center for Human Settlement by UN General Assembly Res. 32/162 of Dec. 19, 1977.

UN Chronicle, Jan., 1978.

NAM. National Association of Manufacturers of USA, founded in 1895; the organization associates the majority of US enterprises, with headquarters in New York, since 1946; reg. with the UIA; Consultative status with ECOSOC. Publ.: *NAM Reports, Industrial Press Service, Program Notes.*

Yearbook of International Organizations.

NAMIBIA. A country in southwest Africa that is to gain independence in April 1990. Name adopted by the UN General Assembly Res. 2332/XXII in accordance with the wish of Namibian people and contrary to the colonial regime of the Republic of South Africa, which uses the colonial name of South West Africa (Suidwes Afrika). Located on the Atlantic, bordering on Angola, Zambia, Zimbabwe, Botswana, Republic of South Africa. Area: 824,269 sq. km. Population (officially estimated at the end of 1986): 1,184,000 including ethnic groups: Ovambo (587,000), Kavango (110,000), Damasa (89,000), Herero (89,000), Whites (78,000), Narna (57,000), Coloured (48,000), Caprivi (44,000), Bushman (34,000), Rehoboh Baster (29,000), Tavana (7,000), others (12,000). Capital: Windhoek, with 75,000 inhabitants. Official languages: Afrikaans and English. Currency: one RSA rand = 100 cents. GNP per capita 1987: US $994.
Member of IAEA, ILO, FAO, UNESCO, ITU and UNIDO. Associate member of WHO.
International relations: from 1802 to 1868 penetration by English and German trading posts and missions; 1868 first rebellions of local population against European missions; from 1884 to 1904 purchases of land by German settlers; from 1904 to 1907 German Reich took over all of Namibia as a protectorate and turned it into a colony. In 1908 rebellion of tribes, to which the Reich responded by issuing the order "to exterminate all natives" (Ausrotten Befehl) following which the most belligerent tribe, the Hereros, were decimated (a mere 55,000 remained in 1970). In July 9, 1915, the territory was taken over by troops of the Republic of South Africa. In 1919, under the Treaty of Versailles, Namibia became a British protectorate as a League of Nations mandate territory, known as South West Africa. It was administered on behalf of the UK by the Union of South Africa. In 1946 Namibia became a UN trusteeship territory under the administration of South Africa; in the same year South Africa applied to the UN for the right to incorporate Namibia. The UN General Assembly Res. 65/I of Dec. 14, 1946 rejected the application stating that African inhabitants of South West Africa had not been granted political autonomy. The stance assumed by the UN in the years 1946–59 is reflected in Resolutions: 65/I, 14/II, 227/III, 337/IV, 449/B/V, 570/VI, 749/VIII, 852/XI, 940/X, 1055/XI, 1141/XII, 1246/XIII, 1359/XVI. The second period in the conflict between the Republic of South Africa (RSA) and the UN marks the years 1960–70, during which the UN sought ways to deprive the RSA of the trusteeship mandate and to restore to Namibia its independence *de jure* and *de facto*, reflected in Res. 1702/XVI, 1761/XVII, 1889/XVIII, 2145/XXI, 2235/XXI and the special session Res. 2248, as well as opinions of the International Court of Justice pronounced at the UN request in 1950, 1956, 1962, 1966. The most important was Res. 2145/XXI of Oct. 27, 1966 passed by 119 votes, with 2 negative votes (RSA and Portugal) and 3 abstentions (USA, France, Malawi). It read in part as follows:

"The General Assembly declares that South Africa has failed to fulfil its obligations in respect of the administration of the Mandated Territory and to ensure the moral and material well-being and security of the indigenous inhabitants of South West Africa and has in fact disavowed the Mandate; and decides that the Mandate is therefore terminated, that South Africa has no further right to administer the Territory and that henceforth South West Africa comes under direct responsibility of the United Nations."

The UN Special Commission for Namibia included Canada, Czechoslovakia, Chile, Egypt, Ethiopia, Finland, Italy, Japan, Mexico, Nigeria, Pakistan, Senegal, the USA and the USSR. At the same time the office of UN Commissioner for Namibia was established to maintain contact between the UN Council for Namibia and the UN Secretary-General. On Apr. 5, 1968, the Council, composed of 11 UN members (Chile, Colombia, Egypt, Guyana, India, Indonesia, Nigeria, Pakistan, Turkey, Yugoslavia and Zambia) set out for Namibia, but was refused admittance by the RSA government. The Council eventually met representatives of the Namibian national-liberation movement in Lusaka. As a result, the UN General Assembly Res. 2372/XXII of June 12, 1968 was published:

"The General Assembly proclaims that in accordance with the desires of its people, South West Africa shall henceforth be known as 'Namibia'; decides that the UN Council for South West Africa shall be called 'UN Council for Namibia'; condemns the government of South Africa for its persistent refusal to comply with the resolutions of the General Assembly and the Security Council, its refusal to withdraw from Namibia and its obstruction of the efforts of the United Nations Council for Namibia to proceed to Namibia; condemns the action of the Government of South Africa designed to consolidate its illegal control over Namibia and to destroy the unity of the people and the territorial integrity of Namibia."

The legal–international question of Namibia was heard by the ICJ on Apr. 21, 1971 at The Hague, which ruled South African annexation illegal and put the RSA under an obligation to "immediately recall its administration from Namibia and thus put an end to the occupation of the territory." UN Security Council Res. 301 of Oct. 20, 1971 fully supported the Court's judgment. The RSA ignored the decisions of the Court and the Council; this resulted in the escalation of the national-liberation struggle carried by ▷ SWAPO (South West Africa People's Organization) founded in 1959. On May 26–28, 1972 SWAPO organized an International Conference for Namibia, which was attended by 500 delegates from 55 countries, and by representatives of the UN, World Council of Churches and other international organizations; it called on the RSA to obey the 1971 decision of the ICJ. SWAPO was recognized in 1971 by the OAU as an official representative of the Namibian national-liberation movement and was granted observer status at the UN Decolonization Committee. In early Mar. 1972, the UN Secretary-General Kurt Waldheim called on RSA Prime Minister in Cape Town and also visited Namibia. In Aug., 1972 the UN Security Council unanimously appointed the UN Commissioner for Namibia as the UN Secretary-General's plenipotentiary. In Oct., 1972, the Commissioner A. Escher, who had previously conferred with SWAPO representatives in Geneva, spent 18 days in Namibia. Refusing to acknowledge the decision of the ICJ and the UN resolutions, the RSA made a purely formal concession by introducing the division of Namibia into administrative units; by a decree of June 26, 1972, the northern province of Ovamboland (center of SWAPO activities) was granted self-government on Jan. 1, 1973, while the regime was preserved in the rich southern provinces.
A commemorative Namibia day proclaimed on Aug. 26, 1973 by the UN Council for Namibia:

"for as long as will be necessary, as a reminder of the critical time of August 26, 1966 when the people of Namibia were forced to begin their resistance against the aggression of the illegal occupation."

The UN Council for Namibia set up a Fund and organized an education and training program. Lengthy negotiations between the UN and the RSA had not produced any results and on Dec. 10, 1976 the UN General Assembly Decolonization Committee, by 108 votes with 6 negative votes (USA, Great Britain, France, FRG, Belgium, Luxembourg) and 12 abstentions, pronounced its support for the armed struggle of SWAPO and called on the Security Council to impose an arms embargo on the RSA. In April, 1978 the ninth special session of UN General Assembly was held, devoted to Namibia. From 1979 to 1984 the issue of independence for Namibia was discussed again by the UN General Assembly and Security Council. The UN Council for Namibia denounced on June 25, 1980 the illegal exploitation, plunder and purchase of Namibian uranium by South Africa and other foreign interests. The International Conference in Support of the Struggle of the Namibia People for Independence, held from Apr. 25 to 29, 1983, in Paris adopted resolutions on assistance to the struggle of the people of Namibia under leadership of the ▷ SWAPO, and on assistance to the ▷ Front-line states with a view to enabling them to sustain their support for the cause of Namibia.

The *UN Chronicle*, 1983, chronology of Namibia, 1884–1983 reads as follows:

1884–1915: South West Africa under German administration.

1915: After outbreak of World War I, South African forces invade and occupy the territory.

1920: League of Nations confers Mandate over South West Africa on "his Brittanic Majesty, to be exercised on his behalf by the Union of South Africa."

1939: Demise of the League of Nations. Till this year South Africa submitted the required annual reports to the Permanent Mandates Commission, which was critical of South African policy on several occasions.

1945: Creation of the United Nations with international Trusteeship System for Territories held under League Mandates.

1946: General Assembly recommends Trusteeship status for South West Africa and invites South Africa to propose agreement.

1947: South Africa submits report on South West Africa for consideration by Trusteeship Council.

1949: South Africa informs the United Nations it will no longer transmit information on the Territory.

1950: International Court of Justice rules that South West Africa is still a Territory under international mandate for which South Africa continues to have international obligations.

1964: South Africa decides to implement policy of separate non-white "homelands" and exclusive white area.

1966: The United Nations terminates South Africa's mandate, assumes responsibility for administering South West Africa. A 14-member Ad Hoc Committee for South West Africa is established to recommend practical means for administering the Territory.

1967: Assembly sets up 11-member United Nations Council for South West Africa to administer the territory until independence.

1968: Assembly renames Territory Namibia, condemns States which, by their political, economic and military collaboration with South Africa, encourage its continued illegal occupation.

1969: The Security Council calls on South Africa to withdraw from Namibia, saying that its establishment of "bantustans" destroyed national unity and territorial integrity and that enactment of the "South West Africa Affairs Bill" violated Assembly resolutions. South Africa replies that it does not intend to leave the Territory. The Security Council calls on states to stop all dealings with the Government of South Africa purporting to act on behalf of the Namibian people.

1970: The Security Council calls on states to refrain from diplomatic and economic relations which imply recognition of South Africa's authority over Namibia. The Assembly calls on South Africa to treat captured Namibian freedom fighters as prisoners of war in accordance with the 1949 Geneva Conventions. A comprehensive assistance Programme, the United Nations Fund for Namibia, is set up.

1971: The International Court of Justice rules that States Members are obliged to recognize the illegality of South Africa's presence in Namibia and refrain from assisting that régime. The Security Council and Assembly call on States to uphold that opinion.

1972: Security Council invites the Secretary-General to initiate contacts with all parties concerned to hasten Namibia's move toward independence. Subsequently, the Secretary-General reports that many issues remain to be clarified, but South Africa is willing to consider removing restrictions on political activity and freedom of movement in the Territory. Security Council condemns repressive measures against African workers

in Namibia, calling for the abolishment of any labour system which violates the Universal Declaration of Human Rights. The Assembly again calls for economic sanctions against South Africa to ensure its immediate withdrawal from Namibia.

1973: The General Assembly recognizes the South West Africa People's Organization (SWAPO) as the authentic representative of the Namibian people. After repeated unsuccessful attempts by the Secretary-General to elicit a "complete and unequivocal clarification" of South Africa's policy regarding Namibian independence, the Security Council and the Assembly decide that contacts between the Secretary-General and the South African Government are detrimental to the interests of the Namibians and should cease.

Council for Namibia's Lusaka Declaration calls on all nations to actively support the Namibian independence struggle. "Namibia Day" (26 August) observed for the first time, commemorating the beginning, in 1966, of resistance to South African occupation.

1974: Council for Namibia enacts Decree for the Protection of the Natural Resources of Namibia. The Assembly endorses the Namibia Council's decision to establish, at Lusaka, Zambia, a research and training institute to equip Namibians to assume positions of responsibility after independence (The institute opened formally in 1979).

1975: Security Council vetoes by France, the United Kingdom and the United States on proposed arms embargo on South Africa. The Assembly urges sanctions against South Africa for military build-up in Namibia, condemns its efforts to consolidate illegal occupation of Namibia by organizing a "constitutional convention" which would create divisions among ethnic groups and further its "bantustanization" policies.

1976: Security Council calls for free elections in Namibia under United Nations supervision, also condemns South Africa's aggression against Angola and Zambia, using Namibia to launch attacks, France, the United Kingdom and the United States again veto a proposal for an arms embargo against South Africa. The Assembly invites SWAPO to participate in its work as an observer and decides that any independence talks on Namibia must be between representatives of South Africa and SWAPO, under United Nations auspices.

1977: Security Council votes unanimously to impose a mandatory arms embargo against South Africa – the first time in the history of the United Nations such action has been taken against a Member State under Chapter VII of the Charter, concerning threats against peace and acts of aggression. Maputo Declaration by the International Conference in Support of the Peoples of Zimbabwe and Namibia calls on Governments to reject all attempts by South Africa to carve up the territory of Namibia. The Council for Namibia and the Assembly condemn South Africa's annexation of Walvis Bay on 31 August as illegal. The Week of Solidarity with the People of Namibia and their Liberation Movement (27 September to 3 October) observed for the first time.

1978: Proposal for settling the Namibia question from five Western members (Canada, France, the Federal Republic of Germany, the United Kingdom and the United States) is accepted by South Africa and SWAPO and presented to the Security Council. The proposal calls for appointment of a Special Representative to ensure establishment of conditions for free and fair elections; release of all Namibian political prisoners and return of all refugees, cessation of hostilities by all parties; and restriction to base of South African and SWAPO armed forces. Martti Ahtisaari, the United Nations Commissioner for Namibia, appointed Secretary-General's Special Representative, visits Territory from 6 to 22 August. The Security Council decides (resolution 435 (1978)) to establish a United Nations Transition Assistance Group (UNTAG) in Namibia, to assist in implementing the settlement plan. Special session of General Assembly on Namibia (24 April to 3 May) fully supports Namibian people's armed liberation struggle under SWAPO.

When South Africa decides to hold unilateral elections in Namibia in December, the Security Council and General Assembly condemn the decision and declare the results null and void. The foreign ministers of the

Western "Contact Group" declare that the unilateral elections by South Africa cannot be reconciled with the terms of the proposed settlement endorsed by the Security Council.

1979: Year of Solidarity with the People of Namibia proclaimed by a decision of the Assembly, which says South Africa acted "deceitfully" in settlement talks on Namibia. South Africa is condemned for continued efforts to destroy SWAPO and impose an "internal settlement" through an illegal "national assembly."

1980: United Nations officials visit southern African States to discuss the proposed demilitarized zone. South Africa reaffirms acceptance of the settlement proposal but asks clarification of how UNTAG would function in the DMZ. Exploitation of the Territory's uranium by South Africa and other foreign interests denounced by the Namibia Council and the General Assembly in 1981. The "collusion" of France, the Federal Republic of Germany, Israel and the United States with South Africa in the nuclear field is condemned by the Assembly. The International Conference on Solidarity with the Struggle of the People of Namibia, held in Paris, calls for comprehensive sanctions against South Africa, including an oil embargo.

1981: SWAPO agrees to sign a cease-fire with South Africa and co-operate with UNTAG, but South Africa is not ready to agree. Sanctions against South Africa again vetoed in the Security Council by France, United Kingdom and United States. The OAU-sponsored international Conference on Sanctions against South Africa in Paris calls for further action to isolate South Africa.

Panama Declaration of Council for Namibia denounces efforts by South Africa and others to introduce issues other than decolonization into the question of Namibia. At its eighth emergency special session, the Assembly reaffirms the United Nations plan for the independence of Namibia as "the only basis for a peaceful settlement" and rejects "manoeuvres" by "certain members" of the Western Contact Group undermining consensus on the plan.

1982: A text of principles for the constituent assembly and constitution of an independent Namibia, submitted by the Western Contact Group, is accepted by "the parties concerned in the negotiations for the implementation of the proposal for a settlement of the Namibian situation in accordance with Security Council resolution 435 (1978)." The Assembly deplores continued military support of South Africa by some Western States and Israel and firmly rejects "persistent attempts" by the United States and South Africa to link Namibian independence to the withdrawal of Cuban forces from Angola.

Arusha Declaration of Council for Namibia condemns South Africa for militarization of Namibia, including forced conscription.

1983: International Conference in Support of the Struggle of the Namibian People for Independence (Paris, 25 to 29 April).

On July 7–11, 1986 a UN sponsored International Conference for the Immediate Independence of Namibia took place in Vienna. The Conference of 120 government representatives demanded "That South Africa withdraw immediately and unconditionally from the entire territory of Namibia, including Walvis Bay and the Penguin and other off-shore islands".

Since Sept. 10, 1986 the UN Decolonization Committee considers Namibia a Non Self-Governing Territory.

The UN Peace-keeping forces were reduced in the spring of 1989. A force of seven infantry batallions (7,500 soldiers) and 2,000 civilian officials and policemen in 1989/1990 remained to ensure the free elections to the Constituent Assembly of an independent Namibia. The first non-racial elections, as provided for by Security Council Res. 435, were held in the presence of UN monitors on Nov. 7–11, 1989. SWAPO won the overall majority of seats, falling short, however, of the 66% which would enable it to draw up a constitution. The country will

Narcotic Drugs and Psychotropic Substances

remain under UN mandate until the end of March, 1990.

M. SCOTT, "The International Status of South West Africa," in: *International Affairs*, No. 34, 1958; *Reports of Judgements Advisory Opinions and Orders, Judgement of 18 July 1956*, ICJ, The Hague, 1967; *South West Africa Cases (Ethiopia vs. South Africa; Liberia vs. South Africa). Pleading, Oral Arguments, Documents*, Vols. 1–5, ICJ, The Hague, 1967; F. CAROLL, *South West Africa and UN*, Lexington, 1967; J.W. WELLINGTON, *South West Africa and Its Human Issues*, New York, 1967; R. VINGE, *A Dwelling Place of Our Own. The Story of the Namibian Nation*, London, 1972; *UN Monthly Chronicle* Nos. 6 and 10, 1975; G. TOTENMEYER, *Namibia Old and New*, New York, 1975; G.M. COCKRAM, *South West African Mandate*, Cape Town, 1976; J.H.P. SERFONTAIN, *Namibia*, London, 1977; W.H. THOMAS, *Economic Development in Namibia*, Munich, 1978; *UN Chronicle*, August 1980; R.H. KILJUNEN (ed.), *Namibia. The Last Colony*, London, 1982; *UN Chronicle*, March., 1983, pp. 17–32; *The Europa Year Book 1984. A World Survey*, Vol. II, pp. 2093–2100, London, 1984; *UN Chronicle*, Jan., 1984, p. 84; Security Council rejects "Interim Government" in Namibia, in: *UN Chronicle*, 985, No. 5, pp. 21–22; Namibia: A Chronology 1884–1986, in: *UN Chronicle*, November 1986, p. 25; KEESING'S Record of World Events, Nov. 1989.

NAMIBIA INSTITUTE. A UN institution, the basis of the UN General Assembly Res. 34/92 G of Dec. 12, 1979,

"to enable Namiblians under the aegis of the UN Council for Namibia, to develop and acquire the necessary skills required for manning the public service of the independent Namibia … to serve as an information and documentation centre on Namibia."

The UN Institute for Namibia was established on Dec. 29, 1979 at Lusaka.

UN Chronicle, March 1980.

NAM NGUM. The river and valley in Laos, subject of international co-operation and agreements. The Committee for Co-ordination of Investigations of the Lower Mekong Basin has recommended 1966 construction of the Nam Ngum hydroelectric Project as "an integral component of the comprehensive development of the Lower ▷ Mekong basin." The Nam Ngum Development Fund Agreement was signed in Washington, May 4, 1966, by the governments of Australia, Canada, Denmark, Japan, Laos, the Netherlands, New Zealand, Thailand and the USA and the IBRD (World Bank); entered into force on Aug. 29, 1966.

UNTS, Vol. 575, p. 50.

NAMSO. ▷ NATO.

NAMUCAR. Naveira Multinacional del Caribes S.A., Multinational Caribbean Fleet, official name of an international joint stock company of Jamaica, Colombia, Costa Rica, Cuba, Mexico, Nicaragua, Panama and Venezuela, established Dec. 1, 1975 in San José de Costa Rica. Until Namucar's establishment 88% of passenger and commercial transport on the Caribbean Sea was in the hands of American and West European shipowners.

NANKIN. *Chinese* = Nansing; a port city in China in the province of Tsiangsu, capital of China from the 14th to the 20th century; place of the signing on Aug. 29, 1842, on the English ship *Cornwallis* of the unequal British–Chinese Treaty.

NANKIN PEACE TREATY, 1842. The peace, friendship and trade treaty, between China and Great Britain, signed Aug. 29, 1842 in Nankin.

Major Peace Treaties of Modern History, New York, 1967, Vol. II, pp. 1059–1064.

NANSEN PASSPORT. The identity cards issued to stateless persons by the League of Nations since 1922 on the initiative of the Arctic explorer and oceanographer, at that time the High Commissioner of the LN for Refugees, Fridtjof Nansen (1861–1930).

W. ROTHOLZ, "Nansenpass", in: *STRUPP-SCHLOCHAUER Wörterbuch des Völkerrechts*, Berlin, 1961, pp. 567–568.

NANSHA ISLANDS. ▷ Spratly Islands.

NAPALM AND PHOSPHORUS ARMS. Naphthenate, palmitate and phosphor, incendiary substances used first time during a World War II and later in wars of Korea and Vietnam, as well as in colonial wars in Angola, Guinea Bissau and Mozambique; it has been included, at the International Conference on Human Rights, held on May 9, 1968, in Teheran, among the weapons the use of which during a war should be condemned and prohibited, together with such other weapons as chemical and bacteriological (▷ B and C arms). The Political Committee of the UN General Assembly adopted on Nov. 17, 1972 a resolution demanding, i.a., that the use of vesicant agents in armed conflicts should be prohibited. According to the report of SIPRI, May 1973, about 14,000 tons of napalm were used during World War II; during the Korean War the US Air Force dropped 32,000 tons; and in Vietnam, in 1964–73, more than 372,000 tons. In June 1973 the Swedish government, basing itself on the evidence collected in Indochina about the effects of the weapons of extreme cruelty, such as napalm, incendiary substances, and cluster and fragmentation bombs, proposed the drafting of an international convention prohibiting all use of these weapons in armed conflicts. The UN Political Committee decided on Nov. 25, 1973 to transfer the question of prohibition or restriction of the use of napalm and other incendiary weapons to the Geneva Conference on Disarmament. The UN Conference on Prohibition or Restriction of Use of Certain Conventional Weapons which may be Deemed to be Excessively Injurious or to have Indiscriminate Effects was held in Geneva in September 1979 and in September 1980.

"Le Napalm", in: *Révue Militaire d'information*, Paris, Jan. 10, 1954, pp. 16–22; *Final Act of the UN Conference for Human Rights*, New York, 1968; M. HASHIMOTO, "The Napalm Bomb", in: *Prevent the Crime of Silence*, London, 1971, pp. 199–202; SIPRI, *World Armaments and Disarmament Yearbook*, 1971, pp. 133–151; 1972, pp. 400–403; *Napalm and other incendiary weapons and all aspects of their possible use*, UN, New York, 1973; *World Armaments and Disarmament. SIPRI Yearbook 1980*, London, pp. 389–392.

NAPOLEONIC AND ANTI-NAPOLEONIC TREATIES. Pro- and anti-Napoleonic treaties in chronological order:

1797 – peace treaty with Austria signed in Campo Formio, Oct. 17, 1797, was the first treaty signed by Napoleon Bonaparte on behalf of the French Republic;
1801 – with Austria and Prussia of Feb. 9, 1801, in Luneville (signed on behalf of France by J. Bonaparte);
1802 – the peace of Amiens, signed on Mar. 27, 1802, by France and Spain;
Dec. 15, 1805, by the treaty signed in Schönbrunn; France concluded an alliance with Prussia; amended on Feb. 15, 1806, by the Treaty of Paris;
Dec. 26, 1805, the peace treaty between Austria and France was signed in Presburg; replaced with the Vienna Protocol signed Oct. 14, 1809.
April 26, 1807, the Prussian–Russian anti-Napoleonic Alliance signed in Bartenstein.
Oct. 12, 1808, the French–Russian alliance signed in Erfurt;

Dec. 30, 1812, the Russian–Prussian convention signed in Taurogi on separation of Prussian armies from French armies in order to maintain neutrality;
Feb. 26/27, 1813, the Russian–Prussian alliance that brought about Prussian declaration of war against France, Mar. 27, 1813.
Apr. 14, 1813, Prussia signed an anti-Napoleonic convention with Great Britain in Reichenbach.
Mar. 9, 1813 the anti-Napoleonic Triple Alliance by Austria, Prussia and Russia; on Oct. 3, 1813, England joined the alliance;
Apr. 11, 1814, Napoleon I abdicates;
Mar. 13, 1815, anti-Napoleonic declaration of Austria, France, Spain, Portugal, Prussia, Russia, Sweden and Great Britain;
Mar. 25, 1815, anti-Napoleonic convention of Austria, Prussia, Russia and Great Britain;
Sept. 26, 1815, the ▷ Holy Alliance.

G.F. DE MARTENS, *Nouveau Recueil des traités depuis 1808 jusqu'à présent*, 1839, 3 Vols., Göttingen, 1817–42; *Konferenzen und Verträge. Vertrags Plötz*, 3 Vols., Würzburg, 1958; J. GODECHOT, *Napoléon*, Paris, 1969.

NARCOTIC DRUGS AND PSYCHOTROPIC SUBSTANCES, UN CONVENTION AGAINST ILLICIT TRAFFIC IN.
Prepared by the Commission on Narcotic Drugs. Adopted unanimously by an ECOSOC Conference of plenipotentiaries convened at Vienna between Nov. 25 and Dec. 20, 1988. The Convention is meant to supplement the Single Convention on Narcotic Drugs of 1961 and the 1971 Convention on Psychotropic Substances.

The Parties to this Convention
Deeply concerned by the magnitude of and rising trend in the illicit production of, demand for and traffic in narcotic drugs and psychotropic substances, which pose a serious threat to the health and welfare of human beings and adversely affect the economic, cultural and political foundations of society,

Deeply concerned also by the steadily increasing inroads into various social groups made by illicit traffic in narcotic drugs and psychotropic substances, and particularly by the fact that children are used in many parts of the world as an illicit drug consumers market and for purposes of illicit production, distribution and trade in narcotic drugs and psychotropic substances, which entails a danger of incalculable gravity,

Recognizing the links between illicit traffic and other related organized criminal activities which undermine the legitimate economies and threaten the stability, security and sovereignty of States,

Recognizing also that illicit traffic is an international criminal activity, the suppression of which demands urgent attention and the highest priority,

Aware that illicit traffic generates large financial profits and wealth enabling transnational criminal organizations to penetrate, contaminate and corrupt the structures of government, legitimate commercial and financial business, and society at all its levels,

Determined to deprive persons engaged in illicit traffic of the proceeds of their criminal activities and thereby eliminate their main incentive for so doing,

Desiring to eliminate the root causes of the problem of abuse of narcotic drugs and psychotropic substances, including the illicit demand for such drugs and substances and the enormous profits derived from illicit traffic,

Considering that measures are necessary to monitor certain substances, including precursors, chemicals and solvents, which are used in the manufacture of narcotic drugs and psychotropic substances, the ready availability of which has led to an increase in the clandestine manufacture of such drugs and substances.

Determined to improve international co-operation in the suppression of illicit traffic by sea,

Recognizing that eradication of illicit traffic is a collective responsibility of all States and that, to that end, co-ordinated action within the framework of international co-operation is necessary,

Acknowledging the competence of the United Nations in the field of control of narcotic drugs and psychotropic substances and desirous that the international organs concerned with such control should be within the framework of that Organization,

Reaffirming the guiding principles of existing treaties in the field of narcotic drugs and psychotropic substances and the system of control which they embody,

Recognizing the need to reinforce and supplement the measures provided in the Single Convention on Narcotic Drugs, 1961, that Convention as amended by the 1972 Protocol Amending the Single Convention on Narcotic Drugs, 1961, and the 1971 Convention on Psychotropic Substances, in order to counter the magnitude and extent of illicit traffic and its grave consequences,

Recognizing also the importance of strengthening and enhancing effective legal means for international co-operation in criminal matters for suppressing the international criminal activities of illicit traffic,

Desiring to conclude a comprehensive, effective and operative international convention that is directed specifically against illicit traffic and that considers the various aspects of the problem as a whole, in particular those aspects not envisaged in the existing treaties in the field of narcotic drugs and psychotropic substances,

Hereby agree as follows:

Article 1

Definitions

Except where otherwise expressly indicated or where the context otherwise requires, the following definitions shall apply throughout this Convention:

(a) "Board" means the International Narcotics Control Board established by the Single Convention on Narcotic Drugs, 1961, and that Convention as amended by the 1972 Protocol Amending the Single Convention on Narcotic Drugs, 1961;

(b) "Cannabis plant" means any plant of the genus Cannabis;

(c) "Coca bush" means the plant of any species of the genus Erythroxylon;

(d) "Commercial carrier" means any person or any public, private or other entity engaged in transporting persons, goods or mails for remuneration, hire or any other benefit;

(e) "Commission" means the Commission on Narcotic Drugs of the Economic and Social Council of the United Nations;

(f) "Confiscation", which includes forfeiture where applicable, means the permanent deprivation of property by order of a court or other competent authority;

(g) "Controlled delivery" means the technique of allowing illicit or suspect consignments of narcotic drugs, psychotropic substances, substances in Table I and Table II annexed to this Convention, or substances substituted for them, to pass out of, through or into the territory of one or more countries, with their knowledge and under the supervision of their competent authorities, with a view to identifying persons involved in the commission of offences established in accordance with article 3, paragraph 1 of the Convention;

(h) "1961 Convention" means the Single Convention on Narcotic Drugs, 1961;

(i) "1961 Convention as amended" means the Single Convention on Narcotic Drugs, 1961, as amended by the 1972 Protocol Amending the Single Convention on Narcotic Drugs, 1961;

(j) "1971 Convention" means the Convention on Psychotropic Substances, 1971;

(k) "Council" means the Economic and Social Council of the United Nations;

(l) "Freezing" or "seizure" means temporarily prohibiting the transfer, conversion, disposition or movement of property or temporarily assuming custody or control of property on the basis of an order issued by a court or a competent authority;

(m) "Illicit traffic" means the offences set forth in article 3, paragraphs 1 and 2, of this Convention;

(n) "Narcotic drug" means any of the substances, natural or synthetic, in Schedules I and II of the Single Convention on Narcotic Drugs, 1961, and that Convention as amended by the 1972 Protocol Amending the Single Convention on Narcotic Drugs, 1961;

(o) "Opium poppy" means the plant of the species *Papaver somniferum* L;

(p) "Proceeds" means any property derived from or obtained, directly or indirectly, through the commission of an offence established in accordance with article 3, paragraph 1;

(q) "Property" means assets of every kind, whether corporeal or incorporeal, movable or immovable, tangible or intangible, and legal documents or instruments evidencing title to, or interest in, such assets;

(r) "Psychotropic substance" means any substance, natural or synthetic, or any natural material in Schedules I, II, III and IV of the Convention on Psychotropic Substances, 1971;

(s) "Secretary-General" means the Secretary-General of the United Nations;

(t) "Table I" and "Table II" means the correspondingly numbered lists of substances annexed to this Convention, as amended from time to time in accordance with article 12;

(u) "Transit State" means a State through the territory of which illicit narcotic drugs, psychotropic substances and substances in Table I and Table II are being moved, which is neither the place of origin nor the place of ultimate destination thereof.

Article 2

Scope of the convention

(1) The purpose of this Convention is to promote co-operation among the Parties so that they may address more effectively the various aspects of illicit traffic in narcotic drugs and psychotropic substances having an international dimension. In carrying out their obligations under the Convention, the Parties shall take necessary measures, including legislative and administrative measures, in conformity with the fundamental provisions of their respective domestic legislative systems.

(2) The Parties shall carry out their obligations under this Convention in a manner consistent with the principles of sovereign equality and territorial integrity of States and that of non-intervention in the domestic affairs of other States.

(3) A Party shall not undertake in the territory of another Party the exercise of jurisdiction and performance of functions which are exclusively reserved for the authorities of that other Party by its domestic law.

Article 3

Offences and sanctions

(1) Each Party shall adopt such measures as may be necessary to establish as criminal offences under its domestic law, when committed intentionally:

(a)(i) The production, manufacture, extraction, preparation, offering, offering for sale, distribution, sale, delivery on any terms whatsoever, brokerage, dispatch, dispatch in transit, transport, importation or exportation of any narcotic drug or any psychotropic substance contrary to the provisions of the 1961 Convention, the 1961 Convention as amended or the 1971 Convention;

(ii) The cultivation of opium poppy, coca bush or cannabis plant for the purpose of the production of narcotic drugs contrary to the provisions of the 1961 Convention and the 1961 Convention as amended;

(iii) The possession or purchase of any narcotic drug or psychotropic substance for the purpose of any of the activities enumerated in (i) above;

(iv) The manufacture, transport or distribution of equipment, materials or of substances listed in Table I and Table II, knowing that they are to be used in or for the illicit cultivation, production or manufacture of narcotic drugs or psychotropic substances;

(v) The organization, management or financing of any of the offences enumerated in (i), (ii), (iii) or (iv) above;

(b)(i) The conversion or transfer of property, knowing that such property is derived from any offence or offences established in accordance with subparagraph (a) of this paragraph, or from an act of participation in such offence or offences, for the purpose of concealing or disguising the illicit origin of the property or of assisting any person who is involved in the commission of such an offence or offences to evade the legal consequences of his actions;

(ii) The concealment or disguise of the true nature, source, location, disposition, movement, rights with respect to, or ownership of property, knowing that such property is derived from an offence or offences established in accordance with subparagraph (a) of this paragraph or from an act of participation in such an offence or offences;

(c) Subject to its constitutional principles and the basic concepts of its legal system;

(i) The acquisition, possession or use of property, knowing, at the time of receipt, that such property was derived from an offence or offences established in accordance with subparagraph (a) of this paragraph or from an act of participation in such offence or offences;

(ii) The possession of equipment or materials or substances listed in Table I and Table II, knowing that they are being or are to be used in or for the illicit cultivation, production or manufacture of narcotic drugs or psychotropic substances;

(iii) Publicly inciting or inducing others, by any means, to commit any of the offences established in accordance with this article or to use narcotic drugs or psychotropic substances illicitly;

(iv) Participation in, association or conspiracy to commit, attempts to commit and aiding, abetting, facilitating and counselling the commission of any of the offences established in accordance with this article.

(2) Subject to its constitutional principles and the basic concepts of its legal system, each Party shall adopt such measures as may be necessary to establish as a criminal offence under its domestic law, when committed intentionally, the possession, purchase or cultivation of narcotic drugs or psychotropic substances for personal consumption contrary to the provisions of the 1961 Convention, the 1961 Convention as amended or the 1971 Convention.

(3) Knowledge, intent or purpose required as an element of an offence set forth in paragraph 1 of this article may be inferred from objective factual circumstances.

(4)(a) Each Party shall make the commission of the offences established in accordance with paragraph 1 of this article liable to sanctions which take into account the grave nature of these offences, such as imprisonment or other forms of deprivation of liberty, pecuniary sanctions and confiscation.

(b) The Parties may provide, in addition to conviction or punishment, for an offence established in accordance with paragraph 1 of this article, that the offender shall undergo measures such as treatment, education, after-care, rehabilitation or social reintegration.

(c) Notwithstanding the preceding subparagraphs, in appropriate cases of a minor nature, the Parties may provide, as alternatives to conviction or punishment, measures such as education, rehabilitation or social reintegration, as well as, when the offender is a drug abuser, treatment and aftercare.

(d) The Parties may provide, either as an alternative to conviction or punishment, or in addition to conviction or punishment of an offence established in accordance with paragraph 2 of this article, measures for the treatment, education, aftercare, rehabilitation or social reintegration of the offender.

(5) The Parties shall ensure that their courts and other competent authorities having jurisdiction can take into account factual circumstances which make the commission of the offences established in accordance with paragraph 1 of this article particularly serious, such as:

(a) The involvement in the offence of an organized criminal group to which the offender belongs;

(b) The involvement of the offender in other international organized criminal activities;

(c) The involvement of the offender in other illegal activities facilitated by commission of the offence;

(d) The use of violence or arms by the offender;

(e) The fact that the offender holds a public office and that the offence is connected with the office in question;

(f) The victimization or use of minors;

(g) The fact that the offence is committed in a penal institution or in an educational institution or social service facility or in their immediate vicinity or in other places to which school children and students resort for educational, sports and social activities;

(h) Prior conviction, particularly for similar offences, whether foreign or domestic, to the extent permitted under the domestic law of a Party.

(6) The Parties shall endeavour to ensure that any discretionary legal powers under their domestic law relating to the prosecution of persons for offences established in accordance with this article are exercised to maximize the effectiveness of law enforcement measures in respect of those offences and with due regard to the need to deter the commission of such offences.

(7) The Parties shall ensure that their courts or other competent authorities bear in mind the serious nature of the offences enumerated in paragraph 1 of this article and the circumstances enumerated in paragraph 5 of this article when considering the eventuality of early release or parole of persons convicted of such offences.

(8) Each Party shall, where appropriate, establish under its domestic law a long statute of limitations period in which to commence proceedings for any offence established in accordance with paragraph 1 of this article, and a longer period where the alleged offender has evaded the administration of justice.

(9) Each Party shall take appropriate measures, consistent with its legal system, to ensure that a person charged with or convicted of an offence established in accordance with paragraph 1 of this article, who is found within its territory, is present at the necessary criminal proceedings.

(10) For this purpose of co-operation among the Parties under this Convention, including, in particular, co-operation under articles 5, 6, 7 and 9, offences established in accordance with this article shall not be considered as fiscal offences or as political offences or regarded as politically motivated, without prejudice to the constitutional limitations and the fundamental domestic law of the Parties.

(11) Nothing contained in this article shall affect the principle that the description of the offences to which it refers and of legal defences thereto is reserved to the domestic law of a Party and that such offences shall be prosecuted and punished in conformity with that law.

Article 4
Jurisdiction

(1) Each Party:
(a) Shall take such measures as may be necessary to establish its jurisdiction over the offences it has established in accordance with article 3, paragraph 1, when:
(i) The offence is committed in its territory;
(ii) The offence is committed on board a vessel flying its flag or an aircraft which is registered under its laws at the time the offence is committed;
(b) May take such measures as may be necessary to establish its jurisdiction over the offences it has established in accordance with article 3, paragraph 1, when:
(i) The offence is committed by one of its nationals or by a person who has his habitual residence in its territory;
(ii) The offence is committed on board a vessel concerning which that Party has been authorized to take appropriate action pursuant to article 17, provided that such jurisdiction shall be exercised only on the basis of agreements or arrangements referred to in paragraphs 4 and 9 of that article;
(iii) The offence is one of those established in accordance with article 3, paragraph 1, subparagraph (c)(iv), and is committed outside its territory with a view to the commission, within its territory, of an offence established in accordance with article 3, paragraph 1.

(2) Each Party:
(a) Shall also take such measures as may be necessary to establish its jurisdiction over the offences it has established in accordance with article 3, paragraph 1, when the alleged offender is present in its territory and it does not extradite him to another Party on the ground:
(i) That the offence has been committed in its territory or on board a vessel flying its flag or an aircraft which was registered under its law at the time the offence was committed; or
(ii) That the offence has been committed by one of its nationals;

(b) May also take such measures as may be necessary to establish its jurisdiction over the offences it has established in accordance with article 3, paragraph 1, when the alleged offender is present in its territory and it does not extradite him to another Party.

(3) This Convention does not exclude the exercise of any criminal jurisdiction established by a Party in accordance with its domestic law.

Article 5
Confiscation

(1) Each Party shall adopt such measures as may be necessary to enable confiscation of:
(a) Proceeds derived from offences established in accordance with article 3, paragraph 1, or property the value of which corresponds to that of such proceeds;
(b) Narcotic drugs and psychotropic substances, materials and equipment or other instrumentalities used in or intended for use in any manner in offences established in accordance with article 3, paragraph 1.

(2) Each Party shall also adopt such measures as may be necessary to enable its competent authorities to identify, trace, and freeze or seize proceeds, property, instrumentalities or any other things referred to in paragraph 1 of this article, for the purpose of eventual confiscation.

(3) In order to carry out the measures referred to in this article, each Party shall empower its courts or other competent authorities to order that bank, financial or commercial records be made available or be seized. A Party shall not decline to act under the provisions of this paragraph on the ground of bank secrecy.

(4)(a) Following a request made pursuant to this article by another Party having jurisdiction over an offence established in accordance with article 3, paragraph 1, the Party in whose territory proceeds, property, instrumentalities or any other things referred to in paragraph 1 of this article are situated shall:
(i) Submit the request to its competent authorities for the purpose of obtaining an order of confiscation and, if such order is granted, give effect to it; or
(ii) Submit to its competent authorities, with a view to giving effect to it to the extent requested, an order of confiscation issued by the requesting Party in accordance with paragraph 1 of this article, in so far as it relates to proceeds, property, instrumentalities or any other things referred to in paragraph 1 situated in the territory of the requested Party.

(b) Following a request made pursuant to this article by another Party having jurisdiction over an offence established in accordance with article 3, paragraph 1, the requested Party shall take measures to identify, trace, and freeze or seize proceeds, property, instrumentalities or any other things referred to in paragraph 1 of this article for the purpose of eventual confiscation to be ordered either by the requesting Party or, pursuant to a request under subparagraph (a) of this paragraph, by the requested Party.

(c) The decisions or actions provided for in subparagraphs (a) and (b) of this paragraph shall be taken by the requested Party, in accordance with and subject to the provisions of its domestic law and its procedural rules or any bilateral or multilateral treaty, agreement or arrangement to which it may be bound in relation to the requesting Party.

(d) The provisions of article 7, paragraphs 6 to 19 are applicable *mutatis mutandis*. In addition to the information specified in article 7, paragraph 10, requests made pursuant to this article shall contain the following:
(i) In the case of a request pertaining to subparagraph (a)(i) of this paragraph, a description of the property to be confiscated and a statement of the facts relied upon by the requesting Party sufficient to enable the requested Party to seek the order under its domestic law;
(ii) In the case of a request pertaining to subparagraph (a)(ii), a legally admissible copy of an order of confiscation issued by the requesting Party upon which the request is based, a statement of the facts and information as to the extent to which the execution of the order is requested;
(iii) In the case of a request pertaining to subparagraph (b), a statement of the facts relied upon by the requesting Party and a description of the actions requested.
(e) Each Party shall furnish to the Secretary-General the text of any of its laws and regulations which give

effect to this paragraph and the text of any subsequent changes to such laws and regulations.
(f) If a Party elects to make the taking of the measures referred to in subparagraphs (a) and (b) of this paragraph conditional on the existence of a relevant treaty, that Party shall consider this Convention as the necessary and sufficient treaty basis.
(g) The Parties shall seek to conclude bilateral and multilateral treaties, agreements or arrangements to enhance the effectiveness of international co-operation pursuant to this article.

(5)(a) Proceeds or property confiscated by a Party pursuant to paragraph 1 or paragraph 4 of this article shall be disposed of by that Party according to its domestic law and administrative procedures.
(b) When acting on the request of another Party in accordance with this article, a Party may give special consideration to concluding agreements on:
(i) Contributing the value of such proceeds and property, or funds derived from the sale of such proceeds or property, or a substantial part thereof, to intergovernmental bodies specializing in the fight against illicit traffic in and abuse of narcotic drugs and psychotropic substances;
(ii) Sharing with other Parties, on a regular or case-by-case basis, such proceeds or property, or funds derived from the sale of such proceeds or property, in accordance with its domestic law, administrative procedures or bilateral or multilateral agreements entered into for this purpose.

(6)(a) If proceeds have been transformed or converted into other property, such property shall be liable to the measures referred to in this article instead of the proceeds.
(b) If the proceeds have been intermingled with property acquired from legitimate sources, such property shall, without prejudice to any powers relating to seizure or freezing, be liable to confiscation up to the assessed value of the intermingled proceeds.
(c) Income or other benefits derived from:
(i) Proceeds;
(ii) Property into which proceeds have been transformed or converted; or
(iii) Property with which proceeds have been intermingled
shall also be liable to the measures referred to in this article, in the same manner and to the same extent as proceeds.

(7) Each Party may consider ensuring that the onus of proof be reversed regarding the lawful origin of alleged proceeds or other property liable to confiscation, to the extent that such action is consistent with the principles of its domestic law and with the nature of the judicial and other proceedings.

(8) The provisions of this article shall not be construed as prejudicing the rights of *bona fide* third parties.

(9) Nothing contained in this article shall affect the principle that the measures to which it refers shall be defined and implemented in accordance with and subject to the provisions of the domestic law of a Party.

Article 6
Extradition

(1) This article shall apply to the offences established by the Parties in accordance with article 3, paragraph 1.

(2) Each of the offences to which this article applies shall be deemed to be included as an extraditable offence in any extradition treaty existing between Parties. The Parties undertake to include such offences as extraditable offences in every extradition treaty to be concluded between them.

(3) If a Party which makes extradition conditional on the existence of a treaty receives a request for extradition from another Party with which it has no extradition treaty, it may consider this Convention as the legal basis for extradition in respect of any offence to which this article applies. The Parties which require detailed legislation in order to use this Convention as a legal basis for extradition shall consider enacting such legislation as may be necessary.

(4) The Parties which do not make extradition conditional on the existence of a treaty shall recognize offences to which this article applies as extraditable offences between themselves.

(5) Extradition shall be subject to the conditions provided for by the law of the requested Party or by

applicable extradition treaties, including the grounds upon which the requested Party may refuse extradition.
(6) In considering requests received pursuant to this article, the requested State may refuse to comply with such requests where there are substantial grounds leading its judicial or other competent authorities to believe that compliance would facilitate the prosecution or punishment of any person on account of his race, religion, nationality or political opinions, or would cause prejudice for any of those reasons to any person affected by the request.
(7) The Parties shall endeavour to expedite extradition procedures and to simplify evidentiary requirements relating thereto in respect of any offence to which this articles applies.
(8) Subject to the provisions of its domestic law and its extradition treaties, the requested Party may, upon being satisfied that the circumstances so warrant and are urgent, and at the request of the requesting Party, take a person whose extradition is sought and who is present in its territory into custody or take other appropriate measures to ensure his presence at extradition proceedings.
(9) Without prejudice to the exercise of any criminal jurisdiction established in accordance with its domestic law, a Party in whose territory an alleged offender is found shall:
(a) If it does not extradite him in respect of an offence established in accordance with article 3, paragraph 1, on the grounds set forth in article 4, paragraph 2, subparagraph (a), submit the case to its competent authorities for the purpose of prosecution, unless otherwise agreed with the requesting Party;
(b) If it does not extradite him in respect of such an offence and has established its jurisdiction in relation to that offence in accordance with article 4, paragraph 2, subparagraph (b), submit the case to its competent authorities for the purpose of prosecution, unless otherwise requested by the requesting Party for the purposes of preserving its legitimate jurisdiction.
(10) If extradition, sought for purposes of enforcing a sentence, is refused because the person sought is a national of the requested Party, the requested Party shall, if its law so permits and in conformity with the requirements of such law, upon application of the requesting Party, consider the enforcement of the sentence which has been imposed under the law of the requesting Party, or the remainder thereof.
(11) The Parties shall seek to conclude bilateral and multilateral agreements to carry out or to enhance the effectiveness of extradition.
(12) The Parties may consider entering into bilateral or multilateral agreements, whether *ad hoc* or general, on the transfer to their country of persons sentenced to imprisonment and other forms of deprivation of liberty for offences to which this article applies, in order that they may complete their sentences there.

Article 7

Mutual legal assistance

(1) The Parties shall afford one another, pursuant to this article, the widest measure of mutual legal assistance in investigations, prosecutions and judicial proceedings in relation to criminal offences established in accordance with article 3, paragraph 1.
(2) Mutual legal assistance to be afforded in accordance with this article may be requested for any of the following purposes:
(a) Taking evidence or statements from persons;
(b) Effecting service of judicial documents;
(c) Executing searches and seizures;
(d) Examining objects and sites;
(e) Providing information and evidentiary items;
(f) Providing originals or certified copies of relevant documents and records, including bank, financial, corporate or business records;
(g) Identifying or tracing proceeds, property, instrumentalities or other things for evidentiary purposes.
(3) The Parties may afford one another any other forms of mutual legal assistance allowed by the domestic law of the requested Party.
(4) Upon request, the Parties shall facilitate or encourage, to the extent consistent with their domestic law and practice, the presence or availability of persons, including persons in custody, who consent to assist in investigations or participate in proceedings.
(5) A Party shall not decline to render mutual legal assistance under this article on the ground of bank secrecy.
(6) The provisions of this article shall not affect the obligations under any other treaty, bilateral or multilateral, which governs or will govern, in whole or in part, mutual legal assistance in criminal matters.
(7) Paragraphs 8 to 19 of this article shall apply to requests made pursuant to this article if the Parties in question are not bound by a treaty of mutual legal assistance. If these Parties are bound by such a treaty, the corresponding provisions of that treaty shall apply unless the Parties agree to apply paragraphs 8 to 19 of this article in lieu thereof.
(8) Parties shall designate an authority, or when necessary authorities, which shall have the responsibility and power to execute requests for mutual legal assistance or to transmit them to the competent authorities for execution. The authority or the authorities designated for this purpose shall be notified to the Secretary-General. Transmission of requests for mutual legal assistance and any communication related thereto shall be effected between the authorities designated by the Parties; this requirement shall be without prejudice to the right of a Party to require that such requests and communications be addressed to it through the diplomatic channel and, in urgent circumstances, where the Parties agree, through channels of the International Criminal Police Organization, if possible.
(9) Requests shall be made in writing in a language acceptable to the requested Party. The language or languages acceptable to each Party shall be notified to the Secretary-General. In urgent circumstances, and where agreed by the Parties, requests may be made orally, but shall be confirmed in writing forthwith.
(10) A request for mutual legal assistance shall contain:
(a) The identity of the authority making the request;
(b) The subject matter and nature of the investigation, prosecution or proceeding to which the request relates, and the name and the functions of the authority conducting such investigation, prosecution or proceeding;
(c) A summary of the relevant facts, except in respect of requests for the purpose of service of judicial documents;
(d) A description of the assistance sought and details of any particular procedure the requesting Party wishes to be followed;
(e) Where possible, the identity, location and nationality of any person concerned;
(f) The purpose for which the evidence, information or action is sought.
(11) The requested Party may request additional information when it appears necessary for the execution of the request in accordance with its domestic law or when it can facilitate such execution.
(12) A request shall be executed in accordance with the domestic law of the requested Party and, to the extent not contrary to the domestic law of the requested Party and where possible, in accordance with the procedures specified in the request.
(13) The requesting Party shall not transmit not use information or evidence furnished by the requested Party for investigations, prosecutions or proceedings other than those stated in the request without the prior consent of the requested Party.
(14) The requesting Party may require that the requested Party keep confidential the fact and substance of the request, except to the extent necessary to execute the request. If the requested Party cannot comply with the requirement of confidentiality, it shall promptly inform the requesting Party.
(15) Mutual legal assistance may be refused:
(a) If the request is not made in conformity with the provisions of this article;
(b) If the requested Party considers that execution of the request is likely to prejudice its sovereignty, security, *ordre public* or other essential interests;
(c) If the authorities of the requested Party would be prohibited by its domestic law from carrying out the action requested with regard to any similar offence, had it been subject to investigation, prosecution or proceedings under their own jurisdiction;
(d) If it would be contrary to the legal system of the requested Party relating to mutual legal assistance for the request to be granted.
(16) Reasons shall be given for any refusal of mutual legal assistance.
(17) Mutual legal assistance may be postponed by the requested Party on the ground that it interferes with an ongoing investigation, prosecution or proceeding. In such a case, the requested Party shall consult with the requesting Party to determine if the assistance can still be given subject to such terms and conditions as the requested Party deems necessary.
(18) A witness, expert or other person who consents to give evidence in a proceeding or to assist in an investigation, prosecution or judicial proceeding in the territory of the requesting Party, shall not be prosecuted, detained, punished or subjected to any other restriction of his personal liberty in that territory in respect of acts, omissions or convictions prior to his departure from the territory of the requested Party. Such safe conduct shall cease when the witness, expert or other person having had, for a period of fifteen consecutive days, or for any period agreed upon by the Parties, from the date on which he has been officially informed that his presence is no longer required by the judicial authorities, an opportunity of leaving, has nevertheless remained voluntarily in the territory or, having left it, has returned of his own free will.
(19) The ordinary costs of executing a request shall be borne by the requested Party, unless otherwise agreed by the Parties concerned. If expenses of a substantial or extraordinary nature are or will be required to fulfil the request, the Party shall consult to determine the terms and conditions under which the request will be executed as well as the manner in which the costs shall be borne.
(20) The Parties shall consider, as may be necessary, the possibility of concluding bilateral or multilateral agreements or arrangements that would serve the purposes of, give practical effect to, or enhance the provisions of this article.

Article 8

Transfer of proceedings

The Parties shall give consideration to the possibility of transferring to one another proceedings for criminal prosecution of offences established in accordance with article 3, paragraph 1, in cases where such transfer is considered to be in the interests of a proper administration of justice.

Article 9

Other forms of co-operation and training

(1) The Parties shall co-operate closely with one another, consistent with their respective domestic legal and administrative systems, with a view to enhancing the effectiveness of law enforcement action to suppress the commission of offences established in accordance with article 3, paragraph 1. They shall, in particular, on the basis of bilateral or multilateral agreements or arrangements:
(a) Establish and maintain channels of communication between their competent agencies and services to facilitate the secure and rapid exchange of information concerning all aspects of offences established in accordance with article 3, paragraph 1, including, if the Parties concerned deem it appropriate, links with other criminal activities;
(b) Co-operate with one another in conducting enquiries, with respect to offences established in accordance with article 3, paragraph 1, having an international character, concerning:
(i) The identity, whereabouts and activities of persons suspected of being involved in offences established in accordance with article 3, paragraph 1;
(ii) The movement of proceeds or property derived from the commission of such offences;
(iii) The movement of narcotic drugs, psychotropic substances, substances in Table I and Table II of this Convention and instrumentalities used or intended for use in the commission of such offences;
(c) In appropriate cases and if not contrary to domestic law, establish joint teams, taking into account the need to protect the security of persons and of operations, to carry out the provisions of this paragraph. Officials of any Party taking part in such teams shall act as authorized by the appropriate authorities of the Party in whose territory the operation is to take place; in all such cases, the Parties involved shall ensure that the sovereignty of the Party on whose territory the operation is to take place is fully respected;

(d) Provide, when appropriate, necessary quantities of substances for analytical or investigative purposes;
(e) Facilitate effective co-ordination between their competent agencies and services and promote the exchange of personnel and other experts, including the posting of liaison officers.
(2) Each Party shall, to the extent necessary, initiate, develop or improve specific training programmes for its law enforcement and other personnel, including customs, charged with the suppression of offences established in accordance with article 3, paragraph 1. Such programmes shall deal, in particular, with the following:
(a) Methods used in the detection and suppression of offences established in accordance with article 3, paragraph 1;
(b) Routes and techniques used by persons suspected of being involved in offences established in accordance with article 3, paragraph 1, particularly transit States, and appropriate countermeasures;
(c) Monitoring of the import and export of narcotic drugs, psychotropic substances and substances in Table I and Table II;
(d) Detection and monitoring of the movement of proceeds and property derived from, and narcotic drugs, psychotropic substances and sustances in Table I and Table II, and instrumentalities used or intended for use in, the commission of offences established in accordance with article 3, paragraph 1;
(e) Methods used for the transfer, concealment or disguise of such proceeds, property and instrumentalities;
(f) Collection of evidence;
(g) Control techniques in free trade zones and free ports;
(h) Modern law enforcement techniques.
(3) The Parties shall assist one another to plan and implement research and training programmes designed to share expertise in the areas referred to in paragraph 2 of this article and, to this end, shall also, when appropriate, use regional and international conferences and seminars to promote co-operation and stimulate discussion on problems of mutual concern, including the special problems and needs of transit States.

Article 10

International co-operation and assistance for transit states

(1) The Parties shall co-operate, directly or through competent international or regional organizations, to assist and support transit States and, in particular, developing countries in need of such assistance and support, to the extent possible, through programmes of technical co-operation on interdiction and other related activities.
(2) The Parties may undertake, directly or through competent international or regional organizations, to provide financial assistance to such transit States for the purpose of augmenting and strengthening the infrastructure needed for effective control and prevention of illicit traffic.
(3) The Parties may conclude bilateral or multilateral agreements or arrangements to enhance the effectiveness of international co-operation pursuant to this article and may take into consideration financial arrangements in this regard.

Article 11

Controlled delivery

(1) If permitted by the basic principles of their respective domestic legal systems, the Parties shall take the necessary measures, within their possibilities, to allow for the appropriate use of controlled delivery at the international level, on the basis of agreements or arrangements mutually consented to, with a view to identifying persons involved in offences established in accordance with article 3, paragraph 1, and to taking legal action against them.
(2) Decisions to use controlled delivery shall be made on a case-by-case basis and may, when necessary, take into consideration financial arrangements and understandings with respect to the exercise of jurisdiction by the Parties concerned.
(3) Illicit consignments whose controlled delivery is agreed to may, with the consent of the Parties concerned, be intercepted and allowed to continue with the narcotic drugs or psychotropic substances intact or removed or replaced in whole or in part.

Article 12

Substances frequently used in the illicit manufacture of narcotic drugs or psychotropic substances

(1) The Parties shall take the measures they deem appropriate to prevent diversion of substances in Table I and Table II used for the purpose of illicit manufacture of narcotic drugs or psychotropic substances, and shall co-operate with one another to this end.
(2) If a Party or the Board has information which in its opinion may require the inclusion of a substance in Table I or Table II, it shall notify the Secretary-General and furnish him with the information in support of that notification. The procedure described in paragraphs 2 to 7 of this article shall also apply when a Party or the Board has information justifying the deletion of a substance from Table I or Table II, or the transfer of a substance from one Table to the other.
(3) The Secretary-General shall transmit such notification, and any information which he considers relevant, to the Parties, to the Commission, and, where notification is made by a Party, to the Board. The Parties shall communicate their comments concerning the notification to the Secretary-General, together with all supplementary information which may assist the Board in establishing an assessment and the Commission in reaching a decision.
(4) If the Board, taking into account the extent, importance and diversity of the licit use of the substance, and the possibility and ease of using alternate substances both for licit purposes and for the illicit manufacture of narcotic drugs or psychotropic substances, finds:
(a) That the substance is frequently used in the illicit manufacture of a narcotic drug or psychotropic substance;
(b) That the volume and extent of the illicit manufacture of a narcotic drug or psychotropic substance creates serious public health or social problems, so as to warrant international action, it shall communicate to the Commission an assessment of the substance, including the likely effect of adding the substance to either Table I or Table II on both licit use and illicit manufacture, together with recommendations of monitoring measures, if any, that would be appropriate in the light of its assessment.
(5) The Commission, taking into account the comments submitted by the Parties and the comments and recommendations of the Board, whose assessment shall be determinative as to scientific matters, and also taking into due consideration any other relevant factors, may decide by a two-thirds majority of its members to place a substance in Table I or Table II.
(6) Any decision of the Commission taken pursuant to this article shall be communicated by the Secretary-General to all States and other entities which are, or which are entitled to become, Parties to this Convention, and to the Board. Such decision shall become fully effective with respect to each Party one hundred and eighty days after the date of such communication.
(7)(a) The decisions of the Commission taken under this article shall be subject to review by the Council upon the request of any Party filed within one hundred and eighty days after the date of notification of the decision. The request for review shall be sent to the Secretary-General, together with all relevant information upon which the request for review is based.
(b) The Secretary-General shall transmit copies of the request for review and the relevant information to the Commission, to the Board and to all the Parties, inviting them to submit their comments within ninety days. All comments received shall be submitted to the Council for consideration.
(c) The Council may confirm or reverse the decision of the Commission. Notification of the Council's decision shall be transmitted to all States and other entities which are, or which are entitled to become, Parties to this Convention, to the Commission and to the Board.
(8)(a) Without prejudice to the generality of the provisions contained in paragraph 1 of this article and the provisions of the 1961 Convention, the 1961 Convention as amended and the 1971 Convention, the Parties shall take the measures they deem appropriate to monitor the manufacture and distribution of substances in Table I and Table II which are carried out within their territory.
(b) To this end, the Parties may:
(i) Control all persons and enterprises engaged in the manufacture and distribution of such substances;
(ii) Control under licence the establishment and premises in which such manufacture or distribution may take place;
(iii) Require that licensees obtain a permit for conducting the aforesaid operations;
(iv) Prevent the accumulation of such substances in the possession of manufacturers and distributors, in excess of the quantities required for the normal conduct of business and the prevailing market conditions.
(9) Each Party shall, with respect to substances in Table I and Table II, take the following measures:
(a) Establish and maintain a system to monitor international trade in substances in Table I and Table II in order to facilitate the identification of suspicious transactions. Such monitoring systems shall be applied in close co-operation with manufacturers, importers, exporters, wholesalers and retailers, who shall inform the competent authorities of suspicious orders and transactions.
(b) Provide for the seizure of any substance in Table I or Table II if there is sufficient evidence that it is for use in the illicit manufacture of a narcotic drug or psychotropic substance.
(c) Notify, as soon as possible, the competent authorities and services of the Parties concerned if there is reason to believe that the import, export or transit of a substance in Table I or Table II is destined for the illicit manufacture of narcotic drugs or psychotropic substances, including in particular information about the means of payment and any other essential elements which led to that belief.
(d) Require that imports and exports be properly labelled and documented. Commercial documents such as invoices, cargo manifests, customs, transport and other shipping documents shall include the names, as stated in Table I or Table II, of the substances being imported or exported, the quantity being imported or exported, and the name and address of the exporter, the importer and, when available, the consignee.
(e) Ensure that documents referred to in subparagraph (d) of this paragraph are maintained for a period of not less than two years and may be made available for inspection by the competent authorities.
(10)(a) In addition to the provisions of paragraph 9, and upon request to the Secretary-General by the interested Party, each Party from whose territory a substance in Table I is to be exported shall ensure that, prior to such export, the following information is supplied by its competent authorities to the competent authorities of the importing country:
(i) Name and address of the exporter and importer and, when available, the consignee;
(ii) Name of the substance in Table I;
(iii) Quantity of the substance to be exported;
(iv) Expected point of entry and expected date of dispatch;
(v) Any other information which is mutually agreed upon by the Parties.
(b) A Party may adopt more strict or severe measures of control than those provided by this paragraph if, in its opinion, such measures are desirable or necessary.
(11) Where a Party furnishes information to another Party in accordance with paragraphs 9 and 10 of this article, the Party furnishing such information may require that the Party receiving it keep confidential any trade, business, commercial or professional secret or trade process.
(12) Each Party shall furnish annually to the Board, in the form and manner provided for by it and on forms made available by it, information on:
(a) The amounts seized of substances in Table I and Table II and, when known, their origin;
(b) Any substance not included in Table I or Table II which is identified having been used in illicit manufacture of narcotic drugs or psychotropic substances, and which is deemed by the Party to be sufficiently significant to be brought to the attention of the Board;
(c) Methods of diversion and illicit manufacture.
(13) The Board shall report annually to the Commission on the implementation of this article and the Commission shall periodically review the adequacy and propriety of Table I and Table II.

(14) The provisions of this article shall not apply to pharmaceutical preparations, nor to other preparations containing substances in Table I or Table II that are compounded in such a way that such substances cannot be easily used or recovered by readily applicable means.

Article 13
Materials and equipment
The Parties shall take such measures as they deem appropriate to prevent trade in and diversion of materials and equipment for illicit production or manufacture of narcotic drugs and psychotropic substances and shall co-operate to this end.

Article 14
Measures to eradicate illicit cultivation of narcotic plants and to eliminate illicit demand for narcotic drugs and psychotropic substances
(1) Any measures taken pursuant to this Convention by Parties shall not be less stringent than the provisions applicable to the eradication of illicit cultivation of plants containing narcotic and psychotropic substances and to the elimination of illicit demand for narcotic drugs and psychotropic substances under the provisions of the 1961 Convention, the 1961 Convention as amended and the 1971 Convention.
(2) Each Party shall take appropriate measures to prevent illicit cultivation of and to eradicate plants containing narcotic or psychotropic substances, such as opium poppy, coca bush and cannabis plants, cultivated illicitly in its territory. The measures adopted shall respect fundamental human rights and shall take due account of traditional licit uses, where there is historic evidence of such use, as well as the protection of the environment.
(3)(a) The Parties may co-operate to increase the effectiveness of eradication efforts. Such co-operation may, *inter alia*, include support, when appropriate, for integrated rural development leading to economically viable alternatives to illicit cultivation. Factors such as access to markets, the availability of resources and prevailing socio-economic conditions should be taken into account before such rural development programmes are implemented. The Parties may agree on any other appropriate measures of co-operation.
(b) The Parties shall also facilitate the exchange of scientific and technical information and the conduct of research concerning eradication.
(c) Whenever they have common frontiers, the Parties shall seek to co-operate in eradication programmes in their respective areas along those frontiers.
(4) The Parties shall adopt appropriate measures aimed at eliminating or reducing illicit demand for narcotic drugs and psychotropic substances, with a view to reducing human suffering and eliminating financial incentives for illicit traffic. These measures may be based, *inter alia*, on the recommendations of the United Nations, specialized agencies of the United Nations such as the World Health Organization, and other competent international organizations, and on the Comprehensive Multidisciplinary Outline adopted by the International Conference on Drug Abuse and Illicit Trafficking, held in 1987, as it pertains to governmental and non-governmental agencies and private efforts in the fields of prevention, treatment and rehabilitation. The Parties may enter into bilateral or multilateral agreements or arrangements aimed at eliminating or reducing demand for narcotic drugs and psychotropic substances.
(5) The Parties may also take necessary measures for early destruction or lawful disposal of the narcotic drugs, psychotropic substances and substances in Table I and Table II which have been seized or confiscated and for the admissibility as evidence of duly certified necessary quantities of such substances.

Article 15
Commercial carriers
The Parties shall take appropriate measures to ensure that means of transport operated by commercial carriers are not used in the commission of offences established in accordance with article 3, paragraph 1; such measures may include special arrangements with commercial carriers.
(2) Each Party shall require commercial carriers to take reasonable precautions to prevent the use of their means of transport for the commission of offences

established in accordance with article 3, paragraph 1. Such precautions may include:
(a) If the principal place of business of a commercial carrier is within the territory of the Party:
(i) Training of personnel to identify suspicious consignments or persons;
(ii) Promotion of integrity of personnel;
(b) If a commercial carrier is operating within the territory of the Party:
(i) Submission of cargo manifests in advance, whenever possible;
(ii) Use of tamper-resistant, individually verifiable seals on containers;
(iii) Reporting to the appropriate authorities at the earliest opportunity all suspicious circumstances that may be related to the commission of offences established in accordance with article 3, paragraph 1.
(3) Each Party shall seek to ensure that commercial carriers and the appropriate authorities at points of entry and exit and other customs control areas co-operate, with a view to preventing unauthorized access to means of transport and cargo and to implementing appropriate security measures.

Article 16
Commercial documents and labelling of exports
(1) Each Party shall require that lawful exports of narcotic drugs and psychotropic substances be property documented. In addition to the requirements for documentation under article 31 of the 1961 Convention, article 31 of the 1961 Convention as amended and article 12 of the 1971 Convention, commercial documents such as invoices, cargo manifests, customs, transport and other shipping documents shall include the names of the narcotic drugs and psychotropic substances being exported as set out in the respective Schedules of the 1961 Convention, the 1961 Convention as amended and the 1971 Convention, the quantity being exported, and the name and address of the exporter, the importer and, when available, the consignee.
(2) Each Party shall require that consignments of narcotic drugs and psychotropic substances being exported be not mislabelled.

Article 17
Illicit traffic by sea
(1) The Parties shall co-operate to the fullest extent possible to suppress illicit traffic by sea, in conformity with the international law of the sea.
(2) A Party which has reasonable grounds to suspect that a vessel flying its flag or not displaying a flag or marks of registry is engaged in illicit traffic may request the assistance of other Parties in suppressing its use for that purpose. The Parties so requested shall render such assistance within the means available to them.
(3) A Party which has reasonable grounds to suspect that a vessel exercising freedom of navigation in accordance with international law and flying the flag or displaying marks of registry of another Party is engaged in illicit traffic may so notify the flag State, request confirmation of registry and, if confirmed, request authorization from the flag State to take appropriate measures in regard to that vessel.
(4) In accordance with paragraph 3 or in accordance with treaties in force between them or in accordance with any agreement or arrangement otherwise reached between those Parties, the flag State may authorize the requesting State to, *inter alia*:
(a) Board the vessel;
(b) Search the vessel;
(c) If evidence of involvement in illicit traffic is found, take appropriate action with respect to the vessel, persons and cargo on board.
(5) Where action is taken pursuant to this article, the Parties concerned shall take due account of the need not to endanger the safety of life at sea, the security of the vessel and the cargo or to prejudice the commercial and legal interests of the flag State or any other interested State.
(6) The flag State may, consistent with its obligations in paragraph 1 of this article, subject its authorization to conditions to be mutually agreed between it and the requesting Party, including conditions relating to responsibility.
(7) For the purposes of paragraphs 3 and 4 of this article, a Party shall respond expeditiously to a request

from another Party to determine whether a vessel that is flying its flag is entitled to do so, and to requests for authorization made pursuant to paragraph 3. At the time of becoming a Party to this Convention, each Party shall designate an authority or, when necessary, authorities to receive and respond to such requests. Such designation shall be notified through the Secretary-General to all other Parties within one month of the designation.
(8) A Party which has taken any action in accordance with this article shall promptly inform the flag State concerned of the results of that action.
(9) The Parties shall consider entering into bilateral or regional agreements or arrangements to carry out, or to enhance the effectiveness of, the provisions of this article.
(10) Action pursuant to paragraph 4 of this article shall be carried out only by warships or military aircraft, or other ships or aircraft clearly marked and identifiable as being on government service and authorized to that effect.
(11) Any action taken in accordance with this article shall take due account of the need not to interfere with or affect the rights and obligations and the exercise of jurisdiction of coastal States in accordance with the international law of the sea.

Article 18
Free trade zones and free ports
(1) The Parties shall apply measures to suppress illicit traffic in narcotic drugs, psychotropic substances and substances in Table I and Table II in free trade zones and in free ports that are no less stringent than those applied in other parts of their territories.
(2) The Parties shall endeavour:
(a) To monitor the movement of goods and persons in free trade zones and free ports, and, to that end, shall empower the competent authorities to search cargoes and incoming and outgoing vessels, including pleasure craft and fishing vessels, as well as aircraft and vehicles and, when appropriate, to search crew members, passengers and their baggage;
(b) To establish and maintain a system to detect consignments suspected of containing narcotic drugs, psychotropic substances and substances in Table I and Table II passing into or out of free trade zones and free ports;
(c) To establish and maintain surveillance systems in harbour and dock areas and at airports and border control points in free trade zones and free ports.

Article 19
The use of the mails
(1) In conformity with their obligations under the Conventions of the Universal Postal Union, and in accordance with the basic principles of their domestic legal systems, the Parties shall adopt measures to suppress the use of the mails for illicit traffic and shall co-operate with one another to that end.
(2) The measures referred to in paragraph 1 of this article shall include, in particular:
(a) Co-ordinated action for the prevention and repression of the use of the mails for illicit traffic;
(b) Introduction and maintenance by authorized law enforcement personnel of investigative and control techniques designed to detect illicit consignments of narcotic drugs, psychotropic substances and substances in Table I and Table II in the mails;
(c) Legislative measures to enable the use of appropriate means to secure evidence required for judicial proceedings.

Article 20
Information to be furnished by the parties
(1) The Parties shall furnish, through the Secretary-General, information to the Commission on the working of this Convention in their territories and, in particular:
(a) The text of laws and regulations promulgated in order to give effect to the Convention;
(b) Particulars of cases of illicit traffic within their jurisdiction which they consider important because of new trends disclosed, the quantities involved, the sources from which the substances are obtained, or the methods employed by persons so engaged.
(2) The Parties shall furnish such information in such a manner and by such dates as the Commission may request.

Narcotic Drugs and Psychotropic Substances

Article 21
Functions of the commission
The Commission is authorized to consider all matters pertaining to the aims of this Convention and, in particular:
(a) The Commission shall, on the basis of the information submitted by the Parties in accordance with Article 20, review the operation of this Convention;
(b) The Commission may make suggestions and general recommendations based on the examination of the information received from the Parties;
(c) The Commission may call the attention of the Board to any matters which may be relevant to the functions of the Board;
(d) The Commission shall, on any matter referred to it by the Board under article 22, paragraph 1(b), take such action as it deems appropriate;
(e) The Commission may, in conformity with the procedures laid down in article 12, amend Table I and Table II;
(f) The Commission may draw the attention of non-Parties to decisions and recommendations which it adopts under this Convention, with a view to their considering taking action in accordance therewith.
Article 22
Functions of the board
(1) Without prejudice to the functions of the Commission under article 21, and without prejudice to the functions of the Board and the Commission under the 1961 Convention, the 1961 Convention as amended and the 1971 Convention:
(a) If, on the basis of its examination of information available to it, to the Secretary-General or to the Commission, or of information communicated by United Nations organs, the Board has reason to believe that the aims of this Convention in matters related to its competence are not being met, the Board may invite a Party or Parties to furnish any relevant information;
(b) With respect to articles 12, 13 and 16:
(i) After taking action under subparagraph (a) of this article, the Board, if satisfied that it is necessary to do so, may call upon the Party concerned to adopt such remedial measures as shall seem under the circumstances to be necessary for the execution of the provisions of articles 12, 13 and 16;
(ii) Prior to taking action under (iii) below, the Board shall treat as confidential its communications with the Party concerned under the preceding subparagraphs;
(iii) If the Board finds that the Party concerned has not taken remedial measures which it has been called upon to take under this subparagraph, it may call the attention of the Parties, the Council and the Commission to the matter. Any report published by the Board under this subparagraph shall also contain the views of the Party concerned if the latter so requests.
(2) Any Party shall be invited to be represented at a meeting of the Board at which a question of direct interest to it is to be considered under this article.
(3) If in any case a decision of the Board which is adopted under this article is not unanimous, the views of the minority shall be stated.
(4) Decisions of the Board under this article shall be taken by a two-thirds majority of the whole number of the Board.
(5) In carrying out its functions pursuant to subparagraph 1(a) of this article, the Board shall ensure the confidentiality of all information which may come into its possession.
(6) The Board's responsibility under this article shall not apply to the implementation of treaties or agreements entered into between Parties in accordance with the provisions of this Convention.
(7) The provisions of this article shall not be applicable to disputes between Parties falling under the provisions of article 32.
Article 23
Reports of the board
(1) The Board shall prepare an annual report on its work containing an analysis of the information at its disposal and, in appropriate cases, an account of the explanations, if any, given by or required of Parties, together with any observations and recommendations which the Board desires to make. The Board may make such additional reports as it considers necessary. The reports shall be submitted to the Council through the

Commission which may make such comments as it sees fit.
(2) The reports of the Board shall be communicated to the Parties and subsequently published by the Secretary-General. The Parties shall permit their unrestricted distribution.
Article 24
Application of stricter measures than those required by this convention
A Party may adopt more strict or severe measures than those provided by this Convention if, in its opinion, such measures are desirable or necessary for the prevention or suppression of illicit traffic.
Article 25
Non-derogation from earlier treaty rights and obligations
The provisions of this Convention shall not derogate from any rights enjoyed or obligations undertaken by Parties to this Convention under the 1961 Convention, the 1961 Convention as amended and the 1971 Convention.
Article 26
Signature
This Convention shall be open for signature at the United Nations Office at Vienna, from 20 December 1988 to 28 February 1989, and thereafter at the Headquarters of the United Nations at New York, until 20 December 1989, by:
(a) All States;
(b) Namibia, represented by the United Nations Council for Namibia;
(c) Regional economic integration organizations which have competence in respect of the negotiation, conclusion and application of international agreements in matters covered by this Convention, references under the Convention to Parties, States or national services being applicable to these organizations within the limits of their competence.
Article 27
Ratification, acceptance, approval or act of formal confirmation
(1) This Convention is subject to ratification, acceptance or approval by States and by Namibia, represented by the United Nations Council for Namibia, and to acts of formal confirmation by regional economic integration organizations referred to in article 26, subparagraph (c). The instruments of ratification, acceptance or approval and those relating to acts of formal confirmation shall be deposited with the Secretary-General.
(2) In their instruments of formal confirmation, regional economic integration organizations shall declare the extent of their competence with respect to the matters governed by this Convention. These organizations shall also inform the Secretary-General of any modification in the extent of their competence with respect to the matters governed by the Convention.
Article 28
Accession
(1) This Convention shall remain open for accession by any State, by Namibia, represented by the United Nations Council for Namibia, and by regional economic integration organizations referred to in article 26, subparagraph (c).
Accession shall be effected by the deposit of an instrument of accession with the Secretary-General.
(2) In their instruments of accession, regional economic integration organizations shall declare the extent of their competence with respect to the matters governed by this Convention. These organizations shall also inform the Secretary-General of any modification in the extent of their competence with respect to the matters governed by the Convention.
Article 29
Entry into force
(1) This Convention shall enter into force on the ninetieth day after the date of the deposit with the Secretary-General of the twentieth instrument of ratification, acceptance, approval or accession by States or by Namibia, represented by the Council for Namibia.
(2) For each State or for Namibia, represented by the Council for Namibia, ratifying, accepting, approving or acceding to this Convention after the deposit of the twentieth instrument of ratification, acceptance, approval or accession, the Convention shall enter into

force on the ninetieth day after the date of the deposit of its instrument of ratification, acceptance, approval or accession.
(3) For each regional economic integration organization referred to in article 26, subparagraph (c) depositing an instrument relating to an act of formal confirmation or an instrument of accession, this Convention shall enter into force on the ninetieth day after such deposit, or at the date the Convention enters into force pursuant to paragraph 1 of this article, whichever is later.
Article 30
Denunciation
(1) A Party may denounce this Convention at any time by a written notification addressed to the Secretary-General.
(2) Such denunciation shall take effect for the Party concerned one year after the date of receipt of the notification by the Secretary-General.
Article 31
Amendments
(1) Any Party may propose an amendment to this Convention. The text of any such amendment and the reasons therefor shall be communicated by that Party to the Secretary-General, who shall communicate it to the other Parties and shall ask them whether they accept the proposed amendment. If a proposed amendment so circulated has not been rejected by any Party within twenty-four months after it has been circulated, it shall be deemed to have been accepted and shall enter into force in respect of a Party ninety days after the Party has deposited with the Secretary-General an instrument expressing its consent to be bound by that amendment.
(2) If a proposed amendment has been rejected by any Party, the Secretary-General shall consult with the Parties and, if a majority so requests, he shall bring the matter, together with any comments made by the Parties, before the Council which may decide to call a conference in accordance with Article 62, paragraph 4, of the Charter of the United Nations. Any amendment resulting from such a Conference shall be embodied in a Protocol of Amendment. Consent to be bound by such a Protocol shall be required to be expressed specifically to the Secretary-General.
Article 32
Settlement of disputes
(1) If there should arise between two or more Parties a dispute relating to the interpretation or application of this Convention, the Parties shall consult together with a view to the settlement of the dispute by negotiation, enquiry, mediation, conciliation, arbitration, recourse to regional bodies, judicial process or other peaceful means of their own choice.
(2) Any such dispute which cannot be settled in the manner prescribed in paragraph 1 of this article shall be referred, at the request of any one of the States Parties to the dispute, to the International Court of Justice for decision.
(3) If a regional economic integration organization referred to in article 26, subparagraph (c) is a Party to a dispute which cannot be settled in the manner prescribed in paragraph 1 of this article, it may, through a State Member of the United Nations, request the Council to request an advisory opinion of the International Court of Justice in accordance with article 65 of the Statute of the Court, which opinion shall be regarded as decisive.
(4) Each State, at the time of signature or ratification, acceptance or approval of this Convention or accession thereto, or each regional economic integration organization, at the time of signature or deposit of an act of formal confirmation or accession, may declare that it does not consider itself bound by paragraphs 2 and 3 of this article. The other Parties shall not be bound by paragraphs 2 and 3 with respect to any Party having made such a declaration.
(5) Any Party having made a declaration in accordance with paragraph 4 of this article may at any time withdraw the declaration by notification to the Secretary-General.
Article 33
Authentic texts
The Arabic, Chinese, English, French, Russian and Spanish texts of this Convention are equally authentic.

N

Article 34
Depositary
The Secretary-General shall be the depositary of this Convention.
By the end of 1989, the Convention had been signed by more than 60 States.

NARCOTICS. The subject of international conventions aimed at suppressing production, trafficking and dissemination of narcotics. The First Conference on the International Control of Narcotics was held in 1909 in Shanghai with the participation of 14 states. Through a number of adopted resolutions the conference started the preparation of the First Hague Convention on Exercising Control over Opium, the so-called Hague Opium Convention of 1912. This first convention, signed on Jan. 23, 1912 in The Hague came into force as late as 1920 when the LN named a permanent organ of the convention, the International Opium Bureau, to study the problem and arbitrate in disputes. The colonial powers, pursuing their interest in the Far East, signed on Jan. 11, 1925, an agreement concerning an international opium trade monopoly and restrictions in the number of opium dens. On the initiative of the LN a new convention expanding the scope of the 1912 convention to include also other narcotics was signed on Feb. 19, 1925 in Geneva. The Permanent Central Narcotics Board, PCNB, became an organ of the convention and later initiated the signing of other agreements and protocols: on July 11, 1931, and June 26, 1936, in Geneva; on Nov. 27, 1931 in Bangkok; in 1931 the Convention to Limit the Manufacture and Regulate the Production of Narcotic Drugs (supplemented by a Protocol of 1948); the Convention for the Suppression of the Illicit Traffic in Dangerous Drugs 1936; and in 1946, 1948 and 1953 the additional Protocols. After World War II the UN General Assembly, on Dec. 11, 1946, adopted a Protocol listing the Conventions and Protocols of 1912, 1925, 1931 and 1936 and also advised ECOSOC to take over all functions of the control organs of the League of Nations. In the same year ECOSOC established the UN Commission for Narcotic Drugs and the Drug Supervisory Body, DSB, and the UN Narcotic Drug Laboratory in Geneva in order to identify confiscated drugs. The UN General Assembly on Nov. 19, 1948, adopted a Protocol expanding the term "narcotics" to include medicaments which, according to WHO, may be used by drug addicts; the Assembly also recommended the working out of an International Convention indiscriminately binding on all states. This was objected to by Great Britain which maintained that it was not in a position to enforce such a convention in its colonies and trusteeship territories. Thirteen years later, along with the process of decolonization, all previous conventions were codified in the so-called Single Convention on Narcotic Drugs adopted on Mar. 25, 1961, by the UN Conference on Narcotics, and came into force Feb. 13, 1964. In 1977, 108 states had become parties to the convention, whose organ is the International Narcotic Control Board, INCB, based in Geneva. In 1972 in Geneva the UN Conference on Narcotics adopted an Auxiliary Protocol to the Single Convention which highlights the need for treatment and rehabilitation of drug addicts. In 1971 the UN Conference on Psychotropic Substances adopted a convention on monitoring and control of such substances, the Convention on Psychotropic Substances. In 1971 the UN created the Fund for Drug Abuse Control, UNFDAC to finance (on the basis of voluntary contributions) a worldwide campaign against narcotics. A WHO Expert Committee on Drug Dependence publishes annual reports on the problem of narcotics throughout the world.

During 1965–70, according to WHO estimates, the USA and Western Europe were afflicted with drug addiction "in epidemic proportions"; this refers to the use of natural narcotics and medicaments by youth (e.g. ▷ LSD-25). WHO put the UN Commission on alert and the latter in effect worked out a number of recommendations for governments to stop new forms of drug dependence. During 1971–76, UNESCO launched a campaign against drug abuse by youth. In 1981 the UN General Assembly initiated a new International Drug Abuse Control Strategy, and in 1983 a program of action for the 1984–85 biennium. ▷ Tranquillizers.
The Report of the UN Secretary General 1984 stated:

"The growing problem of narcotic drugs has become a major international anxiety, not least because of its effect on children and young people. The institutions of the UN system in co-operation with Governments are actively working to deal with it."

The General Assembly in Dec. 1985 (Res. 39/41) called on the Commissions on Narcotic Drugs to begin work on a new Drug Convention.

Organizations reg. with the UIA:

European Society for the Study of Drug Toxicity, f. 1962, Berne.
Institute for the Study of Drug Dependence, f. 1971, London. Publ.: *Drugs and Society*.
International Committee on Alcohol, Drugs and Traffic Safety, f. 1962, Stockholm.
International Council of Alcohol and Addictions, f. 1907, Lausanne. Consultative status with ECOSOC and ILO.

See also ▷ Drug Control.

First Opium Conference 1925, New York, 1947; *Second Opium Conference 1925*, New York, 1927; *Conference on the Suppression of Opium Smoking 1931*, New York, 1947; *Conference for the Limitation of the Manufacture of the Narcotics Drugs 1931*, New York, 1947; *Conference for the Suppression of the Illicit Traffic in Dangerous Drugs 1936*, New York, 1947; H.L. MAY, "Narcotic Drug Control", in: *International Conciliation*, Nov., 1952, pp. 491–536; *UN Opium Conference 1953*, New York, 1953; H.J. ANSLINGER, W.F. TOMPKINS, *The Traffic in Narcotics*, London, 1953; L.M. GOODRICH, "New Trends in Narcotics Control", in: *International Conciliation*, No. 530, 1960; *UN Narcotics Conference 1961*, New York, 1963; *The Unic Convention on Narcotics*, New York, 1962; *UN Narcotic Drugs Under International Control. Multilingual List*, New York, 1962; S.H. SNYDER, *Uses of Marijuana*, London, 1972; *Drug Abuse, Nonmedical Use of Dependence-Producing Drugs. Proceedings of the Sixth Table Conference organized by the Council for International Organization of Medical Sciences, with the Council for International Organization of Medical Sciences, with the participation of UNESCO and WHO, Geneva, Oct. 20–21, 1971*, New York, 1972; T.L. CHRUŚCIEL, "Drug Dependence", in: *Enciclopaedia Medica Italiana*, Roma, 1973; *Youth and Drugs*, Report of a WHO Study Group, WHO Geneva, 1973; D. CARDENAS DE OJEDA, *Toxicomania y narcotrafico, Aspectos legales*, Mexico, DF, 1975; *UN Chronicle*, June 1982, pp. 74–78; *UN Multilingual Directory of Narcotic Drugs and Psychotropic Substances Under International Control*, New York, 1983, January 1984, p. 50 and 88; *Yearbook of International Organizations*.

NARCOTRAFICANTES. Spanish = narcotic traders. An international term since the 1980's in connection with a Latin American cocaine cartel with headquarters in Medellin, Colombia.

O. CALLE, *The Families of Medellin*, in: *Newsweek*, March 14, 1988.

NARODOWY BANK POLSKI. The Polish National Bank. The Central State Bank of Poland, est. Jan. 15, 1945 taking over the issuing functions of the Bank Polski, est. 1924. Within the framework of the restructuring of the economic system, it became the central credit institution as well as the

disposer of gold and currency reserves; it is in continual financial co-operation with the central banks of the socialist countries and some central and trade banks of capitalist countries via Bank Handlowy SA.

NASA. National Aeronautics and Space Administration. The name of an independent US government agency, scientific-research institution, established 1915 as National Advisory Committee for Aeronautics, NACA, which developed aviation legislation and supported technical progress in aviation; after World War II, along with its new name in 1958, it extended the range of its activity to the development of space research and co-ordination of the space program.
See also ▷ DARFA.

A.M. DIN ed., *NASA and Artificial Intelligence*, SIPRI, Oxford, 1987.

NASSAU COMMONWEALTH DECLARATION, 1985. Declaration of the heads of governments, at a meeting on Oct. 2, 1985 in Nassau, commemorating the 40th Anniversary of the United Nations.

KEESING's *Contemporary Archive*, September, 1986.

NASSAU UNDERSTANDING. ▷ CARICOM.

NASSERISM. A Pan-Arabic, anti-imperialist political doctrine formulated by the Arab statesman Gamal Abd el-Nasser (1918–70), co-founder of the nationalistic Egyptian Organization of Free Officers, which on July 23, 1952 dethroned the king and proclaimed Egypt a republic; in 1956, when Egypt nationalized the Suez Canal, Nasser was President of Egypt. In the period 1956–70 Nasserism had a certain influence not only in the Arab world, but also in Latin America.

J. COUBARD, *Nasser*, Paris, 1975.

NATATION. ▷ Swimming.

NATION. An international term having no international definition. ▷ Citizenship, Nationality.

H. SETON-WATSON, *Nations and States. An Enquiry into the Origins of Nations and the Politics of Nationalism*, London, 1972; M. OLSON, *The Rise and Decline of Nations. Economic Growth, Stagflation and Social Rigidities*, New Haven, 1982.

NATIONAL ANTHEMS. Songs elevated to the rank of national hymns. In monarchies their role was to impetrate God's blessing for the ruler ("*God save the King*"; "*Bozhe cara khrani*"; "*Gott behütte, Gott behalte*", ...) the oldest is the Dutch national anthem, "*Wilhelmus van Nassouve*" ...(1568), followed by the British, "*God save the King*" ... (1743). In republics anthems are generally chosen from among revolutionary songs, e.g., *La Marseillaise*, the rallying call of the 1792 French Revolution, became in 1789 the national anthem of the French Republic; the ▷ *International*, 1887 was Soviet Russia's anthem 1917–1944; The *Star-Spangled Banner*, an American folk song of 1814, became the USA's national anthem under President H. Hoover in 1931. It is an international practice to play national anthems at interstate meetings both political and sports (e.g. in honor of winners at Olympic Games).

Hymnen der Völker, Berlin, 1936.

NATIONAL CLAUSE. A formula applied to bilateral or multilateral treaties providing that each party to the agreement should treat ships, commodities, legal persons and nationals of any other member state as equal to its own. The GATT uses the national clause for commodities.

NATIONAL DAYS. The main state anniversaries, officially celebrated as a holiday or holidays; e.g. dates of recovering, gaining or proclaiming independence, or, in monarchist systems – the monarch's birthday. It is an international custom that on a national day heads of other states maintaining friendly relations cable their congratulations.

NATIONAL FLAG. The state flag. In accordance with international courtesy on the occasion of bi- or multinational intergovernmental meetings there is a formal raising of the flags of the states taking part. The merchant vessels in encounters on the open sea and those at anchor in foreign ports have separate etiquettes. In a foreign port a vessel usually flies the flag of the state to which it belongs; in its home port that of the state from which it has most recently come; and during loading the flag of the state to which it is sailing. The flag is a symbol of sovereignty under legal protection in the majority of states. Desecration of a flag is regarded as an intolerable crime in international relations.

E.W. KING, "The Flags of the United Nations", in: *National Geographic Magazine*, February 1951; E.M.C. BARRACLOUGH, *Flags of the World*, London, 1965.

NATIONAL GEOGRAPHIC SOCIETY, THE. f. on Jan. 13, 1888 in Washington DC "for the increase and diffusion of geographic knowledge" started, with charter membership of 165 Americans in Oct. 1888, publ. a National Geographic Magazine; became an "international Juggernaut" with 12 million members in 170 countries on Jan. 1, 1988.

C.D. BRYAN, *The National Geographic Society: 100 Years of Adventure and Discovery*, New York, 1987; *National Geographic*, Vol. 173, January, 1988.

NATIONAL INCOME. The income generated by the entire economy of a given country; is virtually the same as the GNP, stated in forms of all incomes, minus depreciation on capital goods. In UN economic analyses and statistics it is generally accepted that national income is equal to the value of the aggregate production during one year less the costs of materials and amortization. For simplification it is commonly accepted that the term means net national income. A distinction is made between generated and shared income; the latter does not include losses or reflect the financial effects of foreign trade. The amount of national income for each inhabitant (Latin: *per capita*) is accepted as an index of economic development. Regional analyses by the UN Economic Commission make it possible to express national income in such a way as to permit comparisons between states, on the basis of an index of national income per capita, and to determine the rate of economic growth, for which the basic index is the growth of national income. Organization reg. with the UIA:

International Association for Research in Income and Wealth, f. 1947, New Haven, Connecticut. Consultative status with ECOSOC. Publ.: *International Bibliography on Income and Wealth*.

UN Chronicle, October 1982, p. 47; *Yearbook of International Organizations*.

NATIONALISM. An international term for political sentiment, from the end of 18th century, one of the determining factors of history of the 19th and 20th centuries. A subject of international research.

F. ZNANIECKI, *The Modern Nationality. A Sociological Study*, Urbana, 1952; K.S. PIRSON, *A Bibliographical Introduction to Nationalism*, London,

1955; K.W. DEUTSCH, *An Interdisciplinary Bibliography on Nationalism, 1935–1953*, London, 1956; H. KOHN, *American Nationalism*, New York, 1957; B. WARD, *Nationalism and Ideology*, London, 1966; R. McCLINTOCK, "The Development of Nationalism and the Nationalism of Development", in: *The Department of State Bulletin*, No. 1660, Apr. 10, 1971, pp. 517–521; H. SETTON-WATSON, *Nations and States. An Enquiry into the Origins of Nations and the Politics of Nationalism*, London, 1972; W. LINK, W. FELD (eds), *The New Nationalism: Implications for Transatlantic Relations*, New York, 1979.

NATIONALITY. ▷ Citizenship, Nationality.

NATIONALITY OF MARRIED WOMEN. A subject of international agreements. Convention on the Nationality of Married Women, signed in New York on Feb. 20, 1957, by Byelorussia, Canada, Chile, China, Colombia, Cuba, Czechoslovakia, Denmark, the Dominican Republic, Ecuador, Guatemala, Hungary, India, Ireland, Israel, New Zealand, Norway, Pakistan, Portugal, Sweden, Ukraine, the UK, the USSR, Uruguay and Yugoslavia. Came into force on Aug. 11, 1958. The text is as follows:

"The Contracting States,
Recognizing that conflicts in law and in practice to nationality arise as a result of provisions concerning the loss or acquisition of nationality by women as a result of marriage, of its dissolution, or of the change of nationality by the husband during marriage.
Recognizing that, in article 15 of the Universal Declaration of Human Rights, the General Assembly of the United Nations has proclaimed that 'everyone has the right to a nationality' and that 'no one shall be arbitrarily deprived of his nationality nor denied the right to change his nationality',
Desiring to co-operate with the United Nations in promoting universal respect for, and observance of, human rights and fundamental freedoms for all without distinction as to sex,
Hereby agree as hereinafter provided:
Art. 1. Each Contracting State agrees that neither the celebration nor the dissolution of a marriage between one of its nationals and an alien, nor the change of nationality by the husband during marriage, shall automatically affect the nationality of the wife.
Art. 2. Each Contracting State agrees that neither the voluntary acquisition of the nationality of another State nor the renunciation of its nationality by one of its nationals shall prevent the retention of its nationality by the wife of such national.
Art. 3.(1) Each Contracting State agrees that the alien wife of one of its nationals may, at her request, acquire the nationality of her husband through specially privileged naturalization procedures; the grant of such nationality may be subject to such limitations as may be imposed in the interests of national security or public policy.
(2) Each Contracting State agrees that the present Convention shall not be construed as affecting any legislation or judicial practice by which the alien wife of one of its nationals may, at her request, acquire her husband's nationality as a matter of right.
Art. 4.(1) The present Convention shall be open for signature and ratification on behalf of any State Member of the United Nations and also on behalf of any other State which is or hereafter becomes a member of any specialized agency of the United Nations, or which is or hereafter becomes a Party to the Statute of the International Court of Justice, or any other State to which an invitation has been addressed by the General Assembly of the United Nations.
(2) The present Convention shall be ratified and the instruments of ratification shall be deposited with the Secretary-General of the United Nations.
Art. 5.(1) The present Convention shall be open for accession to all States referred to in paragraph 1 of article 4.
(2) Accession shall be effected by the deposit of an instrument of accession with the Secretary-General of the United Nations.

Art. 6.(1) The present Convention shall come into force on the ninetieth day following the date of deposit of the sixth instrument of ratification or accession.
(2) For each State ratifying or acceding to the Convention after the deposit of the sixth instrument of ratification or accession, the Convention shall enter into force on the ninetieth day after deposit by such State of its instrument of ratification or accession.
Art. 7.(1) The present Convention shall apply to all non-self-governing, trust, colonial and other non-metropolitan territories for the international relations of which any Contracting State is responsible; the Contracting State concerned shall, subject to the provisions of paragraph 2 of the present article, at the time of signature, ratification or accession, declare the non-metropolitan territory or territories to which the Convention shall apply ipso facto as a result of such signature, ratification or accession.
(2) In any case in which, for the purpose of nationality, a non-metropolitan territory is not treated as one with the metropolitan territory, or in any case in which the previous consent of a non-metropolitan territory is required by the constitutional laws or practices of the Contracting State or of the non-metropolitan territory for the application of the Convention to that territory, that Contracting State shall endeavour to secure the needed consent of the non-metropolitan territory within the period of twelve months from the date of signature of the Convention by that Contracting State, and when such consent has been obtained the Contracting State shall notify the Secretary-General of the United Nations. The present Convention shall apply to the territory or territories named in such notification from the date of its receipt by the Secretary-General.
(3) After the expiry of the twelve-month period mentioned in paragraph 2 of the present article, the Contracting States concerned shall inform the Secretary-General of the results of the consultations with those non-metropolitan territories whose international relations they are responsible and whose consent to the application of the present Convention may have been withheld.
Art. 8.(1) At the time of signature, ratification or accession, any State may make reservations to any article of the present Convention other than articles 1 and 2.
(2) If any State makes a reservation in accordance with paragraph 1 of the present article, the Convention, with the exception of those provisions to which the reservation relates, shall have effect as between the reserving State and the other Parties. The Secretary-General of the United Nations shall communicate the text of the reservation to all States which are or may become Parties to the Convention. Any State Party to the Convention or which thereafter becomes a Party may notify the Secretary-General that it does not agree to consider itself bound by the Convention with respect to the State making the reservation. This notification must be made, in the case of a State already a Party, within ninety days from the date of the communication by the Secretary-General; and, in the case of a State subsequently becoming a Party, within ninety days from the date when the instrument of ratification or accession is deposited. In the event that such a notification is made, the Convention shall not be deemed to be in effect as between the State making the notification and the State making the reservation.
(3) Any State making a reservation in accordance with paragraph 1 of the present article may at any time withdraw the reservation, in whole or in part, after it has been accepted, by a notification to this effect addressed to the Secretary-General of the United Nations. Such notification shall take effect on the date on which it is received.
Art. 9.(1) Any Contracting State may denounce the present Convention by written notification to the Secretary-General of the United Nations. Denunciation shall take effect one year after the date of receipt of the notification by the Secretary-General.
(2) The present Convention shall cease to be in force as from the date when the denunciation which reduces the number of Parties to less than six becomes effective.
Art. 10. Any dispute which may arise between any two or more Contracting States concerning the interpretation or application of the present Convention, which is

not settled by negotiation, shall, at the request of any one of the Parties to the dispute, be referred to the International Court of Justice for decision, unless the Parties agree to another mode of settlement.

Art. 11. The Secretary-General of the United Nations shall notify all States Members of the United Nations and the non-member States contemplated in paragraph 1 of article 4 of the present Convention of the following:

(a) Signatures and instruments of ratification received in accordance with article 4;

(b) Instruments of accession received in accordance with article 5;

(c) The date upon which the present Convention enters into force in accordance with article 6;

(d) Communications and notifications received in accordance with article 8;

(e) Notifications of denunciation received in accordance with paragraph 1 of article 9;

(f) Abrogation in accordance with paragraph 2 of article 9.

Art. 12.(1) The present Convention, of which the Chinese, English, French, Russian and Spanish texts shall be equally authentic, shall be deposited in the archives of the United Nations.

(2) The Secretary-General of the United Nations shall transmit a certified copy of the Convention to all States Members of the United Nations and to the non-member States contemplated in paragraph 1 of article 4."

UNTS, Vol. 309, pp. 66–74.

NATIONALITY OF SHIPS. An international term for a legal institution linking a ship to a state by ▷ flag or ▷ ships register.

R.L. BLEDSOE, B.A. BOCZEK, *The International Law Dictionary*, Oxford, UK, 1987.

NATIONAL MINORITIES. ▷ Minorities, Protection of.

NATIONAL PARKS. Subject of international co-operation and a UNESCO protection program as the World Heritage of Humanity.

See also ▷ Parks.

The UN List covers about 3600 national parks, nature reserves, natural monuments, protected landscapes, biosphere reserves and ▷ World Heritage Sites.

United Nations List of National Parks and Protected Areas, in English and French, Geneva, 1988.

NATIONAL RECOVERY ACT, 1933. ▷ Anti-Trust Act, 1890.

NATIONAL RESERVES. An international term, defined by the Inter-American Convention on Nature Protection, 1940 as follows:

"Regions established for conservation and utilization of natural resources under government control, on which protection of animal and plant life will be afforded in so far as this may be consistent with the primary purpose of such reserves."

A subject of international co-operation. Organizations reg. with the UIA:

European Association for Free Nature Reserves, f. 1967, Brussels, section of World Wildlife Fund.

Latin American Committee on National Parks, f. 1968, Washington, DC.

OAS Treaty Series No. 31, Washington, DC, 1964; *Yearbook of International Organizations*.

NATIONAL RESOURCES. ▷ Sovereignty over natural resources.

NATIONAL SECURITY AGENCY, NSA. ▷ Intelligence service.

NATIONAL SECURITY COUNCIL. A US President's Office, headed by the President's Adviser for National Security Affairs.

D. ROBERTSON, *Guide to Modern Defense and Strategy*, Detroit, 1988.

NATO. North Atlantic Treaty Organization 1949. The intergovernmental institution established by the North Atlantic Pact signed Apr. 4, 1949 in Washington by the governments of France, the UK and USA as well as Belgium, Canada, Denmark, Iceland, Italy, Luxembourg, the Netherlands, Norway and Portugal; on Feb. 18, 1952 Greece and Turkey joined; on May 8, 1955 the FRG was admitted; seat in London 1949–52, in Paris 1952–66, in Brussels from Oct. 22, 1966. The leading organ is the Atlantic Council, composed of the ministers of defense, foreign affairs and finance (or their deputies) of the member states, hence also called the Ministerial Council. In the period between sessions of the Council the Permanent Representatives Council is in operation, made up of the ambassadors of the member states, accredited in Washington, or vice-ministers. The organizer of the sessions and co-ordinator of their work is a permanent organ, the International Secretariat, headed by the Secretary-General of NATO. On Nov. 2, 1959 General Charles de Gaulle (1890–1969) in the Centre des Hautes Etudes Militaires stated:

"NATO is no longer an alliance; it is subordination. We cannot accept the supremacy of the United States in return for bearing our responsibility. The integrative system is dead. The defence of France must be French. It is an absolute necessity for France to be defended by itself and by its own means. If a nation such as France must wage war, then it must be a French war."

General de Gaulle, as the President of France, informed on Mar. 7, 1966 the President of the USA, L.B. Johnson, of France's intention to withdraw from the military integrative system of NATO on July 1, 1966 (France remained only in the civilian and political institution of NATO). As a result, the NATO Council on Oct. 26, 1966 decided to transfer the seat of NATO from Paris to Brussels. On Dec. 20, 1966 the Nuclear Defence Committee was formed, which France did not join, though the FRG acquired the right to co-participate in setting nuclear policy; the USA retained the right to veto any decision to use American nuclear weapons. In Aug., 1974 Greece also withdrew its forces from NATO on the model of France as a result of the occupation of a part of Cyprus by Turkish armed forces with the tacit consent of the other NATO members. Greece returned to NATO. At the turn of 1975/76 there appeared the possibility of a so-called ▷ historical compromise in Western Europe, i.e. the participation of communist parties in subsequent years in coalition governments in Italy, France and Spain, the principal reaction to which was expressed by the USA in NATO in Feb., 1976, in successive statements of the American Chief of NATO, General Haig, to the effect that "historical compromise" would undermine the (anti-communist) foundations of NATO; Secretary of State H. Kissinger that "the interests of the communist parties are incompatible with the interests of the democratic member states of NATO" as well as by President G. Ford who on Feb. 22, 1976 stated that "I am firmly opposed to the participation of communists in the governments of the NATO member states, especially Italy."

NATO institutions:

NATO Defense Planning Committee, f. 1966 a permanent body in Brussels, deals with questions related to NATO integrated military planning. From the beginning France did not participate in the Committee, and Greece left the DPC in autumn 1974.

NATO Eurogroup, f. 1968 in Brussels, an informal consultative body set up by European NATO members, concentrated on West European co-operation in the fields of armaments, training and logistics. The US which spends about four times as much on armaments as the European NATO states together with France, and bears half the cost of maintaining NATO armed forces in Europe, has been demanding a significant increase in the financial contribution of the European group. Negotiations held in 1970 resulted in a modification of the existing bilateral agreements between the USA and the European NATO states, though politically they led to the consolidation of a group which became *de facto* an autonomous institution within NATO. The practical activity of the NATO Eurogroup aims at standardizing the weapons of the European NATO states and achieving a more effective co-ordination of the infrastructure of the European base of supplies. Belonging to the Eurogroup are all of the European NATO states except France, Iceland, and Turkey; however, France participates in the work of the Eurogroup connected with the production of the armaments industry.

NATO Nuclear Defense Affairs Committee, f. 1966 in Brussels, permanent body at Defense Minister level, meets once a year to inform the non-nuclear members of NATO on nuclear defense affairs of the alliance (not participating: France, Iceland and Luxembourg).

NATO Nuclear Planning Group, established in 1962 to serve as consultant to the NATO member states on the possibility and conditions under which nuclear weapons may be used by the NATO armed forces; on the level of ministers of defense. Consultations at least once a year.

NATO Parliamentarians Conference, official name of the annual (since 1955) meetings of members of the parliaments of the NATO states, initiated by a meeting of 20 deputies of the Advisory Assembly of the Council of Europe with 14 US Congressmen in Nov., 1951; the First Conference took place from July 18 to 23, 1955 in Palais de Chaillot in Paris with the participation of 200 deputies and senators from the parliaments of the NATO states. From then on all sessions have taken place in Paris. The location of the permanent Secretariat of the NATO Parliamentarian Conference is Washington. As a rule each NATO Parliamentarian Conference passes resolutions that are not binding on governments. The number of deputies taking part can and does change, but the number of votes for each delegation remains the same: USA in plenary session 36, in committees 10; France, FRG, Great Britain, and Italy 18 and 5; Canada 12 and 3; Turkey 10 and 3; Belgium, Greece, and The Netherlands 7 and 2; Denmark, Norway, and Portugal 5 and 2; Iceland and Luxembourg 3 and 1.

Agencies responsible to the Council or to the Military Committee:

Allied Communications Security Agency (ACSA), f. 1953, Brussels.

Allied Data System Interoperability Agency (ADSIA), f. 1977, Brussels.

Advisory Group for Aerospace Research and Development (AGARD), f. 1952, Neuilly-sur-Seine.

Allied Long Lines Agency (ALLA), f. 1951, Brussels.

Allied Naval Communications Agency (ANCA), f. 1951, London.

Allied Radio Frequency Agency (ARFA), f. 1951, Brussels.

Allied Tactical Communications Agency (ATCA), f. 1972, Brussels.

Central European Operating Agency (CEOA), f. 1957, Versailles.

Military Agency for Standardization (MAS), f. 1951, Brussels.

NATO Communication and Information Systems Organization (NACISO), f. 1985, Brussels.

NATO Defence College (NADEFCOL), f. 1951, Rome.

NATO Maintenance and Supply Organization (NAMSO), f. 1981, Luxembourg.

NATO MRC Development and Production Management Organization (NAMMO), f. 1969, Munich.

NATO Airborne Early Warning and Control Program Management Organization (NAPMO), f. 1978.

NATO HAWK Production and Logistic Organization (NHPLO), f. 1959, Rueil Malmaison, France.

SACLANT Anti-submarine Warfare Research Center (SANCLANTCEN), f. 1962, La Specia, Italy.

SHAPE Technical Centre (STC), f. 1960, The Hague, Holland.

The NATO publ.: *The NATO Handbook, NATO Facts and Figures, The NATO Review* (bi-monthly), *Aspects of NATO, NATO and Warsaw Pact, NATO Pocket Guide*, and economic and scientific publications.

W.E. BECKETT, *The North Atlantic Treaty, the Brussels Treaty and the Charter of the UN*, London, 1950; C.B. TRELLER, *El Pacto Atlántico*, Madrid, 1950; LORD ISMAY, *OTAN, Les cinq premiers années, 1949–1954*, Paris, 1954; K KNORR, *NATO and American Security*, New York, 1956; A. FONTAINE, *L'Alliance Atlantique à l'heure du dégel*, Paris, 1960, R.E. OZGOOD, *NATO, The Entangling Alliance*, Chicago, 1962; *NATO Bibliography*, Paris, 1964; T. WEINER, *Die Armeen der NATO Staaten: Organisation, Kriegsbild, Waffen und Gerät*, Wien, 1966; R. McNAMARA, *Essence of Security*, New York, 1968; C.H. AMME Jr., *NATO without France*, New York, 1968; D. ACHESON, *Present at the Creation*, New York, 1969; A. BAUFFRE, *L'OTAN et l'Europe*, Paris, 1975; A.J. BROADHURST (ed.), *The Future of European Alliance Systems: NATO and Warsaw Pact*, Boulder, 1980; P. HILL-NORTON, *No Soft Option. The Politico-Military Realities of NATO*, London, 1980; K.A. MYERS (ed.), *NATO. The Next Twenty Years*, Boulder, 1980; *NATO. The Next Thirty Years. The Changing Political, Economic and Military Setting*, London, 1980; L.S. KAPLAN, R.W. CLAWSON, *NATO After 30 Years*, Wilmington, 1981; A. DE STAERCKE, *NATO's Anxious Birth. The Prophetic Vision of the 1940's*, London, 1985; H. HANNING, *NATO–Our Guarantee for Peace*, London, 1986; G. WILLIAMS, A. LEE, *The European Defence Initiative*, London, 1986; R. EAST, *NATO in the 1980's: The European Debate*, London, 1987; D. ROBERTSON, *Guide to Modern Defense and Strategy*, Detroit, 1988.

NATO ALLIED FORCES CENTRAL EUROPE, AFCENT. ▷ NORTHAG.

NATO OTTAWA–BRUSSELS DECLARATION, 1974. The Declaration of the NATO Council on Atlantic relations issued on the 25th Anniversary of NATO, signed on Apr. 19, 1974 in Ottawa by the US President and Canadian Prime Minister, and on Apr. 26, 1974 in Brussels by Prime Ministers of 12 West European countries, following 14 months of negotiations between the USA and the majority of NATO members. On Apr. 23, 1973 the US had put forward the draft of a New Atlantic Charter, which was to bind all NATO members, it had been opposed by France and other West European countries. The Ottawa–Brussels Declaration carried no juridical obligations.

KEESING's *Contemporary Archive*, 1974.

NATO STRATEGICAL DOCTRINES. The military assumptions of members of the North Atlantic Pact, changed many times 1949–84. The first, called Shield and Sword, was replaced on Jan. 12, 1954 by the Doctrine of Massive Retaliation, announced by the US Secretary of State, J.F. Dulles (1888–1959);

this in turn was modified by the foreign policy theoretician of the USA, H. Kissinger, in the Doctrine of Graduated Deterence. In 1961 President J.F. Kennedy introduced the next modification: the conception of a three-staged use of NATO armed forces. In the first phase of the war conventional divisions without the use of tactical nuclear weapons, in the second phase the use of divisions with tactical nuclear weapons, and finally in the third stage attacking with strategic nuclear weapons, which was previously already anticipated in the second phase. In addition the principle was accepted that in nuclear attacks a strategy will be used of destroying the nuclear capability of the opponent, eventually Counterforce Strategy, whereas only in the last resort would the strategy of destroying values of civilization (cities, industry, etc.), called the Countervalue Strategy be applied. F.J. Strauss, Minister of Defense in the FRG Adenauer government, was against this gradualism and favored the immediate use of Countervalue Strategy in the event of a nuclear war. Further modifications of strategic doctrines took place in the decade 1963–73 in connection with experiences from the military defeat in Vietnam and work on anti-ballistic missile systems ▷ Safeguard begun in 1968 and ▷ Sambis, 1970. Appearing in 1971 was the Strategic Deterrent Doctrine, also called the Realistic Deterrent Doctrine; the term was introduced in 1971 by the US Department of Defense for the new stage of US strategy and NATO, SEATO, CENTO military blocs, consisting in having the USA concentrate on the development of strategic weapon systems, especially on multi-warhead ballistic missiles by replacing the Minuteman 1 and 2 missiles with the 3-headed Minuteman 3 and the Polaris missiles with the 10-headed Poseidon. States allied with the USA, on the other hand, are supposed to concentrate on the development of conventional forces. Among others, the FRG obligated itself that by 1980 it would increase its professional cadre from 250,000 to 350,000 officers and non-commissioned officers. The strategic deterrent doctrine implies that the USA assumes a continuation of the arms race. War experiences and technological progress have given rise to further corrections and changes of NATO doctrines in the 1980s with the location of Pershing missiles in Western Europe, in 1984.

On Apr. 6, 1982 US Secretary of State A. Haig rejected the renunciation by the USA of the first use of nuclear weapons, arguing that a No-First-Use policy would be "the end of the credibility of the western strategy of deterrence." The No-First-Use policy was suggested in *Foreign Affairs* by a group of American statesmen: McGeorge Bundy, G.F. Kennan, R.S. McNamara and G. Smith. ▷ No-First-Use.

NATO in 1984 officially opposed the ▷ No-First-Use of Nuclear Weapons formula.

G.F. KENNAN, *American Diplomacy 1900–1950*, New York, 1951; J.F. DULLES, *Containment is not Enough*, New York, 1952; SIR JOHN SLESSOR, *Strategy by the West*, London, 1954; A. ETZIONI, *The Hard Way to Peace. The New Strategy*, New York, 1962; R. ARON, *Le Grand Débat. Initiation à la Stratégie Atomique*, Paris, 1963; J. MOCH, *Destin de la Paix*, Paris, 1969; B. GOLD-SCHMIDT, *Le complexe atomique*. Paris, 1980; *Foreign Affairs*, Spring 1982; KEESING's *Contemporary Archive*, 1975 and 1984.

NATURAL DISASTER DECADE, 1990–1999. Proclaimed by the UN General Assembly on Dec. 11, 1988, with the aim 'to improve the co-ordination of international efforts to predict and research natural disasters, and to improve efforts for the

mitigation of the social and economic disruption caused by these events.'

NATURAL DISASTERS. Floods, hurricanes, earthquakes and tidal waves, droughts, fires, locusts, etc.; the subject of international co-operation. An International Convention on Relief for Countries Afflicted by Natural Disasters was signed on July 12, 1927 in Geneva by Albania, Belgium, Bulgaria, China, Ecuador, Finland, France, Germany, Iraq, Monaco, Sudan, Switzerland, Turkey and Venezuela. The International Relief Union, IRU, was established at the same time by a Diplomatic Conference in Geneva as an organ of the Convention. It controls a center for the documentation and study of the prevention of natural disasters; it is reg. with the UIA and publishes the *IRU Review*.

The First International Conference on the Study of Natural Disasters took place in Paris in 1937. After World War II campaigns were launched to create an Emergency Fund for Disasters. The following periodicals are published: *Matérieaux pour l'étude des calamités* in Geneva, from 1923; and *Résumé annuel d'information sur les catastrophes naturelles*, by UNESCO, from 1970.

L.II. STEPHENS, S.J. GREEN (eds), *Disaster assistance*, New York, 1979; *Yearbook of International Organizations*; UN *Disaster Relief and the Work of UNDRO*, in: *UN Chronicle*, 1985, No. 8, pp. I-XVI.

NATURALIZATION. An international term for granting citizenship to a person not born in the given country and not possessing any citizenship or having a different one. The subject of an international convention. At the Third International Conference of American States on Aug. 13, 1906 in Rio de Janeiro, Argentina, Bolivia, Brazil, Chile, Colombia, Costa Rica, Cuba, Ecuador, El Salvador, Guatemala, Honduras, Mexico, Nicaragua, Panama, Paraguay, Peru, Uruguay and the USA signed a Convention Establishing the Status of Naturalized Citizens who subsequently take up residence in their country of origin. The Convention was not ratified by Bolivia, Cuba, Mexico, Paraguay, Peru and Uruguay; it was later denounced by Brazil on Dec. 1, 1950, and Guatemala on June 13, 1913. The ▷ Bustamante Code of Private International Law, 1928, integrated in arts. 9–21 rules on naturalization, as well as the Convention on the ▷ Nationality of Married Women and on Nationality adopted by the Seventh International Conference of American States in Montevideo, on Dec. 26, 1933. ▷ Citizenship, Nationality.

The Federal Constitutional Court of the Federal Republic of Germany ruled in November 1987 that a person naturalized in the German Democratic Republic also obtains German citizenship as defined in the Basic Law.

US Statute at Large, Washington, DC, 1906; *International Conferences of American States 1899–1928*, Washington, DC, 1931; R.L. BLEDSOE, B.A. BOCZEK, *The International Law Dictionary*, Oxford, 1987.

NATURAL RESERVE. An international term, defined in the ▷ Fauna and Flora Preservation Convention 1933, as follows:

"The term 'strict natural reserve' shall denote an area placed under public control, throughout which any form of hunting or fishing, any undertakings connected with forestry, agriculture, or mining, any excavations or prospecting, drilling, leveling of the ground, or construction, any work involving the alteration of the configuration of the soil or the character of the vegetation, any act likely to harm or disturb the fauna or flora, and the introduction of any species of fauna and flora,

N

whether indigenous or imported, wild or domesticated, shall be strictly forbidden; which it shall be forbidden to enter, traverse or camp in without a special written permit from the competent authorities; and in which scientific investigations may only be undertaken by permission of those authorities."

LNTS, Vol. 172, p. 248.

NATURAL RESOURCES. ▷ Sovereignty over Natural Resources.

NATURAL SCIENCES. A subject of international co-operation. Organization reg. with the UIA:

Joint Committee of the Nordic Natural Sciences Research Council, f. 1967, Stockholm.

Yearbook of International Organizations.

NATURE AND NATURAL RESOURCES. Subject of international co-operation. Organization reg. with the UIA:

International Union for Conservation of Nature and Natural Resources, f. 1988, Gland, Switzerland. Publ.: Red Data Book.

See also ▷ National Parks.

Yearbook of International Organizations, 1986/87; The Europa Yearbook 1988. A World Survey, Vol. I, London, 1988.

NATURE MONUMENTS. An international term defined by the Inter-American Convention on Nature Protection, 1940, as follows:

"Regions, objects, or living species of flora or fauna of aesthetic, historic or scientific interest to which strict protection is given. The purpose of nature monuments is the protection of a specific object, or a species of flora or fauna, by setting aside an area, an object, or a single species, as an inviolate nature monument, except for duly authorized scientific investigations or government inspection."

OAS Treaty Series No. 31, Washington, DC, 1964.

NATURE PROTECTION. A subject of international co-operation and conventions. ▷ Fauna and Flora Preservation Convention, and ▷ Nature Protection and Wildlife Preservation in the Western Hemisphere, Convention on, 1940. Organizations reg. with the UIA:

East African Natural Resources Research Council, f. 1970, Arusha, Tanzania.
European Information Centre for Nature Conservation, f. 1968, Strasbourg. Publ.: *Naturopa.*
International Federation of Friends of Nature, f. 1895, Zurich.
International Naturists Federation, f. 1953, Antwerp. Publ.: *International Naturists Guide.*
International Union for Conservation of Nature and Natural Resources, f. 1948, Morges, Switzerland. Consultative status with ECOSOC, UNESCO, UNIDO, WMO, WHO, Council of Europe and FAO. Members: Governments, institutions and scientific societies. Publ.: *IUCN Bulletin.*
International Youth Federation for Environmental Studies and Conservation, f. 1956, Morges, Switzerland. Publ.: *Taraxacum.*
Joint Committee of the Nordic Natural Science Research Councils, f. 1967, Stockholm.
World Blue Chain for the Protection of Animals and Nature, f. 1964, Brussels. Publ.: *La chaine.*

Yearbook of International Organizations.

NATURE PROTECTION AND WILD LIFE PRESERVATION IN THE WESTERN HEMISPHERE, CONVENTION ON, 1940. The agreement between the member states of the Panamerican Union opened for signature on Oct. 12, 1940 at PAU and ratified by Argentina (1946), the Dominican Republic (1942), Ecuador (1944), El Salvador (1941), Guatemala (1941), Haiti (1942),

Mexico (1942), Nicaragua (1946), Peru (1946) and Venezuela (1941). Art. II to V read as follows:

"Art. II.(1) The Contracting Governments will explore at once the possibility of establishing in their territories national parks, national reserves, nature monuments, and strict wilderness reserves as defined in the preceding article. In all cases where such establishment is feasible, the creation thereof shall be begun as soon as possible after the effective date of the present Convention.
(2) If in any country the establishment of national parks, national reserves, nature monuments, or strict wilderness reserves is found to be impractical at present, suitable areas, objects or living species of fauna or flora, as the case may be, shall be selected as early as possible to be transformed into national parks, national reserves, nature monuments or strict wilderness reserves as soon as, in the opinion of the authorities concerned, circumstances will permit.
(3) The Contracting Governments shall notify the Pan American Union of the establishment of any national parks, national reserves, nature monuments, or strict wilderness reserves, and of the legislation, including the methods of administrative control, adopted in connection therewith.
Art. III. The Contracting Governments agree that the boundaries of national parks shall not be altered, or any portion thereof be capable of alienation, except by the competent legislative authority. The resources of these reserves shall not be subject to exploitation for commercial profit.
The Contracting Governments agree to prohibit hunting, killing and capturing of members of the fauna and destruction or collection of representatives of the flora in national parks except by or under the direction or control of the park authorities, or for duly authorized scientific investigations.
The Contracting Governments further agree to provide facilities for public recreation and education in national parks consistent with the purposes of this Convention.
Art. IV. The Contracting Governments agree to maintain the strict wilderness reserves inviolate, as far as practicable, except for duly authorized scientific investigations or government inspection, or such uses as are consistent with the purposes for which the area was established.
Art. V.(1) The Contracting Governments agree to adopt, or to propose such adoption to their respective appropriate law-making bodies, suitable laws and regulations for the protection and preservation of flora and fauna within their national boundaries, but not included in the national parks, national reserves, nature monuments, or strict wilderness reserves referred to in Article II hereof. Such regulations shall contain proper provisions for the taking of specimens of flora and fauna for scientific study and investigation by properly accredited individuals and agencies.
(2) The Contracting Governments agree to adopt, or to recommend that their respective legislatures adopt, laws which will assure the protection and preservation of the natural scenery, striking geological formations, and regions and natural objects of aesthetic interest or historic or scientific value."

Convention on Nature Protection, OAS Treaty Series No. 31, Washington, DC, 1964.

NATURISTS. An international organization reg. with the UIA:

International Naturists Federation, f. 1953, Antwerp. Publ.: *International Naturists Guide, INF Information.*

Yearbook of International Organizations.

NATZWEILER-STRUTHOF. The German concentration camp, 50 km southwest of Strasbourg, called "Auschwitz in France", with 40 branch-camps and 45,000 prisoners; the majority was murdered, partly in medical experiments. Liberated by General Leclerc's French Army on Nov. 23, 1944.

The Trial of German Major War Criminals. Proceedings of the IMT Sitting at Nuremberg, Germany, 42 Vols., London, 1946–48, Vol. 5, pp. 237–239.

NAUCA. Nomenclatura Aduanera Uniforme de Centroamérica. The Uniform Customs Nomenclature of Central America introduced in 1961 by the Customs Convention, signed and ratified in 1959/60 by the governments of Guatemala, Honduras, Costa Rica, Nicaragua and El Salvador.

NAURU. Republic of Nauru under the aegis of the UN. Atoll in Central Pacific West of the Gilbert Islands. Area: 20,9 sq. km. Pop. 1983 census: 8042 (56% of Nauruans). Capital: Yangor. Official language: English. Currency: one Australian dollar = 100 cents. National Day: Jan. 31, Independence Day, 1968. GNP per capita in 1985: US $9,090. Member of three UN specialized agencies: ICAO, ITU, UPU.
International relations: A German colony from 1888 to 1914. Occupied by Australia 1914–20. Under a mandate of the League of Nations, Dec. 17, 1920–Oct. 31, 1947, administered by the British Empire. Occupied by Japanese troops 1941–45. A UN Trusteeship territory since Nov. 1, 1947, under joint administrative authority of Australia, New Zealand and the UK since Nov. 1, 1947 to Jan. 30, 1968. Independence gained on Jan. 31, 1968 after the UN General Assembly Res. 2347/XXII on Dec. 19, 1967. The phosphate deposit, the main national resource of Nauru, will probably be exhausted by 1993. The Government is planning to change Nauru in the decade 1985–95 into a ▷ tax haven for international business.

UNTS, Vol. 10, pp. 3–9; G.A. PITTMAN, *Nauru, The Phosphate Island,* London, 1959; C.N. PACKETT, *Guide to the Republic of Nauru,* Bradford, 1970; N. VIVIANI, *Phosphate and Political Progress,* Canberra, 1970; *The Europa Year Book 1984. A World Survey,* Vol. II, pp. 2101–2103, London, 1984.

NAUTICAL MILE, INTERNATIONAL. A special unit of distance (1852 m) employed in marine and aerial navigation adopted by the First International Extraordinary Hydrographic Conference, Monaco, 1929, under the name "International Nautical Mile". (▷ SI).

J.-P. VANDENBERGHE, L.Y. CHABALLE (eds), *Elsevier's Nautical Dictionary. In English, French, Spanish, Italian, Dutch and German,* Amsterdam, 1978.

NAVAL AND AIR BASES AGREEMENT, 1941. The Agreement relating to the naval and air bases in Newfoundland, Bermuda, Jamaica, St Lucia, Antigua leased by Great Britain to the USA, signed on Mar. 27, 1941 in London, with Protocol concerning the Defence of Newfoundland; came into force on signature: The General Description of Rights read as follows:

"(1) The United States shall have all the rights, power and authority within the Leased Areas which are necessary for the establishment, use, operation and defence thereof, or appropriate for their control, and all the rights, power and authority within the limits of territorial waters and air spaces adjacent to, or in the vicinity of, the Leased Areas, which are necessary to provide access to and defence of the Leased Areas, or appropriate for control thereof.
(2) The said rights, power and authority shall include, inter alia, the right, power and authority:
(a) To construct (including dredging and filling), maintain, operate, use, occupy and control the said Bases;
(b) To improve and deepen the harbours, channels, entrances and anchorages, and generally to fit the premises for use as naval and air bases;
(c) To control, so far as may be required for the efficient operation of the Bases, and within the limits of military necessity, anchorages, moorings and movements of ships and waterborne craft and the anchorages, moorings, landings, take-offs, movements and operations of aircraft;

(d) To regulate and control within the Leased Areas all communications within, to and from the areas leased;
(e) To install, maintain, use and operate under-sea and other defences, defence devices and controls, including detecting and other similar facilities.
(3) In the exercise of the above-mentioned rights, the United States agrees that the powers granted to it outside the Leased Areas will not be used unreasonably or, unless required by military necessity, so as to interfere with the necessary rights of navigation, aviation or communication to or from or within the Territories, but that they shall be used in the spirit of the fourth clause of the Preamble.
(4) In the practical application outside the Leased Areas of the foregoing paragraphs there shall be, as occasion requires, consultation between the Government of the United States and the Government of the United Kingdom."

LNTS, Vol. 204, 1941–43, pp. 16–17.

NAVAL ARMS. An international term for all arms of naval warships, conventional and nuclear, defensive and offensive. The acronyms used in the 1980's:
▷ ASROC, ▷ SLBM, ▷ SLCM, ▷ SSBN, ▷ SSGN, ▷ SSN, ▷ SUBROC.
See also ▷ ASW, ▷ SOSUS and ▷ SURTASS.

NAVAL COMMISSION OF THE FOUR POWERS, 1947. The Commission was established by a Protocol (with Annex), signed on Feb. 10, 1947 by the USA, USSR, UK and France, in Paris. The aims of the Commission were: the disposal of excess units of the Italian fleet (as listed in Annex XII B of the Treaty of Peace with Italy, 1947) and the return by the USSR of warships on loan to the USA (1 cruiser) and to the UK (1 battleship, 7 destroyers and 3 submarines).

UNTS, Vol. 140, p. 111.

NAVETTE, LA. The international French term for a special procedure in the bicameral parliaments of Australia, Belgium, Canada, France, Italy, Switzerland, and the UK to reach a compromise between two houses on a bill.

Interparliamentary Union, Parliaments of the World, London, 1976, pp. 586–587.

NAVICERT. Navy Certificate, a safe conduct document issued to neutral ships by belligerent parties as a certificate that the ship carries no prohibited cargo.

H. RITCHIE, *The Navicert System during the World War*, London, 1938; M. ROSS, "The Navicert in World War II", in: *American Journal of International Law*, No. 38, 1944; R.L. BLEDSOE, B.A. BOCZEK, *The International Law Dictionary*, Oxford, 1987.

NAVIGATION. The skill of piloting vessels at sea and in the air; subject of international rules and conventions. Up to World War I navigation regulations in international traffic were customary. The General Conference on Communication and Transit in Barcelona drafted and adopted on Apr. 20, 1921 three conventions: (1) Convention on international waterways; (2) Convention and statute on the freedom of transit on international waterways; (3) Declaration relating to the recognition of the right to fly the flag of states with no access to the sea. The First International Conference on Inland Navigation, held in Paris, drafted and adopted on Nov. 27, 1925 a Convention on Measurements of Inland Vessels, extended on Dec. 9, 1930 by the Final Act of the Conference for Codification of International Fluvial Law including three conventions: on collisions of vessels, immatriculation, and the right to fly the flag of inland vessels of states with no direct access to international waterways.

Air Navigation, Washington, DC, 1955; *Navigation Dictionary*, Washington, DC, 1956; C.J. COLOMBOS, *International Law of the Sea*, London, 1959.

NAZI AND FASCIST POSTWAR ACTIVITIES AND THE UN. The postwar activities of Fascist and Nazi groups in Europe and Latin America were a subject of debates in the UN General Assembly in the 1950s and of the UN Res. 2233/XXII, Dec. 18, 1968, unanimously adopted by all members (except of the Republic of South Africa which abstained). The resolution condemned all ideologies based on intolerance on racist grounds, terror including nazism and neo-nazism, and called on all states to use preventive measures to eliminate manifestation of nazism and racial intolerance.
In Sept., 1969 a subcommittee of the Commission on Human Rights dealing with racial discrimination stated that:

"The revival of nazism both in the territory of the former German Third Reich and any other part of the world continues to pose a serious threat to mankind – the movement by use of brutal force, racial discrimination and intolerance still commits grave crimes against humanity and evolves toward a source of a new world war. Governments of many States of all continents, particularly those that had participated in the anti-Hitlerite coalition expressed their deep concern over the growing influence of neo-nazi elements in the Federal Republic of Germany and submitted to the members of the group preparing the report a number of facts evidencing nazi activities in that country."

Further, the report stated that in the light of international law, provisions and treaties concluded by the states of the former anti-Hitlerite coalition, the activities pursued by any kind of nazi groups, political parties and organizations in the Federal Republic of Germany were entirely illegal. On Dec. 15, 1970, the UN General Assembly adopted a resolution expressing concern over the fact that:

"25 years since the foundation of the UN groups and organizations being vehicles of nazism, racism and apartheid continue to operate."

The year 1971 was designated by the UN as the International Year for Action to Combat Racism and Racial Discrimination; Dec. 18, 1971 the UN General Assembly adopted Res. 2839/XXVI concerning measures to be taken to suppress nazism, fascism and other totalitarian ideologies and practices based on fomenting hatred and racial intolerance. On Oct. 5, 1976 the Bishop of Olinda and Recife dom Helder Camara of Brazil, called the rightist military dictatorships in Latin America – neo-nazist:

"... nazism emerged in the Latin American continent ... these are military dictatorships ... believing that for the reason of national security nothing is forbidden, even violation of the law and use of torture."

In 1982 the UN General Assembly Res. 37/179 again condemned nazi, fascist and neofascist ideologies and practices. ▷ Totalitarian ideologies. In 1983 the Third Committee examined a Report of the UN Secretary General on measures to be taken against nazi, fascist and neo-fascist activities and all other forms of totalitarian ideologies and practices based on racial intolerance, hatred and terror.
On Dec. 8, 1988 the GA adopted without vote Res. 43/150 on measures to be taken against Nazi, Fascist and Neo-Nazi activities.

A. GARCIA ROBLES, *El Mundo de la Postguerra*, 2 Vols., México, DF, 1946, pp. 382–383; A. FRYE, *Nazi Germany and the American Hemisphere 1933–41*, New Haven, 1961; D. EISENBERG, *Fascistes et Nazis d'Aujourd'hui*, Paris, 1967; K.T. TAUBER, *Beyond Eagle and Swastika: German Nationalism since 1945*, Middletown, 1967; *Stern*, Hamburg, February 25 and March 7, 1968; *UN Monthly*, January, 1968; J.

NOARES, S. PRIDHAM, *Documents on Nazism 1919–45*, London, 1974, *UN Chronicle*, February, 1983, pp. 85–96, and January, 1984, p. 60; R. WISTRICH, *Who's Who in Nazi Germany*, New York, 1982; *UN Resolutions and Decisions adopted by the General Assembly during First Part of its Forty-Third Session, From 20 September to 22 December 1988*, New York, 1989, pp. 427-428.

N'DJAMENA. The capital of Chad since 1960, formerly Fort Lamy. Seat of two organizations reg. with the UIA: the African Malagasy Sugar Council and Lake Chad Bassin Commission.

Yearbook of International Organizations.

NEAR AND MIDDLE EAST. An international term, not identical in meaning; in British terminology "Near East" is an historical concept including the former African–Arabian territories of the Ottoman Empire, whereas "Middle East" includes Libya, Sudan, Egypt, the Arabian peninsula, Iran and Turkey. The international position of the Near East in the second half of the 20th century was determined by petroleum, whose reserves there in 1939 were estimated at 16.6% of the world total. The discovery in 1950 of the world's largest exploitable oil fields in the Near East increased this total to 58.8% of the world total and together with Libya to 62.8%. In this situation the importance of the Near East increased in direct proportion to the growing world demand for, and production of, petroleum. The world production at this time grew from 4.2 to 86.5 million tons, and the Near East, where the costs of production were the cheapest, shared proportionally in this growth. In the decade since 1971 OPEC policies have ensured the states of the Near East continually rising profits, simultaneously creating the ▷ energy world crisis.

J.C. HUREWITZ, *Diplomacy in the Near and Middle East, Documentary Record*, 6 Vols., London, 1956; Y. SHIMONIN, E. LEVINE, *Political Dictionary of the Middle East in the Twentieth Century*, London, 1972; *The Middle East and North Africa 1979–1980*, London, 1980.

NEGATIVE PRESCRIPTION. An international legal term stating that penal liability of an offence is subject to termination after a specific number of years.

NEGOTIATIONS. An international term for diplomatic or commercial bilateral or multilateral talks, a subject of international rules.

I.S. PARETERKU, *Tolkovanie mezhhdunarodnikh dogovorov*, Moscow, 1959; J. SUBEYROL, "La négociation diplomatique, élément de contact international", in: *Revue de droit international*, Paris, 1968; K. KOCOT, *Rokowania dyplomatyczne* (Diplomatic negotiations), Wroclaw, 1969; R.L. BLEDSOE, B.A. BOCZEK, *The International Law Dictionary*, Oxford, 1987.

NEGROES. A common international name for dark-skinned people originating from Africa. The slave trade in Negroes abducted from Africa resulted in the first international conventions in the 19th century on combatting slavery and in the 20th century on racism and discrimination. The Negro question became a cause of conflicts and international disputes in the Western Hemisphere, to which Negroes had been transported from Africa during the epoch of colonialism. Their descendants in the Caribbean region and South America number c. 40 million and more than 25 million in the USA. There is a non-governmental tendency to treat the American Negroes as a separate national minority. The Havana OLAS Conference, 1967, resolved to celebrate Aug. 18 as a "Day of solidarity with the

Negro nation in the USA." This was the first attempt to internationalize the Negro problem in the Western Hemisphere; the second took place on Mar. 11, 1972 in Gary, Indiana, where the first congress of activists from Negro groups from the Caribbean, North and South America adopted the Black Americans Manifest, stating that the exploitation of Blacks by Whites continued and was a "natural product of a social system which is based on White racism and White capitalism." The aim of the Black American movement was to "unify them and lead to liberation." In the 1980s the US Bureau of census started to use the term Afro-American in ethnic statistics.

See also ▷ Afro-Americans.

G. MYRDAL, *An American Dilemma: the Negro Problem and Modern Democracy*, New York, 1944; E.K. WELSH, *The Negro in the US. A Research Guide*, New York, 1965; E.W. MILLER, *The Negro in America: A Bibliography*, New York, 1966; J.P. DAVIS, *The American Negro Reference Book*, Englewood Cliffs, 1966; P.M. BERGMAN, *The Chronological History of the Negro in America*, New York, 1969; W. GARDNER SMITH, *Return to Black America*, Prentice-Hall, 1970; *The Washington Post*, March 12, 1972; UNESCO, *Specifity and Dynamics of African Negro Cultures*, Paris, 1986.

NEIGHBORHOOD. A term of international law and subject of conventions, and good neighbor doctrines.

NEMINEM CAPTIVABIMUS NISI IURE VICTUM. *Latin* = "nobody will be imprisoned (by us) unless he has had a fair trial." The legal rule applied in Poland to nobility in keeping with the privilege bestowed on gentry by King Wladyslaw Jagiello in Brest (1425), Jedlina (1430) and Cracow (1433). Both acts contributed to the international development of judicature, like ▷ Magna Charta Libertatum 1215, ▷ Habeas Corpus Act 1679 and ▷ Settlement Act 1701. The privilege was granted under King Stanislav August's bill on towns on Apr. 17, 1791 to the propertied townspeople.

NEOCOLONIALISM. An international term for the phenomenon of economic, quasi-colonial dependence of sovereign states on their former colonial rulers.

NEOFASCISM AND NEONAZISM. ▷ Nazi and Fascist Postwar Activities and the UN.

NEO-SLAVISM. An international term for a renascent Pan-Slavistic movement before World War I of a clear anti-German character, aiming at bringing together the Slavic nations under the protectorate of Russia; it had main advocates in the Czech lands (W. Kramar), Poland (R. Dmowski), and Russia (V.A. Bobrinskoy); manifested its aims at two Slavic Congresses: in Prague, 1908, and Sofia, 1909. It was paralyzed by Poland's aspirations toward independence, contrary to the assumptions of Russian Neo-Slavists, which was already expressed in a boycott of the Sofia congress by the Poles.

A.N. PIPIN, *Panslavizm v proshlom i nastoiashchem*, Sankt-Peterburg, 1913; H. KOHN, *Pan-Slavism, Its History and Ideology*, Notre Dame, Indiana, 1953.

NEP. Novaya Ekonomicheskaya Politika = "New Economic Policy". A Soviet system of the 1920s based generally on a socialized economy, but within certain limits also allowing both the individual production of consumer goods as well as free trade in them; in force in the Soviet Union from 1921 to 1928.

A modern kind of NEP was discussed in the USSR at the end of the 1980's in relation with ▷ Perestroika.

Encyclopaedia Britannica, Vol. 22, pp. 519–521, Chicago, London, 1973.

NEPAL. Member of the UN. Kingdom of Nepal. A kingdom in Central Asia, bordered by the Chinese People's Republic (Tibet region) and India. Area: 141,058 sq. km. Pop. 1987 est.: 16,630,000 (1971 census: 11,555,983). Capital: Kathmandu with 393,494 in 1981. GNP per capita 1987: US \$160. Currency: one Nepalese rupee = 100 pice. National Day, Feb. 18, Constitution Day, 1952 and Dec. 28, King Birendra's Birthday.

Member of the UN from Dec. 14, 1959 and of all specialized agencies with exception of the WIPO, IAEA and GATT.

International relations: in 1792 Nepal signed the first commercial treaty with Great Britain. In 1814–16 border war with India. The Friendship Treaty with Great Britain, which affirmed Nepal's full sovereignty, was signed in 1923. In the north of Nepal is the main section of the Himalayas including Mount Everest. Diplomatic relations, 1984, with 86 countries in a spirit of nonaligned foreign policy.

See also ▷ World Heritage UNESCO List.

J.C. OJWA, *Banking and Currency in Nepal*, Kathmandu, 1961; A. GUPTA, *Politics in Nepal*, London, 1964; E.B. MIHALY, *Foreign Aid and Politics in Nepal*, London, 1965; *A Study of Money and Banking Situation in Nepal*, Kathmandu, 1971; T. HASEN, *Nepal: The Kingdom in the Himalayas*, London, 1973; S.D. MAMI, *Foreign Policy of Nepal*, Delhi, 1973; R. SHAHA, *Nepali Politics Retrospect and Prospect*, OUP, 1975; L.S. BARAL, *Political Development in Nepal*, London, 1980; R.L. TURNER, *Nepali Dictionary*, London, 1980; S. BEZRUCHKA, *A Guide to Trekking in Nepal*, Leicester, 1981; D.N. WADHWA, *Nepal Bibliography*, Oxford, 1982; *The Europa Year Book 1984. A World Survey*, Vol. II, pp. 2104–2115, London, 1984.

NEPHROLOGY. A subject of international cooperation. Organizations reg. with the UIA:

European Society for Pediatric Nephrology, f. 1967, Berne.
International Society of Nephrology, f. 1960, Mexico DF. Publ.: *Kidney International*.

Yearbook of International Organizations.

NEPTUNE. One of the ▷ Planets in the Solar System. A subject of international space research. The American unmanned space vehicle Voyager 2 encountered Neptune in 1989.

KEESING'sS *Record of World Events*, 1989.

NERVE GAS. ▷ Binary Chemical Weapon.

NESTORIAN-UNIATE CHURCH. One of the so-called Eastern Christian churches, a branch of the Chaldean church; from the 13th century in union with the Roman Catholic Church while retaining Persian as the liturgical language. The bishop of the Nestorian-Uniate Church has the title Patriarch of Babylonian Chaldea. The national church of the Kurds.

D. ATTWATER, *The Christian Churches of the East*, London, 1948.

NETHERLANDS, THE. Member of the UN. The Kingdom of the Netherlands, Holland. A state in western central Europe on the North Sea. Borders with Belgium and the FRG. Area: 41,863 sq. km. Pop. 1988 est.: 14,669,000; growth of census population: 1892 – 2,613,000; 1909 – 5,858,000; 1920 – 6,865,000; 1947 – 9,625,000; 1960 –

11,461,000; 1971 – 13,060,115. Overseas possessions ▷ Netherlands Antilles. Constitutional capital: Amsterdam with 687,397 inhabitants 1983. Seat of the Government and Royal Court: The Hague with 449,338 inhabitants. GNP per capita 1987: US \$11,680. Official language: Dutch. Currency: one gulden (also called guilder or florin) = 100 cents. National Day: Apr. 30, birthday of Queen Beatrix enthroned 1980.

Founding member of the UN; belongs to all UN specialized organizations. Member of BENELUX, NATO, OECD, EEC and the Council of Europe.

International relations: in the 16th century under Spanish domination; in 1581 the Estates General of the northern provinces proclaimed their separation from Spain. In 1588 the union of these provinces in Utrecht and the proclamation of the Republic of United Provinces of the Netherlands. Recognized by Spain in 1648. Colonial power in southern Asia and in the Caribbean region. Since 1806 called the Kingdom of the Netherlands. Neutral during World War I. In 1920–39 a member of the League of Nations. During World War II occupied by the III Reich, 1940–45. Holland did not recognize the independence of Indonesia, which was proclaimed on Aug. 17, 1945, and then abrogated the treaty of Nov. 15, 1946 (▷ Linggadjati Agreement) on the formation of the ▷ Netherlands–Indonesian Union. In 1947–49 the UN Security Council examined the matter of the conflict between Dutch colonial forces and the partisan movement in Indonesia. On the initiative of the Council a round table conference was held in Nov., 1949 of the representatives of Indonesia, the Netherlands and the UN, ending in December of that year with the granting of independence to Indonesia. The only unsolved problem was the question of West Irian (▷ Irian Barat), which in 1954–62 was the subject of UN mediation; as a result of a Dutch–Indonesian agreement of Aug., 1962 Holland withdrew its forces from West Irian and power there was assumed by the UN Temporary Executive Authority, UNTEA, which in May, 1963 finally transferred West Irian to Indonesia, thereby closing the period of Dutch colonial presence in southern Asia. In 1970 the President of Indonesia, General Suharto, made a visit to Holland and established economic co-operation between both states, expanded in Aug., 1971 during Queen Juliana's return visit to Jakarta. Queen Juliana abdicated in favor of her eldest daughter Beatrix in April 1980.

On Sept. 10, 1984 the FRG signed a border agreement with the Netherlands for cross-border co-operation on the utilization of the estuary of the River Ems.

A yearbook has appeared since 1889: *Pyttersee's Nederlandse Almanak*; since 1967 also in English: *Holland Herald*.

F.E. HUGGETT, *The Modern Netherlands*, London, 1971; D. PIRIDER, *The Netherlands*, Folkestone, 1976; *Netherlands and Netherlands Antilles*, Rotterdam, 1977; G. NEWTON, *The Netherlands, An Historical and Cultural Survey, 1795–1977*, Boulder, 1978; *A Compact Geography of the Netherlands*, Utrecht, 1980; *The Europa Year Book 1984. A World Survey*, Vol. I, pp. 668–689, London, 1984.

NETHERLANDS ANTILLES, THE. A part of the Kingdom of the Netherlands together with Holland and Surinam, former Netherlands colony; comprises the Leeward Islands (Curaçao, Aruba and Bonaire) and the Windward Islands (St Maarten, St Eustatius and Saba). The total area is 993 sq. km; pop. 1980 est. 253,334. The main island is Curaçao, 444 sq. km, with 154,928 inhabitants. Capital:

Willemstad, on Curaçao. Currency: one Netherlands Antilles gulden/guilder = 100 cents.
International relations: a Dutch colony since the 18th century; since Dec., 1954, an Autonomic Territory of the Kingdom of Netherlands, governed by the Island's Council (elective) under the supervision of a Governor (*Gezaghebber*). Member of the UPU, ITU and WMO; included in the Tlatelolco Treaty. On May 30, 1969, riots broke out in Willemstad in connection with a popular protest against a staff reduction and wage freeze in the Royal Dutch Shell oil refinery. On Sept. 16, 1969, the self-rule was extended as a result of popular demands. The Aruba island, seeking independence from Curaçao in March 1983 reached an agreement, that in Jan. 1986 it will be granted separate status and in 1996 full independence.

J. VAN DE VALLE, *De Nederlandse Antillen*, Willemstedt, 1954; *Netherlands and Netherlands Antilles*, Rotterdam, 1977; *The Europa Year Book 1984. A World Survey*, Vol. II, pp. 2114–2120, London, 1984.

NETHERLANDS–INDONESIAN UNION, 1947–56. The Union was formally established on Mar. 25, 1947; earlier basis was the Linggadjati agreement of Sept. 15, 1946, concluded under pressure exerted on the Republic of Indonesia by the Netherlands (Indonesia proclaimed independence on Aug. 17, 1945, despite the Netherlands' objections) which founded the union under the joint authority of the Queen of the Netherlands; in the light of the agreement the Netherlands recognized Indonesia's sovereign rights only to a part of its territory (Java, Sumatra and Madura) and announced the establishment of the United States of Indonesia starting from 1949 (which was to include, apart from the Republic of Indonesia, Borneo and the so-called Great Eastern State: Celebes, Moluccas and Little Sunday Islands); together with the Netherlands and its colonial possessions in America, they were to create the Netherlands–Indonesian Union. Following the formal foundation of the Netherlands–Indonesian Union by the Act of Mar. 25, 1947, and acts obstructing realization of the Union's provisions by the Netherlands in July 1947, an armed conflict between the Netherlands and Indonesia broke out. After two years of fighting a "round table" conference was held Nov. 2–30, 1949 in The Hague, which resulted in the treaty on the sovereignty of the United States of Indonesia with respect to the whole territory of Indonesia save West Irian (which passed under Indonesian administration on May 1, 1963 ▷ Irian Barat) and re-establishment of the Netherlands–Indonesian Union based on the principle of "voluntary access, equity and full independence" under the authority of "Queen Juliana and her successors" (art. 5); the confederated states were to be separate UN members (art. 10). In 1950 the United States of Indonesia were transformed within the Union into the Republic of Indonesia which seceded in Feb., 1956.

C.A. COLLIARD, *Droit international et histoire diplomatique*, Paris, 1950, pp. 275–278.

NEUE ORDNUNG. ▷ New Order.

NEUILLY PEACE TREATY, 1919. The peace treaty between the Principal Allied Powers (France, Great Britain, Italy, Japan and the USA) and the Associated Powers (Belgium, China, Cuba, Czechoslovakia, Greece, the Hedjaz, Poland, Portugal, Romania, the Serb–Croat–Slovene State and Siam) on the one part and Bulgaria on the other, signed on Nov. 27, 1919 in Neuilly-sur-Seine near Paris.

The main points of the Treaty are as follows:
Part I The Covenant of the League of Nations (arts. 1 to 26 and Annex).
Part II Frontiers of Bulgaria (arts. 27 to 33).
Part III Political Clauses (arts. 36 to 63):
"Bulgaria . . . recognizes the Serb-Croat-Slovene State" (art. 36).
"Bulgaria undertakes to assure full and complete protection of life and liberty to all inhabitants of Bulgaria without distinction of birth, nationality, language, race or religion."
Part IV Military, Naval and Air Clause (arts. 64 to 104).
Part V Prisoners of war and graves (arts. 105 to 117).
Part VI Penalties (arts. 118 to 120).
Part VII Reparation (arts. 121 to 131).
Part VIII Financial clauses (arts. 132 to 146).
Part IX Economic clauses (arts. 147 to 203).
Part X Aerial Navigation (arts. 204 to 211).
Part XI Ports, Waterways and Railways (arts. 212 to 248).
Part XII (Part XIII of the Treaty of Versailles: International Labour Organization, arts. 249–289).
Major Peace Treaties of Modern History, New York, 1967, pp. 1727–1861.

NEUROLOGY. A subject of international research and co-operation. Organizations reg. with the UIA:
Asian and Oceanian Association of Neurology, f. 1961, Bangkok. Publ.: *Congress Proceedings*.
Colloquium Internationale Neuro-Psychopharmacologicum, f. 1957, Munich.
European Neurosciences Association, f. 1975, Rijswijk.
European Society of Neuroradiology, f. 1975, Strasbourg.
International Federation of Societies for Electroencephalography and Clinical Neurophysiology, f. 1949, Omaha, Nebr. Publ.: *Electroencephalography and Clinical Neurophysiology* (monthly in English and French).
International Society of Neuropathology, f. 1930, London.
Middle East Neurosurgical Society, f. 1958, Beirut.
Scandinavian Neurosurgical Society, f. 1945, Stockholm.
World Federation of Neurology, f. 1955, London. Official relations with WHO and ECOSOC. Publ.: *Journal of Neurological Sciences*.
World Federation of Neurosurgical Societies, f. 1945, Leyden. Publ.: *Congress Proceedings*.
World Society for Stereotactic and Functional Neurosurgery, f. 1973, Durham, North Car. Publ.: *Applied Neurophysiology*.

Yearbook of International Organizations.

NEUTRAL ARABIC ZONE. A territory on the Arabian peninsula, bounded by Saudi Arabia, Iraq and Kuwait, jointly owned and administered 1922–66 by Kuwait and Saudi Arabia; partitioned between Kuwait and Saudi Arabia in May 1966. Total area: 5700 sq. km.

NEUTRALITY ACTS OF THE USA, 1935–39. The four laws passed in US Congress in 1935, 1936, 1937 and 1939, authorizing the President to embargo the sale of war materials to belligerent countries in Europe and the Far East. The Neutrality Act of 1939 adopted after the outbreak of World War II revised previous Acts and provided that the President could sell arms to Great Britain and France, but all American goods could be shipped to belligerents' ports only on the ▷ Cash-and-carry clause.

NEUTRALITY AT SEA. A subject of international conventions, related to the legal position of third states, which chose to remain uninvolved in the conflict at sea between other states. The Second Hague Conference, 1907, adopted the XIII Convention concerning the rights and duties of neutral Powers in naval war.

P.C. JESSUP (ed), *Neutrality, Its History, Economics and Law*, New York, 1935–36; P.C. JESSUP (ed), *Collection of Neutrality Laws, Regulations and Treaties of Various Countries*, New York, 1939.

NEUTRALITY IS UNMORAL. A formula proclaimed by the US Secretary of State, John Foster Dulles (1888–1959) during the period of the Korean War.

NEUTRALITY OF STATES. The legal, temporary situation, of one state in relation to a conflict between two or more states consisting in non-participation in a direct way in the war through not rendering assistance to any belligerent party. Neutrality of states is not only manifested through unilateral declarations, as in the case of the USA whose neutrality was proclaimed by the first president George Washington, on Apr. 22, 1793, and provided for "friendly and impartial behaviour toward the belligerent parties" (England and France), but also through multilateral treaties, as in the case of Swiss Perpetual Neutrality and the neutrality of Belgium. During the 19th century 172 bi- and multilateral international treaties to guarantee neutrality were concluded; 39 were concluded 1900–38. Guarantees and declarations since 1815 include the following:
1815: The Perpetual Neutrality of Switzerland was guaranteed by the Congress of Vienna; it was reaffirmed by the Versailles Treaty (1919; art. 435) and by an LN Council Res. of May 14, 1933.
1830: The London Conference guaranteed the neutrality of Belgium. Violation of the country's neutrality in World War I and II influenced Belgium's decision to join Benelux and other Western European alliances.
1907: The Second International Hague Peace Conference determined the territorial inviolability of neutral states and the rights and obligations of such states in war at sea (Convention on the Rights and Duties of Neutral Powers in Naval War, signed on Oct. 18, 1907).
1912: Declaration by Denmark, Norway and Sweden of Neutrality and Rules of Neutrality, signed Dec. 21, 1912.
1920: London Declaration, on Feb. 13. The LN Council declaration stated that "perpetual neutrality is justified by the interest of universal peace and therefore is consistent with the Covenant of the League of Nations."
1938: Stockholm Principles of Neutrality of States, on May 27, proclaimed by Denmark, Finland, Iceland, Norway and Sweden.
1939: US Neutrality Act, adopted after the outbreak of World War II. It revised previous acts and provided for the sale of arms to France and the UK, but all goods were to be shipped only on the ▷ cash-and-carry clause.
First Consultative Meeting of Ministers for Foreign Affairs of American Republics. The General Declaration on the Neutrality of American Republics was adopted on Sept. 23. At the request of the USA the Western Hemisphere Neutrality Zone was to be announced. The Inter-American Neutrality Committee, from 1942: Inter-American Juridical Committee, was established to work out "recommendations for neutrality on the basis of experience under different conditions."
1954: After World War II the Indochina Geneva Treaties of 1954.
1955: The State Treaty between the Powers and Austria.

In 1980 Malta declared a status of neutrality 'based on nonalignment'.

LNTS, Vol. 188, 1938, pp. 295–331; *British and Foreign State Papers*, Vol. 100, p. 448; Vol. 106, p. 916; R.L. BLEDSOE, B.A. BOCZEK, *The International Law Dictionary*, Oxford, 1987; D. ROBERTSON, *Guide to Modern Defense and Strategy*, Detroit, 1988.

NEUTRALITY OF WESTERN HEMISPHERE, 1938 ▷ Security of the Western Hemisphere.

NEUTRAL TERRITORIES. An international term for territories, as a rule uninhabited, dividing two states and under their common supervision, such as desert territories between Saudi Arabia and Kuwait of about 5700 sq. km area (divided in 1965 between both states after the discovery of oil deposits); similarly the desert territories on the border of Iraq and Saudi Arabia, of about 7000 sq. km area.

NEUTRAL WATERS. Neutral waters include territorial, offshore waters, gulfs, bays, straits, lakes and rivers neutralized by international agreements.

V. SHEUMER, "Neutrale Gewässer" in: *Strupp-Schlochauer Wörterbuch des Völkerrechts*, Berlin, 1961, Vol. 2, pp. 583–586.

NEUTRAL ZONES. The sanitary or security zones formed during war for civilian population under supervision of the International Red Cross, first established at Madrid, during Civil War 1936, then in Shanghai 1937 (called after the initiator "Jacquinot Zone"), and Jerusalem 1948. The Geneva Convention on Protection of Victims of War, Aug. 12, 1949, provided that the Protecting Powers and the International Red Cross will offer their good services with a view to facilitating the establishment and recognition of sanitary and security zones and localities (art. 14); and that each contracting party will be able directly or through the help of a neutral state or a humanitarian organization, to propose to the adverse party the formation in the region of the fighting of a neutralized zone designed for protection of the following persons indiscriminately: (a) wounded and sick, whether combatants or not, (b) civilian persons not participating in hostilities and not performing any work of a military character (art. 15).

CROIX ROUGE, *Zones sanitaires et Zones de sécurité*, Genève, 1951.

NEUTRON BOMB. A variety of hydrogen bomb causing the emission of rapid neutrons of tremendous energy with a temperature equal to that within the interior of the sun, called in the American armaments industry the Lance Enhanced Radiation Warhead, LERW. The bomb is meant to cause a small amount of radiation fallout, which means that its purpose would be mainly to destroy people and living creatures, while leaving intact military equipment, instruments, buildings, installations, roads, means of transport.
An American nuclear weapon since 1983.

J. GOLDBLAT, *Arms Control Agreements. A Handbook*, New York, 1983.

NEW CALEDONIA. An overseas territory of France, island group in the South Pacific, east of Australia, it comprises New Caledonia, Huon, the Isle of Pines, the Loyalty Islands and Walpole Island. Total area: 19,103 sq. km. Pop. 1986 estimate: 151,400. The major ethnic group Kanaks. The capital Nouméa with 60,112 inhabitants, predominantly French. Annexed by France in 1883. The UN Decolonization Committee demands full autonomy for the population. In July, 1984 the French Government granted an autonomy status until 1989, when a referendum on the future of the territory was to be presented to the French Assemby for approval. In Dec., 1984 a grave conflict between the Melanesian Kanak population of New Caledonia and France after the death of six Kanaks killed by French police during a demonstration for immediate independence of New Caledonia as Kanaky (Land of People).
The UN General Assembly on Dec. 2, 1986, voted by 89 to 24 including France with 34 abstentions in favour of the Kanaks aspiration for independence and affirmed the right of the population to self-determination and independence.
The UN Committee on Decolonization was obliged to act in this direction.

The Europa Year Book 1984. A World Survey, Vol. II, pp. 1583–1585, London, 1984; *Tableau de l'Economie Caledonienne* 1983-85; KEESING's *Record of World Events*, March, 1987; KEESING's *Record of World Events*, March, 1988.

NEW CLASS. An international term for political bureaucracy in socialist classless society; the term was coined 1957 by a Yugoslavian dissident, Milovan Djilas.

M. DJILAS, *The New Class: An Analysis of the Communist System*, London, 1957.

NEW DEAL. An international term, formulated on July 2, 1932 by F.D. Roosevelt (1882–1945), in his speech accepting Presidential nomination:

"I pledge you . . . I pledge myself . . . to a new deal for the American People. This is more than a political campaign; it is a call to arms."

The New Deal program for pulling the US out of the great depression was based on the slogan "Relief, Recovery, Reform."

S.I. ROSENMAN (ed.), *The Public Papers and Addresses of F.D. Roosevelt*, 13 Vols., Washington, 1938–1950; B.M. RAUCH, *History of the New Deal*, New York, 1944; W.E. LEUCHTENBURG, *F.D. Roosevelt and the New Deal 1932–1940*, New York, 1963; J.P. LASH, *Dealers and Dreamers. A New Look at the New Deal*, New York, 1988.

NEW DELHI The capital of India. Population: 273,036 in 1981 census. New Delhi was built 1912-29 to replace ▷ Calcutta as the capital of India, 1931. Seat of 20 international organizations reg. with the UIA, e.g. the Afro-Asian Rural Reconstruction Organization; Asian-African Legal Consultative Committee.

NEW DELHI DECLARATION, 1983. ▷ Nonaligned Countries Declaration, 1983.

NEW DELHI DECLARATION ON THE NUCLEAR ARMS RACE, 1985. Adopted in the capital of India, on Jan. 28, 1985 by the Heads of State or Government of six nations: President Raul Alfonsin of Argentina, Prime Minister Andreas Papandreou of Greece, Prime Minister Rajiv Gandhi of India, President Miguel de la Madrid of Mexico, Prime Minister Olof Palme of Sweden and President Julius Nyerere of the United Republic of Tanzania. The text has been circulated as a document of the General Assembly and Security Council. (A/40/114-S/16921):

"Forty years ago, when atomic bombs were blasted over Hiroshima and Nagasaki, the human race became aware that it could destroy itself, and horror came to dwell among us. Forty years ago, also, the nations of the world gathered to organise the international community, and with the United Nations hope was born for all people.

Almost imperceptibly, over the last four decades, every nation and every human being has lost ultimate control over their own life and death. For all of us, it is a small group of men and machines in cities far away who can decide our fate. Every day we remain alive is a day of grace, as if mankind as a whole were a prisoner in the death cell awaiting the uncertain moment of execution. And like every innocent defendant, we refuse to believe that the execution will ever take place.

We find ourselves in this situation because the nuclear-weapon States have applied traditional doctrines of war in a world where new weapons have made them obsolete. What is the point of nuclear "superiority" or "balance" when each side already has enough weapons to devastate the earth dozens of times over? If the old doctrines are applied in the future, the holocaust will be inescapable sooner or later. But nuclear war can be prevented if our voices are joined in a universal demand in defence of our right to live.

As a result of recent atmospheric and biological studies, there have been new findings which indicate that in addition to blast, heat and radiation, nuclear war, even on a limited scale, would trigger an arctic nuclear winter which may transform the earth into a darkened, frozen planet, posing unprecedented peril to all nations, even those far removed from the nuclear explosions. We are convinced that this makes it still more pressing to take preventive action to exclude forever the use of nuclear weapons and the occurrence of a nuclear war.

In our Joint Statement of May 22, 1984 we called upon the nuclear-weapon States to bring their arms race to a halt. We are encouraged by the world-wide response to our appeal. The international support we received and the responses of the nuclear-weapon States themselves have been such that we deemed it our duty to meet here in New Delhi to consider ways to further our efforts. The nuclear-weapon States have a particular responsibility for the dangerous state of the arms race. We urge them to join us in the search for a new direction. We welcome the agreement in Geneva on January 8, 1985, between the Soviet Union and the United States to start negotiations on "a complex of questions concerning space and nuclear arms—both strategic and intermediate range—with all the questions considered and resolved in their inter-relationship". We attach great importance to the proclaimed objective of these negotiations: to prevent an arms race in space and to terminate it on earth, ultimately to eliminate nuclear arms everywhere. We expect the two major nuclear-weapon Powers to implement, in good faith, their undertaking and their negotiations to produce, at an early date, significant results. We will follow their work closely and we expect tha they will keep the international community informed of its progress. We stress that the agenda for and the outcome of these negotiations is a matter of concern for all nations and all people.

We reiterate our appeal for an all-embracing halt to the testing, production and deployment of nuclear-weapons and their delivery systems. Such a halt would greatly facilitate negotiations. Two specific steps today require special attention: the prevention of an arms race in outer space, and a comprehensive test ban treaty.

Outer space must be used for the benefit of mankind as a whole, not as a battle-ground of the future. We, therefore, call for the prohibition of the development, testing, production, deployment and use of all space weapons. An arms race in space would be enormously costly, and have grave destabilising effects. It would also endanger a number of arms limitation and disarmament agreements.

We further urge the nuclear-weapons States to immediately halt the testing of all kinds of nuclear weapons, and to conclude, at an early date, a treaty on a nuclear-weapon test ban. Such a treaty would be a major step on a nuclear-weapon test ban. Such a treaty would be a major step towards ending the continuous modernisation of nuclear arsenals.

We are convinced that all such steps, in so far as necessary, can be accompanied by adequate and non-discriminatory measures of verification.

A halt to the nuclear arms race is at the present moment imperative. Only thus can it be ensured that nuclear arsenals do not grow while negotiations proceed. However, this halt should not be an end in itself. It must be immediately followed by substantial reductions in nuclear forces, leading to the complete elimination of nuclear-weapons and the final goal of general and complete disarmament. Parallel to this process, it is urgently necessary to transfer precious resources currently wasted in military expenditure to social and economic development. The strengthening of the United Nations must also be an essential part of this endeavour.

It is imperative to find a remedy to the existing situation where hundreds of billions of dollars, amounting to approximately one and a half million per minute, are spent annually on weapons. This stands in dramatic contrast to the poverty, and in some cases misery, in which two-thirds of the world population lives.

The future of all people is at stake. As representatives from non-nuclear-weapon States, we will not cease to express our legitimate concern and make known our demands. We affirm our determination to facilitate agreement among the nuclear-weapon States, so that the required steps can be taken. We will seek to work together with them for the common security of mankind and for peace.

We urge people, parliaments and Governments the world over to lend forceful support to this appeal. Progress in disarmament can only be achieved with an informed public applying strong pressure on Governments. Only then will Governments summon the necessary political will to overcome the many obstacles which lie in the path of peace. The world disarmament campaign launched by the United Nations represents a very important element in generating the political will. For centuries, men and women have fought for their rights and freedoms. We now face the greatest struggle of all—for the right to live, for ourselves and for future generations.

Forty years ago, in Hiroshima and San Francisco, the horror of nuclear war was matched by the hope for peace. We would like this year of 1985 to be the year when hope begins to prevail over terror. We dare to hope that by October 24, 1985, the fortieth anniversary of the United Nations, we might see the first concrete steps to avert the threat to the survival of humanity."

UN Chronicle, 1985, No 1, p. 47.

NEW ENGLAND CONFEDERATION, 1643. The first intercolonial union in America, signed on May 19, 1643 by the colonies of Massachusetts, Connecticut, New Haven and Plymouth.

NEWFOUNDLAND. A province of Canada including the island of Newfoundland and the northeastern part of Labrador peninsula, hence also sometimes called Newfoundland and Labrador. The province consists of the island of Newfoundland and adjacent islands, 112,300 sq. km with *c.* 500,000 inhabitants in 1975, and adjacent islands and mainland area of Labrador, 292,219 sq. km with *c.* 50,000 inhabitants. The capital is St John's. The first British colony, 1583; received the status of a dominion in 1917, but lost it as a result of financial insolvency in 1933; administered since then by a Governmental Commission appointed by the UK; as a result of a plebiscite in July 1948 (78,000 to 71,000) it gave up returning to the independent status of a dominion in favor of integration with Canada, which occurred Apr. 1, 1949. Newfoundland as well as its territorial waters was the subject of a British–French dispute in the 19th century, resolved by the London Treaty of Apr. 8, 1904 by virtue of which France gave up its rights to Newfoundland based on the Peace Treaty in Utrecht of Apr. 11, 1713, but received the right to fish in Newfoundland territorial waters. A separate dispute on fishing rights existed in the 19th century between Great Britain and the USA, resolved by the International Court of Arbitration on Sept. 7, 1910. The agreement respecting defense installations in Newfoundland was signed by the governments of Canada, Newfoundland and the UK, on Mar. 31, 1946.

UNTS, Vol. 17, pp. 160–166.

NEW FREEDOM. American electoral slogan of the Democratic Party, 1912, used by the Democrat W. Wilson during his two terms as President 1913-1918 on the internal and international forum. See also ▷ Wilson Fourteen Points 1918.

I.W. DAVIDSON, *A Crossroads to Freedom,* New York, 1956; A.S. SLINK, *The New Freedom,* New York, 1956.

NEW GUINEA. The world's second largest island after Greenland in the south-west Pacific, north of Australia, politically divided into two parts: Papua–New Guinea and West Irian (▷ Irian Barat). Total area: 885,780 sq. km. The New Guinea Trusteeship Agreement approved by the UN General Assembly, Dec. 13, 1946, expired Sept. 16, 1975 with the independence of ▷ Papua–New Guinea.

P. RYAN ed., *Encyclopedia of Papua and New Guinea,* Melbourne, 1972.

NEW HEBRIDES. ▷ Vanuatu.

NEW HUMAN FRONTIER. Name of the Japanese Oysters programme of World International Scientific Research of Biological Rules of Development.

NEW INTERNATIONAL CULTURAL ORDER. The UNESCO program, introduced by states of the Third World at the Nineteenth General Conference of UNESCO in Nairobi, requesting that a program be worked out on the model of the ▷ New International Economic Order for the preservation and development of the cultural heritage of the Third World.

NEW INTERNATIONAL ECONOMIC ORDER. An international term introduced by a UN Declaration passed May 1, 1974 at the Sixth Special Session of the UN General Assembly. Together with the Declaration a Program of Action was accepted for implementing the New Order and a program of immediate assistance for countries particularly hard-hit by the economic crisis. The Assembly's initiatives were taken during a period marked by a series of crises which threatened the stability of world economic relations. The international monetary system known as the Bretton Woods system, instituted in 1944 and subscribed to by most market economy countries, had broken down in 1971. Soon after the outbreak of hostilities in the Middle East in Oct., 1973, oil prices began to rise. Increased prices of other commodities and manufactured goods, shortages of food and depletion of reserves, imbalances of trade and the growing burdens of debt contributed to the unstable conditions.

The nonaligned countries, at a meeting of their Heads of State or Government in Algiers in September 1973, took the position that the Second Development Decade had failed. On Jan. 30, 1974, the President of the Group of Nonaligned Countries, President Houari Boumédienne of Algeria, called for a special session of the Assembly to discuss the problems of raw materials and development.

The special session, held from Apr. 9 to May 2, 1974, agreed that the current economic order was in direct conflict with current developments in international political and economic relations, and that the crises in the world economy since 1970 had had severe repercussions, especially for the developing countries ▷ Charter of Economic Rights and Duties of States 1974; ▷ Monetary International System and Financing of Development of Developing Countries.

The Program of Action includes sections on raw materials and primary commodities; the international monetary system and financing development; industrialization; transfer of technology; regulation of transnational corporations; co-operation among developing countries; the exercise of permanent sovereignty of states over natural resources; and strengthening the role of the United Nations system in international economic co-operation.

The program, i.a., calls for efforts to further producers' associations including their joint marketing arrangements; to work for a link between the prices of the exports of developing countries and the prices of their imports from developed countries; and to defeat attempts to prevent the free exercise by every state of the right of full permanent sovereignty over its natural resources. It says the international monetary system should be reformed with adequate participation of developing countries in bodies carrying out the reform.

Action is also called for to increase essential food production inputs in developing countries, including fertilizers, obtained from developed countries on favorable terms, as well as efforts to promote exports of food products of developing states through progressive elimination of protective and other measures that constitute unfair competition. The program contains a number of measures aimed at improving the terms of trade of developing nations and at eliminating their chronic trade deficits. These include progressive removal of tariff and non-tariff barriers and restrictive business practice; formulation of commodity agreements where appropriate; preparation of a program for a comprehensive range of commodities of export interest to developing states, and, where developing countries' products compete with domestic production in developed countries, expansion by each developed country of imports from developing nations and provision of a fair opportunity to the developing countries to share in the growth market. At the special session of Sept., 1975, devoted to development and international economic co-operation, the Assembly unanimously adopted a resolution calling for measures to serve as the framework of the work of the United Nations system in international trade; the transfer of real resources for financing development; increased transfer of scientific and technological capacity to developing countries; international monetary reform; industrialization; food and agriculture; and co-operation among developing countries. It established an Ad Hoc Committee of the whole Assembly to make recommendations on restructuring the economic and social sectors of the United Nations system. It reaffirmed the target, originally set in the International Development Strategy for the Second Development Decade, of 0.7% of the gross national product of developed countries for official development assistance to the developing countries.

The resolution also stated that measures should be taken to improve the access of developing countries to the markets and capital of the developed countries and to diversify their manufactured and semi-manufactured exports. It called for the international stocking of commodities to secure stable and equitable prices and for world food reserves to assure grain and food security. It endorsed the recommendation of the Second General Conference of the United Nations Industrial Development Organization (UNIDO) to convert that organization into a specialized agency and said that UNIDO should serve as a forum for consultations and negotiation of agreements in the field of industry between developing and developed countries and among developing countries themselves.

At its regular session in 1975, the Assembly recognized the need to establish a link between the proposed Conference on International Economic Co-operation – also known as the Paris talks of the North–South Dialogue – and the United Nations, in light of the fact that the program of the Conference would have a bearing on the ongoing work on international economic co-operation and development within the United Nations system. The Assembly invited the Conference to report on its conclusions.

The Paris talks were held intermittently from Dec., 1975 to June, 1977 with participants from 27 developing and developed market economy countries, who discussed problems of energy, raw materials, finance, trade and development. Convened at the initiative of the President of France, Valery Giscard d'Estaing, the Conference was intended originally to discuss the problem of energy but its agenda was widened to include subjects of greater concern to developing countries.

At its resumed Thirty-First session in Sept., 1977, the UN General Assembly considered the results of the Paris talks but could come to no agreed assessment of their results. The majority of developing countries took the view that the talks had failed to reach agreements contributing to the goals of the New International Economic Order, while many of the developed countries felt that the negotiations had achieved certain positive results. The UN General Assembly created a Special Committee with the task of evaluating the accomplishment of the Program of Action and preparing materials for the VIII Special Session of the UN General Assembly, held in the spring of 1980. A new Conference on North–South Economic Co-operation was held in Mexico City in June 1981.

On Dec. 9, 1988 GA Res. 43/162 adopted by 129 votes with 24 abstentions "Recognized the need for the codification and progressive development of the principles and norms of international law relating to the new international economic order".

UN Yearbook, 1974; *UN Monthly*, May, 1974, pp. 37–50 and 75–93; *Everyone's United Nations*, New York, 1979; *The New International Economic Order: A Selective Bibliography*, UN, New York, 1980; C. POR-TALES, *La América Latina en el Nuevo Orden Económico Internacional*, México, DF, 1983; R.I. ONWUKA, O. ALUKO, *The Future of Africa and the New International Economic Order*, New York, 1986; *UN Resolutions and Decisions adopted by the General Assembly during the First Part of its Forty-Third Session, From 20 September to 22 December 1988*, New York, 1989, pp. 540-541.

NEW INTERNATIONAL ECONOMIC ORDER, UN DECLARATION ON THE ESTABLISHMENT OF, 1974. Approved without voting by the Special Session of the UN General Assembly, May 1, 1974. The text is as follows:

"We, the Members of the United Nations,
Having convened a special session of the General Assembly to study for the first time the problems of raw materials and development, devoted to the consideration of the most important economic problems facing the world community,
Bearing in mind the spirit, purposes and principles of the Charter of the United Nations to promote the economic advancement and social progress of all peoples,
Solemnly proclaim our united determination to work urgently for the establishment of a new international economic order based on equity, sovereign equality, interdependence, common interest and co-operation among all states, irrespective of their economic and social systems which shall correct inequalities and redress existing injustices, make it possible to eliminate the widening gap between the developed and the developing countries and ensure steadily accelerating economic and social development and peace and justice for present and future generations, and, to that end, declare:

(1) The greatest and most significant achievement during the last decades has been the independence from colonial and alien domination of a large number of peoples and nations which has enabled them to become members of the community of free peoples. Technological progress has also been made in all spheres of economic activities in the last three decades, thus providing a solid potential for improving the well-being of all peoples. However, the remaining vestiges of alien and colonial domination, foreign occupation, racial discrimination, apartheid and neo-colonialism in all its forms continue to be among the greatest obstacles to the full emancipation and progress of the developing countries and all the peoples involved. The benefits of technological progress are not shared equitably by all members of the international community. The developing countries, which constitute 70 per cent of the world's population, account for only 30 per cent of the world's income. It has proved impossible to achieve an even and balanced development of the international community under the existing international economic order. The gap between the developed and the developing countries continues to widen in a system which was established at a time when most of the developing countries did not even exist as independent states and which perpetuates inequality.

(2) The present international economic order is in direct conflict with current developments in international political and economic relations. Since 1970, the world economy has experienced a series of grave crises which have had severe repercussions, especially on the developing countries because of their generally greater vulnerability to external economic impulses. The developing world has become a powerful factor that makes its influence felt in all fields of international activity. These irreversible changes in the relationships of forces in the world necessitate the active, full and equal participation of the developing countries in the formulation and application of all decisions that concern the international community.

(3) All these changes have thrust into prominence the reality of interdependence of all the members of the world community. Current events have brought into sharp focus the realization that the interests of the developed countries and those of the developing countries can no longer be isolated from each other, that there is close interrelationship between the prosperity of the developed countries and the growth and development of the developing countries, and that the prosperity of the international community as a whole depends upon the prosperity of its constituent parts. International co-operation for development is the shared goal and common duty of all countries. Thus the political, economic and social well-being of present and future generations depends more than ever on co-operation between all members of the international community on the basis of sovereign equality and the removal of the disequilibrium that exists between them.

(4) The new international economic order should be founded on full respect for the following principles:
(a) Sovereign equality of states, self-determination of all peoples, inadmissibility of the acquisition of territories by force, territorial integrity and non-interference in the internal affairs of other States;
(b) The broadest co-operation of all the states members of the international community, based on equity, whereby the prevailing disparities in the world may be banished and prosperity secured for all;
(c) Full and effective participation on the basis of equality of all countries in the solving of world economic problems in the common interest of all countries, bearing in mind the necessity to ensure the accelerated development of all the developing countries, while devoting particular attention to the adoption of special measures in favour of the last developed, landlocked and island developing countries as well as those developing countries most seriously affected by economic crises and natural calamities, without losing sight of the interests of other developing countries;
(d) The right to every country to adopt the economic and social system that it deems to be the most appropriate for its own development and not be subjected to discrimination of any kind as a result;
(e) Full permanent sovereignty of every state over its natural resources and all economic activities. In order to safeguard these resources, each State is entitled to exercise effective control over them and their exploitation with means suitable to its own situation, including the right to nationalization or transfer of ownership to its nationals, this right being an expression of the full permanent sovereignty of the state. No state may be subjected to economic, political or any other type of coercion to prevent the free and full exercise of this inalienable right;
(f) The right of all states, territories and peoples under foreign occupation, alien and colonial domination or apartheid to restitution and full compensation for the exploitation and depletion of, and damages to, the natural resources and all other resources of those states, territories and peoples;
(g) Regulation and supervision of the activities of transnational corporations by taking measures in the interest of the national economies of the countries where such transnational corporations operate on the basis of the full sovereignty of those countries;
(h) The right of the developing countries and the peoples of territories under colonial and racial domination and foreign occupation to achieve their liberation and to regain effective control over their natural resources and economic activities;
(i) The extending of assistance to developing countries, peoples and territories which are under colonial and alien domination, foreign occupation, racial discrimination or apartheid or are subjected to economic, political or any other type of coercive measures to obtain from them the subordination of the exercise of their sovereign rights and to secure from them advantages of any kind, and the neo-colonialism in all its forms, and which have established or are endeavouring to establish effective control over their natural resources and economic activities that have been or are still under foreign control;
(j) Just and equitable relationship between the prices of raw materials, primary products, manufactured and semi-manufactured goods exported by developing countries and the prices of raw materials, primary commodities, manufactures, capital goods and equipment imported by them with the aim of bringing about sustained improvement in their unsatisfactory terms of trade and the expansion of the world economy;
(k) Extension of active assistance to developing countries by the whole international community, free of any political or military conditions;
(l) Ensuring that one of the main aims of the reformed international monetary system shall be the promotion of the development of the developing countries and the adequate flow of real resources to them;
(m) Improving the competitiveness of natural materials facing competition from synthetic substitutes;
(n) Preferential and non-reciprocal treatment for developing countries, wherever feasible, in all fields of international economic co-operation whenever possible;
(o) Securing favourable conditions for the transfer of financial resources to developing countries;
(p) Giving to the developing countries access to the achievements of modern science and technology, and promoting the transfer of technology and the creation of indigenous technology for the benefit of the developing countries in forms and in accordance with procedures which are suited to their economies;
(q) The need for all states to put an end to the waste of natural resources, including food products;
(r) The need for developing countries to concentrate all their resources for the cause of development;
(s) The strengthening, through individual and collective actions, of mutual economic, trade, financial and technical co-operation among the developing countries, mainly on a preferential basis;
(t) Facilitating the role which producers' associations may play within the framework of international co-

operation and, in pursuance of their aims, inter alia assisting in the promotion of sustained growth of world economy and accelerating the development of developing countries.

(5) The unanimous adoption of the International Development Strategy for the Second United Nations Development Decade was an important step in the promotion of international economic co-operation on a just and equitable basis. The accelerated implementation of obligations and commitments assumed by the international community within the framework of the Strategy, particularly those concerning imperative development needs of developing countries, would contribute significantly to the fulfilment of the aims and objectives of the present Declaration.

(6) The United Nations as a universal organization should be capable of dealing with problems of international economic co-operation in a comprehensive manner and ensuring equally the interests of all countries. It must have an even greater role in the establishment of a new international economic order. The Charter of Economic Rights and Duties of States, for the preparation of which the present Declaration will provide an additional source of inspiration, will constitute a significant contribution in this respect. All the States Members of the United Nations are therefore called upon to exert maximum efforts with a view to securing the implementation of the present Declaration, which is one of the principal guarantees for the creation of better conditions for all peoples to reach a life worthy of human dignity.

(7) The present Declaration on the Establishment of a New International Economic order shall be one of the most important bases of economic relations between all peoples and all nations."

The United States notified reservations to the point Four of the Declaration.

Together with the Declaration the UN General Assembly approved without voting a *Programme for the Implementation of a New Economic Order:*

"Introduction. (1) In view of the continuing severe economic imbalance in the relations between developed and developing countries, and in the context of the constant and continuing aggravation of the imbalance of the economies of the developing countries and the consequent need for the mitigation of their current economic difficulties, urgent and effective measures need to be taken by the international community to assist the developing countries, while devoting particular attention to the least developed, land-locked and island developing countries and those developing countries most seriously affected by economic crises and natural calamities leading to serious retardation of development processes.

(2) With a view to ensuring the application of the Declaration on the Establishment of a New International Economic Order, it will be necessary to adopt and implement within a specified period a programme of action of unprecedented scope and to bring about maximum economic co-operation and understanding among all states, particularly between developed and developing countries based on the principles of dignity and sovereign equality.

I. *Fundamental problems of raw materials and primary commodities as related to trade and development*

(1) Raw materials. All efforts should be made:

(a) To put an end to all forms of foreign occupation, racial discrimination, apartheid, colonial, neo-colonial and alien domination and exploitation through the exercise of permanent sovereignty over natural resources;

(b) To take measures for the recovery, exploitation, development, marketing and distribution of natural resources, particularly of developing countries, to serve their national interests, to promote collective self-reliance among them and to strengthen mutually beneficial international economic co-operation with a view to bringing about the accelerated development of developing countries;

(c) To facilitate the functioning and to further the aims of producers' associations, including their joint marketing arrangements, orderly commodity trading, improvement in export income of producing developing

countries and in their terms of trade, and sustained growth of the world economy for the benefit of all;

(d) To evolve a just and equitable relationship between the prices of raw materials, primary commodities, manufactured and semi-manufactured goods exported by developing countries and the prices of raw materials, primary commodities, food, manufactured and semi-manufactured goods and capital equipment imported by them, and to work for a link between the prices of exports of developing countries and the prices of their imports from developed countries;

(e) To take measures to reverse the continued trend of stagnation or decline in the real prices of several commodities exported by developing countries, despite a general rise in commodity prices, resulting in a decline in the export earnings of these developing countries;

(f) To take measures to expand the markets for natural products in relation to synthetics, taking into account the interests of the developing countries, and to utilize fully the ecological advantages of these products;

(g) To take measures to promote the processing of raw materials in the producer developing countries.

(2) Food

All efforts should be made:

(a) To take full account of specific problems of developing countries, particularly in times of food shortages, in the international efforts connected with the food problem;

(b) To take into account that, owing to lack of means, some developing countries have vast potentialities of unexploited or underexploited land which, if reclaimed and put into practical use, would contribute considerably to the solution of the food crisis;

(c) By the international community to undertake concrete and speedy measures with a view to arresting desertification, salination and damage by locusts or any other similar phenomenon involving several developing countries, particularly in Africa, and gravely affecting the agricultural production capacity of these countries, and also to assist the developing countries affected by this phenomenon to develop the affected zones with a view to contributing to the solution of their food problems;

(d) To refrain from damaging or deteriorating natural resources and food resources, especially those derived from the sea, by preventing pollution and taking appropriate steps to protect and reconstitute those resources;

(e) By developed countries, in evolving their policies relating to production, stocks, imports and exports of food, to take full account of the interests of:

(i) Developing importing countries which cannot afford high prices for their imports;

(ii) Developing exporting countries which need increased market opportunities for their exports;

(f) To ensure that developing countries can import the necessary quantity of food without undue strain on their foreign exchange resources and without unpredictable deterioration in their balance of payments, and, in this context, that special measures are taken in respect of the least developed, the land-locked and island developing countries as well as those developing countries most seriously affected by economic crises and natural calamities;

(g) To ensure that concrete measures to increase food production and storage facilities in developing countries are introduced, inter alia, by ensuring an increase in all available essential inputs, including fertilizers, from developed countries on favourable terms;

(h) To promote exports of food products of developing countries through just and equitable arrangements, inter alia, by progressive elimination of such protective and other measures as constitute unfair competition.

(3) General trade.

All efforts should be made:

(a) To take the following measures for the amelioration of terms of trade of developing countries and concrete steps to eliminate chronic trade deficits of developing countries:

(i) Fulfilment of relevant commitments already undertaken in the United Nations Conference on Trade and Development and in the international Development Strategy for the Second United Nations Development Decade;

(ii) Improved access to markets in developed countries through the progressive removal of tariff and non-tariff barriers and of restrictive business practices;

(iii) Expeditious formulation of commodity agreements where appropriate, in order to regulate as necessary and to stabilize the world markets for raw materials and primary commodities;

(iv) Preparation of an over-all integrated programme, setting out guidelines and taking into account the current work in this field, for a comprehensive range of commodities of export interest to developing countries;

(v) Where products of developing countries compete with domestic production in developed countries, each developed country should facilitate the expansion of imports from developing countries and provide a fair and reasonable opportunity to the developing countries to share in the growth of the market;

(vi) When the importing developed countries derive receipts from customs duties, taxes and other protective measures applied to imports of these products, consideration should be given to the claim of the developing countries that these receipts should be reimbursed in full to the exporting developing countries or devoted to providing additional resources to meet their development needs;

(vii) Developed countries should make appropriate adjustments in their economies so as to facilitate the expansion and diversification of imports from developing countries and thereby permit a rational, just and equitable international division of labour;

(viii) Setting up general principles for pricing policy for exports of commodities of developing countries, with a view to rectifying and achieving satisfactory terms of trade for them;

(ix) Until satisfactory terms of trade are achieved for all developing countries, consideration should be given to alternative means, including improved compensatory financing schemes for meeting the development needs of the developing countries concerned;

(x) Implementation, improvement and enlargement of the generalized system of preferences for exports of agricultural primary commodities, manufactures and semi-manufactures from developing to developed countries and consideration of its extension to commodities, including those which are processed or semiprocessed; developing countries which are or will be sharing their existing tariff advantages in some developed countries as the result of the introduction and eventual enlargement of the generalized system of preferences should, as a matter of urgency, be granted new openings in the markets of other developed countries which should offer them export opportunities that at least compensate for the sharing of those advantages;

(xi) The setting up of buffer stocks within the framework of commodity arrangements and their financing by international financial institutions, wherever necessary, by the developed countries and, when they are able to do so, by the developing countries, with the aim of favouring the producer developing and consumer developing countries and of contributing to the expansion of world trade as a whole;

(xii) In cases where natural materials can satisfy the requirements of the market, new investment for the expansion of the capacity to produce synthetic materials and substitutes should be made.

(b) To be guided by the principles of non-reciprocity and preferential treatment of developing countries in multilateral trade negotiations between developed and developing countries, and to seek sustained and additional benefits for the international trade of developing countries so as to achieve a substantial increase in their foreign exchange earnings, diversification of their exports and acceleration of the rate of their economic growth.

(4) Transport and insurance.

All efforts should be made:

(a) To promote an increasing and equitable participation of developing countries in the world shipping tonnage;

(b) To arrest and reduce the ever-increasing freight rates in order to reduce the cost of imports to, and exports from, the developing countries;

(c) To minimize the cost of insurance and reinsurance for developing countries and to assist the growth of domestic insurance and reinsurance markets in developing countries and the establishment to this end, where appropriate, of institutions in these countries or at the regional level;

(d) To ensure the early implementation of the code of conduct for liner conferences;

(e) To take urgent measures to increase the import and export capability of the least developed countries and to offset the disadvantages of the adverse geographic situation of land-locked countries, particularly with regard to their transportation and transit costs, as well as developing island countries in order to increase their trading ability;

(f) By the developed countries to refrain from imposing measures or implementing policies designed to prevent the importation, at equitable prices, of commodities from the legitimate measures and policies adopted by the developing countries in order to improve prices and encourage the export of such commodities.

II. *International monetary system and financing of the development of developing countries*

(1) Objectives

All efforts should be made to reform the international monetary system with, inter alia, the following objectives:

(a) Measures to check the inflation already experienced by the developed countries, to prevent it from being transferred to developing countries and to study and devise possible arrangements within the International Monetary Fund to mitigate the effects of inflation in developed countries on the economies of developing countries;

(b) Measures to eliminate the instability of the international monetary system, in particular the uncertainty of the exchange rates, especially as it affects adversely the trade of commodities;

(c) Maintenance of the real value of the currency reserves of the developing countries by preventing their erosion from inflation and exchange rate depreciation of reserve currencies;

(d) Full and effective participation of developing countries in all phases of decision-making for the formulation of an equitable and durable monetary system and adequate participation of developing countries in all bodies entrusted with this reform and, particularly, in the Board of Governors of the International Monetary Fund;

(e) Adequate and orderly creation of additional liquidity with particular regard to the needs of the developing countries through the additional allocation of special drawing rights based on the concept of world liquidity needs to be appropriately revised in the light of the new international environment; any creation of international liquidity should be made through international multilateral mechanisms;

(f) Early establishment of a link between special drawing rights and additional development financing in the interest of developing countries, consistent with the monetary characteristics of special drawing rights;

(g) Review by the International Monetary Fund of the relevant provisions in order to ensure effective participation by developing countries in the decision-making process;

(h) Arrangements to promote an increasing net transfer of real resources from the developed to the developing countries;

(i) Review of the methods of operation of the International Monetary Fund, in particular the terms for both credit repayments and "stand-by" arrangements, the system of compensatory financing, and the terms of the financing of commodity buffer stocks so as to enable the developing countries to make more effective use of them.

(2) Measures

All efforts should be made to take the following urgent measures to finance the development of developing countries and to meet the balance-of-payment crises in the developing world:

(a) Implementation at an accelerated pace by the developed countries of the time-bound programme, as already laid down in the International Development Strategy for the Second United Nations Development Decade, for the net amount of financial resource transfers to developing countries; increase in the official component of the net amount of financial resource transfers

to developing countries so as to meet and even to exceed the target of the Strategy;

(b) International financing institutions should effectively play their role as development financing banks without discrimination on account of the political or economic system of any member country, assistance being untied;

(c) More effective participation by developing countries whether recipients or contributors, in the decision-making process in the competent organs of the International Bank for Reconstruction and Development and the International Development Association, through the establishment of a more equitable pattern of voting rights;

(d) Exemption, wherever possible, of the developing countries from all import and capital outflow controls imposed by the developed countries;

(e) Promotion of foreign investment, both public and private, from developed to developing countries in accordance with the needs and requirements in sectors of their economies as determined by the recipient countries;

(f) Appropriate urgent measures, including international action, should be taken to mitigate adverse consequences for the current and future development of developing countries arising from the burden of external debt contracted on hard terms;

(g) Debt renegotiation on a case-by-case basis with a view to concluding agreements on debt cancellation, moratorium, rescheduling or interest subsidization;

(h) International financial institutions should take into account the special situation of each developing country in reorientating their lending policies to suit these urgent needs; there is also need for improvement in practices of international financial institutions in regard to, inter alia, development financing and international monetary problems;

(i) Appropriate steps should be taken to give priority to the least developed, land-locked and island developing countries and to the countries most seriously affected by economic crises and natural calamities, in the availability of loans for development purposes which should include more favourable terms and conditions.

III. *Industrialization.*

All efforts should be made by the international community to take measures to encourage the industrialization of the developing countries, and, to this end:

(a) The developed countries should respond favourably, within the framework of their official aid as well as international financial institutions, to the requests of developing countries for the financing of industrial projects;

(b) The developed countries should encourage investors to finance industrial production projects, particularly export-oriented production, in developing countries, in agreement with the latter and within the context of their laws and regulations;

(c) With a view to bringing about a new international economic structure which should increase the share of the developing countries in world industrial production, the developed countries and the agencies of the United Nations system, in co-operation with the developing countries, should contribute to setting up new industrial capacities including raw materials and commodity transforming facilities as a matter of priority in the developing countries that produce those raw materials and commodities;

(d) The international community should continue and expand with the aid of the developed countries and the international institutions, the operational and instruction-oriented technical assistance programmes, including vocational training and management development of national personnel of the developing countries, in the light of their special development requirements.

IV. *Transfer of technology*

All efforts should be made:

(a) To formulate an international code of conduct for the transfer of technology corresponding to needs and conditions prevalent in developing countries;

(b) To give access on improved terms to modern technology and to adapt that technology, as appropriate, to specific economic social and ecological conditions and varying stages of development in developing countries;

(c) To expand significantly the assistance from developed to developing countries in research and

development programmes and in the creation of suitable indigenous technology;

(d) To adapt commercial practices governing transfer of technology to the requirements of the developing countries and to prevent abuse of the rights of sellers;

(e) To promote international co-operation in research and development in exploration and exploitation, conservation and the legitimate utilization of natural resources and all sources of energy.

In taking the above measures, the special needs of the least developed and land-locked countries should be borne in mind.

V. *Regulation and control over the activities of transnational corporations*

All efforts should be made to formulate, adopt and implement an international code of conduct for transnational corporations:

(a) To prevent interference in the internal affairs of the countries where they operate and their collaboration with racist regimes and colonial administrations;

(b) To regulate their activities in host countries, to eliminate restrictive business practices and to conform to the national development plans and objectives of developing countries, and in this context facilitate, as necessary, the review and revision of previously concluded arrangements;

(c) To bring about assistance, transfer of technology and management skills to developing countries on equitable and favourable terms;

(d) To regulate the repatriation of the profits accruing from their operations taking into account the legitimate interests of all parties concerned;

(e) To promote reinvestment of their profits in developing countries.

VI. *Charter of Economic Rights and Duties of States*

The Charter of Economic Rights and Duties of States, the draft of which is being prepared by a working group of the United Nations and which the General Assembly has already expressed the intention of adopting at its twenty-ninth regular session, shall constitute an effective instrument towards the establishment of a new system of international economic relations based on equity, sovereign equality, and interdependence of the interests of developed and developing countries. It is therefore of vital importance that the aforementioned Charter be adopted by the General Assembly at its twenty-ninth session.

VII. *Promotion of co-operation among developing countries*

(1) Collective self-reliance and growing co-operation among developing countries will further strengthen their role in the new international economic order. Developing countries, with a view to expanding co-operation at the regional and subregional and interregional levels, should take further steps, inter alia:

(a) To support the establishment and/or improvement of an appropriate mechanism to defend the prices of their exportable commodities and to improve access to and stabilize markets for them. In this context the increasingly effective mobilization by the whole group of oil-exporting countries of their natural resources for the benefit of their economic development is to be welcomed. At the same time there is the paramount need for co-operation among the developing countries in evolving urgently and in a spirit of solidarity all possible means to assist developing countries to cope with the immediate problems resulting from this legitimate and perfectly justified action. The measures already taken in this regard are a positive indication of the evolving co-operation between developing countries;

(b) To protect their inalienable right to permanent sovereignty over their natural resources;

(c) To promote, establish or strengthen economic integration at the regional and subregional levels;

(d) To increase considerably their imports from other developing countries;

(e) To ensure that no developing country accords to imports from developed countries more favourable treatment than that accorded to imports from developing countries. Taking into account the existing international agreements, current limitations and possibilities and also their future evolution, preferential treatment should be given to the procurement of import requirements from other developing countries. Wherever possible, preferential treatment should be given to imports

from developing countries and the exports of those countries;
(f) To promote close co-operation in the fields of finance, credit relations and monetary issues, including the development of credit relations on a preferential basis and on favourable terms;
(g) To strengthen efforts which are already being made by developing countries to utilize available financial resources for financing development in the developing countries through investment, financing of export-oriented and emergency projects and other long-term assistance;
(h) To promote and establish effective instruments of co-operation in the fields of industry, science and technology, transport, shipping and mass communication media.
(2) Developed countries should support initiatives in the regional, subregional and interregional co-operation of developing countries through the extension of financial and technical assistance by more effective and concrete actions, particularly in the field of commercial policy.
VIII. *Assistance in the exercise of permanent sovereignty of states over natural resources*
All efforts should be made:
(a) To defeat attempts to prevent the free and effective exercise of the rights of every state to full and permanent sovereignty over its natural resources;
(b) To ensure that competent agencies of the United Nations system meet requests for assistance from developing countries in connection with the operation of nationalized means of production.
IX. *Strengthening of the role of the United Nations system in the field of international economic co-operation*
(1) In furtherance of the objectives of the International Development Strategy for the Second United Nations Development Decade and in accordance with the aims and objectives of the Declaration on the Establishment of a New International Economic Order, all Member States pledge to make full use of the United Nations system in the implementation of the present Programme of Action, jointly adopted by them, in working for the establishment of a new international economic order and thereby strengthening the role of the United Nations in the field of world-wide co-operation for economic and social development.
(2) The General Assembly of the United Nations shall conduct an over-all review of the implementation of the Programme of Action as a priority item. All the activities of the United Nations system to be undertaken under the Programme of Action as well as those already planned, such as the World Population Conference, 1974, The World Food Conference, the Second General Conference of the United Nations Industrial Development Organization and the mid-term review and appraisal of the International Development Strategy for the Second United Nations Development Decade should be so directed as to enable the special Session of the General Assembly on development, called for under Assembly resolution 3172 (XXVIII) of 17 December 1973, to make its full contribution to the establishment of the new international economic order. All Member States are urged, jointly and individually, to direct their efforts and policies towards the success of that special session.
(3) The Economic and Social Council shall define the policy framework and co-ordinate the activities of all organizations, institutions and subsidiary bodies within the United Nations system which shall be entrusted with the task of implementing the present Programme of Action. In order to enable the Economic and Social Council to carry out its tasks effectively:
(a) All organizations, institutions and subsidiary bodies concerned within the United Nations system shall submit to the Economic and Social Council progress reports on the implementation of the Programme of Action within their respective fields of competence as often as necessary, but not less than once a year;
(b) The Economic and Social Council shall examine the progress reports as a matter of urgency, to which end it may be convened, as necessary, in special session or, if need be, may function continuously. It shall draw the attention of the General Assembly to the problems and difficulties arising in connection with the implementation of the Programme of Action.
(4) All organizations, institutions, subsidiary bodies and conferences of the United Nations system are entrusted with the implementation of the Programme of Action. The activities of the United Nations Conference on Trade and Development as set forth in General Assembly resolution 1995 (XIX) of 30 December 1964, should be strengthened for the purpose of following in collaboration with other competent organizations the development of international trade in raw materials throughout the world.
(5) Urgent and effective measures should be taken to review the lending policies of international financial institutions, taking into account the special situation of each developing country, to suit urgent needs, to improve the practices of these institutions in regard to, inter alia, development financing and international monetary problems, and to ensure more effective participation by developing countries – whether recipients or contributors – in the decision-making process through appropriate revision of the pattern of voting rights.
(6) The developed countries and others in a position to do so should contribute substantially to the various organizations, programmes and funds established within the United Nations system for the purpose of accelerating economic and social development in developing countries.
(7) The present Programme of Action complements and strengthens the goals and objectives embodied in the International Development Strategy for the Second United Nations Development Decade as well as the new measures formulated by the General Assembly at its twenty-eighth session to offset the short-falls in achieving those goals and objectives.
(8) The implementation of the Programme of Action should be taken into account at the time of the mid-term review and appraisal of the International Development Strategy for the Second United Nations Development Decade. New commitments, changes, additions and adaptations in the Strategy should be made, as appropriate taking into account the Declaration on the Establishment of a New International Economic Order and the present Programme of Action.
X. *Special Programme*
The General Assembly adopts the following Special Programme, including particularly emergency measures to mitigate the difficulties of the developing countries most seriously affected by economic crisis, bearing in mind the particular problem of the least developed and land-locked countries:
The General Assembly,
Taking into account the following considerations:
(a) The sharp increase in the prices of their essential imports such as food, fertilizers, energy products, capital goods, equipment and services, including transportation and transit costs has gravely exacerbated the increasingly adverse terms of trade of a number of developing countries, added to the burden of their foreign debt, and, cumulatively, created a situation which, if left untended will make it impossible for them to finance their essential imports and development and result in a further deterioration in the levels and conditions of life in these countries. The present crisis is the outcome of all the problems that have accumulated over the years: in the field of trade, in monetary reform, the world-wide inflationary situation, inadequacy and delay in provision of financial assistance and many other similar problems in the economic and developmental fields. In facing the crisis, this complex situation must be borne in mind so as to ensure that the Special Programme adopted by the international community provides emergency relief and timely assistance to the most seriously affected countries. Simultaneously, steps are being taken to resolve these outstanding problems through a fundamental restructuring of the world economic system, in order to allow these countries while solving the present difficulties to reach an acceptable level of development.
(b) The special measures adopted to assist the most seriously affected countries must encompass not only the relief which they require on an emergency basis to maintain their import requirements, but also, beyond that, steps to consciously promote the capacity of these countries to produce and earn more. Unless such a comprehensive approach is adopted, there is every likelihood that the difficulties of the most seriously affected countries may be perpetuated. Nevertheless, the first and most pressing task of the international community is to enable these countries to meet the short-fall in their balance-of-payments positions. But this must be simultaneously supplemented by additional development assistance to maintain and thereafter accelerate their rate of economic development.
(c) The countries which have been most seriously affected are precisely those which are at the greatest disadvantage in the world economy: the least developed, the land-locked and other low-income developing countries as well as other developing countries whose economies have been seriously dislocated as a result of the present economic crisis, natural calamities, and foreign aggression and occupation. An indication of the countries thus affected, the level of the impact on their economies and the kind of relief and assistance they require can be assessed on the basis, inter alia, of the following criteria:
(i) Low per capita income as a reflection of relative poverty, low productivity, low level of technology and development;
(ii) Sharp increase in their import cost of essentials relative to export earnings;
(iii) High ratio of debt servicing to export earnings;
(iv) Insufficiency in export earnings, comparative inelasticity of export incomes and unavailability of exportable surplus;
(v) Low level of foreign exchange reserves of their inadequacy for requirements;
(vi) Adverse impact of higher transportation and transit costs;
(vii) Relative importance of foreign trade in the development process.
(d) The assessment of the extent and nature of the impact on the economies of the most seriously affected countries must be made flexible, keeping in mind the present uncertainty in the world economy, the adjustment policies that may be adopted by the developed countries and the flow of capital and investment. Estimates of the payments situation and needs of these countries can be assessed and projected reliably only on the basis of their average performance over a number of years. Long-term projections, at this time, cannot but be uncertain.
(e) It is important that, in the special measures to mitigate the difficulties of the most seriously affected countries all the developed countries as well as the developing countries should contribute according to their level of development and the capacity and strength of their economies. It is notable that some developing countries, despite their own difficulties and development needs, have shown a willingness to play a concrete and helpful role in ameliorating the difficulties faced by the poorer developing countries. The various initiatives and measures taken recently by certain developing countries with adequate resources on a bilateral and multilateral basis to contribute to alleviating the difficulties of other developing countries are a reflection of their commitment to the principle of effective economic co-operation among developing countries.
(f) The response of the developed countries which have by far the greater capacity to assist the affected countries in overcoming their present difficulties must be commensurate with their responsibilities. Their assistance should be in addition to the presently available levels of aid. They should fulfil and if possible exceed the targets of the International Development Strategy for the Second United Nations Development Decade on financial assistance to the developing countries, especially that relating to official development assistance. They should also give serious consideration to the cancellation of the external debts of the most seriously affected countries. This would provide the simplest and quickest relief to the affected countries. Favourable consideration should also be given to debt moratorium and rescheduling. The current situation should not lead the industrialized countries to adopt what will ultimately prove to be a self-defeating policy aggravating the present crisis,
Recalling the constructive proposals made by His Imperial Majesty the Shahanshah of Iran and His Excellency Mr. Houari Boumediene, President of the People's Democratic Republic of Algeria,
(1) Decides to launch a Special Programme to provide emergency relief and development assistance to the

developing countries most seriously affected, as a matter of urgency, and for the period of time necessary, at least until the end of the Second United Nations Development Decade, to help them overcome their present difficulties and to achieve self-sustaining economic development;

(2) Decides as a first step in the Special Programme to request the Secretary-General to launch an emergency operation to provide timely relief to the most seriously affected developing countries, as defined in subparagraph (c) above with the aim of maintaining unimpaired essential imports for the duration of the coming 12 months and to invite the industrialized countries and other potential contributors to announce their contributions for emergency assistance, or intimate their intention to do so, by 15 June 1974 to be provided through bilateral or multilateral channels taking into account the commitments and measures of assistance announced or already taken by some countries, and further requests the Secretary-General to report the progress of the emergency operation to the General Assembly at its twenty-ninth session, through the Economic and Social Council at its fifty-seventh session;

(3) Calls upon the industrialized countries and other potential contributors to extend to the most seriously affected countries immediate relief and assistance which must be of an order of magnitude that is commensurate with the needs of these countries. Such assistance should be in addition to the existing level of aid and provided at a very early date to the maximum possible extent on a grant basis and, where not possible, on soft terms. The disbursement and relevant operational procedures and terms must reflect this exceptional situation. The assistance could be provided either through bilateral or multilateral channels, including such new institutions and facilities that have been or are to be set up. The special measures may include the following:

(a) Special arrangements on particularly favourable terms and conditions including possible subsidies for and assured supplies of essential commodities and goods;
(b) Deferred payments for all or part of imports of essential commodities and goods;
(c) Commodity assistance, including food aid, on a grant basis or deferred payments in local currencies, bearing in mind that this should not adversely affect the exports of developing countries;
(d) Long-term suppliers credits on easy terms;
(e) Long-term financial assistance on concessionary terms;
(f) Drawings from special International Monetary Fund facilities on concessional terms;
(g) Establishment of a link between the creation of special drawing rights and development assistance, taking into account the additional financial requirements of the most seriously affected countries;
(h) Subsidies, provided bilaterally or multilaterally, for interest on funds available on commercial terms borrowed by the most seriously affected countries;
(i) Debt renegotiation on a case-by-case basis with a view to concluding agreements on debt cancellation, moratorium or rescheduling;
(j) Provision on more favourable terms of capital goods and technical assistance to accelerate the industrialization of the affected countries;
(k) Investment in industrial and development projects on favourable terms;
(l) Subsidizing the additional transit and transport costs especially of the land-locked countries.

(4) Appeals to the developed countries to consider favourably the cancellation, moratorium or rescheduling of the debts of the most seriously affected developing countries, on their request as an important contribution to mitigating the grave and urgent difficulties of these countries;

(5) Decides to establish a Special Fund under the auspices of the United Nations, through voluntary contributions from industrialized countries and other potential contributors, as a part of the special Programme, to provide emergency relief and development assistance which will commence its operations at the latest by 1 January 1975;

(6) Establishes an *Ad Hoc* Committee on the special Programme, composed of 36 Member States appointed by the President of the General Assembly, after

appropriate consultations, bearing in mind the purposes of the Special Fund and its terms of reference;
(a) To make recommendations, inter alia, on the scope, machinery and modes of operation of the Special Fund, taking into account the need for:
(i) Equitable representation on its governing body;
(ii) Equitable distribution of its resources;
(iii) Full utilization of the service and facilities of existing international organizations;
(iv) The possibility of merging the United Nations Capital Development Fund with the operations of the Special Fund;
(v) A central monitoring body to oversee the various measures being taken both bilaterally and multilaterally; and, to this end, bearing in mind the different ideas and proposals submitted at the sixth special session, including those put forward by Iran and those made at the 2208th plenary meeting and the comments thereon, and the possibility of utilizing the Special Fund to provide an alternative channel for normal development assistance after the emergency period;
(b) To monitor, pending commencement of the operations of the Special Fund, the various measures being taken both bilaterally and multilaterally to assist the most seriously affected countries;
(c) To prepare, on the basis of information provided by the countries concerned and by appropriate agencies of the United Nations system, a broad assessment of:
(i) The magnitude of the difficulties facing the most seriously affected countries;
(ii) The kind and quantities of the commodities and goods essentially required by them;
(iii) Their need for financial assistance;
(iv) Their technical assistance requirements, including especially access to technology;
(7) Requests the Secretary-General of the United Nations, the Secretary General of the United Nations Conference on Trade and Development, the President of the International Bank for Reconstruction and Development, the Managing Director of the International Monetary Fund, the Administrator of the United Nations Development Programme and the heads of the other competent international organizations to assist the Ad Hoc Committee on the Special Programme in performing the functions assigned to it under paragraph 6 above, and to help, as appropriate, in the operations of the Special Fund;
(8) Requests the International Monetary Fund to expedite decisions on:
(a) The establishment of an extended special facility with a view to enabling the most seriously affected developing countries to participate in it on favourable terms;
(b) The creation of special drawing rights and the early establishment of the link between their allocation and development financing;
(c) The establishment and operation of the proposed new special facility to extend credits and subsidize interest charges on commercial funds borrowed by Member States, bearing in mind the interests of the developing countries and especially the additional financial requirements of the most seriously affected countries;
(9) Requests the World Bank group and the International Monetary Fund to place their managerial, financial and technical services at the disposal of Governments contributing to emergency financial relief so as to enable them to assist without delay in channelling funds to the recipients, making such institutional and procedural changes as may be required;
(10) Invites the United Nations Development Programme to take the necessary steps, particularly at the country level, to respond on an emergency basis to requests for additional assistance which it may be called upon to render within the framework of the Special Programme;
(11) Requests the Ad Hoc Committee on the Special Programme to submit its report and recommendations to the Economic and Social Council at its fifty-seventh session and invites the Council, on the basis of its consideration of that report, to submit suitable recommendations to the General Assembly at its twenty-ninth session;
(12) Decides to consider as a matter of high priority at its twenty-ninth session, within the framework of a new international economic order, the question of special measures for the most seriously affected countries."

UN Yearbook 1974; H.S.D. COLE, *Global Models and the New International Economic Order*, London, 1975: E. KÜNG, *Weltwirtschaftspolitik*, Tübingen, 1979. *The New International Economic Order. A Selective Bibliography*, UN, New York, 1980.

NEW INTERNATIONAL HUMANITARIAN ORDER. The codification program of the UN Commission on Human Rights. In 1983 the Third Committee reviewed a report on a New International Humanitarian Order.

UN Chronicle, January, 1984, p. 60.

NEW INTERNATIONAL INFORMATION ORDER. The UNESCO program drafted under the influence of the UN Declaration of 1974 on the New International Economic Order at the V Conference of Nonaligned Countries in Colombo, Aug. 1976; debated at the XIX UNESCO General Conference in Nairobi in the Fall of 1976 and at the following UNESCO General Conferences in Paris in the years 1978–83; subject of symposia concerning the Decolonization of Information in New Delhi and in Baghdad, 1977. Created in New Delhi was the International Council for the Co-ordination of Information (of states of the Third World). This Council on Nov. 24, 1979 formed a permanent pool of press agencies of nonaligned states in Belgrade. The UN General Assembly on Dec. 18, 1978 approved without a vote Res. 33/115A, B, and C, concerning increasing assistance to developing countries in communication technology, the need to establish a new, more just and more effective world information and communication order; and the establishment of a 41-nation Committee to Review UN Public Information Policies and Activities. In 1980 the UNESCO session debated the item of a new international information and communication system and adopted the following recommendations:

"Effective legal measures should be designed to: (a) limit the process of concentration and monopolization; (b) circumscribe the action of transnationals by requiring them to comply with specific criteria and conditions defined by national legislation and development policies."

"Consideration might be given to establishing within the framework of UNESCO an international center for the study and planning of information and communication."

"It would be desirable for the United Nations family to be equipped with a more effective information system, including a broadcast capability of its own and possibly a communications satellite."

In 1983 the Western governments rejected the UNESCO proposals.

Mass Media Policy in Changing Cultures, New York, 1977; *UN Chronicle*, January, 1979, pp. 34–35; *UN Chronicle*, 1985. No. 8, pp 34–36; *UN Chronicle*, 1986, No. 2, pp. 78-81.

NEW MONETARY SYSTEM ▷ Louvre Accord, 1987.

NEW ORDER. An international term for the abolition of status quo in a given region and introduction of hegemony of the strongest power in that region; name adopted in December 1938 by the Japanese Government for the program of gaining hegemony in Eastern Asia, and in June 1940 by Hitler for the program of organizing Europe under the hegemony of the III Reich (Neue Ordnung Europas).

F.C. JONES, *Japan's New Order in East Asia*, London, 1954; L. GRUNDMAN, *Nationalsozialistische Grossraumordnung*, Berlin, 1962; N. RICH, *Hitler's War Aims: The Establishment of the New Order*, New York, 1974.

NEWS DISPATCH. An international term defined in art. 1 of the Convention on the International Right of Correction, 1953:

"News dispatch means news material transmitted in writing or by means of telecommunications, in the form customarily employed by information agencies in transmitting such news material, before publication, to newspapers, news periodicals and broadcasting organizations."

UNTS, Vol. 435, p. 194.

NEW TESTAMENT. A subject of international study. Organization reg. with the UIA:

Society for the Study of New Testament, f. 1938, Old Aberdeen, UK. Publ.: *New Testament Studies*. ▷ Old Testament.

Yearbook of International Organizations.

NEW YORK. City on the East Coast of the USA in the state of New York, permanent seat of the UN since Dec. 14, 1946, and seat of about 70 international organizations reg. with the UN. Population according to the final 1980 census: 7,071,639. Metropolitan area: 9,119,737.

Yearbook of International Organizations; *The World Almanac and Book of Facts*, New York, 1988.

NEW ZEALAND. Member of the UN. Country in Oceania composed of Stewart Island, Chatham Island and outlying islands. Area: 269,057 sq. km. Pop. 1988 est. 3,300,000 (1858 census: 114,000; 1901: 815,000; 1951: 1,939,000; 1971: 2,862,000; 1981 census: 3,175,000). Capital: Wellington with 342,500 inhabitants in 1983. GNP per capita 1986: US $7090. Official language: English. Currency: New Zealand Dollar = 100 cents. National day: Feb. 6, New Zealand Day, 1840.

Founding member of the League of Nations 1919–39 and of the UN, Oct. 24, 1945 as well as all its specialized agencies. Member of the British Commonwealth, ANZUS, ANZAC.

International relations: discovered by Tasman, 1642; small settlement in the 18th century, less than 1000 Europeans in 1800; aborigines – Maoris. Organized British colonization did not start until the 19th century from Australia, institutionalized in 1839–41 by cession of part of the island by a Maori chief (the Waitangi Treaty on Feb. 6, 1840) annexation of the rest; colonial status in May, 1841. Maori resistance broken finally in 1870. In 1907 granted status of British Dominion. In World Wars I and II New Zealand forces under British command. On the American side in Korean War 1951–53 and in Vietnam 1965–69. In 1965–74 formed a common market and military alliance with Australia. In dispute with the USA in Febr. 1985, not accepting US navy ships with nuclear arms to pay a portcall in New Zealand. On 4 June, 1987 the Parliament passed the New Zealand Nuclear Free Zone, Disarmament, and Arms Control Bill enacting into the law of the land provisions to permanently exclude nuclear armed and nuclear powered ships and aircraft from New Zealand. The Bill also makes it illegal to acquire, station or test nuclear explosive devices or to bring them into New Zealand waters, makes similar provisions against biological weapons, and likewise declares dumping of radioactive wastes there as an offence. On Aug. 18, 1988 New Zealand and Australia signed a free trade agreement, with introduction of full trade in goods by July 1, 1990.

The New Zealand Institute of International Affairs, f. 1934, Wellington. Publ. New Zealand International Review.

See also ▷ World Heritage UNESCO List.

W.J. HARRIS, *Guide to New Zealand*, London, 1950; *The Maori Today*, Wellington, 1964; *Oxford New Zealand Encyclopaedia*, 1965; A.H. McLINTOCK, *Encyclopaedia of New Zealand*, 3 Vols., Wellington, 1966; J.W. ROWE, *New Zealand*, New York, 1968; M.H. HOLCROFF, *New Zealand*, Wellington, 1968; A.H. McLINTOCK, *A Descriptive Atlas of New Zealand*, London, 1969; R. KENNAWAY, *New Zealand Foreign Policy 1951–71*, Wellington, 1972; W. ROSENBERG, *Money in New Zealand. Banking, Credit and Inflation*, Wellington, 1973; J. METGE, *The Maoris of New Zealand*, London, 1976; M.F. SHADBOLT, *The Shell Guide to New Zealand*, Christchurch, 1976; *Pacific Island Yearbook 1977*; J.E. TRANE, *Who's Who in New Zealand*, Wellington, 1978; S. LEVING, *The Political System in New Zealand*, London, 1979; D. BEGGOOD, *Rich and Poor in New Zealand*, Sydney, 1980; G. BUSH, *Local Government and Politics in New Zealand*, Sydney, 1980; W.H. OLIVER (ed.), *The Oxford History of New Zealand*, OUP, 1981; *The Europa Year Book 1984. A World Survey*, Vol. II, pp. 2121–2135, London, 1984; KEESING's *Record of World Events*, No. 11, 1988.

NGORONGORO. A natural site of Tanzania, included in the ▷ World Heritage UNESCO List. Around this crater are other craters which are among the largest in the world.

UNESCO, *A Legacy for All*, Paris, 1984.

NHPLO ▷ NATO

NIAGARA FALLS CONFERENCE, 1914. A meeting at Niagara Falls, N.Y, in June 1914 of the representatives of the ABC states (Argentina, Brazil and Chile) offering mediation to Mexico and the US in conflict over the presence of US navy ships in Mexican Vera Cruz harbor and the detention of American sailors in Tampico.

NICARAGUA. Member of the UN. Republic of Nicaragua. A country in Central America, bordered by Costa Rica and Honduras, between the Caribbean Sea and Pacific Ocean. Area: 120,524 sq. km. Pop. 1987 est.: 3,501,000 (1920 census: 1,002,000; 1950 census: 1,437,000; 1971 census: 1,877,952). Capital: Managua with 819,679 inhabitants 1981. GNP per capita 1987: US $830. Currency: one cordoba = 100 centavos. Official language: Spanish. National Day: Sept. 15, Independence Day, 1821.

Original member of the UN, Oct. 24, 1945 and of all specialized organizations. Member of the OAS, the Central America Market and the Tlatelolco Treaty. International relations: Spanish colony from 1523 until 1821; from Sept. 15, 1821 to Apr. 30, 1838 part of the United Provinces of Central America, independent republic from Apr. 30, 1838. In 1835 at war with the army of US adventurer W. Walker. Under British protectorate until 1860. In 1863 at war with Honduras and Guatemala. In 1866 Nicaragua signed a Peace Treaty with Guatemala. In 1875 German military intervention. In 1894 at war with Honduras. In 1895 British military intervention. In 1907 at war with Honduras and El Salvador, terminated with a Peace Treaty 1907. In 1912 US military intervention and occupation until 1933. The partisan war against the American troops under leadership of C.A. Sandino (1893–1934). Under dictatorship of the family clan of General A. Somoza from 1937 until July, 1979, when Nicaragua was liberated by the Sandinista partisans. In the years 1980–84 military intervention from Honduras with support of the USA. In Apr. 1984 Nicaragua accused the USA before the ▷ International Court of Justice of international terrorism (mining of commercial ports of Nicaragua) and before the UN Security Council. In Nov., 1984 the US Congress investigated an instruction book *Operaciones Sicologicas en Guerra de Guerillas* distributed by the CIA in the anti-Sandinists guerillas, called in Nicaragua "*contras*." Direct negotiations between Nicaragua and the USA started in November 1984.

H.L. STIMSON, *American Policy in Nicaragua*, New York, 1927; J. COX, *Nicaragua and the US, 1909 to 1927*, Boston, 1927; R. DE NOGALES, *The Looting of Nicaragua*, New York, 1928; M. TWEEDY, *This is Nicaragua*, New York, 1953; A. VAN WYNAN, A.J. THOMAS, *La Non-Intervención. Sus Normas y Su Significado en las Americas*, Buenos Aires, 1959, pp. 45–55; J. TERAN, J. INCOX, *La geografía de Nicaragua*, Managua, 1964; H. WEBER, *Nicaragua. The Sandinistas Revolution*, New York, 1981; T.W. WALKER, *Nicaragua. The Land of Sandino*, Boulder, 1982; *UN Chronicle*, April 1984, pp. 3–16; *The Europa Year Book 1984. A World Survey*, Vol. II, pp. 2141–2153, London, 1984; *Newsweek*, November 26, 1984, p. 33; D.C. HODGES, *Intellectual Foundation of the Nicaraguan Revolution*, Austin, Tex., 1987; R. GUTMAN, *Banana Diplomacy: The Making of American Policy in Nicaragua, 1981-1987*, New York, 1988.

NICKEL. A subject of international research and agreements; mined on a large scale in Canada, the USSR, Finland, Norway, China, India, the USA, Cuba, the Philippines, Indonesia, Mongolia, Brazil, Korea, South Africa, Burkina Faso, Venezuela and Zimbabwe.

The UN Nickel Conference took place for the first time in Oct.–Nov. 1985 and then in April–May 1986 in Geneva. The second meeting approved the terms of reference of the International Nickel Study Group. 29 states participated in the Conference.

The Nickel Industry and the Developing Countries, UN, New York, 1982; *UN Chronicle*, August 1986, p. 120.

NIEO. ▷ New International Economic Order.

NIGER. Member of the UN. Republic of Niger. Country in West Africa, bordering on Burkina Faso, Mali, Algeria, Libya, Chad, Nigeria and Benin. Area: 1,186,408 sq. km. Pop. 1988 est.: 7,190,000. Capital: Niamey with 225,314 inhabitants, 1982. GNP per capita 1986: UN $260. Official language: French. Currency: one Franc CFA = 100 cents. National Day: Aug. 3, Independence Day, 1960.

Member of the UN since Oct. 20, 1960 and of the UN specialized agencies with exception of the IMO. Member of the OAU and is an ACP state of the EEC.

International relations: occupied by France and Great Britain 1890; since 1904 a territory of French West Africa; independent on Aug. 3, 1960 as a member of the French Community.

P. BONARDI, *La République du Niger*, Paris, 1960; E. SERÈ *Histoire du Niger*, Paris, 1965; P. DONAINT, *Le Niger*, Paris, 1972; *Atlas de Niger*, Paris, 1980; *The Europa Year Book 1984. A World Survey*, Vol. II, pp. 2154–2163, London, 1984.

NIGERIA. Member of the UN. Federal Republic of Nigeria. A state in West Africa on the Atlantic. Bounded by Niger, Chad, Cameroon, Benin. Area: 923,773 sq. km. Pop. 1988 est.: 105,000,000 (1963 census: 55,670,052). Capital: Lagos with 1,060,848 inhabitants in 1976. GNP per capita 1986: US $730. Official language: English. Currency: one Naira = 100 kobo. National day: Oct. 1, Independence Day, 1960.

Member of the UN since Oct. 20, 1960 and of all its specialized agencies except WIPO, Member of the British Commonwealth and OAU. ACP state of the EEC. A signatory of the Lomé Conventions of 1975 and 1980.

International relations: in the mid-19th century under British influence; 1886 under administration of British Royal Niger Company; from Jan. 1, 1914 entire area taken over by Great Britain and named Colony and Protectorate of Nigeria. Cameroon was handed over to Britain by the League of Nations as mandate territory which after World War II was incorporated to Nigeria as a UN trusteeship. During World War II Nigerian troops under British command fought against Italy in East Africa and Japan in Burma. In 1947 granted autonomy, extended in 1953; independence within British Commonwealth on Oct. 1, 1964; the eastern part of Nigeria the ▷ Biafra province left the Federation on May 27, 1967 which caused a civil war, ending with capitulation of Biafra on Jan. 12, 1970. The International Group of Observers set up by the UN and composed of representatives of the UN Secretariat, Algeria and Ethiopia representing the OAU and Canada, Poland, Sweden and the UK was active from Aug., 1968 to Jan., 1970. In 1976 delimitation of frontier with Chad. In 1983 Nigeria expelled over two million illegal immigrants. The deportation affected mainly nationals of the ECOWAS countries: Benin, Ghana, Niger, Togo and Burkina Faso. The UN agencies helped to minimize the suffering of the deportees. In Nov., 1984 Nigeria recognized the ▷ Western Sahara Government "▷ Polisario." In border dispute over a number of islands on Lake Chad, 1983-1984. On May 15, 1984 a joint Chad–Nigeria economic commission was established. Involved in border disputes with ▷ Cameroon 1961–1987. In 1983 Nigeria expelled 120,000 Cameroonians as "illegal aliens".

The Nigerian Institute of International Affairs, f. Lagos. Publ. The Nigerian Journal of International Affairs.

E.O. AWA, *Federal Government in Nigeria*, Berkeley, 1964; C.S. PHYLLIPS, *The Development of Nigerian Foreign Policy*, Chicago, 1964; F.D. SCHWARZ Jr., *Nigeria: The Tribes, the Nation, or the Race. The Politics of Independence*, Cambridge, 1965; S.B. LOCKWOOD, *Nigeria: A Guide to Official Publications*, Washington, DC, 1966; J.P. MACKINTOSH, *Nigerian Government and Politics, Prelude to the Revolution*, Evaston, 1966; F.D. SCHWARZ, *Nigeria*, New York, 1968; H.D. SIEBEL, *Industriearbeit und Kulturwandel in Nigerias*, Opladon, 1968; J. OKPAKU (ed.), *Nigeria: Dilemma of Nationhood. An African Analysis of the Biafran Conflict*, New York, 1972; E. EKUNDARE, *An Economic History of Nigeria 1860–1960*, London, 1973; *Nigeria. Report of a World Bank Mission*, Baltimore, 1974; *Nigeria Yearbook 1975*, Lagos, 1975; *Who's Who in Nigeria?* Lagos, 1975; A.T. OJO, *The Nigerian Financial System*, University of Wales Press, 1976; E. JICHEI, *History of the Igbo People*, London, 1976; S. ARNOLD, *Modern Nigeria*, London, 1977; M. PEIL, *Nigerian Politics, The People's View*, London, 1978; O. OLALOKU, *Structure of the Nigerian Economy*, London, 1980; O. OYEDIRAY, *Nigerian Government and Politics under Military Rule 1966–79*, New York, 1980; J. COMHAIR, *Le Nigeria et ses populations*, Brussels, 1981; O. NNOMI, *Path to Nigerian Development*, Dakar, 1981; M. SIMMONS, O.A. OBBE, *Nigerian Handbook 1982–83*, London, 1982; D. WILLIAMS, *President and Power in Nigeria*, London, 1982; A. MADIEBO, *The Nigerian Revolution and the Biafran War*, Enugu, 1983; *The Europa Year Book 1984. A World Survey*, Vol. II, pp. 2164–2184, London, 1984; Chad–Nigeria, in: A.J. DAY ed., *Border and Territorial Disputes*, London, 1987, pp. 117; Cameroon-Nigeria; in: A.J. DAY ed., *Border and Territorial Disputes*, London, 1987, pp. 111-113; T.J. BIER-STEKER, *Multinational, The State and Control of the Nigerian Economy*, Princeton, NJ, 1987.

NIGER RIVER. The river of West Africa, 4185 km long; the subject of international co-operation between the riparian states: Benin, Cameroon, Chad, Guinea, Côte d'Ivoire, Mali, Niger, Nigeria and Burkina Faso. Agreements: Act regarding Navigation and Economic Co-operation between the States of the Niger Basin, signed on Oct. 26, 1963 in Niamey; came into force on Feb. 1, 1966. Agreement concerning the Niger River Commission and the Navigation and Transport on the River Niger, signed on Nov. 25, 1964, in Niamey, came into force

on Apr. 12, 1966. In the late 1960s a long-term West African drought substantially lowered the water level of the Niger. On Nov. 22, 1983 at Conakry was signed a new Niger River Development Agreement by the Heads of the riparian states.

Organization reg. with the UIA: Niger Basin Authority, f. 1964, Niamey, Niger. Members: Benin, Burkina Faso, Cameroon, Chad, Côte d'Ivoire, Mali, Niger, Nigeria. Publ: Bulletin.

UNTS, Vol. 587, pp. 11 and 21; KEESING's *Contemporary Archive*, 1983; *The Europa Handbook 1988. A World Survey*, Vol I, London 1988.

NIGHT WORK. A subject of ▷ ILO conventions prohibiting night work of children, minors and women.

J. CARPENTIER, P. CARAMIAN, *Night Work: Its Effects on the Health and Welfare of the Worker*, ILO Geneva, 1980.

NIHIL OBSTAT. *Latin* = "there are no obstacles". The Catholic Church formula meaning that Church authorities are not opposed to the publication of a certain work or to the appointment of a cleric to a certain position.

NIJMEGEN PEACE TREATIES, 1678. The Treaties between France and Holland, ending the Dutch War (1672–78), were signed in Nijmegen, on Aug. 10, and Sept. 17, 1678.

Major Peace Treaties 1678–1967, New York, 1967, Vol. I, pp. 129–143.

NILE. African river, the longest in the world, 6695 km long; drains 2,850,000 sq. km, parts in Zaïre, Burundi, Rwanda, Uganda, Kenya, Ethiopia, Sudan, Egypt, from Central Africa to the Mediterranean Sea on the Egyptian coast. The trunk stream is formed in Sudan by the junction of the Blue Nile (1610 km long) and the White Nile (3700 km long). The use of the Nile for irrigation was partially regulated by the Nile Waters Agreement concluded in 1929 and generally regulated by the Agreement between the Republic of the Sudan and the United Arab Republic for the full utilization of the Nile Waters, signed on Nov. 8, 1959 at Cairo; came into force on Dec. 12, 1959. The second Agreement included the project of the ▷ Aswan, High Dam.

H.E. HURST, *The Nile*, London, 1957; *LNTS*, Vol. XCIII, p. 43. *UNTS*, Vol. 453, pp. 64–76; A.H. GARRETSON, "The Nile River System", in: *African Society of International Law*, 1960, pp. 136–144; *The Major Nile Projects*, Cairo, 1966.

NIOKOLO KOBA. A National Park of Senegal, included in the ▷ World Heritage UNESCO List. This reserve lies on the banks of the Gambia River and covers an area of 300,000 hectares. It contains three major ecosystems – Guinean forest, Guinean savannah and Sahelian savannah. There are 329 species of birds, 36 species of reptiles (including three different species of crocodiles) and 70 species of mammals, including leopards, chimpanzees and elephants, as well as lions the population of which is reckoned to be the largest in the world.

UNESCO, *A Legacy for All*, Paris, 1984.

NIUE. A coral Pacific island. Area: 260 sq km. Population: 1989 est. 2,190. Self-governing status in free association with New Zealand since October 1974.

NIXON DOCTRINE. An international term, also known as Guam Doctrine, promoted by US President Richard Nixon as the quintessence of his foreign policy aimed, according to an interview for *New York Times*, at maintaining the US position in

the world by guaranteeing the countries with which US was bound by military obligations assistance if they themselves are militarily prepared, because "we will help those who will help themselves." Nixon also stressed that the US is not, cannot be and ought not to be the policeman of the world. He attached particular significance to the consolidation of conventional marine forces with the aim of performing the role of the guardian of peace in such zones as Latin America, the move considered there as a return to ▷ "big stick" diplomacy of Theodore Roosevelt, 1902. In an interview the US Undersecretary of State for Latin America referred to the Nixon Doctrine and stated that the era of US armed interventions in Latin America belonged to the past, but made a reservation that such intervention could take place only in case of a direct threat to US citizens. This in the past was the formal reason given for US Marine actions. A sequel to the Nixon Doctrine was his own article published in *US News and World Report*, 1972.

"The Nixon Doctrine. A Progress Report", in: *The Department of State Bulletin*, No. 1650, February 8, 1971, pp. 161–166; *New York Times*, March 11, 1971; W.F. HAHN, "The Nixon Doctrine", in: *Orbis*, Summer, 1971; *US News and World Report*, June 26, 1972; *Doktrina Nixona*, Moscow, 1972; R. LITWAK, *Detente and the Nixon Doctrine*, New York, 1986.

NIXON ROUND. The name initially adopted by the GATT for the seventh round of debates of that institution on the successive problem of customs tariffs, begun on the initiative of President R. Nixon in 1973 as a continuation of President J.F. Kennedy's policy of 1962–68 (▷ Kennedy Round). Experts of 81 GATT member states worked out, at the session in Tokyo from Sept. 12 to 14, 1973, the so-called Tokyo Declaration establishing rules for negotiations within the Nixon Round, held at GATT headquarters in Geneva; in the following years named ▷ Tokyo Round.

NKOMATI PACT. ▷ South Africa.

NKWD. ▷ Intelligence Service.

N.N. Latin: *nomen nescio* = "unknown by name". The legal formula for designating a person unknown by first name and surname; introduced by the Church in the baptismal documents of a child in the event it is stated that the father is unknown.

NOBEL LAUREATES SPERM BANK. A laboratory bank, est. 1980 in Escondido, Calif. by American businessman R. Graham attempting to produce highly intelligent babies by inseminating women with sperm from Nobel Laureates. The bank received donations of sperm from five US Nobel Prize science winners. The Sperm Bank offers to: "give bright, young healthy women a choice from five Nobelists of which they would have as the father of their child, providing their husbands agreed also." Nobel Prize winners in America and Europe have denounced the whole idea of engineering birth as biologically and morally unsound, recalling Hitler's "master race" breeding program.

NOBEL PRIZES. Prizes founded by the Swedish scientist inventor of dynamite, Alfred Nobel (1833–96) and awarded annually on the anniversary of his death, Dec. 10. Prizes are awarded in the fields of: physics, chemistry, physiology or medicine, literature, for activities in favor of bringing nations closer together, through disarmament and dissemination of peaceful ideas, the so-called Nobel Peace Prize, and in the field of economy (since 1969 on the initiative of and founded by the Central Bank of Sweden, Sveriges Riksbank). The

Royal Swedish Academy of Sciences grants prizes in the fields of physics, chemistry and economy; the Karolinski Institute of Medicine and Surgery for physiology or medicine. The Swedish Academy for literature and the Norwegian Parliament the Nobel Peace Prize. The value of prizes in 1971 – 450,000 Swedish Krona each (about 90,000 US dollars), was equivalent to about one-third of the value of prizes in 1910. Prize winners also receive a gold medal and diploma. Prizes have been granted since 1910 from the funds of the Swedish–Norwegian Nobel Foundation in Stockholm. The Peace Prize is awarded by a Special Committee of the Norwegian parliament (Storting) not only to persons, but also to international institutions and organizations;

The following international institutions and organizations have received the Nobel Prize: 1904 Institute of International Law; 1910 International Permanent Peace Bureau; 1917, 1944, and 1963 International Committee of the Red Cross; 1938 International Nansen Office for Refugee Problems; 1965 UNICEF; 1969 ILO 1977. Amnesty International, 1981 UN High Commissioner for Refugees, 1988, UN Peace Forces. The list of the Peace Prize winners is as follows:

1901 Jean H. Dunant, Swiss
     Frédéric Passy, French
1902 Elie Ducommun, Swiss and Charles A. Gobat, Swiss
1903 Sir William R. Cremer, British
1904 Institute of International Law
1905 Baroness Bertha von Suttner, Austrian
1906 Theodore Roosevelt, American
1907 Ernesto T. Moneta, Italian; Louis Renault, French
1908 Klas P. Arnoldson, Swedish; Fredrik Bajer, Danish
1909 Auguste M.F. Beernaert, Belgian; Paul H.B.B. d'Estournelles de Constant, French
1910 Permanent International Peace Bureau
1911 Tobias M.C. Asser, Dutch; Alfred H. Fried, Austrian
1912 Elihu Root, American
1913 Henri Lafontaine, Belgian
1914–16 No award
1917 International Committee of the Red Cross
1918 No award
1919 Woodrow Wilson, American
1920 Léon V.A. Bourgeois, French
1921 Karl H. Branting, Swedish; Christian L. Lange, Norwegian
1922 Fridtjof Nansen, Norwegian
1923 No award
1924 No award
1925 Sir J. Austen Chamberlain, British; Charles G. Dawes, American
1926 Aristide Briand, French; Gustav Stresemann, German
1927 Ferdinand Buisson, French; Ludwig Quidde, German
1928 No award
1929 Frank B. Kellogg, American
1930 Lars O.N. Söderblom, Swedish
1931 Jane Addams, American; Nicholas Murray Butler, American
1932 No award
1933 Sir Norman Angell, British
1934 Arthur Henderson, British
1935 Carl von Ossietzky, German
1936 Carlos Saavedra Lamas, Argentina
1937 Viscount Cecil of Chelwood, British
1938 International Office for Refugees
1939–43 No award
1944 International Committee of the Red Cross
1945 Cordell Hull, American
1946 Emily G. Balch, American; John R. Mott, American
1947 Friends Service Council, British; American Friends Service Committee
1948 No award
1949 Lord John Boyd Orr of Brechin, British

1950 Ralph J. Bunche, American
1951 Léon Jouhaux, French
1952 Albert Schweitzer, French (German-born)
1953 George C. Marshall, American
1954 Office of UN High Commissioner for Refugees
1955 No award
1956 No award
1957 Lester B. Pearson, Canadian
1958 Georges Pire, Belgian
1959 Philip J. Noel-Baker, British
1960 Albert J. Luthuli, South African
1961 Dag Hammarskjöld, Swedish (posthumous)
1962 Linus C. Pauling, American
1963 International Committee of the Red Cross; Red Cross Societies League
1964 Martin Luther King Jr., American
1965 United Nations Children's Fund (UNICEF)
1966 No award
1967 No award
1968 René Cassin, French
1969 International Labor Organization (ILO)
1970 Norman E. Borlaug, American
1971 Willy Brandt, German
1972 No award
1973 Henry A. Kissinger, American (German-born); Le Duc Tho, North Vietnamese
1974 Eisaku Sato, Japanese and Sean MacBride, Irish
1975 Andrei D. Sakharov, Russian
1976 Betty Williams and Mairead Corrigan, Irish
1977 Amnesty International
1978 Anwar el-Sadat, Egyptian
     Menachem Begin, Israeli
1979 Mother Teresa, Indian (Albanian-born)
1980 Adolfo Perez Esquivel, Argentinian
1981 UN High Commissioner for Refugees
1982 Alva Myrdal, Swedish and Alfonso Garcia Robles, Mexican
1983 Lech Walesa, Polish
1984 Desmond Tutu, South African
1985 US-USSR International Physicians for the Prevention of Nuclear War (Bernard Lown and Yevgeni Chazov)
1986 Elie Wiesel, (Nazi Death Camp survivor) US writer
1987 Oscar Arias Sanchez, President of Costa Rica
1988 United Nations Peace Forces
1989 Dalai Lama, Tibetan

The Nobel Foundation, Nobelstiftelsen, f. 1900 by Alfred Nobel in Stockholm. publ. *Les Prix Nobel* and *Nobel Lectures.*

R. NOE, *Le prix Nobel de la paix et l'Institut Nobel norvégien*, Oslo, 1932.

NO-FIRST-USE. An international term for the major subject of debate and controversy in the last decades of the 20th century – the problem of first use of nuclear weapons. A SIPRI analysis from spring 1984 stated:

"First use is part of the doctrine of 'flexible response', which has been NATO's strategy since 1967. 'Flexible response' leaves open the option of responding with the use of nuclear weapons to a conventional attack. As early as 1964, China committed itself not to be the first to use nuclear weapons. The Soviet Union made a unilateral declaration of no-first-use at the United Nations Second Special Session on Disarmament in 1982. But there have been no changes in Soviet force posture to support it. On the contrary, recent deployments in Eastern Europe are at odds with the declaration.

Arguments for No-First-Use:
The basic argument is the potentially suicidal nature of making a nuclear response to a conventional attack. If deterrence fails, present NATO strategy carries with it a significant risk that civilization will be destroyed. Nuclear weapons should serve no military purpose other than to deter one's opponent from using them.

Arguments against No-First-Use:
Perceived Soviet superiority in conventional weaponry argues against a no-first-use commitment by NATO. If the risk of a nuclear response to conventional aggression were removed, NATO's defense would become 'predictably inadequate'. A no-first-use policy

would destroy the confidence of Europeans and especially West Germans in the European–American Alliance and would probably lead eventually to US withdrawal from Europe.
SIPRI assessment: steps to a No-First-Use policy:
There is a strong case for Western preparation for a no-first-use commitment and for the Soviet Union's demonstration – through appropriate military deployment – of the seriousness of its declared intent never to be the first to use nuclear weapons.
As for NATO, it could insert a provision in its long-term defense plan, committing the Organization to make the force posture compatible with a future policy of no-first-use, to be declared, say, by the end of its five year planning period.
A no-first-use declaration must be accompanied by changes in the deployment of nuclear weapons. Otherwise it is essentially empty. So long as thousands of tactical nuclear weapons are deployed in close proximity to the borders dividing NATO countries from the Warsaw Pact, statements by the leaders of either side that they will not use them are of little value.
The removal of battlefield nuclear weapons from areas adjacent to the East–West border in Europe would be an obvious first step. It could be followed by the removal of nuclear weapons from the territories of all European countries which do not themselves possess them.
At the same time, the perceived imbalance in conventional forces must be corrected, and the fear of surprise attack reduced. A combined withdrawal of battlefield nuclear weapons and major conventional arms a certain number of kilometers either side of the dividing line, and a system of non-provocative defense within that zone, might alleviate these concerns."

On Oct. 22, 1984, the Secretary General of NATO, Lord Carrington stated that NATO is against the No-First-Use of Nuclear Weapons formula, because it could increase the probability of conventional war with modern conventional arms of multiplied destruction possibilities through microelectronic effectiveness. ▷ NATO Doctrines. ▷ Conventional Arms Ogarkov Doctrine, 1984.

F. BLACKABY, J. GOLDBLAT, S. LODGAARD, (eds), *No-First-Use*, Stockholm, 1984; D. CHARLES, *Nuclear Planning in NATO: Pitfalls of First Use*, Cambridge, Mass., 1987.

NOISE POLLUTION. An international term for sounds harmful to health. A subject of environmental protection initiated by WHO, 1971 and the ILO Convention against occupational hazards in the work environment due to Air Pollution, Noise and Vibration, 1977. In USA the Noise Control Act, 1972 set noise emission standards. In 1980's in the majority of European states there are noise restrictions to protect health.
Organization reg with the UIA: International Association Against Noise, f. 1959, Küssnacht, Switzerland.

UIA, *Yearbook of International Organizations.*

NOMADS. The pastoral and hunting–gathering peoples with a migratory style of life (e.g. Lapps in Europe, Bedouins in Africa), a subject of international studies under the sponsorship of UNESCO.

NO MAN'S LAND. An international term for a territory separating two warring sides after a cease fire.

NOMENCLATURE OF ILLNESSES. An international description, worked out and recommended by the International Commission for Revising the International Nomenclature of Illnesses, Oct. 19, 1929. After World War II the international nomenclature of illnesses was established by the WHO.

LNTS, Vol. 154, pp. 395–399.

NOMENCLATURE OF MERCHANDISE. A subject of an Inter-American Convention on Uniformity of Nomenclature for the Classification of Merchandise, signed by 18 American Republics on May 3, 1923 at Santiago de Chile; came into force on Oct. 8, 1924; ratified by Brazil, Chile, Costa Rica, Cuba, the Dominican Republic, El Salvador, Guatemala, Haiti, Panama, Paraguay, Uruguay and the USA. The USA denounced the Convention May 24, 1955. The Tenth Inter-American Conference, Mar. 1–28, 1954 decreed in Res. LXXXVIII, "that the Convention may be legally abandoned by all the parties" because the nomenclature, based on the Brussels nomenclature of 1913, "has become outdated."

OAS, *Inter-American Treaties and Conventions*, Washington, DC, 1953.

NOMENKLATURA. An international term for the communist states cadre management system. The Nomenklatura system consists of lists of leading positions in the party, and the administration in all state controlled institutions, in the state owned big industry and collective farms, and lists of reserve cadres. Only the party committees exercise the power of appointment to any available position. In practice the system, degenerated into a negative selection super-bureaucracy, was criticised and started to undergo change in the 1980's first in China, then in the USSR and in the majority of communist countries.

J.P BURNS, China's Nomenklatura System, in: *Problems of Communism* September–October, 1987; T.J. COLTON, Moscow's Party Organization, in: *Problems of Communism*, January–February, 1988.

NON AGGRESSION AND DEFENCE AID AGREEMENT OF THE WEST AFRICAN COUNTRIES AND TOGO. ▷ ANAD.

NONAGGRESSION TREATIES. The bilateral and multilateral agreements, called also anti-war treaties, e.g. ▷ Briand–Kellog Treaty 1928, ▷ Saavedra Lamas Treaty 1933; ▷ German–Polish Nonaggression Pact 1934; ▷ German–Soviet Nonaggression Pact 1939.

NONALIGNED COUNTRIES CONFERENCES OF HEADS OF STATE, 1961–1989. The Summit-Meetings of nonaligned countries were held as follows:

I	Belgrade, Yugoslavia 1961 (▷ Nonaligned Countries Declaration, 1961)	
II	Cairo, Egypt, 1964 (▷ Nonaligned Countries Declaration, 1964)	
III	Lusaka, Zambia, 1970 (▷ Nonaligned Countries Declaration, 1970)	
IV	Algiers, Algeria, 1973 (▷ Nonaligned Countries Declaration, 1973)	
V	Colombo, Sri Lanka, 1976 (▷ Nonaligned Countries Declaration, 1976)	
VI	Havana, Cuba, 1979 (▷ Nonaligned Countries Declaration 1979)	
VII	New Delhi, India, 1983 (▷ Nonaligned Countries Declaration, 1983)	
VIII	Harare, Zimbabwe, 1986	
IX	Belgrade, Yugoslavia 1989 (▷ Nonaligned Countries Declaration, 1989)	

NONALIGNED COUNTRIES CO-ORDINATING BUREAU. The Office was est. in 1961 in Colombo with headquarters in New York; its status was revised in 1979 by the Sixth Conference in Havana. The Bureau is composed of the representatives to be chosen by Conferences of Heads of State, membership limited to 36 (17 seats Africa, 12 Asia, 5 Latin America, 2 Europe). The Bureau meets at the level of Ministers of Foreign Affairs or Special Government representatives before a Summit Conference. An Extraordinary Meeting can also be held if necessary. At the level of Permanent Representatives of Nonaligned Countries meetings are held approximately once a month at the UN headquarters in New York. The host country of the most recent Summit Conference serves as Chairman until the next Conference.

"It is recommended that the practice of adopting decisions of the Non-Aligned Countries by consensus be continued"

(Havana Declaration 1979). Members chosen by the Sixth Conference, Sept. 9, 1979 were as follows: Asia: India, Sri Lanka, North Korea, PLO, Jordan, Syria, Iraq, Democratic Republic of Yemen plus Afghanistan or Bangladesh, Vietnam or Laos, Indonesia or Singapore, Iran or Bhutan; Africa: Benin, Ghana, Lesotho, Madagascar, Mauritania, Ethiopia, Somalia, Mozambique, Nigeria, Togo, Zambia plus Uganda or Cyprus; the remaining members to be decided on by the African Group at the UN; Latin America: Cuba, Guyana, Jamaica, Panama plus Peru or Grenada; Europe: Yugoslavia plus Cyprus or Uganda.

Documents of the Gathering of Non-Aligned Countries 1961–1978, Belgrade, 1978; P. WILLETS, *The Non-Aligned Movement*, New York, 1978; *UN Chronicle*, November 1981, p. 24; L. MOJSOV, *Dimensions of Non-Alignment*, Belgrade, 1981; R. JAIPAL, *Non-Alignment Origins, Growth and Potential for World Peace*, New Delhi, 1983.

NONALIGNED COUNTRIES DECLARATION, 1961 OR BELGRADE DECLARATION. The text of the Declaration is as follows:

"The Conference of Heads of State or Government of the following nonaligned countries: Afghanistan, Algeria, Burma, Cambodia, Ceylon, Congo, Cuba, Cyprus, Ethiopia, Ghana, Guinea, India, Indonesia, Iraq, Lebanon, Mali, Morocco, Nepal, Saudi Arabia, Somalia, Sudan, Tunisia, United Arab Republic, Yemen, Yugoslavia, and of the following countries represented by observers: Bolivia, Brazil and Ecuador was held in Belgrade from September 1 to 6, 1961, for the purpose of exchanging views on international problems with a view to contributing more effectively to world peace and security and peaceful co-operation among peoples.
The Heads of State or Government of the aforementioned countries have met at a moment when international events have taken a turn for the worst and when world peace is seriously threatened. Deeply concerned for the future of peace, voicing the aspirations of the vast majority of people of the world, aware that, in our time, no people and no government can or should abandon its responsibilities in regard to the safeguarding of world peace, the participating countries – having examined in detail in an atmosphere of equality, sincerity and mutual confidence, the current state of international relations and trends prevailing in the present-day world – make the following declaration:
The Heads of State or Government of Non-Aligned Countries noting that there are crises that lead towards a world conflict in the transition from an old order based on domination to a new order based on co-operation between nations, founded on freedom, equality and social justice for the promotion of prosperity; considering that the dynamic processes and forms of social change often result in or represent a conflict between the old established and the new emerging nationalist forces; considering that a lasting peace can be achieved only if this confrontation leads to a world where the domination of colonialismimperialism and neo-colonialism in all their manifestations is radically eliminated;
And recognizing the fact

That acute emergencies threatening world peace now exist in this period of conflict in Africa, Asia, Europe and Latin America and big power rivalry likely to result in world conflagration cannot be excluded; that to eradicate basically the source of conflict is to eradicate colonialism in all its manifestations and to accept and practice a policy of peaceful co-existence in the world; that guided by these principles the period of transition and conflict can lay a firm foundation of cooperation and brotherhood between nations, state the following:
I. War has never threatened mankind with graver consequences than today. On the other hand, never before has mankind had at its disposal stronger forces for eliminating war as an instrument of policy in international relations. Imperialism is weakening. Colonial empires and other forms of foreign oppression of peoples in Asia, Africa and Latin America are gradually disappearing from the stage of history. Great successes have been achieved in the struggle of many peoples for national independence and equality. In the same way, the peoples of Latin America are continuing to make an increasingly effective contribution to the improvement of international relations. Great social changes in the world are further promoting such a development. All this not only accelerates the end of the epoch of foreign oppression of peoples, but also makes peaceful co-operation among peoples, based on the principles of independence and equal rights, an essential condition for their freedom and progress.
Tremendous progress has been achieved in the development of science, techniques and in the means of economic development.
Prompted by such developments in the world, the vast majority of people are becoming increasingly conscious of the fact that war between peoples constitutes not only an anachronism but also a crime against humanity. This awareness of peoples is becoming a great moral force, capable of exercising a vital influence on the development of international relations.
Relying on this and on the will of their peoples, the Governments of countries participating in the Conference resolutely reject the view that war, including the 'cold war', is inevitable, as this view reflects a sense both of helplessness and hopelessness and is contrary to the progress of the world. They affirm their unwavering faith that the international community is able to organize its life without resorting to means which actually belong to a past epoch of human history.
However, the existing military blocs, which are growing into more and more powerful military, economic and political groupings, which, by the logic and nature of their mutual relations, necessarily provoke periodical aggravations of international relations.
The cold war and the constant and acute danger of its being transformed into actual war have become a part of the situation prevailing in international relations.
For all these reasons, the Heads of State and Representatives of Government of nonaligned countries wish, in this way, to draw the attention of the world community to the existing situation and to the necessity that all peoples should exert efforts to find a sure road towards the stabilization of peace.
II. The present-day world is characterized by the existence of different social systems. The participating countries do not consider that these differences constitute an insurmountable obstacle for the stabilization of peace, provided attempts at domination and interference in the internal development of other peoples and nations are ruled out.
All peoples and nations have to solve the problems of their own political, economic, social and cultural systems in accordance with their own conditions, needs and potentialities.
Furthermore, any attempt at imposing upon peoples one social or political system or another by force and from outside is a direct threat to world peace. The participating countries consider that under such conditions the principles of peaceful coexistence are the only alternative to the 'cold war' and to a possible general nuclear catastrophe. Therefore, these principles – which include the right of peoples to self-determination, to independence and to the free determination of the forms and methods of economic, social and cultural development – must be the only basis of all international relations.
Active international co-operation in the fields of material and cultural exchanges among peoples is an essential means for the strengthening of confidence in

the possibility of peaceful coexistence among states with different social systems.

The participants in the Conference emphasize, in this connection, that the policy of coexistence amounts to an active effort towards the elimination of historical injustices and the liquidation of national oppression, guaranteeing at the same time, to every people their independent development.

Aware that ideological differences are necessarily a part of the growth of the human society, the participating countries consider that peoples and Governments shall refrain from any use of ideologies for the purpose of waging cold war, exercising pressure, or imposing their will.

III. The Heads of State or Government of nonaligned countries participating in the Conference are not making concrete proposals for the solution of all international disputes, and particularly disputes between the two blocs. They wish, above all, to draw attention to those acute problems of our time which must be solved rapidly, so that they should not lead to irreparable consequences.

In this respect, they particularly emphasize the need for a great sense of responsibility and realism when undertaking the solution of various problems resulting from differences in social systems.

The nonaligned countries represented at this Conference do not wish to form a new bloc and cannot be a bloc. They sincerely desire to cooperate with any Government which seeks to contribute to the strengthening of confidence and peace in the world. The nonaligned countries wish to proceed in this manner all the more so as they are aware that peace and stability in the world depend, to a considerable extent, on the mutual relations of the Great Powers; aware of this, the participants in the Conference consider it a matter of principle that the Great Powers take more determined action for the solving of various problems by means of the negotiations, displaying at the same time the necessary constructive approach and readiness for reaching solutions which will be mutually acceptable and useful for world peace.

The participants in the Conference consider that, under present conditions, the existence and the activities of nonaligned countries in the interests of peace are one of the more important factors for safeguarding world peace. The participants in the Conference consider it essential that the nonaligned countries should participate in solving outstanding international issues concerning peace and security in the world as none of them can remain unaffected by or indifferent to these issues. They consider that the further extension of the noncommitted area of the world constitutes the only possible and indispensable alternative to the policy of total division of the world into blocs, and intensification of cold war policies. The nonaligned countries provide encouragement and support to all peoples fighting for their independence and equality. The participants in the Conference are convinced that the emergence of newly-liberated countries will further assist in narrowing of the area of bloc antagonisms and thus encourage all tendencies aimed at strengthening peace and promoting peaceful cooperation among independent and equal nations.

(1) The participants in the Conference solemnly reaffirm their support to the "Declaration on the Granting of Independence to Colonial Countries and Peoples", adopted at the 15th Session of the General Assembly of the United Nations and recommend the immediate unconditional, total and final abolition of colonialism and resolved to make a concerted effort to put an end to all types of new colonialism and imperialist domination in all its forms and manifestations.

(2) The participants in the Conference demand that an immediate stop be put to armed action and repressive measures of any kind directed against dependent peoples to enable them to exercise peacefully and freely their right to complete independence and that the integrity of their national territory should be respected. Any aid given by any country to a colonial power in such suppression is contrary to the Charter of the United Nations.

The participating countries respecting scrupulously the territorial integrity of all states oppose by all means any aims of annexation by other nations.

(3) The participating countries consider the struggle of the people of Algeria for freedom, self-determination and independence, and for the integrity of its national territory including the Sahara, to be just and necessary and are therefore, determined to extend to the people of Algeria all the possible support and aid. The Heads of State or Government are particularly gratified that Algeria is represented at this Conference by its rightful representative, the Prime Minister of the Provisional Government of Algeria.

(4) The participating countries drew attention with great concern to the developments in Angola and to the intolerable measures of repression taken by the Portuguese colonial authorities against the people of Angola and demand that an immediate end should be put to any further shedding of blood of the Angolan people, and the people of Angola should be assisted by all peaceloving countries, particularly member states of the United Nations, to establish their free and independent state without delay.

(5) The participants in the Conference demand the immediate termination of all colonial occupation and the restoration of the territorial integrity to the rightful people in countries in which it has been violated in Asia, Africa and Latin America as well as the withdrawal of foreign forces from their national soil.

(6) The participating countries demand the immediate evacuation of French armed forces from the whole of the Tunisian territory in accordance with the legitimate right of Tunisia to the exercise of its full national sovereignty.

(7) The participating countries demand that the tragic events in the Congo must not be repeated and they feel that it is the duty of the world community to continue to do everything in its power in order to erase the consequences and to prevent any further foreign intervention in this young African state, and to enable the Congo to embark freely upon the road of its independent development based on respect for its sovereignty, unity and its territorial integrity.

(8) The participants in the Conference resolutely condemn the policy of apartheid practized by the Union of South Africa and demand the immediate abandonment of this policy. They further state that the policy of racial discrimination anywhere in the world constitutes a grave violation of the Charter of the United Nations and the Universal Declaration of Human Rights.

(9) The participating countries declare solemnly the absolute respect of the rights of ethnic or religious minorities to be protected in particular against crimes of genocide or any other violation of their fundamental human rights.

(10) The participants in the Conference declare their support for the full restoration of all the rights of the Arab people of Palestine in conformity with the Charter and resolutions of the United Nations.

(11) The participating countries consider the establishment and maintenance of foreign military bases in the territories of other countries, particularly against their express will, a gross violation of the sovereignty of such states. They declare their full support to countries who are endeavouring to secure the vacation of these bases. They call upon those countries maintaining foreign bases to consider seriously their abolition as a contribution to world peace.

(12) They also acknowledge that the North American military base at Guantanamo, Cuba, to the permanence of which the Government and people of Cuba have expressed their opposition, affects the sovereignty and territorial integrity of that country.

(13) The participants in the Conference reaffirm their conviction that:

(a) All nations have the right of unity, self-determination, and independence by virtue of which right they can determine their political status and freely pursue their economic, social and cultural development without intimidation or hindrance.

(b) All peoples may, for their own ends, freely dispose of their natural wealth and resources without prejudice to any obligations arising out of international economic co-operation, based upon the principle of mutual benefit, and international law. In no case may a people be deprived of its own means of subsistence.

(c) The participating countries believe that the right of Cuba as that of any other nation to freely choose their political and social systems in accordance with their own conditions, needs and possibilities should be respected.

(14) The participating countries express their determination that no intimidation, interference or intervention should be brought to bear in the exercise of the right of self-determination of peoples including their right to pursue constructive and independent policies for the attainment and preservation of their sovereignty.

(15) The participants in the Conference consider that disarmament is an imperative need and the most urgent task of mankind. A radical solution of this problem, which has become an urgent necessity in the present state of armaments, in the unanimous view of participating countries, can be achieved only by means of a general, complete and strictly and internationally controlled disarmament.

(16) The Heads of State or Government point out that general and complete disarmament should include the elimination of armed forces, armaments, foreign bases, manufacture of arms as well as elimination of institutions and installations for military training, except for purposes of internal security; and the total prohibition of the production, possession and utilization of nuclear and thermo-nuclear arms, bacteriological and chemical weapons as well as the elimination of equipment and installations for the delivery and placement and operational use of weapons of mass destruction on national territories.

(17) The participating countries call upon all states in general, and States exploring outer space at present in particular, to undertake to use outer space exclusively for peaceful purposes. They expressed the hope that the international community will, through collective action, establish an international agency with a view to promote and coordinate the human actions in the field of international cooperation in the peaceful uses of outer space.

(18) The participants in the Conference urge the Great Powers to sign without further delay a treaty for general and complete disarmament in order to save mankind from the scourge of war and to release energy and resources now being spent on armaments to be used for the peaceful economic and social development of all mankind. The participating countries also consider that:

(a) The nonaligned Nations should be represented at all future world conferences on disarmament;

(b) All discussions on disarmament should be held under the auspices of the United Nations;

(c) General and complete disarmament should be guaranteed by an effective system of inspection and control, the teams of which should include members of nonaligned Nations.

(19) The participants in the Conference consider it essential that an agreement on the prohibition of all nuclear and thermo-nuclear tests should be urgently concluded. With this aim in view, it is necessary that negotiations be immediately resumed, separately or as part of the negotiations on general disarmament. Meanwhile, the moratorium on the testing of all nuclear weapons should be resumed and observed by all countries.

(20) The participants in the Conference recommend that the General Assembly of the United Nations should, at its forthcoming session, adopt a decision on the convening either of a special session of the General Assembly of the United Nations devoted to discussion of disarmament or on the convening of a world disarmament conference under the auspices of the United Nations with a view to setting in motion the process of general disarmament.

(21) The participants in the Conference consider that efforts should be made to remove economic inbalance inherited from colonialism and imperialism. They consider it necessary to close, through accelerated economic, industrial and agricultural development, the ever-widening gap in the standards of living between the few economically advanced countries and the many economically less-developed countries. The participants in the Conference recommend the immediate establishment and operation of a United Nations Capital Development Fund. They further agree to demand just terms of trade for the economically less-developed countries and, in particular, constructive efforts to eliminate the excessive fluctuations in primary commodity trade and the restrictive measures and practices which adversely affect the trade and revenues of the newly-developing countries. In general to demand that the fruits of the scientific and technological revolution be applied in all fields of economic development to hasten the achievement of international social justice.

(22) The participating countries invite all the countries in the course of development to co-operate effectively in the economic and commercial fields so as to face the policies of pressure in the economic sphere, as well as the harmful results which may be created by the economic blocs of the industrial countries. They invite all the countries concerned to consider to convene, as soon as possible an international conference to discuss their common problems and to reach an agreement on the ways and means of repelling all damage which may hinder their development; and to discuss and agree upon the most effective measures to ensure the realization of their economic and social development.

(23) The countries participating in the Conference declare that the recipient countries must be free to determine the use of the economic and technical assistance which they receive, and to draw up their own plans and assign priorities in accordance with their needs.

(24) The participating countries consider it essential that the General Assembly of the United Nations should, through the revision of the Charter, find a solution to the question of expanding the membership of the Security Council and of the Economic and Social Council in order to bring the composition and work of these two most important organs of the General Assembly into harmony with the needs of the Organization and with the expanded membership of the United Nations.

(25) The unity of the world Organization and the assuring of the efficiency of its work make it absolutely necessary to evolve a more appropriate structure for the Secretariat of the United Nations, bearing in mind equitable regional distribution.

(26) Those of the countries participating in the Conference who recognize the Government of the People's Republic of China recommend that the General Assembly in its forthcoming Session should accept the representatives of the Government of the People's Republic of China as the only legitimate representatives of that country in the United Nations.

(27) The countries participating in the Conference consider that the German problem is not merely a regional problem but liable to exercise a decisive influence on the course of future developments in international relations. Concerned at the developments which have led to the present acute aggravation of the situation in regard to Germany and Berlin, the participating countries call upon all parties concerned not to resort to or threaten the use of force to solve the German question or the problem of Berlin, in accordance with the appeal made by the Heads of State or Government on 5th September, 1961.

The Heads of State of Government of nonaligned countries resolve that this Declaration should be forwarded to the United Nations and brought to the attention of all the Member States of the world Organization. The present Declaration will be also forwarded to all the other states.

Danger of War and Appeal for Peace.

(1) This Conference of the Heads of State or Government of Non-Aligned countries is deeply concerned that even apart from already existing tension the grave and critical situation which, as never before, threatens the world with the imminent and ominous prospect of conflict would almost certainly later develop into a World War. In this age of nuclear weapons and the accumulation of the power of mass destruction, such conflict and war would inevitably lead to devastation on a scale hitherto unknown, if not to world annihilation.

(2) This Conference considers that this calamity must be avoided, and it is therefore urgent and imperative that the parties concerned, and more particularly the United States of America and the USSR, should immediately suspend their recent war preparations and approaches, take no steps that would aggravate or contribute to further deteriorations in the situation, and resume negotiation for a peaceful settlement of any outstanding differences between them with due regard to the principles of the United Nations Charter and continue negotiating until both they and the rest of the world achieve total disarmament and enduring peace.

(3) While decisions leading to war or peace at present rest with these great powers, the consequences affect the entire world. All nations and peoples have, therefore, an abiding concern and interest that the approaches and actions of the great powers should be such as to enable mankind to move forward to peace and prosperity and not to the doom of extinction. In the certain knowledge that they seek peace, this Conference appeals to the President of the United States of America and the Chairman of the Council of Ministers of the USSR to make most immediate and direct approaches to each other to avert the imminent conflict and establish peace.

(4) This Conference expresses the earnest hope that all nations not represented here, conscious of the extreme gravity of the situation will make a similar appeal to the leaders of the Powers concerned thereby proclaiming and promoting the desire and determination of all mankind to see the achievement of lasting peace and security for all nations. Message to President Kennedy and Premier Khrushchev.

The Conference of the Heads of State or Government of Non-Aligned Countries in Belgrade approved the text of the messages sent to President Kennedy of the United States and Premier Khrushchev of the Soviet Union.

The text of both messages is identical and its unofficial translation reads:

Your Excellency,

We, the Heads of State or Government of the countries which took part in the Belgrade Conference held from September 1 to 6, 1961, are taking the liberty of sending you a message treating a question of vital and direct interest to all of us and to the whole of mankind. We are not taking this step in our own name only, but also in the name of the Conference and our peoples – as an expression of their unanimous wishes. We are deeply concerned over the present deterioration of the international situation and a possible war which threatens mankind. Your Excellency has often pointed out the horrors of a modern war and the use of nuclear weapons, which might destroy the human race, and has often appealed for the preservation of world peace.

At present, we find ourselves on the brink of this danger threatening the world and humanity. We are completely aware of the fact that Your Excellency, like all of us, wishes to prevent such an unfortunate development of the international situation which may not only destroy the hopes for prosperity of our peoples, but also endanger the very existence of mankind. It is our deep conviction that Your Excellency will do all that can be done in order to prevent a catastrophe.

Bearing in mind the gravity of the present crisis which threatens the world and the imperative need to avoid developments which may accelerate this crisis, however, we are taking the liberty of appealing to the Great Powers to renew their negotiations, so as to remove the danger of war in the world and enable mankind to embark upon the road of peace.

In the first place, we are asking for direct negotiations between Your Excellency and the President of the United States, Mr. John Kennedy [in the message to President Kennedy this reads: '... between Your Excellency and the President of the Ministerial Council of the Soviet Union, Mr. Nikita Khrushchev ...'], as representatives of the two most powerful nations of our day, in whose hands lies the key to peace and war. Owing to the fact that both of you are devoted to the cause of world peace, we are convinced that your efforts, channeled through constant negotiations, will lead mankind out of the present blind alley, and will enable it to live and create in peace and prosperity.

It is our belief that Your Excellency will understand that, in sending this message, we have been guided by pure love for peace and fear of war, and by an irresistible desire to find solutions to the outstanding problems, before mankind finds itself faced with disaster. Both messages end with a note that a message of identical wording has been sent to President Kennedy, i.e. to Premier Khrushchev."

Documents of the Gatherings of Non-Aligned Countries 1961–1978, Belgrade, 1978, pp. 5–10.

NONALIGNED COUNTRIES DECLARATION, 1964 OR CAIRO DECLARATION. The Second Conference of Heads of State or Government of Nonaligned Countries held at Cairo, Oct. 5–10, 1964, adopted a Programme for Peace and International Co-operation. The text is as follows:

"The Conference undertook an analysis of the international situation with a view to making an effective contribution to the solution of the major problems which are of concern to mankind in view of their effects on peace and security in the world.

To this end, and on the basis of the principles embodied in the Belgrade Declaration of September 1961, the Heads of State or Government of the above mentioned countries proceeded, in an amicable, frank and fraternal atmosphere, to hold detailed discussions and an exchange of views on the present state of international relations and the predominant trends in the modern world. The Heads of State or Government of the participating countries note with satisfaction that nearly half of the independent countries of the world have participated in this Second nonaligned conference.

The Conference also notes with satisfaction the growing interest and confidence displayed by peoples still under foreign domination, and by those whose rights and sovereignty are being violated by imperialism and neo-colonialism, in the highly positive role which the nonaligned countries are called upon to play in the settlement of international problems or disputes.

The Conference expresses satisfaction at the favourable reaction throughout the world to this second meeting of nonaligned countries. This emphasizes the rightness, efficacy and vigour of the policy of nonalignment, and its constructive role in the maintenance and consolidation of international peace and security.

The principles of nonalignment, thanks to the confidence they inspire in the world, are becoming an increasingly dynamic and powerful force for the promotion of peace and the welfare of mankind.

The participating Heads of State or Government note with satisfaction that, thanks to the combined efforts of the forces of freedom, peace and progress, this second Nonaligned Conference is being held at a time when the international situation has improved as compared with that which existed between the two power blocs at the time of the historic Belgrade Conference. The Heads of State or Government of the Nonaligned Countries are well aware, however, that, despite the present improvement in international relations, and notwithstanding the conclusion and signature of the Treaty of Moscow, sources of tension still exist in many parts of the world. This situation shows that the forces of imperialism are still powerful and that they do not hesitate to resort to the use of force to defend their interests and maintain their privileges.

This policy, if not firmly resisted by the forces of freedom and peace, is likely to jeopardize the improvement in the international situation and the lessening of tension which has occurred, and to constitute a threat to world peace.

The policy of active peaceful coexistence is an indivisible whole. It cannot be applied partially, in accordance with special interests and criteria.

Important changes have also taken place within the Eastern and Western blocs, and this new phenomenon should be taken into account in the objective assessment of the current international situation.

The Conference notes with satisfaction that the movements of national liberation are engaged, in different regions of the world, in a heroic struggle against neo-colonialism, and the practices of apartheid and racial discrimination. This struggle forms part of the common striving towards freedom, justice and peace.

The Conference reaffirms that interference by economically developed foreign states in the internal affairs of newly independent, developing countries and the existence of territories which are still dependent constitute a standing threat to peace and security.

The Heads of State or Government of the nonaligned countries, while appreciative of the efforts which resulted in the holding of the United Nations Conference on Trade and Development, and mindful of the results of that Conference, nevertheless note that much ground still remains to be covered to eliminate existing inequalities in the relationship between industrialized and developing countries.

The Heads of State or Government of the nonaligned countries, while declaring their determination to contribute towards the establishment of just and lasting peace in the world, affirm that the preservation of peace and the promotion of the well-being of peoples are a collective responsibility deriving from the natural aspirations of mankind to live in a better world.

The Heads of State or Government have arrived in their deliberations at a common understanding of the various problems with which the world is now faced, and a common approach to them. Reaffirming the basic principles of the Declaration of Belgrade, they express their agreement upon the following points:

I. *Concerted action for the liberation of the countries still dependent; elimination of colonialism, neo-colonialism and imperialism.*

The Heads of State or Government of the Nonaligned Countries declare that lasting world peace cannot be realized so long as unjust conditions prevail and peoples under foreign domination continue to be deprived of their fundamental right to freedom, independence and self-determination.

Imperialism, colonialism and neo-colonialism constitute a basic source of international tension and conflict because they endanger world peace and security.

The participants in the Conference deplore that the Declaration of the United Nations on the granting of independence to colonial countries and peoples has not been implemented everywhere and call for the unconditional, complete and final abolition of colonialism now.

At present a particular cause of concern is the military or other assistance extended to certain countries to enable them to perpetuate by force colonialist and neo-colonialist situations which are contrary to the spirit of the Charter of the United Nations.

The exploitation by colonialist forces of the difficulties and problems of recently liberated or developing countries, interference in the internal affairs of these states, and colonialist attempts to maintain unequal relationships, particularly in the economic field, constitute serious dangers to these young countries. Colonialism has many forms and manifestations.

Imperialism uses many devices to impose its will on independent nations. Economic pressure and domination, interference, racial discrimination, subversion, intervention and the threat of force are neo-colonialist devices against which the newly independent nations have to defend themselves. The Conference condemns all colonialist, neo-colonialist and imperialist policies applied in various parts of the world.

Deeply concerned at the rapidly deteriorating situation in the Congo, the participants:

(1) support all the efforts being made by the Organization of African Unity to bring peace and harmony speedily to that country;

(2) urge the Ad Hoc Commission of the Organization of African Unity to shirk no effort in the attempt to achieve national reconciliation in the Congo, and to eliminate the existing tension between that country and the Republic of Congo (Brazzaville) and the Kingdom of Burundi;

(3) appeal to the Congolese Government and to all combatants to cease hostilities immediately and to seek, with the help of the Organization of African Unity, a solution permitting national reconciliation and the restoration of order and peace;

(4) urgently appeal to all foreign powers at present interfering in the internal affairs of the Democratic Republic of the Congo, particularly those engaged in military intervention in that country, to cease such interference, which infringes the interests and sovereignty of the Congolese people and constitutes a threat to neighbouring countries;

(5) affirm their full support for the efforts being made to this end by the Organization of African Unity's Ad Hoc Commission of good offices in the Congo;

(6) call upon the Government of the Democratic Republic of the Congo to discontinue the recruitment of mercenaries immediately and to expel all mercenaries, of whatever origin who are already in the Congo, in order to facilitate an African solution.

The newly independent countries have, like all other countries, the right of sovereign disposal in regard to their natural resources, and the right to utilize these resources as they deem appropriate in the interest of their peoples, without outside interference.

The process of liberation is irresistible and irreversible. Colonized peoples may legitimately resort to arms to secure the full exercise of their right to self-determination and independence if the colonial powers persist in opposing their natural aspirations.

The participants in the Conference undertake to work unremittingly to eradicate all vestiges of colonialism, and to combine all their efforts to render all necessary aid and support, whether moral, political or material, to the peoples struggling against colonialism and neo-colonialism. The participating countries recognize the

nationalist movements of the peoples which are struggling to free themselves from colonial domination as being authentic representatives of the colonial peoples, and urgently call upon the colonial powers to negotiate with their leaders.

Portugal continues to hold in bondage by repression, persecution and force, in Angola, Mozambique, so-called Portuguese Guinea and the other Portuguese colonies in Africa and Asia, millions of people who have been suffering far too long under the foreign yoke.

The Conference declares its determination to ensure that the peoples of these territories accede immediately to independence without any conditions or reservations.

The Conference condemns the government of Portugal for its obstinate refusal to recognize the inalienable right of the peoples of those territories to self-determination and independence in accordance with the Charter of the United Nations and the Declaration on the granting of independence to colonial countries and peoples.

The Conference:

(1) urges the participating countries to afford all necessary material support – financial and military – to the Freedom Fighters in the territories under Portuguese colonial rule;

(2) takes the view that support should be given to the Revolutionary Government of Angola in exile and to the nationalist movement struggling for the independence of the Portuguese colonies and assistance to the Special Bureau set up by the OAU in regard to the application of sanctions against Portugal;

(3) calls upon all participating states to break off diplomatic and consular relations with the government of Portugal and to take effective measures to suspend all trade and economic relations with Portugal;

(4) calls upon the participating countries to take all measures to compel Portugal to carry out the decisions of the General Assembly of the United Nations;

(5) addresses an urgent appeal to the Powers which are extending military aid and assistance to Portugal to withdraw such aid and assistance.

The countries participating in the Conference condemn the policy of the racist minority regime in Southern Rhodesia, which continues to defy the Charter and the Resolutions of the United Nations in that it denies fundamental freedoms to the people by acts of repression and terror.

The participating countries urge all states not to recognize the independence of Southern Rhodesia if proclaimed under the rule of the racist minority, and instead to give favourable consideration to according recognition to an African nationalist government in exile, should such a government be set up. To this effect, the Conference states its opposition to the sham consultation through tribal chiefs envisaged by the present Minority Government of Southern Rhodesia.

The Conference deplores the British Government's failure to implement the various resolutions of the United Nations relating to Southern Rhodesia and calls upon the United Kingdom to convene immediately a Constitutional Conference, to which all political groups in Southern Rhodesia would be invited, for the purpose of preparing a new constitution based on the 'one man, one vote' principle, instituting universal suffrage, and ensuring majority rule.

The Conference urges the Government of the United Kingdom to call for the immediate release of all political prisoners and detainees in Southern Rhodesia.

The Conference reaffirms the inalienable right of the people of South West Africa to self-determination and independence and condemns the Government of South Africa for its persistent refusal to cooperate with the United Nations in the implementation of the pertinent resolutions of the General Assembly.

It urges all states to refrain from supplying in any manner or form any arms or military equipment or petroleum products to South Africa, and to implement the Resolutions of the United Nations.

The Conference recommends that the United Nations should guarantee the territorial integrity for their speedy accession to independence and for the subsequent safeguarding of their sovereignty.

The participants in the Conference call upon the French Government to take the necessary steps to enable French Somaliland to become free and independent in accordance with paragraph 5 of Resolution 1514 (XV) of the United Nations.

The Conference appeals to all participating countries to lend support and assistance to the Liberation Committee of the Organization of African Unity.

The Conference condemns the imperialistic policy pursued in the Middle East and, in conformity with the Charter of the United Nations, decides to:

(1) endorse the full restoration of all the rights of the Arab people of Palestine to their homeland, and their inalienable right to self-determination;

(2) declare their full support to the Arab people of Palestine in their struggle for liberation from colonialism and racism.

The Conference condemns the continued refusal of the United Kingdom Government to implement the United Nations Resolutions on Aden and the Protectorates, providing for the free exercise by the peoples of the territory of their right to self-determination and calling for the liquidation of the British military base in Aden and the withdrawal of British troops from the territory.

The Conference fully supports the struggle of the people of Aden and the Protectorates and urges the immediate implementation of the Resolutions of the United Nations which are based on the expressed wishes of the people of the territory.

The countries participating in the Conference condemn the continued armed action waged by British colonialism against the people of Oman who are fighting to attain their freedom. The Conference recommends that all necessary political, moral and material assistance be rendered to the liberation movements of these territories in their struggle against colonial rule.

The Conference condemns the manifestations of colonialism and neo-colonialism in Latin America and declares itself in favour of the implementation in that region of the right of peoples to self-determination and independence.

Basing itself on this principle, the Conference deplores the delay in granting full independence to British Guyana and requests the United Kingdom to grant independence speedily to that country. It notes with regret that Martinique, Guadaloupe and other Caribbean Islands are still not self-governing. It draws the attention of the Ad Hoc Decolonization Commission of the United Nations to the case of Puerto Rico and calls upon that commission to consider the situation of these territories in the light of Resolution 1514 (XV) of the United Nations.

II. *Respect for the right of peoples to self-determination and condemnation of the use of force against the exercise of this right.*

The Conference solemnly reaffirms the right of peoples to self-determination and to make their own destiny.

It stresses that this right constitutes one of the essential principles of the United Nations Charter, that it was laid down also in the Charter of the Organization of African Unity, and that the Conference of Bandung and Belgrade demanded that it should be respected, and in particular insisted that it should be effectively exercised.

The Conference notes that this right is still violated or its exercise denied in many regions of the world and results in a continued increase of tension and the extension of the areas of war.

The Conference denounces the attitude of those Powers which oppose the exercise of the right of peoples to self-determination.

It condemns the use of force, and all forms of intimidation, interference and intervention, which are aimed at preventing the exercise of this right.

III. *Racial discrimination and the policy of apartheid.*

The Heads of State or Government declare that racial discrimination – particularly its most odious manifestation, apartheid – constitutes a violation of the Universal Declaration of Human Rights and of the principle of the equality of peoples. Accordingly, all governments still persisting in the practice of racial discrimination should be completely ostracized until they have abandoned their unjust and inhuman policies. In particular the governments and peoples represented at this Conference have decided that they will not tolerate much longer the presence of the Republic of South Africa in the committee of Nations. The inhuman racial policies of South Africa constitute a threat to international peace and security. All countries interested in peace must therefore do everything in their power to ensure that liberty and fundamental freedoms are secured to the people of South Africa.

The Heads of State or Government solemnly affirm their absolute respect for the right of ethnic or religious minorities to protection in particular against the crimes of genocide or any other violation of a fundamental human right.

Sanctions against the Republic of South Africa:

(1) The Conference regrets to note that the Pretoria Government's obstinacy in defying the conscience of mankind has been strengthened by the refusal of its friends and allies, particularly some major powers, to implement United Nations resolutions concerning sanctions against South Africa.

(2) The Conference therefore:

(a) calls upon all states to boycott all South African goods and to refrain exporting goods, especially arms, ammunition, oil and minerals to South Africa;

(b) calls upon all states which have not yet done so to break off diplomatic, consular and other relations with South Africa;

(c) requests the Government represented at this conference to deny airport and overflying facilities to aircraft and port facilities to ships proceeding to and from South Africa, and to discontinue all road or railway traffic with that country;

(d) demands the release of all persons imprisoned, interned or subjected to other restrictions on account of their opposition to the policy of apartheid;

(e) invites all countries to give their support to the special bureau set up by the Organization of African Unity for the application of sanctions against South Africa.

IV. *Peaceful co-existence and the codification of its principles by the United Nations.*

Considering the principles proclaimed at Bandung in 1955, Resolution 1514 (XV) adopted by the United Nations in 1960, the Declaration of the Belgrade Conference, the Charter of the Organization of African Unity, and numerous joint declarations by Heads of State or Government on peaceful coexistence;

Reaffirming their deep conviction that, in present circumstances, mankind must regard peaceful coexistence as the only way to strengthen world peace, which must be based on freedom, equality and justice between peoples within a new framework of peaceful and harmonious relations between the states and nations of the world;

Considering the fact that the principle of peaceful coexistence is based on the right of all peoples to be free and to choose their own political, economic and social systems according to their own national identity and their ideals, and is opposed to any form of foreign domination;

Convinced also that peaceful co-existence cannot be fully achieved throughout the world without the abolition of imperialism, colonialism and neo-colonialism;

Deeply convinced that the absolute prohibition of the threat or use of force, direct or disguised, the renunciation of all forms of coercion in international relations, the abolition of relations of inequality and the promotion of international co-operation with a view to accelerating economic, social and cultural development, are necessary conditions for safeguarding peace and achieving the general advancement of mankind.

The Heads of State or Government solemnly proclaim the following fundamental principles of peaceful coexistence:

(1) The right to complete independence, which is an inalienable right, must be recognized immediately and unconditionally as pertaining to all peoples, in conformity with the Charter and resolutions of the United Nations General Assembly; it is incumbent upon all states to respect this right and facilitate its exercise.

(2) The right to self-determination, which is an inalienable right, must be recognized as pertaining to all peoples, accordingly, all nations and peoples have the right to determine their political status and freely pursue their economic, social and cultural development without intimidation or hindrance.

(3) Peaceful co-existence between states with differing social and political systems is both possible and necessary; it favours the creation of good-neighbourly relations between states with a view to the establishment of lasting peace and general well-being, free from domination and exploitation.

(4) The sovereign equality of states must be recognized and respected. It includes the right of all peoples to the free exploitation of their natural resources.

(5) States must abstain from all use of threat or force directed against the territorial integrity and political independence of other states; a situation brought about by the threat or use of force shall not be recognized, and in particular the established frontiers of states shall be inviolable. Accordingly, every state must abstain from interfering in the affairs of other states, whether openly, or insidiously, or by means of subversion and the various forms of political, economic and military pressure. Frontier disputes shall be settled by peaceful means.

(6) All states shall respect the fundamental rights and freedoms of the human person and the equality of all nations and races.

(7) All international conflicts must be settled by peaceful means, in a spirit of mutual understanding and on the basis of equality and sovereignty, in such a manner that justice and legitimate rights are not impaired, all states must apply themselves to promoting and strengthening measures designed to diminish international tension and achieve general and complete disarmament.

(8) All states must co-operate with a view to accelerating economic development in the world, and particularly in the developing countries. This co-operation, which must be aimed at narrowing the gap, at present widening, between the levels of living in the developing and developed countries respectively, is essential to the maintenance of a lasting peace.

(9) States shall meet their international obligations in good faith in conformity with the principles and purposes of the United Nations.

The Conference recommends to the General Assembly of the United Nations to adopt, on the occasion of its twentieth anniversary, a declaration on the principles of peaceful co-existence. This declaration will constitute an important step towards the codification of these principles.

V. *Respect for the sovereignty of states and their territorial integrity: problems of divided nations.*

(1) The Conference of Heads of State or Government proclaims its full adherence to the fundamental principle of international relations, in accordance with which the sovereignty and territorial integrity of all states, great and small, are inviolable and must be respected.

(2) The countries participating in the Conference, having for the most part achieved their national independence after years of struggle, reaffirm their determination to oppose by every means in their power any attempt to compromise their sovereignty or violate their territorial integrity. They pledge themselves to respect frontiers as they existed when the states gained independence; nevertheless, parts of territories taken away by occupying powers or converted into autonomous bases for their own benefit at the time of independence must be given back to the country concerned.

(3) The Conference solemnly reaffirms the right of all peoples to adopt the form of government they consider best suited to their development.

(4) The Conference considers that one of the causes of international tension lies in the problem of divided nations. It expresses its entire sympathy with the peoples of such countries and upholds their desire to achieve unity. It exhorts the countries concerned to seek a just and lasting solution in order to achieve the unification of their territories by peaceful methods without outside interference or pressure. It considers that the resort to threat or force can lead to no satisfactory settlement, cannot do otherwise than jeopardize international security.

Concerning the situation existing with regard to Cyprus, the Conference calls upon all states in conformity with their obligations under the Charter of the United Nations, and in particular under Article 2, paragraph 4, to respect the sovereignty, unity, independence and territorial integrity of Cyprus and to refrain from any threat or use of force or intervention directed against Cyprus and from any efforts to impose upon Cyprus unjust solutions unacceptable to the people of Cyprus.

Cyprus, as an equal member of the United Nations, is entitled to and should enjoy unrestricted and unfettered sovereignty and independence, and allowing its people to determine freely, and without any foreign intervention or interference, the political future of the country, in accordance with the Charter of the United Nations.

The Conference, considering that foreign pressure and intervention to impose changes in the political, economic and social system chosen by a country are contrary to the principles of international law and peaceful co-existence, requests the Government of United States of America to lift the commercial and economic blockage applied against Cuba.

The Conference takes note of the readiness of the Cuban Government to settle its differences with the United States on an equal footing, and invites these two Governments to enter into negotiations to this end and in conformity with the principles of peaceful co-existence and international co-operation.

Taking into account the principles set forth above and with a view to restoring peace and stability in the Indochina Peninsula, the Conference appeals to the Powers which participated in the Geneva Conference of 1954 and 1962:

(1) to abstain from any action likely to aggravate the situation which is already tense in the Peninsula;

(2) to terminate all foreign interference in the internal affairs of the countries of that region;

(3) to convene urgently a new Geneva Conference on Indochina with a view to seeking a satisfactory political solution for the peaceful settlement of the problems arising in that part of the world namely:

(a) ensuring the strict application of the 1962 agreements on Laos;

(b) recognizing and guaranteeing the neutrality and territorial integrity of Cambodia;

(c) ensuring the strict application of the 1954 Geneva Agreement on Vietnam, and finding a political solution to the problem in accordance with the legitimate aspirations of the Vietnamese people to freedom, peace and independence.

VI. *Settlement of disputes without threat or use of force in accordance with the principles of the United Nations Charter.*

(1) As the use of force may take a number of forms, military, political and economic the participating countries deem it essential to reaffirm the principles that all states shall refrain in their international relations from the threat or use of force against the territorial integrity or political independence of any state, or in any other manner inconsistent with the purposes of the Charter of the United Nations.

(2) They consider that disputes between states should be settled by peaceful means in accordance with the Charter on the bases of sovereign equality and justice.

(3) The participating countries are convinced of the necessity of exerting all international efforts to find solutions to all situations which threaten international peace or impair friendly relations among nations.

(4) The participating countries gave special attention to the problems of frontiers which may threaten international peace or disturb friendly relations among states, and are convinced that in order to settle such problems, all states should resort to negotiation, mediation or arbitration or other peaceful means set forth in the United Nations Charter in conformity with the legitimate rights of all peoples.

(5) The Conference considers that disputes between neighbouring states must be settled peacefully in a spirit of mutual understanding, without foreign intervention or interference.

VII. *General and complete disarmament; peaceful use of atomic energy, prohibition of all nuclear weapon tests, establishment of nuclear-free zones, prevention of dissemination of nuclear weapons and abolition of all nuclear weapons.*

The Conference emphasizes the paramount importance of disarmament as one of the basic problems of the contemporary world, and stresses the necessity of reaching immediate and practical solutions which would free mankind from the danger of war and from a sense of insecurity.

The Conference notes with concern that the continuing arms race and the tremendous advances that have been made in the production of weapons of mass destruction and their stockpiling threaten the world with armed conflict and annihilation.

The Conference urges the Great Powers to take new and urgent steps toward achieving general and complete disarmament under strict and effective international control.

The Conference regrets that despite the efforts of the members of the 18-Nation Committee on Disarmament, and in particular those of the nonaligned countries, the results have not been satisfactory. It urges the Great Powers, in collaboration with the other members of that Committee, to renew their efforts with determination with a view to the rapid conclusion of an agreement on general and complete disarmament.

The Conference calls upon all states to accede to the Moscow treaty partially banning the testing of nuclear weapons, and to abide by its provisions in the interests of peace and the welfare of humanity.

The Conference urges the extension of the Moscow Treaty so as to include underground tests, and the discontinuance of such tests pending the extension of the agreement.

The Conference urges the speedy conclusion of agreements on various other partial and collateral measures of disarmament proposed by the members of the 18-Nation Committee on Disarmament.

The Conference appeals to the Great Powers to take the lead in giving effect to decisive and immediate measures which would make possible substantial reductions in their military budgets.

The Conference requests the Great Powers to abstain from all policies conducive to the dissemination of nuclear weapons and their by-products among those states which do not at present possess them. It underlines the great danger in the dissemination of nuclear weapons and urges all states, particularly those possessing nuclear weapons, to conclude non-dissemination agreements and to agree on measures providing for the gradual liquidation of the existing stock-piles of nuclear weapons.

As part of these efforts, the Heads of State or Government declare their own readiness not to produce, acquire or test any nuclear weapons, and call on all countries including those who have not subscribed to the Moscow Treaty to enter into a similar undertaking and to take the necessary steps to prevent their territories, ports and airfields from being used by nuclear powers for the deployment or disposition of nuclear weapons. This undertaking should be the subject of a treaty to be concluded in an international Conference convened under the auspices of the United Nations and open to accession by all states.

The Conference further calls upon all nuclear Powers to observe the spirit of this declaration.

The Conference welcomes the agreements of the Great Powers not to orbit in outer space nuclear or other weapons of mass destruction and expresses its conviction that it is necessary to conclude an international treaty prohibiting the utilization of outer space for military purposes.

The Conference urges full international co-operation in the peaceful uses of outer space.

The Conference requests those states which have succeeded in exploring outer space, to exchange and disseminate information related to the research they have carried out in this field, so that scientific progress for the peaceful utilization of outer space be of common benefit to all. The Conference is of the view that for this purpose an international conference should be convened at an appropriate time. The Conference considers that the declaration by African States regarding the denuclearization of Africa, the aspirations of the Latin American countries to denuclearize their continent and the various proposals pertaining to the denuclearization of areas in Europe and Asia are steps in the right direction because they assist in consolidating international peace and security and lessening international tensions.

The Conference recommends the establishment of denuclearized zones covering these and other areas and the oceans of the world, particularly those which have been hitherto free from nuclear weapons, in accordance with the desires expressed by the states and peoples concerned.

The Conference also requests the nuclear Powers to respect these denuclearized zones.

The Conference is convinced that the convening of a world disarmament conference under the auspices of the United Nations to which all countries would be invited, would provide powerful support to the efforts which are being made to set in motion the process of disarmament and for securing the further and steady development of this process.

The Conference therefore urges the participating countries to take, at the forthcoming General Assembly of the United Nations, all the necessary steps for the holding of such a conference and of any other special conference for the conclusion of special agreement on certain measures of disarmament.

The Conference urges all nations to join in the co-operative development of the peaceful use of atomic energy for the benefit of all mankind; and in particular, to study the development of atomic power and other technical aspects in which international co-operation might be most effectively accomplished through the free flow of such scientific information.

VIII. *Military pacts, foreign troops and bases.*

The Conference reiterates its conviction that the existence of military blocs, Great Power alliances and pacts arising therefrom has accentuated the cold war and heightened international tensions. The Nonaligned Countries are therefore opposed to taking part in such pacts and alliances.

The Conference considers the maintenance or future establishment of foreign military bases and the stationing of foreign troops on the territories of other countries, against the expressed will of those countries, as a gross violation of the sovereignty of states, and as a threat to freedom and international peace. It furthermore considers as particularly indefensible the existence or future establishment of bases in dependent territories which could be used for the maintenance of colonialism or for other purposes.

Noting with concern that foreign military bases are in practice a means of bringing pressure on nations and retarding their emancipation and development, based on their own ideological, political, economic and cultural ideas, the Conference declares its full support to the countries which are seeking to secure the evacuation of foreign bases on their territory and calls upon all states maintaining troops and bases in other countries to remove them forthwith.

The Conference considers that the maintenance at Guantanamo (Cuba) of a military base of the United States of America, in defiance of the will of the Government and people of Cuba and in defiance of the provisions embodied in the Declaration of the Belgrade Conference, constitutes a violation of Cuba's sovereignty and territorial integrity.

Noting that the Cuban Government expresses its readiness to settle its dispute over the base of Guantanamo with the United States on an equal footing, the Conference urges the United States Government to negotiate the evacuation of this base with the Cuban Government.

The Conference condemns the expressed intention of imperialist powers to establish bases in the Indian Ocean, as a calculated attempt to intimidate the emerging countries of Africa and Asia and an unwarranted extension of the policy of neo-colonialism and imperialism.

The Conference also recommends the elimination of the foreign bases in Cyprus and the withdrawal of foreign troops from this country, except for those stationed there by virtue of United Nations resolutions.

IX. *The United Nations: its role in international affairs, implementation of its resolutions and amendment of its charter.*

The Participating countries declare:

The United Nations Organization was established to promote international peace and security, to develop international understanding and co operation, to safeguard human rights and fundamental freedom and to achieve all the purposes of the Charter. In order to be an effective instrument, the United Nations Organization must be open to all the states of the world. It is particularly necessary that countries still under colonial domination should attain independence without delay and take their rightful place in the community of nations.

It is essential for the effective functioning of the United Nations that all nations should observe its fundamental principles of peaceful co-existence, co-operation, renunciation of the threat or the use of force, freedom and equality without discrimination on grounds of race, sex, language or religion.

The influence and effectiveness of the United Nations also depends upon equitable representation of different geographical regions in the various organs of the United Nations and in the service of the United Nations.

The Conference notes with satisfaction that with Resolution 1991 (XVIII), the General Assembly has taken the initial positive step towards transformation of the structure of the United Nations in keeping with its increased membership and the necessity to ensure a broader participation of states in the work of its Organs. It appeals to all Members of the United Nations to ratify as speedily as possible the amendments to the Charter adopted at the XVIIIth Session of the General Assembly.

The Conference recognizes the paramount importance of the United Nations and the necessity of enabling it to carry out the functions entrusted to it to preserve international cooperation among states.

To this end, the Nonaligned Countries should consult one another at the Foreign Minister or Head of Delegation level at each session of the United Nations.

The Conference stresses the need to adapt the Charter to the dynamic changes and evolution of international conditions.

The Conference expresses the hope that the Heads of State or Government of the States Members of the United Nations will attend the regular Session of the General Assembly on the occasion of the 20th anniversary of the Organization.

Recalling the recommendation of the Belgrade Conference, the Conference asks the General Assembly of the United Nations to restore the rights of the People's Republic of China and to recognize the representatives of its Government as the only legitimate representatives of China in the United Nations.

The Conference recommends to the States Members of the United Nations and to render all assistance necessary for the Organization to fulfil its role in maintaining international peace and security.

X. *Economic development and co-operation.*

The Heads of State or Government participating in this Conference,

Convinced that peace must rest on a sound and solid economic foundation,

that the persistence of poverty poses a threat to world peace and prosperity,

that economic emancipation is an essential element in the struggle for the elimination of political domination,

that respect for the right of peoples and nations to control and dispose freely of their national wealth and resources is vital for their economic development,

Conscious that participating states have a special responsibility to do their utmost to break through the barrier of underdevelopment;

Believing that economic development is an obligation of the whole international community,

that it is the duty of all countries to contribute to the rapid evolution of a new and just economic order under which all nations can live without fear or want or despair and rise to their full stature in the Family of Nations, that the structure of world economy and the existing international institutions of international trade and development have failed either to reduce the disparity in the per capita income of the peoples in developing and developed countries or to promote international action to rectify serious and growing imbalances between developed and developing countries;

Emphasizing the imperative need to amplify and intensify international co-operation based on equality, and consistent with the needs of accelerated economic development;

Noting that as a result of the proposals adopted at Belgrade in 1961 and elaborated in Cairo in 1962, the United Nations Conference on Trade and Development met in Geneva in 1964;

Considering that while the Geneva Conference marks the first step in the evolution of a new international economic policy for development and offers a sound basis for progress in the future, the results achieved were neither adequate for, nor commensurate with, the essential requirements of developing countries;

Support the Joint Declaration of the 'Seventy-Seven' developing countries made at the conclusion of that Conference, and pledge the co-operation of the participating states to the strengthening of their solidarity;

Urge upon all states to implement on an urgent basis the recommendations contained in the Final Act of the United Nations Conference on Trade and Development and in particular to co-operate in bringing into existence as early as possible the new international institutions proposed therein, so that the problems of trade and economic development may be more effectively and speedily resolved;

Consider that democratic procedures, which afford no position of privilege, are as essential in the economic as in the political sphere;

that a new international division of labour is needed to hasten the industrialization of developing countries and the modernization of their agriculture, so as to enable them to strengthen their domestic economies and diversify their export trade,

that discriminatory measures of any kind taken against developing countries on the grounds of different socio-economic systems are contrary to the spirit of the United Nations Charter and constitute a threat to the free flow of trade and to peace and should be eliminated;

Affirm that the practice of the inhuman policy of apartheid or racial discrimination in any part of the world should be eliminated by every possible means, including economic sanctions;

Recommend that the target of economic growth set for the development Decade by the United Nations should be revised upwards,

that the amount of capital transferred to developing countries and the terms and conditions governing the transfer should be extended and improved without political commitments, so as to reinforce the efforts of these countries to build self-reliant economies,

that a programme of action should be developed to increase the income in foreign exchange of developing countries and, in particular, to provide access for primary products from developing countries to the markets of industrialized countries, on an equitable basis and for manufactured goods from developing countries on a preferential basis,

that the establishment of a Specialized Agency for industrial development should be expedited,

that members of regional economic groupings should do their utmost to ensure that economic integration helps to promote the increase of imports from the developing countries either individually or collectively,

that the recommendation of the United Nations Conference on Trade and Development to convene a conference of plenipotentiaries to adopt an International Convention to ensure the right of land-locked countries to free transit and access to the sea be implemented by the United Nations early next year, and that the principles of economic co-operation adopted by the United Nations Conference on Trade and Development in relation to the transit trade of land-locked countries be given consideration;

Call upon participating countries to concert measures to bring about closer economic relations among the developing countries on a basis of equality, mutual benefit and mutual assistance, bearing in mind the obligations of all developing countries to accord favourable consideration to the expansion of their reciprocal trade, to unite against all forms of economic exploitation and to strengthen mutual consultation;

Call upon the members of the 'Seventy-Seven' developing countries, who worked closely together at the United Nations Conference on Trade and Development of 1964 in Geneva to consult together during the next session of the General Assembly of the United Nations in order to consolidate their efforts and harmonize their policies in time for the next Conference on Trade and Development in 1966;

Convinced that progress towards disarmament increases the resources available for economic development; Support proposals for the diversion of resources now employed on armaments to the development of underdeveloped parts of the world and to the promotion of the prosperity of mankind.

XI. Cultural, scientific and educational co-operation and consolidation of the international and regional organizations working for this purpose.

The Heads of State or Government participating in the Conference:

Considering that the political, economic, social and cultural problems of mankind are so interrelated as to demand concerted action;

Considering that co-operation in the fields of culture, education and science is necessary for the deepening of human understanding, for the consolidation of freedom, justice and peace, and for progress and development;

Bearing in mind that political liberation, social emancipation and scientific advancement have effected fundamental changes in the minds and lives of men;

Recognizing that culture helps to widen the mind and enrich life; that all human cultures have their special values and can contribute to the general progress; that many cultures were suppressed and cultural relations

interrupted under colonial domination; that international understanding and progress require a revival and rehabilitation of these cultures, a free expression of their identity and national character, and a deeper mutual appreciation of their values so as to enrich the common cultural heritage of man;

Considering that education is a basic need for the advancement of humanity and that science not only adds to the wealth and welfare of nations but also adds new values to civilization;

Appreciating the work of international and regional organizations in the promotion of educational, scientific and cultural co-operation among nations;

Believing that such co-operation among nations in the educational, scientific and cultural fields should be strengthened and expanded;

Recommend that international co-operation in education should be promoted in order to secure a fair opportunity for education to every person in every part of the world, to extend educational assistance to develop mutual understanding and appreciation of the different cultures and ways of life through the proper teaching of civics, and to promote international understanding through the teaching of the principles of the United Nations at various levels of education;

Propose that a free and more systematic exchange of scientific information be encouraged and intensified and, especially, call upon developed countries to share with developing countries their scientific knowledge and technical knowledge so that the advantages of scientific and technological advance can be applied to the promotion of economic development;

Urge all states to adopt in their legislation the principles embodied in the United Nations Declaration of Human Rights;

Agree that participating countries should adopt measures to strengthen their ties with one another in the fields of education, science and culture;

Express their determination to help, consolidate and strengthen the international and regional organizations working in this direction."

Documents of the Gatherings of Non-Aligned Countries 1961–1978, Belgrade, 1978, pp. 19–28.

NONALIGNED COUNTRIES DECLARATION, 1970 OR LUSAKA DECLARATION.

The Third Conference of Heads of State of Governments of the Nonaligned Countries, held in Lusaka, Sept. 8–10, 1970, adopted a Declaration on Peace, Independence, Development, Co-operation and Democratization of International Relations. The text, without the Preamble and Art 1, is as follows:

"(2) Two and a half decades ago, the peoples of the United Nations inscribed in the Charter their desire to save succeeding generations from the scourge of war; to reaffirm faith in fundamental human rights, in the dignity of the human person, in the equal rights of nations, large and small; to establish conditions under which justice and respect for obligations arising from treaties and other sources of international law can be maintained and to promote social progress and better standards of life in larger freedom for all. The intervening period has confirmed the historic merit of these ideals and aspirations but, it has likewise demonstrated that many expectations have not been fulfilled and many problems have not been solved, notwithstanding the efforts of the nonaligned countries.

(3) The policy of nonalignment has emerged as the result of the determination of independent countries to safeguard their national independence and the legitimate rights of their peoples. The growth of nonalignment into a broad international movement cutting across racial, regional and other barriers, in an integral part of significant changes in the structure of the entire international community. This is the product of the world anticolonial revolution and of the emergence of a large number of newly-liberated countries which, opting for an independent political orientation and development, have refused to accept the replacement of centuries-old forms of subordination by new ones. At the root of these changes lies the ever more clearly expressed aspiration of nations for freedom, independence and equality, and their determination to resist all forms of oppression and exploitation. This has been the substance and meaning of our strivings and actions; this is a confirmation of the validity of the

Belgrade and Cairo Declarations. At a time when the polarization of the international community on a bloc basis was believed to be a permanent feature of international relations, and the threat of a nuclear conflict between the big powers an ever-present spectre hovering over mankind, the nonaligned countries opened up new prospects for the contemporary world and paved the way for relaxation of international tension.

(4) Our era is at the crossroads of history; with each passing day we are presented with fresh evidence of the exceptional power of the human mind and also of the dangerous paths down which its imperfections may lead. The epoch-making scientific and technological revolution has opened up unlimited vistas of progress; at the same time, prosperity has failed to become accessible to all and a major section of mankind still lives under conditions unworthy of man. Scientific discoveries and their application to technology have the possibility of welding the world into an integral whole, reducing the distance between countries and continents to a measure making international co-operation increasingly indispensable and ever more possible; yet the states and nations comprising the present international community are still separated by political, economic and racial barriers. These barriers divide countries into developed and the developing, oppressors and the oppressed, the aggressors and the victims of aggression, into those who act from positions of strength, either military or economic, and those who are forced to live in the shadow of permanent danger of covert and overt assaults on their independence and security. In spite of the great progressive achievements and aspirations of our generation, neither peace, nor prosperity, nor the right to independence and equality, have yet become the integral, indivisible attribute of all mankind. Our age, however, raises the greatest hopes and also presents the greatest challenges.

(5) The immediate danger of a conflict between the super-powers has lessened because their tendency to negotiate in their mutual relations is strengthening; however, it has not yet contributed to the security of the small, medium-sized and developing countries, or prevented the danger of local wars.

(6) The practice of interfering in the internal affairs of other states, and the recourse to political and economic pressure, threats of force and subversion are acquiring alarming proportions and dangerous frequency. Wars of aggression are raging in the Middle East and in Indochina and being prolonged in South Vietnam and extend to Cambodia and the presence of foreign forces in Korea is posing a threat to national independence and international peace and security. The continued oppression and subjugation of the African peoples in southern Africa by the racist and colonial minority regimes, apart from being a blot on the conscience of mankind, poses a serious threat to international peace and security. This situation is becoming dangerously explosive as a result of the collision between certain developed countries of the West and the racist minority regimes in this part of the world. The continuing arms race is causing alarm and concern and rendering nuclear detente extremely precarious and serves as a spur to limited wars. The balance of terror between the superpowers has not brought peace and security to the rest of the world. There are welcome signs of a growing detente between the power blocs but the abatement of the cold war has not yet resulted in the disintegration of the military blocs formed in the context of great power conflicts.

(7) International relations are entering a phase characterized by increasing interdependence and also by the desire of states to pursue independent policies. The democratization of international relations is therefore an imperative necessity of our times. But there is an unfortunate tendency on the part of some of the big powers to monopolize decision-making on world issues which are of vital concern to all countries.

(8) The forces of racism, apartheid, colonialism and imperialism continue to bedevil world peace. At the same time classical colonialism is trying to perpetuate itself in the garb of neo-colonialism – a less obvious, but in no way a less dangerous, means of economic and political domination over the developing countries. These phenomena of present day world tend not only to perpetuate the evils of the past but also to undermine the future; they retard the liberation of many countries still under colonial domination and jeopardize the independence and territorial integrity of many countries,

above all of the nonaligned and developing countries, hampering their advancement, intensifying tension and giving rise to conflicts.
(9) The economic gap between the developed and the developing countries is increasingly widening – the rich growing richer and the poor remaining poor. The developing countries are being denied their right to equality and to effective participation in international progress. The technological revolution, which is now the monopoly of the rich, should constitute one of the main opportunities for progress of developing countries. World solidarity is not only a just appeal but an overriding necessity; it is intolerable today for some to enjoy an untroubled and comfortable existence at the expense of the poverty and misfortune of others.
(10) Concerned by this state of affairs in the world, the participants in this Conference have agreed to take joint action, and to unite their efforts towards that end.
(11) The participants in the Conference of Nonaligned Countries reaffirm and attach special importance to the following principles: the right of the peoples who are not yet free to freedom, self-determination and independence; respect for the sovereignty and territorial integrity of all states; the right of all states to equality and active participation in international affairs, the right of all sovereign nations to determine in full freedom, the paths of their internal political, economic, social and cultural development; the right of all peoples to the benefits of economic development and the fruits of the scientific and technological revolution, refraining from the threat or use of force, and the principle of peaceful settlement of disputes.
(12) The Conference declares that the following continue to be the basic aims of nonalignment: the pursuit of world peace and peaceful co-existence by strengthening the role of nonaligned countries within the United Nations so that it will be a more effective obstacle against all forms of aggressive action and the threat or use of force against the freedom, independence, sovereignty and territorial integrity of any country; the fight against colonialism and racialism which are a negation of human equality and dignity; the settlement of disputes by peaceful means; the ending of the arms race followed by universal disarmament; opposition to great power military bases and foreign troops on the soil of other nations in the context of great powers conflicts and colonial and racist suppression; the universality of and the stating of strengthening of the efficacy of the United Nations and the struggle for economic and mutual cooperation on a basis of equality and mutual benefit. What is needed is not redefinition of nonalignment but a rededication by all nonaligned nations to its central aims and objectives.
(13) The participants in the Conference solemnly declare that they shall consistently adhere to these principles in their mutual relations and in their relations with other states. They have accordingly agreed to take the following measures:
(a) to achieve full solidarity and to initiate effective and concrete measures against all forces that jeopardize and violate the independence and territorial integrity of the nonaligned countries and in this purpose to cooperate with and consult each other as and when necessary.
(b) to continue their efforts to bring about the dissolution of great power military alliances in the interest of promoting peace and relaxing international tensions, under circumstances ensuring the security of all states and peoples; to safeguard international peace and security through the development of social, economic, political and military strength of each country.
(c) to assert the right of all countries to participate in international relations on an equal footing which is imperative for the democratization of international relations.
(d) to offer determined support to the intensification of the work of all international bodies concerned with problems of disarmament, particularly in the preparations for and implementation of the programme of the Disarmament Decade as an integral part of general and complete disarmament.
(e) to intensify and unite efforts among the developing countries and between them and the developed countries for the carrying out of urgent structural changes in the world economy and for the establishment of such international co-operation as will reduce the gap between developed and developing countries.
(f) to intensify joint efforts for the liquidation of colonialism and racial discrimination: to this end to pledge their utmost possible moral, political and material support to national liberation movements and to ensure implementation of international decisions, including measures by the Security Council in accordance with the relevant provisions of the United Nations Charter.
(g) to continue their efforts toward strengthening the role and efficacy of the United Nations, to promote the achievement of the universality of the United Nations and the urgent need for giving the People's Republic of China her rightful place in the organization and the admission of other countries, still outside the United Nations, including those which are still divided, to participate in the activities of the Organization and its Agencies.
(h) to strengthen steadily, and expand the domain of mutual co-operation within the international, regional and bilateral frameworks.
(i) to ensure the continuity of action by holding periodic consultations of representatives of nonaligned countries at different levels and by convening summit conferences more frequently depending on the prevailing international situation.
(14) The Heads of State or Government and leaders of participating countries resolve that this Declaration as well as the statements and resolutions issued by this Conference shall be forwarded to the UN and brought to the attention of all the member states of the World Organization. The present Declaration shall also be forwarded to all other states.
(15) The participants in the Conference appeal to all nations and governments, all peace and freedom-loving forces and to all people the world over for co-operation and joint efforts for the implementation of these objectives. At the same time, they declare that they shall support all international actions that are initiated in the interests of the progress of mankind."

Documents of the Gatherings of Non-Aligned Countries 1961–1978, Belgrade, 1978, pp. 43–45.

NONALIGNED COUNTRIES DECLARATION, 1971. ▷ Lima Group of 77 Declaration, 1971.

NONALIGNED COUNTRIES DECLARATION, 1973 OR ALGIERS DECLARATION. The Fourth Conference of Heads of State and Government of Nonaligned Countries, held in Algiers, Sept. 5–9, 1973 adopted a Political Declaration and Economic Declaration, and an Action Programme of Economic Co-operation. The text, without the Preamble and Art. 1, of the Political Declaration is as follows:

"(2) The participants noted that over half the countries of the world, representing the majority of the world population, attended this Conference. The number and the level of participants and the general tenor of the meeting are an indicator of the vitality and dynamism of nonalignment.
(3) The participants exchanged views on the world situation and the role of nonalignment.
(4) Mankind has always aspired to freedom, well-being and peace. Such ideals are no longer unattainable nor are they accessible only to a minority. All peoples in the world can now seek to achieve them. The creative potentials of our era make this possible, and the urgent needs of nations make it an historical necessity.
(5) The combined power of the movement for national and social emancipation which is constantly being shaken by the obsolete structures of a world undergoing a complete change, together with the constant advances of the scientific and technological revolution, are opening the way to a complete liberation of all mankind.
(6) However, past decades have shown that this scientific progress, unless it is used in the service of peace, can lead mankind to subjugation and even destruction. A clear awareness of such reality has inspired the ever growing movement of nonaligned countries. The succession of conferences held in Belgrade, Cairo, Lusaka and Georgetown have strongly demonstrated the aspirations of peoples for peace in the new world order founded on independence, progress and justice.
(7) The Heads of Government of the nonaligned countries noted with satisfaction that the development of international relations had confirmed the vitality and lasting value of the aims, principles and practice of the policy of nonalignment. They unanimously believe that the policy of nonalignment, together with other peaceful, democratic and progressive forces, was an important and irreplaceable factor in the struggle for freedom and independence of peoples and countries, for general peace and equal security of all states, for the general enforcement of the principles of peaceful, active coexistence, for the democratization of international relations, for overall and just co-operation, for economic development and social progress.
(8) Reviewing contemporary international processes, the Heads of State and Government of nonaligned countries feel that deep changes have occurred in the general balance of power in the world, thanks to the ever greater strengthening of the forces of peace, independence and progress.
(9) Since the Lusaka Conference, developments in the international situation have shown a stronger tendency toward peace in the advanced world, whereas in other areas there are still sources of tension and wars which are becoming more acute because of deteriorating economic conditions in the developing countries.
(10) The current easing of tensions in relations between East and West and progress toward solving European problems inherited from the Second World War are important achievements of the forces of peace in the world. The fear caused by the nuclear threat as well as the resolution of nations are tilting the balance in favour of dialogue rather than confrontation.
(11) This evolution has also been reflected in the greater contacts between the Soviet Union and the United States and between the United States and the People's Republic of China.
(12) The rapprochement of East and West, the negotiations which are presently under way and the negotiations recently concluded and those which are to be completed, are aimed at establishing co-operation in the framework of a system of collective security based on principles which, overcoming ideological differences, are aimed at regulating international relations. In this context, the proposal for the European conference on security and co-operation has been concretized.
(13) The nonaligned countries, which have unceasingly striven to establish peace and to remove tension through negotiations and appeal to international bodies, commend all these efforts and initiatives and consider them to be a positive step in the direction of establishing peace.
(14) Although substantial progress has been made in the easing of tensions between East and West, the fact that nations are faced with colonialism, domination and occupation, neocolonialism, imperialism and Zionism, remains an indisputable reality of our times.
(15) Peace is not even close to being a certainty in all parts of the world as we can see in the situation obtaining in Indochina, despite the Paris Agreements and the cessation of US bombing of Cambodia; in the Middle East, where the situation continues to deteriorate; in Africa, where there has been a new outbreak of colonial wars of extermination and aggression against independent states; and in Latin America, where the colonial situation still exists and where imperialism conspires against the sovereignty and security of states.
(16) So long as there are colonial wars, apartheid, imperialist aggression, power politics and economic exploitation and plundering, peace will be limited both in principle and in scope. In a world which is already divided into the rich and poor countries, it would be dangerous to widen this division by restricting peace to the rich regions in the world, while condemning the rest of mankind to insecurity and the domination of the most powerful. Peace is indivisible; it should not mean simply shifting confrontation from one area to another, nor should it mean reconciling ourselves to the existence of tensions in some areas while striving to remove them from others. Peace will remain precarious unless the interests of other countries are taken into consideration.
(17) In this connection, the nonaligned countries are simply interpreting the aspirations of the majority of peoples, as can be seen in the declarations adopted in Bandung, Belgrade, Cairo, Lusaka and Georgetown. What all peoples want is to be freed from the colonial yoke, where it still exists, to eradicate apartheid,

Zionism and all forms of racial discrimination and segregation and to put an end to regimes which are inspired by and based upon such tendencies.

(18) It is also essential to ensure a genuine independence by eliminating foreign monopolies and taking over control of national resources and utilizing them for the benefit of the people. The peoples of the third world must maintain their identity, revive and enrich their cultural heritage and in all domains promote their authenticity which colonialism seriously alienated. Finally, they must consolidate their independence through the effective exercise of their national sovereignty against any type of hegemony, in other words the rejection of any form of subjugation or dependence and interference or pressure, be it political, economic or military.

(19) In this respect, international security can be achieved only if it includes the economic dimension, which guarantees all countries the right to use their own programmes of development without economic aggression or any other form of pressure.

(20) The nonaligned countries undertake to step up their joint action to promote the principles of economic security in international relations.

(21) On the other hand, the rejection of military alliances which are a part of the rivalry of the great powers and the dismantling of military bases on which such alliances are founded constitute one of the basic goals of national independence and the policy of nonalignment.

(22) The Conference reaffirms the determination of the nonaligned countries to strictly observe the principles of sovereign equality and territorial integrity of all states, to refrain from the threat or use of force, and to settle their disputes by peaceful means, in accordance with the principles of the United Nations Charter, and they call upon all states to do the same.

(23) The evolution of the international situation completely confirms the merit of the principles and motivations of the policy of nonalignment and makes its strengthening necessary.

(24) More and more countries in Asia, Africa, and Latin America are demonstrating a desire for emancipation and willingness to take up the challenges imposed by neocolonialist tutelage and imperialist monopolies.

(25) By the same token, the movement of nonalignment is expanding and is finding an increasing response which demonstrates on an international scale the aspirations of an ever greater number of states, national liberation movements, and all forces for emancipation and progress throughout the world.

(26) In order to undertake the international obligations in totality and to help solve the problems of our times, which concern the fate of all nations of the world, the nonaligned countries should, together with all progressive forces, work to change international relations on the basis of democracy and equality of all states and to make sure that no decision which concerns large and small countries will be made without their full participation, on an equal footing.

(27) In this context, the Conference emphasizes the need for a more decisive action by the nonaligned countries to find a rapid solution to the conflicts taking place in the third world, where imperialist and colonialist power politics clash with the legitimate aspirations of the people.

(28) The situation in the Middle East continues to give cause for great concern. Israel's obstinacy in pursuing the policy of aggression, expansion and annexation, as well as the Israeli policy of oppressing the inhabitants of the territories which they have occupied by force, are a challenge to the international community, to the United Nations and to the universal declaration on human rights and are a threat to international peace and security.

(29) Again calling attention to the inadmissibility of the forcible annexation of territories, the Conference calls upon Israel to withdraw from all occupied territories forthwith and unconditionally, and undertakes the obligation to aid Egypt, Syria and Jordan with all means in the liberation of their occupied territories.

(30) In this connection, the restoration of the national right to the Palestinian peoples is a fundamental precondition for the establishment of an equal and lasting peace in this area. The struggle of the Palestinian people to recover their homeland which was taken from them is an integral part of the struggle of all nations against colonialism and racial discrimination, and their struggle for self-determination. The participants at the Conference call upon all states, particularly the United States of America, to refrain from supplying Israel with weapons, and from any political, economic or financial support which would enable it to continue its aggressive and expansionist policy.

(31) Israel's persistence in defying the international community and the United Nations will force the nonaligned countries themselves, and within the United Nations together with member countries of this organization, to take individual and collective measures against Israel in accordance with the provisions of Chapter VII of the United Nations Charter.

(32) The Conference gives firm support to and expresses solidarity with the Palestinian people in their difficult trials and great sacrifices they are suffering in order to regain their dignity and national identity.

(33) The Conference welcomes the signing of the Paris Agreements on Vietnam and considers them to be the joint victory of the Vietnamese people and the peoples of nonaligned countries, as well as of all peace-loving and freedom-loving nations throughout the world. The Conference expresses concern over the refusal of the United States of America and the Saigon administration to strictly observe the Paris Agreements.

(34) The Conference calls upon the United States to put an immediate end to any military presence or interference in the internal affairs of the peoples of Indochina and to respect the free exercise of the rights of the Indochinese peoples to self-determination, which is a prerequisite for the establishment of a just peace in this region.

(35) The Conference of Heads of State and Government calls upon its member countries to give their diplomatic support to the Provisional Revolutionary Government of South Vietnam, which is the only authentic representative of the South Vietnamese population, and to make a contribution to the reconstruction of war-damaged Vietnam.

(36) The Conference hails the victory of the Cambodian people, who have succeeded in putting a stop to US bombing of Cambodia, and it condemns the persistent policy of aggression of the USA, which is now being demonstrated in broad US support for the regime in Phnom Penh.

(37) It condemns the military intervention of the United States and its allies in Cambodia and US interference in Cambodian internal affairs.

(38) It recognizes the Royal Government of National Unity of Cambodia (GRUNC), with Prince Norodom Sihanouk as Head of State, as the sole legal and rightful government of Cambodia, and calls upon all nonaligned countries to recognize it forthwith.

(39) The Conference endorses the signing of the Vietnam agreement and expresses hope that the signatory parties will sign protocol for the creation of a national coalition government in Laos.

(40) The strict application of the Vietnam agreement is essential for an effective and lasting restoration of peace and national harmony in accordance with the rightful aspirations of the Laotian peoples.

(41) The Conference particularly commends the determination of the countries of this region to continue pursuing the policy of nonalignment.

(42) The Conference endorses the action of the Korean people for an independent and peaceful reunification, calls for the withdrawal of foreign troops from South Korea and feels that the Korean problem must be settled without outside interference.

(43) The Heads of State and Government of the nonaligned countries have very carefully studied the position of peoples in South Africa, Namibia, Zimbabwe, Angola, Mozambique, Guinea (Bissau) and the Cape Verde islands, who are subjected to the worst forms of exploitation, oppression and destruction, inflicted by the forces of colonialism, neocolonialism and racism which enjoy the political, economic and military support of some western governments and of international capitalism. The colonialist and racist regimes which are rampant in this region constitute moreover a direct threat to the free development of all the countries of Africa, particularly Guinea, the People's Republic of the Congo, Senegal, the United Republic of Tanzania, Zaire, Zambia, Botswana, Swaziland and Lesotho.

(44) The collusion between segregationist and colonialistic regimes of Portugal, South Africa and Rhodesia and many forms of assistance which these regimes are receiving from certain NATO countries, reflect the strategical aims of imperialism in this region.

(45) The Heads of State and Government note that colonialist, neocolonialist and racist forces have continued their policy of aggression, domination, and apartheid even after the adoption of the Lusaka Declaration on Southern Africa. The Conference reiterates that armed conflict is the only way to end colonial and racial discrimination in this region.

(46) In this connection, the Conference commends the heroic struggle of the Peoples of Angola, Mozambique, Guinea (Bissau) and the Cape Verde islands, and the struggle of all nations fighting for freedom. It praises the courageous struggle of the peoples of South Africa, Zimbabwe and Namibia which is being waged in particularly difficult conditions.

(47) The Conference considers it urgent to put an end to the colonial presence in the so-called Spanish Sahara, French Somalia (Djibouti), the Comores and Seychelle Islands. The Conference upholds the action programme adopted at the international conference in Oslo for support for the victims of colonialism and apartheid in South Africa, and calls for its effective implementation.

The Conference calls upon the governments of the countries participating in the Conference on European Security and Cooperation to condemn Portuguese colonialism and all other forms of colonialism and racism, to endorse the declarations and resolutions of the United Nations on decolonization and not to allow Portugal, which is waging colonial wars in Africa, to take refuge in the strengthening of security and cooperation in Europe.

(48) The Conference underlines the need for co-operation of nonaligned countries with all countries which oppose colonialism and neocolonialism, for the purpose of lending an active support to the armed struggle of African liberation movements.

(49) The Conference stresses the need to end colonial domination in Latin America wherever it still exists. It reaffirms complete solidarity of the nonaligned countries with the peoples in this region, who are still subject to colonialism and demands that they be recognized their inalienable right to national independence. It supports the struggle of the peoples of Puerto Rico for national independence and supports the resolutions on Puerto Rico adopted by the United Nations Special Committee on decolonization.

(50) It demands that the government of the United States refrain from anything that might directly or indirectly affect this nation in the exercise of its right to independence.

(51) The Conference demands that military bases in the territories of Cuba, Panama and Puerto Rico be returned to the countries which are the true owners of these territories.

(52) It supports the struggle of the peoples of Latin America to confirm the structural changes essential for their development and condemns imperialist aggression and pressure to which these countries are subjected.

(53) The Conference feels that the struggle for the liberation of Latin America is an important factor in the struggle of peoples against colonialism, neocolonialism and imperialism, and is a contribution to the establishment and consolidation of peace and international security.

(54) The Conference commends the government and people of Chile, who are facing the combined aggression of reaction and imperialism in their struggle to strengthen independence and build a new society. It expresses its solidarity with the efforts of Chile to complete the economic and social transformations that have already begun, to avoid civil war and to preserve its national unity.

(55) It commends the government and people of Peru in their struggle to ensure national sovereignty, to regain the resources of the country and to change the economic and social structures of the country.

(56) It hails the victory of the Argentine people in the struggle for an authentic independence and social progress.

(57) It commends the government and people of Panama in laying claim to sovereignty over the Canal Zone.

(58) The nonaligned countries are stressing the need for the relaxation in relations between the great powers, which has already been acclaimed by the Conference, to

lead to the effective dissolution of the military alliances deriving from the cold war.

(59) It endorses the objective determined by the Declaration of the Third Summit Meeting of Nonaligned Countries concerning the dismantling of all military bases and the withdrawal of foreign troops from all parts of the world.

(60) It gives support to countries which are fighting for the liquidation of military bases built on their territory by virtue of unequal agreements and which are maintained on their soil against the wishes of their peoples.

(61) The Heads of State and Government of the nonaligned countries emphasize that the strengthening of international security is an integral part of the programme and actions to achieve peace and progress of all nations and all countries. This objective can only be achieved by the building of international security which would include all parts of the world and would be the same for all peoples and for all countries.

(62) The Conference feels that the creation of a zone of peace and co-operation in various parts of the world on the basis of the principles of the United Nations Charter is liable to reduce tension, eliminate foreign military presence and promote peaceful co-operation among interested countries.

(63) The Heads of State and Government approve the adoption of the Declaration on the Indian Ocean as a zone of peace at the 26th session of the UN General Assembly. They feel that action in promoting the objective of the declaration will help strengthen international peace and security, and they call for the adoption of new measures for the implementation of this resolution.

(64) The Conference expresses its concern because of the growing tension in the Mediterranean following Israel's aggression which is seen in the consolidation of former military bases and in the deployment of foreign naval forces.

(65) In the belief that security in Europe cannot be dissociated from that of the Mediterranean, the Conference endorses the legitimate rights of the nonaligned countries in that region to participate in the decisions concerning their security. On the other hand, it supports their efforts to establish a zone of peace and co-operation, on the basis of respect for the interests of the countries concerned and of non-intervention in their internal affairs.

(66) The Heads of State or Government commend the declaration adopted in Kuala Lumpur, aimed at creating a zone of peace, freedom and neutrality, free from any form of interference from powers outside this region, and note with satisfaction the progress achieved in realizing the goals of the declaration. They consider it to be a positive contribution to the establishment of international peace and security and call upon all states to respect the principles and goals of this declaration. They express the hope that military presence in this region including foreign bases will be eliminated.

(67) The participants have devoted special attention to the strengthening of security and defence of the nonaligned countries from all outside dangers. They have expressed the resolution of their countries to reinforce their solidarity and mutual assistance in the event of threats to their independence and territorial integrity.

(68) The Conference has noted with concern the continuing flow of conventional weapons which threaten the security of nonaligned countries and which create tension in certain regions. It demands that the flow of such weapons should stop.

(69) The Conference calls for a universal and complete disarmament and, in particular, for a complete prohibition of the use of nuclear weapons and the production of atomic weapons and warheads and destruction of existing stockpiles, as well as for a complete prohibition of all nuclear tests in all environments and in all parts of the world.

(70) In this respect, the Conference demands a halt to the nuclear tests which are being carried out at Muroroa in the South Pacific.

(71) The Conference is also in favour of the prohibition of all existing quantities of chemical and bacteriological weapons.

(72) The Conference calls for a speedy convocation of an international conference on disarmament at which all states would take part.

(73) The Conference again emphasizes the enormous benefit to the welfare of all nations and to the social and economic progress of countries of the third world from

peaceful use of nuclear technology and from use of the resources which would be released after disarmament.

(74) The Conference recalls the declaration of the United Nations which was adopted at the Third Summit Conference of Nonaligned Countries and affirms its adherence to the principles and purposes of the Charter. It considers that the United Nations can be an effective instrument in promoting international peace and security, in increasing co-operation among states and in safeguarding fundamental rights and freedoms.

(75) The Conference states that universality of the United Nations is an essential element for its effectiveness. In this connection, it hails the fact that the People's Republic of China has been restored its rights in the United Nations, which the nonaligned countries have been advocating for so long. It also approves the recommendations of the Security Council on the admission of the Federal Republic of Germany and the German Democratic Republic.

(76) The Conference supports the admission to the United Nations of the People's Republic of Bangladesh, a full and sovereign member of the family of nonaligned countries. In this connection it notes the fact that the recently concluded agreements of 23 August 1973 in New Delhi opened the way to solving the humanitarian problems in anticipation of the establishment of a lasting peace in the subcontinent of Southern Asia.

(77) However, the current operative conditions in the international organization are not always in accord with the new reality of international life and prevent it from fully carrying out its mission of peace and development.

(78) Contempt for the decisions of the United Nations and the tendency of the great powers to monopolize the activities of the organization, to paralyze it or to use it for their own particular interests, are in contradiction with the universal nature of the organization and damage its reputation and prestige.

(79) With the aim of ensuring the effectiveness and authority of the United Nations, the nonaligned countries emphasize the need to improve its organization. For this purpose the Security Council, the body primarily responsible for the safeguarding of international peace and security, should not be prevented from exercising all the responsibilities which are conferred upon it by the Charter. In this connection, the Heads of State and Government call upon all those to whom the Charter has conferred a special responsibility, to use wisdom and display moral integrity in the exercise of their functions.

(80) They consider it indispensable for interested bodies of the United Nations to adopt appropriate and unambiguous decisions and resolutions, completely in accordance with the principles of the Charter, and to ensure observance of these decisions and resolutions.

(81) The Conference expresses concern over the constant deterioration in the economic conditions in the developing countries due to the widening gap between the countries of the third world and the industrial countries. Efforts made in the context of the first development decade and the first years of the second decade have not brought any substantial results.

(82) The increased number of cases of violation of the sovereignty of states, neocolonialist exploitation of developing countries, particularly the exploitation by multinational companies, shortcomings in internal structures and the reserves and restrictions by some industrial countries in regard to the execution of the strategy of international development, explain the constant worsening of the situation in developing countries. In addition, the nonaligned countries feel that improved economic relations and greater trade between advanced countries must under no circumstances harm the vital interests of the developing countries by reducing the share of these countries in world trade and international co-operation.

(83) Finally, in respect to the monetary situation and in the light of the negotiations in progress, the Conference notes the absence of sufficient political willingness of industrial countries participating in those negotiations to consider within the framework of the new system the specific needs of the third world in respect to foreign trade and the financing of their development.

(84) In order to create conditions for a genuine development, the Conference affirms the need to put an end to all forms of foreign domination and exploita-

tion. It proclaims the right of states to recover their own natural resources and to develop them in such a way as to serve the people of these countries, within the scope of their freely chosen programme of development.

(85) The Conference feels that sub-regional, regional and international co-operation, on the basis of mutual respect and mutual advantage, is an important contribution to the policy of development.

(86) The Conference calls upon nonaligned countries to step up their joint action in all domains for an active participation in solving international economic problems, particularly in view of the forthcoming monetary and trade negotiations and the Third UN Conference on Law of the Sea.

(87) The Heads of State and Government have agreed to support the adoption of zones of national jurisdiction not exceeding 200 miles, measured from base lines, in which the riparian states would exercise their rights to exploit natural resources and to protect other special rights and interests of the developing countries, with or without coast or otherwise geographically handicapped, without prejudice being made to the freedom of navigation and overflight wherever it may be applicable, and to the regime applying to the continental shelf.

(88) The Heads of State and Government reaffirm the vital importance of a rational utilization of the resources of the seas and oceans for the economic development and promotion of welfare of peoples.

(89) The participants reaffirm their adherence to the fundamental principle according to which the maritime zone and resources located beyond the limits of national jurisdictions constitute a common heritage of mankind and recommend the forming of an international authority with extended powers which would administer this zone for the benefit of the entire international community and particularly of the developing countries.

(90) The participants urgently call upon all the interested parties to comply with the prohibition of exploiting the resources from the international zone before the final adoption of an agreed regime.

(91) They underline that the new rules of the law of the sea must effectively contribute to eliminate the threats to the security of states and to ensure respect for their sovereignty and their territorial integrity.

(92) The Heads of State and Government proclaim the urgency of holding a conference on the Law of the Sea in Santiago de Chile in 1974, as well as the necessity of ensuring its success by an adequate preparation, and regard as indispensable a previous consultation among the nonaligned countries to co-ordinate their positions and actions on the problems of principles and procedure in order to rapidly arrive at satisfactory results.

(93) In bringing the Fourth Summit Conference of Nonaligned Countries to a close, the Heads of State and Government, in order to ensure continuity and effectiveness of the policy of nonalignment which has been vindicated by recent events in the international situation, have resolved to reinforce their action and to co-ordinate their efforts.

(94) This is a necessity which has been made even more imperative by the fact that the principles of nonalignment were adopted as the basis of action of many organs of regional and international co-operation.

(95) The great changes which are now taking place at the political, economic and technological levels in a world which is becoming better organized, the urgency and acuteness of problems of emancipation and development, and the need for a true peace are all factors which today motivate the nonaligned countries to intensify their activities and to organize mutual co-operation both in order to create a new basis for their solidarity and to guarantee their participation in solving the main international problems.''

Documents of the Gatherings of Non-Aligned Countries 1961–1978, Belgrade, 1978, pp. 89–93.

NONALIGNED COUNTRIES DECLARATION, 1975 OR LIMA DECLARATION. The final document of the Conference of Nonaligned Countries, Aug. 23–29, 1975 entitled Lima Program of Solidarity and Mutual Assistance: Political Declaration and Strategy to Strengthen Inter-

national Peace and Security, and Economic Declaration. Fundamental ideas:
– to oppose division of the world into blocs in order to attenuate contradictions in international life,
– to eliminate force and pressure in international relations,
– to base relations between nations on the equality of states, respect for their territorial integrity, national sovereignty, and the right of every country to choose freely its political regime,
– to spread and respect the right of every nation to self-determination and freedom,
– the nonaligned countries are anti-imperialist, anti-colonialist, and anti-racialist.

Documents of the Gatherings of Non-Aligned Countries 1961–1978, Belgrade, 1978.

NONALIGNED COUNTRIES DECLARATION, 1976 OR COLOMBO DECLARATION.

The Fifth Conference of Heads of State or Government of Nonaligned Countries, held in Colombo, Aug. 16–19, 1976, adopted a Political Declaration and Economic Declaration and an Action Programme for Economic Co-operation. The text of the Economic Declaration is as follows:

"I. *Introduction.* The Heads of State or Government of Nonaligned Countries consider that economic problems have emerged as the most acute problems in international relations today. The crisis of the world economic system continues to assume ever-growing proportions. Developing countries are the victims of this worldwide crisis which severely affects political and economic relations. The widening of the gap between developed and developing countries is one of the most threatening sources of tensions and conflicts. It is increasingly evident that the existing system cannot ensure the promotion of the development of the developing countries and hasten the eradication of poverty, hunger, sickness, illiteracy and also the social scourges engendered by centuries of domination and exploitation. Thus the establishment of the New International Economic Order is of the utmost political importance. The struggle for political and economic independence, for the full sovereignty over natural resources and domestic activities and for the greater participation of developing countries in the production and distribution of goods, and the rendering of services and basic changes in the international division of labour assumes the highest priority. Breaking up of the resistance to the struggle for the new order represents the primary task of the Nonaligned and other developing countries. The elimination of foreign aggression, foreign occupation, racial discrimination, apartheid, imperialism, colonialism and neo-colonialism and all other forms of dependence and subjugation, interference in internal affairs, domination and exploitation are crucial to the economics of Nonaligned.

II. *The struggle for liberation and independence.*
(1) The Heads of State or Government of Nonaligned Countries noted the success of developing countries in mobilizing their natural resources as an effective weapon to defend their national security, sovereignty and existence, and in promoting their collective struggle against foreign aggression and occupation, racial discrimination, alien domination, apartheid, Zionism and colonialism which are the greatest threat to world peace and security. This has been amply demonstrated by the triumphs of this struggle in Africa, the Middle East and Asia and in the effective measures taken by the oil exporting countries and other developing countries producers of raw materials to safeguard and control their natural resources.
(2) It is the duty of all states and peoples to work individually and collectively to eliminate those practices and to extend effective support and assistance to the peoples, countries and territories subjected to them, so as to put an immediate end to those major obstacles to their freedom and legitimate aspirations, and in order to promote development and international co-operation, peace and security. Furthermore, these peoples, countries and territories have the right to restitution and full compensation for the exploitation, depletion of and damages to their natural and all other resources in accordance with the principles of the Declaration on the

Establishment of a New International Economic Order, the Charter of Economic Rights and Duties of States and the Dakar Declaration. No state may promote investments that may obstruct or affect the right to political and economic sovereignty and independence of peoples, countries and territories subjected to foreign occupation or domination.

III. *The present international economic situation and the prospects for the developing countries.*
(1) The Heads of State or Government of Nonaligned Countries are deeply perturbed by the glaring inequalities and imbalances in the international economic structure and the ever widening gap between the developed and developing countries. Numerous resolutions were adopted at various international fora concerning the establishment of the New International Economic Order. However, no indication of their implementation is apparent. Despite the growing acceptance of the principles of the New International Economic Order, there has been minimal progress towards their implementation.
(2) The developing countries, and particularly the Least Developed, Land-Locked, Island Developing and other geographically disadvantaged countries, and the Most Seriously Affected countries, are facing an acute crisis both with regard to the attainment or maintenance of minimal living standards of their peoples and their prospects of development. Over the years the economic situation of most developing countries, specially the Least Developed, and the Most Seriously Affected countries has continued to deteriorate and the resultant debt burdens on these countries have reached intolerable levels.
(3) The foreign exchange earnings of the developing countries depend basically on their exports of raw materials and primary commodities. The relative improvement of the level of prices of some of these commodities in 1973/1974, which was shortlived, did not at all compensate for the deterioration in their terms of trade which characterized the post-war period. The decline in their real value is continuing and is today assuming disquieting proportions as a result of the staggering rise in the prices of manufactured goods, foodstuffs, capital goods and services imported by the developing countries. This situation is seriously affecting the efficacy of their efforts and puts a brake on their development.
(4) Despite the continuing assurances given by the developed countries to relax and eliminate barriers to trade for the products of developing countries, progress so far has not been satisfactory. However it should be noted that the agreements concluded between some developed countries and developing countries constitute a sign of hope in this field. The Generalized Scheme of Preferences though a useful scheme of trade liberalization needs substantial improvement. Its limited coverage, particularly in respect of products of export interest to developing countries and especially the Least Developed countries and its temporary nature are a matter of major concern. Progress in the Multilateral Trade Negotiations has been slow and their focus has been narrow. Furthermore, with the exceptions of a few forward looking developed countries there has been no genuine attempt on the part of the developed countries to re-organize and reform the existing inequitable and unbalanced world trade systems to conform to the urgent development requirements and priorities of the developing countries.
(5) There has been a phenomenal rise in the deficit in the balance of payments of developing countries which had increased from about $12.2 billion in 1973 to $33.5 billion in 1974 and to over $40 billion in 1975. Some estimates indicate that this figure could reach $112 billion by 1980 given the present trends. This unprecedented situation is not the product of conjunctural factors, but the reflection of the structural crisis that characterizes the present economic relations which originates in the colonial and neo-colonial policy of imperialism. As a result most developing countries have over the years run down their reserves, accumulated large external debts, a good portion of which carries heavy interest and amortization obligations. It has been estimated that the external indebtedness of these countries which was over $100 billion in 1973 will double itself by the end of 1976.
(6) The continuing diversion of human and material resources from peaceful economic and social pursuits to an unproductive and wasteful arms race, particularly in

the field of nuclear and other weapons of mass destruction, not only heightens the current grave crisis in world economy but also frustrates the purposes and objectives of both the Disarmament Decade and the Second United Nations Development Decade which envisaged a transfer of substantial resources from the developed countries to the developing countries through disarmament. The flow of financial resources to the developing countries amounted to only about $20 billion in 1975 in contrast to the expenditure on armaments that has been increasing at a phenomenal rate and has now reached the staggering figure of $300 million per annum. The Heads of State or Government of the Nonaligned countries reaffirm that much of the development requirements of developing countries would be met if a substantial part of the resources freed by measures in the field of disarmament by the main world military Powers could be used to promote the economic development of developing countries. Such measures would certainly contribute towards a bridging of the gap between developed and developing countries within the foreseeable future.
(7) Industrialization is a dynamic instrument of development for the social and economic progress of the developing countries. It is also linked to the promotion and expansion of trade not only amongst the developing countries. The redeployment of appropriate industries and the provision of the necessary support for building up a sound technological base in the developing countries should be expedited. The monopoly of technology processes by developed countries has led to several unsatisfactory features which call for immediate substantive and institutional remedial action if transfer of technology is to be effected in order to achieve the targets set for the developing countries by the Lima and Manila Declarations. In taking the above measures the special needs of the Least Developed, Land-Locked and Island Developing countries and other geographically disadvantaged countries should be borne in mind.
(8) The inadequate implementation of policy measures embodied in the International Development Strategy due to the lack of political will in most developed countries, compounded with a continuing economic crisis which seriously affects the developing countries because of their greater vulnerability to external economic impulses, produced the most discouraging results. Thus the crisis of poverty, hunger, malnutrition, deprivation and illiteracy has been perpetuating in the developing world and affecting a greater number of countries and peoples.
(9) The developing countries and mainly the Least Developed, Land-Locked and Island Developing countries and other geographically disadvantaged countries have been most seriously affected, inter alia, as a result of shortages in food supplies and the rise in the prices of imported food. The existing deficiency of food grains of 20 million tons annually in the developing countries would increase to 100 million tons in the year 2000 if present trends of production continue as a result of insufficient investment in food production in developing countries. In view of this situation increased investment in food production in developing countries becomes imperative. Loans and other sources of financing investment in food production should therefore be provided to developing countries as grants or on concessionary terms, particularly for the least developed countries. The Conference noted with satisfaction the creation of the International Fund for Agricultural Development. It expresses the hope in the speedy and effective operation of the Fund and calls upon the developed countries to increase their contributions to the Fund. It also urges the early implementation of the other recommendations of the World Food Conference especially the establishment of an international emergency grain reserve.
(10) The lack of an equitable international monetary system is of deep concern, and has aggravated the economic problems of the developing countries. Attempts at reform within the framework of existing monetary relations which is under the control of a few developed capitalist countries have ended in failure. These countries have exerted undue influence in decision-making in matters relating to monetary systems and the solutions of the problems of developing countries are sought on the basis of temporary and inefficient arrangements. The Heads of State or Government of the Nonaligned countries reaffirm that

the solution of the economic problems of developing countries requires the establishment of a new, universal and equitable monetary order.

(11) The efficiency and equitability of the system to be established will depend largely on the influence which the international community will be able to exert collectively on the conditions of creation and utilization of additional liquidity, taking due account of the interests of the developing countries. It is therefore a matter of urgency that liquidity should be created which is automatically tied to the financing needs of development and that the developing countries should be guaranteed their rightful and equitable share in the monetary decision-making process.

(12) The Heads of State or Government of Nonaligned Countries noted with deep concern that there is still a strong resistance from certain developed countries to the implementation of the Declaration and Programme of Action and Resolutions adopted at the Sixth and Seventh Special Sessions of the United Nations General Assembly regarding the establishment of the New International Economic Order, and the resolution adopted at the Twenty-ninth Session of the United Nations General Assembly regarding the Charter of Economic Rights and Duties of States and a continued insistence on solutions aimed at preserving the existing relations of inequality, dependence and exploitation. The resistance to the New International Economic Order by some developed countries has been even intensified.

(13) The Conference notes with anxiety that no headway has been made at the Conference on International Economic Co-operation in Paris. The Heads of State or Government express their full support for the positions taken by the developing countries in the Paris Conference. They observe that the developed countries have not reacted positively to concrete proposals of the developing countries. The failure to agree upon even a work programme at the July Sessions reflects the lack of a political will on the part of the developed countries to effect substantial changes in their economic relations with developing countries. The developed countries will be held responsible for a failure of the Paris Conference which would result from their persistent refusal to accept the proposals concerning a wide range of questions of importance for the developing countries. Such a failure would prompt the developing countries to reconsider their attitudes.

(14) The Heads of State or Government of the Nonaligned Countries in their assessment of the results of the UNCTAD IV noted with satisfaction the exemplary unity maintained by the developing countries throughout the negotiations. At the same time they do not fail to note that UNCTAD IV has fallen far short of the aspirations of the Nonaligned and other developing countries as expressed in the Sixth and Seventh Special Sessions of the United Nations General Assembly and spelt out in the Manila Declaration. Of particular concern is the stand taken by some developed countries in opposing the proposals for the establishment of the Common Fund, measures for the protection of the purchasing power of the developing countries, the urgent and critical external indebtedness of the developing countries, the alleviation of specific and longstanding problems and the implementation of proposals and resolutions including the activation of the fund for the Least Developed, Land-Locked and Island Developing countries. It is therefore of paramount importance that a consensus on the timetable and procedure of all forms of negotiations for the implementation of the integrated programme for commodities including the Common Fund, is acted upon. The continued support given by certain developed countries to the cause of development of the developing countries is a matter for satisfaction.

(15) The Heads of State or Government of Nonaligned Countries are firmly convinced that nothing short of a complete re-structuring of international economic relations through the establishment of the New International Economic Order will place developing countries in a position to achieve an acceptable level of development. They reaffirm their determination to pursue their common efforts to achieve these objectives in particular through the formation of Producer/Exporters' Associations and other means despite threats and repressive economic sanctions.

(16) The Heads of State or Government of Nonaligned Countries express the wish that the negotiations on international economic co-operation and development pursued in various international fora will be integral parts of a mutually reinforcing and convergent process to accelerate the universal implementation of the New International Economic Order. The implementation of agreed decisions is a major responsibility of the international community.

IV. *Nonalignment and economic development.*

(1) The Heads of State or Government of Nonaligned Countries reaffirm that the struggle for political independence and the exercise of their sovereignty cannot be disassociated from the struggle for the attainment of economic emancipation. It is important that the developing countries should use their sovereignty and their independence at the political level as a lever for the attainment of their sovereignty and independence at the economic level. It is the economic issues in international negotiations that will now be the major concern of international politics. No lasting peace and security is possible internationally without the establishment of a just and fair society which provides its citizens the economic and social security which is an inalienable right of every citizen of this planet. The Heads of State or Government of Nonaligned Countries are determined that such a society should be established in the shortest possible time thus ushering in an era of prosperity and dignity for all mankind.

(2) The achievement of the full economic potential rests on the developing countries and entails the following factors:

(a) individual self-reliance in order that developing countries may utilize their economic potential to co operate among themselves to set up the New International Economic Order;

(b) intensification of economic co-operation between developing countries;

(c) strengthening of their solidarity and the co-ordination of the activities of the developing countries in a common front against all attempts of imperialists to sow division and to apply pressure.

(3) At the Summit Conferences held in Belgrade, Cairo and Lusaka, the Heads of State or Government of Nonaligned Countries recognized the close interaction that exists between political and economic relationships. They emphasized the need to accelerate economic development so that world peace and prosperity could be ensured for mankind. At the Georgetown meeting in 1972 the general principles of Nonalignment were translated into concrete programmes of action to promote economic co-operation among Nonaligned countries.

(4) The Fourth Summit Conference in Algiers held in 1973 marked the turning point both with regard to the mutual co-operation among Nonaligned and other developing countries in as much as its decisions and recommendations served as the basis for intensive international negotiations aimed at the establishment of the New International Economic Order. The Algiers Summit affirmed the solidarity of the Nonaligned and other developing countries in the struggle for a better life for their peoples and placed its entire weight and influence behind the actions to be taken by producer countries of raw materials to obtain a remunerative price for their products.

(5) The Declaration and the Programme of Action for the Establishment of the New International Economic Order adopted at the Sixth Special Session of the United Nations General Assembly and the Charter of Economic Rights and Duties of States adopted at the Twenty-ninth Session of the General Assembly of the United Nations on the initiative of the developing countries constitute a clear exposition of the orientation and the economic programme of Nonalignment. The adoption of the Declaration and Programme of Action for the establishment of the New International Economic Order and the Charter of Economic Rights and Duties of States also signify the rejection of the systems of exploitation, which have existed up to now. The international recognition of the principles laid down in these fundamental documents give them universal validity and constitutes a powerful contribution to the efforts for introducing equality in the international economic relations.

(6) The Dakar Conference on Raw Materials first proposed at the Algiers Summit is a prominent landmark in the evolution of international economic relations and solidarity among developing countries. This Conference has embarked on a range of new initiatives which are at the very core of the establishment of the New International Economic Order. The Dakar Declaration has the most important implications for the economic development of developing countries.

(7) The Lima Conference in 1975 set up new guidelines for the Nonaligned countries in its Programme for Mutual Assistance and Solidarity. The programme of economic co-operation of the developing countries has been given concrete shape and form in the Manila Declaration due to the solidarity of the Nonaligned countries and of the other developing countries within the Group of 77.

(8) The Heads of State or Government of Nonaligned Countries recognize with appreciation that the economic content of the Nonaligned Movement has influenced and in turn has been influenced by the articulate and dynamic organization of the Group of 77. The Nonaligned Movement shall continue to maintain and strengthen its solidarity with the Group 77 which has today emerged as a real force of countervailing authority. The Nonaligned countries emphasize the highly constructive role of the Group of 77 in the negotiations for advancing the cause of the developing countries and particularly in the establishment of the New International Economic Order.

V. *The new international economic order.*

(1) The Heads of State or Government of Nonaligned Countries are firmly of the view that nothing short of a complete restructuring of the existing international economic relations will provide an enduring solution to the world economic problems, particularly those of the developing countries. The inadequacy and the recurring failure of the prevailing economic order have been demonstrated in the recent series of crises in the developed market economy countries including inter alia the collapse of the post-war monetary system, emergence of restrictive and protectionist policies in world market trade, spiralling inflation, recession, mounting unemployment and steadily deteriorating levels of real income from exports of primary produce of developing countries and food crisis. These crises have also dramatized the basically dependent character of the constituent elements of the world economy and provided the necessary impetus for the world community to conceive of the New International Economic Order based on equity, sovereign equality, inter-dependence, common interest and co-operation among all states. Faced with this chaotic situation the world has witnessed an unprecedented solidarity among the developing countries and successful assertion of their basic economic and political rights in the international scene.

(2) The Heads of State or Government of Nonaligned Countries view the adoption of the Declaration and the Programme of Action on the Establishment of the New International Economic Order at the Sixth Special Session of the General Assembly of the United Nations as signifying the growing determination of the international community to bring about a fundamental change in the system of international economic relations. The Establishment of the New International Economic Order calls for bold initiative, demands new, concrete and global solution, and is contrary to piecemeal reforms and improvization intended to resolve the present economic difficulties. The fundamental objective of the New Economic Order is to bring about in the international economic relations an equilibrium based on justice through co-operation and human dignity.

(3) The Heads of State or Government of Nonaligned Countries once again denounce the unacceptable policies and practices of transnational corporations which, motivated by exploitative profits, exhaust the resources, distort the economies and infringe the sovereignty of developing countries; violate the principles of non-interference in the affairs of states; infringe the right of peoples to self-determination; and frequently resort to bribery, corruption and other undesirable practices and subordinate the developing countries to the industrialized countries.

(4) The Nonaligned Countries once more reaffirmed the inalienable right of all countries to exercise full permanent sovereignty over their natural and human resources and their economic activities including possession, use and disposal of such resources and their right to nationalization. They further reaffirm the inalienable right of developing countries to exercise supervision, authority, regulation and nationalization of transnational corporations within their national

jurisdiction in accordance with their laws and regulations, as well as in conformity with their national objectives and principles. They further ratify their willingness to lend rapid, efficient and unreserved support to all other developing countries in their struggle for political and economic independence, exercising effective and concrete solidarity in the face of such economic aggression as blockade, discrimination, boycott, pressure and threats or any other form of aggression that may be adopted by imperialist countries.

(5) The Heads of State or Government of Nonaligned Countries reaffirm their view that nothing short of a complete restructuring of existing international economic relations will provide an enduring solution to world economic problems. They reaffirm their determination to secure through collective action the establishment and implementation of the New International Economic Order as it has been manifested and envisaged in various resolutions. Such an order should consist, inter alia, of the following essential elements:

(a) Fundamental restructuring of the entire apparatus of international trade with a view to indexation, improving the terms of trade of developing countries and ensuring fair and remunerative prices in real terms to primary export products and an appropriate share of world trade for developing countries through the expansion of processing, diversification and full participation in transport, marketing and distribution of their products. Urgent and full implementation of the integrated programme of commodities including the measures to ensure that the interest of developing countries particularly the Least Developed and the Most Seriously Affected among them, and those lacking in natural resources, adversely affected by measures under the integrated programme are protected by means of appropriate differential and remedial measures within the programme;

(b) Basic restructuring of world production on the basis of a new international division of labour through improved access to the markets of the developed countries for the manufactured products of developing countries, transfer of appropriate technology on favourable terms and conditions, redevelopment of suitable industries from developed countries to developing countries, harmonization of production of synthetics and substitutes in developed countries with the supply of natural products from developing countries, the elimination of restrictive business practices and effective control of the activities of transnational corporations in conformity with the development objectives of developing countries;

(c) Radical overhauling of the present international monetary arrangements which are characterized by the absence of a rational, equitable and universal system, chaotic currency fluctuations, haphazard growth of international liquidity, widespread inflation, lack of responsiveness to the needs of developing countries and the domination of decision-making by a few developed countries. The new system should remove the dominant role of international currencies in international reserves, ensure parity in decision-making as between developed and developing countries, prevent the domination of any single country over decision-making and forge a link between creation of liquidity and development finance;

(d) Ensuring adequate transfer of resources for development on an assured, continuous and predictable basis with respect to the criteria of independence and in a non-discriminatory manner not likely to create division among developing countries;

(e) Finding urgent and adequate solutions to the problem of official debts particularly for the Least Developed and the Most Seriously Affected countries;

(f) Producing adequate resources and appropriate technologies on favourable terms for investment to ensure increased production of food and agricultural inputs in developing countries;

(g) The right of developing land-locked countries to free access to and from the sea in accordance with resolution No. 2 of the Fourth Conference of the Heads of State or Government of Nonaligned Countries and the Dakar Declaration of February 1975. (Some developing countries expressed their reservation on this.)

VI. *Collective self-reliance.*

(1) The Heads of State or Government of the Nonaligned Countries are of the firm belief that only a confident spirit of collective self-reliance on the part of the developing countries can guarantee the emergence of the New International Economic Order. Self-reliance implies a firm determination on the part of developing nations to secure their legitimate economic rights in international dealings through the use of their collective bargaining strength. It also involves preparedness on their part to follow internally the discipline required of them by the process of economic development with justice. And, most importantly, it means willingness to explore and pursue the immense possibilities of co-operation among themselves in financial, technical, trade, industrial and other fields.

(2) The focal point of this process of growth with social justice will be eradication of unemployment and poverty. It calls for the formulation and implementation of a policy for satisfying the basic minimum needs of the population of the developing world. It is recognized that structural changes where and when necessary will be required to achieve those objectives. The Heads of State or Government of the Nonaligned Countries are determined to use all their energies and resources to achieve this goal in the shortest possible time.

(3) Recent events have generated new complementaries and opened up tremendous opportunities for co-operation among the developing world. The idea that the developing world constitutes only parallel economies is no longer valid, since the developing world reflects a wide variety of resource endowments and stages of development. The Heads of State or Government of the Nonaligned Countries believe that the need of the hour is to develop a common will and evolve suitable mechanisms to fully utilize the complementaries, resources and capabilities within the developing world for mutual benefit and for collective economic advancement. To this end, the Mexico Conference on Economic Co-operation among Developing Countries should examine the various alternative mechanisms and arrangements to achieve that purpose.

(4) The Heads of State or Government of the Nonaligned Countries, in reaffirming their solidarity based on the Principles of collective self-reliance recognize the necessity to give particular consideration to the special problems of the Least Developed, Land-Locked, Island Developing countries and other geographically disadvantaged countries.

(5) The principle of self-reliance, thus seen in its individual and collective aspects, is not only compatible with the aims of the New International Economic Order but is a highly important factor in the strengthening of the solidarity of Nonaligned and other developing countries in their struggle to achieve economic emancipation.

VII. Interdependence within the global economy.

(1) The Heads of State or Government of Nonaligned Countries consider that collective self-reliance within the New International Economic Order is an important and necessary step in the wider process aiming at the establishment of international co-operation which would be a concrete and genuine expression of interdependence within the global economy. International co-operation is nowadays an imperative necessity. It requires the effective participation of all in decision-making and demands that those processes and relationships which lead to increasing inequality and greater imbalance are put to an end. In their strategy of international economic co-operation, concurrently with the intensification of the relations between themselves, it is desirable that the Nonaligned countries diversify their economic relations with the other countries, developed capitalist as well as socialist, on the basis of the principles of respect for national sovereignty, of equality and of mutual benefit.

(2) The Heads of State or Government of Nonaligned Countries recognize that the responsibility for ushering in a new era of just and equitable relationship belong to all but specially to the developed countries. However, such responsibility lies more heavily on those who wield economic power. Moreover, the establishment of the New International Economic Order requires determined and effective action on the part of the developed countries in all the major areas of international economic relations. The developed world as a whole can no longer shy away from its share of responsibility under any pretext, nor can it afford to ignore the fundamentally indivisible nature of the global prosperity.

(3) The Heads of State or Government of Nonaligned Countries, therefore, call upon the developed world to give convincing expression to their faith in the principle of Global Interdependence by adopting a range of measures which alone will lead to true international co-operation and emergence of the New Economic Order.

VIII. *Conclusion.*

(1) The Heads of State or Government note that previous Summits have in the economic field been marked by numerous innovative forward steps. The Belgrade Summit paved the way for the establishment of UNCTAD. The Cairo Summit called upon the international community to restructure the world economy in a manner conducive to the urgent economic development of developing countries. At the Lusaka Summit, Nonaligned countries pledged themselves to actively cultivate the spirit of self-reliance; the initiatives stemming from the Algiers Summit launched Nonaligned countries on a path of asserting that spirit of self-reliance through their collective bargaining strength, based upon the right of permanent sovereignty over natural resources and economic activities, the development of producers' associations and the proclamation in the United Nations of the New International Economic Order.

(2) The Colombo Summit in the view of Heads of State or Government heralds a new phase in which the growing economic potential of Nonaligned and other developing countries, creates a momentum for the establishment of the New International Economic Order with a particular emphasis upon the new international monetary and financial system that is an essential element of that order. In the words of the Chairman of the Conference, Hon. Mrs. Sirimavo Bandaranaike, "If we really and truly want to blunt the weapons of imperialism and colonialism we must surely fashion countervailing weapons in the areas of international money and finance".

(3) The Heads of State or Government declare their commitment to work towards the restructuring of existing systems while inviting the co-operation of the entire international community in the endeavour to develop a democratic equitable and universal monetary and financial system and to establish the New International Economic Order."

Document of the Gatherings of Non-Aligned Countries 1961–1978, Belgrade, 1978.

NONALIGNED COUNTRIES DECLARATION, 1976 OR MANILA DECLARATION. ▷ Manila Group of 77 Declaration, 1976.

NONALIGNED COUNTRIES DECLARATION, 1979 OR HAVANA DECLARATION. The Final Declaration of the Sixth Conference of Heads of State or Government of the Nonaligned Countries, held in Havana, Sept. 3–9, 1979. The Political Part of the Declaration was dedicated to the policy of nonalignment and the strengthening of its independent role. The Economic Part was dedicated to the assessment of the world economic situation and to the New International Economic Order. The Declaration ended with an Action Programme for Economic Co-operation. The text of the preamble of the Declaration follows:

"(1) In its inaugural session the Conference heard an important and wide ranging speech pronounced by his Excellency the President of the Council of State and the Council of Ministers, Commander-in-Chief Fidel Castro, the text of which was included by unanimous decision in the records of the Conference. The speech was an historic contribution to the definition of the objectives of the Movement and an important assistance to the deliberations and final success of the Conference.

(2) The Heads of State or Government welcome the admission of Bolivia, Grenada, Iran, Nicaragua, Pakistan, Surinam and the Patriotic Front of Zimbabwe to the membership of the Movement and of Dominica, the Phillippines, Costs Rica and St. Lucia as observers, and the attendance of Spain as a guest. They consider that these developments are of outstanding historical importance for the strengthening of the policy of nonalignment as the authentic, independent and non-bloc factor. They express their particular satisfaction at the expansion of nonalignment in Latin America and the Caribbean.

(3) The Heads of State or Government of Nonaligned Countries note with particular satisfaction the steady and irreversible growth in the number of nonaligned countries and participants in their gatherings and an ever greater presence and spreading of the policy of nonalignment to all parts of the world. From 25 countries at the First Summit Conference in Belgrade in 1961, the membership of the movement has grown to 95 at the present Sixth Summit in Havana, representing peoples from Africa, Asia, Latin America and Europe and the diversity of economic, social and political systems, thereby confirming the universality of the policy of nonalignment.

(4) It has been confirmed that the spread of nonalignment constitutes, for an ever-increasing number of countries, an indispensable alternative to the policy of total division of the world into blocs. The growth of nonalignment into a broad international movement cutting across racial, regional and other barriers constitutes an integral part of profound changes in the structure of the international community. The fundamental principles of nonalignment, their universal value and the persistent struggle of nonaligned countries for equitable relations among countries and peoples provide, due to their permanent nature inspiration to peoples and countries in their struggle for a world of independence, equality and justice. This is a telling proof of the fact that the policy of nonalignment constitutes a true expression of the interests and aspirations of an ever-larger number of countries and peoples of the world, as well as of the appreciation of the significance and effectiveness of the policy and movement of nonalignment in the entire sphere of international relations.

(5) The Heads of State or Government of the Nonaligned Countries expressed their profound satisfaction at meeting in Latin America for the first time and appreciated the special significance of this singular occasion. They recalled that, at the First Summit Conference held in Belgrade in 1961, when the Movement of Nonaligned Countries was founded, Cuba was the only Latin America and Caribbean country among its members, while Bolivia, Brazil and Ecuador were observers. Latin America has been the scene of constant strife as its peoples have sought to win full independence, eliminate colonialism in the region, affirm their sovereignty, recover their natural resources, promote economic and social development, defend their cultural heritage, and play an active independent role in international life. The battle has deep roots in the history of Latin America, which initiated its efforts to obtain independence at the beginning of the nineteenth century. Marked by victories and setbacks, it has followed an ascending course. In the last few years, Caribbean countries have obtained their independence and have joined the Movement of Nonaligned Countries. The history-making victory of the people of Nicaragua constitutes an encouraging event for the whole region. This has allowed the peoples of Latin America and the Caribbean to play an increasing dynamic role alongside their African and Asian brothers and sisters and with all the peoples of the world in the common struggle against imperialism, colonialism, neo-colonialism, expansionism, racism, including zionism, apartheid, exploitation, power politics and all forms and manifestations of foreign occupation, domination and hegemony. Eleven Latin America and Caribbean countries are now full members of the Movement and 10 participate as observers; the Movement activities evoke attention and respect throughout the area.

(6) Meeting in Havana 18 years after its founding, the Movement of Nonaligned Countries is aware of its responsibilities and has confirmed its perspectives set forth in its Summit Conferences in Belgrade, Cairo, Lusaka, Algiers and Colombo. The Nonaligned Movement represents countries determined to defend interdependence, free national and social development, sovereignty, security, equality, self-determination and to change the existing system of international relations based on injustice, inequality and exploitation. The Movement represents an overwhelming majority of mankind which is struggling to eliminate the inequalities between the developed and developing countries and to eradicate poverty, hunger, sickness and illiteracy and to establish a new world order based on justice, equity and peace instead of the present order in which wealth is still concentrated in the hands of a few powers whose wasteful economies are maintained by the exploitation of the

labour as well as the transfer and plunder of the natural and other resources of the peoples of Africa, Asia, Latin America and other regions of the world.

(7) This contrast means in practice the perpetuation of the old colonial relations in their original form or under various disguises or attempts at the imposition of new relations of dependence and subjugation. The peoples' freedom and independence will not be truly consolidated until the state of domination, dependency and exploitation is ended. Freedom will not be complete until effective control of resources and natural wealth is assured and independent economic development is ensured; and until the peoples are guaranteed suitable and decent living conditions. Security will not be permanent until principles of non-interference in the internal affairs of states, sovereignty, territorial integrity and independence are respected and until the full independence of all countries and peoples is ensured.

(8) The Movement of Nonaligned Countries represents the hopes, aspirations and will of millions of human beings who have been deprived of freedom and the right to decide their own destiny, who have suffered from a long and painful colonial experience and foreign domination and who for centuries have endured servitude and humiliation, tyranny and poverty, hunger and ignorance. Our peoples have struggled generation after generation, with growing success, to emancipate themselves and open the way to a new, free, worthy and prosperous life. They have advanced along the path towards their total aspirations, but there is still a long way to go. The nonaligned countries renew their pledge to continue struggling until they attain a world based on justice and freedom, and establish an international political and economic order governed by peace, independence, equality and co-operation against all obstacles and forces which aim at maintaining old or imposing new forms of unequal relationships and domination, and which have hindered the establishment of the New International Economic Order.

(9) This strong desire reflects the interests of all the peoples and is in accord with the principles and purposes of the United Nations Charter. The Sixth Conference of Heads of State or Government appeals to all peoples of the world to participate in efforts to free the world from war, the policy of force, blocs and bloc politics, military bases, pacts and interlocking alliances, the policy of domination and hegemony, inequalities and oppression, injustice and poverty and to create a new order based on peaceful coexistence, mutual co-operation and friendship, an order in which each people may determine its own future, attain its political sovereignty and promote its own free economic and social development, without interference, pressures or threats of any kind.

(10) The Movement of Nonaligned Countries, which emerged in the midst of the breakdown of the colonial system and during the emancipation struggle of the peoples of Africa, Asia, Latin America and other regions of the world, and at the height of the Cold War, has been an essential factor in the decolonization process that has led to the achievement of freedom and independence by many countries and peoples, the emergence of dozens of sovereign states, and in the preservation of world peace. This struggle for total emancipation received a historic impetus from the emergence of newly liberated countries which have opted for an independent political development and have resolutely rejected polarization on bloc bases, bloc policies, military pacts or military alliances, as well as policies tending to divide the world into spheres of influence or impose any other form of domination. Ever since its inception, the Movement of Nonaligned Countries have waged a constant battle to guarantee that the peoples oppressed by alien occupation and domination may exercise their inalienable right to self-determination and independence; it has joined forces to seek the establishment of a new international economic order that will permit the peoples to enjoy their wealth and natural resources and achieve a higher standard of living, offering a comprehensive platform for a basic change in international economic relations and for full economic emancipation; and it has played a decisive role in the efforts to maintain peace, promote international detente and eliminate focal points of aggression and tension everywhere in the world, and in promoting just solutions to international problems. However, there are still dangerous situations and serious obstacles that oblige them to strengthen their unity, cohesion and co-

operation to face these common dangers and overcome these obstacles.

(11) Taking into consideration the principles on which nonalignment has been based and the elaboration of those principles through the successive Summit Conferences held in Belgrade, Cairo, Lusaka, Algiers and Colombo, the Sixth Conference reaffirmed that the quintessence of the policy of nonalignment, in accordance with its original principles and essential character, involves the struggle against imperialism, colonialism, neo-colonialism, apartheid, racism, including zionism and all forms of foreign aggression, occupation, domination, interference or hegemony, as well as against great-Power and bloc policies. In other words, the rejection of all forms of subjugation, dependency, interference or intervention, direct or indirect, and of all pressures, whether political, economic, military or cultural, in international relations.

(12) Recalling these fundamental goals and purposes of the Movement which have guided it since its inception in 1961 the Heads of State and/or Government reaffirmed their adherence in particular to the following principles:

National independence, sovereignty and territorial integrity, sovereign equality, and the free social development of all countries; independence of nonaligned countries from great-Power or bloc rivalries and influences and opposition to participation in military pacts and alliances arising therefrom; the struggle against imperialism, colonialism, neo-colonialism, racism including zionism and all forms of expansionism, foreign occupation and domination and hegemony; active peaceful co-existence among all States; indivisibility of peace and security; non-interference and non-interference in the internal and external affairs of other countries; freedom of all states to determine their political systems and pursue economic, social and cultural development without intimidation, hindrance and pressure; establishment of a new international economic order and development of international co-operation on the basis of equality; the right to self-determination and independence of all peoples under colonial and alien domination and constant support to the struggle of national liberation movements; respect for human rights and fundamental freedoms; opposition to the division of the world into antagonistic military-political alliances and blocs and rejection of outmoded doctrines such as spheres of influence and balance of terror; permanent sovereignty over natural resources; inviolability of legally established international boundaries; non-use of force or threat of use of force and non-recognition of situations brought about by the threat or use of force; and peaceful settlement of disputes.

Basing themselves on the above-mentioned principles, the Heads of State and/or Government considered the following to be essential objectives of the Nonaligned Movement:

Preservation of the national independence, sovereignty, territorial integrity and security of nonaligned countries; elimination of foreign interference and intervention in the internal and external affairs of states and the use of the threat of force; strengthening of nonalignment as an independent non-bloc factor and the further spread of nonalignment in the world; elimination of colonialism, neo-colonialism and racism, including zionism, and support to national liberation movements struggling against colonial and alien domination and foreign occupation; elimination of imperialistic and hegemonistic policies and all other forms of expansionism and foreign domination; safeguarding international peace and security and the universalization of the relaxation of international tensions; promotion of unity, solidarity and co-operation among nonaligned countries with a view to the achievement of the objectives of nonalignment thus preserving its essential character; ending the arms race, particularly the nuclear arms race and the achievement of general and complete disarmament under effective international control; the early establishment of the New International Economic Order with a view to accelerating the development of developing countries, eliminating the inequality between developed and developing countries and the eradication of poverty, hunger, sickness and illiteracy in the developing countries; participation on the basis of equality in solving international issues; establishment of a democratic system of international relations based on the equality of states, respect for and preservation of human rights and fundamental freedoms; the strengthening of the United Nations as an effective instrument for promoting international peace and security, resolving international problems, the struggle against colonialism, neo-colonialism, racism, zionism, racial discrimination and apartheid and as an important factor in the development of international co-operation and the establishment of equitable economic relations between states; dissolution of great-Power pacts and military alliances and interlocking arrangements arising therefrom, withdrawal of foreign military forces and dismantling of foreign military bases; promotion of economic co-operation among the nonaligned and other developing countries with a view to the achievement of collective self-reliance; establishment of a new international order in the field of information and mass media for the purpose of forging new international relations in general; and revival, preservation and enrichment of the cultural heritage of the peoples of nonaligned countries and promotion of cultural co-operation among them.

(13) The Heads of State or Government of Nonaligned Countries believe that events over the past three decades have demonstrated the validity of the principles of nonalignment. They therefore stress emphatically that adherence to all these principles requires action that is consistent with the objectives underlying the philosophy of the movement.

(14) The Heads of State or Government of Nonaligned Countries, accordingly, rededicate themselves to translating these principles into action. They solemnly pledge to undertake all the necessary steps for the realization of the above objectives. They are convinced that only through concerted action can the objectives be attained.

(15) They stress that the commitment to nonalignment entails respect for and the observance of the above principles as well as the undertaking of concrete measures in order to further reinforce the well-founded principles.

(16) In the context of the above principles and objectives, the Heads of State and/or Government of non-aligned countries reaffirm the following criteria for participation in the Movement as members agreed upon in 1961:

(i) The country should have adopted an independent policy based on the coexistence of states with different political and social systems and on nonalignment or should be showing a trend in favour of such a policy.
(ii) The country concerned should be consistently supporting the movements for national independence.
(iii) The country should not be a member of a multilateral military alliance concluded in the context of great-Power conflicts.
(iv) If a country has a bilateral military agreement with a great Power, or is a member of a regional defence pact, the agreement or pact should not be one deliberately concluded in the context of great-Power conflicts.
(v) If it has conceded military bases to a foreign Power, the concession should not have been made in the context of great-Power conflicts.

(17) The policy of nonalignment, by acting as an independent global factor, represents an important step in mankind's search for freely established, peaceful and equitable relations among nations, irrespective of their size, geographic location, power or social systems.

(18) The Conference considered that unity and mutual solidarity among the nonaligned countries were indispensable for maintaining the independence and strength of the Movement and for the realization of its objectives. Over a period of nearly two decades the Movement of Nonaligned Countries has brought together a growing number of states and liberation movements, which despite their ideological, political, economic, social and cultural diversity, have accepted these fundamental principles and have shown their readiness to translate them into reality.

(19) The nonaligned countries have demonstrated their ability through democratic dialogue, to overcome their differences and to find a common denominator for action leading to mutual co-operation.

(20) Meeting in Havana, the Conference confirmed that the policy of nonalignment constituted an important and indispensable factor in the struggle for freedom and independence of all peoples and countries; for world peace and security for all states; for the universal application of active peaceful co-existence;

for the democratization of international relation; for the establishment for the New International Economic Order; and for economic development and social progress. The Conference acknowledges the co-operation received by nonaligned countries from other peace, freedom and justice-loving, democratic and progressive states and forces in the achievement of their goals and objectives, and expresses its readiness to continue to co-operate with them on the basis of equality."

Final Declaration of the Sixth Conference of Heads of State or Government of the Nonaligned Countries, Havana, 1979.

NONALIGNED COUNTRIES DECLARATION, 1983 OR NEW DELHI DECLARATION.

A final declaration on political and economic issues, adopted with acclamation by the Seventh Conference of the Heads of States or Governments of Nonaligned Countries in New Delhi, March 7-12, 1983. The highlights of the Declaration.

The political part of the summit declaration has demanded an immediate prohibition of use or threat of use of nuclear weapons pending achievement of nuclear disarmament. It asks nuclear powers to give a guarantee that other countries will not be threatened or attacked by nuclear weapons. It says that a treaty should also be concluded to ban chemical weapons.

The economic part of the declaration gives a detailed analysis of the reasons for the present economic crisis and suggests several steps to meet the immediate requirements and long term measures for the economic situation. The summit requested Mrs Gandhi, along with a representative group of non-aligned countries to visit selected capitals of developed countries and to explain to their leaders the substance of the New Delhi declaration.

The summit called for the convening of an international conference on money and finance for development, with universal participation. The summit also decided to propose the convening of a conference within the framework of the United Nations to launch global negotiations. After a review of the worsening world economic situation, Heads of State or Government stressed the need to create a new, equitable and universal international monetary system.

KEESING's *Contemporary Archive; Indian and Foreign Review*, March, 1983.

NONALIGNED COUNTRIES DECLARATION, 1989 OR BELGRADE DECLARATION.

The text is as follows:

The Heads of State or Government of Nonaligned Countries at their Ninth Conference held in Belgrade, September 4–7, 1989.
Aware that the present stage of mankind's development is distinctive for its technological, economic and political changes, making overall progress possible, but at the same time also for its many obstacles, old and new, to the building of a more peaceful, secure, just, equitable, democratic and humane world.
Bearing in mind the role and responsibility of non-aligned countries to make their maximum contribution towards safeguarding peace and promoting co-operation for the development of all countries and thus paving the way for the well-being of nations and peoples based on peace, equity and justice.
Inspired by the principles and objectives of non-alignment, reaffirming their lasting validity, drawing upon the Movement's experience, aware of its invaluable contribution to international developments and of its even greater potentials today.
Declare:

(1) The world is at a crossroads: tension is no longer at breaking point but neither is peace stable; stagnation is not general but neither is development. While there may be reason for hope, there is no cause for undue optimism. The world must decide which way to turn, as we face new challenges as well as new opportunities.
(2) Scientific and technological advances, as well as shared tribulations, increase global interdependence. But they have yet to quench aspirations towards freedom, independence and national identity. Equality rather than domination and subordination should form the basis of interdependence. The irreversible and en-

couraging integration processes now asserting themselves ought to be in the interest of all and not aimed at establishing new hegemonies. The present asymmetry in economic and technological development can only be redressed through a balanced development of the entire international community and through efforts aimed at the broadest possible democratization of international relations.
(3) The world political climate has improved, although not sufficiently. Encouraging progress has been made towards finding solutions to regional and global problems wherein the non-aligned countries have rendered a substantive contribution. There has been a ferment of new economic and political ideas in many parts of the world. These provide a propitious setting for fresh initiatives. On the other hand, if economic imperatives and particularly the requirements of developing countries are not accommodated, the resulting strains may very well undermine the current trends towards global peace and harmony. A detente devoid of economic content is unlikely to endure.
(4) Many countries in the world today are undertaking wide-ranging policy reforms in an effort to adapt to the realities of a rapidly changing world. A greater degree of openness and co-operation is vital for the success of the trend towards global integration.
(5) The pursuit of complete disarmament, especially in weapons of mass destruction, is imperative since it is necessary for securing the very existence of the human race on our planet. The somber contrast between enormous military expenditure and dire poverty underlines the importance of giving concrete shape to the concept of the link between disarmament and development. Given enhanced disarmament prospects, new opportunities are opening for all countries, especially those possessing the largest nuclear and conventional arsenals, for rechannelling additional financial resources, human energy and creativity into development. The close relationship between disarmament and development must be seen as a contribution to the wider efforts to give precedence to economic development over the priorities imposed by the dangerous and irrational race for military might.
(6) The non-aligned countries do not pretend, nor are they in a position, to change the world by themselves; but neither can the world be reshaped without them. The non-aligned favour concordance rather than confrontation, regardless of whether common problems of mankind or issues of regional interests are involved. The non-aligned countries stand ready to take active part in their accommodation and resolution, proceeding from the policy and objectives of non-alignment and from the principles and purposes of the United Nations Charter, which are mankind's historical legacy and the imperative of humanity.
(7) The major military–political alliances, the chief protagonists of the cold war are still present, though their cohesion and continuing relevance are being seriously questioned. Although the threat of bloc confrontation has receded, no stable peace is yet in sight.
(8) The Soviet Union and the United States have embarked upon the path of reducing their huge military arsenals and armed forces. They are also engaged in a wide-ranging dialogue, designed to improve their mutual relations which leads to the easing of world tension. The resulting detente is a window of opportunity for the international community. It is above all based on the realization of the impending danger to the survival of human species posed by the nuclear arms race, by other military and non-military threats to security such as armed conflicts, occupation, use of force, gross economic inequality both within and among nations, poverty, hunger, deprivation, debt burden, disease, drug abuse and all forms of terrorism, as well as by the degradation of the environment. The solution of such vast and complex problems calls for a concreted and coherent approach within a multilateral framework.
(9) Some focal points of crisis in the present day world are of a long-standing nature. These conflicts which more often than not have deep-lying regional causes are aggravated and acquire new dimensions by interference, intervention and involvement of outside powers. The resultant conflicts undermine international relations, cause great human suffering and prevent the international community from addressing the major problems of today. That is why the Non-Aligned Movement is determined to participate actively in all efforts

towards a successful resolution of hot beds of crises in the world, irrespective of their historical or contemporary causes, ensuring that solutions are not imposed by outside powers to the detriment of the interests of the parties directly concerned. In this context, the Nonaligned Countries particularly express the solidarity with all those peoples who have not yet exercised their right to self-determination.

(10) Economic situation in the vast majority of the developing countries has deteriorated dramatically, especially in the least developed ones. They suffocate under the outflow of capital and their diminishing purchasing power. Accelerated economic and social development of developing countries is not only an imperative necessity for them but is also in the interest of the world. Even fifteen years after its proclamation, the New International Economic Order remains a difficult but valid goal. The fruits of development should benefit the largest segments of the population. What is needed are structural adjustments in all spheres, in accordance with the development objectives and priorities, of developing countries in order to respond to the challenges of advanced technology, specially the technology of tomorrow. The developed countries, for their part, should not overlook the fact that their affluence is not assured once and for all nor can it remain stable in an overall impoverished global environment. We appeal to the developed world to face, with maximum will and determination and without prejudice, the conflict which is older and deeper than the cold war and bloc confrontation – the conflict between affluence and poverty.

(11) Growing environmental problems, which pose a threat to the very survival of mankind, testify to the interdependence of interests of all nations. We all suffer the consequences of environmental degradation. There is no doubt that the advanced countries have contributed the most to the dramatic increase of that threat. These countries also have the resources and technology to cope with the problem. In developing countries, protection of the environment has to be seen as an integral part of the development process. Initial, albeit insufficient, international efforts are being made to study and remove the menace to the environment. Our Movement and our countries stand ready to make their fullest possible contribution to this end. It is important, however, that such international co-operation should be based on full respect for the sovereignty of States.

(12) The important process of decolonization from which a large number of sovereign States have emerged – most of whom are members of the Movement today – is entering a decisive stage. While expressing our satisfaction with this epochal achievement to whose inevitable but dearly paid triumph we have contributed a great deal, we cannot but be acutely conscious that not all forms of dependence, particularly economic dependence, have disappeared with the accession of nations to independence and that there are still peoples suffering under colonial bondage or barely disguised non-colonialism. The total eradication of colonialism and economic emancipation of all peoples as an indispensable precondition for maintaining and strengthening their political independence, remains a priority task of our Movement.

(13) Racism and discrimination based on colour, creed, ethnic origin, culture or way of life are still practised in this age which has all the possibilities to become an era of true reason, human dignity and freedom. Racism and discrimination have always been regarded by the Movement as historical anachronisms and a disgrace to our civilization. In the vision of a more humane and more democratic world, there can be no room for any form of racism and of national, religious or any other form of intolerance.

We recognise that Apartheid is a particular and repugnant form of institutionalized racism which civilized nations have rightly condemned as a crime against humanity. We shall accordingly increase, widen, intensify and tighten the sanctions aimed at isolating the abhorent apartheid regime, and eradicating the apartheid system. We call upon the community of nations to join us in this important undertaking.

(14) It is a truism that all forms of terrorism, including state terrorism, violate the fundamental rights of the individual, threaten stability within and among nations and deserve to be universally condemned and countered by every legal means possible.

(15) Illicit drug trafficking, unabated production, demand for drugs, and increased terrorism associated with them, have assumed dangerous proportions. The principle of shared responsibility is a fundamental element in the struggle against this curse.

(16) Notwithstanding all the challenges, the United Nations system has stood the test of time. Even those who tended to ignore the United Nations as a forum for collective action by States, increasingly realize that the World Organization is an irreplaceable instrument for regulating international relations and resolving international problems that concern all. Without the United Nations, it would not be possible to realize the fullest and broadest possible democratization of international relations, which has always been one of the primary objectives of the Movement. Our countries and our Movement have contributed towards expanding the activities of the United Nations aimed at eliminating the causes of war, promoting development and restoring faith in the dignity of the human person and of nations. Peace and harmony among peoples and nations require strict observance and further enhancement of international law. In this context the outcome of the recent meeting of Nonaligned Countries at the Hague and its initiative for the Decade of International Law represents an important contribution.

(17) In the endeavors to formulate a strategy that will enable our movement to exert a more active influence on the world situation and on international relations and to create the best possible conditions for the development of our countries on the eve of the 21st century, the collective vision of the great founding fathers of non alignment continues to serve as an inexhaustible source of inspiration. Strong support for the validity of our action can be found in the contribution we have made to changing the world and in the uninterrupted continuity from Belgrade in 1961, Cairo in 1964, Lusaka in 1970, Algiers in 1973, Colombo in 1976, Havana in 1979, New Delhi in 1983, Harare in 1986, to Belgrade in 1989.

(18) We opposed bloc divisions and confrontation which carried the risk of nuclear annihilation and impeded the struggle of peoples for national liberation. At the time of sharp ideological divisions, we created a movement based on the principle of ideological pluralism and advocated peaceful coexistence in international affairs, which today constitutes the basis of negotiations and accommodation between the great powers and other major actors in international relations. The call given by our Movement to halt and reverse the arms race has in no small measure led to the current actions and efforts aimed at establishing a more stable and peaceful world. Without our historical contribution to the successful implementation of the decolonization process, the emerging multipolarity of the world characterized by growing interdependence of all members of the international community – would be inconceivable. Our faith in the power of negotiations and co-operation is today being brought to bear on the ongoing efforts to resolve focal points of crisis through respect for the legitimate interests of all parties involved. The sense of justice imbuing our peoples and the aspirations of our countries to progress, acting as a driving force in their quest for a better world, cannot countenance inequities and discrimination of any kind, anywhere. Still less can they reconcile themselves to enormous differences in economic development and prosperity becoming the tragic and persisting destiny of mankind.

(19) Following the example of our great predecessors who had the capacity to anticipate and the courage to change, we set ourselves the formidable task to assess critically and comprehensively our position and role in the present-day world of transition and change and to identify a realistic order of priorities in pursuing, on the basis of our principles, the objectives of our Movement.

(20) Guided by the vital interest of our countries to safeguard the freedom of action and to bring about fundamental changes in the existing system of international political and economic relations, our credo during the period of the cold war was not to take part in the divisions that were being imposed.

Now that the world is becoming multipolar and is increasingly integrating, our basic interests and the need to enhance the effectiveness of the Movement, demand that we play an active and direct role in the management of world affairs. Only in such a way can we partake fully in the process of economic and technological advancement leading towards greater interdependence and integration of the world.

(21) Our active participation in and comprehensive contribution to the ongoing development processes and trends at the global, regional and subregional levels, and our widening association, with all countries or groups of countries sharing with us basic perceptions of and aims regarding these processes and trends at the global, regional and sub-regional levels and the concept of nonalignment.

(22) In responding to the challenges of a changing world, we are not to be burdened with prejudice or dogma. That was never a trait of our Movement. We were the first to draw attention to the untenability of the postulates of the cold war. Our approach to the contemporary phenomena and development is to be realistic, far-sighted and creative so that we can live up to the historical mission of our Movement and act as the authentic interpreters of the interests of our countries.

(23) This also calls for more effective actions on our part and for improved functioning. In the past, the Nonaligned Countries shunned the false notion that their action would be strengthened by the creation of a third bloc. They never accepted anything that would endanger the democratic character of the Movement and the relationships of equality inherent in it. It is of vital importance, however, to constantly explore new avenues and improve methods of action in order to enhance the efficiency of our Movement.

II

Strengthened by our past achievements in the struggle against imperialism, colonialism, neo-colonialism, racism, Apartheid and all forms of domination, inspired by the challenges and demands that we face today as nations and as a Movement, and guided by the principles and concept of the policy of nonalignment in our efforts to achieve a world of peace, equality, co-operation and well-being for all, we have agreed to act in conformity with the following priorities in our joint endeavors.

First, until an enduring and stable peace based on a comprehensive, viable and readily implementable structure of international security is established, peace, achievement of disarmament and settlement of disputes by peaceful means, continue to be our first and foremost task.

We have contributed to the creation of international conditions conducive to the elimination of the causes and the horror of war. The general rapprochement between the United States of America and the Union of Soviet Socialist Republics contributes to the relaxation of international tensions and the creation of basic prerequisites for establishing lasting peace. We are encouraged by the positive development in the field of disarmament brought about by the INF treaty. We are however concerned by the recent loss of momentum in nuclear disarmament. The history of disamament negotiations abounds with instances of missed opportunities. The world is still threatened by the massive nuclear arsenals which are being further refined and added to. The only hope for nuclear disarmament lies in discarding the balance of fear and in the nuclear weapon powers embracing the objective of the total elimination of nuclear weapons. We are fully aware of the fact that both nuclear and conventional disarmament cannot be accomplished without the participation of all international factors.

Second, we are desirous to engage in a joint search for effective and acceptable solutions to the outstanding problems in international economic relations. We are prepared to establish a constructive and productive dialogue with the developed world on economic issues affecting not only the interest of our countries but of the international community as a whole. There can be no stability nor better prospects for the world without reducing the disparities in the level of global development.

The task facing us will become much easier if it is undertaken in the context of an expanding and growing world economy. The major challenge is to work out a package of policy which would ensure the return of the world economy to higher rates of growth. Sustained growth in the world economy can be ensured only if all its constituent parts grow in harmony.

Accelerating development requires above all a substantial increase in the net transfer of resources to developing countries, especially to the least developed ones, a lasting and comprehensive solution to the problem of external indebtedness of developing countries, liberation of world trade by the removal of protectionist barriers and remunerative commodity prices and stable monetary conditions.

We are not unmindful of our own responsibility for the efficient functioning of the economies of our countries. Our efforts cannot succeed without strengthening our mutual co-operation. To this end, supportive international economic environment is vital. Also without establishing ties and dialogue with the developed world there can be no solution to economic problems facing our countries. We are looking forward to the contribution of the South Commission on all these issues.

Rapid advances in science and technology are having an enormous impact on overall world developments. Hence it is of paramount importance for the Movement to seek and ensure closer co-operation in this field in the South–South as well as North–South context. Transfer of technology has become imperative for securing rapid economic development.

The management of the world economy needs to be more broad-based so as to reflect the interests of all countries and groups of countries and evolve policies which can be supported by all. The current economic and social problems and needs of the future are such that no single nation or group of nations can solve them in isolation. They call for a collective effort based on a mutuality of interest. Regular North–South consultations at the summit level on international economic issues are essential for ensuring equitable and collective management of global interdependence.

The Nonaligned Countries strongly support the efforts exerted in co-ordination with other developing countries within the Group of 77. They welcome in this regard the readiness of the developing countries, expressed in the Caracas Declaration of 23 June 1989, for integration in the world economy and their commitment to engage in a serious and constructive dialogue with the aim of strengthening international solidarity and co-operation for development. We strongly urge the developed countries to respond positively to this initiative.

Third, we reaffirm our support for the right of all peoples living under colonial or alien domination and foreign occupation to self-determination and independence. It is inconceivable that at the dawn of the 21st century, over twenty territories and millions of people still live under those conditions. Through our Movement's initiative, the United Nations has declared the last decade of the present century as the Decade for the Eradication of Colonialism, a goal which we consider to be a moral obligation for all mankind. We further reaffirm the need to strengthen our solidarity with nonaligned and other countries facing aggression, intervention or interference in their internal affairs.

Fourth, as we approach the 21st century, protection of the environment has emerged as a major global concern, dramatically emphasizing the growing interdependence of the world. This calls for urgent co-operative measures and global compact ensuring a sustainable and environmentally sound development. Such co-operation should take place within the overall framework of the objective of reviving growth, creating a healthy, clean and sound environment and meeting the basic needs of all. Multilateral approaches need to emphasize supportive measures while seeking to redress existing asymmetries. The international community must set aside net additional financial resources for environmental co-operation and facilitate developing countries' access to environmentally safe technologies. A grave danger to our ecosystem comes from indiscriminate dumping of toxic and other hazardous waste on our territories carried out without any regard to their consequential devastating effect on the environment. We demand an immediate halt to such practices. No one should dispose of nuclear nor any other toxic waste on the territories of other countries or in the open seas.

In the conviction that the very future of mankind hinges on the protection of the environment, we are ready to do our own share to check and prevent the pollution of water, land and air. Land degradation, deforestation, water and air pollution, desertification, result from, among other causes, excessive pressure on natural resources, and because of poverty, ignorance and rising population. There exist broad possibilities for joint action aimed at protecting and promoting the environ-

ment at the level of the entire international community within the context of a comprehensive developmental effort. We shall make our contribution to that end.

Fifth, it is only in this century, through the process of decolonization, the effort within the United Nations to apply democratic norms in state relations, and the creation of adequate economic conditions, that the prerequisites for realizing fundamental human rights and freedoms have been provided. In implementing the principles and objectives of our Movement, we have contributed significantly to the creation of conditions conducive to the promotion of human rights in the contemporary international society. We consider the right of every individual to fully enjoy civil, political, economic, social and cultural rights to be the source of the greatest inspiration to our Movement. We reaffirm the valuable contribution of all women, and strongly support their aspirations towards the recognition of their rights. We particularly underscore the need for greater efforts for the full integration of women in our development processes. The promotion of human rights and freedom is one of the basic objectives of our Movement.

Sixth, our countries and our Movement will continue to contribute towards having the United Nations serve as a truly democratic representative of the entire international community, toward expanding its activities aimed at eliminating the causes of war, promoting growth and prosperity and restoring faith in the dignity of the human person and of nations. Together with other member countries, we pledge to strive for the strengthening of the role and effectiveness of the United Nations so that it can fully discharge its legitimate responsibility of resolving all major problems, including those of the rising dangers of drug abuse and all forms of terrorism, facing the world today. For this purpose, we shall endeavor to ensure that the machinery of the United Nations is reinforced, and its activities effectively co-ordinated. Multilateralism, of which the United Nations is the centrepiece has a growing role to play both at the global and regional levels.

Inspired by their great vision, the leaders of the Nonaligned Countries defined in the Belgrade Declaration of 1961 the fundamental goals of the Movement which they founded at that time, as a transition from the old order based on domination, to a new order based on freedom, equality and social justice, and the promotion of the well-being of all. To these goals of non-alignment we, Heads of State or Government, assembled once again in Belgrade after almost three decades, have nothing to add or subtract. We have been striving and will continue to strive for a world of peace, freedom, justice and prosperity for all. We have never assumed to hold the monopoly of these aims. We have never believed that we should be satisfied with what we have accomplished. We have never held the view that these noble goals and ideals can be achieved without dialogue and co-operation with countries outside our Movement. We shall seek every opportunity to engage in such dialogue and co-operation for the realization of the cherished goals of our Movement – and indeed – of entire humankind.

The world must become a common home in which all will have their rights, their obligations and responsibilities.

We are aware of ours.

To achieve these goals, we adopt the following political and economic documents which, together with this Declaration, constitute the Final documents of the Conference and a framework for future action.

Review of International Affairs, Vol. XL, Belgrade 1989.

NONALIGNED COUNTRIES SUMMIT MEETINGS ▷ Nonaligned Countries Conference of Heads of State, 1961–1989.

NONALIGNMENT. An international term for the policy of countries which avoided commitment to any of the military blocs. These countries, called nonaligned countries, since 1961 have been organizing, on the initiative of Egypt, India and Yugoslavia, conferences of nonaligned countries. ▷ Group of 77.

P. WILLETS, *The Non-Aligned Movement*, New York, 1978; *Addresses delivered at the Sixth Conference of Heads of State of Government of Non-Alignment*

Countries, La Habana, 1979; A.W. SINGHAM, S. HUNE, *Non-Alignment in an Age of Alignment*, London, 1986; M.S. RAJAN ed., *The Non-Aligned and the United Nations*, New Delhi, 1988.

NONALIGNMENT POLICY. An international term for the foreign policy of states not belonging to military blocs and which avoid taking any side in international conflicts but are active in peace initiatives.

Documents of the Gatherings of Nonaligned Countries 1961–1978, Belgrade, 1980.

NON-ATOMIC STATES. States which do not possess nuclear weapons, the security of which became an international problem for atomic powers during the preparation of the Agreement on Non-Proliferation of Nuclear Weapons. In 1968 three atomic powers, the UK, USA and USSR, declared their intention to render immediate assistance to any non-atomic state which might become the target of atomic aggression or might be threatened with such aggression; confirmed by the UN Security Council on June 19, 1968. In response to resolutions of the UN General Assembly of Nov. 17 and Dec. 19, 1967, a Conference of Non-Atomic States was held from Aug. 29 to Sept. 28, 1968 in Geneva, with 94 states participating (atomic powers attended as observers), devoted to security matters and use of nuclear energy for peaceful purposes. ▷ Nuclear peace.

UN Monthly Chronicle, No. 10, 1968.

NON-CITIZEN RIGHTS. ▷ Citizenship.

NON-ENTANGLING ALLIANCES DOCTRINE, 1796. The fundamental doctrine of American ▷ isolationism, formulated by George Washington (1732–99) in the Farewell Address of Sept. 19, 1796, not to entangle the peace and prosperity of United States "in the toils of European ambition, rivalship, interest, humor or caprice."

J.C. FITZPATRICK (ed.), *George Washington's Writings*, 39 Vols, Washington, DC, 1931–44; M. CUNLIFFE, *George Washington: Man and Monument*, New York, 1958.

NON-FERROUS METALS. A subject of international co-operation. Organizations reg. with the UIA:

International Conference of Non-Ferrous Metal Manufacturers, f. 1975, London.
Liaison Committee of the Non-Ferrous Metal Trade in the EEC Countries, f. 1961, Brussels.

Yearbook of International Organizations.

NON-GOVERNMENTAL ORGANIZATIONS, NGO. A non-governmental organization, according to the UN, is any international organization not established by intergovernmental agreement. The register of NGOs is run on UN recommendation and in accordance with the ECOSOC criteria by the Union of International Associations, UIA, which publishes *Yearbook of International Organizations*. The organizations registered with the UIA are classified according to their utility to provide Specialized Agencies of the UN with consultation in their particular field in keeping with art. 71 of the UN Charter. ECOSOC set up Committee on Non-Governmental Organizations, whose sessions May 21–Dec. 15, 1946, Mar. 28–Aug. 16, 1949 and Feb. 27, 1950 drew up principles for consultations of NGOs divided hierarchically into three categories, approved by ECOSOC. The preliminary condition to qualify for consultative status is for an NGO to be of service in ECOSOC's field of interest to act in the spirit of the UN, not to act for profit and to possess the means to implement its objectives.

Organizations in Category I are concerned with most of the Council's activities and are entitled to submit written statements to the Council, to be granted hearings and to propose agenda items for consideration by the Council and its subsidiary bodies. Organizations in Category II are internationally known for specific competence in some areas of the Council's activity. They can submit written statements and can be granted hearings. Organizations which are considered to make occasional contributions to the work of the Council are placed in the third category, known as the Roster. They can only submit written statements. Among the main ECOSOC consultants of category I are: the International Chamber of Commerce, International Co-operative Alliance, International Federation of Agricultural Producers, World Federation of Trade Unions, International Federation of Christian Trade Unions, World Confederation of Labour, International Organization of Employers, Inter-Parliamentary Union, World Federation of Associations of Friends of UN, World Veterans Federation, Federation of Twin Cities, International Federation of Local Authorities, Women's Council, International Federation of Democratic Women, League of Red Cross Societies.

The members of the ECOSOC Committee on NGOs, 1984 were: Chile, Costa Rica, Cuba, Cyprus, France, Ghana, India, Kenya, Libyan Arab Jamahiriya, Nicaragua, Nigeria, Pakistan, Rwanda, Sweden, Thailand, USSR, United Kingdom, United States and Yugoslavia.

L.C. WHITE, *The Structure of Private International Organizations*, London, 1933; *Consultation between the UN and the NGO*, New York, 1949; L.L. LEONARD, *International Organization*, New York, 1953; G.P. SPEECKAERT, *International Institution and International Organization. Select Bibliography*, Brussels, 1956; K.C. GARRIGUE, *A Directory of Non-Governmental Organizations*, New York, 1957; M. POBLETE TRONCOSO, *La Comunidad Internacional Contemporanea. Relaciones y Organismos Internacionales*, Santiago de Chile, 1959; *Nations Unies*, Genève, 1964; H.T. ADAM, *Les Organismes Internationaux Spécialisés*, Paris, 1965; D.C. BLAISDELL, *International Organizations*, New York, 1966; M.B. AKEHURST, *The Law Governing Employment in International Organizations*, New York, 1967; R. PAPINI, *Les Relations entre l'UNESCO et les Organisations Non-Gouvernementaux*, Bruxelles, 1967; K. SKELBAK, *The Growth of International Non-Governmental Organizations in the XX Century in Transnational Relations and World Politics*, Cambridge, Mass., 1972; A.J. PEARLE, *International Organizations, Constitutional Documents*, 5 Vols., The Hague, 1975; *UN Chronicle*, April 1981, p. 26, and April 1983, p. 52.

NON-INTERVENTION, NON-INTERFERENCE.

The fundamental principle of peace and international security contained in the UN Charter, article 2, item 4: "All Members of the UN shall refrain in their international relations from the threat or use of force." And item 7 of the same article: "Nothing contained in the present Charter shall authorize the United Nations to intervene in matters which are essentially within the domestic jurisdiction of any state." The principle of non-interference is one of the principles of peaceful co-existence formulated, i.a. in the Chinese–Indian Treaty of 1954 (▷ Pancha Shila). The first legal document formulating the principle of non-interference is the Constitution of the French Republic of June 24, 1793, which in art. 119 proclaimed that "The French people shall not altogether interfere into affairs of other governments and shall not allow other peoples to interfere into affairs of their government." The principle of non-intervention was not recognized by the 19th century governments as a rule of international law. The Monroe Doctrine announced by the US government in 1823 had a great bearing on the

development of the principle of non-interference; it forbade the powers of the Holy Alliance to interfere into the affairs of the Western Hemisphere. In the 20th century the first international convention on non-intervention was initiated by the ▷ Drago Doctrine, 1902, published at the Hague Peace Conference in 1907, which formed the basis for the adopted convention on the limitation of the use of force to collect debts warranted by contracts.

First bilateral treaties based on the principle of non-intervention were prepared by the government of the USSR in 1921 to be signed with Iran, Afghanistan, Turkey and Mongolia. They contained a formula stating that: "Each of the High Contracting Parties shall renounce and unconditionally refrain from interference into internal affairs of the other Party."

The policy of intervention pursued by the Fascist states of Europe during the interwar period (The German and Italian intervention in Spain – 1936–39) and that of Japan in the Far East in the 1930s resulted in the fact that more and more states began to recognize non-interference as a fundamental rule of international law. At the Seventh International Conference of American States, 1933 in Montevideo, the USA, in compliance with the policy of good-neighborly relations proclaimed in 1933, formally accepted the principle of non-interference and signed, together with other Latin American States, the Convention on Rights and Obligations of States on Dec. 26, 1933, which under art. 8 states:

"No state has the right to interfere into internal or external affairs of another state."

The convention was ratified by all American republics except Argentina, Bolivia, Paraguay and by the USA which objected that art. 8 requires interpretation and definition to be binding in special cases. On Dec. 23, 1936, at the Inter-American Conference on the Consolidation of Peace held in Buenos Aires, the Inter-American Peace Covenant and the Additional Protocol relative to Non-Intervention were signed. They provided that:

"The high Contracting Parties announce that they consider interference by any of the Parties, direct or indirect, into internal affairs or external affairs of any other party inadmissible."

The Eighth Inter-American Conference held Dec. 9–27, 1938 in Lima, prepared and adopted the Declaration of American Principles which in Point 1 made a reference to art. 8 of the Convention of 1933.

World War II exerted an influence on the editing of art. 2, item 7, of the UN Charter done in Spring 1945. The first attempt to undermine the principle of non-interference was the ▷ Larreta Doctrine announced on Nov. 21, 1945, allowing intervention in defense of democracy; rejected by the majority of Latin American states which introduced the principle of non-interference in arts. 15 and 16 of the OAS Charter. On Dec. 21, 1965 the UN General Assembly adopted by 109 votes (with one vote against and Great Britain abstaining) the Declaration on the Inadmissibility of Interference into Internal Affairs of States and on the Protection of Their Independence and Sovereignty. On Nov. 29, 1972 the UN General Assembly adopted Resolution 2936/XXVII on non-use of force in international relations and permanent prohibition of use of nuclear arms.

"The principle of obligatory non-interference into matters which are within the domestic jurisdiction of any state in conformity with the UN Charter" was defined in the ▷ International Law Principles, UN Declaration I and adopted on Oct. 24, 1970 by the UN. The total ban on interference into internal

affairs of other states was a subject of Res. 36/103 on Dec. 9, 1981.

A.S. PIRADOV, G.B. STARZSHENKI, "Printsip nevmeshatelstva vo sovremennom mehzdunarodnom prave", in: *Sovietski yezhegodnik mezhdunarodnogo prava*, Moscow, 1958; A. VAN WYNEN, A.J. THOMAS, *La Non-Intervención. Sus Normas y su Significado en las Americas*, Buenos Aires, 1959; Ch.G. FENWICK, *The Organization of American States. The International Regional System*, Washington, 1963; *UN Monthly Chronicle*, November 1970, and December 1972; *Final Act of the Conference on Security and Co-operation in Europe*, Helsinki, 1975, p. 144.

NON-INTERVENTION UN DECLARATION, 1965.

The Declaration was adopted on Dec. 21, 1965 by the UN General Assembly Resolution 2131/XX. The text is as follows:

"The General Assembly,
Deeply concerned at the gravity of the international situation and the increasing threat soaring over universal peace due to armed intervention and other direct or indirect forms of interference threatening the sovereign personality and the political independence of states,
Considering that the United Nations, according to their aim to eliminate war, threats to the peace and acts of aggression, created an Organization, based on the sovereign equality of states, whose friendly relations would be based on respect for the principle of equal rights and self-determination of peoples and on the obligation of its Members to refrain from the threat or use of force against the territorial integrity or political independence of any state.
Recognizing that, in fulfilment of the principle of self-determination, the General Assembly, by the Declaration on the Granting of Independence to Colonial Countries and Peoples contained in Res. 1514/XV of Dec. 15, 1960, stated its conviction that all peoples have an inalienable right to complete freedom, the exercise of their sovereignty and the integrity of their national territory and that, by virtue of that right, they freely determine their political status and freely pursue their economic, social and cultural development.
Recalling that in the Universal Declaration of Human Rights the Assembly proclaimed that recognition of the inherent dignity and of the equal and inalienable rights of all members of the human family is the foundation of freedom, justice and peace in the world, without distinction of any kind.
Reaffirming the principle of non-intervention, proclaimed in the charters of the Organization of American States, OAS, the League of Arab States, LAS, and of the Organization of African Unity, OAU, and affirmed in the Conferences of Montevideo, Buenos Aires, Chapultepec and Bogota, as well as in the decisions of the Afro-Asian Conference in Bandung, the Conference of Non-Aligned Countries in Belgrade, in the Programme for Peace and International Co-operation adopted at the end of the Cairo Conference of Nonaligned Countries, and in the Declaration on subversion adopted in Accra by the Heads of State or Government of the African States.
Recognizing that full observance of the principle of the non-intervention of states in the internal and external affairs of other states is essential to the fulfilment of the purposes and principles of the United Nations,
Considering that armed intervention is synonymous with aggression, and as such is contrary to the basic principles on which peaceful international co-operation between states should be built,
Considering further that direct intervention, subversion, as well as all forms of indirect intervention are contrary to these principles and, consequently a violation of the Charter of the United Nations,
Mindful that violation of the principle of non-intervention poses a threat to the independence and freedom and normal political, economic, social and cultural development of countries, particularly those which have freed themselves from colonialism, and can pose a serious threat to the maintenance of peace,
Fully aware of the imperative need to create appropriate conditions which would enable all states, and in particular the developing countries, to choose without duress or coercion their own political, economic and social institutions,

In the light of the foregoing considerations, the General Assembly of the United Nations solemnly declares:
(1) No state has the right to intervene, directly or indirectly, for any reason whatever, in the internal or external affairs of any other state. Consequently armed intervention as well as all other forms of interference or attempted threats against the personality of the states or against its political, economic and cultural elements, are condemned;
(2) No State may use or encourage the use of economic, political or any other type of measures to coerce another state in order to obtain from it the subordination of the exercise of its sovereign rights or to secure from it advantages of any kind. Also, no state shall organize, assist, foment, finance, incite or tolerate subversive, terrorist or armed activities directed to the violent overthow of the regime of another state, or interfere in civil strife in another state;
(3) The use of force to deprive peoples of their national identity constitutes a violation of their inalienable rights and of the principle of non-intervention;
(4) The strict observance of these obligations is an essential condition to ensure that the nations live together in peace with one another, since the practice of any form of intervention not only violates the spirit and letter of the Charter but also leads to the creation of situations which threaten international peace and security;
(5) Every state has an inalienable right to choose its political, economic, social and cultural systems, without interference in any form by another State;
(6) All states shall respect the right of self-determination and independence of peoples and nations, to be freely exercised without any foreign pressure, and with absolute respect for human rights and fundamental freedoms. Consequently, all states shall contribute to the complete elimination of racial discrimination and colonialism in all its forms and manifestations;
(7) For the purpose of this Declaration, the term 'State' covers both individual states and groups of states;
(8) Nothing in this Declaration shall be construed as affecting in any manner the relevant provisions of the Charter of the United Nations relating to the maintenance of international peace and security, in particular those contained in Chapter VI, VII and VIII."

UN Yearbook, 1965.

NON-NUCLEAR ENERGY AND THE UN. The UN since 1956 has sponsored research on new sources of non-atomic and non-electric energy, such as eolithic, geothermal and solar energy. In Aug., 1961 the First UN Conference on New Sources of Energy took place in Rome; the Second in 1981.

Proceedings of the UN Conference of New Sources of Energy. Solar Energy, Wind Power and Geothermal Energy, Rome, August 21–23, 1961, New York, 1963.

NON-PROLIFERATION OF NUCLEAR WEAPONS. The subject of an international treaty which was initiated by a memorandum submitted Sept. 15, 1965 to the UN General Assembly by the governments of Brazil, Burma, Ethiopia, India, Mexico, Nigeria, Sweden and the UK. The Memorandum stressed the urgent need for an agreement on non-proliferation. The UN General Assembly on Sept. 24, 1965 placed the item on its agenda for the 20th Session, and the Disarmament Committee began to study two proposals for such a treaty: one submitted by the USA Aug. 17, 1965, and one by the USSR, Sept. 24, 1965; however, despite the UN General Assembly Res. 2028/XX, Nov. 23, 1965, the Commission was not able to agree on a draft. In 1968 the USA and the USSR submitted a joint draft to the Commission which was studied in May–June, 1968 at a Special Session of the Assembly. On June 13, 1968 the UK, USA and the USSR submitted a draft to the UN Security Council for guaranteeing the security of states that would renounce the right to produce and use atomic weapons. The UN General Assembly on June 12, 1968 approved the text of the ▷ Non-Proliferation Treaty by 95 votes in favor, 4 against; Albania, Cuba, Tanzania, and Zambia, and 21 abstentions:

Algeria, Argentina, Brazil, Burma, Burundi, Central African Republic, France, Gabon, Guinea, Guyana, India, Malawi, Mali, Morocco, Mauritania, Portugal, Rwanda, Sierra Leone, Spain, Saudi Arabia, and Uganda. On June 19, 1968 the UN Security Council Res. 255/68 adopted the Declaration of the governments of the UK, USA and the USSR on the matter of the Treaty and the above guarantee. The Treaty was effective from Mar. 5, 1970. The IAEA worked out a new system of monitoring approved in 1971 by the parties to the treaty. The European socialist non-nuclear states joined the Treaty and signed the required agreements with the IAEA, as did the majority of the Third World states. In 1973 the West European states ratified the treaty as members of ▷ EURATOM, and signed an agreement with ▷ IAEA, on Apr. 5, 1973 in Brussels, as required in art. 3 of the Treaty. According to the agreement, EURATOM and IAEA would make inspections in the seven non-nuclear EURATOM states to ascertain that fissionable materials intended for peaceful purposes were not being used for military objectives.
On May 5–30, 1975 the International Conference on the implementation of the Treaty was held in Geneva with the participation of the three big powers that had ratified the Treaty: the USA, USSR and Great Britain and 45 states which until May 1975 had also ratified the Treaty: Afghanistan, Austria, Botswana, Bulgaria, Cameroon, Canada, Costa Rica, Cyprus, Czechoslovakia, Denmark, Ecuador, Ethiopia, Finland, the German Democratic Republic, Hungary, Iraq, Iran, Ireland, Iceland, Jamaica, Jordan, Laos, Malaysia, Mali, Malta, Mauritius, Mexico, Mongolia, Nepal, Nigeria, Norway, New Zealand, Paraguay, Peru, Poland, Romania, Somalia, Swaziland, Syria, Sweden, Taiwan, Togo, Tunisia, Upper Volta, Yugoslavia. Twenty-two states which had ratified the Treaty later: Australia, Belgium, Bolivia, the FRG, Gabon, Ghana, Greece, Honduras, Italy, South Korea, Lebanon, Liberia, Luxembourg, Morocco, the Netherlands, Nicaragua, Philippines, San Marino, Senegal, Sudan, Thailand and the Vatican. Representatives of eight states-signatories which had not ratified the Treaty participated in the Conference, however, without the right to vote: Egypt, Japan, Panama, Switzerland, Trinidad-Tobago, Turkey, Venezuela; observers non-signatories: Argentina, Brazil, Cuba, Israel, South Africa, Spain. The Conference adopted the final declaration without a vote. The Second Conference was held in Geneva in 1980. On Mar. 10, 1978 the US President J. Carter signed the Nuclear Non-proliferation Act. The Act introduced more rigorous control over the US export of nuclear fuels for peaceful purposes, ordering the immediate halting of exports to any state which refuses IAEA control or carries out a nuclear explosion. In its preamble the Act appeals to states which have not ratified the Treaty of 1968 to do so.
Among the states which did not sign and did not ratify the Treaty are i.a.: the People's Republic of China, France, Argentina, Brazil, India, Israel, Pakistan, South Africa. For the full list of parties to the NPT ▷ Non Proliferation Treaty 1968.

UNTS, Vol. 729, pp. 169–175, *The Non-Proliferation of Nuclear Weapons*, London, 1971; G. QUESTER, *The Politics of Nuclear Non-Proliferation*, Baltimore, 1973; *UN Monthly Chronicle*, June 1975, pp. 9–14; SIPRI, *Yearbooks of World Armaments and Disarmament 1968–1984; UN Chronicle*, November, 1980, p. 15; *IAEA Bulletin*, December, 1982, p. 40. and September 1984, pp. 37–40.

NON-PROLIFERATION TREATY, 1968. An agreement on the prevention of wider dissemination of nuclear weapons, called the Nuclear Weapons Non-Proliferation Treaty, was adopted on June 12, 1968 by the UN General Assembly and July 1, 1968 signed in London, Moscow and Washington. The text is as follows:

"The States concluding this Treaty, hereinafter referred to as the Parties to the Treaty,
Considering the devastation that would be visited upon all mankind by a nuclear war and the consequent need to make every effort to avert the danger of such a war and to take measures to safeguard the security of peoples,
Believing that the proliferation of nuclear weapons would seriously enhance the danger of nuclear war,
In conformity with resolutions of the United Nations General Assembly calling for the conclusion of an agreement on the prevention of wider dissemination of nuclear weapons,
Undertaking to co-operate in facilitating the application of International Atomic Energy Agency safeguards on peaceful nuclear activities,
Expressing their support for research, development and other efforts to further the application, within the framework of the International Atomic Energy Agency safeguards system, of the principle of safeguarding effectively the flow of source and special fissionable materials by use of instruments and other techniques at certain strategic points,
Affirming the principle that the benefits of peaceful applications of nuclear technology, including any technological by-products which may be derived by nuclear-weapon states from the development of nuclear explosive devices, should be available for peaceful purposes to all Parties to the Treaty, whether nuclear-weapon or non-nuclear-weapon states,
Convinced that in furtherance of this principle, all Parties to this Treaty are entitled to participate in the fullest possible exchange of scientific information for, and to contribute alone or in co-operation with other states to, the further development of the applications of atomic energy for peaceful purposes.
Declaring their intention to achieve at the earliest possible date the cessation of the nuclear arms race and to undertake effective measures in the direction of nuclear disarmament,
Urging the co-operation of all states in the attainment of this objective,
Recalling the determination expressed by the Parties to the 1963 Treaty banning nuclear weapons tests in the atmosphere, in outer space and under water in its Preamble to seek to achieve the discontinuance of all test explosions of nuclear weapons for all time and to continue negotiations to this end,
Desiring to further the easing of international tension and the strengthening of trust between states in order to facilitate the cessation of the manufacture of nuclear weapons, the liquidation of all their existing stockpiles, and the elimination from national arsenals of nuclear weapons and the means of their delivery pursuant to a Treaty on general and complete disarmament under strict and effective international control,
Recalling that, in accordance with the Charter of the United Nations, states must refrain in their international relations from the threat or use of force against the territorial integrity or political independence of any state, or in any other manner inconsistent with the purposes of the United Nations, and that the establishment and maintenance of international peace and security are to be promoted with the least diversion for armaments of the world's human and economic resources;
Have agreed as follows:
Art. I.
Each nuclear-weapon state Party to this Treaty undertakes not to transfer to any recipient whatsoever nuclear weapons or other nuclear explosive devices or control over such weapons or explosive devices directly, or indirectly; and not in any way to assist, encourage, or induce any non-nuclear-weapon state to manufacture or otherwise acquire nuclear weapons or other nuclear explosive devices, or control over such weapons or explosive devices.
Art. II. Each non-nuclear-weapon state Party to this Treaty undertakes not to receive the transfer from any transferor whatsoever of nuclear weapons or other nuclear explosive devices or of control over such weapons or explosive devices directly, or indirectly; not to manufacture or otherwise acquire nuclear weapons

or other nuclear explosive devices; and not to seek or receive any assistance in the manufacture of nuclear weapons or other nuclear explosive devices.

Art. III. (1) Each non-nuclear-weapon state Party to the Treaty undertakes to accept safeguards, as set forth in an agreement to be negotiated and concluded with the International Atomic Energy Agency in accordance with the Statute of the International Atomic Energy Agency and the Agency's safeguards system, for the exclusive purpose of verification of the fulfilment of its obligations assumed under this Treaty with a view to preventing diversion of nuclear energy from peaceful uses to nuclear weapons or other nuclear explosive devices.

Procedures for the safeguards required by this Article shall be followed with respect to source or special fissionable material whether it is being produced, processed or used in any principal nuclear facility or is outside any such facility. The safeguards required by this Article shall be applied on all source or special fissionable material in all peaceful nuclear activities within the territory of such state, under its jurisdiction, or carried out under its control anywhere.

(2) Each State Party to the Treaty undertakes not to provide: (a) source or special fissionable material, or (b) equipment or material especially designed or prepared for the processing, use or production of special fissionable material, to any non-nuclear-weapon state for peaceful purposes, unless the source or special fissionable material shall be subject to the safe-guards required by this Article.

(3) The safeguards required by this article shall be implemented in a manner designed to comply with article IV of this Treaty, and to avoid hampering the economic or technological development of the Parties or international co-operation in the field of peaceful nuclear activities, including the international exchange of nuclear material and equipment for the processing, use or production of nuclear material for peaceful purposes in accordance with the provisions of this Article and the principle of safeguarding set forth in the Preamble.

(4) Non-nuclear-weapon States Party to the Treaty shall conclude agreements, with the International Atomic Energy Agency to meet the requirements of this Article either individually or together with other States in accordance with the Statute of the International Atomic Energy Agency. Negotiations of such agreements shall commence within 180 days from the original entry into force of this Treaty. For States depositing their instruments of ratification or accession after the 180-day period, negotiation of such agreements shall commence not later than the date of such deposit. Such agreements shall enter into force not later than eighteen months after the date of initiation of negotiations.

Art. IV.(1) Nothing in this Treaty shall be interpreted as affecting the inalienable right of all the Parties to the Treaty to develop research, production and use of nuclear energy for peaceful purposes without discrimination and in conformity with Articles I and II of this Treaty.

(2) All the Parties to the Treaty undertake to facilitate, and gave the right to participate in the fullest possible exchange of equipment, materials and scientific and technological information for the peaceful uses of nuclear energy. Parties to the Treaty in a position to do so shall also cooperate in contributing alone or together with other States or international organizations to the further development of the applications of nuclear energy for peaceful purposes, especially in the territories of non-nuclear-weapon States Party to the Treaty, with due consideration for the needs of the developing areas of the world.

Art. V. Each Party to this Treaty undertakes to take appropriate measures to ensure that, in accordance with this Treaty, under appropriate international observation and through appropriate international procedures, potential benefits from any peaceful applications of nuclear explosions will be made available to non-nuclear-weapon States Party to this Treaty on a non-discriminatory basis and that the charge to such Parties for the explosive devices used will be as low as possible and exclude any charge for research and development. Non-nuclear-weapon States Party to this Treaty shall be able to obtain such benefits, pursuant to a special international agreement or agreements, through an appropriate international body with adequate representation of non-nuclear-weapon States. Negotiations on this subject shall commence as soon as possible after the Treaty enters into force. Non-nuclear-weapon States Party to this Treaty so desiring may also obtain such benefits pursuant to bilateral agreements.

Art. VI. Each of the Parties to this Treaty undertakes to pursue negotiations in good faith on effective measures relating to cessation of the nuclear arms race at any early date and to nuclear disarmament, and on a Treaty on general and complete disarmament under strict and effective international control.

Art. VII. Nothing in this Treaty affects the right of any group of States to conclude regional treaties in order to assure the total absence of nuclear weapons in their respective territories.

Art. VIII.(1) Any Party to this Treaty may propose amendments to this Treaty. The text of any proposed amendment shall be submitted to the Depositary Governments which shall circulate it to all Parties to the Treaty. Thereupon, if requested to do so by one-third or more of the Parties to the Treaty, the Depositary Governments shall convene a conference, to which they shall invite all the Parties to the Treaty, to consider such an amendment.

(2) Any amendment to this Treaty must be approved by a majority of the votes of all the Parties to the Treaty, including the votes of all nuclear-weapon States Party to this Treaty and all other Parties which, on the date the amendment is circulated, are members of the Board of Governors of the International Atomic Energy Agency. The amendment shall enter into force for each Party that deposits its instrument of ratification of the amendment upon the deposit of instruments of ratification by a majority of all the Parties, including the instruments of ratification of all nuclear-weapon States Party to this Treaty and all other Parties which, on the date the amendment is circulated, are members of the Board of Governors of the International Atomic Energy Agency. Thereafter, it shall enter into force for any other Party upon the deposit of its instrument of ratification of the amendment.

(3) Five years after the entry into force of this Treaty, a conference of Parties to the Treaty shall be held in Geneva, Switzerland, in order to review the operation of this Treaty with a view to assuring that the purposes of the Preamble and the provisions of the Treaty are being realized. At intervals of five years thereafter, a majority of the Parties to the Treaty may obtain, by submitting a proposal to this effect to the Depositary Governments, the convening of further conferences with the same objective of reviewing the operation of the Treaty.

Art. IX.(1) This Treaty shall be open to all States for signature. Any State which does not sign the Treaty before its entry into force in accordance with paragraph 3 of this Article may accede to it at any time.

(2) This Treaty shall be subject to ratification by signatory States. Instruments of ratification and instruments of accession shall be deposited with the Governments of the Union of Soviet Socialist Republics, the United Kingdom of Great Britain and Northern Ireland, and the United States of America, which are hereby designated the Depositary Governments.

(3) This Treaty shall enter into force after its ratification by the Depositary Governments, and 40 other States signatory to this Treaty and the deposit of their instruments of ratification. For the purposes of this Treaty, a nuclear-weapon State is one which has manufactured and exploded a nuclear weapon or other nuclear-weapon State is one which has manufactured and exploded a nuclear weapon or other nuclear explosive device prior to January 1, 1967.

(4) For the States whose instruments of ratification or accession are deposited subsequent to the entry into force of this Treaty, it shall enter into force on the date of the deposit of their instruments of ratification or accession.

(5) The Depositary Governments shall promptly inform all signatory and acceding States of the date of each signature, the date of deposit of each instrument of ratification or of accession, the date of the entry into force of this Treaty, and the date of receipt of any requests for convening a conference or other notices.

(6) This Treaty shall be registered by the Depositary Governments pursuant to article 102 of the Charter of the United Nations.

Art. X.(1) Each Party shall in exercising its national sovereignty have the right to withdraw from the Treaty if it decides that extraordinary events, related to the subject matter of this Treaty, have jeopardized the supreme interests of its country. It shall give notice of such withdrawal to all other Parties to the Treaty and to the United Nations Security Council three months in advance. Such notice shall include a statement of the extraordinary events it regards as having jeopardized its supreme interests.

(2) Twenty-five years after the entry into force of the Treaty, a Conference shall be convened to decide whether the Treaty shall continue in force indefinitely, or shall be extended for an additional fixed period or periods. This decision shall be taken by a majority of the Parties to the Treaty.

Art. XI. This Treaty, the English, Russian, French, Spanish and Chinese texts of which are equally authentic, shall be deposited in the archives of the Depositary Governments. Duly certified copies of this Treaty shall be transmitted by the Depositary Governments to the Governments of the signatory and acceding States.

In witness whereof the undersigned, duly authorized, have signed this Treaty.''

The Treaty, which entered into force on March 5, 1970 for an intial period of 25 years is a subject of five-year review conferences held in Geneva: first in May 1975, second in August-September 1980, third in August-September 1985 and will again come up to review in 1990. Colombia, Kuwait, Trinidad and Tobago and North Yemen have signed but not ratified the Treaty. Not party to the Treaty are China and France and seven nuclear-threshold countries: Argentina, Brazil, India, Israel, Pakistan, South Africa and Spain. The NPT safeguard agreement with the IAEA was signed until Jan. 1, 1987 by 78 countries.

The full list of 150 parties to the NPT (not including Taiwan which had signed and ratified the treaty as the 'Republic of China') was as follows (with dates of post-1980 accessions, or in the cases of Belize and Dominica technically 'successions' to obligations entered by the UK on their behalf before independence): Afghanistan, Antigua and Barbuda (October 1981), Australia, Austria, Bahamas, Bangladesh, Barbados, Belgium, Belize (August 1985), Benin, Bhutan (May 1985), Bolivia, Botswana, Brunei (March 1985), Bulgaria, Burkina Faso, Burundi, Cameroon, Canada, Cape Verde, Central African Republic, Chad, Congo, Costa Rica, Cyprus, Czechoslovakia, Denmark, Dominica (August 1984), Dominican Republic, Ecuador, Egypt (February 1981), El Salvador, Equatorial Guinea (November 1984), Ethiopia, Fiji, Finland, Gabon, Gambia, East Germany, West Germany, Ghana, Greece, Grenada, Guatemala, Guinea (April 1985), Guinea-Bissau, Haiti, Honduras, Hungary, Iceland, Indonesia, Iran, Iraq, Ireland, Italy, Ivory Coast, Jamaica, Japan, Jordan, Democratic Kampuchea, Kenya, Kiribati (April 1985), South Korea, Laos, Lebanon, Lesotho, Liberia, Libya, Liechtenstein, Luxembourg, Madagascar, Malaysia, Maldives, Mali, Malta, Mauritius, Mexico, Mongolia, Morocco, Nauru (June 1982), Nepal, Netherlands, New Zealand, Nicaragua, Nigeria, North Korea (December 1985), Norway, Panama, Papua New Guinea (January 1982), Paraguay, Peru, Philippines, Poland, Portugal, Romania, Rwanda, St. Lucia, St. Vincent and the Grenadines (November 1984), Samoa, San Marino, Senegal, Seychelles (March 1985), Sierra Leone, Singapore, Solomon Islands (June 1981), Somalia, Soviet Union, Sri Lanka, Sudan, Surinam, Swaziland, Sweden, Switzerland, Syria, Thailand, Togo, Tonga, Tunisia, Turkey, Tuvalu, Uganda (October 1982), United Kingdom, United States, Uruguay, Vatican, Venezuela, Vietnam (June 1982), South Yemen, Yugoslavia and Zaire.

KEESING's Archive 1975 and 1980; UN Chronicle, 1985 No. 8, pp. 32-33; KEESING's Record of World Events, March 1986; UN Yearbook, 1968; UNTS, Vol. 729, pp. 169–175; B. GOLDSCHMIDT, "The Negotiation of the Non-Proliferation Treaty", in: IAEA Bulletin, August, 1980, pp. 73–80; G. DELCOIGNE, C. ROSSI, B. VEENDENDAAL, "Arms-control treaties: review and revision", in: IAEA Bulletin, September 1984, pp. 37–40; SIPRI, Yearbook 1987, Oxford 1988, p. 461; D. ROBERTSON, Guide to Modern Defense and Strategy, Detroit, 1988; UN Resolutions and Decisions adopted by the General Assembly during the First Part of its Forty-Third Session,

N

from 20 September to 22 December, 1988, New York, 1989, p. 202.

NON-PROVOCATIVE DEFENCE. An international term for a conventional defence initiative and unambiguously defensive postures; subject of Vienna negotiations on conventional arms reduction.

In ▷ SIPRI 1987 opinion "Although both sides have shown some signs of reappraisal, the Soviet Union still maintains an offensive force posture in Eastern Europe".

S. LODGAARD, K. BIRNBAUM, *Overcoming Threats to Europe*, SIPRI, Oxford, 1987.

NON-SELF-GOVERNING TERRITORIES. An international term for areas subject to the authority of another state. In pursuance of the obligations determined under art. 11 of the UN Charter, the UN General Assembly Res. 66/I of Dec. 14, 1946, announced a list of 74 non-self-governing territories. Eight UN member States, Australia, Belgium, Denmark, France, Great Britain, the Netherlands, New Zealand and the USA were supervisors of the territories specified in Res. 66/I, and assumed the obligation to submit annual reports on these territories to the UN General Assembly, which South Africa, Portugal and Spain refused to do. Spain submitted reports from 1960. Despite the UN General Assembly Res. 219/III of Nov. 3, 1948, reports on ten territories were not submitted. After a debate on this matter at a session in the fall of 1949, the UN General Assembly established on Dec. 2, 1949, a special committee for non-self-governing territories which operated until 1963, called from 1955 the Committee on Information from Non-Self-Governing Territories. In Dec., 1963, the functions of this Committee, and of the special committees on South West Africa (Namibia) and on Portuguese colonies, were assumed by the Committee of the 24, called the Committee on Decolonization, which prepared a current list of non-self-governing territories including, despite US objections, also Puerto Rico. In 1980, Namibia, the Pacific Islands and Puerto Rico were included on the list. Units which cover rather small areas and have a small population are subject to the same general principle: that all non-self-governing territories should be granted independence.

A. GARCIA ROBLES, *El Mundo de la Postguerra*, Mexico, 1946, Vol. II, pp. 369 and 380–381; *UN Summaries of Non-Self-Governing Territories. Transmitted to the UN Secretary General*, New York, 1946; H.D. HALL, *Mandates, Dependencies and Trusteeship*, London, 1948; J. CORDERO-TORRES, *La evolución de la personalidad internacional de los paises dependientes*, Madrid, 1950; J.L. KUNZ, "Chapter XI of the UN Charter in Action", in: *American Journal of International Law*, No. 48, 1954; Ch.E. TOUSSAINT, *The Trusteeship System of the UN*, New York, 1956; E.J. SADY, *The International Trusteeship System*, London, 1957; T. BARSEGOV, *Territoria v mezhdunarodnom prave*, Moscow, 1958.

NON-TARIFF BARRIERS, NTBs. An international term in the UN system for national legislation including import quotas, health, safety and packaging regulations and customs evaluation methods which intentionally or not, restrict the volume of imports.

UN Chronicle, June and October, 1982.

NON-USE OF FORCE. A principle of international law excluding use of force from international relations and calling for peaceful settlement of disputes. The UN General Assembly decided under Res. 32/150 of Dec. 19, 1978 to establish a Special Committee on Enhancing the Effectiveness of the Principle of Non-Use of Force in International

Relations. The Committee is composed of 35 member states appointed by the Assembly President on the basis of equitable geographical distribution and representing the principal legal systems of the world. The item "conclusion of a world treaty on the non-use of force in international relations" was also allocated by the Assembly to the First Committee. ▷ Use of force.

On Nov. 18, 1987, the General Assembly adopted the Declaration on the Enhancement of the Effectiveness of the Principle of Refraining from the Threat or Use of Force in International Relations. The highlights were are follows:

"Every State has the duty to refrain in its international relations from the threat or use of force against the territorial integrity or political independence of any State, or in any other manner inconsistent with the United Nations purposes. Such a threat or use of force constitutes a violation of international law and the Charter and entails international responsibility.

States should fulfil their obligations under international law to refrain from organizing, instigating, assisting or participating in paramilitary, terrorist or subversive acts, including acts of mercenaries, in other States, or acquiescing in organized activities within their territory directed towards the commission of such acts.

The principle of refraining from the threat or use of force in international relations is universal in character and binding regardless of each State's political, economic, social or cultural system or relations of alliance.

No consideration of whatever nature may be invoked to warrant resorting to the threat or use of force in violation of the Charter.

All peoples have the right freely to determine, without external interference, their political status and to pursue their economic, social and cultural development.

Neither acquisition nor any occupation of territory resulting from the threat or use of force in contravention of international law will be recognised as legal acquisition or occupation."

UN Chronicle, January, 1978; *UN Chronicle*, No. 2, 1987, No. 1, 1988.

NON-VIOLENT ACTION. An international term for a form of political protest, eschewing violence as a matter of principle, applied for the first time on a large scale during the interwar period by Mahatma K. Gandhi (1869–1948) of India, and continued after World War II by many leaders of underprivileged minorities compaigning for equal rights, e.g. Martin Luther King (1929–1968) in the USA.

NON-VIOLENT SOCIETY. An international term for a society free from armaments, warpsychosis, terrorism, civil and moral violence.

NO PASARAN!. History-making cry of *La Pasionaria* (Spanish communist, Dolores Ibarruri) in reply to the attack of General Franco's Fascist troops on the Spanish Republic July 17/18, 1936, in a speech broadcast on July 19, 1936 on Madrid Radio. Full text:

"*No Pasaran. Mejor es morir de pie que vivir de rodillas!*" (They will not pass. It's better to die standing than to live on one's knees!).

Guerra y Revolución en España, Moscú, 1966.

NORAD. North American Aerospace Defence Command. A NORAD agreement between the USA and Canada, 1981, was extended until 1990, on March 19, 1986. A Common American-Canadian military radar and distant early warning system.

J.T. JOCKEL, *No Boundaries Upstairs: Canada, The United States and the Origins of North American Air Defence, 1945-1958*, Vancouver, 1987.

NORDEC. ▷ NORDEK.

NORDEK. Nordec, Nordic Economic Union. The agreement of Denmark, Finland, Norway and Sweden on setting up of a Nordic Economic Union concluded on Feb. 4, 1970. The Union was to operate from Jan. 1, 1972. Among its aims were duty-free trade for 85% of industrial products (the remaining 15% included – iron, steel and electronic elements); a common fund, price control for fish and agricultural products, agricultural restructuring or modernization and the development of common research. The financial organ of NORDEK is the Scandinavian Investment Bank. According to the agreement, each party was authorized to suspend participation in the Union on becoming a member of another economic group. This occurred when Denmark assumed membership of the European Community, and Finland, together with Sweden, stated that their belonging to Union ran counter to the neutrality of both states.

B. SUNDELIUS, *Foreign Policies of Northern Europe*, Boulder, 1982.

NORDEL. The Electric Power Committee of the Nordic Council; it co-ordinates the common system of electric power in Denmark, Finland, Norway and Sweden.

NORDIC COUNCIL. The Scandinavian intergovernmental consultation institution, est. on Jan. 1, 1953 by a statute drawn up by the governments of Denmark, Iceland, Norway, Sweden; Finland became a member in 1955.

Organization: the Council is composed of 69 elected members (16 each from Denmark, Finland, Norway, Sweden and 5 from Iceland) and Cabinet members without voting rights nominated by the Governments. Official languages: Danish, Norwegian, Swedish. Permanent Committees (economic, cultural, legal, social and for communications). Permanent Regional Secretariats in Denmark Nordisk Rad, Christiansborg, Copenhagen; in Finland Nordiska Radet, Riksdagshuset, Helsinki; in Iceland Nordisk Rad, Altinget, Reykjavik; in Norway Det Nordiske Rad, Stortinget, Oslo; Stockholm Nordiska Radet, Riksdagshuset, Stockholm. Organizations under the aegis of the Nordic Council registered with the UIA:

Nordic Association Foreningen Norden, f. 1919, Stockholm.
Scandinavian Council for Applied Research, NORDFORSK, f. 1947, Copenhagen. Publ.: *Scandinavian Research Projects* and *Acta Polytechnica de Scandinaviae*.

E. SOLEM, *The Nordic Council and Scandinavian Integration*, New York, 1977.

NORDIC CULTURAL FUND (Nordisk Kulturfond). The Fund to promote cultural co-operation was established between Denmark, Finland, Iceland, Norway and Sweden. An agreement was signed on Oct. 3, 1966 in Copenhagen, and came into force on July 1, 1967.

"The Fund shall be supplied each year with a total sum of 3 million Danish Kroner (Sweden 37%, Denmark 23%, Finland 22%, Norway 17% and Iceland 1% of the aforementioned sum)."

UNTS, Vol. 610, pp. 174 and 176.

NORDIC POSTAL UNION. Nordiska Postföreningen. The Postal Union established in 1869 by Denmark, Norway and Sweden. An extended agreement to include Finland and Iceland came into force on Jan. 1, 1935; further agreements came into force on Nov. 11, 1946 and April 1, 1972. Publ.: *Nordisk Posttidskrift*. Reg. with the UIA.

Yearbook of International Organizations.

NORDISK BANK. Nordic Investment Bank. The financial organ founded on June 19, 1977 of the Nordic Council, with the initial capital of 1250 million dollars, in which 45% was the share of Sweden, 22% of Denmark, 16% each of Finland and Norway and 1% of Iceland.

NOR-SHIPPING. The International Maritime Exhibition in Oslo; since 1970 the greatest European permanent annual fair of classification societies, shipping agents, bridge- and canal-managing boards, towage enterprises, shipping companies, ship enterprises, shipyards and repair workshops, brokerage houses, stowage, maritime publications.

NORTHAG. Acronym of the Northern Army Group, Central Europe, one of the two land forces under NATO's Allied Forces Central Europe, AFCENT command. Its function is to defend the North German Plains while the Central Army Group, CENTAG covers the southern route. See also the ▷ Northern Flank.

D. ROBERTSON, *Guide to Modern Defense and Strategy*, Detroit, 1988.

NORTH AMERICA. Continent in the Western Hemisphere, north of the Panama isthmus, with an area of 24.2 million sq. km; the southern part of North America is called Central America; politically North America includes: Canada, Mexico, the USA and Central American states.

NORTH ATLANTIC AIRLINE FARES. In the 1980s a subject of international disputes within ▷ IATA between 16 European countries and the USA concerning the policy on air fares in traffic over the North Atlantic, the world's busiest international route.

J. FELDMAN, "IATA is forced to change rigid policy on air fares", in: *International Herald Tribune*, December 1-2, 1984.

NORTH ATLANTIC DRIFT. A continuation of the ▷ Gulf Stream, the warm N. Atlantic ocean current; subject of international research.

NORTH ATLANTIC ICE PATROL. A subject of international agreements. In accordance with the provisions of Chapter V, Regulation 5 and 6, of the 1948 International Convention for the Safety of Life at Sea the US Government has agreed to continue the management of the North Atlantic Ice Patrol and the study and observation of ice conditions in the region affected by icebergs, and to disseminate the information received. On Jan. 4, 1956 in Washington the governments, members of the Convention 1948 (Belgium, Canada, Denmark, France, Italy, the Netherlands, Norway, the UK and USA), signed an Agreement regarding financial support of the Ice Patrol. The Agreement came into force on July 5, 1956.

UNTS, Vol. 164, p. 113 and Vol. 256, p. 172.

NORTH ATLANTIC TREATY, 1949. The Treaty was signed by the governments of Belgium, Canada, Denmark, France, Iceland, Italy, Luxembourg, the Netherlands, Norway, Portugal, the UK and the USA on Apr. 4, 1949 in Washington DC; came into force Aug. 24, 1949.
The text is as follows:

"The Parties to this Treaty reaffirm their faith in the purposes and principles of the Charter of the United Nations and their desire to live in peace with all peoples and all governments.
They are determined to safeguard the freedom, common heritage and civilization of their peoples, founded on the principles of democracy, individual liberty and the rule of law.

They seek to promote stability and well-being in the North Atlantic area.
They are resolved to unite their efforts for collective defense and for the preservation of peace and security. They therefore agree to this North Atlantic Treaty
Art. 1. The Parties undertake, as set forth in the Charter of the United Nations to settle any international disputes in which they may be involved by peaceful means in such a manner that international peace and security, and justice, are not endangered, and to refrain in their international relations from the threat or use of force in any manner inconsistent with the purpose of the United Nations.
Art. 2. The Parties will contribute toward the further development of peaceful and friendly international relations by strengthening their free institutions, by bringing about a better understanding of the principles upon which these institutions are founded, and by promoting conditions of stability and well-being. They will seek to eliminate conflict in their international economic policies and will encourage economic collaboration between any or all of them.
Art. 3. In order more effectively to achieve the objectives of this treaty, The Parties, separately and jointly by means of continuous and effective self-help and mutual aid, will maintain and develop their individual and collective capacity to resist armed attack.
Art. 4. The Parties will consult together whenever, in the opinion of any of them, the territorial integrity, political independence or security of any of the Parties is threatened.
Art. 5. The Parties agree that an armed attack against one or more of them in Europe or North America shall be considered an attack against them all and consequently they agree that, if such an armed attack occurs, each of them, in exercise of the right of individual or collective self-defence recognized by article 51 of the Charter of the United Nations, will assist the Party or Parties so attacked by taking forthwith, individually and in concert with the other Parties, such action as it deems necessary, including the use of armed force, to restore and maintain the security of the North Atlantic area. Any such armed attack and all measures taken as a result thereof shall immediately be reported to the Security Council. Such measures shall be terminated when Security Council has taken the measures necessary to restore and maintain international peace and security.
Art. 6. For the purpose of Article 5 an armed attack on one or more of the Parties is deemed to include an armed attack on the territory of any of the Parties in Europe or North America, on the Algerian Departments of France, on the territory of Turkey or on the islands under the jurisdiction of any of the Parties in the North Atlantic area north of the Tropic of Cancer; on the forces, vessels or aircraft of any of the Parties, when in or over these territories or any other area in Europe in which occupation forces of any of the Parties were stationed on the date when the treaty entered into force or the Mediterranean Sea or the North Atlantic area north of the Tropic of Cancer.
Art. 7. This Treaty does not affect, and shall not be interpreted as affecting, in any way the rights and obligations under the Charter of the Parties which are members of the United Nations, or the primary responsibility of the Security Council for the maintenance of international peace and security.
Art. 8. Each Party declares that none of the international engagements now in force between it and any other of the Parties or any third State is in conflict with the provisions of this Treaty, and undertakes not to enter into any international engagement in conflict with this Treaty.
Art. 9. The Parties hereby establish a council, on which each of them shall be represented, to consider matters concerning the implementation of this Treaty. The council shall be so organized as to be able to meet promptly at any time. The council shall set up such subsidiary bodies as may be necessary; in particular it shall establish immediately a defence committee which shall recommend measures for the implementation of Articles 3 and 5.
Art. 10. The Parties may, by unanimous agreement, invite any other European State in a position to further the principles of this Treaty and to contribute to the security of the North Atlantic area to accede to this Treaty. Any state so invited may become a party to the Treaty by depositing its instrument of accession with

the Government of the United States of America. The Government of the United States of America will inform each of the Parties of the deposit of each such instrument of accession.
Art. 11. This Treaty shall be ratified and its provisions carried out by the Parties in accordance with their respective constitutional processes. The instruments of ratification shall be deposited as soon as possible with the Government of the United States of America, which will notify all the other signatories of each deposit. The Treaty shall enter into force between the States which have ratified it as soon as the ratifications of the majority of the signatories, including the ratifications of Belgium, Canada, France, Luxembourg, the Netherlands, the United Kingdom and the United States, have been deposited and shall come into effect with respect to other States on the date of the deposit of their ratifications.
Art. 12. After the Treaty has been in force for ten years, or at any time thereafter, the Parties shall, if any of them so requests, consult together for the purpose of reviewing the Treaty, having regard for the factors then affecting peace and security in the North Atlantic area, including the development of universal as well as regional arrangements under the Charter of the United Nations for the maintenance of international peace and security.
Art. 13. After the Treaty has been in force for twenty years, any Party may cease to be a party one year after its notice of denunciation has been given to the Government of the United States of America, which will inform the Governments of the other Parties of the deposit of each notice of denunciation.
Art. 14. This Treaty, of which the English and French texts are equally authentic, shall be deposited in the archives of the Government of the United States of America. Duly certified copies thereof will be transmitted by that Government to the Governments of the other signatories.
In witness whereof, the undersigned Plenipotentiaries have signed this Treaty."

Came into force on 24 Aug., 1949 in respect of all the signatory states, by the deposit with the Government of the United States of America of instruments of ratification, in accordance with the provisions of art. 11. Following are the dates in 1949 on which an instrument of ratification was deposited on behalf of each of the signatory states:

Belgium	16 June
Canada	3 May
Denmark	24 Aug.
France	24 Aug.
Iceland	1 Aug.
Italy	24 Aug.
Luxembourg	27 June
Netherlands	12 Aug.
Norway	8 July
Portugal	24 Aug.
United Kingdom	7 June
United States of America	25 June

Greece and Turkey acceded to the Treaty 1952, the Federal Republic of Germany 1955. In 1966 France withdrew from the integrated military structure of NATO. In May, 1982 Spain became a member of NATO.

UNTS, 1949; W.E. BECKETT, *The North Atlantic Treaty, The Brussels Treaty and the Charter of the UN*, London, 1950; *L'avenir de l'Alliance Atlantique*, Paris, 1961; R. OSGOOD, *The Entangling Alliance*, New York, 1962; T. STANLEY, *NATO in Transition*, London, 1965; L. LOGAULT, *Deterrence and the Atlantic Alliance*, Toronto, 1966; D. ACHESON, *Present and the Creation*, New York, 1969; *NATO Facts and Figures*, Brussels, 1972; P. HILL-NORTON, *No Soft Option. The Politico-Military Realities of NATO*, London, 1980; *NATO and the Warsaw Pact*, Brussels, 1983; *The Europa Year Book 1984. A World Survey*, Vol. 1, pp. 180–182, London, 1984.

NORTH ATLANTIC TREATY ORGANIZATION. ▷ NATO.

NORTHEAST PASSAGE. An Arctic sea route along the northern coast of Europe and Asia,

N

between the Atlantic and Pacific Ocean; first traversed in 1878–89. In the beginning of the XX century ice-breakers started to combat heavy ice in the passage. The USSR opened a permanent shipping lane in the 1930's and since World War II maintains a regular Northern Sea Route.

NORTHERN EPIRUS QUESTION. ▷ Albania–Greece Border Dispute.

NORTHERN FLANK. An international military term for the border of Norway with the USSR, a frontier important to the Russians as a sea-way to the North-Atlantic, as well as for NATO UK Royal Marines and the US Marines.

D. ROBERTSON, *Guide to Modern Defense and Strategy,* Detroit, 1988.

NORTHERN IRELAND. ▷ Ireland Northern.

NORTHERN MARIANAS. ▷ Marianas Islands.

NORTH KOREA. ▷ Korea, Democratic People's Republic of.

NORTH POLE. Northern end of the Earth's axis, lat. 90°N and long. 0. The North Pole was first reached by American explorer Robert E. Peary, 1909.

H. HERBERT, *Peary,* London, 1986; W. HERBERT, *Commander Robert E. Peary, Did He Reach the Pole?* in: *National Geographic,* September, 1988.

NORTH SEA. Part of the Atlantic Ocean; area: 574,980 sq. km, 965 km long, and 645 km wide, interconnects with the Norwegian Sea and the Baltic Sea through the Skagerrak, Kattegat and Danish straits. The rivers Elbe, Weser, Rhine and Thames flow into the North Sea; its largest ports are Rotterdam, London, Antwerp, Hamburg. On Apr. 23, 1908 England, France, Germany, the Netherlands and Sweden signed an agreement guaranteeing status quo in the North Sea. After World War II it became the subject of international arguments concerning the delimitation of the continental shelf. The dispute was submitted on Feb. 20, 1968 to the International Court of Justice, ICJ, by the governments of Denmark and the FRG, and by the Netherlands and the FRG; was settled in 1969. In 1959 natural gas was discovered near the Netherlands and in 1965 sea oil fields near England; in 1975 exploitation was started by Great Britain, in 1976 by Norway, the Netherlands and Denmark. Only in the part of the North Sea adjoining the FRG were oil fields not detected.
On Oct. 31–Nov. 1, 1984 the first international conference on the protection of the North Sea, attended by the environment ministers of Belgium, Denmark, the FRG, France, Norway, the Netherlands and the UK to strengthen surveillance resources on ships, to reduce the contamination of rivers, the dumping of radioactive waste and to control air-pollution on the sea was held in Bremen (FRG). The second conference took place in London on Nov. 24–25, 1987 and decided to give the North Sea the status of a special protection area, with a common program for the years 1989–1994. The third conference was scheduled for 1990 in The Hague.
Organization reg. with the UIA:

North Sea Hydrographic Commission, f. 1963, The Hague.

D.I. MAC KAY, *The Political Economy of North Sea Oil,* London, 1975; Q. NORENG, *The Oil Industry and the Government Strategy in the North Sea,* London, 1980; D. HANN, *Governments and North Sea,* London, 1986; KEESING's *Contemporary Archive 1986,* and KEESING's *Record of World Events,* 1988.

NORTH–SOUTH. An international term in the UN system for a division of the world: the political division is called ▷ East–West, the economic North–South. The demand for the New International Economic Order originated from developing countries in Africa, Asia and Latin America. They have been collectively dubbed the "South" of the world in relation to the developed countries of Europe, North America and Japan. The discussion of global economic change between the rich and the poor has come to be known as the North–South dialogue.
The first North–South Conference was held on Dec. 16–19, 1975 in Paris. Participants were: Australia, Canada, Japan, Spain, Sweden, Switzerland, the USA and one common delegation representing the EEC states and representants of 19 developing countries (six from Africa: Algeria, Cameroon, Egypt, Nigeria, Zaïre, and Zambia; six from Latin America: Argentina, Brazil, Jamaica, Mexico, Peru, Venezuela; six from Asia: India, Indonesia, Iraq, Iran, Pakistan, Saudi Arabia; and Yugoslavia). Delegates of Canada and Venezuela were co-chairmen.
The Conference work was carried out in four commissions (on Energy, on Raw materials and Trade, on Development and on Money and Finance) and in Plenary Sessions. The Group of Eight contributed one billion dollars ($385 million by the EEC and $375 million by the USA) for a Special Action Program to help the low-income countries; they also agreed in principle to create a Common Fund to finance raw materials exported by the less-developed countries and committed themselves to increase the amount of their assistance (0.7% of GNP). The Conference disagreed on most of the main issues on energy, raw materials and financial affairs.
In 1978, on the initiative of the World Bank, the Independent Commission for International Development Problems (Brandt Commission) was established to study North–South problems; it has a permanent secretariat in Geneva with Willy Brandt as chairman. In Feb., 1979 the Brandt Commission published a Report which recommended more financial aid and more food for poor countries of the South; a reform of the IMF and a World Bank loan policy to open a larger market in the South for export from the North. In Feb., 1980 the W. Brandt Commission presented to the UN Secretary-General a report called *North–South: A Program for Survival,* concerning (a) the transfer of resources to the less developed countries; (b) an international energy strategy; (c) a global food programme and (d) the reform in the international economic system. In Aug., 1980 a UN Special session was dedicated to the North–South problem. In January 1988 a demographic prognosis of the Institut Français des Relations Internationales for the next century stated that North Africa may have 260.8 million inhabitants (up from 123 million) and the 12 members of the European Community 306.4 million (down from 321 million). Morocco with a 9 million population in 1950 could have a larger army than West Germany. Turkey will have in 1998 as many inhabitants as Italy and West Germany put together. In 2025 some 50 million Muslim immigrants from North Africa are expected to have settled in Western Europe.
See also ▷ Multicultural Societies.

The CIEC Documents, Paris, 1975, 1976, 1977; J. AMUZEGAR, "Requiem for the North–South Conference", in: *Foreign Affairs,* October, 1977, pp. 136–159; *The New International Economic Order: Confrontation on Cooperation between North and South.* West View, New York, 1977; W. BRANDT (ed.), *North–South: A Program for Survival,* London–Boston, 1980; *UN Chronicle,* October, 1982, p. 38;

J. SPRAOS, *Inequalising Trade? A Study of Traditional North–South Specialization in the Context of Terms of Trade Concepts,* Oxford, UK, 1985; K. RAFFER, *Unequal Exchange and the Evolution of the World System: Reconsidering the Impact of Trade on North–South Relations,* London, 1987; G. WILLIAMS, *Third-World Political Organizations,* London, 1987.

NORTHWEST PASSAGE. An Arctic Sea route along the North coast of North America between the Atlantic and Pacific Oceans; first sailed by Roald Amundsen, Norwegian explorer in 1903–06. In the 1960's discovery of oil in Prudhoe Bay, N. Alaska, an inlet of the Arctic Ocean, made the Northwest Passage an important international shipping lane.

NORWAY. Member of the UN. Kingdom of Norway. A kingdom in northern Europe on the Scandinavian Peninsula, on the Norwegian Sea. Borders with Sweden, Finland and the USSR. Area: 323,894 sq. km. Pop. 1983 census: 4,448, 775 (1970 census: 3,874,133). Capital: Oslo with 450,986 inhabitants 1983. GNP per capita 1987: US $17,190. Official language: Norwegian. Currency: one Norwegian krone = 100 öre. National Day: May 14, Constitution Day. 1814.
Founding member of the UN, and all its specialized agencies. Member of the Nordic Council, NATO, EFTA, OECD, Council of Europe. In 1972, as a result of plebiscite, did not join the EEC but concluded a special agreement.
International relations: for centuries part of the United Kingdom of Denmark and Norway, separated by the Vienna Congress 1815 and united with Sweden. Separated from Sweden on June 7, 1905 with the enthronement of Prince Charles of the House of Denmark as King Haakon VII of the Kingdom of Norway. In World War I neutral. Member of the League of Nations 1919–40. In World War II occupied by III Reich 1940–44 (King Haakon VII in exile in London).
Norwegian statesman Trygve Halvdan Lie was the first UN Secretary-General. In 1976 Norway introduced a 200-mile fishing zone. ▷ Spitsbergen. See also ▷ World Heritage UNESCO List.

The Norwegian Institute of International Affairs, Norsk Utenrikspolitisk Institutt, f. 1959, Oslo. Publ.: Annual Report.
K. LARSEN, *History of Norway,* New York, 1948; J.A. STORING, *Norwegian Democracy,* Boston, 1963; J. ANDENAES, *Norway and the World War II,* Oslo, 1966; J. MIDGAARD, *A Brief History of Norway,* Oslo, 1969; N.M. UNGAASD, *Great Power Politics and Norwegian Foreign Policy,* Oslo, 1973; L. EIDE, *The Norwegian Credit and Monetary System,* Oslo, 1973; S. EKELAND, *Norway in the Modern World,* Oslo, 1976; E. GLASSER, *Norwegen. Bibliography,* Darmstadt, 1978; T.K. DERRY, *A History of Scandinavia,* London, 1979; H. ALLEN, *Norway and Europe, 1970's,* New York, 1979; *Facts about Norway,* Oslo, 1982; *The Europa Year Book. A World Survey,* Vol. I, pp. 690–710, London, 1984; *White Papers on Relations with European Community,* March 22, 1987.

NORWEGIAN–SWEDISH UNION, 1814–1905. The Union was established in Aug., 1814 on the basis of the peace treaty signed in Cologne on Jan. 14, 1814 which integrated Norway and Sweden until June 7, 1905 when the Norwegian parliament (Storting) unilaterally dissolved the Union.

NOSTRA AETATE. The Declaration of the Vatican II ▷ Ecumenical Council Oct. 28, 1965; on the Attitude of the Church towards the Non-Christian Religions. The Catholic Church asserted in the Declaration that the Jewish nation cannot be regarded as responsible for the death of Christ. See also ▷ Antisemitism.

NOT AID BUT TRADE. Latin American slogan coined in the 1970s when foreign aid did not compensate losses incurred by Latin American states due to customs barriers and protectionist policy of the USA hindering trade development with the USA. A modification of the above slogan is: Fair Trade the Best Aid.

NOTARIES. Organizations reg. with the UIA:
Conference of Notary Presidents of the EEC, f. 1976, Brussels, Belgium.
International Union of Latin Notaries, f. 1948, Buenos Aires, Argentina. Publ.: Revista Internacional del Notariado.

Yearbook of International Organizations, 1986/87; The Europa Yearbook 1988. A World Survey, Vol. I, London, 1988.

NOTE. An international term for a diplomatic letter, signed by an authorized official, formulated in the third person, handed by a diplomat to a person or institution to which he is accredited. Varieties of general notes are: (1) note collective, drafted and signed by representatives of several states; (2) note verbale, a kind of ▷ aide-mémoire, unsigned but usually bearing the seal and initials of the authorized official; (3) identical notes, directed by one government to several governments on the same matter.
See also ▷ Memoranda and Notes in the UN system.

Dictionnaire de la Terminologie du Droit International, Paris, 1960; *United Nations Editorial Manual,* New York, 1983, pp. 48–51.

NOTIFICATION. An international term for one state informing a second state about an event, decision, or piece of legislation.

D.P. MYERS, "The Name and Scope of Treaties", in *American Journal of International Law,* No. 51, 1957.

NOTIFYING CLAUSE. An international term related to the bill of lading – an obligation of the shipowner to notify the addressee of the cargo of the date of arrival of the ship in a given port.

NPG. ▷ Nuclear Planning Group.

NRMMO. ▷ NATO.

NRT. Netto Register Tonnage. An international term for a unit of net carrying capacity of a ship (brutto ▷ BRT). ▷ Register Tonnage.

NTB. ▷ Non-Tariff Barrier.

NSDAP. Nationalsozialistische Deutsche Arbeiterpartei. German National Socialistic Workers Party
The party was founded after World War I in Munich; from June 29, 1921 to Apr. 30, 1945 under the leadership of Adolf Hitler; it assumed power on Jan. 30, 1933 legally as the most numerous party in Germany. Its leader (Führer der NSDAP), Hitler, was entrusted by President Paul von Hindenburg with the forming of a new Government of the Reich, which initiated during 1933 the introduction of NSDAP dictatorship in Germany. Responsibility of the NSDAP leadership for war crimes, crimes against peace and against mankind was judged by the International Military Tribunal in Nuremberg, which found the activity of heads of all NSDAP organizational levels criminal and ordered suing them for participation in criminal actions. ▷ Nuremberg War Criminals Trial 1945–46. In 1945 the occupation authorities of four powers banned NSDAP activities and ordered dismissal from all posts of its former members, the number of which on Jan. 1, 1920 amounted to 64 persons, 1930 –

125,000; before Jan. 30, 1933, date of assumption of power by Hitler, it increased to about 700,000; in the years 1933–34 to 2.5 million; and in the 1935–44 to 8.5 million. Social composition of the party in 1935: 32.1% workers, 20.6% intellectuals, 20.2% learned professions, 13% clerks, 10.7% peasants, 3.4% others (*Parteistatistik,* as of Jan. 1, 1935, Vol. 4, Berlin, 1935).

A. HITLER, *Mein Kampf,* Munich, 1927; A. ROSENBERG, *Das Programm der NSDAP, Wesen, Grundsätze und Ziele der NSDAP,* Munich, 1930; *Organisationsbuch der NSDAP,* Munich, 1938; A. BULLOCK, *Hitler,* London, 1960; D. ORLOV, *The History of the Nazi Party,* 2 Vols., London, 1973.

NUCLEAR ACCIDENT CONVENTIONS, 1986.
The IAEA General Conference at its special session Sept. 24–26, 1986 in Vienna adopted two conventions:
(1) Convention on Early Notification of a Nuclear Accident;
(2) Convention on Assistance in the Case of a Nuclear Accident or Radiological Emergency. The Conventions designed a communication system to rapidly notify responsible national authorities about nuclear accidents having potential transboundary consequences (like ▷ Chernobyl), based on the Global Telecommunication System of the WHO. The IAEA General Conference in September 1988 endorsed a Joint Protocol establishing a link between the Accident Convention and the Nuclear Damage Conventions on Civil Liability. The IAEA continues in 1988 its studies on the question of State liability for transboundary damage to the environment in the event of a nuclear accident.
The first entered into force on Oct. 24, 1986; the second on Feb. 26, 1987.
The texts:

Convention on Early Notification of a Nuclear Accident
The states parties to this convention,
Aware that nuclear activities are being carried out in a number of States,
Noting that comprehensive measures have been and are being taken to ensure a high level of safety in nuclear activities, aimed at preventing nuclear accidents and minimizing the consequences of any such accident, should it occur,
Desiring to strengthen further international co-operation in the safe development and use of nuclear energy,
Convinced of the need for States to provide relevant information about nuclear accidents as early as possible in order that transboundary radiological consequences can be minimized,
Noting the usefulness of bilateral and multilateral arrangements on information exchange in this area,
Have agreed as follows:
Article 1
Scope of application
(1) This Convention shall apply in the event of any accident involving facilities or activities of a State Party or of persons or legal entities under its jurisdiction or control, referred to in paragraph 2 below, from which a release of radioactive material occurs or is likely to occur and which has resulted or may result in an international transboundary release that could be of radiological safety significance for another State.
(2) The facilities and activities referred to in paragraph 1 are the following:
(a) any nuclear reactor wherever located;
(b) any nuclear fuel cycle facility;
(c) any radioactive waste management facility;
(d) the transport and storage of nuclear fuels or radioactive wastes;
(e) the manufacture, use, storage, disposal and transport of radioisotopes for agricultural, industrial, medical and related scientific and research purposes; and
(f) the use of radioisotopes for power generation in space objects.

Article 2
Notification and information
In the event of an accident specified in article 1 (hereinafter referred to as a "nuclear accident"), the State Party referred to in that article shall:
(a) forthwith notify, directly or through the International Atomic Energy Agency (hereinafter referred to as the "Agency"), those States which are or may be physically affected as specified in article 1 and the Agency of the nuclear accident, its nature, the time of its occurrence and its exact location where appropriate, and
(b) promptly provide the States referred to in subparagraph (a), directly or through the Agency, and the Agency with such available information relevant to minimizing the radiological consequences in those States, as specified in article 5.
Article 3
Other Nuclear Accidents
With a view to minimizing the radiological consequences, States Parties may notify in the event of nuclear accidents other than those specified in article 1.
Article 4
Functions of the Agency
The Agency shall:
(a) forthwith inform States Parties, Member States, other States which are or may be physically affected as specified in article 1 and relevant international intergovernmental organizations (hereinafter referred to as "international organizations") of a notification received pursuant to sub-paragraph (a) of article 2; and
(b) promptly provide any State Party, Member State or relevant international organization, upon request, with the information received pursuant to sub-paragraph (b) of article 2.
Article 5
Information to be provided
(1) The information to be provided pursuant to subparagraph (b) of article 2 shall comprise the following data as then available to the notifying State Party:
(a) the time, exact location where appropriate, and the nature of the nuclear accident;
(b) the facility or activity involved;
(c) the assumed or established cause and the foreseeable development of the nuclear accident relevant to the transboundary release of the radioactive materials;
(d) the general characteristics of the radioactive release, including, as far as is practicable appropriate, the nature, probable physical and chemical form and the quantity, composition and effective height of the radioactive release;
(e) information on current and forecast meteorological and hydrological conditions, necessary for forecasting the transboundary release of the radioactive materials;
(f) the results of environmental monitoring relevant to the transboundary release of the radioactive materials;
(g) the off-site protective measures taken or planned;
(h) the predicted behaviour over time of the radioactive release.
(2) Such information shall be supplemented at appropriate intervals by further relevant information on the development of the emergency situation, including its foreseeable or actual termination.
(3) Information received pursuant to sub-paragraph (b) of article 2 may be used without restriction, except when such information is provided in confidence by the notifying State Party.
Article 6
Consultations
A State Party providing information pursuant to subparagraph (b) of article 2 shall, as far as is reasonably practicable, respond promptly to a request for further information or consultations sought by an affected State Party with a view to minimizing the radiological consequences in that State.
Article 7
Competent authorities and points of contact
(1) Each State Party shall make known to the Agency and to other State Parties, directly or through the Agency, its competent authorities and point of contact responsible for issuing and receiving the notification and information referred to in article 2. Such points of contact and a focal point within the Agency shall be available continuously.
(2) Each State Party shall promptly inform the Agency of any changes that may occur in the information referred to in paragraph 1.

(3) The Agency shall maintain an up-to-date list of such national authorities and points of contact as well as points of contact of relevant international organizations and shall provide it to State Parties and Member States and to relevant international organizations.

Article 8
Assistance to State Parties

The Agency shall, in accordance with its Statute and upon a request of a State Party which does not have nuclear activities itself and borders on a State having an active nuclear programme but not Party, conduct investigations into the feasibility and establishment of an appropriate radiation monitoring system in order to facilitate the achievement of the objectives of this Convention.

Article 9
Bilateral and multilateral arrangements

In furtherance of their mutual interests, States Parties may consider, where deemed appropriate, the conclusion of bilateral or multilateral arrangements relating to the subject matter of this Convention.

Article 10
Relationship to other international agreements

This Convention shall not affect the reciprocal rights and obligations of States Parties under existing international agreements which relate to the matters covered by this Convention, or under future international agreements concluded in accordance with the object and purpose of this Convention.

Article 11
Settlement of dispute

(1) In the event of a dispute between States Parties, or between a State Party and the Agency, concerning the interpretation or application of this Convention, the parties to the dispute shall consult with a view to the settlement of the dispute by negotiation or by any other peaceful means of settling disputes acceptable to them.

(2) If a dispute of this character between States Parties cannot be settled within one year from the request for consultation pursuant to paragraph 1, it shall, at the request of any party to such dispute, be submitted to arbitration or referred to the International Court of Justice for decision. Where a dispute is submitted to arbitration, if, within six months from the date of the request, the parties to the dispute are unable to agree on the organization of the arbitration, a party may request the President of the International Court of Justice or the Secretary-General of the United Nations to appoint one or more arbitrators. In cases of conflicting requests by the parties to the dispute, the request to the Secretary-General of the United Nations shall have priority.

(3) When signing, ratifying, accepting, approving or acceding to this Convention, a State may declare that it does not consider itself bound by either or both of the dispute settlement procedures provided for in paragraph 2. The other States Parties shall not be bound by a dispute settlement procedure provided for in paragraph 2 with respect to a State Party for which such a declaration is in force.

(4) A State Party which has made a declaration in accordance with paragraph 3 may at any time withdraw it by notification to the depositary.

Article 12
Entry into force

(1) This Convention shall be open for signature by all States and Namibia, represented by the United Nations Council for Namibia, at the Headquarters of the International Atomic Energy Agency in Vienna and at the Headquarters of the United Nations in New York, from 26 September 1986 and 6 October 1986 respectively, until its entry into force or for twelve months, whichever period is longer.

(2) A State and Namibia, represented by the United Nations Council for Namibia, may express its consent to be bound by this Convention either by signature, or by deposit of an instrument of ratification, acceptance or approval following signature made subject to ratification, acceptance or approval, or by deposit of an instrument of accession. The instruments of ratification, acceptance, approval or accession shall be deposited with the depositary.

(3) This Convention shall enter into force thirty days after consent to be bound has been expressed by three States.

(4) For each State expressing consent to be bound by this Convention after its entry into force, this Convention shall enter into force for that State thirty days after the date of expression of consent.

(5) (a) This Convention shall be open for accession, as provided for in this article, by international organizations and regional integration organizations constituted by sovereign States, which have competence in respect of the negotiation, conclusion and application of international agreements in matters covered by this Convention.

(b) In matters within their competence such organizations shall, on their own behalf, exercise the rights and fulfil the obligations which this Convention attributes to State Parties.

(c) When depositing its instrument of accession, such an organization shall communicate to the depositary a declaration indicating the extent of its competence in respect of matters covered by this Convention.

(d) Such an organization shall not hold any vote additional to those of its Member States.

Article 13
Provisional application

A State may, upon signature or at any later date before this Convention enters into force for it, declare that it will apply this Convention provisionally.

Article 14
Amendments

(1) A State Party may propose amendments to this Convention. The proposed amendment shall be submitted to the depositary who shall circulate it immediately to all other States Parties.

(2) If a majority of the States Parties request the depositary to convene a conference to consider the proposed amendments, the depositary shall invite all States Parties to attend such a conference to begin not sooner than thirty days after the invitations are issued. Any amendment adopted at the conference by a two-thirds majority of all States Parties shall be laid down in a protocol which is open to signature in Vienna and New York by all States Parties.

(3) The protocol shall enter into force thirty days after consent to be bound has been expressed by three States. For each State expressing consent to be bound by the protocol after its entry into force, the protocol shall enter into force for that State thirty days after the date of expression of consent.

Article 15
Denunciation

(1) A State Party may denounce this Convention by written notification to the depositary.

(2) Denunciation shall take effect one year following the date on which the notification is received by the depositary.

Article 16
Depositary

(1) The Director General of the Agency shall be the depositary of this Convention.

(2) The Director General of the Agency shall promptly notify States Parties and all other States of:

(a) Each signature of this Convention or any protocol of amendment;

(b) each deposit of an instrument of ratification, acceptance, approval or accession concerning this Convention or any protocol of amendment;

(c) any declaration or withdrawal thereof in accordance with article 11;

(d) any declaration of provisional application of this Convention in accordance with article 13;

(e) the entry into force of this Convention and of any amendment thereto; and

(f) any denunciation made under article 15.

Article 17
Authentic texts and certified copies

The original of this Convention, of which the Arabic, Chinese, English, French, Russian and Spanish texts are equally authentic, shall be deposited with the Director General of the International Atomic Energy Agency who shall send certified copies to States Parties and all other States.

In witness whereof the undersigned, being duly authorized, have signed this Convention, open for signature as provided for in paragraph 1 of article 12.

Adopted by the General Conference of the International Atomic Energy Agency meeting in special session at Vienna on the twenty-sixth day of September one thousand nine hundred and eighty-six.

Convention on Assistance in the Case of a Nuclear Accident or Radiological Emergency

The states parties to this convention,

Aware that nuclear activities are being carried out in a number of States.

Noting that comprehensive measures have been and are being taken to ensure a high level of safety in nuclear activities, aimed at preventing nuclear accidents and minimizing the consequences of any such accident, should it occur.

Desiring to strengthen further international co-operation in the safe development and use of nuclear energy,

Convinced of the need for an international framework which will facilitate the prompt provision of assistance in the event of a nuclear accident or radiological emergency to mitigate its consequences,

Noting the usefulness of bilateral and multilateral arrangements on mutual assistance in this area,

Noting the activities of the International Atomic Energy Agency in developing guidelines for mutual emergency assistance arrangements in connection with a nuclear accident or radiological emergency.

Have agreed as follows:

Article 1
General provisions

(1) The States Parties shall cooperate between themselves and with the International Atomic Energy Agency (hereinafter referred to as the "Agency") in accordance with the provisions of this Convention to facilitate prompt assistance in the event of a nuclear accident or radiological emergency to minimize its consequences and to protect life, property and the environment from the effects of radioactive releases.

(2) To facilitate such cooperation States Parties may agree on bilateral or multilateral arrangements or, where appropriate, a combination of these, for preventing or minimizing injury and damage which may result in the event of a nuclear accident or radiological emergency.

(3) The States Parties request the Agency, acting within the framework of its Statute, to use its best endeavours in accordance with the provisions of this Convention to promote, facilitate and support the cooperation between States Parties provided for in this Convention.

Article 2
Provision of assistance

(1) If a State Party needs assistance in the event of a nuclear accident or radiological emergency, whether or not such accident or emergency originates within its territory, jurisdiction or control, it may call for such assistance from any other State Party, directly or through the Agency, and from the Agency, or, where appropriate, from other international intergovernmental organizations (hereinafter referred to as "international organizations").

(2) A State Party requesting assistance shall specify the scope and type of assistance required and, where practicable, provide the assisting party with such information as may be necessary for that party to determine the extent to which it is able to meet the request. In the event that it is not practicable for the requesting State Party to specify the scope and type of assistance required, the requesting State Party and the assisting party shall, in consultation, decide upon the scope and type of assistance required.

(3) Each State Party to which a request for such assistance is directed shall promptly decide and notify the requesting State Party, directly or through the Agency, whether it is in a position to render the assistance requested, and the scope and terms of the assistance that might be rendered.

(4) State Parties shall, within the limits of their capabilities, identify and notify the Agency of experts, equipment and materials which could be made available for the provision of assistance to other States Parties in the event of a nuclear accident or radiological emergency as well as the terms, especially financial, under which such assistance could be provided.

(5) Any State Party may request assistance relating to medical treatment or temporary relocation into the territory of another State Party of people involved in a nuclear accident or radiological emergency.

(6) The Agency shall respond, in accordance with its Statute and as provided for in this Convention, to a requesting State Party's or a Member State's request for assistance in the event of a nuclear accident or radiological emergency by:

(a) Making available appropriate resources allocated for this purpose;

(b) transmitting promptly the request to other States and international organizations which, according to the Agency's information, may possess the necessary resources; and

(c) if so requested by the requesting State, co-ordinating the assistance at the international level which may thus become available.

Article 3

Direction and control of assistance

Unless otherwise agreed:

(a) the overall direction, control, co-ordination and supervision of the assistance shall be the responsibility within its territory of the requesting State. The assisting party should, where the assistance involves personnel, designate in consultation with the requesting State, the person who should be in charge of and retain immediate operational supervision over the personnel and the equipment provided by it. The designated person should exercise such supervision in cooperation with the appropriate authorities of the requesting State;

(b) the requesting State shall provide, to the extent of its capabilities, local facilities and services for the proper and effective administration of the assistance. It shall also ensure the protection of personnel, equipment and materials brought into its territory by or on behalf of the assisting party for such purposes;

(c) ownership of equipment and materials provided by either party during the periods of assistance shall be unaffected, and their return shall be ensured;

(d) a State Party providing assistance in response to a request under paragraph 5 of article 2 shall co-ordinate that assistance within its territory.

Article 4

Competent authorities and points of contact

(1) Each State Party shall make known to the Agency and to other State Parties, directly or through the Agency, its competent authorities and point of contact authorized to make and receive requests for and to accept offers of assistance. Such points of contact and a focal point within the Agency shall be available continuously.

(2) Each State Party shall promptly inform the Agency of any changes that may occur in the information referred to in paragraph 1.

(3) The Agency shall regularly and expeditiously provide to State Parties, Member States and relevant international organizations the information referred to in paragraphs 1 and 2.

Article 5

Functions of the Agency

The States Parties request the Agency, in accordance with paragraph 3 of article 1 and without prejudice to other provisions of this Convention, to:

(a) collect and disseminate to State Parties and Member States information concerning:

(i) experts, equipment and materials which could be made available in the event of nuclear accidents or radiological emergencies;

(ii) methodologies, techniques and available results of research relating to response to nuclear accidents or radiological emergencies;

(b) assist a State Party or a Member State when requested in any of the following or other appropriate matters:

(i) preparing both emergency plans in the case of nuclear accidents and radiological emergencies and the appropriate legislation;

(ii) developing appropriate training programmes for personnel to deal with nuclear accidents and radiological emergencies;

(iii) transmitting requests for assistance and relevant information in the event of a nuclear accident or radiological emergency;

(iv) developing appropriate radiation monitoring programmes, procedures and standards;

(v) conducting investigators into the feasibility of establishing appropriate radiation monitoring systems;

(c) make available to a State Party or a Member State requesting assistance in the event of a nuclear accident or radiological emergency appropriate resources allocated for the purpose of conducting an initial assessment of the accident or emergency;

(d) offer its good offices to the States Parties and Member States in the event of a nuclear accident or radiological emergency;

(e) establish and maintain liaison with relevant international organizations for the purposes of obtaining and exchanging relevant information and data, and make a list of such organizations available to State Parties, Member States and the aforementioned organizations.

Article 6

Confidentiality and public statements

(1) The requesting State and the assisting party shall protect the confidentiality of any confidential information that becomes available to either of them in connection with the assistance in the event of a nuclear accident or radiological emergency. Such information shall be used exclusively for the purpose of the assistance agreed upon.

(2) The assisting party shall make every effort to coordinate with the requesting State before releasing information to the public on the assistance provided in connection with a nuclear accident or radiological emergency.

Article 7

Reimbursement of costs

(1) An assisting party may offer assistance without costs to the requesting State. When considering whether to offer assistance on such a basis, the assisting party shall take into account:

(a) the nature of the nuclear accident or radiological emergency;

(b) the place of origin of the nuclear accident or radiological emergency;

(c) the needs of developing countries;

(d) the particular needs of countries without nuclear facilities; and

(e) any other relevant factors.

(2) When assistance is provided wholly or partly on a reimbursement basis, the requesting State shall reimburse the assisting party for the costs incurred for the services rendered by persons or organizations acting on its behalf, and for all expenses in connection with the assistance to the extent that such expenses are not directly defrayed by the requesting State. Unless otherwise agreed, reimbursement shall be provided promptly after the assisting party has presented its request for reimbursement to the requesting State, and in respect of costs other than local costs, shall be freely transferable.

(3) Notwithstanding paragraph 2, the assisting party may at any time waive, or agree to the postponement of, the reimbursement in whole or in part. In considering such waiver or postponement, assisting parties shall give due consideration to the needs of developing countries.

Article 8

Privileges, immunities and facilities

(1) The requesting State shall afford to personnel of the assisting party and personnel acting on its behalf the necessary privileges, immunities and facilities for the performance of their assistance functions.

(2) The requesting State shall afford the following privileges and immunities to personnel of the assisting party or personnel acting on its behalf who have been duly notified to and accepted by the requesting State:

(a) immunity from arrest, detention and legal process, including criminal, civil and administrative jurisdiction, of the requesting State, in respect of acts or omissions in the performance of their duties; and

(b) exemption from taxation, duties or other charges, except those which are normally incorporated in the price of goods or paid for services rendered, in respect of the performance of their assistance functions.

(3) The requesting State shall:

(a) Afford the assisting party exemption from taxation, duties or other charges on the equipment and property brought into the territory of the requesting State by the assisting party for the purpose of the assistance; and

(b) provide immunity from seizure, attachment or requisition of such equipment and property.

(4) The requesting State shall ensure the return of such equipment and property. If requested by the assisting party, the requesting State shall arrange, to the extent it is liable to do so, for the necessary decontamination of recoverable equipment involved in the assistance before its return.

(5) The requesting State shall facilitate the entry into, stay in and departure from its national territory of personnel notified pursuant to paragraph 2 and of equipment and property involved in the assistance.

(6) Nothing in this article shall require the requesting State to provide its nationals or permanent residents with the privileges and immunities provided for in the foregoing paragraphs.

(7) Without prejudice to the privileges and immunities, all beneficiaries enjoying such privileges and immunities under this article have a duty to respect the laws and regulations of the requesting State. They shall also have the duty not to interfere in the domestic affairs of the requesting State.

(8) Nothing in this article shall prejudice rights and obligations with respect to privileges and immunities afforded pursuant to other international agreements or the rules of customary international law.

(9) When signing, ratifying, accepting, approving or acceding to this Convention, a State may declare that it does not consider itself bound in whole or in part by paragraphs 2 and 3.

(10) A State Party which has made a declaration in accordance with paragraph 9 may at any time withdraw it by notification to the depositary.

Article 9

Transit of personnel, equipment and property

Each State Party shall, at the request of the requesting State or the assisting party, seek to facilitate the transit through its territory of duly notified personnel, equipment and property involved in the assistance to and from the requesting State.

Article 10

Claims and compensation

(1) The States Parties shall closely cooperate in order to facilitate the settlement of legal proceedings and claims under this article.

(2) Unless otherwise agreed, a requesting State shall in respect of death or of injury to persons, damage to or loss of property, or damage to the environment caused within its territory or other area under its jurisdiction or control in the course of providing the assistance requested:

(a) not bring any legal proceedings against the assisting party or persons or other legal entities acting on its behalf;

(b) assume responsibility for dealing with legal proceedings and claims brought by third parties against the assisting party or against persons or other legal entities acting on its behalf;

(c) hold the assisting party or persons or other legal entities acting on its behalf harmless in respect of legal proceedings and claims referred to in sub-paragraph (b); and

(d) compensate the assisting party or persons or other legal entities acting on its behalf for:

(i) death of or injury to personnel of the assisting party or persons acting on its behalf;

(ii) loss of or damage to non-consumable equipment or materials related to the assistance;

except in cases of wilful misconduct by the individuals who caused the death, injury, loss or damage.

(3) This article shall not prevent compensation or indemnity available under any applicable international agreement or national law of any State.

(4) Nothing in this article shall require the requesting State to apply paragraph 2 in whole or in part to its nationals or permanent residents.

(5) When signing, ratifying, accepting, approving or acceding to this Convention, a State may declare:

(a) that it does not consider itself bound in whole or in part by paragraph 2;

(b) that it will not apply paragraph 2 in whole or in part in cases of gross negligence by the individuals who caused the death, injury, loss or damage.

(6) A State Party which has made a declaration in accordance with paragraph 5 may at any time withdraw it by notification to the depositary

Article 11

Termination of assistance

The requesting State or the assisting party may at any time, after appropriate consultations and by notification in writing, request the termination of assistance received or provided under this Convention. Once such a request has been made, the parties involved shall consult with each other to make arrangements for the proper conclusion of the assistance.

Article 12

Relationship to other international agreements

This Convention shall not affect the reciprocal rights and obligations of States Parties under existing international agreements which relate to the matters covered by this Convention, or under future international agreements concluded in accordance with the object and purpose of this Convention.

Article 13

Settlement of disputes

(1) In the event of a dispute between States Parties, or between a State Party and the Agency, concerning the interpretation or application of this Convention, the parties to the dispute shall consult with a view to the

settlement of the dispute by negotiation or by any other peaceful means of settling disputes acceptable to them. (2) If a dispute of this character between States Parties cannot be settled within one year from the request for consultation pursuant to paragraph 1, it shall, at the request of any party to such dispute be submitted to arbitration or referred to the International Court of Justice for decision. Where a dispute is submitted to arbitration, if, within six months from the date of the request, the parties to the dispute are unable to agree on the organization of the arbitration, a party may request the President of the International Court of Justice or the Secretary-General of the United Nations to appoint one or more arbitrators. In cases of conflicting requests by the parties to the dispute, the request to the Secretary-General of the United Nations shall have priority.
(3) When signing, ratifying, accepting, approving or acceding to this Convention, a State may declare that it does not consider itself bound by either or both of the dispute settlement procedures provided for in paragraph 2. The other States Parties shall not be bound by a dispute settlement procedure provided for in paragraph 2 with respect to a State Party for which such a declaration is in force.
(4) A State Party which has made a declaration in accordance with paragraph 3 may at any time withdraw it by notification to the depositary.

Article 14
Entry into force
(1) This Convention shall be open for signature by all States and Namibia, represented by the United Nations Council for Namibia, at the Headquarters of the International Atomic Energy Agency in Vienna and at the Headquarters of the United Nations in New York, from 26 September 1986 and 6 October 1986 respectively, until its entry into force or for twelve months, whichever period is longer.
(2) A State and Namibia, represented by the United Nations for Namibia, may express its consent to be bound by this Convention either by signature, or by deposit of an instrument of ratification, acceptance or approval following signature made subject to ratification, acceptance, or approval, or by deposit of an instrument of accession. The instruments of ratification, acceptance, approval or accession shall be deposited with the depositary.
(3) This Convention shall enter into force thirty days after consent to be bound has been expressed by three States.
(4) For each State expressing consent to be bound by this Convention after its entry into force, this Convention shall enter into force for that State thirty days after the date of expression of consent.
(5) (a) This Convention shall be open for accession, as provided for in this article, by international organizations and regional integration organizations constituted by sovereign States, which have competence in respect of the negotiation, conclusion and application of international agreements in matters covered by this Convention.
(b) In matters within their competence such organizations shall, on their own behalf, exercise the rights and fulfil the obligations which this Convention attributes to States Parties.
(c) When depositing its instrument of accession, such an organization shall communicate to the depositary a declaration indicating the extent of its competence in respect of matters covered by this Convention.
(d) Such an organization shall not hold any vote additional to those of its Member States.

Article 15
Provisional application
A State may, upon signature or at any later date before this Convention enters into force for it, declare that it will apply this Convention provisionally.

Article 16
Amendments
(1) A State Party may propose amendments to this Convention. The proposed amendment shall be submitted to the depositary who shall circulate it immediately to all States Parties.
(2) If a majority of the States Parties request the depositary to convene a conference to consider the proposed amendments, the depositary shall invite all States Parties to attend such a conference to begin not sooner than thirty days after the invitations are issued. Any amendment adopted at the conference by a two-

thirds majority of all States Parties shall be laid down in a protocol which is open to signature in Vienna and New York by all States Parties.
(3) The protocol shall enter into force thirty days after consent to be bound has been expressed by three States. For each State expressing consent to be bound by the protocol after its entry into force, the protocol shall enter into force for that State thirty days after the date of expression of consent.

Article 17
Denunciation
(1) A State Party may denounce this Convention by written notification to the depositary.
(2) Denunciation shall take effect one year following the date on which the notification is received by the depositary.

Article 18
Depositary
(1) The Director General of the Agency shall be the depositary of this Convention.
(2) The Director General of the Agency shall promptly notify States Parties and all other States of:
(a) each signature of this Convention or any protocol of amendment;
(b) each deposit of an instrument of ratification, acceptance, approval or accession concerning this Convention or any protocol of amendment;
(c) any declaration or withdrawal thereof in accordance with articles 8, 10 and 13;
(d) any declaration of provisional application of this Convention in accordance with article 15;
(e) the entry into force of this Convention and of any amendment thereto; and
(f) any denunciation made under article 17.

Article 19
Authentic texts and certified copies
The original of this Convention, of which the Arabic, Chinese, English, French, Russian and Spanish texts are equally authentic, shall be deposited with the Director General of the International Atomic Energy Agency who shall send certified copies to States Parties and all other States.
In witness whereof the undersigned, being duly authorized, have signed this Convention, open for signature as provided for in paragraph 1 of article 14.
Adopted by the General Conference of the International Atomic Energy Agency meeting in special session at Vienna on the twenty-sixth day of September one thousand nine hundred and eighty-six.

IAEA Bulletin, Winter, 1986, pp. 52–58.

NUCLEAR ACCIDENTS AGREEMENTS, 1971-77. Agreements between the USSR and the USA, France and the UK:
(1) Agreement between the USA and the USSR on measures to reduce the risk of outbreak of nuclear war, signed at Washington, DC, on Sept. 30, 1971, entered into force the same day;
(2) Agreement between France and the USSR on the prevention of the accidental or unauthorised use of nuclear weapons, effected by exchange of letters on July 16, 1976 between the foreign ministers, entered into force the same day;
(3) Agreement between the UK and the USSR on the prevention of accidental nuclear war, signed at Moscow on Oct. 10, 1977, entered into force the same day. ▷ Accidental war.

J. GOLDBLAT, *Arms Control Agreements. A Handbook*, New York, 1983, pp. 163, 193 and 197.

NUCLEAR ARMS. Weapons of mass destruction:
(1) atomic weapons whose entire explosive energy comes from a chain reaction of the splitting of atoms of uranium-235, plutonium-239, or uranium-233;
(2) thermonuclear weapons (hydrogen fusion);
(3) nuclear weapons with compound nuclear reaction.
From the military point of view there are two kinds of nuclear weapons, strategic and tactical:
(a) missiles with atomic warheads of intercontinental range and enormous explosive destructive force;

(b) nuclear missiles with limited range from several to several hundred km and limited destructive force. Both of these kinds are included among weapons of mass destruction, since some kinds of tactical nuclear weapons located at extended positions could play the role of strategic weapons.
Subject of international disputes and conventions, one of the main contemporary international problems; which developed in conditions of particularly intense social and political tensions in the 20th century world, emerged from scientific discoveries leading to the harnessing of nuclear energy, initiated 1898–1902 by M. Sklodowska-Curie and P. Curie in France with the isolation of highly radioactive elements from uranium ore and fixing their atomic weight, (Polonium from Latin *Polonia* with the atomic number 84, and Radium from Latin *radius*, ray, with an atomic number 88). In 1905 in Germany A. Einstein published his first work on the theory of relativity: with the equation $E = mc^2$. In 1906–39 the work of A. Einstein, E. Rutheford, N. Bohr, E. Fermi, G. Gamov, L. Pauling, L. Szilard, P.L. Kapitsa, and F. Joliot-Curie developed a new branch of science: atomic physics. In 1933–40 hundreds of scientists from Central and Western Europe emigrated to the USA to escape fascist persecution, i.e. A. Einstein, who on Aug. 2, 1941 proposed to the President F.D. Roosevelt the production of an atomic bomb on the basis of the work of the Italian immigrant E. Fermi and the Hungarian L. Szilard. F.D. Roosevelt gave his consent on Oct. 19, 1941, and the first test explosion took place on July 16, 1945 in Alamogordo, New Mexico, USA, following which (against the petition of L. Szilard, signed by more than two-thirds of the scientists employed in their production) the two remaining atomic bombs were dropped on Aug. 6 and 9, 1945 on ▷ Hiroshima and Nagasaki. On July 10, 1946 the USA near Bikini atoll in the Pacific conducted the next test explosion and on July 25, 1946 the first underwater explosion, also in the Pacific; the USA made three further tests near Enevetak in the Pacific in Apr., 1948.
In the UN Atomic Energy Commission, June 1946, the USA proposed the creation of an international atomic development authority to own and manage atomic production and raw materials; the USSR proposed that priority be given to an agreement prohibiting production and use of atomic weapons. Although nuclear weapons control was deemed feasible, negotiations reached an impasse and the AEC suspended work in 1949. Meanwhile, the USSR conducted on Dec. 28, 1946 the first chain reaction and on Sept. 23, 1949 carried out its first atomic bomb test. Then in 1951 the USA conducted 16 tests, USSR – 2; in 1952 USA – 10, including one hydrogen test on Nov. 10, on Oct. 3, 1952 Great Britain conducted its first test. In 1953 USA – 11, Great Britain – 2, USSR – 2, one of them hydrogen on Aug. 12; simultaneously the USSR renewed its proposal for a complete prohibition of nuclear weapons and the destruction of existing stockpiles. In 1954 USA – 6, USSR – 1; 1955 – USA – 15; USSR – 4; 1956 – USA – 13, USSR – 7, Great Britain – 4; 1957 USA – 21, USSR – 13, Great Britain – 7, including 2 hydrogen on May 17 and Nov. 8; 1958 – USA – 5, USSR – 25, Great Britain – 5; in 1959 and 1960 on the basis of a gentleman's agreement the USA and USSR did not conduct any further tests. However, on Feb. 13, Apr. 1 and Dec. 27, 1960 France began its first tests in the Sahara in Algeria. In 1961 the USA renewed tests – 8, USSR – 31, including one of record force, France – 4; in 1962 USA – 86, USSR – 40, France – 1, Great Britain jointly with the USA – 2 underground tests. In 1963 USA – 10 underground, France – 1 underground. On Oct. 15, 1964 People's Republic of

China conducted its first test, simultaneously issuing the pronouncement that "People's China will never be the first to use this weapon"; on May 14, 1965 – a second test; on May 9, Oct. 27 and Dec. 28, 1966 – the next ones, while on June 17, 1967 – the first hydrogen test, again with the declaration:

"We again solemnly declare that at no time and in no case will China be the first to use atomic weapons. We always abide by our obligations. As in the past, the people and government of China will jointly continue the struggle with all peace-loving nations for the complete prohibition and complete destruction of nuclear weapons."

The Secretary General of the UN, U Thant, reacted with the declaration:

"In light of the UN resolutions declaring for a complete halting of tests with nuclear weapons, each explosion of whatsoever kind of nuclear and thermonuclear weapons in whatsoever part of the world is a fact to be deplored."

However, China continued its tests with hydrogen bombs on Dec. 27, 1968 and Sept. 29, 1969; it conducted its first underground test on Sept. 22, 1969. Up to Jan. 1, 1972 the USA conducted 188 tests in the atmosphere and 351 underground; USSR – 142 and 112; Great Britain 21 and 4 (in co-operation with the USA); France 30 and 43; China 11 and 1. In sum 873 explosions took place in nearly 30 years, not counting Hiroshima and Nagasaki. In June, 1972 a wave of protests was caused by French hydrogen bomb tests in the Pacific, on Mururoa atoll, French Polynesia.

In Nov., 1972 the UN General Assembly again demanded that France cease nuclear tests in the Pacific 105 votes against 4 (including the Chinese People's Republic and France) with 9 abstentions. The chronicle of UN activities in reference to nuclear weapons is as follows:

1946 – in its first Res. 1/I the UN General Assembly unanimously established the Atomic Energy Commission for the purpose of creating a system of control that would prohibit the utilization of nuclear energy for anything other than peaceful purposes.

1947–49 – UN General Assembly examined reports of the Commission, Dec. 14, 1946, Sept. 11, 1947, May 17, 1948 and Feb. 18, 1949. In 1950 the USSR withdrew from the AEC and the Commission on Conventional Armaments over the question of Chinese representation, and both Commissions were dissolved in 1952.

In 1952 – UN General Assembly decided that the problems of nuclear weapons as well as conventional weapons should be examined by the Disarmament Commission, composed of the 11 members of the Security Council and Canada, later enlarged by 11 additional members and in 1958 enlarged again to include all UN member states, in 1953–55 the work of the Disarmament Commission was without result, but in the UN General Assembly a movement in favor of prohibiting hydrogen bomb tests began to take shape. In 1955 Session the UN General Assembly established the Scientific Committee on the Effects of Atomic Radiation, and the information published by it annually from 1958 on the increasing pollution of the earth's atmosphere acted to mobilize world opinion, leading to the signing on Aug. 5, 1963 in Moscow, in the presence of the UN Secretary-General U Thant, of a Treaty banning nuclear weapons tests in the atmosphere, in outer space and under water, 1963 in accordance with UN General Assembly Res. 1378/XIV, 1653/XVI, 1722/XVII, 1976/XXVII, 1801/XVII and 1098, 1909 and 1910/XVIII.

In 1962 the Soviet Union submitted to the Eighteen-Nation Committee on Disarmament a Draft Treaty on general and complete disarmament under strict international control and the United States sub-mitted an Outline of basic provisions for a treaty on general and complete disarmament in a peaceful world. The plans differed significantly on the order of the disarmament measures, verification, and peace-keeping. The differences proved to be obstacles to future progress. The two drafts, as amended from time to time during the following years, were discussed extensively by the General Assembly. Although the debate did not lead to agreement on general and complete disarmament, it was recognized that pragmatic efforts to achieve solutions to partial aspects of the problem should be encouraged. Consequently, the Assembly in several resolutions in the following years called for efforts both towards general and complete disarmament and on specific collateral measures.

In 1964–67 attention was shifting to such questions as the non-proliferation of nuclear weapons and the cessation of nuclear weapons testing, and later to the matter of chemical and bacteriological (biological) weapons, although general and complete disarmament clearly remained the ultimate goal. The concern of member states about the dangerous consequences of a possible spread of nuclear weapons was expressed in a series of resolutions, adopted by the General Assembly from 1959 on, calling for efforts to reach an agreement to prevent such a spread. The wide support for such an agreement was significantly strengthened by a 1967 report on the effects of the possible use of nuclear weapons and the security and economic implications for states of the acquisition and further development of these weapons.

During 1966 and the first half of 1967, intensive negotiations were conducted among the main nuclear powers and their allies, both inside and outside the Eighteen-Nation Committee on Disarmament, in a major effort to work out an agreed text of a non-proliferation treaty. These negotiations resulted in the tabling by the Soviet Union and the United States of separate, identical draft treaties in Aug., 1967. After several revisions the final draft of the treaty was submitted to the resumed 22nd session of the General Assembly in May, 1968. On June 12, the Assembly, by an overwhelming vote, commended the Treaty on the Non-Proliferation of Nuclear Weapons and expressed the hope for the widest possible adherence to it. On July 1, 1968, the Treaty was opened for signature and was signed on the same day by the United Kingdom, the Soviet Union, the United States and more than 50 other countries.

During the negotiations on the Treaty, many non-nuclear-weapon states expressed a desire to receive certain additional assurances with regard to their security against nuclear attack. The United Kingdom, the Soviet Union and the United States agreed to sponsor a resolution on security assurances in the Security Council, which bears primary responsibility for the maintenance of international peace. The resolution was adopted by the Council in June 1968. It stressed that "any aggression accompanied by the use of nuclear weapons would endanger the peace and security of all states." The Council recognized that aggression with nuclear weapons or the threat of such aggression against a non-nuclear-weapon state would create a situation in which the Council, and above all its nuclear-weapon-state permanent members, would have to act immediately in accordance with their obligations under the Charter. The Council reaffirmed in particular the inherent right, recognized under art. 51 of the Charter, of individual and collective self-defence if an armed attack occurred against a member of the United Nations, until the Security Council had taken measures necessary to maintain international peace and security.

The Treaty entered into force on Mar. 5, 1970 and, as of Dec., 1977, about 100 states had become parties to it. In accordance with its art. VIII, the states parties met at Geneva in May 1975 to review the Treaty's operation. A 10-page Final Declaration adopted by the Conference expressed the view that the conclusion of a treaty banning all nuclear weapon tests was one of the most important measures to halt the nuclear arms race. The Conference called on the Soviet Union and the United States, as the nuclear-weapon states signatories of the Treaty on the Limitation of Underground Nuclear Weapon Tests, to keep their underground nuclear weapon tests to a minimum, since this would aid negotiations for a treaty banning all nuclear weapon test explosions for all time.

The Final Declaration stated further that the review undertaken by the Conference confirmed that the Treaty's provisions prohibiting transfer of nuclear weapons and nuclear-weapon technology from nuclear-weapon states to non-nuclear-weapon states had been faithfully observed by all parties. The continued strict observance of those provisions was described as central to the objective of averting the further proliferation of nuclear weapons.

In 1968–72 the USA and USSR, carrying on negotiations called SALT I, reached and concluded the followed agreements connected with nuclear weapons: Treaty on the limitation of anti ballistic missile systems, signed in Moscow on May 26, 1972 (Supplementary protocol signed on July 3, 1974 in Moscow); as well as Temporary agreement on some measures to limit strategic offensive armaments for five years, signed on May 26, 1972 in Moscow; in 1973, on June 22, President R. Nixon and Secretary-General CC CPSU L. Brezhnev in Washington signed the Agreement on the prevention of nuclear war. On July 3, 1974 in Moscow these same statesmen signed the Treaty on the Limitation of Underground Nuclear Weapons Tests, prohibiting the carrying out of any underground nuclear explosions with a yield of more than 150 kilotons for a period of five years from May 31, 1976 to May 30, 1980.

In 1976 on May 28 in Moscow President G. Ford and L. Brezhnev signed the Peaceful Nuclear Explosions Treaty, prohibiting explosions exceeding 150 kilotons or a series of explosions quickly following one another with an aggregate yield of more than 1500 kilotons.

On July 16, 1976 in Moscow the governments of France and the USSR signed an Agreement on the prevention of the accidental or unauthorized use of nuclear weapons.

On Nov. 26, 1976 the heads of state of the Warsaw Pact addressed the remaining signatory states of ▷ Helsinki Final Act, 1975, with an appeal for the signing of a treaty obligating all signatories not to be the first to use nuclear weapons against each other.

The Main Political Committee of the UN General Assembly on Dec. 10, 1976 ratified with 105 votes to 2 (China and Albania) a resolution condemning the carrying out of any kinds of experiments with nuclear weapons in all natural environments.

In 1979 the USA and USSR reached and concluded the SALT II agreement, but it was not ratified. On Sept. 25, 1980 the USA and the USSR reached an agreement to start negotiation in Geneva on reducing nuclear missiles in Europe; suspended by the USSR in November 1983, after the installation of Pershing missiles in Western Europe, and in retaliation of SS 20 missiles in the GDR and Czechoslovakia in January 1984.

The US Defence Department estimates, that in 1965 the US strategic warheads were 1700 and the USSR – 340; in 1975 the US – 6790, the USSR – 3890; in 1984 the US – 11,030, the USSR – 9710.

In 1986 the USA introduced new strategic nuclear weapon systems the MX missile and the B-1B bomber; the USSR–the SS-N-23 missile. On Jan 15, 1986 the USSR proposed a ban on all nuclear weapons by the year 2000.

H. KISSINGER, *Nuclear Weapons and Foreign Policy*, Boston, 1957; G. SCHWARZENBERGER, *The Legality of Nuclear Weapons*, London, 1958; C. DELMAS, *Histoire Politique de la Bombe Atomique*, Paris, 1967; *The Threat of Nuclear Weapons*, UN New York, 1968; A.J. EFREMOV, *Europa i iadernoe oruzhie*, Moscow, 1972; G. BERLIA, *Problèmes nucléaires et relations internationales*, Paris, 1972; E.W. LEFEVER, *Nuclear Arms in the Third World. US Policy Dilemma*, Washington, DC, 1980; J. LIDER, *Towards a Nuclear Doctrine. The 1950s*, Stockholm, 1981; *UN Chronicle*, June 1982, p. 62; J. GOLDBLAT, *Arms Control and Disarmament, A Handbook*, New York, 1983; P. BRACKEN, *The Command and Control of Nuclear Forces*, New Haven, 1983; G.F. KENNAN, *The Nuclear Delusion*, New York, 1983; *Newsweek*, October 1, 1984, pp. 12–14; S. McLEAN, *How Nuclear Weapons Decisions are made*, London, 1986; W. RUDIS, *Anti-Nuclear Movements. A World Survey*, London, 1987; R.K. BETTS, *Nuclear Blackmail and Nuclear Balance*, Washington DC, 1987; *The Soviet Proposals for Complete Nuclear Disarmament*, WPC Helsinki, 1987; R. MCNAMARA, *Blundering Into Disaster; Surveying the First Country of the Nuclear Age*, New York, 1987.

NUCLEAR CLUB. An international military term, since 1948 for the Five Big Nuclear Powers ▷ the USA, the USSR, France, the UK and China.

D. ROBERTSON, *Guide to Modern Defense and Strategy*, London, 1988.

NUCLEAR DAMAGE. ▷ Nuclear Accident Convention 1986.

NUCLEAR DATA CENTERS. There are two international centers dealing with nuclear data; the ▷ IAEA in Vienna (Austria), and the Nuclear Energy Agency of the ▷ OECD at Saclay (France). The major national centers are in the USA and USSR.

NUCLEAR DISENGAGEMENT IN EUROPE ▷ Denuclearized Zones.

NUCLEAR EDUCATION AND TRAINING. The IAEA program of education and training in nuclear sciences and engineering. In many developing countries an insufficient number of qualified personnel is one of the principal constraints to nuclear development. The infrastructure for nuclear education and training consists primarily of universities, technological centres and industry organizations. The nuclear power program activities with national participation considered essential are:

Nuclear power programme planning and co-ordination; Power system planning; Development of a legal and organizational framework; International agreements and arrangements; National participation planning and co-ordination; Manpower development planning and implementation; Feasibility studies; Site evaluation; Preparation of bid specifications; Bid evaluation; Contracting; Project management (utility); Establishment of quality assurance policy; Emergency planning; Public information and public relations; Safeguards and physical protection; Site preparation; Erection of plant buildings and structures; Plant equipment and systems installation; Plant operation and maintenance; Radiological protection and environmental surveillance; Fuel procurement; Fuel management and storage at the power plant; Fuel transport and off-site storage within the country; Waste management; Nuclear licensing and regulation.

IAEA Bulletin, No 2, 1988, pp. 5–50.

NUCLEAR ENERGY AGENCY OF THE OECD. ▷ OECD.

NUCLEAR ENERGY OR NUCLEAR POWER. An international term, subject of international research and control by the ▷ IAEA. The UN Conference on Promotion of International Co-Operation in the Peaceful Uses of Nuclear Energy was convened from March 23 to April 10, 1987 in Geneva.

J.A. HALL, *The International Atomic Energy Agency. Origins and Early Years, in; IAEA Bulletin 1987*, No 2.

NUCLEAR EXPLOSIONS 1945–1986. The SIPRI statistic of known and presumed nuclear explosions give for the period between July 16, 1945 and August 5, 1963 following data: the USA – 216 atmospheric explosions and 115 underground; the USSR – 183 and 2; the UK – 21 and 2; France – 4 and 2; total 545; and in the period between August 6, 1963 and December 31, 1986 the USA – 0 and 484; the USSR – 0 and 412; the UK – 0 and 17; France – 41 and 91; China – 22 and 7; India – 0 and 1; total 1075. Estimated number of nuclear explosions July 16, 1945 – December 31, 1986; the USA – 815; the USSR – 597; the UK – 40; France – 140; China – 29; India – 1; total – 1622. In 1986 the USA conducted 14 explosions, France 8, and the UK (with the USA) 1, China and the USSR – none. A large underground explosion jointly monitored by Soviet and US experts took place in Nevada on Aug. 17, 1988.

SIPRI *Yearbook 1987*, Oxford, 1988, pp. 54–55.

NUCLEAR EXPLOSIONS FOR PEACEFUL PURPOSES. An international problem closely connected with the ▷ Non-Proliferation Treaty, 1968 and the ▷ Denuclearized Zones; i.e. the object of tripartite, Soviet–American–British, negotiations concerning a treaty on the complete prohibition of nuclear weapons tests. At a conference of states not possessing nuclear weapons on Sept. 4, 1968, Mexico submitted a proposal for establishing a Supervising Body for Nuclear Assistance for Peaceful Use, which would enable those states relinquishing atomic weapons to benefit from peaceful nuclear explosions without bearing the additional costs of research and experimentation. To a certain degree such an organ became the system for the supervision of radioactive substances ▷ IAEA. The American–Soviet technical talks on the use of nuclear explosions for peaceful purposes were held in Vienna in Apr., 1969 and in Moscow in Feb., 1970:

"Recognizing an important role to be played by the IAEA in the future in assisting the utilization of potential benefits from peaceful nuclear explosions by non-nuclear weapons countries, the two sides expressed their intention to promote appropriate scientific and technical studies within the framework of the IAEA and in light of Art. 5 of the Non-Proliferation Treaty."

A UN Conference on the peaceful use of nuclear energy, originally scheduled for 1983 was postponed for 1986, by UN General Assembly Res. 38/60 on Dec. 14, 1983.

IAEA, Peaceful Nuclear Explosion, 2 Vols., Vienna, 1970–71; *Recueil de documents*, Varsovie No. 2, 1980; *UN Chronicle*, March, 1983, pp. 27–28.

NUCLEAR FISSION AND NUCLEAR FUSION. The international terms for the physical processes underlying the operation of the ▷ atomic bomb and ▷ hydrogen bomb.

D. ROBERTSON, *Guide to Modern Defense and Strategy*, Detroit, 1988.

NUCLEAR FREE SEA CAMPAIGN. ▷ Greenpeace.

NUCLEAR LAW INTERNATIONAL. The subject of multilateral agreements on atomic energy, elaborated and concluded under the auspices of the UN. International nuclear law developed in three directions: (1) the banning of nuclear weapons tests and of nuclear weapons; (2) the establishment of safe forms of peaceful utilization of nuclear energy and the development of the international co-operation required to this end; (3) civil liability for damages caused by nuclear energy. Multilateral agreements were initiated in 1945 by the Washington Declaration of the governments of Canada, the UK and the USA. In 1953 the Convention on European Organization for Nuclear Research, CERN, was signed. In 1956 the Dubna Joint Institute of Nuclear Research was founded and the Statute of the IAEA was approved. EURATOM was set up in 1958. The Convention on Civil Liability for Nuclear Damages was held in Vienna in 1963, with additional Protocols in 1966. In 1980 the IAEA Convention on ▷ Nuclear Material Protection. The international nuclear law includes also the outer space international law, prohibiting the deployment of nuclear weapons in ▷ outer space (▷ Outer Space Exploration Treaty, 1967).

NUCLEAR MATERIAL PROTECTION. The subject of the IAEA Convention on the Physical Protection of Nuclear Material, opened for signature on Mar. 3, 1980 in Vienna and at the UN headquarters in New York. The Convention applies to the international transport of nuclear material (plutonium and uranium) used for peaceful purposes, 43 states and Euratom have signed the Convention and 21 ratified. The Convention entered into force on Feb. 8, 1987.

SIPRI, *World Armaments and Disarmament Yearbook, 1980*, London, 1980, pp. 335–343; A.F. PANASEN-KOV, "Co-operation among CMEA Member Countries in the Development of Nuclear Energy", in: *IAEA Bulletin*, August, 1980, pp. 95–99; D.L. SLAZON Jr., "The Convention on the Physical Protection of Nuclear Material", in: *IAEA Bulletin*, August, 1980, pp. 57–62; *UN Chronicle*, March, 1983, p. 48; *IAEA Bulletin*, 1987, No 1, p. 55.

NUCLEAR MATERIAL SUPPLIES ASSURANCE. ▷ CAS.

NUCLEAR MEDICINE. The medical application of nuclear technology under supervision of the IAEA and WHO, subject of international co-operation and research.

IAEA Nuclear Medicine and Related Radionuclide Applications in the Developing Countries, Vienna, 1986; R. GANATRA, M. NOFAL, *Promoting Nuclear Medicine in Developing Countries, in: IAEA Bulletin*, Summer, 1986; E. TOUYA, *Nuclear Medicine in Latin America, in: IAEA Bulletin*, 1987, No 1.

NUCLEAR NON-PROLIFERATION ACT, 1978. A US law setting strict controls on the export of nuclear fuel, signed by President Jimmy Carter on Mar. 10, 1978. The law linked the peaceful use of nuclear power for energy needs with the dangers of nuclear proliferation. If a non-nuclear weapons state detonates a nuclear device or violates IAEA safeguards, the US has the right immediately to sever nuclear co-operation. J. Carter said: "Control over the spread of nuclear weapons on our planet is one of the paramount questions of our time." The Act urges other nations to sign the Nuclear ▷ Non-Proliferation Treaty, 1968.

KEESING'S *Contemporary Archive*, 1978.

NUCLEAR PARTIAL TESTS BAN TREATY, 1963. ▷ Outer Space Moscow Treaty, 1963.

NUCLEAR PEACE. The world situation in the late 20th century existing on the basis of nuclear balance, compared to a kind of postprandial feeling when each side realizes it has had enough, though not necessarily bringing any comfort to the nonnuclear Third World.

NUCLEAR PLANNING GROUP, NPG. ▷ An ad hoc committee of NATO established in 1967 as a consulting forum of the USA with its European partners.

D. ROBERTSON, *Guide to Modern Defense and Strategy*, Detroit, 1988.

NUCLEAR POWER PERFORMANCE AND SAFETY, INTERNATIONAL CONFERENCE 1987. Held in relation to the tragedy of ▷ Chernobyl from Sept. 28 to Oct. 2, 1987 in Vienna, attended by 5000 participants from 40 countries and 12 international organizations with the aim to support national and international efforts to improve the performance and safety of nuclear power plants.

IAEA Bulletin, No 4, 1987.

NUCLEAR REACTOR INSPECTIONS. The IAEA inspections since 1982 of safety arrangements in the reactors of civilian atomic power plants. After ▷ Chernobyl the USSR, Czechoslovakia and Hungary invited the IAEA in September 1987 to send inspectors to check the safety of their reactors.

NUCLEAR REACTORS AND NUCLEAR TECHNOLOGY. The IAEA since 1962 keeps a Catalogue of Nuclear Reactors which is updated every six months and also makes inspections of experimental work in laboratories and reactors in countries which have agreed to such control, to ascertain that reactors in a given country are not utilized against the ▷ Non-Proliferation Treaty, 1968.

In Jan., 1976 the governments of Canada, France, the FRG, Japan, the UK, USA and the USSR as states exporting nuclear technology, signed a treaty in the nature of a Gentleman's Agreement setting out the conditions which would make nuclear technology available to other countries. The matter concerned states that had not signed the Non-proliferation Treaty and were not subject to the supervision of the IAEA in Vienna (e.g. Argentina, Brazil). The understanding of the seven exporter states was that each party to the agreement would inform the other six before signing a contract for the sale of nuclear fuel, reactors, or plants for the preparation of uranium or the processing of used fuel. In such transactions each party would impose the same conditions relating to the control of the use of fissile materials as the other partners. None of them would strive to gain an advantage at the expense of the remaining parties to the agreement.

According to IAEA information the first electricity produced by a nuclear reactor came from the EBR-1 power station, USA, on Dec. 20, 1951; then from APS-1 Obninsk, USSR on June 26, 1954.

Largest operating reactor at end of 1985: Ignalino-1 in the USSR, with a net capacity of 1450 megawatts-electric (MWe) and a gross capacity of 1500 MWe. Second is Grohnde, in the Federal Republic of Germany, with net capacity of 1319 MWe and gross capacity of 1391 MWe, followed by two United States entries: Palo verde-1 (1304 MWe net capacity, 1336 MWe gross capacity) and Grand Gulf-1 (1250 MWe net capacity, 1372 MWe gross capacity). Which of these two is in third position depends upon how capacity is measured. (The IAEA always quotes net capacity.)

Largest reactor under construction: Chooz-B1 in France, with net capacity of 1457 MWe (1516 MWe gross). Construction started in January 1984 and when the plant begins scheduled operations in 1991, it will become the world's largest operating nuclear reactor.

Largest nuclear power station: Fukushima in Japan, where nine nuclear units were in operation at the end of 1985 with total net capacity of 7747 MWe (7796 MWe gross). Another unit at Fukushima is scheduled for operation in 1986 that would add 1067 MWe net capacity (1100 MWe gross). Second is Graveline in France, with six nuclear units having net capacity of 5460 MWe (5706 MWe gross). Third is Bruce in Canada, with six units having net capacity of 4606 MWe (4910 MWe gross).

Projected range of nuclear power capacity in Gigawatts-electric:

	1985	1995	2000	2025
OECD Countries	207	320	365–429	555–1150
Developing countries outside CPE	12	22	36– 71	120– 405
CPE countries	35	85	96–146	200– 605
World	254	427	497–646	875–2160

In 1990 40 of the world's 61 operational nuclear research reactors are expected to be in developing countries, which term includes the East European states.

The USSR agreed in February 1985 to allow the IAEA to inspect its nuclear reactors.

W.E. CLASON, *Elsevier's Dictionary of Nuclear Science and Technology. In English/American (with definitions), French, Spanish, Italian, Dutch and German*, Amsterdam, 1978; *WHO. Nuclear Power: Accidental Releases. Principles of Public Health Action*, Geneva, 1984; *IAEA Bulletin*, Spring 1986; *Nuclear Energy and its Fuel Cycle: prospects to 2025*, IAEA, Vienna, 1987; *IAEA Newsbrief*, No. 8, 1987.

NUCLEAR RESEARCH DUBNA JOINT INSTITUTE. Obyedinionniy institut yadiernikh issledovaniy v Dubney. The institute established by the CMEA member states on Mar. 26, 1956 in Moscow with headquarters in Dubna, near Moscow, USSR. Aims: research in developing nuclear physics and the peaceful use of atomic energy. Members: Albania (up to 1967), Bulgaria, China (up to 1967), Czechoslovakia, GDR, Hungary, North Korea, Mongolia, Poland, Romania, Vietnam, USSR. Publ.: *Technical Reports*. Reg. with the UIA.

W.E. BUTLER (ed.), *A Source Book on Socialist International Organizations*, Alphen, 1978, pp. 543–571; *Yearbook of International Organizations*.

NUCLEAR SAFETY STANDARDS, NUSS. The IAEA program for land-based nuclear power plants with thermal neutron reactors. The program is divided into five Codes of Practice and safety guides: Code of Practice on Governmental Organization for the Nuclear Power Plants, Code of Practice on Safety in Nuclear Power Plant Siting, Code of Practice on Design for Safety of Nuclear Power Plants, Code of Safety in Nuclear Power Plant Operation, and Code of Quality Assurance for Safety in Nuclear Power Plants.

In conjunction with an IAEA team of experts the program sponsored the Nuclear Safety Advisory Group, INSAG.

"Nuclear Safety Standards Program", in: *IAEA Bulletin*, October, 1978; M. ROSEN, *New Directions in Nuclear Safety, in: IAEA Bulletin*, Autumn 1986.

NUCLEAR SCIENCE AND TECHNOLOGY. Subject of an IAEA promotion program in the fields of nuclear energy and its peaceful application in agriculture, hydrology, medicine, nuclear physics and nuclear safety. A Regional Co-operative Arrangement for the Promotion of Nuclear Science and Technology in Latin America involved in the IAEA's program since 1984 is known as ARCAL Arreglos Regionales Cooperativos para la Promoción de la Ciencia y a Tecnología Nuclear en América Latina. Members: Argentina, Bolivia, Brazil, Chile, Colombia, Costa Rica, Cuba, Ecuador, Guatemala, Mexico, Paraguay, Peru, Uruguay, and Venezuela. The IAEA holds regional and interregional training courses in nuclear safety, science and technology.

IAEA Newsbriefs, July–August, 1988.

NUCLEAR SUBMARINES. ▷ Submarines.

NUCLEAR SUPPLIERS CLUB. ▷ London Club of Nuclear Suppliers.

NUCLEAR TEST BAN. Subject of negotiations between the atomic powers since 1957, when the USSR in the UN Disarmament Commission demanded a temporary moratorium to start negotiation on a total test ban, independently of other arms control measures. The ▷ Outerspace Moscow Treaty, a Treaty Banning Nuclear Weapon Tests in the Atmosphere, in Outer Space and Under Water, called also the Limited or Partial Test Ban Treaty was signed on Aug. 5, 1963.

On July 3, 1974 the USA and USSR signed the ▷ Threshold Test Ban Treaty, imposing limitation on underground nuclear weapons explosions to a maximum of about 150 kilotons (unratified).

In 1976 the USA and USSR accepted the ▷ Nuclear Explosions for Peaceful Purposes Treaty (unratified).

In October 1986 during the ▷ Reykjavik Summit the USSR (after a testing moratorium initiated by the USSR in July 1985) urged immediate negotiations on a comprehensive or complete nuclear test ban.

The GA has adopted more than fifty resolutions on the subject since 1958 and on eight different occasions it has condemned such tests in the strongest terms in view of their increasing danger of nuclear war. The GA Res. 43/64 on Dec. 7, 1988, adopted by 146 votes to 2 (France, USA) with 6 abstentions (Argentina, Brazil, China, India, Israel, UK) entitled "Urgent need for a comprehensive nuclear-test-ban-treaty":

"(1) Reaffirms its conviction that a treaty to achieve the prohibition of all nuclear-test explosions by all States in all environments for all time is a matter of fundamental importance;
(2) Urges, therefore, that the following actions be taken in order that a comprehensive nuclear-test-ban treaty may be concluded at an early date:
(a) The Conference on Disarmament should intensify its consideration of item 1 of its agenda entitled "Nuclear-test-ban" and initiate substantive work on all aspects of a nuclear-test-ban treaty at the beginning of its 1989 session;
(b) States members of the Conference on Disarmament, in particular the nuclear-weapon States and all other States should co-operate in order to facilitate its 1989 session;
(c) The nuclear-weapon States, especially those that possess the most important nuclear arsenals, should agree promptly to appropriate verifiable and militarily significant interim measures, with a view to realizing a comprehensive nuclear-test-ban treaty;
(d) Those nuclear-weapon States that have not yet done so should adhere to the Treaty Banning Nuclear Weapons Tests in the Atmosphere in Outer Space and under Water."

P. DOTY, *A Nuclear Test Ban, in: Foreign Affairs*, Spring, 1987; *UN Resolutions and Decisions Adopted by the General Assembly during the First Part of its Forty-Third Session, From 20 September to 22 December, 1988*; New York, 1989, p. 120.

NUCLEAR TRANSFER. A subject of international agreement. The Guidelines for Nuclear Transfers were adopted by the member states of the so-called Vienna Club on Jan. 11, 1978. The text is as follows:

"(1) The following fundamental principles for safeguards and export controls should apply to nuclear transfers to any non-nuclear-weapon state for peaceful purposes. In this connection, suppliers have defined an export trigger list and agreed on common criteria for technology transfers.

Prohibition on Nuclear Explosives.

(2) Suppliers should authorize transfer of items identified in the trigger list only upon formal governmental assurances from recipients explicitly excluding uses which would result in any nuclear explosive device.

Physical Protection.

(3)(a) All nuclear materials and facilities identified by the agreed trigger list should be placed under effective physical protection to prevent unauthorized use and handling. The levels of physical protection to be ensured in relation to the type of materials, equipment and facilities, have been agreed by suppliers, taking account of international recommendations.

(b) The implementation of measures of physical protection in the recipient country is the responsibility of the government of that country. However, in order to implement the terms agreed upon amongst suppliers, the levels of physical protection on which these measures have to be based should be the subject of an agreement between supplier and recipient.

(c) In each case special arrangements should be made for a clear definition of responsibilities for the transport of trigger list items.

Safeguards

(4) Suppliers should transfer trigger list items only when covered by IAEA safeguards, with duration and coverage provisions in conformance with the GOV/ 1621 guidelines. Exceptions should be made only after consultation with the parties to this understanding.

(5) Suppliers will jointly reconsider their common safeguards requirements, whenever appropriate.

Safeguards Triggered by the Transfer of Certain Technology.

(6)(a) The requirements of paragraphs 2, 3 and 4 above should also apply to facilities for reprocessing, enrichment, or heavy water production, utilizing technology directly transferred by the supplier or derived from transferred facilities, or major critical components thereof.

(b) The transfer of such facilities, or major critical components thereof, or related technology, should require an undertaking (1) that IAEA safeguards apply to any facilities of the same type (i.e. if the design, construction or operating processes are based on the same or similar physical or chemical processes, as defined in the trigger list) constructed during an agreed period in the recipient country and (2) that there should at all times be in effect a safeguards agreement permitting the IAEA to apply Agency safeguards with respect to such facilities identified by the recipient, or by the supplier in consultation with the recipient, as using transferred technology.

Special Controls on Sensitive Exports

(7) Suppliers should exercise restraint in the transfer of sensitive facilities, technology and weapon-usable materials. If enrichment or reprocessing facilities, equipment or technology are to be transferred, suppliers should encourage recipients to accept, as an alternative to national plants, supplier involvement and/or other appropriate multinational participation in resulting facilities. Suppliers should also promote international (including IAEA) activities concerned with multinational regional fuel cycle centres.

Special Controls on Export of Enrichment Facilities, Equipment and Technology.

(8) For a transfer of an enrichment facility, or technology therefor, the recipient nation should agree that neither the transferred facility, nor any facility based on such technology, will be designed or operated for the production of greater than 20% enriched uranium without the consent of the supplier nation, of which the IAEA should be advised.

Controls on Supplied or Derived Weapons-Usable Material

(9) Suppliers recognize the importance, in order to advance the objectives of these Guidelines and to provide opportunities further to reduce the risks of proliferation, of including in agreements on supply of nuclear materials or of facilities which produce weapons-usable material, provisions calling for mutual agreement between the supplier and the recipient on arrangements for re-processing, storage, alteration, use, transfer or retransfer of any weapons-usable material involved. Suppliers should endeavour to include such provisions whenever appropriate and practicable.

Controls on Retransfer

(10)(a) Suppliers should transfer trigger list items, including technology defined under paragraph 6, only upon the recipient's assurance that in the case of:

(i) retransfer of such items, or

(ii) transfer of trigger list items derived from facilities originally transferred by the supplier, or with the help of equipment or technology originally transferred by the supplier; the recipient of the retransfer or transfer will have provided the same assurances as those required by the supplier for the original transfer.

(b) In addition the supplier's consent should be required for:

(i) any retransfer of the facilities, major critical components, or technology described in paragraph 6; (ii) any transfer of facilities or major critical components derived from those items; (iii) any retransfer of heavy water or weapons-usable material.

Supporting Activities. Physical Security.

(11) Suppliers should promote international co-operation on the exchange of physical security information, protection of nuclear materials in transit, and recovery of stolen nuclear materials and equipment.

Support for Effective IAEA Safeguards.

(12) Suppliers should make special efforts in support of effective implementation of IAEA safeguards. Suppliers should also support the Agency's efforts to assist member states in the improvement of their national systems of accounting and control of nuclear material and to increase the technical effectiveness of safeguards.

Similarly, they should make every effort to support the IAEA in increasing further the adequacy of safeguards in the light of technical developments and the rapidly growing number of nuclear facilities, and to support appropriate initiatives aimed at improving the effectiveness of IAEA safeguards.

Sensitive Plant Design Features.

(13) Suppliers should encourage the designers and makers of sensitive equipment to construct it in such a way as to facilitate the application of safeguards.

Consultations

(14)(a) Suppliers should maintain contact and consult through regular channels on matters connected with the implementation of these Guidelines.

(b) Suppliers should consult, as each deems appropriate, with other Governments concerned on specific sensitive cases, to ensure that any transfer does not contribute to risks of conflict or instability.

(c) In the event that one or more suppliers believe that there has been a violation of supplier/recipient understandings resulting from these Guidelines, particularly on the case of an explosion of a nuclear device, or illegal termination or violation of IAEA safeguards by a recipient, suppliers should consult promptly through diplomatic channels in order to determine and assess the reality and extent of the alleged violation.

Pending the early outcome of such consultations, suppliers will not act in a manner that could prejudice any measure that may be adopted by other suppliers concerning their current contacts with that recipient.

Upon the findings of such consultations, the suppliers, bearing in mind Article XII of the IAEA Statute, should agree on an appropriate response and possible action which could include the termination of nuclear transfers to that recipient.

(15) In considering transfers each supplier should exercise prudence having regard to all the circumstances of each case, including any risk that technology transfers not covered by paragraph 6, or subsequent retransfers, might result in unsafeguarded nuclear materials.

(16) Unanimous consent is required for any changes in these Guidelines, including any which might result from the reconsideration mentioned in paragraph 5".

Recueil de Documents, Varsovie, No. 12, 1978, pp. 7–12.

NUCLEAR UMBRELLA. An international military term for the protection of Central European Warsaw Pact countries by the USSR and Western European NATO countries by the USA.

D. ROBERTSON, *Guide to Modern Defense and Strategy*, Detroit 1988.

NUCLEAR WAR. A military operation with the use of nuclear weapons threatening the complete destruction of human civilization. The subject of numerous treaties and international conventions aiming at the prevention of nuclear war; one of the main problems of disarmament negotiations. Historically, the era of atomic war started by the USA against Japan in Aug. 1945, resulting in the destruction of ▷ Hiroshima and Nagasaki. After World War II the struggle for peace became in the first instance the struggle against the possibility of the outbreak of thermonuclear war. On Aug. 5, 1963 was signed the Treaty Banning Nuclear Weapon Test in the Atmosphere, in Outer Space and Under Water, called the ▷ Outer Space Moscow Treaty, 1963. On Oct. 23, 1967, the UN Secretary-General published a report on the possible consequences of the use of nuclear weapons, drafted and unanimously approved by a group of experts from France, Japan, Mexico, Nigeria, Norway, Poland, Sweden, the USA and the USSR. In the report it was emphasized that:

"No nuclear power can attack another without provoking a nuclear counterattack."

"If a nuclear conflict occurs, regardless of the manner in which it begins, not a single state can feel safe."

The nuclear war risk was the subject of American-- Soviet Agreement on Measure to Reduce the Risk of Outbreak of Nuclear War, signed on Sept. 30, 1971 at Washington; came into force on signature. The text is as follows:

"The United States of America and the Union of Soviet Socialist Republics, hereinafter referred to as the Parties:

Taking into account the devastating consequences that nuclear war would have for all mankind, and recognizing the need to exert every effort to avert the risk of outbreak of such a war, including measures to guard against accidental or unauthorized use of nuclear weapons.

Believing that agreement on measures for reducing the risk of outbreak of nuclear war serves the interests of strengthening international peace and security, and is in no way contrary to the interests of any other country.

Bearing in mind that continued efforts are also needed in the future to seek ways of reducing the risk of outbreak of nuclear war,

Have agreed as follows:

Art. 1. Each Party undertakes to maintain and to improve, as it deems necessary, its existing organizational and technical arrangements to guard against the accidental or unauthorized use of nuclear weapons under its control.

Art. 2. The Parties undertake to notify each other immediately in the event of an accidental, unauthorized or any other unexplained incident involving a possible detonation of a nuclear weapon which could create a risk of outbreak of nuclear war. In the event of such an incident, the Party whose nuclear weapon is involved will immediately make every effort to take necessary measures to render harmless or destroy such weapon without its causing damage.

Art. 3. The Parties undertake to notify each other immediately in the event of detection by missile warning systems of unidentified objects, or in the event of signs of interference with these systems or with related communications facilities, if such occurrences could create a risk of outbreak of nuclear war between the two countries.

Art. 4. Each Party undertakes to notify the other Party in advance of any planned missile launches if such launches will extend beyond its national territory in the direction of the other Party.

Art. 5. Each Party, in other situations involving unexplained nuclear incidents, undertakes to act in such a manner as to reduce the possibility of its actions being misinterpreted by the other Party. In any such situa-

tion, each Party may inform the other Party or request information when, in its view, this is warranted by the interests of averting the risk of outbreak of nuclear war.
Art. 6. For transmission of urgent information, notifications and requests for information in situations requiring prompt clarification, the Parties shall make primary use of the Direct Communications Link between the Governments of the United States of America and the Union of Soviet Socialist Republic.
For transmission of other information, notifications and requests for information, the Parties, at their own discretion, may use any communication facilities, including diplomatic channels, depending on the degree of urgency.
Art. 7. The Parties undertake to hold consultations, as mutually agreed, to consider questions relating to implementation of the provisions of this Agreement, as well as to discuss possible amendments thereto aimed at further implementation of the purposes of this Agreement.
Art. 8. This Agreement shall be of unlimited duration.
Art. 9. This Agreement shall enter into force upon signature."

The USSR and USA in 1973 concluded a ▷ Nuclear War Prevention Treaty. The President of the USA, R. Nixon, on June 5, 1974, justified the necessity of the Treaty as follows:

"From the moment when the Soviet Union reached parity with the USA in the field of strategic weapons all encounters between us would threaten all civilized states with a potential nuclear catastrophe."

Nuclear war and its devastating consequences for mankind remain the major subject of preventive international actions, agreements and UN activities.

C. DELMAS, *Histoire politique de la bombe atomique*, Paris, 1967; J.S. TOMPKINS, *The Weapons of World War III*, London, 1967; *UNTS*, Vol. 807, pp. 57–63; SIPRI, *World Armaments and Disarmament Yearbook*, 1973, pp. 44–46, 1976, pp. 45–48; 1977, pp. 4–5, 14–15, 416–417, 445–449; Office of Technology Assessment, US Congress, *The Effects of Nuclear War*, New York, 1980; A.M. KATZ, *Life After Nuclear War, The Economic and Social Impacts of Nuclear Attacks on the US*, Cambridge, 1981; *Hiroshima and Nagasaki: The Physical, Medical and Social Effects of the Atomic Bombings*, New York, 1981; D. FREI, C. CATRINA, UN Institute for Disarmament Research, *Risks of Unintentional Nuclear War*, New York, 1982; WHO, *Effect of Nuclear War on Health and Health Services*, Geneva, 1984; *UN Prevention of Nuclear War. Three Viewpoints. One: Soviet Scientists' Viewpoints; Two: A United Nations Perspective; Three: An American Perspective*, New York, 1983, 1984, 1985; P. LEVENTHAL, Y. ALEXANDER eds., *Preventing Nuclear Terrorism*, Lexington, Mass., 1987.

NUCLEAR WAR PREVENTION TREATY, 1973.
The Agreement between the USA and USSR on the Prevention of Nuclear War, was signed on June 22, 1973 in Washington, by the President of the USA, Richard Nixon and Leonid Brezhnev, General Secretary of the Communist Party of the Soviet Union. The text read as follows:

"The United States of America and the Union of Soviet Socialist Republics, hereinafter referred to as the parties:
Guided by the objectives of strengthening world peace and international security;
Conscious that nuclear war would have devastating consequences for mankind;
Proceeding from the desire to bring about conditions in which the danger of an outbreak of nuclear war anywhere in the world would be reduced and ultimately eliminated;
Proceeding from their obligations under the Charter of the United Nations regarding the maintenance of peace, refraining from the threat or use of force, and the avoidance of war, and in conformity with the agreements to which either party has subscribed;
Proceeding from the basic principles of relations between the United States of America and the Union of Soviet Socialist Republic signed in Moscow on May 29, 1972;

Reaffirming that the development of relations between the USA and the USSR is not directed against other countries and their interests, have agreed as follows:
Art. I. The United States and the Soviet Union agree that an objective of their policies is to remove the danger of nuclear war and of the use of nuclear weapons.
Accordingly, the parties agree that they will act in such a manner as to prevent the development of situations capable of causing a dangerous exacerbation of their relations, as to avoid military confrontations, and as to exclude the outbreak of nuclear war between them and between either of the parties and other countries.
Art. II. The parties agree, in accordance with Art. I and to realize the objective stated in that Art., to proceed from the premise that each party will refrain from the threat or use of force against the other party, against the allies of the other party and against other countries, in circumstances which may endanger international peace and security. The parties agree that they will be guided by these considerations in the formulation of their foreign policies and in their actions in the field of international relations.
Art. III. The parties undertake to develop their relations with each other and with other countries in a way consistent with the purposes of this Agreement.
Art. IV. If at any time relations between either party and other countries appear to involve the risk of a nuclear conflict, or if relations between countries not parties to this Agreement appear to involve the risk of nuclear war between the USA and the USSR or between either party and other countries, the United States and the Soviet Union, acting in accordance with the provisions of this Agreement, shall immediately enter into urgent consultations with each other and make every effort to avert this risk.
Art. V. Each party shall be free to inform the Security Council of the United Nations, the Secretary General of the United Nations and the Governments of allied or other countries of the progress and outcome of consultations initiated in accordance with Art. IV of this Agreement.
Art. VI. Nothing in this Agreement shall affect or impair:
(a) The inherent right of individual or collective self-defense as envisaged by Art. 51 of the Charter of the United Nations;
(b) The provisions of the Charter of the United Nations, including those relating to the maintenance or restoration of international peace and security; and
(c) The obligations undertaken by either party towards its allies or other countries in treaties, agreements and other appropriate documents.
Art. VII. This Agreement shall be of unlimited duration.
Art. VIII. This Agreement shall enter into force upon signature.
Done at the City of Washington, DC, on June 22, 1973, in two copies, each in the English and in the Russian languages, both texts being equally authentic."

UST 1973; *Recueil de Documents*, No. 6, 1973; F. GRIFFITH (ed.), *The Danger of Nuclear War*, Toronto, 1979.

NUCLEAR WAR UN CONDEMNATION, 1983.
The Res. 38/75 of the UN General Assembly on Dec. 15, 1983 read as follows:

"The General Assembly,
Expressing its alarm at the growing threat of nuclear war, which can lead to the destruction of civilization on earth,
Drawing the attention of all states and peoples to the conclusions arrived at by the most eminent scientists and military and civilian experts to the effect that it is impossible to limit the deadly consequences of nuclear war if it is ever begun and that in a nuclear war there can be no victors,
Convinced that the prevention of nuclear catastrophe is the most profound aspiration of billions of people on earth,
Reaffirming its call for the conclusion of an international convention on the prohibition of the use of nuclear weapons with the participation of all the nuclear-weapon states,
(1) Resolutely, unconditionally and for all time condemns nuclear war as being contrary to human conscience and reason, as the most monstrous crime

against peoples and as a violation of the foremost human right – the right to life;
(2) Condemns the formulation, propounding, dissemination and propaganda of political and military doctrines and concepts intended to provide 'legitimacy' for the first use of nuclear weapons and in general to justify the 'admissibility' of unleashing nuclear war;
(3) Calls upon all states to unite and redouble their efforts aimed at removing the threat of nuclear war, halting the nuclear arms race and reducing nuclear weapons until they are completely eliminated."

F. BLACKABY, J. GOLDBLAT, S. LODGAARD (eds.), *No-First-Use*, Stockholm, 1984, p. 146; *Official Records of the General Assembly*. Thirty-eighth session, No. 27.

NUCLEAR-WEAPON-FREE ZONE ▷ Denuclearized Zones.

NUCLEAR WEAPONS PROHIBITION, UN CONVENTION, 1983.
The Convention adopted by the UN General Assembly Res. 38/73 on Dec. 15, 1983, read as follows:

"The General Assembly, alarmed by the threat to the survival of mankind and to the life-sustaining system posed by nuclear weapons and by their use, inherent in concepts of deterrence,
Conscious of an increased danger of nuclear war as a result of the intensification of the nuclear arms race and the serious deterioration of the international situation,
Convinced that nuclear disarmament is essential for the prevention of nuclear war and for the strengthening of international peace and security,
Further convinced that a prohibition of the use or threat of use of nuclear weapons would be a step towards the complete elimination of nuclear weapons leading to general and complete disarmament under strict and effective international control,
Recalling its declaration, contained in the Final Document of the Tenth Special Session of the General Assembly, that all states should actively participate in efforts to bring about conditions in international relations among states in which a code of peaceful conduct of nations in international affairs could be agreed upon which would preclude the use or threat of use of nuclear weapons,
Reaffirming the declaration, that use of nuclear weapons would be a violation of the Charter of the United Nations and a crime against humanity, contained in its resolutions 1653 (XVI) of 24 November 1961, 33/71 B of 14 December 1978, 34/83 G of 11 December 1979, 35/152 D of 12 December 1980 and 36/92 I of 9 December 1981,
Noting with regret that the Committee on Disarmament, during its session in 1983, was not able to undertake negotiations with a view to achieving agreement on an international convention prohibiting the use or threat of use of nuclear weapons under any circumstances, taking as a basis the text contained in General Assembly resolution 37/100 C of 13 December 1982,
(1) Reiterates its request to the Committee on Disarmament to commence negotiations, as a matter of priority, in order to achieve agreement on an international convention prohibiting the use or threat of use of nuclear weapons under any circumstances, taking as a basis the annexed draft Convention on the Prohibition of the Use of Nuclear Weapons;
(2) Further requests the Committee on Disarmament to report on the results of those negotiations to the General Assembly at its thirty-ninth session."
The GA Res. 43/76E, on Dec. 7, 1988 noted with regret, that "the Conference on Disarmament, during its 1988 session, was not able to undertake negotiations with a view to achieving agreement on an international convention prohibiting the use or threat of use of nuclear weapons under any circumstances, taking as a basis the text annexed to General Assembly resolutions 41/60 F of 3 December, 1986 and 42/39 C of 30 November 1987. The text of the Draft Convention annexed to the Resolution of Dec. 7, 1988 has three main articles:

"Art I The States Parties to this Convention solemnly undertake not to use or threaten to use nuclear weapons under any circumstances.
Art II This Convention shall be of unlimited duration.
Art III (1) This Convention shall be open to all States for signature. Any State that does not sign the Convention

before its entry into force in accordance with paragraph 3 of this article may accede to it at any time.

(2) This Convention shall be subject to ratification by signatory States. Instruments of ratification or accession shall be deposited with the Secretary-General of the United Nations.

(3) This Convention shall enter into force on the deposit of instruments of ratification by twenty-five Governments, including the Governments of the five nuclear-weapon States, in accordance with paragraph 2 of this article.

(4) For States whose instruments of ratification or accession are deposited after the entry into force of this Convention, it shall enter into force on the date of the deposit of their instruments of ratification or accession.

(5) The depository shall promptly inform all signatory and acceding States of the date of each signature, the date of deposit of each instrument of ratification or accession and the date of the entry into force of this Convention, as well as of the receipt of other notices.

(6) This Convention shall be registered by the depository in accordance with Article 102 of the Charter of the United Nations"

F. BLACKABY, J. GOLDBLAT, S. LODGAARD (eds.), *No-First-Use*, Stockholm, 1984, pp. 145–146; *Official Records of the General Assembly. Thirty-eighth session*, No. 27; *UN Resolutions and Decisions adopted by the General Assembly during the First Part of its Forty-Third Session*, from 20 September to 22 December, 1988, New York 1989, pp 173–174.

NUCLEAR WEAPONS TESTS. An international term since July 16, 1945 (the first atomic test at Alamogordo, New Mexico), subject of international agreements on test limitation or prohibition. See ▷ Nuclear Partial Tests Ban Treaty, 1963; ▷ Threshold Test Ban Treaty, 1974; and ▷ Treaty Between the USA and the USSR on Underground Nuclear Explosions for Peaceful Purposes, 1976. See also ▷ Atomic atmospheric tests; ▷ Atomic cosmic tests; ▷ Atomic underground tests; ▷ Atomic underwater tests.

J. GOLDBLAT, D. COX eds., *Nuclear Weapons Tests: Prohibition or Limitation*, SIPRI, CIIPS, Oxford, 1988.

NUCLEAR WINTER. An international military term for a controversial hypothesis (1983) of the American astronomer Carl Sagan, stating that a consequence of nuclear explosions could be a temperature drop, partially or totally annihalating world agriculture. Subject of studies of a UN group of experts (first session in New York in March 1987).

UN Chronicle, May 1987, p. 52; L. GRINSPOON, *The Long Darkness: Psychological and Moral Perspectives on Nuclear Winter*, London 1986; D. ROBERTSON, *Guide to Modern Defense and Strategy*, Detroit 1988.

NUCLEAR YIELD. The explosive power of a nuclear bomb expressed in ▷ kilotons and ▷ megatons.

NUCLEIC ACID. ▷ DNA

NULLA LEX NULLA INIURA. *Latin* = "if there is no law, there is no wrongdoing". An international term for a doctrine stating that something not provided for by law constitutes neither a crime nor wrongdoing; a proposition forwarded by adversaries of the Nuremberg Trials since the Nuremberg Principles were created during the trial and adopted as norms of international law by the UN General Assembly after the trial.

NULLA POENA SINE LEGE. *Latin* = "there is no punishment without law". An international term for a principle stating that no punishment shall be inflicted without a legal norm.

NULLUM CRIMEN NULLA POENA ▷ Nullem Crimen sine Lege.

NULLUM CRIMEN SINE LEGE. Latin = 'there is no crime without law'. An international law doctrine, a subject of controversy between the German defence and the Military International Court at the Nuremberg War Criminals Trial, as was the doctrine ▷ nulla poena sine lege and nullum crimen nulla poena.

P. CALVOCORERSI, *Nuremberg. The Facts, The Law and the Consequences*, London 1947; G.E. GRÜNDLER, A von MANIKOWSKI, *Das Gericht der Sieger*, Oldenberg-Hamburg, 1967; F. RYSZKA, *Norymberga*, Warszawa, 1982; T.M. GELEWSKI, *Proces Norymberski i zasada Nullum Crimen Sine Lege, in: Wyrok Norymberski*, Warszawa 1987.

NUMERUS CLAUSUS. *Latin* = "limited number". An international term for the admittance of a limited number of persons from certain social, religious, racial, class, national or political groups to studies, offices, working places; usually a form of deliberate discrimination.

NUMERUS NULLUS. *Latin* = "no number". An international term for the non-admission of persons from certain groups, nationalities, races, religions, philosophies of life to schools, government employment, associations, residential areas, or certain regions of a country. The practice of *numerus nullus* is a form of discrimination and contrary to the Universal Declaration of Human Rights.

NUMISMATICS. A subject of international cooperation. Organizations reg. with the UIA:

International Association of Professional Numismatics, f. 1951, Geneva. Publ.: *Numismatic Manual for Collectors.*

International Numismatic Commission, f. 1936, Zürich.

P. GRIERSON, *Monnais et monnayage. Une introduction à la numismatique*, Paris, 1976; *Yearbook of International Organizations.*

NUNCIATURE, NUNCIO. The historical name of the diplomatic agency and ambassador of the Apostolic See. The diplomatic regulations of the Congress of Vienna, 1815, and the Vienna diplomatic convention, 1961, recognized the rank of nuncio as a diplomatic rank of a representative of the first class. In some Catholic countries it is customary for the nuncio to be the dean of the diplomatic corps.

In Bonn 1949–75, the representative of the Vatican to the FRG had the title "apostolic nuncio in Germany", but from Aug., 1975, due to the Vatican's having recognized the GDR as a separate state, the title of "apostolic nuncio in the Federal Republic of Germany".

NUREMBERG ANTI-SEMITIC LAWS, 1935. The racial laws issued by German III Reich government, approved by the Reichstag at an outgoing session in Nuremberg on Sept. 15, 1935: on Reich citizenship (Reichsbürgergesetz), and the protection of German blood and German honor (Gesetz zum Schutze des deutschen Blutes und der deutschen Ehre), which brought about a distinction between "Aryan" and "non-Aryan" German citizens, forced dissimilation and gave legal grounds for planned anti-Semitic actions in the III Reich. Nuremberg Anti-Semitic Acts became the epitome of racism and influenced the decison of major powers to choose Nuremberg as the place for the trial of Nazi war criminals.

Lexicon zur Geschichte und Politik im 20 Jahrhundert, Köln, 1971, Vol. 1, p. 297, Vol. 2, pp. 575–576.

NUREMBERG LAW. A set of positive legal norms stemming from verdicts adjudged in international trials after World War II related to war criminals. In the UN the term Nuremberg law was not introduced in common usage, having been replaced by ▷ Nuremberg Principles.

B.F. SMITH, *The Road to Nuremberg*, London, 1981.

NUREMBERG PRINCIPLES. The norms of international law concerning war crimes and war criminals, formulated in the London Agreement of the Four Powers of Aug. 8, 1945 and in the ▷ Charter of International Military Tribunal annexed to it, and then repeated and expressed in the verdicts of the Nuremberg trial in 1946.

Under General Assembly Res. 177(II), 1947 the International Law Commission was directed to "formulate the principles of international law recognized in the Charter of the Nürnberg Tribunal and in the judgment of the Tribunal".

In pursuance of the resolution, the Commission undertook a preliminary consideration of the subject. In the course of this consideration the question arose as to whether or not the Commission should ascertain to what extent the principles contained in the Charter and in the Judgment constituted principles of international law. It was concluded that since the Nuremberg principles had been affirmed by the General Assembly, the task entrusted to the Commission was not to express any appreciation of the principles of international law but merely to formulate them.

The text of the principle is as follows:

"Principle I: Any person who commits an act which constitutes a crime under international law is responsible therefor and liable to punishment.

Principle II: The fact that internal law does not impose a penalty for an act which constitutes a crime under international law does not relieve the person who committed the act from responsibility under international law.

Principle III: The fact that a person who committed an act which constitutes a crime under international law acted as Head of State or responsible government official does not relieve him from responsibility under international law.

Principle IV: The fact that a person acted pursuant to order of his government or of a superior does not relieve him from responsibility under international law, provided a moral choice was in fact possible to him.

Principle V: Any person charged with a crime under international law has the right to a fair trial on the facts and law.

Principle VI: The crimes hereinafter set out are punishable as crimes under international law:

(a) Crimes against peace: (i) Planning, preparation, initiation or waging of a war of aggression or a war in violation of international treaties, agreements or assurances; (ii) Participation in a common plan or conspiracy for the accomplishment of any of the acts mentioned under (i).

(b) War crimes: Violations of the law of customs, of war which include, but are not limited to, murder, ill-treatment or deportation to slave-labour or for any other purpose of civilian population of or in occupied territory, murder or ill-treatment of prisoners of war or persons on the seas, killing of hostages, plunder of public or private property, wanton destruction of cities, towns, or villages, or devastation not justified by military necessity.

(c) Crimes against humanity: Murder, extermination, enslavement, deportation and other inhuman acts done against any civilian population, or persecutions on political, racial or religious grounds, when such acts are done or such persecutions are carried on in execution of or in connexion with any crime against peace or any war crime.

Principle VII: Complicity in the commission of a crime against peace, a war crime, or a crime against humanity as set forth in Principle VI is a crime under international law.

The report containing the text of the above resolution, was considered by the General Assembly at its 320th plenary meeting on Dec. 12, 1950. The Assembly by a

vote of 42 to none, with 6 abstentions, adopted the resolution. Its text (488(V)) was as follows:
The General Assembly,
Having considered part III (Formulation of the Nürnberg principles) of the report of the International Law Commission on the work of its second session,
Recollecting that the General Assembly, by its resolution 95(I) of December 11, 1946, unanimously affirmed the principles of international law recognized by the charter and judgment of the Nürnberg Tribunal, Considering that, by its resolution 177(II) of 21 November 1947, the General Assembly directed the International Law Commission to formulate those principles, and also to prepare a draft code of offences against the peace and security of mankind,
Considering that the International Law Commission has formulated certain principles recognized, according to the Commission, in the charter and judgment of the Nürnberg Tribunal, and that many delegations have made observations during the fifth session of the General Assembly on this formulation. Considering that it is appropriate to give the governments of Member States full opportunity to furnish their observations on this formulation,
(1) Invites the governments of Member States to furnish their observations accordingly;
(2) Requests the International Law Commission, in preparing the draft code of offences against the peace and security of mankind, to take account of the observations made on this formulation by delegations during the fifth session of the General Assembly and of any observations which may be made by governments.''

UN Yearbook 1947–1948, pp. 20, 214–215; *The Charter and Judgment of the Nuremberg Tribunal, History and Analysis*, UN New York, 1949; *UN Yearbook 1950*, pp. 852–857.

NUREMBERG WAR CRIMINALS TRIAL, 1945–46. The case against the principal major German war criminals heard by the International Military Tribunal at Nuremberg Nov. 20, 1945–Oct 1, 1946 as foreseen by the London Agreement and Charter of ▷ International Military Tribunal, 1945. The Tribunal was composed of justices: H. Domedien de Vabres, R. Falco (alternate justice) – for France; G. Lawrence (President of the Tribunal), W. Birkett (alternate) – for Great Britain; F. Biddle, J.J. Parker (alternate) – for the USA; Gen. I.T. Nikitchenko, Col. A.F. Voltchkov (alternate) – for the USSR. The indictment was lodged by four teams of prosecutors with chief prosecutors: A. Champetier de Ribes – for France, R.H. Jackson – for the USA, H. Shawcross – for Great Britain, Gen. A. Rudenko – for the USSR. In the indictment the United States of America, the French Republic, the United Kingdom of Great Britain and Northern Ireland and the Union of Soviet Socialist Republics accused the following 24 defendants:
H.W. Goering, R. Hess, J. von Ribbentrop, R. Ley, W. Keitel, E. Kaltenbrunner, A. Rosenberg, H. Frank, W. Frick, J. Streicher, W. Funk, H. Schacht, G. Krupp von Bohlen und Halbach, K. Doenitz, E. Raeder, B. von Schirach, F. Sauckel, A. Jodl, M. Bormann, F. von Papen, A. Seyss-Inquart, A. Speer, C. von Neurath and H. Fritsche. In addition, the following were named as groups or organizations (since dissolved) which should be declared criminal: the Reich cabinet; the Leadership Corps of the Nazi Party; the Schutzstaffeln, known as the SS; the Sicherheitsdienst, known as the SD; the Geheime Staatspolizei, known as the Gestapo; the Sturmabteilungen, known as the SA; the General Staff and High Command of the German Armed Forces. The indictment consisted of the following four parts: Count One: The common plan or conspiracy against peace – the planning, preparation, initiation and waging of a war of aggression; Count two: Crimes against peace – the seizure of Austria and Czechoslovakia, aggression against Poland, France, Great Britain,

Luxembourg, Denmark, Norway, Belgium, Netherlands, Yugoslavia, Greece, the USSR and USA; the occupation of Poland, France, Denmark, Norway, Luxembourg, Yugoslavia, Greece and part of the USSR; the violation in 64 cases of a total of 36 international treaties and conventions; Count three: War crimes, genocide and the barbarous treatment of civilian population in the occupied territories and of the prisoners of war; Count four: Crimes against humanity perpetrated in the German occupied territories from Sept. 1, 1939 until May 8, 1945: persecution for political, racial or religious reasons in the form of killing, enslaving, deportation, etc. All of the defendants pleaded not guilty. Legal proceedings lasted 216 days: from Nov. 20, 1945 until Aug. 31, 1946. Formal ground of the sentence and the ruling of the responsibility of the accused institutions and organizations were made public on Sept. 30, 1946. On Oct. 1, 1946 the Tribunal justified the general and individual sentences. Groups within the following four organizations were declared criminal in character: the Leadership Corps of the Nazi Party, the SS, the SD and the Gestapo. The Tribunal declined to make that finding with regard to the SA, the Reich Cabinet, and the General Staff and High Command, deciding that membership in those bodies did not prejudge conscious participation in the preparation or perpetration of war crimes. Action was to be taken against all members of organizations declared criminal in character and against those members of other organizations who individually took part in criminal activities. From among the individual defendants, the Tribunal acquitted (with the veto of the Soviet judges) Fritsche, von Papen and Schacht. Sentenced to hang were: Bormann (by default), Frank, Keitel, Goering, Jodl, Kaltenbrunner, Frick, Ribbentrop, Rosenberg, Sauckel, Seyss-Inquart, Streicher. All of them except Bormann and Goering were hanged on the night of Oct. 15–16, 1946, their bodies were then cremated in the former concentration camp Dachau and the ashes scattered in an unknown place. Bormann and Goering escaped the executions; the former missing since Apr. 30, 1945, the latter having committed suicide before the execution by poisoning himself. (Bormann's death on Apr. 30, 1945 was confirmed by the court of West Berlin in Apr., 1973 on the basis of remains found accidentally in West Berlin, identified by experts). Life sentences were passed on: Hess (Soviet veto, demanding death sentence), Raeder and Funk (released 1955 and 1957 respectively due to ill health). Sentenced to 20 years were Speer and Schirach (both released Oct. 1, 1966), to 15 years – Neurath (released 1954 because of ill health); 10 years – Doenitz (released Oct. 1, 1956). Ley committed suicide before the trial. Krupp was excluded from the trial due to ill health. From Oct. 1, 1966 Hess was the only one of those sentenced at the trial who remained in a special prison for Nazi war criminals guarded by troops of the Four Powers – Spandau in West Berlin.
Theses included in the sentence of the trial, confirming and justifying the decisions of the Four Power London Agreement of Aug. 8, 1945 and the appended Statute of the International Military Tribunal were recognized (Dec. 11, 1946) by the UN General Assembly as norms of international law called ▷ Nuremberg Principles.
On Aug. 17, 1987 at the age of 93 Rudolph Hess committed suicide in Spandau prison. After his death work on the demolition of Spandau prison was immediately started.

The Trial of German Major War Criminals, Proceedings of the IMT Sitting at Nuremberg, Germany, 42 Vols., London, 1946–1948; *Prozess gegen die Hauptkriegsverbrecher vor dem Internationalen Militärgerichtshof,*

Nürnberg 1947–49 (Official shorthand report of the German version); W.E. BENTON (ed.), *Nuremberg. German Views of the War Criminals Trial*, Dallas, 1955; J. HEYDECKER, *The Nuremberg Trial. A History of Nazi Germany*, Cleveland, 1962; A. KLAFKOWSKI, *The Nuremberg Principles and the Development of International Law*, Warsaw, 1966; T. CYPRIAN, J. SAWICKI, *Nuremberg in Retrospect*, Warsaw, 1967; P. AZIZ, *Les criminels de guerre*, Paris, 1971; B.F. SMITH, *The Road to Nuremberg*, New York, 1981; R.L. BLEDSOE, B.A. BOCZEK, *The International Law Dictionary*, Oxford, 1987, pp. 82–84; KEESING's *Record of World Events*, 1987.

NUREMBERG WAR CRIMINALS TRIALS, 1947–49. The 12 trials of war criminals following the main Nuremberg Trial of major German war criminals before the International Military Tribunal. These 12 trials were not held before an international court but before exclusively American military tribunals appointed by orders (Oct. 18, 1946 and Feb. 17, 1947) of Chief Commander of the American occupation zone in Germany, General Lucius Clay. All were heard at the International Military Tribunal in Nuremberg headquarters and in pursuance of ▷ Nuremberg Principles. The indictments were lodged against groups of leaders active in the German III Reich. Each trial is known by a Roman number and under a common German name:
The defendants were:
I – Wehrmacht and SS doctors (Arzte-Prozess);
II – E. Milch (Milch-Prozess);
III – senior officials of judicature (Juristen-Prozess);
IV – officials of the main SS Office of Economy and Administration (Pohl-Prozess);
V – F. Flick and heads of Flick concern (Flick-Prozess);
VI – heads of IG Farben-Industrie (IG Farben-Prozess);
VII – generals of Southern Front (Südostgenerals-Prozess);
VIII – officials of Main SS Office for Race and Settlement (SS-Rassen-und-Siedlungshauptampt-Prozess);
IX – O. Ohlendorf and other commanders and special units (Einsatzgruppen-Prozess);
X – A. Krupp and Krupp concern officials (Krupp-Prozess);
XI – Foreign Ministry and other ministerial officials (Wilhelmstrasse-Prozess);
XII – senior officers of Chief Command of Wehrmacht (OKW-Prozess).
35 defendants out of 185 were acquitted. Of the remaining 150, 24 were sentenced to death and 7 of those were hanged; others including those sentenced to imprisonment were released under the amnesty announced by US High Commissioner in West Germany, John McCloy, on Jan. 31, 1951.

T. TAYLOR, "The Nuremberg War Crimes Trials", in: *International Conciliation*, No. 450, Apr., 1949, pp. 234–371; *Trials of War Criminals before the Nuremberg Military Tribunals*, 12 Vols., Washington, DC, 1950–1953; R.K. WOETZEL, *The Nuremberg Trials in International Law with a postlude on the Eichmann-case*, London, 1962.

NURSES DAY, INTERNATIONAL. A day celebrated each year since 1965 on May 12. This date is the anniversary of the birth of Florence Nightingale (1820–1910), the founder of modern nursing.

C. WOODHAM-SMITH, *Florence Nightingale*, London, 1950.

NURSING. The protection of the helpless, sick or injured, a subject of international co-operation. Organizations reg. with the UIA:

Commonwealth Nurses Federation, f. 1971, London.
European Nursing Group, f. 1946, Vienna.
International Committee of Catholic Nurses, f. 1933, Brussels.Consultative status with WHO, UNICEF and Council of Europe.
International Council of Nurses, ICN, f. 1899, London. Executive Director: Geneva. Members: National Associations of Nurses in 84 countries. Consultative status with UNESCO, ECOSOC, WHO, UNICEF, ILO and Council of Europe. The Florence Nightingale International Foundation est. in 1934 became associated with ICN in 1949. NGO Relations with International Hospital Federation, International Committee of the Red Cross, World Medical Association, International Confederation of Midwifes. Publ.: *International Nursing Review, Basic Principles of Nursing Care, Nurses and Nursing.*

Northern Nurses Federation, f. 1920, Stockholm.

F. BECK, *Basic Nursing Education: Principle and Practice*, London, 1958; C. BRIDGES, *A History of the International Council of Nurses 1899–1964*, London, 1967; A.M.C. THOMPSON, *Bibliography of Nursing Literature 1859–1960*, London, 1968; *European Agreement on the Instruction and Education of Nurses, signed on October 25, 1967 in Strasbourg, UNTS*, Vol. 718, pp. 363–384.

NYON AGREEMENT, 1937. The Agreement between Bulgaria, Egypt, France, Greece, Romania, Turkey, the UK, USSR and Yugoslavia, signed on Sept. 14, 1937 in Nyon, concerning Spanish submarine attacks in the Mediterranean against merchant ships not belonging to either of the conflicting Spanish parties. It was decided that "any submarine which attacks such a ship shall be counter-attacked and, if possible, destroyed." A Supplementary Agreement was signed on Sept. 17, 1937 in Geneva.

LNTS, Vol. 181, p. 137 and p. 151.

O

OAMCE. ▷ OCAM.

OAPEC. Organization of Arab Petroleum Exporting Countries. The Arab institution est. on Jan. 9, 1968 in Beirut as an intergovernmental organization open to all Arab states; members: Algeria, Bahrain, Egypt (suspended from Mar. 17, 1979), Iraq, Kuwait, Libya, Qatar, Saudi Arabia, Syria, Tunisia, United Arab Emirates. It works to protect the interests of its members in relations with the importing countries and with foreign oil companies; to develop co-operation between the petroleum industries of the member states. The highest organ of OAPEC is a Council which meets at the ministerial level at least twice a year and its Bureau with the Secretariat and Judical Board. Institutions related to OAPEC:

Arab Drilling and Workover Company, etc. 1981 in Tripoli.
Arab Engineering Company, AREC, est. 1981 in Abu Dhabi.
Arab Maritime Petroleum Transport Company, AMPTC, est. 1973 in Kuwait.
Arab Petroleum Investments Corporation, APICORP, est. 1975 in Dhahran Airport, Saudi Arabia.
Arab Petroleum Services Company, APSC, est. 1977 in Tripoli.
Arab Shipbuilding and Repair Yard Company, est. 1974 in Manama, Bahrain.

The majority of its member states also belong to ▷ OPEC.

The Europa Year Book 1984. A World Survey, Vol. I, p. 193, London, 1984.

OAS. ORGANIZATION OF AMERICAN STATES.
The intergovernmental institution, established on May 2, 1948 in Bogota by the ninth International American Conference as a successor to the International Union of American Republics. (▷ American Republics International Union, 1890.) Headquarters: Washington, DC. The OAS Charter came into force on Dec. 13, 1951; reformed in 1967. Members: Antigua and Barbuda, Argentina, Bahamas, Barbados, Bolivia, Brazil, Chile, Colombia, Costa Rica, Cuba, Dominica, the Dominican Republic, Ecuador, El Salvador, Grenada, Guatemala, Haiti, Honduras, Jamaica, Mexico, Nicaragua, Panama, Paraguay, Peru, Saint Lucia, Saint Vincent and the Grenadines, Suriname, Trinidad and Tobago, Uruguay, the USA and Venezuela. Permanent Observers of the OAS are: Austria, Belgium, Canada, Egypt, France, the Federal Republic of Germany, Greece, Guyana, Israel, Italy, Japan, the Republic of Korea, the Netherlands, Portugal, Saudi Arabia, Spain, Switzerland and Vatican City.

Organization: General Assembly (since 1970), Foreign Ministers Meetings, Permanent Council and General Secretariat in Washington, DC. Specialized Organs of the OAS: Inter-American Council for Education, Science and Culture, Inter-American Economic and Social Council (CIES), Inter-American Juridical Committee, Inter-American Nuclear Energy Commission (IANEC), Pan-American Highway Congresses.

Other organizations of the OAS:
Inter-American Children's Institute, f. 1927, Montevideo.
Inter-American Commission of Women, f. 1928, Washington, DC.
Inter-American Commission on Human Rights, Washington, DC.
Inter-American Defense Board, Washington, DC.
Inter-American Indian Institute, f. 1940, Mexico, DF.
Inter-American Insititute for Co-operation on Agriculture, San José, Costa Rica.
Inter-American Statistical Institute, f. 1940, Santiago.
Inter-American Institute of Geography and History, Mexico, DF.
Pan-American Health Organization, Washington, DC.

On Jan. 31, 1962, in Punta del Este, the Cuban revolutionary government of F. Castro was excluded from participation in the work of the OAS, and on July 25, 1964 a decision of the ministers of foreign affairs of the OAS states recommended the severing of diplomatic and trade relations with Cuba.
In the 1960s there was disagreement between the majority of OAS members and the USA concerning the interpretation of the Charter; the USA wanted to give the OAS the character of a military-police alliance, while the Latin states aimed at making it a vehicle for economic, scientific and technical co-operation and to assist in social reforms. At the Second Special Inter-American Conference in Nov., 1965 in Rio de Janeiro both sides recognized the need for a reform of the Charter. The Third Special Inter-American Conference on this question held in Buenos Aires (Feb. 15–27, 1967) resulted in the passage of a number of amendments relating to changes in the organization and competence of OAS organs, but in the main devoted to the economic and social tasks of the OAS. ▷ Charter of Organization of American States, OAS, 1948, and Protocol, 1967. Since Nov. 16, 1948 the OAS has the status of an observer at the UN and has agreements on co-operation with ECLA – 1948; with WHO – 1949; with ILO and UNESCO – 1950; with FAO – 1952; with GATT – 1959; with IAEA and with ITU – 1963; with EURATOM and OECD – 1963. In 1970 the General Assembly replaced the Inter-American conference as the highest body of the OAS and held every year a session in one of the Member States capitals. All OAS publications are issued by the Panamerican Union in Washington, i.a. *Revista Interamericana de Bibliografía* in Spanish and English.
The 16th annual General Assembly of the OAS took place in Guatemala City on Nov. 10–15, 1986; the 17th in Washington DC on Nov. 9–14, 1987.

Inter-American Juridical Yearbook, Washington, DC, 1947; L.C. DE WOOD, *La OEA y las NU*, Buenos Aires, 1956; A.V. THOMAS, *The OAS*, Cambridge Mass., 1963, T. SZULC, *Wind of Revolution*, New York, 1965; I.L. CLANDE, *The OAS, the UN and the US*, New York, 1964; A. VAN KYNEN, A.J. THOMAS, *The OAS*, Dallas, 1965; J.M. CORDERO TORRES, *Textos básicos de la Organización Internacional*, Madrid, 1966; p. 131–136; INSTITUTO INTERAMERICANO DE ESTUDIOS JURÍDICOS INTERNACIONALES, *El Sistema Interamericano*, Madrid, 1966, pp. 576–582; J. CASTAÑEDA, "Conflicto de Competencia entre las NU y la OEA", in: *Foro Internacional*, México, DF, 1965/66, pp. 303–327; J. SLATAR, *The OAS and US Foreign Policy*, Columbia, 1967; G. PLAZA, *Siete años de evolución, 1968–1975*, Washington, DC, 1975; *Organizations of American States. A Handbook*, Washington, DC, 1977; *OAS. The Americas in the 1980s. An Agenda for the Decade Ahead*, Washington, DC, 1982; *The Europa Year Book 1984. A World Survey*, Vol. I, pp. 190–193, London, 1984; KEESING's *Record of World Events*, March 1988.

OATS. One of the main agricultural products covered by UN international statistics. The main oats-growing countries are the USA, Canada, the Chinese People's Republic and Australia.

OAU. ORGANIZATION OF AFRICAN UNITY.
The African intergovernmental institution established on May 25, 1963 in Addis Ababa, on signature of the ▷ Charter of Organization of African Unity, OAU, by representatives of governments of 32 African states.
Aims: promote unity and development; defend the sovereignty of African states, eradicate colonialism, co-ordinate and harmonize members' economic, diplomatic, educational, health, welfare, scientific and defense policies.
Organizations: Annual Conference of Heads of State; Council of Foreign Ministers (twice a year), Specialized Commission, Commission of Mediation, Secretariat. Official languages: Arabic, French and English.
Flag: horizontally green, white, green, with the white fimbriated yellow and the seal of OAU in the centre.
Members: all African states with exception of the Republic of South Africa.
Publ.: Activities, reports and studies.
The UN General Assembly on Dec. 1, 1978 adopted without a vote Res. 33/27 on co-operation between the UN and the OAU. The co-operation included the elimination of colonialism, racial discrimination and apartheid, social and economic development, establishment of a new international economic order; economic and technical assistance, and assistance to victims of colonialism and apartheid; as well as assistance to liberation movements.
The Assembly of Heads of State and Governments on July 30, 1986 approved an anthem of the OAU.
The OAU Charter of Human and People's Rights 1981, came into force on oct. 21, 1986.
The third extraordinary OAU assembly of Heads of State and government took place in Addis Ababa on Nov. 30–Dec. 1, 1987 to address the $200,000 million African debt.

OAU Basic Documents, Addis Ababa, 1963; B. BOUTROS-GHALI, "The Addis Ababa Charter", in: *International Conciliation*, No. 546, Jan., 1964, p. 5–62; *OAU, What it is? How it Works? What it Does?* Addis Ababa, 1973; *UN Chronicle*, Jan., 1979, p. 27; KEESING's *Record of World Events*, No 6, 1988.

OBERKOMMANDO DER WEHRMACHT, OKW.
High Command of the German III Reich Army, subject of the Nuremberg War Criminals Trial, Nov. 10, 1945–Oct. 1, 1946. The Tribunal declared four German organizations to have been criminal in character: the Leadership Corps of the NSDAP, the SS, SD and Gestapo, but not the OKW "solely because the structure of the particular group was considered by the Tribunal to be too loose to constitute a coherent 'group' or 'organization', and not because of any doubt of its criminality in war plotting." This opinion of the US Justice R.H. Jackson was justified as follows:

"In its judgment the Tribunal condemned the officers who performed General Staff and High Command functions as 'a ruthless military caste' and said they were 'responsible in large measure for the miseries and suffering that have fallen on millions of men, women and children. They have been a disgrace to the honorable profession of arms.' This finding should dispose of any fear that we were prosecuting soldiers just because they fought for their country and lost, but otherwise the failure to hold the General Staff to be a criminal organization is regrettable."

"Final Report of the Prosecution of Major Nazi War Criminals to the President Harry Truman from Supreme Court Justice Robert H. Jackson", in: *The Department of States Bulletin*, No. 382, 1946, pp. 771–776.

O

OBJECTIVE JUSTICE RULE. An international law term formulated by E. Descamp in 1920 in the adoption of art. 38 of the Statute of the Permanent Court of International Justice (PCIJ) which was to demonstrate to judges of the Court that for lack of rules of positive law they should be guided by the "natural objective justice rule."

E. DESCAMP, *Recueil international des traités du XX-e siècle*, Paris, 1904–21.

OBSCENE PUBLICATIONS. A subject of international Agreements. The first Agreement for the Suppression of the Circulation of Obscene Publications, was signed on June 10, 1910 in Paris and amended by a Protocol, signed May 4, 1949 at Lake Success. After World War I an International Convention for the Suppression of the Circulation of and Traffic in Obscene Publications, was concluded on Sept. 12, 1923 in Geneva; and amended by a Protocol signed Nov. 12, 1947 at Lake Success by Afghanistan, Albania, Australia, Belgium, Burma, Canada, China, Czechoslovakia, Denmark, Egypt, Finland, Guatemala, Hungary, India, Italy, Mexico, the Netherlands, New Zealand, Norway, Pakistan, South Africa, the UK, USSR, and Yugoslavia. The amended Convention came into force Feb. 2, 1950. ▷ Pornography.

DE MARTENS, *Nouveau Recueil Général de Traités*, 3éme série, tome VII, p. 266; *LNTS*, Vol. 11, p. 438, *UNTS*, Vol. 30, p. 3 and 366; *UNTS*, Vol. 47, p. 159, *LNTS*, Vol. 27, p. 213, Vol. 200, p. 501; *UNTS*, Vol. 46, pp. 169–200 and 201–213.

OBSERVATION INTERNATIONAL. An international term for the work of the subsidiary organs of the UN consisting of observation and control missions in a certain region of potential trouble or where the current situation threatens peace and security; usually composed of military observers. ▷ UN Observers.

OBSERVATORIES. The astronomical scientific-research stations constructed in elevated locations far removed from air pollution; subject of permanent, organized co-operation under the auspices of the International Astronomical Union. The largest observatory in Europe is the Crimean Astrophysical Observatory in the USSR with a 260-cm. telescope, constructed 1961; in America the International Observatory in La Sarena (Chile) on Mount Tololo 2400 m above sea level and Palomar Mt. NE of San Diego, Calif., at an altitude of 1,680m. The historical Greenwich Observatory in Great Britain, as a result of the industrialization of the region and the pollution of the air, was transferred to Herstmounceaux in the county of Sussex, 1955. In the years 1971–85 the USA as well as the USSR launched space observatories into earth orbit.

Organizations reg. with the UIA:

Boyden Observatory est. 1954 in Bloemfontein in South Africa, Annual symposia in Bloemfontein.
Station Scientifique du Jungfrau, est. 1930, in Berne, affiliates scientific institutes and observatories of Austria, Belgium, France, FRG, the Netherlands, Sweden, and the UK. Publ. *Hochalpine Forschungstation Jungfraujoch*, also in French and English.

Yearbook of International Organizations.

OBSERVER MISSIONS. Special UN Missions sent to areas of potential trouble or where a threat to peace and security may exist; usually consist of military observers. The first such mission was sent to the Middle East in 1978 ▷ UNTSO. ▷ UN Peace-Keeping Operations.

R.S. SYBESMA-KNOL, *The Status of Observers at the UN*, Brussels, 1981.

OBSERVER STATUS. The Observer Status in the UN of National Liberation Movements recognized by regional organizations approved by GA resolutions. The observer status of the ▷ PLO, granted on November 19, 1974 by the GA Res. 3237 (XXIX) was a subject of the GA Res. 43/160 A and B on Dec. 9, 1988, adopted by 117 votes to 2 (Israel and the US) with 31 abstentions (A) and with 124 votes to 9 with 18 abstentions (B).

UN Resolutions and Decisions adopted by the General Assembly during the First Part of its Forty-Third Session, From 20 September to 22 December 1988, New York, 1989, pp 536–538.

OCAM, 1960–1985. Organization Commune Africaine et Mauricienne. Common African and Mauritian Organization. F. in Bangui in 1960 as an inter-govermental institution of economic co-operation of francophonic states under the name, Organization Africaine et Malgache de Coopération Économique, OAMCE; since Feb., 1965 an organization of independent French-speaking states under the name Organisation Commune Africaine et Malgache; after the accession of Mauritius, 1969, the present name was adopted in 1974. Aims: to accelerate within the framework of the OAU the economic, cultural, social and technological development of member states. Organs: Conference of Heads of State and of Government, Council of Ministers, Secretariat-General.

Affiliated organizations:
Bureau africain et mauricien de recherches et d'études législatives, f. 1975, Bangui.
Centre africain et mauricien de perfectionnement des cadres, f. 1975, Abidjan.
Centre interafricain de production de films, CIPROFILM, f. 1974, Ouagadougou.
Consortium interafricain de distribution cinématographique, CIDC, f. 1974, Ouagadougou.
École afrinaine et mauricienne d'architecture et d'urbanisme, f. 1975, Lomé.
École inter-états d'ingénieurs de l'équipment rural, f. 1968, Ouagadougou.
École inter-états des sciences et médecine vétérinaires, f. 1968, Dakar.
Fonds de garantie e de coopération, f. 1977, Cotonou.
Institut africain d'informatique, f. 1971, Libreville.
Institut africain et mauricien de bilinguisme, f. 1975, Curepipe, Mauritius.
Institut africain et mauricien de statistique et d'économie appliquée, f. 1975, Kigali, Rwanda.
Institut culturel africain, f. 1971, Dakar.
Office africain de la propriété, f. 1962, Yaoundé.
Union africaine et mauricienne des banques pour le développement, f. 1962, Cotonou. Publ. *Nations Nouvelles* (bi-monthly), *Chronique Mensuelle.*

The Organization superseded by other African regional Organizations was dissolved on March 23, 1985 in Lomé by the heads of Member-States (Benin, Burkina Faso, Central African Republic, Ivory Coast, Niger, Senegal, Togo and Rwanda).

The Europa Year Book 1984. A World Survey, Vol. I, p. 183, London, 1984.

OCCUPATIONAL DISEASE. An international term for illness resulting from the conditions in work places, defined by ▷ ILO Conventions and recommendations since 1919. A General Workmen's Compensation (Occupational Diseases) Convention was adopted in 1925 (revised 1934). After the II World War the ILO defined occupational hazards caused by ▷ Radiation (Convention 1960), by poisoning arising from ▷ Benzene (Convention 1971), by Carcinogenic Substances and Agents (Conference 1974), and by ▷ Air Pollution (Convention 1977).

ILO Conventions and Recommendations, 1919–1981, Geneva 1982.

OCCUPIED TERRITORIES. The territories of a certain state taken over by another state which administers them on the basis of a treaty of unconditional surrender of the former state, a unilateral act of violence, or a multilateral international agreement. The administration of occupied territories should be in accord with the principles of international law; however, it does not give any rights to the occupier to acquire occupied territories. In the international system a similar principle was defined in the Inter-American Anti-War Treaty, 1933, as well as in art. 11 of the Inter-American Convention on the Laws and Obligations of States, 1933. In Mar., 1932 in connection with the Japanese invasion of Manchuria, the LN Assembly formulated in one resolution the principle of not recognizing territorial acquisitions acquired in a manner contrary to the LN Covenant. On Jan. 1, 1942, in Washington, DC, the representatives of 26 nations fighting the Axis Powers signed the United Nations Declaration on Economic Plunder of Occupied Territories by the Enemy, marking the first formal use of the term "United Nations". Each government pledged itself to employ its full resources, military or economic, against the axis powers and not to make a separate peace with the enemies. On Jan. 4, 1943 the signatories, the governments of Australia, Belgium, China, Czechoslovakia, France, Holland, India, Yugoslavia, Luxembourg, New Zealand, Norway, Poland, Union of South Africa, the USA and USSR, also gave a formal warning to the neutral states against any transactions with Germany and plundering the occupied territories.

A. DEVENCIERE-TERRANDIERE, "Essai historique et critique sur l'occupation comme mode de acquerir les territoires en droit international", in: *Revue de Droit International et de Législation Comparée*, No. 54, 1937; N. HILL, *Claims to Territory in International Law and Relations*, London, 1945; O. LANGER, *Seizure of Territory*, London, 1947; K. SKUBISZEWS-KI, "Currency in Occupied Territory and the Law of War", in: *Jahrbuch für Internationales Recht*, 1961, pp. 162–188; *UN Monthly Chronicle*, No. 11, 1967; R.L. BLEDSOE, B.A. BOCZEK, *The International Law Dictionary,* Oxford, 1987.

OCEANIA. The South Sea Islands, approx. 25,000 islands on the Pacific in tropical areas, including Melanesia, Micronesia, and Polynesia. The problems of Oceania have been discussed since 1946 by the UN Trusteeship Council and at sessions of the UN General Assembly in connection with nuclear tests carried out in that region by the USA and France, and in connection with the colonial status. Held annually since 1970 are Conferences of South Pacific states, called since Nov., 1972 South Pacific Forums, with the governments of Australia, New Zealand, Western Samoa, Cook's and Tonga Islands participating. The following states of Oceania won independence successively: New Zealand, Nauru, Fiji Islands, Tonga Islands, Western Samoa, Papua-New Guinea, Solomon Islands, New Hebrides.

C.H. GRATTAN, *The Southwest Pacific since 1900*, London, 1963.

OCEANS AND OCEANOGRAPHY. The world's oceans comprise 70.8% of the surface of the earth and are the subject of international scientific studies and of international law (▷ Sea Law International). Organizations reg. with the UIA:

European Oceanic Association, f. 1970, Monaco.
Intergovernmental Oceanographic Commission, est. July 1960, Paris, under aegis of UNESCO by the Intergovernmental Conference on Oceanographic Research. Members: governments of 88 states. Publ.: *Reports* in English, French, Russian and Spanish.

International Association for Biological Oceanography, f. 1967, Copenhagen. Publ.: *Proceedings*.

International Association for the Physical Sciences of the Ocean, f. 1919, San Diego, Calif. Consultative status with ECOSOC.

International Association of Medical Oceanography, f. 1975, Nice.

International Ocean Institute Pacem in Maribus, f. 1972, Malta. Publ.: *Proceedings*.

Joint Committee on Atmospheric-Ocean Interaction, f. 1967, Wormley, UK.

Mediterranean Association for Marine Biology and Oceanology, f. 1964, Naples.

Nordic University Group of Physical Oceanography, f. 1965, Copenhagen.

Pacific Scientific Research Institute of Fisheries and Oceanography, f. 1957, Vladivostok.

Scientific Committee on Oceanic Research, f. 1957. Oban, UK. Publ.: *Proceedings*.

H.U. SVERDNYS, M.W. JOHNSON, R. FLEMING, *The Oceans*, London, 1942; L. CARSON, *The Sea Around Us*, London, 1961; J. MCLELLAN, *Elements of Physical Oceanography*, London, 1964; S. ODA, *The International Law of the Ocean Development: Basic Documents*, Leiden, 1972; M.S. MCDOUGAL, W.T. BURK, *The Public Order of the Ocean. A Contemporary International Law of the Sea*, London, 1975; R.W. FAIBRIDGE, *Encyclopaedia of Oceanography*, New York, 1979; *The Law of the Sea*, UN, New York, 1983; C. SANSER, *Ordering the Oceans*, London, 1987.

OCEAN THERMAL ENERGY CONVERSION, OTEC.
An international term for the use of industrial methods to exploit the sea as a source of thermal energy. In 1980 Japan, the USA, the USSR, the UK, Belgium, France, Holland and Taiwan were working on OTEC.

Ocean Thermal Energy in: *The Economist*, June 20, 1987.

OCHO RIOS DECLARATION, 1982. ▷ Caribbean Community, CARICOM.

OCTOBER REVOLUTION, 1917.
The Russian November Revolution, called in Russia the October Revolution, which started on Nov. 7, 1917 (Oct. 24 according to the old Greek calendar) in Petrograd, under the leadership of V.I. Lenin (1870–1924) with an armed uprising signalled from the cruiser *Aurora*; subject of international studies.

E.H. CARR, *The Bolshevik Revolution*, 3 Vols., London, 1950–53; A. ROTHSTEIN, C. DUTT, *History of the Communist Party of the Soviet Union*, London, 1960; *Istoria Velikoi Oktiabr'skoy Sotsyalisticheskoy Revolutsyi*, Moskva, 1962; P. DUKES, *October and World Perspectives on the Russian Revolution*, London, 1979.

ODA. ▷ Official Development Assistance.

ODECA.
Organización de los Estados Centroamericanos, Organization of Central American states. The intergovernmental institution, est. on Oct. 14, 1951 in San Salvador by the governments of El Salvador, Guatemala, Honduras, Costa Rica and Nicaragua. The Convention, which entered into force Jan. 9, 1952 was replaced by a new one signed on Dec. 13, 1963, at Panama City and called the Panama Charter; entered into force on Mar. 30, 1965. A Protocol of Amendment to the Transitory Provisions of the Charter of ODECA was signed on Dec. 13, 1967 at Managua. The first Convention established mutual consultation and the quest for forms of co-operation in all fields; the second in art. 1 stated that "the signatory states comprise an economic–political unity striving toward the integration of Central America."

Aims: strengthen the bonds between the Central American states, prevent any misunderstanding, ensure pacific settlement of any disputes that may arise, assist one another, seek joint solution of their common problems, promote their economic, social and cultural development through co-operation and joint action.

Organizations: Summit Meeting of the Presidents, Meeting of Ministers of Foreign Affairs (every 2 years), Economic Council, Executive Council, Legislative Council, Court of Justice of Central America, Council for Culture and Education, and Central American Defense Council, Central American Bureau, which is the General Secretariat. Headquarters Officina Centroamericana Ciudad de San Salvador, El Salvador.

Publ.: *Boletin Informativo de la ODECA* (monthly).

The American Journal of International Law, Vol. 58, No. 1, 1964; R. VILLAGRAN-KRAMER, *Integración Centroamericana*, Guatemala, 1967; *Instruments relating to the Economic Integration of Latin America*, Washington, DC, 1968; M.L. CHUMAKOVA, *Organizatsya tsentralno-amierikanskikh gosudarstv*, Moscow, 1970.

ODER.
German: Oder; *Polish*: Odra. A river 904 km long, from Stary Bogumin to its estuary forming the frontier between Poland and Czechoslovakia and from the confluence with the Nysa Luzycka (Lusatian Neisse) to the mouth – the frontier between Poland and the German Democratic Republic. It is the subject of international treaties. One of the main European waterways falling within the framework of the valid conventions on the freedom of navigation and transit. Under the Treaty of Versailles of June 28, 1919 (arts. 331–353) it was declared an international river starting from Opawa; the International Oder Commission founded under art. 341 consisted of three representatives of Germany and one representative each from Czechoslovakia, Denmark, France, Poland, Sweden and the UK. Due to the conflicting opinions expressed by Prussia and Poland concerning the Commission's competence with respect to the Oder's tributaries – Warta and Noteć – a verdict of the Permanent Court of International Justice, Sept. 10, 1929, resolved the case in favor of Poland. The Commission ceased to exist when the German III Reich terminated the Treaty of Versailles in 1936. After World War II the Oder was linked with the Vistula by the Bydgoszcz canal and the Warta, and further with the Bug and the East European water system; by the Oder–Spree canal and the Oder–Havela canal with the West European Waterway system; the Gliwice canal links the Oder with the Upper Silesian Industrial Region, thus constituting a waterway to the Baltic sea. Poland, Czechoslovakia and the GDR initiated in 1958 a long-term project for the Danube–Oder–Elbe canal. Since Nov. 12, 1971, the ▷ Silesia Commission, seated in Opole, has operated the Oder Commission which initiates and conducts research into all aspects of the development of the Oder under the project of economic integration of the CMEA member states.

"Kanal Dunaj–Odra–Laba" (Danube–Oder–Elbe Canal), in: *E.J. OSMANCZYK, Encyklopedia ONZ, Warsaw, 1982.*

ODER–LUSATIAN NEISSE.
German: Oder–Lausitzer Neise; *Polish*: Odra–Nysa Luzycka. The frontier rivers between Poland and the German Democratic Republic; subject of the Potsdam Treaty of Aug. 2, 1945, the Zgorzelec Treaty of Dec. 6, 1950 and the Polish–FRG Treaty of Dec. 7, 1970.

Z. JORDAN, *Oder–Neisse Line. A Study of the Political, Economic and European Significance of Poland's Western Frontiers*, London, 1952; J. KOKOT, *The Logic of the Oder–Neisse Frontier*, Poznan, 1959; *Polen, Deutschland und die Oder–Neisse Grenze*, Berlin, 1959; G. BLUHM, *Die Oder–Neisse Linie in der Deutschen Aussenpolitik*, Freiburg, 1963; B. WIEWIÓRA, *German–Polish Frontier from the Standpoint of International Law*, Poznan, 1964; M. LACHS, *The Polish–German Frontier, Law, Life and Logic of History*, Warsaw, 1964; A. KLAFKOWSKI, *Die Deutsch–Polnische Grenze nach dem II Weltkrieg*, Poznan, 1970; A.Z. KRUSZEWSKI, *The Oder–Neisse Boundary and Poland's Modernization*, New York, 1972; S. MEIXLEJOHN TERRY, *Poland's Place in Europe. General Sikorski and the Origin of the Oder–Neisse Line 1939–1943*, Princeton, 1984; East–West Germany – Poland, in: A.J. DAY ed., *Border and Territorial Disputes*, London, 1987.

OECD. ORGANIZATION FOR ECONOMIC CO-OPERATION AND DEVELOPMENT.
An intergovernmental institution, est. in 1961 in Paris, by the Convention on the OECD signed on Dec. 14, 1960; came into force Sep. 30, 1961. Members: Australia, Austria, Belgium, Canada, Denmark, Finland, France, the FRG, Greece, Iceland, Ireland, Italy, Japan, Luxembourg, the Netherlands, New Zealand, Norway, Portugal, Spain, Sweden, Switzerland, Turkey, the UK and the USA. The treaty substituted the Paris Convention of Apr. 16, 1948 on establishment of the European Economic Co-operation Organization (▷ OEEC). The Treaty was acceded to by Australia, Japan and New Zealand 1964, Yugoslavia participates with a special status. The signatories rejected a Soviet proposal to participate in the preparation and adoption of the treaty. They openly aimed to confine their objectives exclusively to western states. These objectives, under art. 2, were: effective use of economic resources of member states, development of scientific and technical research, training of personnel, maintenance of stable finances in external and internal turnover, liberalization of commodity exchange, of services, flow of capital, technical assistance to developing countries.

Aims: achieve the highest sustainable economic growth and employment on a rising standard of living in member countries, with maintaining financial stability; contribute to expansion of world trade on a multilateral, non-disseminatory basis.

Organizations: Council composed of all member countries, elects each year Executive Committee of 10 members. Committees for Agriculture, Consumer Policy, Economic Policy, Environment, Energy Policy, Education, Economic and Development Review, Development Assistance, Financial Markets, Fiscal Affairs, Fisheries, Invisible Transactions, Industry, International Investment and Multinational Enterprises, Maritime Transport, Manpower and Social Affairs, Scientific and Technological Policy, Tourism, Five autonomous or semi-autonomous bodies: International Energy Agency, European Nuclear Energy Agency, Development Centre, Centre for Educational Research and Innovation, Research Project, International Secretariat headed by the Secretary General of the OECD, headquarters Paris. The Commission of the European Communities takes part in OECD's work.

The International Energy Agency, set up by the Council of the OECD in Nov., 1974, including all OECD members with the exception of Finland, Iceland and Yugoslavia: started in Jan., 1976 a program to reduce dependence on oil import, in co-operation with the Commission of the European Communities. Organs: Governing Board with a Coal and Oil Industry Advisory Board and Secretariat, hqs. Paris.

The Nuclear Energy Agency, NEA, est. in Feb., 1958 with hqs. in Paris to further the peaceful uses of nuclear energy; integrates all members of the OECD except New Zealand. Organs: Steering Committee for Nuclear Energy, Secretariat and Committees: for Technical and Economic Studies, on the Safety of Nuclear Installations, on Radiation Protection and Public Heath, on Radioactive Waste Management, on Nuclear Data and on Reactor Physics. Joint projects: Eurochemic, f. 1959 in Mol, Belgium, Halden Project f. 1958 in Halden, Norway and International Project on Food Irradiation, f. 1971, in Karlsruhe, FRG.

O

Publ.: *The OECD Observer* (bi-monthly, from 1962) and *Activities of the OECD* (from 1972).

Yearbook of International Organizations; Convention on the OECD, London, 1960; *The Europa Year Book 1984. A World Survey*, Vol. I, pp. 184–186. London, 1984.

OEEC. Organization for European Economic Co-operation, 1948–61. The ▷ Marshall Plan intergovernmental institution est. on Apr. 16, 1948; in Paris by a European Economic Co-operation Convention. First members: Austria, Belgium, Denmark, Greece, Iceland, Ireland, Italy, Luxembourg, the Netherlands, Norway, Portugal, Sweden, Switzerland, and Turkey, since Oct. 31, 1949, the FRG, since July 1959, Spain. Canada and the USA have been associated members since June 2, 1950. The OEEC was replaced on Sept. 30, 1961 by the ▷ OECD.

Convention for European Economic Co-operation, London, 1948; Annual Reports of the OEEC, 1949–61.

OENOLOGY. A subject of international co-operation. Organization reg. with the UIA:

International Union of Oenologists, f. 1966, Paris. Publ.: *Congress Proceedings*.

Yearbook of International Organizations.

OEOA ▷ Office for Emergency Operation in Africa.

OERLIKON. An international military term for Swiss developed aircraft and antiaircraft guns, produced by the Oerlikon factory near Zurich.

DU PUY, C. JOHNSON, G.P. HAYES, eds., *Dictionary of Military Terms. A Guide of Warfare and Military Institutions*, New York 1986.

OFFENCES AGAINST PEACE. A ▷ Code of Offences against Peace and Security of Mankind.

OFFENSIVE WEAPONS. A definition for those types of weapons which in international agreements have been recognized as aggressive, i.a. in peace treaties signed Feb. 10, 1947 in Paris with Bulgaria, Finland, Hungary, Italy and Romania (e.g. nuclear weapons, missiles, sea mines, bombers).

OFFICE FOR EMERGENCY OPERATION IN AFRICA, OEOA. Existed 1980–86. Since Oct. 31, 1986 its work is carried out by the UNDP, WFP, UNICEF, and UNHCR.

OFFICE OF INTER-AMERICAN AFFAIRS. ▷ Inter-American Affairs Office.

OFFICE OF STRATEGIC SERVICES. ▷ OSS.

OFFICIAL DEVELOPMENT ASSISTANCE, ODA. An international term used in the UN for foreign development assistance, supplied both bilaterally and multilaterally. In the ▷ International Development Strategy, the UN General Assembly asked in 1970 that ODA from the industrialized countries be increased to 7% by 1980. In fact the average figures decreased in the 1970s.

UN Chronicle, October, 1983, p. 48.

OFFICAL GAZETTES Official government journals, a primary source for research in international law.

J.E. ROBERTS, *A Guide to Official Gazettes and their Contents*, Library of Congress, Washington DC, 1985.

OFFICIAL RECORDS. An international term. In the UN system a series of printed publications relating to the proceedings of the principal organs of the UN and, when the General Assembly specifically so decides, of certain UN conferences; verbatim or summary records.

Reports of principal organs (Security Council to the General Assembly) are issued, under Art.15 of the UN Charter, in the series of Official Records.

United Nations Editorial Manual, New York 1983, p. 8.

OFF THE RECORD. An international term dating from F.D. Roosevelt's press conferences for background information not for publication.

OGADEN. A territory, subject of dispute and military conflicts between Ethiopia and Somalia. The OAU Assembly of Heads of State and Government, held in Nairobi on June 24–28, 1981 adopted a resolution reaffirming that the Ogaden area was 'an integral part of Ethiopia'. The continued hostilities 1982-86 led to negotiations 1986 and 1987, which failed to provide a solution.

Ethiopia–Somalia, in: A.J. DAY ed., *Border and Territorial Disputes,* London, 1987, pp 126-132.

OGARKOV DOCTRINE. ▷ Conventional Arms O.D., 1984.

OGASAWARA GUNTŌ ▷ Japan.

OHRID LAKE. A natural site in Macedonia, Yugoslavia, included in the ▷ World Heritage UNESCO List. Lake Ohrid with its transparent water supports a type of fauna dating from the preglacial period. The sponges and molluscs there are living fossils. The historical and aesthetic importance of its shores is due to the monks who founded monasteries there and built churches and schools from the end of the 9th century.

UNESCO, *A Legacy for All*, Paris, 1984.

OIL ▷ Crude Oil.

OIL AND GAS PIPELINES. The subject of international agreements. The first oil and gas pipelines appeared in the USA in 1865 (length 9.7 km, diameter 50 mm), in Russia in 1883, on the Baku–Batum route (length *c.* 800 km, diameter 60 mm); in Iran in 1911, on the Kirkuk–Abadan route (length 215 km). The first international oil pipeline was constructed in 1934 by the Anglo-Persian Oil Co., connecting the Kirkuk oil fields with the Mediterranean Sea. During World War II, in the USA the longest oil pipeline was built linking the oil fields of Texas with the refineries on the Atlantic coast in New Jersey. At the same time more than 16,000 km was laid for military purposes in North Africa and the Far East; in Europe pipeline was laid on the bottom of the English Channel, connecting the Isle of Wight with Cherbourg on the day of invasion, June 6, 1944. After World War II, oil and gas pipelines were constructed between Wilhelmshaven and Cologne 1958 (length 389 km); Rotterdam–Cologne 1960; Marseilles through Strasbourg to Karlsruhe-Mannheim 1962; from Genoa to Ingolstadt, 1966; the so-called Central European Pipeline. The longest pipelines in Europe: "Friendship" and "Brotherhood" from the Western Ukraine to Poland and Czechoslovakia and "Northern Lights" from Tyumen in Siberia to Czechoslovakia and the GDR were constructed 1960–1964. Yugoslavia, Czechoslovakia and Hungary on Feb. 12, 1974 signed an agreement on the construction of an "Adriatic" pipeline from the gulf of Omishala on the island of Krk, where an oil port for Middle East oil was built, through Yugoslavia to Slovakia and Hungary. In the USA oil pipelines totalling nearly 30,000 km in 1900 grew by 1965 to more than 300,000 km; in other countries from approximately 1000 km to more than 100,000 km. Egypt started the construction of an oil pipeline on the route Red Sea–Mediterranean Sea, which is to make the supply of oil independent of the Suez Canal. An oil pipeline Iraq–Turkey, length 1005 km, was put into operation in 1977 to link the Kirkuk oil fields in northern Iraq with the Turkish coast of the Mediterranean. In 1980 in the total length of oil pipelines in the world amounted to 600,000 km; the network of gas pipelines at this time exceeded 1,000,000 km, 90% of them in the USA. In the decade 1970–80 intensive construction of oil and gas pipelines was begun in the USSR and the "contract of the century" was signed by the USSR with the Western European countries on a gas pipeline from Siberia, which was completed in spring, 1984. On the initiative of the UN Economic Commission for Europe, principles were formulated for the legal protection of international oil and gas pipelines.

The gas-pipeline from Siberia, called the Urengoi pipeline started deliveries of Soviet gas to Czechoslovakia and the FRG in Autumn 1983 and to France in January 1984.

International Safety Code for International Transmission of Fuel Gas by Pipeline, IGU Brussels, 1970; L.Y. CHABALLE, L. MASUY, J.P. VANDENBERGHE, *Oil and Gas Field Dictionary*. In English, French, Spanish, Italian, Dutch and German, Amsterdam, 1979; *International Petroleum Encyclopedia*, Tulsa, USA., 1983; B. NASSBAUM, *The World After Oil. The Shifting Axis of Power and Wealth*, New York, 1983; KEESING's *Contemporary Archive*, May, 1985; B.W. JENTLESON, *Pipeline Politics: The Complete Political Economy of East–West Energy*, Ithaca, N.Y., 1986.

OIL COMPANIES. An international term for private and state-owned oil industry enterprises, the major organizers of the energy systems in highly developed countries. ▷ Petroleum Congresses.

L. TURNER, *Oil Companies in the International System*, London, 1978; P.R. ODELL, *Oil and World Power*, London, 1979.

OILSEEDS. A subject of international co-operation. Organizations reg. with the UIA:

African Organization of Oilseed Producers, est. Apr., 1978, Lagos, by the governments of Benin, Cameroon, Chad, Central African Republic, Gabon, Gambia, Guinea, Ethiopia, Kenya, Liberia, Libya, Nigeria, Senegal, Sierra Leone, Somali, Sudan, Togo and Zaïre. European Union for the Grain Oilseed and Fodder Trades, f. 1953, Paris. International Associations of Seed Crushers, f. 1910, London.

Yearbook of International Organizations; International Trade Center UNCTAD/GATT, *The Scope for Increased Trade Between Developing Countries in Vegetable Oils. Other Oilseed Products*, Geneva, 1981.

OIL TEHERAN AGREEMENT, 1971. ▷ Teheran Petroleum Agreement, 1971.

OIL WAR, 1984. The international term for the escalation of the Iran–Iraq war in May 1984, after the Iranian jet attack in the Persian Gulf on two Kuwaiti oil ships, a Saudi Arabian tanker and a Panamian merchant ship.

"The Oil War Flares Up, Will the US intervene?", in: *Newsweek*, May 28, 1984; A. WESTING, *Oil as source of international conflict*, SIPRI, London, Philadelphia, 1985.

OIRT. Organisation internationale de radio-difusion et télévision. The official abbreviation of the International Radio and Television Organization, f. 1946, Prague. ▷ Radio and TV Organizations.

OKINAWA. A Japanese island in the West Pacific in the ▷ Ryukyu islands archipelago. Area: 1176 sq. km. Pop. 1980, estimate 1.1 million. Occupied by US marines after one of the bloodiest battles of World War II in the Pacific area (Apr. 1–June 21, 1945); under US control until May 15, 1972. The Okinawa Reversion Agreement between Japan and the US was signed in June 1971 allowing the retention of US military bases on the island, but without nuclear depot, together with the Voice of America radiostation.

S.E. MORISON, *History of US Naval Operations in World War II*, 15 Vols., Washington, DC 1947–62.

OLADE. Organización Latino-Americana de Energía, Latin American Organization for Energy. An intergovernmental institution, founded on Nov. 1, 1973 in Lima by ministers of the energy industry from 24 Latin American states, with headquarters in Quito.

Yearbook of International Organizations.

OLAS. Organización Latinoamericana de Solidaridad. Latin American Solidarity Organization, LASO. A revolutionary institution founded on Jan. 16, 1966 in Havana during the Three-continental Conference. The First Conference on Latin American Solidarity held July 31–Aug. 10, 1976 in Havana proclaimed:

"The only real road to the solution of economic and social problems is the peoples' revolutionary struggle."

Taking part in the Conference were 27 national committees from independent countries as well as from dependent territories. The Conference ratified the OLAS statute and a Declaration of the Conference, announcing the program of OLAS:

"The situation on the American continent is favorable for revolutionary forces which have to answer the imperialistic violence with revolutionary violence. As it appears from historical analysis, in most Latin American countries conditions are similar to those which prevailed in Russia and in China immediately before the outbreak of revolutions there. Thus, an avant-garde guerilla movement linked with peasant masses and urban proletariat becomes feasible. Latin nations have an inexhaustible revolutionary potential, the full use of which in the proper direction is the task of the revolutionary avant-garde. Revolutionary violence is the highest form of peoples struggle and the most effective weapon in the fight against imperialism, the essential means of revolution in Latin America is armed struggle; all other means should prepare and accelerate the armed struggle. In most Latin American countries the situation is ripe for conducting armed operations, and in other approaches to armed struggle it is an inevitable outlook. The revolution should be directed by united political and military forces. Revolution is the right and the duty of Latin American nations. The duty of each rebel is to make a revolution (*El deber de todo Revolucionario es hacer la Revolución*)."

Actas y Documentos de la I Conferencia de Solidaridad de los Pueblos de América Latina, La Habana, 1967; *The First Conference of the Latin-American Solidarity Organization, LASO–OLAS*, Washington, DC, 1968.

OLD CATHOLICS. Clergy and laymen who broke away from the Catholic Church, rejecting the dogma of papal infallibility, proclaimed by the Vatican Council I, 1870. The old Catholic Churches in Germany, Poland, the UK and the USA are in ecumenical relations with the ▷ World Council of Churches.

C.B. MOSS, *The Old Catholic Movement. Its Origin and History*, London, 1964.

OLD TESTAMENT. A subject of international study. Organization reg. with the UIA:

International Organization for the Study of the Old Testament, f. 1950, Cambridge, UK. Publ.: *Vetus Testamentum* (quarterly) in English, French and German. ▷ New Testament.

Yearbook of International Organizations.

OLIGOPOLIES. A highly concentrated form of market economy, in which a few competing producers determine supply. In the 1980's oligopolists controlled 99% of the US passenger car industry and 90% of the cereal breakfast food, electric lamp, turbine and tubine engine industries.

OLINDA. A town in Brazil, in Pernambuco state. A historic site included in the ▷ World Heritage UNESCO List.

UNESCO. *A Legacy for All*, Paris, 1984.

OLIVA PEACE TREATY, 1660. The peace treaty concluded on May 3, 1660 in the Oliva Monastery near Gdansk between Poland, Brandenburg and Austria on the one side, and Sweden on the other, which put an end to the Polish–Swedish war of 1655–60, with the Polish King, Jan Casimir, giving up the rights to the Swedish crown.

LA MAILLARDIERE, *Abrégé des principaux traités*, 2 Vols., Paris, 1778, Vol. 1.

OLIVE OIL. Subject of international co-operation and conventions. The International Agreement on Olive Oil and Table Oil entered into force on Jan. 1, 1987.

Organizations reg. with the UIA:

International Olive Growers Federation, f. 1934, Rome. Consultative status with FAO, ECOSOC.
International Olive Oil Council, organ of the International Olive Oil Agreement since 1958. Headquarters Madrid. Consultative status with ECOSOC, UNCTAD, FAO, UNDP, GATT and WHO. Members: governments of Algeria, Belgium, Chile, the Dominican Republic, Egypt, France, Greece, Israel, Libya, Lebanon, Luxembourg, Morocco, Panama, Portugal, Spain, Tunisia, Turkey, the UK, and Yugoslavia.

Yearbook of International Organizations; *UN Chronicle*, November 1986, p. 117.

OLYMPIC GAMES. The official name of the ancient sports events resumed late in the 19th century. The First International Sports Congress was convoked at the Paris Sorbonne in June, 1894 on the initiative of Pierre de Coubertin of France and attended by sports activists from Belgium, England, France, Greece, Russia, Spain, Sweden and the USA. The Congress resolved to revive in an international form the Greek sports tournaments organized every four years from 776 BC to 394 BC, and therefore established on June 23, 1894, the International Olympic Committee, IOC, with headquarters in Lausanne to hold Olympic Games every four years in various cities throughout the world promoting peaceful competition of youth and friendship among nations. Olympic teams are selected by national Olympic Committees from among specified amateur sports; these Committees, due to the structure of IOC dating back to 1894, do not have a decisive vote in IOC which often has been the cause of crises, e.g. in 1968 when the chairman of IOC, A. Brundage, failed to consider the opinion expressed by the majority of national Olympic Committees and insisted that teams of states practicing racial discrimination – the Republic of South Africa and Rhodesia – should be admitted to participate in the 19th Olympic Games in Mexico despite the fact that such participation was denounced by the UN, and Mexico refused to grant them an entry visa. In Oct., 1968 the Co-ordinating and Research Committee of the National Olympic Committees, CRC, was founded with headquarters in Rome, the aim of which was to present collective postulates to IOC. Due to the pressure exerted by CRC in May, 1968, the team of the Republic of South Africa was excluded from the Olympic Games on grounds of the racist policy of apartheid pursued by that country; similarly, Rhodesia was prevented from participation in the 1972 Olympic Games in Munich.

Several Olympic Games were scenes of international incidents, generally of a political character:

At the First Olympic Games in Athens, 1896, Irish athletes included in the team of Great Britain, after a victory in high jump contest scored by their fellow countryman raised the Irish instead of the British flag despite the fact that Ireland was not at that time an independent state. The USA team arrived to these Games 11 days late because of their not realizing that the Julian calendar was still in use in Greece.

At the Fourth Olympic Games in London in 1908, US athletes refused to lower their flag before the British King as they marched past the royal stand. At the Fifth Olympic Games in Stockholm in 1912, the Finnish team refused, as they did in London, to march under the banner of Tsarist Russia.

After World War I, the defeated Central Powers were not invited to participate in the Sixth Olympic Games in 1920, nor was revolutionary Russia (the USSR was also not invited to the 1924 Olympic Games, and participated for the first time in 1952). The Tenth Olympic Games in Berlin in 1936 were used by Hitler's government as a political presentation of "the peaceful German Third Reich."

The Republic of South Africa was not invited to the Eighteenth Olympic Games in Tokyo because of its racist policy of apartheid and Indonesia, as well as the People's Democratic Republic of Korea, withdrew their teams.

The Nineteenth Olympic Games in Mexico in 1968 were preceded by violent suppression of a students' rally at the Tlatelolco Square. During the same Olympics black US athletes demonstrated their alignment with the so-called "Black Power" liberation movement.

The Twentieth Olympic Games in Munich took the most tragic course. On Sept. 5, 1972, a group of Palestinians seized the premises occupied by the Israeli team, killed 2 members and tied up and took another 9 hostage, demanding release from Israeli prisons of certain persons involved with the Palestinian liberation movement. Faced with Israeli refusal they demanded a plane which was to take them and the hostages to one of the Arab states. The Government of the Federal Republic of Germany agreed to it but meanwhile undertook an action in which the Palestinians were to be killed at the airport by a team of police marksmen. As a result, all the Israelis, a majority of the Palestinians and one Bavarian policeman died – 17 persons in all. In addition, the Olympics was witness to several political and nationalistic incidents, e.g., an exhibition in memory of European sportsmen murdered during World War II was devastated. Following this, the International Olympic Committee adopted a resolution which obliges hosts of future games to provide maximum security and prevent the occurrence of political provocations.

The Twenty-First Olympic Games in Montreal in 1976 were boycotted by 30 African states and Guyana as a result of participation of New Zealand which maintained contacts with sportsmen of racist South Africa. In addition, the team of Taiwan withdrew because the organizers did not recognize them as representatives of China.

The Twenty-Second Olympic Games in Moscow in 1980 were boycotted by the USA, UK, FRG and 29 other states supporting President J. Carter's

O

initiative in relation with the Afghanistan crisis. On Apr. 13, 1980 the US Olympic Committee voted 1604 : 797 for a boycott of Moscow Games.

The Twenty-Third Olympic Games in Los Angeles in 1984 were boycotted by the USSR, Afghanistan, Bulgaria, Cuba, Czechoslovakia, the GDR, Hungary, Mongolia, Poland and Vietnam.

As a rule since 1896 Olympic Games have been held in summer (June, July): I – in 1896 in Athens (13 states participated); II – in 1900 in Paris (20 states); III – in 1904 in Saint Louis, USA, (28 states), IV – in 1908 in London, (22 states); V – in 1912 in Stockholm (28 states); VI – in 1916 were not held because of the war; VII – in 1920 in Antwerp, Belgium (29 states); VIII – in 1924 in Paris (44 states); IX – in 1928 in Amsterdam (46 states); X – in 1932 in Los Angeles (44 states); XI – in 1936 in Berlin (49 states); XII and XIII – in 1940 and 1944 were not held because of the war; XIV – in 1948 in London (59 states); XV – in 1952 in Helsinki (69 states); XVI – in 1956 in Melbourne (67 states); XVII – in 1960 in Rome (83 states); XVIII – in 1964 in Tokyo (94 states); XIX – in 1968 in Mexico City (108 states); XX – in 1972 in Munich (109 states); XXI – in 1976 in Montreal (93 states); XXII – in 1980 in Moscow (74 states); and XXIII – in 1984 in Los Angeles (146 states). In the Twenty-Fourth Olympiad, held in Seoul, South Korea, on Sep. 17–Oct. 2, 1988, 160 countries participated; seven boycotted the Games: Albania, Cuba, Ethiopia, Madagascar, North Korea, Nicaragua and the Seychelles.

Since 1924 on the initiative of the IOC Winter Olympic Games are also held: I – 1924 in Chamonix; II – 1928 in St. Moritz; III – 1932 in Lake Placid; IV – 1936 in Garmish-Partenkirchen; V – 1948 in St. Moritz; VI – 1952 in Oslo; VII – 1956 in Cortina d'Ampezzo; VIII – 1960 in Squaw Valley; IX – 1964 in Innsbruck; X – 1968 in Grenoble; XI – 1972 in Sapporo; XII – 1976 in Innsbruck; XIII – 1980 in Lake Placid; XIV – 1984 in Sarajevo; XV – 1988 in Calgary.

The Olympic Flag offered by Pierre de Coubertin in 1914 to the Olympic Congress held in Paris may be used only on consent of the IOC and neither the flag nor Olympic symbols may be used for commercial or other ends. Due to absence of an international convention on the protection of the flag and the symbol of IOC, this restriction is not always observed.

The Olympic emblem consists of five circles symbolizing five parts of the world joined in the concept of peaceful competition in the following order of precedence and colors: on top – Europe (blue circle), Africa (black), America (red); at bottom Asia (yellow) and Australia (green).

The composition of the International Olympic Committee was determined at the XXIX session in May 1970 in Amsterdam in the following manner: almost 50% are representatives of Europe (35 out of 74), 20% from America (17 members), about 14% from Asia (10 members), 12% from Africa (9 members) and about 4% from Oceania (3 members).

F.M. MESSERLI, *Histoire des Sports et de l'Olimpisme*, Lausanne, 1950; *Les Jeux Olympiques, Principes Fondamentaux, Status et Règles, Information Générale*, IOC Lausanne, 1958; O. MAYER, *A travers les anneaux Olimpiques*, Genève, 1960; M.T. EYQUEM, *Pierre de Coubertin*, Dortmund, 1972; M.I. FINLEY, H.W. PLEKET, *The Olympic Games*, London, 1976; R. ESPY, *The Politics of the Olympic Games*, Berkeley, 1979; "Olympic Boycott", in: *US Department of State Bulletin*, May 1980, pp. 14–15 and 35.

OLYMPIC MUSEUM. Est. 1965 in Mon Repos, Lausanne, Switzerland under the aegis of the International Olympic Committee.

OLYMPIC NATIONAL PARK. A natural site of the USA, included in the ▷ World Heritage UNESCO List. Among the mountains in this peninsula in the American northwest are some 60 expanding glaciers, some of which are below the 1000 metre level. The forests extend from the rocky and jagged coastline up to the mountain peaks and are of a fantastic variety. Their isolation explains the unique evolution of the many different sub-species of plants and animals found there.

UNESCO, *A Legacy for All*, Paris, 1984.

OMAN. Member of the UN. Sultanate of Oman. Independent state on the Gulf of Oman and the Arabian Sea, bordered by Southern Yemen, Saudi Arabia and the United Arab Emirates. Area: 212,000 sq. km. Pop. 1982 est.: 1,500,000. Capital: Muscat with 50,000 inhabitants 1982. GNP per capita 1987: US $6160. Official language: Arabic. Currency one Omani Rial = 1000 baiza. National Day: Nov. 19, Sultan's Birthday.

Member of UN since Oct. 7, 1971 and of all UN specialized agencies with exception of the IAEA, GATT, WIPO and ILO. Member of the Arab League and since May 1981 of the Gulf Cooperation Council (GCC).

International relations: from 1508 to 1659 under Portuguese control; from 1660 to 1746 Turkish possession. Sultanate of the present dynasty since 1743, known until 1970 as Muscat and Oman. In close ties with Great Britain by a General Peace Treaty 1822 and Treaties of Friendship, Commerce and Navigation, signed in 1891, 1939 and 1951. In 1955 in dispute with the British Petroleum Co. and Shell. In Oct., 1960 ten Arab states at the UN accused Great Britain that its colonial presence in Oman prevented the people from exercising their rights of self-determination. The "Question of Oman" was subject of UN General Assembly Res. 2238/XXI of Dec. 20, 1966 and 2302/XXII of Dec. 14, 1967. The conflict with South Yemen, 1970–76, ended with a normalization agreement in 1982.
See also ▷ World Heritage UNESCO List.

W. PHILIPPS, *Unknown Oman*, London, 1967; WHITEHEAD CONSULTING GROUP, *Sultanate of Oman Economic Survey*, London, 1972; L. SHEET, *Muscat and Oman. The End of an Era*, London, 1974; D. HAWLEY, *Oman and its Renaissance*, London, 1977; J. TOWNSEND, *Oman. The Making of the Modern States*, London, 1977; J.E. PETERSON, *Oman in the Twentieth Century*, London, 1978; M.O. SHANNON, *Oman and South-East Arabia. A Bibliography Survey*, Boston, 1978; F.A. CLEMENTS, *Oman Bibliography*, Oxford, 1981; U. WIKAN, *Behind the Veil in Arabia – Women in Oman*, Baltimore, 1982; *The Europa Year Book 1984. A World Survey*, Vol. II, pp. 2185–2191, London, 1984.

OMBUDSMAN. *Swedish*: ombud = "commission", "recommendation". An international term, for the institution which developed and functioned in the Scandinavian states from the 18th century involving the appointment of a plenipotentiary by the head of state to protect the rights of citizens, e.g. in the administration of justice (*Justitie ombudsman*) or e.g. an office created in Sweden in 1971 to protect the interests of consumers. A UN Report on national institutions for the promotion and protection of human rights, 1983, notes the geographical spread of such institutions as the "ombudsman" and similar bodies. An office of Ombudsman "for the protection of civil rights" was established in Poland on Jan. 2, 1988.

D.C. ROWAT, *The Ombudsman*, London, 1965; W. GELLHORN, *Ombudsman and others citizens' protectors in nine countries*, Cambridge Mass., 1967; S. HURWITZ, *The Ombudsman*, Copenhagen, 1968; J. HANSEN, *Die Institution des Ombudsman*, Kiel, 1972; *UN Chronicle*, January, 1984, p. 51.

OMO. The valley in south-west Ethiopia, near to Lake Turkana, where in 1967 were discovered fragments of the skeletons of two species of *Australopithecus* – one referred to as hardy, which disappeared without trace, while the other, known as slender, could have been a precursor of *Homo sapiens*. However, the lower valley of the Omo is also remarkable for its sediments (sand, clay, alluvium and gravel). As these contain innumerable paleontological remains (boncs of vertebrates, shells, wood and pollen) mixed with the remains of fossil hominids and their implements – the oldest in the world – these deposits have made it possible to reconstitute the environment in which *Australopithecus* lived two million years ago. The Omo deposits are the best distributed, over the longest and most continuous period of time, and have become a reference for the period they illustrate (4 to 1 million years ago). The paleontological Ethiopian sites of the Omo and ▷ Awash were included in the ▷ World Heritage UNESCO List.

UNESCO. *A Legacy for All*, Paris, 1984.

ONE COUNTRY TWO SYSTEMS DOCTRINE, 1984. A Chinese doctrine formulated in 1984 by People's Republic of China's top political leader, Deng Xiaoping, related to the different economic and social systems of ▷ Hong Kong and Taiwan, parts of "one country" – China. Offical Chinese interpretation in Oct., 1984: "The idea of one country, two systems is suitable not only for Hong Kong, but for many other regions. It is definitely suitable for Taiwan." The China-Portugal agreement on the transfer (Dec. 20, 1999) of ▷ Macau signed on April 13, 1987 in Beira was also based upon the "one country two systems doctrine". Macau for a 50 year period – until April 2037 is guaranteed the right to regulate its own autonomy in matters other than foreign policy and defence.

Newsweek, October 8, 1984, pp. 40–43.

ONOMASTICS. A subject of international cooperation. Organizations reg. with the UIA:

International Committee for Outer Space Onomastics, f. 1966, Louvain, Belgium. Consultative status with ECOSOC.
International Committee of Onomastic Sciences, f. 1949, Louvain, Belgium. Publ: *Onoma*.

Yearbook of International Organizations.

ON THE BRINK OF WAR. An international term of the 1950s for the Cold War relations between the USA and the USSR.
See also ▷ Brinkman.

D. ROBERTSON, *Guide to Modern Defense and Strategy*, Detroit 1988.

OPANAL. ▷ Tlatelolco Treaty, 1967.

OPEC. Organization of the Petroleum Exporting Countries. The Organization was established 1960 at a Conference in Baghdad convened on the initiative of Iraq; and its statute ratified at the Second Conference in Jan., 1961 in Caracas. The highest organ is the Conference of government representatives of the member states; there are also the executive – Council of Governors, Economic Commission and Secretariat. The Organization's headquarters are in Vienna. Membership 1984: Algeria, Ecuador, Gabon, Indonesia, Iran, Iraq, Kuwait, Libya, Nigeria, Qatar, Saudi Arabia, United Arab Emirates and Venezuela. In 1973 this represented over 55.5% of world oil production and c. 70% of the then proven oil reserves (remaining: USSR – 9.6%, USA – 8.6% and the rest of the world 11.8%); in 1980 c. 43% and in 1983 some 30%, possessing 67% of known world oil reserves and 32.8% of known natural gas reserves. Production and marketing information is continually exchanged between OPEC members. In 1970 *c.* 85% of OPEC petroleum production was exported to the capitalist world. In 1970 there were three regional groups in OPEC; the strongest – 6 Arab states: Abu Dhabi, Iran, Iraq, Kuwait, Qatar, Saudi Arabia representing 60% of the petroleum exports of all OPEC members (700 million tons out of 1126 million tons); the African group: Libya (160 million tons), Nigeria (50 million tons), and Algeria (46 million tons); members of the third group: Venezuela (180 million tons) and Indonesia (40 million tons). Among the great western exporters, only Canada (exporting 60 million tons) is not a member of OPEC. Among other large exporters not belonging to OPEC is the USSR, which exports petroleum mainly to the socialist countries.

An important stage in the development of OPEC was the formulation in July 1965, at the Conference in Tripoli, of a common policy controlling the level of oil production. In June 1970 it was decided to raise the price of oil, which was finally ratified at the Twenty-First Conference in Caracas (Dec. 10–12, 1970), bringing about an increase of more than 30% and a rise in the base for taxing the net profits of foreign concerns to a minimum of 55%, after the example of Venezuela, which in Dec., 1970, unilaterally raised its tax to 60% from 52% (in the majority of oil-producing states the level of taxation ranged from 35 to 50%), and it was also decided to reduce the differences in the level of ▷ Posted Prices. Also agreed was the standardization in all OPEC countries of posted prices for oil used to calculate the payment of ▷ Royalties, which were pegged to the fluctuations of currency exchange rates. The resolutions of the Twenty-First Conference, published Dec. 27, 1971, were the basis for negotiations with the oil companies in Teheran Jan. 12 –Feb. 14, 1971 and in Tripoli Feb. 14–Apr. 2, 1971, where on the basis of The Teheran Petroleum Agreement (1971) the price rose from US $2.55 to $3.45. In July 1971 at an OPEC ministers conference a plan was developed for the "return of petroleum", modelled on the Venezuelian "*ley sobre el retorno de petrolio*" of June, 1971, assuming the return without compensation by 1983 of the concessions of foreign companies. The OPEC conferences in Beirut Aug. 13 and Sept. 22, 1971 decided to enter into negotiations with the large oil companies on the matter of obtaining 20–51% of those companies shares for their governments. This concerned the governments of Abu Dhabi, Iran, Iraq, Kuwait, Libya, Nigeria, Qatar, and Saudi Arabia. Algeria earlier had received a share of 51%. Indonesia and Venezuela have their own systems for co-operation with the foreign companies. In 1973, OPEC in connection with the devaluation of the dollar by 16%, raised the price of oil in dollars by 11%. On June 1, 1973 the posted prices for crude oil were raised a further 11.9% as the result of an appropriate agreement signed in Geneva by 23 international oil concerns with the OPEC member states.

In Mar., 1974, OPEC temporarily froze the price of oil at US $11.65 for a 159-litre barrel; on Apr. 7, 1974 OPEC created a Compensation Fund for the underdeveloped countries affected by the rise in price of oil.

At the end of 1975 it was decided to create an OPEC Special Fund for this purpose; in operation since 1976. During the Conference in Vienna, the OPEC building was the object of a terrorist attack. In 1976 and in following years, OPEC has annually raised the price of oil in order to equalize losses incurred through the devaluation of the US dollar. These increases have become one of the causes of the continuing ▷ energy world crisis in the decade 1971–80.

The first years of the 1980s were characterized by a reduced consumption of crude oil from OPEC states by many industrialized countries. In Dec., 1981 in Abu Dhabi the OPEC Conference of Oil Ministers started the adjustment of price differential and agreed to the reduction of prices per barrel between US $0.20 and $0.70. In Mar., 1982 an emergency OPEC meeting took place in Vienna. An agreement to limit oil production by the OPEC states was signed. The second Vienna OPEC Conference in Dec., 1982 without agreement on new production quota was followed by an emergency OPEC conference in Mar., 1983 in London, terminated with a compromise agreement on OPEC price cuts and new production quotas; adjusted to the new situation in Nov., 1984. The OPEC pricing system on the basis of output quotas broke down in mid 1985. The collapse of oil prices started on Dec. 10, 1985 from $30 per barrel to $24.40, to $10 in Aug., 1986 for North Sea Brent crude. The Seventy-Sixth conference meeting of OPEC on Dec. 9, 1985 decided generally "to secure and defend for OPEC a fair share in the World oil market consistent with the necessary income for member countries". The conference did not quantify "fair shares". The oil prices had been falling since mid 1986 (until the Persian Gulf crisis in Aug. 1987). On Apr. 26–28, 1988 the 13 OPEC Member States met for the first time with representatives of Non-OPEC petroleum exporting countries: Angola, China, Colombia, Egypt, Malaysia, Mexico, Oman.

The oil price on May 2, 1988 was under $16 per barrel.

The OPEC News Agency publ. *OPEC Bulletin, OPEC Review, OPEC Official Resolutions* and *Press Releases* and booklets.

F. GHADAR, *The Evolution of OPEC Strategy*, Lexington, 1977; F. ABOLATH, *The OPEC Market to 1985*, Lexington, 1977; F. AL-CHALABI, *OPEC and the International Oil Industry*, Oxford, 1980; J. SEYMOUR, *OPEC, Instrument and Change*, London, 1980; *OPEC and Future Energy Markets. The Proceedings of the OPEC Seminar Held in Vienna*, Oct., 1979, London, 1980; Ch. T. SANNDERS (ed.), *East and West in the Energy Squeeze*, London, 1980; J.J. SERVAN-SCHREIBER, *The World Challenge: OPEC and the New Global Order*, New York, 1981; J.M. GRIFFIN (ed.), *OPEC Behavior and World Oil Prices*, Winchester, Mass., 1982; A.M. JAIDAH, *An Appraisal of OPEC Oil Policies*, London, New York, 1983; *The Europa Year Book 1984. A World Survey*, Vol. I, pp. 196–199, London, 1984; M.E. AHRARI, *OPEC: The Failing Giant*, Louisville, 1985; KEESING's *Contemporary Archive*, June 1985; KEESING's *Contemporary Archive*, 1986; J. EVANS, *OPEC, Its Member States and the World Energy Market. A Comprehensive Reference Guide*, London, 1987.

OPEC SPECIAL FUND FOR INTERNATIONAL DEVELOPMENT. The Fund was est. in Aug., 1976, in Vienna, with initial capital of US $800 million, to finance development projects and help cover balance-of-payments deficit of Third World Nations that are not oil-rich. The actual commitments, cumulative to Dec. 31, 1982, were in total US $2,647,100,000.

OPEC Fund Annual Report, Vienna, 1983.

OPEN DIPLOMACY. An international term for diplomatic negotiations open to the press, conducted at international conferences, called also Conference Diplomacy.

OPEN DOOR POLICY. An international term, in the 19th century also known as "the open door doctrine", came into use when the British Empire forced China in 1842 to open its ports to British merchant vessels; in 1854 – the same with respect to Japan. The USA, in turn, signed a treaty with China in Tien Tsin on June 18, 1858; a similar treaty and in the same place was signed by Great Britain on June 26, 1858, both being called "the Treaties of Open Door." In the following decades the same rights were granted to other colonial powers and, as a result of the Berlin Congress of 1885, the open door policy was expanded to include Africa as well. The principles of the open door policy were codified by the US Secretary of State John Hay (1838–1905) in a diplomatic note of Sept. 6, 1899, addressed to France, Japan, Germany, Russia, Great Britain and Italy, referring to equal rights and opportunities in access to China by their vessels and products, while mutually respecting the "interest spheres" of particular states. Similar notes were sent by the USA after the Boxer Uprising of 1900. The John Hay letter concerning the Open Door Policy in China, read as follows:

"In this critical posture of affairs in China it is deemed appropriate to define the attitude of the United States as far as present circumstances permit this to be done. We adhere to the policy initiated by us in 1857, of peace with the Chinese nation, of furtherance of lawful commerce, and of protection of lives and property of our citizens by all means guaranteed under extraterritorial treaty rights and by the law of nations. If wrong be done to our citizens we propose to hold the responsible authors to the uttermost accountability. We regard the condition at Pekin as one of virtual anarchy, whereby power and responsibility are practically devolved upon the local provincial authorities. So long as they are not in overt collusion with rebellion and use their power to protect foreign life and property we regard them as representing the Chinese people, with whom we seek to remain in peace and friendship. The purpose of the President is, as it has been heretofore, to act concurrently with the other powers, first, in opening up communication with Pekin and rescuing the American officials, missionaries, and other Americans who are in danger; secondly, in according all possible protection everywhere in China to American life and property; thirdly, in guarding and protecting all legitimate American interests; and fourthly, in aiding to prevent spread of the disorders to the other provinces of the Empire and a recurrence of such disasters. It is, of course, too early to forecast the means of attaining this last result; but the policy of the government of the United States is to seek a solution which may bring about permanent safety and peace to China, preserve Chinese territorial and administrative entity, protect all rights guaranteed to friendly powers by treaty and international law, and safeguard for the world the principle of equal and impartial trade with all parts of the Chinese Empire.

You will communicate the purport of this instruction to the minister for foreign affairs."

In 1917 a dispute arose between the USA and Japan with regard to the open door policy, a diplomatic conflict resolved at the Washington Conference 1921/22 which drafted the Treaty of Nine Powers (Belgium, China, France, Holland, Japan, Portugal, the United States, Great Britain and Italy), guaranteeing the integrity and independence of China and reaffirming the validity of the open door policy. It was the last international act that sanctioned the open door policy with respect to China. Previously, in Saint Germain-en-Laye on Sept. 10, 1919 a convention was signed which changed some of the decisions of the Berlin Congress of 1885, including annulment of the open door regime. After World War II, full sovereignty of China ruled out the application of the open door policy.

G.Z. WOOD, *Genesis of the Open Door Policy in China*, New York, 1921; M.J. BAN, *The Open Door Policy in China*, New York, 1923; A.A. FURSENKO, *Bor'ba za razdel Kitaya i amerikanskaya doktrina "odkritiy dvereyi"*, Moscow, 1956; M.E. CAMERON, *China, Japan and the Powers*, London, 1960.

OPEN SEA. ▷ Mare Apertum.

O

OPEN SKIES PLAN, 1955. A proposal of the US President Dwight D. Eisenhower during the summit meeting at Geneva in July, 1955 to Premier Nikita S. Khrushchev to open the skies of the United States and the Soviet Union to reciprocal aerial surveillance; rejected by N.S. Khrushchev.

KEESING's *Contemporary Archive*, 1955; B.W. ROSTOW, *Open Skies: Eisenhower's Proposal of July 22, 1955*, Austin, 1983.

OPEN SOCIETY. An international term for democratic systems with all cultural and political freedoms respected.

K. POPPER, *The Open Society and its Enemies*, London, 1985.

OPERATIONAL RESEARCH. A subject of international co-operation. Organizations reg. with the UIA:

International Associations Co-ordinating Committee, f. 1970, Paris. Members: International Association for Analog Computation, International Federation of Automatic Control, International Federation for Information Processing, International Federation of Operational Research Societies and International Measurement Confederation.
International Federation of Operational Research Societies, f. 1959, Lyngby, Denmark.

Yearbook of International Organizations.

OPERATION SAIL. The name of an international gathering of sailing ships and sailing yachts, organized since 1958 every second year by the Sail Association, established 1955.

Yearbook of International Organizations.

OPHTHALMOLOGY. A subject of international co-operation. Organizations reg. with the UIA:

Asia-Pacific Academy of Ophthalmology, f. 1957, Honolulu.
European Ophthalmology Society, f. 1958, Ghent. Publ.: *Congress Acta.*
International Federation of Ophthalmological Societies, f. 1933, Paris. Official relations with WHO. Publ.: *Congress Reports.*
International Society of Geographic Ophthalmology, f. 1970, Montreal.
Ophthalmological Society of East Africa, f. 1976, Nairobi.
Pan American Association of Ophthalmology, f. 1940, Clayton, Mass. Publ.: *Directory.*

Yearbook of International Organizations.

OPIUM. A subject of international conventions. The coagulated juice from the unripe capsule of the poppy plant, used primarily as an important raw material for the licit manufacture of ▷ morphine, codeine and their derivates is also the raw material for the illegal production of ▷ heroin.
The First International Opium Convention was signed in The Hague, 1912; the Second in 1925 in Geneva.
In 1953 the UN adopted The Protocol for Limiting and Regulating the Cultivation of Poppy Plant, the Production of, International and Wholesale Trade in the Use of Opium, which came into force in 1963. Only seven countries – Bulgaria, Greece, India, Iran, Turkey, the USSR and Yugoslavia are authorized to produce opium under state control for export limited to medical and scientific needs.
UN Chronicle, May 1987.

OPIUM CONVENTIONS, 1912 AND 1925. The international agreement signed on Jan. 23, 1912 in The Hague between the governments of China, France, Italy, Japan, Persia, Portugal, Russia, the UK and USA, prohibiting

"the import and export of prepared opium ... determined to bring about the gradual suppression of the abuse of opium, morphine, and cocaine and also of drugs prepared or derived from these substances, which give rise or might give rise to similar abuse."

This was suspended by the Opium Convention, signed on Feb. 19, 1925 at Geneva, establishing the Permanent Control Opium Board. The Convention defined opium as follows:

"By 'prepared opium' is understood: the product of raw opium, obtained by a series of special operations, especially by dissolving, boiling, roasting and fermentation, designed to transform it into an extract suitable for consumption. Prepared opium includes dross and all other residues remaining when opium has been smoked. By 'medical opium' is understood: raw opium which has been heated to 60° centigrade and contains not less than 10% of morphine, whether or not it be powdered or granulated or mixed with indifferent materials."

The International Narcotic Control Board has stated in a report of Jan. 28, 1982 that a bumper crop of poppies in South East Asia threatened to flood the worldwide black market with as much as 600 tons of opium in 1982.
The principal alkaloid of opium is ▷ morphine.

LNTS, Vol. 8, p. 189; L.M. GOODRICH, "New Fronts in Narcotics Control", in: *International Conciliation*, No. 530, 1960; F. BERNHARDT, "Opium Zentralausschuss", in: *STRUPP-SCHLOCHAUER Wörterbuch des Völkerrechts*, Berlin, 1961, Vol. 2, pp. 660–661; *UN Yearbook 1963*, pp. 383–389, 524; G. LAMOUR, M.R. LAMBERT, *Les grandes manoeuvres de l'opium*, Paris, 1972; *UN Chronicle*, April, 1982, p. 33.

OPIUM WARS, 1839–1860. The commonly accepted name for the colonial wars of Great Britain against China 1839–42 and 1856–60. The first Opium War was caused by the introduction in China of a prohibition against the import of opium and the destruction of supplies of opium in the warehouses of British merchants in Canton, which was a defense against the moral destruction of the people and the economic ruin of the country; the British government, which recognized this as a violation of its commercial interests, declared war on China. As a result of military defeat China lost Hongkong and opened its ports for British trading-posts. Two further interventionary wars of Great Britain and France against China 1856–58 and 1859–60, concluded with the further extension of the privileges of the powers, including the dissemination of narcotics in China, which was only brought to an end by the revolution. Opium Treaties 1824–60, resulting from the three Opium wars: the Nankin Peace Treaty, signed on Aug. 29, 1842; the Tientsin Peace Treaty, signed on June 27, 1858; and the Peking Peace Treaty, signed on Oct. 25, 1860.

H.B. MORSE, *International Relations of the Chinese Empire*, 3 Vols., London, 1910–18, SSU-YÜ TONG, J.K. FAIRBANK, *China's Response to the West. A Documentary Survey 1830–1923*, New York, 1954.

OPOLE. A Polish city on the Oder river (1980 est. pop. 113,000). Originally in the Polish Kingdom, Opole passed to Austria (1532–1742) and in 1742 was incorporated by the Prussian state. It was covered by the Upper Silesian Convention 1922–37 and returned to Poland after World War II. Capital of the Opole province. ▷ Colloquium Opole.

L. STRASZEWICZ, *Opole Silesia*, Warsaw, 1965.

OPTICS. A subject of international co-operation. Organizations reg. with the UIA:

Common Market Opticians Group, f. 1960, Paris.
European Association of Industries on Precision Mechanics and Optics. f. 1960, Milan.

International Commission for Optics, f. 1948, Besancon. Publ.: *Newsletter.*
International Guild of Dispensing Opticians, f. 1951, London.
International Optometric and Optical League, f. 1927, London. Publ.: *Interoptics* (quarterly).
Nordic Optical Council, f. 1975, Grevinge.

Yearbook of International Organizations.

OPTION. An indication of the means of acquiring nationality: (1) through voluntary choice between two nationalities and the renouncement of one of them, e.g. in case of marriage when assuming the nationality of the spouse; and (2) as a result of change of state frontiers on the basis of the provisions of a peace treaty. The issue of option and opting persons was disputed by the LN and was also subject to the Peace Treaty with Italy of 1947.

OPTIONAL CLAUSE. An international term linked to ▷ compulsory jurisdiction of the Statute of the Permanent Court of International Justice, 1920, maintained in the ▷ International Court of Justice Statute, 1945 (Art. 36) and approved by the ▷ Bogota Pact, 1948.

G. MASSIS, *La llamada clausula facultativa y su aplicación en el orden internacional*, México, DF, 1961; M. SEARA VAZQUEZ, *Tratado General de la Organización Internacional*, México DF, 1974, pp. 210–214 and 864–865; R.L. BLEDSOE, B.A. BOCZEK, *The International Law Dictionary*, Oxford UK, 1987.

OPUS DEI. *Societas Sacerdotalis Sanctae Crucis et Opus Dei*, Sacerdotal Association of the Holy Cross and *Opus Dei (the Work of God)*. The international Catholic Organization, one of the societies of priests and laymen who, as priests, take monastic vows, yet do not live in orders, but act as laymen. *Opus Dei* was founded in 1928 in Madrid by Father Josemaria Escrivá de Balaguer, "to spread, at every level of society, a profound awakening of consciences to the universal calling to sanctity and apostolate in the course of members own professional work." After World War II the association began its activity mainly in Latin American countries, where it gained considerable political influence. However its greatest influence was in Spain. It also had branches in England, the FRG and USA. The form of lay apostolate introduced by *Opus Dei* was approved by Pope Pius XII in the constitution of *Provida Mater Ecclesia*, 1943.
Opus Dei has two sections: men's and women's, founded in 1930. In 1984 they numbered 72,000 laymen and 1,000 priests from 80 countries. Its seat since 1946 is Rome. A member of *Opus Dei*, Spanish journalist Joaquin Navarro Valls, became in Dec., 1984, a new chief of the Vatican Press Office "Sala Stampa."

V.L. VAILLANT, *La Santa Societa L'Opus Dei in azione*, Milano, 1971; F. SOTO, *Fascismo y Opus Dei en Chile*, Barcelona, 1976; A. KRUCZKOWSKI, *Dzielo Boze w Hiszpanii* (Opus Dei in Spain), Warsaw, 1981; *The Europa Year Book 1984. A World Survey*, Vol. I, p. 249, London, 1984.

ORADOUR-SUR-GLANE. A village in southern France in the departement Haute-Vienne. On June 10, 1944 the whole population, *c.* 1100 persons was murdered by a company of the German police unit SS Der Führer regiment, on the charge of co-operating with partisans; the men were shot, the women and children burned alive in the church. Only one woman escaped. The case of the massacre in Oradour-sur-Glane was presented to the International Military Trial at Nuremburg, 1945.

The Trial of German Major War Criminals. Proceedings of the IMT sitting at Nuremburg, Germany, 42 Vols., London 1946–48, Vol. 37, p. 132 and Vol. 42, p. 128; C.

MOURET, *Oradour, le crime, le procès*, Paris, 1958; G. PAUCHOU, P. MASFRAND, *Oradour-sur-Glane: Vision d'Epouvante*, Limoges, 1966.

ORANGE. A town in southeastern France. A cultural site included in the ▷ World Heritage UNESCO List. A commemorative arch decorated with sculptured trophies and a large theater, one of the best preserved from the Roman world, were both constructed during the reign of Augustus in about 20 BC and evoke the past glory of Arausio from which the name "Orange" is derived.

UNESCO, *A Legacy for All*, Paris, 1984.

ORANIENBURG. ▷ Sachsenhausen-Oranienburg.

ORAVA. ▷ Teschen, Spisz and Orava, 1920.

"ORBITA". A Soviet satellite system of ground stations allowing the reception and retransmission of television programs (▷ Intervision and ▷ Eurovision), radio signals, telephone and teletype messages by telecommunication satellites of the type ▷ Molniya. This system in 1970 encompassed the entire USSR as well as Mongolia.

ORDER OF MALTA. *Ordre souverain et militaire de Malte.* A sovereign institution maintaining diplomatic relations with 42 states, also called the Hospitaliers (*Ordo militiae sancti Joannis Baptistae hospitalis Hierosolimitani*), which came into being during the Crusades, and was recognized by Pope Paschalis II in the Bull of 1113. It cared for sick pilgrims to the Holy Land and in the 13th century performed military functions in defending Christian holy places in Palestine, from whence also called Order of Jerusalemites. In 1291 the Order settled on Cyprus, and in 1310 on Rhodes where its members were known as the Knights of Rhodes. In 1530 received Malta in fief from Charles V (Knights of Malta). It comprised a sovereign administrative unit there until 1798, when Malta fell to the French fleet, and then by the Treaty of Paris, 1814, became a possession of the British Crown. In 1834 Rome became the seat of Order of Malta. From 1888 the Order became an international institution of the European aristocracy while retaining the character of a charitable institution assisting hospitals. Today its official name in French is: *Ordre Souverain Militaire Hospitalier de Saint-Jean de Jérusalem, de Rhodes et de Malte.* Members of the Order are called Knights of Malta. The hierarchy in the Order is two-tiered and the supreme authority is vested in the Grand Master of the Order, *Grand Maitre de l'Ordre.* The Order of Malta retained the status of a sovereign unit accorded to it by Popes in the 15th and 16th centuries and was recognized by 37 states, which enabled it to grant its own passports, maintain its own diplomatic representatives, sign international treaties concerning charitable activities and take part in international conferences. It has diplomatic relations at ambassadorial level with: Argentina, Austria, Bolivia, Brazil, Cameroon, Chile, Colombia, Costa Rica, Cuba, the Dominican Republic, Ecuador, El Salvador, Ethiopia, Gabon, Guatemala, Haiti, Honduras, Iran, Italy, Lebanon, Liberia, Malta, Nicaragua, Niger, Panama, Peru, the Philippines, Senegal, Somalia, Spain, Uruguay and the Vatican. In addition it has delegations to the governments of Belgium, FRG, France, Monaco, Switzerland as well as at the European Council, International Red Cross, International Committee for European Migration, UNESCO, UNHCR and WHO.
It also has local fellowships in states with which it does not maintain diplomatic relations, such as: Hungary, Ireland, Mexico, the Netherlands, Poland, Portugal, Romania, the Scandinavian statutes, the UK, USA and Venezuela.
Institutions which it administers include:

International Aid of the Order of Malta in the Fight Against Famine, Poverty, Illness and Ignorance in the World, seat in Rome; branches in Chile, Colombia, Ethiopia, Japan, Jordan, Kenya, South Korea, Malta, Nigeria, Pakistan, Republic of Central Africa, Romania, Somalia, Vietnam, Yugoslavia.
The International Executive Committee for Assistance to Lepers, seat in Geneva.
The Pediatric Academy of the Order of Malta, seat in Milan. Publ.: *OSM de Malte*, Cahier No. 1, Rome, 1961; No. 2, 1963, *Annales de l'OSM de Malte, Acta Leprologica.*

A.C. BREYCHA-VAUTIER, M. POTULICKI, "The Order of St. John in International Law", in: *American Journal of International Law*, No. 48, 1954; C. D'OLIVIER FARRAN, "The Sovereign Order in Malta in International Law", in *International Law Quarterly*, No. 3, 1954–55; S.B. HAFKEMEYER, *Der Rechtsstatus des Souveraenen Malteser-Ritter-Ordens als Völkerrechtssubjekt ohne Gebietshoheit*, Hamburg, 1955; CH. PEYREFITTE, *Chevalier de Malte*, Paris, 1957; *Charte Constitutionelle*, Rome, 1961; *Code de l'Ordre*, Rome, 1966; *Liste du Corps Diplomatique*, Rome, 1972; B. VALDSTEIN-WALDENBERG, *Rechtsgeschichte des Maltese-Ordens*, Wien, 1969; P. JARIN, *Les Chevaliers de Malte*, Paris, 1974.

ORDER OF PAYMENT. An international term designating paper currency or bank drafts; introduced during the French Revolution in Dec., 1789. The only guarantees of emission of orders of payment were confiscated Catholic Church estates. Successive emissions, beginning with a nominal value of 400 million francs and ending with the value of 45 billion francs, led to the rapid depreciation of orders of payment. In 1796 they were replaced with a new paper currency called "territorial mandates" (equally worthless). However, the name "order of payment" has been preserved and designates a document stating that a cash transaction has been carried out by the bank.

ORDER OF SMILE, THE. ▷ Children's Order of the Smile.

ORDERS. An international term for unions of people professing one religion or world-view and submitting to the specific discipline of their order, usually multi-national. Among catholic orders which played a singular role in international political life were the ▷ Jesuits, and after World War II ▷ Opus Dei.

Annuario Pontificio, 1984.

ORGANISATION COMMUNE AFRICAINE ET MAURICIENNE. ▷ OCAM.

ORGANIZATION FOR THE PROHIBITION OF NUCLEAR WEAPONS IN LATIN AMERICA, OPANAL. ▷ Tlatelolco Treaty, 1967.

ORGANIZATION OF AFRICAN AND MALAGASY STATES. The intergovernmental institution est. on Jan. 30, 1962 in Lagos by the ▷ Monrovia Group, following preliminary conference of the Heads of State in Monrovia May 8–12, 1961. Dissolved 1963 after the foundation of the Organization of African Unity (▷ OAU).

ORGANIZATION OF AFRICAN UNITY. ▷ OAU.

ORGANIZATION OF AFRO-ASIAN AND LATIN-AMERICAN PEOPLES SOLIDARITY. Organización de Solidaridad de los Pueblos de Africa, Asia y América Latina, OSPAAAL. The Organization was established on Jan. 12, 1966 in Havana by the Tricontinental Conference with the task of "unifying, co-ordinating and supporting the struggle of the peoples of Asia, Africa and Latin America against imperialism, colonialism and neo-colonialism directed by North American imperialism"; Headquarters, Havana. Publ.: *Tricontinental Bulletin, Tricontinental Review* in English, French and Spanish. It is reg. with the UIA.

ORGANIZATION OF AFRO-MALAGASY ECONOMIC CO-OPERATION. ▷ OCAM.

ORGANIZATION OF AMERICAN STATES. ▷ OAS.

ORGANIZATION OF ISLAMIC CONFERENCE. ▷ Islamic states.

ORGANIZATIONS, INTERNATIONAL. Any public association or institution assembling legal or physical persons from at least three countries subject to law of international organizations; the LN and UN nomenclature distinguish between inter-governmental organizations and non-governmental organizations. Registers of both kinds are kept by the Union of International Associations. UIA, in Brussels and international organizations formed since the Vienna Congress, 1815 are listed in the Union's history books; the first to be included was the Central Commission for the Navigation of the Rhine, 1815, still operating; this was followed by London's British and Foreign Anti-Slavery Society, 1823; London's Royal Asiatic Society, 1823, active since 1903; St Vincent de Paul religious association in Paris, 1833–1905; New York's International Organization of Good Templars, 1851–1907; Paris International Charity Society Correspondence Internationale 1855–1907; Bologne's Women St Vincent de Paul Community 1856; International Union for the Protection of Trade in Wartime, 1856–1916; European Danube Commission, 1865; International Association for Customs Reform, 1856–1909–1922; International Union of Positivists, 1850; Universal Israelite Alliance, 1861; Universal Ophthalmological Society, 1861; International Union for Social Sciences, 1862–1909–1922; International Committee for Relief of Wounded Soldiers, 1863 (▷ Red Cross); and First International, 1864. The year 1864 marked the beginning of a period of emergence of larger numbers of new governmental and non-governmental organizations, and in 1864–1914 the former totalled 41, the latter – 467. Another wave of increases was recorded between the wars: inter-governmental – 86, non-governmental – 1038, with the largest increase following World War II – 280 and 2470 respectively. Growing at a rate of 3.5% annually the figures for the year 2000 are expected to reach 635 and 6000. A table illustrating formation of international organizations in the period 1893–1954 drawn by Union of International Associations in a study (*Les 1978 Organisations Internationales fondées depuis le Congrés de Vienne*, Bruxelles, 1957) shows the share of individual countries hosting inter-governmental organizations as follows: France – 100, Great Britain – 90, Belgium – 88, FRG – 85, Italy – 77; and the top ten non-governmental organizations according to membership: France – 1,168, FRG – 1,165, Netherlands – 1,088, Belgium – 1,074, Italy – 1,057, Great Britain – 1,039, Switzerland – 1,018, Austria – 901, Denmark – 883, and Sweden – 859. The Fifteen states where most NGO conferences were held in 1970 were: Switzerland – 1,139, France – 124, USA – 121, Great Britain – 83, FRG – 74, Italy – 69, Netherlands – 62, Belgium – 61, Japan – 61, Spain – 43, Denmark – 31, USSR – 31, Sweden – 25, Czechoslovakia – 23, Canada – 22. Host Cities in

O

1970: Geneva – 88, Paris – 65, London – 42, Brussels – 40, New York – 34, Rome – 33, Vienna – 32, Tokyo – 29, Amsterdam – 24, Copenhagen – 24, Washington – 24, Kyoto – 23, Prague – 21, Munich – 18, Stockholm – 18. The headquarters of these organizations are distributed as follows: France – 503, Great Britain – 365, Switzerland – 283, Belgium – 279, USA – 257, Netherlands – 134, FRG – 118, Italy – 100, Poland – 7.

The number of international agreements concluded between international organizations or with states rose rapidly after 1955, as UN Treaty Series records show, to a total of 1280 in 1960; the largest percentage concerned technological assistance from UN agencies; the same occurred in the following decades.

The ▷ Vienna Convention on the representation of states in their relations with international organizations of a universal character, Mar. 14, 1975 provided norms of diplomatic relations between states and international organizations. ▷ Diplomatic law.

A ▷ Non-Governmental Organizations European Convention was signed on Apr. 2–24, 1986.

The ▷ UIA statistics for 1985 registered 5054 ▷ international conventional organizations (1986 – 5018), and others of different character not related directly or indirectly to the UN System: 19,120 in 1985 and 20,100 in 1986.

J. TER MUELEN, *Der Gedanke der Entwicklung der Internationalen Organisation 1300–1800*, 2 Vols. Zürich, 1917–1929; J. TER MEULEN, *Der Gedanke der internationalen Organisationen in seiner Entwicklung 1927–1939*, Zürich, 1940; C.W. JENKS, *The Headquarters of International Institutions*, London, 1945; CH. CHAMON, *Les organisations internationales*, Paris, 1954–55; S.P. SPEEKAERT, *Les Organismes Internationales et l'Organisation Internationale, Bibliographie sélective*, Bruxelles, 1956; S. GOODSPEED, *The Nature and Function of International Organization*, London, 1959; J.D. SINGER, M. WALLACE, "Intergovernmental Organization and the Preservation of Peace, 1816–1964; Some Bivariate Relationships", in *International Organization*, No. 3, 1970; J.G. SINGER, M. WALLACE, "Intergovernmental Organization in the Global System 1815–1964. A Quantative Description", in: *International Organization*, No. 2, 1970: K. SKJELBACK, "Development of the Systems of International Organizations: A Diachronic Study", in: *Proceedings of the International Peace Research Association*, No. 4, 1970; E.H. FEDDAR, (ed.), *The United Nations: Problems and Prospects*, Saint Louis, 1971; B.W. GANIUSHKIN, *Diplomaticheskoye pravo mezhhdunarodnikh organizatsii*, Moscow, 1972; *The Anatomy of Influence. Decision Making in International Organizations*, New Haven--London, 1973; J.E.S. FAWCETTE, R. HIGGINS, *International Organizations Law in Movement*, New York, 1974; W. BAER, *International Organizations 1918–1945. A Guide to Research and Research Material*, Wilmington, 1981; G.J. MOROZOV (ed.), *Aktualniye problemy mezhhdunarodnikh organisatsyi. Tieoriya i praktika*, Moscow, 1982; J. DUFFAR, *Contribution a l'etude des privilèges et immunités des organisations internationales*, Paris, 1982; D. ARMSTRONG, *The Rise of International Organizations*, London, 1982; *Yearbook of International Organizations, 1986/87, Appendix*.

ORGANIZATIONS INTERNATIONAL, CONVENTIONAL.
A UN term for intergovernmental organizations, international non-governmental organizations (NGO) and multinational enterprises.

Yearbook of International Organizations, 1986/87.

ORGANIZATIONS INTERNATIONAL NON-GOVERNMENTAL.
▷ Non-Governmental Organizations.

ORGANIZATIONS MULTINATIONAL.
▷ Multinational Enterprises.

ORGANIZATIONS, NATIONAL ORIENTED INTERNATIONAL.
An international term for non-conventional organizations registered by the UIA, with various forms of international activity or concern such as development, environmental research, peace and relief.

ORGANIZATIONS OF UNIVERSAL CHARACTER.
A term defined in art. 1 of the Vienna Convention 1975 as denoting the UN, its specialized agencies, the International Atomic Energy Agency, and any similar organization whose membership and responsibility are of universal scope.

ORIENTAL CHURCHES.
The Christian churches in the East, formed in the course of the development of Christianity; include many Orthodox churches and the churches separated in the 5th–7th centuries as a result of theological disputes. They are Monophysite churches (recognizing only one divine nature of Christ) to which belong the Armenian, Ethiopian, Jacobite and Coptic churches as well as the group called Nestorian church: Chaldean and East-Syrian (recognizing two persons in Christ: divine and human, and consequently rejecting the cult of Virgin Mary as God's Mother); some oriental churches are in union with Rome, accept the Catholic doctrine and the Pope as the primate, maintaining only their own liturgy and law within their own codes of church discipline.

R. JANIN, *Les Églises orientales et les rites orientaux*, Paris, 1955; R. ETTELDORF, *The Catholic Church in the Middle East*, London, 1959; D. ATTWATER, *The Christian Churches of the East*, London, 1961.

ORIENTAL JEWS.
One of the three major divisions of the Jews (the two others ▷ Ashkenazim, and ▷ Sephardim). The Oriental Jews are the descendants of Assyrian, Babylonian or Roman Jews settled in the Middle Ages in North Africa and in the Middle East, in Arab lands from Lebanon, Syria, Palestine to Morocco speaking Arabic. Many of the communities organizations are in relations with the World Sephardi Federation. See also ▷ Jews.

Yearbook of International Organizations, 1986/87; The Europa Yearbook 1988. A World Survey, Vol. I, London, 1988

ORIENTAL PHILOSOPHY INSTITUTE OF.
Est. 1962 in Tokyo, a research foundation, with the aim of promoting the study of oriental philosophy, thought and culture in particular that of ▷ Buddhism.

Soka Gakkai News, April, 1988.

ORIENT PACT, 1937.
▷ Afghanistan, Iraq, Iran and Turkey Non-Aggression Treaty, 1937.

ORTHODOX CHURCHES.
The largest group of Eastern Christ. churches which in 1054 separated from the Roman Catholic Church and recognized the honorary sovereignty of the ecumenical Patriarch in Constantinople. In 1970 there were 12 independent Autocephalates (▷ Autocephalia):
The Great Church of Christ, called The Ecumenical Patriarchate of Constantinople and the New Rome. The liturgical language is Greek. Official written publ. is *Orthodoksia*. Est. 1980 at around 300,000 believers in dioceses and diaspora. The Patriarchate of Alexandria, with liturgical languages Greek and Arabic, ruled by a Synod and Patriarch in Alexandria; est. 1980 at around 150,000 followers. Publ. *Eklesiastikos Faros i Pantajnos*.
The Patriarchate of Antioch with liturgical languages Greek and Arabic, ruled by a Synod, Patriarch and national assemblies regards itself as a

higher authority than Jerusalem; estimated 1980 at around 60,000 faithful. Publ. *Nea Sion*.
The Patriarchate of Jerusalem, with liturgical languages Greek and Arabic, ruled by a Synod, a Patriarch residing in Jerusalem and the Brotherhood of the Holy Grave; in 1980 had around 40,000 practitioners; regards itself as the supreme authority also for Syria and Arabia (where the Patriarch of Antioch governs).
The Patriarchate of Moscow and all the Russias, with liturgical language Church Slavonic, has two theological academies, in Zagorsk and Leningrad, and six seminaries in Kiev, Luck, Odessa, Saratov, Stavropol and Zhirowice. It is the largest religious community headed by a Patriarch, whose seat is in Moscow, and an eight-member Holy Synod; it is administratively divided into four exarchates: Ukraine with a metropolitan in Kiev, Central Europe, Western Europe and America. The Holy Synod attached to the Patriarch is an advisory body; historically from 1721 to 1917 it was a body governing the Orthodox Church in Russia, and its members were appointed by the tsar. Publ.: *Zhurnal Moskovskoi patriarchii, Tserkovni vieshnik i Blogoslovskije trudy*.
The Patriarchate of Georgia, with liturgical language Georgian, from 1944 autocephalous; governed by a Council and a Patriarch with the title Katholikos of Georgia.
The Albanian Autocephalous Church, with liturgical language Albanian, governed from 1937 by a Synod and the Metropolitan of Tirana. In 1967 when Albania was proclaimed the first completely atheistic state in the world, all of the church institutions and places of worship were closed.
The Autocephalous Church of Cyprus, with liturgical language Greek, ruled by a Synod and the Archbishop of Famagusta, estimated 1980 at around 400,000 followers. Publ.: *Apostolos Varnavas*.
The Greek Autocephalous Church, with liturgical language Greek, governed by a Council of Bishops, Synod and the Archbishop of Athens, estimated 1980 at around 6.5 million believers. Publ.: *Eklesia*.
The Bulgarian Autocephalous Church, with liturgical language Church Slavonic, from 1953 ruled by an Orthodox-People's Council, Synod and the Patriarch of Sofia. Publ.: *Tserloven vestnik*, Godishnik ATP.
The Czechoslovak Orthodox Church, with liturgical language Church Slavonic, from 1951 ruled by a General Council, Metropolitan and Synod.
The Polish Autocephalous Orthodox Church, with liturgical language Church Slavonic, governed by a Council and the Metropolitan of Warsaw and all Poland; estimated at around 400,000 faithful. Publ.: *Tserkovnij viestnik*.
The Romanian Autocephalous Church, with liturgical language Romanian; from 1952 governed by a Synod, National Church Council and Central Spiritual Consistory. Publ.: *Biserice Orthodoxa Romana i Revista Theologica*.
The Serbian Autocephalous Church, with liturgical language Church Slavonic, from 1920 ruled by a Patriarch, assembly of bishops, and a Synod. Publ.: *Glesnik Serpskopatrejarsije i Bogosloje*.
From 1968 – official meetings and theological discussions have been taking place in the Vatican and USSR between representatives of the Russian Orthodox Church and the Roman Catholic Church. ▷ Catholic–Orthodox Patmos Dialogue 1980. In June 5–16, 1988 the 1000th Anniversary of the Conversion of the Ukrainian and Russian People to Orthodox Christianity was celebrated in the Soviet Union. The Russian Orthodox Church with the patriarchate of Moscow since 1448 is ecclesiasticaly independent from the Greek Orthodox Church patriarchate in Constantinople. The Soviet government decided on July 11, 1988 to

build a new Cathedral of the Orthodox Church in Moscow to replace the Old Cathedral of the Saviour destroyed in 1931.

R.A. KLOSTERMANN, *Probleme der Ostkirche*, Göttingen, 1955; J. ELLIS *The Russian Orthodox Church: A Contemporary History*, London, 1986.

ORTHODOX SYNOD. The assembly of the Ukrainian church hierarchy in exile in Western Europe, North America, Australia and Argentina, meeting Oct. 30–Nov. 5, 1971 in Rome on the initiative of Cardinal J. Slipyj, residing there since 1963, to protest against the Vatican policy of normalizing relations with the socialist countries. The ostentatiously organized Synod against the will and in face of the publicly stated disapproval of the Apostolic See, was preceded by the pronouncement of Cardinal Slipyj on Oct. 22, 1971 at a synod of Catholic bishops from the whole world in the Vatican in which he attacked the policy of Paul VI toward East Europe. The dispute terminated in 1980 during the Orthodox Synod, convoked by Pope John Paul II to Rome and the retirement of Cardinal J. Slipyj.

ORTHODOXY. A designation for the doctrine of the Eastern Christian Churches; part of these churches in Russian are called pravoslavniye. ▷ Orthodox Churches.

ORTRAG. Orbital Transport und Raketen Aktiengesellschaft, Orbital Transport and Rocket Company. A West German firm which leased a rocket range in Zaïre with an area of 100,000 sq. km and carried out experiments which led to protests by states bordering on Zaïre. The range was also located by US and USSR reconnoitering satellites, and reference to it was published by the SIPRI, stating that ORTRAG was operating on the basis of an agreement signed 1976 with the FRG government; that in 1977 it began its first rocket tests, and in 1981 envisaged the launching of its first earth satellites. The area of the range was nearly one-twentieth of the area of Zaïre, but more than four-tenths of the territory of the FRG. In 1979 the government of Zaïre under pressure from African states cancelled the agreement with ORTRAG.

SIPRI, *World Armaments and Disarmament Yearbook*, 1976, p. 80.

OSCAR. Film prizes granted annually since May, 1929 by the Academy of Motion Picture Arts and Science in Los Angeles to films and actors of the USA and the world. Prizes are in the form of a small statuette representing a young man standing on a film casette, holding a sword in both hands. The name Oscar was chosen for the statuette in 1931. The first prize winners were Janet Gaynor, American, and Emil Jannings, German, and the American film "Wings".

OSIMO (ANCONA) TREATY, 1975. A treaty with 10 annexes and an additional agreement between Italy and Yugoslavia, signed on Nov. 10, 1975 at Osimo (Ancona); the final settlement of the ▷ Trieste question. The Treaty approved the status quo of Trieste as permanent, with small changes of the frontier in favour of Italy near Gorizia (an area of 3.2 sq. km). The final settlement of the division of Trieste: 233 sq. km with 302,000 inhabitants came to Italy; and 340 sq. km with 73,500 inhabitants to Yugoslavia.

The additional agreement with 4 annexes was an accord on the development of economic relations between the two countries and provided creation of a common industrial zone in the region of Sezana-Fernetti on both sides of the newly agreed frontier. The Treaty and Agreement were ratified by Italy

and Yugoslavia on Oct. 12, 1979 during a visit to Yugoslavia by the Italian President. Both sides agreed in a joint communique of the Heads of State that after the Osimo (Ancona) Treaty border problems between the two countries have ceased to exist.

"Final Solution of the Trieste Dispute", in: A.J. DAY ed., *The Border and Territorial Disputes*, London, 1987, pp. 70–71.

OSLO CUSTOMS CONVENTION, 1930. The Convention was signed in Dec., 1930 in Oslo by Belgium, Denmark, the Netherlands, Norway and Sweden, and by Finland in 1932; introduced mutual reductions in customs duties; precursory to the European Economic Community; elicited the protest of Great Britain which demanded the same ▷ most favored nation clause for itself. Based on its 1930–40 experience was the post-war customs Union of Benelux countries (Belgium, the Netherlands and Luxembourg) and integration processes within EFTA launched by Scandinavian countries.

LNTS, 1932.

OSS. Office of Strategic Services. The governmental US institution established during World War II; after the war became the CIA. ▷ Intelligence service.

A. DULLES, *The Craft of Intelligence*, New York, 1963; R. JEFFREY-JONES, *America's Espionage*, New York, 1977.

OSSERVATORE ROMANO. The official daily of the Vatican, founded in 1861 by Pope Pius IX. Sunday edition: *Osservatore della Dominica*. Since the Vatican Council II foreign-language weekly editions are issued (English, French, German, Portuguese, Spanish and since 1980 also Polish).

OSTASZKÓW. ▷ Katyń Case, 1943.

OSTFLUCHT. *German* = "exodus from the East". An international term for the emigration of German population from East Prussia and the territories East of the Oder–Neisse rivers to Berlin and West Germany since the end of 19th century.

A. BROZEK, "The concept of 'Ostflucht' in Germany", in: *Poland and Germany*, No. 2, 1966, pp. 29–34; A. BROZEK, "Ostflucht aus Schlesien, 1933 bis 1939", in: *Jahrbuch für Wirtschaftsgeschichte*, Berlin, No. 1, 1969, pp. 41–74.

OSTIV. Organization Scientifique et Technique Internationale du Vol à Voile, International Scientific and Technical Organization of Gliding, founded in 1948 as a successor of the ISTUS organization (Internationale Studienkommission für Segelflug) founded in 1930 at the International Congress in Darmstadt affiliated with the International Aeronautic Federation, FIA; organizes Congresses with simultaneous World Gliding Championships; works out international rules of competitions and instructions for equipment building; associates 27 national organizations. Headquarters, Schiphol. In 1963 it established the International Gliding Research Institute. Publishes its bulletins and studies in the *Swiss Aero Revue*.

Yearbook of International Organizations.

OSTPOLITIK. *German* = "the Eastern policy". An international term in the 19th century for the policy of the German Reich with respect to tsarist Russia and in the period between the two World Wars – its policy with respect to Poland, Czechoslovakia and the USSR. After World War II the term was re-introduced on Oct. 18, 1969 in an address by the Chancellor of the FRG W. Brandt, to describe

the policy of normalization of relations with the socialist states. According to the "White Book on the Security of the Federal Republic", published by the FRG government in 1970:

"The Eastern policy of the FRG is strongly anchored in the NATO alliance and if this policy is ever to be effective, the condition for it must be a strong Western alliance. This policy of security forms the basis on which we can develop exchange of views with the East. The Paris Treaties of 1954 and our internal NATO obligations are undisputable. Without continuing Western policy Eastern policy is unthinkable. The federal government carries out its Eastern policy in keeping with its statements made in autumn 1969. It also stems from the assessment of the actual situation in Europe, guiding itself by three factors: first – no matter of importance can occur in the East European region without the consent of Moscow; second – the governments in Warsaw, East Berlin and Prague, as well as in other East European capitals are at the same time sovereign states with their own will and position; third – it would be a mad and highly dangerous thing if someone tried to force a wedge between different states of the Warsaw Treaty."

As a result of this Ostpolitik, also called Realpolitik, Chancellor Brandt went to Erfurt in the GDR in the spring 1970 to meet Premier W. Stoph and on that occasion paid homage to the murdered victims of fascism in the former concentration camp ▷ Buchenwald. Later he negotiated with:
(1) the USSR, ending with the signing in Moscow on Aug. 12, 1970 of a treaty on the renunciation of force in mutual relations between the USSR and the FRG;
(2) Poland, finalized by signing of a treaty on the bases of normalizing international relations between Poland and the FRG (*inter alia*, on the recognition of the Oder–Neisse frontier and its inviolability) in Warsaw on Dec. 7, 1970;
(3) Czechoslovakia, ended with signing of a treaty on principles for normalizing FRG–Czech relations, in Prague on Dec. 21, 1973;
(4) Bulgaria and Hungary in 1974.
The normalization of relations between the FRG and the GDR, partially connected with the regulation of the statute of West Berlin, formed a different chapter of *Ostpolitik*.

R. QUIST, *Ostpolitik, Völkerrecht und Grundgesetz*, Stamberg, 1972; M. GOERTEMAKER, *Die unheilige Allianz. Die Geschichte der Entspannungspolitik 1973–1979*; Munich, 1979; B. ZUENDORF, *Die Ostvertraege*, Munich, 1979.

OST–WEST HANDELSBANK AG. An international merchant bank est. 1971 in Frankfurt M., FRG; 52% shareholder: Gosbank SSSR (State Bank of USSR).

OŚWIĘCIM. ▷ Auschwitz Birkenau.

OTO-RHINO-LARYNGOLOGY. A subject of international co-operation. Organizations reg. with the UIA:

International Collegium for Radiology and Otorhinolaryngology, f. 1976, Bordeaux.
International Federation of Otorhinolaryngological Societies, f. 1928, Osaka.
Pan-American Association of Oto-Rhino-Laryngology and Broncho-Esophagology, f. 1946, Los Angeles. Publ.: *Pan American Review*.

Yearbook of International Organizations.

OTTAWA AGREEMENTS, 1932. The customs agreements arrived at during the Imperial Economic Conference, Ottawa, July 21–Aug. 20, 1932 which established a system of preferences in trade relations between British Commonwealth countries, i.e., imperial relations, providing for total or partial exemption from customs duties in Great

O

Britain of certain goods from various members of the Commonwealth.

OTTAWA CSCE MEETING ON HUMAN RIGHTS, 1985. Held in Ottawa, May 7–June 18, 1985, in closed session on the insistence of the USSR, failed to reach consensus on a Final Act.

KEESING's *Contemporary Archive*, December, 1986.

OTTOMAN EMPIRE. The Ottoman Turkish empire, founded in the beginning of the 14th century by Osman I, called also Othman, dissolved in World War I, formally on Nov. 17, 1922 when Sultan Mohammed VI fled from Turkey. The Ottoman Empire was during the War in alliance with the German Reich (see ▷ German–Ottoman Empire Alliance 1914). In Mar.–Apr., 1915 France, Great Britain and Russia concluded a secret agreement concerning the Black Sea Straits and Constantinople; and in Apr.–Oct., 1916 concluded also a tripartite agreement for the partition of the Ottoman Empire, called the ▷ Sykes–Picot Treaty 1916; succeeded by the ▷ Saint Jean-de-Maurienne Agreement 1917. ▷ Turkey.

W. MILLER, *The Ottoman Empire and its Successors*, London, 1966; H.K. KARPAT ed., *The Ottoman State and its role in World History*, London, 1974; LORD KINROSS, *The Ottoman Centuries. The Rise and Fall of the Turkish Empire*, New York, 1979.

OUCHY PEACE TREATY, 1912. A peace treaty concluded between Turkey and Italy, signed Oct. 18, 1912, in the suburb of Ouchy in Lausanne.

K. STRUPP, *Ausgewählte diplomatische Akten-Stücke zur orientalischen Frage*, Gotha, 1923.

OUEST. ▷ Sud-Aviation.

OUGUIYA. The monetary unit of Mauritania; one ouguiya = 5 khoums; issued (replacing the franc CFA) from June 29, 1973 after withdrawing from the West African currency and the franc zone) by the Banque Centrale de Mauritanie.

OUNCE. The Anglo-Saxon measure of weight and volume. The measure for the weighing of gold: the troy ounce (from the French city of Troyes) = 31.10348 grams, or the commercial ounce = 31.097 grams. Also a measure of volume in Great Britain = 28.4123 g, in the USA = 29.5729 g or 1/128 gallon. The ounce avoirdupois is used in commerce; the measure of magnitude 28.3465 grams. The Final Protocol to the Universal Postal Convention, UPU, 1964, in art. V decided that:

"UPU Member Countries which by reason of their internal system are unable to adopt the metric–decimal system of weight have the option of substituting for it the ounce–avoirdupois taking one ounce as equivalent to 20 grammes for letters and two ounces as equivalent to 40 grammes for printed papers, samples of merchandise, small packets and Phonopost items."

UNTS, Vol. 616, p. 269.

OURO PRETO. The Brazilian historic town of Ouro Preto in the hills of Minas Gerais, included in the ▷ World Heritage UNESCO List, played a leading role in Brazil in the 18th century after the discovery of gold. The churches with their sumptuous decoration, the white houses with colored timberwork, and the bridges and fountains of this mining town all illustrate the originality of its Baroque architecture. The area was cleared by gold diggers at the end of the 17th century and it was gold mining which contributed to its wealth for 100 years. The cultural features, however, are by far the most significant aspect of the town.

UNESCO, *A Legacy for All*, Paris, 1984.

OUTER SPACE. The subject of international space law, conventions, and permanent organized international co-operation under UN auspices, initiated by the International Geophysical Year, 1957/58, during which the first artificial Earth satellite with a UN flag was supposed to be launched jointly by the USSR and USA. The USSR began the space age Oct. 4, 1957 with ▷ Sputnik; on Jan. 31, 1958 the USA launched its first satellite. On Mar. 15, 1958 the USSR requested the UN General Assembly to place on its agenda the "question of the prohibition on using outer space for military purposes, eliminating foreign bases on the territory of other states, and the problem of international co-operation in space research." On Oct. 2, 1958 the USA suggested placing on the same agenda a "program for international co-operation with regard to outer space." The UN General Assembly decided to combine both motions under a common name: "the matter of utilizing outer space for peaceful purposes" and on Dec. 13, 1958 appointed a special UN Committee on the Peaceful Uses of Outer Space, COPUOS. In 1959, the Assembly established the COPUOS to be the focal point of UN's action in this field. The new committee was requested to review, as appropriate, the area of international co-operation, and study practical and feasible means for giving effect to programs in the peaceful uses of outer space which could appropriately be undertaken under UN auspices. Reflecting its interest in both the legal and technical aspects of outer space, the Committee has a Legal Sub-Committee and a Scientific and Technical Sub-Committee.

In Dec., 1961, the General Assembly declared that "the exploration and use of outer space should be only for the betterment of mankind and to the benefit of states irrespective of the stage of their economic or scientific development." States, it said, should be guided by the following principles: "(a) International law, including the Charter of the United Nations, applies to outer space and celestial bodies; (b) Outer space and celestial bodies are free for exploration and use by all states in conformity with international law and are not subject to national appropriation."

The Assembly also took the first steps towards examining legal problems relating to use of outer space, setting up a public registry of objects launched into orbit, providing for exchange of information on space activities, developing weather forecasting capabilities and atmospheric science, and assistance to countries in the field of space communication.

The work of the Outer Space Committee and its Legal Sub-Committee has led to four international instruments dealing with: the exploration and peaceful uses of outer space; the rescue of astronauts and the return of objects launched into outer space; liability for damage caused by space objects; and registration of objects launched into outer space. The UN General Assembly, Oct. 17, 1963, Res. 1884/XVIII, unanimously decided to forbid all states from mounting any nuclear weapons or other weapons of mass destruction on artificial Earth satellites or on other planets. Simultaneously, the Committee submitted a draft for a Declaration on the Peaceful Uses of Outer Space, and the Declaration of Legal Principles Governing the Activities of States in the Exploration and Use of Outer Space, which the Assembly ratified unanimously Dec. 13, 1963, Res. 1962/XVIII. On Jan. 27, 1967 the ▷ Outer Space Exploration Treaty was signed at London, Moscow and Washington, obligating signatory states to refrain from putting into earth orbit any objects with nuclear arms or weapons of mass destruction and prohibiting the establishment of military bases in outer space. The First UN Conference on Research and Peaceful Use of Outer Space was held in Vienna Aug. 14–18, 1968. In Moscow, London and Washington the Agreement on the Rescue of Astronauts, Return of Astronauts and the Return of Objects was signed on Apr. 27, 1968. The UN General Assembly Res. 2777/XXVI, Nov. 29, 1971, ratified the ▷ Space Objects Convention on the International Liability for Damage Caused by Space Objects. In addition a Convention was drafted on the obligatory Register of Objects Launched into Outer Space. Res. 3235/XXIX, on Nov. 19, 1974 and came into force Sept. 15, 1976. In the drafting stage 1976–79 by the legal subcommittee of the Committee on the Peaceful Uses of Outer Space were proposals for treaties relating to the international status of the ▷ Moon and principles relating to the direct transmission of television signals from artificial satellites. A subject of a long dispute is the question of defining outer space in view of the impossibility of agreeing on scientific criteria for fixing the lower boundary of outer space. The provisional Statute on Permanently Functioning Mixed Working Groups for the Basic Orientation of Co-operation of Socialist Countries in the Exploration and Exploitation of Outer Space for Peaceful Purposes, adopted at Moscow, Apr. 13, 1967 by Bulgaria, Cuba, Czechoslovakia, the GDR, Hungary, Mongolia, Poland, Romania and the USSR signed an Agreement on Co-operation in Peaceful Research on the Uses of Outer Space; and on May 19, 1978 a Convention on the Transfer and Use of Data of the Remote Sensing of the Earth from Outer Space. As foreseen in the agreements the citizens of these states have, since 1978, and those of France since 1981, participated in manned flights on Soviet space ships and space stations taking part in carrying out scientific experiments and research there.

The Legal Subcommittee of the UN Outer Space Committee elaborated in 1983 and agreed on a text concerning the form and procedure for notification in case of malfunction of a spacecraft carrying a nuclear power source and in 1984 started the final drafting of principles on remote sensing of the earth from space. According to SIPRI data since 1967 about one third of launched spacecraft have been photographic reconnaissance satellites. The US space shuttle program 1985–1989 (Atlantis, Challenger, Columbia, Discovery) was postponed 1987 by the catastrophe of ▷ Challenger.

Organizations reg. with the UIA:

Aerospace Medical Association, f. 1929, Washington, DC.

Committee on Space Research, f. 1958, Paris, Publ.: *Information Bulletin*.

Commonwealth Consultative Space Research Committee, f. 1960, London. ▷ COSPAR.

European Industrial Space Study Group, f. 1961, Paris.

European Space Agency, f. 1975, Paris.

Ibero–American Institute of Aeronautic and Space Law and Commercial Aviation, f. 1964, Madrid.

International Academy of Aviation and Space Medicine, f. 1959, Paris.

International Committee for Outer Space Onomastics, f. 1966, Leuven. Consultative status with ECOSOC;

International Institute of Space Law, f. 1960, Paris.

The International Telecommunications Union, ITU, took up the question of the legal aspects of ▷ satellite telecommunication. Separate preparatory work for the development of outer space law has been started by three international non-governmental organizations: the Institute of International Law in Brussels, the London Society of International Law and the International Institute of Space Law, f. 1960, Paris. *The Yearbook of Space Law, Annuaire de Droit Aérienne et Spatial*, is published in Montreal.

See also ▷ ASAT.

▷ Outerspace Delimination. ▷ Geostationary Orbit.

A.A. COCCA, *Teoria de Derecho Interplanetario*, Buenos Aires, 1957; CH. CHAMMONT, *Le droit de l'espace*, Paris, 1960; M.S. VASANEZ, *Introducción al Derecho International Cósmico*, México, 1961; G.P. ZHUKOV, *Kosmos i mezhdunarodnye otnosheniia*, Moscow, 1961; F.N. KOVALOV, I.I. CHEPROV, *Na puti k'kosmicheskomu pravu*, Moscow, 1962; M.S. DOUGAL, H.D. LASSWELL, I.A. VLASIC, *Law and Public Order in Space*, New Haven, 1963; Yearbook of the United Nations 1963, New York, 1963, pp. 93–110; E.L. FASAN, *Weltraumrecht*, Mainz, 1965; G.P. ZHUKOV, *Kosmicheskoe pravo*, Moskva, 1966, p. 296; J.E. FAWCETT, *International Law and the Uses of Outer Space*, London, 1968; M. LACHS, *The Law of Outer Space. An Experience in Contemporary Law-Making*, Leiden, 1972; J. KISH, *The Law of International Space*, Leiden, 1973; *UN Chronicle*, October, 1976, p. 350; *UN Chronicle*, October, 1976, p. 350; *Everyone's United Nations*, New York, 1979, pp. 54–59; A. GORBIEL, *Outer Space International Law*, Lódź, 1981; B. JASANI, *Outer Space. A New Dimension of the Arms Race*, SIPRI, Stockholm, 1982; *UN Chronicle*, April, 1984, pp. 32–39; *UN Space Activities of the United Nations and International Organizations*, New York, 1986; "Air, Outer Space and Telecommunication", in: *The International Law Dictionary*, Oxford, 1987; "Military use of Outer Space", in: *SIPRI Yearbook 1987*, Oxtord, 1987; *Europe's Future in Space: A Joint Policy Report*, London, 1988.

OUTER SPACE DELIMITATION. In the Legal-Sub-Committee of the Committee on the Peaceful Uses of Outer-Space some countries started in Mar. 1987 to discuss the definition of Outer Space and the delimitation of Outer Space "as a logical, practical and necessary step to achieve a clear distinction between the legal regime of airspace, with the inherent features of State sovereignty, territorial integrity and security, and that of the Outer Space regime, in which Outer Space Treaties apply".

Other States however maintained the absence of definition and delimitation of Outer Space had not prevented the observance of the Outer Space Treaties nor had it created any practical problems. See also ▷ Geostationary orbit.

UN Chronicle, May 1987, p. 51.

OUTER SPACE DEMILITARIZATION. ▷ Outer Space Exploration Treaty, 1967.

OUTER SPACE DENUCLEARIZATION. A subject of international agreements:
1 Treaty banning Nuclear Tests in the Atmosphere, in Outer Space and Under Water, 1963, called ▷ Outer Space Moscow Treaty, 1963.
2 Treaty on Principles Governing the Activities of States in the Exploration and Use of Outer Space, including the Moon and other Celestial Bodies, 1967, called ▷ Outer Space Exploration Treaty, 1967.

J. GOLDBLAT, *Arms Control Agreements. A Handbook*, New York, 1983, pp. 142 and 145–146.

OUTERSPACE EUROPE. The name of a conference of West European states which on British initiative decided on Mar. 31, 1962 to develop technologies and plans for new artificial Earth satellites; ELDO and ESRO were created for this purpose. On May 30, 1975 both organizations merged under the name ▷ European Space Agency.

OUTER SPACE EXPLORATION. The outer space exploration initiated on Oct. 4, 1957 by the USSR "▷ Sputnik" and on Jan. 31, 1958 by the USA "▷ Explorer", after the failure of the US Navy's Vanguard launcher on Dec. 6, 1957. On April 19, 1971 the USSR launched ▷ Salut-1, a prototype for a manned space station. In May, 1973 the first three-man crew went into space aboard ▷ Skylab, a US manned laboratory; in July, 1975 took place the first international American-Soviet space flight ▷ Soyuz-Apollo. On April 12, 1981 the USA initiated a new era in outer space exploration by the successful launching of the first ▷ space shuttle Columbia. Parallel to the outer space exploration for peaceful scientific research the USA and the USSR started launching military satellites, first for monitoring global violations of treaties, second for developing anti-satellite weapons. According to SIPRI 2,114 militarily orientated satellites were launched from 1958 to 1983. ▷ Apollo; ▷ Intercosmos; ▷ Moon; ▷ NASA; ▷ Soyuz; ▷ Skylab.

B. JASANI, Ch. LEE, *Countdown to Space War*, SIPRI, London, Philadelphia, 1984; F. WHITE, *The Overview Effect: Space Exploration and Human Evolution*, Boston 1987.

OUTER SPACE EXPLORATION TREATY, 1967. Treaty on Principles Governing the Activities of States in the Exploration and use of Outer Space, including the Moon and other Celestial Bodies, opened for signature at Moscow, London and Washington on Jan. 27, 1967; came into force on Oct. 10, 1967, the date of deposit of the instruments of ratification by five governments, including the depositary governments of the UK, the USA and the USSR. The text is as follows:

"The States Parties to this Treaty,
Inspired by the great prospects opening up before mankind as a result of man's entry into outer space,
Recognizing the common interest of all mankind in the progress of the exploration and use of outer space for peaceful purposes,
Believing that the exploration and use of outer space should be carried on for the benefit of all peoples irrespective of the degree of their economic or scientific development,
Desiring to contribute to broad international co-operation in the scientific as well as the legal aspects of the exploration and use of outer space for peaceful purposes,
Believing that such co-operation will contribute to the development of mutual understanding and to the strengthening of friendly relations between States and peoples,
Recalling resolution 1962 (XVIII), entitled Declaration of Legal Principles Governing the Activities of States in the Exploration and Use of Outer Space, which was adopted unanimously by the United Nations General Assembly on 13 December 1963,
Recalling resolution 1884 (XVIII), calling upon States to refrain from placing in orbit around the earth any objects carrying nuclear weapons or any other kinds of weapons of mass destruction or from installing such weapons on celestial bodies, which was adopted unanimously by the United Nations General Assembly on 17 October 1963,
Taking account of United Nations General Assembly resolution 10 (II) of 3 November 1947, which condemned propaganda designed or likely to provoke or encourage any threat to the peace, breach of the peace or act of aggression, and considering that the aforementioned resolution is applicable to outer space,
Convinced that a Treaty on Principles Governing the Activities of States in the Exploration and Use of Outer Space, including the Moon and Other Celestial Bodies, will further the Purposes and Principles of the Charter of the United Nations,
Have agreed on the following:
Art. I. The exploration and use of outer space, including the moon and other celestial bodies, shall be carried out for the benefit and in the interests of all countries, irrespective of their degree of economic or scientific development, and shall be the province of all mankind.
Outer space, including the moon and other celestial bodies, shall be free for exploration and use by all States without discrimination of any kind, on a basis of equality and in accordance with international law, and there shall be free access to all areas of celestial bodies.
There shall be freedom of scientific investigation in outer space, including the moon and other celestial bodies, and States shall facilitate and encourage international co-operation in such investigation.
Art. II. Outer space, including the moon and other celestial bodies, is not subject to national appropriation by claim of sovereignty, by means of use or occupation, or by any other means.
Art. III. States Parties to the Treaty shall carry on activities in the exploration and use of outer space, including the moon and other celestial bodies, in accordance with international law, including the Charter of the United Nations, in the interest of maintaining international peace and security and promoting international co-operation and understanding.
Art. IV. States Parties to the Treaty undertake not to place in orbit around the earth any objects carrying nuclear weapons or any other kinds of weapons of mass destruction, install such weapons on celestial bodies, or station such weapons in outer space in any other manner.
The moon and other celestial bodies shall be used by all States Parties to the Treaty exclusively for peaceful purposes. The establishment of military bases, installations and fortifications, the testing of any type of weapons and the conduct of military manoeuvres on celestial bodies shall be forbidden. The use of military personnel for scientific research or for any other peaceful purposes shall not be prohibited. The use of any equipment or facility necessary for peaceful exploration of the moon and other celestial bodies shall also not be prohibited.
Art. V. States Parties to the Treaty shall regard astronauts as envoys of mankind in outer space and shall render to them all possible assistance in the event of accident, distress, or emergency landing on the territory of another State Party or on the high seas. When astronauts make such a landing, they shall be safely and promptly returned to the State of registry of their space vehicle.
In carrying on activities in outer space and on celestial bodies, the astronauts of one State Party shall render all possible assistance to the astronauts of other States Parties. States Parties to the Treaty shall immediately inform the other States Parties to the Treaty or the Secretary-General of the United Nations of any phenomena they discover in outer space, including the moon and other celestial bodies, which could constitute a danger to the life or health of astronauts.
Art. VI. States Parties to the Treaty shall bear international responsibility for national activities in outer space, including the moon and other celestial bodies, whether such activities are carried on by governmental agencies or by non-governmental entities, and for assuring that national activities are carried out in conformity with the provisions set forth in the present Treaty. The activities of non-governmental entities in outer space, including the moon and other celestial bodies, shall require authorization and continuing supervision by the appropriate State Party to the Treaty. When activities are carried on in outer space, including the moon and other celestial bodies, by an international organization, responsibility for compliance with this Treaty shall be borne both by the international organization and by the States Parties to the Treaty participating in such organization.
Art. VII. Each State Party to the Treaty that launches or procures the launching of an object into outer space, including the moon and other celestial bodies, and each State Party from whose territory or facility an object is launched, is internationally liable for damage to another State Party to the Treaty or to its natural or juridical persons by such object or its component parts on the Earth, in air space or in outer space, including the moon and other celestial bodies.
Art. VIII. A State Party to the Treaty on whose registry an object launched into outer space is carried shall retain jurisdiction and control over such object, and over any personnel thereof, while in outer space or on a celestial body. Ownership of objects launched into outer space, including objects landed or constructed on a celestial body, and of their component parts, is not affected by their presence in outer space or on a celestial body or by their return to the Earth. Such objects or component parts found beyond the limits of the State Party to the Treaty on whose registry they are carried shall be returned to that State Party, which shall, upon request, furnish identifying data prior to their return.
Art. IX. In the exploration and use of outer space, including the moon and other celestial bodies, States

Parties to the Treaty shall be guided by the principle of co-operation and mutual assistance and shall conduct all their activities in outer space, including the moon and other celestial bodies, with due regard to the corresponding interests of all other States Parties to the Treaty. States Parties to the Treaty shall pursue studies of outer space, including the moon and other celestial bodies, and conduct exploration of them so as to avoid their harmful contamination and also adverse changes in the environment of the Earth resulting from the introduction of extraterrestrial matter and, where necessary, shall adopt appropriate measures for this purpose. If a State Party to the Treaty has reason to believe that an activity or experiment planned by it or its nationals in outer space, including the moon and other celestial bodies, would cause potentially harmful interference with activities of other States Parties in the peaceful exploration and use of outer space, including the moon and other celestial bodies, it shall undertake appropriate international consultations before proceeding with any such activity or experiment. A State Party to the Treaty which has reason to believe that an activity or experiment planned by another State Party in outer space, including the moon and other celestial bodies, would cause potentially harmful interference with activities in the peaceful exploration and use of outer space, including the moon and other celestial bodies, may request consultation concerning the activity or experiment.

Art. X. In order to promote international co-operation in the exploration and use of outer space, including the moon and other celestial bodies, in conformity with the purposes of this Treaty, the States Parties to the Treaty shall consider on a basis of equality any requests by other States Parties to the Treaty to be afforded an opportunity to observe the flight of space objects launched by those States. The nature of such an opportunity for observation and the conditions under which it could be afforded shall be determined by agreement between the States concerned.

Art. XI. In order to promote international co-operation in the peaceful exploration and use of outer space, States Parties to the Treaty conducting activities in outer space, including the moon and other celestial bodies, agree to inform the Secretary-General of the United Nations as well as the public and the international scientific community, to the greatest extent feasible and practicable, of the nature, conduct, locations and results of such activities. On receiving the said information, the Secretary General of the United Nations should be prepared to disseminate it immediately and effectively.

Art. XII. All stations, installations, equipment and space vehicles on the moon and other celestial bodies shall be open to representatives of other States Parties to the Treaty on a basis of reciprocity. Such representatives shall give reasonable advance notice of a projected visit, in order that appropriate consultations may be held and that maximum precautions may be taken to assure safety and to avoid interference with normal operations in the facility to be visited.

Art. XIII. The provisions of this Treaty shall apply to the activities of States Parties to the Treaty in the exploration and use of outer space, including the moon and other celestial bodies, whether such activities are carried on by a single State Party to the Treaty or jointly with other States, including cases where they are carried on within the framework of international inter-governmental organizations. Any practical questions arising in connexion with activities carried on by international inter-governmental organizations in the exploration and use of outer space, including the moon and other celestial bodies, shall be resolved by the States Parties to the Treaty either with the appropriate international organization or with one or more States members of that international organization, which are Parties to this Treaty.

Art. XIV.(1) This Treaty shall be open to all States for signature. Any State which does not sign this Treaty before its entry into force in accordance with paragraph 3 of this Article may accede to it at any time.
(2) This Treaty shall be subject to ratification by signatory States. Instruments of ratification and instruments of accession shall be deposited with the governments of the United Kingdom of Great Britain and Northern Ireland, the Union of Soviet Socialist Republics and the United States of America, which are hereby designated the Depositary Governments.

(3) This Treaty shall enter into force upon the deposit of instruments of ratification by five governments including the governments designated as Depositary Governments under this Treaty.
(4) For States whose instruments of ratification or accession are deposited subsequent to the entry into force of this Treaty, it shall enter into force on the date of the deposit of their instruments of ratification or accession.
(5) The Depositary Governments shall promptly inform all signatory and acceding States of the date of each signature, the date of deposit of each instrument of ratification of and accession to this Treaty, the date of its entry into force and other notices.
(6) This Treaty shall be registered by the Depositary Governments pursuant to article 102 of the Charter of the United Nations.
Art. XV. Any State Party to the Treaty may propose amendments to this Treaty. Amendments shall enter into force for each State Party to the Treaty accepting the amendments upon their acceptance by a majority of the States Parties to the Treaty and thereafter for each remaining State Party to the Treaty on the date of acceptance by it.
Art. XVI. Any State Party to the Treaty may give notice of its withdrawal from the Treaty one year after its entry into force by written notification to the Depositary Governments. Such withdrawal shall take effect one year from the date of receipt of this notification.
Art. XVII. This Treaty, of which the English, Russian, French, Spanish and Chinese texts are equally authentic, shall be deposited in the archives of the Depositary Governments. Duly certified copies of this Treaty shall be transmitted by the Depositary Governments to the governments of the signatory and acceding States."

The treaty was signed and ratified until 1982 by following states: Afghanistan, Algeria, Argentina, Australia, Austria, Bahamas, Belgium, Benin, Bhutan, Bolivia, Botswana, Brazil, Bulgaria, Burkina Faso, Burma, Burundi, Byelorussia, Cameroon, Canada, Cape Verde, Central African Republic, Chad, Chile, Colombia, Costa Rica, Cyprus, Czechoslovakia, Denmark, Dominican Republic, Ecuador, Egypt, El Salvador, Ethopia, Fiji, Finland, France, FRG, Gabon, Gambia, GDR, Ghana, Greece, Guatemala, Guinea-Bissau, Haiti, Honduras, Hungary, Iceland, India, Indonesia, Iran, Iraq, Ireland, Israel, Italy, Ivory Coast, Jamaica, Japan, Jordan, Kenya, Korea Republic, Kuwait, Laos, Lebanon, Liberia, Libya, Luxembourg, Madagascar, Malawi, Malaysia, Mali, Malta, Mauritania, Mauritius, Mexico, Mongolia, Morocco, Nepal, Netherlands, New Zealand, Nicaragua, Niger, Nigeria, Norway, Pakistan, Panama, Papua New Guinea, Paraguay, Peru, Philippines, Poland, Portugal, Romania, Rwanda, Samoa, San Marino, Senegal, Sierra Leone, Singapore, Somalia, South Africa, Spain, Sri Lanka, Sudan, Swaziland, Sweden, Switzerland, Syria, Taiwan, Tanzania, Thailand, Togo, Tonga, Trinidad and Tobago, Tunisia, Turkey, Uganda, Ukraine, USSR, UK, USA, Uruguay, Venezuela, Yemen Arab Republic, Yemen Peoples Democratic Republic, Yugoslavia, Zaïre, Zambia. The treaty was ratified until Jan. 1, 1987 by 89 countries.

UNTS, Vol. 610, 1967, pp. 206–212; *UN Monthly Chronicle*, Jan., 1967, pp. 38–50; *UN Yearbook*, 1967; *SIPRI Yearbook 1987*, Oxford, 1988, p. 461.

OUTER SPACE, LAW OF. ▷ Law of Outer Space.

OUTER SPACE MOSCOW CONVENTION, 1978. Convention on the Transfer and Use of Data of the Remote Sensing of the Earth from Outer Space, signed in Moscow, May 19, 1978 by the Representatives of Governments of Bulgaria, Cuba, Czechoslovakia, Hungary, the GDR, Mongolia, Poland, Romania, the USSR. The text is as follows:

"The States Parties to this Convention, hereinafter referred to as the 'Contracting Parties',
considering that outer space is free for use by all States without discrimination of any kind, on a basis of equality and in accordance with international law, including the Charter of the United Nations and the Treaty on Principles Governing the Activities of States in the Exploration and Use of Outer Space, including the Moon and Other Celestial Bodies, for the purpose of carrying on activities in the remote sensing of the Earth from outer space;
believing that in carrying on such activities the sovereign rights of states, in particular their inalienable right to dispose of their natural resources and of information concerning those resources, should be respected;
reaffirming that activities in the field of the remote sensing of the Earth from outer space and international co-operation to this and should promote peace and understanding among States and be carried out for the benefit and in the interests of all peoples irrespective of their degree of economic or scientific development;
convinced that space technology can provide new valuable information necessary for the exploration of the natural resources of the Earth, geology, agriculture, forestry, hydrology, oceanography, geography and cartography, meteorology, environmental control, and for the solution of other problems connected with the systematic exploration of the Earth and its surrounding space in the interests of science and the economic activities of States;
Determined to create favourable conditions and necessary technical and economic prerequisites for expanding co-operation in the effective practical use of data of the remote sensing of the Earth from outer space,
Have agreed as follows:
Art. I. For the Purposes of this Convention:
(a) The term 'remote sensing of the Earth from outer space' means observations and measurements of energy and polarization characteristics of self-radiation and reflected radiation of elements of the land, ocean and atmosphere of the Earth in different ranges of electromagnetic waves which facilitate the location, description of the nature and temporal variations of natural parameters and phenomena, natural resources of the Earth, the environment as well as anthropogenic objects and formations;
(b) The term 'data of the remote sensing of the Earth from outer space' means the initial data obtained by remote sensors installed on space objects and transmitted from them by telemetry in the form of electromagnetic signals or physically in the form of photographic film or magnetic tape, as well as preprocessed data derived from the flow of data which may be used for later analysis;
(c) The term 'information' means the end-product of the analytical process of handling, deciphering and intercepting remote sensing data from outer space, in combination with the data and evidence obtained from other sources;
(d) The term 'natural resources of the Earth' means natural resources forming part of the aggregate of natural conditions of the man habitat and constituting major components of man's natural environment which are used in social production for satisfying the material and cultural requirements of society.
Art. II. The Contracting Parties shall co-operate with each other in the transfer and use of data of the remote sensing of the Earth from outer space.
Art. III. The specific list, technical parameters, the volume of the said data, the time-table of their receipt and conditions of the transfer as well as the degree of participation of the Contracting Parties concerned in their processing and thematic interpretation shall be determined by agreement between the Contracting Parties concerned on a bilateral or multilateral basis.
Art. IV. A Contracting Party in possession of initial data of the remote sensing of the Earth from outer space, with a better than 50 metres resolution on the terrain, relating to the territory of another Contracting Party, shall not disclose or make them available to anyone except with an explicit consent thereto of the Contracting Party to which the sensed territories belong, nor shall it use them or any other data in any way to the detriment of that Contracting Party.
Art. V. A Contracting Party that has obtained as a result of the deciphering and thematic interpretation of any data of the remote sensing of the Earth from outer

space information about the natural resources or the economic potential of another Contracting Party shall not disclose such information or make it available to anyone except with an explicit consent thereto of the Contracting Party to which the sensed territories and natural resources belong, nor shall it use such or any other information in any way to the detriment of that Contracting Party.

Art. VI. The Contracting Parties shall bear responsibility for national activities in the use of data of the remote sensing of the Earth from outer space relating to the territories of other Contracting Parties.

Art. VII. The Contracting Parties shall co-operate, subject to agreement on a bilateral or multilateral basis, in elaborating and developing technical means and methods necessary for taking measurements, the processing and thematic interpretation of the data obtained from the remote sensing of the Earth from outer space, as well as in training appropriate personnel for making an early and most efficient practical use of modern space technology and data of the remote sensing of the Earth from outer space.

Art. VIII.(1) The Contracting Parties shall resolve questions arising in the process of the implementation of this Convention in the spirit of mutual respect by negotiation and consultation.

(2) In order to resolve questions arising in connection with the implementation of this Convention, meetings of representatives of the Contracting Parties concerned may be held, when necessary, by agreement between such Contracting Parties.

Art. IX. Any Contracting Party may propose amendments to this Convention. Amendments shall enter into force for each Contracting Party accepting the amendments upon their approval by two-thirds of the Contracting Parties. An amendment that has entered into force becomes binding upon the other Contracting Parties upon their acceptance of such amendment.

Art. X.(1) This Convention shall be subject to approval of signatory States in accordance with their legislation. The Convention shall enter into force on the deposit of instruments of approval by five Governments, including the Depositary Government of the Convention.

For Contracting Parties whose instruments of approval are deposited after the entry into force of this Convention, it shall enter into force on the date of the deposit of their instruments of approval.

(2) This Convention shall remain in force for five years. For each of the Contracting Parties which does not withdraw from the Convention six months prior to the expiry of the said five-year period and successive five-periods, it shall remain in force for each successive period of five years.

Art. XI.(1) Other states sharing the purposes and principles of the Convention may accede to this Convention. Instruments of accession shall be deposited with the depositary of the Convention.

(2) Accession of a new State shall be considered to have taken effect 30 days from the date of receipt by the depositary of the instrument of accession, who shall promptly notify to all the Contracting Parties.

Art. XII.(1) Each of the Contracting Parties may withdraw from this Convention by giving notice to the depositary of the Convention. Such withdrawal shall take effect 12 months from the date of receipt by the depositary of the notification.

(2) Withdrawal from the Convention shall not affect obligations of co-operating organizations of the Contracting Parties under the working agreements or contracts concluded by them.

Art. XIII.(1) This Convention shall be deposited with the government of the Union of Soviet Socialist Republics, which shall act as the depositary.

(2) The depositary shall transmit certified copies of this Convention to all the Contracting Parties and inform them of all notifications received by him.

(3) This Convention shall be registered by the depositary pursuant to article 102 of the Charter of the United Nations.

Art. XIV. This Convention is drawn up in four copies in the Russian, English, French, and Spanish languages, all of the texts being equally authentic."

Recueil de Documents, Varsovie, No. 5, 1978.

OUTER SPACE MOSCOW TREATY, 1963. The Treaty Banning Nuclear Weapon Tests in the Atmosphere, in Outer Space and Under Water, called also Partial Tests Ban Treaty, Signed on Aug. 5, 1963 in Moscow, in the presence of the UN Secretary General; signed and ratified or only signed (S) by the following states: Afghanistan (S), Argentina, Australia, Austria, Bahamas, Barbados, Belgium, Bolivia, Botswana (S), Brazil, Bulgaria, Burkina Faso, Burma, Burundi (S), Byelorussia, Cameroon (S), Canada, Central African Republic (S), Chile (S), Colombia (S), Cuba, Cyprus, Czechoslovakia, Denmark, Dominican Republic, Ecuador, Egypt, El Salvador, Ethiopia, Fiji, Finland, France, FRG, Gambia (S), GDR, Ghana, Greece, Guinea-Bissau, Guyana (S), Haiti (S), Holy See (S), Honduras (S), Hungary, Iceland, India (S), Indonesia (S), Iran (S), Iraq, Ireland, Israel, Italy, Jamaica, Japan, Jordan (S), Korea Republic, Kuwait, Laos, Lebanon, Lesotho (S), Libya, Luxembourg (S), Madagascar, Malaysia, Mali, Mauritius, Mexico, Mongolia, Morocco, Nepal, Netherlands, New Zealand, Nicaragua, Niger, Nigeria, Norway, Pakistan, Panama (S), Papua New Guinea, Peru, Philippines, Poland, Romania, Rwanda (S), San Marino, Seychelles, Sierra Leone, Singapore, Somalia (S), South Africa, Spain, Sri Lanka (S), Sweden, Switzerland, Syria, Taiwan, Thailand, Togo (S), Tonga, Trinidad and Tobago, Tunisia, Turkey, Uganda, Ukraine, USSR, UK, USA, Uruguay, Venezuela, Vietnam, Yemen Peoples Democratic Republic, Yugoslavia (S), Zaire (S), Zambia (S). As the Treaty does not specifically exclude underground tests, a Treaty banning such tests was recommended by the UN General Assembly by its Res. 2343/XXII of Nov. 19, 1967 and Res. 2604/XXIV of Dec. 16, 1969. The text reads:

"The Governments of the United States of America, the United Kingdom of Great Britain and Northern Ireland, and the Union of Soviet Socialist Republics, hereinafter referred to as the "Original Parties."

Proclaiming as their principal aim the speediest possible achievement of an agreement on general and complete disarmament under strict international control in accordance with the objectives of the United Nations which would put an end to the armaments race and eliminate the incentive to the production and testing of all kinds of weapons, including nuclear weapons.

Seeking to achieve the discontinuance of all test explosions of nuclear weapons for all time, determined to continue negotiations to this end, and desiring to put an end to the contamination of man's environment by radioactive substances.

Have agreed as follows:

Art. I. 1. Each of the Parties to this Treaty undertakes to prohibit, to prevent, and not to carry out any nuclear weapon test explosion, or any other nuclear explosion, at any place under its jurisdiction or control:

(a) in the atmosphere; beyond its limits, including outer space; or under water, including territorial waters or high seas; or

(b) in any other environment if such explosion causes radioactive debris to be present outside the territorial limits of the State under whose jurisdiction or control such explosion is conducted. It is understood in this connection that the provisions of this subparagraph are without prejudice to the conclusion of a treaty resulting in the permanent banning of all nuclear test explosions, including all such explosions underground, the conclusion of which, as the Parties have stated in the Preamble to this Treaty, they seek to achieve.

2. Each of the Parties to this Treaty undertakes furthermore to refrain from causing, encouraging, or in any way participating in, the carrying out of any nuclear weapon test explosion, or any other nuclear explosion, anywhere which would take place in any of the environments described, or have the effect referred to, in paragraph 1 of this article.

Art. II. 1. Any Party may propose amendments to this Treaty. The text of any proposed amendment shall be submitted to the Depositary Governments which shall circulate it to all Parties to this Treaty. Thereafter, if requested to do so by one-third or more of the Parties, the Depositary Governments shall convene a conference, to which they shall invite all the Parties, to consider such amendment.

2. Any amendment to this Treaty must be approved by a majority of the votes of all the Parties to this Treaty, including the votes of all of the Original Parties. The amendment shall enter into force for all Parties upon the deposit of instruments of ratification by a majority of all the Parties, including the instruments of ratification of all of the Original Parties.

Act. III. 1. This Treaty shall be open to all States for signature. Any State which does not sign this Treaty before its entry into force in accordance with paragraph 3 of this article may accede to it at any time.

2. This Treaty shall be subject to ratification by signatory States. Instruments of ratification and instruments of accession shall be deposited with the Governments of the Original Parties – the United States of America, the United Kingdom of Great Britain and Northern Ireland, and the Union of Soviet Socialist Republics – which are hereby designated the Depositary Governments.

3. This Treaty shall enter into force after its ratification by all the Original Parties and the deposit of their instruments of ratification.

4. For States whose instruments of ratification or accession are deposited subsequent to the entry into force of this Treaty, it shall enter into force on the date of the deposit of their instruments of ratification or accession.

5. The Depositary Governments shall promptly inform all signatory and acceding States of the date of each signature, the date of deposit of each instrument of ratification of and accession to this Treaty, the date of its entry into force, and the date of receipt of any requests for conferences or other notices.

6. This Treaty shall be registered by the Depositary Governments pursuant to Article 102 of the Charter of the United Nations.

Art. IV. This Treaty shall be of unlimited duration. Each Party shall in exercising its national sovereignty have the right to withdraw from the Treaty if it decides that extraordinary events, related to the subject matter of this Treaty, have jeopardized the supreme interests of its country. It shall give notice of such withdrawal to all other Parties to the Treaty three months in advance.

Art. V. This Treaty, of which the English and Russian texts are equally authentic, shall be deposited in the archives of the Depositary Governments. Duly certified copies of this Treaty shall be transmitted by the Depositary Governments to the Governments of the signatory and acceding States."

The Treaty was ratified until Jan. 1, 1987 by 116 countries. The Treaty is called Partial Test Ban Treaty, PTBT.

UNTS, Vol. 480, p. 43, *Yearbook of the UN*, 1963; *SIPRI Yearbook 1987*, Oxford, 1988, p. 461.

OUTER SPACE OBJECT. ▷ Space Objects Convention, 1971.

OUTER SPACE PEACEFUL USE, UN COMMITTEE. The UN General Assembly established on Dec. 13, 1958, Res. 1348/XIII an *ad hoc* Committee on the Peaceful Uses of Outer Space composed of the representatives of Argentina, Australia, Belgium, Brazil, Canada, Czechoslovakia, France, India, Iran, Italy, Japan, Mexico, Poland, Sweden, the Union of Soviet Socialist Republics, the United Arab Republic, the United Kingdom of Great Britain and Northern Ireland and the United States of America. The Committee elaborated the legal principles governing the activities of states in the peaceful exploration and use of Outer Space, accepted by the UN General Assembly Res. 1962/XVIII, which reads as follows:

"The General Assembly,
Inspired by the great prospects opening up before mankind as a result of man's entry into outer space,
Recognizing the common interest of all mankind in the progress of the exploration and use of outer space for peaceful purposes,
Believing that the exploration and use of outer space should be carried on for the betterment of mankind and

for the benefit of states irrespective of their degree of economic or scientific development,

Desiring to contribute to broad international co-operation in the scientific as well as in the legal aspects of exploration and use of outer space for peaceful purposes,

Believing that such co-operation will contribute to the development of mutual understanding and to the strengthening of friendly relations between nations and peoples,

Recalling its resolution 110(II) of 3 November, 1947, which condemned propaganda designed or likely to provoke or encourage any threat to the peace, breach of the peace, or act of aggression, and considering that the aforementioned resolution is applicable to outer space, Taking into consideration its resolutions 1721(XVI) of 20 December 1961 and 1802(XVII) of 14 December 1962, adopted unanimously by the States Members of the United Nations,

Solemnly declares that in the exploration and use of outer space States should be guided by the following principles:

(1) The exploration and use of outer space shall be carried on for the benefit and in the interests of all mankind,

(2) Outer space and celestial bodies are free for exploration and use by all States on a basis of equality and in accordance with international law.

(3) Outer space and celestial bodies are not subject to national appropriation by claim of sovereignty, by means of use or occupation, or by any other means.

(4) The activities of States in the exploration and use of outer space shall be carried on in accordance with international law, including the Charter of the United Nations, in the interest of maintaining international peace and security and promoting international co-operation and understanding.

(5) States bear international responsibility for national activities in outer space, whether carried on by governmental agencies or by non-governmental entities, and for assuring that national activities are carried on in conformity with the principles set forth in the present Declaration. The activities of non-governmental entities in outer space shall require authorization and continuing supervision by the State concerned. When activities are carried on in outer space by an international organization, responsibility for compliance with the principles set forth in this Declaration shall be borne by the international organization and by the States participating in it.

(6) In the exploration and use of outer space, States shall be guided by the principle of co-operation and mutual assistance and shall conduct all their activities in outer space with due regard for the corresponding interests of other States. If a State has reason to believe that an outer space activity or experiment planned by it or its nationals would cause potentially harmful interference with activities of other States, in the peaceful exploration and use of outer space, it shall undertake appropriate international consultations before proceeding with any such activity or experiment. A State which has reason to believe that an outer space activity or experiment planned by another State would cause potentially harmful interference with activities in the peaceful exploration and use of outer space may request consultation concerning the activity or experiment.

(7) The State on whose registry an object launched into outer space is carried shall retain jurisdiction and control over such object, and any personnel thereon, while in outer space. Ownership of objects launched into outer space, and of their component parts, is not affected by their passage through outer space or by their return to the earth. Such objects or component parts found beyond the limits of the State of registry shall be returned to that state, which shall furnish identifying data upon request prior to return.

(8) Each State which launches or procures the launching of an object into outer space, and each state from whose territory or facility an object is launched, is internationally liable for damage to a foreign State or to its natural or juridical persons by such objects or its component parts on the earth, in air space, or in outer space.

(9) States shall regard astronauts as envoys of mankind in outer space, and shall render to them all possible assistance in the event of accident, distress, or emergency landing on the territory of a foreign State or on

the high seas. Astronauts who make such a landing shall be safely and promptly returned to the State of registry of their space vehicle."

On Dec. 7, 1988 the GA Res. 43/70 was adopted by 154 votes to 1 (US):

"Welcoming the re-establishment of an Ad Hoc Committee on the Prevention of an Arms Race in Outer Space during the 1988 session of the Conference on Disarmament, in the exercise of the negotiating responsibilities of this sole multilateral negotiating body on disarmament, to continue to examine and to identify through substantive and general consideration issues relevant to the prevention of an arms race in outer space.

(1) Reaffirms that general complete disarmament under effective international control warrants that outer space shall be used exclusively for peaceful purposes and that it shall not become an arena for an arms race;

(2) Recognize as stated in the report of the Ad Hoc Committee of the Conference on Disarmament, that the legal regime applicable to outer space by itself does not guarantee the prevention of an arms race in outer space, that its legal regime plays a significant role in the prevention of an arms race in that environment, the need to consolidate and reinforce that regime and enhance its effectiveness, and the importance of strict compliance with existing agreements, both bilateral and multilateral;

(3) Emphasizes that further measures with appropriate and effective provisions for verification to prevent an arms race in outer space should be adopted by the international community;

(4) Calls upon the States, in particular those with major space capabilities, to contribute actively to the objective of the peaceful use of outer space and to take immediate measures to prevent an arms race in outer space in the interest of maintaining international peace and security and promoting international co-operation and understanding;

(5) Reiterates that the Conference on Disarmament, as the single multilateral disagreement negotiating forum, has the primary role in the negotiation of a multilateral agreement or agreements, as appropriate, on the prevention of an arms race in outer space in all its aspects;

(6) Requests the Conference on Disarmament to consider as a matter of priority the question of preventing an arms race in outer space;

(7) Also requests the Conference on Disarmament to intensifiy its consideration of the question of the prevention of an arms race in outer space in all its aspects, taking into account all relevant proposals and initiatives, including those presented in the Ad Hoc Committee at the 1958 session of the Conference and at the forty-third session of the General Assembly;

(8) Further requests the Conference on Disarmament to re-establish an Ad Hoc Committee with an adequate mandate at the beginning of its 1989 session, with a view to undertaking negotiations for the conclusion of an agreement or agreements, as appropriate, to prevent an arms race in outer space in all its aspects;

(9) Urges the Union of Soviet Socialist Republics and the United States of America to pursue intensively their bilateral negotiations in a constructive spirit aimed at reaching early agreement for preventing an arms race in outer space, and to advise the Conference on Disarmament periodically of the progress of their bilateral sessions so as to facilitate its work;

(10) Calls upon all States, especially those with major space capabilities, to refrain, in their activities relating to outer space, from actions contrary to the observance of the relevant existing treaties or to the objective of preventing an arms race in outer space."

▷ Outer Space Exploration Treaty, 1967.

UN Yearbook, 1958 and 1962; *UN Resolutions and Decisions adopted by the General Assembly during the First Part of its Forty-Third Session, from 20 September to 22 December, 1988*. New York, 1989, pp. 131–132.

OUTER SPACE SOVEREIGNTY FRONTIERS. The international issue considered at the UN Legal Subcommittee for Outer Space in connection with claims of equatorial states for recognition of their sovereign right to respective sections of geostation-

ary orbit at a distance of 36,000 km from the Earth's surface used by telecommunications satellites. In 1979 the Subcommittee started work on a convention to demarcate frontiers of sovereignty of states over their territory at an altitude of up to 100 km above the Earth, estimated from sea level. ▷ Geostationary orbit.

OVERKILL CAPACITY. An international term for the potential for the physical liquidation of an opponent many times over through weapons of mass destruction.

R. LEGER SIVARD, *World Military and Social Expenditures 1987–88*, Washington DC, 1987, p. 16; D. ROBERTSON, *Guide to Modern Defense and Strategy*, Detroit, 1988.

OVERLORD. A cryptonym for the Allied invasion plan of occupied France, realized in June 1944.

CH. CRUICKSHANK, *Deception in World War II*, Oxford, 1979.

OVERSEAS CHINA BANKING CORPORATION. Est. 1932 in Singapore. An international merchant bank with 14 branches in Singapore, 25 in Malaysia, 2 in China, 2 in Hong Kong, 1 in Japan, 1 in the UK.

OWI. The Office of War Information, established during World War II in the USA as the organizer of psychological warfare.

OXFORD AND CAMBRIDGE UNIVERSITIES. The ancient English universities. First to be founded was Oxford, after the migration of English students from Paris, 1167. The University of Cambridge was est. in 1209 after a number of Oxford scholars moved to Cambridge.

Commonwealth University Yearbook; The Oxford University Handbook; The Cambridge University Handbook.

OXFORD, PROVISIONS OF, 1258. The first written constitution of England, known as the Provisions of Oxford (June 10, 1258).

R.F. TREHARNE, *The Baronial Plan of Reform, 1258–1263*, London, 1932.

OXYGEN. A subject of international co-operation: International Oxygen Manufacturers Association (IOMA), f. 1943. Publ.: *IMOA Broadcast*, Reg. with the UIA.

OZONE LAYER. An international term for the belt of rarefied gas some 15–50 km above the surface of the Earth which shields it from the sun's short-wave ultraviolet radiation. Subject of international protection in the frame of the UN Environmental Program and the ▷ Ozone Layer Convention. An expanding hole in stratospheric ozone over the ▷ South Pole as large as the United States is a World ecological problem. According to data from Nimbus 7, an American research satellite that, since 1979, has been taking daily ozone readings around the World, the protective layer of ozone in the Earth's atmosphere declined about 5 per cent from 1979 to 1986. The damage to ozone is a result of cyclical natural processes and of the release of manmade chlorofluorocarbons, CFCs, used as refrigerants and aerosol propellants and in special industrial processes. Ultraviolet light coming to the Earth by "ozone holes" can cause skin cancers, cataracts and immunological system problems. Forecasts of the effects of CFCs estimate depletions of up to 8 per cent over 50 years "more extreme projections hold that the ozone layer could be destroyed in a hundred years".

The US and the USSR which maintain active scientific bases in Antarctica decided on Nov. 2, 1987 to conduct 30 joint climate research projects in 1988. The work will focus on the seasonal depletion of the protective ozone layer over Antarctica. At the World Ozone Conference held in London in Mar. 1989, the EEC countries agreed to stop the production of chlorofluorocarbons by the end of the century. The developing countries are as yet unable to produce alternatives to the gases.

H. TAHA, *Ozone Observations and Their Meteorological Application*, London, 1961. K.P. BOWMAN, "Data from Nimbus 7", in: *Science*, Jan. 1988; B. RENSBERGER, Ozone Level Declined 5% since '79; Study Says, in: *Washington Post*, Jan. 2–3, 1988; KEESING's *Record of World Events*, Jan. 1988.

OZONE LAYER CONVENTION. The Vienna Convention for the protection of the Ozone Layer against man-made chlorofluorcarbons (CFC) reclearing and damping the Earth's ozone layer, adopted on Feb. 27, 1987, under the auspices of the UNEP, signed by: Argentina, Belgium, Byelorussia, Canada, Chile, Denmark, Egypt, Finland, the FRG, Greece, Italy, the Netherlands, Norway, Peru, Sweden, Switzerland, the USA, the USSR and the European Economic Community, EEC. The agreement will freeze the production of CFC by 1990 and then reduce it by 20% in 1991 and 1992.

UN Chronicle, May, 1987.

P

PACEM IN MARIBUS.
Latin = "peace at sea." A proposal put forward at the UN in 1967 by Malta for a program of co-operation for peaceful use of the sea-bed and its resources; later, in 1970 the work of the Special Committee on the Peaceful Uses of the Sea-Bed and Ocean Floor led to the adoption by the UN General Assembly of the Declaration of Principles Governing the Sea-Bed and Ocean Floor, the first set of agreed principles governing the vast area of ocean space. ▷ Sea-Bed and the Ocean Floor.

PACEM IN TERRIS.
Latin = "peace on earth." Two international terms.
(1) A papal encyclical "on peace between all nations, based on truth, justice, mercy, freedom" (*de pace omnium gentium in veritate, iustitia, caritate, libertate, constituenda*). Pope John XXIII announced the encyclical on Apr. 11, 1963, addressing, as stressed by the UN Secretary-General U Thant: "not only members of the Roman Catholic Church, but all people in the world with an appeal that man experience the nuclear age in consciousness that it should not serve death, but the life and dignity of man in a community of mutual understanding."
The encyclical, commonly regarded as a great contribution to the cause of peace, joined Roman Catholics for the first time in the struggle for peace in common with all people of good will of different religions or ideologies. The encyclical for the first time expressed the official support of the Vatican for the UN.
(2) The name of international conventions on behalf of peace. To honor the Year of International Co-operation an International Convention on the Requirement of Peace was held at the Center for the Study of Democratic Institutions on Feb. 17–20, 1965, under the slogan *Pacem in terris*; its aim was to study ways of fostering peace and world co-operation. The inauguration took place in the auditorium of the UN General Assembly in New York, in the presence of the UN Secretary-General U Thant, who stated that: "the very title of the encyclical *Pacem in Terris* is the aim of the UN and all people of good will in the world." A second meeting was held in Geneva on May 29–31, 1967, at which the UN Secretary-General, U Thant, in the face of an escalation of the war in Vietnam and the threat of war between Israel and the Arab states, warned that: "the egoism of some creates the danger of World War III." Both meetings had the character of symposia of statesmen and intellectuals from various regions of the world and from various religions and ideologies (in New York 85 states, in Geneva 70). The basic conclusions on ways to strengthen world peace were as follows: strengthening the UN; promoting the universality of the UN; completely liquidating the Cold War; neutralizing southeast Asia, since the "war in Vietnam is at least a mistake"; "military solutions are not adequate for contemporary problems"; co-existence is a necessary, but not a sufficient, condition for human life; in life co-existence should be transformed into a condition which John XXIII defined as a state of "the common and universal Good."

Encyclica Pacem in Terris, Citta del Vaticano, 1963; E.L. SEVILLA, *La Enciclica Pacem in Terris*, México, DF, 1963; P. JOHNSON, *Pope John XXIII*, London, 1975.

PACIFIC AREA TRAVEL ASSOCIATION. F.
1951, San Francisco for the promotion of tourism in the Pacific area. Publ. *Pacific Travel News; Pacific Area Handbook*.

Yearbook of International Organizations.

PACIFICATION.
Two different international terms. (1) Peace negotiations, (2) The use of armed force to put down demonstrations, or to terrorize or even exterminate the population of a region.

PACIFIC BASIN ECONOMIC COUNCIL. F.
1967, Canberra. A businessmen's organization of Australia, Canada, Japan, New Zealand, the USA and the countries of Pacific Basin.

Yearbook of International Organizations.

PACIFIC BUREAU. ▷ SPEC.

PACIFIC CHARTER, 1954.
The SEATO member states declaration in Manila on Sept. 8, 1954, which reads as follows:
"The Delegates of Australia, France, New Zealand, Pakistan, the Republic of the Philippines, the Kingdom of Thailand, the United Kingdom of Great Britain and Northern Ireland, and the United States of America,
Desiring to establish a firm basis for common action to maintain peace and security in south-east Asia and the south-west Pacific,
Convinced that common action to this end, in order to be worthy and effective, must be inspired by the highest principles of justice and liberty,
Do hereby proclaim:
First, in accordance with the provisions of the United Nations Charter, they uphold the principle of equal rights and self-determination of peoples and they will earnestly strive by every peaceful means to promote self-government and to secure the independence of all countries whose peoples desire it and are able to undertake its responsibilities.
Second, they are each prepared to continue taking effective practical measures to ensure conditions favourable to the orderly achievement of the foregoing purposes in accordance with their constitutional processes;
Third, they will continue to co-operate in the economic, social and cultural fields in order to promote higher living standards, economic progress and social well-being in this region;
Fourth, as declared in the South-East Asia Collective Defense Treaty, they are determined to prevent or counter by appropriate means any attempt in the treaty area to subvert their freedom or to destroy their sovereignty or territorial integrity."

J.A.S. GRENVILLE (ed.), *The Major International Treaties 1914–1973. A History and Guide with Texts*, London, 1974.

PACIFIC FORUM. ▷ South Pacific Forum.

PACIFIC FOUR POWER TREATY. ▷ Pacific
Ocean Washington Treaty, 1921.

PACIFIC ISLANDS, TRUST TERRITORY OF
THE. More than 2000 islands and islets of the Caroline Islands, the Marshall Islands and the Marianas Islands, with a combined land area of 1857 sq. km.; a German colony up to 1914, when they were seized by Japan and since 1922 mandated to Japan by the LN; in 1944 they were occupied by US forces, and on Apr. 2, 1947 the UN accepted a Trusteeship Agreement with the United States. The Administering Authority of the Trust Territory of the Pacific Islands set 1981 as a target date for the termination of the Trusteeship Agreement. The UN Trusteeship in accordance with the wishes of the population terminated on May 28, 1986. The ▷ Marshall Islands, ▷ Micronesia, ▷ Mariana Islands and ▷ Palau adopted, by plebiscites, free association with USA.

UNTS, Vol. 8, p. 190; *UN Chronicle*, July 1980, pp. 49–54; *Pacific Islands Pilot*, 3 Vols., Taunton, UK, 1981; KEESING's *Record of World Events*, 1987.

PACIFIC OCEAN.
The largest ocean in the world, represents 45.8% of the world's seas. A straight navigable line from Guayaquil, Ecuador, on the east to Bangkok, Thailand, on the west is 17,448 km long. In 1986 for the first time the international trade via the Pacific was greater than that via the Atlantic Ocean.

O.W. FREEMAN (ed), *Geography of the Pacific*, New York, 1951; S.W. MIKHAILOV, *Ekonomika Mirovogo Okeana*, Moscow, 1966; D. MACINTYRE, *Sea Power in the Pacific*, London, 1968; *SShA i problemy Tikhogo Okieana*, Moscow, 1979; J.P. CRAVEN, J. SCHNEIDER eds., *Maritime Jurisdiction*, Honolulu, 1988.

PACIFIC OCEAN WASHINGTON TREATY,
1921. The Four Power Treaty related to their insular possessions and dominions in the Pacific, signed on Dec. 13, 1921, in Washington by the British Empire, France, Japan and the USA; accompanying Declaration and identical communication to the Netherlands and Portuguese Government:
"The High Contracting Parties agree as between themselves to respect their rights in relation to their insular possessions and insular dominions in the region of the Pacific Ocean."
In a supplementary Treaty, signed on Feb. 6, 1922 in Washington, France, Japan, the UK and the USA defined that the term "insular possessions and dominions" used in aforesaid Treaty shall, in its application to Japan, include only Karafuto (or the southern portion of Sakhalin), Formosa and the Pescadores, and the islands under the mandate of Japan.

LNTS, Vol. 25, pp. 187 and 197; *US Department of State Conference on the Limitation of Armaments*, 2 Vols., Washington, DC, 1922; Y. ICHICHASKI, *The Washington Conference and After*, New York, 1928; C. VINSON, *The Parchment Peace: The US Senate and the Washington Conference 1921–22*, New York, 1955.

PACIFIC REGION.
A geo-political term for the Pacific rim states and Pacific islands.

J.W. MORLEY, *Security Interdependence in the Asia Pacific Region*, Lexington, Mass., 1986; D. AIKMAN, *Pacific Rim Area of Change, Area of Opportunity*, Boston, 1986; T.P. FENDON, M.J. HEFFRON eds., *Asia and Pacific. A Directory of Resources*, New York, 1986.

PACIFIC SETTLEMENT ACT, 1928.
The General Act for the Pacific Settlement of International Disputes signed at Geneva on Sep. 26, 1928. The text is as follows:
"Chapter I. Conciliation. Art. 1. Disputes of every kind between two or more Parties to the present General Act which it has not been possible to settle by diplomacy shall, subject to such reservations as may be made under article 39, be submitted, under the conditions laid down in the present Chapter, to the procedure of conciliation.
Art. 2. The disputes referred to in the preceding article shall be submitted to a permanent or special Conciliation Commission constituted by the parties to the dispute.
Art. 3. On a request to that effect being made by one of the Contracting Parties to another Party, a permanent

Conciliation Commission shall be constituted within a period of six months.

Unless the parties concerned agree otherwise, the Conciliation Commission shall be constituted as follows:

(1) The Commission shall be composed of five members. The parties shall each nominate one commissioner, who may be chosen from among their respective nationals. The three other commissioners shall be appointed by agreement from among the nationals of third Powers. These three commissioners must be of different nationalities and must not be habitually resident in the territory nor be in the service of the parties. The parties shall appoint the President of the Commission from among them.

(2) The commissioners shall be appointed for three years. They shall be re-eligible. The commissioners appointed jointly may be replaced during the course of their mandate by agreement betweeen the parties. Either party may, however, at any time replace a commissioner whom it has appointed. Even if replaced, the commissioners shall continue to exercise their functions until the termination of the work in hand.

(3) Vacancies which may occur as a result of death, resignation or any other cause shall be filled within the shortest possible time in the manner fixed for the nominations.

Art. 5. If, when a dispute arises, no permanent Conciliation Commission appointed by the parties is in existence, a special commission shall be constituted for the examination of the dispute within a period of three months from the date at which a request to that effect is made by one of the parties to the other party. The necessary appointments shall be made in the manner laid down in the preceding article, unless the parties decide otherwise.

Art. 6.(1) If the appointment of the commissioners to be designated jointly is not made within the periods provided for in articles 3 and 5, the making of the necessary appointments shall be entrusted to a third Power, chosen by agreement between the parties, or on request of the parties, to the Acting President of the Council of the League of Nations.

(2) If no agreement is reached on either of these procedures, each party shall designate a different Power, and the appointment shall be made in concert by the Powers, thus chosen.

(3) If, within a period of three months, the two Powers have been unable to reach an agreement, each of them shall submit a number of candidates equal to the number of members to be appointed. It shall then be decided by lot which of the candidates thus designated shall be appointed.

Art. 7.(1) Disputes shall be brought before the Conciliation Commission by means of an application addressed to the President by the two parties acting in agreement, or in default thereof by one or other of the parties.

(2) The application, after giving a summary account of the subject of the dispute, shall contain the invitation to the Commission to take all necessary measures with a view to arriving at an amicable solution.

(3) If the application emanates from only one of the parties, the other party shall, without delay, be notified by it.

Art. 8.(1) Within fifteen days from the date on which a dispute has been brought by one of the parties before a permanent Conciliation Commission, either party may replace its own commissioner, for the examination of the particular dispute, by a person possessing special competence in the matter.

(2) The party making use of this right shall immediately notify the other party; the latter shall, in such case, be entitled to take similar action within fifteen days from the date on which it received the notification.

Art. 9.(1) In the absence of agreement to the contrary between the parties, the Conciliation Commission shall meet at the seat of the League of Nations, or at some other place selected by its President.

(2) The Commission may in all circumstances request the Secretary-General of the League of Nations to afford it his assistance.

Art. 10. The work of the Conciliation Commission shall not be conducted in public unless a decision to that effect is taken by the Commission with the consent of the parties.

Art. 11.(1) In the absence of agreement to the contrary between the parties, the Conciliation Commission shall lay down its own procedure, which in any case must

provide for both parties being heard. In regard to enquiries, the Commission, unless it decides unanimously to the contrary, shall act in accordance with the provisions of Part III of the Hague Convention of October 18, 1907, for the Pacific Settlement of International Disputes.

(2) The parties shall be represented before the Conciliation Commission by agents, whose duty shall be to act as intermediaries between them and the Commission; they may, moreover, be assisted by counsel and experts appointed by them for that purpose and may request that all persons whose evidence appears to them desirable shall be heard.

(3) The Commission, for its part, shall be entitled to request oral explanations from the agents, counsel and experts of both parties, as well as from all persons it may think desirable to summon with the consent of their Governments.

Art. 12. In the absence of agreement to the contrary between the parties, the decisions of the Conciliation Commission shall be taken by a majority vote, and the Commission may only take decisions on the substance of the dispute if all its members are present.

Art. 13. The parties undertake to facilitate the work of the Conciliation Commission, and particularly to supply it to the greatest possible extent with all relevant documents and information, as well as to use the means at their disposal to allow it to proceed in their territory, and in accordance with their law, to the summoning and hearing of witnesses or experts and to visit the localities in question.

Art. 14.(1) During the proceedings of the Commission, each of the commissioners shall receive emoluments the amount of which shall be fixed by agreement between the parties, each of which shall contribute an equal share.

(2) The general expenses arising out of the working of the Commission shall be divided in the same manner.

Art. 15.(1) The task of the Conciliation Commission shall be to elucidate the questions in dispute, to collect with that object all necessary information by means of inquiry or otherwise, and to endeavor to bring the parties to an agreement. It may, after the case has been examined, inform the parties of the terms settlement which seem suitable to it, and lay down the period within which they are to make their decision.

(2) At the close of the proceedings the Commission shall draw up a proces-verbal stating, as the case may be, either that the parties have come to an agreement and, if need arises, the terms of the agreement, or that it has been impossible to effect a settlement. No mention shall be made in the proces-verbal of whether the Commission's decisions were taken unanimously or by a majority vote.

(3) The proceedings of the Commission must, unless the parties otherwise agree, be terminated within six months from the date on which the Commission shall have been given cognizance of the dispute.

Art. 16. The Commission's proces-verbal shall be communicated without delay to the parties. The parties shall decide whether it shall be published.

Chapter II. Judicial settlement. Art. 17. All disputes with regard to which the parties are in conflict as to their respective rights shall, subject to any reservations which may be made under article 39, be submitted for decisions to the Permanent Court of International Justice, unless the parties agree, in the manner hereinafter provided, to have resort to an arbitral tribunal.

It is understood that the disputes referred to above include in particular those mentioned in article 36 of the Statute of the Permanent Court of International Justice.

Art. 18. If the parties agree to submit the disputes mentioned in the preceding article to an arbitral tribunal, they shall draw up a special agreement in which they shall specify the subject of the dispute, the arbitrators selected, and the procedure to be followed. In the absence of sufficient particulars in the special agreement, the provisions of the Hague Convention of October 18th 1907, for the Pacific Settlement of International Disputes shall apply so far as is necessary. If nothing is laid down in the special agreement as to the rules regarding the substance of the dispute to be followed by the arbitrators, the tribunal shall apply the substantive rules enumerated in article 38 of the Statute of the Permanent Court of International Justice.

Art. 19. If the parties fail to agree concerning the special agreement referred to in the preceding article, or fail to

appoint arbitrators, either party shall be at liberty, after giving three months' notice, to bring the dispute by an application direct before the Permanent Court of International Justice.

Art. 20.(1) Notwithstanding the provisions of article 1, disputes of the kind referred to in article 17 arising between parties who have acceded to the obligations contained in the present chapter shall only be subject to the procedure of conciliation if the parties so agree.

(2) The obligation to resort to the procedure of conciliation remains applicable to disputes which are excluded from judicial settlement only by the operation of reservations under the provisions of article 39.

(3) In the event of recourse to and failure of conciliation, neither party may bring the dispute before the Permanent Court of International Justice or call for the constitution of the arbitral tribunal referred to in article 18 before the expiration of one month from the termination of the proceedings of the Conciliation Commission.

Chapter III. Arbitration. Art. 21. Any dispute not of the kind referred to in article 17 which does not, within the month following the termination of the work of the Conciliation Commission provided for in Chapter I, form the object of an agreement between the parties, shall, subject to such reservations as may be made under article 39, be brought before an arbitral tribunal which, unless the parties otherwise agree, shall be constituted in the manner set out below.

Art. 22. The Arbitral Tribunal shall consist of five members. The parties shall each nominate one member, who may be chosen from among their respective nationals. The two other arbitrators and the Chairman shall be chosen by common agreement from among the nationals of third Powers. They must be of different nationalities and must not be habitually resident in the territory nor be in the service of the parties.

Art. 23.(1) If the appointment of the members of the Arbitral Tribunals is not made within a period of three months from the date on which one of the parties requested the other party to constitute an arbitral tribunal, a third Power, chosen by agreement between the parties, shall be requested to make the necessary appointments.

(2) If no agreement is reached on this point, each party shall designate a different Power, and the appointments shall be made in concert by the Powers thus chosen.

(3) If, within a period of three months, the two Powers so chosen have been unable to reach an agreement, the necessary appointments shall be made by the President of the Permanent Court of International Justice. If the latter is prevented from acting or is a subject of one of the parties, the nominations shall be made by the Vice-President. If the latter is prevented from acting or is a subject of one of the parties, the appointments shall be made by the oldest member of the Court who is not a subject of either party.

Art. 24. Vacancies which may occur as a result of death, resignation or any other cause shall be filled within the shortest possible time in the manner fixed for the nominations.

Art. 25. The parties shall draw up a special agreement determining the subject of the disputes and the details of procedure.

Art. 26. In the absence of sufficient particulars in the special agreement regarding the matters referred to in the preceding article, the provisions of the Hague Convention of October 18th, 1907, for the Pacific Settlement of International Disputes shall apply so far as is necessary.

Art. 27. Failing the conclusion of a special agreement within a period of three months from the date on which the Tribunal was constituted, the dispute may be brought before the Tribunal by any application by one or other party.

Art. 28. If nothing is laid down in the special agreement or no special agreement has been made, the Tribunal shall apply the rules in regard to the substance of the dispute enumerated in article 38 of the Statute of the Permanent Court of International Justice. In so far as there exists no such rule applicable to the dispute, the Tribunal shall decide *ex aequo et bono*.

Chapter IV. General provisions. Art. 29 (1) Disputes for the settlement of which a special procedure is laid down in other conventions in force between the parties to the dispute shall be settled in conformity with the provisions of those conventions.

(2) The present General Act shall not affect any agreements in force by which conciliation procedure is established between the parties or they are bound by obligations to resort to arbitration or judicial settlement which insure the settlement of the dispute. If, however, these agreements provide only for a procedure of conciliation, after such procedure has been followed without result, the provisions of the present General Act concerning judicial settlement or arbitration shall be applied in so far as the parties have acceded thereto.
Art. 30. If a party brings before a Conciliation Commission a dispute which the other party, relying on conventions in force between the parties, has submitted to the Permanent Court of International Justice or an Arbitral Tribunal, the Commission shall defer consideration of the dispute until the Court or the Arbitral Tribunal has pronounced upon the conflict of competence. The same rule shall apply if the Court or the Tribunal is seized of the case by one of the parties during the conciliation proceedings.
Art. 31.(1) In the case of a dispute the occasion of which, according to the municipal law of one of the parties, falls within the competence of its judicial or administrative authorities, the party in question may object to the matter in dispute being submitted for settlement by the different methods laid down in the present General Act until a decision with final effect has been pronounced, within a reasonable time, by the competent authority.
(2) In such a case, the party which desires to resort to the procedures laid down in the present General Act must notify the other party of its intention within a period of one year from the date of the aforementioned decision.
Art. 32. If, in a judicial sentence or arbitral award, it is declared that a judgment, or a measure enjoined by a court of law or other authority of one of the parties to the dispute, is wholly or in part contrary for international law, and if the constitutional law of that party does not permit or only partially permits the consequences of the judgment or measure in question to be annulled, the parties agree that the judicial sentence or arbitral award shall grant the injured party equitable satisfaction.
Art. 33.(1) In all cases where a dispute forms the object of arbitration of judicial proceedings, and particularly if the question on which the parties differ arises out of acts already committed or on the point of being committed, the Permanent Court of International Justice, acting in accordance with article 41 of its Statute, or the Arbitral Tribunal, shall lay down within the shortest possible time the provisional measures to be adopted. The parties to the dispute shall be bound to accept such measures.
(2) If the dispute is brought before a Conciliation Commission, the latter may recommend to the parties the adoption of such provisional measures as it considers suitable.
(3) The parties undertake to abstain from all measures likely to react prejudicially upon the execution of the judicial or arbitral decision or upon the arrangements proposed by the Conciliation Commission and, in general, to abstain from any sort of action whatsoever which may aggravate or extend the dispute.
Art. 34. Should a dispute arise between more than two Parties to the present General Act, the following rules shall be observed for the application of the forms of procedure described in the foregoing provisions:
(a) In the case of conciliation procedure, a special commission shall invariably be constituted. The composition of such commission shall differ according as the parties all have separate interests or as two or more of their number act together.
In the former case, the parties shall each appoint one commissioner and shall jointly appoint commissioners nationals of third Powers not parties to the dispute, whose number shall always exceed by one the number of commissioners appointed separately by the parties.
In the second case, the parties who act together shall appoint their commissioner jointly by agreement between themselves and shall combine with the other party or parties in appointing third commissioners.
In either event, the parties, unless they agree otherwise, shall apply article 5 and the following articles of the present Act, so far as they are compatible with the provisions of the present article.
(b) In the case of judicial procedure, the Statute of the Permanent Court of International Justice shall apply.
(c) In the case of arbitral procedure, if agreement is not secured as to the composition of the tribunal, in the case of the disputes mentioned in article 17, each party shall have the right, by means of an application, to submit the dispute to the Permanent Court of International Justice; in the case of the disputes mentioned in article 21, the above article 22 and following articles shall apply, but each party having separate interests shall appoint one arbitrator and the number of arbitrators separately appointed by the parties to the dispute shall always be one less than that of the other arbitrators.
Art. 35.(1) The present General Act shall be applicable as between the parties thereto, even though a third Power, whether a party to the Act or not, has an interest in the dispute.
(2) In conciliation procedure, the parties may agree to invite such third Power to intervene.
Art. 36.(1) In judicial or arbitral procedure, if a third Power should consider that it has an interest of a legal nature which may be affected by the decision in the case, it may submit to the Permanent Court of International Justice or to the arbitral tribunal a request to intervene as a third party.
(2) It will be for the Court or the tribunal to decide upon this request.
Art. 37.(1) Whenever the construction of a convention to which states other than those concerned in the case are parties is in question, the Registrar of the Permanent Court of International Justice or the arbitral tribunal shall notify all such states forthwith.
(2) Every state so notified has the right to intervene in the proceedings; but if it uses this right, the construction given by the decision will be binding upon it.
Art. 38. Accessions to the present General Act may extend:
A. Either to all the provisions of the Act (Chapters I, II, III and IV);B. Or to those provisions only which relate to conciliation and judicial settlement (Chapters I and II), together with the general provisions dealing with these procedures (Chapter IV);
C. Or to those provisions only which relate to conciliation (Chapter I), together with the general provisions concerning that procedure (Chapter IV).
The Contracting Parties may benefit by the accessions of other parties only in so far as they have themselves assumed the same obligations.
Art. 39 (1) In addition to the power given in the preceding article, a party in acceding to the present General Act, may make his acceptance conditional upon the reservations exhaustively enumerated in the following paragraph. These reservations must be indicated at the time of accession.
(2) These reservations may be such as to exclude from the procedure described in the present Act:
(a) Disputes arising out of facts prior to the accession either of the party making the reservation or of any other party whom the said party may have a dispute;
(b) Disputes concerning questions which by international law are solely within the domestic jurisdiction of states;
(c) Disputes concerning particular cases or clearly specified subject matters, such as territorial status, or disputes falling within clearly defined categories.
(3) If one of the parties to a dispute has made a reservation, the other parties may enforce the same reservation in regard to that party.
(4) In the case of parties, who have acceded to the provisions of the present General Act relating to judicial settlement or to arbitration, such reservations as they may have made shall, unless otherwise expressly stated, be deemed not to apply to the procedure of conciliation.
Art. 40. A party whose accession has been only partial, or was made subject to reservations, may at any moment, by means of a simple declaration, either extend the scope of his accession or abandon all or part of his reservations.
Art. 41. Disputes relating to the interpretation or application of the present General Act, including those concerning the classification of disputes and the scope of reservations, shall be submitted to the Permanent Court of International Justice.
Art. 42. The present General Act, of which the French and English texts shall both be authentic, shall bear the date of the 26th of September, 1928.
Art. 43 (1) The present General Act shall be open to accession by all the Heads of States or other competent authorities of the Members of the League of Nations and the non-Member states to which the Council of the League of Nations has communicated a copy for this purpose.
(2) The instruments of accession and the additional declarations provided for by article 40 shall be transmitted to the Secretary-General of the League of Nations, who shall notify their receipt to all the Members of the League and to the non-Member states referred to in the preceding paragraph.
(3) The Secretary-General of the League of Nations shall draw up three lists, denominated respectively by the letters, A, B and C, corresponding to the three forms of accession to the present Act provided for in article 38, in which shall be shown the accessions and additional declarations of the Contracting Parties. These lists, which shall be continually kept up to date, shall be published in the annual report presented to the Assembly of the League of Nations by the Secretary-General.
Art. 44 (1) The present General Act shall come into force on the ninetieth day following the receipt by the Secretary-General of the League of Nations of the accession of not less than two Contracting Parties.
(2) Accessions received after the entry into force of the Act, in accordance with the previous paragraph, shall become effective as from the ninetieth day following the date of receipt by the Secretary-General of the League of Nations. The same rule shall apply to the additional declaration provided for by article 40.
Art. 45.(1) The present General Act shall be concluded for a period of five years, dating from its entry into force.
(2) It shall remain in force for further successive periods of five years in the case of Contracting Parties which do not denounce it at least six months before the expiration of the current period.
(3) Denunciation shall be effected by a written notification addressed to the Secretary-General of the League of Nations, who shall inform all the Members of the League and the non-Member states referred to in article 43.
(4) A denunciation may be partial only, or may consist in notification of reservations not previously made.
(5) Notwithstanding denunciation by one of the Contracting Parties concerned in a dispute, all proceedings pending at the expiration of the current period of the General Act shall be duly completed.
Art. 46. A copy of the present General Act, signed by the President of the Assembly and by the Secretary-General of the League of Nations, shall be deposited in the archives of the Secretariat; a certified true copy shall be delivered by the Secretary-General to all the Members of the League of Nations and to the non-Member states indicated by the Council of the League of Nations.
Art. 47. The present General Act shall be registered by the Secretary-General of the League of Nations on the date of its entry into force.'

▷ Peaceful Settlements of International Disputes.

LNTS, Vol. 93, 1929, pp. 345–363.

PACIFIC SETTLEMENT ACT, 1949. Revised General Act for the Pacific Settlement of International Disputes, adopted by the UN General Assembly, Apr. 22, 1949; came into force Sept. 20, 1950. The text is as follows:

'Chapter I. Conciliation. Art. 1. Disputes of every kind between two or more parties to the Present General Act which it has not been possible to settle by diplomacy shall, subject to such reservations as may be made under article 39, be submitted, under the conditions laid down in the present chapter, to the procedure of conciliation.
Art. 2. The disputes referred to in the preceding article shall be submitted to a permanent or special conciliation commission constituted by the parties to the dispute.
Art. 3. On a request to that effect being made by one of the Contracting Parties to another party, a permanent conciliation commission shall be constituted within a period of six months.
Art. 4. Unless the parties concerned agree otherwise, the Conciliation Commission shall be constituted as follows:

(1) The Commission shall be composed of five members. The parties shall each nominate one commissioner, who may be chosen from among their respective nationals. The three other commissioners shall be appointed by agreement from among the nationals of third Powers. These three commissioners must be of different nationalities and must not be habitually resident in the territory nor be in the service of the parties. The parties shall appoint the President of the Commission from among them.
(2) The commissioners shall be appointed for three years. They shall be re-eligible. The commissioners appointed jointly may be replaced during the course of their mandate by agreement between the parties. Either party may, however, at any time replace a commissioner whom it has appointed. Even if replaced, the commissioners shall continue to exercise their functions until the termination of the work in hand.
(3) Vacancies which may occur as a result of death, resignation or any other cause shall be filled within the shortest possible time in the manner fixed for the nominations.
Art. 5. If, when a dispute arises, no permanent conciliation appointed by the parties is in existence, a special commission shall be constituted for the examination of the dispute within a period of three months from the date at which a request to that effect is made by one of the parties to the other party. The necessary appointments shall be made in the manner laid down in the preceding article, unless the parties decide otherwise.
Art. 6.(1) If the appointment of the commissioners to be designated jointly is not made within the periods provided for in article 3 and 5, the making of the necessary appointments shall be entrusted to a third Power, chosen by agreement between the parties, or on request of the parties, to the President of the General Assembly, or, if the latter is not in session, to the last President.
(2) If no agreement is reached on either of these procedures, each party shall designate a different Power, and the appointment shall be made in concert by the Powers thus chosen.
(3) If, within a period of three months, the two Powers have been unable to reach an agreement, each of them shall submit a number of candidates equal to the number of members to be appointed. It shall then be decided by lot which of the candidates thus designated shall be appointed.
Art. 7.(1) Disputes shall be brought before the Conciliation Commission by means of an application addressed to the President by the two parties acting in agreement, or in default thereof by one or other of the parties.
(2) The application, after giving a summary account of the subject of the dispute, shall contain the invitation to the Commission to take all necessary measures with a view to arriving at an amicable solution.
(3) If the application emanates from only one of the parties, the other party shall, without delay, be notified by it.
Art. 8.(1) Within fifteen days from the date on which a dispute has been brought by one of the parties before a permanent conciliation commission, either party may replace its own commissioner, for the examination of the particular dispute, by a person possessing special competence in the matter.
(2) The party making use of this right shall immediately notify the other party; the latter shall, in such case, be entitled to take similar action within fifteen days from the date on which it received the notification.
Art. 9.(1) In the absence of agreement to the contrary between the parties, the Conciliation Commission shall meet at the seat of the United Nations, or at some other place selected by its President.
(2) The Commission may in all circumstances request the Secretary-General of the United Nations to afford it his assistance.
Art. 10. The work of the Conciliation Commission shall not be conducted in public unless a decision to that effect is taken by the Commission with the consent of the parties.
Art. 11 (1) In the absence of agreement to the contrary between the parties, the Conciliation Commission shall lay down its own procedure, which in any case must provide for both parties being heard. In regard to enquiries, the Commission, unless it decides unanimously to the contrary, shall act in accordance with the provisions of part III of the Hague Convention of 18 October 1907 for the Pacific Settlement of International Disputes.
(2) The parties shall be represented before the Conciliation Commission by agents, whose duty shall be to act as intermediaries between them and the Commission; they may, moreover, be assisted by counsel and experts appointed by them for that purpose and may request that all persons whose evidence appears to them desirable shall be heard.
(3) The Commission, for its part, shall be entitled to request oral explanations from the agents, counsel and experts of both parties, as well as from all persons it may think desirable to summon with the consent of their Governments.
Art. 12. In the absence of agreement to the contrary between the parties, the decisions of the Conciliation Commission shall be taken by a majority vote, and the Commission may only take decisions on the substance of the dispute if all its members are present.
Art. 13. The parties undertake to facilitate the work of the Conciliation Commission, and particularly to supply it to the greatest possible extent with all relevant documents and information, as well as to use the means at their disposal to allow it to proceed in their territory, and in accordance with their law, to the summoning and hearing of witnesses or experts and to visit the localities in question.
Art. 14.(1) During the proceedings of the Commission, each of the commissioners shall receive emoluments the amount of which shall be fixed by agreement between the parties, each of which shall contribute an equal share.
(2) The general expenses arising out of the working of the Commission shall be divided in the same manner.
Art. 15.(1) The task of the Conciliation Commission shall be to elucidate the questions in dispute, to collect with that object all necessary information by means of enquiry or otherwise, and to endeavour to bring the parties to an agreement. It may, after the case has been examined, inform the parties of the terms of settlement which seem suitable to it, and lay down the period within which they are to make their decision.
(2) At the close of the proceedings the Commission shall draw up a proces-verbal stating, as the case may be, either that the parties have come to an agreement and, if need arises, the terms of the agreement, or that it has been impossible to effect a settlement. No mention shall be made in the proces-verbal of whether the Commission's decisions were taken unanimously or by a majority vote.
(3) The proceedings of the Commission must, unless the parties otherwise agree, be terminated within six months from the date on which the Commission shall have been given cognizance of the dispute.
Art. 16. The Commission's proces-verbal shall be communicated without delay to the parties. The parties shall decide whether it shall be published.
Chapter II. Judicial settlement. Art. 17. All disputes with regard to which the parties are in conflict as to their respective rights shall, subject to any reservations which may be made under article 39, be submitted for decision to the International Court of Justice, unless the parties agree, in the manner hereinafter provided, to have resort to an arbitral tribunal. It is understood that the disputes referred to above include in particular those mentioned in article 36 of the Statute of the International Court of Justice.
Art. 18. If the parties agree to submit the disputes mentioned in the preceding article to an arbitral tribunal, they shall draw up a special agreement in which they shall specify the subject of the dispute, the arbitrators selected and the procedure to be followed. In the absence of sufficient particulars in the special agreement, the provisions of the Hague Convention of 18 October 1907 for the Pacific Settlement of International Disputes shall apply so far as is necessary.
If nothing is laid down in the special agreement as to the rules regarding the substance of the dispute to be followed by the arbitrators, the Tribunal shall apply the substantive rules enumerated in article 38 of the Statute of the International Court of Justice.
Art. 19. If the parties fail to agree concerning the special agreement referred to in the preceding article, or fail to appoint arbitrators, either party shall be at liberty, after giving three months' notice, to bring the dispute by an application direct before the International Court of Justice.
Art. 20.(1) Notwithstanding the provisions of article 1, disputes of the kind referred to in article 17 arising between parties who have acceded to the obligations contained in the present chapter shall only be subject to the procedure of conciliation if the parties so agree.
(2) The obligation to resort to the procedure of conciliation remains applicable to disputes which are excluded from judicial settlement only by the operation of reservations under the provisions of article 39.
(3) In the event of recourse to and failure of conciliation, neither party may bring the dispute before the International Court of Justice or call for the constitution of the arbitral tribunal referred to in article 18 before the expiration of one month from the termination of the proceedings of the Conciliation Commission.
Chapter III. Arbitration. Art. 21. Any dispute not of the kind referred to in article 17 which does not, within the month following the termination of the work of the Conciliation Commission provided for in chapter I, from the object of an agreement between the parties, shall, subject to such reservations as may be made under article 39, be brought before an arbitral tribunal which, unless the parties otherwise agree, shall be constituted in the manner set out below.
Art. 22. The Arbitral Tribunal shall consist of five members. The parties shall each nominate one member, who may be chosen from among their respective nationals. The other arbitrators and the Chairman shall be chosen by common agreement from among the nationals of third Powers. They must be of different nationalities and must not be habitually resident in the territory nor be in the service of the parties.
Art. 23. (1) If the appointment of the members of the Arbitral Tribunal is not made within a period of three months from the date on which one of the parties requested the other party to constitute an arbitral tribunal, a third Power, chosen by agreement between the parties, shall be requested to make the necessary appointments.
(2) If no agreement is reached on this point, each party shall designate a different Power, and the appointments shall be made in concert by the Powers thus chosen.
(3) If, within a period of three months, the two Powers so chosen have been unable to reach an agreement, the necessary appointments shall be made by the President of the International Court of Justice. If the latter is prevented from acting or is a subject of one of the parties, the nominations shall be made by the Vice-President. If the latter is prevented from acting or is subject of one of the parties, the appointments shall be made by the oldest members of the Court who is not a subject of either party.
Art. 24. Vacancies which may occur as a result of death, resignation or any other cause shall be filled within the shortest possible time in the manner fixed for the nominations.
Art. 25. The parties shall draw up a special agreement determining the subject of the disputes and the details of procedure.
Art. 26. In the absence of sufficient particulars in the special agreement regarding the matters referred in the preceding article, the provisions of the Hague Convention of 18 October 1907 for the Pacific Settlement of International Disputes shall apply so far as is necessary.
Art. 27. Failing the conclusion of a special agreement within a period of three months from the date on which the Tribunal was constituted, the dispute may be brought before the Tribunal by an application by one or other party.
Art. 28. If nothing is laid down in the special agreement or no special agreement has been made, the Tribunal shall apply the rules in regard to the substance of the dispute enumerated in article 38 of the Statute of the International Court of Justice. In so far as there exists no such role applicable to the dispute, the Tribunal shall decide *ex aequo et bono*.
Chapter IV. General provisions. Art. 29. (1) Disputes for the settlement of which a special procedure is laid down in other conventions in force between the parties to the dispute shall be settled in conformity with the provisions of those conventions.
(2) The present General Act shall not affect any agreements in force by which conciliation procedure is established between the parties or they are bound by obligations to resort to arbitration or judicial settlement which ensure the settlement of the dispute. If, however, these agreements provide only for a

procedure of conciliation, after such procedure has been followed without result, the provisions of the present General Act concerning judicial settlement or arbitration shall be applied in so far as the parties have acceded thereto.

Art. 30. If a party brings before a Conciliation Commission a dispute which the other party, relying on conventions in force between the parties, has submitted to the International Court of Justice or an arbitral tribunal, the Commission shall defer consideration of the dispute until the Court or the Arbitral Tribunal has pronounced upon the conflict of competence. The same rule shall apply if the Court of the Tribunal is seized of the case by one of the parties during the conciliation proceedings.

Art. 31.(1) In the case of a dispute the occasion of which, according to the municipal law of one of the parties, falls within the competence of its judicial or administrative authorities, the party in question may object to the matter in dispute being submitted for settlement by the different methods laid down in the present General Act until a decision with final effect has been pronounced, within a reasonable time, by the competent authority.

(2) In such a case, the party which desires to resort to the procedures laid down in the present General Act must notify the other party of its intention within a period of one year from the date of the aforementioned decision.

Art. 32. If, in a judicial sentence or arbitral award, it is declared that a judgment, or a measure enjoined by a court of law or other authority of one of the parties to the dispute, is wholly or in part contrary to international law, and if the constitutional law of that party does not permit or only partially permits the consequences of the judgment or measure in question to be annulled, the parties agree that the judicial sentence or arbitral award shall grant the injured party equitable satisfaction.

Art. 33.(1) In all cases where a dispute forms the object of arbitration or judicial proceedings, and particularly if the question on which the parties differ arises out of acts already committed or on the point of being committed, the International Court of Justice, acting in accordance with article 41 of its Statute, or the Arbitral Tribunal, shall lay down within the shortest possible time the provisional measures to be adopted. The parties to the dispute shall be bound to accept such measures.

(2) If the dispute is brought before a conciliation commission, the latter may recommend to the parties the adoption of such provisional measures as it considers suitable.

(3) The parties undertake to abstain from all measures likely to react prejudicially upon the execution of the judicial or arbitral decision or upon the arrangements proposed by the Conciliation Commission and, in general, to abstain from any sort of action whatsoever which may aggravate or extend the dispute.

Art. 34. Should a dispute arise between more than two parties to the present General Act, the following rules shall be observed for the application of the forms of procedure described in the foregoing provisions:

(a) In the case of conciliation procedure, a special commission shall invariably be constituted. The composition of such commission shall differ accordingly as the parties all have separate interests or as two or more or their number act together.

In the former case, the parties shall each appoint one commissioner and shall jointly appoint commissioners nationals of third Powers not parties to the dispute, whose number shall always exceed by one the number of commissioners appointed separately by the parties. In the second case, the parties who act together shall appoint their commissioner jointly by agreement between themselves and shall combine with the other party or parties in appointing third commissioners.

In either event, the parties, unless they agree otherwise shall apply article 5 and the following articles of the present Act so far as they are compatible with the provisions of the present article.

(b) In the case of judicial procedure, the Statute of the International Court of Justice shall apply.

(c) In the case of arbitral procedure, if agreement is not secured as to the composition of the Tribunal, in the case of the disputes mentioned in article 17, each party shall have the right, by means of an application, to submit the dispute to the International Court of Justice; in the case of the disputes mentioned in article 21, the

above article 22 and following articles shall apply, but each party having separate interests shall appoint one arbitrator and the number of arbitrators separately appointed by the parties to the dispute shall always be one less than that of the other arbitrators.

Art. 35.(1) The present General Act shall be applicable as between the parties thereto, even though a third Power, whether a party to the Act or not, has an interest in the dispute.

(2) In conciliation procedure, the parties may agree to invite such third Power to intervene.

Art. 36.(1) In judicial or arbitral procedure, if a third Power should consider that it has an interest of a legal nature which may be affected by the decision in the case, it may submit to the International Court of Justice or to the Arbitral Tribunal a request to intervene as a third party.

(2) It will be for the Court or the Tribunal to decide upon this request.

Art. 37.(1) Whenever the construction of a convention to which states other than those concerned in the case are parties is in question, the Registrar of the International Court of Justice or the Arbitral Tribunal shall notify all such states forthwith.

(2) Every state so notified has the right to intervene in the proceedings but, if it uses this right, the construction given by the decision will be binding upon it.

Art. 38. Accessions to the present General Act may extend:

A. Either to all the provisions of the Act (chapters I, II, III and IV);

B. Or to those provisions only which relate to conciliation and judicial settlement (chapters I and II), together with the general provisions dealing with these procedures (chapter IV);

C. Or to those provisions only which relate to conciliation (chapter I), together with the general provisions concerning that procedure (chapter IV).

The Contracting Parties may benefit by the accessions of other parties only in so far as they have themselves assumed the same obligations.

Art. 39.(1) In addition to the power given in the preceding article, a party, in acceding to the present General Act, may make his acceptance conditional upon the reservations exhaustively enumerated in the following paragraph. These reservations must be indicated at the time of accession.

(2) These reservations may be such as to exclude from the procedure described in the present Act:

(a) Dispute arising out of facts prior to the accession either of the Party making the reservation or of any other party with whom the said party may have a disputes;

(b) Disputes concerning questions which by international law are solely within the domestic jurisdiction of states;

(c) Disputes concerning particular cases or clearly specified subject matters, such as territorial status, or disputes falling within clearly defined categories.

(3) If one of the parties to a dispute has made a reservation, the other parties may enforce the same reservation in regard to that party.

(4) In the case of parties who have acceded to the provisions of the present General Act relating to judicial settlement or to arbitration, such reservations as they may have made shall, unless otherwise expressly stated, be deemed not to apply to the procedure of conciliation.

Art. 40. A party whose accession has been only partial, or was made subject to reservations, may at any moment, by means of a simple declaration, either extend the scope of his accession or abandon all or part of his reservations.

Art. 41. Disputes relating to the interpretation or application of the present General Act, including those concerning the classification of disputes and the scope of reservations, shall be submitted to the International Court of Justice.

Art. 42. The present General Act shall bear the date of 28 April 1949.

Art. 43.(1) The present General Act shall be open to accession by the Members of the United Nations, by non-member states which shall have become parties to the Statute of the International Court of Justice or to which the General Assembly of the United Nations shall have communicated a copy for this purpose.

(2) The instruments of accession and the additional declarations provided for by article 40 shall be trans-

mitted to the Secretary-General of the United Nations, who shall notify their receipt to all the Members of the United Nations and to the non-member states referred to in the preceding paragraph.

(3) The Secretary-General of the United Nations shall draw up three lists, denominated respectively by the letters A, B and C, corresponding to the three forms of accession to the present Act provided for in article 38, in which shall be shown the accessions and additional declarations of the Contracting Parties. These lists, which shall be continually kept up to date, shall be published in the annual report presented to the General Assembly of the United Nations by the Secretary-General.

Art. 44.(1) The present General Act shall come into force on the ninetieth day following the receipt by the Secretary-General of the United Nations of the accession of not less than two Contracting Parties.

(2) Accessions received after the entry into force of the Act, in accordance with the previous paragraph, shall become effective as from the ninetieth day following the date of receipt by the Secretary-General of the United Nations. The same rule shall apply to the additional declarations provided for by article 40.

Art. 45.(1) The present General Act shall be concluded for a period of five years, dating from its entry into force.

(2) It shall remain in force for further successive periods of five years in the case of Contracting Parties which do not denounce it at least six months before the expiration of the current period.

(3) Denunciation shall be effected by a written notification to the Secretary-General of the United Nations, who shall inform all the Members of the United Nations and the non-member states referred to in article 43.

(4) A denunciation may be partial only, or may consist in notification of reservations not previously made.

(5) Notwithstanding denunciation by one of the Contracting Parties concerned in a dispute, all proceedings pending at the expiration of the current period of the General Act shall be duly completed.

Art. 46. A copy of the present General Act, signed by the President of the General Assembly and by the Secretary-General of the United Nations, shall be deposited in the archives of the Secretariat. A certified true copy shall be delivered by the Secretary-General to each of the Members of the United Nations, to the non-member states which shall have become parties to the Statute of the International Court of Justice and to those designated by the General Assembly of the United Nations.

Art. 47. The present General Act shall be registered by the Secretary-General of the United Nations on the date of its entry into force."

▷ Peaceful settlement of International Disputes.

UNTS, Vol. 71, pp. 101–127.

PACIFIC WAR, 1879–1883. A military conflict also called the Saltpeter War, between Chile, Bolivia and Peru over Tarapaca, Arica, Antofagasta and Tacna provinces which contain rich deposits of saltpeter, copper, guano. As result of peace treaties concluded 1883 with Bolivia and with Peru, these provinces were entrusted to Chile, which gained a world-wide saltpeter monopoly and became an important exporter of copper. ▷ Ancon Treaty, 1883, ▷ Tacna-Arica. Since Bolivia by the treaty of 1883 was cut off from the sea coast, until 1888 Chile ran a railway line connecting the capital of Bolivia, La Paz, with the Chilean port of Arica where Bolivia received a duty-free zone. In 1929 Chile returned Tacna province to Peru.

M. LARCO, A. TAURU, *Diccionario enciclopedico del Peru*, 3 Vols., Lima, 1966.

PACIFISM. An international movement from the beginning of 20th century initiated by the Anglican and Methodist Churches, developed after World War I by a group of intellectuals, called "rationalist pacifists" (Bertrand Russell); after World War II an anti-nuclear war world movement and in the 1980's also against ecological industrial disaster.

A.H. FRIED, *Handbuch der Friedensbewegung*, Berlin, 1911; J. TERMEULEN, *Bibliographie du mouvement du la paix avant 1899*, La Haye, 1936; *An Encyclopaedia of Pacifism*, London, 1937; B. MAYER, *Pacifists Conscience*, London, 1966; L.S. WITTNER, *Rebels against war. The American Peace Movement 1941–60*, New York, 1969; M. CEADEL, *Pacifism in Britain 1914–1945*, London, 1980.

PACKAGING. A subject of international co-operation. Organizations reg. with the UIA:

Asian Packaging Federation, f. 1967, Manila. Publ.: *Asian Packaging*.
Asian Packaging Information Center, f. 1974, Hong Kong.
Coordinating CMEA Center for Packaging Materials in the Food Industries, f. 1980, Warsaw, Poland.
European Association of Plastic Packaging Manufacturers, f. 1984, Brussels, Belgium.
European Packaging Federation, f. 1983, Skovunde, Denmark.
European Union of Paper, Board and Packaging Wholesalers, f. 1971, Brussels.
Latin American Packaging Union, f. 1971, Buenos Aires.
North American Packaging Federation, f. 1980, New York, NY, USA.
World Packaging Organization, f. 1968, New York. Liaison status with FAO.

Yearbook of International Organizations, 1986/87; The Europa Yearbook 1988. A World Survey, Vol. I, London, 1988.

PACTA CONVENTA. *Latin* – "agreed treaties." A term for public-legal arrangements between the gentry and the king, in use in Poland since 1573, when Henryk Walezy (Henri de Valois) was elected King of Poland, up to the reign of the last king Stanislaw August; the agreed treaties limited royal rule in favor of civil freedoms for noblemen, and had a considerable influence on Polish international relations; also applicable in Hungary (King Kalman's *pacta conventa* with the Croatian representatives).

W. SOBOCIŃSKI, *Pacta Conventa*, Cracow, 1939; S. GULDESCU, *History of Mediavel Croatia*, London, 1969.

PACTA SUNT SERVANDA. *Latin* = "contracts should be adhered to." The basic principle of international law contained in a declaration on the sanctity of treaties announced on Mar. 13, 1871 at the London Conference on the Black Sea, and the Danube. Representatives of governments of Austria–Hungary, France, Germany, Russia, Turkey, Great Britain and Italy declared that:

"It shall be an important principle of international law that no power may disengage from obligations imposed by a treaty, nor may it alter provisions of treaties unless permission of the contracting parties is obtained by friendly agreement."

The Covenant of the League of Nations in art. 1, par. 2, determined as evident that "meticulous observance of obligations resulting from international treaties" should be the rule. Similarly, the UN Charter in the Preamble and in art. 2 required of UN members "respect for the obligations arising from treaties and other sources of international law". During the Nuremberg Trials the International Military Court frequently emphasized that "pacta sunt servanda" was of great importance, the verdict stressed the violation of this principle by the government of the German Third Reich. The Vienna Convention on the law of treaties includes art. 26 headlined *Pacta sunt servanda*. In turn, art. 27 determines that a party to a treaty may not quote provisions of its domestic laws to justify its failure to adhere to an international treaty.

J.B. WHITTON, "The Sanctity of Treaties" *(Pacta Sunt Servanda)*, in: *International Conciliation*, No. 313,

New York, Oct., 1935, pp. 395–430; J.L. KUNZ, "The Meaning and the range of the norm *Pacta sunt servanda*", in: *American Journal of International Law*, No. 39, 1945; B.G. PAPACOSTAS, "Le principe *Pacta sunt servanda* et l'ONU", in: *Revue Hellenique de Droit International*, No. 6, 1953; H. WEHBERG, "*Pacta sunt servanda*", in: *American Journal of International Law*, No. 53, 1959; G. DELCOIGNE, CH.ROSSI, B. VEEBENDAAL, "Arms Control Treaties: Review and Revision", in: *IAEA Bulletin*, September 1984; R.L. BLEDSOE, B.A. BOCZEK, *The International Law Dictionary*, Oxford, 1987.

PACTA TERTIIS NEC NOCENT, NEC PROSUNT. *Latin* = "agreements should neither harm nor serve third states." An international term for a rule of international law prohibiting the conclusion of bilateral or multilateral agreements to the detriment or benefit of third states without these states' knowledge and willing acceptance.

R.L. BLEDSOE, B.A. BOCZEK, *The International Law Dictionary*, Oxford, 1987.

PACT OF FOUR, 1933. The Agreement of Co-operation signed on July 15, 1933 in Rome on the initiative of B. Mussolini by France, Germany, Great Britain and Italy. The Pact resolved that the signatories "would seek agreement of all matters which concerned them " (art. 1), and especially on matters contained in arts. 10, 16 and 19 of the LN Covenant (art. 2), on matters discussed by the disarmament conferences (art. 3) and on economic matters. Subject of negotiation for 10 years; due to the negative attitude toward the Pact by the states of the Little Entente and the Polish government and its negative appraisal by French public opinion and parliament, it was not ratified by France and never entered into force. The main assumptions of the Pact of Four were reflected in the ▷ Munich Agreement of 1938.

G.F. DE MARTENS, *Nouveau Recueil Général*, 3S. Vol. 28, p. 4.

PACT OF SAN JOSÉ, COSTA RICA, 1969. The ▷ Human Rights American Convention signed at the Inter-American Specialized Conference on Human Rights on Nov. 7–22, 1969 in San José, by the governments of Chile, Colombia, Costa Rica, Ecuador, Guatemala, Honduras, Nicaragua, Panama, Paraguay, El Salvador, Uruguay and Venezuela.

KEESING's *Contemporary Archive*, 1969.

PACT OF THREE, 1940. The war alliance of Germany, Japan and Italy concluded on Sept. 20, 1940 in Berlin for 10 years as a supplement to the ▷ Steel Pact, 1939; it provided the definitive form for the military alliance of Axis countries. The Pact was joined gradually by: Hungary (Nov. 20, 1940), Romania (Nov. 23, 1940), Slovakia (Nov. 24, 1940), Bulgaria (Mar. 1, 1941), Yugoslavia (Mar. 25, 1941 – her accession was annulled after the coup of Mar. 27, 1941), Croatia (June 15, 1941). On Dec. 11, 1941 Germany, Japan and Italy signed an additional agreement in Berlin to declare a state of war against the USA and Great Britain "by all available means of force until the victorious end" (art. 1) and not to conclude separate truce or peace agreements (art. 2), the latter clause was violated by Italy on Sept. 3, 1943, and by Germany on May 8, 1945. The Treaty was appended with a military convention of Jan. 18, 1942 establishing the border of operational theaters at the longitude of the Indian Ocean.

Reichsgesetzblatt 1940, No. 41; KEESING's *Archiv der Gegenwart*, 1940 and 1941.

PACTUM DE CONTRAHENDO. A Latin term in international law to indicate initial agreement

preparing the way for international treaties; it lays down the main principle of a future treaty, a binding international pledge.

PAIN. A subject of international research. Organizations reg. with the UIA:

International Association against Painful Experiments on Animals, f. 1969, London. Consultative status with ECOSOC. Publ.: *Information*.
International Association for the Study of Pain, f. 1975, London.
Nordic Society Against Painful Experiments on Animals, f. 1882, Stockholm.

Yearbook of International Organizations.

PAKHTUNISTAN. The territory on the Pakistan border with Afghanistan separated from Afghanistan 1893 by the ▷ Durand Line. In 1949 Afghanistan demanded the creation of an independent Pakhtunistan, also called Pathan State, which initiated a long series of international disputes between Afghanistan and Pakistan and the suspension of diplomatic relations 1961, resumed 1963.

PAKISTAN. Member of the UN. Islamic Republic of Pakistan. A State in South Asia bordering on Afghanistan, USSR, China, India. Area: 803,943 sq. km. Pop. 1982 est.: 87,125,000 (1972 census: 64,979,732). Capital: Islamabad with 201,000 inhabitants 1981. GNP per capita 1980: US $300. Official language: Urdu and English. Currency: one Pakistani Rupee = 100 paisa. National Day: Aug. 14, Independence Day, 1947.

Member of the UN since Sept. 30, 1947 and all its specialized agencies. Former member of CENTO and SEATO; member of the Colombo Plan. On Jan. 30, 1972 Pakistan withdrew from the Commonwealth. A signatory of a Commercial Co-operation Agreement with the EEC, 1976.

International relations: until Aug., 1947 part of India; on Aug. 15, 1947 Great Britain granted independence to western and eastern Islamic provinces of India divided by the present territory of India. This provoked war between West Pakistan (presently Pakistan) and India in Oct., 1947 over ▷ Kashmir, and in 1948 riots in East Pakistan (presently Bangladesh) sent a wave of refugees to India. In 1949 conflicts between Pakistan and India were examined by the UN. Renewed riots in East Pakistan in 1950: Apr. 2–18 summit meeting of heads of state of East Pakistan and India in Delhi concluded an agreement on East Pakistan; the Kashmir issue was further negotiated in 1951. Mutual defense assistance agreement signed with the USA in Karachi on May 19, 1954. In 1955 Pakistan joined CENTO and in 1956 lodged a complaint against India over Kashmir at the UN Security Council. In Sept., 1960 agreement concluded with India on territorial waters of the ▷ Indus. On May 3, 1962 China signed a treaty with West Pakistan on delimitation of the frontier between Kashmir and Sinkiang, which was protested by Nepal. Treaty of Friendship and Co-operation with China signed on Mar. 2, 1963. In Apr. 1965 Indian-Pakistani fighting in Rann of Kutch Desert. In Jan., 1966 ▷ Tashkent Declaration. In Mar., 1969 state of emergency in East Pakistan and growing crisis in relations between West and East Pakistan. In Mar., 1971 repression by central government caused proclamation of the People's Republic of ▷ Bangladesh. Concurrently, an armed conflict broke out with India, which concluded with an Indian-Pakistani agreement signed in Simla on July 3, 1972 by Indira Ghandi and Ali Bhutto. In its earlier conflict with India and Bangladesh, West Pakistan received the full support of China on Feb. 2, 1972, published in joint Sino-Pakistani communiqué referring to a meeting in Peking between Ali Bhutto and Chou

En-lai. In 1973 separatist demonstrations in north-west border provinces of Pushtunistan and Baluchistan. On July 5, 1977 the Chief of the Army Staff, Gen. M. Zia-ul-Haq, proclaimed martial law and became President. The former Prime Minister Ali Bhutto was hanged on Apr. 4, 1979.

In the first years of 1980s the continuing flow of Afghan refugees were a common problem of Pakistan and the UNHCR (over 2,500,000 persons until mid 1984). Following the death of Gen. Zia-ul-Hag in an airplan accident, Benazir Bhutto, daughter of Ali Bhutto, became on Dec. 3, 1988, the first woman Prime Minister of an Islamic state. See also ▷ World Heritage UNESCO List.

A. NUSHTAG. *The UN and Pakistan*, Karachi, 1955; D.N. WILBER, *Pakistan: Its People, its Society, its Culture*, New Haven, 1955; K.S. HASAN, *Pakistan and the UN*, New York, 1961; A. TAYEEB, *Pakistan: A Political Geography*, New York, 1966; K.B. SAYEED, *The Political System of Pakistan*, Boston, 1967; K.B. SAYEED, *Pakistan: The Formative Phase. 1857–1948*, 4 Vols., New Haven, 1968; W.N. MOSKALENKO, *Problemy sovremennogo Pakistanu*, Moscow, 1970; J. MINHAS, *Analysis of Banking Practices and Policies in Pakistan*, Karachi, 1973; A. HUSSEIN, *China and Pakistan*, Amherst, 1975; G.W. CHOUDHUSY, *The Last Days of United Pakistan*, Bloomington, 1975; S.J. BURKI, *Pakistan under Bhutto*, London, 1980; *The Europa Year Book 1984. A World Survey*, Vol. II, pp. 2192–2215, London, 1984; O. NOMAN, *The Political Economy of Pakistan*, London, 1988.

PAKISTAN INSTITUTE OF INTERNATIONAL AFFAIRS.
The institute was f. 1947 in Karachi, to study international affairs and to promote the scientific study of international politics, economics and jurisprudence. Publ.: *Pakistan Horizons* (quarterly).

PALAIS DES NATIONS. ▷ League of Nations Geneva HQ.

PALAIS DE WILSON. ▷ League of Nations.

PALAPA. ▷ Indonesia.

PALAU OR BELAU.
The Republic of Palau, self-governing Micronesian group of 200 islands in a chain about 600 km long, lying south of Guam; until 1986 one of the Trust Territories of the Pacific Islands was a United Nations Trusteeship administered by the USA. Area: 3057 kq km. Pop. 1980 census: 12,177; in 1987 est. 14,000. The capital is Koror on Koror Island. Languages: Palauan and English. The UN Trusteeship Council terminated the UN trusteeship over what had been the world's last trusteeship territory on Sept. 30, 1986 (France, the UK, the USA voted in favor, the USSR against) noting that the people of Belau had freely exercised their right to self determination in three plebiscites: 1983, 1984, 1986. The Republic of Palau has a free association status with the USA.

KEESING's *Record of World Events*, Mar. 1987; *World Almanac and Book of Facts*, New York 1988; *The Europa Yearbook 1988. A World Survey*, Vol. II, London, 1988.

PALAZZO CHIGI.
The Government Palace in Rome; adopted international term identifying Palazzo Chigi with Italian policy. ▷ Downing Street, ▷ Elysée, ▷ Kremlin, ▷ White House.

PALEOGRAPHY.
Organization reg. with the UIA:

International Committee of Paleography, f. 1986, Vaticano.

Yearbook of International Organizations, 1986/87; The Europa Yearbook 1988. A World Survey, Vol. I, London, 1988.

PALEONTOLOGY.
Subject of international co-operation. Organizations reg. with the UIA:

International Association of Human Paleontology, f. 1985, Paris, France.
International Paleontological Association, f. 1968, Washinton DC, USA. Publ.: *World Directory of Paleontologists Lethaia* (journal).

Yearbook of International Organizations, 1986/87; The Europa Yearbook 1988. A World Survey, Vol. I, London, 1988.

PALESTINE.
An historical land on the eastern Mediterranean Sea, also called The Holy Land by the Christians. Following the dissolution of the Ottoman Empire after World War I, it became one of five League of Nations mandates, entrusted to France (Syria and Lebanon) and Great Britain (Iraq, Jordan and Palestine) in accordance with the decision of a conference in Apr., 1920 in San Remo. The mandate statute was ratified by the LN in 1922; by 1944 all of these states had received independence with the exception of Palestine, whose independence was delayed because of a promise made to the World Zionist movement by the Prime Minister of Great Britain, A.J. Balfour, on Nov. 2, 1917 that a "homeland of the Jewish nation" would be re-established in Palestine, as well as by the mission entrusted to Great Britain by the LN in 1925 to establish conditions for Jewish settlement in Palestine. According to official British figures, in the year of the announcement of the ▷ Balfour Declaration, 1917, the Jewish population in Palestine amounted to 57,000, i.e. 3% of the total population. In 1919 the Jewish Agency initiated the organized immigration of Jews from the entire world to Palestine; in 1936, when the number of Jews had passed 300,000, the first armed Arab uprising took place. In 1939 the population ratio was: 900,000 Arabs, 400,000 Jews, 100,000 Christians; in 1947 – 1,608,000 Jews, 1,159,000 Arabs, 145,000 Christians. On Mar. 22, 1945 the Arab states formed the Arab League. In Jan., 1947 the London Arab–Jewish Conference called by Great Britain reached no agreement on the fate of Palestine. As a result, on a motion of Great Britain of Apr. 2, 1947 a Special Session of the UN General Assembly was convened at Flushing Meadow, Apr. 28–May 15, 1947, which sent a Special Commission on a three-month fact-finding mission to Palestine. In Sept., 1947 seven of its members (Canada, Czechoslovakia, Guatemala, the Netherlands, Peru, Sweden and Uruguay) expressed themselves in favor of dividing Palestine into two states (Arab and Jewish) and detaching ▷ Jerusalem as an independent unit; three members suggested the formation of a federal state made up of an Arab country and a Jewish country with a common capital in Jerusalem; one of the members (Australia) did not submit an opinion. On Nov. 29, 1947 the UN General Assembly, Res. 181/II, resolved to divide Palestine into two independent states: an Arab state with an area of 11,000 sq. km and a Jewish state with an area of 14,000 sq. km, with Jerusalem as an international city under the UN authority. The Res. 181/II was passed by 33 votes in favour, 10 abstentions and 14 against (Afghanistan, Cuba, Egypt, Greece, India, Iran, Iraq, Lebanon, Pakistan, Siam, Saudi Arabia, Syria, Turkey and Yemen, among which Egypt, Iran, Lebanon, Pakistan, Saudi Arabia and Syria announced that they would not recognize the division of Palestine). The *Everyman's United Nations. A Complete Handbook of the Activities and Evolution of the United Nations During its First Twenty Years, 1945–1965*, recorded the crucial years for the history of Palestine as follows:

"On May 14, 1948 the mandate of the United Kingdom over Palestine expired, and a Jewish state was proclaimed under the name of Israel. On the following day, the Arab states instituted armed action in Palestine. The security Council, on May 22, 1948 called on all governments and authorities to abstain from any hostile military action in Palestine, and a week later it requested the observance of a four-week truce. The truce became effective on June 11, 1948. On July 7, 1948 the Security Council urgently appealed to the interested parties to accept the prolongation of the truce for such period as might be decided on in consultation with the Mediator. The Provisional Government of Israel agreed to extend the truce, but the Arab states refused and hostilities broke out anew. On July 15, 1948 the Council, invoking Chapter VII of the Chapter, ordered all authorities and governments concerned to desist from further military action and to issue cease-fire orders. The Council's resolution declared that failure to comply with this order would be construed as a breach of the peace which would require immediate consideration of enforcement measures to be taken under the Charter. In response to an appeal from the Mediator, Count Bernadotte, the Council, on August 19, warned that both Arab and Jewish authorities would be held responsible for any violation of the truce. On September 17, 1948, Count Bernadotte and the Chief of the French observers, Colonel André Sérot, were shot and killed in the Israel-held sector of Jerusalem. In October 1948, large-scale fighting broke out in the Negev area and hostilities were renewed in November and December 1948. The Security Council, in resolutions adopted on October 19, November 4 and 16 and December 29, 1948, called upon the parties to order a cease-fire and to seek an agreement. Following negotiations with the Acting Mediator, Ralph J. Bunche, who succeeded Count Bernadotte, Egypt and Israel signed a General Armistice Agreement at Rhodes on February 24, 1949; Lebanon and Israel at Ras en Naqoura on March 23, 1949; the Hashemite Kingdom of Jordan (including former Transjordan) and Israel at Rhodes on April 3, 1949; and Syria and Israel at Manhanayim on July 20, 1949. The armistice agreements instituted Mixed Armistice Commissions to supervise the implementation of the agreements. Since 1949, the Security Council has been assisted in its consideration of a series of complaints relating to the Palestine question by the United Nations Truce Supervision Organization (UNTSO), an organ composed of international observers and headed by a Chief of Staff who supervises, as Chairman of the four Mixed Armistice Commissions, the implementation of the armistice agreements and also reports to the Security Council as the need arises. Since 1951, the Security Council has been seized of a series of disputes and controversies arising from the unsettled situation in the area and from complaints and protests presented to it by the parties concerning developments along the established Armistice Demarcation Lines and the various demilitarised zones. On December 11, 1948 by a Res. 194/III, the Assembly, following the suggestions in a report which Count Bernadotte had prepared before his death, adopted a resolution which, inter alia, provided for: (a) the establishment of a Conciliation Commission of three members (France, Turkey and the United States) to take steps to assist the parties concerned to achieve a final settlement of all questions; (b) the protection of the Holy Places in Jerusalem and free access to them through arrangements under United Nations supervision; and (c) further steps to be taken by the Security Council to ensure Jerusalem's demilitarization, and instructions to the Conciliation Commission to present detailed proposals for a permanent international regime and to facilitate the repatriation, resettlement and economic and social rehabilitation of the refugees and the payment of compensation".

The Prime Minister of Israel, D. Ben Gurion, made a statement on Nov. 7, 1966 which was repeated by the government of Israel in an official declaration of June 10, 1967:

"The armistice treaties of 1949 are no longer valid, and for this reason Israel cannnot recognize the former status quo."

In the period 1948–1984 the UN Conciliation Commission for Palestine, whose mandate has been renewed annually by the UN General Assembly co-operated fully with other UN bodies associated with the question of Palestine, and since 1975 with the Committee on the Exercise of the Inalienable

Rights of the Palestinian People, est. by the UN General Assembly Res. 3376/XXX on Nov. 10, 1975, by vote of 93 to 18 with 27 abstentions.
▷ West Bank. ▷Intifada.

The Institute for Palestine Studies, f. 1963, Beirut, with Georgetown Station in Washington DC. Publ.: *Journal of Palestine Studies* (quarterly in French, English and Spanish).

UN Social Committee on Palestine, Report to the General Assembly, New York, 1947; J. ROBINSON, *Palestine and the UN; Prelude to Solution*, Washington, DC, 1947; SUMNER WELLES, *We Need Not Fail*, Boston, 1948; F.Ch. SAKRAN, *Palestine Dilemma*, Washington, DC, 1948; B. JOSEPH, *British Rule in Palestine*, Washington, DC, 1949; L.L. LEONARD, "The UN and Palestine", in: *International Conciliation*, Oct., 1949, pp. 603–785; A.M. HYAMSON, *Palestine under the Mandate 1920–1948*, London, 1950; C. ROSNER, *La Fuerza de Emergencia de las NU*, México, DF, 1966; H. CATTAN, *Palestine. The Arabs and Israel. The Search for Justice*, London, 1969; S. KADI, *Basic Political Documents of the Armed Palestinian Resistance Movement*, Cairo, 1969; *Palestine. Le droit du peuple de Palestine à l'autodétermination à la lumière du droit international et de la Déclaration Universelle des Droits de L'Homme*, Le Caire, 1970; M. JANSEN, *The United States and the Palestinian People*, Beyrouth, 1970; E. BERGHEAND, *Les Palestiniens*, Paris, 1972; D. FORSYTHE, *UN Peace. The Conciliation Commission for Palestine*, Baltimore, 1973; H. CATTAN, *Palestine and International Law*, New York, 1973; Y.R. ALTAMENI, *Die Palastina Flüchtlinge und die Vereinten Nationen*, Wien, 1974; *The Origins and Evolution of the Palestine Problem. Part I: 1917–1947, Part II, 1947–1977*, UN New York, 1977; F. ANSPRENGER, *Juden und Araben in einem Land. Die politischen Beziehungen der beiden Völker im Mandatsgebiet Palästina und im Staat Israel*, München, 1978; *An International Law Analysis of the Major UN Resolutions concerning the Palestine Question*, UN, New York. 1979; E.W. SAID, *The Question of Palestine*, New York, 1980; *UN Chronicle*, January, 1981, p. 13; February, 1982, p. 24; June, 1982, p. 39; March 1984, p. 44; W.T. MALLISON, S.V. MALLISON, *The Palestine Problem in International Law and World Order*, Harlow, Essex, 1986; D.K. SHIPLER, *Arab and Jew: Wounded Spirits in a Promised Land*, New York, 1986; B. MORRIS, *The Birth of the Palestinian Refugee Problem, 1947–1949*, Cambridge, 1988; A. SHLAIM, *Collusion Across the Jordan: King Abdullah, the Zionist Movement and the Partition of Palestine*, New York, 1988; KEESING's *Record of World Events*, April 1988.

PALESTINE BRITISH MANDATE, 1922.
In Apr., 1920 the Supreme Allied Council decided that Great Britain would be the mandatory power for Palestine. After 2 years of negotiations the League of Nations Council approved the Mandate on July 24, 1922. The main points of the Mandate are as follows:

'... Whereas the Principal Allied Powers have also agreed that the Mandatory should be responsible for putting into effect the declaration originally made on Nov. 2, 1917, by the Government of His Britannic Majesty, and adopted by the said Powers, in favour of the establishment in Palestine of a national home for the Jewish people, it being clearly understood that nothing should be done which might prejudice the civil and religious rights of existing non-Jewish communities in Palestine, or the rights and political status enjoyed by Jews in any other country; and
Whereas recognition has thereby been given to the historical connection of the Jewish people with Palestine and to the grounds for reconstituting their national home in that country.
Art. 2. The Mandatory shall be responsible for placing the country under such political, administrative and economic conditions as will secure the establishment of the Jewish national home, as laid down in the preamble, and the development of self-governing institutions, and also for safeguarding the civil and religious rights of all the inhabitants of Palestine, irrespective of race and religion.
Art. 4. An appropriate Jewish agency shall be recognized as a public body for the purpose of advising and co-operating with the Administration of Palestine in such economic, social and other matters as may affect the establishment of the Jewish National home and the interests of the Jewish population in Palestine, and, subject always to the control of the Administration, to assist and take part in the development of the country. The Zionist organization, so long as its organization and constitution are in the opinion of the Mandatory appropriate, shall be recognized as such agency. It shall take steps in consultation with His Britannic Majesty's Government to secure the co-operation of all Jews who are willing to assist in the establishment of the Jewish national home.
Art. 6. The Administration of Palestine, while ensuring that the rights and position of other sections of the population are not prejudiced, shall facilitate Jewish immigration under suitable conditions and shall encourage, in co-operation with the Jewish agency referred to in article 4, close settlement by Jews on the land, including state lands and waste lands not required for public purposes."

Great Britain and Palestine, 1915–1945, London, 1946.

PALESTINE LIBERATION ORGANIZATION, PLO.
The PLO was founded in 1964, uniting in 1970 the organizations of Palestine resistance movement.
In the period 1950–70 several groups were formed in the states bordering on Israel propagating programs for the liberation of Palestine, but only five of them became important in the military and political sense: (1) al-Fatah, operating with armed groups of commandos since Jan. 1, 1965, since Feb., 1969 under the leadership of Yassir Arafat; (2) Popular Front for the Liberation of Palestine, operating militarily since Jan., 1967 under the leadership of G. Habash and professing program of struggle "for the liberation of Palestine and all the Arab countries from the yoke of imperialism and its instrument – Zionism"; (3) SAJKA (Arab abbreviation for Avant-garde of the Popular War of Liberation) which has operated since 1958 in association with the Syrian al-Baas party under the leadership of L. Mehsen; (4) the Palestine Liberation Organization was formed in 1970 as the result of an agreement between 10 different organizations of the resistance movement; its armed forces were called the Palestine Liberation Army; the chairman of the Executive Committee of the organization was the leader of al-Fatah, Yassir Arafat; and (5) the organization ▷ Black September.
An agreement was signed in Cairo on Sept. 27, 1970 between the King of Jordan, Hussein II, and the leader of the fedayeen (commandoes), Y. Arafat, on the withdrawal of Jordanian forces from Amman to their garrisons and the simultaneous withdrawal of the fedayeen from the capital to specified border regions. The supplementary Protocol signed Oct. 13, 1970 in Amman specifying the Cairo conditions was not published. In Apr., 1971 the fedayeen accused the King of violating the treaties. In July and Sept. King Hussein's troops massacred groups of fedayeen. This fact together with limitations on the operations of Palestine partisans in Syria and the impossibility of making raids through the Suez Canal resulted in a serious crisis in the Pan-Arab movement. Since then, Lebanon (on the basis of an agreement reached in Nov. 1969 in Cairo) became the main region in which the partisan movement could maintain its bases. In June, 1972 the southern part of Lebanon became the next objective of Israeli attacks. These attacks were renewed in Sept., 1972 in retaliation for the operation of Palestine guerillas of the Black September group against Israeli athletes during the Olympic Games in Munich and in Apr., 1973. In May, 1973 Lebanese-Palestine relations reached a crisis. In Mar., 1975 a civil war started in ▷ Lebanon which paralyzed the Palestine bases. The ideas advanced in Cairo concerning the creation of a government of Palestine, recognized by the states of the Arab League, were not implemented. The only organization which formally includes nearly all the Palestine political groupings is the Palestine National Council, created on June 13, 1968, whose sessions were held up to 1978 on an irregular basis in Cairo. In Sept., 1973 the Conference of Non-Aligned States recognized the PLO "as the sole legal representative of the Palestine people," following which the UN General Assembly, Res. 3236/XXIX of Nov. 22, 1974, confirmed the inalienable rights of the Palestine nation, stating that "the Palestine nation is the major party in the establishment of a just and lasting peace in the Near East" and requesting the UN Secretary-General to "establish contact with the Palestine Liberation Organization in all matters concerning the Palestine question." Since then, the PLO has a permanent office at the UN and in many states, which is a form of diplomatic recognition. In Nov., 1975 the UN General Assembly formed the UN Committee for the Enforcement of the Inalienable Rights of the Palestine Nation. On July 25, 1982, the leader of PLO, Y. Arafat affirmed the UN Resolution 318 and the right of Israel to be sovereign state but with equal right to sovereign Palestine.
In Aug., 1982 the PLO headquarters was removed from Beirut to Tunis and the PLO forces evacuated from Lebanon in Dec., 1983 and Jan., 1984 by Greek passenger ships under the UN flag with a French naval escort to Tunisia or to North Yemen via the Suez Canal. On this occasion on Dec. 22, 1983 Arafat visited in Cairo the President of Egypt, H. Mubarak.
In Nov. 1984 the Palestine National Council, PNC, session in Amman, Jordan, was boycotted by some anti-Arafat fractions. The PNC supported Y. Arafat's continued leadership of the PLO. The reunification of the PLO took place under Al-Fatah leader Yassir Arafat, during the 18th Session of the PNC, held in Algiers in April 1987.

S. KADI, *Basic Political Documents of the Armed Palestinian Resistance Movement*, Cairo, 1969; *An International Law Analysis of the Major UN Resolutions Concerning the Palestine Question*, UN, New York, 1979; *The Europa Year Book 1984. A World Survey*, Vol. II, pp. 1756–1757; K. KIRISCI, *The PLO and World Politics: A Study of the Mobilization of Support for the Palestinian Cause*, London, 1986; S. MISHAL, *The PLO Under Arafat*, New Haven, 1986; T. SZULC. *Suddenly an Audience for Arafat. Arafat's Trials at Tunis: Enemies Inside and Out* in: Los Angeles Times, February 12 and 19 1989.

PALESTINIAN NATIONAL CHARTER, 1968.
The Charter was adopted by the National Congress of the Palestine Liberation Organization held from July 1 to 17, 1968 in Cairo. The main points of the Charter are as follows:

"Art. 1. Palestine is the homeland of the Arab Palestinian People; it is an indivisible part of the Arab Palestinian People; it is an indivisible part of the Arab homeland, and the Palestinian people are an integral part of the Arab Nation.
Art. 2. Palestine with the boundaries it had during the British mandate, is an indivisible unit.
Art. 3. The Palestinian Arab people possesses the legal right to their homeland.
Art. 4. The Palestinian identity is ... transmitted from parents to children.
Art. 5. The Palestinians are those Arab nationals who, until 1947, normally resided in Palestine regardless of whether they were evicted from it or have stayed there. Anyone born, after that date, of a Palestinian father – whether inside Palestine or outside it – is also Palestinian.
Art. 6. The Jews who had normally resided in Palestine until the beginning of the Zionist invasion will be considered Palestinians.
Art. 7. That there is a Palestinian community and that it has material, spiritual and historical connection with Palestine are indisputable facts.

P

Art. 8. The phase in their history ... is that of national struggle for the liberation of Palestine.
Art. 9. Armed struggle is the only way to liberate Palestine.
Art. 10. Commando action constitutes the nucleus of the Palestinian popular liberation War.
Art. 11. The Palestinians will have three motives: national unity, national mobilization and liberation."

S. KADI, *Basic Political Documents*, Cairo, 1969.

PALESTINIAN REFUGEES. One of the greatest groups of ▷ Refugees registered by the ▷ UNHCR, subject of the assistance of the UN Relief and Works Agency for Palestine Refugees in the Near East. The GA Res. 43/57 A, B, C, D, F, G, H, I, J of Dec. 6, 1988 noted with deep regret that repatriation of compensation of the refugees ... "has not been efected" (A), was "deeply concerned at the critical financial situation of the Agency" (B), "alarmed by the Israeli policy of 'demolishing shelters' occupied by refugee families" (E) and urged the Secretary General to continue efforts "in support of the upholding of the safety and security and the legal and human rights of the Palestinian refugees in all the territories under Israeli occupation in 1967 and thereafter" (I).

B. MORRIS, *The Birth of the Palestinian Refugee Problem 1947–1949*, Cambridge, 1988; *UN Resolutions and Decisions adopted by the General Assembly during the First Part of its Forty-Third Session, From 20 September to 22 December 1988*, New York, 1989, pp. 224–236.

PALESTINIAN UPRISING 1987 ▷ Intifada.

PALK STRAIT. ▷ India.

PALLETS. Lifting-transport equipment, on the surface of which a certain quantity of goods can be placed, which form a loading unit; it is used in transporting goods for mechanical loading and unloading, or for storage; subject of the European Convention on Customs Treatment of Pallets Used in International Transport, signed on Dec. 9, 1960 in Geneva, which allows duty-free entry of Pallets provided they are re-exported.

PALMAS OR MIANGAS ISLAND. An Indonesian island on the Pacific Ocean, subject of a dispute between the United States and the Netherlands, 1906–28, decided by the International Court of Arbitration on Apr. 4, 1928 against the American claims.

Ph.C. JESSUP, "The Palmas Island Arbitration," in: *American Journal of International Law*, No. 22, 1928; P. DE VISCHER, "L'arbitrage de l'ile Palmas (Miangas)", in: *Revue de droit international et de legislation comparée*, No. 56, 1929.

PALME CORRIDOR, 1982. One of the ▷ Denuclearized Zones discussed in the 1980's. An international term for a nuclear weapon free corridor of 150 kms on each side of the dividing line between the NATO and Warsaw Pact, formulated by the Independent Commission on Disarmament and Security Issues (Olof Palme Commission) during the UN Special Session on Disarmament, 1982.

UN Chronicle, June and September, 1982.

PALME OLOF COMMISSION. Common name in the 1980's for the Independent Commission for Disarmament and Security established by the Prime Minister of Sweden, Olof Palme (1915–1986), with hqs. in Stockholm.

PALM PRODUCTS. A subject of international cooperation. In the EEC system the ▷ Stabex included palm products of the ACP countries.

PALMYRA. A cultural site of Syria, included in the ▷ World Heritage UNESCO List. Palmyra was an artistic center from the 1st to the 3rd centuries and it contains the remains of colonnades, the walls of sanctuaries, porticoes and the terraces of theaters. Around the city are immense burial grounds.

UNESCO. *A Legacy for All*, Paris, 1984.

PALOMARES. A city on the southwest coast of Spain on the Mediterranean Sea; on Jan. 17, 1966 near Palomares an American military plane crashed, and four atomic bombs were lost with a power 300 times greater than the bombs dropped on Hiroshima and Nagasaki; one of the bombs was retrieved Apr. 7, 1966 after a search of 81 days by ships of the US 6th Fleet. This affair caused a debate in the UN on the danger of flights with nuclear bombs.

T. SZULC, *The Bombs of Palomares*, New York, 1967.

PALOMAR OBSERVATORY ▷ Observatories.

PAL-SECAM ▷ Television.

PANA. Pan-African Press Agency, est. 1982, under aegis of UNESCO.

PAN-AFRICAN CONFERENCE, 1958. A conference convened on the initiative of Ghana, preceded by an introductory meeting in Accra on Apr. 15, 1958 of the governments of Egypt, Ethiopia, Ghana, Liberia, Libya, Morocco, Sudan and Tunisia, which invited all of the governments of the independent states of Africa, except South Africa, as well as all of the liberation committees of African territories dependent on colonial powers. The Conference was held in Accra Dec. 7–13, 1958; it created a permanent Secretariat with the task of supporting the main idea of that time ▷ Pan-Africanism, i.e. liberating all of Africa from colonialism. The Conference made an appeal to the UN, stating that colonialism is contrary to the UN Charter and demanding the restoration of full sovereign rights to all of the peoples of Africa. In the Pan-African Conference Declaration the liberation of all of Africa within the lifetime of the present generation was forecast.

PAN-AFRICAN CONGRESS, 1945. The Fifth Pan-African Congress held in Dec., 1945 in Manchester adopted a Declaration to Colonial Powers and a Declaration to the Colonial Peoples. The texts are as follows:

"Declaration to Colonial Powers
The delegates believe in peace. How could it be otherwise, when for centuries the African peoples have been the victims of violence and slavery? Yet if the Western world is still determined to rule mankind by force, then Africans, as a last resort, may have to appeal to force in the effort to achieve freedom, even if force destroys them and the world.
We are determined to be free. We want education. We want the right to earn a decent living; the right to express our thoughts and emotions, to adopt and create forms of beauty.
We demand for Black Africa autonomy and independence, so far and no further than it is possible in this One World for groups and people to rule themselves subject to inevitable world unity and federation.
We are not ashamed to have been an age-long patient people. We continue willingly to sacrifice and strive. But we are unwilling to starve any longer while doing the world's drudgery, in order to support by our poverty and ignorance a false aristocracy and a discarded imperialism.
We condemn the monopoly of capital and the rule of private wealth and industry for private profit alone. We welcome economic democracy as the only real democracy.

Therefore, we shall complain, appeal and arraign. We will make the world listen to the facts of our condition. We will fight in every way we can for freedom, democracy and social betterment."
"Declaration to the Colonial Peoples
We affirm the right of all colonial peoples to control their own destiny. All colonies must be free from foreign imperialist control, whether political or economic.
The peoples of the colonies must have the right to elect their own governments, without restrictions from foreign powers. We say to the peoples of the colonies that they must fight for these ends by all means at their disposal.
The object of imperialist powers is to exploit. By granting the right to colonial peoples to govern themselves that object is defeated. Therefore, the struggle for political power by colonial and subject peoples is the first step towards, and the necessary prerequisite to, complete social, economic and political emancipation. The Fifth Pan-African Congress therefore calls on the workers and farmers of the Colonies to organize effectively. Colonial workers must be in the front of the battle against imperialism. Your weapons – the strike and the boycott – are invincible.
We also call upon the intellectuals and professional classes of the colonies to awaken to their responsibilities. By fighting for trade union rights, the right to form co-operatives, freedom of the press, assembly, demonstration and strike, freedom to print and read the literature which is necessary for the education of the masses, you will be using the only means by which your liberties will be won and maintained. Today there is only one road to effective action – the organization of the masses. And in that organization the educated colonials must join. Colonial and subject peoples of the World, Unite!"

G. PADMORE, *Panafricanism or Communism?* Dobson, 1956, pp. 170–172.

PAN-AFRICAN INSTITUTE FOR DEVELOPMENT, f. 1964, Douala, Cameroon; to train rural development officers from Africa. Four regional institutes for Central Africa, the Sahel, West Africa, and the Eastern and Western English Speaking African countries.

The Europa Yearbook 1988. A World Survey, Vol. I, London 1988.

PAN-AFRICANISM. An international term for a political trend aiming at uniting the African nations, originated after World War I under the influence of the Pan-European movement, among Arab and Negro students in the universities of Great Britain, Belgium, France, Italy, without defined political purposes, which was reflected in the cultural-philosophical programs of four Pan-African Congresses held in 1928–39 in Great Britain. After World War II the Fifth ▷ Pan-African Congress 1945 in Manchester concentrated on equality of races, and thus equality of rights. In the years which followed, Pan-Africanism began to change into an anti-colonial and anti-imperialist movement; in 1958 the Pan-African Movement for Liberation of Central and East Africa was established, which in 1962 was extended to South Africa under the name Pan-African Freedom Movement of East, Central and Southern Africa. The Seventh Pan-African Congress held in Dar-es-Salaam in June, 1974, declared itself in favor of socialist development for Africa.

C.E. WELCH, *Dream of Unity: Pan-Africanism and Political Unification in West Africa*, Ithaca, 1946; C. LEGUM, *Panafricanism. A Short Political Guide*, New York, 1962; R. COX, *Panafricanism in Practice*, London, 1965; J.S. NYS Jr., *Panafricanism and East African Integration*, Nairobi, 1966; R.H. GREEN, A. SIDMAN, *Unity or Poverty? The Economics of Pan-Africanism*, Baltimore, 1968; CONTERAS GRANGUILHOME, *El Panafricanismo, Evolución y perspectivas*, Mexico, DF, 1971; A. AYALA, *Panafricanism*, London, 1973.

PAN-AFRICAN MILITARY FORCE. A multinational force, proposed May, 1978 by President of France Giscard d'Estaing at a conference of chiefs of state of French Africa in Paris during the time of the intervention of the French Foreign Legion – at the request of the President Mobutu of Zaïre – in the Zaïre civil war in the province of Shaba.

KEESING'S Contemporary Archive, 1978.

PAN-AFRICAN NEWS AGENCY. ▷ Communication.

PAN-AFRICAN PEOPLE'S CONFERENCES, 1958–65. The Pan-African meetings called on the initiative of the leader of Ghana Kwame Nkrumah with the aim of streamlining the process of decolonization.

The First People's Conference of Africa was held on Dec. 7–13, 1958 in Accra, attended by representatives of 29 African states, both independent and dependent, adopted a message to the UN demanding complete liquidation of colonialism in Africa and the world at large as contradictory to the UN Charter; a declaration protesting colonial lawlessness in Africa exercised by Great Britain, France, Portugal, and a number of other resolutions; Permanent Executive Committee and Secretariat were formed.

The Second Conference was held from Jan. 26–31, 1960 in Tunis with the motto "Freedom and Unity of Africa," attended by representatives of 32 African states and 21 observers from other continents; several recommendations were adopted, among others, on the setting up of an independent African Trade Unions Centre.

The Third Conference of African Peoples, was held from Mar. 25–30, 1961 in Cairo, attended by representatives of 35 African states and 21 observers from other continents. The Conference honored Patrice Lumumba, the assassinated leader of the People's Republic of the Congo (now Zaïre) with the title of "African hero"; adopted a number of anti-imperialist resolutions and organizational recommendations for the Pan-African movement.

The Pan-African Conference of the Liberation Movement of East, Central and South Africa, was held from Feb. 2–10, 1962 in Addis Ababa.

The Conference of African Liberation Groups on Subjugated Territories was held from Oct. 21–26, 1965 in Accra.

KEESING's *Contemporary Archives*, 1958–1965.

PAN-AFRICENDERDOM. The official name of the white community of Dutch origin living in the Republic of South Africa.

PANAMA. Member of the UN. Republic of Panama. A state occupying the Isthmus of Panama, which connects Central and South America, bordering with Costa Rica and Colombia; the Panama Canal Zone bisects the country. Area: 77,082 sq. km. Pop. 1987 est.: 2,274,448. Capital: Panama City with 338,683 inhabitants, 1980. GNP per capita 1987: US $2240. Official language: Spanish. Currency: one balboa = 100 centimos. National Day: Nov. 3, Independence Day, 1903.

Member of the UN since Oct. 24, 1945 and of all UN specialized agencies, with the exception of the GATT. Member of the OAS.

International relations: a military coup inspired by the USA led to the separation of Panama province from Colombia and the declaration of independence on Nov. 3, 1903. The USA recognized the de facto government of the Panama Republic on Nov. 18, 1903 by the ▷ Hay-Varilla Treaty; Colombia in 1914. The Colombia–USA Panama agreement was ratified 1921 and on May 8, 1921 diplomatic relations between Colombia and Panama established. For the treaties relating to the relations between Panama and the USA ▷ Panama Canal. Member of the LN 1919–39.

Panama is active member of the ▷ Contadora Group. See also ▷ *World Heritage UNESCO List.* Following the appointments of General Manuel Noriega as President on Dec. 15, 1989, his declaration of war on the United States and the killing of an American soldier, the US, which had since 1986 accused Noriega of various drug-related crimes, invaded Panama on Dec. 20, 1989. Guillermo Endava, whose de facto election as President on May 7, 1989 was rendered void by Noriega's rigging of votes was installed in office. General Noriega gave himself up to US forces and is to stand trial. Casualties of the invasion are estimated at c. 700 dead. The invasion was condemned by GA Res. 240/XLIV.

I.A. SUTO, *An Introduction to Panamania Bibliography*, Panama, 1946; N. GARAY, *Panamá en la Liga de Naciones*, México, DF, 1949; E. CASTILLERO, *Panamá y los Estados Unidos Apendica con textos de Tratados*, Panamá, 1964; E. CASTILLERO, *Historia de Panamá*, Panamá, 1965; D. HOWARTH, *The Golden Isthmus*, London, 1968; *Panamá y Su Sistema Bancario*, Panama, 1975; E. LONGSTAFF, *Panama Bibliography*, Oxford, 1982; S.C. ROPP, *Panamerican Politics*, New York, 1982; *The Europa Year Book 1984. A World Survey*, Vol. II, pp. 2214–2227, London, 1984; KEESING's *Record of World Events*, April 1988; KEESING's *Record of World Events*, May, December 1989.

PANAMA CANAL. The first and up to now the only artificial canal between the Atlantic and Pacific Oceans, traversing the Isthmus of Panama in the territory of the former province of Colombia, from 1903 the Republic of Panama. It was designed by F. de Lesseps 1881–99 and built by the USA 1904–14. The canal became the subject of a conflict between Colombia and the USA, 1900–21. The Panama Canal crosses the so-called Canal Zone with an area of 1432 sq. km and more than 40,000 inhabitants; it was subject to the jurisdiction of the USA on the basis of treaties of Nov. 18, 1903, Mar. 2, 1936, Jan. 25, 1955; which were revised by the treaty of Sept. 7, 1977. The canal was opened to ship traffic on July 15, 1914, but was formally opened only after World War I on July 12, 1920. As its share in the profits from canal traffic Panama received 250,000 dollars per year from the USA and from 1934 – 430,000 dollars. In 1942 the USA and Panama signed a convention on compensation for the use of the services of the Republic of Panama by the American units stationed in the Canal Zone. In 1950 both states negotiated a treaty on free transit roads through the Zone linking both parts of Panama. In 1955 the government of the USA raised the annual compensation from 430,000 to 1.9 million dollars and pledged itself to construct a 20-million-dollar bridge over the canal linking the capital of Panama with the northern part of the country. The nationalization of the Suez Canal in 1956 led to the demand for the nationalization of the Panama Canal by various social groupings. The first massive demonstration took place in Nov, 1959. In June, 1964 bloody encounters took place between Panamanian and American students, who tore down the Panamanian flag, which caused a temporary break in diplomatic relations and a debate on the complaint of Panama in the UN Security Council. In Sept. 1965 the USA and Panama in a joint declaration announced the elaboration of a new treaty. Without waiting for the outcome of the negotiations, Panama in the UN General Assembly proclaimed the assumption of sovereign rights over the Canal Zone, which, nevertheless, changed nothing in the zone, which remained under the administration of the US military. The negotiations in Washington were broken off in Sept., 1968 in protest against the position of the USA, which only agreed to the participation of four representatives of Panama in a Council composed of nine members and did not renounce the validity of the previous treaties to 1999. Negotiations were renewed on June 18, 1971, and on Apr. 17, 1972 the Delegation of Panama at the Third session of UNCTAD in Santiago de Chile called on the government of the USA to withdraw from the canal zone and completely liquidate its military bases so that the Panama Canal "would serve the goals of international socio-economic development, and not any other interests." After the suspension of Panamanian–American negotiations in Dec., 1972, a travelling session of the UN Security Council took place in Panama from Mar. 15–21, 1973, but despite discussing the USA–Panama disagreement the situation remained unchanged. In Jan., 1974 negotiations with the USA on the Panama Canal were resumed, which led to the signing on Feb. 7, 1974 of an essential agreement on the abandonment by the USA of the right to "perpetual leasehold," the gradual transfer of jurisdiction over the Panama Canal to the government of Panama and the raising of rent payments. The American–Panamanian Declaration of Principles was signed Feb. 7, 1974, which served the negotiators of a completely new treaty, framed in eight points of a pactum de contrahendo. See also ▷ Panama Declaration, 1975. After 3 more years of negotiations two agreements on the future status of the Panama Canal were formulated and signed on Sept. 7, 1977 in Washington. On Oct. 1, 1979 the Canal Zone was incorporated into Panama.

Treaty I establishes the sequence of the progressive transfer of the Canal to the government of Panama by Dec. 31, 1999. The Canal and Canal Zone will be governed by a new organization made up of four US and four Panamanian citizens. Until 1990 it will be chaired by a US citizen, then by a Panamanian. The income of Panama from the Canal will grow to 40–50 million dollars annually plus additional bonuses and credits. The USA with Panama will consider the construction of a second canal at sea level. Treaty I will expire Dec. 31, 1999 and simultaneously the presence of US military forces in the Canal Zone will come to an end on the basis of four agreements:

(1) the USA and Panama will guarantee the "continual neutrality" for ships of all states;
(2) the USA will have the "perpetual right" to defend the neutrality of the Canal;
(3) military forces of the USA will remain in the Canal Zone until Dec. 31, 1999;
(4) the government of Panama will assist the armed forces of the USA in the defence of the Canal.

On Dec. 20, 1989, as a result of the American invasion of Panama, the canal was, for the first time in its seventy-year history closed to shipping. Traffic was fully resumed on Dec. 27. Also on Dec. 20, US President G. Bush declared that the invasion would not affect the deadline for handing over the Canal to Panama.

L.I. OPPENHEIM, *Panama Canal Conflict*, Cambridge, 1913; A. ROA, *El Canal de Panamá y el Derecho Internacional*, La Habana, 1926; A. REBOLLEDO, *El Canal de Panamá*, Cali, 1957, *El Canal de Panamá 1914–1964*, Panamá, 1964; W. LA FEBER, *The Panama Canal. The Crisis in Historical Perspective*, New York, 1978; K. LENORTE, *Debate on the Panama Canal Treaties. A Compendium of Major Statements, Documents, Second Votes and Relevant Events*, Washington, DC, 1979; KEESING's *Record of World Events*, December 1989.

PANAMA DECLARATION, 1939. ▷ Security Zone of the Western Hemisphere.

P

PANAMA DECLARATION, 1975. A solidarity declaration of the Heads of States of Colombia: A. Lopez Michelsen, Costa Rica: D. Odubes and Venezuela: C.A. Perez with the Head of Government of Panama: General O. Torijos on his position on the future of Panama Canal, negotiated in that time by Panama with the USA.

"Declaración de Panamá", in: *Venezuela Ahora*, No. 41, 1975; and full Spanish text in: E.J. OSMAŃCZYK, *Encyclopedia Mundial de Relaciones Internacionales y Naciones Unidas*, Madrid, Mexico, DF, 1975, pp. 416–417.

PANAMAX. An international navigation term; a merchant ship meeting size requirements as far as sailing conditions through the Panama Canal are concerned.

PAN-AMAZONIC HIGHWAY. The Organization of American States, ▷ OAS, created in 1965 a Pan-Amazonic Highway Subcommittee for the construction of a highway connecting the Pacific Ocean and the Amazon basin and to take advantage of the river transportation throughout the Amazon River and its tributaries.

The Europa Year Book 1984. A World Survey, Vol. I, p. 192, London, 1984.

PAN-AMERICAN COMMERCIAL CONFERENCE, 1935. A Conference convoked by the Pan-American Union in June, 1935 at Buenos Aires; adopted a Convention for the Creation of Pan-American Commercial Committees, signed on June 19, 1935 by representatives of 21 American Republics, but ratified only by the Dominican Republic and Uruguay.

Inter-American Treaties and Conventions, Washington, DC, 1971, p. 67.

PAN-AMERICAN DAY. The Pan-American Day is celebrated on Apr. 14 in the OAS member states to commemorate the First International Conference of American States, Apr. 14, 1890, in Washington, DC. Another Pan-American Day is ▷ Columbus Day.

PAN-AMERICAN DEVELOPMENT FOUNDATION. The Inter-American institution, f. 1962 in Washington with the task of financing the co-operation of US scientific institutions with those of Latin America. Reg. with the UIA: Publ.: *Newsletter*.

The Europa Yearbook 1988. A World Survey. Vol. I, London 1988.

PAN-AMERICAN GAMES. The games were initiated in Aug., 1940 by the Pan-American Congress at Buenos Aires when it was obvious that the 1940 Olympic London Games would not be held, organized by the National Olympic committees of the American Republics which formed the Pan-American Games Organization. The first games were scheduled for Oct., 1942, the 450th anniversary of Columbus' discovery of America, in the Argentinian capital, but were postponed until Feb. 25–Mar. 9, 1951. The second Pan-American Games were held Mar. 12–26, 1955 in Mexico City, the third Aug. 27–Sept. 7, 1959 in Chicago, the fourth in Sao Paulo Apr. 20–May 5, 1963, the fifth in Winnipeg Canada, 1967, the sixth in Cali, Colombia 1971, the seventh in Mexico City Oct. 15–27, 1975; the eighth in San Juan, Puerto Rico in July 1–14, 1979; the ninth in 1984.
Under aegis of the International Olympic Committee since 1941 are held the quadrennial Bolivarian Games, organized by Bolivia, Colombia, Ecuador, Panama and Venezuela; and since 1973 the Central American Games, organized by ORDECA, the Sport Organization of Central America.

A.J. CUDDON, *Dictionary of Sport and Games*, London, 1980.

PAN-AMERICAN HEALTH ORGANIZATION, PAHO. Organización Panamericana de la Salud, OPAS. International institution est. Jan. 1902, Mexico, DF, as International Sanitary Bureau, changed name to Pan-American Sanitary Bureau, in 1923, which in 1947 became executive organ of the Pan-American Sanitary Organization; finally changed name to PAHO/OPAS in 1958. The executive organ of the PAHO remains the Pan-American Sanitary Bureau in Washington, DC. It is a specialized Agency of the OAS and the regional office for the Americas of WHO. Publ.: *Boletín* (monthly), *Educación Médica y Salud* (quarterly), weekly Epidemiological Report, Health Statistics, Health Conditions in the Americas all in English and Spanish. Reg. with the UIA.

N. HOWARD JONES, "The Pan-American Health Organization: Origins and Evolution", in: *WHO Chronicle*, 1980; *Yearbook of International Organizations*.

PAN-AMERICAN HIGHWAY. ▷ Roads, International and Intercontinental.

PAN-AMERICAN INSTITUTE OF GEOGRAPHY AND HISTORY. Instituto Panamericano de Geografía e Historia. Intergovernmental Specialized Organization of the OAS est. 1928 in Mexico, DF. Publ.: *Revista de Historia de América* (bi-annual), *Revista Geográfica* (bi-annual), *Revista Geofísica* (annual). Reg. with the UIA.

Yearbook of International Organizations.

PAN-AMERICANISM AND PAN-LATIN-AMERICANISM. International terms for two mutually exclusive political systems. The former was first used on Mar. 5, 1888 by the New York newspaper *Evening Post* in a commentary upon the preparations for the First International Conference of American States which in 1899 created the Pan-American Union. The latter term was used as late as the middle of the 20th century, in opposition to Latin-Americanism, which emphasized the spiritual and cultural community of the Latin American States, whereas Pan-Latin-Americanism underlines common economic and political interests. Both ideas have their roots in the 19th century. Pan-Americanism originates in the ▷ Monroe Doctrine of 1823 which, in principle, deprived the European Powers of the possibilities of intervention in the internal affairs of the American continent and, at the same time, entitled the United States, as a protector of that continent, to exercise such intervention, as demonstrated in the 19th century, and in the years from 1889 to 1954, during which the Pan-American System was created under the protection of the USA. A Mexican diplomat, L. Quintanilla, described Pan-Americanism, in 1943, in the following way:

"In the course of 50 years preceding 1933, when the doctrine of 'good neighbourhood' was proclaimed, the USA intervened more than 60 times in internal affairs of its Latin American neighbours ... How can we speak about American solidarity, about Pan-Americanism, about good neighbourhood, when the greatest obstacle to good relations has been none other than the most powerful republic of the Hemisphere? The situation may change only if the United States will renounce once and for ever its imperialistic intervention."

The origin of Pan-Latin-Americanism goes back to conferences and congresses organized between 1826 and 1889 by the Latin American States only, beginning with the Bolivar Congress of 1826 in Panama. The US activities in building, between 1889 and 1954, the Pan-American System hampered the aspirations of the Latin American States to their own economic and political development; however, the crisis of the System revived Bolivarian ideas. J. Castañeda, also a Mexican diplomat, expressed this as follows:

"Pan-Americanism is nothing more than an incoherent society. The only hope of the establishment of a future organic community is Pan-Latin-Americanism. The future regional Latin American organism will be interested in keeping close economic and political ties with the USA. These future ties between Latin America, as a whole, and the United States may become stronger and more productive than those of today."

Thus these two concepts differ basically in that the first aims at establishing political, military and police-protected dependence of the Latin American States upon the USA, whereas the second tends to establish a partnership of Latin America, as a whole, with the USA. In 1976 the establishment of ▷ SELA (Latin-American Economic System) was the strongest manifestation to date of the Pan-Latin-American trends.

C. GARCIA TRELLOS, *Panamericanismo e Iberoamericanismo*, Madrid, 1927; J.M. YEPES, *El Panamericanismo y el derecho internacional*, Bogotá, 1930; J. VASCONCELOS, *Bolivarismo y Monroismo. Temas americanos*, Santiago de Chile, 1937; R.J. ALFARO, *Commentary on Pan-American Problem*, Cambridge, 1938; A. GARCIA ROBLES, *Le Panaméricanisme et la politique de Bon Voisinage*, Paris, 1938; L. QUINTANILLA, *A Latin American Speaks*, New York, 1943; J.G. ROLLAN, *Origen, contenido y alcance del panamericanismo*, Santiago, 1943; P. WHITAKER, "Pan America and World Organization", in: *International Conciliation, Documents for the Year 1946*, New York, 1946, pp. 115–117, and 144–150; A. WHITEAKER, *The Western Hemisphere Idea: It's Rise and Decline*, Ithaca, 1954; P.J. DUPUY, *Le Nouveau Panaméricanisme*, Paris, 1956; J. CASTAÑEDA, *México y el Orden Internacional*, México, DF, 1956; R.A. MARTINEZ, *De Bolivar a Dulles, El Panamericanismo, Doctrina y Práctica Imperialista*, México, DF, 1959; J.J. CALCEDO CASTILLO, *El Panamericanismo*, Buenos Aires, 1961; O.C. STOETZLER, *Panamerika. Idee und Wirklichkeit*, Hamburg, 1964; C. SEPULVEDA, *El Sistema Interamericano. Génesis. Integración. Decadencia*, México, DF, 1974; *El Panamericanismo. In evolución histórica e essencia*, Moscow, 1982.

PAN-AMERICAN L.S. ROVE FUND. The OAS institution, est. 1948 on the initiative of the legate L.S. Rove, who for 25 years was the director of the Pan-American Union; administered by PAU. Annual proceedings in Annual Reports of OAS.

Yearbook of International Organizations.

PAN-AMERICAN OPERATION, 1958. The economic integration project of the Western Hemisphere proposed in a letter by the President of Brazil, J. Kubitschek to the President of the US, D.D. Eisenhower in July, 1958. On Aug. 9, 1958 the government of Brazil presented to the governments of all American countries three *aides-mémoires* stating that the Pan-American Operation is not entirely an economic program but a basic reorientation of the continent's policy enabling Latin America to participate more effectively in the defense of the West through greater economic development. The tasks of the Pan-American Operation included: struggle with underdevelopment aided by international technical and financial help; revision of the fiscal and financial policies by each country; establishment of inter-American institutions within the Pan-American Operation in the spirit of Pan-American solidarity and with full participation of private initiative. The Brazilian proposal was reviewed by a special committee of 21 OAS member countries at three sessions in Washington 1958, Buenos Aires 1959 and Bogota Sept. 1960, elaborating a study entitled: Means of Social and Economic Development Improvement within the Pan-American Operation. This study was adopted by 10 countries on Sept. 12, 1960 as a program called the 1960 Bogota Act. On Mar. 13, 1961 the USA presented to the Latin American governments a program called ▷ Alliance for Progress.

La Operación Panamericana y los Trabajos de la Comisión de los 21. Documentos básicos e informes. Agosto 1958–agosto 1960, OEA, Washington, DC, 1960; INSTITUTO INTER-AMERICANO DE ESTUDIOS JURIDICOS INTERNACIONAL, *El Sistema Interamericano. Estudio sobre Desarrollo y Fortalecimiento*, Madrid, 1966, pp. 533–539; G. CONNEL-SMITH, *The Interamerican System*, New York, 1966, pp. 269–272.

PAN-AMERICAN POSTAL UNION, PRINCIPAL CONVENTION, 1921.
An agreement signed by the American states on Sept. 15, 1921 in Buenos Aires.

"The countries adhering to this Convention shall form a single postal territory. Each of the Contracting Countries is bound to transport freely and gratuitously through its territory ... all correspondence which it receives from any of the said countries destined for any other Contracting Country or for any country forming part of the Universal Postal Union." (Art. 2.)

International Office of the Pan-American Postal Union was established in Montevideo (art. 13). "For the purposes of the Convention the dollar is established as the monetary unit" (art. 18). The Convention came into force on Jan. 1, 1923.

LNTS, Vol. 30, p. 157.

PAN-AMERICAN RAILWAY CONGRESS ASSOCIATION.
Asociación del Congreso Panamericano de Ferrocarrilles, f. 1906, Buenos Aires. Consultative status with the OAS. Publ.: *Boletin*. Reg. with the UIA.

Yearbook of International Organizations.

PAN-AMERICAN SANITARY CODE, 1924.
The sanitary convention, signed on Nov. 14, 1924 in Havana, by the governments of 21 American Republics and came into force with respect to each signatory state on the date of the deposit of its ratification in the years 1925–39; Additional Protocols were signed on Oct. 19, 1927 and on Sept. 24, 1952.

Basic Documents of Pan-American Health Organization, Washington, DC, 1969.

PAN-AMERICAN SPORTS ORGANIZATION.
Organización Deportiva Panamericana, f. 1955, São Paulo. Recognized by the International Olympic Committee. Reg. with the UIA.

Yearbook of International Organizations.

PAN-AMERICAN STANDARDS COMMISSION.
Comisión Panamericana de Normas Técnicas, f. 1961, Buenos Aires. Publ.: *Pan-American Standards Recommendations*. Members: Standardization institutes in Latin America. Reg. with the UIA.

Yearbook of International Organizations.

PAN-AMERICAN TOURIST PASSPORT.
The subject of a Convention relative to the creation of a Pan-American Passport and of a Transit Passport for Vehicles, signed on June 19, 1935 at Buenos Aires, at the Pan-American Commercial Conference, by all Latin American Republics; ratified by Paraguay and Uruguay, and came into force only between them on Apr. 21, 1939.

OAS, *Inter-American Treaties and Conventions*, Washington, DC, 1971.

PAN-AMERICAN TRANSVERSAL HIGHWAY.
▷ Roads, International and Intercontinental.

PAN-AMERICAN TREATY OF CONTINENTAL SOLIDARITY 1915.
The Pan-American Treaty of Continental Solidarity proposed in Jan. 1915 to the States of Latin America by the US President, W.W. Wilson, with the aim of creating a "hemisphere of peace" based on "mutual guarantees of territorial integrity and independence in the form of republican government." Argentina, Brazil and Chile formally rejected the design of the US government; the majority of states did not answer at all in view of US military intervention in Mexico, 1915.

R.S. BAKER, W.E. DODD (eds.), *Wilson's Public Papers*, Washington, DC, 1925; A.S. LINK, *The Struggle for Neutrality, 1914–15*, New York, 1960.

PAN-AMERICAN UNION.
Since 1948 a permanent central organ and general secretariat of the Organization of American States, ▷ OAS. An institution which is a successor to the Interamerican Bureau in Washington, f. on Mar. 29, 1890 and transformed on Feb. 25, 1911 into the Union of American Republics, which on May 3, 1923 by a decision of the Fifth International American Conference in Santiago changed its name to the present one. The new PAU statute was formulated at the Sixth Conference on Feb. 20, 1928, in Havana; modified by Chapter XIII of the OAS Charter, May 2, 1948. Its headquarters is in Washington and it published all documents concerning the OAS and its special organizations.

Conferencias Internacionales Americanas, 1889–1936, Washington, DC, 1938; pp. 268–270, 358–363 and 420–421; A. GARCIA ROBLES, *El Mundo de la Postguerra*, México, DF, 1946, Vol. 2, pp. 314–318; L.S. ROVE, *The PAU and the Pan-american Conferences*, Washington, DC, 1946; *PAU, Governing Board Minutes 1911–48*, Washington, DC, 1948; *Informes Annales del Secretario General de la OEA/OAS*, Washington, DC, 1948–64.

PAN-ARABISM.
The Pan-Arab movement initiated in Syria in the late 19th century as a national liberation movement from the slavery of the Ottoman Empire and European colonial states in Arab Africa; it proclaimed national unity of all Arabs "from the Atlantic Ocean to the Indian Ocean." In the 20th century the Pan-Arab movement was used by competing dynasties of the Hashemites and of the Saudis; nonetheless, it inspired the creation of the League of Arab States in 1945. After the state of Israel came into being, the Pan-Arab movement was characterized by anti-Israelism.

A.W. BELINO, *Panarabism and Labor*, Cambridge Mass., 1960; R. LE TOURNEAU, *L'évolution politique de l'Afrique du Nord, Musulman, 1920–1961*, Paris, 1962; G.S. HAIN (ed.), *Arab Nationalism. An Anthology*, Berkeley, 1962; R.W. MACDONALD, *The League of Arab States. A Study in the Dynamics of Regional Organizations*, Princeton, 1975.

"PANAY" INCIDENT, 1937.
The US gunboat *Panay* and three American oil supply vessels sunk in the Yangtse River in China on Dec. 12, 1937 by Japanese bombers. The incident was settled by a Japanese apology and an indemnity.

PANCHA SHILA OR PANCHSHEEL.
Sanskrit = "Five Rules." A term derived from ancient Asian traditions for five rules of peaceful coexistence, nowadays included in international documents such as the Treaty on Trade and Borders, signed on Apr. 19, 1954 in Delhi, between the People's Republic of China and India. The Treaty was proclaimed on June 28, 1954 by the Prime Minister of the People's Republic of China, Chou En-lai, and the Prime Minister of India, Jawaharlal Nehru, as the foundation of peaceful relations between nations; it includes:

1. Mutual respect for territorial integrity and sovereignty.
2. Mutual non-aggression.
3. Mutual non-interference in internal affairs.
4. Equality and reciprocity of profits.
5. Peaceful coexistence.

The proclamation was approved by the Conference of 29 countries of Asia and Africa in Bandung in Apr., 1955 as the base for the Declaration on Securing Common Peace and Co-operation. ▷ Bandung Conference and Declaration 1955. Jawaharlal Nehru, after the Bandung Conference, stated on Sept. 17, 1955, in Lok Sabha (India's Parliament) as follows:

"At Bandung the Asian-African nations gave serious thought to the question of world peace. The Conference felt that the maintenance of world peace was all the more necessary for the Asian and African countries so that they could achieve 'social progress, better standards of life and greater freedom' The principles of Panchsheel were fully embodied in the ten-point declaration which set out the basis for the governance of relations among the countries represented at the Conference. The ten principles were:
*1. Respect for fundamental human rights and for the purposes and principles of the Charter of the United Nations.
2. Respect for the sovereignty and territorial integrity of all nations.
3. Recognition of the equality of all races and of the equality of all nations, large and small.
4. Abstention from intervention or interference in the internal affairs of other countries.
5. Respect for the right of each nation to defend itself, singly or collectively, in conformity with the Charter of the United Nations.
6. (a) Abstention from the use of arrangements of collective defence to serve the particular interests of any of the Big Powers.
(b) Abstention by any country from exerting pressure on other countries.
7. Refraining from acts or threats of aggression or the use of force against the territorial integrity or political independence of any country.
8. Settlement of all international disputes by peaceful means, such as negotiations, conciliation, arbitration or judicial settlement as well as other peaceful means of the parties' own choice, in conformity with the Charter of the United Nations.
9. Promotion of mutual interest and co-operation.
10. Respect for justice and international obligations.*
Commenting on the Bandung Conference, Prime Minister Nehru, in a statement to the Indian Parliament said:
"We in India have in recent months sought to formulate principles which should govern our relations with other countries and often spoken of them as the 'five principles'. In the Bandung Declaration, we find the full embodiment of these five principles and the addition to them of elaborations which reinforce these principles. The House will remember that when the Five Principles, or Panchsheel, as we have called them, emerged, they attracted much attention as well as opposition from different parts of the world. We have maintained that they contain the essence of the principles of relationship which would promote world peace and co-operation.
The conception of Panchsheel means that there may be different ways of progress, possibly different outlooks, but that, broadly, the ultimate objectives may be the same. It may use another type of analogy, truth is not confined to one country or one people; it has far too many aspects for anyone to presume that he knows all, and each country and each people, if they are true to themselves, have to find out their path themselves,

through trial and error, through suffering and experience. Only then do they grow. If they merely copy others, the result is likely to be that they will not grow. And even though the copy may be completely good, it will be something undertaken by them without a normal growth of mind which really makes it an organic part of themselves.

Our development in the past thirty years or so has been under Mahatma Gandhi. Apart from what he did for us or did not do, the development of this country under his leadership was organic. It was something which fitted in with the spirit and thinking of India. Yet it was not isolated from the modern world, and we fitted in with the modern world. This process of adaptation will go on. It is something which grows out of the mind and spirit of India, though it is affected by our learning many things from outside. Likewise, this idea of Panchsheel lays down the very important truth that each nation must ultimately fend for itself. I am not thinking it in terms of military fending, but in terms of striving intellectually, morally, spiritually, and in terms of opening out all our windows to ideas from others, and learning from the experience of others. Each country should look upon such an endeavour on the part of the other, with sympathy and friendly understanding and without any interference or imposition."

Panchsheel: The Five Principles of Peaceful Co-existence, New Delhi, 1984.

PAN-EUROPE. An international term for a united Europe, introduced after World War I by the anticommunist movement, the Pan European Union, organized in 1923 by the Austrian Coudenhove-Kalergi. After World War II the Pan-European Union resumed its activities, first in its office in Basel and later in Brussels. Reg. with the UIA.

R. COUDENHOVE-KALERGI, *Pan-Europe*, New York, 1926; R. COUDENHOVE-KALERGI, *De la Guerra Permanente a la Paz Universal*, Barcelona, 1958; *L'Histoire du mouvement Paneuropéen de 1929 à 1962*, Basilea, 1964; *Yearbook of International Organizations.*

PAN-GERMANISM. *German* = "Pangermanismus," "Alldeutschtum." The German 19th-century doctrine proclaiming the union of all German tribes, including Germans, Austrians, Dutchmen, Frisians, Swiss, Scandinavians, and German minorities in Europe, and, at the time of Hitler, also the "new German tribes" ("*neu-deutsche Stämme*"), such as Slovenians in Carinthia, Walloons in Belgium, Lorrainians and Alsatians in France. In the Second German Reich of Otto von Bismarck the militant organization of Pan-Germanism and the advocate of new conquests and colonization of the Slav East was the Pan-German Union, *Alldeutscher Verband*, 1891–1939, the organ of which was the weekly *Alldeutsche Blätter*; in the Third Reich the German East Union, *Bund Deutscher Osten*, 1933–45. Pan-Germanism definitely determined Hitler's concepts of the conquest of Europe and of creating Greater Germany, *Gross-Deutschland*.

Collections des documents sur le Pangermanisme, 4 Vols., Paris, 1917; M.S. WERTHEIMER, *The Pan-German League, 1890–1914*, London, 1924; L. WERNER, *Der Alldeutsche Verband 1890–1918*, Berlin, 1935; K. HAUSHOFER, *Geopolitik der Pan-Ideen*, Stuttgart, 1936; F.W. FOERSTER, *Europe and the German Question*, New York, 1940; L. DEHIO, "Gedanken über die deutsche Sendung 1900–1918", in: *Historische Zeitschrift*, October, 1952.

PAN-ISLAMISM. The 19th-century idea of unifying Moslems in order to create a common front of Moslem countries against the colonial penetration of European powers; and, in more remote perspective, establishing a personal union between the sultanate of the common empire and the caliphate. The theoretician of Pan-Islamism was the Persian philosopher, Dshamal ad-Din al-Afghani (1838–97). In the 20th century, particularly after the abolition of the institution of caliphate in 1924,

Pan-Islamism declined, though it still persisted in the form of Pan-Islamism Congresses: 1931 in Jerusalem, 1951 in Karachi, and 1953 in Jerusalem. After World War II the attempts at appealing to the solidarity of Moslem countries on the international forum, particularly at the UN, failed, as a rule, over essential political and economic issues; they influenced, however, the emphasizing of common standpoint as regards Israel. ▷ Islamic States.

S.W. BURY, *Pan-Islam*, London, 1919; A.J. TOYNBEE, *The Islamic World Since the Peace Settlement*, London, 1927; M. KHADDURI, *War and Peace in the Law of Islam*, London, 1955.

PAN-LATIN-AMERICANISM. ▷ Pan-Americanism and Pan-Latin-Americanism.

PANMUNJON ARMISTICE, 1953. The Military Armistice, ending the Korea War, signed on July 27, 1953 at Panmunjon, establishing a military demarcation line and demilitarized zone; a Neutral Nations Supervisory Commission; arrangements relating to prisoners of War and recommending to the Governments of the countries concerned on both sides to "settle through negotiations the question of the withdrawal of all foreign forces from Korea" and the peaceful settlement of the Korean question. After the Geneva Conference on Korea, Apr. 26–June 15, 1954, the Panmunjon zone was the place of negotiations between the members of the Military Armistice Commission and the Neutral Nations Supervisory Armistice Commission; and since 1979 between the representatives of the South and North Korean Red Cross.

KEESING's *Contemporary Archive*, 1953; P.U. VURL (ed.), *Documents on American Foreign Relations 1953/1954*, London, 1955; J.A.S. GRENVILLE (ed.), *The Major International Treaties 1914–1973*, London, 1974, pp. 464–465.

PAN-NEGRITUDE OR PAN-NEGROISM. International term for a world Negro movement for solidarity of the black race, promoted by African Negro leaders.

L.S. SENGHOR, *Negritude and Humanism*, Paris, 1962; K. NKRUMAH, *Africa Must Unite*, London, 1963.

PAN-ORTHODOX COUNCIL. A term for the planned council of all the Orthodox Churches, whose convocation has been under preparation since 1923. In 1961 on the initiative of the Ecumenical Patriarch of Constantinople, Athenagoras I, a standing secretariat was formed that carries on the preparatory work attached to the Ecumenical Center of the Patriarchate in Vhambery, France, where on Nov. 21–29, 1976 a Council of 14 autocephalous churches took place devoted to working out the plan of work of the Council.

R.A. KLOSTERMANN, *Probleme der Ostkirche*, Göteborg, 1955.

PAN-SLAVISM. An international term used for the first time by the Czech writer J. Herkel in 1826; the aspiration of the Slavs for unification. Pan-Slavist movements appeared most strongly in the 19th century in Russia, one of a democratic character was developed by the Association of United Slavs, 1823, and the Cyril and Methodius Association 1846–47, directed by A.I. Herzen and M.A. Bakhunin; the second aimed at the creation of an all-Slav state, also including the Southern Slavs in the Balkans which was to come under the authority of the Tsar, promoted by leading Russian Slavophiles, organizers of the Slav Congress in Moscow, 1867, and solidarity campaigns with the Southern Slavs in their struggles for independence against Turkey. Attempts to create a broader Pan-Slav movement

during World War I under the auspices of Russia, called Neo-Slavism, failed because of the unpopularity of tsardom. During World War II catchwords of Slav solidarity had an anti-fascist character; they were professed by Slav Committees created in 1942 in Canada, USA and USSR. Derived from Pan-Slavism were the trends ▷ Austro-Slavism, ▷ Neo-Slavism, ▷ Slavophilism and ▷ Slavic congresses.

A. FISCHEL, *Der Panslavismus bis zum Weltkrieg*, Berlin, 1919; H. KOHN, *Pan-Slavism. Its History and Ideology*, Notre Dame, 1953; M. PETROVICH-BORO, *The Emergence of Russian Panslavism 1856–70*, New York, 1956; M.B. PETROVITCH, *The Emergence of Russian Panslavism, 1850–1870*, London, 1956; S.N. NIKITIN, *Slavianskiye komiteti v Rossii v 1858–1876 godakh*, Moscow, 1960.

PAPACY. ▷ Vatican.

PAPAL ACADEMY OF SCIENCES. *Pontificia Academia Scientiarum*, f. 1603, under its present name since 1936, gathers 50 academicians of various nationalities nominated by the Pope. On Sept. 10, 1979 during the centennial of the birth of A. Einstein, John Paul II formally rehabilitated the Italian astronomer and philosopher Galileo, who had been condemned by the Church in the 17th century.

PAPAL COMMISSION FOR JUSTICE AND PEACE. *Pontificium Commissionis pro Iustitia et Pax*, est. by Paul VI in 1967 and reorganized by him in Motu proprio on Dec. 10, 1976; its purpose is to deepen studies of the doctrinal and pastoral aspect of justice and peace in the world and to exert an influence on lay Catholics with the aim of teaching them to be responsible for justice and peace in the world.

PAPAL COUNCIL FOR LAY AFFAIRS. Pontificium Consilium pro Laicis, bureau of the Roman Curia founded, under the influence of the postulates of Vatican Council II by Paul VI by *Motu proprio Apostolatus paragendi* on Dec. 10, 1976. Most of the members of the Council which includes women are lay Catholics. The aim of the Council is to inspire and co-ordinate the activity of lay Catholics in the Church. Acting within the framework of the Council is the Committee for Family Affairs est. 1973, by Paul VI.

PAPAL STATES. The historical name of the Pope's territorial possessions on the Italian peninsula from 754 to 1870. ▷ Vatican.

PAPAMIENTO. *Lingua franca* of the population of the Netherlands Antilles which is a mixture of Spanish and Dutch and other languages.

PAPER. A subject of international co-operation. Organizations reg. with the UIA:

European Confederation of Pulp, Paper and Board Industry, f. 1963, Brussels.
European Federation of Paper Bag Manufacturers, f. 1976, Paris.
European Liaison Committee for Pulp and Paper, f. 1956, Paris. Publ.: *Symposia Reports.*
European Union of Paper, Board and Packaging Wholesalers, f. 1971, Brussels.
International Association of Paper Historians, f. 1959, Bamberg, FRG. Publ.: *Information* (quarterly).
International Committee of Paper and Board Converters, Common Market Group, f. 1961, Frankfurt am Main.
International Federation of Manufacturers and Converters of Pressure-Sensitive and Heatseals on Paper and other Materials, f. 1958, The Hague. Publ.: *Bulletin* (quarterly).

Yearbook of International Organizations.

PAPERCLIP PROJECT. The code name for US intelligence operation concerning the location and bringing to the USA, 1945–46, of Nazi scientists who worked in the rocket center at ▷ Peenemünde, where Oct. 3, 1942 the rocket era began with the launching of a missile called V1 carrying one ton of explosives a distance of 300 km. As a result of the operation, 127 specialists (among them the leading German rocket designer Wernher von Braun, along with the plans for ▷ V1, V2) were brought to the experimental center of White Sands near El Paso, New Mexico, USA, and subsequently to the Radstone Arsenal in Alabama, where they participated in the development of the missile industry and in the construction of launch sites for space craft.

E. BERGAUST, *Reaching for the Star*, New York, 1960; T. BOWER, *The Paperclip Conspiracy: The Hunt for the Nazi Scientists*, Boston, 1988; Ch. STIMPSON, *US Recruitment of Nazis and Its Effect on the Cold War*, New York, 1988.

PAPER GOLD. ▷ SDR, Special Drawing Rights.

PAPER TIGER. The description of the atom bomb by Mao Tse-tung in an interview conducted by Anna Louise Strong on Aug. 17, 1946:

"The atom bomb is a paper tiger which the US reactionaries use to scare people. It looks terrible, but in fact it isn't."

The 10th and 20th anniversaries of the event were celebrated by the Chinese press.

W. SAFIRE, *Safire's Political Dictionary*, New York, 1978.

PAPHOS. A cultural site of Cyprus included in the ▷ World Heritage UNESCO List. On the southwest coast of Cyprus stand the ruins of the temples where the cult of Aphrodite, the Mediterranean goddess of beauty and love, was celebrated for more than 1500 years. There are two towns – Paleapaphos, where the foundations of the primitive sanctuary are, and Nea Paphis, where there are two large Roman villas called Dionysos and Theseus on account of their magnificent mosaic pavements.

UNESCO. *A Legacy for All*, Paris, 1984.

PAPIERFETZEN. *German* = "slip of paper." The value definition of treaties, used in the note of the German Reich government to the government of Great Britain on Aug. 5, 1914, when Great Britain went to war because of violation of Belgium's neutrality by the Reich; "for a slip of paper war was declared to the related German nation." A year later, on Dec. 30, 1916, while replying to peace proposals of Germany, the Allies recalled that:

"Belgium had been invaded by a state, which had guaranteed its neutrality, and which did not hesitate to declare that treaties were 'slips of paper,' and that 'need knows no principles' – *Not kennt kein Gebot*."

J. HOCHFELD, *Dokumente der Deutschen Politik und Geschichte von 1848 bis zur Gegenwart, 1848–1951*, 6 Vols., Berlin, 1951–52; W.L. SHIRER, *The Nightmare Years 1930–1940*, Boston, 1984, pp. 491–496.

PAPUA. The southern part of New Guinea, since 1975 part of the independent state ▷ Papua-New Guinea.

PAPUA-NEW GUINEA. Member of the UN. A State near Australia in the eastern part of New Guinea Island (whose western part ▷ Irian Barat, belongs to Indonesia) with Bismarck Archipelago and the northern part of Solomon Islands. Area: 462,840 sq. km. Pop. 1987 est.: 3,700,000 (1971 census: 2,489,935). Capital: Port Moresby with 139,000 inhabitants, 1983. GNP per capita 1987:

US $700. Official languages: English, Pidgin and Motu. Currency: one kina = 100 toca. National Day: Sept. 16, Independence Day, 1975.
Member of the UN since Sept. 17, 1975; and all its specialized agencies with the exception of GATT and WIPO; member of the Commonwealth and Colombo Plan; ACP State of the EEC.
International relations: in 1884 colonized by Germany and Great Britain, the latter conceding its portion to Australia in 1905. As a result of World War I, the German part became League of Nations mandate territory from May 9, 1921, under Australian administration. In 1941–45 occupied by Japan. From Dec. 13, 1946 UN trusteeship under Australian administration. In 1949 assumed common administrative name Papua and New Guinea as a separate unit of Australian External Territories with capital in Port Moresby. The UN Trusteeship Council debated the country's future on June 1, 1967 and decided that its population has the right to free existence and should be given the opportunity to determine its future. Therefore, the name adopted in the official UN terminology was: Territory of Papua and New Guinea. On Sept. 16, 1975 independence was declared. A signatory of the Lomé Conventions, 1977 and 1980. In 1982/83 border incidents with Indonesia.

J. WILKES (ed.), *New Guinea and Australia*, Sydney, 1953; B. ESSAL, *Papua and New Guinea*, Melbourne, 1961; J. RYAN, *The Hot Land*, London, 1970; P. HASTINGS (ed.), *Paper New Guinea*, London, 1971; P. RYAN (ed.), *Encyclopaedia of Papua and New Guinea*, 3 Vols., Melbourne, 1972; *Report of the Committee on Banking in Papua New Guinea*, Port Moresby, 1972; P. HASLUCK, *A Time for Building*, Melbourne, 1976; R. SKELDON (ed.), *Demography of Papua New Guinea*, Melbourne, 1979; *The Europa Year Book 1984. A World Survey*, Vol. II, pp. 2226–2234, London, 1984.

PARACEL ISLANDS. A group of low coral islands and reefs in the oil rich South China Sea. The islands, part of French Indochina until 1945, passed to China but are claimed by Vietnam.

PARAGUAY. Member of the UN. Republic of Paraguay. A country in South America, bordering on Bolivia, Brazil and Argentina. Area: 406,752 sq. km. Pop. 1987 est.: 3,922,000 (1962 census: 1,819,000; 1972 census: 2,557,955). Capital: Asunción with 455,517 inhabitants 1982. Official language: Spanish. Currency: one Guarani = 100 centimos. GNP per capita 1987: US $1000. National Day: May 14, Independence Day, 1811.
Founding member of the UN and its specialized agencies except IMO and GATT; member of the OAS; member of the Tlatelolco Treaty and until 1980 of LAFTA, since 1980 of ALADI.
International relations: from 1537 to 1811 Spanish colony; independence proclaimed on May 14, 1811; from 1864 to 1870 at war with Argentina, Brazil and Uruguay in which 90% of male population was killed. Equally catastrophic was the war with Bolivia over oil regions ▷ Gran Chaco, 1928–29 and 1932–35, ended with a Peace Treaty of July 21, 1938 and delimitation of frontier with Bolivia which was granted part of Gran Chaco and access to River Paraguay. Conflicts with Bolivia were subject of mediation at the League of Nations of which Paraguay was member. In 1973 in conflict with Argentina over a joint dam project with Brazil on the River Parana. Agreement on Parana River signed with Brazil and Argentina on Oct. 19, 1979. ▷ Itaipú. General Alfredo Stroessner, ruling in Paraguay since 1954, became 1984 "the longest-serving dictator in Latin America." On April 8, 1987, the state of siege ended after 40 years. On Feb. 3, 1989, a coup in Paraguay ousted after nearly 35 years the dictator Gen. Alfredo Stroessner.

See also ▷ American Indians.

J. CESAR CHAVEZ, *Compendio de historia paraguaya*, Asunción, 1960; *Paraguay. Síntesis Económica y Financiera*, Buenos Aires, 1965; S. PENDLE, *Paraguay. A Riverside Nation*, London, 1967; L. SANCHEZ NASI, *El marcado de capitales en el Paraguay*, México, DF, 1970; D.L. JONES, *Paraguay. A Bibliography*, New York, 1979; P.H. LEWIS, *Paraguay under Stroessner*, Raleigh N.C., 1980; D. MAYBURY-LEWIS, J. HOWE, *The Indian Peoples of Paraguay*, Cambridge Mass., 1980; *The Europa Year Book 1984. A World Survey*, Vol. II, pp. 2235–2246, London, 1984; KEESING's *Record of World Events*, Feb. 1989.

PARANA. A frontier river of Brazil, Paraguay and Argentina, one of the great rivers of South America, length 3200 km, subject of an agreement between Argentina, Brazil and Paraguay, signed Oct. 19, 1979, on the comprehensive utilization of boundary waters in connection with Brazil's construction of a huge hydroelectric power plant ▷ Itaipú and construction by Argentina of the hydroelectric power plant ▷ Corpus.

PARAPHING. An international term for initialing the text of an agreement by those carrying on the negotiations; the preliminary act following the conclusion of negotiations, prior to signing and ▷ ratification.

PARASITOLOGY. A subject of international co-operation and research. Organizations reg. with the UIA:

Latin American Federation of Parasitologists, f. 1963, San José de Costa Rica.
World Association for the Advancement of Veterinary Parasitology, f. 1963, Thessaloniki.
World Federation of Parasitologists, f. 1962, Bonn, FRG.

M. MERINO-RODRIGUEZ, *Lexicon of Parasites and Diseases in Livestock*. In Latin, English, French, Spanish, Italian and German, Amsterdam, 1964; *Yearbook of International Organizations*; W.D. FOSTER, *A History of Parasitology*, Edinburgh, 1965.

PARDON. An international term for the obligation put down in war conventions to "grant pardon" to the wounded and those surrendering, i.e. to take prisoners. After World War I not granting pardon, or not taking prisoners, was recognized as a war crime.

PARÉAGE ▷ Andorrra.

PARENTHOOD, PLANNING OF. A subject of international co-operation. Organization reg. with the UIA:

International Planned Parenthood Federation, f. 1948, London. Regional Bureaux: Colombo, Kuala Lumpur, Nairobi, New York and Tunis. Consultative status with UNESCO, WHO, UNICEF, ILO, ECOSOC and FAO. Publ.: *People* (quarterly), *IPPF Medical Bulletin* (monthly), *IPPF News* (bi-monthly).

Yearbook of International Organizations.

PAR IN PAREM NON HABET IUDICUM. *Latin* = "equals may not judge themselves." A principle of international law. ▷ Right and Duties of States.

PARIS. The capital of France since the 12th century, city situated on the Seine River; area of the city (Ville de Paris) 105 sq. km; metropolitan area (agglomération Seine-et-Marne, Yvelines, Essone, Hauts-de-Seine, Seine-St. Denis, Val-de-Marne, Val-d'Oise) 12,008 sq. km. Population, 1982 census: 2,188,918 city, metropolitan area: 8,706,963. Seat of UNESCO and over 500 international organizations reg. with the UIA. The site of Peace Conferences

P

after World War I and II. Two UN General Assembly sessions took place in Paris; the Third from Nov. 23–Dec. 12, 1948 and the Fourth from Nov. 6–Dec. 20, 1951, both in the Palais de Chaillot near the Eiffel Tower.

Yearbook of the UN 1947–48 and 1951; H. DE VILLEFOSSE, *Histoire de Paris*, Paris, 1950; P. LAVEDEN, *Histoire de Paris*, Paris, 1960; *Yearbook of International Organizations*; I. SORAGIL, *Urban France*, London, 1983.

PARIS AGREEMENTS, 1954. Common name for the following agreements, signed at Paris on Oct. 23, 1954 by the USA, UK, France and the Federal Republic of Germany: Protocol on the Termination of the Occupation Régime in the FRG.
Convention on the Presence of Foreign Forces in the FRG; Convention (with annexes) on the Rights and Obligations of Foreign Forces and their Members in the FRG; Finance Convention.
Convention (with annex) on the Settlement of Matters Arising out of the War and the Occupation. Agreement on the Tax Treatment of the Foreign Forces and their Members.
The Protocol on Termination provided accession of Germany and Italy to the ▷ Western European Union, which was established by the ▷ Brussels Treaty, 1948, "for collaboration in economic, social and cultural matters and for collective defence" while the other four Protocols, signed also on Oct. 23, 1954 modified the Brussels Treaty, permitting Germany and Italy to accede to NATO in May 1955. The Protocol defined also the limitation of Federal Republic of Germany armaments: "not to manufacture in its territory any atomic weapons, chemical weapons or biological weapons."
The Preamble and the Art. 1 of the Convention on the Rights and Obligation of Foreign Forces and their Members read as follows:

In view of the present international situation and the need to ensure the defence of the free world which require the continuing presence of foreign forces in the Federal Republic of Germany, the United States of America, the United Kingdom of Great Britain and Northern Ireland, the French Republic and the Federal Republic of Germany agree as follows:
Art. 1. (1). From the entry into force of the arrangements for the German Defence Contribution, forces of the same nationality and effective strength as at that time may be stationed in the Federal Republic.
(2). The effective strength of the forces stationed in the Federal Republic pursuant to paragraph 1 of this article may at any time be increased with the consent of the Government of the Federal Republic of Germany.
(3). Additional forces of the States parties to the present Convention may enter and remain in the Federal territory with the consent of the Government of the Federal Republic of Germany for training purposes in accordance with the procedures applicable to forces assigned to the Supreme Allied Commander in Europe, provided that such forces do not remain there for more than thirty days at any one time.
(4). The Federal Republic grants to the French, the United Kingdom and the United States forces the right to enter, pass through and depart from the territory of the Federal Republic in transit to or from Austria (so long as their forces continue to be stationed there) or any country Member of the North Atlantic Treaty Organization, on the same basis as is usual between Parties to the North Atlantic Treaty or as may be agreed with effect for all Member States by the North Atlantic Council.

UNTS Vol. 332 and 334, 1959; R. OSGOOD, *NATO: The Entangling Alliance*, New York, 1962.

PARIS AGREEMENTS, 1973. ▷ Vietnam Agreements, 1973.

PARIS AMERICAN-BRITISH PEACE TREATY, 1783. The Peace treaty signed on Sept. 3, 1783 in Paris between Great Britain and the United States of America. The text of art. 1 reads as follows:

"Art. I. His Britannic Majesty acknowledges the said United States, viz. New Hampshire, Massachusetts Bay, Rhode Island and Providence Plantation, Connecticut, New York, New Jersey, Pennsylvania, Delaware, Maryland, Virginia, North Carolina, South Carolina, and Georgia, to be free, sovereign and independent states."

Major Peace Treaties of Modern History, 1648–1967, New York, 1967, Vol. I, pp. 345–350.

PARIS COAL AND STEEL TREATY, 1951. The Treaty creating the ▷ European Coal and Steel Community, signed at Paris on Mar. 19, 1951.

J. PAXTON, *A Dictionary of the EEC*, London, 1978, pp. 191–200.

PARIS DECLARATION, 1856. The first Convention on the International Law of Sea War adopted in the form of the Paris Declaration by Austria, France, Great Britain, Prussia, Sardinia, Turkey, Russia on Apr. 16, 1856 in Paris, after the termination of the Crimean War in order to introduce unified rules for ships belonging to neutral states. The Paris Declaration suppressed ▷ sea piracy and the medieval right to war booty, and it adopted three principles:

1. Enemy's goods are safeguarded by a neutral flag, unless they are ▷ contraband of war. 2. Neutral goods, unless they are contraband, are inviolable, also under enemy's flag.
3. No one can require other states to comply with war blockade, unless the blockading party is powerful enough to control enemy's coast (invalidity of the "fictitious blockade.")

The Paris Declaration was acceded to for an unlimited period by Argentina, Belgium, Brazil, Denmark, Ecuador, Greece, Guatemala, Japan, Mexico, the Netherlands, Peru, Portugal, Sweden and Norway, Switzerland, Spain, Uruguay.

G. NORADOUNGHIAN, *Recueil d'actes internationaux de l'empire ottoman*, 4 Vols., Paris, 1897–1903, Vol. 3, No. 682, p. 70 and No. 686, p. 88.

PARIS PEACE CONFERENCE, 1919 AND OTHER PARIS PEACE CONFERENCES, 1919–20. The Conference convened by the countries of the Entente to frame the League of Nations Covenant, the peace treaty with Germany, known as ▷ Versailles Treaty 1919 and the peace treaties with Austria, Bulgaria, Hungary and Turkey. The main Conference was held near Paris at Versailles Palace from Jan. 12 to June 28, 1919, attended by the five big powers: France, Italy, Japan, the UK and USA, as well as 22 other countries from the original membership of the League of Nations; the debate on Germany was also attended by the Weimar Republic, but not until the final draft of the treaty was prepared. The most active figures were US President Woodrow T. Wilson who came with 1300 experts, G. Clemenceau for France and British Prime Minister Lloyd George. The main work was done by the Supreme Council of the Five Powers and its 16 commissions, the Commission for the League of Nations headed from Jan. 25, 1919 by Woodrow T. Wilson, after 10 sessions its work wound up at Crillon Hotel, Feb. 13, 1919 with the adoption of the League of Nations Covenant. The Treaty was prepared by June 22, 1919 and signed on June 28, 1919. Russia did not take part in the conference, since the countries of Entente refused to recognize the Soviet government. The total of 10,000 delegates and experts grouped in 58 commissions held 1646 sessions. Plenary sessions had the character of formal ceremonies. The full proceedings were published in Washington during World War II in 12 volumes, with the 13th analyzing the provisions and their execution.
Separate peace negotiations were held in Paris with the allies of the defeated Reich: Austria, Bulgaria, Turkey and Hungary, and concluded individual peace treaties signed in different places: Saint Germain en Laye Treaty, 1919 with Austria; Neuilly sur Seine, 1919, with Bulgaria; Trianon Treaty , 1920, with Hungary; Sèvres Treaty, 1920, with Turkey.

W.T. WILSON, *Wilson and World Settlement*, 3 Vols., London, 1923; CARNEGIE ENDOWMENT, *Treaties of Peace, 1919–1923*, 2 Vols., New York, 1924; G. CLEMENCEAU, *Grandeurs et misères d'une victoire*, Paris, 1930; LLOYD GEORGE, *The Truth about the Peace Treaties*, London, 1938; *The Paris Peace Conference*, 13 Vols., Washington, 1947; A. WALWORTH, *Wilson and His Peacemakers: American Diplomacy at the Paris Conference, 1919*, New York, 1986.

PARIS PEACE CONFERENCE, 1946. A series of peace negotiations held in Paris by the Four Great Powers: France, the UK, USA and USSR, with the allies of the German Third Reich during World War II: Bulgaria, Finland, Hungary, Italy and Romania. Deliberations were held in Luxembourg Palace in the French capital from June 29–Oct. 15, 1946. On the basis of decisions made at Yalta in Jan., 1945 and at the Moscow Conference of Foreign Ministers of the USA, Great Britain and the USSR in Dec., 1945, later approved by France; the foreign ministers of the Four Powers drafted a proposal for a Peace Treaty with Italy; the ministers of Great Britain, the USA and USSR drafted proposals for Treaties with Bulgaria, Hungary and Romania; and the ministers of the USA and USSR, drafted a proposal for a Treaty with Finland; the final texts were then ratified by Council of Ministers of the Four Powers, after which they were submitted to five commissions of various composition as follows:

I. Commission for the Treaty with Italy: Byelorussian SSR, China, France, Great Britain, USA, USSR, as well as Ethiopia, Australia, Belgium, Brazil, Canada, Czechoslovakia, Greece, Holland, India, New Zealand, Poland, South Africa, Ukrainian SSR,
II. Commission for the Treaty with Romania: USA, Great Britain, USSR as well as Australia, Byelorussian SSR, Czechoslovakia, India, New Zealand, South Africa, Ukrainian SSR,
III. Commission for the Treaty with Bulgaria: Great Britain, USA and USSR, as well as Australia, Byelorussian SSR, Czechoslovakia, India, New Zealand, South Africa and Yugoslavia,
IV. Commission for the Treaty with Hungary: Great Britain, USA, USSR and Australia, Byelorussian SSR, Canada, Czechoslovakia, India, New Zealand, South Africa, Ukrainian SSR and Yugoslavia.
V. Commission for the Treaty with Finland: Great Britain and USSR, and Australia, Byelorussian SSR, Canada, Czechoslovakia, India, New Zealand, South Africa, Ukrainian SSR and Yugoslavia.

The texts approved by the Commission were submitted to the Council of Ministers of Foreign Affairs of the Four Powers, which ratified the final text at its session in New York, from Nov. 13–Dec. 12, 1946. Signing of the Treaties took place in Paris in the Luxembourg Palace, on Feb. 10, 1947.

J. KOROWIN, *Parizhkaya mirnaya konferentsya*, Moscow, 1946; M. NICOLSON, "Peace Making at Paris", in: *Foreign Affairs, 1947; Negotiations and texts of Treaties with Italy, Bulgaria, Hungary, Romania and Finland*, Boston, 1954.

PARIS PEACE TREATIES, 1814 AND 1815. Two peace treaties between France and Great Britain, Austria, Prussia and Russia, signed on May 30, 1814 and on Nov. 20, 1815 in Paris. The art. XXXII of the first Treaty convoked the Congress of Vienna 1815.

Major Peace Treaties of Modern History, New York, 1967, Vol. I, pp. 501–512.

PARIS PEACE TREATY, 1856. A Treaty between France, Great Britain, the Ottoman Empire, Sardinia and Russia, signed on Mar. 30, 1856 in Paris, annexed a Convention Prohibiting the Ships of War of Foreign Powers to enter the Straits of the Dardanelles and of the Bosporus; revised by Russian-–Turkish Agreement on Mar. 13, 1871.

Major Peace Treaties of Modern History, New York, 1967, p. 947.

PARIS PEACE TREATY, 1898. A Treaty between Spain and US, signed on Dec. 10, 1898 in Paris.

"Spain relinquishes all claim of sovereignty over and title to Cuba" (Art. I). "Spain cedes to the US the island of Puerto Rico and other islands now under Spanish sovereignty in the West Indies, and the islands of Guam in the Marianas or Ladrones" (Art. II). "Spain cedes to the US the archipelago known as the Philippine Islands … The US will pay to Spain the sum of $20 million" (Art. III).

Major Peace Treaties of Modern History, New York, 1967, Vol. II, pp. 851–859.

PARIS REPARATION CONFERENCE, 1921. A Conference of the Entente states, from Jan. 24–29, 1921, following preliminary talks by Allied and German experts in Brussels, Dec. 15–22, 1920, on final settlement of Germany's reparations. The fixed amount set at 226 billion DM in gold, additional, variable amount – 43 billion DM; during payment of reparations, Germany also pledged to turn over 12% of annual profits from exports.

R. CASTILLON, *Les réparations allemandes. Deux expériences: 1919–1932 el 1945–1952*, Paris, 1953.

PARIS TREATIES, 1954. ▷ Paris Agreements, 1954.

PARIS VIETNAM CONFERENCE, 1973. ▷ Vietnam Agreements, 1973.

PARITY. An international term for the relation of the value of a certain currency to a unit of pure gold (gold parity) or to so-called "hard currencies" (parity established by the government of a given state or by the IMF). Parity forms the basis for the rates of a given currency to other currencies. A separate form of parity is freight parity in the sea transport of goods, setting the limits of costs.

PARITY DOCTRINE. ▷ Schlesinger Nuclear War Doctrine.

PARITY GRID. An international term accepted in the Western European currency system referring to the principles in force in the ▷ currency snake, determining the relationship of particular currencies to each other (the grid of the leading rate with fixed points between the currencies).

J. WALMSLEY, *A Dictionary of International Finance*, London, 1979.

PARKINSON'S LAW. A satirical "law" on the expansibility of bureaucracy, formulated first time 1955 in *The Economist* and in book form in 1957 by the British historian Prof. C. Northcote Parkinson. The "law" is defined as follows:

"For an example of the dangers of democratic finance we need go no further than England. And yet the tendency to build up an enormous civil service, such as existed at Athens, is universal and not even directly connected with democracy. What is distinctively democratic is the force which prevents any reduction in the establishment which has been built up. The increase

in itself is due to law of growth which affects every administrative office; a law which has yet to be fully investigated, the workings of which are manifest although not yet reduced to a satisfactory formula. The obvious fact is that anyone appointing an administrator to do a certain continuing task, assisted by two clerks, will find (after two or three years) that the original official is now assisted by two others, dividing the work between them, and each of these aided in turn by two clerks. A year or two later the official first appointed will need a higher salary in order to control two sub-departments, each of which will comprise a head and two or more assistants, each again with clerks to assist him. By then there will have to be an establishment officer in addition, to deal with problems of emoluments and leave. So much is common knowledge. What is less widely realized is that the increase in staff is governed by a law of growth which is not related in any way to the amount of work to be done. The volume of outside correspondence may be constant, it may have diminished; it may even have increased. But the staff will multiply in any case and at approximately the same speed, all working as hard as (and some working harder than) before. In a commercial concern this process will not continue unchecked for ever and may be reversed promptly in a period of slump. Under a monarchy the process may be undone when the king wants the money for something else, if only for a new mistress. But no one can reduce the civil service in a democracy. No one can economize on staff in a nationalized industry. To do so would be to lose votes on a big scale. There is hardly a modern state not grossly overburdened with unproductive clerks and officials, and Britain perhaps as overburdened as any. But there is no remedy for it under a democratic form of rule."

C. NORTHCOTE PARKINSON, *Parkinson's Law. The Pursuit of Progress*, London, 1957; C. NORTHCOTE PARKINSON, *The Evolution of Political Thought*, New York, 1958, pp. 243–244; C. NORTHCOTE PARKINSON, *The Law*, London, 1980.

PARKS. A subject of international co-operation, sponsored by the International Union for Conservation of Nature and Natural Resources, f. 1948, Morges, Switzerland. Organizations reg. with the UIA:

International Commission on National Parks, f. 1958, Washington, DC.
International Federation of Park and Recreation Administration, f. 1957, London.
Latin American Committee on National Parks, f. 1964, Quito.
National Parks and Conservation Association, f. 1960, Washington, DC. Consultative status with ECOSOC.

Yearbook of International Organizations.

PARLEMENTAIRE French international term defined in the Hague Regulations of the ▷ Hague First Convention 1899, for a representative of belligerent forces ready to negotiate with the enemy commander, advancing within the enemy lines bearing a white flag, symbolic of truce.

R.L. BLEDSOE, B.A. BOCZEK, *The International Law Dictionary*, Oxford, UK, 1987.

PARLIAMENTARY ELECTIONS. An international term for the election of delegates to the legislature, subject of international documentation and research conducted by the International Center of Parliamentary Documentation – Centre internationale de documentation parlementaire, CIDP, est. 1965 in Geneva, which operates on behalf of the Interparliamentary Union publ.: *Chronique des elections parlementaires* (since Aug. 1, 1966) and scholarly studies.

N. WILDING, *An Encyclopaedia of Parliament*, New York, 1971.

PARLIAMENT OF ANDEAN GROUP. The consultatory sessions of the representatives of the ▷ Andean Group countries. On May 6, 1984 the Lima session of the Andean Parliament adopted a

resolution supporting the ▷ Contadora Group and protesting against the mining of territorial waters of Nicaragua.

PARLIAMENT OF CENTRAL AMERICA ▷ Central America Parliament.

PARLIAMENT OF EUROPE. ▷ European Parliament.

PARLIAMENT OF LATIN AMERICA. ▷ Latin America Parliament.

PARLIAMENTS. A subject of international co-operation. Organizations reg. with the UIA:

Association of Secretaries General of Parliament, f. 1938, The Hague.
European Parliament, f. 1958, Strasbourg.
Hansard Society for Parliamentary Government, f. 1944, London. Publ.: *Parliamentary Affairs*.
International Centre for Parliament Documentations, f. 1965, Geneva.
International Parliamentary Consultative Council of Benelux, f. 1955, Brussels.
Interparliamentary Association for Tourism, f. 1948, Brussels.
Interparliamentary Union, f. 1889, Geneva.
Latin-American Parliament, f. 1963, Lima.
NATO Parliamentarian Conference, f. 1955, Brussels.
Parliamentary Association for Euro-Arab Co operation, f. 1974, Paris.
World Parliament Association, f. 1951, London.

V. HERMAN, F. MENDEL (eds.), *Parliaments of the World, A Reference Compendium*, London, 1976; *Yearbook of International Organizations*.

PARTIAL TEST BAN TREATY, PTBT ▷ Outer Space Moscow Treaty 1963.

PARTICIPATION CLAUSE. The observance of rules of a treaty only if all states-signatories of the treaty act accordingly. Art. 2 of the Fourth Hague Convention on Rights and Customs concerning Land Wars of Oct. 18, 1907 may serve as an example: "Provisions drawn up in this Convention are binding only on questions concerning the Contracting Parties and only if all belligerent states participate in the Convention."
The second clause of the sentence above conditions adherence to the rules of the Convention provided that all states taking part in the conflict participate in the Convention. The general participation clause was also contained in the London Declaration of the Sea of 1909. After World War I a departure from the general participation clause was observed: in the Geneva Protocol of 1924, in the question of toxic gasses and in the Geneva Treaties of 1929. A total departure occurred after World War II in the Geneva Treaties of 1949 and in the Hague Convention on the Protection of Cultural Values, 1954, which under art. 18, item 3, provides that "the Powers being parties to this Convention shall remain in mutual relations even if one of the Powers participating in a conflict is not a party."

Convention and Declaration of the First and Second Hague Conference, Washington, DC, 1914.

PARTISAN WAR. An irregular war waged by volunteer units on a territory occupied by an invader or on the area of one's own state against a ruling régime for the purpose of gaining independence or changing the government.
The legal protection of partisans is based on arts. 1 and 2 of Hague Convention (IV), respecting the laws and customs of war on land, 1907, found in its preamble, called the Martens proviso and also by the Geneva Convention, 1949. The Federation of Combatants as well as the International Federation of Members of Resistance Movements (FIR) in

P

1961 began work on a Legal Statute of Partisans and Members of Resistance Movements.

L. NURICK, R. BARRET, "Legality of Guerrilla Forces under the Laws of War", in: *American Journal of International Law*, 1946; I.P. TRAININ, "Voprosy partizanskoi voiny v mezhdunarodnom prave", in: *Izvestiia Akademii Nauk SSSR. Otdelenie ekonomiki i prava*, No. 4, 1954; A. ARMSTRONG, *The Soviet Partisan Movement in World War II*, Chicago, 1964; P. KLEUUT, "Guerre de Partisans et Droit International", in: *Yugoslavenska Reviya za Mezhdunarodno Pravo*, No. 1, 1966; A. CAMBELL, *Guerillas, A History and Analysis*, London, 1967; H. MEYROWITZ, *La Guerilla et le droit de guerres*, Bruxelles, 1971; J. BOND, *The Rules of Riot*, Princeton, 1974; R.B. ASPREY, *War in the Shadows: The Guerrilla in History*, Garden City, 1975; K. MACKSEY, *The Partisans in Europe in World War II*, London 1975; M.K. DZIEWANOWSKI, *War at any Price, World War II in Europe 1939–1945*, Englewood Cliffs, 1987; *Combatants and Noncombatants*, in R.L. BLEDSOE, B.A. BOCZEK, *The International Law Dictionary*, Oxford, 1987.

PAR VALUE SYSTEM. A International Monetary Fund system, 1946–76, of obligatory official value of currencies of the IMF member states, abolished by the Jamaica IMF Agreement in Apr., 1976.

G.N. HALM, *Jamaica and the Par Value System*, Princeton, 1977.

PASCAL. One of the universal international languages for the automatic programming of computers; developed in the 1960s after ▷ Fortran and ▷ Algol.

PASSAROWITZ PEACE TREATY, 1718. A treaty between Austria and Venice on one side and the Ottoman Empire on the other, signed on July 21, 1718 in Passarowitz, East Serbia.

Major Peace Treaties of Modern History, New York, 1967, Vol. II, pp. 883–911.

PASSPORT. *French*: passeporte = "come in through the gate." An identity card permitting travel abroad; issued in various forms: diplomatic (to diplomats), consular (to nationals permanently residing abroad), official (to persons travelling on business) and regular (to nationals making private tours) and finally collective (to package tourists or ship or aircraft crews, the latter called Crew Membership Certificates); the subject of international passport laws and seven Geneva Conferences convened on the initiative of the League of Nations: in 1920, 1922, 1924, 1926, 1927, 1928 and 1929. In order to carry out the recommendations of the conferences of the League of Nations of 1920, Austria, Czechoslovakia, Hungary, the Kingdom of Serbia, Croatia and Slovenia, Poland, Romania and Italy signed on Jan. 27, 1922 in Graz, an agreement providing for uniform rules of issuing passports and visas as well as the reduction of fees for the same. After World War II regional agreements on uniform passports were concluded. Besides passports issued by states, there are passports issued by world and regional intergovernmental organizations, e.g. by the UN ▷ Laissez-Passer; passports for persons having indefinite or questionable nationality, *Titre d'identité et de voyage pour personnes sans nationalité ou de nationalité douteuse*, issued by the International Organization for Refugees, the so-called ▷ Nansen Passport. Navy Certificates issued to neutral ships during wars, and passports of the deceased used for corpses to be transported to another state are not considered passports but "special certificates". Regular passports need visas issued by transit states and visas issued by states which are the travellers' destination unless the state

that issued the passport entered into agreements with those states voiding the obligation to possess visas. The EEC countries signed in Dec. 1975 at Rome an agreement on uniformity of the passports of all member states and decided that their colour will be deep lilac. In 1980 the ICAO suggested the use of machine readable passports to speed the flow of passengers at international airports.

LNTS, Vol. 9, p. 293; C. REALE, "Les problèmes des passeports", in: *Recueil des Cours de l'Académie de Droit International 1934*; *The Right to Travel and United States Passport Policies, US Senate Documents*, No. 120, 1958; D.C. TURACK, *The Passport in International Law*, Lexington, 1972; *UN Chronicle*, 1983, p. 84.

PASSPORTS OF THE DECEASED. The identification cards of corpses transported from one country to another issued in the place of death in accordance with international regulations.

PASTEURIZATION. An international term for treatment of food to destroy disease-causing organisms, developed by French scientist Louis Pasteur in the 1860's; subject of international co-operation, sanitary regulations and obligatory international conventions applying to specified food stuffs after World War II in foreign trade.

PATACA. The local currency of ▷ Macau, since 1977 in a fixed relationship to the Hong Kong dollar with the consent of the authorities of China on whose territory Macau is located.

PATENT COOPERATION TREATY, PCT, 1978, 1985. The Treaty which created the World Intellectual Property Organization (▷ WIPO), became operational in 1978 and has been considerably revised with effect from Jan. 1, 1985. In Nov. 1985 a Seminar organized by the Intellectual Property Unit of the Queen Mary College (University of London) with the ▷ WIPO, the UK Patent Office and The Chartered Institute of Patent Agents was held in London; the papers presented at the Seminar have been edited by J. Lahore.
See also ▷ patents and ▷ trademark.

J. LAHORE ed., *The Patent Cooperation Treaty: A New Era*, London, 1978.

PATENT EUROPEAN OFFICE. An intergovernmental institution, est. 1973 in Munich by the European Patent Convention of the European Community members (Belgium, Denmark, the FRG, France, Great Britain, Ireland, Italy, Luxembourg, the Netherlands) plus Austria, Finland, Greece, Liechtenstein, Monaco, Norway, Portugal, Spain, Sweden, Switzerland, Turkey and Yugoslavia.

PATENTS. A subject of international agreements since 1883 (▷ Industrial Property Protection) and 1886 (▷ Copyright). See also ▷ Inter-American Patents Agreements. International organizations reg. with the UIA not including ▷ WIPO:

Commission of National Institutes of Patent Agents, f, 1956, Eindhoven, the Netherlands.
International Federation of Patent Agents, f, 1906, Turin.
International Patent Institute, f, 1947, The Hague.
See also ▷ Patent Cooperation Treaty 1978.

M. PLAMANT, *Traité de droit international conventional concernant la propriété industrielle*, Paris, 1949; *Yearbook of International Organizations*.

PATENTS INTERNATIONAL INSTITUTE. An intergovernmental institution est. in The Hague by an agreement between Belgium, France, Luxembourg and the Netherlands, signed on June 6, 1947 in The Hague. The International Patents Institute

provides the member governments "with reasoned opinion regarding the novelty of inventions in respect of which applications for patents have been filed with the respective national industrial property services." Publ.: *Documents* in English, French, German and Spanish.

UNTS, Vol. 46, pp. 249–289.

PATERNALISM. A colonial system treating conquered peoples according to the principle that a colonial power is called by God to exercise "paternal authority" over peoples "incapable of governing themselves." In a speech to Congress on Jan. 20, 1973 the US President, R. Nixon, stated: "the time has come to abandon the policy of paternalism." On Apr. 5, 1973 in a letter to the OAS Council, holding its annual session in Washington, President R. Nixon announced that in the future US co-operation with the states of Latin America would be "co-operation without paternalism."

PATHOLOGY. A subject of international co-operation. Organizations reg. with the UIA:

European Society of Pathology, f. 1964, Brussels. Publ.: *Pathologia Europaea*.
International Academy of Pathology, f. 1906, Washington, DC. Publ.: *International Pathology*.
International Council of Societies of Pathology, f. 1962, Washington, DC. Consultative status with WHO and ECOSOC.
International Society of Geographical Pathology, f. 1931, Zurich, Switzerland.
Latin American Society of Pathology, f. 1955, Mexico, DF.
Permanent International Committee of Congresses of Comparative Pathology, f. 1912, Paris. Publ.: *Revue de pathologie comparative* (bi-monthly).
Scandinavian Society of Pathology and Microbiology, f. 1975, Copenhagen.
World Association of Societies of Anatomic and Clinical Pathology, f. 1947, Paris. Official relations with WHO. Publ.: *Journal of Clinical Pathology*.
World Association of Veterinary Pathologists, f. 1952, Zurich.

Yearbook of International Organizations.

PATRIMONIAL POWER. ▷ Protecting Power or Patrimonial Power.

PATRIMONIAL SEA. A name promoted by the spokesman of the states of Latin America at the UN Conference on the Law of the Sea for the 200-mile zone of territorial waters.

PAWNBROKING INSTITUTIONS. A subject of international co-operation. Organization reg. with the UIA:

International Association of Public Pawnbroking Institutions, f. 1957, Milan, Italy. Publ.: *Il Credito Pignoratizo*.

Yearbook of International Organizations.

PAYMENT AGREEMENT. An international term for interstate agreements controlling the principles of settlements between states by virtue of mutual trade; distinct from bilateral and multilateral payments agreement.

PAYMENTS, INTERNATIONAL. A subject of international conventions and similar instruments primarily relating to ▷ Bills of Exchange and ▷ Checks, but also to waybills and bills of lading, exchange invoices, corporate bonds, certificates of deposit and pledge bonds.

PAX AMERICANA. *Latin* = "the American peace." A slogan coined during World War II in the USA saying that as Pax Romana (2nd century BC), *Pax Ecclesiastica* (12th century AD) and *Pax Britan-*

nica (19th century) were landmarks of past epochs, so would *Pax Americana* prevail in the second half of the 20th century. *Pax Americana* was heralded by American publisher Henry R. Luce (1898–1968).

PAX BRITANNICA. *Latin* = "the British peace." An international term for peace on seas and oceans of the world safeguarded in the 19th century by the naval power of Great Britain.

PAX CHRISTI INTERNATIONAL. The catholic peace movement, f. in Mar., 1945, officially consecrated 1950 as Movement of the Church in conjunction with Catholic Hierarchy. Members: National organizations. Publ.: *Bulletin* in English and French. Reg. with the UIA.

Yearbook of International Organizations.

PAX ECCLESIASTICA. *Latin* = "the Church peace." An international term for the period of hegemonistic papal rule over Europe in the 12th century when contestations between Christian states were discontinued and crusades against pagans were undertaken in the name of Christian solidarity.

PAX ROMANA. The catholic international organizations, reg. with the UIA:

Pax Romana. International Catholic Movement for Intellectual Cultural Affairs, f. 1947, Fribourg. Consultative status with UNESCO. Publ.: *Convergence.* Members: national organizations in 60 countries.
Pax Romana. International Movement of Catholic Students, f. 1921, Fribourg. Consultative status with UNESCO and ECOSOC. Publ.: *Newsletter.* Members: National federations in 60 countries.

Yearbook of International Organizations.

PCHS. Population Clearing-House and Information System, one of the information centers of the ▷ UN Economic and Social Commission for Asia and Pacific.

PEACE. The main subject of international law and permanent organized international co-operation. After World War II the UN Charter entrusted to the UN Security Council "responsibility in the first place for the maintenance of peace and international security" based on ▷ unanimity of the great powers in the UN.
The GA Res. 33/73 of Dec. 15, 1978 adopted the Declaration on the Preparation of Societies for Life in Peace.

D. WAINHOUSE, *International Peace Keeping on the Crossroad*, Baltimore, 1973; *World Encyclopedia of Peace*, Vol. 4, Oxford, 1986; *UN Resolutions and Decisions adopted by the General Assembly during the First Part of its Forty-Third Session, from 20 September to 22 December 1988*, New York, 1989, pp. 211-212.

PEACE ACADEMY, INTERNATIONAL. Academie internationale de la paix, f. 1967 by national committees in France and USA. Headquarters New York. Consultative status with ECOSOC and UNITAR. Publ.: *IPA Reports*. Reg. with the UIA.

Yearbook of International Organizations.

PEACE AND LEARNING. The interdependency between education and peace was proclaimed on Nov. 16, 1945 in London in the first phrase of the Constitution of the UNESCO: "that since wars begin in the minds of men, its in the minds of men that the defenses of peace must be constructed." ▷ UNESCO Constitution.

PEACE BUREAU. ▷ International Peace Bureau.

PEACE CORPS. A US governmental volunteer youth organization, established on Sept. 21, 1961 by an act of Congress with the task of rendering economic, technical and cultural assistance to the developing countries at the expense of the US government. In 1966 Senator R. Kennedy made a proposal for establishing a "multinational peace corps composed of members from the highly developed states." The proposal lacked support following the disclosure by the US press of alleged spying activities by members of the Peace Corps.

Bill Making, Peace Corps a Permanent Organization, US Congress, Washington, DC, 1961.

PEACE DAY, 1970. The day was proclaimed by the UN General Assembly, Res. 2526/XXIV of Dec. 17, 1969, to commemorate the 25th anniversary of the founding of the UN Oct. 24, 1945; celebrated in 1970.

UN Yearbook 1969 and 1970.

PEACE, FREEDOM AND NEUTRALITY, ZONE OF, ZOPFAN. A project to convert Southeast Asia into a zone of peace, first broached in 1968 by Malaysia, supported by ▷ ASEAN in 1970, reaffirmed in June 1986 by the ASEAN Foreign Ministers Meeting (Brunei, Indonesia, Malaysia, the Philippines, Thailand and Singapore.) The ministers stated that an ASEAN Working Group was studying the project of a Southeast Asia Nuclear Weapon Free Zone (SEA–NWFZ) as a major component of ZOPFAN.

WPC New Perspective, Helsinki, Nr. 1, 1987.

PEACEFUL CHANGE. An international term promoted in Europe during the 1930s by German revisionists and Anglo-Saxon pacificists, a formula for changing the status quo of post-Versailles Europe by "peaceful means," the realization of which was the ▷ Munich Agreement, 1938. At Conferences on Security and Co-operation in Europe (in Helsinki, 1973, and in Geneva, 1974) the issue became the subject of a basic dispute between the Warsaw Pact countries and the FRG delegation, which made the request for including the right to peaceful change in a declaration of principles on the question of inviolability of the frontiers in Europe. This request was called the "German option" (*deutsche Option*) in support of a revision of frontiers. ▷ Frontiers, Inviolability of.

H. LAUTERPACHT, "L'organisation de la paix et la révision du 'statu quo,'" in: *Recueil des Cours de l'Académie de Droit International*, No. 62, 1930; F.S. DUMM, *Peaceful Change. A Study of International Procedure*, London, 1937; C.A.W. MANNING, *Peaceful Change an International Problem*, London, 1937; H. ROGGE, *Das Revisionsproblem*, Berlin, 1937; International Studies Conference for Peaceful Change. Documents, Paris, 1938; W.G. GRAEVE, "Peaceful Change", in: STRUPP-SCHLOCHAUER *Wörterbuch des Völkerrechts*, Vol. 2, Berlin, 1961, pp. 752–757; R.L. BLEDSOE, B.A. BOCZEK, *The International Law Dictionary*, Oxford, 1987.

PEACEFUL CO-EXISTENCE. An international term for the principle of the peaceful co-existence of states with different social, economic, political and legal systems. At the international level this principle was submitted for the first time to the League of Nations in 1934 by the government of the USSR. Apart from this motion during the same period the Permanent Court of International Justice in The Hague expressed the following view in its decision of Apr. 6, 1935 on the question of minority disputes in Albania:

"The purpose of treaties on the protection of minorities was to ensure these social groups incorporation into a state whose population differs from them with respect to race, language or religion and give them the possibility of peaceful co-existence and broader co-operation with the remaining population, while retaining those characteristic features that distinguish these groups from the majority" (Publications de la CPJI, Series A/B, No. 64, p. 17).

This principle of co-existence thus required the retention by those who co-exist of their own characteristic features. Carrying over this principle to the interstate arena one can assume that "co-existence" from the legal point of view means the totality of relations between states with different structures, where general principles of international law have developed such as sovereignty and territorial integrity, equality and the mutual benefits which ensue. These principles are included in many bilateral and multilateral documents including in the UN Charter.
The principle of co-existence is also reflected in the history of India and China and was expressed in the five rules of ▷ Pancha Shila, 1954, and then in the resolutions of the conference of 29 countries of Asia and Africa in Bandung in 1955 and at conferences of African states in Accra in 1956 and Addis Ababa in 1960. In the UN General Assembly peaceful co-existence was the subject of a general debate from Sept. 20–Dec. 14, 1957, and a series of resolutions in 1960–65 (Res. 1505/XV, Res. 1815/XVII, Res. 1966/XVIII, and 2103/XX) instructed the International Law Commission to form a special committee for the purpose of defining "relations of friendship and co-operation among states." Members of the committee were: Argentina, Australia, Burma, Cameroon, Canada, Czechoslovakia, Dahomey, Egypt, France, Ghana, Great Britain, Guatemala, Holland, India, Italy, Japan, Lebanon, Malagasy Rep., Mexico, Nigeria, Poland, Romania, Sweden, USA, USSR, Venezuela and Yugoslavia. The committee held its first session in Mexico City, from July 24–Oct. 1, 1964, and then debated in New York in Mar.–Apr., 1966, its membership expanded by Algeria, Chile, Kenya, and Syria and in July–Aug., 1967 in Geneva; the result of the first session was the formation of the principle of the sovereign equality of states and the prohibition on the threat to use or the use of force; at the second session the specification of principles for the peaceful resolution of international disputes; at the third session the principles of peaceful co-operation in accordance with the UN Charter. In Latin America toward the end of the 19th century a Cuban scholar, A.S. de Bustamante, recognized peaceful co-existence as the basis of international private law, resulting from the recognition by the international legal community of ever closer ties between people of different nationalities.

A.S. DE BUSTAMANTE Y SIRVEN, *Programas de las Asignaturas de Derecho Internacional Publico y Privado*, Madrid, 1891; S. BERLINA, "Le droit de gens et la coexistence russo-américaine", in: *Journal du droit international*, 1952; R. MARKINS, "Co-existence or Chaos", in: *South Carolina Law Quarterly*, Winter, 1954; O. BOGDANOV, "Peaceful Co-existence and International Law", in: *New Times*, No. 33, 1955; R. PINTO, "Le droit international et la coexistence", in: *Journal du droit international*, 1955; J.N. HAZARD, "Legal Research on Peaceful Co-existence", in: *American Journal of International Law*, 1957; J. RADOJKOVIC "L'aspect juridique de la coexistence pacifique active," in: *Jugoslavenska revija za medunarodno pravo*, 1958; V. ABOLTIN, "Economic Aspects of Peaceful Co-existence of Two Social Systems", in: *American Economic Review*, May, 1958; R.H. FIFIELD, "Five Principles of Peaceful Co-existence", in: *American Journal of International Law*, 1958; N.S. KHRUSHCHEV, "On Peaceful co-existence", in: *Foreign Affairs*, October, 1959; E. SAUER, "Competitive – Co-existence vom Standpunkt des Völkerrechts", in: *Jahrbuch für Internationales Recht*, Juli 1960; A. RANUMDO, *Peaceful*

P

Co-existence, Baltimore, 1970; B.A. ROMANDO, *Peaceful Coexistence, International Law in the Building of Communism*, Baltimore, 1986.

PEACEFUL SETTLEMENT ACT, 1928. ▷
Pacific Settlement Act, 1928.

PEACEFUL SETTLEMENT ACT, 1949. ▷
Pacific Settlement Act, 1949.

PEACEFUL SETTLEMENT OF INTERNATIONAL DISPUTES.
A principle of international law universally in force since 1899, the date of the Hague Conventions, stating that all international disputes and conflicts should be solved in a peaceful way; called in the first half of the 20th century: pacific settlement. Introduced after World War I to the Covenant of the League of Nations (art. 12, 15 and 17) and in the Geneva Protocol of Oct. 2, 1924. The League of Nations on Sept. 26, 1928 approved the ▷ Pacific Settlement Act, 1928, and the UN General Assembly the ▷ Pacific Settlement Act, 1949. The principle that states shall resolve their disputes in a "pacific way" has been defined in the Declaration on the Principles of International Law, adopted by the UN General Assembly on Oct. 24, 1970. It is also the major principle in the adopted Helsinki Final Act of the Conference on Security and Co-operation in Europe of 1974. The Special Committee on the Charter of the UN and the Strengthening of the Role of the Organization had negotiated in the years 1981–1982 the ▷ Manila Declaration on the Peaceful Settlements of Disputes, which was adopted with the consensus on Oct. 27, 1982 by the UN General Assembly.

A ▷ CSCE forum of 120 jurists and diplomats took place in Athens on March 21–April 30, 1984 to discuss the rules of the peaceful settlement of international disputes. A Swiss draft failed to secure consensus.

On Dec. 9, 1988 the GA Res. 43/163 was adopted by 132 votes with 22 abstentions "on Peaceful Settlement of Disputes between States" which read:

"Deeply concerned at the continuation of conflict situations and the emergence of new sources of disputes and tension in international life and especially at the growing tendency to resort to force or the threat of the use of force and to intervention in internal affairs and at the escalation of the arms race, which gravely endanger the independence and security of States as well as international peace and security . . .
Again urges all States to observe and promote in good faith the provisions of the Manila Declaration on the Peaceful Settlement of International Disputes in the Settlement of their international disputes.".

LNTS, Vol. 93, pp. 345 and 361; *UNTS*, Vol. 71, pp. 101–127; J. HYDE, "Peaceful Settlement. A Survey of Studies in the Interim Committee of the UN General Assembly", in: *International Conciliation*, No. 444, Oct., 1948, pp. 531–574; A. PARODI, "Peaceful Settlement of Disputes", in: *International Conciliation*, No. 445, Nov., 1948, pp. 616–632; *UN Chronicle*, Dec., 1982, pp. 79–83; KEESING's *Contemporary Archive*, 1986; *Peaceful Settlement of Disputes*, in R.L. BLEDSOE, B.A. BOCZEK *The International Law Dictionary*, Oxford, 1987; *UN Resolutions and Decisions adopted by the General Assembly during the First Part of its Forty-Third Session, from 20 September to 22 December 1988*, New York, 1989, pp. 541–542.

PEACE INSTRUMENTS.
A term adopted at the UN and in international law, designating all international treaties and bodies serving peaceful settlement of international disputes or conflicts and the strengthening of peace.

PEACE-KEEPING FORCES. ▷
UN Military Forces, and ▷ UN Peace Keeping Operations.

PEACE-KEEPING OPERATION UN SPECIAL COMMITTEE.
Est. 1965, suspended 1983, reactivated on February 10, 1988 to study the growing cost of financing peacekeeping forces.

PEACE-KEEPING TASKS OF THE LEAGUE OF NATIONS AND UN.
In Sept., 1931, the League of Nations Assembly approved the Convention to Improve the Means of Preventing War; the main purpose of the Convention was to create demilitarized zones in an area of conflict and a LN Inspection Commission, whose rights and responsibilities were defined in a Supplementary Protocol. The Convention was never ratified, since in that same year Japan attacked Manchuria, while in following years the German Third Reich and Italy, paralyzed the peace-keeping functions of the LN. After World War II the UN Charter conferred on the UN Security Council "primary responsibility for the maintenance of international peace and security" based on the ▷ unanimity of the great powers in the UN.

D.W. WAINHOUSE, *International Peace Observation*, Baltimore, 1966; A. LEGAULT, *Bibliography of Peace Keeping Organizations*, Paris, 1967; H. WISEMAN, *Peacekeeping. Appraisals and Proposals*, New York, 1983; *United Nations Peace Keeping*, New York, 1988.

PEACE MANIFEST, 1957.
A manifest of the World Meeting of Representatives of Communist and Workers' Parties on Oct. 7, 1957 in Moscow. The main thesis of the Manifesto reads as follows:

"War is not inevitable, war can be avoided, peace can be defended and strengthened. We appeal to the peoples of the world: demand from your governments that they conduct a policy of peace in the United Nations and oppose the politics of Cold War."

PEACE MOVEMENT.
The national and international movements in support of peace. The first peace associations were formed in the USA in 1814 and in England in 1816, and in 1843 the first Anglo-American Peace Congress was organized in London. It was opened to other nationalities in 1848 in Brussels. In 1867 Giuseppe Garibaldi, Charles Lemonnsier, and Victor Hugo formed the International League of Peace and Freedom.

The first Workers' Peace Congress was held in The Hague, from Dec. 10–15, 1922, convened by the International Federation of Trade Unions. Ten years later, French writers, Henri Barbusse and Romain Rolland, suggested that a world meeting be called of intellectuals opposed to Fascist aggression, which took place in Amsterdam on Aug. 27–28, 1932, and was called the Anti-Fascist Peace Congress. After World War II, the World Congress of Intellectuals in Defense of Peace was organized on the initiative of Polish intellectuals in Wroclaw on Aug. 25–30, 1948. On Apr. 25–29, 1949 the First World Peace Congress was held in Paris, and on Nov. 16–22, 1950 the Second Peace Congress in Warsaw, with 1756 delegates from 81 countries participating. The Second Congress was scheduled to be held in Sheffield (Great Britain), but British authorities refused visas to the delegates. The Congresses established the ▷ World Peace Council, which co-ordinates operations of the world peace movement. Its greatest operation was the first world plebiscite in 1950 for a ban on atomic weapons, known as the ▷ Stockholm Appeal. Other Congresses called by the World Peace Council include: Congress of Nations in Defense of Peace was held in Vienna, Dec. 12–19, 1952. The Vienna Appeal issued by the Congress, calling for the immediate ending of the Korean war, was signed by 656 million persons.

A Congress of Nations for Disarmament and International Co-operation was held on July 16–22, 1958 in Stockholm; it appealed for a ban on atomic weapons.

A World Congress for Widespread Disarmament and Peace was held in Moscow on July 9–14, 1962; it proclaimed a Message to the Nations of the World.

A World Congress for Peace, Independence of Nations and Widespread Disarmament was held in Helsinki on Aug. 10–15, 1965; it protested against the war in Vietnam.

A World Congress for Peace in Vietnam was held in Stockholm on Oct. 13–15, 1968.

A World Congress of Peace Forces was held in Moscow in 1973.

The appeal of the World Congress was submitted to the UN General Assembly Chairman and to the UN Secretary-General on Nov. 20, 1973.

A World Convention of Peace Builders was held in Warsaw on May 6–11, 1977.

A meeting to commemorate the 30th anniversary of the World Congress of Intellectuals in Defense of Peace was held in Wroclaw on Oct. 6–10, 1978.

In the years 1980–84 peace movements in Europe organized meetings or congresses against the NATO decision of Dec. 14, 1979 to station Cruise and Pershing rockets with nuclear warheads in the FRG, Italy and Great Britain.

International Peace organizations reg. with the UIA:

Association of Educators for World Peace, f. 1969, Alabama. Publ.: *Peace Progress*.

Carnegie Endowment for International Peace f. 1910 by the American multimillionaire Andrew Carnegie (1835–1919) with a contribution of 10 million dollars. Consultative status with ECOSOC. European office: Geneva.

Council on World Tensions, f. 1950, Paris. Consultative status with UNESCO.

Christian Peace Conference, f. 1958, Geneva. Consultative status with UNESCO.

Christian Movement for Peace, f. 1923, Berne.

EIRENE, International Christian Service for Peace, f. 1957, Königswinter. Publ.: *Newsletter*.

Esperantists' World Peace Movement, f. 1953, Malmö.

Experiment in International Living, f. 1932, Putney, Vermont. Consultative status with UNESCO. Publ.: *The Experiment Newsletter*.

Federation for World Friendship, f. 1948, Copenhagen. Consultative status with UNESCO.

International Catholic Peace Movement, f. 1945, The Hague.

International Confederation for Disarmament and Peace, f. 1964, London. Publ.: *Peace Press*. Consultative status with UNESCO.

International Fellowship of Reconciliation, f. 1919, London. Consultative status with UNESCO.

International Institute for Peace, f. 1958, Vienna. Publ.: *Active Co-existence* and *Peace and the Sciences*.

International Peace Academy Committee, IPAC, f. 1967, New York. Publ.: *IPAC Reports*.

International Peace Bureau, f. 1892, Geneva. Since 1962 known as the Office of the World Union of Peace Organizations. Publ.: *Peace Information Bulletin*.

International Peace Research Assoc., f. 1964, Oslo. Publ.: *International Peace Research Newsletter*.

International Union of Peace Societies, f. 1891, Geneva. Organizes Universal Peace Congresses.

Universities and Quest for Peace, f. 1963, New York. Publ.: *Reports*.

Women's International League for Peace and Freedom, f. 1915, Geneva. Consultative status with ECOSOC and UNESCO. Publ.: *Pax and Libertas*.

World Assoc. of Schools as an Instrument of Peace, f. 1967, Geneva. Consultative status with UNESCO. Publ.: *École et Paix*.

World Conference of Religion for Peace, f. 1970, Kyoto. Publ.: *Beyond Kyoto*.

World Peace Brigade for Non-Violent Action, f. 1962, London.

World Peace Through Law, f. 1963, Geneva. Consultative status with ECOSOC and ILO. Publ.: *Cahier trimestriel*.

J. BENTHAM. "A Plan for an Universal and Perpetual Peace", in: *J. Bentham Works*, 1843, Vol. 2, pp.

546–560; S.E. BALDWIN, "The international congresses and conferences in the last century working toward the solidarity of the World," in: *American Journal of International Law*, July, 1907 and October, 1907; A.H. FRIED, *Handbuch der Friedensbewegung*, Berlin, 1913; I. KANT, *Eternal Peace and Other International Essays*, Boston, 1914. L. QUIDDE, *Völkerbund und Friedensbewegung*, Berlin, 1924; C.J. CADOUX, *Christian Pacifism Re-Examined*, London, 1940; L.S. WITTNER, *Rebels Against War: the American Peace Movements, 1941–1960*, New York, 1969; B.A. CARROLL, C.F. FINK, J. EMOHRAZ, *Peace and War. A Guide to Bibliographies*, Santa Barbara, 1983; A.J. DAY, *Peace Movements of the World: An International Directory*, London, 1987; J. DEWAR, A. PALIWALA, G. PICCIOTTO, M. RWETE, eds., *Nuclear Weapons, the Peace Movements and the Law*, London, 1987.

PEACE OBSERVATION, PEACE SUPERVISION.

International terms introduced by the League of Nations 1919–39 to define actions undertaken by the League, based on arts. 10, 11, 15 and 16 of the League's Covenant, in critical international situations with the help of so-called peace observers or investigators sent by the League to regions of conflict. The League employed this means in the case of German–Lithuanian disputes over Klaypeda (Memel) 1919–24, in the case of the Aaland Islands 1920, in the Polish–Lithuanian conflict over Vilnyus, over the Saar 1920–33, in territorial disputes between Yugoslavia and Greece, in the case of Corfu 1923, Mosul 1925, in the case of the Greek–Bulgarian crisis 1925, in the Chinese–Japanese conflict over Manchuria, in the case of Leticia 1932–35, and in the case of Italy's aggression in Ethiopia 1934–36. The UN adopted the Peace Observation formula and in the years 1946–85 has sent UN observers in over 70 conflict areas in Europe, Africa, Asia and to the Near and Middle East.

D.W. WAINHOUSE, *International Peace Observation*, Baltimore, 1966.

PEACE PROTECTION.

In the years 1950–51 bills were passed on the Protection of Peace in the parliaments of Albania on Jan. 10, 1951, Bulgaria on Dec. 25, 1950, Czechoslovakia on Dec. 20, 1950, the GDR on Dec. 15, 1950, Hungary on Dec. 8, 1950, Mongolia on Feb. 27, 1951, Poland on Dec. 19, 1950, Romania on Dec. 15, 1950 and the USSR on Mar. 12, 1951.
The text of the Polish bill is as follows:

"Propaganda and preparation for a new war are the greatest threat to the peaceful co-operation of nations and are a crime against one's fatherland and all humanity. Expressing the aspirations of millions of Poles who signed the Stockholm Appeal;
Manifesting the unshakable will of the Polish nation to continue peaceful reconstruction and its readiness to defend its security, sovereignty and peace;
Sympathizing with the resolutions of the II World Congress of Defenders of Peace held in Warsaw,
Desiring together with all peace-loving nations to co-operate in neutralizing forces aiming at starting a new world war, the Seym resolves as follows:
Art. 1. Whoever orally or in writing, through the press, radio, film or in any other manner engages in war propaganda commits a crime against peace and is subject to imprisonment for up to 15 years.
Art. 2. Crimes against peace (Art. 1) are committed by one who, specifically:
Promotes war or incites war,
Facilitates the spreading of propaganda conducted by centers waging a campaign to promote war,
Combats or slanders the Movement of Defenders of Peace.
Art. 3. In the event of being judged guilty of the crime defined in this statute, the court may rule as additional punishment: the loss of public and civic honorific rights and the whole or partial confiscation of property."

Stenogram Sejmu PRL, December 19, 1950.

PEACE RESEARCH.

A subject of international co-operation. Organizations reg. with the UIA:

Continuing Committee of the International Conference of Peace Research and Peace Activities, f. 1975, Boston. Publ.: *Conference Reports*.
Stockholm International Peace Research Institute, SIPRI, f. 1966, Stockholm. Publ.: *SIPRI Reports* and *SIPRI Yearbook of World Armaments and Disarmament*.

J.W. BURTON, "Peace Research and International Relations," in: *The Journal of Conflict Resolutions*, No. 3, 1964; UNESCO, "Peace Research," in: *International Science Journal*, No. 3, 1965; UNESCO, *Répertoire international des institutions de recherches sur la paix et les conflits*, Paris, 1974.

PEACE TREATIES.

One of the oldest international terms for bi- and multilateral treaties terminating a dispute, conflict or war. The oldest known text of a peace treaty dates from 1278 BC and was drafted in the Egyptian and Accadian languages by Rameses II and Hattusilis III who promised each other "peace and friendship" and mutually assumed the obligation not to assail the other country but to put up joint defense against mutual enemies. It is estimated that from 1500 BC to AD 1860 about 8000 peace treaties were concluded.

G.F. DE MARTENS, *Recueil de traités d'alliance, de paix, de trêve, de neutralité, de commerce, de limite, d'échange, etc., depuis 1761 jusqu'à present*, Gottingen S., 2 Vols., 1817–35; G. DE GARDEN, *Histoire générale des traités de paix et autres transactions principales entre toutes les Puissances de l'Europe depuis de la Paix de Westphalie*, 15 Vols., Paris, 1848–87; H. TRIEPEL, *Nouveau recueil général de traités. Continuation du Grand Recueil de G. Fr. de Martens*, Leipzig, 1923–35, 10 Vols., 1799–1920, 10 Vols., 1880–1929, 10 Vols., 1859–1935; *Table Générale du Recueil des Traités de G.F. Martens et de ses Continuatoire 1491–1874*, 8 Vols., Göttingen, 1875–76; G. SAUSER HALL, *Les traités de paix et les droits privés de neutre*, Paris, 1924; A.M. VILLALBA, *Los Tratados de Paz*, Madrid, 1927; US State Department, *Making the Peace, 1941–1947*, Washington, DC, 1947; G. BOUTHOUL, *Huit mille Traités de Paix*, Paris, 1948.

PEACE TREATIES AFTER WORLD WAR I.

The treaties in chronological order are:
Peace treaty with Germany, Versailles, June 29, 1919;
Treaty between Main Allied Powers, associated powers and Poland, Versailles, June 28, 1919;
Treaty between Main Allied Powers and Austria, Czechoslovakia and Yugoslavia, Saint-Germain-en-Laye, Sept. 10, 1919;
Treaty of Main Allied Powers with Bulgaria, Neuilly-sur-Seine, Nov. 27, 1919;
Treaty between Main Allied Powers with Romania, Paris, Dec. 9, 1919;
Treaty between Main Allied Powers with Turkey, Sèvres, Aug. 10, 1920;
Treaty of Peace between Poland, Russia and Ukraine, Riga, Mar. 18, 1921.

SOCIÉTÉ DES NATIONS, *Recueil des Traités et des Engagements Internationals, enregistrés par le secrétariat de la SdN*, Genève, 1920–21.

PEACE TREATIES AFTER WORLD WAR II.

The general basis for peace treaties after World War II was the ▷ Potsdam Agreement, 1945.
On Feb. 10, 1947 peace treaties with Bulgaria, Finland, Hungary, Romania and Italy were signed at Paris by the Great Powers and allied states.
On Sept. 8, 1951 – Japan Peace Treaty was signed at San Francisco.
On Mar. 23, 1973 – Vietnam Paris Agreements were signed.
On Mar. 26, 1979 – Egypt–Israel Treaty was signed at Washington.

A. LEISS, R. DEUNEDD, *European Peace Treaties after World War II*, London, 1954.

PEACE, UN DECLARATION ON PREPARATION OF SOCIETIES FOR LIFE IN PEACE, 1978.

A Declaration adopted by the UN General Assembly Res. 33/73 on Dec. 15, 1978 by a vote of 138 in favor, to none against, with abstention by Israel and the USA. The text is as follows:

"The General Assembly, Recalling that in the Charter the peoples of the United Nations proclaimed their determination to save succeeding generations from the scourge of war and that one of the fundamental purposes of the United Nations is to maintain international peace and security,
Reaffirming that, in accordance with General Assembly resolution 95 (I) of 11 December 1946, planning, preparation, initiation or waging of a war of aggression are crimes against peace and that, pursuant to the Declaration on Principles of International Law concerning Friendly Relations and Cooperation among States in accordance with the Charter of the United Nations, of 24 October 1970, and the Definition of Aggression of 14 December 1974, a war of aggression constitutes a crime against the peace,
Reaffirming the right of individuals, states and all mankind to life in peace,
Aware that, since wars begin in the minds of men, it is in the minds of men that the defences of peace must be constructed,
Recognizing that peace among nations is mankind's paramount value, held in the highest esteem by all principal political, social and religious movements,
Guided by the lofty goal of preparing societies for and creating conditions of the common existence and cooperation in peace, equality, mutual confidence and understanding,
Recognizing the essential role of Governments, as well as governmental and non-governmental organizations, both national and international, the mass media, educational processes and teaching methods, in promoting the ideals of peace and understanding among nations,
Convinced that, in the era of modern scientific and technological progress, mankind's resources, energy and creative talents should be directed to the peaceful economic, social and cultural development of all countries, should promote the implementation of the new international economic order and should serve the raising of the living standards of all nations,
Stressing with utmost concern that the arms race, in particular in the nuclear field, and the development of new types and systems of weapons, based on modern scientific principles and achievements, threaten world peace,
Recalling that, in the Final Document of the Tenth Special Session of the General Assembly, the States Members of the United Nations solemnly reaffirmed their determination to make further collective efforts aimed at strengthening peace and international security and eliminating the threat of war, and agreed that, in order to facilitate the process of disarmament, it was necessary to take measures and pursue policies to strengthen international peace and security and to build confidence among states,
Reaffirming the principles contained in the Declaration on the Granting of Independence to Colonial Countries and Peoples, of 14 December 1960, the Declaration on the Strengthening of International Security, of 16 December 1970, and the Declaration on the Deepening and Consolidation of International Detente, of 19 December 1977,
Recalling the Declaration on the Promotion among Youth of the Ideals of Peace, Mutual Respect and Understanding between Peoples, of 7 December 1965,
Further recalling the Universal Declaration of Human Rights, of 10 December 1948, as well as the International Covenant on Civil and Political Rights, of 16 December 1966, and bearing in mind the latter states, inter alia, that any propaganda for war shall be prohibited by law,
I. Solemnly invites all states to guide themselves in their activities by the recognition of the supreme importance and necessity of establishing, maintaining and strengthening a just and durable peace for present and future generations and, in particular, to observe the following principles:

P

(1) Every nation and every human being, regardless of race, conscience, language or sex, has the inherent right to life in peace. Respect for that right, as well as for the other human rights, is in the common interest of all mankind and an indispensable condition of advancement of all nations, large and small, in all fields.

(2) A war of aggression, its planning, preparation or initiation are crimes against peace and are prohibited by international law.

(3) In accordance with the purposes and principles of the United Nations, states have the duty to refrain from propaganda for wars of aggression.

(4) Every state, acting in the spirit of friendship and good-neighbourly relations, has the duty to promote all-round, mutually advantageous and equitable political, economic, social and cultural co-operation with other states, notwithstanding their socio-economic systems, with a view to securing their common existence and co-operation in peace, in conditions of mutual understanding of and respect for the identity and diversity of all peoples, and the duty to take up actions conducive to the furtherance of the ideals of peace, humanism and freedom.

(5) Every state has the duty to respect the right of all peoples to self-determination, independence, equality, sovereignty, the territorial integrity of states and the inviolability of their frontiers, including the right to determine the road of their development, without interference or intervention in their internal affairs.

(6) A basic instrument of the maintenance of peace is the elimination of the threat inherent in the arms race, as well as efforts towards general and complete disarmament, under effective international control, including partial measures with that end in view, in accordance with the principles agreed upon within the United Nations and relevant international agreements.

(7) Every state has the duty to discourage all manifestations and practices of colonialism, as well as racism, racial discrimination and apartheid, as contrary to the right of peoples to self-determination and to other human rights and fundamental freedoms.

(8) Every state has the duty to discourage advocacy of hatred and prejudice against other peoples as contrary to the principles of peaceful co-existence and friendly cooperation.

II. Calls upon all states, in order to implement the above principles:

(a) To act perseveringly and consistently, with due regard for the constitutional rights and the role of the family, the institutions and organizations concerned:

(i) To ensure that their policies relevant to the implementation of the present Declaration, including educational processes and teaching methods as well as media information activities, incorporate contents compatible with the task of the preparation for life in peace of entire societies and, in particular, the young generations;

(ii) Therefore, to discourage and eliminate incitement to racial hatred, national or other discrimination, injustice or advocacy of violence and war;

(b) To develop various forms of bilateral and multilateral cooperation, also in international, governmental and non-governmental organization, with a view to enhancing preparation of societies to live in peace and, in particular, exchanging experiences on projects pursued with that end in view;

III.(1) Recommends that the governmental and non-governmental organizations concerned should initiate appropriate actions towards the implementation of the present Declaration;

(2) States that a full implementation of the principles enshrined in the present Declaration calls for a concerted action on the part of Governments, the United Nations, the specialized agencies, in particular the United Nations Educational, Scientific and Cultural Organization, as well as other interested international and national organizations, both governmental and non-governmental;

(3) Requests the Secretary-General to follow the progress made in the implementation of the present Declaration and to submit periodic reports thereon to the General Assembly, the first such reports to be submitted not later than at the thirty-sixth session, 1981."

UN Yearbook, 1978; UN Chronicle, January, 1979, pp. 23–27; Preparation of Societies for Life in Peace, Warsaw, 1979.

PEANUTS. A subject of international co-operation. Organization reg. with the UIA:

African Peanuts Council, est. 1964, Dakar, by the governments of Gambia, Mali, Niger, Nigeria, Senegal and Sudan representing *c.* 21% of World production and *c.* 35% of export.
In the EEC system peanuts from the ACP states were included in the ▷STABEX.

Yearbook of International Organizations.

PEARL HARBOR. The landlocked natural harbor on Oahu Island, Hawaii, west of Honolulu, on the Pacific Ocean; main US naval base in the Pacific since 1900. On Dec. 7, 1941 the US Pacific fleet moored in Pearl Harbor was attacked by Japanese carrier-based planes. Nineteen naval vessels were sunk or severely damaged (i.a. battleships USS *Arizona, Oklahoma, Utah, Nevada, Pennsylvania*) and US navy and army casualties exceeded 3300, of which over 2200 were killed. Over the sunken hulk of the USS *Arizona* a national memorial was erected.

W. MILLIS, *This is Pearl: The US and Japan 1941*, New York, 1947; W. LORD, *Day of Infamy*, New York, 1957; R. WOHLSTETTER, S.E. MORRISON, *History of US Naval Operations in World War II*, Vol. 1, New York, 1948; *Pearl Harbor: Warning and Decision*, New York, 1962.

PEASANT INTERNATIONAL ORGANIZATIONS. The first peasant organization was established in the late 19th century within the co-operative movement (▷ Co-operativism); between the wars co-operation between various peasant factions of Europe was initiated (▷ Green International); after World War II an international organization was formed under UN auspices devoted to fostering rural development. First conference of European peasant parties and organizations was held in Helsinki from Feb. 6–8, 1976; attended by 34 delegations from 23 countries.
Organization reg. with the UIA:

International Peasant Union, f, 1921, Washington, DC. Members: political peasant parties in exile after World War II. Publ. *Bulletin.*

Yearbook of International Organizations.

PEAT. A subject of international research. Organizations reg. with the UIA:

International Peat Society, f. 1968, Helsinki. Aims: promote study on utilization of peatland, peat and related materials. Consultative status with UNESCO. Publ.: *IPS Bulletin.* Members: national committees in Canada, Denmark, Finland, FRG, GDR, Hungary, Iceland, Norway, Poland, Sweden and the UK.
International Straw, Fodder and Peat Trade Confederation, f. 1967, Paris, France.

Yearbook of International Organizations, 1986/87; The Europa Yearbook 1988. A World Survey, Vol. I, London 1988.

PECUNIARY CLAIMS. A subject of international conventions. The Treaty of Arbitration for Pecuniary Claims was signed by 17 American Republics on Jan. 30, 1902 in Mexico, DF, extended by the Convention on Pecuniary Claims, signed by 19 American Republics on Aug. 13, 1906 in Rio de Janeiro; superseded by the Convention on Pecuniary Claims signed by all 21 American Republics on Aug. 11, 1910 in Buenos Aires; it came into force on Jan. 1, 1913.

OAS Inter-American Treaties and Conventions, Washington, DC, 1971, pp. 3, 13 and 19.

PEDAGOGIC MATERIAL. A subject of international agreement; defined in the Customs Convention on the temporary importation of pedagogic material (with Annex), signed on June 8, 1970 in Brussels. It came into force on Sept. 10, 1971. The Convention's definition of pedagogic material read as follows: "Any material used for purposes of education or vocational training, and especially the models, instruments, apparatus, machines and accessories therefor."

UNTS, Vol. 817, p. 315.

PEDAGOGY. A subject of international co-operation and research. Organizations reg. with the UIA:

International Association for the Advancement of Education Research, f. 1953, Ghent. Aims: research in education sciences and in their teaching at the university level. Consultative status with ECOSOC and UNESCO.
International Council on Education for Teaching, f. 1953, Washington, DC. Consultative status with UNESCO.
International Federation of "École Moderne" Movements (Pedagogy Freinat), Federation internationale des movements d'école moderne (FIMEN), f. 1957, Caen, France. Aims: bringing the school closer to everyday life and transforming it into a co-operative enterprise. Consultative status with UNESCO. Organizes every year Rencontre international Freinet. Publ.: *Vocabularium Pedagogicum.*
International Institute for Education Studies, f. 1969, Brussels. Publ.: *Youth Action.*

Yearbook of International Organizations.

PEDIATRY. A subject of international co-operation. Organizations reg. with the UIA:

African Pediatric Club, f. 1973, Kenema, Sierra Leone.
Afro-Asian Pediatric Association, f. 1975, Karachi.
Asian Association of Pediatric Surgeons, f. 1972, Tokyo.
Association of European Pediatric Cardiologists, f. 1964, Leuven.
Association of Pediatric Societies of the South-east Asian Region, f. 1974, Manila.
European Society for Pediatric Endocrinology, f. 1962, Zurich.
European Society for Pediatric Nephrology, f. 1967, Berne.
European Society for Pediatric Research, f. 1968, Ulm.
International Pediatric Association, f. 1912, Paris. Consultative status with WHO, UNICEF and ESOSOC. Publ.: *Bulletin.*
International Society for Pediatric Neurosurgery, f. 1972, Chicago. Publ.: *Child's Brain* (bi-monthly).
International Society of Pediatric Oncology, f. 1969, Amsterdam.
Latin American Society for Pediatric Research, f. 1975, São Paulo.
Pan-American Association of Pediatric Surgery, f. 1966, Mexico, DF. Publ.: *Panamerican Pediatric Surgery.*
Union of Middle East Mediterranean Pediatric Societies, f. 1966, Athens.

Yearbook of International Organizations.

PEENEMÜNDE. A town in the GDR, on the northwest edge of the Usedom Island in Szczecin Bay, first launching site for ▷ V1, V2 missiles, constructed 1936, extended during World War II, discovered by the intelligence service of the Polish Home Army 1943; the information was passed on to London and resulted in the bombing and a 50% destruction of the Peenemünde center on Aug. 18, 1943.

B. ARCT, *Poles Against the V1 Weapons,* Warsaw, 1972.

PEKING PEACE TREATY, 1860. One of the Opium Treaties, between the Allied Powers and China, signed at Peking on Oct. 25, 1860, concerning the legalization of opium trade in all Chinese provinces and the opening of nine more ports for opium import in relation to the ▷ Tientsin Peace Treaty 1858. ▷ Opium Wars, 1839–60.

Perez de Cuellar Triangular Doctrine, 1987

DE MARTENS, *Nouveau Recueil Général*, Vol. XVII, 1, p. 44.

PEKING TREATY, 1880. ▷ American-Chinese Treaties, 1844–1908.

PELL-MELL. French: *Pêle-Mêle*. An international term for the signing of international documents not according to seniority (rotation in precedence) or alphabetical order, but without any order.

Dictionaire international de terminologie diplomatique, Paris, 1962.

PELOTA VASCA. The Basque ball game, an international sport, popular especially in France, Spain and Latin America, recognized by the International Olympic Committee though not an Olympic competition.

PEMBA. Tanzanian island in the Indian Ocean. Area: 985 sq. km. It was part of the sultanate of ▷ Zanzibar and Pemba until 1964.

PENAL INTERNATIONAL LAW. The term Penal International Law is not defined in any international act, a subject of discussion with regard to the part of International Law, consisting of norms, the violation of which constitute crimes against the law of nations, (crimes against peace, crimes against humanity or war crimes); as opposed to international penal law, which integrates the provisions of internal law, specifying the conditions of application of national penal codes to people who committed crimes abroad. The UN General Assembly recommended on Dec. 11, 1946 the elaboration of an International Penal Code and a statute of International Criminal Court. The first Treaty on International Penal Law was prepared and signed in Montevideo, on Jan. 23, 1889 by the governments of Argentina, Bolivia, Paraguay, Peru and Uruguay. After the revision of the treaty on Mar. 19, 1940, it was signed by Brazil and Colombia.
Organizations reg. with the UIA:

International Association of Penal Law, in 1924, Paris, as successor to International Union of Penal Law (1889), with the task of conducting international studies of the penal law. Publ.: *Revue internationale de droit pénal*.
International Penal and Penitentiary Foundation, f. 1951, Luxembourg. Publ.: *Studies in Penology and of Penal Treatment*.
International Society of Penal Military Law and Law of War, f. 1956, Brussels. Publ.: *Revue de droit penal militaire et de droit de guerre*.
Howard League for Penal Reform, f. 1921, London, as successor to Howard Association (1866) and of Penal Reform League (1907). Consultative status with ECOSOC. Publ.: *Howard Journal of Penology and Crime Prevention*.

D. OEHLER, *Internationales Strafrecht*, Berlin, 1973.

PEN CLUB. (PEN = Poets, Essayists, Novelists.) International Pen, Federation internationale des PEN Clubs, f. 1921 in the UK by Mrs. C.A. Dawson Scott, first President John Galsworthy, as a World Association of Writers, Editors and Translators in all branches and classes of literature, belles lettres, poetry, drama, fiction, history, biography, science, translation and philosophy. International Secretariat: London. Consultative status with UNESCO and ECOSOC. It held 42 international congresses up to 1980. Its secretariat is in London with autonomous centres in over 50 countries and also centres for writers in Catalan, Estonian, Languedoc, Latvian, Yiddish and Writers in Exile (London, New York, Paris, Toronto). Publ.: *International PEN Bulletin of Selected Books, PEN*

Broadsheet (quarterly), *New Poems* (annual). Reg. with the UIA.

Yearbook of International Organizations.

PENICILLIN. A group of antibiotics, discovered in 1929 by the Scottish bacteriologist, Alexander Fleming in the process of growing the fungus *Penicillium notatum* used in therapy since 1942; subject of international co-operation organized since 1947 by WHO in the treatment of many diseases. The WHO in the 1980's was alarmed by the increasing frequency of acquired resistance to antibiotics as a worldwide health problem which demands international attention. An antibiotic-destroying enzyme, penisillinase (*beta-lactamase*) acquired resistance subsequently not only to penicillin, but also to amplicilin, tetraciclina, chloramphenicol and sulfonamides. Antibiotic resistance limits the effectiveness of antibiotics against bacteria. The WHO in 1980 started with a plan of action for worldwide control of the resistant strains and of the ways of using antibiotics.

O. IDSOE, T. GUTHE, R.R. WILCOX, "Pencillin in the Treatment of Syphilis. The Experience of Three Decades", in: *Bulletin of WHO*, No. 47, 1972. N. WILLARD, "Antibiotic. The Resistance Problem", in: *WHO Features*, October 1984.

PENSIONS AND ANNUITIES. The subject of bilateral and multilateral international agreements. On the basis of the principle of mutuality, states as a rule obligate themselves to send to citizens, who have acquired pension rights and settled in another country, the pensions due to them for having worked the number of years stipulated by the law of those states. After World War I the states which succeeded to the Austrian–Hungarian monarchy on Apr. 6, 1922 signed a convention in Rome on pensions awarded by the former government of that monarchy and a supplementary convention followed on Nov. 30, 1923 in Vienna. In Oslo on July 27, 1949 Denmark, Finland, Iceland, Norway and Sweden signed the Scandinavian Convention on the Mutual Payment of Pensions.
On Feb. 10, 1931 in Stockholm the governments of Denmark, Finland, Iceland, Norway and Sweden signed the Scandinavian Convention on Pensions and Annuities, supplemented by a Treaty signed on Apr. 1, 1953, in Oslo.

UNTS, Vol. 47, p. 127 and Vol. 227, p. 169.

PENSION SYSTEM IN THE UN ▷ UN Pension System.

PENTAGON. The common name of the five-sided building of the US Defense Department, constructed in Washington during World War II (ready for use Jan. 15, 1943). Official name of the Pentagon to 1947: the Department of War; 1947–49; the National Military Establishment; from 1950: the Department of Defense. Located also in the Pentagon building are: departments of the various armed forces, Committee of the Joint Chiefs of Staff, intelligence agencies of the armed forces, and other command institutions of the US military. The Pentagon has five stories, its height is 21.7 m, cubic area *c.* 2.2 million m; *c.* 30,000 military and civilian employees work there. In 1958 the Eisenhower administration constructed the so-called Little Pentagon, also on the Potomac River, at a cost of 55 million dollars with offices for the 10,000 employees of the Central Intelligence Agency, CIA.

The Department of Defense, Washington, 1967;

C.R. MOLLENHOF, *The Pentagon Politics. Profit and Plunder*, New York, 1967; J. BOSCH, *El Pentagonismo*, Mexico, DF, 1967.

PENTAGONALISM DOCTRINE, 1973. A US foreign policy formulated by President R. Nixon, assuming that in the pentagon of the USA, Western Europe, Japan, China and the USSR, the USA should play the leading role. ▷ Trilateral Commission.

PENTATHLON. An international sport, Olympic competition since 1948, subject of international co-operation. Organization reg. with the UIA:

International Union of Pentathlon and Biathlon, f. 1948, London. Recognized by International Olympic Committee. Members: National federations in 44 countries.

Yearbook of International Organizations.

PEOPLE'S CAPITALISM ▷ Privatization.

PEOPLE'S DEMOCRACY. An international term, first coined 1905 by the Chinese revolutionary statesman Dr Sun Yat-sen (1866–1925) as one of his Three Principles of the People: People's Rule, People's Democracy and People's Socialism. After the World War II taken up by the communist press to indicate political systems of states that entered "the path of socialism under the leadership of the working class" and on the basis of a "broad national unity front." In 1950 the officially designated "people's democracy" countries list included Albania, Bulgaria, Czechoslovakia, the GDR, Hungary, Poland, Romania and Yugoslavia.

SUN YAT SEN, *Memoirs of Chinese Revolutionary*, London, 1927; SUN YAT SEN *The Three Principles of the People*, London, 1927; J.L. TALMON, *The Rise of Totalitarian Democracy*, New York, 1952; F. FETJO, *A History of the People's Democracies*, London, 1974.

POPULAR FRONT. An international term for the antifascist movement in Europe in the 1930's.

J. DELPERIE DE BAYAC, *Histoire du Front Populaire*, Paris 1972; R. GRAHAM, P. PRESTON, *The Popular Front In Europe*, London, 1987.

PEPPER. A subject of international co-operation. An agreement between the governments of India, Indonesia and Malaysia, was signed on Apr. 16, 1971 in Bangkok and came into force on Mar. 29, 1972, to promote, co-ordinate and harmonize all activities relating to pepper (*piper nigrum*) economy. The Agreement established on Sept. 11, 1972 the Pepper Community in Bangkok. The Community represents *c.* 80% of world pepper production. Reg. with the UIA.

Yearbook of International Organizations; UNTS, Vol. 818, p. 90.

PERESTROIKA. Russian: Restructuring. An international term, coined by M. Gorbachev in the USSR, 1985/86 for the economic and social reforms in countries with a planned economy.

M. GORBACHEV, *Perestroika, New Thinking for Our Country and the World*, New York, 1987; A. AGAN-BEGYAN, *The Challenge: Economics of Perestroika*, London, 1988; J. WINNICKI, *The Distorted World of Soviet Type Economies*, London-New York, 1988; A. NUJKIN, Idealy ili intery, in *Novyi Mir*, No. 1 and 2, 1988 (also in the English edition "New Times").

PEREZ DE CUELLAR TRIANGULAR DOCTRINE, 1987. A doctrine of the Triangular Relationship between Disarmament, Development and Security, formulated by the Secretary General Javier Perez de Cuellar in the opening address to the UN International Conference on the Relationship

687

between Disarmament and Development, held in New York from August 24 to September 11, 1987:

Security is clearly a legitimate and fundamental concern of all States. However, living under the nuclear shadow we have also come to a stage in human affairs where security can no longer be perceived in military terms alone. There is a wide recognition today of a triangular relationship between questions of disarmament, development and security. Non-military threats to human security can endanger national security and in turn threaten international security as well. Moreover, when we talk of disarmament, we are talking of a process which must entail a series of reciprocal, coordinated and verifiable measures that will have the effect of ensuring the security of all at progressively lower levels of armaments.
UN Chronicle, November, 1987.

PERFORMERS OF PHONOGRAMS ▷ Phonograms Conventions.

PERFUMES. Subject of international cooperation. Organizations reg. with the UIA:

European Federation of Perfumery Retailers, f. 1960, Paris, France.
International Fragrance Association, f. 1973, Geneva, Switzerland. Consultative Status: Council of Europe.
Liason Committee of European Association of the Perfume, Cosmetic Products and Toiletries Industries, f. 1962, Brussels, Belgium.

Yearbook of International Organizations, 1986/87; *The Europa Yearbook 1988. A World Survey*, Vol. I, London, 1988.

PERMANENT COURT OF ARBITRATION. ▷ Arbitration, Permanent Court of.

PERMANENT COURT OF INTERNATIONAL JUSTICE. An intergovernmental institution, established under art. 14 of the Covenant of the League of Nations, with the task of examining "all disputes of an international character submitted thereto by the Parties," and of giving "advisory opinions on all disputes and issues presented by the Council or Assembly of the League of Nations." The Statute of the Permanent Court was adopted by 44 member states of the League on Dec. 13, 1920; the Assembly also chose 10 judges and 4 deputy judges for terms of 9 years, and in 1930 the number of judges was increased to 15. Not all member states of the League were also members of the Permanent Court, since it was not compulsory; the Statute was ratified by a total of 51 states. The USA, which signed the Statute, but did not ratify it, was not a member of the Court but was represented indirectly by a judge, a US citizen. The Court began its work on Dec. 15, 1922 in The Hague and ceased to exist formally on Dec. 31, 1945.

LNTS, Vol. 6, pp. 390–401; *Statut de la CPJI*, Genève, 1921; A. DE BUSTAMANTE, *The World Court*, New York, 1925; Q. WRIGHT, "The US and the Court", in: *International Conciliation*, No. 232, September, 1927; *CPJI Série A: Recueil des Arrêts, 1922–1930*, Genève, 1931; *CPJI Série B: Recueil des Avis Consultatifs, 1922–1930*, Geneve, 1931; A.P. FACHIRI, *The Permanent Court of International Justice. Its Constitution, Procedure and Work*, 2 Vols., London, 1932; H. LAUTERPACHT, *The Development of International Law by the PCIJ*, London, 1934; W. JENKS, "La compétence de l OIT. Examen de quatre avis consultatifs rendu pour la Cour Permanente de Justice International", in: *Revue de Droit International et de législation comparée*, No. 64, 1937; M.O. HUDSON, *Handbook of the World Court*, Boston, 1938; *CPJI Série F: Index Généraux 1922–1926, 1927, 1920–1936*, Genève, 1938; *CPJI Série A/B: Recueil des Arrêts, Avis Consultatifs et Ordonnances, 1931–1940*, Geneve, 1941; "The Twentieth Year of the Permanent Court of International Justice", in: *American Journal of International Law*, No. 1, January, 1942; *CPJI Série, C: Plaidoires Exposés Oraux et Documents Relatifs a l Affaire, 1922–1939*, Geneve, 1943; *CPJI Serie D: Actes et Documentation*

relatifs à l'Organisation de la Cour, Geneve, 1943; M.O. HUDSON, *The Permanent Court of International Justice, 1920–1942*, Boston, 1943; *The Permanent Court of International Justice, 1922–1944*, New York, 1944; *CPJI Serie E: Rapports Annuels 1925–1939, 1939–1945*, Geneve, 1946; *Bibliographical List of Official and Unofficial Publications Concerning the PCIJ*, Geneva, 1939 and 1946; "Dissolution de la Cour. Permanente de Justice Internationale et Creation d une nouvelle Cour. Notes et Documents", in: *Revue de Droit international des sciences diplomatiqués et politiques*, No. 24, 1946; R. BERNHARDT, "Rechtsgutachten des Ständigen Internationalen Gerichtshofes", in: STRUPP-SCHLOCHAUER, *Wörterbuch des Völkerrechts*, Berlin, 1962, Vol. III, pp. 37–49; B. WINIARSKI, "The Permanent Court of International Justice", in *UN Review*, March, 1962.

PERMANENT MISSIONS OF THE UN. The official name of permanent governmental delegations to the UN, 1948–54, on the basis of rules and regulations of missions passed by the UN General Assembly, Res. 257/III, Dec. 3, 1948.

Permanent Missions to the UN, New York, 1955; *Delegations to the UN*, New York, 1956; *UN Monthly Chronicle*, No. 11, 1971, pp. 160–161.

PERMANENT OBSERVERS FROM NON-UN MEMBERS. The official name for states which are not UN members but which have permanent accredited representatives at the UN. In 1945 the first permanent observers accredited were: Morocco and Switzerland, 1954 – FRG, South Korea and South Vietnam, 1964 – Vatican.

PERMANENT REVOLUTION DOCTRINE, 1905. An international term, coined in 1905 by L. Trotsky (1879–1940):

"A national revolution is not a self-contained unit, it is just a link in the international chain. The international revolution is a permanent process, in spite of the temporary setbacks and the ebbing of the tide."

The doctrine discussed in the workers movement 1905–06, 1915 and 1921, was repudiated 1924 by Joseph Stalin ▷ Socialism in a single country doctrine.

L. TROTSKY, *Age of Permanent Revolution*, New York, 1947.

PERPETUAL NEUTRALITY. An international term introduced by the Vienna Congress of 1815. ▷ neutrality of states.

PERSEPOLIS. A cultural site of Iran, included in the ▷ World Heritage UNESCO List. Bas-reliefs on the monumental stairways leading to an immense reception hall, columns which conjure up the dazzling proportions of the throne room – these are remains of the inimitable architecture of the imperial city founded by Darius the Great in 518 BC.

UNESCO. *A Legacy for All*, Paris, 1984.

PERSHING II. An American long-range missile. The question of its deployment in NATO countries along with the self-guided Cruise missile, became a subject of international controversy in Europe in the 1980's as did the deployment of Soviet SS-20 missiles in Warsaw Pact countries. The first 91 Pershing II missiles were installed in Western Europe in 1984, out of 572 projected until 1988.

J. GOLDBLAT, *Arms and Disarmament. A Handbook*, New York, 1983. *NATO Press Release*, November 19, 1984; D. ROBERTSON, *Guide to Modern Defense and Strategy*, Detroit, 1988.

PERSIA. The historical name until 1935 of ▷ Iran, since the 7th century BC when the Persian dynasty of the Achemenids began to build an empire.

PERSIAN GULF. An arm of the Arabian Sea, between Saudi Arabia and Iran linking the Strait of Hormuz with the Gulf of Oman. Length: 965 km. Area: 233,110 sq. km. In 19th century the Gulf was under British domination, after temporary truces between Great Britain and the Arab sheikhdoms (Trucial States) in 1820 and 1835, and after the Perpetual Maritime Truce 1853. The British sphere of influence in the Persian Gulf area was accepted in 1907 by the major world powers. Great Britain withdrew her forces from the region in late 1960. The US installed a military base in Bahrain in 1971. Destabilization of the region came in 1979/80 with the US–Iran and USSR–Afghanistan conflicts, as well as with the Iran–Iraq war. ▷ Co-operation Council for the Arab States of the Gulf.

L. MONROE, *The Changing Balance of Power in the Persian Gulf*, Hannover, N.H., 1972.

PERSONAL UNION. An international term for a confederation of states by royal personal union, like Brazil and Portugal 1808–1821 or the Netherlands and Luxembourg 1815–1890.

PERSONA NON GRATA AND PERSONA GRATA. *Latin* = "unacceptable person and acceptable person." International terms used with regard to diplomats. A diplomat is declared persona non grata when the accrediting government, for reasons which do not have to be disclosed, does not agree to accredit him, or decides that a serving diplomat has trespassed his rights and immunities and requires that he be recalled. When the accrediting government has no objections to a candidate for a diplomatic post, that candidate is termed persona grata. ▷ Vienna Diplomatic Convention, 1961.

E. DENZA, *Diplomatic Law, Commentary by Vienna Convention*, New York, 1976, pp. 40–43, 84, 118, 127, 169–174; R.L. BLEDSOE, B.A. BOCZEK, *The International Law Dictionary*, Oxford, 1987.

PERTUSSIS ▷ Immunization.

PERU. Member of the UN. Republic of Peru. A state in South America on the Atlantic, bounded by Ecuador, Colombia, Brazil, Bolivia, Chile. Area: 1,285,215 sq. km. Pop. 1988 est.: 21,300,000 (1876 census: 1,699,000; 1940: 6,207,000; 1961: 9,906,000; 1972: 13,358,208; 1981: 17,005,210). Capital: Lima with 3,968,972 inhabitants, 1981. GNP per capita 1985: US $980. Official language: Spanish. Currency: one Inti = 1,000 soles. National Day: July 28, Independence Day, 1821.
Member of the League of Nations 1919–39. Founding member of the UN and all its specialized agencies. Member of the OAS, Tlatelolco Treaty, Andine Group, SELA and until 1980 LAFTA, since 1980 of ALADI.
International relations: Spanish colony from 1754 to 1821; independent republic since July 28, 1821. In 1836–39 in confederation with Bolivia; in 1864 at war with Spain; 1879 with Chile – ended with loss of Arica, Tarapaca and Tacna (▷ Ancon Treaty Oct. 20, 1883). ▷ Pacific War, 1879–1883. After years of negotiations and arbitration by the US President H. Hoover, Tacna province restored to Peru on June 3, 1929; in 1940–42 in armed conflict with Ecuador – ended with a change in frontiers to the advantage of Peru under the Rio de Janeiro Protocol of Jan 29, 1942, ratified by both parties and guaranteed by Argentina, Brazil, Chile and the USA. Constitutional Assembly of Ecuador of Nov. 25, 1966 annulled the Rio de Janeiro Protocol which Peru refused to acknowledge in a government declaration of Dec. 10, 1966. In 1969 extended territorial waters to 200 miles and joined the ▷ Montevideo Group, 1971. New frontier disputes and border in-

cidents with Ecuador in Jan., 1981, in Jan., 1982 and again in Jan., 1983 over the Cordillera del Condor. See also ▷ *World Heritage* UNESCO List.

B. BERENCHI, *Historia de los Limites del Peru*, Lima, 1930; *Financiera del Peru 1915–1964*, Lima, 1964; J.C. CARREY, *Peru and the United States 1900–1966*, New York, 1964; W.D. HARRIS, H.A. HOSSE, *La Vivienda Peru*, London, 1964; M. BACA, A. TAURO, *Diccionario Enciclopedico del Peru*, 3 Vols., Lima, 1966; F. BOURRICHARD, *Pouvoir et Société dans le Pérou contemporain*, Paris, 1967; J. PIKE, *A Modern History of Peru*, London, 1967; P. VARGAS, *Historia General del Peru*, Lima, 1967; R. MARRET, *Peru*, London, 1969; J. HEMMING, *The Conquest of the Incas*, London, 1970; A. QUIJANO, *Nationalism and Capitalism in Peru. A Study of New-Imperialism*, New York, 1971; D.A. SHARP (ed.), *US Foreign Policy and Peru*, Austin, 1972; *Exposiciones Oficiales Peruanas sobre et Nuevo Derecho del Mar*, Lima, 1973; A.F. LOVENTHAL, *The Peruvian Experiment*, Princeton, 1975; R.C. WEBB, *Government Policy and the Distribution of Income in Peru 1963–1973*, Harvard, 1977; F.B. PIKE, *The US and the Andean Republics: Peru, Bolivia, Ecuador*, Cambridge Mass., 1978; G.D. PHILIP, *The Rise and Fall of the Peruvian Military Radicals, 1968–1976*, London, 1978; R. THORPE, G. BERTRAM, *Peru 1890–1977*, London, 1978; E.V.K. FITZGERALD, *The Political Economy in Peru, 1958–78*, Oxford, 1979; *The Europa Year Book 1984. A World Survey*, Vol. II, pp. 2247–2261, London, 1984; T. SCHEETZ, *Peru and the IMF*, Pittsburgh, PA, 1986.

PESETA. A monetary unit of Spain; one peseta = 100 centimos; issued by the Banco de Espana.

PESO ARGENTINO. A monetary unit of Argentina; one peso = 100 centavos; issued by the Banco Central de la Republica Argentina.

PESO BOLIVIANO. A monetary unit of Bolivia; one peso = 100 centavos; issued by the Banco Central de Bolivia.

PESO CHILENO. A monetary unit of Chile from Sept. 29, 1975, replacing Chilean Escudo (1960–75); one peso = 100 centavos; issued by the Banco Central de Chile.

PESO COLOMBIANO. A monetary unit of Colombia; one peso = 100 centavos; issued by the Banco de la Republica.

PESO CUBANO. A monetary unit of Cuba; one peso = 100 centavos; issued by the Banco Nacional de Cuba.

PESO DOMINICANO. A monetary unit of Dominicana; one peso = 100 centavos; issued by the Banco Central de la Republica Dominicana.

PESO MEXICANO. A monetary unit of Mexico; one peso = 100 centavos; issued by the Banco de Mexico.

PESO PHILIPPINE. A monetary unit of Philippines; one peso = 100 centavos; issued by the Central Bank of the Philippines.

PESO URUGUAYANO. A monetary unit of Uruguay; one peso = 100 centesimos; issued by the Banco Central del Uruguay.

PEST CONTROL. The chemical control of insects, fungi, weeds and other pests; after World War II under the aegis of FAO and WHO.

E.R. DE ONG, *Chemical and Natural Control of Pests*, London, 1960; A. MALLIS, *Handbook of Pest Control*, London, 1960; "Pest Control by Chemical, Biological, Genetic and Physical Means", in: *US Department of Agriculture Bulletin*, 1966.

PESTICIDES. The chemicals used in crop protection such as insecticides, fungicides, herbicides, rodenticides, attractants and repellents; subject of international research. Organizations reg. with the UIA:

Collaborative International Pesticides Analytic Council Ltd., f. 1957, Hamburg. Publ.: *CIPAC Handbook*.
European Group of National Pesticide Manufacturers Associations, f. 1960, Brussels.
International Group of National Pesticide Manufacturers Associations, f. 1967, Brussels. Liaison status with FAO.
Tropical Pesticides Research Institute, f. 1945, Arusha, Tanzania. Publ.: *Annual Report*.

Pesticide Residues on Food. A Joint Report of the FAO Working Party on Pesticide Residues and the WHO Experts Committee on Pesticide Residues, Rome, 1968; IAEA, *Nuclear Technique for Studying Pesticide Residue Problems*, Vienna, 1970; A.R. STILES, *Pesticides: Nomenclature, Specifications, Analysis, Use, and Residues in Food*, Geneva, 1974; R. BOARDMAN, *Pesticides in World Agriculture*, London, 1980; WHO, *Chemistry and Specifications of Pesticides*, Geneva, 1984; *The Europa Handbook 1988. A World Survey*, Vol. I, London, 1988.

PETITION OF RIGHT. The memorandum adopted by the English Parliament in 1628 and submitted to King Charles I reserving to the Parliament the right to pass bills on taxes and to Courts the right to imprison citizens. The Petition, formally accepted by the King but never applied, was a precursory bill to the English Parliament ▷ Habeas Corpus Act of 1679.

J.H. MORGAN, *Remedies against the Crown*, London, 1926.

PETITION, RIGHT OF. Procedure in the LN and in the UN. A system for lodging complaints by persons or minorities; first introduced into practice on Oct. 25, 1920 in the League of Nations under the system of protection of minorities. Such petitions were studied by the Chairman and two members of the Council of the League of Nations and further submitted to all members of the Council; since 1921 to all members of the League of Nations together with commentaries of the states to which they referred. As petitions were used for propaganda, irredentist or even slanderous reasons, on Aug. 5, 1923, the Council of the League of Nations issued regulations forbidding the Secretariat of the League of Nations to accept and disseminate petitions that were irredentist, slanderous, anonymous and irrelevant to the protection of dignity of minorities, provided in treaties, as well as those that repeated facts stated in other petitions submitted to the League of Nations. The Council also limited the circulation of texts with commentaries of states exclusively to the members of the Council. Further limitations were introduced in 1929. Practically, the procedure of lodging petitions was applied only to those European states which were under the obligation to protect minorities (Albania, Austria, Bulgaria, Czechoslovakia, Turkey and Yugoslavia). It was in the UN where the petition procedure, reformed by the Trusteeship Council and further by the Decolonization Commission and by a subcommission of the UN Commission on Human Rights for the protection of minorities, assumed a global character which stemmed not from treaties on the protection of minorities but from the Universal Declaration of Human Rights.
The individual right of petition to the European Commission of Human Rights is recognized by all member countries of the Council of Europe, with the exception of Cyprus.

L.L. BRUN, *Le problème des minorités devant le droit international*, Paris, 1923; *United Nations Editorial Manual*, New York, 1983, pp. 52–53.

PETRODOLLAR. The common name for the dollar reserves of Arab countries deriving from the export of crude oil. The surplus of the balance of payment of the OPEC countries was first put to use on Eurodollar markets, then on markets of the USA, Great Britain and other OECD countries as well as for international organizations and as funds for aid to developing countries. More than half of all petrodollars are returned to markets of highly-developed capitalist countries.

"Recycling the Petrodollar", in: *Newsweek*, July 1, 1974.

PETROLEUM. One of the main energy sources, processed for industrial use from crude oil; subject of constant, organized international co-operation since 1933 (petroleum congresses), as well as international differences caused by conflicts between petroleum companies, e.g. the Bolivian–Paraguayan military conflict regarding Gran Chaco in the interwar period. The use of the "petroleum weapon" by the member states of OPEC in 1973 initiated the world energy crisis.
Organizations reg. with the UIA:

Arab Federation of Petroleum, Mining and Chemicals, f. 1961, Cairo, Egypt. Publ.: *Arab Petroleum* (monthly).
ASEAN Council on Petroleum, f. 1974, Jakarta, Indonesia, Publ.: *ASCOPE Newsletter*.
European Fuel Information Centre, f. 1972, Lausanne, Switzerland. Publ.: *Info-EFIC*.
European Independent Petroleum Union, f. 1962, Paris, France.
International Committee for Coal Petrology, f. 1953, Liège, Belgium.
International Co-operative Petroleum Association, f. 1947, Jersey City, N.J., USA. Publ.: *Action* (monthly).
International Federation of Petroleum and Chemical Workers, f. 1954, Denver, Col, USA. Publ.: Union Builder.
Internefit ▷ Internefitproduct.
Justicial Tribunal of the ▷ OAPEC.
Latin American Federation of Petroleum Workers, f. 1970, Montevideo, Uruguay.
Organization of Arab Petroleum Exporting Countries ▷ OAPEC.
South East Asia Petroleum Exploration Society, f. 1982, Singapore.

S.B. MOODY, *Petroleum Exploration Handbook*, New York, 1961; SIPRI, *Oil and Security*, Stockholm, 1974; ILO *Safety and Health of Fixed Offshore Installations in the Petroleum Industry*, Geneva, 1982; *Yearbook of International Organizations, 1986/87; The Europa Yearbook 1988. A World Survey*, Vol. I, London, 1988.

PETROLEUM ANGLO–AMERICAN AGREEMENT, 1945. An agreement signed on Sept. 24, 1945 at Washington; reads as follows:
"Preamble: The Government of the United States of America and the Government of the United Kingdom of Great Britain and Northern Ireland, whose Nationals hold, to a substantial extent jointly, rights to explore and develop petroleum resources in other countries, recognize:
(1) That ample supplies of petroleum, available in international trade to meet increasing market demands, are essential for both the security and economic well-being of nations;
(2) That for the foreseeable future the petroleum resources of the world are adequate to assure the availability of such supplies;
(3) That the prosperity and security of all nations require the efficient and orderly development of the international petroleum trade;
(4) That the orderly development of the international petroleum trade can best be promoted by international agreement among all countries interested in the petroleum trade, whether as producers or consumers. The two Governments have therefore decided, as a preliminary measure to the calling of an international

conference to consider the negotiation of a multilateral petroleum agreement, to conclude the following agreement.

Art. I: The signatory Governments agree that the international petroleum trade in all its aspects should be conducted in an orderly manner on a worldwide basis with due regard to the considerations set forth in the preamble, and within the framework of applicable laws and concession contracts. To this end and subject always to considerations of military security and to the provisions of such arrangements for the preservation of peace and prevention of aggression as may be in force, the signatory Governments affirm the following general principles with respect to the international petroleum trade:

(A) That adequate supplies of petroleum, which shall in this agreement mean crude petroleum and its derivatives, should be accessible in international trade to the Nationals of all countries on a competitive and nondiscriminatory basis;

(B) That, in making supplies of petroleum thus accessible in international trade, the interests of producing countries should be safeguarded with a view to their economic advancement.

Art. II: In furtherance of the purposes of this agreement, the signatory Governments will so direct their efforts:

(A) That all valid concession contracts and lawfully acquired rights shall be respected and that there shall be no interference directly or indirectly with such contracts or rights;

(B) That with regard to the acquisition of exploration and development rights the principle of equal opportunity shall be respected:

(C) That the exploration for and development of petroleum resources, the construction and operation of refineries and other facilities, and the distribution of petroleum shall not be hampered by restrictions inconsistent with the purposes of this agreement.

Art. III:(1) With a view to the wider adoption of the principles embodied in this agreement, the signatory governments agree that as soon as practicable they will propose to the governments of all interested producing and consuming countries the negotiation of an international petroleum agreement which inter alia would establish a permanent international petroleum council.

(2) To this end the signatory governments agree to formulate at an early date plans for an international conference to negotiate such a multilateral petroleum agreement. They will consult together and with other interested governments with a view to taking whatever action is necessary to prepare for the proposed conference.

Art. IV:(1) Numerous problems of joint immediate interest to the signatory governments with respect to the international petroleum trade should be discussed and resolved on a co-operative interim basis if the general petroleum supply situation is not to deteriorate.

(2) With this end in view, the signatory governments agree to establish an international petroleum commission to be composed of six members, three members to be appointed immediately by each government. To enable the commission to maintain close contact with the operations of the petroleum industry, the signatory governments will facilitate full and adequate consultation with their nationals engaged in the petroleum industry.

(3) In furtherance of and in accordance with the purposes of this agreement, the commission shall consider problems of mutual interest to the signatory governments and their nationals, and with a view to the equitable disposition of such problems it shall be charged with the following duties and responsibilities:

(A) to study the problems of the international petroleum trade caused by dislocations resulting from war;

(B) to study past and current trends in the international petroleum trade;

(C) to study the effects of changing technology upon the international petroleum trade;

(D) to prepare periodic estimates of world demands for petroleum and of the supplies available for meeting the demands, and to report as to means by which such demands and supplies may be correlated so as to further the efficient and orderly conduct of the international petroleum trade;

(E) To make such additional reports as may be appropriate for achieving the purposes of this agree-

ment and for the broader general understanding of the problems of the international petroleum trade.

(4) The Commission shall have power to regulate its procedure and shall establish such organization as may be necessary to carry out its functions under this agreement. The expenses of the Commission shall be shared equally by the signatory governments.

Art. V: The signatory governments agree:

(A) That they will seek to obtain the collaboration of the governments of other producing and consuming countries for the realization of the purposes of this agreement, and to consult with such governments in connection with activities of the Commission;

(B) That they will assist in making available to the Commission such information as may be required for the discharge of its function.

Art. VI: The signatory governments agree:

(A) That the reports of the Commission shall be published unless in any particular case either government decides otherwise;

(B) That no provision in this agreement shall be construed to require either government to act upon any report or proposal made by the Commission, or to require the nationals of either government to comply with any report or proposal made by the Commission, whether or not the report or proposal is approved by that government.

Art. VII: The signatory governments agree:

(A) That the general purpose of this agreement is to facilitate the orderly development of the international petroleum trade, and that no provision in this agreement, with the exception of art. II, is to be construed as applying to the operation of the domestic petroleum industry within the country of either government;

(B) That nothing in this agreement shall be construed as impairing or modifying any law or regulation, or the right to enact any law or regulation, relating to the importation of petroleum into the country of either government;

(C) That, for the purposes of this article, the word 'country' shall mean

(1) In relation to the Government of the United Kingdom of Great Britain and Northern Ireland, the United Kingdom, those British colonies, overseas territories, protectorates, protected states, and all mandated territories administered by that government and

(2) In relation to the Government of the United States of America, the continental United States and all territory under the jurisdiction of the United States, lists of which, as of the date of this agreement, have been exchanged.

Art. VIII: This agreement shall enter into force upon a date to be agreed upon after each government shall have notified the other of its readiness to bring the agreement into force and shall continue in force until three months after notice of termination has been given by either government or until it is superseded by the international petroleum agreement contemplated in art. III."

The Department of State Bulletin, No. 327, September 30, 1945, pp. 481–483.

PETROLEUM BARREL. Universally accepted international unit of measure (1 Amer. p.b. = 158.98 1 or 7 p.b. = 1 t). Despite the fact that in 20th-century statistics the metric system has been universally accepted and the production of petroleum is measured in tons, nevertheless ▷ posted prices of petroleum are still invariably set by the barrel.

PETROLEUM CONGRESSES. International institutions reg. with the UIA:

World Petroleum Congress WPC, with the aim of promoting scientific-technological co-operation and exchange of know-how; delegates, observers and invited guests take part in a series of conferences, discussions and meetings devoted to geological survey techniques, drilling, extraction, storage, and transport of petroleum and its utilization in petrochemistry, medicine, agriculture, etc.; WPC Permanent Council, headquarters London, prepares Congresses and publishes documentation. First WPC was held in London, 1938, second – in Paris, 1939, third – in The Hague, 1951, fourth – in Rome, 1955, fifth – New York, 1959, sixth – Frankfurt am Main, 1963, seventh –

Mexico, 1967, eighth – Moscow, 1971 (6,000 delegates from 70 countries).

Arabian Petroleum Congresses APC, including 15 Arab oil-producing countries and emirates, represent approximately 60% of world oil resources and some 30% of global oil production; first APC meeting – Cairo, 1959, second – Beirut, 1960, third – Alexandria, 1961, fourth – Beirut, 1963, fifth – Cairo, 1965, sixth – Baghdad, 1967, seventh – Kuwait, 1970 (adopted a declaration on the necessity to revise oil prices, implemented Dec. 1970 by ▷ OPEC), eighth – Algiers, 1972; Observers: Burma, Brazil, Canada, Cyprus, USA, France, Hungary (since 1970), India, Indonesia, Japan, Poland (since 1970), GDR (since 1970), FRG, Great Britain, Romania (since 1970), Switzerland, USSR, Venezuela, and members of ▷ OAPEC.

Congresses of State Petroleum Enterprises of Latin America organised by ARPEL; first – Buenos Aires, 1964, then every year in capital cities of its members: Rio de Janeiro, Lima, Mexico, Caracas, La Paz, Bogotá, Montevideo. Observers: Canada, USA, France, Holland, FRG, Great Britain, i.e. countries whose oil companies have concessions in Latin America.

KEESING's *Contemporary Archive*; *Yearbook of International Organizations*.

PETROLEUM STATE MONOPOLIES. The state enterprises dealing with extraction and refining of oil, in socialist states and some capitalist states; they are sole producers and commercial agents in the oil trade. In Latin America, an organization of state petroleum firms, ARPEL, consultative status with the UN.

PETROPOLIS. A Brazilian city in the Rio de Janeiro state, a fashionable resort with a Quintandinha Casino where Aug. 15–Sept. 2, 1947 the American republics held the Pan-American Conference for Maintenance of Peace and Continental Security, called the Conference of Petropolis or Quintandinha.

PHARMACEUTIC SIGNS. International system for making out prescriptions, known since the Middle Ages, making use of unified Latin abbreviations, e.g. *Rp.* ("take") *gtt* (*gutta* = "drop"), *q.s.* (*quantum saris* = "any amount") and signs est. by the Nuremberg Pharmaceutic System of Weights. Many drugs are described by WHO in registers of the *Pharmacopeia Internationalis*.

PHARMACEUTIC SYSTEM OF WEIGHTS. One of the oldest international systems of weights; in the Middle Ages it was based on Roman units of weight, from the 16th to the 18th centuries in most European countries based on the Nuremberg system (adopted 1546 in Nuremberg) which used the pound = 12 ounces, 1 ounce = 8 drachms, 1 drachm = 3 scruples, 1 scruple = 20 grains. Since the end of the 19th century, there has been a general conversion to the metric system, i.e. kilograms, grams, and milligrams (1872 in Germany). Whereas European pharmaceutic systems of weights used the pound = *c.* 360 g, the Asian systems' greatest weight measure was *c.* 15 g, the remaining units being equivalent to several milligrams.

PHARMACOPEA INTERNATIONALIS. An essential list of the most important medicines compiled and published since 1951 by the World Health Organization (WHO). Up to 1951 there existed only governmental descriptions of medicines in individual states, e.g. *Farmakopea Polska, Pharmacopea Helvetica, Pharmacopea Gallica, Pharmocopée Française, Deutsches Arzneibuch, Pharmacopea of the USA.* Within the CMEA system the standardization of pharmaceutic formulas for industry has been introduced. In 1973 the

first multi-lingual volume was published, *Compendium medicamentorum of the CMEA states.*
In 1902 in Paris the first organization was created with the name International Secretariat for the Unification of Pharmacopea. European Pharmacopeias Commission is an organ of the convention of 8 states of Western Europe signed on Apr. 2, 1964, publ. since 1967: *European Pharmacopeia.*

Yearbook of International Organizations.

PHARMACY. A subject of international co-operation. Organizations reg. with the UIA:

American Society of Pharmacognosy, f. 1959, Washington, DC. Publ.: *Newsletter.*
Commonwealth Pharmaceutical Association, f. 1970, London.
Eurocaphar, f. 1974, Paris. Promote pharmaceutical co-operatives in Europe.
Federation of Asian Pharmaceutical Associations, f. 1964, Manila. Publ.: *Asian Journal of Pharmacy.*
Federation of the Pharmaceutical Industry Associations in the EEC, f. 1959, Brussels.
International Academy for the History of Pharmacy, f. 1952, Rotterdam. Publ.: *Acta Pharmaciae. Historia.*
International Bureau for Pharmaceutical Rationalization, f. 1976, Brussels.
International Committee of Military Medicine and Pharmacy, f. 1921, Liège. Publ.: *International Review.*
International Federation of Pharmaceutical Manufacturers Association, f. 1968, Zurich, Switzerland. Consultative status with WHO.
International Group for Pharmaceutical Distribution in the EEC countries, f. 1960, Brussels.
International Pharmaceutical Federation, f. 1912, The Hague. Publ.: *Bulletin d'information.*
International Pharmaceutical Students Federation, f. 1949, London. Publ.: *News Bulletin.*
International Society for the History of Pharmacy, f. 1926, Bremen.
International Society of Clinical Pharmacology, f. 1971, Regensburg.
International Union of Pharmacology, f. 1959, Nutley, NJ.
Latin–Mediterranean Society of Pharmacy, f. 1953, Bologna.
Maghreb Committee for Pharmaceutical Products, f. 1970, Tangier.
Panamerican Federation of Pharmacy and Biochemistry, f. 1970, San Juan de Puerto Rico.
Pharmaceutical Group of the European Community, f. 1959, Brussels.
World Organization of Societies of Pharmaceutical History, f. 1952, Rotterdam.

A. SLIOSBERG, *Elsevier's Dictionary of Pharmaceutical Science and Techniques. In English, French, Italian, Spanish and German.* Vol. 1: *Pharmaceutical Technology*, Amsterdam, 1968, 1974, Vol. 2: *Materia Medica. In English, French, Italian, Spanish, German and Latin*, Amsterdam, 1975; *Yearbook of International Organizations.*

PHEASANT PROTECTION. A subject of international co-operation. Organization reg. with the UIA:

World Pheasant Association, f. 1975, Suffolk, England. Promotes and supports conservation of all species of the order of Galliformes with initial emphasis on the family Phasianidae. Regional programs for Australia, Asia, Central and Latin America.

Yearbook of International Organizations.

PHENOMENOLOGY. A subject of international co-operation. Organization reg. with the UIA:

International Phenomenological Society, f. 1939, Buffalo N.Y. Publ.: *Philosophy and Phenomenological Research.*

Yearbook of International Organizations.

PHILADELPHIA. A city in the USA. The Independence Hall of Philadelphia, included in the ▷ World Heritage UNESCO List, was built in Philadelphia for a provincial assembly, from 1775 onwards this building was the seat of the Continental Congress which sought to achieve the independence of the future United States. George Washington's appointment as commander-in-chief took place there, and it was there, too, that the American Constitution, the oldest in the world, was drawn up.

UNESCO. *A Legacy for All*, Paris, 1984.

PHILADELPHIA ILO DECLARATION, 1944. The official name of a document adopted in Philadelphia, May 12, 1944, at the end of the XXVI International Labor Conference at which ILO was restructured and its aims and objectives took on an anti-fascist character in keeping with the spirit of the anti-fascist alliance of the United Nations. The Declaration provided that the pursuit of social justice must comprise "all people irrespective of race, religion and sex who enjoy the right to material welfare and spiritual development in the conditions of freedom and dignity."

Textos adaptados en la Conferencia Internacional del Trabajo, Montreal, 1944.

PHILAE TEMPLES. A part of the Egyptian monuments of Nubia, subject of a multilateral UNESCO Agreement concerning the voluntary contribution to be given for the execution of the project to save the Temples of Philae; came into force on Dec. 19, 1970.

UNTS, Vol. 798, 1971, pp. 3–27.

PHILATELY. A subject of international co-operation. Organizations reg. with the UIA:

International Association of Philatelic Journalists, f. 1962, Utrecht. Publ.: *Bulletin.*
International Association of Space Philatelists, f. 1968, New York.
International Federation of Aero-Philatelic Societies, f. 1951, Berlin W. Publ.: *Bulletin.*
International Federation of Stamp Dealers Associations, f. 1950, Gravenhage, Publ.: *Handbook.*
International Philatelic Federation, f. 1926, Luxembourg.
International Study Group of Aerogrammes, f. 1966, New York.
United Nations Philatelics Society, f. 1947, New York.
United Nations Study Unit, f. 1963, Brooklyn, NY.
World Union Sain Gabriel, f. 1975, Esher, Surrey, UK. Members: national guilds of collectors of postage stamps with a religious subject. Publ.: *Information.*

Yearbook of International Organizations.

PHILIPPINES, THE. Member of the UN. Republic of the Philippines. A state on the Philippines Archipelago on the Pacific Ocean. Area: 300,000 sq. km; composed of 7100 islands and islets, the largest of which are: Luzon – 105,200 sq. km and Mindanao – 95,300 sq. km. Pop. 1987 est. 58,279,000 (censuses: 1960 – 27,087,000; 1970 – 38,493,000; 1975 – 42,070,600, 1980 – 48,098,400). Constitutional capital: Quezon City with 1,165,865 inhabitants in 1980; seat of the government: Metropolitan Manila with 5,925,884 inhabitants in 1980. Official languages: Pilipino, Spanish and English. Currency: one peso = 100 centavos. GNP per capita in 1985: US $580. National Day: June 12, date of the beginning of the liberation struggles in 1898 and July 4, Philippino-American Friendship Day, 1946.
Original member of the UN and all specialized agencies. Member of the Colombo Plan.
International relations: a Spanish colony from the 16th century to 1896, when the population began a revolutionary struggle for independence; on July 12, 1898 the Philippines proclaimed independence, but Spain on the basis on the Treaty of peace signed with the USA on Dec. 10, 1898 in Paris, ending the Spanish–American war, ceded the Philippines to the USA. During World War II in 1942 the Philippines were occupied by Japan. The USA supported anti-Japanese partisan activities and in 1944 agreed to grant the Philippines independence; the country was completely liberated in the summer of 1945; the USA then recognized the Philippines as an original member of the UN. On July 4, 1946 the Philippines became an independent state; simultaneously, by a treaty signed on that same day they granted the USA the right to station military forces on their territory. The Philippines were a member of SEATO. In June 1983 the Philippines and the USA signed a new agreement on the maintenance of the US naval and air bases until 1989 for US $900 million annually. In March 1986, President F. Marcos fled the country for Hawaii.

C. BENITEZ, *History of the Philippines*, Boston, 1954; A. CHAPMAN, *Philippines Nationalism*, New York, 1955; U.P. ZOFTA, *Philippines Economic Handbook*, Silver Springs Md., 1960; M.W. MAYAR, *A Diplomatic History of the Philippine Republic*, University of Hawaii Press, 1965; F. FRIEND, *Between Two Empires: The Ordeal of the Philippines 1926–1946*, New Haven, 1965; J.E. SPENSER, F.L. WERTENSTADT, *The Philippines Island World*, Berkeley, 1967; K.A. AVESH, *The Matrix of Policy in the Philippines*, Princeton, 1971; *IMF-CBP Banking Survey Commission on the Philippines Financial System. Recommendations*, Manila, 1972; K. LIGHTFORT, *The Philippines*, London, 1973; *The Europa Year Book 1984. A World Survey*, Vol. II, pp. 2262–2280, London, 1984; J. BRESNAN ed., *Crisis in the Philippines: The Marcos Era and Beyond*, Princeton, 1986.

PHILOLOGY. A subject of international co-operation. Organizations reg. with the UIA:

International Committee of Onomastic Sciences, f. 1949, Leuven.
International Federation for Modern Languages and Literatures, f. 1928, Cambridge. Members: Association for Commonwealth Literature and Language Studies, Australasian Universities Language and Literature Association, International Arthurian Society, International Association for Germanic Literature and Language, International Association for Scandinavian Studies, International Association for the Study of Italian Language and Literature, International Association of French Studies, International Association of Hispanists, International Association of Slavonic Languages, and Literatures, International Association of University Professors of English, International Comparative, Literature Association, International Committee of Slavists, International Association for the Study of Anglo–Irish Literature, Linguistic and Philological Association of Latin America, Modern Humanities Research Association, Modern Language Association of America, Society of Romanic Linguistics.
Permanent International Committee of Linguists, f. 1928, Nijmegen. Publ.: *Linguistic Bibliography.*

Yearbook of International Organizations.

PHILOSOPHY. A subject of international co-operation. Organizations reg. with the UIA:

Inter-American Society of Philosophy, f. 1954, São Paulo.
International Association of Philosophy Teachers, f. 1964, Leyden.
International Circle for Philosophical Research by Computer, f. 1972, Paris.
International Council for Philosophy and Humanistic Studies, f. 1949, Paris.
International Federation of Philosophical Societies, f. 1948, Berne. Publ.: *Bibliograpie international de la philosophie.*
International Institute of Philosophy, f. 1937, Paris. Publ.: *Chronique de Philosophie.*
International Jacques Maritain Study Institute, f. 1974, Ancona.
International Society for the Study of Medieval Philosophy, f. 1958, Leuven. Publ.: *Bulletin.*

P

International Society for the History of Ideas, f. 1960, Philadelphia. Publ.: *Journal of the History of Ideas.*
Pythagorean Philosophical Society, f. 1955, Athens.
Society for Asian and Comparative Philosophy, f. 1968, Honolulu.
World Union of Catholic Philosophical Societies, f. 1948, Washington, DC.

See also ▷ Oriental Philosophy Institute.

Yearbook of International Organizations; UNESCO, *Philosophical Foundations of Human Rights,* Paris, 1986; *Teaching and Research in Philosophy: Asia and the Pacific,* Paris, 1986.

PHILOSOPHY OF LAW. A subject of international research. Organization reg. with the UIA:

International Association for the Philosophy of Law and Social Philosophy, f. 190, Torino.

Les biens et les choses en droit. Archives de Philosophie du Droit, Paris, 1979: *Yearbook of International Organizations.*

PHLEBOLOGY. A subject of international research. Organizations reg. with the UIA:

Benelux Phlebology Society, f. 1961, Ghent.
International Union of Phlebology, f. 1960, Paris. Publ.: *Phlebologie.*
Societas Phlebologica Scandinavia f. 1960, Oslo.

Yearbook of International Organizations.

PHONETICS. A subject of international co-operation. Organizations reg. with the UIA:

International Phonetic Association, f. 1886, Paris. Promote the adaptation of the International Phonetic Alphabet to meet the needs of new languages, European, Asiatic and African (publ. 1949 the principles of the Alphabet as applied to 51 languages). Publ.: *Journal of the IPA.*
International Society of Phonetic Studies, f. 1975, Gainsville, Florida.
Permanent Council for the Organization of International Congresses of Phonetics Sciences, f. 1975, Paris.

Yearbook of International Organizations.

PHONOGRAMS AND VIDEOGRAMS. A subject of international co-operation. Organizations reg. with the UIA:

Intergovernmental Committee of the International Convention of Rome for the Protection of Performers, Producers and Phonograms and Broadcasting Organizations, est. Oct. 26, 1961, Rome. Members: governments of Austria, Brazil, Chile, Congo, Costa Rica, Czechoslovakia, Denmark, Ecuador, Fiji, FRG, Italy, Luxembourg, Mexico, Niger, Paraguay, Sweden, the UK.
International Federation of Producers of Phonograms and Videograms, f. 1933, London. Consultative status with UNESCO and Council of Europe. Publ.: *Information.*
Latin American Federation of Manufacturers of Phonograms and Videograms, f. 1965, Buenos Aires.

Yearbook of International Organizations, 1986/87; The Europa Yearbook 1988. A World Survey, Vol. I, London, 1988.

PHONOGRAMS CONVENTIONS Two international Conventions: The Convention for the Protection of Producers of Phonograms Against the Unauthorized Duplication of their Phonograms, signed 1971 under the aegis of WIPO and ▷The Rome Convention for the Protection of Performers, Producers of Phonograms, and Broadcasting Organizations signed Oct. 26, 1961.

PHONOLOGY. A subject of international co-operation. Organization reg. with the UIA:

International College of Experimental Phonology, f. 1955, Paris. Consultative status with UNESCO.

Yearbook of International Organizations.

PHONY WAR. An international term for a war without any de facto military operations, as was the case in fall–winter 1939/40 with England and France (▷ Drôle de guerre) and Germany (▷ Sitzkrieg).

PHOSPHORITES. A subject of international Convention; one of the basic raw materials in the production of mineral fertilizers, phosphorus and phosphoric acid; subject of international statistics. Main producers: USSR, Morocco, USA. In Nov., 1976 the governments of Algeria, Jordan, Morocco, Senegal, Togo and Tunisia signed an agreement on common price policies for phosphorites in export transactions, representing *c.* 34% of world production. The Organ of the Convention is the Organization of Phosphorites Exporting Countries, headquarters Algiers.

Yearbook of International Organizations.

PHOTOBIOLOGY. Subject of international co-operation. Organization reg. with the UIA:

International Committee of Photobiology, f. 1928, London. Promote application of ultra-violet, visible and infra-red radiation effects in biology and medicine. Publ.: *Congress reports.*

Yearbook of International Organizations.

PHOTOGRAMMETRY. A subject of international co-operation. Organizations reg. with the UIA:

International Society for Photogrammetry, f. 1910, Ottawa. Consultative status with UNESCO. Publ.: *International Archives of Photogrammetry.*

Yearbook of International Organizations.

PHOTOGRAPHY. A subject of international co-operation. Organizations reg. with the UIA:

Common Market Committee of Interphoto, f. 1953, Hamburg.
Council of Professional Photographers of Europe, f. 1957, Chalon s. Saone. Publ.: *Europhoto Newsletter.*
European Association of the Photographic Industry, f. 1964, Brussels.
International Committee on High-Speed Photography, f. 1952, Fontenay-aux-Roses. Publ.: *Congress Proceedings.*
International Federation of Photographic Art, f. 1950, St Gallen. Consultative status with UNESCO.
International Fire Photographers Association, f. 1963, Elmhurst, Delaware.

A.S.H. CRAEYBECKX, *Elsevier's Dictionary of Photography.* In English, French and German, Amsterdam, 1965; *Yearbook of International Organizations.*

PHYCOLOGY. A subject of international co-operation. Organization reg. with the UIA:

International Phycological Society, f. 1960, San Francisco. Promotes dissemination of phycological information about algae. Publ.: *Phycologia* (quarterly).

Yearbook of International Organizations.

PHYSICAL EDUCATION. A subject of international co-operation. Organizations reg. with the UIA:

Asian Committee for Standardization of Physical Fitness Tests, f. 1907, Tokyo. Publ.: *News.*
Catholic International Federation for Physical and Sports Education, f. 1962, Liège.
International Association of Physical Education and Sports for Girls and Women, f. 1953, Montreal. Publ.: *Congress Proceedings.*
International Committee on Physical Fitness Research, f. 1964, Tokyo.
International Council of Sport and Physical Education, f. 1956, Paris, under aegis of UNESCO. Consultative status with ECOSOC and UNESCO. Publ.: *Revue Analytique d'Education Physique et Sportive.*

International Council on Health, Physical Education and Recreation, f. 1958, Washington, DC. Publ.: *Gymnasion* (quarterly).
International Federation for Physical Education, f. 1923, Brussels. Publ.: *Bulletin.*

Yearbook of International Organizations.

PHYSICAL REACTOR CMEA RESEARCH. CMEA institution est. 1972 at the Central Institute for Physical Research in Budapest, by an Agreement on the Creation of a Provisional International Scientific Research Collective for Conducting Physical Reactor Research into the Critical Assembly of Water Cooled and Water Moderated Reactors (VVEP), signed on Feb. 23, 1972 at Warsaw.

Recueil de Documents, Varsovie, No. 2, 1972; W.E. BUTLER (ed.), *A Source Book on Socialist International Organizations,* Alphen, 1978, pp. 876–883.

PHYSICAL THERAPY. Subject of international co-operation. Organizations reg. with the UIA:

EEC Liaison Committee of Physical Therapists, f. 1965, Brussels.
European Confederation for Physical Therapy, f. 1938, Paris. Publ.: *Kinesitherapie scientifique.*
Latin American Society for Physical Therapy, f. 1969, São Paulo.
World Federation for Physical Therapy, f. 1951, London. Official relations with WHO and UNICEF. Publ.: *Bulletin.*

Yearbook of International Organizations.

PHYSICIANS. Organizations (see also ▷ Medicine) reg. with the UIA:

European Association of Senior Hospital Physicians, f. 1960, Brussels.
European Federation of Doctors Appointed to Corporate Institutions, f. 1963, Paris.
International Federation of Associations of Catholic Doctors, f. 1936, Brussels. Recognized by Pax Romana.
International Society of Medical Writers, f. 1956, San Remo.
International Union of Associations of Doctor Motorists, f. 1933, Utrecht.
World Organization of National Colleges, Academies and Academic Associations of General Practicioners Family Physicians (WONCA), f. 1970, Chicago.
World Scientific Union of Acupuncture Physicians and Societies of Acupuncture, f. 1973, Marseille.

Yearbook of International Organizations.

PHYSICIANS ETHICS. ▷ Hippocratic Oath. ▷ Medical Ethics.

PHYSICIANS, WAR CRIMINALS. After WWII world public opinion was shocked by the revelation during the trials of war criminals of the complicity of Nazi physicians in crimes of genocide. In the German Third Reich the administration of health services and the German Red Cross was entrusted to SS generals. The Hygienic Institute of the Waffen SS (Higienischer Institut der Waffen SS) subordinate to them carried out genocidal operations in the concentration camps and also made inhuman experiments on people (▷ Guinea pigs). In Poland a periodical, *Przeglad Lekarski–Auschwitz,* documents the crimes of Nazi physicians.

Okupacja i medycyna (Occupation and medicine), 2 Vols., Warsaw, 1971–76; Y. TERNON, S. HELMAN, *Historia medycyny SS,* (The History of SS Medicine), Warsaw, 1973; Y. TERNON, S. HELMAN, *Eksterminacja chorych psychicznie w III Rzeszy,* (The Extermination of the Mentally Ill in the German Third Reich), Warsaw, 1974.

PHYSICS. A subject of international co-operation. Organizations reg. with the UIA:
European Physical Society, f. 1968, Geneva. Publ.: *Europhysics.*

International Association of Meteorology and Atmospheric Physics, f. 1919, Boulder, Colorado. Publ.: *News Bulletin*.

International Centre for Theoretical Physics, f. 1964, Trieste.

International Commission on Cloud Physics, f. 1975, Montreal.

International Commission on Physics Education, f. 1960, Malvern, UK. Publ.: *New Trend for the Teaching of Physics*.

International Institute of Physics and Chemistry, f. 1912, Brussels. Publ.: *Congress Proceedings*.

International Organization for Medical Physics, f. 1963, Stockholm.

International Union of Pure and Applied Physics, f. 1922, London. Publ.: *Reports and Meetings*.

Inter-Union Commission Solar-Terrestrial Physics, f. 1966, Washington, DC.

Latin American Centre for Physics, f. 1962, Rio de Janeiro. Publ.: *Noticia* (monthly).

Nordic Institute for Theoretical Atomic Physics, f. 1957, Copenhagen.

W.E. CLASON, *Elsevier's Dictionary of General Physics. In English/American (with definitions), French, Spanish, Italian, Dutch and German*, Amsterdam, 1962; L. DE VRIES, W.E. CLASON, *Dictionary of Pure and Applied Physics. German–English*, Amsterdam, 1963; *Yearbook of International Organizations*.

PIATILETKA. *Russian* — "Five Year Plan." An international term for a system of economic planning introduced in the USSR 1928. The first Five Year Plan 1928–32 concentrated in 84% on development of heavy industry. Investments equalled 24.8 billion rubles. Increase of total industrial production – 19.2%. The second Five Year Plan 1933–37 with investments of 69.5 billion rubles brought an increase of total industrial production of 120%. The third Five Year Plan 1938–42 was interrupted by World War II (increase of total industrial production within a three and a half year period amounted to 76%). After the War the USSR resumed five year plans, which were also introduced in other socialist countries.

PICTURE AND SOUND. A subject of international co-operation. Organization reg. with the UIA:

Picture and Sound World Organization, Organization mondiale de l'image et du son, f. 1964, Paris.

Yearbook of International Organizations.

PIDGIN. A term, supposedly originating from the Chinese pronunciation of the English word "business", for a jargon used in ports of multilingual regions such as the Caribbean, Asia and Oceania, based on English and other European and Asian languages. The Pidgin language group includes among others Anglo-Creole dialects: Gullah in South Carolina, Negro English in the Antilles, Taki-Taki in Netherlands Guiana and Latin-Creole on Tahiti, Papiamento on Curacao; as well as the lingua franca of New Guinea, Solomon Islands, New Hebrides and the Southern Seas (Beach-la-Mar).

R.A. HALL, *Pidgin and Creole Languages*, London, 1966.

PIEDS-NOIRS. *French*: "Black Feet." An international term defining Europeans born in Algeria.

PIGADD. Permanent Inter-Government Authority on Drought and Development in East Africa, est. Feb. 6, 1964, in Djibouti. See also ▷ Drought.

PIG ON PORK. A British banking term for the signing of a check by persons or institutions closely tied to each other, e.g. the directors of the same company with a limited guarantee or a foreign branch signing a check of its central bank. Checks of this type are usually not honored by large banks, since they arouse the suspicion that in such a case the credit, though doubly secured, is based on the single, limited means of the same firm.

J. WALMSLEY, *A Dictionary of International Finance*, London, 1979.

PILCOMAYO. A South American River 1125 km long, rising in the Bolivian Andes, flowing across the Gran Chaco to the Paraguay River near Asuncion, in part a border river between Argentina and Paraguay, subject of intergovernmental agreement, signed 1941 by Argentina, Bolivia and Paraguay.

Rios y Lagos Internacionales, UPA Washington, DC, 1967, pp. 19 and 134–135.

PILGRIM RECEIPTS. ▷ Rial of Saudi Arabia.

PILGRIMS. An international term for persons journeying in groups to places of religious cult (in Europe and in the Middle East pilgrimages to places of Catholic cult, in Africa and Asia Moslem pilgrimages to Mecca and Medina); subject of sanitary conventions. The ▷ Health International Regulations, IHR, in annex V embracing 26 articles define binding standards of hygiene in conveying pilgrims by vessel and aircraft.

WHO, *International Health Regulations*, Geneva, 1971, pp. 71–78.

PILIPINO. The official national language of the Philippines, since July 4, 1946, based on the Malayan dialect Tagalog.

PIN-BDES AND PIN-PIDS. Patent Information Network Bibliographic Data Exchange System, and Patent Information Network ▷ Patent Information and Documentation System, two institutions of ▷ WIPO.

PING-PONG DIPLOMACY. A name accepted in April, 1971 by the world press for Chinese–American relations, which were resumed after more than 20 years of animosity between the USA and the People's Republic of China initiated by the invitation to an American ping-pong team to take part in an international tournament in China. The American team, accompanied by American correspondents from AP and UPI, met Apr. 14, 1971 with premier Chou En-lai, who stated that "a new chapter had begun in relations between the two nations thanks to your acceptance of the invitation of People's China." President R. Nixon reacted to this ping-pong diplomacy by announcing the cancellation of several restrictions affecting trade, communications and visas with China. Since then, the term ping-pong diplomacy is used for the initial steps toward establishing or renewing relations between quarreling states.

Le Monde, April 15 and 17, 1971.

PIÑOS, ISLA DE (ISLE OF PINES). A Cuban island southwest of Cuba. Area: 1180 sq. km. Pop. 1970 census: 30,103. Spanish possession until 1898; subject of US–Cuba disputes 1904–25 because the definition of Cuba's boundaries in the ▷ Platt Amendment, 1903–34, omitted the Isle of Pines. On Mar. 13, 1925 the US Senate confirmed Cuba's claims.

C. DE LA TORRIENTE, *Mi mission en Washington 1923–25, La soberania de la Isla de Piños*, La Habana, 1952.

PINYIN. The Chinese name for the Latin transcription of Chinese signs (ideograms), officially introduced in China on Jan. 1, 1979 for all foreign language publications and in international telecommunications. This system replaced the Anglo-Saxon Wade system, which was accepted in China in 1958 and used in the Western world alongside the French ETEO system, which was developed in the 19th century, by *l'École Française d'Extrême Orient*. In the Wade transcription, a name read Hua Kuofeng and one of the provinces Kwantung, while in Pinyin transcription, this became: Hua Guofeng, and the province Guangdong. From June 15, 1979 the use of Pinyin is obligatory in the UN Secretariat as the standard method for transcribing into languages using Latin characters the names of Chinese nationals and of places and geographical features of the People's Republic of China. As of that date, the Pinyin form of Chinese names should be used in all documents drafted, translated or issued by the Secretariat.

When the names of Chinese staff members appear in United Nations documents (such as promotion registers), they are converted to Pinyin if the staff members concerned so request.

United Nations Editorial Manual, New York, 1983, p. 351.

PIONEER. An unmanned American space vehicle for space research. See also ▷ Saturn.

PIPELINES. ▷ Oil and gas pipelines.

PIRACY. Air-Piracy, ▷ Sea Piracy.

PIRATE COAST. A historical name of a part of the Arabian Peninsula on the Gulf of Oman and the Arabian Sea, renamed the Trucial Coast following the Maritime Perpetual Truce in 1853. ▷ United Arab Emirates.

PITCAIRN ISLAND. A volcanic island south-east of Tuamotu Archipelago in the South Pacific; area: 4.6 sq. km; pop.: 53 residents in 1983 only settlement Adamstown; uninhabited until 1790, when occupied by 9 mutineers from the HMS *Bounty* with 12 women and 6 men from Tahiti. Under British jurisdiction. The UN Special (Decolonization) Committee in a consensus decision of Aug. 12, 1983, noted the UK statement affirming its policy to encourage as much local initiative and enterprise as possible so that the people could make the most of their own way of life.

The GA Resolution 43/412, adopted without a vote on Nov. 22, 1988, started that:

"The General Assembly, having examined the relevant chapter of the report of the Special Committee on the situation with regard to the Implementation of the Declaration on the Granting of Independence to Colonial Countries and Peoples, reaffirms the inalienable right to the People of Pitcairn to self-determination in conformity with the Declaration on the Granting of Independence to Colonial Countries and Peoples, which fully applies to the Territory. The Assembly further reaffirms the responsibility of the administering Power to promote the economic and social development of the Territory. The Assembly urges the administering Power to continue to respect the life-style that the people of the Territory have chosen and to preserve, and protect it."

I. BALL, *Pitcairn: Children of the Bounty*, London, 1973; *A Guide to Pitcairn*, Suva, Fiji, Auckland, 1976; *UN Chronicle*, January 1984, p. 62; *UN Resolutions and Decisions adopted by the General Assembly during the first Part of its Forty-Third Session, from 20 September to 22 December 1988*, New York, 1989, p. 624.

PITTSBURGH CZECHO-SLOVAK AGREEMENT, 1917. ▷ Czechoslovakia.

P

PLAGUE. The Black Death, murrain, pestilential infection, a communicable or very contagious illness, subject of international health conventions as well as the struggle to prohibit the use of plague germs (discovered 1894 by A. Jerson and K. Shibasaburo, called *Pasteurella pestis*) as weapons in war (▷ B and C arms). The use of plague germs as biological weapons came to light during the trial of 20 higher Japanese officers in Habarovsk (USSR), who were charged with war crimes, i.a. with dropping from planes in the area of the Chinese town Nimpo, 1940, 5 kg of infectious plague fleas and also with spreading in central China during the retreat in 1940 130 kg of plague germs, typhoid fever and anthrax. Subject of International Health Regulation:

"... the incubation period of plague is six days" (art. 51 of IHR).
"Vaccination against plague shall not be required as a condition of admission of any person to a territory" (art. 52 of IHR).
"Each State shall employ all means in its power to diminish the danger from the spread of plague by rodents and their octoparasites." (art. 53 of IHR).

UNTS, Vol. 764, pp. 45–52; "Plague surveillance and control," in: *WHO Chronicle*, No. 34, 1980, pp. 129–143.

PLANETS. The subject of international research by ▷ observatories and ▷ spacelaboratories. The nine planets which revolve around the Sun are: Mercury, Venus, Earth, Mars, Jupiter, Saturn, Uranus, Pluto and Neptune. The minor planets like Apollo, Ceres, Trojan are called asteroids.

F.I. WHIPPLE, *Earth, Moon and Planets*, London, 1963.

PLANKTON. The name of animal and vegetable sea organisms which are the basic nourishment for various sea fauna; subject of international conventions on the protection of the sea environment.

PLANNING, INTERNATIONAL. The development planning of particular regions of the world implemented on the basis of intergovernmental agreements, usually with the co-operation of specialized international institutions. Modern economies are based on planned or programmed developments. The first country to introduce a planned economy was the USSR with its first Five Year Plan 1929–34, (See ▷ Piatiletka). After World War II the majority of world economists accepted not only the necessity to program the development of particular countries, but also to create international regional planning. In the decades that followed various concepts of planning were formed to take into account economic systems and character of particular regions, the integrational associations and the international division of labor. This has become a guideline for the UN Planification and Development Committee established in 1963 by the UN General Assembly. The UN regional economic and social institutions hold annual seminars on economic and communal planning. In Latin America, Mexico was the first country to introduce planned economic development before World War II. The President of Brazil, J. Kubitschek, was the first to initiate regional planning in Latin America 1959 based on his idea of ▷ Pan-American Operation, 1958, in 1961 succeeded by the program of the ▷ Alliance for Progress which provided for "programming national and regional development." Organizations reg. with the UIA:

African Institute for Planification and Economic Development, f. 1962, Dakar, under the auspices of the UN Economic Commission for Africa.

Asiatic Institute for Economic Development and Planification, f. 1964, Bangkok, sponsored by the UN Economic Commission for Asia and Far East.
Interamerican Planification Society, f. 1956, San Juan de Puerto Rico.
Latin American Institute for Economic and Social Planning, Instituto Latino-Americano de Planificatión Económica y Social, f. 1962, Santiago de Chile, under the auspices of the UN Commission for Latin America, CEPAL.

In July 1962 the CMEA Committee for the Co-operation in Planning was established; the Bureau for joint projects on economic planning is seated in Moscow.

Yearbook of International Organizations.

PLAN OF ACCOUNTS. A term used mainly in Western Europe and some states of Africa and Latin America and in the Anglo-Saxon world for a standardized book-keeping system. The International Council for Users of Plan Accounts founded in Brussels in 1959, publ. *Revue internationale de sciences économiques et commerciales*. Reg. with the UIA.

Yearbook of International Organizations.

PLAN OF ACTION OF MAR DEL PLATA. ▷ Mar del Plata, Plan of Action of, 1977.

PLANS, INTERNATIONAL. International term for political or economic regional or global initiatives.

PLANT PROTECTION. A subject of four international conventions. The first International Convention for the Protection of Plants was signed in Rome, Apr. 16, 1929, by the governments of Austria, Belgium, Brazil, Chile, Denmark, Egypt, Finland, France, Haiti, Hungary, Italy, Luxembourg, Morocco, the Netherlands, Norway, Paraguay, Poland, Portugal, Romania, the Serbo-Croat-Slovene State, Spain, Switzerland, Tunisia and in Uruguay. Replaced by the International Plant Protection Convention (with Annex) signed on Dec. 6, 1951 in Rome, and came into force on Apr. 3, 1952. (Art. 1: "to prevent the introduction and spread of pests and diseases of plants and plant products.")
An Agreement on Co-operation in the Quarantine and Protection of Plants from Pests and Diseases signed on Dec. 14, 1959 at Sofia by Albania, Bulgaria, Czechoslovakia, the GDR, Hungary, Korea, Mongolia, Poland, Romania and the USSR; came into force on Oct. 19, 1960.
Convention for the Protection of New Varieties of Plants, signed on Dec. 2, 1961, in Paris by the governments of Belgium, Denmark, France, Germany, Italy, the Netherlands, Switzerland and the UK; came into force Aug. 10, 1968. Organizations reg. with the UIA:

European Association for Research on Plant Breeding, EUCARPIA f. 1956, Wageningen, Netherlands, Publ.: *Bulletin.*
European and Mediterranean Plant Protection Organization, f. 1951, Paris. Recognized by FAO. Publ.: *EMPPO Bulletin.*
International Association for Plant Physiology, f. 1959, Lausanne. Publ.: *Tentative Recommendation of Terminology.*
International Association for Plant Taxonomy, f. 1950, Utrecht. Publ. *Taxon and Regnum Vegetabile.*
International Association for Quality Research on Food Plants, f. 1955, Rüdesheim, FRG. Publ.: *Qualitas Plantarum.*
International Association of Plant Breeders for the Protection of Plant Varieties, f. 1938, Amsterdam.
International Community of Breeders of Asexually Reproduced Ornamentals, f. 1961, Geneva.

International Organization for Biological Control of Noxious Animals and Plants, f. 1955, Zurich. Liaison status with FAO. Publ.: *Entomophaga.*
International Organization for Succulent Plant Study, f. 1950, Zurich. Publ.: *Repertorium plantarum succulentarum* (annual).
International Organization of Paleobotany, f. 1954, Stockholm.
International Organization of Plant Biosystematists, f. 1959, Copenhagen.
International Regional Organization of Plant Protection and Animal Health, Organismo Internacional Regional de Sanidad Agropecuaria, OIRSA, est. by Convention, signed and ratified by Costa Rica, El Salvador, Guatemala, Honduras, Mexico, Nicaragua and Panama; came into force on June 9, 1955. Headquarters: San Salvador.
International Society for Horticultural Science, f. 1959, The Hague. Liaison status with FAO. Publ.: *Cronica Horticulturae.*
International Society for Vegetation Science, f. 1937, Louvain.
International Society of Plant Morphologists, f. 1951, Delhi. Publ.: *Phytomorphology.*
International Union for the Protection of New Varieties of Plants, f. 1961, Geneva. Intergovernmental organization of 9 Western European countries.
Latin American Association of Plant Sciences, f. 1961, Caracas. Publ.: *Fitotecnia Latinoamericana.*
Plant Protection Committee for the South Asia and Pacific Region, f. 1955, Bangkok. Intergovernmental organization of 19 countries.
Scandinavian Society for Plant Physiology, f. 1947, Stockholm. Publ.: *Physiologia Plantarum.*

L. LING, "International Plant Protection Convention: its History, Objectives and Present Status", in: *FAO Plant Protection Bulletin*, No. 1, 1952–53; A.J. PEASLEE (ed.), *International Intergovernmental Organizations*, 2 Vols., The Hague, 1961; M. MERINO-RODRIGUEZ, *Lexicon of Plant Pests and Diseases. In Latin, English, French, Spanish, Italian and German*, Amsterdam, 1966; P. MACURA, *Elsevier's Dictionary of Botany*, Vol. 1: *Plant Names. In English, French, German, Latin and Russian*, Amsterdam, 1979; Vol. II: *General Terms. In English, French, German and Russian*, Amsterdam, 1981; *Yearbook of International Organizations; The Europa Yearbook 1988. A World Survey*, Vol. I, London 1988.

PLASTIC INDUSTRY. A subject of international co-operation. Organizations reg. with the UIA:

European Committee of Machinery Manufacturers for the Plastic and Rubber Industry, f. 1964, Paris.
International Committee of Plastics in Agriculture, f. 1959, Paris. Consultative status with UNIDO. Publ.: *Plastic Culture.*

A.M. WITTFOHT, *The Technical Terms in Plastics Engineering. In English, German, French, Spanish, Italian and Dutch*, Amsterdam, 1976; *Yearbook of International Organizations.*

PLASTIC SURGERY. A subject of international co-operation. Organizations reg. with the UIA:

International Confederation for Plastics and Reconstruction Surgery, f. 1959, Paris. Publ.: *Congress Transaction.*
Scandinavian Association of Plastic Surgeons, f. 1951, Oslo. Publ.: *Congress Papers.*

Yearbook of International Organizations.

PLATA, RIO DE LA. A funnel-shaped estuary of the rivers Parana and Uruguay to the Atlantic Ocean; the estuary is 275 km long, 195 km wide on the Atlantic Ocean; the name La Plata is commonly applied to the river basin of both rivers, which after the Amazon are the greatest water-rich area on the continent – 3.2 million sq. km; including 32% of the territory of Argentina, 19% of Bolivia, 17% of Brazil, 80% of Uruguay and 99% of Paraguay, with a population of *c*. 65 million in 1980; it became the subject of international treaties in view of the great water-power potential of the four major rivers: La Plata, Parana, Paraguay, and Uruguay, estimated by the Institute for the Integration of Latin America at 30–40 million kilowatts. The governments of Argentina, Bolivia, Brazil, Paraguay, and Uruguay, called the River Plata Basin Group, Grupo de la Cuenca del Plata, began in 1967 the subregional integration of the river-basin. At the First Special Meeting of Ministers of Foreign Affairs of the Countries of the River Plata Basin, on Apr. 23, 1969, the five states signed at Brasilia the Treaty on the River Plata Basin. It came into force on Aug. 14, 1970. The historical dispute between Argentina and Uruguay on the division of territorial waters was resolved by a treaty of Nov. 19, 1973.

PAU, *Antecedentes sobre el Derecho de la Cuenca del Plata*, Washington, DC, 1967; INTAL, *Derecho de la integración*, Buenos Aires, No. 5, October, 1969.

PLATINUM. The precious, rare metal found in the Ural region in the USSR, in South Africa, Brazil and Colombia; one of three precious metals ▷ Gold and ▷ Silver used as a metal resource in international clearing.

PLATT AMENDMENT, 1903–34. The US Congress Amendment incorporated in the Permanent Treaty between the US and Cuba on May 23, 1903. The Amendment was first attached to the Army Appropriation Bill of 1901 by Senator O.H. Platt (1827–1905), who made passage of the law dependent on compelling the Cuban government to accept substantially as follows:

"I. That the government of Cuba shall never enter into any treaty or other compact with any foreign power or powers which will impair or tend to impair the independence of Cuba, nor in any manner authorize or permit any foreign power or powers to obtain by colonization or, for military or naval purposes or otherwise, lodgment in or control over any portion of said island.
II. That said government shall not assume or contract any public debt, to pay the interest upon which, and to make reasonable fund provision for the ultimate discharge of which, the ordinary revenues of the island, after defraying the current expenses of government, shall be inadequate.
III. That the government of Cuba consents that the United States may exercise the right to intervene for the preservation of Cuban independence, the maintenance of a government adequate for the protection of life, property, and individual liberty, and for discharging the obligations with respect to Cuba imposed by the treaty of Paris on the United States, now to be assumed and undertaken by the government of Cuba.
IV. That all Acts of the United States in Cuba during its military occupancy thereof are ratified and validated, and all lawful rights acquired thereunder shall be maintained and protected.
V. That the government of Cuba will execute and as far as necessary extend, the plans already devised or other plans to be mutually agreed upon, for the sanitation of the cities of the island, to the end that a recurrence of epidemic and infectious diseases may be prevented, thereby assuring protection to the people and commerce of Cuba, as well as to the commerce of the southern ports of the United States and the people residing therein.
VI. That the Isle of Pines shall be omitted from the proposed constitutional boundaries of Cuba, the title thereto being left to future adjustment by treaty.
VII. That to enable the United States to maintain the independence of Cuba, and to protect the people thereof, as well as for its own defence, the government of Cuba will sell or lease to the United States land necessary for coaling or naval stations at certain specified points, to be agreed upon with the President of the United States.
VIII. That by way of further assurance the government of Cuba will embody the foregoing provisions in a permanent treaty with the United States."

The Cuban parliament accepted the installation of an American military base at ▷ Guantanamo, and included in Cuba's constitution this resolution:

"The government of Cuba grants the United States the right of intervention for the purpose of preserving the independence of Cuba."
The USA made use of the Platt Amendment to intervene militarily in 1906, 1912, and 1924. On May 29, 1934 the US signed a new treaty with Cuba, annulling the Platt formula, but retaining US rights to ▷ Guantanamo.

"Cuba and the Platt Amendment", in: *Information Service of the Foreign Policy Association*, New York, Apr. 17, 1929; "The Platt Amendment," *International Conciliation*, No. 296, January, 1934; D. DE TORIENTE, *La Enmienda Platt y el Tratado Permanente*, La Habana, 1930; R. INFIESTA, "El Proceso histórico de la Enmienda Platt", in: *Anuario de la Facultad de Ciencias Sociales y Derecha Público*, La Habana, 1956.

PLAYBACK. The UN publication on audio-visual projects in which the United Nations and its specialized agencies are involved. Among the featured material are reports on film, radio and television programs, photographs and exhibits, video-taped programs, slide sets, posters, wall charts and education material, available for distribution. *Playback* is distributed by the UN Information Centres and offices of the UNDP.

UN Chronicle, December 1983, p. 95.

PLAZA ACCORD, 1985. Official name of an agreement of the finance ministers and the central banks governors of the five major industrialized countries (France, the FRG, Japan, the UK and the USA) on currency rate stabilization, signed in New York on Sept. 22, 1985 in a building on Rockefeller Plaza. Replaced, 1987 by the ▷ Louvre Accord.

KEESING's *Contemporary Archive*, 1985.

PLEBISCITES. A general voting by a country's or region's population in order to establish its international status, e.g. membership in a union of states or (in the case of a region or area) taking the side of one of two states or pronouncing themselves in favor of establishing their own state. The first modern plebiscites were initiated by the French Revolution: in Avignon in 1791, in Savoy in 1792, in Nice, Belgium and the Rhineland Palatinate in 1795, and also in Mulhouse and Geneva in 1798. Switzerland created its own forms of plebiscite. In the 19th century plebiscites were responsible to a considerable degree for the reunification of Italy, and a number of treaties included a plebiscite clause, *inter alia*, the Treaty between France and Sardinia of Mar. 24, 1860 resulting in plebiscites in Savoy and Nice, which with an overwhelming majority of votes pronounced themselves in favor of France, and the Treaty between Austria and France of Aug. 14, 1866 led Venice almost unanimously to vote for integration with Italy; however, no plebiscite was organized in Schleswig, as provided for in the treaty of Oct. 11, 1787 between Austria and the German Reich, and the regions of Tacna and Arica, as anticipated in the treaty of Oct. 20, 1883 between Chile and Peru. Norway decided its separation from Sweden through a plebiscite organized in 1905. After World War I, on the basis of the Versailles Treaty of May 28, 1919, the following plebiscites took place: in pursuance of articles 32–34 in the regions of Eupen and Malmedy in 1920 (the regions being given to Belgium on Sept. 20, 1920) and in 1935 in the Saar Basin (the majority of citizens voted in favor of unification with Germany, which was done on Mar. 1, 1935); in pursuance of art. 88 a plebiscite was held in Upper Silesia on Mar. 20, 1921, and in keeping with arts. 94–97 in East Prussia and in Western Prussia on July 11, 1920, in accordance with arts. 109 and 110 in Schleswig in 1920. Apart from this, on the basis of arts. 49 and 50

of the Saint Germain-en-Laye Treaty with Austria a plebiscite was held in Klagenfurt and Carinthia in 1920. According to the decision of the Supreme Council of Sept. 27, 1919, the plebiscites that were to be held in the Cieszyn Silesia, Spisz and Orawa did not take place due to the fact that Poland and Czechoslovakia reached an agreement to this end, signed on July 10, 1920, in Spa, on vesting the right of decision on the status of these lands in the Council of Ambassadors, which gave a binding verdict on July 28, 1920. By means of an additional protocol to the Saint Germain-en-Laye Treaty, signed on Oct. 13, 1921 in Venice by Austria and Hungary, both sides agreed to hold a plebiscite in the town of Sorgon (Austrian: Odenburg), the citizens of which declared themselves in favor of union with Hungary in Dec. 1921. After World War II plebiscites were held generally in non-autonomous territories and at the request of the Trusteeship Council of the United Nations.

F. LIEBER, "De la valeur des plébiscites en droit international", in: *Revue de droit international et législation comparative*, Paris, 1871; R. DE CARD, *Les Annexions et les Plébiscites dans l'histoire contemporaine*, Paris, 1881; S. WAMBAUGH, *A Monograph on Plebiscites with a Collection of official Documents*, New York, 1920; *Plebiscite and Referendum*, HMSO, London, 1920; E.O. CRISTI, "La teoria del plebiscito ante la historia y el derecho", in: *Revista de politica international*, Santiago, Julio, 1922; S. WAMBAUGH, *Plebiscites since the World War*, 2 Vols., London, 1933.

PLEDGE BONDS. The notes issued for loans against goods in warehouse. The ▷ Bustamante Code of Private International Law, 1928, includes in Chapter XIII rules on pledges and mortgages. The Treaty on International Commercial Terrestrial Law, signed at Montevideo Mar. 19, 1940 by Argentina, Bolivia, Brazil, Colombia, Paraguay, Peru, Uruguay; came into force on Jan. 29, 1958, includes (arts. 19–22) commercial pledges, and established a rule:

"The rights and obligations of the contracting parties in regard to the object given as a pledge, are governed, whether that object has been moved or not, by the law of its location and the time the pledge was constituted as such."

Register of Texts of Conventions and Other Instruments Concerning International Trade Law, UN, New York, 1973, Vol. I, pp. 252 and 254.

PLEDGING CONFERENCES. An international term introduced by the UN for the meetings of representatives of governments, nongovernmental organizations and finance institutions which pledge payment by a certain date as contribution to a definite goal. This allows planning of ventures within the sums declared.

PLEINS POUVOIRS. French = "full powers." A diplomatic term for the credentials of a diplomatic agent with full powers to conduct negotiations.

Dictionaire international de terminologie diplomatique, Paris, 1961.

PLESETSKAYA. ▷ ICBM.

PLEVEN PLAN, 1950. A draft concerning establishment of supranational West European armed forces within the European Defense Community (EDC) presented on Oct. 26, 1950, by French prime minister, R. Pleven; the draft was to embody the idea presented by W. Churchill on Aug. 11, 1950, at a consultative Assembly of the European Council which postulated the founding of "a European army commanded by a European minister of defense." The Pleven plan was meant to prevent establishment of an independent German army and provided for appropriate contingents to

P

be selected from the then existing armies which were to form a common army to which the Federal Republic of Germany might contribute with contingents of draftees without the right to have its own armed forces and organs of command (ministry and general staff). German Chancellor K. Adenauer on Oct. 29, 1950 supported the Pleven plan on condition that the "German soldiers will have equal rights just as other contingents" and said that "the virtues of German soldiers having been profaned since 1945 should simultaneously be protected." Discussions concerning this issue ended May 27, 1952, when Belgium, France, the Netherlands, Luxembourg, the Federal Republic of Germany and Italy signed a treaty that founded the European Defense Community on the basis of equity of all the six countries and advised establishment of the European Political Community (EPC); as the latter treaty required ratification by all the six states; it was ratified by Bundestag, on Mar. 19, 1953. Its rejection by the French parliament on Aug. 30, 1954 ended further consideration.

A.J. ZURCHER, *A Struggle to United Europe 1940–1958*, New York, 1958.

PLIMSOLL'S CERTIFICATE. A certificate determined by the International Convention on Load Lines of Apr. 5, 1966, obligatory for merchant vessels in international shipping. An evidence that the vessel has been checked and properly marked as to its weight limit under certain conditions; named after the English member of the House of Commons, Samuel Plimsoll (1824–98) who in 1876 was instrumental in the passage of the Merchant Shipping Act, prohibiting the overloading of vessels. Gdansk and Venice had similar regulations in the Middle Ages, but the Plimsoll Line was universally accepted only under pressure from insurance companies.

PLITVICE LAKES. A natural site in Yugoslavia, included in the ▷ World Heritage UNESCO List. The Korana has formed a chain of about twenty clear-water lakes at different levels, joined by waterfalls 20 metres high or more. The mountains which surround the valley are the home of bears, wolves and extremely rare birds. They are covered by a virgin forest of beeches, fir trees and junipers, which is one of the last of its kind in Europe.

UNESCO. *A Legacy for All*, Paris, 1984.

PLO. ▷ Palestine Liberation Organization.

PLOUGHING. Subject of international co-operation. Organization reg. with the UIA:

World Ploughing Organization, f. 1962, Whiteclose, England, to promote World Ploughing Contests and International Soil Cultivation Conferences in a different country each year, to improve techniques and prompt better understanding of soil cultivation practices through research and practical demonstration. Members: national organizations in 28 countries. Publ: *WPO Handbook*.

Yearbook of International Organizations 1986/87.

PLOWSHARE PROJECT. ▷ Atlantic-Pacific Canal Projects.

PLUNDERING OF OCCUPIED TERRITORIES. A subject of a Declaration of the United Nations, 1943 and of investigation by the International Military Tribunal in Nuremberg. The highlights of the Declaration published at London, Moscow and Washington on Jan. 5, 1943 read as follows:

"The systematic spoliation of occupied or controlled territory has followed immediately upon each fresh aggression. This has taken every sort of form, from open looting to the most cunningly camouflaged financial penetration, and it has extended to every sort of property – from works of art to stocks of commodities, from bullion and banknotes to stocks and shares in business and financial undertakings. But the object is always the same – to seize everything of value that can be put to the aggressors' profit and then to bring the whole economy of the subjugated countries under control so that they must slave to enrich and strengthen their oppressors.

It has always been foreseen that when the tide of battle began to turn against the Axis the campaign of plunder would be even further extended and accelerated, and that every effort would be made to stow away the stolen property in neutral countries and to persuade neutral citizens to act as fences or cloaks on behalf of the thieves.

There is evidence that this is now happening, under the pressure of events in Russia and North Africa, and that the ruthless and complete methods of plunder begun in Central Europe are now being extended on a vast and ever-increasing scale in the occupied territories of Western Europe. H.M. Government agree with the Allied Governments and the French National Committee that it is important to leave no doubt whatever of their resolution not to accept or tolerate the misdeeds of their enemies in the field of property, however these may be cloaked, just as they have recently emphasized their determination to exact retribution from war criminals for their outrages against persons in the occupied territories. Accordingly they have made the following joint Declaration, and issued an explanatory Memorandum on its meaning, scope and application: The Governments of the Union of South Africa, the United States of America, Australia, Belgium, Canada, China, the Czechoslovak Republic, the United Kingdom of Great Britain and Northern Ireland, Greece, India, Luxembourg, the Netherlands, New Zealand, Norway, Poland, the Union of Soviet Socialist Republics, Yugoslavia and the French National Committee, hereby issue a formal warning to all concerned, and in particular to persons in neutral countries, that they intend to do their utmost to defeat the methods of dispossession practised by the Governments with which they are at war against the countries and peoples who have been so wantonly assaulted and despoiled."

The New York Times, January 6, 1943.

PLURALISM DOCTRINE, 1970. An international thesis formulated by the President of Chile, the socialist S. Allende, in a message to the nation on Nov. 7, 1970, stating that the existing "political pluralism in international relations" resulting from the co-existence of states with various social systems should not impede the development of good inter-state relations, which should be based on non-intervention in the internal affairs of the other side and on respect for the right of each nation to select its own road of development. The first practical confirmation of this doctrine was the ▷ Salta Declaration of the presidents of Argentina and Chile, July 24, 1971.

Discurso del Presidente Salvadore Allende, de Noviembre 7, 1970, Santiago, 1970.

PLURALISM, IDEOLOGICAL. The co-existence of different ideologies occurring in one country or on one continent, e.g. of a materialistic world outlook alongside an idealistic one. On the American continent, after World War II, the Organization of American States adopted a doctrine of disapproval of any system other than US laissez-faire capitalism; this led to a substantial political controversy when Cuba emerged as a socialist country. The President of Mexico, L. Echeverria on Sept. 1, 1973 in a message addressed to Congress announced: "Ideological pluralism is a reality that should be accepted as a basis for continental co-existence." Since 1980 the problem of an ideological pluralism is the principle international problem in socialist but in the same time catholic Poland. In the 1980's after the ▷ Gdańsk Charter

1980, trade union pluralism was a subject of ideological controversy in the communist parties of the Warsaw Pact Countries. In Sept. 1988 an official speaker of the CP of the USSR declared that the trade union pluralism is not a "heresy" from the communist point of view.

Informe Anual del Presidente L. Echeverria, Sept. 1, 1973, Mexico, DF, 1973; D. NICHOLLS, *Pluralism*, London, 1975; CARDINAL STEFAN WYSZYŃSKI, *Memoires*, Paris, 1982; S. EHRLICH, *Pluralism on and off Course*, New York, 1984; B. GUETTA, *Le pluralisme syndical n'est pas une hérésie nous declare un responsable sovietique*, Le Monde, No. 13584, Sept. 2, 1988.

PLUTO. One of the ▷ Planets in the Solar System. A subject of international space research.

PLUTONIUM. A chemical artificially derived from radioactive chemical particles. The isotope Pu 239 was used in the nuclear bomb dropped on Nagasaki in 1945; used as a reactor fuel. In Apr., 1974 US President J. Carter introduced a ban on the export of plants for the extraction of plutonium and halted their construction.

SIPRI World Armament and Disarmament Yearbook, 1976, pp. 16–42; "The Plutonium Factor", in: *Newsweek*, Mar. 14, 1988.

POALE-ZION. *Hebrew* = "Workers of Zion." The Jewish Social Democratic Workers' Party est. *c*. 1900 in Russia and in 1905 in the Kingdom of Poland; in 1907 in The Hague the World Poale-Zion Federation was formed with a program for building an independent socialist state of Jews in Palestine.

POGROM. *Russian* = "banditry." An international term for ostensibly spontaneous terrorist action directed against religious, national, or racial minorities, usually organized by the ultra-right or by the police of a reactionary government. The name appeared in 1881 after the attempt on the life of Tsar Alexander II, when in the face of rumors spread by the police that the attempt was prepared by Jews, pogroms occurred in the Jewish sections of the majority of Russian cities combined with the plundering of Jewish stores. Similar *pogroms* were organized in Russia in the years 1903–17. After World War I in Turkey *pogroms* were applied in relation to the Armenians. Between wars pogroms were organized by thugs in Germany against the Polish population in Silesia and in East Prussia and from 1933 against the Jewish population. In Feb.-Mar. 1988 anti-Armenian pogroms took place in the ▷ Nagorno-Karabakh Autonomous Region of the Soviet Azerbaidzhan Republic.

The Trial of German Major War Criminals. Proceedings of the International Military Tribunal Sitting at Nuremberg, Germany, 42 Vols., London, 1946–48, Vol. 1, p. 116, Vol. 2, p. 384, Vol. 3, pp. 37, 52 and 218; KEESING's *Record of World Events*, 1988.

POINT. An international banking term in foreign exchange for 0.0001 of a unit.

J. WALMSLEY, *A Dictionary of International Finance*, London, 1979.

POLAND. Member of the UN, Republic of Poland. Central European state on the Baltic Sea, bordering on the German Democratic Republic, the USSR and Czechoslovakia. Area: 312,677 sq. km. Pop. 1989 est. – 37,940,000; (1900 – 25,106,000; 1931 – 32,107,000; 1946 – 23,030,000; 1960 – 29,776,000; 1978 – 35,032,000). Capital: Warsaw with 1,628,900 inhabitants 1983 (in 1939 – 1,289,000; In Dec. 1944 – 162,000). Official language: Polish. GNP per capita in 1980: US $3900.

Currency: one zloty = 100 groszy. National Day: Nov. 11, Proclamation of Liberation, 1918.

A member of the UN since Oct. 24, 1945 and all UN specialized organizations with the exception of IFAD; in dispute with the ILO, 1984–1987. Member of the Warsaw Pact and the CMEA.

International relations: independent kingdom from the 10th century to the last decades of 18th century (▷ Poland, Partitions, 1772, 1793, 1795). Area 733,500 sq. km with 13,800,000 inhabitants, 1772. A Grand Duchy of Warsaw est. by Napoleon existed 1807–1815; partitioned again at the Congress of Vienna, 1815, between Austria, Prussia, Russia and the Free City of Cracow (incorporated by Austria after the revolution of 1846–48). Two Polish uprisings against tsarist Russia, 1830–31 and 1863–64, failed. World War I between the partitioning powers restored the Polish state on Nov. 11, 1918, within new frontiers. Area 382,634 sq. km with 27,177,000 inhabitants in 1921 and 35,100,000 in 1939. The western frontier with Germany was partly decided by the uprisings in Silesia and in the former Grand Duchy of Posen, 1918–21; the eastern frontier after the Polish–Soviet war 1919–20 (▷ Riga Peace Treaty, 1921). The frontier dispute with Lithuania was discussed in the League of Nations, 1927. The frontier disputes with Czechoslovakia were resolved by the decisions of the Conference of Ambassadors on July 28, 1920; and with Romania on Mar. 15, 1923. Poland was member of the League of Nations, 1919–39. Poland signed on June 28, 1919 in Paris a League of Nations obligatory Treaty on Protection of National Minorities. On Sept. 13, 1934, the Polish minister for foreign affairs J. Beck, declared at the XV session of the LN Assembly as follows:

"Until a general and unified system of ethnic minority protection is introduced, the government of Poland is obliged henceforth to cease any co-operation with international organs concerning control over the system of minority protection practiced in Poland."

Occupied by Germany from Sept. 1939 until July, 1944–Mar., 1945. In 1979 the Main Commission for the Investigation of German Crimes in Poland published an encyclopedic guide-book listing in alphabetical order 5877 documented places of imprisonment and execution organized by the Germans in Poland from Sept. 1, 1939 to the spring of 1945. During the war Poland lost 6,028,000 inhabitants.

Poland's alliances after World War I:
Alliance Treaty with France, signed Feb. 19, 1921, in Paris.
Alliance Treaty with Romania, signed Mar. 3, 1921, in Bucharest.
Alliance Treaty with Great Britain, signed Aug. 28, 1939, in London.

Poland's alliances after World War II:
1945 – with the USSR a Treaty of Friendship, Mutual Assistance and Military Co-operation, signed on Apr. 21, 1945, renewed on Apr. 8, 1965 in a Treaty of Friendship, Co-operation and Mutual Assistance.
1947 – with Czechoslovakia a Treaty of Friendship, Co-operation and Mutual Assistance, signed on Mar. 10, 1947, renewed on Mar. 1, 1967.
1948 – with Hungary a Treaty of Friendship, Co-operation and Mutual Assistance, signed on Apr. 18, 1948, renewed on May 16, 1968.
1948 – with Bulgaria a Treaty of Friendship, Co-operation and Mutual Assistance, signed on May 29, 1948, renewed on Apr. 6, 1967.
1949 – with Romania a Treaty of Friendship, Co-operation and Mutual Assistance, signed on Jan. 26, 1949.
1950 – with the GDR a Delimitation Treaty confirming the existing Polish–German frontier, signed on July 6, 1950; expanded on Mar. 15, 1967 to a Treaty of Friendship, Co-operation and Mutual Assistance.

From Sept. 13, 1985 resumed membership in the World Bank (withdrawn 1950).
On May 20, 1986 readmitted to IMF. On July 24, 1986 amnesty for political prisoners.
On Jan. 13, 1987 the President of the Polish Council of State paid an official visit to the Vatican and had an audience with Pope John Paul II.
On Nov. 17, 1987 Poland withdrew its decision of November 1983 to leave the ILO.
On Nov. 29, 1987 the government failed to obtain the endorsement of at least 50% of the total electorate in a referendum on economic and limited political freedom. On June 4, 1989 the re-legalised Solidarity won ⅓ of the seats in the lower chamber of Parliament and 99% in the newly-formed Senate. A Solidarity-led coalition government is in power since Aug. 1989.

See also ▷ World Heritage UNESCO List.
▷ German-Soviet Partition of Poland 1939.

A. BREGMAN, *La Politique de la Pologne dans la Société des Nations*, Paris, 1932; K. SMOGORZEWSKI, *Poland's access to the Sea*, London, 1934; F. ZWEIG, *Poland between two wars*, London, 1944; J. WITTLIN, W. MALINOWSKI, *The Democratic Heritage of Poland*, London, 1944; W. JEDRZEJEWICZ (ed.), *Poland in the British Parliament 1939–1945*, 3 Vols., New York, 1946–59; Z. WOJCIECHOWSKI (ed.), *Poland's place in Europe*, Poznan, 1947; R. DYBOWSKI, *Poland in World Civilization*, New York, 1950; F.W. REDAWAY, *Cambridge History of Poland*, 2 Vols., Cambridge, 1941–50; E. WISKEMAN, *Germany's Eastern Neighbours*, London, 1956; J. KOKOT, *The Logic of Oder-Neisse Frontier*, Warsaw, 1959; F. LEWIS, *The Polish Volcano, A Case History of Hope*, London, 1959; T. CYPRIAN, J. SAWICKI, *Nazi Rule in Poland 1939–1945*, Warsaw, 1961; J. WYTRWAL, *America's Polish Heritage*, New York, 1961; S.J. PAPROCKI, S. HORAK, *Poland and Her Minorities, 1919–1939*, New York, 1961; M. BROSZAT, *Nationalsozialistische Polenpolitik 1939–1945*, Stuttgart, 1961; GEN. SIKORSKI HISTORICAL INSTITUTE, *Documents on Polish-Soviet Relations*, 2 Vols., London, 1961 and 1967; M. DANIELEWICZ, J. NOWAK, *Bibliography of Works by Polish Scholars and Scientists, published outside Poland in languages other than Polish, 1939–1962*, London, 1964; J. SZCZEPAŃSKI, *Polish Society*, New York, 1964; A. GIEYSZTOR (ed.), *History of Poland*, Warsaw, 1967; G.W.S. STROBEL, *Auswahlbibliographie Westsprächigen Schrifttums über Polen*, Köln, 1968; W. MORAWIECKI, "Some Particular Aspects of Poland's Membership in UN, ICAO and GATT," in: *The Polish Yearbook of International Law 1968–1969*, pp. 5–23; K. GRZYBOWSKI, *Poland in the Collections of the Library of Congress; an Overview*, Washington, DC, 1969; M.K. DZIEWANOWSKI, *Poland in the 20th century*, New York, 1977; S. KIENIEWICZ, *History of Poland*, Warsaw, 1979; Zb. ZALUSKI, *Poles on the Fronts of the Second World War*, Warsaw, 1979; Cz. PILICHOWSKI (ed.), *Encyclopaedia of Nazi Genocide Committed Against the Polish Nation*, (in Polish), Warsaw, 1979; J. K. ZAWODNY, *Nothing but Honor*, New York, 1980; P.S. WANDYCZ, *The US and Poland*, Cambridge Mass., 1980; A. POLONSDKY, B. DRUKIER, *The Beginnings of Communist Rule in Poland*, London, 1980; N. ACHERSON, *The Polish August. The Self-Limiting Revolution*, London, 1981; N. DAVIES, *God's Playground. A History of Poland*, Oxford, 1981; M. DOBBS, *Poland Solidarity Walesa*, New York, 1981; D. MACSHANE, *Solidarity, Poland, Independent Trade Union*, Nottingham, 1981; J. WISNIEWSKI, *Who's Who in Poland*, Toronto, 1981; K. RUANE, *The Polish Challenge*, London, 1982; J. WOODALL (ed.), *Policy and Politics in Contemporary Poland: Reform, Failure and Crisis*, London, 1982; K. SMOGORZEWSKI, "Not a single Polish problem can be solved by violence", in: *Britannica Book of the Year 1982*, London, 1982; R.C. LEWANSKI, *Poland, Bibliography*, Oxford, 1983; S. MIKLEJOHN TERRY, *Poland's Place in Europe*, Princeton 1983; N. ANDREWS, *Poland 1980–81*, Washington 1985, The *Europa Yearbook 1985*, Vol. I, London, 1985; J.J. LIPSKI, *KOR. A History of the Workers Defence Committee in Poland 1976–1981*, Berkeley, 1985; J.J. LIPSKI, *KOR. A History of the Workers Defense Committee in Poland 1976–1981*, Berkeley, 1985; J. KLOCZOWSKI, L. MÜLER, J. SKARBEK, *Zarys Dziejów Kościoła Katolickiego w Polsce*, Kraków, 1986; G. SANFORD, *Military Rule in Poland: The Rebuilding of Communist Power, 1981–1983*, New York, 1986; L. WAŁESA, *Un chemin d'espoir ("A Path of Hope")*, Paris, 1987, New York, 1987; S.A. GARRETT, *From Potsdam to Poland. American Policy Toward Eastern Europe*, New York, 1986; J. MOODY, R. BOYER, *The Priest and the Policeman. The Courageous Life and Cruel Murder of Father Jerzy Popiełuszko*, New York, 1987; R.C. LUKAS, *The Forgotten Holocaust: the Poles under German Occupation 1939–1944*, Lexington Ky., 1986; B. SUCHODOLSKI, *A History of Polish Culture*, Warsaw, 1986; E. SMOKTUNOWICZ, *Encyklopedia Obywatela PRL (Citizens Encyclopedia of the PRL Administrative Legal Status)*, Warszawa, 1987; R.C. MONTICONE, *The Catholic Church in Communist Poland, 1945–1985*, New York, 1987; A. PRAZMOWSKA, *Britain, Poland and the Eastern Front 1939*, Cambridge, 1987; P.C. POGONOWSKI, *Poland. A Historical Atlas*, New York, 1987; J. COUTOUVUDIS, J. REYNOLDS, *Poland 1939–1947*, Leicester, 1986; T. TORANSKA, *"Them": Stalin's Polish Puppets*, New York, 1987; T. SZULC, J.L. STANFIELD, "The Hope that Never Dies: Poland", in: *The National Geographic*, January, 1988; T. SZULC, "Poland's Path", in: *Foreign Policy*, Fall, 1988.

POLAND, PARTITIONS, 1772, 1793, 1795. The partitions of the Polish state carried out by the three neighboring powers: Austria, Prussia, and Russia. In the first partition in Aug., 1772 Russia took from Poland Inflanty and part of Byelorussia east of the Dźwina–Druć–Dniepr line; Austria took East Galicia and Lodomeria; Prussia acquired Royal Prussia without Gdańsk and Toruń, the bishopric of Warmia and the Noteć land. In the second partition in Sept., 1793 Russia took part of Byelorussia and the Ukraine along the line Druja–Pinsk–Zbrucz; Prussia – Gdańsk and Toruń as well as Poznań, Kalisz, Gniezno, Dobrzyn, Czestochowa, Dzialdowo; while Austria, which was at war with France, reserved the right to annex Bavaria and resigned from participation in the partition of Poland.

The third partition took place in Jan., 1795 after quelling the uprising by Tadeusz Kościuszko, 1794, and ended with the occupation of remaining Polish lands, Oct. 24, 1795: by Austria along the Pilica, Vistula and Bug; by Prussia along the Pilica, Bug and Niemen; and by Russia along the line Niemen–Grodno–Bug. The delimitation was completed on July 2, 1796. One year later Tsar Paul I, Emperor Francis II and Frederic Wilhelm II on the initiative of the king of Prussia resolved that they would not use the name Poland in their monarchical titles, appreciating: "the necessity for eradicating everything which could reawaken recollection of the existence of the Polish kingdom."

K. LUTOSTANSKI (ed.), *Les partages de la Pologne*, Paris, 1918.

POLAND, PEACE TREATY, 1919. Under art. 93 of the ▷ Versailles Peace Treaty 1919, Poland was obliged to sign a Treaty of Peace with the five Big Powers: the USA, the British Empire, France, Italy and Japan. The Treaty was introduced by a letter addressed to Ignacy Paderewski, Polish Prime Minister, by George Clemenceau, President of the Peace Conference. The text of the letter, dated Paris, June 24, 1919, is as follows:

"On behalf of the Supreme Council of the Principal Allied and Associated Powers, I have the honour to communicate to you herewith in its final form the text of the Treaty which, in accordance with Article 93 of the Treaty of Peace with Germany, Poland will be asked to sign on the occasion of the confirmation of her recognition as an independent State and of the transference to her of the territories included in the former German Empire which are assigned to her by the said Treaty. The principal provisions were communicated to the Polish Delegation in Paris in May last, and were subsequently communicated direct to the Polish Government through the French Minister at Warsaw. The Council have since had the advantage of the suggestions which you were good enough to convey to them in your memorandum of the 16th June, and as the result of a study of these suggestions modifications have been introduced in the text of the Treaty. The Council believe that it will be found that by these modifications the principal points to which attention was drawn in your memorandum have, in so far as they relate to specific provisions of the Treaty, been adequately covered.

In formally communicating to you the final decision of the principal Allied and Associated Powers in this matter, I should desire to take this opportunity of explaining in a more formal manner than has hitherto been done the considerations by which the Principal Allied and Associated Powers have been guided in dealing with the question.

1. In the first place, I would point out that this Treaty does not constitute any fresh departure. It has for long been the established procedure of the public law of Europe that when a State is created, or even when large accessions of territory are made to an established State, the joint and formal recognition by the Great Powers should be accompanied by the requirement that such State should, in the form of a binding international convention, undertake to comply with certain principles of government. This principle, for which there are numerous other precedents, received the most explicit sanction when, at the last great assembly of European Powers – the Congress of Berlin – the sovereignty and independence of Serbia, Montenegro, and Roumania were recognised. It is desirable to recall the words used on this occasion by the British, French, Italian, and German Plenipotentiaries, as recorded in the Protocol of the 28 June, 1878:

'Lord Salisbury recognises the independence of Serbia, but is of opinion that it would be desirable to stipulate in the Principality the great principle of religious liberty.

'Mr Waddington believes that it is important to take advantage of this solemn opportunity to cause the principles of religious liberty to be affirmed by the representatives of Europe. His Excellency adds that Serbia, who claims to enter the European family on the same basis as other States, must previously recognise the principles which are the basis of social organisation in all States of Europe and accept them as a necessary condition of the favour which she asks for.

'Prince Bismarck, associating himself with the French proposal, declares that the assent of Germany is always assured to any motion favourable to religious liberty.

'Count de Launay says that, in the name of Italy, he desires to adhere to the principle of religious liberty, which forms one of the essential bases of the institutions in his country, and that he associates himself with the declarations made on this subject by Germany, France, and Great Britain.

'Count Andrassy expresses himself to the same effect, and the Ottoman Plenipotentiaries raise no objection.

'Prince Bismarck, after having summed up the results of the vote, declares that Germany admits the independence of Serbia, but on condition that religious liberty will be recognised in the Principality. His Serene Highness adds that the Drafting Committee, when they formulate this decision, will affirm the connection established by the Conference between the proclamation of Serbian independence and the recognition of religious liberty.'

2. The Principal Allied and Associated Powers are of opinion that they would be false to the responsibility which rests upon them if on this occasion they departed from what has become an established tradition. In this connection I must also recall to your consideration the fact that it is to the endeavours and sacrifices of the Powers in whose name I am addressing you that the Polish nation owes the recovery of its independence. It is by their decision that Polish sovereignty is being re-established over the territories in question and that the inhabitants of these territories are being incorporated in the Polish nation. It is on the support which the resources of these Powers will afford to the League of Nations that for the future Poland will to a large extent depend for the secure possession of these territories. There rests, therefore, upon these Powers an obligation, which they cannot evade, to secure in the most permanent and solemn form guarantees for certain essential rights which will afford to the inhabitants the necessary protection whatever changes may take place in the internal constitution of the Polish State.

It is in accordance with this obligation that Clause 93 was inserted in the Treaty of Peace with Germany. This clause related only to Poland, but clauses have been inserted in the Treaty of Peace with Austria and will be inserted in those with Hungary and with Bulgaria, under which similar obligations will be undertaken by other States, which under those Treaties receive large accessions of territory.

The consideration of these facts will be sufficient to show that by the requirement addressed to Poland at the time when it receives in the most solemn manner the joint recognition of the re-establishment of its sovereignty and independence and when large accessions of territory are being assigned to it, no doubt is thrown upon the sincerity of the desire of the Polish Government and the Polish nation to maintain the general principles of justice and liberty. Any such doubt would be far from the intention of the Principal Allied and Associated Powers.

3. It is indeed true that the new Treaty differs in form from earlier Conventions dealing with similar matters. The change of form is a necessary consequence and an essential part of the new system of international relations which is now being built up by the establishment of the League of Nations. Under the older system the guarantee for the execution of similar provisions was vested in the Great Powers. Experience has shown that this was in practice ineffective, and it was also open to the criticism that it might give to the Great Powers, either individually or in combination, a right to interfere in the internal constitution of the States affected which could be used for political purposes. Under the new system the guarantee is entrusted to the League of Nations. The clauses dealing with this guarantee have been carefully drafted so as to make it clear that Poland will not be in any way under the tutelage of those Powers who are signatories to the Treaty.

I should desire, moreover, to point out to you that provision has been inserted in the Treaty by which disputes arising out of this provision may be brought before the Court of the League of Nations. In this way differences which might arise will be removed from the political sphere and placed in the hands of a judicial court, and it is hoped that thereby an impartial decision will be facilitated, while at the same time any danger of political interference by the Powers in the internal affairs of Poland will be avoided.

4. The particular provisions to which Poland and the other States will be asked to adhere differ to some extent from those which were imposed on the new States at the Congress of Berlin. But the obligations imposed upon new States seeking recognition have at all times varied with the particular circumstances. The Kingdom of the United Netherlands in 1814 formally undertook precise obligations with regard to the Belgian provinces at that time annexed to the kingdom which formed an important restriction on the unlimited exercise of its sovereignty. It was determined at the establishment of the Kingdom of Greece that the Government of that State should take a particular form, viz., it should be both monarchical and constitutional; when Thessaly was annexed to Greece, it was stipulated that the lives, property, honour, religion and customs of those of the inhabitants of the localities ceded to Greece who remained under the Hellenic administration should be scrupulously respected, and that they should enjoy exactly the same civil and political rights as Hellenic subjects of origin. In addition, very precise stipulations were inserted safeguarding the interests of the Mohammedan population of these territories.

The situation with which the Powers have now to deal is new, and experience has shown that new provisions are necessary. The territories now being transferred both to Poland and to other States inevitably include a large population speaking languages and belonging to races different from that of the people with whom they will be incorporated. Unfortunately, the races have been estranged by long years of bitter hostility. It is believed that these populations will be more easily reconciled to their new position if they know that from the very beginning they have assured protection and adequate guarantees against any danger of unjust treatment or oppression. The very knowledge that these guarantees exist will, it is hoped, materially help the reconciliation which all desire, and will indeed do much to prevent the necessity of its enforcement.

5. To turn to the individual clauses of the present Treaty. Article 2 guarantees to all inhabitants those elementary rights which are, as a matter of fact, secured in every civilised State. Clauses 3 to 6 are designed to insure that all the genuine residents in the territories now transferred to Polish sovereignty shall in fact be assured of the full privileges of citizenship. Articles 7 and 8, which are in accordance with precedent, provide against any discrimination against those Polish citizens who by their religion, their language, or their race, differ from the large mass of the Polish population. It is understood that, far from raising any objection to the matter of these articles, the Polish Government have already, of their own accord, declared their firm intention of basing their institutions on the cardinal principles enunciated therein. The following articles are of rather a different nature in that they provide more special privileges to certain groups of these minorities. In the final revision of these latter articles, the Powers have been impressed by the suggestions made in your memorandum of the 16th June, and the articles have in consequence been subjected to some material modifications. In the final text of the Treaty it has been made clear that the special privileges accorded in Article 9 are extended to Polish citizens of German speech only in such parts of Poland as are, by the Treaty with Germany, transferred from Germany to Poland. Germans in other parts of Poland will be unable under this article to claim to avail themselves of these privileges. They will therefore in this matter be dependent solely on the generosity of the Polish Government, and will in fact be in the same position as German citizens of Polish speech in Germany.

6. Clauses 10 and 12 deal specifically with the Jewish citizens of Poland. The information at the disposal of the Principal Allied and Associated Powers as to the existing relations between the Jews and the other Polish citizens has led them to the conclusion that, in view of the historical development of the Jewish question and the great animosity aroused by it, special protection is necessary for the Jews in Poland. These clauses have been limited to the minimum which seems necessary under the circumstances of the present day, viz., the maintenance of Jewish schools and the protection of the Jews in the religious observance of their Sabbath. It is believed that these stipulations will not create any obstacle to the political unity of Poland. They do not constitute any recognition of the Jews as a separate political community within the Polish State. The educational provisions contain nothing beyond what is in fact provided in the educational institutions of many highly organized modern States. There is nothing inconsistent with the sovereignty of the State in recognising and supporting schools in which children shall be brought up in the religious influences to which they are accustomed in their home. Ample safeguards against any use of non-Polish languages to encourage a spirit of national separation have been provided in the express acknowledgement that the provisions of this Treaty do not prevent the Polish State from making the Polish language obligatory in all its schools and educational institutions.

7. The economic clauses contained in Chapter II of the Treaty have been drafted with the view of facilitating the establishment of equitable commercial relations between independent Poland and the other Allied and Associated Powers. They include provisions for reciprocal diplomatic and consular representation, for freedom of transit, and for the adhesion of the Polish Government to certain international conventions.

In these clauses the Principal Allied and Associated Powers have not been actuated by any desire to secure for themselves special commercial advantages. It will be observed that the rights accorded to them by these clauses are extended equally to all States who are members of the League of Nations. Some of the provisions are of a transitional character, and have been introduced only with the necessary object of bridging over the short interval which must elapse before general regulations can be established by Poland herself or by commercial treaties or general conventions approved by the League of Nations.

In conclusion, I am to express to you on behalf of the Allied and Associated Powers the very sincere satisfaction which they feel at the re-establishment of Poland as an independent State. They cordially welcome the Polish nation on its re-entry into the family of nations. They recall the great services which the ancient Kingdom of Poland rendered to Europe both in public affairs and by its contributions to the progress of mankind which is the common work of all civilised nations. They believe that the voice of Poland will add to the wisdom of their common deliberations in the cause of peace and harmony, that its influence will be used to further the spirit of liberty and justice, both in internal and external affairs, and that thereby it will help in the work of reconciliation between the nations which, with the conclusion of Peace, will be the common task of humanity.

The Treaty by which Poland solemnly declares before the world her determination to maintain the principles of justice, liberty, and toleration, which were the guiding spirit of the ancient Kingdom of Poland, and also receives in its most explicit and binding form the confirmation of her restoration to the family of independent nations, will be signed by Poland and by the Principal Allied and Associated Powers on the occasion of, and at the same time as the signature of the Treaty of Peace with Germany."

The text of the Treaty dated June 28, 1919, is as follows:

"The Principal Allied and Associated Powers, on the one hand; and Poland, on the other hand;

Whereas the Allied and Associated Powers have by the success of their arms restored to the Polish nation the independence of which it had been unjustly deprived; and

Whereas by the proclamation of March 30, 1917, the Government of Russia assented to the re-establishment of an independent Polish State; and

Whereas the Polish State, which now in fact exercises sovereignty over those portions of the former Russian Empire which are inhabited by a majority of Poles, has already been recognised as a sovereign and independent State by the Principal Allied and Associated Powers; and

Whereas under the Treaty of Peace concluded with Germany by the Allied and Associated Powers, a Treaty of which Poland is a signatory, certain portions of the former German Empire will be incorporated in the territory of Poland; and

Whereas under the terms of the said Treaty of Peace, the boundaries of Poland not already laid down are to be subsequently determined by the Principal Allied and Associated Powers;

The United States of America, the British Empire, France, Italy and Japan, on the one hand, confirming their recognition of the Polish State, constituted within the said limits as a sovereign and independent member of the Family of Nations, and being anxious to ensure the execution of the provisions of Article 93 of the said Treaty of Peace with Germany; Poland, on the other hand, desiring to conform her institutions to the principles of liberty and justice, and to give a sure guarantee to the inhabitants of the territory over which she has assumed sovereignty;

For this purpose the High Contracting Parties represented as follows ...

After having exchanged their full powers, found in good and due form, have agreed as follows:

Chapter I. Art. 1. Poland undertakes that the stipulations contained in Articles 2 to 8 of this Chapter shall be recognised as fundamental laws, and that no law, regulation or official action shall conflict or interfere with these stipulations, nor shall any law, regulation or official action prevail over them.

Art. 2. Poland undertakes to assure full and complete protection of life and liberty to all inhabitants of Poland without distinction of birth, nationality, language, race or religion. All inhabitants of Poland shall be entitled to the free exercise, whether public or private, of any creed, religion or belief, whose practices are not inconsistent with public order or public morals.

Art. 3. Poland admits and declares to be Polish nationals ipso facto and without the requirement to any formality German, Austrian, Hungarian or Russian nationals habitually resident at the date of the coming

into force of the present Treaty in territory which is or may be recognised as forming part of Poland, but subject to any provisions in the Treaties of Peace with Germany or Austria respectively relating to persons who became resident in such territory after a specified date.

Nevertheless, the persons referred to above who are over eighteen years of age will be entitled under the conditions contained in the said Treaties to opt for any other nationality which may be open to them. Option by a husband will cover his wife and option by parents will cover their children under eighteen years of age.

Persons who have exercised the above right to opt must, except where it is otherwise provided in the Treaty of Peace with Germany, transfer within the succeeding twelve months their place of residence to the State for which they have opted. They will be entitled to retain their immovable property in Polish territory. They may carry with them their movable property of every description. No export duties may be imposed upon them in connection with the removal of such property.

Art. 4. Poland admits and declares to be Polish nationals ipso facto and without the requirement of any formality persons of German, Austrian, Hungarian or Russian nationality who were born in the said territory of parents habitually resident there, even if at the date of the coming into force of the present Treaty they are not themselves habitually resident there.

Nevertheless, within two years after the coming into force of the present Treaty, these persons may make a declaration before the competent Polish authorities in the country in which they are resident, stating that they abandon Polish nationality, and they will then cease to be considered as Polish nationals. In this connection a declaration by a husband will cover his wife, and a declaration by parents will cover their children under eighteen years of age.

Art. 5. Poland undertakes to put no hindrance in the way of the exercise of the right which the persons concerned have, under the Treaties concluded or to be concluded by the Allied and Associated Powers with Germany, Austria, Hungary or Russia, to choose whether or not they will acquire Polish nationality.

Art. 6. All persons born in Polish territory who are not born nationals of another State shall ipso facto become Polish nationals.

Art. 7. All Polish nationals shall be equal before the law and shall enjoy the same civil and political rights without distinction as to race, language or religion. Differences of religion, creed or confession shall not prejudice any Polish national in matters relating to the enjoyment of civil or political rights, as for instance admission to public employments, functions and honours, or the exercise of professions and industries. No restriction shall be imposed on the free use by any Polish national of any language in private intercourse, in commerce, in religion, in the press or in publications of any kind, or at public meetings.

Notwithstanding any establishment by the Polish Government of an official language, adequate facilities shall be given to Polish nationals of non-Polish speech for the use of their language, either orally or in writing, before the courts.

Art. 8. Polish nationals who belong to racial, religious or linguistic minorities shall enjoy the same treatment and security in law and in fact as the other Polish nationals. In particular they shall have an equal right to establish, manage, and control at their own expense charitable, religious and social institutions, schools and other educational establishments, with the right to use their own language and to exercise their religion freely therein.

Art. 9. Poland will provide in the public educational system in towns and districts in which a considerable proportion of Polish nationals of other than Polish speech are residents adequate facilities for ensuring that in the primary schools the instruction shall be given to the children of such Polish nationals through the medium of their own language. This provision shall not prevent the Polish Government from making the teaching of the Polish language obligatory in the said schools. In towns and districts where there is a considerable proportion of Polish nationals belonging to racial, religious or linguistic minorities, these minorities shall be assured an equitable share in the enjoyment and application of the sums which may be provided out of public funds under the State, municipal or other budget, for educational, religious or charitable pur-

poses. The provisions of this Article shall apply to Polish citizens of German speech only in that part of Poland which was German territory on August 1, 1914.

Art. 10. Educational Committees appointed locally by the Jewish communities of Poland will, subject to the general control of the State, provide for the distribution of the proportional share of public funds allocated to Jewish schools in accordance with Article 9, and for the organisation and management of these schools.

The provisions of Article 9 concerning the use of languages in schools shall apply to these schools.

Art. 11. Jews shall not be compelled to perform any act which constitutes a violation of their Sabbath, nor shall they be placed under any disability by reason of their refusal to attend courts of law or to perform any legal business on their Sabbath. This provision however shall not exempt Jews from such obligations as shall be imposed upon all other Polish citizens for the necessary purposes of military service, national defence or the preservation of public order.

Poland declares her intention to refrain from ordering or permitting elections, whether general or local, to be held on a Saturday, nor will registration for electoral or other purposes be compelled to be performed on a Saturday.

Art. 12. Poland agrees that the stipulations in the foregoing Articles, so far as they affect persons belonging to racial, religious or linguistic minorities, constitute obligations of international concern and shall be placed under the guarantee of the League of Nations. They shall not be modified without the assent of a majority of the Council of the League of Nations. The United States, the British Empire, France, Italy and Japan hereby agree not to withhold their assent from any modification in these Articles which is in due form assented to by a majority of the Council of the League of Nations.

Poland agrees that any Member of the Council of the League of Nations shall have the right to bring to the attention of the Council any infraction, or any danger of infraction, of any of these obligations, and that the Council may thereupon take such action and give such direction as it may deem proper and effective in the circumstances.

Poland further agrees that any difference of opinion as to questions of law or fact arising out of these Articles between the Polish Government and any one of the Principal Allied and Associated Powers or any other Power, a Member of the Council of the League of Nations, shall be held to be a dispute of an international character under Article 14 of the Covenant of the League of Nations. The Polish Government hereby consents that any such dispute shall, if the other party thereto demands, be referred to the Permanent Court of International Justice. The decision of the Permanent Court shall be final and shall have the same force and effect as an award under Article 13 of the Covenant.

Chapter II. Art. 13 Each of the Principal Allied and Associated Powers on the one part and Poland on the other shall be at liberty to appoint diplomatic representatives to reside in their respective capitals, as well as Consuls-General, Consuls, Vice-Consuls, and Consular agents to reside in the towns and ports of their respective territories.

Consuls-General, Consuls, Vice-Consuls and Consular agents, however, shall not enter upon their duties until they have been admitted in the usual manner by the Government in the territory of which they are stationed.

Consuls-General, Consuls, Vice-Consuls and Consular agents shall enjoy all the facilities, privileges, exemptions and immunities of every kind which are or shall be granted to consular officers of the most favoured nation.

Art. 14. Pending the establishment of an import tariff by the Polish Government, goods originating in the Allied and Associated States shall not be subject to any higher duties on importation into Poland than the most favourable rates of duty applicable to goods of the same kind under either the German, Austro-Hungarian or Russian Customs Tariffs on July 1, 1914.

Art. 15. Poland undertakes to make no treaty, convention or arrangement and to take no other action which will prevent her from joining in any general agreement for the equitable treatment of the commerce of other States that may be concluded under the auspices of the League of Nations within five years from the coming into force of the present Treaty.

Poland also undertakes to extend to all the Allied and Associated States any favours or privileges in customs matters which she may grant during the same period of five years to any State with which since August, 1914, the Allies have been at war, or to any State which may have concluded with Austria special customs arrangements as provided for in the Treaty of Peace to be concluded with Austria.

Art. 16. Pending the conclusion of the general agreement referred to above, Poland undertakes to treat on the same footing as national vessels or vessels of the most favoured nation the vessels of all the Allied and Associated States which accord similar treatment to Polish vessels.

By way of exception from this provision, the right of Poland or of any other Allied or Associated State to confine her maritime coasting trade to national vessels is expressly reserved.

Pending the conclusion under the auspices of the League of Nations of a general Convention to secure and maintain freedom of communications and of transit, Poland undertakes to accord freedom of transit to persons, goods, vessels, carriages, wagons and mails in transit to or from any Allied or Associated State over Polish territory, including territorial waters, and to treat them at least as favourably as the persons, goods, vessels, carriages, wagons and mails respectively of Polish or of any other more favoured nationality, origin, importation or ownership, as regards facilities, charges, restrictions, and all other matters.

All charges imposed in Poland on such traffic in transit shall be reasonable having regard to the conditions of the traffic. Goods in transit shall be exempt from all customs or other duties. Tariffs for transit across Poland and tariffs between Poland and any Allied or Associated Power involving through tickets or waybills shall be established at the request of that Allied or Associated Power.

Freedom of transit will extend to postal, telegraphic and telephonic services.

It is agreed that no Allied or Associated Power can claim the benefit of these provisions on behalf of any part of its territory in which reciprocal treatment is not accorded in respect of the same subject matter.

If within a period of five years from the coming into force of the present Treaty no general Convention as aforesaid shall have been concluded under the auspices of the League of Nations, Poland shall be at liberty at any time thereafter to give twelve months' notice to the Secretary General of the League of Nations to terminate the obligations of this Article.

Art. 18. Pending the conclusion of a general Convention on the International Regime of waterways, Poland undertakes to apply to the river system of the Vistula (including the Bug and the Narev) the regime applicable to International Waterways set out in Articles 332 to 337 of the Treaty of Peace with Germany.

Art. 19. Poland undertakes to adhere within twelve months of the coming into force of the present Treaty to the International Conventions specified in Annex I.

Poland undertakes to adhere to any new convention, concluded with the approval of the Council of the League of Nations within five years of the coming into force of the present Treaty, to replace any of the International instruments specified in Annex I.

The Polish Government undertakes within twelve months to notify the Secretary General of the League of Nations whether or not Poland desires to adhere to either or both of the International Conventions specified in Annex II.

Until Poland has adhered to the two Conventions last specified in Annex I, she agrees, on condition of reciprocity, to protect by effective measures the industrial, literary and artistic property of nationals of the Allied and Associated States. In the case of any Allied or Associated State not adhering to the said Conventions Poland agrees to continue to afford such effective protection on the same conditions until the conclusion of a special bi-lateral treaty or agreement for that purpose with such Allied or Associated State.

Pending her adhesion to the other Conventions specified in Annex I, Poland will secure to the nationals of the Allied and Associated Powers the advantages to which they would be entitled under the said Conventions.

Poland further agrees, on condition of reciprocity, to recognise and protect all rights in any industrial, literary or artistic property belonging to the nationals of the

Allied and Associated States in force, or which but for the war would have been in force, in any part of her territories before transfer to Poland. For such purpose she will accord the extensions of time agreed to in Articles 307 and 308 of the Treaty with Germany.

Telegraphic and Radio-Telegraphic Conventions:

International Telegraphic Convention signed at St. Petersburg, July 10–22, 1875.

Regulations and Tariffs drawn up by the International Telegraph Conference, signed at Lisbon, June 11, 1908.

International Radio-Telegraphic Convention, July 5, 1912.

Railway Conventions: Convention and arrangements signed at Berne on October 14, 1890, September 20, 1893, July 16, 1895, June 16, 1898, and September 19, 1906, and the current supplementary provisions made under those Conventions.

Agreement of May 15, 1886, regarding the sealing of railway trucks subject to customs inspection, and Protocol of May 18, 1907.

Agreement of May 15, 1886, regarding the technical standardisation of railways, as modified on May 18, 1907.

Sanitary Convention: Convention of December 3, 1903.

Convention of September 26, 1906, for the suppression of night work for women.

Convention of September 26, 1906, for the suppression of the use of white phosphorus in the manufacture of matches.

Convention of May 18, 1904, and May 4, 1910, regarding the suppression of the White Slave Traffic.

Convention of May 4, 1910, regarding the suppression of obscene publications.

International Convention of Paris of March 20, 1883, as revised at Washington in 1911, for the protection of industrial property.

International Convention of Berne of September 9, 1886, revised at Berlin on November 13, 1908, and completed by the Additional Protocol signed at Berne on March 20, 1914, for the Protection of Literary and Artistic Work.

Annex II. Agreement of Madrid of April 14, 1891, for the Prevention of False Indications of origin on goods, revised at Washington in 1911, and

Agreement of Madrid of April 14, 1891, for the international registration of trade marks, revised at Washington in 1911.

Art. 20. All rights and privileges accorded by the foregoing articles to the Allied and Associated States shall be accorded equally to all States Members of the League of Nations.

Art. 21. Poland agrees to assume responsibility for such proportion of the Russian public debt and other Russian public liabilities of any kind as may be assigned to her under a special convention between the Principal Allied and Associated Powers on the one hand and Poland on the other, to be prepared by a Commission appointed by the above States. In the event of the Commission not arriving at an agreement the point at issue shall be referred for immediate arbitration to the League of Nations. The Present Treaty of which the French and English Texts are both authentic, shall be ratified. It shall come into force at the same time as the Treaty of Peace with Germany.

The deposit of ratifications shall be made at Paris.

Powers of which the seat of the Government is outside Europe will be entitled merely to inform the Government of the French Republic through their diplomatic representative at Paris that their ratification has been given; in that case they must transmit the instrument of ratification as soon as possible. A proces-verbal of the deposit of ratifications will be drawn up.

The French Government will transmit to all the signatory Powers a certified copy of the proces-verbal of the deposit of ratifications.

In Faith Whereof the above-named Plenipotentiaries have signed the present Treaty.

Done at Versailles, the twenty-eighth day of June, one thousand nine hundred and nineteen, in a single copy which will remain deposited in the archives of the French Republic, and of which authenticated copies will be transmitted to each of the Signatory Powers."

LNTS, Vol. 1, 1920.

POLAR BEARS. ▷ Bears.

"POLARIS". The American two-stage ballistic missile belonging to the sea-land class with a nuclear warhead, designed for the destruction of strategic targets, launched from submarines, range 4000–4500 km, a subject of the SALT negotiations. New version ▷ Poseidon. ▷ SALT II Documents, 1979.

D. ROBERTSON, *Guide to Modern Defense and Strategy*, Detroit, 1988.

POLAR RESEARCH. The exploration of the polar regions, subject of international co-operation since the est. in 1879 of the International Polar Commission, on whose initiative the First International Polar Year was held 1882–83; the Second took place 1932–33; the Third called International Geophysical Year, 1957–58. Publ.: *Polar record*.

POLAR SERVICE. ▷ Latitude.

POLENLAGER. *German* = "camp for Poles." A Nazi name for concentration camps established especially for Poles deported 1939–40 mainly from Great Poland, Pomerania and Silesia. In these camps all belongings carried away from homes were confiscated and inmates were forced to perform slave labor. Euthanasia was applied to the old, ill and infirm; fit men were drafted for military service in the Wehrmacht under threat of repression to family members; children were also imprisoned (▷ lebensborn). According to the sentence passed by the Nuremberg Tribunal, all concentration camps as part of the activity of the SS organization were regarded as criminal.

R. HRABAR, *Polenlager*, Katowice, 1972.

POLICE. In the 18th and 19th century state administration, responsible for public order and internal state security; in the 20th century police forces are responsible for the protection of persons and state and private property, for criminal investigation, traffic regulations and public order. International co-operation of police has existed in Europe since the middle of the 19th century. In Dec., 1979 the UN General Assembly approved a Code of Conduct for Law Enforcement Officials.

Organizations reg. with the UIA:

International Association of Chiefs of Police, f. 1893, Caithersburg, Md. Members over 10,000 police executives from 63 nations.

International Association of Women Police, f. 1916, Chicago.

International Conference of Police Associations, f. 1963, Washington, DC.

International Criminal Police Organization ▷ INTERPOL.

International Federation of Senior Police Officers, f. 1950, Münster. Consultative status with ECOSOC, UNESCO and Council of Europe. Publ.: *International Police Information* (monthly in English, French and German), Traffic Safety.

International Police Association, f. 1950, Maidstone, UK. Consultative status with ECOSOC. Publ.: *International Bibliography of Police Literature, Police World, Scholarship Papers*.

International Study Commission for Traffic Police, f. 1960, Essen.

International Union of Police Trade Unions, f. 1953, Hilden.

J.M. HART, *The British Police*, London, 1951; L. RADZINOWICZ, *A History of English Criminal Law and Its Administration*, London, 1956; B. SMITH, *Police Systems in the US*, New York, 1960; J. CRAMER, *The World's Police*, London, 1964.

POLICY FROM A POSITION OF STRENGTH, 1951. An international term for a doctrine equating the foreign policy of a big power with a policy from a position of strength. In the Foreign Affairs Committee of the US Senate on Aug. 6, 1951 the Secretary of State, Dean G. Acheson, formulated the doctrine as follows:

"We should act from a position of strength and should create this strength; if in time we create it, then, I believe the international situation will considerably change. Our position in negotiations will become stronger than the position of the other side, which – as I expect – will force the Kremlin to recognize facts."

The doctrine is also called the Acheson Doctrine.

B. RUSSELL, *Power*, London, 1938; G. SCHWARZENBERGER, "Machtpolitik", in: STRUPP-SCHLOCHAUER, *Wörterbuch des Völkerrechts*, Berlin, 1961, Vol. 2, pp. 449–453.

POLIOMYELITIS. Poliomyelitis was first described by a German doctor Jacob von Heine (1800–79) but recognized as epidemic by Swedish doctor Oscar Medina (1847–1927); American doctor Jonas E. Salk (b. 1914) invented a vaccine against the Heine-Medina disease 1953. A subject of international research. Organization reg. with the UIA:

European Association against Poliomyelitis and other Virus Diseases, f. 1951, Brussels.
See also ▷ Immunization.

M. FISHBEIN, *Bibliography of Infantile Paralysis*, 1789–1949, London, 1951; J.E. SALK, "Principles of Immunization as Applied to Poliomyelitis and Influenza," in: *American Journal of Public Health*, 1953, WHO, *State on Poliomyelitis and the Soviet–American Polio Conference*, Moscow, May 1960.

POLISARIO. Frente Polisario, Frente Popular para la Liberacion de Sanguia el Hamra y Rio de Oro. People's Liberation Front for Western Sahara, est. 1975 as the representative of the Sahrawi people inhabiting the ▷ Western Sahara.
On Nov. 12, 1985 the UN de-colonization Committee adopted a resolution by 91 votes, with 6 against, and 43 abstentions, calling on Morocco to open negotiations with the Polisario.

POLISH–AMERICAN HISTORICAL ASSOCIATION. An institution f. 1942 in New York, as the Polish American Historical Commission of the Polish Institute of Arts and Science; changed its name to the present one 1944, and adopted the statutes of an autonomous scientific association with headquarters in Orchard Lake, Michigan until 1971, when the headquarters was moved to the Polish Museum of America in Chicago. Publ.: *Polish–American Studies*.

A. BROZEK, "The Polish–American Historical Association." in: *Acta Poloniae Historica*, Warsaw, No. 34, 1976; D. DROZDOWSKI, E. KUSIELEWICZ eds., *Polonia Stanow Zjednoczonych Ameryki 1910–1918 (Polish Americans 1910–1918)*, Warsaw, 1988.

POLISH CORRIDOR. An international term for the Polish access to the Baltic 1919–39 by a strip in the Pomerania region, 32–112 km wide, which separated the German Reich from East Prussia; liquidated in Sept., 1939 by German invasion, formally dissolved on Aug. 2, 1945 by the Potsdam Agreement dividing East Prussia between the USSR and Poland and delimiting a new German–Polish Frontier on the ▷ Oder-Lusatian Neisse rivers.

K. SMOGORZEWSKI, *Poland, Germany and the Corridor*, London, 1930.

POLISH HOME ARMY. Polish; Armia Krajowa, AK. Polish underground military forces in occupied Poland 1939–1945. See ▷ Warsaw Uprising 1944.

Armia Krajowa w dokumentach 1939–1945, 3 Vls., London, 1972.

POLISH INSTITUTE OF ARTS AND SCIENCES IN AMERICA. The Institute was established after World War II in New York as an artistic-scientific organization grouping intellectuals of Polish origin permanently residing in the USA and Canada, as a result of prewar, wartime, as well as post-war emigration. Since 1955 publishes a quarterly in English, *The Polish Review*.

J. HOSKINS, *Polish Books in English, 1945–1971*, Library of Congress, Washington, DC, 1972; J.W. ZURAWSKI, *Polish American History and Culture: A Classified Bibliography*, Chicago, 1975; "The Polish Americans," in: *The Polish Review*, New York, No. 3, 1976, pp. 3–288; S. STRZETELSKI, *The Polish Institute of Arts and Sciences in America. Origin and Development*, New York, 1960.

POLISH–ROMANIAN ALLIANCE TREATIES, 1921, 1927 AND 1931. The first Polish–Romanian Treaty was signed on Mar. 3, 1921 in Bucharest under the name: Convention on Defensive Alliance, came to be a defensive alliance, obliging both sides to render each other armed assistance "in case one of the sides is attacked at its present Eastern frontiers" (art. 1.). The Convention concluded for a period of five years was substituted by the Treaty on Mutual Assistance Against Aggression and on Military Aid, signed on Feb. 9, 1927 at Warsaw, and then by a new Guarantee Treaty of Jan. 15, 1931.

Recueil des Documents, Varsovie, 1931.

POLISH–SOVIET AGREEMENT, 1941. A Treaty signed on July 30, 1941 at London; reads as follows:

"The Government of the Republic of Poland and the Government of the Union of Soviet Socialist Republics have concluded the present Agreement and decided as follows:
1. The Government of the Union of Soviet Socialist Republics recognizes that the Soviet–German treaties of 1939 relative to territorial changes in Poland have lost their validity. The Government of the Republic of Poland declares that Poland is not bound by any Agreement with any third state directed against the USSR.
2. Diplomatic relations will be restored between the two Governments upon the signature of this Agreement and an exchange of Ambassadors will follow immediately.
3. The two Governments mutually undertake to render one another aid and support of all kinds in the present war against Hitlerite Germany.
4. The Government of the Union of Soviet Socialist Republics expresses its consent to the formation on the territory of the Union of Soviet Socialist Republics of a Polish army under a commander appointed by the Government of the Republic of Poland, in agreement with the Government of the Union of Soviet Socialist Republics. The Polish army on the territory of Union of Soviet Socialist Republics will be subordinated in operational matters to the Supreme Command of the USSR on which there will be a representative of the Polish army. All details as to command, organization and employment of this force will be settled in a subsequent agreement.
5. This Agreement will come into force immediately upon its signature and without ratification. The present Agreement is drawn up in two copies, each of them in the Russian and Polish languages. Both texts have equal force."
"Secret Protocol
1. Various claims both of public and private nature will be dealt with in the course of further negotiations between the two Governments.
2. This Protocol enters into force simultaneously with the Agreement of the 30th of July, 1941.
Protocol
1. As soon as diplomatic relations are re-established the Government of the Union of Soviet Socialist Republic will grant amnesty to all Polish citizens who are at present deprived of their freedom on the territory of the USSR, either as prisoners of war or on other adequate grounds.

2. The present Protocol comes into force simultaneously with the Agreement of July 30, 1941."

J. DEGRAS (ed.), *Soviet Documents on Foreign Policy 1917–1941*, 3 Vols., London, 1951–53.

POLISH–SOVIET DECLARATION, 1941. The Declaration signed on Dec. 4, 1941, in Moscow by heads of the two governments: General W. Sikorski and Generalissimo J.V. Stalin, also called the Stalin–Sikorski Declaration provided as follows:

"The Government of the Polish Republic and the Government of the Soviet Union animated by the spirit of friendly agreement and wartime co-operation declare:
1. The German–Hitlerite imperialism is the greatest enemy of mankind. It is impossible to find any compromise with it. Both States together with Great Britain and other Allies, supported by the United States of America, shall continue the war until entire victory is achieved and the German invaders are finally destroyed.
2. In the implementation of the treaty concluded on July 30, 1941, both Governments shall render each other full military assistance and the Polish army in the Soviet Union shall carry out the war against the German brigands shoulder to shoulder with the Soviet army. In the peacetime good-neighbourly co-operation, friendship and bilateral honest exercise of the assumed obligations shall be basis for their mutual relations.
3. When the war is over and the Nazi criminals are properly punished, the Allied states shall face the duty of securing stable and just peace. This may be achieved by a new arrangement of international relations based on unification of democratic countries into a firm alliance. In the establishment of such organizations as a decisive factor should be considered respect for international law supported by collective armed forces of all allied states. Only under this condition may Europe be rebuilt from the destruction caused by the German barbarians and guarantees may be obtained that the disaster started by the Nazis shall never repeat."

S. KOT, *Listy z Rosji do Generala Sikorskiego*, (The Letters from Russia to General Sikorski), London, 1955.

POLISH–SOVIET FRIENDSHIP TREATY, 1945. The Treaty was signed on Apr. 21, 1945 in Moscow. The text of the first two articles reads as follows:

"Art. 1: The High Contracting Parties will continue, jointly with all the United Nations, the fight against Germany until final victory. In this fight the High Contracting Parties agree to render each other military and other assistance by all the means in their power.
Art. 2: Believing that it is necessary, in the interests of the security and prosperity of the Polish and Soviet peoples, to maintain and strengthen a firm and lasting friendship both during and after the war, the High Contracting Parties will strengthen friendly co-operation between both countries in accordance with the principles of mutual respect for their independence and sovereignty and also of non-intervention in the internal affairs of the other state."

In keeping with Art. 8 of that Treaty, it was concluded for a duration of 20 years and afterwards was substituted by the Polish–Soviet Friendship treaty of 1965.

UNTS, Vol. 12, p. 392.

POLISH–SOVIET FRONTIER AGREEMENT, 1945. The Agreement was signed Aug. 16, 1945 in Moscow. The text is as follows:

"The Presidium of the Supreme Soviet of the Union of Soviet Socialist Republics and the President of the National Council of the Polish Republic, desiring to settle the problem of the State frontier between the Soviet Union and Poland in a spirit of friendship and accord, have decided to conclude for this purpose the present Treaty, and have appointed their plenipotentiaries:
Who, having exchanged their credentials found in due form and good order, have agreed on the following:
Art. 1. In accordance with the decision of the Crimes Conference, to establish the State frontier between the

P

Union of Soviet Socialist Republics and the Polish Republic along the 'Curzon Line', deviating from that line in Poland's favour in some districts from 5 to 8 kilometres according to the map in the scale 1 : 500,000 annexed hereto, conceding additionally to Poland:

(A) Territory situated to the East of the 'Curzon Line' up to the river Zapadny Bug and the river Solokia south of the town of Krylow with a deviation in Poland's favour up to 30 kilometres at the maximum;

(B) Part of the territory of the Bialowiez Forest in the sector Niemirow–Jalowka situated to the East of the 'Curzon Line', including Niemirow, Gainowka, Bialowieza and Jalowka, with a deviation in Poland's favour up to 17 kilometres at the maximum.

Art. II. In accordance with the provisions of Article I, the State frontier between the Union of Soviet Socialist Republics and the Polish Republic passes along the following line: from a point situated approximately at zero point 6 kilometres to the south-west of the source of the river San, north-eastwards to the source of the river San, and then down the midstream of the river San to a point situated to the south of the inhabited locality of Solina, then east of Przemysl, west of Nowa Russka up to the river Solokia, then along the river Solokia and the river Zapadny Bug in the direction of Niemirow–Jalowka, leaving on the side of Poland part of the territory of the Bialowiez Forest mentioned in Article I, and thence to the meeting-point of the frontiers of the Lithuanian Soviet Socialist Republic, the Polish Republic and East Prussia, leaving Grodno on the side of the USSR.

Delimitation on the spot of the frontier indicated in the present Article will be carried out by a Mixed Soviet–Polish Commission, whose seat will be in Warsaw and which will begin its work not later than 15 days after the date of exchange of ratification instruments.

Art. III. Pending final decision on territorial questions at the peace settlement, part of the Soviet–Polish frontier adjoining the Baltic Sea will pass, in conformity with the decision of the Berlin Conference, along a line leading from a point situated on the eastern shore of Danzig Bay and indicated on the map annexed hereto, eastward to the north of Braunsberg–Goldap to the point where this line meets the frontier line described in Article II of the present Treaty. Done in Moscow, August 16, 1945, in two copies each in the Russian and Polish languages, both texts having equal force."

Entered into force Feb. 5, 1946.

UNTS, Vol. 10, p. 193; *UN Yearbook 1946*, p. 184.

POLISH–SOVIET NON-AGGRESSION PACT, 1932.

The Pact was signed on July 25, 1932 in Moscow and came into force on Dec. 23, 1933, prolonged on May 5, 1934 for the period until Dec. 31, 1945. Its three major articles read as follows:

"Art. 1. Both contracting parties confirming that they have renounced war as an instrument of national policy in their mutual relations, assume the obligation to refrain from all aggressive acts or attack on one another, both individually, or jointly with other powers.

Acts inconsistent with the provision of the present article shall be those, as any act of violence, infringing the entity and inviolability of the territory or of the political independence of the other contracting Party, even if such acts were performed without declaring war and with avoidance of all its possible manifestations.

Art. 2. In case one of the contracting Parties should become an object of an assault on the part of a third state or a group of third states, the other contracting Party assumes the obligation not to render any assistance or support, whether direct or indirect, to the assaulting state through all the period of conflict. If one of the contracting Parties undertakes an assault on a third state, the other Party shall have the right to renounce the present Pact without prior notice.

Art. 3. Each contracting Party assumes an obligation not to participate in any agreements of hostile nature with regard to the other Party from the point of view of aggression."

LNTS, 1933 and 1934.

POLISH-UKRAINIAN AGREEMENT, 1920.

Called also Petlura–Pilsudski Agreement. An agreement between the Polish Republic and Uk-

rainian People's Republic, signed in Warsaw on Apr. 21, 1920. The Polish Government recognized the independence of the Ukraine and the sovereign right of the UPR Government in Kiev, both sides accepted the former East Galicia frontier as definitive. A military convention regulated the military alliance in common defensive action against the Soviet Army. The alliance and the agreement were annulated formally in Sept. 1921 after Soviet Red Army occupation of the Ukraine and proclamation of the Soviet Ukraine.

J. ŁOJEK, "Idea Federacyjna J. Piłsudskiego", in: *Przeglad Powszechny*, No. 11, 1987.

POLISH UPRISING, 1830.

A national uprising of Poles against Russia, beginning on Nov. 29, 1830 in Warsaw, capital of the Kingdom of Poland, whose monarch, Tsar Nicholas I of Russia, was dethroned by the Seym on Jan. 25, 1831; ended with a military defeat in Oct. 1831 and intensified national oppression. In the international aspect the question of the Polish nation's regaining its independence became since then an integral part of the struggles of the peoples of Europe against absolutism.

W. TOKARZ, *Wojna polska–rosyjska 1830–31* (Polish–Russian War 1830–31), Warsaw, 1930; T. LEPKOWSKI, *Warszawa w powstaniu listopadowym* (November Uprising in Warsaw), Warsaw, 1965.

POLISH UPRISING, 1863.

A Polish national uprising against Russia, began Jan. 22, 1863 and ended in the fall of 1864, extended to the Kingdom of Poland, Lithuania, White Russia, and part of the Ukraine. The First International arose from an international campaign of solidarity with the Polish insurgents.

S. KIENIEWICZ, "The January 1863 Insurrection", in: *Polish Perspectives*, No. 3, 1963, pp. 15–22.

POLISH UPRISING, 1918.

The uprising began on Dec. 27, 1918 in Poznan and led to the disarming of Germans and the assumption of authority by Polish administration in the larger part of Western Poland, ended by the armistice in Trier Feb. 16, 1919; it created a new *de facto* state of affairs in the drawing of the western boundary of Poland at the Versailles Conference.

K. PIWARSKI, *Powstanie Wielkopolskie 1918–1919* (The Insurrection in Western Poland, 1918–1919), Poznań, 1958; S. KUBIAK, *Bibliografia historii Powstania Wielkopolskiego 1918–19 (A Bibliography of the History of the Insurrection in Western Poland, 1918–19)*, Poznań, 1963.

POLISH UPRISINGS IN SILESIA, 1919–21.

Three armed risings of Polish people in Upper Silesia aimed at returning Silesia to Poland: the first broke out on Aug. 16/17, 1919, and though not effective in military sense, it facilitated the assumption of power over the plebiscite territory of Upper Silesia by the Inter-Allied Commission; the second broke out on Aug. 19/20, 1920, and resulted in the establishment of a Polish–German plebiscite police; the third began on May 2/3, 1921, and influenced the decision of the League of Nations and of the Council of Ambassadors of Oct. 20, 1921 to give Poland the larger part of Upper Silesia.

T. JEDRUSZCZAK, "Les insurrections silésiennes," in: *Études polonaises d'histoire militaire présentées à l'occupation du XII° Congrès International des Sciences Historique*, Varsovie, 1965; pp. 50–65; *Encyklopedia Powstań Ślaskich* (Encyclopaedia of the Silesia Uprisings), Opole, 1982.

POLISH UPRISINGS IN WARSAW, 1943 AND 1944.

▷ Warsaw Ghetto Uprising, 1943; ▷ Warsaw Uprising, 1944.

POLITICAL ECONOMY.

An international term, introduced 1615 by French dramatist and economist Antoine de Montchretien (1575–1621) in his *Traité de l'économie politique*.

W.Y. ELLIOT, *The Political Economy of American Foreign Policy*, New York, 1955.

POLITICAL INTERNATIONAL BIBLIOGRAPHY.

An instrument developed in the second half of the 20th century which considerably influenced the history of international relations. The International Committee for Social Sciences Documentation under UNESCO auspices started preparation and publication in London of bilingual Anglo–French International Bibliography of Political Science, *Bibliographie de Science Politique*, one volume per year since 1952, as well as annual yearbooks of International Bibliography of Sociology since 1951 and International Bibliography of Social and Cultural Anthropology. The Lenin Library in the USSR issues in Russian bibliographies of political literature dealing with individual regions of the world, e.g. *Strany Latinskoy Amieriki* (The States of Latin America), Moscow 1962; *Strany Evropy, Chast I: Socialisticheskie Strany* (The States of Europe, Part I: Socialist States), Moscow 1965; *Chast II: Kapitalisticheskie Strany* (Part II: Capitalist States).

Bibliographies from particular subject areas are also published, such as L. Paklons, *Bibliographie Européenne*, Bruges 1964, or in Paris by the Centre international de formation européenne, *Répertoire des périodiques consacrés aux questions européennes*. A number of international periodicals carry regular bibliographical departments, some run separate leaflets as does the monthly Scandinavian Political Studies, the *Bibliography of Scandinavian Political Sciences, 1900–1964*.

F. MOUSSA, *Diplomatie Contemporaine. Guide Diplomatique*, Geneva, 1964; J.K. ZAWODNY, *Guide to Study of International Relations*, San Francisco, 1967.

POLITICAL OFFENCE OR DELINQUENCY.

A controversial 19th-century international term, lacking definition in international acts, used in acts and treaties on extradition and asylum. There is a trend to adopt the principle that extradition refers exclusively to criminal offences and war criminals, and asylum is granted not to political "offenders," but to political activists harassed for their struggle for human rights, progress or peace.

C. EAGLETON, *The Responsibility of States in International Law*, London, 1928; P.A. ZAMES, *La responsabilité internationale des états pour les actes de négligence*, Paris, 1952; A. SCHÜLE, "Delikt," in: STRUPP-SCHLOCHAUER, *Wörterbuch des Völkerrechts*, Berlin, 1960, Vol. 1, pp. 326–339; R.L. BLEDSOE, B.A. BOCZEK, *The International Law Dictionary*, Oxford, 1987.

POLITICAL PARTIES AND MOVEMENTS.

An international term for ideologically oriented national groups in multinational co-operation or international solidarity.

A.J. DAY, H.W. DEGENHANDT, *Political Parties of the World*, London, 1984; C.O. MAROLAIN, *Latin American Political Movements*, London, 1986; C. HOBDAY, *Communist and Marxist Parties in the World*, London, 1986; R. SCRUTON, *Thinkers of the New Left*, London, 1986; C.O. MAROLAIN, *The Radical Right. A World Dictionary*, London, 1987.

POLITICAL SCIENCES.

A subject of international co-operation. Organizations reg. with the UIA:

Association for the Development of European Political Science, f. 1964, Paris. Publ.: *Surveys*.

European Consortium for Political Research, f. 1985, University of Essex, UK. Publ.: *European Journal of Political Research.*
International Academy of Political Science and Constitutional History, f. 1936, Paris. Publ.: *Revue internationale d'histoire politique et constitutionnelle* (since 1950) and *Revue internationale de doctrines et des institutions politiques* (since 1958).
International Political Science Association, f. 1949, Paris under aegis of UNESCO. Consultative status with ECOSOC and UNESCO. Publ.: *International Political Science Abstracts* (quarterly), *International Bibliography of Political Science* (annual).

Yearbook of International Organizations; G. DELURY, *World Encyclopedia of Political Systems*, 2 Vls., London, 1983; D. ENGLEFIELD, G. DREWRY, *Information Sources in Politics and Political Science: A Survey Worldwide*, London, 1984; A.S. BANKS ed., *Political Handbook of the World*, Boston, 1928, 1929, 1930–31, New York, 1932–62, 1963–67, 1968, 1970, 1975, 1976–79, 1980–83, 1984–85, 1986, 1987.

POLITOLOGY. An international term for political sciences, coined 1948 by a German historian Eugen Fischer Baling (1881–1958).

Yearbook of International Organizations.

POLITRUK. *Russian:* "Politicheski rukovodityel" = "political guide." A person in charge of political education in a certain social group; the name appeared in 1920 in the Soviet armed forces for political education officers, replaced in 1942 by the term Zampolit (Zamiestitiel Politicheski = Deputy for Political Problems).

T.J. COLTON, *Commissars, Commanders and Civilian Authority: The Structure of Soviet Military Politics*, Cambridge Mass., 1979.

POLLUTION. A subject of international antipollution agreements on ▷ Air Pollution and ▷ Water Pollution.
A "30 percent Club" was established in Mar. 1984, in Ottawa, by Canada, Belgium, Denmark, Finland, the FRG, France, Luxembourg, the Netherlands, Norway and Sweden to reduce 1980 levels of cross-frontier sulfur compound discharges into the air by 1993. In June, 1984 the USSR, GDR and Bulgaria joined the Club. Sulfur dioxide and nitric oxides are dangerous for European forests and mountains. On Nov. 30, 1984 all European countries and the USSR and Canada agreed during the UN Economic Commission plenary session in Geneva to commit themselves to a 30-percent cut in emissions of sulfur dioxide by 1993 in an effort to reduce pollution from acid rain. The UK and the USA declined to join the agreement. The cut was proposed by Canada and the Scandinavian Governments. Canada estimates that the 4,5 million tons of sulfur dioxide emitted yearly by the USA, causes losses equivalent to eight percent of Canada's GNP. Sweden holds the UK partly responsible for the death of fishes in 20 percent of Sweden's 96,000 lakes. See also ▷ Indian Ocean, ▷ Marine Pollution Convention ▷ North Sea.

UN Chronicle, March, 1978, p. 33, May, 1978, pp. 303–331, March, 1979, p. 30; *International Herald Tribune*, October 1, 1984.

POLLUTION CIVIL LIABILITY CONVENTION, 1969. ▷ Maritime Law Conventions, 1882–1978.

POLLUTION FUND CONVENTION, 1971. ▷ Maritime Law Conventions, 1882–1978.

POLYNESIA. The Oceanian islands in the Eastern Pacific: Hawaiian Islands, Samoa, Tonga, Society Islands, Marquesas Islands, Tuamotu Archipelago, Mangareva Islands, Tubnai Islands and Easter Island.

R.C. SUGGS, *The Island Civilization in Polynesia*, London, 1960; G.A. HIGHLAND (ed.), *Polynesian Culture History*, London, 1967; A.P. VAYDA (ed.), *People and Culture of the Pacific*, London, 1968.

POLYNOLOGY. A subject of international co-operation. Organization reg. with the UIA:

International Committee for Polynology, f. 1970, Utrecht. Aims: promote the study of Pollen and spores, whether living or fossil.

Yearbook of International Organizations.

POMERANIA. German: Pommern; Polish: Pomorze. Region by the Baltic Sea. East Pomerania was under Polish rule until 1772; date of Poland's first partition. West Prussia was ruled by Sweden 1648–1814, then until 1919 all Pomerania was held by Prussia. After the ▷ Versailles Treaty, Pomerania was divided between Prussia (West Pomerania and East Prussia) and Poland (in special relations with the Free City of Danzig). After the Potsdam Agreement, 1945 a small part of West Pomerania fell to East Germany, the rest to Poland without the region on the Pregolya River which fell to the USSR (▷ Kaliningrad).

K. SMOGORZEWSKI, *Poland's Access to the Sea*, London, 1934.

POPE. The name for a priest in early Christianity reserved exclusively for the Bishop of Rome by Gregory VII in 1075 *(Dictatus papae)*; presently the position of the pope is associated with the following official titles: Bishop of Rome, Vicar of Jesus Christ, Successor to Peter Prince of the Apostles, Patriarch of the West, Primate of Italy, Archbishop and Metropolitan of the Province of Rome, Sovereign of the Vatican State. From 1523 to 1978 all of the popes were Italians. On Oct. 18, 1978 a non-Italian was elected pope, the Archbishop of Cracow, Cardinal Karol Wojtyla (b. 1920), who took the names John Paul II to honor his predecessors: John XXIII (1958–63), Paul VI (1963–78), and John Paul I (1978). Since 1870, according to a dogma defined by the First Vatican Council, the pope is infallible in matters of faith.

The Catholic Encyclopaedia.

POPLAR. A tree of the willow family, occurring in about 30 species in Eurasia, North Africa and North America, fast growing, and therefore cultivated on a large scale in the second half of the 20th century in connection with the increasing deficit of trees and timber; subject of organized international co-operation. Organization reg. with the UIA:

International Poplar Commission IPC, Commission internationale de peuplier, CIP, f. 1947, under the aegis of FAO, by governments of 28 states of Eurasia, Africa and America, with headquarters attached to the Forestry Division of FAO in Rome.

Yearbook of International Organizations.

POPPY PLANT. *Papaver somniferum.* A plant used for the production of opium, subject of international agreements. ▷ Opium Conventions, 1912 and 1925.

POPULATION. A subject of international laws being one of three constitutive elements, of the state apart from territory and supreme authorities.

POPULATION COUNCIL. Organization reg. with the UIA: f. 1952, New York, N.Y.; conducts research in human reproductive biomedicine and the development of contraceptive methods. In co-operation with the United Nations Fund for Population Activities and with the Program for the Introduction and Adaption of Contraceptive Technology.

Yearbook of International Organizations, 1986/87.

POPULATION OF THE WORLD. A subject of international statistics and research carried on by UN organs. According to these data, in the prehistoric epoch the world population doubled every 10–100,000 years; in the Neolithic every 1000 years; in our era up to 1650 not more than 0.4% annually; then it doubled in the 200 years from 1650 to 1850; in the 100 years from 1850 to 1950; estimates are that it will double in the 40 years from 1950 to 1990 and in the 25–30 years from 1990 to 2020. According to the UN data, the number of inhabitants of the world at the end of 1985 exceeded 5 billion, of which *c.* 57% lived in Asia, *c.* 12% in Europe (without the USSR), *c.* 10% in Africa, *c.* 8% in Latin America, *c.* 6.5% in the USSR, *c.* 6% in North America. In 1950 there were four countries with population over 100 million (China, India, the USSR and the USA); in 1985 five more (Indonesia, Brazil, Japan, Bangladesh and Pakistan). See p. 1085.

"World Population", in: *The Annals*, Philadelphia, Jan., 1967; K. WITHAUER, *Distribution and Dynamics Relating to World Population*, Gotha, 1969; G. LOGIE, *Glossary of Population and Housing*, Amsterdam, 1978; *World Population Trends and Policies, UN Monitoring Report*, New York, 1982; J. VALLIN, "Perspective démographique du monde", in: *Le Monde Diplomatique*, August, 1984.

POPULATION OF THE WORLD IN UN STUDIES. The demographic statistics and analyses of the world population made by the UN Statistical Bureau and the ECOSOC Commission on Population; started with preparations for the first world population census of 1950; followed by the organization of the First World Conference on Population, 1954, and the introduction of standardized statistical questionnaires.
The First World Population Conference was held in Rome, Aug. 31–Sept. 10, 1954, with the participation of *c.* 500 demographers from 68 states who submitted 350 scientific papers. The Second Conference was held in Belgrade, Aug. 30–Sept. 10, 1965, with the participation of 835 demographers from 88 states who presented more than 500 papers. The dominant problem at this Conference was the "demographic explosion," which entailed the doubling of the world population in 35 years. In connection with this prospect sharply debated in the UN was the issue of ▷ family planning, otherwise called birth control. In the UN Declaration on Social Progress and Development drafted by the Commission on Social Development, 1967, it was generally stated that "each family has the right, within the limits of national demographic policy, to know the measures that will enable it to decide on the number of its children."
The Third World Population Conference was held in Bucharest, Aug. 19–30, 1974, with the participation of 1250 delegates from 140 states, which accepted the Bucharest Plan of Action, 1974, and the Resolution on a more just world, stating that the population policy of each state is an integral part of its global policy of economic and social development, and the implementation of such policy, depending on the historical, political, economic and social situation, is an indivisible and incontestable attribute of state sovereignty. The Principles and Recommendations of the Bucharest Plan of Action 1974 are as follows:

"To expand and deepen the capacities of countries to deal effectively with their national and subnational population problems ...

The sovereign right of governments to set their own population policies should take into account ... universal solidarity ... to improve the quality of life of the peoples of the world.

All couples and individuals have the basic human right to decide freely and responsibly the number and spacing of their children and to have the information, education and means to do so.

This right (should take) into account the needs of living and future children, and the responsibilities toward the community.

Women have the right to complete integration in the development process particularly by means of an equal participation in educational, social, economic, cultural and political life.

Governments should integrate population measures and programs into comprehensive social and economic plans and programs. Countries which consider their population growth hampers attainment of their goals should consider adopting population policies through a low level of birth and death rates. Developed countries are urged to adopt appropriate policies in population, consumption, and investment, bearing in mind the need for fundamental improvement in international equity. Highest priority should be given to reduction in mortality and morbidity and increase of life expectancy and programs for this purpose should reach rural areas and underprivileged groups.

Countries should encourage appropriate education concerning responsible parenthood and make available to persons who so desire advice and means of achieving it.

Countries wishing to affect fertility levels should give priority to development programs and health and education strategies which have a decisive effect upon demographic trends, including fertility. International co-operation should give priority to assisting such national efforts. Countries which consider their birth rates detrimental to their national purposes are invited to set quantitative goals and implement policies to achieve them by 1985. Policies and programs should be undertaken to reduce the undesirable consequence of excessively rapid urbanization and to develop opportunities in rural areas and small towns. Agreements should be made to regulate the international migration of workers and to assure nondiscriminatory treatment and social services for these workers and their families; also other measures to decrease the brain drain from developing countries.

Research should be intensified to develop knowledge concerning all aspects of population and family planning.

Medical, paramedical, traditional health personnel, program administrators, senior government officials, labor, community, and social leaders should be trained in population dynamics and administration.

International, intergovernmental, and nongovernmental agencies and national governments should increase their assistance in the population field on request.

The World Population Plan of Action should be closely coordinated with the international development strategy for the Second UN Development Decade, reviewed in depth at 5-year intervals, and modified as appropriate." See pp. 937–963.

UN Proceedings of the World Population Conference, New York, 1954; *UN Proceedings of the II World Population Conference*, New York, 1965; *UN World Population Prospect*, New York, 1967; R. SYMONDS, M. CARDER, *The UN and the Population Question*, New York, 1973; *UN Chronicle*, August, 1980, p. 71; April, 1981, p. 27; July 1982, pp. 77–80; October, 1983, p. 82; ONO, *Informe de la Conferencia International de Población*, México DF, 1984; *UN Population Bulletin*, No. 17, 1984 and No. 18, 1985.

POPULATION STATISTICS. The statistical data concerning births, deaths, diseases, suicides, marriages, divorces, etc. recorded on a domestic scale in Europe and in the USA in the 19th century, on world-wide scale since 1950 based on a UN statistical program. The Statistical Bureau of the UN publishes a monthly, *Bulletin of Statistics*; a quarterly, *Population and Vital Statistics*; and an annual, *Statistical Yearbook*. WHO publishes an *Annual Epidemiological and Vital Statistics*.

POPULATION UN AWARD. An award est. by the UN General Assembly in Res. 36/201 of Dec. 17, 1981, "for the most outstanding contribution to the awareness of population questions."

POPULATION UN TRUSTEESHIP FUND. On Dec. 2, 1966 the Heads of State of Egypt, Colombia, Finland, India, Malaysia, Morocco, Nepal, Singapore, South Korea, Sweden, Tunisia, and Yugoslavia signed a Declaration on population problems. On Dec. 17, 1966 the UN General Assembly Res. 2111/XXI for the first time addressed itself to the matter of the "demographic explosion," professing the thesis that: "the number of children in the family should depend on the free will of each family." On Dec. 11, 1967 the Declaration of Heads of State of 1966 was joined by the heads of government of: Australia, Barbados, Denmark, the Dominican Republic, Ghana, Great Britain, Holland, Indonesia, Iran, Japan, Jordan, Norway, New Zealand, Pakistan, the Philippines, Siam, Trinidad and Tobago and the USA. The Declaration was submitted to the UN Secretary-General U Thant, who took the initiative in establishing a UN Population Fund; ratified in Dec., 1966 by the UN General Assembly Res. 2211/XXI, with the task of assisting the developing countries in the study of demographic problems which have an important influence on economic and social development.

UN Monthly Chronicle, No. 8, 1967, pp. 72–73.

POPULATION WORLD CENSUS, 1950–80. The first World Population census was made in 1950 organized by the majority of UN members on the basis of standardized norms recommended by ECOSOC. The results warned of a demographic explosion. The majority of the UN member states accepted the recommendation of ECOSOC to hold censuses every five years, the others every ten years. In 1960 the UN Statistical Commission initiated a program for the evaluation of 236 national censuses which had been made in the decade 1955–64, entitled the World Population Census Program. The UN and FAO organized regional centers for training census cadres, Regional Census Training Center, i.a. in Lima and Tokyo. Since 1950 in the Americas the Inter-American Statistical Institute has introduced co-ordination of census norms according to ECOSOC recommendations. Up to that time census data were not fully comparable; in particular, US data differed from the Latin American. The first censuses on the American Continent were conducted in the US – 1790, since 1860 every 10 years by the "federal standard" method; Colombia – 1851; Chile – 1854. Other countries: 1860 – Uruguay, 1864 – Costa Rica, 1869 – Argentina, 1872 – Brazil, 1873 – Venezuela, 1876 – Peru, 1880 – Guatemala, 1887 – Honduras, 1895 – Mexico, 1899 – Cuba, 1900 – Bolivia, 1901 – El Salvador, 1911 – Panama, 1920 – Dominican Republic and Nicaragua, 1950 – Ecuador and Haiti.

National Accounting Praxis in Sixty Countries, UN New York, 1964; *Principios y Recomendaciones para los Censos de Población, de 1970*, UN New York, 1968.

POPULORUM PROGRESSIO. *Latin* = "growth of peoples." A papal encyclical published on Mar. 26, 1967, by Paul VI and submitted to the UN Secretary-General, UNESCO and FAO as a statement by the Roman Catholic Church concerning economic and social development of the world today. The paramount aspect of the encyclical was departure of the Church from the doctrines contained in the encyclicals, *Rerum novarum* on May 15, 1891 by Leo VIII and *Quadragesimo anno* of May 15, 1931 by Pius VI concerning inviolability of

private property; following the description of human misery in many parts of the world the *Populorum progressio* encyclical states:

"Private property is no one's unconditional and absolute right" and that "in the circumstances when injustice cries for vengeance, when whole nations deprived of what is necessary live in dependence stripping them of all incentive and responsibility as well as any chance of cultural advance and participation in social and political life, the temptation to oppose violently such an insult to human dignity is extremely strong."

The concepts of economic and social development of the Third World contained in the encyclical were assessed by the UN as similar to a number of theses put forward by UN regional economic commissions.

Populorum Progressio, Citta del Vaticano, 1967; *Sollicitudo Rei Socialis. Encyclical letter of the Supreme Pontiff John Paul II for the Twentieth Anniversary of Populorum Progressio*, London, 1988.

POPUTCHIKI. *Russian* = "fellow travellers." The name appeared in the USSR in the 1920s for non-party and non-communist intellectuals supporting the revolutionary changes; adapted in England and the USA to Fellow Travellers.

PORKKALA-UDD. A small peninsula in the Gulf of Finland near Helsinki; a strategically important naval base; leased to the USSR by Finland for 50 years under art. 8 of the Armistice Agreement signed on Sept. 19, 1944 at Moscow and confirmed under art. 4 of the Treaty of Peace, signed at Paris on Feb. 10, 1947; returned to Finland by an Agreement signed on Sept. 19, 1955 at Moscow; came into force on Oct. 28, 1955.

UNTS, Vol. 48, p. 149; *UNTS*, Vol. 226, pp. 194 and 338.

PORK WAR, 1880–91. Commercial conflict between the United States and the German Empire which banned American pork products, requiring sanitary inspection on trichina worms. After the US Congress passed a microscopic inspection law in 1891, Germany and other European countries lifted their ban. A similar dispute between the European Community and the United States started in 1988 over the import of hormone treated American beef.

S. HOY, W. NUGENT, "The 1880–91 Pork War", in: *The New York Times*, Jan. 13, 1989.

PORNOGRAPHY. A subject of international conventions. The first Convention on Elimination of Pornographic Publications from Circulation was signed on June 10, 1910 in Paris. The second Convention on Elimination of Obscene Publications from Circulation and Sales was signed on Sept. 12, 1923 in Geneva, and a protocol amending the Convention in Lake Success, Nov. 12, 1947. The second Convention and the Protocol keep the first Convention in force. The Conventions and Protocol charge their signatories with the obligation to establish competent organs for the suppression of pornography in publications, books, drawings, pictures or objects; to inform member states about shipments of pornographic commodities, methods of contraband, places of illegal international sales, etc. Competence of courts was also defined in case of conflicting legislation of states prosecuting offenders. During 1969–70 many Western states voided their anti-pornography legislation thus encouraging mass production of obscene publications and objects. In the second phase of the Conference on Co-operation and Security in Europe, the Socialist States opposed free international transfer of obscene publications.

N.S. JOHN-STEVAS, *Obscenity in the Law*, London, 1956; *LNTS*, Vol. 11, p. 438; *UNTS*, Vol. 30, p. 3; *UNTS*, Vol. 47, p. 159; *LNTS*, Vol. 27, p. 213, Vol. 200, p. 501; *UNTS*, Vol. 46, p. 169.

PORT ARTHUR. A temporary name of a Russian naval base 1898–1905 and Japanese naval base 1905–45 in China at the tip of the Liaotung Peninsula. Headquarters of the Sino–Soviet Naval Base administration 1945–55; reincorporated into China in 1955. In 1898 leased for a period of 25 years to Russia. Following the Russian–Japanese War leased along with the whole peninsula to Japan under the peace treaty concluded on Sept. 5, 1905 in Portsmouth. Liberated by the Red Army Aug. 23, 1945. Under the terms of a treaty between the USSR and the Chinese People's Republic, signed on Feb. 5, 1950 in Moscow, Port Arthur was to be returned to China in 1952 but, in connection with anti-Chinese demonstrations of the US navy, and at the request of the Chinese government, the Soviet fleet remained until 1955, when the port was entirely taken over by China after 57 years, initially under its old name Lushun, presently Lu-ta.

PORT LOUIS. The capital of the independent state of Mauritius since 1968. The seat of the Tourist Alliance of Indian Ocean, f. 1967, by tourist authorities of Comoros, Madagascar, Mauritius, Reunion and Seychelles. Reg. with the UIA.

Yearbook of International Organizations.

PORTOBELLO–SAN LORENZO. A historic site of Panama, included in the ▷ World Heritage UNESCO List. The fortifications of San Felipe de Portobello and of San Lorenzo at the mouth of the Chagras River guard the access to the Isthmus of Panama. They are typical examples of Spanish military architecture of the 17th and 18th centuries, and show the development of architectural styles and defensive strategy during the colonial period.

UNESCO. *A Legacy for All*, Paris, 1984.

PORTS AND HARBORS. A subject of international co-operation. Organizations reg. with the UIA:

American Association of Port Authorities, f. 1912, Washington, DC.
Central American Commission of Port Authorities, f. 1960, San Salvador.
Commission for Inter-Mediterranean Port Communications, f. 1975, Marseille.
Co-ordination Committee for North East Mediterranean Ports, f. 1947, Marseille.
International Association of Great Lakes Ports, f. 1955, Toronto.
International Association of Ports and Harbors, f. 1955, Tokyo. Consultative status with ECOSOC, IMCO and UNCTAD. Publ.: *Ports and Harbors* (monthly), *IAPH Membership Directory* (annual).
Latin American Regional Association of Pacific Ports, f. 1960, Valparaiso.
Port Management Association of Eastern Africa, f. 1973, Addis Ababa.
Port Management Association of North Africa, f. 1970, Algiers.
Port Management Association of West and Central Africa, f. 1972, Douala.
South Atlantic Caribbean Ports Association, f. 1960, Georgetown, SC.
In Feb.-Mar. 1986 under the auspices of UNCTAD an expert review of practical problems arising from the development and operation of ports, particularly in developing countries took place in Geneva.

B. NAGORSKI, *Port Problems in Developing Countries. Principles of Port Planning and Organization*, Tokyo, 1972.

PORTSMOUTH JAPAN-RUSSIA PEACE TREATY, 1905. The Peace Treaty between Japan and Russia signed on Aug. 30–Sept. 5, 1905 in Portsmouth; ending the War of 1905. Highlights of the Treaty:

"I. There shall henceforth be peace and amity between their Majesties the Emperor of Japan and the Emperor of All the Russias and between their respective States and subjects.
II. The Imperial Russian Government, acknowledging that Japan possesses in Korea paramount political, military, and economical interests, engages neither to obstruct nor interfere with the measures of guidance, protection, and control which the Imperial Government of Japan may find it necessary to take in Korea ...
III. Japan and Russia mutually engage:
1. To evacuate completely and simultaneously Manchuria, except the territory affected by the lease of the Liao-tung Peninsula, in conformity with the provisions of additional Art. I annexed to this treaty, and
2. To restore entirely and completely to the exclusive administration of China all portions of Manchuria now in the occupation or under the control of the Japanese or Russian troops with the exception of the territory above mentioned ...
IV. Japan and Russia reciprocally engage not to obstruct any general measures common to all countries which China may take for the development of the commerce and industry of Manchuria.
V. The Imperial Russian Government transfer and assign to the Imperial Government of Japan, with the consent of the Government of China, the lease of Port Arthur, Ta-lien, and adjacent territory and territorial waters and all rights, privileges, and concessions connected with or forming part of such lease, and they also transfer and assign to the Imperial Government of Japan all public works and properties in the territory affected by the above- mentioned lease ...
VI. The Imperial Russian Government engage to transfer and assign to the Imperial Government of Japan, without compensation and with the consent of the Chinese Government, the railway between Changchun (Kwang-cheng-tsze) and Port Arthur and all its branches, together with all rights, privileges, and properties appertaining thereto in that region, as well as all coal-mines in the said region, belonging to or worked for the benefit of the railway ...
VII. Japan and Russia engage to exploit their respective railways in Manchuria exclusively for commercial and industrial purposes, and in nowise for strategic purposes ...
VIII. The Imperial Governments of Japan and Russia, with a view to promote and facilitate intercourse and traffic will, as soon as possible, conclude a separate convention for the regulation of their connecting railway services in Manchuria.
IX. The Imperial Russian Government cede to the Imperial Government of Japan in perpetuity and full sovereignty the southern portion of the Island of Sakhalin and all islands adjacent thereto and public works and properties thereon ... Japan and Russia mutually agree not to construct in their respective possessions on the Island of Sakhalin or the adjacent islands any fortifications or other similar military works. They also respectively engage not to take any military measures which may impede the free navigation of the straits of La Perouse and Tartary.
X. It is reserved to the Russian subjects, inhabitants of the territory ceded to Japan, to sell their real property and retire to their country; but if they prefer to remain in the ceded territory they will be maintained and protected in the full exercise of their industries and rights of property on condition of submitting to Japanese laws and jurisdiction. Japan shall have full liberty to withdraw the right of residence or to deport from such territory any inhabitants who labour under political or administrative disability. She engages, however, that the proprietary rights of such inhabitants shall be fully respected.
XI. Russia engages to arrange with Japan for granting to Japanese subjects rights of fishery along the coasts of the Russian possessions in the Japan, Okhotsk, and Bering Seas ...
XII. The treaty of commerce and navigation between Japan and Russia having been annulled by the war, the Imperial Governments of Japan and Russia engage to adopt as the basis of their commercial relations, pending the conclusion of a new treaty of commerce and navigation on the basis of the treaty which was in force before the present war, the system of reciprocal treatment on the footing of the most-favoured nation, in which are included import and export duties, customs formalities, transit and tonnage dues, and the admission and treatment of the agents, subjects, and vessels of one country in the territories of the other.
XIII. As soon as possible after the present treaty comes into force all prisoners of war shall be reciprocally restored ...
XIV. The present Treaty shall be ratified by their Majesties the Emperor of Japan and the Emperor of All the Russias ... The formal exchange of ratifications shall take place in Washington as soon as possible."

The ratifications were exchanged at Washington on Sept. 25, 1905. A Convention implementing the Treaty with reference to Manchuria was signed on Aug. 30, 1907.

Major Peace Treaties of Modern History, New York, 1967, pp. 1149–55.

PORTS OF INTERNATIONAL CONCERN. The sea ports, subject to the international régime defined by multilateral treaty. The ▷ Sèvres Peace Treaty, 1920, included Chapter II. Ports of International Concern. It reads as follows:

"Art. 335. The following Eastern ports are declared ports of international concern and placed under the régime defined in the following Articles of this section:
Constantinople, from St. Stefano to Dolna Bagtchi;
Haidar Pasha;
Smyrna;
Alexandretta;
Haifa;
Basra;
Trebizond (in the conditions laid down in Art. 352);
Batum (subject to conditions to be subsequently fixed).
Free zones shall be provided in these ports.
Subject to any provisions to the contrary in the present Treaty, the régime laid down for the above ports shall not prejudice the territorial sovereignty.
Art. 336. In the ports declared of international concern the nationals, goods and flags of all States Members of the League of Nations shall enjoy complete freedom in the use of the port. In this connection and in all respects they shall be treated on a footing of perfect equality, particularly as regards all port and quay facilities and charges, including facilities for berthing, loading and discharging, tonnage dues and charges, quay, pilotage, lighthouse, quarantine and all similar dues and charges of whatsoever nature, levied in the name of or for profit of the Government, public functionaries, private individuals, corporations or establishments of every kind, no distinction being made between the nationals, goods and flags of the different States and those of the State under whose sovereignty or authority the port is placed. There shall be no restrictions on the movement of persons or vessels other than those arising from regulations concerning customs, police, public health, emigration and immigration and those relating to the import and export of prohibited goods. Such regulations must be reasonable and uniform and must not impede traffic unnecessarily.
Art. 337. All dues and charges for the use of the port or of its approaches, or for the use of facilities provided in the port, shall be levied under the conditions of equality prescribed in Art. 336, and shall be reasonable both as regards their amount and their application, having regard to the expenses incurred by the port authority in the administration, upkeep and improvement of the port and of the approaches thereto, or in the interests of navigation.
Subject to the provisions of Art. 54, Part II (Political Clauses) of the present Treaty all dues and charges other than those provided for in the present Article or in Arts. 338, 342, or 343 are forbidden.
Art. 338. All customs, local octroi or consumption dues, duly authorized, levied on goods imported or exported through a port subject to the international régime shall be the same whether the flag of the vessel which effected or is to effect the transport be the flag of the State exercising sovereignty or authority over the port or any other flag. In the absence of special circumstances justifying an exception on account of economic needs, such dues must be fixed on the same basis and at the same tariffs as similar duties levied on the other

P

customs frontiers of the State concerned. All facilities which may be accorded by such State over other land or water routes or at other ports for the import or export of goods shall be equally granted to imports and exports through the port subject to the international régime."

G.F. DE MARTENS, *Nouveau Recueil Général*, Vol. 12, p. 664 and Vol. 13, p. 342.

PORT SUDAN–JEDDAH TELEGRAPH AGREEMENT, 1929. An Agreement between Hejaz Sudan and the British Empire, signed on Dec. 18, 1926.

LNTS, Vol. 63, p. 185.

PORT TIME. An international term for the difference in time between high and low tide in sea ports calculated for each port.

PORTUGAL. Member of the UN. The Republic of Portugal, borders on Spain and the Atlantic Ocean. Area (with the ▷ Azores islands): 91,632 sq. km. Pop. 1987 est.: 10,212,000 (1970 census: 8,648,369). Capital: Lisbon with 2,061,600 inhabitants, 1981. GNP per capita 1987: US $2830. Currency: one escudo = 100 centavos. Official language: Portuguese. National Day: Apr. 25, Liberation Day, 1974 and Sept. 5, Republic Day, 1910.
Member of the UN from Dec. 4, 1955 and of all specialized agencies with exception of IDA. Member of NATO, EFTA and OECD.
International relations: an independent European State since the 12th century; colonial empire from the 16th century. After the liberation of Brazil, 1822, colonial possessions restricted to Africa and South Asia. In 1933 these ceased to be regarded as colonies, but decreed an "integral part of Portugal." As member of the UN from 1955 Portugal was in standing opposition to the anti-colonial resolutions of the UN General Assembly. In 1963 Portugal was expelled from the UN Economic Commission for Africa; in Nov., 1965 the UN Security Council demanded that Portugal grant freedom to countries under its administration. Portuguese Foreign Minister A.F. Nogueira said on Dec. 14, 1966 that Portugal "does not intend to accept any UN resolutions relating to its overseas territories." In May, 1974 Foreign Minister Mario Soares started negotiations with liberation movements in Angola, Guinea-Bissau and Mozambique which led to ceasefire in June that year. First treaty granting full independence was signed with Guinea-Bissau on Aug. 26, 1974 at Algiers. In 1976/77 normalization of relations with all former colonies. On Mar. 28, 1977 Portugal formally applied for admission to the EEC. On July 19, 1977 introduced a 200-mile fishing zone. In 1977 signed a Treaty of Friendship and Co-operation with Spain. On Nov. 11, 1983, the prime ministers of Portugal and Spain signed a Declaration of Lisbon on co-operation of both States in the Spirit of Friendship. See also ▷ World Heritage UNESCO List.

J. DEFFY, *Portugal in Africa*, Cambridge, 1962; P. WOHLGEMUTH, *The Portuguese Territories and the UN*, New York, 1963; H.V. LIVERMORE, *A New History of Portugal*, New York, 1966; *A Principle of Torment: The UN and Portuguese Territories*, New York, 1973; L.A. SOBEL (ed.), *Portuguese Revolution 1974–76*, New York, 1976; R. HARWEY, *Portugal Birth of a Democracy*, London, 1978; P. RAMOS DE ALMEIDA, *Historia do colonialismo portugues en Africa, Cronologiia*, Lisboa, 1979; F.M. ROGERS, *Atlantic Islanders of the Azores and Madera*, North Quincy, 1979; M. NEWITT, *Portugal in Africa: The Last Hundred Years*, London, 1981; I. ROBERTSON, *Blue Guide, Portugal*, London, 1982; *The Europa Year Book 1984. A World Survey*, Vol. I, pp. 732–752, London, 1984; KEESING's *Record of World Events, 1986*, No. 3.

PORTUGUESE AFRICA. The former possession of Portugal in Africa: ▷ Angola, ▷ Guinea Bissau, ▷ Mozambique.

J. DUFY, *Portuguese Africa*, Cambridge Mass. 1961; D.A. ABSHIRE, M.A. SAMUELS (eds.), *Portuguese Africa, A Handbook*, New York, 1969.

PORTUGUESE INDIA. The former colonial possessions of Portugal in India, 1510–1962. ▷ Goa, Daman and Diu.

POSEIDON. An American strategic missile of the sea–land class launched from submarines and equipped with a split warhead containing several movable warheads with a nuclear payload. Range *c.* 5000 km. It is a new version of the missile ▷ Polaris. Subject of SALT negotiations (▷ SALT II. Documents, 1979).

J. GOLDBLAT, *Arms and Armaments. A Handbook*, New York, 1983; D. ROBERTSON, *Guide to Modern Defense and Strategy*, Detroit, 1988.

POST. A subject of international conventions; a public institution responsible for shipping parcels and mail defined by domestic legislation and by world postal conventions outside and inside the country; subject of continued international co-operation since 1874 when the First World Postal Congress held in Berne established the General Postal Union. The Second Congress in Paris, 1878, changed the name to Universal Postal Union – UPU. Within the CMEA system, the Organization for the Co-operation of Socialist Countries in Electric and Postal Communications was founded in Dec. 1957. The Scandinavian states concluded a number of regional postal treaties.

LNTS, Vol. 12, p. 321; Vol. 30, p. 303; Vol. 105, p. 353; Vol. 158, p. 111 and Vol. 190, p. 299.

POSTAL CHECKS AGREEMENT, 1924. One of the UPU conventions, with Final Protocol and Detailed Regulations for the Execution of the Agreement, concluded on Aug. 28, 1924 at Stockholm, between Albania, Austria, Belgium, Bolivia, Cuba, Czechoslovakia, Denmark, France, Germany, Greece, Hungary, Italy, Japan, Lithuania, Luxembourg, Morocco, the Netherlands, Poland (with Danzig), Portugal, Romania, the Serbo-Croat-Slovene State, Spain, Sweden, Switzerland, Tunis and Venezuela. The same day the Contracting parties signed in Stockholm the Agreement Concerning Payment on Delivery, and Detailed Regulations for the execution of the Agreement Concerning Payment on Delivery.

LNTS, Vol. 41, pp. 9 and 55.

POSTAL CODE. On the initiative of ITU the permanent designation by number and letter-number of rural and urban postal districts was introduced in the 1960s in France, FRG, Italy, UK, USA, Scandinavian countries and others, 1971 in Yugoslavia and the USSR, 1972 in Poland, then in most of the countries of the world.

POSTAL CONVENTIONS. The international agreements and treaties relating to international operation of postal services adopted since 1874 by Postal Congresses, the supreme organs of the Universal Postal Union. The first convention known as the Berne Treaty adopted and signed on Oct. 9, 1874 in Berne, modified on several occasions since World War I, established French as the only official language (maintained by all subsequent agreements); the Seventh Postal Congress on Nov. 30, 1920 in Madrid adopted a Universal Postal Convention (Convention Postale Universelle) and several supplementary agreements which went into

force Jan. 12, 1921; the Eighth Congress adopted on Aug. 28, 1924 in Stockholm, a new Postal Convention which went into force Oct. 1, 1925; modified at the Ninth Congress London, June 28, 1929 and at the Eleventh Congress Mar. 20, 1934 at Cairo. After World War II, on Oct. 3, 1957, the Ottawa Congress adopted a new Universal Postal Convention and the Vienna Congress on July 10, 1964, the new UPU Constitution with final protocol and an agreement with the UN (plus additional clauses) which went into force on Jan. 1, 1966.

LNTS, Vol. 40, pp. 49 and 57; Vol. 46, p. 19; *UNTS*, Vol. 170, pp. 63 and 277; Vol. 611, p. 243.

POSTAL CORRESPONDENCE. The correspondence defined by the art. 33 of the Universal Postal Convention, 1924, as follows:
"The term correspondence means and includes letters, postcards, both single and reply-paid, commercial papers, samples of merchandise, and printed papers of every kind, including articles printed in relief for the use of the blind."

LNTS, Vol. 40, p. 49.

POSTAL IDENTITY CARDS. An identity document, defined in the Universal Postal Constitution 1964, by art. 12 as follows:
"1. Each Postal Administration may issue to persons who apply for them, postal identity cards valid as proof of identity for postal transactions effected in the Member-Countries which have not notified their refusal to admit them."
"2. The Administration which issues a card is authorized to levy, on this account, a charge which must not exceed 1 franc."
"3. Administrations ... are not responsible for consequences arising from the loss ... of a genuine card."
"4. A card is valid for a period of five years."

UNTS, Vol. 611, p. 243.

POSTAL MONEY ORDERS. A subject of international co-operation and conventions: UPU Agreement concerning Postal Money Orders and Postal Traveller's Checks, signed on July 11, 1952. "Each (Postal) Administration is empowered to fix the maximum amount for the money orders which it issues, on condition that this maximum does not exceed 1000 Swiss Francs" (art. 4).

UNTS, Vol. 170, p. 277.

POSTAL PARCELS. A subject of international co-operation and convention: UPU Agreement concerning Postal Parcels, signed on July 11, 1952. The Agreement limited the unit weight of postal parcel items to 20 kilograms maximum.

UNTS, Vol. 170, p. 63.

POSTAL REPLY-COUPONS. The coupons are defined by the art. 44 of the Universal Postal Convention, 1924, as follows:
"Reply-coupons are on sale in the countries of the Universal Postal Union. The selling price of a reply coupon is fixed by the Administration concerned, but may not be less than 40 (Swiss) centimes, or the equivalent of this sum in the money of the country of issue. Each coupon is exchangeable in any country of the Union for a stamp or stamps representing the postage on a single-rate letter for abroad originating in that country. The exchange must, however, be made before the end of six months following the month of issue. Moreover, the right is reserved to each country to demand that reply coupons and the correspondence to be prepaid by means of the stamps received in exchange for these coupons shall be presented at the same time."

LNTS, Vol. 40, p. 57.

POSTAL TRAVELLER'S CHECKS AGREEMENT, 1952. A convention of the UPU concerning money orders and postal traveller's checks, signed on July 11, 1952.

UNTS, Vol. 170, p. 277.

POSTAL UNION, GENERAL. The General Postal Union was established in 1874 by a Treaty concerning the formation of a General Postal Union concluded between Austria–Hungary, Belgium, Denmark, Egypt, France, Germany, Great Britain, Greece, Italy, Norway, the Netherlands, Portugal, Romania, Russia, Serbia, Spain, Sweden, Switzerland, Turkey and the United States. It was signed on Oct. 9, 1874 at Berne; came into force on July 1, 1875. The main first three articles read as follows:

"Art. I. The countries between which the present treaty is concluded shall form, under the title of General Postal Union, a single postal territory for the reciprocal exchange of correspondence between their post-offices. Art. II. The stipulations of this treaty shall extend to letters, post-cards, books, newspapers, and other printed papers, patterns of merchandise, and legal and commercial documents originating in one of the countries of the Union and intended for another of those countries. They shall also apply to the exchange by post of the articles above mentioned between the countries of the Union and countries foreign to the Union whenever such exchange takes place over the territory of two at least of the contracting parties. Art. III. The general Union rate of postage is fixed at 25 centimes for a single prepaid letter.
Nevertheless, as a measure of conversion, the option is reserved to each country, in order to suit its monetary or other requirements, of levying a rate higher or lower than this charge, provided that it does not exceed 32 centimes or go below 20 centimes.
Every letter which does not exceed 15 grammes in weight shall be considered a single letter. The charge upon letters exceeding that weight shall be a single rate for every 15 grammes or fraction of 15 grammes.
The charge on unpaid letters shall be double the rate levied in the country of destination on prepaid letters The prepayment of post-cards is compulsory. The postage to be charged upon them is fixed at one-half of that on paid letters with power to round off the fractions.
For all conveyance by sea of more than 30 nautical miles within the district of the Union, there may be added to the ordinary postage an additional charge which shall not exceed the half of the general Union rate fixed for a paid letter."

J.T. WATKINS, J.W. ROBINSON, *General International Organization*, Princeton, 1956, pp. 14–19; *Everyman's United Nations*, New York, 1971.

POSTAL UNION OF ASIA AND OCEANIA. An intergovernmental institution est. in 1962 in Manila, by the government of the Philippines, Republic of Korea, Taiwan, and Thailand. Members: 20 Asian Pacific countries. Official relations with UPU. Publ.: *Informe annual*.

Yearbook of International Organizations 1986/87; The Europa Yearbook 1988. A World Survey, Vol. I, London, 1988.

POSTAL UNION OF THE AMERICAS AND SPAIN, PUAS. The Union was established in 1931 in Madrid by a Postal Union Convention, with Final Protocol, Detailed Regulations and Provisions relating to the Conveyance of Letter Post by Air. It was signed on Nov. 10, 1931 in Madrid by the governments of 22 American Republics (20 Latin American, the USA and Canada) and Spain. The Contracting Parties "making use of the right accorded them by Art. 5 of the existing Convention of the Universal Postal Union" decided to form "under the title of the Postal Union of the Americas and Spain, a single postal territory" (art. 1).
The Ninth Congress of the Union adopted on July 16, 1966 in Mexico, a new Convention on the

PUAS, together with the Regulations of Executions of the Convention, Regulations of the International Office of PUAS, Regulation of the International Transfer Office, Agreement on Declared Values, Parcel Post Agreement, Regulations of Execution of the Parcel Post Agreement; and Money Order Agreement. It came into force on Mar. 1, 1967. The International Office of PUAS is located in Montevideo.

LNTS, Vol. 131. pp. 327 and 447; *UST*, 1966; *PUAS Congress of Mexico, DC*, Montevideo, 1966.

POSTAL VOTE. The voting in parliamentary or national elections by post, permitted for persons who cannot vote in a voting center. The custom is accepted in Great Britain and the USA and in a few other countries; an international problem in connection with the first multi-state elections to the European Parliament, 1979.

POSTCARDS. A subject of international co-operation. Organization reg. with the UIA:

International Postcard Collectors Association, f. 1969, Los Angeles, USA.

Yearbook of International Organizations.

POSTED PRICES. The contractual prices of raw materials extracted by foreign concerns. Posted prices are the basis for calculating the tax on net profit of companies as well as royalties; foreign companies always attempted to lower posted prices in order to reduce their tax liabilities. OPEC came out in opposition to this and since the Teheran Oil Agreement of 1971 has introduced the unification of principles for determining posted prices, which became the basis for a revision of posted prices in other areas of extractive industries in which foreign concerns have concessions.

POSTE RESTANTE. *French* = "till called for." A postal institution of the Berne convention which obligated the member states to accept letter and parcels for persons not indicated under their own address but only under the address of the post office of a certain town, district, or residential quarter.

POST MORTEM AUCTORIS. *Latin* = "after author's death." A rule providing that ▷ copyright expires after a specified number of years from the author's death. The Universal Convention on Copyright adopted in Geneva in 1952, amended in Paris in 1971, provides for at least 25 years of copyright; reckoned however, in two ways: (a) starting from the date of author's death and (b) starting from the date of first publication (the rule ▷ Post publicationem operis). An international poll taken in 1975 showed that the shortest period of post mortem auctoris is applied in the USSR (15 years), Peru (20 years), Liberia, Mexico, Poland, Salvador (25 years), Bolivia, China, Dominicana, Japan, Jordan, Korea, Liechtenstein, Philippines, Sweden, Thailand, Venezuela (30 years) and Uruguay (40 years). In most countries 50 years is applied: Argentina, Australia, Austria, Belgium, Burma, Canada, Costa Rica, Czechoslovakia, Chile, Denmark, Ecuador, Finland, France, FRG, GDR, Great Britain, Greece, Guatemala, Hungary, Indonesia, Ireland, Iceland, Israel, Lebanon, Luxembourg, Monaco, the Netherlands, Norway, New Zealand, Paraguay, South Africa, Sri Lanka, Syria, Switzerland, Turkey. After 60 years copyright post mortem auctoris expires in Brazil, after 80 years in Colombia and Panama, and never expires in Portugal. In the FRG a 70-year period has been introduced and, as a result, many authors from the German-speaking areas attempt to have their first editions published in the FRG. Only in the USA is a 28-year

period in force counting from the date of the first edition, but with the right to prolong the validity by another 28 years.

World Copyright Encyclopaedia, 4 Vols, Leiden, 1956, supplement 1959.

POST PUBLICATIONEM OPERIS. *Latin* = "after publication of works." A rule of ▷ copyright providing that copyright is invalid after the expiration of a specified period of time counting from the first edition of a work. Vide ▷ Post mortem auctoris.

POTATO. A subject of international co-operation. Organizations reg. with the UIA:

Association of Common Market Potato Breeders, f. 1964, Bonn.
European Association for Potato Research, f. 1956, Wageningen. Publ.: *Potato Research*.
European Union for Wholesale Potato Trade, f. 1952, Paris. Publ.: *Trade Regulations*.
European Union of the Potato Processing Industry, founded 1963, London.
International Potato Center, founded 1971, Lima. Publ.: *Symposium Proceedings*.
International Potato Chip Institute, f. 1937, Cleveland.
Potato Trade Committee of the EEC Countries, f. 1958, Paris.
Specialized Committee on Potatoes of the EEC Countries, f. 1960, Paris.
Union of Professional Groups of the Potato Starch Industry of the EEC, f. 1960, Paris.

Yearbook of International Organizations.

POTSDAM AGREEMENT, 1805. A Treaty concluded on Nov. 3, 1805 by Russian Tsar, Alexander I, and King of Prussia, Friedrich Wilhelm III, in the presence of Queen Luisa by the tomb of Friedrich II in Garnisonkirche in Potsdam. It was a Friendship Treaty between Russia and Prussia under which Prussia was to mediate with Napoleon and to raise under special conditions an 80,000 man army in case he rejected Russian conditions.

F.F. MARTENS, *Recueil des traités et conventions conclus par la Russie*, St. Petersburg, 1874–1905.

POTSDAM AGREEMENT, 1945. An agreement also called the Potsdam Treaty, signed on Aug. 2, 1945 in Potsdam, near Berlin, by the President of USA H. Truman, and Premiers: of the USSR – J.V. Stalin and Great Britain – C. Attlee. The Potsdam Agreement became the foundation for the Peace Treaties: of 1947 with Bulgaria, Finland, Romania, Hungary and Italy, of 1951 with Japan and of 1955 with Austria; also for the quadripartite treaties on West Berlin and the responsibility of the powers for peaceful resolution of German issues of 1971, and also served as the basis for the recognition of the Polish–GDR frontier along the rivers Oder and Neisse in 1950 by the GDR and in 1972 by the FRG. The Potsdam Agreement is in the form of a communiqué on the Potsdam Conference and adopted by its decisions. The text is as follows:

"On July 17, 1945, the President of the United States of America, Harry S. Truman, the Chairman of the Council of People's Commissars of the Union of Soviet Socialist Republics, Generalissimo J.V. Stalin, and the Prime Minister of Great Britain, Winston S. Churchill, together with Mr. Clement R. Attlee, met in the tripartite conference of Berlin. They were accompanied by the Foreign Secretaries of the three Governments, Mr. James F. Byrnes, Mr. V.M. Molotov and Mr. Anthony Eden, the Chiefs of Staff, and other advisers. There were nine meetings between July 17 and July 25. The conference was then interrupted for two days while the results of the British General Election were being declared. On July 28 Mr. Attlee returned to the conference as Prime Minister, accompanied by the new Secretary of State for Foreign Affairs, Mr. Ernest Bevin. Four days of further discussion then took place.

During the course of the conference there were regular meetings of the heads of the three Governments accompanied by the Foreign Secretaries, and also of the Foreign Secretaries alone. Committees appointed by the Foreign Secretaries for preliminary consideration of questions before the conference also met daily. The meetings of the conference were held at the Cecilienhof, near Potsdam. The conference ended on August 2, 1945.

Important decisions and agreements were reached. Views were exchanged on a number of other questions, and considerations of these matters will be continued by the Council of Foreign Ministers established by the conference.

President Truman, Generalissimo Stalin, and Prime Minister Attlee leave this conference, which has strengthened the ties between the three Governments and extended the scope of their collaboration and understanding with renewed confidence that their Governments and peoples, together with the other United Nations, will ensure the creation of a just and enduring peace.

Council of Foreign Ministers

The conference reached an agreement for the establishment of a Council of Foreign Ministers, representing the five principal Powers, to continue the necessary preparatory work for the peace settlements and to take up other matters which from time to time may be referred to the Council by agreement of the Governments participating in the Council. The text of the agreement for the establishment of the Council of Foreign Ministers is as follows:

(1) There shall be established a Council composed of the Foreign Ministers of the United Kingdom, the Union of Soviet Socialist Republics, China, France, and the United States.

(2) (i) The Council shall normally meet in London, which shall be the permanent seat of the joint secretariat which the Council will form. Each of the Foreign Ministers will be accompanied by a highranking deputy, duly authorized to carry on the work of the Council in the absence of his Foreign Minister, and by a small staff of technical advisers. (ii) The first meeting of the Council shall be held in London not later than September 1, 1945. Meetings may be held by common agreement in other capitals as may be agreed from time to time.

(3) (i) As its immediate important task, the Council shall be authorized to draw up, with a view to their submission to the United Nations, treaties of peace with Italy, Romania, Bulgaria, Hungary, and Finland, and to propose settlements of territorial questions outstanding on the termination of the war in Europe. The Council shall be utilized for the preparation of a peace settlement for Germany, to be accepted by the Government of Germany when a government adequate for the purpose is established. (ii) For the discharge of each of these tasks the Council will be composed of the members representing those States which were signatory to the terms of surrender imposed upon the enemy State concerned. For the purpose of the peace settlement for Italy, France shall be regarded as a signatory to the terms of surrender for Italy. Other members will be invited to participate when matters directly concerning them are under discussion. (iii) Other matters may from time to time be referred to the Council by agreement between the member Governments.

(4) (i) Whenever the Council is considering a question of direct interest to a State not represented thereon, such State should be invited to send representatives to participate in the discussion and study of that question. (ii) The Council may adapt its procedure to the particular problem under consideration. In some cases it may hold its own preliminary discussions prior to the participation of other interested States. In other cases the Council may convoke a formal conference of the State chiefly interested in seeking a solution of the particular problem.

In accordance with the decision of the conference, the three Governments have each addressed an identical invitation to the Governments of China and France to adopt this text and to join in establishing the Council. The establishment of the Council of Foreign Ministers for the specific purposes named in the text will be without prejudice to the agreement of the Crimea conference that there should be periodic consultation among the Foreign Secretaries of the United States, the Union of Soviet Socialist Republics, and the United Kingdom.

The conference also considered the position of the European Advisory Commission in the light of the agreement to establish the Council of Foreign Ministers. It was noted with satisfaction that the Commission had ably discharged its principal tasks by the recommendations that it had furnished for the terms of Germany's unconditional surrender, for the zones of occupation in Germany and Austria, and for the interallied control machinery in those countries. It was felt that further work of a detailed character for the co-ordination of allied policy for the control of Germany and Austria would in future fall within the competence of the Allied Control Council at Berlin and the Allied Commission at Vienna. Accordingly, it was agreed to recommend that the European Advisory Commission be dissolved.

Allies and Germany

The allied armies are in occupation of the whole of Germany and the German people have begun to atone for the terrible crimes committed under the leadership of those whom, in the hour of their success, they openly approved and blindly obeyed. Agreement has been reached at this conference on the political and economic principles of a co-ordinated allied policy toward defeated Germany during the period of allied control. The purpose of this agreement is to carry out the Crimea declaration on Germany. German militarism and Nazism will be extirpated and the allies will take in agreement together, now and in the future, the other measures necessary to assure that Germany never again will threaten her neighbours or the peace of the world. It is not the intention of the allies to destroy or enslave the German people. It is the intention of the allies that the German people be given the opportunity to prepare for the eventual reconstruction of their life on a democratic and peaceful basis. If their own efforts are steadily directed to this end it will be possible for them in due course to take their place among the free and peaceful peoples of the world.

The text of the agreement is as follows:

The Political and Economic Principles to govern the Treatment of Germany in the Initial Control Period.

(a) Political Principles

1. In accordance with the agreement on control machinery in Germany, supreme authority in Germany is exercised, on instructions from their respective Governments, by the commanders-in-chief of the armed forces of the United States of America, the United Kingdom, the Union of Soviet Socialist Republics, and the French Republic, each in his own zone of occupation, and also jointly, in matters affecting Germany, as a whole, in their capacity as members of the Control Council.

2. So far as is practicable, there shall be uniformity of treatment of the German population throughout Germany.

3. The purposes of the occupation of Germany by which the Control Council shall be guided are:

(i) The complete disarmament and demilitarization of Germany and the elimination or control of all German industry that could be used for military production. To those ends: (a) All German land, naval and air forces, the S.S., S.A., S.D., and Gestapo, with all their organizations, staffs and institutions, including the General Staff, the Officers' Corps, Reserve Corps, military schools, war veterans' organizations, and all other military and quasi-military organizations, together with all clubs and associations which serve to keep alive the military tradition in Germany, shall be completely and finally abolished in such manner as permanently to prevent the revival or reorganization of German militarism and Nazism; (b) all arms ammunition, and implements of war, and all specialized facilities for their production, shall be held at the disposal of the allies or destroyed. The maintenance and production of all aircraft and all arms, ammunition, and implements of war shall be prevented.

(ii) To convince the German people that they have suffered a total military defeat and that they cannot escape responsibility for what they have brought upon themselves, since their own ruthless warfare and the fanatical Nazi resistance have destroyed German economy and made chaos and suffering inevitable.

(iii) To destroy the National Socialist Party and its affiliated and supervised organizations; to dissolve all Nazi institutions; to ensure that they are not revived in any form; and to prevent all Nazi and militarist activity or propaganda.

(iv) To prepare for the eventual reconstruction of German political life on a democratic basis and for eventual peaceful co-operation in international life by Germany.

4. All Nazi laws which provided the basis of the Hitler regime or established discrimination on grounds of race, creed, or political opinion shall be abolished. No such discriminations, whether legal, administrative, or otherwise, shall be tolerated.

5. War criminals and those who have participated in planning or carrying out Nazi enterprises involving or resulting in atrocities or war crimes shall be arrested and brought to judgment. Nazi leaders, influential Nazi supporters and high officials of Nazi organizations and institutions, and any other persons dangerous to the occupation or its objectives, shall be arrested and interned.

6. All members of the Nazi party who have been more than nominal participants in its activities, and all other persons hostile to allied purposes, shall be removed from public and semi-public office and from positions of responsibility in important private undertakings. Such persons shall be replaced by persons who, by their political and moral qualities, are deemed capable of assisting in developing genuine democratic institutions in Germany.

7. German education shall be so controlled as completely to eliminate Nazi and militarist doctrines and to make possible the successful development of democratic ideas.

8. The judicial system will be reorganized in accordance with the principles of democracy, of justice under law, and of equal rights for all citizens without distinction of race, nationality, or religion.

9. The administration of affairs in Germany should be directed towards the decentralization of the political structure and the development of local responsibility. To this end (i) local self-government shall be restored throughout Germany on democratic principles, and in particular through elective council, as rapidly as is consistent with military security and the purposes of military occupation; (ii) all democratic political parties with rights of assembly and of public discussion shall be allowed and encouraged throughout Germany; (iii) representative and elective principles shall be introduced into regional, provincial, and state (Land) administration as rapidly as may be justified by the successful application of these principles in local self-government; (iv) for the time being no central German government shall be established. Notwithstanding this, however, certain essential central German administrative departments, headed by State Secretaries, shall be established, particularly in the fields of finance, transport, communications, foreign trade, and industry. Such departments will act under the direction of the Control Council.

10. Subject to the necessity for maintaining military security, freedom of speech, press, and religion shall be permitted, and religious institutions shall be respected. Subject likewise to the maintenance of military security, the formation of free trade unions shall be permitted.

(b) Economic Principles

11. In order to eliminate Germany's war potential, the production of arms, ammunition, and implements of war as well as all types of aircraft and sea-going ships shall be prohibited and prevented. Production of metals, chemicals, machinery, and other items that are directly necessary to a war economy shall be rigidly controlled and restricted to Germany's approved post-war peace-time needs to meet the objectives stated in paragraph 15: Productive capacity not needed for permitted production shall be removed in accordance with the reparations plan recommended by the Allied Commission on Reparations and approved by the Governments concerned, or if not removed shall be destroyed.

12. At the earliest practicable date, the German economy shall be decentralized for the purpose of eliminating the present excessive concentration of economic power as exemplified in particular by cartels, syndicates, trusts, and other monopolistic arrangements.

13. In organizing the German economy, primary emphasis shall be given to the development of agriculture and peaceful domestic industries.

14. During the period of occupation Germany shall be treated as a single economic unit. To this end common

policies shall be established in regard to: (a) mining and industrial production and allocation; (b) agriculture, forestry, and fishing; (c) wages, prices, and rationing; (d) import and export programmes for Germany as a whole; (e) currency and banking, central taxation, and Customs; (f) reparation and removal of industrial war potential; (g) transportation and communications. In applying these policies account shall be taken, where appropriate, of varying local conditions.

15. Allied controls shall be imposed upon the German economy, but only to the extent necessary (a) to carry out programmes of industrial disarmament and demilitarization, of reparations, and of approved exports and imports; (b) to assure the production and maintenance of goods and services required to meet the needs of the occupying forces and displaced persons in Germany, and essential to maintain in Germany average living standards not exceeding the average of the standards of living of European countries (European countries means all European countries, excluding the United Kingdom and the Union of Soviet Socialist Republics); (c) to ensure in the manner determined by the Control Council the equitable distribution of essential commodities between the several zones, so as to produce a balanced economy throughout Germany and reduce the need for imports; (d) to control German industry and all economic and financial international transactions, including exports and imports, with the aim of preventing Germany from developing a war potential and of achieving the other objectives named herein; (e) to control all German public or private scientific bodies, research and experimental institutions, laboratories, etc., connected with economic activities.

16. In the imposition and maintenance of economic controls established by the Control Council, German administrative machinery shall be created and the German authorities shall be required to the fullest extent practicable to proclaim and assume administration of such controls. Thus it should be brought home to the German people that the responsibility for the administration of such controls, and any breakdown in these controls, will rest with themselves. Any German controls which may run counter to the objectives of occupation will be prohibited.

17. Measures shall be promptly taken (a) to effect essential repair of transport; (b) to enlarge coal production; (c) to maximize agricultural output; (d) to effect emergency repair of housing and essential utilities.

18. Appropriate steps shall be taken by the Control Council to exercise control and the power of disposition over German-owned external assets not already under the control of the United Nations which have taken part in the war against Germany.

19. Payment of reparations should leave enough resources to enable the German people to subsist without external assistance. In working out the economic balance of Germany the necessary means must be provided to pay for imports approved by the Control Council in Germany. The proceeds of exports from current production and stocks shall be available in the first place for payment for such imports.

The above clause will not apply to the equipment and products referred to in paragraph 4(a) and 4(b) of the Reparations Agreement.

German Reparations

In accordance with the Crimea decision that Germany be compelled to compensate to the greatest possible extent for the loss and suffering that she has caused to the United Nations, and for which the German people cannot escape responsibility, the following agreement on reparations was reached:

1. Reparation claims of the U.S.S.R. shall be met by removals from the zone of Germany occupied by the U.S.S.R. and from appropriate German external assets.
2. The U.S.S.R. undertakes to settle the reparation claims of Poland from its own share of reparations.
3. The reparation claims of the United States, the United Kingdom, and other countries entitled to reparations shall be met from the western zones and from appropriate German external assets.
4. In addition to the reparations to be taken by the U.S.S.R., from its own zone of occupation, the U.S.S.R. shall receive additionally from the western zones: (a) 15% of such usable and complete industrial capital equipment, in the first place from the metallurgical, chemical, and machine manufacturing industries, as is unnecessary for the German peace economy, and

should be removed from the western zones of Germany, in exchange for an equivalent value of food, coal, potash, zinc, timber, clay products, petroleum products, and such other commodities as may be agreed upon. (b) 10% of such industrial capital equipment as is unnecessary for the German peace economy and should be removed from the western zones, to be transferred to the Soviet Government on reparations account without payment or exchange of any kind in return. Removals of equipment as provided in (a) and (b) above shall be made simultaneously.

5. The amount of equipment to be removed from the western zones on account of reparations must be determined within six months from now at the latest.
6. Removals of industrial capital equipment shall begin as soon as possible and shall be completed within two years from the determination specified in paragraph 5. The delivery of products covered by 4(a) above shall begin as soon as possible, and shall be made by the U.S.S.R. in agreed instalments within five years of the date thereof. The determination of the amount and character of the industrial equipment unnecessary for the German peace economy and therefore available for reparation shall be made by the Control Council under policies fixed by the Allied Commission on Reparations, with the participation of France, subject to the final approval of the zone commander in the zone from which the equipment is to be removed.
7. Prior to the fixing of the total amount of equipment subject to removal, advance deliveries shall be made in respect of such equipment as will be determined to be eligible for delivery in accordance with the procedure set forth in the last sentence of paragraph 6.
8. The Soviet Government renounces all claims in respect of reparation to shares of German enterprises which are located in the western zones of occupation in Germany, as well as to German foreign assets in all countries except those specified in paragraph 9 below.
9. The Governments of the U.K. and U.S.A. renounce their claims in respect of reparations to shares of German enterprises which are located in the eastern zone of occupation in Germany, as well as to German foreign assets in Bulgaria, Finland, Hungary, Romania, and eastern Austria.
10. The Soviet Government makes no claims to gold captured by the allied troops in Germany.

Disposal of the Fleet

The conference agreed in principle upon arrangements for the use and disposal of the surrendered German fleet and merchant ships. It was decided that the three Governments would appoint experts to work out together detailed plans to give effect to the agreed principles. A further joint statement will be published simultaneously by the three Governments in due course.

City of Königsberg for Russia

The conference examined a proposal by the Soviet Government that, pending the final determination of territorial questions at the peace settlement, the section of the western frontier of the Union of Soviet Socialist Republics which is adjacent to the Baltic Sea should pass from a point on the eastern shore of the Bay of Danzig to the east, north of Braunsberg-Goldap, to the meeting point of the frontiers of Lithuania, the Polish Republic, and East Prussia.

The conference has agreed in principle to the proposal of the Soviet Government concerning the ultimate transfer to the Soviet Union of the city of Königsberg and the area adjacent to it as described above, subject to expert examination of the actual frontier.

The President of the United States and the British Prime Minister have declared that they will support the proposal of the conference at the forthcoming peace settlement.

War criminals

The three Governments have taken note of the discussions which have been proceeding in recent weeks in London between British, United States, Soviet and French representatives with a view to reaching agreement on the methods of trial of those major war criminals whose crimes under the Moscow declaration of October, 1943, have no particular geographical localization. The three Governments reaffirm their intention to bring these criminals to swift and sure justice. They hope that the negotiations in London will result in speedy agreement being reached for this purpose, and they regard it as a matter of great importance that the trial of these major criminals

should begin at the earliest possible date. The first list of defendants will be published before September 1.

Austria

The conference examined a proposal by the Soviet Government on the extension of the authority of the Austrian Provisional Government to all of Austria. The three Governments agreed that they were prepared to examine this question after the entry of the British and American forces into the city of Vienna.

Poland

The conference considered questions relating to the Polish Provisional Government and the western boundary of Poland.

A. On the Polish Provisional Government of National Unity, they defined their attitude in the following statement:

'We have taken note with pleasure of the agreement reached among representative Poles from Poland and abroad which has made possible the formation, in accordance with the decisions reached at the Crimea conference, of a Polish Provisional Government of National Unity recognized by the three Powers. The establishment by the British and United States Governments of diplomatic relations with the Polish Provisional Government has resulted in the withdrawal of their recognition from the former Polish Government in London, which no longer exists.

'The British and United States Governments have taken measures to protect the interest of the Polish Provisional Government, as the recognized Government of the Polish State, in the property belonging to the Polish State located in their territories and under their control, whatever the form of this property may be. They have further taken measures to prevent alienation to third parties of such property. All proper facilities will be given to the Polish Provisional Government for the exercise of the ordinary legal remedies for the recovery of any property belonging to the Polish State which may have been wrongfully alienated.

'The three Powers are anxious to assist the Polish Provisional Government in facilitating the return to Poland as soon as practicable of all Poles abroad who wish to go, including members of the Polish armed forces and the merchant marine. They expect that those Poles who return home shall be accorded personal and property rights on the same basis as all Polish citizens.

'The three Powers note that the Polish Provisional Government, in accordance with the decisions of the Crimea conference, has agreed to the holding of free and unfettered elections as soon as possible on the basis of universal suffrage and secret ballot, in which all democratic and anti-Nazi parties shall have the right to take part and to put forward candidates, and that representatives of the allied Press shall enjoy full freedom to report to the world upon developments in Poland before and during the elections.'

B. The following agreement was reached on the western frontier of Poland:

In conformity with the agreement on Poland reached at the Crimea conference, the three heads of Government have sought the opinion of the Polish Provisional Government of National Unity in regard to the accession of territory in the north and west which Poland should receive. The President of the National Council of Poland and members of the Polish Provisional Government of National Unity have been received at the conference and have fully presented their views. The three heads of Government reaffirm their opinion that the final delimitation of the western frontier of Poland should await the peace settlement.

The three heads of Government agree that, pending the final determination of Poland's western frontier, the former German territories east of a line running from the Baltic Sea immediately west of Swinemunde, and thence along the Oder River to the confluence of the western Neisse River and along the western Neisse to the Czechoslovak frontier, including that portion of East Prussia not placed under the administration of the Union of Soviet Socialist Republics in accordance with the understanding reached at this conference and including the area of the former free city of Danzig, shall be under the administration of the Polish State and for such purposes should not be considered as part of the Soviet zone of occupation in Germany.

Peace Treaties to be prepared

The conference agreed upon the following statement of common policy for establishing as soon as possible the conditions of lasting peace after victory in Europe:

The three Governments consider it desirable that the present anomalous position of Italy, Bulgaria, Finland, Hungary, and Romania should be terminated by the conclusion of peace treaties. They trust that the other interested allied Governments will share these views. For their part, the three Governments have included the preparation of a peace treaty for Italy as the first among the immediate important tasks to be undertaken by the new Council of Foreign Ministers. Italy was the first of the Axis Powers to break with Germany, to whose defeat she has made a material contribution, and has now joined with the allies in the struggle against Japan. Italy has freed herself from the Fascist regime and is making good progress towards the re-establishment of a democratic Government and institutions. The conclusion of such a peace treaty with a recognized and democratic Italian Government will make it possible for the three Governments to fulfil their desire to support an application from Italy for membership of the United Nations.

The three Governments have also charged the Council of Foreign Ministers with the task of preparing peace treaties for Bulgaria, Finland, Hungary, and Romania. The conclusion of peace treaties with recognized democratic Governments in these States will also enable the three Governments to support applications from them for membership of the United Nations. The three Governments agree to examine each separately in the near future, in the light of the conditions then prevailing, the establishment of diplomatic relations with Finland, Romania, Bulgaria and Hungary to the extent possible prior to the conclusion of peace treaties with those countries.

The three Governments have no doubt that in view of the changed conditions resulting from the termination of the war in Europe, representatives of the allied Press will enjoy full freedom to report to the world upon developments in Romania, Bulgaria, Hungary and Finland.

As regards the admission of other States into the United Nations Organization, Article 4 of the Charter of the United Nations declares that: '1. Membership in the United Nations is open to all other peace-loving States which accept the obligations contained in the present Charter and, in the judgment of the Organization, are able and willing to carry out these obligations. 2. The admission of any such State to membership in the United Nations will be effected by a decision of the General Assembly upon the recommendation of the Security Council.' The three Governments, so far as they are concerned, will support applications for membership from those States which have remained neutral during the war and which fulfil the qualifications set out above.

The three Governments feel bound, however, to make it clear that they for their part would not favour any application for membership put forward by the present Spanish Government, which, having been founded with the support of the Axis Powers, does not, in view of its origins, its nature, its record, and its close association with the aggressor States, possess the qualifications necessary to justify such membership.

Territorial Trusteeship
The conference examined a proposal by the Soviet Government concerning trusteeship territories as defined in the decision of the Crimea conference and in the Charter of the United Nations Organization. After an exchange of views on this question it was decided that the disposition of any former Italian territories was one to be decided in connexion with the preparation of a peace treaty with Italy, and that the question of Italian territory would be considered by the September Council of Ministers of Foreign Affairs.

Romania, Bulgaria and Hungary
The three Governments took note that the Soviet Representatives on the Allied Control Commissions in Romania, Bulgaria, and Hungary had communicated to their United Kingdom and United States colleagues proposals for improving the work of the Control Commissions, now that hostilities in Europe have ceased. The three Governments agreed that the revision of the procedures of the Allied Control Commissions in these countries should now be undertaken, taking into account the interests and responsibilities of the three Governments which together presented the terms of armistice to the respective countries, and accepting as a basis the agreed proposals.

Transfers of German populations

The conference reached the following agreement on the removal of Germans from Poland, Czechoslovakia and Hungary:
The three Governments, having considered the question in all its aspects, recognize that the transfer to Germany of German populations, or elements thereof, remaining in Poland, Czechoslovakia, and Hungary will have to be undertaken. They agree that any transfers that take place should be effected in an orderly and humane manner.
Since the influx of a large number of Germans into Germany would increase the burden already resting on the occupying authorities, they consider that the Allied Control Council in Germany should in the first instance examine the problem with special regard to the question of the equitable distribution of these Germans among the several zones of occupation. They are accordingly instructing their respective representatives on the Control Council to report to their Governments as soon as possible the extent to which such persons have already entered Germany from Poland, Czechoslovakia, and Hungary, and to submit an estimate of the time and rate at which further transfers could be carried out, having regard to the present situation in Germany.
The Czechoslovak Government, the Polish Provisional Government, and the Control Council in Hungary are at the same time being informed of the above, and are being requested meanwhile to suspend further expulsions pending the examination by the Governments concerned of the report from their representatives on the Control Council.
Military talks
During the conference there were meetings between the Chiefs of Staff of the three Governments on military matters of common interest."

The Communiqué on the Potsdam decisions ends with a word "approved by" and with the signatures of J.V. Stalin, Harry S. Truman, C.R. Attlee and bears the date: Berlin, August 2, 1945.
In connection with the 25th anniversary of the Potsdam Agreement the President of the USA, R. Nixon and the Prime Minister of the USSR, A.N. Kosygin exchanged letters.

Journal of the Control Council for Germany, Supplement No. 1, 1945; C.A. COLLIARD, *Droit international et histoire diplomatique*, Paris, 1950; *International Legislation*, Vol. IX, No. 657, 658, p. 580; A. KLAFKOWSKI, *The Potsdam Agreement*, Warsaw, 1963; J. KOKOT, *The Logic of Potsdam*, Warsaw, 1969.

POTSDAM CONFERENCE, 1945. The Conference on the establishment of peace in Europe and the world after World War II, also known as Berlin Conference, held at Potsdam near Berlin, in Cäcilienhof Palace, from July 17 to Aug. 2, 1945; attended by heads of governments of the three victorious powers: US President Harry S. Truman, Soviet Premier Generalissimo Joseph V. Stalin and British Prime Minister Winston L.S. Churchill until July 25 and his successor Clement R. Attlee from July 28. The Protocols of the sessions were published in Washington, DC, and Moscow in 1967 and 1968. Chief resolutions regarded Germany and the ▷ Yalta Declaration; the Allies undertook to bring before court ▷ war crimes and war criminals; a method for setting ▷ reparations was outlined; the Polish Interim Government of National Unity was recognized by all Allies, Polish borderline on the Oder and Neisse demarcated; Poland also obtained the Free City of Gdansk and the part of East Prussia which was not incorporated into the Soviet Union – all these territories excluded from the Soviet occupation zone. An agreement was reached on the displacement of German population from Poland, Czechoslovakia and Hungary to the occupied German territories, and the abolition of ▷ Prussia. In view of continuing war with Japan, the governments of China, Great Britain and the USA drew up an ultimatum, July 25, calling for Japan to unconditionally surrender and specifying main principles of its demilitarization and

democratization. The ultimatum was subscribed to by Soviet Union which declared war on Japan, Aug. 9. Also adopted at the Conference was an agreement regarding formation of the ▷ Council of Foreign Ministers of the Big Powers.
Foreign Relations of the USA Diplomatic Papers, Washington, DC, 1967; W.L. NEUMANN, *After Victory, Churchill, Roosevelt, Stalin and the Making of Peace*, New York, 1967.

POULTRY. Subject of international co-operation. Organizations reg. with the UIA:

Association of Poultry Processors and Poultry Import and Export Trade in the EEC Countries, f. 1966, Copenhagen.
Co-ordinating CMEA Centre for International Testing and Control Stations for Poultry, f. 1970, Prague.
European Unions of the Wholesale Trade in Eggs, Egg Products, Poultry and Game, f. 1959, Milan, Italy.
World Poultry Science Association, f. 1912, Celle, FRG, Publ: *The World Poultry Science Journal*.

Yearbook of International Organizations 1986/87.

POUND, CYPRUS. A monetary unit of Cyprus; one pound = 1000 mils; issued by the Central Bank of Cyprus.

POUND, EGYPTIAN. A monetary unit of Egypt; one pound = 100 piastres = 1000 millièmes; issued by the Central Bank of Egypt.

POUND, INTERNATIONAL (AVOIRDUPOIS). An international unit of weight defined by an agreement on Jan. 1, 1960, between Australia, Canada, New Zealand, South Africa, the UK and the USA: one pound = 453,59237 grammes.

J. PAXTON ed., *The Statesman's Yearbook, 1987–88*, London, 1987.

POUND, IRISH. A monetary unit of Ireland; one pound = 100 pence; issued by the Central Bank of Ireland – Banc Ceannais Na Eireann.

POUND, LEBANESE. A monetary unit of Lebanon; one pound = 100 piastres; issued by the Banque du Liban.

POUND STERLING. A monetary unit of UK; one pound sterling = 100 new pence; issued (replacing the subdivision into 20 shillings on Jan. 15, 1971) by the Bank of England.

POUND, SUDANESE. A monetary unit of Sudan; one pound = 100 piastres = 1000 millièmes; issued from Apr. 8, 1957 by the Bank of Sudan.

POUND, SYRIAN. A monetary unit of Syria; one pound = 100 piastres; issued by the Banque Centrale de Syrie.

POUR LE ROI DE PRUSSE. *French* = "for the King of Prussia"; a figure of speech meaning "for someone else's benefit." An international term which appeared in the 18th century after the Peace of Aix-la-Chapelle, 1748, in which France through her participation in the war of succession failed to receive any significant benefits, whereas Prussia annexed Silesia and the Duchy of Glatz.

POW. ▷ Prisoner of War.

POWER CMEA SYSTEM AGREEMENT, 1962, CDA. An agreement between Bulgaria, Czechoslovakia, GDR, Hungary, Poland, Romania and the Western Ukraine region of the USSR concerning the establishment in Prague of a Central Dispatch Administration, CDA, for Combined Power signed on July 25, 1962 in Moscow; co-ordinate the joint electric power systems of Bulgaria, Czechoslovakia, GDR, Hungary, Poland, Romania and the West Ukraine. The CDA Contracting Parties agree that the CDA will fulfill the following functions: to work out schemes and régimes for the co-ordinated operation of the combined power systems and measures to ensure the parallel work of those systems at normal frequency; to exercise operational supervision over their implementation and to organize mutual assistance among the combined power systems through the use of reserve and of temporary idle capacity, to carry out other functions arising out of the co-ordinated operation of the combined power system. (Art. III.)

UNTS, Vol. 506, pp. 186–188; W.E. BUTLER (ed.), *A Source Book on Socialist International Organizations*, Alphen, 1978, pp. 363–372.

PRAGUE. The capital of Czechoslovakia (pop.: 1985, census 1,141,828), since 1918 on both banks of the Vltava River. The seat of the UN Information Centre, Christian Peace Conference, Esperantist World Peace Movement, International Organization of Journalists, International Radio and TV Organization, International System of Scientific and Technical Information on Agriculture Forestry, International Union of Students, Trade Unions International of Transport Workers, Trade Union International of Workers of Metals Industry, Trade Union International of Workers of Commerce, World Federation of Trade Unions and World Federation of Teachers Unions.

Yearbook of International Organizations.

PRAGUE DECLARATION, 1972. Declaration on Peace, Security and Co-operation in Europe signed on Jan. 26, 1972 in Prague, adopted unanimously at a meeting of the Consultative Political Committee of the states parties to the Warsaw Pact by top level delegations of: Bulgaria, Czechoslovakia, the German Democratic Republic, Hungary, Poland, Romania and the USSR. The states represented at the meeting stated that the European conference should include all European states as well as the USA and Canada, and that the suggestion made by the government of Finland to hold multilateral consultations in Helsinki by the states concerned should be realized.

Recueil de Documents, Varsovie, 1972.

PRAGUE PEACE TREATY, 1635. A treaty concluded by Austria and Saxony, signed on Apr. 30, 1635 in Prague; it unified Saxony with Lusatia.

PRAGUE PEACE TREATY, 1866. A Treaty between Austria and Prussia, concluded on Aug. 23, 1866 in Prague, thus ending the Austrian–Prussian war, on the basis of peace preliminaries signed Jul. 26, 1866 in Nikolsburg, along with an armistice; gave Prussia a free hand in northern Germany, which soon enabled Otto von Bismarck to constitute a Prussian Reich without Austria. According to art. 5, Austria abdicated her rights to Schleswig, while under French pressure Prussia agreed to add a commitment to hold a plebiscite and turn Schleswig over to Denmark if the majority so voted. The German Reich annulled this commitment by an additional Treaty with Austria on Oct. 11, 1878, not enforced until the Treaty of Versailles 1919. Almost simultaneously, Italy also signed on Oct. 3, 1866 at Vienna a Peace Treaty with Austria.

Major Peace Treaties of Modern History, New York, 1967, Vol. I, pp. 629–633.

PRATTS DOCTRINE, 1972. General C. Pratts, commander of Chile's armed forces in 1972, decided in favor of participating in President S. Allende's government and, in order to secure the process of nationalization and reform-making stressed:

"the obligation resting upon the armed forces of the country to safeguard not only the State frontier, but also to protect the nation's natural resources, domestic order and spiritual values."

This extension of the functions discharged by the armed forces was called in Latin America the Pratts Doctrine.

Sintesis Informativo Ibero-americano, Madrid, 1972.

PREAH VIHEAR. A town at the Kampuchea–Thailand frontier in 1904 became a controversial issue, as the mixed French–Siamese delimitation commission granted Preah Vihear to Siam (now Thailand) and later in 1908 amended the decision to give the town to Cambodia (now Kampuchea), the ruins of the Preah Vihear temple being a holy place for Cambodian pilgrims. At the request of Cambodia on Sept. 6, 1959, the International Court of Justice, ICJ, studied the case and on June 15, 1962 decided that Preah Vihear was an integral part of Cambodia and that the Thai armed forces and police forces stationed in Preah Vihear since 1954 were to withdraw from the territory and return the sculptures, taken from the ruins of the Preah Vihear temple. The ICJ verdict, passed by the tribunal chaired by Judge B. Winiarski of Poland, prompted fanatics to kill the Head of the Polish trade mission in the capital of Thailand, Bangkok. The Preah Vihear temple was devastated during the civil war 1976–79. In 1981 UNESCO sponsored an international campaign to save the temple.

International Court of Justice. Documents, The Hague, 1962.

PREAMBLE. The introduction to legal acts (e.g. to a constitution, or a treaty) explaining the reasons and conditions of preparing the act or of concluding the treaty. The importance of a preamble depends on its precision in formulating the principles of the treaty. Under the influence of an extremely well-balanced preamble to the Charter of the United Nations and similar preambles to various other conventions elaborated by the Committee on International Law of the United Nations, the importance of preambles for the interpretation of the agreement's text has significantly increased in the second half of the 20th century.

P. YON, *Le Préambule des traités internationales*, Geneva, 1941.

PREBISH FOUNDATION. Est. 1987 in Argentina, warmly welcomed by the General Assembly. The Foundation will promote the study of development issues. It was set up in honour of the late international economist, who headed ECLAC in its early days and was the first Secretary-General of the United Nations Conference on Trade and Development (UNCTAD).

UN Chronicle, Mar. 1988, p. 90.

PRECEDENCE. The question of seniority in the hierarchy of the diplomatic corps, the source of numerous disputes until the Vienna Congress of 1815, which outlined the hierarchy of diplomatic representations and extraordinary missions, as well as their order depending on the number of years of accreditation, recommending, at the same time, that the order of signing multilateral treaties should be decided by lots, the custom being changed to alphabetical order by the League of Nations.

PREFECT. An international term for two functions: in government administration an official or the chief of police; and in the Roman Catholic Church a catechist; also a cardinal acting as the Head of the Roman Curia.

PREFERENCES. An international term for trade or tariff reductions granted mutually or unilaterally by states, but not extended to third states even in the case where the sides are bound by the ▷ most favoured nation, IMF clause.

The international term "Generalized System of Preference, GSP" is used in the UN for a system under which the exports of developing countries are admitted to the industrialized countries duty-free up to a certain level, or at reduced rates, on a non-reciprocal basis. Preferences are usually granted by the powers to their ex-colonies or dependent territories, but also in other cases. So-called "general" preference, as a departure from the most-favoured-nation clause, is most often applied in the form of unilateral special privileges granted by the rich industrialized countries to the industrial products exported by the developing countries. However, so-called "reversed" preference is usually a neo-colonial granting of privileges in the form of bilateral treaties by the developing countries to the highly developed countries, often the former colonial powers. In Oct., 1970 the EEC states introduced the General Preference System, partially modelled on the System of Generalized and Non-reciprocal and Non-discriminatory Preferences recommended in 1969 by the UN General Assembly Res. 2503/XXIV. The system introduced by the EEC turned out to be unsuccessful, i.a. due to the setting for each country of a rather low upper limit of export free tariffs, which in practice meant that 60% of the goods imported by the EEC states from countries of the Third World did not benefit from preferences. In June, 1972 the Ministerial Council of the EEC states at its session in Luxembourg established the principles for tariff preferences for the UNCTAD member states. In May, 1973 the UNCTAD Committee on Preferences criticized the preferences system in the EEC. On Jan. 1, 1977 a system for tariff preferences in EEC trade with the Third World came into force in compliance with the recommendations of UNCTAD.

The EEC preferences system includes for developing countries: duty-free access for more than 20% of all agricultural products, exports and annually fixed quotas, for industrial products, if no quota applies duty-free entry; and for least developed countries duty-free entry for all agricultural products covered by GSP; exception from quota of cocoa butter, instant coffee and canned pineapple for industrial products; duty-free entry for textile products although the ▷ Multi-Fibre Agreement may apply.

UN Chronicle, October, 1982, p. 47.

PREFERENTIAL TRADE AREA FOR EAST AND SOUTHERN AFRICA, PTA. Est. 1982 by 15 African countries with an action program for the reduction and standardization of tariffs and customs duties, promotion of bilateral trade with clearing house facilities at the Reserve Bank in Zimbabwe.

PRE-INVERSION FUND FOR LATIN AMERICA. The Fund was est. in 1966 by the OAS with the task of financing studies on integration and formulating integrative schemes for the Latin American states.

PRELACY NULLIUS. In the Roman Catholic Church a territory detached from the jurisdiction of a bishop and subject to a Prelate Nullius, performing the duties of an ordinary.

P

PRELATE. In the Roman Catholic Church the name for all higher clerics (bishop, superior of an order, vicar general).

PRELIMINATIONS. An international term for provisional arrangements, preparing the principles of the elaborated treaty.

PRESBYTERIAN ORDER. The Protestants who in Great Britain did not recognize the state ▷ Church of England and, in escaping from persecution, established many religious communities in different countries; not until the 19th century did they begin to create international communities, formally brought into existence on July 21, 1875 in London under the name, Alliance of the Reformed Churches Throughout the World Holding the Presbyterian Order, with headquarters in Geneva; unites 91 national churches in 61 countries of Africa, America, Asia, Australia and Europe. Publ.: *The Reformed and Presbyterian World*. Takes an active part in the ecumenical movement.

Yearbook of International Organizations.

PRESCRIPTION. Subject to varying verdicts by international courts both with respect to prescription of the rights to a territory (▷ *Uti Possidentis*) and cases of prescription of international obligations.

P.A. VERYKIOS, *La prescription en droit internationale*, Paris, 1934; R. PINTO, "La prescription en droit internationale", in: *Recueil des Cours de l'Académie de Droit International*, No. 87, 1955; WHO, *International Health Regulations*, Rioneva, 1971; E. ROELSGARRE, "Health Regulations and International Travel", in: *WHO Chronicle*, June, 1974.

PRESIDENT. An international term for the head of state in a republican political system; in many states the mayor of a city.

PRESIDENTIAL DIRECTIVE 59, 1980. The name of a US nuclear war doctrine, formulated by Harold Brown and Zbigniew Brzezinski, giving priority to strikes at military and political targets in the Soviet Union; suspending the ▷ Schlesinger Nuclear War Doctrine 1975. President Jimmy Carter approved the Directive 59 on July 31, 1980.

R. BUST, "Brown–Brzezinski Tandem Pushed New US Strategy", in: *New York Times*, August, 14, 1980.

PRESIDENT PRO-TEMPORE. The name of the chairman of the US Senate elected in case the Vice President assumes the office of the presidency for the time of the remainder of the Vice President's term.

PRESS. Subject of international co-operation. Organizations reg. with the UIA:

Associations for the Promotion of the International Circulation of the Press, f. 1955, Zürich, Switzerland. Publ.: Distripress.
European Alliance of Press Agencies, f. 1957, Rome, Italy.
Inter American Press Association, f. 1942, Miami, Flo., USA.
International Catholic Union of the Press, 1927, Geneva, Switzerland.
International Federation of the Periodical Press, f. 1925, London, UK.
International Federation of the Socialist and Democratic Press, f. 1953, Milan, Italy.
International Press Institute, f. 1951, London, UK.
Latin American Catholic Press Union, f. 1959, Petropolis, Brazil.
Organization of Asia-Pacific News, Agencies, f. 1961, New Delhi, India.
Press Foundation of Asia, f. 1967, Manila, Philippines.

Union of African News Agencies, f. 1963, Algiers, Algeria.

G.T. KURIAN ed., *World Press Encyclopedia*, 2 vls., New York, 1982; *Yearbook of International Organizations, 1986/87;* ULRICH's *International Periodicals Directory 1987/88*, 2 vls., New York, 1987; *The Europa Yearbook 1988. A World Survey*, Vol. 1, London, 1988.

PRESS AGENCIES. The information agencies defined by the Convention on the International Right of Correction, 1953. Organization reg. with the UIA:

European Alliance of Press Agencies, f. 1957, Brussels. Consultative status with ECOSOC and UNESCO. Members: Press agencies of 23 European countries.

International Periodical Directory, New York, 1980; *Les Agences Mondiales d'Information*, Paris, 1980.

PRESS AND THE UN. At UN headquarters in New York there are premises for news agencies and press, radio and TV correspondents, accredited to cover the activities of the UN for a limited or unlimited period of time. In 1946, the UN General Assembly declared that freedom of information was a "fundamental human right" and "the touchstone of all freedoms to which the UN is consecrated." A draft Convention on ▷ Freedom of Information was originally prepared in 1948 by a UN Conference on the subject and revised in 1951 by an *ad hoc* Committee; meanwhile, the UN General Assembly in 1968 decided to give priority to the consideration and adoption of the draft Declaration on Freedom of Information approved by ECOSOC in 1960 and dealing with the right to seek, receive and impart information, the responsibility of governments to ensure the free flow of information, obligations of the information media, etc. The General Assembly have since deferred further consideration of the question.

J. SZAPIRO, *The Newspaper United Nations. A Guide for Journalists about UN and Special Agencies*, Paris, 1961.

PRESSBURG PEACE TREATY, 1805. A Treaty between Austria and France, signed on Dec. 26, 1805 in Pressburg (now Bratislava).

Major Peace Treaties of Modern History 1648–1967, New York, 1967, Vol. I, pp. 457–468.

PRESS CUTTING AGENCIES. A subject of international co-operation. Organization reg. with the UIA:

International Federation of Press Cutting Agencies, f. 1953, Paris. Publ.: *FIBEP World Newsletter* and *FIBEP Handbook*.

Yearbook of International Organizations.

PRESSURE GROUPS OR LOBBIES. The openly or secretly organized groups whose task is to exert pressure on political authorities, i.a. through the mobilization of public opinion, influencing parliament so that the internal or foreign policies of the government would serve the interests of a certain group in the field with which it is concerned. In the Anglo-Saxon countries a special form of pressure group has developed, called Lobbying; in the USA carried on within the rules defined in the Lobbying Act, 1946. A colloquy entitled 'Interest Groups, a Help or a Hindrance to Parliamentary Democracy' was held at the Council of Europe on Nov. 18–19, 1986 in Strasbourg.

V. LANGBEIN, *Die rechtliche Regelung das Lobbyismus in den Vereinigten Staaten*, Kiel, 1967; G. WOOTTON, *Pressure Groups in Britain 1729–1970*, London, 1975; G. WOOTTON, *Pressure Politics in Contemporary Britain*, Toronto, 1979.

PRETORIA. The administrative capital of South Africa, population, 1985 census: 776,617 city. (The legislative capital since 1910 is ▷ Capetown, and the judicial capital ▷ Bloemfontein). Seat of the African Postal Telecommunication Union and of the South African Regional Commission for Conservation and Utilization of Soil.

Yearbook of International Organizations.

PRETORIA PEACE TREATY, 1902. The Treaty between the Orange Free State and the South Africa Republic with Great Britain, signed on May 31, 1902 in Pretoria. Both states recognized the King of Great Britain "as their lawful Sovereign."

Major Peace Treaties of Modern History, New York, 1967, pp. 1145–47.

PREVENTATIVE OR ENFORCEMENT ACTION. The actions provided for in the Charter of the United Nations in art. 2, par. 5, to be applied within the framework of collective measures undertaken by the United Nations against any state whatsoever. ▷ Sanctions.

PREVENTATIVE WAR. The armed aggression justified by the necessity of anticipating a supposed attack prepared by the opponent.

PREVENTION OF DISPUTES AND SITUATIONS DANGEROUS TO INTERNATIONAL PEACE UN DECLARATION 1988. A Declaration adopted on Dec. 5, 1988 by the GA Res. 43/51. The text is as follows:

Declaration on the Prevention and Removal of Disputes and Situations Which May Threaten International Peace and Security and on the Role of the United Nations in this Field
The General Assembly,
Recognizing the important role that the United Nations and its organs can play in the prevention and removal of international disputes and situations which may lead to international friction or give rise to an international dispute, the continuance of which may threaten the maintenance of international peace and security (hereafter: "disputes" or "situations"), within their respective functions and powers under the Charter of the United Nations,
Convinced that the strengthening of such a role of the United Nations will enhance its effectiveness in dealing with the questions of the maintenance of international peace and security and in promoting the peaceful settlement of international disputes,
Recognizing the fundamental responsibility of States for the prevention and removal of disputes and situations,
Recalling that the peoples of the United Nations are determined to practise tolerance and live together in peace with one another as good neighbours,
Bearing in mind the right of all States to resort to peaceful means of their own choice for the prevention and removal of disputes or situations,
Reaffirming the Declaration on Principles of International Law concerning Friendly Relations and Co-operation among States in accordance with the Charter of the United Nations, the Manila Declaration on the Peaceful Settlement of International Disputes and the Declaration on the Enhancement of the Effectiveness of the Principle of Refraining from the Threat or Use of Force in International Relations, 1987,
Recalling the duty of States to refrain in their international relations from military, political, economic or any other form of coercion aimed at the political independence or territorial integrity of any State,
Calling upon States to co-operate fully with the relevant organs of the United Nations and to support actions taken by them in accordance with the Charter, relating to the prevention or removal of disputes and situations,
Bearing in mind the obligation of States to conduct their relations with other States in accordance with international law, including the principles of the United Nations,
Reaffirming the principle of equal rights and self-determination of peoples.

Recalling that the Charter confers on the Security Council the primary responsibility for the maintenance of international peace and security, and that the Member States have agreed to accept and carry out its decisions in accordance with the Charter.

Recalling also the important role conferred by the Charter on the General Assembly and the Secretary-General in the maintenance of international peace and security.

Solemnly declares that:

(1) States should act so as to prevent in their international relations the emergence or aggravation of disputes or situations, in particular by fulfilling in good faith their obligations under international law.

(2) In order to prevent disputes or situations. States should develop their relations on the basis of sovereign equality of States and in such a manner as to enhance the effectiveness of the collective security system through the effective implementation of the provisions of the Charter of the United Nations.

(3) States should consider the use of bilateral or multilateral consultations in order better to understand each other's views, positions and interests.

(4) States members of regional arrangements or agencies referred to in Art. 52 of the Charter should make every effort to prevent or remove local disputes or situations through such arrangements and agencies.

(5) States concerned should consider approaching the relevant organs of the United Nations in order to obtain advice or recommendations on preventive means for dealing with a dispute or situation.

(6) Any State party to a dispute or directly concerned with a situation, particularly if it intends to request a meeting of the Security Council, should approach directly or indirectly the Council at an early stage, and, if appropriate, on a confidential basis.

(7) The Security Council should consider holding from time to time meetings, including at a high level with the participation, in particular, of Ministers for Foreign Affairs, or consultations to review the international situation and search for effective ways of improving it.

(8) In the course of the preparation for the prevention or removal of particular disputes or situations, the Security Council should consider making use of the various means at its disposal, including the appointment of the Secretary-General as rapporteur for a specified question.

(9) When a particular dispute or situation is brought to the attention of the Security Council without a meeting being requested, the Council should consider holding consultations with a view to examining the facts of the dispute or situation and keeping it under review, when needed with the assistance of the Secretary-General; the States concerned should have the opportunity of making their views known.

(10) In such consultations, consideration should be given to employing such informal methods as the Security Council deems appropriate, including confidential contacts by its President.

(11) The Security Council should consider in such consultations, *inter alia*:

(*a*) Reminding the States concerned to respect their obligations under the Charter.

(*b*) Making an appeal to the States concerned to refrain from any action which might give rise to a dispute or lead to the deterioration of the dispute or situation.

(*c*) Making an appeal to the States concerned to take action which might help to remove or to prevent the continuation or deterioration of, the dispute or situation.

(12) The Security Council should consider sending, at an early stage, fact-finding or good offices missions or establishing appropriate forms of United Nations presence, including observers and peace-keeping operations, as a means of preventing the further deterioration of the dispute or situation in the areas concerned.

(13) The Security Council should consider encouraging and, where appropriate, endorsing efforts at the regional level by the States concerned or by regional arrangements or agencies to prevent or remove a dispute or situation in the region concerned.

(14) Taking into consideration any procedures that have already been adopted by the States directly concerned, the Security Council should consider recommending to them appropriate procedures or methods of settlement of disputes or adjustment of situations, and such terms of settlement as it deems appropriate.

(15) The Security Council, if it is appropriate for promoting the prevention and removal of disputes or situations, should, at an early stage, consider making use of the provisions of the Charter concerning the possibility of requesting the International Court of Justice to give an advisory opinion of any legal question.

(16) The General Assembly should consider making use of the provisions of the Charter in order to discuss disputes or situations, when appropriate, and, in accordance with Art. 11 and subject to Art. 12 of the Charter, making recommendations.

(17) The General Assembly should consider, where appropriate, supporting efforts undertaken at the regional level by the States concerned or by regional arrangements or agencies, to prevent or remove a dispute or situation in the region concerned.

(18) If a dispute or situation has been brought before it, the General Assembly should consider, in accordance with Art. 11 and subject to Art. 12 of the Charter, including in its recommendations the making more use of fact-finding capabilities.

(19) The General Assembly, if it is appropriate for promoting the prevention and removal of disputes or situations, should consider making use of the provisions of the Charter concerning the possiblity of requesting the International Court of Justice to give an advisory opinion on any legal question.

(20) The Secretary-General, if approached by a State or States directly concerned with a dispute or situation, should respond swiftly by urging the States to seek a solution or adjustment by peaceful means of their own choice under the Charter and by offering his good offices or other means at his disposal, as he deems appropriate.

(21) The Secretary-General should consider approaching the States directly concerned with a dispute or situation in an effort to prevent it from becoming a threat to the maintenance of international peace and security;

(22) The Secretary-General should, where appropriate, consider making full use of fact-finding capabilities, including, with the consent of the host State, the sending of a representative or fact-finding missions to areas where a dispute or a situation exists; where necessary, the Secretary-General should also consider making the appropriate arrangements.

(23) The Secretary-General should be encouraged to consider using, at as early a stage as he deems appropriate, the right that is accorded to him under Art. 99 of the Charter.

(24) The Secretary-General should, where appropriate, encourage efforts undertaken at the regional level to prevent or remove a dispute or situation in the region concerned.

(25) Should States fail to prevent the emergence or aggravation of a dispute or situation, they shall continue to seek a settlement by peaceful means in accordance with the Charter.

Declares that nothing in the present Declaration shall be construed as prejudicing in any manner the provisions of the Charter, including those contained in Art. 2, para. 7, thereof, or the rights and duties of States, or the scope of the functions and the powers of the United Nations organs under the Charter, in particular those relating to the maintenance of international peace and security.

Also declares that nothing in the present Declaration could in any way prejudice the right to self-determination, freedom and independence of peoples forcibly deprived of that right and referred to in the Declaration on Principles of International Law concerning Friendly Relations and Co-operation among States in accordance with the Charter of the United Nations, 1970, particularly peoples under colonial or racist régimes or other forms of alien domination.

See also ▷ International Law Principles, UN Declaration, 1970.

UN Resolutions and Decisions adopted by the General Assembly during the First Part of its Forty-Third Session from 20 September to 22 December 1988, New York, 1989, pp. 533–535.

PREVENTION OF FALSE INDICATIONS OF ORIGIN ON GOODS. A subject of international co-operation and international agreements. The first agreement, called the Madrid agreement, was signed on Apr. 14, 1891 in Madrid; revised on June2, 1911 in Washington; on Nov. 6, 1925 in The Hague and on June 2, 1934 in London.

British and Foreign State Papers, Vol. 96, p. 837, and Vol. 104, p. 137; *LNTS*, Vol. 84, p. 319 and Vol. 192, p. 9.

PRICE INDEXES. A subject of national statistics since the end of 19th century, of international statistics after World War I.

F.C. MILLS, *The Behaviour of Prices*, London, 1927; A.H. COLE, *Measures of Business Change*, London, 1957.

PRICES. A subject of international conventions, primarily with respect to prices for basic raw materials; in international terminology the following are distinguished: the CIF price, the FOB price, the monopolistic price, and the world price. In international trade there are in use also the following prices:

the basic price (prix de base);
the guide price or recommended price (prix d'orientation);
the intervention price (prix d'intervention);
the reference price (prix de reference);
the sluicegate price (prix d'exclus);
the target price (prix indicatif) and
the threshold price (prix de seuil).

Price quotations are conducted on an international scale since ILO was called into being in 1919.

I.P. KRAVIS, R.E. LIPSKI, *Price Competitiveness in World Trade*, New York, 1972; "América Latina. Precios de los principales productos de exportación," in: *Notas de la CEPAL sobre la economía y el desarrollo de América Latina*, Jan. 1, 1975; M. ABDEL-FADIL, *La planification des prix en économie socialiste*, Paris, 1975; J. PAXTON, *A Dictionary of the EEC*, London, 1978; R. HOCH, *Consumption and Price*, Budapest, 1979.

PRICES IN THE CMEA SYSTEM. A subject of international adjustments of the CMEA states, one of the most difficult and most essential monetary-financial problems of CMEA for two reasons: the necessity for improving the price system in mutual trade of the CMEA states and simultaneously the necessity of adapting the price system of CMEA states in foreign trade to world prices determined mainly by capitalist states. The accepted model ▷ "stop prices" did not prevent the incursion of fluctuations of world prices on the socialist market.

PRIMATE. the Head archbishop of the Catholic Church in a given country.

PRIMA FACIE. *Latin* = "at first glance." An international term for immediate statement of a definite fact; used in art. 2 of the definition of aggression formulated by the UN (▷ Aggression, UN Definition 1974).

PRIMOGENITURE. *Latin* = "right of the first-born." An international term for the order of inheritance in hereditary monarchies.

PRINTED IN. The formula placed on most publications, indicating the country in which they were printed. In cases of publications protected by ▷ copyright it indicates the country disposing of the Copyright.

PRINTING. A subject of international co-operation. Organizations reg. with the UIA:

Asia-Pacific Printers Federation, f. 1968, Tokyo.
Federation of European Screen-Printers Association, f. 1962, Amsterdam.

P

Gutenberg International Association for Past and Present History of the Art of Printing, f. 1901, Mainz. International Confederation for Printing, f. 1930, Brussels. Publ.: *IMPA Newsletter*.

International Master Printers Association, f. 1923, London.

Screen Printing Association International, f. 1948, Vienna, USA.

F.J.M. WIJNEKUS, *Elsevier's Dictionary of the Printing and Allied Industries*. In English (with definitions), French, Dutch and German, Amsterdam, 1969; *Yearbook of International Organizations, 1986/87*; *The Europa Yearbook 1988. A World Survey*, Vol. I, London, 1988.

PRINTING MEASURES. The subject of the first international unification of measures established in 1889 at the Printers' Congress in Paris, when in Europe the "Parisian height" of 23.56 millimeters was accepted for letters; also approved was the typographical system of measures worked out in 1737 by P.S. Fournier, improved in 1775 by A. Didot and calculated in millimeters by H. Berthold. In the USA, as well as in Great Britain and in the regions under the influence of these two powers, the height of letters of 0.918 inch is in effect. From the mid-19th century in the entire world the ranks of letters (type size) are calculated in points and termed by the number of points, though in some European countries the historical names of certain sizes have been retained. In USA and England the value of points is calculated in inches (one point = 0.01387 inches).

PRISONERS. The subject of international convention elaborated under the authority of the United Nations: Standard Minimum Rules for the Treatment of Prisoners. ECOSOC published studies on the law prohibiting unwarranted arrests and on the right of arrested persons to communicate and the right of condemned persons in foreign countries to decide to stay in the foreign prison or be extradited to their home country. The EEC member states and USA and Canada signed on Mar. 21, 1983, at Strasbourg a Convention on Repatriation Right of the Prisoners. Since July 1, 1985 the European Convention on the Transfer of Sentenced Persons, signed by Belgium, FRG, Greece, Ireland, Italy, Liechtenstein, Norway, Portugal, Switzerland is in force. Contracting States: Austria, Canada, Cyprus, Denmark, Finland, France, Luxembourg, the Netherlands, Spain, Sweden, Turkey, UK, USA. The Annual Report for 1988 of ▷ Amnesty International, surveying 135 countries claimed that during 1987 prisoners of conscience were held in at least 80 countries.

Organization reg. with the UIA:

International Prisoners Aid Association, f. 1950, Louisville, Ky, USA. Publ.: *Newsletter*.

KEESING's *Contemporary Archive*, 1983; N.S. RODLEY, *UN Chronicle*, January 1984, p.69; *Yearbook of International Organizations, 1986/87*; *The Treatment of Prisoners Under International Law*, Oxford 1987; *Council of Europe*, Information Sheet No. 21, Strasbourg, 1988; *The Europa Yearbook 1988. A World Survey*, Vol. I, London, 1988.

PRISONERS OF WAR AND WOUNDED. Since 1864, the date of the establishment of the Red Cross, humanitarian rules for treating prisoners of war and wounded are a subject of international conventions. The first principles were formulated 1874 by the Brussels Conference, and then were expressed in the so-called Hague Conventions 1899 and 1907. After World War I a Conference of 47 states called by the LN drafted the so-called Geneva Convention, relative to the Treatment of Prisoners of War, with Annex signed on July 27, 1929 at Geneva, by Austria, Belgium, Bolivia, Brazil, Bul-

garia, Chile, China, Colombia, Cuba, Czechoslovakia, Denmark, the Dominican Republic, Egypt, Estonia, Finland, France, Germany, Great Britain, Greece, Hungary, Italy, Japan, Latvia, Luxembourg, Mexico, the Netherlands, Nicaragua, Norway, Persia, Poland, Portugal, Romania, Serbo-Croat-Slovene State, Siam, Sweden, Switzerland, Uruguay, USA and Venezuela.

This Convention was criticized on the basis of the racist art. 9 of part III, advising the combatant sides "to avoid placing in the same camp prisoners of different race or nationality." This article enabled the German Third Reich to justify before the International Red Cross the introduction of racial segregation of soldiers of the same country in German prisoner-of-war camps. During World War II Germany and Japan committed crimes of mass extermination of prisoners of war and wounded (more than 3 millions). In 1946 ECOSOC convened a Special Commission on War Prisoners with two tasks: the ongoing study of problems of prisoners of war and wounded and submitting annual reports as well as drafting new conventions on the basis of the previous regulations of 1907, 1909 and 1929 and the experiences of World War II which task was completed in Aug., 1949. These Geneva Conventions on Improving the Conditions of Wounded and Sick in Land Forces, a separate one for Naval Personnel, third on the Treatment of War prisoners, and a fourth one on the Protection of Civilians During War introduced a new principle, namely, that immediately upon conclusion of the war the prisoners should be released; furthermore, all the conventions concern not only interstate conflicts, but also those of a different character, e.g. uprising, and cover not only the regular members of the armed forces, but also insurgents, members of an opposition movement, authorities of a government not recognized by the other side, and noncombatants, such as war correspondents, chaplains, crews of merchant vessels, etc. Prisoners may be punished only for charges proven during a court trial, such as war crimes. Since not all states signed the Convention of 1949, for them the resolutions of the Convention of 1929 remain in force.

Moreover, arts. 4–20 The Hague Regulations, 1907, remain in effect.

Organizations reg. with the UIA, besides the ▷ Red Cross

Consultative Committee for Reading Facilities for Prisoners of War and Internees, Comité consultatif pour la lecture des prisoniers et internés de guerre, f. 1940, Geneva.

International Confederation of Former Prisoners of War, f. 1949, Brussels.

International Prisoners Aid Association, f. 1950, Milwaukee, Wisc., USA. Consultative status with ECOSOC.

LNTS, Vol. 118, pp. 344–411; F. SCHEIDL, *Die Kriegsgefangenschaft von den ältesten Zeiten bis zur Gegenwart. Eine völkerrechtliche Monographie*, Berlin, 1943; J. STONE, *Legal Controls of International Conflicts*, London, 1954; M. GREENSPAN, 'International Law and Its Protection for Participants in Unconventional Warfare," in: *Annals of the American Academy of Political and Social Science*, 1962; "The Geneva Convention of 1949: Application in the Vietnamese Conflict," in: *Virginia Journal of International Law*, 1965; A. KRAMER, *Nazi Prisoners of War in America*, New York, 1980; R.L. BLEDSOE, B.A. BOCZEK, *The International Law Dictionary*, Oxford, 1987.

PRIVATE FOREIGN INVESTMENTS. A subject of legal international disputes in the 19th and 20th centuries, when the colonial powers used diplomatic and even military pressure to ensure privileges for the private investments of their citizens. The states of Latin America drafted the so-called Mexican Convention, 1902, on the Rights of Foreigners

against these privileges; convention not recognized by the USA. In 1966 on the initiative of the USA the World Bank drafted the Washington Convention on the Settlement of Disputes Concerning Private Investments, 1970, guaranteeing privileges to foreign investors. ▷ Aliens' rights.

PRIVATE LAW, INTERNATIONAL. After international public law the second branch of international law, covering civil cases which are not restricted to the boundaries of one state; subject of international civil law proceedings, where provisions are established by agreement or custom. Organizations reg. with the UIA:

The Hague Conference on Private International Law, f. 1893, The Hague, with the task of codifying private international law. Members: governments of 27 states. Publ.: *Actes et Documents. International Institute for the Unification of Private Law*;

UNIDROIT, f. 1926, Rome. An intergovernmental organization of 48 states. Publ.: *Uniform Law Review*.

A.F. SCHNITZER, *Handbuch des Internationalen Privatsrechts*, 2 Vols., Basel, 1957; A.N. MAKAROV, "Internationales Privatrecht und Völkerrecht", in: STRUPP-SCHLOCHAUER *Wörterbuch des Völkerrechts*, Berlin, 1960, Vol. 2, pp. 129–132; J. SZASZY, *Private International Law in the European People's Democracy*, Budapest, 1964; K. ZWEIGERT, J. KROPHOLLER (eds.), *Sources of International Uniform Law*, Leiden, 1971; OEA, *Acta final de la Secunda Conferencia Especializada Interamericana sobre Derecho Internacional Privado, Montevideo, 23 de abril a 8 de mayo de 1979*, Washington, DC.

PRIVATE LIFE. The right to privacy. According to art. 12 of the Universal Declaration of Human Rights:

"No one shall be subjected to arbitrary interference with his privacy, family, home or correspondence, nor to attacks upon his honour and reputation. Everyone has the right to the protection of the law against such interference or attacks."

The UN Human Rights Committee in Geneva in Apr., 1973 started to elaborate similar international provisions on legal protection with respect to the technological development reached in the areas of remote-controlled eavesdropping and photography. According to the report of the technical committee's experts, the technology of eavesdropping and monitoring has become so sophisticated that there exist possibilities to perform "photographic surveillance from a distance of 1500 meters." In many countries the technological means in that area are available not only to state-controlled institutions, but also to pressure groups and criminals, professional blackmailers, etc. In the case of people known to the world public, the materials collected in such a way cannot be sold in the country of the surveillance victim, but are published in "yellow press" in another country. Thus the UN Human Rights Committee suggested that such interference in private life be treated as acts of piracy *sui generis* of international nature, calling for international co-operation in the following fields:

1. Regulating international penal or civil problems arising from publication in one country of information or photographs received as result of using prohibited espionage means in other countries;
2. Regulating international amenability to punishment of and sale of prohibited surveillance means;
3. Establishing international procedures enabling the adoption in another country of appropriate legislation banning publications interfering with other people's privacy;
4. Exchange of technological and judicial experiences related to effective safeguarding of telecommunication secrets. In Italy art. 615 of the penal code forbids "use of telephoto lenses to secretly photograph people on private property."

A US Privacy Act of 1974, protects an individual's constitutional right to private life. Since Oct. 1, 1985 the European Convention for the Protection of Individuals with regard to Automatic Processing of Personal Data, signed by Austria, Belgium, Cyprus, Denmark, Greece, Iceland, Ireland, Italy, Luxembourg, Portugal, Turkey, is in force. Contracting States: France, FRG, Norway, Spain, Sweden, UK.

A.C. BRECKENRIDGE, *The Right to Privacy*, University of Nebraska Press, 1970; *Privacy and Human Rights. Reports and Communications Presented at the Third International Colloquy about the European Convention on Human Rights September 30–October 3, 1970,* Manchester, 1973; P. VEYNE ed., *A History of Private Life*, 5 Vols., Harvard 1987–1992. *Council of Europe*, Information Sheet No. 21, Strasbourg, 1988.

PRIVATE LIFE. USE OF PERSONAL DATA IN THE POLICE SECTOR. The first limitation regulation of the use of personal data by police and security forces was recommended by the Council of Europe to all Member States as Recommendation No R(87) 15 on Sept. 17, 1987. The text is as follows:

The Committee of Ministers, under the terms of Art. 15(b) of the Statute of the Council of Europe.
Considering that the aim of the Council of Europe is to achieve a greater unity between its members.
Aware of the increasing use of automatically processing personal data in the police sector and of the possible benefits obtained through the use of computers and other technical means in this field.
Taking account also of concern about the possible threat to the privacy of the individual arising through the misuse of automated processing methods.
Recognizing the need to balance the interests of society in the prevention and suppression of criminal offences and the maintenance of public order on the one hand and the interests of the individual and his right to privacy on the other.
Bearing in mind the provisions of the Convention for the Protection of Individuals with regard to Automatic Processing of Personal Data of Jan. 28, 1981 and in particular the derogations permitted under Art. 9.
Aware also of the provisions of Art. 8 of the Convention for the Protection of Human Rights and Fundamental Freedoms, recommends the governments of member states to:
– be guided in their domestic law and practice by the principles appended to this recommendation, and
– ensure publicity for the provisions appended to this recommendation and in particular for the rights which its application confers on individuals.

Appendix to Recommendation No. R(87) 15

Scope and definitions

The principles contained in this recommendation apply to the collection, storage, use and communication of personal data for police purposes which are the subject of automatic processing. For the purposes of this recommendation, the expression "personal data" covers any information relating to an identified or identifiable individual. An individual shall not be regarded as "identifiable" if identification requires an unreasonable amount of time, cost and manpower.
The expression "for police purposes" covers all the tasks which the police authorities must perform for the prevention and suppression of criminal offences and the maintenance of public order.
The expression "responsible body" (controller of the file) denotes the authority, service or any other public body which is competent according to national law to decide on the purpose of an automated file, the categories of personal data which must be stored and the operations which are to be applied to them.
A member state may extend the principles contained in this commendation to personal data not undergoing automatic processing.
Manual processing of data should not take place if the aim is to avoid the provisions of this recommendation.
A member state may extend the principles contained in this recommendation to data relating to groups of persons, associations, foundations, companies, corporations or any other body consisting directly or indirectly of individuals, whether or not such bodies possess legal personality.
The provisions of this recommendation should not be interpreted as limiting or otherwise affecting the possiblity for a member state to extend, where appropriate, certain of these principles to the collection, storage and use of personal data for purposes of state security.

Basic Principles

Principle 1 – Control and Notification

1.1 Each member state should have an independent supervisory authority outside the police sector which should be responsible for ensuring respect for the principles contained in this recommendation.
1.2 New technical means for data processing may only be introduced if all reasonable measures have been taken to ensure that their use complies with the spirit of existing data protection legislation.
1.3 The responsible body should consult the supervisory authority in advance in any case where the introducion of automatic processing methods raises questions about the application of this recommendation.
1.4 Permanent automated files should be notified to the supervisory authority. The notification should specify the nature of each file declared, the body responsible for its processing, its purposes, the type of data contained in the file and the persons to whom the data are communicated.
Ad hoc files which have been set up at the time of particular inquiries should also be notified to the supervisory authority either in accordance with the conditions settled with the latter taking account of the specific nature of these files, or in accordance with national legislation.

Principle 2 – Collection of Data

2.1 The collection of personal data for police purposes should be limited to such as is necessary for the prevention of a real danger or the suppression of a specific criminal offence. Any exception to this provision should be the subject of specific national legislation.
2.2 Where data concerning an individual have been collected and stored without his knowledge, and unless the data are deleted, he should be informed, where practicable, the information is held about him as soon as the object of the police activities is no longer likely to be prejudiced.
2.3 The collection of data by technical surveillance or other automated means should be provided for in specific provisions.
2.4 The collection of data on individuals solely on the basis that they have a particular racial origin, particular religious convictions, sexual behaviour or political opinions or belong to particular movements or organizations which are not proscribed by law should be prohibited. The collection of data concerning these factors may only be carried out if absolutely necessary for the purposes of a particular inquiry.

Principle 3 – Storage of Data

3.1 As far as possible, the storage of personal data for police purposes should be limited to accurate data and to such data as are necessary to allow police bodies to perform their lawful tasks within the framework of national law and their obligations arising from international law.
3.2 As far as possible, the different categories of data stored should be distinguished in accordance with their degree of accuracy or reliability and, in particular, data based on facts should be distinguished from data based on opinions or personal assessments.
3.3 Where data which have been collected for administrative purposes are to be stored permanently, they should be stored in a separate file. In any case, measures should be taken so that administrative data are not subject to rules applicable to police data.

Principle 4 – Use of Data by the Police

4. Subject to Principle 5, personnel data collected and stored by the police for police purposes should be used exclusively for those purposes.

Principle 5 – Communication of Data

5.1 Communication within the Police Sector
The communications of data between police bodies to be used for police purposes should only be permissible if there exists a legitimate interest for such communication within the framework of the legal power of these bodies.
5.2(i) Communication in other Public Bodies
Communication of data to other public bodies should only be permissible if, in a particular case:
(a) there exists a clear legal obligation or authorization, or if
(b) these data are indispensable to the recipient to enable him to fulfil his own lawful task and provided that the aim of the collection or processing to be carried out by the recipient is not incompatible with the original processing, and the legal obligations of the communicating body are not contrary to this.
5.2(ii) Furthermore, communication to other public bodies is exceptionally permissible if, in a particular case:
(a) the communication is undoubtedly in the interest of the data subject and either the data subject has consented or circumstances are such as to allow a clear presumption of such consent, or if
(b) the communication is necessary so as to prevent a serious and imminent danger.
5.3(i) Communication to Private Parties
The communication of data to private parties should only be permissible if, in a particular case, there exists a clear legal obligation or authorization, or with the authorization of the supervisory authority.
5.3(ii) Communication to private parties is exceptionally permissible if, in a particular case:
(a) the communication is undoubtedly in the interest of the data subject and either the data subject has consented or circumstances are such as to allow a clear presumption of such consent, or if
(b) the communication is necessary so as to prevent a serious and imminent danger.
5.4 *International Communication*
Communication of data to foreign authorities should be restricted to police bodies. It should only be permissible:
(a) if there exists a clear legal provision under national or international law,
(b) in the absence of such a provision, if the communication is necessary for the prevention of a serious and imminent danger or is necessary for the suppression of a serious criminal offence under ordinary law, and provided that domestic regulations for the protection of the person are not prejudiced.
5.5(i) *Requests for Communication*
Subject to specific provisions contained in national legislation or in international agreements, requests for communication of data should provide indications as to the body or person requesting them as well as the reason for the request and its objective.
5.5(ii) Conditions for Communication
As far as possible, the quality of data should be verified at the latest at the time of their communication. As far as possible in all communications of data, judicial decisions, as well as decisions not to prosecute, should be indicated and data based on opinions or personal assessments checked at source before being communicated and their degree of accuracy or reliability indicated.
If it is discovered that the data are no longer accurate and up to date, they should not be communicated. If data which are no longer accurate or up to date have been communicated, the communicating body should inform as far as possible all the recipients of the data of their non-conformity.
5.5(iii) Safeguards for Communication
The data communicated to other public bodies, private parties and foreign authorities should not be used for purposes other than those specified in the request for communication.
Use of the data for other purposes should, without prejudice to paras. 5.2 to 5.4 of this principle, be made subject to the agreement of the communicating body.
5.6 Interconnection of files and on-line access to files
The interconnection of files with files held for different purposes is subject to either of the following conditions:
(a) the grant of an authorization by the supervisory body for the purposes of an inquiry into a particular offence, or
(b) in compliance with a clear legal provision.
Direct access/on-line access to a file should only be allowed if it is in accordance with domestic legislation which should take account of Principles 3 to 6 of this recommendation.

Principle 6 – Publicity, Right of Access to Police Files, Right to Rectification and Right of Appeal

6.1 The supervisory authority should take measures so as to satisfy itself that the public is informed of the existence of files which are the subject of notification as well as of its rights in regard to these files. Implementation of this principle should take account of the specific nature of *ad hoc* files, in particular the need to avoid serious prejudice to the performance of a legal task of the police bodies.

6.2 The data subject should be able to obtain access to a police file at reasonable intervals and without excessive delay in accordance with the arrangements provided for by domestic law.

6.3 The data subject should be able to obtain, where appropriate, rectification of his data which are contained in a file. Personal data which the exercise of the right of access reveals to be innaccurate or which are found to be excessive, inaccurate or irrelevant in application of any of the other principles contained in this recommendation should be erased or corrected or else be the subject of a corrective statement added to the file.

Such erasure or corrective measures should extend as far as possible to all documents accompanying the police file and, if not done immediately, should be carried out, at the latest, at the time of subsequent processing of the data or of their next communication.

6.4 Exercise of the rights of access, rectification and erasure should only be restricted insofar as a restriction is indispensable for the performance of a legal task of the police or is necessary for the protection of the data subject or the rights and freedoms of others.

In the interests of the data subject, a written statement can be excluded by law for specific cases.

6.5 A refusal or a restriction of those rights should be reasoned in writing. It should only be possible to refuse to communicate the reasons insofar as this is indispensable for the performance of a legal task of the police or is necessary for the protection of the rights and freedoms of others.

6.6 Where access is refused, the data subject should be able to appeal to the supervisory authority or to another independent body which shall satisfy itself that the refusal is well founded.

Principle 7 – Length of Storage and Updating of Data

7.1 Measures should be taken so that personal data kept for police purposes are deleted if they are no longer necessary for the purposes for which they were stored. For this purpose, consideration shall in particular be given to the following criteria: the need to retain data in the light of the conclusion of an inquiry into a particular case; a final judicial decision, in particular an acquittal; rehabilitation; spent convictions; amnesties; the age of the data subject; particular categories of data.

7.2 Rules aimed at fixing storage periods for the different categories of personal data as well as regular checks on their quality should be established in agreement with the supervisory authority or in accordance with domestic law.

Principle 8 – Data Security

8. The responsible body should take all the necessary measures to ensure the appropriate physical and logical security of the data and prevent unauthorized access, communication or alteration.

The different characteristics and contents of files should, for this purpose, be taken into account.

Council of Europe. Information Sheet No. 21, Strasbourg 1988, pp. 162–165.

PRIVATE PROPERTY RIGHT.

The rules safeguarding private property; until the French Revolution private property rights were among "sacred and inviolable" rights, integrated by fundamental laws and papal edicts. The first restrictions were introduced by the Declaration of the Rights of Man of 1789 in art. 17:

"Recognizing property as the sacred and inviolable right that no one can be deprived of, apart from public necessity, but in the form of a just, warranted compensation."

The second revolutionary limitation on private property right was brought about in the 20th century with the establishment of socialist states from 1917 and then with the process of decolonization and subsequent trends for nationalization. In the second half of the 20th century the restrictions put upon private property rights in the name of public, state and social interest became dominant in the majority of states. The UN General Assembly

on Dec. 12, 1958 officially recognized the sovereign right of each nation to make exclusive decisions concerning disposition of its natural resources; on Dec. 18, 1972, following a motion submitted by Iceland, the UN General Assembly expanded this decision to include all natural resources, also those of continental shelf, starting with fish and ending with crude oil.

F. CHALLAYE, *Histoire de la Propriété*, Paris, 1948; K. KATZAROV, *La propriété privée et le Droit International*, Paris, 1957.

PRIVATIZATION.

An international term for the selling off of public enterprises, self-developed or nationalized in different ▷ economic world systems. In the 1980's a noticeable global trend.

S.H. HANRE, "Privatization: Peoples Capitalism", in: *Economic Impact*, No. 2, 1928.

PRIVILEGES AND IMMUNITIES OF THE UN.

Convention on the Privileges and Immunities of the UN, adopted by the UN General Assembly on Feb. 13, 1946; came into force on Sept. 17, 1946, read as follows:

"Whereas Article 104 of the Charter of the United Nations provides that the Organization shall enjoy in the territory of each of its Members such legal capacity as may be necessary for the exercise of its functions and the fulfilment of its purposes and

Whereas Article 105 of the Charter of the United Nations provides that the Organization shall enjoy in the territory of each of its Members such privileges and immunities as are necessary for the fulfilment of its purposes and that representatives of the Members of the United Nations and officials of the Organization shall similarly enjoy such privileges and immunities as are necessary for the independent exercise of their functions in connection with the Organization.

Consequently the General Assembly by a Resolution adopted on the 13 Febuary, 1946, approved the following Convention and proposed it for accession by each Member of the United Nations.

Art. 1. *Juridical Personality*

Section 1. The United Nations shall possess juridical personality. It shall have the capacity:
(a) To contract;
(b) To acquire and dispose of immovable and movable property;
(c) To institute legal proceedings.

Art. II. *Property, Funds and Assets*

Section 2. The United Nations, its property and assets wherever located and by whomsoever held, shall enjoy immunity from every form of legal process except insofar as in any particular case it has expressly waived its immunity. It is however, understood that no waiver of immunity shall extend to any measure of execution.

Section 3. The premises of the United Nations shall be inviolable. The property and assets of the United Nations, wherever located and by whomsoever held, shall be immune from search, requisition, confiscation, expropriation and any other form of interference, whether by executive, administrative, judicial or legislative action.

Section 4. The archives of the United Nations, and in general all documents belonging to it or held by it, shall be inviolable wherever located.

Section 5. Without being restricted by financial controls, regulations or moratoria of any kind,
(a) The United Nations may hold funds, gold or currency of any kind and operate accounts in any currency;
(b) The United Nations shall be free to transfer its funds, gold or currency from one country to another or within any country and to convert any currency held by it into any other currency.

Section 6. In exercising its rights under Section 5 above, the United Nations shall pay due regard to any representation made by the Government of any nation insofar as it is considered that effect can be given to such representations without detriment to the interests of the United Nations.

Section 7. The United Nations, its assets, income and other property shall be:
(a) Exempt from all direct taxes; it is understood, however, that the United Nations will not claim exemp-

tion from taxes which are, in fact, no more than charges for public utility services;
(b) Exempt from customs duties and prohibitions and restrictions on imports and exports in respect of articles imported or exported by the United Nations for its official use. It is understood, however, that articles imported under such exemption will not be sold in the country into which they were imported except under conditions agreed with the Government of that country;
(c) Exempt from customs duties and prohibitions and restrictions on imports and exports in respect of its publications.

Section 8. While the United Nations will not, as a general rule, claim exemption from excise duties and from taxes on the sale of movable and immovable property which form part of the price to be paid, nevertheless when the United Nations is making important purchases for official use of property on which such duties and taxes have been charged or are chargeable, Members will, whenever possible, make appropriate administrative arrangements for the remission or return of the amount of duty or tax.

Art. III. *Facilities in Respect of Communications*

Section 9. The United Nations shall enjoy in the territory of each Member for its official communications treatment not less favourable than that accorded by the Government of that Member to any other Government including its diplomatic mission in the matter of priorities, rates and taxes on mails, cables, telegrams, radiograms, telephotos, telephone and other communications; and press rates for information to the press and radio. No censorship shall be applied to the official correspondence and other official communications of the United Nations.

Section 10. The United Nations shall have the right to use codes and to despatch and receive its correspondence by courier or in bags, which shall have the same immunities and privileges as diplomatic couriers and bags.

Art. IV. *The Representatives of Members*

Section 11. Representatives of Members to the principal and subsidiary organs of the United Nations and to conferences convened by the United Nations, shall, while exercising their functions and during the journey to and from the place of meeting, enjoy the following privileges and immunities:
(a) Immunity from personal arrest or detention and from seizure of their personal baggage, and, in respect of words spoken or written and all acts done by them in their capacity as representatives, immunity from legal process of every kind;
(b) Inviolability for all papers and documents;
(c) The right to use codes and to receive papers or correspondence by courier or in sealed bags;
(d) Exemption in respect of themselves and their spouses from immigration restrictions, aliens registration or national service obligations in the state they are visiting or through which they are passing in the exercise of their functions;
(e) The same facilities in respect of currency or exchange restrictions as are accorded to representatives of foreign governments on temporary official missions;
(f) The same immunities and facilities in respect of their personal baggage as are accorded to diplomatic envoys, and also;
(g) Such other privileges, immunities and facilities not inconsistent with the foregoing as diplomatic envoys enjoy, except that they shall have no right to claim exemption from customs duties on goods imported (otherwise than as part of their personal baggage) or from excise duties or sales taxes.

Section 12. In order to secure, for the representatives of Members to the principal and subsidiary organs of the United Nations and of conferences convened by the United Nations, complete freedom of speech and independence in the discharge of their duties, the immunity from legal process in respect of words spoken or written and all acts done by them in discharging their duties shall continue to be accorded, notwithstanding that the persons concerned are no longer the representatives of Members.

Section 13. Where the incidence of any form of taxation depends upon residence, periods during which the representatives of Members to the principal and subsidiary organs of the United Nations and to conferences convened by the United Nations are present in a state for the discharge of their duties shall not be considered as periods of residence.

Section 14. Privileges and immunities are accorded to the representatives of Members not for the personal benefit of the individuals themselves, but in order to safeguard the independent exercise of their functions in connection with the United Nations. Consequently a Member not only has the right but is under a duty to waive the immunity of its representative in any case where in the opinion of the Member the immunity would impede the course of justice, and it can be waived without prejudice to the purpose for which the immunity is accorded.

Section 15. The provisions of Sections 11, 12, and 13 are not applicable as between a representative and the authorities of the state of which he is a national or of which he is or has been the representative.

Section 16. In this article the expression 'representatives' shall be deemed to include all delegates, deputy delegates, advisers, technical experts and secretaries of delegations.

Art. V. *Officials.*

Section 17. The Secretary-General will specify the categories of officials to which the provisions of this Article and Article VII shall apply. He shall submit these categories to the General Assembly. Thereafter these categories shall be communicated to the Governments of all Members. The names of the officials included in these categories shall from time to time be made known to the Governments of Members.

Section 18. Officials of the United Nations shall:

(a) Be immune from legal process in respect of words spoken or written and all acts performed by them in their official capacity;

(b) Be exempt from taxation on the salaries and emoluments paid to them by the United Nations;

(c) Be immune from national service obligations;

(d) Be immune, together with their spouses and relatives dependent on them, from immigration restrictions and alien registration;

(e) Be accorded the same privileges in respect of exchange facilities as are accorded to the officials of comparable ranks forming part of diplomatic missions to the Government concerned;

(f) Be given, together with their spouses and relatives dependent on them, the same repatriation facilities in time of international crisis as diplomatic envoys;

(g) Have the right to import free of duty their furniture and effects at the time of first taking up their post in the country in question.

Section 19. In addition to the immunities and privileges specified in Section 18, the Secretary-General and all Assistant Secretaries-General shall be accorded in respect of themselves, their spouses and minor children, the privileges and immunities, exemptions and facilities accorded to diplomatic envoys, in accordance with international law.

Section 20. Privileges and immunities are granted to officials in the interests of the United Nations and not for the personal benefit of the individuals themselves. The Secretary-General shall have the right and the duty to waive the immunity of any official in any case where, in his opinion; the immunity would impede the course of justice and can be waived without prejudice to the interests of the United Nations. In the case of the Secretary-General, the Security Council shall have the right to waive immunity.

Section 21. The United Nations shall co-operate at all times with the appropriate authorities of Members to facilitate the proper administration of justice, secure the observance of police regulations and prevent the occurrence of any abuse in connection with the privileges, immunities and facilities mentioned in this Article.

Art. VI. *Experts on Missions for the United Nations*

Section 22. Experts (other than officials coming within the scope of Article V) performing missions for the United Nations shall be accorded such privileges and immunities as are necessary for the independent exercise of their functions during the period of their missions, including the time spent on journeys in connection with their missions. In particular they shall be accorded:

(a) Immunity from personal arrest or detention and from seizure of their personal baggage;

(b) In respect of words spoken or written and acts done by them in the course of the performance of their mission, immunity from legal process of every kind. This immunity from legal process shall continue to be accorded notwithstanding that the persons concerned are not employed on missions for the United Nations;

(c) Inviolability for all papers and documents;

(d) For the purpose of their communications with the United Nations, the right to use codes and to receive papers or correspondence by courier or in sealed bags;

(e) The same facilities in respect of currency or exchange restrictions as are accorded to representatives of foreign governments on temporary official missions;

(f) The same immunities and facilities in respect of their personal baggage as are accorded to diplomatic envoys.

Section 23. Privileges and immunities are granted to experts in the interests of the United Nations and not for the personal benefit of the individuals themselves. The Secretary-General shall have the right and the duty to waive the immunity of any expert in any case where, in his opinion, the immunity would impede the course of justice and it can be waived without prejudice to the interests of the United Nations.

Art. VII. *United Nations Laissez-Passer*

Section 24. The United Nations may issue United Nations laissez-passer to its officials. These laissez-passer shall be recognized and accepted as valid travel documents by the authorities of Members, taking into account the provisions of Section 25.

Section 25. Applications for visas (where required) from the holders of United Nations laissez-passer, when accompanied by a certificate that they are travelling on the business of the United Nations, shall be dealt with as speedily as possible. In addition, such persons shall be granted facilities for speedy travel.

Section 26. Similar facilities to those specified in Section 25 shall be accorded to experts and other persons who, though not the holders of United Nations laissez-passer, have a certificate that they are travelling on the business of the United Nations.

Section 27. The Secretary-General, Assistant Secretaries-General and Directors travelling on United Nations laissez-passer on the business of the United Nations shall be granted the same facilities as are accorded to diplomatic envoys.

Section 28. The provisions of this article may be supplied to the comparable officials of specialized agencies if the agreements for relationship made under Article 63 of the Charter so provide.

Art. VIII. *Settlements of Disputes*

Section 29. The United Nations shall make provisions for appropriate modes of settlement of:

(a) Disputes arising out of contracts or other disputes of a private law character to which the United Nations is a party;

(b) Disputes involving any official of the United Nations who by reason of his official position enjoys immunity, if immunity has not been waived by the Secretary-General.

Section 30. All differences arising out of the interpretation or application of the present convention shall be referred to the International Court of Justice, unless in any case it is agreed by the parties to have recourse to another mode of settlement. If a difference arises between the United Nations on the one hand and a Member on the other hand, a request shall be made for an advisory opinion on any legal question involved in accordance with Article 96 of the Charter and Article 65 of the Statute of the Court. The opinion given by the Court shall be accepted as decisive by the parties.

Final Article. Section 31. This convention is submitted to every Member of the United Nations for accession.

Section 32. Accession shall be affected by deposit of an instrument with the Secretary-General of the United Nations and the convention shall come into force as regards each Member on the date of deposit of each instrument of accession.

Section 33. The Secretary-General shall inform all Members of the United Nations of the deposit of each accession.

Section 34. It is understood that, when an instrument of accession is deposited on behalf of any Member, the Member will be in a position under its own law to give effect to the terms of this convention.

Section 35. This convention shall continue in force as between the United Nations and every Member which has deposited an instrument of accession for so long as that Member remains a Member of the United Nations, or until a revised general convention has been approved by the General Assembly and that Member has become a party to this revised convention.

Section 36. The Secretary-General may conclude with any Member or Members supplementary agreements adjusting the provisions of this convention so far as that Member or those Members are concerned. These supplementary agreements shall in each case be subject to the approval of the General Assembly."

On Dec 21, 1988 the GA without a vote adopted Res. 43/225. Respect for the Privileges and Immunities of Officials of the UN and Specialized Agencies and Related Organizations", in which it:

"(1) Takes note with concern of the report submitted by the Secretary General on behalf of the Administrative Committee on Co-ordination, and of the developments indicated therein, in particular the significant number of new cases of arrest and detention and those regarding previously reported cases under this category.

(2) Also takes note with concern of the restrictions on duty travel of officials as indicated in the report of the Secretary General.

(3) Further takes note with concern of the information in the report of the Secretary General related to taxation and the status, privileges and immunities of officials.

(4) Deplores the increase in the number of cases where the functioning safety and well-being of officials have been adversely affected;

(5) Also deplores the increasing number of cases in which the lives and well-being of officials have been placed in jeopardy during their official functions.

(6) Calls upon all Member States scrupulously to respect the privileges and immunities of all officials of the United Nations, the specialized agencies and related organizations and to refrain from any acts that would impede such officials in the performance of their functions, thereby seriously affecting the proper functioning of the Organization."

UNTS, Vol. 1, pp. 16–32; *UN Resolutions and Decisions adopted by the General Assembly during the First Part of its Forty-Third Session, from 20 September to 22 December, 1988*, New York, 1989, pp. 515–516.

PRIVILEGES AND IMMUNITIES OF THE UN SPECIALIZED AGENCIES. Convention on the Privileges and Immunities of the UN Specialized Agencies, approved by the UN General Assembly, Nov. 31, 1947, came into force on Dec. 2, 1948; read as follows:

"Art. I. Definitions and Scope

Section 1. In this Convention:

(i) The words 'standard clauses' refer to the provisions of Articles II to IX.

(ii) The words 'Specialized agencies' mean:

(a) The International Labour Organizaton;

(b) The Food and Agriculture Organization of the United Nations;

(c) The United Nations Educational, Scientific and Cultural Organization;

(d) The International Civil Aviation Organization;

(e) The International Monetary Fund;

(f) The International Bank for Reconstruction and Development;

(g) The World Health Organization;

(h) The Universal Postal Union;

(i) The International Telecommunications Union; and

(j) Any other agency in relationship with the United Nations in accordance with Articles 57 and 63 of the Charter.

(iii) The word 'Convention' means, in relation to any particular specialized agency, the standard clauses as modified by the final (or revised) text of the annex transmitted by that agency in accordance with sections 36 and 38.

(iv) For the purposes of Article III, the words 'property and assets' shall also include property and funds administered by a specialized agency in furtherance of its constitutional functions.

(v) For the purposes of Articles V and VII, the expression 'representatives of members' shall be deemed to include all representatives; alternates, advisers, technical experts and secretaries of delegations.

(vi) In sections 13, 14, 15 and 25, the expressions 'meetings convened by a specialized agency' means meetings: (1) of its assembly and of its executive body (however designated), and (2) of any commission provided for in its constitution; (3) of any international

conference convened by it; and (4) of any committee of any of these bodies.
(vii) The term 'executive head' means the principal executive official of the specialized agency in question, whether designated 'Director-General' or otherwise.
Section 2. Each State party to this Convention in respect of any specialized agency to which this Convention has become applicable in accordance with section 37 shall accord to, or in connexion with, that agency the privileges and immunities set forth in the standard clauses on the conditions specified therein, subject to any modification of those clauses contained in the provisions of the final (or revised) annex relating to that agency and transmitted in accordance with sections 36 or 38.
Art. II. Juridical Personality
Section 3. The specialized agencies shall possess juridical personality. They shall have the capacity (a) to contract, (b) to acquire and dispose of immovable and movable property, (c) to institute legal proceedings.
Art. III. Property, Funds and Assets
Section 4. The specialized agencies, their property and assets, wherever located and by whomsoever held, shall enjoy immunity from every form of legal process except in so far as in any particular case they have expressly waived their immunity. It is, however, understood that no waiver of immunity shall extend to any measure of execution.
Section 5. The premises of the specialized agencies shall be inviolable. The property and assets of the specialized agencies, wherever located and by whomsoever held, shall be immune from search, requisition, confiscation expropriation and any other form of interference, whether by executive, administrative, judicial or legislative action.
Section 6. The archives of the specialized agencies, and in general all documents belonging to them or held by them, shall be inviolable; wherever located.
Section 7. Without being restricted by financial controls, regulations or moratoria of any kind:
(a) The specialized agencies may hold funds, gold or currency of any kind and operate accounts in any currency;
(b) The specialized agencies may freely transfer their funds, gold or currency from one country to another or within any country and convert any currency held by them into any other currency.
Section 8. Each specialized agency shall, in exercising its rights under section 7 above pay due regard to any representations made by the Government of any State party to this Convention in so far as it is considered that effect can be given to such representations without detriment to the interests of the agency.
Section 9. The specialized agencies, their assets, income and other property shall be:
(a) Exempt from all direct taxes; it is understood, however, that the specialized agencies will not claim exemption from taxes which are, in fact, no more than charges for public utility services;
(b) Exempt from customs duties and prohibitions and restrictions on imports and exports in respect of articles imported or exported by the specialized agencies for their official use; it is understood, however, that articles imported under such exemption will not be sold in the country into which they were imported except under conditions agreed to with the Government of that country;
(c) Exempt from prohibitions and restrictions on imports and exports in respect of their publications.
Section 10. While the specialized agencies will not, as a general rule, claim exemption from excise duties and from taxes on the sale of movable and immovable property which form part of the price to be paid, nevertheless when the specialized agencies are making important purchases for official use of property on which such duties and taxes have been charged or are chargeable, States, parties to this Convention will, whenever possible, make appropriate administrative arrangements for the remission or return of the amount of duty or tax.
Art. IV. Facilities in Respect of Communications
Section 11. Each specialized agency shall enjoy, in the territory of each State party to this Convention in respect of that agency, for its official communications treatment not less favourable than that accorded by the Government of such State to any other Government, including the latter's diplomatic mission in the matter of priorities, rates and taxes on mails, cables, telegrams, radiograms, telephotos, telephone and other communications, and press rates for information to the press and radio.
Section 12. No censorship shall be applied to the official correspondence and other official communications of the specialized agencies.
The specialized agencies shall have the right to use codes and to dispatch and receive correspondence by courier or in sealed bags, which shall have the same immunities and privileges as diplomatic couriers and bags.
Nothing in this section shall be construed to preclude the adoption of appropriate security precautions to be determined by agreement between each State party to this Convention and a specialized agency.
Art. V. Representatives of Members
Section 13. Representatives of members at meetings convened by a specialized agency shall, while exercising their functions and during their journeys to and from the place of meeting, enjoy the following privileges and immunities:
(a) Immunity from personal arrest or detention and from seizure of their personal baggage, and in respect of words spoken or written and all acts done by them in their official capacity, immunity from legal process of every kind;
(b) Inviolability for all papers and documents;
(c) The right to use codes and to receive papers or correspondence by courier or in sealed bags;
(d) Exemption in respect of themselves and their spouses from immigration restrictions, aliens' registration or national service obligations in the State which they are visiting or through which they are passing in the exercise of their functions;
(e) The same facilities in respect of currency or exchange restrictions as are accorded to representatives of foreign Governments on temporary official missions;
(f) The same immunities and facilities in respect of their personal baggage as are accorded to members of comparable rank of diplomatic missions.
Section 14. In order to secure for the representatives of members of the specialized agencies at meeting convened by them complete freedom of speech and complete independence in the discharge of their duties, the immunity from legal process in respect of words spoken or written and all acts done by them in discharging their duties shall continue to be accorded, notwithstanding that the persons concerned are no longer engaged in the discharge of such duties.
Section 15. Where the incidence of any form of taxation depends upon residence, periods during which the representatives of members of the specialized agencies at meetings convened by them are present in a member State for the discharge of their duties shall not be considered as periods of residence.
Section 16. Privileges and immunities are accorded to the representatives of members, not for the personal benefit of the individuals themselves, but in order to safeguard the independent exercise of their functions in connexion with the specialized agencies. Consequently, a member not only has the right but is under a duty to waive the immunity of its representatives in any case where, in the opinion of the member, the immunity would impede the course of justice, and where it can be waived without prejudice to the purpose for which the immunity is accorded.
Section 17. The provisions of sections 13, 14, and 15 are not applicable in relation to the authorities of a State of which the person is a national or of which he is or has been a representative.
Art. VI. Officials
Section 18. Each specialized agency will specify the categories of officials to which the provisions of this Article and of Article VII shall apply. It shall communicate them to the governments of all States parties to this Convention in respect of that agency and to the Secretary-General of the United Nations. The names of the officials included in these categories shall from time to time be made known to the above-mentioned Governments.
Section 19. Officials of the specialized agencies shall:
(a) Be immune from legal process in respect of words spoken or written and all acts performed by them in their official capacity;
(b) Enjoy the same exemptions from taxation in respect of the salaries and emoluments paid to them by the specialized agencies and on the same conditions as are enjoyed by officials of the United Nations;
(c) Be immune, together with their spouses and relatives dependent on them, from immigration restrictions and alien registration;
(d) Be accorded the same privileges in respect of exchange facilities as are accorded to officials of comparable rank of diplomatic missions;
(e) Be given, together with their spouses and relatives dependent on them, the same repatriation facilities in time of international crises as officials of comparable rank of diplomatic missions;
(f) Have the right to import free of duty their furniture and effects at the time of first taking up their post in the country in question.
Section 20. The officials of the specialized agencies shall be exempt from national service obligations, provided that, in relation to the States of which they are nationals, such exemption shall be confined to officials of the specialized agencies whose names have, by reason of their duties, been placed upon a list compiled by the executive head of the specialized agency and approved by the State concerned. Should other officials of specialized agencies be called up for national service the State concerned shall, at the request of the specialized agency concerned grant such temporary deferments in the call-up of such officials as may be necessary to avoid interruption in the continuation of essential work.
Section 21. In addition to the immunities and privileges specified in Sections 19 and 20, the executive head of each specialized agency, including any official action on his behalf during his absence from duty, shall be accorded in respect to himself, his spouse and minor children, the privileges and immunities, exemptions and facilities accorded to diplomatic envoys, in accordance with international law.
Section 22. Privileges and immunities are granted to officials in the interests of the specialized agencies and not for the personal benefit of the individuals themselves. Each specialized agency shall have the right and the duty to waive the immunity of any official in any case where, in its opinion, the immunity would impede the course of justice and can be waived without prejudice to the interests of the specialized agency.
Section 23. Each specialized agency shall co-operate at all times with the appropriate authorities of member States to facilitate the proper administration of justice, secure the observance of police regulations and prevent the occurrence of any abuses in connexion with the privileges, immunities and facilities mentioned in this article.
Art. VII. Abuses of Privilege
Section 24. If any State party to this Convention considers that there has been an abuse of a privilege or immunity conferred by this Convention, consultations shall be held between that State and the specialized agency concerned to determine whether any such abuse has occurred and, if so to attempt to ensure that no repetition occurs. If such consultations fail to achieve a result satisfactory to the State and the specialized agency concerned, the question whether an abuse of a privilege or immunity has occurred shall be submitted to the International Court of Justice in accordance with section 32. If the International Court of Justice finds that such an abuse has occurred, the State party to this Convention affected by such abuse shall have the right, after notification to the specialized agency in question, to withhold from the specialized agency concerned the benefits of the privilege or immunity so abused.
Section 25. 1. Representatives of Members at meetings convened by specialized agencies, while exercising their functions and during their journeys to and from the place of meeting, and officials within the meaning of section 18, shall not be required by the territorial authorities to leave the country in which they are performing their functions on account of any activities by them in their official capacity. In the case, however, of abuse of privileges of residence committed by any such person in activities in that country outside his official functions, he may be required to leave by the Government of that country provided that:
2.(1) Representatives of members, or persons who are entitled to diplomatic immunity under section 21, shall not be required to leave the country otherwise than in accordance with the diplomatic procedure applicable to diplomatic envoys accredited to that country.
(2) In the case of an official to whom section 21 is not applicable, no order to leave the country shall be issued other than with the approval of the Foreign Minister of the country in question, and such approval shall be

given only after consultation with the executive head of the specialized agency concerned; and, if expulsion proceedings are taken against an official, the executive head of the specialized agency shall have the right to appear in such proceedings on behalf of the person against whom they are instituted.

Art. VIII. Laissez-Passer

Section 26. Officials of the specialized agencies shall be entitled to use the United Nations laissez-passer in conformity with administrative arrangements to be concluded between the Secretary-General of the United Nations and the competent authorities of the specialized agencies, to which agencies special powers to issue laissez-passer may be delegated. The Secretary-General of the United Nations shall notify each State party to this Convention of each administrative arrangement so concluded.

Section 27. States parties to this Convention shall recognize and accept the United Nations laissez-passer issued to officials of the specialized agencies as valid travel documents.

Section 28. Applications for visas, where required, from officials of specialized agencies holding United Nations laissez-passer, when accompanied by a certificate that they are travelling on the business of a specialized agency, shall be dealt with as speedily as possible. In addition, such persons shall be granted facilities for speedy travel.

Section 29. Similar facilities to those specified in section 28 shall be accorded to experts and other persons who, though not the holders of United Nations laissez-passer, have a certificate that they are travelling on the business of a specialized agency.

Section 30. The executive heads, assistant executive heads, heads of departments and other officials of a rank not lower than head of department of the specialized agencies, travelling on United Nations laissez-passer on the business of the specialized agencies, shall be granted the same facilities for travel as are accorded to officials of comparable rank in diplomatic missions.

Art. IX. Settlement of Disputes

Section 31. Each specialized agency shall make provision for appropriate modes of settlement of:
(a) Disputes arising out of contracts or other disputes of private character to which the specialized agency is a party;
(b) Disputes involving any official of a specialized agency who by reason of his official position enjoys immunity, if immunity has not been waived in accordance with the provisions of section 22.

Section 32. All differences arising out of the interpretation or application of the present Convention shall be referred to the International Court of Justice unless in any case it is agreed by the parties to have recourse to another mode of settlement. If a difference arises between one of the specialized agencies on the one hand, and a member on the other hand, a request shall be made for an advisory opinion on any legal question involved in accordance with Article 96 of the Charter and Article 65 of the Statute of the Court and the relevant provisions of the agreements concluded between the United Nations and the specialized agency concerned. The opinion given by the Court shall be accepted as decisive by the parties.

Art. X. Annexes and Application to Individual Specialized Agencies

Section 33. In their application to each specialized agency, the standard clauses shall operate subject to any modifications set forth in the final (or revised) text of the annex relating to that agency, as provided in sections 36 and 38.

Section 34. The provisions of the Convention in relation to any specialized agency must be interpreted in the light of the functions with which that agency is entrusted by its constitutional instrument.

Section 35. Draft annexes 1 to 9 are recommended to the specialized agencies named therein. In the case of any specialized agency not mentioned by name in section 1, the Secretary-General of the United Nations shall transmit to the agency a draft annex recommended by the Economic and Social Council.

Section 36. The final text of each annex shall be that approved by the specialized agency in question in accordance with its constitutional procedure. A copy of the annex as approved by each specialized agency shall be transmitted by the agency in question to the

Secretary-General of the United Nations and shall thereupon replace the draft referred to in section 35.

Section 37. The present Convention becomes applicable to each specialized agency when it has transmitted to the Secretary-General of the United Nations the final text of the relevant annex and has informed him that it accepts the standard clauses, as modified by this annex, and undertakes to give effect to sections 8, 18, 22, 23, 24, 31, 32, 42 and 45 (subject to any modification of section 32 which may be found necessary in order to make the final text of the annex consonant with the constitutional instrument of the agency) and any provisions of the annex placing obligations on the agency. The Secretary-General shall communicate to all Members of the United Nations and to other States members of the specialized agencies certified copies of all annexes transmitted to him under this section and of revised annexes transmitted under section 38.

Section 38. If, after the transmission of a final annex under section 36, any specialized agency approves any amendments thereto in accordance with its constitutional procedure, a revised annex shall be transmitted by it to the Secretary-General of the United Nations.

Section 39. The provisions of this Convention shall in no way limit or prejudice the privileges and immunities which have been, or may hereafter be, accorded by any State to any specialized agency by reason of the location in the territory of that State of its headquarters or regional offices. This Convention shall not be deemed to prevent the conclusion between any State party thereto and any specialized agency of supplemental agreements adjusting the provisions of this Convention or extending or curtailing the privileges and immunities thereby granted.

Section 40. It is understood that the standard clauses, as modified by the final text of an annex sent by a specialized agency to the Secretary-General of the United Nations under section 36 (or any revised annex sent under section 38), will be consistent with the provisions of the constitutional instrument then in force of the agency in question and that if any amendment to that instrument is necessary for the purpose of making the constitutional instrument so consistent, such amendment will have been brought into force in accordance with the constitutional procedure of that agency before the final (or revised) annex is transmitted. The Convention shall not itself operate so as to abrogate, or derogate from, any provisions of the constitutional instrument of any specialized agency or any rights or obligations which the agency may otherwise, have, acquire, assume.

Art. XI. Final Provisions

Section 41. Accession to this Convention by a Member of the United Nations and (subject to section 42) by any State member of a specialized agency shall be effected by deposit with the Secretary-General of the United Nations of an instrument of accession which shall take effect on the date of its deposit.

Section 42. Each specialized agency concerned shall communicate the text of the Convention together with the relevant annexes to those of its members which are not Members of the United Nations and shall invite them to accede therein in respect of that agency by depositing an instrument of accession to the Convention in respect thereof either with the Secretary-General of the United Nations or with the executive head of the specialized agency.

Section 43. Each State party to this Convention shall indicate in its instrument of accession the specialized agency or agencies in respect of which it undertakes to apply the provisions of this Convention. Each State party to this Convention may by a subsequent written notification to the Secretary-General of the United Nations undertake to apply the provisions of this Convention to one or more further specialized agencies. This notification shall take effect on the date of its receipt by the Secretary-General.

Section 44. This Convention shall enter into force for each State party to this Convention in respect of a specialized agency when it has become applicable to that agency in accordance with section 37 and the State party has undertaken to apply the provisions of the Convention to that agency in accordance with section 43.

Section 45. The Secretary-General of the United Nations shall inform all Members of the United Nations, as well as all members of the specialized agen-

cies, and executive heads of the specialized agencies, of the deposit of each instrument of accession received under section 41 and of subsequent notifications received under section 43. The executive head of a specialized agency shall inform the Secretary-General of the United Nations and the members of the agency concerned of the deposit of any instrument of accession deposited with him under section 42.

Section 46. It is understood that, when an instrument of accession or a subsequent notification is deposited on behalf of any State, this State will be in a position under its own law to give effect to the terms of this Convention, as modified by the final texts of any annexes relating to the agencies covered by such accessions or notifications.

Section 47. 1. Subject to the provisions of paragraphs 2 and 3 of this section, each State party to this Convention undertakes to apply this Convention in respect of each specialized agency covered by its accession or subsequent notifications until such time as a revised convention or annex shall have become applicable to that agency and the said State shall have accepted the revised convention or annex. In the case of a revised annex, the acceptance of States shall be by a notification addressed to the Secretary-General of the United Nations, which shall take effect on the date of its receipt by the Secretary-General.

2. Each State party to this Convention, however, which is not, or has ceased to be, a member of a specialized agency, may address a written notification to the Secretary-General of the United Nations and the executive head of the agency concerned to the effect that it intends to withhold from that agency the benefits of this Convention as from a specified date, which shall not be earlier than three months from the date of receipt of the notification.

3. Each State party to this Convention may withhold the benefit of this Convention from any specialized agency which ceases to be in relationship with the United Nations.

4. The Secretary-General of the United Nations shall inform all members States parties to this Convention of any notification transmitted to him under the provisions of this section.

Section 48. At the request of one-third of the States parties to this Convention, the Secretary-General of the United Nations will convene a conference with a view to its revision.

Section 49. The Secretary-General of the United Nations shall transmit copies of the Convention to each specialized agency and to the Government of each Member of the United Nations.

Annexes. Annex I. The International Labour Organization, ILO.

The standard clauses shall operate in respect to the International Labour Organization subject to the following provision:

The provisions of article V (other than paragraph (c) of section 16) and of section 25, paragraphs 1 and 2(I) of article VII shall extend to the employers' and workers' member of the Governing Body of the International Labour Office and their alternates and advisers, except that any waiver of the immunity of any such person member under section 16 shall be by the Governing Body.

Annex II. The Food and Agriculture Organization of the United Nations, FAO.

The standard clauses shall operate in respect to the Food and Agriculture Organization of the United Nations (hereinafter called "the Organization") subject to the following provisions:

1. Article V and section 25, paragraphs 1 and 2(I) of article VII shall extend to the Chairman of the Council of the Organization, except that any waiver of the immunity of the Chairman under section 16 shall be by the Council of the Organization.

2.(i) Experts (other than officials coming within the scope of article VI) serving on committees of, or performing missions for, the Organization shall be accorded the following privileges and immunities so far as is necessary for the effective exercise of their functions, including the time spent on journeys in connexion with service on such committees or missions:

(a) Immunity from personal arrest or seizure of their personal baggage;

(b) Immunity from legal process of every kind in respect of words spoken or written or acts done by them in the performance of their official functions, such im-

munity to continue notwithstanding that the persons concerned are no longer serving on committees of, or employed on missions for, the Organization;
(c) The same facilities in respect of currency and exchange restrictions and in respect of their personal baggage as are accorded to officials of foreign Governments on temporary official missions.
(ii) Privileges and immunities are granted to the experts in the interests of the Organization and not for the personal benefit of the individuals themselves. The Organization shall have the right and the duty to waive the immunity of any expert in any case where in its opinion the immunity would impede the course of justice and can be waived without prejudice to the interests of the Organization.

Annex III. The International Civil Aviation Organization, ICAO.

The standard clauses shall operate in respect to the International Civil Aviation Organization (hereinafter called 'the Organization') subject to the following provisions:
1. The privileges, immunities, exemptions and facilities referred to in section 21 of the standard clauses shall also be accorded to the President of the Council of the Organization.
2.(i) Experts (other than officials coming within the scope of article VI) serving on committees of, or performing missions for the Organization shall be accorded the following privileges and immunities so far as is necessary for the effective exercise of their functions, including the time spent on journeys in connexion with service on such committees or missions;
(a) Immunity from personal arrest or seizure of their personal baggage;
(b) Immunity from legal process of every kind in respect of words spoken or written or acts done by them in the performance of their official functions, such immunity to continue notwithstanding that the persons concerned are no longer serving on committees of, or employed on missions for, the Organization;
(c) The same facilities in respect of currency and exchange restrictions and in respect of their personal baggage as are accorded to officials of foreign Governments on temporary official missions;
(d) Inviolability of their papers and documents relating to the work on which they are engaged for the Organization.
(ii) In connexion with (d) or 2 above, the principle contained in the last sentence of section 12 of the standard clauses shall be applicable.
(iii) Privileges and immunities are granted to the experts of the Organization in the interests of the Organization and not for the personal benefit of the individuals themselves. The Organization shall have the right and the duty to waive the immunity of any expert in any case where in its opinion the immunity could impede the course of justice, and it can be waived without prejudice to the interests of the Organization.

Annex IV. The United Nations Educational, Scientific and Cultural Organization, UNESCO.

The standard clauses shall operate in respect to the United Nations Educational, Scientific and Cultural Organization (hereinafter called "the Organization") subject to the following provisions:
1. Article V and section 25, paragraphs 1 and 2(I) of article VII shall extend to the President of the Conference and members of the Executive Board of the Organization, their substitutes and advisers except that any waiver of the immunity of any such person of the Executive Board under section 16 shall be by the Executive Board.
2.(i) Experts (other than officials coming within the scope of article VI) serving on committees of, or performing missions for, the Organization shall be accorded the following privileges and immunities so far as is necessary for the effective exercise of their functions, including the time spent on journeys in connexion with service on such committees or missions:
(a) Immunity from personal arrest or seizure of their personal baggage;
(b) In respect of words spoken or written or acts done by them in the performance of their official functions, immunity of legal process of every kind, such immunity to continue notwithstanding that the persons concerned are no longer serving on committees of, or employed on missions for, the Organization;
(c) The same facilities in respect of currency and exchange restrictions and in respect of their personal baggage as are accorded to officials of foreign Governments on temporary official missions.
(ii) Privileges and immunities are granted to the experts of the Organization in the interests of the Organization and not for personal benefit of the individuals themselves. The Organization shall have the right and duty to waive the immunity of any expert in any case where in its opinion the immunity would impede the course of justice, and it can be waived without prejudice to the interests of the Organization.

Annex V. The International Monetary Fund, IMF.

In their application to the International Monetary Fund (hereinafter called "the Fund"), the standard clauses shall operate subject to the following provisions:
1. The following shall be substituted for section 9:
'(a) The Fund, its assets, property, income and its operations and transactions authorized by its articles of agreement shall be immune from all taxation and from all customs duties. The Fund shall be immune from prohibitions and restrictions on imports and exports in respect of articles imported or exported for its official use and in respect of its publications. It is understood, however, that the Fund will not claim exemption from taxes which are, in fact, no more than charges for public utility services and that articles (other than its publications) imported under this exemption will not be sold in the country into which they were imported except under conditions agreed to with the Government of that country. The Fund shall also be immune from the collection of payment of any tax or duty.
'(b) No taxation of any kind shall be levied on any obligation or security issued by the Fund, including any dividend or interest thereon, by whomsoever held:
'(i) Which discriminates against such obligation or security solely because of its origin; or
'(ii) If the sole jurisdictional basis for each taxation is the place or currency in which it is issued, made payable or paid, or the location of any office or place of business maintained by the Fund.'
2. Section 32 of the standard clauses shall only apply to differences arising out of the interpretation or application of privileges and immunities which are derived by the Fund from this Convention and are not included in those which it can claim under its articles or otherwise.

Annex VI. The International Bank for Reconstruction and Development, IBRD.

In their application to the International Bank for Reconstruction and Development (hereinafter called "the Bank"), the standard clauses shall operate subject to the following provisions:
1. The following shall be substituted for section 4:
'Actions may be brought against the Bank only in a court of competent jurisdiction in the territories of a member in which the Bank has an office, has appointed an agent for the purpose of accepting service or notice of process, or has issued or guaranteed securities. No actions shall, however, be brought by members or persons acting for or deriving claims from members. The property and assets of the Bank shall, wheresoever located and by whomsoever held, be immune from all forms of seizure, attachment or execution before the delivery of final judgment against the Bank.'
2. The following shall be substituted for section 9:
'(a) The Bank, its assets, property income and its operations and transactions authorized by its articles of agreement shall be immune from all taxation and from all customs duties. The Bank shall be immune from prohibitions and restrictions on imports and exports in respect of articles imported or exported for its official use and in respect of its publications. It is understood, however, that the Bank will not claim exemption from taxes which are, in fact, no more than charges for public utility services, and that articles (other than its publications) imported under this exemption will not be sold in the country into which they were imported except under conditions agreed to with the Government of that country.
'The Bank shall also be immune from the collection or payment of any tax or duty.
'(b) No taxation of any kind shall be levied on any obligation or security issued by the Bank (including any dividend or interest thereon) by whomsoever held:
'(i) Which discriminates against such obligation or security solely because it is issued by the Bank; or
'(ii) If the sole jurisdictional basis for such taxation is the place or currency in which it is issued, made payable or paid, or the location of any office or place of business maintained by the Bank.
'(c) No taxation of any kind shall be levied on any obligation or security guaranteed by the Bank (including any dividend or interest thereon) by whomsoever held:
'(i) Which discriminates against such obligation or security solely because it is guaranteed by the Bank; or
'(ii) If the sole jurisdictional basis for such taxation is the location of any office or place of business maintained by the Bank.'
3. Section 32 of the standard clauses shall only apply to differences arising out of the interpretation or application of privileges and immunities which are derived by the Bank from this Convention and are not included in those which it can claim under its articles or otherwise.

Annex VII. The World Health Organization, WHO.

In their application to the World Health Organization (hereinafter called "the Organization") the standard clauses shall operate subject to the following modifications:
1. Article V and section 25, paragraphs 1 and 2(I) of article VII shall extend to persons designated to serve on the executive board of the Organization, their alternates and advisers, except that any waiver of the immunity of any such persons under section 16 shall be by the Board.
2.(i) Experts (other than officials coming within the scope of article VI) serving on committees of, or performing missions for, the Organization shall be accorded the following privileges and immunities so far as is necessary for the effective exercise of their functions, including the time spent on journeys in connexion with service on such committees or missions:
(a) Immunity from personal arrest or seizure of their personal baggage;
(b) Immunity of legal process of every kind, in respect of words spoken or written or acts done by them in the performance of their official functions, such immunity to continue notwithstanding that the persons concerned are no longer serving on committees of, or employed on missions for, the Organization;
(c) The same facilities in respect of currency and exchange restrictions, and in respect of their personal baggage, as are accorded to officials of foreign governments on temporary official missions;
(d) Privileges and immunities are granted to the experts of the Organization in the interests of the Organization and not for the personal benefit of the individuals themselves. The Organization shall have the right and the duty to waive the immunity of any expert in any case where in its opinion the immunity would impede the course of justice and can be waived without prejudice to the interests of the Organization.

Annex VIII. The Universal Postal Union, UPU.

The standard clauses shall apply without modification.

Annex IX. The International Telecommunication Union, ITU.

The standard clauses shall apply without modification."

UNTS, Vol. 33, pp. 262–290.

PRIX ITALIA. An international prize for radio dramas and television films awarded annually since 1955 by Italian Radio and Television.

PRIX JAPON. After the fashion of Prix Italia, Japanese Radio and Television (NHK) organizes each year since 1965 under the name of Prix Japon an International Contest of Radio Programs limited to broadcasts and educational programs.

PRIZE, INTERNATIONAL. International term for regional or world prizes, like ▷ Nobel Prizes or ▷ Bolivar Prize.

PRIZES LAW. The seizure, annexation or confiscation of a ship at sea or seizure of its cargo, a commonly recognized international custom until the mid 19th century, when the Paris Declaration of 1856 on War at Sea finally abolished piracy and established the scope of seizure of alien ships. Further limitations were introduced by the Eleventh Hague Peace Convention of 1907. The

Twelfth Hague Convention, 1907, est. the International Prize Court, but the Convention did not enter into force.

J. BROWN-SCOTT (ed.), *The Hague Conventions and Declarations of 1899 and 1907*, New York, 1978.

PROBLEMS OF PEACE AND SOCIALISM. A periodical established by a resolution of the First Conference of Communist and Workers' Parties in 1958 as a forum for the exchange of information and opinions; published in Prague, initially in 19 languages, then in 34, co-operating with a large number of Communist and Workers' parties. A theoretical-informative monthly.

PROCEDURAL LAW. A subject of international conventions: Treaty concerning the Union of South American States in respect of Procedural Law, signed on Jan. 11, 1889 at Montevideo, at the First South American Congress on Private International Law. General Principles are as follows:

"Art. 1. Trials and their incidents of whatsoever nature shall be conducted in accordance with the procedural law of the States in whose territory the trials are held. Art. 2. Proofs shall be admitted and weighed according to the law applicable to the juridical act which forms the subject-matter of the proceedings. Those proofs are excluded which by their character are not authorized by the law of the place where the trial is held."

The Treaty came into force for Argentina, Bolivia, Colombia, Paraguay, Peru and Uruguay. The Treaty was also signed by Brazil and Chile but ratifications were not deposited.
The Inter-American Treaty on International Procedural Law was signed on Mar. 19, 1940 at Montevideo, at the Second South-American Congress on Private International Law. The Treaty entered into force for Argentina, Paraguay and Uruguay. The Treaty was also signed by Bolivia, Brazil, Colombia and Peru but ratifications were not deposited.

M.A. VIEIRA (ed.), *Tratados de Montevideo 1888–89 y de 1939–40*, Montevideo, 1959; OAS, *Treaty Series*, No. 9.

PROCLAMATION. The name of a declaration or an official public announcement of international or extraordinary state importance.

PROCREATION. ▷ Artificial Procreation.

PRODUCER ASSOCIATIONS. An international term of the UN system for non-governmental and governmental co-operation among countries producing the same commodity.

PRODUCERS OF PHONOGRAMS. ▷ Phonograms Conventions.

PRODUCTION ENGINEERING. A subject of international co-operation. Organizations reg. with the UIA:

International Institution for Production Engineering Research, f. 1951, Paris. Publ.: *Annuals, Dictionary of Production Engineering.*
Scandinavian Committee on Production Engineering Research, f. 1968, Oslo.

Yearbook of International Organizations.

PRODUCTIVITY. Subject of international co-operation. Organizations reg. with the UIA:

Asian Productivity Organization, f. 1961, Tokyo, Japan, Publ.: *APO News.*
European Association of National Productivity Centres, f. 1966, Brussels, Belgium. Publ.: *EURO Productivity* (monthly).
European Federation of Productivity Services, f. 1961, Stockholm, Sweden.

Yearbook of International Organizations, 1986–87; *The Europa Yearbook 1988. A World Survey*, Vol. 1, London, 1988.

PROFINTERN. Russian abbreviation for *Krasnyj Internacjonal Profsojuzov* "Workers' Unions, The International," organization of workers' unions, not admitted to the International Federation of Workers' Unions (the so-called ▷ Amsterdam International); existed in the years 1921–37 and co-operated with the Communist ▷ International. Organized five congresses – 1921, 1922, 1924, 1928 and 1930 – all held in Moscow. The Soviet workers' union was the strongest group within the Profintern and the French Confederation Generale du Travail, CGT, was its counterpart in capitalist countries.

W.S. SWORAKOWSKI, *The Communist International*, Stanford, 1966.

PROGRAMMING LANGUAGE. An international term since the 1950's for the language in which instructions are given to a computer.
See also ▷ Computer Languages.

PROHIBITIONISM. An international term with a double meaning: (1) the extreme protectionism, a total ban on the import of certain categories of goods; (2) a complete or partial ban on the production, import and retailing of alcohol. In the second half of the 19th century temperance movements came into being, united in 1909 in London as the World Prohibition Federation. Publ.: *International Record* (quarterly).

Yearbook of International Organizations.

PROLETARIANS OF ALL COUNTRIES – UNITE! A historic call, words ending the ▷ Communist Manifesto 1848, written in German by K. Marx and F. Engels, reading in German *"Proletarier aller Länder vereinigt Euch!"*

PROLIFERATION. ▷ Non Proliferation Treaty.

PROMOTION. An international term for presenting an article to the public and finding the most favourable markets for it; subject of international co-operation. Organization reg. with the UIA:

International Institute of Promotion and Prestige, f. 1973, Geneva. Presents the International Promotion Award.

Yearbook of International Organizations.

PRONUNCIAMIENTO. *Spanish* = "proclamation." An international term which appeared in Latin America, initially denoting the uprising of a people against colonial authority, later a rebellion of the armed forces, called in the 20th century golpe de estado or coup d'etat.

PRO RUSSIA. A Papal ecumenical commission, co-ordinating in the Catholic Church the ecumenic work of the Congregation for Eastern Churches and the diplomatic initiatives of the Council for Public Questions Concerning the USSR.

PROSTITUTION AND TRAFFIC IN PERSONS. A subject of international conventions and permanent organized international co-operation in combatting prostitution and traffic in persons.

The first Treaty on the Suppression of the Traffic in White Slaves was signed on Mar. 18, 1904 in Paris with the aim of protecting white women against recruitment to foreign countries. Furthermore, the Convention established forms for covering the travel expenses to their native country of foreign women who engaged in prostitution to earn money to pay their way home.
The International Convention on Elimination of the Traffic in White Slaves was signed May 4, 1910, in Paris,

introducing permanent governmental bodies for the suppression of international traffic in white women.
The Paris Convention of Oct. 4, 1921 and the Geneva Convention on the Prohibition of the Traffic in Women and Children of Sept. 30, 1921 and of Oct. 11, 1933 extended terms of the 1910 convention to include persons under the age of 21 and with signatories taking on the obligation to extend control over emigration employment agencies. The Convention signed on Oct. 11, 1933 in Geneva promised to prosecute criminals who kidnap for prostitution abroad women or girls under 21 even with their consent. This convention was replaced by the UN Convention for the Suppression of the Traffic in Persons and of the Exploitation of the Prostitution of Others, signed on Dec. 2, 1949 which came into force Mar. 21, 1950. The UN Social Commission introduced a new questionnaire, based on the Convention, to study prostitution, whose results are published periodically in the International Review of Criminal Policy. Published in 1959 were the UN's practical recommendations for combatting prostitution. The report of UN experts recommended that governments stop treating prostitution as a criminal offense, since such actions push prostitution into the criminal underground and make possible the exploitation of prostitution by professional extortioners.

UNTS, Vol. 96, pp. 271–319: *UN Yearbook 1949; Étude sur la traité des êtres humaines de prostitution*, UN, New York, 1959.

PROTECTING POWER OR PATRIMONIAL POWER. A state which assumes protection of another state's nationals and property in a third state; as a rule it is a state neutral in a dispute or conflict between two parties and takes over protection of embassy or mission buildings after they have been evacuated by diplomatic staff of the state which offers its interest for protection; it may protect sick or wounded persons remaining in the country or take custody over prisoners of war. The first international convention determining rights and obligations of protecting powers was the Geneva Convention on the Protection of the Sick and Wounded of July 27, 1929, art. 86, item 1, which allowed "protecting states to safeguard interests of belligerent parties." During World War II, Chile, Spain, Portugal, Sweden and the USA in several instances acted as protecting powers whereas Switzerland did so much more often (in 1944 it represented the interests of 35 states). The second Geneva Convention of Aug. 12, 1949, art. 11, greatly extended the status of protecting powers; also the Additional Protocol to the Red Cross Conventions, of Dec. 12, 1977.

W. FRANKLIN, *The Protection of Foreign Interests. A Study in Diplomatic and Consular Practice*, London, 1947; J.S. PICTET, "The New Geneva Conventions for the Protection of War Victims", in: *American Journal of International Law*, No. 45, 1952; H.S. LOVIE, "Prisoners of War and the Protecting Power", in: *American Journal of International Law*, No. 55, 1961.

PROTECTIONISM. An international term for a policy of favoring national production in foreign trade in order to protect it against foreign competition; employed in Europe since the 16th century; at its extreme in Europe and America during the years of the great crisis, 1930–39; consists mainly in raising tariffs on identical products imported from abroad and in applying prohibitionism and a system of preferences. Protectionism appeared in new forms during the 1970s, which beside national forms also included regional ones, particularly integrative groupings; used are quotas, compensating payments, complicated import licenses, and also anti-dumping laws. According to GATT figures, *c.* 40% of the total value of foreign trade in 1970s came under protectionist restrictions. The Eighth OAS Session on July 1, 1978 unanimously adopted a resolution condemning protectionism used against the developing

countries. Also in the UN General Assembly sessions many speakers warned that protectionism was intensifying the world economic crisis.
In the 1980's new trends of protectionism have been noted world wide especially in the United States in OECD countries. The ▷ Uruguay Round negotiations of the GATT started in 1986 with a new effort to support the reduction of trade barriers.

R. BLACKHURST, N. MARTIN, J. TUMIR, *Trade Liberalization, Protectionism and Interdependence, GATT*, Geneva, 1978; *Tariffs, Quotas and Trade: The Politics of Protectionism*, San Francisco, 1979; D. GREENWAY, *International Trade Policy. From Tariffs to the New Protectionism*, London, 1983; C.C. COUGHLIN, K.A. CHRYSTAL, G.E. WOOD, *Protectionist Trade Policies: A Survey, in: Economic Impact*, 1988/3; D. SALVATORE, ed., *The New Protectionist Threat to World Welfare*, New York, 1988; J. BHAGWATI, *Protectionism*, London, 1988; H.V. MILNER, *Resisting Protectionism Global Industries and the Politics of International Trade*, Princeton, NJ, 1988.

PROTECTION OF ALL PERSONS UNDER ANY FORM OF DETECTION OR IMPRISONMENT, PRINCIPLES, 1988. Body of Principles for the Protection of All Persons, Under Any Form of Detention or Imprisonment, adopted without a vote with the GA Res. 43/173 on Dec. 9, 1988. The text is as follows:

Body of Principles for the Protection of All Persons under Any Form of Detention or Imprisonment
Scope of the Body of Principles
These Principles apply for the protection of all persons under any form of detention or imprisonment.
Use of terms
For the purposes of the Body of Principles:
(*a*) "Arrest" means the act of apprehending a person for the alleged commission of an offence or by the action of an authority.
(*b*) "Detained person" means any person deprived of personal liberty except as a result of conviction for an offence;
(*c*) "Imprisoned person" means any person deprived of personal liberty as a result of conviction for an offence;
(*d*) "Detention" means the condition of detained persons as defined above;
(*e*) "Imprisonment" means the condition of imprisoned persons as defined above;
(*f*) The words "a judicial or other authority" mean a judicial or other authority under the law whose status and tenure should afford the strongest possible guarantees of competence, impartiality and independence.
Principle 1. All persons under any form of detention or imprisonment shall be treated in a humane manner and with respect for the inherent dignity of the human person.
Principle 2. Arrest, detention or imprisonment shall only be carried out strictly in accordance with the provision of the law and by competent officials or persons authorized for that purpose.
Principle 3. There shall be no restriction upon or derogation from any of the human rights of persons under any form of detention or imprisonment recognized or existing in any State pursuant to law, conventions, regulations or custom on the pretext that this Body of Principles does not recognize such rights or that it recognizes them to a lesser extent.
Principle 4. Any form of detention or imprisonment and all measures affecting the human rights of a person under any form of detention or imprisonment shall be ordered by, or be subject to the effective control of, a judicial or other authority.
Principle 5. (1) These Principles shall be applied to all persons within the territory of any given State, without distinction of any kind, such as race, colour, sex, language, religion or religious belief, political or other opinion, national ethnic or social origin, property, birth or other status.
(2) Measures applied under the law and designed solely to protect the rights and special status of women, especially pregnant women and nursing mothers, children and juveniles, aged, sick or handicapped persons shall not be deemed to be discriminatory. The need for, and the application of, such measures shall always be subject to review by a judicial or other authority.
Principle 6. No person under any form of detention or imprisonment shall be subjected to torture or to cruel, inhuman or degrading treatment or punishment.* No circumstance whatever may be invoked as a justification for torture or other cruel, inhuman or degrading treatment or punishment.
*The term "cruel, inhuman or degrading treatment or punishment" should be interpreted so as to extend the widest possible protection against abuses, whether physical or mental, including the holding of a detained or imprisoned person in conditions which deprive him, temporarily or permanently, of the use of any of his natural senses, such as sight or hearing, or of his awareness of place and the passing of time.
Principle 7. (1) States should prohibit by law any act contrary to the rights and duties contained in these Principles, make any such act subject to appropriate sanctions and conduct impartial investigations upon complaints.
(2) Officials who have reason to believe that a violation of this Body of Principles has occurred or is is about to occur shall report the matter to their superior authorities and, where necessary, to other appropriate authorities or organs vested with reviewing or remedial powers.
(3) Any other person who has ground to believe that a violation of the Body of Principles has occurred or is about to occur shall have the right to report the matter to the superiors of the officials involved as well as to other appropriate authorities or organs vested with reviewing or remedial powers.
Principle 8. Persons in detention shall be subject to treatment appropriate to their unconvicted status. Accordingly, they shall, whenever possible, be kept separate from imprisoned persons.
Principle 9. The authorities which arrest a person, keep him under detention or investigate the case shall exercise only the powers granted to them under the law and the exercise of these powers shall be subject to recourse to a judicial or other authority.
Principle 10. Anyone who is arrested shall be informed at the time of his arrest of the reason for his arrest shall be promptly informed of any charges against him.
Principle 11. (1) A person shall not be kept in detention without being given an effective opportunity to be heard promptly by a judicial or other authority. A detained person shall have the right to defend himself or to be assisted by counsel as prescribed by law.
(2) A detained person and his counsel, if any, shall receive prompt and full communication of any order of detention, together with the reasons therefor.
(3) A judicial or other authority shall be empowered to review as appropriate the continuance of detention.
Principle 12. (1) There shall be duly recorded:
(*a*) The reasons for the arrest;
(*b*) The time of the arrest and the taking of the arrested person to a place of custody as well as that of his first appearance before a judicial or other authority;
(*c*) The identity of the law enforcement officials concerned;
(*d*) Precise information concerning the place of custody.
(2) Such records shall be communicated to the detained person, or his counsel, if any, in the form prescribed by law.
Principle 13. Any person shall, at the moment of arrest and at the commencement of detention or imprisonment, or promptly thereafter, be provided by the authority responsible for his arrest or imprisonment, respectively, with information on and an explanation of his rights and how to avail himself of such rights.
Principle 14. A person who does not adequately understand or speak the language used by the authorities responsible for his arrest, detention or imprisonment is entitled to receive promptly in a language which he understands the information referred to in principle 10, principle 11, paragraph 2, principle 12, paragraph 1, and principle 13 and to have the assistance, free of charge, if necessary, of an interpreter in connection with legal proceedings subsequent to his arrest.
Principle 15. Notwithstanding the exceptions contained in principle 16, paragraph 4, and principle 18, paragraph 3, communication of the detained or imprisoned person with the outside world, and in particular his family or counsel, shall not be denied for more than a matter of days.
Principle 16. (1) Promptly after arrest and after each transfer from one place of detention or imprisonment to another, a detained or imprisoned person shall be entitled to notify or to require the competent authority to notify members of his family or other appropriate persons of his choice of his arrest, detention or imprisonment or of the transfer and of the place where he is kept in custody.
(2) If a detained or imprisoned person is a foreigner, he shall also be promptly informed of his right to communicate by appropriate means with a consular post or the diplomatic mission of the State of which he is a national or which is otherwise entitled to receive such communication in accordance with international law or with the representative of the competent international organization, if he is a refugee or is otherwise under the protection of an intergovernmental organization.
(3) If a detained or imprisoned person is a juvenile or is incapable of understanding his entitlement, the competent authority shall on its own initiative undertake the notification referred to in this principle. Special attention shall be given to notifying parents or guardians.
(4) Any notification referred to in this principle shall be made or permitted to be made without delay. The competent authority may however delay a notification for a reasonable period where exceptional needs of the investigation so require.
Principle 17. (1) A detained person shall be entitled to have the assistance of a legal counsel. He shall be informed of his right by the competent authority promptly after arrest and shall be provided with reasonable facilities for exercising it.
(2) If a detained person does not have a legal counsel of his own choice, he shall be entitled to have a legal counsel assigned to him by a judicial or other authority in all cases where the interests of justice so require and without payment by him if he does not have sufficient means to pay.
Principle 18. (1) A detained or imprisoned person shall be entitled to communicate and consult with his legal counsel.
(2) A detained or imprisoned person shall be allowed adequate time and facilities for consultations with his legal counsel.
(3) The right of a detained or imprisoned person to be visited by and to consult and communicate, without delay or censorship and in full confidentiality, with his legal counsel may not be suspended or restricted save in exceptional circumstances, to be specified by law or lawful regulations, when it is considered indispensable by a judicial or other authority in order to maintain security and good order.
(4) Interviews between a detained or imprisoned person and his legal counsel may be within sight, but not within the hearing, of a law enforcement official.
(5) Communications between a detained or imprisoned person and his legal counsel mentioned in this principle shall be inadmissible as evidence against the detained or imprisoned person unless they are connected with a continuing or contemplated crime.
Principle 19. A detained or imprisoned person shall have the right to be visited by and to correspond with, in particular, members of his family and shall be given adequate opportunity to communicate with the outside world, subject to reasonable conditions and restrictions as specified by law or lawful regulations.
Principle 20. If a detained or imprisoned person so requests, he shall if possible be kept in a place of detention or imprisonment reasonably near his usual place of residence.
Principle 21. (1) It shall be prohibited to take undue advantage of the situation of a detained or imprisoned person for the purpose of compelling him to confess, to incriminate himself otherwise or to testify against any other person.
(2) No detained person while being interrogated shall be subject to violence, threats or methods of interrogation which impair his capacity of decision or his judgement.
Principle 22. No detained or imprisoned person shall, even with his consent, be subjected to any medical or scientific experimentation which may be detrimental to his health.
Principle 23. (1) The duration of any interrogation of a detained or imprisoned person and of the intervals between interrogations as well as the identity of the officials who conducted the interrogations and other

persons present shall be recorded and certified in such form as may be prescribed by law.

(2) A detained or imprisoned person, or his counsel when provided by law, shall have access to the information described above.

Principle 24. A proper medical examination shall be offered to a detained or imprisoned person as promptly as possible after his admission to the place of detention or imprisonment, and thereafter medical care and treatment shall be provided whenever necessary. This care and treatment shall be provided free of charge.

Principle 25. A detained or imprisoned person or his counsel shall, subject only to reasonable conditions to ensure security and good order in the place of detention or imprisonment, have the right to request or petition a judicial or other authority for a second medical examination or opinion.

Principle 26. The fact that a detained or imprisoned person underwent a medical examination, the name of the physician and the results of such an examination shall be duly recorded. Access to such records shall be ensured. Modalities therefor shall be in accordance with relevant roles of domestic law.

Principle 27. Non-compliance with these Principles in obtaining evidence shall be taken into account in determining the admissibility of such evidence against a detained or imprisoned person.

Principle 28. A detained or imprisoned person shall have the right to obtain within the limits of available resources, if from public sources, reasonable quantities of educational, cultural and informational material, subject to reasonable conditions to ensure security and good order in the place of detention or imprisonment.

Principle 29. (1) In order to supervise the strict observance of relevant laws and regulations, places of detention shall be visited regularly by qualified and experienced persons appointed by, and responsible to, a competent authority distinct from the authority directly in charge of the administration of the place of detention or imprisonment.

(2) A detained or imprisoned person shall have the right to communicate freely and in full confidentiality with the persons who visit the places of detention or imprisonment in accordance with paragraph 1, subject to reasonable conditions to ensure security and good order in such places.

Principle 30. (1) The types of conduct of the detained or imprisoned person that constitute disciplinary offences during detention or imprisonment, the description and duration of disciplinary punishment that may be inflicted and the authorities competent to impose such punishment shall be specified by law or lawful regulations and duly published.

(2) A detained or imprisoned person shall have the right to be heard before disciplinary action is taken. He shall have the right to bring such action to higher authorities for review.

Principle 31. The appropriate authorities shall endeavour to ensure, according to domestic law, assistance when needed to dependent and, in particular, minor members of the families of detained or imprisoned persons and shall devote a particular measure of care to the appropriate custody of children left without supervision.

Principle 32. (1) A detained person or his counsel shall be entitled at any time to take proceedings according to domestic law before a judicial or other authority to challenge the lawfulness of his detention in order to obtain his release without delay, if it is unlawful.

(2) The proceedings referred to in paragraph 1 shall be simple and expeditious and at no cost for detained persons without adequate means. The detaining authority shall produce without unreasonable delay the detained person before the reviewing authority.

Principle 33. (1) A detained or imprisoned person or his counsel shall have the right to make a request or complaint regarding his treatment, in particular in case of torture or other cruel, inhuman or degrading treatment, to the authorities responsible for the administration of the place of detention and to higher authorities and, when necessary, to appropriate authorities vested with reviewing or remedial powers.

(2) In those cases where neither the detained or imprisoned person nor his counsel has the possibility to exercise his rights under paragraph 1, a member of the family of the detained or imprisoned person or any other person who has knowledge of the case may exercise such rights.

(3) Confidentiality concerning the request or complaint shall be maintained if so requested by the complainant.

(4) Every request or complaint shall be promptly dealt with and replied to without undue delay. If the request or complaint is rejected or, in case of inordinate delay, the complainant shall be entitled to bring it before a judicial or other authority. Neither the detained or imprisoned person nor any complainant under paragraph 1 shall suffer prejudice for making a request or complaint.

Principle 34. Whenever the death or disappearance of a detained or imprisoned person occurs during his detention or imprisonment, an inquiry into the cause of death or disappearance shall be held by a judicial or other authority, either on its own motion or at the instance of a member of the family of such a person or any person who has the knowledge of the case. When circumstances so warrant, such an inquiry shall be held on the same procedural basis whenever the death or disappearance occurs shortly after the termination of the detention or imprisonment. The findings of such inquiry or a report thereon shall be made available upon request, unless doing so would jeopardize an ongoing criminal investigation.

Principle 35. (1) Damage incurred because of acts or omissions by a public official contrary to the rights contained in these Principles shall be compensated according to the applicable rules on liability provided by domestic laws.

(2) Information required to be recorded under these Principles shall be available in accordance with procedures provided by domestic law for use in claiming compensation under this principle.

Principle 36. (1) A detained persons suspected of or charged with a criminal offence shall be presumed innocent and shall be treated as such until proved guilty according to law in a public trial at which he has had all the guarantees necessary for his defence.

(2) The arrest or detention of such a person pending investigation and trial shall be carried out only for the purposes of the administration of justice on grounds and under conditions and procedures specified by law. The imposition of restrictions upon such a person which are not strictly required for the purpose of the detention or to prevent hindrance to the process of investigation or the administration of justice, or for the maintenance of security and good order in the place of detention shall be forbidden.

Principle 37. A person detained on a criminal charge shall be brought before a judicial or other authority provided by law promptly after his arrest. Such authority shall decide without delay upon the lawfulness and necessity of detention. No person may be kept under detention pending investigation or trial except upon the written order of such an authority. A detained person shall, when brought before such an authority, have the right to make a statement on the treatment received by him while in custody.

Principle 38. A person detained on a criminal charge shall be entitled to trial within a reasonable time or to a release pending trial.

Principle 39. Except in special cases provided for by law, a person detained on a criminal charge shall be entitled, unless a judicial or other authority decides otherwise in the interest of the administration of justice, to release pending trial subject to the conditions that may be imposed in accordance with the law. Such authority shall keep the necessity of detention under review.

General clause. Nothing in the present Body of Principles shall be construed as restricting or derogating from any right defined in the International Covenant on Civil and Political Rights. (The fully text ▷ Human Rights, International Convention on Civil and Political Rights, 1966).

UN Resolutions and Decisions adopted by the General Assembly during the First Part of its Forty-Third Session. From 20 September to 22 December, 1988, New York, 1989, pp. 584–591.

PROTECTION OF MOVABLE PROPERTY OF HISTORIC VALUE, TREATY ON, 1935. ▷ Historic Value Property Protection.

PROTECTION OF STATE TERRITORY. A subject of international law resulting from the principle of the territorial integrity of a state and the inviolability of its borders, the obligation to respect national boundaries in international relations. See principles III and V of the ▷ Helsinki Final Act, 1975.

PROTECTION OF THE AMERICAN NATIONS HERITAGE, 1976. The Convention on the Protection of the Archaeological, Historical and Artistic Heritage of the American Nations, also called the Convention of San Salvador, adopted on June 16, 1976 by the OAS General Assembly. The text is as follows:

"The Governments of the Member States of the Organization of American States,

having seen the continuous looting and plundering of the native cultural heritage suffered by the countries of the hemisphere, particularly the Latin American countries; and considering:

that such acts of pillage have damaged and reduced the archaeological, historical, and artistic wealth, through the national character of their peoples is expressed;

that there is a basic obligation to transmit to coming generations the legacy of their cultural heritage;

that this heritage can only be protected and preserved through mutual appreciation and respect for such properties, within a framework of the soundest inter-American co-operation; and that the member states have repeatedly demonstrated their willingness to establish standards for the protection and surveillance of the archaeological, historical, and artistic heritage, declare:

that it is essential to take steps, at both the national and international levels, for the most effective protection and retrieval of cultural treasures, and

have agreed upon the following:

Art. 1. The purpose of this Convention is to identify, register, protect, and safeguard the property making up the cultural heritage of the American nations in order: (a) to prevent illegal exportation or importation of cultural property; and (b) to promote co-operation among the American states for mutual awareness and appreciation of their cultural property.

Art. 2. The cultural property referred to in the preceding article is that included in the following categories: (a) Monuments, objects, fragments of ruined buildings, and archaeological materials belonging to American cultures existing prior to contact with European culture, as well as remains of human beings, fauna, and flora related to such cultures;

(b) Monuments, buildings, objects of an artistic, utilitarian, and ethnological nature, whole or in fragments, from the colonial era and the Nineteenth Century;

(c) Libraries and archives; incunabula and manuscripts; books and other publications, iconographies, maps and documents published before 1850;

(d) All objects originating after 1850 that the States Parties have recorded as cultural property, provided that they have given notice of such registration to the other parties to the treaty;

(e) All cultural property that any of the States Parties specifically declares to be included within the scope of this convention.

Art. 3. The cultural property included in the above article shall receive maximum protection at the international level, and its exportation and importation shall be considered unlawful, except when the state owning it authorizes its exportation for purposes of promoting knowledge of national cultures.

Art. 4. Any disagreement between the parties to this Convention, regarding application of the definitions and categories of Art. 2. to specific property, shall be resolved definitively by the inter-American Council for Education, Science, and Culture (CIECC), following an opinion by the inter-American Committee on Culture.

Art. 5. The cultural heritage of each state consists of property mentioned in Art. 2, found or created in its territory and legally acquired items of foreign origin.

Art. 6. The control exercised by each state over its cultural heritage and any actions that may be taken to reclaim items belonging to it are imprescriptible.

Art. 7. Regulations on ownership of cultural property and its transfer within the territory of each state shall be

P

governed by domestic legislation. With a view to preventing unlawful trade in such goods, the following measures shall be encouraged:

(a) Registration of collections and of transfer of cultural property subject to protection;

(b) Registration of transactions carried out by establishments engaged in the sale and purchase of such property;

(c) Prohibition of imports of cultural property from other states without appropriate certificate and authorization.

Art. 8. Each state is responsible for identifying, registering, protecting, preserving, and safeguarding its cultural heritage; in fulfillment of these functions each state undertakes to encourage:

(a) Preparation, in accordance with its respective constitutional standards, of rules and legislative provisions required for effective protection of this heritage from destruction resulting from neglect or inadequate preservation work;

(b) Establishment of technical organs entrusted specifically with the protection and safeguarding of cultural property;

(c) Establishment and maintenance of an inventory and record of cultural property, to make it possible to identify and locate it;

(d) The establishment and development of museums, libraries, archives, and other centers for the protection and preservation of cultural property;

(e) The delimitation and protection of archaeological sites and places of historical and artistic interest;

(f) Exploration, excavation, investigation, and preservation of archaeological sites and objects by scientific institutions, in collaboration with the national agency in charge of the archaeological heritage.

Art. 9. Each State Party shall prevent by all available means any unlawful excavation in its territory or any removal of cultural property therefrom."

OAS Annual Report, 1977.

PROTECTORATE. An international term used in two contexts: a colonial protectorate imposed on a weaker state by a colonial power or an international protectorate usually resulting from a compromise between powers over disputed territory, e.g. resolutions of the Congress of Vienna, 1815, that the Polish city of Cracow would remain "a free, independent and strictly neutral city under the protectorate of Russia, Austria and Prussia."

R. KIRCHSCHLAEGER, "Protektorat," in: STRUPP-SCHLOCHAUER *Wörterbuch des Völkerrechts*, Berlin, 1962; R.L. BLEDSOE, B.A. BOCZEK, *The International Law Dictionary*, Oxford, 1987.

PROTEINS. A subject of international WHO action to prevent the danger of a protein crisis in the world; initiated in 1968 by the UN General Assembly Res. 2416/XXIII, in connection with the worldwide hunger problem. The WHO carries on regular research in this domain.

PROTEST. An international term for diplomatic objection of one government against a decision of another government, considered harmful to the interests of the protesting state or to the interest of peace.

J.C.M. GIBSON, "Some Observations on the Part of Protest in International Law," in: *The British Yearbook of International Law*, 1953.

PROTESTANT CHURCHES. ▷ Protestantism.

PROTESTANT EPISCOPAL CHURCH. The name adopted in the USA for the ▷ Church of England, after the US Declaration of Independence, 1776. Organized permanent Executive Council and after World War I, takes an active part in the ecumenical movement. Member of the World Council of Churches.

J. DILLENBERGER, C. WELCH, *Protestant Christianity. Interpreted Through Its Development*, New York, 1954.

PROTESTANTISM. An international term for the creeds which sprang up from the 16th-century religious movement called the Reformation; the name comes from the protest of 18 states of the German Reich, supported by Martin Luther, on Feb. 19, 1529 at Speier against the resolutions of the Catholic majority in the parliament of the Reich. The Protestant Churches are divided into: Church of England, Calvinist, Episcopalian, Evangelical, Presbyterian, and others. In the 19th and 20th centuries they formed many international Christian organizations. They play a leading role in the Ecumenical Movement. (▷ World Council of Churches).

M.E. MARTY, *Protestantism*, London, 1972.

PROTOCOL. An ambiguous international term for (1) a section of the ministry of foreign affairs or of an international organization responsible for diplomatic protocol; for (2) report of an international bi- or multilateral meeting; for (3) bi- or multilateral protocol agreements, e.g. Guatemalan Air Protocol, 1971.

PROTRACTED WAR. An international term for any kind of confrontation between two states or blocks of states in economic, political or cultural fields which results in military competition.

PROVOCATIONS. A planned deceitful international incident triggered to aggravate a dispute or cause a diplomatic or even a military conflict; cited by the Nuremberg Military Tribunal as a crime against peace. The Court heard the case of the so-called Gleivitz provocation, an incident on the eve of the German aggression against Poland, Aug. 31, 1939, involving the overpowering of a broadcast station, then located in Germany by German soldiers wearing Polish military uniforms who broadcast a communiqué to the effect that the Polish army had entered the northeastern part of Silesia and had seized the radio station. An SS Officer, A.H. Naujock, who was in charge of the action coded "Tannenberg," related in detail on Nov. 20, 1945, the preparation and the course of the action before the Nuremberg Court. Another example of diplomatic provocation is the ▷ Ems telegram, 1870 that brought about the French–Prussian war, 1870–1871.

A. SPIESS, H. LICHTENSTEIN, *Das Unternehmen "Tannenberg"*, München, 1971.

PROXYWAR. An international term for a war between two states, supported by two larger powers for many reasons deeply though not directly involved in the conflict.

Sollicitudo Rei Socialis, Encyclical letter of the Supreme Pontiff John Paul II for the Twentieth Anniversary of Populorum Progressio, London, 1988.

PRUSSIA. A German state, abolished formally by the Allied Control Council for Germany on Feb. 25, 1947. The text of the Four Power Act reads as follows:

"Law No. 46. Abolition of the State of Prussia.

The Prussian State which from early days has been a bearer of militarism and reaction in Germany has de facto ceased to exist.

Guided by the interests of preservation of peace and security of peoples and with the desire to assure further reconstruction of the political life of Germany on a democratic basis, the Control Council enacts as follows:

Art. 1. The Prussian State together with its central government and all its agencies is abolished.

Art. II. Territories which were a part of the Prussian State and which are at present under the supreme authority of the Control Council will receive the status of Lander or will be absorbed into Lander.

The provisions of this Article are subject to such revision and other provisions as may be agreed upon by

the Allied Control Authority, or as may be laid down in the future Constitution of Germany.

Art. III. The State and administrative functions as well as the assets and liabilities of the former Prussian State will be transferred to appropriate Lander subject to such agreements as may be necessary and made by the Allied Control Authority.

Art. IV. This law becomes effective on the day of the signature.

Done at Berlin on 25 February 1947."

J. GUTZEIT, *Geschichte der deutschen Polen-Entrechtung*, Danzig, 1928; *Journal Officiel du Conseil de Contrôle en Allemagne*, No. 46, Berlin, 1947; S.A. CRAIG, *The Prussian Army in Politic, 1618–1945*, Oxford, 1957; K. ZEMACK, "Die Geschichte Preussens und das Problem der deutsch-polnischen Beziehungen", in: *Jahrbücher für Geschichte Osteuropas*, Wiesbaden, 1983; S. SALMONOWICZ, *Prusy.Dzieje państwa i społeczeństwa*, Poznań, 1987.

PRUSSIAN WAR, 1866. A military conflict between Prussia and Austria, which started on June 14, 1866 and after the Prussian victory at Königgratz, July 3, ended on July 26, 1866 at Nikolsburg with an armistice and on Aug. 23, 1866 with the ▷ Austro–Prussian Peace Treaty 1866. ▷ German Confederation 1815–1866.

G.F. MARTENS, *Nouveau Recueil Général*, Vol. 18, pp. 316 and 344.

PSYCHIATRY. A subject of international co-operation. Organizations reg. with the UIA:

Association of Psychiatric Treatment of Offenders, f. 1975, London.

Caribbean Psychiatric Association, f. 1967, Wilemstedt, Curacao.

European Union for Child Psychiatry, f. 1954, Vienna.

International Association for Child Psychiatry and Allied Professions, f. 1948, London. Consultative status with WHO and ECOSOC. Publ.: *International Yearbook of Child Psychiatry*.

Latin American Psychiatric Association, f. 1975, Buenos Aires.

Mediterranean Association of Psychiatry, f. 1967, Palma de Mallorca.

Visiting International Psychiatric Teams Inc., f. 1963, Washington, DC. Publ.: *Reports*.

World Psychiatric Association, f. 1961, London. Official relations with WHO and ECOSOC.

Yearbook of International Organizations.

PSYCHO-ANALYSIS. A subject of international co-operation. Organizations reg. with the UIA:

European Psycho-Analytical Federation, f. 1967, London. Publ.: *Bulletin intérieur*.

International Psycho-Analytical Association, f. 1910, London.

Members: National societies in 26 countries. Every 2 years congress. Aims: development of psycho-analysis, scientific branch founded by Freud, as much from the point of view of pure psychology as from that of its applications to medicine or to other scientific fields.

Yearbook of International Organizations.

PSYCHOLOGICAL WAR. The creation through the mass media of international tensions with the aim of helping the state waging psychological war to attain certain ideological, political or economical objectives. Before World War II commonly accepted in the world press was the term "war of nerves," which was supplanted by the more complex psychological war, developed into a modern weapon of cold war. One of the instruments of psychological war is radio-diversion. Organization reg. with the UIA:

Psywar Society, Société d'etude de la guerre psychologique, f. 1958, Kettering, UK. Serves as an international association of psychological warfare historians and collectors of aerial propaganda leaflets. Publ.: *Falling Leaf Magazine*.

M. BALFOUR, *Propaganda in War, 1939–1945: Organizations, Policies and Publics in Britain and Germany*, Boston, 1979; *Yearbook of International Organizations*; D. ROBERTSON, *Guide to Modern Defense and Strategy*, Detroit, 1988.

PSYCHOLOGY. A subject of international co-operation. Organizations reg. with the UIA:

European Association of Experimental Social Psychology, f. 1970, Cambridge. Publ.: *European Journal of Social Psychology*.
Inter-American Society of Psychology, f. 1951, Bogotá. Publ.: *Revista Interamericana de Psicologia* (quarterly).
International Association for Religion and Parapsychology, f. 1972, Tokyo. Publ.: *Religion and Parapsychology* (quarterly).
International Association for Analytical Psychology, f. 1957, Zurich. Publ.: *Congress Proceedings*.
International Association for Cross-Cultural Psychology, f. 1972, Kiriston, Canada. Publ.: *Journal of Cross-Cultural Psychology*.
International Association of Applied Psychology, f. 1920, Liège.
International Association of Individual Psychology, f. 1954, New York. Publ.: *Individual Psychology*.
International Association for Sport Psychology, f. 1965, Rome. Publ. *Journal*.
International Catholic Association for the Study of Medical Psychology, f. 1949, Fribourg.
International Council of Psychologists, f. 1942, New York.
International Society for the Psychology of Writing, f. 1961, Milan, Italy. Publ.: *Revista internazionali di psicologia ipnosi* (quarterly).
International Union of Psychological Science, f. 1951, Austin, Texas. Publ.: *International Journal of Psychology*.
Psywar Society (▷ Psychological War).
Society for Multivariante Experimental Psychology, f. 1960, Manchester.

Yearbook of International Organizations; R. HARRE, R. LAMB eds., *The Encyclopedic Dictionary of Psychology*, MIT, Mass., 1983,

PSYCHOPATHOLOGY. A subject of international research. Organization reg. with the UIA:

International Society of Art and Psychopathology, f. 1959, Paris. Aims: group specialists interested in the problem of expression and artistic activities in relation to psychiatric, sociological and psychological research. Members: at least two-thirds doctors, the rest artists, aestheticians, critics, criminologists, linguists and specialists from other disciplines. Publ.: *Confinia Psychiatrica* (quarterly).

Yearbook of International Organizations.

PSYCHOPHARMACOLOGY. A subject of international co-operation. Organization reg. with the UIA:

Collegium Internationale Neuro-psychopharmacologicum, f. 1957, Munich.

Yearbook of International Organizations.

PSYCHOTRONICS. The science of the energetics of life, subject of international co-operation. The first International Congress of Psychotronic Research was held in July, 1973 in Prague with the participation of 300 scientists from East and West; it established the International Association for Psychotronic Research, in Toronto. Publ.: *Psychotronics*. The second Congress was held in Monte Carlo, 1975, the third in Tokyo.

Yearbook of International Organizations

PSYCHOTROPIC DRUGS. The hallucinogenic drugs such as ▷ LSD-25 acknowledged by UN General Assembly Res. 2584/XXIV of 1970 as a new form of narcotic drugs; subject of international control as stipulated by the WHO Convention of 1971 on Psychotropic Substances, which came into force on Aug. 16, 1976 aimed at protecting humans

against narcotic drugs produced primarily by the pharmaceutic industry. Under its terms WHO is obliged to submit reports to the UN Commission on Narcotic Drugs on medicines containing psychotropic substances and the way they should be controlled nationally or internationally. The WHO evaluation should include "the extent or likelihood of abuse, the degree of seriousness of the public health and social problem and the degree of usefulness of the substance in medical therapy."

"Controlling Psychotropic Substances," in: *WHO Chronicle*, Jan., 1978, pp. 3–8.

PTA. ▷ Preferential Trade Area for East and Southern Africa.

PTBT, PARTIAL TEST BAN TREATY. ▷ Outer Space Moscow Treaty 1963.

PUBLIC ADMINISTRATION. ▷ UN Public Administration Programme.

PUBLICATION. An international term defined by the Copyright Universal Convention 1952, as follows:

"Publication ... means the reproduction in tangible form and the general distribution to the public of copies of a work from which it can be read or otherwise visually perceived." (Art. VI.)

UNTS, Vol. 216, p. 142.

PUBLICATIONS OF THE UN. The UN Department of Conference Services Publishing Division/Sales Section (New York, N.Y. 10017, USA or Palais des Nations, 1211 Geneva 10, Switzerland) publishes an annual Catalogue of United Nations Publications, Catalogue of Periodicals, Annuals and Special Series and Official Records Catalogue.

"The Basic Facts About the United Nations" issued annually or bi-annually since 1948.
The "Everyone's United Nations" (formerly: "Everyman's United Nations") issued irregularly since 1948.
"Yearbook of the United Nations" issued annually since 1946/47.
"Statistic Yearbook" issued since 1949.
"United Nations Treaty Series" began in 1946/47, continues the "League of Nations Treaty Series" which dates back to 1921.
"UN Chronicle" issued monthly since 1964; quarterly since 1987 (English, French, Spanish and Arabic editions).

United Nations Publications, 1990, New York, 1989.

PUBLIC CLEANING. A subject of international co-operation. Organization reg. with the UIA:

International Public Cleaning Association, f. 1931, London.
Members: municipal institutions of Austria, Belgium, Canada, Czechoslovakia, Denmark, Finland, France, FRG, Great Britain, Japan, the Netherlands, Spain, Sweden, Switzerland and Yugoslavia. Holds since May, 1973 every two years an Inter-Clean Exposition in Amsterdam, and an Urban-Exposition in Zagreb.

Yearbook of International Organizations.

PUBLIC EMPLOYEES. A subject of the ILO Convention concerning Protection of the Right to Organize Employment in the Public Service, 1978. The Convention says public employees should have "the civil and political rights which are essential for the normal exercise of freedom of association" and settlement of disputes should be made either through negotiation, or through "independent and impartial machinery, such as mediation, conciliation and arbitration, established in such a manner as to ensure the confidence of the parties." ▷ ILO Conventions.

PUBLIC ENTERPRISE. A subject of international co-operation. On the initiative of the UN the International Centre of Public Enterprises was established on Jan. 1, 1979 in Ljubljana, with the task of training cadres, teaching the principles and procedures of planning and developing various forms of workers' self-management.

PUBLIC OPINION. A subject of international research. Organizations reg. with the UIA:

European Society for Opinion and Marketing Research, f. 1948, Amsterdam. Publ. *ESOMAR Handbook*.
International Survey Library Association, f. 1964, Williamstown, Mass. USA.
World Association for Public Opinion Research, f. 1947, Montreal. Consultative status with ECOSOC and UNESCO. Publ.: *Newsletter*.

G.H. GALLUP, *A Guide to Public Opinion Polls*, New York, 1948; J.W. ALBIG, *Modern Public Opinion*, London, 1956; H.L. CHILDS, *Public Opinion: Nature, Formation and Role*, London, 1965; *Yearbook of International Organizations*.

PUBLIC ORDER CLAUSE. A principle stating that due to special circumstances a foreign law is not applied because of local customs of a country, although it is recognized in that country's private international law (e.g. polygamy, which is accepted in some states, is not respected under the law of the states that make only monogamy legal).

P. LAGARDE, *Recherches sur l'ordre public en Droit International Privé*, Paris, 1959; S. BEITZKE, "*Ordre public*," in: *STRUPP-SCHLOCHAUER Wörterbuch des Völkerrechts*, Berlin, 1961, pp, 665–667.

PUBLIC RELATIONS. A subject of international co-operation. Organizations reg. with the UIA:

European Federation of Public Relations, f. 1959, Brussels.
European Union of Public Relations, f. 1972, Parma, Italy.
Inter-American Federation of Public Relations Associations, f. 1961, Caracas. Consultative status with ECOSOC.
International Conference on University Education for Public Relations, f. 1961, Petit-Enghein, Belgium.
International Public Relations Association, f. 1955, Geneva. Publ.: *Members Newsletters*.
Nuclear Public Relations Contact Group, f. 1961, Rome. Publ.: *The Nuclear Controversy*.
Pan Pacific Public Relations Federation, f. 1958, Honolulu.
Public Relations Centre of the International Union of Railways, f. 1969, Paris. Publ.: *Ferinfor*.

R. SIMON, *Perspectives in Public Relations*, London, 1966; *Yearbook of International Organizations*.

PUBLISHERS' ORGANIZATIONS. Organizations reg. with the UIA:

Association of Publishers of European Legal and Economic Works, f. 1976, Paris.
Association of South East Asian Publishers, f. 1972, Kuala Lumpur.
EEC Community of Associations of Newspaper Publishers, f. 1960, Brussels.
International Association of Scholarly Publishers, f. 1972, Toronto.
International Federation of Newspaper Publishers, f. 1940, Paris. Consultative status with ECOSOC, UNESCO, ITU and Council of Europe. Publ.: *News Bulletin, Newspaper Technique Documentation*.
International Group of Scientific, Technical and Medical Publishers, f. 1969, Amsterdam. Consultative status with UNESCO.
International Publishers Advertising Representatives Association, f. 1964, London. Publ.: *Bulletin*.
International Publishers Association, f. 1896, Geneva. Consultative status with UNESCO, ECOSOC and WIPO. Publ.: *Newsletters*.

P

Yearbook of International Organizations, 1986/87; The Europa Yearbook 1988. A World Survey, Vol. I, London, 1988.

"PUEBLO". An American reconnaissance ship, subject of an international conflict between the USA and North Korea, caused by its incursion into the territorial waters of the Korean People's Democratic Republic, where it was arrested by Korean gunboats and interned. The captain and 82 officers and marines confessed that the ship was carrying out a spying mission. In a letter addressed to the government of the Korean Democratic People's Republic the US government admitted to having violated the territorial sovereignty of the Korean Democratic People's Republic and committed itself to cease such actions; in return, the crew of the *Pueblo* was released on Dec. 22, 1968, but the ship was confiscated by the Korean Democratic People's Republic.

V. MARCHETTI, J.D. MARKS, *The CIA and the Cult of Intelligence*, New York, 1975, pp. 197–204.

PUERTO RICO. Commonwealth of Puerto Rico. An island in the Caribbean between the Dominican Republic and US Virgin Islands. Area: 8,860 sq. km. Pop. 1980 census: 3,196,520. Capital: San Juan with 434,849 inhabitants, 1980. Official languages: English and Spanish. Currency: US dollar.
International relations: Porto Rico was a Spanish colony from 18th century until Dec. 10, 1898, when Spain ceded to the US. The name Puerto Rico was introduced by the US Congress on May 17, 1932. The US territory of Puerto Rico on July 25, 1952 was proclaimed as the Commonwealth of Puerto Rico with its own Senate and House of Representatives. On Nov. 27, 1953 President D. Eisenhower informed the UN General Assembly that, "if at any time the Legislative Assembly of Puerto Rico adopts a resolution in favor of more complete or even absolute independence" he "will immediately thereafter recommend to Congress that such independence be granted." The UN General Assembly's Special Committee on the Situation with regard to the Implementation of the Declaration on the Granting of Independence to Colonial Countries and Peoples continued in the 1980s examination of the statute of Puerto Rico. On Aug. 29, 1983 the UN Decolonization Committee reaffirmed the full right to independence of the Puertorican people; on Aug. 24, 1984 passed a resolution (11 to 2 with 9 abstentions) urging independence for Puerto Rico. The question was never brought before the UN General Assembly due to the veto of the USA.

A. BIRD, *Bibliografía Puertoriqueña 1930–1945*, 2 Vols., San Juan, 1946–47; R.A. CZAMPSAY, *Puerto Rico*, Newton Abbot, 1973; *UN Yearbook*, 1980; *UN Chronicle*, November, 1982, and January, 1984; *The Europa Year Book 1984. A World Survey*, Vol. II, pp. 2281–2290, London, 1984; P.S. FALK ed., *The Political Status of Puerto Rico*, Lexington, Mass., 1986.

PUERTO VALLARTA ANTI-DRUG TRAFFIC DECLARATION. An intergovernmental Declaration of the United States, Belize, Bolivia, Brazil, Colombia, Costa Rica, Ecuador, Guatemala, Jamaica, Mexico, Peru, Venezuela, signed in Puerto Vallarta, Mexico, on October 1986, after three days broad examination of drug trafficking and abuse. The text of the Declaration accepted by consensus expresses the following statement:

(1) A reiteration of the firm political decision to forcefully continue in the struggle against the crimes that endanger the health of the peoples represented at this Meeting, and the permanent determination to prevent and correct drug abuse. The gravity and complexity of these problems that cause severe damage to society and its institutions was stressed. It was added that it is necessary to act against this crime against health at

different stages, beginning with the planning and financing of the narcotics trade and including consumption of drugs and psychotropics.
(2) The unavoidable need for objective in-depth knowledge of the factors that determine or propitiate drug traffic and abuse was recognized. It was stated that an efficient struggle against these problems implies, beyond police and legal measures, a firm and vigorous effort on behalf of social, economic and cultural development, in the belief that this type of factor has a determinant influence on the appearance and development of drug traffic and abuse.
(3) The convenience of favoring legitimate coordination of tasks among the region's countries was recognized, taking into account that drug trafficking is an internationally executed crime. In order to achieve this end the countries will adopt the measures that each considers pertinent to effectively share information and provide adequate assistance in penal matters, all within each country's constitutional and legal framework.
(4) Taking into account the present characteristics of delinquency against the health of the individual, the family and especially against children and youth, note was taken of legislative and institutional reforms undertaken by different countries. It was considered convenient to further update or modernize national legislation on the matter as well as the means and instruments to apply said legislation, all in the terms that each country considers convenient.
(5) It was also noted that several countries lack the necessary resources to strike at these crimes and to correct their causes. Thus, it was considered convenient to favor the use of resources secured by or confiscated from those involved in these delinquent activities in order to support national and international campaigns against drug traffic and abuse. Each participant will review the means and terms of promoting this measure.
(6) The convenience of improving, technical qualifications and equipment for the development of national campaigns against drug traffic and abuse was emphasized. Thus, participants in the Meeting expressed their willingness to support each other in this respect in accordance to measures allowed for by each nation's legislation.
(7) Reports were heard on the significant efforts many nations are carrying out to prevent and remedy drug abuse. Within this framework, it was considered necessary to support broad community mobilization in these countries, respecting prevailing norms and traditions to develop an awareness of the gravity of the problems under examination and of the need to prevent and eradicate them through the joint effort of different social sectors. The development of this awareness in the family, at schools and at the work place is extremely important.
(8) Some of the participants proposed setting up a working group or committee in charge of planning measures to further greater regional cooperation with the purpose of effectively reducing production, trafficking and illicit consumption of drugs and psychotropics. The suggestion was left open with the agreement that it should be acted on as soon as possible, at a future meeting of the region's Ministers of Justice and Attorney Generals represented at Puerto Vallarta.
(9) Likewise, the usefulness of meetings such as this was recognized, as they serve to stimulate free and efficient exchange of points of view in an atmosphere of mutual appreciation, harmony and respect. Suggestions were heard for possible future meetings of this type to be convened by the interested countries following consultations with the nations represented at the Puerto Vallarta Meeting, and if such were the case, with other countries of America whose presence would be useful depending on the state of drug trafficking and abuse in these countries.
(10) The participants stated their recognition of the efforts made by all to be present at the Puerto Vallarta Meeting, as well as everyone's pertinent expositions. They also confirmed their mutually binding and firm resolve to participate in a common struggle against drug trafficking and abuse.

Puerto Vallarta, October 10, 1986.

PUGWASH CONFERENCE ON SCIENCE AND WORLD AFFAIRS. An international institution for peace whose history is the following:

In 1954 the idea was put forward of calling a meeting of scientists of the world for the purpose of presenting international opinion on the final consequences of a nuclear war and the necessity of finding means for preventing it as expressed in two concurrent statements; by the premier of India, Jawaharlal Nehru, and the British philosopher B. Russell. Both were supported by leading physicists such as A. Einstein, M. Born, P. Bridgman, L. Infeld, F. Joliot-Curie, H. Mueller, L. Pauling, C. Powell, J. Rotblat, and Hideki Yukawa in a Manifesto signed in Apr.–May, 1955 and announced in London on July 9, 1955.
The First Conference was scheduled to be held in Delhi at the end of 1956, but world conditions at that time caused postponement; in the end the scientists accepted the invitation of the North American millionaire, C. Eaton, to come to his estate in New Scotland, Canada, called Pugwash, where the First Conference was held in July, 1957 with the participation of 22 scientists from both East and West; it was chaired by Bertrand Russell. The conferences are closed to the press. The organizer is the Permanent Pugwash Committee composed of three representatives each from the USA, Great Britain and the USSR, and one each from Czechoslovakia, France, India, Poland and Italy. The Pugwash group is composed of members from 30 states. Executive Office: Geneva; USA Office: American Academy of Arts and Science, Boston. USSR Office: Soviet Academy of Sciences, Moscow; publ.: *Pugwash Newsletter* (quarterly).

J. ROTBLAT, *Scientists in the Quest for Peace: A History of the Pugwash Conferences*, London, 1972; *Yearbook of International Organizations*; J. HOLDREN, ed., *Strategic Defences and the Future of the Arms Race. A PUGWASH Symposium*, London, 1987; The Chemical Industry and the Projected Chemical Weapons Convention, *Proceedings of a SIPRI-PUGWASH Conference*, London, 1987.

PUNIC WARS. ▷ Carthage-Rome Peace Treaty. ▷ Carthage.

PUNITIVE EXPEDITION. A colonial term for armed attacks of the forces of colonial powers, usually marines, on dependent countries for the purpose of extracting tribute or punishing the population for signs of disobedience against the will of the invader. The authorities of China justified their "self-defensive counterattack" in Vietnam in Apr., 1979 as the application of a "punitive expedition" in retaliation for the participation of the Vietnamese armed forces in Laos in battles against the pro-Chinese régime of Pol Pot.

KEESING's *Contemporary Archive*, 1979.

PUNTA DEL ESTE. The fashionable resort of Uruguay on a narrow peninsula on the Atlantic Ocean. The site of three Inter-American Conferences: Aug., 1961 of the Inter-American Economic and Social Council on the Alliance of Progress; in Jan., 1962 a Consultative Meeting of the Foreign Ministers of the American Republics; and in Apr., 1967 the summit meeting of the Presidents of the American Republics.

PUNTA DEL ESTE CHARTER, 1961. A document containing a program of economic and social development for Latin America, advanced by the US President J.F. Kennedy under the name ▷ Alliance for Progress, signed Aug. 17, 1961, in Punta del Este (Uruguay) by all of the OAS member states with the exception of Cuba at the conclusion of the Punta del Este Conference, Aug. 5–17, 1961. The highlights are as follows:

Objectives 1. To achieve a substantial and sustained growth of per capita incomes at a rate designed to attain levels of income capable of assuring self-sustaining development. In order to reach these objectives within a reasonable time, the rate of economic growth in any country of Latin America should not be less than 2.5 per cent per capita per year.

2. To make the benefits of economic progress available to all through a more equitable distribution of national income.

3. To achieve balanced diversification in national economic structures, while attaining stability in the prices of exports or in income derived from exports.

4. To accelerate the process of rational industrialization so as to increase the productivity of the economy as a whole. Special attention should be given to the establishment and development of capital-goods industries.

5. To raise greatly the level of agricultural productivity and output and to improve storage, transport and marketing services.

6. To encourage programmes of comprehensive agrarian reform.

7. To eliminate adult illiteracy and by 1970 to assure access to six years primary education for each school-age child; to modernize and expand vocational, secondary and higher education; to strengthen basic research and to provide the competent personnel.

8. To increase life expectancy at birth by a minimum of five years by improving individual and public health. To attain this goal to provide potable water and drainage to 70 per cent of the urban and 50 per cent of the rural population; to reduce the mortality rate of children under five by half; to control serious transmissible diseases, to eradicate illnesses for which effective cures are known; to improve nutrition; to train medical and health personnel; to improve basic health services; to intensify scientific research.

9. To increase the construction of low-cost housing and to provide necessary public services.

10. To maintain stable price levels.

11. To strengthen existing agreements with a view to the ultimate fulfilment of a Latin American Common Market.

12. To develop co-operative programmes designed to prevent the harmful effects of excessive fluctuations in foreign exchange earnings and to adopt measures to facilitate exports to international markets.

Economic integration of Latin America

The American Republics recognize that:

1. The Montevideo Treaty and the Central American Treaty on Economic Integration are appropriate instruments for the attainment of these objectives.

2. The integration process can be intensified and accelerated through the use of the agreements for complementary production within economic sections provided for by the Montevideo Treaty.

3. To ensure balanced and complementary economic expansion integration should take into account the condition of less-developed countries.

4. To facilitate economic integration it is advisable to establish effective relationships between LAFTA and the Central American Economic Integration Treaty countries and other countries.

5. The Latin American countries should co-ordinate their actions to meet unfavourable treatment accorded to their trade in world markets.

6. In application of resources under the Alliance, special attention should be given to investment for multi-national projects and expansion of trade in industrial products.

7. To facilitate the participation of countries at a relatively lower stage of economic development in multinational programmes special attention should be given to these countries.

8. Economic integration implies a need for additional investment and funds provided under the Alliance should cover these needs.

9. Latin American countries having their own institutions for financing economic integration should channel financing through them. The co-operation of the Inter-American Development Bank should be sought for inter-regional contributions.

10. To approach the International Monetary Fund and other sources for solving temporary balance-of-payments problems.

11. The promotion and co-ordination of transportation and communications systems, and encourage multinational enterprises.

12. To achieve co-ordination of national plans.

13. To promote the development of national Latin American enterprise.

14. The active participation of the private sector.

15. Countries still under Colonial rule should be invited to participate on achieving independence."

The Punta del Este Charter 1961 was suspended by ▷ Latin American Association of Integration, ALADI, 1980. ▷ Latin American Common Market.

The Europa Yearbook 1974. A World Survey, London, 1974, Vol. 1, pp. 379–380.

PUNTA DEL ESTE DECLARATION, 1967. The Declaration of the Presidents of America, signed on Apr. 17, 1967 at Punta del Este, Uruguay by the Presidents of the member states of OAS and the Prime Minister of Trinidad and Tobago. The highlights of the Declaration:

1. Creation by 1985 of a Latin American Common Market through the progressive convergence of the Latin American Free Trade Association and the Central American Common Market;

2. Lay the physical foundations for Latin American economic integration through multi-national projects;

3. Increase substantially Latin American foreign-trade earnings;

4. Modernize rural living conditions, raise agricultural productivity and increase food production;

5. Promote education for development;

6. Harness science and technology for the service of the peoples;

7. Expand health programmes;

8. Eliminate unnecessary military expenditures.

Declaration of the Presidents of America, Punta del Este, Apr., 1967.

PUPPETRY OR MARIONETTES. A subject of International co-operation. Organizations reg. with the UIA:

International Center for Research on Traditional Puppetry, f. 1958, Musée international de la marionnette, Lyon.

International Puppeteers Union, Union internationale de la Marionnette, UNIMA, f. 1929, Warsaw.

Quand Les Marionnettes du monde se donnent la main, Lyon, 1959; *Yearbook of International Organizations*.

PURPORTED SECESSION. ▷ Cyprus.

PUSH-BUTTON. Since the 1950s synonymous with the possibility of starting an atomic war by "pushing a button."

PYONGYANG. Capital of the Democratic People's Republic of Korea (North Korea) since 1948. During the war in ▷ Korea captured by UN forces (1950). Population, 1981 census: 1,280,000.

PYRAMID FIELDS. The Egyptian historic sites from Giza to Dakshur, included in the ▷ World Heritage UNESCO List.

PYRAMIDOLOGY. A subject of international research. Organization reg. with the UIA:

Institute of Pyramidology, f. 1940, London. Publ.: *Pyramidology Magazine*. Members: individuals in 21 countries.

Yearbook of International Organizations.

PYRENEES. Mountain chain forming the border between France and Spain. Area: 55.374 sq km. Range extends: 435 km. The tallest peak: 3,406 m, Pico de Aneto on the Spanish side. The border demarcated by the ▷ Pyrenees Peace Treaty, 1659.

M. SORRE, *Les Pyrénées*, Paris, 1922; H. BELLOC, *The Pyrenees*, London, 1928; L. SOLE SABARIS, *Los Pireneos*, Barcelona, 1951.

PYRENEES PEACE TREATY, 1659. A Treaty between the King of France and the King of Spain, signed on Nov. 7, 1659.

Major Peace Treaties of Modern History 1648–1967, New York, 1967, Vol. I, pp. 51–116.

PYROTECHNICS. A subject of international co-operation. Organization reg. with the UIA:

European Pyrotechnic Association, f. 1970, Dilbeek, Belgium. Held annually at Cannes, France is the Festival International d'Art Pyrotechnic in which Belgium, France, Italy, Portugal and Spain participate.

Yearbook of International Organizations.

PYRRHIC VICTORY. An international term for doubtful victory due to heavy losses; the Greek King of Epirus, Pyrrhus, in 279 BC won the battle with the Romans at Asculum, but lost his entire army.

PYTHAGOREAN PHILOSOPHY. A subject of international research. Organizations reg. with the UIA:

Pythagorean Philosophical Society, f. 1965, Athens.
World Union of Pythagorean Organizations, f. 1964, Paris.

Yearbook of International Organizations.

Q

Q. The seventeenth letter of the Latin alphabet, accepted as an international mark of ▷ Quality.

QATAR. Member of the UN. State of Qatar. An independent emirate in East Arabia, a desert peninsula on the west coast of the Persian Gulf. Bordered in the south by Saudi Arabia and the United Arab Emirates. Area: 11,437 sq. km. Pop. 1987: 334,000, in majority migrant laborers, only *c.* 100,000 are native Qatars. Capital and main port: Doha with 190,000 inhabitants, 1982. GNP per capita 1987: US $12,360. Official languages: Arabic and English. National Day: Sept. 3, Independence Day, 1971. Member of the UN since Sept. 21, 1971 and of all specialized agencies, with the exception of IFC, IDA and GATT. Member of the Arab League and of the Gulf Co-operation Council (GCC). International relations: until 19th century under Persian rule; from 1868 to 1971 under protectorate of Great Britain ; declared its independence from Britain ending the Treaty of 1916, which was replaced by a Treaty of Friendship on Sept. 1, 1971. The oil and gas resources under national control since Feb. 9, 1977.

Qatar into Seventies, Information Ministry, Doha, 1973; R. EL MALLAKH, *Qatar. The Development of an Oil Economy*, New York, 1979; P.T.H. UNVIN, *Qatar, Bibliography*, Oxford, 1982; *The Europa Year Book 1984. A World Survey*, Vol. II, pp. 2291–2297, London, 1984.

QUADRAGESIMO ANNO, 1931. ▷ Catholic Social Doctrines.

QUADRUPLE ALLIANCE, 1814. The Treaty of Union, Concert and Subsidy, 1814, called also the Chaumont Treaty. Three bilateral coalition anti-Napoleon agreements between Great Britain, Austria, Prussia and Russia, signed on Mar. 1, 1814 at Chaumont en Bassigny; supplementary agreement signed on Nov. 20, 1815. ▷ Holy Alliance.

British and Foreign State Papers. Vol. 1, pp. 121–29 and 273–280.

QUAI D'ORSAY. A street in the center of Paris, where at No. 8 the seat of the French Ministry of Foreign Affairs is located; metaphorically an international term used for French foreign policy.

QUAKERS. The members of the Religious Society of Friends, f. 1650 ("the people of God in scorn called Quakers"). A World Conference of Friends held in Swarthmore, Pa, USA, established on Sept. 8, 1937, the Friends World Committee for Consultation (Quakers) with offices: American Section in Philadelphia, European Section in Edinburgh, African Section in Nairobi and the Friends International Centre in Geneva. Consultative status with ECOSOC, UNESCO and UNICEF. Publ.: *Friends World News*. Reg. with the UIA.

M.E. HIRST, *The Quakers in Peace and War*, London, 1923; *Yearbook of International Organizations*.

QUALITY. A subject of international co-operation. Organizations reg. with the UIA:

European Organization for Quality Control, f. 1956, Berne; it introduced the letter "Q" as an international mark of quality. Publ.: *Quality Newsletter, Glossary of Terms Used in Quality Control* (in fourteen languages). International Academy for Quality, f. 1966, Milan. Aims: Promote research into the philosophy, theory and practice of all activities involved in achieving quality of both products and services. Publ.: *International Calendar of Quality Control Events*. International Association for Quality Research on Food Plants, f. 1955, Geisenheim, FRG. Publ.: *Qualitas Plantarum – Plant Food in Human Nutritions*. International Centre for Quality Promotion and Consumer Information, f. 1975, Frankfurt am Main.

Yearbook of International Organizations, 1986/87; The Europa Yearbook 1988. A World Survey, Vol. I, London 1988.

QUARANTINE. An international term for compulsory separation of persons or merchandise arriving from abroad in sea- or airports for a specified period if a suspicion exists that they can spread contagious diseases. Until World War I periods and forms of quarantine, by way of custom, were: 40 days on board ship lying anchored at a considerable distance from other ships. Since 1926 international conventions have been concluded to distinguish quarantine of sick persons admitted to isolation hospitals from that of healthy persons under observation, based on doctors' suspicion, for a few, ten or more days; new forms of merchandise and plant disinfection have also been introduced. These questions are governed by: the Sanitary Convention of June 21, 1926, amended by the Protocol of Apr. 23, 1946; the Sanitary Convention on Air Navigation of Apr. 12, 1933, amended by the Protocol of Apr. 23, 1946 and the Convention on the Co-operation in Quarantine and Protection of Plants of Dec. 14, 1959.
The International Health Regulation, which came into force on Jan. 1, 1971, defined that "in quarantine" means that state or condition during which measures are applied by a health authority to a ship, an aircraft, a train, road vehicle, or other means of transport or container, to prevent the spread of disease, reservoir of disease or vectors of disease from the object of quarantine.

UNTS, Vol. 764, 1971, p. 10.

QUARANTINE DOCTRINE, 1937. ▷ Roosevelt, Quarantine Doctrine, 1937.

QUARANTINE IN CUBAN MISSILE CRISIS 1962. A controversial international term used by the Council of the OAS in a resolution against Cuba, for a new type of maritime blockade.
See also ▷ Cuban Missile Crisis, 1962.

R.L. BLEDSOE, B.A. BOCZEK, *The International Law Dictionary*, Oxford, UK, 1987.

QUATERNARY RESEARCH. A subject of international geological co-operation. Organization reg. by the UIA:

International Union for Quaternary Research, f. 1928, Brussels. Publ.: *Congress proceedings* and *Guides to excursions*.

Yearbook of International Organizations.

QUEBEC OR QUÉBEC. The largest province of Canada; area: 1,540,668 sq. km. Population, 1985 estimate: 6,582,700. [Capital Quebec] by ethnic origin 80.6% French, 10.8% British; 61.9% of the population speak only French, 11.6% only English, 25.5% are bi-lingual. The capital of the province is the oldest city of Canada, also named Quebec or Québec situated at the confluence of the Saint

Lawrence and St. Charles Rivers, with 539,500 inhabitants, 1985.
International relations: from 1663 to 1763 French royal colony also called New France. By the Treaty of Paris 1763 ceded to Great Britain. The Quebec Act passed by the British Parliament on June 22, 1794 preserved the French Civil Code and the Roman Catholic religion. The successive names of the province were: from 1763 to 1790 the Province of Quebec, from 1791 to 1846 Lower Canada, from 1846 to 1867 Canada East, and after the Confederation of the Dominion of Canada was formed again the Province of Quebec (Québec). A separatist movement formed in the 1970's, advocating an independent Quebec made French in 1977 the official language in administration, education and business. On May 21, 1980 about 40.5% of the Quebec electorate voted for a sovereignty accord and an economic association with the rest of Canada while about 59.5% were in favour of maintaining the status quo. In the Legislative Assembly, consisting 122 members, elected for the period 1981–85, *Parti Québecoise* has the majority (80 seats).
L. BAUDOIN, *Le droit civil de la province de Québec*, Montreal, 1953; R. BLANCHARD, *Le Canada français*, Paris, 1959; T. QUELLET, *Histoire économique et sociale du Québec 1760–1850*, Montreal, 1966; R. COOK, *Canada and the French Canadian Question*, Toronto, 1968; M. WADE (ed.), *The French Canadian*, 2 Vols. London, 1968; M. RIONS, *La question du Québec*, Paris, 1969; *French-Canadian Nationalism Anthology. Toronto*, 1969; *Le terrorisme québecoise*, Montreal, 1970; J. JACOB, *The Question of Separation: Quebec and the Struggle for Sovereignty*, London, 1981; C. PRUTHIER, *Québec ou presque Amérique*, Paris, 1974; *The Europa Year Book 1984. A World Survey*, Vol. II, pp. 1320–1321, London, 1984.

QUEBEC CONFERENCE, 1943. A wartime meeting of the President of the USA, F.D. Roosevelt, with the Prime Minister of the UK, W.S. Churchill, Aug. 11–24, 1943, devoted mainly to the war in the Atlantic as well as preparing for the summit meeting with the Prime Minister of the USSR, J.V. Stalin (▷ Teheran Conference, 1943).
W.L. LANGER, *An Encyclopedia of World History*, Boston, 1968.

QUEEN MAUD LAND. ▷ Antarctica.

QUEMOY ISLANDS. A group of islands in the East China Sea, 240 km west of Taiwan, integrated by Taiwan after the proclamation of the People's Republic of China, 1949; bombarded by China several times in the 1950's, together with ▷ Matsu. The group consists of Quemoy, Little Quemoy and 12 islets in Xiamen Bay.

KEESING's *Contemporary Archive*, **1955.**

QUETZAL.
A monetary unit of Guatemala; one quetzal = 100 centaros; issued by the Banco de Guatemala.

QUIET DIPLOMACY. An international UN term for private talks or negotiations aimed at settling or alleviating international disputes.

QUIET SUN INTERNATIONAL YEAR, 1964–1965. The year was organized under UN patronage by the International Union of Scientific Academies for the period Jan. 1, 1964–Dec. 31, 1965. In 1962, the International Year Committee was formed in London, composed of 30 scientists and 66 representatives of countries on whose territories observations and geophysical measurements were made of the radioactivity of the sun; taking part in the measurements were US and

USSR artificial Earth satellites designed to study the ultraviolet and roentgen rays of the sun.

UN Monthly Chronicle, 1965.

QUINTA COLUMNA. *Spanish* = "Fifth Column." An international term, appeared during the civil war in Spain 1936–39, when in 1936 the fascist forces of General F. Franco marched in four columns on Madrid, while the "fifth," under cover within the city, supported them through diversion, spying, etc. Since then the term "Quinta Columna" means any action by a clandestine group.

A. DE SILVA, *A Quinta Coluna no Brasil. A Conspiraçao nazi no Rio Grande do Sul*, Pôrto Alegre, 1942; L. DE JONG, *The German Fifth Column in the World War*, London 1956.

QUINTAL. An international mass and weight unit = 100,000 grams, or approx. 220.46 pounds.

QUI PRO QUO. *Latin* = "something for something." A principle of reciprocity in foreign trade, used in treaties concluded within GATT, as e.g. in the Kennedy Round.

QUIRIGUA. An Archaeological Park of Guatemala, included in the ▷ World Heritage UNESCO List. In the 9th century, when Quirigua was the center of the export trade in obsidian and jade to the Caribbean coast, some extraordinary buildings and monuments were constructed there, such as: pyramids, terraces and stairways containing stelae and sacred sculptures.

UNESCO. *A Legacy for All*, Paris, 1984.

QUIRINAL. *Italian*: Quirinale. One of the seven hills on which ancient Rome was built. The name of a palace in Rome, the seat since 1870 of Italian kings and since 1946 of presidents; accepted international term identifying the Quirinal with Italian politics.

QUISLINGS. An international term derived from the name of V. Quisling (1887–1945) the Norwegian Prime Minister during the German occupation 1942–45; synonym for collaboration with Hitler's Germany. The UN General Assembly Res. A/45, of Feb. 12, 1946, recognized "the necessity of clearly distinguishing between genuine refugees and displaced persons on the one hand, and the war criminals, quislings and traitors on the other."

The Trial of German Major War Criminals. Proceedings of the IMT Sitting, Nuremberg, Germany, 42 Vols., London 1946–48, Vol. 22, p. 447; W.L. SHIRER, *The Nightmare Years 1930–40*, Boston, 1984, pp. 486–488. Population, 1982 census: 1,110,248.

QUITO. The capital of Ecuador since 1809. Seat of the Intergovernmental Committee of European Migration. The historic part of the city of Quito is included in the ▷ World Heritage UNESCO List. Quito was an Inca capital in the 15th century but a hundred years later became a Spanish city, seat of the colonial government and a political and cultural centre. It was distinguished by the skill of its architects, sculptors and painters who fused indigenous traditions with European techniques.

UNESCO. *A Legacy for All*, Paris, 1984.

QUITO CHARTER, 1948. A treaty between Colombia, Ecuador, Panama and Venezuela, concluded May 8, 1948 in the capital of Ecuador regarding the establishing of a Greater Colombian Economic Union, Union Economica Grancolombiana; referring to the economic unity of the historical territory of Greater Colombia including the above-mentioned countries. Art. 2 of the Charter assumes a gradual movement toward a customs union and co-ordination of production and therefore establishes (art. 3) a Customs Council, a Council for Production, a Council for Trade and Communication and a Finance Council. As none of the signing countries ratified the treaty, the Quito Charter did not enter into effect. Its ideas were taken over by the ▷ Andean Development Corporation.

J.M. CORDERO-TORRES, *Textos Básicos de la Organización Internacional*, Madrid, 1955.

QUITO DECLARATION, 1984. A Declaration and Action Plan for Latin American Economic Recovery, adopted on Jan. 13, 1984 in Quito by the Heads of State or Government of twenty-six Latin American Caribbean Countries, prepared with the assistance of ECLA and SELA. The Quito Conference arose from the "Santo Domingo Pledge", adopted at the meeting in the Dominican Republic in Aug., 1983.

The countries adopted "basic criteria" for renegotiating their external debts, including the following:

Export earnings income should not be committed beyond reasonable percentages consistent with the maintenance of adequate levels of internal productive activity;
Debt service payments should be reduced, and mechanisms should be explored to stabilize the debt servicing of each country in accordance with its payments profile;
Debt renegotiation should be accompanied by commercial measures essential to improving the terms of access for exports from Latin America and the Caribbean in world markets and eliminating increasing protectionism by the developed countries;
The possibility of converting part of the accumulated debt into long-term obligations should be urgently explored;
A net, adequate and increasing flow of new public and private financial resources for all the countries of the region should be an essential component of external debt renegotiations;
Finance ministers and Central Banks should carry out confidential exchanges of information on terms of debt refinancing and rescheduling.

UN Chronicle, March, 1984, pp. 13–17.

QUMRAN. ▷ Dead Sea Scroll.

QUORUM. *Latin: "quorum presentia sufficit"* = "of whom presence is sufficient." An international term for the number of members required by the statute of an organization for a meeting or a session to have legal force. The *quorum presentia sufficit* principle has been adopted by international organizations, e.g. Statute of the International Court of Justice, art. 25: "A *quorum* of nine judges shall suffice to constitute the Court."

QUOTA ACT, 1921. The US Congress Immigration Act of May, 1921, which limited the immigration from Europe to an annual quota equal to 2% of the US residents born in a European country at the time of the 1890 census.

QUOTAS. The import and export measures; quantitative restrictions in foreign trade.

S. HABERLER, M. HILL, *Quantitative Trade Control. Their Causes and Nature*, League of Nations, Geneva, 1943.

QWAQUA. ▷ Bantu Homelands.

R

RA II. A boat, 17 m long and 5 m wide, built of papyrus stalks, named after the Egyptian sun-god, on which the Norwegian, Thor Heyerdahl, with his seven-man crew sailed about 4000 nautical miles in 61 days, May–July 1970, across the Atlantic Ocean, from the Port of Safi in Morocco to the island of Barbados. In 1969 the *RA I* after 58 days of sailing ran aground on July 19 about 600 miles from Barbados.

T. HEYERDAHL, *The Ra Expeditions*, London, 1972.

RABAT. The capital of Morocco since 1956, situated on the Atlantic Ocean at the mouth of Bou Regreg estuary. UN Information Center.

RABIES WORLDWIDE CONTROL. The international group of experts convened by the WHO in Geneva in Sept., 1983 has urged worldwide rabies control to counter the deadly disease of rabies, which has strengthened its hold on the human and animal population of the world in the 1970s and in the first years of the 1980s. The disease, according to the WHO, has followed development of roads, settlement of new areas and human population movement in Latin America, Africa and Asia. In almost all the developing countries, where rabies has been on the increase, the dog has been the carrier of the disease and the principal source of human exposure. Rabies has also extended its hold in many developed countries. In Europe, rabies in foxes has spread westward almost to the Atlantic seaboard. In the USA rabies is spreading in raccoons in the eastern states, while in central USA the disease in skunks increases cyclically; in Central and South America rabies in vampire bats and cattle is increasing. A worldwide rabies control under the aegis of the WHO is recommended, with the formation of national committees and a program of vaccination of the entire dog population.

G.W. BERAN, A.J. CROWLOY, "Toward Worldwide Rabies Control", in: *WHO Chronicle*, Vol. 37, No. 6, 1983, pp. 192–196.

RABBINACAL COURTS, SUPREME. The Court of the Jewish committees ▷ Ashkenazi and ▷ Sephardic in Jerusalem has exclusive jurisdiction in matters of marriage and divorce for the Israeli citizens or residents and in all other matters of personal status. The judgements are executed by the Civil Courts of Israel.

The Europa Yearbook 1987. A World Survey, Vol. I, London, 1987.

RABBIT MEAT. A subject of research and promotion by the International Trade Center UNCTAD/GATT, Geneva.

ITC, *Selected Markets for Rabbit Meat*, Geneva, 1983.

RACE PROTECTION. A racist notion introduced in the 19th and 20th centuries, aimed at justifying segregation of some ethnic population groups from others and granting privileges to one group at the cost of discriminating against others. ▷ Apartheid, ▷ Racial Discrimination, ▷ Rassenschande.

RACES UNIVERSAL CONGRESS, 1911. The first Universal Races Congress was held July 26–29, 1911 at the University of London.

Papers on Inter-Racial Problems, Communicated to the First Universal Races Congress, Boston, 1911.

RACIAL DISCRIMINATION. An international term, defined by the UN International Convention on the Elimination of All Forms of Racial Discrimination, 1965, as

"any distinction, exclusion, restriction or preference based on race, color, descent or national or ethnic origin which has the purpose or effect of nullifying or impairing the recognition, enjoyment or an exercise, on an equal footing, of human rights and fundamental freedoms in the political, economic, social, cultural or any other field of public life."

The struggle against racial prejudice was initiated in the 18th century by the free-thinkers and then continued in the 19th century by liberals, socialists and communists, and in the 20th century by all progressive circles. In 1927 a world movement evolved and created the International League Against Racism and Anti-Semitism. In 1941 the Universal Races Congress was held in London under the motto "there are no superior races", protesting against the racist German war policy which regarded the German nation as a "nation of masters" (Herrenvolk) and the conquered nations as a collection of "subhumans" (Untermenschen). The Allied Powers in 1943 condemned the German racial crimes and created the International Military Tribunal, which in 1946 recognized genocide as a crime against humanity. The UN General Assembly in approving the ▷ Nuremberg principles, initiated the work of UNESCO on eliminating racial discrimination from the national and international scene. The first all-world document on this matter was the ▷ Human Rights, Universal Declaration of, on Dec. 10, 1948.

The United Nations is striving to eliminate all forms of racism, racial discrimination and segregation, considering such discrimination to be a flagrant violation of the principles of the UN Charter and of the obligations member states assumed under it. Despite substantial progress in many countries and Territories, racial discrimination in the political, economic, social and cultural spheres persists, either in law or in fact, in many parts of the world. Various measures aimed at eradicating the evils of racial discrimination have been adopted by the UN General Assembly, the ECOSOC, the Commission on Human Rights and its Sub-Commission on Prevention of Discrimination and Protection of Minorities, and by other competent organs and specialized agencies. These include resolutions, declarations, international conventions, special reports, and programs such as the one for the Decade for Action to Combat Racism and Racial Discrimination.

Among the earlier measures adopted was the UN Declaration on the Elimination of All Forms of Racial Discrimination, proclaimed by the UN General Assembly on Nov. 20, 1963. In it the Assembly affirmed that discrimination between human beings on the grounds of race, colour or ethnic origin is an offence to human dignity, a denial of the Charter principles, a violation of the rights proclaimed in the Universal Declaration of Human Rights and an obstacle to friendly and peaceful relations among nations, capable of disturbing peace and security among peoples. Addressing itself to states as well as to institutions, groups and individuals, the Declaration elaborated upon the provisions of the Universal Declaration and also covered situations not dealt with in it. In order to implement the principles embodied in the Declaration, the UN General Assembly, in December, 1965, adopted the International Convention on the Elimination of All Forms of Racial Discrimination (▷ Racial Discrimination, UN International Convention Against Racism, 1965).

UNESCO on Sept. 26, 1967 ratified a Declaration on Races and Racial Prejudice. The Declaration asserts that the problems which arise from racial relations belong to social, and not biological phenomena, and stem from beliefs and actions based on erroneous views; while discriminatory practices against various groups are falsely justified from a biological point of view, since science in no event provides a basis for ordering ethnic groups hierarchically.

On the proposal of the International Conference of Human Rights, held at Teheran in 1968, the UN General Assembly designated 1971 as International Year for Action to Combat Racism and Racial Discrimination. The purpose of the Year was to intensify and to expand the efforts of states, at national and international levels, and of the United Nations and the specialized agencies towards ensuring the rapid and total eradication of racial discrimination, including apartheid and nazism. The Year was observed in many countries and territories.

"in the name of the ever-growing struggle against racial discrimination in all its forms and manifestations and in the name of international solidarity with those struggling against racism."

A program for observance of the Year called for new measures to eradicate racial discrimination, a world-wide seminar on national efforts to wipe out such discrimination and promote harmonious race relations, and a campaign to promote public awareness of the evils of racial discrimination.

In 1972 the General Assembly decided to launch a Decade for Action to Combat Racism and Racial Discrimination and to inaugurate it on Dec. 10, 1973, the 25th anniversary of the adoption of the Universal Declaration of Human Rights. The Decade was designed as a period for intensified national, regional and international action aimed at achieving the total and unconditional elimination of racism and racial discrimination in all its forms. A detailed Program for the Decade sets forth the goals and policy measures and activities to be undertaken.

The goals of the Decade were to promote human rights and fundamental freedoms for all, without distinction of any kind such as race, color, descent, national or ethnic origin or other status; to arrest any expansion of racist policies, to eliminate their persistence and to counteract the emergence of alliances based on racism and racial discrimination; to resist any policy or practice which strengthens racist régimes and sustains racism; to identify, isolate and dispel the fallacious beliefs, policies and practices that contribute to racism and racial discrimination; and to put an end to racist régimes.

To achieve those objectives, the Program called for appropriate measures to implement fully United Nations instruments and decisions concerning the elimination of racial discrimination; to ensure support for all peoples striving for racial equality, to eradicate all forms of racial discrimination; and to pursue a vigorous world-wide campaign of information designed to dispel racial prejudice.

In conformity with the Program, the UN convened the World Conference to Combat Racism and Racial Discrimination in Geneva from 14–25 Aug., 1978. The conference adopted a Program of Action, including recommendations for elimination of all discriminatory laws and practices, adoption of laws to punish the dissemination of ideas based on racial superiority or hatred, promotion of the rights of indigenous peoples and migrant workers and imposition of sanctions against the racist regimes of Southern Africa.

In 1979 the UN General Assembly approved a program for the remaining four years of the decade and convened the Second World Conference to Combat Racism and Racial Discrimination, which was held in Geneva from Aug. 1–13, 1983. A highlight of the results of the Conference was its call for a Second Decade to extend through 1993. The UN General Assembly declared the Second Decade Against Racism for 1984–93.

UNESCO: *The Race Question in Modern Science*, Paris, 1965; UNESCO, *Le racisme devant la science*, Paris, 1973; SIR RUPERT JOHN, *UN Publications against Apartheid, Racism and its Elimination*, New York, 1979; *Everyone's United Nations*, New York, 1979, pp. 239–245; *UN Chronicle*, July 1982, June, October and December, 1983.

RACIAL DISCRIMINATION, UN INTERNATIONAL CONVENTION AGAINST RACISM, 1965.

The UN General Assembly on Dec. 21, 1965 adopted the International Convention on the Elimination of All Forms of Racial Discrimination. The Convention came into force on Jan. 4, 1969, and as of Sept. 1, 1983, 121 states had ratified (68), acceded (50) or succeeded (3) to it. the text is as follows:

"The States Parties to this Convention,

Considering that the Charter of the United Nations is based on the principles of the dignity and equality inherent in all human beings, and that all Member States have pledged themselves to take joint and separate action, in co-operation with the Organization, for the achievement of one of the purposes of the United Nations which is to promote and encourage universal respect for and observance of human rights and fundamental freedoms for all, without distinction as to race, sex, language or religion,

Considering that the Universal Declaration of Human Rights proclaims that all human beings are born free and equal in dignity and rights and that everyone is entitled to all the rights and freedoms set out therein, without distinction of any kind, in particular as to race, colour or national origin,

Considering that all human beings are equal before the law and are entitled to equal protection of the law against any discrimination and against any incitement to discrimination,

Considering that the United Nations has condemned colonialism and all practices of segregation and discrimination associated therewith, in whatever form and wherever they exist, and that the Declaration on the Granting of Independence to Colonial Countries and Peoples of 14 December 1960 (General Assembly resolution 1514/XV) has affirmed and solemnly proclaimed the necessity of bringing them to a speedy and unconditional end,

Considering that the United Nations Declaration on the Elimination of All Forms of Racial Discrimination of 20 November 1963 (General Assembly resolution 1904/XVIII) solemnly affirms the necessity of speedily eliminating racial discrimination throughout the world in all its forms and manifestations and of securing understanding of and respect for the dignity of the human person,

Convinced that any doctrine of superiority based on racial differentiation is scientifically false, morally condemnable, socially unjust and dangerous, and that there is no justification for racial discrimination, in theory or in practice, anywhere,

Reaffirming that discrimination between human beings on the grounds of race, colour or ethnic origin is an obstacle to friendly and peaceful relations among nations and is capable of disturbing peace and security among peoples and the harmony of persons living side by side even within one and the same State,

Convinced that the existence of racial barriers is repugnant to the ideals of any human society,

Alarmed by manifestations of racial discrimination still in evidence in some areas of the world and by governmental policies based on racial superiority or hatred, such as policies of apartheid, segregation or separation,

Resolved to adopt all necessary measures for speedily eliminating racial discrimination in all its forms and manifestations, and to prevent and combat racist doctrines and practices in order to promote understanding between races and to build an international community free from all forms of racial segregation and racial discrimination,

Bearing in mind the Convention concerning Discrimination in respect of Employment and Occupation adopted by the International Labour Organization in 1958, and the Convention against Discrimination in Education adopted by the United Nations Educational, Scientific and Cultural Organization in 1960,

Desiring to implement the principles embodied in the United Nations Declaration on the Elimination of All Forms of Racial Discrimination and to secure the earliest adoption of practical measures to that end,

Have agreed as follows:

Part I. Art. 1.(1) In this Convention, the term "racial discrimination" shall mean any distinction, exclusion, restriction or preference based on race, colour, descent, or national or ethnic origin which has the purpose or effect of nullifying or impairing the recognition, enjoyment or exercise, on an equal footing, of human rights and fundamental freedoms in the political, economic, social, cultural or any other field of public life.

(2) This Convention shall not apply to distinctions, exclusions, restrictions or preferences made by a State Party to this Convention between citizens and non-citizens.

(3) Nothing in this Convention may be interpreted as affecting in any way the legal provisions of States Parties concerning nationality, citizenship or naturalization, provided that such provisions do not discriminate against any particular nationality.

(4) Special measures taken for the sole purpose of securing adequate advancement of certain racial or ethnic groups or individuals requiring such protection as may be necessary in order to ensure such groups or individuals equal enjoyment or exercise of human rights and fundamental freedoms shall not be deemed racial discrimination, provided, however, that such measures do not, as a consequence, lead to the maintenance of separate rights for different racial groups and that they shall not be continued after the objectives for which they were taken have been achieved.

Art. 2(1) States Parties condemn racial discrimination and undertake to pursue by all appropriate means and without delay a policy of eliminating racial discrimination in all its forms and promoting understanding among all races, and, to this end:

(a) Each State Party undertakes to engage in no act or practice of racial discrimination against persons, groups of persons or institutions and to ensure that all public authorities and public institutions, national and local, shall act in conformity with this obligation;

(b) Each State Party undertakes not to sponsor, defend or support racial discrimination by any persons or organizations;

(c) Each State Party shall take effective measures to review governmental, national and local policies, and to amend, rescind or nullify any laws and regulations which have the effect of creating or perpetuating racial discrimination wherever it exists;

(d) Each State Party shall prohibit and bring to an end, by all appropriate means, including legislation as required by circumstances, racial discrimination by any persons, group or organization;

(e) Each State Party undertakes to encourage, where appropriate, integrationist multi-racial organizations and movements and other means of eliminating barriers between races, and to discourage anything which tends to strengthen racial division.

(2) States Parties shall, when the circumstances so warrant, take, in the social, economic, cultural and other fields, special and concrete measures to ensure the adequate development and protection of certain racial groups or individuals belonging to them, for the purpose of guaranteeing them the full and equal enjoyment of human rights and fundamental freedoms. These measures shall in no case entail as a consequence the maintenance of unequal or separate rights for different racial groups after the objectives for which they were taken have been achieved.

Art. 3. States Parties particularly condemn racial segregation and apartheid and undertake to prevent, prohibit and eradicate all practices of this nature in territories under their jurisdiction.

Art. 4. States Parties condemn all propaganda and all organizations which are based on ideas or theories of superiority of one race or group of persons of one colour or ethnic origin, or which attempt to justify or promote racial hatred and discrimination in any form, and undertake to adopt immediate and positive measures designed to eradicate all incitement to, or acts of, such discrimination and, to this end, with due regard to the principles embodied in the Universal Declaration of Human Rights and the rights expressly set forth in article 5 of this Convention, inter alia:

(a) Shall declare no offence punishable by law all dissemination of ideas based on racial superiority or hatred, incitement to racial discrimination, as well as all acts of violence or incitement to such acts against any race or group of persons of another colour or ethnic origin, and also the provision of any assistance to racist activities, including the financing thereof;

(b) Shall declare illegal and prohibit organizations, and also organized and all other propaganda activities, which promote and incite racial discrimination, and shall recognize participation in such organization or activities as an offence punishable by law;

(c) Shall not permit public authorities or public institutions, national or local, to promote or incite racial discrimination.

Art. 5. In compliance with the fundamental obligations laid down in article 2 of this Convention, States Parties undertake to prohibit and to eliminate racial discrimination in all its forms and to guarantee the right of everyone, without distinction as to race, colour, or national or ethnic origin, to equality before the law, notably in the enjoyment of the following rights:

(a) The right to equal treatment before the tribunals and all other organs administering justice;

(b) The right to security of person and protection by the State against violence or bodily harms, whether inflicted by government officials or by any individual, group or institution;

(c) Political rights, in particular the rights to participate in elections – to vote and to stand for election – on the basis of universal and equal suffrage, to take part in the Government as well as in the conduct of public affairs at any level and to have equal access to public service;

(d) Other civil rights, in particular:

(i) The right to freedom of movement and residence within the border of the State;

(ii) The right to leave any country, including one's own and to return to one's country;

(iii) The right to nationality;

(iv) The right to marriage and choice of spouse;

(v) The right to own property alone as well as in association with others;

(vi) The right to inherit;

(vii) The right to freedom of thought, conscience and religion;

(viii) The right to freedom of opinion and expression;

(ix) The right to freedom of peaceful assembly and association;

(e) Economic, social and cultural rights, in particular:

(i) The right to work, to free choice of employment, to just and favourable conditions of work, to protection against unemployment, to equal pay for equal work, to just and favourable remuneration;

(ii) The right to form and join trade unions;

(iii) The right to housing;

(iv) The right to public health, medical care, social security and social services;

(v) The right to education and training;

(vi) The right to equal participation in cultural activities;

(f) The right of access to any place or service intended for use by the general public, such as transport, hotels, restaurants, cafes, theatres and parks.

Art. 6. States Parties shall assure to everyone within their jurisdiction effective protection and remedies, through the competent national tribunals and other State institutions, against any acts of racial discrimination which violate his human rights and fundamental freedoms contrary to this Convention, as well as the right to seek from such tribunals just and adequate reparation or satisfaction for any damage suffered as a result of such discrimination.

Art. 7. States Parties undertake to adopt immediate and effective measures, particularly in the fields of teaching, education, culture and information, with a view to combating prejudices which lead to racial discrimination and to promoting understanding, tolerance and friendship among nations and racial or ethnical groups, as well as to propagating the purposes and principles of the Charter of the United Nations, the Universal Declaration of Human Rights, the United Nations Declaration on the Elimination of All Forms of Racial Discrimination, and this Convention.

Part II. Art. 8.(1) There shall be established a Committee on the Elimination of Racial Discrimination (hereinafter referred to as the Committee) consisting of eighteen experts of high moral standing and acknowledged impartiality elected by States Parties from among their nationals, who shall serve in their personal capacity, consideration being given to equitable geographical distribution and to the representation of the different forms of civilization as well as of the principal legal systems.

(2) The members of the Committee shall be elected by secret ballot from a list of persons nominated by the States Parties. Each State Party may nominate one person from among its own nationals.

(3) The initial election shall be held six months after the date of the entry into force of this Convention. At least three months before the date of each election the Secretary-General of the United Nations shall address a letter to the States Parties inviting them to submit their nominations within two months. The Secretary-General shall prepare a list in alphabetical order of all persons thus nominated, indicating the States Parties which have nominated them, and shall submit it to the States Parties.

(4) Elections of the members of the Committee shall be held at a meeting of States Parties convened by the Secretary-General at United Nations Headquarters. At that meeting, for which two thirds of the States Parties shall constitute a quorum, the persons elected to the Committee shall be those nominees who obtain the largest number of votes and an absolute majority of the votes of the representatives of States Parties present and voting.

(5)(a) The members of the Committee shall be elected for a term of four years. However, the terms of nine of the members elected at the first election shall expire at the end of two years; immediately after the first election the names of these nine members shall be chosen by lot by the Chairman of the Committee.

(b) For the filling of casual vacancies, the State Party whose expert has ceased to function as a member of the Committee shall appoint another expert from among its nationals, subject to the approval of the Committee.

(6) States Parties shall be responsible for the expenses of the members of the Committee while they are in performance of Committee duties.

Art. 9.(1) States Parties undertake to submit to the Secretary-General of the United Nations, for consideration by the Committee, a report on the legislative, judicial, administrative or other measures which they have adopted and which give effect to the provisions of this Convention:

(a) within one year after the entry into force of the Convention for the State concerned; and

(b) thereafter every two years and whenever the Committee so requests. The Committee may request further information from the States Parties.

(2) The Committee shall report annually, through the Secretary-General, to the General Assembly of the United Nations on its activities and may make suggestions and general recommendations based on the examination of the reports and information received from the States Parties. Such suggestions and general recommendations shall be reported to the General Assembly together with comments, if any, from States Parties.

Art. 10.(1) The Committee shall adopt its own rules of procedure.

(2) The Committee shall elect its officers for a term of two years.

(3) The secretariat of the Committee shall be provided by the Secretary-General of the United Nations.

(4) The meetings of the Committee shall normally be held at United Nations Headquarters.

Art. 11.(1) If a State Party considers that another State Party is not giving effect to the provisions of this Convention, it may bring the matter to the attention of the Committee. The Committee shall then transmit the communication to the State Party concerned. Within

three months, the receiving State shall submit to the Committee written explanations or statements clarifying the matter and the remedy, if any, that may have been taken by that State.

(2) If the matter is not adjusted to the satisfaction of both parties, either by bilateral negotiations or by any other procedure open to them, within six months after the receipt by the receiving State of the initial communication, either State shall have the right to refer the matter again to the Committee by notifying the Committee and also the other State.

(3) The Committee shall deal with a matter referred to it in accordance with paragraph 2 of this article after it has ascertained that all available domestic remedies have been invoked and exhausted in the case, in conformity with the generally recognized principles of international law. This shall not be the rule where the application of the remedies is unreasonably prolonged.

(4) In any matter referred to it, the Committee may call upon the States Parties concerned to supply other relevant information.

(5) When any matter arising out of this article is being considered by the Committee, the States Parties concerned shall be entitled to send a representative to take part in the proceedings of the Committee, without voting rights, while the matter is under consideration.

Art. 12. (1)(a) After the Committee has obtained and collated all the information it deems necessary, the Chairman shall appoint an ad hoc Conciliation Commission (hereinafter referred to as the Commission) comprising five persons who may or may not be members of the Committee. The members of the Commission shall be appointed with the unanimous consent of the parties to the dispute, and its good offices shall be made available to the States concerned with a view to an amicable solution of the matter on the basis of respect for this Convention.

(b) If the States parties to the dispute fail to reach agreement within three months on all or part of the composition of the Commission, the members of the Commission not agreed upon by the States parties to the dispute shall be elected by secret ballot by a two-thirds majority vote of the Committee from among its own members.

(2) The members of the Commission shall serve in their personal capacity. They shall not be nationals of the States parties to the dispute or of a State not Party to this Convention.

(3) The Commission shall elect its own Chairman and adopt its own rules of procedure.

(4) The meetings of the Commission shall normally be held at United Nations Headquarters or at any other convenient place as determined by the Commission.

(5) The secretariat provided in accordance with article 10, paragraph 3, of this Convention shall also service the Commission whenever a dispute among States Parties brings the Commission into being.

(6) The States parties to the dispute shall share equally all the expenses of the members of the Commission in accordance with estimates to be provided by the Secretary-General of the United Nations.

(7) The Secretary-General shall be empowered to pay the expenses of the members of the Commission, if necessary, before reimbursement by the States parties to the dispute in accordance with paragraph 6 of this article.

(8) The information obtained and collated by the Committee shall be made available to the Commission, and the Commission may call upon the States concerned to supply any other relevant information.

Art. 13.(1) When the Commission has fully considered the matter, it shall prepare and submit to the Chairman of the Committee a report embodying its findings on all questions of fact relevant to the issue between the parties and containing such recommendations as it may think proper for the amicable solution of the dispute.

(2) The Chairman of the Committee shall communicate the report of the Commission to each of the States parties to the dispute. These States shall, within three months, inform the Chairman of the Committee whether or not they accept the recommendations contained in the report of the Commission.

(3) After the period provided for in paragraph 2 of this article, the Chairman of the Committee shall communicate the report of the Commission and the declarations of the States Parties concerned to the other States Parties to this Convention.

Art. 14.(1) A State Party may at any time declare that it recognizes the competence of the Committee to receive and consider communications from individuals or groups of individuals within its jurisdiction claiming to be victims of a violation by that State Party of any of the rights set forth in this Convention. No communication shall be received by the Committee if it concerns a State Party which has not made such a declaration.

(2) Any State Party which makes a declaration as provided for in paragraph 1 of this article may establish or indicate a body within its national legal order which shall be competent to receive and consider petitions from individuals within its jurisdiction who claim to be victims of a violation of any of the rights set forth in this Convention and who have exhausted other available local remedies.

(3) A declaration made in accordance with paragraph 1 of this article and the name of any body established or indicated in accordance with paragraph 2 of this article shall be deposited by the State Party concerned with the Secretary-General of the United Nations, who shall transmit copies thereof to the other States Parties. A declaration may be withdrawn at any time by notification to the Secretary-General, but such a withdrawal shall not affect communications pending before the Committee.

(4) A register of petitions shall be kept by the body established or indicated in accordance with paragraph 2 of this article, and certified copies of the register shall be filed annually through appropriate channels with the Secretary-General on the understanding that the contents shall not be publicly disclosed.

(5) In the event of failure to obtain satisfaction from the body established or indicated in accordance with paragraph 2 of this article, the petitioner shall have the right to communicate the matter to the Committee within six months.

(6)(a) The Committee shall confidentially bring any communication referred to it to the attention of the State Party alleged to be violating any provisions of this Convention, but the identity of the individual or groups of individuals concerned shall not be revealed without his or their express consent. The Committee shall not receive anonymous communications.

(b) Within three months, the receiving State shall submit to the Committee written explanations or statements clarifying the matter and the remedy, if any, that may have been taken by that State.

(7)(a) The Committee shall consider communications in the light of all information made available to it by the State Party concerned and by the petitioner. The Committee shall not consider any communication from a petitioner unless it has ascertained that the petitioner has exhausted all available domestic remedies. However, this shall not be the rule where the application of the remedies is unreasonably prolonged.

(b) The Committee shall forward its suggestions and recommendations, if any, to the State Party concerned and to the petitioner.

(8) The Committee shall include in its annual report a summary of such communications and, where appropriate, a summary of the explanations and statements of the States Parties concerned and of its own suggestions and recommendations.

(9) The Committee shall be competent to exercise the functions provided for in this article only when at least ten States Parties to this Convention are bound by declarations in accordance with paragraph 1 of this article.

Art. 15(1) Pending the achievement of the objectives of the Declaration on the Granting of Independence to Colonial Countries and Peoples, contained in General Assembly resolution 1514(XV) of 14 December 1960, the provisions of this Convention shall in no way limit the right of petition granted to these peoples by other international instruments or by the United Nations and its specialized agencies.

(2)(a) The Committee established under article 8, paragraph 1, of this Convention shall receive copies of the petitions from, and submit expressions of opinion and recommendations on these petitions to, the bodies of the United Nations which deal with matters directly related to the principles and objectives of this Convention in their consideration of petitions from the inhabitants of Trust and Non-Self-Governing Territories and all other territories to which General Assembly Resolution 1514(XV) applies, relating to matters covered by this Convention which are before these bodies.

(b) The Committee shall receive from the competent bodies of the United Nations copies of the reports concerning the legislative, judicial, administrative or other measures directly related to the principles and objectives of this Convention applied by the administering Powers within the Territories mentioned in sub-paragraph (a) of this paragraph, and shall express opinions and make recommendations to these bodies.

(3) The Committee shall include in its report to the General Assembly a summary of the petitions and reports it has received from United Nations bodies, and the expressions of opinion and recommendations of the Committee relating to said petitions and reports.

(4) The Committee shall request from the Secretary General of the United Nations all information relevant to the objectives of this Convention and available to him regarding the Territories mentioned in paragraph 2 (a) of this article.

Art. 16. The provisions of this Convention concerning the settlement of disputes or complaints shall be applied without prejudice to other procedures for settling disputes or complaints in the field of discrimination laid down in the constituent instruments of, or in conventions adopted by, the United Nations and its specialized agencies, and shall not prevent the States Parties from having recourse to other procedures for settling a dispute in accordance with general or special international agreements in force between them.

Part III. Art. 17.(1) This Convention is open for signature by any State Member of the United Nations or member of any of its specialized agencies, by any State Party to the Statute of the International Court of Justice, and by any other State which has been invited by the General Assembly of the United Nations to become a Party to this Convention.

(2) This Convention is subject to ratification. Instruments of ratification shall be deposited with the Secretary-General of the United Nations.

Art. 18.(1) This Convention shall be open to accession by any State referred to in article 17, paragraph 1, of the Convention.

(2) Accession shall be effected by the deposit of an instrument of accession with the Secretary-General of the United Nations.

Art. 19.(1) This Convention shall enter into force on the thirtieth day after the date of the deposit with the Secretary-General of the United Nations of the twenty-seventh instrument of ratification or instrument of accession.

(2) For each State ratifying this Convention or acceding to it after the deposit of the twenty-seventh instrument of ratification or instrument of accession, the Convention shall enter into force on the thirtieth day after the date of the deposit of its own instrument of ratification or instrument of accession.

Art. 20.(1) The Secretary-General of the United Nations shall receive and circulate to all States which are or may become Parties to this Convention reservations made by States at the time of ratification or accession. Any State which objects to the reservation shall, within a period of ninety days from the date of the said communication, notify the Secretary-General that it does not accept it.

(2) A reservation incompatible with the object and purpose of this Convention shall not be permitted, nor shall a reservation the effect of which would inhibit the operation of any of the bodies established by this Convention be allowed. A reservation shall be considered incompatible or inhibitive if at least two thirds of the States Parties to this Convention object to it.

(3) Reservations may be withdrawn at any time by notification to this effect addressed to the Secretary-General. Such notification shall take effect on the date on which it is received.

Art. 21. A State Party may denounce this Convention by written notification to the Secretary-General of the United Nations. Denunciation shall take effect one year after the date of receipt of the notification by the Secretary-General.

Art. 22. Any dispute between two or more State Parties with respect to the interpretation or application of this Convention, which is not settled by negotiation or by the procedures expressly provided for in this Convention, shall, at the request of any of the parties to the dispute, be referred to the International Court of

Justice for decision, unless the disputants agree to another mode of settlement.

Art. 23.(1) A request for the revision of this Convention may be made at any time by any State Party by means of a notification in writing addressed to the Secretary-General of the United Nations.

(2) The General Assembly of the United Nations shall decide upon the steps, if any, to be taken in respect of such a request.

Art. 24. The Secretary-General of the United Nations shall inform all States referred to in art. 17, paragraph 1, of this Convention of the following particulars:

(a) Signatures, ratifications and accessions under arts. 17 and 18;

(b) The date of entry into force of this Convention under art. 19;

(c) Communications and declarations received under arts. 14, 20 and 23;

(d) Denunciations under art. 21.

Art. 25.(1) This Convention, of which the Chinese, English, French, Russian and Spanish texts are equally authentic, shall be deposited in the archives of the United Nations.

(2) The Secretary-General of the United Nations shall transmit certified copies of this Convention to all States belonging to any of the categories mentioned in art. 17, paragraph 1, of the Convention.

B. The General Assembly,

Recalling the Declaration on the Granting of Independence to Colonial Countries and Peoples contained in its Res. 1514(XV) of 14 December 1960,

Bearing in mind its Res. 1654(XVI) of 27 November 1961, which established the Special Committee on the Situation with regard to the implementation of the Declaration on the Granting of Independence to Colonial Countries and Peoples to examine the application of the Declaration and to carry out its provisions by all means at its disposal,

Bearing in mind also the provisions of art. 15 of the International Convention on the Elimination of All Forms of Racial Discrimination contained in the annex to resolution A above,

Recalling that the General Assembly has established other bodies to receive and examine petitions from the peoples of colonial countries.

Convinced that close co-operation between the Committee on the Elimination of Racial Discrimination, established by the International Convention on the Elimination of All Forms of Racial Discrimination, and the bodies of the United Nations charged with receiving and examining petitions from the peoples of colonial countries will facilitate the achievement of the objectives of both the Convention and the Declaration on the Granting of Independence to Colonial Countries and Peoples,

Recognizing that the elimination of racial discrimination in all its forms is vital to the achievement of fundamental human rights and to the assurance of the dignity and worth of the human person, and thus constitutes a pre-emptory obligation under the Charter of the United Nations,

(1) Calls upon the Secretary-General to make available to the Committee on the Elimination of Racial Discrimination, periodically or at its request, all information in his possession relevant to article 15 of the International Convention on the Elimination of All Forms of Racial Discrimination;

(2) Requests the Special Committee on the Situation with regard to the implementation of the Declaration on the Granting of Independence to Colonial Countries and Peoples, and all other bodies of the United Nations authorized to receive and examine petitions from the peoples of the colonial countries, to transmit to the Committee on the Elimination of Racial Discrimination, periodically or at its request, copies of petitions from those peoples relevant to the Convention, for the comments and recommendations of the said Committee;

(3) Requests the bodies referred to in paragraph 2 above to include in their annual reports to the General Assembly a summary of the action taken by them under the terms of the present resolution."

On Feb. 10, 1989 the Vatican's Declaration on Racism condemned all forms of Racism:

"South Africa is an extreme case of a vision of racial inequality".

"The most obvious form of racism in the strictest sense of the word to be found today is 'institutionalized racism'. This type is still sanctioned by the constitutions and laws of a country".

See also ▷ Antisemitism; ▷ Genetic Manipulation.

Official Records of the General Assembly. Twentieth Session, Supplement No. 14, pp. 47–52, New York, 1965; *UN Resolutions and Decisions adopted by the General Assembly During the First Part of its Forty-Third Session, from 20 September to 22 December, 1988,* pp. 319–324 and 331–335; *The New York Times,* February 11, 1989.

RACIAL SEGREGATION. A division of people introduced in the colonial epoch according to the color of their skin or other racial criteria, contrary to the principles of the UN Charter and international law. Racial segregation has maintained itself in the second half of the 20th century in the form of racist laws in the Republic of ▷ South Africa. ▷ Apartheid.

RACISM. ▷ Racial discrimination.

RACISM, INTERNATIONAL YEAR AGAINST RACISM AND DISCRIMINATION, 1971. The year was proclaimed by the International Conference for Human Rights in Teheran on May 13, 1968; started under UN aegis a campaign against Racism and Discrimination.

RAD. A special unit employed to express the absorbed dose of ionizing radiation. ▷ SI.

RADAR. Radio Aids for Defense and Reconnaissance or Radio Detection and Ranging. An international term for a radiolocator, a system of co-functioning electronic, electromechanical, and auxiliary units which make it possible to locate and measure the location of both stationary objects (mountains in fog) as well as moving objects (planes, ships); developed by British scientists 1935, improved during the Battle of Britain, 1940; after the war enhanced safety in civil aviation; helpful in the development of guided missiles and rocket technology; and in the development of astronomy. In 1946 radar waves beamed from the earth hit the moon for the first time.

Radiolocation stations connected with an anti-missile defense system (▷ ABM) were the subject of Soviet–American negotiations in ▷ SALT I.

The early warning radar was produced first by the USSR in 1958 and 1960 by the USA, as the Ballistic Missiles Early Warning System. The first aircraft virtually undetectable by radar is the ▷ Stealth Bomber, produced by the USA in 1987.

See also ▷ Space Radar.

A.P. PROVE, *One Story of Radar,* London, 1948; R.M. PAGE, *The Origin of Radar,* New York, 1962; SIPRI *Yearbook 1976,* London, 1976, pp. 115, 117; R. LEGER SILVER, *World Military and Social Expenditures 1987–88,* Washington DC, 1987; D. ROBERT-SON, *Guide to Modern Defense and Strategy,* Detroit, 1988.

RADIATION. A subject of UN control; since 1955 by the UN Scientific Committee on the Effects of Atomic Radiation, UNSCEAR. Since 1957, the IAEA, in consultation with the WHO, issues basic safety standards for radiation protection which served as a reference for national legislation. The UNSCEAR undertakes studies in the following fields: the scientific bases for the evaluation of radiation risk and detriment, doses from natural sources of radiation and from nuclear explosions, the problem of radioactive wastes, doses from the medical uses of radiation, the biological effects of pre-natal irradiation, the early effects of high doses

R

of radiation on man, the genetic effects of irradiation and radiation-induced tumors in man.

The US Scientific Committee on the Effects of Atomic Radiation approved in Vienna, April 14–18, 1986 three major scientific reports, which deal with the genetic effects of radiation, the biological effects of pre-natal radiation, and dose response relationship for radiation induced cancer. After the ▷ Chernobyl accident, 1986, the USSR presented to the IAEA and WHO in May 1987 a study of long-term health effects from exposure to low doses of radiation. The IAEA, WHO, ILO, FAO, UNEP, UNSCEA and ECE initiated in 1987 a global radiation monitoring programme.

See also ▷ Food Irradiation.

IAEA, *Radiation. A Fact of Life*, Vienna, 1979; *UN Chronicle*, May, 1980, pp. 21–22, December, 1983, pp. 40; UNSCEAR, *Ionizing Radiation*, New York, 1982; IAEA, *Radiation Protection Glossary* (English, French, Russian and Spanish), Vienna, 1986; IAIA *Newsbriefs*, Nr 7, 1987; D. ROBERTSON, *Guide to Modern Defense and Strategy*, Detroit, 1988.

RADIATORS. Subject of international co-operation. Organization reg. with the UIA:

European Association of Manufacturers of Radiators, f. 1966, Switzerland.

Yearbook of International Organizations, 1986/87; The Europa Yearbook 1988. A World Survey, Vol. I, London, 1988.

RADIESTHESIA. An international term for sensitivity to radiation of underground mineral deposits, water veins, buried minerals; subject of international research within the field of ▷ Psychotronics. Organization reg. with the UIA:
International Association of Hydrogeologists, f. 1956, Paris. Publ.: *Information Bulletin*.

W.B. GIBSON, "Radiesthesia", in: *The Complete Illustrated Book of the Physical Sciences*, London, 1969; *Yearbook of International Organizations*.

RADIOACTIVE WASTE. An international term, subject of international conventions against air, sea and soil pollution; subject of national legislations (US Nuclear Waste Policy Act of 1982, French Agence nationale pour la gestion des déchats radioactives, ANDRA, 1978; Swedish Radiation Protection Act, 1958 etc.). Subject of the GA Res. 43/74, of Dec. 7, 1988 after a dumping affair of West European nuclear and industrial wastes in Africa:

"Aware of the consideration by the Conference on Disarmament during its 1988 session of the question of dumping of radioactive wastes, which cause destruction, damage or injury by means of radiation produced by decay of such material;
(1) Condemns all nuclear-waste dumping practices that would infringe upon the sovereignty of States;
(2) Expresses profound concern regarding practices of dumping nuclear and industrial wastes in Africa, which have grave implications on the national security of African countries;
(3) Calls upon all States to ensure that no radioactive waste is dumped in the territory of other States in infringement of their sovereignty;
(4) Requests the Conference on Disarmament to take into account, in the ongoing negotiation for a convention on the prohibition of radiological weapons, the dumping of radioactive wastes in the territory of other States,"

J. HEINONEN, F. GERA, *Waste Disposal Management, in: IAEA Bulletin*, Summer, 1985; *UN Resolutions and Decisions adopted by the General Assembly during the First Part of its Forty-Third Session, from 20 September to 22 December, 1988*, New Yok, 1989, p. 161.

RADIOACTIVE WASTE MANAGEMENT. An international term., For safety and technical reasons, the various forms of nuclear wastes are usually categorized by their levels of radioactivity,

heat content, and potential hazard. The IAEA established definitions describing the technical features of radioactive wastes that are applied to their management in many countries. For general purposes, however, more simplified descriptions and explanations of important terms may be useful to a basic understanding:

Half-Life. This term refers to the time it takes for any given radionuclide to lose half of its radioactivity. Most significant fission products, which are highly radioactive, have half-lives of about 30 years or less; for example, caesium-137. A few, such as iodine-129, have half-lives in the thousands of years. For perspective, natural uranium has a half-life of about 4500 million years, or roughly the age of the earth.

Short-Lived and Long-Lived Wastes. These terms refer to a given radioactive element's half-life. Those with half-lives longer than approximately 30 years are generally considered long-lived.

Low-Level Wastes (LLW) contain a negligible amount of long-lived radionuclides. Produced by peaceful nuclear activities in industry, medicine, research, and by nuclear power operations, such wastes may include items such as packaged gloves, rags, glass, small tools, paper, and filters which have been contaminated by radioactive material.

Intermediate-Level Wastes (ILW) contain lower levels of radioactivity and heat content than high-level wastes, but they still must be shielded during handling and transport. Such wastes may include resins from reactor operations or solidified chemical sludges, as well as pieces of equipment or metal fragments. Commercial engineering processes are being used to treat and immobilize these wastes; disposal in surface structures or shallow burial is practiced widely. Some countries have built or plan to build shallow repositories in rock formations on land or under the sea.

High-Level Wastes (HLW) arise from the reprocessing of spent fuel from nuclear power reactors through which uranium and plutonium can be recovered for re-use. These wastes contain trans-uranic elements, and fission products that are highly radioactive, heat-generating, and long-lived. Liquid HLW has been effectively stored in tanks at specially-constructed facilities. Before final disposal and isolation from the biosphere, they require treatment and solidification. Spent fuel that is not reprocessed may be considered a high-level waste.

Alpha-bearing Wastes (also called transuranic, plutonium-contaminated material, or alpha wastes) include wastes that are contaminated with enough long-lived, alpha-emitting nuclides to make disposal at a shallow land burial site unacceptable. They arise principally from spent fuel reprocessing and mixed-oxide fuel fabrication. The wastes may be disposed of in a similar manner to HLW.

IAEA. *Radioactive Waste Management. Status Report*, Vienna, 1985; IAEA *Siting, Design and Construction of Underground Depositories for Radioactive Wastes*, Vienna, 1986; IAEA *New Features*, May 20, 1988.

RADIOACTIVITY OF THE ATMOSPHERE. The radiation from fallout emitted during nuclear bomb explosions or by the leakage of an atomic reactor; pollution of the earth's atmosphere and then land and sea surfaces to a degree dangerous to man and nature. Subject of international research under the aegis of the UN. ▷ Radiation.

RADIOACTIVITY OF THE DEEP-SEA. An international term, subject of the 1972 ▷ Seas and Ocean Protection Treaty, 1972. This Convention on the Prevention of Marine Pollution by Dumping of Wastes and other Matters, known also as the ▷ London Dumping Convention, 1972; under the specific responsibility of the IAEA:
(a) defines high-level radioactive waste that is prohibited from being dumped;
(b) makes recommendations for the dumping of other radioactive waste.

On the IAEA request the scientific group ▷ GESAMP recommended an Oceanographic Model

for the Dispersion of Wastes Disposed of in the Deep-Sea, and the Nuclear Energy Agency of the ▷ OECD has established the Consultation and Surveillance Mechanism for Sea Dumping of Radioactive Waste.

A. HAGAN, B. RUEGGER, *Deep-Sea Disposal: Scientific Bases to Control Pollution, in: IAEA Bulletin*, Spring 1986, pp. 29–32.

RADIO AMERICAN CONVENTIONS. The first Agreement on Radiocommunications for the South American Region was signed on Apr. 10, 1935 in Buenos Aires by Argentina, Bolivia, Brazil, Chile, Paraguay and Uruguay; came into force on Jan. 1, 1936; replaced by Second Regional Agreement, signed on June 20, 1937 in Rio de Janeiro, ratified only by Brazil and Peru; suspended by the Third Regional Agreement signed on Jan. 17, 1940 in Buenos Aires by Argentina, Bolivia, Brazil, Chile, Colombia, Ecuador, Paraguay, Peru, Uruguay, Venezuela; came into force on June 1, 1940. The First Inter-American Radio Conference prepared the Inter-American Radiocommunications Convention, signed on Dec. 13, 1937 at Havana and ratified by Bahamas, Brazil, Canada, Cuba, the Dominican Republic, Haiti, Mexico, Nicaragua, Panama, Peru (denounced 1956) and the USA came into force on Apr. 17, 1939. The same Inter-American Radio Conference prepared the following agreements:

An Inter-American Arrangement Concerning Radio-Communications, signed on Dec. 13, 1937 at Havana and ratified by Brazil, Canada, Chile, the Dominican Republic, Haiti, Mexico, Panama, Peru and the USA; came into force on July 1, 1938; and the North American Regional Broadcasting Agreement, signed on Dec. 13, 1937 at Havana and ratified by Bahamas, Canada, Cuba, the Dominican Republic, Haiti, Mexico and the USA; came into force on Mar. 29, 1940, revised 1946 and replaced by another North American Regional Broadcasting Agreement signed on Nov. 15, 1950 in Washington, DC. A Regional Radio Convention for Central America, Panama and the Canal Zone was signed on Dec. 8, 1938 in Guatemala City and ratified by Guatemala, Honduras, Nicaragua and the United States on behalf of the Canal Zone; came into force on Oct. 8, 1939. An Inter-American Radio Agreement was signed on Jan. 26, 1940 in Santiago and ratified by Brazil, Canada, Chile, the Dominican Republic, the USA and Venezuela; replaced by another Inter-American Radio Agreement, signed on July 9, 1949 in Washington, DC. An Inter-American Telecommunications Convention was signed on Sept. 27, 1945 in Rio de Janeiro, but ratified only by Brazil, Canada and Mexico and did not come into force.

OAS, *Inter-American Treaties and Conventions*, Washington, DC, 1971, pp. 107–118; S.J. DOUGLAS, *Inventing American Broadcasting 1899–1922*, Baltimore, 1988.

RADIO AND TV ORGANIZATIONS. Organizations reg. with the UIA:

Asia-Pacific Broadcasting Union, f. 1964, Kuala Lumpur, Malaysia Broadcasting Organizations of Non-Aligned Countries, f. 1977, Freetown, Sierra Leone.
European Broadcasting Union, f. 1950, Geneva, Switzerland.
International Amateur Radio Union, f. 1925, Paris. Official relations with ITU. Publ.: *IARU Calendar*.
International Association of Broadcasting, f. 1946, Montevideo, Uruguay.
International Catholic Association for Radio and TV, f. 1928, Brussels. Consultative status with UNESCO and FAO. Publ.: *Wide World of Unda*.
International Council of French-Speaking Radio and Television Organizations, f. 1978, Geneva, Switzerland.

International Federation of Radio Officers, f. 1922, Copenhagen. Consultative status with ITU.

International Frequency Registration Board, f. 1947, Geneva.

International Maritime Radio Association, f. 1928, Brussels. Official relations with ITU, ICAO, WMO, IMCO.

International Maritime Radio Committee, f. 1928, London, UK.

International Mission Radio Association, f. 1963, Chicago, USA. Catholic Mission Organization.

International Radio and TV Organization, f. 1946, Prague, Czechoslovakia. Intergovernmental Institution. Members: Afghanistan, Algeria, Bulgaria, Byelorussia, Cuba, Czechoslovakia, Egypt, Estonia, Finland, GDR, Hungary, Iraq, Kampuchea, S. Korea, Laos, Latvia, Lithuania, Mali, Moldavia, Mongolia, Nicaragua, Poland, Romania, Sudan, Ukraine, USSR, Vietnam, Yemen.

International Radio and TV Society, f. 1962, New York.

International Radio Consultative Committee, f. 1927, Geneva.

International Radio-Television University, f. 1949, Paris. Publ.: *Conference reports*.

International Special Committee on Radio Interference, f. 1933, London. Official relations with ITU.

International Union of Radio Science, f. 1919, Brussels, Belgium. Publ.: Review of Radio Science.

Inter-Union Commission on Frequency Allocations for Radio Astronomy and Space Sciences, f. 1960, Slough, UK.

Radio Amateur Satellite Corporation, f. 1969, Washington, DC. Publ.: *AMSAT Newsletter* (quarterly).

Union of National Radio and TV Organizations of Africa, f. 1962, Bamako. Consultative status with ECOSOC, ITU and UNESCO. Publ.: *URTNA Review*.

World Association of Methodists Radio Amateurs and Clubs, f. 1957, Penrith, Cumberl., UK. Publ.: *Circular Letter*.

G. WEDELL, *Making Broadcasting Useful: The African Experience. The Development of Radio and TV in Africa in the 1980's*, Boston, 1986; *Yearbook of International Organizations, 1986/87: The Europa Year book 1988. A World Survey*, Vol. I, London, 1988.

RADIOCOMMUNICATION. The International Radiotelegraph Convention, 1927, defined the term as follows:

"The term 'radiocommunication' or 'radioelectric communication' applies to the wireless transmission of writing, signs, signals, facsimiles, and sounds of all kinds by means of Hertzian waves."

LNTS, Vol. 84, p. 101.

RADIO EUROPE. The first multinational broadcasting service originated in 1977 on the initiative of the BBC, first with programs in English, French and German, and later Danish, Dutch, Icelandic, Italian; aimed at listeners in EEC member countries.

RADIO EUROPEAN CONVENTIONS. Signed on June 19, 1933 in Lucerne by the governments of Austria, Belgium, Czechoslovakia, Denmark, Estonia, France, Greece, Iceland, Ireland, Italy, Latvia, Norway, Poland, Portugal, Romania, Switzerland, the Vatican, the UK and the USSR. Signed on the same day was the Lucerne Plan allocating frequencies for all European radio stations. The Second Radiophonic Convention was signed on Sept. 15, 1948 in Copenhagen; became effective on Mar. 15, 1950, revised in May, 1975 in Montreux. The Convention established obligatory notification of radio wave frequency under consideration of the so-called ▷ Copenhagen Plan, which provided the basis for the international List of Frequencies and defined the European Radiophonic Zone. Since 1933 the International Special Committee on Radio Interference (CISPR) is in operation, with seat in London; in connection with the International Commission for Electrotechnics.

ITU, *Radio Regulations*, Berne, 1971; *World Radio and TV Handbook*, London, 1975.

RADIO FREE EUROPE. An American broadcasting station, in 1950–75 directed and financed by the CIA, similar to ▷ Radio Liberty, broadcasting its programs to Eastern European countries from the FRG, Spain and Portugal. Subject of protests before the UN. In 1975 the USA government merged Radio Free Europe and Radio Liberty into one institution under management of the Council of the Radio Station in Washington, financed from a special budget adopted each year. In Mar., 1977 President J. Carter, and in 1983 President R. Reagan, submitted to Congress a plan for considerable power expansion of the Free Europe station. Radio Free Europe broadcasts its programs in six languages. In Feb. 1987 ▷ radio jamming in the whole area of Warsaw Pact States by the Soviet Union was limited to the Soviet Union area only.

RADIO IN THE CAUSE OF PEACE. An International Convention Concerning the Use of Broadcasting in the Cause of Peace signed on Sept. 23, 1936 in Geneva by the governments of Albania, Argentina, Austria, Belgium, Brazil, Chile, Czechoslovakia, Denmark, the Dominican Republic, Egypt, Estonia, France, Greece, Spain, India, Colombia, Lithuania, Luxembourg, Mexico, the Netherlands, New Zealand, Poland, Romania, Switzerland, Turkey, Uruguay and the USSR.

The Inter-American Conference for the Maintenance of Peace on Dec. 19, 1936 in Buenos Aires approved Res. XV, Radio-Broadcasting in the Service of Peace, "convinced that for the Moral Disarmament of peoples it is necessary to promote the establishment of certain standards, concerning the use of radio-broadcasting in the interest of Peace."

LNTS, 1936; *International Conciliation*, No. 328, New York, March, 1937.

RADIO IN WORLD WAR II. During the war radio was an instrument of international communication as well as diversion and psychological war. The Germans, on the day of the invasion of Poland, Sept. 1, 1939, issued a directive "on extraordinary measures in the area of radiophony," forbidding all inhabitants of Germany from listening to and disseminating foreign radio broadcasts; Eastern Europeans in territories occupied by Germany were forbidden to possess or listen to the radio on pain of death, with the exception of the programs transmitted by loudspeakers in public places. The underground press printed daily transcripts of allied radio programs, London BBC, Moscow Radio and Voice of America.

RADIOISOTOPE TRACERS IN INDUSTRY. Subject of international co-operation, sponsored by the IAEA, which is currently preparing a guidebook on the application of radioisotope tracers in specific industries. Major headings include: the concept of tracers, general tracer technology, tracer methodology, case studies and current trends.

IAEA Bulletin, 1987, No. 2.

RADIO JAMMING. An international term, subject of international discussion. The system of hindering reception of foreign radio programs inside one or more countries, initiated by the USSR during the Cold War after the opening of Radio Free Europe and the foreign language section of the Voice of America in the 1950's, extended in the following years to foreign language programs of the NATO states radio stations in the whole area of Warsaw Pact States. In Feb. 1987 the USSR lifted jamming of the BBC's Russian service and stopped radio-jamming of all western stations in the Warsaw Pact area.

L.C. SOLEY, J.S. NICHOLS, *Clandestine Radio Broadcasting*, New York, 1986; K.R.M. SHORT, *Western Broadcasting Over the Iron Curtain*, New York, 1986.

RADIO LIBERTY. An American broadcasting station (in the years 1950–59 under the name of Radio Liberation) broadcasting programs for different nationalities of the USSR, in 1950–75 directed and financed by CIA. In 1975 merged with ▷ Radio Free Europe; broadcasts its programs in 16 languages.

In 1988 the USSR continued to jam Radio Liberty broadcasts.

RADIOLOGICAL PROTECTION. ▷ ICRP.

RADIOLOGICAL WARFARE. An international term – war with radioactive weapons – a subject of bilateral talks between the USA and the USSR at Geneva 1977–79, resulting in a joint USA–USSR proposal on major elements of Treaty Prohibiting the Development, Production, Stockpiling and Use of Radiological Weapons.

Committee on Disarmament. Doc. CD/31, Geneva, July 9, 1979 SIPRI. *World Armaments and Disarmament Yearbook 1980*, London, 1980, pp. 381–388.

RADIOLOGY. A subject of international research and co-operation. Organizations reg. with the UIA:

Collegium Orbis Radiologiae Docentium, f. 1961, Zurich.

European Association of Radiology, f. 1962, Geneva.

European Society for Cardio-vascular Radiology, f. 1976, Lyon.

European Society of Pediatric Radiology, f. 1961, Paris.

International Commission on Radiological Education and Information, f. 1969, Geneva.

International Commission on Radiological Protection, f. 1928, Sutton, UK. Official relations with WHO and IAEA. Publ.: *Recommendations and Reports*.

International Society of Radiographers and Radiological Technicians, f. 1959, New Delhi. Consultative status with WHO and ECOSOC. Publ.: *Newsletter*.

Scandinavian Radiological Society, f. 1919, Oslo.

Yearbook of International Organizations.

RADIO SIGNALS OF THE SEA SERVICES. A subject of international regulation. The British admiralty publishes annually in five volumes the Admiralty List of Radio Signals, including the signals of (I) coastal radio stations and physicians' services, (II) bearing radio stations and lighthouses, (III) meteorological services, (IV) observational meteorological stations, and (V) radio time signals and radio navigational warnings.

RADIOSUBVERSION. An international term for systems of conducting radio propaganda for subversive purposes directed at a country attacked by armed force or harried by psychological war. Applied for the first time on a large scale by the Axis powers before World War II. In 1936, under the patronage of the International Institute of Cultural Co-operation, a convention was signed in Paris which prohibited spreading of false information by radio and obligated international radio co-operation. ▷ Radio in the cause of peace.

RADIOTELEGRAPH. A subject of international conventions on radiotelegraph communication between ships and naval craft at sea and with the coast. The first, the International Radiotelegraph

Convention, was signed on July 5, 1912 in London; replaced by the Radiotelegraph General Convention with General Regulations and Additional Regulations, signed on Nov. 25, 1927 in Washington by the governments of Argentina, Australia, Austria, Belgium, Bolivia, Brazil, Bulgaria, Canada, Chile, China, Colombia, Costa Rica, Cuba, Czechoslovakia, Denmark, Dominican Republic, Egypt, El Salvador, Estonia, Finland, France, Germany, Greece, Guatemala, Haiti, Honduras, Hungary, Ireland, Italy, Japan, Liberia, Morocco, Mexico, the Netherlands, Nicaragua, Norway, New Zealand, Panama, Paraguay, Peru, Persia, Poland, Portugal, Romania, Serbo–Croat–Slovene State, Sweden, Switzerland, Tunis, Turkey, Uruguay and Venezuela.

Principles of the General Regulations:

"No radiotelegraph station shall be established or worked by an individual person or by a private enterprise without a special licence issued by the Government of the Country to which the station in question subject."

"The holder of a licence must undertake to preserve the secrecy of correspondence."

LNTS, Vol. 1, p. 135 and Vol. 84, p. 129.

RADIO-TREASON. Germ. Radio-Verrat, international term coined in 1944 by J. Goebbels, minister of propaganda of Nazi Germany for listening to enemy radio stations during a war. The first German condemned to death for "radio-treason" was 67 year old Alfred Jacob executed by guillotine in Berlin July 17, 1944.

RADIO VATICANO. The broadcasting station of the Apostolic See, transmitting daily special programs for Africa, America, Asia, Australia, Europe and Oceania.

RADIO VOICE OF AMERICA. The official multilanguage foreign radio service of the US government. The ▷ radio jamming of Voice of America in the USSR and Warsaw Pact States area since 1980 was totally lifted on May 23, 1987. On the same day the USSR started English language broadcasts to the United States from Cuba.

KEESING's *Record of World Events*, June, 1988.

RADON. A product of the radioactive decay of ▷ uranium in rocks and soil. The gas is invisible and odorless. The American Environmental Protection Agency, EPA est. 1988, that 8 million US homes contain a potentially hazardous level of radon, which is blamed for 5,000 to 20,000 deaths annually.

T. MONMANAY, M. NACKER, T. EMERSON, "EPA Urges Testing of all Homes for Deadly Gas", in: *Newsweek*, Sept. 26, 1988.

RAILWAYS. A subject of international co-operation through international train schedules, international railroad organizations, and international conventions on railways transport. The first railroad line was opened on Sept. 27, 1825 in England between two cities, Stockton and Darlington; 24 cars were pulled by a steam locomotive called "Locomotion No. 1", constructed to the specifications of G. Stephenson (1781–1848), with 300 passengers and 90 tons of coal and flour at a speed of 24 km/hr on level ground and 10–12 km/hr uphill. The longest railroad network was built in North America, c. 40% of the world rail lines. The continent with the second longest railroad network is Europe c. 33%. While in America, South Asia, and Africa privately-owned railroads still exist, in Europe the last private stock companies were taken over by the state 1938/39, so that European international railroad organizations are interstate institutions. In Nov., 1972 the state-owned railroads

of the EEC states, now including Great Britain, decided to participate in the formulation of a statute for one common interstate Western European Railroad Company and prepare the complete standardization of all areas of the railroad system. According to UN statistics the longest railroad lines in 1971 were in the USA – 338,000 km, and the USSR – 135,000 km, then in Canada – 70,000 km, France – 35,000 km, FRG – 31,000 km, Poland – 26,000 km, Japan and Italy 20,000 km.

The General Railways Convention with Statute was signed on Dec. 9, 1923 in Geneva by the governments of Austria, Belgium, Brazil, the British Empire, Bulgaria, Chile, Czechoslovakia, Denmark, El Salvador, Estonia, Finland, France, Germany, Greece, Hungary, Italy, Japan, Latvia, Lithuania, Norway, the Netherlands, Poland, Portugal, Romania, Serbo–Croat–Slovene State, Siam, Spain, Sweden, Switzerland and Uruguay. The Statute on the International Regime of Railways constitutes an integral part of the Convention. Part I of the Statute: Intercharge of international traffic by rail; Part II: Reciprocity in the use of Rolling Stock: technical uniformity; Part III: Relations between the railway and its users; Part IV: Tariffs; Part V: Financial Arrangements; Part VI: General Regulations. One year after the Geneva Railways Convention was signed the Berne International Convention concerning the Transport of Passengers and Baggage by Rail, with Annexes and Protocol, signed on Oct. 23, 1924 in Berne, and Procès-Verbal, signed on Oct. 18, 1927 in Berne were concluded between Austria, Belgium, Bulgaria, Czechoslovakia, Denmark, Estonia, Finland, France, Germany, Greece, Hungary, Italy, Latvia, Lithuania, Luxembourg, the Netherlands, Norway, Poland, Portugal, Romania, the Serbo–Croat–Slovene State, Sweden and Switzerland.

LNTS, Vol. 47, p. 55; Vol. 78, p. 17–87; W. HAUSTEIN, "Die Völkerrechtliche Stellung der Eisenbahnrecht", in: STRUPP-SCHLOCHAUER's *Wörterbuch des Völkerrechts*, Berlin, 1960; ONU, *Los ferrocarriles internacionales de Sudamérico y la integración económica regional*, New York, 1972; O.S. NOCK, *World Atlas of Railways*, New York, 1983.

RAILWAYS CMEA ORGANIZATION. The Organization for Railway Co-operation, ORC, est. on Sept. 1, 1957 at Warsaw is a working organ of the three Conventions between Albania, Bulgaria, the People's Republic of China, Czechoslovakia, the GDR, Hungary, Korea, Mongolia, Poland, Romania, the USSR and Vietnam:

The Agreement on International Railway Passengers Communications, AIRPC;

The Agreement on International Railway Freight Communications, AIRFC, concluded in 1951. Cuba acceded in 1966. A co-operation Protocol between ORC and the CMEA concluded on Oct. 16, 1962.

The Agreement on Common Stock of Freight Cars, signed on Dec. 21, 1963 in Bucharest, came into force on Aug. 20, 1964; amended by the Moscow Protocol of Feb. 22, 1973.

Recueil de Documents, Varsovie, No. 9, 1957; W.E. BUTLER (ed.), *A Source Book on Socialist International Organizations*, Alphen, 1978, pp. 455–474.

RAILWAYS INTERNATIONAL ORGANIZATIONS. The inter-governmental organizations, reg. with the UIA:

Arab Union of Railways, f. 1979, Alepro, Syria. Publ.: *Glossary of Railway Terms (Arabic, English, French and German)*.

Asociatión Latinoamericana de Ferrocarriles, Latinamerican Railways Association, f. 1964, Buenos Aires by the governments of Argentina, Bolivia, Brazil, Chile, Columbia, Ecuador, Mexico, Paraguay, Uruguay and Venezuela.

Central Office for International Railway Transport, Office central de transport internationale par chemins de fer, OCTI, f. Oct. 14, 1890, Berne, by First International Convention Concerning the Carriage of Goods by Rail, CIM; extended by International Convention Concerning the Carriage of Passengers and Luggage by Rail, CIV, of Oct. 23, 1924; both Conventions revised on Feb. 17, 1970 at Berne; came into force in 1975. Additional Convention related to Liability of Railways for Death and Personal Injury to Passengers of Feb. 26, 1966, came into force on Jan. 1, 1973. Members: Governments of 32 African, Asian and European Countries. Publ.: *Bulletin for International Railways Transport*.

Common CMEA Wagon Parc Office, f. 1964, Prague.

European Company for the Financing of Railway Rolling Stock, f. 1955, Berne, by International Convention, came into force Nov. 20, 1965; Basel. Members: railways administration of 16 European countries.

European Goods Trains Time-Table Conference, f. 1924, Prague. Publ.: *Livret-indicateur International Marchandises LIM, Livret TEEM, Livret TEC*.

European Passenger Time-Table Conference, f. 1923, Berne. Members: 25 European countries.

European Railway Wagon Pool, f. 1953, Berne, by European Railway Convention, signed by Austria, Belgium, Denmark, France, FRG, Italy, Luxembourg, the Netherlands, Switzerland.

International Association of Rolling Stock Builders, f. 1930, Paris.

International Carriage and Van Union, Union internationale des voitures et fourgons, RIC, f. 1921, Berne. Publ.: *Rules for Reciprocal Use of Carriage and Vans in International Traffic*.

International Organization for Transportation by Rope, f. 1959, Rome.

International Rail Transport Committee, f. 1902, Berne, organ of the CIM and CIV Conventions. Publ.: *Documents and Rules*.

International Railway Congress Association, IRCA, f. Dec. 13, 1884, Brussels, as Commission internationale du congrès des chemin de fer, under present name on Sept. 15, 1919. Members: governments, administrations and railway organizations in 77 countries. Publ. with International Union of Railways: *Selections of International Railway Documentation*.

International Union of Railway Medical Services, f. 1949.

International Union of Railways, Union internationale de chemins de fer, UIC, f. 1922, Paris. Consultative status with ECOSOC. Under aegis of Union: Central Bureau of Compensation, Berne; Information and Publicity Centre of the European Railway, Rome; International Office of Railway Documentation, Paris; International Railway Film Bureau, Paris; and Office for Research and Experiments, Utrecht. Publ.: *International Railway Statistics*.

International Wagon Union, f. 1921, Berne, by governments of Albania, Belgium, Bulgaria, Czechoslovakia, Denmark, France, Germany, Greece, Hungary, Italy, Luxembourg, the Netherlands, Norway, Poland, Romania, the Serb-Croat-Slovene State, Spain, Sweden, Switzerland, Turkey. Consultative status with ECOSOC.

Organization for the Collaboration of CMEA Railway, f. 1956, Warsaw.

Organization internationale des chemins de fer pour les transcontainers, Intercontainer, f. 1967, Basel.

Pan-American Railway Congress Association, Association del Congreso Panamericano de Ferrocarriles, f. 1906, Buenos Aires.

Union of European Railway Industries, f. 1975, Paris, France.

Union of European Railways Road Services, f. 1950, Frankfurt/M.

Yearbook of International Organizations, 1986/87; *The Europa Yearbook 1988. A World Survey*, Vol. 1, London, 1988.

RAILWAYS INTERNATIONAL STATIONS. The stations at border crossings for international railway traffic where, in keeping with the Geneva Convention on the Facilitation of Border-Crossing, Jan. 10, 1952, customs control is carried out either jointly by officers of both neighboring countries or on the delivery–receipt basis using mutual customs and tax privileges, simplification of personnel traffic control on both sides, etc.

RAILWAYS TIME-TABLES, INTERNATIONAL. Twice a year until 1914 (from 1872) European Passenger Time-Table Conferences were held at Berne. They became a registered institution with the League of Nations from Jan. 1, 1923 and met for annual sessions at Berne; from 1946 reg. with the UIA, headquarters, Berne, with biennial sessions held at different capital cities of states parties to conventions on railway transport. Associates 22 European countries. Founded in 1925 was a similar institution, headquarters in Prague, for freight trains, European Goods Trains Time-Table Conference, whose members, 22 European countries, are signatories of the same conventions on railways transport. ▷ Railways.

"RAINBOW WARRIOR". A fishing vessel, belonging to the international environmentalist organization ▷ Greenpeace, that while on an anti-nuclear protest mission in the South Pacific (against nuclear weapons tests in the ▷ Muroroa atoll) was blown up July 10, 1985 in Auckland harbour, New Zealand. One person was killed. New Zealand on July 26, 1985 accused French security officers of being responsible for the explosion. On Sept. 20, 1985 the French Prime Minister L. Fabius stated that the sinking of "Rainbow Warrior" had been carried out by French agents.

KEESING's *Contemporary Archive*, Sept., 1985 and Oct., 1985.

RAISINS (SULTANAS). A subject of world trade, co-operation and agreements:
Agreement between Australia, Greece and Turkey for the stabilization of Raisin (Sultana) Markets, signed on June 9, 1963 in Athens; came into force on June 25, 1963.
Agreement between Australia, Greece and Turkey for the stabilization of Raisin (Sultana) Markets, signed on June 20, 1964 in Munich; came into force on July 15, 1964.

RAISON DE GUERRE. An international doctrine, condemned by the Nuremberg Principles. See also ▷ War necessity.

D. ROBERTSON, *Guide to Modern Defense and Strategy*, Detroit, 1988.

RAISON D'ÉTAT. The reason of state. An international term handed down by the Renaissance (Guicciardini, Machiavelli) for superiority of the interests of the state over other norms.

RAJASTHAN CANAL. The canal constructed 1958–76 in the states of Punjab and Rajasthan, the largest irrigating system of India on the border with Pakistan.

RAMADAN (holy) ninth month of the Islam lunar calendar year, during which all Moslems must fast in the daylight hours. The first revelation of the ▷ Koran took place during Ramadan. Only the sick and soldiers are excluded, but it is an old custom to respect a Ramadan cease-fire during a war. Ramadan, like ▷ Yom Kippur, a Jewish festival, constitutes a period of atonement.

G.E. GRUNBAUM, *Muhammadan Festivals*, London, 1951.

RAMBLING. A subject of international co-operation. Organization reg. with the UIA:
European Ramblers Association, f. 1969, Stuttgart. Promotes a European network of long-distance walking routes.

Yearbook of International Organizations.

RAMBOUILLET. A town in North France, dept. Yvelines, since 1871 official summer residence of French presidents in the old chateau.

RAND. Research and Development Corporation, est. 1948 by the US Air Force, "first of the big American Think-Tanks".

D. ROBERTSON, *Guide to Modern Defense and Strategy*, Detroit, 1988.

RAND. A monetary unit of South Africa; one rand = 100 cents; issued (replacing the South African pound on Feb. 14, 1961) by the South African Reserve Bank.

RANGOON. The capital (Pop. 1983, estimate: 2,458,712) since 1753 of Burma on the Rangoon River, city and the chief port on the Gulf of Martaban. UN Information Center.

The Europa Yearbook, 1937. A World Survey, Vol. I, London, 1987.

RANN OF KUTCH. A salt waste, 23,310 sq. km in the Kutch or Cutch district, 44,030 sq. km in Gujarat State, India, bounded on the north by Pakistan; site of Indo-Pakistani military conflict 1965. On Feb. 19, 1968 the International Court of Justice decided in the Rann of Kutch Case to give about 10% of the border area to Pakistan and about 90% to India.

UN Chronicle, December, 1983.

RAPACKI PLAN, 1957. A plan of the Polish government submitted on Oct. 2, 1957 by the Minister of Foreign Affairs, Adam Rapacki, at the XII Session of the UN General Assembly; the essence of the plan was the creation, under the control of the states of the Warsaw Pact and NATO, of a denuclearized zone in Central Europe, taking in the territory of Czechoslovakia, FRG, GDR, and Poland. The government of Poland on Feb. 14, 1958 formally submitted its proposal in the form of a memorandum to the governments of the Four Powers, Czechoslovakia, FRG, GDR, and also Canada, Belgium, Denmark, Holland and Luxembourg.

On May 8, 1958, a Soviet Memorandum on the agenda of a Summit Meeting, handed to the British, US and French Ambassadors in Moscow, included the following proposals, concerning the Creation in Central Europe of a Zone Free of Atom, Hydrogen and Rocket Weapons:

"In Central Europe at the present time two groupings of States oppose each other, and there is concentrated a quantity not normal for peacetime of armed forces and armaments of various types. This very circumstance alone creates a serious threat to peace, and it is impossible to close one's eyes to the fact that in such a situation, by evil intent or by chance, there can break out the conflagration of a new war with the use of the most modern means of destruction – nuclear and rocket weapons. In order to exclude the danger of such a development of events, the Soviet Government deems it expedient to examine at the Conference the proposal of the Government of the Polish People's Republic about the creation in Europe of a zone free of atom, hydrogen, and rocket weapons which would include the territories of the Polish People's Republic, the Czechoslovak Republic, the German Democratic Republic, and the Federal Republic of Germany. Assumption by these States of the obligation not to produce, or to permit the stationing in their territories of, nuclear weapons of all possible types, and also of sites for the launching of rockets which can bear nuclear warheads, undoubtedly would contribute to the prevention of the possibility of an outbreak of military conflicts in the centre of Europe.

Inasmuch as the Governments of the Polish People's Republic, the Czechoslovak Republic, and the German Democratic Republic have already declared their agreement to enter into an atom-free zone, the creation of such a zone now depends only on the agreement of the Government of the Federal Republic of Germany.

Agreement among the Governments of the USSR, the USA, Great Britain, and France on the expediency of the creation of an atom-free zone in this region of Europe undoubtedly would facilitate attainment of agreement with the Government of the Federal Republic of Germany regarding the adherence of the Federal Republic of Germany to this zone.

Agreement on the creation of an atom-free zone in Europe will be effective if, together with the appropriate obligations of the States included in the zone, the Powers whose armies are equipped with nuclear and rocket weapons, for their part, would assume an obligation to respect the status of this zone, and consider the territory of the States included in it as excluded from the sphere of use of atom, hydrogen, and rocket weapons. As for the Soviet Union, it has already declared its readiness to assume these obligations if the Governments of the United States, Great Britain, and France do the same. The obligations of States included within the zone and also the obligations of the Great Powers could be formulated either in the form of an appropriate international treaty or in the form of appropriate unilateral declarations.

With the aim of ensuring the effectiveness of the obligations and their fulfilment, the interested States would undertake to establish on the territory of the atom-free zone a system of broad and effective control, both ground and aerial, with the establishment of control-points by agreement of the appropriate State.

The creation in the centre of Europe of an atom-free zone would be an important step on the road toward cessation of the dangerous arms race and removal of the threat of atomic war."

On May 17, 1958 the United Kingdom Government's reply to the Polish note read as follows:

"I have the honour to refer to the plan for the establishment of an atom-free zone in Europe which Your Excellency outlined in the General Assembly of the United Nations on the 7th of October 1957, and which was expounded in greater detail in Your Excellency's Note and Memorandum of the 14th of February 1958.

I have now been instructed by her Majesty's Principal Secretary of State for Foreign Affairs to inform Your Excellency that Her Majesty's Government have studied this plan with great care. Her Majesty's Government have every sympathy with the Polish Government in their efforts to ensure and to increase the security of their country, and they share the desire of the Polish Government to see progress in disarmament and the reduction of international tension.

Her Majesty's Government consider, however, that the proposals of the Polish Government raise wider issues to which, nevertheless, they appear to offer no solution. Among these issues is the threat to the security of the Members of the North Atlantic Treaty Organisation which might arise, owing to the preponderant strength of Soviet conventional forces, if the Polish Government's proposals were accepted. If the security of Western European countries was to be maintained, it would be essential that any measures which might be taken to reduce nuclear armaments in Central Europe should be accompanied by measures to reduce the Soviet preponderance in conventional weapons in the whole of Central and Eastern Europe. It would be necessary for all these measures to be subject to control and inspection of the most effective kind. It is also the considered opinion of Her Majesty's Government that the question of German reunification would not be furthered by the adoption of Your Excellency's proposals. Her Majesty's Government have, however, in no way diminished their interest in the solution of the problem of disarmament, European security, and Germany. They have in conjunction with their Allies already made constructive proposals dealing with these problems both at the Geneva Conference in 1955 and in the Disarmament Sub-Committee of the United Nations. Her Majesty's Government hope that progress towards a solution of these major problems may be made at the preparatory discussions for a conference of Heads of Government, at such a conference itself, or in some other."

R

Though the Rapacki Plan was not supported by the NATO states, it did initiate a world-wide debate on the possibilities of establishing ▷ Denuclearized zones in various regions of the world. At a session of the UN General Assembly in June 1978 devoted to disarmament the Soviet delegation made the following proposal:

"Not placing nuclear weapons on the territories of those states which presently do not have such weapons. Such an agreement could be a step forward to the complete withdrawal, at a later time, of nuclear weapons from foreign territories."

This statement was commonly regarded as a return to the Rapacki Plan. ▷ Denuclearized Zones; ▷ Kekkonen Plans, 1963 and 1978; ▷ Tito Plan, 1958.

Selected Documents on Germany and the Question of Berlin 1944–1961, HMSO, London, 1961; A. ALBRECHT, *The Rapacki Plan. New Aspects*, Warsaw, 1963; A. RAPACKI, "Polish Plan of Denuclearization of Europe after 5 years", in: *Foreign Affairs*, Jan., 1967; *UN Chronicle*, July 1978; W. MULTAN, "The Rapacki Plan from the Perspective of a Quarter Century", in: *International Relations*, No. 1, Warsaw, 1984.

RAPALLO TREATY, 1922. The Treaty concluded on Apr. 16, 1922 in Rapallo by the Russian Federative Socialist Soviet Republic and Germany. The treaty settled in art. 1 "differences between Germany and Soviet Russia in questions that arose when the two States were in a state of war against each other"; Germany, under art. 2, renounced claims of indemnity for losses resulting from Russian revolutionary legislation concerning expropriation; under art. 3 both parties resolved to establish diplomatic and consular relations as soon as possible; under art. 4 both parties granted each other the most favored-nation status for the purpose of trade exchange; art. 5 expressed the RFSSR's readiness to establish co-operation with private German firms. The Rapallo Treaty was concluded for an unlimited period of time. On Nov. 5, 1922 in Berlin the Treaty was expanded to include Ukraine, Byelorussia and other Soviet republics and came into force on Jan. 31, 1923. Supplemented by the so-called Berlin Treaty in the form of exchange of notes, Apr. 24, 1926; prolonged June 24, 1931, and May 5, 1933; annulled June 22, 1941, by the German aggression against the USSR. Significance of the treaty derives not from its content but the fact that the two states having opposing political systems, one of them being boycotted by the Entente, the other bound by the Entente's resolutions determined by the Treaty of Versailles, normalized their political and economic relations.

W. RATHENAU, *Cannes and Genua*, Berlin, 1922; W.F. BLÜCHER, *Deutschlands Weg nach Rapallo*, Berlin, 1952; E. FISHER, *The Road to Rapallo*, Madison, 1952; W. WINZER, *Der Rapallo Verlag und seine nationale Bedeutung für Deutschland*, Berlin, 1953; K. KOBLIAKOV, *Od Bresta do Rapallo*, Moscow, 1954.

RAPAT. Radiation Protection Advisory Teams, groups of highly qualified experts from the IAEA; WHO and International Commission on Radiological Protection. Est. 1984 by the IAEA (25 groups until 1987).

IAEA Newsbriefs, 1987, No. 9.

RAPID DEPLOYMENT FORCE, RDF. The US military units organized since 1979, prepared to take immediate action in any region of American interests. On Nov. 29, 1984 six Arab Gulf states, members of the ▷ Co-operation Council for the Arab States of the Gulf, reached agreement on the creation of a rapid deployment force to help each other in case of external aggression against any one of them.

Zb. BRZEZINSKI, *Game Plan. How to Conduct the US–Soviet Contest*, Boston, 1987.

RAROTONGA. Formerly Good-enough's Island, a volcanic island in the South Pacific, capital of the ▷ Cook Islands. Area: 67.3 sq. km. Population 1985 estim. 11,200.

See also ▷ Rarotonga Declaration.

RAROTONGA DECLARATION 1982. The South Pacific Declaration on Natural Resources and the Environment, signed in March 1982, in Rarotonga, under the auspices of UNEP and ESCAP. The Declaration stated that:

"the testing of nuclear devices against the wishes of the people shall not be permitted"; "the storage and release of nuclear wastes in the Pacific regional environment shall be prevented"

KEESING's *Contemporary Archive*, July 1986.

RAROTONGA TREATY, South Pacific Nuclear Free Zone Treaty called Treaty of Rarotonga, signed in Rarotonga, Cook Islands on August 6, 1985, entered into force on Dec. 11, 1986, signed by 13 States: Australia, the Cook Islands, Fiji, Kiribati, Nauru, New Zealand, Niue, Papua New Guinea, the Solomon Islands, Tonga, Tuvalu, Vanuatu and Western Samoa, all member States of the South Pacific Forum, ratified until Jan. 1, 1987 by 9 States. The Treaty forbids its adherents to manufacture, acquire or have control over nuclear weapons and prohibits other countries to station such weapons in the territories of the Treaty parties, but the Treaty does not seek to have nuclear weapon prohibitions applied outside the 12-mile territorial water limits of the Treaty parties. There is also a ban on the dumping of radioactive wastes and other radioactive material at sea within the zone. Like the ▷ Tlatelolco Treaty three protocols annexed to the Treaty were opened for signature to the five atomic powers. Protocol I is related to France, the UK and the USA in respect of the territories in the zone for which they are internationally responsible. Until 1989 not one power had signed Protocol I.

Protocols II and III was signed with reservation on Dec. 15, 1986 by the USSR.

Protocols II and III were signed on Febr. 10, 1987 by China.

KEESING's *Record of World Events*, May 1987; Treaty of Rarotonga, full text and an analysis in: *SIPRI Yearbook 1986*, Oxford, 1987; *SIPRI Yearbook 1987*, Oxford, 1988, pp. 398–400.

RASSENSCHANDE. *German* = "disgrace of a race." A racist term introduced by the German Third Reich, Sept. 15, 1935 in one of the ▷ Nuremberg laws (Law on the protection of German blood, Gesetz zum Schutze des deutschen Blutes), which forbade German ▷ "Aryans" from contracting marriages with "Non-Aryans" or having any sexual relations with them under the penalty of a heavy jail sentence. The racial policy of the German Third Reich was administered by a special office for racial policies (Rassenpolitisches Amt des NSDAP) under Alfred Rosenberg (1893–1946), executed in Nuremberg for crimes against humanity.

O.J. JANOWSKI, M.M. FABEN, *International Aspects of German Racial Policies*, London, 1937; J. ROBINSON, Ph. FRIEDMAN, *Guide to Jewish History Under Nazi Impact*, London, 1960.

RASTADT PEACE TREATY, 1714. A Treaty between the Holy Roman Emperor and the King of France, complementary to the Utrecht Peace Treaty, was signed on Mar. 6, 1774 at Rastadt.

Major Peace Treaties of Modern History 1648–1967, New York, 1967, Vol. I, pp. 241–260.

RATE OF EXCHANGE. The rates for foreign currencies established and announced on money-markets in two variants: buy and sell. The simple quotation of an exchange rate is distinguished from the changing number of foreign units. Depending on the territories taken into consideration, there are various exchange rates. According to the manner of establishing them, there are: (1) official rates (established by agencies designed for that purpose); (2) private rates (not established officially, but usually published in press releases or bank bulletins).

According to the extent of fluctuations, one can distinguish: (1) inflexible rates (official rate not subject to fluctuations); (2) constant rates (where the rate fluctuates under the pressures of supply and demand within certain fixed limits); (3) changeable rates, also called floating (subject to fluctuations depending on supply and demand without fixed limits). After World War I predominant were changeable rates subject to fluctuations depending on supply and demand without fixed limits, such as the French franc 1919–26 and July 1937–May 1938; the pound sterling and Swedish krona 1931–39 and the American dollars Apr., 1933–Jan, 1934. After World War II this phenomenon did not occur, since the IMF member states had their currencies fixed in relation to the American dollar in connection with its unchanged (since 1934) convertibility to gold at the rate of 35 dollars per ounce of pure gold. All devaluations or revaluations could take place only with the consent of the IMF (according to the IMF statute fluctuations on the market were permitted only within the limits of intervention points, plus or minus 1% in relation to the official rate). Not before 1971 did the crisis of the American dollar force the West German mark to move to a changeable rate in May, while on Aug. 15, 1971 – the date of the suspension of the convertibility of the US dollar into gold – other "hard currencies", such as the Japanese yen, the currencies of Benelux and others followed. The French government on Jan. 20, 1974 introduced a floating rate for the so-called commercial franc for a period of 6 months, which served as the basis for international transactions, justifying this i.a. by the conviction that a reform of the Western monetary system would not take place soon. At the end of Jan., 1974 the central banks of Denmark and Benelux fixed a constant exchange rate to the FRG mark in agreement with FRG, which in fact established an FRG mark currency zone, independent of the fluctuating rates in the remaining EEC states. According to the range of application, one distinguishes: (1) uniform rates (applied in all foreign settlements); (2) differentiated rates (various rates used in settlements, e.g. different rates in foreign trade, different rates for foreign tourists, and still others for international institutions); these diverse rates are also the subject of international treaties. ▷ Floating Rate of Exchange.

H.K. HORSEFIELD, *Proposals for Using Objective Indicators as a Guide to Exchange Rate Changes. A Historical Comment*, IMF Staff Papers, Washington, DC, 1973; H.W. MAYER, *The Anatomy of Official Exchange-Rate International System*, Princeton, 1974.

RATE OF INTEREST. An international banking term for the ratio of the amount paid for the use of money capital to the amount of the capital; subject to international agreements and IMF policy. ▷ SDR.

RATIFICATION. An international term for a custom of approving signed international agreements by highest state authorities (Head of State, Council of State or Parliament). After ratification the instruments of ratification are exchanged and the agreement is registered with the UN Secretariat.

R.L. BLEDSOE, B.A. BOCZEK, *The International Law Dictionary*, Oxford, 1987.

RAVENSBRÜCK. The German concentration camp for women in Mecklenburg (today GDR), est. in Mar., 1939. About 130,000 women from 27 countries passed through it and about 90,000 were murdered, partly as victims of medical experiments (▷ "Guinea pigs"). The camp was evacuated in Apr. 1945, over 10,000 prisoners were taken by the Swedish Red Cross to Sweden; liberated by the Soviet Army on May 1, 1945.

The Trial of German Major War Criminals. Proceedings of the International Military Tribunal Sitting at Nuremberg, Germany, Vol. 42, London, 1946–48, Vol. 5, pp. 192–198; Vol. 10, p. 95; Vol. 11, p. 354.

RAWINSONDE OBSERVATION STATIONS. A meteorological stratospheric observation network, subject of international co-operation and agreements. In 1968 the US established a co-operative program for the operation and maintenance of a network of Rawinsonde observation stations in Brazil and in Colombia.

UNTS, Vol. 707, 1970, pp. 12–20; and Vol. 714, 1970, pp. 35–54.

RAW MATERIALS AND PRIMARY COMMODITIES. The basic agricultural and industrial raw materials, subject of international conventions and one of the major problems, particularly of the Third World, which is evidenced by counting topicality of statements and recommendations of the International Conference for Problems of War and Peace, Mar. 8, 1945 stipulating the acknowledgement of the necessity of making up for losses often resulting from differences in prices of basic commodities and manufactures to set a required balance between them. In 1946 the UN launched studies on prices of basic commodities whereas the UN General Assembly, recognizing the necessity of finding effective means of financing economic advance in the developing countries, their problem of basic significance for securing peace of mankind, recommended (in Res. 307/IV, 404/V, 521/VI, 523/VI, etc.) various measures all of which proved failures. ECOSOC, Res. 30/IV, founded the Interim Co-ordinating Committee for International Commodity Arrangements, ICCICA, Mar., 1947; publ. Review of International Commodity. An ECOSOC – Commission for International Commodity Trade was founded in 1954; and a FAO – Committee on Commodity Problems. ICCICA organized several conferences: to deal with rice – Philippines, 1948; tin – Geneva, 1950 and 1953; sugar – London, 1953; New York and Geneva, 1956; olive oil – Geneva, 1955 and 1958; wheat – Geneva, 1955; plus four conferences in Geneva, 1956, on zinc, cocoa, copper and lead. Mutual supplies within the CMEA satisfy demand of member states for basic mineral commodities: coal in 98%, crude oil – 96%, iron ores – 80%.

The question of prices of basic commodities was brought forth at the UN by Third World countries in Spring, 1974 during a debate on the energy crisis at the UN General Assembly special session; on the initiative of, among others, Algeria, nonaligned countries issued a memorandum postulating that the developing countries should assume full control over their natural resources and also that reduction of prices for basic commodities recognizing nationalization of commodities should be a basic condition of development. The UN General Assembly Special Session in Res. 3202/S-VI adopted a Program of Action on the Establishment of a ▷

New International Economic Order. The first part of the Resolution was dedicated to the "fundamental problems related to trade and development." The text is as follows:

"1. All efforts should be made:
(a) To put an end to all forms of foreign occupation, racial discrimination, apartheid, colonial, neocolonial and alien domination and exploitation through the exercise of permanent sovereignty over natural resources;
(b) To take measures for the recovery, exploitation, development, marketing and distribution of natural resources, particularly of developing countries, to serve their national interests, to promote collective self-reliance among them and to strengthen mutually beneficial international economic co-operation with a view to bringing about the accelerated development of developing countries;
(c) To facilitate the functioning and to further the aims of producers' associations, including their joint marketing arrangements, orderly commodity trading, improvement in the export income of producing developing countries and in their terms of trade, and sustained growth of the world economy for the benefit of all;
(d) To evolve a just and equitable relationship between the prices of raw materials, primary commodities, manufactured and semi-manufactured goods exported by developing countries and the prices of raw materials, primary commodities, food, manufactured and semi-manufactured goods and capital equipment imported by them, and to work for a link between the prices of exports of developing countries and the prices of their imports from developed countries;
(e) To take measures to reverse the continued trend of stagnation or decline in the real price of several commodities exported by developing countries, despite a general rise in commodity prices, resulting in a decline in the export earnings of these developing countries;
(f) To take measures to expand the markets for natural products in relation to synthetics, taking into account the interests of the developing countries, and to utilize fully the ecological advantages of these products;
(g) To take measures to promote the processing of raw materials in the producer developing countries."

The First Conference of the Developing Countries on Raw Materials was held Feb. 3–8, 1975 at Dakar and attended by over 100 states; adopted ▷ Dakar Declaration, 1975, providing that Third World countries supply 50% of global commodities and hence have the right to demand a change in existing ▷ Terms of Trade. The Declaration also postulated establishment of a fund for financing reserves of resources. In Mar., 1977, under UNCTAD auspices a conference was held in Geneva on establishment of a fund for stabilization of raw materials' prices. A world commodities market center is London, especially for cocoa, coffee, rubber, soybeans, sugar, vegetable oil and wool, organized by the London Company International Commodities Clearing House, with the Australian Options Market, Hongkong Commodity Exchange, Sydney Futures Exchange and United Terminal Sugar Market Association. In the 1980s the decline in the prices of raw materials was especially sharp.

T. WATLING, J. MORLEY, *Successful Commodity Futures Trading*, London, 1974; *Conference on Economic Co-operation among Developing Countries. Declarations, Resolutions, Recommendation and Decisions adopted in the UN System*; Vol. 1, Mexico, DF, 1976, pp. 45–46 and 511–523; *UN Chronicle*, October, 1983. R.F. MIKESELL, *The Changing Demand for Raw Materials*, in: *Economic Impact*, 1988/3.

RAYON. A subject of international co-operation. Organizations reg. with the UIA:

International Bureau for the Standardization of Man-Made Fibres, f. 1928, Basel. Publ.: *Rules of Standardization*.
International Rayon and Synthetic Fibres Committee, f. 1950, Paris. Consultative status with ECOSOC, FAO and UNCTAD. See also ▷ Fibre.

Yearbook of International Organizations, 1986/87; *The Europa Yearbook 1988. A World Survey, Vol. I*, London, 1988.

RAYTHEON CORPORATION CASE. A case submitted in February 1989 by the US for arbitration to the ▷ International Court of Justice.
The dispute concerns the nationalization in 1968 of a plant at Palermo owned by Raytheon Corporation, an American electronics company.
Washington argues that Italy must pay compensation under a 1948 Treaty of Friendship, Commerce and Navigation with the United States. Italy denies this arguing that the company was incorporated under Italian law and was not covered by the treaty. The Court's verdict will thus determine how much protection the roughly 60 such treaties the United States has signed offer other American investors against expropriation.

The New York Times, February 13, 1989.

REACTORS. ▷ Nuclear reactors.

READING. A subject of international research and co-operation. Organizations reg. with the UIA:

International Institute for Children's Literature and Reading Research, f. 1965, Vienna.
International Reading Association, f. 1955, Paris. Latin American Office Buenos Aires. Consultative status with UNESCO. Publ.: *The Reading Teacher, Journal of Reading, Reading Research*.

Yearbook of International Organizations.

REAGAN DOCTRINE, 1984. A thesis presented by President Ronald R. Reagan on Jan. 16, 1984 in Washington, DC stating that the US and USSR share common interests, and foremost among them is to avoid war and reduce the level of armament.

KEESING'S Contemporary Archive, 1984. L. WOLSY, *Before the Point of No-Return: An Exchange of Views on the Cold War, Reagan Doctrine and What Is To Come*, New York, 1986. W.F. HAHN ed., *Central America and the Reagan Doctrine*, Boston, 1987.

REAL ESTATE. A subject of international co-operation. Organizations reg. with the UIA:

International Real Estate Federation, f. 1948, Paris.
International Union of Land Property Owners, f. 1923, Paris.
International Union for Land Value Taxation and Free Trade, f. 1926, London. Publ.: *Land and Liberty*.

Yearbook of International Organizations.

REALPOLITIK. *German* = "politics based on realities". An international term (1) for internal and external power politics in the German Reich during the Bismarck era; (2) for the foreign policy based on political realities, of the FRG during the social-democrat era (▷ Ostpolitik).

REARMAMENT. An international term for Germany's remilitarization after World Wars I and II.

J.H. MORGAN, *Assize of Arms. Being the Story of Disarmament of Germany and Her Rearmament*, 2 Vols, London, 1944–80.

RÉAUMUR'S SCALE. The thermometric scale, elaborated in 1730 by French physicist, René de Réaumur (1683–1757), establishing the freezing point of chemically pure water at $0°R$, and the boiling point of water at $80°R$; this scale was superseded by the simpler 100-degree Celsius scale. ▷ Temperature, International Scale.

REBUS SIC STANTIBUS. *Latin* = "in that state of affairs." An international term for a controversial doctrine, contradictory to the principle "*pacta sunt servanda*," saying that an international agree-

R

ment is binding only as long as the state of affairs present at the time of its signing continues to exist; indirectly introduced in art. 19 of the Pact of the League of Nations by a recommendation to "study again the treaties which fail to be further applied" used by the German III Reich, 1936, to denounce the Rhine Pact and to introduce militarization in the Rhineland "due to change in situation caused by conclusion of a treaty on mutual assistance between the USSR and France"; disapproved by the Charter of the United Nations, because the USA and the USSR opposed allowing any form of treaty revisions, after the grave experiences with art. 19 of the League of Nations Pact. The Vienna Convention on the Law of Treaties, adopted in 1969, rejects the doctrine of *rebus sic stantibus* as justification for changing interstate frontiers (art. 62). During the ▷ Nuremberg War Criminals Trial, 1945–46, Hitler's interpretation of *Rebus sic stantibus* doctrine was quoted:

"Agreements are to be kept only as long as they serve a purpose."

▷ Revision and Review of Treaties.

The Trial of German Major War Criminals: Proceedings of the IMT at Nuremberg, Germany, London, 1949, Vol. 1, p. 79, Vol. 2, p. 82.

RECALLING LETTER. *French* = "Lettre de rappel." An international term, similar in form to ▷ Credential Letters, advising the termination of a diplomatic mission by a given ambassador or envoy.

RECIDIVISM, INTERNATIONAL. An international term for a principle in penal law stating that an offender who has committed an offence in one country, and then commits the same crime in another country, should be tried as a recidivist, even though in that country he committed the crime for the first time. This principle is not applied in all countries, hence some international conventions include a clause binding for states recognizing international recidivism, such as the 1929 Convention for the Suppression of Counterfeiting Currency, art. 6 stated:

"In countries where the principle of the international recognition of previous convictions is recognized, foreign convictions for the offences referred to in Art. 3 should, within the conditions prescribed by domestic law, be recognized for the purpose of establishing habitual criminality."

Actes de la III Congrès internationale pour l'unification du Droit Pénal, Brussels, 1932.

RECIPROCAL TRADE AGREEMENTS ACT, 1934. An act of the US Congress on trade treaties based on the principle of reciprocity, authorizing the president of the United States to reduce tariffs and customs duties to 50% of their amount on reciprocal principles. This Act had a protectionist clause, the so-called Escape Clause, allowing for withdrawal of the ▷ most favored nation IMF clause, if the reduction of tariffs caused unfavorable competition for American producers. This Act has been substituted by the ▷ Trade Expansion Act, 1962.

KEESING's *Archiv der Gegenwart*, 1934.

RECIPROCITY. An international term for the oldest principle in international law and international trade – receiving the same rights or privileges as the ones granted to another state (e.g. visa-free movement of persons, the most-favored-nation clause in commercial exchange, mutual recognition of scientific titles and diplomas, etc.). The principle is also used in a negative sense in the case of ▷

Boycott. Latin formula: *do ut des* = "I give so that you may give (me)."

M.J. RUSSEL, "Fluctuation in Reciprocity", in: *International Law Quarterly*, 1922; W.S. CULBERTSON, *Reciprocity. A National Policy for Foreign Trade*, London, 1937; A. MALINTOPPI: "L'elemento della reciprocità nel trattamento delle missioni diplomatischi", in: *Revista di diritto internazionale*, 1956.

RECOGNITION OF STATES AND GOVERNMENTS. One of two (constitutive or declarative) forms of reciprocal recognition of states and governments; subject of international disputes concerning both recognition and non-recognition of states and governments as well as international doctrines (▷ Gondra Doctrine, 1983, and ▷ Hallstein Doctrine, 1955). At the UN, the problem of the entry of the People's Republic of China into the UN stirred a general controversy in the early 1950s as the PRC had not been recognized by the USA, which continued to maintain diplomatic relations with the Republic of China on Taiwan. UN Secretary-General Trygve Lie, in a memorandum to the chairman of the Security Council, on Mar. 8, 1950, stated:

"(1) A member could properly vote to accept a representative of a government which it did not recognize, or with which it had no diplomatic relations, and (2) Such a vote did not imply recognition or a readiness to assume diplomatic relations". (Official Record of the Security Council, 1950, Suppl. January–May, p. 18).

In 1970, the US State Department in a Government Instruction (GISD) determined American policy of recognition of states and governments in these terms [excerpts]:

"(1) The decision to recognize a new regime as a government of the country is made with our best national interest in mind. Each instance of recognition or non-recognition has intrinsic factological and political bearing. Finally, it is decided by the administration's assessment. Under the Senate Act of September 1969, recognition by the US of a government need not necessarily imply that we approve of its domestic policy and the way it assumed power.
(2) Traditionally, there are three criteria to decide for or against recognition of a government: – the scope of its effective control over the country's territory and state administration; the scope of public approval for its exercise of power; its eagerness to fulfil the obligations it assumes internationally and toward the USA …
(3) … Since 1965 the US has been trying to avoid making formal declarations on recognition of governments that were formed as a result of a coup or other revolutionary transformations. Often it is best for political reasons rather to continue than discontinue relations with a country where a coup took place. This assures practical, indispensable and effective liaison with such a country and gives hopes for influencing the new regime to restore constitutional processes. It is in our interest to act extremely flexibly in dealing with new regimes.
(4) About 30 States apply the principle of recognizing only States, not governments. This principle was formed for the first time in 1930 by Don Genaro Estrada, Mexican minister of foreign affairs. The US is close to such concepts which provide multiple opportunities to act in the face of a revolt. The opportunities are the following: suspension of formal relations while retaining unofficial contacts; recalling the ambassador and reducing the number of embassy staff; discontinuing relations in a way that does not imply that recognition is withheld. In most cases it is not necessary to take specific actions or to announce decisions concerning recognition of a government. However, this formula cannot be fully applied in case of a prolonged home war when two governments compete for power over the same territory. This refers also to cases of secession when a government claims the right to sovereignty over the seceded territory in spite of another government's claims of sovereignty over the whole country."

▷ Vienna Convention on Diplomatic Relations, 1961.

M.W. GRAHAM, *The League of Nations and the Recognition of States*, Berkeley, 1933; G. VENTURINI, *Il riconoscimento in diritto internazionale*, Roma, 1946; E. JIMENEZ ARECHAGA, *Reconocimiento de Gobiernos*, Madrid, 1947; H. LAUTERPACHT, *Recognition in International Law*, Cambridge, 1947; G. ARÉVALO BLUMENKORN, *La doctrina de reconocimiento en la teoría y práctica de los Estados*, Buenos Aires, 1954; G. SÈPULVEDA, *La teoría y práctica del reconocimiento de los Gobiernos*, México, DF, 1954; B. LANDHERR, J. VAN ESSER, *Recognition in International Law. Selective Bibliography*, 2 Vols, The Hague 1954; M. LACHS, "Recognition in the Law of Nations", in: *British Yearbook of International Law*, 1959; Ch.G. FENWICK, "The Recognition of *de facto* Government", in: *American Journal of International Law*, Vol. 58, 1964; J.J. SALMON, *La Reconnaissance d'État*, Paris, 1971. R.L. BLEDSOE, B.A. BOCZEK, *The International Law Dictionary*, Oxford, 1987.

RECONCILIATION MOVEMENT. Parallel with the Ecumenical movement in Christian churches (▷ World Council of Churches), there came into existence in support of unification with non-Christian religions, in the Roman Catholic Church the Secretariat for Non-Christian Religions. Organizations reg. with the UIA:

Eiren-International Christian Service for Peace, est. 1957, Kaiserslautern.
International Consultative Committee of Organizations for Christian-Jewish Co-operation, est. 1935, London; co-ordinates organizations in Austria, France, FRG, Great Britain, Italy, and Switzerland.
International Fellowship of Reconciliation, IFR, est. 1919, London, and regional centers in New York and Montevideo. Consultative status with UNESCO. Publ.: *Reconciliation Quarterly*.
International Hebrew Christian Alliance, est. 1925, London; its aim is to create a bridge of unification between Judaism and Christianity. Publ.: *The Hebrew Christian*.
World Congress of Faith, est. 1936, London, to spread brotherhood among people of all faiths. Publ.: *World Faith*.

Yearbook of International Organizations.

RECONSTRUCTION OF WAR-DEVASTATED STATES. A subject of the resolution of the UN General Assembly of Feb. 2, 1946 stating that "among postwar problems this is the one deserving high-priority treatment." On Dec. 11, 1946 the Assembly appointed a temporary subcommission for economic reconstruction of devastated regions. Both resolutions were cancelled *de facto* in relation to the most devastated countries in central and Eastern Europe after their rejection of the ▷ Marshall Plan, 1947. The named countries withdraw in 1948 from its Bank (IBRD).

W.O. DAVOREN, *Post-War Reconstruction Conference*, New York, 1945; *Yearbook of the UN 1946–47*, pp. 193–160.

RECORDS. A subject of international co-operation. Organization reg. with the UIA:

International Federation of Record Libraries, f. 1963, Paris.

Yearbook of International Organizations.

RECREATION. A subject of international co-operation. Organizations reg. with the UIA:

European Leisure and Recreation Association, f. 1972, Zurich. Publ.: *Bulletin*.
International Academy for Aquatic Sports and Recreation Facilities, f. 1965, Bremen.
International Council on Health, Physical Education and Recreation, f. 1958, Washington, DC. Publ.: *Gymnasion*.

International Federation of Park and Recreation Administration, f. 1957, London.
World Leisure and Recreation Association, f. 1956, Geneva. Consultative status with UNESCO, UNICEF and ECOSOC. Publ.: *Bulletin.*

Yearbook of International Organizations.

RECYCLING. An international term introduced 1974/5 by the US government in negotiations with the EEC states on the subject of utilizing petrodollars to cover deficits in those countries whose finances were disturbed by price increase of crude oil. The EEC states in Jan., 1975 came out in favor of entrusting the petrodollars to the IMF, whereas the US proposed the creation of a special fund by the highly industrialized countries to the amount of 25 billion dollars. This was opposed by France, which stated that such a special fund would be an instrument of US foreign policy.

RED AID. ▷ Red Secours or MOPR.

RED CRESCENT MOVEMENT. Name of the Red Cross national societies in Muslim countries. Since 1986 incorporated into the International Red Cross and Red Crescent Movement.
See also ▷ Red Cross.

RED CROSS. The world charitable organization including International Committee of the Red Cross, ICRC, Comité international de la Croix Rouge, CICR, est. on July 22, 1864 in Geneva, as an organ of the First International Convention for the Amelioration of the Condition of Soldiers Wounded in Armies in the Field. Initially the International Committee for Relief of Wounded; under the present name from 1880, i.e. after the adoption as a recognition sign for medical personnel and field hospitals the reverse colors of the Swiss flag, in place of a white cross on a red background a red cross on a white background. The new statute took effect on Aug. 1, 1973. The International Committee of the Red Cross became a supporter of the so-called Red Cross Geneva Conventions on the Protection of War Victims 1864, 1906, 1907, 1929, and 1949; it created the Central Prisoners of War Agency, 1870–1, 1914–18, 1939–45, whose name in 1960 was changed to the Central Tracing Agency. Advisory status with ECOSOC. Publ.: *Revue Internationale de la Croix Rouge, Rapport annuel d'activité de la Croix Rouge, Manuel de la Croix Rouge.*
League of Red Cross Societies, World Federation of National Red Cross, Red Crescent and Red Lion and Sun Societies, est. May 5, 1919 with the task of co-ordinating the activities of national societies created in accordance with the recommendation of the First Convention, 1864. Consultative statute with ECOSOC and UNESCO. Headquarters: Geneva. Publ.: monthly *Panorama*; quarterly *The Red Cross World*, and *Annual Reports.*
The two different names of the League resulted from the fact that only in Europe and the Americas do the national societies carry the name Red Cross; in the remaining continents the traditional symbols are employed: in Moslem countries Red Crescent, in Iran Red Lion, in Israel Red Star. The UN General Assembly Res. 55/I of Nov. 19, 1946 established the forms of co-operation of the UN with the International Committee of the Red Cross in Geneva, especially in the assistance in cases of ▷ Natural disasters. The 25th International Conference of the Red Cross held in Geneva, Oct. 28–31, 1986 attended by 137 national and 125 governmental Red Cross and Red Crescent societies adopted a new statute and the name was changed to International Red Cross and Red Crescent Movement (IRC-RCM).

The 26th International Conference should be held in 1990 in Colombia. See also ▷ Holocaust.

UN Yearbook 1946; H. COURSIER, *La Croix Rouge Internationale. Histoire, Organization, Action*, Paris, 1962; A. MARES (ed.), *La Protezione internazionale dei combatantie dei civili*, Milano, 1965; *Yearbook of International Organizations*. ICRC, Geneva, 1986.

RED CROSS CONVENTION, 1864. The Convention for the Amelioration of the Condition of Soldiers wounded in Armies in the Field, signed on Aug. 24, 1864 at Geneva, reads as follows:
"The Swiss Confederation; His Royal Highness the Grand Duke of Baden; His Majesty the King of the Belgians; His Majesty the King of Denmark; Her Majesty the Queen of Spain; His Majesty the Emperor of the French; His Royal Highness the Grand Duke of Hesse; His Majesty the King of Italy; His Majesty the King of the Netherlands; His Majesty the King of Portugal and of the Algarves; His Majesty the King of Prussia; His Majesty the King of Würtenberg, being equally animated with the desire to soften, as much as depends on them, the evils of warfare, to suppress its useless hardships and improve the fate of wounded soldiers on the field of battle, have resolved to conclude a convention to that effect, and have named for their plenipotentiaries, viz:
Who, after having exchanged their powers, and found them in good and due form, agree to the following articles:
Art. I. Ambulances and military hospitals shall be acknowledged to be neuter, and, as such, shall be protected and respected by belligerents so long as any sick or wounded may be therein.
Such neutrality shall cease if the ambulances or hospitals should be held by a military force.
Art. II. Persons employed in hospitals and ambulances, comprising the staff for superintendence, medical service, administration, transport of wounded as well as chaplains, shall participate in the benefit of neutrality, whilst so employed, and so long as there remain any wounded to bring in or to succor.
Art. III. The persons designed in the preceding article may, even after occupation by the enemy, continue to fulfil their duties in the hospital or ambulance which they serve, or may withdraw in order to rejoin the corps to which they belong.
Under such circumstances when these persons shall cease from their functions, they shall be delivered by the occupying army to the outposts of the enemy.
Art. IV. As the equipment of military hospitals remains subject to the laws of war, persons attached to such hospitals cannot, in withdrawing, carry away any articles but such as are their private property.
Under the same circumstances an ambulance shall, on the contrary, retain its equipment.
Art. V. Inhabitants of the country who may bring help to the wounded shall be respected and shall remain free. The generals of the belligerent Powers shall make it their care to inform the inhabitants of the appeal addressed to their humanity, and of the neutrality which will be the consequence of it.
Any wounded man entertained and taken care of in a house shall be considered as a protection thereto. Any inhabitant who shall have entertained wounded men in his house shall be exempted from the quartering of troops, as well as from a part of the contributions of war which may be imposed.
Art. VI. Wounded or sick soldiers shall be entertained and taken care of, to whatever nation they may belong. Commanders-in-chief shall have the power to deliver immediately to the outposts of the enemy soldiers who have been wounded in an engagement, when circumstances permit this to be done, and with the consent of both parties.
Those who are recognized, after their wounds are healed, as incapable of serving, shall be sent back to their country.
The others may also be sent back, on condition of not again bearing arms during the continuance of the war. Evacuations, together with the persons under whose directions they take place, shall be protected by an absolute neutrality.
Art. VII. A distinctive and uniform flag shall be adopted for hospitals, ambulances and evacuations. It must, on every occasion, be accompanied by the nation-

al flag. An arm-badge (brassard) shall also be allowed for individuals neutralized, but the delivery thereof shall be left to military authority.
The flag and the arm-badge shall bear a red cross on a white ground.
Art. VIII. The details of execution of the present convention shall be regulated by the commanders-in-chief of belligerent armies, according to the instructions of their respective governments, and in conformity with the general principles laid down in this convention.
Art. IX. The high contracting Powers have agreed to communicate the present convention to those Governments who have not found it convenient to send plenipotentiaries to the International Conference at Geneva, with an invitation to accede thereto; The protocol is for that purpose left open.
Art. X. The present convention shall be ratified, and the ratifications shall be exchanged at Berne, in four months or sooner, if possible.
In faith whereof the respective Plenipotentiaries have signed it and have affixed their seals thereto.
Done at Geneva, The twenty second day of the month of August of the year one thousand eight hundred and sixty-four."

United States Statutes at Large, Vol. 22, pp. 940–945; A.R. WERNER, *La Croix Rouge et les Conventions de Genève*, Genève, 1945.

RED CROSS CONVENTIONS, 1864–1949. An international term for the military rules of humanitarian warfare embraced by inter-governmental conventions signed in 1864 and 1906 in Geneva. Between the wars replaced by the term ▷ Geneva Humanitarian Conventions, 1864–1949, embracing at present two further intergovernmental agreements concerning protection of military and civilian persons during warfare, signed in 1929 and 1949 in Geneva.

J.S. PICTET, "La Croix Rouge et les Conventions de Genève", in: *Receuil des Cours de l'Académie de Droit International*, 1950.

REDEMPTOR HOMINIS. *Latin* = "redeemer of Man." The encyclical of John Paul II written in Polish and translated into Latin, publ.: Mar. 4, 1979 and directed to the clergy and faithful of the Church as well as "to all men of good will." Based on Christian theological anthropology, it explains the content of the dogma of Redemption; poses and justifies the thesis of Christocentrism in understanding man and the world, and in part III broadly discusses the conditions in which contemporary humanity lives, i.e.: What does modern man fear?, Progress or menace?, The law of man – letter or spirit? Appeals for a concentration of all means and possibilities to develop in man moral sensitivies, the feeling of responsibility, and elimination of dangers to peace.

Redemptor Hominis, Rome, 1979.

RED LOCUST CONVENTION, 1949. An International Convention for the permanent control of outbreak areas of the red locust, signed on Feb. 22, 1949 in London by Belgium, UK, South Africa and Southern Rhodesia.

UNTS, Vol. 93, pp. 129–141.

RED RELIEF, INTERNATIONAL. ▷ Red Secours or MOPR.

RED SEA. The coastal part of the Indian Ocean, between Africa and Arab Peninsula, of 440,300 sq. km area; the Suez Canal since 1869 connects it with the Mediterranean Sea, and the Babel–Mandam Straits with the Arab Sea. The coastal states: Egypt, Sudan, Somalia, Ethiopia, South Yemen, North Yemen and Saudi Arabia. Main ports: Suez and Sudan. The shortest sea way from the Indian Ocean to Europe; subject of international arguments and agreements. Islands on the Red Sea mostly deserted

R

or inhabited by small groups of Arab or Ethiopian fishermen (of 103 islands, 80 belong to Arab countries, 23 to Ethiopia), became an international problem in 1971–3 in connection with the occupation by Israeli commandos of many of them in the region of Bab al-Mandab Straits.

In Febr. 1982 in Jeddah, Saudi Arabia, the Jeddah Convention for the Conservation of the Red Sea and Gulf of Aden Environment was signed by the coastal Countries under UNEP auspices. Organization reg. with the UIA:

Office for Red Sea Ecology, f. 1984. Tunis, Tunisia.

Sailing, Directions Red Sea and Gulf of Aden, US Navy Hydrographic Office Publication No. 157, 1952. *Yearbook of International Organizations*, 1986/87.

RED SEA JEDDA CONVENTION. The Convention for the Conservation of the Red Sea and Gulf of Aden Environment, adopted under the aegis of UNEP in Febr. 1982 in Jedda or Jidda, city on the Red Sea in Saudi Arabia, together with a Protocol Concerning Regional Co-operation in Combating Marine Pollution by Oil and other Harmful Substances in Cases of Emergency.

KEESING's *Contemporary Archive*, 1986.

RED SECOURS OR MOPR. Mezhdunarodnaya Organizatsya Pomoshchi Revolutsyonistom MOPR, International Relief Organizations for Revolutionists, called also Red Aid, Red Relief and Rote Hilfe, est. 1922 in Moscow, international social organization to help political prisoners and their families throughout the world. It was composed of 73 national sections whose operations were interrupted by World War II. The press organ was *Byuletin MOPR* and *Internationale Rote Hilfe*.

Ten Years of International Red Aid in Resolutions and Documents: 1922–1932, Moscow, 1933; C. ZETKIN, *Werk und Weg der Internationalen Roten Hilfe*, Berlin, 1932; J. ZELT, *Und nicht vergessen die Solidarität, Aus der Geschichte der IRH*, Berlin, 1960; W.S. SWORAKOWSKI (ed.), *The Communist International and Its Front Organization*, Stanford, 1965.

REDWOOD NATIONAL PARK. An American natural site in California, included in the ▷ World Heritage UNESCO List. The park covers some 43,000 hectares and contains the giant Californian redwoods which are unique in the world. They are the survivors of a species which extended over a considerable area at the time of the dinosaurs. The height of these trees (80 to 100 meters), their age (many are several centuries old) and the mysterious atmosphere surrounding the trees, shrouded in mist from the ocean, give this forest a most unusual character.

UNESCO, *A Legacy for All*, Paris, 1984.

REED-BULWINKLE ACT, 1948. ▷ Anti-Trust Act, 1890.

RE-EDUCATION. An international term for a system of adapting to international life a society whose education in a past period was based on racist, aggressive, genocidal ideologies. After World War II the term became widespread in connection with the re-education of Germans in the occupied zones and the citizens of Japan.

"Japan and Germany: Problems in Re-education; The Educational US Missions to Japan and Germany", in: *International Conciliation*, No. 427, January, 1947.

RE-EDUCATION CAMPS. ▷ Labour Camps.

REEFS. A subject of the Sea Law Convention 1982 (Art. 6).

RE-ELECTION IN AMERICAN STATES. A subject of the declaration of the Fifth Conference of Foreign Ministers for American Republics, the so-called Santiago Declaration of 1959 on the Principles of Representative Democracy, stating that the prolongation *ad infinitum* of the rule of a president of a state is incompatible with the inter-American system; thus the re-election has to be limited. As a rule, the American states apply this principle. In Mexico the re-election of a president, whose term of office lasts 6 years, is completely prohibited by art. 83 of the Constitution of Feb. 5, 1917 and to emphasize the importance of this provision since 1929 (after the attempt to change art. 83, which had a tragic effect for the candidate who wanted to be re-elected president) each state act signed by the president of Mexico ends with the pledge: "*No reelección.*" Re-election is allowed only once in two subsequent terms of office in the United States and in Panama. Re-election with an intermission of at least one term of office is possible in Bolivia, Brazil, Chile, Columbia, the Dominican Republic, Ecuador, Guatemala, Honduras, Nicaragua, El Salvador and Uruguay. Re-election is possible after 8 years in Costa Rica and after 10 years in Venezuela. The president's term of office lasts 4 years in Ecuador, Columbia, Costa Rica, Panama, Uruguay and in the United States, 6 years in Bolivia, Chile (until 1973), Guatemala, Honduras, Peru, Mexico and Nicaragua. In Haiti, the Constitution of 1964 introduced the office of "the president for life;" in Argentina in 1966 the military junta introduced the title of "the president of the Argentinian People," without stating his term of office, changed in 1983 by the civil administration to 5 years. In three states of Latin America: Honduras, Costa Rica and Mexico, it is also prohibited to re-elect members of parliament and senators.

A. ZAMORA, *Digesto Constitucional Americano*, Buenos Aires, 1958; P.P. CAMARO, *Reelección Presidencial y Reelección Parlamentaria en América y México*, México, DF, 1965.

RE-EXPORT. An international term for the export of products purchased abroad which are immediately resold to foreign contracting parties, called direct re-export or after repackaging and resorting locally, called indirect re-export. In some cases international agreements stipulate that a product cannot be re-exported at all, or only to certain countries; e.g. the Western Powers during the cold war introduced a provision forbidding re-export to socialist countries, which was applied to many goods up to the 1970s.

REFERENDUM. An international term for the surveying of public opinion, voting by all eligible citizens of a commune, province, state or union of states in a particular matter; institutionalized in Switzerland in the 16th century, where all major local, provincial or state decisions were made through referendum; provisionally or temporarily used in other states.

The Treaty of Treaties, in: *American Journal of International Law*, No. 3, 1970.

REFORMATION. An international term for the European social–religious movement in the 16th century which led to a schism in the Roman Catholic Church and the creation of Protestant Churches (▷ Protestantism).

W.E. PEUCKERT, *Die grosse Wende*, Berlin, 1944; G. RITTER, *Die Neugestaltung Europas im 16 Jahrhundert*,, Berlin, 1950; R. BAINTON, *The Reformation of the 16th Century*, London, 1951; E.G. LEONARD, *Histoire générale du Protestantisme*, 2 vls, Genève, 1961.

REFRIGERATION. A subject of international co-operation and conventions. Organizations reg. with the UIA.

European Association of Refrigeration Enterprises, f. 1951, Paris.

European Committee of Manufacturers of Refrigeration Equipment, f. 1959, Paris.

International Institute of Refrigeration, f. 1920, Paris, replacing the International Association of Refrigeration, f. 1908. The main objectives of the Institute, according to art. 3 of the International Convention, signed in Paris on June 21, 1920, are to promote technical and economic studies, collect scientific, technical and economic information and documents; the development of the uses of refrigeration in the field of food and agriculture, in industry and in the domain of health and hygiene; make recommendations to governments and international organizations. Publ.: *Refrigeration Science and Technology*.

International Laboratory of Low Temperatures and Strong Magnetic Fields, f. 1968, Wroclaw, by an agreement between the Academies of Sciences of Bulgaria, GDR, Poland and the USSR.

Transfrigoroute Europe. Central Organization for Road Transport at Controlled Temperature, f. 1955, Geneva.

LNTS, Vol. 8, p. 69; *Yearbook of International Organizations*.

REFUGEES. Persons who for objective or subjective reasons have to leave their countries or are expatriated by force; major international problems that emerged after World War I when the number of refugees in Europe and Asia Minor for the first time was counted in millions. In 1921 the League of Nations established the first world institution to help refugees, the Office of the LN High Commissioner for Refugees headed by F. Nansen, Norwegian scholar and traveler; after his death the institution was named the Nansen Office. One of many actions launched by the Office was assistance to 1.5 million Greeks being resettled from Asia Minor to Greece and about 0.5 million Turks from Greece to Turkey. The victory of Nazism in Germany, Jan. 30, 1933, started another flow of refugees and since the Nansen Office was not allowed by Hitlerite Germany to care for those refugees, the League of Nations created a separate Office of the LN High Commissioner for the Refugees from Germany, "Jews or any other kind." J.G. McDonald, an Englishman, was named the High Commissioner. In May, 1938 his competence was expanded to include refugees from Austria occupied by Germany from Mar. 13, 1938. On Sept. 3, 1938, the LN Assembly combined the Nansen and McDonald Offices into one Office of the High Commissioner for Refugees and named H. Emerson commissioner with a five-year tenure. The unification was preceded by the Conference on Refugees held by 32 states in Evian-les-Bains, France, in July 1938, convened on the initiative of the US President, F.D. Roosevelt; the Conference established the Intergovernmental Committee for Refugees, ICGR, whose secretariat was seated in London and headed by an American, S. Rublee. The ICGR started negotiations with the German government which failed in Aug., 1939. Ruble submitted his resignation and his post was taken over by H. Emerson, thus creating a personal union between the Office of the League of Nations and ICGR. In Apr., 1943 the governments of the USA and Great Britain expanded the competence of the Committee to comprise "all persons who, due to the developments in Europe had to flee their home countries." From 1921 the Office of the High Commissioners enjoyed the right to issue identity and travel documents (▷ Nansen passport). ICGR had a similar right (▷ London Travel Permit).

The Nansen Office in 1938 was awarded with the Nobel Peace Prize. All functions of the Office and

ICGR by a unanimous decision of 44 governments which gathered at the UN Conference held in Washington, Dec. 9, 1944, were taken over by ▷ UNRRA. During World War II and immediately thereafter the American term Displaced Persons, DPs, was used to designate European refugees; however, at its first session in London, Feb. 14, 1946, the UN General Assembly adopted a Resolution which restored the term "refugees." On Dec. 15, 1946, the Assembly adopted the constitution of a new International Refugees Organization, IRO. The IRO Foundation Act was signed by: Australia, Belgium, Canada, China, Denmark, The Dominican Republic, France, Guatemala, Iceland, Luxembourg, the Netherlands, Norway, the UK and USA. The convention entered into force on June 30, 1947, when UNRRA's responsibility for refugees was conferred on IRO. On Oct. 15, 1946 a Refugee Travel Document Agreement was signed in London.

The IRO existed until Feb., 1951 and alone helped 1.5 million refugees in Europe and Asia, and spent 428 million dollars. UNRRA, and subsequently IRO, had the right to issue travel documents and to prolong documents issued earlier.

In 1948, in view of new problems related to refugees in the Middle East, the UN General Assembly established, on Dec. 1, 1948, a new organization independent of IRO, the UN Relief for Palestinian Refugees, whose name on Dec. 8, 1949 was changed to the UN Relief and Works Agency for Palestine Refugees in the Near East, UNRWA, seated in Beirut and financed by voluntary donations, mainly from developed countries. On June 30, 1951 UNRWA registered 904,000 Palestine refugees; June 30, 1971 – 1,506,000 refugees; of that number 821,000 received aid in the form of food accounting for monthly food rations which correspond to 1500 calories daily.

The UN General Assembly on Dec. 5, 1958 proclaimed a World Refugee Year 1959 to attract world public opinion to the refugee problem and to stimulate higher subsidies of governments; 97 countries participated in organizing the year, and payments for the refugee relief fund amounted to nearly 80 million dollars.

The functions of IRO on Jan. 1, 1951 were taken over by a new Office of the UN High Commissioner for Refugees, UNHCR, seated in Geneva and renewed every three years until 1963, then every five years. The office operates on the basis of an international convention signed on July 1951 in Geneva, effected Apr. 22, 1954. The Additional Protocol entered into force on Oct. 4. 1967. The number of states parties to those instruments stands at 95 on Jan. 1, 1984. Total expenditures of UNHCR in 1952 were c. 35 million dollars; the 1982 assistance program US \$407 million. In 1982 the UN General Assembly Res. 37/196, recognizing the "great continuing need for international action on behalf of refugees and displaced persons of concern to the High Commissioner" decided to continue the Office for a further period of five years, from Jan. 1, 1984 to Dec. 31, 1988.

The UNHCR deals with international protection of refugees and with problems arising from mass movements of people forced to seek refuge as a result of civil disturbance or military conflict; in the 1980s especially in Africa, Central America, South East Asia and the Middle East and Near East. In 1982 the UNHCR program focused on aid to refugees in the Horn of Africa and in Somalia, Sudan, Djibouti and Kenya where refugees total almost 1,200,000; in Central America the total number of refugees exceeded 300,000; of the Indo-China refugees some 272,000 were settled in China, more than 36,000 Vietnamese boat people had been rescued since 1980 in the South China Sea; in the

Middle East the largest single problem were the 2,900,000 refugees from Afghanistan in Pakistan. The total number of refugees of concern to UNHCR was estimated on June 30, 1982 at: 10,312,100, plus 1,927,000 Palestinian refugees registered by UNRWA. ▷ Byezhentsy. ▷ Displaced Persons. In July 1984 a Second International Conference on Assistance to Refugees in Africa took place. A UN Group of Governmental Experts on International Co-operation to Avert New Flows of Refugees (set up by the General Assembly Dec. 10, 1982) has concluded (July 1986) its study of the political and natural causes and socio-economic factors leading to massive new flows of refugees. In the 1980s the majority of the refugees were either escaping from famine and misery-ridden regions or from underdeveloped states to obtain the status of economic refugees. See also ▷ Geneva Convention on the Status of Refugees, 1951; and ▷ Migrations.

The 1989 General Programme expenditures for all UNHCR's activities around the world amounted to \$428,700,000. The highest expenditures were in Pakistan (46.3 mln), Ethiopia (42.0 mln), Sudan (37.9 mln), Somalia (34.5 mln), Malawi (22.9 mln), Thailand (21.7 mln), Iran (19.7 mln), Honduras (12.7 mln), Mexico (8.3 mln), Hong-Kong (6.8 mln), Philippines (6.4 mln), Angola (5.2 mln), and Zimbabwe (5.1 mln). UNHCR information systems: Habitat Library and Documentation Centre, UNHCR-HABITAT Doc and Film Library, UNHCR-VISION-HABITAT. The UN statistics: refugees residing in the top 20 host countries on January 1, 1986: Pakistan, 2,702,500; Iran, 2,300,000; Sudan, 1,164,000; USA, 1,000,000; Somalia, 700,000; Canada, 353,000; Zaïre, 283,000; China, 279,800; Burundi, 267,500; Tanzania, 212,900; Mexico, 175,000; France, 174,200; Algeria, 167,000; Uganda, 151,000; India, 136,700; Germany, W., 134,000; Thailand, 130,000; Zambia, 103,000; Malaysia, 99,700. The Association for the Study of the World Refugees Problem, f. 1956, with hqs in Vaduz, Liechtenstein and Secretariat General in Rome, Publ.: AWR Bulletin, quarterly.

J.H. STIMPSON, *The Refugee Problem*, London, 1939; G. POULIN, "Le problème des réfugiés", in: *Schweizerisches Jahrbuch für Internationales Recht*, 1946; R. NATHAN-CHAPOTOT, *Les Nations Unies et les Réfugiés*, Paris, 1949; P. FOINGS, *Das Internationale Flüchtlingsproblem, 1919–1950*, Berlin, 1951; R. RISTELAUBER, *The IRO*, New York, 1951; J.W. HOLBORN, *The IRO*, New York, 1956; M.J. TRONDFOOT, *European Refugees, 1919–1952*, London, 1957; R.E. GARRAY, *The Arab Refugee Problem*, London, 1961; *UNTS*, Vol. 11, pp. 73–105; O. KIMMINICH, *Der internationale Rechtsstatus des Flüchtlings*, Köln, 1962; J.B. SCHECHTMAN, *The Refugee in the World*, New York, 1964; A. GRAHL-MADSON, *The Status of Refugees in International Law*, 2 Vols., Leiden, 1972; *UN Chronicle*, October 1983, p. 88 and January 1984, pp. 48–49; G.S. GOODWIN-GILL, *The Refugee in International Law*, Oxford, UK, 1985; G. KIBREAB, *African Refugees: Reflections on the African Refugee Problem*, Trenton, 1985; *UN Chronicle*, August 1986 p. 62; R. GORMAN, *Coping with Africa's Refugee Burden: A time for Solutions*, New York, 1987; *UN Resolutions and Decisions adopted by the General Assembly during the First Part of its Forty-Third Session, From 20 September to 22 December 1988*, New York, 1989, pp. 374–81.

REGIONAL AGREEMENTS AND THE UN CHARTER. One of the difficult problems encountered in the drawing up of the UN Charter was how to determine the correlation between regional agreements and the Charter. The draft prepared in Dumbarton Oaks did not allow organizations to take up any regional actions in the matter of international peace and security if they had not been approved of by the UN Security Council. This was

objected to by Latin American signatories of the ▷ Chapultepec Act, 1945. Among the big powers the Dumbarton Oaks draft won approval of France, Great Britain and the USSR. N.V. Evatt of Australia, accused Panamericanism of being "isolationism attempting to torpedo the foundation of a world organization." The US Secretary of State, R. Stettinius, in a conversation with ministers for foreign affairs of Bolivia, Brazil, Chile, Colombia, Cuba, Mexico and Peru, May 16, 1945, said that "the USA is ready to sign the Interamerican Regional Treaty, consistent with the Chapultepec Treaty" and simultaneously support the participation of "the Panamerican system in the new world organization." Finally, the big powers agreed to draw up art. 51 of the UN Charter in the spirit of the Dumbarton Oaks draft, but with the restrictions included in arts. 52, 53 and 54 concerning regional arrangements which have never been interpreted unanimously. For authorizations of regional organizations as regards maintenance of international peace and security also see Chapter VIII of the UN Charter.

P. VALLAS, *Le régionalisme international à l'ONU*, Paris, 1948; Ch.G. FENWICK, *The Inter-American Regional System*, Washington, DC, 1949; A.P. WHITAKER, "Development of American Regionalism", in: *International Conciliation*, No. 469, March, 1951, pp. 123–163; A.J. HOVY, *Regionalism and the UN*, London, 1954; E.B. HAAS, "The Challenge of Regionalism", in: *International Conciliation*, No. 513, 1957.

REGIONAL ORGANIZATIONS. An international term for intergovernmental and non-governmental international organizations for a particular continent or region; subject of multilateral agreements.

REGIONAL SECURITY. An international term for the principle that nothing in the UN Charter precludes treaties or regional arrangements whose aim is to settle issues that concern international peace and security and are adapted to regional action under the condition that such treaties or arrangements and their activities are consistent with the aims and principles of the UN (art. 52 UN Charter).

REGISTER OF SERIAL PUBLICATIONS. An information bank est. 1972 in Paris, within the framework of the UNESCO program for a World Science Information System, UNISIST, Centre international d'enregistrement des publications en serie. Registered with the UIA.

Yearbook of International Organizations.

REGISTER TONNAGE. An international term for the measure of the capacity of a vessel, derived from barrels of wine whose number in the cargo hold of a ship determined its dimensions ("tonneau" *French* = "barrel"). In 1854 in England, and then universally, it was accepted that one register ton = 100 cubic feet. This ton = 2,8317 m³ is still in effect. The capacity of a vessel in register tons, if it includes the entire interior, is defined as gross (BRT), and if it includes only the cargo hold as net (NRT). The regulations pertaining to register ton currently in force were formulated and announced in 1966 by IMCO.

REGISTRATION AND PUBLICATION OF INTERNATIONAL AGREEMENTS. The subject of international conventions since 1919; the first initiative regarding registration and publication of agreements by an international institution was considered in 1875 by the Paris Institute of International Law, which in 1891 proposed the

R

establishment of an International Union, the duty of which would be to register and publish such agreements. The proposal was also discussed by the Conference of States held in Berne in 1894. Only after World War I, however, on the initiative of US President W.W. Wilson, an opponent of confidential diplomacy, was art. 18 of the Covenant of the League of Nations adopted:

"Every treaty or international engagement entered into hereafter by any Member of the League of Nations shall be forthwith registered within the Secretariat and shall as soon as possible be published by it. No such treaty or international engagement shall be binding until so registered."

The second sentence of art. 18 caused reservations, mainly on the part of Germany. However, the absolute majority of states agreed to observe the principle of patency in international relations and until the termination of the League's activity, i.e. 1946, there were 4834 international agreements registered in 205 volumes of the League of Nations Treaty Series in French or English versions. Among those not registered were, i.a., the Munich Treaty of 1938 and the German Soviet Non-Aggression Pact of 1939. Somewhat different in wording, but nonetheless containing an identical obligation on the members of the United Nations was introduced by the UN Charter. Under art. 102 of the Charter of the UN every treaty and every international agreement entered into by any member of the UN after the coming into force of the Charter shall, as soon as possible, be registered with the Secretariat and published by it in the original version together with translations in English or French. The Rules of Registration and Publication were adopted by the UN General Assembly in Res. No. 97/I of Dec. 14, 1946.

P.H. Rohn, the author of the *World Treaty Index*, estimates that from Jan. 1, 1946, to Dec. 31, 1965, 12,732 bilateral treaties have been concluded in the world; out of that number 7980 have been registered in the UN Treaty Series and the remaining 4752 in collections of documents of the countries involved. The UN Register, with respect to bilateral treaties, is representative only in part; however, it thoroughly records multilateral treaties.

On Dec. 31, 1975 a total of 20,949 international agreements and 10,719 certified statements relating to those agreements were registered with the UN Secretariat.

UNTS, Vol. 76, p. 18; *Yearbook of the UN 1976*, p. 830; P.H. ROHN, *World Treaty Index and Treaty Profiles*, 5 Vols. Berkeley, 1976. R.L. BLEDSOE, B.A. BOCZEK, *The International Law Dictionary*, Oxford, 1987.

REGISTRATION OF MARKS AGREEMENTS, 1891 AND 1957.
The Agreement concerning the International Registration of Marks, was signed on Apr. 14, 1891 in Madrid; revised on Dec. 14, 1900 in Brussels; on June 2, 1911 in Washington; on Nov. 6, 1925 in The Hague; on June 2, 1934 in London. The Agreement concerning the International Classification of Goods and Services for the Purposes of the Registration of Marks, signed on June 15, 1957 in Nice, revised on July 14, 1967 in Stockholm; came into force on Nov. 12, 1969. The classification consists of (a) a list of classes and (b) an alphabetical list of goods and services with an indication of the classes into which they fall. The list of classes and the alphabetical list of goods are those which were published in 1935 by the International Bureau for the Protection of Industrial Property (art. 1).

UNTS, Vol. 828, p. 191.

REGISTRATION OF SHIPS. ▷ Ships Registration.

REHABILITATION.
A subject of international co-operation. Organizations reg. with the UIA:

Asian Pacific League of Physical Medicine and Rehabilitation, f. 1968, Melbourne. Publ.: *Newsletter*.
European Association for Technical Orthopaedics and Orthopaedic Rehabilitation, f. 1971, Beauvais.
European Federation for Physical Medicine and Rehabilitation, f. 1963, Brussels.
International Association of Rehabilitation Facilities, f. 1969, Washington DC.
International Federation of Physical Medicine and Rehabilitation, f. 1950, London. Consultative status with WHO.
International Rehabilitation Medicine Association, f. 1969, Guaynabo, Puerto Rico. Publ.: *News and Views*.
Latin American Medical Association for Rehabilitation, f. 1976, Caracas.
Rehabilitation International, f. 1922, New York. Consultative status with ECOSOC, ILO, UNICEF, UNESCO and WHO. Publ.: *International Rehabilitation Review* (quarterly in English and Japanese).

Yearbook of International Organizations.

REHABILITATION OF VICTIMS OF POLITICAL REPRESSION.
An international term for a public rehabilitation of political victims condemned to death or long-term prison sentences. In cases related to citizens of foreign countries, subject of international conflicts. A wave of rehabilitation of the victims condemned on the order of J.V. Stalin, took place in the USSR, 1987–1988.

KEESING's *Record of World Events*, 1987 and 1988.

REHOVOT CONFERENCE.
An Israel institution est. Aug. 1960 in the Weizman Institute of Science in Rehovot, Israel as the Rehovot Conference on Science in the Advancement of New States, to stress the importance of science and technology in the development of new independent countries. Reg. with the UIA.

Yearbook of International Organizations.

REICHSDEUTSCHE.
German = "Germans of the Reich." The official term for citizens of the German Reich without regard to their nationality, introduced by a law on Reich citizenship on July 1, 1913 which was Germanizing in its assumptions and whose validity was maintained by the Weimar Republic, the German Third Reich, and the FRG, leading to a conflict with international law in cases of citizens of the Reich of other than German nationality (▷ Minorities, Protection of). Besides this, the German III Reich introduced special legislation for foreign citizens who voluntarily or under compulsion gave their nationality as German (▷ Volksdeutsche) and thereby acquired German citizenship. ▷ Citizenship.

Reichs- und Staatsangehörigkeitgesetz vom 22 Juli 1913, Berlin, 1913.

REICHSSICHERHEITSHAUMPTAMT, RSHA.
Main Security Office of the German III Reich, the central police under the direction of Heinrich Himmler, operated 1939–45, recognized by a judgement of the International Nuremberg Tribunal in 1946 as a criminal organization. Section IV of RHSA was the ▷ Gestapo.

G. CRANKSHAW, *Gestapo. Instrument of Tyranny*, New York, 1956.

REICHSTAG.
German name of the parliament of the German Reich, 1871–1945. The building of the Reichstag in Berlin was erected in 1884–94; its setting on fire on Feb. 27, 1933 served A. Hitler as a pretext to suspend civil liberties in the German III Reich (by the Decree on nation and state protection of Feb. 28, 1933) and for terroristic actions against the communists, which were to be justified also by

one of the Leipzig trials (Reichstagsbrand). The Reichstag building was not reconstructed; meetings of the Reichstag were held in Krolloper in Charlottenburg. During the battle for Berlin, the Reichstag building was captured on Apr. 30, 1945 by the Red Army. After the division of Berlin into occupational sectors in June 1945, the Reichstag building was in the British sector, and was subject to the jurisdiction of the West Berlin Senate. In a consequence of legislation by the FRG parliament of Oct. 26, 1955 on reconstruction of the Reichstag as the seat of the Bundestag, and on removal of historical inscriptions made by Soviet soldiers, a group of West German workers secretly cut out of the Reichstag wall fragments with engraved signatures and slogans and forwarded them in 1963 to the Central Museum of the USSR Military Forces in Moscow. Reconstruction of the Reichstag building was completed in January 1971 for the 100th anniversary of the Bismarck Reich; however, the scheduled formal occupation of the building by the Bundestag did not take place in view of the position of the four powers that West Berlin could not be the seat of central authorities of the Federal Republic of Germany.

"Reikhstag", in: *Woyennoi istoricheskiy zhurnal*, No. 5, 1971; W. HOFER, E. CALIG, K. STEPHAN, *Der Reichstagbrandt*, Berlin West, 1972.

REICHSWEHR.
German = "defence of the Reich." The name of the professional army of Germany, 1919–35, which by the Versailles Treaty was limited to 100,000 men. On Mar. 16, 1935 A. Hitler unilaterally abrogated the provisions of the Treaty and introduced universal military service; simultaneously the name of the army was changed to ▷ Wehrmacht.

G. CASTELLAU, *Le Réarmement clandestin du Reich 1930–1935*, Paris, 1955; H.J. GORDON, *The Reichswehr and the German Republic 1919–1926*, Princeton, 1975.

RELIEF, INTERNATIONAL.
An international term with various meanings: (1) defined by bilateral norms of legal international relief; (2) defined by an International Convention of 1977 on Relief for Countries Affected by Natural Catastrophes; (3) organized international economic or technical assistance, usually under UN auspices, for developing countries, also for saving cultural monuments.

RELIGION.
A subject of international studies, co-operation and agreements.

Organizations reg. with the UIA:

International Association for the History of Religions, f. 1950, Jerusalem, Publ.: *Numen* and *International Bibliography*.
International Association for Religious Freedom, f. 1900, Frankfurt/M. Publ.: *Information Service*.
International Centre for studies in Religious Education, f. 1935, Brussels. Publ.: *Lumen Vitae*.
International Conference of Sociology of Religions, f. 1948, Lille. Publ.: *Bulletin*.
International Federation of Institutes for Socio-Religious Research, f. 1958, Louvain, Belgium. Publ. *International Review of Sociology of Religions* (quarterly).
International Religious Liberty Association, f. 1888, Washington DC.
World Conference on Religion for Peace, f. 1970, New York. Publ.: *Religion to Peace*.
World Fellowship of Religions, f. 1957, New Delhi. Organizes World Religions Conferences.

Yearbook of International Organizations 1986/87; The Europa Yearbook 1988. A World Survey, Vol. I, London, 1988.

RELIGIONS OF THE WORLD.
The most important religions of the world are: ▷ Buddhism, Christianity (▷ Catholicism, ▷ Orthodox Churches, ▷ Protestantism), ▷ Hinduism, ▷ Islam, ▷ Judaism,

▷ Confucianism, ▷ Shinto, ▷ Taoism. The first incomplete studies of the most important religions of the world done in 1810 revealed that of some 658,000,000 people 228,000,000 were Christians, 150,000,000 Buddhists, 110,000,000 Moslems, 60,000,000 Brahmins, 5,000,000 Jews and 100,000,000 other religions. A hundred years later, 1910, of some 1,560,000,000 people the number of Christians was believed to be 617,000,000 among which 293,000,000 Catholics, 186,000,000 Protestants, 127,000,000 Orthodox and 12,000,000 other; Confucianists numbered 240,000,000, Brahmins – 210,000,000, Moslems – 207,000,000, Buddhists – 137,000,000, Shintoists – 49,000,000, Jews – 13,000,000 and others 87,000,000.

In Europe after World War I, according to censuses performed between 1920 and 1927, of 465,000,000 people there were 198,000,000 Catholics, 124,000,000 Orthodox Church believers, 115,000,000 Protestants, 9,300,000 Jews, 7,800,000 Moslems, 2,700,000 other Christians and 7,300,000 other religions. In the Americas after World War I, out of the total 224,000,000 people – 124,000,000 were Catholics, 62,000,000 Protestants, 2,600,000 Jews, 900,000 Orthodox, 760,000 other Christians, 260,000 Hindus, 200,000 of Asian denominations, 50,000 Moslems and 31,000 of other beliefs.

In Asia the population of 989,000,000 was divided into 502,000,000 of Asian denominations, 422,000,000 Hindus, 200,000,000 Moslems, 165,000,000 Catholics, 165,000,000 Orthodox and other Christians, 720,000 Jews and 25,000 of other faiths.

In Africa, of some 135,000,000 people, 48,000,000 were Moslems, 5,400,000 Protestants, 5,100,000 Catholics, 4,500,000 other Christians, 582,000 Jews and 72,000,000 of other believers. In Australia and Oceania out of 8,200,000 people 5,200,000 were Protestants, 1,600,000 Catholics, 70,000 Hindus, 24,000 Jews. After World War II, according to censuses unified by the United Nations in 1960, the Catholics were believed to number 539,000,000 i.e. 18% of the total population of the world, Moslems – 435,000,000 i.e. 14.5%, Buddhists – 392,000,000 i.e. 13%, Hindu – 358,000,000 i.e. 12%, Protestants 212,000,000 i.e. 7.1% and Orthodox – 160,000,000 i.e. 5.4%. Of the remaining 900,000,000 people, i.e. 30%, over 850,000,000 were stated as non-believers, 28,000,000 as members of various sects and 12,000,000 Jews.

At the beginning of 1980s according to UN data, and Catholic, Christian, Islamic, Jewish and other sources there are more than 1,000,000,000 Christians worldwide (606,000,000 Catholics, 353,000,000 Protestants and 67,000,000 Orthodox), then c. 600,000,000 Moslems, 460,000,000 Hindu, 250,000,000 Buddhists and 170,000,000 Confucians. ▷ Jews. Organizations Registered with the UIA.

Agudath Israel ▷ Agudath.
All Agria Conferences of Churches, f. 1958, Nairobi, Kenya.
Alliance Israelite Universelle, f. 1860, Paris.
Baha'i International Community ▷ Baha'i.
Baptist World Alliance ▷ Baptists.
Christian Conference of Asia, f. 1959, New Delhi, India.
Christian Peace Conference, f. 1958, Prague, Czechoslovakia.
Conference of European Churches, f. 1957, Geneva, Switzerland.
Conference of International Catholic Organizations, f. 1927, Geneva, Switzerland.
Consultative Council of Jewish Organizations, f. 1946, London, UK.
European Baptist Federation, f. 1949, Copenhagen, Denmark.
Evangelical Alliance, f. 1846, London, UK.
Friends (Quakers) ▷ Quakers.

General Antroposophical Society, f. 1923, Dornach, Switzerland
International Association of Buddhist Studies, f. 1976, Berkeley, Calif., USA.
International Bible Reading Association, f. 1882, Surrey, UK.
Islamic Council of Europe, f. 1973, London, UK.
Latin American Episcopal Council, f. 1955, Bogota, Colombia.
Lutheran World Federation, f. 1947, Geneva, Switzerland.
Muslim World League, f. 1962, Mecca, South Arabia.
Opus Dei ▷ Opus Dei.
Pax Romana ▷ Pax Romana.
Salvation Army ▷ Salvation Army.
Theosophical Society ▷ Theosophy.
United Bible Societies, f. 1966, Stuttgart, FRG.
United Lodge, of Theosophists, ▷ Theosophy.
Watch Tower Bible ▷ Watchtower Society.
World Alliance of Reformed Churches (Presbytarian and Congregational), f. 1970, Geneva, Switzerland.
World Congress of Faith, f. 1936, London, UK.
World Federation of Christian Life Communities, f. 1963, Rome, Italy.
World Fellowship of Buddhists, f. 1950, Bangkok, Thailand.
World Jewish Congress, f. 1936, New York, N.Y., USA.
World Methodists Congress, f. 1881, Geneva, Switzerland.
World Sephardi Federation, f. 1951, Geneva, Switzerland.
World Student Christian Federation, f. 1896, Geneva, Switzerland
World Union for Progressive Judaism, f. 1926, New York, N.Y., USA.
World Union of Catholic Women's Organizations, f. 1910, Paris, France.

Die Religion in Geschichte und Gegenwart, Handwörterbuch, Tübingen, 1932; J. WACH, *The Comparative Studies of Religions,* London, 1958; *UN Monthly Chronicle,* November, 1967; *The Encyclopaedia Britannica Book of the Year 1983,* Chicago, London, 1983. *Yearbook of International Organizations,* 1986/87; *The Europa Yearbook 1988. A World Survey,* Vol. I, London, 1988. V. FERM ed., *The Encyclopedia of Religion,* New York, 1989.

RELIGIOUS DENOMINATIONS LAW. The legal norms regulating the attitude of the state to religious communities and their members, their rights and obligations; frequently a subject of accords or agreements between the state and a religious community. ▷ Concordat.

RELIGIOUS FREEDOM. One of the basic rights of man to avow or disavow any religion whatsoever, recognized for the first time in an international act in the ▷ Oliva Peace Treaty, 1660; included 1941 by US President F.D. Roosevelt among the Four Freedoms (▷ Roosevelt's Four Freedoms); examined by the UN Commission on the Rights of Man 1955–60 and formulated in the proposal of principles ▷ Freedom of Thought, Conscience and Religion. Also the subject of the UN draft declaration and International Convention on the Elimination of All Forms of Religious Intolerance. In 1977, the General Assembly requested the UN Commission on Human Rights to give the matter the priority necessary to complete the draft declaration.

UN Monthly Chronicle, November, 1967, pp. 43–46, and December, 1967, pp. 95–99; *UN Chronicle,* January, 1979, p. 87.

RELIGIOUS INTERNATIONALISM. The tendencies appearing in the history of religious movements, such as Christianity or Islam, to organize a multinational society on identical legal–moral principles; also the subject of study by historians of international law.

N. BENWITCHER, *The Religious Foundation of Internationalism,* London, 1932; G.F. BENKERT, *The*

Tomistic Conception of an International Society, Washington, DC, 1942.

RELIGIOUS INTOLERANCE. A subject of UN works on the draft of an International Convention on the Elimination of All Forms of Religious Intolerance. The draft was submitted in 1967 to governments of the UN member countries by the UN General Assembly Res. 2295/XXII. On Dec. 8, 1988 the GA adopted Res. 43/108: "Elimination of all forms of religious intolerance".

UN Monthly Chronicle, November and December, 1967. *UN Resolutions and Decisions adopted by the General Assembly during the First Part of its Forty-Third Session, From 20 September to 22 December 1988,* New York, 1989, pp. 359–361.

RELIGIOUS UNIONS. Unions of Christian churches, mainly Roman Catholic and Greek Catholic, but also Protestant groups. The Roman Catholic Church in striving to realize its own interpretation of the idea of Christian unity negotiated, especially in the 15th century, various kinds of unions with churches of the Eastern ritual, allowing them to retain a separate ritual, liturgical language, church calendar, and even marriage for priests, if contracted before final ordination. In connection with the Russian Revolution in 1917 the Pope called a special Cardinal's Congregation on the Eastern Church Congregatio pro Eclesia Orientali, under the leadership of the Pope, conducting its studies through the Papal Instituto Oriental. Publ.: *Orientalia Christiana.* From 1924 the Augustine Order publ.: in Beirut *Écho d'Orient* and *L'Union des Églises.*

REMILITARIZATION. An international term for the rearmament of a state defeated in war which was forbidden to do so by the terms of surrender or the peace treaty. The term appeared after World War I, when Germany violated the Versailles Treaty and at first carried on secret, then open (announced on Mar. 16, 1935), universal military conscription in Germany and on Mar. 7, 1936 denounced the ▷ Versailles Peace Treaty, 1919, the Locarno Treaty 1925 (▷ Locarno Conference and Treaty, 1925), and the ▷ Rhine Pact, 1925. This happened again after World War II under different circumstances in Germany and Japan, whose military expenditures grew from year to year so that 40 years after their surrender both reached a level of armaments second only to the Great Powers.

International Conciliation, No. 310, New York, May 1935, and No. 319, Apr., 1936; J. MOCH, *Histoire du réarmement allemand depuis 1950,* Paris, 1965.

REMOTE SENSING. An international term for acquisition of information, including photographic images, about the earth's surface from instruments aboard airplanes or satellites orbiting the planet. These data are then used to make maps, survey disasters, inventory resources and monitor environmental events. Remote sensing data can be used, in increasing economic productivity of both renewable resources, notably crops and timber, and nonrenewable resources such as oil and minerals; in national or regional planning with the goal of long-term economic and social development; and in monitoring the environment to improve the quality of life. Oil and mining industries – which need to observe vast tracts of the earth for geological exploration and which have the finances and technical expertise needed to make use of the technology – are the major users of satellite data for non-renewable resources. In the area of renewable resources, remote sensing is used to manage forest resources, assess current or potential land use and survey soil and landforms, determine distribution and marketing plans for harvests, and make regional or global crop estimates. Experiments on assessing and monitoring agricultural drought, soil moisture and crop conditions are under way. The technology may also be used in major building projects such as construction of roads or pipelines. Ocean-monitoring satellites may contribute to improved fisheries production by pin-pointing food-rich zones that attract fish or assist in ship routing, to improve the efficiency of commercial shipping. An obstacle in making crop estimates is cloud cover interference with satellite data collection, particularly in countries with a long rainy season. To be useful, crop estimates must be based on information frequently supplied and speedily distributed. Furthermore, a reliable network for disseminating data and an organized data base integrated into national farm distribution and marketing systems must exist. Remote sensing can be helpful in arid and semi-arid regions for tracking brush fires, identifying areas damaged by overgrazing, monitoring range conditions, and studying problems related to desertification. The technology can help monitor air and water quality, identify sources of pollution and elements of climate systems and desertification processes, and provide information on flood water advance and retreat and data for mapping of flood plains. See also ▷ Goestationary Orbit. ▷ Satellite Remote Sensing System.

UN Chronicle, No 2, 1985, pp. 19–20; R.L. BLEDSOE, B.A. BOCZEK, *The International Law Dictionary*, Oxford, UK, 1987.

RENMINBI. The currency of the People's Republic of China. Monetary unit 1 yuan = 10 jiao = 100 feh; issued by the People's Bank of China. In the first years of the People's Republic of China the name of the currency was yen min piao, after a currency reform, Mar. 1, 1955 it was renamed yuan, and in 1969 renminbi, which means – like yen min piao – "people's money."

RENVERSEMENTS DES ALLIANCES. *French* = "reversal of alliances." The abandonment of an ally and entering into an alliance with a recent enemy; an international custom known in history from antiquity to modern times (▷ Washington Doctrine of Unstable Alliances, 1801).

REPARATIONS, RESTITUTIONS, INDEMNITIES. Three international terms of different meaning used to describe the forms of compensating for losses suffered by one state as a result of another state's aggression and occupation: (1) the term "reparations" means compensation of material losses caused by the aggressor; (2) the term "restitutions" means the return of public and private property taken illegally during a war; (3) the term "indemnities" means a compensation for international delicts paid to a state or individual, or to both. The differences between these three forms of compensation for war losses became more precise after World War II, when the Nuremberg trials defined in detail the character of lootings and preplanned devastations and the responsibility for them. The term "reparations" was introduced in the Versailles Treaty, which imposed on conquered Germany not war contribution, as was done by the German Reich with regard to defeated France in 1870 (5 billion francs in gold coins during a two-year period), but as an obligation to pay stated damages caused to the allied states, art. 231–247 with 7 annexes, Chapter VIII under the French title "*Reparations*" and German "*Wiedergutmachung*." The final amount of reparations, as well as the time of payment, was to be specified by the Reparation Committee of the Big Powers, abbreviation REPCO. This amount varied between 90 billion marks in gold paid in the course of 30 years (according to the French proposal of Apr., 1920 tabled at the San Remo Conference) and 269 billion marks payable within 42 years (in keeping with the assessment of real damages caused, as presented by a group of allied experts at the Boulogne Conference in May 1920). In practice, the 11 states entitled to reparations (Belgium, France, Greece, Italy, Japan, Yugoslavia, Poland, Portugal, Romania, UK, USA) between 1921 and 1928 received compensation half in commodities and half in cash amounting to 15 billion marks in gold; after that the payment of reparations was practically suspended through the ▷ Dawes Plan, 1924 and the ▷ Young Plan, 1929. During World War II the governments of Australia, Belgium, Czechoslovakia, China, Greece, the Netherlands, India, Yugoslavia, Luxembourg, Norway, New Zealand, Poland, the USA, the UK, USSR, Union of South Africa and the National Committee of France on Jan. 5, 1943 signed in Moscow, Leningrad and Washington the UN Declaration directed against economic looting of territories occupied by the enemy. In Nov.–Dec., 1945 the Paris Conference on war indemnities from Germany established the Interallied Reparations Agency (IRA) with the task of stating the amount of reparations for its members: Albania, Australia, Belgium, Czechoslovakia, Denmark, Egypt, France, Greece, the Netherlands, India, Yugoslavia, Canada, Luxembourg, Norway, New Zealand, the USA, the UK and the Union of South Africa (Poland and the USSR did not become members of the agency because their reparations were calculated earlier, on Aug. 2, 1945, art. IV, para. 1 and 2 of the Potsdam Treaty which granted Poland reparations through the Soviet Union). In Paris, on Oct. 21, 1947 IRA agreed to the division of reparations into groups A – direct reparations, and B – indirect reparations in disassembled industrial plants, ships, vehicles etc. In practice, the member states of the Agency did not receive any significant reparations and indemnities since the issue was left for consideration at the Peace Conference, the convening of which soon became out-of-date.

Final Act of the Reparation Conference, Paris, 1945; R. CASTILLON, *Les réparations allemandes, Deux expériences: 1919–1932 et 1945–1952*, Paris, 1953; T. HONIG, "The Reparations Agreement between Israel and the FRG," in: *American Journal of International Law*, No. 48, 1954; O. NÖBEL, *Die Amerikanische Reparationspolitik Gegenüber Deutschland*, Frankfurt am M., 1980; R.L. BLEDSOE, B.A. BOCZEK, *The International Law Dictionary*, Oxford, 1987.

REPATRIATION. The return to their Fatherland of persons residing voluntarily or compulsorily for a longer time outside its borders. After World Wars I and II repatriation was the subject of multilateral co-operation and international agreements.

N. TOLSTOY, *Victims of Yalta*, London, 1978; J. CZERNIAKIEWICZ, *Repatriacja ludności polskiej z ZSRR 1944-1948* (The Repatriation of the Polish Population from the USSR in 1944–1948), Warsaw, 1984; A. WALASZEK, *Reemigracja z USA do Polski 1919–1924* (The Repatriation of Polish Emigrants from the USA 1919–1924), Warsaw, 1984.

REPCO. ▷ Reparations, Restitutions, Indemnities.

REPORTS OF THE UNITED NATIONS. A report is a statutory document called for by the UN Charter (Arts. 15 and 98) or authorized by a resolution of the General Assembly or by another principal or subsidiary organ. It is an "account given or opinion formally expressed after investigation or consideration or collation of information" (Concise Oxford Dictionary).

The term "Report of the Secretary General to the General Assembly on the work of the Organization" is used to designate the Annual Report and all documents prepared by the Secretariat that deal with policy questions engaging the responsibility of the Secretary General. The term "report" is also applied in the UN System in a broader sense to documents supplied by a Government or Member State or prepared by the Secretariat at the request of a legislative body.

United Nations Editorial Manual, New York, 1983, p. 5.

REPRESENTATION OF STATES, UN CONFERENCE, 1975. The conference was held from Feb. 4 to Mar. 14, 1975 at the Neue Hofburg in Vienna; 81 states and 16 observers participated in the Conference, which prepared and adopted on Mar. 19, 1975 the ▷ Vienna Convention on the Representation of States in their Relations with International Organizations of a Universal Character.

REPRESENTATIVE DEMOCRACY. A 19th-century international term for a system of appointing legislative and executive authorities through direct or indirect general elections so that these authorities are "representative" for the arrangement of political or class forces in a given state; subject of international conventions and organizations. In the Western Hemisphere the system of representative democracy was recognized in art. 5 of the OAS Charter as the foundation of the inter-American system, which was developed by the Fifth Consultative Council of the Ministers of Foreign Affairs at its session in 1959 in Santiago in a special Declaration on Representative Democracy which defined its special features in 8 points. In Jan., 1961 the Conference of Ministers of Foreign Affairs in Punta del Este reconfirmed the validity of the Declaration of 1959, and in June, 1961 the Inter-American Economic-Social Council recognized representative democracy as the basis for Alliance for Progress. The Inter-American Commission on Human Rights on Apr. 7, 1965, accepted the document entitled Human Rights and Representative Democracy. ▷ Johnson-Mann Doctrine, 1963.

Final Act of the Fifth Consultative Conference of the Ministers of Foreign Relations, PAU, Washington, DC, 1960; *Primer Simposio sobre Democracia Representativa. Informe Final*, PAU, Washington, DC, 1963; *El Sistema Interamericano*, Madrid, 1966, pp. 49–86, 396, 467.

REPRISALS. The retaliation undertaken by one state in response to an action of another state; after World War II the application of retaliatory measures against the citizens of another state or their property e.g. the taking and shooting of ▷ hostages, burning property, etc., was recognized as contrary to international law and prohibited by the Geneva Convention, 1949.

A. HAUMONT, *Les Représailles*, Paris, 1934; E.S. COLBERT, *Retaliation in International Law*, London, 1948; N.A. SCHÜTZE, *Die Repressalien unter besonderer Berücksichtigung der Kriegsverbrecherprozesse*, Berlin, 1950; A.R. ALBRECHT, "War Reprisals in the War Crimes Trials and in the Geneva Conventions of 1948," in: *American Journal of International Law*, No. 47, 1953; F. KALSHOVEN, *Belligerent Reprisals*, Leiden, 1971; R.L. BLEDSOE, B.A. BOCZEK, *The International Law Dictionary*, Oxford, 1987.

REPUBLIC OF NEW AFRICA. The name of a US black-separatist organization, which in 1968 promoted the idea of secession of Alabama, Florida, Georgia, Mississippi and South Carolina.

REPUBLIC OF SOUTH AFRICA. ▷ South Africa.

REPULSION DOCTRINE. A doctrine formulated in 1950 by J.F. Dulles (1888–1959), setting as the goal of American policy the stemming of the formation of socialism in Eastern Europe and the isolation of the USSR.

REQUISITION. In military law the confiscation by the army of food for soldiers, means of transport, fodder for horses, gasoline or other material of immediate need to the army in exchange for a receipt that payment will be made after the war.

RERUM NOVARUM, 1981. ▷ Catholic Social Doctrines.

RES COMMUNIS. *Latin* = "common thing." An international term derived from Roman law; used in contemporary international law to designate territories which have been internationalized. Also an environmentalist term for the environment as a whole.

Dictionnaire de la terminologie du droit international, Paris, 1960.

RESEARCH AND DEVELOPMENT (R&D). An international term uniting basic and applied research, designated in world literature by the English abbreviation "R", and developmental work for the purpose of utilizing "R" studies in production, designated by the English abbreviation "D"; in international statistics R&D is an index of scientific research potential and the level of scientific-technical development. Within CMEA, 1962–71, there existed a Commission for the Coordination of Scientific and Technical Research, transformed in July 1972, into the Committee for Co-operation in Scientific Research. Within OECD the 1961 Committee for Scientific Research was changed in 1966 to the Committee for West European Research Co-operation. Outlays for scientific studies have become a measure of progress and development for particular regions and countries, namely, by the relation of estimated research to the total national income in percentages.

H.M. PALMER, L.E. BRYGANT (eds.), *Research Centers Directory*, Detroit, 1979. *International Research Centers Directory*, Detroit, 1986; *Research Service Directory*, Detroit, 1986; M.M. WATKINS ed., *Research Centers Directory*. A guide to Approximately 9200 University Related and Other Nonprofit Research Organizations Established on a Permanent Basis and Carrying on Continuing Research Programs in Agriculture, Astronomy and Space Sciences, Behavioral and Social Sciences, Biological Sciences and Ecology, Business and Economics, Computers and Mathematics, Education, Engineering and Technology, Government and Public Affairs, Humanities and Religion, Labor and Industrial Relations Law, Medical Sciences and Regional and Areas Studies, Detroit, 11th Edition, 1987.

RESEARCH AND TRAINING. ▷ UNITAR

RESERVATIONS TO TREATIES. A subject of varying states' practice, commonly exercised in the 20th century, codified according to UN General Assembly Res. 478/V of Nov. 16, 1950, by the UN International Law Commission which, on the basis of the definition (with limitations) by the International Court of Justice in 1951 of reservations to the Convention on the Prevention and Punishment of the Crime of Genocide defined the reservations to treaties as:

"unilateral statements made by States and submitted in writing at the signing of an agreement, after its signing or its ratification, in order to waive or change the legal effects arising from application of indicated provisions of a treaty with regard to the country submitting such reservations."

In practice it is possible, due to the number and the kind of reservations, to make an international agreement *de facto* not binding for one of its parties. Reservations to treaties are subject to the same obligation concerning their registration and publication as all international agreements. The practice of individual states with regard to reservations was elaborated by the UN Secretary General and submitted to the UN General Assembly on Jan. 1, 1964.

D.H. MILLER, *Reservations to Treaties*, London, 1919; D. KAPPELER, *Réservations dans les traités internationaux*, Paris, 1957; UN Doc. ST(LRS), Aug. 7, 1959; UN Doc. A/5867, 1964; R.L. BLEDSOE, B.A. BOCZEK, *The International Law Dictionary*, Oxford, 1987.

RESERVE CURRENCIES. The exchangeable and non-exchangeable currencies in banks and the state treasury providing along with gold and bonds a means of stabilising the local currency and financing international trade. Up to World War I about 80% of the settlements in international trade were made in pound sterling; in the interwar period the American dollar was increasingly used along with the pound sterling as a reserve currency and in 1944 in the statute of the IMF it was recognized as the key currency of the world.

After World War II with the strengthening of the "hard currencies" of the highly developed states and with the increasing difficulties for international liquidity, some of these currencies also assumed the character of reserve currencies, but since their value in the IMF was defined not in their relation to gold but to the dollar, the key reserve currency in fact remained the US dollar in accordance with the Statute of the IMF which states that "the standard of the currency of each member country will be expressed in gold as a common denominator or in American dollars of such weight and fineness as were in force on July 1, 1944." In the decade 1961–70 the USA made a suggestion to carry out a general worldwide currency reform by creating an international reserve unit within the framework of the IMF. France, led by General Ch. de Gaulle, strongly opposed this, arguing that this unit was based on Anglo-American majority control in the IMF and would be a continuation of the present key role of the dollar among reserve currencies. Britain, acceding to the wishes of the EEC states, with her entry into EEC resigned from the reserve currency statute of the IMF on June 7, 1971 in Strasbourg.

P.M. BOARMAN, *The World's Money. Gold and Problem of International Liquidity*, Lewisburg, 1965

RESETTLEMENT. The forced migration of population brought about either by wars or occupants' repression, inconsistent with international law, or intergovernmental agreements on exchange of population, or actions based on international agreements; subject of continued organized international co-operation among charity organizations, such as the International Red Cross in Geneva. The first great forced resettlement was made by Turkey after World War I and involved Armenians and Greeks thus becoming subject to an intervention by the League of Nations and the Turkish–Greek Convention on exchange of persons signed on Jan. 30, 1923 in Lausanne.

In 1938 Germany signed a treaty with Italy concerning resettlement of the German population from the Upper Adige. During 1939–44 the German III Reich arranged genocidal resettlements in the occupied territories, mostly in Poland, the USSR and Yugoslavia which was confirmed by the Nuremberg Military Court in the years 1945–46.

After World War II under the Potsdam Treaty the German minorities from Poland, Czechoslovakia, Romania and Hungary were resettled during 1945–47 to the post-Potsdam Germany; from Poland under the agreement between the governments of Great Britain and Poland of Feb. 14, 1946, that determined the procedure of the resettlement of Germans in Poland to the British occupation zone. Simultaneously, under the agreement between the Governments of Poland and the Soviet Union the Polish population in the USSR was resettled; continued under a separate agreement 1957/58.

S.P. LADES, *The Exchange of Minorities: Bulgaria, Greece and Turkey*, London, 1932; W. HÖXTER, *Bevölkerungaustausch als Institut der Völkerrechts*, Berlin, 1932; J.B. SCHECHTMAN, *Population Transfer in Asia*, London, 1949; G. FRUMKIN, *Population Change in Europe since 1942*, London, 1952; K. SKUBISZEWSKI, "Le transfer de la population allemande, était-il conforme au droit international?", in: *Cahiers Pologne-Allemande*, No. 1, 1959.

RESIDENT REPRESENTATIVES TO THE UN. The legal status of the resident representatives to the UN, integrated by the Permanent Missions to the UN in New York, is defined in art. 5 of the Agreement Between the UN and the USA of June 26, 1947, as well as the Convention on the Privileges and Immunities of the UN approved by the UN General Assembly on Feb. 13, 1946. Art. 5 of the 1947 Agreement reads as follows:

"(1) Every person designated by a Member as the principal resident representative to the United Nations of such Member or as a resident representative with the rank of ambassador or minister plenipotentiary,

(2) Such resident members of their staffs as may be agreed upon between the Secretary-General, the Government of the United States and the Government of the Member concerned,

(3) Every person designated by a Member of the specialized agency, as defined in Article 57, paragraph 2, of the Charter, as its principal resident representative, with the rank of ambassador or minister plenipotentiary at the headquarters of such agency in the United States, and

(4) Such other principal resident representatives of members of a specialized agency and such resident members of the staffs of representatives of a specialized agency as may be agreed upon between the principal executive officer of the specialized agency, the Government of the United States and the Government of the Member concerned, shall whether residing inside or outside the headquarters district, be entitled in the territory of the United States to the same privileges and immunities, subject to corresponding conditions and obligations, as it accords to diplomatic envoys accredited to it. In the case of Members whose governments are not recognized by the United States, such privileges and immunities need be extended to such representatives, or persons on the staffs of such representatives, only within the headquarters district, at their residences, and offices outside of the district and such residences and offices, and in transit on official business to or from foreign countries."

International Organization, Vol. 2, 1948, pp. 164–170.

RES INTER ALIAS ACTA. *Latin* = "the matter has bearing only to the parties concerned." An international term for the principle of law that an agreement concluded between two parties gives no rights to third parties, nor does it place them under any obligations.

RES IN TRANSITU. *Latin* = "a thing transported." An international term for something being carried in transit through many states; and also a norm of international law to the effect that things being hauled in transit come under the law in force at the place of loading, in accordance with the following conventions: Brussels, 1924, concerning

R

bills of lading; Berne, 1924, on transport by rail; Warsaw, 1929, on transport by air.

RESISTANCE. A generally adopted term applied to the anti-Hitlerite resistance movement during World War II in Western Europe.

M.R.D. FOOT, *Resistance: European Resistance to Nazism, 1940–1945*, London, 1976; D. STAFFORD, *Britain and European Resistance 1940–1945. A Survey of the Special Operations Executive, with Documents*, London, 1980; J. HAERSTRUP, *European Resistance Movements 1939–1945. A Complete History*, Westport, 1981.

RES NULLIUS. *Latin*: "derelict property." An international term stemming from the Roman law for territory not belonging to any state, also called *Terra* or *Territorium Nullius*. Latin American states, in order to protect the non-discovered territories of the South American continent against their occupation by European powers, on the basis of "*res nullius*," declared in 1810 the principle of "*uti possidentis*," which states that all territories of that continent are the property of states sited in South America.

Dictionnaire de la terminologie du droit international, Paris, 1960.

RESOLUTION. An international term for an act passed by inter-governmental institutions, usually by a majority of votes. Legal validity of a resolution is subject to different interpretations, particularly UN resolutions.

J. CASTAÑEDA, *Valor Jurídico de las Resoluciones de las Naciones Unidas*, México, DF, 1967; R.L. BLEDSOE, B.A. BOCZEK, *The International Law Dictionary*, Oxford, 1987.

RESPONSIBILITY OF THE FOUR POWERS. The joint responsibility shared by France, the UK, USA and USSR for peace in the context of the German issues stemming from the Treaty of Potsdam as well as other decisions and elements of inter-power practice. The continuity of joint responsibility was affirmed in the Declaration of the Four Powers published on Nov. 9, 1972, in the following words:

"Governments of the Union of the Soviet Socialist Republics, the United Kingdom of Great Britain and Northern Ireland, the United States of America and the Republic of France represented by their ambassadors who have held several meetings in the former seat of the Allied Control Council, have mutually agreed to support applications for inclusion into the UN membership if such are furnished by the German Democratic Republic and the Federal Republic of Germany and affirm therefore that the membership may by no means infringe upon the rights and obligations of the Four Powers, as well as relevant decisions and practical actions related thereto."

Simultaneously, in art. 9 of the GDR–FRG treaty published on the same day, both German states declared that:

"The rights and responsibility of the Four Powers and relevant quadripartite agreements, provisions and practice related thereto can not be violated by the present treaty".

KEESING's *Contemporary Archive*, 1972.

RESTITUTION. An international term, defined by the Control Council for Germany at the meeting on Jan. 21, 1946, as follows:

"The question of restitution of property removed by the Germans from Allied countries must be examined in all cases, in the light of the declaration of 5th January, 1943. Restitution will be limited in the first instance, to identifiable goods which existed at the time of occupation of the country concerned and which have been taken by the enemy by force from the territory of the country. Also falling under measures of restitution are identifiable goods produced during the period of occupation and which have been obtained by force. All other property removed by the enemy is eligible for restitution to the extent consistent with reparations. However, the United Nations retain the right receive from Germany compensation for this other property removed as reparations.
As to goods of a unique character, restitution of which is impossible, a special instruction will fix the categories of goods which will be subject to replacement, the nature of these replacements, and the conditions under which such goods could be replaced by equivalent objects."

▷ Reparations, Restitutions, Indemnities.

Documents on Germany 1944–1959, Washington, DC, 1959.

RESTITUTION OF WORKS OF ART. The UN General Assembly, deploring the wholesale removal, virtually without payment, of objets d'art from one country to another, frequently as a result of colonial or foreign occupation, adopted on Dec. 13, 1973, in a recorded vote of 113 in favor to none against with 17 abstentions, Res. 3187/XXVIII which affirmed:

"that prompt restitution to a country of its works of art, monuments, museum pieces, manuscripts and documents by another country, without charge, was calculated to strengthen international co-operation inasmuch as it constituted just reparation for damage done; recognizing the special obligations in that connection of those countries which had access to such objects only as a result of colonial or alien domination." See also ▷ Cultural property return or protection.

UN Monthly Chronicle, January, 1974, pp. 41–42; *UN Yearbook*, 1973 and 1977; *UN Chronicle*, 1986, No. 1, pp. 19–20.

RETALIATION. ▷ Reprisals.

RETORTION. An international term for measures of retaliation applied against hostile steps taken by another state, within the limits permitted by international law; e.g. in return for refusing the right of circulation of another state's press, application of the same action on the principle of reciprocity.

R.L. BLEDSOE, B.A. BOCZEK, *The International Law Dictionary*, Oxford, 1987.

RÉUNION, LA. The overseas department of France, one of the Mascarene Islands, in the Indian Ocean, *c.* 569 miles east of Madagascar; area: 2512 sq. km. Pop. 1982 census: 515,814. Capital: Saint Denis with 109,072 inhabitants 1982. French colony since 1642 with the name Bourbon until the French Revolution. Occupied by the British 1810–16. On Mar. 19, 1946 the colonial status of Réunion was changed to that of Department d'Outre-Mer and during the 1960s the UN Decolonization Committee demanded full autonomy for the population of the island. Since 1974 Réunion has been represented in the French National Assembly by three deputies, in the Senate by two senators, and in the French Economic and Social Council by one councillor.

Statistique et indicateur économique, Saint Denis, 1983; *The Europa Year Book 1984. A World Survey*, Vol. II, pp. 1575–1577, London, 1984.

REUTER. The name of the world's oldest news agency, founded in 1850 in Aix-la-Chapelle (Aachen) by the German financier, P. Reuter (1816–99), moved to London in 1851; initially for information on quotations of West European stock exchanges by means of carrier pigeons; later for collecting and publishing economic, political and sport news from all over the world through about 75 foreign posts. The service exceeds half a million words per 24 hours. It is a joint-stock company of British press concerns.

REVALORIZATION. An international term for restoring monuments to their former state, subject of international co-operation under the auspices of UNESCO.

REVALUATION. An international term for raising the value of a certain currency in relation to others; the opposite of ▷ Devaluation.

REVINDICATION. The right to recover an object stolen usually in times of hostilities, subject of international convention. After World War I the principles of revindication were spelled out in the Versailles Treaty. During World War II United Nations Declaration No. 5 of Jan. 5, 1943 announced that all illegal acts of expropriation shall be annulled after the war (acts enforced by the occupational authorities of the axis states). On Feb. 8, 1947, in Neuchâtel, an agreement on the preservation or restoration of industrial property rights, violated by World War II, together with the Final Protocol and Additional Final Protocol, was signed by the member states of the International Union for the Protection of Industrial Property Rights. These documents came into force on Dec. 3, 1947. ▷ Reparations, restitutions and indemnities.

KEESING's *Contemporary Archive*, 1947.

REVISION AND REVIEW OF TREATIES. The revision of treaties in international law is in contradiction to the basic principle of international law ▷ *pacta sunt servanda*. The states are duty bound to perform in good faith the obligations to which they have consented (art. 26 of the ▷ Vienna Convention on the Law of International Treaties, 1969). Any unilateral revision of any terms of a treaty is prohibited.
However since the 17th century trade treaties incorporated revision clauses especially for prices of commodities and since the 20th century agreements related to arms control and peace also have revision clauses, but in the last decade they have been coupled with review clauses (the ▷ Non-Proliferation Treaty from 1968 comes up for review in 1985). The distinction between revision and review is a subject of discussion in the UN system. See art. 154 *Periodic review*, and art. 155 *The Review Conference* in the ▷ Sea Law Convention, 1982. ▷ Treaties Invalidity.

W.E. STEPHEN, *Revision of the Treaty of Versailles*, New York, 1939; A. VIGNOLI, *La Société des Nations et la révision des Traitées*, Paris, 1952; G. DELCOIGNE, CH. ROSSI, B. VEENDAAL, "Arms Control Treaties: Review and Revision", in: *IAEA Bulletin*, September, 1984.

REVISIONISM. (1) In the international workers' movement trends aimed at undermining the principles of Marxism–Leninism; (2) The territorial claims; demands of the revision of boundaries established by treaties. In a broader sense, the term is used in general for tendencies to change the status quo through revision of concluded peace treaties.

W.E. STEPHENS, *Revision of the Treaty of Versailles*, New York, 1939; A. VIGNOLA, *La Société des Nations et la révision de traités*, Paris, 1952.

REVOLUTION OF RISING EXPECTATIONS. An international term to define public feelings in the countries of the Third World during the decade 1955–65, when aspiration for a rapid improvement of socio-economic conditions collided with post-colonial or neo-colonial reality and resulted in growing frustrations and tensions.

REYKJAVIK. The capital of Iceland since 1904. The site of the Nordic Council Office and Nordic Forestry Union Office. On May 30–31, 1973 place of a summit meeting between the President of France Georges Pompidou and the US President Richard Nixon.

Yearbook of International Organizations; KEESING's *Contemporary Archive*, 1978.

RHEINBUND, 1806–1813. The Rhine Union, founded on June 12, 1806, on the initiative of Talleyrand, by 16 German princes, those of Bavaria included; according to art. 12 the Rheinbund was under Napoleon's patronage. On Oct. 8, 1813 Bavaria left the union by way of the Ried treaty with Austria, and the other principalities followed in Nov., 1813.

F.W. GHILLANY, *Diplomatischer Handbuch 1848–1862*, 2 Vols. Nördlingen, 1868.

RHETO-ROMANIC OR ROMANSH LANGUAGE. The fourth official Swiss national language since 1937. The others: German 65%, French 18.4%, Italian 9.8%. Romansh is spoken by 0.8% of the Swiss population, mostly in the canton Granbünden with 164,641 inhabitants 1980 census. The remaining 6% comprise the non official languages of immigrants.

RHEUMATISM. A subject of international research. Organizations reg. with the UIA:

European League Against Rheumatism, f. 1947, Basel. Publ.: *Zeitschrift für Rheumaforschung*, *Annals of Rheumatic Diseases*.
International League Against Rheumatism, f. 1927, Basel. Consultative status with WHO, UNICEF and ECOSOC. Publ.: *ILAR Handbook*.
South East Asia and Pacific League Against Rheumatism, f. 1963, Melbourne. Publ.: *SEAPAL Bulletin* (quarterly).
In 1977 a WHO Year Against Rheumatism was held.

Yearbook of International Organizations.

RHINE. A European river 1320 km long; it rises in the Alps and flows through Switzerland, Liechtenstein, Austria, FRG, France and The Netherlands into the North Sea. Since Vienna Congress 1815 the Rhine is free to international navigation and since the Mannheim Rhein Convention 1868 for the riparian states free of all navigation dues, including passage through the locks. The Rhine is navigable on a length of 850 km; it has 85 bridges and 11 locks; the tonnage of ships can reach up to 4000 deadweight capacity. The Rhine is connected by canals with the Maas, Rhone-Saone, Marne, and via the Main river with Danube. The main contemporary problem: the increasing pollution of the river by domestic and industrially used water. In 1919 the Versailles Treaty (arts. 354–362) placed the part of Rhine between Basel and Krimpen on the Lek, and Gorinchen, on the Waal, under the Rhine authority of the Central Commission for the Navigation on the Rhine in Palais de Rhine of Strasbourg. Hitler's Germany since 1936 did not respect the Versailles Treaty obligation, but in 1945 the old statute was reestablished. The Agreement Concerning the Social Security of Rhine Boatmen signed on July 27, 1950 at Paris, revised on Feb. 13, 1961 at Geneva came into force on Feb. 1, 1970. On Dec. 3, 1976 a Treaty on Curbing Pollution in the Rhine was signed by France, FRG, Luxembourg, the Netherlands and Switzerland.
Organizations reg. with the UIA:

Administrative Center of Social Security for Rhine Boatmen, f. 1950, Strasbourg.
Central Commission for the Navigation of the Rhine, est. 1815, Strasbourg. Statute modified 1831, 1868, 1919, 1945, 1950, 1963. Publ.: *Annual Reports*.

International Association for the Rhine Ships Register, f. 1947, Strasbourg. Publ.: *The Register*.
International Commission for the Protection of Rhine Against Pollution, f. 1963, Coblenz.
International Study Group for Waterworks in the Rhine Catchment Area, f. 1970, Amsterdam.
Tripartite Commission of the Working Conditions of Rhine Boatmen, f. 1950, Strasbourg.

A. GOELLNER, *Le pont français sur la Rhin*, Paris, 1954; H. KRAUS, U. SCHEUNER, *Rechtsfragen der Rheinschiffahrt*, Köln, 1956; C. BENNET MAURY, *Les Actes du Rhin*, Paris, 1957; U. SCHEUNER, "Rhein", in STRUPP-SCHLOCHAUER, *Wörterbuch des Völkerrechts*, Vol. 2, Berlin, 1962; *UNTS*, Vol. 717, 1970, pp. 3–158; *International Navigable Waterways*, UNITAR, New York, 1975.

RHINELAND. The region of West Germany, along the Rhine River, includes the former Rhine Province of Prussia, the Rheinish Palatinate, Rheinish and Southern Hesse, and Western Baden. Subject of a clause of the Versailles Peace Treaty, 1919, demilitarizing the Rhineland, which reads as follows:

"Art. 42. Germany is forbidden to maintain or construct any fortifications either on the left bank of the Rhine or on the right bank to the west of a line drawn fifty kilometers to the east of the Rhine.
Art. 43. In the area defined above the maintenance and the assembly of armed forces, either permanently or temporarily, and military manoeuvers of any kind, as well as the upkeep of all permanent works for mobilization, are in the same way forbidden.
Art. 44. In case Germany violates in any manner whatever the provisions of Articles 42 and 43, she shall be regarded as committing a hostile act against the Powers signatory of the present treaty and as calculated to disturb the peace of the world."

Together with the remilitarization of Rhineland on Mar. 7, 1936, Germany denounced the Treaty of Versailles and the Locarno Pact called also the Rhine Pact, 1925.

CARNEGIE ENDOWMENT, *Treaties of Peace, 1919–1923*, New York, 1925.

RHINE–MAIN–DANUBE CANAL, THE. The canal also called the European Canal, designed 1921, under construction on the territory of the FRG 1949–82 on the sections Mainz–Bamberg, Bamberg–Kelheim, and Kelheim–Passau, to join the basin of the North Sea with the Black Sea basin, making possible the navigation of ships with a displacement of 1500 t³.

G. JAENICKE, *Die Neue Grosschiffahrtstrasse Rhein–Main–Donau*, Frankfurt am M., 1973; K. ZEMANEK, *Die Schiffahrtsfreiheit auf der Rhein–Main–Donau Grosschiffahrtsstrasse*, Wien, 1976.

RHINE PACT, 1925. The Treaty of Mutual Guarantee concluded between Belgium, France, Great Britain, Italy and Germany, signed on Oct. 16, 1925 in Locarno; so-called Rhine Pact because it related to Belgian and French borders with German Rhineland; the parties guaranteed territorial *status quo* ensuing from the common boundaries of Belgium, France and Germany and the inviolability of these boundaries as fixed by the Treaty of Versailles June 28, 1919. ▷ Locarno Conference and Treaty, 1925.

RHINE POLLUTION ACCIDENT 1986. On November 1, 1986 a fire in the Swiss Chemical factory Sandoz AG., located on the river Rhine, east of Basel, destroyed a store with toxic substances, threatening the ecological balance of the river, killing fish and contaminating the drinking water supply. In two weeks the whole ecological system of the Rhine was destroyed due to this accident. The environment ministers from the FRG, France, Luxembourg, The Netherlands, Switzerland and

the European Community environment commissioner during two meetings in Zürich and Rotterdam criticized the insufficient precautionary measures and elaborated a plan for cleaning the Rhine by the year 2000 and introducing regulations concerning industrial pollution, early warning systems and monetary compensation.

KEESING's *Record of World Events*, 1987, No. 2.

RHODES FORMULA. An international term used in the UN since 1949 to determine procedures of armistice negotiations through a UN representative. From Jan. 12 to 25, 1949 Israeli–Egyptian talks were held on the island of Rhodes to set terms of an armistice agreement stemming from a cease-fire which began on Jan. 7. Since the parties, although staying in the same building, did not agree to conduct talks at one table, a UN representative, American R. Bunche, served as intermediary. The Rhodes Formula was once again applied during the 1970–71 Israeli–Arab conflict when the UN mediator was Swedish ambassador G. Jarring.

KEESING's *Contemporary Archive*, 1949 and 1971.

RHODESIA. ▷ Zimbabwe.

RHOMBOS. *Latin Rhombus macoticus*. A fish under protection as a result of an international convention.

UNTS, Vol. 377, p. 203.

RHONE–RHINE CANAL. French: Canal du Rhone au Rhin, constructed 1784–1833, length 320 km makes possible the transport of coal from the Ruhr Basin to Marseille.

RIAL OF IRAN. Iran's monetary unit, divided into 100 dinars, issued by the Bank Markazi Iran.

RICE. The staple food resource of the world; according to the UN estimates, principal food of one-third of the world's population; subject of international conventions. Main rice-producing countries: China, India, Pakistan, Japan, Indonesia, Thailand, Burma, Brazil and the Philippines. In order to increase rice production, the year 1966 was announced by FAO as the International Rice Year. In 1970 for the first time, the harvest exceeded 30 million tons of which 50% was produced by China and India. The first international conventions were initiated by FAO, which in 1948 called into existence the International Rice Committee, IRC, with seat in Bangkok. It publishes a quarterly: *IRC News Letter*. The International Rice Research Institute with seat in Los Baños near Manila was also established under FAO's sponsorship; at the end of the 1961–70 decade it produced a highly fruitful rice species resistant to vermin. The cost of the experiment equalled $15 million; the value of the additionally obtained rice from planting the IR 20 and IR 22 species in Ceylon, the Philippines, India and Pakistan 1970 alone was estimated at more than $1 billion. Next to the so-called Mexican wheat, Philippine rice became the originator of the Green Revolution. Upon initiative of the UN Economic Commission for Asia and the Far East on June 30, 1973 the Asiatic Rice Trade Fund, ARTF, amounting to $50 million, was established; its task is to promote and facilitate inter-regional rice trade in the Asiatic area, which represents 90% of world rice production and consumption. Since 1951 FAO annually publishes data about worldwide storage of rice according to species, entitled: *World Catalogue of Genetic Stocks Rice*.
Organizations reg. with the UIA:

International Rice Research Institute, f. 1960, Manila. Publ. *The International Bibliography of Rice Research*.

R

West African Rice Development Association, f. 1970, Monrovia.

Rice: Grain of Life, FAO, Rome, 1966; *El Arroz en América Latina*, Santiago, 1966; *National Rice Policies*, FAO, Rome, 1970; *Ten Year Bibliography of Rice Research*, 1960–70, Manila, 1971. International Trade Center UNCTAD/GATT, *Rice: A Survey of Selected Markets in the Middle East*, Geneva, 1984; UNIDO, *Rice Bran: An Under-Utilized Raw Material*, Vienna, 1984; *Yearbook of International Organizations, 1986/87*; *The Europa Yearbook 1988. A World Survey, Vol. I*, London, 1988.

RICHTER'S SCALE. The international scale of earthquake magnitudes, elaborated by American seismologist, Ch. Richter, 1935, according to seismograph records, from 1 to 8 degrees.

RIEL. The monetary unit of Kampuchea: one riel = 100 sen; issued by the Banque Nationale du Cambodge 1950–74, and after the period of liquidation of the monetary system by the Khmer Rouge, since 1980.

RIGA. The capital of Latvia. Population, 1986 census: 890,000.

A. SPEEKE, *History of Latvia*, Stockholm 1948.

RIGA PEACE TREATY, 1921. The peace treaty between Poland on the one hand and Russia and the Ukraine on the other, signed in Riga, Mar. 18, 1921 "putting an end to the war and concluding a final, lasting and honorable peace based on a mutual understanding and in accordance with the peace preliminaries," signed in Riga on Oct. 12, 1920. Highlights of the Treaty:

"The two Contracting Parties declare that a state of war has ceased to exist between them" (art. 1).
"The two Contracting Parties, in accordance with the principle of national self-determination recognize the independence of the Ukraine and of White Ruthenia and agree and decide that the eastern frontier of Poland, that is to say, the frontier between Poland on the one hand, and Russia, White Ruthenia and the Ukraine on the other, shall be as follows ..." (art. 2).
"Russia and the Ukraine abandon all rights and claims to the territories situated to the west of the frontier laid down by Art. 2 of the present Treaty; Poland on the other hand, abandons in favour of the Ukraine and White Ruthenia all rights and claims to the territory situated to the east of this frontier ..." (art. 3).
"(1) Each of the Contracting Parties guarantees to the subjects of the other Party a full amnesty for political crimes and offenses. All acts directed against the system of Government and the security of the state, as well as all acts committed in the interest of the other Party, shall be regarded as political crimes and offenses within the meaning of this Article.
(2) The amnesty shall also apply to acts which have been made the subject of administrative proceedings or proceedings other than before a court of law and to contraventions of provisions in force as regards prisoners of war and interned civilians and, generally, as regards subjects of the other Party.
(3) The putting into effect of the amnesty under Points 1 and 2 of this Article entails the obligation to institute no new judicial investigations, to discontinue proceedings which have already been instituted and to suspend execution of sentences which have already been passed.
(4) The suspension of the execution of a sentence does not necessarily imply that the prisoner shall be set at liberty, but in such an event he must be immediately handed over, with all the papers referring to his case, to the authorities of the state of which he is a national. Nevertheless, if such person states that he desires not to be repatriated, or if the authorities of the country of which he is a national refuse to admit him, such person may be again placed in custody.
(5) Persons against whom legal proceedings have been taken, or a preliminary judicial investigation has been instituted, or who have been summoned to appear before a court of justice for any breach of the law, or who have been sentenced for such an offense, shall forthwith be handed over, on application being made by the state of which they are nationals, together with all the papers relating to their case.
(6) The amnesty referred to in this Article shall also apply to all the above-mentioned offenses that have been committed up to the time when this Treaty is ratified.
Sentence of death passed upon persons found guilty of one of the offenses referred to above shall be suspended as from the date of the signature of this Treaty." (art. 10).
§1. Russia and the Ukraine shall restore to Poland the following objects which were removed from the territory of the Polish Republic to Russia and the Ukraine subsequent to January 1, 1772:
(a) all war trophies (e.g., flags, colors, military insignia of all kinds, cannons, weapons, regimental and other insignia), together with the trophies taken from the Polish nation after 1792, during the struggle for independence which was maintained by Poland against Tsarist Russia. Nevertheless, trophies of the Polish–Russo–Ukrainian war of 1918–21 shall not be restored.
(b) libraries, archaeological collections and archives, collections of works of art, collections of any nature and objects of historical, national, artistic, archaeological, scientific, and general education value.
The collections of objects included under letters (a) and (b) of this Paragraph shall be restored irrespective of the conditions under which, and the pretexts upon which, they were carried off and irrespective of the authorities responsible for such removal and without regard to the person whether physical or legal to whom they belonged prior to, or subsequent to, their removal.
§2. The obligation to make restitution shall not apply to:
(a) objects carried off from the territories situated on the east of the frontiers of Poland, as determined by the present Treaty, in so far as it shall be proved that such objects are a product of White Ruthenian or Ukranian civilization, and that they were subsequently removed to Poland otherwise than as the result of a voluntary transaction or of succession;
(b) objects which passed from the possession of their legal owner into Russian or Ukranian territory as the result of a voluntary transaction or of succession, or were removed to the territories of Russia and the Ukraine by their legal owner.
§3. If there exists in Poland any collections or objects falling within the class specified in letters (a) and (b) of §1 of this Article, which have been removed from Russia or the Ukraine during the same period, such collections and objects shall be restored to Russia and the Ukraine under the conditions laid down in §1 and 2 of this article." (art. 11)
"Immediately after the ratification of the present Treaty, diplomatic relations between the two Contracting Parties shall be resumed." (art. 24)

LNTS, Vol. IV, No. 101, pp. 35–36; *Major Peace Treaties of Modern History*, New York, 1967, pp. 2215–2251.

RIGHT OF ASYLUM. A custom, dating back to ancient times, to grant refuge to persecuted persons. The Decree of April 20, 1793 concerning declaration of war against Austria included a promise of asylum for all aliens who would fight under the French banner. Subsequently, Article 120 of the Constitution of the French Republic of June 20, 1793, granted the right of asylum *"aux étrangers bannis de leur Patrie par la cause de la Liberté"* (to foreigners banished from their homelands due to the cause of liberty). In Europe the right of asylum granted to freedom-fighters for class reasons was voided by the Holy Alliance in 1818 to 1846 and also by a majority of European states, 1872–1914 under special bilateral conventions (such as the Rome convention of 1898 on co-operation between political police organizations and on extradition of revolutionaries). The refusal to grant asylum to freedom-fighters and extradition was upheld after World Wars I and II by a majority of countries on the basis of bilateral or multilateral conventions on police co-operation. Simultaneously, some of these states, despite the fact that international law does not provide for granting the right of asylum to war criminals, sheltered war criminals after World War II. In 1944 the government of the USA obtained assurances of neutral states (Argentina, Ireland, Portugal, Spain, Switzerland, Sweden and Turkey) that they would not grant asylum to war criminals fleeing from the III Reich; nevertheless, as early as 1945 Argentina, Spain, Portugal, also South Africa, Bolivia, Brazil and Paraguay gave shelter to Nazi criminals. Meanwhile, the Convention on Prevention and Punishment of the Crime of Genocide of Dec. 9, 1948 introduced the obligation to extradite war criminals. The ▷ Human Rights, Universal Declaration of, adopted on Dec. 10, 1948 under art. 14 ruled out asylum in case of "acts contrary to the purposes and principles of the UN." The Geneva Convention of July 28, 1951 on the Legal Status of Refugees excluded from the right of asylum persons who commit acts to the detriment of peace, war crimes or genocide. While elaborating on this principle, the UN Commission on Human Rights in the course of preparation for drafting the UN Declaration on Asylum during 1963–67 also discussed the introduction of a total ban on asylum granted to perpetrators of crimes specified in art. 6 of the Statute of the International Military Tribunal and also of a ban on territorial asylum. In 1965 the government of Switzerland issued a ban on entering the country by foreigners suspected of committing acts recognized as war crimes or crimes against humanity. A similar stand was taken by a majority of countries. International law differentiates between territorial asylum and diplomatic asylum. The former, as a rule, is generally accepted and finds expression in art. 14 of the Human Rights Universal Declaration:

"Everyone has the right to seek and to enjoy in other countries asylum from persecution. This right may not be invoked in the case of prosecutions genuinely arising from non-political crimes or from acts contrary to the purposes and principles of the United Nations."

Diplomatic asylum, the ancient custom of granting refuge in ex-territorial premises of diplomatic missions, is not generally recognized, but is observed by a majority of Latin American states. The first international convention on the right of Diplomatic asylum was signed Feb. 20, 1928 in Havana by Brazil, Costa Rica, Cuba, Dominican Republic, Ecuador, Guatemala, Mexico, Nicaragua, Panama, Paraguay and Uruguay. The Conference of American states in Montevideo adopted on Dec. 26, 1933 a Treaty on Asylum, not signed by the USA. In Montevideo, Apr. 8, 1939, the treaty on granting political asylum and refugees was signed by Argentina, Bolivia, Chile, Paraguay and Uruguay. After World War II diplomatic asylum was a subject of dispute between Haiti and Dominican Republic at the OAS and between Colombia and Peru on grounds of granting asylum by the embassy of Colombia in Lima to V.P. Haya de la Torre, the leader of a Peruvian party APRA persecuted by the government of Peru. In this matter the International Court of Justice gave its interpretation of the Havana Convention (Nov. 20, 1950) which under art. 1, in fact, prohibits the granting of asylum in diplomatic premises, on board warships, in military camps and war planes to persons accused of non-political crimes or desertion, however, under art. 2 orders observance of the right of asylum with respect to political offenders; the Court did not accept the statement by the government of Peru that armed rebellion is a non-political crime and thereby rejected the fact of Haya de la Torre being treated as a non-political offender subject to the provisions of art. 1; also, the Court stated that the granting of asylum by the embassy of Colombia was inconsistent with the provisions of the convention on urgency and time limitation. The verdict did not satisfy any of the parties and gave rise to the drafting of two new conventions (only in 1954 was Haya de la Torre permitted to leave the Colombian embassy for Mexico on safe conduct). Asylum granted to ▷ deserters constitutes a separate problem.

The first world debate on the right of asylum was carried out in 1961 and 1962 at the Vienna Conferences on diplomatic relations and consular matters. On Mar. 4, 1960 the Committee on Human Rights approved the draft declaration concerning the right of asylum which was provided with suggestions of 48 governments. On Dec. 14, 1967 the UN General Assembly by Res. 2312/XX adopted the Declaration on Territorial Asylum and recommended governments of member states to be guided by common principles in the matter of the right of asylum.

E. REALE, "Le droit d'asile," in: *Recueil des Cours 1938*, I, pp. 473–601; F. MORGENTHAU, "The Right of Asylum", in: *British Year Book of International Law 1949*, pp. 327–357; L. MORENO QUINTANA, *Derecho de Asilo*, Buenos Aires, 1952; S. PLANAS SUAREZ, *El asilo diplomático*, Buenos Aires, 1953; *El Sistema interamericano. Estudios sobre su Desarrollo y Fortalecimiento*, Madrid, 1966, pp. 447–459.

RIGHT OF CORRECTION, INTERNATIONAL. A subject of international agreement: Convention on the International Right of Correction (of false or distorted news or reports), signed on Mar. 31, 1953 in New York, by the governments of Argentina, Chile, Ecuador, Egypt, El Salvador, Ethiopia, France, Guatemala, Paraguay and Peru. Accessions: Cuba (1954), United Arab Republic (1955), Yugoslavia (1956) and Sierra Leone (1963). Came into force on Aug. 24, 1962.

UNTS, Vol. 435, p. 192.

RIGHT OF FREEDOM OF EXPRESSION. ▷ Right to Free Expression.

RIGHT OF INNOCENT PASSAGE. The commonly recognized rule of international law, allowing merchant ships (not warships) to sail from high sea to a port through territorial waters or vice-versa, in keeping with the interests of international maritime exchanges; subject of the Geneva Convention of 1958 on the Territorial Sea and Contiguous Zone, which in arts. 14–23 granted the right of innocent passage to all merchant ships and fishing vessels, under the condition spelled out in art. 14:

"Passage is innocent as long as it is not prejudicial to the peace, good order or security of the coastal State. Such passage shall take place in conformity with these articles and with other rules of international law."

The Convention does not mention warships, whose passage through territorial waters of alien states takes place depending on the legislation or custom of the state and on the basis of special permission, notification or courtesy. The passage through the territorial waters of Albania, by British warships in May and Oct. 1946 in the Korfu straits, was a subject of proceedings before the International Court of Justice.

R.R. BAXTER, *The Law of International Waterways*, Cambridge, 1961.

RIGHT OF LEGATION. The right vested in a sovereign state to send to another sovereign state envoys with a mission of extraordinary or permanent character as in the case of establishing regular diplomatic relations. However, due to the binding principle of sovereign equality of states, the right of legation may be exercised only upon mutual agreement. In accordance with the Havana Convention of 1928,

"no State may accredit its diplomatic representatives in other States without their previous consent. Such States may refuse to accept a representative of another State or if such a representative has already been accepted, they may request his recall without being obliged to give reasons for such a decision." (art. 8)

According to the Vienna Convention on Diplomatic Relations of 1961, "the establishment of diplomatic relations between states ... takes place by mutual consent" (art. 2). An identical principle for consular relations was included in the Vienna Convention on Consular Relations of 1963, thus resolving the question of the so-called right of consulate. The Vienna Convention on International Organizations of 1975, defined the right of legation of international organizations. In practice, the right of legation is used by the United Nations being, in the opinion of the International Court of Justice of Apr. 11, 1949, a subject of international law; it is also used by intergovernmental regional organizations, such as the EEC. The only non-governmental organization taking advantage of the right of legation is the Maltese Order.

L.T. LEE, *Vienna Convention on Consular Relations*, Leiden, 1966; *The UN and the Human Rights*, New York, 1968.

RIGHT OF PEOPLE TO PEACE, DECLARATION OF, 1984. A Declaration on the Right of People to Peace, was adopted on Nov.12, 1984, with Res.39/11. The Declaration related to ▷ Decolonization was the subject of three GA Resolutions, on Nov. 11, and Nov. 22, 1988.

UN Resolutions and Decisions adopted by the General Assembly during the first Part of its Forty-Third Session, from 20 September to 20 December 1988, New York 1989, p. 65.

RIGHT OF PRESCRIPTION. The right of a state to a territory arising from a long period of control and not from any direct rights (cession, adjudgement, disclosure, discovery, lease or purchase). In keeping with the right of prescription, the Netherlands claimed the mouth of the river Ems; Norway sued Denmark for Greenland; the USA sued the Netherlands for Palmas.

RIGHT OF RESISTANCE. The Ninth International Conference of American States, on May 2, 1948 at Bogota recommended to the Inter American Juridical Community study of the proposal of the Cuban delegation on the right of resistance, expressed in the following terms:

"The right of resistance is recognized in case of manifest acts of oppression or tyranny."

Novena Conferencia Internacional Americana. Actas y Documentos, Bogota, 1953, Vol. VI, p. 307.

RIGHT OF VOTE. A subject of international comparative law and of organized international studies that have been conducted since the 19th century under the auspices of the Inter-Parliamentary Union. In the countries possessing parliamentary systems, as a rule the right of vote is divided into passive and active, with the exception of the Jacobin Constitution 1793 in France. Minimum voting age limit differs, usually being between 18 and 25 years of age. In a few countries women have not received the right to vote, or have received only the passive right. The right to be elected a member of parliament is also generally subject to age limit (minimum 21–25 years of age) and by citizenship requirements of a given state; but rarely by nationality or religious denomination (in Germany until 1848 and in the III Reich Jews could not be elected; in Great Britain until mid 19th century – Jews and Catholics; in Spain – non-Catholics, and in numerous lay countries – clergymen). After World War I treaties on the protection of national minorities indirectly granted the right of such minorities to have their representatives elected to parliament. Many

European countries use the Belgian system of d'Hondt. Austria and Switzerland use the so-called Hagenbach–Bischoff system, and Norway the St. Lague system. After World War II in Western Europe, in connection with the establishment of the European Parliament in Strasbourg and its transformation in 1979 into a parliament elected directly by the citizens of the EEC member states, the concepts of a uniform interstate electoral system have been born.

V. D'HONDT, *Système pratique et raisonné de représentation proportionnelle*, Bruxelles, 1882.

RIGHTS AND DUTIES OF STATES, UN DRAFT DECLARATION, 1949. A subject of international law. At the initiative of the General Assembly Res. 178/II of Nov. 21, 1947, the UN International Law Commission undertook the registration of the international legal norms. The Commission in 1949 drafted a Declaration on Rights and Duties of States. The draft was acknowledged by the UN General Assembly on Dec. 6, 1949, and submitted to member states for comments, but was never adopted.

The highlights of the drafts:

"Art. 1. Each state has the right to sovereignty, to be independent of other states and to fully execute its legitimate rights including the freedom to choose its own form of government.

Art. 2. The state has the right to perform jurisdiction on its territory and with respect to all persons and objects being on this territory. This indicates full domestic jurisdiction of the state which jurisdiction is not dependent on international law as it stems from the sovereignty of the state.

Art. 3. The state assumes the obligation to refrain from interference into domestic affairs or foreign affairs of other states. In international law interference into matters of other states is defined as that having no legal basis and usually in a way incompatible with international law. Interference is a political phenomenon which many a time assumes the character of seemingly legal actions through diplomatic channels.

Art. 4. The state assumes the obligation to refrain from inciting and instigating internal struggles on the territory of another state. It is also prohibited from arranging actions against other states. This article further elaborates on the ban on intervention laid down in art. 3 this draft.

Art. 5. All states have equal rights. This indicates that all states are equal before international law and equally share in the drawing of this law as well as equally participate in international organizations and conferences. From the point of view of international law states must not be divided into small and big as they all are equal before the law. All states are also guaranteed an equal share in the making of international law which, due to a great development of multilateral treaties codifying international law, is of particular importance. Equitable rights of states indicate that one state may not judge another state in keeping with a Roman law principle "par in parem non habet iudicum" (equals may not judge themselves).

Art. 6. The state is obliged to respect human rights and fundamental freedoms indiscriminately of race, language, religion and sex.

Art. 7. It is an obligation of the state to ensure on its territory such conditions which are not detrimental to international peace and order.

Art. 8. It is imposed on all states to settle their disputes in a peaceful manner.

Art. 9. The state is prohibited from resorting to war as an instrument of exercising its policy, from using threats or force against other states' territorial inviolability or political independence.

Art. 10. It is an obligation of the state to refrain from rendering assistance to any state acting in conflict with art. 9 of this draft. It is prohibited, too, to help any state against which UN preventive measures are taken or sanctions applied.

Art. 11. The state is obliged to fail to recognize all territorial gains obtained transgressing art. 9 of this draft.

Art. 12. The state enjoys the right to self-defense, individual or collective, to oppose all kinds of aggression.

Art. 13. Each state is obliged to fulfil its obligations stemming from international treaties concluded. The state may not refuse to carry out its international commitments on the grounds of its constitution or other laws as a justification of the refusal.

Art. 14. Each state is obliged to observe that its relations with other states are congruent with international law and the principle that the sovereignty of the state is subordinated to international law."

The second part of art. 14. was subject to controversies of the Commission.

▷ Charter of Economic Rights and Duties of States, 1975.

UN Yearbook, 1947.

RIGHTS AND OBLIGATIONS OF AMERICAN STATES.
A subject of the convention prepared and adopted at the Seventh International Conference of American States in Montevideo, Dec. 3–26, 1933, and ratified by Brazil, Chile, Colombia, Costa Rica, Cuba, Dominican Republic, Ecuador, Guatemala, Haiti, Honduras, Mexico, Nicaragua, Panama, the USA (conditionally) and Venezuela.

International American Conferences, 1889–1936, Washington, DC, 1938.

RIGHTS AND OBLIGATIONS OF PARENTS.
A subject of international survey undertaken by the UN during 1955–67 to determine which rights and obligations of parents are provided for in the legislations or customs of the UN member states. A summary of the study was published in English, French and Spanish in 1968.

ONU, *Derechos y Deberes de los Padres, Inclusive de la Custodia*, New York, 1968.

RIGHTS INDIVISIBILITY AND INTERDEPENDENCE.
An international term for the indivisibility and interdependence of "economic, social, cultural, civil and political rights". A subject of the GA Res.43/113 of Dec. 8, 1988 (132 votes for 1 against (USA) and 23 abstentions).

UN Resolutions and Decisions adopted by the General Assembly during the First Part of its Forty-Third Session, From 20 September to 22 December 1988, New York, 1989, pp. 365–372.

RIGHTS OF CHILDREN, CONVENTION ON THE, 1989.
Subject of the ▷ Child Declaration of the Rights of 1959, and of the Convention on the Rights of Child, adopted by the UN General Assembly on Nov. 20, 1989 on the thirtieth anniversary of the Declaration. The text is as follows:

PREAMBLE
The States Parties to the present Convention
Considering that, in accordance with the principles proclaimed in the Charter of the United Nations, recognition of the inherent dignity and of the equal and inalienable rights of all members of the human family is the foundation of freedom, justice and peace in the world.

Bearing in mind that the peoples of the United Nations have, in the Charter, reaffirmed their faith in fundamental human rights and in the dignity and worth of the human person, and have determined to promote social progress and better standards of life in larger freedom.

Recognizing that the United Nations has, in the Universal Declaration of Human Rights and in the International Covenants on Human Rights, proclaimed and agreed that everyone is entitled to all the rights and freedoms set forth therein, without distinction of any kind, such as race, colour, sex, language, religion, political or other opinion, national or social origin, property, birth or other status.

Recalling that, in the Universal Declaration of Human Rights, the United Nations has proclaimed that childhood is entitled to special care and assistance.

Convinced that the family, as the fundamental group of society and the natural environment for the growth and well-being of all it members and particularly children, should be afforded the necessary protection and assistance so that it can fully assume its responsibilities within the community.

Recognizing that the child, for the full and harmonious development of his or her personality, should grow up in a family environment, in an atmosphere of happiness, love and understanding.

Considering that the child should be fully prepared to live an individual life in society, and brought up in the spirit of the ideals proclaimed in the Charter of the United Nations, and in particular in the spirit of peace, dignity, tolerance, freedom, equality and solidarity.

Bearing in mind that the need for extending particular care to the child has been stated in the Geneva Declaration on the Rights of the Child of 1924 and in the Declaration of the Rights of the Child adopted by the United Nations in 1959 and recognized in the Universal Declaration of Human Rights, in the International Covenant on Civil and Political Rights (in particular in articles 23 and 24), in the International Covenant on Economic, Social and Cultural Rights (in particular in its article 10) and in the statutes and relevant instruments of specialized agencies and international organizations concerned with the welfare of children.

Bearing in mind that, as indicated in the Declaration of the Rights of the Child adopted by the General Assembly on 20 November 1959, "the child, by reason of his physical and mental immaturity, needs special safeguards and care, including appropriate legal protection, before as well as after birth".

Recalling the provisions of the Declaration on Social and Legal Principles relating to the Protection and Welfare of Children, with Special Reference to Foster Placement and Adoption Nationally and Internationally (General Assembly resolution 41/85 of 3 December 1986); the United Nations Standard Minimum Rules for the Administration of Juvenile Justice (The Beijing Rules) (General Assembly resolution 40/33 of 29 November 1985); and the Declaration on the Protection of Women and Children in Emergency and Armed Conflict (General Assembly resolution 3318 (XXIX) of 14 December 1974).

Recognizing that, in all countries in the world, there are children living in exceptionally difficult conditions, and that such children need special consideration.

Taking due account of the importance of the traditions and cultural values of each people for the protection and harmonious development of the child.

Recognizing the importance of international co-operation for improving the living conditions of children in every country, in particular in the developing countries.

Have agreed as follows:

PART I
Article 1
For the purposes of the present Convention, a child means every human being below the age of eighteen years unless, under the law applicable to the child, majority is attained earlier.

Article 2
(1) The States Parties to the present Convention shall respect and ensure the rights set forth in this Convention to each child within their jurisdiction without discrimination of any kind, irrespective of the child's or his or her parent's or legal guardian's race, colour, sex, language, religion, political or other opinion, national, ethnic or social origin, property, disability, birth or other status.

(2) States Parties shall take all appropriate measures to ensure that the child is protected against all forms of discrimination or punishment on the basis of the status, activities, expressed opinions, or beliefs of the child's parents, legal guardians, or family members.

Article 3
(1) In all actions concerning children, whether undertaken by public or private social welfare institutions, courts of law, administrative authorities or legislative bodies, the best interests of the child shall be a primary consideration.

(2) States Parties undertake to ensure the child such protection and care as is necessary for his or her well-being, taking into account the rights and duties of his or her parents, legal guardians, or other individuals legally responsible for him or her, and, to this end, shall take all appropriate legislative and administrative measures.

(3) States Parties shall ensure that the institutions, services and facilities responsible for the care or protection of children shall conform with the standards established by competent authorities, particularly in the areas of safety, health, in the number and suitability of their staff as well as competent supervision.

Article 4
States Parties shall undertake all appropriate legislative, administrative, and other measures for the implementation of the rights recognized in this Convention. In regard to economic, social and cultural rights, States Parties shall undertake such measures to the maximum extent of their available resources and, where needed, within the framework of international co-operation.

Article 5
States Parties shall respect the responsibilities, rights, and duties of parents or, where applicable, the members of the extended family or community as provided for by local custom, legal guardians or other persons legally responsible for the child, to provide, in a manner consistent with the evolving capacities of the child, appropriate direction and guidance in the exercise by the child of the rights recognized in the present Convention.

Article 6
(1) States Parties recognize that every child has the inherent right to life.

(2) States Parties shall ensure to the maximum extent possible the survival and development of the child.

Article 7
(1) The child shall be registered immediately after birth and shall have the right from birth to a name, the right to acquire a nationality, and, as far as possible, the right to know and be cared for by his or her parents.

(2) States Parties shall ensure the implementation of these rights in accordance with their national law and their obligations under the relevant international instruments in this field, in particular where the child would otherwise be stateless.

Article 8
(1) States Parties undertake to respect the right of the child to preserve his or her identity, including nationality, name and family relations as recognized by law without unlawful interference.

(2) Where a child is illegally deprived of some or all of the elements of his or her identity, States Parties shall provide appropriate assistance and protection, with a view to speedily re-establishing his or her identity.

Article 9
(1) States Parties shall ensure that a child shall not be separated from his or her parents against their will, except when competent authorities subject to judicial review determine, in accordance with applicable law and procedures, that such separation is necessary for the best interests of the child. Such determination may be necessary in a particular case such as one involving abuse or neglect of the child by the parents, or one where the parents are living separately and a decision must be made as to the child's place of residence.

(2) In any proceedings pursuant to paragraph 1, all interested parties shall be given an opportunity to participate in the proceedings and make their views known.

(3) States Parties shall respect the right of the child who is separated from one or both parents to maintain personal relations and direct contact with both parents on a regular basis, except if it is contrary to the child's best interests.

(4) Where such separation results from any action initiated by a State Party, such as the detention, imprisonment, exile, deportation or death (including death arising from any cause while the person is in the custody of the State) of one or both parents or of the child, that State Party shall, upon request, provide the parents, the child or, if appropriate, another member of the family with the essential information concerning the whereabouts of the absent member(s) of the family unless the provision of the information would be detrimental to the well-being of the child. States Parties shall further ensure that the submission of such a request shall of itself entail no adverse consequences for the person(s) concerned.

Article 10
(1) In accordance with the obligation of States Parties under article 9, paragraph 1, applications by a child or his or her parents to enter or leave a State Party for the purpose of family reunification shall be dealt with by States Parties in a positive, humane and expeditious manner. States Parties shall further ensure that the submission of such a request shall entail no adverse

consequences for the applicants and for the members of their family.

(2) A child whose parents reside in different States shall have the right to maintain on a regular basis save in exceptional circumstances personal relations and direct contacts with both parents. Towards that end and in accordance with the obligation of States Parties under article 9, paragraph 2, States Parties shall respect the right of the child and his or her parents to leave any country, including their own, and to enter their own country. The right to leave any country shall be subject only to such restrictions as are prescribed by law and which are necessary to protect the national security, public order (*ordre public*), public health or morals or the rights and freedoms of others and are consistent with the other rights recognized in the present Convention.

Article 11

(1) States Parties shall take measures to combat the illicit transfer and non-return of children abroad.

(2) To this end, States Parties shall promote the conclusion of bilateral or multilateral agreements or accession to existing agreements.

Article 12

(1) States Parties shall assure to the child who is capable of forming his or her own views the right to express those views freely in all matters affecting the child, the views of the child being given due weight in accordance with the age and maturity of the child.

(2) For this purpose, the child shall in particular be provided the opportunity to be heard in any judicial and administrative proceedings affecting the child, either directly, or through a representative or an appropriate body, in a manner consistent with the procedural rules of national law.

Article 13

(1) The child shall have the right to freedom of expression; this right shall include freedom to seek, receive and impart information and ideas of all kinds, regardless of frontiers, either orally, in writing or in print, in the form of art, or through any other media of the child's choice.

(2) The exercise of this right may be subject to certain restrictions, but these shall only be such as are provided by law and are necessary:

(a) For respect of the rights or reputations of others; or

(b) For the protection of national security or of public order (*ordre public*), or of public health or morals.

Article 14

(1) States Parties shall respect the right of the child to freedom of thought, conscience and religion.

(2) States Parties shall respect the rights and duties of the parents and, when applicable, legal guardians, to provide direction to the child in the exercise of his or her right in a manner consistent with the evolving capacities of the child.

(3) Freedom to manifest one's religion or beliefs may be subject only to such limitations as are prescribed by law and are necessary to protect public safety, order, health, or morals or the fundamental rights and freedoms of others.

Article 15

(1) States Parties recognize the rights of the child to freedom of association and to freedom of peaceful assembly.

(2) No restrictions may be placed on the exercise of these rights other than those imposed in conformity with the law and which are necessary in a democratic society in the interests of national security or public safety, public order (*ordre public*), the protection of public health or morals or the protection of the rights and freedoms of others.

Article 16

(1) No child shall be subjected to arbitrary or unlawful interference with his or her privacy, family, home or correspondence, nor to unlawful attacks on his or her honour and reputation.

(2) The child has the right to the protection of the law against such interference or attacks.

Article 17

States Parties recognize the important function performed by the mass media and shall ensure that the child has access to information and material from a diversity of national and international sources, especially those aimed at the promotion of his or her social, spiritual and moral well-being and physical and mental health. To this end, States Parties shall:

(a) Encourage the mass media to disseminate information and material of social and cultural benefit to the child and in accordance with the spirit of article 29;

(b) Encourage international co-operation in the production, exchange and dissemination of such information and material from a diversity of cultural, national and international sources;

(c) Encourage the production and dissemination of children's books;

(d) Encourage the mass media to have particular regard to the linguistic needs of the child who belongs to a minority group or who is indigenous;

(e) Encourage the development of appropriate guidelines for the protection of the child from information and material injurious to his or her well-being, bearing in mind the provisions of articles 13 and 18.

Article 18

(1) States Parties shall use their best efforts to ensure recognition of the principle that both parents have common responsibilities for the upbringing and development of the child. Parents or, as the case may be, legal guardians, have the primary responsibility for the upbringing and development of the child. The best interests of the child will be their basic concern.

(2) For the purpose of guaranteeing and promoting the rights set forth in this Convention, States Parties shall render appropriate assistance to parents and legal guardians in the performance of their child-rearing responsibilities and shall ensure the development of institutions, facilities and services for the care of children.

(3) States Parties shall take all appropriate measures to ensure that children of working parents have the right to benefit from child-care services and facilities for which they are eligible.

Article 19

(1) States Parties shall take all appropriate legislative, administrative, social and educational measures to protect the child from all forms of physical or mental violence, injury or abuse, neglect or negligent treatment, maltreatment or exploitation, including sexual abuse, while in the care of parent(s), legal guardian(s) or any other person who has the care of the child.

(2) Such protective measures should, as appropriate, include effective procedures for the establishment of social programmes to provide necessary support for the child and for those who have the care of the child, as well as for other forms of prevention and for identification, reporting, referral, investigation, treatment, and follow-up of instances of child maltreatment described heretofore, and, as appropriate, for judicial involvement.

Article 20

(1) A child temporarily or permanently deprived of his or her family environment, or in whose own best interests cannot be allowed to remain in that environment, shall be entitled to special protection and assistance provided by the State.

(2) States Parties shall in accordance with their national laws ensure alternative care for such a child.

(3) Such care could include, *inter alia*, foster placement, Kafala of Islamic Law, adoption, or if necessary placement in suitable institutions for the care of children. When considering solutions, due regard shall be paid to the desirability of continuity in a child's upbringing and to the child's ethnic, religious, cultural and linguistic background.

Article 21

States Parties that recognize and/or permit the system of adoption shall ensure that the best interests of the child shall be the paramount consideration and they shall;

(a) Ensure that the adoption of a child is authorized only by competent authorities who determine, in accordance with applicable law and procedures and on the basis of all pertinent and reliable information, that the adoption is permissible in view of the child's status concerning parents, relatives and legal guardians and that, if required, the persons concerned have given their informed consent to the adoption on the basis of such counselling as may be necessary;

(b) Recognize that inter-country adoption may be considered as an alternative means of child's care, if the child cannot be placed in a foster or an adoptive family or cannot in any suitable manner be cared for in the child's country of origin;

(c) Ensure that the child concerned by inter-country adoption enjoys safeguards and standards equivalent to those existing in the case of national adoption;

(d) Take all appropriate measures to ensure that, in inter-country adoption, the placement does not result in improper financial gain for those involved in it;

(e) Promote, where appropriate, the objectives of this article by concluding bilateral or multilateral arrangements or agreements, and endeavour, within this framework, to ensure that the placement of the child in another country is carried out by competent authorities or organs.

Article 22

(1) States Parties shall take appropriate measures to ensure that a child who is seeking refugee status or who is considered a refugee in accordance with applicable international or domestic law and procedures shall, whether unaccompanied or accompanied by his or her parents or by any other person, receive appropriate protection and humanitarian assistance in the enjoyment of applicable rights set forth in this Convention and in other international human rights or humanitarian instruments to which the said States are Parties.

(2) For this purpose, States Parties shall provide, as they consider appropriate, co-operation in any efforts by the United Nations and other competent intergovernmental organizations or non-governmental organizations co-operating with the United Nations to protect and assist such a child and to trace the parents or other members of the family of any refugee child in order to obtain information necessary for reunification with his or her family. In cases where no parents or other members of the family can be found, the child shall be accorded the same protection as any other child permanently or temporarily deprived of his or her family environment for any reason, as set forth in the present Convention.

Article 23

(1) States Parties recognize that a mentally or physically disabled child should enjoy a full and decent life, in conditions which ensure dignity, promote self-reliance, and facilitate the child's active participation in the community.

(2) States Parties recognize the right of the disabled child to special care and shall encourage and ensure the extension, subject to available resources, to the eligible child and those responsible for his or her care, of assistance for which application is made and which is appropriate to the child's condition and to the circumstances of the parents or others caring for the child.

(3) Recognizing the special needs of a disabled child, assistance extended in accordance with paragraph 2 shall be provided free of charge, whenever possible, taking into account the financial resources of the parents of others caring for the child, and shall be designed to ensure that the disabled child has effective access to and receives education, training, health care services, rehabilitation services, preparation for employment and recreation opportunities in a manner conducive to the child's achieving the fullest possible social integration and individual development, including his or her cultural and spiritual development.

(4) States Parties shall promote, in the spirit of international co-operation, the exchange of appropriate information in the field of preventive health care and of medical, psychological and functional treatment of disabled children, including dissemination of and access to information concerning methods of rehabilitation education and vocational services, with the aim of enabling States Parties to improve their capabilities and skills and to widen their experience in these areas. In this regard, particular account shall be taken of the needs of developing countries.

Article 24

(1) States Parties recognize the right of the child to the enjoyment of the highest attainable standard of health and to facilities for the treatment of illness and rehabilitation of health. States Parties shall strive to ensure that no child is deprived of his or her right of access to such health care services.

(2) States Parties shall pursue full implementation of this right and, in particular, shall take appropriate measures:

(a) To diminish infant and child mortality;

(b) To ensure the provision of necessary medical assistance and health care to all children with emphasis on the development of primary health care;

(c) To combat disease and malnutrition, including within the framework of primary health care, through, *inter alia*, the application of readily available technology and through the provision of adequate nutritious foods and clean drinking water, taking into consideration the dangers and risks of environmental pollution;

(d) To ensure appropriate pre- and post-natal health care for mothers;

(e) To ensure that all segments of society, in particular parents and children, are informed, have access to education and are supported in the use of basic knowledge of child health and nutrition, the advantages of breast-feeding, hygiene and environmental sanitation and the prevention of accidents;

(f) To develop preventive health care, guidance for parents, and family planning education and services.

(3) States Parties shall take all effective and appropriate measures with a view to abolishing traditional practices prejudicial to the health of children.

(4) States Parties undertake to promote and encourage international co-operation with a view to achieving progressively the full realization of the right recognized in this article. In this regard, particular account shall be taken of the needs of developing countries.

Article 25

States Parties recognize the right of a child who has been placed by the competent authorities for the purposes of care, protection, or treatment of his or her physical or mental health, to a periodic review of the treatment provided to the child and all other circumstances relevant to his or her placement.

Article 26

(1) States Parties shall recognize for every child the right to benefit from social security, including social insurance, and shall take the necessary measures to achieve the full realization of this right in accordance with their national law.

(2) The benefits should, where appropriate, be granted, taking into account the resources and the circumstances of the child and persons having responsibility for the maintenance of the child, a well as any other consideration relevant to an application for benefits made by or on behalf of the child.

Article 27

(1) States Parties recognize the right of every child to a standard of living adequate for the child's physical, mental, spiritual, moral and social development.

(2) The parent(s) or others responsible for the child have the primary responsibility to secure, within their abilities and financial capacities, the conditions of living necessary for the child's development.

(3) States Parties, in accordance with national conditions and within their means, shall take appropriate measures to assist parents and others responsible for the child to implement this right and shall in case of need provide material assistance and support programmes, particularly with regard to nutrition, clothing and housing.

(4) States Parties shall take all appropriate measures to secure the recovery of maintenance for the child from the parents or other persons having financial responsibility for the child, both within the State Party and from abroad. In particular, where the person having financial responsibility for the child lives in a State different from that of the child, States Parties shall promote the accession to international agreements or the conclusion of such agreements, as well as the making of other appropriate arrangements.

Article 28

(1) States Parties recognize the right of the child to education, and with a view to achieving this right progressively and on the basis of equal opportunity, they shall, in particular:

(a) Make primary education compulsory and available free to all;

(b) Encourage the development of different forms of secondary education, including general and vocational education, make them available and accessible to every child, and take appropriate measures such as the introduction of free education and offering financial assistance in case of need;

(c) Make higher education accessible to all on the basis of capacity by every appropriate means;

(d) Make educational and vocational information and guidance available and accessible to all children;

(e) Take measures to encourage regular attendance at schools and the reduction of drop-out rates.

(2) States Parties shall take all appropriate measures to ensure that school discipline is administered in a manner consistent with the child's human dignity and in conformity with the present Convention.

(3) States Parties shall promote and encourage international co-operation in matters relating to education, in particular with a view to contributing to the elimination of ignorance and illiteracy throughout the world and facilitating access to scientific and technical knowledge and modern teaching methods. In this regard, particular account shall be taken of the needs of developing countries.

Article 29

(1) States Parties agree that the education of the child shall be directed to:

(a) The development of the child's personality, talents, and mental and physical abilities to their fullest potential;

(b) The development of respect for human rights and fundamental freedoms, and for the principles enshrined in the Charter of the United Nations;

(c) The development of respect for the child's parents, his or her own cultural identity, language and values, for the national values of the country in which the child is living, the country from which he or she may originate, and for civilizations different from his or her own;

(d) The preparation of the child for responsible life in a free society, in the spirit of understanding, peace, tolerance, equality of sexes, and friendship among all peoples, ethnic, national and religious groups and persons of indigenous origin;

(e) The development of respect for the natural environment.

(2) No part of this article or article 28 shall be construed so as to interfere with the liberty of individuals and bodies to establish and direct educational institutions, subject always to the observance of the principles set forth in paragraph 1 of this article and to the requirements that the education given in such institutions shall conform to such minimum standards as may be laid down by the State.

Article 30

In those States in which ethnic, religious or linguistic minorities or persons of indigenous origin exist, a child belonging to such a minority or who is indigenous shall not be denied the right, in community with other members of his or her group, to enjoy his or her own culture, to profess and practise his or her own religion, or to use his or her own language.

Article 31

(1) States Parties recognize the right of the child to rest and leisure, to engage in play and recreational activities appropriate to the age of the child and to participate freely in cultural life and the arts.

(2) States Parties shall respect and promote the right of the child to participate fully in cultural and artistic life and shall encourage the provision of appropriate and equal opportunities for cultural, artistic, recreational and leisure activity.

Article 32

(1) State Parties recognize the right of the child to be protected from economic exploitation and from performing any work that is likely to be hazardous or to interfere with the child's education, or to be harmful to the child's health or physical, mental, spiritual, moral or social development.

(2) States Parties shall take legislative, administrative, social and educational measures to ensure the implementation of this article. To this end, and having regard to the relevant provisions of other international instruments, States Parties shall in particular:

(a) Provide for a minimum age or minimum ages for admissions to employment;

(b) Provide for appropriate regulation of the hours and conditions of employment; and

(c) Provide for appropriate penalties or other sanctions to ensure the effective enforcement of this article.

Article 33

States Parties shall take all appropriate measures, including legislative administrative, social and educational measures, to protect children from the illicit use of narcotic drugs and psychotropic substances as defined in the relevant international treaties, and to prevent the use of children in the illicit production and trafficking of such substances.

Article 34

States Parties undertake to protect the child from all forms of sexual exploitation and sexual abuse. For these purposes, States Parties shall in particular take all appropriate national, bilateral and multilateral measures to prevent:

(a) The inducement or coercion of a child to engage in any unlawful sexual activity;

(b) The exploitative use of children in prostitution or other unlawful sexual practices;

(c) The exploitative use of children in pornographic performances and materials.

Article 35

States Parties shall take all appropriate national, bilateral and multilateral measures to prevent the abduction, the sale of or traffic in children for any purpose or in any form.

Article 36

States Parties shall protect the child against all other forms of exploitation prejudicial to any aspects of the child's welfare.

Article 37

States Parties shall ensure that:

(a) No child shall be subjected to torture or other cruel, inhuman or degrading treatment or punishment. Neither capital punishment nor life imprisonment without possibility of release shall be imposed for offences committed by persons below eighteen years of age;

(b) No child shall be deprived of his or her liberty unlawfully or arbitrarily. The arrest, detention or imprisonment of a child shall be in conformity with the law and shall be used only as a measure of last resort and for the shortest appropriate period of time;

(c) Every child deprived of liberty shall be treated with humanity and respect for the inherent dignity of the human person, and in a manner which takes into account the needs of persons of their age. In particular, every child deprived of liberty shall be separated from adults unless it is considered in the child's best interest not to do so and shall have the right to maintain contact with his or her family through correspondence and visits, save in exceptional circumstances;

(d) Every child deprived of his or her liberty shall have the right to prompt access to legal and other appropriate assistance as well as the right to challenge the legality of the deprivation of his or her liberty before a court or other competent, independent and impartial authority and to a prompt decision on any such action.

Article 38

(1) States Parties undertake to respect and to ensure respect for rules of international humanitarian law applicable to them in armed conflicts which are relevant to the child.

(2) States Parties shall take all feasible measures to ensure that persons who have not attained the age of fifteen years do not take a direct part in hostilities.

(3) States Parties shall refrain from recruiting any person who has not attained the age of fifteen years into their armed forces. In recruiting among those persons who have attained the age of fifteen years but who have not attained the age of eighteen years, States Parties shall endeavour to give priority to those who are oldest.

(4) In accordance with their obligations under international humanitarian law to protect the civilian population in armed conflicts, States Parties shall take all feasible measures to ensure protection and care of children who are affected by an armed conflict.

Article 39

States Parties shall take all appropriate measures to promote physical and psychological recovery and social reintegration of a child victim of: any form of neglect, exploitation, or abuse; torture or any other form of cruel, inhuman or degrading treatment or punishment; or armed conflicts. Such recovery and reintegration shall take place in an environment which fosters the health, self-respect and dignity of the child.

Article 40

(1) States Parties recognize the right of every child alleged as, accused of, or recognized as having infringed the penal law to be treated in a manner consistent with the promotion of the child's sense of dignity and worth, which reinforces the child's respect for the human rights and fundamental freedoms of others and which takes into account the child's age and the desirability of promoting the child's reintegration and the child's assuming a constructive role in society.

(2) To this end, and having regard to the relevant provisions of international instruments, States Parties shall, in particular, ensure that:

(a) No child shall be alleged as, be accused of, or recognized as having infringed the penal law by reason of acts or omissions that were not prohibited by national or international law at the time they were committed;

(b) Every child alleged as or accused of having infringed the penal law has at least the following guarantees:

(i) To be presumed innocent until proven guilty according to law;

(ii) To be informed promptly and directly of the charges against him or her, and, if appropriate, through his or her parents or legal guardian, and to have legal or other appropriate assistance in the preparation and presentation of his or her defence;

(iii) To have the matter determined without delay by a competent, independent and impartial authority or judicial body in a fair hearing according to law, in the presence of legal or other appropriate assistance and, unless it is considered not to be in the best interest of the child, in particular, taking into account his or her age or situation, his or her parents or legal guardians;

(iv) Not to be compelled to give testimony or to confess guilt; to examine or have examined adverse witnesses and to obtain the participation and examination of witnesses on his or her behalf under conditions of equality;

(v) If considered to have infringed the penal law, to have this decision and any measures imposed in consequence thereof reviewed by a higher competent, independent and impartial authority or judicial body according to law;

(vi) To have the free assistance of an interpreter if the child cannot understand or speak the language used;

(vii) To have his or her privacy fully respected at all stages of the proceedings.

(3) States Parties shall seek to promote the establishment of laws, procedures, authorities and institutions specifically applicable to children alleged as, accused of, or recognized as having infringed the penal law, and, in particular:

(a) The establishment of a minimum age below which children shall be presumed not to have the capacity to infringe the penal law;

(b) Whenever appropriate and desirable, measures for dealing with such children without resorting to judicial proceedings, providing that human rights and legal safeguards are fully respected.

(4) A variety of dispositions, such as care, guidance and supervision orders; counselling; probation; foster care; education and vocational training programmes and other alternatives to institutional care shall be available to ensure that children are dealt with in a manner appropriate to their well-being and proportionate both to their circumstances and the offence.

Article 41

Nothing in this Convention shall affect any provisions that are more conducive to the realization of the rights of the child and that may be contained in:

(a) The law of a State Party; or

(b) International law in force for that State.

PART II

Article 42

States Parties undertake to make the principles and provisions of the Convention widely known, by appropriate and active means, to adults and children alike.

Article 43

(1) For the purpose of examining the progress made by States Parties in achieving the realization of the obligations undertaken in the present Convention, there shall be established a Committee on the Rights of the Child, which shall carry out the functions hereinafter provided.

(2) The Committee shall consist of ten experts of high moral standing and recognized competence in the field covered by this Convention. The members of the Committee shall be elected by States Parties from among their nationals and shall serve in their personal capacity, consideration being given to equitable geographical distribution, as well as to the principal legal systems.

(3) The members of the Committee shall be elected by secret ballot from a list of persons nominated by States Parties. Each State Party may nominate one person from among its own nationals.

(4) The initial election to the Committee shall be held no later than six months after the date of the entry into force of the present Convention and thereafter every second year. At least four months before the date of each election, the Secretary-General of the United Nations shall address a letter to States Parties inviting them to submit their nominations within two months. The Secretary-General shall subsequently prepare a list in alphabetical order of all persons thus nominated, indicating States Parties which have nominated them, and shall submit it to the States Parties to the present Convention.

(5) The elections shall be held at meetings of States Parties convened by the Secretary-General at United Nations Headquarters. At those meetings, for which two thirds of States Parties shall constitute a quorum, the persons elected to the Committee shall be those who obtain the largest number of votes and an absolute majority of the votes of the representatives of States Parties present and voting.

(6) The members of the Committee shall be elected for a term of four years. They shall be eligible for re-election if renominated. The term of five of the members elected at the first election shall expire at the end of two years; immediately after the first election, the names of these five members shall be chosen by lot by the Chairman of the meeting.

(7) If a member of the Committee dies or resigns or declares that for any other cause he or she can no longer perform the duties of the Committee, the State Party which nominated the member shall appoint another expert from among its nationals to serve for the remainder of the term, subject to the approval of the Committee.

(8) The Committee shall establish its own rules of procedure.

(9) The Committee shall elect its officers for a period of two years.

(10) The meetings of the Committee shall normally be held at United Nations Headquarters or at any other convenient place as determined by the Committee. The Committee shall normally meet annually. The duration of the meetings of the Committee shall be determined, and reviewed, if necessary, by a meeting of the States Parties to the present Convention, subject to the approval of the General Assembly.

(11) The Secretary-General of the United Nations shall provide the necessary staff and facilities for the effective performance of the functions of the Committee under the present Convention.

(12) With the approval of the General Assembly, the members of the Committee established under the present Convention shall receive emoluments from United Nations resources on such terms and conditions as the Assembly may decide.

Article 44

(1) States Parties undertake to submit to the Committee, through the Secretary-General of the United Nations, reports on the measures they have adopted which give effect to the rights recognized herein and on the progress made on the enjoyment of those rights:

(a) Within two years of the entry into force of the Convention for the State Party concerned;

(b) Thereafter every five years.

(2) Reports made under this article shall indicate factors and difficulties, if any, affecting the degree of fulfilment of the obligations under the present Convention. Reports shall also contain sufficient information to provide the Committee with a comprehensive understanding of the implementation of the Convention in the country concerned.

(3) A State Party which has submitted a comprehensive initial report to the Committee need not, in its subsequent reports submitted in accordance with paragraph 1(b), repeat basic information previously provided.

(4) The Committee may request from States Parties further information relevant to the implementation of the Convention.

(5) The Committee shall submit to the General Assembly, through the Economic and Social Council, every two years, reports on its activities.

(6) States Parties shall make their reports widely available to the public in their own countries.

Article 45

In order to foster the effective implementation of the Convention and to encourage international co-operation in the field covered by the Convention:

(a) The specialized agencies, the United Nations Children's Fund, and other United Nations organs shall be entitled to be represented at the consideration of the implementation of such provisions of the present Convention as fall within the scope of their mandate. The Committee may invite the specialized agencies, the United Nations Children's Fund and other competent bodies as it may consider appropriate to provide expert advice on the implementation of the Convention in areas falling within the scope of their respective mandates. The Committee may invite the specialized agencies, the United Nations Children's Fund, and other United Nations organs to submit reports on the implementation of the Convention in areas falling within the scope of their activities;

(b) The Committee shall transmit, as it may consider appropriate, to the specialized agencies, the United Nations Children's Fund and other competent bodies, any reports from States Parties that contain a request, or indicate a need, for technical advice or assistance, along with the Committee's observations and suggestions, if any, on these requests or indications;

(c) The Committee may recommend to the General Assembly to request the Secretary-General to undertake on its behalf studies on specific issues relating to the rights of the child;

(d) The Committee may make suggestions and general recommendations based on information received pursuant to articles 44 and 45 of this Convention. Such suggestions and general recommendations shall be transmitted to any State Party concerned and reported to the General Assembly, together with comments, if any, from States Parties.

PART III

Article 46

The present Convention shall be open for signature by all States.

Article 47

The present Convention is subject to ratification. Instruments of ratification shall be deposited with the Secretary-General of the United Nations.

Article 48

The present Convention shall remain open for accession by any State. The instruments of accession shall be deposited with the Secretary-General of the United Nations.

Article 49

(1) The present Convention shall enter into force on the thirtieth day following the date of deposit with the Secretary-General of the United Nations of the twentieth instrument of ratification or accession.

(2) For each State ratifying or acceding to the Convention after the deposit of the twentieth instrument of ratification or accession, the Convention shall enter into force on the thirtieth day after the deposit by such State of its instrument of ratification or accession.

Article 50

(1) Any State Party may propose an amendment and file it with the Secretary-General of the United Nations. The Secretary-General shall thereupon communicate the proposed amendment to States Parties, with a request that they indicate whether they favour a conference of States Parties for the purpose of considering and voting upon the proposals. In the event that, within four months from the date of such communication, at least one third of the States Parties favour such a conference, the Secretary-General shall convene the conference under the auspices of the United Nations. Any amendment adopted by a majority of States Parties present and voting at the conference shall be submitted to the General Assembly for approval.

(2) An amendment adopted in accordance with paragraph (1) of this article shall enter into force when it has been approved by the General Assembly of the United Nations and accepted by a two-thirds majority of States Parties.

(3) When an amendment enters into force, it shall be binding on those States Parties which have accepted it, other States Parties still being bound by the provisions of this Convention and any earlier amendments which they have accepted.

Article 51

(1) The Secretary-General of the United Nations shall receive and circulate to all States the text of reservations made by States at the time of ratification or accession.

(2) A reservation incompatible with the object and purpose of the present Convention shall not be permitted.

(3) Reservations may be withdrawn at any time by notification to this effect addressed to the Secretary-

R

General of the United Nations, who shall then inform all States. Such notification shall take effect on the date on which it is received by the Secretary-General.

Article 52

A State Party may denounce this Convention by written notification to the Secretary-General of the United Nations. Denunciation becomes effective one year after the date of receipt of the notification by the Secretary-General.

Article 53

The Secretary-General of the United Nations is designated as the depositary of the present Convention.

Article 54

The original of the present Convention, of which the Arabic, Chinese, English, French, Russian and Spanish texts are equally authentic, shall be deposited with the Secretary-General of the United Nations.

RIGHTS OF MAN AND OF THE CITIZEN, DECLARATION OF, 1789.

The French Revolutionary Declaration adopted on Aug. 26, 1789 by the Constituent Assembly of the French Revolution, on a motion by Marquis de Lafayette (1757–1834) referring to certain terms of the ▷ United States Declaration of Independence, 1776; the full name: *Déclaration solennelle des droits naturels, inaliénables et sacrés de l'homme et du citoyen.* Declared "natural, inalienable and sacred" rights of the individual to life, liberty, property, security. Distinguished the rights of the individual and of the state (les droits de l'individu a ceux de l'État), introduced the principles of inadmissibility of prosecution or arrest without legal grounds, the necessity of consent of citizens to the establishment of taxes, freedom of worship and speech. It also asserted the division of authority into legislative, executive, judicial, and the principle of sovereignty of nations (whose effect on the development of international law was considerable) included in Jacobin Constitution of June 24, 1793, art. 119: "The French People do not interfere with governments of other peoples and will not allow other people to interfere with its government."

The principles of the Declaration influenced bourgeois revolutionary movements in the 18th and 19th centuries and were reflected in the constitutions of many European and American republics.

The text is as follows:

"(1) All men are born and remain free, and have equal rights. Social distinctions are unjustifiable except insofar as they may serve the common good.

(2) The purpose of political association is to preserve the natural and inalienable rights of man, i.e., liberty, private property, the inviolability of the person, and the right to resist oppression.

(3) Sovereignty resides essentially in the nation as a whole; no group or individual can exercise any authority not expressly delegated to it or him.

(4) Liberty is the right to do anything which does not harm others. Thus, each man's natural rights are limited only by the necessity to assure equal liberty to others. Only the law can determine what restrictions must be made.

(5) The law can proscribe only those actions which harm society. Any action not forbidden by law cannot be disallowed, nor can anyone be forced to do what the law does not specifically command.

(6) Law is the overt expression of the general will. All citizens have the right to participate in legislation, either in person or through their representatives. The law must be framed to operate completely impartially. Since all are equal before the law, all are equally eligible, in accordance with their abilities, for all public offices and positions.

(7) No man can be indicted, arrested, or held in custody except for offenses legally defined, and according to specified procedures. Those who solicit, transmit, execute or cause to be executed arbitrary commands must be punished; but if a citizen is summoned or arrested in due legal form it is his duty to obey instantly.

(8) The law must impose only penalties that are obviously necessary. No one can be punished except under the correct application of an established law which

must, moreover, have existed before he committed the offense.

(9) Everyone must be presumed innocent until he is pronounced guilty. If his arrest and detention are thought necessary, then no more force may be used than is necessary to secure his person.

(10) No one must suffer for his opinions, even for religious opinions, provided that his advocacy of them does not endanger public order.

(11) Free communication of thought and opinion is one of the most valuable rights of man; thus, every citizen may speak, write, and print his views freely, provided only that he accepts the bounds of this freedom established by law.

(12) Some form of military or police force is necessary to guarantee the maintenance of the rights of man and of the citizen; thus, such a force exists for the benefit of all and not for the particular ends of those who command it.

(13) To maintain the police force and to meet administrative expenses a financial levy is essential; this must be borne equally by all citizens, in accordance with their individual means.

(14) All citizens have the right to decide, either personally or through their representative, the necessity of a financial levy and their free assent to it must be obtained. They can appropriate it, and decide its extent, duration, and assessment.

(15) Society has the right to require of every public official an account of his administration.

(16) A society in which rights are not guaranteed, and in which there is no separation of powers, has no constitution.

(17) Since the right to private property is sacred and inviolable, no one can be deprived of it except in certain cases legally determined to be essential for public security; in such cases a fair indemnity must first of all be granted."

O. JELLINEK, *The Declaration of the Rights of Man and of Citizens*, London, 1901.

RIGHTS TO SOLIDARITY. ▷ Solidarity.

RIGHT TO A FLAG OF STATES HAVING NO SEACOAST, BARCELONA DECLARATION, 1921.

A Declaration signed on Apr. 20, 1921 in Barcelona by the governments of Albania, Austria, Belgium, Bolivia, Bulgaria, Czechoslovakia, Chile, China, Denmark, Estonia, France, Guatemala, Greece, Italy, Japan, Latvia, Lithuania, the Netherlands, Panama, Persia, Poland, Portugal, the Serb-Croat-Slovene State, Spain, Sweden, Switzerland, the UK and Uruguay, proclaiming that they

"recognize the Flag, flown by the vessels of any State having no sea-coast which are registered at some one specified place situated in its territory; such place shall serve as the port of registry of such vessels."

LNTS, Vol. 7, p. 74.

RIGHT TO CONCLUDE TREATIES.

A part of the law of treaties determining which subjects of international law have the right to conclude treaties and which organs of these subjects are entitled to do so. In the 19th century, in principle, states were subjects of international law; some members of federations were also subjects. In the case of dependent states, the agreement of the protector was required for such a state to be a subject of international law. The Vienna Convention of 1969, prepared by the UN International Law Commission confined itself to determining the ability by states to conclude treaties, leaving undefined details of the ability of 'other subjects' to do so; but in the Vienna Convention on International Organizations, 1975, the ability to conclude treaties (*ius tractuum*) was fully granted to international intergovernmental organizations.

UN Law and Practice Concerning the Conclusions of Treaties, New York, 1953; UN, *A Selected Bibliography of the Law of Treaties*, Vienna, 1968.

RIGHT TO DIE.

An international term, introduced in California on Jan. 1, 1977, by means of a legal act permitting doctors to detach an apparatus prolonging heart action from a dying patient, provided that the patient expressed such a request in writing before his death. The law came into force after a lengthy campaign launched by the supporters of euthanasia, maintaining that no moral principles can justify prolonging life beyond its natural end, marked by disappearance of brain action. ▷ Death. ▷ Euthanasia.

KEESING's *Contemporary Archive*, 1970.

RIGHT TO FREE EXPRESSION.

The right defined in art. 19 of the International Covenant on Civil and Political Rights, drafted by the UN Commission on Human Rights and unanimously adopted by the UN General Assembly on Dec. 16, 1966; came into force 1976. Art. 19 reads:

"(1) Everyone shall have the right to hold opinions without interference.

(2) Everyone shall have the right to freedom of expression; this right shall include freedom to seek, receive and impart information and ideas of all kinds, regardless of frontiers, either orally, in writing or in print, in the form of art or through any other media of his choice.

(3) The exercise of the rights provided for in paragraph 2 of this article carries with it special duties and responsibilities. It may therefore be subject to certain restrictions, but these shall only be such as are provided by law and are necessary:

(a) For respect of the rights or reputations of others;

(b) For the protection of national security or of public order (ordre public) or of public health or morals."

In the Human Rights Commission, the Warsaw Pact States voted against the wording of the right to freedom of expression holding that it would allow the freedom to voice racist, fascist opinions or views instigating war.

UN Bulletin, July 1, 1952, p. 50.

RIGHT TO LEAVE AND RETURN. ▷ Strasbourg Declaration, 1986.

RIGHT TO LIFE.

A basic rule of Human Rights differently interpreted throughout the centuries. As late as June, 1952 the Commission on Human Rights prepared and adopted by 11 votes against 4 and 3 abstaining, art. 6 of the Covenant on Human Rights:

"Art. 6.(1) Every human being has the inherent right to life. This law shall be protected by law. No one shall be arbitrarily deprived of his life.

(2) In countries which have not abolished the death penalty, sentence of death may be imposed only for the most serious crimes . . .

(4) Anyone sentenced to death shall have the right to seek pardon or commutation of the sentence . . .

(5) Sentence of death shall not be imposed . . . and shall not be carried out on pregnant women."

The World Congress of the Forces of Peace held in Moscow, on Oct. 25–31, 1973, adopted, i.a., the following provision:

"Every human being has the inalienable right to life which should be protected by law. States should endeavor to totally abolish the death penalty. The right to life is also connected with the right to refuse deprivation of the lives of others."

On Dec. 8, 1988 the GA adopted Res.43/11 "Human rights and technological Developments: the right to life".

UN Bulletin, July 1, 1952; *The UN and Human Rights*, New York, 1968; UN, *La Pena capital*, New York, 1968; *UN Resolutions and Decisions adopted by the General Assembly during the First Part of its Forty-Third Session. From 20 September to 22 December 1988*, New York 1989, pp. 363–364.

RIGHT TO ORGANIZE AND TO BARGAIN COLLECTIVELY. A subject of the ILO Convention No. 98 concerning the Application of the Principles of the Right to Organize and to Bargain Collectively, adopted at Geneva, July 1, 1949; came into force July 18, 1951. The text is as follows:

"The General Conference of the International Labour Organization.
Having been convened at Geneva by the Governing Body of the International Labour Office, and having met in its Thirt -second Session on 8 June 1949, and
Having decided upon the adoption of certain proposals concerning the application of the principles of the right to organise and to bargain collectively, which is the fourth item on the agenda of the session, and
Having determined that these proposals shall take the form of an international Convention,
Adopts this first day of July of the year one thousand nine hundred and forty-nine the following Convention, which may be cited as the Right to Organise and Collective Bargaining Convention, 1949:
Art. 1.(1) Workers shall enjoy adequate protection against acts of anti-union discrimination in respect of their employment.
(2) Such protection shall apply more particularly in respect of acts calculated to
(a) make the employment of a worker subject to the condition that he shall not join a union or shall relinquish trade union membership;
(b) cause the dismissal of or otherwise prejudice a worker by reason of union membership or because of participation in union activities outside working hours or, with the consent of the employer, within working hours.
Art. 2.(1) Workers' and employers' organizations shall enjoy adequate protection against any acts of interference by each other or each other's agents or members in their establishment, functioning or administration.
(2) In particular, acts which are designed to promote the establishment of workers' organizations under the domination of employers' organizations, or to support workers' organizations by financial or other means, with the object of placing such organisations under the control of employers or employers' organisations, shall be deemed to constitute acts of interference within the meaning of this Article.
Art. 3. Machinery appropriate to national conditions shall be established, where necessary, for the purpose of ensuring respect for the right to organise as defined in the preceding Articles.
Art. 4. Measures appropriate to national conditions shall be taken, where necessary, to encourage and promote the full development and utilisation of machinery for voluntary negotiation between employers or employers' organisations and workers' organisations, with a view to the regulation of terms and conditions of employment by means of collective agreements.
Art. 5.(1) The extent to which the guarantees provided for in this Convention shall apply to the armed forces and the police shall be determined by national laws or regulations.
(2) In accordance with the principle set forth in paragraph 8 of article 19 of the Constitution of the International Labour Organisation the ratification of this Convention by any Member shall not be deemed to affect any existing law, award, custom or agreement in virtue of which members of the armed forces or the police enjoy any right guaranteed by this Convention.
Art. 6. This Convention does not deal with the position of public servants engaged in the administration of the State, nor shall it be construed as prejudicing their rights or status in any way.
Art. 7. The formal ratifications of this Convention shall be communicated to the Director-General of the International Labour Office for registration.
Art. 8.(1) This Convention shall be binding only upon those Members of the International Labour Organisation whose ratifications have been registered with the Director-General.
(2) It shall come into force twelve months after the date on which the ratifications of two Members have been registered with the Director-General.(3) Thereafter, this Convention shall come into force for any Member twelve months after the date on which its ratification has been registered.
Art. 9.(1) Declarations communicated to the Director-General of the International Labour Office in accordance with paragraph 2 of article 35 of the Constitution of the International Labour Organisation shall indicate
(a) the territories in respect of which the Member concerned undertakes that the provisions of the Convention shall be applied without modification;
(b) the territories in respect of which it undertakes that the provisions of the Convention shall be applied subject to modifications, together with details of the said modifications;
(c) the territories in respect of which the Convention is inapplicable and in such cases the grounds on which it is inapplicable;
(d) the territories in respect of which it reserves its decision pending further consideration of the position.
(2) The undertakings referred to in subparagraphs (a) and (b) of paragraph 1 of this Article shall be deemed to be an integral part of the ratification and shall have the force of ratification.
(3) Any Member may at any time by a subsequent declaration cancel in whole or in part any reservation made in its original declaration in virtue of subparagraph (b), (c) or (d) of paragraph 1 of this Article.
(4) Any Member may, at any time at which the Convention is subject to denunciation in accordance with the provisions of Article 11, communicate to the Director-General a declaration modifying in any other respect the terms of any former declaration and stating the present position in respect of such territories as it may specify.
Art. 10.(1) Declaration communicated to the Director-General of the International Labour Office in accordance with paragraph 4 or 5 of article 35 of the Constitution of the International Labour Organization shall indicate whether the provisions of the Convention will be applied in the territory concerned without modification or subject to modifications; when the declaration indicates that the provisions of the Convention will be applied subject to modifications, it shall give details of the said modifications.
(2) The Member, Members or international authority concerned may at any time by a subsequent declaration renounce in whole or in part the right to have recourse to any modification indicated in any former declaration.
(3) The Member, Members or international authority concerned may, at any time at which this Convention is subject to denunciation in accordance with the provisions of Article 11, communicate to the Director-General a declaration modifying in any other respect the terms of any former declaration and stating the present position in respect of the application of the Convention.
Art. 11.(1) A Member which has ratified this Convention may denounce it after the expiration of ten years from the date on which the Convention first comes into force, by an act communicated to the Director-General of the International Labour Office for registration. Such denunciation shall not take effect until one year after the date on which it is registered.
(2) Each Member which has ratified this Convention and which does not, within the year following the expiration of the period of ten years mentioned in the preceding paragraph, exercise the right of denunciation provided for in this Article, will be bound for another period of ten years and, thereafter, may denounce this Convention at the expiration of each period of ten years under the terms provided for in this Article.
Art. 12.(1) The Director-General of the International Labour Office shall notify all Members of the International Labour Organization of the registration of all ratifications, declarations and denunciations communicated to him by the Members of the Organization.
(2) When notifying the Members of the Organisation of the registration of the second ratification communicated to him, the Director-General shall draw the attention of the Members of the Organisation to the date upon which the Convention will come into force.
Art. 13. The Director-General of the International Labour Office shall communicate to the Secretary-General of the United Nations for registration in accordance with Article 102 of the Charter of the United Nations full particulars of all ratifications, declarations and acts of denunciation registered by him in accordance with the provisions of the preceding Articles.
Art. 14. At such times as it may consider necessary the Governing Body of the International Labour Office shall present to the General Conference a report on the working of this Convention and shall examine the desirability of placing on the agenda of the Conference the question of its revision in whole or in part.
Art. 15.(1) Should the Conference adopt a new Convention revising this Convention in whole or in part, then, unless the new Convention otherwise provides,
(a) the ratification by a Member of the new revising Convention shall ipso jure involve the immediate denunciation of this Convention, notwithstanding the provisions of Article 11 above, if and when the new revising Convention shall have come into force;
(b) as from the date when the new revising Convention comes into force, this Convention shall cease to be open to ratification by the Members.
(2) This Convention shall in any case remain in force in its actual form and content for those Members which have ratified it but have not ratified the revising Convention.
Art. 16. The English and French versions of the text of this Convention are equally authoritative."

▷ Freedom of Association of Workers and Employers. The ILO General Conference adopted at Geneva, June 28, 1978 a Convention concerning the Protection of the Right to Organize and Procedures for Determining Conditions of Employment in the Public Service.

ILO Conventions, Geneva, 1962, pp. 777–780.

RIGHT TO REFUSE MILITARY SERVICE. ▷ Military Service.

RIGHT TO REPRESENT A STATE IN THE UNITED NATIONS. A subject of international dispute which arose in 1950 due to the fact that China had been taken over by a revolutionary government which requested its rights as the sole and genuine representative of China in the United Nations. UN Secretary-General Trygve Lie, on Mar. 8, 1950, submitted the question to the members of the UN Security Council, who differed in their opinions, a confidential memorial defining the legal aspect of the question who in general has the right to represent a state in the United Nations. UN practice had shown that the question of a state's representation in the United Nations was irrelevant to the question of recognizing the actual government of a given state by the remaining members of the United Nations. Being an organization aspiring to universalism, the United Nations was entitled to allow for a representation of states of different, even contradictory, ideologies. However neither the Charter of the United Nations nor the rules of procedure the UN Security Council established any principle enabling the settlement of a dispute between two governments competing for the right of representation. Western powers used this deficiency on Nov. 28, 1950, when they voted in favor of a Resolution in the General Assembly, with 29 positive votes, 7 against and 15 abstaining, which recommended that:

"Each case should be resolved separately on the basis of the principles and aims of the UN Charter and taking into account the circumstances of each case".

Following this resolution, the government of China was blocked from taking its place in the United Nations for 21 years.

UN Bulletin, April 1, 1950, pp. 339–341 and December 15, 1950, pp. 869–873.

RIGHT TO SELF-DEFENCE. An international term for one of the basic rights vested in states in case of aggression, recognized by the Roman Law, by Papal Verdicts in the Middle Ages and by modern international law, stemming from sovereignty of states; principle formulated in art. 51 of the UN Charter:

"Nothing in the present Charter shall impair the inherent right of individual or collective self-defence if an

R

armed attack occurs against a Member of the United Nations, until the Security Council has taken measures necessary to maintain international peace and security."

R.L. BLEDSOE, B.A. BOCZEK, *The International Law Dictionary*, Oxford, 1987.

RIGHT TO WITHDRAW FROM THE UN. The right to withdraw from the UN was not mentioned in the UN Charter, however it was recognized by the UN Conference in San Francisco in 1945 as an evident right vested in each sovereign state; between 1945 and 1972 used only once by the government of Indonesia, which on Jan. 1, 1965 notified the Secretary-General that Indonesia withdrew from the United Nations due to the fact of Malaysia's election to the Security Council; Malaysia at that time was not recognized by Indonesia. It was formally agreed that Indonesia would withdraw on Mar. 1, 1965. The country's absence in the United Nations lasted until Sept., 1966, when Indonesia informed the Secretary-General that it intended "to resume full co-operation with the United Nations and take part again in its activity starting with the 21st Session of the UN General Assembly." In that precedent-setting case the procedure of renewed admission of Indonesia was not carried out but, with the consent of the UN Security Council and the UN General Assembly, it was tacitly agreed that the period of voluntary absence of Indonesia in the United Nations had come to an end.

UN Monthly Chronicle, April, 1965 and October, 1966.

RIGHT TO WORK. A fundamental human right defined in art. 23 of the Universal Declaration of Human Rights. The term "right to work" was used by factory owners against union membership and against the right to strike.

L. TRACLET, *Législation Sociale Internationale*, Brussels, 1956.

RIJEKA OR FIUME. Yugoslavia's largest sea port. Population, 1971, census: 193,044. In Croatia, on the Adriatic, and the Gulf of Quarnero; subject of international disputes in the 19th century involving Hungary which considered it "*Separatum Corpus Sacrae Hungariae Coronae*" and Croatia and Austria; 1918 reintegrated with Croatia; on Sept. 12, 1919 seized by Italy through a *coup d'état*; established as a free state of Fiume by the Italian–Yugoslav Treaty of Rapallo on Nov. 12, 1920; in view of failure to implement the treaty, partitioned between Italy (which received the larger part with the port of Rijeka) and Yugoslavia under terms of a new treaty of Rome signed on Jan. 27, 1924 and additional agreements signed on July 20, 1925, in Nettuno. After World War II the Paris Peace Treaty 1947 transferred the port of Rijeka to Yugoslavia. Beginning in Rijeka is the Yugoslav–Hungarian– Czechoslovak pipeline "Adria".

S.M. TCHIRITCH, *La question de Fiume*, Paris, 1920; V. DEDIJER, *History of Yugoslavia*, New York, 1984.

RINGGIT OF MALAYSIA. A monetary unit of Malaysia; one ringgit = 100 sen; issued by the Bank Negara Malaysia replacing the Malaysian dollar from Sept. 1975.

RIO BRAVO. The Mexican name for ▷ Rio Grande. In the Mexico–USA Treaty 1970, the Spanish text reads Rio Bravo, the American – Rio Grande.

A. GARCIA ROBLES, *El Mundo de la Postguerra*, Vol. 2, pp. 459–460, México DF, 1947.

RIO DE JANEIRO. The former capital of Brazil, 1822–1961, (superseded by Brasilia), capital of Rio de Janeiro state, on Guanabara Bay of the Atlantic Ocean. City area: 1356 sq. km, state area: 42,912 sq. km. Population, 1980 census: 5,090,700; metropolitan area: 9,014,000. State pop. 1980 census: 11,300,665. Seat of UN Information Center, ILO Regional Office, Interamerican Commercial Arbitration Commission, Latin American Committee of Physics, Latin American Center for Research in the Social Sciences, South American Association of Athletic Referees.

R.B. de MORAES, *Bibliographia Brasiliana 1504–1900*, 2 Vls., Rio de Janeiro, 1958.

RIO DE JANEIRO ACT, 1965. A document adopted by the Special Interamerican Conference for the Strengthening of the System held from Nov. 17 to 30, 1965 in Rio de Janeiro; includes a recommendation for the Interamerican Conference to revise the structure of OAS in order to grant priority status to economic and social aspects of development of Latin American states; the revision was carried out in the so-called Buenos Aires Protocol of Feb. 27, 1967 (OAS Charter 1948 and Protocol 1967) issued by the Third Special Interamerican Conference. Along with the Rio de Janeiro Act, the Rio de Janeiro Declaration 1965 on Alliance for Progress was adopted and postulated accelerated economic integration of Latin America under the Alliance during 1971–80.

OEA, *Fortalecimento del Sistema Interamericano en sus Aspectos Políticos, Jurídicos e Internacionales*, Washington, DC, 1965; M. SEAR VAZQUEZ, *Tratado General de la Organización Internacional*, México, DF, 1974, pp. 844–845.

RIO DE JANEIRO CONFERENCE, 1947. The official name: Interamerican Conference for Maintenance of Peace and Continental Security; convened at the initiative of the USA, held in Rio de Janeiro from Aug. 15 to Sept. 2, 1947; formulated and ratified a Treaty on Mutual Aid, called the Rio de Janeiro Pact.

RIO DE JANEIRO DECLARATION, 1965. The Declaration adopted Nov. 30, 1965 by the Second Special Inter-American Conference; affirmed the socio-economic principles contained in the ▷ Alliance for Progress.

RIO DE JANEIRO PACT. ▷ Inter-American Treaty of Reciprocal Assistance, 1947.

RIO DE LA PLATA. ▷ Plata, Rio de la.

RIO DE ORO. A gulf and territory in West Africa on the Atlantic Ocean. The territory, 184,000 sq. km, was a Spanish colony since 1884 with the name Spanish West Africa, since 1958 South Territory of the Spanish Sahara together with North Territory – Sekia el Hamra; ceased to be a Spanish territory on Dec. 31, 1975. Capital: Villa Cisneros; part of Western Sahara.

UN Yearbook, 1963, p. 435.

RIO GRANDE OR RIO BRAVO. The frontier river of Mexico and the USA, called also Rio Grande del Norte or Rio Bravo del Norte, 2870 km long. Subject of American–Mexican conventions: Convention establishing the International Boundary Commission, signed Mar. 1, 1889.
Convention on Rectification of the Rio Grande, signed Feb. 1, 1933.
The Treaty to resolve pending boundary differences and maintain the Rio Grande and Colorado River as the international boundary between the United Mexican States and the United States of America, signed on Nov. 23, 1970 at Mexico City; came into force on Apr. 17, 1972.

G.F. DE MARTENS, *Nouveau Recueil General*, 25, Vol. 18, p. 553; *British and Foreign State Papers*, Vol. 136, p. 755; *UNTS*, Vol. 830, 1972, pp. 57–77.

RIO PLATANO. A natural site of Honduras, included in the ▷ World Heritage UNESCO List.

UNESCO. *A Legacy for All*, Paris, 1984.

RIOT. An international term for tumult or disorder organized by a group of people against home or foreign institutions.

J.E. BOND, *The Rules of Riot*, Princeton, 1974.

RIVER BASIN. A subject of international co-operation and convention under aegis of the UN system.

Integrated River Basin Development, UN, New York 1958; L.A. TACLAFF, *The River Basin in History and Law*, The Hague, 1967.

RIVER DAMS. A subject of international co-operation and conventions. Organization reg. with the UIA: International Commission on Large Dams, f. 1928, Paris. Organizes international congresses and publ. *Reports, World Register of Dams*, and *Technical Dictionary on Dams* in English, French, German, Italian, Spanish, Portuguese. Members: National committees in 74 countries.

Yearbook of International Organizations.

RIVERS, INTERNATIONALIZED. The internationalization of rivers was first postulated by Hugo Grotius in his *De iure belli ac pacis*; declared by the French Revolution, 1792, which proclaimed all rivers universal and inseparable property of all countries they traverse. Based on this principle, a peace treaty between the French Republic and the United Provinces of Belgium and the Netherlands was signed on May 16, 1795 in The Hague, provided for internationalization of three European rivers: the Rhine, Moselle, and Scheldt. In 1815 the Vienna Congress drew up rules of navigation included in the Final Act (arts. 108–117) and providing that navigation along the entire navigable length of any river up to its mouth is to be completely free and cannot be closed to trade pursued by anyone who observes appropriate regulations of order which will be formulated for all in a way possibly most uniform and most conducive for the trade of all countries (art. 109). Internationalized by the Vienna Congress were the rivers Rhine, Main, Neckar, Moselle, Meuse, Scheldt; also recommended was the setting up of an international commission for river navigation; the first to be founded was the Central Commission for the Navigation of the Rhine. The Paris Congress, 1856, extended international navigation principles to embrace the Danube. The rivers of international status in the Western Hemisphere are the Parana and Uruguay since 1852; a year later status granted to the Colorado and Rio Grande (Rio Bravo del Norte), forming part of natural frontier between Mexico and USA; in 1867 the Amazon; 1871 – the San Lorenzo; 1893 – the Hondo, bordering Mexico and British Honduras.
In Africa the Congo and the Niger were internationalized by the Berlin General Act, 1885.
In Asia the Chinese rivers were open to international navigation in 1857; rivers in Indochina – in 1874.
In Europe the Treaty of Versailles, 1919, further extended international status to include the Elbe, Oder, Nieman, Moldau. Framed on recommendation of the Versailles Conference and on the initiative of the League of Nations was the Conven-

tion and Statute of Navigation Routes of International Importance signed on Apr. 20, 1921 in Barcelona, where the principles of freedom of commercial navigation were broadened to span all navigable water routes, natural as well as artificial. The convention came into force on Oct. 31, 1922. The Eighth International American Conference held in Montevideo, in Dec. 1933, adopted a Declaration on industrial and agricultural utilization of international rivers.

In the second half of the 20th century proper utilization of international rivers and their pollution feature was permanently on agendas of international debates and resolutions of appropriate commissions. At the Potsdam Conference 1945 the USA proposed that all European rivers be opened completely and free to international navigation; the idea was opposed by the USSR as violating sovereignty of European countries. On Nov. 18, 1967 four African states – Senegal, Mauritania, Mali and Guinea – signed an agreement on joint utilization of the River Senegal for economic development of the whole region. In 1967 research was launched in South America into international utilization of the Amazon and the catchment area of the La Plata. In 1969 Warsaw Pact countries issued the Budapest Appeal urging creation of a Pan-European network of navigation routes. On Oct. 17, 1973 the UN General Assembly Legal Commission decided to launch a study project on codification of regulations relating to navigation on international rivers.

International Rivers and Lakes, Official Documents, Washington, DC, 1967.

RIYADH. The political capital of Saudi Arabia (the religious capital is Mecca) with 666,840 inhabitants (census 1974). Headquarters of Arab Investment Company and International Islamic News Agency.

Yearbook of International Organizations.

RIYAL OF QATAR. A monetary unit of Qatar; one riyal = 100 dirhams; issued from 1972 by the Quatar Monetary Agency, replacing the United Arab Emirates Dirham.

RIYAL OF SAUDI ARABIA. Saudi Arabia's monetary unit, divided into 100 halalah, issued by the Saudi Arabian Monetary Agency, since 1960, replacing the "pilgrims' receipts."

RIYAL OF YEMEN. A currency unit of the Yemen Arab Republic; one riyal = 100 fils.; issued by the Central Bank of Yemen.

ROADS. A subject of international conventions on road signals, traffic and statistics related to traffic accidents.

ROAD SIGNS AND SIGNALS. A subject of international co-operation and international agreements. The international system of road signs comprises: danger warning signs, regulatory signs and informative signs. The international system of road signals comprises traffic lights signals in a three-colored system: red indicates "Stop", green "Go", and amber "Caution": when a single amber intermittent light is used it shall indicate "Stop, then proceed with caution." When a single red intermittent light is used, it shall also indicate "Stop, then proceed with caution."

UNTS, Vol. 454, p. 264.

ROADS, INTERNATIONAL AND INTERCONTINENTAL. The subject of international conventions and permanent organized international co-operation.

The First International Congress on International Roads was held in 1909 in Paris, at the beginning of the automobile era; the first regional Congress was held in 1925, in Buenos Aires. In the 1960s regional congresses under UN auspices have been held in Buenos Aires, 1960, Sydney, 1961, and Tokyo, 1964.

Organizations affiliated with the UN:

Asian Highway Co-ordinating Committee, f. under the auspices of ECAFE in 1964, Bangkok;
International Road Federation, f. 1948, Washington and Geneva, publ.: *World Highways* (in English and French) and *Road International*;
International Road Safety, f. 1959, Luxembourg.
Panamerican Highway Congress, f. 1925, Washington, OAS specialized agency;
Permanent International Association of Road Congresses, f. 1909, Paris, publ.: *Bulletin*;

The intercontinental roads include the following routes:

The Trans-African Highway, designed by the UN Economic Commission for Africa in 1971 to join the capitals of Nigeria, Lagos, on the South Atlantic coast with Mombassa in Kenya on the Indian Ocean, Cameroon, the Central African Republic, Zaïre, Uganda and Kenya. Financial credits and know-how were offered by: Belgium, France, the Netherlands, Japan, the Federal Republic of Germany, Sweden, Great Britain, the USA and Italy.

The Asian Highway, designed by the UN Economic Commission for Asia and Far East in 1955, approved by the UN Regional Conference on Roads held in Karachi, 1959, to run through Turkey, Iraq, Iran, Afghanistan, Pakistan, India, Nepal, Bangladesh, Burma, Thailand, Malaysia, Cambodia, China to Hong Kong.

The European Highways, designed by the UN Economic Commission for Europe, include routes from Great Britain to the USSR, from Sweden to Portugal and from Great Britain to Turkey as a European junction with the Asian Highway thereby constituting an intercontinental highway London–Hanoi, 10,800 km long, allowing for regular bus transportation along the highway in 14–20 days;

The Panamerican Highway, designed and approved by the First Panamerican Road Congress, Oct. 5, 1925, held in Buenos Aires. A detailed design of the Highway leading from Alaska, through the USA, Mexico, Central America, Ecuador, Peru, Chile, to Brazila and Argentina, was approved by the Sixth International American Conference held in Havana, 1928. The construction carried out simultaneously in different countries, reached the final stages in the 1970s.

The Trans-American Highways, designed by the UN Economic Commission for Latin America ECLA, 1965–67, composed of three highways: (1) a highway crossing Latin America from Rio de Janeiro to Lima, Peru, 5640 km long, in Spanish called Carretera Transversal Panamericana en Sudamérica; (2) a 5600 km highway from Arcana on the Colombian–Venezuelan border to Santa Cruz de la Sierra in Bolivia; (3) a branch highway connecting Colombia, Ecuador, Peru and Venezuela with Brazil in the catchment area of the Amazon; (4) the Trans-Amazon Highway along the route Recife–Altamira, Nova Brazil, Rio Branco–Cruzeiro do Sul, 5700 km long, related to the exploitation of the Amazon basin.

In May 1973 the presidents of Algeria, Mali, Mauritania and Niger opened the first segment of the Trans-Sahara Highway running from Algeria to the three other countries and named it the "African Unity Highway."

The first International Road Traffic Convention was signed on Apr. 24, 1926 in Paris, by the governments of Austria, Bulgaria, Cuba, Egypt, France, Guatemala, Hungary, Italy, Luxembourg, Morocco, Mexico, Monaco, Peru, Poland, Portugal, Romania, Serbo-Croat-Slovene State, Switzerland, Tunis, Uruguay, Accession: Chile (1929), replaced by the Convention on Road Traffic signed on Sept. 19, 1949 in Geneva.

A Convention concerning the Unification of Road Signals, with Annex was signed on Mar. 30, 1931 in Geneva by the governments of Belgium, Czechoslovakia, Denmark, France, Germany, Hungary, Italy, Luxembourg, the Netherlands, Poland, Spain, Switzerland, Turkey and Yugoslavia.

European Agreement on Road Markings, signed in Geneva, on Dec. 13, 1957, by the governments of Belgium, France, the FRG, Italy, Luxembourg, the Netherlands, Portugal, Switzerland, Turkey and the UK.

LNTS, Vol. 97, p. 83, Vol. 150, p. 247; Vol. 372, p. 159; Vol. 454, p. 264; *Yearbook of International Organizations*, 1986/87; *The Europa Yearbook* 1988. *A World Survey*, Vol. I, London 1988.

ROADS OF LIMIT. The practice since ancient times of designating permitted travel routes for foreigners; currently universally retained for air routes, and also in some states on land roads and territorial waters.

ROAD TRAFFIC ACCIDENTS. A subject of international co-operation and statistics. Organizations reg. with the UIA:

European Liaison Meeting on the Prevention and Control of Road Accidents, f. 1970, Rome.
International Association for Accident and Traffic Medicine, f. 1960, Stockholm. Publ.: *Journal of Traffic Medicine*.
International Prevention of Road Accidents, f. 1957, Bonn. Consultative status with ECOSOC and Council of Europe. Publ.: *Revue*.

Road Traffic Accident Statistics. WHO Report, Copenhagen, 1979.

ROBOT. An international term for machines doing work ordinarily done by humans, coined by Czech writer Karel Capek in his play R.U.R (Rossum's Universal Robots) in 1929.
See also ▷ Automation, Industrial.

W.J. FUNK, *Word Origins and their Romantic Stories*, New York 1978.

ROCBA-LIB. Library of the UNESCO Regional Office for Cultural Book Development in Asia, one of the information systems of the ▷ UNESCO.

ROCK AND ROLL MUSIC. ▷ Music.

ROCKETS. The flying objects propelled by a rocket engine using solid or liquid fuel capable of generating great power. Rockets are used, i.a., for delivering intercontinental missiles and in scientific explorations of space; subject of international treaties on rockets. Here are the American abbreviations for rockets:

AAM	Air–Air Missile
ABM	Anti-Ballistic Missile
ASM	Air–Soil Missile
ICBM	Intercontinental Ballistic Missile
IRBM	Intermediate-Range Ballistic Missile
MIRV	Multiple Independently Targetable Re-entry Vehicle
MRBM	Medium-Range Ballistic Missile
SAM	Soil–Air Missile
SLBM	Submarine-Launched Ballistic Missile
SLCM	Submarine-Launched Cruise Missile
SRBM	Short-Range Ballistic Missile
SSM	Soil–Soil Missile

Besides the above, three main types of American and Soviet intercontinental rockets are recognized:

R

Minuteman, or SS-9 with a range of about 10,000 km; Titan II, or SS-13 with a somewhat lesser range; and the rockets for submarines – Polaris, Poseidon, or SS-M-6 with a range of 4000–5000 km.

J. GOLDBLAT, *Arms Control Agreements. A Handbook*, New York, 1982

ROCK MECHANICS. Subject of international co-operation. Organization reg. with the UIA:

International Society for Rock Mechanics, f. 1962, Lisbon, Portugal. Publ.: News.

Yearbook of International Organizations, 1986/87; *The Europa Yearbook 1988. A World Survey*, Vol. I, London 1988.

RODENTS. A subject of international sanitary conventions. ▷ Deratization. Organization reg. with the UIA:

Asia–Pacific Rodent Control Society, f. 1968, Honolulu. Publ.: *Newsletter*.

Yearbook of International Organizations.

RODŁO, A POLISH SYMBOL. The stylized course of the Vistula on which the city of Cracow is marked – national symbol of Poles on Polish lands which after World War I remained under Prussian administration, as well as the Poles in emigration in the Reich; introduced by the Union of Poles in Germany, est. 1922, to replace the white eagle, symbol of the Polish state, forbidden in the Reich. The Rodło on a white–red background was the badge of the members of the Union and appeared on the flags of Polish organizations in Germany; it expressed the aspiration of the autochthonous Polish population of the Oder region and East Prussia under Prussian rule for union with Poland. On Aug. 5, 1934 during the II Congress of Poles from Abroad in Warsaw, a symbolic union of Rodło banners from the Odra and Baltic region with Vistula took place by immersing the banners in the Vistula at the Kościuszko Bank. In 1972, the 50th anniversary of UPG, the Polish post office issued a stamp and postcards with Rodło.

W. WRZESIŃSKI, "The Union of Poles in Germany 1922–39", in: *Polish Western Affairs*, No. 1, 1968, pp. 19–43; H. LEHR, E. OSMAŃCZYK, *Polacy pod znakiem Rodła* (Poles of the Rodło Sign), Warsaw 1972.

ROERICH PACT. A Russian painter and archeologist, Nicolas K. de Roerich (1874–1947) postulated in the 1920s the universal adoption of a special flag in order to preserve, in any time of danger, nationally and privately owned immovable monuments, from the cultural treasure of peoples. The postulate supported by the Seventh International Conference of America States on Dec. 16, 1933 in Montevideo resulted in the ▷ Inter-American Treaty on the Protection of Artistic and Scientific Institutions and Historic Monuments, 1935, called the Roerich Pact.

N.K. DE ROERICH, *Le poète Roerich, banniére de paix*, Paris, 1931; *LNTS*, Vol. 167, p. 290; CARNEGIE ENDOWMENT, *International Legislation 1922–1945*, 9 Vols. Washington, DC, 1946.

ROGERS PLAN, 1970. A proposal made by US Secretary of State W. Rogers to settle peacefully the conflict between Israel and Egypt and Jordan. The highlights of the plan were drawn in a letter from Rogers to the Ministers of Foreign Affairs of Egypt and Israel on May 19, 1970. The Rogers Plan was approved on July 25, 1970, by the United Arab Republic and Jordan and on Aug. 4, 1970, by Israel. On the basis of the plan a 90-day cease-fire began on Aug. 10, 1970, and was further extended until Feb. 10, 1971.

KEESING's *Contemporary Archive*, 1970.

ROLL-BACK. A term used by the American statesman J.F. Dulles in a book in which he formulated the aims of US foreign policy in relation to the communist world.

J.F. DULLES, *War or Peace*, New York, 1950; D. ROBERTSON, *Guide to Modern Defense and Strategy*, Detroit 1988.

ROLLER SKATING. An international sport, subject of international co-operation. Organization reg. with the UIA:

International Roller Skating Federation, f. 1924, Montreux. Recognized by International Olympic Games. The Federation organizes World and European championships.

Yearbook of International Organizations.

ROLLING STOCK. Subject of international co-operation. Organization reg. with the UIA:

International Association of Rolling Stock Builders, f. 1934, Paris, France.

Yearbook of International Organizations, 1986/87; *The Europa Yearbook 1988. A World Survey*, Vol. I, London 1988.

ROLL-OVER CREDITS. The long-term credits created by banking consortia, e.g. for 10 years, by the renewal 20 times of a six-month short-term credit, with a variable rate of interest based on the

ROMAN CATHOLIC CHURCH. The largest religious organization in the world conducting its international activity from one center in Rome of a dual nature: religious ▷ Apostolic See and political ▷ Vatican. The religious authority of the Roman Catholic Church in the interpretation of the Catholic doctrine has been derived from the Bible, documents of councils, and the Pope – in our times i.a. the encyclical *Mistici Corporis Christi* of Pius XII, 1943, as the Mystical Body of Christ and the documents of ▷ Vatican Council II; the secular character is determined by the politics of the Vatican in relation to international problems. In 1975 according to figures of the Vatican the number of Catholics in the world was 709,500,000 (96,000,000 in Brazil; 54,000,000 in Italy; 47,000,000 in the USA), comprising 18% of the world population. The number of clergy was 1,446,383 among which 986,526 were in convents and monasteries, 404,783 priests, 70,388 other clerics, and 2686 deacons.

J.L. KUNZ, "The Status of the Holy See in International Law", in: *American Journal of International Law*, No. 46, 1952.

ROMAN CURIA. *Latin*: *Curia Romana*. In ancient Rome an administration unit dividing citizens into groups of 30, then 10 tribes, also a military and taxation unit; an international term. In the Catholic Church the whole of the central institutions of the Apostolic See (primarily located within the area of the Vatican) under the leadership of the Pope determining the activity of the Church throughout the world. At the head is the Secretariat of State of the Apostolic See along with the Council for Public Affairs of the Church, the most important role performed by Congregations and Tribunals; also active within the framework of the Curia are Secretariats of Councils, Commissions, Committees as well as varous kinds of bureaus. New organizational principles were given to the Roman Curia by the constitution *Regimini Ecclesiae Universae* of Paul VI on Aug. 15, 1967.

R.A. GRAHAM, *Vatican Diplomacy. A Study of Church and State on the International Plan*, Princeton, 1959.

ROMANIA. Member of the UN. State in South-East Europe on the Black Sea. Borders with the USSR, Hungary, Yugoslavia and Bulgaria. Area: 229,600 sq. km. Pop. 1987 est.: 22,800,000 (1956 census – 17,489,000; 1966 – 19,103,163; 1970 – 20,252,000; 1977 – 21,559,000). Capital: Bucharest with 2,165,000 inhabitants, 1981. GNP per capita in 1980: US $2,340. Official language: Romanian. Currency: one leu = 100 bani. National Day: Aug. 23, anniversary of liberation, 1944.

Member of the League of Nations, 1919–40. Member of the UN since Dec. 14, 1945 and UN specialized organizations with the exception of IFC and IDA. Member of CMEA and the Warsaw Pact. International relations: in the 15th–18th centuries dependent on Ottoman Turkey; from 1881 the independent kingdom of Romania; as a result of the Balkan wars received Dobrudja from Bulgaria, Aug. 10, 1913. During World War I on the side of the Allies. Peace Treaties concluded after the war ceded to Romania: Bessarabia and Bukovina from Russia, Transylvania from Hungary, South Dobrudja from Bulgaria.

In Paris on Dec. 9, 1919 the Great Powers signed the Minority Treaty with Romania. During World War II on the side of Germany, at war with the USSR; surrendered on Aug. 23, 1944. New frontiers were established by the Treaty with the USSR and the Paris Peace Treaty of Feb. 10, 1947. The regime of President Nicolae Ceaucescu, internationally criticized for flagrant abuse of human rights, was overthrown on Dec. 21–25, 1990 by popular revolution. The revolutionaries, enjoying the support of the army, formed a National Salvation Front, composed of former dissidents, some of whom called for the Soviet Union to intervene militarily in support of the revolution. The Soviet Union refused, arguing that the struggle was an internal matter. On Dec. 25 the Ceaucescus were summarily tried and executed, which dampened the morale of pro-Ceaucescu secret police. Casualty estimates were as high as 80,000, but the figure of 5000 is more probable. Dissatisfaction with the National Salvation Front and the vigorous campaigning of numerous political parties emphasizes the need for free elections in the near future.

C.C. GIUSESCU, *Chronological History of Romania*, Bucharest, 1974; I. RATIU, *Contemporary Romania*, Richmond, 1975; T. GILBERG, *Modernization in Romania since World War II*, New York, 1975; D. FRENZKE, *Rümänien, der Sovjetblock und die europäische Sicherheit*, Berlin, 1975; *Romania. An Encyclopedic Survey*, Bucharest, 1980; R.R. KING, *History of the Romanian Communist Party*, Stanford, 1980; D.N. NELSON (ed.), *Romania in the 1980s*, Boulder, 1981; L.S. GRAHAM, *Romania, A Developing Socialist State*, Boulder, 1982; F. CONSTANTINIU, M.E. IONESCU, *200 days early. Romania and the end of World War II*. Bucharest, 1984; *The Europa Year Book 1984. A World Survey*, Vol. I, 753–770, London, 1984; KEESING's *Border and Territorial Disputes*, London, 1987.

ROMANIAN BANK FOR FOREIGN TRADE. A state bank est. 1968 in Bucharest. Foreign operations of the central bank: Banque Nationale de la République Socialiste de Roumanie. Representatives: Frankfurt am M., Rome, Zurich. Associated with Anglo–Romanian Bank Ltd., London.

ROMANIAN MINORITY TREATY, 1919. The Treaty between the Principal Allied and Associatied Powers and Romania, signed on Dec. 9, 1919 at Paris, relating to "full and complete protection of life and liberty to all inhabitants of Romania without distinction of birth, language, race or religion. All inhabitants of Romania shall be entitled to the free exercise, whether public or private, of any creed, religion or belief, whose practices are not inconsistent with public order and public morals." (art. 2)

LNTS, Vol. 5, p. 335.

ROMANIA PARIS PEACE TREATY, 1947.

The Treaty signed on Feb. 10, 1947 in Paris, between the Allied and Associated Powers on the one hand and Romania on the other. The texts of the Preamble and the first 3 articles are as follows:

"The USSR, the UK, the USA, Australia, the Byelorussian SSR, Canada, Czechoslovakia, India, New Zealand, the Ukrainian SSR, and the Union of South Africa, as the States which are at war with Romania and actively waged war against the European enemy States with substantial military forces, hereinafter referred to as 'the Allied and Associated Powers', of the one part, and Romania, of the other part;

Whereas Romania, having become an ally of Hitlerite Germany and having participated on her side in the war against the Union of Soviet Socialist Republics, the United Kingdom, the United States of America, and other United Nations, bears her share of responsibility for this war;

Whereas, however, Romania, on August 24, 1944, entirely ceased military operation against the Union of Soviet Socialist Republics, withdrew from the war against the United Nations, broke off relations with Germany and her satellites and having concluded on September 12, 1944, an Armistice with the Governments of the Union of Soviet Socialist Republics, the United Kingdom and the United States of America, acting in the interests of all the United Nations, took an active part in the war against Germany; and

Whereas the Allied and Associated Powers and Romania are desirous of concluding a treaty of peace, which, conforming to the principles of justice, will settle questions still outstanding as a result of the events hereinbefore recited and form the basis of friendly relations between them, thereby enabling the Allied and Associated Powers to support Romania's application to become a member of the United Nations and also to adhere to any treaty concluded under the auspices of the United Nations;

have therefore agreed to declare the cessation of the state of war and for this purpose to conclude the present Treaty of Peace, and have accordingly appointed the undersigned Plenipotentiaries who, after presentation of their full powers, found in good and due form, have agreed on the following provisions.

Art. 1. The frontiers of Romania, shown on the map annexed to the present Treaty (Annex 1), shall be those which existed on January 1, 1941, with the exception of the Romanian–Hungarian frontier, which is defined in Article 2 of the present Treaty. The Soviet–Romanian frontier is thus fixed in accordance with the Soviet–Romanian Agreement of June 28, 1940, and the Soviet–Czechoslovak Agreement of June 29, 1945.

Art. 2. The decisions of the Vienna Award of August 30, 1940, are declared null and void. The frontier between Romania and Hungary as it existed on January 1, 1938, is hereby restored.

Art. 3. (1) Romania shall take all measures necessary to secure to all persons under Romanian jurisdiction, without distinction as to race, sex, language or religion, the enjoyment of human rights and of the fundamental freedoms, including freedom of expression, of press and publication, of religious worship, of political opinion and of public meeting."

Came into force on Sept. 15, 1947 upon the deposit with the Government of the USSR the instruments of ratification by the USSR, the UK and the USA in accordance with art. 40.

UNTS, Vol. 41, pp. 3–124.

ROMANIA–YUGOSLAVIA ALLIANCE, 1921.

The Treaty on military aid as determined by technical authorities and on mutual assistance in case of attack by Hungary, Bulgaria, or both, with the object of violating the peace settlement, signed on July 8, 1921 at Belgrade, renewed on July 7, 1923, and July 17, 1926.

LNTS, No. 1289.

ROMAN QUESTION.

A dispute 1870–1929 between the Apostolic See and Italy caused by incorporation of Rome into Kingdom of Italy in 1870 and settled Feb. 11, 1929, by the Lateran Treaty where Italy recognized, among others, unlimited property and exclusive and absolute authority and jurisdiction of the sovereign Apostolic See over the Vatican.

S. MOLLAT, *La Questione Romaine de Pie VI à Pie XI*, Paris, 1932.

ROMANSH. ▷ Rheto-Romanic or Romansh.

ROME.

Population, 1985 estimate: 2,826,488. The capital of Italy since 1870; since the 8th century the capital of the Church State (Apostolic Capital), whose head is the pope of the Roman Catholic Church; subject of a dispute between Italy and the papacy up to 1929, when the Vatican State was formed. Headquarters of FAO and *c.* 50 international organizations reg. with the UN, seat of a UN Information Center. The historic centre of Rome is included in the ▷ World Heritage UNESCO List.

Codice topografica della citta di Roma, 4 Vol., Roma, 1940–53; E. CASTAGNOLI, *Topografia e urbanistica di Roma*, Roma, 1958; UNESCO, *A Legacy for All*, Paris, 1984.

ROME–BERLIN AND ROME–BERLIN–TOKYO AXIS, 1936–37.

The two intergovernmental agreements, characterized by Benito Mussolini, Nov. 1, 1936 in a speech concerning the German–Italian agreement signed in Berlin, Oct. 25, 1936 in which Germany recognized Italian annexation of Ethiopia:

"The agreement created a Rome–Berlin axis round which all countries of Europe can gather."

After the agreement with Italy Germany signed on Nov. 25, 1936 an agreement with Japan directed against ▷ Komintern. On Jan. 27, 1937 the organ of the alliance, a Japanese–German commission called ▷ Anti-Comintern was founded. Italy joined the alliance and the commission on Nov. 6, 1937 and the name Rome–Berlin–Tokyo Axis was adopted henceforth.

E. WISKEMANN, *The Rome–Berlin Axis*, London, 1966.

ROME CONVENTION, 1961.

A radio convention on the protection of broadcasting work adopted and signed on Oct. 26, 1961, at a conference held in Rome, under ILO, UNESCO and the International Union for the Protection of Literary and Artistic Works, whose art. 32 set up the Intergovernmental Committee of the International Convention of Rome for the Protection of Performers, Producers of Phonograms and Broadcasting Organizations. The Committee is composed of persons elected by member states and general Directors of ILO, UNESCO and the International Union for the Protection of Literary and Artistic Works.

Manual of Convention of the International Union for Protection of Literary and Artistic Works, Geneva, 1970; *Yearbook of International Organizations*.

ROME NAVAL CONFERENCE, 1924.

The Conference convened under the aegis of the League of Nations on Feb. 14, 1924 at Rome. Naval experts conference of Argentina, Chile, Denmark, Greece, the Netherlands, Norway, Turkey and the USSR, as well as Members of the League of Nations Subcommittee (Belgium, Brazil, Czechoslovakia, France, Great Britain, Italy, Japan and Sweden).

"The Rome Conference", in: *International Conciliaton*, No. 245, Dec. 1928, pp. 595–607.

ROME PROTOCOLS, 1934.

Three agreements concluded in Rome on Mar. 17, 1934, between Austria, Hungary and Italy; first on political co-operation; second on economic co-operation, and third on Austrian–Italian appendix to the second agreement.

LNTS, 1934.

ROME TREATY, 1957.

The Treaty establishing the European Community signed at Rome on Mar. 25, 1957, by Belgium, France, the FRG, Italy, Luxembourg and the Netherlands; came into force on Jan. 1, 1958; concluded for an unlimited period, consists of 248 Articles, 15 Annexes, 4 Declarations of Intentions and 3 Protocols. The text of the essential first 136 Articles is as follows:

"His Majesty the King of the Belgians, the President of the Federal Republic of Germany, the President of the French Republic, the President of the Italian Republic, Her Royal Highness the Grand Duchess of Luxembourg, Her Majesty the Queen of the Netherlands,

Determined to establish the foundations of an ever closer union among the European peoples,

Decided to ensure the economic and social progress of their countries by common action in eliminating the barriers which divide Europe,

Directing their efforts to the essential purpose of constantly improving the living and working conditions of their peoples,

Recognising that the removal of existing obstacles calls for concerted action in order to guarantee a steady expansion, a balanced trade and fair competition,

Anxious to strengthen the unity of their economies and to ensure their harmonious development by reducing the differences existing between the various regions and by mitigating the backwardness of the less favoured,

Desirous of contributing by means of a common commercial policy to the progressive abolition of restrictions on international trade,

Intending to confirm the solidarity which binds Europe and overseas countries, and desiring, to ensure the development of their prosperity, in accordance with the principles of the Charter of the United Nations,

Resolved to strengthen the safeguards of peace and liberty by establishing this combination of resources, and calling upon the other peoples of Europe who share their ideal to join in their efforts,

Have decided to create a European Economic Community and to this end have designated as their plenipotentiaries ...

Who, having exchanged their full powers, found in good and due form, have agreed, as follows:

Part One   Principles

Art. 1. By the present Treaty, the High Contracting Parties establish among themselves a European Economic Community.

Art. 2. It shall be the aim of the Community, by establishing a Common Market and progressively approximating the economic policies of Member States, to promote throughout the Community a harmonious development of economic activities, a continuous and balanced expansion, an increased stability, an accelerated raising of the standard of living and closer relations between its Member States.

Art. 3. For the purposes set out in the preceding art., the activities of the Community shall include, under the conditions and with the timing provided for in this Treaty:

(a) the elimination, as between Member States, of customs duties and of quantitative restrictions in regard to the importation and exportation of goods, as well as of all other measures with equivalent effect;

(b) the establishment of a common customs tariff and a common commercial policy towards third countries;

(c) the abolition, as between Member States, of the obstacles to the free movement of persons, services and capital;

(d) the inauguration of a common agricultural policy;

(e) the inauguration of a common transport policy;

(f) the establishment of a system ensuring that competition shall not be distorted in the Common Market;

(g) the application of procedures which shall make it possible to co-ordinate the economic policies of Member States and to remedy disequilibria in their balances of payments;

(h) the approximation of their respective municipal law to the extent necessary for the functioning of the Common Market;
(i) the creation of a European Social Fund in order to improve the possibilities of employment for workers and to contribute to the raising of their standard of living;
(j)the establishment of a European Investment Bank intended to facilitate the economic expansion of the Community through the creation of new resources; and
(k) the association of overseas countries and territories with the Community with a view to increasing trade and to pursuing jointly their effort towards economic and social development.

Art. 4.(1) The achievement of the tasks entrusted to the Community shall be ensured by: – an Assembly, – a Council, – a Commission, and – a Court of Justice.
Each of these institutions shall act within the limits of the powers conferred upon it by this Treaty.
(2) The Council and the Commission shall be assisted by an Economic and Social Committee acting in a consultative capacity.

Art. 5. Member States shall take all general or particular measures which are appropriate for ensuring the carrying out of the obligations arising out of this Treaty or resulting from the acts of the institutions of the Community.
They shall facilitate the achievement of the Community's aims.
They shall abstain from any measures likely to jeopardise the attainment of the objectives of this Treaty.

Art. 6.(1) Member States, acting in close collaboration with the institutions of the Community, shall coordinate their respective economic policies to the extent that is necessary to attain the objectives of this Treaty.
(2) The institutions of the Community shall take care not to prejudice the internal and external financial stability of Member States.

Art. 7. Within the field of application of this Treaty and without prejudice to the special provisions mentioned therein, any discrimination on the grounds of nationality shall hereby be prohibited.
The Council may, acting by means of a qualified majority vote on a proposal of the Commission and after the Assembly has been consulted, lay down rules in regard to the prohibition of any such discrimination.

Art. 8.(1) The Common Market shall be progressively established in the course of a transitional period of twelve years.
The transitional period shall be divided into three stages of four years each; the length of each stage may be modified in accordance with the provisions set out below.
(2) To each stage there shall be allotted a group of actions which shall be undertaken and pursued concurrently.
(3) Transition from the first to the second stage shall be conditional upon a confirmatory statement to the effect that the essence of the objectives specifically laid down in this Treaty for the first stage has been in fact achieved and that, subject to the exceptions and procedures provided for in this Treaty, the obligations have been observed.
This statement shall be made at the end of the fourth year by the Council acting by means of a unanimous vote on a report of the Commission. The invocation by a Member State of the non-fulfilment of its own obligations shall not, however, be an obstacle to a unanimous vote. Failing a unanimous vote, the first stage shall automatically be extended for a period of one year.
At the end of the fifth year, the Council shall make such confirmatory statement under the same conditions. Failing a unanimous vote, the first stage shall automaticaly be extended for a further period of one year.
At the end of the sixth year, the Council shall make such a statement acting by means of a qualified majority vote on a report of the Commission.
(4) Within a period of one month as from the date of this last vote, each Member State voting in a minority or, if the required majority vote has not been obtained, any Member State, shall be entitled to require the Council to appoint an Arbitration Board whose decision shall bind all Member States and the institutions of the Community. The Arbitration Board shall be composed of three members appointed by the Council acting by means of a unanimous vote on a proposal of the Commission.
If the Council has not within a period of one month from the date of such requirement, appointed the members of the Arbitration Board, they shall be appointed by the Court of Justice within a further period of one month.
The Arbitration Board shall appoint its Chairman.
The Board shall give its award within a period of six months from the date of the vote by the Council referred to in par. 3, last sub-par.
(5) The second and third stages may not be extended or curtailed except pursuant to a decision of the Council acting by means of a unanimous vote on a proposal of the Commission.
(6) The provisions of the preceding pars. shall not have the effect of extending the transitional period beyond a total duration of fifteen years after the date of the entry into force of this Treaty.
(7) Subject to the exceptions or deviations provided for in this Treaty, the expiry of the transitional period shall constitute the final date for the entry into force of all the rules laid down and for the completion of all the measures required for the establishment of the Common Market.

Part Two Bases of the Community
Title I Free Movement of Goods

Art. 9.(1) The Community shall be based upon a customs union covering the exchange of all goods and comprising both the prohibition, as between Member States, of customs duties on importation and exportation and all charges with equivalent effect and the adoption of a common customs tariff in their relations with third countries.
(2) The provisions of Chapter 1, Section 1 and Chapter 2 of this Title shall apply to products originating in Member States and also to products coming from third countries and having been entered for consumption in Member States.

Art. 10.(1) Products having been entered for consumption in a Member State shall be deemed to be products coming from a third country in cases where, in respect of such products, the necessary import formalities have been complied with and the appropriate customs duties or charges with equivalent have been levied in such Member State and where such products have not benefited by any total or partial drawback on such duties or charges.
(2) The Commission shall, before the end of the first year after the date of the entry into force of this Treaty, lay down the methods of administrative co-operation to be adopted for the application of art. 9, par. 2, taking due account of the need for reducing as far as possible the formalities imposed on trade.
Before the end of the first year after the date of the entry into force of this Treaty, the Commission shall lay down the provisions applicable, as regards trade between Member States, to goods originating in another Member State in whose manufacture products have been used on which the appropriate customs duties or charges with equivalent effect in the exporting Member State have not been levied or which have benefited by a total or partial drawback on such duties or charges.
When laying down such provisions, the Commission shall take due account of the rules for the elimination of customs duties within the Community and for the progressive application of the common customs tariff.

Art. 11. The Member States shall take all appropriate measures to enable Governments to carry out, within the time-limits laid down, the obligations with regard to customs duties which are incumbent on them pursuant to this Treaty.

Chapter 1 The Customs Union; Section 1 The Elimination of Customs Duties as between Member States

Art. 12. Member States shall refrain from introducing, as between themselves, any new customs duties on importation or exportation or charges with equivalent effect and from increasing such duties or charges as they apply in their commercial relations with each other.

Art. 13.(1) Customs duties on importation in force between Member States shall be progressively abolished by them in the course of the transitional period under the conditions laid down in arts. 14 and 15.
(2) Charges in force between Member States having an effect equivalent to customs duties on importation shall be progressively abolished by them in the course of the transitional period. The Commission shall, by means of directives, fix the timing of such abolition. It shall be guided by the rules mentioned in art. 14, par. 2 and 3, and by the directives issued by the Council in application of the said par. 2.

Art. 14.(1) In respect of each product, the basic duty which shall be subject to the successive reductions shall be the duty applied on 1 January 1957.
(2) The timing of the reductions shall be as follows:
(a) in the course of the first stage, the first reduction shall be made one year after the date of the entry into force of this Treaty; the second reduction shall be made eighteen months later; the third, at the end of the fourth year after the date of the entry into force of this Treaty;
(b) in the course of the second stage, a reduction shall be made eighteen months after the beginning of that stage; a second reduction, eighteen months after the preceding one; a third reduction shall be made one year later; and
(c) the reductions which still remain to be made shall be carried out in the course of the third stage; the Council, acting by means of a qualified majority vote on a proposal of the Commission, shall fix their timing by means of directives.
(3) At the time of the first reduction, Member States shall, in respect of each product, bring into force as between themselves a duty equal to the basic duty less 10 per cent. At the time of each subsequent reduction, each Member State shall reduce the total of the duties in such a way as to reduce by 10 per cent its total customs receipt as defined in par. 4, it being understood that the reduction in the case of each product shall be equal to at least 5 per cent of the basic duty.
In respect of products, however, on which a duty of more than 30 per cent would still remain, each reduction shall be equal to not less than 10 per cent of the basic duty.
In respect of products, however, on which a duty of more than 30 per cent would still remain, each reduction shall be equal to not less than 10 per cent of the basic duty.
(4) The total customs recipts of each Member State, referred to in par. 3, shall be calculated by multiplying by the basic duties the value of its imports coming from other Member States during the year 1958.
(5) Any special problems raised by the application of the preceding pars. shall be settled by directives issued by the Council acting by means of a qualified majority vote on a proposal of the Commission.
(6) Member States shall report to the Commission as to the manner in which the preceding rules for the reduction of duties are applied. They shall endeavour to ensure that the reduction applied to the duties on each product shall amount:
– at the end of the first stage to at least 25 per cent of the basic duty; and
– at the end of the second stage to at least 50 per cent of the basic duty.
If the Commission finds that there is a danger that the objectives laid down in art. 13 and the percentages fixed in this par. may not be achieved, it shall make any appropriate recommendations to the Member States.
(7) The provisions of this Art. may be amended by the Council acting by means of a unanimous vote on a proposal of the Commission and after the Assembly has been consulted.

Art. 15.(1) Independently of the provisions of art. 14, any Member State may, in the course of the transitional period, suspend in whole or in part the collection of the duties applied by it to products imported from other Member States. It shall inform the other Member States and the Commission thereof.
(2) Member States hereby declare their willingness to reduce their customs duties in regard to other Member States more rapidly than provided for in art. 14 if their general economic situation and the situation of the sector concerned so permit.
The Commission shall make recommendations for this purpose to the Member States concerned.

Art. 16. Member States shall abolish as between themselves, not later than at the end of the first stage, the customs duties on exportation and charges with equivalent effect.

Art. 17.(1) The provisions of arts. 9 to 15, par. 1, shall also apply to customs duties of a fiscal nature. Such duties shall not, however, be taken into consideration for the purpose of calculating either total customs

receipts or the reduction in total duties referred to in art. 14, pars. 3 and 4.
Such duties shall, at each reduction, be lowered by not less than 10 per cent of the basic duty. Member States may reduce their duties more rapidly than is provided for in art. 14.
(2) Member States shall, before the end of the first year after the entry into force of this Treaty, inform the Commission of their customs duties of a fiscal nature.
(3) Member States shall retain the right to substitute for these duties an internal tax in accordance with the provisions of art. 95.
(4) Where the Commission finds that in any Member State the substitution of such duty meets with serious difficulties, it shall authorise such State to retain the said duty provided that the State concerned shall abolish it not later than six years after the date of the entry into force of this Treaty. Such authorisation shall be requested before the end of the first year after the date of the entry into force of this Treaty.
Section 2 Establishment of the Common Customs Tariff
Art. 18. Member States hereby declare their willingness to contribute to the development of international commerce and the reduction of barriers to trade by entering into reciprocal and mutually advantageous arrangements directed to the reduction of customs duties below the general level which they could claim as a result of the establishment of a customs union between themselves.
Art. 19.(1) Under the conditions and within the limits laid down below, the duties under the common customs tariff shall be at the level of the arithmetical average of the duties applied in the four customs territories covered by the Community.
(2) The duties taken into account for calculating this average shall be those applied by Member States on 1 January 1957.
In the case of the Italian tariff, however, the duty applied shall be understood as being that levied before the temporary 10 per cent reduction. Furthermore, in the case of tariff headings in regard to which this tariff contains a conventional duty, this duty shall be substituted for the duty applied as defined above, provided that it does not exceed the latter by more than 10 per cent. If the conventional duty exceeds the applied duty as defined above by more than 10 per cent, the latter duty, increased by 10 per cent, shall be taken into account for calculating the arithmetical average.
With regard to the tariff headings contained in List A, the duties shown in that List shall, for the purpose of calculating the arithmetical average, be substituted for the duties applied.
(3) The duties under the common customs tariff shall not exceed:
(a) 3 per cent in the case of products coming under the tariff headings mentioned in List B;
(b) 10 per cent in the case of products coming under the tariff headings mentioned in List C;
(c) 15 per cent in the case of products coming under the tariff headings mentioned in List D; and
(d) 25 per cent in the case of products coming under the tariff headings mentioned in List E; where, in respect of such products, the tariff of the Benelux countries contains a duty of not more than 3 per cent, such duty shall, for the purpose of calculating the arithmetical average, be raised to 12 per cent.
(4) The duties applicable to products mentioned in List F shall be those laid down therein.
(5) The Lists of tariff headings referred to in this Art. and in art. 20 shall be set out in Annex I to this Treaty.
Art. 20. The duties applicable to the products in List G shall be fixed by means of negotiation between the Member States. Each Member State may add further products to this List up to the limit of 2 per cent of the total value of its imports coming from third countries in the course of the year 1956.
The Commission shall take all appropriate steps in order that such negotiations shall be undertaken before the end of the second year after the date of the entry into force of this Treaty and concluded before the end of the first stage.
If, in the case of certain products, no agreement can be reached within these time-limits, the Council, acting up to the end of the second stage by means of a unanimous vote and subsequently by means of a qualified majority vote on a proposal of the Commission, shall fix the duties under the common customs tariff.
Art. 21.(1) Any technical difficulties which may arise in the application of arts. 19 and 20 shall be settled, within a period of two years after the date of the entry into force of this Treaty, by directives issued by the Council acting by means of a qualified majority vote on a proposal of the Commission.
(2) Before the end of the first stage and, in any case, not later than at the date of the fixing of such duties, the Council, acting by means of a qualified majority vote on a proposal of the Commission, shall decide as to the adjustments required with a view to ensuring the internal harmony of the common customs tariff following the application of the rules laid down in arts. 19 and 20, particular account being taken of the degree of processing undergone by the various goods to which the common tariff applies.
Art. 22. The Commission shall, within a period of two years after the date of the entry into force of this Treaty, determine the extent to which the customs duties of a fiscal nature mentioned in art. 17, par. 2, shall be taken into account for calculating the arithmetical average referred to in art. 19, par. 1. The Commission shall take due account of the protective aspect of such duties.
Within a period of not more than six months after the Commission has so determined, any Member State may request that the procedure provided for in art. 20 shall be applied to the product concerned; the limit prescribed in that article. shall not constitute a valid objection.
Art. 23.(1) For the purpose of the progressive introduction of the common customs tariff, Member States shall amend their duties applicable to third countries in the following manner:
(a) in the case of tariff headings on which the duties in fact applied on 1 January 1957 do not differ by more than 15 per cent in either direction from the duties under the common customs tariff, the latter duties shall be applied at the end of the fourth year after the date of the entry into force of this Treaty;
(b) in the case of the other tariff headings, each Member State shall, as from the same date, apply a duty which reduces by 30 per cent the difference between the duty in fact applied on 1 January 1957 and that under the common customs tariff;
(c) at the end of the second stage this difference shall again be reduced by 30 per cent; and
(d) in the case of tariff headings for which the duties under the common customs tariff are not yet known at the end of the first stage, each Member State shall, within a period of six months after the Council has acted in accordance with the provisions of art. 20, apply such duties as shall result from the application of the rules contained in this par.
(2) Any Member State, which has been granted the authorisation provided for in art. 17, par. 4, shall for as long as that authorisation is valid, be exempted from applying the preceding provisions to the tariff headings covered by the authorisation. At the expiry of such authorisation, the Member State concerned shall apply such duty as would result from the application of the rules contained in the preceding par.
(3) The common customs tariff shall be applied in its entirety not later than at the date of the expiry of the transitional period.
Art. 24. With a view to aligning their duties with the common customs tariff, Member States shall be free to modify these duties more rapidly than is provided for in art. 23.
Art. 25(1) If the Commission finds that the production in the Member States of certain products contained in Lists B, C and D is not sufficient to supply the demands of one of them and that such supply traditionally depends to a considerable extent upon imports coming from third countries, the Council, acting by means of a qualified majority vote on a proposal of the Commission, shall grant to the Member State concerned tariff quotas at a reduced rate of duty or duty free.
Such quotas may not exceed the limits beyond which the transfer of activities to the detriment of other Member States is to be feared.
(2) In respect of the products in List E and those in List G for which the duties shall have been fixed in accordance with the procedure provided for in art. 20, third par., the Commission shall, at the request of any Member State concerned, grant to such State tariff quotas at a reduced rate of duty or duty free, where a change in sources of supply or a shortage of supplies within the Community is of such a nature as to entail harmful consequences for the processing industries of the Member State concerned. Such quotas may not exceed the limits beyond which the transfer of activities to the detriment of other Member States is to be feared.
(3) In respect of the products listed in Annex II to this Treaty, the Commission may authorise any Member State to suspend, in whole or in part, the collection of the duties applicable or may grant to such Member State tariff quotas at a reduced rate or duty free, provided that no serious disturbance in the market or the products concerned may result therefrom.
(4) The Commission shall periodically examine any tariff quotas granted in application of this article.
Art. 26. The Commission may authorise any Member State encountering special difficulties to postpone the lowering or the raising, in accordance with the provisions of art. 23, of the duties on certain headings of its tariff. Such authorisation may only be granted for a limited period and for tariff headings which together represent for such State not more than 5 per cent of the value of its total imports coming from third countries in the course of the latest year for which statistical data are available.
Art. 27. Before the end of the first stage, Member States shall, in so far as may be necessary, take steps to approximate their legislative and administrative provisions in regard to customs matters. The Commission shall for this purpose make all appropriate recommendations to Member States.
Art. 28. Any autonomous modificaton or suspension of duties of the common customs tariff shall be decided upon by the Council acting by means of a unanimous vote. After the expiry of the transitional period, the Council, acting by means of a qualified majority vote on a proposal of the Commission, may, however, decide upon modifications or suspensions not exceeding 20 per cent of the rate of any duty and effective for a maximum period of six months. Such modifications or suspensions may only be extended, under the same conditions, for a second period of six months.
Art. 29. In carrying out the tasks entrusted to it under this Section, the Commission shall be guided by:
(a) the need for promoting commercial exchanges between the Member States and third countries;
(b) the development of competitive conditions within the Community to the extent to which such development will result in the increase of the competitive capacity of the enterprises;
(c) the Community's requirements of supply in raw materials and semi-finished goods, while at the same time taking care not to distort competitive conditions between Member States with regard to finished goods; and
(d) the need for avoiding serious disturbances in the economic life of Member States and for ensuring a rational development of production and an expansion of consumption within the Community.
Chapter 2 The Elimination of Quantitative Restrictions as between Member States.
Art. 30. Quantitative restrictions on importation and all measures with equivalent effect shall, without prejudice to the following provisions, hereby be prohibited between Member States.
Art. 31. Member States shall refrain from introducing as between themselves any new quantitative restrictions or measures with equivalent effect.
This obligation shall, however, only apply to the level of liberalisation attained in application of the decisions of the Council of the Organization for European Economic Co-operation of January 14, 1955. Member States shall communicate to the Commission, not later than six months after the date of the entry into force of this Treaty, the lists of the products liberalised by them in application of these decisions. The lists thus communicated shall be consolidated between Member States.
Art. 32. Member States shall, in their mutual trade, refrain from making more restrictive the quotas or measures with equivalent effect in existence at the date of the entry into force of this Treaty.
Such quotas shall be abolished not later than at the date of the expiry of the transitional period. In the course of this period, they shall be progressively abolished under the conditions specified below.
Art. 33.(1) Each of the Member States shall, at the end of one year after the entry into force of this Treaty, convert any bilateral quotas granted to other Member

States into global quotas open, without discrimination, to all other Member States.

On the same date, Member States shall enlarge the whole of the global quotas so established in such a way as to attain an increase of not less than 20 per cent in their total value as compared with the preceding year. Each global quota for each product shall, however, be increased by not less than 10 per cent.

The quotas shall be increased annually in accordance with the same rules and in the same proportions in relation to the preceding year.

The fourth increase shall take place at the end of the fourth year after the date of the entry into force of this Treaty; the fifth increase shall take place at the end of a period of one year after the beginning of the second stage.

(2) Where, in the case of a product which has not been liberalised, the global quota does not amount to 3 per cent of the national output of the State concerned, a quota equal to not less than 3 per cent of such output shall be established not later than one year after the date of the entry into force of this Treaty. At the end of the second year, this quota shall be raised to 4 per cent and at the end of the third year to 5 per cent. Thereafter, the Member State concerned shall increase the quota by not less than 15 per cent annually.

In the case where there is no such national output, the Commission shall fix an appropriate quota by means of a decision.

(3) At the end of the tenth year, each quota shall be equal to not less than 20 per cent of the national output.

(4) Where the Commission, acting by means of a decision, finds that in the course of two successive years the imports of any products have been below the level of the quota granted, this global quota may not be taken into consideration for the purpose of calculating the total value of the global quotas. In such case, the Member State shall abolish the quota for the product concerned.

(5) In the case of quotas representing more than 20 per cent of the national output of the product concerned, the Council, acting by means of a qualified majority vote on a proposal of the Commission, may reduce the minimum percentage of 10 per cent laid down in par. 1. This modification shall not, however, affect the obligation annually to increase the total value of global quotas by 20 per cent.

(6) Member States which have gone beyond their obligations concerning the level of liberalisation attained in implementation of the decisions of the Council of the Organization for European Economic Co-operation of January 14, 1955 shall, when calculating the annual total increase of 20 per cent provided for in par. 1, be entitled to take into account the amount of imports liberalised by autonomous measures. Such calculations shall be submitted to the Commission for its prior approval.

(7) Directives issued by the Commission shall lay down the procedure and the timing according to which Member States shall abolish as between themselves any measures which exist at the date of the entry into force of this Treaty and which have an effect equivalent to quotas.

(8) If the Commission finds that the application of the provisions of this article and, in particular, of the provisions concerning percentages does not make it possible to ensure the progressive nature of the abolition of quotas provided for in Art. 32, second par., the Council, acting during the first stage by means of a unanimous vote and subsequently by means of a qualified majority vote on a proposal of the Commission, may amend the procedure referred to in this article and may, in particular, raise the percentages fixed.

Art. 34.(1) Quantitative restrictions on exportation and any measures with equivalent effect shall hereby be prohibited as between Member States.

(2) Member States shall abolish, not later than at the end of the first stage, all quantitative restrictions on exportation and any measures with equivalent effect in existence at the date of the entry into force of this Treaty.

Art. 35. Member States hereby declare their willingness to abolish, in relation to other Member States, their quantitative restrictions on importation and exportation more rapidly than is provided for in the preceding articles, if their general economic situation and the situation of the sector concerned so permit.

The Commission shall make recommendations for this purpose to the States concerned.

Art. 36. The provisions of arts. 30 to 34 inclusive shall not be an obstacle to prohibitions or restrictions in respect of importation, exportation or transit which are justified on grounds of public morality, public order, public safety, the protection of human or animal life or health, the preservation of plant life, the protection of national treasures of artistic, historical or archeological value or the protection of industrial and commercial property. Such prohibitions or restrictions shall not, however, constitute either a means of arbitrary discrimination or a disguised restriction on trade between Member States.

Art. 37.(1) Member States shall progressively adjust any State monopolies of a commercial character in such a manner as will ensure the exclusion, at the date of the expiry of the transitional period, of all discrimination between the nationals of Member States in regard to conditions of supply or marketing of goods.

The provisions of this articles shall apply to any body by means of which a Member State shall *de jure* or *de facto* either directly or indirectly control, direct or appreciably influence importation or exportation between Member States. These provisions shall apply also to monopolies by the State.

(2) Member States shall abstain from any new measure which is contrary to the principles laid down in par. 1 or which may limit the scope of the Arts. relating to the abolition, as between Member States, of customs duties and quantitative restrictions.

(3) The timing of the measures referred to in par. 1 shall be adapted to the abolition, as provided for in arts. 30 to 34 inclusive, of the quantitative restrictions on the same products.

In cases where a product is subject to a State monopoly of a commercial character in one Member State or certain Member States only, the Commission may authorize the other Member States to apply, for as long as the adjustment referred to in par. 1 has not been carried out, measures of safeguard of which it shall determine the conditions and particulars.

(4) In the case of a monopoly of a commercial character which is accompanied by regulations designed to facilitate the marketing or the valorisation of agricultural products, it should be ensured that in the application of the rules of this art. equivalent guarantees are provided in respect of the employment and standard of living of the producers concerned, due account taken of the timing in respect of possible adjustments and of necessary specializations.

(5) The obligations incumbent on Member States shall be binding only to such extent as they are compatible with existing international agreements.

(6) The Commission shall, as soon as the first stage has begun, make recommendations as to the particulars and the timing according to which the adjustments referred to in this article shall be carried out.

Title II Agriculture

Art. 38.(1) The Common Market shall extend to agriculture and trade in agricultural products. Agricultural products shall mean the products of the soil, of stockbreeding and of fisheries as well as products after the first processing stage which are directly connected with such products.

(2) Save where there are provisions to the contrary in arts. 39 to 46 inclusive, the rules laid down for the establishment of the Common Market shall apply to agricultural products.

(3) Products subject to the provisions of arts. 39 to 46 inclusive are listed in Annex II to this Treaty. Within a period of two years after the date of the entry into force of this Treaty the Council, acting by means of a qualified majority vote on a proposal of the Commission, shall decide as to the products to be added to that list.

(4) The functioning and development of the Common Market in respect of agricultural products shall be accompanied by the establishment of a common agricultural policy among the Member States.

Art. 39.(1) The common agricultural policy shall have as its objectives:

(a) to increase agricultural productivity by developing technical progress and by ensuring the rational development of agricultural production and the optimum utilization of the factors of production, particularly labour;

(b) to ensure thereby a fair standard of living for the agricultural population, particularly by the increasing of the individual earnings of persons engaged in agriculture;

(c) to stabilize markets;

(d) to guarantee regular supplies; and

(e) to ensure reasonable prices in supplies to consumers.

(2) In working out the common agricultural policy and the special methods which it may involve, due account shall be taken of:

(a) the particular character of agricultural activities, arising from the social structure of agriculture and from structural and natural disparities between the various agricultural regions;

(b) the need to make the appropriate adjustments gradually; and

(c) the fact that in Member States agriculture constitutes a sector which is closely linked with the economy as a whole.

Art. 40.(1) Member States shall gradually develop the common agricultural policy during the transitional period and shall establish it not later than at the end of that period.

(2) With a view to achieving the objectives set out in art. 39, a common organization of agricultural markets shall be effected.

This organization shall take one of the following forms according to the products concerned:

(a) common rules concerning competition;

(b) compulsory co-ordination of the various national market organizations; or

(c) a European market organization.

(3) The common organization in one of the forms mentioned in par. 2 may compromise all measures necessary to achieve the objectives set out in art. 39, in particular, price controls, subsidies as to the production and marketing of various products, arrangements for stockpiling and carryforward, and common machinery for stabilizing importation or exportation.

The organization shall confine itself to pursuing the objectives set out in art. 39 and shall exclude any discrimination between producers or consumers within the Community.

A common price policy, if any, shall be based on common criteria and on uniform methods of calculation.

(4) In order to enable the common organization referred to in par. 2 to achieve its objectives, one or more agricultural orientation and guarantee funds may be established.

Art. 41. In order to permit the achievement of the objectives set out in art. 39, provisions may be made within the framework of the common agricultural policy for, inter alia:

(a) an effective co-ordination of efforts undertaken in the spheres of occupational training, research and the popularization of rural economy, which may involve projects or institutions jointly; and

(b) common action for the development of the consumption of certain products.

Art. 42. The provisions of the Chapter relating to the rules of competition shall apply to the production of and trade in agricultural products, only to the extent determined by the Council within the framework of the provisions and in accordance with the procedure laid down in art. 43, pars. 2 and 3, due account being taken of the objectives mentioned in art. 39.

The Council may, in particular, authorise the granting of aids:

(a) for the protection of enterprises handicapped by structural or natural conditions; and

(b) within the framework of economic development programmes.

Art. 43.(1) In order to formulate the guiding lines of a common agricultural policy, the Commission shall, upon the date of the entry into force of this Treaty, convene a conference of Member States, with a view to comparing their agricultural policies by drawing up, in particular, a statement of their resources and needs.

(2) The Commission, taking due account of the work of the conference provided for in par. 1, shall, after consulting the Economic and Social Committee and within a period of two years after the date of the entry into force of this Treaty, submit proposals concerning the working out and putting into effect of the common agricultural policy, including the substitution of national organizations by one of the forms of common

organization provided for in art. 40, par. 2, as well as concerning the putting into effect of the measures specially mentioned under this Title.

These proposals shall take due account of the interdependence of the agricultural questions raised under this Title.

The Council, acting during the first two stages by means of a unanimous vote and subsequently by means of a qualified majority vote on a proposal of the Commission and after the Assembly has been consulted, shall issue regulations of directives or take decisions, without prejudice to any recommendations which it may make.

(3) The common organization provided for in art. 40, par. 2, may, under the conditions provided for in the preceding par., be substituted for national market organizations by the Council acting by means of a qualified majority vote:

(a) if the common organization offers to Member States which are opposed to this measure and which possess a national organization of their own for the production concerned, equivalent guarantees regarding the employment and standard of living of the producers concerned, due account being taken of the time-factor in respect of possible adjustments and of necessary specializations; and

(b) if such organization ensures for exchanges within the Community conditions similar to those existing in a domestic market.

(4) If a common organization is created for certain raw materials at a time when no common organization yet exists for the corresponding processed products, the raw materials concerned which are used for processed products destined for export to third countries may be imported from outside the Community.

Art. 44.(1) In the course of the transitional period and to the extent that the progressive abolition of customs duties and quantitative restrictions between Member States may result in prices likely to jeopardise the achievement of the objectives set out in art. 39, each Member State shall be permitted to apply to certain products, in a non-discriminatory manner and in substitution for quotas, to such an extent as shall not impede the expansion of the volume of trade provided for in art. 45, par. 2, a system of minimum prices below which imports may be:

– temporarily suspended or reduced; or

– made conditional on their price being above the minimum price fixed for the product concerned.

In the second case, the minimum prices shall not include customs duties.

(2) The minimum prices shall not be such as to lead to a reduction of exchanges existing between Member States at the date of the entry into force of this Treaty and shall not be an obstacle to a progressive expansion of such exchanges. The minimum prices shall not be applied in such a manner as to be an obstacle to the development of a natural preference between the Member States.

(3) Upon the entry into force of this Treaty, the Council, acting on a proposal of the Commission, shall determine objective criteria for the establishment of minimum price systems and for the fixing of such prices. The criteria shall, in particular, take account of average national costs of production in the Member State applying the minimum price, of the situation of the various enterprises in relation to such costs and of the need for promoting both the progressive improvement of agricultural operations and the adjustments and specializations necessary within the Common Market. The Commission shall also propose a procedure for revision of these criteria in order to take into account and accelerate technical progress and in order progressively to approximate prices within the Common Market.

These criteria and the procedure for revision shall be determined by means of a unanimous vote of the Council in the course of the first three years after the date of the entry into force of this Treaty.

(4) Until the Council's decision takes effect, Member States may fix minimum prices on condition that they previously communicate them to the Commission and to the other Member States in order to enable them to submit their comments. As soon as the Council has taken its decision, Member States shall fix minimum prices on the basis of the criteria established under the conditions mentioned above.

The Council, acting by means of a qualified majority vote on a proposal of the Commission, may correct the decisions taken if they do not conform to the criteria so determined.

(5) From the beginning of the third stage and in cases where it has not yet been possible in respect of certain products to establish the above objective criteria, the Council, acting by means of a qualified majority vote on a proposal of the Commission, may modify the minimum prices applied to these products.

(6) At the expiry of the transitional period, a table of minimum prices still in force shall be drawn up. The Council, acting on a proposal of the Commission by means of a majority of nine votes in accordance with the weighting provided for in art. 148, par. 2, first subpar., shall determine the system to be applied within the framework of the common agricultural policy.

Art. 45.(1) Until the substitution of the national organization by one of the forms of common organization provided for in art. 40, par. 2, the development of exchanges in respect of products for which there exist in certain Member States:

– provisions designed to guarantee to national producers a sale of their production, and

– a need of imports,

shall be pursued by the conclusion of long-term agreements or contracts between exporting and importing Member States.

Such agreements or contracts shall be directed towards the progressive abolition of any discrimination in the application of these provisions to the various producers within the Community.

The conclusion of such agreements or contracts shall take place in the course of the first stage; due account shall be taken of the principle of reciprocity.

(2) With regard to quantities, such agreements or contracts shall take as their basis the average volume of exchanges between Member States in the products concerned during the three years preceding the date of the entry into force of this Treaty and shall provide for an increase in that volume within the limit of existing requirements, due account being taken of traditional trade currents.

With regard to prices, such agreements or contracts shall enable producers to dispose of the agreed quantities at prices progressively approximating to those paid to national producers in the home market of the purchasing country. This approximating of prices shall proceed as steadily as possible and shall be completed not later than at the end of the transitional period.

Prices shall be negotiated between the parties concerned within the framework of directives drawn up by the Commission for the implementation of the preceding two sub-pars.

In the event of the first stage being extended, such agreements or contracts shall continue to be carried out under the conditions applicable at the end of the fourth year after the date of the entry into force of this Treaty, while the obligations to increase quantities and to approximate prices shall be suspended until entry on the second stage. Member States shall avail themselves of any possibilities offered to them as a result of their legislative provisions, particularly as regards import policy, with a view to ensuring the conclusion and carrying out of these agreements or contracts.

(3) To the extent that Member States require raw materials for the production of goods destined for export outside the Community in competition with producers in third countries, such agreements or contracts shall not be an obstacle to imports, for this purpose, of raw materials coming from third countries. This provision shall not apply if the Council decides by means of a unanimous vote to grant the payments necessary to compensate, in respect of imports effected for this purpose on the basis of such agreements or contracts, for the excess price paid in comparison with the delivery prices of the same supplies obtained on the world market.

Art. 46. Where in a Member State a product is the object of a national market organization or of any internal regulation with equivalent effect, either of which affects the competitive position of a similar production in another Member State, a countervailing charge on entry shall be applied by Member States in this product when it comes from the Member State where such organization or regulation exists, unless that State levies a countervailing charge on exit.

The Commission shall fix the amount of these charges, to the extent necessary to re-establish the balance; it may also authorise recourse to other measures of which it shall determine the conditions and particulars.

Art. 47. With regard to the functions of the Economic and Social Committee in the application of this Title, its agriculture section shall be at the disposal of the Commission with a view to preparing the conclusions of the Committee in accordance with the provisions of arts. 197 and 198.

Title III   The free movement of persons, services and capital
Chapter 1   Workers

Art. 48.(1) The free movement of workers shall be ensured within the Community not later than at the date of the expiry of the transitional period.

(2) This shall involve the abolition of any discrimination based on nationality between workers of the Member States as regards employment, remuneration and other working conditions.

(3) It shall include the right, subject to limitations justified by reasons of public order, public safety and public health:

(a) to accept offers of employment actually made;

(b) to move about freely for this purpose within the territory of Member States;

(c) to stay in any Member State in order to carry on an employment in conformity with the legislative and administrative provisions governing the employment of the workers of that State; and

(d) to live, on conditions which shall be the subject of implementing regulations to be laid down by the Commission, in the territory of a Member State after having been employed there.

(4) The provisions of this Art. shall not apply to employment in the public administration.

Art. 49. Upon the entry into force of this Treaty, the Council, acting on a proposal of the Commission and after the Economic and Social Committee has been consulted, shall, by means of directives or regulations, lay down the measures necessary to effect progressively the free movement of workers, as defined in the preceding Art., in particular:

(a) by ensuring close collaboration between national labour administrations;

(b) by progressively abolishing according to a plan any such administrative procedures and practices and also any such time-limits in respect of eligibility for available employment as are applied as a result either of municipal law or of agreements previously concluded between Member States and the maintenance of which would be an obstacle to the freeing of the movement of workers;

(c) by progressively abolishing according to a plan all such time-limits and other restrictions provided for either under municipal law or under agreements previously concluded between Member States as impose on workers of other Member States conditions for the free choice of employment different from those imposed on workers of the State concerned; and

(d) by setting up appropriate machinery for connecting offers of employment and requests for employment, with a view to equilibrating them in such a way as to avoid serious threats to the standard of living and employment in the various regions and industries.

Art. 50. Member States shall, under a common programme, encourage the exchange of young workers.

Art. 51. The Council, acting by means of a unanimous vote on a proposal of the Commission, shall, in the field of social security, adopt the measures necessary to effect the free movement of workers, in particular, by introducing a system which permits an assurance to be given to migrant workers and their beneficiaries:

(a) that, for the purposes of qualifying for and retaining the right to benefits and of the calculation of these benefits, all periods taken into consideration by the respective municipal law of the countries concerned, shall be added together; and

(b) that these benefits will be paid to persons resident in the territories of Member States.

Chapter 2 The right of establishment

Art. 52. Within the framework of the provisions set out below, restrictions on the freedom of establishment of nationals of a Member State in the territory of another Member State shall be progressively abolished in the course of the transitional period. Such progressive abolition shall also extend to restrictions on the setting up of agencies, branches or subsidiaries by nationals of any Member State established in the territory of any Member State.

Freedom of establishment shall include the right to engage in and carry on non-wage-earning activities, and also to set up and manage enterprises and, in particular, companies within the meaning of art. 58, second par., under the conditions laid down by the law of the country of establishment for its own nationals, subject to the provisions of the Chapter relating to capital.

Art. 53. Member States shall not, subject to the provisions of this Treaty, introduce any new restrictions on the establishment in their territories of nationals of other Member States.

Art. 54.(1) Before the expiry of the first stage, the Council, acting by means of a unanimous vote on a proposal of the Commission and after the Economic and Social Committee and the Assembly have been consulted, shall lay down a general programme for the abolition of restrictions existing within the Community on freedom of establishment. The Commission shall submit such proposal to the Council in the course of the first two years of the first stage.

The programme shall, in respect of each category of activities, fix the general conditions for achieving freedom of establishment and, in particular, the stages by which it shall be attained.

(2) In order to implement the general programme or, if no such programme exists, to complete one stage towards the achievement of freedom of establishment for a specific activity, the Council, on a proposal of the Commission and after the Economic and Social Committee and the Assembly have been consulted, shall, until the end of the first stage by means of a unanimous vote and subsequently by means of a qualified majority vote, act by issuing directives.

(3) The Council and the Commission shall exercise the functions entrusted to them by the above provisions, in particular:

(a) by according, as a general rule, priority treatment to activities in regard to which freedom of establishment constitutes a specially valuable contribution to the development of production and trade;

(b) by ensuring close collaboration between the competent national authorities with a view to ascertaining the special situation within the Community of the various activities concerned;

(c) by abolishing any such administrative procedures and practice whether resulting from municipal law or from agreements previously concluded between Member States as would if maintained, be an obstacle to freedom of establishment;

(d) by ensuring that wage-earning workers of one Member State employed in the territory of another Member State may remain in that territory for the purpose of undertaking a non-wage-earning activity there, provided that they satisfy the conditions which they would be required to satisfy if they came to that State at the time when they wish to engage in such activity;

(e) by enabling a national of one Member State to acquire and exploit real property situated in the territory of another Member State, to the extent that no infringement of the principles laid down in art. 39, par. 2 is thereby caused;

(f) by applying the progressive abolition of restrictions on freedom of establishment, in each branch of activity under consideration, both in respect of the conditions for setting up agencies, branches or subsidiaries in the territory of a Member State and in respect of the conditions governing the entry of personnel of the main establishment into the managerial or supervisory organs of such agencies, branches and subsidiaries;

(g) by co-ordinating, to the extent that is necessary and with a view to making them equivalent, the guarantees demanded in Member States from companies within the meaning of art. 58, second par., for the purpose of protecting the interests both of the members of such companies and of third parties; and

(h) by satisfying themselves that conditions of establishment shall not be impaired by any aids granted by Member States.

Art. 55. Activities which in any State include, even incidentally, the exercise of public authority shall, in so far as that State is concerned, be excluded from the application of the provisions of this Chapter.

The Council, acting by means of a qualified majority vote on a proposal of the Commission, may exclude certain activities from the application of the provisions of this Chapter.

Art. 56.(1) The provisions of this Chapter and the measures taken in pursuance thereof shall not prejudice the applicability of legislative and administrative provisions which lay down special treatment for foreign nationals and which are justified by reasons of public order, public safety and public health.

(2) Before the expiry of the transitional period, the Council, acting by means of a unanimous vote on a proposal of the Commission and after the Assembly has been consulted, shall issue directives for the co-ordination of the above-mentioned legislative and administrative provisions. After the end of the second stage, however, the Council, acting by means of a qualified majority vote on a proposal of the Commission, shall issue directives for co-ordinating such provisions as, in each Member State, fall within the administrative field.

Art. 57.(1) In order to facilitate the engagement in and exercise of non-wage-earning activities, the Council, on a proposal of the Commission and after the Assembly has been consulted, shall, in the course of the first stage by means of a unanimous vote and subsequently by means of a qualified majority vote, act by issuing directives regarding mutual recognition of diplomas, certificates and other qualifications.

(2) For the same purpose, the Council, acting on a proposal of the Commission and after the Assembly has been consulted, shall, before the expiry of the transitional period, issue directives regarding the co-ordination of legislative and administrative provisions of Member States concerning the engagement in and exercise of non-wage-earning activities. A unanimous vote shall be required on matters which, in at least one Member State, are subject to legislative provisions, and on measures concerning the protection of savings, in particular the allotment of credit and the banking profession, and concerning the conditions governing the exercise in the various Member States of the medical, para-medical and pharmaceutical professions. In all other cases, the Council shall act in the course of the first stage by means of a unanimous vote and subsequently by means of a qualified majority vote.

(3) In the case of the medical, para-medical and pharmaceutical professions, the progressive removal of restrictions shall be subject to the co-ordination of conditions for their exercise in the various Member-States.

Art. 58. Companies constituted in accordance with the law of a Member State and having their registered office, central management or main establishment within the Community shall, for the purpose of applying the provisions of this Chapter, be assimilated to natural persons being nationals of Member States.

The term 'companies' shall mean companies under civil or commercial law including co-operative companies and other legal persons under public or private law, with the exception of non-profit-making companies.

Chapter 3   Services

Art. 59. Within the framework of the provisions set out below, restrictions on the free supply of services within the Community shall be progressively abolished in the course of the transitional period in respect of nationals of Member States who are established in a State of the Community other than that of the person to whom the services are supplied.

The Council, acting by means of a unanimous vote on a proposal of the Commission, may extend the benefit of the provisions of this Chapter to cover services supplied by nationals of any third country who are established within the Community.

Art. 60. Services within the meaning of this Treaty shall be deemed to be services normally supplied for remuneration, to the extent that they are not governed by the provisions relating to the free movement of goods, capital and persons.

Services shall include in particular:

(a) activities of an industrial character;

(b) activities of a commercial character;

(c) artisan activities; and

(d) activities of the liberal professions.

Without prejudice to the provisions of the Chapter relating to the right of establishment, a person supplying a service may, in order to carry out that service, temporarily exercise his activity in the State where the service is supplied, under the same conditions as are imposed by that State on its own nationals.

Art. 61.(1) The free movement of services in respect of transport shall be governed by the provisions of the Title relating to transport.

(2) The liberalization of banking and insurance services connected with movements of capital shall be effected in harmony with the progressive liberalization of the movement of capital.

Art. 62. Except where otherwise provided for in this Treaty, Member States shall not introduce any new restrictions on the freedom which has been in fact achieved, in regard to the supply of services, at the date of the entry into force of this Treaty.

Art. 63.(1) Before the end of this first stage, the Council, acting by means of a unanimous vote on a proposal of the Commission and after the Economic and Social Committee and the Assembly have been consulted, shall lay down a general programme for the abolition of restrictions existing within the Community on the free supply of services. The Commission shall submit such proposal to the Council in the course of the first two years of the first stage.

The programme shall, for each category of services, fix the general conditions and the stages of such liberalization.

(2) In order to implement the general programme or, if no such programme exists, to complete one stage in the liberalization of a specific service, the Council, on a proposal of the Commission and after the Economic and Social Committee and the Assembly have been consulted, shall, before the end of the first stage by means of a unanimous vote and subsequently by means of a qualified majority vote, act by issuing directives.

(3) The proposals and decisions referred to in pars. 1 and 2 shall, as a general rule, accord priority to services which directly affect production costs or the liberalization of which contributes to facilitating the exchange of goods.

Art. 64. Member States hereby declare their willingness to undertake the liberalization of services beyond the extent required by the directives issued in application of art. 63, par. 2, if their general economic situation and the situation of the sector concerned so permit.

The Commission shall make recommendations to this effect to the Member States concerned.

Art. 65. As long as the abolition of restrictions on the free supply of services has not been effected, each Member State shall apply such restrictions without distinction on grounds of nationality or residence to all persons within the meaning of art. 59, first par., who supply services.

Art. 66. The provisions of arts. 55 to 58 inclusive shall apply to the matters governed by this Chapter.

Chapter 4   Capital

Art. 67.(1) Member States shall, in the course of the transitional period and to the extent necessary for the proper functioning of the Common Market, progressively abolish as between themselves restrictions on the movement of capital belonging to persons resident in Member States and also any discriminatory treatment based on the nationality or place of residence of the parties or on the place in which such capital is invested.

(2) Current payments connected with movements of capital between Member States shall be freed from all restrictions not later than at the end of the first stage.

Art. 68.(1) Member States shall, in respect of the matters referred to in this Chapter, grant in the most liberal manner possible such exchange authorization as are still necessary after the date of the entry into force of this Treaty.

(2) Where a Member State applies its domestic provisions in respect of the capital market and credit system to the movement of capital freed in accordance with the provisions of this Chapter, it shall do so in a non-discriminatory manner.

(3) Loans intended for the direct or indirect financing of a Member State or of its territorial sub-divisions may not be issued or placed in other Member States save when the States concerned have reached agreement in this respect. This provision shall not be an obstacle to the implementation of art. 22 of the Protocol on the Statute of the European Investment Bank.

Art. 69. The Council, acting on a proposal of the Commission which for this purpose shall consult the Monetary Committee provided for in art. 105, shall, in the course of the first two stages by means of a unanimous vote and subsequently by means of a qualified majority vote, issue the directives necessary for the progressive implementation of the provisions of art. 67.

Art. 70.(1) The Commission shall propose to the Council measures in regard to the progressive co-ordination of the exchange policies of Member States in respect of the movement of capital between those States and third countries. The Council, acting by means of a unanimous vote, shall issue directives in this connection. It shall endeavour to achieve the highest possible degree of liberalization.

(2) Where the action taken in application of the preceding par. does not permit the abolition of discrepancies between the exchange rules of Member States and where such discrepancies should lead persons resident in one of the Member States to make use of the transfer facilities within the Community, as provided for under art. 67, in order to evade the rules of one of the Member States in regard to third countries, that State may, after consulting the other Member States and the Commission, take appropriate measures to overcome these difficulties.

If the Council finds that such measures restrict the free movement of capital within the Community beyond what is required for the purposes of the preceding sub-par., it may, acting by means of a qualified majority vote on a proposal of the Commission, decide that the State concerned shall modify or abolish these measures.

Art. 71. Member States shall endeavour to avoid introducing within the Community any new exchange restrictions which affect the movement of capital and current payments connected with such movement, and making existing rules more restrictive.

They hereby declare their willingness to go beyond the degree of liberalization of capital provided for in the preceding articles to the extent that their economic situation, and in particular the situation of their balance of payments, permits.

The Commission may, after consulting the Monetary Committee, make recommendations to Member States on this subject.

Art. 72. Member States shall keep the Commission informed of any movements of capital to and from third countries as are known to them. The Commission may address to Member States any opinion which it deems appropriate on this subject.

Art. 73.(1) In the event of movements of capital leading to disturbances in the functioning of the capital market in any Member State, the Commission shall, after consulting the Monetary Committee, authorize such State to take, in regard to such movements of capital, protective measures of which the Commission shall determine the conditions and particulars.

The Council, acting by means of a qualified majority vote, may revoke this authorization and may modify such conditions and particulars.

(2) The Member State which is in difficulty may, however, on the ground of their secret or urgent character, itself take the above-mentioned measures if they should become necessary. The Commission and the other Member States shall be informed of such measures not later than at the date of their entry into force. In this case, the Commission may, after consulting the Monetary Committee, decide that the State concerned shall modify or abolish such measures.

Title IV Transport

Art. 74. The objectives of this Treaty shall, with regard to the subject covered by this Title, be pursued by the Member States within the framework of a common transport policy.

Art. 75.(1) With a view to implementing art. 74 and taking due account of the special aspects of transport, the Council, acting on a proposal of the Commission and after the Economic and Social Committee and the Assembly have been consulted, shall, until the end of the second stage by means of a unanimous vote and subsequently by means of a qualified majority vote, lay down:

(a) common rules applicable to international transport effected from or to the territory of a Member State or crossing the territory of one or more Member States;
(b) conditions for the admission of non-resident carriers to national transport services within a Member State; and
(c) any other appropriate provisions.

(2) The provisions referred to under (a) and (b) of the preceding par. shall be laid down in the course of the transitional period.

(3) Notwithstanding the procedure provided for in par. 1, provisions which relate to the principles governing transport and the application of which might seriously affect the standard of living and the level of employment in certain regions and also the utilization of transport equipment, shall, due account being taken of the need for adaptation to economic developments resulting from the establishment of the Common Market, be laid down by the Council acting by means of a unanimous vote.

Art. 76. Until the provisions referred to in art. 75, par. 1, are enacted and unless the Council gives its unanimous consent, no Member State shall apply the various provisions governing this subject at the date of the entry into force of this Treaty in such a way as to make them less favourable, in their direct or indirect effect, for carriers of other Member States by comparison with its own national carriers.

Art. 77. Aids which meet the needs of transport co-ordination or which constitute reimbursement for certain obligations inherent in the concept of a public utility shall be deemed to be compatible with this Treaty.

Art. 78. Any measure in the sphere of transport rates and conditions, adopted within the framework of this Treaty, shall take due account of the economic situation of carriers.

Art. 79.(1) Any discrimination which consists in the application by a carrier, in respect of the same goods conveyed in the same circumstances, of transport rates and conditions which differ on the ground of the country of origin or destination of the goods carried, shall be abolished in the traffic within the Community not later than at the end of the second stage.

(2) Par. 1 shall not exclude the adoption of other measures by the Council in application of art. 75, par. 1.

(3) The Council, acting by means of a qualified majority vote on a proposal of the Commission and after the Economic and Social Committee has been consulted, shall, within a period of two years after the date of the entry into force of this Treaty, lay down rules for the implementation of the provisions of par. 1.

The Council may, in particular, enact the provisions necessary to enable the institutions of the Community to ensure that the rule stated in par. 1 is observed and that all advantages accruing from it are enjoyed by users.

(4) The Commission shall, on its own initiative or at the request of a Member State, examine the cases of discrimination referred to in par. 1 and shall after consulting any Member State interested, take the necessary decisions within the framework of the rules laid down in accordance with the provisions of par. 3.

Art. 80.(1) The application imposed by a Member State, in respect of transport effected within the Community, of rates and conditions involving any element of support or protection in the interest of one or more particular enterprises or industries shall be prohibited as from the beginning of the second stage, unless authorized by the Commission.

(2) The Commission shall, on its own initiative or at the request of a Member State, examine the rates and conditions referred to in par. 1, taking particular account, on the one hand, of the requirements of a suitable regional economic policy, of the needs of under-developed regions and the problems of regions seriously affected by political circumstances and, on the other hand, of the effects of such rates and conditions on competition between the different forms of transport.

After consulting any interested Member State, the Commission shall take the necessary decisions.

(3) The prohibition referred to in par. 1 shall not apply to competitive tariffs.

Art. 81. Charges or dues collected by a carrier, in addition to the transport rates, for the crossing of frontiers, shall not exceed a reasonable level, due account being taken of real costs actually incurred by such crossing.

Member States shall endeavour to reduce these costs progressively.

The Commission may make recommendations to Member States with a view to the application of this article.

Art. 82. The provisions of this Chapter shall not be an obstacle to the measures taken in the Federal Republic of Germany, to the extent that such measures may be necessary to compensate for the economic disadvantages caused by the division of Germany to the economy of certain regions of the Federal Republic which are affected by that division.

Art. 83. A Committee with consultative status, composed of experts appointed by the Governments of Member States, shall be established and attached to the Commission. The latter shall, whenever it deems it desirable, consult this Committee on transport questions, without prejudice to the competence of the transport section of the Economic and Social Committee.

Art. 84.(1) The provisions of this Title shall apply to transport by rail, road and inland waterway.

(2) The Council, acting by means of a unanimous vote, may decide whether, to what extent and by what procedure appropriate provisions might be adopted for sea and air transport.

Part Three Policy of the Community; Title I Common Rules Chapter I Rules governing competition; Section. 1 Rules applying to enterprises

Art. 85.(1) The following shall be deemed to be incompatible with the Common Market and shall hereby be prohibited: any agreements between enterprises, any decisions by associations of enterprises and any concerted practices which are likely to affect trade between the Member States and which have as their object or result in the prevention, restriction or distortion of competition within the Common Market, in particular those consisting in:

(a) the direct or indirect fixing of purchase or selling prices or of any other trading conditions;
(b) the limitation or control of production, markets, technical development or investment;
(c) market-sharing or the sharing of sources of supply;
(d) the application to parties to transaction of unequal terms in respect of equivalent supplies, thereby placing them at a competitive disadvantage; or
(e) the subjecting of the conclusion of a contract to the acceptance by a party of additional supplies which either by their nature or according to commercial usage, have no connection with the subject of such contract.

(2) Any agreements or decisions prohibited pursuant to this article shall be null and void.

(3) Nevertheless, the provisions of par. 1 may be declared inapplicable in the case of:
– any agreements or classes of agreements between enterprises,
– any decisions or classes of decisions by associations of enterprises, and
– any concerted practices or classes of concerted practices which contribute to the improvement of the production or distribution of goods or to the promotion of technical or economic progress while reserving to users an equitable share in the profit resulting therefrom, and which:
(a) neither impose on the enterprises concerned any restrictions not indispensable to the attainment of the above objectives;
(b) nor enable such enterprises to eliminate competition in respect of a substantial proportion of the goods concerned.

Art. 86. To the extent to which trade between any Member States may be affected thereby, action by one or more enterprises to take improper advantage of a dominant position within the Common Market or within a substantial part of it shall be deemed to be incompatible with the Common Market and shall hereby be prohibited.

Such improper practices may, in particular, consist in:
(a) the direct or indirect imposition of any inequitable purchase or selling prices or of any other inequitable trading conditions;
(b) the limitation of production, markets or technical development to the prejudice of consumers;
(c) the application to parties to transactions of unequal terms in respect of equivalent supplies, thereby placing them at a competitive disadvantage; or
(d) the subjecting of the conclusion of a contract to the acceptance, by a party, of additional supplies which, either by their nature or according to commercial usage, have no connection with the subject of such contract.

Art. 87.(1) Within a period of three years after the date of the entry into force of this Treaty, the Council, acting by means of a unanimous vote on a proposal of the Commission and after the Assembly has been consulted, shall lay down any appropriate regulations or directives with a view to the application of the principles set out in arts. 85 and 86.

If such provisions have not been adopted within the above-mentioned time-limit, they shall be laid down by the Council acting by means of a qualified majority vote on a proposal of the Commission and after the Assembly has been consulted.
(2) The provisions referred to in par. 1 shall be designed, in particular:
(a) to ensure observance, by the institution of fines or penalties, of the prohibitions referred to in art. 85, par. 1, and in art. 86;
(b) to determine the particulars of the application of art. 85, par. 3, taking due account of the need, on the one hand, of ensuring effective supervision and, on the other hand, of simplifying administrative control to the greatest possible extent;
(c) to specify, where necessary, the scope of application in the various economic sectors of the provisions contained in arts. 85 and 86;
(d) to define the respective responsibilities of the Commission and of the Court of Justice in the application of the provisions referred to in this par.; and
(e) to define the relations between, on the one hand, municipal law and, on the other hand, the provisions contained in this Section or adopted in application of this Art.
Art. 88. Until the date of the entry into force of the provisions adopted in application of art. 87, the authorities of Member States shall, in accordance with their respective municipal law and with the provisions of art. 85, particularly par. 3, and of art. 86, rule upon the admissibility of any understanding and upon any improper advantage taken of a dominant position in the Common Market.
Art. 89.(1) Without prejudice to the provisions of art. 88, the Commission shall, upon taking up its duties, ensure the application of the principles laid down in arts. 85 and 86. It shall, at the request of a Member State or ex officio, investigate, in conjunction with the competent authorities of the Member States which shall lend it their assistance, any alleged infringement of the above-mentioned principles. If it finds that such infringement has taken place, it shall propose appropriate means for bringing it to an end.
(2) If such infringement continues, the Commission shall, by means of a reasoned decision, confirm the existence of such infringement of the principles. The Commission may publish its decision and may authorise Member States to take the necessary measures, of which it shall determine the conditions and particulars, to remedy the situation.
Art. 90.(1) Member States shall, in respect of public enterprises to which they grant special or exclusive rights, neither enact nor maintain in force any measure contrary to the rules contained in this Treaty, in particular, to those rules provided for in art. 7 and in arts. 85 to 94 inclusive.
(2) Any enterprise charged with the management of services of general economic interest or having the character of a fiscal monopoly shall be subject to the rules contained in this Treaty, in particular to those governing competition, to the extent that the application of such rules does not obstruct the de jure or de facto fulfilment of the specific tasks entrusted to such enterprise. The development of trade may not be affected to such a degree as would be contrary to the interests of the Community.
(3) The Commission shall ensure the application of the provisions of this article and shall, where necessary, issue appropriate directives or decisions to Member States.
Section 2 Dumping practices.
Art. 91.(1) If, in the course of the transitional period, the Commission, at the request of a Member State or of any other interested party, finds that dumping practices exist within the Common Market, it shall issue recommendations to the originator or originators of such practices with a view to bringing them to an end.
Where such dumping practices continue, the Commission shall authorize the Member State injured to take protective measures of which the Commission shall determine the conditions and particulars.
(2) Upon the entry into force of this Treaty, any products originating or having been entered for consumption in one Member State which have been exported to another Member State shall be admitted free of all customs duties, quantitative restrictions or measures with equivalent effect when re-imported into the territory of the first State. the Commission shall lay down appropriate rules for the application of this par.
Section 3 Aids granted by States.
Art. 92.(1) Except where otherwise provided for in this Treaty, any aid, granted by a Member State or granted by means of State resources, in any manner whatsoever, which distorts or threatens to distort competition by favouring certain enterprises or certain productions shall, to the extent to which it adversely affects trade between Member States, be deemed to be incompatible with the Common Market.
(2) The following shall be deemed to be compatible with the Common Market:
(a) aids of a social character granted to individual consumers, provided that such aids are granted without any discrimination based on the origin of the products concerned;
(b) aids intended to remedy damage caused by natural calamities or other extraordinary events; or
(c) aids granted to the economy of certain regions of the Federal Republic of Germany affected by the division of Germany, to the extent that such aids are necessary in order to compensate for the economic disadvantages caused by such division.
(3) The following may be deemed to be compatible with the Common Market:
(a) aids intended to promote the economic development of regions where the standard of living is abnormally low or where there exists serious underemployment;
(b) aids intended to promote the execution of important projects of common European interest or to remedy a serious disturbance of the economy of a Member State;
(c) aids intended to facilitate the development of certain activities or of certain economic regions, provided that such aids do not change trading conditions to such a degree as would be contrary to the common interest. Any aids to ship-building existing on 1 January 1957 shall, to the extent that such aids merely offset the absence of customs protection, be progressively reduced under the same conditions as apply to the abolition of customs duties, subject to the provisions of this Treaty relating to the common commercial policy in regard to third countries; and
(d) such other categories of aids may be specified by decision of the Council acting by means of a qualified majority vote on a proposal of the Commission.
Art. 93.(1) The Commission shall, together with Member States, constantly examine all systems of aids existing in those States. It shall propose to the latter any appropriate measures required by the progressive development or the functioning of the Common Market.
(2) If, after having given to the parties concerned to submit their comments, the Commission finds that any aid granted by a State or by means of State resources is not compatible with the Common Market within the meaning of art. 92, or that such aid is applied in an improper manner, it shall decide that the State concerned shall abolish or modify such aid within the time-limit prescribed by the Commission.
If the State concerned does not comply with this decision within the prescribed time-limit, the Commission or any other interested State may, notwithstanding the provisions of arts. 169 and 170, refer the matter to the Court of Justice directly.
At the request of any Member State, the Council, acting by means of a unanimous vote, may, if such a decision is justified by exceptional circumstances, decide that any aid instituted or to be instituted by that State shall be deemed to be compatible with the Common Market, notwithstanding the provisions of art. 92 or the regulations provided for in art. 94. If the Commission has, in respect of the aid concerned, already initiated the procedure provided for in the first sub-par. of this par, the request made to the Council by the State concerned shall cause such procedure to be suspended until the Council has made its attitude known.
If, however, the Council has not made its attitude known within a period of three months from such request, the Commission shall act.
(3) The Commission shall be informed, in due time to enable it to submit its comments, of any plans to institute or modify aids. If it considers that any such plan is not compatible with the Common Market within the meaning of art. 92, it shall without delay initiate the procedure provided for in the preceding par. The Member State concerned may not put its proposed measures into effect until such procedure shall have resulted in a final decision.
Art. 94. The Council, acting by means of a qualified majority vote on a proposal of the Commission, may make any appropriate regulations with a view to the application of arts. 92 and 93 and may, in particular, fix the conditions of the application of art. 93, par. 3, and the categories of aids which are exempted from this procedure.
Chapter 2 Fiscal provisions
Art. 95. A Member State shall not impose, directly or indirectly, on the products of other Member States any internal charges of any kind in excess of those applied directly or indirectly to like domestic products.
Furthermore, a Member State shall not impose on the products of other Member States any internal charges of such a nature as to afford indirect protection to other productions.
Member States shall, not later than at the beginning of the second stage, abolish or amend any provisions existing at the date of the entry into force of this Treaty which are contrary to the above rules.
Art. 96. Products exported to the territory of any Member State may not benefit from any drawback of internal charges in excess of those charges imposed directly or indirectly on them.
Art. 97. Any Member States which levy a turnover tax calculated by a cumulative multi-stage system may, in the case of internal charges imposed by them on imported products or of drawbacks granted by them on exported products, establish average rates for specific products or groups of products, provided that such States do not infringe the principles laid down in arts. 95 and 96. Where the average rates established by a Member State do not conform with the above-mentioned principles, the Commission shall issue to the State concerned appropriate directives or decisions.
Art. 98. With regard to charges other than turnover taxes, excise duties and other forms of indirect taxation, exemptions and drawbacks in respect of export to other Member States may not be imposed, save to the extent that the measures contemplated have been previously approved for a limited period by the Council acting by means of a qualified majority vote on a proposal of the Commission.
Art. 99. The Commission shall consider in what way the law of the various Member States concerning turnover taxes, excise duties and other forms of indirect taxation, including compensatory measures applying to exchanges between Member States, can be harmonized in the interest of the Common Market.
The Commission shall submit proposals to the Council which shall act by means of a unanimous vote, without prejudice to the provisions of arts. 100 and 101.
Chapter 3 Approximation of Laws
Art. 100. The Council, acting by means of a unanimous vote on a proposal of the Commission, shall issue directives for the approximation of such legislative and administrative provisions of the Member State as have a direct incidence on the establishment or functioning of the Common Market. The Assembly and the Economic and Social Committee shall be consulted concerning any directives whose implementation in one or more of the Member States would involve amendment of legislative provisions.
Art. 101. Where the Commission finds that a disparity existing between the legislative or administrative provisions of the Member States distorts the conditions of competition in the Common Market and thereby causes a state of affairs which must be eliminated, it shall enter into consultation with the interested Member States.
If such consultation does not result in an agreement which eliminates the particular distortion, the Council, acting during the first stage by means of a unanimous vote and subsequently by means of a qualified majority vote on a proposal of the Commission, shall issue the directives necessary for this purpose. The Commission and the Council may take any other appropriate measures as provided for in this Treaty.
Art. 102.(1) Where there is reason for fear that the enactment or amendment of a legislative or administrative provision will cause a distortion within the meaning of the preceding Article, the Member State desiring to proceed therewith shall consult the Commission. After consulting the Member States, the Commission shall recommend to the States concerned such

measures as may be appropriate to avoid the particular distortion.

(2) If the State desiring to enact or amend its own provisions does not comply with the recommendation made to it by the Commission, other Member States may not be requested, in application of art. 101 to amend their own provisions in order to eliminate such distortion. If the Member State which has ignored the Commission's recommendation causes a distortion to its own detriment only, the provisions of Art. 101 shall not apply.

Title II Economic policy. Chapter 1 Policy relating to economic trends.

Art. 103.(1) Member States shall consider their policy relating to economic trends as a matter of common interest. They shall consult with each other and with the Commission on measures to be taken in response to current circumstances.

(2) Without prejudice to any other procedures provided for in this Treaty, the Council may, by means of a unanimous vote on a proposal of the Commission, decide on measures appropriate to the situation.

(3) The Council, acting by means of a qualified majority vote on a proposal of the Commission, shall, where necessary, issue any requisite directives concerning the particulars of application of the measures decided upon under the terms of par. 2.

(4) The procedures provided for in this article shall apply also in the event of difficulties arising in connection with the supply of certain products.

Chapter 2 Balance of Payments

Art. 104. Each Member State shall pursue the economic policy necessary to ensure the equilibrium of its overall balance of payments and to maintain confidence in its currency, while ensuring a high level of employment and the stability of the level of prices.

Art. 105.(1) In order to facilitate the attainment of the objectives stated in art. 104, Member States shall co-ordinate their economic policies. They shall for this purpose institute a collaboration between the competent services of their administrative departments and between their central banks.

The Commission shall submit to the Council recommendations for the bringing into effect of such collaboration.

(2) In order to promote the co-ordination of the policies of Member States in monetary matters to the full extent necessary for the functioning of the Common Market, a Monetary Committee with consultative status shall hereby be established with the following tasks:

– to keep under review the monetary and financial situation of Member States and of the Community and also the general payments system of Member States and to report regularly thereon to the Council and to the Commission; and

– to formulate opinions, at the request of the Council or of the Commission or on its own initiative, for submission to the said institutions.

The Member States and the Commission shall each appoint two members of the Monetary Committee.

Art. 106.(1) Each Member State undertakes to authorize, in the currency of the Member State in which the creditor or the beneficiary resides, any payments connected with the exchange of goods, services or capital, and also any transfers of capital and wages, to the extent that the movement of goods, services, capital and persons is freed as between Member States in application of this Treaty.

Member States hereby declare their willingness to free payments beyond the extent provided for in the preceding sub-par., in so far as their economic situation in general and the situation of their balance of payments in particular so permit.

(2) To the extent that exchanges of goods and services and movements of capital are limited only by restrictions on payments connected therewith, the provisions of the Chapters relating to the abolition of quantitative restrictions, to the freeing of services and to the free movement of capital shall, for the purposes of the progressive abolition of such restrictions, apply by analogy.

(3) Member States undertake not to introduce as between themselves any new restrictions on transfers connected with the invisible transactions listed in Annex III to this Treaty.

The progressive abolition of existing restrictions shall be effected in accordance with the provisions of arts. 63 to 65 inclusive, in so far as such abolition is not governed by the provisions contained in pars. 1 and 2 or by the Chapter relating to the free movement of capital.

(4) Member States shall, where necessary, seek agreement concerning the measures to be taken in order to enable the payments and transfers mentioned in this Art. to be effected. These measures shall not adversely affect the attainment of the objectives laid down in this Chapter.

Art. 107.(1) Each Member State shall treat its policy with regard to exchange rates as a matter of common interest.

(2) If a Member State alters its exchange rate in a manner which is incompatible with the objectives laid down in art. 104 and which seriously distorts the conditions of competition, the Commission may, after consulting the Monetary Committee, authorize other Member States to take for a strictly limited period the necessary measures, of which it shall determine the conditions and particulars, in order to deal with the consequences of such alteration.

Art. 108.(1) Where a Member State is in difficulties or seriously threatened with difficulties as regards its balance of payments as a result either of overall disequilibrium of the balance of payments or of the kinds of currency at its disposal and where such difficulties are likely, in particular, to prejudice the functioning of the Common Market or the progressive establishment of the common commercial policy, the Commission shall without delay examine the situation of such State and the action which, in making use of all the means at its disposal, that State has taken or may take in conformity with the provisions of art. 104. The Commission shall indicate the measures which it recommends to the State concerned to adopt.

If the action taken by a Member State and the measures suggested by the Commission do not prove sufficient to overcome the difficulties encountered or threatening, the Commission shall, after consulting the Monetary Committee, recommend to the Council the granting of mutual assistance and the approriate methods therefor. The Commission shall keep the Council regularly informed of the situation and of its development.

(2) The Council, acting by means of a qualified majority vote, shall grant mutual assistance; it shall issue directives or decisions laying down the conditions and particulars thereof. Mutual assistance may take the form, in particular, of:

(a) concerted action in regard to any other international organizations to which Member States may have recourse;

(b) any measure necessary to avoid diversions of commercial traffic where the State in difficulties maintains or reestablishes quantitative restrictions with regard to third countries; or

(c) the granting of limited credits by other Member States, subject to the agreement of the latter.

Furthermore, during the transitional period, mutual assistance may also take the form of special reductions in customs duties or enlargements of quotas, for the purpose of facilitating the increase of imports from the State in difficulties, subject to the agreement of the States by which such measures would have to be taken.

(3) If the mutual assistance recommended by the Commission is not granted by the Council or if the mutual assistance granted and the measures taken are insufficient, the Commission shall authorize the State in difficulties to take measures of safeguard of which the Commission shall determine the conditions and particulars.

Such authorization may be revoked and such conditions and particulars may be amended by the Council acting by means of a qualified majority vote.

Art. 109.(1) Where a sudden crisis in the balance of payments occurs and if a decision, within the meaning of art. 108, par. 2, is not immediately taken, the Member State concerned may provisionally take the necessary measures of safeguard. Such measures shall cause the least possible disturbance in the functioning of the Common Market and shall not exceed the minimum strictly necessary to remedy the sudden difficulties which have arisen.

(2) The Commission and the other Member States shall be informed of such measures of safeguard not later than at the time of their entry into force. The Commission may recommend to the Council mutual assistance under the terms of art. 108.

(3) On the basis of an opinion of the Commission and after consulting the Monetary Committee, the Council, acting by means of a qualified majority vote, may decide that the State concerned shall amend, suspend or abolish the measures of safeguard referred to above.

Chapter 3 Commercial policy.

Art. 110. By establishing a customs union between themselves the Member States intend to contribute, in conformity with the common interest, to the harmonious development of world trade, the progressive abolition of restrictions on international exchanges and the lowering of customs barriers. The common commercial policy shall take into account the favourable incidence which the abolition of customs duties as between Member States may have on the increase of the competitive strength of the enterprises in those States.

Art. 111. In the course of the transitional period and without prejudice to arts. 115 and 116, the following provisions shall apply:

(1) Member States shall co-ordinate their commercial relations with third countries in such a way as to bring about, not later than at the expiry of the transitional period, the conditions necessary to the implementation of a common policy in the matter of external trade.

The Commission shall submit to the Council proposals regarding the procedure to be applied, in the course of the transitional period, for the establishment of common action and regarding the achievement of a uniform commercial policy.

(2) The Commission shall submit to the Council recommendations with a view to tariff negotiations with third countries concerning the common customs tariff.

The Council shall authorize the Commission to open such negotiations.

The Commission shall conduct these negotiations in consultation with a special Committee appointed by the Council to assist the Commission in this task and within the framework of such directives as the Council may issue to it.

(3) The Council shall, when exercising the powers conferred upon it under this article, act during the first two stages by means of a unanimous vote and subsequently by means of a qualified majority vote.

(4) Member States shall, in consultation with the Commission, take all necessary measures with the object, in particular, of adjusting their tariff agreements in force with third countries in order that the entry into force of the common customs tariff may not be delayed.

(5) Member States shall aim at securing uniformity between themselves at as high a level as possible of their lists of liberalization in regard to third countries or groups of third countries. For this purpose the Commission shall make any appropriate recommendations to Member States. If Member States abolish or reduce quantitative restrictions in regard to third countries, they shall inform the Commission beforehand and shall accord identical treatment to the other Member States.

Art. 112.(1) Without prejudice to obligations undertaken by Member States within the framework of other international organizations, their measures to aid exports to third countries shall be progressively harmonized before the end of the transitional period to the extent necessary to ensure that competition between enterprises within the Community shall not be distorted.

On a proposal of the Committee, the Council, acting until the end of the second stage by means of a unanimous vote and subsequently by means of a qualified majority vote, shall issue the directives necessary for this purpose.

(2) The preceding provisions shall not apply to such drawbacks on customs duties or charges with equivalent effect nor to such refunds of indirect charges including turnover taxes, excise duties and other indirect taxes as are accorded in connection with exports of goods from a Member State to a third country, to the extent that such drawbacks or refunds do not exceed the charges which have been imposed, directly or indirectly, on the products exported.

Art. 113.(1) After the expiry of the transitional period, the common commercial policy shall be based on uniform principles, particularly in regard to tariff amendments, the conclusion of tariff or trade agreements, the alignment of measures of liberalization, export policy and protective commercial measures including measures to be taken in cases of dumping or subsidies.

(2) The Commission shall submit proposals to the Council for the putting into effect of this common commercial policy.

(3) Where agreements with third countries require to be negotiated, the Commission shall make recommendations to the Council, which will authorize the Commission to open the necessary negotiations.

The Commission shall conduct these negotiations in consultation with a special Committee appointed by the Council to assist the Commission in this task and within the framework of such directives as the Council may issue to it.

(4) The Council shall, when exercising the powers conferred upon it by this article, act by means of a qualified majority vote.

Art. 114. The agreements referred to in art. 111, par. 2, and in art. 113 shall be concluded on behalf of the Community by the Council acting during the first two stage by means of a unanimous vote and subsequently by means of a qualified majority vote.

Art. 115. In order to ensure that the execution of measures of commercial policy taken in conformity with this Treaty by any Member State shall not be prevented by diversions of commercial traffic, or where disparities between such measures lead to economic difficulties in one or more of the Member States, the Commission shall recommend the methods whereby the other Member States shall provide the necessary co-operation. Failing this, the Commission shall authorize the Member States to take the necessary protective measures of which it shall determine the conditions and particulars.

In cases of emergency and during the transitional period, Member States may themselves take such necessary measures and shall notify them to the other Member States and also to the Commission which may decide that the State concerned shall amend or revoke such measures.

In choosing such measures, priority shall be given to those which cause the least disturbance to the functioning of the Common Market and which take due account of the necessity for expediting, as far as possible, the introduction of the common customs tariff.

Art. 116. As from the end of the transitional period, Member States shall in respect of all matters of particular interest in regard to the Common Market, within the framework of any international organizations of an economic character, only proceed by way of common action. The Commission shall for this purpose submit to the Council, which shall act by means of a qualfied majority vote, proposals concerning the scope and implementation of such common action.

During the transitional period, Member States shall consult with each other with a view to concerting their action and, as far as possible, adopting a uniform attitude.

Title III Social Policy. Chapter 1 Social provisions
Art. 117. Member States hereby agree upon the necessity to promote improvement of the living and working conditions of labour so as to permit the equalization of such conditions in an upward direction.

They consider that such a development will result not only from the functioning of the Common Market which will favour the harmonization of social systems, but also from the procedures provided for under this Treaty and from the approximation of legislative and administrative provisions.

Art. 118. Without prejudice to the other provisions of this Treaty and in conformity with its general objectives, it shall be the aim of the Commission to promote close collaboration between Member States in the social field, particularly in matters relating to:
– employment,
– labour legislation and working conditions,
– occupational and continuation training,
– social security,
– protection against occupational accidents and diseases,
– industrial hygiene,
– the law as to trade unions, and collective bargaining between employers and workers.

For this purpose, the Commission shall act in close contact with Member States by means of studies, the issuing of opinions, and the organizing of consultations both on problems arising at the national level and on those of concern to international organizations.

Before issuing the opinions provided for under this Art., the Commission shall consult the Economic and Social Committee.

Art. 119. Each Member State shall in the course of the first stage ensure and subsequently maintain the application of the principle of equal remuneration for equal work as between men and women workers.

For the purposes of this Art., remuneration shall mean the ordinary basic or minimum wage or salary and any additional emoluments whatsoever payable directly or indirectly, whether in cash or in kind, by the employer to the worker and arising out of the workers' employment.

Equal remuneration without discrimination based on sex means:(a) that remuneration for the same work at piece-rates shall be calculated on the basis of the same unit of measurement; and

(b) that remuneration for work at time-rates shall be the same for the same job.

Art. 120. Member States shall endeavour to maintain the existing equivalence of paid holiday schemes.

Art. 121. The Council, acting by means of a unanimous vote after consulting the Economic and Social Committee, may assign to the Commission functions relating to the implementation of common measures, particularly in regard to the social security of the migrant workers referred to in arts. 48 to 51 inclusive.

Art. 122. The Commission shall, in its annual report to the Assembly, include a special chapter on the development of the social situation within the Community.

The Assembly may invite the Commission to draw up reports on special problems concerning the social situation.

Chapter 2. The European Social Fund.
Art. 123. In order to improve opportunities of employment of workers in the Common Market and thus contribute to raising the standard of living, a European Social Fund shall hereby be established in accordance with the provisions set out below; it shall have the task of promoting within the Community employment facilities and the geographical and occupational mobility of workers.

Art. 124. The administration of the Fund shall be incumbent on the Commission.

The Commission shall be assisted in this task by a Committee presided over by a member of the Commission and composed of representatives of Governments, trade unions and employers' associations.

Art. 125.(1) At the request of a Member State, the Fund shall, within the framework of the rules provided for in art. 127, cover 50 per cent of expenses incurred after the entry into force of this Treaty by that State or by a body under public law for the purpose of:
(a) ensuring productive re-employemnt of workers by means of:
– occupational re-training,
– resettlement allowances; and

(b) granting aids for the benefit of workers whose employment is temporarily reduced or wholly or partly suspended as a result of the conversion of their enterprise to other productions, in order that they may maintain the same wage-level pending their full re-employment.

(2) The assistance granted by the Fund towards the cost of occupational retraining shall be conditional upon the impossibility of employing the unemployed workers otherwise than in a new occupation and upon their having been, in productive employment, for a period of at least six months in the occupation for which they have been re-trained.

The assistance granted in respect of resettlement allowances shall be conditional upon the unemployed workers having been obliged to change their residence within the Community and upon their having been in productive employment for a period of at least six months in their new place of residence.

The assistance given for the benefit of workers in cases where an enterprise is converted shall be subject to the following conditions:
(a) that the workers concerned have again been fully employed in that enterprise for a period of at least six months;

(b) that the Government concerned has previously submitted a plan, drawn up by such enterprise, for its conversion and for the financing thereof; and

(c) that the Commission has given its prior approval to such conversion plan.

Art. 126. At the expiry of the transitional period, the Council, on the basis of an opinion of the Commission and after the Economic and Social Committee and the Assembly have been consulted, may:
(a) acting by means of a qualified majority vote, rule that all or part of the assistance referred to in art. 125 shall no longer be granted; or

(b) acting by means of a unanimous vote, determine the new tasks which may be entrusted to the Fund within the framework of its mandate as defined in art. 123.

Art. 127. On a proposal of the Commission and after the Economic and Social Committee and the Assembly have been consulted, the Council, acting by means of a qualified majority vote, shall lay down the provisions necessary for the implementation of arts. 124 to 126 inclusive; in particular, it shall fix details concerning the conditions under which the assistance of the Fund shall be granted in accordance with the terms of arts. 125 and also concerning the categories of enterprises whose workers shall benefit from the aids provided for in art. 125, par. 1(b).

Art. 128. The Council shall, on a proposal of the Commission and after the Economic and Social Committee has been consulted, establish general principles for the implementation of a common policy of occupational training capable of contributing to the harmonious development both of national economies and of the Common Market.

Title IV The European Investment Bank
Art. 129. A European Investment Bank having legal personality shall hereby be established.

The members of the European Investment Bank shall be the Member States.

The Statute of the European Investment Bank shall form the subject of a Protocol annexed to this Treaty.

Art. 130. The task of the European Investment Bank shall be to contribute, by calling on the capital markets and its own resources, to the balanced and smooth development of the Common Market in the interest of the Community. For this purpose, the Bank shall be granting loans and guarantees on a non-profit-making basis facilitate the financing of the following projects in all sectors of the economy:
(a) projects for developing less developed regions,

(b) projects for modernizing or converting enterprises or for creating new activities which are called for by the proegressive establishment of the Common Market where such projects by their size or nature cannot be entirely financed by the various means available in each of the Member States; and

(c) projects of common interest to several Member States which by their size or nature cannot be entirely financed by the various means available in each of the Member States.

Part Four The Association of Overseas Countries and Territories
Art. 131. The Member States hereby agree to bring into association with the Community the non-European countries and territories which have special relations with Belgium, France, Italy and the Netherlands. These countries and territories, hereinafter referred to as 'the countries and territories', are listed in Annex IV to this Treaty. The purpose of this association shall be to promote the economic and social development of the countries and territories and to establish close economic relations between them and the Community as a whole. In conformity with the principles stated in the Preamble to this Treaty, this association shall in the first place permit the furthering of the interests and prosperity of the inhabitants of these countries and territories in such a manner as to lead them to the economic, social and cultural development which they expect.

Art. 132. Such association shall have the following objects:
(1) Member States shall, in their commercial exchanges with the countries and territories, apply the same rules which they apply among themselves pursuant to this Treaty.

(2) Each country or territory shall apply to its commercial exchanges with Member States and with the other countries and territories the same rules which it applies in respect of the European State with which it has special relations.

(3) Member States shall contribute to the investments required by the progressive development of these countries and territories.

(4) As regards investments financed by the Community, participation in tenders and supplies shall be open, on equal terms, to all natural and legal persons being nationals of Member States or of the countries and territories.

(5) In relations between Member States and the countries and territories, the right of establishment of nationals and companies shall be regulated in accordance with the provisions, and by application of the procedures, referred to in the Chapter relating to the right of establishment and on a non-discriminatory basis, subject to the special provisions made pursuant to art. 136.

Art. 133.(1) Imports originating in the countries or territories shall, on their entry into Member States, benefit by the total abolition of customs duties which shall take place progressively between Member States in conformity with the provisions of this Treaty.

(2) Customs duties imposed on imports from Member States and from countries or territories shall, on the entry of such imports into any of the other countries or territories, be progressively abolished in conformity with the provisions of arts. 12, 13, 14, 15 and 17.

(3) The countries and territories may, however, levy customs duties which correspond to the needs of their development and to the requirements of their industrialization or which, being of a fiscal nature, have the object of contributing to their budgets.

The duties referred to in the preceding sub-par. shall be progressively reduced to the level of those imposed on imports of products coming from the Member State with which each country or territory has special relations. The percentages and the timing of the reductions provided for under this Treaty shall apply to the difference between the duty imposed, on entry into the importing country or territory, on a product coming from the Member State which has special relations with the country or territory concerned and the duty imposed on the same product coming from the Community.

(4) Par. 2 shall not apply to countries and territories which, by reason of the special international obligations by which they are bound, already apply a non-discriminatory customs tariff at the date of the entry into force of this Treaty.

(5) The establishment or amendment of customs duties imposed on goods imported into the countries and territories shall not, either de jure or de facto, give rise to any direct or indirect discrimination between imports coming from the various Member States.

Art. 134. If the level of the duties applicable to goods coming from a third country on entry into a country or territory is likely, having regard to the application of the provisions of art. 133, par. 1, to cause diversions of commercial traffic to the detriment of any Member State, the latter may request the Commission to propose to the other Member States the measures necessary to remedy the situation.

Art. 135. Subject to the provisions relating to public health, public safety and public order, the freedom of movement in Member States of workers from the countries and territories, and in the countries and territories of workers from Member States shall be governed by subsequent conventions which shall require unanimous agreement of Member States.

Art. 136. For a first period of five years as from the date of the entry into force of this Treaty, an Implementing Convention annexed to this Treaty shall determine the particulars and procedure concerning the association of the countries and territories with the Community. Before the expiry of the Convention provided for in the preceding sub-par., the Council, acting by means of a unanimous vote, shall, proceeding from the results achieved and on the basis of the principles set out in this Treaty, determine the provisions to be made for a further period."

Part Five defines the Institution of the Community (arts. 137–209) and Part Six General and Final Provisions (arts. 210–248), The Annexes: Lists of tariff headings referred to in arts. 19 and 20; Protocol on the Statute of the European Investment Bank; Protocol relating to German Internal Trade and Connected Problems (▷ Interzonenhandel); Protocol relating to certain provisions of concern to France; Protocol concerning Italy; Protocol concerning Luxembourg; Protocol relating to goods originating in and coming from certain countries; Protocol relating to Algeria; Protocol concerning oil minerals; Protocol relating to the Netherlands overseas possessions; Protocol on the Privileges and Immunities of the EEC; Protocol on the Status of the Court of Justice; Convention relating to the association with the Community of the overseas countries and territories; Protocol concerning bananas; and Protocol concerning unroasted coffee.

In Dec. 1985 the EEC started discussion of proposed measures to reform the Treaty; continued in the following years.

UNTS, Vol. 298, 1958, pp. 11–266.

RONGELAP ATOLL. ▷ Bikini.

RÖNTGEN. The international unit of exposure to radiation. ▷ SI.

ROOSEVELT'S COROLLARY TO THE MONROE DOCTRINE, 1904. A doctrine formulated by the US President Th.R. Roosevelt (1858–1919) first in May, 1904 and reiterated in his message to Congress on Dec. 6, 1904 as follows:

"... It is not true that the United States feels any land hunger or entertains any projects as regards the other nations of the Western Hemisphere save such as are for their welfare. All that this country desires is to see the neighboring countries stable, orderly, and prosperous. Any country whose people conduct themselves well can count upon our hearty friendship. If a nation shows that it knows how to act with reasonable efficiency and decency in social and political matters, if it keeps order and pays its obligations, it need fear no interference from the United States. Chronic wrongdoing, or an impotence which results in a general loosening of the ties of civilized society, may in America, as elsewhere, ultimately require intervention by some civilized nation, and in the Western Hemisphere the adherence of the United States to the Monroe Doctrine may force the United States, however reluctantly, in flagrant cases of such wrongdoing or impotence, to the exercise of an international police power. If every country washed by the Caribbean Sea would show the progress in stable and just civilization which with the aid of the Platt amendment Cuba has shown since our troops left the island, and which so many of the republics in both Americas are constantly and brilliantly showing, all question of interference by this Nation with their affairs would be at an end. Our interests and those of our southern neighbors are in reality identical. They have great natural riches, and if within their borders the reign of law and justice obtains, prosperity is sure to come to them. While they thus obey the primary laws of civilized society they may rest assured that they will be treated by us in a spirit of cordial and helpful sympathy. We would interfere with them only in the last resort, and then only if it became evident that their inability or unwillingness to do justice at home and abroad had violated the rights of the United States or had invited foreign aggression to the detriment of the entire body of American nations. It is a mere truism to say that every nation, whether in America or anywhere else, which desires to maintain its freedom, its independence, must ultimately realize that the right of such independence can 'not be separated from the responsibility of making good use of it.

In asserting the Monroe Doctrine, in taking such steps as we have taken in regard to Cuba, Venezuela, and Panama, and in endeavoring to circumscribe the theater of war in the Far East, and to secure the open door in China, we have acted in our own interest as well as in the interest of humanity at large."

In the Annual Message to the Congress in Dec. 1905, President T.R. Roosevelt stated again:

"... It must be understood that under no circumstances will the United States use the Monroe Doctrine as a cloak for territorial aggression. We desire peace with all the world, but perhaps most of all with the other peoples of the American Continent. There are, of course, limits to the wrongs which any self-respecting nation can endure. It is always possible that wrong actions toward this Nation, or toward citizens of this Nation, in some State unable to keep order among its own people, unable to secure justice from outsiders, and unwilling to do justice to those outsiders who treat it well, may result in our having to take action to protect our rights; but such action will not be taken with a view to territorial aggression, and it will be taken at all only with extreme reluctance and when it has become evident that every other resource has been exhausted.

Moreover, we must make it evident that we do not intend to permit the Monroe Doctrine to be used by any nation on this Continent as a shield to protect it from the consequences of its own misdeeds against foreign nations. If a republic to the south of us commits a tort against a foreign nation, such as an outrage against a citizen of that nation, then the Monroe Doctrine does not force us to interfere to prevent punishment of the tort, save to see that the punishment does not assume the form of territorial occupation in any shape. The case is more difficult when it refers to a contractual obligation. Our own Government has always refused to enforce such contractual obligations on behalf of its citizens by an appeal to arms. It is much to be wished that all foreign governments would take the same view. But they do not; and in consequence we are liable at any time to be brought face to face with disagreeable alternatives. On the one hand, this country would certainly decline to go to war to prevent a foreign government from collecting a just debt; on the other hand, it is very inadvisable to permit any foreign power to take possesssion, even temporarily, of the custom houses of an American Republic in order to enforce the payment of its obligations; for such temporary occupation might turn into permanent occupation. The only escape from these alternatives may at any time be that we must ourselves undertake to bring about some arrangement by which so much as possible of a just obligation shall be paid. It is far better that this country should put through such an arrangement, rather than allow any foreign country to undertake it. To do so insures the defaulting republic from having to pay debt of an improper character under duress, while it also insures honest creditors of the republic from being passed by in the interest of dishonest or grasping creditors. Moreover, for the United States to take such a position offers the only possible way of insuring us against a clash with some foreign power. The position is, therefore, in the interest of peace as well as in the interest of justice. It is of benefit to our people; it is of benefit to the people of the country concerned ..."

The corollary was made void in 1933 on the basis of an opinion presented by Undersecretary of State R.J. Clark, prepared in Dec., 1928, announced in 1930, which stated that from the legal point of view the corollary was not justified and cannot be contained in the Monroe doctrine.

A.P. WHITAKER, *The Western Hemisphere Idea. Its Rise and Decline*, New York, 1954; D. PERKINS, *A History of the Monroe Doctrine* (Chapter IV. The Policeman of the West: The Evolution of the Roosevelt T.R. Corollary), Boston, 1955.

ROOSEVELT'S FOUR FREEDOMS, 1941. The US President F.D. Roosevelt's (1882–1945) statement in his message to the US Congress on Jan. 6, 1941 regarding the future of the world after World War II:

"In the future days, which we seek to make secure, we look forward to a world founded upon four essential human freedoms.

The first is freedom of speech and expression – everywhere in the world.

The second is freedom of every person to worship God in his own way – everywhere in the world.

The third is freedom from want – which, translated into world terms, means economic understandings which will secure to every nation a healthy peace time life for its inhabitants – everywhere in the world.

The fourth is freedom from fear – which, translated into world terms, means a world-wide reduction of armaments to such a point and in such a thorough fashion that no nation will be in a position to commit an act of physical aggression against any neighbor – anywhere in the world.

That is no vision of a distant millennium. It is a definite basis for a kind of world attainable in our own time and

R

generation. That kind of world is the very antithesis of the so-called new order of tyranny which the dictators seek to create with the crash of a bomb."

C. EAGLETON, "The US and the Statement of War-Aims", in: *American Journal of International Law*, No. 35, 1941.

ROOSEVELT'S QUARANTINE DOCTRINE, 1937. A suggestion that aggressive forces of fascist states in Europe and of imperialistic Japan be quarantined, like a contagious physical disease; made by the US President F.D. Roosevelt on Oct. 5, 1937 in a speech in Chicago; without political consequences as a result of the strong isolationism of the US Congress. The highlights of the Chicago speech:

"... Those who cherish their freedom and recognize and respect the equal right of their neighbors to be free and live in peace must work together for the triumph of law and moral principles in order that peace, justice and confidence may prevail in the world.
There must be a return to a belief in the pledged word, in the value of a signed treaty. There must be a recognition of the fact that national morality is as vital as private morality ...
... When an epidemic of physical disease starts to spread, the community approves and joins in a quarantine ...
War is a contagion, whether it be declared or undeclared ..."

S.J. ROSENMAN, *The Public Papers and Addresses of F.D. Roosevelt*, New York, 1950.

ROROS. A Norwegian village, north of Oslo, whose cultural monuments are included in the ▷ World Heritage UNESCO List. This small town was begun in 1644 by the workers drawn there by the copper mines which had just been discovered in a hitherto hardly explored mountain site. The rugged history of these miners is revealed in the monuments of Roros – a church in neo-classical style, a hundred or so wooden houses on stone foundations and the slag-heaps dotted here and there.

UNESCO, *A Legacy for All*, Paris, 1984.

ROSICRUCIAN ORDER. The Ancient Mystical Order Rosae Crucis, AMORC, Fraternitatis Rosae Crucis, supposedly originated in Egypt 1500 BC; there is reference to it in Europe in AD 1115; known since the 16th century in France, Germany, and America (1694); a theosophical doctrine interpreting the Christian religion; organizationally a precursor of masonry; has its center in San Jose, California, where the mother lodge of the Rosicrucian Order is located, propagating

"a system of metaphysical and physical philosophy to help the individual student utilize to a better advantage his natural talents. Rosicrucian teaching unites into one liveable philosphy, science, art and mysticism."

Maintains Rose-Croix University, Egyptian Museum, Rosicrucian Science Museum, Rosicrucian Research Library, Rosicrucian Planetarium, Rosicrucian Art Salon, Lectorium Rosicrucianum in Haarlem (Holland). Organizes annual international conferences in San Jose and through more than 300 lodges in 53 countries. Publ.: *The Rosicrucian Digest, El Rosacruz* and *La Rose-Croix*. Since 1946 reg. with the UIA.

Yearbook of International Organization.

ROSS DEPENDENCY AND THE ROSS ICE SHELF. A part of Antartica, discovered in 1841 by Sir James Clark Ross; the Ross Sea's frozen extension is the Ross Ice Shelf; New Zealand's territorial claims in the Antarctic.

F.M. AUBURN, *The Ross Dependency*, The Hague, 1972.

ROSSING URANIUM MINE. The world's largest uranium mine, in the Namib Desert in Namibia, near the Atlantic coast town of Swakopmund, Production capacity: about 5000 tons a year. The uranium-308 is exported to Austria, France, the FRG, Iran, South Africa, Switzerland and the USA.

ROTARY, INTERNATIONAL. The Rotary Club was f. 1905, London. An International Association of Rotary Clubs are active in 151 countries. Reg. with the UIA. Aims:

"Encourage and foster the Ideal of Service as a basis of worthy enterprise and, in particular, encourage and foster the development of acquaintance as an opportunity for service; high ethical standards in business and profession; recognition of the worthiness of all useful occupations; the dignifying by each Rotary of his occupation as an opportunity to serve society."

Consultative status with UNESCO. Annual Conventions. Publ.: *The Rotaries* and *Revista Rotaria*.

Yearbook of International Organizations.

ROTE HILFE. ▷ Red Secours or MOPR.

ROUBLE OR RUBLE. The monetary unit of the Soviet Union; one rouble = 100 kopecks; issued by Gosbank of SSSR, State Bank of the USSR.

ROUBLES, TRANSFERABLE. An accounting unit of the CMEA states created on Oct. 22, 1963 by the Agreement on Multilateral Settlements among CMEA States. Art. 1 of which reads:

"Settlements resulting from bilateral or multilateral agreements and individual contracts for the mutual exchange of goods as well as agreements on other payments between the Agreeing Parties from Jan. 1, 1964 will be made in t.r. The gold content of t.r. is 0.987412 g of pure gold. Each of the Agreeing Parties which has an account in t.r. may freely dispose of these funds in settlements with other Agreeing Parties. With the signing of trade treaties each of the Agreeing Parties will ensure the equalization, with the limits of a calendar year, of recipts and payments in t.r. with all of the remaining Agreeing Parties as a whole. The creation of the exploitation of eventual reserves in t.r. as well as credit operations will also be taken into consideration."

The Agreement charged the ▷ International Bank for Economic Co-operation, which was founded for this purpose, among others, with the task of handling multilateral settlements. The states participating in the Agreement reached an understanding on July 28, 1971 in Bucharest on keeping an invoice on non-trade payments and established a ratio for calculating the sum of non-trade payments. Transfer roubles are also applied to settlements with other countries outside CMEA which signed appropriate agreements. The transfer rouble is not exchangeable into other currencies, since it is not an international transaction money, but is exclusively a clearing account unit of CMEA countries. The name "transfer" is connected with the form of using the new money – namely it can be freely transferred from the accounts of one country which is a member of the International Bank for Economic Co-operation to the account of another country. Each country can utilize the financial means in transfer roubles acquired through the export of its goods in payment for imports from another country which participates in the multilateral settlements of CMEA. To a certain extent the transfer rouble also functions as a means of accumulation, for the system of multilateral settlements assumes the accumulation of reserves in the common currency. Each year CMEA gives its member countries short-term credits in this currency – from 1.5 billion to 2.8 billion. The Complex Program for the Further Intensification and Improvement of Co-operation, as well as the development of the economic integra-

tion of CMEA countries, outlined perspectives for increasing the role of transfer rouble in the international arena.

UNTS, Vol. 506, pp. 216–218, J.S. GARLAW, *Financing Foreign Trade in Eastern Europe*, New York, 1976.

ROUND TABLE. An international term for the meetings of diplomats, scientists, experts, etc., in which there is no established hierarchy of chairmen, deputies, etc., or strict agenda; in round table seating there are no superior or inferior places. They are organized, as a rule, for preliminary discussion of some special problem.

ROUTE CHARGES. Charges for the use of air-route navigation facilities and services in the airspace; subject of international agreements relating to the ICAO Convention on International Civil Aviation. The ▷ Eurocontrol member states signed on Sept. 8, 1970 at Brussels a Multilateral Agreement relating to the Collection of Route Charges; came into force on Dec. 15, 1971.

UNTS, Vol. 830, 1972, pp. 30–33.

ROWING. An Olympic sport since 1900, organized in the International Federation of Rowing Societies, Fédération internationale des sociétés d'aviron, FISA, est. 1892, which since 1893 has patronized the annual European championships and since 1962 the world championships (every four years).

Yearbook of International Organizations.

ROYAL INSTITUTE OF INTERNATIONAL AFFAIRS. An Institute f. 1920, London, called Chattam House, to facilitate the scientific study of international questions, affiliated Institutes in Canada, Australia, New Zealand, India, Sri Lanka, Singapore, Nigeria, Trinidad and Tobago and Guyana. Publ.: *British Yearbook of International Law* (annually), *International Affairs* (quarterly), *The World Today* (monthly), individual studies.

ROYALTIES. A term defined by a OECD Model Convention for the avoidance of double taxation, as follows:

"The term 'royalties' means payments of any kind received as a consideration for the use of, or the right to use, any copyright of literary, artistic or scientific work including cinematograph films, any patent, trade mark, design or model, plan, secret formula or process, or for the use of, or the right to use, industrial, commercial or scientific equipment, or for information concerning industrial, commercial or scientific experience."

W.H. and D.B. DIAMOND, *International Tax Treaties of All Nations*, New York, 1976, Vol. 1, p. 11.

RPV. Remotely Piloted Vehicles. An international military term for the reconnaissance planes, fighters, unmanned bombers, guided from the ground whose mass production was scheduled for the 1980s.

RUBBER. A subject of international co-operation. Organizations reg. with the UIA:

Association of Natural Rubber Producing Countries, f. 1970, Kuala Lumpur. Members: governments of India, Indonesia, Malaysia, Singapore, Sri Lanka, Thailand and Vietnam.
Eurpean Committee of Machinery Manufacturers for the Plastic and Rubber Industries, f. 1964, Paris.
International Institute of Synthetic Rubber Producers, f. 1972, New York.
International Rubber and Plastic Federation, f. 1957, London.
International Rubber Research and Development Board, f. 1960, London.
International Rubber Study Group, f. 1944, London.

Rubber Growers Association, f. 1907, London. Publ.: *Current Information Bulletin.*
Rubber Industries Liaison Bureau of the EEC, f. 1959, Brussels.

The first International Natural Rubber Convention entered into force on Oct. 24, 1980. The International Natural Rubber Council started to work on Nov. 17, 1980 at Geneva. An International Natural Rubber Agreement, adopted by the UN Conference on Natural Rubber in Oct. 1979 was prolonged until 1991 in Oct. 1986, under the auspices of UNCTAD. Some 50 countries representing all major producers and consumers participate in it.

RUBBER FOUNDATION, *Elsevier's Rubber Dictionary.* In English/American, French, Spanish, Italian, Portuguese, German, Dutch, Swedish, Indonesian and Japanese, Amsterdam, 1959; *Yearbook of International Organizations*; *UN Chronicle*, August 1986, p. 121.

RUBICON. Name of a stream separating the province of Cisalpine Gaul from the Appenine peninsula. In 49 B.C. Julius Caesar in order to start a civil war against Pompey the Great and the Senate had to cross the stream with his armies. He did so, reportedly saying "The die is cast". Hence an international term: "to cross the Rubicon" – to take an irrevocable step.

RUBLE. ▷ Rouble.

RUGBY. A ballgame, originated in 1823 in the Midlands of England, in the town of Rugby, near Birmingham; distinct from football (soccer) as the ball can also be carried, and an adversary can be stopped in any manner whatever. Although rugby is not admitted to the Olympic Games, the International Amateur Rugby Federation, founded in 1934, is acknowledged by the International Olympic Committee.

Yearbook of International Organizations.

RUHR. The right tributary of the Rhine in the province of Rhineland Westphalia; the territory through which it flows is called the Ruhr District; contained the greatest concentration of German heavy industry in the 19th century, it was the forge of the German armaments industry; after World War I occupied by France and Belgium from Jan., 1923 to Nov., 1925 in connection with the refusal of Germany to pay war reparations. At the end of World War II again occupied by allied forces; from June 1945 the Ruhr District became part of the British zone of occupation but with a special statute. The question of the internationalization of the main center of German heavy industry and coal mining was debated by the four occupation powers of Germany at Conferences of Ministers of Foreign Affairs in Paris, from Apr. 25 to July 12, 1946, and in London, from Nov. 25 to Dec. 15, 1947 and then at Conferences of the Ministers of Foreign Affairs of the Western Powers and Benelux, from Feb. 23 to Mar. 5, from Apr. 20 to May 31 and from Nov. 11 to Dec. 29, 1948 in London. As a result of these meetings, France, USA and Great Britain and Belgium, the Netherlands and Luxembourg on Apr. 28, 1949 signed a treaty on the International Statute of the Ruhr District, whose executive organ was the International Authority for the Ruhr, IAR, which was given the task of "dividing coal, coke and steel from the Ruhr District between German consumption and export" (art. 14); with the right "to investigate transport, customs and trade practices" and decide whether export agreements could be accepted (art. 15). In addition to the signatories, also participating in IAR since Nov. 30, 1949 was the FRG government in accordance with a treaty signed with the Western Powers on Nov. 22, 1949 in Petersberg near Bonn. The IAR was completely

dissolved when the FRG assumed total economic independence on May 8, 1955.

U. SAHM. "Die internationale Kontrolle des Ruhrgebietes", in: *Europa Archiv*, No. 5, 1950; A. TOBLER, "Internationale Ruhrbehörde", in: STRUPP-SCHLOCHAUER, *Wörterbuch des Völkerrechts*, Berlin, 1960.

RULE OF LAW. The adherence on the part of authorities and citizens to the laws and rules of international law in force in a given state; drastic cases of violation of law and order in a state entail international protests and boycott actions.

RULE OF THE WAR OF 1756. In international law the principle that trade with a hostile country in wartime is prohibited. This principle was introduced for the first time in 1756, during the war between Great Britain and France.

RULES OF THE RED CROSS. The principles on protecting civilian population in wartime, elaborated by the International Committee of the Red Cross in 1956.

RULES OF WAR. The right to wage a war, banned in the 20th century and rights and obligations imposed on belligerent parties and neutral states involved in an armed conflict. Commonly accepted international law denounces and bans invasive wars; however, national liberation wars are treated differently. In the development of rules of war, a separate place is occupied by the medieval tenet of just wars.

RUMICHACA ACT, 1966. A Treaty on Integration of Borderland of Colombia and Ecuador, signed at Rumichaca, Colombia, on Mar. 12, 1966.

Acto de Rumichaca, Bogotá, 1966.

RUMOURS INTERNATIONAL REGISTER. ▷ Smallpox.

RUPEE, INDIAN. The monetary unit of India; one rupee = 100 paisa; issued by the Reserve Bank of India.

RUPEE, NEPALESE. The monetary unit of Nepal; one rupee = 100 pice; issued by the Nepal Rastra Bank; linked to the Indian Rupee.

RUPEE, PAKISTANI. The monetary unit of Pakistan; one rupee = 100 paisa; issued by the State Bank of Pakistan.

RUPEE, SRI LANKA. The monetary unit of Sri Lanka; 1 rupee = 100 cents; issued (name changed from Ceylon rupee Apr. 1, 1973) by the Central Bank of Sri Lanka (Ceylon).

RUPIAH, INDONESIAN. The monetary unit of Indonesia; one rupiah = 100 sen; issued by the Bank of Indonesia.

RURAL DEVELOPMENT. A subject of international co-operation. Organizations reg. with the UIA:

Afro–Asian Rural Reconstruction Organization, f. 1962, New Delhi. Publ.: *Rural Reconstruction.*
Agency for Co-operation in Rural Development, f. 1975, Geneva. Centre for the Development of Human Resources in Rural Asia, f. 1974, Manila.
European Committee for Rural Law, f. 1960, Paris.
International Association for Rural Development, f. 1964, Brussels. Publ.: *Reports.*
International Association for Rural Family Houses, f. 1975, Paris.

International Research Centre on Rural Co-operative Committees, f. 1965, Tel Aviv. Working relations with FAO and ILO.
Regional Center for Functional Literacy in Rural Areas in Latin America, Centro Regional de Alfabetizacion Funcional en las Zonas Rurales de America Latina, CRETAL, f. 1951, Patzcuaro, Mexico.

Yearbook of International Organizations.

RURAL EDUCATION. A subject of international co-operation and agreements. The Treaty, called in Spanish *Convenio Andres Bello*, between the governments of Bolivia, Chile, Columbia, Ecuador, Peru and Venezuela, was signed in 1969 in Lima, relating to the educational, scientific and cultural rural integration of the Andean Region. The Executive Secretariat in Lima, the Andean Regional Centre for Research and Promotion of Rural Education in La Paz.

RUSH–BAGOT CONVENTION ON DEMILITARIZATION OF THE AMERICAN–CANADIAN BORDER, 1817. A Convention signed on Apr. 28, 1817 at Washington by the Secretary of State, R. Rush (1780–1859), and the British ambassador to the US, Ch. Bagot (1781–1843). The Convention established permanent demilitarization of the entire American–Canadian border between the Great Lakes and the Saint Lawrence River.

W.M. MALLOYS, *Treaties, Conventions, International Acts, Protocols and Agreements between the USA and other Powers*, 4 Vols., Washington, DC, 1909–38, Vol. I, p. 628; T. GLAZEBROOK, *Sir Charles Bagot in Canada*, London, 1929; J.H. POWELL, *Richard Rush: Republican Diplomat*, New York, 1942.

RUSSELL'S (BERTRAND) INTERNATIONAL TRIBUNALS. Two international institutions, under the aegis of English philosopher and mathematician Bertrand Arthur 3rd Earl of Russell, (1872–1970):
(1) International Tribunal on War Crimes in Vietnam f. 1966 by Bertrand Russell. Members: J.P. Sartre (France) president, G. Andres (FRG), L. Basso (Italy), S. de Beauvoir (France), L. Cardenas (Mexico), S. Carmichel (US), A. Carpentier (Cuba), J. de Castro (Brazil), V. Dedijer (Yugoslavia), D. Dellinger (US), I. Deutscher (UK), A. Hernandez (Philippines), M. Ali Kasusi (Pakistan), S. Sachati (Japan), L. Schwartz (France), P. Weiss (FRG). After two sessions (in Stockholm May 2–10, 1967 and in Roskilde near Copenhagen Nov. 20–Dec. 1, 1967), the Russell Tribunal published a unanimous judgment: the United States together with Australia, New Zealand, South Korea, Thailand and the Philippines were charged with a crime against peace, violation of the Briand–Kellogg Pact, the UN Charter and the Geneva Indochina Agreements.
(2) Bertrand Russell second International Tribunal on Crimes Against Human Rights in Latin America convened by the ex-members of the First Bertrand Russell Tribunal as a result of the growing fascization of many countries in the region, the use of terror and torture, mass murders, extermination of Indians and Gypsies, burning of books, destruction of cultural treasures. At the session of the Tribunal from Apr. 1 to 4, 1974 in Rome witnesses were heard who told of the tragic situation of political prisoners in Chile, Bolivia, Brazil, Paraguay and Uruguay. The Tribunal condemned the violation of human rights.

B. RUSSELL, *War Crimes in Vietnam*, London, 1967; J. DUFFET ed., *Against the Crime of Silence: Proceedings of the Russell International War Crimes Tribunal*, Stockholm, New York, 1968; T. TAYLOR, *Nuremberg and Vietnam*, New York, 1970.

R

RUSSIA. A Euro-Asiatic country whose name was adopted in 1721 by the Great Russian State (previously called the Grand Duchy of Moscow) in the 18th and 19th centuries annexed non-Russian lands; in 1914 its area was 22,556,520 sq. km with 140,600,000 inhabitants. The history of the international relations of Tsarist Russia ended with the outbreak of the October Revolution on Nov. 7, 1917 which introduced the name Russian Soviet Federated Socialist Republic.

Mezhdunarodnie otnoshenia v epokhu imperialisma. Dokumenti iz arkhivov tsarskiego i vriemiennego pravitielstva. I, 1878–1899; II, 1900–1913; III, 1914–1917; Moscow, 1923; H. SMITH, *The Russians,* New York, 1981; *The Cambridge Encyclopedia of Russia and the Soviet Union,* Cambridge, London, New York, 1982.

RUSSIA, DECLARATION OF THE RIGHTS OF THE PEOPLES OF, 1917. The document adopted by the Soviet of People's Commissars on Nov. 15, 1917, in Petrograd, announced in 215th issue of the *Isvestia* daily. The Declaration contained the following four principles adopted by Soviet Russia in keeping with the right of nations to self-determination, proclaimed at the initiative of V.I. Lenin by the First Congress of the Soviets of Workers' and Soldiers' Delegates:

"(1) The equality and sovereignty of the peoples of Russia.
(2) The right of the peoples of Russia to free self-determination, even to the point of separation and the formation of an independent state.
(3) The abolition of any and all national and national–religious privileges and disabilities.
(4) The free development of national minorities and ethnographic groups inhabiting the territory of Russia".

Dokumienty vnieshniey politiki SSSR, Moscow, 1957, Vol. 1; "Russian Documents", in: *International Conciliation,* No. 136, Mar. 1919, p. 419.

RUSSIAN AMERICA. Before the ▷ Alaska purchase by the United States in 1867 a common name for Alaska and North California.

RUSSIAN–AMERICAN COMPANY. The Russian trading company operating under a tsarist privilege 1799–1867, initially in Irkutsk and then in Petersburg, administering the Russian dominions in North America, then called Russian America. After Russia relinquished Alaska to the USA, the company was dissolved. ▷ Alaska Agreement, 1867.

RUSSIAN ASIA. IN the XIX century a common name for ▷ Siberia.

RUSSIAN LANGUAGE. One of the official and working languages of the UN, subject of international co-operation. On June 2, 1988 the Latvian Writer's Union called in an official declaration for a re-evaluation of the status of the Russian Language in the Soviet Union in non-Russian Republics. The status of the first-official language should be changed into 'a communication language between nationalities of the Soviet Union'. Organization reg. with the UIA:

International Association of Russian Language and Literature Teachers, f. 1948 in Moscow; under its aus-

pices International Russian Language Competitions are held in Moscow annually since 1972.

Yearbook of International Organizations; B. KELER, *Latvian Writers Publish a Call for Sovereignty, in: Internatoinal Herald Tribune,* June 23, 1988.

RUSSIAN MANIFESTO, 1832. An infraction of the ▷ Vienna Congress, 1814–1815 agreements (art. 1 of the Treaty on the Kingdom of Poland). By the Russian Manifesto of Feb. 14/26, 1832, the Kingdom of Poland was declared to be perpetually united to the Russian Empire and to form an integral part thereof. The British Government protested against this on July 3, 1832.

G.F. MARTENS, *Recueil des traités et conventions conclus par la Russie,* Petersburg, 1874–1905.

RUSSIAN ORTHODOX CHURCH. The largest religious institution in tsarist Russia (believers comprised two-thirds of the population); in the USSR the majority of the followers are in the Russian, Byelorussian and Ukrainian SSR. The constitution of the Church was accepted by the Council of 1945, amended by the Council of 1971. The Moscow Patriarch is recognized not only in the USSR, but also by three exarchates: for Western Europe with seat in West Berlin, for Central America with seat in New York, and for South America with seat in Buenos Aires and by church groups in Australia, Canada, Hungary, Japan and USA. Member of the World Council of Churches and the Christian Conference for Peace. Publ.: *Zhurnal Moskovskoi Patriarkhiy* since 1943.

R.A. KLOSTERMANN, *Probleme der Ostkirche,* Göttingen, 1956.

RUSSIAN REFUGEES, 1922. An arrangement with respect to the issue of certificates of identity to Russian refugees, signed on July 5, 1922 at Geneva by Austria, the British Empire, Bulgaria, France, Czechoslovakia, Germany, Greece, Hungary, Poland, Romania, the Kingdom of Serbs, Croats and Slovenes, Spain, and Switzerland, accepting the ▷ Nansen Passport. The following states adhered later to the agreement: Bolivia, Estonia, Finland, Guatemala, Italy, Latvia, Norway, the Union of South Africa. ▷ Byezhentsy.

LNTS, Vol. 13, p. 238.

RUSSIAN SOVIET FEDERATED SOCIALIST REPUBLIC, RSFSR. The constituent republic of the USSR, which occupies over 76% of the total area with 65% of the total USSR population. In consequence of the October Revolution, Nov. 7, 1917, a new revolutionary system in Russia was proclaimed on Nov. 10, 1917, by the Central Committee of the Soviets of Workmen's, and Soldiers' Deputies:

"(1) All classes and class divisions of citizens, class privileges and disabilities, class organizations and institutions which have until now existed in Russia, as well as all civil ranks, are abolished.
(2) All designations (as merchant, nobleman, burgher, peasant, etc.), titles (as Prince, Count, etc.), and distinctions of civil ranks (Privy, State, and other Councillors), are abolished, and one common designation is established for all the population of Russia – citizen of the Russian Republic."

Russia was declared

"to be a Republic of the Soviets of Workers', Soldiers', and Peasants' Deputies. All the central and local power belongs to these Soviets. The Russian Soviet Republic is organized on the basis of a free union of free nations, as a federation of Soviet national Republics."

Area: 17,070,649 sq. km. Pop. 1970 census: 130,079,000; est. 1982 – 140,000,000 of which *c.* 83% Russian, the rest being 38 national minorities, living in 16 autonomous republics; 6 krays, 5 autonomous oblasts, 10 national okrugs and 49 oblasts. Capital: Moscow (also of the USSR) with 8,203,000 inhabitants 1981. The Republic extends for *c.* 8000 km from the Baltic Sea in the West (Kaliningrad) to the Pacific Ocean in the east (Vladivostok). The RSFSR is bounded in Europe by Poland, Norway, Finland, Estonia, Lithuania, Latvia, Byelorussia, Ukraine, Georgia, and Azerbaidzhan; in Asia by the Kazakh Republic, Mongolia and China.

"Russian Documents", in: *International Conciliation,* No. 136, Mar. 1919, pp. 482–485.

RUSSO-JAPANESE WAR 1904–1905. ▷ Japanese Russian Treaties 1858–1916.

RUSSO-TURKISH WAR 1877–88. ▷ San Stefano Peace Treaty, 1878.

RWANDA. Member of the UN. Republic of Rwanda. An East African state, bordered by Zaïre, Uganda, Tanzania and Burundi. Area: 26,338 sq. km. Pop. 1987 est. 6,454,000 (1978 census: 4,819,317). Capital: Kigali with 698,063 inhabitants in 1978. GNP per capita 1987 US $310. Official languages: Kinya-Rwanda and French. Currency: one Rwanda franc = 100 centimes. National Day: July 1, Independence Day, 1962.
Member of the UN since Sept. 18, 1962 and of UN specialized agencies with exception of IAEA and IMO. Member of the OAU and is an ACP state of the EEC.
International relations: powerful kingdom in the 19th century until 1890, when it became part of German East Africa; occupied by Belgian troops 1916; a mandate of the League of Nations, 1920–45 under Belgian administration with the name Ruanda-Urundi, and after World War II as a UN trusteeship territory, 1946–62. Independence on July 1, 1962. Internal conflicts between the Hutu and Tutsi tribes, and external disputes with Burundi, Uganda and Zaïre.

UNTS, Vol. 8, pp. 105–117; B. LACROIX, *Le Rwanda,* Montreal, 1966; *The Europa Year Book 1984. A World Survey,* Vol. II, pp. 2296–2304, London, 1984.

RYE. One of the main agricultural products included in UN international statistics and the UNCTAD program for the development of staples.

RYSWICK PEACE TREATY, 1697. A Treaty between the King of Great Britain, and the King of France, ending the war of Grande Alliance, signed on Sept. 20, 1697 at Ryswick, with a separate article of the Treaty between the King of France and the King of Spain.

Major Peace Treaties 1648–1967, New York, 1967, Vol. 1, pp. 145–176.

RYUKYU ISLANDS. ▷ Japan, ▷ Okinawa.

S

SA. Sturmabteilungen der NSDAP. Storm Troops of the Nazi Party in Germany (▷ NSDAP) armed, uniformed and organized along military lines, since 1920 directly subordinate to A. Hitler; was the main instrument of terror during the period of Hitler's struggle to seize and consolidate power; in 1933 i.a. organized the concentration camps. On June 30, 1934 the leaders of the SA were murdered by the ▷ SS and units of the SA were transformed into paramilitary units without any significant influence on the development of the state. The Military Tribunal of Nuremberg admitted that, in contrast to the SS and Gestapo, the SA did not generally participate in war crimes, and as a result it was not included among the war criminal organizations.

E. RÖHM, *Die Memoiren des Stabschefs Röhm*, Saarbrücken, 1934; K.D. BRACHER, W. SANAR, G. SCHULZ, *Die National-sozialistische Machtergreifung*, Köln, 1960.

SAARC. ▷ South-Asian Association for Regional Co-operation.

SAARLAND. Since 1956 a state of the Federal Republic of Germany; area: 2569 sq. km; pop. 1985 census: 1,048,300; capital: Saarbrücken with 187,600 inhabitants, 1985. The territory has been the subject of conflict between France and Germany since June 28, 1919, when under art. 45 of the Treaty of Versailles the coal mines located in the Saarland basin were ceded to France with the exclusive right to use them as "absolute and exclusive property, free of any debts and liabilities" and being "compensation for the devastation of coal in Northern France and a part of dues that Germany should pay as war reparations." Arts. 46-50, together with the Annex, determined the border of Saarland and excluded the area from German jurisdiction, thereby establishing "the Government of the territory of the Saarland basin" subordinated to a special Commission of the League of Nations consisting of five members named by the LN Council. On the basis of a plebiscite on Jan. 12, 1935 favoring reunification of Saarland with Germany, the provisions of the Versailles Treaty were annulled and on Mar. 1, 1935, Saarland was incorporated into the German Reich. After the liberation by the US VII Army on March 21, 1945 in keeping with the Declaration of the Four Powers of June 5, 1945, France again occupied the territory on July 26, 1945. On Aug. 22, 1946, France formed a custom frontier between Saarland and the rest of Germany and on Dec. 15, 1947, established the government of Saarland based on the pro-French parliament which had been elected on Oct. 5, 1947. France was the official representative of Saarland at the Paris Conference that established the European Coal and Steel Community, Apr. 18, 1951. In the face of claims by the Federal Republic of Germany on Apr. 23, 1954, the French–German convention on the "European status of Saarland" was signed. Two years later, following a plebiscite which resulted in rejection of the status by the people of Saarland, France ceded Saarland to the Federal Republic of Germany. The customs union with France was dissolved, and Saarland was integrated into the Federal Republic of Germany as the tenth *Land* on Jan. 1, 1957.

Bassin de la Sarre. Documents. Geneva, 1920; J. FREYMOND, *The Saar 1945–1955*, New York, 1960; M. MERLE, "Le règlement de la question sarroise et la liquidation du contentieux france-allemande", in: *Annuaire Français de droit international*, Paris, 1956; *The Europa Yearbook 1987. A World Survey*, Vol. I, London, 1987.

SAAVEDRA LAMAS TREATY, 1933. The name adopted for the Non-aggression and Conciliation Anti-war Treaty prepared by the minister of foreign affairs of Argentina, C. Saavedra Lamas (1880–1954), on the basis of the ▷ Briand–Kellogg Treaty, 1928, in the League of Nations and the ▷ Stimson Non-Recognition Doctrine, 1931, presented to governments of American republics on Sept. 10, 1932. On Oct. 10, 1933 the following six Latin American states signed the Saavedra Lamas Treaty in Rio de Janeiro: Argentina, Brazil, Chile, Mexico, Paraguay and Uruguay. The closing art. 16 made the Saavedra Lamas Treaty "accessible to all states" without the limitation to "American" used in other inter-American treaties. In the years 1934–38 the treaty was signed not only by all other Latin American states, but also by 11 European states (Bulgaria, Czechoslovakia, Finland, Greece, Italy, Norway, Portugal, Romania, Spain, Turkey and Yugoslavia), thereby making the Saavedra Lamas Treaty the only inter-American treaty with the membership of states from outside the hemisphere. Seven states did not ratify the treaty (in brackets the year of signing): Bolivia (1934), Greece (1935), Costa Rica (1934), Norway (1936), Portugal (1934), Turkey (1935) and Italy (1934). For American states the Treaty has been suspended by the ▷ Bogota Pact, 1948. The text is as follows:

"The States hereinafter named, in an endeavor to contribute to the consolidation of peace, and in order to express their adherence to the effort that all civilized nations have made to further the spirit of universal harmony;

To the end of condemning aggression and territorial acquisitions secured by means of armed conquest and of making them impossible, of sanctioning their invalidity through the positive provisions of this Treaty, and in order to replace them with pacific solutions based upon lofty concepts of justice and equity;

Being convinced that one of the most effective means of insuring the moral and material benefits the world derives from peace is through the organization of a permanent system of conciliation of international disputes, to be applied upon a violation of the hereinafter mentioned principles;

Have decided to record, in conventional form, these aims of non-aggression and concord, through the conclusion of the present Treaty, to which end they have appointed the undersigned Plenipotentiaries, who, after having exhibited their respective full powers, which were found in good and due form, have agreed on the the following provisions:

Art. I. The High Contracting Parties solemnly declare that they condemn wars of aggression in their mutual relations or against other States and that the settlement of disputes and controversies shall be effected only through the pacific means established by International Law.

Art. II. They declare that between the High Contracting Parties territorial questions must not be settled by resort to violence and that they shall recognize no territorial arrangement not obtained through pacific means, nor the validity of an occupation or acquisition of territory brought about by armed force.

Art. III. In case any of the States engaged in the dispute fails to comply with the obligations set forth in the foregoing Articles, the Contracting States undertake to make every effort in their power for the maintenance of peace. To that end, and in their character of neutrals, they shall adopt a common and solidary attitude; they shall exercise the political, juridical or economic means authorized by International Law; they shall bring the influence of public opinion to bear; but in no case shall they resort to intervention either diplomatic or armed. The attitude they may have to take under other collective treaties of which said States are signatories is excluded from the foregoing provisions.

Art. IV. The High Contracting Parties, with respect to all controversies which have not been settled through diplomatic channels within a reasonable period, obligate themselves to submit to the conciliatory procedure created by this Treaty, the disputes specifically mentioned, and any other that may arise in their reciprocal relations, without any further limitations than those recited in the following Article.

Art. V. The High Contracting Parties and the States which may hereafter accede to this Treaty may not formulate at the moment of signing, ratifying or adhering thereto limitations to the procedure of conciliation other than those indicated below:

(a) Controversies for the settlement of which pacifist treaties, conventions, covenants, or agreements, of any nature, have been concluded. These shall in no case be deemed superseded by this Treaty; to the contrary, they shall be considered as supplemented thereby insofar as they are directed to insure peace. Questions or issues settled by previous treaties are also included in the exception.

(b) Disputes that the Parties prefer to settle by direct negotiation or through submission to an arbitral or judicial procedure by mutual consent.

(c) Issues that International Law leaves to the exclusive domestic jurisdiction of each State, under its constitutional system. On this ground the Parties may object to their being submitted to the procedure of conciliation before the national or local jurisdiction has rendered a final decision. Cases of manifest denial of justice or delay in the judicial proceedings are excepted, and should they arise, the procedure of conciliation shall be started not later than within the year.

(d) Questions affecting constitutional provisions of the Parties to the controversy. In case of doubt, each Party shall request its respective Tribunal or Supreme Court, whenever vested with authority therefor, to render a reasoned opinion on the matter.

(e) At any time, and in the manner provided for in art. XV, any High Contracting Party may communicate the instrument stating that it has partially or totally dropped the limitations set thereby to the procedure of conciliation.

The Contracting Parties shall deem themselves bound to each other in connection with the limitations made by any of them, only to the extent of the exceptions recorded in this Treaty.

Art. VI. Should there be no Permanent Commission of Conciliation, or any other international body charged with such a mission under previous treaties in force, the High Contracting Parties undertake to submit their controversies to examination and inquiry by a Commission of Conciliation to be organized in the manner hereinafter set forth, except in case of an agreement to the contrary entered into by the Parties in each instance: The Commission of Conciliation shall consist of five members. Each Party to the controversy shall appoint one member, who may be chosen from among its own nationals. The three remaining members shall be appointed by agreement of the Parties from among nationals of third nations. The latter must be of different nationalities, and shall not have their habitual residence in the territory of the Parties concerned, nor be in the service of either one of them. The Parties shall select the President of the Commission of Conciliation from among these three members.

Should the Parties be unable to agree, they may request a third nation or any other existing international body to make those designations. Should the nominees so designated be objected to by the Parties, or by any of them, each Party shall submit a list containing as many names as vacancies are to be filled, and the names of those to sit on the Commission of Conciliation shall be determined by lot.

Art. VII. Those Tribunals or Supreme Courts of Justice vested by the domestic law of each State with authority to interpret, as a Court of sole or final recourse and in matters within their respective jurisdiction, the Constitution, the treaties or the general principles of the Law of Nations, may be preferred for designation by the High Contracting Parties to discharge the duties

S

entrusted to the Commission of Conciliation established in this Treaty. In this event, the Tribunal or Court may be constituted by the whole bench or may appoint some of its members to act independently or in Mixed Commissions organized with justices of other Courts or Tribunals, as may be agreed by the Parties to the controversy.

Art. VIII. The Commission of Conciliation shall establish its own Rules of Procedure. Those shall provide, in all cases, for hearing both sides.

The Parties to the controversy may furnish, and the Commission may request from them, all the antecedents and data necessary. The Parties may be represented by agents, with the assistance of counsellors or experts, and may also submit every kind of evidence.

Art. IX. The proceedings and discussions of the Commission of Conciliation shall not be made public unless there is a decision to that effect, assented to by the Parties. In the absence of any provision to the contrary, the Commission shall adopt its decisions by a majority vote; but it may not pass upon the substance of the issue unless all its members are in attendance.

Art. X. It is the duty of the Commission to procure a conciliatory settlement of the disputes submitted to it. After impartial consideration of the questions involved in the dispute, it shall set forth in a report the outcome of its work and shall submit to the Parties proposals for a settlement on the basis of a just and equitable solution. The report of the Commission shall, in no case, be in the nature of a decision or arbitral award, either in regard to the exposition or interpretation of facts or in connection with juridical consideration or findings.

Art. XI. The Commission of Conciliation shall submit its report within a year to be reckoned from the day of its first sitting, unless the Parties decide, by common accord, to shorten or extend that term.

Once started, the procedure of conciliation may only be interrupted by a direct settlement between the Parties, or by their later decision to submit, by common accord, the dispute to arbitration or to an international court.

Art. XII. On communicating its report to the Parties, the Commission of Conciliation shall fix a period of time, which shall not exceed six months, within which the Parties shall pass upon the bases of settlement it has proposed. Once this period of time has expired the Commission shall set forth in a final act the decision of the Parties. Should the period of time elapse without the Parties having accepted the settlement, nor adopted by common accord another friendly solution, the Parties to the controversy shall regain their freedom of action to proceed as they may see fit within the limitations set forth in Articles I and II of this Treaty.

Art. XIII. From the outset of the procedure of conciliation until the expiration of the term set by the Commission for the Parties to make a decision, they shall abstain from any measure which may prejudice the carrying out of the settlement to be proposed by the Commission and, in general, from every act capable of aggravating or prolonging the controversy.

Art. XIV. During the procedure of conciliation the members of the Commission shall receive honoraria in the amount to be agreed upon by the Parties to the controversy. Each Party shall bear its own expenses and a moiety of the joint expenses or honoraria.

Art. XV. This Treaty shall be ratified by the High Contracting Parties, as soon as possible, in conformity with their respective constitutional procedures.

The original Treaty and the instruments of ratification shall be deposited in the Ministry of Foreign Affairs and Worship of the Argentine Republic, which shall give notice of the ratifications to the other signatory States. The Treaty shall enter into effect for the High Contracting Parties thirty days after deposit of the respective ratifications and in the order in which the same may be made.

Art. XVI. This Treaty remains open to the adherence of all the States.

The adherence shall be made through the deposit of the respective instrument with the Ministry of Foreign Affairs and Worship of the Argentine Republic, which shall give notice thereof to the other States concerned.

Art. XVII. This Treaty is concluded for an indefinite period, but it may be denounced by means of one year's previous notice, at the expiration of which it shall cease to be in force as regards the Party denouncing the same, but shall remain in force as regards the other States

which may be Parties thereto under signature or adherence. Notice of the denunciation shall be addressed to the Ministry of Foreign Affairs and Worship of the Argentine Republic, which will transmit it to the other States concerned."

LNTS, Vol. 163, 1935–36, p. 403; CARNEGIE ENDOWMENT, *International Conferences of American States, First Supplement, 1933–1940*, Washington, DC, 1940.

SABA. Island in the Leeward Islands group in the ▷ Netherlands Antilles. Area: 13 sq. km. Pop. 1985 estim. 10,300. Since Jan. 1, 1986 special status with ▷ Curaçao.

SABAH. One of the federal states of Malaysia since Sept. 16, 1963. Formerly British North Borneo, 1882–1963. Area: 73,613 sq. km. Pop. 1980 census: 998,827.

J. PAXTON ed., *The Statesman's Yearbook 1987–88*, London, 1987.

SABMIS. Seabased Anti-Ballistic Missile Intercept System, the sea anti-ballistic system of the USA, experimental studies undertaken 1970; its land counterpart is ▷ Safeguard.

SACCHARIN. A chemical sugar substitute. In therapy a sweetening agent for diabetics. A subject of international dispute 1977/78 between WHO and Canadian and American experts, who found saccharin harmful and requested its prohibition. According to the WHO, tests carried out in other countries did not confirm North American experts' evidence.

SACCO–VANZETTI CASE, 1921–27. A murder trial in Massachusetts, USA, from May 31, 1921 to Apr. 19, 1927, of two American workers of Italian descent, Nicola Sacco (1891–1927) and Bartolomeo Vanzetti (1888–1927), supposed anarchists who were falsely accused and on Apr. 19, 1927 sentenced to death. Their execution on Aug. 23, 1927 caused protest throughout the entire world. In the 1970s in the USA there was a campaign for their rehabilitation. In 1977 the Congress of the state of Massachusetts rehabilitated Sacco and Vanzetti.

N.D. BAKER (ed.), *The Sacco–Vanzetti Case: A Transcript of the Record of the Trial*, New York, 1928; H.B. EHRMANN, *The Untried Case: the Sacco–Vanzetti Case and the Morelli Gang*, New York, 1933; R.P. WEEKS (ed.), *Commonwealth v. Sacco and Vanzetti*, New York, 1958.

SACEUR. Supreme Allied Commander Europe. The supreme commander of allied armed forces in Europe NATO and CINCCHAN. He is always an American general, and his deputies are British and West German generals.

D. ROBERTSON, *Guide to Modern Defense and Strategy*, Detroit, 1988.

SACHSENHAUSEN–ORANIENBURG. One of the largest German concentration camps near Berlin, on the Havel river. In 1933 the Gestapo established on the periphery of the city the Concentration Camp Oranienburg, in 1936 extended to Sachsenhausen, named Konzentrations-Lager Sachsenhausen–Oranienburg and divided into 53 sub-camps for about 50,000 persons. Of some 200,000 persons of different nationalities that passed through Sachsenhausen–Oranienburg, half died. In Oct., 1939, 184 professors of the Jagiellonian University in Cracow were placed in the camp. It was liberated by the Soviet army Apr. 22, 1945. Since 1961 it is an International Museum of the Resistance Movement, under the care of the GDR government.

The Trial of German Major War Criminals. Proceedings of the International Military Tribunal Sitting at Nurem-

berg, Germany, 42 Vols. London, 1946–48, Vol. 9, p. 371, Vol. 11, pp. 334, 351, 358, 363; Vol. 12, pp. 36, 126, Vol. 15, p. 309; Vol. 17, p. 268; Vol. 21 pp. 120, 121, 124, 127, 130, 134, 137; H. KUNN, *Der KZ-Staat. Rolle und Entwicklung der faschistischen Konzentrationslager 1938 bis 1945*, Berlin, 1960; G. ZYCH, *Oranienburg*, Warsaw, 1962; E. KOGON, *Der SS-Staat, Das System der deutschen Konzentrationslager*, München, 1974.

SACKS. A subject of international co-operation. Organization reg. with the UIA:

European Federation of Manufacturers of Multiwall Paper Sacks, f. 1952, Paris. Members: Manufacturers of 16 western European countries. Publ.: *Flash d'information*.

Yearbook of International Organizations.

SACLANT. Supreme Allied Commander Atlantic, the supreme commander of allied armed forces in the Atlantic NATO, besides SACEUR and CINCCHAN. He is always an American general and his deputy is a British general.

SACLANTCEN. ▷ NATO.

SACRED PLACES. An international term for places of worship, covered by international protection, ▷ Jerusalem, for example, or Mecca, which is accessible only to followers of one religion. The Catholic Church established strict regulations for its sacred places in *Codex Juris Canonici*.

SADCC. ▷ Southern African Development Coordination Conference.

SADOVA. A village in Bohemia, near Hradec Kralove (Czechoslovakia), the site of the Battle of Sadova or Battle of Königgratz, July 3, 1866, between Austria and Prussia with heavy losses on both sides. The armistice signed July 22 ending the war resulted in the ▷ Austro–Prussian Peace Treaty, signed in Prague, Aug. 23, 1866.

SADR. Sahrawi Democratic Arab Republic. ▷ Western Sahara.

SAF. Structural Adjustment Facility, est. March 26, 1986 by the IMF to provide balance-of-payments assistance to low-income developing countries on concessional terms. About ▷ SDR 2,700 million would be available to the SAF (repayment to the IMF over the period 1985–91 of loans made from the Trust Fund in 1976–81.) Interest rate would be charged at ½ per cent per annum.

KEESING's *Record of World Events*, 1987, No. 1.

SAFE-CONDUCT. An international term for a document also called an iron letter assuring the safe-conduct of a person, vehicle, or ship during a conflict; in the 20th century issued mainly to persons benefiting from asylum in foreign embassies (a practice most frequently occurring in Latin America) or to persons sent to another country for whatever other reasons which require a guarantee of safe-conduct. ▷ Vienna Convention on Diplomatic Relations, 1961.

Dictionnaire de la terminologie du Droit International, Paris, 1960; R.L. BLEDSOE, B.A. BOCZEK, *The International Law Dictionary*, Oxford, 1987.

"SAFEGUARD". A name of the land anti-rocket system of the USA, whose construction was begun 1968. Its sea counterpart is ▷ SABMIS.

SAFEGUARDS. An international term, used in the UN, also known as "escape clause", for a provision in most trade agreements permitting special measures to protect an industry from undue injury

776

caused by increased import of a product subject to a trade concession.

UN Chronicle, October, 1982, p. 48.

SAFEGUARDS AGREEMENTS. A name for all agreements on peaceful use of atomic energy in the UN system. According to the *IAEA Bulletin* "for the first time in the history of the law of nations – sovereign states have accepted that an international organization (▷ IAEA) may carry out on their territory systematic inspections of installations that are highly important and sensitive." ▷ Tlatelolco Treaty, 1974.

IAEA Bulletin, September, 1984, pp. 27–28.

SAFEGUARDS IAEA SYSTEM. A system which originated with the Agency's Statute and which has been given further recognition by the Treaty on the Non-Proliferation of Nuclear Weapons (NPT), the Treaty for the Prohibition of Nuclear Weapons in Latin America (The Treaty of Tlatelolco), and the Treaty establishing a Nuclear Weapon Free Zone in the South Pacific (the Treaty of Rarotonga), constitutes the main part of the non-proliferation regime.

The technical IAEA definition:

A verification system within the framework of international non-proliferation policy applied to peaceful uses of nuclear energy designed to ensure that special fissionable and other materials, services, equipment, facilities, and information made available by the Agency or at its request or under its supervision or control are not used in such a way as to further any military purpose.

In the opinion of the IAEA:

The safeguards system serves, not rules, world interests. On the one hand, it eases transfers of nuclear technology for peaceful applications. On the other hand, it is firmly bound by the desire and willingness of governments not to acquire nuclear weapons and to demonstrate that conviction by opening their nuclear activities to continued outside inspection by a multinational institution. This initiative is revolutionary in the history of international relations.

IAEA Statute, 1957; *IAEA Safeguards Glossary*, 1987; *IAEA News Feature*, July 15, 1988.

SAFETY AND HYGIENE AT WORK. An international term describing a set of conditions under which workers are protected against accidents and professional diseases; subject of an ILO international convention, i.a. Convention No. 62 Concerning Safety Provisions in the Building Industry, signed on June 28, 1930 in Geneva and specifying e.g. rules of constructing scaffolds, hoisting devices, protective and first aid equipment. First inspections of factories in the context of safety and hygiene of work were introduced by England (1833), France (1841), Germany (1869), Russia (1882). The first international conference on safety and hygiene at work was held in Berlin in 1892 and in 1902 at the Paris Congress the International Society for the Protection of Workers was established in Basel; in 1921 the ILO established the Workers' Health Protection Section thereby assuming the functions of the Basel Society.

LEAGUE OF NATIONS HEALTH ORGANIZATION, *Bibliography of the Technical Work of the Health Organization 1920–1945*, Geneva, 1945.

SAFETY OF INTERNATIONAL CIVIL AVIATION. A subject of international conventions and UN Resolutions:
Convention on Offences and Certain Other Acts Committed on Board Aircraft, signed on Sept. 14, 1963 at Tokyo.
Convention for the Suppression of Unlawful Seizure of Aircraft, signed on Dec. 16, 1970 at The Hague.

Convention for the Suppression of Unlawful Acts against the Safety of Civil Aviation, signed on Sept. 23, 1971 at Montreal.
UN General Assembly Res. 2551 (XXIV) of Dec. 12, 1969.
UN General Assembly Res. 2645 (XXV) of Nov. 25, 1970.
UN General Assembly Res. 32/8 of Nov. 3, 1977.

UN Yearbook, 1963, 1969, 1970, 1971, 1977.

SAFETY OF LIFE AT SEA. A subject of international co-operation and conventions:
International Convention for the Safety of Life at Sea, between Australia, Belgium, Canada, Czechoslovakia, Denmark, France, Germany, Great Britain, India, Ireland, Italy, Japan, the Netherlands, Norway, Spain, Sweden, USA, USSR, signed on May 31, 1929 in London. Exchange of Notes relating to the Application of the Convention, London, Jan.–Feb., 1933. Replaced by the International Convention for the Safety of Life at Sea (with annexed Regulations), signed on June 10, 1948 in London, by the governments of Argentina, Australia, Belgium, Brazil, Canada, Chile, China, Denmark, Egypt, Finland, France, Greece, Iceland, India, Ireland, Italy, the Netherlands, New Zealand, Norway, Pakistan, Panama, Philippines, Poland, Portugal, Sweden, UK, USA, Union of South Africa, USSR and Yugoslavia.
Art. V. Carriage of Persons in Emergency states:

"(a) For the purpose of moving persons from any territory in order to avoid a threat to the security of their lives a Contracting Government may permit the carriage of a larger number of persons in its ships than is otherwise permissible under the present Convention.
(b) Such permission shall not deprive other Contracting Governments of any right of control under the present Convention over such ships which come within their posts.
(c) Notice of any such permission, together with the statement of the circumstances, shall be sent to IMCO by the Contracting Government granting such permission".

LNTS, Vol. 136, p. 81; *UNTS*, Vol. 164, p. 126.

"SAGAN BEFEHL". A description of the Hamburg Trial, Jul. 1–Sept. 3, 1947, conducted by the British martial court and concerning the murder of the 50 officers of the Royal Air Force who, captured after their escape from the ▷ POW camp at Sagan, were murdered by the Gestapo in 1944.

T. SOJKA, *Sagan Befehl*, Warsaw, 1983.

SAGARMATHA NATIONAL PARK. A natural site of Nepal, included in the ▷ World Heritage UNESCO List. This park contains the world's highest mountain, six other peaks rising to more than 7000 meters and the glaciers which feed the headwaters of the Ganges. Both the forest and the fauna need protection, as does the culture of the people, the Sherpas, who have come from Tibet at various times since the 16th century.

UNESCO, *A Legacy for All*, Paris, 1984.

SAHARA. *Arabic* = "wilderness". The largest desert in the world, 9,065,000 sq. km stretching 4830 km from the Atlantic Ocean to the Red Sea and 1930 km from Sahel to the Atlas Mts and the Mediterranean Sea. Pop. *c.* 2 million nomads. Following the colonial domination by European powers, divided between African states: Algeria, Chad, Egypt, Libya, Mali, Morocco, Mauritania, Niger and Sudan. An international event was the construction of the first trans-Saharan highway, connecting Algeria with Mali and Nigeria, built with UN technical aid (agreement with the UNDP was signed 1968). Organization reg. with the UIA:

Trans Sahara Liason Committee called Trans-Sahara Road, f. 1946. Algiers, Algeria. Members: governments of Algeria, Mali, Niger, Tunisia.

H.P. EYDOUX, *L'exploration du Sahara*, Paris, 1948; R. TURON, *Le Sahara*, Paris, 1952; B. VEHLET, *Le Sahara*, Paris, 1958; L.C. BRIGGS, *Tribes of the Sahara*, London, 1960; D. PORCH, *The Conquest of the Sahara*, New York, 1987; *Yearbook of International Organizations*, 1986/87.

SAHEL. The semi-arid region of Africa from Senegal, through Mauritania, Mali, Burkina Faso, Niger, Nigeria, Sudan to Ethiopia. Area of recent devastating drought. The UN General Assembly designated the UN Sahelian Office, responsible for assisting, on behalf of UNEP, the efforts of the countries of the Sudano-Sahelian region, to implement the UN Plan of Action to Combat ▷ Desertification. The heaviest rainstorms in 50 years between Sept. 4–13, 1988 led to severe flooding of the Blue and White Nile and the Atbara and Gash Rivers in Sudan. An estimated 1,500,000 people were left homeless. Organizations reg. with the UIA:

European Institute for the Development of African Sahel, f. 1975, Honilles, France.
International Training and Technological Support Service for West Africa and the Sahel, f. 1983, Dakar, Senegal.
Permanent Interstate Committee for Drought Control in the Sahel f. 1973, Ougadougou. Members: governments of Burkina Faso, Cape Verde, Chad, Gambia, Guinea-Bissau, Mali, Mauritania, Niger, Senegal.
Sahel Intergovernmental Institute, f. 1977, Bamako, Mali. Publ. *INSAH-Info*.
SOS Sahel International, f. 1976, Dakar, Senegal. Members: Burkina Faso, Mali, Mauritania, Niger, Senegal, Belgium, France, Italy, Luxembourg, UK.
United Nations Sudano-Sahelian Office, f. 1976, New York, NY, USA.
United Nations Trust Fund for Sudano-Sahelians, f. 1981, New York, NY, USA.

UN Chronicle, March, 1978, p. 19 and January, 1979, p. 52, and March, 1984, pp. I–XXVIII; L.H. MACDONALD, *Natural Resources Development in the Sahel. The Role of the United Nations System*, UNU Press, Tokyo, 1986; *Yearbook of International Organizations*, 1986/87; F. BEUDOT, *Elements for a Bibliography on the Sahelian Countries*. In English and French, Paris, 1987; W.S. ELLIS, Africa's Sahel. The Stricken Land, in: *National Geographic*, August 1987.

SAHRAWI DEMOCRATIC ARAB REPUBLIC. Proclaimed by ▷ Polisario on Feb. 27, 1976 in the ▷ Western Sahara.

SAIGON. A city in South Vietnam, since 1976 officially ▷ Ho Chi Minh City, on the right bank of the Saigon River, 80 km from the South China Sea; occupied by the French 1859–1954; first capital of Cochin-China, then from 1887 capital of the Union of Indochina, from 1954 to 1975 capital of South Vietnam (Republic of Vietnam).

SAIKAN TUNNEL. The World's longest (54 km) undersea railroad tunnel between Japan's main island of Honshu and the northernmost island Hokkaido, built 1964–88, opened to traffic on March 13, 1988. The second longest tunnel is the ▷ Chunnel.

R. GARNER, The Saga of the Saikan Tunnel, Boring Beneath Turbulent Seas, in: *International Herald Tribune*, March 16, 1988.

SAIL FOR EUROPE. An international association formed in 1977 in Brussels with the object of promoting the European Community idea through the sport of sailing, and to encourage the development of this sport. Participates in the Whitbread Round the World race.

SAIMAA. A lake system in central Finland, connecting more than 120 lakes, 4790 sq. km; the

S

largest Lake Saimaa 1295 sq. km connected with the Gulf of Finland by the Saimaa Canal, constructed 1856 in Finnish territory; 60 km long; from 1944 in accordance with the Soviet–Finnish Peace Treaty, two-thirds of Saimaa Canal is in the USSR; by virtue of the Supplementary Agreement to the Treaty from 1962 Finland leased the Soviet part of Saimaa Canal for 50 years. The canal is open to international navigation, but only for unarmed ships. Saimaa Canal is also called the Lappeenranta–Vyborg Canal, since it connects those two port cities.

R. CALVERT, *Inland Waterways of Europe*, London, 1963.

SAINT CHRISTOPHER (SAINT KITTS) – NEVIS. Member of the UN. An independent state in the Leeward Islands in the Caribbean Sea. Area: 261 sq. km (St Kitts, 168; Nevis, 93). Pop. 1986 estimate: 43,700. Capital: Basseterre, St Kitts, with 14,725 inhabitants, 1980. Official language: English. GNP 1986 per capita: US $1700. Currency: one East Caribbean dollar = 100 cents. National Day: September 19, Independence Day, 1983.
Member of the UN, Sept. 23, 1983 and of FAO, UNESCO, WHO, IBRD, IDA, IMF, IFAD, UNIDO and UPU. Member of the Commonwealth and OAS.
International relations: discovered and named St Christopher by Columbus, 1492. British and French settlements in 17th century. British territory 1913, part, together with ▷ Anguilla, of the Leeward Islands Federation from 1871 to 1958, then part of the Federation of the West Indies until 1962, when the colony achieved self-government as an associated state of the UK. Independent on Sept. 19, 1983.

UN Chronicle, January, 1984, p. 63; *The Europa Yearbook, 1984. A World Survey*, Vol. II, pp. 2305–2308, London, 1984; J. GORDON, *Nevis: Queen of the Caribes*, London, 1985.

SAINT EUSTATIUS. ▷ Curaçao.

SAINT-GERMAIN-EN-LAYE AUSTRIA PEACE TREATY, 1919 AND GENEVA PROTOCOL, 1922. A town in north-central France on the Seine River, suburb of Paris, with 37,509 inhabitants in 1975. Following World War I, on Sept. 10, 1919, the Peace Treaty with Austria was signed in St Germain, separating Austria from Hungary and creating the new Czechoslovak state, granting Upper Adiga to Italy and a number of provinces to Yugoslavia and Romania; came into force July 16, 1920. The Protocol to the Treaty, signed on Oct. 4, 1922 in Geneva prevented Austria from concluding political (▷ Anschluss) and economic agreements with Germany. The issue was brought before the League of Nations, which ordered the annulment of the Austrian–German customs union 1922.

LNTS, 1920 and 1922; J. VINER, *The Customs Union Issue*, New York, 1950.

SAINT HELENA. The British colony of St Helena since 1834 together with the islands Ascension and Tristan da Cunha, island in the south Atlantic Ocean, 1930 km from the west coast of Africa. Area: 121.7 sq. km. Pop. 1985, census: 5,895. Capital: Jamestown with 1,516 inhabitants. The place of exile of Napoleon I in 1815 until his death on May 5, 1821. In April–June, 1982, during the ▷ Falkland Islands–Malvinas Crisis the 3000-meter long airfield, built during World War II, temporarily became one of the busiest airports in the world. The UN Special Decolonization Committee on Sept. 14, 1983 reaffirmed the right of the people of St Helena to self-determination and independence. The GA Res.43/413

adopted by 123 votes to 2 (UK, USA) with 30 abstentions on Nov. 22, 1988 stated that:
"The General Assembly, on recommendation of the Fourth Committee, having examined the relevant chapters of the report of the Special Committee on the Situation with regard to the Implementation of the Declaration on the Granting of Independence to Colonial Countries and Peoples, reaffirmed the inalienable right of the people of St. Helena to self-determination and independence in conformity with the Declaration on the Granting of Independence to Colonial Countries and Peoples, contained in Assembly resolution 1514 (XV) of 14 December 1960. The Assembly urged the administering power, in consultation with the Legislative Council and other representatives of the People of St. Helena, to continue to take all necessary steps to ensure the speedy implementation of the Declaration in respect of the Territory and, in that connection, reaffirmed the importance of promoting an awareness among the people of St. Helena of the possibilities open to them in the exercise of their right to self-determination".

O. BLAKESTONE, *Isle of St. Helena*, London, 1957; A. CROSS, *Saint Helena*, Newton Abbot, 1981; *UN Chronicle, January, 1984, p. 62; The Europa Year Book 1984. A World Survey*, Vol. I. pp. 1263–1264, London, 1984; *UN Resolutions and Decisions adopted by the General Assembly during the First Part of its Forty-Third Session from 20 September to 22 December 1988*, New York, 1989, pp. 625–626.

SAINT JEAN-DE-MAURIENNE AGREEMENT, 1917. An agreement concluded between France, Great Britain and Italy on the division of Turkish territorial estates after World War I, signed on Apr. 19, 1917 in Saint Jean-de-Maurienne in France; confirmed by an exchange of relevant instruments on Aug. 18, 1917 in London, and on Aug. 21, 1917 in Paris.

C.A. COLLIARD, *Droit international et histoire diplomatique*, Paris, 1950.

SAINT KITTS–NEVIS. ▷ Saint Christopher and Nevis.

SAINT LAWRENCE RIVER. The principal US–Canadian river of North America, 1197 km long; it rises in the northeastern end of Lake Ontario and flows northeast along the US–Canadian border (183 km), then to the Gulf of St Lawrence. Together with the Great Lakes forms the international ▷ Saint Lawrence Seaway system.

SAINT LAWRENCE SEAWAY SYSTEM. The Great Lakes and St Lawrence Basin, a vast drainage system covering an area of 788,800 sq. km in Canada, and 288,000 sq. km in the United States, totals 1,076,800 sq. km. It includes Lake Superior, Lake Michigan, Lake Huron, Lake Saint Clair, Lake Erie and Lake Ontario, together with all tributary rivers and streams. Canada–US co-operation began in 1895 with the creation of the International Deep Waterways Commission. The Commission investigated all possible waterways which would connect the Great Lakes to the Atlantic Ocean. In 1903 a new International Waterways Commission was formed for the purpose of studying the feasibility and usefulness of a deep waterway, between the Great Lakes and Montreal. In 1909 the International Boundary Treaty between Canada and the US established the International Joint Boundary Water Commission. In 1932 Canada and the US signed in Washington a treaty providing for the construction of a waterway 27 ft (9 m) deep from the sea to all Canadian and American points on the Great Lakes, but the US Congress failed to approve. Subsequently, the Great Lake–Saint Lawrence Basin Agreement was drafted and signed on Mar. 19, 1941 in Ottawa. After World War II Canada decided to establish in

Dec. 1951 the Canadian St Lawrence Seaway Authority. In May, 1954 the US Congress approved the American St Lawrence Seaway Development Corporation. The Seaway, as the first part of the Great Lakes–St Lawrence Basin System, was officially opened on June 26, 1959 by HM Queen Elizabeth II and President Dwight D. Eisenhower. A system of dams and locks in the river, permits entry of oceangoing vessels into Canada and the USA. Under anti-pollution protection of the US–Canada Water Quality Agreement, 1972.

Correspondence and Documents Relating to St Lawrence Deep Waterways Treaty of 1932, Washington, DC, 1932; *St Lawrence Seaway Manual*, US Senate Doc. No. 165, Washington, DC, 1955; R.D. SCOTT, "The Canadian–American Boundary Waters Treaty", in: *Canadian Bar Review*, No. 36, 1958; *International Navigable Waterways*, UNITAR, New York, 1975, pp. 115–124.

SAINT LUCIA. Member of the UN. The state of St Lucia in the Caribbean Sea. One of the Windward Islands, West Indies. Area: 616 sq. km. Pop. 1988, estimate: 146,600. Capital: Castries with 47,600 inhabitants. Official language: English. Currency: one East Caribbean dollar = 100 cents. National Day: Feb. 22, Independence Day, 1979. Member of all UN specialized agencies except ITU and WIPO. International relations: settled by the French 1660; ceded to Britain in 1814. Part of the British Windward Islands Colony. In 1967 self-government in the Associated states of the West Indies. Member of the UN, Sept. 18, 1979. Member of the Organization of East Caribbean States, participated in the US-led invasion of Grenada, Oct., 1983.

The Europa Year Book 1984. A World Survey, Vol. II. pp. 2309–2313, London, 1984; G. ELLIS, *St. Lucia: Helen of the West Indies*, London, 1985.

SAINT MAARTEN OR SAINT MARTIN. Island in the Leeward Islands group in the ▷ Netherlands Antilles. Area: 95.8 sq. km. Pop. 1985, estimate: 10,000. Since Jan. 1, 1986 special status with ▷ Curaçao.

SAINT PETERSBOURG. Russian: Sankt-Petersburg. The name in tsarist Russia from 1703–1914 of the city and port on the Neva River at the head of the Gulf of Finland, renamed 1914–24 Petrograd, since then Leningrad; built in 1703 by Peter I.

SAINT PETERSBOURG DECLARATION, 1868. A Declaration on the matter of small-caliber explosive shells; adopted at an International Conference convened at the initiative of Russia in Petersburg, Nov. 29–Dec. 11, 1868, attended by Austria, Bavaria, Belgium, Denmark, France, Great Britain, Greece, Hungary, the Netherlands, Persia, Portugal, Russia, Sweden, Switzerland, Turkey, Wirtemberg and the North German Union. The Saint Petersbourg Declaration imposed on the contracting parties an obligation that "in case of war between them they shall renounce reciprocally the use by their armies on land and sea of any explosive shells and those containing shattering or incendiary matter which weigh less than 400 grammes each."

G.F. MARTENS, *Nouveau Recueil, General*, Vol. 18, p. 479.

SAINT PIERRE AND MIQUELON. Departement de Saint-Pierre-et-Miquelon (Iles). French archipelago in the north Atlantic in the Gulf of St Lawrence, a group of eight small islands off the south coast of Newfoundland. Area of St-Pierre group 242 sq. km. Pop. 1988 est.: 6400; Miquelon-Langlade group 216 sq. km. Pop. 1982 census: 6,041. The UN Decolonization Committee demanded in 1974 full autonomy for the population. In July, 1976 the department changed its status from that of French Overseas Territory and is represented in the National Assembly of France by one deputy, in the Senate by one senator and in the Economic and Social Council by one councillor.

J.Y. RIBAULT, *Histoire de Saint-Pierre et Miquelon: Des Origines à 1814*, Paris, 1962; E.A. DE LA RUE, *Saint-Pierre et Miquelon*, Paris, 1963; *The Europa Yearbook 1984. A World Survey*, Vol. II, pp. 1577–1578, London, 1984.

SAINT VINCENT AND THE GRENADINES.
Member of the UN. A state in the Windward Islands, West Indies. Area: 389 sq. km together with the Grenadine islands. Pop. 1987, est.: 112,614 (about 10,000 of which live on the Grenadines). 1979 census: 119,942. Capital: Kingstown with 33,694 inhabitants. GNP per capita 1986: US $960. Official currency: pound sterling. National Day: Oct. 27, Independence Day 1979.
Member of the UN Sept. 16, 1980 and of all its specialized agencies except ILO, IFC, WMO and WIPO. "Special Member" of the Commonwealth not represented at meetings of Heads of Government.
International relations: British colony 1762–1958. Member of the West Indies Federation 1958–79. Independent on Oct. 27, 1979.

UN Chronicle, March 1980, pp. 17–19; *The Europa Yearbook 1984, A World Survey*, Vol. II, pp. 2314–2318. London, 1984.

SAKHALIN.
Formerly Saghalien. The USSR island between the Sea of Okhotsk and the Sea of Japan, separated from the Japanese island of Hokkaido by the Soya Strait and from the USSR mainland by the Tatar Strait; colonized by Russia and Japan since the 17th century until 1875, when by a Japan–Russian agreement it was ceded to Tsarist Russia in exchange for the Kuriles; then after the Japanese–Russian war 1905 the southern part of Sakhalin returned to Japan by the Treaty of Portsmouth, Sept. 5, 1905; occupied entirely by Japan 1920–25. Divided again along the 50th parallel, in Aug., 1945, when it was occupied by the Soviet fleet in accordance with a resolution in Yalta of the Great Powers of Feb. 11, 1945 that "the southern part of Sakhalin as well as all of the adjacent islands will be returned to the Soviet Union." Japan renounced "all rights, titles and claims to the southern part of Sakhalin and its adjacent islands" by the Peace Treaty in San Francisco of Sept. 8, 1951. ▷ Pacific Ocean Washington Treaty, 1921.

The International Geographic Encyclopedia and Atlas, London, 1979.

SALAMI TACTICS.
An international term for an imperialistic method relying on small military steps to change the balance of power such as Adolf Hitler's 1935–1938 policy, from the remilitarization of ▷ Rhineland to the ▷ Anschluss and München Pact.

D. ROBERTSON, *Guide to Modern Defense and Strategy*, Detroit, 1988.

SALE GUERRE.
French = "Dirty War". French denomination after World War II of colonial wars in Vietnam and Algeria.

SALES OF GOODS, INTERNATIONAL.
A subject of international conventions and similar instruments:
Convention on the Law Applicable to International Sales of Goods, signed on June 15, 1955 at The Hague; came into force on May 3, 1964; ratified by Belgium, Denmark, Finland, France, Italy, Norway, Sweden; not ratified by Luxembourg, the Netherlands and Spain:
"Art. 1. This Convention shall apply to international sales of goods.
It shall not apply to sales of securities, to sales of ships and of registered boats or aircraft, or to sales upon judicial order or by way of execution. It shall apply to sales based on documents.
For the purposes of this Convention, contracts to deliver goods to be manufactured or produced shall be placed on the same footing as sales, provided the party who assumes delivery is to furnish the necessary raw materials for their manufacture or production.
The mere declaration of the parties, relative to the application of a law or the competence of a judge or arbitrator, shall not be sufficient to confer upon a sale the international character provided for in the first paragraph of this article." (*UNTS*, Vol. 510, p. 149).
Convention on the Jurisdiction of the Selected Form in the Case of International Sales of Goods, signed on Apr. 15, 1958 at The Hague, by Austria, Belgium, FRG and Greece, has not entered into force. (*Register of Texts of Conventions and Other Instrument Concerning International Trade Law*, UN, New York, 1973, Vol. I, p. 9.)
Convention on the Law Applicable to the Transfer of Title in International Sales of Goods, signed on Apr. 15, 1958 at The Hague by Greece and Italy; has not entered into force (*Register of Texts ...*, Vol. I, p. 13).
Convention relating to a Uniform Law on the International Sale of Goods, signed on July 1, 1964 at The Hague, ratified by Belgium, San Marino and UK, not ratified by FRG, France, Greece, Holy See, Hungary, Israel, Italy, Luxembourg, the Netherlands; has not entered into force (*Register of Texts ...*, Vol. I, p. 39).
Convention relating to a Uniform Law on the formation of Contracts for the International Sale of Goods, signed on July 1, 1964 at The Hague, ratified by San Marino and UK, signed but not ratified by Belgium, FRG, Greece, Holy See, Hungary, Israel, Luxembourg, the Netherlands; has not entered into force (*Register of Texts ...*, Vol. I, p. 64).
The Council for Mutual Economic Assistance, CMEA, has elaborated and approved three instruments on sale of goods between foreign trade organizations of the CMEA Member-States:
General Conditions of Assembly and Provision of Other Technical Services in connection with Reciprocal Deliveries of Machinery and Equipment, 1962.
General Conditions for the Technical Servicing of Machinery, Equipment and Other Items, 1962.
General Conventions of Delivery of Goods, 1968. (*Register of Texts ...*, Vol. I, pp. 17, 31 and 74).
▷ Goods Delivery in the CMEA Member-States.
The UNCITRAL elaborated and adopted in June, 1974 the Convention on the Limitation Period in the International Sale of Goods, 1974.
The International Institute for the Unification of Private Law, elaborated and adopted 1960 a Draft Uniform Law on the Contract of Commission on the International Sale or Purchase of Goods including articles on the relations between the principal and the commission agent (*UNIDROIT Yearbook*, 1960, p. 304); and in 1968 a Draft Uniform Law on the Protection of the Bona Fide Purchaser of Corporeal Movables, primarily concerned with the protection of the good faith purchaser against third parties (*UNIDROIT Yearbook*, 1968, p. 222).
The Inter-American Juridical Committee elaborated 1960 a Draft Convention on a Uniform Law on the International Sale of Tangible Personal Property, but in Sept., 1967 decided that there was no reason for promoting the adoption of a regional instrument to regulate the international sale of personal property. The Draft contains provisions defining the scope of law, and stating the types of transaction to which it applies (*Publication OAS* CIJ-46).
The UN Conference on Contracts for the International Sale of Goods, in Vienna, Mar. 10–Apr. 11, 1980 adopted a Convention providing uniform rules to govern the sale of goods between parties in different countries, replacing the two Hague Conventions 1964.

Register of Conventions and Other Instruments Concerning International Trade Law, UN, New York, 1973; *UN Monthly Chronicle*, July 1974, p. 35; *UN Chronicle*, June, 1980, p. 52.

SALIC LAW.
Latin: Lex Salica. A code of laws for the Salian Franks, one of the Teutonic laws issued in Gaul in the 5th century by Clovis.

K.A. ECKHARDT, *Pactus legis Salicae*, 2 Vols., 1954–56; Encyclopedia Britannica, Vol. 19, Chicago – London, 1973.

SALIC LAW OF SUCCESSION.
The monarchistic rule that women should not succeed to the crown, formulated in France in the XV century on the basis of ▷ Salic Law.

Encyclopedia Britannica, Vol. 19, Chicago – London, 1973.

SALMON.
Common name of fishes of the family *Salmonidae*; those living in the Atlantic Ocean are called in Latin *Salmo Salar* and those living in the Pacific are called *Oncorhynchus*. Subjects of international protection. ▷ Fishery.

SALO.
A town in northern Italy (Lombardy) on lake Garda; provisional capital of Italy during World War II from Sept., 1943 to Apr., 1945, during the Fascist rule of Benito Mussolini (1883–1943), who after losing power in the Kingdom of Italy on June 25, 1943 found shelter in Salo with the aid of A. Hitler's army and there proclaimed the pro-Hitler *Republica Sociale Italiana*. On Apr. 10, 1945 Salo was liberated by guerrillas who executed B. Mussolini outside Salo, near Lake Como.

SALONICA.
▷ Thessaloniki.

SALTPETER WAR.
▷ Pacific War, 1879–1883.

SALT. STRATEGIC ARMAMENTS LIMITATION TALKS.
The talks between the USA and USSR which began Nov. 17, 1969 in Helsinki on the question of retarding and limiting strategic armaments, above all in the area of atomic missiles, anti-missile systems, various types of strategic bombers, atomic submarines and systems for defense against them. The first two agreements concluded in the SALT talks were signed May 26, 1972 in Moscow on the limitation of anti-missile defense systems ▷ ABM and on some measures in the area of limiting strategic offensive weapons ▷ ICBM. The chronology of the talks which led to the signing of the first agreements was the following:
On Nov. 10, 1966 US Secretary of Defense R. McNamara informed the press that in the USSR near Moscow an ABM system was under construction. On Jan., 1967 US President L.B. Johnson sent a note to the government of the USSR with the proposition of suspending the costly construction of anti-ballistic missile systems. On Mar. 2, 1967 the government of the USSR agreed to begin talks on limiting the construction of "both offensive as well as defensive" rocket systems. After signing on July 1, 1968 the agreement on the non-proliferation of nuclear weapons the decision of both governments was announced at the beginning of SALT talks Nov. 17, 1969 in Helsinki. After a 1-year period of tension the first round began, conducted by the vice-minister of foreign affairs, V.S. Syemyonov and the director of the US Agency on Disarmament and Control, G. Smith; it lasted until Dec. 22, 1969; the second round was held in Vienna from Apr. 16 until July 14, 1970; the third in Helsinki from Nov. 2 until Dec. 18, 1970; the fourth round in Vienna from Mar. 15 until May 28, 1971 and fifth in Helsinki from July 7–Nov. 14, 1971, concluded with an understanding signed on Sept. 30, 1971, in Washington on measures for reducing the danger of an accidental nuclear war and improving communication between Moscow and Washington through

the ▷ Hot Line. The sixth round took place in Vienna from Nov. 15, 1971 until Feb. 4, 1972; the seventh in Helsinki – May 26–28, 1972 and ended with the signing in Moscow of the two above mentioned agreements. The second phase of talks in Geneva called SALT II, with the task of working out permanent agreements, began Oct. 21, 1972. Within the framework of SALT II on Dec. 27, 1972 a consultative committee was established on limiting the number of ballistic missile launchers. On June 21, 1973 during the visit of L. Brezhnev in Washington the document on the basic principles of American–Soviet talks on SALT was signed, and June 22, 1973 the understanding on the prevention of nuclear war was signed. Then, during the visit of US President R. Nixon to Moscow on July 3, 1974 the Protocol on the limitation of anti-missile defense systems and the Agreement on the limitation of underground atomic tests were signed. Two further agreements were signed Nov. 1, 1976 in Geneva: Protocol on putting into effect the understandings of 1971 on measures to decrease the risk of nuclear war, as well as Protocol on procedures for exchange, disassembly or destruction of antimissile defense systems. The third phase of SALT II talks lasted 1977–79 and ended with the signing June 15, 1979 in Vienna of a new agreement by J. Carter and L. Brezhnev, not ratified by the US Congress. The new negotiations called Strategic Arms Reduction Talks, START, were initiated on June 30, 1982, by President R. Reagan and L. Brezhnev. The chiefs of the delegations were the same as in the 1972 SALT negotiations, Edward Rowny (USA) and Vladimir Karpov (USSR). The negotiations were suspended in December 1983; reinitiated under the name ▷ START, March 15, 1985.

SIPRI, *World Armaments and Disarmament Yearbooks*, 1968–84; *SALT II Treaty: Background documents*, Washington DC, 1979; M.B. DONLEY, *The SALT Handbook*, Washington, DC, 1979; S. TALBOT, *Endgame: The Inside Story of SALT II*, New York, 1979; D. ROBERTSON, *Guide to Modern Defense and Strategy*, Detroit, 1988.

SALT I. AGREEMENT AND PROTOCOL, 1972.

The Interim Agreement between the USA and the USSR on Certain Measures with Respect to the Limitation of Strategic Offensive Arms, called SALT I Agreement, signed on May 26, 1972 in Moscow; came into force on Oct. 3, 1972. The text is as follows:

"The United States of America and the Union of Soviet Socialist Republics, hereinafter referred to as the Parties, Convinced that the Treaty on the Limitation of Anti-Ballistic Missile Systems and this Interim Agreement on Certain Measures with Respect to the Limitation of Strategic Offensive Arms will contribute to the creation of more favorable conditions for active negotiations on limiting strategic arms as well as to the relaxation of international tension and the strengthening of trust between states, Taking into account the relationship between strategic offensive and defensive arms, Mindful of their obligations under Art. VI of the Treaty on the Non-Proliferation of Nuclear Weapons, Have agreed as follows:
Art. I. The Parties undertake not to start construction of additional fixed land-based intercontinental ballistic missile (ICBM) launchers after July 1, 1972.
Art. II. The Parties undertake not to convert land-based launchers for light ICBMs, or for ICBMs of older types deployed prior to 1964, into land-based launchers for heavy ICBMs of types deployed after that time.
Art. III. The Parties undertake to limit submarine-launched ballistic missile (SLBM) launchers and modern ballistic missile submarines to the numbers operational and under construction on the date of signature of this Interim Agreement, and in addition to launchers and submarines constructed under procedures established by the Parties as replacements for an equal number of

ICBM launchers of older types deployed prior to 1964 or for launchers on older submarines.
Art. IV. Subject to the provisions of this Interim Agreement, modernization and replacement of strategic offensive ballistic missiles and launchers covered by this Interim Agreement may be undertaken.
Art. V.(1) For the purpose of providing assurance of compliance with the provisions of this Interim Agreement, each Party shall use national technical means of verification at its disposal in a manner consistent with generally recognized principles of international law.
(2) Each Party undertakes not to interfere with the national technical means of verification of the other Party operating in accordance with paragraph 1 of this Article.
(3) Each Party undertakes not to use deliberate concealment measures which impede verification by national technical means of compliance with the provisions of this Interim Agreement. This obligation shall not require changes in current construction, assembly, conversion, or overhaul practices.
Art. VI. To promote the objectives and implementation of the provisions of this Interim Agreement, the Parties shall use the Standing Consultative Commission established under art. XIII of the Treaty on the Limitation of Anti-Ballistic Missile Systems in accordance with the provisions of that Article.
Art. VII. The Parties undertake to continue active negotiations for limitations on strategic offensive arms. The obligations provided for in this Interim Agreement shall not prejudice the scope or terms of the limitations on strategic offensive arms which may be worked out in the course of further negotiations.
Art. VIII.(1) This Interim Agreement shall enter into force upon exchange of written notices of acceptance by each Party, which exchange shall take place simultaneously with the exchange of instruments of ratification of the Treaty on the Limitation of Anti-Ballistic Missile Systems.
(2) This Interim Agreement shall remain in force for a period of five years unless replaced earlier by an agreement on more complete measures limiting strategic offensive arms. It is the objective of the Parties to conduct active follow-on negotiations with the aim of concluding such an agreement as soon as possible.
(3) Each Party shall, in exercising its national sovereignty, have the right to withdraw from this Interim Agreement if it decides that extraordinary events related to the subject matter of this Interim Agreement have jeopardized its supreme interests. It shall give notice of its decision to the other Party six months prior to withdrawal from this Interim Agreement. Such notice shall include a statement of the extraordinary events the notifying Party regards as having jeopardized its supreme interests".

The text of the Protocol to the Interim Agreement is as follows:

"The United States of America and the Union of Soviet Socialist Republics, hereinafter referred to as the Parties,
Having agreed on certain limitations relating to submarine-launched ballistic missile launchers and modern ballistic missile submarines, and to replacement procedures, in the Interim Agreement.
Have agreed as follows:
The Parties understand that, under article III of the Interim Agreement, for the period during which that Agreement remains in force:
The US may have no more than 710 ballistic missile launchers on submarines (SLBMs) and no more than 44 modern ballistic missile submarines. The Soviet Union may have no more than 950 ballistic missile launchers on submarines and no more than 62 modern ballistic missile submarines. Additional ballistic missile launchers on submarines up to the above-mentioned levels, in the U.S. – over 656 ballistic missile launchers on nuclear-powered submarines, and in the U.S.S.R – over 740 ballistic missile launchers on nuclear-powered submarines, operational and under construction, may become operational as replacements for equal numbers of ballistic missile launchers of older types deployed prior to 1964 or ballistic missile launchers on older submarines.
The deployment of modern SLBMs on any submarine, regardless of type, will be counted against the total level of SLBMs permitted for the U.S. and the U.S.S.R.

This Protocol shall be considered an integral part of the Interim Agreement."

The text of Agreed Interpretations and Unilateral Statements regarding the Interim agreements are as follows:

1. Agreed interpretations
(a) Initialed Statements. The document set forth below was agreed upon and initialed by the Heads of the Delegations on May 26, 1972:
(A) The Parties understand that land-based ICBM launchers referred to in the Interim Agreement are understood to be launchers for strategic ballistic missiles capable of ranges in excess of the shortest distance between the north-eastern border of the continental U.S. and the north-western border of the continental U.S.S.R.
(B) The Parties understand that fixed land-based ICBM launchers under active construction as of the date of signature of the Interim Agreement may be completed.
(C) The Parties understand that in the process of modernization and replacement the dimensions of land-based ICBM silo launchers will not be significantly increased.
(D) The Parties understand that during the period of the Interim Agreement there shall be no significant increase in the number of ICBM or SLBM test and training launchers, or in the number of such launchers for modern land-based heavy ICBMs. The Parties further understand that construction or conversion of ICBM launchers at test ranges shall be undertaken only for purposes of testing and training.
(E) The Parties understand that dismantling or destruction of ICBM launchers of older types deployed prior to 1964 and ballistic missile launchers on older submarines being replaced by new SLBM launchers on modern submarines will be initiated at the time of the beginning of sea trials of a replacement submarine, and will be completed in the shortest possible agreed period of time. Such dismantling or destruction, and timely notification thereof, will be accomplished under procedures to be agreed in the Standing Consultative Commission.
(b) Common Understandings. Common understanding of the Parties on the following matters was reached during the negotiations:
A. Increase in ICBM silo dimensions
Ambassador Smith made the following statement on May 26, 1972:
The Parties agreed that the term 'significantly increased' means that an increase will not be greater than 10–15 per cent of the present dimensions of land-based ICBM silo launchers.
Minister Semenov replied that this statement corresponded to the Soviet understanding.
B. Standing Consultative Commission
Ambassador Smith made the following statement on May 22, 1972:
The United States proposes that the sides agree that, with regard to initial implementation of the ABM Treaty's Article XIII on the Standing Consultative Commission (SCC) and of the consultation Articles to the Interim Agreement on offensive arms and the Accidents Agreement, agreement establishing the SCC will be worked out early in the follow-on SALT negotiations; until that is completed, the following arrangements will prevail: when SALT is in session, any consultation desired by either side under these Articles can be carried out by the two SALT Delegations; when SALT is not in session, ad hoc arrangements for any desired consultations under these Articles may be made through diplomatic channels.
Minister Semenov replied that, on an ad referendum basis, he could agree that the U.S. statement corresponded to the Soviet understanding.
C. Standstill
On May 6, 1972, Minister Semenov made the following statement:
In an effort to accommodate the wishes of the U.S. side, the Soviet Delegation is prepared to proceed on the basis that the two sides will in fact observe the obligations of both the Interim Agreement and the ABM Treaty beginning from the date of signature of these two documents.
In reply, the U.S. Delegation made the following statement on May 20, 1972:

The U.S. agrees in principle with the Soviet statement made on May 6 concerning observance of obligations beginning from date of signature but we would like to make clear our understanding that this means that, pending ratification and acceptance, neither side would take any action prohibited by the agreements after they had entered into force. This understanding would continue to apply in the absence of notification by either signatory of its intention not to proceed with ratification or approval.

The Soviet Delegation indicated agreement with the U.S. statement.

2. Unilateral statements

(a) The following noteworthy unilateral statements were made during the negotiations by the United States Delegation:

A. Withdrawal from the ABM Treaty

On May 9, 1972, Ambassador Smith made the following statement:

The U.S. Delegation has stressed the importance the U.S. Government attaches to achieving agreement on more complete limitations on strategic offensive arms, following agreement on an ABM Treaty and on an Interim Agreement on certain measures with respect to the limitation of strategic offensive arms. The U.S. Delegation believes that an objective of the follow-on negotiations should be to constrain and reduce on a long-term basis threats to the survivability of our respective strategic retaliatory forces. The USSR Delegation has also indicated that the objectives of SALT would remain unfulfilled without the achievement of an agreement providing for more complete limitations on strategic offensive arms. Both sides recognize that the initial agreements would be steps toward the achievement of more complete limitations on strategic arms. If an agreement providing for more complete strategic offensive arms limitations were not achieved within five years, U.S. supreme interests could be jeopardized. Should that occur, it would constitute a basis for withdrawal from the ABM Treaty. The U.S. does not wish to see such a situation occur, nor do we believe that the USSR does. It is because we wish to prevent such a situation that we emphasize the importance the U.S. government attaches to achievement of more complete limitations on strategic offensive arms. The U.S. Executive will inform the Congress, in connection with Congressional consideration of the ABM Treaty and the Interim Agreement, of this statement of the U.S. position.

B. Land-mobile ICBM launchers

The U.S. Delegation made the following statement on May 20, 1972:

In connection with the important subject of land-mobile ICBM launchers, in the interest of concluding the Interim Agreement the U.S. Delegation now withdraws its proposal that Article I or an agreed statement explicitly prohibit the deployment of mobile land-based ICBM launchers. I have been instructed to inform you that, while agreeing to defer the question of limitation of operational land-mobile ICBM launchers to the subsequent negotiations on more complete limitations on strategic offensive arms, the U.S. would consider the deployment of operational land-mobile ICBM launchers during the period of the Interim Agreement as inconsistent with the objectives of that Agreement.

C. Covered facilities

The U.S. Delegation made the following statement on May 20, 1972:

I wish to emphasize the importance that the United States attaches to the provisions of Article V, including in particular their application to fitting out or berthing submarines.

D. 'Heavy' ICBM's

The U.S. Delegation made the following statement on May 26, 1972:

The U.S. Delegation regrets that the Soviet Delegation has not been willing to agree on a common definition of a heavy missile. Under these circumstances, the U.S. Delegation believes it necessary to state the following: The United States would consider any ICBM having a volume significantly greater than that of the largest light ICBM now operational on either side to be a heavy ICBM. The U.S. proceeds on the premise that the Soviet side will give due account to this consideration.

(b) The following noteworthy unilateral statement was made by the Delegation of the U.S.S.R. and is shown here with the U.S. reply:

On May 17, 1972, Minister Semenov made the following unilateral 'Statement of the Soviet Side':

Taking into account that modern ballistic missile submarines are presently in the possession of not only the U.S., but also of its NATO allies, the Soviet Union agrees that for the period of effectiveness of the Interim "Freeze" Agreement the U.S. and its NATO allies have up to 50 such submarines with a total of up to 800 ballistic missile launchers thereon (including 41 U.S. submarines with 656 ballistic missile launchers). However, if during the period of effectiveness of the Agreement U.S. allies in NATO should increase the number of their modern submarines to exceed the numbers of submarines they would have operational or under construction on the date of signature of the Agreement, the Soviet Union will have the right to a corresponding increase in the number of its submarines. In the opinion of the Soviet side, the solution of the question of modern ballistic missile submarines provided for in the Interim Agreement only partially compensates for the strategic imbalance in the deployment of the nuclear-powered missile submarines of the USSR and the U.S. Therefore, the Soviet side believes that this whole question, and above all the question of liquidating the American missile submarine bases outside the U.S., will be appropriately resolved in the course of follow-on negotiations.

On May 24, Ambassador Smith made the following reply to Minister Semenov:

The United States side has studied the "statement made by the Soviet side" of May 17 concerning compensation for submarine basing and SLBM submarines belonging to third countries. The United States does not accept the validity of the considerations in that statement.

On May 26 Minister Semenov repeated the unilateral statement made on May 24. Ambassador Smith also repeated the U.S. rejection on May 26."

US DEPARTMENT OF STATE, *Treaties and Other International Acts*, Series 7504, Washington, DC, 1972; J. GOLDBLAT, *Arms Control Agreements*, New York, 1983, pp. 172–175.

SALT II. DOCUMENTS, 1979. The text of the Joint Statement, Joint Communiqué, SALT II Treaty with Agreed or Common Statements, Memorandum of Understanding on the Numbers of Strategic Offensive Arms and other additional statements are as follows:

I JOINT STATEMENT

1. Joint Statement by the USA and the USSR of principles and basic guidelines for subsequent negotiations on the limitation of strategic arms, signed on June 18, 1979, in Vienna:

The United States of America and the Union of Soviet Socialist Republics, hereinafter referred to as the Parties,

Having concluded the Treaty on the Limitation of Strategic Offensive Arms,

Reaffirming that the strengthening of strategic stability meets the interests of the Parties and the interests of international security,

Convinced that early agreement on the further limitation and further reduction of strategic arms would serve to strengthen international peace and security and to reduce the risk of outbreak of nuclear war,

Have agreed as follows:

First. The Parties will continue to pursue negotiations, in accordance with the principle of equality and equal security, on measures for the further limitation and reduction in the numbers of strategic arms, as well as for their further qualitative limitation.

In furtherance of existing agreements between the Parties on the limitation and reduction of strategic arms, the Parties will continue, for the purposes of reducing and averting the risk of outbreak of nuclear war, to seek measures to strengthen strategic stability by, among other things, limitations on strategic offensive arms most destabilizing to the strategic balance and by measures to reduce and to avert the risk of surprise attack.

Second. Further limitations and reductions of strategic arms must be subject to adequate verification by national technical means, using additionally, as appropriate, co-operative measures contributing to the effectiveness of verification by national technical means. The Parties will seek to strengthen verification and to perfect the operation of the Standing Consultative Commission in order to promote assurance of compliance with the obligations assumed by the Parties.

Third. The Parties shall pursue in the course of these negotiations, taking into consideration factors that determine the strategic situation, the following objectives:

1. significant and substantial reductions in the numbers of strategic offensive arms;
2. qualitative limitations on strategic offensive arms, including restrictions on the development, testing, and deployment of new types of strategic offensive arms and on the modernization of existing strategic offensive arms;
3. resolution of the issues included in the Protocol to the Treaty between the United States of America and the Union of Soviet Socialist Republics on the Limitation of Strategic Offensive Arms in the context of the negotiations relating to the implementation of the principles and objectives set out herein.

Fourth. The Parties will consider other steps to ensure and enhance strategic stability, to ensure the equality and the equal security of the Parties, and to implement the above principles and objectives. Each Party will be free to raise any issue relative to the further limitation of strategic arms. The parties will also consider further joint measures, as appropriate, to strengthen peace and security and to reduce the risk of outbreak of nuclear war.

II JOINT COMMUNIQUÉ

2. Joint US-Soviet Communiqué in Connection with the Signing of the SALT II Treaty, issued on June 18, 1979, in Vienna (excerpt)

I. General Aspects of US-Soviet Relations

There is agreement between the sides that the state of relations between the United States and the Soviet Union is of great importance for the fundamental interests of the peoples of both countries and that it significantly affects the development of the international situation as a whole. Recognizing the great responsibility connected with this, the sides have expressed their firm intent to continue working toward the establishment of a more stable and constructive foundation for US Soviet relations. To this end, the two sides acknowledged the necessity of expanding areas of cooperation between them.

Such cooperation should be based on the principles of complete equality, equal security, respect for sovereignty and non-intervention in each other's internal affairs, and should facilitate the relaxation of international tension and the peaceful conduct of mutally beneficial relations between states, and thereby enhance international stability and world peace.

The sides reaffirmed their conviction that full implementation of each of the provisions of the "Basic Principles of Relations between the United States of America and the Union of Soviet Socialist Republics" as well as other treaties and agreements concluded between them would contribute to a more stable relationship between the two countries.

The two sides stressed the importance of peaceful resolution of disputes, respect for the sovereignty and territorial integrity of states, and of efforts so that conflicts or situations would not arise which could serve to increase international tensions. They recognize the right of the peoples of all states to detemine their future without outside interference.

Recognizing that an armed world conflict can and must be avoided, the sides believe that at the present time there is no more important and urgent task for mankind than ending the arms race and preventing war. They expressed their intention to make every effort to attain that goal. To that end, they also recognized the value of consultation between themselves and with other governments, at the United Nations and elsewhere, in order to prevent and eliminate conflict in various regions of the world.

The sides note with satisfaction the growing practice of contacts between government officials of the USA and the USSR in the course of which key questions of US-Soviet relations and pressing international issues are discussed. The process of developing useful ties between the US Congress and the Supreme Soviet of the USSR and of exchanges between non-governmental organizations is continuing. The talks again confirmed the specific significance of personal meetings between the leaders of the USA and the USSR in resolving the basic questions in the relations between the two states. In principle, it has been agreed that such meetings will be held in the future on a regular basis, with the understanding that the specific timing will be determined by mutual agreement.

Agreement has also been reached on broadening the practice of consultations and exchanges of opinion between representatives of the sides on other levels.

II. Limitations of Nuclear and Conventional Arms

The two sides reaffirmed their deep conviction that special importance should be attached to the problems of the prevention of nuclear war and to curbing the competition in strategic arms. Both sides recognized that nuclear war would be a disaster for all mankind. Each stated that it is not striving and will not strive for military superiority, since that can only result in dangerous instability, generating higher levels of armaments with no benefit to the security of either side.

Recognizing that the USA and the USSR have a special responsibility to reduce the risk of nuclear war and contribute to world peace. President Carter and President Brezhnev committed themselves to take major steps to limit nuclear weapons with the objective of ultimately eliminating them, and to complete successfully other arms limitation and disarmament negotiations.

SALT. In the course of the meeting, President Carter and President Brezhnev confirmed and signed the Treaty Between the USA and the USSR on the Limitation of Strategic Offensive Arms, the Protocol thereto, the Joint Statement of Principles and Basic Guidelines for Subsequent Negotiations on the Limitation of Strategic Arms and the document entitled Agreed Statements and Common Understandings Regarding the Treaty Between the USA and USSR on the Limitation of Strategic Offensive Arms.

At the same time, the sides again stressed the great significance of the Treaty on the Limitation of Anti-Ballistic Missile Systems and strict compliance with its provisions and of other agreements previously concluded between them in the field of strategic arms limitations and reducing the danger of nuclear war.

Both sides express their deep satisfaction with the process of the negotiations on strategic arms limitations and the fact that their persistent efforts for many years to conclude a new treaty have been crowned with success. This treaty sets equal ceilings on the nuclear delivery systems of both sides; to begin the process of reductions it requires the reduction of existing nuclear arms; to begin to limit the threat represented by the qualitative arms race it also places substantial constraints on the modernization of strategic offensive systems and the development of new ones.

The new Treaty on the Limitation of Strategic Offensive Arms and the Protocol thereto represent a mutually acceptable balance between the interests of the sides based on the principles of equality and equal security. These documents are a substantial contribution to the prevention of nuclear war and the deepening of detente, and thus serve the interests not only of the American and Soviet peoples, but the aspirations of mankind for peace.

The two sides reaffirmed their commitment strictly to observe every provision in the treaty.

President Carter and President Brezhnev discussed questions relating to the SALT II negotiations and in this connection expressed the firm intention of the sides to act in accordance with the Joint Statement of Principles and Basic Guidelines for Subsequent Negotiations on the Limitation of Strategic Arms.

Comprehensive Test Ban Treaty. It was noted that there has been definite progress at the negotiations, in which the UK is also participating, on an international treaty comprehensively banning test explosions of nuclear weapons in any environment and an associated protocol. They confirmed the intention of the USA and the USSR to work, together with the UK, to complete preparation of this treaty as soon as possible.

Non-proliferation. The two sides reaffirmed the importance they attach to nuclear non-proliferation. They consistently advocate the further strengthening of the regime of non-proliferation of nuclear weapons and confirm their resolve to continue to comply strictly with the obligations they have assumed under the Treaty on the Non-Proliferation of Nuclear Weapons. They stressed the importance of applying comprehensive international safeguards under the International Atomic Energy Agency and pledged to continue their efforts to strengthen these safeguards.

They noted the profound threat posed to world security by the proliferation of nuclear weapons, and agreed that the states already possessing nuclear weapons bear a special responsibility to demonstrate restraint. To this end, they affirmed their joint conviction that further efforts are needed, including on a regional basis, and expressed the hope that the conclusion of the SALT II Treaty will make an important contribution toward non-proliferation objectives. Both sides further committed themselves to close cooperation, along with other countries, to insure a successful conclusion to the Non-Proliferation Treaty Review Conference in 1980, and called upon all states which have not already done so to sign and ratify the Non-Proliferation Treaty.

Vienna Negotiations. President Carter and President Brezhnev emphasized the great importance the sides attached to the negotiations on the mutual reduction of forces and armaments and associated measures in Central Europe in which they are participating with other states. A reduction of the military forces of both sides and the implementation of associated measures in Central Europe would be a major contribution to stability and security.

ASAT. It was also agreed to continue actively searching for mutually acceptable agreement in the ongoing negotiations on anti-satellite systems.

Conventional Arms Transfers. The two sides agreed that their respective representatives will meet promptly to discuss questions related to the next round of negotiations on limiting conventional arms transfers.

Chemical Weapons. The two sides reaffirmed the importance of a general, complete and verifiable prohibition of chemical weapons and agreed to intensify their efforts to prepare an agreed joint proposal for presentation to the Committee on Disarmament.

Radiological Weapons. President Carter and President Brezhnev were pleased to be able to confirm that bilateral agreement on major elements of a treaty banning the development, production, stockpiling and use of radiological weapons has been reached. An agreed joint proposal will be presented to the Committee on Disarmament this year.

Indian Ocean. The two sides agreed that their respective representatives will meet promptly to discuss the resumption of the talks on questions concerning arms limitation measures in the Indian Ocean.

Other Questions of Arms Limitations and General Disarmament. In discussing other questions connected with solving the problems of limiting the arms race and of disarmament, the sides expressed their support for the Final Document adopted at the Special Session of the UN General Assembly on Disarmament. The sides noted their support for a second special session of the UN General Assembly devoted to disarmament and for that session to be followed by the convocation of a World Disarmament Conference with universal participation, adequately prepared and at an appropriate time.

The USA and the USSR will continue to cooperate between themselves and with other member states of the Committee on Disarmament with its enlarged membership for the purpose of working out effective steps in the field of disarmament in that forum.

In summing up the exchange of views on the state of negotiations being conducted between the USA and the USSR, or with their participation, on a number of questions connected with arms limitation and disarmament, the sides agreed to give new impetus to the joint efforts to achieve practical results at these negotiations.

III SALT II TREATY

(3) Treaty between the USA and the USSR on the Limitation of Strategic Offensive Arms (SALT II Treaty), signed on June 18, 1979, in Vienna; and Agreed Statements and common understanding:

These documents were signed separately. However, for the convenience of the reader, the Treaty and the Protocol are reproduced jointly with the Agreed Statements and Common Understandings, as they pertain to particular article paragraphs.

Treaty

The United States of America and the Union of Soviet Socialist Republics, hereinafter referred to as the Parties,

Conscious that nuclear war would have devastating consequences for all mankind,

Proceedings from the Basic Principles of Relations Between the United States of America and the Union of Soviet Socialist Republics of 29 May 1972.

Attaching particular significance to the limitation of strategic arms and determined to continue their efforts begun with the Treaty on the Limitation of Anti-Ballistic Missile Systems and the Interim Agreement on Certain Measures with Respect to the Limitation of Strategic Offensive Arms, of 26 May 1972,

Convinced that the additional measures limiting strategic offensive arms provided for in this Treaty will contribute to the improvement of relations between the Parties, help to reduce the risk of outbreak of nuclear war and strengthen international peace and security.

Mindful of their obligations under art. VI of the Treaty on the Non-Proliferation of Nuclear Weapons,

Guided by the principle of equality and equal security,

Recognizing that the strengthening of strategic stability meets the interests of the Parties and the interests of international security,

Reaffirming their desire to take measures for the further limitation and for the further reduction of strategic arms, having in mind the goal of achieving general and complete disarmament,

Declaring their intention to undertake in the near future negotiations further to limit and further to reduce strategic offensive arms,

Have agreed as follows:

Art. I. Each Party undertakes, in accordance with the provisions of this Treaty, to limit strategic offensive arms quantitatively and qualitatively, to exercise restraint in the development of new types of strategic offensive arms, and to adopt other measures provided for in this Treaty.

Art. II. For the purposes of this Treaty:

(1) Intercontinental ballistic missile (ICBM) launchers are land-based launchers of ballistic missiles capable of a range in excess of the shortest distance between the northeastern border of the continental part of the territory of the United States of America and the northwestern border of the continental part of the territory of the Union of Soviet Socialist Republics, that is, a range in excess of 5,500 kilometres.

Agreed Statements and Common Understandings
Paragraph 1 of Article II of the Treaty

First Agreed Statement. The term 'intercontinental ballistic missile launchers', as defined in paragraph 1 of art. II of the Treaty, includes all launchers which have been developed and tested for launching ICBMs. If a launcher has been developed and tested for launching an ICBM, all launchers of that type shall be considered to have been developed and tested for launching ICBMs.

First Common Understanding. If a launcher contains or launches an ICBM, that launcher shall be considered to have been developed and tested for launching ICBMs.

Second Common Understanding. If a launcher has been developed and tested for launching an ICBM, all launchers of that type, except for ICBM test and training launchers, shall be included in the aggregate numbers of strategic offensive arms provided for in art. III of the Treaty, pursuant to the provisions of art. VI of the Treaty.

Third Common Understanding. The 177 former Atlas and Titan I ICBM launchers of the United States of America, which are no longer operational and are partially dismantled, shall not be considered as subject to the limitations provided for in the Treaty.

Second Agreed Statement. After the date on which the Protocol ceases to be in force, mobile ICBM launchers shall be subject to the relevant limitations provided for in the Treaty which are applicable to ICBM launchers, unless the Parties agree that mobile ICBM launchers shall not be deployed after that date.

(2) Submarine-launched ballistic missile (SLBM) launchers are launchers of ballistic missiles installed on any nuclear-powered submarine or launchers of modern ballistic missiles installed on any submarine, regardless of its type.

To Paragraph 2 of Article II of the Treaty

Agreed Statement. Modern submarine-launched ballistic missiles are: for the United States of America, missiles installed in all nuclear-powered submarines; for the Union of Soviet Socialist Republics, missiles of the type installed in nuclear-powered submarines made operational since 1965; and for both Parties, submarine-launched ballistic missiles first flight-tested since 1965 and installed in any submarine, regardless of its type.

(3) Heavy bombers are considered to be:

(a) currently, for the United States of America, bombers of the B-52 and B-1 types, and for the Union of Soviet Socialist Republics, bombers of the Tupolev-95 and Myasishchev types;

(b) in the future, types of bombers which can carry out the mission of a heavy bomber in a manner similar or superior to that of bombers listed in sub-paragraph (a) above;

(c) types of bombers equipped for cruise missiles capable of a range in excess of 600 kilometres; and

(d) types of bombers equipped for ASBMs.

To Paragraph 3 of Article II of the Treaty

First Agreed Statement. The term 'bombers', as used in paragraph 3 of art. II and other provisions of the Treaty, means airplanes of types initially constructed to be equipped for bombs or missiles.

Second Agreed Statement. The parties shall notify each other on a case-by-case basis in the Standing Consultative Commission of inclusion of types of bombers as heavy bombers pursuant to the provisions of paragraph 3 of art. II of the Treaty; in this connexion the Parties shall hold consultations, as appropriate, consistent with the provisions of paragraph 2 of art. XVII of the Treaty.

Third Agreed Statement. The criteria the Parties shall use to make case-by-case determinations of which types of bombers in the future can carry out the mission of a heavy bomber in a manner similar or superior to that of current heavy bombers, as referred to in subparagraph 3(b) of art. II of the Treaty, shall be agreed upon in the Standing Consultative Commission.

Fourth Agreed Statement. Having agreed that every bomber of a type included in paragraph 3 of art. II of the Treaty is to be considered a heavy bomber, the Parties further agree that:

(a) airplanes which otherwise would be bombers of a heavy bomber type shall not be considered to the bomber type if they have functionally related observable differences which indicate that they cannot perform the mission of a heavy bomber;

(b) airplanes which otherwise would be bombers of a type equipped for cruise missiles capable of a range in excess of 600 kilometres shall not be considered to be bombers of a type equipped for cruise missiles capable of a range in excess of 600 kilometres if they have functionally related observable differences which indicate that they cannot perform the mission of a bomber equipped for cruise missiles capable of a range in excess of 600 kilometres, except that heavy bombers of current types, as designated in subparagraph 3(a) of art. II of the Treaty, which otherwise would be of a type equipped for cruise missiles capable of a range in excess of 600 kilometres shall not be considered to be heavy bombers of a type equipped for cruise missiles capable of a range in excess of 600 kilometres if they are distinguishable on the basis of externally observable differences from heavy bombers of a type equipped for cruise missiles capable of a range in excess of 600 kilometres; and

(c) airplanes which otherwise would be bombers of a type equipped for ASBMs shall not be considered to be bombers of a type equipped for ASBMs if they have functionally related observable differences which indicate that they cannot perform the mission of a bomber equipped for ASBMs, except that heavy bombers of current types, as designated in subparagraph 3(a) of art. II of the Treaty, which otherwise would be of a type equipped for ASBMs shall not be considered to be heavy bombers of a type equipped for ASBMs if they are distinguishable on the basis of externally observable differences from heavy bombers of a type equipped for ASBMs.

First Common Understanding. Functionally related observable differences are differences in the observable features of airplanes which indicate whether or not these airplanes can perform the mission of a heavy bomber, or whether or not they can perform the mission of a bomber equipped for cruise missiles capable of a range in excess of 600 kilometres or whether or not they can perform the mission of a bomber equipped for ASBMs. Functionally related observable differences shall be verifiable by national technical means. To this end, the Parties may take, as appropriate, co-operative measures contributing to the effectiveness of verification by national technical means.

Fifth Agreed Statement. Tupolev-142 airplanes in their current configuration, that is, in the configuration for anti-submarine warfare, are considered to be airplanes of a type different from types of heavy bombers referred to in subparagraph 3(a) of art. II of the Treaty and not subject to the Fourth Agreed Statement to paragraph 3 of art. II of the Treaty. This Agreed Statement does not preclude improvement of Tupolev-142 airplanes as an anti-submarine system, and does not prejudice or set a precedent for designation in the future of types of airplanes as heavy bombers pursuant to subparagraph 3(b) of art. II of the Treaty or for application of the Fourth Agreed Statement to paragraph 3 of art. II of the Treaty to such airplanes.

Second Common Understanding. Not later than six months after entry into force of the Treaty the Union of Soviet Socialist Republics will give its 31 Myasishchev airplanes used as tankers in existence as of the date of signature of the Treaty functionally related observable differences which indicate that they cannot perform the mission of a heavy bomber.

Third Common Understanding. The designations by the United States of America and by the Union of Soviet Socialist Republics for heavy bombers to in subparagraph 3(a) of art. II of the Treaty correspond in the following manner: Heavy bombers of the types designated by the United States of America as the B-52 and the B-1 are known to the Union of Soviet Socialist Republics by the same designations; Heavy bombers of the type designated by the Union of Soviet Socialist Republics as the Tupolev-95 are known to the United States of America as heavy bombers of the Bear type; and Heavy bombers of the type designated by the Union of Soviet Socialist Republics as the Myasishchev are known to the United States of America as heavy bombers of the Bison type.

(4) Air-to-surface ballistic missiles (ASBMs) are any such missiles capable of a range in excess of 600 kilometres and installed in an aircraft or on its external mountings.

(5) Launchers of ICBMs and SLBMs equipped with multiple independently targetable re-entry vehicles (MIRVs) are launchers of the types developed and tested for launching ICBMs or SLBMs equipped with MIRVs.

To paragraph 5 of Article II of the Treaty

First Agreed Statement. If a launcher has been developed and tested for launching an ICBM or an SLBM equipped with MIRVs, all launchers of that type shall be considered to have been developed and tested for launching ICBMs or SLBMs equipped with MIRVs.

First Common Understanding. If a launcher contains or launches an ICBM or an SLBM equipped with MIRVs, that launcher shall be considered to have been developed and tested for launching ICBMs or SLBMs equipped with MIRVs.

Second Common Understanding. If a launcher has been developed and tested for launching an ICBM or an SLBM equipped with MIRVs, all launchers of that type, except for ICBM and SLBM test and training launchers, shall be included in the corresponding aggregate numbers provided for in art. V of the Treaty, pursuant to the provisions of art. VI of the Treaty.

Second Agreed Statement. ICBMs and SLBMs equipped with MIRVs are ICBMs and SLBMs of the types which have been flight-tested with two or more independently targetable re-entry vehicles, regardless of whether or not they have also been flight-tested with a single re-entry vehicle or with multiple re-entry vehicles which are not independently targetable. As of the date of signature of the Treaty, such ICBMs and SLBMs are: for the United States of America, Minuteman III ICBMs, Poseidon C-3 SLBMs, and Trident C-4 SLBMs; and for the Union of Soviet Socialist Republics, RS-16, RS-18, RS-20 ICBMs and RSM-50 SLBMs.

Each Party will notify the other Party in the Standing Consultative Commission on a case-by-case basis of the designation of the one type of light ICBM, if equipped with MIRVs, permitted pursuant to paragraph 9 of art. IV of the Treaty when first flight-tested; of designations of additional types of SLBMs equipped with MIRVs when first installed on a submarine; and of designations of types of ASBMs equipped with MIRVs when first flight-tested.

Third Common Understanding. The designations by the United States of America and by the Union of Soviet Socialist Republics for ICBMs and SLBMs equipped with MIRVs correspond in the following manner:

Missiles of the type designated by the United States of America as the Minuteman III and known to the Union of Soviet Socialist Republics by the same designation, a light ICBM that has been flight-tested with multiple independently targetable re-entry vehicles;

Missiles of the type designated by the United States of America as the Poseidon Socialist Republics by the same designation, an SLBM that was first flight-tested in 1968 and that has been flight-tested with multiple independently targetable re-entry vehicles;

Missiles of the type designated by the United States of America as the Trident C-4 and known to the Union of Soviet Socialist Republics by the same designation, an SLBM that was first flight-tested in 1977 and that has been flight-tested with multiple independently targetable re-entry vehicles;

Missiles of the type designated by the Union of Soviet Socialist Republics as the RS-16 and known to the United States of America as the SS-17, a light ICBM that has been flight-tested with a single re-entry vehicle and with multiple independently targetable re-entry vehicles;

Missiles of the type designated by the Union of Soviet Socialist Republics as the RS-18 and known to the United States of America as the SS-19, the heaviest in terms of launch-weight and throw-weight of light ICBMs, which has been flight-tested with a single re-entry vehicle and with multiple independently targetable re-entry vehicles;

Missiles of the type designated by the Union of Soviet Socialist Republics as the RS-20 and known to the United States of America as the SS-18, the heaviest in terms of launch-weight and throw-weight of heavy ICBMs, which has been flight-tested with a single re-entry vehicle and with multiple independently targetable re-entry vehicles;

Missiles of the type designated by the Union of Soviet Socialist Republics as the RSM-50 and known to the United States of America as the SS-N-18, an SLBM that has been flight-tested with a single re-entry vehicle and with multiple independently targetable re-entry vehicles.

Third Agreed Statement. Re-entry vehicles are independently targetable:

(a) if, after separation from the booster, manoeuvring and targeting of the re-entry vehicles to separate aim points along trajectories which are unrelated to each other are accomplished by means of devices which are installed in a self-contained dispensing mechanism or on the re-entry vehicles, and which are based on the use of electronic or other computers in combination with devices using jet engines, including rocket engines, or aerodynamic systems;

(b) if manoeuvring and targeting of the re-entry vehicles to separate aim points along trajectories which are unrelated to each other are accomplished by means of other devices which may be developed in the future.

Fourth Common Understanding. For the purposes of this Treaty, all ICBM launchers in the Derazhnya and Pervomaysk areas in the Union of Soviet Socialist Republics are included in the aggregate numbers provided for in Article V of the Treaty.

Fifth Common Understanding. If ICBM or SLBM launchers are converted, constructed or undergo significant changes to their principal observable structural design features after entry into force of the Treaty, any such launchers which are launchers of missiles equipped with MIRVs shall be distinguishable from launchers of missiles not equipped with MIRVs, and any such launchers which are launchers of missiles not equipped with MIRVs shall be distinguishable from launchers of missiles equipped with MIRVs, on the basis of externally observable design features of the launchers. Submarines with launchers of SLBMs equipped with MIRVs shall be distinguishable from submarines with launchers of SLBMs not equipped with MIRVs on the basis of externally observable design features of the submarines.

This Common Understanding does not require changes to launcher conversion or construction programmes, or to programmes including significant changes to the principal observable structural design features of launchers, under way as of the date of signature of the Treaty.

(6) ASBMs equipped with MIRVs are ASBMs of the types which have been flight-tested with MIRVs.

To Paragraph 6 of Article II of the Treaty

First Agreed Statement. ASBMs of the types which have been flight-tested with MIRVs are all ASBMs of the types which have been flight-tested with two or more independently targetable re-entry vehicles, regardless of whether or not they have also been flight-tested with a single re-entry vehicle or with multiple re-entry vehicles which are not independently targetable.

Second Agreed Statement. Re-entry vehicles are independently targetable:

(a) if, after separation from the booster, manoeuvring and targeting of the re-entry vehicles to separate aim points along trajectories which are unrelated to each other are accomplished by means of devices which are installed in a self-contained dispensing mechanism or on the re-entry vehicles, and which are based on the use of electronic or other computers in combination with devices using jet engines, including rocket engines, or aerodynamic systems;

(b) if manoeuvring and targeting of the re-entry vehicles to separate aim points along trajectories which are unrelated to each other are accomplished by means of other devices which may be developed in the future.

(7) Heavy ICBMs are ICBMs which have a launch-weight greater or a throw-weight greater than that of the heaviest, in terms of either launch-weight or throw-weight, respectively of the light ICBMs deployed by either Party as of the date of signature of this Treaty.

To Paragraph 7 of Article II of the Treaty

First Agreed Statement. The launch-weight of an ICBM is the weight of the fully loaded missile itself at the time of launch.

Second Agreed Statement. The throw-weight of an ICBM is the sum of the weight of:

(a) its re-entry vehicle or re-entry vehicles;

(b) any self-contained dispensing mechanisms or other appropriate devices for targeting one re-entry vehicle, or for releasing or for dispensing and targeting two or more re-entry vehicles; and

(c) its penetration aids, including devices for their release.

Common Understanding. The term "other appropriate devices", as used in the definition of the throw-weight of an ICBM in the Second Agreed Statement to paragraph 7 of art. II of the Treaty, means any devices for dispensing and targeting two or more re-entry vehicles; and any devices for releasing two or more re-entry vehicles or for targeting one re-entry vehicle, which cannot provide their re-entry vehicles or re-entry vehicle with additional velocity of more than 1,000 metres per second.

(8) Cruise missiles are unmanned, self-propelled, guided, weapon-delivery vehicles which sustain flight through the use of aerodynamic lift over most of their flight path and which are flight-tested from or deployed on aircraft, that is, air-launched cruise missiles or such vehicles which are referred to as cruise missiles in subparagraph 1(b) of art. IX.

To Paragraph 8 of Article II of the Treaty

First Agreed Statement. If a cruise missile is capable of a range in excess of 600 kilometres, all cruise missiles of that type shall be considered to be cruise missiles capable of a range in excess of 600 kilometres.

Second Common Understanding. Cruise missiles not capable of a range in excess of 600 kilometres shall not be considered to be of a type capable of a range in excess of 600 kilometres if they are distinguishable on the basis of externally observable design features from cruise missiles of types capable of a range in excess of 600 kilometres.

Second Agreed Statement. The range of which a cruise missile is capable is the maximum distance which can be covered by the missile in its standard design mode flying until fuel exhaustion, determined by projecting its flight path onto the Earth's sphere from the point of launch to the point of impact.

Third Agreed Statement. If an unmanned, self-propelled, guided vehicle which sustains flight through the use of aerodynamic lift over most of its flight path has been flight-tested or deployed for weapon delivery, all vehicles of that type shall be considered to be weapon-delivery vehicles.

Third Common Understanding. Unmanned, self-propelled, guided vehicles which sustain flight through the use of aerodynamic lift over most of their flight path and are not weapon-delivering vehicles, that is, unarmed, pilotless, guided vehicles, shall not be con-

sidered to be cruise missiles if such vehicles are distinguishable from cruise missiles on the basis of externally observable design features.

Fourth Common Understanding. Neither Party shall convert unarmed, pilotless, guided vehicles into cruise missiles capable of a range in excess of 600 kilometres nor shall either Party convert cruise missiles capable of a range in excess of 600 kilometres into unarmed, pilotless, guided vehicles.

Fifth Common Understanding. Neither Party has plans during the term of the Treaty to flight-test from or deploy on aircraft unarmed, pilotless, guided vehicles which are capable of a range in excess of 600 kilometres. In the future, should a Party have such plans, that Party will provide notification thereof to the other Party well in advance of such flight-testing or deployment. This Common Understanding does not apply to target drones.

Art. III.(1) Upon entry into force of this Treaty, each Party undertakes to limit ICBM launchers, SLBM launchers, heavy bombers, and ASBMs to an aggregate number not to exceed 2,400.

(2) Each Party undertakes to limit, from 1 January, 1981, strategic offensive arms referred to in paragraph 1 of this article to an aggregate number not to exceed 2,250, and to initiate reductions of those arms which as of that date would be in excess of this aggregate number.

(3) Within the aggregate numbers provided for in paragraphs 1 and 2 of this article and subject to the provisions of this Treaty, each Party has the right to determine the composition of these aggregates.

(4) For each bomber of a type equipped for ASBMs, the aggregate numbers provided for in paragraphs 1 and 2 of this article shall include the maximum number of such missiles for which a bomber of that type is equipped for one operational mission.

(5) A heavy bomber equipped only for ASBMs shall not itself be included in the aggregate numbers provided for in paragraphs 1 and 2 of this article.

(6) Reductions of the numbers of strategic offensive arms required to comply with the provisions of paragraphs 1 and 2 of this article shall be carried out as provided for in art. XI.

Article IV.(1) Each Party undertakes not to start construction of additional fixed ICBM launchers.

(2) Each Party undertakes not to relocate fixed ICBM launchers.

(3) Each Party undertakes not to convert launchers of light ICBMs, or of ICBMs of older types deployed prior to 1964, into launchers of heavy ICBMs of types deployed after that time.

(4) Each Party undertakes in the process of modernization and replacement of ICBM silo launchers not to increase the original internal volume of an ICBM silo launcher by more than thirty-two per cent. Within this limit each Party has the right to determine whether such an increase will be made through an increase in the original diameter or in the original depth of an ICBM silo launcher, or in both of these dimensions.

To Paragraph 4 of Article IV of the Treaty

Agreed Statement. The word 'original' in paragraph 4 of art. IV of the Treaty refers to the internal dimensions of an ICBM silo launcher, including its internal volume, as of 26 May 1972, or as of the date on which such launcher becomes operational, whichever is later.

Common Understanding. The obligations provided for in paragraph 4 of art. IV of the Treaty and in the Agreed Statement thereto mean that the original diameter or the original depth of an ICBM silo launcher may not be increased by an amount greater than that which would result in an increase in the original internal volume of the ICBM silo launcher by 32 per cent solely through an increase in one of these dimensions.

(5) Each Party undertakes:

(a) not to supply ICBM launcher deployment areas with intercontinental ballistic missiles in excess of a number consistent with normal deployment, maintenance, training, and replacement requirements;

(b) not to provide storage facilities for or to store ICBMs in excess of normal deployment requirements at launch sites of ICBM launchers;

(c) not to develop, test, or deploy systems for rapid reload of ICBM launchers.

To Paragraph 5 of Article IV of the Treaty

Agreed Statement. The term "normal deployment requirements", as used in paragraph 5 of art. IV of the Treaty, means the deployment of one missile at each ICBM launcher.

(6) Subject to the provisions of this Treaty, each Party undertakes not to have under construction at any time strategic offensive arms referred to in paragraph 1 of art. III in excess of numbers consistent with a normal construction schedule.

To Paragraph 6 of Article IV of the Treaty

Common Understanding. A normal construction schedule, in paragraph 6 of art. IV of the Treaty, is understood to be one consistent with the past or present construction practices of each Party.

(7) Each Party undertakes not to develop, test, or deploy ICBMs which have a launch-weight greater or a throw-weight greater than that of the heaviest, in terms of either launch-weight or throw-weight, respectively, of the heavy ICBMs deployed by either Party as of the date of signature of this Treaty.

To Paragraph 7 of Article IV of the Treaty

First Agreed Statement. The launch-weight of an ICBM is the weight of the fully loaded missile itself at the time of launch.

Second Agreed Statement. The throw-weight of an ICBM is the sum of the weight of:

(a) its re-entry vehicle or re-entry vehicles;

(b) any self-contained dispensing mechanisms or other appropriate devices for targeting one re-entry vehicle, or for releasing or for dispensing and targeting two or more re-entry vehicles; and

(c) its penetration aids, including devices for their release.

Common Understanding. The term 'other appropriate devices', as used in the definition of the throw-weight of an ICBM in the Second Agreed Statement to paragraph 7 of art. IV of the Treaty, means any devices for dispensing and targeting two or more re-entry vehicles; and any devices for releasing two or more re-entry vehicles or for targeting one re-entry vehicle, which cannot provide their re-entry vehicles or re-entry vehicle with additional velocity of more than 1,000 metres per second.

(8) Each Party undertakes not to convert land-based launchers of ballistic missiles which are not ICBMs into launchers for launching ICBMs, and not to test them for this purpose.

To Paragraph 8 of Article IV of the Treaty

Common Understanding. During the term of the Treaty, the Union of Soviet Socialist Republics will not produce, test, or deploy ICBMs of the type designated by the Union of Soviet Socialist Republics as the RS-14 and known to the United States of America as the SS-16, a light ICBM first flight-tested after 1970 and flight-tested only with a single re-entry vehicle; this Common Understanding also means that the Union of Soviet Socialist Republics will not produce the third stage of that missile, the re-entry vehicle of that missile, or the appropriate device for targeting the re-entry vehicle of that missile.

(9) Each Party undertakes not to flight-test or deploy new types of ICBMs, that is, types of ICBMs not flight-tested as of 1 May 1979, except that each party may flight-test and deploy one new type of light ICBM.

To Paragraph 9 of Article IV of the Treaty

First Agreed Statement. The term "new types of ICBMs", as used in paragraph 9 of art. IV of the Treaty, refers to any ICBM which is different from those ICBMs flight-tested as of 1 May 1979 in any one or more of the following respects:

(a) the number of stages, the length, the largest diameter, the launch-weight, or the throw-weight, of the missile;

(b) the type of propellant (that is, liquid or solid) of any of its stages.

First Common Understanding. As used in the First Agreed Statement to paragraph 9 of art. IV of the Treaty, the term 'different', referring to the length, the diameter, the launch-weight, and the throw-weight, of the missile, means a difference in excess of 5 per cent.

Second Agreed Statement. Every ICBM of the one new type of light ICBM permitted to each Party pursuant to paragraph 9 of art. IV of the Treaty shall have the same number of stages and the same type of propellant (that is, liquid or solid) of each stage as the first ICBM of the one new type of light ICBM launched by that Party. In addition, after the twenty-fifth launch of an ICBM of that type, or after the last launch before deployment begins of ICBMs of that type, whichever occurs earlier,

ICBMs of the one new type of light ICBM permitted to that Party shall not be different in any one or more of the following respects: the length, the largest diameter, the launch-weight, or the throw-weight, of the missile. A Party which launches ICBMs of the one new type of light ICBM permitted pursuant to paragraph 9 of art. IV of the Treaty shall promptly notify the other Party of the date of the first launch and of the date of either the twenty-fifth or the last launch before deployment begins of ICBMs of that type, whichever occurs earlier.

Second Common Understanding. As used in the Second Agreed Statement to paragraph 9 of art. IV of the Treaty, the term 'different', referring to the length, the diameter, the launch-weight, and the throw-weight, of the missile, means a difference in excess of 5 per cent from the value established for each of the above parameters as of the twenty-fifth launch or as of the last launch before deployment begins, whichever occurs earlier. The values demonstrated in each of the above parameters during the last 12 of the 25 launches or during the last 12 launches before deployment begins, whichever 12 launches occur earlier, shall not vary by more than 10 per cent from any other of the corresponding values demonstrated during those 12 launches.

Third Common Understanding. The limitations with respect to launch-weight and throw-weight, provided for in the First Agreed Statement and the First Common Understanding to paragraph 9 of art. IV of the Treaty, do not preclude the flight-testing or the deployment of ICBMs with fewer re-entry vehicles, or fewer penetration aids, or both, than the maximum number of re-entry vehicles and the maximum number of penetration aids with which ICBMs of that type have been flight-tested as of May 1, 1979, even if this results in a decrease in launch-weight or in throw-weight in excess of 5 per cent.

In addition to the aforementioned cases, those limitations do not preclude a decrease in launch-weight or in throw-weight in excess of 5 per cent, in the case of the flight-testing or the deployment of ICBMs with a lesser quantity of propellant, including the propellant of a self-contained dispensing mechanism or other appropriate device, than the maximum quantity of propellant, including the propellant of a self-contained dispensing mechanism or other appropriate device, than the maximum quantity of propellant, including the propellant of a self-contained dispensing mechanism or other appropriate device, with which ICBMs of that type have been flight-tested as of 1 May 1979, provided that such an ICBM is at the same time flight-tested or deployed with fewer re-entry vehicles, or fewer penetration aids, or both, than the maximum number of re-entry vehicles and the maximum number of penetration aids with which ICBMs of that type have been flight-tested as of 1 May 1979, and the decrease in launch-weight and throw-weight in such cases results only from the reduction in the number of re-entry vehicles, or penetration aids, or both, and the reduction in the quantity of propellant.

Fourth Common Understanding. The limitations with respect to launch-weight and throw-weight, provided for in the Second Agreed Statement and the Second Common Understanding to paragraph 9 of art. IV of the Treaty, do not preclude the flight-testing or the deployment of ICBMs of the one new type of light ICBM permitted to each Party pursuant to paragraph 9 of art. IV of the Treaty with fewer re-entry vehicles, or fewer penetration aids, or both, than the maximum number of re-entry vehicles and the maximum number of penetration aids with which ICBMs of that type have been flight-tested, even if this results in a decrease in launch-weight or in throw-weight in excess of 5 per cent.

In addition to the aforementioned cases, those limitations do not preclude a decrease in launch-weight or in throw-weight in excess of 5 per cent, in the case of the flight-testing or the deployment of ICBMs of that type with a lesser quantity of propellant, including the propellant of a self-contained dispensing mechanism or other appropriate device, than the maximum quantity of propellant, including the propellant of a self-contained dispensing mechanism or other appropriate device, with which ICBMs of that type have been flight-tested, provided that such an ICBM is at the same time flight-tested or deployed with fewer re-entry vehicles, or fewer penetration aids, or both, than the maximum number of re-entry vehicles and the maximum number of penetration aids with which ICBMs of that type have been flight-tested, and the decrease in launch-weight and throw-weight in such cases results only from the reduction in the number of re-entry vehicles, or penetration aids, or both, and the reduction in the quantity of propellant.

(10) Each Party undertakes not to flight-test or deploy ICBMs of a type flight-tested as of 1 May 1979, with a number of re-entry vehicles greater than the maximum number of re-entry vehicles with which an ICBM of that type has been flight-tested as of that date.

To Paragraph 10 of Article IV of the Treaty

First Agreed Statement. The following types of ICBMs and SLBMs equipped with MIRVs have been flight-tested with the maximum number of re-entry vehicles set forth below:

For the United States of America:

ICBMs of the Minuteman II type	– 7 re-entry vehicles;
SLBMs of the Poseidon C-3 type	– 14 re-entry vehicles;
SLBMs of the Trident C-4 type	– 7 re-entry vehicles;

For the Union of Soviet Socialist Republics:

ICBMs of the RS-16 type	– 4 re-entry vehicles;
ICBMs of the RS-18 type	– 6 re-entry vehicles;
ICBMs of the RS-20 type	– 10 re-entry vehicles;
SLBMs of the RSM-50 type	– 7 re-entry vehicles;

Common Understanding. Minuteman III ICBMs of the United States of America have been deployed with no more than three re-entry vehicles. During the term of the Treaty, the United States of America has no plans to and will not flight-test or deploy missiles of this type with more than three re-entry vehicles.

Second Agreement Statement. During the flight-testing of any ICBM, SLBM, or ASBM after 1 May 1979 the number of procedures for releasing or for dispensing may not exceed the maximum number of re-entry vehicles established for missiles of corresponding types as provided for in paragraphs 10, 11, 12, and 13 of art. IV of the Treaty. In this Agreed Statement 'procedures for releasing or for dispensing' are understood to ing mean manoeuvres of a missile associated with targeting and releasing or dispensing its re-entry vehicles to aim points, whether or not a re-entry vehicle is actually released or dispensed. Procedures for releasing anti-missile defence penetration aids will not be considered to be procedures for releasing or for dispensing a re-entry vehicle so long as the procedures for releasing anti-missile defence penetration aids differ from those for releasing or for dispensing re-entry vehicles.

Third Agreed Statement. Each Party undertakes:

(a) not to flight-test or deploy ICBMs equipped with multiple re-entry vehicles, of a type flight-tested as of 1 May 1979, with re-entry vehicles the weight of any of which is less than the weight of the lightest of those re-entry vehicles with which an ICBM of that type has been flight-tested as of that date;

(b) not to flight-test or deploy ICBMs equipped with a single re-entry vehicle and without an appropriate device for targeting a re-entry vehicle, of a type flight-tested as of 1 May 1979, with a re-entry vehicle the weight of which is less than the weight of the lightest re-entry vehicle on an ICBM of a type equipped with MIRVs and flight-tested by that Party as of 1 May 1979; and

(c) not to flight-test or deploy ICBMs equipped with a single re-entry vehicle and with an appropriate device for targeting a re-entry vehicle, of a type flight-tested as of 1 May 1979, with a re-entry vehicle the weight of which is less than 50 per cent of the throw-weight of that ICBM.

(11) Each Party undertakes not to flight-test or deploy ICBMs of the one new type permitted pursuant to paragraph 9 of this article with a number of re-entry vehicles greater than the maximum number of re-entry vehicles with which an ICBM of either Party has been flight-tested as of 1 May 1979, that is, ten.

To Paragraph 11 of Article IV of the Treaty

First Agreed Statement. Each Party undertakes not to flight-test or deploy the one new type of light ICBM permitted to each Party pursuant to paragraph 9 of art. IV of the Treaty with a number of re-entry vehicles greater than the maximum number of re-entry vehicles with which an ICBM of that type has been flight-tested as of the twenty-fifth launch or the last launch before deployment begins of ICBMs of that type, whichever occurs earlier.

Second Agreed Statement. During the flight-testing of any ICBM, SLBM, or ASBM after 1 May 1979 the number of procedures for releasing or for dispensing may not exceed the maximum number of re-entry vehicles established for missiles of corresponding types as provided for in paragraphs 10, 11, 12 and 13 of art. IV of the Treaty. In this Agreed Statement 'procedures for releasing or for dispensing' are understood to mean manoeuvres of a missile associated with targeting and releasing or dispensing its re-entry vehicles to aim points, whether or not a re-entry vehicle is actually released or dispensed. Procedures for releasing anti-missile defence penetration aids will not be considered to be procedures for releasing or for dispensing a re-entry vehicle so long as the procedures for releasing anti-missile defence penetration aids differ from those for releasing or for dispensing re-entry vehicles.

(12) Each Party undertakes not to flight-test or deploy SLBMs with a number of re-entry vehicles greater than the maximum number of re-entry vehicles with which an SLBM of either party has been flight-tested as of 1 May 1979, that is, 14.

To Paragraph 12 of Article IV of the Treaty

First Agreed Statement. The following types of ICBMs and SLBMs equipped with MIRVs have been flight-tested with the maximum number of re-entry vehicles set forth below:

For the United States of America:

ICBMs of the Minuteman III type	– 7 re-entry vehicles;
SLBMs of the Poseidon C-3 type	14 re-entry vehicles;
SLBMs of the Trident C-4 type	–7 re-entry vehicles;

For the Union of Soviet Socialist Republics:

ICBMs of the RS-16 type	– 4 re-entry vehicles;
ICBMs of the RS-18 type	– 6 re-entry vehicles;
ICBMs of the RS-20 type	– 10 re-entry vehicles;
SLBMs of the RSM-50 type.	– 7 re-entry vehicles.

Second Agreed Statement. During the flight-testing of any ICBM, SLBM, or ASBM after 1 May 1979 the number of procedures for releasing or for dispensing may not exceed the maximum number of re-entry vehicles established for missiles of corresponding types as provided for in paragraphs 10, 11, 12 and 13 of art. IV of the Treaty. In this Agreed Statement "procedures for releasing or for dispensing" are understood to mean manoeuvres of a missile associated with targeting and releasing or dispensing its re-entry vehicles to aim points, whether or not a re-entry vehicle is actually released or dispensed. Procedures for releasing anti-missile defence penetration aids will not be considered to be procedures for releasing or for dispensing a re-entry vehicle so long as the procedures for releasing anti-missile defence penetration aids differ from those for releasing or for dispensing re-entry vehicles.

(13) Each Party undertakes not to flight-test or deploy SSBMs with a number of re-entry vehicles greater than the maximum number of re-entry vehicles with which an ICBM of either Party has been flight-tested as of 1 May 1979, that is, ten.

To Paragraph 13 of Article IV of the Treaty

Agreed Statement. During the flight-testing of any ICBM, SLBM, or ASBM after 1 May 1979 the number of procedures for releasing or for dispensing may not exceed the maximum number of re-entry vehicles established for missiles of corresponding types as provided for in paragraphs 10, 11, 12 and 13 of art. IV of the Treaty. In this Agreed Statement 'procedures for releasing or for dispensing' are understood to mean manoeuvres of a missile associated with targeting and releasing or dispensing its re-entry vehicle is actually released or dispensed. Procedures for releasing anti-missile defence penetration aids will not be considered to be procedures for releasing or for dispensing a re-entry vehicle so long as the procedures for releasing anti-missile defence penetration aids differ from those for releasing or for dispensing re-entry vehicles.

(14) Each Party undertakes not to deploy at any one time on heavy bombers equipped for cruise missiles capable of a range in excess of 600 kilometres a number of such cruise missiles which exceeds the product of 28 and the number of such heavy bombers.

To Paragraph 14 of Article IV of the Treaty

First Agreed Statement. For the purposes of the limitation provided for in paragraph 14 of art. IV of the Treaty, there shall be considered to be deployed on each heavy bomber of a type equipped for cruise missiles capable of a range in excess of 600 kilometres the maximum number of such missiles for which any bomber of that type is equipped for one operational mission.

Second Agreed Statement. During the term of the Treaty no bomber of the B-52 or B-1 types of the United States of America and no bomber of the Tupolev-95 or Myasishchev types of the Union of Soviet Socialist Republics will be equipped for more than 20 cruise missiles capable of a range in excess of 600 kilometres.

Art. V.(1) Within the aggregate numbers provided for in paragraphs 1 and 2 of art. III, each Party undertakes to limit launchers of ICBMs and SLBMs equipped with MIRVs, ASBMs equipped with MIRVs, and heavy bombers equipped for cruise missiles capable of a range in excess of 600 kilometres to an aggregate number not to exceed 1,320.

(2) Within the aggregate number provided for in paragraph 1 of this article, each Party undertakes to limit launchers of ICBMs and SLBMs equipped with MIRVs, and ASBMs equipped with MIRVs to an aggregate number not to exceed 1,200.

(3) Within the aggregate number provided for in paragraph 2 of this article, each Party undertakes to limit launchers of ICBMs equipped with MIRVs to an aggregate number not to exceed 820.

(4) For each bomber of a type equipped for ASBMs equipped with MIRVs, the aggregate numbers provided for in paragraphs 1 and 2 of this article shall include the maximum number of ASBMs for which a bomber of that type is equipped for one operational mission.

To Paragraph 4 of Article V of the Treaty

Agreed Statement. If a bomber is equipped for ASBMs equipped with MIRVs, all bombers of that type shall be considered to be equipped for ASBMs equipped with MIRVs.

(5) Within the aggregate numbers provided for in paragraphs 1, 2, and 3 of this article and subject to the provisions of this Treaty, each Party has the right to determine the composition of these aggregates.

Article VI.(1) The limitations provided for in this Treaty shall apply to those arms which are:
(a) operational;
(b) in the final stage of construction;
(c) in reserve, in storage, or mothballed;
(d) undergoing overhaul, repair, modernization, or conversion.

(2) Those arms in the final stage of construction are:
(a) SLBM launchers on submarines which have begun sea trials;
(b) ASBMs after a bomber of a type equipped for such missiles has been brought out of the shop, plant, or other facility where its final assembly or conversion for the purpose of equipping it for such missiles has been performed;
(c) other strategic offensive arms which are finally assembled in a shop, plant, or other facility after they have been brought out of the shop, plant, or other facility where their final assembly has been performed.

(3) ICBM and SLBM launchers of a type not subject to the limitation provided for in art. V, which undergo conversion into launchers of a type subject to that limitation, shall become subject to that limitation as follows:
(a) fixed ICBM launchers when work on their conversion reaches the stage which first definitely indicates that they are being so converted;
(b) SLBM launchers on a submarine when that submarine first goes to sea after their conversion has been performed.

To Paragraph 3 of Article VI of the Treaty

Agreed Statement. The procedures referred to in paragraph 7 of art. VI of the Treaty shall include procedures determining the manner in which mobile ICBM launchers of a type not subject to the limitation provided for in art. V of the Treaty, which undergo conversion into launchers of a type subject to that

limitation, shall become subject to that limitation, unless the Parties agree that mobile ICBM launchers shall not be deployed after the date on which the Protocol ceases to be in force.

(4) ASBMs on a bomber which undergoes conversion from a bomber of a type equipped for ASBMs which are not subject to the limitation provided for in art. V into a bomber of a type equipped for ASBMs which are subject to that limitation shall become subject to that limitation when the bomber is brought out of the shop, plant, or other facility where such conversion has been performed.

(5) A heavy bomber of a type not subject to the limitation provided for in paragraph 1 of art. V shall become subject to that limitation when it is brought out of the shop, plant, or other facility where it has been converted into a heavy bomber of a type equipped for cruise missiles capable of a range in excess of 600 kilometres. A bomber of a type not subject to the limitation provided for in paragraph 1 or 2 of art. III shall become subject to that limitation and to the limitation provided for in paragraph 1 of art. V when it is brought out of the shop, plant or other facility where it has been converted into a bomber of a type equipped for cruise missiles capable of a range in excess of 600 kilometres.

(6) The arms subject to the limitations provided for in this Treaty shall continue to be subject to these limitations until they are dismantled, are destroyed, or otherwise cease to be subject to these limitations under procedures to be agreed upon.

To Paragraph 6 of Article VI of the Treaty

Agreed Statement. The procedures for removal of strategic offensive arms from the aggregate numbers provided for in the Treaty, which are referred to in paragraph 6 of art. VI of the Treaty, and which are to be agreed upon in the Standing Consultative Commission, shall include:
(a) procedures for removal from the aggregate numbers, provided for in art. V of the Treaty, of ICBM and SLBM launchers which are being converted from launchers of a type subject to the limitation provided for in art. V of the Treaty, into launchers of a type not subject to that limitation;
(b) procedures for removal from the aggregate numbers, provided for in arts. III and V of the Treaty, of bombers which are being converted from bombers of a type subject to the limitations provided for in art. III of the Treaty or in arts. III and V of the Treaty into airplanes or bombers of a type not so subject.

Common Understanding. The procedures referred to in subparagraph (b) of the Agreed Statement to paragraph 6 of art. VI of the Treaty for removal of bombers from the aggregate numbers provided for in art. III and V of the Treaty shall be based upon the existence of functionally related observable differences which indicate whether or not they can perform the mission of a heavy bomber, or whether or not they can perform the mission of a bomber equipped for cruise missiles capable of a range in excess of 600 kilometres.

(7) In accordance with the provisions of art. XVII, the Parties will agree in the Standing Consultative Commission upon procedures to implement the provisions of this article.

Art. VII.(1) The limitations provided for in art. III shall not apply to ICBM and SLBM test and training launchers or to space vehicle launchers for exploration and use of outer space. ICBM and SLBM test and training launchers are ICBM and SLBM launchers used only for testing or training.

To Paragraph 1 of Article VII of the Treaty

Common Understanding. The term 'testing', as used in art. VII of the Treaty, includes research and development.

(2) The Parties agree that:
(a) there shall be no significant increase in the number of ICBM or SLBM test and training launchers or in the number of such launchers of heavy ICBMs;
(b) construction or conversion of ICBM launchers at test ranges shall be undertaken only for purposes of testing and training;
(c) there shall be no conversion of ICBM test and training launchers or of space vehicle launchers into ICBM launchers subject to the limitations provided for in art. III.

To Paragraph 2 of Article VII of the Treaty

First Agreed Statement. The term 'significant increase', as used in subparagraph 2(a) of art. VII of the Treaty, means an increase of 15 per cent or more. Any new

ICBM test and training launchers which replace ICBM test and training launchers at test ranges will be located only at test ranges.

Second Agreed Statement. Current test ranges where ICBMs are tested are located: for the United States of America near Santa Maria, California, and at Cape Canaveral, Florida; and for the Union of Soviet Socialist Republics, in the areas of Tyura-Tam and Plesetskaya. In the future, each Party shall provide notification in the Standing Consultative Commission of the location of any other test range used by that Party to test ICBMs.

First Common Understanding. At test ranges where ICBMs are tested, other arms, including those not limited by the Treaty, may also be tested.

Second Common Understanding. Of the 18 launchers of fractional orbital missiles at the test range where ICBMs are tested in the area of Tyura-Tam, 12 launchers shall be dismantled or destroyed and six launchers may be converted to launchers for testing missiles undergoing modernization.

Dismantling or destruction of the 12 launchers shall begin upon entry into force of the Treaty and shall be completed within eight months, under procedures for dismantling or destruction of these launchers to be agreed upon in the Standing Consultative Commission. These 12 launchers shall not be replaced.

Conversion of the six launchers may be carried out after entry into force of the Treaty. After entry into force of the Treaty, fractional orbital missiles shall be removed and shall be destroyed pursuant to the provisions of subparagraph 1(c) of ar. IX and of art. XI of the Treaty and shall not be replaced by other missiles, except in the case of conversion of these six launchers for testing missiles undergoing modernization. After removal of the fractional orbital missiles, and prior to such conversion, any activities associated with these launchers shall be limited to normal maintenance requirements for launchers in which missiles are not deployed. These six launchers shall be subject to the provisions of art. VII of the Treaty and, if converted, to the provisions of the Fifth Common Understanding to paragraph 5 of art. II of the Treaty.

Art. VIII.(1) Each Party undertakes not to flight-test cruise missiles capable of a range in excess of 600 kilometres or ASBMs from aircraft other than bombers or to convert such aircraft into aircraft equipped for such missiles.

To Paragraph 1 of Article VIII of the Treaty

Agreed Statement. For purposes of testing only, each Party has the right, through initial construction or, as an exception to the provisions of paragraph 1 of art. VIII of the Treaty, by conversion, to equip for cruise missiles, capable of a range in excess of 600 kilometres or for ASBMs no more than 16 airplanes, including airplanes which are prototypes of bombers equipped for such missiles. Each Party also has the right, as an exception to the provisions of paragraph 1 of art. VIII of the Treaty, to flight-test from such airplanes cruise missiles capable of a range in excess of 600 kilometres and, after the date on which the Protocol ceases to be in force, to flight-test ASBMs from such airplanes as well, unless the Parties agree that they will not flight-test ASBMs after that date. The limitations provided for in art. III of the Treaty shall not apply to such airplanes.

The aforementioned airplanes may include only:
(a) airplanes other than bombers which, as an exception to the provisions of paragraph 1 of art. VIII of the Treaty, have been converted into airplanes equipped for cruise missiles capable of a range in excess of 600 kilometres or for ASBMs;
(b) airplanes considered to be heavy bombers pursuant to subparagraphs 3(c) or (d) of art. II of the Treaty; and
(c) airplanes other than heavy bombers which, prior to 7 March 1979 were used for testing cruise missiles capable of a range in excess of 600 kilometres.

The airplanes referred to in subparagraphs (a) and (b) of this Agreed Statement shall be distinguishable on the basis of functionally related observable differences from airplanes which otherwise would be of the same type but cannot perform the mission of a bomber equipped for cruise missiles capable of a range in excess of 600 kilometres or for ASBMs.

The airplanes referred to in subparagraph (c) of this Agreed Statement shall not be used for testing cruise missiles capable of a range in excess of 600 kilometres after the expiration of a six-month period from the date of entry into force of the Treaty, unless by the expiration of that period they are distinguishable on the basis of functionally related observable differences from airplanes which otherwise would be of the same type but cannot perform the mission of a bomber equipped for cruise missiles capable of a range in excess of 600 kilometres.

First Common Understanding. The term 'testing', as used in the Agreed Statement to paragraph 1 of art. VIII of the Treaty includes research and development.

Second Common Understanding. The Parties shall notify each other in the Standing Consultative Commission of the number of airplanes, according to type, used for testing pursuant to the Agreed Statement to paragraph 1 of art. VIII of the Treaty. Such notification shall be provided at the first regular session of the Standing Consultative Commission held after an airplane has been used for such testing.

Third Common Understanding. None of the 16 airplanes referred to in the Agreed Statement to paragraph 1 of art. VIII of the Treaty may be replaced, except in the event of the involuntary destruction of any such airplane or in the case of the dismantling or destruction of any such airplane. The procedures for such replacement and for removal of any such airplane from that number, in case of its conversion, shall be agreed upon in the Standing Consultative Commission.

(2) Each Party undertakes not to convert aircraft other than bombers into aircraft which can carry out the mission of a heavy bomber as referred to in subparagraph 3 (b) of art. II.

Art. IX.(1) Each Party undertakes not to develop, test, or deploy:

(a) ballistic missiles capable of a range in excess of 600 kilometres for installation on waterborne vehicles other than submarines, or launchers of such missiles;

(b) fixed ballistic or cruise missile launchers for emplacement on the ocean floor, on the seabed, or on the beds of internal waters and inland waters, or in the subsoil thereof, or mobile launchers of such missiles, which move only in contact with the ocean floor, the seabed, or the beds of internal waters and inland waters, or missiles for such launchers;

(c) systems for placing into Earth orbit nuclear weapons or any other kind of weapons of mass destruction, including fractional orbital missiles;

(d) mobile launchers of heavy ICBMs;

(e) SLBMs which have a launch-weight or throw-weight greater than that of the heaviest, in terms of either launch-weight or throw-weight, respectively, of the light ICBMs deployed by either Party as of the date of signature of this Treaty, or launchers of such SLBMs; or

(f) ASBMs which have a launch-weight greater or a throw-weight greater than that of the heaviest, in terms of either launch-weight or throw-weight, respectively, of the light ICBMs deployed by either Party as of the date of signature of this Treaty.

To Paragraph 1 of Article IX of the Treaty.

Common Understanding to subparagraph (a). The obligations provided for in subparagraph 1(a) of art. IX of the Treaty do not affect current practices for transporting ballistic missiles

Agreed Statement to subparagraph (b). The obligations provided for in subparagraph 1(b) of art. IX of the Treaty shall apply to all areas of the ocean floor and the seabed, including the seabed zone referred to in arts. I and II of the 1971 Treaty on the Prohibition of the Emplacement of Nuclear Weapons and Other Weapons of Mass Destruction on the Seabed and the Ocean Floor and in the Subsoil Thereof.

Common Understanding to subparagraph (c). The provisions of subparagraph 1(c) of art. IX of the Treaty do not require the dismantling or destruction of any existing launchers of either Party.

First Agreed Statement to subparagraphs (e) and (f). The throw-weight of an SLBM or of an ASBM is the weight of the fully loaded missile itself at the time of launch.

Second Agreed Statement to subparagraphs (e) and (f). The throw-weight of an SLBM or of an ASBM is the sum of the weight of:

(a) its re-entry vehicle or re-entry vehicles;

(b) any self-contained dispensing mechanisms or other appropriate devices for targeting one re-entry vehicle, or for releasing or for dispensing and targeting two or more re-entry vehicles; and

(c) its penetration aids, including devices for their release.

Common Understanding to subparagraphs (e) and (f). The term 'other appropriate devices', as used in the definition of the throw-weight of an SLBM or of an ASBM in the Second Agreed Statement to subparagraphs 1(e) and 1(f) of art. IX of the Treaty, means any devices for dispensing and targeting two or more re-entry vehicles; and any devices for releasing two or more re-entry vehicles or for targeting one re-entry vehicle, which cannot provide their re-entry vehicles or re-entry vehicle with additional velocity of more than 1,000 metres per second.

(2) Each Party undertakes not to flight-test from aircraft cruise missiles capable of a range in excess of 600 kilometres which are equipped with multiple independently targetable warheads and not to deploy such cruise missiles on aircraft.

To Paragraph 2 of Article IX of the Treaty

Agreed Statement. Warheads of a cruise missile are independently targetable if manoeuvring or targeting of the warheads to separate aim points along ballistic trajectories or any other flight paths, which are unrelated to each other, is accomplished during a flight of a cruise missile.

Art. X. Subject to the provisions of this Treaty, modernization and replacement of strategic offensive arms may be carried out.

Art. XI.(1) Strategic offensive arms which would be in excess of the aggregate numbers provided for in this Treaty as well as strategic offensive arms prohibited by this Treaty shall be dismantled or destroyed under procedures to be agreed upon in the Standing Consultative Commission.

(2) Dismantling or destruction of strategic offensive arms which would be in excess of the aggregate number provided for in paragraph 1 of art. III shall begin on the date of the entry into force of this Treaty and shall be completed within the following periods from that date: four months for ICBM launchers; six months for ICBM launchers; and three months for heavy bombers.

(3) Dismantling or destruction of strategic offensive arms which would be in excess of the aggregate number provided for in paragraph 2 of art. III shall be initiated no later than 1 January 1981, shall be carried out throughout the ensuing twelve-month period, and shall be completed no later than 31 December 1981.

(4) Dismantling or destruction of strategic offensive arms prohibited by this Treaty shall be completed within the shortest possible agreed period of time, but not later than six months after the entry into force of this Treaty.

Art. XII. In order to ensure the viability and effectiveness of this Treaty, each Party undertakes not to circumvent the provisions of this Treaty, through any other state or states, or in any other manner.

Art. XIII. Each Party undertakes not to assume any international obligations which would conflict with this Treaty.

Art. XIV. The Parties undertake to begin, promptly after the entry into force of this Treaty, active negotiations with the objective of achieving, as soon as possible, agreement on further measures for the limitation and reduction of strategic arms. It is also the objective of the Parties to conclude well in advance of 1985 an agreement limiting strategic offensive arms to replace this Treaty upon its expiration.

Art. XV.(1) For the purpose of providing assurance of compliance with the provisions of this Treaty, each Party shall use national technical means of verification at its disposal in a manner consistent with generally recognized principles of international law.

(2) Each Party undertakes not to interfere with the national technical means of verification of the other Party operating in accordance with paragraph 1 of this article.

(3) Each Party undertakes not to use deliberate concealment measures which impede verification by national technical means of compliance with the provisions of this Treaty. This obligation shall not require changes in current construction, assembly, conversion, or overhaul practices.

To Paragraph 3 of Article XV of the Treaty

First Agreed Statement. Deliberate concealment measures, as referred to in paragraph 3 of art. XV of the Treaty, are measures carried out deliberately to hinder or deliberately to impede verification by national tech-

nical means of compliance with the provisions of the Treaty.

Second Agreed Statement. The obligation not to use deliberate concealment measures, provided for in paragraph 3 of art. XV of the Treaty, does not preclude the testing of anti-missile defence penetration aids.

First Common Understanding. The provisions of paragraph 3 of art. XV of the Treaty and the First Agreed Statement thereto apply to all provisions of the Treaty, including provisions associated with testing. In this connexion, the obligation not to use deliberate concealment measures includes the obligation not to use deliberate concealment measures associated with testing, including those measures aimed at concealing the association between ICBMs and launchers during testing.

Second Common Understanding. Each party is free to use various methods of transmitting telemetric information during testing, including its encryption, except that, in accordance with the provisions of paragraph 3 of art. XV of the Treaty, neither Party shall engage in deliberate denial of telemetric information, such as through the use of telemetry encryption, whenever such denial impedes verification of compliance with the provisions of the Treaty.

Third Common Understanding. In addition to the obligations provided for in paragraph 3 of art. XV of the Treaty, no shelters which impede verification by national technical means of compliance with the provisions of the Treaty shall be used over ICBM silo launchers.

Art. XVI.(1) Each Party undertakes, before conducting each planned ICBM launch, to notify the other party well in advance on a case-by-case basis that such a launch will occur, except for single ICBM launches from test ranges or from ICBM launcher deployment areas, which are not planned to extend beyond its national territory.

To Paragraph 1 of Article XVI of the Treaty

First Common Understanding. ICBM launches to which the obligations provided for in art. XVI of the Treaty apply, include, among others, those ICBM launches for which advance notification is required pursuant to the provisions of the Agreement on Measures to Reduce the Risk of Outbreak of Nuclear War Between the United States of America and the Union of Soviet Socialist Republics signed 30 September 1971, and the Agreement Between the Government of the United States of America and the Government of the Union of Soviet Socialist Republics on the Prevention of Incidents On and Over the High Seas, signed 25 May 1972. Nothing in art. XVI of the Treaty is intended to inhibit advance notification, on a voluntary basis, of any ICBM launches not subject to its provisions, the advance notification of which would enchance confidence between the Parties.

Second Common Understanding. A multiple ICBM launch conducted by a Party, as distinct from single ICBM launches referred to in art. XVI of the Treaty, is a launch which would result in two or more of its ICBMs being in flight at the same time.

Third Common Understanding. The test ranges referred to in art. XVI of the Treaty are those covered by the Second Agreed Statement to paragraph 2 of art. VII of the Treaty.

(2) The Parties shall agree in the Standing Consultative Commission upon procedures to implement the provisions of this article.

Art. XVII.(1) To promote the objectives and implementation of the provisions of this Treaty, the Parties shall use the Standing Consultative Commission established by the Memorandum of Understanding Between the Government of the United States of America and the Government of the Union of Soviet Socialist Republics Regarding the Establishment of a Standing Consultative Commission of 21 December 1972.

(2) Within the framework of the Standing Consultative Commission, with respect to this Treaty, the Parties will:

(a) consider questions concerning compliance with the obligations assumed and related situations which may be considered ambiguous;

(b) provide on a voluntary basis such information as either Party considers necessary to assure confidence in compliance with the obligation assumed;

(c) consider questions involving unintended interference with national technical means of verification, and questions involving unintended impeding of verification by national technical means of compliance with the provisions of this Treaty;

(d) consider possible changes in the strategic situation which have a bearing on the provisions of this Treaty;

(e) agree upon procedures for replacement, conversion, and dismantling or destruction, of strategic offensive arms in cases provided for in the provisions of this Treaty and upon procedures for removal of such arms from the aggregate numbers when they otherwise cease to be subject to the limitations provided for in this Treaty, and at regular sessions of the Standing Consultative Commission, notify each other in accordance with the aforementioned procedures, at least twice annually, of actions completed and those in process;

(f) consider, as appropriate, possible proposals for further increasing the viability of this Treaty, including proposals for amendments in accordance with the provisions of this Treaty;

(g) consider, as appropriate, proposals for further measures limiting strategic offensive arms.

(3) In the Standing Consultative Commission the Parties shall maintain by category the agreed data base on the numbers of strategic offensive arms established by the Memorandum of Understanding Between the United States of America and the Union of Soviet Socialist Republics Regarding the Establishment of a Data Base on the Numbers of Strategic Offensive Arms of 18 June 1979.

To Paragraph 3 of Article XVII of the Treaty

Agreed Statement. In order to maintain the agreed data base on the numbers of strategic offensive arms subject to the limitations provided for in the Treaty in accordance with paragraph 3 of art. XVII of the Treaty, at each regular session of the Standing Consultative Commission the Parties will notify each other of and consider changes in those numbers in the following categories: launchers of ICBMs; fixed launchers of ICBMs; launchers of ICBMs equipped with MIRVs; launchers of SLBMs; launchers of SLBMs equipped with MIRVs; heavy bombers; heavy bombers equipped for cruise missiles capable of a range in excess of 600 kilometres; heavy bombers equipped only for ASBMs; ASBMs; and ASBMs equipped with MIRVs.

Art. XVIII. Each Party may propose amendments to this Treaty. Agreed amendments shall enter into force in accordance with the procedures governing the entry into force of this Treaty.

Art. XIX.(1) This Treaty shall be subject to ratification in accordance with the constitutional procedures of each Party. This Treaty shall enter into force on the day of the exchange of instruments of ratification and shall remain in force through 31 December 1985, unless replaced earlier by an agreement further limiting strategic offensive arms.

(2) This Treaty shall be registered pursuant to art. 102 of the Charter of the United Nations.

(3) Each Party shall, in exercising its national sovereignty, have the right to withdraw from this Treaty if it decides that extraordinary events related to the subject matter of this Treaty have jeopardized its supreme interests. It shall give notice of its decision to the other party six months prior to withdrawal from the Treaty. Such notice shall include a statement of the extraordinary events the notifying Party regards as having jeopardized its supreme interests.

Protocol. The United States of America and the Union of Soviet Socialist Republics, hereinafter referred to as the Parties,

Having agreed on limitations on strategic offensive arms in the Treaty,

Have agreed on additional limitations for the period during which this Protocol remains in force, as follows:

Art. I. Each Party undertakes not to deploy mobile ICBM launchers or to flight-test ICBMs from such launchers.

Art. II.(1) Each Party undertakes not to deploy cruise missiles capable of a range in excess of 600 kilometres on sea-based launchers or on land-based launchers.

(2) Each Party undertakes not to flight-test cruise missiles capable of a range in excess of 600 kilometres which are equipped with multiple independently targetable warheads from sea-based launchers or from land-based launchers.

To Paragraph 2 of Article II of the Protocol.

Agreed Statement. Warheads of a cruise missile are independently targetable if manoeuvring or targeting of the warheads to separate aim points along ballistic trajectories or any other flight paths, which are unrelated to each other, is accomplished during a flight of a cruise missile.

(3) For the purposes of this Protocol, cruise missiles are unmanned, self-propelled, guided, weapon-delivery vehicles which sustain flight through the use of aerodynamic lift over most of their flight path and which are flight-tested from or deployed on sea-based or land-based launchers, that is, sea-launched cruise missiles and ground-launched cruise missiles, respectively.

To Paragraph 3 of Article II of the Protocol.

First Agreed Statement. If a cruise missile is capable of a range in excess of 600 kilometres, all cruise missiles of that type shall be considered to be cruise missiles capable of a range in excess of 600 kilometres.

First Common Understanding. If a cruise missile has been flight-tested to a range in excess of 600 kilometres, it shall be considered to be a cruise missile capable of a range in excess of 600 kilometres.

Second Common Understanding. Cruise missiles not capable of a range in excess of 600 kilometres shall not be considered to be a type capable of a range in excess of 600 kilometres if they are distinguishable on the basis of externally observable design features from cruise missiles of types capable of a range in excess of 600 kilometres.

Second Agreed Statement. The range of which a cruise missile is capable is the maximum distance which can be covered by the missile in its standard design mode flying until fuel exhaustion, determined by projecting its flight path onto the Earth's sphere from the point of launch to the point of impact.

Third Agreed Statement. If an unmanned, self-propelled, guided vehicle which sustains flight through the use of aerodynamic lift over most of its flight path has been flight-tested or deployed for weapon delivery, all vehicles of that type shall be considered to be weapon-delivery vehicles.

Third Common Understanding. Unmanned, self-propelled, guided vehicles which sustain flight through the use of aerodynamic lift over most of their flight path and are not weapon-delivery vehicles, that is, unarmed, pilotless, guided vehicles, shall not be considered to be cruise missiles if such vehicles are distinguishable from cruise missiles on the basis of externally observable design features.

Fourth Common Understanding. Neither Party shall convert unarmed, pilotless, guided vehicles into cruise missiles capable of a range in excess of 600 kilometres, nor shall either Party convert cruise missiles capable of a range in excess of 600 kilometres into unarmed, pilotless, guided vehicles.

Fifth Common Understanding. Neither Party has plans during the term of the Protocol to flight-test from or deploy on sea-based or land-based launchers unarmed, pilotless, guided vehicles which are capable of a range in excess of 600 kilometres. In the future, should a Party have such plans, that Party will provide notification thereof to the other Party well in advance of such flight-testing or deployment. This Common Understanding does not apply to target drones.

Art. III. Each Party undertakes not to flight-test or deploy ASBMs.

Art. IV. This Protocol shall be considered an integral part of the Treaty. It shall enter into force on the day of the entry into force of the Treaty and shall remain in force through 31 December 1981, unless replaced earlier by an agreement on further measures limiting strategic offensive arms.

IV MEMORANDUM

Memorandum of Understanding Between the USA and the USSR Regarding the Establishment of a Data Base on the Numbers of Strategic Offensive Arms.

Signed at Vienna on 18 June 1979

For the purposes of the Treaty between the United States of America and Union of Soviet Socialist Republics on the Limitation of Strategic Offensive Arms, the Parties have considered data on numbers of strategic offensive arms and agree that as of 1 November 1978 there existed the following numbers of strategic offensive arms subject to the limitations provided for in the Treaty which is being signed today.

	United States	USSR
Launchers of ICBMs	1,054	1,398
Fixed Launchers of ICBMs	1,054	1,398
Launchers of ICBMs equipped with MIRVs	550	576
Launchers of SLBMs	656	950
Launchers of SLBMs equipped with MIRVs	496	128
Heavy bombers	574	156
Heavy bombers equipped for cruise missiles capable of a range in excess of 600 kilometres	0	0
Heavy bombers equipped only for ASBMs	0	0
ASBMs	0	0
ASBMs equipped with MIRVs	0	0

At the time of entry into force of the Treaty the Parties will update the above agreed data in the categories listed in this Memorandum.

Statement by the USA of Data on the Numbers of Strategic Offensive Arms as of the Date of Signature of the Salt II Treaty

The United States of America declares that as of 18 June 1979, it possesses the following number of strategic offensive arms subject to the limitations provided for in the Treaty which is being signed today:

Launchers of ICBMs	1,054
Fixed launchers of ICBMs	1,054
Launchers of ICBMs equipped with MIRVs	550
Launchers of SLBMs	656
Launchers of SLBMs equipped with MIRVs	496
Heavy bombers	573
Heavy bombers equipped for cruise missiles capable of a range in excess of 600 kilometres	3
Heavy bombers equipped only for ASBMs	0
ASBMs	0
ASBMs equipped with MIRVs	0

Statement by the USSR of Data on the Numbers of Strategic Offensive Arms as of the Date of Signature of the Salt II Treaty

The Union of Soviet Socialist Republics declares that as of 18 June 1979 it possesses the following numbers of strategic offensive arms subject to the limitations provided for in the Treaty which is being signed today:

Launchers of ICBMs	1,398
Fixed launchers of ICBMs	1,398
Launchers of ICBMs equipped with MIRVs	608
Launchers of SLBMs	950
Launchers of SLBMs equipped with MIRVs	144
Heavy bombers	156
Heavy bombers equipped for cruise missiles capable of a range in excess of 600 kilometres	0
Heavy bombers equipped only for ASBMs	0
ASBMs	0
ASBMs equipped with MIRVs	0

Statement by the USSR on the TU-22M called Backfire Bomber

On June 16, 1979, President Brezhnev handed President Carter the following written statement: 'The Soviet side informs the United States side that the Soviet "TU-22M" airplane, called "Backfire" in the United States, is a medium-range bomber and that it does not intend to give this airplane the capability of operating at intercontinental distance. In this connexion, the Soviet side states that it will not increase the radius of action of this airplane in such a way as to enable it to strike targets on the territory of the United States. Nor does it intend to give it such a capability in any other manner, including by in-flight refuelling. At the same time, the Soviet side states that it will not increase the production rate of this airplane as compared to the present rate.' President Brezhnev confirmed that the Soviet Backfire production rate would not exceed 30 per year.

Statement of President Carter
President Carter stated that the United States enters into the SALT II agreement on the basis of the commitments contained in the Soviet statement and that it considers the carrying out of these commitments to be essential to the obligations assumed under the Treaty.'

The SALT II Treaty was as of 1985 not ratified and did not come into force.

Committee on Disarmament. Doc. CD 128, June 27, 1979 and CD 129, July 2, 1979; US DEPARTMENT OF STATE, *Vienna Summit*, Washington, DC, 1979; J. GOLDBLAT, *Arms Control Agreements. A Handbook*, New York, 1983, pp. 212–229.

SALTA DECLARATION, 1971. A document signed by the presidents of Argentina and Chile, Gen. A.A. Lanusse and S. Allende, July 24, 1971, in Salta (Argentina) following a two-day conference. The Declaration provided that the two states desired to continue the bonds of friendship and co-operation without interference into internal affairs and the development of the other party.

Sintesis Información Iberoamericana, 1971, Madrid, 1972.

"SALUT" OR "SALYUT". A type of Soviet orbital station. The launching of Salut-1 occurred on Apr. 19, 1971; the spaceship Soyuz-11 joined up with the station July 7, 1971. During the return to earth, due to the unsealing of the cabin, the crew of Soyuz-11 (T.T. Dobrovolsky, V.N. Volkov, V.I. Patsayev) was lost. Salut-1 burned up Oct. 11, 1971 after it was guided into the heavy layers of the atmosphere.
Salut-2 was launched June 23, 1971; Soyuz-14 linked up with the station July 5, and its crew returned to earth July 19; Oct. 24 the station sent a container of research materials to earth; Jan. 24, 1975 Salut-3 burned up. Salut-4 was launched Dec. 26, 1974; Soyuz-17 joined up with the station Jan. 12, 1975; Feb. 9 the crew returned to earth; May 26 Soyuz-18 linked up with the station; the crew returned to earth July 26; the station burned up Feb. 3, 1975. Salut-5 was launched June 22, 1976; Soyuz-21 joined up with the station July 7; Aug. 24 the crew returned to earth; Feb. 8, 1977 Soyuz-24 linked up with the station; the crew returned to earth Feb. 25; Feb. 26 the station sent a container of research materials to earth; the station burned up Aug. 8, 1977.
Salut-6 was launched Sept. 29, 1977; Soyuz-26 joined up with the station Dec. 11, 1977; the crew (V. Romanyenko and G.M. Grechko) remained in space 96 days; during this time on Jan. 11, 1978 Soyuz-27 linked up with the station, and its crew (V.A. Dzhanibekov and O.G. Makarov) returned to earth Jan. 16 in Soyuz-26. In the 1980's astronauts from Cuba, Czechoslovakia, France, GDR, Hungary, India and Poland have flown with Soviet astronauts on Salut–Soyuz. ▷ Soyuz. ▷ Skylab.

KEESING's *Contemporary Archive, 1971–78; World Armaments and Disarmament SIPRI Yearbook 1984*, London, Philadelphia, 1984, p. 367.

SALVADOR. ▷ El Salvador.

SALVAGE. The assistance rendered to ships in distress at sea, in the air and in outer space. International norms on sea salvage were specified in the Brussels Conventions of Sept. 23, 1910, unifying some of the provisions related to sea salvage procedures, ratified by 37 states. The Convention adopted the rule on remuneration for assistance rendered, but on the principle of "no cure – no pay", French: "*pas de résultat – pas de payement*", Spanish: "*sin salvar – no se paga*". The salvage money is fixed at a percentage of the object's value. Salvage money is not paid for rescuing a crew or passenger.
International provisions on salvage in outer space are laid out in the ▷ Law of Outer Space.

KENNEDY's *Civil Salvage*, London, 1958; M.J. NORRIS, *The Law of Salvage*, London, 1958; G.D. SHMISELSKI, *Pravovoie voprosi okazania pomoshchi i spaseniya na more*, Moscow, 1961; A. MARESCA, *Le relazioni consulares*, Milano, 1968; Spanish edition, *Las relaciones consulares*, Madrid, 1974, pp. 368–376.

SALVATION ARMY. An international religious and charitable organization, est. 1865 in London working among the underprivileged, organized on military lines in corps, divisions, with its own uniforms and ranks; from 1880 of an international character. Consultative status with ECOSOC, UNICEF and UNESCO. Headquarters London. Retains permanent representative at the UN in New York. Publ. The weekly *War Cry* and many periodicals. Registered with the UIA.

Yearbook of International Organizations.

SALZBURG MOZART FESTIVAL. ▷ Music International Festivals.

SAMARITANS, THE. An ancient Jewish sect, which recognizes only the Thorah from the Judaic canon. In the 1980's the community in Israel numbers about 500. The majority live in Holon where a Samaritan synagogue stands, the remainder including the High Priest live in Nablus, near Mt. Garizim.

The Europa Yearbook 1987. A World Survey, Vol. I, London, 1987.

SAMOA. Islands in the South Pacific midway between Hawaii and Australia. Total area: 3110 sq. km, divided into the eastern islands of ▷ American Samoa under US control and of the independent State of ▷ Western Samoa.

SAN'A'. Capital of North Yemen. The old walled city of San'a' is a subject of the UNESCO International Campaign to Safeguard the City of San'a'.

R. LEWCOCK, *The Old Walled City of San'a'*. UNESCO, Paris, 1986.

SANCTIONS. International sanctions are divided into political, economic and military sanctions. Political sanctions include severance of diplomatic relations, suspension or expulsion of a state from the UN or other governmental organizations. Economic sanctions or trade sanctions may involve the total severance of all economic and financial relations or selected embargoes on imports or exports, ▷ boycotts or ▷ blockade. Military sanctions were colonial ▷ punitive expeditions and were never accepted by international law. The term "sanctions" was introduced by the Versailles Treaty to denote two things: in art. 16 as means of exerting pressure; in arts. 227–230 as punishment of war criminals; art. 16 referred to all members of the League of Nations violating commitments undertaken and provided for in the League's Pact. Art. 16 was generally interpreted by the founders of the

League of Nations in such a way that the military sanctions provided for in the Treaty were of a facultative character; however, economic and financial sanctions were compulsory. This found its expression in the statement of the Council of the League of Nations of Feb. 13, 1920 exempting Switzerland from participating in military sanctions that might be applied by the League of Nations, in light of that country's perpetual neutrality but, at the same time, keeping in force its obligation to take part in economic and financial sanctions enforced by the League. The League of Nations never adopted or applied military sanctions. However, the Council of the League of Nations on Oct. 3, 1935 and the Assembly of the League of Nations on Oct. 10, 1935 adopted a decision to apply economic sanctions against Italy, due to its aggression on another member of the League – Ethiopia, which "remained incompatible with obligations adopted and provided for in art. 16 of the Pact of the League of Nations." The sanctions were opposed by France and Great Britain, and on May 9, 1936 Italy occupied Ethiopia, a fact which according to the interpretation of other member states made the League sanctions pointless.
The Union Council of Switzerland on Apr. 29, 1938 tabled a Memorandum at the 101st Session of the Council of the League, requesting recognition of the full neutrality of Switzerland, which was accepted by the Council of the League on May 14, 1938. In turn, on July 24, 1938, the foreign ministers of Belgium, Denmark, Finland, Luxembourg, the Netherlands, Norway and Sweden meeting in Copenhagen stated that:

"the sanction system of the League of Nations in current conditions and as a result of practice used in the past years has received a non-obligatory character; in our opinion this non-obligatory character of sanctions shall spread to include not only a particular group of States, but all member States of the League of Nations; we are convinced that explicit ascertainment of this right to free assessment is in the interest of the League of Nations itself".

Due to the failure of sanctions of the League of Nations, the Charter of the United Nations does not contain the term "sanctions", but refers to "effective collective measures" (art. 1, para 1) and "preventive or enforcement measures" (art. 2, para 5) in application of which "all members shall give the United Nations every assistance". The cases in which the United Nations applied sanctions were the following:
(1) against the People's Republic of China in the form of a trade embargo, the decision being taken on Feb. 1, 1951 by the Security Council in the absence of one of the big powers – the USSR.
(2) against Southern Rhodesia in the form of an embargo enforced on maritime and air transportation of all kinds of armament, crude oil and oil products to Rhodesia and on carriage of Rhodesian products; this decision was adopted by means of Res. 232/1962 of the Security Council with 11 votes in its favor, none against and 4 abstaining due to the allegedly imprecise wording of the resolution: Bulgaria, France, Mali and USSR. The decision was openly ignored by the Union of South Africa. As regards regional organizations, the League of Arab States on many occasions tried to apply sanctions against Israel, and the Organization of African Unity – against Rhodesia; in both cases these attempts were not effective due to the lack of solidarity.

Other instances of economic sanctions:

The Hostage Incident between the USA and Iran, 1979; The Falkland/Malvinas conflict between Argentina and Great Britain, 1982; EEC economic sanctions after the military intervention, 1979, in ▷ Afghanistan.

In Dec., 1981 the USA and the EEC Western European proclaimed economic sanctions against the USSR and Poland; suspended against the USSR in 1983, against Poland partly 1984. A Polish White Book on the US sanctions was published in Apr., 1984.

J. DUMAS, *Les sanctions de l'arbitrage international*, Paris, 1905; E. MILHAUD, *Les sanctions de droit international*, Paris, 1912; D.N. HADISCOS, *Les sanctions internationaled de la Société des Nations*, Paris, 1920; W. ARNOLD-FOSTER, "Sanctions", in: *Journal of British and International Affairs*, Jan., 1926; S.O. LEVINSON, *The Sanction of Peace*, London, 1930; G. de RESSEQUIER, *Les sanctions de la Societe de Nations*, Paris, 1930; P. BARTHOLIN, *Les conséquences économiques des sanctions*, Paris, 1939; H. KELSEN, "Sanctions in International Law under the Charter of the UN", in: *Iowa Law Review*, No. 31, 1946; J.L. KUNZ, "Sanctions in International Law", in: *American Journal of International Law*, No. 54, 1960; B. SEPULVEDA, "L'ONU, el Tratado de Rio y la OEA", in: *Foro Internacional*, No. 25–26, 1966; V. VASILEN-KO, *Mezhdunarodno-pravoviye sankstii*, Kiev, 1982; M.S. DAOUDI, M.S. DAJANI, *Economic Sanctions*, Boston, 1983; S. WAJDA, *EEC and its Member States Economic Sanctions under International and Community Law*, Europe Institute, University of Amsterdam, Opole, 1984; M.P. DOXEY, *International Sanctions in Contemporary Perspective*, London, 1987; M. LIPTON, *Sanctions and South Africa: The Dynamics of Economic Isolation*, London, 1988.

SANCTUARY MOVEMENT. An international term for a church-based movement to provide aid to refugees from war-affected Central America wishing to enter the USA. On May 1, 1986 the federal jury in Tucson, Arizona convicted a presbyterian minister, a Roman Catholic priest and a nun, and Christian lay workers of a conspiracy to smuggle illegal aliens from Central America. The movement started in Arizona, the San Francisco area, and New Mexico. In 1986, 20 cities (Berkeley, San Francisco, Seattle, etc.) had declared themselves to be sanctuary cities about 300 churches as 'sanctuary churches' and New Mexico as the first 'sanctuary state'.

KEESING's *Contemporary Archive*, 1986.

SANCTUM OFFICIUM. *Latin* = "Holy Office". The name of the congregation of the Roman Catholic Church on questions of doctrine, faith and morality; historical synonym of the ▷ Inquisition.

SANCTUM SANCTORUM. *Latin* = "holy of holies". The name of the sanctuary in the Temple of Solomon in Jerusalem.

SANDINISTAS. The Nicaraguan underground organization carrying on armed struggle against the dictatorship of the Somosa clan in Nicaragua. Toppled the regime and came to power in 1979. The name Sandinistas comes from the leader of the people's uprising against military intervention of the USA, 1928, Augusto Cesaro Sandino (1893–1934), murdered by order of Somosa. ▷ Nicaragua.

T.W. WALKER, *Nicaragua, The Land of Sandino*, Boulder, 1982.

SANDOZ. ▷ Rhine pollution accident, 1986.

SAN FRANCISCO. The US city and port in West California on the tip of two peninsulas between the Pacific Ocean and San Francisco Bay, connected by the Golden Gate Strait. Area: 335 sq. km. The site of the Conference on UN Charter, Apr. 25–June 26, 1945; and of the Peace Conference with Japan, Sept. 4–8, 1951. The site of the UN Special Anniversary Sessions in June, 1955 and in June, 1985.

The United Nations Conference on International Organization, San Francisco, California, April 25–June 26, 1945, Selected Documents, Washington 1946; A. DE LA PRADELLE, *La paix moderne 1899–1945*. De la Haye à San Francisco, Paris, 1947.

SAN FRANCISCO CONFERENCE OF THE UNITED NATIONS, 1945. The official name: United Nations Conference on International Organization, UNCIO, the founding conference of the United Nations Organization, held from Apr. 25 until June 26, 1945 which drafted the final Charter of the United Nations, accepted and signed on June 26, 1945 and came into force on Oct. 24, 1945. The first international document preceding the creation of a world international organization was the ▷ Atlantic Charter, 1941 whose principles were shortly thereafter recognized in the ▷ United Nations Declaration, 1942; following this the Moscow Conference, 1943, anticipated the creation of such an organization, which was confirmed by the ▷ Teheran Conference, 1943 (Teheran Declaration) and made explicit in the form of a plan for a UN Charter ▷ Dumbarton Oaks Conference Declaration, 1944; the date and place for convening the conference was established by the ▷ Yalta Conference, 1945. Before the start of the San Francisco Conference, the Dumbarton Oaks proposals were studied and discussed by 51 nations of the world both collectively and individually. From Feb. 21–Mar. 8, 1945, for instance, the representatives of 20 Latin American nations met in Mexico City and adopted a resolution suggesting points to be taken into consideration in the drawing up of the charter of the proposed international organization. From Apr. 4–13, 1945, talks were held in London among representatives of the British Commonwealth. A statement issued at the close of the meetings indicated agreement that the Dumbarton Oaks proposals provided the basis for a Charter while recognizing that clarification, improvement and expansion were called for in certain respects.
On Apr. 25, delegates of 50 nations met in San Francisco for the conference known officially as the United Nations Conference on International Organization. Working on the Dumbarton Oaks proposals, the Yalta Agreement and amendments proposed by various governments, the delegates, meeting both in plenary sessions and in committees, drew up the 111-Article Charter.
On June 25, the delegates met in full session in the Opera House in San Francisco and unanimously adopted the Charter. The next day they signed it at a ceremony in the auditorium of the Veterans' Memorial Hall.
The Charter came into force on Oct. 24, 1945, when China, France, the USSR, the United Kingdom and the United States and a majority of the other signatories had filed their instruments of ratification. In 1953 the Security Council initiated the publication of the complete collection of documents concerning the founding of the UN, which was accomplished 1954/55.

Documents of the UN Conference on International Organizations, San Francisco 1945, 16 Vols., UN London–New York, 1946; *Postwar Foreign Policy Preparation 1939–1945*, Washington, DC, 1949, pp. 408–434; *The United Nations Conference on International Organization, San Francisco, California, April. 25–June 26, 1945, Selected Documents*, Washington, DC, 1946; A. GARCIA ROBLES, *La conferencia de San Francisco y su Obra*, México, DF, 1946; S.G. KRYLOV, *Materialy po istorii OON*, Moskva, 1948; *United Nations Conference on International Organizations*, 12 Vols., New York, 1954–55; J.A. HOUSTON, *Latin America in the UN*, New York, 1956; *Everyone's United Nations*, UN, New York, 1979; *The Story of the UN Conference on International Organization, 1945, in: UN Chronicle*, 1985, No. 4, pp. 9–11.

SANITARY CONTROL. The international control of passengers and goods in accordance with the recommendations of the International Health Rules, IHR, formulated by WHO; subject of international bilateral and regional agreements. In Stockholm on Mar. 19, 1955, Denmark, Norway, and Sweden signed the Scandinavian Treaty on Sanitary Control.

UNTS, Vol. 228, 1956, p. 95.

SANITARY ENGINEERING. A subject of international co-operation. Organizations reg. with the UIA:

European Federation of Cermanic Sanitary Ware Manufacturers, f. 1954, Milan.
Inter-American Association of Sanitary Engineering, f.1946, Caracas. Publ.: *Journal of Sanitary Engineering*. International Union of Roofing, Plumbing, Sanitary Installations, Gas and General Hydraulics, f. 1949, Paris.

Yearbook of International Organizations.

SANITARY INTERNATIONAL CONFEREN-CES, 1851–1938. An international institution created July 23, 1851 on the initiative of the governments of Austria, France, Great Britain, Greece, Portugal, Spain, Russia and Turkey as well as the four Italian states; operated until World War II (the last conference took place in 1938); under its auspices the first International Sanitary Conventions were formulated, and the Pan-American Sanitary Bureau, International Bureau of Hygiene, and the Health Organization of the League of Nations were established; after World War II the functions were assumed by World Health Organization, WHO.

SANITARY INTERNATIONAL CONVENTIONS, 1903–65. The multilateral agreements for co-operation in preventing the dissemination and proliferation of contagious diseases of human beings and animals. Initiated by the International Sanitary Conference (1851–1938); first convention framed in Paris, 1881; Rome Convention of Dec. 9, 1907 established l'Office International d'Hygiene Publique, OIHP, as an organ of the Paris convention, replaced Apr. 12, 1926 under official French name Convention Sanitaire Internationale. Art. 1 makes it incumbent on the participating states to immediately notify other governments and OIHP of the first established case of plague, cholera, yellow fever, typhoid and smallpox. Art. 171 specifies sanitary regulations relating to the prevention of incidence and proliferation of these diseases. Since 1945 sanitary conventions are supervised by WHO which worked out in 1969 the International Health Regulations, IHR, in operation since Jan 1, 1971 and abrogating the following previous conventions:
International Sanitary Convention, signed on Dec. 3, 1903 in Paris;
Pan-American Sanitary Convention, signed on Oct. 14, 1905 in Washington;
International Sanitary Convention, signed on Jan. 17, 1912 in Paris;
International Sanitary Convention, signed on June 21, 1926 in Paris;
International Sanitary Convention for Aerial Navigation, signed on Apr. 12, 1933 at The Hague;
International Agreement for dispensing with Bills of Health, on Dec. 22, 1934 signed in Paris;
International Agreement for dispensing with Consular Visas on Bills of Health, signed on Dec. 22, 1934 in Paris;
Convention modifying the International Sanitary Convention of 21 June 1926, signed on Oct. 31, 1938 in Paris;
International Sanitary Convention, 1944, modifying the International Sanitary Convention of 21

June 1926, opened for signature on Dec. 15, 1944 in Washington;
International Sanitary Convention for Aerial Navigation, 1944, modifying the International Sanitary Convention of Apr. 12, 1933, opened for signature on Dec. 15, 1944 in Washington;
Protocol of Apr. 23, 1946 to prolong the International Sanitary Convention, 1944, signed in Washington;
Protocol of Apr. 23, 1946 to prolong the International Sanitary Convention for Aerial Navigation, 1944, signed in Washington;
International Sanitary Regulations 1951, and the Additional Regulations of 1955, 1956, 1960, 1963 and 1965.
The Pan-American Sanitary Code, signed on Nov. 14, 1924 at Havana, remains in force with the exceptions of arts. 2, 9, 10, 11, 16 to 53 inclusive, 61, and 62.
In Argentina, Brazil, Paraguay, and Uruguay the Sanitary Convention signed on Apr. 21, 1914 at Montevideo is still in force.

British and Foreign State Papers, p. 1085; G.F. DE MARTENS, *Nouveau Recueil général de Traités*, 3S., Vol. 2, p. 277; *LNTS*, Vol. 4, p. 281; Vol. 5, p. 394; Vol. 24, p. 150; Vol. 78, p. 229; Vol. 92, p. 409; Vol. 104, p. 513; Vol. 107, p. 524; Vol. 161, p. 65; Vol. 181, p. 430; Vol. 183, p. 145 and 153; Vol. 198, p. 205; *UNTS*, Vol. 16, p. 180 and 217; Vol. 17, p. 9; Vol. 175, p. 215; Vol. 252, p. 338; *LNTS*, Vol. 5, p. 394; Vol. 86, p. 43.

SANITATION DECADE, 1981–90. The International Drinking-Water Supply and Sanitation Decade was launched at a special meeting of the UN General Assembly on Nov. 10, 1980.

SAN JOSÉ. The capital of Costa Rica, population, 1984 census: 241,464, since 1823. The site of the Seventh Consultative Meeting of the Foreign Ministers of American Republics, 1960 (▷ San José Declaration, 1960).

SAN JOSÉ DECLARATION, 1960. A document adopted Aug. 8, 1960 by the Seventh Conference of Ministers of Foreign Affairs of the American Republics which stated that the American continent was endangered with an intervention from outside the continent by "Sino-Soviet powers". Here are major issues of the Declaration:

"(1) The Conference resolutely denounces intervention or a threat of intervention in any form by extra-continental powers in the affairs of American republics and declares that the acceptance of the threat of extra-continental intervention against one state exposes American solidarity and security which binds the Organization of American States to disapprove and repulse the threat with equal vigor.
(2) Simultaneously, the Conference denounces the claims made by Sino-Soviet powers to take advantage of the political, economic or social situation in any American state, as such claims may corrupt continental unity and threaten peace and security of the Hemisphere.
(3) The Conference reaffirms the principle of non-interference into internal or external affairs of other American states, emphasizes that each state enjoys the right to free and unhampered development of its cultural, political and economic life with due respect for human rights and the principles of public morality; therefore, as a consequence, no American state must interfere to impose on another American state its ideology, or its political, economic or social principles.
(4) The Conference reaffirms that the inter-American system cannot be reconciled with any form of totalitarianism, and that only through democracy it may fully reach its goals on the continent when all American republics adapt their conduct to the principles contained in the Santiago de Chile Declaration adopted at Fifth Conference of Ministers of Foreign Affairs and whose observance is recommended in the shortest possible time.

(5) The Conference proclaims that all OAS member States are obliged to submit to the discipline of the inter-American system, voluntarily and willfully chosen, as observance of the provisions of the Charter of the Organization of American States is the most powerful guarantee of sovereignty and political independence of the states.
(6) The Conference declares that any dispute between member States should be settled by peaceful means incumbent on the inter-American system.
(7) The Conference affirms its faith in the regional system and its confidence in OAS founded to establish order, peace and justice to eliminate any possible aggression, to further co-operation and to safeguard sovereignty, territorial integrity and political independence; so that in the Organization its members may find a better warranty of their reconstruction and progress."

SAN JOSÉ PACT, 1969. The official name of the American Convention on Human Rights signed on Nov. 22, 1969 in the Capital of Costa Rica. ▷ Human Rights American Convention, 1969.

SAN MARINO. Not a member of the UN. Republic of San Marino. Enclave state in Italy, in the Apennines near the Adriatic Sea. Area: 60.5 sq. km. Population 1982 census 21,240, but some 20,000 citizens of San Marino live abroad. Capital: San Marino City with 4344 inhabitants 1982. Official language: Italian. Currency: Italian lira. National Day: Sept. 3, Constitution Anniversary, 1600. International relations: the world's oldest republic (early 4th century); the republican constitution (*Leges Statuae*) proclaimed on Sept. 2, 1600 was recognized by the papacy 1631. In 1798 signed first Treaty of Friendship and Commerce with the Roman Republic. On Mar. 22, 1862 concluded a Treaty of Friendship and Co-operation with the Kingdom of Italy, renewed on Mar. 27, 1872, on June 28, 1897; on Mar. 31, 1913; and on Mar. 31, 1939, with seven amendments in 1942–71. Extradition treaties with Belgium, France, the Netherlands, UK and USA. San Marino is a member of six UN specialized agencies: ILO, UNESCO, ICAO, WHO, ITU and UPU. Since 1982 women born in San Marino have the right to keep their citizenship if they marry a foreign citizen.

G. ROSSI, *San Marino*, San Marino, 1954; A. GARBALETTO, *Evoluzione storica della constituzione di San Marino*, Milano, 1956; C.N. PACKETT, *Guide to the Republic of San Marino*, Bradford, 1970; *The Europa Year Book 1984. A World Survey*, Vol. I, pp. 771–773, London, 1984.

SAN REMO. A city in northwestern Italy on the Ligurian Sea and on the Italian Riviera. The site of the Conference of the Entente States on Germany and Balkan Problems on Apr. 19–26, 1920.

SAN SALVADOR. The capital of the El Salvador Republic since 1821, population, 1984, census: 452,614, (1831–38 capital of the Central American Federation). The seat of a UN Information Center and OCAS Office.

Yearbook of International Organizations; J. DIDION, *Salvador*, London, 1983.

SAN SALVADOR CHARTER, 1951. A treaty concluded on Oct. 14, 1951 in the capital of El Salvador by heads of the governments of Guatemala, Honduras, Costa Rica, Nicaragua and El Salvador in order to initiate economic integration, and integration in the sphere of social affairs and culture of the region. The San Salvador Charter replaced the ▷ Charter of the Organization of Central American States, ODECA, 1962.

J.M. CORDERO TORRES, *Textos Básicos de la Organización Internacional*, Madrid, 1955, pp. 131–136.

SAN STEFANO PEACE TREATY, 1878. A Treaty between the Ottoman Empire and Russia, signed on Feb. 19/Mar. 3, 1878 in San Stefano. Recognition by the Ottoman Emperor of the independence of Bulgaria, Montenegro, Serbia and Romania.

Major Peace Treaties of Modern History, New York, 1967, pp. 959–974.

SANTA MARIA. ▷ ICBM.

SANTIAGO. The capital of Chile, population, 1982 census: 4,318,305, since 1810; on the Mapocho River. The seat of a UN Information center. UNESCO Office, ILO Office, UN Economic Commission for Latin America, Christian Democratic Organization of America, Inter-American Federation of Construction Industry, Inter-American Savings and Loans Union, Latin American Demographic Center and Pan-American Medical Confederation.

Yearbook of International Organizations.

SANTIAGO DE CHILE DECLARATION, 1959. A document adopted unanimously by the Fifth Conference of Ministers of Foreign Affairs of American Republics in Aug., 1959 in the capital of Chile concerning principles of continental democracy. Here are its major issues:

"Dictatorship cannot be reconciled with the American system; governments of American states should result from general elections. Human rights and fundamental civic freedoms should be guaranteed."

PAU/UPA, *Actas y Documentos de la V Reunión Consulta de los Ministros de Relaciones de las Repúblicas Americanas*, Washington, DC, 1960.

SANTO DOMINGO GROUP. A group of nine Caribbean states (Barbados, Colombia, the Dominican Republic, Guyana, Haiti, Jamaica, Mexico, Trinidad and Tobago, Venezuela) which in 1972 at a conference held in the capital of the Dominican Republic, Santo Domingo, made a formal statement in support of the 12-mile territorial waters zone, however, recognized as "patrimonial sea", subject to jurisdiction of coastal states, the 200-mile zone favored by the ▷ Montevideo Group. In 1972 negotiations between the two groups moved toward a common stand for the UN International Maritime Conference, 1974/75.

SANTO DOMINGO PLEDGE. ▷ Quito Declaration, 1984.

SANTO OR ESPIRITU SANTO. The volcanic South Pacific island 1280 km east of Australia, largest island of the New Hebrides (▷ Vanuatu) with about 10,000 inhabitants; area: 3846 sq. km. A Separatist movement proclaimed independence in June 1980, supported by an international group of businessmen, seeking to create a ▷ tax haven of the island.

SAO PAULO CONFERENCE, 1963. The Conference of the Inter-American Economic–Social Council in São Paulo in Nov., 1963 devoted to problems of the Alliance for Progress.

IA-ECOSOC, *Report of the II Annual Meeting at the Ministerial Level Held in São Paulo, Brazil, November 11–16, 1963*, São Paulo, 1963.

SAO TOMÉ AND PRINCIPE. Member of the UN. Democratic Republic of the Islands of São Tomé and Principe. Islands in the Gulf of Guinea about 240 km off the Gabonian coast of Africa. Total area: 1001 sq. km. Population, 1988, estimate: 115,600 (1970 census: 73,631). Capital; São Tomé

S

City, a port on São Tomé Island with 34,997 inhabitants, 1984. Official language: Portuguese. Currency: one dobra = 100 centavos. GNP per capita 1986 US $340. National Day: June 12, Independence Day, 1975.

Member of the UN on Aug. 16, 1975, and of all UN specialized agencies except: IFC, IMO and WIPO. Member of OAU and is an ACP state of the EEC. International relations: Portuguese colony 1552 to 1951; overseas province (provincia ultramarina) of Portugal, not accepted by the UN, 1951–75. Independent June 12, 1975. A member of the Lomé Convention in 1977 and signatory of the Lomé Convention of 1980. In close links with Angola and Portugal.

São Tomé e Principe, Lisboa, 1964; *UN Monthly Chronicle,* No. 10, 1975; *The Europa Year Book 1984. A World Survey,* Vol. II, pp. 2319–2321, London, 1984.

SAR. ▷ Maritime Search and Rescue Convention.

SARAJEVO. ▷ Serajevo.

SARC. ▷ South Asia Regional Commission.

SARGASSO SEA. A part of the North Atlantic Ocean, length *c.* 2000 km, width *c.* 5000 km, located between 20° and 35° latitude N, and 30° and 70° longitude W, distinguished by clear, warm salt water as well as thick seaweed, called by Portuguese sailors, Sargaçao, after the variety of grapes called "sarga"; subject of international research since the first oceanographic expedition in 1910 which discovered that this seaweed serves as a spawning ground for eels from America and Europe.

The International Encyclopedia and Atlas, London, 1979.

SARK. One of the islands of the Bailiwick of Guernsey, UK Crown Dependencies in the English Channel. Area: 5,5 sq km. Population: 420 in 1984.

The Europa Yearbook. A World Survey, Vol. II, London, 1988.

SASAKAVA-UNDRO DISASTER PREVENTION AWARD. ▷ Disaster Relief.

SASONOV–MOTONO TREATY, 1916. Signed on July 3, 1916 by diplomats of Russia and Japan, S.D. Sasonov and M. Motono; a confidential document referring to the confidential pacts the two Parties had signed on July 30, 1907, June 4, 1910 and June 8, 1912 on "vital interests of each side in the protection of China against political domination by a third party, expressing hostile attitude to Russia or Japan" and on joint steps relating thereto.

MAC MURRAY, *Treaties and Agreements with and Concerning China, 1894–1919,* Washington, DC, 1921, Vol. 2.

SASONOV PLAN, 1914. A plan presented on Sept. 14, 1914 by the Russian minister of foreign affairs, Sergei D. Sasonov, to the ambassador of France, M.G. Paleologue; an introductory proposal for changing the frontiers of states in Europe (after the defeat of Austria and Germany) based on the principle of nationality: Russia was to receive eastern Galicia and the northeast part of East Prussia, the Kingdom of Poland, western Galicia with Cracow, Silesia, and Poznan province; France was assured the return of Alsace-Lorraine and part of the Rhineland and Palatinate, at its discretion; Belgium – districts which it claimed; Denmark – Schleswig-Holstein. The Kingdom of Hannover was to be revived. Austria was to become the Triple Monarchy of Austria, Bohemia and Hungary.

Serbia was to combine with Bosnia, Hercegovina, Dalmatia and North Albania. Bulgaria was to receive part of Macedonia from Serbia; Greece South Albania, except the city of Valona (Vlora) granted to Italy. Great Britain, France, and Japan were to divide the German colonies. Finally, Austria and Germany were to pay the allies war reparations.

M.G. PALEOLOGUE, *La Russia de Tzars pendant la Grande Guerre,* 3 Vols., Paris, 1924.

SATELLITE REMOTE SENSING SYSTEM, UN PROJECT. The UNISPACE 82 Conference discussed how all States could take advantage of space technology for economic and social development and benefit from using satellite remote sensing systems to develop and monitor their natural resources and the environment.

A first step towards its establishment could be creation of a group of interested countries, both space powers and major users of satellite information, to discuss organizational and financial arrangements of the system.

By the mid-1990s, if remote sensing activities were pursued nationally and co-operatively in a vigorous manner, the technology would be firmly established. Plans are already under way for a second-generation of regionally and nationally owned remote sensing satellite systems to be in place by the mid-1990s.

Preparations for a third-generation high resolution remote sensing satellite system for use in the late 1990s or during the first decade of the 21st century should be undertaken now, taking into consideration identified needs and existing and planned satellite systems.

The report of the Conference also recommended:

Consideration of a proposal for a three-year United Nations project to define remote sensing systems to satisfy developing countries needs, possibly followed by establishment of an international consortium to build and operate remote sensing systems.

Compiling a regularly updated catalogue on how satellite remote sensing is being used, including such information as project description, sponsors and major results, which could form a part of the United Nations directory of space information and data services;

Creating a world-wide or regional archive for remote sensing data for research in developing countries.

Setting up "centres of excellence" in nations or regions to advise scientists and institutions in developing countries on processing, applications, distribution and verification of remote sensing data.

The Technology Application Center of the New Mexico University Albuquerque publishes since 1979 a Quarterly Review of Remote Sensing and since 1986 a Remote Sensing Yearbook.

Spreading the Benefits of Space Technology, in: UN Chronicle, 1985, No. 2, pp. 18–21; R. CRACNELL, L. HAYES eds., *Remote Sensing Yearbook 1987,* London, 1987.

SATELLITES IN OUTER SPACE. According to the SIPRI research, an average of about 120 spacecraft were launched each year in the 1980s. About 25% of them are used for scientific or telecommunication purposes, while 75% are for military purposes. Most of the spacecraft are launched either by the Soviet Union or the United States. The satellites are of several types: for military reconnaissance, communications, navigation, meteorological, geodetic and mapping missions. They continue to enhance the land-, sea- and air-based military forces of these countries. Satellites are used for gaining accurate targeting information. They are used for accurately guiding, for example, missiles, aircraft and naval ships carrying nuclear warheads to their targets. They are used for communications between military forces, over both

short and long distances. On 28 Dec., 1982 a Soviet military ocean-surveillance satellite, Cosmos 1402, was split up during its 1926th orbit, into three components – the rocket, the main satellite, and the nuclear reactor. In such cases the reactor is usually placed into a higher orbit where it circles the earth for some 500 years, a sufficient time for the short-lived radioactive fission products generated within the reactor to decay. But on this occasion attempts to do this failed, and the section carrying the nuclear reactor has entered into an ever-decreasing circular orbit which will bring it back into the earth's atmosphere.

Such accidents have occurred before. The most recent one was on 24 Jan., 1978, when a similar Soviet satellite, Cosmos 954, entered the earth's atmosphere and partially burned up, contaminating the atmosphere with radioactivity. The remaining debris landed in northern Canada, contaminating parts of the land there. Another accident, resulting in substantial contamination of the atmosphere and the earth's surface, involved a US satellite. A US Navy satellite launched on 21 Apr., 1964 carried a nuclear power generator which used plutonium-238. The spacecraft failed to orbit and the payload re-entered the earth's atmosphere in the Southern Hemisphere. The power generator was completely burned up during re-entry, and the resulting radioactive particles were distributed at about 50 km above the earth's surface. Some 95% of the radioactivity eventually landed on the earth.

Nuclear reactors have been developed both in the Soviet Union and in the USA for use in satellites. The first reactor ever to be placed in space, the American SNAP-10A, was orbited on 3 Apr., 1965 at 13,000 km, but it failed after 45 days. This reactor will re-enter the earth's atmosphere after about 4000 years. Currently the USA is working on a reactor, SP-100, capable of producing 100 kilowatts compared to the power from SNAP-10A of about 30 kilowatts.

By the end of 1982 the Soviet Union had launched about 25 satellites carrying nuclear reactors. Their early reactors were known as *Romashka* and the recent ones are known as *Topaz*. Such reactors produce about 40 kW of thermal power and they are fuelled with about 50 kg of highly enriched uranium. Since 1974 the Soviet Union has been operating two satellites at a time. Satellites are orbited in the same orbital plane but about 25 minutes apart. The USA uses four ocean-surveillance satellites at a time. Again, the satellites are in the same orbital plane, but they are separated from each other in time and distance along their orbital paths. The use of such groups of satellites indicates that they are probably used to determine the position and velocity of the naval vessels being surveyed.

In response to concerns expressed during the first week of Jan., 1983 regarding the re-entry of Cosmos 1402 into the earth's atmosphere, the Soviet news agency Tass announced on Jan. 7 that the satellite "was divided into separated fragments by commands from earth in order to isolate the active part of the reactor, which ensured its subsequent complete combustion in the dense atmospheric strata." While this may be so, the radioactivity, however small, eventually will fall on the earth's surface, as past experience has shown. Contamination of the earth's environment from such sources is small at present, but in future this may not be the case as there are plans to orbit much larger nuclear reactors in space.

As a result of the Cosmos 954 accident, President Carter pledged that the United States would pursue a ban on nuclear power in space. However, this position of the USA was later abandoned. The United Nations Sub-Committee on the Peaceful

Uses of Outer Space examined the issues of nuclear power sources on board satellites. Both the United States and the USSR participated in this technical study. The main recommendation of the Sub-Committee was that appropriate measures for adequate radiation protection during all phases of a spacecraft carrying a nuclear power source should be mainly based on existing and internationally recognized standards recommended by the International Commission on Radiological Protection (ICRP). The first photo reconnaissance satellite was produced by the USA in 1959, by the USSR 1962 and by China 1983.

SIPRI, *Fact Sheet*, January, 1983; *World Armaments and Disarmement, SIPRI Yearbook 1984*, London, Philadelphia, 1984; B. JASANI, T. SAKATA, *Satellites for Arms Control and Crises Monitoring*, SIPRI, Oxford, 1987.

SATELLITE INTERNATIONAL MONITORING UN AGENCY. ▷ Satellite Telecommunication.

SATELLITE TELECOMMUNICATION. The utilization of artificial Earth satellites as transmitting stations for telegraph, telex, telephones, television, the subject of international conventions and organized international co-operation. A UN Working Group on Direct Broadcast Satellites has been studying since 1968 the technical feasibility of telecommunication by direct broadcast from satellites and on current and foreseeable developments in that form of communication. The Group in 1974 started to discuss the principles that might be adopted to govern the use by states of artificial earth satellites for direct TV broadcasting in interests of international peace and security, co-operation among all states and peoples, development, exchange of information and enhancement of education. In 1977 the annual ITU conference in Geneva established for each country frequency channels for the transmission of TV programs via satellites. The establishment of global satellite communications through two systems ▷ Intelsat and ▷ Molniya has created many problems in international space law in view of the possibility of interfering in the internal affairs of other states through satellite telecommunication. Satellite television is the sphere of activity since the 1960s of two global organizations ▷ INTELSAT and ▷ INTERSPUTNIK. A satellite system on the sea was introduced in the 1970s by the International Sea Satellite Organization, ▷ INMARSAT, which includes moving and stationary land stations as well as an outer space station.

In 1978 the President of France V. Giscard d'Estaing presented to the UN the idea of UN Blue Satellite for peace telecommunication.

The UN General Assembly Res. 34/83E of Dec. 11, 1979 initiated to study the implications of the establishment of an International Satellite Monitoring Agency under aegis of the UN. On Feb. 7, 1984 the President of France, J. Mitterrand, presented to the European Community a draft of an European Cosmics Unity, building its own satellites.

A regional telecommunication satellite was launched 1984/85 for Arab countries by the Arab Satellite Communication Organization, ARABSAT (▷ League of Arab States Satellite).

UN Monthly Chronicle, April, 1974, p. 11; SIPRI, *World Armaments and Disarmament Yearbook*, 1968–80; *UN Chronicle*, April, 1980, p. 23.

SATISFACTION. An international term for the material or non-material settlement of damages in international disputes, in the latter case usually in the form of a letter of apology or regret or an oral statement by the side responsible for an incident.

C. EAGLETON, "Measures of Damage in International Law", in: *Yale Law Journal*, No. 39, 1929; P.A. BISONNETTE, *La satisfaction comme mode de réparation en droit international*, Paris, 1952; A. SCHULE, "Genugtuung", in: STRUPP-SCHLOCHAUER, *Wörterbuch des Völkerrechts*, Berlin, 1960, Vol. 1, pp. 660–661.

SATO. South Atlantic Treaty Organization, an institution planned since 1976 by the military authorities of South Africa, Argentina, Brazil and Uruguay.

SATURN. One of the ▷ Planets in the Solar System. A subject of international space research. Three American unmanned vehicles encountered Saturn: Pioneer 11 in 1979, Voyager 1 in 1980 and Voyager 2 in 1981.

SAUDI ARABIA. member of the UN. Kingdom of Saudi Arabia. State in southwestern Asia on the Arabian peninsula on the Persian Gulf and the Red Sea. Borders with Jordan, Iraq, Kuwait, Oman, Qatar, United Arab Emirates, Yemen and South Yemen; northern frontiers were established by a British–Saudi treaty signed May 20, 1927 in Jedda; the southern frontiers with Yemen were established in Nov., 1939; the delimitation of the continental shelf in the Persian Gulf occurred as a result of a treaty signed with Iran on Oct. 24, 1968 in Teheran. ▷ Neutral Arabic Zone.

Area: 2,240,000 sq. km. Pop. in 1986 est.: 11,520,000 (1974 census: 7,012,642). Capital: Riyadh with 666,840 inhabitants, 1974. Center of the cult of Islam is Mecca with 366,801 inhabitants, 1974. Official language: Arabic. Currency: one Saudi riyal = 20 qurush = 100 halalah. GNP per capita in 1986: US $6930. National Day: Mar. 26, anniversary of king Khalid's accession to the throne, 1975. Founding member of the UN, and of all specialized agencies, except GATT.

International relations: the Arabian monarchy was formed after World War I by the proclamation of the kingdom of Hejaz on Jan. 8, 1926 by Great Britain, recognized in a treaty signed on May 20, 1927 in Jedda with king Ibn Saud. Since Sept. 23, 1932 the official name is the Kingdom of Saudi Arabia. Treaties: with Yemen signed in May 1934 and extended in Mar., 1953; with Kuwait in 1942; with Jordan in Aug., 1962. During World War II Saudi Arabia in 1941 broke off diplomatic relations with Germany and Italy; in 1944 the US built an air base near the city of Az-Zaharan. In 1952–55 in conflict with Great Britain, which annexed the oasis Al-Buraymi. In 1956 Saudi Arabia broke off diplomatic relations with France and Great Britain in connection with the attack on Suez and with Israel in connection with the occupation of the Gulf of Accaba. Since 1939 connected with the oil company ARAMCO, whose assets she purchased in 1977/78. The state institution of Saudi Arabia is PETROMIN (General Petroleum and Mineral Organization). A pipeline 1900 km long leading to Port Saida (Sidon) in Lebanon is under the management of the Transarabian Pipeline Co. In 1978 in conflict with South Yemen. Member of the OAU. Member of the Arab League and OPEC. Saudi Arabia plays a special role in the Moslem world, since located on her territory is Mecca, Mohamed's birth-place and the goal of pilgrimages of followers of Islam.

In Sept., 1982 the Crown Prince Fahd at a summit conference of Arab States presented the "Fahd Peace Plan" for the Middle East. In 1983 Saudi Arabian diplomacy helped to achieve cease-fire between factions of the PLO; and in 1984 to prepare elaboration of agreements in the Lebanon crisis.

H. PHILBY, *Saudi Arabia*, London, 1955; D. HOWARTH, *The Desert King. Ibn Saud and his Arabia*, New York, 1964; J.G. SOULIE, W.R. BAILY, *Saudi Arabia in the 19th Century*, London, 1965; L. CHAMPENOIS, *Le Royaume d'Arabie Saoudite face à l'Islam Révolutionnaire 1953–1964*, Paris, 1966; P. HOBDAY, *Saudi Arabia Today*, London, 1978; F.A. CLEMENTS, *Saudi Arabia, Bibliography*, Oxford, 1979; B. McMASTER, *The Definitive Guide to Living in Saudi Arabia*, London, 1980; C.M. HELNY, *The Cohesion of Saudi Arabia*, Baltimore, 1981; D. HOLDEN, R. JOHNS, *The House of Saud*, New York, 1981; W.B. QUANDT, *Saudi Arabia in the 1980's: Foreign Policy, Security and Oil*, Washington, DC, 1981; T. NIBLOCK, *State, Society and Economy in Saudi Arabia*, New York, 1981; R. LACEY, *The Kingdom*, New York, 1981; W. POWELL, *Saudi Arabia and its Royal Family*, Secanus, N.J., 1982; R.E. LOONEY, *Saudi Arabia's Development Potential*, Lexington, 1982; *The Europa Year Book 1984. A World Survey*, Vol. II, pp. 2322–2335, London, 1984; M.A. HAMEED, *Saudi Arabia, the West and the Security of the Gulf*, London, 1986.

"SAVANNAH" NS. The first freighter (10,000 DWT) with nuclear propulsion (NS = nuclear ship), built 1961, in the USA; named after the seaport of the state of Georgia, USA, as was in 1818 the first American ship with steam and sail propulsion, which crossed the Atlantic on the route Savannah–Liverpool and later visited Baltic ports.

SAVINGS ASSOCIATIONS. The co-operative savings and loan institutions, building societies, savings banks, investment trusts. Organizations reg. with the UIA:

Africa Co-operative Savings and Credit Association, ACOSCA, f. 1968, Nairobi. Publ.: *Courier*.
EEC Group of Savings and Credit Co-operatives, f. 1963, Brussels.
EEC Savings Banks Group, f. 1963, Brussels. Publ.: *EEC-Épargne Europe*.
European Federation of Savings and Loan Institutions for Constructions, f. 1962, Brussels.
Interamerican Union of Savings and Loan for Housing, f. 1964, Santiago.
International Savings Bank Institute, ISBI, f. 1925, Geneva. Publ.: *Savings Bank International*.
International Union of Building Societies and Savings Association, IUBSSA, f. 1914, London. Publ.: *The Union Newsletter*.

Yearbook of International Organizations.

SCANDINAVIA. A territory in northern Europe whose name comes from the Scandinavian peninsula; in world press the name usually refers not only to the territory of Norway and Sweden, but also Denmark, Finland, Iceland and the Faroe Islands. The area of the Scandinavian Peninsula amounts to 770,000 sq. km; it is 1850 km long and from 370 to 805 km wide. Because of the reservations on the part of Finland to the term Scandinavia, which implies the policies of ▷ Scandinavianism, integrational organizations of the above states have been called "Nordic" (northern), as e.g. the Nordic Council. However, common conventions are called Scandinavian.

F. SCOTT, *Scandinavia*, Cambridge Mass., 1979; G. FERNE, *Science and Technology in Scandinavia*, London, 1988.

SCANDINAVIAN ACCIDENT INSURANCE LAW CONVENTION, 1937. A Convention between Denmark, Finland, New Zealand, Norway and Sweden, restricting the Application of the Accident Insurance Law of the various states to cases where an employer in one of the contracting states carries on a business or employs workers in another of the said states, signed in Oslo, Mar. 3, 1937.

LNTS, Vol. 182, p. 127.

S

SCANDINAVIAN AGREEMENT FOR THE READMITTANCE OF ALIENS, 1952. Agreement between Denmark, Finland, Norway and Sweden for the readmittance of aliens who have illegally entered the territory of another contracting party, signed on July 14, 1952 in Stockholm.

UNTS, Vol. 198, p. 47.

SCANDINAVIAN AGREEMENT ON PERSONS INSURED FOR SICKNESS, 1967. Agreement between Denmark, Finland, Iceland, Norway and Sweden concerning transfer of persons insured for sickness benefits and sickness benefits during temporary residence, signed on Feb. 24, 1967 in Copenhagen.

UNTS, Vol. 596, p. 164.

SCANDINAVIAN AIRLINES SYSTEM, SAS. The Agreement between Denmark, Norway and Sweden regarding co-operation in the field of Civil aviation, signed on Dec. 20, 1951 in Oslo, approving a consortial agreement concluded between Det Danske Luftfartselskab A/S, Det Norske Luftfartselskap A/S and Aktiebolaget Aerotransport of Sweden, under which the three air transport companies agreed to carry on air transport through a joint consortium designated the Scandinavian Airlines System, called SAS. Came into force May 28, 1952. In 1955 and 1959 Denmark, Norway and Sweden signed two Scandinavian Airlines Agreements regarding financial guarantees to certain airlines, on Sept. 29, 1955 in Copenhagen and on Aug. 20, 1959 in Oslo.

UNTS, Vol. 163, p. 303; Vol. 222, p. 313; Vol. 376, p. 99.

SCANDINAVIAN ANTI-POLLUTION AGREE-MENT, 1967. An Agreement concerning co-operation to ensure compliance with the regulations for preventing the pollution of the sea by oil, signed on Dec. 8, 1967 in Copenhagen, by the governments of Denmark, Finland, Norway and Sweden.

UNTS, Vol. 620, p. 225.

SCANDINAVIAN BANKRUPTCY CONVEN-TION, 1933. The convention between Denmark, Finland, Iceland, Norway and Sweden, regarding Bankruptcy, signed on Nov. 7, 1933 in Copenhagen.

LNTS, Vol. 155, p. 115.

SCANDINAVIAN CHILD ALLOWANCES CONVENTION, 1951. A Convention between Finland, Iceland, Norway and Sweden, regarding the reciprocal payment of child allowances, signed on Aug. 28, 1951 in Helsinki.

UNTS, Vol. 198, p. 17.

SCANDINAVIAN CITIZENS CONVENTION, 1928. A Convention between Denmark, Finland, Norway and Sweden concerning mutual Relief to Indigent Citizens of those Countries, signed on Oct. 25, 1928 in Stockholm.

LNTS, Vol. 84, p. 7.

SCANDINAVIAN CITIZENSHIP LEGISLA-TION. Denmark, Norway and Sweden guarantee that in their legislation on citizenship they will treat each other's nationals in an equal way. This was expressed in the Scandinavian Convention on Citizenship, signed on May 26, 1914 in Stockholm, expanded to include Finland by means of a protocol signed on July 11, 1923 in Stockholm and by means of a Scandinavian Treaty on Citizenship signed on Dec. 1950 in Copenhagen.

LNTS, Vol. 18, p. 85, and Vol. 90, p. 3.

SCANDINAVIAN CLAUSE. A reservation in a trade agreement introduced by the Scandinavian states, invalidating the most-favored-nation clause, in cases of preferences to Scandinavian states to a degree not applied to third states.

SCANDINAVIAN COMMON LABOR MARKET AGREEMENT, 1954. A Convention (with Protocol) between Denmark, Finland, Norway and Sweden, signed on May 22, 1954 in Copenhagen, relating to the free movement of labor between the Scandinavian countries. "None of the contracting states shall require a work permit in respect of the nationals of any other contracting state" (art. 1).

UNTS, Vol. 199, p. 20.

SCANDINAVIAN CONVENTION ON DISTRESSED PERSONS, 1951. A Convention between Denmark, Finland, Iceland, Norway and Sweden concerning the reciprocal granting of assistance to distressed persons, signed on Jan. 9, 1951 in Stockholm.

UNTS, Vol. 197, p. 341.

SCANDINAVIAN CONVENTION RESPECT-ING TRANSFERS OF INSURED PERSONS, 1953. A Convention between Denmark, Iceland, Norway and Sweden respecting transfers of insured persons from one sick fund to another and respecting sickness benefit during temporary residence. Signed on July 20, 1953 in Reykjavik, and Supplementary Agreement to the above-mentioned Convention, signed on Dec. 30, 1954 in Stockholm.

UNTS, Vol. 227, p. 217.

SCANDINAVIAN CO-OPERATION AGREE-MENT, 1962. An Agreement between Denmark, Finland, Iceland, Norway and Sweden concerning co-operation, signed on Mar. 23, 1962 in Helsinki.

"Art. 1. The Contracting Parties shall strive to maintain and intensify co-operation between countries in the juridical, cultural, social and economic fields and in communications matters."

UNTS, Vol. 434, p. 145.

SCANDINAVIAN CULTURAL CO-OPERA-TION AGREEMENTS, 1962 AND 1971. The Scandinavian Treaty between Denmark, Finland, Iceland, Norway and Sweden on Co-operation in the Fields of Culture, Economy, Transportation and Law, signed on Mar. 23, 1962 in Helsinki and the Scandinavian Cultural Convention signed on Mar. 15, 1971 in Helsinki, came into force on Jan. 1, 1972.

UNTS, Vol. 434, p. 145 and Vol. 825, p. 392.

SCANDINAVIAN FISHERY CONVENTIONS, 1937–66. The Conventions between Denmark, Norway and Sweden concerning the Preservation of Plaice and Dab in the Skagerrak, Kattegat and Sound, with Final Protocol, signed on Sept. 6, 1937 in Oslo.
Agreement between Denmark, Norway and Sweden concerning measures for the protection of stocks of deep-sea prawns (*Pandalus borealis*), European lobsters (*Homarus vulgaris*), Norway lobsters (*Nephrops norvegicus*) and crabs (*Cancer pagurus*), signed on Mar. 7, 1952 in Oslo.
Agreement between Denmark, Norway and Sweden on reciprocal access to the Skagerrak and the Kattegat, signed on Dec. 19, 1966 in Copenhagen.

LNTS, Vol. 186, p. 419; *UNTS*, Vol. 175, p. 205; Vol. 605, p. 313.

SCANDINAVIAN ICE-BREAKING CO-OPERATION, 1961. An Agreement between Denmark, Finland, Norway and Sweden concerning co-operation in ice-breaking, signed on Dec. 20, 1961 in Helsinki.

UNTS, Vol. 419, p. 79.

SCANDINAVIAN INHERITANCE CONVEN-TION, 1934. A Convention between Denmark, Finland, Iceland, Norway and Sweden, regarding Inheritance and the Settlement of the Devolution of Property, and Final Protocol, signed on Nov. 19, 1934 in Copenhagen.

LNTS, Vol. 164, p. 243.

SCANDINAVIAN INSURANCE CONVEN-TIONS AND AGREEMENTS, 1937–1967. Four Conventions concluded by Denmark, Finland, Iceland, Norway and Sweden:
Convention on accident insurance, signed on Mar. 3, 1937 in Oslo;
Convention on transfer of insured persons from one sick fund to another respecting sickness benefits during temporary residence signed on July 20, 1953 in Reykjavik;
Agreement on unemployment insurance, signed on Sept. 8, 1959 in Reykjavik.
Convention on sickness insurance, signed on Feb. 24, 1967 in Copenhagen.

LNTS, Vol. 182, p. 127; *UNTS*, Vol. 227, p. 217; Vol. 383, p. 203; Vol. 596, p. 164.

SCANDINAVIAN INVESTMENT BANK. ▷ Banks of Scandinavia.

SCANDINAVIANISM. An international term for a political trend striving toward the cultural, economic and political unity of the Scandinavian nations, initiated 1845 by the Congress of Scandinavian Students in Copenhagen; in the second half of the 20th century it played a certain role in re-awakening national feelings in Schleswig against policies of germanization. After World War II was institutionalized in interstate form in the Nordic Council, 1953.

Nordeuropa Positionen zur Entspannung, Berlin, 1979.

SCANDINAVIAN JURIDICAL CONVEN-TIONS, 1932 AND 1948. The first Convention between Denmark, Finland, Iceland, Norway and Sweden, regarding the Juridical Recognition and Enforcements, was signed on Mar. 16, 1932 in Copenhagen. The second agreement between Denmark, Norway and Sweden, regarding the Recognition and Enforcement of Judgements in Criminal Matters, was signed on Mar. 8, 1948 in Copenhagen.

LNTS, Vol. 139, p. 165; *UNTS*, Vol. 27, pp. 119–133.

SCANDINAVIAN LABOUR MARKET FOR NURSES AGREEMENT, 1968. An Agreement between Denmark, Finland, Norway and Sweden concerning a common Scandinavian labor market for nurses signed on Dec. 5, 1968 in Oslo; came into force Aug. 15, 1970.

UNTS, Vol. 763, p. 265.

SCANDINAVIAN MAINTENANCE ALL-OWANCES CONVENTION, 1931. A Convention between Denmark, Finland, Iceland, Norway and Sweden, signed on Feb. 10, 1931 in Stockholm, regarding the collection of maintenance allowances;

and Agreement concerning amendments to this Convention, signed on Apr. 1, 1953 in Oslo.

LNTS, Vol. 126, p. 51; *UNTS*, Vol. 227, p. 169.

SCANDINAVIAN MAINTENANCE CONTRIBUTIONS RECOVERY CONVENTION, 1962.
A Convention between Denmark, Finland, Iceland, Norway and Sweden concerning the recovery of maintenance contributions, signed on Mar. 23, 1962 in Oslo.

UNTS, Vol. 470, p. 25.

SCANDINAVIAN MARRIAGE AND ADOPTION CONVENTION, 1931.
A Convention between Denmark, Finland, Iceland, Norway and Sweden containing certain provisions of private international law regarding Marriage, Adoption and Guardianship, signed on Feb. 6, 1931 in Stockholm and Agreement, changing the text of arts. 2, 7 and 9 of the above-mentioned Convention, signed on Mar. 23, 1953 in Stockholm.

UNTS, Vol. 202, p. 241.

SCANDINAVIAN MATERNITY ASSISTANCE CONVENTION, 1953.
A Convention (with Final Protocol) between Denmark, Finland, Iceland, Norway and Sweden, respecting reciprocity in the granting of Maternity Assistance, signed on July 20, 1953 in Reykjavik.

UNTS, Vol 228, p. 3.

SCANDINAVIAN MEDICAL CENTRE IN KOREA.
An Agreement between Denmark, Sweden and Norway regarding co-operation in the establishment and operation of a Scandinavian Medical Centre for Treatment and Training in Korea, signed on Dec. 21, 1956 in Oslo in collaboration with the Republic of Korea and the UN Korea Reconstruction Agency

UNTS, Vol. 427, p. 81.

SCANDINAVIAN MILITARY SERVICE AGREEMENT, 1956.
An Agreement between Denmark, Norway and Sweden concerning the relationship between compulsory military service and nationality in Norway, Denmark and Sweden, signed on Mar. 3, 1956 in Oslo.

UNTS, Vol. 243, p. 169.

SCANDINAVIAN MONETARY CONVENTION, 1873.
An Agreement on monetary union between Denmark and Sweden signed on May 27, 1873 and extended to Norway by the supplementary Convention of Oct. 16, 1875; enlarged by an additional article on May 11, 1920 ("... each contracting state shall be permitted to mint, on its own account, coins of copper-nickel"); enlarged Mar. 22, 1924.

LNTS, Vol. 1, p. 15; Vol. 25, pp. 171–177.

SCANDINAVIAN NATIONALITIES AGREEMENT, 1950.
Agreement between Denmark, Norway and Sweden on the implementation of the provisions in section 10 of the Danish Nationality Act No. 252 of May 27, 1950, in section 10 of the Norwegian Nationality Act of Dec. 8, 1950 and in section 10 of the Swedish Nationality Act (No. 382) of June 22, 1950, signed at Copenhagen on Dec. 1, 1950.

UNTS, Vol. 90, pp. 3–17.

SCANDINAVIAN NATIONALS CONVENTION, 1914.
A Convention concluded in Stockholm, May 26, 1914, between Denmark, Norway and Sweden, regarding the assistance to be granted to nationals of one of the contracting states on the territory of another of those states. Protocol concerning the adhesion of Finland was signed on July 11, 1923 in Stockholm.

LNTS, Vol. 18, p. 85.

SCANDINAVIAN NAVIGABLE WATERS MARKING AGREEMENT, 1962.
Agreement between Denmark, Finland, Norway and Sweden, concerning uniform rules for the marking of navigable waters, signed in Helsinki, Sept. 18, 1962.

UNTS, Vol. 442, p. 215.

SCANDINAVIAN NEUTRALITY DECLARATION, 1938.
Common Declaration of the Governments of Denmark, Finland, Iceland, Norway and Sweden for the Purpose of establishing Similar Rules of Neutrality, with five Annexes, signed in Stockholm, May 27, 1938.

The text is as follows:

"The Governments of Denmark, Finland, Iceland, Norway and Sweden,
Considering it to be highly desirable that, in the event of war between foreign Powers, they should all apply similar rules of neutrality,
Have drawn up, on the basis of the Declaration in this matter made by Denmark, Norway and Sweden on December 21st, 1912, Rules of Neutrality, the texts of which are appended hereto, to be enacted by the said Governments, each in so far as concerns itself,
And have agreed that, should any of them desire, in the light of their own experience, to modify the said Rules, as contemplated by the Convention on the Rights and Duties of Neutral Powers in Naval War, signed at The Hague on October 18th, 1907, they shall not do so without first giving, if possible, sufficient notice to the other four Governments to permit of an exchange of views in the matter.

Denmark. Rules of Neutrality.

Concerning the neutrality of Denmark in the event of war between foreign Powers, the following provisions shall apply, as from the date and to the extent to be fixed by the King:

Art. 1. Belligerent warships shall be granted admission to the ports and other territorial waters of the Kingdom subject to the following exceptions, restrictions, and conditions.

Art. 2.(1) Belligerent warships shall not be allowed access to the port and roadstead of Copenhagen or to ports and maritime areas proclaimed to be naval ports or to form part of the protection zones of coast defence works.

(2) Belligerent warships shall, further, not be allowed access to inner waters, the entrance to which is closed by submarine mines or other means of defence.

For the purposes of the present Decree, 'Danish inner waters' shall be deemed to include ports, the approaches to ports, gulfs and bays, and the waters between those Danish islands, islets and reefs which are not constantly submerged, and between the said islands, islets and reefs and the mainland; nevertheless, in those parts of the Danish territorial waters in the Kattegat, the Great and Little Belt, and the Sound which form the natural routes for traffic between the North Sea and the Baltic Sea, only the ports and approaches to ports and the roadstead of Copenhagen shall be regarded as inner waters.

(3) Belligerent submarines ready for service shall be prohibited from navigating or remaining in Danish territorial waters.

The foregoing prohibition shall not apply, however, to passage without unnecessary stops through the zone of the Danish outer waters which forms part of the neutral route for traffic between the North Sea and the Baltic Sea in the Kattegat, the Great and Little Belt, and the Sound, with the exception of the roadstead of Copenhagen, which, falling within the category of waters, shall be entirely closed to such passage or to submarines forced to enter prohibited waters by stress of weather or by damage, provided always that they indicate by means of an international signal their reason for entering such waters. Such submarines shall be required to leave the prohibited waters as soon as the circumstances which are the cause of their presence there have ceased. While in Danish territorial waters, submarines shall continuously fly their national flag and, save in the case of extreme necessity, shall navigate on the surface.

(4) The King may in special circumstances, for the purpose of safeguarding the sovereign rights and maintaining the neutrality of the Kingdom, while at the same time observing the general principles of international law, prohibit access to Danish ports and other stated zones of Danish territorial waters other than those to which access is prohibited by the foregoing provisions.

(5) The King may likewise prohibit the access to Danish ports and anchorages of any belligerent warships which may have failed to comply with the rules and regulations laid down by the competent Danish authorities, or have violated the neutrality of the Kingdom.

Art. 3.(1) Privateers shall not be permitted to enter Danish ports or to remain in Danish territorial waters.

(2) The armed merchant vessels of belligerents shall, if their armaments are intended for purposes other than their own defence, likewise be forbidden access to Danish ports or to remain in Danish territorial waters.

Art. 4.(1) Belligerent warships shall not be permitted to remain in Danish ports and anchorages or in other Danish territorial waters for more than twenty-four hours, save in the event of their having suffered damage or run aground, or under stress of weather, or in the cases enumerated in paragraphs 3 and 4 below. In such cases, they shall leave as soon as the cause of the delay has ceased. In the case of vessels having suffered damage or run aground, the competent Danish authority shall fix such time-limit as may be deemed sufficient to repair the damage or refloat the vessel. No vessel shall, however, be permitted to prolong its stay for more than twenty-four hours if it is clear that the said vessel cannot be rendered seaworthy within a reasonable time, or if the damage was caused by an enemy act of war. The above restrictions on the stay of vessels shall not apply to warships used exclusively for religious, scientific or humanitarian purposes, or to naval and military hospital ships.

(2) Not more than three warships of a belligerent power or of several allied belligerent Powers shall be permitted to remain in a Danish port or anchorage at the same time, or, the coast having been divided into districts for the purpose, in the ports or anchorages of the same coastal district of Denmark.

(3) In the event of warships belonging to both belligerents being present in a Danish port or anchorage at the same time, a period of not less than twenty-four hours shall elapse between the departure of a ship belonging to one belligerent and the departure of a ship belonging to the other. The order of departure shall be determined by the order of arrival, unless the ship which arrived first is so circumstanced that an extension of its stay is permitted.

(4) No belligerent warship shall leave a Danish port or anchorage in which there is a merchant vessel flying an enemy flag within less than twenty-four hours after the departure of such merchant vessel. The competent authorities shall make such arrangements for the departure of merchant vessels that the stay of warships is not unnecessarily prolonged.

Art. 5.(1) In Danish ports and anchorages belligerent warships shall only be permitted to effect such repairs as may be essential to seaworthiness, and they shall not increase their warlike strength in any manner whatsoever. In repairing damage manifestly caused by enemy acts of war, damaged vessels shall not be permitted to avail themselves of any assistance which they may have procured in Danish territory. The competent Danish authorities shall determine the nature of the repairs to be carried out. Such repairs shall be effected as rapidly as possibly within the time-limit laid down in Article 4, paragraph 1.

(2) Belligerent warships shall not make use of Danish ports or other Danish territorial waters to replace or augment their warlike stores or armament, or to complete their crews.

(3) Belligerent warships shall only be permitted to revictual in Danish ports or anchorages to the extent necessary to bring their supplies up to the normal peace standard.

(4) As regards refuelling, belligerent warships shall be subject, in Danish ports and anchorages, to the same provisions as other foreign vessels. They shall, nevertheless, only be permitted to ship sufficient fuel to enable them to reach the nearest port in their own country and in no case shall they ship more than is

necessary to fill their coal bunkers, strictly so called, or their liquid fuel bunkers. After obtaining fuel in any Danish port or anchorage, they shall not be permitted to obtain further supplies in Danish ports and anchorages within a period of three months.

Art. 6. Belligerent warships shall be required to employ the officially licensed pilots in Danish territorial waters whenever the assistance of a pilot is compulsory, but otherwise they shall only be permitted to make use of the services of such pilots when in distress, in order to escape perils of the sea.

Art. 7.(1) Prizes of foreign nationality shall not be brought into a Danish port or anchorage save on account of unseaworthiness, under stress of weather or for lack of fuel or provisions. Prizes brought into a Danish port or anchorage in any of the above circumstances shall leave as soon as such circumstances are at an end.

(2) No prize court shall be set up by a belligerent in Danish territory or on any vessel in Danish territorial waters. The sale of prizes in a Danish port or anchorage shall likewise be prohibited.

Art. 8.(1) Belligerent military aircraft, with the exception of air ambulances and aircraft carried on board warships shall not be admitted to Danish territory, save in so far as may be otherwise provided in regulations applied, or to be applied, in accordance with the general principles of international law in regard to certain spaces.

Such aircraft shall be permitted to cross, without unnecessary stops, the Danish outer territorial waters connecting the North Sea and the Baltic Sea through the Kattegat, the Great and Little Belt and the Sound, and the air space above such waters. They shall on no account traverse the Copenhagen roadstead and the air space above. In all circumstances, they shall be required, while so crossing, to keep as far as possible from the coast.

(2) Aircraft carried on board belligerent warships shall not leave such vessels while in Danish territorial waters.

Art. 9.(1) Belligerent warships and military aircraft shall be required to respect the sovereign rights of the Kingdom and to refrain from all acts infringing its neutrality.

(2) Within the limits of Danish territory all acts of war, including the stopping, visit and search and capture of vessels and aircraft, whether neutral or of enemy nationality, shall be prohibited. Any vessel or aircraft captured within such limits shall be released immediately, together with its officers, crew and cargo.

Art. 10. The sanitary, pilot, Customs, navigation, air traffic, harbour and police regulations shall be strictly observed.

Art. 11. Belligerents shall not use Danish territory as a base for warlike operations against the enemy.

Art. 12.(1) Belligerents and persons in their service shall not install or operate in Danish territory wireless-telegraph stations or any other apparatus to be used for the purpose of communication with belligerent military, naval or air forces.

(2) Belligerents shall not use their mobile wireless-telegraph stations, whether belonging to their combatant forces or not, in Danish territory, for the transmission of messages, save when in distress or for the purpose of communicating with the Danish authorities through a Danish inland or coastal wireless-telegraph station or a wireless-telegraph station on board a vessel belonging to the Danish navy.

Art. 13. The observation, by any person whatsoever, either from aircraft or in any other manner in Danish territory, of the movements, operations or defence works of one belligerent with a view to the information of the other belligerent shall be prohibited.

Art. 14.(1) Belligerents shall not establish fuel depots within the territory of the Kingdom, whether upon land or on vessels stationed in its territorial waters.

(2) Vessels and aircraft cruising with the manifest purpose of furnishing fuel or other supplies to the combatant forces of the belligerents shall not ship such fuel or other supplies in Danish ports or anchorages in quantities exceeding their own requirements.

Art. 15.(1) No vessel shall be fitted or armed in Danish territory for cruising or taking part in hostile operations against either of the belligerents. Nor shall any vessel intended for such uses, which has been partly or wholly adapted in Danish territory for warlike purposes, be permitted to leave such territory.

(2) Aircraft equipped to carry out an attack on a belligerent or carrying apparatus or material the mounting or use of which would enable it to carry out such an attack shall not be permitted to leave Danish territory if there are grounds for presuming that it is intended for use against a belligerent Power. Any work on aircraft to prepare it for departure for the above-mentioned purpose shall likewise be prohibited.

ANNEX I Finland. Rules of Neutrality.

Concerning the neutrality of Finland in the event of war between foreign Powers, the following provisions shall apply as from the date and to the extent to be fixed by the President of the Republic:

Art. 1. Belligerent warships shall be granted admission to the ports and other territorial waters of the Republic subject to the following exceptions, restrictions and conditions.

Art. 2.(1) Belligerent warships shall not be allowed access to ports and maritime areas proclaimed to be naval ports or to form part of the protection zones of coast defence works.

(2) Belligerent warships shall, further, not be allowed access to inner waters, the entrance to which is closed by submarine mines or other means of defence.

For the purposes of the present Decree, 'Finnish inner waters' shall be deemed to include ports, entrances to ports, gulfs and bays, and the waters between those Finnish islands, islets and reefs which are not constantly submerged, and between the said islands, islets and reefs and the mainland.

(3) Belligerent submarines ready for service shall be prohibited from navigating or remaining in Finnish territorial waters.

The foregoing prohibition shall not apply, however, to submarines forced to enter prohibited waters by stress of weather or by damage, provided always that they indicate by means of an international signal their reason for entering these waters. Such submarines shall be required to leave the prohibited waters as soon as the circumstances which are the cause of their presence there have ceased. While in Finnish territorial waters, submarines shall continuously fly their national flag and, save in the case of extreme necessity, shall navigate on the surface.

(4) The President of the Republic may, in special circumstances, for the purpose of safeguarding the sovereign rights and maintaining the neutrality of the Republic, while at the same time observing the general principles of international law, prohibit access to Finnish ports and other stated zones of Finnish territorial waters other than those to which access is prohibited by the foregoing provisions.

(5) The President of the Republic may likewise prohibit the access to Finnish ports and anchorages of any belligerent warships which may have failed to comply with the rules and regulations laid down by the competent Finnish authorities, or have violated the neutrality of the Republic.

Art. 3.(1) Privateers shall not be permitted to enter Finnish ports or to remain in Finnish territorial waters.

(2) The armed merchant vessels of belligerents shall, if their armaments are intended for purposes other than their own defence, likewise be forbidden access to Finnish ports or to remain in Finnish territorial waters.

Art. 4.(1) Belligerent warships shall not be permitted to remain in Finnish ports and anchorages or in other Finnish territorial waters for more than twenty-four hours, save in the event of their having suffered damage or run aground, or under stress of weather, or in the cases enumerated in paragraphs 3 and 4 below. In such cases, they shall leave as soon as the cause of the delay has ceased. In the case of vessels having suffered damage or run aground, the competent Finnish authority shall fix such time-limit as may be deemed sufficient to repair the damage or refloat the vessel. No vessel shall, however, be permitted to prolong its stay for more than twenty-four hours if it is clear that the said vessel cannot be rendered seaworthy within a reasonable time, or if the damage was caused by an enemy act of war.

The above restrictions on the stay of vessels shall not apply to warships used exclusively for religious, scientific or humanitarian purposes, or to naval and military hospital ships.

(2) Not more than three warships of a belligerent Power or of several allied belligerent Powers shall be permitted to remain in a Finnish port or anchorage at the same time or, the coast having been divided into

districts for the purpose, in ports or anchorages of the same coastal district of Finland.

(3) In the event of warships belonging to both belligerents being simultaneously present in a Finnish port or anchorage, a period of not less than twenty-four hours shall elapse between the departure of a ship belonging to one belligerent and the departure of a ship belonging to the other. The order of departure shall be determined by the order of arrival, unless the ship which arrived first is so circumstanced that an extension of its stay is permitted.

(4) No belligerent warship shall leave a Finnish port or anchorage in which there is a merchant vessel flying an enemy flag within less than twenty-four hours after the departure of such merchant vessel. The competent authorities shall make such arrangements for the departure of merchant vessels that the stay of warships is not unnecessarily prolonged.

Art. 5.(1) In Finnish ports and anchorages belligerent warships shall only be permitted to effect such repairs as may be essential to seaworthiness, and they shall not increase their warlike strength in any manner whatsoever. In repairing damage manifestly caused by enemy acts of war, damaged vessels shall not be permitted to avail themselves of any assistance which they may have procured in Finnish territory. The competent Finnish authorities shall determine the nature of the repairs to be carried out. Such repairs shall be effected as rapidly as possible within the time-limit laid down in art. 4, paragraph 1.

(2) Belligerent warships shall not make use of Finnish ports or other Finnish territorial waters to replace or augment their warlike stores or armament, or to complete their crews.

(3) Belligerent warships shall only be permitted to revictual in Finnish ports or anchorages to the extent necessary to bring their supplies up to the normal peace standard.

(4) As regards refuelling, belligerent warships shall be subject, in Finnish ports and anchorages, to the same provisions as other foreign vessels. They shall, nevertheless, only be permitted to ship sufficient fuel to enable them to reach the nearest port in their own country and in no case shall they ship more than is necessary to fill their coal bunkers, strictly so called, or their liquid fuel bunkers. After obtaining fuel in any Finnish port or anchorage, they shall not be permitted to obtain further supplies in Finnish ports and anchorages within a period of three months.

Art. 6. Belligerent warships shall be required to employ the officially licensed pilots in the Finnish inner waters in accordance with the rules applied, or to be applied, to warships in time of peace, but otherwise they shall only be permitted to make use of the services of such pilots when in distress, in order to escape perils of the sea.

Art. 7.(1) Prizes of foreign nationality shall not be brought into a Finnish port or anchorage save on account of unseaworthiness, under stress of weather, or for lack of fuel or provisions. Prizes brought into a Finnish port or anchorage in any of the above circumstances shall leave as soon as such circumstances are at an end.

(2) No prize court shall be set up by a belligerent in Finnish territory or on any vessel in Finnish territorial waters. The sale of prizes in a Finnish port or anchorage shall likewise be prohibited.

Art. 8.(1) Belligerent military aircraft, with the exception of air ambulances and aircraft carried on board warships, shall not be admitted to Finnish territory save in so far as may be otherwise provided in regulations applied, or to be applied, in accordance with the general principles of international law in regard to certain spaces.

(2) Aircraft carried on board belligerent warships shall not leave such vessels while in Finnish territorial waters.

Art. 9.(1) Belligerent warships and military aircraft shall be required to respect the sovereign rights of the Republic and to refrain from all acts infringing its neutrality.

(2) Within the limits of Finnish territory, all acts of war, including the stopping, visit and search and capture of vessels and aircraft, whether neutral or of enemy nationality, shall be prohibited. Any vessel or aircraft captured within such limit shall be released immediately, together with its officers, crew and cargo.

Art. 10. The sanitary, pilot, Customs, navigation, air traffic, harbour and police regulations shall be strictly observed.

Art. 11. Belligerents shall not use Finnish territory as a base for warlike operations against the enemy.

Art. 12.(1) Belligerents and persons in their service shall not install or operate in Finnish territory wireless-telegraph stations or any other apparatus to be used for the purpose of communication with belligerent military, naval or air forces.

(2) Belligerents shall not use their mobile wireless-telegraph stations, whether belonging to their combatant forces or not, in Finnish territory, for the transmission of messages, save when in distress or for the purpose of communicating with the Finnish authorities through a Finnish inland or coastal wireless-telegraph station on board a vessel belonging to the Finnish navy.

Art. 13. The observations, by any person whatsoever, either from aircraft or in any other manner in Finnish territory, of the movements, operations or defence works of one belligerent with a view to the information of the other belligerent shall be prohibited.

Art. 14.(1) Belligerents shall not establish fuel depots within the territory of the Republic, whether on land or on vessels stationed in its territorial waters.

(2) Vessels and aircraft cruising with the manifest purpose of furnishing fuel or other supplies to the combatant forces of the belligerents shall not ship such fuel or other supplies in Finnish ports or anchorages in quantities exceeding their own requirements.

Art. 15.(1) No vessel shall be fitted or armed in Finnish territory for cruising or taking part in hostile operations against either of the belligerents. Nor shall any vessel intended for such uses, which has been partly or wholly adapted in Finnish territory for warlike purposes, be permitted to leave such territory.

(2) Aircraft equipped to carry out an attack on a belligerent or carrying apparatus or material the mounting or use of which would enable it to carry out such an attack shall not be permitted to leave Finnish territory if there are grounds for presuming that it is intended for use against a belligerent Power. Any work on aircraft to prepare it for departure for the above-mentioned purpose shall likewise be prohibited.

ANNEX II Iceland. Rules of Neutrality.

Concerning the neutrality of Iceland in the event of war between foreign Powers, the following provisions shall apply as from the date and to the extent to be fixed by the King:

Art. 1. Belligerent warships shall be granted admission to the ports and other territorial waters of the Kingdom subject to the following exceptions, restrictions and conditions.

Art. 2.(1) Belligerent submarines ready for service shall be prohibited from navigating or remaining in Icelandic territorial waters.

The foregoing prohibition shall not apply, however, to submarines forced to enter prohibited waters, by stress of weather or by damage, provided always that they indicate by means of an international signal their reason for entering such waters. Such submarines shall be required to leave the prohibited waters as soon as the circumstances which are the cause of their presence there have ceased. While in Icelandic territorial waters, submarines shall navigate on the surface and shall continuously fly their national flag.

(2) The King may, in special circumstances, for the purpose of safeguarding the sovereign rights and maintaining the neutrality of the Kingdom, while at the same time observing the general principles of international law, prohibit access to Icelandic ports and other stated zones of Icelandic territorial waters.

(3) The King may likewise prohibit the access to Icelandic ports and anchorages of any belligerent warships which may have failed to comply with the rules and regulations laid down by the competent Icelandic authorities, or have violated the neutrality of the Kingdom.

Art. 3.(1) Privateers shall not be permitted to enter Icelandic ports or to remain in Icelandic territorial waters.

(2) The armed merchant vessels of belligerents shall, if their armaments are intended for purposes other than their own defence, likewise be forbidden access to Icelandic ports or to remain in Icelandic territorial waters.

Art. 4.(1) Belligerent warships shall not be permitted to remain in Icelandic ports and anchorages or in other Icelandic territorial waters for more than twenty-four hours, save in the event of their having suffered damage or run aground, or under stress of weather, or in the cases enumerated in paragraphs 3 and 4 below. In such cases, they shall leave as soon as the cause of the delay has ceased. In the case of vessels having suffered damage or run aground, the competent Icelandic authority shall fix such time-limit as may be deemed sufficient to repair the damage or refloat the vessel. No vessel shall, however, be permitted to prolong its stay for more than twenty-four hours if it is clear that the said vessel cannot be rendered seaworthy within a reasonable time, or if the damage was caused by an enemy act of war.

The above restrictions on the stay of vessels shall not apply to warships used exclusively for religious, scientific or humanitarian purposes, or to naval and military hospital ships.

(2) Not more than three warships of a belligerent Power or of several allied belligerent Powers shall be permitted to remain in an Icelandic port or anchorage at the same time or, the coast having been divided into districts for the purpose, in ports or anchorages of the same coastal district of Iceland.

(3) In the event of warships belonging to both belligerents being simultaneously present in an Icelandic port or anchorage, a period of not less than twenty-four hours shall elapse between the departure of a ship belonging to one belligerent and the departure of a ship belonging to the other. The order of departure shall be determined by the order of arrival, unless the ship which arrived first is so circumstanced that an extension of its stay is permitted.

(4) No belligerent warship shall leave an Icelandic port or anchorage in which there is a merchant vessel flying an enemy flag within less than twenty-four hours after the departure of such merchant vessel. The competent authorities shall make such arrangement for the departure of merchant vessels that the stay of warships is not unnecessarily prolonged.

Art. 5.(1) In Icelandic ports and anchorages belligerent warships shall only be permitted to effect such repairs as may be essential to seaworthiness, and they shall not increase their warlike strength in any manner whatsoever. In repairing damage manifestly caused by enemy acts of war, damaged vessels shall not be permitted to make use of any materials or labour which they may have procured in Icelandic territory. The competent Icelandic authorities shall determine the nature of the repairs to be carried out. Such repairs shall be effected as rapidly as possible within the time-limit laid down in art. 4, paragraph 1.

(2) Belligerent warships shall not make use of Icelandic ports or other Icelandic territorial waters to replace or augment their warlike stores or armament, or to complete their crews.

(3) Belligerent warships shall only be permitted to revictual in Icelandic ports or anchorages to the extent necessary to bring their supplies up to the normal peace standard.

(4) As regards refuelling, belligerent warships shall be subject, in Icelandic ports and anchorages, to the same provisions as other foreign vessels. They shall, nevertheless, only be permitted to ship sufficient fuel to enable them to reach the nearest port in their own country and in no case shall they ship more than is necessary to fill their coal bunkers, strictly so called, or their liquid fuel bunkers. After obtaining fuel in any Icelandic port or anchorage, they shall not be permitted to obtain further supplies in Icelandic ports and anchorages within a period of three months.

Art. 6. Belligerent warships shall be required to employ the officially licensed pilots in Icelandic territorial waters whenever the assistance of a pilot is compulsory, but otherwise they shall only be permitted to make use of the services of such pilots when in distress, in order to escape perils of the sea.

Art. 7.(1) Prizes of foreign nationality shall not be brought into an Icelandic port or anchorage save on account of unseaworthiness, under stress of weather, or for lack of fuel or provisions. Prizes brought into an Icelandic port or anchorage in any of the above circumstances shall leave as soon as such circumstances are at an end.

(2) No prize court shall be set up by a belligerent in Icelandic territory or on any vessel in Icelandic territorial waters. The sale of prizes in an Icelandic port or anchorage shall likewise be prohibited.

Art. 8.(1) Belligerent military aircraft, with the exception of air ambulances and aircraft carried on board warships, shall not be admitted to Icelandic territory save in so far as may be otherwise provided in regulations applied, or to be applied, in accordance with the general principles of international law in regard to certain spaces.

(2) Aircraft carried on board belligerent warships shall not leave such vessels while in Icelandic territorial waters.

Art. 9.(1) Belligerent warships and military aircraft shall be required to respect the sovereign rights of the Kingdom and to refrain from all acts infringing its neutrality.

(2) Within the limits of Icelandic territory all acts of war, including the stopping, visit and search and capture of vessels and aircraft, whether neutral or of enemy nationality, shall be prohibited. Any vessel or aircraft captured within such limit shall be released immediately, together with its officers, crew and cargo.

Art. 10. The sanitary, pilot, Customs, navigation, air traffic, harbour and police regulations shall be strictly observed.

Art. 11. Belligerents shall not use Icelandic territory as a base for warlike operations against the enemy.

Art. 12.(1) Belligerents and persons in their service shall not install or operate in Icelandic territory wireless-telegraph stations or any other apparatus to be used for the purpose of communication with belligerent military, naval or air forces.

(2) Belligerents shall not use their mobile wireless-telegraph stations, whether belonging to their combatant forces or not, in Icelandic territory for the transmission of messages, save when in distress or for the purpose of communicating with the Icelandic authorities through an Icelandic wireless-telegraph station on land or on board a vessel used by the Icelandic police.

Art. 13. The observation, by any person whatsoever, either from aircraft or in any other manner in Icelandic territory, of the movements, operations or defence works of one belligerent with a view to the information of the other belligerent shall be prohibited.

Art. 14.(1) Belligerents shall not establish fuel depots within the territory of the Kingdom, whether on land or on vessels stationed in its territorial waters.

(2) Vessels and aircraft cruising with the manifest purpose of furnishing fuel or other supplies to the combatant forces of the belligerents shall not ship such fuel or other supplies in Icelandic ports or anchorages in quantities exceeding their own requirements.

Art. 15.(1) No vessel shall be fitted or armed in Icelandic territory for cruising or taking part in hostile operations against either of the belligerents. Nor shall any vessel intended for such uses, which has been partly or wholly adapted in Icelandic territory for warlike purposes, be permitted to leave such territory.

(2) Aircraft equipped to carry out an attack on a belligerent, or carrying apparatus or material the mounting or use of which would enable it to carry out such an attack, shall not be permitted to leave Icelandic territory if there are grounds for presuming that it is intended for use against a belligerent Power. Any work on aircraft to prepare it for departure for the above-mentioned purpose shall likewise be prohibited.

ANNEX III Norway. Rules of Neutrality.

Concerning the neutrality of Norway in the event of war between foreign Powers, the following provisions shall apply as from the date and to the extent to be fixed by the King:

Art. 1. Belligerent warships shall be granted admission to the ports and other territorial waters of the Kingdom subject to the following exceptions, restrictions and conditions.

Art. 2.(1) Belligerent warships shall not be allowed access to ports and maritime areas proclaimed to be naval ports or to form part of the protection zones of coast defence works.

(2) Belligerent warships shall, further, not be allowed access to inner waters the entrance to which is closed by submarine mines or other means of defence.

For the purpose of the present Decree, 'Norwegian inner waters' shall be deemed to include ports, the approaches to ports, gulfs and bays, and the waters between those Norwegian islands, islets and reefs which are not constantly submerged, and between the said islands, islets and reefs and the mainland.

(3) Belligerent submarines ready for service shall be prohibited from navigating or remaining in Norwegian territorial waters.

The foregoing prohibition shall not apply, however, to submarines forced to enter prohibited waters by stress of weather or by damage, provided always that they indicate by means of an international signal their reason for entering such waters. Such submarines shall be required to leave the prohibited waters as soon as the circumstances which are the cause of their presence there have ceased. While in Norwegian territorial waters, submarines shall continuously fly their national flag and, save in the case of extreme necessity, shall navigate on the surface.

(4) The King may, in special circumstances, for the purpose of safeguarding the sovereign rights and maintaining the neutrality of the Kingdom while at the same time observing the general principles of international law, prohibit access to Norwegian ports and other stated zones of Norwegian territorial waters other than those to which access is prohibited by the foregoing provisions.

(5) The King may likewise prohibit the access to Norwegian ports and anchorages of any belligerent warships which may have failed to comply with the rules and regulations laid down by the competent Norwegian authorities or have violated the neutrality of the Kingdom.

Art. 3.(1) Privateers shall not be permitted to enter Norwegian ports or Norwegian territorial waters.

(2) The armed merchant vessels of belligerents shall, if their armaments are intended for purposes other than their own defence, likewise be forbidden access to Norwegian ports or Norwegian territorial waters.

Art. 4.(1) Belligerent warships shall not be permitted to remain in Norwegian ports and anchorages, or in other Norwegian territorial waters, for more than twenty-four hours, save in the event of their having suffered damage or run aground, or under stress of weather, or in the cases enumerated in paragraphs 3 and 4 below. In such cases, they shall leave as soon as the cause of the delay has ceased. In the case of vessels having suffered damage or run aground, the competent Norwegian authority shall fix such time-limit as may be deemed sufficient to repair the damage or refloat the vessel. No vessel shall, however, be permitted to prolong its stay for more than twenty-four hours if it is clear that the said vessel cannot be rendered seaworthy within a reasonable time or if the damage was caused by an enemy act of war. The above restrictions on the stay of vessels shall not apply to warships used exclusively for religious, scientific or humanitarian purposes, or to naval and military hospital ships.

(2) Not more than three warships of a belligerent Power or of several allied belligerent Powers shall be permitted to remain in a Norwegian port or anchorage at the same time or, the coast having been divided into districts for the purpose, in ports or anchorages of the same coastal district of Norway.

(3) In the event of warships belonging to both belligerents being simultaneously present in a Norwegian port or anchorage, a period of not less than twenty-four hours shall elapse between the departure of a ship belonging to the one belligerent and the departure of a ship belonging to the other. The order of departure shall be determined by the order of arrival, unless the ship which arrived first is so circumstanced that an extension of its stay is permitted.

(4) No belligerent warship shall leave a Norwegian port or anchorage in which there is a merchant vessel flying an enemy flag within less than twenty-four hours after the departure of such merchant vessel. The competent authorities shall make such arrangements for the departure of merchant vessels that the stay of warships shall not be unnecessarily prolonged.

Art. 5.(1) In Norwegian ports and anchorages, belligerent warships shall only be permitted to effect such repairs as may be essential to seaworthiness, and they shall not increase their warlike strength in any manner whatsoever. In repairing damage manifestly caused by enemy acts of war, damaged vessels shall not be permitted to avail themselves of any assistance which they may have procured in Norwegian territory. The competent Norwegian authorities shall determine the nature of the repairs to be carried out. Such repairs shall be effected as rapidly as possible within the time-limit laid down in art. 4, paragraph 1.

(2) Belligerent warships shall not make use of Norwegian ports or other Norwegian territorial waters to replace or augment their warlike stores or armament, or to complete their crews.

(3) Belligerent warships shall only be permitted to revictual in Norwegian ports or anchorages to the extent necessary to bring their supplies up to the normal peace standard.

(4) As regards refuelling, belligerent warships shall be subject, in Norwegian ports and anchorages, to the same provisions as other foreign vessels. They shall, nevertheless, only be permitted to ship sufficient fuel to enable them to reach the nearest port in their own country and in no case shall they ship more than is necessary to fill their coal bunkers, strictly so called, or their liquid fuel bunkers. After obtaining fuel in any Norwegian port or anchorage, they shall not be permitted to obtain further supplies in Norwegian ports and anchorages within a period of three months.

Art. 6. Belligerent warships shall be required to employ the officially licensed pilots in Norwegian territorial waters whenever the assistance of a pilot is compulsory, but otherwise they shall only be permitted to make use of the services of such pilot when in distress, in order to escape perils of the sea.

Art. 7.(1) Prizes of foreign nationality shall not be brought into a Norwegian port or anchorage save on account of unseaworthiness, under stress of weather, or for lack of fuel or provisions. Prizes brought into a Norwegian port or anchorage in any of the above circumstances shall leave as soon as such circumstances are at an end.

(2) No prize court shall be set up by a belligerent in Norwegian territory or on any vessel in Norwegian territorial waters. The sale of prizes in a Norwegian port or anchorage shall likewise be prohibited.

Art. 8.(1) Belligerent military aircraft, with the exception of air ambulances and aircraft carried on board warships, shall not be admitted to Norwegian territory save in so far as may be otherwise provided in regulations applied, or to be applied, in accordance with the general principles of international law in regard to certain spaces.

(2) Aircraft carried on board belligerent warships shall not leave such vessels while in Norwegian territorial waters.

Art. 9.(1) Belligerent warships and military aircraft shall be required to respect the sovereign rights of the Kingdom and to refrain from all acts infringing its neutrality.

(2) Within the limits of Norwegian territory all acts of war, including the stopping, visit and search and capture of vessels and aircraft, whether neutral or of enemy nationality, shall be prohibited. Any vessel or aircraft captured within such limit shall be released immediately, together with its officers, crew and cargo.

Art. 10. The sanitary, pilot, Customs, navigation, air traffic, harbour and police regulations shall be strictly observed.

Art. 11. Belligerents shall not use Norwegian territory as a base for warlike operations against the enemy.

Art. 12.(1) Belligerents and persons in their service shall not install or operate in Norwegian territory wireless-telegraph stations or any other apparatus to be used for the purpose of communication with belligerent military, naval or air forces.

(2) Belligerents shall not use their mobile wireless-telegraph stations, whether belonging to their combatant forces or not, in Norwegian territory for the transmission of messages, save when in distress or for the purpose of communicating with the Norwegian authorities through a Norwegian inland or coastal wireless-telegraph station or a wireless-telegraph station on board a vessel belonging to the Norwegian navy.

Art. 13. The observation, by any person whatsoever, either from aircraft or in any other manner in Norwegian territory, of the movements, operations or defence works of one belligerent with a view to the information of the other belligerent shall be prohibited.

Art. 14.(1) Belligerents shall not establish fuel depots within the territory of the Kingdom, whether upon land or on vessels stationed in its territorial waters.

(2) Vessels and aircraft cruising with the manifest purpose of furnishing fuel or other supplies to the combatant forces of the belligerents shall not ship such fuel or other supplies in Norwegian ports or anchorages in quantities exceeding their own requirements.

Art. 15.(1) No vessel shall be fitted or armed in Norwegian territory for cruising or taking part in hostile operations against either of the belligerents. Nor shall any vessel intended for such uses, which has been partly or wholly adapted in Norwegian territory for warlike purposes, be permitted to leave such territory.

(2) Aircraft equipped to carry out an attack on a belligerent, or carrying apparatus or material the mounting or use of which would enable it to carry out such an attack, shall not be permitted to leave Norwegian territory if there are grounds for presuming that it is intended for use against a belligerent Power. Any work on aircraft to prepare it for departure for the above-mentioned purpose shall likewise be prohibited.

ANNEX IV Sweden. Rules of Neutrality.

Concerning the neutrality of Sweden in the event of war between foreign Powers, the following provisions shall apply as from the date and to the extent to be fixed by the King:

Art. 1. Belligerent warships shall be granted admission to the ports and other territorial waters of the Kingdom subject to the following exceptions, restrictions and conditions.

Art. 2.(1) Belligerent warships shall not be allowed access to ports and maritime areas proclaimed to be naval ports or to form part of the protection zones of coast defence works.

(2) Belligerent warships shall, further, not be allowed access to inner waters the entrance to which is closed by submarine mines or other means of defence.

For the purpose of the present Decree, 'Swedish inner waters' shall be deemed to include ports, the approaches to ports, gulfs and bays, and the waters between those Swedish islands, islets and reefs which are not constantly submerged, and between the said islands, islets and reefs and the mainland; nevertheless, in the Sound to the north of the parallel of latitude drawn through the Klagshamn lighthouse, only the ports and approaches to ports shall be regarded as inner waters.

(3) Belligerent submarines ready for service shall be prohibited from navigating or remaining in Swedish territorial waters.

The foregoing prohibition shall not apply, however, to passage without unnecessary stops through the zone of the Swedish outer waters in the Sound bounded to the North by a line drawn from Kullen to Gilbjerghoved, and to the South by a line drawn from Falsterbo Point to Stevn lighthouse, or to submarines forced to enter prohibited waters by stress of weather or by damage, provided always that they indicate by means of an international signal their reason for entering such waters. Such submarines shall be required to leave the prohibited waters as soon as the circumstances which are the cause of their presence there have ceased. While in Swedish territorial waters, submarines shall continuously fly their national flag and, save in the case of imperative necessity, shall navigate on the surface.

(4) The King may, in special circumstances, for the purpose of safeguarding the sovereign rights and maintaining the neutrality of the Kingdom while at the same time observing the general principles of international law, prohibit access to Swedish ports and other stated zones of Swedish territorial waters other than those to which access is prohibited by the foregoing provisions.

(5) The King may likewise prohibit the access to Swedish ports and anchorages of any belligerent warships which may have failed to comply with the rules and regulations laid down by the competent Swedish authorities or have violated the neutrality of the Kingdom.

Art. 3.(1) Privateers shall not be permitted to enter Swedish ports or to remain in Swedish territorial waters.

(2) The armed merchant vessels of belligerents shall, if their armaments are intended for purposes other than their own defence, likewise be forbidden access to Swedish ports or to remain in Swedish territorial waters.

Art. 4.(1) Belligerent warships shall not be permitted to remain in Swedish ports and anchorages or in other Swedish territorial waters for more than twenty-four hours, save in the event of their having suffered damage or run aground, or under stress of weather, or in the cases enumerated in paragraphs 3 and 4 below. In such cases, they shall leave as soon as the cause of the delay has ceased. In the case of vessels having suffered damage or run aground, the competent Swedish authority shall fix such time-limit as may be deemed sufficient to repair the damage or refloat the vessel. No vessel shall, however, be permitted to prolong its stay for more than twenty-four hours if it is clear that the said vessel cannot be rendered seaworthy within a reasonable time, or if the damage was caused by an enemy act of war.

The above restrictions on the stay of vehicles shall not apply to warships used exclusively for religious, scientific or humanitarian purposes, or to naval and military hospital ships.

(2) Not more than three warships of a belligerent Power or of several allied belligerent Powers shall be permitted to remain in a Swedish port or anchorage at the same time or, the coast having been divided into districts for the purpose, in the ports or anchorages of the same coastal district of Sweden.

(3) In the event of warships belonging to both belligerents being simultaneously present in a Swedish port or anchorage, a period of not less than twenty-four hours shall elapse between the departure of a ship belonging to one belligerent and the departure of a ship belonging to the other. The order of departure shall be determined by the order of arrival, unless the ship which arrived first is so circumstanced that an extension of its stay is permitted.

(4) No belligerent warship shall leave a Swedish port or anchorage in which there is a merchant vessel flying an enemy flag within less than twenty-four hours after the departure of such merchant vessel. The competent authorities shall make such arrangements for the departure of merchant vessels that the stay of warships is not unnecessarily prolonged.

Art. 5.(1) In Swedish ports and anchorages, belligerent warships shall only be permitted to effect such repairs as may be essential to seaworthiness, and they shall not increase their warlike strength in any manner whatsoever. In repairing damage manifestly caused by enemy acts of war, damaged vessels shall not be permitted to avail themselves of any assistance they may have procured in Swedish territory. The competent Swedish authorities shall determine the nature of the repairs to be carried out. Such repairs shall be effected as rapidly as possible within the time-limit laid down in art. 4, paragraph 1.

(2) Belligerent warships shall not make use of Swedish ports or other Swedish territorial waters to replace or augment their warlike stores or armament or to complete their crews.

(3) Belligerent warships shall only be permitted to revictual in Swedish ports or anchorages to the extent necessary to bring their supplies up to the normal peace standard.

(4) As regards refuelling, belligerent warships shall be subject, in Swedish ports and anchorages, to the same provisions as other foreign vessels. They shall, nevertheless, only be permitted to ship sufficient fuel to enable them to reach the nearest port in their own country and in no case shall they ship more than is necessary to fill their coal bunkers, strictly so called, or their liquid fuel bunkers. After obtaining fuel in any Swedish port or anchorage, they shall not be permitted to obtain further supplies in Swedish ports and anchorages within a period of three months.

Art. 6. Belligerent warships shall be required to employ the officially licensed pilots in the Swedish inner waters in accordance with the rules applied, or to be applied, to warships in time of peace, but otherwise they shall only be permitted to make use of the services of such pilots when in distress, in order to escape perils of the sea.

Art. 7.(1) Prizes of foreign nationality shall not be brought into a Swedish port or anchorage save on account of unseaworthiness, under stress of weather or for lack of fuel or provisions. Prizes brought into a Swedish port or anchorage in any of the above circumstances shall leave as soon as such circumstances are at an end.

(2) No prize court shall be set up by a belligerent in Swedish territory or on any vessel in Swedish territorial waters. The sale of prizes in a Swedish port or anchorage shall likewise be prohibited.

Art. 8.(1) Belligerent military aircraft, with the exception of air ambulances and aircraft carried on board warships, shall not be admitted to Swedish territory save in so far as may be otherwise provided in regulations applied, or to be applied, in accordance with the general principles of international law in regard to certain spaces.

In the Sound, such aircraft shall be permitted to cross, without unnecessary stops, the outer territorial waters of Sweden, bounded as stated in art. 2, paragraph 3, and

the air space above. While so crossing, they shall be required to keep as far as possible from the coast.

(2) Aircraft carried on board belligerent warships shall not leave such vessels while in Swedish territorial waters.

Art. 9.(1) Belligerent warships and military aircraft shall be required to respect the sovereign rights of the Kingdom and to refrain from all acts infringing its neutrality.

(2) Within the limits of Swedish territory all acts of war, including the stopping, visit and search and capture of vessels and aircraft, whether neutral or of enemy nationality, shall be prohibited. Any vessel or aircraft captured within such limit shall be released immediately, together with its officers, crew and cargo.

Art. 10. The sanitary pilot, Customs, navigation, air traffic, harbour and police regulations shall be strictly observed.

Art. 11. Belligerents shall not use Swedish territory as a base for warlike operations against the enemy.

Art. 12.(1) Belligerents and persons in their service shall not install or operate in Swedish territory wireless-telegraph stations or any other apparatus to be used for the purpose of communication with belligerent military, naval or air forces.

(2) Belligerents shall not use their mobile wireless-telegraph stations, whether belonging to their combatant forces or not, in Swedish territory for the transmission of messages, save when in distress or for the purpose of communicating with the Swedish authorities through a Swedish inland or coastal wireless-telegraph station or a wireless-telegraph station on board a vessel used by the Swedish navy.

Art. 13. The observation, by any person whatsoever, either from aircraft or in any other manner in Swedish territory, of the movements, operations or defence works of one belligerent with a view to the information of the other belligerent shall be prohibited.

Art. 14.(1) Belligerents shall not establish fuel depots within the territory of the Kingdom, whether upon land or on vessels stationed in its territorial waters.

(2) Vessels and aircraft cruising with the manifest purpose of furnishing fuel or other supplies to the combatant forces of the belligerents shall not ship such fuel or other supplies in Swedish ports or anchorages in quantities exceeding their own requirements.

Art. 15.(1) No vessel shall be fitted or armed in Swedish territory for cruising or taking part in hostile operations against either of the belligerents. Nor shall any vessel intended for such uses, which has been partly or wholly adapted in Swedish territory for warlike purposes, be permitted to leave such territory.

(2) Aircraft equipped to carry out an attack on a belligerent, or carrying apparatus or material the mounting or use of which would enable it to carry out such an attack, shall not be permitted to leave Swedish territory if there are grounds for presuming that it is intended for use against a belligerent Power. Any work on aircraft to prepare it for departure for the above-mentioned purpose shall likewise be prohibited.

LNTS, Vol. 188, 1938, p. 295.

SCANDINAVIAN OCEAN WEATHER STATION AGREEMENT, 1949. An agreement between Norway, Sweden and UK, relating to a joint ocean weather station in the North Atlantic, signed on Feb. 28, 1949 in Oslo.

UNTS, Vol. 29, pp. 54–81.

SCANDINAVIAN OLD-AGE CONVENTION, 1949. An agreement between Denmark, Finland, Iceland, Norway and Sweden regarding mutual payment of old-age pensions, signed on Aug. 27, 1949 in Oslo.

UNTS, Vol. 47, pp. 127–157.

SCANDINAVIAN PASSPORT AGREEMENT, 1954. A Protocol concerning the exemption of nationals of Denmark, Finland, Norway and Sweden from the obligation of having a passport or residence permit while resident in a Scandinavian country other than their own, signed on May 22, 1954 in Copenhagen.

UNTS, Vol. 199, p. 29.

SCANDINAVIAN POSTAL AGREEMENTS AND CONVENTIONS, 1919–37. The postal instruments in chronological order:

Scandinavian Postal Convention between Denmark, Norway and Sweden regarding postal communication, adopted Dec. 15, 1919, modified Jan. 18, 1920.
Scandinavian Postal Agreement, signed on July 26, 1924 at Christiania, Copenhagen and Stockholm by Denmark, Norway and Sweden.
Scandinavian Postal Agreement between Denmark, Norway and Sweden, regarding Postal Exchanges and Detailed Regulations annexed thereto, signed on May 14, 1930 in Stockholm.
Scandinavian Postal Exchanges Agreement signed on Dec. 31, 1934 in Copenhagen, Helsinki, Reykjavik, Oslo and Stockholm by Denmark, Finland, Iceland, Norway and Sweden.
Scandinavian Postal Vouchers Convention regarding Booklets of Travellers' Postal Vouchers in the Relations between Denmark, Finland, Iceland, Norway and Sweden, with Final Protocol and Detailed Regulations, signed on Sept. 23, 1937 in Stockholm.

LNTS, Vol. 12, p. 321; Vol. 30, p. 303; Vol. 105, p. 353; Vol. 158, p. 111; Vol. 190, p. 299.

SCANDINAVIAN ROAD TRANSPORT AGREEMENTS, 1955 AND 1958. Agreement between Denmark, Norway and Sweden concerning Road Transport, signed in Oslo, Mar. 2, 1955; and Agreement between Denmark, Finland, Norway and Sweden, concerning the carriage of persons and goods by road, signed in Oslo, Nov. 5, 1958.

UNTS, Vol. 211, p. 26; Vol. 428, p. 73.

SCANDINAVIAN SANITARY CONTROL AGREEMENT, 1955. An Agreement between Denmark, Norway and Sweden to facilitate the sanitary control of traffic between those countries, signed on Mar. 19, 1955 in Stockholm.

UNTS, Vol. 228, p. 95.

SCANDINAVIAN SHIPS CONVENTION, 1926. A Convention concerning the Seaworthiness and Equipment of Ships, signed on Jan. 28, 1926 in Copenhagen by Denmark and Iceland, Finland, Norway and Sweden.

LNTS, Vol. 51, p. 9.

SCANDINAVIAN SICK FUNDS AGREEMENT, 1956. An Agreement between Denmark, Iceland, Norway and Sweden concerning transfers between sick funds and sickness benefits during temporary residence, signed on Dec. 19, 1956 in Copenhagen.

UNTS, Vol. 427, p. 114.

SCANDINAVIAN SOCIAL SECURITY CONVENTION, 1955. A Convention respecting Social Security, with Final Protocol, signed on Sept. 15, 1955 in Copenhagen.

UNTS, Vol. 254, p. 55.

SCANDINAVIAN–TANGANYIKAN AGREEMENT, 1963. An Agreement between Tanganyika and the Scandinavian States (Denmark, Finland, Norway and Sweden) on technical co-operation, signed on Jan. 15, 1963 in Helsinki.

UNTS, Vol. 456, p. 409.

SCANDINAVIAN TELEPHONIC AND TELEGRAPHIC AGREEMENTS, 1920–37. The postal instruments in chronological order:

Agreement regarding telephonic and telegraphic correspondence between Denmark and Norway via Sweden, signed on Dec. 16, 1920 in Stockholm, on Dec. 23, 1920 in Copenhagen and on Dec. 29, 1920 in Christiania, together with an additional regulation, signed on

S

Mar. 29, 1922 in Stockholm, on June 20, 1922 in Christiania and on Aug. 8, 1922 in Copenhagen.

Agreement regulating the Radio section of Telegrams free of charge between Denmark, Finland, Iceland, Norway and Sweden, signed on Apr. 1, 1931 in Oslo, on Apr. 10, 1931 in Copenhagen, on Apr. 14, 1931 in Helsinki, on Apr. 24 in Stockholm, and on May 6, 1931 in Reykjavik.

Agreement between the Telegraph Administrations of Denmark, Finland, Iceland, Norway and Sweden regarding Telecommunications between those countries, signed on Dec. 15, 19, 21, and 30, 1936, Jan. 13 and Feb. 11, 1937 in Stockholm with 3 Annexes regarding Telephonic Correspondence.

LNTS, Vol. 13, p. 289; Vol. 120, p. 217; Vol. 186, pp. 55, 99, 109 and 135.

SCANDINAVIAN UNEMPLOYMENT INSURANCE AGREEMENT, 1959.
An Agreement between Denmark, Finland, Iceland, Norway and Sweden regarding rules on recognition of contribution periods and periods of employment in the case of persons covered by unemployment insurance who move from one country to another, signed on Sept. 8, 1959 in Fevik.

UNTS, Vol. 383, p. 203.

SCANDINAVIAN WORKING CAPACITY CONVENTION, 1953.
A Convention between Denmark, Finland, Iceland, Norway and Sweden respecting reciprocity in the granting of benefits for reduced working capacity, signed on July 20, 1953 in Reykjavik. Came into force on Sept. 1, 1954.

UNTS, Vol. 228, p. 72.

SCAPA FLOW.
The British main naval base in landlocked anchorage in the Orkney Islands north of Scotland, 24 km long and 12.9 km wide. During World War I the British Fleet was based there and after the surrender of the German Fleet, the High Sea Fleet was interned in Scapa Flow, but the German crews sank the ships on June 21, 1919. During World War II a German submarine on Oct. 14, 1939 entered the Flow from the east and sank the HMS *Royal Oak*; on Mar. 31, 1940 the Luftwaffe bombed HMS *Norfolk*. A Churchill Barrier was built in 1940 at the eastern entrance by sinking 250,000 tons of rock. The naval base was closed in 1956.

R. VON REUTER, *Scapa Flow das Grab der deutschen Flotte*, Berlin, 1923.

SCHILLING.
A monetary unit of Austria; one schilling = 100 groschen; issued by the Oesterreichische National-Bank.

SCHISM.
Greek: "division" or "dissension". An international term – division in Christian religious institutions. The "great schism" or "East–West schism" took place in the year 1054. ▷ Catholic–Orthodox Patmos Dialogue, 1980.

T.A. LACEY, *Unity and Schism*, London, 1918; S.L. GREENSLADE, *Schism in the Early Church*, London, 1964; Y. CONGAR, *Chrétiens en Dialogue*, Genève, 1964; *Osservatore Romano*, December 1, 1979 and June 4, 1980.

SCHISTOSOMIASIS.
An endemic illness in Africa, Asia, the Eastern Mediterranean region and South America, subject of international actions directed by the WHO. The global prevalence was set in 1980 at some 200 million cases in 74 developing countries. According to WHO schistosomiasis has become after malaria, the second most common tropical disease.

Epidemiology and control of schistosomiasis, WHO Geneva, 1980; "Schistosomiasis. From Research to Control", in: *World Health*, December 1983; *WHO Press Release*, November 13, 1984.

SCHIZOPHRENIA.
A mental disease, subject of international studies carried out under WHO auspices in nine countries in the 1970s under so-called International Pilot Study of Schizophrenia Program.

SCHLESINGER NUCLEAR WAR DOCTRINE, 1975.
A nuclear war doctrine, formulated by the US Secretary of Defense James Schlesinger during President G. Ford's administration, known as National Security Decision Memorandum 242, to the effect that US missiles needed to be capable of threatening a wide range of civilian and military targets in the Soviet Union; suspended by the ▷ Presidential Directive 59, 1980. The doctrine was also called Countervailing Strategy, or Parity Doctrine.

R. BUST, "Brown–Brzezinski Tandem Pushed New US Strategy", in: *New York Times*, Aug. 14, 1980.

SCHLESWIG.
A historic region, former duchy, divided between Denmark and the FRG. Annexed by Prussia 1866 together with the Duchy of Holstein. The north part of Schleswig in accordance with arts. 109–114 of the Versailles Treaty, 1919, passed to Denmark by a plebiscite in Mar. 1920. In south Schleswig there remained the Danish minority, whose rights were debated in the League of Nations in 1925 (▷ Minorities, Protection of).

A. TARDIEU, F. DE JESSEN, *Le Schleswig et la Paix*, Paris, 1928; L.T. STEEFEL, *The Schleswig-Holstein Question*, London, 1932; S. WAMBAUCH, *Plebiscites since the World War, With a Collection of Official Documents*, Washington, DC, 1933; F. DE JESSEN, *Manuel historique de la question du Schleswig 1906–1938*, Paris, 1939; "Die Ergebnisse der deutsch-dänischen Besprechungen. Die Rechte der beiderseitigen Minderheiten", in: *Jahrbuch für Internationales Rechts*, 1956, pp. 308–311; E. JACKEL, *Die Schleswig-Frage seit 1945*, Dokumente Band 29, 1959; E. JACKEL, *Die Schleswig Frage Seit 1945, Dokumente zur Rechtsstellung der Minderheiten beiderseits der deutsch-dänischen Grenze*, Frankfurt a.M., 1959.

SCHLESWIG PEACE TREATY, 1864.
A Treaty concluded Oct. 30, 1864, in Vienna, also called the Vienna Peace, by Austria and Prussia with Denmark which, on Aug. 1, 1864, was forced to give up its claims to Schleswig, Holstein and Lauenburg. The treaty entered into force on Nov. 16, 1864. The Schleswig conflict erupted on Mar. 21, 1848, when Denmark formally integrated the Duchy of Schleswig, until then independent in keeping with the law of succession of the Danish royal family, and on Apr. 12, 1848, the Frankfurt Parliament formally integrated Schleswig into the German Union and ordered Prussia to seize it by force. The war started Apr. 20 and ended Aug. 26, 1848; was resumed after a wintertime truce on Apr. 3 to July 10, 1849, when in Malmö another armistice was signed. A number of international conferences were subsequently held on the subject, ending with the adoption of the Second London Protocol on May 8, 1852, which established the right to succession of Schleswig and Holstein by the Danish line. In Nov., 1863 the Third London Protocol was opposed by Prussian chancellor O. von Bismarck who, on January 16, 1864, confronted Denmark with an ultimatum and, following its rejection, commenced military actions which ended with the Schleswig Peace Treaty of 1864.

O. JAGER, F. MOLDENHAUER, *Auswahl wichtiger Aktenstücke zur Geschichte des 19 Jahrhunderts*, Berlin, 1989.

SCHLESWIG TREATY, 1920.
Treaty between the Principal Allied Powers and Denmark with regard to Schleswig, signed on July 5, 1920 in Paris, fixing a new frontier between Denmark and Germany in conformity with the wishes of population (Plebiscite in Schleswig in Mar., 1920 in accordance with art. 109 of the Versailles Treaty 1919).

LNTS, Vol. 2, p. 241.

SCHLIEFFEN PLAN, 1905.
A plan prepared in 1905 by head of the Prussian General Staff, General A. von Schlieffen, who mapped out a war on two fronts with smashing attacks: in the east from Eastern Prussia toward Russia and in the west through Belgium, Luxemburg, and the Netherlands toward France; it was the basis for the German concept of the invasion of France violating neutrality of Belgium in 1914 and 1940.

G. RITTER, *Der Schlieffenplan*, Berlin, 1956; J.E. WALLACH, *Das Dogma der Vernichtungsschlacht*, München, 1967.

SCHMIDT PLAN, 1978.
A plan for West European currency reform, aiming at the creation of a West ▷ European Monetary System (EMS), presented in June 1978 to the President of France and the Prime Minister of Great Britain by the Chancellor of FRG, Helmut Schmidt. The plan in its assumption was based on the fact that the nine EEC states represent 40% of the world's trade, which entitles them to create their own monetary unit independent of the fluctuations of the American dollar.

KEESING's *Contemporary Archive*, 1978.

SCHOLARSHIP, INTERNATIONAL.
The first international scholarships for artists and scholars were in the form of patronage of feudal lords over the development of the sciences and fine arts; modern forms of international scholarship founded by the state, national and international foundations and industrial concerns and financial institutions initiated in the 19th century developed into an important element of international co-operation after World War II, when the establishment of international scholarship by individual countries, special organizations and institutions is constantly encouraged by the UN and its special organizations, especially by UNESCO. Many countries award international scholarship annually both within the framework of bilateral agreements on cultural--scientific–technical exchange as well as within the framework of agreements with UNESCO and other UN specialized organizations.

Informacion sobre la UNESCO, Madrid, 1975, pp. 35–41.

SCHOOL OF PHYSICISTS, INTERNATIONAL.
An institution f. 1968, Zakopane, Poland, on the initiative of the ▷ Nuclear Research Dubna Joint Institute and the Geneva based ▷ CERN as a school for highly advanced scientific specialists in the field of nuclear energy; lecturers are scientists from the East and West. Reg. with the UIA.

Yearbook of International Organizations.

SCHOOLS.
A subject of international co-operation. Organizations reg. with the UIA:

Association mondiale pour l'école instrument de paix, EIP, f. 1967, Geneva; promotes instruction in the service of peace by means of the school. Consultative status with UNESCO. Publ.: *École et paix* (quarterly).

Association of Schools of Public Health in the European Region, f. 1966, Zagreb.

International Association of Schools in Advertising, f. 1965, Brussels.

International Association of Schools of Social Work, f. 1929, New York. Consultative status with ECOSOC, UNICEF, UNESCO. Council of Europe and OAS. Publ.: *International Social Work*.

International Federation of Organizations for School Correspondence and Exchange, f. 1929, Paris. Consul-

tative status with UNESCO and ECOSOC. Publ.: *Bulletin*.
International Liaison Centre for Cinema and TV Schools, f. 1955, Brussels.
International Schools Association, f. 1951, Geneva, Consultative status with ECOSOC and UNESCO. Publ.: *ISA Bulletin*.
United Schools International, f. 1961, New Delhi. Consultative status with UNESCO and FAO.

Yearbook of International Organizations.

SCHOOLS, INTERNATIONALLY-MINDED.

The national schools with programs in foreign languages, subject of international co-operation, since 1951, date of the first conference of Internationally-Minded Schools, IMS, and the foundation of International Schools Association, ISA, in Geneva. Consultative status with ECOSOC and UNESCO. The ISA develops close co-operation among existing internationally-minded schools by means of consultation and co-ordination of curricula. Since 1964 directs the International Baccalaureate Office in Geneva. Publ.: *ISA Bulletin*. Reg. with the UIA.

Yearbook of International Organizations.

SCHOOL TEXTBOOKS.
A subject of international co-operation, conventions and interstate agreements, concerning contents of textbooks. The Convention concerning Peaceful Orientation of Public Instruction approved at the Inter-American Conference for the Maintenance of Peace, signed by 20 Latin American Republics, entered into force on Mar. 16, 1938, included the problem of public education.
The ▷ Chapultepec Conference of American States, 1945, adopted a Resolution on Revision of School Textbooks.
In Oct., 1972 the UNESCO Committees of Poland and the FRG concluded in Brunswick, FRG, an Agreement on Revision of Textbook Contents.
In 1975 the FRG concluded a similar agreement with the USSR.
▷ History, Teaching of.
CARNEGIE ENDOWMENT, *International Conferences of American States. First Supplement, 1933–1940*, Washington, DC, 1940; A. GARCIA ROBLES, *El Mundo de la Postguerra*, México, DF, 1946, Vol. 2, p. 396.

SCHUMAN PLAN, 1950.
A plan proposed May 9, 1950 by the French minister of foreign affairs, Robert Schuman (1886–1963), and named after him; it contained the proposition for combining the entire Franco–German coal and steel production and subordinating it to a common authority – an organization which other European countries could also join. As a result of the Plan, a treaty was signed Apr. 18, 1951 on forming the ▷ European Coal and Steel Community, one of the three Western European integrative economic communities.

P. REUTER, "La conception du pouvoir politique dans le Plan Schuman", in: *Revue Française de Science Politique*, No. 3, 1951.

SCHUTZHAFT.
German = "protective arrest". An international term for a Nazi form of mass terror used in the German III Reich, initially in relation to Germans and national minitories in Germany, during World War II in relation to citizens in the occupied countries. The term was described in a Decree signed Feb. 28, 1933 by the German Reich's President, P. von Hindenburg, concerning the establishment of a system of ▷ Concentration camps; extended by an enactment of the Reich's Interior Minister, Jan. 25, 1938, stating that:

"protective arrest would be the Gestapo's means of compulsion for protecting against hostile acts directed at the nation and state applied to persons, who by their behavior threatened the existence and safety of the nation and State."

Arrest took place without any adjudication, upon the Gestapo's decision, and commitment to a concentration camp was termless.

Law Report of Trials of War Criminals, UN, New York, 1948.

SCHWEITZER HOSPITAL.
The hospital created 1913 by Albert Schweitzer (1875–1965), Alsatian philosopher, theologian, musician, mission doctor and winner of the Nobel Peace Prize in 1952 at Lambarene, Gabon. In 1966 was founded the International Association for the Schweitzer Hospital at Lambarene to continue and improve the work of Albert Schweitzer. Reg. with the UIA.

N. COUSIN, *Dr Schweitzer of Lambarene*, New York, 1960; *Yearbook of International Organizations.*

SCIENCES.
A subject of international research, agreements and co-operation under aegis of UNESCO. Organizations reg. with the UIA:

Commonwealth Science Council, f. 1946, London.
International Centre for Scientific and Technical Information, f. 1969, Moscow. Intergovernmental institution of the CMEA Member States.
International Co-ordinating Committee for the Presentation of Science and the Development of Out-of-School Scientific Activities, f. 1962, Brussels. Consultative status with UNESCO, Publ.: *Information Bulletin, Journal*.
International Council for Science Policy Studies, f. 1971, Paris.
International Council of Scientific Unions, f. 1919, Brussels. Consultative status with UNESCO, ECOSOC, FAO and IAEA. Working arrangements with WMO, ITU and WHO. Publ.: *ICSU Bulletin, ICSU Yearbook* (since 1954)
International Foundation for Science, f. 1972, Stockholm.
International Union of the History and Philosophy of Science, London.
Pacific Science Association, f. 1920, Honolulu, USA. Consultative Status with UNESCO. Publ.: *Information Bulletin*.
Pugwash Conference on Science and World Affairs, f. 1957, Geneva. Publ.: *Pugwash Newsletter* (quarterly).
Universal Movement for Scientific Responsibility, f. 1974, Paris. Publ. *Bulletin de liaison*.
West African Science Association, f. 1953, Legon, Ghana. Consultative Status with OAU. Publ.: *Journal of the WASA*.
World Academy of Art and Science, f. 1960, New York. Consultative Status with UNESCO. Publ.: *WAAS Newsletter*.
World Federation of Scientific Workers, f. 1946, Paris. Consultative Status with UNESCO and ECOSOC. Publ.: *Scientific World* (quarterly in English, French, German and Russian) and *Impact of Science on Society* (quarterly in English and French).

Yearbook of International Organizations; W.F. BYNUM, E.J. BROWNE, R. PORTER, *Dictionary of the History of Science*, Princetown, 1985.

SCIENTIFIC AND TECHNICAL INTERNATIONAL CO-OPERATION.
A subject of few international agreements between the wars and of many after World War II. The NATO council at the end of 1957 formed the NATO Scientific Committee on the grounds that

"the development of science and technology in the NATO states is the cultural, political, economic and military foundation of the strength and unity of the Atlantic Community."

In the decades 1961–80 the institutionalization of scientific–technical co-operation of the NATO states advanced considerably. At the same time, UNESCO carried on a comprehensive campaign to develop this type of co-operation on a regional and global basis by organizing conferences and symposia.
The UN General Assembly appointed 1960 an Advisory Committee on Sciences and Technology for Development. Feb. 4–20, 1963, the First UN Conference on Sciences and Technology was held in Geneva with 1800 delegates from 87 countries. Report was published in eight volumes in English, French and Spanish.
In 1965 UNESCO initiated all types of informative–documentary services related to the development of sciences and technology of significance to the developing countries in particular. An intergovernmental special conference under UNESCO auspices, Oct. 4–8, 1971 in Paris, worked out a world system of scientific information, called ▷ UNISIST. A Scientific and Technical Services for the Asian and Pacific Region, est. by Agreement on Registry of Scientific and Technical Services for the Asian and Pacific Region, signed on July 16, 1971 in Manila, by Australia, Republic of China, Japan, South Korea, Malaysia, Philippines, Thailand, Republic of Vietnam; came into force upon signature. An International Centre of Scientific and Technical Information, was est. 1969 at Moscow, by a CMEA Agreement signed on Feb. 27, 1969. The Committee for Scientific and Technical Co-operation, which is the main organ of CMEA, is composed of Chairmen of the National Committees or Ministers of Science and Technology. Subordinate to the Committee are the special CMEA committees which organize research and carry out joint scientific–technical research in their special fields.

UNTS, Vol. 789, p. 284; Vol. 808, p. 10; W.E. BUTLER (ed.), *A Source Book on Socialist International Organizations*, Alphen, 1978.

SCIENTIFIC AND TECHNICAL SERVICES FOR THE ASIAN AND PACIFIC REGION.
An institution est. by ASPAC Agreement on Registry of Scientific and Technical Services for the Asian and Pacific Region, signed on July 16, 1971 in Manila by Australia, Republic of China, Japan, South Korea, Malaysia, Philippines, Thailand, Vietnam Republic; came into force with signature.

UNTS, Vol. 808, p. 10.

SCIENTIFIC AND TECHNOLOGICAL PROGRESS, UN DECLARATION, 1975.
The UN Declaration on the Use of Scientific and Technological Progress in the Interests of Peace and for the Benefit of Mankind, adopted by the UN General Assembly Res. 3384 (XXX) on Nov. 8, 1975. The text is as follows:

"(1) All States shall promote international cooperation to ensure that the results of scientific and technological developments are used in the interests of strengthening international peace and security, freedom and independence, and also for the purpose of the economic and social development of peoples and the realization of human rights and freedoms in accordance with the Charter of the United Nations.
(2) All States shall take appropriate measures to prevent the use of scientific and technological developments, particularly by the State organs, to limit or interfere with the enjoyment of the human rights and fundamental freedoms of the individual as enshrined in the Universal Declaration of Human Rights, the International Convenants on Human Rights and other relevant international instruments.
(3) All States shall take measures to ensure that scientific and technological achievements satisfy the material and spiritual needs of all sectors of the population.
(4) All States shall refrain from any acts involving the use of scientific and technological achievements for the purposes of violating the sovereignty and territorial integrity of other States interfering in their internal affairs, waging aggressive wars, suppressing national liberation movements or pursuing a policy of racial

discrimination. Such acts are not only a flagrant violation of the Charter of the United Nations and principles of international law, but constitute an inadmissible distortion of the purposes that should guide scientific and technological developments for the benefit of mankind.

(5) All States shall cooperate in the establishment, strengthening and development of the scientific and technological capacity of developing countries with a view to accelerating the realization of the social and economic rights of the peoples of those countries.

(6) All States shall take measures to extend the benefits of science and technology to all strata of the population and to protect them, both socially and materially, from possible harmful effects of the misuse of scientific and technological developments, including their misuse to infringe upon the rights of the individual or of the group, particularly with regard to respect for privacy and the protection of the human personality and its physical and intellectual integrity.

(7) All States shall take the necessary measures, including legislative measures, to ensure that the utilization of scientific and technological achievements promotes the fullest realization of human rights and fundamental freedoms without any discrimination whatsoever on grounds of race, sex, language or religious beliefs.

(8) All States shall take effective measures, including legislative measures, to prevent and preclude the utilization of scientific and technological achievements to the detriment of human rights and fundamental freedoms and the dignity of the human person.

(9) All States shall, whenever necessary, take action to ensure compliance with legislation guaranteeing human rights and freedom in the conditions of scientific and technological developments''.

UN Chronicle, December, 1975, pp. 58–59; *UN Yearbook*, 1975.

SCIENTIFIC AND TECHNOLOGICAL REVOLUTION. An international term, formulated in 1939 by the English scientist J.D. Bernal in the thesis that "characteristic of the scientific and technological revolution is the outstripping rate of development of science in comparison with economic development." The thesis was generally accepted after World War II as the universal influence of the sciences on the economic–social development of humanity grew in connection with the possibilities which the incessant progress of human productive forces opened up in the second phase of the industrial revolution, which spread to all highly developed countries of the world, regardless of their socio-economic order. From the 1980's products of the scientific and technological revolution are called High-Technology or High-Tech.

J.D. BERNAL, *The Social Functions of Science*, London, 1939; T.S. KUHN, *The Structure of Scientific Revolutions*, Chicago, 1962; J. MACHOWSKI, "The Scientific and Technological Revolution as a Factor of Development of International Law", in: *Polish Yearbook of International Law*, 1970, pp. 273–292; J. FILIOES, *Kritika nekotorikh burzhuasiinikh interpretatsii nauchno tekhnicheskoi revolutsii*, Moscow, 1974. LONGMAN *Guide to World Science and Technology*, London, 1988.

SCIENTIFIC DIPLOMAS. A subject of international conventions which permit the recognition of graduation certificates from secondary and higher schools, as a rule on the principle of reciprocity. A West European Convention signed on Dec. 1, 1953 in Paris became effective Mar. 20, 1960.

A Convention on the Mutual Recognition of the Equivalency of Graduation Documents from Secondary Schools, Secondary Vocational Schools and Higher Schools, as well as documents on attainment of degrees and scientific titles in the socialist countries was signed June 7, 1972 in Prague by Bulgaria, Cuba, Czechoslovakia, GDR, Hungary, Mongolia, Poland, Romania, the USSR and North Vietnam. A convention affecting 24 Latin American states was signed in July, 1974 in Mexico under UNESCO auspices, and in Dec. 6, 1976 in Nice a Convention of the States of the Mediterranean basin: Albania, Algeria, Cyprus, Egypt, France, Greece, Lebanon, Libya, Malta, Monaco, Morocco, Spain, Syria, Tunisia, and Turkey.

In accordance with the ▷ Helsinki Final Act, 1975, negotiations were started on the question of a European Convention on the mutual recognition of scientific diplomas.

▷ Academic Degrees.

R.J. DUPUY, G. TURKIN, *Comparabilité des diplomes en Droit International*, UNESCO, Paris, 1972, *Études sur les équivalences internacionales des diplomes*, UNESCO, Paris, 1973; *Les études supérieures. Présentations comparative des régimes d'enseignement supérieurs et des diplomes*, UNESCO, Paris, 1973; A.J. BOGOMOLOV, *Comparabilité des régimes d'Études et de diplomes en science de l'ingénieur*, UNESCO, Paris, 1975.

SCIENTIFIC FORUM OF THE CSCE, 1980. The Scientific Forum of the Conference on Security and Co-operation in Europe (▷ Helsinki Final Act, 1975) took place from Feb. 18 to Mar. 3, 1980, in Hamburg, FRG. It was held in the form of a meeting of leading personalities in science from the CSCE participating states. The Forum discussed international problems concerning current and future development in Exact and Natural Sciences, Medicine, the Humanities and Social Sciences. The Forum also discussed the problems of alternative energy sources (utilization of fossil fuels, solar energy and other renewable energy sources) of food production and co-operative research.

A.D. ROTFELD (ed.), *From Helsinki to Madrid. Documents*, Warsaw, 1984, pp. 237–264.

SCIENTIFIC LITERATURE. A subject of international co-operation since July 26, 1905, date of the signing of the first International Convention for the International Catalogue of Scientific Literature. After World War II the functions of the convention were assumed by UNESCO with the co-operation of the Council of International Scientific Unions and the International Center of Scientific and Technical Information.

Yearbook of International Organizations.

SCIENTIFIC ORGANIZATION OF LABOUR AND MANAGEMENT. An international term for a theory elaborated at the turn of 19th and 20th centuries by an American, F.W. Taylor (1856–1915) and the Frenchmen, H. Fayol (1841–1925) and H.L. de Chatelier (1850–1936). After World War I, under the auspices of the League of Nations, the First International Congress of Organization of Labour and Management was held in 1924 in Prague, and in 1926 the International Council for Labour Organization and Management was established. Organizations reg. with the UIA:

European Association of Management Training Centers, f. 1959, Brussels;
Institute of Management Sciences, f. 1953, New York. Publ.: *Management Science* and *Management Technology* (quarterly);
International Council for Scientific Management, f. 1926, Geneva. Consultative statute with ECOSOC and UNESCO;
International University Contact for Management Education, f. 1952, Delft.

Yearbook of International Organizations.

SCIENTISTS. ▷ Church of Christ.

SCLEROSIS. A subject of international research. Organization reg. with the UIA:

International Federation of Multiple Sclerosis Societies, f. 1966, Vienna. Consultative status with WHO and ECOSOC. Publ.: *Newsletter*.

Yearbook of International Organizations.

SCOTLAND. Part of the United Kingdom of Great Britain since 1707 together with England and Wales. Area together with Orkney Islands, Shetland Islands and Western Isles 78,772 sq. km. Pop.: 5,116,000 in 1981. Capital: Edinburgh. Bounded on the north and west by the Atlantic Ocean and on the east by the North Sea; separated in south from England by the Tweed River, Cheviot Hills, the Liddel River and Solway Firth. After the discovery of oil in the North Sea shelf, a national movement in the 1970s urged greater autonomy.

H.W. MIEBLE, *Scotland, A Select Bibliography*, London, 1950; P.D. HANCOCK, *A Bibliography of Works Relating to Scotland*, 2 Vols., Edinburgh, 1960; W. FERGUSON, *Scotland: 1689 to the Present*, London, 1968; J.G. KELLAS, *Modern Scotland: The Nation since 1870*, London, 1968.

SCOUTING. An organized youth movement; its idea was formulated by British General Baden Powell (1857–1941) at the beginning of the 20th century in South Africa during the British colonial war against the ▷ Boers. There he observed the possibility of sending children on scouting patrols, thereby accustoming them to paramilitary service for the British Empire. In 1908 B. Powell published a book on the subject entitled *Scouting for Boys*, which became a bestseller in prewar Europe and in the Anglo-American world; in many countries it inspired the establishment of scouting organizations as centers of civic education for youth in the spirit of the country's form of government. The first meeting of British scouts took place 1913 in Birmingham; also participating were 20 delegations from other countries; this initiated International Meetings, called Jamborees, organized by the Scouts International Bureau, established 1920, with headquarters in London; I – 1924 in Denmark, II – 1929 in Great Britain, III – 1933 in Hungary, IV – 1937 in the Netherlands; after World War II under the name of Scouts Gatherings.

Organizations reg. with the UIA:

Boy Scouts World Bureau, est. 1920, since 1961 the Boy Scouts International Bureau, Ottawa; publ.: *World Scouting Bulletin*.
International Conference of Catholic Scouting, est. 1948, Paris.
International Fellowship of Former Scouts and Guides, est. 1953, Brussels;
Scouts' Esperanto League, est. 1918, Antwerp.
World Association of Girl Guides and Girl Scouts, est. 1928, London.

R. BADEN-POWELL, *Scouting and Youth Movement*, London, 1929; *Yearbook of International Organizations*.

SDI. US Strategic Defence Initiative, official name of the US program of research into a system of antimissile defence, announced by President Ronald Reagan on March 23, 1983 called the 'Star Wars' program by the press.

A subject of principal disputes between the USSR and the USA during the Reykjavik 1986 pre-summit and the Washington 1987 summit.

The United Kingdom was the first to sign an agreement with the USA on co-operation in research into the feasibility of SDI, on Dec. 6, 1985; West Germany, on March 27, 1986; Israel on May 6, 1986 and Italy on Sept. 19, 1986; Japan signed an agreement for the participation of Japanese companies on July 21, 1987. Australia, Canada, Denmark, France and Norway were not ready to sign bilateral agreements with the USA but did not exclude participation by companies on a private basis. The total cost of research, development and deployment for SDI was estimated in 1985 around $1,000,000 million, since then the amount has grown, due to the weak US dollar.

KEESING's *Contemporary Archive*, 1985 and 1986; KEESING's *Record of World Events*, 1987 and 1988; L. PRESSLER, *Star Wars, The Strategic Defense Initiative Debates in Congress*, New York, 1986; H.G. BRAUCH, *Star Wars and European Defence*, New York, 1987; D. CARLTON, C. SCHAERF, *The Arms Race in the Era of Star Wars*, London, 1987; R.M. LAWRENCE, *Strategic Defence Initiative: Bibliography and Research Guide*, London, 1987; H. WALDMAN, *The Dictionary of SDI*, Wilmington, Del., USA, 1988.

SDR, SPECIAL DRAWING RIGHTS. A new international monetary reserve currency to supplement traditional reserve assets: gold and hard currency. Like gold, they may be used for settlement of international accounts, created in 1967 by the ▷ IMF. The IMF General Assembly in Sept. 1967, in Rio de Janeiro, adopted a SDR Convention; came into force on Jan. 2, 1970, giving the Fund in arts. XXI and XII of its amended statute "special drawing rights," allowing the member states to replenish their currency reserves in cases of inadequate international liquidity or the need to make up balance of payments deficits. Also known as "paper gold", SDR are assigned to the accounts of IMF members in proportion to their contribution to the Fund. Participating countries agree to accept SDRs exchangeable for gold or reserve currencies in the settlement of international accounts. Practically, for an IMF member state the SDR is a supplement to the statutory right to draw, by the right to receive through the mediation of the IMF from other members, a certain sum of foreign currency, so-called "hard currency", defined by the regulations not for its own currency but for SDR units set aside for it (as its share) from a "special drawing account" which was est. Jan. 1, 1970 in the sum of 31,114 million dollars. This is the total sum of shares for the 104 members of the IMF which joined the SDR (11 states refused their share). Payment of an SDR credit begins from the time when a given country regains a favorable balance of payments. Since the SDR is proportional to the level of participation of particular states in the IMF, the highly developed member countries can benefit from high credit, whereas the developing countries, which have low levels of participation, benefit from very low sums. IMF member states are obligated without exception to accept SDR funds as a means of payment for the settlement of international obligations. A report of IMF experts, Sept. 6, 1972, on the question of the reform of the international monetary system came out in favor of the staged takeover by the IMF of the practical function of currency reserves and international means of payment (1972 SDR issues amounted to 9.5 billion dollars); also examined was the idea of using the SDR as a replacement for gold in establishing a standard for currencies, so that the price of gold would not be expressed in dollars, but in SDR units, since 1969 equal to 0.888671 grams of pure gold. Since July 1, 1974 the IMF has introduced a new system for pegging the value of an SDR on the basis of a "basket of 16 currencies," among which the American dollar received a weight of 33% of an SDR, the FRG Mark – 12.5%, British pound – 9%, French franc – 7.5%, Japanese yen – 7.5%, Canadian dollar – 6%, Italian Lire – 6%. Since July 1, 1974 the daily currency rates in the "basket" became the basis for calculating the value of an SDR on a given day. Simultaneously, the interest rate for an SDR was raised Aug. 1, 1974 from 1.5% to 5%. The IMF on Sept. 18, 1980 decided to change the method of valuing its Special Drawing Right, not using the 16-currency basket, but only a 5-currency basket.

The composition of the New SDR currency basket, effective from Jan. 1, 1981 is as follows:

US dollar	42%
Deutsche mark	19%
French franc	13%
Japanese yen	13%
Pound sterling	13%

According to the IMF 1983 report, compensatory financing facility purchases of SDR rose most dramatically from 1.2 billion SDR in 1981 to 2.6 billion SDR in 1982 (35% of total purchases, reflecting the severe drop in the export earning of community producers).

The UNCIFRAL draft Convention on International Bills of Exchange 1987, allows international ▷ bills of exchange and promisory notes to be payable in monetary units of account such as ECU or SDR.

J. GOLD, *SDR: Character and Use*, IMF, Washington, DC, 1970; R.M. SCHUSTER, *The Public International Law of Money*, Oxford, 1973; O. EMMINGER, *Inflation and the International Monetary System*, Basel, 1973; J. GOLD, *SDR's Gold and Currencies, IMF, Third Survey of New Legal Developments*, Washington, DC, 1979; L.D. WRANG, "Again SDR's Could Grow Into a Global Currency", in: *International Herald Tribune*, Euromarket 1980, November, 1980; *UN Chronicle*, February, 1983, p. 122; *UN Chronicle*, November, 1987.

SEA AND NUCLEAR WASTE MANAGEMENT. One of the main environmental problems, subject of the ▷ Seas and Oceans Protection Treaty, 1972 against the ▷ radioactivity of the deep sea, under control of the IAEA International Laboratory of Marine Radioactivity.

R. FUKAI, *Report from Monaco: Waste Management and the Sea, in: IAEA Bulletin*, Spring, 1986, pp. 33–36.

SEA ANIMALS PROTECTION. Under the protection of international conventions are the following salt water creatures:

Beluga (White Whale), *Delphinapterus leucas*.
Crabs, *Crustacea*.
Flounder (Flatfish), *Heterosomatos*.
Haddock, *Melanogrammus aeglefinus*.
Halibut, *Rheinhardtius hippoglossoiden*.
Herring, *Clupea harengus*.
Lemon Soles, *Microstomus Kitt*.
Lobster, *Homarus vulgaris*.
Lobster, *Nephrops norvegicus*.
Negrims, *Lepidorhombus whiff*.
Plaice, *Pleuronectes platessa*.
Prawns, *Pandalus borealis*.
Rhombos, *Rhombus maeoticus*.
Scad, *Alosa Kentari pontica*.
Sole, *Soles*.
Sprat, *Clupea sprattus*.
Sturgeon, *Acipenseridæ*.
Turbot, *Rhombus maeoticus*.
Whiting, *Gadus merlangus*.

Yearbook of International Organizations.

SEA-BED AND THE OCEAN FLOOR. A subject of international co-operation under UN auspices for the peaceful utilization of the natural resources of sea-beds not only in coastal regions (▷ Continental shelf), but in all places where the development of technology already makes this possible. In Nov., 1947 the UN General Assembly charged the International Law Commission with the study of the legal problems of sea-bed of the open sea and the "utilization of its resources for the good of humanity." The Fourth Geneva Convention on the Continental Shelf, 1958, determined the exclusive right of a coastal state to exploitation of the sea-bed to a place where the depth is not greater than 200 m, or beyond this line if the sea-bed permits the exploitation of natural resources. This last principle soon caused objections due to the rapid development of technology, making it possible for coastal states to dominate the majority of the seas. The UN General Assembly in Res. 2340/XII, Feb. 18, 1967, created a Special Committee on the Peaceful Uses of Sea-bed and Ocean Floors composed of 42 states. It began work in Mar., 1968 on the legal definition of principles for using the undersea areas in accordance with art. 2 of the Geneva Convention on the Open Sea, 1958, that freedom of the seas must be based on respect for the rights and interests of all of the interested states. The question of an international agreement to limit military use of the seabed and ocean floor was revised in 1968 by the USA and USSR at the meeting of the Eighteen Nations Disarmament Committee, ENDC. This led to the adoption by the UN General Assembly Res. 2660/XXV, Dec. 7, 1970, of the ▷ Sea-bed Treaty on the Denuclearization of the 1971, and on Dec. 17, 1970 of a Declaration of Principles Governing the Seabed and the Ocean Floor, and the Subsoil Thereof, beyond the Limits of National Jurisdiction. The text of the Declaration is as follows:

"The General Assembly,
Recalling its resolutions 2340 (XXII) of 18 December 1967, 2467 (XXIII) of December 21, 1968 and 2574 (XXIV) of December 15, 1969, concerning the area to which the title of the item refers,
Affirming that there is an area of the sea-bed and the ocean floor, and the subsoil thereof, beyond the limits of national jurisdiction, the precise limits of which are yet to be determined,
Recognizing that the existing legal regime of the high seas does not provide substantive rules for regulating the exploration of the aforesaid area and the exploitation of its resources,
Convinced that the area shall be reserved exclusively for peaceful purposes and that the exploration of the area and the exploitation of its resources shall be carried out for the benefit of mankind as a whole,
Believing it essential that an international regime applying to the area and its resources and including appropriate international machinery should be established as soon as possible,
Bearing in mind that the development and use of the area and its resources shall be undertaken in such a manner as to foster the healthy development of the world economy and balanced growth of international trade, and to minimize any adverse economic effects caused by the fluctuation of prices of raw materials resulting from such activities,
Solemnly declares that:
(1) The sea-bed and ocean floor, and the subsoil thereof, beyond the limits of national jurisdiction (hereinafter referred to as the area), as well as the resources of the area, are the common heritage of mankind.
(2) The area shall not be subject to appropriation by any means by States or persons, natural or juridical, and no State shall claim or exercise sovereignty or sovereign rights over any part thereof.
(3) No State or person, natural or juridical, shall claim, exercise or acquire rights with respect to the area or its resources incompatible with the international regime to be established and the principles of this Declaration.
(4) All activities regarding the exploration and exploitation of the resources of the area and other related activities shall be governed by the international regime to be established.
(5) The area shall be open to use exclusively for peaceful purposes by all States, whether coastal or landlocked, without discrimination, in accordance with the international regime to be established,
(6) States shall act in the area in accordance with the applicable principles and rules of international law, including the Charter of the United Nations and the Declaration on Principles of International Law concerning Friendly Relations and Co-operation among States in accordance with the Charter of the United Nations, adopted by the General Assembly on October

24, 1970, in the interests of maintaining international peace and security and promoting international co-operation and mutual understanding.

(7) The exploration of the area and the exploitation of its resources shall be carried out for the benefit of mankind as a whole, irrespective of the geographical location of States, whether land-locked or coastal, and taking into particular consideration the interests and needs of the developing countries.

(8) The area shall be reserved exclusively for peaceful purposes without prejudice to any measures which have been or may be agreed upon in the contexts of international negotiations undertaken in the field of disarmament and which may be applicable to a broader area. One or more international agreements shall be concluded as soon as possible in order to implement effectively this principle and to constitute a step towards the exclusion of the sea-bed, the ocean floor and the subsoil thereof from the arms race.

(9) On the basis of the principles of this Declaration, an international regime applying to the area and its resources and including appropriate international machinery to give effect to its provisions shall be established by an international treaty of a universal character, generally agreed upon. The regime shall, inter alia, provide for the orderly and safe development and rational management of the area and its resources and for expanding opportunities in the use thereto and ensure the equitable sharing by States in the benefits derived therefrom, taking into particular consideration the interests and needs of the developing countries, whether land-locked or coastal.

(10) States shall promote international co-operation in scientific research exclusively for peaceful purposes:
(a) By participation in international programmes and by encouraging co-operation in scientific research by personnel of different countries;
(b) Through effective publication of research programmes and dissemination of the results of research through international channels;
(c) By co-operation in measures to strengthen research capabilities of developing countries, including the participation of their nationals in research programmes. No such activity shall form the legal basis for any claims with respect to any part of the area or its resources.

(11) With respect to activities in the area and acting in conformity with the international regime to be established, States shall take appropriate measures for and shall co-operate in the adoption and implementation of international rules, standards and procedures for, inter alia:
(a) The prevention of pollution and contamination, and other hazards to the marine environment, including the coastline, and of interference with the ecological balance of the marine environment;
(b) The protection and conservation of the natural resources of the area and the prevention of damage to the flora and fauna of the marine environment.

(12) In their activities in the area, including those relating to its resources, States shall pay due regard to the rights and legitimate interests of coastal States in the region of such activities, as well as of all other States, which may be affected by such activities. Consultations shall be maintained with the coastal States concerned with respect to activities relating to the exploration of the area and the exploitation of its resources with a view to avoiding infringement of such rights and interests.

(13) Nothing herein shall affect:
(a) The legal status of the waters superjacent to the area or that of the air space above those waters;
(b) The rights of coastal States with respect to measures to prevent, mitigate or eliminate grave and imminent danger to their coastline or related interests from pollution or threat thereof or from other hazardous occurrences resulting from or caused by any activities in the area, subject to the international regime to be established.

(14) Every State shall have the responsibility to ensure that activities in the area, including those relating to its resources, whether undertaken by governmental agencies, or non-governmental entities or persons under its jurisdiction, or acting on its behalf, shall be carried out in conformity with the international regime to be established. The same responsibility applies to international organizations and their members for activities undertaken by such organizations or on their behalf. Damage caused by such activities shall entail liability.

(15) The parties to any dispute relating to activities in the area and its resources shall resolve such dispute by the measures mentioned in art. 33 of the Charter of the United Nations and such procedures for settling disputes as may be agreed upon in the international regime to be established".

On Nov. 16, 1973, the UN General Assembly adopted Res. 3067/XXVIII on the Reservation Exclusively for Peaceful Purposes of the Sea-bed and Ocean Floor and the Subsoil Thereof Underlying the High Seas Beyond the Limits of Present National Jurisdiction and Use of Their Resources in the Interests of Mankind and Convening of the Third UN Conference on the Law of the Sea.

The Third UN Conference on the Law of the Sea, July 28–Aug. 29, 1980, in Geneva, agreed on a new package of proposals on seabed exploration. The Fourth UN Conference in Sept., 1983 discussed the protection of the seabed from the storage of nuclear weapons. ▷ Sea Law Convention, 1982 (arts. 56, 76, 77, 186).

UN Yearbook, 1970; A. COLLIARD, *Le Fond des Mers*, Paris, 1971; W.G. VITZTHUM, *Der Rechtsstatus des Meeresboden*, Berlin, 1972; *UN Yearbook*, 1973; SIPRI, *World Armaments and Disarmament Yearbook*, 1970, pp. text 537–541, 578–590; 1971, pp. 437–471; 1972, pp. 457–491; 1973, pp. 553–583; 1974, pp. 429–461; 1977, pp. 579–617; J.N. BARKENBUS, *Deep Seabed Resources*, New York, 1979; *UN Chronicle*, September–October, 1980, pp. 40–41 and 74–75; and April 1984, p. 44.

SEA-BED AUTHORITY.
The ▷ Sea Law Convention 1982 called for the establishment of the Sea-Bed Authority to govern and regulate sea-bed mining in areas designated as the common heritage of mankind. A Preparatory Commission for the International Sea-Bed Authority, elaborated a draft of the Authority Statute.

UN Chronicle, 1985, No 3, pp. 27–28.

SEA-BED, TREATY ON DENUCLEARIZATION OF THE, 1971.
Treaty on the Prohibition of the Emplacement of Nuclear Weapons and Other Weapons of Mass Destruction on the Sea-bed and the Ocean Floor and in the Subsoil Thereof, approved by the UN General Assembly, Res. 2660/XXV, Dec. 7, 1970; signed on Feb. 11, 1971; entered into force on May 18, 1972. The text is as follows:

"The States Parties to this Treaty.
Recognizing the common interest of mankind in the progress of the exploration and use of the sea-bed and the ocean floor for peaceful purposes,
Considering that the prevention of a nuclear arms race on the sea-bed and the ocean floor serves the interests of maintaining world peace, reduces international tensions, and strengthens friendly relations among States,
Convinced that this Treaty constitutes a step towards the exclusion of the sea-bed, the ocean floor and the subsoil thereof from the arms race,
Convinced that this Treaty constitutes a step towards a treaty on general and complete disarmament under strict and effective international control, and determined to continue negotiations to this end,
Convinced that this Treaty will further the purposes and principles of the Charter of the United Nations, in a manner consistent with the principles of international law and without infringing the freedoms of the high seas,
Have agreed as follows:
Art. I.(1) The States Parties to this Treaty undertake not to emplant or emplace on the sea-bed and the ocean floor and in the subsoil thereof beyond the outer limit of a sea-bed zone as defined in art. II any nuclear weapons or any other types of weapons of mass destruction as well as structures, launching installations or any other facilities specifically designed for storing, testing or using such weapons.
(2) The undertakings of paragraph 1 of this article shall also apply to the sea-bed zone referred to in the same paragraph, except that within such sea-bed zone, they

shall not apply either to the coastal State or to the sea-bed beneath its territorial waters.
(3) The States Parties to this Treaty undertake not to assist, encourage or induce any State to carry out activities referred to in paragraph 1 of this article and not to participate in any other way in such actions.
Art. II. For the purpose of this Treaty the outer limit of the sea-bed zone referred to in art. I shall be coterminous with the twelve-mile outer limit of the zone referred to in Part II of the Convention on the Territorial Sea and the Contiguous Zone, signed in Geneva on April 29, 1958, and shall be measured in accordance with the provisions of Part I, Section II, of this Convention and in accordance with international law.
Art. III.(1) In order to promote the objectives of and ensure compliance with the provisions of this Treaty, each State Party to the Treaty shall have the right to verify through observation the activities of other States Parties to the Treaty on the sea-bed and the ocean floor and in the subsoil thereof beyond the zone referred to in art. I, provided that observation does not interfere with such activities.
(2) If after such observation reasonable doubts remain concerning the fulfilment of the obligations assumed under the Treaty, the State Party having such doubts and the State Party that is responsible for the activities giving rise to the doubts shall consult with a view to removing the doubts. If the doubts persist, the State Party having such doubts shall notify the other States Parties, and the Parties concerned shall co-operate on such further procedures for verification as may be agreed, including appropriate inspection of objects, structures, installations or other facilities that reasonably may be expected to be of a kind described in art. I. The Parties in the region of the activities, including any coastal State, and any other Party so requesting, shall be entitled to participate in such consultation and co-operation. After completion of the further procedures for verification, an appropriate report shall be circulated to other Parties by the Party that initiated such procedures.
(3) If the State responsible for the activities giving rise to the reasonable doubts is not identifiable by observation of the object, structure, installation or other facility, the State Party having such doubts shall notify and make appropriate inquiries of States Parties in the region of the activities and of any other State Party. If it is ascertained through these inquiries that a particular State Party is responsible for the activities, that State Party shall consult and co-operate with other Parties as provided in paragraph 2 of this article. If the identity of the State responsible for the activities cannot be ascertained through these inquiries, the further verification procedures, including inspection, may be undertaken by the inquiring State Party, which shall invite the participation of the Parties in the region of the activities, including any coastal State, and of any other Party desiring to co-operate.
(4) If consultation and co-operation pursuant to paragraphs 2 and 3 of this article have not removed the doubts concerning the activities and there remains a serious question concerning fulfilment of the obligations assumed under this Treaty, a State Party may, in accordance with the provisions of the Charter of the United Nations, refer the matter to the Security Council, which may take action in accordance with the Charter.
(5) Verification pursuant to this article may be undertaken by any State Party using its own means, or with the full or partial assistance of any other State Party, or through appropriate international procedures within the framework of the United Nations and in accordance with its Charter.
(6) Verification activities pursuant to this Treaty shall not interfere with activities of other States Parties and shall be conducted with due regard for rights recognized under international law including the freedoms of the high seas and the rights of coastal States with respect to the exploration and exploitation of their continental shelves.
Art. IV. Nothing in this Treaty shall be interpreted as supporting or prejudicing the position of any State Party with respect to existing international conventions, including the 1958 Convention on the Territorial Sea and the Contiguous Zone, or with respect to rights or claims which such State Party may assert, or with respect to recognition or non-recognition of rights or claims asserted by any other State, related to waters off

its coasts; including inter alia territorial seas and contiguous zones, or to the sea-bed and the ocean floor, including continental shelves.

Art. V. The Parties to this Treaty undertake to continue negotiations in good faith concerning further measures in the field of disarmament for the prevention of an arms race on the sea-bed, the ocean floor and the subsoil thereof.

Art. VI. Any State Party may propose amendments to this Treaty. Amendments shall enter into force for each State Party accepting the amendments upon their acceptance by a majority of the States Parties to the Treaty and thereafter for each remaining State Party on the date of acceptance by it.

Art. VII. Five years after the entry into force of this Treaty, a conference of Parties to the Treaty shall be held in Geneva, Switzerland, in order to review the operation of this Treaty with a view to assuring that the purposes of the preamble and the provisions of the Treaty are being realized. Such review shall take into account any relevant technological developments. The review conference shall determine in accordance with the views of a majority of those Parties attending whether and when an additional review conference shall be convened.

Art. VIII. Each State Party to this Treaty shall in exercising its national sovereignty have the right to withdraw from this Treaty if it decides that extraordinary events related to the subject matter of this Treaty have jeopardized the supreme interests of its country. It shall give notice of such withdrawal to all other States Parties to the Treaty and to the United Nations Security Council three months in advance. Such notice shall include a statement of the extraordinary events it considers to have jeopardized its supreme interests.

Art. IX. The provisions of this Treaty shall in no way affect the obligations assumed by States Parties to the Treaty under international instruments establishing zones free from nuclear weapons.

Art. X.(1) This Treaty shall be open for signature to all States. Any State which does not sign the Treaty before its entry into force in accordance with paragraph 3 of this article may accede to it at any time.

(2) This Treaty shall be subject to ratification by signatory States. Instruments of ratification and of accession shall be deposited with the Governments of the Union of Soviet Socialist Republics, the United Kingdom of Great Britain and Northern Ireland and the United States of America, which are hereby designated the Depositary Governments.

(3) This Treaty shall enter into force after the deposit of instruments of ratification by twenty-two Governments, including the Governments designated as Depositary Governments of this Treaty.

(4) For States whose instruments of ratification or accession are deposited after the entry into force of this Treaty it shall enter into force on the date of the deposit of their instruments of ratification or accession.

(5) The Depositary Governments shall promptly inform the Governments of all signatory and acceding States of the date of each signature, of the date of deposit of each instrument of ratification, or of accession, of the date of the entry into force of this Treaty, and of the receipt of other notices.

(6) This Treaty shall be registered by the Depositary Governments pursuant to art. 102 of the Charter of the United Nations.

Art. XI. This Treaty, the Chinese, English, French, Russian and Spanish texts of which are equally authentic, shall be deposited in the archives of the Depositary Governments. Duly certified copies of this Treaty shall be transmitted by the Depositary Governments to the Governments of the States signatory and acceding thereto.

In witness whereof the undersigned, being duly authorized thereto, have signed this Treaty.

Done in triplicate, at the cities of Moscow, London and Washington DC, this eleventh day of February 1971."

The Treaty was ratified until Jan. 1, 1987 by 78 countries.

UN Yearbook, 1970; *The UN and Disarmament, 1970–1975*, New York, 1976; SIPRI *Yearbook 1987*, Oxford, 1988, p. 461.

SEA CHARTER. An international term for the renting of cargo vessels for the transport of specific goods. International maritime conferences worked out standard charter agreements for the transport of various goods (▷ Charter Agreements).

SEA EXPLORATION. A subject of international co-operation. Organization reg. with the UIA:

International Council for the Exploration of the Sea, est. 1902, Copenhagen, to carry out oceanographic research programs. It was adopted at intergovernmental conferences in 1899, 1901 and 1964. The latter adopted a Convention on Sea Exploration signed and ratified by Belgium, Canada, Denmark, Finland, France, FRG, GDR, Iceland, Ireland, the Netherlands, Norway, Poland, Portugal, Spain, Sweden, the UK and the USSR. Collaborates with FAO and WMO. Publ.: *Journal du Conseil Annales Biologiques, Rapports*; Headquarters, Charlottenlund, Denmark.

SEAFARERS CONVENTION, 1984. The International Convention on Standards of Training, Certification and Watchkeeping for Seafarers, adopted in 1978 by the IMCO Conferences, entered into force on Apr. 28, 1984, having been ratified by 33 countries, whose combined merchant fleets represent two-thirds of world gross tonnage. The Convention has established specific minimum professional standards applicable worldwide for seafarers.

UN Chronicle, March, 1984, p. 34.

SEA FISHING CONVENTIONS. The first convention to regulate sea fisheries was the Geneva Convention on whaling, signed Sept. 24, 1931. The rapid increase of sea fisheries after World War II prompted further conventions aimed at protecting living resources of the sea. Among the major conventions:
International Fisheries Convention, signed 1946 in London;
North West Atlantic Fisheries Convention, signed 1949 in London, Additional Protocol signed 1956 in Washington;
North East Atlantic Fisheries Convention, signed 1959 in London; went into force 1963;
International Convention for the High Seas of the North Pacific Ocean Fisheries signed 1952 in Tokyo, by Japan, Canada, and USA;
Convention on Fisheries and Conservation of High Sea Resources, signed on Apr. 29, 1958 in Geneva, went into force Mar. 20, 1966;
Convention on Fishing and Conservation of the Living Resources of the High Sea, signed on Apr. 29, 1958 in Geneva.
Scandinavian Fishing Convention on Conservation of Flatfish (*Pleuronectes* and *Pleuronectes platessa*) in the region of Skagerrak, Kattegat and the Sound, signed by Denmark, Norway, and Sweden, Sept. 6, 1957 in Oslo.
Scandinavian Agreement on Fishing Regarding Conservation of *Pandalus borealis, Homarus vulgaris, Nephrops norvegicus*, and *Cancer pugurus*, signed Mar. 7, 1952 in Oslo by the same countries.
Another Scandinavian Agreement on Fisheries granting fishing grounds in the region of Skagerrak and Kattegat to all ships, was signed Dec. 19, 1966 in Copenhagen, also by Denmark, Norway and Sweden.
Convention on Fishing and Conservation of the Living Resources in the Baltic Sea, signed Sept. 13, 1973 in Gdansk, by Denmark, Finland, GDR, FRG, Poland, Sweden, and USSR. (Preamble and 20 articles specifying aims and duties of the signatories relating to conservation and multiplication of the living resources in the Baltic and their rational and effective utilization); this convention also spanned the region of Danish Belts which separates the Baltic from the Kattegat; signed for a 5-year term, it was open to any country interested in

protection and rational utilization of Baltic resources. The International Commission for Fishing on the Baltic Sea was set up with headquarters in Warsaw for implementation of the Convention.
On Dec. 18, 1951, the International Court of Justice examined a dispute involving Great Britain and Norway on the latter's expartite demarcation of territorial waters in the North Pole fishing regions and pronounced a verdict to the advantage of Norway.
Within the CMEA in the field of fishing co-operation, Bulgaria, GDR, Poland, Romania, and USSR have agreed since 1962 on the joint supply of food, fresh water and fuel to fishing grounds and transport of catches from fishing grounds; joint repair centres on the basis of CMEA Bank credits; and joint research on fishing technologies.

LNTS, Vol. 186, p. 413; *UST*, Vol. 175, p. 205; *UNTS*, Vol. 605, p. 313; *ICJ Reports 1951*, p. 116.

SEA FISHING LAW. The national legislation and international conventions outlining the principles of legal protection of fishing, both in territorial seas and the high seas. ▷ Sea Fishing Conventions.

SEA FREIGHT. An international term for payment due a sea carrier for the transport of cargo. One of the main problems of international transport after World War II is the excessive cost of sea freight for the basic raw materials of developing countries. According to UNCTAD statistics, the average sea freight is 10% of the value of the goods on the basis of ▷ FOB prices; for heavy mass raw materials it exceeds 20%. The first International Freight Conference took place in 1875 in Calcutta.

Las fletas marítimas en el comercio exterior de América Latina, UN, New York, 1969.

SEA FRONTIERS. An international term for boundaries of internal seas; for boundaries of territorial seas; and for boundaries of open seas. A subject of international conventions on the Law of the Sea under which all three sea boundaries are determined through the delineation of limits of territorial seas together with internal waters and their width in order to establish borders of open seas. The issue of the width has not been settled by any treaty. For centuries it was adopted by custom that borders of territorial waters should be determined 6, 9 or 12 nautical miles off shore. A separate controversial issue is the belt of territorial waters claimed by states either for the reason of fish resources or natural resources found in coastal shelves. The delineation of the coastal basic boundaries of territorial seas as well as their external limits is open to a variety of solutions related to geographical conditions.

J.K. ONDENIJE, *Statute and Extent of Adjacent Waters*, Amsterdam, 1970.

SEA INTERNAL WATERS. The sea area between the lowest water level during ebb-tide and the coast; also sea waters in ports and entry to ports, bays and other waters under specified conditions. The First Geneva Convention of 1958 in art. 5 para. 1 states that

"waters on the side of the basic line of territorial waters facing land form a part of internal waters of the state." The Second Geneva Convention provides in art. 3 for an agreement on receiving free access to the sea for states having no such access. The Convention on the Law of the Sea, 1981 defined in art. 8 the internal waters as follows:
"waters on the landward side of the baseline of the territorial sea form part of the internal waters of the State."

R.R. BAXTER, *The Law of International Waterways with Particular Regard to Interoceanic Canals*, Cambridge, 1964; UNITA, *International Waterways*, New York, 1975.

SEA LABOUR LAW. A subject of 34 international conventions of the international law of the Sea, prepared by the ILO between 1920–1980. ▷ ILO Conventions 1919–1980.

SEA-LAUNCHED CRUISE MISSILE. ▷ SLCM.

SEA LAW CONFERENCES. The intergovernmental meetings under the auspices of the League of Nations and the UN, devoted to the codification and development of the law of the sea. (▷ Sea Law Convention, 1982).

Third United Nations Conference on the Law of the Sea. Official Records, New York, 1985; *The Law of the Sea: Master File Containing References to Official Documents of the Third UN Conference*, New York, 1985.

SEA LAW CONVENTION, 1982. The UN Convention on the Law of the Sea was signed on Dec. 10, 1982 at Montego Bay, Jamaica. The Convention was the product of nine years of work by the Third United Nations Conference on the Law of the Sea. A Statement by Javier Perez de Cuellar, Secretary-General of the UN, underlined that on this day "International Law is irrevocably transformed:
With the signing of the Final Act of the Third United Nations Conference on the Law of the Sea, and with the opening for signature of the United Nations Convention on the Law of the Sea, the efforts begun almost 14 years ago to establish a new legal order for ocean space are now reaching their culmination. In order to affirm that international law is now irrevocably transformed, so far as the seas are concerned, we need not wait for the process of ratification of the Convention to begin."
The text of the Convention reads as follows:

"*The States Parties to this Convention,*
Prompted by the desire to settle, in a spirit of mutual understanding and co-operation, all issues relating to the law of the sea and aware of the historic significance of this Convention as an important contribution to the maintenance of peace, justice and progress for all peoples of the world,
Noting that the developments since the United Nations Conferences on the Law of the Sea held at Geneva in 1958 and 1960 have accentuated the need for a new and generally acceptable Convention on the law of the sea,
Conscious that the problems of ocean space are closely interrelated and need to be considered as a whole,
Recognizing the desirability of establishing through this Convention, with due regard for the sovereignty of all States, a legal order for the seas and oceans which will facilitate international communication, and will promote the peaceful uses of the seas and oceans, the equitable and efficient utilization of their resources, the conservation of their living resources, and the study, protection and preservation of the marine environment.
Bearing in mind that the achievement of these goals will contribute to the realization of a just and equitable international economic order which takes into account the interests and needs of mankind as a whole and, in particular, the special interests and needs of developing countries, whether coastal or land-locked,
Desiring by this Convention to develop the principles embodied in resolution 2749 (XXV) of 17 December 1970 in which the General Assembly of the United Nations solemnly declared *inter alia* that the area of the sea-bed and ocean floor and the subsoil thereof, beyond the limits of national jusridiction, as well as its resources, are the common heritage of mankind, the exploration and exploitation of which shall be carried out for the benefit of mankind as a whole, irrespective of the geographical location of States,
Believing that the codification and progressive development of the law of the sea achieved in this Convention will contribute to the strengthening of peace, security, co-operation and friendly relations among all nations in conformity with the principles of justice and equal rights and will promote the economic and social advancement of all peoples of the world, in accordance with the Purposes and Principles of the United Nations as set forth in the Charter,
Affirming that matters not regulated by this Convention continue to be governed by the rules and principles of general international law,
Have agreed as follows:

Part I   Introduction
Art. 1. Use of terms and scope
1. For the purposes of this Convention:
(1) 'Area' means the sea-bed and ocean floor and subsoil thereof, beyond the limits of national jurisdiction;
(2) 'Authority' means the International Sea-Bed Authority;
(3) 'activities in the Area' means all activities of exploration for, and exploitation of, the resources of the Area;
(4) 'pollution of the marine environment' means the introduction by man, directly or indirectly, of substances or energy into the marine environment, including estuaries, which results or is likely to result in such deleterious effects as harm to living resources and marine life, hazards to human health, hindrance to marine activities, including fishing and other legitimate uses of the sea, impairment of quality for use of sea water and reduction of amenities;
(5) (a) 'dumping' means:
(i) any deliberate disposal of wastes or other matter from vessels, aircraft, platforms or other man-made structures at sea;
(ii) any deliberate disposal of vessels, aircraft, platforms or other man-made structures at sea;
(b) 'dumping' does not include:
(i) the disposal of wastes or other matter incidental to, or derived from the normal operations of vessels, aircraft, platforms or other man-made structures at sea and their equipment, other than wastes or other matter transported by or to vessels, aircraft, platforms or other man-made structures at sea, operating for the purpose of disposal of such matter or derived from the treatment of such wastes or other matter on such vessels, aircraft, platforms or structures;
(ii) placement of matter for a purpose other than the mere disposal thereof, provided that such placement is not contrary to the aims of this Convention.
2 (1) 'States parties' means States which have consented to be bound by this Convention and for which this Convention is in force.
(2) This Convention applies *mutatis mutandis* to the entities referred to in article 305, paragraph 1(b), (c), (d), (e) and (f), which become Parties to this Convention in accordance with the conditions relevant to each, and to that extent 'States Parties' refers to those entities.

Part II   Territorial Sea and Contiguous Zone
Section 1. General
Art. 2. Legal status of the territorial sea, of the air space over the territorial sea and of its bed and subsoil
1. The sovereignty of a coastal State extends, beyond its land territory and internal waters and, in the case of an archipelagic State, its archipelagic waters, to an adjacent belt of sea, described as the territorial sea.
2. This sovereignty extends to the air space over the territorial sea as well as to its bed and subsoil.
3. The sovereignty over the territorial sea is exercised subject to this Convention and to other rules of international law.

Section 2. Limits of the territorial sea
Art. 3. Breadth of the territorial sea
Every State has the right to establish the breadth of its territorial sea up to a limit not exceeding 12 nautical miles, measured from baselines determined in accordance with this Convention.
Art. 4. Outer limit of the territorial sea
The outer limit of the territorial sea is the line every point of which is at a distance from the nearest point of the baseline equal to the breadth of the territorial sea.
Art. 5. Normal baseline
Except where otherwise provided in this Convention, the normal baseline for measuring the breadth of the territorial sea is the low-water line along the coast as marked on large-scale charts officially recognized by the coastal State.
Art. 6. Reefs
In the case of islands situated on atolls or of islands having fringing reefs, the baseline for measuring the breadth of the territorial sea is the seaward low-water line of the reef, as shown by the appropriate symbol on charts officially recognized by the coastal State.
Art. 7. Straight baselines
1. In localities where the coastline is deeply indented and cut into, or if there is a fringe of islands along the coast in its immediate vicinity, the method of straight baselines joining appropriate points may be employed in drawing the baseline from which the breadth of the territorial sea is measured.
2. Where because of the presence of a delta and other natural conditions the coastline is highly unstable, the appropriate points may be selected along the furthest seaward extent of the low-water line and, notwithstanding subsequent regression of the low-water line, the straight baselines shall remain effective until changed by the coastal State in accordance with this Convention.
3. The drawing of straight baselines must not depart to any appreciable extent from the general direction of the coast, and the sea areas lying within the lines must be sufficiently closely linked to the land domain to be subject to the régime of internal waters.
4. Straight baselines shall not be drawn to and from low-tide elevations, unless lighthouses or similar installations which are permanently above sea level have been built on them or except in instances where the drawing of baselines to and from such elevations has received general international recognition.
5. Where the method of straight baselines is applicable under paragraph 1, account may be taken, in determining particular baselines, of economic interests peculiar to the region concerned, the reality and the importance of which are clearly evidenced by long usage.
6. The system of straight baselines may not be applied by a State in such a manner as to cut off the territorial sea of another State from the high seas or an exclusive economic zone.
Art. 8. Internal waters
1. Except as provided in Part IV, waters on the landward side of the baseline of the territorial sea form part of the internal waters of the State.
2. Where the establishment of a straight baseline in accordance with the method set forth in article 7 has the effect of enclosing as internal waters areas which had not previously been considered as such, a right of innocent passage as provided in this Convention shall exist in those waters.
Art. 9. Mouths of rivers
If a river flows directly into the sea, the baseline shall be a straight line across the mouth of the river between points on the low-water line of its banks.
Art. 10. Bays
1. This article relates to bays the coasts of which belong to a single State.
2. For the purposes of this Convention, a bay is a well-marked indentation whose penetration is in such proportion to the width of its mouth as to contain landlocked waters and constitute more than a mere curvature of the coast. An indentation shall not, however, be regarded as a bay unless its area is as large as, or larger than, that of the semi-circle whose diameter is a line drawn across the mouth of that indentation.
3. For the purpose of measurement, the area of an indentation is that lying between the low-water mark around the shore of the indentation and a line joining the low-water mark of its natural entrance points. Where, because of the presence of islands, an indentation has more than one mouth, the semi-circle shall be drawn on a line as long as the sum total of the lengths of the lines across the different mouths. Islands within an indentation shall be included as if they were part of the water area of the indentation.
4. If the distance between the low-water marks of the natural entrance points of a bay does not exceed 24 nautical miles, a closing line may be drawn between these two low-water marks, and the waters enclosed thereby shall be considered as internal waters.
5. Where the distance between the low-water marks of the natural entrance points of a bay exceeds 24 nautical miles, a straight baseline of 24 nautical miles shall be drawn within the bay in such a manner as to enclose the maximum area of water that is possible with a line of that length.
6. The foregoing provisions do not apply to so-called 'historic' bays, or in any case where the system of straight baselines provided for in article 7 is applied.
Art. 11. Ports

For the purpose of delimiting the territorial sea, the outermost permanent harbour works which form an integral part of the harbour system are regarded as forming part of the coast. Off-shore installations and artificial islands shall not be considered as permanent harbour works.

Art. 12. Roadsteads
Roadsteads which are normally used for the loading, unloading and anchoring of ships, and which would otherwise be situated wholly or partly outside the outer limits of the territorial sea, are included in the territorial sea.

Art. 13. Low-tide elevations
1. A low-tide elevation is a naturally formed area of land which is surrounded by and above water at low tide but submerged at high tide. Where a low-tide elevation is situated wholly or partly at a distance not exceeding the breadth of the territorial sea from the mainland or an island, the low-water line on that elevation may be used as the baseline for measuring the breadth of the territorial sea.
2. Where a low-tide elevation is wholly situated at a distance exceeding the breadth of the territorial sea from the mainland or an island, it has no territorial sea of its own.

Art. 14. Combination of methods for determining baselines
The coastal State may determine baselines in turn by any of the methods provided for in the foregoing articles to suit different conditions.

Art. 15. Delimitation of the territorial sea between States with opposite or adjacent coasts
Where the coasts of two States are opposite or adjacent to each other, neither of the two States is entitled, failing agreement between them to the contrary, to extend its territorial sea beyond the median line every point of which is equidistant from the nearest points on the baselines from which the breadth of the territorial seas of each of the two States is measured. The above provision does not apply, however, where it is necessary by reason of historic title or other special circumstances to delimit the territorial seas of the two States in a way which is at variance therewith.

Art. 16. Charts and lists of geographical co-ordinates
1. The baselines for measuring the breadth of the territorial sea determined in accordance with articles 7, 9 and 10, or the limits derived therefrom, and the lines of delimitation drawn in accordance with articles 12 and 15 shall be shown on charts of a scale or scales adequate for ascertaining their position. Alternatively, a list of geographical co-ordinates of points, specifying the geodetic datum, may be substituted.
2. The coastal State shall give due publicity to such charts or lists of geographical co-ordinates and shall deposit a copy of each such chart or list with the Secretary-General of the United Nations.

Section 3. Innocent passage in the territorial sea
Subsection A. Rules applicable to all ships

Art. 17. Right of innocent passage
Subject to this Convention, ships of all States, whether coastal or land-locked, enjoy the right of innocent passage through the territorial sea.

Art. 18. Meaning of passage
1. Passage means navigation through the territorial sea for the purpose of:
(a) traversing that sea without entering internal waters or calling at a roadstead or port facility outside internal waters; or
(b) proceeding to or from internal waters or a call at such roadstead or port facility.
2. Passage shall be continuous and expeditious. However, passage includes stopping and anchoring, but only in so far as the same are incidental to ordinary navigation or are rendered necessary by *force majeure* or distress or for the purpose of rendering assistance to persons, ships or aircraft in danger or distress.

Art. 19. Meaning of innocent passage
1. Passage is innocent so long as it is not prejudicial to the peace, good order or security of the coastal State. Such passage shall take place in conformity with this Convention and with other rules of international law.
2. Passage of a foreign ship shall be considered to be prejudicial to the peace, good order or security of the coastal State if in the territorial sea it engages in any of the following activities:
(a) any threat or use of force against the sovereignty, territorial integrity or political independence of the coastal State, or in any other manner in violation of the principles of international law embodied in the Charter of the United Nations;
(b) any exercise or practice with weapons of any kind;
(c) any act aimed at collecting information to the prejudice of the defence or security of the coastal State;
(d) any act of propaganda aimed at affecting the defence or security of the coastal State;
(e) the launching, landing or taking on board of any aircraft;
(f) the launching, landing or taking on board of any military device;
(g) the loading or unloading of any commodity, currency or person contrary to the customs, fiscal, immigration or sanitary laws and regulations of the coastal State;
(h) any act of wilful and serious pollution contrary to this Convention;
(i) any fishing activities;
(j) the carrying out of research or survey activities;
(k) any act aimed at interfering with any systems of communication or any other facilities or installations of the coastal State;
(l) any other activity not having a direct bearing on passage.

Art. 20. Submarines and other underwater vehicles
In the territorial sea, submarines and other underwater vehicles are required to navigate on the surface and to show their flag.

Art. 21. Laws and regulations of the coastal State relating to innocent passage
1. The coastal State may adopt laws and regulations, in conformity with the provisions of this Convention and other rules if international law, relating to innocent passage through the territorial sea, in respect of all or any of the following:
(a) the safety of navigation and the regulation of maritime traffic;
(b) the protection of navigational aids and facilities and other facilities or installations;
(c) the protection of cables and pipelines;
(d) the conservation of the living resources of the sea;
(e) the prevention of infringement of the fisheries laws and regulations of the coastal State;
(f) the preservation of the environment of the coastal State and the prevention, reduction and control of pollution thereof;
(g) marine scientific research and hydrographic surveys;
(h) the prevention of infringement of the customs, fiscal, immigration or sanitary laws and regulations of the coastal State.
2. Such laws and regulations shall not apply to the design, construction, manning or equipment of foreign ships unless they are giving effect to generally accepted international rules or standards.
3. The coastal State shall give due publicity to all such laws and regulations.
4. Foreign ships exercising the right of innocent passage through the territorial sea shall comply with all such laws and regulations and all generally accepted international regulations relating to the prevention of collisions at sea.

Art. 22. Sea lanes and traffic separation schemes in the territorial sea
1. The coastal State may, where necessary having regard to the safety of navigation, require foreign ships exercising the right of innocent passage through its territorial sea to use such lanes and traffic separation schemes as it may designate or prescribe for the regulation of the passage of ships.
2. In particular, tankers, nuclear-powered ships and ships carrying nuclear or other inherently dangerous or noxious substances or materials may be required to confine their passage to such sea lanes.
3. In the designation of sea lanes and the prescription of traffic separation schemes under this article, the coastal State shall take into account:
(a) the recommendations of the competent international organization;
(b) any channels customarily used for international navigation;
(c) the special characteristics of particular ships and channels; and
(d) the density of traffic.
4. The coastal State shall clearly indicate such sea lanes and traffic separation schemes on charts to which due publicity shall be given.

Art. 23. Foreign nuclear-powered ships and ships carrying nuclear or other inherently dangerous or noxious substances
Foreign nuclear-powered ships and ships carrying nuclear or other inherently dangerous or noxious substances shall, when exercising the right of innocent passage through the territorial sea, carry documents and observe special precautionary measures established for such ships by international agreements.

Art. 24. Duties of the coastal State
1. The coastal State shall not hamper the innocent passage of foreign ships through the territorial sea except in accordance with this Convention. In particular, in the application of this Convention or of any laws or regulations adopted in conformity with this Convention, the coastal State shall not:
(a) impose requirements on foreign ships which have the practical effect of denying or impairing the right of innocent passage; or
(b) discriminate in form or in fact against the ships of any State or against ships carrying cargoes to, from or on behalf of any State.
2. The coastal State shall give appropriate publicity to any danger to navigation, of which it has knowledge, within its territorial sea.

Art. 25. Rights of protection of the coastal State
1. The coastal State may take the necessary steps in its territorial sea to prevent passage which is not innocent.
2. In the case of ships proceeding to internal waters or a call at a port facility outside internal waters, the coastal State also has the right to take the necessary steps to prevent any breach of the conditions to which admission of those ships to internal waters or such a call is subject.
3. The coastal State may, without discrimination in form or in fact among foreign ships, suspend temporarily in specified areas of its territorial sea the innocent passage of foreign ships if such suspension is essential for the protection of its security, including weapons exercises. Such suspension shall take effect only after having been duly published.

Art. 26. Charges which may be levied upon foreign ships
1. No charge may be levied upon foreign ships by reason only of their passage through the territorial sea.
2. Charges may be levied upon a foreign ship passing through the territorial sea as payment only for specific services rendered to the ship. These charges shall be levied without discrimination.

Subsection B. Rules applicable to merchant ships and government ships operated for commercial purposes.
Art. 27. Criminal jurisdiction on board a foreign ship
1. The criminal jurisdiction of the coastal State should not be exercised on board a foreign ship passing through the territorial sea to arrest any person or to conduct any investigation in connection with any crime committed on board the ship during its passage, save only in the following cases:
(a) if the consequences of the crime extend to the coastal State;
(b) if the crime is of a kind to disturb the peace of the country or the good order of the territorial sea;
(c) if the assistance of the local authorities has been requested by the master of the ship or by a diplomatic agent or consular officer of the flag State; or
(d) if such measures are necessary for the suppression of illicit traffic in narcotic drugs or psychotropic substances.
2. The above provisions do not affect the right of the coastal State to take any steps authorized by its laws for the purpose of an arrest or investigation on board a foreign ship passing through the territorial sea after leaving internal waters.
3. In the cases provided for in paragraphs 1 and 2, the coastal State shall, if the master so requests, notify a diplomatic agent or consular officer of the flag State before taking any steps, and shall facilitate contact between such agent or officer and the ship's crew. In cases of emergency this notification may be communicated while the measures are being taken.
4. In considering whether or in what manner an arrest should be made, the local authorities shall have due regard to the interests of navigation.
5. Except as provided in Part XII or with respect to violations of laws and regulations adopted in accordance with Part V, the coastal State may not take any steps on board a foreign ship passing through the territorial sea to arrest any person or to conduct any investigation in connection with any crime committed before

the ship entered the territorial sea, if the ship, proceeding from a foreign port, is only passing through the territorial sea without entering internal waters.

Art. 28. Civil jurisdiction in relation to foreign ships

1. The coastal State should not stop or divert a foreign ship passing through the territorial sea for the purpose of exercising civil jurisdiction in relation to a person on board the ship.
2. The coastal State may not levy execution against or arrest the ship for the purpose of any civil proceedings, save only in respect of obligations or liabilities assumed or incurred by the ship itself in the course or for the purpose of its voyage through the waters of the coastal State.
3. Paragraph 2 is without prejudice to the right of the coastal State, in accordance with its laws, to levy execution against or to arrest, for the purpose of any civil proceedings, a foreign ship lying in the territorial sea, or passing through the territorial sea after leaving internal waters.

Subsection C. Rules applicable to warships and other government ships operated for non-commercial purposes.

Art. 29. Definition of warships

For the purposes of this Convention, 'warship' means a ship belonging to the armed forces of a State bearing the external marks distinguishing such ships of its nationality, under the command of an officer duly commissioned by the government of the State and whose name appears in the appropriate service list or its equivalent, and manned by a crew which is under regular armed forces discipline.

Art. 30. Non-compliance by warships with the laws and regulations of the coastal State

If any warship does not comply with the laws and regulations of the coastal State concerning passage through the territorial sea and disregards any request for compliance therewith which is made to it, the coastal State may require it to leave the territorial sea immediately.

Art. 31. Responsibility of the flag State for damage caused by a warship or other government ship operated for non-commercial purposes

The flag State shall bear international responsibility for any loss or damage to the coastal State resulting from the non-compliance by a warship or other government ship operated for non-commercial purposes with the laws and regulations of the coastal State concerning passage through the territorial sea or with the provisions of this Convention or other rules of international law.

Art. 32. Immunities of warships and other government ships operated for non-commercial purposes

With such exceptions as are contained in subsection A and in articles 30 and 31, nothing in this Convention affects the immunities of warships and other government ships operated for non-commercial purposes.

Section 4. Contiguous zone

Art. 33. Contiguous zone

1. In a zone contiguous to its territorial sea, described as the contiguous zone, the coastal State may exercise the control necessary to:
(a) prevent infringement of its customs, fiscal, immigration or sanitary laws and regulations within its territory or territorial sea;
(b) punish infringement of the above laws and regulations committed within its territory or territorial sea.
2. The contiguous zone may not extend beyond 24 nautical miles from the baselines from which the breadth of the territorial sea is measured.

Part III Straits used for international navigation

Section 1. General Provisions

Art. 34. Legal status of waters forming straits used for international navigation

1. The régime of passage through straits used for international navigation established in this Part shall not in other respects affect the legal status of the waters forming such straits or the exercise by the States bordering the straits of their sovereignty or jurisdiction over such waters and their air space, bed and subsoil.
2. The sovereignty or jurisdiction of the States bordering the straits is exercised subject to this Part and to other rules of international law.

Art. 35. Scope of this Part

Nothing in this Part affects:
(a) any areas of internal waters within a strait, except where the establishment of a straight baseline in accordance with the method set forth in article 7 has the effect of enclosing as internal waters areas which had not previously been considered as such;
(b) the legal status of the waters beyond the territorial seas of States bordering straits as exclusive economic zones or high seas; or
(c) the legal régime in straits in which passage is regulated in whole or in part by long-standing international conventions in force specifically relating to such straits.

Art. 36. High seas routes or routes through exclusive economic zones through straits used for international navigation

This Part does not apply to a strait used for international navigation if there exists through the strait a route through the high seas or through an exclusive economic zone of similar convenience with respect to navigational and hydrographical characteristics; in such routes, the other relevant Parts of this Convention, including the provisions regarding the freedoms of navigation and overflight, apply.

Section 2. Transit passage

Art. 37. Scope of this section

This section applies to straits which are used for international navigation between one part of the high seas or an exclusive economic zone and another part of the high seas or an exclusive economic zone.

Art. 38. Right of transit passage

1. In straits referred to in article 37, all ships and aircraft enjoy the right of transit passage, which shall not be impeded; except that, if the strait is formed by an island of a State bordering the strait and its mainland, transit passage shall not apply if there exists seaward of the island a route through the high seas or through an exclusive economic zone of similar convenience with respect to navigational and hydrographical characteristics.
2. Transit passage means the exercise in accordance with this Part of the freedom of navigation and overflight solely for the purpose of continuous and expeditious transit of the strait between one part of the high seas or an exclusive economic zone and another part of the high seas or an exclusive economic zone. However, the requirement of continuous and expeditious transit does not preclude passage through the strait for the purpose of entering, leaving or returning from a State bordering the strait, subject to the conditions of entry to that State.
3. Any activity which is not an exercise of the right of transit passage through a strait remains subject to the other applicable provisions of this Convention.

Art. 39. Duties of ships and aircraft during transit passage

1. Ships and aircraft, while exercising the right of transit passage, shall:
(a) proceed without delay through or over the strait;
(b) refrain from any threat or use of force against the sovereignty, territorial integrity or political independence of States bordering the strait, or in any other manner in violation of the principles of international law embodied in the Charter of the United Nations;
(c) refrain from any activities other than those incident to their normal modes of continuous and expeditious transit unless rendered necessary by *force majeure* or by distress;
(d) comply with other relevant provisions of this Part.
2. Ships in transit passage shall:
(a) comply with generally accepted international regulations, procedures and practices for safety at sea, including the International Regulations for Preventing Collisions at Sea;
(b) comply with generally accepted international regulations, procedures and practices for the prevention, reduction and control of pollution from ships.
3. Aircraft in transit passage shall:
(a) observe the Rules of the Air established by the International Civil Aviation Organization as they apply to civil aircraft; state aircraft will normally comply with such safety measures and will at all times operate with due regard for the safety of navigation;
(b) at all times monitor the radio frequency assigned by the competent internationally designated air traffic control authority or the appropriate international distress radio frequency.

Art. 40. Research and survey activities

During transit passage, foreign ships, including marine scientific research and hydrographic survey ships, may not carry out any research or survey activities without the prior authorization of the States bordering straits.

Art. 41. Sea lanes and traffic separation schemes in straits used for international navigation

1. In conformity with this Part, States bordering straits may designate sea lanes and prescribe traffic separation schemes for navigation in straits where necessary to promote the safe passage of ships.
2. Such States may, when circumstances require, and after giving due publicity thereto, substitute other sea lanes or traffic separation schemes for any sea lanes or traffic separation schemes previously designated or prescribed by them.
3. Such sea lanes and traffic separation schemes shall conform to generally accepted international regulations.
4. Before designating or substituting sea lanes or prescribing or substituting traffic separation schemes, States bordering straits shall refer proposals to the competent international organization with a view to their adoption. The organization may adopt only such sea lanes and traffic separation schemes as may be agreed with the States bordering the straits, after which the States may designate, prescribe or substitute them.
5. In respect of a strait where sea lanes or traffic separation schemes through the waters of two or more States bordering the strait are being proposed, the States concerned shall co-operate in formulating proposals in consultation with the competent international organization.
6. States bordering straits shall clearly indicate all sea lanes and traffic separation schemes designated or prescribed by them on charts to which due publicity shall be given.
7. Ships in transit passage shall respect applicable sea lanes and traffic separation schemes established in accordance with this article.

Art. 42. Laws and regulations of States bordering straits relating to transit passage.

1. Subject to the provisions of this section, States bordering straits may adopt laws and regulations relating to transit passage through straits, in respect of all or any of the following:
(a) the safety of navigation and the regulation of maritime traffic, as provided in article 41;
(b) the prevention, reduction and control of pollution, by giving effect to applicable international regulations regarding the discharge of oil, oily wastes and other noxious substances in the strait;
(c) with respect to fishing vessels, the prevention of fishing, including the stowage of fishing gear;
(d) the loading or unloading of any commodity, currency or person in contravention of the customs, fiscal, immigration or sanitary laws and regulations of States bordering straits.
2. Such laws and regulations shall not discriminate in form or in fact among foreign ships or in their application have the practical effect of denying, hampering or impairing the right of transit passage as defined in this section.
3. States bordering straits shall give due publicity to all such laws and regulations.
4. Foreign ships exercising the right of transit passage shall comply with such laws and regulations.
5. The flag State of a ship or the State of registry of an aircraft entitled to sovereign immunity which acts in a manner contrary to such laws and regulations or other provisions of this Part shall bear international responsibility for any loss or damage which results to States bordering straits.

Art. 43. Navigational and safety aids and other improvements and the prevention, reduction and control of pollution

User States and States bordering a strait should by agreement co-operate:
(a) in the establishment and maintenance in a strait of necessary navigational and safety aids or other improvements in aid of international navigation; and
(b) for the prevention, reduction and control of pollution from ships.

Art. 44. Duties of States bordering straits

States bordering straits shall not hamper transit passage and shall give appropriate publicity to any danger to navigation or overflight within or over the strait of which they have knowledge. There shall be no suspension of transit passage.

Section 3. Innocent passage

Art. 45. Innocent passage

1. The régime of innocent passage, in accordance with Part II, section 3, shall apply in straits used for international navigation:
(a) excluded from the application of the régime of transit passage under article 38, paragraph 1; or
(b) between a part of the high seas or an exclusive economic zone and the territorial sea of a foreign State.
2. There shall be no suspension of innocent passage through such straits.

Part IV   Archipelagic States
Art. 46. Use of terms
For the purposes of this Convention:
(a) 'archipelagic State' means a State constituted wholly by one or more archipelagos and may include other islands;
(b) 'archipelago' means a groups of islands, including part of islands, inter-connecting waters and other natural features which are so closely inter-related that such islands, waters and other natural features form an intrinsic geographical, economic and political entity, or which historically have been regarded as such.
Art. 47. Archipelagic baselines
1. An archipelagic State may draw straight archipelagic baselines joining the outermost points of the outermost islands and drying reefs of the archipelago provided that within such baselines are included the main islands and an area in which the ratio of the area of the water to the area of the land, including atolls, is between 1 to 1 and 9 to 1.
2. The length of such baselines shall not exceed 100 nautical miles, except that up to 3 per cent of the total number of baselines enclosing any archipelago may exceed that length, up to a maximum length of 125 nautical miles.
3. The drawing of such baselines shall not depart to any appreciable extent from the general configuration of the archipelago.
4. Such baselines shall not be drawn to and from low-tide elevations, unless lighthouses or similar installations which are permanently above sea level have been built on them or where a low-tide elevation is situated wholly or partly at a distance not exceeding the breadth of the territorial sea from the nearest island.
5. The system of such baselines shall not be applied by an archipelagic State in such a manner as to cut off from the high seas or the exclusive economic zone the territorial sea of another State.
6. If a part of the archipelagic waters of an archipelagic State lies between two parts of an immediately adjacent neighbouring State, existing rights and all other legitimate interests which the latter State has traditionally exercised in such waters and all rights stipulated by agreement between those States shall continue and be respected.
7. For the purpose of computing the ratio of water to land under paragraph 1, land areas may include waters lying within the fringing reefs of islands and atolls, including that part of a steep-sided oceanic plateau which is enclosed or nearly enclosed by a chain of limestone islands and drying reefs lying on the perimeter of the plateau.
8. The baselines drawn in accordance with this article shall be shown on charts of a scale adequate for ascertaining their position. Alternatively, lists of geographical co-ordinates of points, specifying the geodetic datum, may be substituted.
9. The archipelagic State shall give due publicity to such charts or lists of geographical co-ordinates and shall deposit a copy of each such chart or list with the Secretary-General of the United Nations.
Art. 48. Measurement of the breadth of the territorial sea, the contiguous zone, the exclusive economic zone and the continental shelf
The breadth of the territorial sea, the contiguous zone, the exclusive economic zone and the continental shelf shall be measured from archipelagic baselines drawn in accordance with article 47.
Art. 49. Legal status of archipelagic waters, of the air space over archipelagic waters and of their bed and subsoil
1. The sovereignty of an archipelagic State extends to the waters enclosed by the archipelagic baselines drawn in accordance with article 47, described as archipelagic waters, regardless of their depth or distance from the coast.

2. This sovereignty extends to the air space over the archipelagic waters, as well as to their bed and subsoil, and the resources contained therein.
3. This sovereignty is exercised subject to this Part.
4. The regime of archipelagic sea lanes passage established in this Part shall not in other respects affect the status of the archipelagic waters, including the sea lanes, or the exercise by the archipelagic State of its sovereignty over such waters and their air space, bed and subsoil, and the resources contained therein.
Art. 50. Delimitation of internal waters
Within its archipelagic waters, the archipelagic State may draw closing lines for the delimitation of internal waters, in accordance with articles 9, 10 and 11.
Art. 51. Existing agreements, traditional fishing rights and existing submarine cables
1. Without prejudice to article 49, an archipelagic State shall respect existing agreements with other States and shall recognize traditional fishing rights and other legitimate activities of the immediately adjacent neighbouring States in certain areas falling within archipelagic waters. The terms and conditions for the exercise of such rights and activities, including the nature, the extent and the areas to which they apply, shall, at the request of any of the States concerned, be regulated by bilateral agreements between them. Such rights shall not be transferred to or shared with third States or their nationals.
2. An archipelagic State shall respect existing submarine cables laid by other States and passing through its waters without making a landfall. An archipelatgic State shall permit the maintenance and replacement of such cables upon receiving due notice of their location and the intention to repair or replace them.
Art. 52. Right of innocent passage
1. Subject to article 53 and without prejudice to article 50, ships of all States enjoy the right of innocent passage through archipelagic waters, in accordance with Part II, section 3.
2. The archipelagic State may, without discrimination in form or in fact among foreign ships, suspend temporarily in specified areas of its archipelagic waters the innocent passage of foreign ships if such suspension is essential for the protection of its security. Such suspension shall take effect only after having been duly published.
Art. 53. Right of archipelagic sea lanes passage
1. An archipelagic State may designate sea lanes and air routes thereabove, suitable for the continuous and expeditious passage of foreign ships and aircraft through or over its archipelagic waters and the adjacent territorial sea.
2. All ships and aircraft enjoy the right of archipelagic sea lanes passage in such sea lanes and air routes.
3. Archipelagic sea lanes passage means the exercise in accordance with this Convention of the rights of navigation and overflight in the normal mode solely for the purpose of continuous, expeditious and unobstructed transit between one part of the high seas or an exclusive economic zone and another part of the high seas or an exclusive economic zone.
4. Such sea lanes and air routes shall traverse the archipelagic waters and the adjacent territorial sea and shall include all normal passage routes used as routes for international navigation or overflight through or over archipelagic waters and, within such routes, so far as ships are concerned, all normal navigational channels, provided that duplication of routes of similar convenience between the same entry and exit points shall not be necessary.
5. Such sea lanes and air routes shall be defined by a series of continuous axis lines from the entry points of passage routes to the exit points. Ships and aircraft in archipelagic sea lanes passage shall not deviate more than 25 nautical miles to either side of such axis lines during passage, provided that such ships and aircraft shall not navigate closer to the coasts than 10 per cent of the distance between the nearest points on islands bordering the sea lane.
6. An archipelagic State which designates sea lanes under this article may also prescribe traffic separation schemes for the safe passage of ships through narrow channels in such sea lanes.
7. An archipelagic State may, when circumstances require, after giving due publicity thereto, substitute other sea lanes or traffic separation schemes for any sea lanes or traffic separation schemes previously designated or prescribed by it.

8. Such sea lanes and traffic separation schemes shall conform to generally accepted international regulations.
9. In designating or substituting sea lanes or prescribing or substituting traffic separation schemes, an archipelagic State shall refer proposals to the competent international organization with a view to their adoption. The organization may adopt only such sea lanes and traffic separation schemes as may be agreed with the archipelagic State, after which the archipelagic State may designate, prescribe or substitute them.
10. The archipelagic State shall clearly indicate the axis of the sea lanes and the traffic separation schemes designated or prescribed by it on charts to which due publicity shall be given.
11. Ships in the archipelagic sea lanes passage shall respect applicable sea lanes and traffic separation schemes established in accordance with this article.
12. If an archipelagic State does not designate sea lanes or air routes, the right of archipelagic sea lanes passage may be exercised through the routes normally used for international navigation.
Art. 54. Duties of ships and aircraft during their passage, research and survey activities, duties of the archipelagic State and laws and regulations of the archipelagic State relating to archipelagic sea lanes passage
Articles 39, 40, 42 and 44 apply *mutatis mutandis* to archipelagic sea lanes passage.

Part V.   Exclusive economic zone
Art. 55. Specific legal régime of the exclusive economic zone
The exclusive economic zone is an area beyond and adjacent to the territorial sea, subject to the specific legal régime established in this Part, under which the rights and jurisdiction of the coastal State and the rights and freedoms of other States are governed by the relevant provisions of this Convention.
Art. 56. Rights, jurisdiction and duties of the coastal State in the exclusive economic zone
1. In the exclusive economic zone, the coastal State has:
(a) sovereign rights for the purpose of exploring and exploiting, conserving and managing the natural resources, whether living or non-living, of the waters superjacent to the sea-bed and of the sea-bed and its subsoil, and with regard to other activities for the economic exploitation and exploration of the zone, such as the production of energy from the water, currents and winds;
(b) jurisdiction as provided for in the relevant provisions of this Convention with regard to:
(i) the establishment and use of artificial islands, installations and structures;
(ii) marine scientific research;
(iii) the protection and preservation of the marine environment;
(c) other rights and duties provided for in this Convention.
2. In exercising its rights and performing its duties under this Convention in the exclusive economic zone, the coastal State shall have due regard to the rights and duties of other States and shall act in a manner compatible with the provisions of this Convention.
3. The rights set out in this article with respect to the sea-bed and subsoil shall be exercised in accordance with Part VI.
Art. 57. Breadth of the exclusive economic zone
The exclusive economic zone shall not extend beyond 200 nautical miles from the baselines from which the breadth of the territorial sea is measured.
Art. 58. Rights and duties of other States in the exclusive economic zone
1. In the exclusive economic zone, all States, whether coastal or land-locked, enjoy, subject to the relevant provisions of this Convention, the freedoms referred to in article 87 of navigation and overflight and of the laying of submarine cables and pipelines, and other internationally lawful uses of the sea related to these freedoms, such as those associated with the operation of ships, aircraft and submarine cables and pipelines, and compatible with the other provisions of this Convention.
2. Articles 88 to 115 and other pertinent rules of international law apply to the exclusive economic zone in so far as they are not incompatible with this Part.
3. In exercising their rights and performing their duties under this Convention in the exclusive economic zone, States shall have due regard to the rights and duties of the coastal State and shall comply with the laws and

regulations adopted by the coastal State in accordance with the provisions of this Convention and other rules of international law in so far as they are not incompatible with this Part.

Art. 59. Basis for the resolution of conflicts regarding the attribution of rights and jurisdiction in the exclusive economic zone

In cases where this Convention does not attribute rights or jurisdiction to the coastal State or to other States within the exclusive economic zone, and a conflict arises between the interests of the coastal State and any other State or States, the conflict should be resolved on the basis of equity and in the light of all the relevant circumstances, taking into account the respective importance of the interests involved to the parties as well as to the international community as a whole.

Art. 60. Artificial islands, installations and structures in the exclusive economic zone

1. In the exclusive economic zone, the coastal State shall have the exclusive right to construct and to authorize and regulate the construction, operation and use of:
(a) artificial islands;
(b) installations and structures for the purposes provided for in article 56 and other economic purposes;
(c) installations and structures which may interfere with the exercise of the rights of the coastal State in the zone.
2. The coastal State shall have exclusive jurisdiction over such artificial islands, installations and structures, including jurisdiction with regard to customs, fiscal, health, safety and immigration laws and regulations.
3. Due notice must be given of the construction of such artificial islands, installations or structures, and permanent means for giving warning of their presence must be maintained. Any installations or structures which are abandoned or disused shall be removed to ensure safety of navigation, taking into account any generally accepted international standards established in this regard by the competent international organization. Such removal shall also have due regard to fishing, the protection of the marine environment and the rights and duties of other States. Appropriate publicity shall be given to the depth, position and dimensions of any installations or structures not entirely removed.
4. The coastal State may, where necessary, establish reasonable safety zones around such artificial islands, installations and structures in which it may take appropriate measures to ensure the safety both of navigation and of the artificial islands, installations and structures.
5. The breadth of the safety zones shall be determined by the coastal State, taking into account applicable international standards. Such zones shall be designed to ensure that they are reasonably related to the nature and function of the artificial islands, installations or structures, and shall not exceed a distance of 500 metres around them, measured from each point of their outer edge, except as authorized by generally accepted international standards or as recommended by the competent international organization. Due notice shall be given of the extent of safety zones.
6. All ships must respect these safety zones and shall comply with generally accepted international standards regarding navigation in the vicinity of artificial islands, installations, structures and safety zones.
7. Artificial islands, installations and structures and the safety zones around them may not be established where interference may be caused to the use of recognized sea lanes essential to international navigation.
8. Artificial islands, installations and structures do not possess the status of islands. They have no territorial sea of their own, and their presence does not affect the delimitation of the territorial sea, the exclusive economic zone or the continental shelf.

Art. 61. Conservation of the living resources

1. The coastal State shall determine the allowable catch of the living resources in its exclusive economic zone.
2. The coastal State, taking into account the best scientific evidence available to it, shall ensure through proper conservation and management measures that the maintenance of the living resources in the exclusive economic zone is not endangered by over-exploitation. As appropriate, the coastal State and competent international organizations, whether subregional, regional or global, shall co-operate to this end.
3. Such measures shall also be designed to maintain or restore populations of harvested species at levels which can produce the maximum sustainable yield, as qualified by relevant environmental and economic factors, including the economic needs of coastal fishing communities and the special requirements of developing States, and taking into account fishing patterns, the interdependence of stocks and any generally recommended international minimum standards, whether subregional, regional or global.
4. In taking such measures the coastal State shall take into consideration the effects on species associated with or dependent upon harvested species with a view to maintaining or restoring populations of such associated or dependent species above levels at which their reproduction may become seriously threatened.
5. Available scientific information, catch and fishing effort statistics, and other data relevant to the conservation of fish stocks shall be contributed and exchanged on a regular basis through competent international organizations, whether subregional, regional or global, where appropriate and with participation by all States concerned, including States whose nationals are allowed to fish in the exclusive economic zone.

Art. 62. Utilization of the living resources

1. The coastal State shall promote the objective of optimum utilization of the living resources in the exclusive economic zone without prejudice to article 61.
2. The coastal State shall determine its capacity to harvest the living resources of the exclusive economic zone. Where the coastal State does not have the capacity to harvest the entire allowable catch, it shall, through agreements or other arrangements and pursuant to the terms, conditions, laws and regulations referred to in paragraph 4, give other States access to the surplus of the allowable catch, having particular regard to the provisions of articles 69 and 70, especially in relations to the developing States mentioned therein.
3. In giving access to other States to its exclusive economic zone under this article, the coastal State shall take into account all relevant factors, including, *inter alia*, the significance of the living resources of the area to the economy of the coastal State concerned and its other national interests, the provisions of articles 69 and 70, the requirements of developing States in the subregion or region in harvesting part of the surplus and the need to minimize economic dislocation in States whose nationals have habitually fished in the zone or which have made substantial efforts in research and identification of stocks.
4. Nationals of other States fishing in the exclusive economic zone shall comply with the conservation measures and with the other terms and conditions established in the laws and regulations of the coastal State. These laws and regulations shall be consistent with this Convention and may relate, *inter alia*, to the following:
(a) licensing of fishermen, fishing vessels and equipment, including payment of fees and other forms of remuneration, which, in the case of developing coastal States, may consist of adequate compensation in the field of financing, equipment and technology relating to the fishing industry;
(b) determining the species which may be caught, and fixing quotas of catch, whether in relation to particular stocks or groups of stocks or catch per vessel over a period of time or to the catch by nationals of any State during a specific period;
(c) regulating seasons and areas of fishing, the types, sizes and amount of gear, and the types, sizes and number of fishing vessels that may be used;
(d) fixing the age and size of fish and other species that may be caught;
(e) specifying information required of fishing vessels, including catch and effort statistics and vessel position reports;
(f) requiring, under the authorization and control of the coastal State, the conduct of specified fisheries research programmes and regulating the conduct of such research, including the sampling of catches, disposition of samples and reporting of associated scientific data;
(g) the placing of observers or trainees on board such vessels by the coastal State;
(h) the landing of all or any part of the catch by such vessels in the ports of the coastal State;
(i) terms and conditions relating to joint ventures or other co-operative arrangements;
(j) requirements for the training of personnel and the transfer of fisheries technology, including enhancement of the coastal State's capability of undertaking fisheries research;
(k) enforcement procedures.
5. Coastal States shall give due notice of conservation and management laws and regulations.

Art. 63. Stocks occurring within the exclusive economic zones of two or more coastal States or both within the exclusive economic zone and in an area beyond and adjacent to it

1. Where the same stock or stocks of associated species occur within the exclusive economic zones of two or more coastal States, these States shall seek, either directly or through appropriate subregional or regional organizations, to agree upon the measures necessary to co-ordinate and ensure the conservation and development of such stocks without prejudice to the other provisions of this Part.
2. Where the same stock or stocks of associated species occur both within the exclusive economic zone and in an area beyond and adjacent to the zone, the coastal State and States fishing for such stocks in the adjacent area shall seek, either directly or through appropriate subregional or regional organizations, to agree upon the measures necessary for the conservation of these stocks in the adjacent area.

Art. 64. Highly migratory species

1. The coastal State and other States whose nationals fish in the region for the highly migratory species listed in Annex I shall co-operate directly or through appropriate international organizations with a view to ensuring conservation and promoting the objective of optimum utilization of such species throughout the region, both within and beyond the exclusive economic zone. In regions for which no appropriate international organization exists, the coastal State and other States whose nationals harvest these species in the region shall co-operate to establish such an organization and participate in its work.
2. The provisions of paragraph 1 apply in addition to the other provisions of this Part.

Art. 65. Marine mammals

Nothing in this Part restricts the right of a coastal State or the competence of an international organization, as appropriate, to prohibit, limit or regulate the exploitation of marine mammals more strictly than provided for in this Part. States shall co-operate with a view to the conservation of marine mammals and in the case of cetaceans shall in particular work through the appropriate international organizations for their conservation, management and study.

Art. 66. Anadromous stocks

1. States in whose rivers anadromous stocks originate shall have the primary interest in and responsibility for such stocks.
2. The State of origin of anadromous stocks shall ensure their conservation by the establishment of appropriate regulatory measures for fishing in all waters landward of the outer limits of its exclusive economic zone and for fishing provided for in paragraph 3(b). The State of origin may, after consultations with the other States referred to in paragraphs 3 and 4 fishing these stocks, establish total allowable catches for stocks originating in its rivers.
3. (a) Fisheries for anadromous stocks shall be conducted only in waters landward of the outer limits of exclusive economic zones, except in cases where this provision would result in economic dislocation for a State other than the State of origin. With respect to such fishing beyond the outer limits of the exclusive economic zone, States concerned shall maintain consultations with a view to achieving agreement on terms and conditions of such fishing giving due regard to the conservation requirements and the needs of the State of origin in respect of these stocks.
(b) The State of origin shall co-operate in minimizing economic dislocation in such other States fishing these stocks, taking into account the normal catch and the mode of operations of such States, and all the areas in which such fishing has occurred.
(c) States referred to in subparagraph (b), participating by agreement with the State or origin in measures to renew anadromous stocks, particularly by expenditures for that purpose, shall be given special consideration by the State of origin in the harvesting of stocks originating in its rivers.

(d) Enforcement of regulations regarding anadromous stocks beyond the exclusive economic zone shall be by agreement between the State of origin and the other States concerned.

4. In cases where anadromous stocks migrate into or through the waters landward of the outer limits of the exclusive economic zone of a State other than the State of origin, such State shall co-operate with the State of origin with regard to the conservation and management of such stocks.

5. The State of origin of anadromous stocks and other States fishing these stocks shall make arrangements for the implementation of the provisions of this article, where appropriate, through regional organizations.

Art. 67. Catadromous species

1. A coastal State in whose waters catadromous species spend the greater part of their life cycle shall have responsibility for the management of these species and shall ensure the ingress and egress of migrating fish.

2. Harvesting of catadromous species shall be conducted only in waters landward of the outer limits of the exclusive economic zones. When conducted in exclusive economic zones, harvesting shall be subject to this article and other provisions of this Convention concerning fishing in these zones.

3. In cases where catadromous fish migrate through the exclusive economic zone of another State, whether as juvenile or maturing fish, the management, including harvesting, of such fish shall be regulated by agreement between the State mentioned in paragraph 1 and the other State concerned. Such agreement shall ensure the rational management of the species and take into account the responsibilities of the State mentioned in paragraph 1 for the maintenance of these species.

Art. 68. Sedentary species

This Part does not apply to sedentary species as defined in article 77, paragraph 4.

Art. 69. Right of land-locked States

1. Land-locked States shall have the right to participate, on an equitable basis, in the exploitation of an appropriate part of the surplus of the living resources of the exclusive economic zones of coastal States of the same sub-region or region, taking into account the relevant economic and geographical circumstances of all the States concerned and in conformity with the provisions of this article and of articles 61 and 62.

2. The terms and modalities of such participation shall be established by the States concerned through bilateral, subregional or regional agreements taking into account, *inter alia*:

(a) the need to avoid effects detrimental to fishing communities or fishing industries of the coastal State;

(b) the extent to which the land-locked State, in accordance with the provisions of this article, is participating or is entitled to participate under existing bilateral, subregional or regional agreements in the exploitation of living resources of the exclusive economic zones of other coastal States;

(c) the extent to which other land-locked States and geographically disadvantaged States are participating in the exploitation of the living resources of the exclusive economic zone of the coastal State and the consequent need to avoid a particular burden for any single coastal State or a part of it;

(d) the nutritional needs of the populations of the respective States.

3. When the harvesting capacity of a coastal State approaches a point which would enable it to harvest the entire allowable catch of the living resources in its exclusive economic zone, the coastal State and other States concerned shall co-operate in the establishment of equitable arrangements on a bilateral, sub-regional or regional basis to allow for participation of developing land-locked States of the same subregion or region in the exploitation of the living resources of the exclusive economic zones of coastal States of the subregion or region, as may be appropriate in the circumstances and on terms satisfactory to all parties. In the implementation of this provision the factors mentioned in paragraph 2 shall also be taken into account.

4. Developed land-locked States shall, under the provisions of this article, be entitled to participate in the exploitation of living resources only in the exclusive economic zones of developed coastal States of the same subregion or region having regard to the extent to which the coastal State, in giving access to other States to the living resources of its exclusive economic zone, has taken into account the need to minimize detriment-al effects on fishing communities and economic dislocation in States whose nationals have habitually fished in the zone.

5. The above provisions are without prejudice to arrangements agreed upon in subregions or regions where the coastal States may grant to land-locked States of the same subregion or region equal or preferential rights for the exploitation of the living resources in the exclusive economic zones.

Art. 70. Right of geographically disadvantaged States

1. Geographically disadvantaged States shall have the right to participate, on an equitable basis, in the exploitation of an appropriate part of the surplus of the living resources of the exclusive economic zones of coastal States of the same subregion or region, taking into account the relevant economic and geographical circumstances of all the States concerned and in conformity with the provisions of this article and of articles 61 and 62.

2. For the purposes of this Part, 'geographically disadvantaged States' means coastal States, including States bordering enclosed or semi-enclosed seas, whose geographical situation makes them dependent upon the exploitation of the living resources of the exclusive economic zones of other States in the subregion or region for adequate supplies of fish for the nutritional purposes of their populations or parts thereof, and coastal States which can claim no exclusive economic zones of their own.

3. The terms and modalities of such participation shall be established by the States concerned through bilateral, subregional or regional agreements taking into account, *inter alia*:

(a) the need to avoid effects detrimental to fishing communities or fishing industries of the coastal State;

(b) the extent to which the geographically disadvantaged State, in accordance with the provisions of this article, is participating or is entitled to participate under existing bilateral, subregional or regional agreements in the exploitation of living resources of the exclusive economic zones of other coastal States;

(c) the extent to which other geographically disadvantaged States and land-locked States are participating in the exploitation of the living resources of the exclusive economic zone of the coastal State and the consequent need to avoid a particular burden for any single coastal State or a part of it;

(d) the nutritional needs of the populations of the respective States.

4. When the harvesting capacity of a coastal State approaches a point which would enable it to harvest the entire allowable catch of the living resources in its exclusive economic zone, the coastal State and other States concerned shall co-operate in the establishment of equitable arrangements on a bilateral, subregional or regional basis to allow for participation of developing geographically disadvantaged States of the same subregion or region in the exploitation of the living resources of the exclusive economic zones of coastal States of the subregion or region, as may be appropriate in the circumstances and on terms satisfactory to all parties. In the implementation of this provision the factors mentioned in paragraph 3 shall also be taken into account.

5. Developed geographically disadvantaged States shall, under the provisions of this article, be entitled to participate in the exploitation of living resources only in the exclusive economic zones of developed coastal States of the same subregion or region having regard to the extent to which the coastal State, in giving access to other States to the living resources of its exclusive economic zone, has taken into account the need to minimize detrimental effects on fishing communities and economic dislocation in States whose nationals have habitually fished in the zone.

6. The above provisions are without prejudice to arrangements agreed upon in subregions or regions where the coastal States may grant to geographically disadvantaged States of the same subregion or region equal or preferential rights for the exploitation of the living resources in the exclusive economic zones.

Art. 71. Non-applicability of articles 69 and 70

The provisions of articles 69 and 70 do not apply in the case of a coastal State whose economy is overwhelmingly dependent on the exploitation of the living resources of its exclusive economic zone.

Art. 72. Restrictions on transfer of rights

1. Rights provided under articles 69 and 70 to exploit living resources shall not be directly or indirectly transferred to third States or their nationals by lease or licence, by establishing joint ventures or in any other manner which has the effect of such transfer unless otherwise agreed by the State concerned.

2. The foregoing provision does not preclude the States concerned from obtaining technical or financial assistance from third States or international organizations in order to facilitate the exercise of the rights pursuant to articles 69 and 70, provided that it does not have the effect referred to in paragraph 1.

Art. 73. Enforcement of laws and regulations of the coastal State

1. The coastal State may, in the exercise of its sovereign rights to explore, exploit, conserve and manage the living resources in the exclusive economic zone, take such measures, including boarding, inspection, arrest and judicial proceedings, as may be necessary to ensure compliance with the laws and regulations adopted by it in conformity with this Convention.

2. Arrested vessels and their crews shall be promptly released upon the posting of reasonable bond or other security.

3. Coastal State penalties for violations of fisheries laws and regulations in the exclusive economic zone may not include imprisonment, in the absence of agreements to the contrary by the States concerned, or any other form of corporal punishment.

4. In cases of arrest or detention of foreign vessels the coastal State shall promptly notify the flag State, through appropriate channels, of the action taken and of any penalties subsequently imposed.

Art. 74. Delimitation of the exclusive economic zone between States with opposite or adjacent coasts

1. The delimitation of the exclusive economic zone between States with opposite or adjacent coasts shall be effected by agreement on the basis of international law, as referred to in Article 38 of the Statute of the International Court of Justice, in order to achieve an equitable solution.

2. If no agreement can be reached within a reasonable period of time, the States concerned shall resort to the procedures provided for in part XV.

3. Pending agreement as provided for in paragraph 1, the States concerned, in a spirit of understanding and co-operation, shall make every effort to enter into provisional arrangements of a practical nature and, during this transitional period, not to jeopardize or hamper the reaching of the final agreement. Such arrangements shall be without prejudice to the final delimitation.

4. Where there is an agreement in force between the States concerned, questions relating to the delimitation of the exclusive economic zone shall be determined in accordance with the provisions of that agreement.

Art. 75. Charts and lists of geographical co-ordinates

1. Subject to this Part, the outer limit lines of the exclusive economic zone and the lines of delimitation drawn in accordance with article 74 shall be shown on charts of a scale or scales adequate for ascertaining their position. Where appropriate, lists of geographical co-ordinates of points, specifying the geodetic datum, may be substituted for such outer limit lines or lines of delimitation.

2. The coastal State shall give due publicity to such charts or lists of geographical co-ordinates and shall deposit a copy of each such chart or list with the Secretary-General of the United Nations.

Part VI. Continental shelf

Art. 76. Definition of the continental shelf

1. The continental shelf of a coastal State comprises the sea-bed and subsoil of the submarine areas that extend beyond its territorial sea throughout the natural prolongation of its land territory to the outer edge of the continental margin, or to a distance of 200 nautical miles from the baselines from which the breadth of the territorial sea is measured where the outer edge of the continental margin does not extend up to that distance.

2. The continental shelf of a coastal State shall not extend beyond the limits provided for in paragraphs 4 to 6.

3. The continental margin comprises the submerged prolongation of the land mass of the coastal State, and consists of the sea-bed and subsoil of the shelf, the slope and the rise. It does not include the deep ocean floor with its oceanic ridges or the subsoil thereof.

4. (a) For the purposes of this Convention, the coastal State shall establish the outer edge of the continental margin wherever the margin extends beyond 200 nautical miles from the baselines from which the breadth of the territorial sea is measured, by either:

(i) a line delineated in accordance with paragraph 7 by reference to the outermost fixed points at each of which the thickness of sedimentary rocks is at least 1 per cent of the shortest distance from such point to the foot of the continental slope; or

(ii) a line delineated in accordance with paragraph 7 by reference to fixed points not more than 60 nautical miles from the foot of the continental slope.

(b) In the absence of evidence to the contrary, the foot of the continental slope shall be determined as the point of maximum change in the gradient at its base.

5. The fixed points comprising the line of the outer limits of the continental shelf on the sea-bed, drawn in accordance with paragraph 4 (a)(i) and (ii), either shall not exceed 350 nautical miles from the baselines from which the breadth of the territorial sea is measured or shall not exceed 100 nautical miles from the 2,500 metre isobath, which is a line connecting the depth of 2,500 metres.

6. Notwithstanding the provisions of paragraph 5, on submarine ridges, the outer limit of the continental shelf shall not exceed 350 nautical miles from the baselines from which the breadth of the territorial sea is measured. This paragraph does not apply to submarine elevations that are natural components of the continental margin, such as its plateaux, rises, caps, banks and spurs.

7. The coastal State shall delineate the outer limits of its continental shelf, where that shelf extends beyond 200 nautical miles from the baselines from which the breadth of the territorial sea is measured, by straight lines not exceeding 60 nautical miles in length, connecting fixed points, defined by co-ordinates of latitude and longitude.

8. Information on the limits of the continental shelf beyond 200 nautical miles from the baselines from which the breadth of the territorial sea is measured shall be submitted by the coastal State to the Commission on the Limits of the Continental Shelf set up under Annex II on the basis of equitable geographical representation. The Commission shall make recommendations to coastal States on matters related to the establishment of the outer limits of their continental shelf. The limits of the shelf established by a coastal State on the basis of these recommendations shall be final and binding.

9. The coastal State shall deposit with the Secretary-General of the United Nations charts and relevant information, including geodetic data, permanently describing the outer limits of its continental shelf. The Secretary-General shall give due publicity thereto.

10. The provisions of this article are without prejudice to the question of delimitation of the continental shelf between States with opposite or adjacent coasts.

Art. 77. Rights of the coastal State over the continental shelf

1. The coastal State exercises over the continental shelf sovereign rights for the purpose of exploring it and exploiting its natural resources.

2. The rights referred to in paragraph 1 are exclusive in the sense that if the coastal State does not explore the continental shelf or exploit its natural resources, no one may undertake these activities without the express consent of the coastal State.

3. The rights of the coastal State over the continental shelf do not depend on occupation, effective or notional, or on any express proclamation.

4. The natural resources referred to in this Part consist of the mineral and other non-living resources of the sea-bed and subsoil together with living organisms belonging to sedentary species, that is to say, organisms which, at the harvestable stage, either are immobile on or under the sea-bed or are unable to move except in constant physical contact with the sea-bed or the subsoil.

Art. 78. Legal status of the superjacent waters and air space and the rights and freedoms of other States

1. The rights of the coastal State over the continental shelf do not affect the legal status of the superjacent waters or of the air space above those waters.

2. The exercise of the rights of the coastal State over the continental shelf must not infringe or result in any unjustifiable interference with navigation and other rights and freedoms of other States as provided for in this Convention.

Art. 79. Submarine cables and pipelines on the continental shelf

1. All States are entitled to lay submarine cables and pipelines on the continental shelf, in accordance with the provisions of this article.

2. Subject to its right to take reasonable measures for the exploration of the continental shelf, the exploitation of its natural resources and the prevention, reduction and control of pollution from pipelines, the coastal State may not impede the laying or maintenance of such cables or pipelines.

3. The delineation of the course for the laying of such pipelines on the continental shelf is subject to the consent of the coastal State.

4. Nothing in this Part affects the right of the coastal State to establish conditions for cables or pipelines entering its territory or territorial sea, or its jurisdiction over cables and pipelines constructed or used in connection with the exploration of its continental shelf or exploitation of its resources or the operations of artificial islands, installations and structures under its jurisdiction.

5. When laying submarine cables or pipelines, States shall have due regard to cables or pipelines already in position. In particular, possibilities of repairing existing cables or pipelines shall not be prejudiced.

Art. 80. Artificial islands, installations and structures on the continental shelf

Article 60 applies *mutatis mutandis* to artificial islands, installations and structures on the continental shelf.

Art. 81. Drilling on the continental shelf

The coastal State shall have the exclusive right to authorize and regulate drilling on the continental shelf for all purposes.

Art. 82. Payments and contributions with respect to the exploitation of the continental shelf beyond 200 nautical miles

1. The coastal State shall make payments or contributions in kind in respect of the exploitation of the non-living resources of the continental shelf beyond 200 nautical miles from the baselines from which the breadth of the territorial sea is measured.

2. The payments and contributions shall be made annually with respect to all production at a site after the first five years of production at that site. For the sixth year, the rate of payment or contribution shall be 1 per cent of the value or volume of production at the site. The rate shall increase by 1 per cent for each subsequent year until the twelfth year and shall remain at 7 per cent thereafter. Production does not include resources used in connection with exploitation.

3. A developing State which is a net importer of a mineral resource produced from its continental shelf is exempt from making such payments or contributions in respect of that mineral resource.

4. The payments or contributions shall be made through the Authority, which shall distribute them to States Parties to this Convention, on the basis of equitable sharing criteria, taking into account the interests and needs of developing States, particularly the least developed and the land-locked among them.

Art. 83. Delimitation of the continental shelf between States with opposite or adjacent coasts

1. The delimitation of the continental shelf between States with opposite or adjacent coasts shall be effected by agreement on the basis of international law, as referred to in Article 38 of the Statute of the International Court of Justice, in order to achieve an equitable solution.

2. If no agreement can be reached within a reasonable period of time, the States concerned shall resort to the procedures provided for in Part XV.

3. Pending agreement as provided for in paragraph 1, the States concerned, in a spirit of understanding and co-operation, shall make every effort to enter into provisional arrangements of a practical nature and, during this transitional period, not to jeopardize or hamper the reaching of the final agreement. Such arrangements shall be without prejudice to the final delimitation.

4. Where there is an agreement in force between the States concerned, questions relating to the delimitation of the continental shelf shall be determined in accordance with the provisions of that agreement.

Art. 84. Charts and lists of geographical co-ordinates

1. Subject to this Part, the outer limit lines of the continental shelf and the lines of delimitation drawn in accordance with article 83 shall be shown on charts of a scale or scales adequate for ascertaining their position. Where appropriate, lists of geographical co-ordinates of points, specifying the geodetic datum, may be substituted for such outer limit lines or lines of delimitation.

2. The coastal State shall give due publicity to such charts or lists of geographical co-ordinates and shall deposit a copy of each such chart or list with the Secretary-General of the United Nations and, in the case of those showing the outer limit lines of the continental shelf, with the Secretary-General of the Authority.

Art. 85. Tunnelling

This part does not prejudice the right of the coastal State to exploit the subsoil by means of tunnelling, irrespective of the depth of water above the subsoil.

Part VII. High seas

Section 1. General

Art. 86. Application of the provisions of this Part

The provisions of this Part apply to all parts of the sea that are not included in the exclusive economic zone, in the territorial sea or in the internal waters of a State, or in the archipelagic waters of an archipelagic State. This article does not entail any abridgement of the freedoms enjoyed by all States in the exclusive economic zone in accordance with article 58.

Art. 87. Freedom of the high seas

1. The high seas are open to all States, whether coastal or land-locked. Freedom of the high seas is exercised under the conditions laid down by this Convention and by other rules of international law. It comprises, *inter alia*, both for coastal and land-locked States:

(a) freedom of navigation;

(b) freedom of overflight;

(c) freedom to lay submarine cables and pipelines, subject to Part VI;

(d) freedom to construct artificial islands and other installations permitted under international law, subject to Part VI;

(e) freedom of fishing, subject to the conditions laid down in section 2;

(f) freedom of scientific research, subject to Parts VI and XIII.

2. These freedoms shall be exercised by all States with due regard for the interests of other States in their exercise of the freedom of the high seas, and also with due regard for the rights under this Convention with respect to activities in the Area.

Art. 88. Reservation of the high seas for peaceful purposes

The high seas shall be reserved for peaceful purposes.

Art. 89. Invalidity of claims of sovereignty over the high seas

No State may validly purport to subject any part of the high seas to its sovereignty.

Art. 90. Right of navigation

Every State, whether coastal or land-locked, has the right to sail ships flying its flag on the high seas.

Art. 91. Nationality of ships

1. Every State shall fix the conditions for the grant of its nationality to ships, for the registration of ships in its territory, and for the right to fly its flag. Ships have the nationality of the State whose flag they are entitled to fly. There must exist a genuine link between the State and the ship.

2. Every State shall issue to ships to which it has granted the right to fly its flag documents to that effect.

Art. 92. Status of ships

1. Ships shall sail under the flag of one State only and, save in exceptional cases expressly provided for in international treaties or in this Convention, shall be subject to its exclusive jurisdiction on the high seas. A ship may not change its flag during a voyage or while in a port of call, save in the case of a real transfer of ownership or change of registry.

2. A ship which sails under the flags of two or more States, using them according to convenience, may not claim any of the nationalities in question with respect to any other State, and may be assimilated to a ship without nationality.

Art. 93. Ships flying the flag of the United Nations, its specialized agencies and the International Atomic Energy Agency

The preceding articles do not prejudice the question of ships employed on the official service of the United Nations, its specialized agencies or the International Atomic Energy Agency, flying the flag of the organization.

Art. 94. Duties of the flag State

1. Every State shall effectively exercise its jurisdiction and control in administrative, technical and social matters over ships flying its flag.

2. In particular every State shall:

(a) maintain a register of ships containing the names and particulars of ships flying its flag, except those which are excluded from generally accepted international regulations on account of their small size; and

(b) assume jurisdiction under its internal law over each ship flying its flag and its master, officers and crew in respect of administrative, technical and social matters concerning the ship.

3. Every State shall take such measures for ships flying its flag as are necessary to ensure safety at sea with regard, *inter alia*, to:

(a) the construction, equipment and seaworthiness of ships;

(b) the manning of ships, labour conditions and the training of crews, taking into account the applicable international instruments;

(c) the use of signals, the maintenance of communications and the prevention of collisions.

4. Such measures shall include those necessary to ensure:

(a) that each ship, before registration and thereafter at appropriate intervals, is surveyed by a qualified surveyor of ships, and has on board such charts, nautical publications and navigational equipment and instruments as are appropriate for the safe navigation of the ship;

(b) that each ship is in the charge of a master and officers who possess appropriate qualifications, in particular in seamanship, navigation, communications and marine engineering, and that the crew is appropriate in qualification and numbers for the type, size, machinery and equipment of the ship;

(c) that the master, officers and, to the extent appropriate, the crew are fully conversant with and required to observe the applicable international regulations concerning the safety of life at sea, the prevention of collisions, the prevention, reduction and control of marine pollution, and the maintenance of communications by radio.

5. In taking the measures called for in paragraphs 3 and 4 each State is required to conform to generally accepted international regulations, procedures and practices and to take any steps which may be necessary to secure their observance.

6. A State which has clear grounds to believe that proper jurisdiction and control with respect to a ship have not been exercised may report the facts to the flag State. Upon receiving such a report, the flag State shall investigate the matter and, if appropriate, take any action necessary to remedy the situation.

7. Each State shall cause an inquiry to be held by or before a suitably qualified person or persons into every marine casualty or incident of navigation on the high seas involving a ship flying its flag and causing loss of life or serious injury to nationals of another State or serious damage to ships or installations of another State or to the marine environment. The flag State and the other State shall co-operate in the conduct of any inquiry held by that other State into any such marine casualty or incident of navigation.

Art. 95. Immunity of warships on the high seas

Warships on the high seas have complete immunity from the jurisdiction of any State other than the flag State.

Art. 96. Immunity of ships used only on government non-commercial service

Ships owned or operated by a State and used only on government non-commercial service shall, on the high seas, have complete immunity from the jurisdiction of any State other than the flag State.

Art. 97. Penal jurisdiction in matters of collision or any other incident of navigation

1. In the event of a collision or any other incident of navigation concerning a ship on the high seas, involving the penal or disciplinary responsibility of the master or of any other person in the service of the ship, no penal or disciplinary proceedings may be instituted against such person except before the judicial or administrative authorities either of the flag State or of the State of which such person is a national.

2. In disciplinary matters, the State which has issued a master's certificate or a certificate of competence or licence shall alone be competent, after due legal process, to pronounce the withdrawal of such certificates, even if the holder is not a national of the State which issued them.

3. No arrest or detention of the ship, even as a measure of investigation, shall be ordered by any authorities other than those of the flag State.

Art. 98. Duty to render assistance

1. Every State shall require the master of a ship flying its flag, in so far as he can do so without serious danger to the ship, the crew or the passengers:

(a) to render assistance to any person found at sea in danger of being lost;

(b) to proceed with all possible speed to the rescue of persons in distress, if informed of their need of assistance, in so far as such action may reasonably be expected of him;

(c) after a collision, to render assistance to the other ship, its crew and its passengers and, where possible, to inform the other ship of the name of his own ship, its port of registry and the nearest port at which it will call.

2. Every coastal State shall promote the establishment, operation and maintenance of an adequate and effective search and rescue service regarding safety on and over the sea and, where circumstances so require, by way of mutual regional arrangements co-operate with neighbouring States for this purpose.

Art. 99. Prohibition of the transport of slaves

Every State shall take effective measures to prevent and punish the transport of slaves in ships authorized to fly its flag and to prevent the unlawful use of its flag for that purpose. Any slave taking refuge on board any ship, whatever its flag, shall *ipso facto* be free.

Art. 100. Duty to co-operate in the repression of piracy

All States shall co-operate to the fullest possible extent in the repression of piracy on the high seas or in any other place outside the jurisdiction of any State.

Art. 101. Definition of piracy

Piracy consists of any of the following acts:

(a) any illegal acts of violence or detention, or any act of depredation, committed for private ends by the crew or the passengers of a private ship or a private aircraft, and directed:

(i) on the high seas, against another ship or aircraft, or against persons or property on board such ship or aircraft;

(ii) against a ship, aircraft, persons or property in a place outside the jurisdiction of any State;

(b) any act of voluntary participation in the operation of a ship or of an aircraft with knowledge of facts making it a pirate ship or aircraft;

(c) any act of inciting or of intentionally facilitating an act described in subparagraph (a) or (b).

Art. 102. Piracy by a warship, government ship or government aircraft whose crew has mutinied

The acts of piracy, as defined in article 101, committed by a warship, government ship or government aircraft whose crew has mutinied and taken control of the ship or aircraft are assimilated to acts committed by a private ship or aircraft.

Art. 103. Definition of a pirate ship or aircraft

A ship or aircraft is considered a pirate ship or aircraft if it is intended by the persons in dominant control to be used for the purpose of committing one of the acts referred to in article 101. The same applies if the ship or aircraft has been used to commit any such act, so long as it remains under the control of the persons guilty of that act.

Art. 104. Retention or loss of the nationality of a pirate ship or aircraft

A ship or aircraft may retain its nationality although it has become a pirate ship or aircraft. The retention or loss of nationality is determined by the law of the State from which such nationality was derived.

Art. 105. Seizure of a pirate ship or aircraft

On the high seas, or in any other place outside the jurisdiction of any State, every State may seize a pirate ship or aircraft, or a ship or aircraft taken by piracy and under the control of pirates, and arrest the persons and seize the property on board. The courts of the State which carried out the seizure may decide upon the penalties to be imposed, and may also determine the action to be taken with regard to the ships, aircraft or property, subject to the rights of third parties acting in good faith.

Art. 106. Liability for seizure without adequate grounds

Where the seizure of a ship or aircraft on suspicion of piracy has been effected without adequate grounds, the State making the seizure shall be liable to the State the nationality of which is possessed by the ship or aircraft for any loss or damage caused by the seizure.

Art. 107. Ships and aircraft which are entitled to seize on account of piracy

A seizure on account of piracy may be carried out only by warships or military aircraft, or other ships or aircraft clearly marked and identifiable as being on government service and authorized to that effect.

Art. 108. Illicit traffic in narcotic drugs or psychotropic substances

1. All States shall co-operate in the suppression of illicit traffic in narcotic drugs and psychotropic substances engaged in by ships on the high seas contrary to international conventions.

2. Any State which has reasonable grounds for believing that a ship flying its flag is engaged in illicit traffic in narcotic drugs or psychotropic substances may request the co-operation of other States to suppress such traffic.

Art. 109. Unauthorized broadcasting from the high seas

1. All States shall co-operate in the suppression of unauthorized broadcasting from the high seas.

2. For the purposes of this Convention, 'unauthorized broadcasting' means the transmission of sound radio or television broadcasts from a ship or installation on the high seas intended for reception by the general public contrary to international regulations, but excluding the transmission of distress calls.

3. Any person engaged in unauthorized broadcasting may be prosecuted before the court of:

(a) the flag State of the ship;

(b) the State of registry of the installation;

(c) the State of which the person is a national;

(d) any State where the transmissions can be received; or

(e) any State where authorized radio communication is suffering interference.

4. On the high seas, a State having jurisdiction in accordance with paragraph 3 may, in conformity with article 110, arrest any person or ship engaged in unauthorized broadcasting and seize the broadcasting apparatus.

Art. 110. Right of visit

1. Except where acts of interference derive from powers conferred by treaty, a warship which encounters on the high seas a foreign ship, other than a ship entitled to complete immunity in accordance with articles 95 and 96, is not justified in boarding it unless there is reasonable ground for suspecting that:

(a) the ship is engaged in piracy;

(b) the ship is engaged in the slave trade;

(c) the ship is engaged in unauthorized broadcasting and the flag State of the warship has jurisdiction under article 109;

(d) the ship is without nationality; or

(e) though flying a foreign flag or refusing to show its flag, the ship is, in reality, of the same nationality as the warship.

2. In the cases provided for in paragraph 1, the warship may proceed to verify the ship's right to fly its flag. To this end, it may send a boat under the command of an officer to the suspected ship. If suspicion remains after the documents have been checked, it may proceed to a further examination on board the ship, which must be carried out with all possible consideration.

3. If the suspicions prove to be unfounded, and provided that the ship boarded has not committed any act justifying them, it shall be compensated for any loss or damage that may have been sustained.

4. These provisions apply *mutatis mutandis* to military aircraft.

5. These provisions also apply to any other duly authorized ships or aircraft clearly marked and identifiable as being on government service.

Art. 111. Right of hot pursuit

1. The hot pursuit of a foreign ship may be undertaken when the competent authorities of the coastal State have good reason to believe that the ship has violated the laws and regulations of that State. Such pursuit must be commenced when the foreign ship or one of its boats is within the internal waters, the archipelagic waters, the territorial sea or the contiguous zone of the pursuing State, and may only be continued outside the territorial sea or the contiguous zone if the pursuit has

not been interrupted. It is not necessary that, at the time when the foreign ship within the territorial sea or the contiguous zone receives the order to stop, the ship giving the order should likewise be within the territorial sea or the contiguous zone. If the foreign ship is within a contiguous zone, as defined in article 33, the pursuit may only be undertaken if there has been a violation of the rights for the protection of which the zone was established.
2. The right of hot pursuit shall apply *mutatis mutandis* to violations in the exclusive economic zone or on the continental shelf, including safety zones around the continental shelf installations, of the laws and regulations of the coastal State applicable in accordance with this Convention to the exclusive economic zone or the continental shelf, including such safety zones.
3. The right of hot pursuit ceases as soon as the ship pursued enters the territorial sea of its own State or of a third State.
4. Hot pursuit is not deemed to have begun unless the pursuing ship has satisfied itself by such practicable means as may be available that the ship pursued or one of its boats or other craft working as a team and using the ship pursued as a mother ship is within the limits of the territorial sea, or, as the case may be, within the contiguous zone or the exclusive economic zone or above the continental shelf. The pursuit may only be commenced after a visual or auditory signal to stop has been given at a distance which enables it to be seen or heard by the foreign ship.
5. The right of hot pursuit may be exercised only by warships or military aircraft, or other ships or aircraft clearly marked and identifiable as being on government service and authorized to that effect.
6. Where hot pursuit is effected by an aircraft:
(a) the provisions of paragraphs 1 to 4 shall apply *mutatis mutandis*;
(b) the aircraft giving the order to stop must itself actively pursue the ship until a ship or another aircraft of the coastal State, summoned by the aircraft, arrives to take over the pursuit, unless the aircraft is itself able to arrest the ship. It does not suffice to justify an arrest outside the territorial sea that the ship was merely sighted by the aircraft as an offender or suspected offender, if it was not both ordered to stop and pursued by the aircraft itself or other aircraft or ships which continue the pursuit without interruption.
7. The release of a ship arrested within the jurisdiction of a State and escorted to a port of that State for the purposes of an inquiry before the competent authorities may not be claimed solely on the ground that the ship, in the course of its voyage, was escorted across a portion of the exclusive economic zone or the high seas, if the circumstances rendered this necessary.
8. Where a ship has been stopped or arrested outside the territorial sea in circumstances which do not justify the exercise of the right of hot pursuit, it shall be compensated for any loss or damage that may have been thereby sustained.

Art. 112. Right to lay submarine cables and pipelines
1. All States are entitled to lay submarine cables and pipelines on the bed of the high seas beyond the continental shelf.
2. Article 79, paragraph 5, applies to such cables and pipelines.

Art. 113. Breaking or injury of a submarine cable or pipeline
Every State shall adopt the laws and regulations necessary to provide that the breaking or injury by a ship flying its flag or by a person subject to its jurisdiction of a submarine cable beneath the high seas done wilfully or through culpable negligence, in such a manner as to be liable to interrupt or obstruct telegraphic or telephonic communications, and similarly the breaking or injury of a submarine pipeline or high-voltage power cable, shall be a punishable offence. This provision shall apply to conduct calculated or likely to result in such breaking or injury. However, it shall not apply to any break or injury caused by persons who acted merely with the legitimate object of saving their lives or their ships, after having taken all necessary precautions to avoid such break or injury.

Art. 114. Breaking or injury by owners of a submarine cable or pipeline of another submarine cable or pipeline
Every State shall adopt the laws and regulations necessary to provide that, if persons subject to its jurisdiction who are the owners of a submarine cable or pipeline beneath the high seas, in laying or repairing that cable or pipeline, cause a break in or injury to another cable or pipeline, they shall bear the cost of the repairs.

Art. 115. Indemnity for loss incurred in avoiding injury to a submarine cable or pipeline
Every State shall adopt the laws and regulations necessary to ensure that the owners of ships who can prove that they have sacrificed an anchor, a net or any other fishing gear, in order to avoid injuring a submarine cable or pipeline, shall be indemnified by the owner of the cable or pipeline, provided that the owner of the ship has taken all reasonable precautionary measures beforehand.

Section 2. Management and conservation of the living resources of the high seas

Art. 116. Right to fish on the high seas
All States have the right for their nationals to engage in fishing on the high seas subject to:
(a) their treaty obligations;
(b) the rights and duties as well as the interests of coastal States provided for *inter alia*, in article 63, paragraph 2, and articles 64 to 67; and
(c) the provisions of this section.

Art. 117. Duty of States to adopt with respect to their nationals measures for the conservation of the living resources of the high seas
All States have the duty to take, or to co-operate with other States in taking, such measures for their respective nationals as may be necessary for the conservation of the living resources of the high seas.

Art. 118. Co-operation of States in the conservation and management of living resources
States shall co-operate with each other in the conservation and management of living resources in the areas of the high seas. States whose nationals exploit identical living resources, or different living resources in the same area, shall enter into negotiations with a view to taking the measures necessary for the conservation of the living resources concerned. They shall, as appropriate, co-operate to establish subregional or regional fisheries organizations to this end.

Art. 119. Conservation of the living resources of the high seas
1. In determining the allowable catch and establishing other conservation measures for the living resources in the high seas, States shall:
(a) take measures which are designed, on the best scientific evidence available to the States concerned, to maintain or restore populations of harvested species at levels which can produce the maximum sustainable yield, as qualified by relevant environmental and economic factors, including the special requirements of developing States, and taking into account fishing patterns, the interdependence of stocks and any generally recommended international minimum standards, whether subregional, regional or global;
(b) take into consideration the effects on species associated with or dependent upon harvested species with a view to maintaining or restoring populations of such associated or dependent species above levels at which their reproduction may become seriously threatened.
2. Available scientific information, catch and fishing effort statistics, and other data relevant to the conservation of fish stocks shall be contributed and exchanged on a regular basis through competent international organizations, whether subregional, regional or global, where appropriate and with participation by all States concerned.
3. States concerned shall ensure that conservation measures and their implementation do not discriminate in form or in fact against the fishermen of any State.

Art. 120. Marine mammals
Article 65 also applies to the conservation and management of marine mammals in the high seas.

Part VIII. Régime of islands

Art. 121. Régime of islands
1. An island is a naturally formed area of land, surrounded by water, which is above water at high tide.
2. Except as provided for in paragraph 3, the territorial sea, the contiguous zone, the exclusive economic zone and the continental shelf of an island are determined in accordance with the provisions of this Convention applicable to other land territory.
3. Rocks which cannot sustain human habitation or economic life of their own shall have no exclusive zone or continental shelf.

Part IX. Enclosed or semi-enclosed seas

Art. 122. Definition
For the purposes of this Convention, 'enclosed or semi-enclosed sea' means a gulf, basin or sea surrounded by two or more States and connected to another sea or the ocean by a narrow outlet or consisting entirely or primarily of the territorial seas and exclusive economic zones of two or more coastal States.

Art. 123. Co-operation of States bordering enclosed or semi-enclosed seas
States bordering an enclosed or semi-enclosed sea should co-operate with each other in the exercise of their rights and in the performance of their duties under this Convention. To this end they shall endeavour, directly or through an appropriate regional organization:
(a) to co-ordinate the management, conservation, exploration and exploitation of the living resources of the sea;
(b) to co-ordinate the implementation of the rights and duties with respect to the protection and preservation of the marine environment;
(c) to co-ordinate their scientific research policies and undertake where appropriate joint programmes of scientific research in the area;
(d) to invite, as appropriate, other interested States or international organizations to co-operate with them in futherance of the provisions of this article.

Part X. Right to access of land-locked states to and from the sea and freedom of transit

Art. 124. Use of terms
1. For the purposes of this Convention:
(a) 'land-locked State' means a State which has no sea-coast;
(b) 'transit State' means a State, with or without a sea-coast, situated between a land-locked State and the sea, through whose territory traffic in transit passes;
(c) 'traffic in transit' means transit of persons, baggage, goods and means of transport across the territory of one or more transit States, when the passage across such territory, with or without trans-shipment, warehousing, breaking bulk or change in the mode of transport, is only a portion of a complete journey which begins or terminates within the territory of the land-locked State;
(d) 'means of transport' means:
(i) railway rolling stock, sea, lake and river craft and road vehicles;
(ii) where local conditions so require, porters and pack animals.
2. Land-locked States and transit States may, by agreement between them, include as means of transport pipelines and gas lines and means of transport other than those included in paragraph 1.

Art. 125. Right of access to and from the sea and freedom of transit
1. Land-locked States shall have the right of access to and from the sea for the purpose of exercising the rights provided for in this Convention including those relating to the freedom of the high seas and the common heritage of mankind. To this end, land-locked States shall enjoy freedom of transit through the territory of transit States by all means of transport.
2. The terms and modalities for exercising freedom of transit shall be agreed between the land-locked States and transit States concerned through bilateral, subregional or regional agreements.
3. Transit States, in the exercise of their full sovereignty over their territory, shall have the right to take all measures necessary to ensure that the rights and facilities provided for in this Part for land-locked States shall in no way infringe their legitimate interests.

Art. 126. Exclusion of application of the most-favoured-nation clause
The provisions of this Convention, as well as special agreements relating to the exercise of the right of access to and from the sea, establishing rights and facilities on account of the special geographical position of land-locked States, are excluded from the application of the most-favoured-nation clause.

Art. 127. Customs duties, taxes and other charges
1. Traffic in transit shall not be subject to any customs duties, taxes or other charges except charges levied for specific services rendered in connection with such traffic.
2. Means of transport in transit and other facilities provided for and used by land-locked States shall not be subject to taxes or charges higher than those levied for the use of means of transport of the transit State.

Art. 128. Free zones and other customs facilities
For the convenience of traffic in transit, free zones or other customs facilities may be provided at the ports of entry and exit in the transit States, by agreement between those States and the land-locked States.

Art. 129. Co-operation in the construction and improvement of means of transport
Where there are no means of transport in transit States to give effect to the freedom of transit or where the existing means, including the port installations and equipment, are inadequate in any respect, the transit States and land-locked States concerned may co-operate in constructing or improving them.

Art. 130. Measures to avoid or eliminate delays or other difficulties of a technical nature in traffic in transit
1. Transit States shall take all appropriate measures to avoid delays or other difficulties of a technical nature in traffic in transit.
2. Should such delays or difficulties occur, the competent authorities of the transit States and land-locked States concerned shall co-operate towards their expedition elimination.

Art. 131. Equal treatment in maritime ports
Ships flying the flag of land-locked States shall enjoy treatment equal to that accorded to other foreign ships in maritime ports.

Art. 132. Grant of greater transit facilities
This Convention does not entail in any way the withdrawal of transit facilities which are greater than those provided for in this Convention and which are agreed between States Parties to this Convention or granted by a State Party. This Convention also does not preclude such grant of greater facilities in the future.

Part XI. The Area

Section 1. General Provisions

Art. 133. Use of terms
For the purposes of this Part:
(a) 'resources' means all solid, liquid or gaseous mineral resources *in situ* in the Area at or beneath the sea-bed, including polymetallic nodules;
(b) resources, when recovered from the Area, are referred to as 'minerals'.

Art. 134. Scope of this Part
1. This Part applies to the Area.
2. Activities in the Area shall be governed by the provisions of this Part.
3. The requirements concerning deposit of, and publicity to be given to, the charts or lists of geographical co-ordinates showing the limits referred to in article 1, paragraph 1 (1), are set forth in Part VI.
4. Nothing in this article affects the establishment of the outer limits of the continental shelf in accordance with Part VI or the validity of agreements relating to delimitation between States with opposite or adjacent coasts.

Art. 135. Legal status of the superjacent waters and air space
Neither this Part nor any rights granted or exercised pursuant thereto shall affect the legal status of the waters superjacent to the Area or that of the air space above those waters.

Section 2. Principles governing the area

Art. 136. Common heritage of mankind
The Area and its resources are the common heritage of mankind.

Art. 137. Legal status of the Area and its resources
1. No State shall claim or exercise sovereignty or sovereign rights over any part of the Area or its resources, nor shall any State or natural or juridical person appropriate any part thereof. No such claim or exercise of sovereignty or sovereign rights nor such appropriation shall be recognized.
2. All rights in the resources of the Area are vested in mankind as a whole, on whose behalf the Authority shall act. These resources are not subject to alienation. The minerals recovered from the Area, however, may only be alienated in accordance with this Part and the rules, regulations and procedures of the Authority.
3. No State or natural or juridical person shall claim, acquire or exercise rights with respect to the minerals recovered from the Area except in accordance with this Part. Otherwise, no such claim, acquisition or exercise of such rights shall be recognized.

Art. 138. General conduct of States in relation to the Area
The general conduct of States in relation to the Area shall be in accordance with the provisions of this Part, the principles embodied in the Charter of the United Nations and other rules of international law in the interests of maintaining peace and security and promoting international co-operation and mutual understanding.

Art. 139. Responsibility to ensure compliance and liability for damage
1. States Parties shall have the responsibility to ensure that activities in the Area, whether carried out by States Parties, or state enterprises or natural or juridical persons which possess the nationality of States Parties or are effectively controlled by them or their nationals, shall be carried out in conformity with this Part. The same responsibility applies to international organizations for activities in the Area carried out by such organizations.
2. Without prejudice to the rules of international law and Annex III, article 22, damage caused by the failure of a State Party or international organization to carry out its responsibilities under this Part shall entail liability; States Parties or international organizations acting together shall bear joint and several liability. A State Party shall not however be liable for damage caused by any failure to comply with this Part by a person whom it has sponsored under article 153, paragraph 2(b), if the State Party has taken all necessary and appropriate measures to secure effective compliance under article 153, paragraph 4, and Annex III, article 4, paragraph 4.
3. States Parties that are members of international organizations shall take appropriate measures to ensure the implementation of this article with respect to such organizations.

Art. 140. Benefit of mankind
1. Activities in the Area shall, as specifically provided for in this Part, be carried out for the benefit of mankind as a whole, irrespective of the geographical location of States, whether coastal or land-locked, and taking into particular consideration the interests and needs of developing States and of peoples who have not attained full independence or other self-governing status recognized by the United Nations in accordance with General Assembly resolution 1514 (XV) and other relevant General Assembly resolutions.
2. The Authority shall provide for the equitable sharing of financial and other economic benefits derived from activities in the Area through any appropriate mechanism, on a non-discriminatory basis, in accordance with article 160, paragraph 2(f)(i).

Art. 141. Use of the Area exclusively for peaceful purposes
The Area shall be open to use exclusively for peaceful purposes by all States, whether coastal or land-locked, without discrimination and without prejudice to the other provisions of this Part.

Art. 142. Rights and legitimate interests of coastal States
1. Activities in the Area, with respect to resource deposits in the Area which lie across limits of national jurisdiction, shall be conducted with due regard to the rights and legitimate interests of any coastal State across whose jurisdiction such deposits lie.
2. Consultations, including a system of prior notification, shall be maintained with the State concerned, with a view to avoiding infringement of such rights and interests. In cases where activities in the Area may result in the exploitation of resources lying within national jurisdiction, the prior consent of the coastal State concerned shall be required.
3. Neither this Part nor any rights granted or exercised pursuant thereto shall affect the rights of coastal States to take such measures consistent with the relevant provisions of Part XII as may be necessary to prevent, mitigate or eliminate grave and imminent danger to their coastline, or related interests from pollution or threat thereof or from other hazardous occurrences resulting from or caused by any activities in the Area.

Art. 143. Marine scientific research
1. Marine scientific research in the Area shall be carried out exclusively for peaceful purposes and for the benefit of mankind as a whole, in accordance with Part XIII.
2. The Authority may carry out marine scientific research concerning the Area and its resources, and may enter into contracts for that purpose. The Authority shall promote and encourage the conduct of marine scientific research in the Area, and shall co-ordinate and disseminate the results of such research and analysis when available.

3. States Parties may carry out marine scientific research in the Area. States parties shall promote international co-operation in marine scientific research in the Area by:
(a) participating in international programmes and encouraging co-operation in marine scientific research by personnel of different countries and of the Authority;
(b) ensuring that programmes are developed through the Authority or other international organizations as appropriate for the benefit of developing States and technologically less developed States with a view to:
(i) strengthening their research capabilities;
(ii) training their personnel and the personnel of the Authority in the techniques and applications of research;
(iii) fostering the employment of their qualified personnel in research in the Area;
(c) effectively disseminating the results of research and analysis when available, through the Authority or other international channels when appropriate.

Art. 144. Transfer of technology
1. The Authority shall take measures in accordance with this Convention:
(a) to acquire technology and scientific knowledge relating to activities in the Area; and
(b) to promote and encourage the transfer to developing States of such technology and scientific knowledge so that all States Parties benefit therefrom.
2. To this end the Authority and States Parties shall co-operate in promoting the transfer of technology and scientific knowledge relating to activities in the Area so that the Enterprise and all States Parties may benefit therefrom. In particular they shall initiate and promote:
(a) programmes for the transfer of technology to the Enterprise and to developing States with regard to activities in the Area, including, *inter alia*, facilitating the access of the Enterprise and of developing States to the relevant technology, under fair and reasonable terms and conditions;
(b) measures directed towards the advancement of the technology of the Enterprise and the domestic technology of developing States, particularly by providing opportunities to personnel from the Enterprise and from developing States for training in marine science and technology and for their full participation in activities in the Area.

Art. 145. Protection of the marine environment
Necessary measures shall be taken in accordance with this Convention with respect to activities in the Area to ensure effective protection for the marine environment from harmful effects which may arise from such activities. To this end the Authority shall adopt appropriate rules, regulations and procedures for *inter alia*:
(a) the prevention, reduction and control of pollution and other hazards to the marine environment, including the coastline, and of interference with the ecological balance of the marine environment, particular attention being paid to the need for protection from harmful effects of such activities as drilling, dredging, excavation, disposal of waste, construction and operation or maintenance of installations, pipelines and other devices related to such activities;
(b) the protection and conservation of the natural resources of the Area and the prevention of damage to the flora and fauna of the marine environment.

Art. 146. Protection of human life
With respect to activities in the Area, necessary measures shall be taken to ensure effective protection of human life. To this end the Authority shall adopt appropriate rules, regulations and procedures to supplement existing international law as embodied in relevant treaties.

Art. 147. Accommodation of activities in the Area and in the marine environment
1. Activities in the Area shall be carried out with reasonable regard for other activities in the marine environment.
2. Installations used for carrying out activities in the Area shall be subject to the following conditions:
(a) such installations shall be erected, emplaced and removed solely in accordance with this Part and subject to the rules, regulations and procedures of the Authority. Due notice must be given of the erection, emplacement and removal of such installations, and permanent means for giving warning of their presence must be maintained;

(b) such installations may not be established where interference may be caused to the use of recognized sea lanes essential to international navigation or in areas of intense fishing activity;

(c) safety zones shall be established around such installations with appropriate markings to ensure the safety of both navigation and the installations. The configuration and location of such safety zones shall not be such as to form a belt impeding the lawful access of shipping to particular maritime zones or navigation along international sea lanes;

(d) such installations shall be used exclusively for peaceful purposes;

(e) such installations do not possess the status of islands. They have no territorial sea of their own, and their presence does not affect the delimitation of the territorial sea, the exclusive economic zone or the continental shelf.

3. Other activities in the marine environment shall be conducted with reasonable regard for activities in the Area.

Art. 148. Participation of developing States in activities in the Area

The effective participation of developing States in activities in the Area shall be promoted as specifically provided in this Part, having due regard to their special interests and needs, and in particular to the special need of the land-locked and geographically disadvantaged among them to overcome obstacles arising from their disadvantaged location, including remoteness from the Area and difficulty of access to and from it.

Art. 149. Archaeological and historical objects

All objects of an archaeological and historical nature found in the Area shall be preserved or disposed of for the benefit of mankind as a whole, particular regard being paid to the preferential rights of the State or country of origin, or the State of cultural origin, of the State of historical and archaeological origin.

Section 3. Conduct of activities in the Area

Art. 150. Policies relating to activities in the Area

Activities in the Area shall, as specifically provided for in this Part, be carried out in such a manner as to foster healthy development of the world economy and balanced growth of international trade, and to promote international co-operation for the over-all development of all countries, especially developing States, and with a view to ensuring:

(a) the development of the resources of the Area;

(b) orderly, safe and rational management of the resources of the Area, including the efficient conduct of activities in the Area and, in accordance with sound principles of conservation, the avoidance of unnecessary waste;

(c) the expansion of opportunities for participation in such activities consistent with articles 144 and 148;

(d) participation in revenues by the Authority and the transfer of technology to the Enterprise and developing States as provided for in this Convention;

(e) increased availability of the minerals derived from the Area as needed in conjunction with minerals derived from other sources, to ensure supplies to consumers of such minerals;

(f) the promotion of just and stable prices remunerative to producers and fair to consumers for minerals derived both from the Area and from other sources, and the promotion of long-term equilibrium between supply and demand;

(g) the enhancement of opportunities for all States Parties, irrespective of their social and economic systems or geographical location, to participate in the development of the resources of the Area and the prevention of monopolization of activities in the Area;

(h) the protection of developing countries from adverse effects on their economies or on their export earnings resulting from a reduction in the price of an affected mineral, or in the volume of exports of that mineral, to the extent that such reduction is caused by activities in the Area, as provided in article 151;

(i) the development of the common heritage for the benefit of mankind as a whole; and

(j) conditions of access to markets for the imports of minerals produced from the resources of the Area and for imports of commodities produced from such minerals shall not be more favourable than the most favourable applied to imports from other sources.

Art. 151. Production policies

1. (a) Without prejudice to the objectives set forth in article 150 and for the purpose of implementing sub-

paragraph (h) of that article, the Authority, acting through existing forums or such new arrangements or agreements as may be appropriate, in which all interested parties, including both producers and consumers, participate, shall take measures necessary to promote the growth, efficiency and stability of markets for those commodities produced from the minerals derived from the Area, at prices remunerative to producers and fair to consumers. All States Parties shall co-operate to this end.

(b) The Authority shall have the right to participate in any commodity conference dealing with those commodities and in which all interested parties including both producers and consumers participate. The Authority shall have the right to become a party to any arrangement or agreement resulting from such conferences. Participation of the Authority in any organs established under those arrangements or agreements shall be in respect of production in the Area and in accordance with the relevant rules of those organs.

(c) The Authority shall carry out its obligations under the arrangements or agreements referred to in this paragraph in a manner which assures a uniform and non-discriminatory implementation in respect of all production in the Area of the minerals concerned. In doing so, the Authority shall act in a manner consistent with the terms of existing contracts and approved plans of work of the Enterprise.

2. (a) During the interim period specified in paragraph 3, commercial production shall not be undertaken pursuant to an approved plan of work until the operator has applied for and has been issued a production authorization by the Authority. Such production authorizations may not be applied for or issued more than five years prior to the planned commencement of commercial production under the plan of work unless, having regard to the nature and timing of project development, the rules, regulations and procedures of the Authority prescribe another period.

(b) In the application for the production authorization, the operator shall specify the annual quantity of nickel expected to be recovered under the approved plan of work. The application shall include a schedule of expenditures to be made by the operator after he has received the authorization which are reasonably calculated to allow him to begin commercial production on the date planned.

(c) For the purposes of subparagraphs (a) and (b), the Authority shall establish appropriate performance requirements in accordance with Annex III, article 17.

(d) The Authority shall issue a production authorization for the level of production applied for unless the sum of that level and the levels already authorized exceeds the nickel production ceiling, as calculated pursuant to paragraph 4 in the year of issuance of the authorization, during any year of planned production falling within the interim period.

(e) When issued, the production authorization and approved application shall become a part of the approved plan of work.

(f) If the operator's application for a production authorization is denied pursuant to subparagraph (d), the operator may apply again to the Authority at any time.

3. The interim period shall begin five years prior to 1 January of the year in which the earliest commercial production is planned to commence under an approved plan of work. If the earliest commercial production is delayed beyond the year originally planned, the beginning of the interim period and the production ceiling originally calculated shall be adjusted accordingly. The interim period shall last 25 years or until the end of the Review Conference referred to in article 155 or until the day when such new arrangements or agreements as are referred to in paragraph 1 enter into force, whichever is earliest. The Authority shall resume the power provided in this article for the remainder of the interim period if the said arrangements or agreements should lapse or become ineffective for any reason whatsoever.

4. (a) The production ceiling for any year of the interim period shall be the sum of:

(i) the difference between the trend line values for nickel consumption, as calculated pursuant to subparagraph (b), for the year immediately prior to the commencement of the interim period; and

(ii) sixty per cent of the difference between the trend line values for nickel consumption, as calculated pursuant

to subparagraph (b), for the year immediately prior to the year of the earliest commercial production.

(b) For the purposes of subparagraph (a):

(i) trend line values used for computing the nickel production ceiling shall be those annual nickel consumption values on a trend line computed during the year in which a production authorization is issued. The trend line shall be derived from a linear regression of the logarithms of actual nickel consumption for the most recent 15-year period for which such data are available, time being the independent variable. This trend line shall be referred to as the original trend line;

(ii) if the annual rate of increase of the original trend line is less than 3 per cent, then the trend line used to determine the quantities referred to in subparagraph (a) shall instead be one passing through the original trend line at the value for the first year of the relevant 15-year period, and increasing at 3 per cent annually; provided however that the production ceiling established for any year of the interim period may not in any case exceed the difference between the original trend line value for that year and the original trend line value for the year immediately prior to the commencement of the interim period.

5. The Authority shall reserve to the Enterprise for its initial production a quantity of 38,000 metric tonnes of nickel from the available production ceiling calculated pursuant to paragraph 4.

6. (a) An operator may in any year produce less than or up to 8 per cent more than the level of annual production of minerals from polymetallic nodules specified in his production authorization, provided that the over-all amount of production shall not exceed that specified in the authorization. Any excess over 8 per cent and up to 20 per cent in any year, or any excess in the first and subsequent years following two consecutive years in which excesses occur, shall be negotiated with the Authority, which may require the operator to obtain a supplementary production authorization to cover additional production.

(b) Applications for such supplementary production authorizations shall be considered by the Authority only after all pending applications by operators who have not yet received production authorizations have been acted upon and due account has been taken of other likely applicants. The Authority shall be guided by the principle of not exceeding the total production allowed under the production ceiling in any year of the interim period. It shall not authorize the production under any plan of work of a quantity in excess of 46,500 metric tonnes of nickel per year.

7. The levels of production of other metals such as copper, cobalt and manganese extracted from the polymetallic nodules that are recovered pursuant to a production authorization should not be higher than those which would have been produced had the operator produced the maximum level of nickel from those nodules pursuant to this article. The Authority shall establish rules, regulations and procedures pursuant to Annex III, article 17, to implement this paragraph.

8. Rights and obligations relating to unfair economic practices under relevant multilateral trade agreements shall apply to the exploration for and exploitation of minerals from the Area. In the settlement of disputes arising under this provision, States Parties which are Parties to such multilateral trade agreements shall have recourse to the dispute settlement procedures of such agreements.

9. The Authority shall have the power to limit the level of production of minerals from the Area, other than minerals from polymetallic nodules, under such conditions and applying such methods as may be appropriate by adopting regulations in accordance with article 161, paragraph 8.

10. Upon the recommendation of the Council on the basis of advice from the Economic Planning Commission, the Assembly shall establish a system of compensation or take other measures of economic adjustment assistance including co-operation with specialized agencies and other international organizations to assist developing countries which suffer serious adverse effects on their export earnings or economies resulting from a reduction in the price of an affected mineral or in the volume of exports of that mineral, to the extent that such reduction is caused by activities in the Area. The Authority on request shall initiate studies on the problems of those States which

are likely to be most seriously affected with a view to minimizing their difficulties and assisting them in their economic adjustment.

Art. 152. Exercise of powers and functions by the Authority

1. The Authority shall avoid discrimination in the exercise of its powers and functions, including the granting of opportunities for activities in the Area.

2. Nevertheless, special consideration for developing States, including particular consideration for the landlocked and geographically disadvantaged among them, specifically provided for in this Part shall be permitted.

Art. 153. System of exploration and exploitation

1. Activities in the Area shall be organized, carried out and controlled by the Authority on behalf of mankind as a whole in accordance with this article as well as other relevant provisions of this Part and the relevant Annexes, and the rules, regulations and procedures of the Authority.

2. Activities in the Area shall be carried out as prescribed in paragraph 3:

(a) by the Enterprise, and

(b) in association with the Authority by States Parties, or state enterprises or natural or juridical persons which possess the nationality of States Parties or are effectively controlled by them or their nationals, when sponsored by such States, or any group of the foregoing which meets the requirements provided in this Part and in Annex III.

3. Activities in the Area shall be carried out in accordance with the formal written plan of work drawn up in accordance with Annex III and approved by the Council after review by the Legal and Technical Commission. In the case of activities in the Area carried out as authorized by the Authority by the entities specified in paragraph 2(b), the plan of work shall, in accordance with Annex III, article 3, be in the form of a contract. Such contracts may provide for joint arrangements in accordance with Annex III, article 11.

4. The Authority shall exercise such control over activities in the Area as is necessary for the purpose of securing compliance with the relevant provisions of this Part and the Annexes relating thereto, and the rules, regulations and procedures of the Authority, and the plans of work approved in accordance with paragraph 3. States Parties shall assist the Authority by taking all measures necessary to ensure such compliance in accordance with article 139.

5. The Authority shall have the right to take at any time any measures provided for under this Part to ensure compliance with its provisions and the exercise of the functions of control and regulation assigned to it thereunder or under any contract. The Authority shall have the right to inspect all installations in the Area used in connection with activities in the Area.

6. A contract under paragraph 3 shall provide for security of tenure. Accordingly, the contract shall not be revised, suspended or terminated except in accordance with Annex III, articles 18 and 19.

Art. 154. Periodic review

Every five years from the entry into force of this Convention, the Assembly shall undertake a general and systematic review of the manner in which the international régime of the Area established in this Convention has operated in practice. In the light of this review the Assembly may take, or recommend that other organs take, measures in accordance with the provisions and procedures of this Part and the Annexes relating thereto which will lead to the improvement of the operation of the régime.

Art. 155. The Review Conference

1. Fifteen years from 1 January of the year in which the earliest commercial production commences under an approved plan of work, the Assembly shall convene a conference for the review of those provisions of this Part and the relevant Annexes which govern the system of exploration and exploitation of the resources of the Area. The Review Conference shall consider in detail, in the light of the experience acquired during that period:

(a) whether the provisions of this Part which govern the system of exploration and exploitation of the resources of the Area have achieved their aims in all respects, including whether they have benefited mankind as a whole;

(b) whether, during the 15-year period, reserved areas have been exploited in an effective and balanced manner in comparison with non-reserved areas;

(c) whether the development and use of the Area and its resources have been undertaken in such a manner as to foster healthy development of the world economy and balanced growth of international trade;

(d) whether monopolization of activities in the Area has been prevented;

(e) whether the policies set forth in articles 150 and 151 have been fulfilled; and

(f) whether the system has resulted in the equitable sharing of benefits derived from activities in the Area, taking into particular consideration the interests and needs of the developing States.

2. The Review Conference shall ensure the maintenance of the principle of the common heritage of mankind, the international régime designed to ensure equitable exploitation of the resources of the Area for the benefit of all countries, especially the developing States, and an Authority to organize, conduct and control activities in the Area. It shall also ensure the maintenance of the principles laid down in this Part with regard to the exclusion of claims or exercise of sovereignty over any part of the Area, the rights of States and their general conduct in relation to the Area, and their participation in activities in the Area in conformity with this Convention, the prevention of monopolization of activities in the Area, the use of the Area exclusively for peaceful purposes, economic aspects of activities in the Area, marine scientific research, transfer of technology, protection of the marine environment, protection of human life, rights of coastal States, the legal status of the waters superjacent to the Area and that of the air space above those waters and accommodation between activities in the Area and other activities in the marine environment.

3. The decision-making procedure applicable at the Review Conference shall be the same as that applicable at the Third United Nations Conference on the Law of the Sea. The Conference shall make every effort to reach agreement on any amendments by way of consensus and there should be no voting on such matters until all efforts at achieving consensus have been exhausted.

4. If, five years after its commencement, the Review Conference has not reached agreement on the system of exploration and exploitation of the resources of the Area, it may decide during the ensuing 12 months, by a three-fourths majority of the States Parties, to adopt and submit to the States Parties for ratification or accession such amendments changing or modifying the system as it determines necessary and appropriate. Such amendments shall enter into force for all States Parties 12 months after the deposit of instruments of ratification or accession by three fourths of the States Parties.

5. Amendments adopted by the Review Conference pursuant to this article shall not affect rights acquired under existing contracts.

Section 4. The Authority
Subsection A. General Provisions
Art. 156. Establishment of the Authority

1. There is hereby established the International Sea-Bed Authority, which shall function in accordance with this Part.

2. All States Parties are *ipso facto* members of the Authority.

3. Observers at the Third United Nations Conference on the Law of the Sea who have signed the Final Act and who are not referred to in article 305, paragraph 1(c), (d), (e) or (f), shall have the right to participate in the Authority as observers, in accordance with its rules, regulations and procedures.

4. The seat of the Authority shall be in Jamaica.

5. The Authority may establish such regional centres or offices as it deems necessary for the exercise of its functions.

Art. 157. Nature and fundamental principles of the Authority

1. The Authority is the organization through which States Parties shall, in accordance with this Part, organize and control activities in the Area, particularly with a view to administering the resources of the Area.

2. The powers and functions of the Authority shall be those expressly conferred upon it by this Convention. The Authority shall have such incidental powers, consistent with this Convention, as are implicit in and necessary for the exercise of those powers and functions with respect to activities in the Area.

3. The Authority is based on the principle of the sovereign equality of all its members.

4. All members of the Authority shall fulfil in good faith the obligations assumed by them in accordance with this Part in order to ensure to all of them the rights and benefits resulting from membership.

Art. 158. Organs of the Authority

1. There are hereby established, as the principal organs of the Authority, an Assembly, a Council and a Secretariat.

2. There is hereby established an Enterprise, the organ through which the Authority shall carry out the functions referred to in article 170, paragraph 1.

3. Such subsidiary organs as may be found necessary may be established in accordance with this Part.

4. Each principal organ of the Authority and the Enterprise shall be responsible for exercising those powers and functions which are conferred upon it. In exercising such powers and functions each organ shall avoid taking any action which may derogate from or impede the exercise of specific powers and functions conferred upon another organ.

Subsection B. The Assembly.
Art. 159. Composition, procedure and voting

1. The Assembly shall consist of all the members of the Authority. Each member shall have one representative in the Assembly, who may be accompanied by alternates and advisers.

2. The Assembly shall meet in regular annual sessions and in such special sessions as may be decided by the Assembly, or convened by the Secretary-General at the request of the Council or of a majority of the members of the Authority.

3. Sessions shall take place at the seat of the Authority unless otherwise decided by the Assembly.

4. The Assembly shall adopt its rules of procedure. At the beginning of each regular session, it shall elect its President and such other officers as may be required. They shall hold office until a new President and other officers are elected at the next regular session.

5. A majority of the members of the Assembly shall constitute a quorum.

6. Each member of the Assembly shall have one vote.

7. Decisions on questions of procedure, including decisions to convene special sessions of the Assembly, shall be taken by a majority of the members present and voting.

8. Decisions on questions of substance shall be taken by a two-thirds majority of the members present and voting, provided that such majority includes a majority of the members participating in the session. When the issue arises as to whether a question is one of substance or not, that question shall be treated as one of substance unless otherwise decided by the Assembly by the majority required for decisions on questions of substance.

9. When a question of substance comes up for voting for the first time, the President may, and shall, if requested by at least one fifth of the members of the Assembly, defer the issue of taking a vote on that question for a period not exceeding five calendar days. This rule may be applied only once to any question, and shall not be applied so as to defer the question beyond the end of the session.

10. Upon a written request addressed to the President and sponsored by at least one fourth of the members of the Authority for an advisory opinion on the conformity with this Convention of a proposal before the Assembly on any matter, the Assembly shall request the Sea-Bed Disputes Chamber of the International Tribunal for the Law of the Sea to give an advisory opinion thereon and shall defer voting on that proposal pending receipt of the advisory opinion by the Chamber. If the advisory opinion is not received before the final week of the session in which it is requested, the Assembly shall decide when it will meet to vote upon the deferred proposal.

Art. 160. Powers and functions

1. The Assembly, as the sole organ of the Authority consisting of all the members, shall be considered the supreme organ of the Authority to which the other principal organs shall be accountable as specifically provided for in this Convention. The Assembly shall have the power to establish general policies in conformity with the relevant provisions of this Convention on any question or matter within the competence of the Authority.

2. In addition, the powers and functions of the Assembly shall be:

(a) to elect the members of the Council in accordance with article 161;

(b) to elect the Secretary-General from among the candidates proposed by the Council;

(c) to elect, upon the recommendation of the Council, the members of the Governing Board of the Enterprise and the Director-General of the Enterprise;

(d) to establish such subsidiary organs as it finds necessary for the exercise of its functions in accordance with this Part. In the composition of these subsidiary organs due account shall be taken of the principle of equitable geographical distribution and of special interests and the need for members qualified and competent in the relevant technical questions dealt with by such organs;

(e) to assess the contributions of members to the administrative budget of the Authority in accordance with an agreed scale of assessment based upon the scale used for the regular budget of the United Nations until the Authority shall have sufficient income from other sources to meet its administrative expenses;

(f) (i) to consider and approve, upon the recommendation of the Council, the rules, regulations and procedures on the equitable sharing of financial and other economic benefits derived from activities in the Area and the payments and contributions made pursuant to article 82, taking into particular consideration the interests and needs of developing States and peoples who have not attained full independence or other self-governing status. If the Assembly does not approve the recommendations of the Council, the Assembly shall return them to the Council for reconsideration in the light of the views expressed by the Assembly;

(ii) to consider and approve the rules, regulations and procedures of the Authority, and any amendments thereto, provisionally adopted by the Council pursuant to article 162, paragraph 2 (o)(ii). These rules, regulations and procedures shall relate to prospecting, exploration and exploitation in the Area, the financial management and internal administration of the Authority, and, upon the recommendation of the Governing Board of the Enterprise, to the transfer of funds from the Enterprise to the Authority;

(g) to decide upon the equitable sharing of financial and other economic benefits derived from activities in the Area, consistent with this Convention and the rules, regulations and procedures of the Authority;

(h) to consider and approve the proposed annual budget of the Authority submitted by the Council;

(i) to examine periodic reports from the Council and from the Enterprise and special reports requested from the Council or any other organ of the Authority;

(j) to initiate studies and make recommendations for the purpose of promoting international co-operation concerning activities in the Area and encouraging the progressive development of international law relating thereto and its codification;

(k) to consider problems of a general nature in connection with activities in the Area arising in particular for developing States, as well as those problems for States in connection with activities in the Area that are due to their geographical location, particularly for land-locked and geographically disadvantaged States;

(l) to establish, upon the recommendation of the Council, on the basis of advice from the Economic Planning Commission, a system of compensation or other measures of economic adjustment assistance as provided in article 151, paragraph 10;

(m) to suspend the exercise of rights and privileges of membership pursuant to article 185;

(n) to discuss any question or matter within the competence of the Authority and to decide as to which organ of the Authority shall deal with any such question or matter not specifically entrusted to a particular organ, consistent with the distribution of powers and functions among the organs of the Authority.

Subsection C. The Council

Art. 161. Composition, procedure and voting

1. The Council shall consist of 36 members of the Authority elected by the Assembly in the following order:

(a) four members from among those States Parties which, during the last five years for which statistics are available, have either consumed more than 2 per cent of total world consumption or have had net imports of more than 2 per cent of total world imports of the commodities produced from the categories of minerals to be derived from the Area, and in any case one State from the Eastern European (Socialist) region, as well as the largest consumer;

(b) four members from among the eight States Parties which have the largest investments in preparation for and in the conduct of activities in the Area, either directly or through their nationals, including at least one State from the Eastern European (Socialist) region;

(c) four members from among States Parties which on the basis of production in areas under their jurisdiction are major net exporters of the categories of minerals to be derived from the Area, including at least two developing States whose exports of such minerals have a substantial bearing upon their economies;

(d) six members from among developing States Parties, representing special interests. The special interests to be represented shall include those of States with large populations, States which are land-locked or geographically disadvantaged, States which are major importers of the categories of minerals to be derived from the Area, States which are potential producers of such minerals, and least developed States;

(e) eighteen members elected according to the principle of ensuring an equitable geographical distribution of seats in the Council as a whole, provided that each geographical region shall have at least one member elected under this subparagraph. For this purpose, the geographical regions shall be Africa, Asia, Eastern European (Socialist), Latin America and Western European and Others.

2. In electing the members of the Council in accordance with paragraph 1, the Assembly shall ensure that:

(a) land-locked and geographically disadvantaged States are represented to a degree which is reasonably proportionate to their representation in the Assembly;

(b) coastal States, especially developing States, which do not qualify under paragraph 1 (a), (b), (c) or (d) are represented to a degree which is reasonably proportionate to their representation in the Assembly;

(c) each group of States Parties to be represented on the Council is represented by those members, if any, which are nominated by that group.

3. Elections shall take place at regular sessions of the Assembly. Each member of the Council shall be elected for four years. At the first election, however, the term of one half of the members of each group referred to in paragraph 1 shall be two years.

4. Members of the Council shall be eligible for re-election, but due regard should be paid to the desirability of rotation of membership.

5. The Council shall function at the seat of the Authority, and shall meet as often as the business of the Authority may require, but not less than three times a year.

6. A majority of the members of the Council shall constitute a quorum.

7. Each member of the Council shall have one vote.

8. (a) Decisions on questions of procedure shall be taken by a majority of the members present and voting.

(b) Decisions on questions of substance arising under the following provisions shall be taken by a two-thirds majority of the members present and voting, provided that such majority includes a majority of the members of the Council: article 162, paragraph 2, subparagraphs (f); (g); (h); (i); (n); (p); (v); article 191.

(c) Decisions on questions of substance arising under the following provisions shall be taken by a three-fourths majority of the members present and voting, provided that such majority includes a majority of the members of the Council: article 162, paragraph 1; article 162, paragraph 2, subparagraphs (a); (b); (c); (d); (e); (l); (q); (r); (r); (s); (t); (u) in cases of non-compliance by a contractor or a sponsor; (w) provided that orders issued thereunder may be binding for not more than 30 days unless confirmed by a decision taken in accordance with subparagraph (d); article 162, paragraph 2, subparagraphs (x); (y); (z); article 163, paragraph 2; article 174, paragraph 3; Annex IV, article 11.

(d) Decisions on questions of substance arising under the following provisions shall be taken by consensus: article 162, paragraph 2(m) and (o); adoption of amendments to Part XI.

(e) For the purposes of subparagraphs (d), (f) and (g), 'consensus' means the absence of any formal objection. Within 14 days of the submission of a proposal to the Council, the President of the Council shall determine whether there would be a formal objection to the adoption of the proposal. If the President determines that there would be such an objection, the President shall establish and convene, within three days following such determination, a conciliation committee consisting of not more than nine members of the Council, with the President as chairman, for the purpose of reconciling the differences and producing a proposal which can be adopted by consensus. The committee shall work expeditiously and report to the Council within 14 days following its establishment. If the committee is unable to recommend a proposal which can be adopted by consensus, it shall set out in its report the grounds on which the proposal is being opposed.

(f) Decisions on questions not listed above which the Council is authorized to take by the rules, regulations and procedures of the Authority or otherwise shall be taken pursuant to the subparagraphs of this paragraph specified in the rules, regulations and procedures or, if not specified therein, then pursuant to the subparagraph determined by the Council if possible in advance, by consensus.

(g) When the issue arises as to whether a question is within subparagraph (a), (b), (c) or (d), the question shall be treated as being within the subparagraph requiring the higher or highest majority or consensus as the case may be, unless otherwise decided by the Council by the said majority or by consensus.

9. The Council shall establish a procedure whereby a member of the Authority not represented on the Council may send a representative to attend a meeting of the Council when a request is made by such member, or a matter particularly affecting it is under consideration. Such a representative shall be entitled to participate in the deliberations but not to vote.

Art. 162. Powers and functions

1. The Council is the executive organ of the Authority. The Council shall have the power to establish, in conformity with this Convention and the general policies established by the Assembly, the specific policies to be pursued by the Authority on any question or matter within the competence of the Authority.

2. In addition, the Council shall:

(a) supervise and co-ordinate the implementation of the provisions of this Part on all questions and matters within the competence of the Authority and invite the attention of the Assembly to cases of non-compliance;

(b) propose to the Assembly a list of candidates for the election of the Secretary-General;

(c) recommend to the Assembly candidates for the election of the members of the Governing Board of the Enterprise and the Director-General of the Enterprise;

(d) establish, as appropriate, and with due regard to economy and efficiency, such subsidiary organs as it finds necessary for the exercise of its functions in accordance with this Part. In the composition of subsidiary organs, emphasis shall be placed on the need for members qualified and competent in relevant technical matters dealt with by those organs provided that due account shall be taken of the principle of equitable geographical distribution and of special interests;

(e) adopt its rules of procedure including the method of selecting its president;

(f) enter into agreements with the United Nations or other international organizations on behalf of the Authority and within its competence, subject to approval by the Assembly;

(g) consider the reports of the Enterprise and transmit them to the Assembly with its recommendations;

(h) present to the Assembly annual reports and such special reports as the Assembly may request;

(i) issue directives to the Enterprise in accordance with article 170;

(j) approve plans of work in accordance with Annex III, article 6. The Council shall act upon each plan of work within 60 days of its submission by the Legal and Technical Commission at a session of the Council in accordance with the following procedures:

(i) if the Commission recommends the approval of a plan of work, it shall be deemed to have been approved by the Council if no member of the Council submits in writing to the President within 14 days a specific objection alleging non-compliance with the requirements of Annex III, article 6. If there is an objection, the conciliation procedure set forth in article 161, paragraph 8 (e), shall apply. If, at the end of the conciliation procedure, the objection is still maintained, the plan of work shall be deemed to have been approved by the Council unless the Council disapproves it by consensus among its members excluding any State or States making the application or sponsoring the applicant;

(ii) if the Commission recommends the disapproval of a plan of work or does not make a recommendation, the Council may approve the plan of work by a three-fourths majority of the members present and voting, provided that such majority includes a majority of the members participating in the session;

(k) approve plans of work submitted by the Enterprise in accordance with Annex IV, article 12, applying, *mutatis mutandis*, the procedures set forth in sub-paragraph (j);

(l) exercise control over activities in the Area in accordance with article 153, paragraph 4, and the rules, regulations and procedures of the Authority;

(m) take, upon the recommendation of the Economic Planning Commission, necessary and appropriate measures in accordance with article 150, subparagraph (h), to provide protection from the adverse economic effects specified therein;

(n) make recommendations to the Assembly, on the basis of advice from the Economic Planning Commission, for a system of compensation or other measures of economic adjustment assistance as provided in article 151, paragraph 10;

(o) (i) recommend to the Assembly rules, regulations and procedures on the equitable sharing of financial and other economic benefits derived from activities in the Area and the payments and contributions made pursuant to article 82, taking into particular consideration the interests and needs of the developing States and peoples who have not attained full independence or other self-governing status;

(ii) adopt and apply provisionally, pending approval by the Assembly, the rules, regulations and procedures of the Authority, and any amendments thereto, taking into account the recommendations of the Legal and Technical Commission or other subordinate organ concerned. These rules, regulations and procedures shall relate to prospecting, exploration and exploitation in the Area and the financial management and internal administration of the Authority. Priority shall be given to the adoption of rules, regulations and procedures for the exploration for and exploitation of polymetallic nodules. Rules, regulations and procedures for the exploration for and exploitation of any resource other than polymetallic nodules shall be adopted within three years from the date of a request to the Authority by any of its members to adopt such rules, regulations and procedures in respect of such resource. All rules, regulations and procedures shall remain in effect on a provisional basis until approved by the Assembly or until amended by the Council in the light of any views expressed by the Assembly;

(p) review the collection of all payments to be made by or to the Authority in connection with operations pursuant to this Part;

(q) make the selection from among applicants for production authorizations pursuant to Annex III, article 7, where such selection is required by that provision;

(r) submit the proposed annual budget of the Authority to the Assembly for its approval;

(s) make recommendations to the Assembly concerning policies on any question or matter within the competence of the Authority;

(t) make recommendations to the Assembly concerning suspension of the exercise of the rights and privileges of membership pursuant to article 185;

(u) institute proceedings on behalf of the Authority before the Sea-Bed Disputes Chamber in cases of non-compliance;

(v) notify the Assembly upon a decision by the Sea-Bed Disputes Chamber in proceedings instituted under sub-paragraph (u), and make any recommendations which it may find appropriate with respect to measures to be taken;

(w) issue emergency orders, which may include orders for the suspension or adjustment of operations, to prevent serious harm to the marine environment arising out of activities in the Area;

(x) disapprove areas for exploitation by contractors or the Enterprise in cases where substantial evidence indicates the risk of serious harm to the marine environment;

(y) establish a subsidiary organ for the elaboration of draft financial rules, regulations and procedures relating to:

(i) financial management in accordance with articles 171 to 175; and

(ii) financial arrangements in accordance with Annex III, article 13 and article 17, paragraph 1 (c);

(z) establish appropriate mechanisms for directing and supervising a staff of inspectors who shall inspect activities in the Area to determine whether this Part, the rules, regulations and procedures of the Authority, and the terms and conditions of any contract with the Authority are being complied with.

Art. 163. Organs of the Council

1. There are hereby established the following organs of the Council:

(a) an Economic Planning Commission;

(b) a Legal and Technical Commission.

2. Each Commission shall be composed of 15 members, elected by the Council from among the candidates nominated by the States Parties. However, if necessary, the Council may decide to increase the size of either Commission having due regard to economy and efficiency.

3. Members of a Commission shall have appropriate qualifications in the area of competence of that Commission. States Parties shall nominate candidates of the highest standards of competence and integrity with qualifications in relevant fields so as to ensure the effective exercise of the functions of the Commissions.

4. In the election of members of the Commissions, due account shall be taken of the need for equitable geographical distribution and the representation of special interests.

5. No State party may nominate more than one candidate for the same Commission. No person shall be elected to serve on more than one Commission.

6. Members of the Commissions shall hold office for a term of five years. They shall be eligible for re-election for a further term.

7. In the event of the death, incapacity or resignation of a member of a Commission prior to the expiration of the term of office, the Council shall elect for the remainder of the term, a member from the same geographical region or area of interest.

8. Members of Commissions shall have no financial interest in any activity relating to exploration and exploitation in the Area. Subject to their responsibilities to the Commissions upon which they serve, they shall not disclose, even after the termination of their functions, any industrial secret, proprietary data which are transferred to the Authority in accordance with Annex III, article 14, or any other confidential information coming to their knowledge by reason of their duties for the Authority.

9. Each Commission shall exercise its functions in accordance with such guidelines and directives as the Council may adopt.

10. Each Commission shall formulate and submit to the Council for approval such rules and regulations as may be necessary for the efficient conduct of the Commission's functions.

11. The decision-making procedures of the Commissions shall be established by the rules, regulations and procedures of the Authority. Recommendations to the Council shall, where necessary, be accompanied by a summary on the divergencies of opinion in the Commission.

12. Each Commission shall normally function at the seat of the Authority and shall meet as often as is required for the efficient exercise of its functions.

13. In the exercise of its functions, each Commission may, where appropriate, consult another commission, any competent organ of the United Nations or of its specialized agencies or any international organizations with competence in the subject-matter of such consultation.

Art. 164. The Economic Planning Commission

1. Members of the Economic Planning Commission shall have appropriate qualifications such as those relevant to mining, management of mineral resource activities, international trade or international economics. The Council shall endeavour to ensure that the membership of the Commission reflects all appropriate qualifications. The Commission shall include at least two members from developing States whose exports of the categories of minerals to be derived from the Area have a substantial bearing upon their economies.

2. The Commission shall:

(a) propose, upon the request of the Council, measures to implement decisions relating to activities in the Area taken in accordance with this Convention;

(b) review the trends of and the factors affecting supply, demand and prices of materials which may be derived from the Area, bearing in mind the interests of both importing and exporting countries, and in particular of the developing States among them;

(c) examine any situation likely to lead to the adverse effects referred to in article 150, subparagraph (h), brought to its attention by the State Party or States Parties concerned, and make appropriate recommendations to the Council;

(d) propose to the Council for submission to the Assembly, as provided in article 151, paragraph 10, a system of compensation or other measures of economic adjustment assistance for developing States which suffer adverse effects caused by activities in the Area. The Commission shall make the recommendations to the Council that are necessary for the application of the system or other measures adopted by the Assembly in specific cases.

Art. 165. The Legal and Technical Commission

1. Members of the Legal and Technical Commission shall have appropriate qualifications such as those relevant to exploration for and exploitation and processing of mineral resources, oceanology, protection of the marine environment, or economic or legal matters relating to ocean mining and related fields of expertise. The Council shall endeavour to ensure that the membership of the Commission reflects all appropriate qualifications.

2. The Commission shall:

(a) make recommendations with regard to the exercise of the Authority's functions upon the request of the Council;

(b) review formal written plans of work for activities in the Area in accordance with article 153, paragraph 3, and submit appropriate recommendations to the Council. The Commission shall base its recommendations solely on the grounds stated in Annex III and shall report fully thereon to the Council;

(c) supervise, upon the request of the Council, activities in the Area, where appropriate, in consultation and collaboration with any entity carrying out such activities or State or States concerned and report to the Council;

(d) prepare assessments of the environmental implications of activities in the Area;

(e) make recommendations to the Council on the protection of the marine environment, taking into account the views of recognized experts in that field;

(f) formulate and submit to the Council the rules, regulations and procedures referred to in article 162, paragraph 2(o), taking into account all relevant factors including assessments of the environmental implications of activities in the Area;

(g) keep such rules, regulations and procedures under review and recommend to the Council from time to time such amendments thereto as it may deem necessary or desirable;

(h) make recommendations to the Council regarding the establishment of a monitoring programme to observe, measure, evaluate and analyse, by recognized scientific methods, on a regular basis, the risks or effects of pollution of the marine environment resulting from activities in the Area, ensure that existing regulations are adequate and are complied with and co-ordinate the implementation of the monitoring programme approved by the Council;

(i) recommend to the Council that proceedings be instituted on behalf of the Authority before the Sea-Bed Disputes Chamber, in accordance with this Part and the relevant Annexes taking into account particularly article 187;

(j) make recommendations to the Council with respect to measures to be taken, upon a decision by the Sea-Bed Disputes Chamber in proceedings instituted in accordance with subparagraph (i);

(k) make recommendations to the Council to issue emergency orders, which may include orders for the suspension or adjustment of operations, to prevent serious harm to the marine environment arising out of activities in the Area. Such recommendations shall be taken up by the Council on a priority basis;

(l) make recommendations to the Council to disapprove areas for exploitation by contractors or the Enterprise in cases where substantial evidence indicates the risk of serious harm to the marine environment;

(m) make recommendations to the Council regarding the direction and supervision of a staff of inspectors

who shall inspect activities in the Area to determine whether the provisions of this Part, the rules, regulations and procedures of the Authority, and the terms and conditions of any contract with the Authority are being complied with;
(n) calculate the production ceiling and issue production authorizations on behalf of the Authority pursuant to article 151, paragraphs 2 to 7, following any necessary selection among applicants for production authorizations by the Council in accordance with Annex III, article 7.
3. The members of the Commission shall, upon request by any State Party or other party concerned, be accompanied by a representative of such State or other party concerned when carrying out their function of supervision and inspection.

Subsection D. The Secretariat
Art. 166. The Secretariat
1. The Secretariat of the Authority shall comprise a Secretary-General and such staff as the Authority may require.
2. The Secretary-General shall be elected for four years by the Assembly from among the candidates proposed by the Council and may be re-elected.
3. The Secretary-General shall be the chief administrative officer of the Authority, and shall act in that capacity in all meetings of the Assembly, of the Council and of any subsidiary organ, and shall perform such other administrative functions as are entrusted to the Secretary-General by these organs.
4. The Secretary-General shall make an annual report to the Assembly on the work of the Authority.
Art. 167. The staff of the Authority
1. The staff of the Authority shall consist of such qualified scientific and technical and other personnel as may be required to fulfil the administrative functions of the Authority.
2. The paramount consideration in the recruitment and employment of the staff and in the determination of their conditions of service shall be the necessity of securing the highest standards of efficiency, competence and integrity. Subject to this consideration, due regard shall be paid to the importance of recruiting the staff on as wide a geographical basis as possible.
3. The staff shall be appointed by the Secretary-General. The terms and conditions on which they shall be appointed, remunerated and dismissed shall be in accordance with the rules, regulations and procedures of the Authority.
Art. 168. International character of the Secretariat
1. In the performance of their duties the Secretary-General and the staff shall not seek or receive instructions from any government or from any other source external to the Authority. They shall refrain from any action which might reflect on their position as international officials responsible only to the Authority. Each State Party undertakes to respect the exclusively international character of the responsibilities of the Secretary-General and the staff and not to seek to influence them in the discharge of their responsibilities. Any violation of responsibilities by a staff member shall be submitted to the appropriate administrative tribunal as provided in the rules, regulations and procedures of the Authority.
2. The Secretary-General and the staff shall have no financial interest in any activity relating to exploration and exploitation in the Area. Subject to their responsibilities to the Authority, they shall not disclose, even after the termination of their functions, any industrial secret, proprietary data which are transferred to the Authority in accordance with Annex III, article 14, or any other confidential information coming to their knowledge by reason of their employment with the Authority.
3. Violations of the obligations of a staff member of the Authority set forth in paragraph 2 shall, on the request of a State party affected by such violation, or a natural or juridical person, sponsored by a State Party as provided in article 153, paragraph 2(b), and affected by such violation, be submitted by the Authority against the staff member concerned to a tribunal designated by the rules, regulations and procedures of the Authority. The Party affected shall have the right to take part in the proceedings. If the tribunal so recommends, the Secretary-General shall dismiss the staff member concerned.
4. The rules, regulations and procedures of the Authority shall contain such provisions as are necessary to implement this article.
Art. 169. Consultation and co-operation with international and non-governmental organizations
1. The Secretary-General shall, on matters within the competence of the Authority, make suitable arrangements, with the approval of the Council, for consultation and co-operation with international and non-governmental organizations recognized by the Economic and Social Council of the United Nations.
2. Any organization with which the Secretary-General has entered into an arrangement under paragraph 1 may designate representatives to attend meetings of the organs of the Authority as observers in accordance with the rules of procedure of these organs. Procedures shall be established for obtaining the views of such organizations in appropriate cases.
3. The Secretary-General may distribute to States Parties written reports submitted by the non-governmental organizations referred to in paragraph 1 on subjects in which they have special competence and which are related to the work of the Authority.

Subsection E. The Enterprise
Art. 170. The Enterprise
1. The Enterprise shall be the organ of the Authority which shall carry out activities in the Area directly, pursuant to article 153, paragraph 2(a), as well as the transporting, processing and marketing of minerals recovered from the Area.
2. The Enterprise shall, within the framework of the international legal personality of the Authority, have such legal capacity as is provided for in the Statute set forth in Annex IV. The Enterprise shall act in accordance with this Convention and the rules, regulations and procedures of the Authority, as well as the general policies established by the Assembly, and shall be subject to the directives and control of the Council.
3. The enterprise shall have its principal place of business at the seat of the Authority.
4. The Enterprise shall, in accordance with article 173, paragraph 2, and Annex IV, article 11, be provided with such funds as it may require to carry out its functions, and shall receive technology as provided in article 144 and other relevant provisions of this Convention.

Subsection F. Financial Arrangements of the Authority
Art. 171. Funds of the Authority
The funds of the Authority shall include:
(a) assessed contributions made by members of the Authority in accordance with article 160, paragraph 2(e);
(b) funds received by the Authority pursuant to Annex III, article 13, in connection with activities in the Area;
(c) funds transferred from the Enterprise in accordance with Annex IV, article 10;
(d) funds borrowed pursuant to article 174;
(e) voluntary contributions made by members or other entities; and
(f) payments to a compensation fund, in accordance with article 151, paragraph 10, whose sources are to be recommended by the Economic Planning Commission.
Art. 172. Annual budget of the Authority
The Secretary-General shall draft the proposed annual budget of the Authority and submit it to the Council. The Council shall consider the proposed annual budget and submit it to the Assembly, together with any recommendations thereon. The Assembly shall consider and approve the proposed annual budget in accordance with article 160, paragraph 2(h).
Art. 173. Expenses of the Authority
1. The contributions referred to in article 171, subparagraph (a), shall be paid into a special account to meet the administrative expenses of the Authority until the Authority has sufficient funds from other sources to meet those expenses.
2. The administrative expenses of the Authority shall be a first call upon the funds of the Authority. Except for the assessed contributions referred to in article 171, subparagraph (a), the funds which remain after payment of administrative expenses may, *inter alia*:
(a) be shared in accordance with article 140 and article 160, paragraph 2(g);
(b) be used to provide the Enterprise with funds in accordance with article 170, paragraph 4;
(c) be used to compensate developing States in accordance with article 151, paragraph 10, and article 160, paragraph 2(l).
Art. 174. Borrowing power of the Authority
1. The Authority shall have the power to borrow funds.
2. The Assembly shall prescribe the limits on the borrowing power of the Authority in the financial regulations adopted pursuant to article 160, paragraph 2(f).
3. The Council shall exercise the borrowing power of the Authority.
4. States Parties shall not be liable for the debts of the Authority.
Art. 175. Annual Audit
The records, books and accounts of the Authority, including its annual financial statements, shall be audited annually by an independent auditor appointed by the Assembly.

Subsection G. Legal status, privileges and immunities
Art. 176. Legal status
The Authority shall have international legal personality and such legal capacity as may be necessary for the exercise of its functions and the fulfilment of its purposes.
Art. 177. Privileges and immunities
To enable the Authority to exercise its functions, it shall enjoy in the territory of each State party the privileges and immunities set forth in this subsection. The privileges and immunities relating to the Enterprise shall be those set forth in Annex IV, article 13.
Art. 178. Immunity from legal process
The Authority, its property and assets, shall enjoy immunity from legal process except to the extent that the Authority expressly waives this immunity in a particular case.
Art. 179. Immunity from search and any form of seizure
The property and assets of the Authority, wherever located and by whomsoever held, shall be immune from search, requisition, confiscation, expropriation or any other form of seizure by executive or legislative action.
Art. 180. Exemption from restrictions, regulations, controls and moratoria
The property and assets of the Authority shall be exempt from restrictions, regulations, controls and moratoria of any nature.
Art. 181. Archives and official communications of the Authority
1. The archives of the Authority, wherever located, shall be inviolable.
2. Proprietary data, industrial secrets or similar information and personnel records shall not be placed in archives which are open to public inspection.
3. With regard to its official communications, the Authority shall be accorded by each State Party treatment no less favourable than that accorded by that State to other international organizations.
Art. 182. Privileges and immunities of certain persons connected with the Authority
Representatives of States Parties attending meetings of the Assembly, the Council or organs of the Assembly or the Council, and the Secretary-General and staff of the Authority, shall enjoy in the territory of each State Party:
(a) immunity from legal process with respect to acts performed by them in the exercise of their functions, except to the extent that the State which they represent or the Authority, as appropriate, expressly waives this immunity in a particular case;
(b) if they are not nationals of that State Party, the same exemptions from immigration restrictions, alien registration requirements and national service obligations, the same facilities as regards exchange restrictions and the same treatment in respect of travelling facilities as are accorded by that State to the representatives, officials and employees of comparable rank of other States Parties.
Art. 183. Exemption from taxes and customs duties
1. Within the scope of its official activities, the Authority, its assets and property, its income, and its operations and transactions, authorized by this Convention, shall be exempt from all direct taxation and goods imported or exported for its official use shall be exempt from all customs duties. The Authority shall not claim exemption from taxes which are no more than charges for services rendered.
2. When purchases of good or services of substantial value necessary for the official activities of the Authority are made by or on behalf of the Authority, and when the price of such goods or services includes taxes or duties, appropriate measures shall, to the extent practicable, be taken by States Parties to grant exemption from such taxes or duties or provide for their reim-

bursement. Goods imported or purchased under an exemption provided for in this article shall not be sold or otherwise disposed of in the territory of the State Party which granted the exemption, except under conditions agreed with that State party.

3. No tax shall be levied by States Parties on or in respect of salaries and emoluments paid or any other form of payment made by the Authority to the Secretary-General and staff of the Authority, as well as experts performing missions for the Authority who are not their nationals.

Subsection H. Suspension of the exercise of rights and privileges of members
Art. 184. Suspension of the exercise of voting rights
A State Party which is in arrears in the payment of its financial contributions to the Authority shall have no vote if the amount of its arrears equals or exceeds the amount of the contributions due from it for the preceding two full years. The Assembly may, nevertheless, permit such a member to vote if it is satisfied that the failure to pay is due to conditions beyond the control of the member.

Art. 185. Suspension of exercise of rights and privileges of membership
1. A State party which has grossly and persistently violated the provisions of this Part may be suspended from the exercise of the rights and privileges of membership by the Assembly upon the recommendation of the Council.
2. No action may be taken under paragraph 1 until the Sea-Bed Disputes Chamber has found that a State Party has grossly and persistently violated the provisions of this Part.

Section 5. Settlement of disputes and advisory opinions
Art. 186. Sea-Bed Disputes Chamber of the International Tribunal for the Law of the Sea
The establishment of the Sea-Bed Disputes Chamber and the manner in which it shall exercise its jurisdiction shall be governed by the provisions of this section, of Part XV and of Annex VI.

Art. 187. Jurisdiction of the Sea-Bed Disputes Chamber
The Sea-Bed Disputes Chamber shall have jurisdiction under this Part and the Annexes relating thereto in disputes with respect to activities in the Area falling within the following categories:
(a) disputes between States Parties concerning the interpretation or application of this Part and the Annexes relating thereto;
(b) disputes between a State Party and the Authority concerning:
(i) acts or omissions of the Authority or of a State Party alleged to be in violation of this Part or the Annexes relating thereto or of rules, regulations and procedures of the Authority adopted in accordance therewith; or
(ii) acts of the Authority alleged to be in excess of jurisdiction or a misuse of power;
(c) disputes between parties to a contract, being States Parties, the Authority or the Enterprise, state enterprises and natural or juridical persons referred to in article 153, paragraph 2(b), concerning:
(i) the interpretation or application of a relevant contract or a plan of work; or
(ii) acts or omissions of a party to the contract relating to activities in the Area and directed to the other party or directly affecting its legitimate interests;
(d) disputes between the Authority and a prospective contractor who has been sponsored by a State as provided in article 153, paragraph 2(b), and has duly fulfilled the conditions referred to in Annex III, article 4, paragraph 6, and article 13, paragraph 2, concerning the refusal of a contract or a legal issue arising in the negotiation of the contract;
(e) disputes between the Authority and a State Party, a state enterprise or a natural or juridical person sponsored by a State Party as provided for in article 153, paragraph 2(b), where it is alleged that the Authority has incurred liability as provided in Annex III, article 22;
(f) any other disputes for which the jurisdiction of the Chamber is specifically provided in this Convention.
Art. 188. Submission of disputes to a special chamber of the International Tribunal for the Law of the Sea or an ad hoc chamber of the Sea-Bed Disputes Chamber or to binding commercial arbitration
1. Disputes between States Parties referred to in article 187, subparagraph (a), may be submitted:

(a) at the request of the parties to the dispute, to a special chamber of the International Tribunal for the Law of the Sea to be formed in accordance with Annex VI, articles 15 and 17; or
(b) at the request of any party to the dispute, to an *ad hoc* chamber of the Sea-Bed Disputes Chamber to be formed in accordance with Annex VI, article 36.
2. (a) Disputes concerning the interpretation or application of a contract referred to in article 187, subparagraph (c)(i), shall be submitted, at the request of any party to the dispute, to binding commercial arbitration, unless the parties otherwise agree. A commercial arbitral tribunal to which the dispute is submitted shall have no jurisdiction to decide any question of interpretation of this Convention. When the dispute also involves a question of the interpretation of Part XI and the Annexes relating thereto, with respect to activities in the Area, that question shall be referred to the Sea-Bed Disputes Chamber for a ruling.
(b) If, at the commencement of or in the course of such arbitration, the arbitral tribunal determines, either at the request of any party to the dispute or *proprio motu*, that its decision depends upon a ruling of the Sea-Bed Disputes Chamber, the arbitral tribunal shall refer such question to the Sea-Bed Disputes Chamber for such ruling. The arbitral tribunal shall then proceed to render its award in conformity with the ruling of the Sea-Bed Disputes Chamber.
(c) In the absence of a provision in the contract on the arbitration procedure to be applied in the dispute, the arbitration shall be conducted in accordance with the UNCITRAL Arbitration Rules or such other arbitration rules as may be prescribed in the rules, regulations and procedures of the Authority, unless the parties to the dispute otherwise agree.
Art. 189. Limitation on jurisdiction with regard to decisions of the Authority
The Sea-Bed Disputes Chamber shall have no jurisdiction with regard to the exercise by the Authority of its discretionary powers in accordance with this Part; in no case shall it substitute its discretion for that of the Authority. Without prejudice to article 191, in exercising its jurisdiction pursuant to article 187, the Sea-Bed Disputes Chamber shall not pronounce itself on the question of whether any rules, regulations and procedures of the Authority are in conformity with this Convention, nor declare invalid any such rules, regulations and procedures. Its jurisdiction in this regard shall be confined to deciding claims that the application of any rules, regulations and procedures of the Authority in individual cases would be in conflict with the contractual obligations of the parties to the dispute or their obligations under this Convention, claims concerning excess of jurisdiction or misuse of power, and to claims for damages to be paid or other remedy to be given to the party concerned for the failure of the other party to comply with its contractual obligations or its obligations under this Convention.
Art. 190. Participation and appearance of sponsoring States Parties in proceedings
1. If a natural or juridical person is a party to a dispute referred to in article 187, the sponsoring State shall be given notice thereof and shall have the right to participate in the proceedings by submitting written or oral statements.
2. If an action is brought against a State party by a natural or juridical person sponsored by another State Party in a dispute referred to in article 187, subparagraph (c), the respondent State may request the State sponsoring that person to appear in the proceedings on behalf of that person. Failing such appearance, the respondent State may arrange to be represented by a juridical person of its nationality.
Art. 191. Advisory opinions
The Sea-Bed Disputes Chamber shall give advisory opinions at the request of the Assembly or the Council on legal questions arising within the scope of their activities. Such opinions shall be given as a matter of urgency.

Part XII. Protection and preservation of the marine environment

Section 1. General provisions
Art. 192. General obligation
States have the obligation to protect and preserve the marine environment.
Art. 193. Sovereign right of States to exploit their natural resources

States have the sovereign right to exploit their natural resources pursuant to their environmental policies and in accordance with their duty to protect and preserve the marine environment.
Art. 194. Measures to prevent, reduce and control pollution of the marine environment
1. States shall take, individually or jointly as appropriate, all measures consistent with this Convention that are necessary to prevent, reduce and control pollution of the marine environment from any source, using for this purpose the best practicable means at their disposal and in accordance with their capabilities, and they shall endeavour to harmonize their policies in this connection.
2. States shall take all measures necessary to ensure that activities under their jurisdiction or control are so conducted as not to cause damage by pollution to other States and their environment, and that pollution arising from incidents or activities under their jurisdiction or control does not spread beyond the areas where they exercise sovereign rights in accordance with this Convention.
3. The measures taken pursuant to this Part shall deal with all sources of pollution of the marine environment. These measures shall include, *inter alia*, those designed to minimize to the fullest possible extent:
(a) the release of toxic, harmful or noxious substances, especially those which are persistent, from land-based sources, from or through the atmosphere or by dumping;
(b) pollution from vessels, in particular measures for preventing accidents and dealing with emergencies, ensuring the safety of operations at sea, preventing intentional and unintentional discharges, and regulating the design, construction, equipment, operation and manning of vessels;
(c) pollution from installations and devices used in exploration or exploitation of the natural resources of the sea-bed and subsoil, in particular measures for preventing accidents and dealing with emergencies, ensuring the safety of operations at sea, and regulating the design, construction, equipment, operation and manning of such installations or devices;
(d) pollution from other installations and devices operating in the marine environment, in particular measures for preventing accidents and dealing with emergencies, ensuring the safety of operations at sea, and regulating the design, construction, equipment, operation and manning of such installations or devices.
4. In taking measures to prevent, reduce or control pollution of the marine environment, States shall refrain from unjustifiable interference with activities carried out by other States in the exercise of their rights and in pursuance of their duties in conformity with this Convention.
5. The measures taken in accordance with this Part shall include those necessary to protect and preserve rare or fragile ecosystems as well as the habitat of depleted, threatened or endangered species and other forms of marine life.
Art. 195. Duty not to transfer damage or hazards or transform one type of pollution into another
In taking measures to prevent, reduce and control pollution of the marine environment, States shall act so as not to transfer, directly or indirectly, damage or hazards from one area to another or transform one type of pollution into another.
Art. 196. Use of technologies or introduction of alien or new species
1. States shall take all measures necessary to prevent, reduce and control pollution of the marine environment resulting from the use of technologies under their jurisdiction or control, or the intentional or accidental introduction of species, alien or new, to a particular part of the marine environment, which may cause significant and harmful changes thereto.
2. This article does not affect the application of this Convention regarding the prevention, reduction and control of pollution of the marine environment.

Section 2. Global and regional co-operation
Art. 197. Co-operation on a global or regional basis
States shall co-operate on a global basis and, as appropriate, on a regional basis, directly or through competent international organizations, in formulating and elaborating international rules, standards and recommended practices and procedures consistent with this Convention, for the protection and preservation of

the marine environment, taking into account characteristic regional features.

Art. 198. Notification of imminent or actual damage
When a State becomes aware of cases in which the marine environment is in imminent danger of being damaged or has been damaged by pollution, it shall immediately notify other States it deems likely to be affected by such damage, as well as the competent international organizations.

Art. 199. Contingency plans against pollution
In the cases referred to in article 198, States in the area affected, in accordance with their capabilities, and the competent international organizations shall co-operate, to the extent possible, in eliminating the effects of pollution and preventing or minimizing the damage. To this end, States shall jointly develop and promote contingency plans for responding to pollution incidents in the marine environment.

Art. 200. Studies, research programmes and exchange of information and data
States shall co-operate, directly or through competent international organizations, for the purpose of promoting studies, undertaking programmes of scientific research and encouraging the exchange of information and data acquired about pollution of the marine environment. They shall endeavour to participate actively in regional and global programmes to acquire knowledge for the assessment of the nature and extent of pollution, exposure to it, and its pathways, risks and remedies.

Art. 201. Scientific criterial for regulations
In the light of the information and data acquired pursuant to article 200, States shall co-operate, directly or through competent international organizations, in establishing appropriate scientific criteria for the formulation and elaboration of rules, standards and recommended practices and procedures for the prevention, reduction and control of pollution of the marine environment.

Section 3. Technical assistance
Art. 202. Scientific and technical assistance to developing States
States shall, directly or through competent international organizations:
(a) promote programmes of scientific, educational, technical and other assistance to developing States for the protection and preservation of the marine environment and the prevention, reduction and control of marine pollution. Such assistance shall include, *inter alia*:
(i) training of their scientific and technical personnel;
(ii) facilitating their participation in relevant international programmes;
(iii) supplying them with necessary equipment and facilities;
(iv) enhancing their capacity to manufacture such equipment;
(v) advice on and developing facilities for research, monitoring, educational and other programmes;
(b) provide appropriate assistance, especially to developing States, for the minimization of the effects of major incidents which may cause serious pollution of the marine environment;
(c) provide appropriate assistance, especially to developing States, concerning the preparation of environmental assessments.

Art. 203. Preferential treatment for developing States
Developing States shall, for the purposes of prevention, reduction and control of pollution of the marine environment or minimization of its effects, be granted preference by international organizations in:
(a) the allocation of appropriate funds and technical assistance; and
(b) the utilization of their specialized services.

Section 4. Monitoring and environmental assessment
Art. 204. Monitoring of the risks or effects of pollution
1. States shall, consistent with the rights of other States, endeavour, as far as practicable, directly or through the competent international organizations, to observe, measure, evaluate and analyse, by recognized scientific methods, the risks or effects of pollution of the marine environment.
2. In particular, States shall keep under surveillance the effects of any activities which they permit or in which they engage in order to determine whether these activities are likely to pollute the marine environment.

Art. 205. Publication of reports

States shall publish reports of the results obtained pursuant to article 204 or provide such reports at appropriate intervals to the competent international organizations, which should make them available to all States.

Art. 206. Assessment of potential effects of activities
When States have reasonable grounds for believing that planned activities under their jurisdiction or control may cause substantial pollution of or significant and harmful changes to the marine environment, they shall, as far as practicable, assess the potential effects of such activities on the marine environment and shall communicate reports of the results of such assessments in the manner provided in article 205.

Section 5. International rules and national legislation to prevent, reduce and control pollution of the marine environment
Art. 207. Pollution from land-based sources
1. States shall adopt laws and regulations to prevent, reduce and control pollution of the marine environment from land-based sources, including rivers, estuaries, pipelines and outfall structures, taking into account internationally agreed rules, standards and recommended practices and procedures.
2. States shall take other measures as may be necessary to prevent, reduce and control such pollution.
3. States shall endeavour to harmonize their policies in this connection at the appropriate regional level.
4. States, acting especially through competent international organizations or diplomatic conference, shall endeavour to establish global and regional rules, standards and recommended practices and procedures to prevent, reduce and control pollution of the marine environment from land-based sources, taking into account characteristic regional features, the economic capacity of developing States and their need for economic development. Such rules, standards and recommended practices and procedures shall be re-examined from time to time as necessary.
5. Laws, regulations, measures, rules, standards and recommended practices and procedures referred to in paragraphs 1, 2 and 4 shall include those designed to minimize, to the fullest extent possible, the release of toxic, harmful or noxious substances, especially those which are persistent, into the marine environment.

Art. 208. Pollution from sea-bed activities subjet to national jurisdiction
1. Coastal States shall adopt laws and regulations to prevent, reduce and control pollution of the marine environment arising from or in connection with sea-bed activities subject to their jurisdiction and from artificial islands, installations and structures under their jurisdiction, pursuant to articles 60 and 80.
2. States shall take other measures as may be necessary to prevent, reduce and control such pollution.
3. Such laws, regulations and measures shall be no less effective than international rules, standards and recommended practices and procedures.
4. States shall endeavour to harmonize their policies in this connection at the appropriate regional level.
5. States, acting especially through competent international organizations or diplomatic conference, shall establish global and regional rules, standards and recommended practices and procedures to prevent, reduce and control pollution of the marine environment referred to in paragraph 1. Such rules, standards and recommended practices shall be re-examined from time to time as necessary.

Art. 209. Pollution from activities in the Area
1. International rules, regulations and procedures shall be established in accordance with Part XI to prevent, reduce and control pollution of the marine environment from activities in the Area, Such rules, regulations and procedures shall be re-examined from time to time as necessary.
2. Subject to the relevant provisions of this section, States shall adopt laws and regulations to prevent, reduce and control pollution of the marine environment from activities in the Area undertaken by vessels, installations, structures and other devices flying their flag or of their registry or operating under their authority, as the case may be. The requirements of such laws and regulations shall be no less effective than the international rules, regulations and procedures referred to in paragraph 1.

Art. 210. Pollution by dumping
1. States shall adopt laws and regulations to prevent, reduce and control pollution of the marine environment by dumping.

2. States shall take other measures as may be necessary to prevent, reduce and control such pollution.
3. Such laws, regulations and measures shall ensure that dumping is not carried out without the permission of the competent authorities of States.
4. States, acting especially through competent international organizations or diplomatic conference, shall endeavour to establish global and regional rules, standards and recommended practices and procedures to prevent, reduce and control such pollution. Such rules, standards and recommended practices and procedures shall be re-examined from time to time as necessary.
5. Dumping within the territorial sea and the exclusive economic zone or onto the continental shelf shall not be carried out without the express prior approval of the coastal State, which has the right to permit, regulate and control such dumping after due consideration of the matter with other States which by reason of their geographical situation may be adversely affected thereby.
6. National laws, regulations and measures shall be no less effective in preventing, reducing and controlling such pollution than the global rules and standards.

Art. 211. Pollution from vessels
1. States, acting through the competent international organization or general diplomatic conference, shall establish international rules and standards to prevent, reduce and control pollution of the marine environment from vessels and promote the adoption, in the same manner, wherever appropriate, of routeing systems designed to minimize the threat of accidents which might cause pollution of the marine environment, including the coastline, and pollution damage to the related interests of coastal States. Such rules and standards shall, in the same manner, be re-examined from time to time as necessary.
2. States shall adopt laws and regulations for the prevention, reduction and control of pollution of the marine environment from vessels flying their flag or of their registry. Such laws and regulations shall at least have the same effect as that of generally accepted international rules and standards established through the competent international organization or general diplomatic conference.
3. States which establish particular requirements for the prevention, reduction and control of pollution of the marine environment as a condition for the entry of foreign vessels into their ports or internal waters or for a call at their off-shore terminals shall give due publicity to such requirements and shall communicate them to the competent international organization. Whenever such requirements are established in identical form by two or more coastal States in an endeavour to harmonize policy, the communication shall indicate which States are participating in such co-operative arrangements. Every State shall require the master of a vessel flying its flag or of its registry, when navigating within the territorial sea of a State participating in such co-operative arrangements, to furnish, upon the request of that State, information as to whether it is proceeding to a State of the same region participating in such co-operative arrangements and, if so, to indicate whether it complies with the port of entry requirements of that State. This article is without prejudice to the continued exercise by a vessel of its right of innocent passage or to the application of article 25, paragraph 2.
4. Coastal States may, in the exercise of their sovereignty within their territorial sea, adopt laws and regulations for the prevention, reduction and control of marine pollution from foreign vessels, including vessels exercising the right of innocent passage. Such laws and regulations shall, in accordance with Part II, section 3, not hamper innocent passage of foreign vessels.
5. Coastal States, for the purpose of enforcement as provided for in section 6, may in respect of their exclusive economic zones adopt laws and regulations for the prevention, reduction and control of pollution from vessels conforming to and giving effect to generally accepted international rules and standards established through the competent international organization or general diplomatic conference.
6. (a) Where the international rules and standards referred to in paragraph 1 are inadequate to meet special circumstances and coastal States have reasonable grounds for believing that a particular, clearly defined area of their respective exclusive economic zones is an area where the adoption of special mandatory measures for the prevention of pollution from

vessels is required for recognized technical reasons in relation to its oceanographical and ecological conditions, as well as its utilization or the protection of its resources and the particular character of its traffic, the coastal States, after appropriate consultations through the competent international organization with any other States concerned, may, for that area, direct a communication to that organization, submitting scientific and technical evidence in support and information on necessary reception facilities. Within 12 months after receiving such a communication, the organization shall determine whether the conditions in that area correspond to the requirements set out above. If the organization so determines, the coastal States may, for that area, adopt laws and regulations for the prevention, reduction and control of pollution from vessels implementing such international rules and standards or navigational practices as are made applicable, through the organization, for special areas. These laws and regulations shall not become applicable to foreign vessels until 15 months after the submission of the communication to the organization.

(b) The coastal States shall publish the limits of any such particular, clearly defined area.

(c) If the coastal States intend to adopt additional laws and regulations for the same area for the prevention, reduction and control of pollution from vessels, they shall, when submitting the aforesaid communication, at the same time notify the organization thereof. Such additional laws and regulations may relate to discharges or navigational practices but shall not require foreign vessels to observe design, construction, manning or equipment standards other than generally accepted international rules and standards; they shall become applicable to foreign vessels 15 months after the submission of the communication to the organization, provided that the organization agrees within 12 months after the submission of the communication.

7. The international rules and standards referred to in this article should include *inter alia* those relating to prompt notification to coastal States, whose coastline or related interests may be affected by incidents, including maritime casualties, which involve discharges or probability of discharges.

Art. 212. Pollution from or through the atmosphere

1. States shall adopt laws and regulations to prevent, reduce and control pollution of the marine environment from or through the atmosphere, applicable to the air space under their sovereignty and to vessels flying their flag or vessels or aircraft of their registry, taking into account internationally agreed rules, standards and recommended practices and procedures and the safety of air navigation.

Section 6. Enforcement

Art. 213. Enforcement with respect to pollution from land-based sources

States shall enforce their laws and regulations adopted in accordance with article 207 and shall adopt laws and regulations and take other measures necessary to implement applicable international rules and standards established through competent international organizations or diplomatic conference to prevent, reduce and control pollution of the marine environment from land-based sources.

Art. 214. Enforcement with respect to pollution from sea-bed activities

States shall enforce their laws and regulations adopted in accordance with article 208 and shall adopt laws and regulations and take other measures necessary to implement applicable international rules and standards established through competent international organizations or diplomatic conference to prevent, reduce and control pollution of the marine environment arising from or in connection with sea-bed activities subject to their jurisdiction and from artificial islands, installations and structures under their jurisdiction, pursuant to articles 60 and 80.

Art. 215. Enforcement with respect to pollution from activities in the Area

Enforcement of international rules, regulations and procedures established in accordance with Part XI to prevent, reduce and control pollution of the marine environment from activities in the Area shall be governed by that Part.

Art. 216. Enforcement with respect to pollution by dumping

1. Laws and regulations adopted in accordance with this Convention and applicable international rules and standards establishing through competent international organizations or diplomatic conference for the prevention, reduction and control of pollution of the marine environment by dumping shall be enforced:

(a) by the the coastal State with regard to dumping within its territorial sea or its exclusive economic zone or onto its continental shelf;

(b) by the flag State with regard to vessels flying its flag or vessels or aircraft of its registry;

(c) by any State with regard to acts of loading of wastes or other matter occurring within its territory or at its off-shore terminals.

2. No State shall be obliged by virtue of this article to institute proceedings when another State has already instituted proceedings in accordance with this article.

Art. 217. Enforcement by flag States

1. States shall ensure compliance by vessels flying their flag of their registry with applicable international rules and standards, established through the competent international organization or general diplomatic conference, and with their laws and regulations adopted in accordance with this Convention for the prevention, reduction and control of pollution of the marine environment from vessels and shall accordingly adopt laws and regulations and take other measures necessary for their implementation. Flag States shall provide for the effective enforcement of such rules, standards, laws and regulations, irrespective of where a violation occurs.

2. States shall, in particular, take appropriate measures in order to ensure that vessels flying their flag of their registry are prohibited from sailing, until they can proceed to sea in compliance with the requirements of the international rules and standards referred to in paragraph 1, including requirements in respect of design, construction, equipment and manning of vessels.

3. States shall ensure that vessels flying their flag or of their registry carry on board certificates required by and issued pursuant to international rules and standards referred to in paragraph 1. States shall ensure that vessels flying their flag are periodically inspected in order to verify that such certificates are in conformity with the actual condition of the vessels. These certificates shall be accepted by other States as evidence of the condition of the vessels and shall be regarded as having the same force as certificates issued by them, unless there are clear grounds for believing that the condition of the vessel does not correspond substantially with the particulars of the certificates.

4. If a vessel commits a violation of rules and standards established through the competent international organization or general diplomatic conference, the flag State, without prejudice to articles 218, 220 and 228, shall provide for immediate investigation and where appropriate institute proceedings in respect of the alleged violation irrespective of where the violation occurred or where the pollution caused by such violation has occurred or has been spotted.

5. Flag States conducting an investigation of the violation may request the assistance of any State whose co-operation could be useful in clarifying the circumstances of the case. States shall endeavour to meet appropriate requests of flag States.

6. States shall, at the written request of any State, investigate any violation alleged to have been committed by vessels flying their flag. If satisfied that sufficient evidence is available to enable proceedings to be brought in respect of the alleged violation, flag States shall without delay institute such proceedings in accordance with their laws.

7. Flag States shall promptly inform the requesting State and the competent international organization of the action taken and its outcome. Such information shall be available to all States.

8. Penalties provided for by the laws and regulations of States for vessels flying their flag shall be adequate in severity to discourage violations wherever they occur.

Art. 218. Enforcement by port States

1. When a vessel is voluntarily within a port or at an off-shore terminal of a State, that State may undertake investigations and, where the evidence so warrants, institute proceedings in respect of any discharge from that vessel outside the internal waters, territorial sea or exclusive economic zone of that State in violation of applicable international rules and standards established through the competent international organization or general diplomatic conference.

2. No proceedings pursuant to paragraph 1 shall be instituted in respect of a discharge violation in the internal waters, territorial sea or exclusive economic zone of another State unless requested by that State, the flag State, or a State damaged or threatened by the discharge violation, or unless the violation has caused or is likely to cause pollution in the internal waters, territorial sea or exclusive economic zone of the State instituting the proceedings.

3. When a vessel is voluntarily within a port or at an off-shore terminal of a State, that State shall, as far as practicable, comply with requests from any State for investigation of a discharge violation referred to in paragraph 1, believed to have occurred in, caused, or threatened damage to the internal waters, territorial sea or exclusive economic zone of the requesting State. It shall likewise, as far as practicable, comply with requests from the flag State for investigation of such a violation, irrespective of where the violation occurred.

4. The records of the investigation carried out by a port State pursuant to this article shall be transmitted upon request to the flag State or to the coastal State. Any proceedings instituted by the port State on the basis of such an investigation may, subject to section 7, be suspended at the request of the coastal State when the violation has occurred within its internal waters, territorial sea or exclusive economic zone. The evidence and records of the case, together with any bond or other financial security posted with the authorities of the port State, shall in that event be transmitted to the coastal State. Such transmittal shall preclude the continuation of proceeding in the port State.

Art. 219. Measures relating to seaworthiness of vessels to avoid pollution

Subject to section 7, States which, upon request or on their own initiative have ascertained that a vessel within one of their ports or at one of their offshore terminals is in violation of applicable international rules and standards relating to seaworthiness of vessels and thereby threatens damage to the marine environment shall, as far as practicable, take administrative measures to prevent the vessel from sailing. Such States may permit the vessel to proceed only to the nearest appropriate repair yard and, upon removal of the causes of the violation, shall permit the vessel to continue immediately.

Art. 220. Enforcement by coastal States

1. When a vessel is voluntarily within a port or at an off-shore terminal of a State, that State may, subject to section 7, institute proceedings in respect of any violation of its laws and regulations adopted in accordance with this Convention or applicable international rules and standards for the prevention, reduction and control of pollution from vessels when the violation has occurred within the territorial sea or the exclusive economic zone of that State.

2. Where there are clear grounds for believing that a vessel navigating in the territorial sea of a State has, during its passage therein, violated laws and regulations of that State adopted in accordance with this Convention or applicable international rules and standards for the prevention, reduction and control of pollution from vessels, that State, without prejudice to the application of the relevant provisions of Part II, section 3, may undertake physical inspection of the vessel relating to the violation and may, where the evidence so warrants, institute proceedings, including detention of the vessel, in accordance with its laws, subject to the provisions of section 7.

3. Where there are clear grounds for believing that a vessel navigating in the exclusive economic zone or the territorial sea of a State has, in the exclusive economic zone, committed a violation of applicable international rules and standards for the prevention, reduction and control of pollution from vessels or laws and regulations of that State conforming and giving effect to such rules and standards, that State may require the vessel to give information regarding its identity and port of registry, its last and its next port of call and other relevant information required to establish whether a violation has occurred.

4. States shall adopt laws and regulations and take other measures so that vessels flying their flag comply with requests for information pursuant to paragraph 3.

5. Where there are clear grounds for believing that a vessel navigating in the exclusive economic zone or the territorial sea of a State has, in the exclusive economic zone, committed a violation referred to in paragraph 3 resulting in a substantial discharge causing or threaten-

ing significant pollution of the marine environment, that State may undertake physical inspection of the vessel for matters relating to the violation if the vessel has refused to give information or if the information supplied by the vessel is manifestly at variance with the evident factual situation and if the circumstances of the case justify such inspection.

6. Where there is clear objective evidence that a vessel navigating in the exclusive economic zone or the territorial sea of a State has, in the exclusive economic zone, committed a violation referred to in paragraph 3 resulting in a discharge causing major damage or threat of major damage to the coastline or related interests of the coastal State, or to any resources of its territorial sea or exclusive economic zone, that State may, subject to section 7, provided that the evidence so warrants, institute proceedings, including detention of the vessel, in accordance with its laws.

7. Notwithstanding the provisions of paragraph 6, whenever appropriate procedures have been established, either through the competent international organization or as otherwise agreed, whereby compliance with requirements for bonding or other appropriate financial security has been assured, the coastal State if bounded by such procedures shall allow the vessel to proceed.

8. The provisions of paragraphs 3, 4, 5, 6 and 7 also apply in respect of national laws and regulations adopted pursuant to article 211, paragraph 6.

Art. 221. Measures to avoid pollution arising from maritime casualties

1. Nothing in this Part shall prejudice the right of States, pursuant to international law, both customary and conventional, to take and enforce measures beyond the territorial sea proportionate to the actual or threatened damage to protect their coastline or related interests, including fishing, from pollution or threat of pollution following upon a maritime casualty or acts relating to such a casualty, which may reasonably be expected to result in major harmful consequences.

2. For the purposes of this article, 'maritime casualty' means a collision of vessels, stranding or other incident of navigation, or other occurrence on board a vessel or external to it resulting in material damage or imminent threat of material damage to a vessel or cargo.

Art. 222. Enforcement with respect to pollution from or through the atmosphere

States shall enforce, within the air space under their sovereignty or with regard to vessels flying their flag or vessels or aircraft of their registry, their laws and regulations adopted in accordance with article 212, paragraph 1, and with other provisions of this Convention and shall adopt laws and regulations and take other measures necessary to implement applicable international rules and standards established through competent international organizations or diplomatic conference to prevent, reduce and control pollution of the marine environment from or through the atmosphere, in conformity with all relevant international rules and standards concerning the safety of air navigation.

Section 7. Safeguards
Art. 223. Measures to facilitate proceedings

In proceedings instituted pursuant to this Part, States shall take measures to facilitate the hearing of witnesses and the admission of evidence submitted by authorities of another State, or by the competent international organization, and shall facilitate the attendance at such proceedings of official representatives of the competent international organization, the flag State and any State affected by pollution arising out of any violation. The official representative attending such proceedings shall have such rights and duties as may be provided under national laws and regulations or international law.

Art. 224. Exercise of powers of enforcement

The powers of enforcement against foreign vessels under this Part may only be exercised by officials or by warships, military aircraft, or other ships or aircraft clearly marked and identifiable as being on government service and authorized to that effect.

Art. 225. Duty to avoid adverse consequences in the exercise of the powers of enforcement

In the exercise under this Convention of their powers of enforcement against foreign vessels, States shall not endanger the safety of navigation or otherwise create any hazard to a vessel, or bring it to an unsafe port or anchorage, or expose the marine environment to an unreasonable risk.

Art. 226. Investigation of foreign vessels

1. (a) States shall not delay a foreign vessel longer than is essential for purposes of the investigations provided for in articles 216, 218 and 220. Any physical inspection of a foreign vessel shall be limited to an examination of such certificates, records or other documents as the vessel is required to carry by generally accepted international rules and standards or of any similar documents which it is carrying; further physical inspection of the vessel may be undertaken only after such an examination and only when:

(i) there are clear grounds for believing that the condition of the vessel or its equipment does not correspond substantially with the particulars of those documents;

(ii) the contents of such documents are not sufficient to confirm or verify a suspected violation; or

(iii) the vessel is not carrying valid certificates and records.

(b) If the investigation indicates a violation of applicable laws and regulations or international rules and standards for the protection and preservation of the marine environment, release shall be made promptly subject to reasonable procedures such as bonding or other appropriate financial security.

(c) Without prejudice to applicable international rules and standards relating to the seaworthiness of vessels, the release of a vessel may, whenever it would present an unreasonable threat of damage to the marine environment, be refused or made conditional upon proceeding to the nearest appropriate repair yard. Where release has been refused or made conditional, the flag State of the vessel must be promptly notified, and may seek release of the vessel in accordance with Part XV.

2. States shall co-operate to develop procedures for the avoidance of unnecessary physical inspection of vessels at sea.

Art. 227. Non-discrimination with respect to foreign vessels

In exercising their rights and performing their duties under this Part, States shall not discriminate in form or in fact against vessels of any other State.

Art. 228. Suspension and restrictions on institution of proceedings

1. Proceedings to impose penalties in respect of any violation of applicable laws and regulations or international rules and standards relating to the prevention, reduction and control of pollution from vessels committed by a foreign vessel beyond the territorial sea of the State instituting proceedings shall be suspended upon the taking of proceedings to impose penalties in respect of corresponding charges by the flag State within six months of the date on which proceedings were first instituted, unless those proceedings relate to a case of major damage to the coastal State or the flag State in question has repeatedly disregarded its obligation to enforce effectively the applicable international rules and standards in respect of violations committed by its vessels. The flag State shall in due course make available to the State previously instituting proceedings a full dossier of the case and the records of the proceedings, whenever the flag State has requested the suspension of proceedings in accordance with this article. When proceedings instituted by the flag State have been brought to a conclusion, the suspended proceedings shall be terminated. Upon payment of costs incurred in respect of such proceedings, any bond posted or other financial security provided in connection with the suspended proceedings shall be released by the coastal State.

2. Proceedings to impose penalties on foreign vessels shall not be instituted after the expiry of three years from the date on which the violation was committed, and shall not be taken by any State in the event of proceedings having been instituted by another State subject to the provisions set out in paragraph 1.

3. The provisions of this article are without prejudice to the right of the flag State to take any measures, including proceedings to impose penalties, according to its laws irrespective of prior proceedings by another State.

Art. 229. Institution of civil proceedings

Nothing in this Convention affects the institution of civil proceedings in respect of any claim for loss or damage resulting from pollution of the marine environment.

Art. 230. Monetary penalties and the observance of recognized rights of the accused

1. Monetary penalties only may be imposed with respect to violations of national laws and regulations or applicable international rules and standards for the prevention, reduction and control of pollution of the marine environment, committed by foreign vessels beyond the territorial sea.

2. Monetary penalties only may be imposed with respect to violations of national laws and regulations or applicable international rules and standards for the prevention, reduction and control of pollution of the marine environment, committed by foreign vessels in the territorial sea, except in the case of a wilful and serious act of pollution in the territorial sea.

3. In the conduct of proceedings in respect of such violations committed by a foreign vessel which may result in the imposition of penalties, recognized rights of the accused shall be observed.

Art. 231. Notification to the flag State and other States concerned

States shall promptly notify the flag State and any other State concerned of any measures taken pursuant to section 6 against foreign vessels, and shall submit to the flag State all official reports concerning such measures. However, with respect to violations committed in the territorial sea, the foregoing obligations of the coastal State apply only to such measures as are taken in proceedings. The diplomatic agents or consular officers and where possible the maritime authority of the flag State, shall be immediately informed of any such measures taken pursuant to section 6 against foreign vessels.

Art. 232. Liability of States arising from enforcement measures

States shall be liable for damage or loss attributable to them arising from measures taken pursuant to section 6 when such measures are unlawful or exceed these reasonably required in the light of available information. States shall provide for recourse in their courts for actions in respect of such damage or loss.

Art. 233. Safeguards with respect to straits used for international navigation

Nothing in sections 5, 6 and 7 affects régime of straits used for international navigation. However, if a foreign ship other than those referred to in section 10 has committed a violation of the laws and regulations referred to in article 42, paragraph 1(a) and (b), causing or threatening major damage to the marine environment of the straits, the States bordering the straits may take appropriate enforcement measures and if so shall respect *mutatis mutandis* the provisions of this section.

Section 8. Ice-covered areas
Art 234. Ice-covered areas

Coastal States have the righ to adopt and enforce nondiscriminatory laws and regulations for the prevention, reduction and control of marine pollution from vessels in ice-covered areas within the limits of the exclusive economic zone, where particularly severe climate conditions and the presence of ice covering such areas for most of the year obstructions or exceptional hazards to navigation, and pollution of the marine environment could cause major harm to or irreversible disturbance of the ecological balance. Such laws and regulations shall have due regard to navigation and the protection and preservation of the marine environment based on the best available scientific evidence.

Section 9. Responsibility and liability
Art. 235. Responsibility and liability

1. States are responsible for the fulfilment of their international obligations concerning the protection and preservation of the marine environment. They shall be liable in accordance with international law.

2. States shall ensure that recourse is available in accordance with their legal systems for prompt and adequate compensation or other relief in respect of damage caused by pollution of the marine environment by natural or juridical persons under their jurisdiction.

3. With the objective of assuring prompt and adequate compensation in respect of all damage caused by pollution of the marine environment, States shall co-operate in the implementation of existing international law and the further development of international law relating to responsibility and liability for the assessment of and compensation for damage and the settlement of related disputes, as well as, where appropriate, development of criteria and procedures for payment of

adequate compensation, such as compulsory insurance or compensation funds.

Section 10. Sovereign immunity
Art. 236. Sovereign immunity
The provisions of this Convention regarding the protection and preservation of the marine environment do not apply to any warship, naval auxiliary, other vessels or aircraft owned or operated by a State and used, for the time being, only on government non-commercial service. However, each State shall ensure, by the adoption of appropriate measures not impairing operations or operational capabilities of such vessels or aircraft owned or operated by it, that such vessels or aircraft act in a manner consistent, so far as is reasonable and practicable, with this Convention.

Section 11. Obligations under other conventions on the protection and preservation of the marine environment
Art. 237. Obligations under other conventions on the protection and preservation of the marine environment
1. The provisions of this Part are without prejudice to the specific obligations assumed by States under special conventions and agreements concluded previously which relate to the protection and preservation of the marine environment and to agreements which may be conducted in furtherance of the general principles set forth in this Convention.
2. Specific obligations assumed by States under special conventions, with respect to the protection and preservation of the marine environment, should be carried out in a manner consistent with the general principles and objectives of this Convention.

Part XIII. Marine scientific research.
Section 1. General provisions.
Art. 238. Right to conduct marine scientific research
All States, irrespective of their geographical location, and competent international organizations have the right to conduct marine scientific research subject to the rights and duties of other States as provided for in this Convention.
Art. 239. Promotion of marine scientific research
States and competent international organizations shall promote and facilitate the development and conduct of marine scientific research in accordance with this Convention.
Art. 240. General principles for the conduct of marine scientific research
In the conduct of marine scientific research the following principles shall apply:
(a) marine scientific research shall be conducted exclusively for peaceful purposes;
(b) marine scientific research shall be conducted with appropriate scientific methods and means compatible with this Convention;
(c) marine scientific research shall not unjustifiably interfere with other legitimate uses of the sea compatible with this Convention and shall be duly respected in the course of such uses;
(d) marine scientific research shall be conducted in compliance with all relevant regulations adopted in conformity with this Convention including those for the protection and preservation of the marine environment.
Art. 241. Non-recognition of marine scientific research activities as the legal basis for claims
Marine scientific research activities shall not constitute the legal basis for any claim to any part of the marine environment or its resources.

Section 2. International co-operation
Art. 242. Promotion of international co-operation
1. States and competent international organizations shall, in accordance with the principle of respect for sovereignty and jurisdiction and on the basis of mutual benefit, promote international co-operation in marine scientific research for peaceful purposes.
2. In this context, without prejudice to the rights and duties of States under this Convention, a State, in the application of this Part, shall provide, as appropriate, other States with a reasonable opportunity to obtain from it, or with its co-operation, information necessary to prevent and control damage to the health and safety of persons and to the marine environment.
Art. 243. Creation of favourable conditions
States and competent international organizations shall co-operate, through the conclusion of bilateral and multilateral agreements, to create favourable conditions for the conduct of marine scientific research in the marine environment and to integrate the efforts of scientists in studying the essence of phenomena and processes occurring in the marine environment and the interrelations between them.
Art. 244. Publication and dissemination of information and knowledge
1. States and competent international organizations shall, in accordance with this Convention, make available by publication and dissemination through appropriate channels information on proposed major programmes and their objectives as well as knowledge resulting from marine scientific research.
2. For this purpose, States, both individually and in co-operation with other States and with competent international organizations, shall actively promote the flow of scientific data and information and the transfer of knowledge resulting from marine scientific research, especially to developing States, as well as the strengthening of the autonomous marine scientific research capabilities of developing States through, *inter alia*, programmes to provide adequate education and training of their technical and scientific personnel.
Section 3. Conduct and promotion of marine scientific research
Art. 245. Marine scientific research in the territorial sea
Coastal States, in the exercise of their sovereignty, have the exclusive right to regulate, authorize and conduct marine scientific research in their territorial sea. Marine scientifc research therein shall be conducted only with the express consent of and under the conditions set forth by the coastal State.
Art. 246. Marine scientific research in the exclusive economic zone and on the continental shelf
1. Coastal States, in the exercise of their jurisdiction, have the right to regulate authorize and conduct marine scientific research in their exclusive economic zone and on their continental shelf in accordance with the relevant provisions of this Convention.
2. Marine scientific research in the exclusive economic zone and on the continental shelf shall be conducted with the consent of the coastal State.
3. Coastal States shall, in normal circumstances, grant their consent for marine scientific research projects by other States or competent international organizations in their exclusive economic zone or on their continental shelf to be carried out in accordance with this Convention exclusively for peaceful purposes and in order to increase scientific knowledge of the marine environment for the benefit of all mankind. To this end, coastal States shall establish rules and procedures ensuring that such consent will not be delayed or denied unreasonably.
4. For the purposes of applying paragraph 3, normal circumstances may exist in spite of the absence of diplomatic relations between the coastal State and the researching State.
5. Coastal States may however in their discretion withhold their consent to the conduct of a marine scientific research project of another State or competent international organization in the exclusive economic zone or on the continental shelf of the coastal State if that project:
(a) is of direct significance for the exploration and exploitation of natural resources, whether living or non-living;
(b) involves drilling into the continental shelf, the use of explosives or the introduction of harmful substances into the marine environment;
(c) involves the construction, operation or use of artificial islands, installations and structures referred to in articles 60 and 80;
(d) contains information communicated pursuant to article 248 regarding the nature and objectives of the project which is inaccurate or if the researching State or competent international organization has outstanding obligations to the coastal State from a prior research project.
6. Notwithstanding the provisions of paragraph 5, coastal States may not exercise their discretion to withhold consent under subparagraph (a) of that paragraph in respect of marine scientific research projects to be undertaken in accordance with the provisions of this Part on the continental shelf, beyond 200 nautical miles from the baselines from which the breadth of the territorial sea is measured, outside those specific areas which coastal States may at any time publicity designate as areas in which exploitation or detailed exploratory operations focused on those areas are occurring or will occur within a reasonable period of time. Coastal States shall give reasonable notice of the designation of such areas, as well as any modifications thereto, but shall not be obliged to give details of the operations therein.
7. The provisions of paragraph 6 are without prejudice to the rights of coastal States over the continental shelf as established in article 77.
8. Marine scientific research activities referred to in this article shall not unjustifiably interfere with activities undertaken by coastal States in the exercise of their sovereign rights and jurisdiction for in this Convention.
Art. 247. Marine scientific research projects undertaken by or under the auspices of international organizations
A coastal State which is a member of or has a bilateral agreement with an international organization, and in whose exclusive economic zone or on whose continental shelf that organization wants to carry out a marine scientific research project, directly or under its auspices, shall be deemed to have authorized the project to be carried out in conformity with the agreed specifications if that State approved the detailed project when the decision was made by the organization for the undertaking of the project, or is willing to participate in it, and has not expressed any objection within four months of notification of the project by the organization to the coastal State.
Art. 248. Duty to provide information to the coastal State
States and competent international organizations which intend to undertake marine scientific research in the exclusive economic zone or on the continental shelf of a coastal State shall, not less than six months in advance of the expected starting date of the marine scientific research project, provide that State with a full discription of:
(a) the nature and objectives of the project;
(b) the method and means to be used, including name, tonnage, type and class of vessels and a description of scientific equipment;
(c) the precise geographical areas in which the project is to be conducted;
(d) the expected date of first appearance and final departure of the research vessels, or deployment of the equipment and its removal, as appropriate;
(e) the name of the sponsoring institution, its director, and the person in charge of the project; and
(f) the extent to which it is considered that the coastal State should be able to participate or to be represented in the project.
Art. 249. Duty to comply with certain conditions
1. States and competent international organizations when undertaking marine scientific research in the exclusive economic zone or on the continental shelf of a coastal State shall comply with the following conditions:
(a) ensure the right of the coastal State, if it so desires, to participate or be represented in the marine scientific research project, especially on board research vessels and other craft or scientific research installations, when practicable, without payment of any remuneration to the scientists of the coastal State and without obligation to contribute towards the costs of the project;
(b) provide the coastal State, at its request, with preliminary reports, as soon as practicable, and with the final results and conclusions after the completion of the research;
(c) undertake to provide access for the coastal State, at its request, to all data and samples derived from the marine scientific research project and likewise to furnish it with data which may be copied and samples which may be divided without detriment to their scientific value;
(d) if requested, provide the coastal State with an assessment of such data, samples and research results or provide assistance in their assessment or interpretation;
(e) ensure, subject to paragraph 2, that the research results are made internationally available through appropriate national or international channels, as soon as practicable;
(f) inform the coastal State immediately of any major change in the research programme;
(g) unless otherwise agreed, remove the scientific research installations or equipment once the research is completed.

2. This article is without prejudice to the conditions established by the laws and regulations of the coastal State for the exercise of its discretion to grant or withhold consent pursuant to article 246, paragraph 5, including requiring prior agreement for making internationally available the research results of a project of direct significance for the exploration and exploitation of natural resources.

Art. 250. Communications concerning marine scientific research projects
Communications concerning the marine scientific research projects shall be made through appropriate official channels, unless otherwise agreed.

Art. 251. General criteria and guidelines
States shall seek to promote through competent international organizations the establishment of general criteria and guidelines to assist States in ascertaining the nature and implications of marine scientific research.

Art. 252. Implied consent
States or competent international organizations may proceed with a marine scientific research project six months after the date upon which the information required pursuant to article 248 was provided to the coastal State unless within four months of the receipt of the communication containing such information the coastal State has informed the State or organization conducting the research that:
(a) it has withheld its consent under the provisions of article 246; or
(b) the information given by that State or competent international organization regarding the nature or objectives of the project does not conform to the manifestly evident facts; or
(c) it requires supplementary information relevant to conditions and the information provided for under articles 248 and 249; or
(d) outstanding obligations exist with respect to a previous scientific research project carried out by that State or organization, with regard to conditions established in article 249.

Art. 253. Suspension or cessation of marine scientific research activities
1. A coastal State shall have the right to require the suspension of any marine scientific research activities in progress within its exclusive economic zone or on its continental shelf if:
(a) the research activities are not being conducted in accordance with the information communicated as provided under article 248 upon which the consent of the coastal State was based; or
(b) the State or competent international organization conducting the research activities fails to comply with the provisions of article 249 concerning the rights of the coastal State with respect to the marine scientific research project.
2. A coastal State shall have the right to require the cessation of any marine scientific research activities in case of any non-compliance with the provisions of article 248 which amounts to a major change in the research project or the research activities.
3. A coastal State may also require cessation of marine scientific research activities if any of the situations contemplated in paragraph 1 are not rectified within a reasonable period of time.
4. Following notification by the coastal State of its decision to order suspension or cessation, States or competent international organizations authorized to conduct marine scientific research activities shall terminate the research activities that are the subject of such a notification.
5. An order of suspenslion under paragraph 1 shall be lifted by the coastal State and the marine scientific research activities allowed to continue once the researching State or competent international organization has complied with the conditions required under articles 248 and 249.

Art. 254. Rights of neighbouring land-locked and geographically disadvantaged States
1. States and competent international organizations which have submitted to a coastal State a project to undertake marine scientific research referred to in article 246, paragraph 3, shall give notice to the neighbouring land-locked and geographically disadvantaged States of the proposed research project, and shall notify the coastal State thereof.
2. After the consent has been given for the proposed marine scientific research project by the coastal State concerned, in accordance with article 246 and other relevant provisions of this Convention, States and competent international organizations undertaking such a project shall provide to the neighbouring land-locked and geographically disadvantaged States, at their request and when appropriate, relevant information as specified in article 248 and article 249, paragraph 1(f).
3. The neighbouring land-locked and geographically disadvantaged States referred to above shall, at their request, be given the opportunity to participate, whenever feasible, in the proposed marine scientific research project through qualified experts appointed by them and not objected to by the coastal State, in accordance with the conditions agreed for the project, in conformity with the provisions of this Convention, between the coastal State concerned and the State or competent international organizations conducting the marine scientific research.
4. States and competent international organizations referred to in paragraph 1 shall provide to the above-mentioned land-locked and geographically disadvantaged States, at their request, the information and assistance specified in article 249, paragraph 1(d), subject to the provisions of article 249, paragraph 2.

Art. 255. Measures to facilitate marine scientific research and assist research vessels
States shall endeavour to adopt reasonable rules, regulations and procedures to promote and facilitate marine scientific research conducted in accordance with this Convention beyond their territorial sea and, as appropriate, to facilitate, subject to the provisions of their laws and regulations, access to their harbours and promote assistance for marine scientific research vessels which comply with the relevant provisions of this Part.

Art. 256. Marine scientific research in the Area
All States, irrespective of their geographical location, and competent international organizations have the right, in conformity with the provisions of Part XI, to conduct marine scientific research in the Area.

Art. 257. Marine scientific research in the water column beyond the exclusive economic zone
All States, irrespective of their geographical location, and competent international organizations have the right, in conformity with this Convention, to conduct marine scientific research in the water column beyond the limits of the exclusive economic zone.

Section 4. Legal status of scientific research installations or equipment in the marine environment
Art. 258. Deployment and use
The deployment and use of any type of scientific research installations or equipment in any area of the marine environment shall be subject to the same conditions as are prescribed in this Convention for the conduct of marine scientific research in any such area.

Art. 259. Legal status
The installations or equipment referred to in this section do not possess the status of islands. They have no territorial sea of their own, and their presence does not affect the delimitation of the territorial sea, the exclusive economic zone or the continental shelf.

Art. 260. Safety zones
Safety zones of a reasonable breadth not exceeding a distance of 500 metres may be created around scientific research installations in accordance with the relevant provisions of this Convention. All States shall ensure that such safety zones are respected by their vessels.

Art. 261. Non-interference with shipping routes
The deployment and use of any type of scientific research installations or equipment shall not constitute an obstacle to established international shipping routes.

Art. 262. Identification markings and warning signals
Installations or equipment referred to in this section shall bear identification markings indicating the State of registry or the international organization to which they belong and shall have adequate internationally agreed warning signals to ensure safety at sea and the safety of air navigation, taking into account rules and standards established by competent international organizations.

Section 5. Responsibility and liability
Art. 263. Responsibility and liability
1. States and competent international organizations shall be responsible for ensuring that marine scientific research, whether undertaken by them or on their behalf, is conducted in accordance with this Convention.
2. States and competent international organizations shall be responsible and liable for the measures they take in contravention of this Convention in respect of marine scientific research conducted by other States, their natural or juridical persons or by competent international organizations, and shall provide compensation for damage resulting from such measures.
3. States and competent international organizations shall be responsible and liable pursuant to article 235 for damage caused by pollution of the marine environment arising out of marine scientific research undertaken by them or on their behalf.

Section 6. Settlement of disputes and interim measures
Art. 264. Settlement of disputes
Disputes concerning the interpretation or application of the provisions of this Convention with regard to marine scientific research shall be settled in accordance with Part XV, sections 2 and 3.

Art. 265. Interim measures
Pending settlement of a dispute in accordance with Part XV, sections 2 and 3, the State or competent international organization authorized to conduct a marine scientific research project shall not allow research activities to commence or continue without the express consent of the coastal State concerned.

Part XIV. Development and transfer of marine technology

Section 1. General provisions
Art. 266. Promotions of the developing and transfer of marine technology
1. States, directly or through competent international organizations, shall cooperate in accordance with their capabilities to promote actively the development and transfer of marine science and marine technology on fair and reasonable terms and conditions.
2. States shall promote the development of the marine scientific and technological capacity of States which may need and request technical assistance in this field, particularly developing States, including land-locked and geographically disadvantaged States, with regard to the exploration, exploitation, conservation and management of marine resources, the protection and preservation of the marine environment, marine scientific research and other activities in the marine environment compatible with this Convention, with a view to accelerating the social and economic development of the developing States.
3. States shall endeavour to foster favourable economic and legal conditions for the transfer of marine technology for the benefit of all parties concerned on an equitable basis.

Art. 267. Protection of legitimate interests
States, in promoting co-operation pursuant to article 266, shall have due regard for all legitimate interests including, *inter alia*, the rights and duties of holders, suppliers and recipients of marine technology.

Art. 268. Basic objectives
States, directly or through competent international organizations, shall promote:
(a) the acquisition, evaluation and dissemination of marine technological knowledge and facilitate access to such information and data;
(b) the development of appropriate marine technology;
(c) the development of the necessary technological infrastructure to facilitate the transfer of marine technology;
(d) the development of human resources through training and education of nationals of developing States and countries and especially the nationals of the least developed among them;
(e) international co-operation at all levels, particularly at the regional, sub-regional and bilateral levels.

Art. 269. Measures to achieve the basic objectives
In order to achieve the objectives referred to in article 268, States, directly or through competent international organizations, shall endeavour, *inter alia*, to:
(a) establish programmes of technical co-operation for the effective transfer of all kinds of marine technology to States which may need and request technical assistance in this field, particularly the developing land-locked and geographically disadvantaged States, as well as other developing States which have not been able either to establish or develop their own technological capacity in marine science and in the exploration and exploitation of marine resources or to develop the infrastructure of such technology;

(b) promote favourable conditions for the conclusion of agreements, contracts and other similar arrangements, under equitable and reasonable conditions;
(c) hold conferences, seminars and symposia on scientific and technological subjects, in particular on policies and methods for the transfer of marine technology;
(d) promote the exchange of scientists and of technological and other experts;
(e) undertake projects and promote joint ventures and other forms of bilateral and multilateral co-operation.

Section 2. International co-operation
Art. 270. Ways and means of international co-operation
International co-operation for the development and transfer of marine technology shall be carried out, where feasible and appropriate, through existing bilateral, regional or multilateral programmes, and also through expanded and new programmes in order to facilitate marine research, the transfer of marine technology, particularly in new fields, and appropriate international funding for ocean research and development.

Art. 271. Guidelines, criteria and standards
States, directly or through competent international organizations, shall promote the establishment of generally accepted guidelines, criteria and standards for the transfer of marine technology on a bilateral basis or within the frame-work of international organizations and other fora, taking into account, in particular, the interests and needs of developing States.

Art. 272. Co-ordination of international programmes
In the field of transfer of marine technology, States shall endeavour to ensure that competent international organizations co-ordinate their activities, including any regional or global programmes, taking into account the interests and needs of developing States, particularly land-locked and geographically disadvantaged States.

Art. 273. Co-operation with international organizations and the Authority
States shall co-operate actively with competent international organizations and the authority to encourage and facilitate the transfer to developing States, their nationals and the Enterprise of skills and marine technology with regard to activities in the Area.

Art. 274. Objectives of the Authority
Subject to all legitimate interests including, *inter alia* the rights and duties of holders, suppliers and recipients of technology, the Authority, with regard to activities in the Area, shall ensure that:
(a) on the basis of the principle of equitable geographical distribution, nationals of developing States, whether coastal, land-locked or geographically disadvantaged, shall be taken on for the purposes of training as members of the managerial, research and technical staff constituted for its undertakings;
(b) the technical documentation on the relevant equipment, machinery, devices and processes is made available to all States, in particular developing States which may need and request technical assistance in this field;
(c) adequate provision is made by the Authority to facilitate the acquisition of technical assistance in the field of marine technology by States which may need and request it, in particular developing States, and the acquisition by their nationals of the necessary skills and know-how, including professional training,
(d) States which may need and request technical assistance in this field, in particular developing States, are assisted in the acquisition of necessary equipment, processes, plant and other technical know-how through any financial arrangements provided for in this Convention.

Section 3. National and regional marine scientific and technological centres
Art. 275. Establishment of national centres
1. States, directly or through competent international organizations and the Authority, shall promote the establishment, particularly in developing coastal States, of national marine scientific and technological research centres and the strengthening of existing national centres, in order to stimulate and advance the conduct of marine scientific research by developing coastal States and to enhance their national capabilities to utilize and preserve their marine resources for their economic benefit.
2. States, through competent international organizations and the Authority, shall give adequate support to facilitate the establishment and strengthening of such national centres so as to provide for advanced training

facilities and necessary equipment, skills and know-how as well as technical experts to such States which may need and request such assistance.

Art. 276. Establishment of regional centres
1. States, in co-ordination with the competent international organizations, the Authority and national marine scientific and technological research institutions, shall promote the establishment of regional marine scientific and technological research centres, particularly in developing States, in order to stimulate and advance the conduct of marine scientific research by developing States and foster the transfer technology.
2. All States of a region shall co-operate with the regional centres therein to ensure the more effective achievement of their objectives.

Art. 277. Functions of regional centres
The functions of such regional centres shall include, *inter alia*:
(a) training and educational programmes at all levels on various aspects of marine scientific and technological research, particularly marine biology, including conservation and management of living resources, oceanography, hydrography, engineering, geological exploration of the sea-bed, mining and desalination technologies;
(b) management studies;
(c) study programmes related to the protection and preservation of the marine environment and the prevention, reduction and control of pollution;
(d) organization of regional conferences, seminars and symposia;
(e) acquisition and processing of marine scientific and technological data and information;
(f) prompt dissemination of results of marine scientific and technological research in readily available publications;
(g) publicizing national policies with regard to the transfer of marine technology and systematic comparative study of those policies;
(h) compilation and systematization of information on the marketing of technology and on contracts and other arrangements concerning patents;
(i) technical co-operation with other States of the region.

Section 4. Co-operation among international organizations
Art. 278. Co-operation among international organizations
The competent international organizations referred to in this Part and in Part XIII shall take all appropriate measures to ensure, either directly or in close co-operation among themselves, the effective discharge of their functions and responsibilities under this Part.

Part XV. Settlement of disputes

Section 1. General provisions and general obligations
Art. 279. Obligation to settle disputes by peaceful means
States Parties shall settle any dispute between them concerning the interpretation or application of this Convention by peaceful means in accordance with article 2, paragraph 3, of the Charter of the United Nations and, to this end, shall seek a solution by the means indicated in article 33, paragraph 1, of the Charter.

Art. 280. Settlement of disputes by any peaceful means chosen by the parties
Nothing in this Part impairs the right of any States Parties to agree at any time to settle a dispute between them concerning the interpretation or application of this Convention by any peaceful means of their own choice.

Art. 281. Procedure where no settlement has been reached by the parties
1. If the States Parties which are parties to a dispute concerning the interpretation or application of this Convention have agreed to seek settlement of the dispute by a peaceful means of their own choice, the procedures provided for in this Part apply only where no settlement has been reached by recourse to such means and the agreement between the parties does not exclude any further procedure.
2. If the parties have also agreed on a time-limit, paragraph 1 applies only upon the expiration of that time-limit.

Art. 282. Obligations under general, regional or bilateral agreements
If the States Parties which are parties to a dispute concerning the interpretation or application of this Con-

vention have agreed, through a general, regional or bilateral agreement or otherwise, that such dispute shall, at the request of any party to the dispute, be submitted to a procedure that entails a binding decision, that procedure shall apply in lieu of the procedures provided for in this Part, unless the parties to the dispute otherwise agree.

Art. 283. Obligation to exchange views
1. When a dispute arises between States Parties concerning the interpretation or application of this Convention, the parties to the dispute shall proceed expeditiously to an exchange of views regarding its settlement by negotiation or other peaceful means.
2. The parties shall also proceed expeditiously to an exchange of views where a procedure for the settlement of such a dispute has been terminated without a settlement or where a settlement has been reached and the circumstances require consultation regarding the manner of implementing the settlement.

Art. 284. Conciliation
1. A State Party which is a party to a dispute concerning the interpretation or application of this Convention may invite the other party or parties to submit the dispute to conciliation in accordance with the procedure under Annex V, section 1, or another conciliation procedure.
2. If the invitation is accepted and if the parties agree upon the conciliation procedure to be applied, any party may submit the dispute to that procedure.
3. If the invitation is not accepted or the parties do not agree upon the procedure, the conciliation proceedings shall be deemed to be terminated.
4. Unless the parties otherwise agree, when a dispute has been submitted to conciliation, the proceedings may be terminated only in accordance with the agreed conciliation procedure.

Art. 285. Application of this section to disputes submitted pursuant to Part XI
This section applies to any dispute which pursuant to Part XI, section 5, is to be settled in accordance with procedures provided for in this Part. If an entity other than a State Party is a party to such a dispute this section applies *mutatis mutandis.*

Section 2. Compulsory procedures entailing binding decisions
Art. 286. Application of procedures under this section
Subject to section 3, any dispute concerning the interpretation or application of this Convention shall, where no settlement has been reached by recourse to section 1, be submitted at the request of any party to the dispute to the court or tribunal having jurisdiction under this section.

Art. 287. Choice of procedure
1. When signing, ratifying or acceding to this Convention or at any time thereafter, a State shall be free to choose, by means of a written declaration, one or more of the following means for the settlement of disputes concerning the interpretation or application of this Convention:
(a) the International Tribunal for the Law of the Sea established in accordance with Annex VI;
(b) the International Court of Justice;
(c) an arbitral tribunal constituted in accordance with Annex VII;
(d) a special arbitral tribunal constituted in accordance with Annex VIII for one or more of the categories of disputes specified therein.
2. A declaration made under paragraph 1 shall not affect or be affected by the obligation of a State Party to accept the jurisdiction of the Sea-Bed Disputes Chamber of the International Tribunal for the Law of the Sea to the extent and in the manner provided for in Part XI, section 5.
3. A State Party, which is a party to a dispute not covered by a declaration in force, shall be deemed to have accepted arbitration in accordance with Annex VII.
4. If the parties to a dispute have accepted the same procedure for the settlement of the dispute, it may be submitted only to that procedure, unless the parties otherwise agree.
5. If the parties to a dispute have not accepted the same procedure for the settlement of the dispute, it may be submitted only to arbitration in accordance with Annex VII, unless the parties otherwise agree.
6. A declaration made under paragraph 1 shall remain in force until three months after notice of revocation

has been deposited with the Secretary-General of the United Nations.
7. A new declaration, a notice of revocation or the expiry of a declaration does not in any way affect proceedings pending before a court or tribunal having jurisdiction under this article, unless the parties otherwise agree.
8. Declarations and notices referred to in this article shall be deposited with the Secretary-General of the United Nations, who shall transmit copies thereof to the States Parties.

Art. 288. Jurisdiction

1. A court or tribunal referred to in article 287 shall have jurisdiction over any dispute concerning the interpretation or application of this Convention which is submitted to it in accordance with this Part.
2. A court or tribunal referred to in article 287 shall also have jurisdiction over any dispute concerning the interpretation or application of an international agreement related to the purposes of this Convention, which is submitted to it in accordance with the agreement.
3. The Sea-Bed Disputes Chamber of the International Tribunal for the Law of the Sea established in accordance with Annex VI, and any other chamber or arbitral tribunal referred to in Part XI, section 5, shall have jurisdiction in any matter which is submitted to it in accordance therewith.
4. In the event of a dispute as to whether a court or tribunal has jurisdiction, the matter shall be settled by decision of that court or tribunal.

Art. 289. Experts

In any dispute involving scientific or technical matters, a court or tribunal exercising jurisdiction under this section may, at the request of a party or *proprio motu*, select in consultation with the parties no fewer than two scientific or technical experts chosen preferably from the relevant list prepared in accordance with Annex VIII, article 2, to sit with the court or tribunal but without the right to vote.

Art. 290. Provisional measures

1. If a dispute has been duly submitted to a court or tribunal which considers that *prima facie* it has jurisdiction under this Part or Part XI, section 5, the court or tribunal may prescribe any provisional measures which it considers appropriate under the circumstances to preserve the respective rights of the parties to the dispute or to prevent serious harm to the marine environment, pending the final decision.
2. Provisional measures may be modified or revoked as soon as the circumstances justifying them have changed or ceased to exist.
3. Provisional measures may be prescribed, modified or revoked under this article only at the request of a party to the dispute and after the parties have been given an opportunity to be heard.
4. The court or tribunal shall forthwith give notice to the parties to the dispute, and to such other State Parties as it considers appropriate, of the prescription, modification or revocation of provisional measures.
5. Pending the constitution of an arbitral tribunal to which a dispute is being submitted under this section, any court or tribunal agreed upon by the parties or, failing such agreement within two weeks from the date of the request for provisional measures, the International Tribunal for the Law of the Sea or, with respect to activities in the Area, the Sea-Bed Disputes Chamber, may prescribe, modify or revoke provisional measures in accordance with this article if it considers that *prima facie* the tribunal which is to be constituted would have jurisdiction and that the urgency of the situation so requires. Once constituted, the tribunal to which the dispute has been submitted may modify, revoke or affirm those provisional measures, acting in conformity with paragraphs 1 to 4.
6. The parties to the dispute shall comply promptly with any provisional measures prescribed under this article.

Art. 291. Access

1. All the dispute settlement procedures specified in this Part shall be open to State Parties.
2. The dispute settlement procedures specified in this Part shall be open to entities other than State Parties only as specifically provided for in this Convention.

Art. 292. Prompt release of vessels and crews

1. Where the authorities of a State Party have detained a vessel flying the flag of another State Party and it is alleged that the detaining State has not complied with the provisions of this Convention for the prompt release of the vessel or its crew upon the posting of a reasonable bond or other financial security, the question of release from detention may be submitted to any court or tribunal agreed upon by the parties or, failing such agreement within 10 days from the time of detention, to a court or tribunal accepted by the detaining State under article 287 or to the International Tribunal for the Law of the Sea, unless the parties otherwise agree.
2. The application for release may be made only by or on behalf of the flag State of the vessel.
3. The court or tribunal shall deal without delay with the application for release and shall deal only with the question of release, without prejudice to the merits of any case before the appropriate domestic forum against the vessel, its owner or its crew. The authorities of the detaining State remain competent to release the vessel or its crew at any time.
4. Upon the posting of the bond or other financial security determined by the court or tribunal, the authorities of the detaining State shall comply promptly with the decision of the court or tribunal the release of the vessel or its crew.

Art. 293. Applicable law

1. A court or tribunal having jurisdiction under this section shall apply this Convention and other rules or international law not incompatible with this Convention.
2. Paragraph 1 does not prejudice the power of the court or tribunal having jurisdiction under this section to decide a case *ex aequo et bono*, if the parties so agree.

Art. 294. Preliminary proceedings

1. a court or tribunal provided for in article 287 to which an application is made in respect of a dispute referred to in article 297 shall determine at the request of a party, or may determine *proprio motu*, whether the claim constitutes an abuse of legal process or whether *prima facie* it is well founded. If the court or tribunal determines that the claim constitutes an abuse of legal process or is *prima facie* unfounded, it shall take no further action in the case.
2. Upon receipt of the application, the court or tribunal shall immediately notify the other party or parties of the application, and shall fix a reasonable time-limit within which they may request it to make a determination in accordance with paragraph 1.
3. Nothing in this article affects the right of any party to a dispute to make preliminary objections in accordance with the applicable rules of procedure.

Art. 295. Exhaustion of local remedies

Any dispute between States Parties concerning the interpretation or application of this Convention may be submitted to the procedures provided for in this section only after local remedies have been exhausted where this is required by international law.

Art. 296. Finality and binding force of decisions

1. Any decision rendered by a court or tribunal having jurisdiction under this section shall be final and shall be complied with by all the parties to the dispute.
2. Any such decision shall have no binding force except between the parties and in respect of that particular dispute.

Section 3. Limitations and exceptions to applicability of section 2

Art. 297. Limitations on applicability of section 2

1. Disputes concerning the interpretation or application of this Convention with regard to the exercise by a coastal State of its sovereign rights or jurisdiction provided for in this Convention shall be subject to the procedures provided for in section 2 in the following cases:
(a) when it is alleged that a coastal State has acted in contrvention of the provisions of this Convention in regard to the freedom and rights of navigation, overflight or the laying of submarine cables and pipelines, or in regard to other internationally lawful uses of the sea specified in article 58;
(b) when it is alleged that a State in exercising the aforementioned freedoms, rights or uses has acted in contravention of this Convention or of laws or regulations adopted by the coastal State in conformity with this Convention and other rules of international law not compatible with this Convention; or
(c) when it is alleged that a coastal State has acted in contravention of specified international rules and standards for the protection and preservation of the marine environment which are applicable to the coastal State and which have been established by this Convention or through a competent international organization or diplomatic conference in accordance with this Convention.
2. (a) Disputes concerning the interpretation or application of the provisions of this Convention with regard to marine scientific research shall be settled in accordance with section 2, except that the coastal State shall not be obliged to accept the submission to such settlement of any dispute arising out of:
(i) the exercise by the coastal State of a right or discretion in accordance with article 246; or
(ii) a decision by the coastal State to order suspension or cessation of a research project in accordance with article 253.
(b) a dispute arising from an allegation by the researching State that with respect to a specific project the coastal State is not exercising its rights under articles 246 and 253 in a manner compatible with this Convention shall be submitted, at the request of either party, to conciliation under Annex V, section 2, provided that the conciliation commission shall not call in question the exercise by the coastal State of its discretion to designate specific areas as referred to in article 246, paragraph 6, or of its discretion to withhold consent in accordance with article 246, paragraph 5.
3. (a) Disputes concerning the interpretation or application of the provisions of this Convention with regard to fisheries shall be settled in accordance with Section 2, except that the coastal State shall not be obliged to accept the submission to such settlement of any dispute relating to its sovereign rights with respect to the living resources in the exclusive economic zone or their exercise, including its discretionary powers for determining the allowable catch, its harvesting capacity, the allocation of surpluses to other States and the terms and conditions established in its conservation and management laws and regulations.
(b) Where no settlement has been reached by recourse to section 1 of this Part, a dispute shall be submitted to conciliation under Annex V, section 2, at the request of any party to the dispute, when it is alleged that:
(i) a coastal State has manifestly failed to comply with its obligations to ensure through proper conservation and management measures that the maintenance of the living resources in the exclusive economic zone is not seriously endangered;
(ii) a coastal State has arbitrarily refused to determine, at the request of another State, the allowable catch and its capacity to harvest living resources with respect to stocks which that other State is interested in fishing; or
(iii) a coastal State has arbitrarily refused to allocate to any State, under articles 62, 69 and 70 and under the terms and conditions established by the coastal State consistent with this Convention, the whole or part of the surplus it has declared to exist.
(c) In no case shall the conciliation commission substitute its discretion for that of the coastal State.
(d) The report of the conciliation commission shall be communicated to the appropriate international organizations.
(e) In negotiating agreements pursuant to articles 69 and 70, State Parties, unless they otherwise agree, shall include a clause on measures which they shall take in order to minimize the possibility of a disagreement concerning the interpretation or application of the agreement, and on how they should proceed if a disagreement nevertheless arises.

Art. 298. Optional exceptions to applicability of section 2

1. When signing, ratifying or acceding to this Convention or at any time thereafter, a State may, without prejudice to the obligations arising under section 1, declare in writing that it does not accept any one or more of the procedures provided for in section 2 with respect to one or more of the following categories of disputes:
(a) (i) disputes concerning the interpretation or application of articles 15, 74 and 83 relating to sea boundary delimitations, or those involving historic bays or titles, provided that a State having made such a declaration shall, when such a dispute arises subsequent to the entry into force of this Convention and where no agreement within a reasonable period of time is reached in negotiations between the parties, at the request of any party to the dispute, accept submission of the matter to conciliation under Annex V, section 2; and provided further that any dispute that necessarily involves the concurrent consideration of any unsettled

dispute concerning sovereignty or other rights over continental or insular land territory shall be excluded from such submission;
(ii) after the conciliation commission has presented its report, which shall state the reasons on which it is based, the parties shall negotiate an agreement on the basis of that report; if these negotiations do not result in an agreement, the parties shall, by mutual consent, submit the question to one of the procedures provided for in section 2, unless the parties otherwise agree;
(iii) this subparagraph does not apply to any sea boundary dispute finally settled by an arrangement between the parties, or to any such dispute which is to be settled in accordance with a bilateral or multilateral agreement binding upon those parties;
(b) disputes concerning military activities, including military activities by government vessels and aircraft engaged in non-commercial service, and disputes concerning law enforcement activities in regard to the exercise of sovereign rights or jurisdiction excluded from the jurisdiction of a court or tribunal under article 297, paragraph 2 or 3;
(c) disputes in respect of which the Security Council of the United Nations is exercising the functions assigned to it by the Charter of the United Nations, unless the Security Council decides to remove the matter from its agenda or calls upon the parties to settle it by the means provided for in this Convention.
2. A State Party which has made a declaration under paragraph 1 may at any time withdraw it, or agree to submit a dispute excluded by such declaration to any procedure specified in this Convention.
3. A State Party which has made a declaration under paragraph 1 shall not be entitled to submit any dispute falling within the excepted category of disputes to any procedure in this Convention as against another State Party, without the consent of that party.
4. If one of the States Parties has made a declaration under paragraph 1(a), any other State Party may submit any dispute falling within an excepted category against the declarant party to the procedure specified in such declaration.
5. A new declaration, or the withdrawal of a declaration, does not in any way affect proceedings pending before a court or tribunal in accordance with this article, unless the parties otherwise agree.
6. Declarations and notices of withdrawal of declarations under this article shall be deposited with the Secretary-General of the United Nations, who shall transmit copies thereof to the State Parties.

Art. 299. Right of the parties to agree upon a procedure
1. A dispute excluded under article 297 or excepted by a declaration made under article 298 from the dispute settlement procedures provided for in section 2 may be submitted to such procedures only by agreement of the parties to the dispute.
2. Nothing in this section impairs the right of the parties to the dispute to agree to some other procedure for the settlement of such dispute or to reach an amicable settlement.

Part XVI. General provisions

Art. 300. Good faith and abuse of rights
States Parties shall fulfil in good faith the obligations assumed under this Convention and shall exercise the rights, jurisdiction and freedoms recognized in this Convention in a manner which would not constitute an abuse of right.

Art. 301. Peaceful uses of the seas
In exercising their rights and performing their duties under this Convention, States Parties shall refrain from any threat or use of force against the territorial integrity or political independence of any State, or in any other manner inconsistent with the principles of international law embodied in the Charter of the United Nations.

Art. 302. Disclosure of information
Without prejudice to the right of a State Party to resort to the procedures for the settlement of disputes provided for in this Convention, nothing in this Convention shall be deemed to require a State Party, in the fulfilment of its obligations under this Convention, to supply information in the disclosure of which is contrary to the essential interests of its security.

Art. 303. Archaeological and historical objects found at sea
1. States have the duty to protect objects of an archaeological and historical nature found at sea and shall co-operate for this purpose.
2. In order to control traffic in such objects, the coastal State may, in applying article 33, presume that their removal from the sea-bed in the zone referred to in that article without its approval would result in an infringement within its territory or territorial sea of the laws and regulations referred to in that article.
3. Nothing in this article affects the rights of identifiable owners, the law of salvage or other rules of admiralty, or laws and practices with respect to cultural exchanges.
4. This article is without prejudice to other international agreements and rules of international law regarding the protection of objects of an archaeological and historical nature.

Art. 304. Responsibility and liability for damage
The provisions of this Convention regarding responsibility and liability for damage are without prejudice to the application of existing rules and the development of further rules regarding responsibility and liability under international law.

Part XVII. Final clauses

Art. 305. Signature
1. This Convention shall be open for signature by:
(a) all States;
(b) Namibia, represented by the United Nations Council for Namibia;
(c) all self-governing associated States which have chosen that status in an act of self-determination supervised and approved by the United Nations in accordance with General Assembly resolution 1514 (XV) and which have competence over the matters governed by this Convention, including the competence to enter into treaties in respect of those matters;
(d) all self-governing associated States which, in accordance with their respective instruments of association, have competence over the matters governed by this Convention, including the competence to enter into treaties in respect of those matters;
(e) all territories which enjoy full internal self-government, recognized as such by the United Nations, but have not attained full independence in accordance with General Assembly resolution 1514 (XV) and which have competence over the matters governed by this Convention, including the competence to enter into treaties in respect of those matters;
(f) international organizations, in accordance with Annex IX.
2. This Convention shall remain open for signature until 9 December 1984 at the Ministry of Foreign Affairs of Jamaica and also, from 1 July 1983 until 9 December 1984, at United Nations Headquarters in New York.

Art. 306. Ratification and formal confirmation
This Convention is subject to ratification by States and the other entities referred to in article 305, paragraph 1(b), (c), (d) and (e), and to formal confirmation, in accordance with Annex IX, by the entities referred to in article 305, paragraph 1(f). The instruments of ratification and of formal confirmation shall be deposited with the Secretary-General of the United Nations.

Art. 307. Accession
This Convention shall remain open for accession by States and the other entities referred to in article 305. Accession by the entities referred to in article 305, paragraph 1(f), shall be in accordance with Annex IX. The instruments of accession shall be deposited with the Secretary-General of the United Nations.

Art. 308. Entry into force
1. This Convention shall enter into force 12 months after the date of deposit of the sixtieth instrument of ratification or accession.
2. For each State ratifying or acceding to this Convention after the deposit of the sixtieth instrument of ratification or accession, the Convention shall enter into force on the thirtieth day following the deposit of its instrument of ratification or accession, subject to paragraph 1.
3. The Assembly of the Authority shall meet on the date of entry into force of this Convention and shall elect the Council of the Authority. The first Council shall be constituted in a manner consistent with the purpose of article 161 if the provisions of that article cannot be strictly applied.
4. The rules, regulations and procedures drafted by the Preparatory Commission shall apply provisionally pending their formal adoption by the Authority in accordance with Part XI.
5. The Authority and its organs shall act in accordance with resolution II of the Third Nations Conference on the Law of the Sea relating to preparatory investment and with decisions of the Preparatory Commission taken pursuant to that resolution.

Art. 309. Reservations and exceptions
No reservations or exceptions may be made to this Convention unless expressly permitted by other articles of this Convention.

Art. 310. Declarations and statements
Article 309 does not preclude a State, when signing, ratifying or acceding to this Convention, from making declarations or statements, however phrased or named, with a view, *inter alia*, to the harmonization of its laws and regulations with the provisions of this Convention, provided that such declarations or statements do not purport to exclude or to modify the legal effect of the provisions of this Convention in their application to that State.

Art. 311. Relation to other conventions and international agreements
1. This Convention shall prevail, as between States Parties, over the Geneva Conventions on the Law of the Sea of 29 April 1958.
2. This Convention shall not alter the rights and obligations of States Parties which arise from other agreements compatible with this Convention and which do not affect the enjoyment by other States Parties of their rights or the performance of their obligations under this Convention.
3. Two or more States Parties may conclude agreements modifying or suspending the operation of provisions of this Convention, applicable solely to the relations between them, provided that such agreements do not relate to a provision derogation from which is incompatible with the effective execution of the object and purpose of this Convention, and provided further that such agreements shall not affect the application of the basic principles embodied herein, and that the provisions of such agreements do not affect the enjoyment by other States Parties of their rights or the performance of their obligations under this Convention.
4. States Parties intending to conclude an agreement referred to in paragraph 3 shall notify the other States Parties through the depository of this Convention of their intention to conclude the agreement and of the modification or suspension for which it provides.
5. This article does not affect international agreements expressly permitted or preserved by other articles of this Convention.
6. States Parties agree that there shall be no amendments to the basic principle relating to the common heritage of mankind set forth in article 136 and that they shall not be party to any agreement in derogation thereof.

Art. 312. Amendment
1. After the expiry of a period of 10 years from the date of entry into force of this Convention, a State Party may, by written communication addressed to the Secretary-General of the United Nations, propose specific amendments to this Convention, other than those relating to activities in the Area, and request the convening of a conference to consider such proposed amendments. The Secretary-General shall circulate such communication to all States Parties. If, within 12 months from the date of the circulation of the communication, not less than one half of the States Parties reply favourably to the request, the Secretary-General shall convene the conference.
2. The decision-making procedure applicable at the amendment conference shall be the same as that applicable at the Third United Nations Conference on the Law of the Sea unless otherwise decided by the conference. The conference should make every effort to reach agreement on any amendments by way of consensus and there should be no voting on them until all efforts at concensus have been exhausted.

Art. 313. Amendment by simplified procedure
1. A State Party may, by written communication addressed to the Secretary-General of the United Nations, propose an amendment to this Convention, other than an amendment relating to activities in the Area, to be adopted by the simplified procedure set forth in this article without convening a conference. The Secretary-General shall circulate the communication to all States Parties.
2. If, within a period of 12 months from the date of the circulation of the communication, a State Party objects

to the proposed amendment or to the proposal for its adoption by the simplified procedure, the amendment shall be considered rejected. The Secretary-General shall immediately notify all States Parties accordingly.

3. If, 12 months from the date of the circulation of the communication, no State Party has objected to the proposed amendment or to the proposal for its adoption by the simplified procedure, the proposed amendment shall be considered adopted. The Secretary-General shall notify all States parties that the proposed amendment has been adopted.

Art. 314. Amendments to the provisions of this Convention relating exclusively to activities in the Area

1. A State Party may, by written communication addressed to the Secretary-General of the Authority, propose an amendment to the provisions of this Convention relating exclusively to activities in the Area, including Annex VI, section 4. The Secretary-General shall circulate such communication to all States Parties. The proposed amendment shall be subject to approval by the Assembly following its approval by the Council. Representatives of States Parties in those organs shall have full powers to consider and approve the proposed amendment. The proposed amendment as approved by the Council and the Assembly shall be considered adopted.

2. Before approving any amendment under paragraph 1, the Council and the Assembly shall ensure that it does not prejudice the system of exploration for and exploitation of the resources of the Area, pending the Review Conference in accordance with article 155.

Art. 315. Signature, ratification of, assession to and authentic texts of amendments

1. Once adopted, amendments to this Convention shall be open for signature by State Parties for 12 months from the date of adoption, at United Nations Headquarters in New York, unless otherwise provided in the amendment itself.

2. Articles 306, 307 and 320 apply to all amendments to this Convention.

Art. 316. Entry into force of amendments

1. Amendments to this Convention, other than those referred to in paragraph 5, shall enter into force for the States Parties ratifying or acceding to them on the thirtieth day following the deposit of instruments of ratification or accession by two thirds of the States Parties or by 60 States Parties, whichever is greater. Such amendments shall not affect the enjoyment by other States Parties of their rights or the performance of their obligations under this Convention.

2. An amendment may provide that a larger number of ratifications or accessions shall be required for its entry into force than are required by this article.

3. For each State Party ratifying or acceding to an amendment referred to in paragraph 1 after the deposit of the required number of instruments of ratification or accession, the amendment shall enter into force on the thirtieth day following the deposit of its instrument of ratification or accession.

4. A State which becomes a Party to this Convention after the entry into force of an amendment in accordance with paragraph 1 shall, failing an expression of a different intention by that State:
(a) be considered as a Party to this Convention as so amended; and
(b) be considered as a Party to the unamended Convention in relation to any State Party not bound by the amendment.

5. Any amendment relating exclusively to activities in the Area and any amendment to Annex VI shall enter into force for all States Parties one year following the deposit of instruments of ratification or accession by three fourths of the States Parties.

6. A State which becomes a Party to this Convention after the entry into force of amendments in accordance with paragraph 5 shall be considered as a Party to this Convention as so amended.

Art. 317. Denunciation

1. A State Party may, by written notification addressed to the Secretary-General of the United Nations, denounce this Convention and may indicate its reasons. Failure to indicate reasons shall not affect the validity of the dununciation. The denunciation shall take effect one year after the date of receipt of the notification, unless the notification specifies a later date.

2. A State shall not be discharged by reason of the denunciation from the financial and contractual obligations which accrued while it was a Party to this Conven-

tion, nor shall the denunciation affect any right, obligation or legal situation of that State created through the execution of this Convention prior to its termination for that State.

3. The denunciation shall not in any way affect the duty of any State Party to fulfil any obligation embodied in this Convention to which it would be subject under international law independently of this Convention.

Art. 318. Status of Annexes

The Annexes form an integral part of this Convention and, unless expressly provided otherwise, a reference to this Convention or to one of its Parts includes a reference to the Annexes relating thereto.

Art. 319. Depositary

1. The Secretary-General of the United Nations shall be the depositary of this Convention and amendments thereto.

2. In addition to his functions as depositary, the Secretary-General shall:
(a) report to all States Parties, the Authority and competent international organizations on issues of a general nature that have arisen with respect to this Convention;
(b) notify the Authority of ratifications and formal confirmations of an accessions to this Convention and amendments thereto, as well as of denunciations of this Convention;
(c) notify States Parties of agreements in accordance with article 311, paragraph 4;
(d) circulate amendments adopted in accordance with this convention to States Parties for ratification or accession;
(e) convene necessary meetings of States Parties in accordance with this Convention.

3. (a) The Secretary-General shall also transmit to the observers referred to in article 156:
(i) reports referred to in paragraph 2(a);
(ii) notifications referred to in paragraph 2(b) and (c); and
(iii) texts of amendments referred to in paragraph 2(d), for their information.
(b) The Secretary-General shall also invite those observers to participate as observers at meetings of States Parties referred to in paragraph 2(e).

Art. 320. Authentic texts

The original of this Convention, of which the Arabic, Chinese, English, French, Russian and Spanish texts are equally authentic, shall, subject to article 305, paragraph 2, be deposited with the Secretary-General of the United Nations.

In witness whereof, the undersigned Plenipotentiaries, being duly authorized thereto, have signed this Convention.

Done at Montego Bay, this tenth day of December, one thousand nine hundred and eighty-two.

The Convention has nine Annexes:

Annex I. Highly Migratory Species. Annex II. Commission on the limits of the continental shelf, Annex III. Basic conditions of prospecting, exploration and exploitation. Annex IV. Statue of the enterprise. Annex V. Conciliation. Annex VI. Statue of the International Tribunal for the Law of the Sea. Annex VII. Arbitration. Annex VIII. Special Arbitration. Annex IX. Participation by International Organizations.

Signatories of the Convention, as at December 10, 1982, when the Convention was opened for signature at Montego Bay, Jamaica:

Algeria	Chad
Angola	Chile
Australia	China
Austria	Colombia
Bahamas	Congo
Bahrain	Cook Islands
Bangladesh	Costa Rica
Barbados	Cuba
Belize	Cyprus
Bhutan	Czechoslovakia
Brazil	Democratic People's
Bulgaria	Republic of Korea
Burma	Democratic Yemen
Burundi	Denmark
Byelorussian SSR	Djibouti
Canada	Dominican Republic
Cape Verde	Egypt

Ethiopia	Norway
Fiji	Pakistan
Finland	Panama
France	Papua New
Gabon	Guinea
Gambia	Paraguay
German Democratic	Philippines
Republic	Poland
Ghana	Portugal
Greece	Romania
Grenada	Rwanda
Guinea-Bissau	Saint Lucia
Guyana	Saint Vincent and
Haiti	the Grenadines
Honduras	Senegal
Hungary	Seychelles
Iceland	Sierra Leone
India	Singapore
Indonesia	Solomon
Iran	Islands
Iraq	Somalia
Ireland	Sri Lanka
Ivory Coast	Sudan
Jamaica	Suriname
Kenya	Sweden
Kuwait	Thailand
Laos	Togo
Lesotho	Trinidad and
Liberia	Tobago
Malaysia	Tunisia
Maldives	Tuvalu
Malta	Uganda
Mauritania	Ukrainian SSR
Mauritius	USSR
Mexico	United Arab
Monaco	Emirates
Mongolia	United Republic
Morocco	of Cameroon
Mozambique	United Republic
Namibia (United	of Tanzania
Nations Council	Upper Volta
for Namibia)	Uruguay
Nauru	Vanuatu
Nepal	Viet Nam
Netherlands	Yemen
New Zealand	Yugoslavia
Niger	Zambia
Nigeria	Zimbabwe

Signatories of the Final Act. The Final Act was signed by all 119 delegations which signed the Convention, as well as by the following full participants.

Belgium	Libya
Benin	Luxembourg
Botswana	Oman
Ecuador	Peru
Equatorial Guinea	Republic of Korea
Federal Republic	Samoa
of Germany	Spain
Holy See	Switzerland
Israel	United Kingdom
Italy	United States
Japan	Venezuela
Jordan	Zaire

States and territories with observer status: Netherlands Antilles and the Trust Territory of the Pacific Islands. Intergovernmental organization: European Economic Community. National liberation movements: African Congress of South Africa, Palestinian Liberation Organization, Pan Africanist Congress of Azania, South West Africa People's Organization. Until Dec. 9, 1984 the Convention was signed by 159 states (except, among others, FRG, Israel, the UK and the USA) and ratified by 14 states. The Convention will come into force after ratification by 60 states.

B. J. DUPUY, *L'océan partagé*, Paris, 1979; *UN Chronicle*, November, 1980, p. 4; UN, *The Law of the Sea*, New York, 1983; J.L. DE AZCARAGA, *Derecho del Mar*, Madrid, 1983; B. ZULETA TORRES, *El Nuevo Derecho del Mar*, Bogota, 1984; P.P. CARGO, *La Convención Sobre el Derecho del Mar*, Mexico DF, 1984; UN, *The Law of the Sea: Multilateral Treaties Relevant to the United Nations Conventions. A Chronological and Subject Index to the Treaties*, New York, 1985; N.S. FRANO, *Aspectos Actuales de Derecho del Mar, Reseña Histórion-Jurídica*, Bogota, 1986; Th.A. CLINGAN ed., *The Law of the Sea: What Lies Ahead?* Honolulu, 1988; E.D. BROWN, R.R. CHURCHILL eds., *The UN Convention on the Law of the Sea: Impact and Implementation*, Honolulu, 1988.

SEA LAW, INTERNATIONAL. A subject of private codification procedures in the 19th and 20th centuries, a subject of The Hague Conferences of 1899 and 1907, of the League of Nations and of the United Nations Commission on the Law of the Sea. The first international convention on the Law of the Sea was the Paris Declaration of 1856, which banned sea piracy and established the principles of an "effective blockade" and of property seizure. The first codification work was started by two private scientific associations: Institut de Droit International, IDI, in Paris and the International Law Association, ILA:

1879–IDI, at the Brussels session on the protection of undersea cable.
1883–ILA, at the Milan session on collisions at sea.
1894–IDI, at the Venice session on the nationality of sea vessels.
1898–IDI, at The Hague session on the legal status of sea vessels and their crews in alien seaports.
1924–ILA, at a Stockholm session on the principles of jurisdiction in territorial sea, in open sea, in straits and channels.
1926–ILA, at a Vienna session on the legal situation of sea vessels in seaports.
1927–IDI, at a Lausanne session on the legal status of territorial waters.
1928–IDI, at a Stockholm session, the same subjects as in 1898 and 1927.
1934–IDI, at a Paris session, establishment of Office International des Eaux.
1937–IDI, at a Luxembourg session on the protection of biological resources of the sea.
1954–ILA, at an Edinburgh session on the legal status of the ocean bed and the minerals under the sea bed.
1957–IDI, at an Amsterdam session on differences between the legal status of territorial waters and internal waters.

Apart from these conferences, codification work was also carried out by the American International Conference, the League of Nations, the Barcelona Declaration of 1921, and a convention and Geneva statute on the international status of sea-ports of 1923. The establishment, in 1924, of the League Commission of Experts on the Codification of International Law was the beginning of preliminary work on the following issues: territorial sea, use of biological resources of seas, legal status of registered sea vessels used for commercial transportation and the suppression of sea piracy. At the codification conference in The Hague held between Mar. 13 and Apr. 12, 1930, with the participation of 47 States, the width of the territorial sea, its boundaries and its legal status were discussed, but without reaching agreement. In 1931, under the auspices of the League of Nations, a convention was concluded on the protection of whales. In the United Nations, the Commission of International Law, at eight sessions held between 1949 and 1956, prepared codification material regarding territorial sea, open sea, the continental shelf and other questions to be presented at the International Conference on the Codification of the Law of the Sea, convened according to Resolution 1105/XI of Feb. 21, 1957. The Conference was preceded by a Conference of twelve land-locked states: Afghanistan, Austria, Byelorussian SSR, Bolivia, Czechoslovakia, Luxembourg, Nepal, San Marino, Switzerland, Vatican and Hungary, held from Feb. 10 to Feb. 14, 1950, which introduced the issue of free access to the sea for non-coastal states (included in article 3 of the First Geneva Conference on the Open Sea). The Conference also adopted an optional protocol on the obligatory resolution of disputes and resolutions concerning (1) nuclear tests in open sea, (2) pollution of open sea with radio-active pollutants, (3) protection of fish resources, (4) cooperation with regard to the measures of protection, (5) application of humanitarian methods concerning the killing of the sea fauna, (6) coastal fishery, (7) legal status of historical waters.

The chronology of the Conferences on the Law of the Sea, 1958–1984, is as follows:

1958–First United Nations Conference on the Law of the Sea: 86 States meet in Geneva and adopt four international conventions covering the territorial sea, the high seas, the continental shelf and fishing and conservation of living resources.
1960–Second United Nations Conference on the Law of the Sea fails to produce any substantive agreement on the limits of the territorial zone and fishing rights.
1967–The United Nations General Assembly decides that technological and other changes in the world require the international community to address the matter of laws governing the seas beyond national jurisdiction. A 35-member *ad hoc* committee is set up by the Assembly to study the matter.
1968–The *ad hoc* committee grows to 41 members and is renamed *Committee on the Peaceful Uses of the Sea-Bed and the Ocean Floor beyond the Limits of National Jurisdiction.*
1970–As a result of the Sea Bed Committee's work the General Assembly adopts a *Declaration of Principles Governing the Sea-Bed and Ocean Floor, and the Subsoil Thereof, beyond the Limits of National Jurisdiction.* These areas are declared the "common heritage of mankind." The Assembly also decides to convene the Third United Nations Conference on the Law of the Sea and the Sea-Bed Committee, enlarged to 91 members, is given the job of preparing for the Conference. By 1973 it puts out a 6-volume report.
1973–First session of the Conference (organizational, New York) elects officers, begins work on rules of procedure. Hamilton Shirley Amerasinghe of Sri Lanka is elected President of the Conference.
1974–Second session, Caracas. Adopts rules of procedure; 115 countries speak in general debate. First attempt to deal with alternate texts submitted by Sea-Bed Committee.
1975–Third session, Geneva. A "single negotiating text" produced by Committee Chairmen, sets out in treaty language the provisions to be included.
1976–Fourth session, New York. The results of negotiations set out in a "revised single negotiating text."
1976–Fifth session, New York. Further progress in some areas, impasse on how deep-sea mining should be organized and regulated.
1977–Sixth session, New York. An "informal composite negotiating text" marks continuing deliberations.
1978–Seventh session, first Geneva, then New York. Seven negotiating groups created to tackle "hard core" differences.
1979–Eighth session, first Geneva, then New York. First revision of the 1977 negotiating text emerges. Decision taken to complete work on Convention by 1980.
1980–Ninth session, first New York, then Geneva. "Informal text" of Draft Convention produced. Plans to hold final session in 1981.
1981–Tenth session, first New York, then Geneva. First official text of Draft Convention issued. Jamaica and Federal Republic of Germany chosen as seats for the International Sea-Bed Authority and the International Tribunal for the Law of the Sea respectively. United States cites difficulties in sea-bed provisions. "Final decision-making session" set for 1982.
1982–Eleventh session (Part I. Mar. 8–Apr. 30). New York. All efforts at reaching general agreement having been exhausted, the Conference votes on a number of amendments to the Draft Convention. At the end, at the request of the United States, there is a recorded vote. The Convention is adopted on Apr. 30 by 130 votes to 4 against, with 17 abstentions.

Eleventh session (Part II Sept. 22–24), New York. Approves Drafting Committee changes in the Convention, adopts draft Final Act, selects Jamaica as site of signing session.
1982 (Dec. 6–10)–Convention and Final Act are signed at Montego Bay, Jamaica, by 119 delegations.
1983–Preparatory Commission is convened in Kingston, Jamaica, to begin work on the creation of International Sea-Bed Authority and International Tribunal for the Law of the Sea.
1984–The second session of the Preparatory Commission is convened in Kingston, Jamaica, Mar. 19 to Apr. 13.

International organizations reg. with the UIA, participating in the codification of the law of the sea:

International Maritime Consultative Organization. ▷ IMCO.
Diplomatic Conference on the International Law of the Sea, Conference Diplomatique de Droit Maritime International, convened by the government of Belgium, on a regular basis, starting in 1905. In the years 1905–70, the Conference held twelve sessions.
International Maritime Committee, established in 1897, seat: Antwerp. Its task is to promote codification of the law of the sea; associates national associations.
Permanent Commission for the Conservation of the Maritime Resources of the South Pacific, established in 1952 on the basis of an agreement between the governments of Chile, Ecuador and Peru. Seat: Santiago.
Since 1980 the Dalhouse Law School in Halifax, Canada publishes the *Marine Affairs Bibliography. A Comprehensive Index to Marine Law and Policy Literature.*
The Law of the Sea Institute of the University of Hawaii, Honolulu publishes reports on international Sea Law.

Acts of the Conference for the Codification of International Law of 1930, 3 Vols., Geneva, 1930; A. GARCIA ROBLES, *La Conferencia de Ginebra y la Anchura del Mar Territorial*, Mexico, DF, 1959; *Official Documents of the Second Sea Law Conference*, 3 Vols., Geneva, 1960; M. MAC DOUGAL, W.T. BURKE, *The Public Order of the Ocean. A Contemporary International Law of the Sea*, London, 1962; S. ODA, *International Control of Sea Resources*, Leiden, 1963; A.N. SILLING, *Morskoie pravo*, Moscow, 1964; W.A. RAYNALD, *Traité de Droit Maritime Général*, Geneva, 1964; M.R. SIMMONET, *La Convention sur la Haute Mer*, 1958, Paris, 1966; *New Director of the Law of the Sea. Documents*, London 1973; *The Sea. A Select Bibliography on the Legal, Political, Economic and Technological Aspects, 1974–75*; UN, New York, 1975; E.VARGAS, *América Latina y el Derecho del Mar*, México, DF, 1975; *The Sea: Bibliography on Legal, Political, Economic and Technological Aspects 1976–1978*, UN, New York, 1979; "The Third UN Conference on the Law of Sea", in: *UN Yearbook 1980*, pp. 136–158; *The Law of the Sea: Multilateral Treaties Relevant to the United Nations Convention. A Chronological and Subject Index to Treaties*, UN, New York, 1985; Yu.G. BARSEGOV ed., *Slovar Mezhdunarodnogo morskogo prava*, Moskva, 1985; The Law of the Sea, in: R.L. BLEDSOE, B.A. BOCZEK, *International Law Dictionary*, Oxford, 1987; Ch. PARK, J.K. PARK, eds., *The Law of the Sea: Problems from the East Asia Perspective*, Honolulu, 1988.

SEA-LIFT. An international military term, like ▷ Air-Lift, for moving troops, equipment and supplies to or from a conflict zone by ship.

D. ROBERTSON, *Guide to Modern Defense and Strategy*, Detroit, 1988.

SEAL OF THE UN. ▷ Flag Emblem and Seal of the UN.

SEALS. A subject of international protection, including bearded seals, Greenland and hooded seals, walruses and sea lions; initiated by exchange of notes between the US, Canada and Japan, constituting an agreement relating to scientific investigations of the fur seals in the North Pacific Ocean. Tokyo, Jan. 31, and Feb. 8, 1952, and Ottawa, Feb. 7 and Mar. 1, 1952.

S

The international convention signed Feb. 9, 1957 in Washington created the North Pacific Fur Seal Commission, established 1958, seat in Washington, affiliating the governments of Japan, Canada, USA, and USSR. The convention took effect Oct. 14, 1957; supplemented by a protocol which entered into force Apr. 10, 1964. The first task was a 12-year program (1958–70) of research on seals protection, guaranteeing the maintenance of the species and a high quality of furs; the next – the establishment of reservations and formulating common norms. Each year the Proceeding Meetings are held in the capital of a different member state. The first international dispute on the right to catch seals in the region of Alaska was examined by the Court of Arbitration Aug. 15, 1893 between the USA and Great Britain. The first laws on the protection of seals were passed by the USA and Great Britain 1894–95; they turned out to be ineffective, and the number of seals in the region of Alaska, estimated in the middle of the 19th century at 2 million, fell to 0.2 million when the USA and Great Britain signed the first treaty Feb. 7, 1911 on the international protection of seals in Washington and July 7, 1911 with Japan and Russia. The hunting of seals was prohibited in the region of the Pacific Ocean, north of the 30° parallel and permitted only on islands. By 1941 the number of seals had increased to 1.6 million. Japan refused to obey the treaty Oct. 23, 1941, but by the Peace Treaty in San Francisco, 1951, was compelled to enter into a new one, signed Mar. 9, 1957 by Japan, Canada, USA, and USSR. This treaty guarantees Japan and Canada a share of 15% each in the catches made by the USA and USSR on their islands.

The Council of Fisheries of the EEC introduced in 1983 and renewed in 1985 a four years ban on European Community imports of hides and products of white coat pups of harp seals and the blue-black pups of hooded seals.

In July 1986 the Royal Seals Commission of Canada recommended putting a permanent end to the killing of white-coats or seal pups and the recompensation of Canadian $100 million permitting sealers to find new jobs.

On Dec. 31, 1987 Canada announced the banning of all offshore commercial hunting of white coated baby harp seals and blueback hooded seals and imposed a ban for 1988 on the hunting of grey seals. In summer 1988 the worsening ecological conditions of the North Sea caused the mass death of seals washed up on the coast of Denmark and the FRG. Bilateral intergovernmental organizations are:

Canadian–Norwegian Sealing Commission for the Northwest Atlantic, est. 1971.
North Pacific Fur Sea Commission, f. 1958, Washington DC, Members: Canada, Japan, USSR and USA.
Norwegian–Soviet Sealing Commission for the Northeast Atlantic, est. 1957.

UNTS, Vol. 168, p. 9; G.F. DE MARTENS, *Nouveau Recueil Général*, 2 s. Vol. 11, p. 293 S; Vol. 6, p. 320; *US Department of State Bulletin*, 1957, p. 377; *European Council and Commission*, 1985; *Canadian News Facts*, 1986; *The Europa Yearbook 1988. A World Survey*, Vol. I, London, 1988; KEESING's *Record of World Events*, June, 1988.

SEAMEO. ▷ Southeast Asian Ministers of Education Organization.

SEA MILE. The international unit of length for measuring distances at sea: the length of an arc corresponding to one-sixtieth of a degree of the southern circumference of the earth = 1852 meters.

SEA PIRACY. An international term for sea robbery; in international law, initially applied only to those acts of violence which were committed by private ships not bound by agreements with any state. In the 19th century it referred to all acts of violence committed on high seas and pirates were generally considered *hostes humani generis* – enemies of mankind. Questions of sea piracy were debated at the Paris Conference of 1856 following the Crimean War and a declaration on sea piracy was adopted. In the USA in the 19th century participation in acts of sea piracy was punishable by life-time imprisonment. In 1926 the Committee of Experts for codification of international law prepared a Report on Piracy. The UN began codificaton work on sea piracy in 1952 and concluded with the adoption of the Geneva Convention on Open Seas of Apr. 29, 1958 (it entered into force on Sept. 30, 1962) defining (in art. 15) what should be considered as acts of piracy committed on the open seas:

"(1) Any unlawful act of violence, seizure or robbery committed for personal reasons by private ship or aircraft's passengers or crew and aimed at: (a) a vessel or aircraft at open seas or against persons or property on board; (b) against a ship or aircraft, persons or property in places being outside jurisdiction of any State. (2) Any act of voluntary participation in actions taken by an aircraft or ship if the agent is conscious that what is being done on board the ship or aircraft is considered piracy. (3) Any action aimed to do or albeit acts determined under items 1 and 2".

Arts. 16–21 codified international rules applying to piracy on the open seas. ▷ Air piracy constitutes a separate problem also raised at the UN.

P. GOSSE, *The Pirates Who's Who?*, New York, 1924; "Piracy", in: *American Journal of International Law*, Special Supplement, 1926; N.W. MALKIN, "The inner history of the Declaration of Paris (1856)", in: *The British Yearbook of Internatonal Law*, 1927; P. GOSSE, *The History of Piracy*, New York, 1932; "A Collection of Piracy Law of Various Countries", in: *American Journal of International Law*, 1932; N.N., "The Nyon Arrangements. Piracy to Treaty?", in: *The British Yearbook of International Law*, 1938; R. GENET, "The Charge of Piracy in the Spanish Civil War", in: *American Journal of International Law*, No. 32, 1938; R.L. BLEDSOE, B.A. BOCZEK, *The International Law Dictionary*, Oxford, 1987.

SEA POWER. An international term for a state with a considerable merchant fleet or a large merchant fleet with warships, aircraft carriers, cruisers, destroyers and submarines.

JANE'S *Fighting Ships*, British Annual; G. MODELSKI, W.R. THOMPSON, *Seapower in Global Politics 1494–1993*, London, 1987.

SEA RESEARCH. A subject of international co-operation and agreements. The first conferences on exploration of the sea were held in Stockholm in 1899 and in Christiania (Oslo) in 1901 and established in Copenhagen in 1902 the International Council for the Exploration of the Sea initiating a programme of international investigation of the sea. A new constitution for the Council was signed in Copenhagen, Sept. 12, 1964. Members: The governments of Belgium, Canada, Denmark, Finland, France, GDR, FRG, Iceland, Ireland, the Netherlands, Norway, Poland, Portugal, Spain, Sweden, UK and USSR; came into force on July 22, 1968. Publ. *Research Reports, Journal du Conseil* and *Annales Biologiques*.

"It shall be the duty of the Council (a) to promote and encourage research and investigations for the study of the sea particularly those related to the living resources thereof; (b) to draw up programmes required for these purposes; (c) to publish the results of research . . ." (art. 1).

"The Council shall be concerned with the Atlantic Ocean and its adjacent seas and primarily concerned with the North Atlantic" (art. 2).

UNTS, Vol. 652, pp. 238 and 240.

SEA RESOURCES. The living resources in sea waters and geological resources on and under the sea bed, subject of international disputes and co-operation, as well as a subject of conventions related to resources and continental shelf.

The first disputes occurred at the end of the 19th century, when Scottish and Portuguese fishermen sought to expand their exclusive fishing zones exceeding the boundaries of their territorial waters. In Stockholm in 1899 and in Christiania (Oslo) in 1901 the first inter-governmental conferences were held which initiated studies on sea resources. To this end the inter-governmental International Council for the Utilization of Sea Resources was established in 1902. In the period between the two world wars, the Council suggested the creation of protective zones for some species of fish and limiting the use of trollnets, both of which were opposed by major fishing companies. Only after World War II, under the auspices of the United Nations, both the Council and FAO undertook expanded studies and initiatives aimed at preparing conventions on biological protection of sea resources. At the same time there has been an increase of international disputes regarding the width of territorial sea and fishing rights on adjoining waters. The UN General Assembly by force of its Res. 900/17 of Dec. 14, 1954, convened the first International Technical Conference on Conservation of Living Sea Resources, held in Rome Apr. 18–May 10, 1955. As a result of recommendations of this Conference, the UN General Assembly initiated preparations for the UN Conference on the Law of the Sea and for a Convention on fishing and protection of biological resources of high seas, adopted in Geneva on Apr. 29, 1958 and entered into force on Mar. 20, 1966. In art 1 it guarantees all states free fishing on the high seas putting on them the obligation to "observe legal norms regulating conservation of biological resources of the high seas"; arts 3, 8 and 13 specifying these norms with regard to specific cases. Intergovernmental organization reg. with the UIA; International Council for the Exploitation of the Sea ICES, established in 1902 in Copenhagen, linking governments of 17 states: Belgium, Canada, Denmark, Finland, France, the FRG, Great Britain, Holland, Iceland, Italy, Norway, Poland, Portugal, Spain, Sweden and the USSR. Seat: Helrup (Denmark). Publ.: *Journal du Conseil, Annales Biologiques, Fiches d'identification du Zooplancton, Fiches d'identification des Oeufs et Larves des Poissons, ICES Oceanographic Data Lists* and other.

The Conference of Ministers of Fisheries, held on July 6–7, 1972 in Moscow adopted a Declaration on Principles of Rational Exploitation of the Living Resources of the Seas and Oceans in the Common Interests of the Peoples of the World.

V.T. HOOFT, *Les Nations Unies et la conservation des resources de la mer*, Paris, 1958; F.V.G. AMADOR, *The Exploitation and Conservation of the Resources of the Sea*, Leiden, 1959; S. ODA, *International Control of Sea Resources*, Leiden, 1963; *Informe de la Conferencia Técnica International para la Conservación de los Recursos Vivos del Mar*, Roma, 1965, New York, 1967; *La Comisión de Derecho International y su Obra*, UN, New York, 1968, pp. 129–135; *UN Yearbook*, 1972, pp. 32–40; *UN Yearbook*, 1978, pp. 144–151.

SEA SAFETY. ▷ Safety of Life on Sea.

SEAS AND OCEANS PROTECTION TREATY, 1972. A Treaty signed on Nov. 13, 1972 in London by 57 States, including France, Japan, the USA, Great Britain and the USSR, specified which kinds of substance and chemical compounds must not be dumped into seas and oceans: first and foremost compounds of mercury and cadmium, several pesticides of organic origin, solid plastics, synthetics, oil, gas, mazut, highly radioactive waste and any composites of biological and chemical weapons. The treaty vested in a special conference the duty of monitoring how the provisions are implemented and advised a system of penalties to be inflicted on states violating the treaty.

IAEA, *Definition and Recommendation for the Convention on the Prevention of Marine Pollution 1972–1986*, Vienna, 1986.

SEA SIGNALIZATION. Universally introduced at the beginning of the 20th century. The initiator of the codification of sea signalization was the British Admiralty, which in 1857 published the first code of sea signals "for the use of all nations," then accepted by all sea states in an international convention of 1901 as the International Code of Signals, including visual signalling with international alphabets, flags and semaphore, and signalling by sound and radio-telegraph. Since 1958 a modernized International Code of Signals is administered by IMCO.

T.B. GRAVELY, *The Second World War: Signal Communications*, London, 1950; D.L. WOODS, *A History of Tactical Communicative Techniques*, London, 1965.

SEATO. Southeast Asia Treaty Organization. The Organ of the Southeast Asia Collective Defence Treaty, called ▷ SEATO Treaty, signed on Sept. 8, 1954 in Manila by the governments of Australia, France, Great Britain, New Zealand, Pakistan, Philippines, Thailand, USA; SEATO was one of the military instruments organized by the USA, 1945–55, in close communication with NATO 1949, ANZUS 1951 and CENTO 1955–59.

In 1967 France and Pakistan withdrew from participation in the work of the military organs of the pact due to the war in Vietnam. Pakistan withdrew completely from SEATO on Nov. 7, 1972. From Jan. 1, 1974 the government of France suspended the payment of membership contributions. Simultaneously Australia and New Zealand decided not to participate in the sessions of SEATO. On June 30, 1977 in Bangkok, SEATO was formally dissolved.

UNTS, Vol. 209, 1955, pp. 28–38; W.M. BALL, "A Political Reexamination of SEATO", in: *International Organization*, No. 12, 1958; G. MODELSKI, *SEATO*, Melbourne 1962; *SEATO, Select Documents*, Canberra, 1966; *SIPRI Yearbook*, 1977.

SEATO MANILA CHARTER, 1954. ▷ Pacific Charter, 1954.

SEATO TREATY, 1954. The Southeast Asia Defence Treaty, called Manila Pact. A Treaty between Australia, France, New Zealand, Pakistan, Philippines, Thailand, UK and USA, signed on Sept. 8, 1954 in Manila, together with the ▷ Pacific Charter, 1954; entered into force on Feb. 19, 1955. The text of the Treaty is as follows:

"The Parties to this Treaty,
Recognizing the sovereign equality of all the Parties, Reiterating their faith in the purposes and principles set forth in the Charter of the United Nations and their desire to live in peace with all peoples and all governments,
Reaffirming that, in accordance with the Charter of the United Nations, they uphold the principle of equal rights and self-determination of peoples, and declaring that they will earnestly strive by every peaceful means to promote self-government and to secure the independence of all countries whose peoples desire it and are able to undertake its responsibilities.

Desiring to strengthen the fabric of peace and freedom and to uphold the principles of democracy, individual liberty and the rule of law, and to promote the economic well-being and development of all peoples in the treaty area,
Intending to declare publicly and formally their sense of unity, so that any potential aggressor will appreciate that the Parties stand together in the area, and
Desiring further to co-ordinate their efforts for collective defense for the preservation of peace and security,
Therefore agree as follows:
Art. I. The Parties undertake, as set forth in the Charter of the United Nations, to settle any international disputes in which they may be involved by peaceful means in such a manner that international peace and security and justice are not endangered, and to refrain in their international relations from the threat or use of force in any manner inconsistent with the purpose of the United Nations.
Art. II. In order more effectively to achieve the objectives of this Treaty, the Parties separately and jointly, by means of continuous and effective self-help and mutual aid, will maintain and develop their individual and collective capacity to resist armed attack and to prevent and counter subversive activities directed from without against their territorial integrity and political stability.
Art. III. The Parties undertake to strengthen their institutions and to co-operate with one another in further development of economic measures, including technical assistance, designed both to promote economic progress and social well-being and to further the individual and collective efforts of governments toward these ends.
Art. IV.(1) Each Party recognizes that aggression by means of armed attack in the treaty area against any of the Parties or against any State or territory which the Parties by unanimous agreement may hereafter designate, would endanger its own peace and safety, and agrees that it will in that event act to meet the common danger in accordance with its constitutional processes. Measures taken under this paragraph shall be immediately reported to the Security Council of the United Nations.
(2) If, in the opinion of any of the Parties, the inviolability or the integrity of the territory or the sovereignty or political independence of any Party in the treaty area or of any other State or territory to which the provisions of paragraph 1 of this article from time to time apply is threatened in any way other than by armed attack or is affected or threatened by any fact or situation which might endanger the peace of the area, the Parties shall consult immediately in order to agree on the measures which should be taken for the common defense.
(3) It is understood that no action on the territory of any State designated by unanimous agreement under paragraph 1 of this article or on any territory so designated shall be taken except at the invitation or with the consent of the Government concerned.
Art. V. The Parties hereby established a Council, on which each of them shall be represented, to consider matters concerned the implementation of this Treaty. The Council shall provide for consultation with regard to military and any other planning as the situation obtaining in the treaty area may from time to time require. The Council shall be so organized as to be able to meet at any time.
Art. VI. This Treaty does not affect and shall not be interpreted as affecting in any way the rights and obligations of any of the Parties under the Charter of the United Nations or the responsibility of the United Nations for the maintenance of international peace and security. Each Party declares that none of the international engagements now in force between it and any other of the Parties or any third party is in conflict with the provisions of this Treaty, and undertakes not to enter into any international engagement in conflict with this Treaty.
Art. VII. Any other State in a position to further the objectives of this Treaty and to contribute to the security of the area may, by unanimous agreement of the Parties, be invited to accede to this Treaty. Any State so invited may become a Party to the Treaty by depositing its instrument of accession with the Government of the Republic of the Philippines. The Government of the Republic of the Philippines shall inform each of the

Parties of the deposit of each such instrument of accession.
Art. VIII. As used in this Treaty, the 'treaty area' is the general area of South-east Asia, including also the entire territories of the Asian Parties, and the general area of the South-west Pacific not including the Pacific area north of 21 degrees 30 minutes north latitude. The Parties may, by unanimous agreement, amend this Article to include within the treaty area the territory of any State acceding to this Treaty in accordance with Art. VII or otherwise to change the treaty area.
Art. IX.(1) This Treaty shall be deposited in the archives of the Government of the Republic of the Philippines. Duly certified copies thereof shall be transmitted by that Government to the other signatories.
(2) The Treaty shall be ratified and its provisions carried out by the Parties in accordance with their respective constitutional processes. The instruments of ratification shall be deposited as soon as possible with the Government of the Republic of the Philippines, which shall notify all of the other signatories of such deposit.
(3) The Treaty shall enter into force between the States which have ratified it as soon as the instruments of ratification of a majority of the signatories shall have been deposited, and shall come into effect with respect to each other State on the date of the deposit of its instrument of ratification.
Art. X. This Treaty shall remain in force indefinitely, but any Party may cease to be a Party one year after its notice of denunciation has been given to the government of the Republic of the Philippines, which shall inform the Governments of the other Parties of the deposit of each notice of denunciation.
Art. XI. The English text of this Treaty is binding on the Parties, but when the Parties have agreed to the French text thereof and have so notified the Government of the Republic of the Philippines, the French text shall be equally authentic and binding on the Parties."

A protocol annexed to the Treaty reads as follows:

"The United States of America in executing the present Treaty does so with the understanding that its recognition of the effect of aggression and armed attack and its agreement with reference thereto in art. IV, paragraph 1, apply only to communists aggression but affirms that in the event of other aggression or armed attack it will consult under the provision of art. IV, paragraph 2."

UNTS, Vol. 209, pp. 28–34 and p. 36.

SEA TRANSPORT. A subject of international conventions and disputes in connection with the 85% dominance of world sea transport by 12 highly developed states. Thus e.g. in the foreign trade of Africa and Latin America 80% of the cargoes are transported under a foreign flag. In the opinion of ALAMAR:

"At 35 conferences of merchant fleets which have their headquarters in the great sea ports – London, New York, Rotterdam, Hamburg, Tokyo – not one has paid the least attention to the interests of the developing countries."

The countries of the Third World hence demanded a basic revision of international conventions of sea transport, arguing that "conventions on sea commerce practices and customs were established in epochs in which the interests of developing countries were of little importance." ▷ Tequendama Charter, 1967. The developing countries also demanded the "right to participate in all merchant fleet conferences as an equal partner of shipowners of the developed countries". ▷ Algiers Group of 77 Charter, 1967. The States of the so-called Group of 77 presented these problems at the First and Second UNCTAD Conferences, 1965 and 1968, which established a permanent Maritime Transport Committee, headquarters in Geneva, as a mediating institution on sea freight charges between users and shipowners and also with the task of studying the possibility of building up merchant fleets and ports in the developing countries.

S

UN Monthly Chronicle, April 1967, pp. 53–54; *Consultation in Shipping*, UN, New York, 1968; H. MAYERS, *The Nationality of Ships*, New York, 1970; "La OCMI (IMCO) y el Desarrollo del Transporte Maritimo", in: *Bolatin Económico de América Latina*, No. 2, 1972.

SEA WAR. A military action at sea; the practices of waging sea war were framed in the 19th and 20th centuries in a series of international norms. In 1856 in the so-called Paris Declaration the powers condemned piracy as against the law of sea war; in 1907 the Second Hague Conference introduced a series of rules, whose complete codification was accomplished 1910 at the London Conference. After World War I the Washington Conference 1922 and London Conference 1936 worked out the norms of undersea warfare. The attitude towards castaways, wounded and sick in sea war was defined in the Tenth Hague Convention 1907, superseded by the Second Geneva Convention, 1949.

S.W. ROSKILL, *The War at Sea*, 3 Vols., London 1954–65; S.E. MORISON, *History of US Naval Operations in World War II*, 5 vols., 1947–62.

SEA WATERWAY LAW. The international rules on the principles of ships passing each other and on their illumination from sunset until sunrise and also on emergency lights, shallow waters illumination, tugging, pilot, water works, mine-sweeping and fishing lights. ▷ Sea Law Convention, 1982.

SEAWEED INDUSTRY. A subject of research and promotion by the International Trade Center UNCTAD/GATT, Geneva.

ITC *Pilot Survey of the World Seaweed Industry and Trade*, Geneva, 1981.

SECAM. ▷ Television.

SECOND. Symbol: s. The international unit of time, originally until 1960 defined as the fraction 1/86400 of the "mean solar day." Since 1960 one of base units of the International System of Units (▷ SI); definition adopted by the General Conference of Weights and Measures, 1967, as follows:

"The second is the duration of 9,192,631,770 periods of the radiation corresponding to the transition between the two hyperfine levels of the ground state of the caesium–133 atom."

This provisional definition is based on the atomic (caesium) standard of frequency and is called the "atomic second"; distinct from the defintion of 1956 formulated by the International Astronomical Union based orbital movements of the solar system (ephemerid time) and on the rotation of the earth (universal time) and called "ephemerid second". The leading organ of the International Bureau of Weights and Measures, XIII General Conference of Measures, deliberating Oct. 10–16, 1967 in Paris, taking into consideration the objections to the "atomic" definition of both the International Astronomical Union, IAU, as well as some delegations, recognized the possibility of obtaining a higher precision of the caesium standard of frequency and called on organizations and laboratories specializing in this field to continue their work on the definition of the second. Simultaneously, IAU, while recognizing the definition of the second as a unit of SI "on the principle of atomic transition", stated: "measurements of time for purposes of astronomy and related fields should be continued based on the natural observation of phenomena which are the foundation of ephemerid and universal time".

Work on the most precise definition of the second possible is co-ordinated by the International Bureau of Time, subordinate to IAU and the International Union of Geodesy and Geophysics, in close co-operation with the International Committee of Measures and International Advisory Committee for Radio Communication.

Yearbook of International Organizations.

SECRETARIAT OF INTERNATIONAL ORGANIZATIONS. An intergovernmental institution, accepted after World War I: the permanent staff of international organizations, beginning with the League of Nations Secretariat (1919–46). In the 19th century permanent secretariats were active at the Vienna Congress 1815, at the Paris Congress 1856 and at the Hague Peace Conferences 1899 and 1907; they were closely related to intergovernmental councils but were not organizations. The UN Secretariat is the general international staff since Aug. 1, 1946; and maintains permanent contact with international secretariats of specialized UN agencies and other intergovernmental institutions.

A. GAGUA, *Le Secretariat Général de la Société des Nations*, 1926, Paris, 1926.

SECRETARY-GENERAL OF THE UN. ▷ UN Secretary-General.

SECRET DIPLOMACY. An international term used in the 19th century, meaning, above all, the practice of not making public international treaties which, as a rule, were concluded at the expense of third states, or in case of bribery or compulsion clearly detrimental to one of the parties, and for that reason secret. The Covenant of the League of Nations (Art. 18) introduced the obligation concerning registration and publication of international agreements by the Secretariat of the League and since 1945 by the UN Secretariat. These rules in no way limit the right of states to use secret diplomacy in negotiations leading to the signing of treaties, by contrast called more and more often "quiet diplomacy".

CH. DANRAT, "Conventions et Traités secret", in: *Revue politique et parlamentaire*, 1912; J. SEVENS, *Le Régime nouveau des traités internationaux. L'article 18 du Pacte de la SdN et la suppression des tractations diplomatiques secrètes*, Paris, 1925; M. BRANDON, "The Validity of Non-Registered Treaties", in: *The British Yearbook of International Law*, No. 29, 1952.

SECT. A derogatory name introduced into international relations mostly by Christian churches, used for minor Christian groups which reject certain dogmas.

SECULARIZATION. An international term for limitation or liquidation of church influence on political, social and customary life of the state; in addition a term in Catholic Church for release by the Pope of a monk from monastic vows.

SECURITIES. An international term for obligations defining the property rights which belong to their owners (orders of payment, stocks, bonds, checks, bills of exchange; the last two covered by international conventions); divided into securities with a constant and variable income.

SECURITY. ▷ Mutual Strategic Security.

SECURITY AND CO-OPERATION IN EUROPE. An international term for the Helsinki Conference of Security and Co-operation in Europe, CSCE.

Z. WOJCIECHOWSKI, "Le Problème de la securité collective en Euorpe entre 1919 et 1939", in: *Securité Collective en Europe. Conférence fermée à Varsovie du 3 au 6 avril 1955*, Varsovie, 1955; A. ROTFELD, *From Helsinki to Madrid, Documents*, Warsaw, 1983; J.

SYMONIDES, "The Balance of Forces System and European Security", in: *International Relations*, No. 1, Warsaw, 1984.

SECURITY AND DISARMAMENT, LEAGUE OF NATIONS RESOLUTION, 1922. The first act of the League of Nations Assembly to strengthen the security provisions of the League of Nations Covenant, was the adopting of a Res. XIV, Sept. 27, 1922, which read as follows:

"XIV. (a) The Assembly, having considered the report of the Temporary Mixed Commission on the question of a general Treaty of Mutual Guarantee, being of opinion that this report can in no way affect the complete validity of all the Treaties of Peace or other agreements which are known to exist between States; and considering that this report contains valuable suggestions as to the methods by which a Treaty of Mutual Guarantee could be made effective, is of the opinion that:

(1) No scheme for the reduction of armaments, within the meaning of art. 8 of the Covenant, can be fully successful unless it is general.

(2) In the present state of the world many Governments would be unable to accept the responsibility for a serious reduction of armaments unless they received in exchange a satisfactory guarantee of the safety of their country.

(3) Such a guarantee can be found in a defensive agreement, which should be open to all countries, binding them to provide immediate and effective in accorance with a prearranged plan in the event of one of them attacked, provided that the obligation to render assistance to a country attacked shall be limited in principle to those countries situated in the same part of the globe. In cases, however, where, for historical, geographical, or other reasons, a country is in special danger of attack, detailed arrangements should be made for its defence in accordance with the above-mentioned plan.

(4) As a general reduction of armaments is the object of three preceding statements, and the Treaty of Mutual Guarantee the means of achieving that object, previous consent to this reduction is therefore the first condition for the Treaty. This reduction could be carried out either by means of a general Treaty, which is the most desirable plan, or by means of partial treaties designed to be extended and open to all countries. In the former case, the Treaty will carry with it a general reduction of armaments. In the latter case, the reduction should be proportionate to the guarantees afforded by the Treaty. The Council of the League, after having taken the advice of the Temporary Mixed Commission, which will examine how each of these two systems could be carried out, should further formulate and submit to the Governments for their consideration and sovereign decision the plan of the machinery, both political and military, necessary to bring them clearly into effect.

(b) The Assembly requests the Council to submit to the various Governments the above proposals for their observations, and requests the Temporary Mixed Commission to continue its investigations, and, in order to give precision to the above statements, to prepare a draft Treaty embodying the principles contained therein."

League of Nations Assembly. Records of the Plenary Meetings, III Session, Geneva, 1922, p. 291; B. WINIARSKI, *Security, Arbitration, Disarmament*, The Hague, 1928.

SECURITY COUNCIL OF THE UN. ▷ UN Security Council.

SECURITY, DISARMAMENT AND DEVELOPMENT. ▷ Perez de Cuellar Triangular Doctrine 1988.

SECURITY, INTERNATIONAL. A UN system term introduced by the UN, similar to collective security introduced by the League of Nations. The UN General Assembly Res. 2734/XXV, of Dec. 16, 1970 called the Declaration on the Strengthening of International Security reads as follows:

"The General Assembly,

Recalling the determination of the peoples of the United Nations, as proclaimed by the Charter, to save succeeding generations from the scourge of war, and to this end to live together in peace with one another as good neighbours and to unite their strength to maintain international peace and security.

Considering that in order to fulfil the purposes and principles of the United Nations Member States must strictly abide by all provisions of the Charter,

Recalling its resolution 2606 (XXIV) of 16 December 1969 in which the General Assembly, inter alia, expressed the desire that the twenty-fifth year of the Organization's existence should be marked by new initiatives to promote peace, security, disarmament and economic and social progress for all mankind and the conviction of the urgent need to make the United Nations more effective as an instrument for maintaining international peace and security,

Mindful of the observations, proposals and suggestions advanced during the debate at the twenty-fourth session of the General Assembly or presented subsequently by Governments of Member States concerning the attainment of this objective, and of the report submitted by the Secretary-General in conformity with paragraph 5 of resolution 2606 (XXIV),

Having in mind the Declaration on Principles of International Law concerning Friendly Relations and Co-operation among States in accordance with the Charter of the United Nations, adopted unanimously at the current session,

Conscious of its duty to examine in depth the present international situation and to study the means and recourses provided by the relevant provisions of the Charter in order to build peace, security and co-operation in the world,

(1) Solemnly reaffirms the universal and unconditional validity of the purposes and principles of the Charter of the United Nations as the basis of relations among States irrespective of their size, geographical location, level of development or political, economic and social systems and declares that the breach of these principles cannot be justified in any circumstances whatsoever;

(2) Calls upon all States to adhere strictly in their international relations to the purposes and principles of the Charter, including the principle that States shall refrain in their international relations from the threat or use of force against the territorial integrity or political independence of any State or in any other manner inconsistent with the purposes of the United Nations; the principle that States shall settle their international disputes by peaceful means in such a manner that international peace and security and justice are not endangered; the duty not to intervene in matters within the domestic jurisdiction of any State, in accordance with the Charter; the duty of States to co-operate with one another in accordance with the Charter; the principle of equal rights and self-determination of peoples; the principle of sovereign equality of States; and the principle that States shall fulfil in good faith the obligations assumed by them in accordance with the Charter;

(3) Solemnly reaffirms that, in the event of a conflict between the obligation of the Members of the United Nations under the Charter and their obligations under any other international agreement, their obligations under the Charter shall prevail;

(4) Solemnly reaffirms that States must fully respect the sovereignty of other States and the right of peoples to determine their own destinies, free of external intervention, coercion or constraint, especially involving the threat or use of force, overt or covert, and refrain from any attempt aimed at the partial or total disruption of the national unity and territorial integrity of any other State or country;

(5) Solemnly reaffirms that every State has the duty to refrain from the threat or use of force against the territorial integrity and political independence of any other State, and that the territory of a State shall not be the object of military occupation resulting from the use of force in contravention of the provisions of the Charter, that the territory of a State shall not be the object of acquisition by another State resulting from the threat or use of force, that no territorial acquisition resulting from the threat or use of force shall be recognized as legal and that every State has the duty to refrain from organizing, instigating, assisting or participating in acts of civil strife or terrorist acts in another State;

(6) Urges Member States to make full use and seek improved implementation of the means, and methods provided for in the Charter for the exclusively peaceful settlement of any dispute or any situation, the continuance of which is likely to endanger the maintenance of international peace and security, including negotiation, inquiry, mediation, conciliation, arbitration, judicial settlement, resort to regional agencies or arrangements, good offices including those of the Secretary-General, or other peaceful means of their own choice, it being understood that the Security Council in dealing with such disputes or situations should also take into consideration that legal disputes should as a general rule be referred by the parties to the International Court of Justice in accordance with the provisions of the Statute of the Court;

(7) Urges all Member States to respond to the immediate need to agree on guidlines for more effective peace-keeping operations in accordance with the Charter, which could increase the effectiveness of the United Nations in dealing with situations endangering international peace and security, and consequently to support the efforts of the Special Committee on Peacekeeping Operations to reach agreement on all questions relating to such operations, as well as on provisions for their appropriate and equitable financing;

(8) Recognizes the need for effective, dynamic and flexible measures, in accordance with the Charter, to prevent and remove threats to the peace, suppress acts of aggression or other breaches of the peace, and in particular for measures to build, maintain and restore international peace and security;

(9) Recommends that the Security Council take steps to facilitate the conclusion of the agreements envisaged in Article 43 of the Charter in order fully to develop its capacity for enforcement action as provided for under Chapter VII of the Charter;

(10) Recommends that the Security Council consider, in conformity with art. 29 of the Charter, whenever appropriate and necessary, the desirability of establishing subsidiary organs, on an ad hoc basis, and with the participation of the parties concerned, when conditions so warrant, to assist the Council in the performance of its functions as defined in the Charter;

(11) Recommends that all States contribute to the efforts to ensure peace and security for all nations and to establish, in accordance with the Charter, an effective system of universal collective security without military alliances;

(12) Invites Member States to do their utmost to enhance by all possible means the authority and effectiveness of the Security Council and of its decisions;

(13) Calls upon the Security Council, including the permanent members, to intensify efforts to discharge, in conformity with the Charter, its primary responsibility for the maintenance of international peace and security;

(14) Recommends that Member States support the efforts of the Special Committee on the Question of Defining Aggression to brings its work to a successful conclusion, thus achieving the definition of aggression as soon as possible;

(15) Reaffirms its competence under the Charter to discuss and recommend measures for the peaceful adjustment of any situation which it deems likely to impair the general welfare or friendly relations among States, including situations resulting from a violation of the provisions of the Charter setting forth the purposes and principles of the United Nations;

(16) Urges all Member States to implement the decisions of the Security Council in accordance with their obligations under art. 25 of the Charter and to respect, as provided for in the Charter, the resolutions of United Nations organs responsible for the maintenance of international peace and security and the peaceful settlement of disputes;

(17) Urges Member States to reaffirm their will to respect fully their obligations under international law in accordance with the relevant provisions of the Charter and to continue and intensify the efforts towards the progressive development and codification of international law;

(18) Call upon all States to desist from any forcible or other action which deprives peoples, in particular those still under colonial or any other form of external domination, of their, inalienable right to self-determination, freedom and independence and to refrain from military and repressive measures aimed at preventing the attainment of independence by all dependent peoples in accordance with the Charter and in furtherance of the objectives of General Assembly resolution 1514 (XV) of 14 December 1960, and render assistance to the United Nations and, in accordance with the Charter, to the oppressed peoples in their legitimate struggle in order to bring about the speedy elimination of colonialism or any other form of external domination;

(19) Affirms its belief that there is a close connexion between the strengthening of international security, disarmament and the economic development of countries, so that any progress made towards any of these objectives will constitute progress towards all of them;

(20) Urges all States, particularly the nuclear-weapon States, to make urgent and concerned efforts within the framework of the Disarmament Decade and through other means for the cessation and reversal of the nuclear and conventional arms race at an early date, the elimination of nuclear weapons, and other weapons of mass destruction and the conclusion of a treaty on general and complete disarmament under effective international control, as well as to ensure that the benefits of the technology of the peaceful use of nuclear energy shall be available to all States, to the maximum extent possible, without discrimination;

(21) Emphatically reiterates the need to undertake, within the framework of the Second United Nations Development Decade, urgent and concerted international action based on a global strategy aimed at reducing and eliminating as soon as possible the economic gap between developed and developing countries, which is closely and essentially correlated to the strengthening of the security of all nations and the establishment of lasting international peace;

(22) Solemnly reaffirms that universal respect for all full exercise of human rights and fundamental freedom and the elimination of the violation of those rights are urgent and essential to the strengthening of international security, and hence resolutely condemns all forms of oppression, tyranny and discrimination, particularly racism and racial discrimination, wherever they occur;

(23) Resolutely condemns the criminal policy of apartheid of the Government of South Africa and reaffirms the legitimacy of the struggle of the oppressed peoples to attain their human rights and fundamental freedoms and self-determination;

(24) Expresses its conviction that the achievement of universality of the United Nations, in accordance with the Charter, would increase its effectiveness in strengthening international peace and security;

(25) Considers that the promotion of international co-operation, including regional, subregional and bilateral co-operation among States, in keeping with the provisions of the Charter and based on the principle of equal rights and on strict respect for the sovereignty and independence of States, can contribute to the strengthening of international security;

(26) Welcomes the decision of the Security Council to hold periodic meetings in accordance with art. 28, paragraph 2, of the Charter and expresses the hope that these meetings will make an important contribution to the strenthening of international security."

On Dec. 14, 1976 the UN General Assembly adopted the following Resolution:

"The General Assembly,

Having considered the item entitled 'Implementation of the Declaration on the Strengthening of International Security,'

Bearing in mind the Declaration on the Strengthening of International Security, contained in General Assembly resolution 2734 (XXV) of 16 December 1970, and the relevant resolutions of the Assembly concerning the implementation of the Declaration,

Welcoming new achievement and trends in international relations and all other efforts contributing to the strengthening of international security and the promoting of peaceful co-operation in accordance with the Charter of the United Nations,

Welcoming also, in this context, the successful results of the Fifth Conference of Heads of State or Government of Non-Aligned Countries, held at Colombo from 16 to 19 August 1976, which represents a further significant contribution to the strengthening of international security and development of equitable international relations,

Noting the successful outcome of the Conference on Security and Co-operation in Europe, emphasizing that

S

the security of Europe should be considered in the broader context of world security and is closely inter-related, in particular, to the security of the Mediter-ranean, the Middle East and to other regions of the world, and expressing its conviction that the imple-mentation of the Final Act of that Conference though agreed means will contribute to the strengthening of international peace and security,

Noting however with grave concern the continuing existence of focal points of crises and tensions in various regions endangering international peace and security, the continuation of the arms race as well as acts of aggression, the threat or use of force, foreign occupation and alien domination and the existence of colonialism, neo-colonialism, racial discrimination and apartheid, which remain the main obtacles to the strengthening of international peace and security,

Reaffirming the close link existing between the strengthening of international security, disarmament, decolonization, development and the need for a more intensive national and international effort to narrow the widening gap between the developed and the developing countries, and also stressing, in this con-nexion, the importance of the early implementation of the decisions adopted at its sixth and seventh special sessions,

Emphasizing the need constantly to strengthen the peace-keeping and peace-making role of the United Nations in accordance with the Charter as well as its role in promoting development through equitable co-operation,

(1) Solemnly calls upon all States to seek strict and consistent implementation of the purposes and the principles of the Charter of the United Nations and of all the provisions of the Declaration on the Strengthen-ing of International Security;

(2) Reaffirms the legitimacy of the struggle of peoples under colonial and alien domination to achieve self-determination and independence and appeals to all States to increase their support and solidarity with them in their struggle against colonialism, racial discrimina-tion and apartheid;

(3) Also calls upon all States to extend the process of relaxation of tensions, which is still limited both in scope and geographical extent, to all regions of the world, in order to help bring about just and lasting solutions to international problems with the participa-tion of all States so that peace and security will be based on effective respect for the sovereignty and indepen-dence of all States and the inalienable rights of all peoples to determine their own destiny freely and without outside interference, coercion or pressure;

(4) Reaffirms that any measure or pressure directed against any State while exercising its sovereign right freely to dispose of its natural resources constitutes a flagrant violation of the right of self-determination of peoples and the principles of non-intervention, as set forth in the Charter, which, if pursued, could constitute a threat to international peace and security;

(5) Reaffirms its opposition to any threats or use of force, intervention, aggression, foreign occupation and measures of political and economic coercion which attempts to violate the sovereignty, territorial integrity, independence and security of States;

(6) Recommends urgent measures to stop the arms race and promote disarmament, the dismantling of foreign military bases, the creation of zones of peace and co-operation and the achievement of general and complete disarmament and strengthening the role of the United Nations, in accordance with the Charter, in order to eliminate the causes of international tensions and ensure international peace, security and co-opera-tion;

(7) Recommends that the Security Council should con-sider appropriate steps towards carrying out effectively, as provided in the Charter and the Declaration on the Strengthening of International Security, its primary responsibility for the maintenance of international security and peace;

(8) Invites the States parties to the Conference on Security and Co-operation in Europe to implement fully and urgently all the provisions of the Final Act, including those relating to the Mediterranean, and to consider favourably the conversion of the Mediter-ranean into a zone of peace and co-operation in the interests of international peace and security;

(9) Takes note of the report of the Secretary-General, requests him to submit to the General Assembly at its

thirty-second session a report on the implementation of the Declaration on the Strengthening of International Security and decides to include in the provisional agenda of its thirty-second session the item entitled 'Im-plementation of the Declaration on the Strengthening of International Security.'

UN Yearbooks, 1970 and 1976. A. GARCIA ROBLES, "Consideraciones Constitucionales sobre las funciones y poderes de la NU y de las organizaciones regionales en el mantenimiento de la paz y la seguridad internacion-al", in: *Jurídica*, No. 6, 1974.

SECURITY NUCLEAR DOCTRINE. A doctrine of security based on nuclear deterrence. In the opinion of the UN Secretary-General, J. Perez de Cuellar, on Sept. 5, 1984, "this doctrine was not taken into account when the Charter was drafted in San Francisco."

Official Record of the General Assembly, 39th Session, Supplement No. 1, New York, 1984.

SECURITY ZONE OF THE WESTERN HEMISPHERE. The zone was defined for the first time by the Meeting of the Ministers of Foreign Affairs of the American Republics Sept. 23–Oct. 3, 1939 in Panama City in a General Declaration of Neutrality as a zone of coastal waters 30 miles from the shore of the continent; then defined from the north to the south pole as "a geographical safety zone" in art. 40 of the Inter-American Treaty on Mutual Assistance, 1947; this description was ac-cepted by the Tlateldco Treaty, 1967. During World War II German and Japanese submarines violated the zone many times; in Oct., 1939 Germany and Great Britain made official statements on the occasion of the affair connected with the battleship ▷ "Admiral Graf Spee" denying the need for res-pecting a unilaterally established zone.

A. GARCIA ROBLES, *El Mundo de la Postguerra*, México, DF, 1946, Vol. 2, pp. 368–370; *The Final Act of the Rio de Janeiro Conference*, 1947, Washington, DC, 1947.

SEDAN. A town in northeastern France, Depart-ment des Ardennes, on the Meuse River. The site of the Battle of Sedan on Sept. 1, 1870, between the French army of the Emperor Napoleon III and the Prussian army; Napoleon III surrendered with nearly 82,000 officers and men after the loss of 17,000 French (Prussian losses about 9000). The second Franco-German Battle of Sedan took place on May 13, 1940 and terminated with a defeat of French troops.

La guerre de 1870–71. L'année de Chalons: Sedan, Paris, 1907.

SEEDS. A subject of international co-operation. Organizations reg. with the UIA:

Association of Growing Stations for Fodder Seed in the EEC, f. 1969, Brussels.
Expert Committee on Seeds of the EEC, f. 1960, Brussels.
Federation of the Seed Crushers and Oil Processors in the EEC, f. 1957, Brussels.
Fluoroselect, f. 19/0, The Hague. Testing organization for new varieties of flower seeds.
International Association of Seed Crushers, f. 1910, London. Liaison status with FAO.
International Association of Seed Trade, f. 1924, Paris, Publ.: *Bulletin*.
International Seed Testing Association, f. 1924, Cam-bridge, UK. Publ.: *Seed Science and Technology*.

Yearbook of International Organizations.

SEISMOLOGY. A subject of international co-operation. Organizations reg. with the UIA:

European Mediterranean Seismological Centre, f. 1976, Strasbourg.
Federation of Astronomical and Geophysical Services, f. 1956, Greenwich Observatory, UK.

International Associations of Seismology and Physics of the Earth Interior, f. 1901, Rome. Publ.: *Inter-national Seismological Summary* (quarterly).
International Institute of Seismology and Earthquake Engineering, f. 1960, Tokyo.
International Seismological Centre, f. 1964, Newbury Berks, UK. Publ.: *Bulletin, Regional Catalogue of Earthquakes, Bibliography of Seismology.*
Seismological Society of the South-West Pacific, f. 1967, Wellington. Publ.: *News Sheet.*

The UN General Assembly, Res. 2604/XXIV, Dec. 16, 1969, initiated the creation of a worldwide ex-change of seismological data by conventional seismograph stations and array stations which would facilitate the achievement of a comprehen-sive underground nuclear test ban.

UN Yearbook, 1969; *Yearbook of International Organizations, 1986/87; The Europa Yearbook 1988. A World Survey*, Vol. I, London, 1988.

SEKIA EL HAMRA. A territory in West Africa on the Atlantic Ocean, 83,000 sq. km, part of Western Sahara since Jan. 1976; before then a Spanish colonial province (part of the Spanish Sahara). Capital: Smara.

SELA. Sistema Económico Latinoamericano. Latin American Economic System, insti-tutionalized by the ▷ SELA Panama Convention, 1975, signed on Oct. 17, 1975, in the capital of Panama, by Argentina, Barbados, Bolivia, Brazil, Chile, Colombia, Costa Rica, Cuba, the Dominican Republic, Ecuador, El Salvador, Grenada, Guatemala, Guyana, Haiti, Honduras, Jamaica, Mexico, Nicaragua, Panama, Paraguay, Peru, Trinidad and Tobago, Uruguay and Venezuela.
Structure: Latin-american Council (Consejo Latinoamericano) composed of representatives of the signatory states. Action Committee (Comitee de Accion) and Permanent Secretariat (Secretaria Per-manente).
Headquarters: Caracas. The main task of SELA is "the promotion of regional co-operation for the purpose of achieving universal autonomous and in-dependent development".
SELA began its operations Jan. 13–15, 1976 with a session of the Council in Caracas.
In the intention of its founders, whose main movers were the presidents of Mexico and Venezuela, Luis Echeverria and Jose Luis Perez, SELA is to be an instrument of Latin America in preparing the ▷ New International Economic Order.
In Nov., 1978 at a Conference of SELA in Punta del Este a common position of the states of Latin America was formulated with respect to the EEC states in connection with the continual drop in the share of Latin foreign trade with the EEC, from 10% in 1958 to 5% in 1978. In the middle of 1979 direct EEC–SELA negotiations began in Brussels. In 1979–80 negotiations began with CMEA. In May 1983 SELA and ECLA published a joint survey: *Bases for Latin American Responses to the International Economic Crisis.*

"La Construtión del SELA", in: *Commercio Exterior*, México, DF, August, 1975.

SELA PANAMA CONVENTION, 1975. The con-vention establishing the Latin American Economic System, called the SELA Convention (Convención del Sistema Económico Latino-americano), signed at Panama City, Oct. 17, 1975 by Argentina, Bar-bados, Bolivia, Brazil, Chile, Colombia, Costa Rica, Cuba, Dominican Republic, Ecuador, El Sal-vador, Grenada, Guatemala, Guyana, Haiti, Hon-duras, Jamaica, Mexico, Nicaragua, Panama, Paraguay, Peru, Trinidad and Tobago, Uruguay and Venezuela; entered into force June 7, 1976. The text is as follows:

"The Latin American States represented at the ministerial meeting convened to establish the Latin American States whereas,

There is a need to establish a permanent system of intra-regional economic and social co-operation, of consultation and co-ordination of the positions of Latin America in international bodies as well as before third countries and groups of countries;

The present dynamics of international relations and socio-economic fields also make it necessary that all initiatives and efforts for co-ordination among Latin American countries be converted into a permanent system which for the first time will include all States of the region and be responsible for all agreements and principles which up to now have been jointly adopted by all countries of Latin America and which will ensure their implementation through concerted actions;

This co-operation must be realized in the spirit of the Declaration and the Program of Action on the Establishment of a New International Economic Order and of the Charter of Economic Rights and Duties of States; and in a manner consistent with the commitments for integration which the majority of Latin American countries have assumed;

It is imperative to promote greater unity among Latin American countries in order to ensure concerted action in the field of intraregional economic and social co-operation, to increase the bargaining power of the region and to ensure that Latin America occupies its rightful position in the international community;

The action of a permanent system of intraregional co-ordination, consultation and co-operation of Latin America should be carried out on the basis of the principles of equality, sovereignty, independence of States, solidarity, non-intervention in internal affairs, reciprocal benefits, non-discrimination, and full respect for the social and economic systems freely chosen by States;

There is a need to strengthen and complement the various Latin American integration processes through the joint promotion of specific development programs and projects; Consequently, it is advisable and appropriate to establish a regional body to achieve these ends; and

In the Panama Meeting held from July 31 to August 2, 1975, a consensus was reached to establish the Latin American Economic System, and to agree to the following convention:

Art. 1. The Latin American Economic System, hereinafter referred to as SELA, is established by the signatories, with the membership, powers, and functions specified in this Convention.

Art. 2. SELA is a permanent regional body for consultation, co-ordination, co-operation and joint economic and social promotion, with its own international juridical personality. It is composed of sovereign Latin American States.

Art. 3. The fundamental purposes of SELA are:

(a) To promote intraregional co-operation in order to accelerate the economic and social development of its members;

(b) To provide a permanent system of consultation and coordination for the adoption of common positions and strategies on economic and social matters in international bodies and forums as well as before third countries and groups of countries.

Art. 4. The activities of SELA shall be based on the principles of equality, sovereignty and independence of States; on solidarity, non-intervention in internal affairs, with due respect for the differences in political, economic and social systems. Likewise, the actions of SELA shall duly respect the characteristics inherent to the various regional and sub-regional integration processes as well as their basic mechanisms and juridical structure.

Art. 5. The objectives of SELA are:

(1) To promote regional co-operation, with a view to attaining self-sustained, independent and integral development, particularly through actions designed to:

(a) Encourage the optimum use of natural, human, technical and financial resources of the region, by creating and fostering Latin American multinational enterprises. These enterprises could be established with statal, parastatal, private or mixed capital whose national character is guaranteed by the respective Member States and whose activities are subject to their jurisdiction and supervision.

(b) Stimulate satisfactory levels of production and supply of agricultural products, energy, and other commodities, with emphasis on the specific supply of foodstuffs; and to encourage co-ordination of national policies for production and supply with a view to establishing a Latin American policy in this area;

(c) Stimulate throughout the region the processing of raw materials of the Member States, industrial complementation, intraregional trade and the export of manufactured goods;

(d) Design and strengthen mechanisms and forms of association which will enable Member States to obtain adequate prices, ensure stable markets for the export of their commodities and manufactures and increase their bargaining power, without prejudice to the support necessary to the systems and mechanisms of co-ordination and protection raw material prices to which the countries of the area may already belong;

(e) Improve the bargaining power for the acquisition and utilization of capital goods and technology;

(f) Encourage the channelling of financial resources toward projects and programs which stimulate the development of the countries of the region;

(g) Foster co-operation in Latin America for the creation, development, adaptation and exchange of technology and scientific information, as well as the optimum use and development of human, educational, scientific and cultural resources;

(h) Study and propose measures which will ensure that the activities of transnational enterprises comply with the development objectives of the region and with the national interests of the Member States, and to exchange information on the activities of those enterprises;

(i) Promote the development and co-ordination of transportation and communication, particularly within the region;

(j) Promote co-operation among the member countries in the area of tourism;

(k) Encourage co-operation for the protection, conservation and improvement of the environment;

(l) Support all efforts to assist those countries which face emergency situations of an economic nature, as well as those resulting from natural disasters;

(m) Support any other measures related to the foregoing, which may contribute to the achievement of the economic, social and cultural development of the region.

(2) To support the integration processes of the region and encourage co-ordination among them, or with Member States of SELA, particularly with respect to those activities aimed at promoting greater harmonization, with due regard for the commitments made within the framework of such processes.

(3) To promote the formulation and implementation of economic and social programs and projects of interest to the Member States.

(4) To act as a mechanism for consultation and co-ordination within Latin America for the purpose of formulating common positions and strategies on economic and social matters before third countries, groups of countries and in international organizations and forums.

(5) To promote within the context of the objectives of SELA relating to intraregional co-operation means to ensure preferential treatment for the relatively less developed countries and special measures for countries with limited markets and for those whose landlocked condition affects their development, taking into account the economic situation of each of the Member States.

Art. 6. Sovereign Latin American States which sign and ratify the present Convention shall be members of SELA.

Art. 7. The present Convention is open to accession by all other sovereign Latin American States which did not originally sign it. To this end, they shall deposit the appropriate instrument of accession with the Government of Venezuela. The Convention shall enter into force for the acceding State, thirty days after the appropriate instrument is depositied.

Art. 8. The organs of SELA are:

(a) The Latin American Council

(b) The Action Committees

(c) The Permanent Secretariat

Art. 9. The Latin American Council is the supreme organ of SELA and shall be composed of one representative from each Member State. It shall normally meet at the headquarters of the Permanent Secretariat.

Art. 10. Each Member State has the right to one vote.

Art. 11. The Latin American Council shall hold an annual regular session, at the ministerial level, and may hold special sessions at ministerial or non-ministerial level whenever it is to decided by a regular session or requested by at least one third of the Member States. The Council, by consensus, may change the proportion mentioned in the preceding paragraph.

Art. 12. Regular sessions of the Latin American Council, at the ministerial level, shall be preceded by a preparatory meeting. In the event of special sessions, the notice convening the session shall state whether or not a preparatory meeting is to be held.

Art. 13. The Council may meet when at least a majority of the Member States is present.

Art. 14. The Latin American Council shall elect a Chairman, two Vice-Chairmen and one Rapporteur for each session.

Art. 15. The Latin American Council has the following functions:

(1) To establish the general policies of SELA.

(2) To elect and remove the Permanent Secretary and the Deputy Permanent Secretary.

(3) To adopt its Rules of Procedure as well as those of the other permanent bodies of SELA.

(4) To consider and approve, as the case may be, the Annual Report submitted by the Permanent Secretariat.

(5) To approve the budget and financial statements of SELA, and to fix the quotas of the Member States.

(6) To consider and approve the work program of SELA.

(7) To consider the reports of the Action Committees.

(8) To decide on the interpretation of this Convention.

(9) To approve amendments to this Convention proposed by Member States.

(10) To study, direct, and approve the activities of the organs of SELA.

(11) To approve the common positions and strategies of the Member States with respect to economic and social matters, in international and regional organizations and forums, and before third countries or groups of countries.

(12) To consider proposals and reports submitted by the Permanent Secretariat on matters within its competence.

(13) To decide on the holding of special sessions.

(14) To designate the site of its sessions whenever they are not held at the headquarters of the Permanent Secretariat.

(15) To approve operational agreements entered into by the Permanent Secretary, pursuant to the provisions of Article 31, sub-paragraph 8.

(16) To adopt measures necessary for the implementation of this Convention and to evaluate the results of such implementation.

(17) To decide on all other matters of interest to it which are related to the objectives of SELA.

Art. 16. The functions set forth in sub-paragraphs 11 to 17 of the preceding Article may be performed by a special meeting at the non-ministerial level whenever agreed to by the Member States.

Art. 17. The Latin American Council shall adopt its decisions:

(a) By consenus, in the case of the functions set forth in sub-paragraphs 1, 8, 9 and 11 of art. 15 of this Convention and

(b) By majority of two-thirds of the Members present, or by an absolute majority of the Member States, whichever is greater, in the case of the functions set forth in the remaining sub-paragraphs of art. 15.

With respect to any issue arising for decision under art. 15, sub-paragraph 17, if a member state informs the Council that it considers the issue to be one of fundamental importance which has implications for its own national interest, the decision on that issue shall be by consensus.

Art. 18. The specific agreements and projects dealing with regional cooperation shall be binding only on those countries participating therein.

Art. 19. The Latin American Council shall not take decisions adversely affecting national policies of the Member States.

Art. 20. Action committees composed of representatives of the Member States concerned shall be established to carry out specific studies, programs and

S

projects and to prepare and adopt joint negotiating positions of interest to more than two Member States.
Art. 21. The Committees may be established by decision of the Council or by decision of the States concerned, which shall so notify the Secretariat and the latter shall inform the other Member States. The Committees shall be of a temporary nature and shall cease to function upon completion of their specified tasks. They will be open to participation by all Member States.
Art. 22. Financing of the Action Committees shall be the responsibility of the Member States participating therein.
Art. 23. Each Action Committee shall establish its own Secretariat. The functions of the Secretariat shall be performed insofar as possible by an official of the Permanent Secretariat with a view to supporting the work and contributing to the coordination of the Action Committees. These shall at all times keep the Permanent Secretariat informed of the progress and results of their work.
Art. 24. Compliance with the objectives relating to regional cooperation through the Action Committees shall be compulsory only for those Member States participating therein.
Art. 25. Activities of the Action Committees operating within the general objectives of SELA shall not discriminate against or create conflicts detrimental to other Member States of SELA.
Art. 26. Action Committees shall submit annual reports of their activities for consideration by the Latin American Council. When required, the Member States may request that the Permanent Secretariat provide them with information on the activities of the Action Committees.
Art 27. The Permanent Secretariat is the technical administrative organ of SELA, with Headquarters in Caracas, Venezuela.
Art 28. The Secretariat shall be under the direction of a Permanent Secretary. He shall be responsible for the technical and administrative personnel necessary for the performance of the functions of the Permanent Secretariat. The Permanent Secretary shall be the legal representative of the permanent Secretariat and in specific cases as determined by the Latin American Council, he shall act as legal representative of SELA. The Permanent Secretary shall be elected for a four-year term. He may only be re-elected once, but not for consecutive terms. He may not be replaced by a person of the same nationality.
The foregoing also applies to the election of the Deputy Permanent Secretary, who can not be of the same nationality as the Permanent Secretary.
Art. 29. The Permanent Secretary shall be a citizen of one of the Member States and will participate with voice but without vote in the sessions of the Latin American Council
Art. 30. The Permanent Secretary shall be responsible to the Latin American Council for the proper performance of the functions of the Permanent Secretariat. In the performance of their duties, the Permanent Secretary and the personnel of the Secretariat shall not seek or receive instructions from any government, or national or international body.
Art. 31. The functions of the Permanent Secretariat shall be as follows:
(1) To perform the functions assigned to it by the Latin American Council and, when appropriate, implement its decisions.
(2) To encourage and carry out preliminary studies and take the measures necessary to identify and promote projects of interest to two or more Member States. Whenever such actions have budgetary implications, their implementation shall be subject to the availability of funds.
(3) To facilitate the activities of the Action Committees and contribute to their coordination, including the provision of assistance for carrying out the appropriate studies.
(4) To propose to the Council programs and projects of common interest and to suggest ways in which they may be carried out, including meetings of experts and other measures which may better contribute to the attainment of the objectives of SELA.
(5) To prepare and submit for consideration by Member States the draft agenda for sessions of the Council and to prepare and distribute all related documents.

(6) To prepare the draft budget and work programs to be submitted to the Council for its approval.
(7) To submit the financial statements of SELA for consideration by the Council, at its regular session.
(8) To promote and conclude, subject to the approval of the Council, arrangements with international organizations and agencies, national agencies of Member States and third countries, to carry out studies, programs and projects, especially those of a regional nature.
(9) To formally convene the sessions and meetings of the organs of SELA.
(10) To receive the contributions of the Member States, to administer the resources and to execute the budget of SELA.
(11) To prepare the annual report on its activities for consideration by the Council at its regular session; and to coordinate the submission of the annual reports of the Action Committees, without prejudice to the reports they may submit directly to the Council.
(12) To recruit and hire the technical and administrative personnel of the Secretariat.
Art. 32. Each signatory State shall ratify the Convention in accordance with its laws. The instrument of ratification shall be deposited with the Government of Venezuela, which shall notify the Governments of signatory and acceeding States of the date of deposit.
Art. 33. This Convention shall enter into force for the ratifying States when an absolute majority of the signatory States have deposited their respective instruments of ratification; and for the other signatory States, from the date of deposit of their respective instruments of ratification in the order in which they were deposited.
Art. 34. Amendments to this Convention proposed by any Member State shall be approved by the Latin American Council. The amendments shall enter into force for the ratifying States when two-thirds of the Member States have deposited their respective instruments of ratification.
Art. 35. This Convention shall remain in force indefinitely. It may be denounced by any of the Member States by written notification addressed to the Government of Venezuela, which shall forward such notification without delay to the other Member States. After ninety (90) days have elapsed from the date on which the Government of the host country receives such notification, this Convention shall cease to be binding on the denouncing State. The denouncing member State shall fulfill all obligations undertaken prior to its notification of withdrawal, notwithstanding the fact that such obligations may extend beyond the effective date of withdrawal.
Art. 36. The Member States of SELA shall defray the cost of its operation. The Council, upon approving the annual budget, shall establish the quotas of the Members in accordance with the formula agreed upon.
Art. 37. SELA, its organs, staff members of the Permanent Secretariat and governmental representatives shall enjoy, in the territory of each Member State, such legal status, privileges and immunities as are necessary for the exercise of their functions. To this end, appropriate agreements shall be entered into with the Government of Venezuela and other Member States.
Art. 38. The official languages of SELA shall be: English, French, Portuguese and Spanish.
Art. 39. This Convention shall remain open for signature for a period of thirty (30) days from October 17, 1975.
Art. 40. This Convention shall be registered with the Secretariat of the United Nations by the Government of Venezuela.
In Witness Whereof, the undersigned Plenipotentiaries, having deposited their Full Powers, found to be in due and proper order, do hereby sign this Convention on behalf of their respective Governments.
Done at the City of Panama, Republic of Panama, on the seventeenth day of October, nineteen hundred and seventy five (1975), with original copies in the English, French, Portuguese and Spanish languages, whose texts are equally authentic.
The Government of Venezuela shall be the depository of the present Convention and shall forward duly authenticated copies of the Convention to the Government of the other signatory and acceeding countries."

Convention Establishing The Latin American Economic System, SELA, Panama City, 1975.

SELF-DEFENCE OBLIGATION. A doctrine formulated in 1758 by the Swiss lawyer E. de Vattel (1714–1767):

"One's own defence against unlawful assault is not only rightful, but the obligation of a nation, and one of the most sacred."

▷ Law of Nations, Vattel's principles, 1758.

In contemporary times there are two meanings of the term "self defence": (1) an institution of common international law, according to which each state has the right to individual or collective self defence; (2) civil defence.

In 1919 the Covenant of the League of Nations introduced the obligation of rendering assistance to a state which undertook self-defensive steps against aggression, with the provision that aggression on one member of the League of Nations constituted an aggression against other members. The same interpretation was explicit during World War II, and was expressed in the UN Charter Art. 51, stating that:

"Nothing in the present Charter shall impair the inherent right of individual or collective self-defence if an armed attack occurs against a Member of the United Nations until the Security Council has taken measures necessary to maintain peace and security."

In Aug., 1967 the governments of Argentina, Chile, Guatemala and Venezuela submitted to the UN Special Committee on the Principles of International Law a Draft Declaration and commitments of states on refraining from use of threats against territorial integrity or independence of any state. The declaration proposed the following formula:

"Execution of the right to justified individual or collective self-defence, as expressed in Art. 51 of the UN Charter, refers solely to armed attack, which does not restrict the capacity of a state affected by subversive actions or terrorist actions, supported by other states, to apply reasonable and adequate measures in order to rescue its institutions."

B.C. RODICK, *The Doctrine of Necessity in International Law*, London, 1928; E. GIRANDZ, "La théorie de légitime défense", in: *Recueil des Cours*, No. 49, 1934; L.J. KUNZ, "Individual and Collective Self-Defence in Art. 51 of the Charter of the UN", in: *American Journal of International Law*, No. 41, 1947; E.T. HAZAN, *L'état de nécessité en droit penal interéstatique et international*, Paris, 1949; D.W. BOWETT, "Collective Self-Defence under the Charter of the UN", in: *British Yearbook of International Law*, 1958; G.V. SHARMAZANSHVILI, "Kontseptsiia samoobroni v mezhdunarodnym prave", in: *Yezhigodnik mezhdunarodnogo prava*, 1958, Moscow, 1959.

SELF-DETERMINATION AND THE UN. A principle of international law which found full expression in art. 1 of the UN Charter on the purposes and principles of the World organization "... friendly relations among nations based on respect for the principle of equal rights and self-determination of peoples ...".

In Apr., 1952 the Human Rights Committee of the United Nations elaborated and adopted art. 5 of the Human Rights Code of the following wording:

"(1) All peoples and all nations shall have the right to self-determination, namely, the right freely to determine their political, economic, social and cultural status.
(2) All States, including those having responsibility for the administration of Non-Self-Governing and Trust Territories and those controlling in whatsoever manner the exercise of that right by another people, shall promote the realization of that right in all their territories, and shall respect the maintenance of that right in other States, in conformity with the provisions of the United Nations Charter.
(3) The right of peoples to self-determination shall also include permanent sovereignty over their national wealth and resources. In no case may a people be

deprived of its own means of subsistence on the grounds of any rights that may be claimed by other States."

The first resolutions on equality and the right of a nation to unrestricted self-determination was adopted by the UN General Assembly on Dec. 16, 1952, over the opposition of the colonial states. The text of the Res. 673 A, B and C/VIII is as follows;

"A. Whereas the right of peoples and nations to self-determination is a prerequisite to the full enjoyment of all fundamental human rights,
Whereas the Charter of the United Nations, under arts. 1 and 55, aims to develop friendly relations among nations based on respect for the equal rights and self-determination of peoples in order to strengthen universal peace,
Whereas the Charter of the United Nations recognize that certain Members of the United Nations are responsible for the administration of Territories whos peoples have not yet attained a full measure of self-government, and affirms the principles which should guide them,
Whereas every Member of the United Nations, in conformity with the Charter, should respect the maintenance of the right of self-determination in other States,
The General Assembly recommends that:
(1) The States Members of the United Nations shall uphold the principle of self-determination of all peoples' nations;
(2) The States Members of the United Nations shall recognize and promote the realization of the right of self-determination of the peoples of Non-Self-Governing and Trust Territories who are under their administration and shall facilitate the exercise of this right by the peoples of such Territories according to the principles and spirit of the Charter of the United Nations in regard to each Territory and to the freely expressed wishes of the peoples concerned, the wishes of the people being ascertained through plebiscites or other recognized democratic means, preferably under the auspices of the United Nations;
(3) The States Members of the United Nations responsible for the administration of Non-Self-Governing and Trust Territories shall take practical steps, pending the realization of the right of self-determination and in preparation thereof, to ensure the direct participation of the indigenous populations in the legislative and executive organs of government of those Territories, and to prepare them for complete self-government or independence.
B. The General Assembly,
Considering that one of the conditions necessary to facilitate United Nations action to promote respect for the right of self-determination of peoples and nations, in particular with regard to the peoples of Non-Self-Governing Territories, is that the competent organs of the United Nations should be in possession of official information on the government of these Territories,
Recalling its Res. 144(II) of November 3, 1947 in which it declared that the voluntary transmission of such information was entirely in conformity with the spirit of Article 73 of the Charter, and should therefore be encouraged,
Recalling its Res. 327(IV) of 2 December 1949 in which it expressed the hope that such of the Members of the United Nations as had not done so might voluntarily include details on the government of Non-Self-Governing Territories in the information transmitted by them under art. 73e of the Charter,
Considering that at the present time such information has not yet been furnished in respect of a large number of Non-Self-Governing Territories,
(1) Recommends States Members of the United Nations responsible for the administration of Non-Self-Governing Territories, voluntarily to include in the information transmitted by them under art. 73e of the Charter details regarding the extent to which the right of peoples and nations to self-determination is exercised by the peoples of those Territories, and in particular regarding their political progress and the measures taken to develop their capacity for self-administration, to satisfy their political aspirations and to promote the progressive development of their free political institutions;

(2) Decides to place the present resolution on the agenda of the Committee on information from Non-Self-Governing Territories for its next session in 1953.
C. The General Assembly,
Considering that it is necessary to continue the study of ways and means of ensuring international respect for the right of peoples to self-determination,
Considering that the recommendations it had adopted at its seventh session do not represent the only steps that can be taken to promote respect for such right,
(1) Requests the Economic and Social Council to ask the Commission on Human Rights to continue preparing recommendations concerning international respect for the right of peoples to self-determination, and particularly recommendations relating to the steps which might be taken, within the limits of their resources and competence, by the various organs of the United Nations and the specialized agencies to develop international respect for the right of peoples to self-determination;
(2) Requests the Commission on Human Rights to submit through the Economic and Social Council its recommendations to the General Assembly".

The UN General Assembly on Dec. 12, 1958 expanded the right of peoples to self-determination to include economy, recognizing the right of peoples to self-determine the use of their natural resources; the voting being 52 for, 15 against and 8 abstaining. The questions on self-determination were treated in the most precise and comprehensive way in Res. 1514/XV of Dec. 14, 1960, in the Declaration on the Granting of Independence to Colonial Countries and Peoples, which was adopted by 89 votes for, none against and 8 abstaining: Australia, Belgium, the Dominican Republic, France, Spain, Portugal, Great Britain, the USA and the Union of South Africa.
On Nov. 30, 1966 the General Assembly of the United Nations after a lengthy debate on the issue of "the duty to strictly respect the ban on the use of force or threat to use force in international relations and on the right of peoples to free self-determination" adopted, with 98 votes for, 2 against (Portugal and Great Britain) and 8 abstaining, Res. 2160/XX, calling upon states administering non-autonomous territories to "promptly employ all necessary means for enabling the peoples living under colonial domination to exercise the right of free self-determination."
The International Conference on Human Rights, held at Teheran in 1968, adopted a resolution on "the importance of the universal realization of the right of peoples to self-determination and of the speedy granting of independence to colonial countries and peoples for the effective guarantee and observance of human rights."
Every year since then, the General Assembly has adopted a resolution on the question. It has expressed indignation at the continued violation of the sovereignty and territorial integrity of countries and the human rights and fundamental freedoms of their peoples, and it has reaffirmed the legitimacy of the people's struggle for liberation from colonial and foreign domination and alien subjugation by all available means including armed struggle. The Association has condemned all governments that denied the right to self-determination of peoples, notably to the peoples of Africa and the Palestinian people, and has demanded full respect for the basic human rights of all individuals detained or imprisoned as a result of their struggle for self-determination and independence.
In 1970, the Assembly considered that the acquisition and retention of territory in contravention of the right of the people of that territory to self-determination was inadmissible and a gross violation of the Charter. One year later, the Assembly condemned the policy of certain states members of the North Atlantic Treaty Organization that contributed to the creation in southern Africa of a

military–industrial complex whose aim was to suppress the peoples struggling for self-determination and to interfere in the affairs of independent African states. It also urged the Security Council as well as members of the United Nations or of the specialized agencies to ensure the implementation of the relevant United Nations resolutions on the elimination of colonialism and racism.
The Assembly, in 1972, strongly deplored the intensification of armed repression and wanton slaughter of peoples under colonial and alien domination and acts of aggression committed by colonialists and alien forces against a number of sovereign states.
In 1974 it reaffirmed that the independence of Southern Rhodesia should not be negotiated with the illegal régime but with the authentic and recognized representatives of the Rhodesian people, and it called upon countries to sever all links with South Africa and Southern Rhodesia.
In 1976 the Assembly condemned South Africa's policy of bantustanization (creation of tribal homelands) as being incompatible with genuine independence, unity and national sovereignty and perpetuating the power of the white minority and the racist system of apartheid there. In 1977, it strongly condemned the "ever increasing massacres of innocent and defenceless people" by the racist minority régimes of southern Africa in their attempt to thwart the legitimate demands of the people, and it demanded the immediate release of all persons detained or imprisoned as a result of their struggle for self-determination and independence.
Two special studies were prepared and submitted to the Sub-Commission on Prevention of Discrimination and Protection of Minorities in 1978. One dealt with the historical and current development of the right to self-determination on the basis of the United Nations Charter and other instruments adopted by United Nations organs, with particular reference to the promotion and protection of human rights and fundamental freedoms. The other was concerned with the implementation of United Nations resolutions relating to the right of people under colonial and alien domination to self-determination.
On Dec. 8, 1988 the GA Res. 43/105 called for universal realisation of the right of people to self-determination.

UN Bulletin, No. 1, 1953, pp. 22–25; C. EAGLETON, "Excesses of Self-Determination", in: *Foreign Affairs*, 1953; *UN Review*, No. 208, 1959, pp. 30–71; L.V. SPIRIDINSKAYA, *Princip samopriedielenia natsyi v mezhdunarodnom pravie*, Moscow, 1961, *UN Review*, No. 316, 1961, pp. 5–11; S. STARUSHENKO, *El Principio de Autodeterminación de los Pueblos y las Naciones*, Moscú, 1962; *UN Monthly Chronicle*, No. 11, 1966, pp. 58–67; O.U. UMOZURIKE, *Self-Determination in International Law*, Hamden, Conn., 1973; W. HELDERMEYER, *Das Selbstbestimmungsrecht der Völker*, Padernborn, 1973; *Everyone's United Nations*, UN, New York, 1979, pp. 236–237; *UN Chronicle*, January 1981, p. 39; R.L. BLEDSOE, B.A. BOCZEK, *The International Law Dictionary*, Oxford, 1987; UN *Resolutions and Decisions adopted by the General Assembly during the First Part of its Forty-Third Session from 20 September to 22 December, 1988*, New Yor, 1989, pp. 349–359.

SELOUS GAME RESERVE. A historic site of Tanzania, included in the ▷ World Heritage UNESCO List.

UNESCO, *A Legacy for All*, Paris, 1984.

SEMANTICS. A subject of international research. Organization rep. with the UIA:

International Society for General Semantics, f. 1942, San Franciso. Publ.: *A Review of General Semantics*.

S

Yearbook of International Organizations, 1986/87; The Europa Yearbook 1988. A World Survey, Vol. I, London, 1988.

SEMI-MANUFACTURES. An international term, used in the UN for products, such as rubber and steel which have been processed from raw materials and are intended for use in manufactured articles. The developing countries, seeking to expand their own industrial capacities, are asking for tariff concessions on semi-manufactures as well as on raw materials.

UN Chronicle, October 1982, p. 48.

SENEGAL. Member of the UN. Republic of Senegal. A country in West Africa on the Atlantic bordering on Mauritania, Mali, Guinea, Guinea-Bissau, Gambia. Area: 196,192 sq. km. Pop. 1988 est.: 6,980,000 (1976 census: 5,085,388). Capital: Dakar with 978,553 inhabitants 1979. GNP per capita 1986: US $420. Official language: French. Currency: one CFA Franc = 100 centimes. National day: Apr. 4, Independence Day, 1960.

Member of the UN since Apr. 18, 1960 and all its specialized agencies except IDA. ITU and WIPO; member of OCAM, OAU and Senegal Riparian States Organization; ACP state of the EEC.

International relations: colonized by France in the 18th century; 1854–1959 French colony; became autonomous territory within French Union Nov. 25, 1958. From Jan. 17 to Aug. 30, 1959 part of the Mali Federation. Independent republic: Aug. 20, 1960. On Oct. 21–23, 1972, the UN Security Council examined Senegal's charge against Portugal for armed assault on borderland between Senegal and Guinea-Bissau.

A signatory of the Yaoundé Conventions of 1965 and of 1970, and of the Lomé Conventions of 1975 and of 1980. In November 1980 and in July 1981 Sengalese troops intervened in Gambia. On February 1, 1982 Senegal formed a Confederation with Gambia ▷ Senegambia, but in the UN preserved the individual membership of Gambia and Senegal. See also ▷ World Heritage UNESCO List.

M. CROWDER, *Senegal: a Study in French Assimilation Policy*, London, 1962; H. DESCHAMPS, *Le Senegal et la Gambia*, Paris, 1964; *Social and Economic Development in Senegal*, New York, 1964; E. MILCENT, *Au Carrefour des Options Africaines: Le Sénégal*, Paris, 1965; P. DOLL, *Der Senegalische Weg zum Afrikanischen Sozialismus*, Hamburg, 1966; J.C. GAUTEON, *L'administration senegalaise*, Paris 1971; M. SAMB (ed.), *Spotlight on Senegal*, Dakar, 1972; S. GELLAR, *Senegal*, Boulder, 1982; *The Europa Year Book 1984. A World Survey*, Vol. II, pp. 2336–2349, London, 1984.

SENEGAL RIVER. An African river 1610 km long, rises in south-western Mali and north Guinea, forms the Mauritania–Senegal border and flows into the Atlantic Ocean; area of river basin 441,000 sq. km; subject of international co-operation of the river basin states which in 1960 established the Organization of the Inshore States of the Senegal River, Organisation des États riverains du fleuve Sénégal, OERS, with the task of improving navigation on the river and furthering the economic co-operation among the inshore states. In Nov., 1971 OERS suspended its operations due to a political conflict between Guinea and the other members which led to the resignation of Senegal. On Mar. 11, 1972 the governments of Mali, Mauritania, and Senegal signed a Convention concerning the Status of the Senegal river, establishing as a common organ the Organisation pour le Mise en Valeur du Fleuve Senegal, OMVS, as an open institution. The highlights of the Convention:

"Art. 1. The Senegal River is declared to be, within the national territory of the Republics of Mali, of the Islamic Republic of Mauritania and the Republic of Senegal, together with its tributaries, an international river within the framework of this Convention.

Art. 2. The States of Mali, Mauritania and Senegal, hereafter called the Contracting States, solemnly affirm their will to develop close co-operation to permit the rational exploitation of the resources of the Senegal River and to guarantee freedom of navigation and equality of treatment to those who use it.

Art. 3. The utilization of the Senegal River is open to each Contracting State in accordance with the principles defined in the present Convention."

On May 28, 1974 a long-range program was signed involving the joint investment of *c.* 16 billion French francs.

Organization reg. with the UIA:

Organization for the Development of the Senegal River, f. 1972, Dakar.

Convention relative au Status du Fleuve Sénégal, Dakar, 1974; A.J. PEASLE (ed.), *International Governmental Organizations, Constitutional Documents*, The Hague, 1976, Part V, pp. 587–590; *The Europa Yearbook 1986. A World Survey*, Vol. I, London, 1988.

SENEGAMBIA. The Confederation of ▷ Senegal and ▷ Gambia, est. on Feb. 1, 1982. The principles of the Confederation: Each of the Confederal States maintains its independence and sovereignty. The institutions of the Confederation: the President of the Confederation (the President of Senegal) and Vice-President of the Confederation (the President of Gambia); the Confederal Council of Ministers and the Confederal Assembly. The official languages are African languages chosen by the President and the Vice-President along with English and French. The integration is based on co-operation of the armed and security forces, on economic and monetary union, on joint jurisdiction, communication and external relations.

The Europa Year Book 1984. A World Survey, Vol. II, p. 1604, London, 1984.

SENKAKU. Japanese name accepted in 20th century atlases for five uninhabited islands in the south part of the East China Sea *c.* 80 km from the Ryukyu islands and *c.* 145 km from Taiwan, subject of an international dispute. After World War II formally under US occupation along with part of the Ryukyu archipelago and the island of Okinawa. With the return of Okinawa May 15, 1972 to Japan, the latter also laid claim to the Senkaku islands, but at the same time the Chinese People's Republic and Taiwan announced their claims, pointing out that they have historic Chinese names: Tiayu, Hunagvey, Chicvey, Nansiao, and Peysiao. This dispute is connected with the discovery of rich oil reserves in the East China Sea, especially in the region of the Senkaku islands.

SEPARATE BUT EQUAL. A doctrine followed by the US Supreme Court in the case of *Plessy versus Fergusson*, 1896; the court accepted as constitutional states' laws requiring Negroes to use segregated railroad facilities; indirectly overturned by the Supreme Court decision in the *Brown versus Board of Education of Topeka* case 1954 holding that separate but equal facilities for Negroes in public schools do not need equal constitutional protection. "Separate educational facilities are inherently unequal." The same kind of Supreme Court decision in *Swann versus Mecklenburg Board of Education* on busing of pupils, 1971, definitely overcame the racial imbalance of 1896.

C.H. S. JOHNSON, *Pattern of Negro Segregation*, New York, 1943; L. MILLER, *The Petitioners; The Story of the Supreme Court of the US and the Negro*, New York, 1950; J. D. WEAWER, *Warren: the Man, the Court, the Era*, New York, 1969.

SEPARATION OF CHURCH AND STATE. Up to the 17th century all of the state systems of Europe were characterized by a connection of secular and spiritual authority in various forms and to varying degrees, which was associated with the existence of state or dominant religions. A different situation was introduced in North America on the territory colonized by the adherents of various religions and philosophies who saw no need for granting the clergy of the minority Anglican state religion the privileges which it had acquired in the motherland. Separation of Church and State was implemented for the first time in 1636 in the English colony of Rhode Island, then 1682 in Pennsylvania, and finally in all of the United States in the Constitution of 1787. In time the influence of the free-thinking ideas of the French Revolution brought about the separation of church and state in France, which was carried out 1794–1801 and then again in 1905; in Belgium in 1831, in the states of Latin America during the 19th century, and in the majority of European states in the 20th century. In 1980, in Europe only Andorra maintained a church–state connection; in Latin America: Argentina, Bolivia, Colombia, Ecuador, Guatemala, Peru and Venezuela. The Second Vatican Council approved of the separation of church and state in examining the question of adopting the church to contemporary international conditions. The constitution, *Gaudium et spes*, accepted by the Second Vatican Council, stated in p. 76 that:

"the political community and the Church in their areas are independent of each other and autonomous."

The interpretation of this principle was contained in the statement of Pope Paul VI in *Motu proprio: Sollicitudo omnium ecclesiarum*, June 24, 1969:

"It cannot be denied that the goal facing the Church and public authority is different and that the Church as well as the State, each in its system are perfect communities, and thus possessing their own powers and means, guided by such laws as their nature requires. However, it is also true that both communities work toward the benefit of a common subject, namely, man ... From this it follows that sometimes the Church and the State have common aims and that for the attainment of the good of either single individuals or that of the human community should conduct an open dialogue and attain unity so that their mutual relations would be established, develop and strengthen in co-operation and mutual association and, simultaneously, the divergences of opinion which sometimes might arise should be either avoided or clarified."

J.B. SAGMÜLLER, *Der rechtliche Begriff der Trennung von Kirche und Staat*, Berlin, 1916; J. BENNETT, *Christians and the State*, London, 1958; L. PFEIFER, *Church and State in the United States*, New York, 1964.

SEPHARDIC COMMUNITY. One of the two (▷ Ashkenazi) historical Jewish communities, comprising Jews from the Balkan countries, North Africa and the Middle East. The Chief Rabbi has his headquarters in Jerusalem and is member together with the Ashkenazi Chief Rabbi of the Supreme ▷ Rabbinacal Council.

The Europa Yearbook 1987. A World Survey, Vol. I, London, 1987.

SEPHARDIM. Hebrew: Sephard = Spain. One of the three major divisions of the Jews, whose ancestors resided in the Middle Ages in the Iberian Peninsula. After their expulsion from Spain, 1492–1497, transferred to North Africa and the Middle East where they continue to practice the sephardic ritual and liturgy and use dialect called Iadino or Spanioli (Judeo-Spanish).

Organization reg. with the UIA:

World Sephardi Federation, f. 1951, Geneva, Switzerland; to strengthen the unity of Jewry and Judaism among Sephardic and oriental Jewish communities. Members in 33 countries.

See also ▷ Jews.

Yearbook of International Organizations, 1986/87; The Europa Yearbook 1988. A World Survey, Vol. I, London, 1988.

SERAJEVO OR SARAJEVO. The Capital of Bośnia and Hercegovina. A center of the Serbian independence movement in the beginning of 20th century. On June 28, 1914 in Serajevo the Austrian Archduke Francis Ferdinand and his wife were assassinated, which was the immediate cause of World War I.

R.W. SETTON-WATSON, *Serajevo*, London, 1926.

SERBIA. Federal unit of Yugoslavia, together with the autonomous provinces Vojvodina and Kosovo; area 88,361 sq. km; pop. 1971 census: 8,447,000. Capital of Serbia and Yugoslavia: Belgrade. Annexed by the Turks in 1459, initiated the liberation struggle in 1804, gained autonomy under Russian protection with the Treaty of Adrianople, 1829; evacuation of Turkish troops 1867, and complete independence 1878. In 1912 and 1913 in the Balkan War; Aug. 3, 1914 attacked by Austria. Since 1918 in union with Croatia and Slovenia (▷ Yugoslavia).

S. STANOJEVIC, *Istorija srpskaga naroda*, Beograd, 1910; *Istoriya Yugoslavii*, 2 Vols., Moscow, 1963; M. de VOS, *Histoire de Yougoslavie*, Paris, 1965; V. DEDIJER, *History of Yugoslavia*, New York, 1974.

SERBIA–USA TRADE AGREEMENT, 1881. The first agreement of Serbia, independent since 1878, with the USA, concluded in Belgrade on Oct. 14, 1881. The highlights of the agreement:

"Art. 1. There will be full reciprocal freedom of trade and navigation between the subjects and citizens of the high contractual parties which will, both the ones and the others, be able freely to settle in the area of the other country."

The Agreement guarantees the freedom to engage in industry and trade, to possess and dispose of moveable and real property.

"Art. 3. No obstacles will be raised in the free movement of subjects, while administrative formalities relative to travel documents will be confined only to what is absolutely essential for the public in crossing frontiers."

"Art. 12. The United States agrees to give up the privileges and immunity enjoyed so far by its citizens in Serbia on the strength of the capitulation of the Ottoman Empire which were granted to the USA and confirmed under the Treaties of 1830 and 1862."

The observance of the 1881 Trade Agreement was not affected by the USA–Yugoslavia relations between the two World Wars. The agreement was never cancelled despite the new trade agreements between the US and Yugoslavia.

S. AVRAMOR, "Trade Agreement of 1881 in the Light of Present Day Relations", in: *Review of International Relations*, Belgrade, Nov. 20, 1981.

SERENGETTI. A national park of Tanzania, included in the ▷ World Heritage UNESCO List. Over this immense area roam herbivorous animals which can be counted in tens of thousands (antelopes, topis, buffaloes, giraffes and water hogs) or in hundreds of thousands (gnus, gazelles and zebras) pursued by their predators (lions, leopards, hyenas, etc.) of which, although less abundant, there are about 20 different species. The whole area represents an ecosystem similar to that of the Pleistocene.

UNESCO, *A Legacy for All*, Paris, 1984.

SERICULTURE. A subject of international co-operation and conventions. Organization reg. with the UIA:

International Sericultural Commission, f. 1948, Paris by resolution of the 7th Congress of Sericulture. New status on the basis of an intergovernmental convention, signed on July 1, 1957 in Paris, came into force on Sept. 18, 1960. Members: Algeria, Central African Republic, Ecuador, Egypt, France, India, Japan, Lebanon, Madagascar, Romania, Spain, Thailand and Tunisia. Publ.: *Journal of Silkworm*.

UNTS, Vol. 724, p. 236; *Yearbook of International Organization*.

SERVICES. An international term for one of the economic sectors of national and international business; subject of international co-operation:

Institute of Development and Economic Affairs Services, IDEAS
Magnolia Star Route, Nederlan, USA.
International Institutional Services, New York, NY, USA.
World Council of Service, St. Anna's-on-Sea, UK.

D.L. RIDDLE, *Service Led Growth: The Role of the Service Sector in World Development*, New York, 1987; S.E. VEALE, J.M. SPIEGELMAN, I. RONKAINEN eds., *Trade in Services: The US Position*; J.N. BHAGWATI, *Trade in Services: Developing Countries Concerns, in: Economic Impact*, Washington DC, 1988/1.

SERVICES AND DEVELOPMENT. The labour intensive service industries are one of the most important elements of the new economic order especially for the developing countries. The national and international services in 1980's were a subject of international co-operation under the auspices of UN specialized agencies.

J.D. ARONSON, *Services and Development, in: Economic Impact* 1988/3.

SETTLEMENT ACT, 1701. An English law on succession to the throne, passed by Parliament in 1701; bound the English monarch to adhere to the Anglican Church (▷ Habeas Corpus Act), creating at the same time the independence of the law courts on the King's authority and, consequently, contributed to the international development of judicature.

SETTLEMENT OF CIVIL LAW DISPUTES IN THE CMEA SYSTEM. A Convention on Settlement by Arbitration of Civil Law Disputes arising from Relations of Economic, Scientific and Technical Co-operation, signed by the governments of Bulgaria, Czechoslovakia, GDR, Hungary, Mongolia, Poland, Romania and USSR at Moscow, May 26, 1972; adopted a Uniform Regimen for Arbitration Tribunals attached to Chambers of Commerce of Member Countries of CMEA and a Statute on Arbitration Fees, Expenses and Cost of Parties.

W.E. BUTLER (ed.), *A Source Book on Socialist International Organizations*, Alphen, 1978, pp. 607–630.

SETTLEMENT PEACEFUL. ▷ Peaceful Settlement of International Disputes.

SETTLEMENTS, HUMAN. ▷ UN Center for Human Settlements.

SETTLEMENTS, MULTILATERAL SYSTEM OF. A multilateral clearance system initiated after World War I, a system simplifying international financial operations and promoting international liquidity by comprehensive intergovernmental or bilateral treaties between central banks; expanded after World War II. Members of the treaties are obligated to avoid bilateral payment arrangements. The first international bank for multilateral settlements is the International Clearance Bank, est. 1930; in the EEC system the International Bank for Economic Co-operation. Constant units are introduced in the settlements system for simplification, e.g. the transfer rouble or the European Accounting Unit, EAU.

SEVEN SISTERS. An international term for seven petroleum companies dominant on the World market: Exxon, Socal, Texaco, Mobil, Gulf, Royal Dutch Shell, British Petroleum; in 1975 they produced 77% of the petroleum in the OPEC member countries and 40% of the petroleum in the USA.

C. TUGENDHAT, *The Chronological History of the Petroleum and Natural Gas Industries*, New York, 1963; T. SZULC, *The Oil Crisis*, New York, 1974, pp. 59–64; A. SAMPSON, *The Seven Sisters*, London, 1975; D.S. PAINTER, *Private Power and Public Policy. Multinational Oil Corporations and US Foreign Policy 1941–1954*, London, 1986.

SÈVRES. City in France; a suburb of Paris: seat of the International Bureau of Weights and Measures (▷ Weights and Measure, International Bureau of) and the International Pedagogical Center. Place of the signing of the Peace Treaty of Allied and Associated Powers with Turkey on Aug. 10, 1920 called the Treaty of Sèvres.

SÈVRES PEACE TREATY, 1920. A Treaty between the Allied Powers (France, Great Britain, Italy, Japan and Armenia, Belgium, Czechoslovakia, Greece, the Hedjaz, Poland, Portugal, Romania and the Serb-Croat-Slovene State) of the one part and Turkey of the other part, signed in Sèvres, Aug. 10, 1920. Highlights of the Treaty:

Part. I. The Covenant of the League of Nations (art. 1 to 26 and Annex).

Part II. Frontiers of Turkey (art. 27 to 35).

Part III. Political Clauses (art. 36 to 139). Art. 37:

"The navigation of the straits, including the Dardanelles, the Sea of Marmara and the Bosporus, shall in future be open, both in peace and war, to every vessel of commerce or of war and to military and commercial aircraft, without distinction of flag. These waters shall not be subject to blockade, nor shall any belligerent right be exercised nor any act of hostility be committed within them, unless in pursuance of a decision of the Council of League of Nations."

Part IV. Protection of Minorities (art. 140 to 151).

Part V. Military, Naval and Air Clauses (art. 152 to 207).

Part VI. Prisoners of War and Graves (art. 208 to 225).

Part VII. Penalties (art. 226 to 230). Art 226:

"The Turkish Government recognizes the right of the Allied Powers to bring before military tribunal persons accused of having committed acts in violation of the laws and customs of war."

Part VIII. Financial Clauses (art. 231 to 260).

Part IX. Economic Clauses (art. 261 to 317).

Part X. Aerial Navigation (art. 318 to 327).

Part XI. Ports, Waterways and Railways (art. 328 to 373).

Part XII. (Part XIII of the Versailles Treaty: International Labour Organisation).

Part XIII. Miscellaneous Provisions (art. 415 to 433).

Major Peace Treaties of Modern History, New York, 1967, pp. 2055–2213.

SEWING MACHINES. A subject of international co-operation. Organizations reg. with the UIA:

Association of Sewing Machine Manufacturers of the EEC, f. 1959, Milan.

European Liaison Committee for the Sewing Machine Industries, f. 1956, Milan.

Yearbook of International Organizations.

SEXOLOGY. A subject of organized international co-operation. The first international organization active before World War I was Association Internationale pour la protection de la mère et pour la réforme de la vie sexuelle, International Association for the Protection of Mother and for the Reform of Sexual Life, f. 1911 in Paris; and between the wars: Ligue universelle de la réforme sexuelle, Universal League for Sexual Reform, f. 1927, Paris. Its 1st international congress was held in Paris in 1974.

Yearbook of International Organizations.

SEXUALLY TRANSMITTED DISEASES. ▷ STD

SEYCHELLES. Member of the UN. The territory of the Seychelles State consists of 112 islands and islets in the Indian Ocean, north of Madagascar. Area: 455 sq. km. Pop. 1983 census: 64,314. Capital: Victoria with 23,334 inhabitants, 1977, on the principal island Mahé. GNP 1988 per capita: US $3590. Currency: one Seychelles rupee = 100 cents. Official language: English and French. National Day: June 29, Independence Day, 1976.
Member of the UN from Sept. 21, 1976; and all its specialized agencies. Member of the Commonwealth, OAU and is an ACP state of the EEC.
International relations: the Seychelles were colonized by the French 1768–94; occupied by the British as a dependency of Mauritius, 1903–76 a separate colony. Independent on June 29, 1976. Member of the Lomé Conventions, 1977, 1980 and 1985.
See also ▷ World Heritage UNESCO List.

B. BENEDICT, *People of the Seychelles*, London, 1966; G. LIONNET, *The Seychelles*, Newton Abbot, 1972; *Seychelles Handbook*, Victoria, 1976; *UN Chronicle*, February, June and July, 1982; M. FRANDA, *The Seychelles; Unquiet Islands*, Boulder, 1982; *The Europa Year Book 1984. A World Survey*, Vol. II, pp. 2350–2354, London, 1984.

SEYM. The Polish Parliament, one of the oldest in Europe, with two houses 1483–1793 and 1919–39. One House from 1946 until Jun 4 1989, when the Senate was reinstated. Member of the Inter-Parliamentary Union.

W. KONOPCZYŃSKI, *Chronologia sejmów polskich, 1483–1793*, Kraków, 1948; J. JĘDRUCH, *Constitutions, Elections and Legislatures of Poland 1493–1977. A Guide to their History*, Washington, DC, 1982.

SHABA. One of the richest mining regions of Africa, up to 1973 called Katanga; in southeastern Zaïre on the border of Angola, Zambia, and Lake Tanganyika. Area 496,965 sq. km, with 3,823,172 inhabitants 1981; administrative center Lumbumbashi (up to 1973 Elisabethville) with 451,332 inhabitants 1976. Main subject of the international crisis 1960–64 in the Congo (▷ Zaïre). After declaring the independence of the Congo July 10, 1960, Katanga separatists financed by the Belgian company Union Minière de Haute Katanga, announced Katanga an independent state headed by M. Tshombe. As a result of the outbreak of civil war Sept. 13, 1961, UN forces entered Katanga and remained there to June 1964, when the separation of Katanga was ended with M. Tshombe's assumption of power over the entire Congo (deprived of power in 1969, he left the country, was sentenced to death in absentia and died in prison in Algeria). In Mar., 1977 an armed *coup d'état* in Katanga by partisan

units stationed on the Angola border was put down by forces of the central government.

C. C. O'BRIEN, *To Katanga and Back*, London, 1962; C. YOUNG, *Politics in the Congo: Decolonization and Independence*, Princeton, 1963; G. VAN DE MEERSH, *Fin de la souverainete Belge au Congo*, Bruxelles, 1965; B. URQUHART, *A Life in Peace and War*, New York, 1987.

SHANGHAI. A city and seaport of East China; area 5800 sq. km; opened to foreign trade by the Treaty of Nankin in 1842 and a year after the major part of the city was incorporated into the British concession, enlarged 1849 by French and 1862 by US concessions, renamed 1863 the International Settlement under extraterritorial administration and controlled by its own police and troops. Occupied by Japan Dec. 7, 1941, liberated Sept. 2, 1945. The UK and the US formally renounced their claims in 1943, France in 1946.

E.M. DYCÉ, *Personal Reminiscenses of Thirty Years' Residence in the Model Settlement, Shanghai 1870–1900*, London, 1906; G.E. MILLER, *Shanghai, Paradise of Adventures*, London, 1937; R. MURPHY, *Shanghai, Key to Modern China*, London, 1953; L. TAIRE, *Shanghai Episode*, London, 1957.

SHANGHAI CHINA–USA COMMUNIQUÉ, 1972. A joint Sino-American statement issued by US President R. Nixon and China's Prime Minister Chou En-lai on Feb. 28, 1972. The text is as follows:

"President Richard Nixon of the United States of America visited the People's Republic of China at the invitation of Premier Chou En-lai of the People's Republic of China from February 21 to February 28, 1972. Accompanying the President were Mrs Nixon, United States Secretary of State William Rogers, Assistant to the President Dr Henry Kissinger, and other American officials.
President Nixon met with Chairman Mao Tse-tung of the Communist Party of China on February 21. The two leaders had a serious and frank exchange of views on Sino–United States relations and world affairs.
During the visit, extensive, earnest and frank discussions were held between President Nixon and Premier Chou En-lai on the normalization of relations between the United States of America and the People's Republic of China, as well as on other matters of interest to both sides. In addition, Secretary of State William Rogers and Foreign Minister Chi Peng-fei held talks in the same spirit.
President Nixon and his party visited Peking and viewed cultural, industrial and agricultural sites, and they also toured Hangchow and Shanghai where, continuing discussions with Chines leaders, they viewed similar places of interest.
The leaders of the People's Republic of China and the United States of America found it beneficial to have this opportunity, after so many years without contact, to present candidly to one another their views on a variety of issues. They reviewed the international situation, in which important changes and great upheavals are taking place, and expounded their respective positions and attitudes.
The United States side stated: Peace in Asia and peace in the world requires efforts both to reduce immediate tensions and to eliminate the basic causes of conflict. The United States will work for a just and secure peace: just, because it fulfils the aspirations of peoples and nations for freedom and progress; secure, because it removes the danger of foreign aggression. The United States supports individual freedom and social progress for all the peoples of the the world, free of outside pressure or intervention.
The United States believes that the effort to reduce tensions is served by improving communication between countries that have different ideologies so as to lessen the risk of confrontation through accident, miscalculation or misunderstanding. Countries should treat each other with mutual respect and be willing to compete peacefully, letting performance be the ultimate judge. No country should claim infallibility and each country should be prepared to re-examine its own attitudes for the common good.

The United States stressed that the peoples of Indo-China should be allowed to determine their destiny without outside intervention; its constant primary objective has been a negotiated solution; the eight-point proposal put forward by the Republic of Vietnam and the United States on January 27, 1972, represents a basis for the attainment of that objective; in the absence of a negotiated settlement the United States envisages the ultimate withdrawal of all United States forces from the region consistent with the aim of self-determination for each country of Indo-China. The United States will maintain its close ties with and support for the Republic of Korea; the United States will support efforts of the Republic of Korea to seek a relaxation of tension and increased communication in the Korean peninsula.
The United States places the highest value on its friendly relations with Japan; it will continue to develop the existing close bonds.
Consistent with the United Nations Security Council Resolution of December 21, 1971, the United States favours the continuation of the ceasefire between India and Pakistan and the withdrawal of all military forces to within their own territories and to their own sides of the ceasefire line in Jammu and Kashmir; the United States supports the right of the peoples of South Asia to shape their own future in peace, free of military threat, and without having the area become the subject of Great Power rivalry.
The Chinese side stated: Wherever there is oppression, there is resistance. Countries want independence, nations want liberation and the people want revolution – this has become the irresistible trend of history. All nations, big or small, should be equal; big nations should not bully the small and strong nations should not bully the weak. China will never be a Superpower and it opposes hegemony and power politics of any kind.
The Chinese side stated that it firmly supports the struggles of all the oppressed people and nations for freedom and liberation and that the people of all countries have the right to choose their social systems, according to their own wishes, and the right to safeguard the independence, sovereignty and territorial integrity of their own countries and oppose foreign aggression, interference, control and subversion. All foreign troops should be withdrawn to their own countries.
The Chinese side expressed its firm support to the peoples of Vietnam, Laos and Cambodia in their efforts for the attainment of their goal and its firm support to the seven-point proposal of the Provisional Revolutionary Government of the Republic of South Vietnam and the elaboration of February this year on the two key problems in the proposal, and to the Joint Declaration of the summit conference of the Indo-Chinese peoples.
It firmly supports the eight-point programme for the peaceful unification of Korea put forward by the Government of the Democratic People's Republic of Korea on April 12, 1971, and the stand for the abolition of the 'United Nations Commission for the unification and rehabilitation of Korea'.
It firmly opposes the revival and outward expansion of Japanese militarism and firmly supports the Japanese people's desire to build an independent, democratic, peaceful and neutral Japan.
It firmly maintains that India and Pakistan should, in accordance with the United Nations resolutions on the India–Pakistan question, immediately withdraw all their forces to their respective territories and to their own sides of the ceasefire line in Jammu and Kashmir, and firmly supports the Pakistan Government and people in their struggle to preserve their independence and sovereignty and the people of Jammu and Kashmir in their struggle for the right of self-determination.
There are essential differences between China and the United States in their social systems and foreign policies. However, the two sides agreed that countries, regardless of their social systems, should conduct their relations on the principles of respect for the sovereignty and territorial integrity of all States, non-aggression against other States, non-interference in the internal affairs of other States, equality and mutual benefit, and peaceful coexistence. International disputes should be settled on this basis, without resorting to the use or threat of force. The United States and the People's Republic of China are prepared to apply these principles to their mutual relations.

With these principles of international relations in mind, the two sides stated that: Progress towards the normalization of relations between China and the United States is in the interests of all countries.

Both wish to reduce the danger of international military conflict.

Neither should seek hegemony in the Asia–Pacific region and each is opposed to efforts by any other country or group of countries to establish such hegemony.

Neither is prepared to negotiate on behalf of any third party or to enter into agreements or understandings with the other directed at other States.

Both sides are of the view that it would be against the interests of the peoples of the world for any major country to collude with another against other countries, or for major countries to divide up the world into spheres of interest.

The two sides reviewed the long-standing serious disputes between China and the United States.

The Chinese side reaffirmed its position: The Taiwan question is the crucial question obstructing the normalization of relations between China and the United States; the Government of the People's Republic of China is the sole legal Government of China; Taiwan is a province of China which has long been returned to the motherland; the liberation of Taiwan is China's internal affair in which no other country has the right to interfere; and all United States forces and military installations must be withdrawn from Taiwan. The Chinese Government firmly opposes any activities which aim at the creation of 'one China, one Taiwan', 'one China, two Governments', 'two Chinas' and 'independent Taiwan', or advocate that 'the status of Taiwan remains to be determined'.

The United States side declared: The United States acknowledges that all Chinese on either side of the Taiwan Strait maintain there is but one China and that Taiwan is a part of China. The United States Government does not challenge that position. It reaffirms its interest in a peaceful settlement of the Taiwan question by the Chinese themselves.

With this prospect in mind, it affirms the ultimate objective of the withdrawal of all United States forces and military installations from Taiwan. In the meantime, it will progressively reduce its forces and military installations on Taiwan as the tension in the area diminishes.

The two sides agreed that it is desirable to broaden the understanding between the two peoples. To this end, they discussed specific areas in such fields as science, technology, culture, sports and journalism, in which people-to-people contacts and exchanges would be mutually beneficial. Each side undertakes to facilitate the further development of such contacts and exchanges.

Both sides view bilateral trade as another area from which mutual benefit can be derived, and agreed that economic relations based on equality and mutual benefit are in the interest of the peoples of the two countries. They agree to facilitate the progressive development of trade between their two countries.

The two sides agreed that they will stay in contact through various channels, including the sending of a senior United States representative to Peking from time to time for concrete consultations to further the normalization of relations between the two countries and continue to exchange views on issues of common interest.

The two sides expressed the hope that the gains achieved during this visit would open up new prospects for the relations between the two countries. They believe that the normalization of relations between the two countries is not only in the interest of the Chinese and American peoples but also contributes to the relaxation of tension in Asia and the world.

President Nixon, Mrs Nixon and the American party expressed their appreciation for the gracious hospitality shown them by the Government and people of the People's Republic of China.

J.A.S. GRENVILLE, *The Major International Treaties 1914–1973, A History and Guide with Texts*, London, 1974, pp. 524–527.

SHANTUNG OR SHANDONG. A province in East China, area: 153,300 sq. km, pop. (1978) *c.* 70,000,000; capital: Tsinam (Finan); region of German penetration in the 19th century; on basis of the Chinese–German Treaty, Mar. 6, 1898, the Reich was granted a concession to build a railway line, to lay underwater cables and to exploit mines: June 28, 1919 under art. 156–158 of the Versailles Treaty Germany abdicated all its rights to movable and immovable properties in Shantung and privileges granted by China, 1898, in favor of Japan. This took place without the consent of China and became the subject of a Chinese–Japanese dispute, settled in China's favor but not until Japan's defeat in 1945 and the founding of the Chinese People's Republic, 1949.

SHAPE. Supreme Headquarters Allied Powers in Europe. The supreme organ of NATO armed forces in Europe, subordinate to the Chiefs of Staff and Supreme Allied Commander Atlantic (▷ SACLANT), Channel Command, CHANCOM, and other commands or military institutions of NATO; subordinate to it are the commands of individual West European regions and the special air–sea command for the Mediterranean.

D. ROBERTSON, *Guide to Modern Defense and Strategy*, Detroit, 1988.

SHARIAH. Arabic name of the Islamic legal code based on the Koran and Hadith.

SHARJAH. A sheikdom, one of the former Trucial States, part of the federation of ▷ United Arab Emirates.

SHARM AL-SHEIK. A promontory on the peninsula of Sinai, at the mouth of the Gulf of Aqaba, overlooks the Strait of Tiran, occupied by Israeli military forces Oct. 29, 1956–Mar. 8, 1957 and from June 6, 1967 to Feb. 18, 1976. During the period from Mar. 8, 1957 to May 20, 1967 controlled by the UN Emergency Force, and again since Feb. 18, 1976.

UN Review No. 261, 1957; *UN Chronicle*, July, 1967.

SHARPEVILLE. A city of South Africa, place in which on Mar. 21, 1960, 69 demonstrators against the pass laws of the apartheid system were shot and killed and 180 others wounded. The UN General Assembly proclaimed the International Mobilization against Apartheid in Res. 33/1836, and the UN Special Committee against Apartheid has annually held a solemn meeting on Mar. 21.

UN Chronicle, April, 1979, p. 49–50; and April, 1984, p.56; *Sharpeville twenty-fifth anniversary, in UN Chronicle*, 1985, No. 3, pp. 3–6.

SHEKEL. A monetary unit of Israel; one shekel = 100 new agorot; issued by the Bank of Israel.

SHELLFISH POISONING. A subject of WHO studies in connection with international trade in shellfish and with serious forms of human intoxication, called paralytic shellfish or dinoflagellate poisoning, resulting from the ingestion of bivalve molluscs (e.g. mussels, clams, scallops, oysters).

WHO *Guide to Shellfish Hygiene*, Geneva, 1976; B.W. HALSTEAD, E.J. SCHANTZ, *Paralytic Shellfish Poisoning*, Geneva, 1984.

SHELTER FOR THE HOMELESS. A UN World Program in the International Year of Shelters for the Homeless, 1987. It aims to set in motion policies and strategies that will see the world's population adequately housed by the year 2000. By then 13 out of the 15 largest cities in the world will be in developing countries and for the first time in history more people will be living in urban than in rural areas. By the start of 1987, 135 countries had designed national focal points to co-ordinate domestic shelter program.

The European Parliamentary Assembly on June 16, 1987 adopted a Resolution on Shelter for the Homeless in the European Community.

The GA adopted on Dec. 20 1988, a Res. 43/181 on "Global Strategy for Shelter to the Year 2000" with Annex (Guidelines for steps to be taken at the national level). The highlights of the Resolution:

"Decides that the main objective of the Strategy is to facilitate adequate shelter for all by the year 2000, that the main focus should therefore be on improving the situation of the disadvantaged and the poor, and that the following fundamental objectives and principles should form the basis of the Strategy:

(a) Enabling policies, whereby the full potential and resources of all governmental and non-governmental factors in the field of human settlements are utilized, must be at the heart of national and international efforts;

(b) Women, as income-earners, home-makers and heads of households, and women's organizations fulfil a crucial role as contributors to the solution of human settlements problems, which should be fully recognized and reflected in equal participation of women in the elaboration of housing policies, programmes and projects, and that specific interests and capabilities of women should be adequately represented in human settlement policy formulation and in government mechanisms employed at all levels for the implementation of housing policies, programmes and projects;

(c) Shelter and development are mutually supportive and interdependent, and policies must be developed in full recognition of the important links between shelter and economic development;

(d) The concept of sustainable development implies that shelter provision and urban development must be reconciliable with a sustainable management of the environment."

See also ▷ UN Center for Human Settlements (HABITAT); and ▷ HABITAT Vancouver Declaration, 1976.

Council of Europe. Human Rights, *Information Sheet No. 21*, Strasbourg, 1988, pp. 225–229; *UN Resolutions and Decisions adopted by the General Assembly during the First Part of its Forty-Third Session, From 20 September to 22 December 1988*, New York, 1989, p. 270.

SHENYANG. ▷ Manchuria.

SHIBAM. A historic site of Democratic Yemen, included in the ▷ World Heritage UNESCO List. See ▷ Wadi Hadramavi.

UNESCO. *A Legacy for All*, Paris, 1984.

SHI'ISM. One of the two branches of Islam with its main base in Iran, organized on a national basis around mosques; many times in history it assumed the form of a politico-religious movement, usually directed against invaders of foreign influences on the monarchy. In 1978/79 it played a key role in dethroning the Shah in Iran. In 1977 there were 33 million Shi'ites in Iran, 17 million in India, 15 million in Pakistan, 7.2 million in Afghanistan, 4.8 million in Iraq, 1.1 million in Lebanon, and 5.7 million in dispersion; in total more than 86 million.

D.M. DONALDSON, *The Shi'ite Religion*, London, 1933; J.R.I. COLE, N.R. KEDDI eds., *Shi'ism and Social Protest*, London, 1986; M. KRAMER ed., *Shi'ism, Resistance and Revolution*, London, 1987.

SHILLING. A monetary unit of Kenya; one shilling = 100 cents, first issued Sept. 14, 1966 (replacing the East African shilling) by the Central Bank of Kenya – Banki Kuu Ya Kenya.

SHILLING. A monetary unit of Tanzania; one shilling = 100 cents; issued (replacing the East African shilling) since June 14, 1966 by the Bank of Tanzania.

S

SHILLING. A monetary unit of Uganda; one shilling = 100 cents; issued (replacing the East African Shilling Dec. 15, 1966) by the Bank of Uganda.

SHIMONOSEKI. A port city in Japan in the province of Yamaguchi; place of the attack by the French fleet 1863 and the signing of peace treaty between China and Japan, 1895.

SHIMONOSEKI PEACE TREATY, 1895. A Treaty between China and Japan, signed on Apr. 17, 1895 in Shimonoseki, Japan. China recognized the full and complete independence and autonomy of Korea (art. I); China ceded to Japan "the southern portion of the Province of Fêg-Tien, the Island of Formosa and the Pescadores Islands" (art. II) and China agreed to pay Japan a war indemnity (art. V).

Major Peace Treaties of Modern History, New York, 1968, pp. 1101–1110.

SHINTO. *Japanese* = "way of the Gods." The *de facto* state religion of Japan, in Europe called Shintoism, expressing itself in the worship of nature and the cult of deceased ancestors, particularly that of the ancestors of the imperial line, which gave it the character of a state religion.

GENCHI KATÔ, *A Study of Shinto, the Religion of the Japanese Nation*, 1926; GENCHI KATÔ, *A Bibliography of Shinto in Western Languages from the Oldest Time until 1952*, London, 1952.

SHIPOWNERS' LIABILITY CONVENTION, 1976. ▷ Maritime Law Conventions, 1882–1978.

SHIPPERS. Individual or legal persons sending or receiving goods via sea as their present or future owners; thus the term does not include forwarding agents, but solely the real owners of cargoes transported by sea. They form national shippers councils, Reg. with the UIA:

European National Shippers Council, f. 1975, The Hague.

Yearbook of International Organizations.

SHIPPING. A subject of international co-operation and agreements. International organizations reg. with the UIA:

Arab Shipbuilding and Repair Company, f. 1974, Kuwait.
Association of West European Shipbuilders, f. 1970, Copenhagen.
Baltic and International Maritime Council, f. 1905, Copenhagen, Denmark; to unite shipowners and shipbuilders.
Committee of European Shipowners Associations, f. 1970, London.
Committee on Shipping of the ▷ UNCTAD.
Eastern African National Shipping Line, f. 1966, Dar-es-Salaam.
European Committees Shipowners Associations Organization, f. 1966, Brussels.
European National Shippers Council, f. 1975, The Hague.
Federation of National Associations of Ship Brokers and Agents, f. 1969, London. Consultative status with UNCTAD.
International Chamber of Shipping, f. 1921, London. Consultative status with ITU, IMCO, WHO, ECOSOC, UNCTAD and UPU. Aim: to promote internationally the interests of its members in general shipping matters, including marine safety, navigation, insurance, maritime law, documentation and pollution control.
International Passenger Ship Association, f. 1972, New York.
International Ship Electric Service Association, ISES, est. 1964, Manchester.
International Shipowners Association, f. 1970, Gdynia, Poland. Consultative status with UNCTAD, and

IMCO. Agreement of Co-operation with Vessels CMEA Chartering Bureau, Members: State-owned and private shipowning enterprises and shipowner associations in Bulgaria, Cuba, Czechoslovakia, GDR, Hungary, India, Poland, USSR and Yugoslavia.
The International Shipping Federation Ltd., f. 1909, London. Consultative status with ECOSOC, IMCO and ILO. Aims: considers all question of the shipping industry particularly within the sphere of ILO and IMCO.
International Ship Suppliers Association, ISSD, est. 1955, The Hague, secretariat in Hamburg. Publ.: *ISSA Conditions*.
Latin American Shipowner Association, Asociación Latino-Americana de Armadores, ALAMAR, f. 1963, Montevideo. Members: National associations of Argentina, Brazil, Chile, Colombia, Ecuador, Mexico, Paraguay, Peru, Uruguay, Venezuela. Consultative status with UNCTAD, ECOSOC AND IMCO.
Northern Shipowners Defence Club, f. 1889, Oslo, Norway; to assist members in dispute over contracts. Members; Scandinavian shipowners. Publ.: A Law Report of Scandinavian Maritime Cases (annually).
World Ship Society, f. 1946, Haywards Heath, UK.

On Oct. 28, 1988 The International Maritime Organization ▷ IMO approved new safety standards aimed at reducing the possibility of passenger ships capsizing after being damaged. The measures are to apply to all ships built after April 1990.

Yearbook of International Organizations, 1986/87; The Europa Yearbook 1988. A World Survey, Vol. I, London, 1988; KEESING's *Record of World Events*, No. 11, 1988.

SHIPPING BLACK SEA LINE. A regular shipping line between the Black Sea ports of the USSR, Romania, Bulgaria and also the ports of Albania, est. Aug. 20, 1954 at Moscow by an Agreement in order to maintain regular cargo and passenger maritime carriage between the ports of Odessa, Constanza, Varna and Durres.

W.E. BUTLER (ed.), *A Source Book on Socialist International Organizations*, Alphen, 1978, pp. 1060–1062.

SHIPPING CONFERENCES OR LINER CONFERENCES. The meetings of two or more shipping lines with the aim of establishing sailing schedules, tariffs, cargo transport etc. ▷ Liner Conferences Code.

SHIPPING EXCHANGE. International meeting place of the members of s.e., shipowners and ship-brokers seeking cargo as well as buyers seeking suitable tonnage. In Europe the world's largest s.e. for shipping transactions is the London Baltic Mercantile and Shipping Exchange (in short Balticex-change).

SHIPPING LAW AND INTERNATIONAL LEGISLATION. A branch of law, subject of international law since 1897, when the International Maritime Committee was established with the task of carrying out codification of shipping law; subject of international conventions prepared mainly by the aforementioned committee or by ILO. After the wreckage of the *Titanic* in 1912, work was initiated on preparing international conventions on the safety of life at sea. The same year saw the introduction of the London Convention concerning security of life at sea, signed in 1914, and entered into force with amendments in 1929; modernized in 1960. The general principles concerning safety of life at sea are included in the Geneva Convention on the High Sea, concluded in 1958.
Initially, the codification of the shipping law referred only to capitalist states and their shipping laws (American, British, French, Scandinavian etc.). Starting in 1929, when the first codification of

shipping law of socialist countries was introduced (The Code of Seagoing Merchant Shipping of the USSR), other socialist states also began their codification work to this end. In general, international conventions on the subject of shipping law fall into three travel categories: (1) property shipping law, initiated in 1905 with the participation of 13 coastal states, held in 1961 and 1962 with the participation of over 50 states; (2) concerning labor law at sea – the conventions prepared and adopted by Conferences of the ILO; (3) concerning administrative law of the sea, including also provisions on international law of the sea, as e.g. Barcelona Convention on the Banner of a ship of each state without access to sea; London Shipping Conventions: Convention of 1930 concerning shipping lines; convention of May 12, 1954 on water pollution, on preservation of undersea cables, etc.
All conventions and international agreements on the shipping law were concluded in the 20th century.
The science of shipping law has been developing since the 19th century. The first collection of texts on shipping law was published in Paris 1828–45. In Paris, the Institut de droit has been publishing since 1929 shipping codes of coastal states, as e.g. in 1970 *Codex maritime polonais*. In Great Britain, the publication entitled *The Library of Shipping Law* has become an institution.
The source of socialist shipping law is the *Kodeks torghovogo moryueplavanyia SSR* of July 14, 1929.
The international conventions, uniform rules and similar instruments dealing with international legislation on shipping are as follows:
Convention for the Unification of Certain Rules with respect to assistance and Salvage at Sea, signed on Sept. 23, 1910 at Brussels.
International Convention for the Unification of Certain Rules of Law with respect to Collision between Vessels, signed on Sept. 23, 1910 at Brussels, entered into force on March 1, 1912, ratified by: Argentina, Australia, Austria, Barbados, Belgium, Brazil, Canada, Ceylon, Cyprus, Danzig, Denmark, East Africa, Egypt, Estonia, Federated Malay States, Fiji, Finland, France, Gambia, Germany, Ghana, Greece, Guyana, Haiti, Hungary, India, Ireland, Iran, Italy, Jamaica, Japan, Latvia, Madagascar, Malta, Mauritius, Mexico, the Netherlands, New Zealand, Newfoundland, Nicaragua, Nigeria, Norway, Paraguay, Poland, Portugal, Romania, Sierra Leone, Somalia, Spain, Sweden, Switzerland, Trinidad and Tobago, Turkey, UK, USSR, Uruguay, Yugoslavia, Zaïre.
The Convention was signed but not ratified by Chile, Cuba, and the USA. The text of the first articles are as follows:
"Art. 1. Where a collision occurs between sea-going vessels or between sea-going vessels and vessels of inland navigation, the compensation due for damages caused to the vessels, or to any things or persons on board thereof, shall be settled in accordance with the following provisions, in whatever waters the collision takes place.
Art. 2. If the collision is accidental, if it is caused by force majeure, or if the cause of the collision is left in doubt, the damages are borne by those who have suffered them. This provision is applicable notwithstanding the fact that the vessels, or any one of them, may be at anchor (or otherwise made fast) at the time of the casualty.
Art. 3. If the collision is caused by the fault of one of the vessels, liability to make good the damages attaches to the one which has committed the fault.
Art. 4. If two or more vessels are in fault the liability of each vessel is in proportion to the degree of the faults respectively committed. Provided that if, having regard to the circumstances, if is not possible to establish the degree of the respective faults, or if it appears that the faults are equal, the liability is apportioned equally."

(*Great Britain Treaty Series*, 1913, p. 41).
International Convention for the Unification of Certain Rules relating to Bills of Lading, signed on Aug. 25, 1925 at Brussels; entered into force on June 2, 1931; ratified by Algeria, Argentina, Australia, Barbados, Cameroon, Ceylon, Cyprus, Denmark, Egypt, Fiji, Finland, France, Gambia, Germany, Ghana, Guyana, Hungary, Iran, Ireland, Israel, Italy, Ivory Coast, Jamaica, Japan, Kenya, Kuwait, Madagascar, Malay States, Mauritius, Monaco, the Netherlands, Norway, Paraguay, Peru, Poland, Portugal, Romania, Spain, Sweden, Switzerland, Tanzania, UK, USA, Yugoslavia, Zaïre. The Convention was signed but not ratified by Chile and Estonia (*LNTS*, Vol. 120, p. 157). The ▷ Bustamante Code of Private International Law, 1928, includes (arts. 274–294) rules on shipping.
International Convention for the Unification of Certain Rules relating to the Immunity of State-Owned Ships, signed on Apr. 10, 1926 at Brussels, (*International Legislation*, Hudson, Vol. 3, p. 1837).
International Convention for the Unification of Certain Rules relating to the Limitation of the Liability of Owners of Seagoing Vessels, signed on Aug. 25, 1924 at Brussels; entered into force on June 2, 1931; ratified by Belgium, Brazil, Dominican Republic, France, Hungary, Madagascar, Monaco, Poland, Portugal, Spain and Turkey. The Convention was signed but not ratified by Argentina, Chile, Denmark, Estonia, Italy, Japan, Latvia, Norway, Romania, UK, Sweden and Yugoslavia (*LNTS*, Vol. 120, p. 125).
International Convention for the Unification of Certain Rules relating to Maritime Liens and Mortgages, signed Apr. 10, 1926 at Brussels; entered into force on June 2, 1931; ratified by: Algeria, Argentina, Belgium, Brazil, Democratic Republic of the Congo, Estonia, France, Haiti, Hungary, Iran, Italy, Lebanon, Madagascar, Monaco, Poland, Portugal, Romania, Spain, Switzerland, Syria, Turkey.
International Convention between Belgium, Denmark, Finland, France, Iceland, the Netherlands, Norway and Sweden, for a Uniform System of Tonnage Measurement of ships, signed (with Final Protocol and International Regulations and Figures) on June 10, 1947 in Oslo. (*UNTS*, Vol. 208, p. 3).
Treaty on International Commercial Navigation Law, signed on March 19, 1940, at Montevideo, ratified by Argentina, Paraguay and Uruguay. The Treaty was signed but not ratified by Bolivia, Brazil, Chile, Colombia and Peru (*OAS Treaty*, Series, No. 9).
The ▷ Warsaw–Oxford Rules, 1932.
The ▷ York–Antwerp Rules, 1950.
International Convention relating to the Arrest of Seagoing Ships, signed on May 10, 1952 at Brussels; entered into force on Feb. 24, 1956, ratified by Algeria, Belgium, Cameroon, Costa Rica, Egypt, Fiji, France, Greece, Guyana, Haiti, Holy See, Khmer Republic, Madagascar, Mauritius, Nigeria, Paraguay, Portugal, Spain, Switzerland, Syrian Arab Republic, Togo, UK. The Convention was signed but not ratified by Brazil, Italy, Lebanon, Mexico, Nicaragua (*UNTS*, Vol. 439, p. 195).
International Convention on Certain Rules Concerning Civil Jurisdiction in Matters of Collision, signed on May 10, 1952 at Brussels, entered into force on Sept. 14, 1955; ratified by Algeria, Argentina, Belgium, Cameroon, Costa Rica, Egypt, Fiji, France, Greece, Guyana, Holy See, Khmer Republic, Madagascar, Mauritius, Nigeria, Paraguay, Portugal, Spain, Switzerland, Togo, UK. The Convention was signed but not ratified by Brazil, Denmark, FRG, Italy, Lebanon, Monaco, Nicaragua (*UNTS*, Vol. 439, p. 219).
International Convention relating to the Limitation of the Liability of Owners of Sea-Going Ships, signed on Oct. 10, 1957 at Brussels, entered into force May 31, 1968, ratified by Algeria, Denmark, Egypt, Fiji, Finland, France, Ghana, Guyana, Iceland, India, Iran, Israel, Madagascar, Mauritius, the Netherlands, New Hebrides, Norway, Portugal, Singapore, Spain, Sweden, Switzerland, Syrian Arab Republic, the UK and Zaïre. The Convention was signed but not ratified by Belgium, Brazil, Canada, FRG, Holy See, Italy, Peru, Poland and Yugoslavia (*UNIDROIT Yearbook*, 1957, p. 303).
Convention relating to the Unification of Certain Rules concerning Collision in Inland Navigation, signed Mar. 15, 1960 at Geneva (*UNTS*, Vol. 572, p. 147).
Convention on the Liability of Operators of Nuclear Ships, signed on May 25, 1962 at Brussels (N. Singh

(ed.), *British Shipping Law; International Conventions*, Vol. 8, p. 1071).
Convention on the Registration of Inland Navigation Vessels with annexed two Protocols, signed on Jan. 25, 1965 at Geneva (Doc. E/ECE/579).
Convention on the Facilitation of International Maritime Traffic, signed Apr. 19, 1965 at London (*UNTS*, Vol. 591, p. 266).
International Convention relating to the Registration of Rights in respect of Vessels under Construction, signed at Brussels May 27, 1967 (*Le Droit Maritime Français*, Vol. 19, p. 596).
International Convention for the Unification of Certain Rules relating to Maritime Liens and Mortgages, signed on May 27, 1967 at Brussels, has not entered into force; signed by Austria, Belgium, Republic of China, Congo, Denmark, Finland, FRG, Greece, Holy See, India, Iran, Ireland, Israel, Italy, Liberia, Monaco, Poland, Portugal, Sweden, Switzerland, the UK, Uruguay, and Yugoslavia. Protocol to amend the International Convention for the Unification of Certain Rules of Law relating to Bills of Lading, 1924, signed of Feb. 23, 1968 at Brussels, by Argentina, Belgium, Cameroon, Canada, Finland, France, Federal Republic of Germany, Greece, Holy See, Italy, Liberia, Mauritania, Paraguay, Philippines, Poland, Republic of China, United Kingdom of Great Britain and Northern Ireland, United States of America, Uruguay, Sweden, Switzerland, Zaïre; has not entered into force. (*Register of Texts of Conventions and Other Instruments Concerning International Trade Law*, UN New York, 1973, Vol. II, p. 180).
Convention on a Code of Conduct for Liner Conferences, adopted on Apr. 6, 1974, came into force Apr. 6, 1983. (▷ Liner Conferences Codes).
The International Institute for the Unification of Private Law prepared 1958, a Preliminary Draft Convention to the Limitation of Liability of Boat Owners; and in 1970 a Draft Convention on the International Combined Transport of Goods (TCM Convention). The second Draft Convention was adopted by IMCO in Nov., 1971, and relates to the transport of goods between at least two states by at least two different modes of transport (*UNIDROIT Yearbook*, 1958; *IMCO Doc. CTC*, Jan. 24, 1972).

J.M. PARDESSUS, *Collection des lois maritimes antérieures au XVIII siècle*, 6 Vols., Paris 1828–45; A.D. KEILIN, *Sovietskoe morskoe pravo*, Moscow, 1954; W.E. BUTLER, *The Soviet Union and the Law of Sea*, Baltimore, 1971; *Instrumentos nacionales e internacionales sobre el Derecho del mar*, Lima, 1971; *UN Chronicle*, November 1980, p. 50.

SHIPPING MARKETS. The sea or interland shipping centers where freight transactions take place between ship owners and cargo owners.

SHIPS NATIONALITY. ▷ Nationality of Ships.

SHIPS REGISTRATION. A subject of international agreements, relating to the commercial ships insurance. In 1984 the UN Conference on Conditions for Registration of Ships concluded an Informational Agreement on Conditions for the Registration of Ships.

UN Chronicle, January, 1984, pp. 92–93; *UN Chronicle*, 1985, No. 2, p. 16.

SHIP, VESSEL. Two international terms used to distinguish two basic types of sea-going craft: merchant ships and warships. In international treaties the following definition of a ship is accepted: "Any floating mechanism authorized to fly the flag of one of the Agreeing Parties, but does not include warships."

SHIPWRECK AT SEA. Any serious damage of a vessel as a result of collision with another vessel, or an iceberg, break-up, running aground, fire or explosion on board; subject of international regulations and conventions.

SHIPYARDS AND SHIPBUILDERS. International organizations reg. with the UIA:

Arab Shipbuilding and Repair Company, f. 1974, Kuwait.
Association of West European Shipbuilders, f. 1970, Copenhagen.
International Brotherhood of Boilermakers, Iron Shipbuilders, Blacksmiths, Forgers, f. 1880, Kansas City.

R. POLLARD, P. ROBERTSON, *British Shipbuilding 1870–1914*, Harvard, 1979.

SHOE. A subject of international co-operation. Organizations reg. with the UIA:

International Federation of the Independent Shoe Trade, f. 1958, Geneva.
Latin American Federation of Workers of the Textile, Clothing, Leather and Shoe Industry, f. 1972, Montevideo.

Yearbook of International Organizations.

SHOOTING. An Olympic sport since the First Olympic Games 1896, organized in the International Shooting Union, f. 1907 in London. Recognized by the International Olympic Committee. World Championships. Publ.: *International Shooting Sport*. Reg. with the UIA.

Yearbook of International Organizations.

SHOPPING CENTRES. Subject of international co-operation. Organization reg. with the UIA:

International Council of Shopping Centres, f. 1957, New York, N.Y., USA.

Yearbook of International Organizations 1986/87; The Europa Yearbook 1988. A World Survey, Vol. I, London, 1988.

SHORTHAND AND TYPING. A subject of international co-operation. Organization reg. with the UIA:

International Federation of Shorthand and Typewriting, f. 1954, Berne.

Yearbook of International Organizations.

SHRIMPS. A subject of research and promotion by the International Trade Center UNCTAD/GATT, Geneva.

ITC, *Shrimps: A Survey of the World Market*, Geneva, 1983.

SHULTZ DOCTRINE, 1984. The thesis of the USA Secretary of State, George Shultz, after the tragic death of Indira Gandhi on Oct. 30, 1984, that ▷ terrorism is an international problem that requires antiterroristic international action.

SI. The International System of Units, adopted by the General Conference of Weights and Measures, 1960 with the international abbreviation SI; published by the International Bureau of Weights and Measures. SI units are divided into three classes: base units, derived units and supplementary units.
SI base units: unit of length (▷ meter), unit of mass (▷ kilogram), unit of time (▷ second), unit of electric current (▷ ampère), unit of thermodynamic temperature (▷ kelvin), unit of amounts of substance (▷ mole) and unit of luminous intensity (▷ candela).
SI base units symbols are shown in the table.

Quantity	Name	Symbol
Length	meter	m
Mass	kilogram	kg
Time	second	s
Electric current	ampere	A
Thermodynamic temperature	kelvin	K
Amount of substance	mole	mol
Luminous intensity	candela	cd

Roman type, in general lower case, is used for symbols of units; if, however, the symbols are

S

derived from proper names, capital roman type is used (for the first letter). Unit symbols do not change in the plural.

SI derived units are expressed algebraically in terms of base units by means of the mathematical symbols of multiplication and division. Several derived units have been given special names and symbols which may themselves be used to express other derived units in a simpler way than in terms of the base units. Derived units may therefore be classified under three headings:

(1) SI derived units expressed in terms of basic units (example: luminance – candela per square meter – cd/m^2).

(2) SI derived units with special name (example frequency – hertz – s^{-1}).

(3) SI derived units expressed by means of special names (example: power density – watt per W/m^2 – $kg \cdot s^{-3}$).

The International Committee of Weights and Measures recognized that users of SI will also wish to employ with it certain units not part of it, but which are important and are widely used. These units are: minute, hour, day, degree, liter, ton. The Committee recognized also units whose values in SI are obtained experimentally (electronvolt, unified mass unit, astronomical unit, parsec) or units to be used temporarily with the SI system (nautical mile, knot, ångström, acre, hectare, barn, bar, standard atmosphere, gallon, curie, röntgen, rad).

Units which the Committee considers that it is generally preferable to avoid (using instead units of the SI system) are the following: erg. fermi, gauss, micron, stere, torr.

Ch.H. PAGE, P. VIGOREUX, *SI. The International System of Units*. London, HMSO, 1977.

SIBERIA. Vast geographical region of Asian Russia; colonized 1581–1890 by the Russian empire; used as a penal and a resettlement colony for political prisoners also under the Soviet administration. In 1918–20 during the civil war a part of Siberia with Orush was in the hands of Adm. A.V. Kolchak of the White Forces, supported by expeditionary British, French, Japanese and US forces. In the 1980's connected by ▷ oil and gas piplines with Western Europe. Border problems with the People's Republic of China (▷ Ussuri River).

H.H. FISHER ed., *The Testimony of Kolchak and Other Siberian Materials*, New York, 1935; D.W. TREDGOLD, *The Great Siberian Migration*, London, 1957; R. SWERRINGEN ed., *Siberia and the Soviet Far East: Strategic Dimensions in Multinational Perspectives*, Stanford, Ca., 1987.

SIBCM. ▷ Midgetman.

SICHERHEITSPOLIZEI. *German:* "security police". A political police unit of the German Reich, for short called SIPO, dissolved Oct. 4, 1920 at the demand of the Allies. In 1936 in the III Reich the political and criminal police were combined into one uniform security police by H. Himmler (1900–45) with the return of the historical name and abbrev. SIPO "to emphasize the German police tradition." At the Nuremberg Trial it was recognized as a criminal organization. ▷ Gestapo.

SICK MAN OF EUROPE. A name applicated to Turkey in the 19th century.

SIDI-IFNI. Formerly Ifni. A region of Morocco, 1502 sq. km on the Atlantic Ocean, with *c.* 100,000 inhabitants 1980; subject of dispute involving Morocco and Spain. The latter under the terms of a Treaty of Tetuan 1860, assumed administrative control over the enclave of Ifni confirmed by the 1912 Madrid Convention. After regaining independence in 1956, Morocco commenced negotiations with Spain which refused to return Ifni and annexed it formally in 1958 as its overseas province, an action not recognized by the UN. On Dec. 20, 1966, the UN General Assembly ordered a plebiscite resulting in the incorporation of Ifni into Morocco on June 30, 1969 under the name Sidi-Ifni.

R. PELISSIER, *Les territoires espagnoles d'Afrique*, Paris, 1963.

SIEGFRIED LINE. A defense line constructed after Hitler's accession to power in the years 1936–39 on the western border of Germany in the section from the Netherlands to Switzerland, with a length of 500 km and a depth of from 35 to 100 km.

SIERRA LEONE. Member of the UN. Republic of Sierra Leone. A country in West Africa on the Atlantic, bordering on Guinea and Liberia. Area: 71,740 sq. km. Pop. 1988 est.: 3,880,000 (1974 census: 2,735,159). Capital: Freetown, with 274,000 inhabitants (1974). Official language: English. Currency: one Leone = 100 cents. GNP per capita 1986: US \$310. National day: Apr. 19, proclamation of republic, 1971.

Member of the UN since Sept. 18, 1961 and all its specialized agencies; member of the OAU; member of the Commonwealth; ACP state of the EEC.

International relations: from 1787 to 1928 British colony and protectorate. 1928 abolition of slavery and new colonial status; republic within British Commonwealth since Apr. 27, 1961; full independence since Apr. 19, 1971.

A signatory of the Lomé Conventions of 1975, 1980 and 1985.

D.T. JACK, *Economic Survey of Sierra Leone*, Freetown, 1958; C. TYFE, *A History of Sierra Leone*, Freetown, 1962; R.S. SAYLOR, *The Economic System of Sierra Leone*, Duke University Press, 1968; B.A. WAPENSKY, *Banking and Finance in Sierra Leone. A Developing Economy*, Atlanta, 1968; A.P. KUP, *Sierra Leone*, Newton Abbot, 1975; *The Europa Year Book 1984. A World Survey*, Vol. II, pp. 2355–2364, London, 1984.

SIFIDA. Société internationale financière pour les investissements et le développement en Afrique, an investment company, incorporated in Luxembourg 1970, with headquarters in Geneva, by an international group of investors, including the African Development Bank, the IFC and other institutions from 13 developed countries. Aim: "Promoting of private investment in Africa, particularly in manufacturing, mining and tourism."

Yearbook of International Organizations.

SIGNALS BY SATELLITE CONVENTION. Est. 1988 as the Convention Relating to Distribution of Program-Carrying Signals Transmitted by Sattelite.

Economic Impact, Washington DC., 1988/3, p. 20.

SIGNALS CODE. A book of agreed signs used at sea, in the air and on the ground by voice, sound, sight, or radio signal. Each signal has a specific meaning written in the book. Signal codes were introduced at the beginning of the 19th century in France (1818) and Great Britain (1820), and the first international code was introduced in 1855, then revised in 1897 and 1934. Presently in force from Jan. 1, 1969 is the International Signals Code, a flag alphabet introduced by IMCO that does not require knowledge of foreign languages. The present code is greatly simplified, for it only goes up to 3 letters, while previous ones had signals up to 7 letters. One-letter signals are of great importance, two-letter ones are general signs, three-letter ones only medical. Cipher signals are used to supplement letter signals. The IMCO International Code was published in 9 language versions.

IMCO, *International Code*, Geneva, 1969.

SIGNATURE AND SIGNATURE AD REFERENDUM. A subject of the ▷ Vienna Convention on the Law of Treaties, 1969 (Art 12).

R.L. BLEDSOE, B.A. BOCZEK, *The International Law Dictionary*, Oxford, UK, 1987.

SIKHISM AND SIKHS. Religion combining Islamic and Hindu beliefs. The Sikhs (from Sanscrit: Sikh = disciple) believe in the ten guru and in the sacred book Granth Sahib. The Sikh empire, founded 1799 in the Punjab region was destroyed by British colonial troops during the Sikh wars 1845–46 and 1848–49. Under British rule the Sikhs served in the colonial army; in independent India after the partition of the Punjab the majority of Sikhs live in India, the minority in Pakistan. In the 1980's in conflict with the Indian government; in 1986 proclamation of ▷ Khalistan.

Sir C. GOUGH and A.D. INNES, *The Sikhs and the Sikh Wars*, London, 1987.

SIKKIM. A state of the Indian Union since Apr., 1975, south central Asia, in the eastern Himalayas, bounded on the north by Tibet, east by Tibet and Bhutan, south by West Bengal and west by Nepal. Area: 7,096 sq. km. Pop. 1981 census: 316,385. Under British protectorate 1839-1886 then integrated by the British Empire until 1947. Indian protectorate 1950–74 as constitutional monarchy. In 1974 Sikkim became a state associated with the Indian Union, and by the India Constitution Act 1975 the 22nd state of the Indian Union. The monarchy (Chogyal) was abolished. The capital: Gangtok. China on Apr. 26, 1975 filed a protest against the India Constitution Act 1975.

V.H. COELHO, *Sikkim and Bhutan*, New Delhi, 1970; F. MELE, *Sikkim*, Paris, 1975, *Peking Review*, May 2, 1975; *The Europa Year Book 1984. A World Survey*, Vol. II, pp. 1676–1679, London, 1984.

SILA. Servicio de Informacion de America Latina, Information Service of Latin America, name of a Latin American press agency; f. 1978 in Caracas for the purpose of making Latin American press less dependent on the foreign agencies.

SILESIA. Polish region of Central Europe, on both banks of the Oder River, bounded in the south by Sudetes and Carpathians mountain ranges, bordered in the west by the GDR, in the south by Czechoslovakia. Integral part of Poland since the 10th century; in 1335 posession of the king of Bohemia; 1526 passed to the house of Hapsburg: 1740 was taken by Prussia, 1919–39 divided between German Reich and Poland, returned to Poland by the Potsdam Agreement 1945. The German Democratic Republic accepted the Potsdam frontier by the Zgorzelec Treaty 1949 and the Federal Republic of Germany relinquished all claims in a 1972 Warsaw agreement with Poland. The German "Provinz Schlesien" covered until 1939 an area of 36,696 sq. km with 4,815,000 in habitants (census of May 17, 1939). The Polish "Województwo Śląskie" until 1939 covered 4216 sq. km with 1,312,000 inhabitants (est. Sept. 1, 1939). The population of Silesia in 1960 passed the prewar number of inhabitants, reaching 6,440,378 and in 1980 – c. 8,000,000.

J. PARTSCH, *Schlesien*, 2 Vols., Breslau, 1896–1911; S. KUTRZEBA, W. SEMKOWICZ *et al.*, *Historia Śląska* (History of Silesia), 3 Vols., Kraków, 1933–1936; K. POPIOŁEK, *Silesia in German Eyes 1939–1945*, Katowice, 1964; K. SMOGORZEWSKI,

"Silesia", in: *The Encyclopedia Britannica*, 1973, Vol. 20, pp. 509–511.

SILESIA INSTITUTE. *Polish*: Instytut Śląski w Opolu. A scientific society, f. 1934 in Katowice, during the war in underground in Cracow, reactivated in 1957 in Opole under direction of Prof. J. Kokot (1916–75), author of the *Logic of Potsdam*. Publ. *Przegląd Stosunków Międzynarodowych* (Review of International Relations) and *Studia Śląskie* (Silesia Study).

SILESIA UPRISINGS. ▷ Polish Uprisings in Silesia, 1919–21.

SILK. Subject of international research and co-operation. Organization registered with the UIA:

International Silk Association, f. 1949, Lyon, France, Publ. *Bulletin*, in English and French.

Yearbook of International Organizations.

SILO. An international military term for shelters storing ballistic missiles in holes in the ground protected by a thick layer of concrete and steel shell. In the 1980's the great vulnerability of the silo caused by the development of high accuracy ICBM's is a problem for both NATO and the Warsaw Pact.

D. ROBERTSON, *Guide to Modern Defense and Strategy*, Detroit, 1988.

SILVER. A subject of international agreements. One of the oldest, besides ▷ Gold, means of payment; from the times of ancient Egypt 3000 B.C. until the end of the 19th century together with gold formed a bimetallic system; devalued in the 19th century as a result of mass mining of silver; became more of an industrial than a monetary metal, though in Asia, Africa and Latin America many silver coins remained in circulation up to the middle of the 20th century. The term "silver standard" was a general name for all of the international monetary systems which had a fixed relation between the value of their currency and a specific amount of silver in grams. The main countries producing silver: Mexico, USA, USSR, Canada, Peru, Australia, Bolivia, Japan, Honduras, Zaïre, Yugoslavia. The relation of silver to gold in antiquity was 12:1, at the beginning of the 19th century 16:1, at the end of the 19th century 22:1.

In the 20th century the use of silver for industrial purposes increased considerably, which resulted in a rising trend for the price of silver (more than three-fold in the period 1950–75) and a continual increase in production (more than 50% in the period 1950–75).

The Netherlands and the FRG witnessed a thesaurization of silver coins as having a greater value as metal than their nominal value, and their replacement with nickel coins.

Organizations reg. with the UIA.

Silver League, Argentarius Ligae, est. 1973, Paris. International Federation of Watch, Jewellery, Gold and Silverware Retailers of the EEC Countries, f. 1959, Brussels.

Silver coins were the subject of a monetary Convention of the governments of Belgium, France, Greece, Italy, and Switzerland, signed on Nov. 6, 1885 and a supplementary Convention, signed on Mar. 25, 1920 in Paris.

In Jan., 1955 silver was selling at about $1 an ounce; in Jan., 1979 at about $6.5 and in Oct. 1979 $17.6 an ounce. In the same period 1979 the gold price had risen *c.* 84%. The bullish factors for silver are heavy industrial demand, especially in the photographic industry, and the issue of silver coins in 80 countries, consuming 30 million ounces yearly.

F.X. CASTELLANOS, M.A. CORREA, *La Plata en el Mercado Mundial 1900–1961*, México, DF, 1962; F. PICK, *Silver, How and Where to Buy and Hold It*, New York, 1965.

SIMEN NATIONAL PARK. An Ethiopian natural site, included in the ▷ World Heritage UNESCO List. In the north-west of the Ethiopian plateau, erosion on a gigantic scale has produced sharply chiselled peaks, gouged-out valleys and carved sheer precipices a thousand metres high. In this region live animals which are now extremely rare, such as the Walia Ibex, the Gelada Baboon and the Simen Fox.

UNESCO. *A Legacy for All*, Paris, 1984.

SIMLA. A town in northwest India, capital of Himachal Pradesh state, summer resort and the headquarters of the Indian Army in the Western Himalayas on a ridge 2165 m high, linked with Delhi by railroad (282 km); place of the summit meeting of the President of Pakistan, Zulfikar Ali Bhutto, and the Premier of India, Indira Gandhi, July 1–3, 1972, which ended with the Simla Agreement, by which both sides agreed to refrain from the use of force in mutual relations and pledged themselves to the peaceful solution of disputed problems, i.e. the problems of ▷ Kashmir.

Pakistan ratified the agreement July 15, 1972, India on July 28, 1972.

E.F. BUCK, *Simla Past and Present*, London, 1904.

SINAI. The peninsula in northeastern Egypt; area: 59,570 sq. km; 370 km long and 240 km wide; bounded on the east by the Gulf of Aqaba, on the west by the Gulf of Suez. Occupied by Israel from Oct. 29, 1956 to Mar. 8, 1957, controlled by the UN Emergency Force until May 20, 1967, and again occupied by Israel from June 6, 1967 to Feb. 18, 1976; subject of the Egypt–Israel–USA agreement signed in Sept. 1975. Since Feb. 18, 1976 again controlled by UNEF.

"SINATRA DOCTRINE". Jocular term for the new non-interventionist policy of the Warsaw Pact States, whose foreign ministers officially renounced the ▷ Brezhnev Doctrine on Oct 26, 1989. The term was coined by Soviet government spokesman G. Gerasimov, who summed up the absolute right accorded each state to determine its own socio-political development in the phrase "They can do it their way" – a reference to F. Sinatra's hit song "My Way".

KEESING's *Record of World Events* Oct. 1989.

SINGAPORE. Member of the UN. Republic of Singapore. A country in Southeast Asia on Singapore Island and 54 adjacent islets. Area: 618 sq. km. Population 1987 est.: 2,610,000 (1970 census: 2,074,500 with 1,579,866 Chinese, 311,379 Malays, 145,196 Indians, and 38,093 others). Capital: Singapore City. Official languages: Chinese, Malay, Tamil, English. GNP per capita 1987: US $7464. Currency: one Singapore dollar = 100 cents. National day: Aug. 9, independence anniversary, 1965.

Member of the UN since Sept. 20, 1965 and all its specialized agencies except FAO, IDA, UNESCO, WIPO, IFAD and UNIDO; member of the Commonwealth, Colombo Plan, ASEAN.

International relations: the first "Lion City" (from Sanskrit *Singapura*), was a seaport erected 1297, destroyed 1376, rebuilt 1819 by East India Company; British colony from 1824 till 1959. In World War II occupied by Japan (Feb. 12, 1942–Sept. 5, 1945). Granted autonomous and 1959 independent status within British Commonwealth. In Sept., 1962 the population voted in plebiscite for union with the Malay Federation; on July 8, 1965 separated from Malaysia and proclaimed an independent republic. In 1971 Great Britain handed over its air base to Singapore and announced withdrawal of its navy from military bases in Singapore. Australia, Malaysia, New Zealand, Singapore and Great Britain signed an agreement on Apr. 16, 1971 on defense of Malaysia and Singapore, in which they obliged themselves to immediate consultation in case of aggression. Common air defense system in Malaysia and Singapore came into force on Sept. 1, 1971. Singapore City is the seat of seven international organizations reg. with the UIA (among others South-East Asia Iron–Steel Institute).

H.A.R. CRESHMAN, *Bibliography of Malaya*, London, 1959; I.P. TRUFANOV, *Singapur*, Moscow, 1967; J.B. OOI, *Modern Singapore*, Singapore, 1969; *The Statute of the Republic of Singapore*, 8 Vols., Singapore, 1970; *The Far East and Australasia, 1972*, London, 1972, pp. 593–620; YOU POH SING, LIM CHONG YAH, *The Singapore Economy*, Eastern Universities Press, 1972; A. JOSEY, *Lee Kuan Yew. The Struggle for Singapore*, 1972; R. WILSON, *The Future of Singapore. The Global City*, Singapore, 1973; R. CLUTTEBUCK, *Riot and Revolution in Singapore and Malaya, 1945–63*, London, 1973; T.J.S. GEORGE, *Lee Kuan Yew's Singapore*, London, 1973; S.Y. LEE, *The Monetary and Banking Development of Malaysia and Singapore*, Singapore, 1974; *Singapore and Finances*, Singapore, 1977; S.Y. LOE, *Public Finance and Public Investment in Singapore*, Singapore, 1978; C.H. TAN, *Financial Institutions in Singapore*, Singapore, 1978; S.H. SHAW, *Population Control for Zero Growth in Singapore*, Singapore, 1980; *The Europa Year Book 1984. A World Survey*, Vol. II, pp. 2365–2380, London, 1984.

SINHUA. The official Chinese press agency, f. 1944 in Yenan, since 1948 with headquarters in Peking; known abroad as the New China Agency.

SIPRI. Stockholm International Peace Research Institute, an independent Institute for research into problems of peace and conflict, especially those of disarmament and arms regulation. It was established in 1966 to commemorate Sweden's 150 years of unbroken peace. The Institute is financed by the Swedish Parliament.

SIPRI is a problem-oriented research institute: that is, it starts by considering what the topics of importance are in the area of world armaments and disarmament, and then considers what research approach is appropriate to these problems. The Institute is international. The research staff, Governing Board members and management are recruited from different geographical regions and economic systems. Thus SIPRI is not biased in favor of any one political or economic system or regional interest group. The Governing Board is responsible for the general direction of SIPRI's activities. In its decisions about the research it undertakes and publishes, SIPRI is entirely independent of Swedish state authorities.

It has a continuing interest in certain subjects, on which it has built up data banks. It has the only publicly accessible data bank in the world on transfers of major weapons; it reports every year on the arms trade, and has produced a major study on arms sales to Third World countries. It also maintains a unique data bank on launches of military satellites and one on world military expenditure, and comments on trends annually. The range of subjects with which SIPRI deals is indicated by the list of books which have been published. They cover, for example, a wide range of weapon developments – such as a six-volume study of chemical and biological warfare, and books on the militarization of outer space; a substantial quantity of background work on the Non-Proliferation Treaty; handbooks on arms control; studies of military research and development expenditure. The Institute's main publication is its yearbook of Armament and Disarmament.

It is a basic rule of the Institute that SIPRI's research should be based on open sources. Contacts are maintained with other research institutes and individual researchers throughout the world; and SIPRI researchers participate when appropriate in conferences and symposia organized elsewhere.

Researchers work either individually or in research on SIPRI projects: project proposals are considered by the Research Collegium and the Governing Board, and publications are refereed by independent experts outside the Institute. In addition to the researchers recruited for some years, there is a flow of guest researchers who spend a short time at SIPRI, and the Institute also uses consultants who work in their own countries on SIPRI's behalf.

SIPRI convenes symposia on various subjects, in order to bring in a wide range of expertise and views on some of the subjects which it studies. The purpose of the symposia is to improve the range and quality of the studies which SIPRI publishes.

SIPRI has been entirely financed by grants from the Swedish Parliament (though the statutes do not prevent SIPRI from seeking other sources of finance if it judges this to be necessary for its work). SIPRI is not a teaching institute. Its function is to produce and publish research work. There are thus no facilities for students to combine graduate work with research at the Institute. However, short-term research fellowships are available for scholars who can contribute to SIPRI's published output. SIPRI does not run courses. The seminars which it holds are primarily for the benefit of the resarch staff.

SIPRI started its activities in July, 1966. The first Director of the Institute was Professor Robert Neild, from the United Kingdom, now Professor of Economics at the University of Cambridge. In 1971 he was succeeded by Dr Frank Barnaby, nuclear physicist from the United Kingdom. The present Director, Mr Frank Blackaby, also from the UK, is an economist.

SPIRI's research programme basically covers eight areas: Arms Trade, Military Expenditure, Weapons Technology and Arms Control, Multilateral Arms Control, Chemical and Biological Weapons, European Security and Arms Control, The US-Soviet Strategic Relationship, Third World Countries, Development and Military Expenditure.

"Statute of the SIPRI", in: *SIPRI Information*, No. 1, 1983.

SIS. Secret Intelligence Service, the official name of the intelligence department of the UK.

SISAL. A subject of international co-operation and agreements. In the EEC system the ▷ STABEX includes sisal in the ACP countries.

SITZKRIEG. *German* = "sitting war". An international term for a war that has been declared, but *de facto* proceeds without any military action, coined to define the state of war in the fall and winter 1939/40 between Germany and France: *French* ▷ Drôle de guerre.

SI VIS PACEM PARA BELLUM. *Latin* = "if you desire peace, prepare for war". A Roman doctrine in modern formulation, based on the statement of the Roman military theorist Renatus Flavius Vegetius in a work published c. A.D. 375 entitled, *Epitoma institutionum rei militaris*: "*qui desiderat pacem, praeparet bellum*" (who desires peace, let him prepare for war).

T.R. PHILLIPS, *Roots of Strategy*, London, 1940.

SKAGERRAK. ▷ Danish straits.

SKAL CLUBS. An International Association of Skäl Clubs, f. 1934, Brussels. Aim: to develop friendship and common purpose between executives of the tourist industry. Clubs in 86 countries. Reg. with the UIA.

Yearbook of International Organizations.

SKANSEN. International term – ethnographic museum under the open sky, also an ethnographic park. Name accepted in 1891, the year in which the first museum was opened, its exhibits – characteristic Swedish country and town buildings as well as sacral monuments (totalling 160 objects) were amassed in a Stockholm park, called Skansen.

SKATING. An Olympic sport since 1908, organized by the International Skating Union, Union Interntionale de Patinage, UIP, f. in 1892, sponsoring world championships.

Yearbook of International Organizations.

SKIING. An Olympic sport since the First Winter Olympic Games, 1924, in Chamonix, organized by the International Skiing Federation, Fédération Internationale de Ski, FIS, in 1924; sponsoring world championships.

Yearbook of International Organizations.

SKIN BURNS. A subject of international co-operation under aegis of WHO. In 20th century the highly dangerous skin burns are caused not only by flames and hot fluids but also by chemicals (▷ napalm) and ▷ radiation. ▷ Burn Injuries.

J.F. BURKE, J.D. CONSTABLE, "Systematic Changes and Replacement Therapy in Burns", in: *Journal of Trauma*, 1965; W. RUDOWSKI, *Burns Therapy and Research*, Baltimore, 1976.

SKINS. A subject of international agreements. In the EEC system the ▷ STABEX includes skins and furs in the ACP countries.

SKOPJE OR SKOPLJE. Yugoslavian city (1971 pop. 312,092), capital of the Macedonian province; 80% destroyed July 26, 1967 by an earthquake, was rebuilt under the aegis of the UN.

UNDP, *Skopje Resurgent. The Story of a UN Special Fund Town Planning Project*, UN, New York, 1970.

"SKYLAB". Abbreviation for sky laboratory, term introduced by the American ▷ NASA for a three-person satellite laboratory, whose construction was begun in the USA in 1968 with a double safety feature: with a space ship by means of which the crew could return to Earth and a Saturn L-B rocket ready for launching in the event of the need for rescue efforts. In May, 1973, the first three-man crew went aboard Skylab orbiting more than 400 km above the Earth. ▷ Salut or Salyut.

SLAVERY. A system for keeping people in servile dependency, combatted internationally since the Congress of Vienna, 1815; subject of international conventions aimed at completely liquidating slavery in the world, which according to the UN Commission on Human Rights has still not been achieved. The chronology of the international struggle against slavery, is as follows:

1688 – Anti-slavery proclamation of American ▷ Mennonites.

1794 – The Jacobin Convention of the Republic of France announced the abolition of slavery in all French colonies; this resolution was repealed in 1809, and not until 1848 did France again abolish slavery.

1801 – the abolition of slavery in Haiti, repealed 1803.

1812 – in the Ghent Peace Treaty between the US and Great Britain both parties declared that the slave trade is "irreconcilable with the principles of Humanity" and therefore the two governments agreed to use their best endeavors to promote its abolition.

1814 – in the Treaty of Peace signed in Paris, France and Great Britain agreed to submit jointly to the Congress of Vienna a draft of a convention on the abolition of slavery by all of the Christian powers.

1815 – at the Congress of Vienna 8 European states decided to put an end to slavery "a plague which has so greatly depopulated Africa, debased Europe, and saddened Humanity."

1823 – the formal abolition of slavery in Chile. In London the first international organization, the British and Foreign Anti-Slavery Society, was established. In 1909 it changed its name to ▷ Anti-Slavery Society for the Protection of Human Rights.

1824 – the formal abolition of slavery by the Congress of the United Provinces of Central America.

1826 – the abolition of slavery in Mexico.

1833 – Great Britain calls for the abolition of slavery in all her colonies.

1841 – Austria, France, Great Britain, Prussia and Russia signed a Treaty on combined operations on the open sea against ships suspected of carrying slaves. Officers and men could be punished as pirates.

1842 – the Ashberston–Webster Treaty between Great Britain and the USA on co-operation on the Coast of Africa against slave ships flying their flag.

1848 – France abolished slavery in her colonies.

1851 – the abolition of slavery in Colombia.

1859 – a white US abolitionist, J. Brown, led a raid at Harpers Ferry, on behalf of freedom for Negroes; wounded, captured, tried and hung.

1860 – Holland abolished slavery in her colonies.

1863 – the president of the USA, A. Lincoln, proclaimed the emancipation of Negroes and accorded them the right to bear arms against the slavery states. About 186,000 Negroes joined the Army of the North; 68,000 were killed or wounded.

1873 – Spain and Portugal abolished slavery in their colonies.

1877 – the abolition of slavery on Madagascar.

1881 – the abolition of slavery in Cuba and Brazil.

1885 – the Colonial Conference on the Congo in Berlin resolved "to do everything possible to preserve the nomadic population in Africa ... and to combat slavery, and specially the traffic in Negro slaves."

1890 – Belgium abolished slavery in her colonies. The Colonial Conference in Brussels drafted and passed the General Act for the Repression of African Slave Trade, a convention on the use of military, economic and legal measures in the struggle to eliminate the traffic in slaves from Africa. (Full text in *International Conciliation*, No. 236, Jan., 1928, pp. 36–67).

1904 – in Paris on Mar. 18, 1904 the governments of Belgium, Denmark, France, Germany, Great Britain, Holland, Italy, Portugal, Russia, Sweden, and Switzerland signed the treaty on traffic in white slaves (*LNTS*, Vol. 1, p. 83).

1909 – the abolition of slavery in Zanzibar.

1910 – signed in Paris on May 4, 1910 the International Convention on the abolition of traffic in white slaves (*LNTS*, Vol. 3, p. 278); the supplementary protocol was signed at Lake Success May 4, 1949 by Brazil, China, Canada, Cuba, Great Britain, Luxembourg, Norway, Turkey, Yugoslavia and the USA (*LNTS*, Vol. 30, pp. 24–44).

1919 – after World War I the first Convention of Saint-Germain-en-Laye on the complete elimination of slavery in whatsoever form and on the treatment of slavery on land and at sea.

1921 – on Nov. 30, 1921 in Geneva the convention on the prohibition of traffic in women and children was signed by Albania, Austria, Belgium, Brazil, Chile, China, Colombia, Costa Rica, Czechoslovakia, Estonia, Germany, Great Britain, Greece, Holland, Italy, Japan, Lithuania, Norway, Persia, Poland, Portugal, Romania, Siam, Sweden, and Switzerland (*LNTS*, Vol. 9, p. 415).

1922 – the League of Nations created the Temporary Commission on Slavery, with special reference to Abyssinia.

1923 – the abolition of slavery in Rwanda.

1924 – the Temporary Commission on Slavery of the LN submitted to the LN Council the following syllabus of the matters to be considered by the Commission:

(1)(a) Enslaving of persons; slave raiding and the slave trade;

(b) Slave dealing (including transfer by exchange, sale, gift or inheritance);

(c) Slavery or serfdom (domestic or predial).

(2) Practices restrictive of the liberty of the person, or tending to acquire control of the person in conditions analogous to slavery, as for example:

(a) Acquisition of girls by purchase disguised as payment of dowry, it being understood that this does not refer to normal marriage customs;

(b) Adoption of children, of either sex, with a view to their virtual enslavement or the ultimate disposal of their persons;

(c) All forms of pledging or reducing to servitude of persons for debt or other reason.

(3) Measures taken to check practices under (1) and (2) and results obtained.

(4) System of compulsory labor, public, or private, paid or unpaid.

(5) Measures taken or contemplated to facilitate the transition from service or compulsory labor to free wage labor or independent production.

1926 – on Nov. 26, in Geneva 36 states signed the Slavery Convention. The Preamble and the Arts. 1 and 2 read as follows:

"Albania, Germany, Austria, Belgium, the British Empire, Canada, the Commonwealth of Australia, the Union of South Africa, the Dominion of New Zealand, India, Bulgaria, China, Colombia, Cuba, Denmark, Spain, Estonia, Abyssinia, Finland, France, Greece, Italy, Latvia, Liberia, Lithuania, Norway, Panama, the Netherlands, Persia, Poland, Portugal, Romania, the Kingdom of the Serbs, Croats and Slovenes, Sweden, Czechoslovakia, and Uruguay.

Whereas the signatories of the Convention of Saint-Germain-en-Laye of 1919 to revise the General Act of Berlin of 1885 and the General Act and Declaration of Brussels of 1890 affirmed their intention of securing the complete suppression of slavery in all its forms and of the slave trade by land and sea;

Taking into consideration the report of the Temporary Slavery Commission appointed by the Council of the League of Nations on June 12, 1924;

Desiring to complete and extend the work accomplished under the Brussels Act and to find a means of giving practical effect throughout the world to such intentions as were expressed in regard to slave trade and slavery by the signatories of the Convention of Saint-Germain-en-Laye, and recognizing that it is necessary to conclude to that end more detailed arrangements than are contained in that Convention;

Considering moreover, that it is necessary to prevent forced labor from developing into conditions analogous to slavery; Have decided to conclude a Convention and have accordingly appointed as their Plenipotentiaries:

Who, having communicated their full powers, have agreed as follows:

Art. 1. For the purpose of the present Convention, the following definitions are agreed upon:

(1) Slavery is the status or condition of a person over whom any or all of the powers attaching to the right of ownership are exercised.

(2) The slave trade includes all acts involved in the capture, acquisition, or disposal of a person with intent to reduce him to slavery; all acts involved in the acquisition of a slave with a view to selling or exchanging him; all acts of disposal by sale or exchange of a slave acquired with a view to being sold or exchanged, and, in general, every act of trade or transport in slaves.

Art. 2. The high contracting parties undertake, each in respect of the territories placed under its sovereignty, jurisdiction, protection, suzerainty or tutelage, so far as they have not already taken the necessary steps:

(a) To prevent and suppress the slave trave.

(b) To bring about, progressively and as soon as possible, the complete abolition of slavery in all its forms. (*LNTS*, Vol. 60, p. 263).

1928 – the abolition of slavery in Sierra Leone.

1932 – the LN created the Permanent Advising Committee on Slavery.

1948 – the Universal Declaration on Human Rights proclaimed that "it is forbidden to make anyone a slave or to impose servitude on anyone; slavery is forbidden in all of its forms."

1949 – the UN General Assembly charged ECOSOC to study the problem of slavery in the contemporary world. The data received from 75 states were published in 1967.

1953 – the UN General Assembly ratified the Protocol on modifying the Slavery Convention of 1926.

1956 – the UN Conference in Geneva ratified the supplementary Convention on the Abolition of Slavery traffic in Slaves, and Institutions and Practices Akin to Slavery; signed Sept. 7, 1956, entered into force April 30, 1957. ▷ Slavery Convention 1956.

1957 – the abolition of slavery in Oman.

1958 – the Convention on the Open Sea drafted in Geneva resolved in art. 13;

"All states will take effective measures not to allow the transport of slaves on ships having the right to sail under their flags and to mete out punishment for such transport and not to allow the use of their flags for such illegal purpose. Each slave who escapes to the deck of whatsoever ship irregardless of under which flag the ship is sailing ipso facto becomes a free man."

1962 – the abolition of slavery in Saudi Arabia with indemnity from the State treasury of 3000 dollars for each slave.

1967 – the UN Human Rights Commission during its session Feb. 23–Mar. 23 in Geneva stated that to this day slavery has still not been completely eliminated in the world; according to UN estimates *c.* 12 million people still live in servitude in Latin America, Africa, and South Asia.

1980 – Commission report to the XXXV Session of the UN General Assembly.

1982 – Report on slavery and slavery-like practices in Geneva session (Aug. 16–Sept. 10) of the Subcommission of the Commission on Human Rights. In 1987–88 the Government of Sudan was accused of tolerating the slave trade in Southern Sudan.

A Chronological Summary of the Work of the British and Foreign Anti-Slavery Society 1839–1900, London, 1950; *Provisional Bibliography on Slavery*, Washington, DC, 1950; M.P. FRONCOZO, *Institutions, Practices and Customs Similar to Slavery in Latin America*, UN Doc. E/AC 33/6, 1950; UN, *La répression de l'esclavage*, New York, 1951; M. SCHREIBER, "Convention supplémentaire des Nations Unies relative à l'abolition de l'esclavage", in: *Annuaire Français de Droit International*, 1956; *Conferencia de las UN sobre la Abolición de la Esclavitud*, 1956, New York, 1957; UN, *Informe sobre la Esclavitud*, New York, 1967; H. TINKER, *A New System of Slavery: The Export of Indian Labour Overseas 1830–1920*, Oxford, 1974; J.T. SELLIN, *Slavery and the Penal System*, Amsterdam, 1976; *Yearbook of the UN 1980*, New York, 1982, p. 883; *UN Chronicle*, November, 1982, p. 29–30; UN, *Slavery*, New York, 1984; R. SAWYER, *Slavery in the Twentieth Century*, London, 1986; P. KOLCHIN, *Unfree Labour. American Slavery and Russian Serfdom*, Boston, 1987.

SLAVERY CONVENTION, 1926 AND 1956. The Slavery Convention, signed at Geneva on Sept. 26, 1926 and by the Supplementary Convention on the Abolition of Slavery, the Slave Trade, and Institutions and Practices Similar to Slavery adopted at Geneva, Sept. 7, 1956; "Slavery" means the status or condition of a person over whom any or all of the powers attaching to the right of ownership are exercised, and "slave" means a person in such condition or status.

A "person of servile status" means a person in the condition of status resulting from any of the following institutions or practices, mentioned in Art. 1 of the Supplementary Convention 1956;

"(a) debt bondage, that is to say, the status or condition arising from a pledge by a debtor of his personal service or of those of a person under his control as security for a debt, if the value of those services as reasonably assessed is not applied towards the liquidation of the debt or the length and nature of those services are not respectively limited and defined;

(b) serfdom, that is to say, the condition or status of a tenant who is by law, custom or agreement bound to live and labour on land belonging to another person and to render some determinate service to such other person, whether for reward or not, and is not free to change his status;

(c) any institution or practices whereby:

(i) a woman, without the right to refuse, is promised or given in marriage on payment of a consideration in money or in kind to her parents, guardian, family or any other person or group; or

(ii) the husband of a woman, his family, or his clan, has the right to transfer her to another person for value received or otherwise; or

(iii) a woman on the death of her husband is liable to be inherited by another person;

(d) any institution or practice whereby a child or young person under the age of eighteen years is delivered by either or both of his natural parents or by his guardian to another person, whether for reward or not, with a view to the exploitation of the child or young person or of his labour."

The Supplementary Convention 1956 stated:

"The act of conveying or attempting to convey slaves from one country to another by whatever means of transport, or of being accessory thereto, shall be a criminal offence under the laws of the States Parties to this Convention and persons convicted thereof shall be liable to very severe penalties.

Any slave who takes refuge on board any vessel of a State Party to this Convention shall ipso facto be free. The act of enslaving another person or of inducing another person to give himself or a person dependent upon him into slavery, or of attempting these acts, or being accessory thereto, or being a party to a conspiracy to accomplish any such acts, shall be a criminal offence under the laws of the States Parties to this Convention and persons convicted thereof shall be liable to punishment."

This Convention entered into force July 1, 1957.

UN Conference on Slavery Abolition 1956, New York, 1957.

SLAVE TRADE. Defined in the Art. 7 of the Slavery Convention, 1926, as follows:

"The slave trade includes all acts involved in the capture, acquisition or disposal of a person with intent to reduce him to slavery; all acts involved in the acquisition of a slave with a view to selling or exchanging him; all acts of disposal by sale or exchange of a slave acquired with a view to being sold or exchanged, and, in general, every act of trade or transport in slaves."

S

LNTS, Vol. 60, p. 263; Ph.D: CURTIN, *The Atlantic Slave Trade: A Census*, Madison, Wis. 1969.

SLAVIC CONGRESSES. The First Slavic Congress was held in Prague Apr. 2–12, 1848 as a manifestation of Austro-Slavism, with the participation of 340 delegates of Slavic groups living in Austria, among them 42 Serbs, Croats and Slovenes, 61 Poles and Ruthenians, and 237 Czechs, Moravians and Slovaks; M.I. Bakunin of Russia attended as a guest and came out in favor of democratic Pan-Slavism. The Second Slavic Congress took place in Moscow in 1867 and had a conservative Pan-Slavistic character. The two Congresses of 1908 in Prague and 1909 in Sofia, promoting Neo-Slavism, were of a similar character.

A.N. PYPIN, *Panslavism v proshlom i nastoiashchem*, Saint Petersburg, 1913; J.S. ROUČEK (ed.), *Slavonic Encyclopedia*, New York, 1949.

SLAVONIC BANK COMPANY. *Polish*: Bank Słowiański; *German*: Slawische Bank, central financial institution of Polish co-operative societies in the German Reich 1933–39; est. at the suggestion of the Union of Poles in Germany and the Union of Polish Co-operative Societies in Germany, with headquarters in Berlin. The bank was closed Sept., 1939 and its property was confiscated by the Gestapo.

SLAVONIC CULTURES. Subject of international research. Organizations reg. with the UIA:

International Association for Research and Promotion of Slavonic Cultures, f. 1976, Paris. Consultative status: UNESCO.
International Association of Slavonic Languages and Literature, f. 1951, Stockholm.
International Committee of Slavists, f. 1951, Warsaw. Member of International Federation for Modern Languages and Literature.

Yearbook of International Organizations.

SLAVOPHILISM. The 19th century international term, initially signifying love for Slavic culture, later expressing ideas of cultural community and political solidarity of the Slavic nations, becoming the main element of ▷ Pan-slavism, and then ▷ Neo-slavism.

SLBM. Submarine-launched ballistic missiles, defined by the SALT agreement: "Launches installed on any nuclear-powered submarine or launches of modern ballistic missiles installed on any submarine regardless of its type." ▷ SALT I; ▷ SALT II.
The first SLBM was launched by the USA in 1960, the second in 1968 by the USSR.

J. GOLDBLAT, *Arms and Disarmament, A Handbook*, New York, 1983.

SLCM, SEA-LAUNCHED CRUISE MISSILE. (Pronounced: 'Slickum'). An international military term for all cruise missiles fired from submarines and/or surface ships. The first SLCM with multiple warheads was produced in 1971 by the USSR and in 1982 by the USA.

D. ROBERTSON, *Guide to Modern Defense and Strategy*, Detroit, 1988.

SLEEPING-CARS. A subject of international co-operation. Organization reg. with the UIA:

International Group for the Study and Utilization of Railway, Sleeping Cars in Europe, f. 1972, Brussels.

Yearbook of International Organizations.

SLOGANS, CATCHWORDS, FIGURATIVE REPRESENTATIONS. Subject of national and international protection, by copyright law, trademark law and the law on industrial models and design.

PRINNER'S *World Unfair Competition Law. An Encyclopedia*, Alphen, 1978.

SLOVAK SOCIALIST REPUBLIC. Member of the UN together with the ▷ Czech Socialist Republic. A federal state in eastern Czechoslovakia. Area: 49,000 sq. km. Pop. 4.8 million (1976). Capital: Bratislava. ▷ Czechoslovakia.

SLOVAKIA. A historical land in Czechoslovakia, inhabited by Slovaks, 1526–1918 in the Habsburg monarchy and from 1919 the eastern part of ▷ Czechoslovakia, with the exception of the years 1938–44.

SLOVAK STATE. 1938–44. The Slovak State was formed on the initiative of the German government with the aim of dividing Czechoslovakia, by a resolution of the parliament of Slovakia in Bratislava, Mar. 14, 1938; this decision was co-ordinated on the previous day in Berlin with the Chancellor, A. Hitler, by the Catholic priest J. Tiso, former head of the government of Slovakia (removed from this position on Mar. 10, 1938 by the central authorities of the republic). The resolution of the parliament and the election of Father Tiso as president and premier of the Slovak State enabled A. Hitler to send armed forces into Czech territory on Mar. 15, 1939 and establish the ▷ Bohemian and Moravian protectorate. The satellite status of the Slovak State was expressed in a note from Tiso to Hitler, Mar. 16, 1939, handing over the Slovak State to the protection of Germany and in a German–Slovak Treaty signed in Berlin on Mar. 23, 1939, stating that:

"In order to ensure the protection of the political independence of the Slovak State and the inviolability of its territory accepted by the German Reich, German armed forces have the right at any time to establish military installations and to maintain in such force as the Reich regards as necessary."

In addition, the Slovak State was obliged to conduct foreign policy "in strict understanding with the German government." The boundaries of the Slovak state were established in accordance with a decision of the German government of the Reich; in the west the administrative federal boundary remained unchanged, in the north the border with Poland was fixed by the Delimitation Protocol signed in Zakopane, Nov. 30, 1938; in the east and south by a Hungarian–Slovak agreement of Apr. 3, 1939, according to which Hungary shared a common border with Poland in the region of the river Ung, simultaneously cutting off the eastern province of Slovakia, so-called ▷ Transcarpathia. The Treaty of the Slovak State with the III Reich, valid for 25 years, was annulled by the liberation of Slovakia in Apr. 1945, when authority over the territory was simultaneously returned to the Republic of Czechoslovakia.

Akten zur Deutschen Auswärtigen Politik 1918–1945, Serie D. Vol. 4, Baden-Baden 1950.

SLOVENIA. A federal unit of Yugoslavia, situated in the Karst plateau and in the Julian Alps; area: 20,251 sq. km; pop. (1971) 1,727,000; capital: Ljubljana; a Balkan country whose fate from the 13th century until the fall of the Habsburg monarchy was connected with the international politics of the Habsburgs, with the exception of a short period of dependence on Napoleonic France. On Dec. 2, 1918 became part of the Kingdom of Serbia, Croatia, and Slovenia/SHS, which in 1929 took the name Yugoslavia. During World War II, in May 1941 occupied by Germany and divided between the Reich and Italy. A strong anit-fascist resistance movement was organized by the Communist Party of Yugoslavia. Liberated in May, 1945 and on Nov. 29, 1945 joined Yugoslavia as one of six federal republics.

V. DEDIJER, *History of Yugoslavia*, New York, 1974.

SLUMS. An international term for residental areas of poverty, usually in the suburbs of large cities; in French called *bidonvilles* or tandies; in Spanish *barriadas* (Peru), *callampas* (Chile), *favelas* (Brazil); in Russian *trushchoby*. In 1963 ECOSOC recognized that the use of the pejorative term "slums" in UN publications devoted to housing problems and social areas of poverty is improper and recommended the use of term ▷ transitory settlement.

SMALL INTERCONTINENTAL BALLISTIC MISSILE. ▷ Midgetman.

SMALLPOX. Subject of International Health Regulations:

"… the incubation period of smallpox is 14 days" (Art. 83 of IHR).

The total eradication of smallpox from the globe was proclaimed at a ceremonial session of the Thirty-third World Health Assembly in Geneva, May 8, 1980. The Assembly in a resolution declared that:

"the world and all its peoples have won freedom from smallpox, which was a most devastating disease sweeping in epidemic form through many countries since earliest times, leaving death, blindness and disfigurement in its wake and which only a decade ago was rampant in Africa, Asia and South America, [and expressed] deep gratitude to all nations and individuals who contributed to the success of this noble and historic endeavour."

The resolution said it wished to call

"this unprecedented achievement in the history of public health to the attention of all nations, which by their collective action have freed mankind of this ancient scourge and, in so doing, have demonstrated how nations working together in a common cause may further human progress."

The last case of endemic smallpox was recorded on 26 Oct., 1977 in Meka, Somalia. Since smallpox vaccination is no longer justified and may even be dangerous 164 countries stopped vacinnation. The smallpox virus exists since 1977 in only two places: high security laboratories in Moscow and at the Centers for Disease Control in Atlanta. Since 1987 the WHO registers all rumours of smallpox in an International Rumours Register.

UNTS, Vol. 764, pp. 66–70; I. ARITA, "How technology contributed to the success of global smallpox eradication", in: *WHO Chronicle*, No. 5, 1980; "Smallpox is dead", in: WHO, *World Health*, May, 1980, pp. 1–38; "Smallpox: Post-Eradication Vigilance Continues", in: *WHO Chronicle*, No. 3, 1982; J. WICKETT, "Smallpox: a happy ending", in: *WHO World Health*, November, 1984; F. FENNER, Can Smallpox Return? in: *World Health Organization*, August/September, 1987; H.M. SCHMECK, Last Samples of Smallpox Pose a Quandary. On 10th Anniversary of the Eradication of the Disease, Should the Virus be Destroyed? in: *The New York Times, Science Times*, November 3, 1987.

SMALL-SCALE INDUSTRIES. ▷ Microenterprises.

SMITHSONIAN INSTITUTION. An American institution, est. 1846, Washington, DC, by congressional act for the "increase and diffusion of knowledge among men" by request of James Smithson (1765–1829). His fortune was willed to the United States. Publ. *Smithsonian Year, Smithsonian Annuals of Flight, Smithsonian Studies* and serial publications.

W.P. TRUE, *The First Hundred Years of the Smithsonian Institution*, Washington DC, 1946.

SMOKERS PIPE CLUBS. International Association of Pipe Smokers Clubs, f. 1949, Ballstron Lake, N.Y. USA. Members: clubs in Brazil, Canada, FRG, Israel, Japan, the Netherlands and USA. Reg. with the UIA.

Yearbook of International Organizations.

SMOKING OF TOBACCO. A habit of American Indians in Middle Ages, introduced into Spain, 1600, and in 19th century in other European and American countries. The industrial production of cigars and cigarettes begin in middle of 19th century. The Spanish name *cigarro* was an adaptation of the Mexican Indian, Mayan term for smoking. In the second half of 20th century WHO started an international campaign against the smoking epidemic. The World production was 5,679,000 metric tons (farm weight) in 1976, projected 6,308,000 by 1985. Consumption per capita of tobacco 1976 (kg dry weight): Poland 2.97, Bulgaria 2.90, Canada, Belgium and Luxembourg 2.84, the Netherlands 2.81, Switzerland 2.79, Denmark 2.70, Japan 2.57, Greece 2.54, FRG 2.52, USA 2.50, Cuba 2.40, Hungary 2.35, Argentina 2.34, Ireland 2.30, France 2.15, Burma 2.11, Australia 2.10, Syria 2.11, Yugoslavia 1.91, Spain and UK 1.90, Austria 1.83, Norway 1.71, Italy 1.70, USSR 1.55, Czechoslovakia 1.54, GDR 1.54, Turkey 1.51.

In USA official warning against cigarettes started in 1965 with obligatory warnings on cigarette packages and advertising: "Cigarette smoking may be hazardous to your health", but since 1970: "It is dangerous to your health"; in 1984 a legislation making the language of warnings more precise (smoking causes: lung cancer, heart disease, emphysema and may complicate pregnancy) was considered and later passed by the US Congress.

Every year in the last decades of the 20th century more than a million people around the world die prematurely because of cigarette smoking.

WHO's first clear commitment to anti-smoking action came in 1970, when the World Health Assembly in a resolution called on governments to take action in the field of smoking control. Since then two WHO Expert Committees have been convened to advise the Organization (1974 and 1978), the WHO International Clearinghouse on Smoking and Health Information was established, and WHO cosponsored the Third, Fourth and Fifth World Conferences on Smoking and Health. The Organization has also collaborated with FAO on a study of the economic benefits and social and medical costs of tobacco production and consumption. The Health Assembly in 1980 has analyzed the content of cigarettes from developing countries, conducted educational seminars, collaborated with developing countries in the implementation of national smoking control program and convened a WHO Expert Committee on Smoking Control Strategies in Developing Countries, whose main findings and recommendations are summarized as follows:

– Cigarettes marketed in China and India have been shown to have high tar (21–33 mg/cigarette) and high nicotine yields compared with Western cigarettes.

– Lung cancer rates in Chinese men (e.g., 50.2 per 100,000 in Shanghai) are higher than in many North American and European populations.

– A case–control study conducted in Cuba revealed that the risk of developing lung cancer was considerable for female as well as male smokers.

– The developing countries now account for 63% of world tobacco production, compared with 58% in 1971–74 and only 50% in 1961–63.

– Smokers have higher annual rates of medical care utilization than non-smokers. In Canada, for instance, health care costs and losses in productivity due to smoking are together estimated to account for at least US $3000 million.

The Committee expressed particular concern at reports that imported cigarettes sold and promoted in developing countries had been shown to yield much higher levels of tar and nicotine than similar brands (and even brands of the same name) sold in developed countries, including the countries of origin. Most of the work undertaken so far on emission products has been carried out with western-style cigarettes.

Cigarettes with high nicotine and tar yields may be more addictive than other brands; the promotion of such brands in developing countries is to be deplored, and governments should be alerted to the dangers they face in this area.

The Committee considered two main categories of smoking control measures:

(1) those leading to changes in practice among those engaged in the manufacture, promotion, or sale of cigarettes (e.g., promotional bans, reduction in tar, nicotine and carbon monoxide yield);

(2) those leading to changes in practice among smokers (e.g., restrictions on smoking in public places).

The World's First No Tobacco Day was announced by the WHO on April 7, 1988, with the slogan: Tobacco or Health: Choose Health.

"Legislative action to combat smoking around the world: a survey of existing legislation", in: *WHO International Digest of Health Legislation*, Geneva, 1967; "Controlling the smoking epidemic", in: *Report of a WHO Expert Committee*, Geneva, 1979; C. VAN PROOSDY, *Smoking*, Amsterdam, 1980: *UN Chronicle*, May, 1980; R. ROENER, *Legislative Action to Combat Smoking*, WHO, Geneva, 1980; *World Health*, October, 1984; *Tobacco or Health Programme*, WHO Geneva, 1988.

SMOOT–HAWLEY TARIFF ACT, 1930. A protectionist law adopted by the US Congress on June 13, 1930, signed by President H. Hoover; it brought US tariffs to the highest level on all imported goods; was jointly sponsored by Senator R. Smoot and Representative J.P. Hawley; it was a reaction to the Black Friday of 1929 and Black Week of 1930, which started the world economic crisis. The act brought retaliatory tariff acts from other countries; and US foreign trade as well as the world foreign trade, suffered a sharp decline.

J.K. GALBRAITH, *The Great Crash 1929*, London 1955.

SMUGGLING. Illegal importation or exportation of goods prohibited to be imported or exported; subject of international conventions and international co-operation, particularly on combatting narcotics contraband. War smuggling forms a separate part or part of the international law of war. A number of European states participate in the Convention on combatting the contraband of alcoholic beverages, signed in Helsingfors on Aug. 19, 1925.

The governments of 21 American Republics at Buenos Aires, on June 19, 1935, at the Pan-American Commercial Conference, signed a Convention on the Repression of Smuggling; entered into force on Jan. 27, 1939; ratified until 1981 only by Brazil, Chile, Ecuador and Uruguay.

OAS, *Inter-American Treaties and Conventions*, Washington DC, 1971.

SOBIBÓR. A village in Chełm province in Poland on the river Bug (300 inhabitants 1970); from May, 1942 to Oct., 1943 location of a death camp in which more than 250,000 prisoners in the majority Jews from Belgium, France, Germany, the Netherlands, Baltic States and Byelorussia, and Soviet prisoners of war were gassed. The camp was liquidated after a rebellion by several hundred prisoners Oct. 14, 1943 many of whom escaped. In 1965 a monument was erected in honor of those murdered.

Z. ŁUKASZEWICZ, "Obóz zagłady w Sobiborze" (The Sobibór Death Camp), in: *Biuletyn Głównej Komisji Badania Zbrodni Hitlerowskich w Polsce*, Warsaw, 1947, Vol. 3, pp. 109–124. A. PIECZARSKI, "Powstanie w Sobiborze" (The Sobibór Uprising), in *Biuletyn Żydowskiego Instytutu Historycznego*, Warsaw, 1952, Vol. 3.

SOCIAL CENTERS. A subject of international co-operation. Organization reg. with the UIA:

International Federation of Settlements and Neighbourhood Centres, f. 1926, Utrecht. Consultative status with ECOSOC and UNICEF. Publ.: *Newsletter*.

Yearbook of International Organizations.

SOCIAL DEFENCE. Subject of international co-operation. Organizations reg. with the UIA:

International Society of Social Defence, f. 1945, Paris, France. Publ.: *Cahier de defense sociale*.

Yearbook of International Organizations, 1986/87; The Europa Yearbook 1988. A World Survey, Vol. I, London, 1988.

SOCIAL DEFENCE RESEARCH INSTITUTE OF THE UNITED NATIONS (UNSDRI). F. May 8, 1968 in Rome by agreement between the United Nations and the Italian Government. The UNSDRI is dedicated to the problems of prevention and control of juvenile delinquency and adult criminality.

SOCIAL DEMOCRATIC PARTIES. The national political organizations in Europe, Latin America, North Africa and the Near East; organized in the ▷ Socialist International.

SOCIAL INTERNATIONAL WELFARE. An international term for the organized assistance to the needy, provided by international relief bodies. (▷ Red Cross; ▷ UNICEF; ▷ UNRRA).

SOCIALISM. An international term of early 19th century having different definitions in 19th and 20th centuries either as a social ideology, or as a social system; a target of international actions for dissemination of socialist ideology and construction of socialist systems (The ▷ International).

SOCIALISM IN A SINGLE COUNTRY DOCTRINE, 1924. Doctrine of Joseph Stalin (1879–1953) opposed to the Leon Trotsky doctrine of ▷ Permanent revolution, 1905; saying that the USSR with a large population, extensive territory and vast natural resources has sufficient forces for building up an integral socialist system within its borders.

L. TROTSKY, *La révolution permanente*, Paris 1932, pp. 210–214; M. PRELOT, G. LESENYER, *Histoire des idées politiques*, Paris, 1977, pp. 656–657.

SOCIALISMO MORENO. Portuguese = Black Socialism or Tropical Socialism. An international term coined by Lionel do Mouro Brizola, a Brazilian statesman, for a socialist democracy adequate to the conditions of tropical countries.

SOCIALIST COUNTRIES. ▷ Socialist states.

SOCIALIST DEMOCRACY. An international term coined in the USSR characterized by M. Gor-

S

bachev, secretary general of the CP USSR, on Jan. 27, 1987, as follows:

"What I have in view is an organic combination of democracy and discipline, of independence and responsibility, of the rights and duties of officials, and of every citizen. Socialist democracy has nothing in common with permissiveness, irresponsibility, anarchy. Real democracy serves every person, protecting his political and social rights, and it simultaneously serves every collective and society as a whole, upholding their interests. Democratization of all spheres of life in Soviet society is important first of all because we link with it the further development of the working people's initiative and the revelation of the entire potential of the socialist system. We need democratization in order to move ahead, in order to ensure that legality grows stronger and justice triumphs in society and that a moral atmosphere, in which man can live freely and work fruitfully, is asserted in it".

KEESING's *Record of World Events*, 1987.

SOCIALIST INTERNATIONAL. *German*: Sozialistische Internationale, historical joint name for various organs of the Social Democratic Party in the international workers' movement since 1889, date of the formation of the first Socialist International in Paris, called, at that time, The Second International, with reference to the ▷ International Working Men's Association, est. 1864 in London. It existed up to the outbreak of World War I and affiliated the Social Democratic Parties of Europe, Argentina, Uruguay and the USA. It organized 9 congresses: in Paris, 1889, Brussels, 1891; Zurich, 1893; London, 1896; Paris, 1900; Amsterdam, 1904; Stuttgart, 1907; Copenhagen, 1920; and Basel, 1912 (a special one). Since 1900 the headquarters of the International Socialist Bureau was Brussels. In 1919 it was reactivated in Berne, and at the Congress in Hamburg changed its name to Workers' and Socialist International; united the main parties of Europe and four American ones: Argentina, Chile, Uruguay and the USA. Headquarters: London to 1926, Zurich to 1935 and Brussels to 1940, when it was dissolved after the entry of Nazi forces into Belgium. Formed for the third time in 1946 as Committee of International Socialistic Conferences (COMISCO); transformed in 1951 once again into Socialist International. Socialist International has the statute of an extra-governmental organization attached to the UN; activities are directed by a Council selected by Congresses held every three years. Headquarters: London. Official languages: English, French and German. Publ. the monthly *Socialist Affairs*.
Emigrant groups from 12 countries work under the Socialist International. The main mass organizations connected with the International are the organizations registered with the UIA:

International Confederation of Free Trade Unions in Brussels.
International Council of Social Democratic Women in London.
International Union of Social Democratic Teachers in Arnim, FRG.
International Union of Socialist Youth in Vienna.

L.L. LORVIN, *Historia del Internacionalismo Obrero*, Santiago, 1947; J. JOLL, *The Second International 1889–1914*, London, 1955; V. ALBA, *Historia del Movimiento Obrero en América Latina*, México, DF, 1963; J. BRAUNTHAL, *History of the International*, London, 2 Vols., 1966–67.

Yearbook of International Organizations.

SOCIALIST INTERNATIONAL OF MEDITERRANEAN COUNTRIES. International term – common name of the Conference of Socialist Mediterranean Parties, initiated by the Socialist Arab League of Libya. The I Conference was held with the participation of 14 parties (out of 24 invited) in Barcelona in Nov., 1976 at the same time

that the historic ▷ Socialist International was meeting in Geneva. The Socialist International of Mediterranean Countries has a permanent secretariat in Tripoli, capital of Libya. The II Conference was held in 1977 on Malta.

SOCIALIST LAW. International term – law established according to the Marxist–Leninist theory of the state and the law; formulated in legal acts of socialist states; subject of international research in comparative legislation. ▷ Socialist states.

SOCIALIST MARKET. International term – in the wider meaning an international market of all of the socialist states in the world, in the narrower, accepted name in the press for the market of the CMEA states.

SOCIALIST PLURALISM. International term coined in the USSR in the 1980's as characteristic of "democratic socialism" ("more socialism – more democracy").

SOCIALIST STATES. In the UN system common name for states which undertook the task of constructing socialism with a centrally planned economy: Russia, 1917; Mongolia, 1930; and after World War II successively – Poland, Yugoslavia, Albania, Bulgaria, Romania, Hungary, Czechoslovakia, China, North Korea, GDR, North Vietnam and Cuba.

R. CHARVIN, *Les états socialistes aux Nations Unies*, Paris, 1970; A. KLAFKOWSKI, "Rola państw socjalistycznych w ONZ (Role of the Socialist States in the UN), in: *Studia polsko-radzieckie* (Polish–Soviet Studies), No. 9, 1972, pp. 139–149; P.M. LEIDERETZ, *Key to the study of Eastern European Law* (Bibliography of Bibliographies and Location guide), Kluwer, 1978; R. A. REMINGTON, *The International Relations of Eastern Europe. A Guide to Information Sources*, Detroit, 1978.

SOCIALIST WORLD SYSTEM. A subject of international research:

International Institute for the Study of Economic Problems of the Socialist World System, f. 1970, Moscow, Reg. with the UIA.

Yearbook of International Organizations.

SOCIAL PROGRESS AND DEVELOPMENT, UN DECLARATION 1969. Adopted by the UN General Assembly Res. 2542/XXIV, on Dec. 11, 1969. The text is as follows:

"The General Assembly solemnly proclaims this Declaration on Social Progress and Development and calls for national and international action for its use as a common basis for social development policies:
Part I. Principles.
Art. 1. All peoples and all human beings without distinction as to race, colour, sex, language, religion, nationality, ethnic origin, family or social status, or political or other conviction, shall have the right to live in dignity and freedom and to enjoy the fruits of social progress and should, on their part, contribute to it.
Art. 2. Social progress and development shall be founded on respect for the dignity and value of the human person and shall ensure the promotion of human rights and social justice, which requires:
(a) The immediate and final elimination of all forms of inequality, exploitation of peoples and individuals, colonialism and racism, including nazism and apartheid and all other policies and ideologies opposed to the purpose and principles of the United Nations;
(b) The recognition and effective implementation of civil and political rights as well as of economic, social and cultural rights without any discrimination.
Art. 3. The following are considered primary conditions of social progress and development:
(a) National independence based on the right of peoples to self-determination;

(b) The principle of non-interference in the internal affairs of States;
(c) Respect for the sovereignty and territorial integrity of States;
(d) Permanent sovereignty of each nation over its natural wealth and resources;
(e) The right and responsibility of each State and, as far as they are concerned, each nation and people to determine freely its own objectives of social development, to set its own priorities and to decide in conformity with the principles of the Charter of the United Nations the means and methods of their achievement without any external interference;
(f) Peaceful coexistence, peace, friendly relations and co-operation among States irrespective of differences in their social, economic or political systems.
Art. 4. The family as a basic unit of society and the natural environment for the growth and well-being of all its members, particularly children and youth, should be assisted and protected so that it may fully assume its responsibilities within the community. Parents have the exclusive right to determine freely and responsibly the number and spacing of their children.
Art. 5. Social progress and development require the full utilization of human resources, including, in particular:
(a) The encouragement of creative initiative under conditions of enlightened public opinion;
(b) The dissemination of national and international information for the purpose of making individuals aware of changes occurring in society as a whole;
(c) The active participation of all elements of society, individually or through associations, in defining and in achieving the common goals of development with full respect for the fundamental freedoms embodied in the Universal Declaration of Human Rights;
(d) The assurance to disadvantaged or marginal sectors of the population of equal opportunities for social and economic advancement in order to achieve an effectively integrated society.
Art. 6. Social Development requires the assurance to everyone of the right to work and the free choice of employment. Social progress and development require the participation of all members of society in productive and socially useful labour and the establishment, in conformity with human rights and fundamental freedoms and with the principles of justice and the social function of property, of forms of ownership of land and of the means of production which preclude any kind of exploitation of man, ensure equal rights to property for all and create conditions leading to genuine equality among people.
Art. 7. The rapid expansion of national income and wealth and their equitable distribution among all members of society are fundamental to all social progress, and they should therefore be in the forefront of the preoccupations of every State and Government. The improvement in the position of the developing countries in international trade resulting, among other things, from the achievement of favourable terms of trade and of equitable and remunerative prices at which developing countries market their products is necessary in order to make it possible to increase national income and in order to advance social development.
Art. 8. Each Government has the primary role and ultimate responsibility of ensuring the social progress and well-being of its people, of planning social development measures as part of comprehensive development plans, of encouraging and coordinating or integrating all national efforts towards this end and of introducing necessary changes in the social structure. In planning social development measures, the diversity of the needs of developing and developed areas, and of urban and rural areas, within each country, shall be taken into due account.
Art. 9. Social progress and development are the common concerns of the international community, which shall supplement, by concerted international action, national efforts to raise the living standards of peoples.
Social progress and economic growth require recognition of the common interest of all nations in the exploration, conservation, use and exploitation, exclusively for peaceful purposes and in the interests of all mankind, of those areas of the environment such as outer space and the sea-bed and ocean floor and the subsoil thereof, beyond the limits of national jurisdiction, in accordance with the purposes and principles of the Charter and of the United Nations.

Part II. Objectives.
Social progress and development shall aim at the continuous raising of the material and spiritual standards of living of all members of society, with respect for and in compliance with human rights and fundamental freedoms, through the attainment of the following main goals:
Art. 10.(a) The assurance at all levels of the right to work and the right of everyone to form trade unions and workers' associations and to bargain collectively; promotion of full productive employment and elimination of unemployment and underemployment, establishment of equitable and favourable conditions of work for all, including the improvement of health and safety conditions; assurance of just remuneration for labour without any discrimination as well as a sufficiently high minimum wage to ensure a decent standard of living; the protection of the consumer;
(b) The elimination of hunger and malnutrition and the guarantee of the right to proper nutrition;
(c) The elimination of poverty; the assurance of a steady improvement in levels of living and of a just and equitable distribution of income;
(d) The achievement of the highest standards of health, and the provision of health protection for the entire population, if possible free of charge;
(e) The eradication of illiteracy and the assurance of the right to universal access to culture, to free compulsory education at the elementary level and to free education at all levels; the raising of the general level of life-long education;
(f) The provision for all, particularly persons in low-income groups and large families, of adequate housing and community services.
Social progress and development shall aim equally at the progressive attainment of the following main goals:
Art. 11. (a) The provision of comprehensive social security schemes and social welfare services, the establishment and improvement of social security and insurance schemes for all persons who, because of illness, disability or old age, are temporarily or permanently unable to earn a living, with a view to ensuring a proper standard of living for such persons and for their families and dependants;
(b) The protection of the rights of the mother and child; concern for the upbringing and health of children; the provision of measures to safeguard the health and welfare of women and particularly of working mothers during pregnancy and the infancy of their children, as well as of mothers whose earnings are the sole source of livelihood for the family; the granting to women of pregnancy and maternity leave and allowances without loss of employment or wages;
(c) The protection of the rights and the assuring of the welfare of children, the aged and the disabled; the provision of protection for the physically or mentally disadvantaged;
(d) The education of youth in, and promotion among them of, the ideals of justice and peace, mutual respect and understanding among peoples; the promotion of full participation of youth in the process of national development;
(e) The provision of social defense measures and the elimination of conditions leading to crime and delinquency, especially juvenile delinquency;
(f) The guarantee that all individuals without discrimination of any kind, are made aware of their rights and obligations and receive the necessary aid in the exercise and safeguarding of their rights.
Social progress and development shall further aim at achieving the following main objectives:
Art. 12.(a) The creation of conditions for rapid and sustained social and economic development, particularly in the developing countries; change in international economic relations, new and effective methods of international co-operation in which equality of opportunity should be as much a prerogative of nations as of individuals within a nation;
(b) The elimination of all forms of discrimination and exploitation and all other practices and ideologies contrary to the purposes and principles of the Charter of the United Nations;
(c) The elimination of all forms of foreign economic exploitation, particularly that practised by international monopolies, in order to enable the people of every country to enjoy in full the benefits of their natural resources.
Social progress and development shall finally aim at the attainment of the following main goals:
Art. 13.(a) Equitable sharing of scientific and technological advances by developed and developing countries, and a steady increase in the use of science and technology for the benefit of the social development of society;
(b) The establishment of a harmonious balance between scientific, technological and material progress and the intellectual, spiritual, cultural and moral advancement of humanity;
(c) The protection and improvement of the human environment.
Part III. Means and methods
On the basis of the principles set forth in this Declaration the achievement of the objectives of social progress and development requires the mobilization of the necessary resources by national and international action, with particular attention to such means and methods as:
Art. 14.(a) Planning for social progress and development, as an integral part of balanced over-all development planning;
(b) The establishment, where necessary, of national systems for framing and carrying out social policies and programmes, and the promotion by the countries concerned of planned regional development, taking into account differing regional conditions and needs, particularly the development of regions which are less favoured or under-developed by comparison with the rest of the country;
(c) The promotion of basic and applied social research, particularly comparative international research applied to the planning and execution of social development programmes.
Art. 15.(a) The adoption of measures to ensure the effective participation, as appropriate, of all the elements of society in the preparation and execution of national plans and programmes of economic and social development;
(b) The adoption of measures for an increasing rate of popular participation in the economic, social, cultural and political life of countries through national governmental bodies, non-governmental organizations, co-operatives, rural associations, workers' and employers; organizations and women's and youth organizations, by such methods as national and regional plans for social and economic progress and community development, with a view to achieving a fully integrated national society, accelerating the process of social mobility and consolidating the democratic system;
(c) Moblization of public opinion, at both national and international levels, in support of the principles and objectives of social progress and development;
(d) The dissemination of social information, at the national and at the international level, to make people aware of changing circumstances in society as a whole, and to educate the consumer.
Art. 16.(a) Maximum mobilization of all national resources and their national and efficient utilization; promotion of increased and accelerated productive investment in social and economic fields and of employment; orientation of society towards the development process;
(b) Progressively increasing provision of the necessary budgetary and other resources required for financing the social aspects of development;
(c) Achievement of equitable distribution of national income, utilizing, inter alia, the fiscal system and government spending as an instrument for the equitable distribution and redistribution of income in order to promote social progress;
(d) Adoption of measures aimed at prevention of such an outflow of capital from developing countries as would be detrimental to their economic and social development.
Art. 17.(a) Adoption of measures to accelerate the process of industrialization, especially in developing countries, with due regard for its social aspects, in the interest of the entire population; development of an adequate organizational and legal framework conducive to an uninterrupted and diversified growth of the industrial sector; measures to overcome the adverse social effects which may result from urban development and industrialization, including automation; maintenance of a proper balance between rural and urban development, and in particular measures designed to ensure healthier living conditions in large industrial centres;
(b) Integrated planning to meet the problems of urbanization and urban development;
(c) Comprehensive rural development schemes to raise the levels of living of the rural populations and to facilitate such urban-rural relationships and population distribution as will promote balanced national development and social progress;
(d) Measures for appropriate supervision of the utilization of land in the interests of society.
The achievement of the objectives of social progress and development equally requires the implementation of the following means and methods:
Art. 18(a) Adoption of appropriate legislative, administrative and other measures ensuring to everyone not only political and civil rights, but also the full realization of economic, social and cultural rights without any discrimination;
(b) The promotion of democratically based social and institutional reforms and motivation for change basic to the elimination of all forms of discrimination and exploitation conducive to high rates of economic and social progress, to include land reform, in which the ownership and use of land will be made to serve best the objectives of social justice and economic development;
(c) The adoption of measures to boost and diversify agricultural production through inter alia, the implementation of democratic agrarian reforms, to ensure an adequate and well-balanced supply of food, its equitable distribution among the whole population and the improvement of nutritional standards;
(d) The adoption of measures to introduce, with the participation of the Government, low-cost housing programmes in both rural and urban areas;
(e) Development and expansion of the system of transportation and communications, particularly in developing countries.
Art. 19.(a) The provision of free health services to the whole population and of adequate preventive and curative facilities and welfare medical services accessible to all;
(b) The enactment and establishment of legislative measures and administrative regulations with a view to the implementation of comprehensive programmes of social security schemes and social welfare services and to the improvement and coordination of existing services;
(c) The adoption of measures and the provision of social welfare services to migrant workers and their families, in conformity with the provisions of Convention No. 97 of the International Labour Conference and other international instruments relating to migrant workers;
(d) The institution of appropriate measures for the rehabilitation of mentally or physically disabled persons, especially children and youth, so as to enable them to the fullest possible extent to be useful members of society – these measures shall include the provision of treatment and technical appliances, education, vocation and social guidance, training and selective placement, and other assistance required – and the creation of social conditions in which the handicapped are not discriminated against because of their disabilities.
Art. 20(a) The provision of full democratic freedoms to trade unions; freedom of association for all workers, including the right to bargain collectively and to strike, recognition of the right to form other organizations of working people; the provision for the growing participation of trade unions in economic and social development; effective participation of all members of trade unions in the deciding of economic and social issues which affect their interests;
(b) The improvement of health and safety conditions for workers, by means of appropriate technological and legislative measures and the provision of the material prerequisites for the implementation of those measures, including the limitation of working hours;
(c) Adoption of appropriate measures for the development of harmonious industrial relations.
Art. 21.(a) The training of national personnel and cadres, including administrative, executive, professional and technical personnel needed for social development and for over-all development plans and policies;
(b) The adoption of measures to accelerate the extension and improvement of general, vocational and technical education and of training and retraining, which should be provided free at all levels;

(c) Raising the general level of education; development and expansion of national information media, and their rational and full use towards continuing education of the whole population and towards encouraging its participation in social development activities; the constructive use of leisure, particularly that of children and adolescents;

(d) The formulation of national and international policies and measures to avoid the 'brain drain' and obviate its adverse effects.

Art. 22.(a) Development and coordination of policies and measures designed to strengthen the essential functions of the family as a basic unity of society;

(b) The formulation and establishment, as needed, of programmes in the field of population, within the framework of national demographic policies and as part of the welfare medical services including education, training of personnell and the provision to families of the knowledge and means necessary to enable them to exercise their right to determine freely and responsibly the number and spacing of their children;

(c) Establishment of appropriate child-care facilities in the interest of children and working parents.

The achievement of the objectives of social progress and development finally requires the implementation of the following means and methods:

Art. 23.(a) The laying down of economic growth rate targets for the developing countries within the United Nations policy for development, high enough to lead to a substantial acceleration of their rates of growth;

(b) The provision of greater assistance of better terms; the implementation of the aid volume target of a minimum of 1 per cent of the gross national product at market prices of economically advanced countries; the general easing of the terms of lending to the developing countries through low-interest rates on loans and long grace periods for the repayment of loans, and the assurance that the allocation of such loans will be based strictly on socio-economic criteria free of any political considerations;

(c) The provision of technical, financial and material assistance, both bilateral and multilateral, to the fullest possible extent and on favourable terms, and improved co-ordination of international assistance for the achievement of the social objectives of national development plans;

(d) The provision to the developing countries of technical, financial and material assistance and of favourable conditions to facilitate the direct exploitation of their national resources and natural wealth by those countries with a view to enabling the peoples of those countries to benefit fully from their national resources;

(e) Expansion of international trade based on principles of equality and non-discrimination; the rectification of the position of developing countries in international trade by equitable terms of trade; a general non-reciprocal and non-discriminatory system of preferences for the exports of developing countries to the developed countries; the establishment and implentation of general and comprehensive commodity agreements; and the financing of reasonable buffer stocks by international institutions.

Art. 24.(a) Intensification of international co-operation with a view to ensuring the international exchange of information, knowledge and experience concerning social progress and development;

(b) The broadest international technical scientific and cultural co-operation and reciprocal utilization of the experience of countries with different economic and social systems and different levels of development, on the basis of mutual advantage and strict observance of an respect for national sovereignty;

(c) Increased utilization of science and technology for social and economic development; arrangements for the transfer and exchange of technology, including know-how and patents to the developing countries.

Art. 25.(a) Establishment of legal and administrative measures for the protection and improvement of the human environment of both national and international levels;

(b) The use and exploitation, in accordance with the appropriate international regimes, of the resources of areas of the environment such as outer space and the sea-bed and ocean floor and the subsoil thereof beyond the limits of national jurisdiction, in order to supplement national resources available for the achievement of economic and social progress and development, in every country irrespective of its geographical location,

special consideration being given to the interests and needs of the developing countries.

Art. 26. Compensation for damages, be they social or economic in nature, including restitution and reparations – caused as a result of aggression and of illegal occupation of territory by the aggressor.

Art. 27.(a) The achievement of general and complete disarmament and the channelling of the progressively released resources to be used for economic and social progress for the welfare of people everywhere and, in particular, for the benefit of developing countries;

(b) The adoption of measures contributing to disarmament, including, inter alia, the complete prohibition of tests of nuclear weapons, the prohibition of the development, production and stockpiling of chemical and bacteriological (biological) weapons and the prevention of the pollution of oceans and inland waters by nuclear wastes.

UN Yearbook, 1969.

SOCIAL REVOLUTION. International term – transformation of social-economic system as the result of assumption of power by a new social class.

SOCIAL SCIENCE. ▷ Sociology.

SOCIAL SECURITY. International term, subject of international co-operation. Organizations reg. with the UIA:

Administration Centre of Social Security for Rhine Boatmen, f. 1950, Strasbourg, France.
Ibero-American Social Security Organizations, f. 1951, Madrid. Publ.: *Revista Iberoamericana de Seguridad Social*. Inter-American Conference on Social Security, f. 1942, Mexico, DF. Publ.: *Seguridad Social*.
International Security Social Association, f. 1927, Geneve. Publ.: *International Social Security Review* (quarterly), *World Bibliography of Social Security* (quarterly).
International Society for Labour Law and Social Security, f. 1958, Geneva. Consultative Status ILO.

Yearbook of International Organizations.

SOCIAL SECURITY, EUROPEAN AGREEMENT, 1961. Signed on Oct. 18, 1961, in Turin, by Belgium, France, the Netherlands, Luxembourg, the FRG, Italy – members of the European Council in keeping with the Convention on the Protection of Human Rights and Fundamental Freedoms, signed Nov. 4, 1950, in Rome together with the Auxiliary Protocol, signed Mar. 20, 1952 in Rome. Part I of the agreement puts forth the principles of social care. Part II defines the following rights: to work, to just conditions at work, to the safety and hygiene of work, to fair pay, to the freedom of association in labor unions, to collective bargaining, to the protection of the work of juveniles, to the protection of health, to professional training, to social and health care, to public services, to social, economic and legal protection of the family, to social and economic protection of motherhood, to work on the territory of other member states.

G. LYON-CAEN, *Droit social européenne*, Paris, 1972, 400 pp.

SOCIAL SECURITY INTERNATIONAL ASSISTANCE. Subject of international agreements establishing the principle of equal treatment for the national of each Contracting Party in the application of Social Security legislation in whichever of the territories of the Contracting Parties such nationals are or become resident.
Convention between Belgium, France, Luxembourg, the Netherlands and UK to extend co-ordinate Social Security schemes in their application to the nationals of the Parties to the Brussels Treaty of 1948, signed in Paris, Nov. 9, 1949.

UNTS, Vol. 132, p. 31.

SOCIAL SERVICE. International term, subject of international co-operation. Organizations reg. with the UIA:

Altrusa International, f. 1917, Chicago, USA. Publ.: *International Altrusan* (monthly).
Catholic International Union for Social Service, f. 1960, Rome. Consultative Status ECOSOC, UNESCO, FAO, OAS, ILO, Publ.: *Service social dans le monde* (quarterly).
International Social Service, f. 1921, Geneva, by the World ▷ YWCA as the International Migration Service, present name adopted 1946. Consultative Status ECOSOC, UNESCO, UNICEF, ILO. Publ.: *Annual Activity Report*.
Travellers Aid – International Social Service of America, f. 1956, New York.

Yearbook of International Organizations.

SOCIAL WELFARE. An international term for assistance rendered by state or social institutions to persons who are temporarily or permanently unable to provide maintenance for themselves; subject of international conventions prepared by the International Labour Organization in striving for a universal social welfare system. On the initiative of the ILO, the UN Conference of Social Welfare Ministers was held in New York, Sept. 3–11, 1968.

SOCIETIES, INTERNATIONAL. An international term for mostly scientific usually non-governmental organizations, while in other areas of international life the term "associations" predominates. It has become an international custom to call organizations of scientific co-operation – societies; also organizations for economy, finances, development.

SOCIETY FOR WORLDWIDE INTERBANK FINANCIAL TELECOMMUNICATION. ▷ SWIFT.

SOCIOLOGY. Subject of international co-operation and research. Organizations reg. with the UIA:

Committee for International Co-operation in Rural Sociology, f. 1962, Rome.
European Society for Rural Sociology, f. 1957, Giessen, FRG. Publ.: *Sociologia Ruralis*.
Institute of Sociology of Law for Europe, f. 1972, Brussels. Publ.: *Newsletter*.
International Association of French-Language Sociologists, f. 1956, Paris.
International Conference of Sociology of Religion, f. 1948, Louvain, Belgium. Publ. *Bulletin*.
International Institute of Sociology, f. 1893, Paris. Constituted as an academy. Publ.: *Revue international de sociologie*.
International Sociological Association, on the initiative of UNESCO, f. 1949, Montreal. Consultative Status: UNESCO, ECOSOC. Publ.: *Current Sociology*.
Latin American Association of Sociology, f. 1951, México, DF, Publ.: *Boletín de ALAS*.
Scandinavian Sociological Association, f. 1970, Copenhagen.

UNESCO publ. *International Social Science Journal* (quarterly in English and French); *Yearbook of International Organizations*. J. SZCZEPAŃSKI, *Introduction to Sociology*, Warsaw, 1963; UNESCO, *World List of Social Science Periodicals*, Paris, 1986.

SODEPAX. Committee on Society, Development and Peace of the World Council of Churches and the Pontifical Commission Iustitia et Pax, f. 1968 by mutual agreement of the World Council of Churches and Holy See on an experimental basis. A significant ecumenical instrument, SODEPAX bases its program on social thinking and teaching of the World Council of Churches and Roman Catholic Church. Headquarters in Ecumenical Center, Geneva. Publ. documentary magazine, *Church Alert*.

Yearbook of International Organizations.

SOE. Special Operations Executive. A British government institution during World War II est. by the British Ministry of War Economy with the task of carrying out special actions in enemy territory.

J. GARLINSKI, *Poland, SOE and the Allies*, London, 1969; M.R.D. FOOT, *SOE, An Outline History of the Special Operations Executive, 1940–46*, London, 1984; M.K. DZIEWANOWSKI, *War at any Price, World War II in Europe 1939–1945*, Englewood Cliffs, 1987.

SOFIA. Capital of Bulgaria since 1879; area: 1038 sq. km, pop. (1976) 1,084,000. The seat of organizations reg. with the UIA:
Balkan and Near East Railway Rates Union, Trade Unions International of Food, Tobacco, Hotel and Allied Industries Workers.

SOFT DRINKS. Subject of international co-operation. Organization reg. with the UIA:
Confederation of European Soft Drinks Associations, f. 1961, Brussels, Belgium.

Yearbook of International Organizations, 1986/87; The Europa Yearbook 1988. A World Survey, Vol. I, London 1988.

SOIL. Subject of organized international research, co-ordinated by FAO, which publishes together with UNESCO soil maps of the whole world, specifying geological, physiographic, vegetal, climatic, topographic conditions and degree of their utilization. Work is being conducted on a world scientific soil map in a 1:5,000,000 scale in 10 volumes: I, Elements of the Legend; II, North America; III, Mexico, Central America; IV, South America; V, Europe; VI, Africa; VII, Coastal Asia; VIII, Central and North Asia; IX, South-East Asia; and X, Australia. The first 4 volumes published by UNESCO appeared in Paris, 1966–72. Each volume, besides a map, includes a detailed geological description of the region. 1954 FAO published (edition revised 1960) the *Multilingual Vocabulary of Soil Science* (English, French, Spanish, German, Italian, Dutch, Swedish and Russian).
The struggle with erosion is one of FAO's international actions. In collaboration with the IAEA agricultural laboratory at Selbersdorf, Austria, scientists are studying various nuclear, isotopic and related techniques to establish better conditions for crop cultivation, maintaining soil fertility and production. The research program is conducted by the Soil Fertility, Irrigation and Crop Production Institute of the Joint Division of the IAEA and FAO. Organizations reg. with the UIA:

Interafrican Bureau for Soils, f. 1968, Nairobi;
International Association of Soil Science, f. 1924, Rome. Consultative Status UNESCO and WHO. Publ.: *Bulletin*;
International Society for Soil Mechanics and Foundation Engineering, f. 1936, London;
International Working Group on Soilless Culture, f. 1958, Wageningen, the Netherlands;
Southeast Asian Society of Soil Engineering, f. 1967, Bangkok.

A.D. VISSER, ELSEVIER's *Dictionary of Soil Mechanics. In English/American, French, Dutch and German*, Amsterdam, 1965; *Yearbook of International Organizations*; *FAO Multilingual Vocabulary of Soil Science*, Rome, 1970; *The IAEA in Soil Research*, in: IAEA Bulletin 1987, No. 2.

SOILLESS CULTURE. Subject of international co-operation. Organization reg. with the UIA:

International Society for Soilless Culture, f. 1955, Wageningen, The Netherlands. Pub.: Bibliography on Hydroponic, Soilless Culture.

The Europa Yearbook, 1988. A World Survey, Vol. I, London, 1988.

SOJUZKARTU. ▷ Glavkosmos.

SOKOL, ATHLETIC CLUB. An independence youth movement in Slavic countries initiated in 1860 by the Czechs: M. Tyrs (1832–82) and J. Funger (1822–65) who founded a gymnastics society, called Sokol, with the following slogan: *Mens sana in corpore sano* (Sound mind in a sound body). The independence-minded character of the movement was emphasized by red shirts called Garibaldi shirts, after an Italian hero, also by Slavic national patterns in girls' and boys' garb. Following the example of Bohemia, the movement soon spread over Slovakia (since 1896 called *Swaz česko-slovenskeho sokolstwa*), Bulgaria, Croatia, Dalmatia, Serbia, Lusatia and Poland, thereby becoming the most strongly organized slavonophilic movement among Western Slavs and Slavic emigrants in the German Reich, France and the USA before World War I. It played a significant role in stirring national feelings and solidarity among Slavs, which was expressed in Panslavonic Sokol Rallies.

J. ROUČEK (ed.), *Slavonic Encyclopedia*, New York, 1949.

SOL. A monetary unit of Peru; 1 sol = 100 centavos; issued by the Banco Central de Reserva del Peru.

SOLAR ENERGY. A subject of international co-operation under the aegis of the UN in the framework of UN Conference, on New and Renewable Sources of Energy in the 1980s.

The Solar Energy Institute, SERI of the US Department of Energy publ. Solar Energy Bibliography and Solar Energy Legal Bibliography. See ▷ ASSET.

UN Yearbook, 1981.

SOLAS CONVENTIONS. Four successive Conventions on Safety of Life at Sea; the first of which was prepared in 1913 by the so-called *Titanic* Conference convened in London and signed on Jan. 20, 1914; however, did not enter into force due to the outbreak of World War I. It was modified and signed on May 31, 1929, in London (valid till Nov. 19, 1952); Third Convention of June 10, 1948 (valid from Nov. 19, 1952 to May 26, 1965) and Fourth Convention of June 17, 1960 (valid since May 26, 1965). The English acronym SOLAS indicates Safety of Life at Sea. The first three London Conferences were convened by the government of Great Britain, the fourth by IMCO. The fifth convention adopted by IMCO 1974 entered into force in 1980; a set of amendments adopted by IMO in June 1983 entered into force on July 1986.

IMCO, *Maritime Conventions*, Geneva, 1970; *UN Chronicle*, November, 1986.

SOLIDARITY. The solidarity of ethnic, religious or professional groups one of the human rights UNESCO organized Aug. 12–15, 1980 in Mexico City a Colloquium on the Rights of Solidarity. ▷ *Laborem exercens*. ▷ Gdańsk 1986. The Christian solidarity doctrine defines 'peace as the fruit of solidarity'; 'Opun solidaritis pax' (▷ Sollicitudo Rei Socialis).

UNESCO, *Colloquium on the New Human Rights. The Rights of Solidarity: The Rights to be Different*, by F. Hassan, Paris, May 23, 1980; SS-80/Conf. 806/9. Original: English; and *The Right to Communicate*, by M. Paillet, Paris, August 7, 1980, SS-80/Conf. 806/10. Original: French.; J. TISCHNER, *The Spirit of Solidarity*, New York, 1984; E. TEAGUE, *Solidarity and the Soviet Workers*, London, 1988; Sollicitudo Rei Socialis, *Encyclical Letter of the Supreme Pontiff John Paul II for the Twentieth Anniversary of Populorum Progressio*, London, 1988, p. 78.

SOLIDARITY CONFERENCES. Meetings of countries of the Third World in the 2nd half of the 20th century for the purpose of manifesting unity against colonialism and imperialism as well as making decisions on actions to be taken to completely eliminate colonialism and neocolonialism. Despite many political and other differences separating countries of the Third World, these conferences revealed the existence of many common aims and formed the first global ties among the developing countries. A similar function was performed by conferences of the nonaligned countries. A Solidarity Conference of Three Continents (Africa, Asia and Latin America) was held in Havana, Jan. 3–14, 1966; adopted Havana General Declaration.

E.J. OSMAŃCZYK, *Enciclopedia Mundial de Relaciones Internacionales y Naciones Unidas*, México, DF, 1976, pp. 398–399.

SOLIDARITY FUND, INTERNATIONAL. A Fund est. 1963, in Rome; an international organization of the European Christian-democratic parties with the task of assisting Christian Democratic parties in Latin America, especially in Chile, Brazil, Colombia, and Venezuela.

SOLLICITUDO REI SOCIALIS. The seventh encyclical of Pope John Paul II whose English title is 'The Social Concerns of the Church' published February 19, 1987 providing a Roman Catholic analysis of global political and social issues. The highlights:

"Collaboration in the development of the whole person and of every human being is in fact a duty *of all towards all*, and must be shared by the four parts of the world: East and West, North and South; or, as we say today, by the different 'worlds'. If, on the contrary, people try to achieve it in only one part, or in only one world, they do so at the expense of the others; and, precisely because the others are ignored, their own development becomes exaggerated and misdirected.
Peoples or *nations* too have a right to their own full development, which while including–as already said–the economic and social aspects should also include individual cultural identity and openness to the transcendent. Not even the need for development can be used as an excuse for imposing on others one's own way of life or own religious belief.
33. Nor would a type of development which did not respect and promote *human rights*–personal and social, economic and political, including the *rights of nations and of peoples*–be really *worthy of man*.
39. The exercise of solidarity within each Society is valid when its members recognize one another as persons ... The same criterion is applied by analogy in international relations. Interdependence must be transformed into solidarity, based upon the principle that the goods of creation are meant for all. That which human industry produces through the processing of raw material, with the contribution of work must serve equally for the good of all ...
The motto of the pontificate of my esteemed predecessor Pius XII was Opus iustitice pax, peace as the fruit of justice. Today one could say with the same exactness and the same power of biblical inspiration (cf. *Is* 32:17; *Jas* 3:18): *Opus solidaritatis pax*, peace as the fruit of solidarity.
The goal of peace, so desired by everyone, will certainly be achieved through the putting into effect of social and international justice, but also through the practice of the virtues which favour togetherness, and which teach us to live in unity, so as to build in unity, by giving and receiving, a new society and a better world ...
40. *Solidarity* is undoubtedly a *Christian virtue*. In what has been said so far it has been possible to identify many points of contact between solidarity and *charity*, which is the distinguishing mark of Christ's disciples (cf. *Jn* 13:35).
In the light of faith, solidarity seeks to go beyond itself, to take on the *specifically Christian* dimensions of total gratuity, forgiveness and reconciliation. One's neighbour is then not only a human being with his or her own

rights and a fundamental equality with everyone else, but becomes the *living image* of God the Father, redeemed by the blood of Jesus Christ and placed under the permanent action of the Holy Spirit. One's neighbour must therefore be loved, even if an enemy, with the same love with which the Lord loves him or her; and for that person's sake one must be ready for sacrifice, even the ultimate one: to lay down one's life for the brethren (cf. *1 Jn* 3:16)."

Sollicitudo Rei Socialis. Encyclical Letter of the Supreme Pontiff John Paul II for the Twentieth Anniversary of Populorum Progressio, London, 1988.

SOLOMON ISLANDS. Member of the UN. An islands group in the Pacific. Total area: 27,556 sq. km. Pop. 1986 est. 286,000 (1976 census: 196,823). Capital on the larger island Guadalcanal: Honiara with 18,346 inhabitants 1979. GNP 1986 per capita: US $530. Currency: one Solomon Island dollar = 100 cents. Official language: English. National Day: July 7, Independence Day, 1978.
Member of the UN from Sept. 19, 1978 and all its specialized agencies except UNESCO, UPU, WIPO, UNIDO, IAEA and GATT; and is an ACP state of the EEC.
International relations: the Solomon Islands, discovered in 1586 by the Spanish explorer Alvaro de Mendana; occupied by German New Guinea Company 1885, the southern islands placed under British protectorate in 1895; the eastern islands 1898; in 1900 Germany transferred all rights to the UK in return for British withdrawal from Western Samoa; placed under Australian mandate by the League of Nations, 1920. In 1942 occupied by the Japanese, liberated by the US Navy 1944. From 1978 independent constitutional monarchy, with the British Sovereign, represented by a Governor-General, who must be a Solomon Islands citizen. A maritime border agreement was signed in June 1987 with Papua-New Guinea.

J. KENT, *The Solomon Islands*, Newton Abbot, 1972; *UN Chronicle*, Oct., 1978, pp. 27–30; *The Europa Year Book 1984. A World Survey*, Vol. II, pp. 2381–2384, London, 1984.

SOMALIA. Member of the UN. Democratic Republic of Somalia. Country in northeast Africa on the Indian Ocean. Borders with Kenya, Ethiopia and Djibouti. Area: 637,657 sq. km. Pop. 1988 est.: 6,260,000 (1980 est.: 4,637,000). Capital: Mogadishu with 350,000 inhabitants. Official language: Somali. GNP per capita in 1986: US $280. Currency: one Somali Shilling = 100 centesimi. National Day: July 1, Independence Day, 1960.
Member of the UN since Oct. 28, 1960, and all its specialized agencies except IAEA, GATT. Member of the OAU, of the Arab League, ACP state of the EEC. International relations: partitioned by Great Britain and Italy into (since 1905) British Somaliland and Italian Somaliland. The latter occupied by British troops in 1942; in 1948 British Somaliland became a British Protectorate and Italian Somaliland was given UN trusteeship status. By a UN General Assembly decision of Nov. 21, 1959 both Somalilands were united on June 1, 1960, and a month later the country was granted independence as Somalia (July 1, 1960). Somalia claims a major portion of Djibouti and Ogaden in Ethiopia, as well as other territories inhabited by the Somalis. In 1973 an OAU commission for the Ethiopian--Somali dispute was set up; in 1977 armed conflict broke out, which led to Somalia renouncing Treaty of Friendship and co-operation with the USSR signed in 1974 and breaking diplomatic relations with Cuba. On Oct. 18, 1977, a West German unit recaptured a Lufthansa plane hijacked to Mogadishu. A signatory of the Yaoundé Conventions of 1963 and 1969, and of the Lomé Conventions of 1975 and of 1980. A Naval and Air bases

agreement negotiated by the United States in 1980 was signed. The Ethiopia–Somalia border dispute 1960 referred to the area of ▷ Ogaden. It escalated into a military conflict 1982–1987; negotiations were held in Djibouti and Addis Ababa and Mogadishu in January, May and August 1986 and in Addis Ababa in April 1987, without arriving at a solution. The conflict ended on April 3, 1988 (▷ Ethiopia–Somalia peace agreement). The GA Res. 43/206 of Dec. 20, 1988 decided to provide emergency assistance to the Northern provinces of Somalia to help the Government cope with the large numbers of displaced persons and the repair, rehabilitation and reconstruction of vital public facilities and installations, destroyed as a result of attacks by armed bandits on towns and villages and on public installations.

UN Bulletin, Feb. 15 and Dec. 15, 1950; A.A. CASTAGNO Jr., *Somalia*, New York, 1959; I.M. LEWOS, *The Modern History of Somaliland. From Nation to State*. New York, 1965, 234 pp; R.L. HESS, *Italian Colonialism in Somalia*, Chicago, 1966, 234 pp.; *The Agricultural Economy of Somalia*, Washington, 1971; *Background to the Liberation Struggle of the Western Sahara*, Mogadiscio, 1978; *The Europa Year Book 1984. A World Survey*, Vol. II, pp. 2385–2395, London, 1984; Ethiopia–Somalia, in: A.J. DAY ed., *Border and Territorial Disputes*, London, 1987, pp. 126–132; *UN Resolutions and Decisions adopted by the General Assembly during its Forty Third Session, from 20 September to 22 December 1988*, pp. 309–310.

SONAR. Sound navigation and ranging. An instrument for deep-water surveying with sound for navigational, fishing, scientific and military purposes.

SONATRACH. Société Nationale pour le Transport et la Commercialisation des Hydrocarbures, the petroleum company of Algeria, established 1963 as an international Algerian–French company, with seat in Algiers; since 1968 possesses a monopoly for petroleum marketing in Algeria. A part-owner of SNREPAS (Societé Nationale de Recherche et d'Exploitation des Petrole au Sahara), CEP (Compagnie d'Exploitation Petroliere) and COPEFA (Compagnie des Petroles France-Afrique). On Feb. 24, 1971 the government of Algeria nationalized 51% of shares of all the abovementioned foreign companies and transferred them to Sonatrach. This led to a crisis in Algerian-French relations, ending June 30, 1971 upon the signing of an agreement by Compagnie Française des Pétroles (CFP) with Sonatrach, under which CFP received compensation for the nationalized shares to repay outstanding taxes and to invest a considerable part of its profits (until the end of 1975 – *c*. $550 million) in new research and drillings, and agreed to a higher catalogue price, which is a base for taxation; this agreement meant practically the end of the decolonization stage of Algerian crude oil, at the same time putting an end to illusions bolstered by the agreements regarding Algerian–French co-operation of July, 1965.

Le Monde, July 2, 1971; *The Middle East and North Africa 1972–73*, London, 1972.

SOPRON. Formerly Ödenburg, Austrian-Hungarian borderland territory, area: 356 sq. km, subject of international dispute 1921, settled Dec. 14–16, 1921 by a plebiscite in favor of Hungary (65%), recognized by the Conference of Ambassadors Dec. 23, 1921.

SORBONNE. Historical name of the Paris University from the middle of the 13th century. The number of students, about 12,000 in 1885, was ten times larger in 1980. The reform in the 1970s split

the Sorbonne into 13 interdisciplinary universities in the Paris area.

SOS. supposed abbrev. for "Save Our Ship" or "Save Our Souls", in the Morse alphabet: · · · — — — · · · (three dots, three dashes, three dots) by ships at sea calling for help; introduced by the London International Radiotelegraphic Convention 1912; in fact the selection of letters does not stand for any abbreviation but is derived from the ease of sending a telegraphic message by Morse alphabet; It corresponds to the broadcast distress signal MEDEA; MAY DAY is used by the British Air Force and MD (m'aider) is its French analogue. The International Federation of Blood Donors' Organizations, est. 1955 also accepted SOS as its abbreviation.

Yearbook of International Organizations.

SOSUS. NATO Sound Surveillance System. An international naval term for an underwater network of passive acoustic listening devices, primarily long arrays of hydrophones, fixed in place and designed to track Soviet submarines and surface ships.

SOUTH AFRICA. Member of the UN. The Republic of South Africa, country in Southern Africa on the Indian and Atlantic Ocean, bordering on Namibia, Botswana, Mozambique, Swaziland and Zimbabwe. Area: 1,221,037 sq. km. Pop. 1988 est.: 29,600,000 (1978 est. 23,894,000, divided by racist statistics into the four following groups: Whites – 4,408,000; Coloreds – 2,494,000; Asians – 778,000 and Blacks – 16,214,000 (1960 census total pop. 17,122,000 of whom Whites – 3,069,000; Coloreds – 1,500,000; Asians – 476,000 and Blacks 12,077,000). Administrative Capital: Pretoria, 1985 census: 443,059 city, 882,925 metropolitan area. Legislative capital: Cape Town, 1985 census: 776,617, city, 1.911,521 metropolitan area. Judicial capital: Bloemfontein, 1985 census: 104,381 city; 232,984 metropolitan area. GNP per capita of total pop. 1986, US $1800. Official languages: Afrikaans and English. Currency: one rand = 100 cents. National Day: May 31, Proclamation of Republic, 1961.
Member of the UN since Oct. 24, 1945 and of UN specialized organizations, with the exception of ILO, FAO, UNESCO, UPU, IFAD, UNIDO and IMO. International relations: 1652–1815 Dutch settlements (Dutch East India Company). The Congress of Vienna assigned to Great Britain the Cape of Good Hope territory. The Dutch colonists, called Boers, left the Cape in the years 1835–43 and established two republics in the interior: Orange Free State and Transvaal, 1850. After the discovery of diamond fields in the Orange river valley, 1867, and gold on the Witwatersrand, 1886, the British first annexed the Orange valley, 1871, and in 1889 began to integrate the two Boer republics in a customs union with The Cape Colony. The Boer War, 1899–1902, was lost by the Dutch. The Union of South Africa was formed in 1910 by the British and given dominion status. In 1925 the Afrikaans language was made an official language equal with English. The Union was a member of the British Commonwealth until it became a republic on May 31, 1961. Member of the League of Nations 1919–45. On the side of the Allies and of the United Nations in World Wars I and II. The racist segregation system, called ▷ Apartheid, was condemned by the UN General Assembly and by the International Court of Justice. (▷ Namibia.) In Dec., 1983 South African troops invaded the south provinces of Angola.

In April 1975 South Africa was suspended as a member of the WMO, and in July 1984 was expelled from the UPU.

Dec. 14, 1983 the UN General Assembly unanimously condemned the South African raid on Dec. 9, 1982 against the homes of alleged African National Congress members in Maseru, the capital of Lesotho, which resulted in the death of 42 people reported to be South African refugees. In Feb., 1984 South Africa agreed to a cease-fire with Angola.

On Mar. 16, 1984, South Africa signed with Mozambique a Non-aggression Pact, called also the Nkomati Pact. Both countries agreed to prevent their land, water or air space from being "used as a base, thoroughfare or in any other way by another state, government, foreign military forces organizations or individuals which plan or prepare acts of violence, terrorism or aggression against the other country."

The official ceremony at Komatiport on the border river Nkomati was boycotted by the invited Black African countries, with the exception of Swaziland. In 1984 the absolute majority of inhabitants protested against a new racist Constitution.

The UN General Assembly Res. 39/2, Sept. 18, 1984 by 133 votes to none with 2 abstentions (the UK and the USA) declared "the so called 'new constitution' of 1983 as null and void".

In July 1987, in Dakar, the first anti-apartheid meeting of the representatives of the white liberal opposition groups in South Africa with members of the outlawed African National Congress took place. (▷ Dakar anti-apartheid meeting 1987).

On Nov. 20, 1987, the GA Res. 42/23 supported an oil-embargo against South Africa, directed by the Intergovernmental Group to Monitor the Supply and Shipping of Oil and Petroleum Products to South Africa.

On November 25 and December 23, 1987 the Security Council adopted unanimously resolutions 602(1987) and 606(1987) condemning South Africa for its occupation of Angolan frontier territory.

The General Assembly on Dec. 7, 1988 expressed its "grave disappointment that, despite repeated appeals by the international community, certain Western States and Israel have continued to collaborate with the regime of South Africa in the military and nuclear fields and that some of these States have, by a ready recourse to use of veto, consistently frustrated every effort in the Security Council to deal decisively with the question of South Africa'. (Res. 43/71B, adopted by 138 votes to 4 (France, Israel, UK, US) with 12 abstentions). The unconditional release on Feb. 11, 1990 of Nelson Mandela, leader of the African National Congress, after 27 years in jail, and the lifting of the ban on the ANC's activities, brought hope for a gradual renouncement of apartheid and the introduction of a democratic "One man – One vote" electoral system.

The Africa Institute of South Africa, f. 1960, Pretoria. Publ.: *Journal of Contemporary African Studies* (2 a year), The South African Institute of International Affairs, f. 1934, Johannesburg. Publ.: *Southern Africa Record*.

M.J. HAIGHT, M. PALMER, *South Africa and India*, Johannesburg, 1949; *Immigration to South Africa*, Johannesburg, 1949; E. ROSENTHAL, *Encyclopaedia of Southern Africa*, London, 1961; F.A. JAARSVELD, *The Afrikaaners Interpretation of South-African History*, Cape Town, 1964; R. SEGAL (ed.), *Sanctions against South Africa*, Baltimore, 1964; A. HEPPLE, *South Africa. A Political and Economic History*, New York, 1966; D. BROWN, *Against the War Attitudes of White South Africa*, Garden City, 1968; N. PHILLIPS, *Racismo en Sudáfrica. La Tragedia del Apartheid*, México, DF, 1969; *The Oxford History of South Africa*, 3 Vols., Oxford, 1969; J. BARBER, *South Africa's Foreign Policy 1945–70*, Oxford, 1973; J. HOAGLAND, *South Africa. Civilizations in Conflict*, London, 1973; J. CARBSON, *No Neutral Ground*, New York, 1974; A. SACHS, *Justice in South Africa*, University of California, 1974; H. ADAM, *Modernizing Racial Domination: The Dynamics of South African Politics*, University of California, 1974; P. RANDALL, *A Taste of Power*, Johannesburg, 1974; *Bantustans in Sechab*, London, June–July 1975, pp. 12–14; L. DE VILLIERS, *South Africa. A Skunk Among Nations*, London, 1975; T.H.R. DAVENPORT, *South Africa: A Modern History*, London, 1977; H. BROTZ, *The Politics of South Africa: Democracy and Racial Diversity*, London, 1977; S. BIKO, *Black Consciousness in South Africa*, New York, 1978; *UN Chronicle*, March, May, July, 1981; *UN Chronicle*, February, 1982, p. 42; O.A. OZGUNT, *Apartheid, the UN and Peaceful Change in South Africa*, Dobbs Ferry, N.Y., 1982; *UN Chronicle*, February, 1982, p. 42; J. BARBER, *The Uneasy Relationship: Britain and South Africa*, London, 1983; R. LEONARD, *South Africa at War. White Power and the Crisis in Southern Africa*, Westport, 1983; *The Europa Year Book 1984. A World Survey*, Vol. II, pp. 2395–2423, London, 1984; Ch.COOKER, *The United States and South Africa, 1968–1985*, Durham N.C., 1986; I.D.I. MOORE, *South Africa and Nuclear Proliferation*, London, 1987; *International Herald Tribune*, July 10, 1987; J. BLUMENFIELD ed., *South Africa in Crisis*, London, 1987; M. MURRAY, *South Africa. Time of Agony, Time of Destiny*, New York, 1987; *UN Sanctions Against South Africa, A Selective Bibliography*, New York, 1988; N. GORDIMER, *The Essential Gesture: Writing, Politics and Places*, London, 1988; *UN Resolutions and Decisions adopted by the General Assembly during the First Part of its Forty-Third Session, from 20 September to 22 December 1988*, New York, 1989, p. 89, p. 135.

SOUTH AFRICAN INSTITUTE OF INTERNATIONAL AFFAIRS. f. 1934, Johannesburg, to facilitate the scientific study of international questions, particularly African questions. Publ.: *Quarterly Newsletter*.

SOUTH AFRICA PARIS DECLARATION, 1981. The International Conference on Sanctions against South Africa, organized by the United Nations in co-operation with the Organization of African Unity, was held at UNESCO House in Paris, from May 20 to 27, 1981. The Conference was attended by representatives of 124 governments, the United Nations, the Organization of African Unity, the movement of nonaligned countries, the specialized agencies of the United Nations, intergovernmental organizations, national liberation movements, and international and national non-governmental organizations, as well as a number of experts and leading statesmen. The national liberation movements of South Africa and Namibia – the African National Congress of South Africa, the Pan-Africanist Congress of Azania and the South West Africa People's Organization – were represented by high-level delegations led by their respective Presidents.

After reviewing the situation in South Africa, and in southern Africa as a whole, and after an extensive exchange of views on the feasibility of sanctions and other means as credible measures not involving force, which the world community can employ to exert diplomatic, economic and other pressures against the racist regime of South Africa, thereby averting the grave danger to international peace and security arising from the policy and action of the racist régime of South Africa, the international Conference adopted the following declaration which it commends for the earnest and urgent attention of all Governments, organizations and peoples for appropriate action to secure the expeditious eradication of apartheid and the liberation of Namibia from illegal occupation by South Africa's racist régime.

"The Conference expresses its profound concern over the situation in South Africa, and in southern Africa as a whole, resulting from the policies and actions of the South African régime of racism, repression and terrorism.

The stubborn efforts of that régime to perpetuate racist domination by an ever increasing dependence on violence and repression and to continue its illegal occupation of Namibia, in defiance of repeated appeals by the international community and in flagrant contravention of the United Nations Charter, the Universal Declaration of Human Rights, and the Declaration on the Granting of Independence to Colonial Countries and Peoples, have created an explosive situation in southern Africa and constitute no longer a threat to, but a manifest breach of international peace and security.

The Pretoria régime is, moreover, continuing its illegal occupation of Namibia in defiance of the United Nations and the Advisory Opinion of the International Court of Justice, thereby undermining the authority of the United Nations and violating the principles of the Charter of the United Nations. It has resorted to the militarization of the Territory, for which the United Nations has assumed direct responsibility, and to brutal repression of the Namibian people. It has frustrated the implementation of the United Nations Plan for the independence of Namibia through free and fair elections. To this end, the South African racist régime deliberately caused the collapse of the preimplementation meeting held at Geneva from 7 to 19 January 1981. The result has been a continuing and escalating armed conflict against the people of Namibia and its sole and authentic representative – the South West Africa People's Organization.

In pursuance of its policies seeking to perpetuate racist domination in South Africa and to maintain illegal occupation of Namibia, as well as expand its imperialist influence beyond its borders, the Pretoria régime has resorted to constant acts of aggression, subversion, destabilization and terrorism against neighbouring independent African States, thereby aggravating existing international tensions.

It has built up a massive military machine and repressive apparatus and has embarked on acquisition of nuclear weapon capability in an attempt to suppress resistance by the oppressed people and terrorize neighbouring States into effective subservience.

Acquisition of military equipment and nuclear weapon capability by the racist régime of South Africa, with its record of violence and aggression, poses a grave menace to humanity. The situation in southern Africa is, therefore, characterized by repeated breaches of the peace and acts of aggression and an ever-growing threat of a wider conflict with grave repercussion in Africa and the world.

The continuing political, economic and military collaboration of certain Western States and their transnational corporations with the racist régime of South Africa encourages its persistent intransigence and definace of the international community and constitutes a major obstacle to the elimination of the inhuman and original system of apartheid in South Africa and the attainment of self determination, freedom and national independence by the people of Namibia.

The United Nations and the international community must take energetic and concerted action because the oppressed people of South Africa and Namibia deserve full support in their legitimate struggle for self-determination, freedom and national independence. The independent sovereign States of southern Africa have a right to protection from the repeated armed attacks, act of aggression and depredations by a racist régime which acts as an international outlaw.

The United Nations and the international community must take action to stop the continuing breaches of the peace, and to avert a wider conflict. Such action is urgent and indispensable for the maintenance of international peace and security, for the elimination of apartheid and illegal occupation, for the discharge of the solemn obligations to the people of Namibia, for ensuring the emancipation of Africa after centuries of oppression, exploitation and humiliation, and for promoting genuine international co-operation.

The Conference strongly condemns the minority racist régime of South Africa for its criminal policies and actions.

The Conference declares that the racist régime of South Africa – by its repression of the great majority of the people of the country and their national liberation movements, by its illegal occupation of Namibia, and by its acts of aggression against neighbouring States – bears full responsibility for the present conflict and for its inevitable escalation.

The Conference further stresses that this responsibility of South Africa is shared by those States whose assistance and multifaceted support encourage the aggressive policy of the Pretoria racist régime.

It expresses its deep conviction that the situation in South Africa, and in southern Africa as a whole, is of deep concern to all Governments and organizations and to humanity as a whole.

The Conference affirms that the sanctions provided under Chapter VII of the United Nations Charter, universally applied, are the most appropriate and effective means to ensure South Africa's compliance with the decisions of the United Nations. The choice is between an escalation of conflict and the imposition of international sanctions, when all other attempts to reach a peaceful settlement have failed.

The Conference notes that an overwhelming majority of States, as well as most governmental and non-governmental organizations, including trade unions and religious organizations, share this view. It notes with appreciation the sacrifices by many States, especially the developing States, in accordance with the decisions of the United Nations, OAU and the Movement of non-aligned countries to promote freedom and peace in southern Africa. It urges those Powers which have so far opposed sanctions to head the views of the rest of the international community and harmonize their policies in order to facilitate concerted action.

The purpose of sanctions is: (a) to force South Africa to abandon its racist policy of apartheid and to put an end to its illegal occupation of Namibia; (b) to demonstrate, by action, the universal abhorrence of apartheid and solidarity with the legitimate aspirations and struggles of the people of South Africa and Namibia; (c) to deny the benefits of international cooperation to the South African régime so as to oblige it and its supporters to heed world opinion, to abandon the policy of racist domination and to seek a solution by consultation with the genuine leaders of the oppressed people; (d) to undermine the ability of the South African régime to repress its people, commit acts of aggression against independence States and pose a threat to international peace and security; (e) to remove economic support from apartheid so as to mitigate suffering in the course of the struggle of the people of South Africa and Namibia for freedom, and thereby promote as peaceful a transition as possible.

In the light of the above, the Conference urgently calls for a programme of sanctions and related measures against South Africa.

UN Chronicle, July, 1981, pp. 44–48.

SOUTH AMERICA. Continent in the Western Hemisphere, part of America south of the isthmus of Panama, with an area of 17,800,000 sq. km; politically comprises Argentina, Bolivia, Brazil, Chile, Colombia, Ecuador, French Guyana, Guyana, Paraguay, Peru, Suriname, Uruguay and Venezuela.

SOUTHASIA. An international geopolitical term for the southern region, of the Asian continent, with a sub-region of Southeast Asia a broad peninsula including the Malaya and the Indonesian archipelagoes. ▷ ASEAN.

C.A. FISHER, *Southeast Asia*, London, 1964; J. HARRIS, H. ALAVI eds., *South Asia*, London, 1986.

SOUTH ASIA ECONOMIC COOPERATION TREATY, 1967. Signed in Bangkok on Aug. 8, 1967, by the governments of Philippines, Indonesia, Malaysia, Singapore and Siam, for the purpose of promoting the growth of the South Asia region.

SOUTH-ASIAN ASSOCIATION FOR REGIONAL CO-OPERATION, SAARAC, est. in Dec. 1985 in Bangladesh by the leaders of Bangladesh,

Bhutan, India, the Maldives, Nepal, Pakistan and Sri Lanka. The first meeting was dedicated to economic problems.

The second meeting in Bangalore, the capital of the Indian state of Karnataka took place in Nov. 1986 and adopted a Bangalore Declaration.

The third summit was held in Katmandu, the capital of Nepal in Nov. 1987. The Final Document included an action program for the protection of the environment and for food security reserves for combating the effects of natural disasters. The summit accepted the Convention for the Supression of Terrorism and Extradition of Convicted Terrorists.

KEESING's *Contemporary Archive*, 1985 and 1986; KEESING's *Record of World Events*, 1987.

SOUTH ASIAN INTEGRATION. Economic integration of South Asia was started when, in 1963, the Philippines, Indonesia and Thailand opened a Free Trade Zone and by the Treaty on South Asian Economic Co-operation signed by the Philippines, Indonesia, Malaysia, Singapore and Thailand, 1967.

SOUTH ASIAN REGIONAL COMMISSION, SARC. An intergovernmental organization est. on Aug. 2, 1983 in New Delhi by the governments of Bangladesh, Bhutan, India, the Maldives, Nepal, Pakistan and Sri Lanka.

KEESING's *Contemporary Archive*, 1983.

SOUTH ATLANTIC ZONE OF PEACE. A Brazilian Proposal of a 'zone of peace and co-operation' between Africa and South America was adopted on Oct. 27, 1986 with 124 votes, – one (USA) against, and 8 abstentions (Belgium, France, FRG, Italy, Japan, Luxembourg, the Netherlands and Portugal). By the UN Resolution 41/11 all states of the South Atlantic Zone were called to ensure 'the protection of the environment, the conservation of living resources, the non-introduction of nuclear weapons or other weapons of mass destruction'.

KEESING's *Record of World Events*, March 1987; SIPRI *Yearbook 1987*, London, 1988, pp. 404–408.

SOUTH CHINA SEA. West arm of the Pacific Ocean, 2,590,000 sq. km, separating South-East Asia from the Taiwan, Luzon, Palawan and Borneo islands. Main sea ports: Hong Kong, Kuangeron, Manila, Haiphong and Saigon. Four archipelagos of the Paracel Islands are subject of dispute among the Peoples' Republic of China, the Philippines, Taiwan and Vietnam. The islands, the majority of them uninhabited, most probably have deposits of crude oil, and the government of the People's Republic of China, having carried through trial drillings in that region, officially laid claim to all four archipelagos within China's 320 km coastal zone June 15, 1976, maintaining that they were part of Chinese territory.

SOUTHEAST ASIA TREATY ORGANIZATION. ▷ SEATO.

SOUTHEAST ASIAN MINISTERS OF EDUCATION ORGANIZATION, SEAMEO. An intergovernmental institution, est. 1965, in Bangkok, "to promote co-operation among the southeast Asian nations through education, sciences and culture to further respect for justice, for the rule of law and for human rights and fundamental freedoms."

The Charter of the SEAMEO was signed in Singapore, Feb. 7, 1968, and came into force on Mar. 6, 1969. Members: Indonesia, Khmer Republic, Laos, Malaysia, Philippines, Singapore, Thailand,

Vietnam. Associated members: Australia, France and New Zealand.

UNTS, Vol. 669, p. 32.

SOUTHERN AFRICAN DEVELOPMENT CO-OPERATION CONFERENCE, est. 1979 by Angola, Botswana, Malawi, Mozambique, Tanzania, Zambia and Zimbabwe to elaborate economic strategy aiming to reduce dependence on South Africa. The annual conferences on the level of heads of state elaborated over 400 projects for the period 1986–1990.

KEESING's *Record of World Events*, April, 1986.

SOUTH KOREA. ▷ Korea, Republic of.

SOUTH PACIFIC BUREAU FOR ECONOMIC CO-OPERATION. ▷ SPEC.

SOUTH PACIFIC COMMISSION AGREEMENT, 1947. Agreement between Australia, France, the Netherlands, New Zealand, UK and US, establishing the South Pacific Commission, signed in Canberra, Feb. 6, 1947; came into force July 29, 1948.

UNTS, Vol. 97, pp. 227–269.

SOUTH PACIFIC COMMISSION, PERMANENT (CPPS). Comisión Permanente del Pacífico Sur, an intergovernmental agency, which was established by the Convention of Aug. 18, 1952 signed and ratified by the Government of Chile, Ecuador and Peru, and by virtue of the Incorporation Convention signed in Quito on Aug. 9, 1979 by Colombia. Purpose: co-ordination of maritime policies among the member States, promotion of scientific research, protection of the marine environment and resources.

The CPS signed agreements on co-operation with OAS, 1979; UNESCO, 1979; ECLA, 1983; FAO, 1985; UNEP, 1985.

Comisión Permanente del Pacífico Sur, Estructura, objetivos, actividades y programas (in Spanish and English) Quito 1985.

SOUTH PACIFIC DECLARATION, 1982. ▷ Rarotonga Declaration, 1982.

SOUTH PACIFIC FORUM. The official name since 1971 for inter-governmental meetings of five islands of Oceania: Fiji, Nauru, Tonga, Western Samoa and Cook Islands, also Australia and New Zealand. The first took place in Wellington, New Zealand, in Aug., 1971; the second in Canberra one year later, subsequent ones in the capitals of the member islands. In 1975 Papua-New Guinea and Niue island were accepted into the Forum; in the following years also: Kiribati, Solomon Islands, Tuvalu, Vanuatu and Federated States of Micronesia (observer).

KEESING's *Contemporary Archive*, 1971.

SOUTH PACIFIC LIMA CONVENTION 1981. The Convention for the Protection of Marine Environment and Coastal Areas of the South Pacific, signed in November 1981 in Lima, under the aegis of UNEP, together with an Agreement on Regional Co-operation in Combating Pollution of the South-East Pacific by Hydrocarbons and other Harmful Substances in Cases of Emergency.

In March 1982, in Rarotonga, capital of the Cook Islands, also under the aegis of UNEP the South Pacific countries adopted the South Pacific Declaration on Natural Resources and the Environment, called the Rarotonga Declaration.

KEESING's *Contemporary Archive*, 1986.

SOUTH PACIFIC MARINE ENVIRONMENT CONVENTIONS, 1981. ▷ South-Pacific Lima Convention, 1981.

SOUTH POLE. Southern end of the Earth's axis lat. 90°S and long. 0. The South Pole was first reached by the Norwegian explorer Roald Amundsen, 1911.

The US Amundsen Scott Station was rebuilt in 1974. In the 1980's a thousand tourists a year were visiting the South Pole on nine ships. The National Geographic Magazine published in April 1987 a map of Antarctica with many new details on the coastline and other information about the continent, that thirty years ago had been explored only in one third.

In the scientific station Esperanza on the Antarctic Peninsula, Argentina set up a post office and in 1978 a pregnant woman coming from Argentina gave birth in Esperanza to a son, Emilio Marcos Palina who was declared under ▷ ius soli an Argentinian citizen. In 1982 a convention to protect ▷ marine living resources was signed.

See also ▷ Antarctica:, and ▷ Ozone.

R. AMUNDSEN, *My Life*, London, 1929.

SOUTH-SOUTH COMMISSION. Established in 1986 in Kuala Lumpur, as a "think tank" consisting of 20 intellectuals and former politicians, acting independently of governments, to identify the causes of underdevelopment and to produce common strategies to combat poverty and hunger and economic stagnation, modelled on the Independent Commission on International Development (▷ Brandt Commission).

KEESING's *Record of World Events*, 1987.

SOUTH TYROL ▷ Austria–Italy Border Dispute.

SOVEREIGNTY OF STATES IN THE UN. Doctrine of international law, recognized by the signatories of the Charter of the United Nations that all the states members of the United Nations are sovereign states and their international relations are regulated in accordance with the principle of ▷ Equality of States in the UN. The UN General Assembly Res. 3016/XXVII on Dec. 18, 1972, recalling its previous resolutions of Dec. 14, 1962, of Nov. 25, 1966, of Nov. 19, 1968 and of Dec. 11, 1970, reaffirmed the sovereignty of States over natural resources:

"The General Assembly of the United Nations reaffirms the right of States to permanent sovereignty over all natural resources on land within their national boundaries, as well as over such resources that are placed on the sea-bed and under it within the boundaries of their state jurisdiction and in the waters over such sea-bed."

Ch.E. MERRIAM, *History of the Theory of Sovereignty since Rousseau*, New York, 1900; H.J. LASKI, *Studies in the Problem of Sovereignty*, New Haven, 1917; M. METTATIS, R. BOTTINI, R.J. DUPUY, *La souveraineté au XX-e siècle*, Paris, 1971; A. JAMES, *Sovereign Statehood: The Basis of International Society*, London, 1986; M.S. SORODS, *Beyond the Sovereignty, The Challenge of Global Policy*, Colombia, S.C., 1986; C.A. ERHARDT, *Europa Zwischen nationaler Souveränität und Integration*, in: Aussenpolitik, 1987, 2; R.L. BLEDSOE, B.A. BOCZEK, *The International Law Dictionary*, Oxford, 1987.

SOVEREIGNTY OVER NATURAL RESOURCES. The UN General Assembly Res. 1803/XVII, Dec. 14, 1962, on Permanent Sovereignty over National Resources declared as follows:

"The General Assembly,
Recalling its resolutions 523(VI) of 12 January 1952 and 626(VII) of 21 December 1952.

Bearing in mind its resolution 1314(XIII) of 12 December 1958, by which it established the Commission on Permanent Sovereignty over Natural Resources and instructed it to conduct a full survey of the status of permanent sovereignty over natural wealth and resources as a basic constituent of the right to self-determination, with recommendations, where necessary, for its strengthening, and decided further that, in the conduct of the full survey of the status of the permanent sovereignty of peoples and nations over their natural wealth and resources, due regard should be paid to the rights and duties of States under international law and to the importance encouraging international co-operation in the economic developing countries,
Bearing in mind its resolution 1515(XV) of 15 December 1960, in which it recommended that the sovereign right of every State to dispose of its wealth and its natural resources should be respected,
Considering that any measure in this respect must be based on the recognition on the inalienable right of all States freely to dispose of their natural wealth and resources in accordance with their national interests, and on respect for the economic independence of States,
Considering that nothing in paragraph 4 below in any way prejudices the position of any Member State on any aspect of the question of the rights and obligations of successor States and Governments in respect of property acquired before the accession to complete sovereignty of countries formerly under colonial rule,
Noting that the subject of succession of States and Governments is being examined as a matter of priority by the International Law Commission,
Considering that it is desirable to promote international co-operation for the economic development of developing countries, and that economic and financial agreements between the developed and the developing countries must be based on the principles of equality and of the right of peoples and nations to self-determination,
Considering that the provision of economic and technical assistance, loans and increased foreign investment must not be subject to conditions which conflict with the interests of the recipient State,
Considering the benefits to be derived from exchanges of technical and scientific information likely to promote the development and use of such resources and wealth, and the important part which the United Nations and other international organizations are called upon to play in that connexion,
Attaching particular importance to the question of promoting the economic development of developing countries and securing their economic independence,
Noting that the creation and strengthening of the inalienable sovereignty of States over their natural wealth and resources reinforces their economic independence,
Desiring that there should be further consideration by the United Nations of the subject of permanent sovereignty over natural resources in the spirit of international co-operation in the field of economic development, particularly that of the developing countries,
Declares that:
I(1) The right of peoples and nations to permanent sovereignty over their natural wealth and resources must be exercised in the interest of their national development and of the well-being of the people of the State concerned.
(2) The exploration, development and disposition of such resources, as well as the import of the foreign capital required for these purposes, should be in conformity with the rules and conditions which the peoples and nations freely consider to be necessary or desirable with regard to the authorization, restriction or prohibition of such activities.
(3) In cases where authorization is granted, the capital imported and the earnings on that capital shall be governed by the terms thereof, by the national legislation in force, and by international law. The profits derived must be shared in the proportions freely agreed upon, in each case, between the investors and the recipient State, due care being taken to ensure that there is no impairment, for any reason, of that State's sovereignty over its natural wealth and resources.
(4) Nationalization, expropriation or requisitioning shall be based on grounds or reasons of public utility, security or the national interest which are recognized as overriding purely individual or private interests, both domestic and foreign. In such cases the owner shall be paid appropriate compensation, in accordance with the rules in force in the State taking such measures in the exercise of its sovereignty and in accordance with international law. In any case where the question of compensation gives rise to a controversy, the national jurisdiction of the State taking such measures shall be exhausted. However, upon agreement by sovereign States and other parties concerned, settlement of the dispute should be made through arbitration or international adjudication.
(5) The free and beneficial exercise of the sovereignty of peoples and nations over their natural resources must be furthered by the mutual respect of States based on their sovereign equality.
(6) International co-operation for the economic development of developing countries, whether in the form of public or private capital investments, exchange of goods and services, technical assistance, or exchange of scientific information, shall be such as to further their independent national development and shall be based upon respect for their sovereignty over their natural wealth and resources.
(7) Violation of the rights of peoples and nations to sovereignty over their natural wealth and resources is contrary to the spirit and principles of the Charter of the United Nations and hinders the development of international co-operation and the maintenance of peace.
(8) Foreign investment agreements freely entered into by or between sovereign States shall be observed in good faith; States and international organizations shall strictly and conscientiously respect the sovereignty of peoples and nations over their natural wealth and resources in accordance with the Charter and the principles set forth in the present resolution.
II. Welcomes the decision of the International Law Commission to speed up its work on the codification of the topic of responsibility of States for the consideration of the General Assembly;
III. Requests the Secretary-General to continue the study of the various aspects of permanent sovereignty over natural resources, taking into account the desire of Member States to ensure the protection of their sovereign rights while encouraging international co-operation in the field of economic development, and to report to the Economic and Social Council and to the General Assembly, if possible at its eighteenth session."

UN Yearbook, 1962; G. ELIAN, *The Principle of Sovereignty over Natural Resources*, Alphen, 1979, *UN Chronicle*, September–October, 1983.

SOVETSK. Formerly Tilsit, a town on the Niemen river in the northwestern European part of the USSR. Pop. 1970 census: 38,456. ▷ Tilsit Peace Treaties, 1807.

SOVIET. *Russian*: "council", a principal organ of the Soviet Union system initiated by the October Revolution 1917 in Russia, which was declared to be "a Republic of Soviets of Workmen's, Soldiers' and Peasants' Deputies. All the power in the center and in the provinces belongs to these Soviets." On Jan. 9, 1918 the collegium under the People's Commissary for Internal Affairs adopted the following Instruction regarding the Organization of Soviets of Workmen's, Soldiers' and Peasants' Deputies:

"In all Soviets, in place of the old, antiquated government institutions, the following departments or commissariats must first be organized:
(1) Administration, in charge of the domestic and foreign relations of the Republic and technically unifying all the other departments.
(2) Finances, whose duty is the compilation of the local budget, the collection of local and state taxes, the carrying out of measures for the nationalization of the banks, the administration of the People's Bank, control over the disbursements of national funds, etc.
(3) Board of National Economy, which organizes the manufacture of most necessary products of factory, mill, and home industries, determines the amount of raw materials and fuel obtains and distributes them, organizes and supplies the rural economy, etc.

(4) Land, whose duty is make an exact survey of the land, forests, waters, and other resources, and their distribution for purposes of utilization.

(5) Labor, which must organize and unite trade unions, factory and mill committees, peasant associations, etc., and also create insurance organizations of all kinds.

(6) Ways of Communication, whose duty is the taking of measures for the nationalization of the railways and steam-ship enterprises, the direction of this most important brance of the national economy, the building of new roads of local importance, etc.

(7) Post, Telegraph, and Telephone, which must aid and develop these state enterprises.

(8) Public Education, which looks after the education and instruction of the population in the school and out of school, establishes new schools, kindergartens, universities, libraries, clubs, etc., carries out measures for the nationalization of printing-shops, the publication of necessary periodicals and books and their circulation among the population, etc.

(9) Legal, which must liquidate the old courts, organize people's and arbitration courts, take charge of places of detention, reform then, etc.

(10) Medical-Sanitary, whose duty is sanitary-hygienic supervision, the organization of medical aid accessible to all, sanitary equipment of urban and rural settlements, etc.

(11) Public Realty, whose duty is the regulation of the housing problem, supervision over confiscated and public buildings, the construction of new ones, etc."

"Russian Documents", in: *International Conciliation*, No. 136, March, 1919, pp. 434–435.

SOVIET BLOC. International term, coined after World War II by the Western press for the new socialist countries and the Soviet Union.

Z. BRZEZINSKI, *The Soviet Bloc: Unity and Conflict*, Cambridge, Mass., 1960.

SOVIET CONTROL COMMISSION IN GERMANY. Est. Oct. 10, 1949 by the USSR in place of the Soviet Military Administration in Germany (one of the four Allied military governments in Germany); in operation from June 9, 1945 to Oct. 10, 1949, when the Soviet government transferred its functions to the GDR government. The creation of the Soviet Control Commission followed the establishment in June (and legalization in Sept.), 1949 by the governments of France, Great Britain, and USA of a trilateral ▷ Allied High Commission for Germany.

SOVIET DECLARATION OF RIGHTS OF THE LABORING AND EXPLOITED PEOPLE, 1918. The Declaration approved in Jan., 1918 by the third All-Russian Congress of Soviet, which together with the Constitution of the Russian Soviet Federated Socialist Republic adopted by the fifth All-Russian Congress of Soviets on July 10, 1918, formed the preamble of the Constitution:

"(1) Russia is declared to be a Republic of the Soviets of Workers', Soldiers', and Peasants' Deputies. All the central and local power belongs to these Soviets.

(2) The Russian Soviet Republic is organized on the basis of a free union of free nations, as a federation of Soviet National Republics.

(3) Bearing in mind as its fundamental problem the abolition of exploitation of men by men, the entire abolition of the division of the people into classes, the suppression of exploiters, the establishment of a Socialist society, and the victory of socialism in all lands, the third All-Russian Congress of Soviets of Workers', Soldiers', and Peasants' Deputies further resolves:

(a) for the purpose of realizing the socialization of land, all private property in land is abolished, and the entire land is declared to be national property and is to be apportioned among husbandmen without any compensation to the former owners, in the measure of each one's ability to till it.

(b) all forests, treasures of the earth, and waters of general public utility, all implements whether animate or inanimate, model farms and agricultural enterprises, are declared to be national property.

(c) as a first step towards complete transfer of ownership to the Soviet Republic of all factories, mills, mines, railways, and other means of production and transportation, the Soviet law for the control by workmen and the establishment of the Supreme Soviet of National Economy is hereby confirmed, so as to assure the power of the workers over the exploiters.

(d) with reference to international banking and finance, the third Congress of Soviets is discussing the Soviet decree regarding the annulment of loans made by the Government of the Czar, by landowners and the bourgeoisie, and it trust that the Soviet Government will firmly follow this course until the final victory of the international workers' revolt against the oppression of capital.

(e) the transfer of all banks into the ownership of the Workers' and Peasants' Government, as one of the conditions of the liberation of the toiling masses from the yoke of capital, is confirmed.

(f) universal obligation to work is introduced for the purpose of eliminating the parasitic strata of society and organizing the economic life of the country.

(g) for the purpose of securing the working class in the possession of the complete power, and in order to eliminate all possibility of restoring the power of the exploiters, it is decreed that all toilers be armed, and that a Socialist Army be organized and the propertied class be disarmed.

(4) Expressing its absolute resolve to liberate mankind from the grip of capital and imperialism, which flooded the earth with blood in this present most criminal of all wars, the third Congress of Soviets fully agrees with the Soviet Government in its policy of breaking secret treaties, of organizing on a wide scale the fraternization of the workers and peasants of the belligerent armies, and of making all efforts to conclude a general democratic peace without annexations or indemnities, upon the basis of the free determination of the peoples.

(5) It is also to this end that the third Congress of Soviets insists upon putting an end to the barbarous policy of the bourgeois civilization which enables the exploiters of a few chosen nations to enslave hundreds of millions of the toiling population of Asia, of the colonies, and of small countries generally.

(6) The third Congress of Soviets hails the policy of the Council of People's Commissars in proclaiming the full independence of Finland, in withdrawing troops from Persia, and in proclaiming the right of Armenia to self-determination.

(7) The third All-Russian Congress of Soviets of Workers', Soldiers', and Peasants' Deputies believes that now, during the progress of the decisive battle between the proletariat and its exploiters, the exploiters cannot hold a position in any branch of the Soviet Government. The power must belong entirely to the toiling masses and to their plenipotentiary representatives – the Soviets of Workers', Soldiers', and Peasants' Deputies.

(8) In its effort to create a league – free and voluntary, and for that reason all the more complete and secure – of the working classes of all the peoples of Russia, the third Congress of soviets merely establishes the fundamental principles of the federation of Russian Soviet Republics, leaving to the workers and peasants of every people to decide the following question at their plenary sessions of their Soviets: whether or not they desire to participate, and on what basis, in the federal government and other federal Soviet institutions."

"Russian Documents", in: *International Conciliation*, No. 136, March, 1919, pp. 485–487.

SOVIET MILITARY DEFENCE DOCTRINE 1987. According to US Pentagon experts the USSR in 1987 made a fundamental change in its strategic military doctrine. The old doctrine: 'offense is the main form of battle' was replaced by the formula: 'Soviet military doctrine considers defence as the main form of military operations', published in a book by the Soviet Minister of Defence, General Dymitriy Yazov called 'In Defence of Socialism and Peace',

B.E. TRAINOR, *A Strategic Shift Observed in Moscow*, in: International Herald Tribune, March 8, 1988.

SOVIET NATION. An international term introduced by Joseph Stalin for the commonwealth of 190 nationality groups in the USSR (census 1929, but 62, census 1939 and 109, census 1959); defined by L. Brezhnev in 1980: as a concept extending to all nations in the Soviet Union:

'The Soviet nation is a social phenomenon whose significance is determined not only by influence on life in our society, but also on international relations and on the entire historical process'.

The doctrine of 'socialistic nationality' linked with the term 'Soviet Nation' is criticized since 1987 by Soviet demographers as being in contradiction with the doctrine of ▷ Self-determination.

S. SHESMUKHAMIED, *'Sovietskiy Narod'*, in: Woprosy Filosofyi, No. 5, 1980; M. KRIUKOV, *Socialistic Nationality*, in: Moskovskaye Novosti, Nr. 32, 1987.

SOVIET PROPOSAL ON ATOMIC ENERGY, 1947. A Soviet project of an International Control Commission of Atomic Energy in the framework of the Security Council, presented on June 19, 1947 to the ▷ UNAEC. Rejected on April 5, 1947, by 9:2. The text is as follows:

The Government of the USSR, "in addition and in development of" its proposal of June 19, 1946, calling for an international convention prohibiting atomic and other major weapons of mass destruction, presented for the consideration of the Commission the following "basic provisions" on which an international agreement for convention on atomic energy should be based:

"(1) For ensuring the use of atomic energy only for peaceful purposes, in accordance with the international convention on the prohibition of atomic and other major weapons of mass destruction and also with the purpose of preventing violations of the convention on the prohibition of atomic weapons and for the protection of complying States against hazards of violations and evasions, there shall be established strict international control simultaneously over all facilities engaged in mining of atomic raw materials and in production of atomic materials and atomic energy.

(2) For carrying out measures of control of atomic energy facilities, there shall be established, within the framework of the Security Council, an international commission for atomic energy control, to be called the International Control Commission.

(3) The International Control Commission shall have its own inspectorial apparatus.

(4) Terms and organizational principles of international control of atomic energy, and also composition, rights and obligations of the International Control Commission, as well as provisions on the basis of which it shall carry out its activities, shall be determined by a special international convention on atomic energy control, which is to be concluded in accordance with the convention on the prohibition of atomic weapons.

(5) With the purpose of ensuring the effectiveness of international control of atomic energy, the convention on the control of atomic energy shall be based on the following fundamental provisions:

(a) The International Control Commission shall be composed of the Representatives of States Members of the Atomic Energy Commission established by the General Assembly decision of 24 January 1946, and may create such subsidiary organs which it finds necessary for the fulfilment of its functions.

(b) The International Control Commission shall establish its own rules of procedure.

(c) The personnel of the International Control Commission shall be selected on an international basis.

(d) The International Control Commission shall periodically carry out inspection of facilities for mining of atomic raw materials and for the production of atomic materials and atomic energy.

(6) While carrying out inspection of atomic energy facilities, the International Control Commission shall undertake the following actions:

(a) Investigates the activities of facilities for mining atomic raw materials, for the production of atomic materials and atomic energy as well as verifies their accounting.

(b) Checks existing stocks of atomic raw materials, atomic materials, and unfinished products.

(c) Studies production operations to the extent necessary for the control of the use of atomic materials and atomic energy.

(d) Observes the fulfilment of the rules of technical exploitation of the facilities described by the convention on control as well as works out and prescribes the rules of technological control of such facilities.

(e) Collects and analyses data on the mining of atomic raw materials and on the production of atomic materials and atomic energy.

(f) Carries on special investigations in cases when suspicion of violations of the convention on the prohibition of atomic weapons arises.

(g) Makes recommendations to Governments on the questions relating to production, stockpiling and use of atomic materials and atomic energy.

(h) Makes recommendations to the Security Council on measures for prevention and suppression in respect to violators of the conventions on the prohibition of atomic weapons and on the control of atomic energy.

(7) For the fulfilment of the tasks of control and inspection entrusted to the International Control Commission, the latter shall have the right of:

(a) Access to any facilities for mining, production, and stockpiling of atomic raw materials and atomic materials, as well as to the facilities for the exploitation of atomic energy.

(b) Acquaintance with the production operations of the atomic energy facilities, to the extent necessary for the control of use of atomic materials and atomic energy.

(c) The carrying out of weighing, measurements, and various analyses of atomic raw materials, atomic materials, and unfinished products.

(d) Requesting from the Government of any nation, and checking of, various data and reports on the activities of atomic energy facilities.

(e) Requesting of various explanations on the questions relating to the activities of atomic energy facilities.

(f) Making recommendations and presentations to Governments on the matters of the production and use of atomic energy.

(g) Submitting recommendations for the consideration of the Security Council on measures in regard to violators of the conventions on the prohibition of atomic weapons and on the control of atomic energy.

(8) In accordance with the tasks of international control of atomic energy, scientific research activities in the field of atomic energy shall be based on the following provisions:

(a) Scientific research activities in the field of atomic energy must comply with the necessity of carrying out the convention on the prohibition of atomic weapons and with the necessity of preventing its use for military purposes.

(b) Signatory States to the convention on the prohibition of atomic weapons must have a right to carry on unrestricted scientific research activities in the field of atomic energy, directed toward discovery of methods, of its use for peaceful purposes.

(c) In the interests of an effective fulfilment of its control and inspectorial functions, the International Control Commission must have a possibility to carry out scientific research activities in the field of discovery of methods of the use of atomic energy for peaceful purposes. The carrying out of such activities will enable the Commission to keep itself informed on the latest achievements in this field and to have its own skilled international personnel, which is required by the Commission for practical carrying out of the measures of control and inspection.

(d) In conducting scientific research in the field of atomic energy, one of the most important tasks of the International Control Commission should be to ensure a wide exchange of information among nations in this field and to render necessary assistance, through advice, to the countries parties to the convention, which may request such assistance.

(e) The International Control Commission must have at its disposal material facilities including research laboratories and experimental installations necessary for the proper organization of the research activities to be conducted by it."

B. GOLDSCHMIDT, *A Forerunner of the NPT? The Soviet Proposals of 1947*, in: IAEA BULLETIN, Spring, 1986, pp. 58–64.

SOVIET RUSSIA. The abbreviation of the ▷ Russian Soviet Federated Socialist Republic, often used in the world press to mean the whole Union of Soviet Socialist Republics, of which RSFSR occupies over three-fourths of the total area.

SOVIET SPACE AGENCY. ▷ Glavkosmos.

SOVIET UNION. ▷ Union of Soviet Socialist Republics, USSR.

SOVIET UNION DRAFT FOR A GENERAL AND COMPLETE DISARMAMENT, 1927. On Nov. 30, 1927 the Soviet Delegation to the Preparatory Commission for the Disarmament Conference presented for the first time in the League of Nations forum its own proposals for world disarmament. The highlights of the Soviet statement are as follows:

"The Soviet Government has systematically endeavoured to get the question of disarmament definitely and practically formulated. Its endeavours have, however, always encountered determined resistance from other States. The Soviet Government – the only one to show in deeds its will to peace and disarmament – was not admitted to the Washington Conference of 1921–1922, devoted to questions of the curtailment of naval armaments. The proposal of general disarmament made by the Soviet delegation to the Genoa Conference on April 10th, 1922, was rejected by the Conference. Despite this opposition, the Soviet Government has never relaxed in its determined endeavours with regard to disarmament. In December 1922 a Conference was called in Moscow, by the Soviet Government, of representatives of the border States for the joint discussion of the problem of proportional curtailment of armaments. The Soviet Government agreed to a considerable diminution of its armaments despite the fact that this would not affect many great Powers always ready, whether under the obligation of treaties or not, to come to the assistance of the other countries represented at the Moscow Conference should these be involved in conflicts with the Soviet State. A definite scheme for the limitation of armaments was proposed at that Conference by the Soviet Government. This scheme was, however, rejected.

Despite the sceptical attitude of the Government of the Union of Socialist Soviet Republic towards the labours of the League of Nations, it accepted the invitation of December 12th, 1925, to attend the coming Disarmament Conference, and only the Soviet–Swiss conflict, evoked by the assassination of M. Vorovsky, Minister Plenipotentiary, and the subsequent acquittal of the assassins by the Swiss Court, prevented the Union of Socialist Soviet Republics from attending the previous sessions of the Preparatory Commission.

In now sending its delegation to the fourth session of the Preparatory Commission on Disarmament, the Government of the Union of Socialist Soviet Republic has authorized it to present a scheme for general and complete disarmament.

II. The delegation of the Union of Socialist Soviet Republics is authorized by its Government to propose the complete abolition of all land, naval and air forces. The Government of the Union suggests the following measures for the realisation of this proposal:

(a) The dissolution of all land, sea and air forces and the non admittance of their existence in any concealed from whatsoever.

(b) The destruction of all weapons, military supplies, means for chemical warfare and all other forms of armament and means of destruction in the possession of troops or in military or general stores.

(c) The scrapping of all warships and military air vessels.

(d) The discontinuance of calling up citizens for military training either in armies or public bodies.

(e) Legislation for the abolition of military service, either compulsory, voluntary or recruited.

(f) Legislation prohibiting the calling up of trained reserves.

(g) The destruction of fortresses and naval and air bases.

(h) The scrapping of military plants and factories and of war industry equipment in general industrial works.

(i) The discontinuance of assigning funds for military purposes both on State budgets and those of public bodies.

(k) The abolition of military, naval and air ministries, and the dissolution of general staffs and military administrations, departments and institutions of every kind.

(l) The legislative prohibition of military propaganda and military training of the population and of military education both in State and public bodies.

(m) The legislative prohibition of the patenting of all kinds of armaments and means of destruction with a view to the removal of incentives to the invention of the same.

(n) Legislation making the infringement of any of the above stipulations a grave crime against the State.

(o) The withdrawal or corresponding alteration of all legislative acts, both of national or international scope, infringing the above stipulations.

III. The delegation of the Union is empowered to propose the execution of the above programme of complete disarmament as soon as the Convention in question comes into force, in order that all the necessary measures for the destruction of military stores be completed in a year's time.

The Soviet Government considers that the above scheme for the execution of complete disarmament is the simplest and the most conducive to peace.

In the case, however, of capitalist States rejecting immediate actual abolition of standing armies, the Soviet Government, in its desire to facilitate the achievement of a practical agreement on complete disarmament, is prepared to make a proposal for complete disarmament to be carried out simultaneously by all contracting States, by gradual stages, during a period of four years, the first stage to be accomplished in the course of the coming year.

National funds, freed from war expenditure, to be employed by each State at its own discretion, but exclusively for productive and cultural purposes.

IV. Whilst insisting upon the views just stated, the delegation of the Union of Socialist Soviet Republics is nevertheless ready to participate in any and every discussion of the question of the limitation of armaments whenever practical measures really leading to disarmament are proposed."

The Soviet Delegation on Feb. 28, 1928 submitted to the Commission a Draft Convention for Immediate, Complete and General Disarmament.

League of Nations Documents of the Preparatory Commission for the Disarmament Conference entrusted with the Preparation for the Reduction and Limitation of Armaments. Geneva, 1928, Vol. IX, pp. 9–12; M. SALVIN, "Soviet Policy toward Disarmament", in: *International Conciliation*, No. 428, February, 1947, pp. 42–112.

SOVIET UNION DRAFT FOR A GENERAL REDUCTION OF ARMAMENTS, 1946. The draft was presented in the United Nations on Nov. 28, 1946; read as follows:

"(1) With a view to strengthening peace and international security in conformity with the aims and principles of the United Nations, the General Assembly recognizes the necessity of a general reduction of armaments.

(2) The implementing of the decision concerning the reduction of armaments should include as primary object the prohibition to produce and use atomic energy for military purposes.

(3) To insure the adoption of measures for the reduction of armaments and prohibition of the use of atomic energy for military purposes, there shall be established within the framework of the Security Council, which has the primary responsibility for international peace and security, international control operating on the basis of a special provision which should provide for the establishment of special organs of inspection, for which purpose there shall be formed:

(a) A commission for the control of the execution of the decision regarding the reduction of armaments;

(b) A commission for the control of the execution of the decision regarding the prohibition of the use of atomic energy for military purposes."

The New York Times, November. 29, 1946.

S

SOVIET-YUGOSLAV DECLARATION, 1988. A Joint Declaration of the leaders of the Communist Party of the USSR and the Yugoslav League of Communists, signed by Mikhail S. Gorbachev and Stanislav Stojanovic in Belgrade on March 18, 1988.

The declaration, intended to reaffirm agreements of 1955 and 1956 establishing Yugoslav independence from Moscow, said the two Communist states "have no pretensions of imposing their concepts of social development on anyone" and accepted the prohibition of "any threat and use of force and interference in the internal affairs of other states under any pretext whatsover."

International Herald Tribune, March 19–20, 1988.

SOVIET–YUGOSLAVIA FRIENDSHIP TREA-TY, 1945. The treaty was concluded on June 11, 1945 in Moscow. A Treaty of Friendship, Mutual Aid and Postwar Co-operation, committing to a defense alliance in the case of a repeated German aggression or of any other country, which would be allied directly with Germany or in any other form. Valid for a period of 20 years; came into force June 15, 1945; annulled 1948.

KEESING's *Contemporary Archive*, 1945, p. 173D.

SOVKHOZ. Sovyetskoye hozyastvo – "soviet farm" in the Soviet Union a farm administrated by the state. ▷ Kolkhoz.

SOWETO DAY. The International Day – June 16 – of Solidarity with the Struggling People of South Africa. The observance marks the massacre of hundreds of unarmed school children, demonstrating on June 16, 1976, against the forcible imposition of the ▷ Afrikaans language and the so-called Bantu education; commemorated every year at UN Hqs.

SOYBEAN. *Glycine maxima.* The oil plant, containing *c.* 50% proteins, up to 25% fats, cultivated for oil from its seeds and for its fodder value for cattle (oil cake), subject of international statistics. World production 1972: 52.8 million tons. Principal producers: the USA (34.9 million t.), the Chinese Peoples' Republic (11.5 million t.), Brazil (3.3 million t.). The USA is the main exporter of soybean oil and oil cake (90%); restraining its export in 1974 caused a grave fodder crisis in Europe.

Between 1945 and 1985 the US soybean harvest increased in volume 11 times; in 1985 the US exported 3.7 billion dollars worth of soybean.

In the 1980's the United Nations supported the international campaign for introducing soya into the diet of children with protein deficiency.

K.S. MARKLEY (ed.), *Soybeans and Soybean Products*, 2 Vols., London, 1950–51; A.G. NORMAN (ed.), *The Soybean*, New York, 1963; F. HAPGOOD, *Soybean. A Weapon Against World Hunger*, in: National Geographic, July, 1987.

"SOYUZ". The Soviet spaceships launched into orbit around the earth from Apr. 23, 1967, when Soyuz 1 took off with the pilot-cosmonaut, V.M. Komarov. Soyuz II without a crew made a flight Oct. 25, 1968. Succeeding flights were always made with crews. The crews of Soyuz 4 and 5, launched Jan. 14 and 15, 1969, made an in-flight transfer from one ship to the other. In July, 1973 joint American–Soviet meetings of astronauts preparing for a joint flight in 1975 on the ship Soyuz with the American "Apollo" began in the center for manned space flight in Houston. ▷ "Apollo–Soyuz". After the completion of the first international flight with astronauts from the USA, the USSR invited the governments of other countries to participate in space expeditions on ships of the "Soyuz" type. The first flight took place Mar. 2, 1978 with the cosmonaut from Czechoslovakia, Vlasdislav Romek, the second with a Pole, Władysław Hermaszewski, June 27, 1978. French cosmonauts took part in Soyuz flights 1981, a cosmonaut from India 1984. On Apr. 20, 1983, the Soyuz T8 met the Salut 7-Kosmos. ▷ Salut or Salyut.

"SOYUZ–APOLLO". The first international space flight, initiated by the governments of the USA and the USSR July 17, 1975, when two spaceships were joined: the American "Apollo" commanded by astronauts T. Stafford and D. Sleyton and the Soviet "Soyuz 19" under the command of A. Leonov and V. Kubasov. After a two-day linkage and joint experiments, the ships separated and returned to Earth.

Apollo–Soyuz. Test Project, Houston, 1975.

SOZOLOGY. *Greek:* "sozo = protect". An international term created in 1970 by the Polish scientist W. Goetel (1889–1972) for science of the protection of the environment and its resources. Its character was defined by W. Goetel as follows:

"This is a composite science including those elements of the natural, technical, and humanistic sciences which are necessary for solving today's complex problems of the protection of nature and its resources and ensuring the permance of their utilization. Since for the prevention of damages, which in many cases reach catastrophic levels, effective action is necessary, we have created the concept of 'sozotechnics', whose task is to implement the injunctions of sozology. These names are ever more widely accepted. And one should emphasize that sozology and sozotechnics can acquire greater possibilities of realization with the help of industry, whose rational development requires a more fundamental attention to the protection and safeguarding of nature, and thereby the human environment."

K. KOCOT, *Prawno-międzynarodowe zasady sozologii* (The Principles of Sozology Relating to International Law), Wroclaw, 1975.

SPACE AGE. ▷ Space Scientific Co-operation.

SPACE EXPLORATION. ▷ Outer Space Exploration.

SPACELAB. Space Laboratory, space vehicle whose construction was undertaken July, 1974 by nine states of Western Europe (Belgium, Denmark, France, FRG, Italy, the Netherlands, Spain, Switzerland and the UK) with the help of American ▷ NASA. The placement of Spacelab into earth orbit was projected for the 1980s. The USA started to build in 1984–92 a permanent manned orbiting space laboratory station. On Nov. 28, 1983, the Western European Spacelab used the Columbia ▷ space shuttle for space research. On Jan. 31, 1986 the space shuttle Challenger with its crew exploded 73 seconds after launch.

Newsweek, February 4, 1986.

SPACE MEDICINE. An international term for the study of medical and biological effects of space travel of men, women, animals (▷ Laika) and plants.

SPACE OBJECTS CONVENTION, 1971. Convention on International Liability for Damage Caused by Space Objects, adopted Nov. 29, 1971 by the UN General Assembly, Res. 277/XXVI. The text is as follows:

"The States Parties to this Convention,
Recognizing the common interest of all mankind in furthering the exploration and use of outer space for peaceful purposes,
Recalling the Treaty on Principles Governing the Activities of States in the Exploration and Use of Outer Space, including the Moon and Other Celestial Bodies, Taking into consideration that, notwithstanding the precautionary measures to be taken by States and international intergovernmental organizations involved in the launching of space objects, damage may on occasion be caused by such objects,
Recognizing the need to eleaborate effective international rules and procedures concerning liability for damage caused by space objects and to ensure, in particular, the prompt payment under the terms of this Convention of a full and equitable measure of compensation to victims of such damage,
Believing that the establishment of such rules and procedures will contribute to the strengthening of international co-operation in the field of the exploration and use of outer space for peaceful purposes,
Have agreed on the following:
Art. I. For the purposes of this Convention:
(a) The term 'damage' means loss of life, personal injury or other impairment of health; or loss of or damage to property of States or of persons, natural or juridical, or property of international intergovernmental organizations;
(b) The term 'launching' includes attempted launching;
(c) The term 'launching State' means:
(i) A State which launches or procures the launching of a space object;
(ii) A State from whose territory or facility a space object is launched;
(d) The term 'space object' includes component parts of a space object as well as its launch vehicle and parts thereof.
Art. II. A launching State shall be absolutely liable to pay compensation for damage caused by its space object on the surface of the earth or to aircraft in flight.
Art. III. In the event of damage being caused elsewhere than on the surface of the earth to a space object of one launching State or to persons or property on board such a space object by a space object of another launching State, the latter shall be liable only if the damage is due to its fault or the fault of persons for whom it is responsible.
Art. IV(1) In the event of damage being caused elsewhere than on the surface of the earth to a space object of one launching State or to persons or property on board such a space object by a space object of another launching State, and of damage thereby being caused to a third State or to its natural or juridical persons, the first two States shall be jointly and severally liable to the third State, to the extent indicated by the following:
(a) If the damage has been caused to the third State on the surface of the earth or to aircraft in flight, their liability to the third State shall be absolute;
(b) If the damage has been caused to a space object of the third State or to persons or property on board that space object elsewhere than on the surface of the earth, their liability to the third State shall be based on the fault of either of the first two States or on the fault of persons for whom either is responsible.
(2) In all cases of joint and several liability referred to in paragraph 1 of this article, the burden of compensation for the damage shall be apportioned between the first two States in accordance with the extent to which they were at fault; if the extent of the fault of these States cannot be established, the burden of compensation shall be apportioned equally between them. Such apportionment shall be without prejudice to the right of the third State to seek the entire compensation under this Convention from any or all of the launching States which are jointly and severally liable.
Art. V.(1) Whenever two or more States jointly launch a space object, they shall be jointly and severally liable for any damage caused.
(2) A launching State which has paid compensation for damage shall have the right to present a claim for indemnification to other participants in the joint launching. The participants in a joint launching may conclude agreements regarding the apportioning among themselves of the financial obligation in respect of which they are jointly and severally liable. Such agreements shall be without prejudice to the right of a State sustaining damage to seek the entire compensation due under this Convention from any or all of the launching States which are jointly and severally liable.

(3) A State from whose territory or facility a space object is launches shall be regarded as a participant in a joint launching.

Art. VI.(1) Subject to the provisions of paragraph 2 of this article, exoneration from absolute liability shall be granted to the extent that a launching State establishes that the damage has resulted either wholly or partially from gross negligence or from an act or omission done with intent to cause damage on the part of a claimant State or of natural or juridical persons it represents.

(2) No exoneration whatever shall be granted in cases where the damage has resulted from activities conducted by a launching State which are not in conformity with international law including, in particular, the Charter of the United Nations.

Art. VII. The provisions of this Convention shall not apply to damage caused by a space object of a launching State to:

(a) Nationals of that launching State;

(b) Foreign national during such time as they are participating in the operation of that space object from the time of its launching or at any stage thereafter until its descent, or during such time as they are in the immediate vicinity of a planned launching or recovery area as the result of an invitation by that launching State.

Art. VIII.(1) A State which suffers damage, or whose natural or juridical persons suffer damage, may present to a launching State a claim for compensation for such damage.

(2) If the State of nationality has not presented a claim, another State may, in respect of damage sustained in its territory by any natural or juridical person, present a claim to a launching State.

(3) If neither the State of nationality nor the State in whose territory the damage was sustained has presented a claim or notified its intention of presenting a claim, another State may, in respect of damage sustained by its permanent residents, present a claim to a launching State.

Art. IX. A claim for compensation for damage shall be presented to a launching State through diplomatic channels. If a State does not maintain diplomatic relations with the launching State concerned, it may request another State to present its claim to that launching State or otherwise represent its interests under this Convention. It may also present its claim through the Secretary-General of the United Nations, provided the claimant State and the launching State are both Members of the United Nations.

Art. X.(1) A claim for compensation for damage may be presented to a launching State not later than one year following the date of the occurrence of the damage or the identification of the launching State which is liable.

(2) If, however, a State does not know of the occurrence of the damage or has not been able to identify the launching State which is liable, it may present a claim within one year following the date on which it learned of the aforementioned facts; however, this period shall in no event exceed one year following the date on which the State could reasonably be expected to have learned of the facts through the exercise of due diligence.

(3) The time-limits specified in paragraphs 1 and 2 of this article shall apply even if the full extent of the damage may not be known. In this event, however, the claimant State shall be entitled to revise the claim and submit additional documentation after the expiration of such time-limits until one year after the full extent of the damage is known.

Art. XI.(1) Presentation of a claim to a launching State for compensation for damage under this Convention shall not require the prior exhaustion of any local remedies which may be available to a claimant State or to natural or juridiclal persons it represents.

(2) Nothing in this Convention shall prevent a State, or natural or juridical persons it might present, from pursuing a claim in the courts or administrative tribunals or agencies of a launching State. A State shall not, however, be entitled to present a claim under this Convention in respect of the same damage for which a claim is being pursued in the courts or administrative tribunals or agencies of a launching State or under another international agreement which is binding on the States concerned.

Art. XII. The compensation which the launching State shall be liable to pay for damage under this Convention shall be determined in accordance with international law and the principles of justice and equity, in order to provide such reparation in respect of the damage as will restore the person, natural or juridical, State or international organization on whose behalf the claim is presented to the condition which would have existed if the damage had not occurred.

Art. XIII. Unless the claimant State and the State from which compensation is due under this Convention agree on another form of compensation, the compensation shall be paid in the currency of the claimant State or, if that State so requests, in the currency of the State from which compensation is due.

Art. XIV. If no settlement of a claim is arrived at through diplomatic negotiations as provided for in article IX, within one year from the date on which the claimant State notifies the launching State that it has submitted the documentation of its claim, the parties concerned shall establish a Claims Commission at the request of either party.

Art. XV.(1) The Claims Commission shall be composed of three members: one appointed by the claimant State, one appointed by the launching State and the third member, the Chairman, to be chosen by both parties jointly. Each party shall make its appointment within two months of the request for the establishment of the Claims Commission.

(2) If no agreement is reached on the choice of the Chairman within four months of the request for the establishment of the Commission, either party may request the Secretary-General of the United Nations to appoint the Chairman within a further period of two months.

Art. XVI.(1) If one of the parties does not make its appointment within the stipulated period, the Chairman shall, at the request of the other party, constitute a single-member Claims Commission.

(2) Any vacancy which may arise in the Commission for whatever reason shall be filled by the same procedure adopted for the original appointment.

(3). The Commission shall determine its own procedure.

(4) The Commission shall determine the place or places where it shall sit at and all other administrative matters.

(5) Except in the case of decisions and awards by a single-member Commission, all decisions and awards of the Commission shall be by majority vote.

Art. XVII. No increase in the membership of the Claims Commission shall take place by reason of two or more claimant States or launching States being joined in any one proceeding before the Commission. The claimant States so joined shall collectively appoint one member of the Commission in the same manner and subject to the same conditions as would be the case for a single claimant State. When two or more launching States are so joined, they shall collectively appoint one member of the Commission in the same way. If the claimant States or the launching States do not make the appointment within the stipulated period, the Chairman shall constitute a single-member Commission.

Art. XVIII. The Claims Commission shall decide the merits of the claim for compensation and determine the amount or compensation payable, if any.

Art. XIX.(1) The Claims Commission shall act in accordance with the provisions of article XII.

(2) The decision of the Commission shall be final and binding if the parties have so agreed; otherwise the Commission shall render a final and recommendatory award, which the parties shall consider in good faith. The Commission shall state the reasons for its decision or award.

(3) The Commission shall give its decision or award as promptly as possible and no later than one year from the date of its establishment, unless an extension of this period is found necessary by the Commission.

(4) The Commission shall make its decision or award public. It shall deliver a certified copy of its decision or award to each of the parties and to the Secretary-General of the United Nations.

Art. XX. The expenses in regard to the Claims Commission shall be borne equally by the parties, unless otherwise decided by the Commission.

Art. XXI. If the damage caused by a space object presents a large-scale danger to human life or seriously interferes with the living conditions of the population or the functioning of vital centres, the States Parties, and in particular the launching State, shall examine the possibility of rendering appropriate and rapid assistance to the State which has suffered the damage, when it so requests. However, nothing in this article shall affect the rights or obligations of the States Parties under this Convention.

Art. XXII.(1) In this Convention, with the exception of articles XXIV to XXVII, references to States shall be deemed to apply to any international intergovernmental organization which conducts space activities if the organization declares its acceptance of the rights and obligations provided for in this Convention and if a majority of the States members of the organization are States Parties to this Convention and to the Treaty on Principles Governing the Activities of States in the Exploration and Use of Outer Space, including the Moon and Other Celestial Bodies.

(2) States members of any such organization which are States Parties to this Convention shall take all appropriate steps to ensure that the organization makes a declaration in accordance with the preceding paragraph.

(3) If an international intergovernmental organization is liable for damage by virtue of the provisions of this Convention, that organization and those of its members which are States Parties to this Convention shall be jointly and severally liable; provided, however, that:

(a) Any claim for compensation in respect of such damage shall be first presented to the organization;

(b) Only where the organization has not paid, within a period of six months, any sum agreed or determined to be due as compensation for such damage, may the claimant State invoke the liability of the members which are States Parties to this Convention for the payment of that sum.

(4) Any claim, pursuant to the provisions of this Convention, for compensation in respect of damage caused to an organization which has made a declaration in accordance with paragraph 1 of this article shall be presented by a State member of the organization which is a State Party to this Convention.

Art. XXII.(1) The provisions of this Convention shall not affect other international agreements in force in so far as relations between the States Parties to such agreements are concerned.

(2) No provisions of this Convention shall prevent States from concluding international agreements reaffirming, supplementing or extending its provisions.

Art. XXIV.(1) This Convention shall be open to all States for signature. Any State which does not sign this Convention before its entry into force in accordance with paragraph 3 of this articles may accede to it at any time.

(2) This Convention shall be subject to ratification by signatory States. Instruments of ratification and instruments of accession shall be deposited with the Governments of the Union of Soviet Socialist Republics, the United Kingdom of Great Britain and Northern Ireland and the United States of America, which are hereby designated the Depositary Governments.

(3) This Convention shall enter into force on the deposit of the fifth instrument of ratification.

(4) For States whose instruments of ratification or accession are deposited subsequent to the entry into force of this Convention, it shall enter into force on the date of the deposit of their instruments of ratification or accession.

(5) The Depositary Governments shall promptly inform all signatory and acceding States of the date of each signature, the date of deposit of each instrument of ratification of and accession to this Convention, the date of its entry into force and other notices.

(6) This Convention shall be registered by the Depositary Governments pursuant to Article 102 of the Charter of the United Nations.

Art. XXV. Any State Party to the Convention may propose amendments to this Convention. Amendments shall enter into force for each State Party to the Convention accepting the amendments upon their acceptance by a majority of the States Parties to the Convention and thereafter for each remaining State Party to the Convention on the date of acceptance by it.

Art. XXVI. Ten years after the entry into force of this Convention, the question of the review of this Convention shall be included in the provisional agenda of the United Nations General Assembly in order to consider, in the light of past application of the Convention, whether it requires revision. However, at any time after the Convention has been in force for five years, and at the request of one third of the States Parties to the Convention, and with the concurrence of the majority of the States Parties, a conference of the States Parties shall be convened to review this Convention.

Art. XXVII. Any State Party to this Convention may give notice of its withdrawal from the Convention one year after its entry into force by written notification to the Depositary Governments. Such withdrawal shall take effect one year from the date of receipt of this notification.

Art. XXVIII. This Convention, of which the Chinese, English, French, Russian and Spanish texts are equally authentic, shall be deposited in the archives of the Depositary Governments. Duly certified copies of this Convention shall be transmitted by the Depositary Governments to the Governments of the signatory and acceding States."

UN Yearbook, 1971.

SPACEPLANE. An unmanned computer-controlled airplane to be produced in the 21st century. Construction started in the 1980's in the USA, the UK, the FRG and Japan. The name of the US project announced by President R. Reagan in his 1986 State of the Union address is X-30; the British Aerospace Co-Hotol. The X-30 will fly at speeds of more than 25 times the speed of sound.

The Economist, September 3, 1988.

SPACE PLATFORM OR STATION. An international term for artificial Earth satellites capable of being manned. See American ▷ Skylab, and the Soviet spacecrafts ▷ Mir and ▷ Salut.

SPACE PROBE. An international term for an unmanned space vehicle, designed to explore the solar system.

SPACE RADAR. A joint US Air Force and Navy space based radar program started in 1988 to lead to a first launch in the mid-1990's of a sensor platform in the Earth's orbit for surveillance of ships, aircraft and cruise missiles.

SPACE SCIENTIFIC CO-OPERATION. The theoretical and technical co-operation of scientific institutions and of cosmonauts during flights into outer space; subject of international agreements. The continual organized international co-operation dated from the foundation of the International Astronautic Federation, IFA, 1950, made up of the governments of the member states of NATO, with the task of supporting preparations for cosmic flights; headquarters Paris. In 1955 at the annual Congress of IFA in Copenhagen the representative of the USSR Prof. L.I. Syedov announced on Aug. 1, 1955 that the USSR was so advanced in its preparations that it foresaw the launching of the first space craft in 1957 and offered to accomplish this jointly with the USA under the patronage of the UN. The chairman of the IFA, a representative of the US space industry, A.G. Hall, did not support the Soviet proposal. In Sept., 1959 at the IFA Congress in London Prof. L.I. Syedov was elected chairman of the IFA. On Sept. 25, 1967 at the Congress of the IFA in Belgrade it was unanimously decided to recognize Oct. 4, 1957, the date of the launching of the first Sputnik, as the beginning of the Space Age. At the XXIVth IFA Congress Oct. 8–13, 1978 in Baku, possibilities were discussed for applying the results of space research for the peaceful needs of science and technology. IFA has consultative status with ECOSOC, UNESCO, WHO, ITO and WMO; pub.: *Astronautica Acta.* Reg. with the UIA. Institutions created by IFA since 1960 are: International Academy of Astronautics, bringing scientists together and awarding The International Astronautic Prize founded by Daniel and Florence Guggenheim; headquarters Paris. International Institute of Space Law, headquarters Dallas, Texas.

Yearbook of International Organizations.

SPACE SHUTTLE. An American spacecraft used since 1981 in manned flights. The first space shuttle *Columbia* was successfully launched and recovered on Apr. 12, 1981. With the space shuttle program the USA initiated a new era in outer space exploration. The most important feature of the space shuttle is that it can be re-used and it not only launch satellites but also retrieve them.

The space shuttles Challenger and Discovery were launched in 1984 and the Atlanta in 1985. The three were on 24 shuttle missions, twice carrying secret military payloads. On the 25th shuttle mission on Jan. 28, 1986 the Challenger exploded 73 seconds after lift-off from Cape Canaveral killing all seven members of the crew including one woman, Judith A. Resnick, a teacher.

KEESING's *Record of World Events,* March, 1986.

SPACE STRIKE WEAPONS. An international term discussed but not defined by the Ad Hoc Committee of the UN Committee on Disarmament in 1986.

SPIRI *Yearbook,* 1987, Oxford, 1988, p. 395.

SPACE TELECOMMUNICATION. The use of artificial satellites as telegraph, telex, telephone and television relay stations; subject to international conventions and organized international cooperation under the aegis of the Legal Subcommittee of the UN Outer Space Committee.

SPACE WAR. A subject of international studies and research. On Jan. 6, 1984 President R. Reagan signed National Security Directive 119 to start a multibillion dollar research program. The program will determine if high-energy lasers and other advanced ballistic missile defense systems can be used to stop enemy attack. On Jan. 21, 1984 the USA carried out its first test of an air-launched anti-satellite missile, called MHV (miniature homing vehicle). This weapon could be used to destroy satellites in orbit. The SIPRI fact sheet published in Feb., 1984, outlines the implications of these events. In the tested system, the MHV is carried on a two-stage rocket which is launched by an F-15 fighter flying at an altitude of 10–15 km under the orbit of the target satellite. By 1987 some 28 of the weapons will be ready for use on a squadron F-15s. Two squadrons will be fitted for Anti Satellite Missile System, ASAT, missions by 1989.

Negotiations in 1978 and 1979 between the superpowers for a treaty banning ASAT weapons broke down. Since then the USSR has made two proposals for a treaty banning the placing of weapons in space and prohibiting use of force from or in space. According to the SIPRI opinion, though at first glance the idea of rendering nuclear weapons obsolete is attractive, it is doubtful that such a system can ever give adequate protection against ballistic missile attack. In the meantime a costly arms race would follow between the two powers. Though the Anti-Ballistic Missile (ABM) Treaty apparently allows research into new BMD systems based on other physical principles (such as lasers) the treaty would be violated in spirit; it represented a commitment to maintain mutual vulnerability and enhance the deterrent effect of nuclear weapons. Furthermore, the chances are that one of the most feasible beam weapons will be the X-ray laser, which, powered by a nuclear explosion, is labeled as a third-generation nuclear weapon. If such a laser were tested it would violate the 1963 Partial Test Ban Treaty, since the Treaty bans the testing of any kind of nuclear explosives in outer space (or in the atmosphere or underwater). Of course, on deployment of an X-ray laser, the 1967 Outer Space Treaty would be totally violated, since

the Treaty prohibits placing nuclear weapons and other weapons of mass destruction in orbit round the earth.

It should be emphasized, according to the SIPRI opinion, that the systems for defense against ballistic missiles have much in common with those for offense against satellites in orbit. A space-based BMD laser, for example, turned 90°, would threaten satellites. Furthermore, past developments emphasize the communality of ASAT and ballistic missile defence systems. In the USA, for example, the early land-based ASAT missiles were originally ABM missiles. In the ASAT form they were slightly modified. Then again, the MHV, under development for ASAT purposes, was in the early days designed as a warhead for defence against ballistic missiles. In fact, it is still being developed for more advanced BDM systems. Thus defensive developments give impetus to the offensive ones, which becomes all the more obvious when one realizes that a laser system being developed for BDM would be adequate for ASAT purposes before it had reached the stage of sophistication necessary for defense against ballistic missiles.

This brings another arms control difficulty hinted at above. Further negotiations for an ASAT Treaty would be complicated by the fact that the offensive weapons also have defensive purposes.

According to SIPRI, new BDM efforts would not only encourage an expensive arms race, and give impetus to the development of weapons for attacking objects in space, but would have adverse arms control implications. On the other hand, the deployment of ASAT systems that could also be used for BMD would jeopardize the ABM Treaty. The capability to shoot down objects in orbit, far from implying a nice clean war up in space without human casualties, increases the danger of nuclear war on earth, for its use could trigger war, invite escalation of war, and/or result in destruction of those very satellites that might enable a crisis situation to be kept under control.

The SIPRI 1983 conclusions: if any meaningful control on militarization of space is to be achieved, it is essential that an ASAT Treaty be negotiated soon. Ideally, the Treaty should prohibit possession, but in view of the need for adequate verification, a ban on testing might be the most useful form for the Treaty to take. ▷ "Star War".

B. JASANI, Ch. LEE, *Outer Space Threat for the Eighties,* SIPRI, London, Philadelphia, 1984; B. JASANI, *Space Weapons: The Arms Control Dilemma,* SIPRI, London, Philadelphia, 1984; B. JASANI, Ch. LEE, *Countdown to Space War,* SIPRI, London, Philadelphia, 1984.

SPA CONFERENCE, 1920. An intergovernmental conference held in the Belgian health resort of Spa, July 5–16, 1920, attended by representatives of Entente and Reich governments, which considered the delay of Germany in the implementation of military restrictions ensuing from the provisions of the Treaty of Versailles and Germany's failure to deliver coal within reparations payments. The deadline for demilitarization was set for Jan. 1, 1921, with the reservation that, in case the scheduled date was not kept, occupation zones would be extended; volume of monthly deliveries of coal for Germany was established and reparations apportioned between individual Allies: France – 52.5%. Great Britain – 22%, Italy – 10%, Belgium – 8%, Yugoslavia – 5%, the rest going to Romania, Japan and Greece.

LNTS, 1920.

SPAIN. Member of the UN. Kingdom of Spain. State on the Iberian Peninsula on the Atlantic Ocean and Mediterranean Sea. Area: 499,542 sq.

km including the Balearic, Canary and other islands. Spanish North Africa comprises two enclaves within Moroccan territory: ▷ Ceuta and Melilla. Pop.: 37,746,260 census1981 (according to censuses: 1860 – 15,655,000, 1910 – 19,927,000, 1930 – 23,363,000, 1950 – 27,976,000, 1960 – 30,903,000, 1970 – 34,032,000). Capital: Madrid, 3,188,297 inhabitants. Official languages: ▷ Spanish language. GNP per capita 1986: US $5,198; currency: one Spanish peseta = 100 centimos. National Day: Oct. 12, Colombus Day, 1492.

Member of the UN since Dec. 14, 1955 and of all specialized agencies, the Council of Europe, NATO and OECD.

International relations: in the 16th–18th centuries one of the world's colonial powers; in the 19th century divested of all colonies in the Western Hemisphere; Spain recognized the independence of Mexico – 1845, Bolivia – 1847, Nicaragua – 1850, Argentina and Chile – 1858, Costa Rica – 1859, Guatemala – 1863, El Salvador – 1865, Peru – 1866, Paraguay – 1880, Colombia – 1881, Uruguay – 1882, Honduras – 1894, Cuba – 1900. Spanish decolonization in Africa occurred in the second half of the 20th century. Neutral during World War I; 1920–39 a member of the League of Nations. In the period July 17, 1936–Mar. 28, 1939 a civil war was fought in Spain. A Treaty of Friendship and Nonaggression was signed in Lisbon on Mar. 17, 1939 between Spain and Portugal which obligated both sides "to absolutely respect their frontiers and territories and not to commit any act of aggression or invasion against the other side." In Mar., 1939 Spain joined the ▷ Anti-comintern Pact, 1936 and, though formally neutral in World War II (maintained diplomatic relations with both the Axis states as well as with Great Britain and the USA), from June 27, 1941 Spain's volunteer "Blue Division" (Division Azul) participated in the war against the USSR. At the Potsdam Conference, on Aug. 2, 1945, the heads of government of the UK, USA, and the USSR resolved "not to support the admission to the UN of the present Spanish government which came into power with the help of the Axis states." On Feb. 9, 1946 the UN General Assembly recommended that members of the UN break off diplomatic relations with Spain, which i.a. was done by all of the Latin-American states with the exception of Argentina. The UN General Assembly Res. 39/1 of Dec. 12, 1946, resolved not to admit Spain to any UN specialized agencies and again called upon UN members to immediately withdraw their representatives from Madrid. On Jan. 31, 1955 Spain and the FRG were given the status of permanent observers at the UN over Gibraltar. On Nov. 20, 1975 General F. Franco died, and power was assumed on Nov. 22, 1975 by King Juan Carlos I. On Jan. 26, 1976 the government of Spain signed a treaty with the USA on friendship and co-operation; on July 28, 1976 the government of Spain signed an agreement with the Vatican on a partial revision of the concordat of 1953. The constitution of 1978 established i.a. the following:

"Art. 1. Spain constitutes a state of social and democratic laws which as the highest values of its legal order recognizes freedom, justice, equality and political pluralism. The political form of the Spanish state is a parliamentary monarchy".

"Art. 3. The constitution is based on the inseparable unity of the Spanish nation, on a common and indivisible Fatherland of all Spaniards, and recognizes and guarantees the right of autonomy to nationalities and regions which comprise it and solidarity between them."

"Castilian is the official Spanish state language ... Other Spanish languages are also official languages in their Autonomous Communities in accordance with their Statutes."

In fishing dispute with France since 1976 in the Bay of Biscay. In Mar., 1984 a French patrol boat closed in on two unarmed Spanish trawlers in the Bay of Biscay and chased the boats, injuring six Spanish fishermen.

On Jan. 17, 1986 Spain established diplomatic ties with Israel, announcing its determination "To maintain the traditional policy of friendship and solidarity with the Arab World".

On Nov. 10, 1987 Spain announced its decision not to renew the agreement with the USA of 1982 on American Military Airbases, near Madrid.

See also ▷ World Heritage UNESCO List.

B. SANCHEZ ALONSO, *Fuentes de la historia española e hispanoamericana*, 3 Vols., Madrid, 1945–52; E.K. LINDLEY, E. WEINTAL "American Diplomacy at Madrid 1940–1944", in: *International Conciliation*, No. 408, Feb., 1945, pp. 103–125; P. BROUE, E. TEMINE, *La Revolución y la guerra en España*, México DF, 1963; G. JACKSON, *The Spanish Republic and the Civil War*, London, 1965; R. CARR, *Spain 1808–1939*, New York, 1966; F. GARCIA, *Spaniya dvatsatogo vieka*, Moscow, 1967; S.P. POZARSKAJA, *Taynaya Diplomatisiya Madrida*, Moscow, 1971; R.M. CORTINA, *Crédito y Banca en España*, Madrid, 1971; T. SZULC, *Portrait of Spain*, New York, 1972; J. GOYTISOLO, *España y los Españoles*, Barcelona, 1980; R. CARR, *Modern Spain 1875–1980*, Oxford, 1980; J. MASAVALL, *The Transition to Democracy in Spain*, London, 1982; S. LIEBERMAN, *The Contemporary Spanish Economy. A Historical Perspective*, London, 1982; D. BELLED, *Democratic Politics in Spain*, London, 1983; *The Europa Year Book 1984. A World Survey*, Vol. I, pp. 774–804, and Vol. II, p. 2425, London, 1984; KEESING's *Record of World Events*, 1986, No. 3; P. PRESTON, *The Triumph of Democracy in Spain*, London, 1986; G. SANI, G. SHABAD, *Spain After Franco: The Making of the Competitive Party System*, Berkeley, Calif., 1986; F. FERNANDEZ-ORDOÑEZ, *Política exterior de España 1987–1990*, in: Política Exterior, No. 1, 1987; B. POLLACK, G. HUNTER, *The Paradox of Spanish Foreign Policy: Spain's International Relations from Franco to Democracy*, London, 1987; P.J. DONACHY, M.T. NEWTON, *Spain: A Guide to Political and Economic Institutions*, Cambridge, UK, 1987.

SPANDAU. District of West Berlin with a major fortress built in the XVIth century, which served in the years 1947–1987 as a prison for the German War Criminals sentenced at the ▷ Nuremberg Military Trial. See also ▷ Allied Control Council for Germany.

The International Geographical Encyclopedia and Atlas, 1979; KEESING's *Record of World Events*, January, 1988.

SPANISH AMERICA. A term derived from the colonial era referring to those areas of the American continent which were ruled by the Spanish kingdom; indicates the Spanish-speaking region of Latin America.

SPANISH CIVIL WAR, 1936–39. The military action in Spain directed by Gen. Franco, started July 17/18, 1936 supported by the fascist governments of Italy and the German Third Reich, first with equipment and ammunition and then with special units and airforce (▷ Condor Legion) object of sharp controversies in League of Nations, ended with the capitulation of Madrid Mar. 27, 1939 and the entry of Franco's Spain on the same day into ▷ Anti-comintern Pact, 1936.

A. RAMOS OLIVEIRA, *Historia de España*, Vol. III: *Le segunda república y la guerra civil*, México, DF, 1952; H. THOMAS, *The Spanish Civil War*, London, 1961; R. CARR, *Spain 1808–1939*, Oxford, 1966; P. ARTAD, *Cuadernos bibliográficos de la guerra de España*, Universidad de Madrid, 1967; G. JACKSON, *La República Española y la Guerra Civil, 1931–1939*, México, DF, 1967; M. GALLO, *Histoire de l'Espagne franquiste*, Vol. I: *De la prise du pouvoir à 1950*; Vol. II:

De 1951 à aujourd'hui, Paris, 1969; P. BROUE, E. TEMINE, *La Revolución y la Guerra de España*, México, DF, 1971; M. TUÑON DE LARA, *La España del siglo XX*, Barcelona, 1976; C.M. RAMA, *La crisis española del siglo XX*, Madrid, 1976.

SPANISH ENCLAVES IN MOROCCO. The Spanish possessions within the territory of Morocco or its territorial waters (200 miles from shore according to a Moroccan government declaration of 1972); they include: in North Morocco, two harbor towns ▷ Ceuta and Melilla and islets on the Moroccan coast: Alhucemas, Chafarinas and Peñon de Vàlez. Subject of a dispute between Morocco and Spain.

The Europa Year Book 1984. A World Survey, Vol. II, p. 2425, London, 1984.

SPANISH LANGUAGE. A language called in Spain "castellano", one of the six official UN languages. Subject of international conventions. The Spanish Constitution, 1978, which recognizes the language of the province of Castile as the national standard form of official Spanish also acknowledges as Spanish all languages used in offices and schools in semiautonomous areas such as the Basque provinces, Galicia, or Catalonia. Organizations reg. with the UIA:

European Association of Teachers of Spanish, f. 1967, Madrid.

Spanish Language Academies Association, intergovernmental organization, est. by the Congress of Spanish Academies held in Mexico, DF, in 1951 and by a multilateral convention, signed in Bogota, July 28, 1960 by Argentina, Bolivia, Colombia, Costa Rica, Chile, Ecuador, El Salvador, Guatemala, Honduras, Nicaragua, Panama, Paraguay, Peru, Spain, Uruguay and Venezuela.

"Every Signatory Government undertakes to give moral and economic support to its own National Spanish Language Academy" (art. 2).

UNTS, Vol. 485, p. 10.

SPANISH–NORTHAMERICAN ALLIANCE. Alianza Hispano–Norteamericana, est. 1967, first organizations in US history to group US citizens of Mexican and African origin. Headquarters: Alberquerque (New Mexico, USA).

SPANISH–PORTUGUESE TREATY, 1977. Treaty of friendship and co-operation signed Nov. 23, 1977, in Madrid by prime ministers of Spain, A. Suarez, and Portugal, P. Soares. The treaty replaced the fascist ▷ Iberic Pact, 1939.

KEESING's *Contemporary Archive*, 1977.

SPANISH SAHARA. The colonial name for ▷ Western Sahara during the period of its rule by Spain 1884–1976.

SPANISH SECRET TREATY WITH GERMANY, 1937. A Treaty concluded Mar. 20, 1937, in Salamanca by the German ambassador and Gen. F. Franco; it called for joint defense against communism (art. 1) for consultation in matters of foreign policy (arts. 2 and 3), for a friendly attitude in case of a war (art. 4) and for intensified economic co-operation (art. 5). Expanded by the protocol of July 16, 1937, on settlement of "accounts on special deliveries" and by the treaty of Mar. 31, 1939.

Akten zur deutschen auswärtigen Politik, 1918–1945, Baden-Baden, 1950, Serie D, Vol. 3, Document No. 245.

SPARTA PROJECT, 1966. A subject of international agreement between the USA, Australia and the UK, signed on Mar. 30, 1966 in Canberra; came into force the same day upon signature. The

S

project, known as Sparta, concerned the firing of certain re-entry vehicles from the Australian test range at Woomera and the use of special instrumentation to observe re-entry phenomena, conducted by three co-operating agencies on behalf of the three governments: the US Advanced Research Projects Agency, the UK Ministry of Aviation and the Australian Department of Supply.

UNTS, Vol. 593, p. 262.

SPEC. South Pacific Bureau for Economic Co-operation, est. by an agreement signed on Apr. 17, 1973, at the third meeting of the ▷ South Pacific Forum in Apia, Western Samoa. The SPEC work program includes regional activities in the following areas: trade; trade promotion; transport (shipping and civil aviation); telecommunication; tourism; agriculture; industrial development; aid and air co-ordination; Law of the Sea; fisheries and seabed resources; the environment; energy.

Associated and affiliated organizations:
Association of South Pacific Airlines, f. 1979, hqs. Suva, Fiji;
Pacific Forum Line, f. 1977, hqs. Apia, Western Samoa;
South Pacific Forum Fisheries Agency, FFA, f. 1978, hqs. Honiara, Solomon Islands;
South Pacific Trade Commission, f. 1979, hqs. Sydney.
Publ. *Annual Report, SPEC Activities* (monthly) and *Trade and Industry Scene* (monthly).

The Europa Year Book 1984. A World Survey, Vol. I, pp. 203–204, London, 1984.

SPECIAL DEVELOPMENT ASSISTANCE FUND. The Fund was est. 1964 with the task of financing the program of the Inter-American Economic and Social Council, CIES, in reference of the Alliance for Progress.

SPECIAL DRAWING RIGHTS. ▷ SDR.

SPECIALIZED AGENCIES WITHIN THE UN SYSTEM. The intergovernmental specialized agencies related to the UN are as follows: ▷ FAO; ▷ GATT; ▷ IBRD/World Bank; ▷ IDA; ▷ IFC; ▷ ICAO; ▷ IFAD; ▷ ILO; ▷ IMO; ▷ IMF; ▷ ITU; ▷ UNESCO; ▷ UPU; WHO; ▷ WIPO and WHO. (Other United Nations Bodies, which are not Specialized UN Agencies: ▷ IAEA; International Seabed Authority – ▷ Sea Law Convention, 1982); ▷ UNDRO; ▷ HABITAT; ▷ UNICEF; ▷ UNCTAD; ▷ UNDP; ▷ UNEP; ▷ UNFPA; ▷ UNHCR; ▷ UNIDO; ▷ UNITAR; United Nations Observer Mission and Peace-keeping Forces in the Middle East: ▷ UNDOF, ▷ UNFICYP, ▷ UNIFIL, ▷ UNTSO; ▷ UNRWA; ▷ UNRISD; ▷ WFC and ▷ WFP).
The United Nations Charter provides that the

"various specialized agencies, established by intergovernmental agreement and having wide international responsibilities, as defined in their basic instruments, in economic, social, cultural, educational, health, and related fields, shall be brought into relationship with the United Nations".

The instruments defining this relationship are the individual agreements between the United Nations and the specialized agencies.

Although not a specialized agency, the International Atomic Energy Agency (IAEA) is an autonomous intergovernmental organization under the aegis of the United Nations, established to further the peaceful uses of atomic energy. An agreement on the Agency's working relationship with the United Nations was approved by the General Conference of the Agency on Oct. 23, 1957, and by the General Assembly of the United Nations on Nov. 14, 1957.

The agreements between the United Nations and the specialized agencies generally follow a standard pattern. As a rule they provide for reciprocal representation at meetings; reciprocal inclusion of agenda items when requested; exchange of information and documents; uniformity of personnel arrangements; and co-ordination of statistical services as well as budgetary and financial arrangements. Each specialized agency has agreed to consider any recommendation made to it by the United Nations and to report to the Organization on the action taken to give effect to any such recommendation. In the case of the agreements with the International Bank for Reconstruction and Development (IBRD) and the International Monetary Fund (IMF), the United Nations has agreed to consult with these agencies prior to making any recommendation.

To implement the agreements relating the agencies with the United Nations, to avoid overlapping of activities, and, in general, to promote co-ordination of efforts, an Administrative Committee on Co-ordination (ACC) was established in Feb., 1947 by the Economic and Social Council; it reports to the Council periodically. This Committee is composed of the Secretary-General of the United Nations, who acts as Chairman, and the executive heads of the specialized agencies, the Director General of IAEA, the Executive Chairman of the Technical Assistance Board (TAB), the Managing Director of the Special Fund, the Executive Director of UNICEF, the Commissioner-General of the United Nations Relief and Works Agency for Palestine Refugees, the High Commissioner for Refugees, and the Executive-Secretary of the General Agreement on Tariffs and Trade (GATT), who participate in the work of ACC as observers.

Consultations in ACC take place on subjects of common interest to the different organizations within the United nations system, for example, on the Expanded Program of Technical Assistance, and on United Nations programs in science and technology, education and training, rural and industrial development, public administration, atomic energy, oceanography, the peaceful uses of outer space, and public information.

In addition to meetings of ACC, ad hoc consultations take place between the United Nations and the agencies, in order to improve administrative and budgetary co-ordination. Arrangements have been made concerning, among other questions: a joint system of external audit; the common collection of contributions; mutual problems affecting the currency of contributions; common financial regulations; a Joint Staff Pension Fund; uniform recruitment policies; personnel regulations, salary; allowance, and leave systems; the International Civil Service Advisory Board; and certain common administrative services.

Among its subsidiary bodies are the Consultative Committee on Administrative Questions (CCAQ) and the Consultative Committee on Public Information (CCPI), in which the United Nations itself, its operating agencies, the specialized agencies, IAEA, GATT, and TAB are represented. CCAQ, established in 1947 and normally meeting once a year, deals with personnel, budgetary, and financial questions as well as with administrative questions such as common services, records, and other administrative matters. CCPI, established in 1949, seeks to form a common information policy and to co-ordinate the information services involved.

The UN statute of the Specialized agencies provides that,

"the specialized agencies shall possess juridical personality. They shall have the capacity (a) to contract, (b) to acquire and dispose of immovable and movable property, (c) to institute legal proceedings.

The specialized agencies, their property and assets, wherever located and by whomsoever held, shall enjoy immunity from every form of legal process except in so far as in any particular case they have expressly waived their immunity. It is, however, understood that no waiver of immunity shall extend to any measure of execution.

The premises of the specialized agencies shall be inviolable. The property and assets of the specialized agencies, wherever located and by whomsoever held, shall be immune from search, requisition, confiscation, expropriation and any other form of interference, whether by executive, administrative, judicial or legislative action".

W. SHARP, "The Specialized Agencies and the UN", in: *International Organization*, No. 1, 1947; J.A. SHYBAYEVA, *Spetsializirovannye uchrezhdenia OON*, Moskva, 1966; M. SEARA-VASQUEZ, *Tratado General de la Organización Internacional*, México, DF, 1974; H.T. ADAM, *Les organismes internationaux specialisés*, Paris, 1977; *International Organization. Organizations related to the UN*, Vol. I B, The Hague, 1982; D. WILLIAMS, *The Specialized Agencies and the United Nations: The System in Crisis*, London, New York, 1987.

SPECIAL MISSIONS. An international term, defined by the Convention on Special Missions prepared by the UN International Law Commission and adopted by the UN General Assembly Res. 2530/XXIV, Dec. 16, 1969. The Preamble and the first 20 articles are as follows:

"The States Parties to the present Convention,
Recalling that special treatment has always been accorded to special missions,
Having in mind the purposes and principles of the Charter of the United Nationa concerning the sovereign equality of States, the maintenance of international peace and security and the development of friendly relations and co-operation among States,
Having in mind the purposes and principles of the Charter of the United Nations concerning the sovereign equality of States, the maintenance of international peace and security and the development of friendly relations and co-operation among States,
Recalling that the importance of the question of special missions was recognized during the United Nations Conference on Diplomatic Intercourse and Immunities and in resolution I adopted by the Conference on April 10, 1961,
Considering that the United Nations Conference on Diplomatic Intercourse and Immunities adopted the Vienna Convention on Diplomatic Relations which was opened for signature on April 18, 1961,
Considering that the United Nations Conference on Consular Relations adopted the Vienna Convention on Consular Relations, which was opened for signature on April 24, 1963,
Considering that the United Nations Conference on Diplomatic Intercourse and Immunities adopted the Vienna Convention on Diplomatic Relations which was opened for signature on April 18, 1961,
Considering that the United Nations Conference on Consular Relations adopted the Vienna Convention on Consular Relations, which was opened for signature on April 24, 1963,
Believing that an international convention on special missions would complement those two Conventions and would contribute to the development of friendly relations among nations, whatever their constitutional and social systems,
Realizing that the purpose of privileges and immunities relating to special missions is not to benefit individuals but to ensure the efficient performance of the functions of special missions as missions representing the State,
Affirming that the rules of customary international law continue to govern questions not regulated by the provisions of the present Convention,
Have agreed as follows:
Art. 1. For the purposes of the present Convention:
(a) a 'special mission' is a temporary mission, representing the State, which is sent by one State to another State with the consent of the latter for the purpose of dealing with it on specific questions or of performing in relation to it a specific task;
(b) a 'permanent diplomatic mission' is a diplomatic mission within the meaning of the Vienna Convention on Diplomatic Relations;

(c) a 'consular post' is any consulate-general, consulate, vice-consulate or consular agency,

(d) the 'head of a special mission' is the person charged by the sending State with the duty of acting in that capacity;

(e) a 'representative of the sending State in the special mission' is any person on whom the sending State has conferred that capacity;

(f) the 'members of a special mission' are the head of the special mission, the representatives of the sending State in the special mission and the members of the staff of the special mission;

(g) the 'members of the staff of the special mission' are the members of the diplomatic staff, the administrative and technical staff and the service staff of the special mission;

(h) the 'members of the diplomatic staff' are the members of the staff of the special mission who have diplomatic status for the purposes of the special mission;

(i) the 'members of the administrative and technical staff' are the members of the staff of the special mission employed in the administrative and technical service of the special mission:

(j) the 'members of the service staff' are the members of the staff of the special mission employed by it as household workers or for similar tasks;

(k) the 'private staff' are persons employed exclusively in the private service of the members of the special mission.

Art. 2 A State may send a special mission to another State with the consent of the latter, previously obtained through the diplomatic or another agreed or mutually acceptable channel.

Art. 3. The functions of a special mission shall be determined by the mutual consent of the sending and the receiving State.

Art. 4. A State which wishes to send the same special mission to two or more States shall so inform each receiving State when seeking the consent of that State.

Art. 5. Two or more States which wish to send a joint special mission to another State shall so inform the receiving State when seeking the consent of that State.

Art. 6. Two or more States may each send a special mission at the same time to another State, with the consent of that State obtained in accordance with article 2, in order to deal together with the agreement of all of these States, with a question of common interest to all of them.

Art. 7. The existence of diplomatic or consular relations is not necessary for the sending or reception of a special mission.

Art. 8. Subject to the provisions of articles 10, 11 and 12, the sending State may freely appoint the members of the special mission after having given to the receiving State all necessary information concerning the size and composition of the special mission, and in particular the names and designations of the persons it intends to appoint. The receiving State may decline to accept a special mission of a size that is not considered by it to be reasonable, having regard to circumstances and conditions in the receiving State and to the needs of the particular mission. It may also, without giving reasons, decline to accept any person as a member of the special mission.

Art. 9.(1) A special mission shall consist of one or more representatives of the sending State from among whom the sending State may appoint a head. It may also include diplomatic staff, administrative and technical staff and service staff.

(2) When members of a permanent diplomatic mission or of a consular post in the receiving State are included in a special mission, they shall retain their privileges and immunities as members of their permanent diplomatic mission or consular post in addition to the privileges and immunities accorded by the present Convention.

Art. 10.(1) The representatives of the sending State in the special mission and the members of its diplomatic staff should in principle be of the nationality of the sending State.

(2) Nationals of the receiving State may not be appointed to a special mission except with the consent of that State, which may be withdrawn at any time.

(3) The receiving State may reserve the right provided for in paragraph 2 of this article with regard to nationals of a third State who are not also nationals of the sending State.

Art. 11.(1) The Ministry of Foreign Affairs of the receiving State, or such other organ of that State as may be agreed, shall be notified of:

(a) the composition of the special mission and any subsequent changes therein;

(b) the arrival and final departure of members of the mission and the termination of their functions with the mission;

(c) the arrival and final departure of any person accompanying a member of the mission;

(d) the engagement and discharge of persons resident in the receiving State as members of the mission or as private staff;

(e) the appointment of the head of the special mission or, if there is none, of the representative referred to in paragraph 1 of article 14, and of any substitute for them;

(f) the location of the premises occupied by the special mission and of the private accommodation enjoying inviolability under articles 30, 36 and 39, as well as any other information that may be necessary to identify such premises and accommodation.

(2) Unless it is impossible, notification of arrival and final departure must be given in advance.

Art. 12.(1) The receiving State may, at any time and without having to explain its decision, notify the sending State that any representative of the sending State in the special mission or any member of its diplomatic staff is persona non grata or that any other member of the staff of the mission is not acceptable. In any such case, the sending State shall, as appropriate, either recall the person concerned or terminate its functions with the mission. A person may be declared non grata or not acceptable before arriving in the territory of the receiving State.

(2) If the sending State refuses, or fails within a reasonable period, to carry out its obligations under paragraph 1 of this article, the receiving State may refuse to recognize tye person concerned as a member of the special mission.

Art. 13.(1) The functions of a special mission shall commence as soon as the mission enters into official contact with the Ministry of Foreign Affairs or with such other organ of the receiving State as may be agreed.

(2) The commencement of the functions of a special mission shall not depend upon presentation of the mission by the permanent diplomatic mission of the sending State or upon the submission of letters of credence or full powers.

Art. 14.(1) The head of the special mission or, if the sending State has not appointed a head, one of the representatives of the sending State designated by the latter is authorized to act on behalf of the special mission and to address communications to the receiving State. The receiving State shall address communications concerning the special mission, or, if there is none, to the representative referred to above, either direct or through the permanent diplomatic mission.

(2) However, a member of the special mission may be authorized by the sending State, by the head of the special mission or, if there is none, by the representative referred to in paragraph 1 of this article, either to substitute for the head of the special mission or for the aforesaid representative or to perform particular acts on behalf of the mission.

Art. 15. All official business with the receiving State entrusted to the special mission by the sending State shall be conducted with or through the Ministry of Foreign Affairs or with such other organ of the receiving State as may be agreed.

Art. 16.(1) Where two or more special missions meet in the territory of the receiving State or of a third State, precedence among the missions shall be determined, in the absence of a special agreement, according to the alphabetical order of the names of the States used by the protocol of the State in whose territory the missions are meeting.

(2) Precedence among two or more special missions which meet on a ceremonial or formal occasion shall be governed by the protocol in force in the receiving State.

(3) Precedence among the members of the same special mission shall be that which is notified to the receiving State or to the third State in whose territory two or more special missions are meeting.

Art. 17.(1) A special mission shall have its seat in the locality agreed by the States concerned.

(2) In the absence of agreement, the special mission shall have its seat in the locality where the Ministry of Foreign Affairs of the receiving State is situated.

(3) If the special mission performs its functions in different localitites, the States concerned may agree that it shall have more than one seat from among which they may choose one as the principal seat.

Art. 18.(1) Special missions from two or more States may meet in the territory of a third State only after obtaining the express consent of that State, which retains the right to withdraw it.

(2) In giving its consent, the third State may lay down conditions which shall be observed by the sending States.

(3) The third State shall assume in respect of the sending States the rights and obligations of a receiving State to the extent that it indicates in giving its consent.

Art. 19.(1) A special mission shall have the right to use the flag and emblem of the sending State on the premises occupied by the mission, and on its means of transport when used on official business.

(2) In the exercise of the right accorded by this article, regard shall be had to the laws, regulations and usages of the receiving State.

Art. 20.(1) The functions of a special mission shall come to an end, inter alia, upon:

(a) the agreement of the States concerned;

(b) the completion of the task of the special mission;

(c) the expiry of the duration assigned for the special mission, unless it is expressly extended;

(d) notification by the sending State that it is terminating or recalling the special mission;

(e) notification by the receiving State that it considers the special mission terminated.

(2) The severance of diplomatic or consular relations between the sending State and the receiving State shall not of itself have the effect of terminating special missions existing at the time of such severance."

The further arts. 21–55 are dedicated to the status of the high ranking persons in a special mission, general facilities, inviolability of the premises and documents, freedom of movement and communication, exemption from dues and taxes, etc.

UN Yearbook, 1969.

SPECIAL OPERATIONS EXECUTIVE. ▷ SOE.

SPELEOLOGY. A subject of international co-operation: International Speleological Union, f. 1965, Vienna. Aims: develop relations between speleologists in all countries and co-ordinate their activities at the international level. Publ. *International Speleological Bibliography*.

Yearbook of International Organizations.

SPEYER. A German city in Rhineland-Palatinate, a historical site. The Speyer Cathedral is included in the ▷ World Heritage UNESCO List, built in the 11th century on the orders of the Emperor Conrad and continued by his grandson Henry IV, the "Kaiserdom" is the largest Romanesque building still in existence. It suffered war damage in 1689 but was very faithfully reconstructed in the 18th century. Its crypt, which has remained unaltered since 1050, contains the tombs of the emperors.

UNESCO, *A Legacy for All*, Paris, 1984.

SPHERE OF INFLUENCE. In the 19th century an international term introduced to multilateral treaties in the colonial division of Africa in the case when one of the powers reserved for itself the exclusive right to a certain territory before occupying it; the territorial range of the influence of a given power based on an existing state of affairs or agreed upon with other powers in a treaty or by a gentlemen's agreement. ▷ German–Soviet Non-Aggression Pact, 1939.

During the meeting of W. Churchill with J. Stalin in Moscow, Oct. 9, 1944, Churchill was ready to propose to the USSR a division into "spheres of influence of Eastern Europe, namely: the USSR was to have 90% influence in Romania, 75% in Bulgaria, 50% in Yugoslavia, but 10% in Greece, while Great Britain 90% in Greece, 50% in Yugoslavia, 25% in Bulgaria and 10% in Romania".

A memo containing the British proposal was discovered in the personal papers of the chief of staff of the British army, Gen. H. Ismay, and published by the historian D.D. Yergin.

D.D. YERGIN, *The Shattered Peace*, London, 1977.

SPICES. A subject of research and promotion by the International Trade Center UNCTAD/GATT, Geneva.

ITC. *Spices: A Survey of the World Market*, 2 Vls. Geneva, 1982.

SPIRITISTS. Persons who believe in the possibility of communication with spirits, particularly those of the dead. Spiritists form strong open and secret associations, especially in Latin America: Argentina, Brazil, Costa Rica, Cuba, Haiti, Mexico and Puerto Rico; on the west coast of Africa and in Europe. Spiritists organizations are divided into three groups: (1) believers in reincarnation and occultism; (2) umbandists; (3) kardacists, i.e. believers in a book entitled, *Le Livre des Esprits Contenant Les Principes de la Doctrine Spiritiste*, written by the Frenchman Hippolite Leon Denizart-Rovail, published under the pseudonym Allan Kardac in Paris, 1857, and then translated into many languages and republished many times also in the 20th century. Organizations reg. with the UIA:

Greater World Christian Spiritualist Association, f. 1921, London.
International General Assembly of Spiritualists, f. 1949, Norfolk, Virginia.
International Spiritualist Federation, f. 1923, Stockholm.

N. BLUNSDON, *A Popular Dictionary of Spiritualism*, London, 1962; C. PAPE, *Katholizismus in Latin America*, Santiago de Chile, 1963.

"SPIRIT OF ST. LOUIS". A Ryan monoplane in which American Charles A. Lingbergh (1902–78), air-mail pilot on the route St. Louis–Chicago, in 1926 made the first non-stop flight between New York and Paris in 33½ hours on May 20–21, 1927. The monoplane is exhibited at the Smithsonian Museum in Washington, DC.

Ch.A. LINDBERGH, *The Spirit of St. Louis*, New York, 1953.

SPIRITUALISM. ▷ Spiritists.

SPISZ. ▷ Teschen, Spisz and Orava Conference of Ambassadors, 1920.

SPITSBERGEN OR SVALBARD. An archipelago of the Norwegian Islands in the Arctic Sea; area: 61,229 sq. km: 3910 inhabitants, 1981, of which 1400 Norwegian, 2498 Soviet citizens and 12 Poles. A subject of international dispute in the 19th century as Tierra Nullus between Norway, Russia, Great Britain and Holland, finally ruled in favor of Norway by force of the Paris Treaty of Feb. 9, 1920 concluded by the governments of Denmark, France, Italy, Japan, the Netherlands, Sweden, the UK and the USA with the government of Norway,

"recognizing the full and absolute sovereignty of Norway over the Archipelago of Spitsbergen, including Bear Island; seeing these territories are provided with an equitable regime, in order to assure their development and peaceful utilization."

In art. 9 of this Treaty government of Norway was obligated:

"not to establish or allow establishment of any naval base ... nor to build any fortifications ..."

The Treaty, which entered into force on Aug. 14, 1920, reserved for its signatories the right to natural resources and fishing in the waters of the archipelago, as well as the right to demilitarize the whole territory.

On Aug. 14, 1925 Norway integrated the archipelago, creating a new province called Svalbard. During World War II the archipelago was occupied by Germany between 1941 and 1943.

The USSR filed claims to a part of the archipelago (Bear Island), requesting revision of the Treaty in the fall of 1944, which was expressed in a joint declaration of the governments of Norway and the USSR of Apr. 9, 1945 and in an exchange of notes dated Jan. 14 and 17, 1947. As a result of the agreement, which considered the Russian claims from before World War I, the USSR continues excavation of coal in Spitsbergen. Barensburg is the reloading terminal, where Soviet miners also reside, making up a significant part of the 4000 people inhabiting the archipelago. The USSR proposed for a joint defense of Spitsbergen, but Norway and the Western Powers refused. On Feb. 15, 1947 Norway expressed its readiness to discuss only the economic provisions of the Treaty. In 1951, due to the fact that Norway put the territory of Spitsbergen at the disposal of the NATO headquarters, the government of the USSR placed an official protest; in reply the government of Norway on Oct. 15, 1951 assured that no fortifications shall be installed in Spitsbergen. In 1977 Norway announced the establishment of a 200-mile economic zone for fishing around Spitsbergen. In the years 1932/33 Barents Island was the scientific base for the expedition of the Second International North Pole Year, and in 1957/58 it was the base for the Third International North Pole Year.

LNTS, Vol. 2, p. 7; M. CONWAY, *No Man's Land; A History of Spitsbergen from its Discovery in 1596 to the Beginning of the Scientific Exploration of the Country*, London, 1907; *Svalbard, a Norwegian Outpost*, Bergen, 1920; M.O. HUDSON, *International Legislation*, Washington, DC, 1931; R. MAURACH, "Spitsbergen zwischen Osten und Westen", in: *Geopolitik*, 1951; A.K. ORVIN, "Twenty-five Years of Norwegian Sovereignty in Svalbard 1925–1950", in: *The Polar Record*, 1951; T. MATHISEN, *Svalbard in International Politics, 1871–1925*, Oslo, 1954; T. GREVE, *Svalbard Norway in the Arctic*, Oslo, 1975; V. HISDAL, *Geography of Svalbard*, Oslo, 1976; *The Europa Year Book 1984. A World Survey*, Vol. I, p. 710, London, 1984.

SPLENDID ISOLATION. A British term coined during the period of imperial power of the UK, when British governments believed that they did not need allies to maintain Britain's authority as the strongest power.

SPLIT. A city of Croatia in Yugoslavia. The historic complex of Split, with the Palace of Diocletian, is included in the ▷ World Heritage UNESCO List. This is a whole town inside a Roman palace. Over the centuries the architecture has been transformed and adapted, and a harmonious town has been built inside the walls, leaving in place the peristyle, the mausoleum of the emperor, the temple of Jupiter and even the colonnades along the streets.

UNESCO, *A Legacy for All*, Paris, 1984.

SPORT. One of the oldest and most common forms of organized international co-operation; since the 19/20th centuries subject to all kinds of competitions under the sponsorship of international organizations and international meetings; in principle, an area covered by the universal Olympic formula: All Nations–All Games; factor in inter-

national relations; subject of disputes, and open international conflicts (football war between Honduras and Salvador, 1969). Despite the First Principle of the Olympic Charter, stating that sport does not approve of any discrimination against a country or person on racial, religious or political grounds, between the wars and after the World War II different types of discrimination occurred, evoking protests of many countries. The Sport Manifesto, 1964, elaborated under UNESCO's auspices, defined the main tasks of sport in international life. On the initiative of the International Sport and Physical Education Council, the Scientific Congress for worldwide popularization of sport was held 1972 in Munich. The First European Sport Conference, under UNESCO sponsorship, was held May 12–17, 1973, in Vienna, with the participation of sporting organizations and institutions from all European countries; the Second in Dresden 1975 and the Third in Copenhagen 1977. An international symposium on the matter of youth participation in sporting organizations took place in Warsaw in 1973; the First Scientific Congress of Physical Education and Sport in 1974 in Moscow; the Conference of Sport Ministers in 1975 in Paris, EUROSPORT. The UN General Assembly Res. 32/105 of Dec. 14, 1977 condemned apartheid in sport.

Besides ▷ Olympic Games, particular federations of different disciplines organize world championships, the most popular, in alphabetical order are:
Cycling – held since 1921, in two amateur categories: road and track, organized by the International Cyclist Federation, Union Cycliste Internationale, UCI.
Football – world championships are organized by the International Federation of Football Associations, Federation Internationale de Football-Associations. FIFA, est. 1904, Zurich. The game rules are based on the English system called the Cambridge Regulations, developed 1862–94. World Championships for professional and amateur teams are organized every 4 years since 1930. Its challenge prize is the Rimet Cup; in 1970 Brazil won the exclusive right to its possession and founded a new trophy. Upon the Federation's decision 1971 it was given an official name: the FIFA World Cup. Also held are:
– the Europe Championships since 1958 called Cup of Nations, in which amateur and professional national teams participate;
– the European League Champions' Cup since 1955;
– matches for the Cup Winners' Cup were initiated since 1961;
– European championships of those teams, which in the past season won championships in games for home cups.
Rowing – championships organized within Olympic Games by the International Federation of Rowing Associations, Federation des Societès d'Aviron, est. 1892, Montreux. The tradition of rowing races existed on all continents: among American Indians, among African tribes, among Polynesians. The Venetian races on Lake Bolzano became the best known in Europe in the 16th century and on the Thames River in Great Britain since 1775, where annually since 1892 races of eights, with crews from the two leading British universities, Oxford and Cambridge, take place.
Skiing – organized by the International Skiing Federation, FIS. One of the permanent prizes at skiing contests is the challenge Kandahara Cup, founded 1906.
Sports Aviation – one of the fields of international competition involving gliding, engine-powered and balloon aviation started in 1908 with Michelin Cup competition won by the American W. Wright who

covered airborne the distance of 66.6 km in 1 hour 31 min. All world records have been certified and registered, since 1905, with the International Aeronautical Federation, f. 1905, headquarters Paris, associating national federations in five continents.

Tennis – international matches have been held since 1877 in Wimbledon, a district of London, initially between champions of the Anglo-Saxon world, and since 1924 in an international competition considered as unofficial world championships. International tennis matches for the Davis Cup, founded by the American, D.F. Davis, have been held since 1900 between national representations (first match between the USA and Great Britain in Boston). Since 1920 eliminations for the Davis Cup take place in three zones: American, European and Eastern.

All world amateur sport records are subject of international rules elaborated by international amateur movement unions in different sport fields. These regulations describe conditions which must be met so that the best results obtained at home or at international sporting meetings can be recognized by international federations of the given field of sport as world records. These regulations are usually based on Olympic Games rules. The results are published in official announcements or special annuals, e.g. of the IAAF – International Amateur Athletic Federation.

The notion of "amateur" in contrast to "professional" was introduced in sports formally by England through the creation of the Amateur Football Association (1863) and the Amateur Athletic Club (1866). In 1894 the First Olympic Games Congress, held at the Paris Sorbonne, adopted a principle derived from the ancient Greek tradition of crowning winners with laurel wreaths, signifying that Olympic awards should be merely symbolic as they bestow "immortal glory". Nevertheless, even then historians reminded the organizers of the modern games that winners in ancient Greece benefited from a number of privileges, such as exemption from taxes and increased state pensions. This had caused the Ancient Games to evolve into a competition between well-coached athletes kept by rich families in the hope of obtaining valuable economic privileges. The warning of the historians moved the father of the modern Games, Baron de Coubertin, aware of the difficulty of defining "amateur" in sports of different cultural, customary and political milieux to appeal to subjective factors: "Being an amateur indicates not a book of rules but a feeling, the state of the soul."

After World War I the question was again raised up in international debates. During the Olympic Congress in Prague, 1925, the final formula in the wording proposed by Henri de Baillet-Latour was adopted: "An amateur is a person who obtains no material gains from sports and is ready to give his word of honor in writing to prove this." Thus a professional is a person "who directly or indirectly obtains material gains from engaging in sports."

Two years later, the formula of "word of honor in writing" proved to be insufficient. Therefore, concrete circumstances under which an amateur may be barred from competition were continuously added, first at the Paris Congress in 1927, later Vienna in 1933, Warsaw in 1937 and Cairo in 1938. After World War II the discussion started anew in 1950 in Copenhagen, when Mr Avery Brundage made a declaration entitled "Stop" and closed with the following statement:

"An athlete who is paid or compensated for his participation in the Games; who is paid for learning or training sports; who is maintained by a government or his club in terms of sports; who intends to become a professional and who is paid for writing press releases or broadcast statements on sports – he is no longer an amateur and no sports organization has a right to issue the amateur license to him."

In the years 1950–70 such views were revised under the influence of the growth of sports everywhere in the world, by the tremendous growth of the number of states participating in the Games, by modern forms of physical education and by different social systems. Such problems were on the agenda of the First International Congress of Law of Sports held in June, 1968 in Mexico City. There it was recognized that adherence to the old rules of the IOC was impossible primarily for social reasons insofar as: "an athlete in poverty will never obtain world results, doomed together with his family to malnutrition he will forever stand in the shadow of mediocrity". Thus, "an athlete cannot be a pariah." As a result, the First International Congress of Law of Sports expressed three opinions on the matter:
(1) amateurism in sports based on the word of honor or irrealistic provisions is a fiction that should be discarded;
(2) among the most commonly applied solutions, none can be recognized as taking account of all the social benefits of sports, except the world development of military sports, which, however, is limited to the duration of service;
(3) the most reasonable pattern is offered by the practice of socialist states.

At the 75th Olympic Congress in Vienna, Oct., 1974, IOC submitted new rules for amateur sports by revising art. 26 of the Olympic Rules. ▷ Law of Sport.

Organizations reg. with the UIA:

Arab Sport Conference, f. 1976, Riyadh, Saudi Arabia.
General Association of International Sports Federations, f. 1966, Monte Carlo, Monaco. Publ.: Calendar of International Sports Competitions (2 a year).
International Amateur Athletic Federation, f. 1912, London, UK. Publ.: IAAF Handbook (biannual), IAAF Bulletin (quarterly).
International Amateur Boxing Association, f. 1946, Creshill, NJ, USA. Publ.: World Amateur Boxing (quarterly).
International Amateur Swimming Federation, f. 1908, Vancouver, Canada. Publ.: Handbook (every 4 years), FINA News (quarterly).
International Amateur Wrestling Federation, f. 1912, Lausanne, Switzerland. Publ.: News Bulletin, Theory and Practice of Wrestling.
International Cricket Conference, f. 1909, London, UK.
International Cycling Union, f. 1900, Geneva, Switzerland. Publ.: Le monde cycliste magazine (quarterly).
International Federation of Association Football, f. 1904, Zürich, Switzerland. Publ.: IFA News.
International Gymnastic Federation, f. 1881, Lyss, Switzerland. Publ.: Bulletin (quarterly).
International Hockey Federation, f. 1924, Brussels, Belgium. Publ.: World Hockey (quarterly).
International Judo Federation, f. 1949, Tokyo, Japan.
International Rowing Federation, f. 1892, Neuchâtel, Switzerland.
International Shooting Union, f. 1907, München, FRG. Publ.: International Shooting Sport (bi-monthly).
International Skating Union, f. 1892, Davos, Switzerland.
International Ski Federation, f. 1924, Berne, Switzerland. Publ. FIS Bulletin (quarterly).
International Table Tennis Federation, f. 1926, London, UK. Publ.: Handbook of Regulations.
International Tennis Federation, f. 1913, London, UK. Publ.: Rules of Tennis (annually), World of Tennis (annually), Newsletter (monthly).
International Weightlifting Federation, f. 1920, Budapest, Hungary. Publ.: IWF Constitution and Rules (every 4 years), World Weightlifting (quarterly).
International Yacht Racing Union, f. 1907, London, UK.
World Underwater Federation, f. 1959, Paris, France. Publ.: Bulletin News.

See also ▷ Physical Education; ▷ Recreation ▷ Violence in Sports.

Geschichte des Sports aller Zeiten und Völker, 2 Vols., Leipzig, 1925–26; O. BECHMANN, Sportlexikon, Berlin, 1933; F.G. MONKE, New Encyclopaedia of Sports, New York, 1953; I Congreso Internacional del Derecho del Deporte. Materiales y Documentos. México, DF, 1968; BROCKHAUS, Sport Enzyklopaedie, Stuttgart, 1972; UN Chronicle, January 1978, pp. 122–123; J.A. CUDDON, Dictionary of Sport and Games, London, 1980; Yearbook of International Organizations 1986/87; The Europa Yearbook 1988. A World Survey, Vol. I, London, 1988.

SPORT AID. ▷ Hunger.

SPORT HOOLIGANISM INTERNATIONAL. An international term for hooligan riots during international sporting events such as football competitions in Belgium and West Germany and the Seoul Olympic Games (1988).

SPOT. The French satellite, taking space photos of Earth for sale in the world market.

SPRATLY ISLANDS. Chinese = Nanshan. Uninhabited islands in the South China Sea, subject of an international dispute since Feb. 1974, when the People's Republic of China proclaimed that they are an integral part of Chinese territory; at the same time, the Philippines and Vietnam also laid claim to these islands. These tripartite claims were repeated in the following years. On June 7, 1976 the Vietnamese government, protesting against drillings by foreign companies near the coast of the Spratly Archipelago, stated that this infringes upon its sovereign rights. On June 14, 1976 a spokesman for the Chinese government announced that the Spratly Archipelago, as well as other islands in the region of the South China Sea, are part of China. Aug. 10, 1980 a part of Spratly Islands was occupied by Philippines troops, Vietnam protested.

KEESING's Contemporary Archive, 1974 and 1980.

"SPUTNIK". The first Soviet artificial Earth satellites, launched on Oct. 4, 1957 marking the beginning of the Space Age, as the International Astronautical Federation unanimously asserted, 1967, Sputnik 1 was a polished ball of aluminum alloy with a diameter of 58 cm and mass of 83.6 kg, together with its equipment, i.e. a four-antenna radio sending station located inside the ball. Two transmitters sent signals with a frequency of 20,005 megacycles/s and 40,002 megacycles/s, which were received throughout the world since Sputnik 1 was placed in an orbit slanting toward the equator at a 65° angle. After 92 days in orbit, on Jan. 4, 1968 Sputnik 1 burned out when it re-entered the Earth's atmosphere. Sputnik 2, launched Nov. 3, 1957, was shaped like a missile with a length of nearly 5 m, diameter 1 m, mass 508.3 kg. and besides radio transmitters carried the first living creature, the dog Laika. The Sputnik burned out after 161 days, Apr. 14, 1958. Sputnik 3 launched May 15, 1958 was cone-shaped with a height of 357 cm, diameter at the base 173 cm, mass 1327 kg. Sputnik 4, launched May 15 1960 was a prototype of a space ship with a mass of more than 4.5 t. Sputnik 5 was a space ship launched with two dogs on board; after a one-day space flight it returned to Earth Aug. 19–20, 1960, ushering in the successful travels of living beings in space.

Five more improved Sputniks were launched: Dec. 1, 1960, Feb. 4, 1961 (Sputnik served as a starting platform for the space probe ASM2 directed at Venus), Mar. 9, 1961 and Mar. 25, 1961; launched on Apr. 12, 1961 was ▷ Vostok 1 with J.A. Gagarin.

S

▷ Explorer.

M. VASILIEV, *Sputnik into Space*, New York, 1958.

SRI LANKA. Member of the UN. Republic of Sri Lanka. Country in South Asia on Ceylon Island in the Indian Ocean, separated from India by the Palk Strait, 64 km wide. Area: 65,610 km. Pop. 1988 est.: 16,600,000 (1963 census: 10,582,000; 1971 census: 12,689,897; 1981 census: 14,850,001). Capital Colombo with 585,776 inhabitants, 1981. Official languages: since 1961 Singhalese (*c.* 75% of population) and since 1966 – Tamil in the southwest region (English in 1947–61). GNP per capita 1986: US $400. Currency: one Ceylon rupee = 100 cents. National day, Feb. 4, Independence Day, 1948.
Member of the UN since Dec. 14, 1956 and all its specialized agencies. Member of the Commonwealth and the Colombo Plan.
International relations: since the 6th century Singhalese Kingdom in union with India; 1547–1638 Portuguese colony; 1639–1796 Dutch colony; 1802–1948 British colony; Feb. 4, 1948 granted independence within British Commonwealth. Cofounder of ▷ Colombo Plan for joint economic development of South and Southeast Asia drawn up at Colombo on Nov. 28, 1950 by a member of British Commonwealth of Nations; advocate of nonalignment.
On July 29, 1987 in Colombo the leaders of India and Sri Lanka signed an agreement called the Tamil Pact, ending four years of war with separatist Tamil groups in the Northern and Eastern Provinces.
See also ▷ World Heritage UNESCO List.

E.F.C. LUDOWYK, *The Modern History of Ceylon*, New York, 1966; D.R. SNOTGRASS, *Ceylon: An Export Economy in Transportation*, Homewood, 1966; H.N.S. KARUNATILAKE, *Banking and Financial Institutions in Ceylon*, Colombo, 1968; A.J. WILSON, *Politics in Sri Lanka 1947–73*, New York, 1974; M.S. ROBINSON, *Political Structure in a Changing Singhalese Village*, London, 1975; K.M. DE SILVA, *A History of Sri Lanka*, London, 1980; A.J. WILSON, *The Gaullist System in Asia: The Constitution of Sri Lanka*, London, 1980; S. PANNAMBALAM, *Dependent Capitalism in Crisis: the Sri Lankan Economy 1948–1980*; London, 1981; P. RICHARDS, W. GOONERATUE, *Basic Needs, Poverty and Government Policy in Sri Lanka*, Geneva, 1981; *The Europa Year Book 1984. A World Survey*, Vol. II, pp. 2426–2440, London, 1984; S.J. TAMBIAH, *Sri Lanka: Ethnic Fratricide and the Dismantling of Democracy*, London, 1986; A.J. WILSON, *The Break up of Sri Lanka. Sinhalese Versus Tamil*, London, 1988.

SRINF. ▷ Intermediate Nuclear Forces.

SS. Schutz-Staffeln der NSDAP. Defense Units of ▷ NSDAP, formed 1923; received name SS in 1925, in 1926 subordinated to the leadership of ▷ SA; from Jan 6, 1929 directed by Heinrich Himmler (Reichsführer SS), performed inter-party police functions. After the assumption of power by NSDAP 1933 its leaders occupied key positions in the Gestapo; special SS Death Skull Units, SS-Totenkopfverbände, took over the concentration camps from the ▷ SA. In 1936 the entire German police came under the leadership of the SS, and in 1939 the complete integration of the police and SS took place through the creation of the Main Security Bureau of the Reich (RSHA) led by H. Himmler. After the outbreak of World War II the rapid formation of Waffen SS, separate military forces besides the Wehrmacht, took place. The dominant role of the SS in organizing and carrying out war crimes was established at the Nuremberg Trial 1945/46. By the judgement of the International Military Tribunal in Nuremberg all persons belonging to any divisions of the SS (with the exception of the riding club – SS Reiterei) were recognized as war criminals who should be tried in court. The incomplete balance sheet of SS crimes established by the International Military Tribunal included the participation of the SS in the murder of 5,721,800 Jews, 2,700,000 Poles, 520,000 Gypsies, 473,000 Russian war prisoners, and 100,000 mentally ill. In FRG a Union of former SS men was formed (HIAG) which undertook a broad campaign of rehabilitating and glorifying the SS. The government of K. Adenauer on Sept. 1, 1956 allowed the Bundeswehr to accept former officers and non-commissioned officers of the Waffen SS with the recognition of their rank, and the Bundestag on June 26, 1961 ratified a law granting all former SS men, including those convicted, retirement benefits from the state.

G. REITLINGER, *The SS: Alibi of a Nation*, London, 1956; R. SCHNABEL, *Macht ohne Moral. Eine Dokumentation über die SS*, Frankfurt am Main, 1957; H. BUCHKEIM, M. BROSZAT, H.A. JACOBSON, H. KRAUSCHNICK, *Anatomie des SS-Staates*, Olten-Freiburg, 1965; A. RAMME, *Der Sichersheitsdienst der SS. Zu seiner Funktion im faschistische Machtapparat in Generalgouvernement Polen*, Berlin, 1970; E. KOGON, *Der SS Staat*, München, 1974.

SS–20. A Soviet mobile missile with multiple nuclear warheads. In Mar. 1977 the US government proposed to the USSR the abandonment of the US mobile MX together with the Soviet SS–20.
The largest Soviet missile of this type is the SS-18; the SS-22 and SS-23 have shorter ranges than the SS-20.

D. ROBERTSON, *Guide to Modern Defense and Strategy*, Detroit, 1988.

SSBN. Submersible Ship, Ballistic, Nuclear. An international naval term for a nuclear-powered submarine carrying ballistic missiles.

SSGN. Submersible Ship, Guided, Nuclear. An international naval term for a nuclear powered submarine armed with cruise guided missiles.

SSN. Submersible Ship, Nuclear. An international naval term for a nuclear-powered attack submarine.

STABEX. Stabilization of Export. A system introduced by the ▷ Lomé Convention, 1975, concluded between the EEC and ACP states for guaranteeing to countries exporting certain raw materials stable incomes from exports despite price fluctuations.
STABEX includes 13 products (cotton, copra, coffee, cocoa, coconuts, peanuts and their oils, palm products, skins and furs, lumber, bananas, tea, sisal, iron ore). In the event the income of an exporter dependent on one of these products falls more than 7.5%, and in the case of the 24 poorest countries by 2.5%, below the average of the last four years, then the EEC will make up the difference from a special fund; Other so-called International Commodities Agreements in effect concern: cocoa, coffee and sugar. The STABEX was a reaction by the EEC states to the appearance of raw material cartels.

J. PAXTON, *A Dictionary of the EEC*, London, 1978, pp. 229–330; J.D. CUDDY, "Compensatory Financing in the North-South Dialogue: The IMF and STABEX Schemes", in: *Journal of World Trade Law*, London, Jan–Feb., 1979.

STABILIZATION FUND, INTERNATIONAL. A fund suggested by the US government for an international monetary institution which, at the ▷ Bretton Woods Conference in 1944 was finally named the International Monetary Fund (▷ IMF).

STABILIZATION, INTERNATIONAL. An international term for a state of balance of forces. The international stabilizer *sui generis* is the UN through the constant confrontation of power configurations in specific regions of the world and sounding a warning when a threat to peace and destabilization appears.

STAGFLATION. A neologism, originating in the 1970s from the words "stagnation" and "inflation", for a new economic phenomenon in which rapid price increases take place simultaneously with economic stagnation as the result of declining free market competition and monopolization of the market by great corporations that impose higher prices.

STAKHANOVITE. A term applied in the USSR to highly productive workers; introduced in 1930 from the name of a Donets coal miner, Aleksei Stakhanov, who set a coal-mining record.

STALIN AWARD. ▷ Lenin International Award.

STALINGRAD. Former Tsaritsyn until 1925, since 1961 Volgograd. City and port on the Volga River in south-east European USSR, terminus of the Volga-Don Canal; the site of the ▷ Battle of Stalingrad, Sept., 1942–Feb., 1943.

STALINISM. An international term since the 1930's, accepted in the late 1980's by Soviet officials (▷Glasnost). The New York Times' definition, published on Sept. 18, 1939 following the ▷ German-Soviet Partition of Poland, read:

"Germany having killed the prey, Soviet Russia will seize that part of the carcass that Germany cannot use. It will play the noble role of hyena to the German lion. At last the issue stands clear, Hitlerism is the Brown Communism. Stalinism is the Red Facism. The world will now understand that the only real ideological issue is the one between democracy, liberty and peace on the one hand, and despotism, terror and war on the other".

On Feb. 2, 1989 the Soviet weekly "Argumenti i Fakti" published an essay by historian Roi Medvedev entitled "The Number of Victims of Stalinism is about 40 Million People". The author puts the amount of those actually killed at 20 million, with the remainder suffering various forms of persecution such as: false accusation, show trials, punitive famine, forcible relocation, unlawful arrest, deportation, forced labour, torture and terror.

B. KELLER, Major Soviet Paper says 20 million Died as Victims of Stalinism, in: *The New York Times*, Feb. 4, 1989.

STAMP LAWS CONVENTION, 1931. An International Convention on Stamp Laws in connection with Cheques and Protocol, signed on Mar. 19, 1931 in Geneva, by the governments of Austria, Belgium, Czechoslovakia, Ecuador, Finland, France, Germany, Great Britain, Greece, Hungary, Italy, Japan, Luxembourg, Mexico, Monaco, the Netherlands, Norway, Poland, Portugal, Romania, Spain, Sweden, Switzerland, Turkey and Yugoslavia.

LNTS, 1931.

STAMPS. Postal charges introduced in the form of stamps pasted on letters and cards according to tariffs set since 1875 by the Universal Postal Union, UPU. The first stamps, initially for circulation within one country, were introduced May 6, 1840 in Great Britain together with a nation-wide system of tariffs developed by the author of an idea for a new type of postal services, the general director of the British Post Office, Rowland Hill (1795–1879). In

1843 Britain's example was followed by Switzerland (Mar. 1) and Brazil (Aug. 1); in 1849 France (Jan 1), Belgium (July 2) and Bavaria (Nov. 1); in 1850 Spain (Jan 1) and Austria (June 1) and Prussia (Nov. 15); in 1851 Denmark, in 1852 Holland (Jan. 1), the Papal states (Jan. 1) and Luxembourg (Sept, 5); in 1853 Portugal; in 1855 Norway (Jan. 1) and Sweden (July 1); in 1856 Finland; in 1857 Russia; 1858 Romania.

The first international convention on mutual recognition of postal stamps and a system for settling accounts was ratified 1874 at the First World Postal Congress, I Congrès Mondiale du Poste, in Brno. A New World Postal Convention, Convention Postale Universelle de UPU, was signed on Oct. 3, 1957 in Ottawa. In point 44 it determined that stamps intended for the payment of postal charges are issued by the post offices of the member states, which are to inform all of the other offices about each new issue through the International Bureau of UPU along with the required explanations. The executory regulations of the Convention in art. 186 determined that supplementary stamps printed by postage metering machines are to be bright red in color; the stamps should contain the name of the country and insofar as possible be written in Latin letters and the value in Arabic numerals. During the second half of the 19th century international non-governmental organizations began to be formed devoted to the collection of stamps. ▷ UN Stamps. Organizations reg. with the UIA:

International Federation of Stamp Dealers' Associations, f. 1950, London. Publ.: *IFSDA Handbook* devoted to stamp-collecting.
Scouts on Stamps Society International, f. 1951, St. Westbury NY, USA.

R.J. SUTTON, *The Stamp Collectors Encyclopaedia*, London, 1959; *Enciclopedia del Sello*, Madrid, 1975; *Yearbook of International Organizations*.

STANAFORCHAN. Standing Naval Force for Channel, combined naval forces, mainly minesweeper of the British, Belgian, Dutch and West German fleets in the English Channel, est. May 11, 1973 within NATO with headquarters in Northwood, UK.

STANDARD. An international term accepted in metrology for an international or national unit of measure of the highest attainable preciseness. International standards of measures and weights, les etalons internationaux, are kept in the International Bureau of Measures and Weights in the pavilion de Bretuil in Sevres near Paris. The first standards were established for the ▷ meter and ▷ kilogram in 1799 by the Paris Academy of Science. Due to their insufficient preciseness they were replaced in 1874 by new ones in accordance with a resolution of the International Commission of Measures and Weights, which deliberated in Paris. After the signing of the first International Metric Convention on May 20, 1875, the International Bureau of Measures and Weights was established 1878, and subsequently sent member states the standards for the meter and kilogram. In 1969 the International Committee of Measures, one of the organs of the Metric Convention, jointly with the National Bureau of Standards of the USA, formed a working group with the task of preparing an international organization devoted to setting standards for industrial materials.

STANDARD CLASSIFICATION OF EDUCATION. Introduced by UNESCO for the purpose of standardizing school statistics and introducing generally accepted divisions into elementary, secondary, higher, extra-school education, etc.

STANDARDIZATION. A term adopted in 20th century designed to apply in technology unified international standards in keeping with the rules of ▷ metrology; initiated in Great Britain where a national institution called the Committee of Standards was founded 1901; since 1928 – the British Standard Institution.
Organizations registered with the UIA:

African Regional Organization for Standardization, f. 1977, Nairobi, Kenya.
Arab Organization for Standardization and Metrology, f. 1965, Cairo.
European Committee for Standardization, f. 1961, Paris.
European Committee for Standards Coordination, f. 1960, Paris.
International Committee for Standardization in Human Biology, f. 1958, Paris. Publ.: *Handbook of Standard Methods in Human Biology*.
International Organization for Standardization, ISO, f. 1946, Geneva. Consultative Status with UNESCO, ECOSOC, FAO, IAEA, ICAO, ILO, IMCO and ITU. One of ISO organs since 1975 – the Permanent Committee for the Study of Scientific Foundation of Standardization. Publ.: *ISO Journal*, monthly, and *ISO Memento*, yearly.
Pan American Standards Commission, f. 1961, Buenos Aires. Publ.: *Bulletin COPANT*;
Permanent Standardization Committee, f. 1961, Moscow, attached to CMEA.

Yearbook of International Organizations, 1986/87; The Europa Yearbook 1988, A World Survey, Vol. I, London, 1988.

STANDARDIZATION CMEA INSTITUTE. An intergovernmental institution est. in June 1962 at Moscow, by the CMEA countries. The Institute of Standardization of CMEA carries out the following functions: conducts theoretical and experimental research, work out draft recommendations on the unification of national standards, publishes studies and information bulletins.

Recueil de Documents, Varsovie, No. 6, 1962; W.E. BUTLER (ed.), *A Source Book on Socialist International Organizations*, Alphen, 1978, pp. 259–268.

STANDARDS, INTERNATIONAL. Uniform technical sample standards recognized by international conventions or by metrology and by standardizing organizations; distinct from domestic standards set up by state standardizing commissions and bearing their own names:
ASA - American Standard, USA; BS – British Standard, Great Britain; CSA – Canadian Standard, Canada; CSN – Czechoslovenska Statni Norma, Czechoslovakia; DIN – Deutsche Industrie Norm, FRG; GOST – Gosudarstviennij Obshchesnosojuznij Standard, USSR; JIS – Japanese Standard, Japan; JUS – Jugoslovenski Standard, Yugoslavia; NBN – Norma Belge, Belgium; NF – Norme Francaise, France; PN – Polska Norma, Poland; TGL – Technische Normen, Gütervorschriften und Lieferbedingungen, GDR; UNE – Unificacion Español, Spain; UNI – Unificazione Italiana, Italy.
At the 28th session of the CMEA countries June 21, 1974 in Sofia a convention concerning usage of CMEA standards was signed by Bulgaria, Cuba, Czechoslovakia, the GDR, Hungary, Mongolia, Poland and the USSR.

STARCH. A subject of international co-operation. Organizations reg. with the UIA:

Association of Maize-Starch Manufacturers of the EEC, f. 1959, Brussels.
European Committee for Trade in Starch Products and Derivatives, f. 1963, Milan, Italy.
Liaison Committee of the Rice-Starch Manufacturers of the EEC, f. 1960, Bonn.
Union of Professional Groups of the Potato-Starch Industry of the EEC, f. 1960, Brussels.

Wheat-Starch Manufacturers Association of the EEC, f. 1959, Bonn.
Yearbook of International Organizations.

STARI RAS AND SOPOCANI. A historic site of Serbia, Yugoslavia, included in the ▷ World Heritage UNESCO List. Between 1000 and 1400 the distinctive culture of the newly-formed Serbian nation grew up around this rocky crag, Stari Ras, where the princes built churches and castles. At the foot of the fortress are two 12th-century monasteries, one of which, Sopocani, is decorated with paintings which are among the finest examples of Byzantine art in the Balkans.

UNESCO, *A Legacy for All*, Paris, 1984.

STAROBIELSK. ▷ Katyń Case, 1943.

STARS AND STRIPES. The flag of the USA, metaphorically the United States. The US flag was adopted June 14, 1777 by a resolution of the Second Continental Congress in Philadelphia, representing 13 states:

"It is resolved that the flag of the United States shall be thirteen stripes, alternating red and white; that the Union shall be thirteen white stars on a blue field, representing a new constellation."

With the territorial expansion of the states, each new state, in accordance with a resolution of Congress of July 4, 1818, added one star to the symbol of the Union, but the number of stripes remained unchanged. By 1912 the number of stars had grown to 48, when New Mexico and Arizona acquired statehood. In 1959 Alaska became the 49th state, and in 1960 Hawaii became the 50th.

START. Strategic Arms Reduction Talks. The continuation of ▷ SALT negotiations, began on June 30, 1982, suspended *sine die* on Dec. 8, 1983. The new nuclear arms talks, initiated by the US Secretary of State, G. Shultz and the Soviet Foreign Minister, A. Gromyko, on Jan. 7 and 8, 1985 in Geneva, resumed the Strategic Arms Reduction Talks (START), the negotiations on Intermediate Nuclear Forces (INC) and on the Antisatellite weapons (ASAT).

Newsweek, December 3, 1984 and January 14, 1985; S. TALBOTT, Why START stopped, in: *Foreign Affairs*, Fall, 1988.

STAR WARS. ▷ SDI.

STATE. A term defined in the Inter-American Convention on Rights and Duties of States, 1933, as follows:

"Art. 1. The state as a person of International Law should possess the following qualifications: (a) a permanent population; (b) a defined territory; (c) government; and (d) capacity to enter into relations with the other States."

LNTS, Vol. 165, p. 25; States as Subjects of International Law, in: R.L. BLEDSOE, B.A. BOCZEK, *International Law Dictionary*, Oxford, 1987.

STATE AMERICAN DOCTRINE, 1897. The US Supreme Court Doctrine (Underhill v. Hernandez, 168 US, 250, 1897):

"Every sovereign state is bound to respect the independence of every other sovereign state, and the courts of one country will not sit in judgement on the acts of the government of another done within its own territory".

STATE EASEMENT. A term in international law for a part of the territory of a sovereign state put at the service of another state (*Latin: territorium serviens*; e.g. Chinese concessions granted to European states and the United States at the end of the 19th century), or a territory which has restricted rights because of obligations with respect to another state (e.g. the authorities of Rome were not allowed to build edifices higher than those in the Vatican around the Holy See, on the basis of the Lateran Treaties), or a territory serving the purposes of international organizations (e.g. the headquarters and offices of the United Nations in New York and Geneva), or for the purposes of international road, river or sea traffic; also a territory for the purposes of foreign military bases; subject of international agreements.

SHIH SHUM ZIN, *Extraterritoriality. Its Rise and Decline*, London, 1925.

STATE FRONTIERS. The frontiers of states delineated on land or underground, waters, depths, seabeds, air, formally through delimitation or, as the case may be, demarcation; subject to bilateral or multilateral agreements. In international practice, the setting of state frontiers resulted from natural geographical or ethnographical divisions; only in the era of colonial conquests were scientific frontiers sought for and were usually astronomical frontiers – ideally straight lines running along meridians or parallels, e.g. between Libya and Egypt or between Egypt and Sudan, etc. The Conference on Secuirty and Co-operation in Europe worked out the principle of ▷ frontiers, inviolability of.

S.B. JOHNSON, *Boundary Making. A Handbook for Statesmen, Treaty Editors and Boundary Commissioners*, New York, 1945; B.M. KLIMIENKO, *Gosudarstvinnie granitsy*, Moscow, 1964; K. SKUBISZEWSKI, "Les traités sur les frontières en Europe Centrale, 1970–73", in: *Polish Yearbook of International Law*, Warsaw, 1974.

STATE FUNCTIONARIES. The government civil service workers, subject of an international ILO convention, accepted in Geneva by the 64th Session of the General ILO Conference May 7–28, 1978 on the conditions of work of state functionaries.

STATE INTERNATIONAL RESPONSIBILITY. A practice pursued by states aiming at the recognition of other states' right to due reparations of damages suffered by these states; subject to codification on the adoption of a uniform principle of the definitive international law in this matter. Such works were initiated by the League of Nations on the basis of the verdict of the Permanent Court of International Justice of July 26, 1927, stating that the violation of other states' rights involves the obligation to provide "appropriate reparations." The initiative of the League of Nations was taken up by the Seventh International Conference of American States in Montevideo, Dec. 26, 1933, which ordered the International Law Commission to work out norms of international responsibility of states which were to include works in this field done by the League of Nations. After World War II the International Court of Justice issued, Apr. 11, 1949, an advisory opinion stating that the infringement of other states' rights causes "an obligation to repair damages in an appropriate manner." Under Res. 779/VII of Dec. 7, 1953, the UN General Assembly initiated the International Law Commission to prepare five documentations of the problem during 1955–1960: Jan. 20, 1956 – A/CN.4/96; Feb. 15, 1957 – A/CN.4/106; Jan. 2, 1958 – A/CN.4/111; Feb. 20, 1950 – A/CN.4/119; Feb. 9, 1960 – A/CN.4/125; and in 1962 it established a special commission for this purpose. Until then the UN General Assembly took a stand in these matters in resolutions 1968/XVI of Dec. 18, 1961; 1902/XVIII of Nov. 18, 1963 and 2167/XXI of Dec. 5, 1966. In international practice direct and indirect international responsibility of the state is distinguished.

The former is related to acts forbidden by international law and committed on the territory of another state by the ruling organs of a state; the latter refers to acts committed by the state's nationals. In terms of rules adopted by the UN International Law Commission such acts are recognized as "internationally illegal." The International Law Commission on July 25, 1980 adopted by acclamation the draft articles of the general principles of the state international responsibility; elaborated by the Commission on State Responsibility:

"Art. 1. Every internationally wrongful act of a State entails the international responsibility of that State.
Art. 2. Every State is subject to the possibility of being held to have committed an internationally wrongful act entailing its international responsibility.
Art. 3. There is an internationally wrongful act of a State when:
(a) conduct consisting of an action or omission is attributable to the State under international law; and
(b) that conduct constitutes a breach of an international obligation of the State.
Art. 4. An act of a State may only be characterized as internationally wrongful by international law. Such characterization cannot be affected by the characterization of the same act as lawful by internal law."

The other 31 articles of the draft are concerned with determining on what grounds and under what circumstances a state may be held to have committed an internationally wrongful act which, as such, is a source of international responsibility.

In the International Law Commission there was general agreement that the determination of all legal consequences of all internationally wrongful acts was a formidable task since virtually the whole field of international law was involved. Nevertheless, the main trend in the discussions was that the Commission should, at least for the time being, work in the perspective of drafting articles which would ultimately be embodied in a general convention on state responsibility, covering every aspect of the topic and, in particular, dealing with the legal consequences of aggression, of other international crimes, as well as of simple breaches of bilateral obligations.

Several members of the Commission drew attention to the connection between the work of the Commission on state responsibility and that on the Code of Offences against the Peace and Security of Mankind. While it was recognized that the final responsibility of individuals fell inside the scope of the Code of Offences and outside that of state responsibility, a certain overlap between the two topics would be inevitable if it were decided to include in the Code of Offences the crimes committed by states as such.

C. EAGLETON, "The Responsibility of States", in: *International Law*, New York, 1928; P.M. KURIS, *Mezhdunarodniye pravonanishenia i otvietstviennosti gosudarstva*, Moscow, 1973; Responsibility of States, UN General Assembly A/10010, Aug. 8, 1975, pp. 5–53; J.M. KOLOSOV, *Otviestviennost' v. miezhdunarodnim pravie*, Moskva, 1975; B. GRAEFRATH, E. OESER, P. STEINIGER, *Völkerrechtliche Verantvortlichkeit der Staaten*, Berlin, 1977; *Report of the ILC on the Work of its 32nd Session, May 5–July 25, 1980*, UN New York, 1980, pp. 49–136; *UN Chronicle*, October 1983, pp. 23–26; R.L. BLEDSOE, B.A. BOCZEK, *The International Law Dictionary*, Oxford, 1987.

STATELESS PERSONS. Persons who do not possess nationality of any state (have lost the nationality of one state without having acquired the nationality of another, or are born without any nationality); defined by the UN Conference on the Status of Stateless Persons, New York 1954, as "a person who is not considered as a national by any state under the operation of its law." A subject of international conventions and bilateral agreements

concluded after World War I when, in consequence of the October Revolution in Russia, disintegration of Austria–Hungary, defeat of Germany, and emergence of new states in Europe, problems arose for those without legally defined national status, to whom neither the principle of *jus sanguinis*, nor that of *jus soli*, nor a combination of both systems, were applicable. International treaties on this subject are aimed – apart from problems arising from conflicting internal laws (*jus sanguinis* as against *jus soli*) – at resolving the cases of destitute children of any nationality and cases of loss of nationality as a result of specific circumstances. The status of stateless persons is highly disadvantageous as, while being subject to the laws of the states of their residence, they are at the same time deprived of any civic rights, enjoy no diplomatic protection and may be deported at any time. It was the League of Nations that first took up the question of stateless persons. On the initiative of the polar explorer and Norwegian delegate to the LN, Fridjof Nansen, the LN set up, under Art. 24/1 of its Convenant, the Nansen International Office for Refugees with the right of issuing the so-called Nansen passports. Then, on Apr. 12, 1930, the Convention on Conflicts of Nationality Laws and Statelessness was signed at The Hague.

The principle that every man has a right to nationality was first formulated after World War II in Art. 15 of the Universal Declaration of Human Rights, 1948. In 1951 the UN General Assembly entrusted the UN Human Rights Commission with the task of preparing a convention aimed at the liquidation of statelessness. A convention relating to the Status of Stateless Persons was drafted by the abovementioned UN Commission and signed Sept. 28, 1954 in New York, by the governments of Belgium, Brazil, Colombia, Costa Rica, Denmark, Ecuador, El Salvador, France, FRG, Guatemala, Honduras, Israel, Italy, Liechtenstein, Luxembourg, the Netherlands, Norway, Philippines, Sweden, Switzerland, UK and Vatican City. It came into force on June 6, 1960.

In May, 1959 at Geneva and in Aug., 1961 in New York, two UN Conferences debated the liquidation or reduction of statelessness. The New York Conference approved on Aug. 30, 1961 the Convention on the Elimination or Reduction of Statelessness and, moreover, adopted a resolution recommending *de jure* recognition of *de facto* stateless persons so as to enable them to apply for a national status. In summing up the debates of the Conference it was stated that no agreement had been achieved with respect to three principles: that every man shall acquire his nationality in a settled uniform manner and under specific conditions; that nobody can be deprived of his nationality acquired by birth unless he has previously acquired another nationality; and that a person who in his lifetime has lost contact with his home state and is residing in another, shall acquire the nationality of the latter.

UNTS, Vol. 360, p. 117; J. FRANÇOIS, "Le problème des apatrides", in: *Recueil des Cours*, 1935, pp. 288–376; REUT-NICOLUSSI, "Displaced Persons and International Law", in: *Recueil des Cours*, 1948, II, pp. 5–68; PAU, *Inter-American Juridical Committee, Report and Draft Convention on the Nationality and Status of Stateless Persons*, Washington, DC, 1952; *UN Review*, Dec., 1954, pp. 48–50; P. VIGOR, "Après les réfugiés, les apatrides ou leur Status", in: *Revue politique et parlementaire*, No. 126, 1959; P. WEIS, "Convention Relating to the Status of Stateless Persons", in: *International Quarterly*, No. 10, 1961; ONU, *La Comisión de Derecho Internacional y su Obra*, New York, 1967, pp. 33, 78 and 156–163: R.L. BLEDSOE, B.A. BOCZEK, *The International Law Dictionary*, Oxford, 1987.

STATE LIABILITY FOR NUCLEAR DAMAGE.
▷ Nuclear Accident Convention, 1986.

STATE ORDERS AND DECORATIONS OF INTERNATIONAL INSTITUTIONS. State orders have existed since the 14th century and are awarded to foreigners according to the customs and regulations that apply in a given country. International decorations have existed since the end of the 19th century i.a.: Médaille Florence Nightingale, instituted by the International Red Cross, Médaille interalliée dite "de la Victoire" established by the Versailles Conference in 1919 and others.

STATE RESPONSIBILITY. ▷ State International Responsibility.

STATE SERVITUDE. ▷ State Easement.

STATES OF THE THIRD WORLD. A term accepted in the UN 1955 for states of economically underdeveloped regions; these states in the decade 1955–65 became a majority in the UN General Assembly; in 1966 they formed the ▷ Group of 77.

STATES, UNION OF. A federation or confederation of states based on common interest (Switzerland), language (FRG) or religion (West and East Pakistan 1947–72).

STATE TERRITORY PROTECTION. A protection, resulting from the principle of the territorial integrity of a state and the inviolability of its borders, the obligation to respect national boundaries in international relations. See principles III and V of Helsinki Final Accords, 1975.

STATISTICS. A subject of international co-operation and agreements. The first institution for international statistics was the International Statistics Institute, est. 1885. An International Convention on Economic Statistics was signed on Dec. 14, 1928 in Geneva and supplemented by a protocol signed on Dec. 9, 1948 in Paris. In the Western Hemisphere, the Inter-American Statistical Institute was established in 1940, since 1948 a special OAS organization having consultative status with ECOSOC.
The first world organization dealing officially with international statistics is the ILO Labor Statistics Bureau, est. 1919. Within CMEA a Statistical Committee with headquarters in Moscow has operated since June 1962.
Organizations reg. with the UIA:

Inter-American Centre of Biostatistics, f. 1960, Santiago de Chile.
Inter-American Centre of Economic and Financial Statistics Education, f. 1952.
International Statistic Institute, f. 1885, The Hague. Consultative status with ECOSOC and UNESCO. Prior to establishment of the UN the Institute assumed the character of an international organization which sought international uniformity in statistical procedures and practices and formulated recommendations to national governments in this connection. Reconstituted itself in 1948 as an international professional society. Publ. *International Statistical Review, Bulletin of the ISI* and studies.

▷ Morbidity statistics.

LNTS, Vol. 11C, p. 171 and *UNTS*, Vol. 20, pp. 230–237; J. W. NIXON, *A History of the ISI*, The Hague, 1960; *ISI Dictionary of Statistical Terms*, The Hague, 1971; G. KURIAN, *Source-book of Global Statistics*, London 1986; THE ECONOMIST, *The World in Figures*, London 1976, 1978, 1981, 1984, 1987; J. WASSERMAN O'BRIEN, S.R. WASSERMAN eds., *Statistic Sources. A Subject Guide to Data on Industrial, Business, Social, Educational, Financial and Other Topics for the United States and Internationally*, 2 Vols., Detroit, 1988.

STATUS QUO. *Latin* = "existing state". An international term for legal and political state of things, (frontiers, for example), the preservation of which is the subject of international agreements. Other international formulae are also used: *status quo ante* = "existing previously (legal or political) state", and *status ante bellum* = "existing before the war (legal or political) state".

STATUTE. An international term for a collection of legal prescriptions defining the structure and activities of a national or international organization; or for a legal international document defining an administrative unit subordinated to international rule; in Anglo-Saxon countries Statutory Law indicates constituted law in contrast with customary common law.

STAVKA. "Stavka Glavnego Komendovaniya" = Supreme Headquarters of the Russian army during World War I, and during World War II the supreme headquarters of all Soviet armed forces. ▷ Teheran Conference, 1943.

STC. ▷ NATO.

STD. Sexually transmitted diseases. An international term introduced in 1974 by WHO to define generally a group of infectious illnesses spread mainly through sexual contacts; this includes not only the traditional venereal diseases, but also virus infections of the sexual organs, which have assumed epidemic proportions in some countries. Subject of international conventions, joint action in combatting STD and international organizations; under continual statistical surveillance by WHO. The first international convention was concluded Dec. 1, 1924 in the Brussels Agreement on facilities for merchant sailors to treat venereal diseases. After World War II a "V" campaign was waged under UN sponsorship, requiring the treatment of some illnesses with penicillin. Organization reg. with the UIA:

International Union Against Venereal Diseases and Treponematosis, f. 1923, Paris; united national associations of several dozen states. Consultative status with WHO and UNICEF; is a founding member of the Council of International Organizations of Medical Sciences; co-operates with the International League of Dermatology Societies. Publ.: *Bulletin*.

WHO. *Venereal Disease Treatment Centres and Ports*, Geneva, 1972; *Yearbook of International Organizations*.

STEALTH BOMBER. A US long range heavy bomber virtually undetectable by radar, in production since 1987, first unveiled on Nov. 20, 1988.

D ROBERTSON, *Guide to Modern Defense and Strategy*, London, 1987.

STEEL. A subject of international agreements, defined in Annex I of the Treaty Constituting the ▷ European Coal and Steel Community. ▷ Iron.

STEEL PACT, 1939. *Italian = Patto d'acciao; German = Stahlpakt*. A name given by the fascist press to the Pact on Friendship and Alliance, concluded in Berlin on May 22, 1939, for a duration of 10 years by Germany and Italy. Its major provisions:

"The Parties shall make an obligation to remain … in constant mutual contact, so as to communicate on all their common interests or on the general situation in Europe" (art. 1).
"In the case one of the Parties should be drawn into war with another power the other Party shall immediately manifest itself as its ally and support it with all its land, naval and air forces" (art. 3).

Measures on fulfilling in the most rapid way allied obligations were specified in general terms in art. 4, and in a specific way by the secret additional protocol, revealed in the Nuremberg Trial (1945–46). The "Steel Pact" was an extra link in the military alliance between Germany, Italy and Japan, the so-called ▷ Rome–Berlin–Tokyo Axis, begun by the ▷ Anti-comintern Pact, 1936.

Dokumente der Deutschen Politik, 2 Vols., Berlin, 1940.

STENOGRAPHY. Shorthand, Stenotype (machine recorded shorthand). A subject of international co-operation. First International Congress of Stenography took place 1887 (▷ Intersteno).

H. GEATTE, *Shorthand Systems of the World*, London, 1959; *Yearbook of International Organizations*.

STERILIZATION. A subject of international co-operation under the aegis of WHO, in connection with the demographic explosion especially in Latin America and South-East Asia. The International Planned Parenthood Federation, IPPF, f. 1948 in Stockholm 1977 elaborated Recommendations on Voluntary Sterilization for National Family Planning Associations:

"… Each person being sterilized should sign an informed consent form in duplicate, one copy to be kept at the clinic where the sterilization operation is performed, the other to be kept centrally in each country.
The consent form should make clear that each person being sterilized:
(a) knows that he or she will not be able to have any more children,
(b) is aware of the surgical nature of the procedure and of its possible complications and failures,
(c) is aware of other contraceptive methods and their risks and benefits,
(d) knows that he or she can withdraw consent to the operation at any time before it is undertaken.
Where young people or those without children request sterilization, special care should be taken to discuss the lifetime consequences of infertility after the operation. FPAs should ensure that local medical committees review in detail all serious complications and deaths following sterilization and report them to the Regional Medical Committee. Every six months each FPA should provide the following information on sterilization programs to the IPPF Regional and Central offices: (a) name and number of the hospital, clinic or mobile team carrying out voluntary sterilization procedures, (b) number and type of operations carried out by each unit, (c) analysis of those undergoing sterilization procedures by age, sex and number of living children, (d) number of failures."

The IPPF has a Consultative Status with ECOSOC, WHO, UNICEF, ILO, FAO and UNESCO.

WHO Chronicle, January, 1978.

STIMSON NON-RECOGNITION DOCTRINE, 1931. A principle of the foreign policy of the US formulated by H.L. Stimson (1867–1950), Secretary of State (1929–33), first in identical notes to the governments of China and Japan, Feb. 6, 1931:

"With the recent military operations about Chinchow, the last remaining administrative authority of the Government of the Chinese Republic in South Manchuria, as it existed prior to September 18, 1931, has been destroyed. The American Government continues confident that the work of the neutral commission recently authorized by the Council of the League of Nations will facilitate an ultimate solution of the difficulties now existing between China and Japan. But in view of the present situation and of its own rights and obligations therein, the American Government deems it to be its duty to notify both the Governments of the Chinese Republic and the Imperial Japanese Government that it can not admit the legality of any situation de facto nor does it intend to recognize any treaty or agreement entered into between those governments, or agents thereof, which may impair the treaty rights of the United States or its citizens in China, including those which relate to the sovereignty, the independence, or the territorial and administrative integrity of the Republic of China, or to the international policy relative to China, commonly known as the open-door policy; and that it does not intend to recognize any situation, treaty, or agreement which may be brought about by means contrary to the covenants and obligations of the pact of Paris of August 27, 1928, to which treaty both China and Japan, as well as the United States, are parties".

The doctrine was defined on Dec. 1, 1931 as follows:

"The American nation will not recognize any territorial changes which are not the result of peaceful means nor the validity of an occupation or acquisition of some territory if it has been achieved through the use of armed force".

This formula, extended to all of the American States, was included in art. 2 of the Anti-War Treaty of Nonagression and Reconciliation, called the ▷ Saavedra Lamas Treaty, 1933.

Q. WRIGHT, "The Note of January 7, 1932", in: *American Journal of International Law*, No. 26, 1932; A.D. MCNAIR, "The Stimson Doctrine of Nonrecognition. A Note on its Legal Aspects", in: *The British Yearbook of International Law*, 1933; Q. WRIGHT, "The Legal Foundation of the Stimson Doctrine", in: *Pacific Affairs*, No. 8, 1935; R. LANGER, *Seizure of Territory. The Stimson Doctrine and Related Principles in Legal Theory and Diplomatic Practice*, Baltimore, 1947; H. WEHBERG, *Die Stimson Doktrin. Festschrift* Spiropoulos, 1957; Ch.G. FENWICK, *The OAS. The International System*, Washington, DC, 1963.

STINGER. An anti-aircraft missile, developed during the late 1970's for US foot soldiers as the last line of defence against fighter planes. The missile is shot from the shoulder from a launcher that resembles a bazooka with a computerized viewfinder attached, and is guided to its target by a device sensitive to the infrared heat of aircraft engines. The Stinger missiles were supplied by the USA to the guerilla units in Afghanistan until March 1988.

J.H. CUSHMAN Jr., *In Afghanistan, Stinger is More Than a Missile*, in: *The New York Times*, January 18, 1988. KEESING's *Record of World Events*, June, 1988.

STIPENDIARIES OF CMEA FROM DEVELOPING COUNTRIES. A subject of an Agreement of the CMEA countries on the General Conditions for the Admission and Study of Stipendiaries from Developing Countries in Institutions of Higher Education of CMEA Member Countries. The highlights of the conditions for admission:

citizens of developing countries up to 30 years of age and who have documents or certificates concerning the completion of secondary education, recommended by the appropriate agencies of their countries shall submit the following documents through these agencies before 15 June of each year: an officially certified copy of an education document; an official medical opinion concerning state of health; a questionnaire of the established form; six photographs; and official copy of a birth document. The studies are free of charge. A stipend shall be paid by the CMEA country in the currency of the CMEA country. The stipendiary shall be provided with communal housing and shall be granted the possibility to dine in student lunchrooms on the same basis as students of the CMEA country where they are studying.

W.E. BUTLER (ed.), *A Source Book on Socialist International Organizations*, Alphen, 1978, pp. 919–922.

STOCK EXCHANGE. An institution of an international nature where buying and selling transactions of various currencies, securities and gold and silver, take place if this is not prohibited by the law of a given country (e.g. USA, 1933). The first

stock exchange appeared in the 14th century in the home of the patrician family Van der Burse in Bruges (thus in French *Bourse*, German *Börse*). The Stock exchange in Great Britain and USA is an institution with private legal status closed to outsiders; in other countries it is more or less under the control of the state. The quotations of stock exchange transactions are the basis for publishing the daily market prices. Among the oldest stock exchanges are: Antwerp – 1541, Lyon and Toulouse – 1549, Hamburg – 1558, London – 1566, Amsterdam 1608. The stock exchanges of advanced capitalist countries considered world exchanges are located: in France – La Bourse de Paris, branches in Bordeaux, Lille, Lyon, Marseille, Nancy and Nantes; In Japan – in Tokyo, Hiroshima, Fukuoka, Nagoyi and Osaka;
in FRG – Bremen, Düsseldorf, Hamburg, Frankfurt am Main, Hanover, Munich and Stuttgart; West Berlin has its own stock exchange;
in Switzerland – Berne, Geneva, Lausanne and two in Zurich (Bourse de Valeurs and Bourse Suisse de Commerce);
in Great Britain – The Stock Exchange in London, the Northern Stock Exchange in Oldham; the Scottish Stock Exchange in Glasgow, Aberdeen, Edinburgh and Dundee; and the Council of Associated Stock Exchanges in Belfast, Corcaigh and Dublin; in the USA – American Stock Exchange and the New York Stock Exchange in New York City; in Baltimore, Boston, Cincinnati, Colorado Springs, Detroit, Philadelphia, Honolulu, Chicago, Cleveland, Los Angeles, Minneapolis, San Francisco, Pittsburgh, Richmond, Salt Lake City and Spokane.
In Nov., 1972 the president of The New York Stock Exchange visited Moscow for the first time and expressed interest in the "universal internationalization" of stock exchange shares in connection with the growing importance of East–West commercial transactions.

C.A. DICE, W.J. EITEMAN, *Leading World Stock Exchanges: Practice and Organization*, London, 1964; B.L.L.M. THOLE, *Lexicon of Stock-Market Terms, in English/American, French, German and Dutch*, Amsterdam, 1965.

STOCKHOLM. The capital of Sweden, city and port. Founded in the 13th century; was important center of the Hanseatic League. Headquarters of about 40 international organizations reg. with the UIA.

Yearbook of International Organizations.

STOCKHOLM APPEAL, 1950. A document drawn up by the World Peace Council at its Third Session, Mar. 15–21, 1950, in the capital of Sweden in the form of an appeal to the peoples of the world to hold an international plebiscite concerning nuclear weapons ban and individual signing of the following text:

"We demand unconditional prohibition of nuclear arms as instruments of aggression and mass-annihilation of people, we demand strict international control over this resolution's implementation. We will consider as a war criminal each government which will first use nuclear weapons against any other country.
We call on all people of good will to endorse this appeal".

STOCKHOLM APPEAL, 1975. A Declaration on Detente, Peace and Security in Europe adopted by the World Peace Council at Stockholm on June 2, 1975.

STOCKHOLM CONFERENCE 1984–1986. On the basis of the ▷ Helsinki Final Act, the Conference on Confidence and Security Building

Measures and Disarmament in Europe opened in Stockholm, on Jan. 17, 1984. Sessions of the Conference, at which 35 European countries were represented, took place from May 8 to July 6, from Sept. 11 to Oct. 12 and from Nov. 6 to Dec. 14; in 1985 from Jan. 29 to March 23, from May 14 to July 5, from Sept. 10 to Oct. 18 and from Nov. 5 to Dec. 20; and in 1986 from Jan. 28 to March 15, from April 15 to May 23, from June 10 to July 18 and from Aug. 19 until Sept. 19, closed with a ▷ Stockholm Declaration 1986.

KEESING'S *Contemporary Archive*, 1986.

STOCKHOLM DECLARATION, 1986. The Final Act of the ▷ Stockholm Conference 1984–1986, which came into force on Jan. 1, 1987 and is binding on all 35 participant countries. The agreement covered military activities in Europe, the advanced exchange of information about all significant activities, rules of inspection and verifications.

KEESING'S *Contemporary Archive*, 1986.

STOCKHOLM DECLARATION ON HUMAN ENVIRONMENT, 1972. A Declaration adopted by the Stockholm Conference on the Human Environment, June 16, 1972:

"The United Nations Conference on the Human Environment, having met in Stockholm from 5 to 16 June, 1972, having considered the need for a common outlook and for common principles to inspire and guide the peoples of the world in the preservation and enhancement of the human environment, proclaims:
(1) Man is both creature and moulder of his environment, which gives him physical sustenance and affords him an opportunity for intellectual, moral, social and spiritual growth. In the long and tortuous evolution of the human race on this planet a stage has been reached when, through the rapid acceleration of science and technology, man has acquired the power to transform his environment in countless ways and on an unprecedented scale. Both aspects of man's environment, the natural and the man-made, are essential to his well-being and to the enjoyment of basic life itself.
(2) The protection and improvement of the human environment is a major issue which affects the well-being of peoples and economic development throughout the world; it is the urgent desire of the peoples of the whole world and the duty of all governments.
(3) Man has constantly to sum up experience and go on discovering, inventing, creating and advancing. In our time man's capability to transform his surroundings, if used wisely, can bring to all peoples the benefits of development and the opportunity to enhance the quality of life. Wrongly or heedlessly applied, the same power can do incalculable harm to human beings and the human environment. We see around us growing evidence of man-made harm in many regions of the earth: dangerous levels of pollution in water, air, earth and living beings; major and undesirable disturbances to the ecological balance of the biosphere; destruction and depletion of irreplaceable resources; and gross deficiencies harmful to the physical, mental and social health of man, in the manmade environment, particularly in the living and working environment.
(4) In the developing countries most of the environmental problems are caused by under-development. Millions continue to live far below the minimum levels required for a decent human existence, deprived of adequate food and clothing, shelter and education, health and sanitation. Therefore, the developing countries must direct their efforts to development, bearing in mind their priorities and the need to safeguard and improve the environment. For the same purpose the industrialized countries should make efforts to reduce the gap between themselves and the developing countries. In the industrialized countries, environmental problems are generally related to industrialization and technological development.
(5) The natural growth of population continuously presents problems on the preservation of the environment and adequate policies and measures should be adopted, as appropriate, to face these problems. Of all things in the world, people are the most precious. It is the people that propel social progress, create social

wealth, develop science and technology and, through their hard work, continuously transform the human environment. Along with social progress and the advance of production, science and technology, the capability of man to improve environment increases with each passing day.

(6) A point has been reached in history when we must shape our actions throughout the world with a more prudent care for their environmental consequences. Through ignorance or indifference we can do massive and irreversible harm to the earthly environment on which our life and well-being depend. Conversely, through fuller knowledge and wiser action, we can achieve for ourselves and our posterity a better life in an environment more in keeping with human needs and hopes. There are broad vistas for the enhancement of environmental quality and the creation of a good life. What is needed is an enthusiastic but calm state of mind and immense but orderly work. For the purpose of attaining freedom in the world of nature, man must use knowledge to build, in collaboration with nature, a better environment. To defend and improve the human environment for present and future generations has become an imperative goal for mankind – a goal to be pursued together with, and in harmony with, the established and fundamental goals of peace and of world-wide economic and social development.

(7) To achieve this environmental goal will demand the acceptance of responsibility by citizens and communities and by enterprises and institutions at every level, all sharing equitably in common efforts. Individuals in all walks of life as well as organizations in many fields, by their values and the sum of their actions, will shape the world environment of the future. Local and national governments will bear the greatest burden for large-scale environmental policy and action within their jurisdictions. International cooperation is also needed in order to raise resources to support the developing countries in carrying out their responsibilities in this field. A growing class of environmental problems, because they are regional or global in their extent or because they effect the common international realm, will require extensive cooperation by nations and action by international organizations in the common interest. The Conference calls upon the governments and peoples to exert common efforts for the preservation and improvement of the human environment for the benefit of all the people and their prosperity."

The Conference then laid down the following 26 principles:

"(1) Man had the fundamental right to freedom, equality and adequate conditions of life, in an environment of a quality that permitted a life of dignity and well-being, and he bore a solemn responsibility to protect and improve the environment for present and future generations. In this respect, policies promoting or perpetuating apartheid, racial segregation, discrimination, colonial and other forms of oppression and foreign domination stood condemned and had to be eliminated.

(2) The natural resources of the earth, including the air, water, land, flora and fauna and, especially, representative samples of natural ecosystems, were to be safeguarded for the benefit of present and future generations through careful planning or management, as appropriate.

(3) The capacity of the earth to produce vital renewable resources was to be maintained and, wherever practicable, restored or improved.

(4) Man had a special responsibility to safeguard and wisely manage the heritage of wildlife and its habitat which were now gravely imperilled by a combination of adverse factors. Nature conservation, including wildlife, was therefore to receive importance in planning for economic development.

(5) The non-renewable resources of the earth were to be employed in such a way as to guard against the danger of their future exhaustion and to ensure that benefits from such employment were shared by all mankind.

(6) The discharge of toxic substances or of other substances and the release of heat, in such quantities or concentrations as to exceed the capacity of the environment to render them harmless, had to be halted in order to ensure that serious or irreversible damage was not inflicted upon ecosystems. The just struggle of the peoples of all countries against pollution should be supported.

(7) States were to take all possible steps to prevent pollution of the seas by substances that were liable to create hazards to human health, to harm living resources and marine life, to damage amenities or to interfere with other legitimate uses of the sea.

(8) Economic and social development was essential for ensuring a favourable living and working environment for man and for creating conditions on earth that were necessary for the improvement of the quality of life.

(9) Environmental deficiencies generated by the conditions of under-development and natural disasters posed grave problems and could best be remedied by accelerated development through the transfer of substantial quantities of financial and technological assistance as a supplement to the domestic effort of the developing countries and such timely assistance as might be required.

(10) For the developing countries, stability of prices and adequate earnings for primary commodities and raw material were essential to environmental management, since economic factors as well as ecological processes had to be taken into account.

(11) The environmental policies of all States should enhance and not adversely affect the present or future development potential of developing countries, nor should they hamper the attainment of better living conditions for all, and appropriate steps should be taken by States and international organizations with a view to reaching agreement on meeting the possible national and international economic consequences resulting from the application of environmental measures.

(12) Resources should be made available to preserve and improve the environment, taking into account the circumstances and particular requirements of developing countries and any costs which might emanate from their incorporating environmental safeguards into their development planning and the need for making available to them, upon their request, additional international technical and financial assistance for this purpose.

(13) In order to achieve a more rational management of resources and thus to improve the environment, States should adopt an integrated and coordinated approach to their development planning so as to ensure that development was compatible with the need to protect and improve the human environment for the benefit of their population.

(14) Rational planning constituted an essential tool for reconciling any conflict between the needs of development and the need to protect and improve the environment.

(15) Planning was to be applied to human settlements and urbanization with a view to avoiding adverse effects on the environment and obtaining maximum social, economic and environmental benefits for all. In this respect, projects which were designed for colonialist and racist domination had to be abandoned.

(16) Demographic policies which were without prejudice to basic human rights and which were deemed appropriate by Governments concerned should be applied in those regions where the rate of population growth or excessive population concentrations were likely to have adverse effects on the environment or development, or where low population density might prevent improvement of the human environment and impede development.

(17) Appropriate national institutions were to be entrusted with the task of planning, managing or controlling the environmental resources of States, with the view to enhancing environmental quality.

(18) Science and technology, as part of their contribution to economic and social development, were to be applied to the identification, avoidance and control of environmental risks and the solution of environmental problems and for the common good of mankind.

(19) Education in environmental matters, for the younger generation as well as adults, giving due consideration to the underprivileged, was essential in order to broaden the basis for an enlightened opinion and responsible conduct by individuals, enterprises ad communities in protecting and improving the environment in its full human dimension. It was also essential that mass media of communications avoid contributing to the deterioration of the environment, but, on the contrary, disseminate information of an educational nature, on the need to protect and improve the environment in order to enable man to develop in every respect.

(20) Scientific research and development in the context of environmental problems, both national and multinational, were to be promoted in all countries, especially the developing countries. In this connexion, the free flow of up-to-date scientific information and transfer of experience was to be supported and assisted to facilitate the solution of environmental problems; environmental technologies should be made available to developing countries on terms which would encourage their wide dissemination without constituting an economic burden on the developing countries.

(21) States had, in accordance with the Charter of the United Nations and the principles of international law, the sovereign right to exploit their own resources pursuant to their own environmental policies, and the responsibility to ensure that activities within their jurisdiction or control did not cause damage to the environment of other States or of areas beyond the limits of national jurisdiction.

(22) States were to co-operate to develop further the international law regarding liability and compensation for the victims of pollution and other environmental damage caused by activities within the jurisdiction or control of such States to areas beyond their jurisdiction.

(23) Without prejudice to such criteria as might be agreed upon by the international community, or to standards which would have to be determined nationally, it was essential in all cases to consider the systems of values prevailing in each country, and the extent of the applicability of standards which were valid for the most advanced countries but which might be inappropriate and of unwarranted social cost for the developing countries.

(24) International matters concerning the protection and improvement of the environment should be handled in a co-operative spirit by all countries, big or small, on an equal footing. Co-operation through multilateral or bilateral arrangements or other appropriate means was essential to effectively control, prevent, reduce and eliminate adverse environmental effects resulting from activities conducted in all spheres, in such a way that due account was taken of the sovereignty and interests of all States.

(25) States were to ensure that international organizations played a co-ordinated, efficient and dynamic role for the protection and improvement of the environment.

(26) Man and his environment had to be spared the effects of nuclear weapons and all other means of mass destruction. States were to strive to reach prompt agreement, in the relevant international organs, on the elimination and complete destruction of such weapons."

The Conference adopted the Declaration by acclamation, subject to observations and reservations made by a number of governments. Among these were the following:

A number of states – including Canada, Chile, Egypt, India, Kenya, Pakistan, Sudan, the United Kingdom and Yugoslavia – held that the Declaration, while not perfect, represented a first step in developing international environmental law. Kenya, however, expressed concern at the emphasis the Conference had given to the physical, as opposed to social, environment of man; it regretted that no explicit reference had been made to the pollution of the minds of men, which resulted in policies such as apartheid. The Philippines also felt that the Declaration should have affirmed the primacy of human over physical factors.

China stated that the Declaration had failed to point out the main reason for the pollution of the environment – namely, the policy of plunder, aggression and war carried out by imperialist, colonialist and neo-colonialist countries, especially by the super-powers. China, therefore, did not agree with a number of views embodied in the Declaration.

Algeria declared that the environmental despoliation of colonialism was still going on. Although a considerable evolution of the concept of the environment had occurred during the Conference, the

S

Declaration should have affirmed the need to end the misuse of natural resources by certain powers. The United Kingdom considered that there were certain references to highly political matters in the Declaration which were out of place. The purpose of the Conference was to reach a consensus on priorities for action, not to discuss strategic issues, the United Kingdom held.

The following reservations or comments were made with regard to specific principles.

South Africa stated that the first principle – which called for the condemnation and elimination of policies promoting or perpetuating apartheid, racial segregation, discrimination, and colonial and foreign domination – constituted interference by the Conference in the internal affairs of states.

With regard to the second principle, concerning the preservation of representative ecosystems, the United States said that in its view the phrase meant retention of a complete system, with all the complex interrelationships intact. Uruguay also stressed it was necessary to preserve ecosystems as a whole.

A number of comments were made with regard to the final principle, concerning nuclear weapons. China maintained that the principle should have called for the prohibition and destruction of biological, chemical and nuclear weapons.

Peru, the Philippines, Sweden and the United Republic of Tanzania also felt that the principle did not condemn the use of such weapons in strong enough terms.

Japan said that, in its interpretation, the wording of the principle definitely implied prohibition of nuclear weapon testing.

The United States said it fully supported the purpose behind the principle but that the international agreements referred to therein must be adequately verifiable.

After considering the reports of its three main committees, the Conference adopted 109 recommendations for environmental action at the international level.

Included were 18 recommendations concerning planning and management of human settlements.

UN Yearbook, 1972, pp. 319–330.

STOCKHOLM EFTA CONVENTION, 1960. A
Convention on Jan. 1, 1960 signed at Stockholm by Austria, Iceland, Norway, Portugal, Sweden and Switzerland. The Convention establishing the European Free Trade Association came into force on May 3, 1960. The main provisions of the Convention: elimination of tariffs on industrial goods and progressive reduction of quantitative restrictions on all imports from member states, special arrangements have been made for fish and other marine products as also for agricultural goods.

J.S. LABRINDIS, *The Structure, Functions and Law of the EFTA*, London, 1965.

STOCKHOLM PLAN, 1952. The European
Broadcasting Agreement, signed in Stockholm June 30, 1952; entered into force July 1, 1953, defined the ▷ European Broadcasting Area and modified the ▷ Copenhagen Plan, 1948.

European Broadcasting Conference 1952, Final Act, ITU, Geneva, June 1952.

STOCK MARKET. ▷ Stock Exchange.

STOCKPILING. A policy of accumulation of
strategic materials for use in event of war, blockade or disruption in world transport. The United States in 1950 started stockpiling about eighty strategic materials.

STOMATOLOGY. A subject of international co-
operation. Organizations reg. with the UIA:

European Group for Scientific Research on Stomato-Odontology, f. 1957, Brussels. Publ.: *Bulletin.*
International Stomatological Association, f. 1907, Rome.

Yearbook of International Organizations.

"STOP PRICES". A system for determining prices
in mutual trade between the CMEA states, established in the 1950s for the purpose of insulating them from the passing fluctuations of world prices. Initially from 1951 to 1953 prices in the trade among socialist states were frozen, modified somewhat in bilateral treaties of 1954–57. In 1958 at its IX session CMEA adopted the system of "stop prices", based on the acceptance of the mean world prices for the past 5-year period in calculating the turnover of the member states, i.e. in the years 1960–65 the average world prices during the past 5-year period 1954–59 were in force, then in the years 1966–70 the average world prices for 1960–65, and in the period 1971–75 the average for the years 1966–70. However, in the first half of the 1970s there was a sudden increase in prices on the capitalistic market, caused i.a. by the energy crisis, and then the difference between the level of prices on the CMEA market and world prices began to increase greatly: in 1971 – 15%, in 1972 – 24%, in 1973 – 52%, and in 1974 – 110%. In this situation the Executive Committee of CMEA, in Jan., 1975 adopted the principle of annual updating, while retaining as the basis for updating the "stop prices" or the average for the last 5-year period, with the difference that each year one takes a new average for the last 5-year period, thus in 1978 for the years 1972–77, and in 1979 for the years 1973–78. This system is not regarded as final, and the need for further reform was recognized, especially in the 1980s, when the "stop prices" started to be higher than the world prices. The Havana Conference of CMEA in Nov., 1984 discussed this problem.

STORE. An international volume unit = 1 cubic
meter, or approximately 1.31 cubic yards.

STORE BAELT OR GREAT BELT. ▷ Danish
Straits.

STOWAWAYS. A subject of one of the ▷
Maritime Brussels Conventions: the International Convention relating to Stowaways, signed on Oct. 10, 1957 at Brussels by Belgium, Finland, France Greece, Israel, Norway, Peru, Sweden, Switzerland and the Vatican City, stating that

"Stowaway means a person who, at any port or place in the vicinity thereof, secretes himself in a ship without the consent of the shipowner or the master or any other person in charge of the ship and who is on board after the ship has left that port or place."

The highlights of the Convention:

"If on any voyage of a ship registered in or bearing the flag of a Contracting State a stowaway is found in a port or at sea, the master of the ship may deliver the stowaway to the appropriate authority at the first port.
This authority may return him to any State of which it considers that he is a national and is admitted as such by that State.
The costs of maintenance of a stowaway at his port of disembarkation as well as those for returning him to the country of which he is a national shall be defrayed by the shipowner, without prejudice to the right of recovery, if any, from the State of which the stowaway is a national. In all other cases the shipowner shall defray the costs of returning the stowaway but he will not be liable to defray the maintenance costs of a period exceeding three months from the time when the stowaway is delivered to the appropriate authority.

Any obligation to provide a deposit or bail as a guarantee for payment of the above costs shall be determined by the law of the port of disembarkation."

▷ Carriage of Passengers by Sea.

IMCO, *Maritime Conventions*, Geneva, 1970.

STRAITS. A narrow strip of sea joining two seas, a
sea with an ocean, two oceans, or a bay with a sea; subject of international conventions related to strategic significance of straits. The first international treaty concerning straits was signed in 1774 by Russia and Turkey in Küczük Kaynargy; the first multilateral agreement was the so-called London convention of July 13, 1841, concluded by Austria, Prussia, Russia, Great Britain, Ottoman Turkey; slightly amended and renewed in Paris, Mar. 30, 1856, and then replaced by the treaty on the Black Sea and the Danube signed on Mar. 18, 1871, in London; affirmed by art. 64 of the Berlin Treaty of July 13, 1878. Each of these treaties concerned ▷ Turkish straits. The question of the ▷ Danish straits was debated at an international conference in Copenhagen where Austria, Belgium, France, the Netherlands, Norway, Prussia, Russia, Sweden, Great Britain and Bremen, Hamburg, Hannover, Meklemburg, Lübeck and Oldenburg signed on Mar. 14, 1857, a treaty with Denmark (in force from June, 1868) eliminating customs in those straits, and granting Denmark one-time compensation to the amount of 30 million thalers. Denmark retained the obligation to maintain navigation safety equipment.

The Chile–Argentina agreement of 1881 determined neutrality of the coast along the ▷ Magellan Strait and full freedom of navigation.

A declaration concerning Egypt and Morocco, signed on Apr. 8, 1904, in London in which the governments of Great Britain and France guaranteed free passage through the Gibraltar Strait, was reaffirmed by the Anglo-Spanish convention signed on Nov. 27, 1912 in Madrid.

Free passage through the La Perouse Strait and the Tartar Strait was guaranteed by the Russian–Japanese Peace Treaty signed on Sept. 5, 1903 in Portsmouth.

Hostilities in Danish and Turkish straits, 1914–18, prompted Bulgaria, France, Greece, Japan, Yugoslavia, Romania, Turkey and the USSR to sign on July 24, 1923 in Lausanne, the Convention on Straits which provided for "the principle of free passage and navigation, by sea and air, in the Dardanelles, the Marmara Sea and Bosporus" (art. 1); a special annex to art. 2 specified regulations for "passage and navigation of sea and air craft, merchant and war craft, in both peace and war time", demilitarized the straits and adjacent zones, and imposed limits on the tonnage of war fleets which were to be supervised by a Straits Commission acting under the auspices of the League of Nations. The convention came into force in 1924 after having been ratified by all signatories except the USSR which objected to the granting to non-coastal states of the right to bring their fleets to the Black Sea.

The Lausanne Convention was replaced by a Montreux Convention regarding the Régime of the Straits, with Annexes and Protocol, signed on July 20, 1936 in Montreux, by Australia, Bulgaria, France, Great Britain, Greece, Japan, Romania, Turkey, USSR and Yugoslavia. The highlights of the Convention:

"Art. 1. In time of Peace merchant vessels shall enjoy complete freedom of transit and navigation in the Straits, by day and by night, under any flag and with any kind of cargo, without any formalities, except as provided in art. 3 below."
"Art. 3. All ships entering the Straits by the Aegean Sea or by the Black Sea shall stop at a sanitary station near the entrance to the Straits."

The Convention eliminated the demilitarization clauses concerning the Turkish straits and introduced limitations on the right of passage of battleships of states not located on the Black Sea coast (arts. 1 and 12) tonnage limits for such ships (art. 13), and a total ban on the passage of ships of belligerent parties in case of war. In 1938 Denmark, on the basis of the Montreux Convention, unilaterally introduced limitations on the passage of war ships through the Danish Straits.

The problem of innocent passage of warships through straits was discussed in 1923 by the Permanent Court of International Justice in the context of the ship "Wimbledon". The Court stated that the passage of a warship of a belligerent state through a territorial strait did not constitute a violation of neutrality of the state having jurisdiction over the strait, in 1946 the International Court of Justice declared in the matter of the Corfu Strait that:

"In time of peace States have the right to navigate their warships through straits serving international sea-going transport as waterways between two parts of open sea without prior permit obtained from a coastal State provided that the passage is not harmful. Unless international treaties state otherwise, the coastal state has no right to refuse permit of passage in time of peace."

This was reaffirmed in the Convention on Territorial Sea signed on Apr. 29, 1958 in Geneva, which in art. 16, stated the principle that

"harmless passage of alien vessels may not be suspended in straits used for international navigation between one part of open sea and another or in the territorial sea of an alien State."

R.M. OGELVIE, *International Waterways*, New York, 1920; E. BROEL, *International Straits*, New York, 1947; R.R. BAXTER, *The Law of International Waterways*, Cambridge, 1961; P.D. BARABOLYI, *Mezhdunarodno-pravovoi rezhim vazhneyshikh prolivov i kanalov*, Moscow, 1965; S. ALEXANDERSON, *The Baltic Straits*, London, 1982; R.L. BLEDSOE, B.A. BOCZEK, *The International Law Dictionary*, Oxford, 1987.

STRAITS SETTLEMENTS. The name of English East India Company trading emporia in Penang (1786), Singapore (1819), Malacca (1824) and Labuan (1912). The Straits Settlements status ceased to exist during World War II. Penang, Malacca and Labuan are now part of Malaysia; Singapore in 1965 become an independent state.

R.L. BLEDSOE, B.A. BOCZEK, *The International Law Dictionary*, Oxford, 1987.

STRASBOURG. A French city, with 355,262 inhabitants, census 1975; capital of the Bas-Rhine department, on the Ill River near its junction with the Rhine River. From 1871 to 1919 and 1940–44 under German occupation. In 1949 the seat of the Council of Europe, and from 1958 the seat of European Parliament.

STRASBOURG DECLARATION 1986 ON THE RIGHT TO LEAVE AND TO RETURN. Adopted on November 26, 1986 by the European Parliamentary Assembly. The text is as follows:

Preamble – The Meeting of Experts on the Right to Leave and Return.
Recognising that respect for human rights and fundamental freedoms is essential for peace, justice and well-being and is necessary to ensure the development of friendly relations and co-operation among all states;
Recalling that the Universal Declaration of Human Rights, the International Covenant on Civil and Political Rights, and the International Convention on the Elimination of All Forms of Racial Discrimination, as well as regional conventions, recognize the fundamental principle, based on general international law, that everyone has the right to leave any country, including one's own, and to return to one's own country;
Emphasizing that the right of everyone to leave any country and to enter one's own country is indispensable for the full enjoyment of all civil, political, economic, social and cultural rights;
Concerned that the denial of this right is the cause of widespread human suffering, a source of international tensions, and an object of international concern;
Adopts the following Declaration:
Article 1 – Everyone has the right to leave any country, including one's own, temporarily or permanently, and to enter one's own country, without distinction as to race, colour, sex, language, religion, political or other opinion, national or social origin, property, birth, marriage, age (except for unemancipated minors independently of their parents), or other status.
Article 2 – Every state shall adopt such legislative or other measures as may be necessary to ensure the full and effective enjoyment of the rights set forth in this Declaration.
All laws, administrative regulations or other provisions affecting the enjoyment of these rights shall be published and made easily accessible.
The Right to Leave – Article 3 – a) No person shall be subjected to any sanction, penalty, reprisal or harassment for seeking to exercise or for exercising the right to leave a country, such as acts which adversely affect, inter alia, employment, housing, residence status or social, economic or educational benefits.
b) No person shall be required to renounce his or her nationality in order to leave a country, nor shall a person be deprived of nationality for seeking to exercise or for exercising the right to leave a country.
c) No person shall be denied the right to leave a country on the grounds that that person wishes to renounce or has renounced his or her nationality.
Article 4 – a) No restriction may be imposed on the right to leave except those which are:
– provided by law;
– necessary to protect national security, public order, public health, or morals or the rights and freedoms of others; and
– consistent with internationally recognized human rights and other international legal obligations.
Any such restriction shall be narrowly construed.
b) Any restriction on the right to leave shall be clear, specific and not subject to arbitrary application.
c) A restriction shall be considered 'necessary' only if it responds to a pressing public and social need, pursues a legitimate aim and is proportionate to that aim.
d) A restriction based on 'national security' may be invoked only in situations where the exercise of the right poses a clear, imminent and serious danger to the State. When this restriction is invoked on the grounds that an individual acquired military secrets, the restriction shall be applicable only for a limited time, appropriate to the specific circumstances, which should not be more than five years after the individual acquired such secrets.
e) A restriction based on 'public order' shall be directly related to the specific interest which is sought to be protected. 'Public order' means the universally accepted fundamental principles, consistent with respect for human rights, on which a democratic society is based.
f) A restriction based on 'the rights and freedoms of others' shall not imply that relatives (except for parents with respect to unemancipated mirrors), employers or other persons may prevent, by withholding their consent, the departure of any person seeking to leave a country.
g) No fees, taxes or other exactions shall be imposed for seeking to exercise or exercising the right to leave a country, with the exception of nominal fees related to travel documents.
h) Permissibility of restriction on the right to leave is subject to international scrutiny. The burden of justifying any such restriction lies with the state.
Article 5 – a) Any person leaving a country shall be entitled to take out of that country:
1. his or her personal property, including household effects and property connected with the exercise of that person's profession or skill;
2. all other property or the proceeds thereof, subject only to the satisfaction of legal monetary obligations, such as maintenance obligations to family members, and to general controls imposed by law to safeguard the national economy, provided that such controls do not have the effect of denying the exercise of the right.
b) Property or the proceeds thereof which cannot be taken out of the country shall remain vested in the departing owner, who shall be free to dispose of such property or proceeds within the country
Right to enter or Return – Article 6 – a) No one shall be deprived of the right to enter his or her own country.
b) No person shall be deprived of nationality or citizenship in order to exile or to prevent that person from exercising the right to enter his or her country.
c) No entry visa may be required to enter one's own country.
Article 7 – Permanent legal residents who temporarily leave their country of residence shall not be arbitrarily denied the right to return to that country.
Article 8 – On humanitarian grounds, a state should give sympathetic consideration to permitting the return of a former resident, in particular a stateless person, who has maintained strong bona fide links with that state.
Procedural Safeguards – Article 9 – Everyone has the right to obtain such travel or other documents as may be necessary to leave any country or to enter one's own country. Such documents shall be issued free of charge or subject only to nominal fees.
Article 10 – a) Any national procedures or requirements affecting the exercise of the rights set forth in this Declaration shall be established by law or administrative regulations adopted pursuant to law.
b) Everyone shall have the right to communicate as necessary with any person, including foreign consular or diplomatic officials, for the realisation of the rights set forth in this Declaration.
c) No state shall refuse to issue the documents referred to in Article 9 or shall otherwise impede the exercise of the right to leave, on the grounds of the applicant's inability to present authorization to enter another country.
d) Procedures for the issuance of the documents referred to in Article 9 shall be expeditious and shall not be unreasonably lengthy or burdensome.
e) Everyone filing an application for any document referred to in Article 9 shall be entitled to obtain promptly a duly certified receipt for the application filed. Decisions regarding issuance of such documents shall be taken within a reasonable period of time specified by law. The applicant shall be promptly informed in writing of any decision denying, withdrawing, cancelling or postponing issuance of any such document; the specific reasons therefor; the facts upon which the decision is based and the administrative or other remedies available to appeal the decision.
f) The right to appeal to a higher administrative or judicial authority shall be provided in all instances in which the right to leave or enter is denied. The appellant shall have a full opportunity to present the grounds for the appeal, to be represented by counsel of his or her choice, and to challenge the validity of any fact upon which a denial or restriction has been founded. The results of any appeal, specifying the reasons for the decision, shall be communicated promptly in writing to the appellant.
Final Clauses – Article 11 – Any person claiming a violation of his or her rights set forth in this Declaration shall have effective recourse to a judicial or other independent tribunal to seek enforcement of those rights.
Article 12 – No state may impede communication by any person with an international organization or other bodies or persons outside the state with regard to the rights set forth in this Declaration, and no sanction, penalty, reprisal or harassment may be imposed on anyone exercising this right of communication.
Article 13 – The enjoyment of the rights set forth in this Declaration shall not be limited because of activities protected under internationally recognized human rights or other international legal obligations.
Article 14 – Nothing in this Declaration shall be interpreted as implying for any state, group or person any right to engage in any activity or perform any act aimed at destroying any of the rights set forth herein or at limiting them to a greater extent than is provided for in this Declaration.
Article 15 – The present Declaration shall not be interpreted to limit the enjoyment of any human right protected by international law.

Council of Europe. Human Rights. Information Sheet No 21, Strasbourg 1988, pp. 204–208.

S

STRATEGIC AND TACTICAL WEAPONS. A differentiation of the kinds of weapons according to their tasks, applied in negotiations concerning the limitation of weapons or disarmament. Among strategic weapons are included long-range weapons, e.g. nuclear and thermonuclear weapons.

J. GOLDBLAT, *Arms and Disarmament. A Handbook*, New York, 1983; D. ROBERTSON, *Guide to Modern Defense and Strategy*, Detroit, 1988; S.D. DRELL, T.H. JOHNSON, Managing Strategic Weapons, in: *Foreign Affairs*, Summer 1988.

STRATEGIC ARMS LIMITATION, 1973. An Agreement between the USA and USSR on Limiting Strategic Arms, signed at Washington, June 21, 1973; read as follows:

"The President of the United States of America, Richard Nixon, and the General Secretary of the Central Committee of the CPSU, L.I. Brezhnev.
Having thoroughly considered the question of the further limitation of strategic arms, and the progress already achieved in the current negotiations.
Reaffirming their conviction that the earliest adoption of further limitations of strategic arms would be a major contribution in reducing the danger of an outbreak of nuclear war and in strengthening international peace and security.
First. The two sides will continue active negotiations in order to work out a permanent agreement on more complete measures on the limitation of strategic offensive arms, as well as their subsequent reduction, proceeding from the basic principles of relations between the United States of America and the Union of Soviet Socialist Republics signed in Moscow on May 29, 1972, and from the interim agreement between the United States of America and the Union of Soviet Socialist Republics of May 26, 1972, on certain measures with respect to the limitation of strategic offensive arms.
Over the course of the next year the two sides will make serious efforts to work out the provisions of the permanent agreement on more complete measures on the limitation of strategic offensive arms with the objective of signing it in 1974.
Second. New agreements on the limitation of strategic offensive armaments will be based on the principles of the American–Soviet documents adopted in Moscow in May 1982 and the agreements reached in Washington in June 1973, and in particular, both sides will be guided by the recognition of each other's equal security interests and by the recognition that efforts to obtain unilateral advantage, directly or indirectly, would be inconsistent with the strengthening of peaceful relations between the United States of America and the Union of Soviet Socialist Republics.
Third. The limitations place on strategic offensive weapons can apply both to their quantitative aspects as well as to their qualitative improvement.
Fourth. Limitations on strategic offensive arms must be subject to adequate verification by national technical means.
Fifth. The modernization and replacement of strategic offensive arms would be permitted under conditions which will be formulated in the agreements to be concluded.
Sixth. Pending the completion of a permanent agreement on more complete measures of strategic offensive arms limitation, both sides are prepared to reach agreements on separate measures to supplement the existing interim agreement of May 26, 1972.
Seventh. Each side will continue to take necessary organizational and technical measures for preventing accidental or unauthorized use of nuclear weapons under its control in accordance with the agreement of September 30, 1971 between the United States of America and the Union of Soviet Socialist Republics."

UST, 1973; J. GOLDBLAT, *Arms and Disarmament. A Handbook*, New York, 1983; D. ROBERTSON, *Guide to Modern Defense and Strategy*, Detroit, 1988; S.D. DRELL, T.H. JOHNSON, "Managing Strategic Weapons" in: *Foreign Affairs*, Summer, 1988.

STRATEGIC DEFENCE INITIATIVE. ▷ SDI.

STRATEGIC SECURITY. ▷ Mutual Strategic Security.

STRATEGIC STUDIES. A subject of international co-operation Organization reg. with the UIA: International Institute for Strategic Studies, f. 1958 in London. A center for information and research on problems of international security, defense and arms control in the nuclear age. Members in 57 countries. Publ.: *Studies in International Security, Adelphi Papers, Military Balance*, and *Strategic Survey*.

Yearbook of International Organizations; D. ROBERTSON, *Guide to Modern Defense and Strategy*, Detroit, 1988.

STRATEGIC TERRITORIES. A UN term – under arts. 82 and 83 of UN Charter there may be designated in any ▷ trusteeship agreement "a strategic area or areas which may include part or all of the trust territory" and in relation to which "all functions of the UN . . . shall be exercised by the Security council." The designation of strategic territories occurred at the San Francisco Conference, 1945 on the initiative of the USA which sought to establish military bases on the Pacific Island trust territories.

Documents of the UN Conference on International Organizations, San Francisco, 1945, Vols. 1, 3 and 11; J.W. COULTER, *The Pacific Dependencies of the United States*, New York, 1957.

STRAUSS PLAN. A draft providing for the establishment of joint West European nuclear forces in NATO independent from the US nuclear forces, promoted by a Bavarian Christian-Democratic politician, F.J. Strauss, Minister of Defence of the Federal Republic of Germany during 1955–62. The draft was opposed by France. The guidelines of the Strauss Plan were presented in 1965 in a book published in London as follows: due to a variety of factors, the influence exerted by the USA in Europe would decrease; simultaneously, the fulcrum of Soviet policy in face of the Chinese threat would shift toward Asia and the East European socialist camp would disintegrate; under such circumstances there would be no need to maintain recognition of the European status quo agreed in Potsdam; on the contrary, the aim should be to unite Europe up the the Bug river "through exerting influence on people's democracies as well as peremptory negotiations with Moscow in the framework of a long-term process." As a consequence of such policy, a unified Europe under the leadership of Germany would become a third nuclear and economic superpower and a worthy partner of the USA. The Strauss Plan was drawn up after a political defeat that Strauss suffered in 1962 when trying to influence US strategic doctrines. This plan was also completely rejected by France, opposed to German hegemony in Europe.

F.J. STRAUSS, *The Grand Design*, London, 1965; F.J. STRAUSS, *Entwurf für Europa*, Stuttgart, 1966; F.J. STRAUSS, *Herausforderung und Antwort ein Program für Europa*, Stuttgart, 1968.

STRAW. ▷ Fodder.

STRESA CONFERENCE, 1935. A meeting of the heads of states of France, (Prime Minister P. Flandin), Great Britain (Prime Minister J. R. MacDonald) and Italy (Duce B. Mussolini) in Stresa, North Italy, Apr. 11–14, 1935, as a result of the German III Reich's decision concerning compulsory conscription in violation of the Versailles Treaty. The three powers in anticipation of ▷ Anschluss by Hitler issued a joint guarantee of sovereignty of Austria and expressed dissatisfaction at the Reich's *ex-parte* decisions. Six months later Italy by ex-parte decision launched its occupation of Ethiopia.

KEESING's *Archiv der Gegenwart*, 1935.

STRIKE. A work stoppage by a factory crew or the employees of an institution for economic or political purposes; subject of organized co-operation of international trade unions and international conventions: one signed in Geneva, Oct. 12, 1921 on the organization and coalition of agricultural workers and one signed on July 9, 1948 in San Francisco on the freedom to unionize and protection of the rights of unions, guaranteeing trade unions the right to organize strikes; ratified by the majority of ILO member states. The first state to recognize the right to strike was France in 1864. The first strike in the UN system was in March, 1976 in Palais des Nations in Geneva.

M. PERROT, *Les ouvriers en grève, France, 1871–1891*, 2 Vols. Mouton, 1900; "La grève du Palais de Nations à Genève a fait rentrer l'ONU dans son siècle", in: *Le Monde*, Mar. 5. 1976.

STRIKES, INTERNATIONAL. International political solidarity strikes or international economic solidarity strikes in multi-state regions which have been integrated economically, e.g. in the European Economic Community, confirmed in June, 1971 in Brussels by the Conference of Metal-workers Trade Unions of six EEC states, establishing the European Metalworkers Trade Union with the task of "representing and defending the economic social and cultural interests of workers of the metal industry at all levels of the EEC." International strikes of purely economic character occurred in the 1960s not only in the EEC region, such as the successful 1967 strike of 300,000 employees of Philips Company in Belgium, France, FRG, Great Britain, the Netherlands and Italy in protest against the closing of the Philips factory in West Berlin, but also in the territory of the NATO states, such as the 1969 strike of workers of the chemical industry in France, FRG, Italy and USA against the signing of identical labor contracts in the glass industry in those four countries. The largest international strike was the 25-hour strike protesting against air piracy, June 19, 1972, by pilots organized in the International Federation of Air Line Pilots' Associations, IFALPA. In June, 1972 an international strike took place simultaneously in the plants of the Pirelli–Dunlop company in Italy and Great Britain. In 1976, UN employees in the Palace of Nations in Geneva went on strike and received a wage increase, which was then also granted to UN specialized organizations headquartered in Geneva whose employees did not take part in the strike.

M. PERROT, *Les ouvriers en grève, France 1871–1891*, 2 Vols. Mouton, 1900; "La grève du Palais des Nations à Genève, a fait rentrer l'ONU dans son siècle", in: *Le Monde*. Mar. 5, 1976.

STRUCTURAL ADJUSTMENT FACILITY. ▷ SAF.

STRUTHOF. A Nazi concentration camp near Strasbourg, 1940–44; branch camp of Natzweiler. The ▷ Natzweiler–Struthof KZ Lager was called "Auschwitz in France."

The Trial of German Major War Criminals; Proceedings of the IMT Sitting at Nuremberg, Germany, 42 Vols., London, 1946–48, Vol. 5, p. 237.

STUDENTS. International Student organizations, reg. with the UIA:

Asian Student's Association, f. 1969, Hong Kong. Publ.: Asian Student News.

Council on International Educational Exchange, f. 1947, New York, NY, USA. Publ.: Whole World Handbook, Campus Update.

International Association for the Exchange of Students for Technical Experience, f. 1945, Lisbon, Portugal.

International Association of Dental Students, f. 1951, London, UK.

International Association of Students in Economic and Business Management, f. 1948, Brussels, Belgium. Publ.: Compendium.

International Federation of Medical Students Association, f. 1951, Vienna, Austria. Publ.: Medical Students.

International Pharmaceutical Students' Federation, f. 1949, Kiryat Rishon, Israel.

International Union of Students, f. 1946, Prague, Czechoslovakia.

International Youth and Student Movement for the United Nations, f. 1948, Geneva, Switzerland. Publ.; IYSMUN Newsletter (monthly)

World Union of Jewish Students, f. 1924, Jerusalem, Israel. Publ.: Shofar.

Yearbook of International Organizations, 1986/87; The Europa Yearbook 1988. A World Survey, Vol. I, London, 1988.

STUDENTS EXCHANGE. A subject of international co-operation and conventions, after World War II under the aegis of UNESCO. First international agreement was a Convention for Reciprocal Exchange of Central American Students, signed on Feb. 7, 1923 at Washington, DC, by Costa Rica, El Salvador, Guatemala, Honduras and Nicaragua; came into force on Mar 24, 1925; not ratified by Costa Rica and El Salvador, denounced by Honduras on Mar. 26, 1953.

The Brussels Convention of 1950 on the Employment of Students for Foreign Training defined the students employees as follows:

"... nationals (of either sex, up to 30 years of age) of one Contracting Party going to the territory of another Contracting Party in order to improve their linguistic and occupational knowledge by taking (manual or non-manual) employment with an employer."

UNTS, Vol. 126, p. 286; UNESCO. *Study Abroad 1987–1988*. In English, French and Spanish, Paris, 1987.

STUTTGART AMERICAN POLICY ON GERMANY DECLARATION, 1946. Speech of the US Secretary of State, J.F. Byrnes at Stuttgart (West Germany) on Sept. 6, 1946. The text is as follows:

"I have come to Germany to learn at first hand the problems involved in the reconstruction of Germany and to discuss with our representatives the views of the United States Government as to some of the problems confronting us.

We in the United States have given considerable time and attention to these problems because upon their proper solution will depend not only the future well-being of Germany but the future well-being of Europe. We have learned, whether we like it or not, that we live in one world, from which we cannot isolate ourselves. We have learned that peace and well-being cannot be purchased at the price of peace or the well-being of any other country.

I hope that the German people will never again make the mistake of believing that because the American people are peace-loving they will sit back hoping for peace if any nation uses force or the threat of force to acquire dominion over other peoples and other governments.

In 1917 the United States was forced into the first World War. After that war we refused to join the League of Nations. We thought we could stay out of Europe's wars and we lost interest in the affairs of Europe. That did not keep us from being forced into a second world war.

We will not again make that mistake. We intend to continue our interest in the affairs of Europe and of the world. We have helped to organize the United Nations. We believe it will stop aggressor nations from starting wars. Because we believe it we intend to support the

United Nations organization with all the power and resources we possess.

The American people want peace. They have long since ceased talk of a hard or a soft peace for Germany. This never has been the real issue. What we want is a lasting peace. We will oppose soft measures which invite breaking of the peace.

In agreeing at Potsdam that Germany should be disarmed and demilitarized, and in proposing that the four major powers should by treaty jointly undertake to see that Germany is kept disarmed and demilitarized for a generation, the United States is not unmindful of the responsibility resting upon it and its major allies to maintain and enforce peace under the law.

Freedom from militarism will give the German people the opportunity, if they will but seize it, to apply their great energies and abilities to the works of peace. It will give them the opportunity to show themselves worthy of the respect and friendship of peace-loving nations and, in time, to take an honorable place among Members of the United Nations.

It is not in the interest of the German people or in the interest of world peace that Germany should become a pawn or a partner in a military struggle for power between the East and the West.

German militarism and nazism have devastated twice in our generation the lands of German neighbors. It is fair and just that Germany should do her part to repair that devastation. Most of the victims of Nazi aggression were before the war less well off than the Germans. They should not be expected by Germany to bear, unaided, the major costs of Nazi aggression.

The United States, therefore, is prepared to carry out fully the principles outlined in the Potsdam Agreement on demilitarization and reparations. However, there should be changes in the levels of industry agreed upon by the Allied Control Commission if Germany is not to be administered as an economic unit as the Potsdam Agreement contemplates and requires.

The basis of the Potsdam Agreement was that, as part of a combined program of demilitarization and reparations, Germany's war potential should be reduced by elimination and removal of her war industries and the reduction and removal of heavy industrial plants. It was contemplated this should be done to the point that Germany would be left with levels of industry capable of maintaining in Germany average European living standards without assistance from other countries.

The plants so to be removed were to be delivered as reparations to the Allies. The plants to be removed from the Soviet zone would go to the Soviet Union and Poland, and the plants to be removed from the western zones would go in part to the Soviet Union, but in the main to the western Allies. Provision was also made for the distribution of Germany's foreign assets among the Allies.

After considerable discussion, the Allies agreed upon levels to which the principal German industries should be reduced to carry out the Potsdam Agreement. These levels were agreed to upon the assumption that the indigenous resources of Germany were to be available for distribution on an equitable basis for all Germans in Germany and that products not necessary for use in Germany would be available for export in order to pay for necessary imports.

In fixing the levels of industry, no allowance was made for reparations from current production. Reparations from current production would be wholly incompatible with the levels of industry now established under the Potsdam Agreement.

Obviously, higher levels of industry would have had to be fixed if reparations from current production were contemplated. The levels of industry fixed are only sufficient to enable the German people to become self-supporting and to maintain living standards approximating the average European living conditions. That principle involved serious hardships for the German people, but it only requires them to share the hardships which Nazi aggression imposed on the average European.

The German people were not denied, however, the possibility of improving their lot by hard work over the years. Industrial growth and progress were not denied them. Being obliged to start again like the people of other devastated countries with a peacetime economy not able to provide them more than the average European standard, the German people were not to be denied the right to use such savings as they might be

able to accumulate by hard work and frugal living to build up their industries for peaceful purposes.

That was the principle of reparations we agreed to at Potsdam. And the United States will not agree to the taking from Germany of greater reparations than was provided by the Potsdam Agreement.

The carrying out of the Potsdam Agreement has, however, been obstructed by the failure of the Allied Control Council to take the necessary steps to enable the German economy to function as an economic unit. Essential central German administrative departments have not been established, although they are expressly required by the Potsdam Agreement.

The equitable distribution of essential commodities between the several zones, so as to produce a balanced economy throughout Germany and reduce the need for imports, has not been arranged, although that, too, is expressly required by the Potsdam Agreement.

The working out of a balanced economy throughout Germany to provide the necessary means to pay for approved imports has not been accomplished, although that, too, is expressly required by the Potsdam Agreement.

The United States is firmly of the belief that Germany should be administered as an economic unit, and that zonal barriers should be completely obliterated so far as the economic life and activity in Germany are concerned.

The conditions which now exist in Germany make it impossible for industrial production to reach the levels which the occupying powers agreed were essential for a minimum German peacetime economy. Obviously, if the agreed levels of industry are to be reached, we cannot continue to restrict the free exchange of commodities, persons, and ideas throughout Germany. The barriers between the four zones of Germany are far more difficult to surmount than those between normal independent States.

The time has come when the zonal boundaries should be regarded as defining only the areas to be occupied for security purposes by the armed forces of the occupying powers, and not as self-contained economic or political units.

That was the course of development envisaged by the Potsdam Agreement, and that is the course of development which the American Government intends to follow to the full limit of its authority. It has formally announced that it is its intention to unify the economy of its own zone with any or all of the other zones willing to participate in the unification.

So far only the British Government has agreed to let its zone participate. We deeply appreciate their co-operation. Of course, this policy of unification is not intended to exclude the governments not now willing to join. The unification will be open to them at any time they wish to join.

We favor the economic unification of Germany. If complete unification cannot be secured, we shall do everything in our power to secure the maximum possible unification.

Important as economic unification is for the recovery of Germany and of Europe, the German people must recognize that the basic cause of their suffering and distress is the war which the Nazi dictatorship brought upon the world.

But just because suffering and distress in Germany is inevitable, the American Government is unwilling to accept responsibility for the needless aggravation of economic distress that is caused by the failure of the Allied Control Council to agree to give the German people a chance to solve some of their most urgent economic problems.

So far as many vital questions are concerned, the Control Council is neither governing Germany nor allowing Germany to govern itself.

A common financial policy is essential for the successful rehabilitation of Germany. Runaway inflation accompanied by economic paralysis is almost certain to develop unless there is a common financial policy directed to the control of inflation. A program of drastic fiscal reform to reduce currency and monetary claims, to revise the debt structure, and to place Germany on a sound financial basis is urgently required. The United States has worked hard to develop such a program, but fully coordinated measures must be accepted and applied uniformly to all zones if ruinous inflation is to be prevented. A central agency of finance is obviously necessary to carry out any such program effectively.

It is also essential that transportation, communications, and postal services should be organized throughout Germany without regard to zonal barriers. The nation-wide organization of these public services was contemplated by the Potsdam Agreement. Twelve months have passed and nothing has been done.

Germany needs all the food she can produce. Before the war she could not produce enough food for her population. The area of Germany has been reduced. The population in Silesia, for instance, has been forced back into a restricted Germany. Armies of occupation and displaced persons increased demands while the lack of farm machinery and fertilizer reduces supplies. To secure the greatest possible production of food and the most effective use and distribution of food that can be produced, a central administrative department for agriculture should be set up and allowed to function without delay.

Similarly, there is urgent need for the setting up of a central German administrative agency for industry and foreign trade. While Germany must be prepared to share her coal and steel with the liberated countries of Europe dependent upon these supplies, Germany must be enabled to use her skills and her energies to increase her industrial production and to organize the most effective use of her raw materials.

Germany must be given a chance to export goods in order to import enough to make her economy self-sustaining. Germany is a part of Europe and recovery in Europe, and particularly in the adjoining States, will be slow if Germany, with her great resources of iron and coal, is turned into a poorhouse.

When the ruthless Nazi dictatorship was forced to surrender unconditionally, there was no German government with which the Allies could deal. The Allies had temporarily to take over the responsibilities of the battered German State, which the Nazi dictatorship had cut off from any genuine accountability to the German people. The Allies could not leave the leaders or minions of nazism in key positions, ready to reassert their evil influence at first opportunity. They had to go.

But it never was the intention of the American Government to deny to the German people the right to manage their own internal affairs as soon as they were able to do so in a democratic way, with genuine respect for human rights and fundamental freedoms.

The Potsdam Agreement, concluded only a few months after the surrender, bound the occupying powers to restore local self-government and to introduce elective and representative principles into the regional, provincial, and State administration as rapidly as was consistent with military security and the purposes of the military occupation.

The principal purposes of the military occupation were and are to demilitarize and denazify Germany, but not to raise artificial barriers to the efforts of the German people to resume their peacetime economic life.

The Nazi war criminals were to be punished for the suffering they brought to the world. The policy of reparations and industrial disarmament prescribed in the Potsdam Agreement was to be carried out. But the purpose of the occupation did not contemplate a prolonged alien dictatorship of Germany's peacetime economy or a prolonged alien dictatorship of Germany's internal political life. The Potsdam Agreement expressly bound the occupying powers to start building a political democracy from the ground up.

The Potsdam Agreement did not provide that there should never be a central German government; it merely provided that for the time being there should be no central German government. Certainly this only meant that no central government should be established until some sort of democracy was rooted in the soul of Germany and some sense of local responsibility developed.

The Potsdam Agreement wisely provided that administration of the affairs of Germany should be directed toward decentralization of the political structure and the development of local responsibility. This was not intended to prevent progress toward a central government with the powers necessary to deal with matters which would be dealt with on a nation-wide basis. But it was intended to prevent establishment of a strong central government dominating the German people instead of being responsible to their democratic will.

It is the view of the American Government that the German people throughout Germany, under proper safeguards, should not be given the primary responsibility for the running of their own affairs. More than a year has passed since hostilities ceased. The millions of German people should not be forced to live in doubt as to their fate. It is the view of the American Government that the Allies should, without delay, make clear to the German people the essential terms of the peace settlement which they expect the German people to accept and observe. It is our view that the German people should now be permitted and helped to make the necessary preparations for the setting up of a democratic German government which can accept and observe these terms.

From now on the thoughtful people of the world will judge Allied action in Germany not by Allied promises but by Allied performances. The American Government has supported and will continue to suport the necessary measures to denazify and demilitarize Germany, but it does not believe that large armies of foreign soldiers or alien bureaucrats, however well motivated and disciplined, are, in the long run, the most reliable guardians of another country's democracy.

All that the Allied governments can and should do is to lay down the rules under which Germany can govern itself. The Allied occupation forces should be limited to the number sufficient to see that these rules are obeyed.

But the question for us will be: What force is needed to make certain that Germany does not rearm as it did after the first World War. Our proposal for a treaty with the major powers to enforce for twenty-five or even forty years the demilitarization plan finally agreed upon in the peace settlement would have made possible a smaller army of occupation. For enforcement we could rely more upon a force of trained inspectors and less upon infantry.

For instance, if an automobile factory, in violation of the treaty, converted its machinery to the production of weapons of war, inspectors would report it to the Allied Control Council. They would call upon the German Government to stop production and punish the offender. If the German Government failed to comply then the Allied nations would take steps to enforce compliance by the German Government. Our proposal for the treaty was not agreed to.

Security forces will probably have to remain in Germany for a long period. I want no misunderstanding. We will not shirk our duty. We are not withdrawing. As long as an occupation force is required in Germany the Army of the United States will be a part of that occupation army.

The United States favors the early establishment of a provisional German government for Germany. Progress has been made in the American zone in developing local and State self-government in Germany and the American Government believes similar progress is possible for all zones.

It is the view of the American Government that the provisional government should not be hand-picked by other governments. It should be a German national council composed of democratically responsible minister-presidents or other chief officials of the several States or provinces which have been established in each of the four zones.

Subject to the reserved authority of the Allied Control Council, the German national council should be responsible for the proper functioning of central administrative agencies. Those agencies should have adequate power to assure the administration of Germany as an economic unit, as was contemplated by the Potsdam Agreement.

The German national council should also be charged with the preparation of a draft of a federal constitution for Germany which, among other things, should insure the democratic character of the new Germany and the human rights and fundamental freedoms of all its inhabitants.

After approval in principle by the Allied Control Council, the proposed constitution should be submitted to an elected convention for final drafting and then submitted to the German people for ratification.

While we shall insist that Germany observe the principles of peace, good-neighborliness and humanity, we do not want Germany to become the satellite of any power or powers or to live under a dictatorship, foreign or domestic. The American people hope to see peaceful, democratic Germans become and remain free and independent.

Austria has already been recognized as a free and independent country. Her temporary forced union with Germany was not a happy event for either country, and the United States is convinced that it is in the interest of both countries and the peace of Europe that they should pursue their separate ways.

At Potsdam specific areas which were part of Germany were provisionally assigned to the Soviet Union and to Poland, subject to the final decisions of the peace conference. At that time these areas were being held by Soviet and Polish armies. We were told that Germans in large numbers were fleeing from these areas and that it would in fact, because of the feelings aroused by the war, be difficult to reorganize the economic life of these areas if they were not administered as integral parts in the one case of the Soviet Union and in the other of Poland.

The heads of government agreed to support at the peace settlement the proposal of the Soviet Government concerning the ultimate transfer to the Soviet Union of the city of Koenigsberg and areas adjacent to it. Unless the Soviet Government changes its views on the subject we will certainly stand by our agreement.

With regard to Silesia and other eastern German areas, the assignment to Poland by Russia for administrative purposes had taken place before the Potsdam meeting. The heads of government agreed that, pending the final determination of Poland's western frontier, Silesia and other eastern German areas should be under the administration of the Polish State and, for such purposes, should not be considered as a part of the Soviet zone of occupation in Germany. However, as the protocol of the Potsdam Conference makes clear, the heads of government did not agree to support at the peace settlement the cession of any particular area.

The Soviets and the Poles suffered greatly at the hands of Hitler's invading armies. As a result of the agreement at Yalta, Poland ceded to the Soviet Union territory east of the Curzon Line. Because of this, Poland asked for revision of her northern and western frontiers. The United States will support revision of these frontiers in Poland's favor. However, the extent of the area to be ceded to Poland must be determined when the final settlement is agreed upon.

The United States does not feel that it can deny to France, which has been invaded three times by Germany in seventy years, its claim to the Saar territory, whose economy has long been closely linked with France. Of course, if the Saar territory is integrated with France she should readjust her reparation claims against Germany.

Except as here indicated, the United States will not support encroachment on territory which is indisputably German or any division of Germany which is not genuinely desired by the people concerned. So far as the United States is aware the people of the Ruhr and the Rhineland desire to remain united with the rest of Germany. And the United States will not oppose their desire.

While the people of the Ruhr were the last to succumb to nazism, without the resources of the Ruhr nazism could never have threatened the world. Never again must those resources be used for destructive purposes. They must be used to rebuild a free, peaceful Germany and a free, peaceful Europe.

The United States will favor such control over the whole of Germany, including the Ruhr and the Rhineland, as may be necessary for security purposes. It will help to enforce those controls. But it will not favor any controls that would subject the Ruhr and the Rhineland to political domination or manipulation of outside powers.

The German people are now feeling the devastating effects of the war which Hitler and his minions brought upon the world. Other people felt those devastating effects long before they were brought home to the German people.

The German people must realize that it was Hitler and his minions who tortured and exterminated innocent men, women, and children and sought with German arms to dominate and degrade the world. It was the massed, angered forces of humanity which had to fight their way into Germany to give the world the hope of freedom and peace.

The American people who fought for freedom have no desire to enslave the German people. The freedom Americans believe in and fought for is freedom which must be shared with all willing to respect the freedom of others.

The United States has returned to Germany practically all prisoners of war that were in the United States. We are taking prompt steps to return German prisoners of war in our custody in other parts of the world.

The United States cannot relieve Germany from the hardships inflicted upon her which the war leaders started. But the United States has no desire to increase those hardships or to deny the German people an opportunity to work their way out of those hardships so long as they respect human freedom and cling to the paths of peace.

The American people want to return the government of Germany to the German people. The American people want to help the German people to win their way back to an honourable place among the free and peace-loving nations of the world.

The Department of State Bulletin, No. 376, Sept. 15, 1946; J. BYRNES, *Speaking Frankly*, New York, 1947.

STUTTHOF. A German concentration camp, near Gdansk in northern Poland, est. Sept. 2, 1939. About 110,000 prisoners, in the majority Poles and since 1941 also Russians, passed through it and *c.* 85,000 were murdered. The bodies of the victims were used by the Hygienic Institute in Danzig for soap production. Evacuated Jan. 25, 1945 (the "death march" for *c.* 15,000 prisoners).

K. DUNIN-WASOWICZ, *Stutthof*, Warsaw, 1946; T. SKUTNIK, *Stutthof Historischer Informator*, Warsaw, 1979; *Obozy hitlerowskie na ziemiach polskich, 1939–1945* (Nazi concentration camps on Polish territories 1939–1945), Warsaw, 1979, pp. 492–506; E. STEYER ed., *Stutthof: Hitlerowski obóz koncentracyjny (Stutthof: Nazi Concentration Camp)*, Warsaw, 1988.

SUBMARINE CABLES AND PIPELINES. A subject of international co-operation and conventions. The first submarine telegraphic cable was laid between Dover and Calais in 1885; between Europe and North and South America 1858–61. The first Convention was signed by 24 European and American states on Mar. 14. 1884 at Paris. The protection of submarine cables and pipelines was integrated in the Geneva Convention on High Sea, 1958.

A.P. HIGGINS, "Submarine Cables and International Law", in: *The British Year-Book of International Law*, 1921.

SUBMARINE-LAUNCHED BALLISTIC MISSILES. ▷ SLBM.

SUBMARINE MINES. A subject of international laws. The first rules and limitations in the use of submarine mines in sea wars were introduced by the Eighth Hague Convention of Oct. 18, 1907.

SUBMARINES. Warships capable of navigating under water and attacking the enemy with torpedoes or missiles; subject of international law, examined from the aspect of using submarines in torpedo attacks against enemy and neutral merchant vessels at the Washington Conference, 1922, and the London Conference 1930 and 1935/36, which discussed the problems of disarmament or the limitation of naval armaments. The most important agreement was the so-called London Protocol on Submarines concerning the rules of submarine warfare established in Part IV, Art. 22, of the London Treaty, Apr. 22, 1930, signed on Nov. 6, 1936 in London. The Protocol, taking into consideration the fact that the London Treaty was not ratified by all of the signatories, appealed to all states which had not been parties to the Treaty to accept two basic rules of International Law:

(1) In their action with regard to merchant ships, submarines must conform to the rules to which surface vessels are subject.

(2) In particular, except in the case of persistent refusal to stop on being duly summoned, or of active resistance to visit or search, a warship, whether surface vessel or submarine, may not sink or render incapable of navigation a merchant vessel without having first placed passengers, crew and ship's papers in a place of safety. For this purpose the ship's boats are not regarded as a place of safety unless the safety of the passengers and crew is assured, in the existing sea and weather conditions, by the proximity of land, or the presence of another vessel which is in a position to take them on board.

The Protocol was not respected by the Axis powers during World War II.

After World War II the German submarine potential was completely eliminated. Reconstruction took place within the framework of successive permissions granted to the FRG government by the Ministerial Council of the West European Union: 1954 a displacement of 350 tonnes, 1960 of 900 tonnes, 1965 of 1100 tonnes, 1973 of 1800 tonnes (armed with conventional weapons).

As a result of the development of nuclear weapons submarines became one of the most important kinds of strategic weapons; subject of SALT negotiations. In the world press atomic powered submarines with ballistic missiles on board are referred to by the American abbreviation – ASBN, the Anti-Submarine Rocket – ASROC, and the Anti-Submarine Torpedo – ASTOR.

The first nuclear powered submarine was produced in 1955 by the USA and in 1958 by the USSR, but the high speed attack submarine called the ▷ Hunter Killer Submarine was first produced in 1970 by the USSR and in 1976 by the USA.

See also ▷ SLBM.

LNTS, Vol. 112, 1931, p. 88; SIPRI *Yearbook 1979*; *World Armaments and Disarmaments*, London, 1979, pp. 391–394; D.C. DANIEL, *Anti-submarine Warfare and Superpower Strategic Stability*, London, 1986; J.E. MOORE, R.C. HALL, *Submarine Warfare: today and tomorrow*, London, 1986; R. LEGER SIVARD, *World Military and Social Expenditures 1987–88*, Washington DC, 1987.

SUBMARINE UNRESTRICTED WARFARE, 1917. Unrestricted warfare was ordered on Jan. 31, 1917 by the German government against all merchant vessels, whether armed or not, around the British Isles and in the Mediterranean Sea. The order was a violation of the ▷ "Sussex" Pledge, 1916.

SUBROCK. Submarine Rocket. An international naval term for a submarine launched rocket-propelled nuclear depth bomb used in antisubmarine warfare.

SUBVERSIVE ACTIVITY. An international term for activity of political groups of foreign agents in a state, with the aim of destabilizing it and bringing about a change of its government or political system. The term was introduced in 19th-century Europe by the Holy Alliance Powers into international conventions and agreements on co-operation of political police in combating anarchists, communists and also – in some states – liberals. In the 20th century the term is applied to revolutionary and reformist groups and to counter-revolutionary forces (▷ Quinta Columna). On Apr. 8, 1970 the Commission of Faith of the Conference of the Latin-American Episcopacy, CELAM, declared publicly that the existence of poverty was the source of subversive activity in Latin America. A similar opinion was expressed earlier by the US President, John F. Kennedy, in his speech of June 1963 at Washington University.

Conferencias Internacionales Americanas Primer Suplemento, 1938–42, Washington, DC, 1943, pp. 195–197; W. GOLLHOM, *The States and Subversion*, London, 1952; L. OPPENHEIMER, *International Law*, London, 1955, Vol. 1, p. 259.

SUCCESSION. A subject of international private law pursuing the so-called principle of one statute, i.e. one law that governs inheritance (resulting from ▷ domicile) having priority over the principle of two statutes (separate for immovable and movable property). Some socialist states, such as Poland, the USSR and the German Democratic Republic, as well as some Scandinavian, Iberian and other states, pursue the principle of domicile, whereas Anglo-Saxon states and Austria, Belgium, France, Hungary, Romania are guided by the dualism of succession. The law of succession is the subject of a convention the preparation of which was undertaken by the Hague Conferences of International Private Law held during 1925–28 and in 1961. In case of heirless succession the property falls to the Treasury of the State on whose territory, in principle, it is located.

SUCCESSION OF STATES AND GOVERNMENTS. A term of international law for recognition of the commitments of a state that has ceased to exist due to the loss of one of the three basic elements of a state: sovereignty, population or territory, and also recognition of a government's obligations after changes in its political system. After World War I, due to the emergence of a number of successive states, a number of issues relating to the succession of states and governments remained uncodified. The UN General Assembly, due to widespread decolonization and the emergence of numerous new successive states, requested the UN International Law Commission to elaborate uniform principles and norms for the succession of states. The UN General Assembly by a Res. 3496/XXX of Dec. 15, 1975 and by a Res. 31/18 of Nov. 24, 1976 decided to convene a conference of plenipotentiaries to consider a set of draft articles on succession of states in respect of treaties. The UN Conference on Succession of States in Respect of Treaties took place in Vienna from Apr. 4 to May 6, 1977; and adopted on Aug. 23, 1978, the ▷ Vienna Convention on Succession of States in Respect of Treaties.

L. GUGGENHEIM, *Beiträge zur völkerrechtlichen Lehre vom Staatenwechsel*, Leipzig, 1925; K. MAREK, *Identity and Continuity of States in Public International Law*, Geneva, 1954; K. ZEMANEK, "State Succession after Decolonization", in: *Recueil des Cours, 1955–III*; "Preemstvennost' gosudarstv subiekt mezhdunaordnogo prava", in: *Sovestkoe gosudarstvo y pravo*, Moscow, 1958; UN General Assembly Doc. A/5 209, 1962, annex. No 9; H. SZEGO-BOKER, "Succession of New States and International Law", in: *Questions of International Law*, Budapest, 1964; *Yearbook of the UN*, 1976; pp. 820–821; *Official Records of the UN Conference on Succession of States in Respect of Treaties, New York, 1978. Report of the International Law Commission*, New York 1980, pp. 6–49; *UN Chronicle*, September–October, 1981; p. 61; K.H. NEUMAYER (ed), *International Encyclopedia of Comparative Law*, Vol. V, Succession, The Hague, 1985; R.L. BLEDSOE, B.A. BOCZEK, *The International Law Dictionary*, Oxford, 1987.

SUCCESSION TO THE CROWN. ▷ Salic Law of Succession.

SUCRE. The capital of Bolivia. Seat of the Parliament.

SUCRE. A monetary unit of Ecuador; one sucre = 100 centavos; issued by the Banco Central del Ecuador.

S

SUDAN. Member of the UN. Democratic Republic of Sudan.Country in northeast Africa on the Red Sea, bordering on Libya, Egypt, Ethiopia, Kenya, Uganda, Zaïre, Central Africa, and Chad. Area: 2,505,813 sq. km. Pop. 1987 est.: 23,200,000 (1956 census: 10,262,000; 1973: 14,819,271). Capital: Khartoum with 476,218 inhabitants 1983. GNP per capita 1987: US $330. Official language: Arabic. Currency: one Sudanese pound = 100 piastre. National day: Jan. 1, proclamation of independence, 1956.

Member of the UN since Nov. 12, 1956 and all its specialized agencies except GATT. Member of the Arab League, OAU and is an ACP state of the EEC. International relations: from 1899 to 1956 under British rule; liberation struggle in 1950–55 led to full independence as of Jan. 1, 1956. South Sudanese separatism constitutes a hotbed of internal conflicts with repercussion in other African countries. In 1977–78 tensions with Ethiopia over Sudanese support of Eritrean separatists and Ethiopian support for South Sudanese separatists. Good neighborly relations provided for in treaty of 1980. A signatory of the Lomé Convention of 1975, 1980, and 1985. In Oct., 1982 Sudan and Egypt signed a Charter of Integration, creating the common Nile Valley Parliament, convened in May, 1983 with 60 Egyptian and 60 Sudanese members. In August 1988 disastrous rains and floods devastated Khartoum and the North of the country. (GA Res. 43/52 of Dec. 6, 1988 on Emergency Assistance to the Sudan).

E.M. CORBYN, *Survey of the Anglo-Egyptian Sudan 1898–1944*, London, 1946; M. ABBAS, *The Sudan Question: the Dispute about the Anglo-Egyptian Condominium 1884–1951*, London, 1952; M. SHIBEIKA, *The Independent Sudan*, New York, 1960; P.M. HOLT, *A Modern History of the Sudan*, London, 1962; J. ODUHE, W. DENG, *The Problem of Southern Sudan*, London, 1963; D. PENZIG, *Sudan. Sotsialno-ekonomicheskie problemy rozvivaiushchikhsia stran*, Moscow, 1964; K.D. HENDERSON, *The Sudan Republic*, London, 1965; M.O. BASHIR, *The Southern Sudan: Background to Conflict*, London, 1968; ABIDEL RAHIM, *Imperialism and Nationalism in the Sudan: A Study in Constitutional and Political Developments 1899–1956*, Oxford, 1969; D.M. WAI, (ed.), *The Southern Sudan: The Problem of National Integration*, London, 1973; F.A. LEES, *The Economic and Political Development of the Sudan*, London, 1977; P.M. HOLT, *A Modern History of the Sudan*, New York, 1979; P. WOODWARD, *Condominium and Sudanese Nationalism*, London, 1979; M.W. DALY, *Sudan, Bibliography*, Oxford, 1983; *UN Chronicle*, April, 1984, p. 27; *The Europa Year Book 1984. A World Survey*, Vol. II, pp. 2441–2454, London, 1984; C.H. GORDON, *Sudan in Transition*, London, 1986; T. NIBLOCK, *Class and Power in Sudan, The Dynamics of Sudanese Politics 1898–1985*, London, New York, 1987; *UN Resolutions and Decisions adopted by the General Assembly during the First Part of its Forty-Third Session From 20 September to 22 December 1988*, New York, 1989, pp. 262–263.

SUDAN STATE BANK FOR FOREIGN TRADE.
A bank est. 1970 in Khartoum, Sudan. A state merchant international bank with 25 branches in Sudan and correspondents in London and New York.

SUD-AVIATION.
One of three great French aircraft companies; established 1957 by the merger of Société Nationale de Construction Aéronautique Sud-Est and Société Nationale de Construction Aéronautique Sud-Ouest (the latter separated and created the independent company Ouest). In 1962 Sud Aviation signed an agreement with ▷ BAC for the construction of a four-engine supersonic passenger plane ▷ Concorde.

SÜDBAHN AGREEMENTS, 1923.
One agreement and one convention. Agreement between Austria, Hungary, Italy, the Kingdom of the Serbs, Croats and Slovenes and the Southern Railway Company (Südbahn), drawn up with the concurrence of the Committee representing the holders of bonds issued by the above Company with a view to the administrative and technical reorganization of the Südbahn's system, signed on Mar. 29, 1923 in Rome.

Convention for the Regulation of Transit and Communications on the System of the Danube–Save–Adriatic Railway Company (formerly the Südbahn), signed on Mar. 29, 1923 in Rome, by Austria, Hungary, Italy and the Kingdom of the Serbs, Croats and Slovenes.

LNTS, Vol. 23, pp. 336–375 and 377–431.

SUDETEN.
A European mountain range between the Erzgebirge and the Carpathian, since 1945 forms 300 km of the border of Czechoslovakia and Poland.

SUDETEN CRISIS, 1938.
A conflict between the German III Reich and Czechoslovakia regarding the northern part of Czechoslovakia in the years 1933–38, ended by the ▷ Munich Agreement, 1938.

"The Crisis in Czechoslovakia, April 24–Oct. 13, 1938", in: *International Conciliation*, No. 344, Nov., 1938; H. RÖNNER-FAHRT, *Die Sudetenkrise in der internationalen Politik*, 2 Vols., Würzburg, 1969.

SUEZ ANGLO-EGYPTIAN AGREEMENT, 1954.
An Agreement between the government of the UK and the Egyptian government regarding the Suez Canal Base, was signed on Oct. 19, 1954 at Cairo. The highlights of the Agreement:

"Art. 1. Her Majesty's Forces shall be completely withdrawn from Egyptian territory."

"Art. 2. The Treaty of Alliance, signed Aug. 26, 1936, is terminated."

B. AVRAM, *The Evolution of the Suez Canal Status from 1869 up to 1956*, London, 1958.

SUEZ CANAL.
The canal which connects the Mediterranean Sea with the Red Sea; located in Egypt, constructed by F. de Lesseps, 1859–69, under the protectorate of Great Britain; administered by an international joint stock company est. in 1858 in Paris, Compagnie Universelle du Canal Maritime de Suez, to 1875; next by an international consortium, Suez Canal Company, seat in London, to 1956; from 1882 to 1956 British military forces were stationed in the Suez Canal zone; subject of agreements, debates, and international conflicts. The legal status of the Suez Canal was defined by an International Convention signed on Oct. 29, 1888 in Istanbul by Austro–Hungary, France, Germany, Great Britain, Italy, Luxembourg, the Netherlands, Russia, Spain and Turkey in accordance with the principles of international navigation.

Art. 1. of the original French text stated:

"Le Canal Maritime de Suez sera toujours libre et ouvert, en temps de guerre comme en temps de paix, à tout navire de commerce ou de guerre sans distinction de pavillon. Le Canal ne sera jamais assujetti à l'exercice du droit de biens."

After the establishment of the Egyptian state on Feb. 28, 1922 Great Britain retained its colonial privileges in the Suez Canal zone; affirmed by the Egyptian–British Treaty on Aug. 26, 1936. During World War I the canal was the object of two German attacks Feb. 3, and Apr. 28, 1915; during World War II it was bombed by German planes in the period from Aug. 28, 1940 to July 27, 1942, causing a dozen or so brief closings of the Canal, totaling a period of 66 days.

After World War II on Oct. 8, 1951 the revolutionary government of Egypt renounced the Suez provisions of the Treaty of 1936, which in the light of British objections led to armed incidents in Nov., 1951 and the partial evacuation of British units from the Suez Canal zone. On the basis of the agreement of Oct. 19, 1954 complete evacuation began, which was concluded on June 13, 1956. Shortly thereafter, July 26, 1956 the President of Egypt, G. A. Nasser, announced the nationalization of the Canal; in response on Oct. 29–31, 1956 France, Great Britain, and Israel occupied the Canal Zone by force, which was condemned by the UN General Assembly on Nov. 5, 1956 and led to the withdrawal of foreign forces from Egypt on Dec. 22, 1956. The unblocking of the Canal took place with the help of UN experts on Apr. 24, 1957. The Suez Canal again became an international waterway, but under the administration of the government of Egypt, which acceded to the Istanbul Convention of 1888.

In June, 1967 navigation on the Suez Canal was halted as a result of a renewed invasion of Egyptian territory by Israel and the occupation of the East bank by the Israeli army. The issue of the renewed opening of the Suez Canal became part of the problem of ending the Israeli–Arabic war and the withdrawal of Israeli forces from occupied Arab territories in accordance with Res. 242/1967 of the UN Security Council of Nov. 1, 1967.

In Mar., 1974 after the withdrawal of the Israel army from the region of the Suez Canal and the occupation of the Canal along the length of its east bank by the UN armed forces, the government of Egypt began the work of clearing the canal and opening it for international navigation, which took place on June 15, 1975.

W. ALEKSEYENKO, "Suezkii kanal", in: *Mezhdunarodnaia zhizn*, No. 9, 1956; B. AVRAM, *The Evolution of the Suez Canal Status from 1869 up to 1956*, London, 1958; H. FEIS, "Suez Scenario, A Lamentable Tale", in: *Foreign Affairs*, No. 38, 1959–60; E. LAUTERPACHT, *The Suez Canal Settlement: A Selection of Documents 1956–1959*, London, 1960; H.T., R.D. MATTHEWS, "The Suez Canal Dispute. A Case Study in Peaceful Settlement", in: *International Organization*, No. 21, 1967; H. THOMAS, *The Suez Affair*, London, 1967; UNITAR, *Rios y canales navegables Internacionales*, Buenos Aires, 1971; *The Middle East and North Africa 1973–74*, London, 1973, pp. 82–84; D. NEFF, *Warriors at Suez*, New York, 1980; R.L. BLEDSOE, B.A. BOCZEK, *The International Law Dictionary*, Oxford, 1987; The Suez Crisis, in: B. URQUHART, *A Life in Peace and War*, New York, 1987.

SUEZ CANAL NATIONALIZATION DECREE, 1956.
The Decree Law No. 285 of 1956 Respecting the Nationalization of the Universal Suez Maritime Canal Company, stated in art. 1:

"The Suez Canal Maritime Company, S.A.E., is nationalized. All money, rights and obligations of the company are transferred to the State. All organizations and committees now operating the company are dissolved.

Shareholders and holders of constituent shares shall be compensated in accordance to the value of the shares on the Paris Stock Market on the day preceding the enforcement of this law. Payment of compensation shall take place immediately the State receives all the assets and property of the nationalized company."

Official Gazette, Cairo, July 26, 1956.

SUEZ TREATY, 1888.
A Treaty concluded on the initiative of Great Britain on Oct. 29, 1888 in Istanbul, by Austro-Hungary, France, Great Britain, the Netherlands, Italy, Germany, Luxembourg, Russia, Spain and Turkey guaranteeing free navigation for vessels from "all states for all time" on the Suez Canal. Art. I excluded the right to blockade the Canal; art. II stipulated that Canal and the

Canal Zone would be neutral with regard to the Parties in war, so as to remain open in wartime, provided that naval vessels not stay in harbors or waters of the Canal more than 24 hours. The treaty came into force on July 22, 1889.

Egypt, occupied by Great Britain in 1887, was not a party to the treaty. When Great Britain, on Aug. 26, 1936 signed a friendship pact with Egypt and removed its troops from the country, it left them in the Canal Zone, thus limiting the rights of Egypt. Only the British–Egyptian pact of June 27, 1954, made Egypt a formal Party to the Suez Pact, which was annulled on July 29, 1956, following a decision by the Egyptian government to nationalize the Canal.

G. NORODOUNGHAN, *Recueil d'actes internationals de l'Empire Ottoman*, 4 Vols. Paris, 1897–1903; C.A. COLLIARD, *Droit international et histoire diplomatique*, Paris, 1950.

SUEZ TUNNEL. A tunnel 5.1 km long under the Suez Canal was opened on Oct. 26, 1980 at the southern end of the waterway, ten miles north of the port of Suez. The tunnel carries cars and trucks as well as electricity and water pipes into Sinai.

KEESING's *Contemporary Archive*, 1980.

SUFFRAGETTES. An international term, from suffrage = the right to vote, for female militants for women's right to vote; in the USA the suffragette movement began in 1848, in Great Britain in 1869. The suffragettes won the right to vote in the USA and England after World War I.

In 1920 the National American Women's Suffrage Association established a public service organization: League of Women Voters, The League organized educational campaigns in the 1980's on state and national level and co-operates with the special ECOSOC Commission on the Status of Women.

I.H. HARPER, *The History of Women's Suffrage*, 6 Vols., 1881–1922; K.H. PORTER, *A History of Suffrage in the United States*, New York, 1918; *Inter American Convention on the Granting of Political Rights to Women*, Washington, DC, 1948; W.M. MORTON, *Women Suffrage in Mexico*, New York, 1962; C. ROVER, *Women's Suffrage and Party Politics in Britain, 1866–1914*, London, 1967; D. BOUCHIER, *The Feminist Challenge. The Movement for Women's Liberation in Britain and the USA*, London, 1983; R. GATLIN, *American Women since 1945*, London, 1987.

SUGAR. One of the basic raw materials of the food industry, subject of international conventions. The first convention, the so-called Brussels Convention, was signed in 1902 by Austria–Hungary, Belgium, France, Holland, Germany and Great Britain and until 1908 was an intra-European one, from 1908 to 1914 it also included the colonies and British dominions. In 1931 Belgium, Cuba, Czechoslovakia, Germany, Java, Peru, Poland, and Yugoslavia concluded a convention, Chadbourne Plan, but since the main producers of sugar – Great Britain, USA, USSR – did not enter it, the agreement was cancelled in 1935. Attempts at mediation by the League of Nations 1933/34 failed. In 1937 in London a World Sugar Agreement was reached with the participation of the then main producers of sugar, a total of 21 states. This agreement was extended 1942 and 1947 in modified form. The hierarchy of the main producing countries of sugar cane after World War II was: India, Cuba, Brazil, Philippines, Pakistan, Mexico, Puerto Rico, and countries producing sugar from cane as well as from sugar beets, so-called raw sugar: Cuba, India, USSR, Brazil, USA, France, FRG.

In Oct., 1953 the International Agreement for the Regulation of the Production and the Marketing of Sugar was signed establishing a permanent organ, the International Sugar Council, with seat in London. Members of the Convention: Argentina, Australia, Belgium, Brazil, Canada, Colombia, Costa Rica, Cuba, Czechoslovakia, Denmark, Dominican Republic, Ecuador, FRG, Ghana, Great Britain, Guatemala, Haiti, Holland, India, Indonesia, Ireland, Italy, Jamaica, Japan, Morocco, Nigeria, Nicaragua, New Zealand, Panama, Paraguay, Peru, Philippines, Poland, Portugal, South Africa, Taiwan, Trinidad and Tobago, USA, USSR. The convention was supplemented with the protocol of Dec. 1, 1956 and extended 1958, 1965, 1968. From 1965 the council meetings of sugar exporting states take place under the auspices of UNCTAD and all member governments of UNCTAD are invited to participate in the International Sugar Conferences, which previously were reserved only for the members of the Convention. The most difficult problem is ensuring sugar producing countries of the Third World free access to world markets. A sugar agreement for the years 1974–79 was negotiated in Geneva under the auspices of UNCTAD. The largest importers of sugar: USA, USSR, Japan, Canada, and countries of Western Europe. The world sugar market centre is London. The United Terminal Sugar Market Association, which administers the London Terminal Sugar Market, provides standard contracts, called London World Sugar Contracts, related to the International Commodities Clearing House in London. The European states: Austria, Belgium, Czechoslovakia, Denmark, France, FRG, GDR, Greece, Holland, Ireland, Italy, Poland, Portugal, Spain, Sweden, Switzerland, Turkey, and USSR established in 1949 the International Commission of Sugar Technology, ICST, with seat in Tienen, Belgium.

The ▷ Lomé Convention 1980 in chapter 2, art. 48 defined special undertaking on sugar in the period Mar. 1, 1980–Feb. 28, 1985.

The International Sugar Organization, sponsored by UNCTAD, after the collapse of World sugar prices, 1985 ($0.11 per pound) started talks in Geneva on replacing the 1979 agreement with a new system of management.

Organizations with the UIA:
Caribbean Cane Farmers Association, f. 1960, Kingston, Jamaica.

In 1975 the Group of Countries of Latin America and Caribbean Exporters of Sugar was formed, Grupo de Paises Latinoamericanos y del Caribe Exportadores de Azúcar, GEPLACEA.

European Committee of Sugar Manufacturers, f. 1954, Paris. International Association of Confectionery Manufacturers, f. 1953, Paris.

International Commission of Sugar Technology, f. 1948, Rome.

International Confederation of European Sugar-Beet Growers, est. 1925, Brussels, reorganized in 1947. Publ.: *Betteraviers Européens*.

International Institute of Sugar-Beet Researchers, est. 1931, Tienen, Belgium; Publ.: *Sugar-Beet Lexicon*.

International Society of Sugar Cane Technologists, f. 1924, São Paulo.

International Sugar Organization, f. 1950, London, Publ.: *Statistical Bulletin* and *Pocket Sugar Yearbook*.

L.M. PEREZ, *El Convenio Internacional del Azúcar, 1954–1959*, La Habana, 1959; C.A. MULLER, *Glossary of Sugar Technology*. In English, French, Spanish, Swedish, Dutch, German, Italian and Danish, Amsterdam, 1970; *International Sugar Agreement 1977*, Washington, DC, 1978; *UN Chronicle*, February, 1978, p. 30; E. HUGOT, *Handbook of Cane Sugar*, Amsterdam, 1979; *Yearbook of International Organizations*; N. DEERT, *The History of Sugar*, 2 vols., London, 1979; *The Europa Yearbook 1988. A World Survey*, Vol. I, London, 1988.

SUICIDES. A subject of international studies carried out under the aegis of the WHO and international statistics. In 1970 c. 1000 persons daily committed suicide according to WHO statistics. In European countries in the age group 15–44 suicides were the fourth most frequent cause of death after accidents, cancer and heart disease. Since the beginning of the 20th century a continual growth in the number of suicides has been taking place, which in the majority of countries in 1970 reached an average of 10 for each 100,000 population.

Organization reg. with the UIA:
International Association for Suicide Prevention, f. 1960, Burlingame, Calif., USA.

WHO, *Prevention of Suicide*, Geneva, 1968; *Suicide and Attempted Suicide*, Stockholm, 1972; A.R. MAY, "Suicide: A World Problem", in: *World Health*, May 1973; L.R. SALA, *Suicidios y suicides de la sociedad Mexicana*, Mexico, DF, 1974; *Yearbook of International Organizations, 1986/87; The Europa Yearbook 1988. A World Survey*, Vol. I, London, 1988.

SULPHUR. A subject of international co-operation, ▷ Pollution. Airborne sulphur pollution is the source of transboundary ▷ Air Pollution in Europe.

Subject of a Protocol of the Geneva Convention on Long-range Transboundary Air Pollution ("30 per cent sulphur club") on 30% or more reduction of national annual sulphur emissions.

Organization reg. with the UIA:
The Sulphur Institute, f. 1960, Washington, DC. Aims: develop and promote new uses for sulphur in all forms. Liaison statute with FAO. Publ.: *The SI Journal, The Sulphur Research Newsletter*.

Yearbook of International Organizations; KEESING's *Contemporary Archive*, Nov. 1986.

SUMED. Suez–Mediterranée. The oil pipeline leading from the Gulf of Suez to Sidi Krir near Alexandria on the coast of the Mediterranean Sea; constructed by the government of Egypt jointly with an international banking consortium representing the Union of Arab–French Banks, L'Union des banques arabes et françaises, UBAT, on the basis of an agreement of April, 13, 1972; completed Dec., 1976.

Le Monde, April 15, 1972.

SUMMIT CONFERENCES. A chronicle of post-war summits:

1955 July, ▷ Geneva Conference. End of the ▷ Cold war. ▷ Detente.
1959 September, D. Eisenhower, N. Khrushchev. Spirit of ▷ Camp David.
1960 May, D. Eisenhower, N. Khrushchev in Paris. ▷ U2.
1961 June, J.F. Kennedy, N. Khrushchev in Vienna. No formal agreement.
1967 June, L. Johnson, A. Kosygin in ▷ Glassboro.
1972 May, R. Nixon, L. Brezhnev in Moscow. First treaties.
1973 June, R. Nixon, L. Brezhnev in Washington. Agreements.
1974 June-July, R. Nixon, L. Brezhnev in Moscow and Yalta. Treaties.
1974 November, G. Ford, L. Brezhnev in Vladivostok. Pact.
1979 June, J. Carter, L. Brezhnev in Vienna. ▷ SALT II.
1985 November, R. Reagan, M. Gorbachev in Geneva. Agreements.

K. ENBANK, *The Summit Conferences, 1919–1960*, Oklahoma, 1966.

SUMMIT MEETING USA–USSR 1988. A summit meeting of the US President Ronald Reagan and the Soviet Leader Mikhail Gorbachev took place in Moscow on May 29–June 2, 1988. An agreement was signed on the joint verification of underground nuclear weapons tests at various test sites.

KEESING's *Record of World Events*, June, 1988.

SUMMIT OF INDUSTRIALIZED NATIONS. ▷ London Declaration, 1979.

SUNDAY SCHOOLS. An international term for a 19th-century school system, created by Christian Churches in Anglo-Saxon countries; subject of international co-operation since 1907, when the World's Sunday School Association was founded with headquarters in New York, London and Geneva; in 1947 adopted the name World Council of Christian Education and Sunday School Associations; merged Jan. 1972 with the ▷ World Council of Churches.

Yearbook of International Organizations.

SUNFED, UN SPECIAL FUND. In Dec., 1952 the UN General Assembly initiated studies on the possibilities of raising funds for economic development. In Dec., 1955 the UN General Assembly Res. 923/X decided to formulate a statute for the UN Special Fund for Economic Development. The work took three years. The UN General Assembly on Dec. 14, 1958 ratified the statute and on Jan. 1, 1959 the Fund began operations with a capital of 26 million American dollars, voluntary contributions from member states. The Fund became a new financial institution within the UN which, unlike the World Bank, financed neither production nor direct technical assistance, but made possible the study of possibilities for the economic development of a country or region, as well as the education of staff for these types of studies. The Fund was administered by an Administrative Council with the assistance of the UN Secretary General, the President of the Bank for International Development, the head of the UN Program for Technical Assistance, and the director-general of the Fund. The Fund, as well as the UN Program for Technical Assistance, were combined Jan. 1, 1966 to form one ▷ UNDP.

UN Yearbook, 1958 and 1966.

SUN, THE. A neutral body of the solar system, object of international scientific research under the auspices of the International Astronomical Union, as the main source of energy reaching the Earth. Observation of the Sun was begun by the USSR on Feb. 1, 1959 with the aid of Luna I and by the USA Mar. 3, 1959 with Pioneer IV; Mar. 11, 1960 Pioneer V was the first to circle the Sun. In 1962–67, acting within the International Council for Scientific Unions, was the International Quiet Sun Years Committee, called IQYS Committee, joining 66 states; publ.: *IQYS Reports*. In July, 1973 a scientific congress took place at UNESCO headquarters in Paris with the participation of 300 scientists from 60 states; devoted to the utilization of solar energy under the slogan: "The Sun in the service of man." From Apr. 1975 a satellite of the CMEA states, Intercosmos 13, has been engaged in research of the Sun.

A. SOBEL, *Space: From Sputnik to Gemini*, New York, 1965; "Le Soleil un des espoirs du XXI siècle", in: *Le Monde*, Mar. 7–8, 1976; S.D. GOMKALE, T. KURIAN, *Enriching Seeds with the Sun*, Bhanagava, India, 1988; UNU Work in Progress, May, 1988.

SUPERCARGO. An international term for a person protecting a cargo on a vessel on behalf of the charterer and making decisions in his name in unforeseen circumstances.

SUPERPOWERS. An international term for the most powerful great powers in terms of military potential.

A. HARTLEY, "Europe between the Superpowers", in: *Foreign Affairs*, Jan., 1971; W.H. PARKER, *The Superpowers. The US and USSR compared*, London, 1972; C. HOLBREAD, *Superpowers and International Conflict*, London, 1979; W. GOLDSTEIN, The Erosion of the Superpowers, in: *SAIS Review*, Summer-Fall, 1988.

SUPRANATIONALITY. A form of integration requiring multinational organs having legislative and international legal authorization in not one but in many states. In the integrative process of the EEC there are two opposing tendencies: (1) retaining the political sovereignty of each of the member states with full economic integration; (2) limiting the sovereignty of the member states in favor of supranational, multinational, economic, political and military institutions. The first tendency in the EEC was most strongly reflected in France during the period of General Charles de Gaulle's governments, the second by the government of FRG.

SUPRANATIONAL ORGANS. A term coined by a French statesman R. Schuman in 1951 for e.g. the European Community of Steel and Coal.

SUPREME SOVIET OF THE USSR. Verkhovny Soviet SSSR. The highest legislative body in the USSR since the Soviet Constitution 1936; consists of two chambers: the Soviet of the Union elected in a general election (one deputy for every 300,000 citizens) and the Soviet of Nationalities (32 deputies for each union republic, 11 deputies for each autonomous republic, 5 deputies for each autonomous region, and one deputy for each national area).
Both chambers have a jointly elected Presidium of the Supreme Soviet (chairmen, 15 deputy chairmen from each union republic, 20 members and secretary).

Interparliamentary Union, Parliaments of the World, London, 1976.

SURGERY. A subject of international co-operation and research. Organizations reg. with the UIA:

Asian Association of Pediatric Surgeons, f. 1972, Tokyo.
Collegium Internationale Chirurgiae Digestivae, f. 1969, Rome. Publ.: *Chirurgia Gastroenterologica*.
European Association for Maxillo-Facial Surgery, f. 1970, Zurich. Publ.: *Journal of Maxillo-Facial Surgery*.
European Society for Surgical Research, f. 1966, Rotterdam.
European Society of Cardiovascular Surgery, f. 1951, Zurich.
International Association of Oral Surgeons, f. 1962, Copenhagen. Publ.: *International Journal of Oral Surgery*.
International College of Surgeons, f. 1935, Washington, DC. Publ.: *International Surgery*.
International Confederation for Plastic and Reconstructive Surgery, f. 1959, Paris.
International Federation of Surgical Colleges, f. 1958, Edinburgh, UK. Consultative status with WHO and ECOSOC. Publ.: *News Bulletin*.
International Society of Orthopaedic Surgery and Traumatology, f. 1929, Brussels. Consultative status with WHO.
International Society of Surgery, f. 1902, Brussels.
Panamerican Association of Pediatric Surgery, f. 1966, São Paulo. Publ.: *Panamerican Pediatric Surgery*.
Pan-Pacific Surgical Association, f. 1929, Honolulu.
Scandinavian Association of Plastic Surgeons, f. 1951, Stockholm.
Scandinavian Association of Thoracic Surgery, f. 1949, Oslo. Publ.: *Scandinavian Journal of Thoracic and Cardio-vascular Surgery*.
Scandinavian Surgical Society, f. 1955, Oslo. Publ.: *Acta Chirurgica Scandinavica*.

West African College of Surgeons, f. 1960, Ibadan, Nigeria. Publ.: *West African Medical Journal*.

Yearbook of International Organizations.

SURINAME. Member of the UN. State of Suriname in South America on the Atlantic Ocean. Area: 163,265 sq. km. Pop.: 1987 est.: 415,000 (1971 census 384,900 including 39,500 Bush Negroes and 10,200 aboriginal Indians; 1980 census: 352,041). Capital: Paramaribo with 67,718 inhabitants, 1980. Official languages: Dutch and English. GNP 1986 per capita US $2,510. Currency: one Suriname guilder = 100 cents. National Day: Nov. 25, Independence Day, 1975.
Member of the UN since Dec. 4, 1975 and of all UN specialized agencies: except IAEA, IFC and IDA. Member of the OAS and is an ACP state of the EEC.
International relations: Dutch colony since 1667, by the Breda Anglo-Dutch Peace Treaty. Achieved full independence on Nov. 25, 1975. Member of the Lomé Convention in 1977, 1980, 1985. In territorial dispute with Guyana on the Corentyne region.
In Nov. 1985 Suriname signed with Brazil an agreement to purchase aluminium (130,000 tons) up to 1990. In Feb. 1986 signed an agreement granting Venezuela fishing rights in Suriname territorial waters. In Nov. 1986 signed an economic co-operation agreement with Guyana.

UN Monthly Chronicle, No. 12, 1975; *The Europa Year Book 1984. A World Survey*, Vol. II, pp. 2455–2460, London, 1984; KEESING's *Record of World Events*, 1987, No. 2.

SURTASS. Surveillance Towed Array Sensor System. International naval term for an underwater hydrophone acoustic array, used to listen for submarine activity, that is towed behind a specially configured ship.

SURVEYORS ORGANIZATION. An organization reg. the UIA:

International Federation of Surveyors, f. 1898, Malmö. Consultative status with ECOSOC. Member: National associations. Publ.: *Bulletin*.

Yearbook of International Organizations.

SUSSEX PLEDGE, 1916. During World War I on May 4, 1916, after a French steamer *Sussex* was sunk with Americans on board in the English Channel by a German submarine, the German government promised that American merchant ships would not be attacked without warning by German submarines. The pledge was violated in Jan., 1917. ▷ Submarine unrestricted warfare.

SVALBARD. ▷ Spitsbergen.

SWAP. A quick purchase of foreign currency; swap operations do not extend beyond 90 days.

H. RIEHL, R.M. RODRIGUEZ, *Foreign Exchange Markets*, New York, 1977.

SWAPO. The South West Africa People's Organization (SWAPO) was established as a national liberation movement on 19 Apr., 1960 by the Namibian people "in response to their need for an organizational framework through which the masses could articulate their problems and aspirations and weather the storm of apartheid repression".
With provisional headquarters in Luanda, Angola, and offices in several other countries, SWAPO's stated objective is to liberate the Namibian people from colonial oppression and exploitation in all its forms. At a meeting of its Central Committee in

Lusaka (1976), it adopted a Constitution, as well as a Political Programme, in which it aims

"(a) to liberate and win independence for the people of Namibia, by all possible means and to establish a democratic Government based on the will and participation of all the Namibian people; (b) to realize genuine and total independence of Namibia in the spheres of politics, economy, defense, social and cultural affairs."

SWAPO has always expressed its readiness to have the Namibian issue settled through negotiations, but in 1966, in response to measures of repression designed to thwart the growth of the movement, it felt the need to formally establish a military wing – the People's Liberation Army of Namibia (PLAN). Since its formation, PLAN has been waging an armed liberation struggle against South Africa.

SWAPO is active both internally and externally. While it has never been officially banned in Namibia by the South African government, the organization's supporters have been the subjects of arrests and repression, making open political activity impossible. The movement was declared the sole and authentic representative of the people of Namibia at home and abroad by the UN General Assembly in its resolution 31/146 (1976) and was

"invited to participate in the sessions and the work of all international conferences convened under the auspices of the General Assembly in the capacity of Observer (GA Resolution 31/152)"

Sam Nujoma has been SWAPO's President and Chief Executive Officer since its formation. Besides the President, SWAPO has a Vice-President, A National Chairperson, 15 Secretaries, a Regional Conference and a Regional Committee.

In July, 1984, the first official contact between SWAPO and the South African Republic took place in Green Hope Peninsula. Democratic elections were held in Namibia on Nov. 6–11, 1989, under the supervision of the UN.

UN Chronicle, March, 1983, p. 32.

SWAZILAND. Member of the UN. Kingdom of Swaziland. A country in southeast Africa, bordered by the South African Republic and by Mozambique. Area: 17,363 sq. km. Pop. 1986 census 676,049 (1976 census: 494,534). The administrative capital: Mbabane with 36,636 inhabitants, 1982. GNP per capita 1984 US $730. Official languages: English and siSwati. Currency: one lilangeni (plural: emalangeni) = 100 cents and South African rand. National Day: Sept. 6, Independence Day, 1968.
Member of the UN from Sept. 24, 1968 and of the UN specialized agencies with exception of IAEA, IMO and GATT; ACP state of the EEC.
International relations: under British protection from 1884 to 1968. Complete independence achieved on Sept. 6, 1968 within the Commonwealth.
A signatory of the Lomé Conventions of 1975 and of 1980.
In August and Dec. 1986 South African security forces entered Swaziland, terrorizing the border population.

C.P. POTHOLM, *Swaziland, The Dynamics of Political Modernization*, University of California Press, 1972; J.S.M. MATSEBULA, *A History of Swaziland*, London, 1972; J.J. GROTPETER, *Historical Dictionary of Swaziland*, Methuen, 1975; B. NYCHO, *Swaziland. Bibliography*, Oxford, 1982; *The Europa Year Book 1984. A World Survey*, Vol. II, pp. 2461–2466, London, 1984.

SWEDEN. Member of the UN. Kingdom of Sweden. European constitutional monarchy in the eastern part of the Scandinavian peninsula, bordering on Norway, Finland, Gulf of Bothnia and on the Baltic. Area: 449,964 sq. km. Pop.: 1982 census: 8,327,484 (1975 census: 8,208,544). Capital: Stockholm with 1,544,454 inhabitants 1982. GNP 1987 per capita US $18,607. Currency: one krona = 100 ore. Official language: Swedish. National Day: June 6, Independence Day, 1523.
Member of the UN from Nov. 19, 1946 and of all UN specialized agencies. Member of EFTA and the Nordic Council.
International relations: independent kingdom; in personal union with Norway 1319, and with Norway and Denmark 1397–1523. Neutral since 1818, also during World War I and II.
On Feb. 28, 1986 Prime Minister Olof Palme was assassinated by an unknown gunman in a street in the centre of Stockholm.
▷ Scandinavia.

Sweden and the United Nations, New York, 1956; I. ANDERSON, *A History of Sweden*, Stockholm, 1962; R. NORDING, *Suède socialiste et libre entreprise*, Paris, 1970; J. PARENT, *Le Monde Suedois*, Paris, 1970; *The Swedish Economy 1971–75 and the general outlook up to 1990*, Ministry of Finance Stockholm, 1971; W. CARLGREN, *Svensk utrikespolitik 1939–1945*, Stockholm, 1974; *Constitutional Documents of Sweden, The Instrument of Government. The Riksdag Act; The Act of Succession; The Freedom of the Prys Act*, Stockholm, 1975; *Documentation on Sweden*, Stockholm, 1976; B. TURNER, *Sweden*, London, 1976; F.D. SCOTT, *Sweden: The Nation's History*, Minnesota, 1977; *The Europa Year Book 1984. A World Survey*. Vol. I, pp. 805–825, London, 1984; L.B. SATHER, A. SWANSON, *Sweden*, Oxford, 1987.

SWEDISH–SOVIET ATOMIC ENERGY AGREEMENT, 1970. An Agreement concerning co-operation on the peaceful uses of atomic energy, signed at Moscow on Jan. 12, 1970.

UNTS, Vol. 787, 1971, pp. 273–303.

SWIFT. Society for Worldwide Interbank Financial Telecommunication, f. 1973 with hqs. in Brussels (World Trade Center). Members: 1046 banks in 49 countries.

SWIMMING. One of the Olympic competitions, since 1908. Organizations reg. with the UIA:

Amateur Swimming Union of the Americas, f. 1948, London. Sanctioned by the International Olympic Committee. Publ.: *Rule Book* (every 4 years).
International Swimming Federation, f. 1908, London. Recognized by International Olympic Committee. Draws up rules for amateur swimming, recognizes world records, manages and controls swimming competitions at Olympic Games and World Championships. Members: National federations. Publ.: *Official Handbook*.

Yearbook of International Organizations.

SWISS TIMING. A technical measurement of time during international sports events with instruments produced by the Swiss firms Longines, Omega and Heuer-Leonidas, which called into being the Swiss Association of Time Measurement (Schweizerische Zeitmessung A.G.). The instruments are marked with words Swiss Timing.

SWITZERLAND. Non-member of the UN. Swiss Confederation. Central European state bordered by France, FRG, Austria, Liechtenstein and Italy. Area: 41,293 sq. km. Pop.: 1987 est.: 6,600,000; census 1970: 6,269,782. Capital: Bern (Berne) with 289,200 inhabitants 1982; in 1970: 983,296. Currency: one Swiss franc = 100 centimes. GNP 1986 per capita: US $17,840. Official languages: French, German, Italian and Romansch. National Day: Aug. 1, Confederation Day, 1291.
Member of the League of Nations 1919, whose headquarters was Geneva. Member of FAO, GATT, IAEA, ICAO, IFAD, ILO, IMO, ITU, UPU, UNESCO, UNIDO, WIPO, WHO, WMO and of about 300 international organizations registered with the UIA.
International relations: Confederation from 1291; neutral during the Thirty-years war 1618–48; neutrality confirmed by the Treaty of Westphalia 1648 and by the Vienna Congress 1815. Neutral during World War I and II.
In a referendum on March 16, 1986 voters rejected (3:1) a plan to join the United Nations.
See also ▷ World Heritage UNESCO List.

C. VON WALDKRICH, *Art. 435 des Versailler Vertrages und seine Bedeutung für dauernde Neutralität der Schweiz*, Basel, 1924; P. GUGGENHEIM, *Völkerbund. Dumbarton Oaks und die Schweizerische Neutralität*, Zürich, 1945; D. SCHINDLER, "Relations de la Suisse avec les puissances alliés et les puissances de l'axe avant et après la capitulation", in: *Schweizerisches Jahrbuch für Internationales Recht*, 1946; A. SIEGFRIED, *La Suisse. Démocratie-création*, Neuchâtel, 1956; T. SHRAFARD, *Der Weg der Schweitz. Aspect du Devenir Helvétique 1914–1964*, Bern, 1964; *Unser Schweizer Standpunkt 1914, 1939, 1964*, Bern, 1964; G. PERRIN, *La neutralité permanente de Suisse et les organisations internationales*, Genève 1964; G. SALSER-HALLA, *Guide politique suisse*, Lausanne, 1965; J. BELIN, *La Suisse et les Nations Unies*, New York, 1966; J. DIERAUER, *Geschichte der Schweizerischen Eidgenossenschaft*, Zürich, 1967; E. BREMEIER, *Struktur des Bankwesens in der Schweiz*, Frankfurt am Main, 1968; SCHWEIZERISCHER BANK VEREIN, *The Role of the Swiss Commercial Banks*, Geneva 1970; "Documents Concerning the Accession of Switzerland to the League of Nations", in *International Conciliation*, No. 152, July, 1970; E. BONJOUR, *Geschichte der schweizerischen Neutralität, Vier Jahrhunderte eidgenossische Aussenpolitik*, Basel, 1970; P. CHAUDET, *La Suisse et notre temps*, Paris, 1970; M. IKLE, *Switzerland; An International Banking and Finance Center*, Strasbourg, 1972; J. ROHR, *La Suisse contemporaine*, Paris, 1972; F. RITZMANN, *Die Schweizer Banken: Geschichte Theorie, Statistik*, Bern, 1973; D. BOURGEOIS, *Le Troisième Reich et la Suisse*, Paris, 1974; *Switzerland, Economic Survey*, OEC, March, 1975; H.J. BAR, *The Banking System of Switzerland*, London, 1975; A. RIKLIN, *Handbuch der Schweizerischen Aussenpolitik*, Bern, 1975; H. BROWN, *Complete Guide to Swiss Banks*, New York, 1976; J.W.M. CHAPMAN, *German Intelligence Reports on Switzerland 1939–1944*, Brighton, 1979; U. SCHWARK, *The Eye of the Hurricane. Switzerland in World War II*, Boulder, 1980; J. GARLINSKI, *The Swiss Corridor*, London, 1981; *The Europa Year Book 1984. A World Survey*, Vol. I, pp. 826–856, London, 1984; *Zero inflation in 1986. La grande illusion*, in: *Tribune de Genève*, July 9, 1987.

SYKES–PICOT TREATY, 1916. A Treaty signed on May 16, 1916, on behalf of England by Sir Mark Sykes and on behalf of France by Georges Picot; a confidential pact on the division of the zones of interest of both powers in the Middle East after the defeat of Turkey and the dissolution of the Ottoman Empire. On the basis of this Treaty, which provided for the international administration of Palestine, on Nov. 2, 1917 the ▷ Balfour Declaration was announced. In 1919 the Sykes–Picot Treaty was amended by submitting Palestine to British administration and excluding ▷ Mosul from the French zone of influence.

Documents on British Foreign Policy, London, 1947.

SYLI. A monetary unit of the Guinea Republic; one syli = 100 cauris; issued from Oct. 2, 1972 by the Banque Centrale de la République de Guinée replacing the Guinea Franc 1960–72.

SYMBOLS AND SIGNS, INTERNATIONAL. An international term for touristic, railroad, airline, road international symbols and signs standardized by conventions. The work of standardizing international symbols and signs of various areas is sponsored by UNESCO and several international organizations.

A. DE VRIES, *Dictionary of Symbols and Imagery*, Amsterdam, 1976.

SYMBOLS OF INTERNATIONAL ORGANIZATIONS. The UN symbols and those of its special agencies are the subject of legal safeguard by the member states, which does not apply to the symbols of non-governmental organizations, e.g. the Olympic Committee.

SYMMETRY AND ASYMMETRY IN DISARMAMENT TALKS. An international term introduced in the negotiations on the mutual reduction of military forces and armaments in Europe, which have been taking place since 1973 in Vienna; the states of the Warsaw Pact came out in favor of the symmetrical reduction of military forces, the NATO states for asymmetrical. The essence of the debate hinged on a fundamental question – which method could truly guarantee the maintenance of the existing balance of power in Central Europe. ▷ Asymmetry.

"SYMPHONY". A telecommunications satellite of France and FRG launched from Cape Canaveral, USA; the exchange of television programs was initiated on Jan. 22, 1975. In Peking Apr. 12, 1978 China signed with France and FRG an agreement that permits the People's Republic of China to use both "Symphony" satellites for scientific research purposes. Previously similar agreements were signed by Canada, Egypt, India, Indonesia, Iran, Spain, and the UN.

SYMPOSIA, INTERNATIONAL. A form of international meetings of scholars and artists, often under the auspices of UNESCO or leading international organizations of the world of learning and the arts.

SYNAGOGUES, WORLD COUNCIL OF. An international organization reg. with the UIA, f. 1962, New York.

SYNDICALISM. A sociopolitical trend in the trade union movement, precisely defined in the so-called Amiens Charter, ratified at the Congress of the French General Confederation of Labor, CGT, in Amiens, 1906, proclaiming that the main form of workers' organizations should be trade unions and the only successful form of class struggle the indirect activities of trade unions. During the interwar period syndicalism gained influence in trade unions in South and North America and came to be known as anarchosyndicalism.

G.D.N. COLE, *A History of Socialist Thought*, London, 1954.

SYNDICATE. An international term open to various interpretations – in the Anglo-Saxon world an agreement among the companies of one branch of the economy, usually temporary (a form of ▷ cartel); in many countries the term is a synonym for trade unions.

M. PRELOT, G. LESEUYER, *Histoire des idées politiques*, Paris, 1977, pp. 623–636.

SYNDICATE RIGHTS. A subject of international conventions prepared by ILO in 1947. The Freedom of Association Convention and the Right to Organize adopted by ILO in 1948 was the first of them, the next, the Right to Organize and Collective Bargaining Convention, 1949. In Jan., 1955 the UN Commission on Human Rights established a group of experts to study labor laws and syndicate rights and the application of these rights in UN member states.

UN Monthly Chronicle, No. 8, 1967, pp. 51–52; No. 9, 1967, pp. 36–37; No. 2, 1968, pp. 42–43.

SYNOD. An assembly of the clergy of Christian churches, with either the character of standing ruling colleges, as in the autocephalous Orthodox Churches or in Protestant Churches and others stemming from them – or with the character of an advisory body, as when in 1965 Paul VI convened the Synod of Bishops of the Roman Catholic Church.

SYNTHETIC FIBERS. A subject of international co-operation. Organization reg. with the UIA: International Rayon and Synthetic Fibres.

SYRIA. Member of the UN. Syrian Arab Republic. State of western Asia, bordering on Lebanon and the Mediterranean Sea, on Turkey, Iraq, Jordan and Israel. Area: 184,050 sq. km. Pop. 1988 est. 11,400,000 (1960 census: 5,565,121; 1970 census: 6,304,685; 1981 census: 9,171,622). Capital Damascus with 923,253 inhabitants, census 1970. GNP 1984 per capita US $2,000. Currency: one Syrian pound = 100 piastres. Official language: Arabic. National Day: Apr. 17, Independence Day, 1946.
Member of the UN from Oct. 24, 1945 and of all UN specialized agencies with the exception of GATT and WIPO. Member of the Arab League.
International relations: from 1515 to 1918 under Turkish Ottoman Empire domination. 1919–45 League of Nations mandate administrated by France. Independent on Apr. 17, 1946. In Union with Egypt (▷ United Arab Republic) from Feb. 1, 1958 to Oct. 5, 1961. A Signatory of a Co-operation Agreement with the EEC, 1977. In the 1980s in conflict with Israel over Lebanon. On the side of Iran in the Gulf War with Iraq.
Relations with Jordan renewed in Dec. 1985 (visit of King Hussein in Damascus).
See also ▷ World Heritage UNESCO List.

A.F. SULTANOV, *Sovremennaia Siriia*, Moscow, 1950; M. HOMET, *L'Histoire secrète du traité franco-syrien*, Paris, 1951; IBRD, *The Economic Development of Syria*, Baltimore, 1955; S.H. KONGRIGG, *Syria and Lebanon under French Mandate*, Oxford, 1958; A.L. TIBARI, *Syria*, London, 1962; S.H. TORREY, *Syrian Politics and the Military*, Ohio, 1964; *A Bibliographical List of Works about Syria*, Cairo, 1965; L.Z. YAMAK, *The Syrian Social Nationalist Party*, Cambridge, 1966; K.S. ABU JABER, *The Arab Baath Socialist Party*, New York, 1966; A.K. TIBAWI, *A Modern History of Syria including Lebanon and Palestine*, London, 1969; A.T. SAID, *Die Bedeutung des Bankwesens in Wirtschaftlichen Wachstumsprozess Syriens*, Berlin, 1972; T. PETRAN, *Syria*, London, 1972; *Inside on the Middle East War, Team of the Sunday Times*, London, 1974; *The October War, An-Nahar Arab Report*, Beirut, 1974; *The Europa Year Book 1984. A World Survey*, Vol. II, pp. 2467–2477, London, 1984; N.J. WEINBERGER, *Syrian Intervention in Lebanon: the 1975–76 Civil War*, New York, 1987.

SYRIA–USSR TREATY, 1980. A 20-year Treaty of Friendship and Co-operation, signed on Oct. 8, 1980 at Moscow. The text is similar to the ▷ Afghanistan–USSR Friendship Treaty, 1978.

KEESING's *Contemporary Archive*, 1980.

SYSTEM ANALYSIS. A subject of international co-operation through the International Institute for Applied System Analysis, f. 1972, London on signature of Charter by representatives of research institutes of Austria, Bulgaria, Canada, Czechoslovakia, France, FRG, GDR, Italy, Japan, Poland, UK, USA and USSR. Aims: to encourage research on problems of modern societies arising from scientific and technological development. Reg. with the UIA.

Yearbook of International Organizations.

SYSTEMS MANAGEMENT. A subject of international co-operation through the Association for System management, f. 1947, Cleveland, Publ.: *Journal of System Management*. Reg. with the UIA.

Yearbook of International Organizations.

SYSTEMS RESEARCH. A subject of international co-operation under aegis of UNESCO. Organization reg. with the UIA:

Society for General Systems Research, f. 1954, Washington, DC. Consultative status with UNESCO and ECOSOC. Publ.: *Behavioural Science* (bi-monthly), *General Systems Bulletin* (3 a year), *General Systems Yearbook.*

Yearbook of International Organizations.

T

TABLE TENNIS. Game also called ping-pong, organized within the International Table Tennis Federation, ITTF, 1926, which since then has sponsored world championships every two years. Publ.: *Handbook of Regulations.*

Yearbook of International Organizations.

TABULA RASA. *Latin* = scraped tablet. A principle that a newly independent state is under no international obligations arising from its colonial period; accepted by the Vienna Convention on Succession of States in Respect to Treaties, 1978, providing in Art. 16 that: "A newly independent state is not bound to maintain in force, or to become a party to, any treaty by reason only of the fact that at the date of the succession of states the treaty was in force in respect of the territory to which the succession of states relates."

UN Yearbook, 1978.

TACIT APPROVAL. The tacit recognition of a legal act having international implications by failure to submit any objections or remarks; subject of an opinion by the International Court of Justice.

ICJ Reports, 1951.

TACNA–ARICA. Two provinces on the borderland of Chile and Peru, subject of international dispute in 1883–1929; in consequence of a four-year war between Chile and Peru the two Peruvian provinces were granted to Chile for 10 years by the treaty signed in 1883 at Ancón (▷ Ancón Treaty, 1883; ▷ Pacific War, 1879–83); afterwards a plebiscite was to determine their future. Since the Chilean government did not hold the plebiscite, Peru and Chile in 1922 agreed to the arbitration of the President of the USA, whose suggestions were finally accepted by both sides on Aug. 28, 1929; by virtue of the agreement Tacna was returned to Peru together with a part of the Arica bay, whereas Arica remained with Chile, which paid Peru 6 million dollars of compensation.

U. SOARES, *A Questão Chileno–Peruano, 1840–1923*, Rio de Janeiro, 1925; *Documentos del Plebiscito*, Santiago, 1926; *El Processo de Tacna y Arica (1925–27)*, Lima, 1927; W.J. DENNIS, *Documentary History of the Tacna–Arica Dispute*, Iowa City, 1927; G.H. STUART, *The Tacna–Arica Dispute*, New York, 1927; L.H. WOOLSEY, "The Tacna–Arica Settlement", in: *American Journal of International Law*, No. 23, 1929; S. WAMBAUGH, *Plebiscites since the World War With a Collection of Official Documents*, Vol. 2, Washington, DC, 1933; C. RIOS GALLARD, *Chile y Perú Los Pactos de 1929*, Santiago, 1959.

TAFT TREATIES, 1911. The arbitration treaties concluded by the USA with France and Great Britain on Aug. 3, 1911, on the initiative of a US President W.H. Taft (1909–1913); they replaced the arbitration treaties of 1897 and 1908.

"The Treaties of Arbitration with Great Britain and France", in: *American Journal of International Law*, No. 6, 1912.

TAIWAN. Republic of China. A seaport meaning "terrace port"; also known as Formosa: colonial Portuguese name meaning "pretty." A Chinese island on the Pacific, between the East and South China Seas, just off the southeast coast of Asia, separated from China by Taiwan Strait (Formosa Strait). The area of Taiwan Island with the Penghu (Pescadores) Archipelago including the islands Quemoy and Manchu totals 35,989 sq. km. Pop. 1987 est.: 19,700,000 (1976 census: 16,426,386; 1980 est.: 17,805,067). Capital: Taipei with 2,327,641 inhabitants 1982. GNP 1987 per capita US $5,075. Currency: one New Taiwan dollar = 100 cents. Official language: Chinese. National Day: Oct. 10, Anniversary of the Revolution, 1911. International relations: subject of international conflicts and disputes in the 19th century when its annexation was attempted by the USA (1867), Japan (1874) and France (1885). Declared a separate province by China in 1887, occupied 10 years later and colonized by Japan 1897–1945. Returned to China by Potsdam Agreements of Aug. 2, 1945, in the act of surrender of Japan of Aug. 13, 1945 and in the Peace Treaty with Japan signed on Sept. 8, 1951 in San Francisco. From Oct. 1, 1949 the seat of the Republic of China, which aspired to represent all of China and was recognized as such by the US President H. Truman, who on June 27, 1950 announced that his Cabinet had decided not to admit into Taiwan the Chinese People's Liberation Army of Mao-Tse-tung for which purpose the 7th US Fleet entered the Formosa Strait and US air and marine military bases were built on Taiwan.

In 1971–72 the Republic of China was removed from the UN and its specialized agencies as a representative of China.

Another issue involved Taiwan's evasion for many years of UN membership fees which came to a total of 27 million US dollars. On Oct. 25, 1971 the People's Republic of China took over the Republic of China seat in the UN. On Dec. 16, 1972 the UN General Assembly Budgetary Commission passed by 47 votes the Chinese motion that debt would not burden its account. A joint Sino–American communiqué of Feb. 27, 1972, after US President R. Nixon's visit to Peking, stated US recognition of all the Chinese on both sides of the Taiwan Strait, claiming that there was only one China and that Taiwan was part of China. On Mar. 2, 1973 People's China sent an official note to the Chang-Kai-shek regime to start official negotiations on the unification of the country. An American–Chinese rapprochement in 1978 led to formal recognition by USA of the rights of People's China to Taiwan, followed by the establishment of diplomatic relations between the USA and People's China on Jan. 1, 1979 and the USA breaking off diplomatic relations with the Chinese Republic in Taiwan and the announcement that the USA will maintain relations with Taiwan through the American Institute on Taiwan in Washington, DC and the Taiwan Co-ordination Council for North American Affairs in Taipei. In April, 1979 the US Congress passed a law on commercial cultural and other relations with Taiwan. The USA in Oct., 1980 accorded to the representatives of the Taiwan Council diplomatic status in Washington, DC. In 1979 China annulled all customs barriers for Taiwan products, and Taiwan supported trade with China. In 1983 the People's Republic of China suggested reunification with Taiwan as "a special adminstrative region" under a guarantee to maintain the *status quo* in Taiwan for next 100 years.

W.G. GODDARD, *Formosa: A Study of Chinese History*, London, 1966; H. CHIN (ed.), *China and the Question of Taiwan: Documents and Analysis*, New York, 1973; V.H. LI, *De-recognizing Taiwan*, New York, 1977; R.N. CONGH, *Island China*, Cambridge Mass., 1978; H. CHIO (ed.), *China and the Taiwan issue*, New York, 1979; J. TIEMEY (ed.), *About Face, The China decision and its Consequences*, New Rochelle, 1979; J.C. ITSINNG (ed.), *Contemporary Republic of China*, New York, 1981; J.K. JAVITS, "Taiwan Relations Act", in: *Foreign Affairs*, Fall, 1981; *The Europa Year Book 1984. A World Survey*, Vol. II, pp. 1409–1419, London, 1984.

TAIWAN STRAIT. A sea lane between continental China and the island of Taiwan, length *c.* 360 km; connecting the East China Sea with the South China Sea; from 1950 controlled by the US VII Pacific fleet.

TAKA. A monetary unit of Bangladesh; one taka = 100 poisha; issued on Jan. 1, 1972 by the Bangladesh Bank, replacing the Pakistan rupee.

TAKESHIMA. The Japanese name of an island situated between Japan and Korea (Korean name Tok Do), in the 12-mile belt of territorial waters of Japan, with sentry station of South Korean police, subject of Japanese–Korean dispute.

TAKHT-i-BAHI. A cultural site of Pakistan, included in the ▷ World Heritage UNESCO List. Takht-i-Bahi, in the valley of Peshawar, was a center of monastic life for nearly 700 years, beginning in the early 1st century AD. Spread out on a hill, the architectural complex remains the same as when it was seen by the last pilgrims to the Kingdom of Ghandara. On the neighboring site of Sahr-i-Bahlol stand the ruins of a fortified city of the same period.

UNESCO. *A Legacy for All*, Paris, 1984.

TALA. A monetary unit of Western Samoa since 1966, issued by Bank of Western Samoa in co-operation with Bank of New Zealand. One tala = one New Zealand dollar.

TALLINN. The Capital of Estonia. Population, 1986 census: 472,000.

A. KUNG, *A Dream of Freedom*, Cardiff, 1980.

TAMILS. A people, chiefly inhabiting India (Tamil Nadu and parts of Kerala, Mysore, Andhra Pradesh) and northern and eastern Sri Lanka. The Tamil language, one of the principal Dravidian languages spoken in South India and parts of Sri Lanka for more than 2500 years is one of the 14 official languages of India and since 1966 is one of the national languages of Sri Lanka (together with Sinhala and English). The population of Tamil Nadu province is according to the 1981 census 48,297,456; the capital Madras 4,277,000; the Tamil population in Sri Lanka (1981 census) 1,877,000 (15% of Sri Lanka's population). Since 1983 the Sri Lankan Tamils are fighting for a Tamil homeland in the Northern and Eastern province. The majority of Tamils are Hindus while the Sinhalese are Buddhists, but this is not a religious conflict. In July 1987 an agreement between India and Sri Lanka brought Indian peacekeeping forces to the Northern and Eastern provinces.
See also ▷ Sri Lanka.

E.A.N. SASTRI, *The Culture and History of the Tamils*, London, 1964; J. PAXTON, *The Statesman's Yearbook 1987–88*, London 1988; KEESING's *Record of World Events*, 1988; A.J. WILSON. *The Break-Up of Sri Lanka. Sinhalese Versus Tamil*, London, 1988.

TANANARIVE. The capital of the Democratic Republic of Madagascar since 1960. Seat of the International Catholic Conference of Scouting.

Yearbook of International Organizations.

T

TANGANYIKA. Member of the UN, 1961–64. From Apr. 22, 1964 part of ▷ Tanzania.

"The Mandate for German East Africa", in: *League of Nations Official Journal*, July 20, 1922; "Trusteeship Agreement for the Territory of Tanganyika, December 13, 1946", in: *UNTS*, 1947, pp. 92–102.

TANGIER. A seaport in northwest Morocco, at the Strait of Gibraltar; subject of international disputes and agreements in the 19th and 20th century. Turned into an international zone (350 sq. km) under the treaty signed on Nov. 27, 1912 in Madrid by France and Spain; demilitarized under the Tangier Convention of Dec. 18, 1923, signed by Belgium, France, Italy, the Netherlands, Portugal, Spain, the UK and USA.

"The Tangier Zone shall be placed under a regime of permanent neutrality." (Art. 3.)
"... the international legislative Assembly shall be composed of 4 French Members, 4 Spanish, 3 British, 2 Italian, 1 American Member, 1 Belgian, 1 Dutch, 1 Portuguese, nominated by their respective consulates, and in addition 6 Mussulman and 3 Jewish subjects of the Sultan." (Art. 34.)

The Tangier Zone coast was seized on June 14, 1940 and incorporated by Spain Nov. 3, 1940. International status restored by the British–French treaty of Aug. 31, 1945, revised by the British–French protocol of Nov. 10, 1952, annulled by sovereignty granted Moroccan Sultan on July 5, 1956 and formally reinstated at the Conference in Fedali on Oct. 29, 1956. Under Moroccan administration since Nov. 4, 1957.

LNTS, Vol. 28, pp. 545 and 546; R.F. FITZGERALD, *L'organization judiciaire de Tanger sur le régime international*, Paris, 1927; *Documents relatifs aux réformes de statut de Tanger mise en application le 1-er août 1953*; G.H. STUART, *The International City of Tangier*, New York, 1955.

TANK. A conventional combat vehicle, first used by the French and British Army along the Aisne in September 1914 and during the battle of St. Quentin in March 1918 by the German Army and by the Soviet Red Army in the II World War. A modern battle tank with wire guided anti-tank missiles was produced by the USSR 1955 and by the USA 1972. In 1979 the price of a main battle tank has risen from US $55,000 to US $1,100,000. Subject of NATO-Warsaw Pact negotions in the end of the 1980s.

R.J. ICKS, *Tanks and Armoured Vehicles*, London 1945; SIPRI *World Armaments and Disarmament Yearbook*, 1970, pp. 205–206; 1977, pp. 183–184; R. LEGER SIVARD, *World Military and Social Expenditures 1987–1988*, Washington, 1987.

TANKERS. The merchant vessels designed to transport mainly liquid fuels as well as alcohols and chemicals; subject of organized international cooperation and international conventions concerning protection of the oceans against water pollution. The largest tanker fleet sails under the flag of Liberia, followed by England, Norway and Japan. Since 1960 many shipyards began to build supertankers, called in short VLCC (Very Large Crude Carriers), initially with a draught of 30,000 tons, then 50,000 tons, 100,000 tons, etc. In 1971 there were already 241 VLCC with a draught of 160,000 tons and 83 of more than 200,000 tons. In Sept., 1971 the Japanese *Nisski Maru* was launched with a draught of 372,000 tons; in 1972 Japanese shipyards began to build the first VLCC with a draught of 477,000 tons. This created the necessity for adapting ports. In Europe in 1973 only Rotterdam-Europort was able to accept VLCC with a capacity of 500–600,000 tons, and the port of Bantry in Ireland to 372,000 tons. Organizations reg. with the UIA:

International Tanker Nominal Freight Scale Association, f. 1969, London.
International Tanker Owners Pollution Federation, f. 1962, London UK; to protect coastal zones, harbours, estuaries against oil pollution. Publ.: *ITOPF Newsletter*. Members: owners of the world tanker fleet.
International Towing Tank Conference, f. 1932, Osaka.
Oil Companies Institute for Marine Pollution Compensation, f. 1971, Bermuda.

Yearbook of International Organizations, 1986/87; The Europa Yearbook 1988. A World Survey, Vol. I, London 1988.

TANK FREE ZONE IN CENTRAL EUROPE. A disarmament doctrine, discussed by NATO and the Warsaw Pact since November 1987. The zone was delimited to include West Germany and the Benelux states in the West, and East Germany, Poland, Czechoslovakia and Hungary in the East. The doctrine was linked to the ▷ Jaruzelski Plan on reduction of conventional arms.

TANNERS. Organization reg. with the UIA:

International Council of Tanners, f. 1926, East Sussex, England.

Yearbook of International Organizations, 1986/87; The Europa Yearbook 1988. A World Survey, Vol. I, London 1988.

TANZAM. The international railroad line, TANzania–ZAMbia, built between Jan. 2, 1970 and Oct. 25, 1975, with the assistance of People's China (500 million dollar credit for 30 years); 1919 km long, from Kapiri Mpashi station in Zambia to Dar-es-Salam in Tanzania, with 22 tunnels, 300 bridges and 147 stations. It opened the road to the Indian Ocean for Zambia.

TANZANIA. Member of the UN. United Republic of Tanzania. A state in East Africa formed by the Union of Tanganyika and Zanzibar, 1964; bounded by Mozambique, Malawi, Zambia, Zaïre, Burundi, Rwanda, Uganda, Kenya and the Indian Ocean. Area: 945,087 sq. km. Pop. 1987 est. 23,200,000; census 1978: 17,551,925 (17,076,270 in the mainland and 475,655 in Zanzibar). Capital: Dar-es-Salam with 870,020 inhabitants 1978. (To be moved to Dodoma.) Official languages: Swahili and English. GNP per capita 1986: US $240. Currency: one Tanzanian shilling = 100 cents. National Day: Apr. 26, Union Day, 1964.
Member of the UN from Dec. 21, 1961 (Tanganyika) and from Dec. 17, 1963 (Zanzibar and Pemba). Member of all UN specialized agencies. Member of the Commonwealth, OAU and is an ACP state of the EEC.
International relations: 1890–1919 Tanganyika was under German protectorate: 1919–1945 League of Nations Mandate administered by Great Britain together with Zanzibar and Pemba; 1946–61 UN trusteeship. After the independence proclamations of Tanganyika on Dec. 9, 1961 and of Zanzibar and Pemba on Mar. 10, 1963, both states on Apr. 26, 1964 combined to form the United Republic of Tanganyika and Zanzibar, named Tanzania on Oct. 29, 1964. In 1979–80 the Tanzanian troops supported the Uganda National Liberation Front in the overthrow of President Amin. In 1983 normalization of relations with Kenya.
See also ▷ World Heritage UNESCO List.

A. MACDONALD, *Tanzania: Young Nation in a Hurry*, New York, 1966; W. BIENEN, *Tanzania*, Princeton, 1967; V.V. PAVLOVA, *Tanzania, ekonomicheskaia politika provitelstva*, Moscow, 1973; J. NYERERE, *Freedom and Development*, New York, 1976; B. MWANSASU, *Towards Socialism in Tanzania*, Toronto, 1979; A. COULSON, *Tanzania, A Political Foreign Policy of Tanzania, 1961–1981*, Dar-

es-Salam, 1981; *The Europa Year Book 1984. A World Survey*, Vol. II, pp. 2478–2490, London, 1984.

TAOISM. One of the religions of Asia, originated in the 6th century B.C. simultaneously with ▷ Confucianism, based on the book *On Truth and Virtue* (Tao-te-ching) which proclaims that man's acts of kindness and of mischief are rewarded on earth and punished by the spirits of Earth and Heaven; it is professed mainly in China by the rural people.

M. GRANET, *La religion de Chinois*, Paris, 1922; M. GRANET, *La pensée chinoise*, Paris, 1934.

TAPRI, Tampere Peace Research Institute in Finland, f. 1985, Helsinki, Finland. Publ.: *TAPRI Yearbook*.

Yearbook of International Organizations, 1986/1987.

TARA. *Arab*: "tarha" = "what was taken away." An international term for the difference between gross and net weight, the weight of the packaging.

TARAPUR REACTOR. ▷ India.

TARBELA DAM DEVELOPMENT FUND. A fund est. by Agreement between the IBRD, Canada, France, Italy, UK, US and Pakistan, signed in Washington and came into force on May 2, 1968. The Fund served for the construction of Tarbela Dam on the Indus River in northeast Pakistan.

UNTS, Vol. 638, p. 42.

TARIFF BARRIER. An international term, used in the foreign trade, for the tariff system of a state which practices protectionism in defence of local industry; depending on the general level of customs duties, one speaks of a country with a high or low tariff barrier.

D. GREENWAY, *International Trade Policy. From Tariffs to the New Protectionism*, London, 1983.

TARIFFS. An international term, used in the UN for a system or schedule of duties imposed by a government on imports. The duty is the tax itself, paid by the importer on a particular shipment.

UN Chronicle, October, 1982, p. 48.

TARTU TREATIES, 1920. Two peace treaties:
A Peace Treaty between Estonia and Soviet Russia, signed on Feb. 2, 1920 in Tartu, Estonia.
"Art. 5. Should the perpetual neutrality of Estonia be internationally recognized, Russia undertakes to respect such neutrality and to join in guaranteeing it."
A Peace Treaty between Finland and Soviet Russia, signed on Oct. 14, 1920 in Tartu.

LNTS, Vol. XI, pp. 29–72; pp. 121–142.

TASHKENT DECLARATION, 1966. The agreement between India and Pakistan relating to Kashmir, signed Jan. 10, 1966 by the Prime Minister of India, Lala Bahadura Shastri and the President of Pakistan, Ayub Khan, in the presence of the Soviet Prime Minister, A.N. Kosygin in the Soviet city of Tashkent, capital of Uzbekistan, following mediation effort by the government of the USSR. The Declaration entered into force on Mar. 22, 1966; it was repudiated in 1972 by Pakistan during the Indian–Pakistani crisis.

Monthly Chronicle, No. 4, 1966, pp. 41–43.

TASS. The official abbreviation of the Russian, Tielegrafnoie Agientstwo Sowietskogo Sojuza, Telegraphic Agency of the Soviet Union, a state institution of the USSR, one of the largest press agencies, of worldwide range, founded in 1925 to replace the Russian Telegraphic Agency, ROSTA, established in 1918.

TATAR STRAIT. A strait 565 km long and from 8 to 129 km wide, between Sakhalin and the Asian mainland, connecting the Sea of Japan with the Sea of Okhotsk.

TA TZY PAO. *Chinese*: ta = "great," tzy = "sign," pao = "news-paper." In People's China the large handwritten newspapers-posters, informing the population about national and international events, with commentary; introduced as a political-educational device before the Chinese revolution.

TAX. The compulsory material obligations collected by the state or by a legally empowered public institution. In the 20th century income taxes (introduced for the first time in England in 1799) and estate taxes are the most common form of national revenue; both have become the subject of bilateral and multilateral international agreements for the prevention of double taxation. Subject of studies and recommendations by ECOSOC and the United Nations regional economic commissions. UN technical experts provide assistance to the developing countries in preparing tax reforms or in creating the rudiments of modern tax systems. The UN Secretary-General, in a report (E.1980.11) on international taxation issues, recommended the establishment of a direct tax co-operation council to work towards combating international tax evasion and avoidance, and towards increased and closer international co-operation in the tax field. The report also recommended: approval of a series of studies and surveys relating to tax evasion and avoidance; that the name of the Group of Experts on Tax Treaties between Developed and Developing Countries be changed to the Group of Experts on International Taxation and that a new membership be appointed; and the organization of symposia at a regional level for dissemination of two documents containing guidelines on international taxation – the Manual for the Negotiation of Bilateral Tax Treaties between Developed and Developing Countries, and the United Nations Model Double Taxation Convention between Developed and Developing Countries.
In this recommendation the Secretary-General said that he believed a particular merit of the proposed council would be that it would associate developing countries with international efforts towards combating international tax evasion and avoidance to the benefit of the international community as a whole.
The membership of the Group is drawn from the following countries: Argentina, Brazil, Chile, France, FRG, Ghana, India, Israel, Japan, the Netherlands, Norway, Pakistan, Philippines, Sri Lanka, Sudan, Switzerland, Tunisia, Turkey, UK and US.
▷ Tax treaties.
Organizations reg. with the UIA:

European Tax Confederation, f. 1959, Paris.
European Taxpayers Association, ETA Institute, f. 1969, Munich.
Inter-American Center of Tax Administrators, f. 1967, Panama.
International Tax Institute, f. 1961, New York.
International Union for Land Value Taxation and Free Trade, f. 1926, London. Publ.: *Land and Liberty* (monthly).

UN Chronicle, May, 1980, p. 30; *Yearbook of International Organizations*.

TAXATION OF FOREIGN MOTOR VEHICLES. A subject of international convention, signed on Mar. 30, 1931, in Geneva, by the governments of Belgium, Czechoslovakia, Denmark, Great Britain, Italy, Luxembourg, the Netherlands, Poland, Portugal, Spain, Sweden, Switzerland, Turkey.
LNTS, Vol. 138, p. 149.

TAX HAVEN. An international term for a state (▷ Liechtenstein, ▷ Vanuatu) with absolute bank secrecy and low fiscal charges for foreign private businessmen, companies and holding corporations. See also ▷ Delaware.

TAXICABS. A subject of international co-operation. Organizations, reg. with the UIA:
International Taxicab Association, f. 1966, Lake Forest, Illinois.
Nordic Taxi Owners' Council, f. 1958, Oslo.
Yearbook of International Organizations.

TAXILA. A cultural site of Pakistan, included in the ▷ World Heritage UNESCO List, remains of Buddhist temples and monasteries lie scattered around Taxila in the Indus region. Excavations at the most famous of these sites, Dharmarajika, have brought to light sculptures in stone and stucco work, which historians have used to establish the chronology of Gandhara art.
UNESCO. *A Legacy for All*, Paris, 1984.

TAX TREATIES. The international agreements between two or more nations, concerning administrative or legal protection and assistance in matters of taxation; avoidance of double taxation, and the establishment of rules of assistance in the case of succession duties; tax exemption on royalties, etc. Two model conventions were adopted 1967 by the Organization for Economic Cooperation and Development, OECD: one for the avoidance of double taxation with respect to taxes on estates and inheritances; the second on income and capital. The first OECD Model Convention "shall apply to estates of deceased persons whose domicile at their death was in one or both of the Contracting States." The second "shall apply to persons who are residents of one or both of the Contracting States." On Jan. 1, 1979 a multilateral agreement among the eight member states of CMEA (Bulgaria, Czechoslovakia, GDR, Hungary, Poland, Romania and USSR) concerning the prevention of double taxation (income and estate) of private individual residents of states which are parties to the Convention was implemented. Previously, Bulgaria, Czechoslovakia, GDR, Hungary, Romania, and USSR signed an agreement on the prevention of the double taxation of airline and sea transport companies, as well as the salaries and bonuses of workers and employees in such transport.
International organizations are exempted from paying taxes, however, they have the right to draw taxes in the form of membership contributions, specified by their supreme bodies (in the United Nations – by the General Assembly, according to art. 17). ▷ Tax.

International Tax Agreements, 4 Vols. UN, New York, 1948–56. W.H. DIAMOND, D.B. DIAMOND (eds.), *International Tax Treaties of All Nations Containing English Texts of All Tax Treaties Between Two or More Nations*, 10 Vols., Series A, 2 Vols., Series B, New York, 1975–78.

TAYLOR SYSTEM. The scientific management, defined by the American F.W. Taylor (1856–1915), founder of the Society to Promote the Sciences of Management, 1911, New York.

F.W. TAYLOR, *The Principles of Scientific Management*, New York, 1911; F.B. COPLEY, *F.W. Taylor. Father of Scientific Management*, Boston, 1923.

TBILISI DECLARATION, 1977. A Declaration accepted at Tbilisi, USSR, by an UNESCO–UNEP Intergovernmental Conference on Education Relative to the Environment, in Oct., 1977. The Declaration defines the role of education in relation to the environment.
Yearbook of the United Nations, 1977, New York, 1979, pp. 505 and 1091.

TCHOGA ZAMBIL. A historic site of Iran, included in the ▷ World Heritage UNESCO List. This consists of three concentric walls. Within the first wall are three palaces, five tombs and a shrine dedicated to Nusku, the God of fire. Within the second are seven temples, and at the center is the ziggurat decorated with cuneiform inscriptions in the Elamite language. The whole complex dates from the 13th century BC.
UNESCO. *A Legacy for All*, Paris, 1984.

TDW. Ton Deadweight. An international term, defining the carrying capacity of a vessel in metric or English tons.

TEA. A subject of international agreements and co-operation. Organizations reg. with the UIA:
East African Tea Trade Association, f. 1975, Nairobi.
European Tea Committee, f. 1975, Rotterdam.
International Association of Tea Producing and Exporting Countries, est. 1979, Colombo, by a Convention signed in Dec. 1978 by India, Indonesia, Kenya, Malawi, Mauritius, Sri Lanka, Tanzania, and Uganda.
International Tea Committee, f. 1933, London under terms of International Tea Agreement signed by the representatives of the tea industries in India, Ceylon and the Netherlands East Indies. Members: Bangladesh, India, Indonesia, Kenya, Malawi, Mozambique, Sri Lanka, Tanzania, Uganda. Publ.: *Bulletin of Statistics* (annually).

In the EEC system the ▷ STABEX includes tea in the ACP countries.

V.D. VICKIZER, *Tea Under International Regulation*, London, 1949; V.D. VICKIZER, *Coffee, Tea and Cocoa*, London, 1951; *UN Chronicle*, February, 1978, p. 31; UNDP, *Review of International Action and Discussion on Tea*, Geneva, 1978.

TEACHER SHORTAGE. A world problem, especially in the developing countries, a subject of international co-operation under the aegis of ILO and UNESCO. An expert meeting convened by the ILO from Oct. 27 to Nov. 4, 1981 at Geneva with Government delegates and representatives of teacher organizations in Africa, Asia and Europe, proposed measures for improving work conditions of teachers.
UN Chronicle, January, 1982, p. 31.

TEACHING ABOUT THE UNITED NATIONS. The UN General Assembly resolution of Nov. 17, 1947, recommended member states to introduce in schools teaching about the tasks, structure and activities of the UN and its specialized organizations. The teaching program was elaborated by ECOSOC and UNESCO, which every three years submit to the UN General Assembly reports on disseminating teaching about the UN.

TECHNICAL UN ASSISTANCE. A major program of the UN to assist economic, social and cultural development of less developed countries to which the UN allocates 80% of its financial resources and employs about 17–20,000 technicians and experts; subject of international conventions. Pur-

T

suant to the General Assembly's decision on the restructuring of the economic and social sectors of the UN, the Department of Technical Co-operation for Development was formed in 1978 as the organizational entity responsible for carrying out technical co-operation activities in areas of UN specialization. Carrying out about 1800 technical co-operation projects, it is the second largest executive agency in the UN system (FAO being first) for UNDP-financed projects.

In addition, the Department of Technical Co-operation for Development manages the UN regular program of technical co-operation financed from the assessed contributions to the regular budget of the UN. Although the amount of assistance is relatively small, the Department has been able to launch innovative and pioneering activities. The UN regular program was the first to concentrate its resources in the least-developed countries. One of its unique features is use of interregional advisers who, on short notice, provide consultancy services to developing countries. The UNDP Governing Council provides general policy guidance for the regular program. ▷ UN Technical Aid.

Everyone's United Nations, UN, New York, 1979, pp. 135–139; P. ENGBERG-PETERSEN, *The UN and Political Intervention in International Economic Processes. The Transfer of Technology*, Copenhagen, 1982.

TECHNOLOGICAL PROGRESS. The process of perfecting means of production, methods of manufacture and conditions of labor; a subject of international meetings devoted to seeking ways of disseminating and popularizing technical progress among developing countries, e.g. through the scientific-technological information system UNISIS. The UN General Assembly Res. 3384/XXX Nov. 10, 1975, adopted a Declaration on the Use of Scientific and Technological Progress in the Interests of Peace and for the Benefit of Mankind. The international term "appropriate technology" is used in the UN for production methods in agriculture and industry suitable to local resources, the skills of the available manpower, amount of capital and degree of development of the individual country concerned.

Under the auspices of the UNCTAD, the UN Conference on an International Code of Conduct on the Transfer of Technology was held in Geneva, Oct. 16–Nov. 11, 1978. The UN Centre for Science and Technology for Development publ. since 1985, The Advance Technology Alert System, ATAS, Bulletin designed to alert planners and policy makers in developing countries to the potential impact and implication of emerging technology.

UNIDO Abstracts on Technology Transfer, Geneva, May, 1977; A.F. DORIAN, *Dorian's Dictionary of Science and Technology*, English and German, Amsterdam, 1978; *UN Chronicle*, 1985, No 3, p. 53.

TECHNOLOGY. Subject of international co-operation. Organizations reg. with the UIA:

Union of International Technical Associations, UATI, f. 1951, under the auspices of UNESCO, Paris, France. Members: 30 organizations:
International: Association for Hydraulic Research, f. 1935, Delft, Netherlands. Publ.: *Directory of Hydraulic Research Institutes and Laboratories, Journal of Hydraulic Research, Proceeding of Congresses and Symposia, List of Papers*. Member of UATI.
International Association of Lighthouse Authorities, f. 1957, Paris, France. Member of UATI. Publ.: *Bulletin* (quarterly), technical dictionary (in English, French, German and Spanish).
International Bridge, Tunnel and Turnpike Association. Member of UATI, f. 1932, Washington DC, USA.

International Commission of Agricultural Engineering, f. 1930, Paris, France. Member of the UATI. Publ.: *Yearbook*, technical reports.
International Commission on Irrigation and Drainage, f. 1950, New Delhi, India. Member of the UATI. Publ.: *Bulletin, Bibliography* (annually), *World Irrigation, Multilingual Technical Dictionary, World Flood Control*, technical books.
International Commission on Large Dams, f. 1928, Paris, France. Publ.: *Technical Bulletin, World Register of Dams, World Register of Mine and Industrial Wastes, Technical Dictionary on Dams*, studies. Member of the UATI.
International Committee of Foundry Technical Associations, f. 1960, Zürich, Switzerland. Member of UATI.
International Congress on Fracture, f. 1965, Sendai, Japan. Member of the UATI. Publ.: *Proceedings*.
International Federation for the Theory of Machines and Mechanisms, f. 1965, Budapest, Hungary. Member of the UATI.
International Federation of Automatic Control – IFAC, f. 1957, Laxenburg, Austria. Member of the UATI. Publ.: *Automatica* (bi-monthly), *Newsletter*.
International Federation of Industrial Energy, f. 1965, Courbevoie, France. Member of the UATI.
International Fertilizer Industry Association, f. 1960, Paris, France. Member of the UATI.
International Gas Union, f. 1931, Paris, France. Member of the UATI.
International Institute of Welding, f. 1948, London, UK. Member of the UATI. Publ.: *Welding in the World* (6 a year).
International Institution for Production Engineering Research, f. 1951, Paris, France. Publ.: *Annuals*. Member of the UATI.
International Measurement Confederation, f. 1965, Budapest, Hungary. Member of the UATI.
International Society for Soil Mechanics and Foundation Engineering, f. 1936, Cambridge, England. Member of the UATI. Publ: *Newsletter* (quarterly), *Conference Proceedings* (every 2 years), *Lexicon of Soil Mechanics Terms* (in 8 languages).
International Solid Wastes and Public Cleansing Association, f. 1965, Paris, France. Member of the UATI.
International Union for Electro-heat, f. 1953, Paris, France. Member of the UATI.
International Union of Air Pollution Prevention Association, f. 1974, Brighton, England. Member of the UATI.
International Union of Producers and Distributors, of Electrical Energy, f. 1925, Paris, France. Publ.: reports on periodical congresses, periodical circulars on statistical matters. Member of the UATI.
International Union of Testing and Research Laboratories for Materials and Structures, f. 1947, Paris, France. Member of the UATI. Publ.: *Materials and Structures – Testing and Research* (bi-monthly).
Permanent International Association of Navigation Congresses – PIANC, f. 1885, Brussels, Belgium. Member of the UATI. (Present form adopted in 1902). Publ.: *Papers and Proceedings of Congresses, Bulletin* (quarterly), *Illustrated Technical Dictionary* (in 6 languages), final reports of international study commissions and working groups.
Permanent International Association of Road Congresses, f. 1909, Paris, France. Member of the UATI. Publ.: *Bulletin, Technical Dictionary, Reports and Proceedings of Congresses, Reports of Technical Committees*.
World Energy Conference, f. 1924, London, England. Member of the UATI.

Yearbook of International Organizations 1986/87; The Europa Yearbook 1988. A World Survey, Vol. I, London 1988.

TEHERAN. The capital of Iran since 1788, called also Tehran, seat of organizations registered with the UIA: Asian Clearing Union, Asian Games Federation, Asian Weightlifting Federation, International Congress on Tropical Medicine and Malaria, International Federation of Women Lawyers, Regional Co-operation for Development, UN Information Center.

Yearbook of International Organizations.

TEHERAN CONFERENCE, 1943. The first meeting during World War II of the leaders of the United Nations coalition, British Prime Minister Winston S. Churchill, US President Franklin D. Roosevelt and Soviet Premier Joseph V. Stalin, held on Nov. 27–Dec. 1, 1943 at the Iranian capital adopted the Teheran Declaration 1943 and five secret military agreements regarding:
(1) the widest possible support for Yugoslav guerillas; (2) recognition of the need for Turkey to join the war on the Allied side; (3) Soviet readiness to immediately declare war against Bulgaria if it assails Turkey; (4) decision that the Western invasion in Normandy should take place in May 1944 at the same time as the Soviet offensive on the eastern front; (5) reorganization of close co-operation between Supreme Headquarters of the Army Expeditionary Forces, SHAEF, and the Soviet Supreme Headquarters called STAVKA within the planned operations in the European theatre.
The highlights of the Teheran Declaration:

"As to peace, we are confident that our accord will make it lasting. We fully recognize that on us and all United Nations rests a high responsibility to achieve such a peace that would win approval of an overwhelming majority of nations of the world and would avert peril and horror of war for many generations."

War Documents, Washington, DC, 1944, p. 27; A. GARCIA ROBLES, *El Mundo de la Postguerra*, México, DF, 1946, Vol. 2, p. 265; *A Decade of American Foreign Policy. Basic Documents 1941–49*, Washington, DC, 1950.

TEHERAN DECLARATION, 1943. ▷ Teheran Conference, 1943.

TEHERAN PETROLEUM AGREEMENT, 1971. An unprecedented agreement concluded by 6 states and emirates of the Persian Gulf represented by ▷ OPEC on the one hand and on the other by a group of 22 concerns licensed to extract oil in those countries, on Feb. 14, 1971, in the capital of Iran and seriously curtailing the profit of these companies. The treaty proposed on Dec. 12, 1970 by the XXI OPEC Conference was finally concluded under pressure of the resolution of the OPEC Special Conference, on Feb. 7, 1971, which stipulated that if the concerns have not reached an agreement by Feb. 15, 1971, the OPEC member states would issue a decree on a unilateral oil price increase and embargo those concerns that would have failed to comply by Feb. 22, 1971. Here are the major points of the agreement:
(1) net corporate profit is taxed 55% and up; (2) posted prices being theoretically the basis of calculation of companies' net profit are unified and set at the level of the country most favored in this respect; (3) the posted price of each barrel of oil extracted in any country of the Persian Gulf is raised by 33 cents; (4) new principles of pricing oil of a higher quality are applied tying the price to density; this indicated another raise of four cents per barrel; (5) any bonus prices for exported oil are annulled; (6) the posted price of oil is to be increased by 2.5% annually in the five year period starting June 1, 1971, to compensate the losses of the Persian Gulf countries caused by inflation which unfavorably affects the price structure of oil sold and goods purchased, both consumer goods and investment goods; (7) it is decided that from June, 1971 to 1975 the price of one barrel will be raised by another five cents to adjust it to world level which is in an upward trend as a result of increased demand; (8) an additional two cents per barrel went to balance the difference in overseas freight of the oil exported by the Persian Gulf countries.
The total increase of the posted price of oil agreed in Teheran amounted to c. 39 cents per barrel, the total

price of one barrel now being 2.17 dollars. But since the bonus prices applied until then were voided, the real increase was 46 cents on average. It was estimated that by the year 1975 the Persian Gulf countries would increase their oil sales profit by three billion dollars. In exchange, they pledged to the concerns making concessions that within the five ensuing years the agreed prices would be observed and maintained on the same level even if other OPEC member states negotiated more favorable conditions.

In turn, Algeria, Saudi Arabia, Libya and Iraq, Apr. 2, 1971, signed a similar agreement in Tripoli, which i.a. stipulated an increase of the price of one barrel from 2.55 US dollars to 3.75 US dollars for five years.

The Teheran Petroleum Agreement was unprecedented as the states of the Persian Gulf were the most disadvantaged with respect to sharing the profit from their natural resources. In order to co-ordinate their policy toward OPEC member states, 21 Western oil companies prior to the Teheran Petroleum Agreement on Jan. 22, 1971 concluded an agreement in New York on the foundation of the Permanent Co-ordination Office in London.

Financial Times, 1971, No. 25355, 25357.

TEHERAN PROCLAMATION, 1968. The official name of a declaration adopted on May 13, 1968, by unanimous vote of the UN International Conference on Human Rights held in Teheran, Apr. 22–May 13, 1968. The proclamation urged all peoples and governments to dedicate themselves to the principles of the Universal Declaration of Human Rights, adopted 20 years earlier, and to redouble their efforts to provide for all humanity a life consonant with freedom and dignity and conducive to physical, mental, social and spiritual welfare.

UN Yearbook, 1968.

TEHERAN TREATY, 1937. The treaty on non-aggression signed by Afghanistan, Iraq, Iran and Turkey on July 8, 1937 in Teheran.

LNTS, Vol. 190, p. 21.

TEHUANTEPEC, THE ISTHMUS OF. The natural frontier between North and South America. Gulf of Tehuantepec, an arm of the Pacific. The town Tehuantepec in Oaxaca state in South Mexico, on the Tehuantepec River, near the Gulf of Tehuantepec, with 15,000 inhabitants, 1988 estimate, near the Mexico–Guatemala highway.

J. BROOKS, *South American Handbook*, Bath, UK, 1988.

TELECOMMUNICATION. The term "telecommunication" was defined by the ITU Convention, 1947 as "any transmission, emission or reception of signs, signals, writing, images and sounds or intelligence of any nature by wire, radio, visual or other electromagnetic waves (hertzian waves) of frequencies between 10 kilocycles per second (kc/s) and 3,000,000 megacycles per second (Mc/s)." The term "telecommunication" was introduced at the first International Telecommunication Convention, signed on Dec. 9, 1932, in Madrid; the second, signed on Dec. 22, 1952 at Buenos Aires, established the ITU.

A Central American Telecommunication Treaty was signed on Apr. 26, 1966 at Managua.

The CMEA countries founded in 1971 in Moscow the CMEA Permanent Telecommunications Commission for co-ordinating the integration of member states in the field of telephone, telegraph, telex, TV and satellites (through ▷ Molniya) as well as co-ordination of production of telecommunications equipment. The International Telecommunication Day is celebrated on May 17 since 1965 to commemorate the First Telegraphic Convention adopted on May 17, 1865; each year has a motto worded by ITU e.g. 1970 in the context of International Education Year – "Telecommunication at the service of Education." Organizations reg. with the UIA:

African Post, and Telecommunication Union, f. 1961, Brazzaville, Congo.
European Conference of Postal and Telecommunications Administration, f. 1959, Copenhagen.
Pacific Telecommunication Council, f. 1981, Honolulu.

UNTS, Vol. 781, pp. 71–86; D.D. SMITH, *International Telecommunication Control*, Leyden, 1969; M.D. LAIVE, *International Telecommunication and International Law*, Leiden, 1970; W.E. CLASON, *Elsevier's Telecommunication Dictionary. In English/American, French, Spanish, Italian, Dutch and German*, Amsterdam, 1976; S. ROBERTS, T. HAY, *International Directory of Telecommunications*. London, 1986; E. SCIBERRAS, B.D. PAYNE, *Telecommunications Industry*, London 1986; *Yearbook of International Organizations, 1986/87; The Europa Yearbook 1988. A World Survey*, Vol. I, 1988.

TELECOMMUNICATION WORLD NETWORK. A subject of an international agreement prepared in 1961 by ITU, implemented from 1961 to 1975. For purposes of the network the world was divided into seven automatic continental exchanges: Moscow for socialist countries in Europe and Asia, Paris and London for Western Europe, Tokyo for the Far East, Singapore for South Asia, Sydney for Australia and Oceania, New York for North America, Brasilia for South America. Simultaneously, construction of 70 intercontinental telex and telephone relay stations was recommended: 21 in Asia, 16 in Africa, 12 in both Americas, 7 in Europe, 5 in Australia and Oceania; also 9 submerged cables. The ITU forecasts that the 400,000,000 telephones in 1980 will increase to one billion in the next 20 years.

TELEDETECTION. An international term for the study of the globe from airplanes and satellites orbiting the earth, the subject of international co-operation.

TELEGRAPHIC NORTH EAST EUROPEAN AGREEMENT, 1921. A special agreement concerning telegraphic relations between Finland, Norway and Soviet Union, signed on Sept. 19, 1921 in Riga.

LNTS, Vol. 15, p. 191.

TELEOBSERVATION. A system of controlling or acquiring data at a distance, the object of common international work under the aegis of the UN. The UN General Assembly permitted a research group to collect data on the natural resources of the Earth with teleobservation systems, UN Panel on Remote Sensing Systems for Earth Resources Surveys.

TELEPHONES AND TELEGRAPH. A subject of international conventions. The first international world agreements were signed on July 10–22, 1875 in Petersburg; on Nov. 3, 1906 in Berlin; in July, 1912 in London; on Nov. 25, 1927 in Washington; on Dec. 9, 1932 in Madrid; on Oct. 2, 1947 in Atlantic City; on Apr. 10, 1949 in Mexico; and on Dec. 22, 1952 in Buenos Aires. ▷ Telecommunication. Organizations reg. with the UIA:

International Congresses on the Application of the Theory of Probability in Telephone Engineering and Administration, f. 1955, Copenhagen.
International Federation for Services of Emergency Telephonic Help, f. 1960, Geneva publ.: *Liste de postes de Téléphone Secours.*

International Telegraph and Telephone Consultative Committee, f. 1957, Geneva.
Postal Telegraph and Telephone International, f. 1920, Geneva. Regional offices: Lagos, Singapore, Washington, DC.

H.N. CASSON, *The History of the Telephone*, New York, 1910; "Übersicht über internationale Funk und Rundfunkverträge", in: *Jahrbuch für Internationales Recht*, 1954, Vol. 3, pp. 211–219 and Vol. 4, pp. 190–211; H. SCHIVECK, *Telegraphentechnik*, Hamburg, 1955; J. KIEVE, *The Electro Telegraph*, London, 1973; *Yearbook of International Organizations.*

TELEPHONE SERVICE AGREEMENTS. The bilateral and multilateral agreements, signed in Europe after the World War I relating to the first European Telephone Cable System (in chronological order):

The first telephone service agreements, signed on Sept. 8, Oct. 30, and Nov. 26, 1913 in Paris, Berne and London by Great Britain, France and Switzerland, contained rules for the organization of the Anglo-Swiss Telephonic Service via France. It was replaced by a new one signed on Dec. 28, 1922 in Paris, on Jan. 5, 1923 in London. (*LNTS*, Vol. 28, p. 411.)

Agreement respecting telephone service between Great Britain and Germany via the Netherlands, with schedule signed on Sept. 18 in Berlin, on Oct. 18 in London, and on Oct. 30, 1926 in the Hague. (*LNTS*, Vol. 61, p. 65.)

Agreement between Germany and Norway via Denmark and Sweden, 1926, signed on Sept. 14 in Oslo, on Sept. 20 in Stockholm, on Oct. 8 in Copenhagen, and on Nov. 1, 1926 in Berlin. (*LNTS*, Vol. 78, p. 109.)

Agreement between Austria and Sweden via Germany and Czechoslovakia, signed on Jan. 12 in Stockholm, on Jan. 20 in Vienna, on Feb. 10 in Prague, and on Feb. 25, 1927 in Berlin. (*LNTS*, Vol. 78, p. 123.)

Agreement between the Netherlands and Switzerland via Germany, signed on Feb. 1 in Berne, on Feb. 11 in The Hague, and on Feb. 19, 1927 in Berlin. (*LNTS*, Vol. 68, p. 139.)

Agreement between Denmark and the Netherlands via Germany, signed Feb. 10 in Copenhagen, Feb. 17 in The Hague, Feb. 24, 1927 in Berlin. (*LNTS*, Vol. 68, p. 159.)

Agreement between Luxembourg and the Netherlands via Belgium signed on Feb. 28 in The Hague, on Mar. 7 in Luxembourg; and on Mar. 18, 1927 in Brussels. (*LNTS*, Vol. 68, p. 179.)

Agreement between France and the Netherlands via Belgium, signed on Apr. 5 in The Hague, on Apr. 14 in Brussels, and on May 2, 1927 in Paris. (*LNTS*, Vol. 68, p. 211.)

Agreement between France and Sweden via Germany, signed on July 1 in Paris, on Aug. 4 in Stockholm, and on Aug. 16, 1927 in Berlin. (*LNTS*, Vol. 78, p. 141.)

Agreement between Norway and Switzerland via Sweden and Germany, signed on Sept. 30 in Oslo, on Oct. 7 in Stockholm, on Oct. 14 in Berne, and on Nov. 11, 1927 in Berlin. (*LNTS*, Vol. 78, p. 153.)

Agreement between Austria and Norway via Germany and Sweden, signed on Oct. 19 in Oslo, on Oct. 28 in Stockholm, on Nov. 11 in Berlin, and on Nov. 21, 1927 in Vienna. (*LNTS*, Vol. 78, p. 163.)

Agreement between Belgium and Norway via Germany and Sweden, signed on Nov. 21 in Oslo, on Nov. 26 in Brussels, on Jan. 10 in Berlin, and on Mar. 19, 1927 in Stockholm. (*LNTS*, Vol. 78, p. 177.)

Agreement between Czechoslovakia and the Netherlands via Germany, signed on Dec. 8, 1926 in The Hague, on Feb. 11 in Prague, and on Feb. 22, 1927 in Berlin. (*LNTS*, Vol. 68, p. 149.)

Agreement between Austria and the Netherlands via Germany, signed on Dec. 17, 1926 in The Hague, on Jan. 12 in Vienna, and on Jan. 22, 1927 in Berlin. (*LNTS*, Vol. 68, p. 129.)

Agreement between Italy and the Netherlands via Germany and Switzerland, signed on Jan. 14 in The Hague, on Mar. 21 in Rome, on Apr. 24 in Berlin, and on May 1, 1928 in Berne. (*LNTS*, Vol. 132, p. 415.)

Agreement between Finland, Norway and Sweden, signed on Dec. 29, 1928 in Oslo, on Jan. 22 in Stockholm, and on Jan. 14, 1929 in Helsinki. (*LNTS*, Vol. 87, p. 169.)

Agreement between Hungary and the Netherlands via Austria and Germany, signed on Feb. 5 in Budapest, on Feb. 21 in The Hague, on Mar. 4 in Berlin, and on Mar. 10, 1928 in Vienna. (*LNTS*, Vol. 132, p. 405.)

Agreement between Great Britain and Switzerland via France, signed on Feb. 14 in London, on Feb. 18 in Berne, and on Mar. 8, 1928 in Paris. (*LNTS*, Vol. 80, p. 241.)

Agreement between Norway and Czechoslovakia via Germany and Sweden, signed on Feb. 15 in Oslo, on Mar. 1 in Prague, on Mar. 24 in Berlin, and on Apr. 23, 1928 in Stockholm. (*LNTS*, Vol. 78, p. 197.)

Agreement between Belgium and Sweden via Germany, signed on Apr. 11 in Stockholm, on Apr. 17 in Brussels, and on Apr. 25, 1928 in Berlin. (*LNTS*, Vol. 78, p. 207.)

Agreement between Norway and the Netherlands via Sweden and Germany, signed on May 11 in The Hague, on May 16 in Oslo, on May 24 in Stockholm, and on June 9, 1928 in Berlin. (*LNTS*, Vol. 78, p. 219.)

Agreement between Germany, Finland and Sweden, signed on Nov. 7 in Helsinki, and Nov. 30, 1928 in Berlin. (*LNTS*, Vol. 87, p. 119.)

Agreement between Great Britain and the Free City of Danzig via the Netherlands and Germany, signed Apr. 18 in London, on May 8 in The Hague, on May 16 in Berlin, and on May 22, 1928 in Danzig. (*LNTS*, Vol. 85, p. 99.)

Agreement between Great Britain and Luxembourg via Belgium, signed on Nov. 13 in London, on Nov. 22 in Brussels, and on Nov. 27, 1928 in Luxembourg. (*LNTS*, Vol. 92, p. 321.)

Agreement between Great Britain and the administration of the Saar via France, signed on Nov. 16, 1928 in Paris, on Jan. 2 in London, and on Feb. 2, 1929 in Saarbrücken. (*LNTS*, Vol. 93, p. 12.)

Agreement between the Netherlands and Sweden via Germany, signed on Dec. 17 in The Hague, on Dec. 30, 1927 in Stockholm, and Jan. 7, 1928 in Berlin. (*LNTS*, Vol. 78, p. 187.)

Agreement between Lithuania and the Netherlands via Germany, signed on Dec. 18, 1928 in The Hague, on Dec. 27, 1928, in Kaunas, and on Jan. 5, 1929 in Berlin. (*LNTS*, Vol. 132, p. 425.)

Agreement between Finland and Switzerland via Sweden–Germany, signed on Sept. 19 in Helsinki, on Sept. 25 in Stockholm, on Oct. 1 in Berlin, and on Oct. 8, 1929 in Berne. (*LNTS*, Vol. 98, p. 409.)

Agreement between Finland and Poland via Sweden–Germany, signed on Aug. 30 in Helsinki, on Sept. 6 in Stockholm, on Sept. 20 in Berlin, and on Oct. 1, 1929 in Warsaw. (*LNTS*, Vol. 98, p. 197.)

Agreement between Finland and Luxembourg via Sweden–Germany, signed on Aug. 30 in Helsinki, on Sept. 6 in Stockholm, on Sept. 20 in Berlin, and Sept. 25, 1929 in Luxembourg. (*LNTS*, Vol. 98, p. 361.)

Agreement between Finland and Netherlands via Sweden–Germany, signed on Sept. 2 in Helsinki, on Sept. 10 in Stockholm, on Sept. 24 in Berlin, and on Sept. 30, 1929 in The Hague. (*LNTS*, Vol. 98, p. 183.)

Agreement between Finland and Latvia, via Estonia, signed on Oct. 16 in Helsinki, on Oct. 24 in Tallin, and on Oct. 28, 1929 in Riga. (*LNTS*, Vol. 97, p. 71.)

Agreement between Finland and Hungary via Sweden, Germany and Czechoslovakia, signed on Sept. 2 in Helsinki, on Sept. 10 in Stockholm, Sept. 26 in Berlin, on Oct. 18 in Prague, and Oct. 29, 1929 in Budapest. (*LNTS*, Vol. 99, p. 85.)

Agreement between Finland and France via Sweden–Germany, signed on May 23 in Paris, Aug. 20 in Helsinki, Aug. 26 in Stockholm, on Sept. 7, 1929 in Berlin. (*LNTS*, Vol. 98, p. 345.)

Agreement between Finland and Czechoslovakia, via Sweden–Germany, signed on Aug. 30 in Helsinki, on Sept. 6, 1929 in Stockholm, on Sept. 21, in Berlin, and Oct. 10, 1929, in Prague. (*LNTS*, Vol. 98, p. 375.)

Agreement between Estonia, Finland, Latvia and Sweden, signed on Mar. 25 in Stockholm, on Apr. 27, in Helsinki, on May 4 in Tallin, and on May 8, 1929 in Riga. (*LNTS*, Vol. 91, p. 337.)

Agreement between Estonia and Sweden via Finland, signed on Mar. 18 in Tallin, on June 14 in Stockholm, and Aug. 30, 1929 in Helsinki. (*LNTS*, Vol. 96, p. 117.)

Agreement between Denmark, Finland, and Sweden, signed on Dec. 22, 1928 in Helsinki, on Jan. 14, 1929 in Stockholm, and on Jan. 16, 1929 in Copenhagen. (*LNTS*, Vol. 87, p. 155.)

Agreement between Denmark and Italy via Germany and Switzerland signed on July 31 in Copenhagen, on Oct. 16 in Rome, on Oct. 20 in Berlin, and on Nov. 18, 1929 in Berne. (*LNTS*, Vol. 99, p. 415.)

Agreement between Denmark and Estonia via Finland and Sweden, signed on July 17 in Tallin, on July 29 in Copenhagen, on Aug. 3 in Stockholm, and on Aug. 30, 1929 in Helsinki. (*LNTS*, Vol. 96, p. 129.)

Agreement between Belgium and Finland via Germany and Sweden, signed on Sept. 2 in Helsinki, on Sept. 10 in Stockholm, on Sept. 23 in Berlin, and on Sept. 30, 1929 in Brussels. (*LNTS*, Vol. 99, p. 71.)

Agreement between Austria and Finland via Germany–Sweden, signed on Aug. 30 in Helsinki, on Sept. 6 in Stockholm, Sept. 19 in Berlin, and on Sept. 26, 1929 in Vienna. (*LNTS*, Vol. 98, p. 395.)

Agreement between the Netherlands and Poland, via Germany, signed on June 20 in The Hague, on Aug. 22 in Warsaw, and on Aug. 28, 1930 in Berlin. (*LNTS*, Vol. 133, p. 21.)

Agreement between Latvia and the Netherlands, via Lithuania and Germany, signed on June 3 in The Hague, on June 12 in Riga, on June 14 in Kaunas, and on June 26, 1930 in Berlin. (*LNTS*, Vol. 133, p. 9.)

Agreement between Finland and Lithuania via Estonia and Latvia, signed on Dec. 29 in Helsinki, on Dec. 31, 1929 in Tallin, on Jan. 2, 1930 in Riga, and on Jan. 14, 1930, at Kaunas. (*LNTS*, Vol. 99, p. 343.)

Agreement between Finland and Great Britain via Sweden, Germany and the Netherlands, signed on Nov. 9 in Helsinki, on Dec. 4 in Stockholm, on Dec. 17 in Berlin, on Dec. 30, 1929 in The Hague, and on Apr. 10, 1930 in London. (*LNTS*, Vol. 101, p. 465.)

Agreement between Denmark and Latvia via Sweden, Finland and Estonia, signed on Jan. 7 in Copenhagen, on Jan. 17 in Stockholm, on Feb. 10 in Helsinki, on Feb. 15 in Tallin, and on Feb. 25, 1930 in Riga. (*LNTS*, Vol. 101, p. 343.)

TELEVISION. The international abbreviation: TV. A subject of international conventions and permanent, organized intergovernmental and non-governmental co-operation. The first TV station began operation in New York in 1939 during the World Fair; however, the integration of all states of the USA by a television network was not achieved until 1952. In Western Europe TV integration was implemented in 1953 through Eurovision; in Central-Eastern Europe in 1957 by way of Intervision. These two organizations, co-operating with each other, also cover the European part of Soviet Union and constitute the world's largest TV network. TV development is co-ordinated under the UNESCO International Film and TV Council, IFTC, founded in 1958. The era of telecasting TV programs through man-made earth satellites began in 1962 with the development of satellite telecommunication. During the 18th Olympic Games in Tokyo in 1964 satellite communication on an intercontinental scale was initiated. According to the UNESCO data, in 1971 there were the following numbers of TV sets per one thousand inhabitants: in North America – 397, Europe – 188, Oceania – 175, East Asia – 138, the USSR – 128, South America – 54, Africa – 3.2, South Asia – 2.3. There were some 251 million TV sets and 1470 TV stations worldwide. In the CMEA countries in 1973 a permanent Commission for Standardization began work on a complex standardization of black-and-white and color TV sets in CMEA member countries.

Color TV programs are broadcast by three different systems: American NTSX (used by the USA, Canada, Mexico and Japan), French SECAM (used within the organization Intersecam by France, Switzerland and Luxembourg as well as Bulgaria, Czechoslovakia, GDR, Poland, Hungary and the USSR), and the West German system PAL (used by Austria, Belgium, Brazil, Denmark, Finland, FRG, Holland, Hong Kong, Iceland, Ireland, Norway, Sweden, Thailand and Yugoslavia).

In 1972 the UN began work on a draft convention concerning rules for using man-made earth satellites for direct TV broadcasting. In 1992 the current PAL-SECAM standard of 625 lines will be doubled to 1,250, and the HD-MAC, a single standard for high-definition television, will be implemented throughout the European Community. Organizations (besides ▷ Eurovision and ▷ Intervision) reg. with the UIA:

International Radio and TV University, f. 1949, Paris.
Union of Film and TV Technicians, f. 1952, Paris.
Union of National Radio and TV Organizations of Africa, INTRA, f. 1962, Conakry; has advisory status with UNESCO.

UN Bulletin, July, 1952, p. 123; *World Radio and TV Handbook*, London, 1975; UNESCO, *IFTC Directory of International Film and TV Organizations and their National Branches*, Paris, 1975; *Yearbook of International Organizations*; B. SENDALL, *The History of Independent Television in Britain*, 4 Vls., London, 1982–89.

TELSTAR. First television satellite launched on July 23, 1962 by the USA. ▷ Intelsat; ▷ Molniya; ▷ Intersputnik.

TEMPERATURE, GLOBAL WARMTH. A subject of international research in the XX century. The average temperature around the world in 1988 was the highest in the century, according to the British Meteorological Office and the University of East Anglia's Climatic Research Unit. A scientific theory explains the phenomenon, by saying that a build-up of heat-trapping pollutants in the atmosphere is warming the earth. The warming trend could disrupt the agriculture and raise the sea levels, by melting glaciers, causing the inundation of coastal areas.

Ph. SHABECOFF, "Global Warmth in 88 Found to set a Record", in: *The New York Times*, Feb. 4th, 1989.

TEMPERATURE, INTERNATIONAL SCALE. The scale, generally in effect since 1948, is the improved Celsius scale in which the interval between the freezing point and the boiling point of water is divided into 100 degrees with 0° representing the freezing point and 100° the boiling point. Other improvements relate to the temperatures of phasic equilibrium between: liquid oxygen and its steam (−182.970°C), liquid sulphur and its steam (444.600°C), liquid silver and its steam (960.8°C), and liquid gold and its steam (1063.0°C). In use up to 1948 besides the Celsius scale in some countries were the ▷ Fahrenheit's, (still used in Anglo-Saxon countries) ▷ Kelvin, and ▷ Réaumur's scales.

TEMPLARS. *Latin*: *Fratres Militiae Templi, Pauperes Commilitiones Christi Templique Salomonis*, knightly Christian order, came into being 1119 with seat near the ruins of Solomon's Temple in Jerusalem; abolished by Clement V, 1312, after the burning at the stake in Paris on Oct. 13, 1307 of 54 leaders of the order together with the Grand Master, Jacques de Molay on the order of Philip IV, The Fair. The Templars as a Masonic order appeared for the first time in France in the 18th century. The existing international Masonic lodge of Templars bases itself on the tradition of the order of Templars with the legend that de Molay was not burned, but fled to England, where he founded four mother lodges.

M. DESSUBRE, *Bibliographie de l'Ordre de Templiers*, Paris, 1929; L. DALLIER, *Les Temples, ces inconnues*, Paris, 1972; G. ZIEGLER, *Les Templiers*, Paris, 1973.

TENDE AND LA BRIGUE. Territory on the French–Italian border, ceded to France by the Italian Peace Treaty 1947. A plebiscite was held on Oct. 12, 1947.

UN Yearbook, 1947/48, p. 801.

TENNIS. An Olympic sport 1896–1926, organized within the International Lawn Tennis Federation, ILTF, est. 1922 sponsoring international tournaments (the Wimbledon) which have unofficially evolved from English championships to individual world championships and the Davis Cup team tournament. Tennis was excluded from World Olympics 1926 as the result of a dispute over professionalism.

Yearbook of International Organizations.

TEQUENDAMA CHARTER, 1967. The declaration on the principles and policies of Latin American States in international trade, prepared and adopted unanimously by the Special Commission on Latin American Coordination, Commission Especial de Coordination Latinoamericana, CECLA, Sept. 25–30, 1967 in Bogota, Colombia, as guidelines for the first session on UNCTAD. Basic provisions of the Tequendama Charter included:

1. The importance for the developing countries to have highest priorities and best conditions of access with their basic natural resources to highly industrialized countries and planned economy markets.
2. In order to promote exportation of reprocessed and semi-finished products, as a dynamic method of improving the finances and technology in developing states, the highest priority should be given to establishing a system of preferences for the exported products from developing countries and for opening the markets of developed countries for developing countries' manufactured products.

The provisions of the Tequendama Charter were further developed in accordance with the decisions of UNCTAD and in the light of new factors in the economic situation of Latin America, in the ▷ Viña del Mar Charter.

"Carta de Tequendama", in: *Boletin de CEMLA*, México, DF, No. 10, 1967, pp. 553–560.

TERCERISM. An international term for nationalist trend of social and economic policy in Third World countries, proclaiming the "third road of development" intermediate between capitalism and socialism.

L. SACHS, *Le découverte du Tiers Monde*, Paris, 1971.

TERMINOLOGY, INTERNATIONAL. The vocabulary adopted in international relations and international organizations which facilitates formulation of international agreements and their interpretations. Standardization of international terminology was initiated by the League of Nations in connection with the necessity for precise translation of the texts into the official languages of those organizations. In the UN Secretariat, the Office of Conference Services includes a Terminology Section which publishes terminology bulletins. At present, the UN terminology has been adopted by other organizations as well as by research centers. The School of Interpreters at the University of Geneva, École d'Interprètes de l'Université de Geneve, publishes a series of dictionaries entitled, *Glossaria Interpretum*, in six languages: English, French, Spanish, German, Russian and Italian. UNESCO publishes the monthly, *Bibliographie, Documentation, Terminologie*. The Elsevier Publishing Company in Amsterdam, London and New York, specializing in Multilingual Dictionaries, published in 1965 a *Dictionary of International Relations and Politics*, prepared by I. Heansch, in four languages: English, French, Spanish and German, covering 5778 international terms divided into different fields and historical periods. A dictionary by H. Back, H. Cirullies and G. Marquard, entitled, *Polec, Dictionary of Politics and Economics*, published in West Berlin in 1964 in English, French and German, includes 14,000 international terms. The Banker's Almanac and Yearbook, published in London since 1845, ran a section in 11 languages entitled, *Cardinal Numbers and Commercial Terms*.

In 1958 the UN published the *Dictionaire Démographique Multilingue*, prepared by the Commission for a Demographic Dictionary of International Union for Demographic Research (▷ Demography).

In 1971 under the aegis of UNESCO an International Center for Terms, ▷ INFOTERM, was founded in Vienna.

In 1975 a Symposium on International Co-operation in Terminology was held in Vienna; and in 1984 in Luxembourg. ▷ Lexicography.

Most of the UN specialized agencies have their own terminology centers for the various fields in which they work. The UN Secretariat publ.: *Current Terminology English–French–Spanish*.

Glossary of Interamerican Maritime Terminology, Washington, DC, 1966; M. ORELLANA, *Glossario Internacional*. (*Cerca de 5,000 terminos usados par organizaciones de las Naciones Unidas. Ingles. Castellano.*) Santiago, 1967; E. GHALEB, *Dictionnaire des Sciences de la Nature* (*Agriculture, Botanique, Zoologie, Ornitologie, Ichtiologie, Entomologie, Parasitologie, Bactériologie, Microbiologie, Affections animales et végétables. Termes techniques: Physique, Chimie, Mathématique, Géologie, Astronomie, Droit*), 3 Vols., Beirut 1970; E. PIENKOS, J. PIENKOS, *Dictionnaire juridique et économique français-polonais*, 2 Vols., Varsovie, 1970; Z. STOBERSKI, "Guidelines for the Adoption of New Scientific and Technical Terms", in: *International Journal of Translation "Babel"*, No. 1, 1975. J.C. SAGER, "International Scientific Terminology. Prospects and Limitation", on: *Neoterm*, No. 1, 1984.

TERMINOLOGY OF INTERNATIONAL LAW. A subject of codification efforts in the 20th century as laws of nations and concepts, which were formulated in centers of international thinking, approached closer to each other in juridical circles of Europe and USA. Latin America and Asia (▷ Pancha Shila).

In Sept., 1938 the International Academic Union, Union Académique Internationale, in Paris decided to compile a dictionary of public international law based on international documents starting from the Paris Congress of 1856. This work, continued after World War II under UNESCO sponsorships, has resulted in a lexicon with examples of the use of terms in French together with a dictionary of the terms themselves in English, German, Italian and Spanish; with an introduction by J. Basdevant.

Dictionaire de la terminologie du droit international, anglais, espagnol, italien, allemand, Paris, 1960; J. PAENSON, *Manual of the Terminology of Public International Law (Law of Peace) and International Organizations, Multilingual Edition: English, French, Russian, Spanish*, The Hague, 1983.

TERM OF OFFICE. The term defined by an act or statute of an organization: a limited time of performing an office by an elected person. In intergovernmental organizations this may be a period from one year (e.g. the President of the UN General Assembly) to three (e.g. the President of ICJ) or five (e.g. the Secretary General of the UN) and in special cases up to nine years (e.g. the Judges of ICJ). In some countries a re-election is not possible by law (▷ re-election in American States); in international organizations there is no regulation as to the number of terms of office (e.g. in ICJ the President can preside only once for three years, while the Secretary-General of the UN can remain in office for several terms).

TERMS OF TRADE. The ratio of the index of export prices to the index of import prices. Terms of trade can be calculated for the foreign trade with all of a country's partners totally (total terms of trade) or separately for individual partners (bilateral terms of trade).

R.A. ALLEN, R.N. BROWN, "The Terms of Trade", in: *Bank of England Quarterly Bulletin*, September, 1978. S.E. STIEGELER (ed.), *A Dictionary of Economics and Business*, London, 1985.

TERRE ADÉLIE. The French part of the Antarctic continent, between 136° and 142° E long., south of 60° S lat.; part of the French Southern and Antarctic Territories. Situated at Base Dumont d'Urville, since 1949 is the research station for French Polar Expeditions. ▷ Antarctica.

Expéditions Polaires Français. Études et Rapports, Paris, 1949–59.

TERRITORIAL ASYLUM CONVENTION, 1954. A Convention signed at Caracas Mar. 28, 1954 at the Tenth Inter-American Conference, by Brazil, Chile, Colombia, Costa Rica, Cuba, the Dominican Republic, Ecuador, El Salvador, Guatemala, Haiti (denounced on Aug. 1, 1967), Honduras, Mexico, Nicaragua, Panama, Paraguay, Peru, Uruguay.

The text is as follows:

"The governments of the Member States of the Organization of American States, desirous of concluding a Convention regarding Territorial Asylum, have agreed to the following articles:

Art. 1. Every State has the right, in the exercise of its sovereignty, to admit into its territory such persons as it deems advisable, without, through the exercise of this right, giving rise to complaint by any other State.

Art. 2. The respect which, according to international law, is due the jurisdictional right of each State over the

inhabitants in its territory, is equally due, without any restriction whatsoever, to that which it has over persons who enter it proceeding from a State in which they are persecuted for their beliefs, opinions, or political affiliations, or for acts which may be considered as political offenses.
Any violation of sovereignty that consists of acts committed by a government or its agents in another State against the life or security of an individual, carried out on the territory of another State, may not be considered attenuated because the persecution began outside its boundaries or is due to political considerations or reasons of state.
Art. 3. No State is under the obligation to surrender to another State, or to expel from its own territory persons persecuted for political reasons or offenses.
Art. 4. The right of extradition is not applicable in connection with persons who, in accordance with the qualifications of the solicited State, are sought for political offenses, or for common offenses committed for political ends, or when extradition is solicited for predominantly political motives.
Art. 5. The fact that a person has entered into the territorial jurisdiction of a State surreptitiously or irregularly does not affect the provisions of this Convention.
Art. 6. Without prejudice to the provisions of the following articles, no State is under the obligation to establish any distinction in its legislation, or in its regulations or administrative acts applicable to aliens, solely because of the fact that they are political asylees or refugees.
Art. 7. Freedom of expression of thought, recognized by domestic law for all inhabitants of a State, may not be ground of complaint by a third State on the basis of opinions expressed publicly against it or the government by asylees or refugees, except when these concepts constitute systematic propaganda through which they incite to the use of force or violence against the government of the complaining State.
Art. 8. No State has the right to request that another State restrict for the political asylees or refugees the freedom of assembly or association which the latter State's internal legislation grants to all aliens within its territory, unless such assembly or association has as its purpose fomenting the use of force or violence against the government of the soliciting State.
Art. 9. At the request of the interested State, the State that has granted refuge or asylum shall take steps to keep watch over, or to intern at a reasonable distance from its border, those political refugees or asylees who are notorious leaders of a subversive movement, as well as those against whom there is evidence that they are disposed to join it.
Determination of the reasonable distance from the border, for the purpose of internment, shall depend upon the judgment of the authorities of the State of refuge.
All expenses incurred as a result of the internment of political asylees and refugees shall be chargeable to the State that makes the request.
Art. 10. The political internees referred to in the preceding article shall advise the government of the host State whenever they wish to leave its territory. Departure therefrom will be granted, under the condition that they are not to go to the country from which they came and the interested government is to be notified.
Art. 11. In all cases in which a complaint or request is permissible in accordance with this Convention, the admissibility of evidence presented by the demanding State shall depend on the judgment of the solicited State.
Art. 12. This Convention remains open to the signature of the Member States of the Organization of American States, and shall be ratified by the signatory States in accordance with their respective constitutional procedures. Art. 13. The original instrument, whose texts in the English, French, Portuguese, and Spanish languages are equally authentic, shall be deposited in the Pan American Union, which shall send certified copies to the governments for the purpose of ratification. The instruments of ratification shall be deposited in the Pan American Union; this organization shall notify the signatory governments of said deposit.
Art. 14. This Convention shall take effect among the States that ratify it in the order in which their respective ratifications are deposited.
Art. 15. The Convention shall remain effective indefinitely, but may be denounced by any of the signatory States by giving advance notice of one year, at the end of which period it shall cease to have effect for the denouncing State, remaining, however, in force among the remaining signatory States. The denunciation shall be forwarded to the Pan American Union which shall notify the other signatory States thereof.

The Convention entered into force on Dec. 29, 1954; ratified by Brazil, Colombia, Costa Rica, Ecuador, El Salvador, Haiti, Panama, Paraguay, Uruguay and Venezuela.

Inter-American Asylum Conventions, 1928–54,, Washington, DC, 1956; *International Conferences of American States. Second Supplement 1942–1954*, Washington, DC, 1958; OAS, *Treaty Series*, Washington, DC, 1967.

TERRITORIAL CESSION. An international legal term for a legal act by one state of renouncing its sovereign rights over a territory in favor of another state. As a rule this is carried out by giving the rights to a territory to another state under a peace treaty (e.g. by Austro-Hungary in the Treaty of Versailles to Poland, Czechoslovakia and Yugoslavia) or under a treaty determining payment (e.g. the United States purchasing in 1867 Alaska from Russia and in 1917 the Virgin Islands from Denmark), or under any other bilateral agreement.

G. SCHWARZENBERG, "Title in Territory: Response to a Challenge", in: *American Journal of International Law*, 1957.

TERRITORIAL DISPUTES. ▷ Frontier Litigation; ▷ Frontier Inviolability.

TERRITORIAL INTEGRITY. The inviolability of territories of states; subject of international law. In modern history denotes one of the five principles of ▷ Pancha Shila in South Asia; in Europe, employed in the Vienna Congress resolutions of Apr. 9, 1815 warranting territorial integrity of Switzerland; subsequently used by several other treaties, e.g.: the London Protocol of May 8, 1852 on succession in the Kingdom of Denmark; the Peace of Paris of Mar. 30, 1856 between France, Prussia, Russia, Kingdom of Sardinia, Great Britain and Turkey; the treaty between Japan and Korea of Feb. 23, 1904; in the Scandinavian agreement of Nov. 2, 1907 on independence and territorial integrity of Norway. After World War I, the League of Nations Covenant of 1919 referred to territorial integrity and political independence as a combined notion. The UN Charter in art. 2, para. 4 contains this broadened formula which has since appeared in all bi- and multi-lateral treaties, e.g.: In art. 20 of the Charter of the OAS. The obligation to respect territorial integrity is also included in the Declaration of Principles of International Law adopted by the UN General Assembly on Oct. 24, 1970. The term territorial integrity embraces the principle of inviolability of frontiers.

T. KOMARNICKI, *La Question de l'Intégrité Territoire dans le Pacte de la Société des Nations*, Varsovie, 1923; A.A.H. STRUYCKEN, *La Société des Nations et l'Intégrité Territoire*, Paris, 1923.

TERRITORIAL SEA. The sea waters adjoining the coast, of varying width; subject of international disputes and conventions. In the 19th century a three-mile wide belt was generally recognized as the territorial sea between the coast (i.e. between the line of lowest water in ebb-tide) and the open sea. In 1930, during the Conference of the League of Nations on the Codification of the International Law in The Hague, only three states favored a three-mile wide territorial sea, with the majority of states requesting an expanded territorial sea. At the beginning of World War II, at a Meeting of Foreign Ministers of the American Republics held in Panama City, the boundaries of the territorial sea of the South American continent were expanded to 300-miles under the name of the Security Zone of the Western Hemisphere. The American States again took up the issue in June, 1950 at the Inter-American Legal Council Conference in Rio de Janeiro which, on Aug. 30, 1952, adopted a draft international convention on the territorial sea and related problems, introducing the principle of full sovereignty over the territorial sea, the width of which, due to economic interests, could be expanded to 200 nautical miles. In its final form the first Geneva Convention of Apr. 29, 1958 on the Territorial Sea and Contiguous Zone, does not include any provisions regarding the width of the territorial sea, giving only a general statement:

"The sovereignty of a State extends, beyond its land territory and its internal waters, to a belt of sea adjacent to its coast, described as the territorial sea." (Art. 1 p. 1.)
"The sovereignty over a coastal State extends to the air space over the territorial sea as well as to its bed and subsoil." (Art. 2.)
"... ships of oil States, whether coastal or not, shall enjoy the right of innocent passage through the territorial sea." (Art. 14 p. 1.)
"The Coastal State is required to give appropriate publicity to any danger to navigation, of which it has knowledge, within the territorial sea." (Art. 15.)
"No charge may be levied upon foreign ships by reason only of their passage through the territorial sea." (Art. 18 p. 1.)
"In a zone of the high seas contiguous to its territorial sea, the coastal State may exercise the control necessary to:
(a) prevent infringement of its customs, fiscal, immigration or sanitary regulations within its territory or territorial sea;
(b) punish infringement of the above regulations committed within its territory or territorial sea. The contiguous zone may not extend beyond twelve miles from the baseline from which the breadth of the territorial sea is measured." (Art. 24.)

The convention entered into force on Sept. 10, 1964. The second Geneva conference in 1960 also failed to resolve disagreements over the breadth of the territorial sea. In Jan. and Feb., 1964 the countries of Western Europe deliberated at the Special London Conference on the width of the territorial sea, on the boundaries of fishing zones in the North Sea and in the Northeast Atlantic, without however, reaching any agreement. In July, 1965 the Inter-American Legal Council adopted the "Mexican principle" that "each American state shall have the right to establish the width of its territorial sea within the 12-mile limit." In 1966 the USA expanded its territorial waters from 6 to 12 miles, then shortly after, Mexico from 9 to 12 miles. All countries of the Latin America Free Trade Zone, ALALC, LAFTA, on June 15, 1967, at a Regional Conference on the Conservation of Sea Resources held in Montevideo, adopted a declaration on their right to sovereignty over a territorial sea of 200 miles. In 1970, the USSR and a number of other States submitted the issue on the width of the territorial sea to the UN General Assembly for reconsideration. In the general debate at the third World Conference on the Law of the Sea, in July, 1974, the USA, the USSR and France favored a 12-mile territorial sea zone expressing, at the same time, their readiness to recognize under specific conditions the 200 mile zone as "an economic zone" (▷ Fisheries, Economic Zones). In 1977 the major powers introduced the 200-mile exclusive, economic zone. ▷ Sea Law Convention, 1982, Part II.

UNTS, Vol. 516, pp. 204–224; Ph. C. JESSUP, *The Laws of Territorial Waters and Maritime Jurisdiction*, London, 1927; A.S. BUSTAMANTE, *La Mer territoriale*, Paris, 1930; *League of Nations Acts of Conferences for the Codification of International Law 1930*, Geneva, 1931; W. WALKER, "Territorial Waters: The Cannon Shot Rule", in: *The British Yearbook of International Law*, No. 22, 1945; UN Legislative Series

I. *Laws and Regulations on the Regime of the High Seas. Contiguous Zones*, New York, 1951; H.S.K. KENT, "The Historical Origins of the Three-Mile Limit", in: *American Journal of International Law*, No. 48, 1954; A. NIKOLAJEV, *Problema territorialnikh vod w mezh-dunarodnim pravie*, Moscow, 1954; A. GARCIA ROBLES, *La Conferencia de Ginebra y la Anchura del Mar*, México, DF, 1959; *Actas de la I y II Conferencias del Derecho Maritimo Internacional, 1958 y 1960*, Geneva, 1959, 1961; A. GARCIA ROBLES, *La Anchura del Mar Territorial*, México, DF, 1966; *Actas de la Conferencia Extraordinaria sobre Explotación y Conservación de las Riquezas Maritimas del Pacífico del Sur*, Quito, Mayo 1967; *Instrumentos Nacionales y Internacionales sobre Derecho del Mar*, Lima, 1971, pp. 359–368; *Everyone's United Nations*, UN, New York 1979; *The Law of the Sea*, UN, New York, 1983, pp. 3–11; KEESING's *Contemporary Archive*, November 1985; R.L. BLEDSOE, B.A. BOCZEK, *The International Law Dictionary*, Oxford, 1987.

TERRITORIES UNDER FOREIGN RULES OR DEPENDENT TERRITORIES. UN terms for territories on the list of UN Special Committee on the Situation With Regard to the Implementation of the Declaration on the Granting of Independence to Colonial Countries, in Peoples. The list for 1984 was as follows:

Administering country	Territory	Area (sq. km.)	Population (approx.)
Australia	Cocos Islands	14	600
Disputed[1]	Western Sahara	305,240	165,000
Indonesia	East Timor	14,874	555,000
New Zealand	Tokelau	1,210 ha	1,570
South Africa	Namibia	824,269	1,000,000
United Kingdom	Bermuda	53	54,700
	British Virgin Islands	153	11,200
	Cayman Islands	259	16,700
	Falkland Islands	12,173	1,800
	Gibraltar	5.5	31,200
	Montserrat	102	11,700
	Pitcairn Islands	4,5	60
	St Helena	122	5,300
	Anguilla	96	7,700
	Turks and Caicos Islands	430	7,400
United States	American Samoa	194,8	32,300
	Guam	541	106,000
	Micronesia	1,300	117,600
	U.S. Virgin Islands	344,5	96,600

[1] disputed between Morocco and the Algerian-backed Polisario Front

TERRITORY. One of the three basic elements in the definition of a state; subject of international law, differentiating between various forms of determining territory, stemming from: sovereignty of a state, lease or purchase, occupation, discovery, cession, right of prescription, adjudgement and internationalization.

A. LANGER, *Seizure of Territory*, London, 1947; S. BASTID, *Le territoire dans le droit international contemporain*, Paris, 1954; R. BACK, *Die internationalisierung von Territorien*, Stuttgart, 1962; Territory, in: R.L. BLEDSOE, B.A. BOCZEK, *The International Law Dictionary*, Oxford, 1987.

TERRORISM. An international term for the use of force to attain political or economic objectives in international relations, a form of intervention through violence committed by special military or police units or by terrorist organizations. Following debate in the UN General Assembly, the Legal Committee in Dec., 1972, initiated work on an international definition, taking into consideration i.a. the following elements: (1) actions against persons who are under the protection of interna-

tional law, such as heads of state or members of the diplomatic service; (2) actions aimed at highjacking civilian passenger planes; (3) "the export of terrorism, the export of violence."

Failure to agree on a common definition was the result of reluctance on the part of African and Arab states, which were not in favor of a precise definition claiming that this would harm national liberation movements. On the other hand, many states attempted to identify as terrorism self-defensive actions of armed units of national independence movements. This position was criticized by other states which noted that wars of national liberation were regarded by the UN as acts of war, and not acts of terrorism. In 1976, the UN General Assembly expressed deep concern over increasing acts of terrorism and urged states to seek just and peaceful solutions to its underlying causes. The subject remained on the agenda of the UN General Assembly in the 1980s. A UN Secretary-General Report on Measures to Prevent International Terrorism, 1983, stated that the terrorism "endangers or takes innocent human lives or jeopardizes fundamental freedoms and study of the underlying causes of those forms of terrorism and acts of violence which lie in misery, frustration, grievance and despair which cause some people to sacrifice human lives, including their own, in an attempt to effect radical changes."

In 1981 the Assembly had re-endorsed the recommendations submitted by the Ad Hoc Committee on International Terrorism in 1979 relating to practical measures of co-operation for the speedy elimination of the problem of international terrorism.

The Secretary-General's report, which followed up the implementation of those recommendations, stated that as at Nov. 29, 1983, replies had been received from Byelorussian SSR, Czechoslovakia, Democratic People's Republic of Korea, Ireland, Israel, Republic of Korea, Ukrainian SSR, USSR, Yemen, the Universal Postal Union, the Council of Europe and the Organization of American States. In addition, an annex reflects the state of signatures, ratifications or accessions, as at Aug. 19, 1983, of international conventions relating to various aspects of the problem of international terrorism. The conventions listed are: Convention on the Prevention and Punishment of Crimes against Internationally Protected Persons, including Diplomatic Agents; International Convention against the Taking of Hostages: Convention on Offences and Certain Other Acts Committed on Board Aircraft; Convention for the Suppression of Unlawful Acts against the Safety of Civil Aviation; and Convention for the Suppression of Unlawful Seizure of Aircraft.

The European Convention on the Suppression of Terrorism was drafted and signed on Jan. 27, 1977 by 17 member states of the Council of Europe (Ireland and Malta abstained) and ratified by the end of 1978 by Austria, Denmark, FRG, Great Britain, and Sweden. The Convention recognized as criminal offences: the hijacking of airplanes, the taking of hostages, attempts on the life or rendering bodily harm and infringing on the freedoms of functionaries with diplomatic status. ▷ Shultz Doctrine, 1984.

The 1977 Convention was not ratified until April 1987 by Malta (signed Nov. 5, 1986), France and Greece.

See also ▷ East-West Agreement on the Protection of Human Rights, 1989.

H. DOMREDIN, de VARRES, "La répression international du terrorisme, Les Conventions de Genève, 1937", in: *Revue de droit international public*, No. 65, 1938; R. SOTTLE, "La terrorisme international", in: *Recueil des Cours de l'Académie de Droit*

International, No. 65, 1938; V.V. PELLA, "La répression des crimes contre la personnalité de l'état", in: *Recueil des Cours de l'Académie de Droit International*, No. 33, 1950; *International Terrorism. A Select Bibliography*, UN DOC., Sept. 21, 1973; E. HYAMS, *Terrorists and Terrorism*, New York, 1975; P. WILKINSON, *Political Terrorism*, New York, 1975; *US News and World Report*, Sept. 29, 1975; E. EVANS, *Calling a Truce to Terror: The American Response to International Terrorism*, Westport Conn., 1979; J. LODGE, *Terrorism: A Challenge to the State*, New York, 1981. *UN Chronicle*, January, 1984, p. 70; Ch.H. PYLE, "Defining Terrorism", in: *Foreign Policy*, Fall, 1986; J. ADAMS, *The Financing of Terror*, London, 1986; L. FREEDMAN, *Terrorism and International Order*, London, 1986; S. SEGALIER, *Invisible Armies: Terrorism into the 1990's*, London, 1986, San Diego, 1987; R.S. CHINE, Y. ALEXANDER, *Terrorism as State-sponsored Covert Warfare*, Washington DC, 1986; P. WILKINSON, R.N. STEWART, *Contemporary Research on Terrorism*, Aberdeen, 1987; R.E. RUBENSTEIN, *Alchemists of Revolution: Terrorism in the Modern World*, New York, 1987; R. OAKLEY, "International Terrorism", in: *Foreign Affairs*, No. 3, 1987; W. LAQUER, *The Age of Terrorism*, Boston, London, 1987; S. AUST, *The Baader-Meinhof Group*, London, 1987; A. LAKOS, *International Terrorism: A Bibliography*, London, 1987; Ch. DOBSON, R. PAYNES, *The Never Ending War: Terrorism in the 1990's*, New York, 1987; P. LEVENTHAL, Y. ALEXANDER eds., *Preventing Nuclear Terrorism: The Report and Papers of the International Task Force on Prevention of Nuclear Terrorism*, Lexington, 1987, A. TAHERI, *Holy Terror: Inside the World of Islamic Terrorism*, Washington DC, 1987.

TESCHEN, SPISZ AND ORAVA, 1920. "The arbitration decision of the USA, UK, France, Italy and Japan over the former Duchy of Teschen and the territories of Orava and Spisz, dated Paris, July 28, 1920, considering the Polish–Czechoslovakian convention signed on July 10, 1920, at Spa, that their respective frontiers in these regions should be determined by the Principal Allied and Associated Powers. The Decree fixed a frontier line in the district of Teschen, of Orava and Spisz.

LNTS, Vol. 5, p. 49.

TESIN. ▷ Cieszyn.

TESTAMENT. An international term for a legal act specifying inheritors in the case of death of a person, who notifies his last will in accordance with legal provisions in force in the state; subject of bilateral and multilateral international agreements.

TETANUS. ▷ Immunization.

"TET VICTORY", 1968. An international term, coined by Vietnamese military forces, after the liberation of Saigon in the days of Tet, the Lunar New Year of the Monkey.

TEXTBOOKS. A subject of international co-operation, conventions and inter-state agreements, under the aegis of UNESCO, concerning contents of textbooks. The first document recommending the revision of history textbooks, was the declaration of member states of the League of Nations (Afghanistan, Argentina, Belgium, Chile, Colombia, Dominican Republic, Egypt, Estonia, Greece, Holland, Iran, Norway, South Africa and Sweden), signed on Oct. 20, 1937 in Geneva; became effective on Nov. 20, 1937.

In 1982 Japan, by publishing new schoolbooks on history provoked a controversy with China, Taiwan and the two Korean states.

LNTS, Vol. 182, p. 263; A. ROTFELD, *From Helsinki to Madrid*, Warsaw, 1983, p. 321.

TEXTILES. A subject of international co-operation. Organizations reg. with the UIA:

Co-ordinating Committee for the Textile Industries in the EEC, f. 1961, Brussels.
EFTA Textiles Steering Committee, f. 1965, London.
European Association of National Textile Retailers Organizations, f. 1958, Köln.
European Committee of Textile Machinery Manufacturers, CEMATEX, f. 1953, Zürich.
European Co-ordinating Group for the Textile Industry, f. 1976, Paris.
Inter-American Textile, Garment and Leather Workers Federation, f. 1966, Mexico DF, Publ.: *Aguja* (monthly in Spanish).
Intercolor, f. 1962, Berne.
International Association of Textile Dyers and Printers, f. 1967, Bonn.
International Association of Wood Textile Laboratories, f. 1969, Brussels.
International Federation of Associations of Textile Chemists and Colourists, f. 1930, Pratteln, Switzerland.
International Group for Textile Care Labeling, f. 1965, Paris.
International Textile Care and Rental Association, f. 1950, London.
International Textile Garment and Leather Workers Federation, f. 1970, Brussels.
International Textile Manufacturers Federation, f. 1904, Zürich, Switzerland. Publ.: International Textile Manufacturing, International Cotton Industry Statistics (annually).
International Research Centre on Ancient Textiles, CIETA, f. 1954, Lyon, France. Publ.: *Bulletin de Liaison*.
Scandinavian Textile Retailers Union, f. 1950, Copenhagen.
Textile Institute, f. 1909, Manchester, UK. Publ.: *Journal of the Textile Institute*.
Textile Workers Asian Regional Organization, f. 1960, Tokyo.
Trade Union International of Textile, Clothing, Leather and Fur Workers, f. 1958, Prague.

Textile Dictionary. In English, French, German and Spanish. Amsterdam, 1979; *Yearbook of International Organizations, 1986/87; The Europa Yearbook 1988. A World Survey*, Vol. I, London, 1988.

TEXTILES INTERNATIONAL TRADE. A subject of an Arrangement regarding International Trade in Textiles called the Multifibre Arrangements, MFA, concluded in December 1973, extended in 1981 and 1986 to July 31, 1991. The signatories made up the International Textiles Committee: Argentina, Austria, Bangladesh, Brazil, Canada, China, Colombia, Czechoslovakia, Dominican Republic, Egypt, El Salvador, The European Community (representing the 12 member countries), Finland, Guatemala, Haiti, Hong Kong, Hungary, India, Indonesia, Israel, Jamaica, Japan, South Korea, Malaysia, Maldives, Mexico, Norway, Pakistan, Panama, Peru, the Philippines, Poland, Portugal (on behalf of Macao), Romania, Singapore, Sri Lanka, Sweden, Switzerland, Thailand, Turkey, the United States, Uruguay and Yugoslavia.

Organizations reg. with the UIA:

Committee of the Cotton and Allied Textile Industries of the EEC (EUROCOTTON), f. 1957, Brussels.
Common Market Committee of the European Association of National Textile Retailers Organizations, f. 1958, Köln (FRG).
Coordinating Committee for Textile Salvage in the EEC, f. 1960, Brussels.
Coordination Committee for the Textile Industries in the EEC, f. 1961, Brussels. Consult. Status: ECOSOC, UNCTAD. Publ.: Bulletin du COMITEXTIL.
International Textile Manufacturers Federation, f. 1904, Zürich, Switzerland. Consult. Status: ECOSOC, FAO, IBRD, ILO, UNCTAD, UNDP, GATT, OECD, ICAC, ICC. Publ.: ITMF Newsletter; State of Trade Report.

W.R. CLINE, *The Future of World Trade in Textiles and Apparel*, Washington DC., 1987; KEESING's *Record of World Events*, No. 3, 1987.

THAILAND. Member of the UN. State of Thais. A state in south-east Asia on the Indochina Peninsula, bordering on Burma, Laos, Kampuchea, Malaysia. The historical name up to 1949 was Siam. Area: 513,115 sq. km. Pop. 1987 est. 5,390,000 (1970 census: 34,397,000; 1980 census: 44,278,000). Capital Bangkok with 5,535,048 inhabitants 1983. Official language: Siamese. GNP per capita 1986: US $810. Currency: one Baht = 100 satangs. National Day: Dec. 5, King's birthday, 1927.
Member the UN since Dec. 16, 1946 and all its specialized agencies except WIPO. Member of the Colombo Plan and ASEAN.
International relations: Siam was an independent kingdom since the 12th century. In the early 19th century in conflict with the British East India Company; 1826 first trade agreement with Great Britain, extended by the British–Siamese Treaty of 1856. In 1893 in conflict with France, concluded with cession of parts of territories of Laos and Cambodia to French Indochina in 1904–07, and in 1909 of part of Malay to Great Britain. During World War I on the side of the Allies. Member of the League of Nations 1934–39. In World War II in alliance with Japan against the Allies. A secret pro-American grouping in touch with the USA through the Siamese ambassador to Washington (never conveyed his government's declaration of war) led to change of government in Sept., 1945 and establishment of relations with the United Nations which allowed the country to accede to the UN, 1946. In May, 1954 alarmed the UN Security Council about the possibility of escalation of the Indochina War into Thailand; the issue settled by the provisions of Indochina Treaties signed in Geneva on July 22, 1954. In conflict with Cambodia over ▷ Preah Vihear, a borderline shrine. In 1962 a treaty with the USA allowed the latter to build naval and air bases for up to 50,000 troops in 1967. After US withdrawal from Vietnam, military bases in Thailand were liquidated entirely by July 20, 1976. In 1980 the Red Khmer troops evacuation from Kampuchea together with part of the civilian population resulted in serious frontier incidents and political disputes in following years.

D. INSOR, *Thailand: A Political, Social and Economic Analysis*, New York, 1963; F.C. DARLING, *Thailand and the United States*, Washington, DC, 1965; N.F. BUSCH, *Thailand: An Introduction to Modern Siam*, New York, 1965; P. FISTIE, *L'évolution de la Thaïlande contemporaine*, Paris, 1967; D.E. NEUCHTERNLEIN, *Thailand and the Struggle for Southeast Asia*, New York, 1967; R.O. NAIRN, *International Aid to Thailand. The New Colonialism*, New York, 1967; P.B. TRESCOTT, *Thailand's Monetary Experience: the Economics of Stability*, New York, 1971; *The Far East and Australasia 1974*, London, 1974, pp. 611–636; P. SONDYSURAN, "Finance, Trade and Economic Development", in *Thailand*, Bangkok, 1975; W. DONNER, *The Five Faces of Thailand*, London, 1978; *Thailand in the 1980s*, Bangkok, 1979; D. MORELLI, C. SAMUDAVANIJA, *Political Conflict in Thailand*, Cambridge Mass., 1981; *The Europa Year Book 1984. A World Survey*, Vol. II, pp. 2491–2505, London, 1984.

THALAR. *German*: Thaler. A silver coin. Weight *c.* 27.4 g, minted from the end of the 15th to the 19th centuries in Europe, initially in Jachymov, from which it was called Joachimsthaler and then anglicized in the United States to ▷ Dollar.

THALASOTHERAPY. The seaside climatotherapy and balneotherapy, subject of international co-operation. Organization reg. with the UIA:

International Association of Thalasotherapy, f. 1907, Paris.

Yearbook of International Organizations.

THALWEG. *German* "road in a valley." An international term since Feb. 9, 1801, when it was introduced in the French text of the Treaty of Luneville in arts. 3 and 6, as a definition of a border demarcation line:

"Art. III. ... le *thalweg* de l'Adige servant de ligne de delimination ... Art. VI. ... de maniere que ... le *thalweg* du Rhin soit desormait la limite entre la Republique Française et l'Empire Germanique."

Since then the term has been used to define the frontier line on rivers in their main current; sometimes used with regard to straits.

Dictionnaire de la terminologie internationale, Paris, 1960.

THANKSGIVING DAY. The American national holiday on the fourth Thursday in November, accepted for all states by act of Congress in 1941, remembering the day of thanks in 1621 of the Pilgrims.

THATTA. A historic site of Pakistan, included in the ▷ World Heritage UNESCO List. Thatta was once the capital of Sind and still possesses two fine mosques from the 16th and 17th centuries. It also contains a necropolis, one of the most astonishing in the Orient. Two kilometers outside the town are 500,000 tombs arranged in lines and entirely decorated with sculptures or covered with enamelled tiles. The oldest date from the 14th century.

UNESCO. *A Legacy for All*, Paris, 1984.

THAVRA. Arabic = Revolution.

THEATRE. A subject of international co-operation under the aegis of UNESCO. Organizations reg. with the UIA:

International Amateur Theatre Association, f. 1952, Amsterdam.
International Association for Children's and Youth Theatres, f. 1965, Paris. Publ.: *Théâtre Enfance et Jeunesse* (quarterly in English and French).
International Association of Theatre Critics, f. 1956, Paris.
International Centre of Theatre Research, f. 1971, Paris.
International Federation for Theatre Research, f. 1957, Paris. Publ.: *Theatre Research International*.
International Institute for Music, Dance and Theatre in the Audio-visual Media, f. 1969, Vienna.
International Organization of Scenographers and Theatre Technicians, f. 1968, Prague.
International Student Theatre Union, f. 1962, Amsterdam.
International Theatre Institute, f. 1948, Paris. Consultative Status with UNESCO and ECOSOC. Publ.: *International Theatre Information* (quarterly in English and French).
Scandinavian Amateur Theatre Council, f. 1967, Grasten, Denmark.

Encyclopédie du Théâtre Contemporaine, Paris, 1966; *Enciclopedia dello Spettacolo*, Roma, 1954–66; *Tieatralnaya Enciclopediya*, Moscow, 1961–68; K.R.M. BAND-KURMANY, *Glossary of the Theatre, in English, French, Italian and German*, Amsterdam 1969.

THEBES. A historic site of Egypt, included in the ▷ World Heritage UNESCO List. Two thousand years before Christ, Thebes, the capital of an empire which stretched as far as the Euphrates, lavished its wealth on the construction of temples – the monuments of Karnak and Luxor. The temple of Amon-Re was repeatedly extended westwards towards the Nile and southwards towards the sanctuary of the Goddess Mut. At Luxor, bas-relief and porticoes provide illustrations of the artistic refinement of the 14th and 13th centuries BC.

Nubian monuments from Abu Simbel to Philae. The temples of Abu Simbel were carved into the cliff in honor of Ramses II, Queen Nefertari and the great divinities of Egypt. Philae is an island of sanctuaries sculpted with devotion, where the Nubians maintained the cult of Isis until the 6th century AD.

UNESCO. *A Legacy for All*, Paris, 1984.

THEOLOGY OF LIBERATION. A concept which emerged among the radical clergy of Latin America, advocating the need for the active engagement of the faithful on the side of social national liberation movements, not excluding military and guerilla activities. (▷ Encuentro Latinoamericano Camillo Torres.) The content and limits of this engagement (mainly in reference to priests) was defined by John Paul II in Mexico in Jan. 1979 and by the Congregation of Faith in Fall 1984 and Spring 1986.
On April 5, 1986 the Sacred Congregation for the Doctrine of the Faith of the Catholic Church issued an 'Instruction on Christian Freedom and Liberation', which stated:

"Because of the continual development of the technology of violence and the increasingly serious dangers implied in its recourse, what is known today as 'passive resistance' points out a way which is more in line with moral principles and no less likely to succeed."

See also ▷ Kairos Document.

G. GUTIEREZ, *Teología de la Liberación*, Salamanca, 1972; W.I. BRODERICK, *A Biography of the Priest Guerillo Camilo Torres*, Garden City, 1973; SANTA CONGREGAZIONE PER LA DOCTRINA DELLA FIDE, *Instruzione su alcuni aspetti della "Teologia della liberazione,"* Citta del Vaticano, 1984; *Instruction on Christian Freedom and Liberation (also in French, German, Italian, Latin, Polish, Russian and Spanish)*, Citta del Vaticano, 1986. *Newsweek*, April 14, 1986; Catholic Truth Society. *Instruction on Certain aspects of the Theology of Liberation (Libertatis Nuntices)*, London, 1986; M. NOVAK, *Will It Liberate? Questions About Liberation Theology*, New York, 1986; Ph. BERRYMAN, *Liberation Theology: Essential Facts about the Revolutionary Movement in Latin America and Beyond*, London, 1987.

THEOSOPHY. A mystical doctrine of a universal principle, subject of international promotion. Organizations reg. with the UIA:

Theosophical Society, f. Nov. 17, 1875 in New York by Helena P. Blavatska (1831–91); headquarters since 1882 in Adyar, Madras, India. Aims: to form a nucleus of a universal brotherhood without distinction as to race, creed, sex, caste or color, and to encourage the study of comparative religion, philosophy and science. Members organized in lodges in 62 countries. Library, Research Center and School of Wisdom in Adyar for Students. Publ.: *The Theosophist* (monthly).
Theosophical Society in Europe, f. 1903, London. Publ.: *The Theosophical Journal* (English), *Le Lotus Bleu* (French) and *Adyar* (German).
United Lodge of Theosophists, f. 1909, Los Angeles, since 1929 Bombay. Publ.: *Theosophical Movement* (monthly), *Theosophy* (monthly).

H.P. BLAVATSKA, *The Key to Theosophy*, New York, 1900; C.W. LEADBEATER, *Textbook to Theosophy*, New York, 1946; *Yearbook of International Organizations*.

THERMONUCLEAR BOMB. ▷ Hydrogen Bomb.

THESSALONIKI. A city and port on the Gulf of Thessaloniki in northeast Greece, subject of conflicts and international disputes after the first Balkan war, when Thessaloniki, after 482 years of Turkish rule, was ceded to Greece in 1912, becoming the cause of the second Balkan war because of the claims of Bulgaria and Austria supported by Germany. In World War I an Allied base 1915–18,

during World War II – a German base 1941–44; liberated on Oct. 31, 1944.

"THIRD BASKET," THE. A term adopted during the many years of preparations for the Conference on Security and Co-operation in Europe; a name for a set of problems concerning co-operation in the exchange of persons, information, ideas, occupying third place after political and economic problems.

"THIRD WINDOW." A financing facility under which poorer developing countries can receive loans on terms intermediate between the standard terms of the World Bank and the highly concessional terms of its affiliate, the IDA. The "Third Window" subsidized from 1975 by the Interest Subsidy Fund, supplements interest payments due the World Bank from borrowers. The Fund is financed by governments on a voluntary basis.

UN Chronicle, August–September., 1975, p. 42.

"THIRD WORLD." A term coined by the press (First world – capitalist, Second world – socialist), generally adopted by the UN during 1955–60, when a number of new states, formed as a result of decolonization, became members of the UN, and gained majority in the organization. Attempts were made to unite the "Third World" politically, such as the Afro-Asian Conferences and the Tri Continental Conference, and economically by joint postulates advanced at meetings of Group 77 and UNCTAD. UN demographic prognoses in 1972 predicted that by the year 2000 the population of the Third World would reach 4.5–5 billion people and in the remaining countries about 1.5 billion people. These economic forecasts warned that an extremely wide gap in living standards was bound to appear and that the population of the Third countries would be 20–30 times worse off than in industrialized countries. In Dec., 1984 in Rome a new UN agency was established: UN Agency for Research on Utilization of Energy Sources in the Third World. Since 1978 a *Third World Quarterly*, publ. in London, presents Third World opinions on contemporary issues. Organization reg. with the UIA:

Third World Association, f. 1975, Brussels. A non-profit association, made up of European Community officials who together finance small development projects. Publ.: *Reports on Third World Problems*.

G. KURIAN, *Encyclopedia of the Third World*, New York, 1978; M. NOELKE, *Europe – Third World. Interdependence. Facts and Figures*, Brussels, 1979; D.K. WHYNES, *The Economics of Third World Military Expenditure*, Austin, 1979; A.G. FRANK, *Crisis in the Third World*, New York, 1981; *Eastern Europe and the Third World*, New York, 1981; T. OHLSON, M. BRZOSKA, *Arms Production in Third World*, SIPRI, London, Philadelphia, 1985, Oxford, 1986; R.S. LITWAK, S.F. WELLS eds., *Superpower Competition and Security in the Third World*, Cambridge, 1987; *Yearbook of International Organizations*.

THIRD WORLD PRIZE. The award created 1980 by the Third World Foundation for Social and Economic Studies to honor outstanding contributions to the development of Asian, African and Latin American Countries. The first laureate 1980 was Dr Raul Prebisch, Argentina.

THIRD WORLD UNIVERSITY. A project initiated in Mexico, DF in Sept., 1976 by a Center of Economic and Social Studies of the Third World, Centro de Estudios Económicos y Sociales del Terces Mundo, promoted by President Luis Echeverría.

THRACE. The historic territory of the Thracians in the Balkan peninsula on the southern coast of the

Aegean Sea; subject of international conflicts. From the 14th to the 19th centuries under Turkish rule. As a result of the Balkan wars, in 1912 divided between Bulgaria and Greece. After World War I Bulgaria was deprived of her part of Thrace called the western part, which was given to Greece by the Thrace Treaty 1920, and Thrace Frontier Convention 1923, but received eastern Thrace from Turkey. During the years of the German occupation of Greece, from the spring of 1941 to the fall of 1944, this part of Thrace was temporarily again under Bulgarian administration. The Paris Peace Treaty of Feb. 10, 1947 restored the state of affairs before 1941.
The highlights of the Treaty, signed on Aug. 10, 1920 at Sèvres:
"The Principal Allied and Associated Powers hereby transfer to Greece, who accept the said transfer, all rights and titles which they hold, under Art. 48 of the Treaty of Peace with Bulgaria, signed on 27 Nov., 1919 in Neuilly-sur-Seine, over the territories in Thrace which belonged to the Bulgarian Monarchy and are dealt with in the said Article." (Art. 1.)
"In order to ensure to Bulgaria free access to the Aegean Sea, freedom of transit is accorded to her over the territories and in the ports assigned to Greece under the present Treaty." (Art. 4.)
"Dedeagatch is declared a point of international concern." (Art. 6.)
"Greece must not undertake any works liable to prejudice the facilities for the use of port of Dedeagatch or of its approaches." (Art. 10.)
Greek name of Dedeagatch is Alexandroupolis.
The Thracian Frontier Convention, respecting the Thracian Frontier was signed on July 24, 1923 in Lausanne and decided that "from the Aegean Sea to the Black Sea the territories on both sides of the frontiers separating Turkey from Bulgaria and from Greece shall be demilitarized to a depth of about 30 kilometres." (Art. 1.)

LNTS, Vol. 28, pp. 143 and 235.

THRACIAN TOMB OF KAZANLAK. A Bulgarian cultural monument, included in the ▷ World Heritage UNESCO List. The Thracians were the ancient inhabitants of Bulgaria and have left numerous tombs which display the originality of their art. The tomb of Kazanlak, dating from the 4th century BC, is decorated with frescoes which occupy an important place in the history of art.

UNESCO. *A Legacy for All*, Paris, 1984.

THRESHOLD TEST BAN TREATY, 1974. The official name of the American–Soviet agreement signed on July 3, 1974, imposing limitations on the USA and the USSR's underground nuclear weapon tests; both countries were not to exceed in their military testing an agreed threshold for explosion yield.

SIPRI, *World Armaments and Disarmament Yearbook*, 1975, pp. 405–408.

TIAS. Treaties and other International Acts Series. US Department of State, Washington DC.

TIBET. The Himalayan region of western China, autonomous since Sept. 9, 1965; bounded in the south by India, Nepal and Bhutan. Area: 1,221,600 sq. km; pop. 1982 census: 1,892,393. Capital: Lhasa with c. 120,000 inhabitants. Subject of dispute in the UN when, after the formation of the People's Republic of China, the Tibetan ruler, ▷ Dalai Lama, demanded on Oct. 7, 1950 a UN protectorate over the region, and the UN General Assembly General Commission refused to interfere in internal Chinese affairs, expressing hopes for a peaceful Chinese solution of the problem, which was finally reached under an agreement between the Dalai

T

Lama and Mao-Tse-tung signed May 23, 1951. The matter was again brought before the UN after the Dalai Lama fled to India, Mar., 1959. On Oct. 21, 1959 the UN General Assembly adopted by 45 votes, with 9 vetoes and 26 abstentions, Res. 1533/XIV calling for respect for basic human rights of the Tibetan people, which was confirmed by Res. 1723/XVI of Dec. 20, 1961 and 2079/XX of Dec. 18, 1965, the latter failing to obtain an absolute majority (43 for, 23 against, 22 abstentions). ▷ China. In 1983 the Tibet-India border was open to repatriation or family visits of the 1959 Tibetan refugees in India. In 1984 China invited the Dalai Lama to visit Peiping. Pro-independence rioting in Lhassa on March 5, 1988 and March 1989.

The Tibet-Institut Rikon, Tibetan Monastic Institute in Rikon, f. 1967 to take care of the Tibetans living in exile in Switzerland, in Rikon Zürich, publ. Opuscula Tibetana.

THE DALAI LAMA, *My Land and My People*, London, 1962; J.N. THUBTEN, C. TUMBULL, *Tibet. Its History, Religion and People*, Harmondsworth, 1974; *Tibet*, London, 1974; F. MELE, *Tibet*, Paris, 1975; B.R. BURMAN, *Religion and Politics in Tibet*, New Delhi, 1979; *The Europa Year Book 1984. A World Survey*, Vol. II, pp. 1385–1387, London, 1984; KEESING's *Contemporary Archive*, 1986, No. 9; A.T. GRUNFELD, *The Making of Modern Tibet*, London, 1987.

TIENTSIN. A city in north China in the province of Hopei on the river Hai-ho; pop. 1970 est.: 4,500,000. During the ▷ opium wars occupied in 1858 by English and French forces, place of the signing, June 26, 1858, of the Treaty of Peace, Friendship, and Trade between Great Britain and China, the so-called Treaty of Tientsin; and of a similar Treaty of Friendship, Trade, and Shipping between France and China, the former renewing and confirming the Nankin Treaty, 1842; since 1860 one of the open ports of China. An additional Treaty of Peace and Friendship between France and China was signed on Oct. 20, 1861. Tientsin was occupied by the European powers 1900 during the Boxer Rebellion and 1937–45 by Japan.

G.E. HESTLER, *Treaties and Conventions between Great Britain and China and between China and Foreign Powers*, London, 1908; *Major Peace Treaties of Modern History*, New York, 1967, Vol. II, pp. 763–776 and 1065–1080.

TIENTSIN TREATY, 1858. ▷ American-Chinese Treaties, 1844–1908.

TIGRIS. Turkish–Iraqi River 1850 km long; rising in the Taurus Mountains in Turkey and flowing through Iraq forming with the Euphrates River the Shatt al Arab, which flows into the Persian Gulf.

TIKAL. The National Park of Guatemala, included in the ▷ World Heritage UNESCO List. In a nature reserve covering 576 sq. km are the remains of temples and stelae, ballgame courts, dams and highways. More than 3000 structures bear witness to the past splendor of Tikal, which was undoubtedly the most important religious center of Mayan civilization.

UNESCO. *A Legacy for All*, Paris, 1984.

TILE AND BRICK. Subject of international co-operation. Organizations reg. with the UIA:

Common Market Group of Ceramic Tile Producers, f. 1959, Brussels, Belgium.
European Federation of Tile and Brick Manufacturers, f. 1952, Zürich, Switzerland.
European Union of Tile Fixers Associations, f. 1982, London, UK.
International Committee for the Conservation of Mud-Brick, f. 1986, Rome, Italy.

Nordic Cooperative of Brick and Tilemakers Association, f. 1970, Stockholm, Sweden.

Yearbook of International Organizations, 1986/87; The Europa Yearbook 1988. A World Survey, Vol. I, London, 1988.

TILSIT PEACE TREATIES, 1807. Two Peace Treaties, between France and Russia, and between France and Prussia, signed on July 7 and July 9, 1807 respectively in Tilsit.

Major Peace Treaties of Modern History, New York, 1967, Vol. I, pp. 469–486.

TIMBER. A subject of international co-operation and agreements:

Agreement on Scientific Technical Co-operation for the Problem "Comprehensive Use of Timber," signed on Apr. 28, 1971 at Moscow by the CMEA states.
International Timber Agreement, approved on June 11, 1982 at Geneva, under aegis of UNCTAD. In Dec., 1982 an International Tropical Timber Organization was established under the Agreement.

On April 1, 1985 the International Tropical Timber Agreement entered into force, after eight years of negotiations between producers and consumer countries.

Organization reg. with the UIA:
African Timber Organization, f. 1976, Libreville, Gabon.

Recueil de Documents, Varsovie, No. 4, 1971; W.E. BUTLER (ed.), *A Source Book on Socialist International Organizations*, Alphen, 1978, pp. 888–896; *UN Chronicle*, September, 1982, p. 77; *UN Chronicle*, 1985, No. 3, pp. 52–53; *The Europa Yearbook 1988. A World Survey*, Vol. I, London, 1988.

TIME. The international measurement of time is a subject of international co-operation in view of the existence of various calendar systems for reckoning time introduced by religious groups (Judaic, Christian, Moslem and others) and the desire to create a uniform ▷ World calendar.

Organizations reg. with the UIA:
International Commission on Time, f. 1985, Potsdam, GDR.
International Federation of Time-Keepers, f. 1982, Rome, Italy.
International Society for the Study of Time, f. 1966, Westport, Ct., USA.

Yearbook of International Organizations, 1986/87.

TIME, INTERNATIONAL. An international term for the time used in international transport given in the form of plus or minus so many hours in relation to ▷ GMT.

Organization reg. with the UIA:
International Time Bureau, f. 1912, Sèvres, France. Publ.; Annual Report.

Yearbook of International Organizations, 1986/87.

TIME UNIT, INTERNATIONAL. A subject of international co-operation initiated by the International Time Bureau, Bureau International de l'Heure, BIH, the International Astronomical Union, LAU, and the International Union of Geodesy and Geophysics, IUGG; from 1956 integrated by the Federation of Astronomical and Geophysical Services, FAGS, and the International Council of Scientific Unions, ICSU. Work on establishing an international scale of time led to the introduction beside the "ephemeron second" of the "atomic second," both defined by the Advisory Committee for the Definition of a Second est. 1956 attached to the International Committee of Measures, which directs the International Bureau of Weights and Measures. Simultaneously in 1967 with the passage to an inner atomic scale of time two further scales of time came into being: UTC

(Universal Time Coordinated) as well as SAT (Stepped Atomic Time) used by radio stations of the world in accordance with experiments carried on by the International Advisory Committee on Radio Communication, one of the organs of ITU with its seat in Geneva.

Yearbook of International Organizations.

TIME ZONES. The Zero Meridian at ▷ Greenwich; the 60° Meridian West of Greenwich determines Atlantic Standard Time; 75° Meridian Eastern Standard Time; 90° Central Time; 105° Mountain Time; 120° for Pacific; 135° for Yukon, 150° for part of Alaska. The International ▷ Date Line is a modification of the line of the 180° Meridian.

"Time Measurement", in: *Encyclopedia Britannica.*

TIMOR ISLAND. The largest island of the Lesser Sundas on the Timor Sea, ancillary to the Pacific. Area: 34,190 sq. km (14,874 sq. km of which is East Timor). Pop. 1976: 3,726,000 (690,000 of which live in East Timor), both parts of the island administered since 1976 by Indonesia, under the name Timor Timur (East Timor), even though the UN Security Council of Apr. 22, 1976 recognized the right to sovereignty and independence of the community of East Timor.

International relations: a Portuguese colony from 1586 until 1857, when Portugal ceded the western part to Holland, confirmed under treaty of Oct. 1, 1904; occupied by Japan 1942–45; overseas province (Provincia ultramarina) of Portugal from June 11, 1957, the inhabitants having Portuguese citizenship from Sept. 6, 1961; subject of dispute between Portugal and Indonesia. From the three major political parties in the territories one, FRETILIN, on Nov. 28, 1975 declared the full independence of the Territory and the establishment of the Democratic Republic of East Timor; two others, APODETI, UDT, also proclaimed the independence of the Territory but in integration with Indonesia.

On Dec. 7, 1975, Portugal informed the Security Council that Indonesian naval, air and land forces had launched an offensive action against East Timor. On Dec. 17, the pro-Indonesian parties declared the establishment of a Provisional Government of East Timor at Dili, the Territory's capital. The Provisional Government called on the people of East Timor to help fight FRETILIN and appealed to Indonesia for military and economic aid. In Apr., 1976, the Security Council, after consideration of the report of the Secretary-General containing information on the efforts undertaken by his special representative, called upon Indonesia to withdraw without further delay. On July 17, 1976, the President of Indonesia promulgated a law providing for the integration of East Timor into Indonesia and the establishment of East Timor as its 27th province with the name Timor Timur.

In Dec., 1976 and Nov., 1977, the General Assembly adopted resolutions rejecting the claim that East Timor had been integrated into Indonesia, inasmuch as the people of the Territory had not been able to exercise freely their right to self-determination and independence. On Jan. 20, 1978 Australia officially recognized East Timor as a province of Indonesia. The UN General Assembly reaffirmed on Nov. 21, 1979 the inalienable right of the people of East Timor to self-determination and independence, by a vote of 62 in favour to 31 against with 45 abstentions; and on Nov. 24, 1981 by a vote of 54 in favour, 42 against, with 46 abstentions.

Indonesian Handbook, Jakarta, 1975; *UN Chronicle*, January, 1980, p. 53, January, 1981, pp. 18–19, and

Tlatelolco Conference, 1974

January, 1982, p. 19; *The Europa Year Book 1984. A World Survey*, Vol. II, pp. 1710–1712, London, 1984.

TIN. One of the basic raw materials on world markets, subject of international conventions. Main producers: Bolivia, Brazil, China, Indonesia, Zaïre, Malaysia, Nigeria, Thailand. Main consumer – USA. The first agreement called Pool de Bandung was reached 1921–24; the second – Tin Producers Pool, 1935. In 1931–40 there was an international tin cartel controlling 90% of the production at that time. After World War II periodic UN Tin Conferences took place in Geneva: I – 1950, II – 1953, III – 1956, IV – 1961, V – 1965, VI – 1970, VII – 1975, VIII – 1981. From 1965 under the auspices of UNCTAD. A permanent organ is the International Tin Research Group, which every five years works out revised international conventions. The first took effect in July, 1956. Brazil, China, and USA did not enter the fifth revision up to the period June 30, 1980. The sixth International Tin Agreement adopted on June 26, 1981 at Geneva, and came into force for five years on June 30, 1982. The size of the buffer stock was set at 50,000 tons (before 20,000), of which 30,000 were to be financed by government-al contributions and an additional 20,000 by borrowing. The financing would be shared up to 1987 equally between producers and consumers. A new mechanism of determining the trigger points at which export control might be applied automatic-ally subjected the duration of the control to the market situation and price of tin, thus introducing a much greater degree of flexibility. The organ of the convention is the International Tin Council with seat in London. Representatives of the producing states make up the Council: Bolivia, Indonesia, Zaïre, Malaysia, Nigeria, and Rwanda as well as the consuming states: Australia, Belgium, Canada, Denmark, France, FRG, Great Britain, India, Italy, Liberia, Luxembourg, the Netherlands, Mexico, Panama, South Korea, Spain, Turkey, USA and Yugoslavia. Publ.: *Bulletin of ITC, Notes of Tin*, and *ITC Statistical Yearbook*. The Council co-operates with the International Tin Research Council, est. 1932 with seat in Greenford, UK, whose members are: Bolivia, France, Indonesia, Zaïre, Malaysia, and Nigeria. Publ.: *Tin and Its Uses*, (quarterly). Registered with the UIA.
In Oct. 1985 the increasing disorder in the tin market in relation with sharp price fluctuation forced the London Metal Exchange LME, to suspend tin contracts for short periods and on March 7, 1986 the LME closed down the London Tin Market altogether.

UN Chronicle, August, 1981, pp. 42–44; *Yearbook of International Organizations*; KEESING's *Contemporary Archive*, 1986; KEESING's *Record of World Events*, 1986, No. 7; KEESING's *Contemporary Archive*, July, 1987.

TINDEMANS' REPORT, 1976. A comprehensive report on an overall concept of the European Union, prepared by the Belgian Prime Minister, Leo Tindemans for the heads of government of the EEC Countries, published on Jan. 7, 1976 in Brussels. The highlights of Tindemans' recom-mendations were as follows:
"(I) Member states should accept an obligation to reach a common foreign policy on major issues, if necessary by majority rather than unanimous voting. It was suggested that such a policy could begin with the less developed countries and the United States, defence, and crises affecting non-EEC European countries.
(II) There should be faster progress towards economic and monetary union, with economically stronger member states possibly moving towards closer integration at a faster rate initially than the weaker countries, although the latter would be expected to catch up eventually. The 'snake' of linked currencies should be

consolidated by joint action on monetary, budgetary, and short-term economic policy, but member states not yet belonging to the 'snake' should be brought into these discussions. Machinery for short- and medium-term support, the European Monetary Co-operation Fund, should be made automatic and strengthened. The 'snake' countries should gradually abolish the remaining barriers to capital movements between them, and 'non-snake' countries should be helped to join it. (III) The development of common policies in impor-tant fields such as industry, energy and research should be regarded as a priority."
R. FORNELL, *The Common Agricultural Policy of the European Community*, London, 1979; *The Agricultural Situation in the Community*, Brussels, 1982.

TIPASA. An Algerian cultural site included in the ▷ World Heritage UNESCO List.

UNESCO, *A Legacy for All*, Paris, 1984.

TIRAN. The strait of Tiran between the Red Sea and the Gulf of Akaba, subject of disputes between Egypt and Israel, 1967–79.

TIRANA. The capital of Albania on the Ishm river.

TIR BOOK. Transport Internationaux Routiers, International Road Transport. The standardization of the international transport of goods by the Geneva Customs Convention of Jan. 15, 1959 through the issuance of a TIR Book, a blank which simplifies customs formalities in the import, export, and transit of goods. Special regulations of the TIR Book state that the international languages of customs is French, but a translation in the language of the issuing country may be appended to a TIR Book by the issuing country.

TIS. Trade Information Service, one of the in-formation systems of the ▷ UN Economic and Social Commission for Asia and Pacific.

"TITANIC." The largest British White Star liner (Cunard Line) *Titanic*, 47,000 BRT, sunk on the night of Apr. 14–15, 1912 after striking an iceberg in the North Atlantic on her maiden voyage, drowning 1563 of the 2224 passengers. The cause of so many casualties was an insufficient number of lifeboats and the non-reception of SOS signals by the ship *Californian* sailing nearby. *Titanic*'s disaster resulted in the drafting of the first convention on safety at sea, Jan. 12, 1914. The broken wreck of the "Titanic" was found on Sept. 1, 1985.

"Shipping Casualties (*Titanic*)", in: *British Parliamen-tary Papers*, 1912; W. LORD, *A Night to Remember*, London, 1956; P. PADFIELD, *The "Titanic" and the "Californian"*, London, 1965; J.P. EATON, Ch.A. HAAS, *Titanic, Triumph and Tragedy*, New York, 1987.

TITO PLAN, 1958. A plan proposed by Yugo-slavia's President Tito (1892–1980) of a nuclear-weapon-free zone of the Balkan region and Italy, presented in the United Nations, 1958, by Yugo-slavia, called the Tito Plan; supported 1959 by Romania and 1960 by the USSR. ▷ Denuclearized Zones; ▷ Kekkonen Plans, 1963 and 1978; ▷ Rapacki Plan, 1957.

P. AUTY, *Tito. A Biography*, London, 1970; D. WILSON, *Tito's Yugoslavia*, Cambridge, 1979.

TIYS. A historic site of Ethiopia, included in the ▷ World Heritage UNESCO List.

UNESCO, *A Legacy for All*, Paris, 1984.

TLATELOLCO. The oldest district of Mexico City with the Office of Mexican Foreign Ministry, where on Feb. 14, 1967 the first regional treaty on

denuclearization, called the ▷ Tlatelolco Treaty, 1967 was signed.

F. BORGIA STECK, R.H. BORLOW, *El Primer Colegio de América. Santa Cruz de Tlatelolco. Con un estudio del Códice de Tlatelolco*, México, DF, 1944; "Tlatelolco", in: *Diccionario Porua de Historia, Biografia y Geografia de México*, México, DF, 1971, Vol. 2, pp. 2129–2130.

TLATELOLCO CONFERENCE, 1974. Official name of a meeting of the Ministers of Foreign Affairs of Latin America (with the exception of Cuba) and the USA Secretary of State, H. Kissin-ger, in Mexico City, Feb. 21–24, 1974, in the build-ing of the Mexican ministry of foreign affairs located on Tlatelolco square. This was the first meeting since 1967 at this level of the represen-tatives of the member states of OAS and the first attempt at a dialogue of the states of Latin America with the USA on mainly economic subjects. The Conference goes on record as follows:
"(1) The Foreign Ministers recognized that the success of the Conference of Tlatelolco emphasizes the value of the new dialogue of the Americas. Mindful of the growing interaction between themselves and the rest of the world and that their countries have different needs and different approaches on foreign policy, the Foreign Ministers were nevertheless agreed that the relations between their countries, which history, geography and sentiment have produced and continued to sustain, call for an expansion of the process of consultation between their governments.
(2) The Conference welcomes the agreement reached in Panama City on February 7, 1974, by the Governments of Panama and the United States of America, by which they established the guiding principles for their current negotiations leading to a new Canal treaty.
(3) The Foreign Ministers agreed that, if progress toward a new inter-American solidarity is to be made, solutions must be found not only to existing differences, but means also be provided for the solution of problems that may arise.
(4) In this spirit, the Foreign Ministers of Latin America have taken due note and will continue to examine the suggestion advanced by the Secretary of State of the United States of America with respect to the controversies that may arise from matters involving private foreign investment.
The Secretary of State of the United States proposed the establishment of a fact-finding or conciliation procedure that would limit the scope of such controver-sies by separating the issues of fact from those of law. This could provide an objective basis for the solution of disputes without detriment to sovereignty.
He further proposed the creation of an inter-American working group to study the appropriate procedures that might be adopted.
(5) With regard to the problems of transnational cor-porations, the Foreign Ministers discussed the different aspects of their operation in Latin America and have agreed to continue the examination of the matter at a later meeting.
(6) The Foreign Ministers agreed on the need for inten-sifying work on the restructuring of the inter-American system.
(7) The Foreign Ministers agreed that one of the prin-cipal objectives is the accelerated development of the countries of the Americas and the promotion of the welfare of all their peoples. In this regard, the United States accepts a special responsibility; and the more developed countries of the Americas recognize that special attention should be paid to the needs of the lesser developed.
They further agreed that development should be integral, covering the economic, social and cultural life of their nations.
(8) The United States offered to promote the integral development of the region in the following fields:
Make maximum efforts to secure passage of the legisla-tion on the system of generalized preferences during the present session of Congress, and then work with the other countries of the hemisphere to apply these preferences in the most beneficial manner.
Avoid, as far as possible, the implementation of any new measures that would restrict access to the United

899

States market. Maintain, as a minimum, present aid levels despite growing costs. Cooperate throughout the region and in international institutions to facilitate the flow of new concessional and conventional resources toward those countries most affected by growing energy costs.

Examine with others in the Committee of Twenty and the Inter-American Development Bank all restrictions on the entry of hemispheric countries to capital markets in the United States and other industrialized countries.

(9) The Foreign Ministers further declare:

They reaffirm the need of Latin American and Caribbean countries for an effective participation of their countries in an international monetary reform.

It was acknowledged that the net transfer of real resources is basic, and that ways to institutionalize transfers through adequate mechanisms should be considered.

It was reaffirmed that external financial cooperation should preferably be channeled through multilateral agencies and respect the priorities established for each country, without political ties or conditions.

With respect to 'transfers of technology', the Foreign Ministers agreed to promote policies facilitating transfers of both patented and unpatented technical knowledge among the respective countries in the fields of industry as well as education, housing and agriculture, taking into account conditions prevailing in each country and in particular the needs of the Latin American and Caribbean countries for introduction of new manufactures for greater utilization of the human and material resources available in each country, for increased local technical development and for creation of products for export. It was further agreed that transfers of technology should be on fair and equitable terms without restraint upon the recipient country. Particular emphasis is to be placed upon sharing knowledge and technology for development of new sources of energy and possible alternatives.

(10) The Foreign Ministers agreed that it would be desirable to establish an Inter-American Commission of Science and Technology. They left over for later decision whether this Commission should be adapted from existing institutions or whether a new body should be formed.''

US Department of State Bulletin, No. 1812, 1974.

TLATELOLCO TREATY, 1967. Treaty for the Prohibition of Nuclear Weapons in Latin America, with Additional Protocols, signed in Mexico, Feb. 14, 1967; came into force on Apr. 22, 1968. The text is as follows:

"Preamble. In the name of their peoples and faithfully interpreting their desires and aspirations, the Governments of the States which sign the Treaty for the Prohibition of Nuclear Weapons in Latin America,

Desiring to contribute, so far as lies in their power, towards ending the armaments race, especially in the field of nuclear weapons, and towards strengthening a world at peace, based on the sovereign equality of States, mutual respect and good neighbourliness,

Recalling that the United Nations General Assembly, in its Resolution 808/IX, adopted unanimously as one of the three points of a coordinated programme of disarmament 'the total prohibition of the use and manufacture of nuclear weapons and weapons of mass destruction of every type',

Recalling that militarily denuclearized zones are not an end in themselves but rather a means for achieving general and complete disarmament at a later stage,

Recalling United Nations General Assembly Resolution 1911/XVIII, which established that the measures that should be agreed upon for the denuclearization of Latin America should be taken "in the light of the principles of the Charter of the United Nations and of regional agreements",

Recalling United Nations General Assembly Resolution 2028/XX, which established the principle of an acceptable balance of mutual responsibilities and duties for the nuclear and non-nuclear powers, and

Recalling that the Charter of the Organization of American States proclaims that it is an essential purpose of the Organization to strengthen the peace and security of the hemisphere,

Convinced:

That the incalculable destructive power of nuclear weapons has made it imperative that the legal prohibition of war should be strictly observed in practice if the survival of civilization and of mankind itself is to be assured,

That nuclear weapons, whose terrible effects are suffered, indiscriminately and inexorably, by military forces and civilian population alike, constitute, through the persistence of the radioactivity they release, an attack on the integrity of the human species and ultimately may even render the whole earth uninhabitable,

That general and complete disarmament under effective international control is a vital matter which all the peoples of the world equally demand,

That the proliferation of nuclear weapons, which seems inevitable unless States, in the exercise of their sovereign rights, impose restrictions on themselves in order to prevent it, would make any agreement on disarmament enormously difficult and would increase the danger of the outbreak of a nuclear conflagration,

That the establishment of militarily denuclearized zones is closely linked with the maintenance of peace and security in the respective regions,

That the military denuclearization of vast geographical zones, adopted by the sovereign decision of the States comprised therein, will exercise a beneficial influence on other regions where similar conditions exist,

That the privileged situation of the signatory States, whose territories are wholly free from nuclear weapons, imposes upon them the inescapable duty of preserving that situation both in their own interests and for the good of mankind,

That the existence of nuclear weapons in any country of Latin America would make it a target for possible nuclear attacks and would inevitably set off, throughout the region, a ruinous race in nuclear weapons which would involve the unjustifiable diversion, for warlike purposes, of the limited resources required for economic and social development,

That the foregoing reasons, together with the traditional peace-loving outlook of Latin America, give rise to an inescapable necessity that nuclear energy should be used in that region exclusively for peaceful purposes, and that the Latin American countries should use their right to the greatest and most equitable possible access to this new source of energy in order to expedite the economic and social development of their peoples,

Convinced finally:

That the military denuclearization of Latin America – being understood to mean the undertaking entered into internationally in this Treaty to keep their territories forever free from nuclear weapons – will constitute a measure which will spare their peoples from the squandering of their limited resources on nuclear armaments and will protect them against possible nuclear attacks on their territories, and will also constitute a significant contribution towards preventing the proliferation of nuclear weapons and a powerful factor for general and complete disarmament, and

That Latin America, faithful to its tradition of universality, must not only endeavour to banish from its homelands the scourge of a nuclear war, but must also strive to promote the well-being and advancement of its peoples, at the same time co-operating in the fulfilment of the ideals of mankind, that is to say, in the consolidation of a permanent peace based on equal rights, economic fairness and social justice for all, in accordance with the principles and purposes set forth in the Charter of the United Nations and in the Charter of the Organization of American States,

Have agreed as follows:

Obligations

Art. 1.(1) The Contracting Parties hereby undertake to use exclusively for peaceful purposes the nuclear material and facilities which are under their jurisdiction, and to prohibit and prevent in their respective territories:

(a) The testing, use, manufacture, production or acquisition by any means whatsoever of any nuclear weapons by the Parties themselves, directly or indirectly, on behalf of anyone else or in any other way, and

(b) The receipt, storage, installation, deployment and any form of possession of any nuclear weapons, directly or indirectly, by the Parties themselves, by anyone on their behalf or in any other way.

(2) The Contracting Parties also undertake to refrain from engaging in, encouraging or authorizing, directly or indirectly, or in any way participating in the testing, use, manufacture, production, possession or control of any nuclear weapon.

Definition of the Contracting Parties.

Art. 2. For the purposes of this Treaty, the Contracting Parties are those for whom the Treaty is in force.

Definition of Territory

Art. 3. For the purposes of this Treaty, the term 'territory' shall include the territorial sea, air space and any other space over which the State exercises sovereignty in accordance with its own legislation.

Zone of application.

Art. 4.(1) The zone of application of this Treaty is the whole of the territories for which the Treaty is in force.

(2) Upon fulfilment of the requirements of article 28, paragraph 1, the zone of application of this Treaty shall also be that which is situated in the western hemisphere within the following limits (except the continental part of the territory of the United States of America and its territorial waters): starting at a point located at 35° north latitude, 75° west longitude; from this point directly southward to a point at 30° north latitude, 75° west longitude; from there, directly eastward to a point at 30° north latitude, 50° west longitude; from there, along a loxodromic line to a point at 5° north latitude, 20° west longitude; from there, directly southward to a point at 60° south latitude, 20° west longitude; from there, directly westward to a point at 60° south latitude, 115° west longitude; from there, directly northward to a point at 0 latitude, 115° west longitude; from there, along a loxodromic line to a point at 35° north latitude, 150° west longitude; from there, directly eastward to a point at 35° north latitude, 75° west longitude.

Definition of nuclear weapons

Art. 5. For the purposes of this Treaty, a nuclear weapon is any device which is capable of releasing nuclear energy in an uncontrolled manner and which has a group of characteristics that are appropriate for use for warlike purposes. An instrument that may be used for the transport or propulsion of the device is not included in this definition if it is separable from the device and not an indivisible part thereof.

Meeting of signatories.

Art. 6. At the request of any of the signatory States or if the Agency established by article 7 should so decide, a meeting of all the signatories may be convoked to consider in common questions which may affect the very essence of this instrument, including possible amendments to it. In either case, the meeting will be convoked by the General Secretary.

Organization.

Art. 7.(1) In order to ensure compliance with the obligations of this Treaty, the Contracting Parties hereby establish an international organization to be known as the Agency for the Prohibition of Nuclear Weapons in Latin America, hereinafter referred to as 'the Agency'. Only the Contracting Parties shall be affected by its decisions.

(2) The Agency shall be responsible for the holding of periodic or extraordinary consultations among Member States on matters relating to the purposes, measures and procedures set forth in this Treaty and to the supervision of compliance with the obligations arising therefrom.

(3) The Contracting Parties agree to extend to the Agency full and prompt co-operation in accordance with the provisions of this Treaty, of any agreements they may conclude with the Agency and of any agreements the Agency may conclude with any other international organization or body.

(4) The headquarters of the Agency shall be in Mexico City.

Organs.

Art. 8.(1) There are hereby established as principal organs of the Agency a General Conference, a Council and a Secretariat.

(2) Such subsidiary organs as are considered necessary by the General Conference may be established within the purview of this Treaty.

The General Conference.

Art. 9.(1) The General Conference, the supreme organ of the Agency, shall be composed of all the Contracting Parties; it shall hold regular sessions every two years, and may also hold special sessions whenever this Treaty so provides or, in the opinion of the Council, the circumstances so require.

(2) The General Conference:

(a) May consider and decide on any matters or questions covered by this Treaty, within the limits thereof, including those referring to powers and functions of any organ provided for in this Treaty;

(b) Shall establish procedures for the control system to ensure observance of this Treaty in accordance with its provisions;

(c) Shall elect the Members of the Council and the General Secretary;

(d) May remove the General Secretary from office if the proper functioning of the Agency so requires;

(e) Shall receive and consider the biennial and special reports submitted by the Council and the General Secretary.

(f) Shall initiate and consider studies designed to facilitate the optimum fulfilment of the aims of this Treaty, without prejudice to the power of the General Secretary independently to carry out similar studies for submission to and consideration by the Conference.

(g) Shall be the organ competent to authorize the conclusion of agreements with Governments and other international organizations and bodies.

(3) The General Conference shall adopt the Agency's budget and fix the scale of financial contributions to be paid by Member States, taking into account the systems and criteria used for the same purpose by the United Nations.

(4) The General Conference shall elect its officers for each session and may establish such subsidiary organs as it deems necessary for the performance of its functions.

(5) Each Member of the Agency shall have one vote. The decisions of the General Conference shall be taken by a two thirds majority of the Members present and voting in the case of matters relating to the control system and measures referred to in article 20, the admission of new Members, the election or removal of the General Secretary, adoption of the budget and matters related thereto. Decisions on other matters, as well as procedural questions and also determination of which questions must be decided by a two-thirds majority of the Members present and voting.

(6) The General Conference shall adopt its own rules of procedure.

The Council.

Art. 10.(1) The Council shall be composed of five Members of the Agency elected by the General Conference from among the Contracting Parties, due account being taken of equitable geographic distribution.

(2) The Members of the Council shall be elected for a term of four years. However, in the first election three will be elected for two years. Outgoing Members may not be re-elected for the following period unless the limited number of States for which the Treaty is in force so requires.

(3) Each Member of the Council shall have one representative.

(4) The Council shall be so organized as to be able to function continuously.

(5) In addition to the functions conferred upon it by this Treaty and to those which may be assigned to it by the General Conference, the Council shall, through the General Secretary, ensure the proper operation of the control system in accordance with the provisions of this Treaty and with the decisions adopted by the General Conference.

(6) The Council shall submit an annual report on its work to the General Conference as well as such special reports as it deems necessary or which the General Conference requests of it.

(7) The Council shall elect its officers for each session.

(8) The decisions of the Council shall be taken by a simple majority of its Members present and voting.

(9) The Council shall adopt its own rules of procedure.

The Secretariat.

Art. 11.(1) The Secretariat shall consist of a General Secretary, who shall be the chief administrative officer of the Agency, and of such staff as the Agency may require. The term of office of the General Secretary shall be four years and he may be re-elected for a single additional term. The General Secretary may not be a national of the country in which the Agency has its headquarters. In case the office of General Secretary becomes vacant, a new election shall be held to fill the office for the remainder of the term.

(2) The staff of the Secretariat shall be appointed by the General Secretary, in accordance with rules laid down by the General Conference.

(3) In addition to the functions conferred upon him by this Treaty and to those which may be assigned to him by the General Conference, – the General Secretary shall ensure, as provided by article 10, paragraph 5, the proper operation of the control system established by this Treaty, in accordance with the provisions of the Treaty and the decisions taken by the General Conference.

(4) The General Secretary shall act in that capacity in all meetings of the General Conference and of the Council and shall make an annual report to both bodies on the work of the Agency and any special reports requested by the General Conference or the Council or which the General Secretary may deem desirable.

(5) The General Secretary shall establish the procedures for distributing to all Contracting Parties information received by the Agency from governmental sources and such information from non-governmental sources as may be of interest to the Agency.

(6) In the performance of their duties the General Secretary and the staff shall not seek or receive instructions from any Government or from any other authority external to the Agency and shall refrain from any action which might reflect on their position as international officials responsible only to the Agency; subject to their responsibility to the Agency, they shall not disclose any industrial secrets or other confidential information coming to their knowledge by reason of their official duties in the Agency.

(7) Each of the Contracting Parties undertakes to respect the exclusively international character of the responsibilities of the General Secretary and the staff and not to seek to influence them in the discharge of their responsibilities.

Control system.

Art. 12.(1) For the purpose of verifying compliance with the obligations entered into by the Contracting Parties in accordance with article 1, a control system shall be established which shall be put into effect in accordance with the provisions of articles 13–18 of this Treaty.

(2) The control system shall be used in particular for the purpose of verifying:

(a) That devices, services and facilities intended for peaceful uses of nuclear energy are not used in the testing or manufacture of nuclear weapons;

(b) That none of the activities prohibited in article 1 of this Treaty are carried out in the territory of the Contracting Parties with nuclear materials or weapons introduced from abroad, and

(c) That explosions for peaceful purposes are compatible with article 18 of this Treaty.

IAEA safeguards.

Art. 13. Each Contracting Party shall negotiate multilateral or bilateral agreements with the International Atomic Energy Agency for the application of its safeguards to its nuclear activities. Each Contracting Party shall initiate negotiations within a period of 180 days after the date of the deposit of its instrument of ratification of this Treaty. These agreements shall enter into force, for each Party, not later than eighteen months after the date of the initiation of such negotiations except in case of unforeseen circumstances or force majeure.

Reports of the Parties.

Art. 14.(1) The Contracting Parties shall submit to the Agency and to the International Atomic Energy Agency, for their information, semi-annual reports stating that no activity prohibited under this Treaty has occurred in their respective territories.

(2) The Contracting Parties shall simultaneously transmit to the Agency a copy of any report they may submit to the International Atomic Energy Agency which relates to matters that are the subject of this Treaty and to the application of safeguards.

(3) The Contracting Parties shall also transmit to the Organization of American States, for its information, any reports that may be of interest to it, in accordance with the obligations established by the Inter-American System.

Special reports requested by the General Secretary.

Art. 15.(1) With the authorization of the Council, the General Secretary may request any of the Contracting Parties to provide the Agency with complementary or supplementary information regarding any event or circumstance connected with compliance with this Treaty, explaining his reasons. The Contracting Parties under-

take to co-operate promptly and fully with the General Secretary.

(2) The General Secretary shall inform the Council and the Contracting Parties forthwith of such requests and of the respective replies.

Special inspections.

Art. 16.(1) The International Atomic Energy Agency and the Council established by this Treaty have the power of carrying out special inspections in the following cases:

(a) In the case of the International Atomic Energy Agency, in accordance with the agreements referred to in article 13 of this Treaty;

(b) In the case of the Council:

(i) When so requested, the reasons for the request being stated, by any Party which suspects that some activity prohibited by this Treaty has been carried out or is about to be carried out, either in the territory of any other Party or in any other place on such latter Party's behalf, the Council shall immediately arrange for such an inspection in accordance with article 10, paragraph 5;

(ii) When requested by any Party which has been suspected of or charged with having violated this Treaty, the Council shall immediately arrange for the special inspection requested in accordance with article 10, paragraph 5.

The above requests will be made to the Council through the General Secretary.

(2) The costs and expenses of any special inspection carried out under paragraph 1, sub-paragraph (b), sections (i) and (ii) of this article shall be borne by the requesting Party or Parties, except where the Council concludes on the basis of the report on the special inspection that, in view of the circumstances existing in the case, such costs and expenses should be borne by the Agency.

(3) The General Conference shall formulate the procedures for the organization and execution of the special inspections carried out in accordance with paragraph 1, sub-paragraph (b), sections (i) and (ii) of this article.

(4) The Contracting Parties undertake to grant the inspectors carrying out such special inspections full and free access to all places and all information which may be necessary for the performance of their duties and which are directly and intimately connected with the suspicion of violation of this Treaty. If so requested by the authorities of the Contracting Party in whose territory the inspection is carried out, the inspectors designated by the General Conference shall be accompanied by representatives of said authorities, provided that this does not in any way delay or hinder the work of the inspectors.

(5) The Council shall immediately transmit to all the Parties, through the General Secretary, a copy of any report resulting from special inspections.

(6) Similarly, the Council shall send through the General Secretary to the Secretary-General of the United Nations, for transmission to the United Nations Security Council and General Assembly, and to the Council of the Organization of American States, for its information, a copy of any report resulting from any special inspection carried out in accordance with paragraph 1, sub-paragraph (b), sections (i) and (ii) of this article.

(7) The Council may decide, or any Contracting Party may request, the convening of a special session of the General Conference for the purpose of considering the reports resulting from any special inspection. In such a case, the General Secretary shall take immediate steps to convene the special session requested.

(8) The General Conference, convened in special session under this article, may make recommendations to the Contracting Parties and submit reports to the Secretary-General of the United Nations to be transmitted to the United Nations Security Council and the General Assembly.

Use of nuclear energy for peaceful purposes.

Art. 17. Nothing in the provisions of this Treaty shall prejudice the rights of the Contracting Parties, in conformity with this Treaty, to use nuclear energy for peaceful purposes, in particular for their economic development and social progress.

Explosions for peaceful purposes.

Art. 18.(1) The Contracting Parties may carry out explosions of nuclear devices for peaceful purposes – including explosions which involve devices similar to those used in nuclear weapons – or collaborate with third parties for the same purpose, provided that they do so in accordance with the provisions of this article and the other articles of the Treaty, particularly articles 1 and 5.

(2) Contracting Parties intending to carry out, or to co-operate in carrying out, such an explosion shall notify the Agency and the International Atomic Energy Agency, as far in advance as the circumstances require, of the date of the explosion and shall at the same time provide the following information:

(a) The nature of the nuclear device and the source from which it was obtained;

(b) The place and purpose of the planned explosion;

(c) The procedures which will be followed in order to comply with paragraph 3 of this article;

(d) The expected force of the device, and

(e) The fullest possible information on any possible radioactive fall-out that may result from the explosion or explosions, and measures which will be taken to avoid danger to the population, flora, fauna and territories of any other Party or Parties.

(3) The General Secretary and the technical personnel designated by the Council and the International Atomic Energy Agency may observe all the preparations, including the explosion of the device, and shall have unrestricted access to any area in the vicinity of the site of the explosion in order to ascertain whether the device and the procedures followed during the explosion are in conformity with the information supplied under paragraph 2 of this article and the other provisions of this Treaty.

(4) The Contracting Parties may accept the collaboration of third parties for the purpose set forth in paragraph 1 of the present article, in accordance with paragraphs 2 and 3 thereof.

Relations with other international organizations.

Art. 19.(1) The Agency may conclude such agreements with the International Atomic Energy Agency as are authorized by the General Conference and as it considers likely to facilitate the efficient operation of the control system established by this Treaty.

(2) The Agency may also enter into relations with any international organization or body, especially any which may be established in the future to supervise disarmament or measures for the control of armaments in any part of the world.

(3) The Contracting Parties may, if they see fit, request the advice of the Inter-American Nuclear Energy Commission on all technical matters connected with the application of this Treaty with which the Commission is competent to deal under its Statute.

Measures in the event of violation of the Treaty.

Art. 20.(1) The General Conference shall take note of all cases in which, in its opinion, any Contracting Party is not complying fully with its obligations under this Treaty and shall draw the matter to the attention of the Party concerned, making such recommendations as it deems appropriate.

(2) If, in its opinion, such non-compliance constitutes a violation of this Treaty which might endanger peace and security, the General Conference shall report thereon simultaneously to the United Nations Security Council and the General Assembly through the Secretary-General of the United Nations, and to the Council of the Organization of American States. The General Conference shall likewise report to the International Atomic Energy Agency for such purposes as are relevant in accordance with its Statute.

United Nations and Organization of American States.

Art. 21. None of the provisions of this Treaty shall be construed as impairing the rights and obligations of the Parties under the Charter of the United Nations or, in the case of States Members of the Organization of American States, under existing regional treaties.

Privileges and immunities.

Art. 22.(1) The Agency shall enjoy in the territory of each of the Contracting Parties such legal capacity and such privileges and immunities as may be necessary for the exercise of its functions and the fulfilment of its purposes.

(2) Representatives of the Contracting Parties accredited to the Agency and officials of the Agency shall similarly enjoy such privileges and immunities as are necessary for the performance of their functions.

(3) The Agency may conclude agreements with the Contracting Parties with a view to determining the

details of the application of paragraphs 1 and 2 of this article.

Notification of other agreements.

Art. 23. Once this Treaty has entered into force, the Secretariat shall be notified immediately of any international agreement concluded by any of the Contracting Parties on matters with which this Treaty is concerned; the Secretariat shall register it and notify the other Contracting Parties.

Settlement of disputes.

Art. 24. Unless the Parties concerned agree on another mode of peaceful settlement, any question or dispute concerning the interpretation or application of this Treaty which is not settled shall be referred to the International Court of Justice with the prior consent of the Parties to the controversy.

Signature.

Art. 25.(1) This Treaty shall be open indefinitely for signature by:

(a) All the Latin American Republics, and

(b) All other sovereign States situated in their entirety south of latitude 35° north in the western hemisphere; and except as provided in paragraph 2 of this article, all such States which become sovereign, when they have been admitted by the General Conference.

(2) The General Conference shall not take any decision regarding the admission of a political entity part or all of whose territory is the subject, prior to the date when this Treaty is opened for signature, of a dispute or claim between an extra-continental country and one or more Latin American States, so long as the dispute has not been settled by peaceful means.

Ratification and deposit.

Art. 26.(1) This Treaty shall be subject to ratification by signatory States in accordance with their respective constitutional procedures.

(2) This Treaty and the instruments of ratification shall be deposited with the Government of the Mexican United States, which is hereby designated the Depositary Government.

(3) The Depositary Government shall send certified copies of this Treaty to the Governments of signatory States and shall notify them of the deposit of each instrument of ratification.

Reservations.

Art. 27. This Treaty shall not be subject to reservations.

Entry into force.

Art. 28.(1) Subject to the provisions of paragraph 2 of this article, this Treaty shall enter into force among the States that have ratified it as soon as the following requirements have been met:

(a) Deposit of the instruments of ratification of this Treaty with the Depositary Government by the Governments of the States mentioned in article 25 which are in existence on the date when this Treaty is opened for signature and which are not affected by the provisions of article 25, paragraph 2;

(b) Signature and ratification of Additional Protocol I annexed to this Treaty by all extra-continental or continental States having de jure or de facto international responsibility for territories situated in the zone of application of the Treaty;

(c) Signature and ratification of the Additional Protocol II annexed to this Treaty by all powers possessing nuclear weapons;

(d) Conclusion of bilateral or multilateral agreements on the application of the Safeguards System of the International Atomic Energy Agency in accordance with article 13 of this Treaty.

(2) All signatory States shall have the imprescriptible right to waive, wholly or in part, the requirements laid down in the preceding paragraph. They may do so by means of a declaration which shall be annexed to their respective instrument of ratification and which may be formulated at the time of deposit of the instrument or subsequently. For those States which exercise this right, this Treaty shall enter into force upon deposit of the declaration, or as soon as those requirements have been met which have not been expressly waived.

(3) As soon as this Treaty has entered into force in accordance with the provisions of paragraph 2 for eleven States, the Depositary Government shall convene a preliminary meeting of those States in order that the Agency may be set up and commence its work.

(4) After the entry into force of this Treaty for all the countries of the zone, the rise of a new power possessing nuclear weapons shall have the effect of suspending the execution of this Treaty for those countries which have

ratified it without waiving requirements of paragraph 1, sub-paragraph (c) of this article, and which request such suspension; the Treaty shall remain suspended until the new power, on its own initiative or upon request by the General Conference, ratifies the annexed Additional Protocol II.

Amendments

Art. 29.(1) Any Contracting Party may propose amendments to this Treaty and shall submit its proposals to the Council through the General Secretary, who shall transmit them to all the other Contracting Parties and, in addition, to all other signatories in accordance with article 6. The Council, through the General Secretary, shall immediately following the meeting of signatories convene a special session of the General Conference to examine the proposals made, for the adoption of which a two-thirds majority of the Contracting Parties present and voting shall be required.

(2) Amendments adopted shall enter into force as soon as the requirements set forth in article 28 of this Treaty have been complied with.

Duration and denunciation.

Art. 30.(1) This Treaty shall be of a permanent nature and shall remain in force indefinitely, but any Party may denounce it by notifying the General Secretary of the Agency if, in the opinion of the denouncing State, there have arisen or may arise circumstances connected with the content of this Treaty or of the annexed Additional Protocols I and II which affect its supreme interests or the peace and security of one or more Contracting Parties.

(2) The denunciation shall take effect three months after the delivery to the General Secretary of the Agency of the notification by the Government of the signatory State concerned. The General Secretary shall immediately communicate such notification to the other Contracting Parties and to the Secretary-General of the United Nations for the information of the United Nations Security Council and the General Assembly. He shall also communicate it to the Secretary-General of the Organization of American States.

Authentic texts and registration.

Art. 31. This Treaty, of which the Spanish, Chinese, English, French, Portuguese and Russian texts are equally authentic, shall be registered by the Depositary Government in accordance with article 102 of the United Nations Charter. The Depositary Government shall notify the Secretary-General of the United Nations of the signatures, ratifications and amendments relating to this Treaty and shall communicate them to the Secretary-General of the Organization of American States for its information.

Transitional Article.

Denunciation of the declaration referred to in article 28, paragraph 2, shall be subject to the same procedures as the denunciation of this Treaty, except that it will take effect on the date of delivery of the respective notification."

Additional Protocol I:

"The undersigned Plenipotentiaries, furnished with full powers by their respective Governments,

Convinced that the Treaty for the Prohibition of Nuclear Weapons in Latin America, negotiated and signed in accordance with the recommendations of the General Assembly of the United Nations in Resolution 1911 (XVIII) of 27 November 1963, represents an important step towards ensuring the non-proliferation of nuclear weapons,

Aware that the non-proliferation of nuclear weapons is not an end in itself but, rather, a means of achieving general and complete disarmament at a later stage, and

Desiring to contribute, so far as lies in their power, towards ending the armaments race, especially in the field of nuclear weapons, and towards strengthening a world at peace, based on mutual respect and sovereign equality of States,

Have agreed as follows:

Art. 1. To undertake to apply the statute of denuclearization in respect of warlike purposes as defined in articles 1, 3, 5 and 13 of the Treaty for the Prohibition of Nuclear Weapons in Latin America in territories for which, de jure or de facto, they are internationally responsible and which lie within the limits of the geographical zone established in that Treaty.

Art. 2. The duration of this Protocol shall be the same as that of the Treaty for the Prohibition of Nuclear

Weapons in Latin America of which this Protocol is an annex, and the provisions regarding ratification and denunciation contained in the Treaty shall be applicable to it.

Art. 3. This Protocol shall enter into force, for the States which have ratified it, on the date of the deposit of their respective instruments of ratification."

Additional Protocol II:

"The undersigned Plenipotentiaries, furnished with full powers by their respective Governments,

Convinced that the Treaty for the Prohibition of Nuclear Weapons in Latin America, negotiated and signed in accordance with the recommendations of the General Assembly of the United Nations in Resolution 1911 (XVIII) of 27 November 1963, represents an important step towards ensuring the non-proliferation of nuclear weapons,

Aware that the non-proliferation of nuclear weapons is not an end in itself but, rather, a means of achieving general and complete disarmament at a later stage, and Desiring to contribute, so far as lies in their power, towards ending the armaments race, especially in the field of nuclear weapons, and towards promoting and strengthening a world at peace, based on mutual respect and sovereign equality of States,

Have agreed as follows:

Art. 1. The statute of denuclearization of Latin America in respect of warlike purposes, as defined, delimited and set forth in the Treaty for the Prohibition of Nuclear Weapons in Latin America of which this instrument is an annex, shall be fully respected by the Parties to this Protocol in all its express aims and provisions.

Art. 2. The Governments represented by the undersigned Plenipotentiaries undertake, therefore, not to contribute in any way to the performance of acts involving a violation of the obligations of article 1 of the Treaty in the territories to which the Treaty applies in accordance with article 4 thereof.

Art. 3. The Governments represented by the undersigned Plenipotentiaries also undertake not to use or threaten to use nuclear weapons against the Contracting Parties of the Treaty for the Prohibition of Nuclear Weapons in Latin America.

Art. 4. The duration of this Protocol shall be the same as that of the Treaty for the Prohibition of Nuclear Weapons in Latin America of which this Protocol is an annex, and the definitions of territory and nuclear weapons set forth in articles 3 and 5 of the Treaty shall be applicable to this Protocol, as well as the provisions regarding ratification, reservations, denunciation, authentic texts and registration contained in articles 26, 27, 30 and 31 of the Treaty.

Art. 5. This Protocol shall enter into force, for the States which have ratified it, on the date of the deposit of their respective instruments of ratification.

In Witness whereof, the undersigned Plenipotentiaries, having deposited their full powers, found to be in good and due form, hereby sign this Additional Protocol on behalf of their respective Governments."

The Protocol I was signed by UK on Dec. 20, 1967; by Netherlands on Mar. 15, 1968.

The Protocol II was signed by UK on Dec. 20, 1967; by USA on Apr. 1, 1968, declaring:

"In signing Protocol II of the Treaty of Tlatelolco, the United States Government makes the following statement:

I. The United States understands that the Treaty and its Protocols have no effect upon the international status of territorial claims.

The United States takes note of the Preparatory Commission's interpretation of the Treaty, as set forth in the Final Act, that, governed by the principles and rules of international law, each of the Contracting Parties retains exclusive power and legal competence, unaffected by the terms of the Treaty, to grant or deny non-Contracting Parties transit and transport privileges.

As regards the undertaking in Article 3 of Protocol II not to use or threaten to use nuclear weapons against the Contracting Parties, the United States would have to consider that an armed attack by a Contracting Party, in which it was assisted by a nuclear-weapon State, would be incompatible with the Contracting Party's corresponding obligations under Article 1 of the Treaty.

II. The United States wishes to point out again the fact that the technology of making nuclear explosive devices

for peaceful purposes is indistinguishable from the technology of making nuclear weapons and the fact that nuclear weapons and nuclear explosive devices for peaceful purposes are both capable of releasing nuclear energy in an uncontrolled manner and have the common group of characteristics of large amounts of energy generated instantaneously from a compact source. Therefore we understand the definition contained in Article 5 of the Treaty as necessarily encompassing all nuclear explosive devices. It is our understanding that Articles 1 and 5 restrict accordingly the activities of the Contracting Parties under paragraph 1 of Article 18. The United States further notes that paragraph 4 of Article 18 of the Treaty permits, and that United States adherence to Protocol II will not prevent, collaboration by the United States with Contracting Parties for the purpose of carrying out explosions of nuclear devices for peaceful purposes in a manner consistent with our policy of not contributing to the proliferation of nuclear weapons capabilities. In this connection, the United States reaffirms its willingness to make available nuclear explosion services for peaceful purposes on a non-discriminatory basis under appropriate international arrangements and to join other nuclear-weapon States in a commitment to do so.

III. The United States also wishes to state that, although not required by Protocol II, it will act with respect to such territories of Protocol I adherents as are within the geographical area defined in paragraph 2 of Article 4 of the Treaty in the same manner as Protocol II requires to act with respect to the territories of Contracting Parties." The Treaty was ratified until Jan. 1, 1987 by 23 countries, the Additional Protocol I by 3, and Additional Protocol II by 5.

UNTS, Vol. 634, pp. 326–356, 362–366 and 419–421; J. MARTINEZ COBO, "The Tlatelolco Treaty: An update," in: *IAEA Bulletin,* no. 3, 1984, pp. 25–30; SIPRI *Yearbook 1987,* Oxford, 1988.

TLATELOLCO TREATY, THE GREAT POWERS AND THE UN. The first regional treaty on the creation of an atom free zone, named officially Tlatelolco Treaty was signed on Feb. 14, 1967, by Bolivia, Chile, Colombia, Costa Rica, Ecuador, Guatemala, Haiti, Mexico, Nicaragua, Panama, Salvador, Uruguay and Venezuela. The treaty was later signed by Argentina – Sept. 27, 1967; Brazil – May 9, 1967; the Dominican Republic – July 28, 1967; Honduras – Mar. 14, 1967; Jamaica – Oct. 27, 1967; and Barbados – Oct. 18, 1968. The Netherlands with her territories in the Western Hemisphere signed the additional Protocol I on Mar. 15, 1968; ratified on July 20, 1971. The first states to ratify the Tlatelolco Treaty were: Mexico on Sept. 20, 1967; Brazil (with important reservations) on Jan. 29, 1968; Salvador Apr. 22, 1968; the Dominican Republic on June 14, 1968 and Uruguay on Aug. 20, 1968. Up to Jan. 1, 1980 the following had ratified it without reservations: Barbados, Bolivia, Costa Rica, Ecuador, Guatemala, Haiti, Honduras, Jamaica, Nicaragua, Panama, Paraguay and Venezuela. The only Latin American country which refused to sign the Treaty was Cuba in protest against the maintenance by the USA of bases with nuclear weapons in the Caribbean region: in Guantanamo, Puerto Rico and on the American Virgin Islands. The UN General Assembly Res. 2286/XXII of Dec. 5, 1967 approved the Treaty by 82 votes in favor, none against and 27 abstentions in solidarity with Cuba (Algeria, Botswana, Bulgaria, Burundi, Byelorussian SSR, Cameroon, Cuba, Czechoslovakia, France, Ghana, Guyana, Kenya, Lesotho, Liberia, Mali, Mauritania, Mongolia, Poland, Syria, Taiwan, Togo, Uganda, Ukrainian SSR, Upper Volta, the USSR, Yemen and Zambia). The resolution obligates states to "universal respect" for the Tlatelolco Treaty and called on the nuclear Powers to sign and ratify Supplementary Protocols as quickly as possible, which guarantees their respect for the non-nuclear zone. The UK was the first to sign Protocols I and II on Dec. 20, 1967; ratification followed on Dec. 11, 1969. The USA

signed Protocol II on Apr. 1, 1968, but with very important reservations: (1) that the Tlatelolco Treaty does not prohibit the USA from transporting atomic weapons by air or sea through the non-nuclear zone; (2) the Latin American signatory states to the Treaty can receive services permitting atomic explosions for peaceful purposes; (3) the USA guarantees that it will not use or threaten to use nuclear weapons against any of the signatory states to the Treaty, but this guarantee loses force should any of the states with the help of another nuclear power launch an armed attack on the USA. The USA ratified Protocol II on May 12, 1971 and signed Protocol I on May 26, 1977, announcing that this obligates the United States not to make atomic experiments, not to use nuclear weapons and also not to stockpile them in the region of Latin America, for which the USA bears responsibility. However, this will not concern the right of US naval vessels to put in at ports in these territories and to freedom of navigation on the open seas around Latin America. The USA ratified the Protocol I on Nov. 23, 1981. France signed Protocol II on July 18, 1976, and ratified on March 22, 1974; and the Protocol I on March 2, 1979, not ratified until 1985. The People's Republic of China signed the Protocol II on Aug. 21, 1973 and ratified on June 12, 1974. The USSR signed Protocol II on Apr. 28, 1978.

The institution of the Treaty, with headquarters in Mexico City is the OPANAL, Organismo para la Proscripcion de las Armas Nucleares en la America Latin, Organization for the Prohibition of Nuclear Weapons in Latin America, est. Sept. 2, 1969. Members: states which ratified the Treaty. OPANAL is in permanent contact with IAEA and OAS. Each year it organizes General Conferences in Mexico. Publ.: *OPANAL Documents.* The architect of the Treaty, the Mexican diplomat Alfonso Garcia Robles was honored with the Nobel Peace Prize in 1982.

A. GARCIA ROBLES, *El Tratado de Tlatelolco, Génesis, Alcance y Propositos de la Proscripción de las Armas Nucleares in América Latina,* México, DF, 1967; *UN Monthly Chronicle,* January, 1968, pp. 27–28; A. GARCIA ROBLES, "Mesures de désarmement dans les zones particulieres du Traité visant l'interdiction des armes nucleaires en Amérique Latine," in: *Recueil des Cours,* Vol. I, 1971, pp. 45–134; H. GROS ESPIELL, "The Non-Proliferation of Nuclear Weapons in Latin America," in: *IAEA Bulletin,* August, 1980. pp. 81–86; J.R. MARTINEZ COBO, "The Tlatelolco Treaty: An Update", in: *IAEA Bulletin,* September, 1984, pp. 26–30.

TNF ▷ Intermediate Nuclear Force.

TOBACCO. A subject of international agreement (▷ Smoking of Tobacco.) Organizations reg. with the UIA:

Afro–Asian Federation for Tobacco-Producers and Manufacturers, f. 1971, Cairo.
Co-operation Centre for Scientific Research Relative to Tobacco, f. 1956, Paris. Liaison status with FAO. Publ.: *Information Bulletin* (quarterly).
European Federation of Tobacco Retail Organizations, f. 1963, Hamburg, FRG.
Tobacco Specialist Group in the EEC, f. 1961, Brussels.
Tobacco Workers International Union, f. 1895, Washington, DC.

A World WHO campaign against ▷ Smoking of Tobacco, was started in the 1970's.

According to the 1986 WHO report, about 90% of all cases of lung cancer are caused by cigarette smoking. The habit is spreading in developing countries, because of intensive campaigns by the transnational tobacco companies, the report states.

W.F. FORBES, M.E. THOMPSON, "The Economies of Tobacco," in: *World Health,* February–March., 1980; *Yearbook of International Organizations; UN*

Chronicle, 1986, No. 3, p. 89; L.C. WHITE, Merchants of Death, The American Tobacco Industry, New York, 1988.

TOBAR DOCTRINE, 1907. The counter-revolutionary principle formulated by the Minister of Foreign Affairs of Ecuador, C.R. Tobar: "Each American state should refuse recognition to governments which have emerged from revolution."
This doctrine was behind two Central American Treaties 1907 and 1923, signed and ratified by Costa Rica, El Salvador, Guatemala, Honduras, Nicaragua, but denounced by Costa Rica and El Salvador on Dec. 23 and 26, 1935 and by Honduras on Mar. 26, 1953.

American Journal of International Law, No. 7, 1923; *Conference on Central American Affairs,* Washington, DC, 1923; Ch. G. FENWICK, *International Law,* New York, 1952.

TOGO. Member of the UN. Republic of Togo. West African state on the Gulf of Guinea, bordered by Ghana, Upper Volta and Benin. Area: 56,785 sq. km. Pop. 1988 est.: 3,250,000 (1970 census: 1,997,109). Capital: Lomé with 247,000 inhabitants, 1979. GNP per capita 1986: US $250. Official language: French. Currency: one franc CFA = 100 centimes. National Day: Apr. 28, Independence Day, 1960.
Member of the UN since Sept. 18, 1960 and of UN specialized agencies with the exception of IAEA. Member of OAU, Conseil d'entente and is an ACP state of the EEC.
International relations: a German protectorate from 1894 to 1914; a mandate of the League of Nations from 1922 to 1945 divided between France and Great Britain; a trusteeship territory of the United Nations administered by France from Dec. 14, 1946 to Apr. 26, 1960. Autonomous republic within the French Union in 1956; achieved full independence on Apr. 28, 1960. The British part was integrated by Ghana. A signatory of the Yaoundé Conventions of 1963 and 1969, and of the Lomé Conventions of 1975, 1980 and 1985. Involved in border disputes with ▷ Ghana.

UNTS, Vol. 8, pp. 152–163; J.S. COLEMAN, "Togoland," in: *International Conciliation,* September., 1956, pp. 3–85; R. CORNEVIN, *Histoire du Togo,* Paris, 1959; C. FENILLET, *Le Togo en général,* Paris, 1976; M. PIRAUS, *Le Togo aujourd'hui,* Paris, 1977; *The Europa Year Book 1984. A World Survey,* Vol. II, pp. 2506–2514, London, 1984; Ghana–Togo, in: A.J. DAY ed., *Border and Territorial Disputes,* London, 1987, p. 138–144.

TOK DO. ▷ Takeshima.

TOKELAU. An island group situated 480 km to the north of Western Samoa; area: 1,210 ha with 1572 inhabitants, 1981; formerly part of the British Gilbert and Ellice Islands Colony, from Feb. 11, 1926 under New Zealand jurisdiction, integrated within the territorial boundaries of the Tokelau Islands Act 1948.
The UN Special Committee on the situation with regard to the Implementation of the Declaration on the Granting of Independence to Colonial Countries and People, on Aug. 12, 1983, reaffirmed the right of the Tokelau people to independence and stated that it was the responsibility of New Zealand, the administrating Power, to keep the people fully informed of that right. The Special Committee noted that the Territory's people had said that at present they did not wish to alter the nature of the existing relationship between Tokelau and New Zealand.

The Europa Year Book 1984. A World Survey, Vol. II, p. 2140, London, 1984. *UN Chronicle,* January, 1984, p. 61.

TOKYO. The capital of Japan at the head of Tokyo Bay. The seaport is Yokohama. Headquarters of c. 30 international organizations reg. with the UIA.

Yearbook of International Organizations.

TOKYO MILITARY TRIAL, 1946–48. After the start of ▷ Nuremberg War Criminals Trial, 1945–1946, which dealt with major German war criminals, the International Military Tribunal for the Far East was established on Jan. 19, 1946 in Tokyo to try Japanese war criminals. The trial started on May 3, 1946 and lasted until Nov. 4, 1948. The procedure of the trial was different to the one applied in Nuremberg: the judges (there were 11 of them) and the Chief Justice of the Tribunal, the Australian, Sir William Webb, as well as the main prosecutor and his ten attorneys were appointed by the American supreme commander in the Far East, General MacArthur. On Nov. 4, 1948 the Tribunal rendered its verdict sentencing 25 of the defendants, including 7 to capital punishment (6 former army-generals: Hidoki Tojo, Konoi Doihara, Ivano Matsui, Seishoro Itagaki, Atiro Muto, Haitaro Kimura; and the Minister of Foreign Affairs, Koki Hirota); 16 other defendants were given life sentences, including, inter alia, Counsellor to the Emperor, Koichi Kido, signatory of the act of capitulation of Japan, General Joshiro Umezo, the commander of the attack on Pearl Harbor, General Shigentaro Shimada, General Kuntaki Koiso, Minister of War, Sado Araki, Ambassador in Germany, Hiroshi Oshima; a term of 20 years' imprisonment was given to Shigenoro Togo and 7 years imprisonment to Namure Shihemitsu, both high representatives of the Foreign Office. French judge H. Bernard and Dutch judge B.V.A. Rolling placed *votum separatum* with regard to some of the basic points of the prosecution, stating that before World War II aggression was not considered a crime in the understanding of international law. *Votum separatum* was also placed by Indian judge Binod Pal against the thesis of the existence of a conspiracy, claiming that if the anti-communist intervention of the USA in China was not considered a crime, then equally Japan could not be punished for waging war against communism in China; similar position was manifested by the Dutch judge and a judge from Philippines. Due to opposition on the part of the USA, the highest commander of the Japanese armed forces, Emperor Hirohito, did not stand trial. However, Justice Sir William Webb in his sentencing statement said that: "The emperor perhaps did not want war, but he approved of it and everything else depended on it. He misused his duties, even if it were true that in case of his refusal he was to be murdered. A ruler has to risk his life if he is willing to save his people and country from a war. Thus, the Emperor has to be recognized as the most guilty of the crime."
The death sentences were executed on 7 defendants on Dec. 22, 1948; as regards the other defendants, they were included in an amnesty announced on the same day by General MacArthur. The Japanese press, during the whole period of the trial, did not once use the words "war criminals" and after the execution of the sentences, it called the executed "victims on the altar of peace." (The Library of Congress, Washington, DC, has mimeographic copies of the trial's shorthand notes.)
▷ Military Tribunal International for Far East, 1946–48.

Trial of Japanese War Criminals, Washington, DC, 1948; S. HOREWITZ, "The Tokyo Trial," in: *International Conciliation,* No. 465, 1950; *The Tokyo Trials: A Functional Index to the Proceedings of the IMT for the Far East,* Ann Arbor, 1957; H. MINEAR, *Victory Justice. The Tokyo War Crimes Trial,* London, 1971.

TOKYO ROUND. The multilateral negotiations on further trade liberalization within GATT, after the ▷ Kennedy Round; initially named in 1973–74 Nixon Round, after his resignation (Aug. 9, 1974), named Tokyo Round after the place of negotiations. Negotiations delayed due to the passing by USA Congress of the US Trade Act 1974, and by the energy crisis, resumed in 1975, ended in 1979. The agreements signed in Tokyo on Dec. 13, 1979 came into force Jan. 1, 1980.

W.R. CLINE, *Trade Negotiations in the Tokyo Round,* Washington, DC, 1978; *The Tokyo Round of Multilateral Trade Negotiations, GATT,* Geneva, 1980: R. BALASSA, "The Tokyo Round and the Developing Countries," in: *Journal of World Trade Laws,* No. 2, 1980; G.R. WINHAM, *International Trade and the Tokyo Round Negotiation,* Princeton, 1987.

TOKYO SUMMIT 1986. The summit meeting of the major industrialized countries (Canada, France, FRG, Italy, Japan, the UK and the USA) was held in Tokyo on May 4–6, 1986.
The political declaration ended as follows:
"We proclaim our conviction that ... our countries cannot enjoy lasting stability and prosperity without stability and prosperity in the developing world and without the co-operation among us that can achieve these aims. We pledge ourselves afresh to fight against hunger, disease and poverty ...
We owe it to future generations to pass on a healthy environment and a culture rich in both spiritual and material values. We are resolved to pursue effective international action to eliminate the abuse of drugs. We proclaim our commitment to work together for a world which respects human beings in the diversity of their talents, beliefs, cultures and tradition. In such a world based upon peace, freedom and democracy, the ideals of social justice can be realised and employment opportunities can be available for all.
We must harness wisely the potential for science and technology and enhance the benefits through co-operation and exchange. We have a solemn responsibility to so educate the next generation as to endow them with the creativity befitting the 21st century and to convey to them the value of living in freedom and dignity."

KEESING's *Contemporary Archive,* 1986.

TOLA. The Indian unit of weight for gold and other precious metals = 0.375 troy ounces.

TOMAHAWK. An American system of missiles with nuclear warheads destinated for battle ships.

JANE'S *Yearbook 1984,* London, 1984.

TON. A metric tonne of 1000 kilograms. In Anglo-Saxon countries one ton = 2240 pounds or 907 kilograms.

TONGA, FRIENDLY ISLANDS. A member of the Commonwealth. The Kingdom of Tonga. Islands in the South Pacific near Fiji and Western Samoa. A total area of some 169 islands and islets: 748 sq.km. Pop. 1988 est. 95,200 inhabitants. Capital: Nuku'alofa on Tongapatu Island with 20,564 inhabitants 1983. Currency: pa'anga = 100 seniti. GNP per capita 1987: US $580. Official language: Tonga and English. National Day: June 4, Emancipation Day, 1970.
Tonga is not a member of the UN but is a member of its specialized agencies with the exception of: ILO, IAEA, GATT, WMO, IMO and WIPO. Member of the Commonwealth and is an ACP state of the EEC.
International relations: the last 18th-century kingdom in the South Pacific; in friendly co-operation with Great Britain in the 19th century; under British protectorate since May 18, 1900 by a Treaty of Friendship and Protection until June 4, 1970, the day of restoration of independence. A signatory of the Lomé Conventions of 1975 and 1980. In March

1982 cyclone Isaac caused extensive damage. Since June 30, 1986 member of the World Bank. Since 1986 member of the IMF.

A.H. WOOD, *A History of Geography of Tonga*, Nuku'alofa, 1963; K.R. BAIN, *The Friendly Islanders*, London, 1967; *The Europa Year Book 1984. A World Survey*, Vol. II, pp. 2515–2517, London, 1984.

TONKIN, GULF OF. The northwest arm of the South China Sea, 480 km long and 240 km wide, between North Vietnam and China. In 1964 the place of the alleged Vietnamese attack on two American destroyers, which became the justification for a decision by the US Congress permitting the US President to commence the bombardment of the Gulf of Tonkin on Nov. 18, 1964, while simultaneously imposing a long sea blockade of the Democratic Republic of Vietnam. In 1974 it was revealed in the US Congress that the story of the Vietnamese attack in the Gulf of Tonkin was untrue.

KEESING's *Contemporary Archive*, 1964.

TOPONOMY. The science on place names, part of cartography, a subject of the UN conferences on the standardization of geographical names, held in Geneva 1967, London 1972, Athens 1977, Geneva 1983, and Montreal 1987. The aim of the Toponomy Conferences is to accelerate national standardization of geographical names in order to achieve international standardization on maps and in a variety of textual material. A UN Group of Experts on Geographical Names, UNGEGN, since 1960 meets every two years, develops programs designed to help countries resolve the technical and linguistic problems of standardization and publishes *Toponymic Guidelines for Cartography*.

UN Chronicle, November, 1982, pp. 74–75.

TORDESILLAS TREATY, 1494. The Treaty on the division of the New World, concluded June 7, 1494 at the castle Tordesillas in the Spanish province of Valladolid between Ferdinand of Aragon and Isabella of Castille in the name of Spain and John II, King of Portugal, based on a decision of Pope Alexander VI, expressed in the Bull of May 4, 1494, *Inter caetera divinae*, dividing the just discovered Western Hemisphere "100 miles to the Azores along the line of the North Pole–South Pole" so that everything to the east of this line was to belong to Portugal, and everything to the west, to Spain; the Treaty shifted the line 370 miles to the west of Azores, and the Pope in his edict of Sept. 26, 1493, *Dudum siquidem*, approved this change; reconfirmed June 24, 1506. This division determined that the Amazon Valley, or the eastern region of South America, became a Portugese possession, while the western Andean America–Spanish. In the 18th century Spain on the basis of the Tordesillas Treaty carried on a territorial dispute with Portugal concerning part of Paraguay, Peru and Guiana, which were granted to her, but she had to renounce claims to the mouth of the La Plata by the Treaties of Madrid of Jan. 13, 1750 and San Ildefonso of Oct. 1, 1777.

Bullarum Magnum Romanum, Vol. 5, Turin, 1857; G.F. DE MARTENS; *Supplément en Recueil*, Vol. 1. Göttingen, 1891.

TORGAU. A town on the Elbe in the German Democratic Republic, historic site of the meeting, Apr. 25, 1945, between Soviet soldiers of the First Ukrainian Front and US troops of the 12th Army Group. Since 1965, at the initiative of an American editor of the *Saturday Review*, N. Cousins, and a Soviet writer B. Polevoy, annual meetings of veterans of World War II of both armies have been held at Dartmouth College in Hanover, New Hampshire; called also Dartmouth meetings.

B. POLEVOY, "Veterani nie zabudiut," in: *Pravda*, Moscow, April 25, 1973.

TORPEDO. ▷ ASROC.

TORPEDOES SALVAGE CONVENTION, 1934. An international convention relating to the Salvage of Torpedoes, signed on June 12, 1934 in Paris, by the governments of Belgium, France, Great Britain, Ireland, Italy, Netherlands, Portugal and Spain.

LNTS, Vol. 155, p. 367.

TORTURE AND INHUMAN OR DEGRADING TREATMENT OR PUNISHMENT, EUROPEAN CONVENTION FOR THE PREVENTION OF, 1987. Signed at Strasbourg on Nov. 26, 1987 by the Member States of the European Community. The text is as as follows:

"The member States of the Council of Europe, signatory hereto, having regard to the provisions of the Convention for the Protection of Human Rights and Fundamental Freedoms, recalling that, under Article 3 of the same Convention, 'no one shall be subjected to torture or to inhuman or degrading treatment or punishment'.
Noting that the machinery provided for in that Convention operates in relation to persons who allege that they are victims of violations of Article 3.
Convinced that the protection of persons deprived of their liberty against torture and inhuman or degrading treatment or punishment could be strengthened by non-judicial means of a preventive character based on visits, have agreed as follows:

CHAPTER I
Art. 1. There shall be established a European Committee for the Prevention of Torture and Inhuman or Degrading Treatment or Punishment (hereinafter referred to as 'the Committee'). The Committee shall, by means of visits, examine the treatment of persons deprived of their liberty with a view to strengthening, if necessary, the protection of such persons from torture and from inhuman or degrading treatment or punishment.
Art. 2. Each Party shall permit visits, in accordance with this Convention, to any place within its jurisdiction where persons are deprived of their liberty by a public authority.
Art. 3. In the application of this Convention, the Committee and the competent national authorities of the Party concerned shall co-operate with each other.
CHAPTER II
Art. 4.(1) The Committee shall consist of a number of members equal to that of the Parties.
(2) The members of the Committee shall be chosen from among persons of high moral character, known for their competence in the field of human rights or having professional experience in the areas covered by this Convention.
(3) No two members of the Committee may be nationals of the same State.
(4) The members shall serve in their individual capacity, shall be independent and impartial, and shall be available to serve the Committee effectively.
Art. 5.(1) The members of the Committee shall be elected by the Committee of Ministers of the Council of Europe by an absolute majority of votes, from a list of names drawn up by the Bureau of the Consultative Assembly of the Council of Europe; each national delegation of the Parties in the Consultative Assembly shall put forward three candidates, of whom two at least shall be its nationals.
(2) The same procedure shall be followed in filling casual vacancies.
(3) The members of the Committee shall be elected for a period of four years. They may only be re-elected once. However, among the members elected at the first election, the terms of three members shall expire at the end of two years. The members whose terms are to expire at the end of the initial period of two years shall be chosen by lot by the Secretary General of the Council of Europe immediately after the first election has been completed.

Art. 6(1) The Committee shall meet in camera. A quorum shall be equal to the majority of its members. The decisions of the Committee shall be taken by a majority of the members present, subject to the provisions of Article 10, paragraph 2.
(2) The Committee shall draw up its own rules of procedure.
(3) The Secretariat of the Committee shall be provided by the Secretary General of the Council of Europe.
CHAPTER III
Art. 7.(1) The Committee shall organise visits to places referred to in Art. 2. Apart from periodic visits, the Committee may organise such other visits as appear to it to be required in the circumstances.
(2) As a general rule, the visits shall be carried out by at least two members of the Committee. The Committee may, if it considers it necessary, be assisted by experts and interpreters.
Art. 8(1) The Committee shall notify the Government of the Party concerned of its intention to carry out a visit. After such notification it may at any time visit any place referred to in Article 2.
(2) A Party shall provide the Committee with the following facilities to carry out its task:
(a) access to its territory and the right to travel without restriction;
(b) full information on the places where persons deprived of their liberty are being held;
(c) unlimited access to any place where persons are deprived of their liberty, including the right to move inside such places without restriction;
(d) other information available to the Party which is necessary for the Committee to carry out its task. In seeking such information, the Committee shall have regard to applicable rules of national law and professional ethics.
(3) The Committee may interview in private persons deprived of their liberty.
(4) The Committee may communicate freely with any person whom it believes can supply relevant information.
(5) If necessary, the Committee may immediately communicate observations to the competent authorities of the Party concerned.
Art. 9.(1) In exceptional circumstances, the competent authorities of the Party concerned may make representations to the Committee against a visit at the time or to the particular place proposed by the Committee. Such representations may only be made on grounds of national defence, public safety, serious disorder in places where persons are deprived of their liberty, the medical condition of a person or that an urgent interrogation relating to a serious crime is in progress.
(2) Following such representations, the Committee and the Party shall immediately enter into consultations in order to clarify the situation and seek agreement on arrangements to enable the Committee to exercise its functions expeditiously. Such arrangements may include the transfer to another place of any person whom the Committee proposed to visit. Until the visit takes place, the Party shall provide information to the Committee about any person concerned.
Art. 10(1) After each visit, the Committee shall draw up a report on the facts found during the visit, taking account of any observations which may have been submitted by the Party concerned. It shall transmit to the latter its report containing any recommendations it considers necessary. The Committee may consult with a Party with a view to suggesting, if necessary, improvements in the protection of persons deprived of their liberty.
(2) If the Party fails to co-operate or refuses to improve the situation in the light of the Committee's recommendations, the Committee may decide, after the Party has had an opportunity to make known its views, by a majority of two-thirds of its members to make a public statement on the matter.
Art. 11.(1) The information gathered by the Committee in relation to a visit, its report and its consultations with the Party concerned shall be confidential.
(2) The Committee shall publish its report, together with any comments of the Party concerned, whenever requested to do so by that Party.
(3) However, no personal data shall be published without the express consent of the person concerned.
Art. 12. Subject to the rules of confidentiality in Article 11, the Committee shall every year submit to the Committee of Ministers a general report on its activities

which shall be transmitted to the Consultative Assembly and made public.

Art. 13. The members of the Committee, experts and other persons assisting the Committee are required, during and after their terms of office, to maintain the confidentiality of the facts or information of which they have become aware during the discharge of their functions.

Art. 14.(1) The names of persons assisting the Committee shall be specified in the notification under Article 8, paragraph 1.

(2) Experts shall act on the instructions and under the authority of the Committee. They shall have particular knowledge and experience in the areas covered by this Convention and shall be bound by the same duties of independence, impartiality and availability as the members of the Committee.

(3) A Party may exceptionally declare that an expert or other person assisting the Committee may not be allowed to take part in a visit to a place within its jurisdiction.

CHAPTER IV

Art. 15. Each Party shall inform the Committee of the name and address of the authority competent to receive notifications to its Government, and of any liaison officer it may appoint.

Art. 16. The Committee, its members and experts referred to in Article 7, paragraph 2 shall enjoy the privileges and immunities set out in the Annex to this Convention.

Art. 17.(1) This Convention shall not prejudice the provisions of domestic law or any international agreement which provide greater protection for persons deprived of their liberty.

(2) Nothing in this Convention shall be construed as limiting or derogating from the competence of the organs of the European Convention on Human Rights or from the obligations assumed by the Parties under that Convention.

(3) The Committee shall not visit places which representatives or delegates of Protecting Powers or the International Committee or the Red Cross effectively visit on a regular basis by virtue of the Geneva Conventions of August 12, 1949 and the Additional Protocols of June 8, 1977 thereto.

CHAPTER V

Art. 18. This Convention shall be open for signature by the member States of the Council of Europe. It is subject to ratification, acceptance or approval. Instruments of ratification, acceptance or approval shall be deposited with the Secretary General of the Council of Europe.

Art. 19.(1) This Convention shall enter into force on the first day of the month following the expiration of a period of three months after the date on which seven member States of the Council of Europe have expressed their consent to be bound by the Convention in accordance with the provisions of Article 18.

(2) In respect of any member State which subsequently expresses its consent to be bound by it, the Convention shall enter into force on the first day of the month following the expiration of a period of three months after the date of the deposit of the instrument of ratification, acceptance or approval.

Art. 20(1) Any State may at the time of signature or when depositing its instrument of ratification acceptance or approval, specify the territory or territories to which this Convention shall apply.

(2) Any State may at any later date, by a declaration addressed to the Secretary General of the Council of Europe, extend the application of this Convention to any other territory specified in the declaration. In respect of such territory the Convention shall enter into force on the first day of the month following the expiration of a period of three months after the date of receipt of such declaration by the Secretary General.

(3) Any declaration made under the two preceding paragaphs may, in respect of any territory specified in such declaration, be withdrawn by a notification addressed to the Secretary General. The withdrawal shall become effective on the first day of the month following the expiration of a period of three months after the date of receipt of such notification by the Secretary General.

Art. 21. No reservation may be made in respect of the provisions of this Convention.

Art. 22.(1) Any Party may, at any time, denounce this Convention by means of a notification addressed to the Secretary General of the Council of Europe.

(2) Such denunciation shall become effective on the first day of the month following the expiration of a period of twelve months after the date of receipt of the notification by the Secretary General.

Art. 23. The Secretary General of the Council of Europe shall notify the member States of the Council of Europe of:

(a) any signature;

(b) the deposit of any instrument of ratification, acceptance or approval;

(c) any date of entry into force of this Convention in accordance with Article 19 and 20;

(d) any other act, notification or communication relating to this Convention, except for action taken in pursuance of Articles 8 and 10.

In witness whereof, the undersigned, being duly authorised thereto, have signed this Convention.

Done at Strasbourg, this November 26, 1987, in English and French, both texts being equally authentic, in a single copy which shall be deposited in the archives of the Council of Europe. The Secretary General of the Council of Europe shall transmit certified copies to each member State of the Council of Europe.

Council of Europe, *Human Rights, Information Sheet No. 21*, Strasbourg, 1988, pp. 150–157 and 171–172.

TORTURE AND THE UN DECLARATION, 1975.

The method of forcing confessions by inflicting pain on the witness; subject of international conventions prohibiting the use of torture on war prisoners or the civilian population in an occupied country. The use of torture on political prisoners by dictatorial régimes became so widespread in the 1960s and 1970s in South Asia, Africa and Latin America that "the problem of tortures used in the world" was addressed in 1974 by the Interparliamentary Union and the so-called Bertrand Russell Tribunal, which labeled torture used by the régimes of Chile, Brazil, Paraguay and Uruguay a crime against humanity. The UN General Assembly Res. 3218, of Nov. 6, 1974 condemned the use of tortures. The UN General Assembly Res. 3452/XXX, of Dec. 9, 1975, passed without a vote the UN Declaration on the Protection of All Persons from Being Subjected to Torture and Other Cruel, Inhuman or Degrading Treatment or Punishment. The text is as follows:

"Art. 1.(1) For the purpose of this Declaration, torture means any act by which severe pain or suffering, whether physical or mental, is intentionally inflicted by or at the instigation of a public official on a person for such purposes as obtaining from him or a third person information or confession, punishing him for an act he has committed or is suspected of having committed, or intimidating him or other persons. It does not include pain or suffering arising only from, inherent in or incidental to lawful sanctions to the extent consistent with the Standard Minimum Rules for the Treatment of Prisoners. (2) Torture constitutes an aggravated and deliberate form of cruel, inhuman or degrading treatment or punishment.

Art. 2. Any act of torture or other cruel, inhuman or degrading treatment or punishment is an offence to human dignity and shall be condemned as a denial of the purposes of the Charter of the United Nations and as a violation of human rights and fundamental freedoms proclaimed in the Universal Declaration of Human Rights.

Art. 3. No State may permit or tolerate torture or other cruel, inhuman or degrading treatment or punishment. Exceptional circumstances such as a state of war or a threat of war, internal political instability or any other public emergency may not be invoked as a justification of torture or other cruel, inhuman or degrading treatment or punishment.

Art. 4. Each State shall, in accordance with the provisions of this Declaration, take effective measures to prevent any other cruel, inhuman or degrading treatment or punishment from being practised within its jurisdiction.

Art. 5. The training of law enforcement personnel and of other public officials who may be responsible for persons deprived of their liberty shall ensure that full account is taken of the prohibition against torture and other cruel, inhuman or degrading treatment or punishment. This prohibition shall also, where appropriate, be included in such general rules or instructions as are issued in regard to the duties and functions of anyone who may be involved in the custody or treatment of such persons.

Art. 6. Each state shall keep under systematic review interrogation methods and practices as well as arrangements for the custody and treatment of persons deprived of their liberty in its territory, with a view to preventing any cases of torture or other cruel, inhuman or degrading treatment or punishment.

Art. 7. Each State shall ensure that all acts of torture as defined in Art. 1 are offences under its criminal law. The same shall apply in regard to acts which constitute participation in, complicity in, incitement to or an attempt to commit torture.

Art. 8. Any person who alleges he has been subjected to torture or other cruel, inhuman or degrading treatment or punishment by or at the instigation of a public official shall have the right to complain to, and to have his case impartially examined by, the competent authorities of the State concerned.

Art. 9. Wherever there is reasonable ground to believe that an act of torture as defined in Art. 1 has been committed, the competent authorities of the State concerned shall promptly proceed to an impartial investigation even if there has been no formal complaint.

Art. 10. If an investigation under Art. 8 or Art. 9 establishes that an act of torture as defined in Art. 1 appears to have been committed, criminal proceedings shall be instituted against the alleged offender or offenders in accordance with national law. If an allegation of other forms of cruel, inhuman or degrading treatment or punishment is considered to be well founded, the alleged offender or offenders shall be subject to criminal, disciplinary or other appropriate proceedings.

Art. 11. Where it is proved that an act of torture or other cruel, inhuman or degrading treatment or punishment has been committed by or at the instigation of a public official, the victim shall be afforded redress and compensation, in accordance with national law.

Art. 12. Any statement which is established to have been made as a result of torture or other cruel, inhuman or degrading treatment or punishment may not be invoked as evidence against the person concerned or against any other person in any proceedings."

The Commission on Human Rights of the ECOSOC in 1978 completed a body of principles for the protection of all persons under any form of detention or imprisonment. The Committee reaffirmed that many countries still train their police in the practice of torture. The most frequently used methods are prolonged beatings, electric shocks, isolation, denial of sleep, starvation, and dehydration, sexual torture, mock examinations, pharmacological poisoning, dental pain and torture by the use of water and of light.

The UN General Assembly adopted on Dec. 18, 1981 Principles of Medical Ethics relevant to the role of health personnel, particularly physicians in the protection of prisoners and detainees against torture. ▷ Medical Ethics.

In 1982 an International Rehabilitation and Research Centre for Torture Victims started work in Copenhagen. The Chile Fund was renamed the UN Voluntary Fund for Victims of Torture, which informed in 1983 the Third Committee of the UN General Assembly that in spite UN efforts to eliminate torture, such practices were still present in various parts of the world. The bequest to the Fund for assistance, already considerable, could be expected to increase as it became known that something could be done for torture victims. Pledges on contributions to the Voluntary Fund totalling US $707,000 were received by Nov. 15, 1983 from Canada, Cyprus, Denmark, Finland, France, FRG, Greece, Luxembourg, the Netherlands, Norway and Sweden.

On June 26, 1987 the Parliamentary Assembly of the Council of Europe invited the Council of Ministers to adopt the draft European Convention Against Torture. The new Convention establishes a system of visits to places of detention within the jurisdiction of the Contracting Parties. The visits will be organised by a Committee of Experts in the field of human rights, serving in their individual capacity and consisting 'of a number of members equal to that of the Parties'. They will be elected by an absolute majority vote of the Committee of Ministers of the Council of Europe from a list to which each Contracting Party will have nominated three candidates. The visits will be made by members of the Committee of Experts who may be assisted by experts and interpreters.

From April 6 to 9, 1987 in Montevideo, the ICJ and the Swiss Committee against Torture co-sponsored a seminar to consider a draft of an Inter-American Convention for the Prevention of Torture.

Amnesty International's 1988 annual report surveying 135 countries, revealed that during 1987 torture and ill-treatment of prisoners was reported in 90 countries.

The United Nations and Human Rights, New York, 1970, pp. 26–27; *UN Monthly Chronicle*, December, 1974; *UN Chronicle*, January, 1976, January, 1978, March, 1982, January, 1984; J. MILWETZ, "Victims of Torture," in: *World Health*, August, 1983; "UN Human Rights Commission Requests Monitoring of Torture Cases", in: *UN Chronicle*, 1985, No. 3, pp. 19–24; *ICJ Newsletter*, No. 33, 1987, p. 17; *UN Resolutions and Decisions adopted by the General Assembly during the First Part of its Forty-Third Session. From 20 September to 22 December 1988*, New York, 1989, pp. 402–405.

TORTURE, CONVENTION AGAINST. After seven years work, the General Assembly adopted on Dec. 10, 1984 the Convention Against Torture and other Cruel, Inhuman or Degrading Treatment or Punishment; opened for signature and signed by 23 countries in a formal ceremony at UN Hqs, on Feb. 4, 1985 (Afghanistan, Argentina, Austria, Belgium, Bolivia, Costa Rica, Denmark, Dominican Republic, Ecuador, Finland, France, Greece, Iceland, Italy, Luxembourg, Netherlands, Norway, Portugal, Senegal, Spain, Sweden, Switzerland and Uruguay). The Convention enter into force on June 26, 1987, on Nov. 26, 1987 the States parties to the Convention established the UN Committee Against Torture, which will be responsible for monitoring the implementation of the Convention.

The General Assembly,

Recalling the Declaration on the Protection of All Persons from Being Subjected to Torture and Other Cruel Inhuman or Degrading Treatment or Punishment, adopted by the General Assembly in its resolution 3452 (XXX) of 9 December 1975.

Recalling also its resolution 32/62 of 8 December 1977, in which it requested the Commission on Human Rights to draw up a draft convention against torture and other cruel, inhuman or degrading treatment or punishment, in the light of the principles embodied in the Declaration.

Recalling further that, in its resolution 38/19 of 16 December 1983 it requested the Commission on Human Rights to complete, at its fortieth session, as a matter of highest priority, the drafting of such a convention, with a view to submitting a draft, including provisions for the effective implementation of the future convention, to the General Assembly at its thirty-ninth session,

Noting with satisfaction Commission on Human Rights resolution 1984/21 of 6 March 1984, by which the Commission decided to transmit the text of a draft convention against torture and other cruel, inhuman or degrading treatment or punishment, contained in the annex to the report of the Working Group, to the General Assembly for its consideration.

Desirous of achieving a more effective implementation of the existing prohibition under international and national laws of the practice of torture and other cruel, inhuman or degrading treatment or punishment.

(1) *Expresses its appreciation* for the work achieved by the Commission on Human Rights in preparing the text of a draft convention against torture and other cruel, inhuman or degrading treatment or punishment;

(2) *Adopts* and opens for signature, ratification and accession the Convention against Torture and Other Cruel, Inhuman or Degrading Treatment or Punishment contained in the annex to the present resolution;

(3) *Calls upon* all Governments to consider signing and ratifying the Convention as a matter of priority.

ANNEX

Convention against Torture and Other Cruel, Inhuman or Degrading Treatment or Punishment

The States parties in this Convention,

Considering that, in accordance with the principles proclaimed in the Charter of the United Nations, recognition of the equal and inalienable rights of all members of the human family is the foundation of freedom, justice and peace in the world,

Recognizing that those rights derive from the inherent dignity of the human person,

Considering the obligation of States under the Charter, in particular Article 55, to promote universal respect for, and observance of, human rights and fundamental freedom,

Having regard to article 5 of the Universal Declaration of Human Rights and article 7 of the International Covenant on Civil and Political Rights, both of which provide that no one shall be subjected to torture or to cruel, inhuman or degrading treatment or punishment,

Having regard also to the Declaration on the Protection of All Persons from Being Subjected to Torture and Other Cruel, Inhuman or Degrading Treatment or Punishment, adopted by the General Assembly on 9 December 1975,

Desiring to make more effective the struggle against torture and her cruel, inhuman or degrading treatment or punishment throughout the world,

Have agreed as follows:

PART I

Art. 1. (1) For the purposes of this Convention, the term "torture" means any act by which severe pain or suffering, whether physical or mental, is intentionally inflicted on a person for such purposes as obtaining from him or a third person information or a confession, punishing him for an act he or a third person has committed or is suspected of having committed, or intimidating or coercing him or a third person, or for any reason based on discrimination of any kind, when such pain or suffering is inflicted by or at the instigation of or with consent or acquiescence of a public official or other person acting in an official capacity. It does not include pain or suffering arising only from, inherent in or incidental to lawful sanctions.

(2) This article is without prejudice to any international instrument or national legislation which does or may contain provisions of wider application.

Art. 2. (1) Each State party shall take effective legislative, administrative, judicial or other measures to prevent acts of torture in any territory under its jurisdiction.

(2) No exceptional circumstances whatsoever, whether a state of war of a threat of war, may be invoked as a justification of torture.

(3) An order from a superior officer or a public authority may not be invoked as a jurisdiction of torture.

Art. 3. (1) No State Party shall expel, return ("refouler") or extradite a person to another State where there are substantial grounds for believing that he would be in danger of being subjected to torture.

(2) For the purpose of determining whether there are such grounds, the competent authorities shall take into account all relevant considerations including, where applicable, the existence in the State concerned of a consistent pattern of gross, flagrant or mass violations of human rights.

Art. 4. (1) Each State Party shall ensure that all acts of torture are offences under its criminal law. The same shall apply to an attempt to commit torture and to an act by any person which constitutes complicity or participation in torture.

(2) Each State Party shall make these offences punishable by appropriate penalties which take into account their grave nature.

Art. 5. (1) Each State Party shall take such measures as may be necessary to establish its jurisdiction over the offences referred to in article 4 in the following cases:

(a) When the offences are committed in any territory under its jurisdiction or on board a ship or aircraft registered in that State;

(b) When the alleged offender is a national of that State;

(c) When the victim is a national of that State if that State considers it appropriate.

(2) Each State party shall likewise take such measures as may be necessary to establish its jurisdiction over such offences in cases where the alleged offender is present in any territory under its jurisdiction and it does not extradite him pursuant to article 8 to any of the States mentioned in paragraph 1 of this article.

(3) This Convention does not exclude any criminal jurisdiction exercised in accordance with internal law.

Art. 6. (1) Upon being satisfied, after an examination of information available to it, that the circumstances so warrant, any State Party in whose territory a person alleged to have committed any offence referred to in article 4 is present shall take him into custody or take other legal measures shall be as provided in the law of that State but may be contained only for such time as is necessary to enable any criminal or extradition proceedings to be instituted.

(2) Such State shall immediately make a preliminary inquiry into the facts.

(3) Any person in custody pursuant to paragraph 1 of this article shall be assisted in communicating immediately with the nearest appropriate representative of the State of which he is a national, or if he is stateless person, with the representative of the State where he usually resides.

(4) When a State, pursuant to this article, has taken a person into custody, it shall immediately notify the States referred to in article 5, paragraph 1, of the fact that such person is in custody and of the circumstances which warrant his detention. The State which makes the preliminary inquiry contemplated in paragraph 2 of this article shall promptly report its findings to the said States and shall indicate whether it intends to exercise jurisdiction.

Art. 7. (1) The State Party in the territory under whose jurisdiction a person alleged to have committed any offence referred to in article 4 is found shall in the cases contemplated in article 5, if it does not extradite him, submit the case to its competent authorities for the purpose of prosecution.

(2) These authorities shall take their decision in the same manner as in the case of any ordinary offence of a serious nature under the law of that State. In the cases referred to in article 5, paragraph 2, the standards of evidence required for prosecution and conviction shall in no way be less stringent than those which apply in the cases referred to in article 5, paragraph 1.

(3) Any person regarding whom proceedings are brought in connection with any of the offences referred to in article 4 shall be guaranteed fair treatment at all stages of the proceedings.

Art. 8. (1) The offences referred to in article 4 shall be deemed to be included as extraditable offences in any extradition treaty existing between States Parties. States Parties undertake to include such offences as extraditable offences in every extradition treaty to be concluded between them.

(2) If a State Party which makes extradition conditional on the existence of a treaty receives a request for extradition from another State Party which it has no extradition treaty, it may consider this Convention as the legal basis for extradition in respect of such offences. Extradition shall be subject to the other conditions provided by the law of the requested State.

(3) States Parties which do not make extradition conditional on the existence of a treaty shall recognize such offences as extraditable offences between themselves subject to the conditions provided by the law of the requested State.

(4) Such offences shall be treated, for the purpose of extradition between States parties, as if they had been committed not only in the place in which they occurred but also in the territories of the States required to establish their jurisdiction in accordance with article 5, paragraph 1.

Art. 9. (1) State Parties shall afford one another the greatest measure of assistance in connection with criminal proceedings brought in respect of any of the ces referred to in article 4, including the supply of all evidence at their disposal necessary for the proceedings.

(2) States Parties shall carry out their obligations under paragraph 1 of this article in conformity with any treaties on mutual judicial assistance that may exist between them.

Art. 10. (1) Each State Party shall ensure that education and information regarding the prohibition against torture are fully included in the training of the law enforcement personnel, civil or military, medical personnel, public officials and other persons who may be involved in the custody, interrogation or treatment of any individual subjected to any form of arrest, detention or imprisonment.

(2) Each State Party shall include this prohibition in the rules or instructions issued in regard to the duties and functions of any such persons.

Art. 11. Each State Party shall keep under systematic review interrogation rules, instructions, methods and practices as well as arrangements for the custody and treatment of persons subjected to any form of arrest, detention or imprisonment in any territory under its jurisdiction, with a view to preventing any cases of torture.

Art. 12. Each State Party shall ensure that its competent authorities proceed to a prompt and impartial investigation, wherever there is reasonable ground to believe that an act of torture has been committed in any territory under its jurisdiction.

Art. 13. Each State Party shall ensure that any individual who alleges he has been subject to torture in any territory under its jurisdiction has the right to complain to, and to have his case promptly and impartially examined by, its competent authorities. Steps shall be taken to ensure that the complainant and witnesses are protected against all ill-treatment or intimidation as a consequence of his complaint or any evidence given.

Art. 14. (1) Each State Party shall ensure in its legal system that the victim of an act of torture obtains redress and has an enforceable right to fair and adequate compensation, including the means for a full rehabilitation as possible. In the event of the death of the victim as a result of an act of torture, his dependants shall be entitled to compensation.

(2) Nothing in this article shall affect any right of the victim or other persons to compensation which may exist under national law.

Art. 15. Each State Party shall ensure that any statement which is established to have been made as a result of torture shall not be invoked as evidence in any proceedings, except against a person accused of torture as evidence that the statement was made.

Art. 16. (1) Each State Party shall undertake to prevent in any territory under its jurisdiction other acts of cruel, inhuman or degrading treatment or punishment which do not amount to torture as defined in article 1, when such acts are committed by or at the instigation of or with the consent or acquiescence of a public official or other person acting in an official capacity. In particular, the obligations contained in articles 10, 11, 12 and 13 shall apply with the substitution for references to torture of references to other forms of cruel, inhuman or degrading treatment or punishment.

(2) The provisions of this Convention are without prejudice to the provisions of any other international instrument or national law which prohibits cruel, inhuman or degrading treatment or punishment or which relates to extradition or expulsion.

PART III

Art. 17. (1) There shall be established a Committee against Torture (hereinafter referred to as the Committee) which shall carry out the functions hereinafter provided. The Committee shall consist of ten experts of high moral standing and recognized competence in the field of human rights, who shall serve in their personal capacity. The experts shall be elected by the States Parties, consideration being given to equitable geographical distribution and to the usefulness of the participation of some persons having legal experience.

(2) The members of the Committee shall be elected by secret ballot from a list of persons nominated by States Parties. Each State Party may nominate one person from among its own nationals. States Parties shall bear in mind the usefulness of the Human Rights Committee established under the International Covenant on Civil and Political Rights and who are willing to serve on the Committee against Torture.

(3) Elections of the members of the Committee shall be held at biennial meetings of States Parties convened by the Secretary-General of the United Nations. At those meetings, for which two thirds of the States Parties shall constitute a quorum, the persons elected to the Committee shall be those who obtain the largest number of votes and an absolute majority of votes of the representatives of States Parties present and voting.

(4) The initial election shall be held no later than six months after the date of the entry into force of this Convention. At least four months before the date of each election, the Secretary-General of the United Nations shall address a letter to the States Parties inviting them to submit their nominations within three months. The Secretary-General shall prepare a list in alphabetical order of all persons thus nominated them, and shall submit it to the States Parties.

(5) The members of the Committee shall be elected for a term of four years. They shall be eligible for re-election if renominated. However, the term of five of the members elected at the first election shall expire at the end of two years, immediately after the first election the names of these five members shall be chose by lot by the chairman of the meeting referred to in paragraph 3 of this article.

(6) If a member of the Committee dies or resigns or for any other cause can no longer perform his Committee duties, the State Party which nominated thim shall appoint another expert from among its nationals to serve for the remainder of his term, subject to the approval of the majority of the States Parties. The approval shall be considered given unless half or more of the States Parties respon negatively within six weeks after having been informed by the Secretary-General of the United Nations of the proposed appointment.

(7) States Parties shall be responsible for the expenses of the members of the Committee while they are in performance of Committee duties.

Art. 18. (1) The Committee shall elect its officers for a term of two years. They may be re-elected:

(2) The Commitee shall establish its own rules of procedure, but these rules shall provide, inter alia, that:

(a) Six members shall constitute a quorum;

(b) Decisions of the Committee shall be made by a majority vote of the members present.

(3) The Secretary-General of the United Nations shall provide the necessary staff and facilities for the effective performance of the functions of the Committee under this Convention.

(4) The Secretary-General of the United Nations shall convene initial meeting of the Committee. After its initial meeting, the Committee shall meet at such times as shall be provided in its rules of procedure.

(5) The States Parties shall be responsible for expenses incurred in connection with the holding of meetings of the States Parties and of the Committee, including reimbursement to the United Nations for any expenses, such as the cost of staff and facilities, incurred by the United Nations pursuant to paragraph 3 of this article.

Art. 19. (1) The States Parties shall submit to the Committee, through the Secretary-General of the United Nations, reports on the measures they have taken to give effect to their undertakings under this Convention, within one year after the entry into force of the Convention for the State Party concerned. Thereafter the States Parties shall submit supplementary reports every four years on any new measures taken and such other reports as the Committee may request.

(2) The Secretary-General of the United Nations shall transmit the reports to all States Parties.

(3) Each report shall be considered by the Committee which may take such general comments on the report as it may consider appropriate and shall forward these to the State Party concerned. That State Party may respond with any observations it chooses to the Committee.

(4) The Committee may, at its discretion, decided to include any comments made by it in accordance with paragraph 3 of this article, together with the observations thereon received from the State Party concerned, in its annual report made in accordance with article 24. If so requested by the State Party concerned, the Committee may also include a copy of the report submitted under paragraph 1 of this article.

Art. 20. (1) If the Committee receives reliable information which appears to it to contain well-founded indications that torture is being systematically practised in the territory of a State Party, the Committee shall invite that State Party to co-operate in the examination of the information and to this end to submit observations with regard to the information concerned.

(2) Taking into account any observations which may have been submitted by the State Party concerned, as well as any relevant information available to it, the Committee may, if it decides that this is warranted, designate one or more of its members to make a confidential inquiry and to report to the Committee urgently.

(3) If an inquiry is made in accordance with paragraph 2 of this article, the Committee shall seek the co-operation of the State Party concerned. In agreement with that State Party, such an inquiry may include a visit to its territory.

(4) After examining the findings of its members or members submitted in accordance with paragraph 2 of this article, the Committee shall transmit these findings to the State Party concerned together with any comments or suggestions which seem appropriate in view of the situation.

(5) All proceedings of the Committee referred to in paragraphs 1 to 4 of this article shall be confidential, and at all stages of the proceedings the co-operation of the State Party shall be sought. After such proceedings have been completed with regard to an inquiry made in accordance with paragraph 2, the Committee may, after consultations with the State Party concerned, decide to include a summary account of the results of the proceedings in its annual report made in accordance with article 24.

Art. 21. (1) A State Party to this Convention may at any time declare under this article that it recognizes the competence of the Committee to receive and consider communications to the effect that a State Party claims that another State Party is not fulfilling its obligations under this Convention. Such communications may be received and considered according to the procedures laid down in this article only if submitted by a State Party which has made a declaration recognizing in regard to itself the competence of the Committee. No communication shall be dealt with by the Committee under this article if it concerns a State Party which has not made such a declaration. Communications received under this article shall be dealt with in accordance with the following procedure:

(a) If a State Party considers that another State Party is not giving effect to the provisions of this Convention, it may, by written communication, bring the matter to the attention of that State Party. Within three months after the receipt of the communication the receiving State shall afford the State which sent the communication an explanation or any other statement in writing clarifying the matter, which should include, to the extent possible and pertinent or available in the matter;

(b) If the matter is not adjusted to the satisfaction of both States Parties concerned within six months after the receipt by the receiving State of the initial communication, either State shall have the right to refer the matter to the Committee, by notice given to the Committee and to the other State;

(c) The Committee shall deal with a matter referred to it under this article only after it has ascertained that all domestic remedies have been invoked and exhausted in the matter, in conformity with the generally recognized principles of international law. This shall not be the rules where the application of the remedies is unreasonably prolonged or is unlikely to bring effective relief to the person who is the victim of the violation of this Convention;

(d) The Committee shall hold closed meetings when examining communications under this article;

(e) Subject to the provisions of subparagraph (c), the Committee shall make available its good offices to the States Parties concerned with a view to a friendly solution of the matter on the basis of respect for the obligations provided for in this Convention. For this purpose, the Committee may, when appropriate, set up an *ad hoc* conciliation commission;

(f) In any matter referred to it under this article, the Committee may call upon the States Parties concerned, referred to in subparagraph (b), to supply any relevant information;

(g) The States Parties concerned, referred to in subparagraph (b), shall have the right to be represented when the matter is being considered by the Committee and to make submission orally and/or in writing;

(h) The Committee shall, within twelve months after the date of receipt of notice under subparagraph (b), submit a report:
(i) If a solution within the terms of subparagraph (e) is reached, the Committee shall confine its report to brief statement of the facts and of the solution reached;
(ii) If a solution within the terms of subparagraph (e) is not reached, the Committee shall confine its report to a brief statement of the facts; the written submissions and record of the oral submission made by the States Parties concerned shall be attached to the report.
In every matter, the report shall be communicated to the States Parties concerned.
(2) The provisions of this article shall come into force when five States Parties to this Convention have made declarations under paragraph 1 of this article. Such declarations shall be deposited by the States Parties with the Secretary-General of the United Nations, who shall transmit copies thereof to the other States Parties. A declaration may be withdrawn at any time by notification to the Secretary-General. Such a withdrawal shall not prejudice the consideration of any matter which is the subject of a communication already transmitted under this article; no further communciation by any State Party shall be received under this article after the notification of withdrawal of the declaration has been received by the Secretary-General, unless the State Party concerned has made a new declaration.
Art. 22. (1) A State Party to this Convention may at any time declare under this article that it recognizes the competence of the Committee to receive and consider communications from or on behalf of individuals subject to its jurisdiction who claim to be victims of a violation by a State Party of the provisions of the Convention. No communication shall be received by the Committee if it concerns a State Party which has not made such a declaration.
(2) The Committee shall consider inadmissible any communication under this article which is anonymous or which it considers to be an abuse of the right of submission of such communications or to be incompatible with the provisions of this Convention.
(3) Subject to the provisions of paragraph 2, the Committee shall bring any communications submitted to it under this article to the attention of the State Party to this Convention which has made a declaration under Paragraph 1 and is alleged to be violating any provisions of the Convention. Within six months, the receiving State shall submit to the Committee written explanation or statements clarifying the matter and the remedy, if any, that may have been taken by that State.
(4) The Committee shall consider communications received under this article in the light of all information made available to it by or on behalf of the individual and by the State Party concerned.
(5) The Committee shall not consider any communications from an individual under this article unless it has ascertained that:
(a) The same matters has not been, and is not being, examined under another procedure of international investigation or settlement;
(b) The individual has exhausted all available domestic remedies; this shall not be the rule where the application of the remedies is unreasonably prolonged or is unlikely to bring effective relief to the person who is the victim of the violation of this Convention.
(6) The Committee shall hold closed meetings when examining communications under this article.
(7) The Committee shall forward its views to the State Party concerned and to the individual.
(8) The provisions of this article shall come into force when five States Parties to this Convention have made declarations under paragraph 1 of this article. Such declarations shall be deposited by the States Parties with the Secretary-General of the United Nations, who shall transmit copies thereof to the other States Parties. A declaration may be withdrawn at any time by notification to the Secretary-General. Such a withdrawal shall not prejudice the consideration of any matter which is the subject of a communication already transmitted under this article; no further communication by or on behalf of an individual shall be received under this article after the notification of withdrawal of the declaration has been received by the Secretary-General, unless the State Party has made a new declaration.
Art. 23. The members of the Committee and of the *ad hoc* conciliation commissions which may be appointed under article 21, paragraph 1 (e), shall be entitled to the facilities, privileges and immunities of experts on mission for the United Nations as laid down in the relevant sections of the Convention on the Privileges and Immunities of the United Nations.
Art. 24. The Committee shall submit an annual report on its activities under this Convention to the States Parties and to the General Assembly of the United Nations.
PART III
Art. 25. (1) This Convention is open for signature by all States.
(2) This Convention is subject to ratification. Instruments of ratification shall be deposited with the Secretary-General of the United Nations.
Art. 26. This Convention is open to accession by all States. Accession shall be effected by the deposit of an instrument of accession with the Secretary-General of the United Nations.
Art. 27. (1) This Convention shall enter into force on the thirtieth day after the date of the deposit with the Secretary-General of the United Nations of the twentieth instrument of ratification or accession.
(2) For each State ratifying this Convention or acceding to it after the deposit of the twentieth instrument of ratification of accession, the Convention shall enter into force on the thirtieth day after the date of the deposit of its own instrument of ratification or accession.
Art. 28. (1) Each State may, at the time of signature or ratification of this Convention or accession thereto, declare that it does not recognize the competence of the Committee provided for in article 20.
(2) Any State Party having made a reservation in accordance with paragraph 1 of this article may, at any time, withdraw this reservation by notification to the Secretary-General of the United Nations.
Art. 29. (1) Any State Party to this Convention may propose an amendment and file it with the Secretary-General of the United Nations. The Secretary-General shall thereupon communicate the proposed amendment to the States Parties with a request that they notify him whether they favour a conference of States Parties for the purpose of considering and voting upon the proposal. In the event that within four months from the date of such communication at least one third of the States Parties favours such a conference, the Secretary-General shall convene the conference under auspices of the United Nations. Any amendment adopted by a majority of the States Parties present and voting at the conference shall be submitted by the Secretary-General to all the States Parties for acceptance.
(2) An amendment adopted in accordance with paragraph 1 of this article shall enter into force when two thirds of the States Parties to this Convention have notified the Secretary-General of the United Nations that they have accepted it in accordance with their respective constitutional processes.
(3) When amendments enter into force, they shall be binding on those States Parties which have accepted them, other States Parties still being bound by the provisions of this Convention and any earlier amendments which they have accepted.
(1) Any dispute between two or more States parties concerning the interpretation or application of this Convention which cannot be settled through negotiation shall, at the request of one of them, be submitted to arbitration. If within six months from the date of the request for arbitration the Parties are unable to agree on the organization of the arbitration, any one of these Parties may refer the dispute to the International Court of Justice by request in conformity with the Statute of the Court.
(2) Each State may, at the time of signature or ratification of this Convention or accession thereto, declare that it does not consider itself bound by paragraph 1 of this article. The other States Parties shall not be bound by paragraph 1 of this article with respect to any State Party having made such a reservation.
(3) Any State Party having made a reservation in accordance with pargraph 2 of this article may at any time withdraw this reservation by notification to the Secretary-General of the United Nations.
Art. 31. (1) A State Party may denounce this Convention by written notification to the Secretary-General of the United Nations. Denunciation becomes effective one year after the date of receipt of the notification by the Secretary-General.
(2) Such a denunciation shall not have the effect of releasing the State Party from its obligations under this Convention in regard to any act or omission which occurs prior to the date at which the denunciation becomes effective, nor shall denunciation prejudice in any way the continued consideration of any matter which is already under the consideration by the Committee prior to the date at which the denunciation becomes effective.
(3) Following the date at which the denunciation of a State Party becomes effective, the Committee shall not commence consideration of any new matter regarding that State.
Art. 32. The Secretary-General of the United Nations shall inform all States Members of the United Nations and all States which have signed this Convention or acceded to it of the foloowing:
(a) Signature, ratifications and accessions under articles 25 and 26;
(b) The date of entry into force of this Convention under article 27 and the date of the entry into force of any amendments under article 29;
(c) Denunciations under article 31.
Art. 33. (1) This Convention, of which the Arabic, Chinese, English, French and Spanish texts are equally authentic, shall be deposited with the Secretary-General of the United Nations.
(2) The Secretary-General of the United Nations shall transmit certified copies of this Convention to all States.
Many States viewed universal jurisdiction as an essential element to ensure the effectiveness of the convention. That concept, as the nordic countries put it, would ensure there would be 'no safe haven for torturers in the territories of States Parties'. Some added that universal jurisdiction must be complemented by effective implementation procedures.
A few Governments found the universal jurisdiction provisions as envisaged in the text 'problematic', mainly as a result of doubts about their 'practical implementation'.

UN Chronicle 1985, No. 1, pp. 31–35 and 48–52.

TOTALITARIAN IDEOLOGIES. A subject of UN General Assembly Res. 36/162 of Dec. 16, 1981, adopted without vote. The Assembly "condemned all totalitarian or other ideologies and practices, in particular nazi, facist and neo-fascist, based on ethnic exclusiveness or intolerance, hatred, terror, the systematic denial of human rights and fundamental freedom, or those which had such consequencies."
States were urged to draw attention to the threats to democratic institutions by such ideologies and practices, and to consider taking measures, in accordance with their national constitutional systems and with the provisions of the Universal Declaration of Human Rights prohibiting or deterring such activities. They were also invited to adopt, as a matter of high priority, measures declaring punishable by law any dissemination of ideas based on racial superiority and of war propaganda.
The Assembly further called upon the appropriate specialized agencies, as well as intergovernmental and international non-governmental organizations, to initiate or intensify measures against such ideologies and practices; and requested the Commission on Human Rights to continue consideration of the subject.
According to the *UN Chronicle* report: "Speaking after the consensus, Japan said it had voted in favor of the resolution, but had reservations on some of its paragraphs.
The USSR said it supported the resolution because it had borne the brunt of the struggle of the Second World War and could not resign itself to the growing dangers of facist and nazi forces. Parties and groups which espoused fascist ideas were coming out more strongly against those who supported the fight against racism and apartheid. They were acting openly and participating in terrorist activities on an international scale.

Sweden said that its vote in favor of the resolution was not to be interpreted as an expression of any intention to allow unconstitutional limitation of freedom of opinion and expression of the press. Norway said it was fully aware of the threat posed to democratic institutions by certain ideologies and felt that measures should be taken in the context of established democratic practices. It had reservations on any paragraph which might be interpreted as threatening freedom of speech and of the press. Stating that it had supported the resolution because it was directed against nazism which had made the Jewish people its most tragic victims, Israel said nazism was a danger to democracy and human decency. However, nazism was not the only form of totalitarianism or the sole purveyor of anti-semitism.

Dissociating itself from the consensus, the United States said the resolution, introduced by totalitarian states, was cynical and propagandistic. Unlike some countries, the United States had always opposed nazism, fascism and totalitarianism, including communism.

Recommended by the Third Committee (Social, Humanitarian and Cultural), which had adopted it by a recorded vote of 125 in favor to none against, with 13 abstentions, the resolution, in draft form, was sponsored by Afghanistan, Angola, Bulgaria, the Congo, Cuba, Czechoslovakia, the German Democratic Republic, Grenada, Hungary, the Laos People's Democratic Republic, Poland, the Ukranian SSR, Vietnam and Zimbabwe."

UN Chronicle, March, 1982, pp. 54–55; G. HERMET, P. HASSNER, J. RUPNIK, *Totalitarismes*, Paris, 1984.

TOTAL WAR. An international term formulated 1935 by the German General E. Luddendorff, it assumed the use by the state of all of the human, material and moral resources at its disposal for the purpose, in some cases, of not only destroying the armed forces of the enemy but also the entire nation by all means without any legal or moral restraints. The idea of total war was put into effect by the German Third Reich during World War II.

E. LUDDENDORFF, *Der Totale Krieg*, Berlin, 1935; D. ROBERTSON, *Guide to Modern Defense and Strategy*, Detroit, 1988.

TOURISM, INTERNATIONAL. A subject of permament organized international co-operation since 1898 marking the inception of the International Alliance of Tourism at Geneva. The International Congress of Official Tourist Organizations was f. 1927 in The Hague, name changed 1930 to Union internationale des organismes officiels de propagande touristique with headquarters in Paris. In 1947 became the International Union of Official Travel Organizations, IUOTO. In 1939 the first Inter-American Travel Congress was held in San Francisco.

First studies on problems of tourism were initiated by the UN General Assembly in 1947 which recommended simplification and uniformization of travel documents and passport–customs regulations for tourists and their vehicles implemented in Conventions on Tourism worked out by the First UN World Conference on Tourism, Aug. 25–Sept. 5, 1963 in Rome, ended with adoption of the Rome Charter of Tourism specifying significance of international tourism for the maintenance of peace, development of freedom of travelling, acquaintance with other cultural and civilized regions and economic development.

In 1966, the General Assembly designated 1967 as International Tourist Year, dedicated to facilitating understanding among peoples everywhere, to promoting international co-operation and to a greater awareness of the wealth and diversity of different civilizations. Activities for the observance of the Year were largely carried out by the IUOTO. The Intergovernmental Conference on Tourism, held at Sofia, Bulgaria, in May, 1969, recommended the creation of an intergovernmental tourism organization to promote and develop tourism. In Nov., 1969, the IUOTO decided to amend its statutes in order to give the organization an intergovernmental character. The UN General Assembly decided that an agreement should be concluded which would establish close co-operation and relationships between the United Nations and the future World Tourism Organization, WTO, and recognize the decisive and central role that the ▷ WTO would play in world tourism in co-operation with the existing machinery within the United Nations system.

The statutes of the WTO, adopted at Mexico City on Sept. 27, 1970, entered into force on Jan. 2, 1975 after 51 states had formally signified their approval. The IUOTO was thus transformed into an intergovernmental organization with headquarters in Madrid.

In 1977, the General Assembly approved a formal agreement on co-operation and relationships between the United Nations and the WTO and requested the latter to intensify its efforts to promote tourism, particularly in developing countries, and invited those United Nations member states which had not yet joined WTO to consider becoming members.

In addition to a number of research studies, member states and territories in all regions have been aided by the execution of a large number of technical assistance projects ranging from limited advisory services, physical planning and environmental impact evaluations to tourism projects which were integral parts of large-scale urban and regional planning and human settlement development efforts.

The UN launched a special program to foster development of international tourism in the developing countries of Latin America, Africa, South Asia and the Balkan Peninsula. The OECD publ. *Tourism Policy and International Tourism in OECD Member Countries*, 1955 ff.

Organizations reg. with the UIA:

Alliance Internationale de Tourisme, f. 1898, Geneva, Switzerland.
Arab Tourism Union, f. 1954, Jordan. Publ.: Arab Tourism Magazine (bi-monthly), and Research Supplements.
Caribbean Tourism Association–CTA, f. 1951, New York, N.Y., USA.
International Academy of Tourism, f. 1951, Monte Carlo, Monaco. Publ.: Revue Dictionnaire Touristique International.
International Association of Scientific Experts in Tourism, f. 1949, St. Gallen, Switzerland. Publ.: The Tourist Review (quarterly).
International Federation of Tourist Centres, f. 1949, Linz, Austria.
Latin-American Confederation of Tourist Organizations, f. 1957, Buenos Aires, Argentina. Publ.: Revista COTAL (monthly), Aqui COTAL Newsletter.
World Tourism Organization, f. 1975, Madrid, Spain. Publ.: World Tourism Statistics, World Travel/Tourisme Mondial (every 2 months), Tourist Bibliography (annually), Travel Abroad (annually), manuals studies.

The Economic Impact of Tourism on National Economies and International Trade, Geneva, 1966; K. LIBERA, "Le tourisme et le droit international." in: *Polish Yearbook of International Law*, Warsaw, 1975, pp. 179–214; A.J. PEASLEE, *International Governmental Organizations Constitutional Documents*, The Hague, 1976, Vol. 5, pp. 366 and 574–575; E. DE KADT, *Tourism, Passport to Development*, New York, 1979; *Everyone's United Nations*, UN, New York, 1979, pp. 165–166; *Yearbook of International Organizations 1986/87; The Europa Yearbook 1988. A World Survey*, Vol. I, London, 1988.

TOVALOP. ▷ Water Pollution.

TOWNS. ▷ Urbanization.

TOXIC CHEMICALS. A subject of WHO concern over environmental pollution and effects on health.

TOXICOLOGY. A subject of international research. Organizations reg. with the UIA:

European Committee for the Protection of the Population Against the Hazards of Chronic Toxicity, EUROTOX, f. 1957, Paris. Publ.: *Reports. European Society of Toxicology*, f. 1962, Basel.
International Association for Forensic Toxicologists, f. 1963, London.
International Association for Research in Toxicological Information, f. 1973, Paris.
International Association on Toxicology, f. 1962, Tokyo. Publ.: *Toxicon*.
World Federation of Associations of Clinical Toxicology and Anti-Poison Centres, f. 1976, Lyon.

Yearbook of International Organizations.

TOXINS. An international term in the UN system for biological and synthetically produced or modified compounds that can be used as warfare agents; prohibited by the ▷ BW Convention, 1972, "whatever their origin or method of production."

J. GOLDBLAT, *Arms Control Agreements. A Handbook*, New York, 1983, p. 47.

TOYS. A subject of international co-operation. Organizations reg. with the UIA:

European Federation of Groups of Toy Manufacturers, f. 1975, Paris.
European Federation of Toy Manufacturers Associations, f. 1961, Nuremberg.
European Federation of Toy Wholesalers and Importers Association, f. 1961, Nuremberg.
European Toy Institute, f. 1961, Nuremberg.
International Doll Association, f. 1963, Dallas. Publ.: *World Wide Doll News*.

Yearbook of International Organizations; G. CHANAN, H. FRANCIS, *Juegos e juguetes de los niños del mundo*, UNESCO, Barcelona, 1984 (also in English).

TRACERS. ▷ Radioisotope tracers.

TRACHOMA. A subject of international action since 1924 against this infectious disease.

The WHO estimated that in 1988 approximately 360 million people are affected, the vast majority of them in the developing countries. Trachoma has blinded approximately six million people and an even larger number suffer from partial loss of vision because of the disease. Trachoma can be transmitted by direct or indirect contact. Overcrowding, lack of clean water, insanitary habits, all contribute to its spread. Repeated exposure to sources of infection, causing reinfection and relapse, increases the severity of the disease.

The burden of trachoma on the community is heavy: human suffering as a result of the disease requires treatment and assistance, and the loss of sight is a severe handicap for education and work. A disease which used to be universal, present in all continents and under almost all types of climates, trachoma has now practically disappeared as a public health problem from the more developed countries, but is still prevalent in some of the less developed ones.

Recommended methods and criteria for trachoma control are described in two WHO technical publications entitled "Trachoma Control" (Geneva

1981) and "Strategies for the Prevention of Blindness in National Programmes" (Geneva 1984). Organization reg. with the UIA:

International Organization Against Trachoma, f. 1924, Creteil, France, Official relations WHO and ECOSOC. Aims: research, diagnosis and prevention of trachoma. Publ.: *Revue international du trachoma*.

Yearbook of International Organizations; WHO *In Point of Fact*, May, 1988.

TRACING SERVICE. A subject of international co-operation. In 1945 the Allied High Commission for Germany established in Arolsen, FRG, an International Tracing Service "for the purpose of tracing missing persons and collecting, classifying, preserving and rendering accessible to governments and interested individuals documents relating to Germans and non-Germans who were interned in German concentration or labor camps or the non-Germans who were displaced as a result of the World War II" (▷ Displaced Persons). After the Allied High Commission ceased to exist, an Agreement between Belgium, France, FRG, Israel, Italy, Luxembourg, Netherlands, UK and USA constituting an International Commission for the International Tracing Service (with Annex) was signed in Bonn on June 6, 1955. ▷ Arolsen.

UNTS, Vol. 219, p. 80.

TRADE. Subject of international co-operation. Organizations reg. with the UIA:

Association of African Trade Promotion Organizations, f. 1975, Tangier, Morocco. Publ.: African Trade (monthly).
International Organization for Motor Trade and Repairs, f. 1947, Rijswijk, Netherlands.
World Trade Centers Association, f. 1968, New York, NY, USA. Publ.: World Traders (quarterly).

Yearbook of International Organizations, 1986/87; The Europa Yearbook 1988. A World Survey, Vol. I, London, 1988.

TRADE AGREEMENTS ACT, 1934. The US Congress of June 12, 1934 adopted in the form of an amendment to the Tariff Act 1930, the Trade Agreements Act (for a period of three years, extended 1937, 1940 and 1943), under which the US has concluded reciprocal trade agreements with 27 countries.

S. WELLES, "Reciprocal Trade Agreements: Postwar Policies of the US" and A. STEVENSON, "Reciprocal Trade Agreements Program," in: *International Conciliation*, May, 1943. FAO, *Trade Yearbook*, Rome, 1947 ff.

TRADE, BALANCE OF. ▷ Balance of trade.

TRADE CENTER UNCTAD/GATT. ▷ Trade Terms International.

TRADE CO-OPERATION ORGANIZATION, OTC. An intergovernmental institution est. in Mar., 1955, at Geneva, the Organization for Trade Co-operation, to administer the General Agreement on Tariffs and Trade, GATT, and facilitate its operation, conduct intergovernmental consultation on trade matters, sponsor international trade negotiations and make recommendations on trade questions.

GATT, *Basic Instruments and Selected Documents: US Department of State Bulletin*, No. 823, April 4, 1955, pp. 579–582; R. VERMON, "Organizing for World Trade," in: *International Conciliation*, November, 1955, pp. 163–222.

TRADE EXPANSION ACT, 1962. A bill passed on June 30, 1962, by the US Congress concerning expansion of foreign trade of the USA for the first time since the Reciprocal Trade Agreement Act of 1934; the 1962 Act allowed for reduced tariffs on the basis of reciprocity up to 50% within five years; it became a foundation of the negotiations carried out by GATT member states during the so-called Kennedy Round.

KEESING'S *Contemporary Archive*, 1962.

TRADE FAIRS. ▷ Fairs, International.

TRADE GENEVA CENTER OF GATT AND UNCTAD. An intergovernmental institution f. under UN auspices in May, 1964, in Geneva, as the Trade Center of GATT, since Jan., 1968 in conjunction with UNCTAD; assists developing countries in organizing their exports, marketing and in training foreign trade cadres. Members are the member states of UNCTAD and GATT. Publ.: *International Trade Forum*.

Yearbook of International Organizations.

TRADE IN ARMS. ▷ Arms Trade International.

TRADE IN ARMS AND AMMUNITION, CONVENTION FOR THE CONTROL OF, 1919. An agreement between the USA, Belgium, Bolivia, the British Empire, China, Cuba, Czechoslovakia, Ecuador, France, Greece, Guatemala, Haiti, the Hedjaz, Italy, Japan, Nicaragua, Panama, Peru, Poland, Portugal, Romania, the Serb-Croate-Slovene State and Siam, signed on Sept. 10, 1919 at Saint-Germain-en-Laye, prohibiting the export of the following arms of war:

"Artillery of all kinds, apparatus for the discharge of all kinds of projectiles explosive or gas-diffusing, flame throwers, bombs, grenades, machine guns and rifled smallbore breech loading weapons of all kinds, as well as the exportation of the ammunition for use with such arms. The prohibition of exportation shall apply to all such arms and ammunition, whether complete or in parts." (Art. 1.)

According to art. 6, the import of arms and ammunition was prohibited in the whole of the Continent of Africa (with the exception of Algeria, Libya and the Union of South Africa), Transcaucasia, Persia, Gwadar, the Arabian Peninsula and the maritime zone (Red Sea, the Gulf of Aden, the Persian Gulf and the Sea of Oman).

LNTS, Vol. 7, pp. 340–343.

TRADE INTERNATIONAL ORGANIZATION, ITO. An institution planned in Mar., 1945 by GATT under the condition that the convention would be ratified by countries representing 85% of international trade. Such ratification did not take place.

TRADE INTERNATIONAL TREATIES. A subject of centuries of international practices adopted in the 19th and 20th centuries, regional formulas and international conventions concerning specific goods, transport, customs charges, packaging, etc. In Mar., 1950 in Geneva the ▷ Trade Co-operation Organization, OTC, was established to administer ▷ GATT and to sponsor international trade organizations.

R. VERMON, "Organizing for World Trade," in: *International Conciliation*, November, 1955, pp. 163–222; J.A.C. CONYBEAR, *Trade Wars: The Theory and Practice of International Commercial Rivalry*, New York, 1987.

TRADE IN WORKS OF ART. A subject of UNESCO international convention 1970 to foster co-operation between states in the suppression of illegal trade in works of art. An international meeting of archaeologists in Nicosia, Cyprus, Sept., 1972, devoted to theft and illegal trade in objects of art recalled the UNESCO conference held in Palermo in 1956 that worked out regulations for archaeological missions in the world but which failed to produce expected results. It was agreed that the best remedy against theft and illegal trade in works of art was fast dissemination of photographic reproductions of newly discovered objects as well as a reverting to the formerly applied principle of discoveries being shared by countries where archaeological surveys were made and countries represented by archaeological missions. Archaeologists attending the Nicosia conference adopted a resolution to the effect that illegal trade in works of art was a crime liable to legal prosecution on a par with trade in narcotics.

B. HOLLANDER, *The International Law of Art*, London, 1959; K.E. MEYER, *The Plundered Past*, New York, 1973.

TRADE LAW, INTERNATIONAL. A subject of codification work carried out by the United Nations. On Dec. 17, 1966 the UN General Assembly, unanimously adopted Res. 2205/XXI setting up the UN Commission of International Trade Law, UNCITRAL, with the task of gradually "harmonizing and standardizing" this law, which should include "a number of norms that govern trade relations and have the character of private law in force in different countries."

The Commission is composed of representatives of 29 states, appointed by the General Assembly for a period of 6 years, including 7 representatives from Africa, 5 from Asia, 4 from socialist Europe and 8 from Western Europe and other states. The Commission commenced its activities in Jan., 1968, concentrating its attention initially on the following 4 issues:

(1) International sale of goods, due to the need for revising the Hague Conventions in that area of 1964, which have not entered into force because of reservations expressed by numerous countries. A new version of the convention was prepared on termination of international sale of goods. At the same time, in the area of standardizing the customs and practices of international sales, UNCITRAL began to co-ordinate work with regional Economic Commissions of the United Nations and with the International Chamber of Commerce.

(2) International payments (multilateral payments), due to the need for rapprochement between the two major world systems, that of the bill of exchange and check law, the system of exchange and check law, system of Geneva Conventions on the Bills of Exchange of 1930 and on checks of 1971, and that of the Anglo-Saxon system. The Commission also works on creating a new type of security which would be used exclusively in international turnover.

(3) International Trade arbitration. The Commission, recognizing the tested value of the New York Convention on the recognition and execution of foreign arbitration verdicts, 1958, and the European Convention on international trade arbitration, 1961, favored maximum expansion of the number of states participating in these conventions.

(4) International maritime legislation for merchant vessels. The Commission initiated codification work to this end. The Commission's activities are reported in the *Journal of World Trade* published bimonthly in Geneva.

In 1976 UNCITRAL elaborated a Convention on Maritime Transportation of Goods and on the Principles of Arbitration in International Trade Relations; in 1977 a Convention on International Sale of Goods.

V.A.S. MUHAMMED, *The Legal Framework of World Trade*, London, 1958; C.N. SCHMITHOFF, *The Unification of the Law of International Trade*, Stockholm, 1964; *UN Monthly Chronicle*, February, 1966, April, 1967, November, 1967; March, 1968; O.C. GILES, *Uniform Commercial Law. An Essay on International Conventions in National Courts*, Leiden,

1970; *Register of Texts of Conventions and other Instruments Concerning International Trade Law*, 2 Vols., UN, New York, 1971–73; *Informe de la Comisión de las NU para el Derecho Mercantil Internacional*, UN, New York, 1975; *UN Conference on Prescription (Limitation) in the International Sale of Goods*, New York, 1975; *UN Chronicle*, October, 1982, p. 54; *UN Handbook of International Trade and Development Statistics*, New York, 1983; *UN Commission on International Trade Law Yearbook*, New York, 1985 (issued irregularly since 1968); F.J. HARPER ed., *Trade Unions of the World*, London, 1987.

TRADE MARK. A subject of international agreements; commercial name, symbol, figure, letter, word, abbreviation, or mark adopted since the Middle Ages by craftsmen, merchants, settlements, or manufacturers to designate their goods. Along with the development of manufactures it became, since 1883, the subject of legal protection by the International Union for Protection of Industrial Property seated in Geneva; publ.: *Les Marques Internationales* (monthly).

The designation, reserved and registered under international law, is also an indication of guarantee of good quality of a product; trade marks do not apply to markings by assay offices (gold or silver hallmarks), food inspection units, etc. The first International Registration of Marks was signed on Apr. 14, 1891 in Madrid, revised in Brussels, Dec. 14, 1900, in Washington, June 2, 1911, in The Hague, Nov. 6, 1925, in London, June 2, 1934. The second international Agreement on Suppression of False Certificates of Origin of Goods was signed on Apr. 14, 1891 in Madrid, modified Aug. 2, 1911 in Washington; extended June 6, 1925. The agreement stipulates to participating states that:

"Each product labeled with a counterfeit trade mark indicating, directly or indirectly, one of the contracting countries or a place in any of the countries, shall be sequestered upon importation to any of these countries. Sequestration shall be made in the state in which the counterfeit trade mark was attached or in the state to which the commodity bearing a counterfeit trade mark was imported."

Agreement Concerning the International Classification of Goods and Services for the Purposes of the Registration of Marks, was signed on June 15, 1957 in Nice, revised in Stockholm, July 14, 1967; came into force on Nov. 12, 1969. The classification consists of (a) a list of classes and (b) an alphabetical list of goods and services with an indication of the classes into which they fall. The list of classes and the alphabetical list of goods are those which were published in 1935 by the International Bureau for the Protection of Industrial Property (art. 1.)

The CMEA countries concluded an agreement on legal protection of inventions, industrial designs and trade marks on Apr. 12, 1973 in Moscow.

In the Western Hemisphere the first Convention on trademarks was adopted at the First South American Congress on Private International Law, Montevideo, 1889. The first Inter-American Convention for the Protection of Commercial Industrial and Agricultural Trade Marks and Commercial Names, signed on Apr. 28, 1928 at Santiago de Chile, by the governments of 18 American Republics, came into force on Sept. 19, 1926; ratified by Brazil, Cuba, the Dominican Republic, Haiti, Paraguay, USA and Uruguay.

The General Inter-American Convention for Trade Marks and Commercial Protection, and Protocol on the Inter-American Registration of Trade Marks, signed at Washington, DC, on Feb. 20, 1929, at the Pan-American Trade Mark Conference by the governments of 19 American Republics, came into force on Apr. 2, 1930; ratified by Colombia, Cuba, Guatemala, Haiti, Honduras, Nicaragua, Panama, Paraguay, Peru, USA. The Protocol was denounced 1944–46 by USA and other signatory states.
▷ Industrial Property Protection.

CARNEGIE ENDOWMENT. *International Conferences of American states, 1889–1928*, Washington, DC, 1931; *UNTS*, Vol. 828, p. 191; D.M. KERLY, *Law of Trade Marks and Trade Names*, London, 1951; R. CALLMAN, *The Law of Unfair Competition and Trademarks*, 5 vols., New York, 1950–65; W.E. BUTTLER, (ed.), *A Source Book on Socialist International Organizations*, Alphen, 1978, pp. 1036–1045; *Yearbook of International Organizations*; A.M. GREENE, *Trademarks Throughout the World*, New York, 1980.

TRADE RELATED ASPECTS OF INTELLECTUAL PROPERTY. The ▷ GATT General Agreement, 1947 contains two types of provisions of relevance to the trade aspects of intellectual property.

(1) Some provisions, while not specifically mentioning intellectual property rights, nevertheless define general rules or principles that may affect some aspects of these rights. These are, specifically, Article III, which in substance provides that imported products shall be accorded treatment no less favourable than that accorded to like products of national origin in respect of all laws, regulations, requirements or internal charges; general most-favoured-nation treatment (Article I), which applies not only to import and export formalities but also to internal regulations; Article XI, which lays down the principle of the general elimination of quantitative restrictions; and Article XIII concerning the non-discriminatory application of authorized quantitative restrictions.

In addition, some general provisions may apply in certain situations, in particular Article V on freedom of transit, Article VIII on fees and formalities connected with importation and exportation, Article X on the publication and administration of trade regulations, Articles XXII and XXIII on dispute settlement, and Article XXV:1 on joint action by the Contracting Parties.

(2) Intellectual property rights mentioned in the General Agreement:

Article XX (d) provides a general exception; it enables measures which would otherwise be inconsistent with the General Agreement to be taken to secure compliance with laws and regulations on intellectual property (protection of patents, trademarks and copyrights) or 'the prevention of deceptive practices'.
Article IX essentially seeks to ensure that marking requirements are not used in such a way as to hamper unnecessarily international trade or discriminate contracting parties.
The Contracting Parties adopted, in 1958, a recommendation on marks of origin with the objective of further reducing the difficulties and inconveniences that marking requirements may cause to the commerce and industry of the exporting country. It provides in particular for a consultation procedure in the event of difficulties.
In addition, several instruments negotiated under GATT auspices explicitly refer to intellectual property rights: the Agreement on Technical Barriers to Trade, the Agreement on Implementation of Article VII of the GATT (Customs valuation) and the 1986 version of the ▷ Multifibre.
GATT's *Newsletter Focus*, September/October, 1987.

TRADE TERMS INTERNATIONAL. A subject of research and promotion of the International Trade Center UNCTAD/GATT, f. 1964 in Geneva, Palais des Nations. Publ.: Trade Promotion Handbooks, Directories and Bibliographies, Market Surveys, Monographs on Trade Channels, Monographs on Trade Functions, Training Material and others, in English, French and Spanish. In English: International Trade Documentation: Annotated List of Publications Received by ITC (monthly).

ITC *Twenty Year History 1964–1984*, Geneva, 1984; ITC UNCTAD/GATT *Thesaurus of International Terms*, Geneva, 1985; *World Directory of Trade Promotion Organizations and Other Foreign Trade Bodies*, Geneva, 1985.

TRADE UNIONS. The social institutions for the protection of the interests of the working class; originated from the class struggle waged by the European and American proletariat in the 19th century; first legalized in Great Britain in 1871; before World War I organized into the Trade Unions International. In America, on the initiative of the American Federation of Labor, AFL, and the Revolutionary Confederation of Mexican Workers – Confederación Revolucionario de Obreros Mexicanos, CROM, the Panamerican Workers Confederation – Confederación Obrera Panamericana, was established in 1918 which split after 6 congresses (Jan., 1918, Laredo, USA; Feb., 1919, New York; Mar., 1921 and Apr., 1924, Mexico; May, 1927, Washington; June, 1930, Havana) in face of a conflict between the interests of the USA and Latin America. An independent Confederation of Latin American Workers – Confederación de Trabajadores de America Latina, CTAL, was established in 1938 in Mexico; after World War II the European trade union movement established three central international organizations: the International Confederation of Trade Unions (1919), popularly called the Amsterdam International; the International Confederation of Christian Trade Unions (1920) and the Red Trade Union International (1921), commonly called Profitern. At the same time, ILO initiated studies on the international development of trade union laws. After World War II an event of historic significance was the unification of the international trade union movement into one organization called the World Federation of Trade Unions whose statute provided, i.a., that:

"The World Federation shall strive to improve living and working conditions of peoples of all countries and to consolidate them in order to obtain goals set by all peace-loving nations and laid down in the Declaration of the World Confederation of Trade Unions in London, February, 1945. These and other objectives may be fully implemented only if such an order is established in the world that all resources are used to the benefit of every nation consisting to a considerable extent of manual and clerical workers. The unification of organized domestic and international forces is essential for the protection of their interests and for progress."

In 1948 the International Conference of Labor seated in Geneva laid down principles of union laws and prepared a convention on the freedom of association by working people to form trade unions; adopted in Res. 84/V by ECOSOC and in Res. 128/II by the UN General Assembly.

In 1948 the world Federation of Trade Unions disintegrated. The International Confederation of Free Trade Unions was established. In 1966 the French trade union organization CGT and its Italian counterpart CGIL formed a permanent liaison committee with the World Federation of Trade Unions in Brussels. In 1969 the American trade union organizations AFL–CIO left the International Confederation of Free Trade Unions. In 1968 the International Confederation of Christian Trade Unions changed its name to the World Confederation of Labor with headquarters in Brussels. The largest trade union is the World Federation of Trade Unions, WFTU, with a membership of 150 million, the second largest is the International Confederation of Free Trade Unions, ICFTU, 47 million members, about 27 million members in Western Europe, about 7.6 million in Asia and Oceania, about 3 million in Latin America and 1.5 million in Canada. The next is the World Federation of Labor with headquarters in Brussels and 14 million members, i.e. 3 million members in Western Europe, about 7 million in Latin America, the remaining 4 million in Canada, Africa and South Asia. Besides the trade unions mentioned above, in 1972 the UN registered the following organizations and institutions of the trade union movement (according to the date of establishment):

International Organization of Employees, f. 1919, Geneva; advisory status with ECOSOC and ILO; Publ.: *IOE Information Bulletin.*
International Confederation of Intellectual Workers, f. 1923, Paris; consultative status with ECOSOC and UNESCO.
International Federation of Social Workers, f. 1932, New York, Consultative status with ECOSOC.
World Union of Liberal Trade Union Organizations, f. 1948, Zurich.
International Center of Free Trade Unions In Exile, f. 1948, Paris.
Inter-American Regional Confederation of Workers, f. 1951, Mexico, as a successor to the Interamerican Confederation of Workers. Publ.: *Noticiero Obrero Interamericano.*
Scandinavian Bank Employees Union, f. 1953, Helsinki.
International Federation of Arab Trade Unions, f. 1956, Cairo.
All-African Trade Union Federation, f. 1961, Casablanca.
Inter-American Institute for Trade Union Research, f. 1962, Mexico.
Federation of Workers in the Banana Industry in Latin America and the Caribbean, f. 1963, Lima.

On May 1, 1960 the Cuban trade unions initiated the unification of Latin American trade unions; Jan. 24–28, 1964 the first Permanent Congress of Unity of Latin American Workers, Congresso Permanente de Unidad Sindical de Trabajadores en América Latina, CPUSTAL, was held in Brasilia. Santiago de Chile was chosen as the headquarters of the secretariat and since Sept., 1973 – Havana.

In Jan., 1977 CPUSTAL signed a joint declaration in Havana with the World Federation of Trade Unions. In Western Europe, as a result of the establishment of large multinational corporations, trade unions early in the 70s also started to organize their struggle on the multinational level. This problem was considered by ILO, the only international organization including government and trade unions representatives. In the 60s multinationals began to transfer their enterprises to countries with cheaper labor. In 1967 the American Automobile Workers Union forced three companies: General Motors, Ford and Chrysler to pay the same wages both in Canadian and US factories. In Western Europe, where the tradition of solidarity strikes among dockers prevails, similar forms of struggle were adopted by automotive and steel industry trade unions.
In Feb., 1973 at the Congress of Free Trade Unions held in Brussels and associated with social democratic parties the Confederation of European Trade Unions was established. It incorporated headquarters of trade unions of all EEC and EFTA countries as an organization open to other trade unions included either in the World Confederation of Labor or the World Federation of Trade Unions. The VIIIth World Congress of Trade Unions held in Varna on Sept. 15–22, 1973 under the slogan: Unity and solidarity for future progress, freedom and peace, for the first time gathered 86 countries representing 200 trade union headquarters and organizations, including 120 non-members of the World Federation of Trade Unions.
In 1979 ECOSOC initiated the preparation of an international convention on the protection of the

rights of all migrant workers. In 1980 the ILO adopted an International Recommendation on Older Workers (aged 45 or over) for equality of opportunity and treatment and initiation of retirement problems.
The International Confederation of Free Trade Unions, publ.: *Free Labour World* (bimonthly), *ITU News* (fortnightly), and *Economic and Social Bulletin* (bimonthly).
The World Federation of Trade Unions, publ.: *World Trade Union Movement* (monthly, in 9 languages) and *Trade Unions Press* (fortnightly, in 6 languages).
World Confederation of Labour, publ.: *Labour Press and Information* (monthly, in 5 languages).

S. WEBB, B. WEBB, *History of Trade Unionism*, London, 1920; S. PERLMAN, *History of Trade Unionism in the United States*, New York, 1922; H.E. MARQUAND, *Organized Labour in Four Continents*, London, 1930; J. PRICE, *International Labour Movement*, London, 1945; I. DEUTSCHER, *Soviet Trade Unions, Their Place in Soviet Labour Policy*, London, 1950; H.A. MILLIS, E.C. BROWN, *From the Wagner Act to the Taft Hartley*, New York, 1950; W. GALNSON, (ed.), *Comparative Labour Movements*, London, 1952; F.R. DULLAS, *Labour in America, A History*, New York, 1960; V. ALBA, *Historia del Movimiento Obrero en America Latina*, Mexico, DF, 1964; A. DEL ROSAL, *Los Congresos Obreros Interamericanos en el Siglo XX, des 1900 a 1950*, 2 Vols., México, DF, 1964; K.A. SUSIEYNOV, *Internatsionalnie sviazi profsoyuzov SSSR*, Moscow, 1965; J. DAVIES, *Trade Unions*, Harmondsworth, 1966; A.P. COLDRICK, P.H. JONES, *International Directory of the Trade Union Movement*, London, 1979; *Yearbook of International Organizations.*

TRADE UNIONS, INTERNATIONAL. The world trade unions organizations since the end of the 19th century. The first Congresses of the Trade Unions International were held before World War I: 1900 in Paris, 1901 in Copenhagen, 1902 in Stuttgart, 1903 in Dublin, 1905 in Amsterdam, 1907 in Oslo, 1909 in Paris, 1910 in Budapest, 1913 in Zurich. During World War I three congresses were held: 1916 in Leeds (Great Britain), and in 1917 in Stockholm and in Berlin. There was a break in the movement after World War I: in 1919/20 the Amsterdam International was set up and in 1920/21 the Profintern. After World War II a new Trade Unions International came into being under the name of the World Federation of Trade Unions; some West European Unions have left the World Federation of Trade Unions in 1949 and formed the Confederation of International Free Trade Unions.

L.L. LORVIN, *Labor and Internationalism*, London, 1929; J. PRICE, *International Labour Movement*, London, 1945; F.J. HARPER, *Trade Unions in the World*, London, 1987.

TRAFFIC ARTERIES IN EUROPE. A subject of a Declaration on the Construction of Main International Traffic Arteries, signed on Sept. 16, 1950, at Geneva, by Albania, Austria, Belgium, Bulgaria, Byelorussian SSR, Czechoslovakia, Denmark, Egypt, Finland, France, FRG, GDR, Greece, Hungary, Iceland, Iraq, Ireland, Israel, Italy, Jordan, the Netherlands, Norway, Poland, Romania, Sweden, Switzerland, Turkey, the UK, Ukrainian SSR, the USSR, Yugoslavia.

UNTS, 1951.

TRAFFIC IN WHITE SLAVES. A subject of international treaties:
(1) the Treaty on the Suppression of the Traffic in White Slaves concluded on Mar. 18, 1904; (2) the International Convention on Elimination of the traffic in White Slaves of May 4, 1910; and (3) the Auxiliary Protocol of May, 1949. ▷ Slavery.

Provisional Bibliography on Slavery, Washington, DC, 1950.

TRAFFIC IN WOMEN AND CHILDREN. A subject of two conventions: The Convention on the Prohibition of the Traffic in Women and Children, signed on Sept. 30, 1921, in Geneva. The Convention for the Suppression of the Traffic in Persons and of the Exploitation of the Prostitution of Others, adopted by the UN General Assembly Res. 317/IV of Dec. 2, 1949.
See also ▷ Child Exploitation.

LNTS, Vol. 9, p. 415; *Yearbook of the UN 1948–49*, p. 613.

TRAFFICKING IN LABOUR. The usually illegal or clandestine recruitment and shipment under highly inhuman conditions of foreign labor from the developing to the developed countries where firms employing such labor profiteer on their exploitation. Because of their clandestine arrival such workers have no right to welfare or other social benefits. Known in interwar Central Europe the practice spread in Western Europe 1960–80; 53rd ECOSOC session, July 28, 1972, defined exploitation of foreign labor through illegal clandestine trafficking as close to ▷ Slavery.

W. TINKER, *A Law System of Slavery The Export of Indian Labour Overseas 1830–1920*, Oxford, 1974.

TRAINING. The vocational and technical education. In the UN system promoted by the ILO's programs. The highlights of the ILO training program for the 1980s are as follows:
"In 1979 the ILO's expenditure on technical co-operation activities in the field of training had reached the record amount of US $38.2 million (representing the expenditure incurred on projects financed through the ILO's Regular Budget, UNDP, multilateral and trust fund arrangements; it constitutes 50% of the ILO's total expenditure on technical co-operation in 1979). Apart from the increasing demand on the ILO to provide support for training activities, at the national and regional levels, the concern of the Organisation and its membership with training is based on two major sets of interlinked considerations.
The first are economic considerations. Training provides people with knowledge, skills and attitudes which enable them to produce goods and services. It raises their productivity, increases the profits of undertakings and thus contributes to general economic development.
The second series of considerations are the social ones. They are based on the recognised fact that economic development can no longer be an end in itself and that it is only a means to achieve the social objectives of our societies. What we have to seek is the freedom and dignity of man and his right to live and work in better conditions than hitherto. The role of training in achieving these social objectives is crucial.
Training helps people to break out of the poverty trap by raising their productivity and increasing their incomes. Millions of workers, though employed, find themselves in low-productivity jobs which they cannot change unless they have acquired additional knowledge and skills.
Training improves people's ability to choose freely an employment and contributes to their mobility.
Training protects the employability of the worker and reduces his vulnerability to unemployment in a time of depression.
Training opens the door to workers to develop their careers and leads to job and personal satisfaction.
Training promotes self-reliance and self-respect.
Training is an important key to unlocking the potential for an improved quality of life.
Viewed as such, training is a basic right and a basic need to which every person, man or woman, boy or girl, should have access if he or she so desires. It is a life-long process which is not limited to initial training but is a continuous process extending throughout the working life of an individual.

Obviously training must be seen within the context of the total learning system of a country. This is a system which, despite the enormous efforts which have been made, still does not reach millions of people in developing countries, nor does it provide equal opportunities; and it often perpetuates prevailing economic and social injustices.

The extensive discussions on the reform of education and training which started some two decades ago and which still continue are the best evidence that important and probably drastic changes are still needed.

The ILO has always played the leading role within the United Nations system in supporting national endeavours which aim at promoting or bringing about reforms in training in close collaboration with the International Centre for Advanced Technical and Vocational Training in Turin.

The first ILO training initiative dates back to 1921 when the Vocational Education (Agriculture) Recommendation (No. 15) was adopted. Since then, more than 15 international instruments directly related to training have been adopted; there are also a number of other instruments which, though not directly related to training, have an impact on training policies.

The long history of the ILO's involvement in training and the accumulated experience which the Organisation has gained enabled it to widen the scope of its activities. Today, these activities cover policy issues at the sectoral and inter-sectoral levels and training activities at all levels of skill, from unskilled worker to manager and for all sectors of the economy.

The tripartite structure of the ILO has given these activities much strength. The interest in training is shared not only by governments but also by employers' and workers' organisations, which see in training a means of ensuring the participation of people in the development process of their nations."

"Training: Challenge of the 1980s," in: *Report of the Director General of the ILO*, Geneva, 1980, pp. 3–52.

TRAINMARK. ▷ World Maritime University.

TRAMP NAVIGATION. ▷ Line shipping.

TRANCHE. An international term, used in the UN system for a credit granted by the IMF to its member nations. Each country is entitled to a series of four tranches under increasingly difficult conditions. The first tranche usually carries conditions, the fourth might be contingent on stringent economic reforms such as reduced or eliminated budget deficit.

UN Chronicle, October, 1982, p. 48.

TRANQUILLIZERS. A subject of international control. In Feb., 1983 the UN Commission on Narcotic Drugs, on the basis of a recommendation by the WHO decided to place 33 widely prescribed tranquillizers, known as *benzodiazepines*, under international control, requiring, among other restrictions, that they be dispensed only by prescription. Foremost on the list is *diazepam*, a psychotropic drug sold under dozens of brand names, including *Valium*. Among other brand names are: *Alboral* in Mexico, *Anding* in China, *Anzepam* and *Calmpose* in India, *Dialag* in Switzerland, *Pacitran* in Brazil, *Saromet* in Argentina, *Sedavil* in Japan, and *Sedapam* and *Tensium* in the United Kingdom.

UN Chronicle, No. 3, 1984.

TRANS-ANDEAN RAILROADS. The longest, 500 km, links Buenos Aires on the Atlantic with Valparaiso on the Pacific, running through the Tunnel La Cumbra at a height of 3200 m. The Argentine–Chilean railroad Salta–Antofagasta runs through the mountain pass Socompo at 3858 m. Two railroad lines link Chile with Bolivia: Antofagasta–Oruro–La Paz and Arica–La Paz.

Los ferrocarriles internacionales de Sudamerica y la integración económica regional, UN, New York, 1972.

TRANSATLANTIC CABLE LINE. The cable line constructed 1956 by the American Telephone and Telegraph Company, British Post Office and Canadian Overseas Telecommunication Corporation along a line 3600 km long on the bottom of the North Atlantic from the town of Oban in western Scotland (where the telephone exchange connecting to London is located) to Clarenville in Newfoundland, then a further 600 km by land and again along the ocean bottom to Sidney Mines, location of the telephone exchange switchboard to New York and Montreal; connected to cables linking Great Britain with Europe. It was the first and longest transoceanic line carrying intercontinental conversations, constructed one year before the flight into orbit of the first satellite, which opened new possibilities of ▷ Satellite telecommunication.

The Post Office Engineers Journal, London, Jan., 1957.

TRANSATLANTIC SINGLE-HANDED RE-GATTAS. The international boat races, organized by the Royal Western Yacht Club of England and by the editorial office of the English daily *Observer* every 4 years since June 11, 1960, when four yachts each with a one-man crew started from Plymouth (Great Britain) for Newport (USA). The winner was a 58-year-old Englishman F. Chichester, who completed the journey in 40 days, 12 hours and 30 minutes.

KEESING'S *Contemporary Archive*, 1960.

TRANSCARPATHIA. The name of a territory subject of international disputes between Hungary, Czechoslovakia and the Ukraine: for centuries under the Hungarian rule; in 1919 was given to Czechoslovakia but in Oct., 1938 became subject of political strife as a result of the post-Munich crisis in that country. Under the Vienna Arbitration agreement of Nov., 1938 an autonomous government of Transcarpathia was formed and given rights to two towns, Hust and Svalva. The area was occupied by Hungary from 1939 until 1945, when it became the Transcarpathian province of the Ukrainian Soviet Socialist Republic on the basis of the CSR–USSR treaty signed on June 29, 1945, in Moscow, in which Czechoslovakia renounced its rights to Transcarpathia. The treaty was ratified Nov., 1945 and entered into force on Jan. 30, 1946.

TRUS *Diplomatic Papers 1945*, Europe, Vol. IV, p. 521; C.A. COLLIARD, *Droit internationale et histoire diplomatique*, Paris, 1950.

TRANSCAUCASIA. An historical region of the USSR, between the Black and Caspian Seas from the Greater Caucasus to Iran and Turkey. After the October Revolution 1917, divided between three independent republics: Armenia, Azerbaidzhan and Georgia; in Dec., 1922, united in the Transcaucasian SFSR until 1936, when again three republics were proclaimed, but as Soviet Socialist Republics, a part of the USSR.

TRANSCONTAINER. A common commercial agency of the European railway administrations, under the name International Company for the Transport by Transcontainers, Intercontainer, f. 1967, Brussels. Publ.: *International Transcontainer Tariff*. Reg. with the UIA.

Yearbook of International Organizations.

TRANS-EUROPEAN MOTORWAY, TEM. A road network, linking the north and south of Europe. ▷ Traffic arteries in Europe.

UN Chronicle, December, 1982, p. 103.

TRANS-EUROPE EXPRESS, TEE. A railroad network of the EEC countries of express trains with frontier formalities reduced to minimum.

J. PAXTON, *A Dictionary of the European Economic Community*, London, 1978.

TRANSFER. The unilateral movement of funds from one country to another in a certain exchangeable currency as well as in stocks and bonds. The free transfer of capital from country to country took place without limitations in the 19th century in western and central Europe and in North America. After World War I, in connection with the destabilization of currencies, many states introduced limitations on transfer.

J.M. KEYNES, "The German Transfer Problem," in: *Economic Journal*, 1929.

TRANSFER OF CONVICTS EC CONVENTIONS, 1987. Signed on May 9, 1987 by the EC Member States allowing Community citizens sentenced in another member country to serve their sentence in their home country.

KEESING's *Record of World Events*, May, 1988.

TRANSFER OF TECHNOLOGY. The transfer of modern technology achievements from highly developed countries to developing countries. The UN General Assembly Special Session, 1974, in the Res. 3202/S-VI, adopted a Program of Action on the Establishment of a ▷ New International Economic Order. The fourth chapter of this Program was dedicated to the transfer of technology. The text is as follows:

"All efforts should be made:
(a) To formulate an international code of conduct for the transfer of technology corresponding to needs and conditions prevalent in developing countries;
(b) To give access on improved terms to modern technology and to adapt that technology, as appropriate, to specific economic, social and ecological conditions and varying stages of development in developing countries;
(c) To expand significantly the assistance from developed to developing countries in research and development programmes and in the creation of suitable indigenous technology;
(d) To adapt commercial practices governing transfer of technology to the requirements of the developing countries and to prevent abuse of the rights of sellers;
(e) To promote international co-operation in research and development in exploration and exploitation, conservation and the legitimate utilization of natural resources and all sources of energy.
In taking the above measures, the special needs of the least-developed and land-locked countries should be borne in mind."

Conference on Economic Co-operation among Developing Countries. Declarations, Resolutions, Recommendations and Decisions adopted in the UN System. México, DF, 1976, Vol. I, pp. 57–88; *UN Chronicle*, October, 1982, p. 48.

TRANSFER ROUBLE. ▷ Roubles, transferable.

TRANSFUSIOLOGY. A subject of international co-operation since the 1st Congress of Blood Transfusion, 1935 in Rome. Organization reg. with the UIA:

International Society for Blood Transfusion, f. 1937, Paris. Official relations with WHO and ECOSOC. Publ.: *Vox Sanguinis* (six a year in English).

Yearbook of International Organizations.

TRANSIT. A carriage of persons, objects and products by water, air or land across a specified area on the basis of international conventions, as well as carriage of persons or cargo from one country to another across the territory of a third country under terms of bilateral or multilateral agreements. First

International Convention and Statute on Free Transit was signed on Apr. 20, 1921 in Barcelona, and came into force Oct. 31, 1922. Its major provisions defined traffic in transport as meaning the passage of persons, luggage, cargo, sea-going and river vessels, passenger and freight railway stock, as well as other means of transport, across territories under supervision or authority of any contracting state whether the passage includes transshipment or not, warehousing or not, breaking bulk or not, assembly, disassembly or reassembly of cargo, with or without a change in the mode of transport, and is a portion of a complete journey which begins or terminates outside the territory of that state. Such transit traffic charges may be levied solely to cover the cost of maintaining in good condition the road used by the object or person in transit. No country shall be bound to grant transit to persons or goods whose admission or exit is prohibited on its territory (the convention allows temporary suspension of its provisions under exceptional circumstances and does not apply to the rights and duties of belligerents in the time of war). On July 8, 1965 the UN Conference of Trade and Development adopted a Convention on Transit for Land Locked Countries, which came into force June 9, 1967. (▷ Sea Law Convention, 1982, Art. 125.)

In Europe since 1960 transit is free for persons with identity cards as well as for objects and products in transit between Scandinavian countries and within EEC countries. A similar process took place in the 60s and 70s between the European Warsaw Pact countries. In the Western Hemisphere free transit of persons has been in force since 1900 between USA and Canada, whereas in Latin America the matter is regulated since Dec. 12, 1966 by the Protocol on the Transit of Persons, signed in Montevideo by foreign ministers of ALALC countries providing (art. 1) that holders of passports or valid identity cards of one of ALALC countries are allowed to enter, pass through or leave the territory of any other member country without the necessity of obtaining a visa or special permission; the Protocol limits the period of stay to 90 days (Art. 3).

R. OCHSNER, *Der Transit von Personen und Gütern durch ein neutrales Land im Falle des Landkrieges*, Zürich, 1948; *UN Bulletin*, 1949, p. 402, and 1952, p. 329; *UNTS*, Vol. 597, pp. 42-58.

TRANSIT LAW. The right of transit of foreign troops, granted by one state to another state on the basis of bilateral or multilateral agreements; recognized by the United Nations in art. 43 of the Charter of the UN, obliging all UN members to make available to the call of the Security Council, "armed forces, assistance, and facilities, including the rights of passage, necessary for the purpose of maintaining international peace and security."

TRANSITORY SETTLEMENT. An international term introduced in 1963 by ECOSOC in the UN publications and replacing the depreciatory term ▷ slums.

TRANSJORDAN. A historical name (a land across the Jordan) of an Arab emirate, founded after the defeat of Turkey in 1921 from a part of Palestine on the eastern bank of the Jordan by Great Britain, which exercised power over this territory under League of Nations mandate. After the mandate's expiry on Mar. 15, 1946, Transjordan was proclaimed an independent kingdom, and on Jan. 24, 1949 assumed the official name of the Hashemite Kingdom of ▷ Jordan.

U. BAR-JOSEPH, *The Best of Enemies/Israel and Jordan in the War of 1948*, London, 1987.

TRANSKEI. One of the Bantustans in the Republic of South Africa on the coast of the Indian Ocean. Area: 42,000 sq. km. Pop. 1971: 1,751,000. On Oct. 25, 1976 the government of South Africa proclaimed the "independence" of Transkei, an action which the UN General Assembly on Oct. 27, 1976 recognized as "null and invalid." At the same time, the government of South Africa forced the members of the Khosa tribe living outside the territory of Transkei in the approx. number of 1.3 million to take citizenship of that bantustan, or else they would lose their jobs. UN Secretary-General, Kurt Waldheim, stated that: "the world community shall never recognize transformation of Bantustans into separate political entities."

KEESING'S *Contemporary Archive*, 1975.

TRANSLATIONS. A subject of international co-operation under the aegis of UNESCO (▷ Index). Official translation in the United Nations is formally into five (Chinese, English, French, Russian and Spanish) or six (Arabic) official languages; in the majority of institutions of the UN System two working languages (English–French or English–Spanish) in regional intergovernmental organizations from one (EFTA–English only) up to nine (EEC–Danish, Dutch, English, French, German, Greek, Italian, Portuguese, Spanish). The cost of translation swallows up to a third of the UN's annual budget ($2 billion) at a cost of over $500 a page into the nine languages.

Organizations reg. with the UIA:

International Association of Conference Interpreters, f. 1953, Geneva, Publ.: *Yearbook with Conference Interpreters Directory*.
International Association of Conference Translators, f. 1962, Geneva, Publ.: *Practical Guide for Users of Conference Language Services*.
International Federation of Translators, f. 1953, Paris. Consultative status with UNESCO and ECOSOC. Publ.: *Babel, International Journal of Translation* (quarterly, in English and French).
International Translation Centre, f. 1961, Delft, Netherlands. Provides for Western industry and research translation of Russian and East European and Oriental scientific and technical literature. Publ.: *World Index of Scientific Translations, Translation News and Translation Journal*.
Leibnitz Group, Groupe d'étude pour la traduction automatique, f. 1974, Grenoble. Under EEC aegis at the University of Grenoble co-ordinates procedures for automatic language translation to facilitate multilingual translations.
Standing International Conference of the Directors of University Institutes for the Training of Translators and Interpreters, f. 1961, Geneva.

ELSEVIER's, *Glossarium Interpretum*, Amsterdam, since 1957; *International Bibliography of Translation*, München, 1972, *Yearbook of International Organizations, 1986/87*. *The Economist*, July 18, 1987, p. 20.

TRANSLITERATION. An international term for rendering the written elements of one language by means of the written elements of another, i.e. conversion of letters consisting in the graphic reproduction of the letters of one alphabet by using the corresponding letters of another alphabet, if necessary with diacritical marks without considering the phonetic properties of the vowels corresponding to the transliterated letters ("Transcription" considers the phonetic qualities of vowels corresponding to individual letters), subject of international standardizations introduced by UNESCO.

British Standard for Transliteration of Cyrillic and Greek Characters, London, 1958; *International System for the Transliteration of Slavic Cyrillic Characters*, London, 1968; P. CALONGE, *Transcripción del ruso al español*, Madrid, 1969.

TRANSNATIONAL BANKS. An international term for commercial and investment banks with major expansions of their foreign networks. In 1975 there were 84 deposit-taking banks with branches or with majority-owned subsidiaries in five or more different countries or territories. About three-quarters of the assets in the transnational banking community were from the US, the UK, Japan, France, the FRG and Canada.

"Transnational Banks and Developing Countries," in: *The CTC Reporter*, No. 8, Spring, 1980.

TRANSNATIONAL CORPORATIONS. The term was introduced in the second half of the 20th century by large international concerns, which had developed a network of foreign branches employing local manpower.

In July, 1972, the ECOSOC unanimously called for action regarding the role of transnational corporations in the world economy, especially their impact on development and on international relations. The relevant resolution noted that the international community had yet to formulate a positive policy and to establish effective machinery for dealing with the issues raised by the activities of those corporations. That resolution led to a comprehensive study entitled Multinational Corporations in World Development.

Subsequently, the UN Secretary-General established a Group of Eminent Persons, intimately acquainted with international economic, trade and social problems, which met during 1973–74. The Group concluded that fundamental new problems had arisen as a direct result of the growing internationalization of production carried out by transnational corporations. It recommended that the international community, through the United Nations, tackle those problems without delay in order to ease tensions and fully realize the benefits to be derived from those corporations.

On that basis, the Economic and Social Council decided, in 1974, to establish an intergovernmental Commission on Transnational Corporations to act "as the forum within the United Nations system for the comprehensive and in-depth consideration of issues relating to transnational corporations." The 48-member Commission, which meets annually, held its first meeting in New York in 1975. The Commission's work program gives the highest priority to formulating a code of conduct for transnational corporations. To this end it has established an intergovernmental working group which has made substantial progress in its work. Other important areas of activity include: establishing a comprehensive information system; research on the economic, political, legal and social effects of the activities of transnational corporations; and technical co-operation.

The Economic and Social Council also established a Center on Transnational Corporations, which became functional in Nov., 1975, to provide the necessary support to the Council and the Commission. The Center was to develop a comprehensive information system on the activities of transnational corporations, to organize and co-ordinate technical co-operation programs, and to conduct research. The Commission requested the Center to collect publicly available information on transnationals, including the preparation of profiles on individual corporations. Other areas of study include the impact of transnationals on the balance of payments, particularly of developing countries, corrupt practices, the effects of investments by transnationals on investment and production by domestic enterprises, and the effects on employment. The Commission has also requested the Center to examine the role and impact of transnationals in a number of sectors, notably in banking, insurance, shipping, tourism and the extractive, food and pharmaceutical industries.

The Center organizes training workshops for government officials, responds to inquiries from Governments for specific information, and makes advisers available to assist Governments. This is aimed at strengthening the negotiating capacity of developing countries in questions relating to transnational corporations. The Center publ. in New York *The OTC Reporter*.

A comprehensive report on the impact of transnationals on the world economy was completed in Mar., 1978. It examined how transnationals could contribute more to the growth and improvement of conditions in developing countries. The report stated that direct investments by transnationals in foreign countries rose by 80% between 1971 and 1976, from $158 billion to $287 billion. Nearly three-quarters of their capital investment was in the developed countries. The one quarter in the developing countries was increasingly concentrated in the more industrialized nations, underlining, in the view of the report, the limited contribution of transnationals towards fulfilling the basic needs of developing countries. The report concluded that national and international action was still needed if transnationals were to play a more constructive role.

A UN Commission on Transnational Corporations established in 1978 a 48-member Intergovernmental Working Group on a Code of Conduct on Transnational Corporations. The draft of the Code, according to a statement made by UN Secretary-General Javier Perez de Cuellar, on Mar. 17, 1983, "will be the most comprehensive instrument dealing with a wide variety of issues in international economic relations on a global basis."

The members of the Commission for 1984 were: Algeria, Argentina, Bahama, Bangladesh, Brazil, Canada, Central African Republic, China, Congo, Costa Rica, Cuba, Egypt, France, FRG, GDR, Ghana, Guatemala, Guinea, India, Indonesia, Iran, Italy, Jamaica, Japan, Kenya, Korea Republic, Libya, Mexico, the Netherlands, Nigeria, Norway, Pakistan, Peru, Romania, Sierra Leone, Swaziland, Switzerland, Thailand, Turkey, Uganda, UK, Ukrainian SSR, USA, USSR, Venezuela and Yugoslavia.

On July 29, 1983, the ECOSOC plenary session adopted a resolution by a vote (36 in favor, 3 against, with 11 abstentions) condemning those Transnational Corporations which collaborated with the "racist minority régime" in South Africa and Namibia.

B. McLENNAN, *The Impact of Transnational Corporations on Developing Countries, A Selected Literature and Annotated Bibliography*, UNESCO, Paris, 1978; *UN Bibliography on Transnational Corporations*, New York, 1978; G. MODELSKI (ed.), *Transnational Corporations and World Order*, San Francisco, 1979; *UN Chronicle*, March, 1982, p. 57, and July, 1982, pp. 105–106; March, 1983, p. 2, March, 1983, pp. 65–68; and October, 1983, p. 63; *Transnational Corporations in World Development, UN Third Survey*, New York, 1983; *UN National Legislation and Regulations Relating to Transnational Corporations*, 5 Vls., New York, 1986.

TRANSNATIONAL LAW. An international term coined in the 1950's for public and private transnational transactions, in the 1980's applicable to ▷ multinational (or transnational) corporations.

R.L. BLEDSOE, B.A. BOCZEK, *The International Law Dictionary*, Oxford, 1987.

TRANS-PACIFIC AGREEMENT, 1947. An agreement between the governments of the UK, Australia and New Zealand, concerning the formation of the British Commonwealth Pacific Airlines Limited, signed on Aug. 4, 1947, for the purpose "of establishing, operating and developing Trans-Pacific Air Service between Australia and North America and between New Zealand and North America."

UNTS, Vol. 28, pp. 42–44 and Vol. 53, pp. 236–245.

TRANSPORT. A subject of international co-operation and agreements.

TRANSPORT AND COMMMUNICATIONS IN THE UN, The UN General Assembly decision made ECOSOC responsible in the years 1946–59 for working out instruments of international co-operation and international conventions in the field of transport and communications. The ECOSOC commission convened the following specialized conferences: in Apr 1947– on passports, visas and transit documents, called Meeting of experts on Passport and Frontier Formality: in Aug.–Sept., 1949–the UN Conference on Road and Motor Transport, which adopted Conventions on Road Traffic (came into force Mar. 26, 1952) and Protocol on Road Signs and Signals (came into force Mar. 26, 1952); another meeting in Sept., 1957 was the Conference on Customs Formalities for the Temporary Importation of Private Road Motor Vehicles and for Tourism; adopted Convention on Customs Tourism Facilities (came into force Sept. 11, 1957) and Convention on the Temporal Import of Private Road Vehicles (came into force Dec. 15, 1957). Other activities of this ECOSOC commission include: 1953–draft protocol on unified system of road signs and signals; 1956–recommendations for transportation of explosives, inflammable materials, etc., 1958–recommendations for food transportation., By an ECOSOC decision in 1959 the work of the commission was terminated, its functions assumed by ECOSOC Council, while some functions passed on to UN regional economic commissions.

In May, 1980 a UN Conference on International Multimodal Transport was held in Geneva and elaborated the Convention on International Multimodal Transport of Goods, to be mandatorily applicable to international multimodal contracts, imposed an agreed system of liability over existing unimodal regimes governing the contractual relationship between consignor and the multimodal transport operator (MTO) for the entire transport of goods from the time the MTO took them in charge until delivery; irrespective of the different modes of transport involved.

UN List of Multilateral Conventions, Agreements etc. Relating to Transport and Communications Questions, New York, 1948; *Conferencia de las NU sobre Transporte par Carreterra y Transporte par Vehiculos Automotores*, New York, 1950; *UN Customs Convention on the International Transport of Goods by Road*, New York, 1950; *Transport de Mercadorias Peligrosas*, New York, 1956; *Transport of Perishable Foodstuffs*, New York, 1958; R.T. BROWNS, *Transport and the Economic Integration of South America*, Washington, DC, 1966; *UN Chronicle*, August 1980, p. 80; W. RYBCZYNSKI, *Transportation and Water: Low-cost Options for Sanitation*, Washington, DC, World Bank, 1982; R. RODIERE (ed.), *International Encyclopedia of Comparative Law*, Vol. IV, *Law of Transport*, The Hague, 1985.

TRANSPORT ESCAP DECADE 1985–1994. The Transport and Communication Decade 1985–1994 was launched by Asia–Pacific Governments that adopted on Jan. 25, 1985, during an ESCAP conference, a Declaration recommending a transport and communication program for the region inhabited by some 2.6 billion people.

UN Chronicle, 1985, No. 2, p. 26.

TRANSPORTATION LAW. The civil law rules on transportation, integrated by international private law; subject of international bilateral and multilateral conventions in the areas of railroads, aviation and shipping.

TRANSPORT IN THE CMEA SYSTEM. One of the fundamental branches of economy embraced by the process of integration of socialist countries; subject of work carried out since June, 1958 by the CMEA Permanent Commission for Transport with a view to co-ordinating development and unification on the most modern level of international railway, air, coach, water transport, as well as transport through pipelines of oil, gas, petrochemicals, chemical products and minerals; the commission co-ordinates research into a dozen or so key problems of transport, among others–organization of the system of container transport, optimization of transport through computerization, automation of air traffic, exploitation of railway track and ways of increasing track resistance. The commission works in close co-operation with the CMEA Normalization Institute aiming at standardization, unification and normalization of transport stock. A comprehensive program adopted at the 25th session envisages, among other things, providing technical, economic and technological foundations for container transport system in domestic and international transport of CMEA member countries and application of analytical techniques and mathematical methods in planning and management of transport processes.

The CMEA transport agreements, in alphabetical order are as follows:

Agreement on International Direct Mixed Rail––Water Freight Transport, signed on Dec. 14, 1959 at Sofia, by the governments of Bulgaria, Czechoslovakia, GDR, Hungary, Poland, Romania, USSR.

Agreement on Introducing a Uniform Container Transport System, signed on Dec. 3, 1971 at Budapest by the governments of Bulgaria Czechoslovakia, GDR, Hungary, Mongolia, Poland and USSR.

Agreement on Joint Use of Containers in International Transport signed on June 24, 1974 at Karl-Marx-Stadt, by Bulgaria, Czechoslovakia, Cuba, GDR, Hungary, Mongolia, Poland, Romania and USSR.

Agreement on the Joint Planning of the Material Technical Base of the Container Transport System and Co-operation in the Creation of Future Development, signed on Apr. 20, 1972 at Moscow, by the governments of Bulgaria, Czechoslovakia, GDR, Hungary, Poland and USSR.

Agreement on Questions of Co-operation in the Operational, Commercial and Financial Activity between Air Transport Enterprises, signed on Dec. 14, 1959 at Sofia, by the Bulgarian Civil Air Transport Board, TABSO; the Czechoslovak Air Line, CSA; the GDR Geselschaft für Internationalen Flug-Verkehr, INTERFLUG; the Air Transport Board of Mongolia, MBH; the Polish Air Line, LOT; the Romanian Air Transport, TAROM; and the International Civil Aviation Airline of the USSR, AEROFLOT. ▷ Railways.

W.E. BUTLER (ed.), *A Source Book on Socialist International Organizations*, Alphen, 1978, pp. 511–524 and 1063–1094.

TRANSPORT IN THE INTER-AMERICAN SYSTEM. After World War II in the Western Hemisphere rapid integration of transport and communications occurred in North America (Canada, USA, Mexico); alongside integrational progress of transport and communications in Central America; and chronic disintegration of South American transport and communications.

There were air and sea links between North and Central America and South America but hardly any roads and railways to connect South American republics. It was not until the construction of the new capital of Brazil and a star-shaped system of south- north- and west-bound motorways from Brasilia, as well as the Trans-Amazon project in 1971–80, that the possibility opened for the creation in South America of a uniform system of internal connections, motor roads in particular. The efforts of Latin American countries started in 1960–65 with the establishment of special organs for Central America and for Latin America as a whole, such as the Asociacion Latino-Americana de Armadores, ALAMAR (Latin American Shipowners Association, LASA) and Asociacion Latino-Americana de Ferrocarriles, ALAF (Latin-American Railways Association, LARA). Earlier only an intercontinental railways project had been debated on by Inter-American conferences, 1899–1928. In 1928 construction of the Pan-American Motorway was started and in 1933 the Permanent Inter-American Committee on Fluvial Navigation was founded; the first Inter-American Port and Harbor Conference held in 1956 discussed improvement of port conditions in Latin America for the use of international sea transport.

El Transporte en el Istmo Centroamericano, CEPAL, Santiago, 1953; *El Transporte Aereo en la América Latina, PAU*, Washington, DC, 1962; Ch.G. FENWICK, *The OAS*, Washington, DC, 1963, pp. 412–423; *El Transporte en América Latina, CEPAL*, Santiago, 1965; *Estudio Económico de América Latina 1965, CEPAL*, New York, 1966, pp. 387–429; R.T. BROWN, *Transport and the Economic Integration of South America*, Washington, DC, 1966; F. HENNING, *Intra-Kontinentaler Verkehr in Lateinamerika*, Hamburg, 1966; *Notas de la CEPAL sobre la economia y el desarrollo de América Latina*, December 1, 1974.

TRANSPUTER. A microprocessor, developed in the late 1970's in Great Britain, "designed for parallel processing, working on several tasks at the same time". Like ▷ computers, subject of international co-operation or competition of the world electronic industries.

Transputers. Fast Movers, in: *The Economist*, December 12, 1987.

TRANS SAHARA ROAD. ▷ Sahara.

TRANS-SIBERIAN RAILWAY. The railroad constructed 1891–1916, linking European Russia with Siberia and the Pacific, from Chelyabinsk via Omsk–Novosibirsk–Irkutsk–Khabarovsk to Vladivostok. In 1974–84 construction of northern leg called ▷ BAM.

TRANSYLVANIA. A historical land and province of Romania, area 55,146 sq. km, subject of international conflicts and disputes; in the 17th century between Turkey and Hungary; in the 19th century between Austria and Hungary, whose province it was in 1848 and 1867–1918; in the 20th century between Hungary and Romania, to which Transylvania was ceded June 4, 1920 by the Treaty of Trianon; and on Aug. 30, 1940 by the Arbitration of Vienna the northwest part of Transylvania returned to Hungary, which was anulled by the Paris Peace Treaty of Feb. 10, 1947, and all of Transylvania returned to Romania.

Transylvania with the largest national minority group in Europe (around 2.5 million Romanian citizens of Hungarian extraction) was the subject of a Hungarian–Romanian dispute in Nov. 1986 in Vienna, during the ▷ Conference on Security and Co-operation in Europe. In Spring 1988 thousands of refugees from Transylvania settled in Hungary.

L. MAKKON, *Histoire de Transylvanie*, Paris, 1946; KEESING's *Record of World Events*, 1987, No. 5; *The Economist*, April 23, 1988.

TRAVEL AGENTS ORGANIZATIONS. International organizations reg. with the UIA:

Arab Association of Tourist and Travel Agents, f. 1950, Beirut.
East Asia Travel Association, f. 1966, Tokyo, Japan.
EEC Group of National Unions of Travel Agents, f. 1967, Brussels.
European Travel Commission, f. 1956, Deventer, Netherlands.
International League of Commercial Travelers and Agents, f. 1947, Geneva.
Pacific–Asia Travel Association, f. 1951, San Francisco, Geneva, Switzerland.
Universal Federation of Travel Agents Association, f. 1966, Brussels. Consultative status with ECOSOC and IMCO. Publ.: *Courrier*.
World Association of Travel Agencies, f. 1949, Geneva, Switzerland.

Yearbook of International Organizations, 1986/87; The Europa Yearbook 1988. A World Survey, Vol. I, London, 1988.

TRAVEL BY UN OFFICIALS. A subject of the UN General Assembly Resolutions, establishing two principles, (1) that travel expenses should be limited to the least costly air-fare structure regularly available or its equivalent, by recognized public carrier via the shortest and most direct route; (2) the use of first class is permitted only when the duration of a particular flight exceeds nine hours (by the most direct and economical route), including scheduled stops for such purposes as change of planes or refueling, but excluding travel time to and from airports.

UN Chronicle, January, 1978.

TRAVELER'S CHECKS. An international term for checks for specific sums bearing the signature of the purchaser, which after being signed a second time are honored by national and foreign banks honoring the financial institutions issuing traveler's checks.

TREASON. The crime of betraying one's homeland, state, sovereign, recognized since antiquity both by law and by custom as the most grave offence against a country's security. Usually, penal codes recognize as treason transmission of secret documents, information of highest value to the alien side (espionage), activities harmful to the security of a country (sabotage) and escape to the enemy state (defection) as well as – in some codes – armed rebellion against the supreme authority (coup d'état, golpe de estado).

M. BOVERI, *Treason in the 20th Century*, London, 1961; B. CHAPIN, *The American Law of Treason*, New York, 1964.

TREATIES. According to the definition in the Vienna Convention on the Law of Treaties of 1969:

"Treaty means an international agreement concluded between States in written form and governed by international law, whether embodied in a single instrument or in two or more related instruments and whatever its particular designation."

Catalogue of Treaties 1814–1918, Washington, DC, 1919 (Reprinted New York, 1964); League of Nations Treaty Series, 1920–46; D.P. MYERS, *Manual of Collections of Treaties and of Collections Relating to Treaties*, London, 1922; *LNTS General Index*, 9 Vols., Geneva, 1946; *UNTS*, 1946–85; J.A.S. GREENVILLE, *The Major International Treaties 1914–1945. A History and Guide with Texts*, London, 1987; R.L. BLEDSOE, B.A. BOCZEK, *The International Dictionary of Law*, Oxford, 1987.

TREATIES AND THIRD STATES. A subject of international law which since ancient times recognizes the principle that each international treaty bears consequences only for the parties (*res inter alies acta*), but does not concern third states, on which it places no obligations nor grants any rights (*pacta tertiis neo nocent neo prosunt*); at the same time, however, in international practice many deviations from the principle *pacta tertiis* appeared, expressing themselves in international agreements by a formula in favor of a third party (*in favorens tertii*), e.g. by leaving a treaty between a group of states open to third states, or by a formula to their disadvantage (*in odium tertii*) by designating a negative relationship to a third state or states.

In accordance with art. 2 par. 1 of the Vienna Convention on the Law of International Treaties, the validity of international treaties is independent of the name given them or whether they were formulated in one, two, or more documents. The essence of a treaty is the intention with which it was made.

R.F. ROXBURGH, *International Conventions and Third States*, London, 1917; J. DE ARECHAGA, "Treaty Stipulations in Favour of Third States," in: *American Journal of International Law*, No. 50, 1956; I.S. PERETERSKI, "Znachenie mezhdunarodnogo dogovora dlia tretego (ne zakluchivshego v etot dogovor) gosudarstva," in: *Sovetskoe gosudarstwo i prawo*, No. 4, 1957.

TREATIES BETWEEN STATES AND INTERNATIONAL ORGANIZATIONS. A subject of draft articles adopted by the International Law Commission during its 32nd session, May 5–July 25, 1980.

Report of the International Law Commission, UN, New York, 1980, pp. 136–181.

TREATIES, BILATERAL. An international term for the oldest form of international agreements concluded between two states; already known in the ancient world; up to the 19th century they were mainly peace and trade treaties; since the Congress of Vienna, 1815, they cover ever more areas of co-operation; in the second half of the 20th century they ever more frequently have the character not only of "state–state" agreements, but also of "state–international organizations," particularly where the field of technical assistance is concerned. Simultaneously, a tendency to limit their number through multilateral treaties has appeared in the integrative processes. As a rule, bilateral treaties are made in writing, but they can also be made orally; according to a judgment of the PCIJ of May 5, 1933 (so-called Ihlen case) on the case of Denmark's treaty with Norway on Greenland. The Norwegian Minister of Foreign Affairs, M. Ihlen, on Dec. 22, 1919, made an oral agreement with the Danish representative that Denmark would not oppose the granting of the archipelago of Spitsbergen to Norway by the Treaty of Paris (signed on Feb. 9, 1920), if the convention would not voice opposition to Denmark's extending its sovereignty to all of Greenland. However, in 1924 Norway did oppose this, making a complaint to the PCIJ, which rejected it, stating that a declaration of a Minister of Foreign Affairs in the name of his government is binding on a state regardless of whether it was made orally or in writing.

E. SATOW, *Guide to Diplomatic Practice*, London, 1957; L. WILDHABER, *Treaty Making Power and Constitution. An International and Comparative Study*, Basel, 1971.

TREATIES DENUNCIATION. A subject of international disputes, not defined in the ▷ Vienna

Convention on the Law of International Treaties, 1969.

B.P. SINKO, *Unilateral Denunciation of Treaty*, The Hague, 1965; S.E. NAHLIK, "Grounds of Invalidity and Termination of Treaties," in: *American Journal of International Law*, No. 65, 1971; H. BRIGGS, *Unilateral Denunciation of Treaties, The Vienna Convention and the ICJ*; M. FRANKOWSKA, *Wypowiedzenie umowy miedzynarodowej* (Denunciation of International Treaty), Wroclaw, 1976.

TREATIES INTERPRETATION. A subject of international law, which recognizes the principle, *eius est interpretari cuius est condere*, which assumes that interpretation of treaties is reserved for the states parties to an agreement and only their concordant position creates an interpretation binding on both sides. An exception is the Statute of the ICJ which, according to art. 38, may make judgments in disputes also based on "juridical decisions and the teachings of the most highly qualified publicists of the various nations." The task of interpretation of the treaties is to determine the exact content of an agreement and to explain the purpose and conditions for implementing the resolutions of the agreement. One of the basic principles of treaty interpretation was formulated by the Swiss jurist and diplomat E. de Vattel (1714–67): "what does not require interpretation should not be interpreted." Many scholars worked on the formulation of principles for the interpretation of international treaties as did the Institute of International Law, Association of International Law, OAS, etc. The result of these efforts are resolutions contained in the ▷ Vienna Convention on the Law of International Treaties, 1969, in Section IV, part 3, Interpretation of Treaties, arts. 31–33.
The jurisdiction of the ICJ had a great influence on the process of formulating principles for the interpretation of international treaties, principles particularly important in a period when multilateral international agreements became the basic instrument of international relations, replacing bilateral treaties. Following the drafting of the Vienna Convention another document relevant to the interpretation of international agreements was the opinion of the ICJ in the Southwest Africa Case, 1970.

L. EHRLICH, "L'interprétation des traités," in: *Recueil des Cours*, La Haye, 1928; M. JOKL, *De l'interprétation des traités normatives d'après la doctrine et la jurisprudence international*, Paris, 1936; S. NERI, *Sull'interpretazione dei Trattai nel Diritto Internazionale*, Roma, 1958; Y. RENOUX, *Glossary of International Treaties. In French, English, Spanish, Italian, Dutch, German and Russian*, Amsterdam, 1970; Ch.L. WIKTOR, *Unperfected Treaties of the USA, 1776–1976*, Vol. 1, 1776–1855, New York, 1976; R.L. BLEDSOE, B.A. BOCZEK, *The International Law Dictionary*, Oxford, 1987.

TREATIES INVALIDITY. A subject of complex disputes and manifold interpretations and codifications carried out by the UN Diplomatic Conference which prepared and adopted the ▷ Vienna Convention on the Law of International Treaties, 1969, whose Chapter V was entitled Invalidity, Termination and Suspension of Application of Treaties. The convention determined causes of formal invalidity: lack of treaty-making ability (art. 6), lack of competence (art. 8), lack of full powers (art. 8), lack of registration in the League of Nations or the UN (art. 80) and reasons for basic invalidity: excess of competence (art. 46), excess of full powers (art. 47), error (art. 48), stratagem (art. 49), corruption (art. 50), a representative of a state acting under duress (art. 51) or state under duress (art. 58), incompatibility with ▷ jus cogens (art. 53).

W.E. STEPHEN, *Revision of the Treaty of Versailles*, New York, 1939; A. VIGNOLI, *La Société des Nations et la révision des Traitées*, Paris, 1952; *Report of the International Law Commission on the Work of Its 32nd Session, May 5–July 25, 1980*, UN, New York, 1980, pp. 182–214; R.L. BLEDSOE, B.A. BOCZEK, *The International Law Dictionary*, Oxford, 1987.

TREATIES LAW. ▷ Law of Treaties.

TREATIES, MULTILATERAL. The treaties concluded by a number of states for the purpose of ending a conflict or dispute or initiating an alliance or co-operation. Up to the 19th century bilateral treaties predominated, while multilateral ones were usually either wartime alliances or peace treaties after the ending of a common war. In the second half of the 19th century (1864–99) the number of multilateral treaties was 133; by 1919 it grew to 257; in the period 1920–37, some 550 were signed throughout the world; in the postwar register of the UN for one decade (1946–56) 576 multilateral treaties were recorded. The largest increase recorded in the UN Secretariat is for the decade 1961–70, which was connected with the processes of the disintegration of colonial systems and the formation of regional integration. The most important multilateral treaty for the contemporary world is the UN Charter. The multilateral treaties are subject to ▷ Law of Treaties. In 1984 a Special UN Working group completed the review of Multilateral Treaty-Making Process.

UN Chronicle, February, 1983, p. 520; *Handbook of Final Clauses and the Summary of the Practice of the Secretary General as Depositary of Multilateral Agreements*, UN, New York, 1984; *Multilateral Treaties Deposited with the Secretary General: Status as of 31 December 1986*, New York, 1986.

TREATIES REGISTRATION. ▷ Registration and Publication of International Agreements.

TREATIES RESERVATION. ▷ Reservations to treaties.

TREATIES REVIEW. ▷ Revision and Review of Treaties.

TREATIES REVISION. ▷ Revision and Review of Treaties.

TREATIES SCOPE. An international term distinguishing treaty from non-treaty countries; that is states participating in international conventions and for that reason benefiting from the rights and privileges established by the convention on the principle of mutuality, e.g. from the ▷ Most Favored Nation IMF Clause in international trade; from non-member states of a treaty which eo ipso are not entitled to these rights and privileges, but which may benefit from them under specified conditions.

TREATIES, SIGNATURE. ▷ Signature.

TREATIES TERMINATION. Termination of treaties by ▷ Treaties denunciation, ▷ Treaties invalidity, or other methods.

Termination of Treaties: The Constitutional Allocation of Power. Materials compiled by the Committee on Foreign Relations, Senate, Washington 1979; R.L. BLEDSOE, B.A. BOCZEK, *The International Law Dictionary*, Oxford, 1987.

TREATY AND NON TREATY COUNTRIES. ▷ Treaties Scope.

TREATY BANNING NUCLEAR TEST, 1963. ▷ Outer Space Moscow Treaty, 1963.

TREATY OF LOMÉ. ▷ Lomé Conventions.

TREBLINKA. One of the German death camps est. in July 1941 near Lublin, a mass annihilation camp with toxic ▷ Zyklon B gas, built for about 700,000 Jews (▷ Endlösung), from Austria, Belgium, Czechoslovakia, France, Germany, Greece, Poland, USSR and Yugoslavia. The heroic uprising of the prisoners on Aug. 2, 1943 stopped the mass annihilation and the camp was liquidated in Sept., 1943.

Das Menschenschlachthaus Treblinka, Wien, 1946; *The Trial of German Major War Criminals. Proceedings of the International Military Tribunal Sitting at Nuremberg, Germany*, 42 vols., London, 1946–48, Vol. 2, pp. 416–417; Vol. 8, pp. 16–19, Vol. 11, p. 317.

TRETTNER PLAN, 1964. A draft suggesting a belt of nuclear mines to be laid along the frontier of the Federal Republic of Germany with the German Democratic Republic and Czechoslovakia. The draft submitted in Dec., 1964 at a NATO session in Paris was authored by the Inspector-General of the Bundeswehr, General H. Trettner. The plan's objective was anticipating the character of a possible armed conflict between NATO and the Warsaw Alliance which from the very outset was supposed to be a nuclear war and, as a consequence, the Bundeswehr was to be equipped with nuclear arms. The Trettner Plan was not approved by the NATO council, nevertheless since Dec., 1965 members of the Bundeswehr were allowed to participate in the NATO Nuclear Planning Group which formulates the premises for a nuclear war.

KEESING's *Contemporary Archive*, 1964.

TREUGA DEI. *Latin*: "divine peace (armistice)." An international term for the temporary suspension of all military operations during Advent, Christmas, Holy Week and other holidays under threat of ▷ excommunication. The custom of ceasing fire during great religious holidays has been retained into the 20th century, e.g. in the Vietnam war (*Trêve de Dieu*).

Dictionnaire de la terminologie de droit international, Paris, 1960.

TRIANONS. Two chateaux in the park of ▷ Versailles, Grand Trianon and Petit Trianon, which was place of the signature of the Hungarian Peace Treaty, July 26, 1921, called the ▷ Hungary Peace Treaty, 1921.

"TRIDENT." An American strategic missile of the class Water–Earth, equipped with a partitioned head composed of a dozen or so movable warheads with a nuclear payload. Range: 9–10,000 km. Launched from submarines equipped with 24 rocket launchers (previous version ▷ Polaris and ▷ Poseidon with 16 rockets launchers). The weapon is expected to be part of the armament of the American strategic underwater fleet to the end of the 20th century. The first ship of this type was launched for experimental purposes in Apr., 1979. Subject of negotiations in ▷ SALT II, counted as MIRV missiles.
On Dec. 10, 1987, at the end of the American-Soviet Summit both sides agreed that they should work out rules to count the number of ▷ warheads. By agreeing to new rules the United States may shelve its plans to develop a new version of the Trident submarine-launched missile that would carry 12 warheads. During the summit the Soviet experts presented new ideas on how to verify a limit on sea-launched nuclear Cruise missiles.

J. GOLDBLAT, *Arms Control Agreements. A Handbook*, New York, 1983; *The New York Times*, December 11, 1987; D. ROBERTSON, *Guide to Modern Defense and Strategy*, Detroit, 1988.

TRIESTE. The main port of northeastern Italy, from 1918 to 1954, subject of controversy between Yugoslavia and Italy, resolved by the Treaty of Versailles, June 27, 1919, in favor of Italy, reaffirmed by peace treaties signed in Saint-Germain-en-Laye, 1919, and Rapallo, 1920; during 1943–45 occupied by the German Third Reich; May, 1945 liberated by the Yugoslavian national-liberation army; 1945–47 divided into A center zone (Italian) and B suburban zone (Yugoslavian). On Feb. 10, 1947, under arts. 11 and 12 of the Paris Peace Treaty, both zones were integrated into the Free Town of Trieste. Under the London Italian–Yugoslavian Treaty of Oct. 5, 1954, rearranged. A zone was given to Italy and B zone incorporated into the Yugoslavian province of Istria. The frontier delineated in London was not recognized by Italy as final; the talks concerning this question held in Mar., 1973 in Dubrovnik by Ministers of Foreign Affairs of Italy and Yugoslavia were a fiasco. In a note to the government of Yugoslavia the Italian government, on Apr. 11, 1974, again took a stance that: "Yugoslavian sovereignty has never been expanded on the Italian territory determined as zone 'B' of the undeveloped vacant area of Trieste."
This brought about a Yugoslavian protest.
The ultimate solution was a settlement formalized in the ▷ Osima (Ancona) Treaty, 1975 On Oct. 12, 1979 a Belgrade Declaration during a visit to Yugoslavia by the Italian President stated that since the Treaty of Osima border disputes between the two countries have ceased to exist.

J. MARTIN-CHAUFFIER, *Trieste*, Paris, 1947; A. GERVAIS, *Le Status Libre de Triest*, Paris, 1947; J.L. KUNZ, "The Territory of Trieste," in: *The Western Political Quarterly*, No. 1, 1948; J. LEPRETTE, *Le Statut International de Triest*, Paris, 1949; H. KELSEN, "The Free Territory of Trieste under the United Nations," in: *Yearbook of World Affairs*, 1950; D. DE CASTRO, *Il Problema di Trieste: Genesi a Sviluppi della Questione Giuliana in Relazione agli Avvenimenti Internazionale dal 1943 al 1952*, Bologna, 1953; W. HILDEBRAND, *Der Triest Konflikt und die Italienisch–Jugoslawische Frage*, Göttingen, 1953; "Memorandum of Understanding between the governments of Italy, the UK, the US and Yugoslavia regarding the free territory of Trieste," in: *Jahrbuch für internationales Völkerrecht*, 1956, pp. 314–317; Italy–Yugoslavia (Trieste), in A.J. DAY, (ed.) *Border and Territorial Disputes*, London, 1987.

TRILATERAL COMMISSION. A private international institution established in New York in 1973 on the initiative of David Rockefeller, president of Chase Manhattan Bank, with the task of strengthening co-operation among the three main regions of the capitalist world and developing a joint strategy of North America, Western Europe, and Japan. Participating in the work of the Commission were leading statesmen, businessmen and financiers, economists and political scientists who at that time occupied no government position. The first director-general 1973–75 was Zbigniew Brzezinski, subsequently special adviser to the US President Jimmy Carter, who himself was a member of the Commission as were future members of his administration: Michael Blumenthal, Fred Bergston, Harold Brown, Richard Copper, and Cyrus Vance, as well as US vice-president, Walter Mondale. West Europe is represented in the Commission by some 70 representatives, Japan by about 60. The Commission published reports on its studies in a quarterly, *Trialog*.

R. ENINGER, *The Global Manipulation*, Boston, 1980; *Trilateral Commission Task Force Reports*, 3 Vols., New York, 1981; *Yearbook of International Organizations 1986/87*; *The Europa Yearbook 1988. A World Survey*, Vol. I, London, 1988; R. MURATA, Japan, America and Europe. Political Relations Between the United States and Europe: Their implication for Japan, in: *International Affairs*, Winter 1987/88.

TRIMMING CERTIFICATE. A document officially attesting to the trimming capacity of a vessel, protecting it against dangerous listing, in the case of vessels freighting coal and coke according to international trimming classifications for this type of ship.

TRINIDAD AND TOBAGO. Member of the UN. A state in West Indies occupying five islands: Trinidad (4828 sq. km with 892,317 inhabitants, 1970 census) and Tobago (300 sq. km, 38,754 inhabitants). Pop. 1988 est.: 1,240,000. Capital: Port of Spain with 65,906 inhabitants 1980. GNP per capita 1986: US $5,120. Official language: English. Currency: one dollar of Trinidad–Tobago = 100 cents. National Day: Aug. 31, Independence Day, 1962.
Member of the UN since Sept. 18, 1962 and of UN specialized agencies with the exception of IAEA and IFAD. Member of the Commonwealth, of the Tlatelolco, CARICOM and is an ACP state of the EEC.
International relations: Trinidad was a Spanish colony 1783–1802; ceded to Great Britain by the Treaty of Amiens 1802; joined with Tobago in 1889; part of the West Indies Federation 1958–62. Independent on Aug. 31, 1962.
An agreement on maritime boundaries with Venezuela was signed on Sept. 14, 1986.
Since Jan. 1, 1987 Tobago enjoys full internal self-government.
The Trinidad and Tobago Institute of International Affairs, was f. in 1964 in Port-of-Spain.

Report of the Trinidad and Tobago Independence Conference, 1962, HMSO, London, 1962; E. WILLIAMS, *History of the People of Trinidad and Tobago*, New York, 1964; *Trade Dictionary of Trinidad and Tobago*, London, 1966; M. ANTHONY, *Profile Trinidad: A Historical Survey from the Discovery to 1900*, London, 1976; *Facts on Trinidad and Tobago*, Port of Spain, 1978; *Oil and Energy, Trinidad and Tobago*, Port of Spain 1980; St. G.C. COOPER, P.R. BACON (eds.), *The Natural Resources of Trinidad and Tobago*, London, 1981; *The Europa Year Book 1984. A World Survey*, Vol. II, pp. 25-18-2522, London, 1984; KEESING's *Record of World Events*, 1987, No. 6.

TRIPARTITE PACT, GERMANY, ITALY AND JAPAN, 1940. The Pact was signed on Sept. 27, 1940 in Berlin. The text is as follows:
"The Governments of Germany, Italy and Japan, considering it as a condition precedent of any lasting peace that all nations of the world be given each its own proper place, have decided to stand by and co-operate with one another in regard to their efforts in Greater East Asia and the regions of Europe respectively wherein it is their prime purpose to establish and maintain a new order of things calculated to promote the mutual prosperity and welfare of the peoples concerned.
Furthermore, it is the desire of the three Governments to extend co-operation to such nations in other spheres of the world as may be inclined to put forth endeavours along lines similar to their own, in order that their ultimate aspirations for world peace may thus be realised.
Accordingly, the Governments of Germany, Italy and Japan have agreed as follows:
I. Japan recognises and respects the leadership of Germany and Italy in the establishment of a new order in Europe.
II. Germany and Italy recognise and respect the leadership of Japan in the establishment of a new order in Greater East Asia.
III. Germany, Italy and Japan agree to co-operate in their efforts on the aforesaid lines. They further undertake to assist one another with all political, economic and military means when one of the contracting Powers is attacked by a Power at present not involved in the European war or in the Chinese–Japanese conflict.
IV. With a view to implementing the present pact, joint technical commissions, the members of which are to be appointed by the respective Governments of Germany, Italy, and Japan, will meet without delay.
V. Germany, Italy and Japan affirm that the aforesaid terms do not in any way affect the political status which exists at present as between each of the three contracting parties and Soviet Russia.
VI. The present pact shall come into effect immediately upon signature and shall remain in force ten years from the date of its coming into force. At the proper time before the expiration of the said term the high contracting parties shall at the request of any one of them enter into negotiations for its renewal."
Accessions: Hungary Nov. 20, 1940, Romania Nov. 23, 1940, Slovakia Nov. 24, 1940, Bulgaria Mar. 1, 1941, Croatia June 15, 1941, Yugoslavia, which signed the Pact on Mar. 25, 1941, later refused to ratify.
Referred to in the ▷ United Nations Declaration, 1942.

Reichsgesetzblatt, No. 41, 1940; *LNTS*, Vol. 204, 1941–43, p. 386.

TRIPOLI. The capital and port of Libya on the Mediterranean Sea. Place of the first ▷ Catholic–Moslem meeting, 1976.

TRIPOLITANIAN CHARTER, 1969. A treaty signed on Dec. 27, 1969 by Egypt, Sudan and Libya to which Syria acceded Nov. 27, 1970; reaffirmed by the conference of the above-mentioned states held in Benghazi, Apr. 14–17, 1971; not entered into force.

KEESING'S *Contemporary Archive*.

TRIPLE ALLIANCE, 1887. The tripartite Anglo–Austro–Italian alliance concluded secretly through an exchange of notes, Dec. 12, and 16, 1887, between governments of Austro–Hungary, Great Britain and Italy; art. 2 guaranteed *status quo* in the Middle East; art. 4 granted independence to Turkey as the guardian of important European interests; arts. 5–8 defined Turkish obligations towards Bulgaria and the Dardanelles.

H. RONNENFAHRT, *Konferenzen und Verträge*, Vol. 3, Würzburg, 1958.

TRIPLE ALLIANCE, 1907. The tripartite alliance founded on the basis of the alliance between Great Britain and France of 1904 and the British–Russian alliance of 1907. Its opposite ▷ Dreibund, 1882.

TRIPLE ALLIANCE OF EMPERORS, 1873. The Alliance, called also Three Emperors' League, initiated on June 6, 1873 by Austro–Hungarian Emperor Francis Joseph I and the Russian Tsar Alexander II at a meeting at Schönbrunn, with a Treaty on Mutual Consultation in Case of Threat of War from other European powers; also signed on Oct. 22, 1873, by German Emperor William II; extended in Berlin, on June 18, 1881, by a new treaty, art. 1 of which guaranteed "benevolent neutrality" in case any of them were involved in a war with a fourth power other than Turkey. A separate agreement would be required to consult the positions of the three on the subject of war with Turkey; art. 2 obliged the parties to respect their mutual interests on the Balkan Peninsula; art. 3 provided for a joint watch on Turkey's conduct regarding navigation in the Dardanelles and Bosphorus; the Alliance concluded for three years was renewed Mar. 27, 1884.

Grosse Politik der Europäischen Kabinette, 1871–1914, 40 Vols., Berlin, 1926, Doc. 129, p. 206.

TRISTAN DA CUNHA. A small group of volcanic islands in the South Atlantic with est. 1978 pop. of 300. Since 1942, it has been the site of a British meteorological and radio station. In Oct., 1961 the volcano of the Tristan island erupted, and the population was evacuated, but in 1963 the majority returned. The islands annexed in 1816 by Great Britain and since 1938 have been a dependency of the British colony of St. Helena.

R.A. MUNCH, *Sociology of Tristan da Cunha*, Oslo, 1945; D.M. BOOY, *Rock of Exile: A Narrative of Tristan da Cunha*; London, 1957; P.A. MUNCH, *Crisis in Utopia*, New York, 1971; A. CRAWFORD, *Tristan da Cunha and the Roaring Forties*, Edinburgh, 1982.

TRI-ZONE OR TRIZONIA. An unofficial name given to occupied West Germany after annexation of the French occupation zone to the American–British Bi-Zone. On Sept. 7, 1949 the Tri-Zone was transformed into the Federal Republic of Germany.

TROIKA KHRUSHCHEV PLAN, 1960. A proposal of Premier of the Soviet Union, N. S. Khrushchev, during the Congo crisis, 1960, to replace the office of UN Secretary-General by a three-man presidium, called by N. S. Khrushchev "troika" (Russian name for a three-horsed vehicle), representing the Capitalistic World, the Socialistic World and the Third World. The majority of the UN member states did not support the Soviet proposal and the tragic death of UN Secretary-General Dag Hammarskjold in the Congo, 1961, terminated the dispute.

KEESING'S *Contemporary Archive*, 1960.

TROMELIN ISLAND. A French possession in the Indian Ocean since 1814, between ▷ Mauritius and ▷ Réunion, about 450 km east of Madagascar and 550 km north of Mauritius, a coral plateau seven meters above sea level, with a total area of about one sq km, a subject of dispute since 1976 between Mauritius and France. On April 4, 1983 France declared the readiness to review the question of French sovereignty over the island in favour of Mauritius.

France–Mauritius (Tromelin Island), in: A.J. DAY ed., *Border and Territorial Disputes*, London, 1987, pp. 136–137.

TROPICAL AGRICULTURE. Subject of international co-operation.
Organization reg. with the UIA:
International Centre for Tropical Agriculture, f. 1969, Cali, Colombia.

The Europe Yearbook 1988. A World Survey, Vol. I, London, 1988.

TROPICAL CYCLONES. A subject of international co-operation to mitigate damage caused by tropical cyclones in the Bay of Bengal and the Arabian Sea, organized by a WMO-ESCAP Panel on Tropical Systems, f. 1973, with hqs. in Colombo, Sri Lanka. Members: Bangladesh, Burma, India, Maldives, Pakistan, Sri Lanka, Thailand.

Yearbook of International Organizations.

TROPICAL DISEASES. The infectious, endemic human and animal diseases in tropical regions of the world, subject of the UNDP, World Bank and WHO Special Program for Research and Training in Tropical Diseases. WHO and FAO are collaborating closely on public health and veterinary services in tropical regions, organizing continuous surveillance and control. Six diseases are estimated to afflict more than one billion people in the developing world: filiarasis, leishmaniasis, leprosy, malaria, schistosomiasis and trypanosomiasis (sleeping sickness). A special program of research and training against the six tropical diseases was launched in 1977 by the WHO, UNDP and the World Bank.

E.A. GREGORY, "The Burden of Tropical Diseases," in: *World Health*, December, 1983; Progress in Combating Tropical Diseases, in: *WHO Chronicle*, 1985, No. 5, pp. 176–180.

TROPPAU CONGRESS, 1820. A meeting in Troppau (presently Opava in Czechoslovakia) in Oct., 1820 of Austrian Emperor Francis I, Russian Tsar Alexander I, Prussian King Frederick William III, as well as representatives from France and Great Britain; adopted note de circulation which recognized revolutionary changes in Spain, Naples and Portugal as a "new threat to Europe" and resolved to take joint action to protect Europe from the plague of new revolutions.

G.F. MARTENS, *Recueil des traitées et Conventions conclus par la Russie*, 14 Vols., Petersburg, 1874–1905, Vol. 4.

TRUCE. An international term for cessation of hostilities, or cessation of all acts of armed force for a period of the armistice negotiations. According to the ▷ Hague Rules, 1907, during the truce "no aggressive action by the armed forces – land, sea, or air – of either party shall be undertaken, planned, or threatened against the people or the armed forces of the other."

P. MOHN, "Problem of Truce Supervision," in: *International Conciliation*, February, 1952, pp. 51–98.

TRUCIAL OMAN. Arabic Oman al Mutasali, historical name of an Arabic territory, formerly called ▷ Pirate Coast, today part of the ▷ United Arab Emirates.

TRUCIAL STATES. The name in the 19th century of the Arab Sheikhdoms in the Persian gulf area.

TRUMAN ATOM THREAT, 1952. The US President Harry Truman (1884–1972) on Jan. 27 and May 18, 1952 considered using the threat of nuclear war against China and the USSR as a means of ending the stalemated Korean War. The text of the Truman handwritten memoranda dated Jan. 27 and May 18, 1952 was first published by Prof. Fr. Loevenheim in the *Houston Chronicle* on Aug. 2, 1980. The text of the first memorandum is as follows:

"It seems to me that the proper approach now would be an ultimatum with a 10-day expiration limit, informing Moscow that we intend to blockade the China coast from the Korean border to Indochina, and that we intend to destroy every military base in Manchuria by means now in our control – and if there is further interference we shall eliminate any ports or cities necessary to accomplish our purposes. This means all-out war. It means that Moscow, St. Petersburg, Mukden, Vladivostok, Peking, Shanghai, Port Arthur, Darien, Odessa, Stalingrad and every manufacturing plant in China and the Soviet Union will be eliminated."

In the second memorandum, dated May 18, 1952, Truman wrote that the Korean truce talks, begun in July, 1951, were "propaganda sounding boards for the Commies."
Then, writing as if he was addressing his enemies directly, he said:

"Now do you want an end to hostilities in Korea or do you want China and Siberia destroyed? You may have one or the other; whichever you want, these lies of yours at this conference have gone far enough. You either accept our fair and just proposal or you will be completely destroyed."

The memoranda were part of an intermittent journal, that President H. Truman kept – all handwritten – during his White House years, 1945–56. *The New York Times* noted, that: "several former officials who served under Truman said they doubted that he had considered a nuclear strike."

The US State Department released in June, 1984 unpublished documents dealing with the Korean War. Among them the following from the record of the National Security Council meeting on May 20, 1953:

"After further discussion of various military aspects of the problem the President summed up the views presented by the Joint Chiefs as indicating their belief that if we went over to more positive action against the enemy in Korea, it would be necessary to use the atomic bomb."

In both cases the US President was against the use of atomic bomb.

A. CABE BROWN (ed.), *"Dropshot." The United States Plan for War with the Soviet Union in 1952*, New York, 1978; "Truman Weighed Using Atom Threat, Story Says," in: *The New York Times*, August 3, 1980.

TRUMAN DOCTRINE, 1947. The main line of US foreign policy formulated on Mar. 12, 1947 by the US President Harry Truman (1884–1972) in a message to a joint session of the Congress to grant "military and economic aid to states threatened by communism"; accepted by the Senate 67:23 on Apr. 22 and on May 10, by the House 277:107, in reference to two states in particular: Greece and Turkey.
The highlights of the Message:

"One of the primary objectives of the foreign policy of the United States is the creation of conditions in which we and other nations will be able to work out a way of life free from coercion. This was a fundamental issue in the war with Germany and Japan. Our victory was won over countries which sought to impose their will, and their way of life, upon other nations.
To insure the peaceful development of nations, free from coercion, the United States has taken a leading part in establishing the United Nations. The United Nations is designed to make possible lasting freedom and independence for all its members. We shall not realize our objectives, however, unless we are willing to help free peoples to maintain their free institutions and their national integrity against aggressive movements that seek to impose upon them totalitarian regimes.
This is no more than a frank recognition that totalitarian regimes imposed upon free peoples, by direct or indirect aggression, undermine the foundations of international peace and hence the security of the United States.
The peoples of a number of countries of the world have recently had totalitarian regimes forced upon them against their will. The Government of the United States had made frequent protests against coercion and intimidation in violation of the Yalta agreement, in Poland, Romania, and Bulgaria. I must also state that in a number of other countries there have been similar developments.
At the present moment in world history nearly every nation must choose between alternative ways of life. The choice is too often not a free one.
One way of life is based upon the will of the majority, and is distinguished by free institutions, representative government, free elections, guaranties, of individual liberty, freedom of speech and religion, and freedom from political oppression.
The second way of life is based upon the will of a minority forcibly imposed upon the majority. It relies upon terror and oppression, a controlled press and radio, fixed elections, and the suppression of personal freedoms.
I believe that it must be the policy of the United States to support free peoples who are resisting attempted subjugation by armed minorities or by outside pressures. I believe that we must assist free peoples to work out their own destinies in their own way.
I believe that our help should be primarily through economic and financial aid which is essential to economic stability and orderly political processes.
The world is not static, and the status quo is not sacred. But we cannot allow changes in the status quo in violation of the Charter of the United Nations by such methods as coercion, or by such subterfuges as political infiltration. In helping free and independent nations to maintain their freedom, the United States will be giving

effect to the principles of the Charter of the United Nations. It is necessary only to glance at a map to realize that the survival and integrity of the Greek nation are of grave importance in a much wider situation. If Greece should fall under the control of an armed minority, the effect upon its neighbour, Turkey, would be immediate and serious. Confusion and disorder might well spread throughout the entire Middle East. Moreover, the disappearance of Greece as an independent state would have a profound effect upon those countries in Europe whose peoples are struggling against great difficulties to maintain their freedoms and their independence while they repair the damages of war.

It would be an unspeakable tragedy if these countries, which have struggled so long against overwhelming odds, should lose that victory for which they sacrificed so much. Collapse of free institutions and loss of independence would be disastrous not only for them but for the world. Discouragement and possible failure would quickly be the lot of neighboring peoples striving to maintain their freedom and independence.

Should we fail to aid Greece and Turkey in this fateful hour, the effect will be far reaching to the West as well as to the East.

We must take immediate and resolute action."

Ten years later the Truman doctrine was replaced by the ▷ Eisenhower doctrine, 1957, extending the Truman doctrine to all of the countries of the Near and Middle East. ▷ Carter's Persian Gulf Doctrine, 1980.

Congressional Record, 80th Congress, 1st Session, pp. 535–537; *US Department of State Bulletin*, March 23, 1947, D. ROBERTSON, *Guide to Modern Defense and Strategy*, Detroit, 1988.

TRUMAN'S FOURTH POINT. The name used for a US government technical aid project directed to countries lagging in development, proclaimed by the US President Harry Truman in his Inaugural Address before Congress on Jan. 20, 1949, and repeated in his speech on Feb. 23, 1950, contained in four points. The first three were political theses: first – on the communist danger, second – on the impossibility to exercise control over nuclear weapons, third – on the need to disseminate the ideas of freedom and self-determination, and the fourth announced technical aid financed by the US state treasury to be rendered to developing countries. Such aid, for the first time approved by the US Congress on Aug. 29, 1950, totalling 26.9 million dollars, later became an inherent part of the US foreign aid. The Fourth Point of Inaugural Address, read as follows:

"We must embark on a bold new program for making the benefits of our scientific advances and industrial progress available for the improvement and growth of underdeveloped areas.

More than half the people of the world are living in conditions approaching misery. Their food is inadequate. They are victims of disease. Their economic life is primitive and stagnant. Their poverty is a handicap and a threat both to them and to more prosperous areas.

For the first time in history, humanity possesses the knowledge and the skill to relieve the suffering of these people.

The United States is preeminent among nations in the development of industrial and scientific techniques. The material resources which we can afford to use for the assistance of other peoples are limited. But our imponderable resources in technical knowledge are constantly growing and are inexhaustible.

I believe that we should make available to peace-loving peoples the benefits of our store of technical knowledge in order to help them realize their aspirations for a better life. And, in co-operation with other nations, we should foster capital investment in areas needing development. Our aim should be to help the free peoples of the world, through their own efforts, to produce more food, more clothing, more materials for housing, and more mechanical power to lighten their burdens.

We invite other countries to pool their technological resources in this undertaking. Their contributions will be warmly welcomed. This should be a co-operative enterprise in which all nations work together through the United Nations and its specialized agencies wherever practicable. It must be a world-wide effort for the achievement of peace, plenty, and freedom.

With the cooperation of business, private capital, agriculture, and labor in this country, this program can greatly increase the industrial activity in other nations and can raise substantially their standards of living. Such new economic developments must be devised and controlled to benefit peoples of the areas in which they are established. Guarantees to the investor must be balanced by guarantees in the interest of the people whose resources and whose labor go into these developments.

The old imperialism – exploitation for foreign profit – has no place in our plans. What we envisage is a program of development based on the concepts of democratic fair dealing.

All countries, including our own, will greatly benefit from a constructive program for the better use of the world's human and natural resources. Experience shows that our commerce with other countries expands as they progress industrially and economically.

Greater production is the key to prosperity and peace. And the key to greater production is a wider and more vigorous application of modern scientific and technical knowledge. Only by helping the least fortunate of its members to help themselves can the human family achieve the decent, satisfying life that is the right of all people.

Democracy alone can supply the vitalizing force to stir the peoples of the world into triumphant action, not only against their human oppressors, but also against their ancient enemies – hunger, misery, and despair."

US Department of State Bulletin, January 30, 1949, pp. 123–126; A. BAKER FOX, "President Truman's Fourth Point and the UN," in: *International Conciliation*, No. 452, June, 1949, pp. 459–503.

TRUMAN'S TWELVE POINTS, 1945. A statement of the US President Harry Truman, on Oct. 27, 1945, defining the principles of American foreign policy in the post-war era:

"I. We seek no territorial expansion or selfish advantage. We have no plane for aggression against any other State, large or small. We have no objective which need clash with the peaceful aims of any other nation.

II. We believe in the eventual return of sovereign right and self-government to all peoples who have been deprived of them by force.

III. We shall approve no territorial changes in any friendly part of the world unless they accord with the freely expressed wishes of the people concerned.

IV. We believe that all peoples who are prepared for self-government should be permitted to choose their own form of government by their own freely expressed choice without interference from any foreign source. This is true in Europe, in Asia, and in Africa, as well as in the western hemisphere.

V. In co-operative action with our war allies we shall help the defeated enemy States to establish peaceful democratic governments of their own free choice, and we shall try to attain a world in which Nazism, Fascism, and military aggression cannot exist.

VI. We shall refuse to recognise any government imposed on any nation by force of any foreign Power. In some cases it may be impossible to prevent the forceful imposition of such government, but the United States will not recognise any such government.

VII. We believe that all nations should have the freedom of the seas and of rivers and waterways passing through more than one country.

VIII. We believe that all States which are accepted in the society of nations should have access to the trade and raw materials of the world.

IX. We believe that the sovereign States of the western hemisphere without interference from outside the hemisphere, must work together as good neighbours in the solution of their common problems.

X. We believe that full economic collaboration between all nations great and small is essential to the improvement of living conditions all over the world and

the establishment of freedom from fear and freedom from want.

XI. We shall continue to strive to promote freedom of expression and freedom of religion throughout the peace-loving areas of the world.

XII. We are convinced that the preservation of peace between the nations requires a United Nations Organization composed of all the peace-loving nations of the world who are willing jointly to use force if necessary to ensure peace.

The New York Times, Oct. 28, 1945; *A Decade of American Foreign Policy. Basic Documents 1941–49*, Washington, DC, 1950.

TRUONGA ISLANDS. ▷ Spratly Islands.

TRUST. An international term for one of many forms of the monopolistic enterprise which exists in lieu of several firms merging into a new enterprise either by way of purchase or by arrangement made by trustees, having its own board of trustees and issuing trust certificates that replace the stock of each formerly separate firm; the certificates are allotted to firms by the board of trustees to the amount corresponding to their share; profits of such merged firms are collected by the trust and it is the trust that divides profit into parts equivalent to the share endorsed in the trust certificate. To challenge this form of capital concentration, being like ▷ cartel, a union of independent firms in many capitalist states, anti-trust legislation has been passed; e.g. in the USA, Sherman Act in 1890, Clayton Act, 1914; in Great Britain in 1907, 1929, 1948, 1967, Companies Act; in France in 1953 a permanent anti-trust commission was appointed, Commission Technique des Entente. The occupation authorities in 1945 banned trusts in Germany; as a consequence the ban was transferred into the Common Market of Western Europe where regional, international anti-trust legislation was made.

D. KENT, *Common Market Antitrust Law. A Guide to the Law, Procedure and Literature*, The Hague, 1964; L.C.B. GOWER, *Modern Company Law*, London, 1967; D. ZWARENSTEYN, *Some aspects of the extraterritorial reach of the American Antitrust Law*, New York, 1970.

TRUSTEESHIP. In the UN system the trusteeship indicates international rule over a territory; in civil law, tutelage.

"International Trusteeship System," in: *International Conciliation*, February, 1949, pp. 97–180.

TRUSTEESHIP FUND FOR SOCIAL PROGRESS. A Fund est. on May 27, 1961 by a resolution of the US Congress; had the task of supporting the social development of Latin America in the spirit of the program of ▷ Alliance for Progress. The administrator of the Fund is the Interamerican Development Bank on the basis of an agreement with the Bank of June 19, 1961.

TRUSTEESHIP TERRITORIES. A name adopted in the UN Charter, Chapters XII and XIII, to determine so-called mandate territories of the League of Nations; since Oct., 1945 taken over by the UN Trusteeship Administration whose states-mandataries were Australia, Belgium, France, Great Britain, New Zealand and the USA. On Sept. 30, 1986 the world's last territory ▷Palau was granted independence by the UN Trusteeship Committee.

H.D. HALL, *Mandates, Dependencies and Trusteeship*, New York, 1948; M. BARONDI, *Les problèmes juridique concernant l'administration des communautés mandat*, Paris, 1949; Ch.E. TONSSAINT, *The Trusteeship System of the UN*, New York, 1956; J. MALENZIC, *La tutelle internationale et les problèmes de l'union administrative*, Paris, 1958; J.N. MURRAY, *The UN Trusteeship System*, New York, 1968; *Pacific Islands:*

Last of the Trust Territories, in: *UN Chronicle,* 1985, No. 5, p. 27–31; *World's Almanac,* New York, 1988.

TRYGVE LIE PLAN, 1950. A Plan prepared by UN Secretary-General Trygve Lie, and submitted to UN member states in a June, 1950 "Memorandum on matters that should be considered in the preparation of a 20-year plan on the strengthening of peace through the UN." The memorandum consisted of the following ten points:

(1) meetings, in keeping with the UN Charter, at the level of ministers of foreign affairs or heads of governments should be started in the Security Council;
(2) new efforts should be made to create a system of international supervision over nuclear energy which would prevent its use for hostile purposes and would promote its peaceful uses;
(3) new studies should be undertaken to determine whether it is possible to control the arms race, not only with respect to nuclear arms, but also other mass-destruction weapons, as well as conventional armaments;
(4) new efforts should be made to prepare a treaty on emergency forces put up by UN members at the disposal of the Security Council, thereby being capable of effecting its decisions in keeping with the UN Charter;
(5) the principle that it is reasonable and adequate to strive urgently for universality of the UN should be accepted and effected;
(6) a program of technical assistance should be worked out with the aim of testhering economic development on the basis of large-scale capital investment making use of private, governmental and intergovernmental resources;
(7) the governments of the member states of UN specialized agencies should strive most effectively to "enhance the standard of living, provide jobs for everyone and to advance economic and social progress" in keeping with the UN Charter;
(8) UN activities for fundamental human rights and freedoms to make them respected and observed worldwide should be dynamically expanded and continued;
(9) the UN should be used to promote by peaceful means and "if necessary, by force" the growth of dependent, colonial and semi-colonial peoples in order to achieve equality of all peoples in the world;
(10) the UN Charter should be applied actively and systematically and the UN mechanism should be involved in the development of international law to reach as far as universal laws generally binding on world community.

UN Bulletin, April 1 and June 15, 1950, and February 15, 1952.

TRYPANOSOMIASES. A parasitic disease caused by flagellate protozoans of the Trypanosoma Cruzi; subject of WHO Special Program for Research and Training in Tropical Diseases:
(1) African trypanosomiases, called sleeping sickness, transmitted by tsetse flies (*glossina palpalis*); "is still a grave threat to human health and an obstacle to the development of agriculture in 35 African countries."
(2) American trypanosomiases, or "endemic Chagas" disease in rural areas of Central and South America. The parasite was discovered in 1909 by the Brazilian epidemiologist Carlos Chagas (1879–1934).

P.A. BUXTON,*The Natural History of Tsetse Flies,* London, 1955; *WHO Report on the African Trypanosomiases,* Geneva, 1979; P. EATTAND, *Sleeping Sickness–Re-awakes,* in: *World Health Organization,* July, 1988.

TSETSE FLY. ▷ Trypanosomiases.

TSUNAMIS. Japanese = Seaquake. A disaster similar to an earthquake, provoked by tremors of the sea-bed and tidal waves, typical of the Pacific Ocean shelves, subject of UN ▷ international disaster relief.

TSUSHIMA. A group of five Japanese islands in a strait between Japan and Korea; the strait is divided by the islands in the Eastern and Western Channels, called Tsushima Strait and Chosen or Korean Strait, both *c.* 90 km wide. The total area of the rocky islands is 698 sq. km. On May 27–28, 1905 in the Battle of Tsushima the Russian Baltic fleet was destroyed by the Japanese fleet.

H. TOGO, *La bataille de Tsouchima,* Paris, 1905.

TUBERCULOSIS. A subject of international action against this infectious disease.
The World Health Assembly in May, 1980 expressed concern that:

"tuberculosis remained one of the most important health problems in developing countries and that efforts in control programmes and resources for research on the application of control measures were still inadequate or had been reduced. Technology in tuberculosis control had been simplified to such an extent that it was now applicable even at the community and individual levels as part of primary health care. The discovery of new, potent, bactericidal drugs facilitated a considerable shortening of the duration of antituberculosis chemotherapy, although the danger of drug resistance remained. Member States were urged to give earliest attention to the integration of tuberculosis control within primary health care. The Director-General was requested to:
– take steps to ensure that antituberculosis drugs became more widely available in developing countries, within the essential drugs programme, at the lowest possible cost;
– take measures to increase the extrabudgetary support for health research on integrated tuberculosis control programmes."

Organizations reg. with the UIA:

East African Tuberculosis Investigation Centre, f. 1953, Nairobi.
International Union Against Tuberculosis, f. 1920, Paris. Official relations with WHO and UNICEF. Publ.: *Bulletin.*

WHO Chronicle, No. 7/8, 1980; *Vaccination Against Tuberculosis. WHO Technical Report Series,* No. 651, 1981; "Tuberculosis in the Developing World," in: *World Health Forum,* No. 2, 1984. *Yearbook of International Organizations;* M.CALDWELL, *The Last Crusade, 1862–1954,* New York, 1988; J. LEOWSKIŁ, *Tuberculosis Control. The Past, The Present, The Future,* in: *WHO Features,* January, 1988.

TUGHRIK. The Mongolian monetary unit. One tughrik = 100 mongos; issued since 1924 by the State Bank of Mongolian People's Republic.

TU-22M AIRPLANE CALLED BACKFIRE. The subject of a Statement by the USSR, signed on June 16, 1979, in Vienna. The text may be found in ▷ SALT II. Documents 1979.

J. GOLDBLAT, *Arms Control Agreements. A Handbook,* New York, 1983.

TUMORS. A subject of international research, under the the aegis of WHO. The WHO publ. from 1967 books and slides on Tumors in English, French, Russian and Spanish.

The International Histological Classification of Tumors, Rome, 1980.

TUNA. Subject of international co-operation. Organizations reg. with the UIA:

Inter-American Tropical Tuna Commission, f. 1950, La Jolla, Calif., USA. Members: France, Japan, Nicaragua, Panama, USA. Publ.: Annual Report.
International Commission for the Conservation of Atlantic Tunas, f. 1971, Madrid.

The Europa Yearbook 1988. A World Survey, Vol. I, London, 1988.

TUNA WAR. The argument between the USA and Ecuador caused by the widening of the control coastal zone by Ecuador up to 200 nautical miles and limitation of fishing for American fishing boats, 1971–72. ▷ Ecuador.

TUNISIA. Member of the UN. Republic of Tunisia. A northern African state on the Mediterranean Sea, bordered by Algeria and Libya. Area: 163,610 sq. km. Pop. 1986 est.: 7,320,000 (1975 census: 5,527,193). Capital: Tunis with 550,404 inhabitants, 1975. GNP per capita 1986: US $1310. Official language: Arabic. Currency: one Tunisian dinar = 1000 millimes. National Day: June 1, Victory Day, 1955.
Member of the UN since Nov. 12, 1966 and of the UN specialized agencies with the exception of GATT. Member of the OAU and the Arab League. International relations: from 1869 to 1880 under financial control of France, Great Britain and Italy; from 1881 to 1946 under protectorate of France (during the World War II, 1940–44, under rules of the French régime of Vichy; associated state of the French Union 1946–56; the republic was proclaimed in July, 1957; the French military forces were evacuated in June, 1958 after a UN Security Council debate, and the French naval forces from the port of Bizerta in Oct., 1963. In 1966 Tunis signed an economic and cultural co-operation agreement with France; in 1971 signed with the USSR an agreement on cultural and scientific co-operation. The union with Libya proclaimed on Jan. 1, 1974 never came into force.
A Signatory of a Preferential Trade Agreement with the EEC, 1976. On Mar. 20, 1983 Tunisia signed with Algeria a Treaty of Brotherhood and Concordance and Agreement on Final Delimitation of Frontiers.
The ICJ rejected on Jan. 10, 1986 a Tunisian application for a revision of the 1982 delimitation of the Tunisian–Libyan continental shelf.
See also ▷ World Heritage UNESCO List.

H. BOURGUIBA, *La Tunisie et la France,* Paris, 1954; F. GARAS, *Bourguiba et la naissance d'une nation,* Paris, 1956; Ch. MICOT, *Tunisia: The Politics of Modernization,* New York, 1964; D.L. LING, *Tunisia: From Protectorate to Republic,* Indiana University Press, 1967; A. SYLVESTER, *Tunisia,* London, 1969; L. RUDEBECK, *The Tunisian Experience, Party and People,* London, 1970; Gh. DUVAJI, *Economic Development in Tunisia. The Impact and Course of Government Planning,* New York, 1972; A.A. FINDLAY, R.L. LAWLESS, *Tunisia, Bibliography,* Oxford, 1982; *The Europa Year Book 1984. A World Survey,* Vol. II, pp. 2528–2539, London, 1984; L ANDERSON, *The State and Social Transformation in Tunisia and Libya,* 1830–1980, Princeton, 1986.

TUNNELS, INTERNATIONAL. The tunnels connecting in order of their construction: Italy–France, 1857–71, the Tunnel Mont Cenis, length 13.63 km, and 1959–65 the Mont Blanc Tunnel, 11.6 km; Switzerland–Italy, 1898–1906 the Simplon I Tunnel; 1912–22 the Simplon II Tunnel, both 19.8 km, and 1978 the S. Gothard Tunnel, 16.3 km; Argentina–Chile, 1951 the Transandes Tunnel, length 8.1 km.
In the planning stage is a sea tunnel under the English Channel, called the ▷ Chunnel; the project was reaffirmed by France and the UK in Nov., 1984, and is to be completed by 1993.

E.M. WHITE, *Famous Subways and Tunnels of the World,* New York, 1953; G.E. SANDSTRÖM, *Tunnels,* London, 1963.

TUPAMAROS. A partisan movement in Uruguay active mainly in towns, particularly in the capital Montevideo, 1963–73.

After the restoration of democratic order in Uruguay, the first legal convention of the Tupamaros National Liberation Movement was held in Montevideo on Dec. 20–23, 1985.

R. GOTT, *Guerrilla Movements in America Latina*, London, 1970; *Nous les Tupamaros*, Paris, 1971; *Actas Tupamaros*, Montevideo, 1972; A.C. PORZECAN-SKI, *Uruguay's Tupamaros. The Urban Guerrilla*, New York, 1974.

TURKEY. Member of the UN. Turkish Republic. A state on the borderline of Europe and Asia on the Mediterranean, Aegean, Greek and Black Seas, bordered by the USSR, Iraq, Iran, Syria. Greece, Bulgaria. Area: 779,452 sq. km, with European part – Thracia: 23,764 sq. km, Asiatic part – Anatolia: 755,688 sq. km. Population 1980 census: 44,736,000; 1985 census: 51,428,000. Capital: Ankara with 1,877,775 inhabitants, 1980 census. GNP per capita 1986: US $1020. Official language: Turkish. Currency: one Lira (Turkish Pound) = 100 kurus. National day: Oct. 29, anniversary of proclamation of republic, 1923.
Founding member of the UN and all its specialized agencies. Founding member of the Balkan Alliance, NATO, OECD, Council of Europe. A signatory of an Association Agreement with the EEC 1963.
International relations: The European–Asiatic Ottoman Empire from 1299 to 1918; lost almost all its European possessions during Balkan wars 1912–13 and after World War I in which it fought on the German and Austrian side. Proclamation of republic on Oct. 29, 1923 ushered in a new era of Turkish history, the state covering *c.* 30% of the former Ottoman Empire. Frontier with USSR established by Moscow and Cairo treaties of 1921, demarcated in 1926, re-demarcated following changes in frontier river-beds in 1973 under the Ankara Protocol of Mar. 24, 1972; borderline with USSR on the Black Sea mapped out by Protocol of Apr. 14, 1973. In 1924–25 border dispute with Iraq over ▷ Mosul. Concluded treaty with Afghanistan, Iran, Iraq on July 8, 1937, extended in Dec., 1942. After the outbreak of World War II a British–French–Turkish treaty was signed on Oct. 19, 1939 on the neutrality of Turkey. In World War II Turkey supplied goods to both fighting parties; deliveries to Germany stopped in Apr., 1944; diplomatic relations with Germany terminated on Aug. 2, 1944; remained neutral until Mar. 1, 1945, then waged war against Germany and Japan. Member of the League of Nations 1934–39. Since Aug., 1954 in dispute with Greece in the UN Security Council over the status of ▷ Cyprus. On July 20, 1974 Turkish troops landed on Cyprus and established Turkish administration over one-third of the island. The Greek–Turkish dispute over Cyprus was examined by the UN Security Council on several occasions but remains unsettled. On July 25, 1975 the Turkish government assumed control over 26 American military bases in relation to a Congress ban on arms supplies to Turkey. Turkish control confirmed in American–Turkish agreement of Mar., 1976. In 1976 Turkey applied to the ICJ for delimitation of continental shelf it shared with Greece which the Court refused to settle as an incompetent body. Turkey attended the Balkan Conference in Athens, Jan. 26–Feb. 5, 1975. Greek and

Turkish heads of state met at Montreux, Switzerland, on Mar. 10–11, 1978. In dispute with Greece over sovereignty in the Aegean Sea. On Jan. 9, 1980 Turkey concluded a new agreement on the status of American military bases on Turkish territory.
On March 26, 1986 a family planning campaign to lower the high birth rate (2.8 per cent) was started. In 1986–87 increased tensions with Greece (▷ Aegean Sea). On March 17, 1987 in Washington Turkey and the USA extended until 1990 the defence and economic co-operation agreement.
On Sept. 31, 1988 the only border crossing between Turkey and the USSR was reopened after 51 years.
See also ▷ World Heritage UNESCO List.

E. KORAY, *Turkiye Bibliografyasi 1729–1950. A Bibliography of Turkey*, Ankara, 1952; C.H. DODDA, *Politics and Government in Turkey*, Manchester University Press, 1970; A.F. VALI, *Bridge across the Bosphorus; The Foreign Policy of Turkey*, Baltimore, 1970; J.C. DOVONNEY, *Turkey*, London, 1971; F. ALMAD, *The Turkish Experiment in Democracy*, London, 1977; F.G. WEBER, *The Evasive Neutral: Germany, Britain and the Quest for a Turkish Alliance in the II World War*, Columbia University Press, 1979; M. GUCHU, *Turkey. Bibliography*, Oxford, 1981; W. HALE, *The Political and Economic Development of Modern Turkey*, London, 1981; A. KAZANCIGIL, F. OZBUDUN, *Atatürk, Founder of a Modern State*, London, 1981; D.B. SEZER, *Turkey's Security Policies*, London, 1981; W. WEIKER, *The Modernization of Turkey*, New York, 1981; *The Europa Year Book 1984. A World Survey*, Vol. I, pp. 847–865, London, 1984; L.A. RUSTOW, *Turkey: Americas Forgotten Ally*, New York, 1987; I.C. SCHICK, E.A. TOMAK eds., *Turkey in Transition: New Perspectives*, New York, 1987.

TURKEY–ITALY TREATY, 1912. ▷ Ouchy Peace Treaty, 1912.

TURKISH REPUBLIC OF NORTHERN CYPRUS. ▷ Cyprus.

TURKISH STRAITS. The Black Sea straits, ▷ Bosporus and ▷ Dardanelles, connecting the Black Sea with the Mediterranean Sea. The Turkish Straits were internationalized with the Treaty of Adrianople, 1829 (earlier, from 1774 they were open to Russian merchant vessels on the basis of a Russian–Turkish treaty and from 1833 also for Russian war ships, while Turkey was simultaneously obligated not to admit foreign war ships into the Black Sea); demilitarization was annulled by the ▷ Montreux Convention signed in 1936.

TURKS AND CAICOS ISLANDS. A dependency of the UK, in the Caribbean Sea, British West Indies, geographically a part of the Bahamas; 30 cays and islands of which only 6 are inhabited: Grand Caicos, Grand Turk, South Caicos, Middle Caicos, North Caicos and Providenciales. Area: 430 sq. km. Pop. 1980 census: 7436. The capital is Grand Turk. Associated since the 18th century with the colonies of Bahamas and Jamaica; since 1973 a separate British Crown colony.
The UN Special (Decolonization) Committee on Aug. 12, 1983 reiterated that it is the UK obligation to create conditions in the Territory to enable the people to exercise freely and without interference their right to self-determination and independence.

The Europa Year Book 1984. A World Survey, Vol. I, pp. 1266–1267, London, 1984; *UN Chronicle*, January, 1984, p. 63.

TUTELAGE. The patronage *ex officio* over orphaned children, incapacitated or handicapped persons, absent persons and their property and also derelict property; subject of the Convention on Incapacitation and Other Tutorial Rules, signed on July 17, 1905, in The Hague.

CARNEGIE ENDOWMENT, *Signatures, Ratifications, Adhevious and Reservations to the Conventions and Declarations of the First and Second Hague Conference*, Washington, DC, 1914.

TUVALU. Member of the Commonwealth. An island group in Polynesia, formerly the Ellice Islands, Area: 26 sq. km. Pop. 1985 census: 8229. Capital: Fongafale. Official language: English. GNP per capita 1984: US $500. Currency: Australian dollars and Tuvaluan coins up to one dollar. National Day: Oct. 1; Independence Day, 1978. Member of one UN specialized agency: the UPU. International relations: from 1882 until 1976 under British Protectorate together with the Gilbert Islands. Separated from the Gilbert Islands in Oct., 1975, independent on Oct. 1, 1975. Member of the Commonwealth and is an ACP State of the EEC.

The Europa Year Book 1984. A World Survey, Vol. II, pp. 2540–2541, London, 1984.

TWO-TIER-MARKET. An international financial term for a market in which, besides the free exchange of currencies, there are officially fixed, permanent rates for certain transactions in foreign trade; in 1971 France introduced e.g. separate rates for commercial and financial transactions as a protection against an excessive inflow of "unwanted" dollars.

J. WALMSLEY, *A Dictionary of International Finance*, London, 1979.

TYNRA TAM. ▷ ICBM.

TYPHOONS. The tropical cyclones in the northwest part of the Pacific Ocean along the southeast China coastline, in Japan and the Philippines; a subject of an organized international warning service under UN auspices; attached to WMO is a Typhoon Committee.

Yearbook of International Organizations.

TYPOGRAPHY. International term – subject of international co-operation. Organizations reg. with the UIA:

International Center for the Typographic Arts, f. 1961, Stuttgart, FRG.
International Typographical Association, f. 1957, Frankfurt M., FRG. Publ.: *Studies*.
International Typographical Union, f. 1976, Colorado Springs, Col., USA.
International Typographic Composition Association, f. 1920, Washington, DC.

Yearbook of International Organizations.

TYROL. ▷ Austria–Italy Border Dispute.

U

U2. An American military reconnaissance plane produced in the 1950s by the Lockheed Aircraft Co. One plane of this type was shot down May 1, 1960 over the USSR, resulting in the cancellation of the conference of Chiefs of State of the Big Four in Paris, when US President D. Eisenhower refused to apologize to Premier N.S. Khrushchev for violating the sovereign territory of the USSR and guaranteeing that the United States would suspend further U2 flights over the USSR; the subject of debates in the Security Council May 23, 1960.

V. MARCHETTI, J.D. MARKS, *The CIA and the Cult of Intelligence*, New York, 1975.

UBANGI RIVER. A border river between Zaïre, the Central African Republic and Congo, 1125 km. The river, formed by the confluence of the Zaïrian Uele and Bili, flows into the Congo River.

UEBERMENSCH. *German* = "Superman." Initially a philosophical-literary term used for the first time by the theologian H. Muller from Rostock in the 17th century, then F.W. Nietzsche as the ideal man of "master morality," the opposite to "slave morality": the conception of the "superman" was usurped by German fascism as the ideal for Germans called to govern and dominate the world (Herrenvolk, *German*: "Nation of Masters") and to oppress "lower races," so-called "submen" (▷ Untermensch).

UFO. Unidentified Flying Object. An international term. Introduced in the 1960s for so-called flying saucers. The UN General Assembly on Dec. 13, 1977 reached a consensus that a Grenada item – Establishment of a UN agency for undertaking, coordinating and disseminating the results of research into unidentified flying objects and related phenomena – be transmitted to the UN member states and to the specialized agencies so that they might communicate their views to the Secretary-General.

C. SAGAN (ed.), *UFO. A Scientific Debate*, Cornell University Press, 1978; *UN Chronicle*, January, 1978, p. 97.

UGANDA. Member of the UN. Republic of Uganda. Country in East Africa bounded by Sudan, Kenya, Tanzania, Rwanda, and Zaïre. Area: 236,860 sq. km. Pop. 1987 est.: 15,500,000 (1959 census: 6,449,558; 1969 census: 9,548,847). Capital Kampala with 332,000 inhabitants 1975. Official language: English. Currency: one Ugandan Shilling = 100 cents. GNP per capita 1984: US $230. National Day: Oct. 9, proclamation of independence, 1962.
Member of the UN since Oct. 25, 1962 and all its specialized agencies except IMO. Member of the OAU and the Commonwealth; ACP state of the EEC. International relations: from 1894 to 1962 colonial dependency of Great Britain. Popular rebellion in 1955 prompted limited self-rule. In 1958 first direct elections in part and in 1961–62 in the whole country. Independence granted on Oct. 9, 1962. Founding member of the ▷ East African Community incepted by the governments of Kenya, Tanzania, Uganda in Dec., 1963. In armed conflict with Tanzania in Sept. 1972 which ended with the assistance of the OAU. In Apr., 1979 General Amin's régime was abolished with military support from Tanzania. A signatory of the Arusha Conventions of 1968 and of 1969, and of the Lome Conventions of 1975, 1980, 1985. In 1982–84 an estimated 200,000 Ugandans have fled to Sudan and Zaïre and in 1984 a number of ethnic Rwandans living in Uganda have fled to Tanzania.

P.M. GUKIINA, *Uganda*, University of Notre Dame Press, 1972; J. GERSHENBERG, *Commercial Banking in Uganda*, Kampala, 1973; J. LISTOREL, *Amin*, Irish University Press, 1973; J. BROWNLIE, *African Boundaries*, London, 1979; J.J. JORGENSEN, *Uganda: A Modern History*, London, 1981; R.L. COLLISON, *Uganda. Bibliography*, Oxford, 1981; *The Europa Year Book 1984. A World Survey*, Vol. II, pp. 2543–2554, London, 1984; A. OMARA-OTUNNU, *Politics and the Military in Uganda 1890–1985*, London, 1987.

UIA. Union of International Associations, f. 1907, Brussels, from 1950 the UIA in co-operation with the UN, publishes the *Yearbook of International Organizations*.
The UIA became a federation in 1900 at the 1st World Congress of International Organizations; after WWI an International Federation for Documentation related to the League of Nations International Institute of Intellectual Cooperation. During the 1920's the UIA created the International University.
The statue was modified in 1951, recognized by the ESOSOC. The HQ is in Brussels.
A chronology of UIA publications:
1908–1909–1910–1911 *Annuaire de la UIA internationale* (In the years 1910–1911 with the support of the ▷ Carnegie endowment);
1926–1929–1939 *Repertoire des Organisations internationaux* (in cooperation with the League of Nations); English editions: *Handbook of International Organizations*.
Publ. since 1948 was a bimestrial revue *International Transnational Associations* in English and French.
1948–1949–1950 *Annuaire des Organizations internationaux. Yearbook of International Organizations*, published by the Editions de l'Annuaire des Organizations internationaux (Geneva).
On the basis of an agreement in 1951 with the UN resulting from a resolution of the ECOSOC, the UIA with HQ in Brussels, published the *Yearbook of International Organizations*. (1951/52, 4th eds.; 1954/55, 5th ed.; 1956/57, 6th ed.; 1958/59, 7th ed.; 1960/61, 8th ed.; 1962/63, 9th ed.; 1964/65, 10th ed.; 1966/67, 11th ed.; 1968/69, 12th ed.; 1970/71, 13th ed.; 1972/73, 14th ed.; 1974/75 15th ed.; (in English and French); 1976/77, 16th ed.; 1978/79, 17th and 18th ed.).
In 1981 on the basis of an agreement with the UN, published jointly with the International Chamber of Commerce (Paris): the *Yearbook of International Organizations* 1981, 19th ed.
Since 1983 based on an agreement with the UN published in Säur München, New York, London, Paris: 1983, 20th ed.; 1984, 21st ed.; 1985, 22nd ed.; 1986/87, 23rd ed. with two supplementary volumes:
Geographic Volume of International Organization Participation, 1983, 1st ed.; 1984, 2nd ed.; 1985, 3rd ed.; 1986/87, 4th ed.
Global Action Network, ditto.
Related publications of the UIA:
African International Organization Directory, 1984/86, 1st ed.
Arab-Islamic International Organizations Directory, 1984/86, 1st ed.
International Organizations Abbreviation and Addresses, 1984/86, 1st ed.
Intergovernmental Organization Directory, 1984/85, 1st ed. *Yearbook of World Problems and Human Potential*, 1978, 1st ed; and with changed title:
Encyclopedia of World Problems and Human Potential, 1985, 2nd ed. *International Congress Calendar*, 1986, quarterly. *International Association Statute Series*, since 1986.
Yearbook of International Organizations, 1986/87.

UK. ▷ United Kingdom of Great Britain and Northern Ireland.

UKRAINE. Member of the UN. The Ukrainian Soviet Socialist Republic. Federal republic in the southwestern part of the USSR on the Black Sea and Sea of Azov. Borders with Poland, Czechoslovakia, Hungary, Romania and the Russian SFSR, Byelorussian SSR and Moldavian SSR. Area: 603,700 sq. km. Pop. 1983 est.: 50,456,000 (of these 74.9% are Ukrainians, 19.4% Russians, 0.8% Byelo-russians, 0.6% Moldavians and 0.6% Poles); growth of census population: 1913 – 32,210,000; 1939 – 40,469,000; 1959 – 41,869,000; 1960 – 45,516,000. Capital: Kiev with 1,632,000 inhabitants in 1970. Official languages: Ukrainian and Russian. Currency: one USSR rouble. National Day: Nov. 7, anniversary of the October Revolution, 1917.
The Ukraine is a founding member of the UN, and a member of all UN special organizations with the exception of FAO, IBRD, IDA, IMF, IFC, IFAD, IMO and GATT. As part of the USSR it is a member of the Warsaw Pact and the CMEA. See also ▷ Polish–Ukrainian Agreement, 1920.

W.E. ALLEN, *The Ukraine*, London, 1940; W.H. CHAMBERLAIN, *The Ukraine*, New York, 1945; I. MIRCHUK (ed.), *Ukraine and its People*, London, 1949; *Vossoedinenie Ukrainy s Rossiey. Dokumenty i materialy*, 3 Vols., Moscow, 1954; V. HOLUBNYCH, *The Industrial Output of the Ukraine 1913–1956*, Munich, 1957; R. ILNYTZKYJ. *Deutschland und die Ukraine 1934–1945*, München, 1958; N.L. CHIROVSKY, *The Ukrainian Economy*, New York, 1965; O.K. KOSYMENKO, *Istoriya Ukrainskoy SSR*, Kiev, 1965; K.S. ZABIGAYLO, *K'istorii uchastiya Ukrainskoy SSR w wyrabotkie ustava OON*, Moscow, 1966; *Soviet Ukraine, Ukrainian Soviet Encyclopaedia.* English edition, Kiev, 1970; *Ukraine. A Concise Encyclopaedia*, 2 Vols., Toronto, 1971; *History of the Ukrainian SSR*, 8 Vols., Kiev, 1980; T. KIS (ed), *Studia Ucrainica*, Ottawa, 1984: *The Europa Year Book 1984. A World Survey*, Vol. I, pp. 933–934, London, 1984; N.L. CHIROVSKY, *An Introduction to Ukrainian History*, 3 Vls, New York, 1981–1986; P.J. POINTCHNYJ, Y. SHTENDERA, eds., *Political Thought of the Ukrainian Underground 1943–1951*, Edmonton, 1986.

ULAN BATOR. The capital since 1921 of the Mongolian People's Republic, on the Tola River in central Outer Mongolia.

ULSTER. The historic region of Ireland, divided since Dec. 6, 1922 between Ireland (counties: Cavan, Donegal and Monaghan) and the UK province of Northern Ireland (six counties: Antrim, Armagh, Down, Fermanagh, Londonderry and Tyrone). ▷ Ireland, Northern.

ULTIMATUM. Under the Third Hague Convention of 1907 it is equal to a conditional declaration of war; subject of controversial interpretations in international laws; after World War II the UN Charter obliged member states to refrain from threat or use of force and indirectly recognized that ultimatum is an inadmissible instrument of aggression unless it has an anti-war character as that made by Great Britain in relations with Germany, Sept. 3, 1939, demanding that German aggression against Poland be discontinued.

W. BRAUN, *Démarche, Ultimatum, Sommation*, Paris, 1930; H. ASBECK, *Das Ultimatum im modernen Völkerrecht*, Berlin, 1933.

UMM AL-QAIWAIN. A sheikhdom, part of the United Arab Emirates, 1971. Until 1971 a British protectorate.

UMPIRE. In the international arbitration procedure the chairman of the mixed arbitration commission.

UN. ▷ United Nations.

UN ADMINISTRATIVE TRIBUNAL. A UN institution established on Nov. 24, 1949 by the UN General Assembly to hear and pass judgement upon applications alleging non-observance of contracts of employment of UN staff members and those of several UN agencies. It is composed of seven members from different countries, three of whom may constitute the Tribunal for consideration of a particular case. In the political issue of ▷ McCarthyism at the UN in 1952/53, the Tribunal declared itself against the policy of the UN Secretariat of dismissing UN workers on request of the FBI, and granted high compensation to those dismissed. The UN General Assembly, modified on Nov. 6, 1951 the Statutes of the Tribunal. The manner and methods of proceedings of the Tribunal are covered in detail by its Statute and Rules. Under a procedure established by the General Assembly on Nov. 8, 1955, either party to a case, or the Government of any Member State, may contest a judgement within 30 days of its date and request an advisory opinion of the International Court of Justice. Such requests are reviewed in the first instance by a committee of Member States whose representatives served on the General Committee of the most recent regular session of the General Assembly. (Committee on Application for Review of Administrative Tribunal Judgements, est. by UN General Assembly Res. 957/X of 1955). This committee decides whether there is a substantial basis for submitting the matter to the Court.

UN Bulletin, December 1, 1949, pp. 701–702; H. WRIGGINS, E.A. BOCK, *The Status of the UN Secretariat. The Role of the Administrative Tribunal*, New York, 1955; G. LANGROD, "La réforme 1955 du Tribunal Administratif des Nations Unies", in: *Zeitschrift für ausländisches öffentliches Recht, 1956–57; Judgement of the UN Administrative Tribunal 1950–57*, New York, 1958; *UN Administrative Tribunal Statute and Rules*, New York, 1962; B.C. KOTZ, *The UN Administrative Tribunal*, Baton Rouge, 1966; *Everyone's United Nations*, New York, 1979; *Judgements of the UN Administrative Tribunal*, New York, 1983.

UNAEC. United Nations Atomic Energy Commission, unanimously est. on Jan. 24, 1946 by the General Assembly Res. 1 (1), suspended de facto on June 22, 1948 after an absolute disagreement between the USA and USSR.
The UNAEC was composed of the States represented in the Security Council and of Canada when the latter was not a member of the Security Council. The UNAEC was established to deal with the problems "raised by the discovery of atomic energy and other related matters". The Commission was to receive instruction from and report to the Security Council. The UNAEC prepared for the Security Council three reports on December 31, 1946, on September 8, 1947 and on June 22, 1948.
See also ▷ Atomic energy and the UN.

The Yearbook of the United Nations, 1946–1947, pp. 64–66; *The Yearbook of the United Nations*, 1947–1948, pp. 463–480. "The UN Atomic Energy Commission. An Historical Survey of the Period June 1946 to March 1947", in: *International Conciliation*, No. 430, April, 1947, pp. 166–288.

UN AFRICA DECLARATION, 1984. a Declaration on the Critical Economic Situation in Africa adopted by consensus on Dec. 3, 1984 by UN General Assembly. The Declaration stated, that "despite its enormous potential Africa remains the least developed of all continents" and expressed alarm over "the specter of widespread famine hanging over many African countries and the threat of hunger and malnutrition facing more than 150 million of Africans."

KEESING'S *Contemporary Archive*, 1984.

UN AGENCY FOR RESEARCH ON UTILIZATION OF ENERGY SOURCES IN THE THIRD WORLD. A United Nations institution established in Rome on Dec. 5, 1984.

UNANIMITY IN THE LEAGUE OF NATIONS. Principle binding in all essential decisions both in the Assembly as well as in the Council of the LN in accordance with Art. 5 of the Covenant of the League of Nations. The principle of absolute unanimity as "the most certain guarantee of the just interests of the Members of the League of Nations, which should remain an organization of sovereign states free in their decisions," was rejected by the founders of the UN, who only retained the duty of unanimity of states defined in the Covenant of the LN as applying to the Major Powers. The five permanent members of the UN Security Council – China, France, USSR, UK and USA – must concur in all decisions that are not procedural.

A.C. RICHET, *The Unanimity Rule and the League of Nations*, London, 1933.

UNANIMITY OF THE GREAT POWERS IN THE UN. A fundamental principle of UN activities on behalf of maintaining peace and security based on a harmony of views on matters essential for peace by the five permanent members of the UN Security Council; included in Art. 27 of the UN Charter. De facto this UN Charter provision gives each of the five powers the right to veto, which was opposed at the UN Conference in San Francisco, Apr., 1945, by a number of states, mainly from Latin America. ▷ Veto in UN Security Council.

W.T. FOX, *Las Super potencias: Estados Unidos, Inglaterra y la Unión Soviética, Su responsabilidad ante la Paz*, México, DF, 1944; G.M. UBARTAZZI, *Il principio di unanimita regli organi collegiali internazionali*, Roma, 1953; E.A. GROSS, *The United Nations: Structure for Peace*, New York, 1962; M. LACHS, "Zasada jedności Wielkich Mocarstw", in: *Sprawy Miedzynarodowe*, No. 6, 1963; M. SEARA VAZQUEZ, *Tratado General de la Organización Internacional*, México, DF, 1974, pp. 36–38 and 160–168.

UN AS INTERNATIONAL LEGAL PERSON. ▷ UN Juridical International Personality.

UN ATOMIC ENERGY COMMISSION. ▷ UNAEC.

UNAVEM. United Nations Angola Verification Mission, est. by the Security Council on Dec. 22, 1988 with effect from April 1, 1989 on the initiative of Angola and Cuba.

"The mandate of the observer mission would be to verify the redeployment northwards and phased and total withdrawal of Cuban troops from the territory of Angola in accordance with the timetable agreed between Angola and Cuba. It is recommended that, if the Council decides to accede to the request of Angola and Cuba, an observer group should be set up to carry out this mandate in the manner described in the following paragraphs."

UN Security Council s/20338, 17 December 1988.

UNBIS. United Nations Bibliographic Information System based on a multidisciplinary indexing vocabulary in English, French and Spanish, reflecting the wide-ranging concerns of the UN. The system now includes members outside the Dag Hammarskjöld Library (DHL), notably the Library of the United Nations Office at Geneva, as well as various other units; indexing and cataloguing practices have been brought in line with international standards in the areas of bibliographic description, name authority and computer record format; the single descriptor indexing method has been adopted.
The UNBIS serves as:
(a) The basis source of descriptors for indexers and cataloguers in various units of the DHL and other members of the UNBIS network, to ensure consistency in subject analysis throughout the system;
(b) A guide for structuring searches in the Library's data bases;
(c) A device for automatically finding broader, narrower and related terms (through linkages between the bibliographic data files and the Thesaurus File);
(d) A means of verifying the accuracy of input into the data bases (through computer matching of approved terms against the descriptor field of the bibliographic records).
UNBIS Thesaurus, Trilingual List of Terms Used in Subject Analysis of Documents and Other Material Relevant to United Nations Programmes and Activities, New York, 1985.

UN BLUE SATELLITE.
▷ Satellite Telecommunication.

UN BOARD OF AUDITORS. UN General Assembly body, est. by Res. 74/I of 1986, to serve as external auditor of the accounts of the UN, FAO, ILO, UNESCO, WHO and the ICJ. The members appointed by the UN General Assembly for 3 years have to right to be re-elected.

United Nations Handbook, Wellington, 1986, p. 12.

UN BONDS. The UN Secretary-General on instructions of the UN General Assembly, Res. 1739/XVI of Dec. 21, 1961, in order to cover deficits in the UN budget, issued in 1962 the UN Bonds, which paid interest at the annual rate of 2 per cent.

UN BUDGET. ▷ Budget of the UN.

UNCA. The United Nations Correspondents Association, f. 1948 at Lake Success. Its aims and purposes as stated in its Constitution are as follows:
1. To maintain and protect the freedom and prestige of Press, Radio and Television correspondents in all their relations with the United Nations.
2. To promote the interest of its members and to facilitate their personal and professional relationships.
3. To take whatever measures possible to protect the rights of bona fide correspondents to secure accreditation and unhindered access to the United Nations headquarters or regional offices, and to their normally available facilities, without discrimination.
4. To undertake any other action, when required, on behalf of Press, Radio and Television correspondents accredited to the United Nations, either at its headquarters or at any of its regional offices.
5. To facilitate social contact between its members, delegates from member nations or the United Nations, officials of the Secretariat, and distinguished personalities connected with international affairs.

After the death of Secretary-General Dag Hammarskjöld in a plane crash on Sept. 8, 1961 UNCA decided to establish a Scholarship Fund to perpetuate his memory.
A Dag Hammarskjöld Fellowship Program was created under which working journalists from developing countries are brought to the United Nations every year to cover the regular session of the General Assembly.

U

The UNCA publ. periodically from Oct., 1980: *The UN Correspondent and UNCA Membership Directory.*

UN CENTRE FOR DISARMAMENT, UNCD. A UN institution est. Jan. 1, 1977 by resolution of the UN General Assembly with the task of strengthening the role of the UN in the field of disarmament by collecting information, making studies, and initiating action in support of disarmament. The director of the centre is one of the Assistant Secretaries-General of the UN.

UN CENTRE FOR HUMAN SETTLEMENTS (HABITAT). Est. 1978 within the UN System. It assists in improving human habitats, and managing national programmes, particularly in developing countries (▷ Shelter for the Homeless). Habitat is a subsidiary body of the UN General Assembly. It also serves as the secretariat for the UN Commission on Human Settlements, consisting of 58 government representatives. The Habitat technical programme is funded mainly by the UNDP Hq, Nairobi and liaison office at UN Hq, New York.

UN CENTRE ON TRANSNATIONAL CORPORATIONS. ▷ Transnational Corporations.

UNCIO. United Nations Conference of International Organization. The official name of the ▷ San Francisco Conference of the United Nations, 1945.

UNCITRAL. United Nations Commission on International Trade Law. The Commission elaborated in the years 1974–77 the following conventions:
Convention on the Limitation Period in the International Sale of Goods, adopted in 1974 by a UN Conference;
Convention on the Carriage of Goods by Sea, elaborated 1976;
UNCITRAL Arbitration Rules in international commercial relations, drafted by the Commission and recommended by UN General Assembly in 1976;
Convention on the International Sale of Goods, elaborated 1977.
See also ▷ UNCITRAL Convention, 1988.

UNCITRAL, Arbitration Rules, New York, 1977; *UN Chronicle*, December, 1983, p. 76; UNCITRAL, *Legal Guide on Drawing up International Contracts for Construction of Industrial Works*, New York, 1988.

UNCITRAL CONVENTION, 1988. Official name of the UN Convention on International ▷ Bills of Exchange and International Promissory Notes, adopted without a vote, Dec. 9, 1988, (Res. 43/165). The text is as follows:
United Nations Convention on International Bills of Exchange and International Promissory Notes
Chapter I. *Sphere of Application and Form of the Instrument.*
Art. 1.(1) This Convention applies to an international bill of exchange when it contains the heading "International bill of exchange (UNCITRAL Convention)" and also contains in its text the words "International bill of exchange (UNCITRAL Convention)".
(2) This Convention applies to an international promissory note when it contains the heading "International promissory note (UNCITRAL Convention)" and also contains in its text the words "International promissory note (UNCITRAL Convention)".
(3) This Convention does not apply to cheques.
Art. 2.(1) An international bill of exchange is a bill of exchange which specifes at least two of the following places and indicates that any two so specified are situated in different States:
(a) The place where the bill is drawn;
(b) The place indicated next to the signature of the drawer;
(c) The place indicated next to the name of the drawee;
(d) The place indicated next to the name of the payee;
(e) The place of payment:
provided that either the place where the bill is drawn or the place of payment is specified on the bill and that such place is situated in a Contracting State.
(2) An international promissory note is a promissory note which specifies at least two of the following places and indicates that any two so specified are situated in different States:
(a) The place where the note is made;
(b) The place indicated next to the signature of the maker;
(c) The place indicated next to the name of the payee;
(d) The place of payment:
provided that the place of payment is specified on the note and that such place is situated in a Contracting State.
(3) This Convention does not deal with the question of sanctions that may be imposed under national law in cases where an incorrect or false statement has been made on an instrument in respect of a place referred to in paragraph (1) or (2) of this article. However, any such sanctions shall not affect the validity of the instrument or the application of this Convention.
Art. 3.(1) A bill of exchange is a written instrument which:
(a) Contains an unconditional order whereby the drawer directs the drawee to pay a definite sum of money to the payee or to his order;
(b) Is payable on demand or at a definite time;
(c) Is dated;
(d) Is signed by the drawer.
(2) A promissory note is a written instrument which:
(a) Contains an unconditional promise whereby the maker undertakes to pay a definite sum of money to the payee or to his order;
(b) Is payable on demand or at a definite time;
(c) Is dated;
(d) Is signed by the maker.
Chapter II. *Interpretation, Section 1. General provisions.*
Art. 4. In the interpretation of this Convention, regard is to be had to its international character and to the need to promote uniformity in its application and the observance of good faith in international transaction.
Art. 5. In this Convention:
(a) "Bill" means an international bill of exchange governed by this Convention;
(b) "Note" means an international promissory note governed by this Convention;
(c) "Instrument" means a bill or a note;
(d) "Drawee" means a person on whom a bill is drawn and who has not accepted it;
(e) "Payee" means a person in whose favour the drawer directs payment to be made or to whom the maker promises to pay;
(f) "Holder" means a person in possession of an instrument in accordance with article 15;
(g) "Protected holder" means a holder who meets the requirements of article 29;
(h) "Guarantor" means any person who undertakes an obligation of guarantee under article 46, whether governed by subparagraph (b) ("guaranteed") or subparagraph (c) ("aval") of paragraph (4) of article 47;
(i) "Party" means a person who has signed an instrument as drawer, maker, acceptor, endorser or guarantor;
(j) "Maturity" means the time of payment referred to in paragraphs (4), (5), (6) and (7) of article 9;
(k) "Signature" means a handwritten signature, its facsimile or an equivalent authentication effected by any other means; "forged signature" includes a signature by the wrongful use of such means;
(l) "Money" or "currency" includes a monetary unit of account which is established by an intergovernmental institution or by agreement between two or more States, provided that this Convention shall apply without prejudice to the rules of the intergovernmental institution or to the stipulations of the agreement.
Art. 6. For the purposes of this Convention, a person is considered to have knowledge of a fact if he has actual knowledge of that fact or could not have been unaware of its existence.
Section 2. Interpretation of formal requirements.
Art. 7. The sum payable by an instrument is deemed to be a definite sum although the instrument states that it is to be paid:
(a) With interest;
(b) By instalments at successive dates;
(c) By instalments at successive dates with a stipulation in the instrument that upon default in payment of any instrument the unpaid balance becomes due;
(d) According to a rate of exchange indicated in the instrument or to be determined as directed by the instrument; or
(e) In a currency other than the currency in which the sum is expressed in the instrument.
Art. 8.(1) If there is a discrepancy between the sum expressed in words and the sum expressed in figures, the sum payable by the instrument is the sum expressed in words.
(2) If the sum is expresed more than once in words, and there is a disrcrepancy, the sum payable is the smaller sum. The same rule applies if the sum is expressed more than once in figures only, and there is a discrepancy.
(3) If the sum is expressed in a currency having the same description as that of at least one other State than the State where payment is to be made, as indicated in the instrument, and the specified currency is not identified as the currency of any particular State, the currency is to be considered as the currency of the State where payment is to be made.
(4) If an instrument states that the sum is to be paid with interest, without specifying the date from which interests is to run, interest runs from the date of the instrument.
(5) A stipulation stating that the sum is to be paid with interest is deemed not to have been written on the instrument unless it indicates the rate at which interest is to be paid.
(6) A rate at which interest is to be paid may be expressed either as a definite rate or as a variable rate. For a variable rate to qualify for this purpose, it must vary in relation to one or more reference rates of interest in accordance with provisions stipulated in the instrument and each such reference must be published or otherwise available to the public and not be subject, directly or indirectly, to unilateral determination by a person who is named in the instrument at the time the bill is drawn or the note is made, unless the person is named only in the reference rate provisions.
(7) If the rate at which interest is to be paid is expressed as a variable rate, it may be stipulated expressly in the instrument that such rate shall not be less than or exceed a specified rate of interest, or that the variations are otherwise limited.
(8) If a variable rate does not qualify under paragraph (6) of this article or for any reason it is not possible to determine the numerical value of the variable rate for any period, interest shall be payable for the relevant period at the rate calculated in accordance with paragraph (2) of article 70.
Art. 9.(1) An instrument is deemed to be payable on demand:
(a) If it states that it is payable at sight or on demand or on presentment or if it contains words of similar import; or
(b) If no time of payment is expressed.
(2) An instrument payable at a definite time which is accepted or endorsed or guaranteed after maturity is an instrument payable on demand as regards the acceptor, the endorser or the guarantor.
(3) An instrument is deemed to be payable at a definite time if it states that it is payable:
(a) On a stated date or at a fixed period after a stated date or at a fixed period after the date of the instrument; or
(b) At a fixed period after sight; or
(c) By instalments at successive dates; or
(d) By instalments at successive dates with the stipulation in the instrument that upon default in payment of any instalment the unpaid balance becomes due.
(4) The time of payment of an instrument payable at a fixed period after date is determined by reference to the date of the instrument.
(5) The time of payment of a bill payable at a fixed period after sight is determined by the date of acceptance or, if the bill is dishonoured by non-acceptance, by the date of protest or, if protest is dispensed with, by the date of dishonour.
(6) The time of payment of an instrument payable on demand is the date of which the instrument is presented for payment.
(7) The time of payment of a note payable at a fixed period after sight is determined by the date of the visa

signed by the maker on the note or, if his visa is refused, by the date of presentment.

(8) If an instrument is drawn, or made, payable one or more months after a stated date or after the date of the instrument or after sight, the instrument is payable on the corresponding date of the month when payment must be made. If there is no corresponding date, the instrument is payable on the last day of that month.

Art. 10.(1) A bill may be drawn:
(a) By two more more drawers;
(b) Payable to two or more payees.
(2) A note may be made:
(a) By two or more makers;
(b) Payable to two or more payees.
(3) If an instrument is payable to two or more payees in the alternative, it is payable to any one of them and any one of them in possession of the instrument may exercise the rights of a holder. If any other case the instrument is payable to all of them and the rights of a holder may be exercises only by all of them.

Art. 11. A bill may be drawn by the drawer:
(a) On himself;
(b) Payable to his order.

Section 3. Completion of an incomplete instrument.

Art. 12.(1) An incomplete instrument which satisfies the requirements set out in paragraph (1) of article 1 and bears the signature of the drawer or the acceptance of the drawee, or which satisfies the requirements set out in paragraph (2) or article 1 and subparagraph (d) of paragraph (2) of article 3, but which lacks other elements pertaining to one or more of the requirements set out in articles 2 and 3, may be completed, and the instrument so completed is effective as a bill or a note.
(2) If such an instrument is completed without authority or otherwise than in accordance with the authority given:
(a) A party who signed the instrument before the completion may invoke such lack of authority as a defence against a holder who had knowledge of such lack of authority when he became a holder;
(b) A party who signed the instrument after the completion is liable according to the terms of the instrument so completed.

Chapter III. Transfer.

Art. 13. An instrument is transferred:
(a) By endorsement and delivery of the instrument by the endorser to the endorsee; or
(b) By mere delivery of the instrument if the last endorsement is in blank.

Art. 14.(1) An endorsement must be written on the instrument or on a slip affixed thereto ("*allonge*"). It must be signed.
(2) An endorsement may be:
(a) In blank, that is, by a signature alone or by a signature accompanied by a statement to the effect that the instrument is payable to a person in possession of it;
(b) Special, that is, by a signature accompanied by an indication of the person to whom the instrument is payable.
(3) A signature alone, other than that of the drawee, is an endorsement only if placed on the back of the instrument.

Art. 15.(1) A person is a holder if he is:
(a) The payee in possession of the instrument; or
(b) In possession of an instrument which has been endorsed to him, or on which the last endorsement is in blank, and on which there appears an uninterrupted series of endorsements, even if any endorsement was forged or was signed by an agent without authority.
(2) If an endorsement in blank is followed by another endorsement, the person who signed this last endorsement is deemed to be an endorsee by the endorsement in blank.
(3) A person is not prevented from being a holder by the fact that the instrument was obtained by him or any previous holder under circumstances, including incapacity or fraud, duress or mistake of any kind, that would give rise to a claim to, or a defence against liability on, the instrument.

Art. 16. The holder of an instrument on which the last endorsement is in blank may:
(a) Further endorse it either by an endorsement in blank or by a special endorsement; or
(b) Convert the blank endorsement into a special endorsement by indicating in the endorsement that the instrument is payable to himself or to some other specified person; or

(c) Transfer the instrument in accordance with sub-paragraph (b) of article 13.

Art. 17.(1) If the drawer or the maker has inserted in the instrument such words as "not negotiable", "not transferable", "not to order", "pay (X) only", or words of similar import, the instrument may not be transferred except for purposes of collection, and any endorsement, even if it does not contain words authorizing the endorsee to collect the instrument, is deemed to be an endorsement for collection.
(2) If an endorsement contains the words, "not negotiable", "not transferable", "not to order", "pay (X) only", or words of similar import, the instrument may not be transferred further except for purposes of collection, and any subsequent endorsement, even if it does not contain words authorizing the endorsee to collect the instrument, is deemed to be an endorsement for collection.

Art. 18.(1) An endorsement must be unconditional.
(2) A conditional endorsement transfers the instrument whether or not the condition is fulfilled. The condition is ineffective as to those parties and transferees who are subsequent to the endorsee.

Art. 19. An endorsement in respect of a part of the sum due under the instrument is ineffective as an endorsement.

Art. 20. If there are two or more endorsements, it is presumed, unless the contrary is proved, that each endorsement was made in the order in which it appears on the instrument.

Art. 21.(1) If an endorsement contains the words "for collection", "for deposit", "value in collection", "by procuration", "pay any bank", or words of similar import authorizing the endorsee to collect the instrument, the endorsee is a holder who:
(a) May exercise all rights arising out of the instrument;
(b) May endorse the instrument only for purposes of collection;
(c) Is subject only to the claims and defences which may be set up against the endorser.
(2) The endorser for collection is not liable on the instrument to any subsequent holder.

Art. 22.(1) If an endorsement contains the words "value in security", "value in pledge", or any other words indicating a pledge, the endorsee is a holder who:
(a) May exercise all rights arising out of the instrument;
(b) May endorse the instrument only for purposes of collection;
(c) Is subject only to the claims and defences specified in article 28 or 30.
(2) If such an endorsee endorses for collection, he is not liable on the instrument to any subsequent holder.

Art. 23. The holder of an instrument may transfer it to a prior party or to the drawee in accordance with article 13; however, if the transferee has previously been a holder of the instrument, no endorsement is required, and any endorsement which would prevent him from qualifying as a holder may be struck out.

Art. 24. An instrument may be transferred in accordance with article 13 after maturity, except by the drawee, the acceptor or the maker.

Art. 25.(1) If an endorsement is forged, the person whose endorsement is forged, or a party who signed the instrument before the forgery, has the right to recover compensation for any damage that he may have suffered because of the forgery against:
(a) The forger;
(b) The person to whom the instrument was directly transferred by the forger;
(c) A party or the drawee who paid the instrument to the forger directly or through one or more endorsees for collection.
(2) However, an endorsee for collection is not liable under paragraph (1) of this article if he is without knowledge of the forgery;
(a) At the time he pays the principal or advises him of the receipt of payment, or
(b) At the time he received payment, if this is later, unless his lack of knowledge is due to his failure to act in good faith or to exercise reasonable care.
(3) Furthermore, a party or the drawee who pays an instrument is not liable under paragraph (1) of this article if, at the time he pays the instrument, he is without knowledge of the forgery, unless his lack of knowledge is due to his failure to act in good faith or to exercise reasonable care.

(4) Except as against the forger, the damages recoverable under paragraph (1) of this article may not exceed the amount referred to in article 70 or 71.

Art. 26.(1) If an endorsement is made by an agent without authority or power to bind his principal in the matter, the principal, or a party who signed the instrument before such endorsement, has the right to recover compensation for any damage that he may have suffered because of such endorsement against:
(a) The agent;
(b) The person to whom the instrument was directly transferred by the agent;
(c) A party or the drawee who paid the instrument to the agent directly or through one or more endorsees for collection.
(2) However, an endorsee for collection is not liable under paragraph (1) of this article if he is without knowledge that the endorsement does not bind the principal:
(a) At the time he pays the principal or advises him of the receipt of payment, or
(b) At the time he receives payment, if this is later, unless his lack of knowledge is due to his failure to act in good faith or to exercise reasonable care.
(3) Furthermore, a party or the drawee who pays an instrument is not liable under paragraph (1) of this article if, at the time he pays the instrument, he is without knowledge that the endorsement does not bind the principal, unless his lack of knowledge is due to his failure to act in good faith or to exercise reasonable care.
(4) Except as against the agent, the damages recoverable under paragraph (1) of this article may not exceed the amount referred to in article 70 or 71.

Chapter IV. Rights and Liabilities. Section 1. The rights of a holder and of a protected holder.

Art. 27.(1) The holder of an instrument has all the rights conferred on him by this Convention against the parties to the instrument.
(2) The holder may transfer the instrument in accordance with article 13.

Art. 28.(1) A party may set up against a holder who is not a protected holder:
(a) Any defence that may be set up against a protected holder in accordance with paragraph (1) of article 30;
(b) Any defence based on the underlying transaction between himself and the drawer or between himself and his transferee, but only if the holder took the instrument with knowledge of such defence or if he obtained the instrument by fraud or theft or participated at any time in a fraud or theft concerning it;
(c) Any defence arising from the circumstances as a result of which he became a party, but only if the holder took the instrument with knowledge of such defence or if he obtained the instrument by fraud or theft or participated at any time in a fraud or theft concerning it;
(d) Any defence which may be raised against an action in contract between himself and the holder;
(e) Any other defence available under this Convention.
(2) The rights to an instrument of a holder who is not a protected holder are subject to any valid claim to the instrument on the part of any person, but only if he took the instrument with knowledge of such claim or if he obtained the instrument by fraud or theft or participated at any time in a fraud or theft concerning it.
(3) A holder who takes an instrument after the expiration of the time-limit for presentment for payment is subject to any claim to, or defence against liability on, the instrument to which his transferor is subject.
(4) A party may not raise as a defence against a holder who is not a protected holder the fact that a third person has a claim to the instrument unless:
(a) The third person asserted a valid claim to the instrument; or
(b) The holder acquired the instrument by theft or forged the signature of the payee or an endorsee, or participated in the theft or the forgery.

Art. 29. "Protected holder" means the holder of an instrument which was complete when he took it or which was incomplete within the meaning of paragraph (1) of article 12 and was completed in accordance with authority given, provided that when he became a holder:
(a) He was without knowledge of a defence against liability on the instrument referred to in subparagraphs (a), (b), (c) and (e) of paragraph (1) of article 28;
(b) He was without knowledge of a valid claim to the instrument of any person;

(c) He was without knowledge of the fact that it had been dishonoured by non-acceptance or by non-payment;

(e) The time-limit provided by article 55 for presentment of that instrument for payment had not expired; and

(e) He did not obtain the instrument by fraud or theft or participate in a fraud or theft concerning it.

Art. 30.(1) A party may not set up against a protected holder any defence except:

(a) Defences under articles 33 (1), 34, 35 (1), 36 (3), 53 (1), 57 (1), 63 (1) and 84 of this Convention;

(b) Defences based on the underlying transaction between himself and such holder or arising from any fraudulent act on the part of such holder in obtaining the signature on the instrument of that party;

(c) Defences based on his incapacity to incur liability on the instrument or on the fact that he signed without knowledge that his signature made him a party to the instrument, provided that his lack of knowledge was not due to his negligence and provided that he was fraudulently induced so to sign.

(2) The rights to an instrument of a protected holder are not subject to any claim to the instrument on the part of any person, except a valid claim arising from the underlying transaction between himself and the person by whom the claim is raised.

Art. 31.(1) The transfer of an instrument by a protected holder vests in any subsequent holder the rights to and on the instrument which the protected holder had.

(2) Those rights are not vested in a subsequent holder if:

(a) He participated in a transaction which gives rise to a claim to, or a defence against liability on, the instrument;

(b) He has previously been a holder, but not a protected holder.

Art. 32. Every holder is presumed to be a protected holder unless the contrary is provided.

Section 2. Liabilities of the parties. A. General provisions.

Art. 33.(1) Subject to the provisions of articles 34 and 36, a person is not liable on an instrument unless he signs it.

(2) A person who signs an instrument in a name which is not his own is liable as if he had signed it in his own name.

Art. 34. A forged signature on an instrument does not impose any liability on the person whose signature was forged. However, if he consents to be bound by the forged signature or represents that it is his own, he is liable as if he had signed the instrument himself.

Art. 35.(1) If an instrument is materially altered:

(a) A party who signs it after the material alteration is liable according to the terms of the altered text;

(b) A party who signs it before the material alteration is liable according to the terms of the original text. However, if a party makes, authorizes or assents to a material alteration, he is liable according to the terms of the altered text.

(2) A signature is presumed to have been placed on the instrument after the material alteration unless the contrary is proved.

(3) Any alteration is material which modifies the written undertaking on the instrument of any party in any respect.

Art. 36(1) An instrument may be signed by an agent.

(2) The signature of an agent placed by him on an instrument with the authority of his principal and showing on the instrument that he is signing in a representative capacity for that named principal, or the signature of a principal placed on the instrument by an agent with his authority, imposes liability on the principal and not on the agent.

(3) A signature placed on an instrument by a person as agent but who lacks authority to sign or exceeds his authority, or by an agent who has authority to sign but who does not show on the instrument that he is signing in a representative capacity for a named person, or who shows on the instrument that he is signing in a representative capacity but does not name the person whom he represents, imposes liability on the person signing and not on the person whom he purports to represent.

(4) The question whether a signature was placed on the instrument in a representative capacity may be determined only by reference to what appears on the instrument.

(5) A person who is liable pursuant to paragraph (3) of this article and who pays the instrument has the same rights as the person for whom he purported to act would have had if that person had paid the instrument.

Art. 37. The order to pay contained in a bill does not of itself operate as an assignment to the payee of funds made available for payment by the drawer with the drawee.

B. The drawer.

Art. 38.(1) The drawer engages that upon dishonour of the bill by non-acceptance or by non-payment, and upon any necessary protest, he will pay the bill to the holder, or to any endorser or any endorser's guarantor who takes up and pays the bill.

(2) The drawer may exclude or limit his own liability for acceptance or for payment by an express stipulation in the bill. Such a stipulation is effective only with respect to the drawer. A stipulation excluding or limiting liability for payment is effective only if another party is or becomes liable on the bill.

C. The maker.

Art. 39.(1) The maker engages that he will pay the note in accordance with its terms to the holder, or to any party who takes up and pays the note.

(2) The maker may not exclude or limit his own liability by a stipulation in the note. Any such stipulation is ineffective.

D. The drawee and the acceptor.

Art. 40.(1) The drawee is not liable on a bill until he accepts it.

(2) The acceptor engages that he will pay the bill in accordance with the terms of his acceptance to the holder, or to any party who takes up and pays the bill.

Art. 41(1) An acceptance must be written on the bill and may be effected:

(a) By the signature of the drawee accompanied by the word "accepted" or by words of similar import; or

(b) By the signature alone of the drawee.

(2) An acceptance may be written on the front or on the back of the bill.

Art. 42.(1) An incomplete bill which satisfies the requirements set out in paragraph (1) of article 1 may be accepted by the drawee before it has been signed by the drawer, or while otherwise incomplete.

(2) A bill may be accepted before, at or after maturity, or after it has been dishonoured by non-acceptance or by non-payment.

(3) If a bill drawn payable at a fixed period after sight, or a bill which must be presented for acceptance before a specified date, is accepted, the acceptor must indicate the date of his acceptance; failing such indication by the acceptor, the drawer or the holder may insert the date of acceptance.

(4) If a bill drawn payable at a fixed period after sight is dishonoured by non-acceptance and the drawee subsequently accepts it, the holder is entitled to have the acceptance dated as of the date of which the bill was dishonoured.

Art. 43(1) An acceptance must be unqualified. An acceptance is qualified if it is conditional or varies the terms of the bill.

(2) If the drawee stipulates in the bill that his acceptance is subject to qualification:

(a) He is nevertheless bound according to the terms of his qualified acceptance;

(b) The bill is dishonoured by non-acceptance.

(3) An acceptance relating to only a part of the sum payable is a qualified acceptance. If the holder takes such an acceptance, the bill is dishonoured by non-acceptance only as to the remaining part.

(4) An acceptance indicating that payment will be made at a particular address or by a particular agent is not a qualified acceptance, provided that:

(a) The place in which payment is to be made is not changed;

(b) The bill is not drawn payable by another agent.

E. The endorser.

Art. 44.(1) The endorser engages that upon dishonour of the instrument by non-acceptance or by non-payment, and upon any necessary protest, he will pay the instrument to the holder, or to any subsequent endorser or any endorser's guarantor who takes up and pays the instrument.

(2) An endorser may exclude or limit his own liability by an express stipulation in the instrument. Such a stipulation is effective only with respect to that endorser.

F. The transferor by endorsement or by mere delivery.

Art. 45.(1) Unless otherwise agreed, a person who transfers an instrument, by endorsement and delivery or by mere delivery, represents to the holder to whom he transfers the instrument that:

(a) The instrument does not bear any forged or unauthorized signature;

(b) The instrument has not been materially altered;

(c) At the time of transfer, he has no knowledge of any fact which would impair the right of the transferee to payment of the instrument against the acceptor of a bill or, in the case of an unaccepted bill, the drawer, or against the maker of a note.

(2) Liability of the transferor under paragraph (1) of this article is incurred only if the transferee took the instrument without knowledge of the matter giving rise to such liability.

(3) If the transferor is liable under paragraph (1) of this article, the transferee may recover, even before maturity, the amount paid by him to the transferor, with interest calculated in accordance with article 70, against return of the instrument.

G. The guarantor.

Art. 46.(1) Payment of an instrument, whether or not it has been accepted, may be guaranteed, as to the whole part of its amount, for the account of a party or the drawee. A guarantee may be given by any person, who may or may not already by a party.

(2) A guarantee must be written on the instrument or on a slip affixed thereto ("*allonge*").

(3) A guarantee is expressed by the words "guaranteed", "*aval*", "good as *aval*" or words of similar import, accompanied by the signature of the guarantor. For the purposes of this Convention, the words "prior endorsements guaranteed" or words of similar import do not constitute a guarantee.

(4) A guarantee may be effected by a signature alone on the front of the instrument. A signature alone on the front of the instrument, other than that of the maker, the drawer or the drawee, is a guarantee.

(5) A guarantor may specify the person for whom he has become guarantor. In the absence of such specification, the person for whom he has become guarantor is the acceptor or the drawee in the case of a bill, and the maker in the case of a note.

(6) A guarantor may not raise as a defence to his liability the fact that he signed the instrument before it was signed by the person for whom he is a guarantor, or while the instrument was incomplete.

Art. 47.(1) The liability of a guarantor on the instrument is of the same nature as that of the party for whom he has become guarantor.

(2) If the person for whom he has become guarantor is the drawee, the guarantor engages:

(a) To pay the bill at maturity to the holder, or to any party who takes up and pays the bill;

(b) If the bill is payable at a definite time, upon dishonour by non-acceptance and upon any necessary protest, to pay it to the holder, or to any party who takes up and pays the bill.

(3) In respect of defences that are personal to himself, a guarantor may set up:

(a) Against a holder who is not a protected holder only those defences which he may set up under paragraphs (1), (3) and (4) of article 28;

(b) Against a protected holder only those defences which he may set up under paragraph (1) of article 30.

(4) In respect of defences that may be raised by the person for whom he has become a guarantor:

(a) A guarantor may set up against a holder who is not a protected holder only those defences which the person for whom he has become a guarantor may set up against such holder under paragraphs (1), (3) and (4) of article 28;

(b) A guarantor who expresses his guarantee by the words 'guaranteed", "payment guaranteed" or "collection guaranteed", or words of similar import, may set up against a protected holder only those defences which the person for whom he has become a guarantor may set up against a protected holder under paragraph (1) of article 30;

(c) A guarantor who expresses his guarantee by the words "*aval*" or "good as *aval*" may set up against a protected holder only:

  (i) The defence, under subparagraph (b) of paragraph (1) of article 30, that the protected holder obtained the signature on the instrument of the person for whom he has become a guarantor by a fraudulent act;

(ii) The defence, under article 53 or 57, that the instrument was not presented for acceptance or for payment;
(iii) The defence, under article 63, that the instrument was not duly protested for non-acceptance or for non-payment;
(iv) The defence, under article 84, that a right of action may no longer be exercised against the person for whom he has become guarantor;
(d) A guarantor who is not a bank or other financial institution and who expresses his guarantee by a signature alone may set up against a protected holder only the defences referred to in subparagraph (b) of this paragraph;
(e) A guarantor which is a bank or other financial institution and which expresses its guarantee by a signature alone may set up against a protected holder only the defences referred to in subparagraph (c) of this paragraph.
Art. 48.(1) Payment of an instrument by the guarantor in accordance with article 72 discharges the party for whom he became guarantor of his liability on the instrument to the extent of the amount paid.
(2) The guarantor who pays the instrument may recover from the party for whom he has become guarantor and from the parties who are liable on it to that party the amount paid and any interest.
Chapter V. Presentment, Dishonour by Non-Acceptance or Non-Payment, and Recourse. Section 1. Presentment for acceptance and dishonour by non-acceptance.
Art. 49.(1) A bill may be presented for acceptance.
(2) A bill must be presented for acceptance:
(a) If the drawer has stipulated in the bill that it must be presented for acceptance;
(b) If the bill is payable at a fixed period after sight; or
(c) If the bill is payable elsewhere than at the residence or place of business of the drawee, unless it is payable on demand.
Art. 50.(1) The drawer may stipulate in the bill that it must not be presented for acceptance before a specified date or before the occurrence of a specified event. Except where a bill must be presented for acceptance under subparagraph (b) or (c) of paragraph (2) of article 49, the drawer may stipulate that it must not be presented for acceptance;
(2) If a bill is presented for acceptance notwithstanding a stipulation permitted under paragraph (1) of this article and acceptance is refused, the bill is not thereby dishonoured.
(3) If the drawee accepts a bill notwithstanding a stipulation that it must not be presented for acceptance, the acceptance is effective.
Art. 51. A bill is duly presented for acceptance if it is presented in accordance with the following rules:
(a) The holder must present the bill to the drawee on a business day at a reasonable hour;
(b) Presentment for acceptance may be made to a person or authority other than the drawee if that person or authority is entitled under the applicable law to accept the bill;
(c) If a bill is payable on a fixed date, presentment for acceptance must be made before or on that date;
(d) A bill payable on demand or at a fixed period after sight must be presented for acceptance within one year of its date;
(e) A bill in which the drawer has stated a date or time-limit for presentment for acceptance must be presented on the stated date or within the stated time-limit.
Art. 52.(1) A necessary or optional presentment for acceptance is dispensed with if:
(a) The drawee is dead, or no longer has the power freely to deal with his assets by reason of his insolvency, or is a fictitious person, or is a person not having capacity to incur liability on the instrument as an acceptor; or
(b) The drawee is a corporation, partnership, association or other legal entity which has ceased to exist.
(2) A necessary presentment for acceptance is dispensed with if:
(a) A bill is payable on a fixed date, and presentment for acceptance cannot be effected before or on that date due to circumstances which are beyond the control of the holder and which he could neither avoid nor overcome; or
(b) A bill is payable at a fixed period after sight, and presentment for acceptance cannot be effected within one year of its date due to circumstances which are beyond the control of the holder and which he could neither avoid nor overcome.
(3) Subject to paragraphs (1) and (2) of this article, delay in a necessary presentment for acceptance is excused, but presentment for acceptance is not dispensed with, if the bill is drawn with a stipulation that it must be presented for acceptance within a stated time-limit, and the delay in presentment for acceptance is caused by circumstances which are beyond the control of the holder and which he could neither avoid nor overcome. When the cause of the delay ceases to operate, presentment must be made with reasonable diligence.
Art. 53.(1) If a bill which must be presented for acceptance is not so presented, the drawer, the endorsers and their guarantors are not liable on the bill.
(2) Failure to present a bill for acceptance does not discharge the guarantor of the drawee of liability on the bill.
Art. 54. (1) A bill is considered to be dishonoured by non-acceptance.
(2) A bill is considered to be dishonoured by non-acceptance:
(a) If the drawee, upon due presentment, expressly refuses to accept the bill or acceptance cannot be obtained with reasonable diligence or if the holder cannot obtain the acceptance to which he is entitled under this Convention;
(b) If presentment for acceptance is dispensed with pursuant to article 52, unless the bill is in fact accepted.
(2) (a) If a bill is dishonoured by non-acceptance in accordance with subparagraph (a) of paragraph (1) of this article, the holder may exercise an immediate right of recourse against the drawer, the endorsers and their guarantors, subject to the provisions of article 59.
(b) If a bill is dishonoured by non-acceptance in accordance with subparagraph (b) of paragraph (1) of this article, the holder may exercise an immediate right of recourse against the drawer, the endorsers and their guarantors.
(c) If a bill is dishonoured by non-acceptance in accordance with paragraph (1) of this article, the holder may claim payment from the guarantor of the drawee upon any necessary protest.
(3) If a bill payable on demand is presented for acceptance, but acceptance is refused, it is not considered to be dishonoured by non-acceptance.
Section 2. *Presentment for payment and dishonour by non-payment.*
Art. 55. An instrument is duly presented for payment if it is presented in accordance with the following rules:
(a) The holder must present the instrument to the drawee or to the acceptor or to the maker on a business day at a reasonable hour;
(b) A note signed by two or more makers may be presented to any one of them, unless the note clearly indicates otherwise;
(c) If the drawee or the acceptor or the maker is dead, presentment must be made to the persons who under the applicable law are his heirs or the persons entitled to administer his estate;
(d) Presentment for payment may be made to a person or authority other than the drawee, the acceptor or the maker if that person or authority is entitled under the applicable law to pay the instrument;
(e) An instrument which is not payable on demand must be presented for payment on the date of maturity or on one of the two business days which follow;
(f) An instrument which is payable on demand must be presented for payment within one year of its date;
(g) An instrument must be presented for payment:
(i) At the place of payment specified on the instrument; or
(ii) If no place of payment is specified, and the address of the drawee or the acceptor or the maker indicated in the instrument; or
(iii) If no place of payment is specified and the address of the drawee or the acceptor or the maker is not indicated, at the principal place of business or habitual residence of the drawee or the acceptor or the maker;
(h) An instrument which is presented at a clearing-house is duly presented for payment if the law of the place where the clearing-house is located or the rules or customs of that clearing-house so provide.
Art. 56.(1) Delay in making presentment for payment is excused if the delay is caused by circumstances which are beyond the control of the holder and which he could neither avoid nor overcome. When the cause of the delay ceases to operate, presentment must be made with reasonable diligence.
(2) Presentment for payment is dispensed with:
(a) If the drawer, an endorser or a guarantor has expressly waived presentment; such waiver:
(i) If made on the instrument by the drawer, binds any subsequent party and benefits any holder;
(ii) If made on the instrument by a party other than the drawer, binds only that party but benefits any holder;
(iii) If made outside the instrument, binds only the party making it and benefits only a holder in whose favour it was made;
(b) If an instrument is not payable on demand, and the cause of delay in making presentment referred to in paragraph (1) of this article continues to operate beyond 30 days after maturity;
(c) If an instrument is payable on demand, and the cause of delay in making presentment referred to in paragraph (1) of this article continues to operate beyond 30 days after the expiration of the time-limit for presentment for payment;
(d) If the drawee, the maker or the acceptor has no longer the power freely to deal with his assets by reason of his insolvency, or is a fictitious person or a person not having capacity to make payment, or if the drawee, the maker or the acceptor is a corporation, partnership, association or other legal entity which has ceased to exist;
(e) If there is no place at which the instrument must be presented in accordance with subparagraph (g) of article 55.
(3) Presentment for payment is also dispensed with as regards a bill, if the bill has been protested for dishonour by non acceptance.
Art. 57.(1) If an instrument is not duly presented for payment, the drawer, the endorsers and their guarantors are not liable on it.
(2) Failure to present an instrument for payment does not discharge the acceptor, the maker and their guarantors or the guarantor of the drawee of liability on it.
Art. 58.(1) An instrument is considered to be dishonoured by non-payment:
(a) If payment is refused upon due presentment or if the holder cannot obtain the payment to which he is entitled under this Convention;
(b) If presentment for payment is dispensed with pursuant to paragraph (2) of article 56 and the instrument is unpaid at maturity.
(2) If a bill is dishonoured by non-payment, the holder may, subject to the provisions of article 59, exercise a right or recourse against the drawer, the endorsers and their guarantors.
(3) If a note is dishonoured by non-payment, the holder may, subject to the provisions of article 59, exercise a right of recourse against the endorsers and their guarantors.
Section 3. *Recourse*
Art. 59. If an instrument is dishonoured by non-acceptance or by non-payment, the holder may exercise a right of recourse only after the instrument has been duly protested for dishonour in accordance with the provisions of articles 60 to 62.
A. *Protest*
Art. 60.(1) A protest is a statement of dishonour drawn up at the place where the instrument has been dishonoured and signed and dated by a person authorized in that respect by the law of that place. The statement must specify:
(a) The person at whose request the instrument is protested;
(b) The place of protest; and
(c) The demand made and the answer given, if any, or the fact that the drawee or the acceptor or the maker could not be found.
(2) A protest may be made:
(a) On the instrument or on a slip affixed thereto *("allonge")*; or
(b) As a separate document, in which case it must clearly identify the instrument that has been dishonoured.
(3) Unless the instrument stipulates that protest must be made, a protest may be replaced by a declaration written on the instrument and signed and dated by the drawee or the acceptor or the maker, or, in the case of an instrument domiciled with a named person for payment, by that named person; the declaration must be to the effect that acceptance or payment is refused.
(4) A declaration made in accordance with paragraph (3) of this article is a protest for the purpose of this Convention.

Art. 61. Protest for dishonour of an instrument by non-acceptance or by non-payment must be made on the day on which the instrument is dishonoured or on one of the four business days which follow.

Art. 62.(1) Delay in protesting an instrument for dishonour is excused if the delay is caused by circumstances which are beyond the control of the holder and which he could neither avoid nor overcome. When the cause of the delay ceases to operate, protest must be made with reasonable diligence.

(2) Protest for dishonour by non-acceptance or by non-payment is dispensed with:

(a) If the drawer, an endorser or guarantor has expressly waived protest; such waiver:

(i) If made on the instrument by the drawer, binds any subsequent party and benefits any holder;

(ii) If made on the instrument by a party other than the drawer, binds only that party but benefits any holder;

(iii) If made outside the instrument, binds only the party making it and benefits only a holder in whose favour it was made;

(b) If the cause of the delay in making protest referred to in paragraph (1) of this article continues to operate beyond 30 days after the date of dishonour;

(c) As regards the drawer of a bill, if the drawer and the drawee or the acceptor are the same person;

(d) If presentment for acceptance or for payment is dispensed with in accordance with article 52 or paragraph (2) of article 56.

Art. 63.(1) If an instrument which must be protested for non-acceptance or for non-payment is not duly protested, the drawer, the endorsers and their guarantors are not liable on it.

(2) Failure to protest an instrument does not discharge the acceptor, the maker and their guarantors or the guarantor of the drawee of liability on it.

B. *Notice of dishonour*

Art. 64.(1) The holder, upon dishonour of an instrument by non-acceptance or by non-payment, must give notice of such dishonour:

(a) To the drawer and the last endorser, and

(b) To all other endorsers and guarantors whose addresses the holder can ascertain on the basis of information contained in the instrument.

(2) An endorser or a guarantor who receives notice must give notice of dishonour to the last party preceding him and liable on the instrument.

(3) Notice of dishonour operates for the benefit of any party who has a right of recourse on the instrument against the party notified.

Art. 65.(1) Notice of dishonour may be given in any form whatever and in any terms which identify the instrument and state that has been dishonoured. The return of the dishonoured instrument is sufficient notice, provided it is accompanied by a statement indicating that it has been dishonoured.

(2) Notice of dishonour is duly given if it is communicated or sent to the party to be notified by means appropriate in the circumstances, whether or not it is received by that party.

(3) The burden of proving that notice has been duly given rests upon the person who is required to give such notice.

Art. 66. Notice of dishonour must be given within the two business days which follow:

(a) The day of protest or, if protest is dispensed with, the day of dishonour; or

(b) The day of receipt of notice of dishonour.

Art. 67.(1) Delay in giving notice of dishonour is excused if the delay is caused by circumstances which are beyond the control of the person required to give notice, and which he could neither avoid nor overcome. When the cause of the delay ceases to operate, notice must be given with reasonable diligence.

(2) Notice of dishonour is dispensed with:

(a) If, after the exercise of reasonable diligence, notice cannot be given;

(b) If the drawer, an endorser or a guarantor has expressly waived notice of dishonour; such waiver:

(i) If made on the instrument by the drawer, binds any subsequent party and benefits any holder;

(ii) If made on the instrument by a party other than the drawer, binds only that party but benefits any holder;

(iii) If made outside the instrument, binds only the party making it and benefits only a holder in whose favour it was made;

(c) As regards the drawer of the bill, if the drawer and the drawee or the acceptor are the same person.

Art. 68. If a person who is required to give notice of dishonour fails to give it to a party who is entitled to receive it, he is liable for any damages which that party may suffer from such failure, provided that such damages do not exceed the amount referred to in article 70 or 71.

Section 4. *Amount payable*

Art. 69.(1) The holder may exercise his rights on the instrument against any one party, or several or all parties, liable on it and is not obliged to observe the order in which the parties have become bound. Any party who takes up and pays the instrument may exercise his rights in the same manner against parties liable to him.

(2) Proceedings against a party do not preclude proceedings against any other party, whether or not subsequent to the party originally proceeded against.

Art. 70.(1) The holder may recover from any party liable:

(a) At maturity: the amount of the instrument with interest, if interest has been stipulated for;

(b) After maturity:

(i) The amount of the instrument with interest, if interest has been stipulated for, to the date of maturity;

(ii) If interest has been stipulated to be paid after maturity, interest at the rate stipulated, or, in the absence of such stipulation, interest at the rate specified in paragraph (2) of this article, calculated from the date of presentment on the sum specified in sub-paragraph (b)(i) of this paragraph;

(iii) Any expenses of protest and of the notices given by him;

(c) Before maturity:

(i) The amount of the instrument with interest, if interest has been stipulated for, to the date of payment; or, if no interest has been stipulated for, subject to a discount from the date of payment to the date of maturity, calculated in accordance with paragraph (4) of this article;

(ii) Any expenses of protest and of the notices given by him.

(2) The rate of interest shall be the rate that would be recoverable in legal proceedings taken in the jurisdiction where the instrument is payable.

(3) Nothing in paragraph (2) of this article prevents a court from awarding damages or compensation for additional loss caused to the holder by reason of delay in payment.

(4) The discount shall be at the official rate (discount rate) or other similar appropriate rate effective on the date when recourse is exercised at the place where the holder has his principal place of business, or, if he does not have a place of business his habitual residence, or, if there is no such rate, then at such rate as is reasonable in the circumstances.

Art. 71. A party who pays an instrument and is thereby discharged in whole or in part of his liability on the instrument may recover from the parties liable to him:

(a) The entire sum which he has paid;

(b) Interest on that sum at the rate specified in paragraph (2) of article 70, from the date on which he made payment;

(c) Any expenses of the notices given by him.

Chapter VI. *Discharge. Section 1. Discharge by payment*

Art. 72.(1) A party is discharged of liability on the instrument when he pays the holder, or a party subsequent to himself who has paid the instrument and is in possession of it, the amount due pursuant to article 70 or 71:

(a) At or before maturity; or

(b) Before maturity, upon dishonour by non-acceptance.

(2) Payment before maturity other than under sub-paragraph (b) of paragraph (1) of this article does not discharge the party making the payment of his liability on the instrument except in respect of the person to whom payment was made.

(3) A party is not discharged of liability if he pays a holder who is not a protected holder, or a party who has taken up and paid the instrument, and knows at the time of payment that the holder or that party acquired the instrument by theft or forged the signature of the payee or an endorsee, or participated in the theft or the forgery.

(4) (a) A person receiving payment of an instrument must, unless agreed otherwise, deliver:

(i) To the drawee making such payment, the instrument;

(ii) To any other person making such payment, the instrument, a receipted account, and any protest.

(b) In the case of an instrument payable by instalments at successive dates, the drawee or a party making a payment, other than payment of the last instalment, may require that mention of such payment be made on the instrument or on a slip affixed thereto ("*allonge*") and that a receipt therefor be given to him.

(c) If an instrument payable by instalments at successive dates is dishonoured by non-acceptance or by non-payment as to any of its instalments and a party, upon dishonour, pays the instalment, the holder who receives such payment must give the party a certified copy of the instrument and any necessary authenticated protest in order to enable such party to exercise a right on the instrument.

(d) The person from whom payment is demanded may withhold payment if the person demanding payment does not deliver the instrument to him. Withholding payment in these circumstances does not constitute dishonour by non-payment under article 58.

(e) If payment is made but the person paying, other than the drawee, fails to obtain the instrument, such person is discharged but the discharge cannot be set up as a defence against a protected holder to whom the instrument has been subsequently transferred.

Art. 73.(1) The holder is not obliged to take partial payment.

(2) If the holder who is offered partial payment does not take it, the instrument is dishonoured by non-payment.

(3) If the holder takes partial payment from the drawee, the guarantor of the drawee, or the acceptor or the maker:

(a) The guarantor of the drawee, or the acceptor or the maker is discharged of his liability on the instrument to the extent of the amount paid; and

(b) The instrument is to be considered as dishonoured by non-payment as to the amount unpaid.

(4) If the holder takes partial payment from a party to the instrument other than the acceptor, the maker or the guarantor of the drawee:

(a) The party making payment is discharged of his liability on the instrument to the extent of the amount paid; and

(b) The holder must give such party a certified copy of the instrument and any necessary authenticated protest in order to enable such party to exercise a right on the instrument.

(5) The drawee or a party making partial payment may require that mention of such payment be made on the instrument and that a receipt therefor be given to him.

(6) If the balance is paid, the person who receives it and who is in possession of the instrument must deliver to the payor the receipted instrument and any authenticated protest.

Art. 74.(1) The holder may refuse to take payment at a place other than the place where the instrument was presented for payment in accordance with article 55.

(2) In such case if payment is not made at the place where the instrument was presented for payment in accordance with article 55, the instrument is considered to be dishonoured by non-payment.

Art. 75.(1) An instrument must be paid in the currency in which the sum payable is expressed.

(2) If the sum payable is expressed in a monetary unit of account within the meaning of subparagraph (1) of article 5 and the monetary unit of account is transferable between the person making payment and the person receiving it, then, unless the instrument specifies a currency of payment, payment shall be made by transfer of monetary units of account. If the monetary unit of account is not transferable between those persons, payment shall be made in the currency specified in the instrument or, if no such currency is specified, in the currency of the place of payment.

(3) The drawer or the maker may indicate in the instrument that it must be paid in a specified currency other than the currency in which the sum payable is expressed. In that case:

(a) The instrument must be paid in the currency so specified;

(b) The amount payable is to be calculated according to the rate of exchange indicated in the instrument. Failing such indication, the amount payable is to be calculated according to the rate of exchange for sight drafts (or, if there is no such rate, according to the

appropriate established rate of exchange) on the date of maturity:
(i) Ruling at the place where the instrument must be presented for payment in accordance with subparagraph (g) of article 55, if the specified currency is that of that place (local currency); or
(ii) If the specified currency is not that of that place, according to the usages of the place where the instrument must be presented for payment in accordance with subparagraph (g) of article 55;
(c) If such an instrument is dishonoured by non-acceptance, the amount payable is to be calculated:
(i) If the rate of exchange is indicated in the instrument, according to that rate;
(ii) If no rate of exchange is indicated in the instrument, at the option of the holder, according to the rate of exchange ruling on the date of dishonour or on the date of actual payment;
(d) If such an instrument is dishonoured by non-payment, the amount payable is to be calculated:
(i) If the rate of exchange is indicated in the instrument, according to that rate;
(ii) If no rate of exchange is indicated in the instrument, at the option of the holder, according to the rate of exchange ruling on the date of maturity or on the date of actual payment.
(4) Nothing in this article prevents a court from awarding damages for loss caused to the holder by reason of fluctuations in rates of exchange if such loss is caused by dishonour for non-acceptance or by non-payment.
(5) The rate of exchange ruling at a certain date is the rate of exchange ruling, at the option of the holder, at the place where the instrument must be presented for payment in accordance with subparagraph (g) of article 55 or at the place of actual payment.
Art. 76.(1) Nothing in this Convention prevents a Contracting State from enforcing exchange control regulations applicable in its territory and its provisions relating to the protection of its currency, including regulations which it is bound to apply by virtue of international agreements to which it is a party.
(2) (a) If, by virtue of the application of paragraph (1) of this article, an instrument drawn in a currency which is not that of the place of payment must be paid in local currency, the amount payable is to be calculated according to the rate of exchange for sight drafts (or, if there is no such rate, according to the appropriate established rate of exchange) on the date of presentment ruling at the place where the instrument must be presented for payment in accordance with subparagraph (g) of article 55.
(b) (i) If such an instrument is dishonoured by non-acceptance, the amount payable is to be calculated, at the option of the holder, at the rate of exchange ruling on the date of dishonour or on the date of actual payment.
(ii) If such an instrument is dishonoured by non-payment, the amount is to be calculated, at the option of the holder, according to the rate of exchange ruling on the date of presentment or on the date of actual payment.
(iii) Paragraphs (4) and (5) of article 75 are applicable where appropriate.

Section 2. *Discharge of other parties*

Art. 77.(1) If a party is discharged in whole or in part of his liability on the instrument, any party who has a right on the instrument against him is discharged to the same extent.
(2) Payment by the drawee of the whole or a party of the amount of a bill to the holder, or to any party who takes up and pays the bill, discharges all parties of their liability to the same extent, except where the drawee pays a holder who is not a protected holder, or a party who has taken up and paid the bill, and knows at the time of payment that the holder or that party acquired the bill by theft or forged the signature of the payee or an endorsee, or participated in the theft or the forgery.

Chapter 4. *Lost Instruments*

Art. 78.(1) If an instrument is lost, whether by destruction, theft or otherwise, the person who lost the instrument has, subject to the provisions of paragraph (2) of this article, the same right to payment which he would have had if he had been in possession of the instrument. The party from whom payment is claimed cannot set up as a defence against liability on the instrument the fact that the person claiming payment is not in possession of the instrument.
(2) (a) The person claiming payment of a lost instrument must state in writing to the party from whom he claims payment:
(i) The elements of the lost instrument pertaining to the requirements set forth in paragraph (1) or (2) of articles 1, 2 and 3; for this purpose the person claiming payment of the lost instrument may present to that party a copy of that instrument;
(ii) The facts showing that, if he had been in possession of the instrument, he would have had a right to payment from the party from whom payment is claimed;
(iii) The facts which prevent production of the instrument.
(b) The party from whom payment of a lost instrument is claimed may require the person claiming payment to give security in order to indemnify him for any loss which he may suffer by reason of the subsequent payment of the lost instrument.
(c) The nature of the security and its terms are to be determined by agreement between the person claiming payment and the party from whom payment is claimed. Failing such an agreement, the court may determine whether security is called for and, if so, the nature of the security and its terms.
(d) If the security cannot be given, the court may order the party from whom payment is claimed to deposit the sum of the lost instrument, and any interest and expenses which may be claimed under article 70 or 71, with the court or any other competent authority or institution, and may determine the duration of such deposit. Such deposit is to be considered as payment to the person claiming payment.
Art. 79.(1) A party who has paid a lost instrument and to whom the instrument is subsequently presented for payment by another person must give notice of such presentment to the person whom he paid.
(2) Such notice must be given on the day the instrument is presented or on one of the two business days which follow and must state the name of the person presenting the instrument and the date and place of presentment.
(3) Failure to give notice renders the party who has paid the lost instrument liable for any damages which the person whom he paid may suffer from such failure, provided that the damages do not exceed the amount referred to in article 70 or 71.
(4) Delay in giving notice is excused when the delay is caused by circumstances which are beyond the control of the person who has paid the lost instrument and which he could neither avoid nor overcome. When the cause of the delay ceases to operate, notice must be given with reasonable diligence.
(5) Notice is dispensed with when the cause of delay in giving notice continues to operate beyond 30 days after the last day on which it should have been given.
Art. 80.(1) A party who has paid a lost instrument in accordance with the provisions of article 78 and who is subsequently required to, and does, pay the instrument, or who, by reason of the loss of the instrument, then loses his right to recover from any party liable to him, has the right:
(a) If security was given, to realize the security; or
(b) If an amount was deposited with the court or other competent authority or institution, to reclaim the amount so deposited.
(2) The person who has given security in accordance with the provisions of subparagraph (b) of paragraph (2) of article 78 is entitled to obtain release of the security when the party for whose benefit the security was given is no longer at risk to suffer loss because of the fact that the instrument is lost.
Art. 81. For the purpose of making protest for dishonour by non-payment, a person claiming payment of a lost instrument may use a written statement that satisfies the requirements of subparagraph (a) of paragraph (2) of article 78.
Art. 82. A person receiving payment of a lost instrument in accordance with article 78 must deliver to the party paying the written statement required under subparagraph (a) of paragraph (2) of article 78, reeceipted by him, and any protest and a receipted account.
Art. 83.(1) A party who pays a lost instrument in accordance with article 78 has the same rights which he would have had if he had been in possession of the instrument.
(2) Such party may exercise his rights only if he is in possession of the receipted written statement referred to in article 82.

Chapter VIII. *Limited (Prescription)*

Art. 84.(1) A right of action arising on an instrument may no longer be exercised after four years have elapsed:
(a) Against the maker, or his guarantor, of a note payable on demand, from the date of the note:
(b) Against the acceptor or the maker or their guarantor of an instrument payable at a definite time, from the date of maturity;
(c) Against the guarantor of the drawee of a bill payable at a definite time, from the date of maturity or, if the bill is dishonoured by non-acceptance, from the date of protest for dishonour or, where protest is dispensed with, from the date of dishonour;
(d) Against the acceptor of a bill payable on demand or his guarantor, from the date on which it was accepted or, if no such date is shown, from the date of the bill;
(e) Against the guarantor of the drawee of a bill payable on demand, from the date on which he signed he bill or, if no such date is shown, from the date of the bill;
(f) Against the drawer or an endorser or their guarantor, from the date of protest for dishonour by non-acceptance or by non-payment or, where protest is dispensed with, from the date of dishonour.
(2) A party who pays the instrument in accordance with article 70 or 71 may exercise his right of action against a party liable to him within one year from the date on which he paid the instrument.

CHAPTER IX. Final Provisions

Art. 85. The Secretary-General of the United Nations is hereby designated as the depositary for this Convention.
Art. 86. (1) This Convention is open for signature by all States at the Headquarters of the United Nations, New York until 30 June 1990.
(2) This Convention is subject to ratification, acceptance or approval by the signatory States.
(3) This Convention is open for access by all States which are not signatory States as from the date it is open for signature.
(4) Instruments of ratification, acceptance, approval and accession are to be deposited with the Secretary-General of the United Nations.
Art. 87.(1) If a Contracting State has two or more territorial units in which, according to its constitution, different systems of law are applicable in relation to the matters dealt with in this Convention, it may, at the time of signature, ratification, acceptance, approval or accession, declare that this Convention is to extend to all its territorial units or only to one or more of them, and may amend its declaration by submitting another declaration at any time.
(2) These declarations are to be notified to the depositary and are to state expressly the territorial units to which the Convention extends.
(3) If a Contracting State makes no declaration under paragraph (1) of this article, the Convention is to extend to all territorial units of that State.
Art. 88. (1) Any State may declare at the time of signature, ratification, acceptance, approval or accession that its courts will apply the Convention only if both the place indicated in the instrument where the bill is drawn, or the note is made, and the place of payment indicated in the instrument are situated in Contracting States.
(2) No other reservations are permitted.
Art. 89. (1) This Convention enters into force on the first day of the month following the expiration of twelve months after the date of deposit of the tenth instrument of ratification, acceptance, approval or accession.
(2) When a State ratifies, accepts, approves or accedes to this Convention after the deposit of the tenth instrument of ratification, acceptance, approval or accession, this Convention enters into force in respect of that State on the first day of the month following the expiration of twelve months after the date of deposit of its instrument of ratification, acceptance, approval or accession.
Art. 90.(1) A Contracting State may denounce this Convention by a formal notification in writing addressed to the depositary.
(2) The denunciation takes effect on the first day of the month following the expiration of six months after the notification is received by the depositary. Where a longer period for the denunciation to take effect is specified in the notification, the denunciation takes effect upon the expiration of such longer period after the notification is received by the depositary. The Convention remains applicable to instruments drawn or

U

made before the date at which the denunciation takes effect.

Done at New York this 9th day of Dec., one thousand nine hundred and eighty-seven in a single original, of which the Arabic, Chinese, English, French, Russian and Spanish texts are equally authentic.

In Witness Whereof the undersigned plenipotentiaries being duly authorized by their respective Governments, have signed this Convention.

UN Resolutions and Decisions adopted by the General Assembly during the First Part of its Forty-Third Session, From 20 September to 22 December 1988, New York, 1989, pp. 545–571.

UNCLE SAM. A common international term used to designate the US government, appeared in the United States during the war of 1812, when soldiers for the first time wore the initials US (United States) on their uniforms and may have been used derisively by those opposing the war. Other sources attribute its origin to Samuel Wilson (1766–1854) of Troy, New York, who as inspector of Army supplies, was referred to as "Uncle Sam" by workmen. Regardless of origin, the term found wide acceptance and has been used permanently ever since.

UN COMMISSION FOR CONVENTIONAL ARMAMENTS. An organ of the UN created on Dec. 14, 1946 with the same membership as the Security Council and instructed to consider measures for the reduction of conventional armaments. No agreement could be reached and in 1950 the Soviet Union withdrew from the Commission as it had done from the Atomic Energy Commission over the question of the representation of China. The Commission for Conventional Armaments was dissolved in early 1952. In 1974, 1976 and 1978 the International Committee of the Red Cross elaborated a number of draft proposals for the prohibition or restriction of the use of certain conventional weapons.

Everyone's United Nations, New York, 1979, pp. 28, 48 and 265.

UN COMMISSION ON HUMAN RIGHTS. One of the functional commissions of the ▷ ECOSOC.

UN COMMISSION ON INTERNATIONAL COMMODITY TRADE. One of the functional commissions of the ▷ ECOSOC.

UN COMMISSION ON NARCOTIC DRUGS. One of the functional Commissions of the ▷ ECOSOC.

UN COMMISSION ON STATUS OF WOMEN. One of the functional Commissions of ▷ ECOSOC.

UN COMMITTEE FOR INDUSTRIAL DEVELOPMENT. One of standing Committees of ▷ ECOSOC.

UN COMMITTEE ON ADMINISTRATIVE AND BUDGETARY QUESTIONS. One of two standing Committees of the UN General Assembly.

UN COMMITTEE ON HOUSING, BUILDING AND PLANNING. One of the standing Committees of the ▷ ECOSOC.

UN COMMITTEE ON HUMAN RIGHTS. An organ of ▷ Human Rights Covenants, 1966, which has specified authority and operates independently of the UN Commission on Human Rights.

UN COMMITTEE ON INFORMATION. The UN General Assembly on Dec. 18, 1979 decided to maintain the Committee to Review UN Public In-

formation Policies but under the name UN Committee on Information and to increase the membership from 42 to 66.

UN Chronicle, January, 1980, pp. 55–56.

UN COMPUTERING INTERNATIONAL CENTRE. An instrument of the UN Statistical Office came into operation in Nov., 1965. The Centre provides electronic data processing and computing services to all units of the UN and, on request and against payment of costs, to specialized agencies as well as to governments and private institutions. In 1978 started the ▷ UN Treaty Information System.

Everyman's United Nations, 1945–65, New York, 1966, p. 267.

UNCONDITIONAL SURRENDER. ▷ Germany's Unconditional Surrender; ▷ Japan's Unconditional Surrender.

UN CONFERENCES. The intergovernmental conferences of UN member states convened on the basis of special resolutions adopted by UN General Assembly and other organs. The right to call UN Conferences is also granted to ECOSOC (under Art. 62 of UN Charter) in consultation with the UN Secretary-General and specialized agencies in cases where the work to be done by a Conference falls within its competence.

UN CONFERENCES SERVICE OFFICE. A permanent institution in the UN Secretariat in New York, which has, among others, a staff of translators available, and is running a section of international terminology.

UN CORRESPONDENTS ASSOCIATION. ▷ UNCA.

UN COUNCIL COMMITTEE ON NON-GOVERNMENTAL ORGANIZATIONS. One of the standing Committees of the ▷ ECOSOC.

UN COUNCIL FOR NAMIBIA. A council est. in June, 1968 by the Special Session of the UN General Assembly. ▷ Namibia.

UNCTAD. United Nations Conference on Trade and Development. The first conference was held from Mar. 23 to June 16, 1964 in Geneva, and on Dec. 30, 1964 the UN General Assembly decided to establish UNCTAD as one of its permanent organs. In its resolution the Assembly expressed the view that international trade was an important instrument for economic development and noted a widespread desire among developing countries for a comprehensive trade organization.

The main purposes of UNCTAD are to promote international trade with a view to accelerating economic development, to formulate principles and policies on international trade, to initiate action for the adoption of multilateral trade agreements, and to act as a center for harmonizing trade and development policies of Governments and regional economic groups.

To carry out the functions of the Conference between sessions, the Assembly established a 55-member Trade and Development Board (expanded in 1976 to include all UNCTAD members) to take action to implement Conference decisions and to make or initiate studies and reports on trade and related development problems. The Board, which reports annually to the General Assembly through the Economic and Social Council, serves also as the preparatory body for sessions of the Conference.

The Trade and Development Board has seven committees, which are open to all UNCTAD members: the Committee on Commodities, the Committee on Manufactures, the Committee on Invisibles and Financing related to Trade, the Committee on Shipping, the Committee on Preferences, the Committee on Transfer of Technology, and the Committee on Economic Co-operation among Developing Countries. Other subsidiary bodies include special committees and intergovernmental groups.

UNCTAD has a full-time secretariat, which services the Conference, the Board and its subsidiary bodies. Located at Geneva, it is headed by the Secretary-General of UNCTAD, who is appointed by the United Nations Secretary-General and confirmed by the Assembly. Gamani Corea of Sri Lanka has been Secretary-General of UNCTAD since Apr., 1974.

Since the initial session of the Conference in Geneva in 1964, sessions have been held at four-year intervals, at New Delhi (1968), Santiago (1972) and Nairobi (1976). This pattern was changed, however, with the holding of the fifth session at Manila from May 7 to June 1, 1979, three years after the Nairobi meeting.

UNCTAD membership is open to all countries that are Members of the United Nations or of any of the agencies related to the Organization. At the end of 1984, UNCTAD had 159 members.

Although UNCTAD's work touches on all aspects of international development policy, it is concerned mainly with primary commodities, manufactures and semi-manufactures, transfer of technology, development of finance, shipping and invisibles, trade between socialist and non-socialist countries, trade expansion and economic integration among developing countries, and special measures in favour of the least developed countries.

With regard to commodities, a major achievement was the adoption at Nairobi in 1976 of an Integrated Programme for Commodities. The proposal, initiated by the UNCTAD secretariat and supported by the developing countries, envisages the setting of remunerative and just prices which would take account of world inflation, monetary changes and cost of manufactured imports. As part of the program, the Nairobi session agreed that steps would be taken for the negotiation of a common fund for the financing of buffer stocks which could be held or sold as conditions required, thus helping to end the wide fluctuations in commodity prices that have plagued developing countries dependent on their commodity exports. Five international commodity agreements – on coffee, tin, olive oil, sugar and wheat – are in operation.

UNCTAD's efforts to bring about a transfer of technological knowhow to developing countries have concentrated on helping to change national laws and international agreements governing the industrial property system as well as on strengthening the technological capacity of developing countries. A major goal was the adoption of an international code of conduct on the transfer of technology aimed at ending restrictive business practices and increasing access of developing countries to technology.

Restructuring the international financial and monetary system to make it more responsive to the needs of the developing countries is an UNCTAD concern, since it touches on many aspects of development. In this area, UNCTAD has concentrated on four key issues: relieving the external debt burden of the developing countries; meeting the large payments deficits that they continue to experience; providing them with an adequate long-term flow of financial resources; and reforming the international monetary system to make its effects on different groups of countries more uniform as well as more universal in membership. UNCTAD recommendations on the terms and conditions of aid seek to improve techniques of lending, including measures to soften the terms of both bilateral assistance and multilateral lending. A major objective is to eliminate the practice of tying aid to developing countries to purchases in the donor country.

UNCTAD promotes the expansion of trade and other exchanges among countries having different economic and social systems. Both the number of trade and economic co-operation agreements between individual developing and socialist countries, as well as the volume of overall trade beteen these two groups, have been rising continuously in recent years. Further acceleration can be expected, particularly if some of the problems that affect those trade flows can be overcome. UNCTAD has suggested more flexible means of settling payments and increasing the multilateral elements in mutual trade.

Under UNCTAD auspices, global policies on insurance and reinsurance are negotiated and adopted in order to promote the national insurance markets of developing countries and to enable those markets to cover locally the risks associated with their economic activities. As a result, developing countries have experienced a gradual decrease in insurance services purchased abroad followed by substantial savings in foreign exchange.

UNCTAD has pioneered in providing special measures in favor of the least developed and the geographically disadvantaged developing countries, such as landlocked and island countries. At its fourth session, the Conference emphasized special consideration for them in commercial policy, shipping, technical assistance, development and insurance, and transfer of technology. It approved a series of measures aimed at expanding their exports and lowering import costs.

UNCTAD is also active in maritime transport, since shipping practices have a major effect on world trade. In 1974, an UNCTAD-sponsored conference adopted the Convention on a Code of Conduct for Liner Conferences, aimed at bringing about significant changes in the working arrangements of shipping conferences (associations of shipping lines active along particular trade routes). So far, 29 countries have expressed consent to be bound by the treaty.

Export promotion and marketing are the responsibility of the International Trade Centre which is operated jointly by UNCTAD and the GATT. Complementing the work of UNCTAD and other United Nations organizations, the Centre focuses attention on export market opportunities and helps developing countries to train personnel in marketing and export promotion techniques and to set up the institutions and training programmes necessary to build up modern export promotion services.

The UNCTAD VII Conference held in Geneva 1987, in its Final Act recommended revitalizing development, introducing new policy to deal with debt crisis, resources for development, commodities, international trade.

Everyone's United Nations, New York, 1979; UN Yearbook, 1964–80; UN Chronicle, December, 1983, p. 81; E. DELL, The Common Fund, in: International Affairs, Nr. 1, 1987; T.G. WEISS, Multilateral Development Diplomacy in UNCTAD. The Lessons of Group Negotiations 1964–1984, New York, 1987.

UNCTAD CHRONOLOGY 1964–1989. The Conference on Trade and Development was initiated 1961 at the XVI Session of the General Assembly by the Latin American and African States and Indonesia.

The I Conference of 124 states was held in Geneva, from March 23 to June 16, 1964 under the slogan: 'trade not aid'.

The II Conference of 121 member states was held in New Delhi from February 1, to March 25, 1986. A total of 43 intergovernmental bodies and NGO's took part in the Conference.

The III Conference of 146 member states was held in Santiago de Chile, from April 13 to March 20, 1972; adopted a project of the ▷ Charter of Economic Rights and Duties of States.

The IV Conference of 153 member states was held in Nairobi, from May 5 to May 31, 1976; adopted an integrated commodities program.

The V Conference of 144 member states was held in Manila, from May 7 to June 3, 1979. A total of 79 intergovernmental bodies and NGO's took part in the Conference.

The VI Conference of 162 member states was held in Belgrade, from June 6 to July 3, 1983. The Final Act was accepted with reservations by FRG, Japan and UK and not accepted by the USA.

The VII Conference of 143 member states was held in Geneva, from July 9 to Aug. 3, 1987. A total of 98 intergovernmental bodies and NGO's took part in the Conference. The Final Act was adopted by consensus.

G. WILLIAMS, Third World Political Organizations, London 1981; KEESING's Contemporary Archive, 1983; UN Chronicle, November, 1987.

UN DAG HAMMARSKJÖLD LIBRARY. ▷ Hammarskjöld Dag Library.

UN DEATH CERTIFICATE. ▷ UN International Office for Death Certificates.

UN DEMOGRAPHIC YEAR, 1950. In 1950 for the first time, on UN initiative, general censuses were held in most of the member countries in the standard form recommended by the UN Population Committee.

UNDERDEVELOPED COUNTRIES. A term adopted by the UN in 1956; abolished from the UN documents under pressure of Third World countries as pejorative and replaced by the now commonly accepted term: Developing Countries.

UNDERWATER MINES. A subject of international law; the first rules and limitations on the use of underwater mines in sea war were introduced by the VIIIth Hague Convention of Oct. 18, 1907.

UN DEVELOPMENT DECADES, 1961–70, 1971–80, 1981–1990. The official name given to the successive ten-year programs aimed at accelerating economic and social progress in developing countries. One of the goals of the program was to achieve in developing countries a production growth in excess of 5% yearly, which proved unworkable. UNCTAD Secretary-General, R. Prebisch, warned in 1966 that "the Development Decade had become ever more an illusion." The Second UNCTAD Conference in 1968, declared it an unquestionable failure which "changed the Development Decade into a frustration decade." Among other things, it blamed the unfavorable terms of trade for developing countries which "allowed a blood transfusion from the weaker to the stronger." In 1970, the UN General Assembly in proclaiming the second decade adopted an international development strategy that outlined goals and objectives, and measures needed to achieve them.

Conference on Economic Cooperation Among Developing Countries, Declarations, Resolutions, Recommen-

dations and Decisions adopted in the UN System, 3 Vols., México, DF, September 13, 1976.

UN DISARMAMENT COMMISSION. The UN General Assembly commission est. Feb. 11, 1952 composed of 11 members of the Security Council and Canada. In accordance with a recommendation of the Assembly disarmament negotiations, in the years 1954–57, were carried on in a disarmament commission composed of the representatives of five states: USSR, USA, Great Britain, France and Canada. In 1958 the UN General Assembly made a decision to extend the membership of the commission to all UN member states. (▷ Disarmament.)

Everyone's United Nations, New York, 1979.

UN DOCUMENTATION. The system of filing the documents of the UN and its specialized agencies recorded in the only index, issued in English, entitled *United Nations Documents Index*. The tremendous amount and variety of documents produced each year posed ever more difficult problems for the UN Secretariat even after the introduction of microfilm records which led to the UN Secretary-General submitting to the General Assembly in 1967 a new restrictive system of UN documentation approved on Dec. 8, 1967, Res. 2292/XXII.

A Guide to the Use of UN Documents, Including Reference to the Specialized agencies and Special UN Bodies, New York, 1962; UN Monthly Chronicle, January, 1968, p. 121.

UNDOF. United Nations Disengagement Observer Force. On May 13, 1974, an agreement on the disengagement of forces between Israel and Syria was signed at a meeting of the Military Working Group of the Geneva Peace Conference on the Middle East. The agreement provided for a redeployment of the Israeli and Syrian forces, the establishment of areas of limited forces and armaments on both sides of the buffer zone and the establishment of a United Nations force to supervize its implementation.

On May 31, 1974 the Security Council took note of this agreement and decided to set up the UNDOF. The cease-fire became effective upon the conclusion of the disengagement agreement and the area has remained generally quiet since then. The mandate of UNDOF, initially for a duration of six months, has been extended as necessary by the Security Council.

As of May, 1980, the Force comprised 1289 troops from Austria (532), Canada (220), Finland (388) and Poland (129), including 20 Military Observers detailed from UNTSO.

UN Chronicle, January, 1984, p. 80.

UNDP. United Nations Development Programme. A Program, which has headquarters in New York and local field offices in more than 100 countries, was established in 1965 through the General Assembly's decision to merge two United Nations organizations: the Expanded Programme of Technical Assistance (EPTA), set up in 1949, and the Special fund which was set up in 1958 to provide pre-investment assistance to relatively large development projects. UNDP is financed by voluntary annual contributions from Member States of the United Nations or of its related agencies as its predecessor organizations were. UNDP is the world's largest multilateral technical assistance program. It has been designated as the central coordinating organization of the United Nations for development activities.

UN Yearbook, 1965; UN Monthly Chronicle, December, 1965; Everyone's United Nations New York, 1979; pp. 137–139. UN Chronicle, January, 1984.

U

UNDP VOLUNTARY SERVICE. A service established on Dec. 7, 1970 within the framework of the UN Development Program by virtue of UN General Assembly Res. 2659/XXV. Headquarters Geneva.

UN Chronicle, May 1982, pp. 61–62.

UNDRO. United Nations Disaster Relief Office, est. 1971, Geneva ▷ Disaster Relief, International.

UN Chronicle, May, 1981, p. 29, October, 1983, p. 57 and January, 1984, p. 43.

UN ECONOMIC AND SOCIAL COMMISSION FOR ASIA AND THE PACIFIC, ESCAP. Former, 1947–1974, ▷ UN Economic Commission for Asia and the Far East, ECAFE. Est. on Aug. 1, 1974, by a Colombo Declaration of new principles, priorities and approaches for Commission Action. The most urgent priorities for action in the region concerned food, energy, raw materials and external financial resources.

Members (1984): Afghanistan, Australia, Bangladesh, Bhutan, Brunei, Burma, Chinese People's Republic, Fiji, France, India, Indonesia, Iran, Japan, Kampuchea, Korea Republic, Laos, Malaysia, Maldives, Mongolia, Nauru, Nepal, the Netherlands, New Zealand, Pakistan, Papua New Guinea, Philippines, Singapore, Solomon Islands, Sri Lanka, Thailand, Tonga, UK, USA, USSR, Vanuatu, Viet-Nam, Western Samoa. Associate members (1984): Cook Islands, Guam, Hong Kong, Kiribati, Niue, Trust Territory of the Pacific Islands, Tuvalu.

Organization: the Commission holds annual sessions and meetings of the nine main legislative Committees: agriculture; development planning; industry, technology and environment; natural resources; population; shipping, transport and communications; social development; statistics; trade. Executive Secretary with hqs in Bangkok and Pacific Liaison Office in Nauru. Institutions related to regional projects: Asian and Pacific Coconut Community, f.1969, Jakarta; Asian and Pacific Development Centre, f.1980, Kuala Lumpur; Asian Clearing Union, f.1974, Teheran; Asian Free Trade Zone, est. 1976 by the Bangkok Agreement, signed by Bangladesh, India, Korea Rep., Laos and Sri Lanka; Asian Highway Network Project, est. in 1980's, comprises a network of 65,000 km of highway from the Iranian-Turkish border to Viet-Nam and to Indonesia with a linking route to Sri Lanka; Asian Pacific Telecommunity, f.1979, Bangkok; Asian Reinsurance Corporation, f.1979, Bangkok; Committee for Co-ordination of Joint Prospecting for Mineral Resources in Asian Offshore Areas, f.1966, Bangkok (the same Committee in the South Pacific Area with hqs in Suva, Fiji); ESCAP/WMO Typhoon Committee, f.1968, Manila; International Pepper Committee, f.1972, Jakarta; Regional Co-ordinating Centre for Research and Development of Coarse Grains, Pulses, Roots and Tuber Crops, f.1981, Bogor, Indonesia; Regional Energy Development Programme, f.1982, Bangkok; Regional Mineral Resources Development Centre, f.1973, Bandung; South-East Asia Tin Research and Development Centre, f.1977, Ipoh, Malaysia; Statistical Institute for Asia and the Pacific, f.1970, Tokyo; WMO-ESCAP Panel on Tropical Cyclones, f.1973, Colombo.

ESCAP information systems: Group of Experts on Urban and Regional Research, ESCAP-GEURR, Fertilizer Advisory, Development and Information Network for Asia and Pacific, ESCAP-FADINAP, Population Clearing-House and Information System, ESCAP-PCHIS and Trade Information Service, ESCAP-TIS.

Publ.: *ESCAP Annual Report, Agricultural Development Bulletin, Agro-chemicals, fertilizers and agro-pesticides news-in-brief, Economic and Social Survey of Asia and the Pacific, Economic Bulletin for Asia and the Pacific, Small Industry Bulletin for Asia and the Pacific, Electric Power in Asia and the Pacific, Water Resources Series, Oil and Natural Gas Map of Asia, Mineral Resources Development Series, Asian Population Programme News, Energy Resources Development Series, Asia Population Studies Series, Statistical Yearbook for Asia and the Pacific, Quarterly Bulletin of Statistics for Asia and the Pacific, Statistical Indicators in ESCAP Countries, Foreign Trade Statistics of Asia and the Pacific, Transport and Communication Bulletin for Asia and the Pacific.*

Yearbook of the United Nations, 1974, pp. 534–538, New York, 1976; *The Europa Year Book 1984. A World Survey*, Vol. I, pp. 24–26, London, 1984.

UN ECONOMIC COMMISSION FOR AFRICA, ECA. The Commission was formed in 1958 on the recommendation of the UN General Assembly by the ECOSOC resolution. Members: Algeria, Angola, Benin, Botswana, Burkina Faso, Burundi, Cameroon, Cape Verde, Central African Republic, Chad, Comores, Congo, Côte d'luoire, Djibouti, Egypt, Equatorial Guinea, Ethiopia, Gabon, Ghana, Guinea, Guinea-Bissau, Kenya, Lesotho, Liberia, Libya, Madagascar, Malawi, Mali, Mauretania, Mauritius, Morocco, Mozambique, Niger, Nigeria, Rwanda, Sao Tome and Principe, Senegal, Seychelles, Sierra Leone, Somalia, South Africa (suspended since 1963), Sudan, Swaziland, Tanzania, Togo, Tunisia, Uganda, Zaïre, Zambia, Zimbabwe. Publ.: *Investment Africa* (quarterly); *Survey of Economic Conditions in Africa* (annually); *African Census Programme Newsletter* (irregular); *African Trade* (quarterly); *African Target* (quarterly); *Rural Progress* (quarterly).

The Europa Yearbook 1984. A World Survey, Vol. I, pp. 27–31, London, 1984.

UN ECONOMIC COMMISSION FOR ASIA AND THE FAR EAST, ECAFE, 1947–1974. The Commission was created on the recommendation of the UN General Assembly, Feb. 2, 1947 by the ECOSOC Res. 37/IV, Mar. 28, 1947; began its work in June, 1948 with seat in Bangkok. The Commission initiated i.a. a plan for development of the delta of the ▷ Mekong river and the construction of a trans-asiatic highway, whose Teheran–Saigon stretch was completed 1973. Institutions created by the Commission were the Asiatic Development Bank, est, 1966, and the Institute for Asiatic Development and Planning, est. 1964. Publ. i.a.: *Economic Survey of Asia and the Pacific, Economic Bulletin of Asia and Far East, Statistical Yearbook for Asia and Far East, Asian Industrial Development News, Asian Population Studies Series, Regional Economic Co-operation Series, Foreign Trade Statistics of Asia and Far East,*
The ECAFE was reorganized at the 30th session in Colombo, on Apr. 6, 1974, and adopted the name ▷ UN Economic and Social Commission for Asia and the Pacific, ESCAP.

UN ECONOMIC COMMISSION FOR EUROPE, ECE. A Commission created on a recommendation of UN General Assembly on Feb. 2, 1946, and by a decision of ECOSOC, Res. 36/IV of Mar., 1947 with seat in Geneva; began work on May 3, 1947. Members: Albania, Austria, Belgium, Bulgaria, Byelorussian SSR, Canada, Cyprus, Czechoslovakia, Denmark, Finland, France, FRG (since 1955), GDR (1955–72 "in a consultative capacity"), Greece, Hungary, Iceland, Ireland, Luxembourg, Malta, Netherlands, Norway, Poland, Portugal, Romania, Spain, Sweden, Switzerland, Turkey, Ukrainian SSR, USSR, UK, USA, Yugoslavia. Publ.: *The Annual Economic Survey of Europe, The Economic Bulletin for Europe*, and besides statistical and economic studies the Anglo-French monthly, *ECE News Nouvelles.*

UN, *Fifteen Years of ECE Activities, 1947–1962*, New York, 1963; G. MYRDAL, "20 years of the UN ECE", in: *International Organization*, Summer, 1968; *Travaux de la Commission économique de l'Europe, 1947–1972.*

UN ECONOMIC COMMISSION FOR LATIN AMERICA AND THE CARIBBEAN. Comisión Económica de la ONU para América Latina, CEPAL. One of the UN regional economic commissions created by ECOSOC Res. 106/VI, Mar. 5, 1948; began activities in June, 1948 with seat in Santiago. Members: Antigua and Barbuda, Argentina, Bahamas, Barbados, Belize, Bolivia, Brazil, Canada, Chile, Colombia, Costa Rica, Cuba, Dominica, Dominican Republic, Ecuador, El Salvador, France, Grenada, Guatemala, Guyana, Haiti, Honduras, Jamaica, Mexico, Montserrat, Netherlands, Nicaragua, Panama, Paraguay, Peru, Saint Christopher and Nevis, Saint Lucia, Saint Vincent and the Grenadines, Spain, Suriname, Trinidad and Tobago, UK, Uruguay, USA, Venezuela. Associated member: Netherlands Antilles. Besides its seat in Santiago (in the Latin-American Institute of Economic and Social Planning) has its regional or special centers in Bogota, Mexico City, Montevideo, Rio de Janeiro and Washington. The Commission celebrated the 25th anniversary of its operation at its XV Session in Quito, Mar. 20–30, 1973. At this Session the delegate of Chile, H. Santa Cruz, expressed the view that the non-Latin American states – France, Great Britain, the Netherlands and USA, which have been members of CEPAL since 1948, should be deprived of their membership in this regional Organization. "The membership of CEPAL – Santa Cruz stated – reflects the political situation which existed 25 years ago. Presently Latin America needs its own international body." ECLAC institutions: Latin American Centre for Economic and Social Documentation (ECLAC-CLADES); Latin American Population Documentation System (ECLAC-DOCPAL). Publ.: *Yearbook Economic Survey of Latin America* (semi-annual), *Economic Bulletin for America Latina and Statistical Bulletin for Latin America.*

UN, ECLA. *A Basic Guide to the Commission and its Secretariat*, Santiago, 1966.

UN ECONOMIC COMMISSION FOR WESTERN ASIA, ECWA. One of the regional organizations of ECOSOC, est. Jan. 1, 1974 with membership of 12 Arab countries, which up to that time had benefited from the services of the UN Economic and Social Bureau, UNESOB, in Beirut. Members: Bahrain, Egypt, Iraq, Iran, Jordan, Kuwait, Lebanon, Oman, Palestine Liberation Organization, Qatar, Saudi Arabia, Syria, United Arab Emirates, Yemen Arab Republic, Yemen People's Democratic Republic.
Headquarters Baghdad, Iraq. Publ.: *Agriculture and Development* (annually), *Population Bulletin* (2 a year), *Middle East* (annually), *Statistical Abstract* (annually), *Economic and Social Development in the ECWA Region* (annually).

The Europa Year Book 1984. A World Survey, Vol. I, p. 32, London, 1984.

UNEMPLOYMENT. A subject of international conventions: designation for an economic phenomenon where part of those capable of working cannot find employment for economic, political or social reasons; unemployment is included in national statistics: in England – since 1860, in Germany – since 1895, in France – since 1900, and international ILO statistics – since 1920. On the basis of statistical analysis ILO states that at the end of 1910 in the 20 largest countries of the world, unemployment had reached 10.835 million persons, in Europe alone – 8.5 million; at the end of 1919 – 32.680 million, in Europe – more than 26 million. The second period of high unemployment were the years of world crisis, when in the USA (1932/33) more than 24% of the total labor force was without permanent employment. In Germany the peak period of unemployment was 1932, when it reached more than 30% and in 1933 fell to 25.8%. In the ▷ Human Rights, Universal Declaration of, 1948, the principle was accepted that "each person has the right to work ... and to protection against unemployment," amplified in the Convention on Employment, 1964. Two conventions concerning unemployment were formulated by the ILO: the Washington Convention on unemployment of Nov. 28, 1919 and the Geneva Convention on Compensation in the Case of Unemployment Resulting from a Shipwreck, signed on June 15, 1920.

H. CLAY, *The Post-War Unemployment Problems*, London, 1930; ILO, *The Campaign Against Unemployment*, Geneva, 1950; M. GODFREY, *Global Unemployment. A New Challenge to Economic Theory*, Brighton, 1988.

UNEP. United Nations Environment Programme, est. 1972 by the UN General Assembly, after the Stockholm UN Conference on the Human Environment (▷ Stockholm Declaration, 1972). Hqs. in Nairobi. Organization: Governing Council (16 African, 13 Asian, 10 Latin American, 6 Eastern European and 13 Western European and other states), which provides general policy within the UN system; Secretariat with Liaison Office in New York and Regional Offices in Geneva, Bangkok, Mexico, DF, and Beirut; the Environment Fund administered by the Secretariat, under the Chairmanship of the UN General Secretary, an Administrative Committee on Co-ordination, composed of heads of organizations within the UN system, ensures co-operation in the implementation of environmental programmes. ▷ Environmental Protection; ▷ Environmental Protection, UNEP World Report, 1983.

UNEP Information systems: International Referral System for Sources of Environmental Information, UNEP–INFOTERRA and International Register of Potentially Toxic Chemicals, UNEP-IRPTC.

UNEPTA. United Nations Expanded Programme of Technical Assistance, a specialized institution of the UN, 1950–1965; integrated by ▷ UNDP.

UNESCAP. ▷ UN Economic and Social Commission for Asia and the Pacific.

UNESCO. United Nations Educational Scientific and Cultural Organization. Organisation des Nations Unies pour l'éducation, la science et la culture. Organizatsya Obyedinionnikh Natsyi po voprosam provieshcheniya nauki i kultury, YUNESKO, Organización de las Naciones Unidas para la Educación, la Ciencia y la Cultura; official English, French, Russian and Spanish names of a UN specialized agency, est. by the ▷ UNESCO Constitution, adopted on Nov. 16, 1945 in London by representatives of 44 governments; also established was a Preparatory Commission to function until the Organization came into being on Nov. 4, 1946. Headquarters: Paris. An Agreement between UN and UNESCO was approved by the UN General Assembly in Dec., 1946. As a

Specialized Agency of the UN, UNESCO has established Agreements with ILO, FAO, WHO, WIPO, IAEA, UNRWA and co-operates closely with the other specialized agencies. It also has Agreements with Intergovernmental Organizations not belonging to the UN system: African Development Bank; Council of Europe; Customs Co-operation Council; European Organization for Nuclear Research; Ibero-American Bureau of Education; Inter-American Development Bank; Intergovernmental Bureau for Information; International Bureau of Weights and Measures; International Organization of Legal Metrology; Joint Afro-Malagasy-Mauritian Organization; Latin American Center for Physics; League of Arab States (The Arab Educational, Cultural and Scientific Organization); Organization of African Unity; Organization of American States; Organization of Central American States.

UNESCO has working relations with 7 intergovernmental organizations; and exchanges information with 27 such organizations. The purpose of UNESCO, as defined in its Constitution, is to contribute to peace and security by promoting collaboration among the nations through education, science, culture and communications in order to further universal respect for justice, for the rule of law, and for the human rights and fundamental freedoms for all, which are affirmed by the United Nations Charter. To realize this aim, UNESCO collaborates in the work of advancing mutual knowledge and understanding of people through all means of mass communication. It gives fresh stimuli to popular education and to the spread of culture, and it maintains, increases and diffuses knowledge. Organization: UNESCO works through a General Conference, an Executive Board and a Secretariat. The General Conference, consisting of representatives from each member state, convenes every two years to fix policies and to approve the program and budget for the next two years. It elects a 45-member Executive Board to oversee the program; it meets three times a year. The Secretariat headed by a Director-General is responsible for carrying out the program. National commissions, composed of representatives of the Government and of Non-Governmental Organizations in each of the member states, link UNESCO with the educational, scientific and cultural life in each country, and assist in carrying out UNESCO's program.

The general conference on Nov. 7, 1987 endorsed the nomination of Federico Mayor Zaragoz (Spain) as the organization's Director General in succession of Armadon M. M'Bow.

Publications: *UNESCO Chronicle* (monthly), English, French, Spanish, Arabic: *UNESCO Courier* (monthly illustrated), Arabic, Dutch, English, French, German, Hebrew, Hindi, Italian, Japanese, Persian, Portuguese, Russian, Spanish, Tamil, Turkish; *UNESCO Features* (24 a year), English, French, Spanish; Arabic and Russian (monthly); *International Social Science Journal* (quarterly), English, French; *Museum* (quarterly), bilingual English–French; *Unesco Bulletin for Libraries* (bimonthly), English, French, Spanish; *Copyright Bulletin* (2 a year), trilingual English–French–Spanish; *Study Abroad* (annual), trilingual English–French–Spanish; *Impact of Science on Society* (quarterly), bilingual English–French; *Prospects*; *Statistical Yearbook*; *Index Translatorium*. General information material on activities and on various world-wide aspects of education, science and culture. A catalogue of publications is printed each year.

All publications can be obtained from UNESCO, Place de Fontenay, 75700 Paris, France.

In Dec., 1984 Singapore, the USA and the UK decided to resign from the UNESCO membership.

UN, *Everyman's United Nations*, UIA, *Yearbook of International Organizations*; R.A. JOHNSON, "The Origin of the UNESCO", in: *International Conciliation*, No. 242, 1946, pp. 441–449; A. GARCIA ROBLES, *El Mundo de la Postguerra*, México, DF, 1946, Vol. 2, pp. 121–127; W.H.C. LAVES, Ch.A. THOMPSON, UNESCO: *Purpose, Progress, Prospect*, Bloomington, 1957; T.V. SATHYAMURTHY, *The Politics of International Cooperation Contrasting Conception of UNESCO*, Geneva, 1964; R. PAPINI, *Les relations entre l'UNESCO et les Organisations Non-Gouvernementales*, Bruxelles, 1967; U. CAMPAGNOLO, *Petit Dictionnaire pour une politique de la culture*, Neuchâtel, 1969; D. MYLONAS, *La genèse de l'UNESCO, 1942–1945*, Bruxelles, 1976; *Everyone's United Nations*, New York, 1979; *Basic Facts About the United Nations*, New York, 1983; C. WELLS, *The UN, UNESCO and the Politics of Knowledge*, New York, 1987.

UNESCO CONSTITUTION. The Constitution of the United Nations Educational and Cultural Organization, adopted on Nov. 16, 1945 at the UN Conference in London; entered into force on Nov. 4, 1946.

The Text as amended in 1976 reads as follows:

"The Governments of the States parties to this Constitution on behalf of their peoples declare:
That since wars began in the minds of men, it is in the minds of men that the defences of peace must be constructed;
That ignorance of each other's ways and lives has been a common cause, throughout the history of mankind, of that suspicion and mistrust between the peoples of the world through which their differences have all too often broken into war;
That the great and terrible war which has now ended was a war made possible by the denial of the democratic principles of the dignity, equality and mutual respect of men, and by the propagation, in their place, through ignorance and prejudice, of the doctrine of the inequality of men and races;
That the wide diffusion of culture, and the education of humanity for justice and liberty and peace are indispensable to the dignity of man and constitute a sacred duty which all the nations must fulfil in a spirit of mutual assistance and concern;
That a peace based exclusively upon the political and economic arrangements of governments would not be a peace which could secure the unanimous, lasting and sincere support of the peoples of the world, and that the peace must therefore be founded, if it is not to fail, upon the intellectual and moral solidarity of mankind.
For these reasons, the States parties to this Constitution, believing in full and equal opportunities for education for all, in the unrestricted pursuit of objective truth, and in the free exchange of ideas and knowledge, are agreed and determined to develop and to increase the means of communication between their peoples and to employ these means for the purposes of mutual understanding and a truer and more perfect knowledge of each others' lives;
In consequence whereof they do hereby create the United Nations Educational, Scientific and Cultural Organization for the purpose of advancing, through the educational, scientific and cultural relations of the peoples of the world, the objectives of international peace and of the common welfare of mankind for which the United Nations Organization was established and which its Charter proclaims.
Purposes and functions
Art. I.(1) The purpose of the Organization is to contribute to peace and security by promoting collaboration among the nations through education, science and culture in order to further universal respect for justice, for the law and for the human rights and fundamental freedoms which are affirmed for the peoples of the world, without distinction of race, sex, language or religion by the Charter of the United Nations.
(2) To realize this purpose the Organization will:
(a) collaborate in the work of advancing the mutual knowledge and understanding of peoples, through all means of mass communication and to that end promote such international agreements as may be necessary to promote the free flow of ideas by word and image;

(b) Give fresh impulse to popular education and to the spread of culture;
By collaborating with members, at their request, in the development of educational activities;
By instituting collaboration among the nations to advance the ideal of equality of educational opportunity without race, sex or any distinctions, economic or social;
By suggesting educational methods best suited to prepare the children of the world for the responsibilities of freedom;
(c) Maintain, increase and diffuse knowledge;
By assuring the conservation and protection of the world's inheritance of books, works of arts and monuments of history and science, and recommending to the nations concerned the necessary international conventions;
By encouraging co-operation among the nations in all branches of intellectual activity, including the international exchange of persons active in the fields of education, science and culture, and the exchange of publications, objects of artistic and scientific interest and other materials of information;
By initiating methods of international co-operation calculated to give the people of all countries access to the printed and published materials produced by any of them.
(3) With a view to preserving the independence, integrity and fruitful diversity of the cultures and educational systems of the member States of this Organization, the Organization is prohibited from intervening in matters which are essentially within their domestic jurisdiction.

Membership

Art. II.(1) Membership of the United Nations Organization shall carry with it the right to membership of the United Nations Educational, Scientific and Cultural Organization.
(2) Subject to the conditions of the Agreement between this Organization and the United Nations Organization, approved pursuant to Art. X of this Constitution, States not members of the United Nations Organization may be admitted to membership of the Organization upon recommendation of the Executive Board, by a two-thirds majority vote of the General Conference.
(3) Territories or groups of territories which are not responsible for the conduct of their international relations may be admitted as associate members by the General Conference by a two-thirds majority of members present and voting, upon application made on behalf of such territory or group of territories by the member or other authority having responsibility for their international relations. The nature and extent of the rights and obligations of associate members shall be determined by the General Conference.
(4) Members of the Organization which are suspended from the exercise of the rights and privileges of membership of the United Nations Organization shall upon the request of the latter, be suspended from the rights and privileges of this Organization.
(5) Members of the Organization which are expelled from the United Nations Organization shall automatically cease to be members of this Organization.
(6) Any member state or associate member of the Organization may withdraw from the Organization by notice addressed to the Director General. Such notice shall take effect on 31 December of the Year following that during which the notice was given. No such withdrawal shall affect the financial obligation owed to the Organization on the date the withdrawal takes effect. Notice of withdrawal by an associate member shall be given on its behalf by the member State or other authority having responsibility for its international relations.

Organs

Art. III. The Organization shall include a General Conference, an Executive Board and a Secretariat.

The General Conference

Art. IV. A. Composition
(1) The General Conference shall consist of the representatives of the States members of the Organization. The Government of each member State shall appoint not more than 5 delegates, who shall be selected after consultation with the National Commission, if established, or with educational, scientific and cultural bodies.

B. Functions
(2) The General Conference shall determine the policies and the main lines of work of the Organization. It shall take decisions on programs submitted to it by the Executive Board.
(3) The General Conference shall, when it deems desirable and in accordance with the regulations to be made by it, summon international conferences of States on education, the sciences and the humanities for the dissemination of knowledge; non-governmental conferences on the same subjects may be summoned by the General Conference or by the Executive Board in accordance with such regulations.
(4) The General Conference shall, in adopting proposals for submission to the member States, distinguish between recommendations and international conventions submitted for their approval. In the former case a majority vote shall suffice; in the latter case a two-thirds majority shall be required. Each of the member States shall submit recommendations or conventions to its competent authorities within a period of one year from the close of the session of the General Conference at which they were adopted.
(5) Subject to the provisions of Art. V, paragraph 5(c), the General Conference shall advise the United Nations Organization on the educational, scientific and cultural aspects of matters of concern to the latter; in accordance with the terms and procedure agreed upon between the appropriate authorities of the two Organizations.
(6) The General Conference shall receive and consider the reports sent to the Organization by member States on the action taken upon the recommendations and conventions referred to in paragraph 4 above or, if it so decides, analytical summaries of these reports.
(7) The General Conference shall elect the members of the Executive Board and, on the recommendation of the Board, shall appoint the Director General.
C. Voting
(8) (a) Each memnber State shall have one vote in the General Conference. Decisions shall be made by a simple majority except in cases in which a two-thirds majority is required by the provisions of this constitution, or of the Rules of Procedure of the General Conference. A majority shall be a majority of the members present and voting.
(b) A member State shall have no vote in the General Conference if the total amount of contributions due from it exceeds the total amount of contributions payable by it for the current year and the immediately preceding calendar year.
(c) The General Conference may nevertheless permit such a member State to vote, if it is satisfied that failure to pay is due to conditions beyond the control of the member Nation.
D. Procedure
(9) (a) The General Conference shall meet in ordinary session every two years. It may meet in extraordinary session if it decides to do so itself or if summoned by the Executive Board, or on the demand of at least one third of the member States.
(b) At each session the location of its next ordinary session shall be designated by the General Conference. The location of an extraordinary session is summoned by it, or otherwise by the Executive Board.
(10) The General Conference shall adopt its own rules of procedure. It shall at each session elect a President and other officers.
(11) The General Conference shall set up special and technical committees and such other subordinate bodies as may be necessary for its purposes.
(12) The General Conference shall cause arrangements to be made for public access to meetings, subject to such regulations as it shall prescribe.
E. Observers
(13) The General Conference, on the recommendation of the Executive Board and by a two-thirds majority may, subject to its rules of procedure, invite as observers at specified sessions of the Conference or of its Commissions representatives of international organizations, such as those referred to in Art. XI, paragraph 4.
(14) When consultative arrangements have been approved by the Executive Board for such international non-governmental or semigovernmental organizations in the manner provided in Art. XI, paragraph 4, those organizations shall be invited to send observers to sessions of the General Conference and its Commissions.

Executive Board

Art. V. A. Composition
(1) The Executive Board shall be elected by the General Conference from among the delegates appointed by the member States and shall consist of forty-five members each of whom shall represent the Government of the State of which he is a national. The President of the General Conference shall sit ex officio in an advisory capacity on the Executive Board.
(2) In electing the members of the Executive Board the General Conference shall endeavor to include persons competent in the arts, the humanities, the sciences, education and the diffusion of ideas, and qualified by their experience and capacity to fulfil the administrative and executive duties of the Board. It shall also have regard to the diversity of cultures and a balanced geographical distribution. Not more than one national of any member State shall serve on the Board at any one time, the President of the Conference excepted.
(3) Members of the Board shall serve from the close of the session of the General Conference which elected them until the close of the second ordinary session of the General Conference following that election. They shall not be immediately eligible for a second term. The General Conference shall, at each of its ordinary sessions, elect the number of members required to fill the vacancies occurring at the end of the session.
(4) (a) In the event of the death or resignation of a member of the Executive Board, his replacement for the remainder of his term shall be appointed by the Executive Board on the nomination of the Government of the State the former member represented.
(b) The Government making the nomination and the Executive Board shall have regard to the factors set forth in paragraph 2 of this Article.
(c) When exceptional circumstances arise, which, in the considered opinion of the represented State, make it indispensable for its representative to be replaced, even if he does not tender his resignation, measures shall be taken in accordance with the provisions of subparagraph (a) above.
B. Functions
(5) (a) The Executive Board shall prepare the agenda for the General Conference. It shall examine the program of work for the Organization and corresponding budget estimates submitted to it by the Director General in accordance with paragraph 3 of Art. VI and shall submit them with such recommendations as it considers desirable to the General Conference.
(b) The Executive Board, acting under the authority of the General Conference, shall be responsible for the execution of the program adopted by the Conference. In accordance with the decisions of the General Conference and having regard to circumstances arising between two ordinary sessions, the Executive Board shall take all necessary measures to ensure the effective and rational execution of the program by the Director General.
(c) Between ordinary sessions of the General Conference, the Board may discharge the functions of adviser to the United Nations, set forth in Art. IV, paragraph 5, whenever the problem upon which advice is sought has already been dealt with in principle by the Conference, or when the solution is implicit in decisions of the Conference.
(6) The executive Board shall recommend to the General Conference the admission of new members to the Organization.
(7) Subject to the decisions of the General Conference, the Executive Board shall adopt its own rules of procedure. It shall elect its officers from among its members.
(8) The Executive Board shall meet in regular session at least twice a year and may meet in special session if convoked by the Chairman on his own initiative or upon the request of six members of the Board.
(9) The Chairman of the Executive Board shall present, on behalf of the Board, to each ordinary session of the General Conference, with or without comments, the reports of the activities of the Organization which the

Director General is required to prepare in accordance with the provisions of Art. VI.3(b).

(10) The Executive Board shall make all necessary arrangements to consult the representatives of international organizations or qualified persons concerned with questions within its competence.

(11) Between sessions of the General Conference, the Executive Board may request advisory opinions from the International Court of Justice on legal questions arising within the field of the Organization's activities.

(12) Although the members of the Executive Board are representative of their respective Governments they shall exercise the powers delegated to them by the General Conference on behalf of the Conference as a whole.

C. Transitional Provisions

(13) Notwithstanding the provisions of paragraph 3 of this Art.

(a) members of the Executive Board elected prior to the seventeenth session of the General Conference shall serve until the end of the term for which they were elected.

(b) members of the Executive Board appointed, prior to the seventeenth session of the General Conference, by the Board in accordance with the provision of paragraph 4 of this Art. to replace members with a four year term shall be eligible for a second term of four years.

Secretariat

Art. VI.(1) The Secretariat shall consist of a Director General and such staff as may be required.

(2) The Director General shall be nominated by the Executive Board and appointed by the General Conference for a period of six years, under such conditions as the Conference approve, and shall be eligible for reappointment. He shall be the chief administrative officer of the Organization.

(3) (a) The Director General, or a deputy designated by him, shall participate, without the right to vote, in all meeting of the General Conference, of the Executive Board, and of the Committees of the Organization. He shall formulate proposals for appropriate action by the Conference and the Board, and shall prepare for submission to the Board a draft program of work for the Organization with corresponding budget estimates.

(b) The Director General shall prepare and communicate to member States and to the Executive Board periodical reports on the activities of the Organization. The General Conference shall determine the periods to be covered by these reports.

(4) The Director General shall appoint the staff of the Secretariat in accordance with staff regulations to be approved by the General Conference. Subject to the paramount consideration of securing the highest standards of integrity, efficiency and technical competence, appointment to the staff shall be on as wide a geographical basis as possible.

(5) The responsibilities of the Director General and of the staff shall be exclusively international in character. In the discharge of their duties they shall not seek or receive instructions from any Government or from any authority external to the Organization. They shall refrain from any action which might prejudice their position as international officials. Each member State of the Organization undertakes to respect the international character of the responsibilities of the Director General and the staff, and not to seek to influence them in the discharge of their duties.

(6) Nothing in this Art. shall preclude the Organization from entering into special arrangements within the United Nations Organization from common services and staff and for the interchange of personnel.

National Co-operating Bodies

Art. VII.(1) Each member State shall make such arrangements as suits its particular conditions for the purpose of associating its principal bodies interested in educational, scientific and cultural matters with the work of the Organization, preferably by the formation of a National Commission broadly representative of the Government and such bodies.

(2) National Commissions or National Co-operating Bodies, where they exist, shall act in an advisory capacity to their respective delegations to the General Conference and to their Governments in matters relating to the Organization and shall function as agencies of liaison in all matters of interest to it.

(3) The Organization may, on the request of a member State, delegate, either temporarily or permanently, a member of its Secretariat to serve on the National Commission of that State, in order to assist in the development of its work.

Reports by Member States

Art. VIII. Each member State shall submit to the Organization, at such times and such manner as shall be determined by the General Conference, reports on the laws, regulations and statistics relatiing to its educational, scientific and cultural institutions and activities, and on the action taken upon the recommendations and conventions referred to in Art. IV, paragraph 4.

Budget

Art. IX.(1) The Budget shall be administered by the Organization,

(2) The General Conference shall approve and give final effect to the budget and to the apportionment of financial responsibility among the member States of the Organization subject to such arrangement with the United Nations as may be provided in the agreement to be entered into pursuant to Art. X.

(3) The Director General, with the approval of the Executive Board, may receive gifts, bequests, and subventions directly from Governments, public and private institutions, associations and private persons.

Relations with the United Nations Organization

Art. X. This Organization shall be brought into relation with the United Nations Organization, as soon as practicable, as one of the Specialized Agencies referred to in Art. 57 of the Charter of the United Nations. This relationship shall be effected through an agreement with the United Nations Organization under Art. 63 of the Charter, which agreement shall be subject to the approval of the General Conference of this Organization. The agreement shall provide for effective co-operation between the two Organizations in the pursuit of their common purposes, and at the same time shall recognize the autonomy of this Organization, within the fields of its competence as defined in this Constitution. Such agreement may, among other matters, provide for the approval and financing of the budget of the Organization by the General Assembly of the United Nations.

Relations with other Specialized International Organizations and Agencies

Art. XI.(1) This Organization may co-operate with other Agencies, intergovernmental organizations and agencies whose interests and activities are related to its purposes. To this end the Director General, acting under the general authority of the Executive Board, may establish effective working relationships with such organizations and agencies and establish such joint committees as may be necessary to assure effective co-operation. Any formal arrangements entered into with such organizations or agencies shall be subject to the approval of the Executive Board.

(2) Whenever the General Conference of this Organization and the competent authorities of any other specialized intergovernmental organizations or agencies whose purpose and functions lie within the competence of this Organization, deem it desirable to effect a transfer of their resources and activities to this Organization, the Director General, subject to the approval of the Conference, may enter into mutually acceptable arrangements for this purpose.

(3) This Organization may make appropriate arrangements with other intergovernmental organizations for reciprocal meetings.

(4) The United Nations Educational, Scientific and Cultural Organization may make suitable arrangements for consultation and co-operation with non-governmental international organizations concerned with matters within its competence, and may invite them to undertake specific tasks. Such co-operation may also include appropriate participation by representatives of such organizations on advisory committees set up by the General Conference.

Legal Status of the Organization

Art. XII. The provisions of Art. 104 and 105 of the Charter of the United Nations Organization concerning the legal status of that Organization, its privileges and immunities, shall apply in the same way to this Organization.

Amendments

Art. XIII.(1) Proposal for amendments to this constitution shall become effective upon receiving the approval of the General Conference by a two-thirds majority; provided, however, that those amendments which involve fundamental alterations in the aims of the Organization or new obligations for the member States shall require subsequent acceptance on the part of two thirds of the member States before they come into force. The draft texts of proposed amendments shall be communicated by the Director General to the member States at least six months in advance of their consideration by the General Conference.

(2) The General Conference shall have power to adopt by a two-thirds majority rules of procedure for carrying out the provisions of this Art.

Interpretation

Art. XIV.(1) The English and French texts of this Constitution shall be regarded as equally authoritative.

(2) Any question or dispute concerning the interpretation of this Constitution shall be referred for determination to the international Court of Justice or to an arbitral tribunal, as the General Conference may determine under its rule of procedure.

Entry into force

Art. XV.(1) This Constitution shall be subject to acceptance. The instrument of acceptance shall be deposited with the Government of the United Kingdom.

(2) This Constitution shall remain open for signature in the archives of the Government of the United Kingdom. Signature may take place either before or after the deposit of the instrument of acceptance. No acceptance shall be valid unless preceded or followed by signature.

(3) This Constitution shall come into force when it has been accepted by twenty of its signatories. Subsequent acceptances shall take effect immediately.

(4) The Government of the United Kingdom will inform all members of the United Nations of the receipt of all instruments of acceptance and of the date on which the Constitution comes into force in accordance with the preceding paragraph.

In faith whereof, the undersigned, duly authorized to that effect, have signed this Constitution in the English and French languages, both texts being equally authentic.

Done in London the sixteenth day of November, one thousand nine hundred and forty-five, in a single copy, in the English and French languages, of which certified copies will be communicated by the Government of the United Kingdom to the Governments of all the Members of the United Nations."

Constitution of the UNESCO, Paris, 1977.

UNESCO HERITAGE PROTECTION. Intergovernmental Committee for the Protection of Cultural and Natural Heritage of Exceptional Universal Value, created by the UNESCO Convention on the Protection of the World Cultural and Natural Heritage, 1972. The task of the Committee is to organize co-operation and international assistance for identifying and preserving this heritage. One of the initial tasks is to catalogue the list of objects of "world cultural and natural heritage" whose preservation is an obligation of mankind and also a list of monuments of this type threatened with destruction for the purpose of undertaking rescue operations under the aegis of UNESCO; ▷ World Heritage UNESCO List. The precursor of the International Committee is the International Federation of Associations for the Protection of Europe's Cultural and Natural Heritage, est. 1963, in London, reg. with the UIA.

UN Yearbook, 1972 Yearbook of International Organizations.

UNESCO INFORMATION SERVICES. In alphabetical order: Clearing-House for Thesaurus and Classification, UNESCO-CLEARIBE World-Wide Network for Education Information, UNESCO-IBE-NETWORK.

International Education Reporting Service, UNESCO-IERS.

International Information System on Research in Documentation, UNESCO-ISORID.

International Serials Data System, UNESCO-ISDS.

Library of the UNESCO Regional Office for Culture and Book Development in Asia, UNESCO-ROCBA-LIB.

Marine Environmental Data and Information Referral System, UNESCO-IOC-MEDI.

Directory of United Nations Information Services, New York, 1980.

UNESOB. United Nations Economic and Social Office in Beirut, est. 1963 to assist in the implementation of the UN resolutions aimed at fostering economic growth and social development of the region, with particular reference to the objectives of the Development Decades, integrated in Aug. 1973 into the ▷ UN Economic Commission for Western Asia, ECWA.

UN EUROPEAN OFFICE. The official name since 1946 for the European seat of the UN in the Palais des Nations in Geneva.

UN EXPERTS ON RULE AND PROCEDURE. A special Committee of the Security Council of Experts on Rule and Procedure, encompassing all Members of the Security Council like the ▷ Admission of New Members UN Committee.

UNFAIR COMPETITION. A subject of national and international acts against unfair competition, boycott, black listing, picketing, discrimination, by national and international bribery etc.

H. DAVID (ed.), *Pinners World Unfair Competition Law. An Encyclopaedia*, Alphen, 1978.

UNFDAC. ▷ Narcotics.

UNFICYP. United Nations Peace-keeping Force in Cyprus, created in pursuance of Security Council Res. 186 (1964) of Mar. 4, 1964. In it the Council recommended the establishment of the Force in order to prevent a recurrence of fighting between the Greek Cypriot and Turkish Cypriot communities and to contribute to the maintenance of law and order and a return to normal conditions in the Island. UNFICYP also supports relief operations co-operating with the World Food Programme. Following the hostilities of 1974, cease-fire lines were established between the area controlled by the Cyprus National Guard and the Turkish forces. UNFICYP supervises these lines and provides security for civilians of both communities living or working in the area between cease-fire lines.

As of 31 May, 1980, the Force comprised 2457 troops; from Austria (314), Canada (515), Denmark (365), Finland (11), Ireland (7), Sweden (428) and the United Kingdom (817) and 34 civilian police: from Australia (20) and Sweden (14). A Special Representative of the Secretary-General is in Cyprus to deal with the political aspects of the mission and to assist in the search for a peaceful settlement of the conflict between Greek Cypriot and Turkish Cypriot communities. In 1975 the Security Council entrusted the Secretary-General with a mission of good offices to facilitate negotiations between the parties concerned. Under this mission, seven rounds of intercommunal talks and two high-level meetings have been held under the UN Secretary-General's auspices. ▷ Cyprus.

According to the report of UN Secretary General, the accumulated deficit of the UNFICYP had reached US$166 million on March 8, 1988.

UN Yearbook, 1964, 1974, 1975, 1980, 1983; KEESING's *Contemporary Archive*, 1984.

UN FILM BOARD. A subsidiary body of the UN Public Information Department, which co-ordinates film operations connected with the UN and its specialized agencies.

UN FINANCES. The first provisional UN financial statute was ratified on Dec. 11, 1946 by the UN General Assembly on the basis of Res. 80/I and revised by Res. 163/II of Nov. 20, 1947. The final text of the UN Financial Statute was ratified by the UN General Assembly on Nov. 16, 1950, and amended by it on Nov. 3, 1955 and Dec. 15, 1955 including Financial Rules issued by the Secretary General in UN *Bulletin*, May 1, 1970.

The rules apply not only to the UN financial administration, but also to the International Court of Justice; it contains budgetary, credit, settlement principles, etc. Finances connected with ▷ Budget of the UN are a subject of debate both in the Committees of the Assembly as well as in the plenary sessions of the Assembly.

UN Doc. ST/SGB/ Financial Rules 1/Rev. 1, 1970.

UNFPA. United Nations Fund for Population Activities.

UN Chronicle, January, 1984, p. 88.

UN GENERAL ASSEMBLY. The first of the six UN principal organs; established under Chapters III and IV of the UN Charter it consists of all UN members; however, the number of each state's representatives in the General Assembly may not exceed five. The function and competence of the General Assembly is determined in Arts. 10–17; the procedure of voting – in Arts. 18 and 19. Under the UN Charter the General Assembly may discuss any question or any matters within the scope of the Charter itself. It has become a rule that annual regular sessions are held in mid-September through December and seldom last longer than January or February. Special sessions are convoked at the request of the UN Security Council or a majority of the Members of the Assembly. It consists of seven principal committees (six numbered): 1 – the Political and Security Committee, II – the Economic and Financial Committee, III - the Social, Humanitarian and Cultural Committee, IV – the Trusteeship Committee, V – the Administrative and Budgetary Committee, VI – Legal Committee and VII called only the Special Political Committee. The seven Main Committees correspond to the General Assembly's major areas of responsibility. In each of the committees all member States are represented; therefore, the voting in the committees is usually decisive for the voting at General Assembly plenary sessions.

Each session of the Assembly begins with a rite of ceremonial initiation. The head of the delegation from which the President was selected the preceding year, in his role as temporary President, gavels the Assembly to order and asks for a minute of prayer or silent meditation. The silence over, the temporary President proposes the names of the nine people he has selected, after consultation with various groups of countries, to be members of the Credentials Committee. The names are usually accepted without further ado and the Assembly passes on to the election of a President.

The President is elected by secret ballot and there are no nominations. This means that any name can be written in by any delegation. But the results are usually pre-determined by consultations within and among regional groups. Since 1963 the post of President has rotated among the different regional groups. And as the regional groups decide firmly who it is to be, Presidents of the Assembly have been elected by acclamation (i.e. without a vote at all),

since 1977. The only exception to this was in 1981 when there was no agreement within the Asian Group on who its candidate would be.

After the election of the President and his opening statement, the Assembly moves to elect the chairmen of its seven Main Committees. These too are predetermined by consultations within groups and rotate according to a set pattern, so there is usually no vote. The chairmen are elected by acclamation. After the chairmen comes the election of the 21 Vice-Presidents of the Assembly, again, usually by acclamation.

The General Assembly with its 159 members has an intricate structure of committees to perform its many and varied tasks. At the center of the structure is the plenary with its President and 21 Vice-Presidents who hold office until the close of the session at which they are elected. (In practice the term of the President has come to run a full year, with the incumbent during each regular session of the Assembly retaining that role till the next session.)

The Assembly plenary has four types of committees:

Procedural Committees; Main Committees; Standing Committees; Ad Hoc Committees.

The General Committee consists of the President, the 21 Vice-Presidents and the Chairmen of the Assembly's seven Main Committees. The General Committee recommends to the Assembly the items to be included in the agenda. It also recommends the priority of items and their allocation among the Main Committees.

There are two standing committees whose members are experts appointed in their personal capacities for three-year terms. They are the Advisory Committee on Administrative and Budgetary Questions (ACABQ) and the Committee on Contributions. The ACABQ is a 16-member body that examines closely all budgetary proposals made to the Assembly. The 18-member Committee on Contributions has the job of advising the Assembly on the apportionment of the United Nations expenses among its member States.

Ad Hoc Committees are set up, as the name implies, whenever the Assembly needs to devote special consideration to any matter. Ad Hoc committees have been established to deal with such issues as disarmament, information, apartheid, decolonization, economic negotiations and international years related to the disabled, the aging and youth.

The rules of the General Asssembly were adopted in a preliminary form on Feb. 11, 1946, and in the final form on Nov. 17 and Nov. 21, 1947 under Res. 173/II and 176/II.

They entered into force on Jan. 1, 1948; modified several times: Dec. 11, 1948 – Res. 262/III, Apr. 2, 1949 – Res. 271/III, Oct. 22, 1949 – Res. 362/IV, Nov. 3, 1950 – Res. 457/V, Nov. 20, 1951 – Res. 689/VII, Oct. 23, 1953 – Res. 791/VIII, Oct. 11, 1954 – Res. 844/IX, Dec. 18, 1956 – Res. 1104/XI, Dec. 12, 1957 – Res. 1192/XII, Dec. 8, 1965 – Res. 2101/XX.

An index in the English language to all documents issued by a recent General Assembly Session is published annually. During 1946–49 a separate Index of Resolutions Adopted by the UN General Assembly was published.

Due to a tremendous ammount of documents issued by each session (in 1970 there were about 600 pages per day of the session), documents to be kept in archives are prepared in the form of microfilms. In 1954 the first Index to Microfilm of UN Documents during 1946–50 was published.

P.A. LADAME, *L'Assemblée Général de l'ONU*, Paris, 1949; H.F. HAVILAND, *The Political Role of the UN General Assembly*, New York, 1951; P.F. BRUGIER, *Les pouvoirs de l'Assemblée Générale des Nations Unies en matière politique et de sécurité*, Paris, 1955; D.S. BAYLEY, *The General Assembly of the UN. A Study of Procedure and Praxis*, London, 1960; H.R. ALKER, B.M. RUSSET, *World Politics in the General Assembly*, New Haven, 1965; J. KOLASA, *Rules of Procedure of the UN General Assembly. A Legal Analysis*, Wroclaw, 1967; *UN Rules of Procedure the General Assembly*, New York, 1972; *UN Chronicle*, September, 1982, pp. 33–48; M.J. PETERSON, *The General Assembly in World Politics*, Boston, Mass, 1986.

UN GENERAL ASSEMBLY DECLARATIONS. The statements made by UN's main deliberative organ specifying principles concerning any field of international relations and adopted by the majority of votes cast by UN member states, e.g. the Universal Declaration of Human Rights, or the Declaration of Principles of International Law. The principles laid down in UN declarations are often integrated by the UN member states as well as non-member states into their national constitutions and statutes of intergovernmental institutions.

L.M. GOODRICH, "Development of the General Assembly", in: *International Conciliation*, No. 471, May, 1951, pp. 231–278.

UN GENERAL ASSEMBLY PRESIDENT OF THE SESSION. The official title of chairmen of the UN General Assembly regular sessions elected by the Assembly to preside over such sessions in keeping with Art. 21 of the UN Charter and to exercise functions determined by the UN General Assembly rules of procedure. In case of Extraordinary Sessions the function of president is exercised as a rule by the president of regular sessions. The rules assign to the President the function of presiding over plenary sessions, putting motions to vote, announcing resolutions, etc., also, supervising the work of ancillary organs of the Assembly. The President is assisted by 21 deputies also elected by the Assembly who, together with chairmen of seven main UN Committees, from the General Committee make decisions on procedural matters and not political ones.

The names of the presidents 1946–89 ▷ UN General Assembly Sessions. ▷ UN General Assembly.

UN. *Rules of Procedure of the General Assembly*, New York, 1972.

UN GENERAL ASSEMBLY SESSIONS. According to Art. 20 of the UN Charter, the General Assembly meets in regular annual sessions and, when circumstances require it, at special sessions. In 1950 the Assembly established under the Resolution ▷ Uniting for Peace, the third possibility of calling emergency sessions in 24 hours by decision of any nine members of the Security Council or, in cases where unanimity was lacking among the Council's permanent members, by one member state with the concurrence of the majority of the UN members. The first session of the UN Preparatory Commission was held in 1945, in the Church House, in Westminster Abbey, London, with 51 states participating.

Regular sessions traditionally take place each year on the third Thursday of September:

I Inauguration Session started formally on Jan. 11, 1946 in London, but carried on its work in New York at the site of the former fair ground (World's Fair 1939) in a section of Flushing Meadow, from Sept. 23–Dec. 19, 1946, under the chairmanship of H. Spaak (Belgium);

II at Lake Success (USA), Oct. 1–Dec. 6, 1947, under the chairmanship of O. Aranha (Brazil);

III in Paris Sept. 23–Dec. 12, 1948, under the chairmanship of H.V. Evatt (Australia);

IV in Flushing Meadow, Sept. 28–Dec. 14, 1949, under the chairmanship of C.P. Romulo (Republic of the Philippines);

V in Flushing Meadow, Sept. 19–Dec. 15, 1950, under the chairmanship of N. Entezam (Iran);

VI in Paris, Nov. 6–Dec. 20, 1951, under the chairmanship of Luis Padilla Nervo (Mexico);

VII in New York, Oct. 14–Dec. 21, 1952, under the chairmanship of L.B. Pearson (Canada);

VIII in New York, Sept. 15–Dec. 10, 1953, under the chairmanship of V. Lakshmi Pandit (India);

IX in New York, Sept. 21–Dec. 18, 1954, and in San Francisco June 20–26, 1955 (a jubilee session on the tenth anniversary of passing the UN Charter), under the chairmanship of E.N. van Kleffens (Netherlands);

X in New York, Sept. 20–Dec. 20, 1955, under the chairmanship of J. Maza (Chile);

XI in New York, Nov. 12, 1956–Mar. 8, 1957, under the chairmanship of V. Vaithayokon (Thailand);

XII in New York, Sept. 17–Dec. 14, 1957, under the chairmanship of L. Munro (New Zealand);

XIII in New York, Sept. 16–Dec. 13, 1958, under the chairmanship of Ch. Malik (Indonesia);

XIV in New York, Sept. 15–Dec. 12, 1959, under the chairmanship of V.A. Belaunde (Peru);

XV in New York, Sept. 20, 1960–Apr. 22, 1961, under the chairmanship of F.H. Boland (Ireland);

XVI in New York, Sept. 23–Dec. 21, 1961, Jan. 15–Feb. 23, 1962, June 7–29, 1962, under the chairmanship of M. Slim (Tunisia);

XVII in New York, Sept. 18–Dec. 21, 1962, under the chairmanship of M. Zafrulla Khan (Pakistan);

XVIII in New York, Sept. 17–Dec. 17, 1963, under the chairmanship of S. Rodriguez (Venezuela);

XIX in New York, Dec. 1–30, 1964 and Jan. 18–Feb. 18, 1965, under the chairmanship of A. Quaison Sackey (Ghana);

XX in New York, Sept. 21–Dec. 21, 1965, under the chairmanship of A. Fanfani (Italy);

XXI in New York, Sept. 20–Dec. 20, 1966, under the chairmanship of A.R. Rahman Pashwak (Afghanistan);

XXII in New York, Sept. 16–Dec. 19, 1967 and Apr. 15–June 15, 1968, under the chairmanship of C. Manescu (Romania);

XXIII in New York, Sept. 24–Dec. 20, 1968, under the chairmanship of A. Arenales (Guatemala);

XXIV in New York, Sept. 16, 1969, under the chairmanship of Mme. A. Brooks (Liberia);

XXV in New York, Sept. 15–Dec. 17, 1970, under the chairmanship of E. Hambro (Norway);

XXVI in New York, Sept. 21–Dec. 22, 1971, under the chairmanship of A. Malik (Indonesia);

XXVII in New York, Sept. 19–Dec. 19, 1972, under the chairmanship of S. Trepczyński (Poland);

XXVIII in New York, Sept. 18–Dec. 21, 1973, under the chairmanship of L. Benitez (Ecuador); formally the session was not closed due to the unsettled crisis in the Middle East.

XXIX in New York, Sept. 17–Dec. 18, 1974, under the chairmanship of A. Bouteflika (Algeria);

XXX in New York, Sept. 16–Dec. 17, 1975, under the chairmanship of S. Thon (Luxembourg);

XXXI in New York, Sept. 21–Dec. 22, 1976, under the chairmanship of H.S. Amerasinghe (Sri Lanka);

XXXII in New York, Sept. 20–Dec. 21, 1977, under the chairmanship of L. Mojsov (Yugoslavia);

XXXIII in New York, Sept. 17–Sept. 20, 1978 and Jan. 7–21, 1979, under the chairmanship of I. Llevano (Columbia);

XXXIV in New York, Sept.–Dec. 19, 1979, under the chairmanship of A. Salim (Tanzania);

XXXV in New York, Sept. 16–Dec. 18, 1980 and Jan. 15–21, 1981, under the chairmanship of B. von Wechmar (FRG).

XXXVI in New York, Sept. 15–Dec. 18, 1981 and March 16–19, 1982 and Apr. 28, 1982 and Aug. 20, 1982, under the chairmanship of Ismat T. Kittani (Iraq);

XXXVII in New York, Sept. 21–Dec. 21, 1982 and in May, 1983, under the chairmanship of Imre Hollai (Hungary);

XXXVIII in New York Sept. 20–Dec. 20, 1983, under the chairmanship of Jorge Illueca (Panama);

XXXIX in New York, Sept. 24–Dec. 20, 1984 and Jan. 1985, Paul Lusaka (Zambia)

XL in New York, Sept 17–Dec. 20, 1985, Jaime de Pinies (Spain).

XLI in New York, Sept. 16–Dec. 20, 1986, Humayem Rashid Chowdhury (Bangladesh).

XLII in New York, Sept. 15–Dec. 21, 1987, Peter Florin (GDR).

XLIII in New York, Sept. 20–Dec. 22, 1988, under the chairmanship of Dante Caputo (Argentina).

XLIV in New York, opened Sept. 19, 1989, J. N. Garba (Nigeria).

In addition, on the basis of Art. 9 of the UN Charter, in the years 1947–85 eight special Sessions and five Emergency Sessions were held. Below are the Special and Emergency Sessions in chronological order:

1947 – I Special Session (Apr. 28–May 15) in Flushing Meadow, on Palestine, under the chairmanship of O. Aranha (Brazil).

1948 – II Special Session (Apr. 16–May 14) in Lake Success, on Palestine and protection of sacred places in Jerusalem; under the chairmanship of J. Aros (Argentina).

1956 – 1 Emergency Session (Nov. 1–10), in New York, on the attack of France, Israel and Great Britain on Egypt; under the chairmanship of R. Ortega (Chile).

1956 – II Emergency Session (Nov. 4–11) in New York, on Hungary; under the chairmanship of R. Ortega (Chile).

1958 – III Emergency Session (Aug. 8–21) in New York, on military intervention of the USA in Lebanon, and of Great Britain in Jordan; under the chairmanship of L. Munro (New Zealand).

1960 – IV Emergency Session (Sept. 17–19) in New York, on Congo; under the chairmanship of V. Belaunde (Peru).

1961 – III Special Session (Aug. 21–25) in New York, on bombardment of the port of Bizerta in Tunisia by the air force of France, under the chairmanship of H. Boland (Ireland).

1963 – IV Special Session (June 14–27) in New York, on the UN financial crisis; under the chairmanship of M. Zafrulla Khan (Pakistan).

1967 – V Special Session (Apr. 21–June 13) in New York, on South-West Africa (Namibia), and on UN military forces; under the chairmanship of A. Rahman (Afghanistan).

1967 – V Emergency Session (June 17–July 22) in New York, on "consequences of Israeli aggression against Arab countries"; under the chairmanship of A. Rahman (Afghanistan).

1974 – VI Special Session (Apr. 9–May 2) in New York, on World raw-material economy; under the chairmanship of L. Benites (Ecuador). Resolution of the Session ▷ New International Economic Order.

1975 – VIII Special Session (Sept. 1–16) in New York, on development of international economic co-operation, under the chairmanship of A. Bouteflika (Algeria).

1978 – VIII Special Session May 23–June 30, in New York, on disarmament; under the chairmanship of L. Mojsov (Yugoslavia).

1980 – IX Special Session, Aug. 7– Sept. 5, in New York, on the North–South problems; under the chairmanship of A. Salim (Tanzania).

UN Yearbooks, 1946–80.

UNHCR. United Nations High Commissioner for Refugees. ▷ Refugees.

UN HEADQUARTERS. ▷ United Nations Headquarters.

UN HUMAN RIGHTS COMMITTEE. An organ of the Covenant on Civil and Political Rights, 1976, to consider reports by states on measures taken to implement Covenant provisions, and communications alleging violations under Optional Protocol. Committee held first two sessions in 1977.

UN HYMN. A song performed for the first time on Oct. 24, 1971 at the annual concert at the UN New York headquarters to celebrate the anniversary of UN inception; music by Spanish composer and virtuoso Pablo Cassals to a poem by American poet of British descent, W.H. Auden.

UNIAPAC. The International Christian Union of Business Executives, f. 1949, Brussels, as the successor to the International Conference of Catholic Employers Association, f. 1931. Aims: propagate the Christian social doctrine in economic and social life. Consultative status with ECOSOC, UNESCO, UNIDO, UNCTAD, Council of Europe, and ILO. Publ. UNIAPAC *Reflexions* (quarterly, in English, French and Spanish). Reg. with the UIA.

UNIAPAC *Programme 1977–80*, Brussels, 1977; *Yearbook of International Organizations*.

UNICEF. United Nations Children's Fund, created by the UN General Assembly on Dec. 11, 1946 as the United Nations International Children's Emergency Fund. By 1953, when the General Assembly extended UNICEF's mandate indefinitely and the words "International" and "Emergency" were dropped from its name, the Fund had begun to focus its attention on the widespread malnutrition, disease and illiteracy afflicting millions of children throughout the developing world. In 1965, UNICEF was awarded the Nobel Peace Prize because "it has fulfilled the condition of Alfred Nobel's will, the promotion of brotherhood among the nations." Headquarters: New York.

UNICEF has semi-autonomous status within the United Nations, reporting to the Economic and Social Council and the General Assembly. An Executive Board, composed of representatives of 41 states chosen by the Economic and Social Council, establishes UNICEF policies and meets annually to review the Fund's programmes. UNICEF depends entirely on voluntary contributions to finance its activities. Approximately three quarters of its income derives from Governments; the remainder comes from the general public through greeting card sales and various fund-raising campaigns. Currently, UNICEF assists programmes for children in more than 100 countries in Africa, the Americas, Asia and the Eastern Mediterranean, with a combined child population of approximately 960 million. UNICEF-assisted countries are divided into three categories: *Group I* – countries that require "special assistance": those designated by the United Nations as least developed countries; others in which temporary circumstances necessitate extra assistance; and small nations, each with a child population under 500,000, which require special consideration. *Group II* – countries which receive UNICEF's "normal" level of assistance. These are in the middle range of development (although they include a number of countries "most seriously affected" by current economic problems). Their child population represents about two thirds of all the children in UNICEF-assisted countries. *Group III* –

countries which have reached a more advanced stage of development, but which still require outside assistance due to particular needs such as lack of trained personnel.

While UNICEF assistance is directed primarily towards long-range programmes for children in developing countries, it also moves swiftly to meet the immediate needs of children and mothers in emergencies arising from major natural disasters, civil strife or epidemics. In the early stages of an emergency, UNICEF provides relief in the form of children's food, medicines, vaccines, clothing, blankets and, when required, transport. This is followed by long-range rehabilitation operations of lasting impact.

The UN General Assembly resolution which proclaimed 1979 the International Year of the Child – dedicated to the well-being of all children in all countries – designated UNICEF as the "lead agency" of the United Nations system responsible for co-ordinating the activities of the Year.

Publ.: *UNICEF Annual Report; Facts about UNICEF* (annually); *State of the World's Children Report* (annually); *UNICEF News* (quarterly); *Les Carnets de l'Enfance; Assignment Children; Ideas Forum*.

Yearbook of the United Nations, 1946; *Everyone's United Nations*, pp. 200–203, New York, 1979; *The Europa Year Book 1984. A World Survey*, Vol. I, pp. 39–40, London, 1984.

UNIDIR. United Nations Institute for Disarmament Research, est. 1980 in Geneva. Publishes, since 1981, studies on disarmament in English, French and German; distributed through the Sales Section of the UN Office in Geneva.

UNIDO. One of the UN specialized agencies. United Nations Industrial Development Organization, est. with headquarters in Vienna by the ▷ UNIDO Resolution 1966. In 1975 the UN General Assembly decided that UNIDO be transformed into a specialized agency. The Constitution of UNIDO as a specialized agency of the UN system, opened for signature on Apr. 8, 1979 in Vienna, remained open in 1980 in New York; by Dec. 31, 1980, the Constitution had been signed by 97 countries. By 1982, the Constitution had been ratified by 80 States, thus paving the way for UNIDO to become one of the specialized agencies related to the United Nations when the 80 States have agreed, after consultations among themselves, that the Constitution shall enter into force.

On Dec. 13, 1985 after 120 ratifications (138 signatories) the constitution entered into force. In the elected Industrial Development Board the developing countries have 33 seats, Western industrialized countries 15, and socialist bloc countries 5.

On June 21, 1985 UNIDO became the 16th Specialized Agency of the United Nations.

UNIDO's primary objective, its Constitution stipulates, is the promotion of industrial development in developing countries with a view to assisting the establishment of a new international economic order. It will also promote industrial development and co-operation on global, regional, national and sectoral levels.

UNIDO shall, among other things, assist developing countries in establishing and operating industries; provide a forum and act as an instrument to serve developing and industrialized countries in their contacts, consultations and negotiations; and develop special measures designed to promote co-operation among developing countries and between the developed and developing countries.

UNIDO's principal organs are: the General Conference, which would meet every two years unless it decided otherwise; the IDB, consisting of 53

members (33 from developing countries, 15 from Western Industrialized countries and five from Eastern European socialist countries); and the secretariat, consisting of a Director-General, as well as such Deputy Director-Generals and other staff as the organization might require.

On 21 June the Secretary-General had been notified by the following 82 countries of their agreement that UNIDO's Constitution should enter into force:

Afghanistan, Algeria, Argentina, Australia, Austria, Barbados, Belgium, Bolivia, Brazil, Bulgaria, Byelorussian SSR, Cameroon, Canada, Cape Verde, Chile, China, Cuba, Cyprus, Czechoslovakia, Denmark, Dominican Republic, Ecuador, Egypt, Ethiopia, Finland, France, German Democratic Republic, Germany, Federal Republic of, Greece, Guatemala, Guinea, Guinea-Bissau, Honduras, India, Indonesia, Ireland, Israel, Italy, Ivory Coast, Jamaica, Japan, Kenya, Lesotho, Luxembourg, Madagascar, Malaysia, Malta, Mauritius, Mexico, Mongolia, Netherlands, Niger, Nigeria, Norway, Oman, Pakistan, Panama, Peru, Philippines, Poland, Portugal, Republic of Korea, Romania, Rwanda, Senegal, Spain, Sri Lanka, Sweden, Switzerland, Syrian Arab Republic, Thailand, Tunisia, Turkey, Ukranian SSR, USSR, United Kingdom, United Republic of Tanzania, United States, Uruguay, Venezuela, Yugoslavia, Zambia.

Members: members of the United Nations. Organization: Industrial Development Board, composed of 45 members, elected annually for three-year periods by the UN General Assembly; the Secretariat in Vienna and a network of Senior Industrial Development Field Advisers, reinforced with Junior Professional Officers, co-operating with 60 UNIDO National Committees. UNIDO information systems: Industrial and Technological Information Bank, UNID-INTIB and Industrial Information System, UNIDO-INDIS. Publ. *UNIDO Newsletter* (monthly), *Industrial Development Survey* (annually), *Guide to Information Sources* (bi-monthly), *Transfer of Technology Series*.

UN Yearbook, 1966, pp. 297–299 and 1102–1103; *UN Chronicle*, January, 1980, pp. 63–64 and February, 1983, p. 123; *Basic Facts About the United Nations*, New York, 1983; *The Europa Year Book 1984. A World Survey*, Vol. I, pp. 47–48, London, 1984.

UNIDO RESOLUTION, 1966. The United Nations Industrial Development Organization was established on Jan. 1, 1967 by UN General Assembly Res. 2152/XXI adopted on Nov. 17, 1966 by 109 votes to 0. The text of the Resolution with Annex reads as follows:

"The General Assembly,

Recognizing that the industrialization of developing countries is essential for their economic and social development and for the expansion and diversification of their trade,

Conscious of the fact that the acceleration of industrial development, especially in the developing countries, depends largely on the broadest international co-operation.

Considering the widespread desire for a comprehensive organization capable of intensifying, coordinating and expediting the efforts of the United Nations system in the field of industrial development,

Bearing in mind the need for special measures designed to give additional impetus to the industrialization of the less advanced of the developing countries,

Recalling its resolution 2089/XX of 20 December 1965, by which it established within the United Nations an autonomous organization for the promotion of industrial development,

Having considered the report of the Ad Hoc Committee on the United Nations Organization for Industrial Development,

I. Decides that the United Nations Industrial Development Organization (hereinafter referred to as the Organization), established as an organ of the General Assembly, shall function as an autonomous organization within the United Nations in accordance with the provisions set forth in section II below;

II. Purpose.

1. The purpose of the Organization shall be to promote industrial development, in accordance with Article 1, paragraph 3, and Articles 55 and 56 of the Charter of the United Nations, and by encouraging the mobilization of national and international resources to assist in, promote and accelerate the industrialization of the developing countries, with particular emphasis on the manufacturing sector.

Functions.

2. In the fulfilment of its purpose, the Organization shall undertake:

(a) Operational activities, including in particular:

(i) Encouragement and promotion of and making of recommendations for national, regional and international action to achieve more rapid industrialization of developing countries;

(ii) Contribution to the most effective application in the developing countries of modern industrial methods of production, programming and planning, taking into account the experience of States with different social and economic systems;

(iii) Building and strengthening of institutions and administration in the developing countries in the matter of industrial technology, production, programming and planning;

(iv) Dissemination of information on technological innovation originating in various countries and, for the developing countries, assistance in the implementation of practical measures for the application of such information, the adaptation of existing technology and the development of new technology especially suited to the particular physical, social and economic conditions of developing countries through the establishment and improvement, inter alia, of technological research centres in these countries;

(v) Assistance, at the request of Governments of developing countries, in the formulation of industrial development programs and in the preparation of specific industrial projects, including, as necessary, technical and economic feasibility studies;

(vi) Co-operation with regional economic commissions and the United Nations Economic and Social Office in Beirut in assisting the regional planning of industrial development of developing countries within the framework of regional and sub-regional economic groupings among those countries, where such groupings exist;

(vii) Making recommendations, in connexion with the objectives stated under (vi) above, for special measures for adapting and co-ordinating the measures adopted so that, in particular, the less advanced of the developing countries will receive a strong impetus to their growth;

(viii) Offering advice and guidance, in close co-operation with the appropriate bodies of the United Nations, the specialized agencies and the International Atomic Energy Agency, on problems relating to the exploitation and efficient use of natural resources, industrial raw materials, by-products and new products of developing countries, with a view to increasing their industrial productivity and contributing to the diversification of their economies;

(ix) Assistance to the developing countries in the training of technical and other appropriate categories of personnel needed for their accelerated industrial development in co-operation with the specialized agencies concerned, in conformity with the principles of collaboration and co-ordination set forth in paragraphs 33 and 34 below;

(x) Proposing, in co-operation with the international bodies or inter-governmental regional bodies concerned with industrial property, measures for the improvement of the international system of industrial property, with a view to accelerating the transfer of technical know-how to developing countries and to strengthening the role of patents consistent with national interests as an incentive to industrial innovations;

(xi) Assistance, at the request of Governments of developing countries, in obtaining external financing for specific industrial projects, by giving guidance in the preparation of requests, by providing information on the terms and conditions of the various financing agencies and by advising the financing agencies on the technical and economic soundness of the projects submitted for financing;

(b) Action-oriented studies and research programs designed especially to facilitate the activities outlined in sub-paragraph (a) above, including in particular the compilation, analysis, publication and dissemination of information concerning various aspects of the process of industrialization, such as industrial technology, investment, financing, production, management techniques, programming and planning.

Industrial Development Board.

Composition.

3. The Industrial Development Board (hereinafter referred to as the Board), established as the principal organ of the Organization, shall consist of forty-five members, elected by the General Assembly from among States Members of the United Nations and members of the specialized agencies and of the International Atomic Energy Agency for a term of three years, provided, however, that of the members elected at the first election the terms of fifteen members shall expire at the end of one year and the terms of fifteen other members at the end of two years.

4. In electing the members of the Board, the General Assembly shall have due regard to the principle of equitable geographical representation and shall accordingly observe the following distribution of seats:

(a) Eighteen from the States listed in part A of the annex to the present resolution;

(b) Fifteen from the States listed in part B of the annex;

(c) Seven from the States listed in part C of the annex;

(d) Five from the States listed in part D of the annex.

The List of States contained in the annex shall be reviewed by the Board in the light of changes in the membership of the United Nations or of the specialized agencies or of the International Atomic Energy Agency.

5. Retiring members shall be eligible for immediate re-election.

6. Each member of the Board shall have one representative with such alternates and advisers as may be required.

Functions and powers.

7. The principal functions and powers of the Board shall be:

(a) To formulate principles and policies to achieve the purpose of the Organization;

(b) To make proposals for putting those principles and policies into effect and to take such other steps within its competence as may be conducive to this end;

(c) To initiate such other action as may be necessary and appropriate to the fulfilment of the purpose of the Organization;

(e) To review and facilitate the coordination of activities within the United Nations system in the field of industrial development;

(f) To exercise control over the effective utilization of resources available to the Organization;

(g) To keep the activities of the Organization under review and to request its Executive Director to prepare such reports, studies and other documents as it may deem appropriate;

(h) To report annually to the General Assembly through the Economic and Social Council; the Council may transmit to the Organization and to the General Assembly such comments on the report as it may deem necessary.

Voting.

8. Each member of the Board shall have one vote.

9. Decisions of the Board shall be taken by a simple majority of the members present and voting.

Procedures.

10. The Board shall adopt its own rules of procedure.

11. The Board shall meet as required in accordance with its rules. It shall normally hold one regular session a year.

12. The Board shall elect its President, three Vice-Presidents and a Rapporteur to hold office for a period of one year. In electing its officers, it shall pay due regard to the principle of equitable geographical representation.

13. The Board may invite any State Member of the United Nations or member of a specialized agency or of the International Atomic Energy to participate, without a vote, in its deliberations on any matter of particular concern to that State.

Subsidiary organs.

14. The Board may establish such subsidiary organs on a permanent or ad hoc basis as may be necessary for the effective discharge of its functions, including, as

required, expert groups to consider specific problems and to make recommendations.

15. The Board shall determine the terms of reference and rules of procedure of its subsidiary organs.

16. In electing the members of its subsidiary organs, the Board may include any State Member of the United Nations or member of a specialized agency or of the International Atomic Energy Agency, whether or not that State is represented on the Board.

Secretariat.

17. The Organization shall have an adequate permanent and full-time secretariat, which will be appointed in accordance with Article 101 of the Charter of the United Nations, and which will avail itself of the other appropriate facilities of the Secretariat of the United Nations.

18. The secretariat shall be headed by the Executive Director, who shall be appointed by the Secretary-General of the United Nations and whose appointment shall be confirmed by the General Assembly. He shall be appointed for four years and shall be eligible for re-appointment.

19. The Executive Director shall have over-all responsibility for the administrative and research activities of the Organization. He shall also be responsible for all operational activities of the Organization, including activities executed by the Organization as a participating organization of the United Nations Development Program. He shall make arrangements for meetings of the Board and shall prepare such reports, studies or other documents as may be necessary for the functioning of the Board and its subsidiary organs and shall perform such other functions as may be entrusted to him by the Board.

Financial arrangements.

20. The expenditure of the Organization shall be classified under the following categories:

(a) Expenses for administrative and research activities;

(b) Expenses for operational activities.

21. Expenses for administrative and research activities shall be borne by the regular budget of the United Nations, which shall include a separate budgetary provision for such expenses.

22. Expenses for operational activities shall be met:

(a) From the voluntary contributions made to the Organization, in cash or in kind, by Governments of the States Members of the United Nations, members of the specialized agencies and of the International Atomic Energy Agency;

(b) Through participation in the United Nations Development Program on the same basis as other participating organizations;

(c) By the utilization of the appropriate resources of the United Nations regular program of technical assistance.

23. Voluntary contributions to the Organization for its operational activities under paragraph 22 (a) above may be made, at the option of the Governments, either:

(a) Through announcement at a pledging conference to be convened by the Secretary-General of the United Nations on the recommendation of the Board; or

(b) In accordance with regulations 7.2 and 7.3 of the Financial Regulations of the United Nations; or

(c) By both of these methods.

24. The voluntary contributions referred to in paragraph 22

(a) above shall be governed by the Financial Regulations of the United Nations, except for such modifications as may be approved by the General Assembly on the recommendation of the Board.

25. Disbursement of the funds referred to in paragraph 22 (b) above shall be for purposes consistent with the policies, aims and functions of the Organization, including such policies and programmes as may be established by the Board, and shall be made by the Secretary-General of the United Nations in consultation with the Executive Director of the Organization.

26. All States Members of the United Nations, members of the specialized agencies and of the International Atomic Energy Agency, and in particular the industrially advanced countries, when considering contributions for the operational activities of the Organization under paragraph 22 (a) above, are urged to bear in mind the pressing need for the industrial development of the developing countries.

Coordination and co-operation with United Nations bodies and other organizations.

27. The Organization shall play the central role in and be responsible for reviewing and promoting the coordination of all activities of the United Nations system in the field of industrial development.

28. In its relations with organs and agencies within the United Nations system, the Board shall act in conformity with the responsibilities of the Economic and Social Council under the Charter of the United Nations, particularly those of coordination, and with the relationship agreements with the agencies concerned.

29. There shall be a close and continuous working relationship between the Organization and the United Nations Conference on Trade and Development, in accordance with the general principle that the former shall be competent to deal with the general and technical problems of industrialization, including the establishment and expansion of industries in developing countries, and the latter with the foreign trade aspects of industrialization, including the expansion and diversification of exports of manufactures and semi-manufactures by developing countries.

30. The Organization shall establish a close and continuous working relationship with the regional economic commissions and the United Nations Economic and Social Office in Beirut.

31. The Organization shall be a participating agency in the United Nations Development Program and there shall be close co-operation and coordination between the Organization and the United Nations Development Program. The Executive Director shall be a member of the Inter-Agency Consultative Board of the United Nations Development Program.

32. Adequate arrangements shall be made by the Secretary-General of the United Nations for close co-operation and coordination between the secretariat of the Organization and the other departments of the United Nations Secretariat.

33. The Organization shall exercise its functions, when appropriate, in close co-operation with the specialized agencies concerned and the International Atomic Energy Agency.

34. The coordination between the Organization and the specialized agencies concerned and the International Atomic Energy Agency shall be carried out at the inter-governmental level by the Board. Adequate arrangements shall also be made by the Secretary-General of the United Nations for such coordination at the secretariat level.

35. The Organization may establish appropriate working relationships with relevant inter-governmental organizations.

36. The Organization may, when it considers it appropriate, establish a working relationship with international non-governmental organizations concerned with the promotion of industrial development.

Future institutional arrangements.

37. The General Assembly shall review, in the light of experience, the effectiveness and further evolution of these institutional arrangements, with a view to deciding upon such changes and improvements as might be necessary in order to meet fully the growing needs in the field of industrial development.

Transitional arrangements.

38. The provisions approved by the General Assembly under the appropriate sections of the budget for the activities of the Centre for Industrial Development shall be transferred to the Organization.

39. The post of Commissioner for Industrial Development shall be abolished.

40. The Secretary-General of the United Nations, in establishing the secretariat of the Organization under paragraph 17 above, shall make arrangements, in consultation with the Executive Director:

(a) To transfer to the secretariat of the Organization such of the existing staff of the Center for Industrial Development as is appropriate to the functions of the Organization;

(b) To transfer to the secretariat of the Organization the staff at present servicing the operational activities of the Center for Industrial Development for which the Organization will assume full operational responsibility;

(c) To recruit such additional staff as may be required to fill the existing posts in the establishment for the purpose of industrial development.

41. After the adoption of the present resolution, the Economic and Social Council is requested to abolish the Committee for Industrial Development.

42. The Executive Director shall submit to the Board at its first session a report on the activities so far carried out by the United Nations system in the field of industrial development and proposals for a work program for the Organization, by sectors and areas of activities.

Annex. A. *List of States indicated in section II, paragraph 4 (a):*

Afghanistan
Algeria
Botswana
Burma
Burundi
Cambodia
Cameroon
Central African Republic
Ceylon
Chad
China
Congo (Brazzaville)
Congo (Democratic Republic of)
Dahomey
Ethiopia
Gabon
Gambia
Ghana
Guinea
India
Indonesia
Iran
Iraq
Israel
Ivory Coast
Jordan
Kenya
Kuwait
Laos
Lebanon
Lesotho
Liberia
Libya
Madagascar
Malawi
Malaysia
Maldive Islands
Mali
Mauritania
Mongolia
Morocco
Nepal
Niger
Nigeria
Pakistan
Philippines
Republic of Korea
Republic of Vietnam
Rwanda
Saudi Arabia
Senegal
Sierra Leone
Singapore
Somalia
South Africa
Sudan
Syria
Thailand
Togo
Tunisia
Uganda
United Arab Republic
United Republic of Tanzania
Upper Volta
Western Samoa
Yemen
Yugoslavia
Zambia

B. *List of States indicated in section II, paragraph 4 (b):*

Australia
Austria
Belgium
Canada
Cyprus
Denmark
Federal Republic of Germany
Finland
France
Greece
Holy See
Iceland
Ireland
Italy
Japan
Liechtenstein
Luxembourg
Malta
Monaco
Netherlands
New Zealand
Norway
Portugal
San Marino
Spain
Sweden
Switzerland
Turkey
United Kingdom of Great Britain and Northern Ireland
United States of America

C. *List of States indicated in section II, paragraph 4 (c):*

Argentina
Bolivia
Brazil
Chile
Colombia
Costa Rica
Cuba
Dominican Republic
Ecuador
El Salvador
Guatemala
Guyana
Haiti
Honduras
Jamaica
Nicaragua
Panama
Paraguay
Peru
Trinidad and Tobago
Uruguay
Venezuela

D. *List of States indicated in section II, paragraph 4 (d):*

Albania
Bulgaria
Byelorussian Soviet Socialist Republic
Czechoslovakia
Hungary
Poland
Romania
Ukrainian Soviet Socialist Republic
Union of Soviet Socialist Republics

UN Yearbook, 1966, pp. 302–307.

UNIFICATION OF INTERNATIONAL STANDARDS. An intergovernmental codification, dealt with by metrology (▷ metric system) and international ▷ standardization.

Union, League and Permanent Confederation Treaty, 1826

UNIFIL. United Nations Interim Force in Lebanon. On Mar. 15, 1978, following a Palestinian raid in Israel, Israeli forces invaded southern Lebanon. On Mar. 19 the Security Council adopted Res. 425, 1978 in which it called upon Israel immediately to cease its military action against Lebanese territory. It also decided to establish immediately under its authority the UNIFIL for the purpose of confirming withdrawal of Israeli forces, restoring international peace and security and assisting the Government of Lebanon in ensuring the return of its effective authority in the area. The mandate of UNIFIL, which was initially set up for a period of six months, has been extended as necessary by the Security Council.

At the end of May 1980, the Force comprised 5917 troops: from Fiji (865), France (668), Ghana (865), Ireland (672), Italy (34), Netherlands (816), Nigeria (700), Norway (952) and Senegal (577). On February 25, 1982 the Security Council decided on a 1000-man increase stating that the Force was seriously over-strained.

On Sept. 22, 1986, 132 soldiers in the Force had died in the line of duty. The Security Council on Sept. 23, 1986 condemned in the 'strongest terms' the attacks committed against the UNIFIL.

UN Yearbook, 1978; *UN Chronicle*, February, 1979, pp. 20–25 and April, 1982, pp. 13–19; *UN Chronicle*, November, 1986, pp. 58–64.

UNIFORM CHARTER, standard contracts concerning overseas freight of commodities; blank contracts are prepared by competent international organizations. One of the first blanks concerning naval transportation of coal was prepared by the International Baltic Conference (in full: the Baltic International Maritime Coal Charter Conference – Baltcon) in 1921. In 1972 the International Maritime Uniform Charter Conference – Gencon, held in Genoa, prepared patterns of contracts on shipment of i.a. sugar, salt, ore, cereals, scrap, artificial fertilizers. In 1926 the Baltic Wood Charter – Baltwood agreement was signed.

K. RORDAM, *Treaties on the Baltcon Charter Parties*, Copenhagen, 1950; J. BES, *Chartering Practice, Analyses of Charter Parties*, Amsterdam, 1960.

UN IMMUNITIES AND PRIVILEGES, subject of Convention adopted by the UN General Assembly Feb. 13, 1946:

"The UN shall possess juridical personality. It shall have the capacity: (a) To contract; (b) To acquire and dispose of immovable and movable property; (c) To institute legal proceedings" (Art. I).

"The UN, its property and assets wherever located and by whomsoever held, shall enjoy immunity from every form of legal process except insofar as in any particular case it has expressly waived its immunity ..." (Art. II).

Art. IV Lists all privileges.

UNTS, Vol. I, pp. 15–33.

UN INCOMES. The main source of UN incomes are membership fees varying as to the amount (▷ UN Members Contributions Scale, 1989–1990). Other sources of income, apart from the fees, are modest: *c*. 20 million dollars, two thirds of which are taxes paid by UN personnel. Other sources: stamps (*c*. 2 million US dollars), interest rates on capital and return on services rendered to other institutions; small amounts come from UN publications, the restaurant and sightseeing of the UN Headquarters.

UN INFORMATION CENTRES. Official name of *c*. 60 centres of the UN organized by the UN Department of Public Information and located in UN member states.

UN INFORMATION COMMITTEE. ▷ UN Committee on Information.

UN INFORMATION OFFICE. The office est. 1940 in New York to publicize allied war aims of the United Nations, initially called Inter-Allied Information Center, from Jan. 1, 1942 to fall 1945 under its new name. In its last year the Office concentrated on work in preparation for the creation of the UN and became its first publicity agency: integrated by the UN 1946 under the name, UN Department of Public Information.

UN INFORMATION SYSTEM. ▷ Information UN System.

UN INFORMATION SYSTEMS AND SERVICES DIRECTORY. A guide to UN libraries, bibliographic services, referral centers and other data collections prepared by the UN Inter-Organization Board for Information Systems, published 1978.

UN INTERIM COMMITTEE. One of the Standing Committees of the ▷ ECOSOC.

UN INTERNATIONAL LAW COMMISSION. The Commission was est. under Art. 13 of the UN Charter on Nov. 21, 1947 to promote "gradual development of international law" through "drawing up agreements in matters not yet determined by international law or with respect to which international law has not been developed sufficiently" and to codify international law. One of the standing bodies of the UN General Assembly. The Commission meets annually in Geneva and is composed of 25 members who serve in their individual capacity as experts in international law. They are elected by the UN General Assembly for five-year terms in a manner so as to reflect the main forms of civilization and the principal legal systems of the world.

The Commission has prepared drafts on a number of topics of international law, some chosen by the Commission and others referred to it by the UN General Assembly or the ECOSOC. Most of its work has taken the form of draft articles on the basis of which international conferences of plenipotentiaries convened by the General Assembly have adopted Conventions and opened them for States to become Parties thereto. Drafts prepared by the Commission include: draft Declaration on the Rights and Duties of States (prepared in 1949); ways and means for making the evidence of customary international law more readily available; formulation of the Nuremberg Principles (1950); question of international criminal jurisdiction; reservations to multilateral conventions; question of defining aggression in the draft Code of Offences against the Peace and Security of Mankind (1954); model rules of arbitral procedure (1958); in 1958 a United Nations conference approved four Conventions on the law of the sea, all of which are now in force. These are the Convention on the High Seas, the Convention on the Territorial Sea and Contiguous Zone, the Convention on Fishing and Convention of the Living Resources of the High Seas, and the Convention on the Continental Shelf.

In 1961, a Conference approved a Convention on the Reduction of Statelessness. Two conferences, held in Vienna in 1961 and 1963, respectively, approved the Vienna Convention on Diplomatic Relations and the Vienna Convention on Consular Relations. Both Conventions are now in force. A conference which held two sessions in Vienna in 1968 and 1969 approved a Convention on the Law of Treaties.

The draft articles prepared by the Commission on Special Missions and on the Prevention and Punishment of Crimes against Internationally Protected Persons, including Diplomatic Agents, however, were not referred to an international conference but were considered directly by the UN General Assembly, which adopted Conventions on those subjects in 1969 and 1973, respectively. In 1975 a conference held in Vienna approved the Vienna Conventions on the Representation of States in their Relations with International Organizations of a Universal Character and Succession of States in Respect of Treaties (1977).

UN International Law Commission, New York, 1967.

UN INTERNATIONAL LOTTERY. Name of a project passed Dec. 16, 1972 by the Administrative and Budgetary Committee of the UN General Assembly to draw up a plan of the UN International Lottery by the UN Secretariat. The Lottery's profits would contribute partly to overcoming the constant financial shortages of the UN. The project was not put into effect.

UN INTERNATIONAL OFFICE FOR DEATH CERTIFICATES. The Office est. by the UN General Assembly in 1952 with the task of recording deaths of persons during war, migrations, or natural calamities. Seat: UN Secretariat, New York.

UN Yearbook, 1952.

UN INTERNATIONAL SCHOOL. A school for children of UN delegates and international UN staff, founded in 1947 in Lake Success near New York; since the fall of 1961 in New York City in three different locations in Manhattan. On Dec. 21, 1965, the UN General Assembly (Res. 2123/XX) authorized acceptance of the offer of the City of New York of a site for school construction on the East River at 25th Street. The School, completed in 1972 by means of a $7.5-million grant from the Ford Foundation, had in 1977 an enrollment of over 1400 pupils from 103 countries.

UN Yearbook, 1965.

UN INTERVENTION. A term used to describe UN joint action called for by the Security Council "necessary to maintain or restore international peace and security" under Chapter VII of the UN Charter: "Action with respect to threats to the peace, breaches of the peace, and acts of aggression."

UN INVESTMENT COMMITTEE. One of the Standing Committees of the ▷ ECOSOC.

UNION CARBIDE. A US pesticide company in Charleston, W.Va., which built in the 1970's a factory in Bhopal, the capital of Madhya Pradesh state of India, under the name Union Carbide Chemical Plant. The Indian company was set up with 51 percent of ownership by Union Carbide and 49 percent in private hands of Indian companies or individuals. On Dec. 8, 1984 a poison gas leak (of phosgen type) from the factory killed over 3,000 Bhopal inhabitants, the majority of them children and youths and injured over 100,000 "in the worst industrial accident in history."

Newsweek, December 17, 1984, pp. 10–20.

UNION, LEAGUE AND PERMANENT CONFEDERATION TREATY, 1826. Spanish Tratado de Union, Liga y Confederacion Permanente, elaborated by the American Assembly in Panama and concluded there on July 15, 1826 by the heads of governments of Greater Colombia, Republic of Central America, Peru and Mexico.

It never came into force since it was ratified by only one government, Greater Colombia. Formulated by S. Bolivar, it was the essential document of pan-Latin-Americanism. The treaty was, in essence, an anti-Spanish defense alliance (arts. 1–22), but it also introduced joint political and economic consultations and obligated all member countries to a "full ban on, and strict fight against, slave trade from Africa."

A. DE LA PENA Y REYES, *El Congreso de Panamá y Algunos otros Proyectos de Unión Hispano-Americana*, México, DF, 1926; J.M. YEPES, *Del Congreso de Panamá a la Conferencia de Caracas, 1826–1954*, Caracas, 1955, Vol. 6, pp. 81–136; E.J. OSMAŃCZYK, *Enciclopedia Mundial de Relaciones Internacionales y de la ONU*, México, DF, 1976, pp. 1057–1060 (the full text in Spanish).

UNION OF INTERNATIONAL ASSOCIATIONS. ▷ UIA.

UNION OF SOUTH AFRICA. From 1910 until 1961 name of the Republic of South Africa. ▷ South Africa.

UNION OF SOVIET SOCIALIST REPUBLICS, USSR. Member of the UN. Permanent Member of the UN Security Council. The largest state in the world, including the eastern part of Europe (25% of the territory of the USSR) and part of Asia (75% of the territory). Area: 22,402,200 sq. km. Soviet population 1988 est. 284 million; growth of census population: 1913 – 159,000,000; 1940 – 194,000,000; 1959 – 208,000,000; 1970 – 241,000,000; the population exceeded 250,000,000 in Aug., 1973. Borders with 12 states: in the west – with Norway, Finland, Poland, Czechoslovakia, Hungary, Romania; in the south – with Turkey, Iran, Afghanistan, China, Mongolia and Korea. The total length of the frontiers of the USSR is 60,000 km, of which two-thirds are coastline and one-third land frontiers, the longest with China 7500 km. The delimitation of frontiers occurred at various times with all of the neighbors with the exception of China, with whom the delimitation of frontiers was taken up by both sides in 1924, 1926, 1964 and since Sept., 1969 (not concluded by 1985). Capital: Moscow with 8,203,000 inhabitants in 1981. Official language of the USSR: Russian; in particular republics, districts and autonomous regions, the local language and Russian. GNP per capita 1980: US $4550. Currency: one rouble = 100 kopecks. National Day: Nov. 7, anniversary of the October Revolution, 1917. Original Member of the UN, and of specialized agencies with exception of GATT, IDA, IFAD, FAO, IBRD, IFC, IMF. Member of CMEA and the Warsaw Pact.

International relations: the October Socialist Revolution began on Nov. 7, 1917 in Russia. The Declaration on the formation of the Union of Soviet Socialist Republics was adopted in Moscow on Dec. 30, 1922 at the First Congress of the Soviets of the USSR. The USSR began diplomatic activity with the normalization of its relations with its European and South Asian neighbors in 1920/21:
Feb. 2, 1920 Tartu Treaty with Estonia;
July 12, 1920 Riga Treaty with Latvia;
Oct. 14, 1920 Tartu Treaty with Finland;
Feb. 26, 1921 Moscow Treaty with Persia;
March 16, 1921 Treaty of Friendship with Turkey, extended on Oct. 18, 1921 to Azerbaidzhan, Armenia and Georgia;
March 18, 1921 Riga Treaty with Poland;
The first international conference in which the USSR participated was the Geneva Conference (Apr.–May, 1922). The diplomatic boycott was breached by

the establishment of relations with Germany and the signing of the ▷ Rapallo Treaty with that state on Apr. 16, 1922 (expanded by the Berlin Treaty of Apr. 24, 1926); in the next period, up to 1924, diplomatic relations with Great Britain, Italy, Austria, Norway, Sweden, Denmark and France; and in Peking on May 31, 1924 a Treaty on the General Principles for Settling Disputed Issues between the USSR and China, supplemented on Sept. 20, 1924 by the Mukden Treaty on implementation of the Peking resolutions (and on Dec. 22, 1929 the Khabarovsk Treaty on the Eastern Chinese Railroad).

After this normalization in the period 1920–24, the USSR successively concluded the following treaties:
1925 – a Treaty on the establishment of diplomatic relations with Japan;
1925, Dec. 7 – a treaty of friendship and neutrality with Turkey, extended on Nov. 7, 1935 for 10 years;
1926, Apr. 24 – the Berlin Treaty with Germany, extended without limit by the Protocol of June 24, 1931;
1926, Sept. 28 – a Treaty of Non-aggression with Lithuania, extended by the Prolongation Protocol of Apr. 4, 1933 to Dec. 31, 1945;
1927, Oct. 1 – a Treaty on the Guarantee of Neutrality with Persia;
1931, Apr. 24 – a Treaty of Neutrality and Non-aggression with Afghanistan;
1932, May 21 – a Treaty of Non-aggression and Peaceful Settlement of Disputes with Finland; extended on Apr. 7, 1934 to Dec. 31, 1945;
1932, Feb. 4 – a Pact of Non-aggression with Estonia, extended on Apr. 4, 1934 with a validity to Dec. 31, 1945;
1932, July 25 – a Pact of Non-aggression with Poland;
1932, Nov. 29 – a Pact of Non-aggression with France;
1933, Sept. 2 – a Pact of Friendship, Non-aggression and Neutrality with Italy;
1934 – the USSR joined the League of Nations;
1935, May 2 – a Treaty on Mutual Assistance with France;
1935, May 16 – a Treaty on Mutual Assistance with Czechoslovakia;
1937, Aug. 21 – a Treaty of Non-aggression with China.

On Aug. 29, 1939 the USSR signed a non-aggression pact with Germany. Following the Nazi aggression on June 21, 1941, the USSR entered the great coalition of United Nations. After World War II a founding member of the UN on Oct. 24, 1945 and a permanent member of the Security Council. The political heads of the Soviet Union 1917–90:

Vladimir I. Lenin	1917–24
Joseph V. Stalin	1924–53
Nikita S. Khrushchev	1953–64
Leonid I. Brezhnev	1964–82
Juriy V. Andropov	1982–84
Konstantin U. Chernenko	1984–85
M.S. Gorbachev	1985–

After World War II the USSR signed the Potsdam Agreement on Aug. 2, 1945, the Paris Treaties, 1947, with Italy, Romania, Hungary, Bulgaria and Finland, and treaties of alliance with Czechoslovakia (1943), Yugoslavia (1945), Poland (1945) and in 1948 with Hungary, Bulgaria, Romania and Finland. On Oct. 7, 1949, the GDR was proclaimed in the Soviet occupation zone. An alliance treaty USSR-GDR was signed on June 12, 1964. In 1948 the USSR denounced the 1945 Treaty with Yugoslavia. On Oct. 2, 1949 the USSR broke off relations with the Chiang-Kai-shek Nationalist Government of China and recognized the Mao Tse-tung Communist Government. The death of Stalin on March 5, 1953 changed in the following years the relations with Yugoslavia. In Apr. 1954 the USSR joined

UNESCO. On May 1955 the USSR together with France, the UK and the USA signed the Austria Treaty. In Aug. 1970 the USSR signed a non-aggression treaty with the FRG, in Aug. 1971 a friendship treaty with India. Other treaties of the USSR with Afghanistan, Albania, Bulgaria, China, Cuba, Czechoslovakia, Egypt, Ethiopia, GDR, Hungary, Korea North, Mongolia, Poland, Romania, Vietnam.

On March 7, 1986 the USA demanded that the USSR reduce the number of the Soviet Byelorussan, and Ukranian Missions personnel from 275 to 170 by April 1, 1988.

On April 29, 1986 the USA and USSR resumed commercial air links, cancelled in Dec. 1981, after the imposition of martial law in Poland.

The USSR on October 15, 1987 announced that it would pay all its outstanding debts to the UN including debts for regular budget ($28 million) and for peacekeeping operations (UNIFIL $172 million and Golan Heights and Sinai $25 millions), $225 million altogether. In the late 1980's the USSR, like the USA, continued developing its nuclear weapons system concurrently with the first disarmament agreements and further negotiations on nuclear and conventional weapons.

See also ▷ Armenia; ▷ Azerbaidzhan; ▷ Estonia; ▷ Latvia; ▷ Lithuania; ▷ Nagorno-Karabakh.

SOVIETISCHE AKADEMIE DER WISSENSCHAFTEN *Geschichte der Völker der Sowjetunion*, Basel, 1945; *Bolshaya Sovietskaya Entsiklopedia*, 65 Vols., Moscow, 1926–47; 2nd ed. 51 Vols., Moscow, 1949–58; W.P. and Z.H. COATES, *A History of Anglo–Soviet Relations*, 2 Vols., London, 1944–55; M. BELOFF, *The Foreign Policy of Soviet Russia 1929–1941*, 2 Vols., Oxford, 1947–49; *Documents on Soviet Foreign Policy 1917–1941*, 3 Vols., London, 1950; J.V. STALIN, *Collected Works*, 13 Vols., London, 1952–55; L. SHAPIRO ed., *Soviet Treaty Series. A Collection of Bilateral Treaties, Agreements and Conventions, etc Concluded Between the Soviet Union and Foreign Powers*, Vol. I, 1917–1928, Vol. II, 1929–1939, Washington, DC., 1950–55; G.F. KENNAN, *Soviet–American Relations 1917–1920*, 2 Vols., Princeton, 1956–58; P. DALLIN, *German Rule in Russia 1941–1945*, London, 1957; E.H. CARR, *The Bolshevik Revolution*, 14 Vols., London, 1951–78; R.M. SCHLUSSER, J.F. TRISKA, *A Calendar of Soviet Treaties, 1917–1957*, Stanford, 1959; *SSSR i Arabskie Strany 1947–1960*, Moskva, 1960; W.G. TRUCHANOWSKI, *Istoria Mezhdunarodnyi Otnosheni Vneshney Politiki SSSR, 1917–1939*, Moscow, 1961; *SSSR i Strany Afriki 1946–1962*, Moskva, 1963; V. TURAIEV, *Sovietsko–Amerikanskie Otnoshenia 1917–1939*, Moscow, 1964; *Velikaya Otiechestviennaya Voina Sovietskogo Soyuza*, Moscow, 1965; A. GROMYKO, P. PONOMARIOV, *Istoria Vnieshney Politiki SSSR*, Vol. I, 1917–45, Moscow, 1966; *Vielikaia Oktiabrska Revolutsya*, Moscow, 1968; A.F. GONCHAROV (ed.), *Istoria Gosudarstva i Prava SSSR*. *Sbornik dokumentov*, Moscow, 1968; V.I. LENIN, *Collected Works*, 45 Vols., London, 1960–70; M. MENDELSOHN, *Banking in Russia*, New York, 1970; A. GROMYKO, B.N. PONOMARIOV, *Istoria Vnieshney Politiki SSSR*, Vol. 2., 1945–70, Moscow, 1971; *Sovietsko-Afganskie Otnoshenia 1919–1969*, Moskva, 1971; E.J.M. FELDBRUGGE, *Encyclopedia of Soviet Law*, 2 Vols., Leiden, 1973; *Sovietsko-Czekhoslovatskie Otnoshenia 1945–1971*, 2 Vols., Moskva, 1973; *Sovietski Soyuz-Narodnaia Polsha 1944–1974*, Moskva, 1974; *SSSR-Vengersko Otnoshenia 1948–1976*, 2 Vols., Moskva, 1978; G. GINSBURG, C.F. PINKELE, *The Sino-Soviet Territorial Dispute 1949–1964*, New York, 1978; *Sovietskiy Soyuz na mezhdunarodnikh konfierentsyakh pieroda Vielikoy Otiechestviennoy Voyni, 1941–1945. Sbornik Dokumientov*, 4 Vols., Moscow, 1978; L.I. BREZHNEV, *Selected Works*, Oxford, 1979; A. THOMPSON, *Russia/USSR. A Selective Annotated Bibliography of Books in English*, Oxford, 1979; V. SIVACHEV, N.N. YAKOVLEV, *Russia and the United States: US–Soviet Relations from the Soviet Point of View*, Chicago, 1979; McCAVLEY, *The Soviet Union Since 1917*, London, 1981; G. GINSHARGS, R.M. SCHLUSSER, *A Calen-*

dar of Soviet Treaties 1958–73, Alphen, 1981; B. NYGREN, D. LAVERY, Co-operation Between the Soviet Union and Three Western Great Powers 1950–1975, Stockholm, 1981; R.H. McNEAL ed., Resolutions and Decisions of the Communist Party of the Soviet Union, 5 Vols., Toronto, 1974–1982; A. BROWN, J. FENNELL, M. KASER, H.T. WILLETS (eds.), The Cambridge Encyclopedia of Russia and the Soviet Union, Cambridge, 1982; Narodnoye Khoziaistwo SSSR, 1922–1982, Moscow, 1982; R.A. CLARKE, D.J.I. MATKO (eds.), Soviet Economic Facts 1917–1980, London, 1983; R.G. JENSEN, TH. SHABAD, A.W. WRIGHT (eds.), Soviet Natural Resources in the World Economy, Chicago, 1983; R. WIXMAN, Peoples of Russia and the USSR. An Ethnographic Handbook, London, 1984; The Europa Year Book 1984. A World Survey, Vol. I, pp. 866–936, London, 1984; O. BERNER, Sovyet och Norden, The Soviet Union and the Nordic Countries, Stockholm, Boston, 1985; J. HASLAM, Soviet Foreign Policy, 4 Vols. (1930–1945). London 1980–87; M. KATZ, Russian and Arabia, Baltimore, 1986; R.D. LAIRD, B.A. LAIRD, A Soviet Lexicon: Important Terms, Concepts and Phrases; R.H. SOLOMON, M. KOSAKA eds., The Soviet Far East Military Buildup: Nuclear Dilemma and Asian Security, Dover, Mass., 1986; M.J. BERRY, Science and Technology in the USSR, London, 1987; M. GORBACHEV, Perestroika, New Thinking for our Country and the World, New York, 1987; G. SCHÖPFLIN, ed., The Soviet Union and Eastern Europe, London, 1987; SIPRI Yearbook, 1987, Oxford, 1988, pp. 16–24.

UNION RIGHTS. A subject of international conventions; prepared at the request of the UN General Assembly in 1947; the first of these was the Freedom of Association Convention and the Right to Organize (by the working class) of 1949; the next was the Right to Organize and Collective Bargaining Convention. In Jan., 1955 the UN Human Rights Commission established the Group of Experts on labor and union rights to observe the application of Union Rights by UN member states.

UNIPOM. Acronym of United Nations India-Pakistan Observation Mission. ▷ Jammu and Kashmir.

UNISIST. United Nations International System of Information on Science and Technology, elaborated under the aegis of UNESCO and ICSU by the First Intergovernmental UNISIST Conference, Oct. 4–9, 1971 in Paris. Program for a ▷ World Science Information System.

UNISPACE. United Nations Conference on the Exploration and Peaceful Uses of Outer Space. The Second Conference was held in August, 1982 in Vienna.

R. CHIPMAN, The World in Space. A Survey of Space Activities and Issues. Prepared for Unispace 82, Englewood Cliffs, N.J., 1982; UN Chronicle, July, 1982, pp. 49–64, and October., 1982, pp. 28–32.

UNITAR. United Nations Institute for Training and Research, est. Dec. 11, 1963 by virtue of UN General Assembly Res. 1934/VII as an autonomous institution within the framework of the UN. Its training and research activities since Jan. 1, 1965 are designed to enhance "the effectiveness of the UN in achieving the major object of the Organization. Since 1975, special emphasis placed on issues relating to the ▷ New International Economic Order. Financed by voluntary contributions and/or grants from governments, intergovernmental organizations and non-governmental sources. Headquarters, New York. Organization: Board of Trustees, composed of 24 members appointed by the UN Secretary-General for three-year period; Executive Director appointed by the Secretary-General. The Institute organizes seminars for delegates to the UN

and publishes many studies. A special programme since 1975 is a Project on the Future for the continuous examination of major trends and developments having implications for the future of mankind which may require responses from the United Nations system.
Publ.: UNITAR News (annually) and Important for the Future (quarterly).

Everyone's United Nations, pp. 146–148, New York, 1979; The Europa Year Book 1984. A World Survey, Vol. I, p 49, London, 1984.

UNITARIANS. One of the Protestant groups of Christian religions, disavowing the Trinity dogma; organized in 1813 by the British and Foreign Unitarian Association. In 1900 the first International Council of Unitarian and other Liberal Religious Thinkers and Workers was established, transformed in 1930 into the International Association for Religious Freedom and Liberal Christianity, IARF, with headquarters in The Hague; registered with the UN since 1946 and has advisory status with UNESCO. It publishes IARF News Digest, sponsors the International Union of Liberal Christian Women, founded in 1910 with headquarters in The Hague.

A.M. WILBUR, A History of Unitarianism, The Hague, 1945; Yearbook of International Organizations.

UNITED ARAB EMIRATES. Member of the UN. Federation of seven Trucial States in the Arabian Peninsula on the Persian Gulf and Gulf of Oman; bordering with Oman, Saudi Arabia and Qatar. Area: 83,657 sq. km. Pop. 1988 est.: 1,600,000 (only 322,800 females); 1976 census: 652,846. Pop. 1982 est. in Abu Dhabi – 516,000; Ajman – 42,000; Dubai – 296,000; Fujairah – 38,000; Ras al Khaimah – 83,000; Sharjah – 184,000; Umm al Quawain – 14,000. Capital: Abu Dhabi. Official language: Arabic. GNP per capita 1986: US $14,410 (1980 – $30,070). Currency: one UAE dirham = 1000 fils. National Days: Moslem holidays.
Member of the UN since Dec. 7, 1971. Member of all UN specialized agencies with exception of GATT. Member of the Arab League since Dec. 6, 1971. Founder member of the Gulf Co-operation Council, 1981.
International relations: territory known in the 18th century as the Pirate Coast, and since the Maritime Perpetual Truce 1833 with Great Britain as the Trucial Coast or Trucial Oman or Trucial States; since Mar., 1892 (the Exclusive Agreements) under British protection until Dec. 1, 1971, when Great Britain terminated all treaties with the Trucial States and withdrew all British troops. On Dec. 2, 1971 the States proclaimed the independent United Arab Emirates, and signed with Great Britain a Treaty of Friendship. Protector of the Abu Dhabi Fund for Arab Economic Development.

K.G. FENELON, The United Arab Emirates: An Economic and Social Survey, London, 1973; R.S. ZAHLEN, The Origins of the UAE, London, 1978; R.S. MALLAKH, The Economic Development of the United Arab Emirates, New York, 1981; United Arab Emirates. A Record of Archives 1979–1981, Abu Dhabi, 1981; F.H. BAY, From Trucial States to United Arab Emirates, 1982; The Europa Year Book 1984. A World Survey, Vol. II, pp. 2555–2565, London, 1984.

UNITED ARAB REPUBLIC. Name officially used for: (1) union of Egypt and Syria in the years 1958–61 (also at the UN); (2) Egypt in the years 1961–71 (also at the UN); (3) Federation of Arab Republics 1972.

UNITED ARAB STATES, UAS. The official name of a confederation between (North) Yemen and the

United Arab Republic, concluded on Mar. 8, 1958; dissolved on Dec. 25, 1961.

UNITED BRANDS. An American concern for production and distribution of bananas, founded in 1975, by merging of the United Fruit Co. and AKM Corp., headquarters in New York, controlling over 40% of banana production and trade. In 1978 it was accused by the EEC Tribunal of Justice of breaking the Common Market rules of free competition in the EEC area and fined 900,000 dollars.

UNITED FRUIT CO. Until 1975 the name of the largest concern of Southern fruit plantations; founded in the late 19th century in Boston. It was owned by one of the 10 largest USA financial groups, the Boston Group, the co-ordinator of which is the First National Bank of Boston. It exercised a decisive influence on the administration of Central American States and of Panama. It had at its disposal its own merchant marine, railway lines and ports in Central America. In 1975 it became United Brands after merger with AKM Corporation.

UNITED KINGDOM OF GREAT BRITAIN AND NORTHERN IRELAND. Member of the UN. Permanent Member of the UN Security Council. State in western Europe on islands in the Atlantic Ocean. Borders with Ireland. Area: 244,103 sq. km. Pop.: 56,340,800 inhabitants in 1982; growth of census population: 1901 – 36,999,000; 1931 – 44,937,000; 1951 – 50,383,000; 1961 – 52,867,000; 1971 – 55,506,650; 1981 – 55,775,650. Capital: London with 2,145,185 inhabitants in Registration London and 6,765,100 in Greater London, 1982. Official language: English. Currency: one pound sterling = 100 pence. GNP per capita in 1986: US $8970. National Day flexible: birthday of the reigning monarch, celebrated on the second Saturday of June.
Original UN Member and Permanent member of the UN Security Council and all UN specialized agencies with the exception of UNESCO. Member of the Commonwealth, EEC, OECD, Council of Europe and the Colombo Plan.
International relations: from the 16th century to World War I the most powerful colonial empire. Since the 19th century under the name British Empire, changed by the Imperial Conferences of 1923, 1926 and 1931 into the British Commonwealth and following this into the ▷ Commonwealth of Nations. After World War I, Great Britain was co-author of the Versailles Treaty and the League of Nations.
In the late 1980's the UK defense program was closely coordinated with the US strategic system. See also ▷ World Heritage UNESCO List.
The Royal Institute of International Affairs, f. 1919, London. Publ.: The World Today, Chattam House Papers and International Affairs.

KEESING's UK Record, London, published since March, 1988.

The Cambridge History of the British Empire, 8 Vols., Cambridge, 1929; Sir E.E. WOODWARD, R. BUTTLER, Documents on British Foreign Policy 1919–1939, London, 1952–57; D. BUTLER, J. FREEMAN, British Political Facts 1900–1960, London, 1963; J.E. FAWCETT, The British Commonwealth in International Law, London, 1963; J.W.L. ADAMS, The Financial Mechanism of the UK, London, 1969; H. DUNCAN HALL, Commonwealth, A History of the British Commonwealth of Nations, London, 1971; C.J. BARNETT, The Collapse of British Power, London, 1972; C.J. BARTLETT, The Long Retreat. A Short History of British Defence Policy 1945–1970, London, 1972; M. CHARLOT, Naissance d'un probleme racial-minorites de couleur en Grande Bretagne, Paris, 1972; A.H. HALSEY, Trends in British

Society since 1900, London, 1972; *Britain, an Official Handbook*, London, 1972; C.P. COOK, *British Historical Facts 1830–1900*, London, 1974; J. CALLAGHAN, *Challenges and Opportunities for British Foreign Policy*, London, 1976; J. REVELL, *Financial Structure and Government Regulation in the United Kingdom, 1952–1980*, London, 1982; *The Europa Year Book 1984. A World Survey*, Vol. I, pp. 937–1008, London, 1984; D. BUTLER, G. BUTLER, *British Political Facts 1900–1985*, London, 1986; Ch.P. COOK, *Sources in British Political History, 1900–1951*, 6 Vols., London, 1975–85; *SIPRI Yearbook*, 1987, Oxford, 1988, pp. 24–28.

UNITED NATIONS. The name was suggested in Dec., 1941 by the US President Franklin Delano Roosevelt (1882–1945) as a common name for all states at war with the Axis Powers (as during World War I Allies against the Central States). The new term was first used in the Declaration by the United Nations in 1942. It was unanimously adopted at the San Francisco Conference Apr. 25, 1945 as the name of the postwar world organization in tribute to the late President of the United States.

"The UN and the Future", in: *The Annals*, Philadelphia, July, 1946, *Yearbook of the UN 1945–46*, p. 2; MIN-CHUAN KU (ed.), *A Comprehensive Handbook of the United Nations*, New York, 1978; H. BOKOR-SZEGO, *The Role of the United Nations in International Legislation*, Amsterdam, 1978; *The United Nations Organizations*, The Hague, 1981; E. LUARD, *A History of the UN*, London, 1982; M. GAUDIER, *Les Nations Unies et l'avenir: un itinéraire bibliographique en trois décênnies*, Genève, 1984; Directory of United Nations, *Data Bases and Information Systems*, New York, 1985; M. ALLESBROOK, *Prototypes of Peacemaking. The First Forty Years of the United Nations*, London, 1986; L.S. FINKELSTEIN, *Politics in the United Nations System*, Durham, N.C., 1988; J. WORONIECKI, *Przysłość ONZ, in: Sprawy Miezynarodowe*, No. 10, Warsaw, 1988; B. KINGSBURY, A. ROBERTS eds., *United Nations, Divided World: The UN's Roles in International Relations*, Oxford, UK, 1988.

UNITED NATIONS BIBLIOGRAPHIC SYSTEM. ▷ UNBIS.

UNITED NATIONS CHARTER, 1945. Adopted by the ▷ San Francisco Conference of the United Nations, Apr. 25–June 26, 1945, entered into force on Oct. 24, 1945; amended Dec. 17, 1963 (arts. 23, 27 and 61); entered into force Aug. 31, 1965; amended Dec. 20, 1965 (art. 23 changed number of Security Council from 11 to 15 and art. 27), entered into force June 12, 1968. The text with amendments reads as follows:

"We the Peoples of the United Nations determined to save succeeding generations from the scourge of war, which twice in our life-time has brought untold sorrow to mankind, and
to reaffirm faith in fundamental human rights, in the dignity and worth of the human person, in the equal rights of men and women and of nations large and small, and
to establish conditions under which justice and respect for the obligations arising from treaties and other sources of international law can be maintained, and
to promote social progress and better standards of life in larger freedom,
and for these ends
to practice tolerance and live together in peace with one another as good neighbors, and
to unite our strength to maintain international peace and security, and
to ensure, by the acceptance of principles and the institution of methods, that armed force shall not be used, save in the common interest, and
to employ international machinery for the promotion of the economic and social advancement of all peoples,
have resolved to combine our efforts to accomplish these aims
Accordingly, our respective Governments, through representatives assembled in the city of San Francisco, who have exhibited their full powers found to be in good and due form, have agreed to the present Charter of the United Nations and do hereby establish an international organization to be known as the United Nations.

Chapter I. *Purposes and principles.*

Art. 1. The Purposes of the United Nations are:
(1) To maintain international peace and security, and to that end: to take effective collective measures for the prevention and removal of threats to the peace, and for the suppression of acts of aggression or other breaches of the peace, and to bring about by peaceful means, and in conformity with the principles of justice and international law, adjustment or settlement of international disputes or situations which might lead to a breach of the peace;
(2) To develop friendly relations among nations based on respect for the principle of equal rights and self-determination of peoples, and to take other appropriate measures to strengthen universal peace;
(3) To achieve international co-operation in solving international problems of an economic, social, cultural, or humanitarian character, and in promoting and encouraging respect for human rights and for fundamental freedoms for all without distinction as to race, sex, language, or religion; and
(4) To be a center for harmonizing the actions of nations in the attainment of these common ends.

Art. 2. The Organization and its Members, in pursuit of the Purposes stated in Article 1, shall act in accordance with the following Principles.
(1) The Organization is based on the principle of the sovereign equality of all its Members.
(2) All Members, in order to ensure to all of them the rights and benefits resulting from membership, shall fulfil in good faith the obligations assumed by them in accordance with the present Charter.
(3) All Members shall settle their international disputes by peaceful means in such a manner that international peace and security, and justice, are not endangered.
(4) All Members shall refrain in their international relations from the threat or use of force against the territorial integrity or political independence of any state, or in any other manner inconsistent with the Purposes of the United Nations.
(5) All Members shall give the United Nations every assistance in any action it takes in accordance with the present Charters and shall refrain from giving assistance to any state against which the United Nations is taking preventive or enforcement action.
(6) The Organization shall ensure that states which are not Members of the United Nations act in accordance with these Principles so far as may be necessary for the maintenance of international peace and security.
(7) Nothing contained in the present Charter shall authorize the United Nations to intervene in matters which are essentially the domestic jurisdiction of any state or shall require the Members to submit such matters to settlement under the present Charter; but this principle shall not prejudice the application of enforcement measures under Chapter VII.

Chapter II. *Membership.*

Art. 3. The original Members of the United Nations shall be the states which, having participated in the United Nations Conference on International Organization at San Francisco, or having previously signed the Declaration by United Nations of 1 January 1942, sign the present Charter and ratify it in accordance with Article 110.

Art. 4.(1) Membership in the United Nations is open to all other peaceloving states which accept the obligations contained in the present Charter and, in the judgment of the Organization, are able and willing to carry out these obligations.
(2) The admission of any such state to membership in the United Nations will be effected by a decision of the General Assembly upon the recommendation of the Security Council.

Art. 5. A Member of the United Nations against which preventive or enforcement action has been taken by the Security Council may be suspended from the exercise of the rights and privileges of membership by the General Assembly upon the recommendation of the Security Council. The exercise of these rights and privileges may be restored by the Security Council.

Art. 6. A Member of the United Nations which has persistently violated the Principles contained in the present Charter may be expelled from the Organization by the General Assembly upon the recommendation of the Security Council.

Chapter III. *Organs.*

Art. 7.(1) There are established as the principal organs of the United Nations: a General Assembly, a Security Council, an Economic and Social Council, a Trusteeship Council, an International Court of Justice, and a Secretariat.
(2) Such subsidiary organs as may be found necessary may be established in accordance with the present Charter.

Art. 8. The United Nations shall place no restrictions on the eligibility of men and women to participate in any capacity and under conditions of equality in its principal and subsidiary organs.

Chapter IV. *The General Assembly.*

Composition.

Art. 9.(1) The General Assembly shall consist of all the Members of the United Nations.
(2) Each Member shall have not more than five representatives in the General Assembly.

Functions and Powers.

Art. 10. The General Assembly may discuss any questions or any matters within the scope of the present Charter or relating to the powers and functions of any organs provided for in the present Charter, and, except as provided in Article 12, may make recommendations to the Members of the United Nations or to the Security Council or to both on any such questions or matters.

Art. 11.(1) The General Assembly may consider the general principles of co-operation in the maintenance of international peace and security, including the principles governing disarmament and the regulation of armaments, and may make recommendations with regard to such principles to the Members or to the Security Council or to both.
(2) The General Assembly may discuss any questions relating to the maintenance of international peace and security brought before it by any Member of the United Nations, or by the Security Council, or by a state which is not a Member of the United Nations in accordance with Article 35, paragraph 2, and, except as provided in Article 12, may make recommendations with regard to any such questions to the state or states concerned or to the Security Council or to both. Any such question on which action is necessary shall be referred to the Security Council by the General Assembly either before or after discussion.
(3) The General Assembly may call the attention of the Security Council to situations which are likely to endanger international peace and security.
(4) The powers of the General Assembly set forth in this Article shall not limit the general scope of Article 10.

Art. 12.(1) While the Security Council is exercising in respect of any dispute or situation the functions assigned to it in the present Charter, the General Assembly shall not make any recommendation with regard to that dispute or situation unless the Security Council so requests.
(2) The Secretary-General, with the consent of the Security Council, shall notify the General Assembly at each session of any matters relative to the maintenance of international peace and security which are being dealt with by the Security Council and shall similarly notify the General Assembly, or the Members of the United Nations if the General Assembly is not in session, immediately the Security Council ceases to deal with such matters.

Art. 13.(1) The General Assembly shall initiate studies and make recommendations for the purpose of:
(a) promoting international co-operation in the political field and encouraging the progressive development of international law and its codification;
(b) promoting international co-operation in the economic, social, cultural, educational, and health fields, and assisting in the realization of human rights and fundamental freedoms for all without distinction as to race, sex, language, or religion.
(2) The further responsibilities, functions and powers of the General Assembly with respect to matters mentioned in paragraph 1(b) above are set forth in Chapters IX and X.

Art. 14. Subject to the provisions of Article 12, the General Assembly may recommend measures for the peaceful adjustment of any situation, regardless of origin, which it deems likely to impair the general welfare or friendly relations among nations, including situations resulting from a violation of the provisions of the present Charter setting forth the Purposes and Principles of the United Nations.

Art. 15.(1) The General Assembly shall receive and consider annual and special reports from the Security Council; these reports shall include an account of the measures that the Security Council has decided upon or taken to maintain international peace and security.

(2) The General Assembly shall receive and consider reports from the other organs of the United Nations.

Art. 16. The General Assembly shall perform such functions with respect to the international trusteeship system as are assigned to it under Chapters XII and XIII, including the approval of the trusteeship agreements for areas not designated as strategic.

Art. 17.(1) The General Assembly shall consider and approve the budget of the Organization.

(2) The expenses of the Organization shall be borne by the Members as apportioned by the General Assembly.

(3) The General Assembly shall consider and approve any financial and budgetary arrangements with specialized agencies referred to in Article 57 and shall examine the administrative budgets of such specialized agencies with a view to making recommendations to the agencies concerned.

Voting.

Art. 18.(1) Each member of the General Assembly shall have one vote.

(2) Decisions of the General Assembly on important questions shall be made by a two-thirds majority of the members present and voting. These questions shall include: recommendations with respect to the maintenance of international peace and security, the election of the non-permanent members of the Security Council, the election of the members of the Economic and Social Council, the election of members of the Trusteeship Council in accordance with paragraph 1(c) of Article 86, the admission of new Members to the United Nations, the suspension of the rights and privileges of membership, the expulsion of Members, questions relating to the operation of the trusteeship system, and budgetary questions.

(3) Decisions on other questions, including the determination of additional categories of questions to be decided by a two-thirds majority, shall be made by a majority of the members present and voting.

Art. 19. A Member of the United Nations which is in arrears in the payment of its financial contributions to the Organization shall have no vote in the General Assembly if the amount of its arrears equals or exceeds the amount of the contributions due from it for the preceding two full years. The General Assembly may, nevertheless, permit such a Member to vote if it is satisfied that the failure to pay is due to conditions beyond the control of the Member.

Procedure.

Art. 20. The General Assembly shall meet in regular annual sessions and in such special sessions as occasion may require. Special sessions shall be convoked by the Secretary-General at the request of the Security Council or of a majority of the Members of the United Nations.

Art. 21. The General Assembly shall adopt its own rules of procedure. It shall elect its President for each session.

Art. 22. The General Assembly may establish such subsidiary organs as it deems necessary for the performance of its functions.

Chapter V. *The Security Council.*

Composition.

Art. 23.(1) The Security Council shall consist of fifteen Members of the United Nations. The Republic of China, France, the Union of Soviet Socialist Republics, the United Kingdom of Great Britain and Northern Ireland, and the United States of America shall be permanent members of the Security Council. The General Assembly shall elect ten other Members of the United Nations to be non-permanent members of the Security Council, due regard being specially paid, in the first instance, to the contribution of Members of the United Nations to the maintenance of international peace and security and to the other purposes of the Organization, and also to equitable geographical distribution.

(2) The non-permanent members of the Security Council shall be elected for a term of two years. In the first election of the non-permanent members after the increase of the membership of the Security Council from eleven to fifteen, two of the four additional members shall be chosen for a term of one year. A retiring member shall not be eligible for immediate re-election.

(3) Each member of the Security Council shall have one representative.

Functions and Powers.

Art. 24.(1) In order to ensure prompt and effective action by the United Nations, its Members confer on the Security Council primary responsibility for the maintenance of international peace and security, and agree that in carrying out its duties under this responsibility the Security Council acts on their behalf.

(2) In discharging these duties the Security Council shall act in accordance with the Purposes and Principles of the United Nations. The specific powers granted to the Security Council for the discharge of these duties are laid down in Chapters VI, VII, VIII and XII.

(3) The Security Council shall submit annual and, when necessary, special reports to the General Assembly for its consideration.

Art. 25. The Members of the United Nations agree to accept and carry out the decisions of the Security Council in accordance with the present Charter.

Art. 26. In order to promote the establishment and maintenance of international peace and security with the least diversion for armaments of the world's human and economic resources, the Security Council shall be responsible for formulating, with the assistance of the Military Staff Committee referred to in Article 47, plans to be submitted to the Members of the United Nations for the establishment of a system for the regulation of armaments.

Voting.

Art. 27.(1) Each member of the Security Council shall have one vote.

(2) Decisions of the Security Council on procedural matters shall be made by an affirmative vote of nine members.

(3) Decisions of the Security Council on all other matters shall be made by an affirmative vote of nine members including the concurring votes of the permanent members; provided that, in decisions under Chapter VI, and under paragraph 3 of Article 52, a party to a dispute shall abstain from voting.

Procedure.

Art. 28.(1) The Security Council shall be so organized as to be able to function continuously. Each member of the Security Council shall for this purpose be represented at all times at the seat of the Organization.

(2) The Security Council shall hold periodic meetings at which each of its members may, if it so desires, be represented by a member of the government or by some other specially designated representative.

(3) The Security Council may hold meetings at such places other than the seat of the Organization as in its judgement will best facilitate its work.

Art. 29. The Security Council may establish such subsidiary organs as it deems necessary for the performance of its functions.

Art. 30. The Security Council shall adopt its own rules of procedure, including the method of selecting its President.

Art. 31. Any Member of the United Nations which is not a member of the Security Council may participate, without vote, in the discussion of any question brought before the Security Council whenever the latters considers that the interests of that Member are specially affected.

Art. 32. Any Member of the United Nations which is not a member of the Security Council or any state which is not a Member of the United Nations, if it is a party to a dispute under consideration by the Security Council, shall be invited to participate, without vote, in the discussion relating to the dispute. The Security Council shall lay down such conditions as it deems just for the participation of a state which is not a Member of the United Nations.

Chapter VI. *Pacific Settlement of Disputes.*

Art. 33.(1) The parties to any dispute, the continuance of which is likely to endanger the maintenance of international peace and security, shall, first of all, seek a solution by negotiation, enquiry, mediation, conciliation, arbitration, judicial settlement, resort to regional agencies or arrangements, or other peaceful means of their own choice.

(2) The Security Council shall, when it deems necessary, call upon the parties to settle their dispute by such means.

Art. 34. The Security Council may investigate any dispute, or any situation which might lead to international friction or give rise to a dispute, in order to determine whether the continuance of the dispute or situation is likely to endanger the maintenance of international peace and security.

Art. 35.(1) Any Member of the United Nations may bring any dispute, or any situation of the nature referred to in Article 34, to the attention of the Security Council or of the General Assembly.

(2) A state which is not a Member of the United Nations may bring to the attention of the Security Council or of the General Assembly any dispute to which it is a party if it accepts in advance, for the purposes of the dispute, the obligations of pacific settlement provided in the present Charter.

(3) The proceedings of the General Assembly in respect of matters brought to its attention under this Article will be subject to the provisions of Articles 11 and 12.

Art. 36.(1) The Security Council may, at any stage of a dispute of the nature referred to in Article 33 or of a situation of like nature, recommend appropriate procedures or methods of adjustment.

(2) The Security Council should take into consideration any procedures for the settlement of the dispute which have already been adopted by the parties.

(3) In making recommendations under this Article the Security Council should also take into consideration that legal disputes should as a general rule be referred by the parties to the International Court of Justice in accordance with the provisions of the Statute of the Court.

Art. 37.(1) Should the parties to a dispute of the nature referred to in Article 33 fail to settle it by the means indicated in that Article, they shall refer it to the Security Council.

(2) If the Security Council deems that the continuance of the dispute is in fact likely to endanger the maintenance of international peace and security, it shall decide whether to take action under Article 36 or to recommend such terms of settlement as it may consider appropriate.

Art. 38. Without prejudice to the provisions of Articles 33 to 37, the Security Council may, if all the parties to any dispute so request, make recommendations to the parties with a view to a pacific settlement of the dispute.

Chapter VII. *Action with respect to threats to the peace, breaches of the peace, and acts of aggression.*

Art. 39. The Security Council shall determine the existence of any threat to the peace, breach of the peace, or act of aggression and shall make recommendations, or decide what measures shall be taken in accordance with Articles 41 and 42, to maintain or restore international peace and security.

Art. 40. In order to prevent an aggravation of the situation, the Security Council may, before making the recommendations or deciding upon the measures provided for in Article 39, call upon the parties concerned to comply with such provisional measures as it deems necessary or desirable. Such provisional measures shall be without prejudice to the rights, claims, or position of the parties concerned. The Security Council shall duly take account of failure to comply with such provisional measures.

Art. 41. The Security Council may decide what measures not involving the use of armed force are to be employed to give effect to its decisions, and it may call upon the Members of the United Nations to apply such measures. These may include complete or partial interruption of economic relations and of rail, sea, air, postal, telegraphic, radio, and other means of communication, and the severance of diplomatic relations.

Art. 42. Should the Security Council consider that measures provided for in Article 41 would be inadequate or have proved to be inadequate, it may take such action by air, sea, or land forces as may be necessary to maintain or restore international peace and security. Such action may include demonstrations, blockade, and other operations by air, sea, or land forces of Members of the United Nations.

Art. 43.(1) All Members of the United Nations, in order to contribute to the maintenance of international peace and security, undertake to make available to the Security Council, on its call and in accordance with a special agreement or agreements, armed forces, assistance, and facilities, including rights of passage, necessary for the purpose of maintaining international peace and security.

(2) Such agreement or agreements shall govern the numbers and types of forces, their degree of readiness

and general location, and the nature of the facilities and assistance to be provided.
(3) The agreement or agreements shall be negotiated as soon as possible on the initiative of the Security Council. They shall be concluded between the Security Council and Members or between the Security Council and groups of Members and shall be subject to ratification by the signatory states in accordance with their respective constitutional processes.
Art. 44. When the Security Council has decided to use force it shall, before calling upon a Member not represented on it to provide armed forces in fulfilment of the obligations assumed under Article 43, invite that Member, if the Member so desires, to participate in the decisions of the Security Council concerning the employment of contingents of that Member's armed forces.
Art. 45. In order to enable the United Nations to take urgent military measures, Members shall hold immediately available national air-force contingents for combined international enforcement action. The strength and degree of readiness of these contingents and plans for their combined action shall be determined, within the limits laid down in the special agreement or agreements referred to in Article 43, by the Security Council with the assistance of the Military Staff Committee.
Art. 46. Plans for the application of armed force shall be made by the Security Council with the assistance of the Military Staff Committee.
Art. 47.(1) There shall be established a Military Staff Committee to advise and assist the Security Council on all questions relating to the Security Council's military requirements for the maintenance of international peace and security, the employment and command of forces placed at its disposal, the regulation of armaments, and possible disarmament.
(2) The Military Staff Committee shall consist of the Chiefs of Staff of the permanent members of the Security Council or their representatives. Any Member of the United Nations not permanently represented on the Committee shall be invited by the Committee to be associated with it when the efficient discharge of the Committee's responsibilities requires the participation of that Member in its work.
(3) The Military Staff Committee shall be responsible under the Security Council for the strategic direction of any armed forces placed at the disposal of the Security Council. Questions relating to the command of such forces shall be worked out subsequently.
(4) The Military Staff Committee, with the authorization of the Security Council and after consultation with appropriate regional agencies, may establish regional sub-committees.
Art. 48.(1) The action required to carry out the decisions of the Security Council for the maintenance of international peace and security shall be taken by all the Members of the United Nations or by some of them, as the Security Council may determine.
(2) Such decisions shall be carried out by the Members of the United Nations directly and through their action in the appropriate international agencies of which they are members.
Art. 49. The Members of the United Nations shall join in affording mutual assistance in carrying out the measures decided upon by the Security Council.
Art. 50. If preventive or enforcement measures against any state are taken by the Security Council, any other state, whether a Member of the United Nations or not, which finds itself confronted with special economic problems arising from the carrying out of those measures shall have the right to consult the Security Council with regard to a solution of those problems.
Art. 51. Nothing in the present Charter shall impair the inherent right of individual or collective self-defence if an armed attack occurs against a Member of the United Nations, until the Security Council has taken measures necessary to maintain international peace and security. Measures taken by Members in the exercise of this right of self-defence shall be immediately reported to the Security Council and shall not in any way affect the authority and responsibility of the Security Council under the present Charter to take at any time such action as it deems necessary in order to maintain or restore international peace and security.
Chapter VIII. *Regional arrangements.*
Art. 52.(1) Nothing in the present Charter precludes the existence of regional arrangements or agencies for dealing with such matters relating to the maintenance of international peace and security as are appropriate for regional action, provided that such arrangements or agencies and their activities are consistent with the Purposes and Principles of the United Nations.
(2) The Members of the United Nations entering into such arrangements or constituting such agencies shall make every effort to achieve pacific settlement of local disputes through such regional arrangements or by such regional agencies before referring them to the Security Council.
(3) The Security Council shall encourage the development of pacific settlement of local disputes through such regional arrangements or by such regional agencies either on the initiative of the states concerned or by reference from the Security Council.
(4) This Article in no way impairs the application of articles 34 and 35.
Art. 53.(1) The Security Council shall, where appropriate, utilize such regional arrangements or agencies for enforcement action under its authority. But no enforcement action shall be taken under regional arrangements or by regional agencies without the authorization of the Security Council, with the exception of measures against any enemy state, as defined in paragraph 2 of this Article, provided for pursuant to Article 107 or in regional arrangements directed against renewal of aggressive policy on the part of any such state, until such time as the Organization may, on request of the Governments concerned, be charged with the responsibility for preventing further aggression by such a state.
(2) The term enemy state as used in paragraph 1 of this Article applies to any state which during the Second World War has been an enemy of any signatory of the present Charter.
Art. 54. The Security Council shall at all times be kept fully informed of activities undertaken or in contemplation under regional arrangements or by regional agencies for the maintenance of international peace and security.
Chapter IX. *International economic and social co-operation.*
Art. 55. With a view to the creation of conditions of stability and wellbeing which are necessary for peaceful and friendly relations among nations based on respect for the principle of equal rights and self-determination of peoples, the United Nations shall promote:
(a) higher standards of living, full employment, and conditions of economic and social progress and development;
(b) solutions of international economic, social, health, and related problems; and international cultural and educational co-operation; and
(c) universal respect for, and observance of, human rights and fundamental freedoms for all without distinction as to race, sex, language, or religion.
Art. 56. All Members pledge themselves to take joint and separate action in co-operation with the Organization for the achievement of the purposes set forth in Article 55.
Art. 57.(1) The various specialized agencies, established by inter-governmental agreement and having wide international responsibilities, as defined in their basic instruments, in economic, social, cultural, educational, health, and related fields, shall be brought into relationship with the United Nations in accordance with the provisions of Article 63.
(2) Such agencies thus brought into relationship with the United Nations are hereinafter referred to as specialized agencies.
Art. 58. The Organization shall make recommendations for the co-ordination of the policies and activities of the specialized agencies.
Art. 59. The Organization shall, where appropriate, initiate negotiations among the states concerned for the creation of any new specialized agencies required for the accomplishment of the purposes set forth in Article 55.
Art. 60. Responsibility for the discharge of the functions of the Organization set forth in this Chapter shall be vested in the General Assembly and, under the authority of the General Assembly, in the Economic and Social Council, which shall have for this purpose the powers set forth in Chapter X.
Chapter X. *The Economic and Social Council.*
Composition.
Art. 61.(1) The Economic and Social Council shall consist of twenty-seven Members of the United Nations elected by the General Assembly.
(2) Subject to the provisions of paragraph 3, nine members of the Economic and Social shall be elected each year for a term of three years. A retiring member shall be eligible for immediate re-election.
(3) At the first election after the increase in the membership of the Economic and Social Council from eighteen to twenty-seven members, in addition to the members elected in place of the six members whose term of office expires at the end of that year, nine additional members shall be elected. Of these nine additional members, the term of office of three members so elected shall expire at the end of one year, and of three other members at the end of two years, in accordance with arrangements made by the General Assembly.
(4) Each member of the Economic and Social Council shall have one representative.
Functions and Powers.
Art. 62.(1) The Economic and Social Council may make or initiate studies and reports with respect to international economic, social, cultural, educational, health, and related matters and may make recommendations with respect to any such matters to the General Assembly, to the Members of the United Nations, and to the specialized agencies concerned.
(2) It may make recommendations for the purpose of promoting respect for, and observance of, human rights and fundamental freedoms for all.
(3) It may prepare draft conventions for submission to the General Assembly, with respect to matters falling within its competence.
(4) It may call, in accordance with the rules prescribed by the United Nations, international conferences on matters falling within its competence.
Art. 63.(1) The Economic and Social Council may enter into agreements with any of the agencies referred to in Article 57, defining the terms on which the agency concerned shall be brought into relationship with the United Nations. Such agreements shall be subject to approval by the General Assembly.
(2) It may coordinate the activities of the specialized agencies through consultation with and recommendations to such agencies and through recommendations to the General Assembly and to the Members of the United Nations.
Art. 64.(1) The Economic and Social Council may take appropriate steps to obtain regular reports from the specialized agencies. It may make arrangements with the Members of the United Nations and with the specialized agencies to obtain reports on the steps taken to give effect to its own recommendations and to recommendations on matters falling within its competence made by the General Assembly.
(2) It may communicate its observations on these reports to the General Assembly.
Art. 65. The Economic and Social Council may furnish information to the Security Council and shall assist the Security Council upon its request.
Art. 66.(1) The Economic and Social Council shall perform such functions as fall within its competence in connexion with the carrying out of the recommendations of the General Assembly.
(2) It may, with the approval of the General Assembly, perform services at the request of Members of the United Nations and at the request of specialized agencies.
(3) It shall perform such other functions as are specified elsewhere in the present Charter or as may be assigned to it by the General Assembly.
Voting.
Art. 67.(1) Each member of the Economic and Social Council shall have one vote.
(2) Decisions of the Economic and Social Council shall be made by a majority of the members present and voting.
Procedure.
Art. 68. The Economic and Social Council shall set up commissions in economic and social fields and for the promotion of human rights, and such other commissions as may be required for the performance of its functions.
Art. 69. The Economic and Social Council shall invite any Member of the United Nations to participate, without vote, in its deliberations on any matter of particular concern to that Member.

Art. 70. The Economic and Social Council may make arrangements for representatives of the specialized agencies to participate, without vote, in its deliberations and in those of the commissions established by it, and for its representatives to participate in the deliberations of the specialized agencies.

Art. 71. The Economic and Social Council may make suitable arrangements for consultation with non-governmental organizations which are concerned with matters within its competence. Such arrangements may be made with international organizations and, where appropriate, with national organizations after consultation with the Member of the United Nations concerned.

Art. 72.(1) The Economic and Social Council shall adopt its own rules of procedure, including the method of selecting its President.

(2) The Economic and Social Council shall meet as required in accordance with its rules, which shall include provision for the convening of meetings on the request of a majority of its members.

Chapter XI. *Declaration regarding non-self-governing territories.*

Art. 73. Members of the United Nations which have or assume responsibilities for the administration of territories whose peoples have not yet attained a full measure of self-government recognize the principle that the interests of the inhabitants of these territories are paramount, and accept as a sacred trust the obligation to promote to the utmost, within the system of international peace and security established by the present Charter, the well-being of the inhabitants of these territories, and, to this end:

(a) to ensure, with due respect for the culture of the peoples concerned, their political, economic, social, and educational advancement, their just treatment, and their protection against abuses;

(b) to develop self-government, to take due account of the political aspirations of the peoples, and to assist them in the progressive development of their free political institutions, according to the particular circumstances of each territory and its peoples and their varying stages of advancement;

(c) to further international peace and security;

(d) to promote constructive measures of development, to encourage research, and to co-operate with one another and, when and where appropriate, with specialized international bodies with a view to the practical achievement of the social, economic, and scientific purposes set forth in this Article; and

(e) to transmit regularly to the Secretary-General for information purposes, subject to such limitation as security and constitutional considerations may require, statistical and other information of a technical nature relating to economic, social, and educational conditions in the territories for which they are respectively responsible other than those territories to which chapters XII and XIII apply.

Art. 74. Members of the United Nations also agree that their policy in respect of the territories to which this Chapter applies, no less than in respect of their metropolitan areas, must be based on the general principle of goodneighborliness, due account being taken of the interests and well-being of the rest of the world, in social, economic, and commercial matters.

Chapter XII. *International trusteeship system.*

Art. 75. The United Nations shall establish under its authority an international trusteeship system for the administration and supervision of such territories as may be placed thereunder by subsequent individual agreements. These territories are hereinafter referred to as trust territories.

Art. 76. The basic objectives of the trusteeship system in accordance with the Purposes of the United Nations laid down in Article 1 of the present Charter, shall be:

(a) to further international peace and security;

(b) to promote the political, economic, social, and educational advancement of the inhabitants of the trust territories, and their progressive development towards self-government or independence as may be appropriate to the particular circumstances of each territory and its peoples and the freely expressed wishes of the peoples concerned, ans as may be provided by the terms of each trusteeship agreement;

(c) to encourage respect for human rights and for fundamental freedoms for all without distinction as to race, sex, language, or religion, and to encourage recognition of the interdependence of the peoples of the world; and

(d) to ensure equal treatment in social, economic, and commercial matters for all Members of the United Nations and their nationals, and also equal treatment for the latter in the administration of justice, without prejudice to the attainment of the foregoing objectives and subject to the provisions of Article 80.

Art. 77.(1) The trusteeship system shall apply to such territories in the following categories as may be placed thereunder by means of trusteeship agreements:

(a) territories now held under mandate;

(b) territories which may be detached from enemy states as a result of the Second World War; and

(c) territories voluntarily placed under the system by states responsible for their administration.

(2) It will be a matter for subsequent agreement as to which territories in the foregoing categories will be brought under the trusteeship system and upon what terms.

Art. 78. The trusteeship system shall not apply to territories which have become Members of the United Nations, relationship among which shall be based on respect for the principle of sovereign equality.

Art. 79. The terms of trusteeship for each territory to be placed under the trusteeship system, including any alteration or amendment, shall be agreed upon by the states directly concerned, including the mandatory power in the case of territories held under mandate by a Member of the United Nations, and shall be approved as provided for in Articles 83 and 85.

Art. 80.(1) Except as may be agreed upon in individual trusteeship agreements, made under Articles 77, 79 and 81, placing each territory under the trusteeship system, and until such agreements have been concluded, nothing in this Chapter shall be construed in or of itself to alter in any manner the rights whatsoever of any states or any peoples or the terms of existing international instruments to which Members of the United Nations may respectively be parties.

(2) Paragraph 1 of this Article shall not be interpreted as giving grounds for delay or postponement of the negotiation and conclusion of agreements for placing mandated and other territories under the trusteeship system as provided for in Article 77.

Art. 81. The trusteeship agreement shall in each case include the terms under which the trust territory will be administered and designate the authority which will exercise the administration of the trust territory. Such authority, hereinafter called the administering authority, may be one or more states or the Organization itself.

Art. 82. There may be designated, in any trusteeship agreement, a strategic area or areas which may include part or all of the trust territory to which the agreement applies, without prejudice to any special agreement or agreements made under Article 43.

Art. 83.(1) All functions of the United Nations relating to strategic areas, including the approval of the terms of the trusteeship agreements and of their alteration or amendment, shall be exercised by the Security Council.

(2) The basic objectives set forth in Article 76 shall be applicable to the people of each strategic area.

(3) The Security Council shall, subject to the provisions of the trusteeship agreements and without prejudice to security considerations, avail itself of the assistance of the Trusteeship Council to perform those functions of the United Nations under the trusteeship system relating to political, economic, social, and educational matters in the strategic areas.

Art. 84. It shall be the duty of the administering authority to ensure that the trust territory shall play its part in the maintenance of international peace and security. To this end the administering authority may make use of volunteer forces, facilities, and assistance from the trust territory in carrying out the obligations towards the Security Council undertaken in this regard by the administering authority, as well as for local defence and the maintenance of law and order within the trust territory.

Art. 85.(1) The functions of the United Nations with regard to trusteeship agreements for all areas not designated as strategic, including the approval of the terms of the trusteeship agreements and of their alteration or amendment, shall be exercised by the General Assembly.

(2) The Trusteeship Council, operating under the authority of the General Assembly, shall assist the General Assembly in carrying out these functions.

Chapter XIII. *The Trusteeship Council.*
Composition.

Art. 86.(1) The Trusteeship Council shall consist of the following Members of the United Nations:

(a) those Members administering trust territories;

(b) such of those Members mentioned by name in Article 23 as are not administering trust territories; and

(c) as many other Members elected for three-year terms by the General Assembly as may be necessary to ensure that the total number of members of the Trusteeship Council is equally divided between those Members of the United Nations which administer trust territories and those which do not.

(2) Each member of the Trusteeship Council shall designate one specially qualified person to represent it therein.

Functions and Powers.

Art. 87. The General Assembly and, under its authority, the Trusteeship Council, in carrying out their functions, may:

(a) consider reports submitted by the administering authority;

(b) accept petitions and examine them in consultation with the administering authority;

(c) provide for periodic visits to the respective trust territories at times agreed upon with the administering authority; and

(d) take these and other actions in conformity with the terms of the trusteeship agreements.

Art. 88. The Trusteeship Council shall formulate a questionnaire on the political, economic, social, and educational advancement of the inhabitants of each trust territory, and the administering authority for each trust territory within the competence of the General Assembly shall make an annual report to the General Assembly upon the basis of such questionnaire.

Voting.

Art. 89.(1) Each member of the Trusteeship Council shall have one vote.

(2) Decisions of the Trusteeship Council shall be made by a majority of the members present and voting.

Procedure.

Art. 90.(1) The Trusteeship Council shall adopt its own rules of procedure, including the method of selecting its President.

(2) The Trusteeship Council shall meet as required in accordance with its rules, which shall include provisions for the convening of meetings on the request of a majority of its members.

Art. 91. The Trusteeship Council shall, when appropriate, avail itself of the assistance of the Economic and Social Council and of the specialized agencies in regard to matters with which they are respectively concerned.

Chapter XIV. *The International Court of Justice.*

Art. 92. The International Court of Justice shall be the principal organ of the United Nations. It shall function in accordance with the annexed Statute, which is based upon the Statute of the Permanent Court of International Justice and forms an integral part of the present Charter.

Art. 93.(1) All Members of the United Nations are ipso facto parties to the Statute of the International Court of Justice.

(2) A state which is not a Member of the United Nations may become a party to the Statute of the International Court of Justice on conditions to be determined in each case by the General Assembly upon the recommendation of the Security Council.

Art. 94.(1) Each Member of the United Nations undertakes to comply with the decision of the International Court of Justice in any case to which it is a party.

(2) If any party to a case fails to perform the obligations incumbent upon it under a judgment rendered by the Court, the other party may have recourse to the Security Council, which may, if it deems necessary, make recommendations or decide upon measures to be taken to give effect to the judgment.

Art. 95. Nothing in the present Charter shall prevent Members of the United Nations from entrusting the solution of their differences to other tribunals by virtue of agreements already in existence or which may be concluded in the future.

Art. 96.(1) The General Assembly or the Security Council may request the International Court of Justice to give an advisory opinion on any legal question.

(2) Other organs of the United Nations and specialized agencies, which may at any time be so authorized by the General Assembly, may also request advisory opinions of the Court on legal questions arising within the scope of their activities.

Chapter XV. *The Secretariat.*

Art. 97. The Secretariat shall comprise a Secretary-General and such staff as the Organization may require. The Secretary-General shall be appointed by the General Assembly upon the recommendation of the Security Council. He shall be the chief administrative officer of the Organization.

Art. 98. The Secretary-General shall act in that capacity in all meetings of the General Assembly, of the Security Council, of the Economic and Social Council, and of the Trusteeship Council, and shall perform such other functions as are entrusted to him by these organs. The Secretary-General shall make an annual report to the General Assembly on the work of the Organization.

Art. 99. The Secretary-General may bring to the attention of the Security Council any matter which in his opinion may threaten the maintenance of international peace and security.

Art. 100.(1) In the performance of their duties the Secretary-General and the staff shall not seek or receive instructions from any government or from any other authority external to the Organization. They shall refrain from any action which might reflect on their position as international officials responsible only to the Organization.

(2) Each Member of the United Nations undertakes to respect the exclusively international character of the responsibilities of the Secretary-General and the staff and not to seek to influence them in the discharge of their responsibilities.

Art. 101.(1) The staff shall be appointed by the Secretary-General under regulations established by the General Assembly.

(2) Appropriate staffs shall be permanently assigned to the Economic and Social Council, the Trusteeship Council, and, as required, to other organs of the United Nations. These staffs shall form a part of the Secretariat.

(3) The paramount consideration in the employment of the staff and in the determination of the conditions of service shall be the necessity of securing the highest standards of efficiency, competence, and integrity. Due regard shall be paid to the importance of recruiting the staff on as wide a geographical basis as possible.

Chapter XVI. *Miscellaneous provisions.*

Art. 102.(1) Every treaty and every international agreement entered into by any Member of the United Nations after the present Charter comes into force shall as soon as possible be registered with the Secretariat and published by it.

(2) No party to any such treaty or international agreement which has not been registered in accordance with the provisions of paragraph 1 of this Article may invoke that treaty or agreement before any organ of the United Nations.

Art. 103. In the event of a conflict between the obligations of the Members of the United Nations under the present Charter and their obligations under any other international agreement, their obligations under the present Charter shall prevail.

Art. 104. The Organization shall enjoy in the territory of each of its Members such legal capacity as may be necessary for the exercise of its functions and the fulfilment of its purposes.

Art. 105.(1) The Organization shall enjoy in the territory of each of its Members such privileges and immunities as are necessary for the fulfilment of its purposes.

(2) Representatives of the Members of the United Nations and officials of the Organization shall similarly enjoy such privileges and immunities as are necessary for the independent exercise of their functions in connexion with the Organization.

(3) The General Assembly may make recommendations with a view to determining the details of the application of paragraphs 1 and 2 of this Article or may propose conventions to the Members of the United Nations for this purpose.

Chapter XVII. *Transitional security arrangements.*

Art. 106. Pending the coming into force of such special agreements referred to in Article 43 as in the opinion of the Security Council enable it to begin the exercise of its responsibilities under Article 42, the parties to the Four-Nation Declaration, signed at Moscow, 30 October 1943, and France, shall, in accordance with the provisions of paragraph 5 of that Declaration, consult with one another and as occasion requires with other Members of the United Nations with a view to such joint action on behalf of the Organization as may be necessary for the purpose of maintaining international peace and security.

Art. 107. Nothing in the present Charter shall invalidate or preclude action, in relation to any state which during the Second World War has been an enemy of any signatory to the present Charter, taken or authorized as a result of that war by the Governments having responsibility for such action.

Chapter XVIII. *Amendments.*

Art. 108. Amendments to the present Charter shall come into force for all Members of the United Nations when they have been adopted by a vote of two thirds of the members of the General Assembly and ratified in accordance with their respective constitutional processes by two thirds of the Members of the United Nations, including all the permanent members of the Security Council.

Art. 109.(1) A General Conference of the Members of the United Nations for the purpose of reviewing the present Charter may be held at a date and place to be fixed by a two-thirds vote of the members of the General Assembly and by a vote of any nine members of the Security Council. Each Member of the United Nations shall have one vote in the conference.

(2) Any alteration of the present Charter recommended by a two-thirds vote of the conference shall take effect when ratified in accordance with their respective constitutional processes by two thirds of the Members of the United Nations including all the permanent members of the Security Council.

(3) If such a conference has not been held before the tenth annual session of the General Assembly following the coming into force of the present Charter, the proposal to call such a conference shall be placed on the agenda of that session of the General Assembly, and the conference shall be held if so decided by a majority vote of the members of the General Assembly and by a vote of any seven members of the Security Council.

Chapter XIX. *Ratification and signature.*

Art. 110.(1) The present Charter shall be ratified by the signatory states in accordance with their respective constitutional processes.

(2) The ratifications shall be deposited with the Government of the United States of America, which shall notify all the signatory states of each deposit as well as the Secretary-General of the Organization when he has been appointed.

(3) The present Charter shall come into force upon the deposit of ratifications by the Republic of China, France, the Union of Soviet Socialist Republics, the United Kingdom of Great Britain and Northern Ireland, and the United States of America, and by a majority of the other signatory states. A protocol of the ratifications deposited shall thereupon be drawn up by the Government of the United States of America which shall communicate copies thereof to all the signatory states.

(4) The states signatory to the present Charter which ratify it after it has come into force will become original Members of the United Nations on the date of the deposit of their respective ratifications.

Art. 111. The present Charter, of which the Chinese, French, Russian, English, and Spanish texts are equally authentic, shall remain deposited in the archives of the Government of the United States of America. Duly certified copies thereof shall be transmitted by that Government to the Governments of the other signatory states.

In Faith Whereof the representatives of the Governments of the United Nations have signed the present Charter. Done at the city of San Francisco the twenty-sixth day of June, one thousand nine hundred and forty-five."

Charter of the UN and Statute of the ICJ, New York, 1960; L.M. GOODRICH, *UN Charter-Commentary and Documents*, New York, 1969.

UNITED NATIONS CHARTER, REVISION OF. A possibility provided for in Chapter XVII of the UN Charter, following a decision taken by the UN General Assembly or by a General Conference of All Members of the United Nations. Agreed amendments enter into force after their adoption and ratification by two thirds of all members of the United Nations, including in this number all five permanent members of the Security Council, i.e. China, France, USA, Great Britain and USSR. This latter condition, based on the principle of unanimity of the big powers, was attacked at the Conference of the United Nations in San Francisco, 1945, by Latin American states, as introducing inequitable membership rights. Opposition also occurred at the general debate of the UN General Assembly in 1946. In July, 1947 Argentina submitted a motion on revision of the UN Charter "in order to abolish the privilege of veto in the United Nations." In 1948 the Small General Assembly was convened in the spirit of the slogan "Change without amendment to the Charter," Argentina again requested the convening of the General Conference. In 1949 the Senate of the United States appointed a special sub-committee to study the possibility of revising the Charter of the United Nations. On Apr. 27, 1950 two leaders of the Republican Party of the USA, H. Hoover and J.F. Dulles, published a draft amendment to the Charter of the United Nations which excluded communist states from the United Nations. In 1953 Argentina, Egypt, the Netherlands, Cuba, New Zealand and Pakistan submitted their drafts of amendments to the UN Charter to the UN General Assembly. On Jan. 19, 1954 Secretary of State J.F. Dulles stated that the Charter of the United Nations had to be revised in order to abolish the right to veto by the Soviet Union, and the debate on this proposal was held on Nov. 17–21, 1955. Rapporteur, the representative of Philippines, requested not only abolishment of the veto and permanent seats in the Security Council, but also "to limit national sovereignty," which was a reflection of the idea of transforming the United Nations into "a supranational Federation of States" with their internal jurisdiction and sovereignty restricted in favor of the Federation.

The UN General Assembly by force of its Res. 992/X appointed a Committee for the Preparation of a General Conference on introduction of amendments to the Charter of the United Nations. This committee each year submits reports to the General Assembly on the work of UN bodies, but since 1957 it has not recommended the convening of such a Conference; however, in 1963 it univocally recommended that the composition of the Security Council be increased from 11 to 15 states and of ECOSOC from 18 to 27 members, which called for the approval of the UN General Assembly, which came on Dec. 17, 1963 by introducing amendments to arts. 23, 27 and 61 of the UN Charter, entered into force on Aug. 31, 1965. In 1970 the General Assembly of the United Nations called on its member states to express their opinions on revision of the UN Charter. At its 1974 session, the Assembly established an Ad Hoc Committee with the aims, among others, of discussing the observations received from Governments on the question of review of the Charter; and of considering suggestions for the more effective functioning of the United Nations that may not require amendment to the Charter.

In December, 1975, the General Assembly decided to reconvene the Ad Hoc Committee as a 47-member Special Committee on the Charter of the United Nations and on the Strengthening of the Role of the Organization. The Special Committee was instructed to examine in detail the obser-

United Nations 40th Anniversary

vations, suggestions and proposals by Governments regarding the Charter and the strengthening of the role of the United Nations. The Committee met in 1976 and 1977.

Amendments to the Charter come into force when they have been adopted by a vote of two thirds of the members of the General Assembly and ratified by two thirds of the members of the United Nations, including all the permanent members of the Security Council.

The amendments adopted and ratified up to the end of 1977 provided for or related to increases in the membership of the Security Council and the Economic and Social Council. Amendments to arts. 23 and 27 were approved by the Assembly in 1963 and came into force in 1965. The amendment to art. 23 increased the membership of the Security Council from 11 to 15. The amended article 27 provides that decisions of the Security Council shall be made by an affirmative vote of nine members (formerly seven), including the concurring votes of the five permanent members for all matters other than procedural.

Under an amendment to art. 61 which took effect in 1965, the Economic and Social Council was enlarged from 18 to 27 members. In 1971 the Assembly approved a further amendment to increase the Council's membership to 54. The amendment entered into force in 1973.

An amendment of art. 109 entered into force in 1968. It increased from seven to nine the number of votes of members of the Security Council that would have to concur in convening a General Conference of member states for the purpose of reviewing the Charter, but left unchanged the requirement of a two-thirds vote in the General Assembly on that question.

A. GARCIA ROBLES, *El Mundo de la Postguerra*, Vol. 1, México, DF, 1946, pp. 145–147; *US Congress Committee on Foreign Relations Revision of the UN Charter*, Washington, DC, 1950. *The Future of the UN: Issue of Charter*, Washington, DC, 1950; "The Future of the UN: Issue of Charter Revision", in: *The Annals*, November., 1954; M. YEPES, "La réforme de la Charte des Nations Unies", in: *Revue Général de Droit International Public*, No. 4, 1954; S. BORISOV, "Protiv proektov peresmotra Ustava OON", in *Sovetskoe gosudarstvo i pravo*, No. 6, 1955; C. EAGLETON, "Preparation for Review of the UN Charter", in: *American Journal of International Law*, No. 2, 1955; M. UDINA, "Verfahren zur Revision der Satzung der Vereinten Nationen", in: *Jahrbuch fur Internationales Recht*, No. 6, 1955; G. FISCHER, "France and the Proposed Revision of the UN Charter", in: *Indian Quarterly*, No. 8, 1955; *UN Monthly Chronicle*, No. 1, 1975, p. 118 and No. 8, 1975, pp. 21–22; *Everyone's United Nations*, New York, 1979; M. BERTRAND, *Some Reflections on the Reform of the United Nations*, Geneva, 1985.

UNITED NATIONS DAY. The UN Day celebrated since 1948 on Oct. 24 to commemorate the entry into force of the UN Charter 1945 following its ratification by the Five Powers and a majority of states-signatories.

UNITED NATIONS DECLARATION, 1942. An intergovernmental document signed on Jan. 1, 1942 in Washington, DC by the representatives of 26 states that were fighting against the Axis states. The Declaration obliged the signatories to co-operate in winning the war in the spirit of the Atlantic Charter 1941 and not to make a separate peace. The full text of the Declaration is as follows:

"A Joint Declaration by the United States of America, the United Kingdom of Great Britain and Northern Ireland, the Union of Soviet Socialist Republics, China, Australia, Belgium, Canada, Costa Rica, Cuba, Czechoslovakia, Dominican Republic, El Salvador, Greece, Guatemala, Haiti, Honduras, India, Luxem-

bourg, Netherlands, New Zealand, Nicaragua, Norway, Panama, Poland, South Africa, Yugoslavia. The Governments signatory hereto,

Having subscribed to a common programme of purposes and principles embodied in the Joint Declaration of the President of the United States of America and the Prime Minister of the United Kingdom of Great Britain and Northern Ireland, dated August 14th, 1941, known as the Atlantic Charter.

Being convinced that complete victory over their enemies is essential to defend life, liberty, independence and religious freedom, and to preserve human rights and justice in their own lands as well as in other lands, and that they are now engaged in a common struggle against savage and brutal forces seeking to subjugate the world, declare:

(1) Each Government pledges itself to employ its full resources, military or economic, against those members of the Tripartite Pact (Germany, Japan, Italy) 1940 and its adherents with which such Government is at war.

(2) Each Government pledges itself to co-operate with the Governments signatory hereto and not to make a separate armistice or peace with the enemies.

The foregoing declaration may be adhered to by other nations which are, or which may be, rendering material assistance and contributions in the struggle for victory over Hitlerism."

The Declaration was later signed by 21 more states: Mexico June 5, 1942, Philippines June 20, 1942, Ethiopia June 28, 1942, Iraq Jan. 16, 1943, Brazil Feb. 8, 1943, Bolivia June 27, 1943, Iran Oct 10, 1943, Colombia Dec. 22, 1943, Liberia Feb. 26, 1944, France Dec. 26, 1944, Ecuador Feb. 7, 1945, Peru Feb. 11, 1945, Chile and Paraguay Feb. 12, 1945, Venezuela Feb. 16, 1945, Uruguay Feb. 23, 1945, Turkey Feb. 24, 1945, Egypt Feb. 27, 1945, Saudi Arabia, Lebanon and Syria Mar. 1, 1945.

UNTS, Vol. 382, 1941–43, pp. 382–387; *Yearbook of the UN*, 1946–47, p. 2.

UNITED NATIONS FOR A BETTER WORLD. The General Assembly on Dec. 11, 1984 adopted Res. 39/161A concerning the 40th Anniversary of the Organization and chose as the theme of the year of the United Nations, 1985: "United Nations for a Better World".

UN Chronicle, 1985, No. 1.

UNITED NATIONS 40TH ANNIVERSARY. The fortieth anniversary of the signing of the UN Charter was commemorated on June 23–26, 1985 in San Francisco with an address by the Secretary General Javier Perez de Cuellar, entitled "The first forty years of the United Nations and the next". The text is as follows:

Forty years ago vast cities lay in ruins. An appreciable portion of the world's economic productive capacity was destroyed. Millions of people were dispossessed and homeless. Many more millions were dead, victims of the most terrible war that had ever occurred. The devastation was such as to make clear that recurrence would entail the impermissible risk of the total destruction of civilization.

The San Francisco Conference, which opened on 26 April 1945, was not a conference to end that war. The purpose of the governmental and non-governmental representatives gathered in this city was to end all wars–to save succeeding generations from the scourge of war–words that were drafted by two American women, Virginia Gildersleeve and Elizabeth Reynard, who were members of the United States delegation. There was no disagreement on this objective nor, in the course of the lengthy negotiations, was failure ever contemplated. San Francisco was frequently referred to then as "the capital of tomorrow" because the decisions taken here were seen as of decisive influence in assuring a future with all the promise for the world that peace could impart.

Thus, 40 years ago today the hopes and aspirations of Governments and peoples around the world were focused on this city, where the representatives of 51 States signed the document which defined the means whereby peace might be assured–the Charter of the

United Nations. These means are essentially twofold in nature: a code of international behaviour in the form of purposes and principles to which all Member States of the United Nations are committed and a multilateral organization–the United Nations.

The purposes and principles represent a culmination of human efforts to define how nations should behave to attain lasting peace. The United Nations Organization is the practical machinery for transforming these purposes and principles into the reality of global relationships.

This, then is the basis of the most ambitious effort ever undertaken to establish the conditions and the machinery which would bring lasting peace to the world–a world that from its earliest history has seldom been free from war. The United Nations has enjoyed a large investment of hope, of ideals, of visionary statesmanship and of material resources. We are now at the beginning of its fortieth year, the span of a generation. It is a time to look back and to look forward, to assess what the effect of the United Nations has been and to conclude what it can, and should be, in the future.

No United Nations?

In sharing my thoughts with you on these subjects, I would suggest, as a beginning, that we imagine the results if suddenly on this anniversary day the United Nations system should disappear–swallowed up in the western sea that lies so close at hand in San Francisco. Let me list only a small number:

– Children and mothers in the neediest countries would be without the major emergency and long-term assistance that makes for millions of them the difference between life and death, between productive lives and lives wasted through malnutrition and disease.

– The over-all co-ordination of emergency aid to the drought-stricken countries of Africa would cease to the peril of the millions of people whose lives depend on the effective utilization of available resources.

– Some 10 million refugees would be without the protection and assistance now afforded by the United Nations High Commissioner for Refugees.

– Multilateral negotiations on such vital disarmament objectives as the complete prohibition of chemical weapons and of nuclear testing would stop.

– Syrian and Israeli forces would be in direct confrontation on the Golan Heights with the disappearance of the peace-keeping forces positioned between them.

– The presently viable channel to resolve certain key international problems, including Afghanistan, Cyprus and the Iran-Iraq war, would cease to exist.

– The options available in time of crisis to prevent or restrict conflict would immediately diminish.

This list is far from comprehensive, but it is sufficient to illustrate in a rather dramatic way the present importance of the United Nations to the global community. Peace involves continued common engagement in the betterment of the human condition. For 40 years now, the United Nations has provided the catalyst, the framework and the machinery for such common engagement. Despite political and ideological differences, despite distrust and tension in bilateral relations, new horizons of hope and achievement have opened for the majority of the world's inhabitants as a result.

None of the functions which I have listed as ceasing with the disappearance of the United Nations could be successfully undertaken by any one country acting unilaterally, or even by a limited or exclusive grouping of States. This is characteristic of many of today's major issues. Environmental pollution, population growth, the existence of extensive malnutrition and hunger, the traffic in illicit drugs are examples of problems that affect the well-being of people the world over and require co-operative efforts of all countries for their solution. There must be structures within which nations can work together for the progress which no nation acting alone can accomplish. Multilateralism, as represented by the United Nations, is the necessary response to this interdependence of countries and peoples. It is a compelling need of our times.

Terrorism

In these past days and weeks, the world has faced repeated instances of terrorism in the form of bombings, hijackings and the taking of hostages. The victims have been hundreds of innocent people who have harmed no persons and no cause. Mere condemnation of such acts is insufficient. Effective international action is required. Resolutions and conventions have been adopted in the past by the General Assembly and the International Civil Aviation Organization, outlawing hijackings and the taking of hostages. These provide a vital framework for counter-measures. It is tragically evident, however, that new, multilaterally co-ordinated efforts are urgently required to deal with this terrible phenomenon, which is beyond the capacity of any one country to handle alone.

Human Rights

The promotion of human rights, one of the principal purposes of the United Nations, as we have seen, and a major concern during these four decades, is also dependent on multilateral co-operation. Within three years of the founding of the United Nations agreement had been reached by its members on the Universal Declaration of Human Rights. This Declaration is accepted as the authoritative definition of the basic rights to which all people are entitled precisely because it is a multilaterally agreed document. Its provisions admittedly are frequently disregarded. However, with it and the subsequent United Nations instruments in the human rights field, a measure has been set for the behaviour of Governments that can no longer be ignored.

These United Nations documents validate in specific terms the principle in the Charter, which is new in history, that deprivation of human rights is the legitimate concern of the international community. This is a significant element in an increasing effectiveness of the United Nations in the promotion and protection of human rights. It is a result that could be obtained only on a multilateral basis.

An Interdependent World

There can be no serious doubt that since its establishment the United Nations has alleviated many needs of an interdependent world. It has left marks on these 40 years of a superior norm for international conduct, of the validation of multilateral enterprise, of the resolution or restriction of disputes, of peace-keeping, and of substantial improvement in the human condition. These are necessary elements in a lasting peace. These years bear other marks as well, however: the deep scars of armed conflict and violence, of fear and tension between nations, of economic inequity and social injustice and of an arms race which burdens the human spirit no less than the global economy, feeds distrust and, in its nuclear dimension, threatens the very existence of life itself. These are realities which, in their persistence, pose questions as to the capacity of the United Nations to meet adequately the purposes defined in its Charter. These questions cannot and should not be ignored for they are directly relevant to our common destiny. As Secretary-General, I have tried to face them squarely in the realization that to the extent that this capacity is inadequate, the means should be found to strengthen it while there is time. Let me put before you a number of conclusions.

Resolving Disputes

The power of enforcement is largely lacking in the United Nations. The Charter foresees the use of enforcement measures only by the Security Council for the maintenance or restoration of international security. The utilization of a multilateral armed force made up of contingents from Member States is the principal means provided in the Charter for this purpose. Because of differences between the major States, the force has never been established. Realistically, I do not think this situation is likely to change in the near future, as desirable as that would be. The lack of effective means of enforcement has unquestionably weakened the capacity of the United Nations to deal with threats to the peace. Yet, even if an armed force existed, its use for enforcement purposes would be highly problematical as long as there are profound differences between the most powerful permanent members of the Security Council and between countries closely associated with them.

How then can there be collective security if there is no force through which it can be multilaterally assured? How under these circumstances can one reach the point where Governments will feel able to rely less than now on national armed strength for their security?

The answer, I believe, lies first in the resolution of the acute differences, or at least in the establishment of a constructive working relationship, between the major Powers who have a unique responsibility for the security of the world as a whole. Directly related to this is the achievement of solutions to the disputes and the conflicts that cause distrust and instability at the regional

level and tend to exacerbate relations between the two great Powers. The United Nations has a unique potential for dealing with this most difficult task, a potential which has not until now been fully exploited and perhaps not adequately understood.

I am convinced that, contrary to what is often stated by critics of the Organization, the great advantage of the United Nations is that it is not a national government or a body with a specific ideological or political identity. In accepting the assistance or mediation of United Nations instrumentalities, countries need not feel that they are bending to the will of another country or placing themselves under an obligation to another Power or Powers. The effectiveness of the United Nations in the resolution of disputes requires general recognition of, and respect for, this special attribute.

It should be accepted that the Organization must function in accordance with the Charter rather than the will of any one State or group of States. Especially in the Security Council, Member States must act for the common advantage that can accrue from the elimination of a cause of friction or a threat to peace. In pragmatic terms Security Council members—and I speak especially of the two most powerful—when participating in the Council's responsibilities must be motivated less by bilateral differences and more by the objective of resolving disputes for which their common support is needed. Implementation of the Council's decisions can be more successfully achieved if the influence of the permanent members is exercised in co-ordination towards that objective.

The Security Council must deal with incipient disputes at an early stage, which, until now, has too often not been the case. It may seek facts, consult with the parties, make suggestions, appoint a mediator. The Secretary-General has a role in this regard in ensuring that information is available on crisis situations in a timely fashion and that his good offices are available to assist, within his mandate under the Charter, in encouraging understanding and in assuring a channel of communication between parties on the brink of conflict, I have sought to do this.

It may be that in the future, United Nations peace-keeping forces can be employed for preventive purposes. These lightly-armed soldiers, who have stood valiantly between adversaries after conflict has occurred, could, under certain conditions, I believe, be deployed in situations of tension to discourage the transgression of borders or the exchange of fire.

American-Soviet Teams?

American and Soviet officers have served in the past and serve now on military observation teams which are part of United Nations peace-keeping efforts. These efforts might gain in effectiveness if, in some circumstances, American and Soviet soldiers, who fought together to gain victory in the Second World War, were included in the actual peace-keeping contingents. Until now this has not been done, but it would be completely in harmony with the intent of the Charter.

Should there be conflict between the Soviet Union and the United States, it would be tantamount to a new world conflagration. I believe the United Nations has served to reduce this possibility and can do so in the future by providing a channel of communication in crisis, by affording opportunities for issues to be defused, by helping to generate the time and atmosphere in which the consequences of actions can be considered with a full sense of responsibility to all humanity.

And, as I have said, the United Nations role will be of extreme importance during the coming years in bringing peaceful resolutions to those disputes between other parties, which if unsettled, could bring the major nuclear Powers into direct confrontation.

Arms Reduction

The reduction of both conventional and nuclear arms is also vital as a means of achieving the collective security which the world so badly needs. Balanced and adequately verifiable arms reduction can increase the security of all parties by clarifying intentions, reducing the likelihood of aggression, and decreasing the threat inherent in the mere existence of large stockpiles of lethal weapons, particularly, of course, of nuclear weapons.

The United Nations has long provided the only fully representative, multilateral forum for disarmament negotiations within which most existing disarmament agreements, aside from those on strategic nuclear

weapons, have been developed. It has mobilized understanding of the necessity of disarmament and has served to bring Governments into broad agreements on disarmament ends.

The United Nations, while continuing to afford these services, can do more. It can provide an objective capacity to monitor agreements, and it can furnish expertise often needed in the formulation of treaties. If communication falters between parties, the Secretary-General will always be available as a quiet channel.

The building of international confidence must be seen as a progressive process, entailing concrete and constructive steps. The resolution of conflict and disputes can facilitate progress in the reduction of arms. Reduction in arms can, in turn, encourage yet another element in international security—equitable economic progress for the global population.

Social Justice

As we look to the next 40 years, collective security must be seen as dependent on these broad elements. I would add yet another: the defence of social justice. In each of these the United Nations has played an important role during the past 40 years.

The Organization—the machinery for peace—has been inadequately fueled in terms of national support for the maintenance of security, of compliance with the principles of the Charter and of resources for economic development. It is less than perfect in its operation. But the United Nations Organization is in place. It is, in practical terms, universal. It has functioned with much good effect for 40 years. It is equipped for service well beyond the coming biennium into the next century. The continuing need is already evident.

On this fortieth anniversary day, when negative perceptions of the capacity of the United Nations are too often voiced, I have given a relatively optimistic evaluation of the benefit which the United Nations has brought and can bring in the future. Much will depend, however, on the steadfastness with which the vision is maintained that was defined 40 years ago in San Francisco in the United Nations Charter.

The statesmen of that time were not dreamers. They were entirely conscious of the difficulties entailed in developing an effective system of international security when States retained their sovereign status.

In his address to the final session of the San Francisco Conference, Andrei Gromyko, as head of the Soviet delegation, said that the very best and most perfect Charter is not yet a guarantee of peace. There will be required, in addition, unity and co-ordination of action by Member States, especially by the most powerful.

In his report at the end of the San Francisco Conference the head of the American delegation, Edward Stetinius, wrote that measured against the magnitude of the task to which the United Nations have committed themselves, the instruments agreed upon may seem inadequate to the labour to be done. But, he said, they have behind them the history of humanity's long effort to suppress disorder that anarchy and the rule of violence.

Vision of Peace

The vision of peace shared by the signers of the Charter was based on an understanding of reality—the reality that the risk of widespread war was no longer tolerable, that without common security for all, there could well be a future for none. The reality remains unchanged, only intensified in its significance by the ongoing developments of nuclear weapons. In this situation there is evidence of a widening understanding of the need for a strong United Nations. Almost 60 Heads of State and Government have indicated their intention to participate in the fortieth anniversary session of the General Assembly this autumn. Today, on the anniversary of the signing of the Charter, the leaders of nine countries—Argentina, Austria, Canada, Jordan, Malaysia, Senegal, Spain, Sweden and Tanzania—have issued a solemn, joint appeal for the international community to unite "efforts to enable the United Nations to play its unique and vital role in promoting peace, justice, freedom and progress for all humanity". Other countries have made statements expressing similar views.

As Secretary-General, I would, on this fortieth anniversary, call on all Governments and peoples alike to affirm their determination to build on the achievements of the United Nations and to overcome such weaknesses as has been evident, so that its full potential for the maintenance of peace will be realized. The interests of tomorrow, of which San Francisco for this day can again be called the capital, leave us no other choice.

UN Chronicle 1985, No. 4 pp. 13–16; M. NERFIN, The Future of the United Nations Systems. Some Questions on the Occasion of an Anniversary, in: *Development Dialogue*, Uppsala, 1985.

UNITED NATIONS HEADQUARTERS. The UN Charter did not mention where the headquarters of the United Nations were to be located. However, the UN Preparatory Commission, on Oct. 4, 1945 decided that the permanent headquarters should be sited on the territory of the United States and the US Congress on Dec. 10 unanimously invited the UN to do so. On Feb. 14, 1946, the UN General Assembly accepted the invitation and decided that the permanent headquarters should be established in the Westchester County region, New York State, or in the Fairfield County region, Connecticut State, that is, in the vicinity of New York City, where the provisional headquarters would be located. Philadelphia and San Francisco also offered possible sites. Early in 1946, the Secretariat was established provisionally at Hunter College in the Bronx, New York, and in the middle of August the United Nations moved to the Sperry Gyroscope plant at Lake Success on Long Island.

On Dec. 14, 1946, the UN General Assembly accepted an offer by John D. Rockefeller, Jr., of $8.5 million for the purchase of the present 18-acre site between 42nd and 48th streets on Manhattan's East Side, bounded on the west by United Nations Plaza (formerly part of First Avenue) and on the east by the East River. Concurrently with the Rockefeller gift, the City of New York offered certain lands within and adjacent to the site, together with waterfront rights and easements. The City also undertook a $30-million improvement program in the immediate area, including the construction of a vehicular tunnel under First Avenue.

Once the site was decided on, the first Secretary-General, Trygve Lie, appointed the architect, Wallace K. Harrison, of the United States, to guide the architectural and development plans in co-operation with an international board of design consultants from 10 countries: W.K. Harrison (USA) as president and N.D. Bassov (USSR), G. Brunfaut (Belgium), E. Cornier (Canada), Ch.E. Le Corbusier (France), L. Chu-Cheng (China), S. Marhelius (Sweden), O. Niemeyer (Brazil), H. Robertson (Great Britain), G.A. Soilleux (Australia) and J. Vilamayo (Uruguay).

The plans prepared by the international board of consultants were unanimously adopted by the General Assembly on Nov. 20, 1947. Construction work costing $65 million was financed by the US repayable in yearly installments between 1951 and 1982. The corner-stone was laid on Oct. 24, 1949 – United Nations Day – at an open-air plenary meeting of the General Assembly at which the President of the United States, among others, spoke. Occupancy of the Secretariat building began in Aug., 1950 and was completed the following June. The Security Council held its first meeting in its new chamber early in 1952, and in October of the same year the General Assembly convened for the first time in the new Assembly Hall.

The four main structures, all interconnected, that comprise Headquarters, are: the 39-storey office building of the Secretariat; the long, low Conference Building paralleling the East River; the General Assembly Hall; and the Dag Hammarskjöld Library.

The international statute: Agreement between the UN and the USA regarding the Headquarters of the UN, signed at Lake Success, June 26, 1947, and approved by the UN General Assembly, Res. 169/II, Oct. 31, 1947 with the Exchange of Notes, Nov.

21, 1947, bringing the Agreement into effect; First Supplemental Agreement, signed at New York, Feb. 9, 1966; Second Supplemental Agreement, signed at New York, Aug. 28, 1969; Regulations to give Effect to art. 3, Sect. 8 of the 1947 Agreement, adopted by the UN General Assembly, Dec. 12, 1950.

By May 14, 1964 the first ten million persons had visited the UN headquarters which had become a major tourist attraction. On June 11, 1964, Secretary-General U Thant unveiled before the Secretariat building an abstract sculpture of bronze, 7 m high, placed on a granite plinth, and made according to the wishes of the late UN Secretary-General, Dag Hammarskjöld.

The official address is United Nations, New York 10017. Telephone: (212) 754-1234.

UN Yearbook, 1947–48, pp. 199–207; C.W. JENKS, *The Headquarters of International Institutions*, London, 1954; O.W. BOGDANOV, *Pravoviye voprosy prebyvanya OON w SSzA, Privilegyi i immunitety OON*, Moscow, 1962; *Everyone's United Nations*, New York, 1979.

UNITED NATIONS INSTITUTE FOR DISARMAMENT RESEARCH. ▷ UNIDIR.

UNITED NATIONS INSTITUTE FOR TRADING AND RESEARCH. Est. 1987 by the GA Res. 42/187; being organized in 1988/89.

UN Resolutions and Decisions adopted by the General Assembly during its Forty-Third Session, from 20 September to 22 December 1988, New York, 1989, pp. 301–303.

UNITED NATIONS, MOSCOW DECLARATION ON. ▷ Moscow Declaration on General International Organization, 1943.

UNITED NATIONS PARTICIPATION ACT, 1945. The name of the US law, adopted by the Congress Dec. 20, 1945, providing legislative authority for executive action in relations with the United Nations. The text reads as follows:

"Be it enacted by the Senate and House of Representatives of the United States of America in Congress assembled, That this Act may be cited as the 'United Nations Participation Act of 1945.'

Sec. 2.(a) The President, by and with the advice and consent of the Senate, shall appoint a representative and a deputy representative of the United States to the United Nations, both of whom shall have the rank and status of envoy extraordinary and ambassador plenipotentiary and shall hold office at the pleasure of the President. Such representative and deputy representative shall represent the United States in the Security Council of the United Nations and may serve ex officio as United States representative on any organ, commission, or other body of the United Nations other than specialized agencies of the United Nations, and shall perform such other functions in connection with the participation of the United States in the United Nations as the President may from time to time direct.

(b) The President, by and with the advice and consent of the Senate, shall appoint an additional deputy representative of the United States to the Security Council who shall hold office at the pleasure of the President. Such deputy representative shall represent the United States in the Security Council of the United Nations in the event of the absence or disability of both the representative and the deputy representative of the United States to the United Nations.

(c) The President, by and with the advice and consent of the Senate, shall designate from time to time to attend a specified session or specified sessions of the General Assembly of the United Nations not to exceed five representatives of the United States and such number of alternates as he may determine consistent with the rules of procedure of the General Assembly. One of the representatives shall be designated as the senior representative.

(d) The President may also appoint from time to time such other persons as he may deem necessary to represent the United States in the organs and agencies of the United Nations, but the representative of the United States in the Economic and Social Council and in the Trusteeship Council of the United Nations shall be appointed only by and with the advice and consent of the Senate, except that the President may, without the advice and consent of the Senate, designate any officer of the United States to act, without additional compensation, as the representative of the United States in either such council (A) at any specified session thereof, where the position is vacant or in the absence or disability of the regular representative, or (b) in connection with a specified subject matter at any specified session of either such Council in lieu of the regular representative. The President may designate any officer of the Department of State, whose appointment is subject to confirmation by the Senate, to act, without additional compensation, for temporary periods as the representative of the United States in the Security Council of the United Nations in the absence or disability of the representative and deputy representatives appointed under section 2(a) and (b) or in lieu of such representatives in connection with a specified subject matter. The advice and consent of the Senate shall be required for the appointment by the President of the representative of the United States in any commission that may be formed by the United Nations with respect to atomic energy or in any other commission of the United Nations to which the United States is entitled to appoint a representative.

(e) Nothing contained in this section shall preclude the President or the Secretary of State, at the direction of the President, from representing the United States at any meeting or session of any organ or agency of the United Nations.

(f) All persons appointed in pursuance of authority contained in this section shall receive compensation at rates determined by the President upon the basis of duties to be performed but not in excess of rates authorized by sections 411 and 412 of the Foreign Service Act of 1946 (Public Law 724, Seventy-ninth Congress) for chiefs of mission and Foreign Service officers occupying positions of equivalent importance, except that no Member of the Senate or House of Representatives or officer of the United States who is designated under subsections (c) and (d) of this section as a representative of the United States or as an alternate to attend any specified session or specified sessions of the General Assembly shall be entitled to receive such compensation.

Sec. 3. The representatives provided for in section 2 hereof, when representing the United States in the respective organs and agencies of the United Nations, shall, at all times, act in accordance with the instructions of the President transmitted by the Secretary of State unless other means of transmission is directed by the President, and such representatives shall, in accordance with such instructions, cast any and all votes under the Charter of the United Nations.

Sec. 4. The President shall, from time to time as occasion may require, but not less than once each year, make reports to the Congress of the activities of the United Nations and of the participation of the United States therein. He shall make special current reports on decisions of the Security Council to take enforcement measures under the provisions of the Charter of the United Nations, and on the participation therein under his instructions, of the representative of the United States.

Sec. 5.(a) Notwithstanding the provisions of any other law, whenever the United States is called upon by the Security Council to apply measures, which said Council has decided, pursuant to article 41 of said Charter, are to be employed to give effect to its decisions under said Charter, the President may, to the extent necessary to apply such measures, through any agency which he may designate, and under such orders, rules, and regulations as may be prescribed by him, investigate, regulate, or prohibit, in whole or in part, economic relations or rail, sea, air, postal, telegraphic, radio, and other means of communication between any foreign country or any national thereof or any person therein and the United States or any person subject to the jurisdiction thereof, or involving any property subject to the jurisdiction of the United States.

(b) Any person who willfully violates or evades or attempts to violate or evade any order, rule, or regulation issued by the President pursuant to paragraph (a) of this section shall, upon conviction, be fined not more than $10,000 or, if a natural person, be imprisoned for not more than ten years, or both; and the officer, director, or agent of any corporation who knowingly participates in such violation or evasion shall be punished by a like fine, imprisonment, or both, and any property, funds, securities, papers, or other articles or documents, or any vessel, together with her tackle, apparel, furniture, and equipment, or vehicle or aircraft, concerned in such violation shall be forfeited to the United States.
Sec. 6. The President is authorized to negotiate a special agreement or agreements with the Security Council which shall be subject to the approval of the Congress by appropriate Act or joint resolution, providing for the numbers and types of armed forces, their degree of readiness and general location, and the nature of facilities and assistance, including rights of passage, to be made available to the Security Council on its call for the purpose of maintaining international peace and security in accordance with article 43 of said Charter. The President shall not be deemed to require the authorization of the Congress to make available to the Security Council on its call in order to take action under article 42 of said Charter and pursuant to such special agreement or agreements the armed forces, facilities, or assistance provided for therein: Provided, That except as authorized in section 7 of this Act, nothing herein contained shall be construed as an authorization to the President by the Congress to make available to the Security Council for such purpose armed forces, facilities, or assistance in addition to the forces, facilities, and assistance provided for in such special agreement or agreements.
Sec. 7.(a) Notwithstanding the provisions of any other law, the President upon the request by the United Nations for cooperative action, and to the extent that he finds that it is consistent with the national interest to comply with such request, may authorize, in support of such activities of the United Nations as are specifically directed to the peaceful settlement of disputes and not involving the employment of armed forces contemplated by chapter VII of the United Nations Charter.
(1) the detail to the United Nations, under such terms and conditions as the President shall determine, of personnel of the armed forces of the United States to serve as observers, guards, or in any noncombatant capacity, but in no event shall more than a total of one thousand of such personnel be so detailed at any one time: Provided, That while so detailed, such personnel shall be considered for all purposes as acting in the line of duty, including the receipt of pay and allowances as personnel of the armed forces of the United States, credit for longevity and retirement, and all other perquisites appertaining to such duty: Provided further, That upon authorization or approval by the President, such personnel may accept directly from the United Nations (a) any or all of the allowances or perquisites to which they are entitled under the first proviso hereof, and (b) extraordinary expenses and perquisites incident to such detail;
(2) the furnishing of facilities, services, or other assistance and the loan of the agreed fair share of the United States of any supplies and equipment to the United Nations by the National Military Establishment, under such terms and conditions as the President shall determine;
(3) the obligation, insofar as necessary to carry out the purposes of clauses (1) and (2) of this subsection, of any funds appropriated to the National Military Establishment or any department therein, the procurement of such personnel, supplies, equipment, facilities, services, or other assistance as may be made available in accordance with the request of the United Nations, and the replacement of such items, when necessary, where they are furnished from stocks.
(b) Whenever personnel or assistance is made available pursuant to the authority contained in subsection (a) (1) and (2) of this section, the President shall require reimbursement from the United Nations for the expense thereby incurred by the United States: Provided, That in exceptional circumstances, or when the President finds it to be in the national interest, he may waive, in whole or in part, the requirement of such reimbursement: Provided further, That when any such reimbursement is made, it shall be credited, at the option of the appropriate department of the National Military Establishment, either to the appropriation, fund, or account utilized in incurring the obligation, or to an appropriate appropriation, fund, or account currently available for the purposes for which expenditures were made.
(c) In addition to the authorization of appropriations to the Department of State contained in section 8 of this Act, there is hereby authorized to be appropriated to the National Military Establishment, or any department therein, such sums as may be necessary to reimburse such Establishment or department in the event that reimbursement from the United Nations is waived in whole or in part pursuant to authority contained in subsection (b) of this section.
(d) Nothing in this Act shall authorize the disclosure of any information or knowledge in any case in which such disclosure is prohibited by any other law of the United States.
Sec. 8. There is hereby authorized to be appropriated annually to the Department of State, out of any money in the Treasury not otherwise appropriated, such sums as may be necessary for the payment by the United States of its share of the expenses of the United Nations as apportioned by the General Assembly in accordance with article 17 of the Charter, and for all necessary salaries and expenses of the representatives provided for in section 2 hereof, and of their appropriate staffs."

United States Statutes at Large, Washington, DC, 1945, Vol. 59, p. 619.

UNITED NATIONS PEACE ROLE RESOLUTION, 1973.

Adopted by the UN General Assembly, on Nov. 20, 1973. The text is as follows:

"The General Assembly,
Having further considered the item entitled 'Strengthening of the role of the United Nations with regard to the maintenance and consolidation of international peace and security, the development of co-operation among all nations and the promotion of the rules of international law in relations between States,'
Recalling its resolution 2925/XXVII of November 27, 1972,
Taking note of the report of the Secretary-General prepared on the basis of that resolution, as well as of the views and suggestions expressed in the debate on this item,
Considering that new steps taken towards achieving the universality of the United Nations are likely to contribute to an increase in the capacity of the Organization to take effective action for the strengthening of international peace and security and for the development of international co-operation,
Aware that the affirmation of a new course in international life, aimed at the establishment of an atmosphere of confidence and understanding between States and at the settlement of international problems of general interest with the broadest possible participation of States, requires an adequate strengthening of the role of the United Nations as a center for harmonizing the actions of nations,
Concerned about the insufficient use of the framework, provided by the United Nations for the settlement of problems affecting the interest of all Member States.
1. Reaffirms that it is imperative that the United Nations should become a more effective instrument in safeguarding and strengthening the independence and sovereign equality of all States, as well as the inalienable rights of every people to decide its own fate without any outside interference, and that it should take firm action, in accordance with the Charter of the United Nations, to oppose foreign domination and to prevent and suppress acts of aggression or any other acts which, in violating the Charter, may jeopardize international peace and security;
2. Reiterates its appeal to all Member States to take full advantage of the framework and means provided by the United Nations in order to prevent the perpetuation of situations of tension, crisis and conflict, avert the creation of such new situations which endanger international peace and security, and settle international problems exclusively by peaceful means;
3. Believes that the United Nations can bring an increased contribution to the strengthening of general peace and security by taking actions aimed at establishing the relations between all States on the basis of the principles of the Charter, and at using more actively the machinery and possibilities provided by the Charter with a view to preventing conflicts and encouraging the peaceful settlement of disputes between States;
4. Considers that the strengthening of the role of the United Nations requires continuous improvement of the functioning and effectiveness of its principal organs in the exercise of their responsibilities under the Charter;
5. Considers further that, in the context of endeavours to strengthen the role of the United Nations, it is important to study and agree upon ways and means of enhancing, in accordance with the Charter, the effectiveness of the resolutions of the General Assembly and other organs of the United Nations, inter alia, by actively promoting the method of consultation among all Member States interested in their elaboration and adoption, and by evaluating, as appropriate, their practical effects;
6. Emphasizes that the active participation of all Member States in the efforts aimed at strengthening the United Nations and enhancing its role in contemporary international relations is essential for the success of these efforts;
7. Urges all Member States, in furtherance of these efforts, to fulfill their obligations under the Charter and, in accordance with its provisions, to implement the resolutions of the General Assembly and the Security Council;
8. Invites all Member States to communicate and further elaborate on their views, suggestions and proposals concerning the strengthening of the role of the United Nations, not later than April 30, 1974;
9. Believes that the efforts aimed at strengthening the role of the United Nations will be greatly assisted by grouping the views, suggestions and proposals made on this subject by Member States, so as to facilitate their consideration by the appropriate existing organs of the United Nations;
10. Requests the Secretary-General to prepare a report presenting, in a systematized manner, those views, suggestions and proposals formulated at the twenty-seventh and twenty-eighth sessions of the General Assembly, as well as in the relevant communications received from Member States, and to submit that report to the Assembly at its twenty-ninth session;
11. Decides to include in the provisional agenda of its twenty-ninth session the item entitled 'Strengthening of the role of the United Nations with regard to the maintenance and consolidation of international peace and security, the development of co-operation among all nations and the promotion of the rules of international law in relations between States.'"

UN Yearbook, 1973.

UNITED NATIONS PUBLIC ADMINISTRATION PROGRAMME.

A national and international UN programme, initiated by ECOSOC in 1967, supported by the UN General Assembly Res. 2561/XXIV. A Meeting of Experts on the UN Programme in Public Administration with hq. in New York reviews issues and priorities in public administration and finance for the 1980's.

Yearbook of the UN 1969 and 1980.

UNITED NATIONS REPORTS.

▷ Reports of the United Nations.

UNITED NATIONS VOLUNTEERS.

▷ UNDP Voluntary Service.

UNITED STATES DECLARATION OF INDEPENDENCE, 1776.

The name of an historic document adopted on July 4, 1776, in Philadelphia by representatives of 13 colonies of Great Britain in America as "Representatives of the United States of America ... free from any ties with the British Crown." The Declaration was drafted by T. Jefferson (1743–1826) and amended by B. Franklin (1706–1790). It has influenced the growth of revolutionary movements in Europe and Latin America, particularly through its doctrine of the "self-evident truth" that "all men are created equal" ... "they are endowed by their Creator with certain unalienable Rights, that among these are Life, Liberty and the pursuit of Happiness." The text is as follows:

"When, in the course of human events, it becomes necessary for one people to dissolve the political bands which have connected them with another, and to assume, among the powers of the earth, the separate and equal station to which the laws of nature and of nature's God entitle them, a decent respect to the opinions of mankind requires that they should declare the causes which impel them to the separation.

We hold these truths to be self-evident, that all men are created equal; that they are endowed by their Creator with certain unalienable rights; that among these, are life, liberty, and the pursuit of happiness. That, to secure these rights, governments are instituted among men, deriving their just powers from the consent of the governed; that, whenever any form of government becomes destructive of these ends, it is the right of the people to alter or to abolish it, and to institute a new government, laying its foundation on such principles, and organizing its powers in such form, as to them shall seem most likely to effect their safety and happiness. Prudence, indeed, will dictate that governments long established, should not be changed for light and transient causes; and, accordingly, all experience hath shown, that mankind are more disposed to suffer, while evils are sufferable, than to right themselves by abolishing the forms to which they are accustomed. But, when a long train of abuses and usurpations, pursuing invariably the same object, evinces a design to reduce them under absolute despotism, it is their right, it is their duty, to throw off such government and to provide new guards for their future security. Such has been the patient sufferance of these colonies, and such is now the necessity which constrains them to alter their former systems of government. The history of the present King of Great Britain is a history of repeated injuries and usurpations, all having, in direct object, the establishment of an absolute tyranny over these States. To prove this, let facts be submitted to a candid world:-
He has refused his assent to laws the most wholesome and necessary for the public good.
He has forbidden his governors to pass laws of immediate and pressing importance, unless suspended in their operation till his assent should be obtained; and, when so suspended, he has utterly neglected to attend to them.
He has refused to pass other laws for the accommodation of large districts of people, unless those people would relinquish the right of representation in the legislature: a right inestimable to them, and formidable to tyrants only.
He has called together legislative bodies at places unusual, uncomfortable, and distant from the depository of their public records, for the sole purpose of fatiguing them into compliance with his measures.
He has dissolved representative houses repeatedly for opposing, with manly firmness, his invasions on the rights of the people.
He has refused, for a long time after such dissolutions, to cause others to be elected; whereby the legislative powers, incapable of annihilation, have returned to the people at large for their exercise; the state remaining, in the meantime, exposed to all the danger of invasion from without, and convulsions within.
He has endeavored to prevent the population of these States; for the purpose, obstructing the laws for naturalization of foreigners, refusing to pass others to encourage their migration hither, and raising the conditions of new appropriations of lands.
He has obstructed the administration of justice, by refusing his assent to laws for establishing judiciary powers. He has made judges dependent on his will alone, for the tenure of their offices, and the amount and payment of their salaries.
He has erected a multitude of new offices, and sent hither swarms of officers to harass our people, and eat out their substance.
He has kept among us, in time of peace, standing armies, without the consent of our legislatures.
He has affected to render the military independent of, and superior to, the civil power.
He has combined, with others, to subject us to a jurisdiction foreign to our Constitution, and unacknowledged by our laws; giving his assent to their acts of pretended legislation:
For quartering large bodies of armed troops among us:
For protecting them by a mock trial, from punishment, for any murders which they should commit on the inhabitants of these States:
For cutting off our trade with all parts of the world:
For imposing taxes on us without our consent:
For depriving us, in many cases, of the benefit of trial by jury:
For transporting us beyond seas to be tried for pretended offences:
For abolishing the free system of English laws in a neighboring province, establishing therein an arbitrary government, and enlarging its boundaries, so as to render it at once an example and fit instrument for introducing the same absolute rule into these colonies:
For taking away our charters, abolishing our most valuable laws, and altering, fundamentally, the powers of our governments:
For suspending our own legislatures, and declaring themselves invested with power to legislate for us in all cases whatsoever.
He has abdicated government here, by declaring us out of his protection, and waging war against us.
He has plundered our seas, ravaged our coasts, burnt our towns, and destroyed the lives of our people.
He is, at this time, transporting large armies of foreign mercenaries to complete the works of death, desolation, and tyranny, already begun, with circumstances of cruelty and perfidy scarcely paralleled in the most barbarous ages, and totally unworthy the head of a civilized nation.
He has constrained our fellow citizens, taken captive on the high seas, to bear arms against their country, to become the executioners of their friends, and brethren, or to fall themselves by their hands.
He has excited domestic insurrections amongst us, and has endeavored to bring on the inhabitants of our frontiers, the merciless Indian savages, whose known rule of warfare is an undistinguished destruction of all ages, sexes, and conditions.
In every stage of these oppressions, we have petitioned for redress, in the most humble terms; our repeated petitions have been answered only by repeated injury. A prince, whose character is thus marked by every act which may define a tyrant, is unfit to be the ruler of a free people.
Nor have we been wanting in attention to our British brethren. We have warned them, from time to time, of attempts made by their legislature to extend an unwarrantable jurisdiction over us. We have reminded them of the circumstances of our emigration and settlement here. We have appealed to their native justice and magnanimity, and we have conjured them, by the ties of our common kindred, to disavow these usurpations, which would inevitably interrupt our connections and correspondence. They, too, have been deaf to the voice of justice and consanguinity. We must, therefore, acquiesce in the necessity which denounces our separation, and hold them, as we hold the rest of mankind, enemies in war, in peace, friends.
We, therefore, the representatives of the United States of America, in general Congress assembled, appealing to the Supreme Judge of the world for the rectitude of our intentions, do, in the name, and by the authority of the good people of these colonies, solemnly publish and declare, that these united colonies are, and of right ought to be, free and independent states: that they are absolved from all allegiance to the British Crown, and that all political connection between them and the state of Great Britain is, and ought to be, totally dissolved; and that, as free and independent states, they have full power to levy war, conclude peace, contract alliances, establish commerce, and to do all other acts and things which independent states may of right do. And, for the support of this declaration, with a firm reliance on the protection of Divine Providence, we mutually pledge to each other our lives, our fortunes, and our sacred honor."

J.P. BOYD, *The Declaration of Independence; The Evolution of the Text*, New York, 1945; D. MALONE, *The Story of the Declaration of Independence*, Oxford, Mass., 1975.

UNITED STATES DOCTRINE ON COMMUNIST PARTICIPATION IN WESTERN EUROPEAN GOVERNMENTS, 1978.

An official US Department of State statement on Jan. 12, 1978:

"US Ambassador to Italy Richard N. Gardner's visit to Washington has provided an occasion for a general policy review with senior Administration officials.
There has been no change in the Administration's attitude toward Western European Communist Parties, including that of Italy, although recent developments in Italy have increased the level of our concern.
As the President and other members of the Administration have publicly stated on a number of occasions, our Western European allies are sovereign countries and, rightly and properly, the decision on how they are governed rests with their citizens alone. At the same time, we believe we have an obligation to our friends and allies to express our views clearly.
Administration leaders have repeatedly expressed our views on the issue of Communist participation in Western European governments. Our position is clear: We do not favor such participation and would like to see Communist influence in any Western European country reduced.
As we have said in the past, we believe the best way to achieve these goals rests with the efforts of democratic parties to meet the aspirations of their people for effective, just, and compassionate government.
The United States and Italy share profound democratic values and interests, and we do not believe that the Communists share those values and interests.
As the President said last week in Paris: 'It's precisely when democracy is up against difficult challenges that its leaders must show firmness in resisting the temptation of finding solutions in non democratic forces.'"

Department of State Bulletin, No. 2011, 1978.

UNITED STATES FOREIGN AID.

The bilateral credits and loans, leases or transfer or raw materials, manufactured goods, military material or rendering of services by the USA to different countries of the world; in the years 1918–21 on the basis of the so called Hoover program, in the years 1941–45 on the basis of ▷ Lend-Lease Act for the United Nations; then according to annual decisions of the Congress, given on the request of the US government. The first law initiating this system was the Foreign Assistance Act of Apr. 3, 1948, providing formal basis for ▷ the Marshall Plan, 1947, and the ▷ Military Assistance Program of Oct. 28, 1949 giving legal grounds for arming NATO states and anti-communist states of South Asia by the United States and also the Congress decision of July 29, 1950, on the implementation of ▷ Truman's Fourth Point on technological assistance for the developing countries; on Oct. 31, 1951 US Congress adopted the Mutual Security Appropriation Bill, which extended United States arming of other states to include all those which declared themselves as anti-communist, in exchange for providing United States with military bases for their armed forces or in exchange for strategic obligations in case of the "communist threat." In the years 1945–65, from the total amount of 116 billion dollars of US foreign aid for civil and military purposes 40.2% was received by the European NATO states, 22.04% by the Far East, 10.3% by the Middle East and 8.9% by Latin America. UNCTAD on principle argued against US bilateral foreign aid in 1968, stating that in the majority of cases it was linked to superfluous armaments and anachronistic political preconditions. The standpoint of UNCTAD of May 19, 1968 was supported by the Secretary-General of the Organization of American States, Galo Plaza, requesting that all assistance for Latin American states be administered "through multi-national organizations, such as the International Bank for the Development, which has been established for such purposes."
Due to the opposition of the US Congress to the multinational system, the aforementioned postulates have not been implemented. The US Senate on Nov. 2, 1971, decided that foreign aid shall be

rendered separately for military purposes, and separately for humanitarian and developmental purposes. According to Senator J.F. Fulbright, this was necessary because "even the war in Vietnam was begun with our foreign aid." The Foreign Aid Act of 1973 in art. 32 introduced a new precondition: "The Congress is of the opinion that the President should deny all economic or military assistance to a government of any foreign state whatsoever which due to political reasons detains or imprisons its citizens."

US Department Bulletin, 1973.

UNITED STATES NEUTRALITY ACTS. ▷ Neutrality Acts of the USA, 1935–39.

UNITED STATES NEUTRALITY PROCLAMATION, 1939. The Neutrality and Arms Embargo Proclamation and Rules Governing Ship Travel of American Citizens, issued Sept. 5, 1939 by the President F.D. Roosevelt. The text of the Preamble is as follows:

Whereas a state of war unhappily exists between Germany and France; Poland; and the United Kingdom, India, Australia, and New Zealand;
And whereas the United States is on terms of friendship and amity with the contending Powers, and with the persons inhabiting their several dominions; and whereas there are nationals of the United States residing within the territories or dominions of each of the said belligerents, and carrying on commerce, trade, or other business or pursuits therein; and whereas there are nationals of each of the said belligerents residing within the territory or jurisdiction of the United States, and carrying on commerce, trade, or other business or pursuits therein; and whereas the laws and treaties of the United States, without interfering with the free expression of opinion and sympathy, nevertheless impose upon all persons who may be within their territory and jurisdiction the duty of an impartial neutrality during the existence of this contest; and whereas it is the duty of a neutral government not to permit or suffer the making of its territory or territorial waters subservient to the purposes of war;
Now, therefore, I, Franklin D. Roosevelt, President of the United States of America, in order to preserve the neutrality of the United States and of its citizens and of persons within its territory and jurisdiction, and to enforce its laws and treaties, and in order that all persons, being warned of the general tenor of the laws and treaties of the United States in this behalf, and of the law of nations, may thus be prevented from any violation of the same, do hereby declare and proclaim that by certain provisions of the act approved on the fourth day of March, AD 1909, commonly known as the Penal Code of the United States and of the act approved on the fifteenth day of June, AD 1917, the following acts are forbidden to be done, under severe penalties, within the territory and jurisdiction of the United States, to wit.

US Department of State Bulletin, No. 11, 1939; F. DEAK, "The US Neutrality Acts. Theory and Practice. Text of the Neutrality Act of 1939", in: *International Conciliation*, No. 358, March, 1940.

UNITED STATES OF AFRICA. A term for co-operation of Ghana, Guinea and Mali, 1961–65, on the basis of the Charter of African States Union, signed on Apr. 29, 1961 in Accra by the presidents of those countries.

UNITED STATES OF AMERICA, USA. Member of the UN. Permanent Member of the UN Security Council. After World War II the major capitalist power. State on the Atlantic and Pacific Oceans. Borders with Canada and Mexico. Area: 9,369,885 sq. km. Pop. 1985 est.: 255,000,000. Growth of census population: 1790 – 3,929,000; 1800 – 5,308,000; 1850 – 23,191,000; 1900 – 75,994,000; 1920 – 105,710,000; 1940 – 131,669,000; 1950 – 150,697,000; 1960 – 179,323,000; 1970 – 203,302,031; 1980 – 226,504,825 (▷ Melting Pot).

Capital: Washington, DC., with 637,651 inhabitants in 1980 (1970 – 756,668). GNP per capita in 1985: US $16,710. Official language: English. Currency: one dollar = 100 cents. National Day: July 4, Independence Day, 1776.
Original Member of the UN, and of all specialized organizations with the exception of UNESCO.
Member of OAS, NATO, OECD and the Colombo Plan.
International relations: in the 17th–18th centuries a British colony established through settlement, which began in May, 1607. In the fall of 1774 the 13 British colonies called the Continental Congress in Philadelphia. On July 4, 1776 they announced the Declaration of Independence. Territorially the States expanded the area of their state in stages: by the Treaty of Paris in 1783 with Great Britain, by the Continental Congress with the North-West Ordinance; by a Treaty with France in 1803 they acquired Louisiana, by the American-British agreement on demilitarization of the Canadian border, 1818 and on Northwest territories, 1869; by a Treaty with Spain in 1819, by Texas' proclamation of independence from Mexico, 1836, Florida; by a Treaty with Great Britain in 1842 and 1846. Part of Mexico was annexed in 1845, confirmed by Treaties with Mexico in 1848 and 1853. The territory divided by the Civil War was reintegrated 1867–1877. By a Treaty with Russia Alaska was acquired in 1867. In 1898 the States annexed Hawaii, in 1901 the Panama Canal zone, in 1902 the base at Guantanamo in Cuba. From 1917 the States participated in World War I on the side of the Allies, and President W. Wilson (▷ Wilson's Fourteen Points, 1918) was instrumental in the formation of the League of Nations but the USA remained outside the League. On Dec. 7, 1941 Japan attacked the American naval base at Pearl Harbor, and on Dec. 11, 1941 Germany and Italy declared war on the United States. In the years 1942–45 the USA, USSR, Great Britain and the other United Nations defeated the axis states. One of the five Great Powers, a founder of the UN and permanent member of the UN Security Council. At war in Korea, 1950–53, and in Vietnam, 1964–73.
On Dec. 14, 1984 the USA signed the first agreement with Cuba on the normalization of migration procedure.
The new US strategic concept related to the ▷ SDI program remained without change during President R. Reagan's administration.
On March 18, 1988 the new immigration law legalized the status of 1,400,000 illegal aliens in the USA.
After the USSR's November 1987 decision to pay all its outstanding debts, the top debtor was the United States with $352,5 million owed to the regular budget and $61,4 million owed for its share of peacekeeping operations in the Middle East.
On Febr. 1, 1989 the US Census Bureau predicted that the US population would grow from 246 million to 302 million in 50 years, and then trail off to 292 million by the year 2080.
The solidarity with the US in voting in the 41st UN General Assembly Sessions, analized by the State Department was as follows: in 88.8% by Israel, 88.2% by UK, 87.3% by FRG, 79.2% by Luxembourg, 78.9% by Belgium, 78.3% by France, 77.3% by Italy, 75.5% by Holland, and 74.3% by Portugal.
The 41 Presidents of the USA 1789–1989:

George Washington (1732–99)	1789–97
John Adams (1735–1826)	1797–1801
Thomas Jefferson (1743–1826)	1801–09
James Madison (1751–1836)	1809–17
James Monroe (1759–1831)	1817–25
John Quincy Adams (1767–1848)	1825–29
Andrew Jackson (1767–1845)	1829–37
Martin van Buren (1782–1862)	1837–41
William H. Harrison (1773–1841)	1841
John Tyler (1790–1862)	1841–45
James K. Polk (1795–1849)	1845–49
Zachary Taylor (1784–1850)	1849–50
Millard Fillmore (1800–74)	1850–53
Franklin Pierce (1804–69)	1854–57
James Buchanan (1791–1861)	1857–61
Abraham Lincoln (1809–65)	1861–65
Andrew Johnson (1808–75)	1865–69
Ulysses S. Grant (1822–85)	1869–77
Rutherford B. Hayes (1822–93)	1877–81
James A. Garfield (1831–81)	1881
Chester A. Arthur (1830–86)	1881–85
Grover Cleveland (1837–1908)	1885–89
Benjamin Harrison (1833–1901)	1889–93
Grover Cleveland (1837–1908)	1893–97
William McKinley (1843–1901)	1897–1901
Theodore Roosevelt (1858–1919)	1901–09
William H. Taft (1857–1930)	1909–13
Woodrow Wilson (1856–1924)	1913–21
Warren G. Harding (1865–1923)	1921–23
Calvin Coolidge (1872–1933)	1923–29
Herbert C. Hoover (1874–1964)	1929–33
Franklin D. Roosevelt (1882–1945)	1933–45
Harry S. Truman (1884–1972)	1945–53
Dwight D. Eisenhower (1890–1969)	1953–61
John F. Kennedy (1917–63)	1961–63
Lyndon B. Johnson (1908–73)	1963–69
Richard M. Nixon (1913–)	1969–74
Gerald F. Ford (1913–)	1974–77
James E. Carter (1924–)	1977–81
Ronald Reagan (1911–)	1981–89
George Bush (1924–)	1989–

See also ▷ World Heritage UNESCO List.

M. MALLOY (ed.), *Treaties, Conventions Between the US and other Powers, 1776–1937*, Washington, DC, 1909–38; "Treaties of Peace between the US and Germany, Austria, Hungary", in: *International Conciliation*, No. 170, January, 1922; H. MILLER (ed.), *Treaties and other International Acts of the United States of America*, 8 Vols., Washington, DC, 1929–48; T.A. BAILEY, *A Diplomatic History of the American People*, New York, 1947; *Postwar Foreign Preparation 1939–1945. Department of State*, Washington, DC, 1949; *US Treaties and Other International Agreements*, Washington, DC, 1950; *Harvard Guide to American History*, Cambridge Mass., 1954; A.M. SCHLESINGER, *The Rise of Modern America, 1865–1951*, New York, 1954; J.W. PRATT, *A History of the US Foreign Policy*, New York, 1955; LIBRARY OF CONGRESS, *Guide to the Study of the USA*, Washington, DC, 1960; P.M. HAMMER (ed.), *Guide to Archives and Manuscripts in the US*, Yale, 1961; A. MAUROIS, *Histoire des États-Unis de 1917 à 1961*, Paris, 1961; F.B. GROSS, *The US and the UN*, Oklahoma, 1964; D. WATSON, *American Agencies Interested in International Affairs*, New York, 1964; J. LLOYD MECCHAM, *A Survey of US Latinamerican Relations*, Boston, 1965; *Regional and other Documents Concerning US Relations with Latin America, US Congress*, Washington DC, 1966; H.S. COMMAGER (ed.), *Documents of American History*, New York, 1966; J.W. FULBRIGHT, *The Arrogance of Power*, London, 1967; L.D. WEYLER, A.P. SIMONS, *The US and the UN*, New York, 1967; S.E. MORRISON, *Oxford History of the American People*, Oxford, 1968; R.B. RUSSEL, *The UN and the US Security Policy*, Washington, DC, 1968; F.W. FULLBRIGHT, *The Crippled Giant: American Foreign Policy and the Domestic Consequences*, New York, 1972; H.V. PROCHNOW, *The Changing World of Banking*, New York, 1974; H. GUNTHER, *Banking in the US*, London, 1976; A.W. ROVINE, *Digest of US Practice in International Law, 1973*, Washington, DC, 1974; T. TIMITRICHEV, *Amierikanskaya diplomatiya w OON*, Moscow, 1977; A. DE CONDE, *Encyclopedia of American Foreign Policy*, 3 Vols., New York, 1978; A. GROMYKO, *Wnieshnaya politika SSha*, Moscow, 1978; T. SZULC, *The Illusion of Peace. Foreign Policy in the Nixon Years*, New York, 1978; N.V. SIVACHOV, N.N. YAKOVLEV, *Russia and the United States*, Chicago, 1979; P. DUIGNON, A. RABUSHKA (eds.), *The United States in the 1980s*, Stanford, 1980; S.R. HENTEIN, *USA, Bibliography*, Santa Barbara, 1982; A. DECONDE ed., *Encyclopedia of American Foreign Policy*, 3 Vol., 1982; *The Europa*

Year Book 1984. A World Survey, Vol. II, pp. 2566–2637, London, 1984; J.P. GREENE, *Encyclopedia of American Political History*, London, 1984; A.M. SCHLESINGER Jr., *The Cycles of American History*, Boston, 1986; G. CARRUTH, *The Encyclopedia of American Facts and Dates*, New York, 1987; J. CHACE, C. CARR, *America Invulnerable. The Quest for Absolute Security From 1812 to Star Wars*, New York, 1988; M. NIEZABITOWSKA, T. TOMASZEWSKI, Discovering America, in: *National Geographic*, January, 1988; C.F. BERGSTEN, *America in the World Economy: A Strategy for the 1990's*, Washington, DC, 1988; *SIPRI Yearbook 1987*, Oxford, 1988, pp. 4–16; *The New York Times*, Feb. 1 and 2, 1989.

UNITED STATES OF EUROPE. Name of a political integration proposed in May 1930 to all European member states of the League of Nations in a memorandum of the French government signed by Prime Minister Aristides Briand (1862–1932). The aim of the union was the elimination of the armaments race in international relations in order to ensure a lasting peace for Western Europe. In view of internal conflicts and the world economic crisis, as well as of national Fascist movements, Briand's idea became unrealistic and the memorandum had no practical consequences.

G. SUAREZ, *Aristide Briand*, 3 Vols., Paris, 1938–39.

UNITED STATES PROCLAMATION OF NEUTRALITY, 1793. Proclamation done at Philadelphia, Apr. 22, 1793 by the President George Washington. The text is as follows:

"Whereas it appears that a state of war exists between Austria, Prussia, Sardinia, Great Britain, and the United Netherlands, on the one part, and France on the other, and the duty and interest of the United States require, that they should with sincerity and good faith adopt and pursue a conduct friendly and impartial toward the belligerent powers:

I have therefore thought fit by these presents to declare the disposition of the United States to observe the conduct aforesaid towards those powers respectively; and to exhort and warn the citizens of the United States carefully to avoid all acts and proceedings whatsoever, which may in any manner tend to contravene such disposition.

And I do hereby also make known that whosoever of the citizens of the United States shall render himself liable to punishment or forfeiture under the law of nations, by committing, aiding or abetting hostilities against any of the said powers, or by carrying to any of them those articles, which are deemed contraband by the modern usage of nations, will not receive the protection of the United States against such punishment or forfeiture: and further, that I have given instructions to those officers, to whom it belongs, to cause prosecutions to be instituted against all persons who shall, within the cognizance of the courts of the United States, violate the Law of Nations, with respect to the powers at war, or any of them."

America State Papers Foreign Relations, Vol. 1, p. 140.

UNITED STATES PROCLAMATION OF NEUTRALITY, 1914. Proclamation done at Washington, DC, Aug. 4, 1914 by the President W. Wilson. The highlights of the Proclamation:

"Whereas a state of war unhappily exists between Austria–Hungary and Servia and between Germany and Russia and between Germany and France; and whereas the United States is on terms of friendship and amity with the contending powers, and with the persons inhabiting their several dominions;

And whereas there are citizens of the United States residing within the territories or dominions of each of the said belligerents, and carrying on commerce, trade, or other business or pursuits therein;

And whereas there are subjects of each of the said belligerents residing within the territory or jurisdiction of the United States, and carrying on commerce, trade, or other business or pursuits therein;

And whereas the laws and treaties of the United States, without interfering with the free expression of opinion and sympathy, or with the commercial manufacture or sale of arms or munitions of war, nevertheless impose upon all persons who may be within their territory and jurisdiction the duty of an impartial neutrality during the existence of the contest;

And whereas it is the duty of a neutral government not to permit or suffer the making of its waters subservient to the purposes of war;

Now, therefore, I, Woodrow Wilson, President of the United States of America, in order to preserve the neutrality of the United States and of its citizens and of persons within its territory and jurisdiction, and to enforce its laws and treaties, and in order that all persons, being warned of the general tenor of the laws and treaties of the United States in this behalf, and of the law of nations, may thus be prevented from any violation of the same, do hereby declare and proclaim that by certain provisions of the act approved on the 4th day of March, AD 1909, commonly known as the "Penal Code of the United States," the following acts are forbidden to be done, under severe penalties, within the territory and jurisdiction of the United States, to wit:

1. Accepting and exercising a commission to serve either of the said belligerents by land or by sea against the other belligerent.

2. Enlisting or entering into the service of either of said belligerents as a soldier, or as a marine, or seaman on board of any vessel of war, letter of marque, or privateer.

3. Hiring or retaining another person to enlist or enter himself in the service of either of the said belligerents as a soldier, or as a marine, or seaman on board of any vessel of war, letter of marque, or privateer.

4. Hiring another person to go beyond the limits or jurisdiction of the United States with intent to be enlisted as aforesaid.

5. Hiring another person to go beyond the limits of the United States with intent to be entered into service as aforesaid.

6. Retaining another person to go beyond the limits of the United States with intent to be enlisted as aforesaid.

7. Retaining another person to go beyond the limits of the United States with intent to be entered into service as aforesaid. (But the said act is not to be construed to extend to a citizen or subject of either belligerent who, being transiently within the United States, shall, on board of any vessel of war, which, at the time of its arrival within the United States, was fitted and equipped as such vessel of war, enlist or enter himself or hire or retain another subject or citizen of the same belligerent, who is transiently within the United States, to enlist or enter himself to serve such belligerent on board such vessel of war, if the United States shall then be at peace with such belligerent.)

8. Fitting out and arming, or attempting to fit out and arm, or procuring to be fitted out and armed, or knowingly being concerned in the furnishing, fitting out, or arming of any ship or vessel with intent that such ship or vessel shall be employed in the service of either of the said belligerents.

9. Issuing or delivering a commission within the territory or jurisdiction of the United States for any ship or vessel to the intent that she may be employed as aforesaid.

10. Increasing or augmenting, or procuring to be increased or augmented, or knowingly being concerned in increasing or augmenting, the force of any ship of war, cruiser, or other armed vessel, which at the time of her arrival within the United States was a ship of war, cruiser, or armed vessel in the service of either of the said belligerents, or belonging to the subjects of either, by adding to the number of guns of such vessels, or by changing those on board of her for guns of a larger caliber, or by the addition thereto of any equipment solely applicable to war.

11. Beginning or setting on foot or providing or preparing the means for any military expedition or enterprise to be carried on from the territory or jurisdiction of the United States against the territories or dominions of either of the said belligerents."

International Law Documents, Washington, DC, 1916, p. 83.

UNITED STATES TARIFF COMMISSION. An independent agency observing American foreign trade, est. 1916, Washington, DC, especially the impact of imports on American production. The six commissioners are appointed by the US President for six-year terms. The Tariff Commission investigates and recommendations are presented to the President, to the Senate Committee on Finance and to the House Committee on Ways and Means. The Commission initiated the Reciprocal Trade Agreements Act of 1934 (▷ Escape Clause) and the Trade Expansion Act of 1962 and other tariff legislation.

UNITED STATES TRADE ACT, 1975. ▷ Jackson Amendment, 1975.

UNITED TOWN ORGANIZATION. Federation mondiale des villes jumelees, f. 1957, Paris. Aims: develop understanding between peoples whatever their race, language, religion or political system. Consultative Status ECOSOC, UNESCO. Publ.: *Cités Unies* (quarterly in English and French). Reg. with the UIA.

Yearbook of International Organizations.

"UNITING FOR PEACE," 1950. A UN General Assembly resolution during the Korea War, proposed by the US Secretary of State Dean Acheson, so-called "Acheson Plan," adopted as Res. 337 A, B and C, Nov. 3, 1950. The Res. A was adopted by 51 votes against 5 (Byelorussia, Czechoslovakia, Poland, Ukrainian SSR and USSR) and 2 abstaining (Argentina and India); the Res. B by 50:0 with 6 abstaining; the Res. 6 by 57:0. The text is as follows:

Resolution A
The General Assembly,
Recognizing that the first two stated Purposes of the United Nations are:
"To maintain international peace and security, and to that end: to take effective collective measures for the prevention and removal of threats to the peace, and for the suppression of acts of aggression or other breaches of the peace, and to bring about by peaceful means, and in conformity with the principles of justice and international law, adjustment or settlement of international disputes or situations which might lead to a breach of the peace;
"To develop friendly relations among nations based on respect for the principle of equal rights and self-determination of peoples, and to take other appropriate measures to strengthen universal peace";
Reaffirming that it remains to the primary duty of all Members of the United Nations, when involved in an international dispute, to seek settlement of such a dispute by peaceful means through the procedures laid down in Chapter VI of the Charter, and recalling the successful achievements of the United Nations in this regard on a number of previous occasions,
Finding that international tension exists on a dangerous scale. Recalling its resolution 290 (IV) entitled "Essentials of peace," which states that disregard of the principles of the Charter of the United Nations is primarily responsible for the continuance of international tension, and desiring to contribute further to the objectives of that resolution,
Reaffirming the importance of the exercise by the Security Council of its primary responsibility for the maintenance of international peace and security, and the duty of the permanent members to seek unanimity and to exercise restraint in the use of the veto,
Reaffirming that the initiative in negotiating the agreements for armed forces provided for in Article 43 of the Charter belongs to the Security Council, and desiring to ensure that, pending the conclusion of such agreements, the United Nations has at its disposal means for maintaining international peace and security,
Conscious that failure of the Security Council to discharge its responsibilities on behalf of all the Member States, particularly those responsibilities referred to in the two preceding paragraphs, does not relieve Member States of their obligations or the United Nations of its responsibility under the Charter to maintain international peace and security,

Recognizing in particular that such failure does not deprive the General Assembly of its rights or relieve it of its responsibilities under the Charter in regard to the maintenance of international peace and security,

Recognizing that discharge by the General Assembly of its responsibilities in these respects calls for possibilities of observation which would ascertain the facts and expose aggressors; for the existence of armed forces which could be used collectively; and for the possibility of timely recommendation by the General Assembly to Members of the United Nations for collective action which, to be effective, should be prompt,

A. 1. Resolves that if the Security Council because of lack of unanimity of the permanent members, fails to exercise its primary responsibility for the maintenance of international peace and security in any case where there appears to be a threat to the peace, breach of the peace, or act of aggression, the General Assembly shall consider the matter immediately with a view to making appropriate recommendations to Members for collective measures, including in the case of a breach of the peace or act of aggression the use of armed force when necessary, to maintain or restore international peace and security. If not in session at the time, the General Assembly may meet in emergency special session within twenty-four hours of the request therefor. Such emergency special session shall be called if requested by the Security Council on the vote of any seven members, or by a majority of the Members of the United Nations,

2. Adopts for this purpose the amendments to its rules of procedure set forth in the annex to the present resolution;

B. 3. Establishes a Peace Observation Commission for which the calendar years 1951 and 1952, shall be composed of fourteen Members, namely: China, Colombia, Czechoslovakia, France, India, Iraq, Israel, New Zealand, Pakistan, Sweden, the Union of Soviet Socialist Republics, the United Kingdom of Great Britain and Northern Ireland, the United States of America and Uruguay, and which could observe and report on the situation in any area where there exists international tension the continuance of which is likely to endanger the maintenance of international peace and security. Upon the invitation or with the consent of the State into whose territory the Commission would go, the General Assembly, or the Interim Committee when the Assembly is not in session, may utilize the Commission if the Security Council is not exercising the functions assigned to it by the Charter with respect to the matter in question. Decisions to utilize the Commission shall be made on the affirmative vote of two-thirds of the members present and voting. The Security Council may also utilize the Commission in accordance with its authority under the Charter;

4. The Commission shall have authority in its discretion to appoint subcommissions and to utilize the services of observers to assist it in the performance of its functions;

5. Recommends to all governments and authorities that they co-operate with the Commission and assist it in the performance of its functions;

6. Requests the Secretary-General to provide the necessary staff and facilities, utilizing, where directed by the Commission, the United Nations Panel of Field Observers envisaged in General Assembly resolutions 297 B (IV);

C. 7. Invites each Member of the United Nations to survey its resources in order to determine the nature and scope of the assistance it may be in a position to render in support of any recommendations of the Security Council or of the General Assembly for the restoration of international peace and security;

8. Recommends to the Member States of the United Nations that each Member maintain within its national armed forces elements so trained, organized and equipped that they could promptly be made available, in accordance with its constitutional processes, for service as a United Nations unit or units, upon recommendation by the Security Council or General Assembly, without prejudice to the use of such elements in exercise of the right of individual or collective self-defence recognized in Article 51 of the Charter;

9. Invites the Members of the United Nations to inform the Collective Measures Committee provided for in paragraph 11 as soon as possible of the measures taken in implementation of the preceding paragraph;

10. Requests the Secretary-General to appoint, with the approval of the Committee provided for in paragraph 11, a panel of military experts who could be made available, on request, to Member States wishing to obtain technical advice regarding the organization, training, and equipment for prompt service as United Nations units of the elements referred to in paragraph 8;

D. 11. Establishes a Collective Measures Committee consisting of fourteen Members, namely: Australia, Belgium, Brazil, Burma, Canada, Egypt, France, Mexico, Philippines, Turkey, the United Kingdom of Great Britain and Northern Ireland, the United States of America, Venezuela and Yugoslavia, and directs the Committee, in consultation with the Secretary-General and with such Member States as the Committee finds appropriate, to study and make a report to the Security Council and the General Assembly, not later than 1 September 1951, on methods, including those in Section C of the present resolution, which might be used to maintain and strengthen international peace and security in accordance with the Purposes and Principles of the Charter, taking account of collective self-defence and regional arrangements (Articles 51 and 52 of the Charter);

12. Recommends to all Member States that they co-operate with the Committee and assist it in the performance of its functions;

13. Requests the Secretary-General to furnish the staff and facilities necessary for the effective accomplishment of the purposes set forth in sections C and D of the present resolution;

E. 14. The General Assembly, in adopting the proposals set forth above, is fully conscious that enduring peace will not be secured solely by collective security arrangements against breaches of international peace and acts of aggression, but that a genuine and lasting peace depends also upon the observance of all the Principles and Purposes established in the Charter of the United Nations, upon the implementation of the resolutions of the Security Council, the General Assembly and other principal organs of the United Nations intended to achieve the maintenance of international peace and security, and especially upon respect for and observance of human rights and fundamental freedoms for all and on the establishment and maintenance of conditions of economic and social well-being in all countries; and accordingly

15. Urges Member States to respect fully, and to intensify, joint action, in co-operation with the United Nations, to develop and stimulate universal respect for and observance of human rights and fundamental freedoms, and to intensify individual and collective efforts to achieve conditions of economic stability and social progress, particularly through the development of underdeveloped countries and areas.

Annex. The rules of procedure of the General Assembly are amended in the following respects:

1. The present text of rule 8 shall become paragraph (a) of that rule, and a new paragraph (b) shall be added to read as follows:

"Emergency special sessions pursuant to resolution – (V) shall be convened within twenty-four hours of the receipt by the Secretary-General of a request for such a session from the Security Council, on the vote of any seven members thereof, or of a request from a majority of the Members of the United Nations expressed by vote in the Interim Committee or otherwise, or of the concurrence of a majority of Members as provided in rule 9."

2. The present text of rule 9 shall become paragraph (a) of that rule and a new paragraph (b) shall be added to read as follows:

"This rule shall apply also to a request by any Member for an emergency special session pursuant to resolution – (V). In such a case the Secretary-General shall communicate with other Members by the most expeditious means of communication available."

3. Rule 10 is amended by adding at the end thereof the following:

"In the case of an emergency special session convened pursuant to rule 8 (b), the Secretary-General shall notify the Members of the United Nations at least twelve hours in advance of the opening of the session."

4. Rule 16 is amended by adding at the end thereof the following:

"The provisional agenda of an emergency special session shall be communicated to the Members of the United Nations simultaneously with the communication summoning the session."

5. Rule 19 is amended by adding at the end thereof the following:

"During an emergency special session additional items concerning the matters dealt with in resolution – (V) may be added to the agenda by a two-thirds majority of the Members present and voting."

6. There is added a new rule to precede rule 65 to read as follows:

"Notwithstanding the provisions of any other rule and unless the General Assembly decides otherwise, the Assembly in case of an emergency special session, shall convene in plenary session only and proceed directly to consider the item proposed for consideration in the request for the holding of the session, without previous reference to the General Committee or to any other Committee; the President and Vice-Presidents for such emergency special sessions shall be, respectively, the Chairman of those delegations from which were elected the President and Vice-Presidents of the previous session."

Resolution B

For the purpose of maintaining international peace and security, in accordance with the Charter of the United Nations, and, in Particular, with Chapters V, VI and VII of the Charter,

The General Assembly

Recommends to the Security Council:

That it should take the necessary steps to ensure that the action provided for under the Charter is taken with respect to threats to the peace, breaches of the peace or acts of aggression and with respect to the peaceful settlement of disputes or situations likely to endanger the maintenance of international peace and security;

That it should devise measures for the earliest application of Articles 43, 45, 46 and 47 of the Charter of the United Nations regarding the placing of armed forces at the disposal of the Security Council by the Member States of the United Nations and the effective functioning of the Military Staff Committee.

The above dispositions should in no manner prevent the General Assembly from fulfilling its functions under resolution – (V).

Resolution C

The General Assembly,

Recognizing that the primary function of the United Nations Organization is to maintain and promote peace, security and justice among all nations,

Recognizing the responsibility of all Member States to promote the cause of international peace in accordance with their obligations as provided in the Charter,

Recognizing that the Charter charges the Security Council with the primary responsibility for maintaining international peace and security,

Reaffirming the importance of unanimity among the permanent members of the Security Council on all problems which are likely to threaten world peace,

Recalling General Assembly resolution 190 (III) entitled

"Appeal to the Great Powers to renew their efforts to compose their differences and establish a lasting peace,"

Recommends to the permanent members of the Security Council that:

(a) They meet and discuss, collectively or otherwise, and, if necessary, with other States concerned, all problems which are likely to threaten international peace and hamper the activities of the United Nations, with a view to their resolving fundamental differences and reaching agreement in accordance with the spirit and letter of the Charter;

(b) They advise the General Assembly and, when it is not in session, the Members of the United Nations, as soon as appropriate, of the results of their consultations."

UN General Assembly, Official Records, 1950, Supplement No. 20, p. 10; *Uniting for Peace*, UN, New York, 1952; K.S. PETERSEN, "The Uses of the Uniting for Peace Resolution since 1950", in: *International Organization*, No. 13, 1959.

UNIVERSAL DECIMAL CLASSIFICATION.

The international system of decimal classification of book registration in public libraries started in 1876 by a work of an American Librarian M. Dewey entitled, "Decimal Classification", adopted and developed into a system of universal classification during 1905–1933 by the International Bibliographical Institute in Brussels, generally applied ever since. According to the Book Encyclopedia:

"The principle of Universal Decimal Classification consists in the division of the whole literature classified into ten major segments marked from 0 to 9. By adding further digits from 0 to 9 to the digits of major segments second-order segments are obtained, this time double digit marks (e.g. 01, 02, 03, etc.) By the same token, higher-order divisions are made composed, if need be, of several or more than ten digits. For example:

6 – applied sciences
621 3 – electrotechnics
62 – engineering
621 39 – telecommunications"
621 – machinery construction
621 396 – radiocommunications

R. DUBUL, *La Classification Décimal Universelle, Manual pratique d'utilisation*, Paris, 1965.

UNIVERSALITY PRINCIPLE OF THE WORLD ORGANIZATION.

During World War I as well as during World War II the promotors of the League of Nations as well as of the United Nations debated the problem of universality of the world organization. In both cases the Versailles Conference, 1919, as well as the San Francisco Conference, 1945, rejected the principles of universality as "scarcely compatible with the actual conditions of the world" and accepted the principle of selected membership.

The Latin American countries were in favor of universality in 1919 and 1945 demanding that all sovereign states recognized by the community of nations be admitted to the Organization, and that their participation must be obligatory, "that is to say that it will not be left to the choice of any nation whether to become a member of the Organization or to withdraw from it; thus the question of expulsion will not be raised." The proposal of the North American internationalists, 1944, was as follows:

"The Community of States should be organized on a universal basis. All states which exist or which may come into existence in the future should be included. No provision should be made for the expulsion or withdrawal of any state."

This principle stipulating that the UN should include all states in the world irrespective of their political systems was voiced for the first time during World War II in a session at Dumbarton Oaks and in London in 1944 in a memorial called Future International Law. (Suggestion 1. Item 1 of the American-Canadian Plan.) Despite such ideas, the UN was organized on the pattern of the League of Nations, not in the spirit of universalism but in the atmosphere of victory in a war by one group of nations over the other. In turn the Cold War that came almost immediately after the hot one paralyzed co-operation between the West and the East and limited to a minimum affiliation of new members after 1955. Lack of recognition by the USA of People's China prevented China from restoring her place in the UN until 1972. Accession of the two German states took place in 1973. In the International Co-operation Year, 1965, UN Secretary-General U Thant invited a number of statesmen to UN Headquarters to let them express their views of the future of the UN. One of them was W. Lippman, American commentator, who devoted his paper to proving the necessity of UN universalism and said in his closing remarks:

"... no sooner than in this century we became aware that it is possible and necessary to organize a universal community. ... because modern war has taken the shape of a universal disaster, and necessity is the mother of invention." At the end of the period 1945–80 the universality principle *de facto* dominates in the United Nations.

A.W. RUDZINSKI, "Admission of New Members. The UN and the LN", in: *International Conciliation*, No. 480, April 1952, pp. 143–186.

UNIVERSAL LANGUAGES.

The first attempts at working out a universal language were made in ancient times in the form of ideographic languages; the 17th century brought the first phonetic universal languages (*Characteristica Universalis* 1696). Most popular is Esperanto (1887) propagated by 27 international organizations, and reg. within UIA. Other universal languages: Volapük 1879, Interlingua (*Latino sine flexione*) 1905, Ido 1907, Occidental 1922, failed to be disseminated. In 1960, UNESCO commenced a research project on international ideographic writing and the possibility of its being universally understood.

I. COUTOURAT, L. LEON, *Histoire de la langue universelle*, Paris, 1903; J. BAUDOUIN DE COURTENAY, *Zur Kritik künstlicher Weltsprachen*, Berlin, 1937.

UNIVERSAL POSTAL CONVENTION, 1929.

Constitution of the Universal Postal Union, with Final Protocol, Detailed Regulations and Final Protocol, and Provisions relating to the Conveyance of Letter Post by Air, with Final Protocol, signed in London, June 28, 1929.

"The countries between which the present Convention is concluded form, under the title of the Universal Postal Union, a single postal territory for the reciprocal exchange of correspondence. It is also the object of the UPU to secure the organization and improvement of the various international postal services."
▷ UPU.

LNTS, Vol. 102, p. 245.

UNIVERSITIES.

International term for higher education institutions; in the UN system under aegis of UNESCO.

Organizations reg. with the UIA:

Association of African Universities, f. 1967, Accra.
Association of Arab Universities, f. 1964, Amman.
Association of Caribbean Universities, and Research Institutes, f. 1968, San Juan, Puerto Rico.
Association of Partially or Wholly French Language Universities, f. 1961, Montreal.
Association of South-East Asian Institutions of Higher Learning, f. 1956, Bangkok.
International Associations of Universities, f. 1950, Paris.
International Federation of Universities for Women, f. 1919, Geneva.
Organization of Catholic Universities of Latin America, f. 1953, Buenos Aires.
Union of Latin American Universities.

O. AKINGUBE, "Universities in Developing Countries", in: *World Health Forum*, No. 4, 1984; *The Europa Year Book 1984. A World Survey*, Vol. II, p. 2140, London, 1984; *Yearbook of International Organizations 1986/87*.

UNIVERSITY FOR DEVELOPMENT, INTERNATIONAL.

The name of a plan by the Brazilian scholar, J. de Castro, and a French scholar, M. Guernier, 1967, for an international university for training economists and planners from the Third World in close co-operation with local universities in those countries. The draft was submitted to UNESCO but, despite UNCTAD's support, was not implemented due to the lack of financial resources.

UNIVERSITY FOR PEACE.

Universidad para la Paz, est. Dec. 14, 1979 by Res. 34/111 of the UN General Assembly in Costa Rica as a university of international character and a part of the system of the UN University.

UN Chronicle, January, 1980, pp. 72–73.

UNIVERSITY INTERNATIONAL. ▷ UN University.

UNIVERSITY OF JERUSALEM "AL-QUDS".

The GA Res. 35/13 B of Nov. 3, 1980 decided to establish a University ("Al Qud") for Palestinian Refugees in Jerusalem. In 1989 the project was still not realized, owing to US and Israeli opposition.

UN Resolutions and Decisions adopted by the General Assembly during the First Part of its Forty-Third Session, From 20 September to 22 December, 1988, New York, 1989, pp. 232–236.

UNIVERSITY OF THE AMERICAS.

Universidad de las Americas, the higher educational institution f. in 1940 in the capital of Mexico with the name Mexico City College, training youth from all the American states; present name since 1963. Seat: Puebla, Mexico. Publ. *Meso-Americas Notes*.

The World of Learning, London, 1975.

UNIVERSITY OF THE PEOPLE.

An international term for institutions for spreading education, organized in Europe in late 19th century, subject of international co-operation since 1910, when the International Confederation of Universities of the People, Confederation internationale des universites populaires, was founded in Paris.

Yearbook of International Organizations.

UNIVERSITY OF THE UN. ▷ UN University.

UNIVERSITY SERVICE. ▷ World University Service.

UN JOINT STAFF PENSION FUND.

A Fund established for the benefit of employees of the UN and its specialized and related organizations created Dec. 7, 1948 by a resolution of the UN General Assembly of Dec. 15, 1946. The rules and regulations of UN JSPF took effect Jan. 23, 1949 and have been amended on a number of occasions by the Assembly.

UN Bulletin, January, 1949.

UN JURIDICAL INTERNATIONAL PERSONALITY.

The legal grounds provided on Apr. 11, 1949 by International Court of Justice on the request of UN General Assembly for the claiming of reparation for injuries suffered in the UN service, unanimously recognized international personality of UN (in spite of it being neither a state nor a supra-state) which is thus capable of having international rights and duties, including the right to lodge international claims with regard to member states as well as non member states. The ICJ decision referred to a similar decision taken by the Permanent Tribunal of Justice on July 23, 1926, with regard to ILO.

United Nations Juridical Yearbook, New York, 1984 (issued irregularly since 1962).

UNKNOWN SOLDIER'S TOMB.

The first memorial to fallen soldiers containing ashes of an unknown soldier was erected after World War I in Paris under the Arc de Triomphe and became a place where tribute to victims of war was paid and peaceful manifestations arranged. In Warsaw the unknown soldier's tomb was built in 1925 under the colonnade of the former Saxon Palace; damaged by the Nazis it was rebuilt and unveiled on May 8, 1946. Similar memorials are to be found in e.g.

Brussels, Belgrade, Berlin, Moscow, Rio de Janeiro, Washington.

UN LANGUAGES. Under the UN Charter the official languages of the United Nations are Chinese, English, French, Russian and Spanish. Arabic has been added as an official language of the General Assembly, the Security Council and the Economic and Social Council.

UN Bulletin, No. 1, 1949, pp. 18–20, and No. 11, 1949, p. 532; *Basic Facts About the United Nations*, New York, 1983.

UN LIBRARIES. Three main UN libraries are: the Dag Hammarskjöld Library and the UN Archives in New York; the UN Library in Geneva; and the Library of the International Court of Justice in the Hague. In addition there are the libraries of UN specialized organizations and UN Regional Economic Commissions. The latter contain the largest collections of economic-social literature for those regions. The UN every few years publishes a bibliographical guide; however, the Geneva Public Library publ. a monthly, *Liste mensuelle d'ouvrages catalogué à la Bibliothèque des Nations Unies* and information on the content of *c.* 2500 periodicals, *Liste mensuelle d'articles sélectionnés*; the New York Public Library: *New Publications* in the Dag Hammarskjöld Library.

UN LITTLE GENERAL ASSEMBLY. An Interim Committee of the General Assembly on Peace and Security, established by the General Assembly, Nov. 13, 1947, Res. 111/II by a vote of 41 to 6 (USSR, Byelorussian SSR, Czechoslovakia, Poland, Ukraine and Yugoslavia), with 6 abstentions. The text of the Resolution is as follows:

"The General Assembly,
Conscious of the responsibility specifically conferred upon it by the Charter in relation to matters concerning the maintenance of international peace and security (Arts. 11 and 35), the promotion of international co-operation in the political field (Art. 13) and the peaceful adjustment of any situations likely to impair the general welfare or friendly relations among nations (Art. 14);
Deeming it necessary for the effective performance of these duties to establish an interim committee to consider and report with its conclusions on such matters to the General Assembly during the period between the closing of the present session and the opening of the next regular session of the General Assembly;
Recognizing fully the primary responsibility of the Security Council for prompt and effective action for the maintenance of international peace and security (Art. 24):
Resolves that
1. There shall be established, for the period between the closing of the present session and the opening of the next regular session of the General Assembly, an Interim Committee on which each Member of the General Assembly shall have the right to appoint one representative;
2. The Interim Committee, as a subsidiary organ of the General Assembly established in accordance with Art. 22 of the Charter, shall assist the General Assembly in the performance of its functions by discharging the following duties:
(a) To consider and report, with its conclusions, to the General Assembly on such matters as have been referred to it by the General Assembly;
(b) To consider and report with its conclusions to the General Assembly on any dispute or any situation which, in virtue of Arts. 11 (paragraph 2), 14 or 35 of the Charter, has been proposed for inclusion in the agenda of the General Assembly by any Member of the United Nations or brought before the General Assembly by the Security Council, provided the Committee previously determines the matter to be both important and requiring preliminary study. Such determination shall be made by a majority of two-thirds of the members present and voting, unless the matter is one referred by the Security Council under Art. 11 (par. 2), in which case a simple majority will suffice;

(c) To consider, as it deems useful and advisable, and report with its conclusions to the General Assembly on methods to be adopted to give effect to that part of Art. 11 (par. 1), which deals with the general principles of co-operation in the maintenance of international peace and security, and to that part of Art. 13 (par. 1a) which deals with the promotion of international co-operation in the political field;
(d) To consider, in connection with any matter under discussion by the Interim Committee, whether occasion may require the summoning of a special session of the General Assembly and, if it deems that such session is required, so to advise the Secretary-General in order that he may obtain the view of the Members of the United Nations thereon;
(e) To conduct investigations and appoint commissions of enquiry within the scope of its duties, as it may deem useful and necessary, provided that decisions to conduct such investigations or enquiries shall be made by a two-thirds majority of the members present and voting. An investigation or enquiry elsewhere than at the headquarters of the United Nations shall not be conducted without the consent of the State or States in whose territory it is to take place;
(f) To report to the next regular session of the General Assembly on the advisability of establishing a permanent committee of the General Assembly to perform the duties of the Interim Committee as stated above with any changes considered desirable in the light of experience.
3. In discharging its duties the Interim Committee shall at all times take into account the responsibilities of the Security Council under the Charter for the maintenance of international peace and security as well as the duties assigned by the Charter or by the General Assembly or by the Security Council to other Councils or to any committee or commission. The Interim Committee shall not consider any matter of which the Security Council is seized.
4. Subject to par. 2 (b) and 2 (e) above, the rules of procedure of the General Assembly shall, so far as they are applicable, govern the proceedings of the Interim Committee and such sub-committees and commissions as it may set up. The Interim Committee shall, however, have authority to adopt such additional rules as it may deem necessary provided that they are not inconsistent with any of the rules of procedure of the General Assembly. The Interim Committee shall be convened by the Secretary-General not later than six weeks following the close of the second regular session of the General Assembly. It shall meet as and when it deems necessary for the conduct of its business.
5. The Secretary-General shall provide the necessary facilities and assign appropriate staff as required for the work of the Interim Committee, its sub-committees and commissions."

UN Yearbook 1947/48, pp. 75–81; *UN Bulletin*, December 1, 1947, August 15, 1948, December 1, 1949 and April 1, 1950.

UN MEDAL. A UN decoration, approved in Dec. 1950, granted for the first time in 1950–53 to soldiers of the troops which took part in the Korean war under the UN banner. On one side of the medal is the emblem of UN, on the other the inscription in English: "For service in defense of UN Charter principles."

UN Bulletin, Aug. 15, 1951.

UN MEDITATION HALL. A special space in the UN Headquarters in New York; on Oct. 24, 1952 in the western part of the vestibule a hall was inaugurated in the shape of a letter V, length 10 m, 6 m wide at its broadest point, whose central point is a block of mineral iron ore illuminated by a shaft of light from above. Since 1957 on the frontal wall there is an abstract fresco 3 × 2 m by the Swedish artist Bo Beskov. In this hall, open to delegates and visitors, absolute silence is in force. The text of the information handed to visitors before entering the UN M.H. reads:
"This building dedicated to work and debate in the service of peace also has its place of concentration

and quiet, in which the space of infinity is open for reflections or prayers."
This symbolic common temple of believers of many faiths and non-believers of many philosophies of life is mainly frequented by visitors to the UN building.

UN Review, January, 1958.

UN MEMBERS, 1945–85. The UN Members historically are divided into:
51 Original Members, i.e. those states which on Jan. 1, 1942 signed the Declaration of the United Nations or participated in the ▷ San Francisco Conference of the United Nations, 1945; or signed and ratified the UN Charter before Oct. 24, 1945, when the UN Charter took effect;
Members accepted on the motion of the Security Council of the UN with the consent of the UN General Assembly after Oct. 24, 1945.
Politically both the former and the latter have identical rights and obligations in the UN.
The membership of United Nations has grown over the years as follows:

1945 Argentina, Australia, Belgium, Bolivia, Brazil, Byelorussian SSR, Canada, Chile, China, Colombia, Costa Rica, Cuba, Czechoslovakia, Denmark, Dominican Republic, Ecuador, Egypt, El Salvador, Ethiopia, France, Greece, Guatemala, Haiti, Honduras, India, Iran, Iraq, Lebanon, Liberia, Luxembourg, Mexico, Netherlands, New Zealand, Nicaragua, Norway, Panama, Paraguay, Peru, Philippines, Poland, Saudi Arabia, South Africa, Syrian Arab Republic, Turkey, Ukrainian SSR, USSR, United Kingdom, United States, Uruguay, Venezuela, Yugoslavia
1946 Afghanistan, Iceland, Sweden, Thailand
1947 Pakistan, Yemen
1948 Burma
1949 Israel
1950 Indonesia
1951
1952
1953
1954
1955 Albania, Austria, Democratic Kampuchea, Finland, Hungary, Ireland, Italy, Jordan, Lao People's Democratic Republic, Libyan Arab Jamahiriya, Nepal, Portugal, Romania, Spain, Sri Lanka
1956 Japan, Morocco, Sudan, Tunisia
1957 Ghana, Malaysia
1958 Guinea
1959
1960 Benin, Central African Republic, Chad, Congo, Cyprus, Gabon, Ivory Coast (now Côte d'Iuoire), Madagascar, Mali, Niger, Nigeria, Senegal, Somalia, Togo, United Republic of Cameroon, Upper Volta (now Burkina Faso), Zaïre
1961 Mauritania, Mongolia, Sierra Leone, United Republic of Tanzania
1962 Algeria, Burundi, Jamaica, Rwanda, Trinidad and Tobago, Uganda
1963 Kenya, Kuwait
1964 Malawi, Malta, Zambia
1965 Bulgaria, Gambia, Maldives, Singapore
1966 Barbados, Botswana, Guyana, Lesotho
1967 Democratic Yemen
1968 Equatorial Guinea, Mauritius, Swaziland
1969
1970 Fiji
1971 Bahrain, Bhutan, Oman, Qatar, United Arab Emirates
1972
1973 Bahamas, German Democratic Republic, Germany, Federal Republic of
1974 Bangladesh, Grenada, Guinea-Bissau
1975 Cape Verde, Comoros, Mozambique, Papua New Guinea, Sao Tome and Principe, Suriname
1976 Angola, Samoa, Seychelles
1977 Djibouti, Vietnam
1978 Solomon Islands
1979 Dominica, Saint Lucia
1980 Saint Vincent and the Grenadines, Zimbabwe

1981 Antigua and Barbuda, Belize, Vanuatu
1982
1983 Saint Christopher and Nevis
1984 Brunei Darussalam

UN Chronicle, September, 1982, and September, 1984.

UN MEMBERS CONTRIBUTIONS SCALE 1989–1990. On Dec. 21, 1988 the GA adopted without a vote a Res. 43/223 "Scale of assessment for the apportionment of the expenses of the United Nations", stating that:

The General Assembly, Recognizing the obligation of Member States, under Article 17 of the Charter of the United Nations, to bear the expenses of the Organization as apportioned by the General Assembly.

Bearing in mind rule 160 of the rules of procedure of the General Assembly,

(1) *Resolves* that the scale of assessments for the contributions of Member States to the United Nations regular budget for 1989 and 1990, and also 1991 unless a new scale is approved earlier by the General Assembly on the recommendation of the Committee on Contributions in response to resolution B below, shall be:

Member State	Per cent
Afghanistan	0.01
Albania	0.01
Algeria	0.15
Angola	0.01
Antigua and Barbuda	0.01
Argentina	0.66
Australia	1.57
Austria	0.74
Bahamas	0.02
Bahrain	0.02
Bangladesh	0.01
Barbados	0.01
Belgium	1.17
Belize	0.01
Benin	0.01
Bhutan	0.01
Bolivia	0.01
Botswana	0.01
Brazil	1.45
Brunei Darussalam	0.04
Bulgaria	0.15
Burkina Faso	0.01
Burma	0.01
Burundi	0.01
Byelorussian Soviet Socialist Republic	0.33
Cameroon	0.01
Canada	3.09
Cape Verde	0.01
Central African Republic	0.01
Chad	0.01
Chile	0.08
China	0.79
Colombia	0.14
Comoros	0.01
Congo	0.01
Costa Rica	0.02
Côte d'Ivoire	0.02
Cuba	0.09
Cyprus	0.02
Czechoslovakia	0.66
Democratic Kampuchea	0.01
Democratic Yemen	0.01
Denmark	0.69
Djibouti	0.01
Dominica	0.01
Dominican Republic	0.03
Ecuador	0.03
Egypt	0.07
El Salvador	0.01
Equatorial Guinea	0.01
Ethiopia	0.01

Fiji	0.01
Finland	0.51
France	6.25
Gabon	0.03
Gambia	0.01
German Democratic Republic	1.28
Germany, Federal Republic of	8.08
Ghana	0.01
Greece	0.40
Grenada	0.01
Guatemala	0.02
Guinea	0.01
Guinea-Bissau	0.01
Guyana	0.01
Haiti	0.01
Honduras	0.01
Hungary	0.21
Iceland	0.03
India	0.37
Indonesia	0.15
Iran (Islamic Republic of)	0.69
Iraq	0.12
Ireland	0.18
Israel	0.21
Italy	3.99
Jamaica	0.01
Japan	11.38
Jordan	0.01
Kenya	0.01
Kuwait	0.29
Lao People's Democratic Republic	0.01
Lebanon	0.01
Lesotho	0.01
Liberia	0.01
Libyan Arab Jamahiriya	0.28
Luxembourg	0.06
Madagascar	0.01
Malawi	0.01
Malaysia	0.11
Maldives	0.01
Mali	0.01
Malta	0.01
Mauritania	0.01
Mauritius	0.01
Mexico	0.94
Mongolia	0.01
Morocco	0.04
Mozambique	0.01
Nepal	0.01
Netherlands	1.65
New Zealand	0.24
Nicaragua	0.01
Niger	0.01
Nigeria	0.20
Norway	0.55
Oman	0.02
Pakistan	0.06
Panama	0.02
Papua New Guinea	0.01
Paraguay	0.03
Peru	0.06
Philippines	0.09
Poland	0.56
Portugal	0.18
Qatar	0.05
Romania	0.19
Rwanda	0.01
Saint Kitts and Nevis	0.01
Saint Lucia	0.01
Saint Vincent and the Grenadines	0.01
Samoa	0.01
Sao Tome and Principe	0.01
Saudi Arabia	1.02
Senegal	0.01
Seychelles	0.01
Sierra Leone	0.01
Singapore	0.11
Solomon Islands	0.01

Somalia	0.01
South Africa	0.45
Spain	1.95
Sri Lanka	0.01
Sudan	0.01
Suriname	0.01
Swaziland	0.01
Sweden	1.21
Syrian Arab Republic	0.04
Thailand	0.10
Togo	0.01
Trinidad and Tobago	0.05
Tunisia	0.03
Turkey	0.32
Uganda	0.01
Ukranian Soviet Socialist Republic	1.25
Union of Soviet Socialist Republics	9.99
United Arab Emirates	0.19
United Kingdom of Great Britain and Northern Ireland	4.86
United Republic of Tanzania	0.01
United States of America	25.00
Uruguay	0.04
Vanuatu	0.01
Venezuela	0.57
Viet Nam	0.01
Yemen	0.01
Yugoslavia	0.46
Zaire	0.01
Zambia	0.01
Zimbabwe	0.02
	100.00

(2) *Requests* the Committee on Contributions, in accordance with its mandate and the rules of procedure of the General Assembly, to consider representations made by Member States during the forty-third session of the General Assembly on their respective assessments and to advise the Assembly of its recommendations for possible adjustments to allow the Assembly to take a decision at its forty-fourth session;

(3) *Resolves further* that:

(a) In accordance with rule 160 of the rules of procedure of the General Assembly, the scale of assessments given in paragraph 1 above shall be reviewed by the Committee on Contributions in 1991, or earlier as specified in paragraph 1, when a report shall be submitted to the Assembly for its consideration at its forty-sixth session;

(b) Notwithstanding the terms of regulation 5.5 of the Financial Regulations of the United Nations, the Secretary-General shall be empowered to accept, at his discretion and after consultation with the Chairman of the Committee on Contributions, a portion of the contributions of Member States for the calendar years 1989, 1990 and 1991 in currencies other than United States dollars;

(c) In accordance with rule 160 of the rules of procedure of the General Assembly, States which are not members of the United Nations but which participate in certain of its activities shall be called upon to contribute towards the 1989, 1990 and 1991 expenses of such activities on the basis of the following rates, unless modified as specified in paragraph 1:

Non-member State	Per cent
Democratic People's Republic of Korea	0.05
Holy See	0.01
Liechtenstein	0.01
Monaco	0.01
Nauru	0.01
Republic of Korea	0.22
San Marino	0.01
Switzerland	1.08
Tonga	0.01
Tuvalu	0.01

The General Assembly,

Recalling all its previous resolutions on the scale of assessments and, in particular, resolutions 39/247 B of 12 April 1985 and 42/208 of 11 December 1987.

Having considered the report of the Committee on Contributions and noting with appreciation the efforts of the Committee.

Bearing in mind the evolution of the world economic situation and its impact on the capacity to pay of Member States.

Taking into account the views expressed in the Fifth Committee during the forty-third session of the General Assembly, in particular on the need for a substantial improvement of the existing methodology and criteria for the determination of the scale of assessments, and the need for information on the steps taken in the preparation of the scale of assessments.

Also taking into account the views expressed in the Fifth Committee during the forty-third session on the ceiling and floor levels;

(1) *Reconfirms* that the capacity to pay of Member States is the fundamental criterion for determining the scale of assessments;

(2) *Requests* the Committee on Contributions, in order to ensure fairness and equity in the scale and to make the methodology transparent, easily understandable, stable over time and as simple as possible, to undertake a comprehensive review of all aspects of the existing methodology, and to this end:
(a) To continue to monitor the improvements in the area of the availability and comparability of national income data, and to continue its work on the PARE methodology;
(b) To seek more comprehensive and systematic information on external debt with a view to ensuring that this factor is adequately taken into account in the calculations for determining the capacity to pay;
(c) To undertake a comprehensive review of the upper limit of the low per capita income allowance formula and the application of the formula;
(d) To review, in the light of the proposals made in the Fifth Committee:
(i) The statistical base period and its application;
(ii) The scheme to avoid excessive variations of individual rates between successive scales;
(iii) The possibility of excluding allocation of any additional points as a result of the application of the scheme of limits to those Member States with a very low per capita income;
and to include in its report the implications of the various options considered;
(e) To limit the use of *ad hoc* adjustments in the preparation of the scale to the minimum possible, keeping in mind that in case such *ad hoc* adjustments are necessary, they should be made on the basis of objective, rational and transparent considerations, applied uniformly, and to include in its reports on the preparation of future scales of assessments explicit information on the basis of which such *ad hoc* adjustments were made;

(3) *Requests* the Committee on Contributions to examine, as a means of improving the current methodology, the possible use of other factors, including the situation of those countries:
(a) Whose economies depend on one or a few products or income sources;
(b) Which suffered a real loss of income as a result of deteriorating terms of trade;
(c) Which experience serious balance-of-payments (trade) problems or a negative net flow of resources;
(d) Which have limited capacity to acquire convertible currencies;

(4) *Also requests* the Committee on Contributions to continue its study on the concept of national income, as indicated in paragraph 47 of its report;
100/

(5) *Further requests* the Committee on Contributions, in conducting the studies and reviews

indicated in paragraphs 2 and 3 above, to examine also the interrelationship of each of the elements as part of the overall methodology, bearing in mind the need to avoid duplication and negative impact of each individual element on the others in order to reflect capacity to pay;

(6) *Requests* the Committee on Contributions to submit a report on the above-mentioned reviews and their implications for future scales of assessments, with illustrative examples, to the General Assembly at its forty-fourth session;

(7) *Requests* the Secretary-General to provide the Committee on Contributions with the facilities it requires to carry out its work, including supplementary assistance if necessary.

UN Resolutions and Decisions adopted by the General Assembly during the First Part of its Forty-Third Session. From 20 September to 22 December 1988, New York, 1989, pp. 506–510.

UN MILITARY FORCES. In accordance with Chapter VII of the UN Charter on action with respect to threats to the peace, breaches of the peace, and acts of aggression the Security Council may call upon members of the UN to place at its disposal the military forces required to maintain international peace. According to art. 43 this obligation requires the negotiation and ratification of additional agreements by the member states "as soon as possible." To the middle of 1960s these agreements still had not been negotiated as a result of basic differences of opinion in the Military Staff Committee of the UN; however, in Apr., 1967 on the initiative of the USSR and with the support of Mexico the UN Special Committee for the Maintenance of Peace began work on an agreement defining the manner and conditions of supplying military contingents by the member states to the disposition of the UN. In 1945–80 the Security Council organized:

In 1948 in Palestine a 100-man military observer group composed of contingents from Belgium, France, Sweden, and USA.

In June, 1950 the Security Council of the UN (without the consent of all 5 permanent members – the USSR was not present) organized the UN Military Forces (UNMF) which took part in the war in Korea.

On Nov. 4, 1956 during the Suez crisis the Council formed the UN-Emergency Forces (UNEF) for the region of the Near East, located on the Egyptian–Israeli border. Their withdrawal at the demand of Egypt May 18–July 17, 1967 became an indirect cause of the renewal of the Israeli–Arab war June 5, 1967.

On July 22, 1960 during the civil war in the Congo the Council called into being military forces under the French name Operation des Nations Unies Congo (ONUC) whose action was terminated June 30, 1964.

On Mar. 4, 1964 the Council in order to end the civil war on Cyprus sent in military forces, UN-Forces in Cyprus (UNFICYP), whose tour there is extended every half year.

The Institute of International Law at its session in Zagreb Sept. 3, 1971 accepted the resolution on the conditions for applying humanitarian rules to military conflicts to war operations in which UN Military Forces are engaged.

On Oct. 25, 1973 the Council formed the UN Emergency Forces, UNEF, in connection with the new situation in the Near East, composed of units from Canada, Finland, Poland, and Sweden.

In the fall of 1973 a special committee for peaceful operations of the UN worked out a proposal of principles concerning the duties and area of competence of the UN Security Council in summoning UN m.f. and their peace-keeping function. Of the 16

principles 12 were agreed upon, among others the key principle that the Security Council alone is the only authoritative organ of the UN for the UN m.f. Of the 5 powers only China refused to take part in the work of the committee.

On June 1, 1974 part of the units of UNEF were directed to the territorial strip of the Syrian–Israeli cease-fire line and received the name, UN Demilitarization Observatory Forces. Both there as well as on the Egyptian–Israeli cease-fire line UN military forces served on duty. In 1976 the UN Temporary Forces in Lebanon were directed to Lebanon. In 1979 the UN Auxiliary Group for Namibia was formed.

On Sept. 29, 1988 the Swedish Nobel Committee honoured the UN Peace Keeping Forces with the Nobel Peace Prize, recognizing that "they represent the manifest will of the community of nations to achieve peace".

W.R. FRYE, *A United Nations Peace Force*, New York, 1957; K.H. KUNZMANN, "Aktuelle Vorschläge für eine Friedenstruppe der Vereinten Nationen", in: *Europa Archiv*, No. 13, 1958; R.B. RUSSEL, *UN Experience with Military Forces; Political and Legal Aspects*, Washington, DC, 1963; L. BLUMFIELD, *International Military Forces. The Questions of Peace keeping in Armed and Disarming World*, Cambridge, 1964; D.W. BOWETT, *UN Force: A Legal Study*, New York, 1964; E.S. KRIVCHITSOV, *Wooruzhonniye sili OON*, Moscow, 1965; F. SEYERSTAD, *UN Forces in the Law of Peace and War*, Leiden, 1966; D.W. WAINHOUSE, *International Peace Observation*, Baltimore, 1966; W.S. SIEMIONOV, "Niekotoriye problemy ispolsovaniya woorushonnikh sil OON", in: *Sovietskiy yezhegodnik mezhdunarodnogo prava*, No. 65, 1964; S. LAZAREFF, *Status of Military Forces under Current International Law*, Leiden, 1971; W.L. WILLIAMS, *Intergovernmental military forces and world public order*, The Hague, 1971; *Annuaires de l'Institut de Droit International 1971*, Vol. 2, pp. 449–470; A. VERRIER, *International Peacekeeping: UN Forces in a Troubled World*, New York, 1981.

UN MILITARY STAFF COMMITTEE. An institution with whose assistance the UN Security Council in accordance with Chapter VII of the UN Charter may carry out military actions in the event of a threat to peace, breaking of the peace, or acts of aggression.

"The task of the Military Staff Committee – according to Art. 47 of the UN Charter – is to advise and assist the Security Council on all questions relating to the Security Council's military requirements for the maintenance of international peace and security, the employment and command of forces placed at its disposal, the regulation of armaments, and possible disarmament."

The Military Staff Committee is composed of the Chiefs of Staff (or their deputies) of the permanent members of the Security Council or of the Five Great Powers. According to a report of the UN Secretary General, Trygve Lie, on June 10, 1947, the UN Military Staff Committee during its session of 1946/47, at which the question of establishing UN military forces was discussed, reached only partial agreement. In view of the impossibility of achieving unanimity by the permanent members of the Security Council on this matter, which the Council debated in June and July, 1947, the issue was never returned to and therewith the functions of the Military Staff Committee were suspended.

UN Bulletin, June 15, 1948.

UNMOGIP. United Nations Military Observer Group in India and Pakistan. The origin of UNMOGIP derives from Security Council Res. 39, 1948, which established the United Nations Commission for India and Pakistan, and Res. 47, 1948, by which the Council laid down a procedure for the restoration of peace and order in Jammu and

Kashmir. The latter resolution authorized the Commission to establish such observers as it might require in discharging the tasks entrusted to it. The terms of reference for UNMOGIP were changed over the years as was made necessary by developments in the area. It supervised a Line of Control, agreed upon by India and Pakistan in July, 1972, which generally follows the same course as the cease-fire line established between the two countries in 1949. While the activities of UNMOGIP since 1971 have been restricted on the Indian side of the Line, it has continued its observation operation and continues to report on it to the Secretary-General. As of May 1, 1980, 39 military observers were serving with UNMOGIP. They were provided by the Governments of Australia, Belgium, Chile, Denmark, Finland, Italy, Norway, Sweden and Uruguay.

UN Yearbook, 1948, 1972, 1980.

UN OBSERVERS. The official name for UN military observers assigned to areas of conflict or possible conflict in order to collect information on the spot and forward it to the UN Security Council or the Secretary-General. Among the UN Observers Missions were the following:

1949	– in Pakistan and India over Kashmir
1948/49	in Palestine, to supervise truce
1956–67	– in Gaza
1958	– in Lebanon, to check on cases of illegal border crossing
1963	– in Yemen, to check on the implementation of withdrawal of Great Britain troops;
1965–66	– in Pakistan and India
1974	– in Israel and Syria
1980	– in Cyprus
1984	in Lebanon

UN OFFICE AT GENEVA. The European bureau of the UN in Palais de Nations in Geneva, in the former building of League of Nations.

UN OFFICIAL DOCUMENTS. The records, documents, studies and resolutions of the UN General Assembly, Security Council, ECOSOC, Trusteeship Council, and other UN organs, since 1945; the majority published in English and French; a part also in Spanish, Russian and Chinese; each year a bibliography of all UN documents is published in English: United Nations Documents Index, and various bibliographical guides for longer periods are published by the Dag Hammarskjöld Library.

J.K. ZAWODNY, *Guide to the Study of International Relations*, San Francisco, 1966, pp. 73–80.

UN OFFICIALS. In accordance with the Convention on the Privileges and Immunities of the UN, art. V, Sect. 18;

"Officials of the United Nations shall:
(a) Be immune from legal process in respect of words spoken or written and all acts performed by them in their official capacity;
(b) Be exempt from taxation on the salaries and emoluments paid to them by the United Nations;
(c) Be immune from national service obligations;
(d) Be immune, together with their spouses and relatives dependent on them, from immigration restrictions and alien registration;
(e) Be accorded the same privileges in respect of exchange facilities as are accorded to the officials of comparable ranks forming part of diplomatic missions to the Government concerned;
(f) Be given, together with their spouses and relatives dependent on them, the same repatriation facilities in time of international crisis as diplomatic envoys;
(g) Have the right to import free of duty their furniture and effects at the time of first taking up their post in the country in question."

UNTS, Vol. 1, pp. 18–19.

UN, ONU, OON, ONU. Official abbreviations in four official UN languages: English – United Nations, French – Organisation des Nations Unies, Russian – Organizatsiya Obyedinionnikh Natsyi, Spanish – Organización de las Naciones Unidas.

S.D. VOYTOVICH, *OON i Strany Sotsializma*, Minsk, 1983.

UN PEACE-KEEPING OPERATIONS. In accordance with Chapter VII of the UN Charter on action with respect to threats to the peace, breaches of the peace, and acts of aggression, the Security Council may call upon members of the UN to place at its disposal military forces required to maintain international peace. Under art. 43 such a call would be in accord with a special agreement or agreements governing the manpower and types of forces, their degree of readiness, location, etc. which should be negotiated as soon as possible. These agreements have never been finalized; rather the UN has engaged in a number of operations which may be classified into two categories: observer missions consisting of a group of military observers, and peace-keeping forces composed of national contingents. Because of difficulties encountered in financing the first two peace-keeping operations, in the Middle East and Congo, the General Assembly est. in Feb., 1965 a Special Committee to study the question in all its aspects. The Committee has met annually since 1966 to elaborate agreed guidelines for the conduct of such operations but has not been able so far to complete them. The first peace-keeping operation was an observer mission, the United Nations Truce Supervision Organization in Palestine, UNTSO, set up in May, 1948. Later, other observer missions were set up according to the same principles as UNTSO: the United Nations Military Observer Group in India and Pakistan, UNMOGIP in Aug., 1949, the United Nations Yemen Observation Mission UNYOM in June, 1963, and the Mission of the Representative of the Secretary-General in the Dominican Republic DOMREP, in Apr., 1965. Two of those missions, UNTSO and UNMOGIP, are still in operation. There have been seven peace-keeping forces in all. The first one was the United Nations Emergency Force UNEF(I), which was in operation in the Egypt–Israel sector from Nov. 1956 until May, 1967. The United Nations Force in the Congo, ONUC, was deployed in the Republic of the Congo (now Zaïre) from July 1960 until June 1964. The United Nations Security Force in West Irian, was in operation from Sept., 1962 until Apr., 1963. The United Nations Force in Cyprus UNFICYP, est. in Mar., 1964; the United Nations Emergency Force, UNEF(II), established in Oct., 1973; the United Nations Disengagement Observer Force UNDOF, est. in May, 1974; and the United Nations Interim Force in Lebanon UNIFIL, est. in Mar., 1978.
All the peace-keeping operations have been under the command of the United Nations, vested in the Secretary-General, under the authority of either the Security Council or the General Assembly. Military personnel for the operations are placed at the disposal of the United Nations by member states.
Although the terms of reference and functioning of the peace-keeping operations have varied to meet the specific needs of each situation, there have emerged a number of common practices and characteristics. A United Nations peace-keeping operation is not an enforcement action as envisaged in Art. 42 of the Charter, and it is carried out with the consent and co-operation of the parties concerned. Its main function is to prevent the resumption or expansion of a conflict through impartial supervision of cease-fires, truce or armistice agreements

and troops withdrawals and through the stabilizing influence of a United Nations "presence." The peace-keeping operations seek to achieve their objective by negotiation and persuasion, rather than by force. The military observers are never armed. The soldiers of the peace-keeping forces are provided with weapons of a defensive character, but they are authorized to use them only in self-defense and with the utmost restraint. In most cases, United Nations peace-keeping operations are coupled with a peace-making effort to seek a peaceful solution of the political problems at the root of the conflict.
Until Oct. 1987 the USSR refused to finance 'the peacekeeping UN force in the Middle East after the 1973 Arab-Israeli war; the UN monitoring the Golan Heights between Israel and Syria, since 1974 and the Southern Lebanon force established in 1978. On Oct. 15, 1987 the USSR announced that 'it will meets its arrears in full for peacekeeping operations without any exceptions'. The USSR decided to pay $197 million in accumulated arrears toward the cost of United Nations peacekeeping operation acting on the belief that 'wide use' should be made of multinational UN forces 'in disengaging the troops of warring sides and observing cease fire and armistice agreements'.
In the years 1948–1988 there have been fifteen peace-keeping operations involving some 500,000 soldiers and civilians from all regions of the world. About 730 UN peace keepers have lost their lives while in the service of the United Nations. In 1989 there were more than 10,500 men and women from 35 countries in peace-keeping field operations. They served in the three peace keeping forces (▷ UNIFICYP, ▷ UNDOF and ▷ UNIFIL) and five observer missions (▷ UNTSO, ▷ UNMOGIP, ▷ UNGOMAP, ▷ UNITMOG and ▷ UNAVEM). The Nobel Peace Prize Committee awarded the UN Peace Keeping Forces in 1988 with the Nobel Peace Prize:

"The peace-keeping forces of the United Nations have under extremely difficult conditions contributed to reducing tensions where an armistice has been negotiated but a peace treaty has yet to be established. In situations of this kind the UN forces represent the manifest will of the community of nations to achieve peace through negotiations, and the forces have by their presence made a decisive contribution towards the initiation of actual peace negotiations.
It is the considered opinion of the Committee that the peace-keeping forces through their efforts have made important contributions towards the realization of one of the fundamental tenets of the United Nations. Thus the world organization has come to play a more central part in world affairs and has been invested with increasing trust".

The Peace Prize – a diploma, a gold medal and a cheque for $390,000 was handed to the Secretary General at a ceremony in Oslo on Dec. 10, the anniversary of Alfred Nobel's death in 1896.

Everyone's United Nations, 1979; *Pravda*, Moscow, Oct. 13; *Disarmament Newsletter*, December 1988; L. ZAPAŁOWSKI, *Operacje Pokojowe ONZ (UN Peacekeeping Operations)*, Krakow, 1989.

UN PENSION SYSTEM. The UN pension scheme directed by the UN Joint Staff Pension Board is related to the UN Joint Staff Pension Fund.

UN Resolutions and Decisions adopted by the General Assembly during the First Part of its Forty-Third Session. From 20 September to 22 December 1988, New York, 1989.

UN POSTAL ADMINISTRATION. In 1951, through an agreement between the United States and the United Nations, an international organization – not a country or territory – was allowed for the first time in history to have its own postal service and to issue its own stamps. A similar agreement was signed in 1968 between the United Nations Postal Administration, UNPA, and the Swiss Postal, Telephone and Telegraph Enterprise (PTT). That led to the opening of a second United Nations post office, located at the Palais des Nations in Geneva. Five commemorative stamps were issued in an average year from 1966 through 1977, together with a number of definitives and pieces of postal stationery which are periodically issued to meet revised postage rates. Fourteen definitive stamps and three pieces of postal stationery in Swiss denominations were issued in 1969 and 1970 to meet the postal requirements specified by the United Nations agreement with the Swiss PTT. United Nations commemorative stamps are valid for postage only from the United Nations buildings in New York and Geneva respectively, they can also be purchased by collectors in more than 100 other countries.

Among commemorative stamps issued were those paying tribute to various organs and agencies of the United Nations, such as WHO, UNICEF, UNDP, UNIDO and ILO, or to various United Nations activities or observances such as the World Weather Watch, International Year for Human Rights, Fight Cancer, Human Environment, World Population Year, Peaceful Uses of Outer Space, International Women's Year, United Nations Peace-keeping Operations and the World Food Council. Other commemorative stamps were issued in the "Art at the United Nations" series which depicted works of art contributed to the United Nations by different Governments.

Designs are chosen from a panel of nearly 400 artists, including some of the world's foremost, from 58 countries. Designs have even been reproduced from the works of Marc Chagall and Pablo Picasso. Printing is done all over the world by firms offering the best security printing at the most reasonable rates. Finland, Switzerland, Japan, the United States and nine other countries have so far printed United Nations stamps.

Printing quantities are low, usually around 2 million. As a result, some of the issues have become extremely valuable. In addition, commemorative stamps remain on sale for only 12 months unless supplies become exhausted beforehand. They are never reprinted.

The returns from postage stamps sales are not all profit. The UNPA pays the United States and the Swiss postal services for all stamps used for mailing. On the other hand, the proceeds of sales to collectors are retained by the United Nations and are credited annually to the budget and decrease accordingly the contributions of Member States.

Everyone's United Nations, New York, 1978, pp. 346–347.

UN PROGRAM OF UNIVERSAL ALPHABETIZATION. A world campaign for universal alphabetization adopted unanimously on Dec. 11, 1963, by UN General Assembly Res. 1937/XVIII following a study by UNESCO which reported that on the basis of available statistics over 700 million persons over 15 are illiterate, i.e. two-fifths of the world population; in some African, Latin American and Asian countries the percentage of illiterate persons in proportion to total population is as high as 70–90%. From 1966 to 1969 the UN program was an experiment based on recommendations by an international Committee of Experts for Alphabetization established in 1964. In 1970 a UNESCO General Conference reviewed collected experience and worked out a comprehensive program for a world campaign of universal alphabetization. International Universal Alphabetization Day is celebrated each year on Sept. 8.

A. MEISTER, *Alphabetization et developpement*, Paris, 1973.

UN PUBLICATIONS BOARD. Permanent body of the UN Secretariat; supervises the publishing activities of the UN.

UN Publications 1945–1963. A Reference Catalogue, New York, 1964 (Supplement, every year).

UN RADIO. A UN institution established by the decision of the UN General Assembly of Nov. 20, 1947 on setting up a temporary radio station in Lake Success and permanent ones in New York and Geneva. Experimental broadcasts were started on May 17, 1948, and daily ones began in Aug. 1948. The UN General Assembly on Nov. 18, 1948 resolved to set up a world system for UN station programs, which was implemented in the decade 1950–60. In the decade 1971–80 broadcasting by means of man-made earth satellites was initiated.

UN REGISTER OF EXPERTS. The register is kept in various fields of international co-operation by the UN Secretariat, ECOSOC and the UN specialized agencies, according to the resolutions of the UN General Assembly, which regulate the forms of keeping and using registers (e.g. Res. 2329/XXII of the UN General Assembly on the register of legal experts). Names of experts are submitted by governments, and, in case the UN institutions need an expert opinion on a specific matter, the experts are invited at the cost of the UN to examine the problem in common and work out suggestions.

UN REGISTER OF INTERNATIONAL INTERGOVERNMENTAL ORGANIZATIONS. Kept by the UN since 1946; new regulations for the register were adopted by the UN General Assembly in 1969 (Res. 2502/XXIV). While the UN Secretariat keeps the register of all intergovernmental organizations, the ECOSOC keeps a register of non-governmental organizations; both co-operate closely with the Union of International Associations (UIA) which publishes the *Yearbook of International Organizations.*

UN REGISTER OF OBJECTS LAUNCHED IN SPACE. The UN General Assembly Res. 3235/XXIX of Nov. 12, 1974 ratified the Convention on the registration of objects launched in space. The Convention came into force on Sept. 15, 1976.

UN Yearbook, 1974 and 1976.

UN REPARATIONS. A term adopted by the UN to determine claims by the UN against member states or non-member states for damages suffered by persons serving the UN. Under the General Assembly decision of Dec. 3, 1948, such claims based on the international legal status of the UN are lodged with the party guilty of causing damage as determined by the Secretary-General upon the authorization of the General Assembly.

UN Bulletin, December 15, 1948.

UN RESOLUTIONS. Decisions taken by the UN General Assembly, the Security Council, the ECOSOC and bodies of specialized organizations. Resolutions, together with the Declarations adopted by the General Assembly, have great importance for the development of the international law and frequently set precedents in international relations; subject of scientific research.

J. CASTAÑEDA, *Valor Juridico de las Resoluciones de las Naciones Unidas*, México DF, 1967.

UNRIP. United Nations Representative for India and Pakistan, appointed in connection with the Indian–Pakistani conflict over Kashmir.

UNRISD. English abbreviation for United Nations Research Institute for Social Development, established in 1963, began operation on July 1, 1964, with headquarters in the Palais des Nations, Geneva; one of the autonomous UN bodies called upon to carry out international research on problems and policy of social development in different phases of economic development. It is headed by the chairman of the Institute, appointed by the UN Secretary-General, and by seven members of the Institute, appointed by the UN Commission for Social Development.

UNRRA. English abbreviation for United Nations Relief and Rehabilitation Administration, international organization of 44 countries, founded on Nov. 9, 1943 in Washington to render emergency assistance in food, clothing, medicines, housing, etc. to UN countries liberated after World War II. It operated in Europe from Dec. 31, 1946; in Africa, China and Far East from June 30, 1947. The value of UNRRA distributed goods: food – 1232 million dollars, clothing – 419 million dollars, medicines and sanitary equipment – 116 million dollars. Surpluses in UNRRA warehouses were allocated, according to a decision of the UN General Assembly of Nov. 19, 1948, to FAO, ILO, WHO and UNICEF.

"Draft Agreement for UNRRA", in: *International Conciliation*, September, 1943, pp. 534–540; G. WOODBRIDGE, *UNRRA: The History*, 3 Vols., New York, 1950.

UNRRA TRAVEL PERMIT. Travel document for refugees issued by ▷ UNRRA under the international convention, signed on Oct. 15, 1946, in London, by Argentina, Australia, Belgium, Bolivia, Chile, Czechoslovakia, Denmark, Dominican Republic, Ecuador, France, Great Britain, Greece, India, Luxembourg, the Netherlands, Norway, Poland, Sweden, Switzerland, the Union of South Africa, the United States and Venezuela. When the UNRRA discontinued its activities, the right to issue travel documents to refugees was given to the International Refugee Organization and on Jan. 1, 1951 to the Office of the UN High Commissioner for Refugees, UNHCR (▷ Refugees).

UNTS, Vol. 11, pp. 73.

UNRWA. United Nations Relief and Works Agency for Palestine Refugees in the Near East, est. by the UN General Assembly on Dec. 8, 1949. Hqs. in Vienna and Amman. Since May 1950, the Agency, supported by voluntary contributions, has provided relief, education, training and other services to Arab refugees from Palestine. In 1967 UNRWA's functions were expanded to include humanitarian assistance, as far as practicable, on an emergency basis and as a temporary measure, to other displaced persons in serious need of immediate assistance as a result of hostilities. According to the 1983 UNRWA report "although UNRWA was set up as a temporary institution, its perpetuation, through the renewal of its mandate, reflected the nature of the political framework in which the problem of the Palestine refugees was embedded. Its substantial accomplishments should be measured primarily in humanitarian terms, and its shortcomings should be judged against the background of the lack of prospects for a political solution and a just settlement of the question of the Palestine refugees."

Publ.: *Annual Report of the Commissioner-General of UNRWA; UNRWA – a survey of United Nations Assistance to Palestine Refugees* (every 2 years); *Palestine Refugees Today – the UNRWA Newsletter* (quarterly). ▷ Palestine.

UN Chronicle, January, 1984, p. 33; *The Europa Year Book 1984. A World Survey*, Vol. I, pp. 51–52, London, 1984; "UNRWA in Figures", in: *UN Chronicle*, June 1988, p. 35.

UN SALES AGENTS. A world-wide network of UN booksales agents to disseminate publications on the UN and its specialized agencies, organized by the UN Secretariat.

UNSCEAR. United Nations Scientific Committee on the Effects of Atomic Radiation, est. by the UN General Assembly Res. 913/X on Dec. 3, 1955; publ. at irregular intervals comprehensive reports with detailed scientific annexes.

"Radiation risk assessment: the 1982 UNSCEAR Report", in: *IAEA Bulletin*, December 1982; *United Nations Handbook*, Wellington, 1986, p. 14.

UNSCOB, UN SPECIAL COMMITTEE ON THE BALKANS. A Committee created by UN General Assembly Res. 10/II of Oct. 21, 1947 with the task of studying the problems of the civil war in Greece on the border with Albania, Bulgaria, and Yugoslavia. The functions of the Committee were extended by Res. 193/II of Nov. 27, 1948 and 288/IV of Nov. 18, 1949; ended by Res. 508/VI of Dec. 7, 1951. ▷ Balkans: Problems in the UN.

UN SECRETARIAT. According to arts. 7, 12, 97–101 of the UN Charter, the organ which administers and co-ordinates UN activities and signals to the Security Council problems that might imperil world peace is the UN Secretariat headed by the ▷ UN Secretary-General. The structure of the UN Secretariat underwent many changes while being adjusted to ever greater tasks, resulting from the UN assuming features of a universal international organization. The percentage of women employed at the UN is small, only 16.3% (including the least number from Eastern Europe – 3.1%, and the biggest from North America and the Caribbean Islands – 29.1%). In the UN specialized organizations the highest percentage of women – 23.7%, is employed by UNESCO, the lowest – 5.7% by FAO. On Dec. 8, 1988 the GA Res. 43/103 and on Dec. 21, 1988 GA Res. 43/224A,B, and C (adopted without a vote) was dedicated to the Personal Question of the Secretariat: Composition of Secretariat (A), Administration of Justice in the Secretariat (B), Improvement of the Status of Women in the Secretariat (Res. 43/103 and 43/224, C) and Working Languages of the Secretariat and Languages Training (D).

O. SCHACHTER, "The Development of International Law through the Legal Opinions of the UN Secretariat", in: *The British Yearbook of International Law*, 1948; M. COHEN, "The UN Secretariat", in: *American Journal of International Law*, No. 49, 1955; E. GIRAUD, "La structure et le fonctionnement du Secrétariat de l'ONU", in: *Archiv für Völkerrecht 1956–57*; R.N. SWIFT, "Personnel Problem of the UN Secretariat", in: *International Organization*, No. 11, 1957; S.D. BAILEY, *The Secretariat of the UN*, New York, 1962; N.M. VASILEV, *Sekretariat OON*, Moskva, 1965; *UN Personnel Question. Composition of the Secretariat. Report of the Secretary-General*, New York, 1967; T. MERON, *The UN Secretariat*, Lexington, 1977. *UN Yearbook*, 1980; D. PITT, T.C. WEISS, *The Nature of United Nations Bureaucracy*, London, 1986; *UN Resolutions and Decisions adopted by the General Assembly during the First Part of its Forty-Third Session, From 20 September to 22 December 1988*, New York, 1989, pp. 511–514.

UN SECRETARY-GENERAL. Under art. 97 of the UN Charter, the UN Secretary-General is appointed by the UN General Assembly upon the recommendation of the UN Security Council. "He shall be the chief administrative officer of the Organization" (art. 97) and he "shall act in that capacity in all meetings of the General Assembly, of the Security Council, of the Economic and Social Council and the Trusteeship Council, and shall perform such other functions as are entrusted to him by those organs (art. 98). Art. 99 enables the UN Secretary-General to put before the Security Council "any matter which in his opinion may threaten the maintenance of international peace and security." Arts. 100 and 101 of the UN Charter define the obligation to maintain and respect the "exclusively international character of the responsibilities of the Secretary-General" and the Organization.

The ▷ UN Secretariat, an international staff of more than 16,000 men and women from some 150 countries, carries out the day-to-day work of the UN both at Hqs in New York as well as in offices and centres all over the world.

The Secretary-General exercises depositary functions of multilateral treaties prepared under the aegis of the UN. By the end of 1980 the number of multilateral treaties for which the Secretary-General performed depositary function rose to over 290. The UN secretariat published periodically a List of Signature, Ratification, Accession etc. of the Multilateral Treaties in respect of which the Secretary-General Performs Depositary functions. The UN Secretaries-General in the first 40 years of the Organizations, 1946–1965:

A Norwegian, Trygve Lie, was the first Secretary-General of the UN; he was appointed on Feb. 1, 1946 for a five-year term of office, prolonged for a further three-year period on Nov. 1, 1950. On Apr. 10, 1953, a new Secretary-General was appointed, a Swede – Dag Hammarskjöld, whose term of office was extended on Sept. 26, 1957 for a further five-year period, beginning Apr. 10, 1958. He did not complete his second term of office having died on Sept. 18, 1961 in mysterious circumstances during an official flight to Africa, connected with the civil war in the Congo. The third Secretary-General was a Burmese, U Thant, first as Acting Secretary-General, and then as Secretary-General from Nov. 3 1961 for a five-year period; was re-appointed on Dec. 2, 1966 for a further five-year term ending on Dec. 31, 1971. On Dec. 22, 1971, an Austrian, Kurt Waldheim, official of the Austrian diplomatic service and representative of Austria to the UN, was appointed the fourth Secretary-General. He was re-elected in 1976 for further five-year period, ending on Dec. 31, 1981. On Dec. 15, 1981 Javier Perez de Cuellar of Peru was appointed by the UN General Assembly as the fifth Secretary-General of the United Nations for a five-year term beginning Jan. 1, 1982. In his statement Mr Perez de Cuellar said that he could not separate himself from his origins in a developing country, and he was very much aware of the need to provide an impetus to the renewal of global negotiations. On Apr. 4, 1986 the UN Secretariat made available to Israel, Austria and the USA the confidential UN War Crimes Commission file on former UN Secretary General, Kurt Waldheim. The Justice Department's Office of Special Investigation recommended on Apr. 24, 1986 that Kurt Waldheim be banned from entering the US as a private citizen. On Oct. 10, 1986 the Security Council decided unanimously in closed session to recommend the renewal of the mandate of Javier Perez de Cuellar for a second five year term as UN Secretary General, effective from Jan. 1, 1987.

L.L. KUNZ, "The Legal Position of the Secretary-General of the UN", in: *American Journal of International Law*, No. 40, 1946; E. JACKSON, "The Developing Role of the Secretary-General", in: *International Organization*, No. 11, 1957; M. VIRALLY, "Le rôle politique du Secrétaire Général des Nations Unies", in: *Annuaire Français de Droit International*, 1958; *Dag Hammarskjöld, A Selection of the speeches and the statements of Secretary-General of the UN 1953–1961*, New York, 1962; S.M. SCHWEBEL, *The Secretary-General of the UN, His Powers and Practice*, New York, 1967; L. GORDENKER, *The UN Secretary-General and the Maintenance of Peace*, New York, 1967, 380 pp.; J. BINGHAM, U THANT, *The Search of Peace*, New York, 1967, 300 pp.; W.A. ROVINE, *The First Fifty Years, The Secretary-General in World Politics 1920–1970*, Leiden, 1970; M. SMOOTS, *Le Secrétaire Général des Nations Unies – son role dans la solution des conflits internationaux*, Paris, 1971, p. 2899; B. URQUHART, *Hammarskjöld*, London, 1973; *Everyone's United Nations*, UN, New York, 1979; R.S. JORDAN (ed.), *Dag Hammarskjöld revisited. The UN Secretary General as a Force in World Politic*, Durham, 1983; R. NASSIF, *U Thant in New York 1961–1971*, London, 1988.

UN SECURITY COUNCIL. The UN organ primarily responsible for the maintenance of peace and security, consists of 15 members (5 permanent: China, France, UK, USA and USSR); 10 non-permanent elected for a 2 year term by a two thirds majority of the General Assembly.

The Provisional Rules of Procedure of the Security Council, adopted on Apr. 9, 1946 and amended by the Council up to Jan. 24, 1969 and effective Jan. 31, 1969 read as follows:

"Chapter 1. *Meetings*
Rule 1. Meetings of the Security Council shall, with the exception of the periodic meetings referred to in rule 4, be held at the call of the President at any time he deems necessary, but the interval between meetings shall not exceed fourteen days.
Rule 2. The President shall call a meeting of the Security Council at the request of any member of the Security Council.
Rule 3. The President shall call a meeting of the Security Council if a dispute or situation is brought to the attention of the Security Council under Article 35 or under Article 11 (3) of the Charter, or if the General Assembly makes recommendations or refers any question to the Security Council under Article 11 (2), or if the Secretary-General brings to the attention of the Security Council any matter under Article 99.
Rule 4. Periodic meetings of the Security Council called for in Article 28 (2) of the Charter shall be held twice a year, at such times as the Security Council may decide.
Rule 5. Meetings of the Security Council shall normally be held at the seat of the United Nations.
Any member of the Security Council or the Secretary-General may propose that the Security Council should meet at another place. Should the Security Council accept any such proposal, it shall decide upon the place, and the period during which the Council shall meet at such place.
Chapter II. *Agenda*.
Rule 6. The Secretary-General shall immediately bring to the attention of all representatives on the Security Council all communications from States, organs of the United Nations, or the Secretary-General concerning any matter for the consideration of the Security Council in accordance with the provisions of the Charter.
Rule 7. The provisional agenda for each meeting of the Security Council shall be drawn up by the Secretary-General and approved by the President of the Security Council. Only items which have been brought to the attention of the representatives on the Security Council in accordance with rule 6, items covered by rule 10, or matters which the Security Council has previously decided to defer, may be included in the provisional agenda.
Rule 8. The provisional agenda for a meeting shall be communicated by the Secretary-General to the representatives on the Security Council at least three days before the meeting, but in urgent circumstances it may be communicated simultaneously with the notice of the meeting.

Rule 9. The first of the provisional agenda for each meeting of the Security Council shall be the adoption of the agenda.
Rule 10. Any item of the agenda of a meeting of the Security Council, consideration of which has not been completed at that meeting, shall, unless the Security Council otherwise decides, automatically be included in the agenda of the next meeting.
Rule 11. The Secretary-General shall communicate each week to the representatives on the Security Council a summary statement of matters of which the Security Council is seized and of the stage reached in their consideration.
Rule 12. The provisional agenda for each periodic meeting shall be circulated to the members of the Security Council at least twenty-one days before the opening of the meeting. Any subsequent change in or addition to the provisional agenda shall be brought to the notice of the members at least five days before the meeting. The Security Council may, however, in urgent circumstances, make additions to the agenda at any time during a periodic meeting.
The provisions of rule 7, paragraph 1, and of rule 9, shall apply also to periodic meetings.
Chapter III. *Representation and credentials.*
Rule 13. Each member of the Security Council shall be represented at the meetings of the Security Council by an accredited representative. The credentials of a representative on the Security Council shall be communicated to the Secretary-General not less than twenty-four hours before he takes his seat on the Security Council. The credentials shall be issued either by the Head of the State or of the Government concerned or by its Minister of Foreign Affairs. The Head of Government or Minister of Foreign Affairs of each member of the Security Council shall be entitled to sit on the Security Council without submitting credentials.
Rule 14. Any Member of the United Nations not a member of the Security Council and any State not a Member of the United Nations, if invited to participate in a meeting or meetings of the Security Council, shall submit credentials for the representative appointed by it for this purpose. The credentials of such a representative shall be communicated to the Secretary-General not less than twenty-four hours before the first meeting which he is invited to attend.
Rule 15. The credentials of representatives on the Security Council and of any representative appointed in accordance with rule 14 shall be examined by the Secretary-General who shall submit a report to the Security Council for approval.
Rule 16. Pending the approval of the credentials of a representative on the Security Council in accordance with rule 15, such representative shall be seated provisionally with the same rights as other representatives.
Rule 17. Any representative on the Security Council, to whose credentials objection has been made within the Security Council, shall continue to sit with the same rights as other representatives until the Security Council has decided the matter.
Chapter IV. *Presidency.*
Rule 18. The presidency of the Security Council shall be held in turn by the members of the Security Council in the English alphabetical order to their names. Each President shall hold office for one calendar month.
Rule 19. The President shall preside over the meetings of the Security Council and, under the authority of the Security Council, shall represent it in its capacity as an organ of the United Nations.
Rule 20. Whenever the President of the Security Council deems that for the proper fulfillment of the responsibilities of the presidency he should not preside over the Council during the consideration of a particular question with which the member he represents is directly connected, he shall indicate his decision to the Council. The presidential chair shall then devolve, for the purpose of the consideration of that question, on the representative of the member next in English alphabetical order, it being understood that the provisions of this rule shall apply to the representatives on the Security Council called upon successively to preside. This rule shall not affect the representative capacity of the President as stated in rule 19, or his duties under rule 7.
Chapter V. *Secretariat.*
Rule 21. The Secretary-General shall act in that capacity in all meetings of the Security Council. The Secretary-General may authorize a deputy to act in his place at meetings of the Security Council.
Rule 22. The Secretary-General, or his deputy acting on his behalf, may make either oral or written statements to the Security Council concerning any question under consideration by it.
Rule 23. The Secretary-General may be appointed by the Security Council, in accordance with rule 28, as rapporteur for a special question.
Rule 24. The Secretary-General shall provide the staff required by the Security Council. This staff shall form a part of the Secretariat.
Rule 25. The Secretary-General shall give to representatives on the Security Council notice of meetings of the Security Council and of its commissions and committees.
Rule 26. The Secretary-General shall be responsible for the preparation of documents required by the Security Council and shall, except in urgent circumstances, distribute them at least forty-eight hours in advance of the meeting at which they are to be considered.
Chapter VI. *Conduct of business.*
Rule 27. The President shall call upon representatives in the order in which they signify their desire to speak.
Rule 28. The Security Council may appoint a commission or committee or a rapporteur for a specified question.
Rule 29. The President may accord precedence to any rapporteur appointed by the Security Council.
The Chairman of a commission or committee, or the rapporteur appointed by the commission or committee to present its report, may be accorded precedence for the purpose of explaining the report.
Rule 30. If a representative raises a point of order, the President shall immediately state his ruling. If it is challenged, the President shall submit his ruling to the Security Council for immediate decision and it shall stand unless overruled.
Rule 31. Proposed resolutions, amendments and substantive motions shall normally be placed before the representatives in writing.
Rule 32. Principal motions and draft resolutions shall have precedence in the order of their submission.
Parts of a motion or of a draft resolution shall be voted on separately at the request of any representative, unless the original mover objects.
Rule 33. The following motions shall have precedence in the order named over all principal motions and draft resolutions relative to the subject before the meeting:
1. To suspend the meeting;
2. To adjourn the meeting;
3. To adjourn the meeting to a certain day or hour;
4. To refer any matter to a committee, to the Secretary-General or to a rapporteur;
5. To postpone discussion of the question to a certain day or indefinitely; or
6. To introduce an amendment.

Any motion for the suspension or for the simple adjournment of the meeting shall be decided without debate.
Rule 34. It shall not be necessary for any motion or draft resolution proposed by a representative on the Security Council to be seconded before being put to a vote.
Rule 35. A motion or draft resolution can at any time be withdrawn so long as no vote has been taken with respect to it.
If the motion or draft resolution has been seconded, the representative on the Security Council who has seconded it may require that it be put to the vote as his motion or draft resolution with the same right of procedure as if the original mover had not withdrawn it.
Rule 36. If two or more amendments to a motion or draft resolution are proposed, the President shall rule on the order in which they are to be voted upon. Ordinarily, the Security Council shall first vote on the amendment furthest removed in substance from the original proposal and then on the amendment next furthest removed until all amendments have been put to the vote, but when an amendment adds to or deletes from the text of a motion or draft resolution, that amendment shall be voted on first.
Rule 37. Any Member of the United Nations which is not a member of the Security Council may be invited, as the result of a decision of the Security Council, to participate, without vote, in the discussion of any question brought before the Security Council when the Security Council considers that the interests of that Member are specially affected, or when a Member brings a matter to the attention of the Security Council in accordance with Article 35 (1) of the Charter.
Rule 38. Any Member of the United Nations invited in accordance with the preceding rule, or in application of Article 32 of the Charter, to participate in the discussions of the Security Council may submit proposals and draft resolutions. Thesc proposals and draft resolutions may be put to a vote only at the request of a representative on the Security Council.
Rule 39. The Security Council may invite members of the Secretariat or other persons, whom it considers competent for the purpose, to supply it with information or to give other assistance in examining matters within its competence.
Chapter VII. *Voting.*
Rule 40. Voting in the Security Council shall be in accordance with the relevant Articles of the Charter and of the Statute of the International Court of Justice.
Chapter VIII. *Languages.*
Rule 41. Chinese, English, French, Russian and Spanish shall be the official languages of the Security Council, and English, French, Russian and Spanish the working languages.
Rule 42. Speeches made in one of the working languages shall be interpreted into the other working languages.
Rule 43. Speeches made in the official languages shall be interpreted into the working languages.
Rule 44. Any representative may make a speech in a language other than the official languages. In this case he shall himself provide for interpretation into one of the working languages. Interpretation into the other working languages by an interpreter of the Secretariat may be based on the interpretation given in the first working language.
Rule 45. Verbatim records of meetings of the Security Council shall be drawn up in the working languages. At the request of any representative a verbatim record of any speech made in an official language other than the working languages shall be drawn up in the original language.
Rule 46. All resolutions and other important documents shall forthwith be made available in the official languages. Upon the request of any representative any other document shall be made available in any or all of the official languages.
Rule 47. Documents of the Security Council shall, if the Security Council so decides, be published in any language other than the official languages.
Chapter IX. *Publicity of meetings, records.*
Rule 48. Unless it decides otherwise, the Security Council shall meet in public. Any recommendation to the General Assembly regarding the appointment of the Secretary-General shall be discussed and decided at a private meeting.
Rule 49. Subject to the provisions of rule 51, the verbatim record of each meeting of the Security Council shall be made available in the working languages to the representatives on the Security Council and to the representatives of any other States which have participated in the meeting not later than 10 a.m. of the first working day following the meeting. The verbatim record of any speech made in any other of the official languages, which is drawn up in accordance with the provisions of rule 45, shall be made available in the same manner to any of the above-mentioned representatives at his request.
Rule 50. The representatives of the States which have participated in the meeting shall, within two working days after the time indicated in rule 49, inform the Secretary-General of any corrections they wish to have made in the verbatim record.
Rule 51. The Security Council may decide that for a private meeting the record shall be made in a single copy alone. This record shall be kept by the Secretary-General. The representatives of the States which have participated in the meeting shall, within a period of ten days, inform the Secretary-General of any corrections they wish to have made in this record.
Rule 52. Corrections that have been requested shall be considered approved unless the President is of the opinion that they are sufficiently important to be submitted to the representatives on the Security Council. In the latter case, the representatives on the Security Council shall submit within two working days any comments they may wish to make. In the absence of

objections in this period of time, the record shall be corrected as requested.
Rule 53. The verbatim record referred to in rule 49 or the record referred to in rule 51, in which no corrections have been requested in the period of time required by rules 50 and 51, respectively, or which has been corrected in accordance with the provisions of rule 52, shall be considered as approved. It shall be signed by the President and shall become the official record of the Security Council.
Rule 54. The official record of public meetings of the Security Council, as well as the documents annexed thereto, shall be published in the official languages as soon as possible.
Rule 55. At the close of each private meeting the Security Council shall issue a communiqué through the Secretary-General.
Rule 56. The representatives of the Members of the United Nations which have taken part in a private meeting shall at all times have the right to consult the record of that meeting in the office of the Secretary-General. The Security Council may at any time grant access to this record to authorized representatives of other Members of the United Nations.
Rule 57. The Secretary-General shall, once each year, submit to the Security Council a list of the records and documents which up to that time have been considered confidential. The Security Council shall decide which of these shall be made available to other Members of the United Nations, which shall be made public, and which shall continue to remain confidential.
Chapter X. *Admission of new Members*.
Rule 58. Any State which desires to become a Member of the United Nations shall submit an application to the Secretary-General. This application shall contain a declaration made in a formal instrument that it accepts the obligations contained in the Charter.
Rule 59. The Secretary-General shall immediately place the application for membership before the representatives on the Security Council. Unless the Security Council decides otherwise, the application shall be referred by the President to a committee of the Security Council upon which each member of the Security Council shall be represented. The committee shall examine any application referred to it and report its conclusions thereon to the Council not less than thirty-five days in advance of a regular session of the General Assembly or, if a special session of the General Assembly is called, not less than fourteen days in advance of such session.
Rule 60. The Security Council shall decide whether in its judgement the applicant is a peaceloving State and is able and willing to carry out the obligations contained in the Charter and, accordingly, whether to recommend the applicant State for membership.
If the Security Council recommends the applicant State for membership, it shall forward to the General Assembly the recommendation with a complete record of the discussion.
If the Security Council does not recommend the applicant State for membership or postpones the consideration of the application, it shall submit a special report to the General Assembly with a complete record of the discussion.
In order to ensure the consideration of its recommendation at the next session of the General Assembly following the receipt of the application, the Security Council shall make its recommendation not less than twenty-five days in advance of a regular session of the General Assembly, nor less than four days in advance of a special session.
In special circumstances, the Security Council may decide to make a recommendation to the General Assembly concerning an application for membership subsequent to the expiration of the time limits set forth in the preceding paragraph.
Chapter XI. *Relations with other United Nations Organs*.
Rule 61. Any meeting of the Security Council held in pursuance of the Statute of the International Court of Justice for the purpose of the election of members of the Court shall continue until as many candidates as are required for all the seats to be filled have obtained in one or more ballots an absolute majority of votes.
Appendix. Provisional procedure for dealing with communications from private individuals and non-governmental bodies.
A. A list of all communications from private individuals and non-governmental bodies relating to matters of which the Security Council is seized shall be circulated to all representatives on the Security Council.
B. A copy of any communication on the list shall be given by the Secretariat to any representative on the Security Council at his request."

The number of meetings held in the years 1946–76 was as follows:
1946 – 88, 1947 – 137, 1948 – 168, 1949 – 62, 1950 – 73, 1951 – 39, 1952 – 42, 1953 – 42, 1954 – 32, 1955 – 23, 1956 – 50, 1957 – 49, 1958 – 36, 1959 – 5, 1960 – 71, 1961 – 68, 1962 – 38, 1963 – 59, 1964 – 104, 1965 – 81, 1966 – 70, 1967 – 46, 1968 – 76, 1969 – 54, 1970 – 38, 1971 – 59, 1972 – 60, 1973 – 77, 1974 – 52, 1975 – 57, 1976 – 113.
A private meeting of the permanent members of the Security Council with the Secretary General took place twice in the years 1946–1987; first in London with Trygve Lie to discuss the civil war in Greece, the second time with Javier Perez de Cuellar to discuss the Iran-Iraq conflict.

Yearbook of the UN 1946–47; T. LIE, *In the Cause of Peace*, London, 1955; *UN Yearbook*, 1969; R. HISCOCKS, *The Security Council. A Study in Adolescence*, New York, 1974; R.D. BAILEY, *The Politics of the UN Security Council*, Oxford, 1975; A. DAVIDSON, *The UN Security Council. Towards Greater Effectiveness*, New York, 1982.

UNSO. United Nations Sahelian Office. ▷ Sahel.

UN SOCIAL COMMISSION. One of the functional Commissions of the ▷ ECOSOC.

UN SPECIALIZED AGENCIES. ▷ Specialized Agencies within the UN System.

UN STAFF PENSION COMMITTEE. One of the standing bodies of the UN General Assembly.

UN STAFF RULES. Internal rules of the UN. The Staff Regulations of the UN, which are established by the General Assembly according to art. 101 of the Charter of the UN by Res. 590/VI of Feb. 2, 1952, were amended by General Assembly Res. 2990/XXVII on Dec. 15, 1972; Res. 3008/XXVII of Dec. 18, 1972; Res. 34/219 on Dec. 20, 1979 and Res. 35/214 B and Annex on Dec. 17, 1980.
The duties, obligations and privileges (art. 1) are as follows:

"Regulation 1.1: Members of the Secretariat are international civil servants. Their responsibilities are not national but exclusively international. By accepting appointment, they pledge themselves to discharge their functions and to regulate their conduct with the interests of the United Nations only in view.
Regulation 1.2: Staff members are subject to the authority of the Secretary-General and to assignment by him to any of the activities or offices of the United Nations. They are responsible to him in the exercise of their functions. The whole time of staff members shall be at the disposal of the Secretary-General. The Secretary-General shall establish a normal working week.
Regulation 1.3: In the performance of their duties members of the Secretariat shall neither seek nor accept instructions from any Government or from any other authority external to the Organization.
Regulation 1.4: Members of the Secretariat shall conduct themselves at all times in a manner befitting their status as international civil servants. They shall not engage in any activity that is incompatible with the proper discharge of their duties with the United Nations. They shall avoid any action and in particular any kind of public pronouncement which may adversely reflect on their status, or on the integrity, independence and impartiality which are required by that status. While they are not expected to give up their national sentiments or their political and religious convictions, they shall at all times bear in mind the reserve and tact incumbent upon them by reason of their international status.
Regulation 1.5: Staff members shall exercise the utmost discretion in regard to all matters of official business. They shall not communicate to any person any information known to them by reason of their official position which has not been made public, except in the course of their duties or by authorization of the Secretary-General. Nor shall they at any time use such information to private advantage. These obligations do not cease upon separation from the Secretariat.
Regulation 1.6: No staff member shall accept any honour, decoration, favour, gift or remuneration from any Government excepting for war service; nor shall a staff member accept any honour, decoration, favour, gift or remuneration from any source external to the Organization, without first obtaining the approval of the Secretary-General. Approval shall be granted only in exceptional cases and where such acceptance is not incompatible with the terms of regulation 1.2 of the Staff Regulations and with the individual's status as an international civil servant.
Regulation 1.7: Staff members may exercise the right to vote but shall not engage in any political activity which is inconsistent with or might reflect upon the independence and impartiality required by their status as international civil servants.
Regulation 1.8: The immunities and privileges attached to the United Nations by virtue of Article 105 of the Charter are conferred in the interests of the Organization. These privileges and immunities furnish no excuse to the staff members who enjoy them for non-performance of their private obligations or failure to observe laws and police regulations. In any case where these privileges and immunities arise, the staff member shall immediately report to the Secretary-General, with whom alone it rests to decide whether they shall be waived.
Regulation 1.9: Members of the Secretariat shall subscribe to the following oath or declaration:
'I solemnly swear (undertake, affirm, promise) to exercise in all loyalty, discretion and conscience the functions entrusted to me as an international civil servant of the United Nations, to discharge these functions and regulate my conduct with the interests of the United Nations only in view, and not to seek or accept instructions in regard to the performance of my duties from any Government or other authority external to the Organization.'
Regulation 1.10: The oath or declaration shall be made orally by the Secretary-General at a public meeting of the General Assembly. All other members of the Secretariat shall make the oath or declaration before the Secretary-General or his authorized representative."

UN Doc. ST/SGB/ Staff Regulations /Rev. 7/ Amend 2, 1972; *Yearbook of the United Nations 1979*, New York, 1980; *Yearbook of the United Nations 1982*, New York, 1983.

UN STAFF SALARIES AND RELATED ALLOWANCES, defined 1972 by the art. III, Regulations of the UN, as follows:

"Regulation 3.1: Salaries of staff members shall be fixed by the Secretary-General in accordance with the provisions of annex I to the present regulations.
Regulation 3.2: The Secretary-General shall establish terms and conditions under which an education grant shall be available to a staff member serving outside his recognized home country whose dependent child under the age of 21 is in full-time attendance at a school, university or similar educational institution of a type which will, in the opinion of the Secretary-General, facilitate the child's re-assimilation in the staff member's recognized home country. The maximum amount of the grant shall be $1500 per scholastic year for each child (in 1980 over $2000). Travel costs of the child may also be paid for an outward and return journey once in each scholastic year between the educational institution and the duty station, by a route approved by the Secretary-General, but not in an amount exceeding the cost of such a journey between the home country and the duty station.
The Secretary-General shall also establish terms and conditions under which an education grant shall be available to a staff member serving in a country whose language is different to his own and who is obliged to

pay tuition for the teaching of the mother tongue to a dependent child attending a local school in which the instruction is given in a language other than his own. The Secretary-General may decide in each case whether the education grant shall extend to adopted children or step-children.

Regulation 3.3: (a) An assessment at the rates and under the conditions specified below shall be applied to the salaries and such other emoluments of staff members are computed on the basis of salary, excluding post adjustments, provided that the Secretary-General may, where he deems it advisable, exempt from the assessment the salaries and emoluments of staff engaged at locality rates.

(b) The assessment shall be calculated according to the following rates:

Total assessable payments (in United States dollars)	Assessment %
First $1000 per year	5
Next $1000 per year	10
Next $1000 per year	15
Next $1000 per year	20
Next $6000 per year	25
Next $6000 per year	30
Next $8000 per year	35
Next $8000 per year	40
Next $8000 per year	45
Remaining assessable payments	50

The resulting net salary may be rounded to the nearest $10.

In the case of staff whose salary scales are established in currencies other than United States dollars, the relevant amounts to which the assessment rates apply shall be fixed at the local currency equivalent of the above-mentioned dollar amount at the time the salary scales of the staff concerned are approved.

(c) In the case of a person who is not employed by the United Nations for the whole of a calendar year or in cases where there is a change in the annual rate of payments made to a staff member, the rate of assessment shall be governed by the annual rate of each such payment made to him.

(d) The assessment computed under the foregoing provisions of the present regulation shall be collected by the United Nations by withholding it from payments. No part of the assessment so collected shall be refunded because of cessation of employment during the calendar year.

(e) Revenue derived from staff assessment not otherwise disposed of by specific resolution of the General Assembly shall be credited to the Tax Equalization Fund established by General Assembly resolution 973 A (X).

(f) Where a staff member is subject both to staff assessment under this plan and to national income taxation in respect of the salaries and emoluments paid to him by the United Nations, the Secretary-General is authorized to refund to him the amount of staff assessment collected from him provided that:

(i) The amount of such refund shall in no case exceed the amount of his income taxes paid and payable in respect of his United Nations income;

(ii) If the amount of such income taxes exceeds the amount of staff assessment, the Secretary-General may also pay to the staff member the amount of such excess;

(iii) Payments made in accordance with the provisions of the present regulation shall be charged to the Tax Equalization Fund;

(iv) A payment under the conditions prescribed in the three preceding subparagraphs is authorized in respect of dependency benefits and post adjustments, which are not subject to staff assessment but may be subject to national income taxation.

Regulation 3.4: (a) Staff members whose salary rates are set forth in paragraphs 1 and 4 of annex I to these regulations shall be entitled to receive dependency allowances as follows:

(i) At $400 per year for a dependent wife or dependent husband and $300 per year for each dependent child; or

(ii) Where there is no dependent spouse, a single annual allowance of $200 per year for either a dependent parent, a dependent brother or a dependent sister;

(b) If both husband and wife are staff members, one may claim, for dependent children, under (i) above, in which case the other may claim only under (ii) above, if otherwise entitled;

(c) With a view to avoiding duplication of benefits and in order to achieve equality between staff members who receive dependency benefits under applicable laws in the form of governmental grants and staff members who do not receive such dependency benefits, the Secretary-General shall prescribe conditions under which the dependency allowance for a child specified in (a) (i) above shall be payable only to the extent that the dependency benefits enjoyed by the staff member or his spouse under applicable laws amount to less than such a dependency allowance;

(d) Staff members whose salary rates are set by Secretary-General under paragraph 6 or paragraph 7 of annex to these regulations shall be entitled to receive dependency allowances at rates and under conditions determined by the Secretary-General, due regard being given to the circumstances in the locality in which the office is located;

(e) Claims for dependency allowances shall be submitted in writing and supported by evidence satisfactory to the Secretary-General. A separate claim for dependency allowances shall be made each year."

UN Doc. /ST/SGB/ Staff Regulations /Rev. 7/ Amend 2, 1972.

UN STAFF WORKING HOURS AND OFFICIAL HOLIDAYS. A regulation defined 1952 by the Rules 101.2 and 101.3 of the Staff Regulations of the UN:

"(a) Normal working hours at Headquarters shall be from 9.30 a.m. to 6 p.m., Monday through Friday, with an interruption of one hour for lunch. Exceptions may be made by the Secretary-General as the needs of the service may require.

(b) The Secretary-General shall set the normal working hours for each duty station away from Headquarters and notify the staff of these hours.

(c) A staff member shall be required to work beyond the normal tour of duty whenever requested to do so."

"(a) Official holidays at Headquarters shall be New Year's Day (1 January), Washington's Birthday (third Monday in February), Memorial Day (last Monday in May), Independence Day (4 July), Labor Day (first Monday in September), Thanksgiving Day (fourth Thursday in November), Christmas Day (25 December) and one further day during Christmas season designated each year by the Secretary-General. If any such day occurs on a Saturday or Sunday, the preceding Friday shall be considered an official holiday in lieu of Saturday and the following Monday in lieu of Sunday.

(b) The Secretary-General shall set the official holidays for each duty station away from Headquarters and notify the staff of these holidays.

(c) Staff members who are nationals of any country which observes a national day may be excused from work on that day."

UN Doc. ST/SGB/ Staff Regulations /Rev. 7/ Amend 2, 1972.

UN STAMPS. ▷ UN Postal Administration.

UN STATISTICAL COMMISSION. One of the functional commissions of the ▷ ECOSOC.

UNTAG. United Nations Temporary Auxiliary Group, called for under Security Council Res. 435 in Mar., 1979 for the purpose of ensuring free elections to the Constitutional Assembly of Namibia. Up to early 1981 UNTAG was not operational.

UNTAS. United Nations Transitional Assistance Group for Namibia provided for under UN Res. 435/1978, founded 1989/90 in relation with the withdrawal of Cuban troops from ▷ Angola.

UN TECHNICAL AID. The major aim of the UNO in the field of assisting economic, social and cultural development to which the UN allocate 80% of their financial means and employ about 17–20,000 officers and experts as technical aides; subject to international conventions. The first UN technical aid project was adopted by the UN General Assembly on Dec. 4, 1948 under the Resolution 198

and 200/III with respect to "underdeveloped countries." Previously, during 1947–48 the UN Secretariat rendered technical aid in three cases: on request of Haiti it studied economic problems of that country; on request of Uruguay it analysed budgetary problems of that country; on request of the OAS it helped establish the International Institute of Statistics. A comprehensive project on technical aid prepared by ECOSOC was unanimously adopted by the UN General Assembly on Nov. 16, 1949. The first session of the UN Council of Technical Aid was held on Feb. 23, 1950. The UN Expanded Program of Technical Assistance ▷ UNEPTA financed by voluntary donations made by UN member states was enacted on July 1, 1950.

The Technical Assistance Board, TAB, is the co-ordinating organ that holds its periodical meetings in New York and Geneva; it names permanent representatives in countries benefiting from technical aid. All specialized organs of the UN participate in the works of UNEPTA. The works are supervised by the Committee for Technical Aid of ECOSOC which also prepares reports and suggestions to the UN General Assembly. During 1949–59 in the UN Secretariat the Technical Assistance Administration, TAA, was operated and in 1959 it was included into the Economic and Social Department of the UN Secretariat. The principles and rules of technical aid worked out throughout the years are the following:

(1) Organizations participating in the UN Technical Aid projects may do so only on request of governments; (2) the aid is given exclusively to governments or through governments and must meet interests of countries; (3) the aid may not serve interference into economic and political life of the country; (4) experts may not be involved in any kind of commercial or political activities and should be selected not only on the basis of professional skills but also knowledge of cultural traditions and specificity of the host country; (5) in principle experts are paid by the UN.

In 1958 the UN General Assembly assisted by IBRD and IFC established the Special UN Fund for Economic Development, SUNFED, headed by a triumvirate composed of the UN Secretary-General, the Director of TAB and the President of IBRD. The fund was started in 1959.

In the decades 1960–80 the activities have been insufficient when compared to the enormous needs of the developing countries. Three forms of technical aid were dominant: 80% accounted for expertise, 10% for scholarship projects and 10% for equipment. Voluntary donations hardly exceeded 500 million dollars within the first 15 years of the project's operation. The aid has been given to 135 states and non-autonomous territories with the use of 13,500 experts contracted by 99 states (experts have been paid about 450 million dollars); 31 thousand scholarships to persons from 138 states and territories. November 22, 1965, the UN General Assembly by the Resolution 2029/XX decided to unite UNEFTA and SUNFED under the UNDP (UN Development Program) whose rules and principles of activities remained substantially unchanged as those of the UN Technical Aid.

Everyone's United Nations, New York, 1979.

UN TECHNICAL ASSISTANCE COMMITTEE. One of the Standing Committees of the ECOSOC.

UN TECHNICAL CO-OPERATION PROGRAMME. Part of UN Development Program, ▷ UNDP.

UN TELEVISION A part of the telecommunication system of the United Nations. Its tasks cover the preparation of programs on activities of the UN and its specialized organizations for TV of member countries; granting assistance to TV correspondents accredited to the UN. The first program prepared by UN TV, entitled Las Naciones Unidas en Accion, in Spanish, was broadcast on July 9, 1952 by UN Radio and TV Division to TV stations of Argentina, the Dominican Republic, Cuba, Mexico and Venezuela.

UNTERGANG DES ABENDLANDES. German: "Fall of Western Civilization," international term – a philosophy of history on the morphology of cultures whose lifespan – as the history of humanity indicates – as a rule does not extend beyond one thousand years, heralding the fall of West European culture and the defeat of europocentrism, formulated after World War I by the German philosopher Oswald Spengler (1880–1936), author i.a. of the two-volume work published in Berlin in 1918 and 1927 entitled *Untergang des Abendlandes*.

UNTERMENSCH. German: "subman," term of the German Reich which grew out of the rascist, colonial separation of nations and people into "nations of masters" (Herrenvolk) composed of "supermen" (▷ Uebermensch) and "lower races" composed of "submen."

UN TRADE AND DEVELOPMENT BOARD. Est. by the UN General Assembly. A standing body of the UN Conference on Trade and Development ▷ UNCTAD est. by the UN General Assembly on Dec. 1964 to carry out functions of the Conference between sessions and to implement Conference decisions.

UN TREATY INFORMATION SYSTEM, TIS. A computerized system of treaty information, established in 1978 in the UN Hqs. ▷ UN Computering International Centre.

UN TRUSTEESHIP ADMINISTRATION. An institution est. in 1945 under the UN Charter (Chapters XII and XIII) for the so-called League of Nations mandatory areas, those detached from enemy states as a result of World War II and areas embodied in the UN trusteeship system by will of states responsible for their administration. Such non-self-governing territories were termed trusteeship territories in the UN Charter. The states supervising them (art. 76 of the UN Charter) pledged to support local people in their striving for self-government or independence. The UN Charter (Chapter XIII) founded the Trusteeship Council, the General Assembly established the Trusteeship Administration and Information about Non-Self-Governing Territories Committee while the UN Secretariat established a special department headed by one of the Secretary General's deputies. During the ▷ San Francisco Conference of the United Nations, 1945, the government of the USSR insisted that the system of trusteeship be provisional and a deadline be drawn for the countries to receive independence. But the Western powers put through the formula of "self-government or independence" without giving specific dates. The Western Powers established the UN Trusteeship Administration as early as Oct. 19, 1945, i.e. five days prior to the installation of major UN organs. During 1945–60 the administrating countries were: Australia, Belgium, France, New Zealand, Great Britain and the USA, and, during 1956–60: Italy which exercised control over Somalia. In 1960, following decolonization of these areas, France and Italy terminated their administrative functions, as did

Belgium in 1961. On Nov. 12, 1961 the USSR demanded total dissolution of the UN Trusteeship Administration; this however, was impossible because Great Britain and the USA vetoed the move. Nevertheless, the competence of the UN Trusteeship Council was considerably limited through subordinating it to the Decolonization Committee, called the Committee of 24 ▷ Decolonization). From 1966 to 1970 the composition of the Council was as follows: Australia, New Zealand, Great Britain, the USA as administrators, permanent members of the Security Council: China, France, the USSR and in keeping with article 86 of the UN Charter – Liberia was co-opted to maintain a balance in the voting. In face of the process of decolonization in 1980 the UN Trusteeship Administration performed its functions only with regard to the US Trust Territory of the Pacific Islands, whose independence is demanded by the UN Decolonization Committee.

A. GARCIA ROBLES, *El Mundo de la Postguerra*, Vol. I, pp. 141–143, México, DF, 1946; C.V. NARAYAN, *Analysis of the Principles and System of international Trusteeship in the Charter*, Geneva, 1951; Q. WRIGHT, *Mandate under the League of Nations*, Chicago, 1959, p. 218; S. THULLEN, *Problems of the Trusteeship System: A Study of Political Behavior in the UN*, Geneva, 1964; S.M. ALLEN, *Decolonization in Small Island Territories*, New York, 1966.

UNTS. United Nations Treaty Series. ▷ Registration and Publication of International Agreements.

UNTSO. United Nations Truce Supervision Organization. UNTSO was initially established in June, 1948 for the purpose of supervising the truce called for by the Security Council in Palestine (resolution 50 (1948)). After the conclusion of armistice agreements between Israel and four Arab states in 1949, UNTSO was given the task of assisting the parties in the supervision of those agreements (Security Council resolution 73 (1949)). Under each agreement, mixed armistice commissions were set up which are chaired by the Chief of Staff of UNTSO or his representative.

At present, observers of UNTSO assist and cooperate with UNDOF and UNIFIL in the performance of their tasks. They also maintain a presence in Egypt, in accordance with existing decisions of the Security Council. UNTSO continues to maintain the mixed armistice commissions machinery although, owing to the lack of co-operation among the parties, they no longer function as stipulated in the Armistice Agreements.

The authorized strength of UNTSO observers is 298. The following countries provide military observers for UNTSO: Argentina, Australia, Austria, Belgium, Canada, Chile, Denmark, Finland, France, Ireland, Italy, Netherlands, New Zealand, Norway, Sweden, USSR and USA.

UN UNIVERSITY. The UN General Assembly Res. 2951/XXVII est. on Dec. 19, 1972 the University. The UN University Charter was adopted on Dec. 6, 1975. The seat of the University headquarters is in Tokyo, where in spring 1975 the University Council was constituted, headed by the rector, appointed *ad personam* for 6 years by the UN Secretary-General and the UNESCO Director General. The first rector appointed was Professor James Hester, former President of the New York University (1962–75). The Tokyo University Center does not teach students, but inspires and co-ordinates the work of a network of research institutes in all continents. The aims of the UN University are both humanistic and utilitarian, and its work aims at finding new methods for improving

man's existence worldwide. The University is not organized on the traditional basis of academic structure of faculties. The institutes of the University adopted a multi-disciplinary approach to the leading world problems. The works of the University are, to a high degree, set on meeting the requirements of developing countries. The statute of the University names, among others, the following subjects to be included in research programs: "Co-existence of nations of different cultures and languages, of different social structures; peaceful relations between countries, and maintenance of peace and security; human rights; socio-economic changes and development; environment and proper use of resources; basic scientific research and application of scientific and technical results for development; universal human values connected with improvement of the quality of life."

High priority was given by the University Council to the following problems: hunger in the world; management and use of natural resources; development of the individual and social development. The University is trying to gather the most prominent experts from all corners of the world, the most promising young scientists, in order to carry out common studies of maximum mutual benefit, which could be used in the world scale. The University is to become a center for "anti brain drain" (▷ Brain-Drain), aiming at enrichment of intellectual resources in the developing world regions. As an international organization the University is to serve as a center of data on the situation in various fields of science.

In 1982 the University had 28 associated institutions and 112 research and training units, carrying out University work in more than 60 countries.

The three main activities of the University – research, post-graduate training and dissemination of knowledge – would be carried out by three divisions whose work would be closely integrated:
– The Development Studies Division would be concerned with empirical specific country and comparative country research involving field-work and experimentation as well as policy research and related post-graduate training;
– The Regional and Global Studies Division would carry out transnational studies and dialogue designed to close gaps between different academic disciplines and learning traditions; and
– The Global Learning Division, in disseminating the results of the University's research in both traditional and innovative ways, would promote a more even global distribution of the capacities to create and have access to knowledge and extend the outreach of the University to centers of learning, policy-makers and concerned citizens.

The UN University Office for Europe is in London (Ship House, 20 Buckingham Gate). The construction of a permanent headquarters for the University is being financed by the Government of Japan. The Government of Finland lent financial support to the first research and training centre, established by the UN University in Helsinki, the World Institute for Development Economic Research. The Government of the Netherlands offered to establish the Research and Training Centre of New Technologies. In 1988/89 ways of securing the funding for the commencement of the activities of the Institute for Natural Resources in Africa were being discussed.

UN Monthly Chronicle, February, 1975, pp. 38–42; *UN Chronicle*, February, 1982, p. 57; August, 1983, p. 80; "How Unique is UNU, in: *UN Chronicle*, November, 1986, pp. 114–115; *UN Resolutions and Decisions adopted by the General Assembly during the First Part of its Forty-Third Session, from 20 September to 22 December 1988*, New York, 1989, pp. 300–301.

U

UN VOLUNTEERS. Part of the UN Development Program. ▷ Voluntary services.

UN WORLD YEARS. International term for memorial years, proclaimed by the UN General Assembly.

UPPER ADIGA. A territory in south Italy in the autonomous region of Trentino–Upper Adiga, including the provinces of Bolzano and Trydent; subject of a dispute between Italy and Austria, the latter claiming the right to U.A. as a historical part of south Tirol with a German-speaking majority. Upper Adiga was separated from Austria and ceded to Italy by the Treaty of Saint-Germain, Sept. 10, 1919. The issue of cultural autonomy for the German minority was examined many times in the LN 1923–38. After the Anschluss Germany and Italy on June 23, 1939 signed an agreement on an option which aimed at a "final and complete solution of the problem of Upper Adiga". After the plebiscite, in which 185,000 voted for Germany, 38,000 for Italy and 48,000 did not express themselves on the option and were recognized as Italians, guidelines for the repatriation and resettlement of Volksdeutsche from Upper Adiga were signed Oct. 21, 1939. The repatriation operation began in Nov., 1939, but was halted July 26, 1943 due to the fall of the Mussolini government. The number repatriated was more than 80,000, among whom more than half returned to Upper Adiga in 1945. In Sept. and Nov., 1945 the government of Austria made claim to U.A. with the Council of Ministers of Foreign Affairs of the Four Powers, which was unanimously rejected on the basis of art. 2 of the Atlantic Charter, which excluded the possibility of a change of boundaries in the case of Austria and Italy; this was confirmed by the Peace Treaty with Italy, Nov. 5, 1946. The question of the German-speaking minority in Upper Adiga was presented to the UN by Austria in 1960. In July, 1971 the governments of Austria and Italy signed an agreement on submitting the dispute to the ICJ in The Hague.

C. BATTISTI, *L'Italie l'Alto Adige*, Firenze, 1957; A. SOTTILE, "Le différend italo-autrichien à l'Assemblée Générale des NU", en: *Revue de droit international*, No. 38, 1960; *UN Review*, November, 1960, and December, 1961; *Lutante Adige, actions terroristes et responsabilités autrichennes*, Roma, 1961; C. LATOUR, *Südtirol und die Achse Berlin–Rom 1938–45*, Stuttgart, 1962; *UN Monthly Chronicle*, November, 1967; R. STEININGER, *Los von Rom: die Südtirolfrage 1945–1946 und das Gruber-de Gasperi Abkommen*, Innsbruck, 1987.

UPPER SAVOY. French Haute Savoie, department of France on the Swiss border south of Lake Geneva; neutralized along with the region ▷ Gex by art. 92 of the Final Act of the Congress of Vienna and art. 3 of the Treaty of Paris Nov. 20, 1815. These decisions were cancelled by art. 435 of the Versailles Treaty of June 28, 1919 with reservations by Switzerland announced before the signing of the Treaty May 5, 1919; subject of a dispute and verdict of PICJ/1929.

UPPER SILESIA. Polish territory, subject of a dispute between Poland and the German Reich examined by the Major Powers, 1919–21. Initially, the Powers took the position that Poland should be granted nearly the entire region of Upper Silesia, with nearly the entire Opole region, as also resulted from the peace conditions submitted to Germany May 7, 1919 in a *Lettre d'envoi* and from the reply May 29, 1919 to the remarks of the German delegation:

"... one must solemnly declare that it is untrue that Poland has no rights which could not be defended on the basis of president Wilson's principles. In the districts whose cession is under discussion the population is incontestably Polish. All of the special German works, all of the school textbooks teach the German children that the inhabitants of Upper Silesia are Poles by descent and language. The Allied and Associated Powers would violate the principles recognized by the German Government itself if they were not to recognize the right of Poles to this land."

The change in the position of the Major Powers took place under the pressure of the representative of Great Britain, Lloyd George. Finally, art. 88 of the Versailles Treaty, June 28, 1919, recommended the holding of a plebiscite in Upper Silesia, which took place Mar. 20, 1921 (preceded by two uprisings of the indigenous Polish population, protesting against the Prussian administrative terror, which made it impossible to freely express oneself). The result of the plebiscite reflected the unfavorable conditions for Poland under which it was held: 59.6% of the qualified voters approved remaining within the Reich, of which number around 10% were Germans brought into Upper Silesia from other parts of the Reich in virtue of supposedly having been born locally. In view of the tendency to retain all of Upper Silesia within the boundaries of the Reich after the plebiscite, a third uprising broke out May 3, 1921, which led the Conference of Ambassadors, after requesting the opinion of the LN, to make a decision Oct. 20, 1921 on the division of Upper Silesia ceding to Poland 3221 km² of the 10,753 km² plebiscite region. A special status for the plebiscite region was established for 15 years by the Upper Silesia Convention, 1922. With the Potsdam resolutions of Aug. 2, 1945 the Great Powers awarded all of Upper Silesia to Poland.

J.F. HARRINGTON JR., "Upper Silesia and the Paris Peace Conference", in: *The Polish Review*, New York, No. 2, 1974, pp. 25–46; J.F. HARRINGTON JR., "The League of Nations and the Upper Silesian Boundary Dispute 1921–1922", in: *The Polish Review*, New York, No. 3, 1978, pp. 86–101.

UPPER SILESIA CONVENTION, 1922–37. A Convention signed on May 15, 1922 in Geneva by Poland and Germany, effective for 15 years in accordance with art. 93 of the Versailles Treaty of June 28, 1919 as well as after the plebiscite on Mar. 20, 1921, by a decision of the Conference of Ambassadors of Oct. 20, 1921 on the division of Upper Silesia: it established i.a. protection of minorities as well as a system for resolving contested issues and complaints of the Polish population in the plebiscite area of Opole, Silesia (Regierunsbezirk Oppeln), and of the German population in the territory of Upper Silesia (Województwo Śląskie) ceded to Poland.
Organs of the Convention:
Mixed Commission for Upper Silesia, MCUS; operated with seat in Katowice until July 15, 1937, resolved disputes of a public-legal nature. The competence of the MCUS defined by the convention included: (1) preparing Polish–German agreements consistent with the convention, (2) settling interstate disputes, (3) pronouncements on submitting cases to the Permanent Court of International Justice in The Hague. The membership of the MCUS was made up of two citizens each of Poland and Germany. The chairman, appointed by the LN Council, was the former president of Switzerland, P. Calonder, to whom was entrusted supervision over the implementation of the norms of the convention and the right to issue general guidelines and establishment of principles and who, on the basis of the MCUS by-laws, was obligated to express his view (*avis*) on every matter submitted to him by the Polish Bureau for Minority Affairs in Katowice and the German Bureau for Minority Affairs in Oppeln.

Upper Silesian Arbitration Court in Bytom (called at that time Beuthen), effective from June 23, 1923 till July 15, 1937, acted as an arbitrary body for physical and legal persons of the Upper Silesian Convention, for resolving private–legal disputes arising from the Convention's implementation; it also issued permits for crossing the German–Polish frontier, honored by both sides.
With the Potsdam resolutions of Aug. 2, 1945 the Great Powers awarded all of Upper Silesia to Poland.

Das Ultimatum der Entente. Vollständiger französischer Text der Mantelnote (Lettre d'envoi) und der Antwort auf die deutschen Gegenvorschläge (Réponse aux remarques de la délégation allemande sur les conditions de paix), Berlin, 1919; CH. FIRICH, *Le Caractère Polonais de la Haute-Silésie d'après des Statistiques Oficielles Prussiens et le Résultat du Plébiscite*, Varsovie, 1921; S. WAMBAUGH, *Plebiscites since the World War*. With a Collection of Official Documents, Vol. 2, Washington, DC, 1933; W.J. ROSE, *The Drama of Upper Silesia*, Brattleboro, 1935; S. KAECKEN-BEECK, *The International Experiment of Upper Silesia*, New York, 1943; E. WISKEMAN, *Germany's Eastern Neighbours. Problems Relating to the Oder-Neise Line and Czech Frontier Region*, London, 1956; J. KOKOT, *Der Schutz der Nationalen Minderheiten auf Grund des deutsch-polnischen Genfer Alkommen über Oberschlesien in den Jahren 1922–1937*, Opole, 1970; J.F. HARRINGTON JR., "Upper Silesia and the Paris Peace Conference", in: *The Polish Review*, New York, No. 2, 1974, pp. 25–46; J.F. HARRINGTON JR., "The League of Nations and the Upper Silesian Boundary Dispute 1921–1922", in: *The Polish Review*, New York, No. 3, 1978, pp. 86–101.

UPPER VOLTA. ▷ Burkina Faso.

UPU, UNIVERSAL POSTAL UNION. Union postale universelle, Vsiemirniy pochtoviy soyuz, Union Postal Universal. Official English, French, Russian and Spanish names of a UN specialized agency, est. Oct. 9, 1874 in Berne, Switzerland, under the Treaty concerning the Establishment of a General Postal Union (Berne Treaty). The Convention came into force July 1, 1875. The present name adopted in 1878. The Constitution of the UPU and other Acts which have developed from the Berne Treaty of 1874 are periodically revised at International Postal Congresses.
The aim of the UPU is to form a single postal territory of countries for the reciprocal exchange of letter-post items, to secure the organization and improvement of postal services, to promote in this sphere international collaboration and to take part in postal technical assistance sought by the member countries of the Union. Every member agrees to transmit the mail of all other members by the best means used for its own mail.
The principal organs of UPU are the Universal Postal Congress, the Executive Council, the Consultative Council for Postal Studies and the International Bureau.
The Universal Postal Congress, which usually meets at five-year intervals, reviews the Acts of UPU, including the subsidiary agreements, and fixes the place of meeting of the following Congress. The Executive Council, which normally holds one session a year at Berne, consists of 40 members elected by the Congress on an equitable geographical basis. The Council ensures the continuity of the work of UPU in the interval between Congresses. For this purpose, it maintains close contact with postal administrations, exercises certain control over the activities of the International Bureau, ensures working relations with the United Nations and other international organizations, promotes the development of postal technical assistance, and makes studies and submits proposals to the Congress.

The Consultative Council for Postal Studies, composed of 35 members elected by the Congress, meets annually at Berne. The Council organizes studies of major problems affecting postal administrations in all UPU member countries in the technical, operational and economic fields and in the sphere of technical co-operation; it also examines teaching and training problems in the newly independent and developing countries.

The International Bureau, located at Berne, coordinates, publishes and disseminates information about the international postal service. At the request of the parties concerned, it gives opinions on disputes and can act as a clearing house for the settlement of debts between postal administrations. It considers requests for amendments to the Acts of the Union, gives notice of changes adopted, and takes part in the preparation of the work of Congress; it provides secretariat services for UPU bodies and promotes technical co-operation of all types.

As of 31 July 1978, there were 159 UPU Members. The basic activity of the Union is to make provisions for the various international postal services carried out by the postal administrations of its members. The Universal Postal Convention and other legislation of UPU allow international postal exchanges to be made under principles and practices which are largely standardized.

UPU, a participating agency in the United Nations Development Programme (UNDP), manages postal projects approved by UNDP, thereby assisting on request in the modernization of existing postal services as well as in the introduction of new postal and financial services, such as postal cheques and postal savings banks.

During the Second United Nations Development Decade, UPU objectives are to enable postal administrations to speed up the conveyance and delivery of mail, especially in rural areas; to enlarge the number of post offices; to expand the use of airmail for forwarding parcels in the international postal service, up to 30% of the total, and to maximize air conveyance in all categories; to introduce financial services such as money orders and savings banks where they do not already exist, and to improve staff management.

The aid has been rendered in three forms: recruiting and supplying experts; awarding fellowships for vocational training; and furnishing minor equipment or training and demonstration material.

Member countries of UPU have also been aided on a bilateral basis by technical assistance from other members, usually by means of professional training courses, the provision of experts and exchanges of information, documents and results of tests or experiments. The Union has encouraged, in particular, joint projects among countries for the more rational and less costly solution of an area's problems. The International Bureau has supplemented as far as possible this bilateral assistance and has also managed some of the technical projects.

French is the sole official language of the UPU.

Headquarters: Case Postale, 3000 Berne 15, Switzerland.

J.F. SLY, "The Genesis of the UPU", in: *International Conciliation*, October, 1927; *UPU Convention*, Paris, 1948; *The UPU. Its Foundation and Development*, Berne, 1959; *UPU, Documents of the Lausanne Congress, 1974*, Berne, 1975; *UN Everyone's United Nations*, UN, New York, 1979, pp. 370–371.

UPU, UNIVERSAL POSTAL UNION CONSTITUTION. Constitution of Vienna, signed on July 10, 1964, amended by a Tokyo Protocol on Nov. 14, 1969, reads as follows:

"Preamble

With a view to developing communication between peoples by the efficient operation of the postal services, and to contributing to the attainment of the noble aims of international collaboration in the cultural, social and economic fields,

the Plenipotentiaries of the Governments of the contracting countries have, subject to ratification, adopted this Constitution.

Section I. Organic Provisions

Chapter I. General

Scope and Objectives of the Union

Art. 1.1. The countries adopting this Constitution comprise, under the title of the Universal Postal Union, a single postal territory for the reciprocal exchange of letter post items. Freedom of transit is guaranteed throughout the entire territory of the Union.

2. The aim of the Union is to secure the organization and improvement of the postal services and to promote in this sphere the development of international collaboration.

3. The Union takes part, as far as possible, in postal technical assistance sought by its member countries.

Members of the Union

Art. 2. Member countries of the Union are:

(a) Countries which have membership status at the date on which this Constitution comes into force.

(b) Countries admitted to membership in accordance with Art. 11.

Art. 3. The Union has within its jurisdiction:

(a) the territories of member countries;

(b) post offices set up by member countries in territories not included in the Union;

(c) territories which, without being members of the Union, are included in it because from the postal point of view they are dependent on member countries.

Exceptional Relations

Art. 4. Postal Administrations which provide a service with territories not included in the Union are bound to act as intermediaries for other Administrations. The provisions of the Convention and its Detailed Regulations are applicable to such exceptional relations.

Seat of the Union

Art. 5. The seat of the Union and of its permanent organs shall be at Berne.

Official Language of the Union

Art. 6. The official language of the Union is French.

Monetary Standard

Art. 7. The franc adopted as the monetary unit in the Acts of the Union is the gold franc of 100 centimes weighing 10/31 of a gram and a fineness of 0.900.

Restricted Unions. Special Agreements

Art. 8.1. Member countries, or their Postal Administrations if the legislation of those countries so permits, may establish Restricted Unions and make Special Agreements concerning the international postal service, provided always that they do not introduce provisions less favorable to the public than those provided for by the Acts to which the member countries concerned are parties.

2. Restricted Unions may send observers to Congresses, Conferences and meetings of the Union, to the Executive Council and to the Consultative Committee for Postal Studies.

3. The Union may send observers to Congresses, Conferences and meetings of Restricted Unions.

Relations with the United Nations

Art. 9. The relations between the Union and the United Nations are governed by the Agreements whose texts are annexed to this Constitution.

Relations with International Organizations

Art. 10. In order to secure close co-operation in the international postal sphere, the Union may collaborate with international organizations having related interests and activities.

Chapter II. Accession or Admission to the Union. Withdrawal from the Union

Accession or Admission to the Union. Procedure

Art. 11.1. Any member of the United Nations may accede to the Union.

2. Any sovereign Country which is not a member of the United Nations may apply for admission as a member country of the Union.

3. Accession or application for admission to the Union entails a formal declaration of accession to the Constitution and to the obligatory Acts of the Union. It shall be addressed through diplomatic channels to the Government of the Swiss Confederation and by that Government to member countries.

4. A country which is not a member of the United Nations will be deemed to be admitted as a member country if its application is approved by at least two thirds of the member countries of the Union. Member countries which have not replied within a period of four months are considered as having abstained.

5. Accession or admission to membership shall be notified by the Government of the Swiss Confederation to the Government of member countries. It shall take effect from the date of such notification.

Withdrawal from the Union. Procedure

Art. 12.1. Each member country may withdraw from the Union by notice of denunciation of the Constitution given through diplomatic channels to the Government of the Swiss Confederation and by that Government to the Governments of member countries.

2. Withdrawal from the Union becomes effective one year after the day on which the notice of denunciation provided for in paragraph 1 is received by the Government of the Swiss Confederation.

Chapter III. Organization of the Union

Organs of the Union

Art. 13.1. The organs of the Union are Congress, Administrative Conferences, the Executive Council, the Consultative Committee for Postal Studies, Special Committees and the International Bureau.

2. The permanent organs of the Union are the Executive Council, the Consultative Committee for Postal Studies and the International Bureau.

Congress

Art. 14.1. Congress is the supreme organ of the Union.

2. Congress consists of the representatives of member countries.

Extraordinary Congresses

Art. 15. An Extraordinary Congress may be convened at the request or with the consent of at least two thirds of the member countries of the Union.

Administrative Conferences

Art. 16. Conferences entrusted with the examination of questions of an administrative nature may be convened at the request or with the consent of at least two thirds of the Postal Administrations of member countries.

Executive Council

Art. 17.1. Between Congresses the Executive Council (EC) ensures the continuity of the work of the Union in accordance with the provisions of the Acts of the Union.

2. Members of the Executive Council carry out their functions in the name and in the interests of the Union.

Consultative Committee for Postal Studies

Art. 18. The Consultative Committee for Postal Studies (CCPS) is entrusted with carrying out studies and giving opinion on technical, operational and economic questions concerning the postal service.

Special Committees

Art. 19. Special Committees may be entrusted by a Congress or by an Administrative Conference with the study of one or more specific questions.

International Bureau

Art. 20. A central office operating at the seat of the Union under the title of the International Bureau of the Universal Postal Union, directed by a Director-General and placed under the general supervision of the Government of the Swiss Confederation, serves as an organ of liaison, information and consultation for Postal Administrations.

Chapter IV. Finances of the Union

Expenditure of the Union. Contributions of Member Countries

Art. 21.1. Each Congress shall fix the maximum amount which the ordinary expenditure of the Union may reach annually.

2. The maximum amount for ordinary expenditure referred to in paragraph 1 may be exceeded if circumstances so require, provided that the relevant provisions of the General Regulations are observed.

3. The extraordinary expenses of the Union are those occasioned by the convening of a Congress, an Administrative Conference or a Special Committee as well as special tasks entrusted to the International Bureau.

4. The ordinary expenses of the Union, including where applicable the expenditure envisaged in paragraph 2, together with the extraordinary expenses of the Union, shall be borne in common by member countries, which shall be divided by Congress for this purpose into a specific number of contribution classes.

5. In the case of accession or admission to the Union under art. 11, the Government of the Swiss

Confederation shall fix, by agreement with the Government of the country concerned, the contribution class into which the latter country is to be placed for the purpose of apportioning the expenses of the Union.

Section II. Acts of the Union

Chapter I. General

Acts of the Union

Art. 22.1. The Constitution is the basic Act of the Union. It contains the organic rules of the Union.

2. The General Regulations embody those provisions which ensure the application of the Constitution and the working of the Union. They shall be binding on all member countries.

3. The Universal Postal Convention and its Detailed Regulations embody the rules applicable throughout the international postal service and the provisions concerning the letter post services. These Acts shall be binding on all member countries.

4. The Agreements of the Union, and their Detailed Regulations, regulate the service other than those of the letter post between those member countries which are parties to them. They shall be binding on those countries only.

5. The Detailed Regulations, which contain the rules of application necessary for the implementation of the Convention and of the Agreements, shall be drawn up by the Postal Administration of the member countries concerned.

6. The Final Protocols annexed to the Acts of the Union referred to in paragraphs 3, 4 and 5 contain the reservations to those Acts.

Application of the Acts of the Union to Territories for whose International Relations a Member Country is Responsible

Art. 23.1. Any country may declare at any time that its acceptance of the Acts of the Union includes all the Territories for whose international relations it is responsible, or certain of them only.

2. The Declaration provided for in paragraph 1 must be addressed to the Government.

(a) of the country where Congress is held, if made at the time of signature of the Act or Acts in question;

(b) of the Swiss Confederation in all other cases.

3. Any member country may at any time address to the Government of the Swiss Confederation a notification of its intention to denounce the application of those Acts of the Union in respect of which it has made the declaration provided for in paragraph 1. Such notification shall take effect one year after the date of its receipt by the Government of the Swiss Confederation.

4. The declarations and notifications provided for in paragraphs 1 and 3 shall be communicated to member countries by the Government of the country which has received them.

5. Paragraphs 1 to 4 shall not apply to Territories having the status of a member of the Union and for whose international relations a member country is responsible.

National Legislation

Art. 24. The provisions of the Acts of the Union do not derogate from the legislation of any member country in respect of anything which is not expressly provided for by those Acts.

Chapter II. Acceptance and Denunciation of the Acts of the Union Signature, Ratification and other Forms of Approval of the Acts of the Union

Art. 25.1. Signature of the Acts of the Union by Plenipotentiaries shall take place at the end of Congress.

2. The Constitution shall be ratified as soon as possible by the signatory countries.

3. Approval of the Acts of the Union other than the Constitution is governed by the constitutional regulations of each signatory country.

4. When a country does not ratify the Constitution or does not approve the other Acts which it has signed, the Constitution and other Acts shall be no less valid for the countries that have ratified or approved them.

Notification of Ratifications and Other Forms of Approval of the Acts of the Union

Art. 26. The instruments of ratification of the Constitution and, where appropriate, of approval of the other Acts shall be addressed as soon as possible to the Government of the Swiss Confederation and by that Government to the Governments of member countries.

Accession to the Agreements

Art. 27.1. Member countries may, at any time, accede to one or more of the Agreements provided for in Art. 22, paragraph 4.

2. Accession of member countries to the Agreements is notified in accordance with Art. 11, paragraph 3.

Denunciation of an Agreement

Art. 28. Each member country may cease being a party to one or more of the Agreements, under the conditions laid down in Art. 12.

Chapter III. Amendment of the Acts of the Union Presentation of Proposals

Art. 29.1. The Postal Administration of a member country has the right to present, either to Congress or between Congresses, proposals concerning the Acts of the Union to which its country is a party.

2. However, proposals concerning the Constitution and the General Regulations may be submitted only to Congress.

Amendment of the Constitution

Art. 30.1. To be adopted, proposals submitted to Congress and relating to this Constitution must be approved by at least two thirds of the member countries of the Union.

2. Amendments adopted by a Congress shall form the subject of an additional protocol and, unless that Congress decides otherwise, shall enter into force at the same time as the Acts renewed in the course of the same Congress. They shall be ratified as soon as possible by member countries and the instruments of such ratification shall be dealt with in accordance with the procedure laid down in Art. 26.

Amendment of the Convention, the General Regulations and the Agreements

Art. 31.1. The Convention, the General Regulations and the Agreements define the conditions to be fulfilled for the approval of proposals which concern them.

2. The Acts referred to in paragraph 1 shall enter into force simultaneously and shall have the same duration. As from the day fixed by Congress for the entry into force of these Acts the corresponding Acts of the preceding Congress shall be abrogated.

Chapter IV. Settlement of Disputes

Arbitration

Art. 32. In the event of a dispute between two or more Postal Administrations of member countries concerning the interpretation of the Acts of the Union or the responsibility imposed on a Postal Administration by the application of those Acts, the question at issue shall be settled by arbitration.

Section III. Final Provisions

Coming into Operation and Duration of the Constitution

Art. 33. This Constitution shall come into operation on 1st January, 1966 and shall remain in force for an indefinite period. In witness whereof, the Plenipotentiaries of the Governments of the contracting countries have signed this Constitution in a single original which shall be deposited in the Archives of the Government of the country in which the seat of the Union is situated. A copy thereof shall be delivered to each party by the Government of the country in which Congress is held."

Constitution of the Universal Postal Union, UPU Berne, 1970.

URALS. The Ural Mountains and the Ural River in the USSR, called the boundary between Europe and Asia; extending from the Arctic to the Caspian Sea. *c.* 2400 km.

URANCO. A British–Dutch–West German consortium for processing uranium, co-operates with Brazil.

URANIUM. Basic raw material for atomic energy, subject of international debates in the International Atomic Energy Agency, IAEA, on a scheme for creating an international uranium pool. The main known reserves are possessed by Canada, USA, USSR, Australia, Congo, China, France; other reserves are in Angola, Argentina, Gabon, Greenland, India, Japan, Morocco, Niger, Republic of South Africa, Spain, Sweden and others. The industrial preparation of uranium by gas diffusion or centrifugal machines became the subject of widespread international co-operation. Main producers are the USA and USSR. In Western Europe the production of enriched uranium was started by the ultracentrifugal method on the basis of an agreement, Mar. 13, 1971 between Holland, FRG and Great Britain, and by the gas diffusion method on the basis of an agreement, Feb. 15, 1972, between Benelux, France, FRG, Italy and Great Britain (EURODIF S.A.). On June 12, 1975 the Uranium Institute was formed in London as an intergovernmental association of five states which supply 60% of the production of uranium in the Western world (Australia, Canada, France, Great Britain, Republic of South Africa). The USA and Canada in 1976/77 suspended the export of uranium, demanding a guarantee of control over the use of fissionable materials. Organization registered with the UIA.

Gas Centrifuge Study Association, f. 1973 by URANCO and CENTE, two companies set up to further the industrial exploitation of the gas centrifuge process for uranium enrichment with the support of the government of the FRG. Headquarters c/o CENTEC, Bensberg/Köln (FRG).

The IAEA publishes *Uranium Resources, Production and Demand* called the "Red Book", with information on 46 countries. the twelfth edition (1988) in English and French presents results of a review of uranium supply and demand for the period through the year 2000. Since Mar. 1987 the IAEA publishes the *Uranium Newsletter.*

IAEA, *Tratamiento de minerales de Uranio,* Vienna, 1962; OECD, *Uranium. Resources, Production and Demand,* Paris, December, 1979; *UN Transnational Corporations and Contractual Relations in the World Uranium Industry,* New York, 1983; *Uranium and Nuclear Energy: 1986,* London, 1987; *IAEA Newsbrief,* June 1, 1988; OECD, *Uranium Resources, Production and Demand,* Paris 1988.

URANUS. One of the ▷ Planets in the Solar System. A subject of international space research. The American unmanned vehicle Voyager 2 encountered Uranus in 1986.

URBANIZATION. A process, characteristic of the 20th century, of the expansion of cities due to industrialization and mass migration of the rural population to towns; a complex process taking four basic forms: demographic, spatial, economic and social; subject of international research conducted by the Social Affairs Bureau of the UN Secretariat and by UN specialized agencies. From July 29 to Sept. 2, 1967 a UN Committee of Experts in demography and urbanization met in Sydney and declared that the problem of urbanization was the most important for developing countries. The greatest migration of people from villages to towns occurred in Latin America, where in 1940 65% lived in rural districts, whereas in 1970 only 47.4% did. Venezuela showed a record-breaking urbanization: in 1940 62.1% of its population lived in the country, while in 1970 the urban population amounted to 69.9%. A record increase of urban population also occurred in Brazil, where in the two decades, 1950–70, the population of Sao Paulo increased from 2.4 million to 8.4 million, and that of Rio de Janeiro from 3 million to 7.2 million. Similarly great demographic changes, in percentage terms, also occurred in cities such as Belo Horizonte, Salvador and Recife. The same occurred in Mexico, where the percentage of urban population was the following: 1800 – 3%, 1850 – 6%, 1900 – 14%, 1950 – 28%, 1970 – 40%, 2000 – estimated 50%. In 1970 there were world-wide some 174 cities with over 1 million population, 50 of which had more than 2.5 million.

In 1933 the French architect Le Corbusier (1887–65), known for his model for a "contemporary city of 3,000,000 inhabitants", together with other urbanists proclaimed in Athens a document called the Charter of Athens, which recognized "the essential unity of cities and their surrounding regions." In 1977 a group of urbanists, members of the International Union of Architects, UIA, on the initiative of Peruvian universities, proclaimed during the XIIIth World Congress of UIA in Mexico City, the Machu Picchu Charter, related to the demographic explosion and chaotic growth of cities in the major populated regions of the world.

"The phenomenon can not be solved, not even controlled, by the usual tools and techniques of urban planning. Such techniques can barely try to incorporate the marginated areas into the urban organism and, in many occasions, measures adopted to regularize marginality (introduction of public services, paving, housing, etc.) contribute paradoxically to aggravate the problem making the migratory movements more attractive. Quantitative changes produce, thus, fundamental qualitative transformations and the urban problem appears to be totally different.

The Charter of Athens suggests that the keys to urban planning encompass four basic functions; housing, employment, recreation and transport, and that master plan should define the structure and location of these functions.

This has led to the functional division of cities where analysis has been used as a synthetic process to create urban order. As a result, interpersonal relationships in the life of the city have been hampered to such an extent that each work of architecture becomes an isolated object and spatial interrelations have been determined largely by human mobility. Over the ensuing years it has become evident that urban development should not encourage the division of cities into distinct functional sectors but rather should attempt to create well-integrated multifunctional areas.

In contrast to the Charter of Athens we consider that human communication is a predominant factor in determining the very existence of the city. Consequently city planning and housing must recognize this fact. We consider likewise that the quality of life and its integration with the natural environment ought to be a fundamental goal in the formulation of living spaces.

Cities must plan for and maintain a massive public transport system, considering it to be a basic aspect of urban planning. The social cost of a transport system must be correctly evaluated and properly considered in the planning for the future growth of our cities.

One of the most serious threats against nature today is the environmental pollution that has progressed to unprecedented and potentially catastrophic proportions as a direct consequence of unplanned urbanization and excessive exploitation of resources.

Public politics that affect development must include immediate measures to prevent further degradation of the environment in urban areas and the restoration of basic integrity of the environment in balance with recognized standards for human health and well-being. The identity and character of a city is composed, obviously, not only of its physical structure but also of sociological characteristics. Because of this it is necessary to save and maintain inherited historical landmarks."

In 1980 a World Congress of Urbanization at Rome adopted a recommendation of reglamentation of influx of country population to the cities. ▷ Population of the world. The United Nations Fund for Population, Activities, UNFRA, in its 1986 report stated that more than half of the world population will live in cities by year 2000.

J.M. MILLER, *New Life for Cities around the World: International Handbook on Urban Renewal*, London, 1959; R. QUINTERO, *Antropología de las Ciudades Latinoamericanas*, Caracas, 1964; *Informe Final de la IV Reunión del CIES, 1966*, Washington, DC, 1966, VI. I, pp 175–176; M.H. SABLE, *Latinamerican Urbanization: A Guide to the Literature and Organizations in the Field*, Los Angeles, 1966; CEPAL, *Desarrollo Social de América Latina en la Postguerra*, Buenos Aires, 1966; *UN Monthly Chronicle*, No. 8, 1967, p. 72 and No. 9, 1967, p. 33; G.H. BAYER, *The Urban Explosion in Latin America, A Continent in Process of Modernization*, New York, 1967; C. MEILASSOUX, *Urbaniza-*

tion of African Community, Washington, DC, 1968; *UN Urbanization Development and Planning*, New York, 1968; D. KINGSLEY, *World Urbanization 1950–1970*, Los Angeles, 1970; B.J.L. BERRY, *The Human Consequences of Urbanization*, London, 1973; *The Machu Picchu Charter*, Lima, 1977; Ch. ALEXANDER, *A Pattern Language. Towns, Buildings, Construction*, New York, 1977; *Architektura* (Special English Edition), Warsaw, September-October, 1978; CENTRO OIKOS, *Halina Skibniewska, Architetto dell Uomo e dell'ambiante*, Bologna, 1979; M. DERYCKE, *Économie et planification urbaine*, Paris, 1979; UNFPA, *1986 State of World Population*, New York, 1986; *UN Chronicle*, Aug. 1986, p. 92.

URENGOI PIPELINE. ▷ Oil and gas pipelines.

URNES STAVE CHURCH. A cultural site of Norway, included in the ▷ World Heritage UNESCO List. Among the 30 wooden churches preserved in Norway the Urnes Stave Church is considered to be the finest. It was built in the 12th century but incorporates material which is even older, such as the Romanesque sculptures (interlaced fighting animals) which decorate three of its walls.

UNESCO. *A Legacy for All*, Paris, 1984.

UROLOGY. A subject of international co-operation. Organizations registered with the UIA:

International Society of Urology, f. 1910, Paris. Members: National Committees of 57 countries. Publ.: *Congress Reports*.

Scandinavian Association of Urology, f. 1976, Djusholm, Sweden. Publ.: *Scandinavian Journal of Urology and Nephrology*.

Yearbook of International Organizations.

URUGUAY. Member of the UN. Oriental Republic of Uruguay. Country in southeast South America, bordering with Argentina and Brazil. Area: 176,215 sq. km. Pop. 1988 est.: 3,080,000 (1963 census: 2,595,510; 1975 census: 2,778,429). Capital: Montevideo: 1,229,748 inhabitants. Official language: Spanish. GNP per capita 1987: US $1,860. Currency: one peso Uruguayo = 100 centimos. National Day: Aug. 25, Proclamation of Independence, 1825.

Member of the UN since Oct. 24, 1945 and of all UN specialized agencies with exception of IDA. Member of the OAS and ALADI (ex LAFTA).

International relations: a part of the Spanish Vice-Royalty of Rio de la Plata and subsequently a province of Brazil, proclaimed its independence on Aug. 25, 1825, recognized by a treaty between Argentina and Brazil, signed at Rio de Janeiro Aug. 27, 1828. During World War I neutral until Oct. 7, 1917, in war with Central States 1917–18. Member of the LN 1919–39. During World War II neutral until Feb. 22, 1945, then in war with Germany and Japan. On Apr. 6, 1988 Uruguay signed 16 integration agreements with Argentina and Brazil (▷ Alvorado Act, 1988).

J. SALGADO, *Historia de la República Oriental del Uruguay*, 8 Vols., Montevideo, 1943; I.A. ARCAS, *Historia del Siglo XX Uruguayo, 1897–1943*, Montevideo, 1950; R.H. FITZGIBBON, *Uruguay, Portrait of a Democracy*, London, 1956; G. PENDLE, *Uruguay*, London, 1963; A.C. PORZECANSKI, *Uruguay. Tupamaros*, London, 1973; *UN Chronicle*, January, 1980, pp. 80 and 97; M.H.J. FINCH, *A Political Economy of Uruguay since 1870*, London, 1981; A.P. WHITAKER, *The US and the Southern Cone: Argentina, Chile, Uruguay*, Cambridge Mass., 1981; *The Europa Year Book 1984. A World Survey*, Vol. II, pp. 2648–2661, London, 1984; M. WEINSTEIN, *Uruguay: Democracy at the Crossroads*, Boulder, Colorado, 1988.

URUGUAY RIVER. 1610 km long, rising in south Brazil and flowing to the Rio de la Plata; forms the border river between Brazil and Argentina, and between Argentina and Uruguay; subject of bilateral conventions; Argentina–Brazil on Aug. 27, 1828 and on Nov. 20, 1857; Argentina–Uruguay on Dec. 30, 1946 and on Apr. 7, 1964.

H.M. MONTARO, *El Rio Uruguay, Geografía, historia y geopolítica de sus aguas y sus islas*, Montevideo, 1957; UNITAR, *Ríos y Canales Navegables Internacionales*, Buenos Aires, 1971, pp. 202–222.

URUGUAY ROUND. The multilateral trade negotiations within the framework of GATT started after the ▷ Tokyo Round 1973–79 on Sept. 15, 1986 in Punta del Este, expected to last until 1990. The subjects of negotiations are trade in services and trade in goods principles and rules for trade in service, tariffs, non-tariff measures, tropical products, natural resource based products, textiles and clothing, agriculture, trade related aspects of intellectual property rights (including trade in counterfeit goods), trade related investment measures and dispute settlements.

KEESING's *Record of World Events*, No. 3, 1987; Ch.E.HANDRAHAN, *Agriculture in the Uruguay Round*; A. VALDES, "Third World Interests in the Uruguay Round", in: *The Economic Impact*, Washington DC, No. 5, 1987.

USA. ▷ United States of America.

USAREUR. Acronym of the US Army in Europe.

USA–USSR COMMUNIQUÉ, 1972. ▷ Moscow Communiqué, 1972.

USA–USSR GENEVA ARMS TALKS STATEMENT, 1985. A joint US–Soviet Statement released in Geneva after the meeting of A. Gromyko and G. Shultz on Jan. 7–8, 1985. The text is as follows:

"As previously agreed, a meeting was held on January 7 and 8, 1985 in Geneva between Andrei A. Gromyko, Member of the Politbureau of the Central Committee of the CPSU, First Deputy Chairman of the Council of Ministers of the USSR and Minister of Foreign Affairs of the USSR, and George P. Shultz, the US Secretary of State.

During the meeting they discussed the subject and objectives of the forthcoming Soviet–US negotiations on nuclear and space arms.

The sides agree that the subject of the negotiations will be a complex of questions concerning space and nuclear arms – both strategic and intermediate-range – with all these questions considered and resolved in their interrelationship. The objective of the negotiations will be to work out effective agreements aimed at preventing an arms race in space and terminating it on earth, at limiting and reducing nuclear arms, and at strengthening strategic stability. The negotiations will be conducted by a delegation from each side divided into three groups.

The sides believe that ultimately the forthcoming negotiations, just as efforts in general to limit and reduce arms, should lead to the complete elimination of nuclear arms everywhere.

The date of the beginning of the negotiations and the site of these negotiations will be agreed through diplomatic channels within one month."

The negotiations started on March 12, 1985 in Geneva.

USA-USSR SUMMIT 1988. ▷ Summit Meeting USA-USSR, 1988.

USA–USSR TREATY ON NUCLEAR SUBTERRANEAN EXPLOSIONS, 1976. *Russian*: Dogovor SSSR–SSA o yadiernikh podpolnikh eksplozyiakh, 1976, signed in Moscow and

Washington on May 28, 1976, by L. Brezhnev and G. Ford.

US CONGRESS. The two chamber parliament of the United States: the House of Representatives and Senate. Member of the Inter-parliamentary Union.

F. RIDDICK, *The United States Congress Organization and Procedure*, Washington, DC, 1949; G.B. GALLOWAY, *History of the House of Representatives*, Washington, DC, 1962; W.S. WHITE, *Citadel: The Story of the US Senate*, Washington, DC, 1968.

US DEVELOPMENT FUND. Est. 1957 as an institution of the US ▷ Mutual Security Program, directly subordinate to the president of the US and responsible for granting credits to the developing countries. Loans are repayable in the currency of the borrowing country.

USE OF FORCE. "Any forcible action, direct or indirect which deprives peoples under foreign domination of their rights." A UN definition.
The UN General Assembly on Dec. 1, 1949 adopted an appeal to every nation

"to refrain from threatening to use force contrary to the Charter;
To refrain from any threats or acts, direct or indirect, aimed at impairing the freedom, independence or integrity of any State, or at fomenting civil strife and subverting the will of the people in any State."

On Nov. 30, 1966 the UN General Assembly adopted by Res. 2160/XXII another appeal for strict observance of the prohibition of the threat or use of force:

"I. Drawing the attention of States to the fundamental obligations incumbent upon them in accordance with the Charter of the United Nations to refrain in their international relations from the threat or use of force against the territorial integrity or political independence of any State, or in any other manner inconsistent with the purposes of the United Nations and to develop friendly relations among nations based on respect for the principle of equal rights and self-determination of peoples.
Deeply concerned at the existence of dangerous situations in the world constituting a direct threat to universal peace and security, due to the arbitrary use of force in international relations.
Reaffirming the right of peoples under colonial rule to exercise their right to self-determination and independence and the right of every nation, large or small, to choose freely and without any external interference its political, social and economic system,
Recognizing that peoples subjected to colonial oppression are entitled to seek and receive all support in their struggle which is in accordance with the purposes and principles of the Charter.
Firmly convinced that it is within the power and in the vital interest of the nations of the world to establish genuinely sound relations between States, based on justice, equality, mutual understanding and co-operation.
Recalling the declarations contained in its resolutions 1514 (XV) of 14 December 1960 and 2131 (XX) of 21 December 1965,
1. Reaffirms that:
(a) States shall strictly observe, in their international relations, the prohibition of the threat or use of force against the territorial integrity or political independence of any State, or in any other manner inconsistent with the purposes of the United Nations. Accordingly, armed attack by one State against another or the use of force in any other form contrary to the Charter of the United Nations constitutes a violation of international law giving rise to international responsibility.
(b) Any forcible action, direct or indirect, which deprives peoples under foreign domination of their right to self-determination and freedom and independence and of their right to determine freely their political status and pursue their economic, social and cultural development constitutes a violation of the Charter of the United Nations. Accordingly, the use of force to deprive peoples of their national identity, as prohibited

by the Declaration on the Inadmissibility of Intervention in the Domestic Affairs of States and the Protection of Their Independence and Sovereignty contained in General Assembly resolution 2131 (XX), constitutes a violation of their inalienable rights and the principle of non-intervention.
2. Urgently appeals to States:
(a) To renounce and to refrain from any action contrary to the above-states fundamental principles and to assure that their activities in international relations are in full harmony with the interests of international peace and security;
(b) To exert every effort and to undertake all necessary measures with a view to facilitating the exercise of the right of self-determination of peoples under colonial rule, lessening international tension, strengthening peace and promoting friendly relations and co-operation among States;
3. Reminds all Members of their duty to give their fullest support to the endeavours of the United Nations to ensure respect for and the observance of the principles enshrined in the Charter and to assist the Organization in discharging its responsibilities as assigned to it by the Charter for the maintenance of international peace and security;
II. Considering that the above principles, together with the other five principles of friendly relations and cooperation among States, have been the object of a study with a view to their progressive development and codification on the basis of General Assembly resolutions 1815 (XVII) of 18 December 1962, 1966 (XVIII) of 16 December 1963 and 2103 (XX) of 20 December 1965,
Requests the Secretary-General to include the present resolution and the records of the debate on the item entitled 'Strict observance of the prohibition of the threat or use of force in international relations and of the right of peoples to self-determination' in the documentation to be considered in the further study of the principles of international law concerning friendly relations and co-operation among States in accordance with the Charter of the United Nations, with a view to the early adoption of a declaration containing an enunciation of these principles."

The Stockholm Conference 1984–86 on Confidence and Security-Building Measures and Disarmament in Europe, convened in accordance with the relevant provisions of the concluding document of the ▷ Madrid CSCE Meeting 1980–83, and adopted on Sept. 19, 1986 a Declaration on Refraining From the Threat or Use of Force.
Consequently the participating States have declared the following:

Refraining from the Threat or Use of Force
(9) The participating States, recalling their obligation to refrain, in their mutual relations as well as in their international relations in general, from the threat or use of force against the territorial integrity or political independence of any State, or in any other manner inconsistent with the purposes of the United Nations, accordingly reaffirm their commitment to respect and put into practice the principle of refraining from the threat or use of force, as laid down in the Final Act.
(10) No consideration may be invoked to serve to warrant resort to the threat or use of force in contravening of this principle.
(11) They recall the inherent right of individual or collective self-defence if an armed attack occurs, as set forth in the Charter of the United Nations.
(12) They will refrain from any manifestation of force for the purpose of inducing any other State to renounce the full exercise of its sovereign rights.
(13) As set forth in the Final Act, no occupation or acquisition of territory resulting from the threat or use of force in contravention of international law, will be recognized as legal.
(14) They recognize their commitment to peace and security. Accordingly they reaffirm that they will refrain from any use of armed forces inconsistent with the purposes and principles of the Charter of the United Nations and the provisions of the Declaration on Principles Guiding Relations between Participating States, against another Participating State, in particular from invasion of or attack on its territory.
(15) They will abide by their commitment to refrain from the threat or use of force in their relations with any

State, regardless of that State's political, social, economic or cultural system and irrespective of whether or not they maintain with that State relations of alliance.
(16) They stress that non-compliance with the obligation of refraining from the threat or use of force, as recalled above, constitutes a violation of international law.
(17) They stress their commitment to the principle of peaceful settlement of disputes as contained in the Final Act, convinced that it is an essential complement to the duty of States to refrain from the threat or use of force, both being essential factors for the maintenance and consolidation of peace and security. They recall their determination and the necessity to reinforce and to improve the methods at their disposal for the peaceful settlement of disputes. They reaffirm their resolve to make every effort to settle exclusively by peaceful means any dispute between them.
(18) The participating States stress their commitment to the Final Act and the need for full implementation of all its provisions, which will further the process of improving security and developing co-operation in Europe, thereby contributing to international peace and security in the world as a whole.
(19) They emphasize their commitment to all the principles of the Declaration on Principles Guiding Relations between Participating States and declare their determination to respect and put them into practice irrespective of their political, economic or social systems as well as of their size, geographical location or level of economic development.
(20) All these ten principles are of primary significance and, accordingly, they will be equally and unreservedly applied, each of them being interpreted taking into account the others.
(21) Respect for the application of these principles will enhance the development of friendly relations and co-operation among the participating States in all fields covered by the provisions of the Final Act.
(22) They reconfirm their commitment to the basic principle of the sovereign equality of States and stress that all States have equal rights and duties within the framework of international law.
(23) They reaffirm the universal significance of human rights and fundamental freedoms. Respect for and the effective exercise of these rights and freedoms are essential factors for international peace, justice and security, as well as for the development of friendly relations and co-operation among themselves as among all States, as set forth in the Declaration on Principles Guiding Relations between Participating States.
(24) They reaffirm that, in the broader context of world security, security in Europe is closely linked with security in the Mediterranean area as a whole; in this context, they confirm their intention to develop good neighbourly relations with all States in the region, with due regard to reciprocity, and in the spirit of the principles contained in the Declaration on Principles Guiding Relations between Participating States, so as to promote confidence and security and make peace prevail in the region in accordance with the provisions contained in the Mediterranean chapter of the Final Act.
(25) They emphasize the necessity to take resolute measures to prevent and to combat terrorism, including terrorism in international relations. They express their determination to take effective measures, both at the national level and through international co-operation, for the prevention and supression of all acts of terrorism. They will take all appropriate measures in preventing their respective territories from being used for the preparation, organization or commission of terrorist activities. This also includes measures to prohibit on their territories illegal activities, including subversive activities, of persons, groups and organizations that instigate, organize or engage in the perpetration of acts of terrorism, including those directed against other States and their citizens.
(26) They will fulfil in good faith their obligations under international law; they also stress that strict compliance with their commitments within the framework of the CSCE is essential for building confidence and security.
(27) The participating States confirm that in the event of a conflict between the obligations of the members of the United Nations under the Charter of the United Nations and their obligations under any treaty or other

international agreement, their obligations under the Charter will prevail, in accordance with Article 103 of the Charter of the United Nations.

(28) The participating States have adopted the following measures:

Prior Notification of Certain Military Activities

(29) The participating States will give notification in writing through diplomatic channels in an agreed form of content, to all other participating States 42 days or more in advance of the start of notifiable* military activities in the zone of application for confidence- and security-building measures (CSBMs).**

(30) Notification will be given by the participating State on whose territory the activity in question is planned to take place even if the forces of that State are not engaged in the activity or their strength is below the notifiable level. This will not relieve other participating States of their obligation to give notification, if their involvement in the planned military activity reaches the notifiable level.

(31) Each of the following military activities in the field conducted as a single activity in the zone of application for CSBMs at or above the levels defined below, will be notified:

(31.1) The engagement of formations of land forces*** of the participating States in the same exercise activity conducted under a single operational command independently or in combination with any possible air or naval components.

(31.1.1) This military activity will be subject to notification whenever it involves at any time during the activity:
– at least 13,000 troops, including support troops, or
– at least 300 battle tanks
if organized into a divisional structure or at least two brigades/regiments, not necessarily subordinate to the same division.

(31.1.2) The participation of air forces of the participating States will be included in the notification if it is foreseen that in the course of the activity 200 or more sorties by aircraft, excluding helicopters, will be flown.

(31.2) The engagement of military forces either in an amphibious landing or in a parachute assault by airborne forces in the zone of application for CSBMs.

(31.2.1) These military activities will be subject to notification whenever the amphibious landing involves at least 3000 troops or whenever the parachute drop involves at least 3000 troops.

(31.3) The engagement of formations of land forces of the participating States in a transfer from outside the zone of application for CSBMs to arrival points in the zone, or from inside the zone of application for CSBMs to points of concentration in the zone, to participate in a notifiable exercise activity or to be concentrated.

(31.3.1) The arrival or concentration of these forces will be subject to notification whenever it involves, at any time during the activity:
– at least 13,000 troops, including support troops, or
– at least 300 battle tanks
if organized into a divisional structure or at least two brigades/regiments, not necessarily subordinate to the same division.

(31.3.2) Forces which have been transferred into the zone will be subject to all provisions of agreed CSBMs when they depart their arrival points to participate in a notifiable exercise activity or to be concentrated within the zone of application for CSBMs.

(32) Notifiable military activities carried out without advance notice to the troops involved, are exceptions to the requirements for prior notification to be made 42 days in advance.

* In this document, the term notifiable means subject to notification.
** See Annex I.
*** In this context, the term land forces includes amphibious, airmobile and airborne forces.

(32.1) Notification of such activities, above the agreed thresholds, will be given at the time the troops involved commence such activities.

(33) Notification will be given in writing of each notifiable military activity in the following agreed form:

(34) A—*General Information*
(34.1) The designation of the military activity;
(34.2) The general purpose of the military activity;

(34.3) The names of the States involved in the military activity;
(34.4) The level of command, organizing and commanding the military activity;
(34.5) The start and end dates of the military activity.

(35) B—*Information on Different Types of Notifiable Military Activities*

(35.1) The engagement of formations of land forces of the participating States in the same exercise activity conducted under a single operational command independently or in combination with any possible air or naval components:

(35.1.1) The total number of troops taking part in the military activity (i.e., ground troops, amphibious troops, airmobile and airborne troops) and the number of troops participating for each State involved, if applicable;

(35.1.2) Number and type of divisions participating for each State;

(35.1.3) The total number of battle tanks for each State and the total number of anti-tank guided missile launchers mounted on armoured vehicles;

(35.1.4) The total number of artillery pieces and multiple rocket launchers (100 mm calibre or above);

(35.1.5) The total numbers of helicopters, by category;

(35.1.6) Envisaged number of sorties by aircraft, excluding helicopters;

(35.1.7) Purpose of air missions;

(35.1.8) Categories of aircraft involved;

(35.1.9) The level of command, organizing and commanding the air force participation;

(35.1.10) Naval ship-to-shore gunfire;

(35.1.11) Indication of other naval ship-to-shore support;

(35.1.12) The level of command, organizing and commanding the naval force participation.

(35.2) The engagement of military forces either in an amphibious landing or in a parachute assault by airborne forces in the zone of application for CSBMs;

(35.2.1) The total number of amphibious troops involved in notifiable parachute assaults;

(35.2.2) In the case of a notifiable amphibious landing, the point or points of embarkation, if in the zone of application for CSBMs.

(35.3) The engagement of formations of land forces of the participating States in a transfer from outside the zone of application for CSBMs to arrival points in the zone, or from inside the zone of application for CSBMs to points of concentration in the zone, to participate in a notifiable exercise activity or to be concentrated;

(35.3.1) The total number of troops transferred;

(35.3.2) Number and type of divisions participating in the transfer;

(35.3.3) The total number of battle tanks participating in a notifiable arrival or concentration;

(35.3.4) Geographical co-ordinates for the points of arrival and for the points of concentration.

(36) C—*The Envisaged Area and Timeframe of the Activity*

(36.1) The area of the military activity delimited by geographic features together with geographic co-ordinates, as appropriate;

(36.2) The start and end dates of each phase (transfers, deployment, concentration of forces, active exercise phase, recovery phase) of activities in the zone of application for CSBMs of participating formations, the tactical purpose and corresponding geographical areas (delimited by geographical co-ordinates) for each phase;

(36.3) Brief description of each phase.

(37) D—*Other Information*

(37.1) Changes, if any, in relation to information provided in the annual calendar regarding the activity;

(37.2) Relationship of the activity to other notifiable activities.

Observation of Certain Military Activities

(38) The participating States will invite observers from all other participating States to the following notifiable military activities:

(38.1) – The engagement of formations of land forces* of the participating States in the same exercise activity conducted under a single operational command independently or in combination with any possible air or naval components.

(38.2) – The engagement of military forces either in an amphibious landing or in a parachute assault by airborne forces in the zone of applications for CSBMs.

(38.3) – In the case of the engagement of formations of land forces of the participating States in a transfer from outside the zone of application for CSBMs to arrival points in the zone, or from inside the zone of application for CSBMs to points of concentration in the zone, to participate in a notifiable exercise activity or to be concentrated, the concentration of these forces. Forces which have been transferred into the zone will be subject to all provisions of agreed confidence- and security-building measures when they depart their arrival points to participate in a notifiable exercise activity or to be concentrated within the zone of application for CSBMs.

* In this context, the term land forces includes amphibious, airmobile and airborne forces.

(38.4) The above-mentioned activities will be subject to observation whenever the number of troops engaged meets or exceeds 17,000 troops except in the case of either an amphibious landing or a parachute assault by airborne forces, which will be subject to observation whenever the number of troops engaged meets or exceeds 5000 troops.

(39) The host State will extend the invitations in writing through diplomatic channels to all participating States at the time of notification. The host State will be the participating State on whose territory the notified activity will take place.

(40) The host State may delegate some of its responsibilities as host to another participating State engaged in the military activity on the territory of the host State. In such cases, the host State will specify the allocation of responsibilities in its invitation to observe the activity.

(41) Each participating State may send up to two observers to the military activity to be observed.

(42) The invited State may decide whether to send military and/or civilian observers, including members of its personnel accredited to the host State. Military observers will, normally, wear their uniforms and insignia while performing their tasks.

(43) Replies to the invitation will be given in writing not later than 21 days after the issue of the invitation.

(44) The participating States accepting an invitation will provide the names and ranks of their observers in their reply to the invitation. If the invitation is not accepted in time, it will be assumed that no observers will be sent.

(45) Together with the invitation the host State will provide a general observation programme, including the following information:

(45.1) – the date, time and place of assembly of observers;

(45.2) – planned duration of the observation programme;

(45.3) – languages to be used in interpretation and/or translation;

(45.4) – arrangements for board, lodging and transportation of the observers;

(45.5) – arrangements for observation equipment which will be issued to the observers by the host State;

(45.6) – possible authorization by the host State of the use of special equipment that the observers may bring with them.

(45.7) – arrangements for special clothing to be issued to the observers because of weather or environmental factors.

(46) The observers may make requests with regard to the observation programme. The host State will, if possible, accede to them.

(47) The host State will determine a duration of observation which permits the observers to observe a notifiable military activity from the time that agreed thresholds for observation are met or exceeded until, for the last time during the activity, the thresholds for observation are no longer met.

(48) The host State will provide the observers with transportation to the area of the notified activity and back. This transportation will be provided from either the capital or another suitable location to be announced in the invitation, so that the observers are in position before the start of the observation programme.

(49) The invited State will cover the travel expenses for its observers to the capital, or another suitable location specified in the invitation, of the host State, and back.

(50) The observers will be provided equal treatment and offered equal opportunities to carry out their functions.

(51) The observers will be granted, during their mission, the privileges and immunities accorded to diplomatic agents in the Vienna Convention on Diplomatic Relations.

(52) The host State will not be required to permit observation of restricted locations, installations or defence sites.

(53) In order to allow the observers to confirm that the notified activity is non-threatening in character and that it is carried out in conformity with the appropriate provisions of the notification, the host State will:

(53.1) – at the commencement of the observation programme give a briefing on the purpose, the basic situation, the phases of the activity and possible changes as compared with the notification and provide the observers with a map of the area of the military activity with a scale of 1 to not more than 500,000 and an observation programme with a daily schedule as well as a sketch indicating the basic situation;

(53.2) – provide the observers with appropriate observation equipment; however, the observers will be allowed to use their personal binoculars, which will be subject to examination and approval by the host State;

(53.3) – in the course of the observation programme give the observers daily briefings with the help of maps on the various phases of the military activity and their development and inform the observers about their positions geographically; in the case of a land force activity conducted in combination with air or naval components, briefings will be given by representatives of these forces;

(53.4) – provide opportunities to observe directly forces of the State/States engaged in the military activity so that the observers get an impression of the flow of the activity; to this end, the observers will be given the opportunity to observe major combat units of the participating formations of a divisional or equivalent level and, whenever possible, to visit some units and communicate with commanders and troops; commanders or other senior personnel of participating formations as well as of the visited units will inform the observers of the mission of their respective units;

(53.5) – guide the observers in the area of the military activity; the observers will follow the instructions issued by the host State in accordance with the provisions set out in the document;

(53.6) – provide the observers with appropriate means of transportation in the area of the military activity;

(53.7) – provide the observers with opportunities for timely communication with their embassies or other official missions and consular posts; the host State is not obligated to cover the communication expense of the observers;

(53.8) – provide the observers with appropriate board and lodgings in a location suitable for carrying out the observation programme and, when necessary, medical care.

(54) The participating States need not invite observers to notifiable military activities which are carried out without advance notice to the troops involved unless these notifiable activities have a duration of more than 72 hours. The continuation of these activities beyond this time will be subject to observation while the agreed thresholds for observation are met or exceeded. The observation programme will follow as closely as practically possible all the provisions for observation set out in this document.

Annual Calendars

(55) Each participating State will exchange, with all other participating States, an annual calendar of its military activities subject to prior notification*, within the zone of application for CSBMs, forecast for the subsequent calendar year. It will be transmitted every year, in writing, through diplomatic channels, not later than 15 November for the following year.

(56) Each participating State will list the above-mentioned activities chronologically and will provide information on each activity in accordance with the following model:

(56.1) – type of military activity and its designations;

(56.2) – general characteristics and purpose of the military activity;

(56.3) – States involved in the military activity;

(56.4) – area of military activity, indicated by appropriate geographic features and/or defined by geographic co-ordinates;

*as defined in the provisions on Prior Notification of Certain Military Activities.

(56.5) – planned duration of the military activity and the 14-day period, indicated by dates, within which it is envisaged to start;

(56.6) – the envisaged total number of troops* engaged in the military activity;

(56.7) – the types of armed forces involved in the military activity;

(56.8) – the envisaged level of command, under which the military activity will take place;

(56.9) – the number and type of divisions whose participation in the military activity is envisaged;

(56.10) – any additional information concerning, *inter alia*, components of armed forces, which the participating State planning the military activity considers relevant.

(57) Should changes regarding the military activities in the annual calendar prove necessary, they will be communicated to all other participating States no later than in the appropriate notification.

(58) Information on military activities subject to prior notification not included in an annual calendar will be communicated to all participating States as soon as possible, in accordance with the model provided in the annual calendar.

Constraining Provisions

(59) Each participating State will communicate, in writing, to all other participating States, by 15 November each year, information concerning military activities subject to prior notification* involving more than 40,000 troops*, which it plans to carry out in the second subsequent calendar year. Such communication will include preliminary information on each activity, as to its general purpose, timeframe and duration, area, size and States involved.

(60) Participating States will not carry out military activities subject to prior notification involving more than 75,000 troops, unless they have been the object of communication as defined above.

(61) Participating States will not carry out military activities subject to prior notification involving more than 40,000 troops unless they have been included in the annual calendar, not later than 15 November each year.

(62) If military activities subject to prior notification are carried out in addition to those contained in the annual calendar, they should be as few as possible.

(63) According to the Madrid Mandate, the confidence- and security-building measures to be agreed upon 'will be provided with adequate forms of verification which correspond to their content'.

(64) The participating States recognize that national technical means can play a role in monitoring compliance with agreed confidence- and security-building measures.

(65) In accordance with the provisions contained in this document each participating State has the right to conduct inspections on the territory of any other participating State within the zone of application for CSBMs.

(66) Any participating State will be allowed to address a request for inspection to another participating State on whose territory, within the zone of application for CSBMs, compliance with the agreed confidence- and security-building measures is in doubt.

(67) No participating State will be obliged to accept on its territory within the zone of application for CSBMs, more than three inspections per calendar year.

(68) No participating State will be obliged to accept more than one inspection per calendar year from the same participating State.

(69) An inspection will not be counted if, due to *force majeure*, it cannot be carried out.

(70) The participating State which requests an inspection will state the reasons for such a request.

(71) The participating State which has received such a request will reply in the affirmative to the request within the agreed period of time, subject to the provisions contained in paragraphs (67) and (68).

(72) Any possible dispute as to the validity of the reasons for a request will not prevent or delay the conduct of an inspection.

(73) The participating State which requests an inspection will be permitted to designate for inspection on the territory of another State within the zone of application for CSBMs, a specific area. Such an area will be referred to as the 'specific area'. The specified area will comprise terrain where notifiable military activities are conducted or where another participating State believes a notifiable military activity is taking place. The specified area will be

defined and limited by the scope and scale of notifiable military activities but will not exceed that required for an army level military activity.

(74) In the specified area the representatives of the inspecting State accompanied by the representatives of the receiving State will be permitted access, entry and unobstructed survey, except for areas or sensitive points to which access is normally denied or restricted, military and other defence installations, as well as naval vessels, military vehicles and aircraft. The number and extent of the restricted areas should be as limited as possible. Areas where notifiable military activities can take place will not be declared restricted areas, except for certain permanent or temporary military installations which, in territorial terms, should be as small as possible, and consequently those areas will not be used to prevent inspection of notifiable military activities. Restricted areas will not be employed in a way inconsistent with the agreed provisions on inspection.

(75) Within the specified area, the forces of participating States other than the receiving State will also be subject to the inspection conducted by the inspecting State.

(76) Inspection will be permitted on the ground, from the air, or both.

(77) The representatives of the receiving State will accompany the inspection team, including when it is in land vehicles and an aircraft from the time of their first employment until the time they are no longer in use for the purpose of inspection.

(78) In its request, the inspecting State will notify the receiving State of:

(78.1) – the reasons for the request;

(78.2) – the location of the specified area defined by geographical co-ordinates;

(78.3) – the preferred point(s) of entry for the inspection team;

(78.4) – mode of transport to and from the point(s) of entry and, if applicable, to and from the specified areas;

(78.5) – where in the specified area the inspection will begin;

(78.6) – whether the inspection will be conducted from the ground, from the air, or both simultaneously;

(78.7) – whether aerial inspection will be conducted using an airplane, a helicopter or both;

(78.8) – whether the inspection team will use land vehicles provided by the receiving State or, if mutually agreed, its own vehicles;

(78.9) – information for the issuance of diplomatic visas to inspectors entering the receiving State.

(79) The reply to the request will be given in the shortest possible period of time, but within not more than twenty-four hours. Within thirty-six hours after the issuance of the request, the inspection team will be permitted to enter the territory of the receiving State.

(80) Any request for inspection as well as the reply thereto will be communicated to all participating States without delay.

(81) The receiving State should designate the point(s) of entry as close as possible to the specified area. The receiving State will ensure that the inspection team will be able to reach the specified area without delay from the point(s) of entry.

(82) All participating States will facilitate the passage of the inspection teams through their territory.

(83) Within 48 hours after the arrival of the inspection team at the specified area, the inspection will be terminated.

(84) There will be no more than four inspectors in an inspection team. While conducting the inspection the inspection team may divide into two parts.

(85) The inspectors and, if applicable, auxiliary personnel, will be granted during their mission the privileges and immunities in accordance with the Vienna Convention on Diplomatic Relations.

(86) The receiving State will provide the inspection team with appropriate board and lodging in a location suitable for carrying out the inspection, and, when necessary, medical care; however this does not exclude the use by the inspection team of its own tents and rations.

(87) The inspection team will have use of its own maps, own photo cameras, own binoculars and own dictaphones, as well as own aeronautical charts.

(88) The inspection team will have access to appropriate telecommunications equipment of the receiving State, including the opportunity for continuous communication between the members of an inspection team in an aircraft and those in a land vehicle employed in the inspection.

(89) The inspecting State will specify whether aerial inspection will be conducted using an airplane, a helicopter or both. Aircraft for inspection will be chosen by mutual agreement between the inspecting and receiving States. Aircraft will be chosen which provide the inspection team a continuous view of the ground during the inspection.

(90) After the flight plan, specifying, inter alia, the inspection team's choice of flight path, speed and altitude in the specified area, has been filed with the competent air traffic control authority the inspection aircraft will be permitted to enter the specified area without delay. Within the specified area, the inspection team will, at its request be permitted to deviate from the approved flight plan to make specific observations provided such deviation is consistent with paragraph (74) as well as flight safety and air traffic requirements. Directions to the crew will be given through a representative of the receiving State on board the aircraft involved in the inspection.

(91) One member of the inspection team will be permitted, if such a request is made, at any time to observe data on navigational equipment of the aircraft and to have access to maps and charts used by the flight crew for the purpose of determining the exact location of the aircraft during the inspection flight.

(92) Aerial and ground inspectors may return to the specified area as often as desired within the 48-hour inspection period.

(93) The receiving State will provide for inspection purposes land vehicles with cross country capability. Whenever mutually agreed taking into account the specific geography relating to the area to be inspected, the inspecting State will be permitted to use its own vehicles.

(94) If land vehicles or aircraft are provided by the inspecting State, there will be one accompanying driver for each land vehicles, or accompanying aircraft crew.

(95) The inspecting State will prepare a report of its inspection and will provide a copy of that report to all participating States without delay.

(96) The inspection expenses will be incurred by the receiving State except when the inspecting State uses its own aircraft and/or land vehicles. The travel expenses to and from the point(s) of entry will be borne by the inspecting State.

(97) Diplomatic channels will be used for communications concerning compliance and verification.

(98) Each participating State will be entitled to obtain timely clarification from any other participating State concerning the application of agreed confidence- and security-building measures. Communications in this context will, if appropriate, be transmitted to all other participating States.

(99) The participating States stress that these confidence- and security-building measures are designed to reduce the dangers of armed conflict and of misunderstanding or miscalculation of military activities and emphasize that their implementation will contribute to these objectives.

(100) Reaffirming the relevant objectives of the Final Act, the participating States are determined to continue building confidence, to lessen military confrontation and to enhance security for all. They are also determined to achieve progress in disarmament.

(101) The measures adopted in this document are politically binding and will come into force on 1 January 1987.

(102) The Government of Sweden is requested to transmit the present document to the follow-up meeting of the CSCE in Vienna and to the Secretary-General of the United Nations. The Government of Sweden is also requested to transmit the present document to the Governments of the non-participating Mediterranean States.

(103) The text of this document will be published in each participating State, which will disseminate it and make it known as widely as possibly.

(104) The representatives of the participating States express their profound gratitude to the Government and people of Sweden for the excellent arrangements made for the Stockholm Conference and the warm hospitality extended to the delegations which participated in the Conference.

Stockholm, 19 September, 1986

Annex I

Under the terms of the Madrid mandate, the zone of application for CSBMs is defined as follows:

"On the basis of equality of rights, balance and reciprocity, equal respect for the security interests of all CSCE participating States, and of their respective obligations concerning confidence- and security-building measures and disarmament in Europe, these confidence- and security-building measures will cover the whole of Europe as well as the adjoining sea area* and air space. They will be of military significance and politically binding and will be provided with adequate forms of verification which correspond to their content.

As far as the adjoining sea area* and air space is concerned, the measures will be applicable to the military activities of all the participating States taking place there whenever these activities affects security in Europe as well as constitute a part of activities taking place within the whole of Europe as referred to above, which they will agree to notify. Necessary specifications will be made through the negotiations on the confidence- and security-building measures at the Conference.

Nothing in the definition of the zone given above will diminish obligations already undertaken under the Final Act. The confidence- and security-building measures to be agreed upon at the Conference will also be applicable in all areas covered by any of the provisions in the Final Act relating to confidence-building measures and certain aspects of security and disarmament.

*In this context, the notion of adjoining sea area is understood to refer also to ocean areas adjoining Europe.

Wherever the term 'the zone of application for CSBMs' is used in this document, the above definition will apply.

Annex II

Chairman's Statement

It is understood that, taking into account the agreed date of entry into force of the agreed confidence- and security-building measures and the provisions contained in them concerning the timeframes of certain advance notifications, and expressing their interest in an early transition to the full implementation of the provisions of this document, the participating States agree to the following:

The annual calendars concerning military activities subject to prior notification and forecast for 1987 will be exchanged not later than 15 December 1986. Communications, in accordance with agreed provisions, concerning military activities involving more than 40,000 troops planned for the calendar year 1988 will be exchanged by 15 December 1986. Participating States may undertake activities involving more than 75,000 troops during the calendar year 1987 provided that they are included in the annual calendar exchanged by 15 December 1986. Activities to begin during the first 42 days after 1 January 1987 will be subject to the relevant provisions of the Final Act of the CSCE. However, the participating States will make every effort to apply to them the provisions of this document to the maximum extent possible.

This statement will be an annex to the Document of the Stockholm Conference and will be published with it.

Stockholm, 19 September 1986

Annex III
Chairman's Statement

It is understood that each participating State can raise any question consistent with the mandate of the Conference on Confidence- and Security-Building Measures and Disarmament in Europe at any stage subsequent to the Vienna CSCE Follow-up Meeting.

This statement will be an annex to the Document of the Stockholm Conference and will be published with it.

Stockholm, 19 September 1986

Annex IV
Chairman's Statement

It is understood that the participating States recall that they have the right to belong or not to belong to international organizations, to be or not to be a party to bilateral or multilateral treaties including the right to be or not to be a party to treaties of alliance; they also have the right of neutrality. In this context, they will not take advantage of these rights to circumvent the purposes of the system of inspection, and in particular the provision that no participating State will be obliged to accept on its territory within the zone of application for CSBMs, more than three inspections per calendar year.

Appropriate understandings between participating States on this subject will be expressed in interpretative statements to be included in the journal of the day.

This statement will be an annex to the Document of the Stockholm Conference and will be published with it.

Stockholm, 19 September 1986

UN Yearbook 1966, pp. 61–68; *SIPRI Yearbook 1987*, Oxford, 1988, pp. 356–369 and 371–381.

US FOREIGN AID. ▷ United States Foreign Aid.

USIA. United States Information Agency, 1953–78 subordinated to the President; in charge of cultural and scientific exchange directed and supervised by the State Department, also co-ordinating official mass media and foreign broadcasts; USIA libraries outside USA distributed publications, films, materials for radio and TV broadcasting stations. USIA was also in charge of multilingual broadcasting: the Voice of America and West Berlin RIAS (Rundfunk im Amerikanischer Sektor). In content all materials reflect to a large extent current lines of US government policy. Similar roles are performed in France by ▷ Alliance Française, in Great Britain by ▷ British Council, institutions also dealing with cultural and scientific exchange. In these latter fields USIA was supplemented by the Institute of International Education, based in New York, whose scholarship projects are financed by the US government, corporations, foundations, institutions and private persons. In 1978 the functions of USIA were taken over by ▷ ICA.

See also ▷ Worldnet.

US INTERNATIONAL COOPERATION ADMINISTRATION. US institution, est. 1957 as part of the US Mutual Security Program; directly subordinate to the US President and responsible for the administration of US economic, technical and military foreign aid, as well as for granting investment guarantees to American private firms abroad and monetary grants to central banks of countries with which US has bilateral agreements to support international fluctuations.

US ISOLATIONISM. ▷ Isolationism.

USSR. ▷ Union of Soviet Socialist Republics.

USSR–YUGOSLAV FRIENDSHIP TREATY, 1945. Concluded in Moscow, June 11, 1945, a treaty of friendship, mutual aid and postwar co-operation; committing both parties to a defense alliance in the case of a repeated German aggression or aggression by any other country, which might be allied directly with Germany. Valid for a period of 20 years. Became effective June 15, 1945; annulled 1948.

UST, *United States Treaties and other International Agreements*, US Department of State, Washington, DC.

USSURI RIVER. 590 km long, forms the border of USSR and China in the Far East, covered by the agreement between both countries of 1951 on shipping on the border rivers Amur, Argun, Sungari, Tasta, Ussuri, and Chanka lake; in 1969 subject of disputes between China–USSR in connection with the incident on Damanskij Island (named Tchenpao in Chinese notes), aggravated by further incidents in that year on the Tasta river, and on Soviet–Chinese Goldinskij Island (Patcho) on the Amur river. The argument was referred by both governments to the mixed Chinese–Soviet Commission for Shipping on Border Rivers which convened in Khabarovsk from 1951 to 1964, when it suspended its activity. In May, 1978 the Commission resumed meeting following repeated incidents on the Ussuri river.

USTASHES. *Croatian*: "insurgents." A nationalistic Croatian terrorist organization formed 1929 by Ante Pavelic; co-operated with the fascist governments of Italy and Germany and sponsored a program for separating Croatia from Yugoslavia; one of the Ustashes terrorist operations was the murder of the king of Yugoslavia, Alexander I, and the Minister of Foreign Affairs of France, L. Barthou, in Marseilles, to which the LN reacted Dec. 10, 1934 with a resolution condemning the activities of Ustashes. The Ustashes program was executed during World War II with the help of the Third Reich, 1941–45 (▷ Croatia), in exchange for co-operating with the Germans in combatting the Yugoslavian resistance movement and participating in the murder of *c.* 700,000 Yugoslavs in the death camp at Jasenovac; regular Ustashes units fought on the Nazi side in the war against the USSR. After the war Ustashes established their terrorist headquarters initially in Munich, organizing bombings of diplomatic and consular posts of Yugoslavia in the NATO states, and then after the death of Pavelic (1959) – in Stockholm. In Apr., 1971 Ustashes murdered the Yugoslavian ambassador to Sweden, J. Rolovic, and in Sept., 1972 highjacked a SAS plane, extracting from the Swedish government the release from prison of the 6 participants in this murder. In 1970 it was estimated that *c.* 40 Ustashes terrorist groups, comprising several hundred members, were active in the world. In June, 1972 a 10-man group of Ustashes terrorists was transferred to Yugoslavia, but was shortly thereafter liquidated.

UTA. Union de Transport Aeriens, a French passenger and cargo airline, connecting France with francophone States in Africa and with French Overseas possessions. Headquarters Paris.

UTI POSSIDENTIS. *Latin*: "if (you) are in possession," international term – controversial international doctrine stating that being in possession of a territory occupied in wartime becomes prescribed after some period of time, thus it becomes not only *de facto*, but also *de jure* a legitimate possession of the formerly occupying state. In the conflict between Peru and Ecuador in 1942 and 1944, Peru referred to the principle of uti possidentis.

UTRECHT PEACE TREATIES, 1713. Treaties ending the Spanish Succession War, were signed Apr. 12 and July 13, 1713 between the Queen of Great Britain and the King of France and between the Queen of Great Britain and the King of Spain in Utrecht (Holland).

Major Peace Treaties 1648–1679, New York, 1967, Vol. I, pp. 177–239.

UZHGOROD. Capital of Zakarpatskaya oblast in the Ukraine. Capital of the Trans-Carpathian province in Hungary until 1919, when ceded to Czechoslovakia; returned to Hungary 1938–44 ceded together with Trans-Carpathia to the Ukrainian SSR by the Paris Peace Treaty of Feb. 10, 1947; ▷ Paris Peace Conference, 1946.

V

V1, V2. *German*: Vergeltungswaffe = "retaliatory weapon". The names of two successive types of German guided missiles with which London was bombed during World War II. The first V1 tests took place in late fall 1942 in Peenemünde. V1 was directed at London for the first time on June 13, 1944, V2 on Sept. 8, 1944. V1 was an airplane type missile which reached 550–640 km/h and carried 850 kg of explosives at an altitude of 200–2000 m to targets at a distance of 240–300 km; V2, on the other hand, was a ballistic rocket missile with a warhead weighing 980 kg, range 300 km, speed 5700 km/h.

M. KOZACZUK, *Enigma*, New York, 1984.

VACCINATION, WHO ACTIONS AND CERTIFICATES.

According to the World Health Organization the new biotechnology may facilitate the development of vaccines against certain parasitic bacteria and virus diseases, which are a major cause of mortality and disability of the world's population. The greatest hope of reducing this toll in the 1980s lies in ▷ immunization, widely disseminated due to the new era in the technology of vaccine development and production. The Sanitary International Regulations of the WHO are obligatory for the WHO member states. e.g. the vaccination certificates for international travel.

WHO Certificate Requirement for International Travel and Health Advice to Travellers, Geneva, 1983; *Viral Vaccines and Antiviral Drugs*, WHO, Geneva, 1983; G.C. SHILD, F. ASSAD, "Vaccines: the Way Ahead", in *World Health Forum*, No. 4, 1983.

VALLETTA.

The capital of Malta, included in the ▷ World Heritage UNESCO List. This fortified city, with its winding streets and fine 16th, 17th and 18th century buildings, is an outstanding example of the late Renaissance which has almost completely preserved its original appearance.

UNESCO, *A Legacy for All*, Paris, 1984.

VALLETTA CSCE MEETING, 1979.

▷ Mediterranean Conference, 1979, and ▷ Mediterranean States.

VALUE ADDED TAX, VAT.

An international term for a common system of indirect taxation by harmonization of the member states of the European Community, based on a method of imposing a general tax on the use of goods and services by the final consumer. The VAT system, according the EEC opinion, is competitively neutral; at equal prices the same kind of goods carry the same amount of tax; tax already paid on investment goods being deductible.

J. PAXTON, *A Dictionary of the EEC*, London, 1978, pp. 271–272.

VANDENBERG RESOLUTION, 1948.

A resolution approved by the US Senate on June 11, 1948, proposed by Republican senator, Arthur H.

Vandenberg (1884–1952) advising the US government to pursue a new line of foreign policy "within the UN Charter." The text is as follows:

"Whereas peace with justice and the defense of human rights and fundamental freedoms require international cooperation through more effective use of the United Nations: Therefore be it.

Resolved, That the Senate reaffirms the policy of the United States to achieve international peace and security through the United Nations so that armed force shall not be used except in the common interest, and that the President be advised of the sense of the Senate that this Government, by constitutional process, should particularly pursue the following objectives within the United Nations Charter:

(1) Voluntary agreement to remove the veto from all questions involving pacific settlements of international disputes and situations, and from the admission of new members.

(2) Progressive development of regional and other collective arrangements for individual and collective self-defense in accordance with the purposes, principles, and provisions of the Charter.

(3) Association of the United States, by constitutional process, with such regional and other collective arrangements as are based on continuous and effective self-help and mutual aid, and as affect its national security.

(4) Contributing to the maintenance of peace by making clear its determination to exercise the right of individual or collective self-defense under article 51 should any armed attack occur affecting its national security.

(5) Maximum efforts to obtain agreements to provide the United Nations with armed forces as provided in the Charter, and to obtain agreement among member nations upon universal regulation and reduction of armaments under adequate and dependable guaranty against violation.

(6) If necessary, after adequate effort toward strengthening the United Nations, review of the Charter at an appropriate time by a General Conference called under Art. 109 or by the General Assembly."

Congressional Record, 80th Congress, 2nd session, May 19, 1948, p. 6053.

"VANGUARD".

The American artificial Earth satellites. Vanguard 1 was launched into orbit on Mar. 17, 1958 after ▷ Explorer, and before ▷ Discoverer.

VANUATU.

Member of the UN. Republic of Vanuatu. A state of the New Hebrides islands group in South Pacific 1280 km east of Australia. It comprises a 724 km long chain of 80 islands. Area: 14,760 sq. km. Pop. 1988 est.: 149,400 (1979 census: 11,251). Capital: Port Vila with 14,598 inhabitants in 1983. GNP per capita 1980: US $530. Currency: one vatu = 100 centimes. Official languages: English and French. National Day: July 30, Independence Day, 1980.

Member of the UN since Sept. 18, 1980 and of all its specialized agencies except ILO, UNESCO, IAEA, GATT, IMO and WIPO.

International relations: from 1906 to 1980 British–French condominium, administered by France and Great Britain as provided in Anglo-French Convention of Feb. 27, 1906, came into force on Oct. 20, 1906, and a Protocol signed at London on Aug. 6, 1911 and ratified on Mar. 22, 1929. On July 30, 1980 France and Great Britain handed full powers of independence to the New Hebrides, which as an independent state was renamed Vanuatu. The main town on Espiritu ▷ Santo was still controlled by the French-speaking separatists, supported by a group of international businessmen seeking to create a ▷ tax haven on the island, but in Sept., 1980 the separatist movement was dissolved. A new currency, the *vatu*, was introduced on Jan. 1, 1981, replacing the Australian dollar with the effective rate from Mar. 1984 in the IMF system in relation

to US dollars. A major international tax haven: no corporate or personal incomes tax, no exchange controls, no inheritance duties and capital-gains taxes. On Jan. 27, 1987 Vanuatu signed a fishing agreement with the USSR permitting it to fish within a 200 mile exclusive economic zone but without the right to enter the 12 mile territorial waters. On Febr. 7, 1987 Cyclon Lima swept through Vanuatu leaving 45 people dead and 3,000 homeless.

"A Tax-Free Paradise in the Pacific", in: *Newsweek*, November 19, 1984; *The Europa Year Book 1984. A World Survey*, Vol. II, pp. 2662–2665, London, 1984; KEESING's *Record of World Events*, May, 1988.

VAT.

▷ Value Added Tax.

VATICAN.

Vatican City State. Not a member of the UN. Called the Apostolic See or the Holy Capital. A church enclave state in the territory of Rome. Area: 0.44 sq. km. Pop. 738 inhabitants (1978) of whom 370 had Italian citizenship (1980 est.: 830). The boundaries were established by the Lateran Treaty signed Feb. 11, 1929. Besides the area included in the Vatican, the state is also composed of many buildings in other parts of Rome, i.a. the Lateran church-palace complex, several palaces, institutes, churches, the summer papal residence Castel Gandolfo and the radio station in Santa Maria di Galeria near Rome.

The Vatican City State has a permanent observer at the UN in New York and Geneva, at UNESCO in Paris and at FAO in Rome. The Holy See is a member of IAEA, UPU, ITU and WIPO.

International relations: the Vatican State, after having regained its political sovereignty by the Lateran Treaty of 1929, reverted back to medieval tradition of the ▷ Church State (*Patrimonium Sancti Petri*), which had existed in mid-Italy until 1870, when Rome, regarded in the Catholic Church as the Apostolic See, was occupied by the king of Italy and made the capital of the Kingdom; from 1870 to 1929 the popes regarded themselves as prisoners locked within the confines of Vatican Palace. Since 1929 the pope, as the absolute ruler of the Vatican state representing legislative, executive and judicial authority, also personally conducted foreign policy until the entry into force on Aug. 15, 1967 of the new constitution of the Vatican (*Regimini Ecclesiae Universae*) by which a Council for Secular Affairs was established which henceforth formulated foreign policy, executed by a reorganized Secretary of State (since Jan. 1, 1968 called *Consilium Pro Publicis Ecclesiae*); subordinate to the latter are diplomatic representatives throughout the world, Nunciatures. The Vatican did not join the League of Nations or any special organization of the League, patronizing only the Conference of International Catholic Organizations, founded in 1927 in Freiburg. The foreign policy of Pius XII (1939–58) was the subject of international controversy. A subject of international controversy was a directive of the Holy Office of July 1, 1949 excommunicating communists and all persons co-operating with communists; it was annulled by John XXIII.

The foreign policy of the Vatican during the pontificate of John XXIII who gave the impetus to the Vaticanum Council II (▷ Ecumenical Councils), was formulated in the encyclical ▷ *Pacem in Terris*, 1963. One copy of the encyclical, dedicated to the UN, was given to the UN Secretary-General U Thant by John XXIII on May 13, 1963. On June 3, 1963, the day of John XXIII's death, the death of a head of the Vatican State was honored for the first time in the UN headquarters by a lowering of the flag to half-mast and a declaration of the UN Secretary-General. On July 11, 1963 the latter made a visit in the Vatican to the new pope, Paul VI, who on Mar. 21, 1964 appointed a new permanent observer to the UN with the task of "concentrating on the problems of peace, disarmament and the Third World."

Paul VI paid a visit to UN headquarters on Oct. 4, 1965 and made a speech before the UN General Assembly against war: "never more war, never again"; elevating the services and authority of the UN: "you have and are continuing to do great work: teaching people peace; the UN is a great school in which the art of peace is learned."

Paul VI on Dec. 31, 1965 addressed an appeal for peace connected with the war in Vietnam to the governments of the People's Republic of China, USA, Democratic Republic of Vietnam and the USSR. On Mar. 28, 1967 Paul VI published the encyclical ▷ *Populorum Progressio* and sent copies with personal dedications to the UN Secretariat, UNESCO and FAO as well as to two Catholic organizations: ▷ Caritas Internationalis and ▷ Iustitia et Pax. In 1967 a representative of the Vatican affixed his signature in the UN headquarters to the Treaty on the Peaceful Uses of Outer Space. The Vatican proclaimed Jan. 1, 1968 as Peace Day. Paul VI, 1965–70, visited many states in the Southern and Northern Hemispheres. During this same time Paul VI was visited in the Vatican by numerous statesmen both from the West and the East. The UN Secretary-General K. Waldheim paid a visit to the Vatican in Feb. 1972. On this occasion Paul VI said:

"Today we wish once again to repeat what we said from the platform of the UN: we believe in the possibility of establishing peace and respect for human rights in this so-troubled world. We are ready to give this organization our full moral support."

In international politics the Apostolic See does not take formal part in international conferences, as stipulated in art. 24 of the Lateran Treaty that:

"... in view of the sovereignty vested in it also in the international arena ... wishes to and will remain beyond all mundane competitions between other states and international congresses convened for this purpose, unless the competing sides agree to appeal to its mission of peace."

In Feb., 1972, in the Center for Studies of International Politics in Milan, the secretary of the Council on Public Affairs of the Church, Archbishop Agostino Cassaroli, presented the position of the Apostolic See on preparations for the Conferences in Helsinki, formulating the thesis that "in view of the truly new socio-political situation in Europe" and "the opening of the road to broader peaceful co-operation between the European nations, the Apostolic See is not limiting its support to words only – but is offering its co-operation." The spokesman of the Vatican in Helsinki expressed this as follows:

"During the discussion on point 5 of the procedural rules at the preparatory conference in Helsinki concerning unanimous agreement (*ius cogens*) the representative of the Apostolic See asserted that on the question of voting in discussions on the subject of specific political problems the representative of the Apostolic See, taking into consideration its specific nature, concerning which the delegation reserves the right to make a separate declaration, recognizes as its duty to abstain from taking a position. Such action should not be interpreted either as agreement or as opposition nor will it impede the attainment of the required general agreement. The Apostolic See reserves the right to request that its explanation be included among the documents of the present consultations."

The Vatican was one of the 35 signatories of the ▷ Helsinki Final Act, 1975. Among the five Great Powers the Vatican maintains official diplomatic relations with three: France, Great Britain and the

USA (since 1984). The Vatican maintains relations with Taiwan; a representative of the Vatican made the first visit to the People's Republic of China in Apr., 1980.

In principle the USSR was not recognized by the Vatican until 1961, when John XXIII and Premier N.S. Khrushchev exchanged congratulatory New Year's messages. In 1965 Paul VI in New York received Minister of Foreign Affairs A.A. Gromyko, who then made successive visits to the Vatican in 1966, 1967, 1970, 1979, 1985. Recognized in the world press as the normalization *de facto* of Vatican–Soviet relations was the visit of the chairman of the Supreme Soviet of the USSR, N.V. Podgorny, to the Vatican in 1967. Archbishop A. Cassaroli paid a visit to Moscow in Feb., 1971 in connection with the Conference on Security and Co-operation in Europe. The process of the normalization of relations with the other Warsaw Pact countries, called in the world press the "eastern policy" of the Vatican, began during the pontificate of John XXII with the conclusion of a treaty with Hungary on Sept. 15, 1964. The establishment of diplomatic relations with Yugoslavia took place on June 25, 1966 at the level of legations (since 1970 – ambassadorial level). Then the Vatican entered into negotiations with Bulgaria (First Secretary of the Bulgarian Communist Party T. Zhivkov paid a visit to Paul VI in 1975), Czechoslovakia, GDR, Romania (President N. Ceausescu paid a visit to Paul VI in June, 1978). The First Secretary of the Hungarian Socialist Workers Party, J. Kadar, visited Paul VI in June, 1977. The Vatican established diplomatic relations with Poland on Mar. 30, 1919, appointing as the first nuncio on June 6, 1919 Msgr. Achilles Ratti, later Pius XI. The Polish legation at the Apostolic See established on July 1, 1919 was raised to the level of an embassy on Dec. 11, 1924. The Concordat of Poland with the Vatican signed in 1925 was broken in 1945 when the Vatican did not accept the Potsdam resolutions establishing the Oder–Neisse frontier. On June 28, 1972 Paul VI ordered with the bulla *Episcoporum Poloniae coetus* that Church administrative boundaries in Poland be adjusted to her Potsdam frontiers. In Sept., 1974 formal working contacts were established between the Vatican and Poland. On Dec. 1, 1977 The First Secretary of the Polish United Workers Party Edward Gierek paid a visit to Paul VI.

An historical event in Vatican–Polish relations was the election of the Archbishop of Cracow, Cardinal Karol Wojtyla, as successor to Pope John Paul I on Oct. 16, 1978, the first non-Italian pope in 456 years. An official delegation from the Polish People's Republic was present at the inauguration of John Paul II led by the chairman of the Council of State, Henryk Jabłoński.

In Jan., 1979 John Paul II attended the Conference of the Latin American Episcopate in Mexico, CELAM, stressing at the beginning of his trip that "the future of the Church is in Latin America", which was universally interpreted as a recognition of the demographic explosion of the Third World in the second half of the 20th century which changed the proportions of representation in the Church of specific regions of the world; whereas at the beginning of the 20th century Europeans and North Americans were preponderant in the Church, at the end of the 20th century South Americans (c. 600 million in the year 2000), Africans and Asiatics became the majority.

On the 30th anniversary of the Universal Declaration of Human Rights on Dec. 10, 1978 John Paul II sent a Speech on Human Rights to the UN Secretary-General. On World Peace Day, Jan. 1, 1979, John Paul II made an address entitled "We Shall Attain Peace by Educating for Peace." John

Paul II made an official visit to Poland, June 2–10, 1979, visiting Warsaw, Gniezno, Czestochowa, Auschwitz, Wadowice and Cracow. When leaving Poland, Pope John Paul II at the Cracow airport said i.a. the following:

"The visit of a pope to Poland is certainly an event without precedent not only in this century, but also in the entire millennium. All the more so in that this is the visit of a Polish pope who has the holy right and duty to continue to feel deeply tied to his nation. This unprecedented event was certainly an act of certain courage on both sides, but just such an act of courage was required by our times. Sometimes one must also dare to go in a direction in which no one has gone before. Our times have great need of such testimony in which there is a clear expression of the will for a rapprochement between nations and political systems as an indispensable condition of peace in the world."

Two attempts were made on the life of John Paul II, on May, 13, 1981 at St Peters Place in Rome and in May, 1983. In the years 1979–1985 John Paul II visited the following countries:

1979, Jan. 25–Feb. 1 Mexico; June 2–10 Poland; Sept. 29–Oct. 1 Ireland; Oct. 1–8 UN Hqs and USA; Nov. 28–30 Turkey;

1980, May 2–4 Zaire; May 5 Congo; May 6–7 Kenya; May 8–9 Ghana; May 10 Upper Volta (now Burkina Faso); May 11 Ivory Coast; May 30–June 2 France; June 30–July 12 Brazil, Nov. 15–19 FRG;

1981, Febr. 17 Pakistan; Febr. 17–22 Philippines; Febr. 22 Guam; Febr. 23–26 Japan; Febr. 26 Alaska;

1982, Febr. 12–17 Nigeria; Febr. 17 Gabon; Febr. 18 Guinea Equatorial; Febr. 19 Gabon; May 12–15 Portugal; May 28–June 2 Great Britain, June 11–12 Argentina; June 15 Geneva; Oct. 31–Nov. 9 Spain;

1983, March 2–3 Costa Rica; March 4–5 Nicaragua; March 5 Panama; March 6 El Salvador; March 7 Guatemala; March 8 Honduras; March 9 Belize and Haiti;

1984, May 2–12 South Korea, Papua New Guinea, Solomon Islands and Thailand; May 12–14 Switzerland; Sept. 6–18 Canada; Oct. 11–14 Spain (Saragossa), Santo Domingo and Puerto Rico; 1985, Jan. 26–27 Venezuela; Jan. 28 Ecuador; Jan. 29–30 Peru.

A new Concordat with Italy was signed in Feb., 1984. On Nov. 29, 1984 Argentina and Chile signed in Vatican a Vatican-mediated Treaty over the ▷ Beagle Channel. On April 13, 1986, John Paul II paid the first papal visit to a Jewish synagogue. On Oct. 27, 1986 John Paul II led a Day of Prayer in Assisi, Italy with leaders of 12 World religions.

Diplomatic missions accredited to the Holy See as at Jan. 1, 1985: Argentina, Australia, Austria, Belgium, Bolivia, Brazil, Canada, Central African Republic, Chile, Colombia, Costa Rica, Cuba, Denmark, Dominican Republic, Ecuador, Egypt, El Salvador, Finland, France, FRG, Guatemala, Haiti, Honduras, Indonesia, Iran, Ireland, Italy, Ivory Coast, Japan, Korea Republic, Lebanon, Liberia, Lithuania, Luxembourg, Monaco, the Netherlands, Nicaragua, Panama, Paraguay, Peru, Philippines, Poland, Portugal, San Marino, Senegal, Spain, Turkey, UK, USA, Uruguay, Venezuela, Yugoslavia and Zaïre. Diplomatic relations: in 1916 – with 9 States, 1922 – 28, 1962 – 48, 1987 – 113.

The official title of the Supreme Pontiff elected for life by a conclave of the Sacred College of Cardinals is as follows: His Holiness Pope John Paul II, Bishop of Rome, Vicar of Christ, Successor of the Prince of the Apostles, Supreme Pontiff of the Universal Church, Patriarch of the West, Primate of Italy, Archbishop and Metropolitan of the Province of Rome, Sovereign of the Vatican City State, Servant of the Servants of God; acceded on Oct. 16, 1978, as the 266th Roman Pontiff.

The only daily of the Apostolic See is *L'Osservatore Romano* (Sunday edition published as *L'Osservatore della Domenica*), established 1861 as the private property of the Pope and since 1871 the property of the Apostolic See. Circulation on weekdays (only in Italian) c. 50,000. The Sunday edition, since 1968, is also published in English, French, Spanish and German (and since 1980 in Polish); together c. 100,000 copies. The only official organ is *Acta Apostolicae Sedis*.

G.P. CANSACCHI, *Il Papa e la Societa delle Nazioni*, Roma, 1929; Y. DE LA BRIERE, *L'Organisation Internationale du Monde Contemporain et la Papauté Souveraine*, 3 Vols., Paris, 1930; D. DONATI, *La Citta del Vaticano nella teoria generale dello Stato*, Roma, 1930; J.L. KUNZ, "The Status of the Holy See in International Law", in: *American Journal of International Law*, No. 46, 1952; W.S. KERR, *A Handbook on the Papacy*, London, 1950; E. HALES, *The Catholic Church and the Modern World*, London, 1958; R.A. GRAHAM, *Vatican Diplomacy. A Study of Church and State on the International Plane*, Princeton, 1959; CARDINAL IGINO, *Le Saint-Siège et la Diplomatie*, Tournai, 1962; *Encyclopédie catholique du monde chrétien*, Tournai, 1964; N.A. KOVALEVSKIY, *Vatikan y mirovaia politika*, Moscow, 1964; *UN Review*, No. 335, 1965; *UN Monthly Chronicle*, No. 10, 1965; M.M. SHEINAM, *Ot Piya IX do Ioanna XXIII. Watikan za 100 let*, Moscow, 1966; *La visita di Pablo VI alle Nazioni Unite*, Vaticano, 1966; W. PARDY, *The Church on the Move*, London, 1966; P. NICHOLS, *The Politics of the Vatican*, London, 1968; C. PALLENBORG, *Vatican Finances*, Harmondsworth 1971; L. WEI TSING SING, *Le Saint-Siège et la Chine (1922–1966)*, Paris, 1972; E. WINTER, *Die Sowjetunion und der Vatikan*, Berlin, 1972; A. RHODES, *The Vatican in the Age of Dictators: 1922–1945*, New York, 1974; R.S. CASTAÑO, "La posición del Vaticano en materia de desarrollo económico en la UNCTAD", in: *Relaciones Exteriores*, No. 4, México, DF, 1974; J.J. STEHLE, *Die Ostpolitik des Vatikans 1917–1975*, Munich, 1975; H.F. KOCK, *Die Völkerrechtliche Stellung des Heiligen Stuhls*, Berlin, 1975; CARDINAL IGINO, *The Holy See and the International Order*, New York, 1976; F. MAYER, *The Vatican, Portrait of a State and a Community*, Dublin, 1980; *The Europa Year Book 1984. A World Survey*, Vol. I, pp. 1009–1014, London, 1984; K.C. ELLIS, *The Vatican: Islam and the Middle East*, New York, 1987; L.R. ROKACH, *The Catholic Church and the Question of Palestine*, London, 1987; E.O. HANSON, *The Catholic Church in World Politics*, Princetown, N.J., 1987.

VATICANUM COUNCIL II. The name of the XXI universal council, 1962–65. ▷ Ecumenical Councils.

VATTEL DOCTRINE, 1758. A principle of international law concerning the interpretation of international treaties, formulated by the Swiss philosopher Emerich Vattel (1714–67) in a work published 1758 entitled *Droit des gens ou principes de la loi naturelle appliquée à la conduite et aux affaires des nations et des souverains*, expressed in five principles:

(1) One is not free to interpret what does not require interpretation ("One cannot assume that rational people did not want to achieve anything through the making of a treaty ... hence, an interpretation which would render the document invalid and ineffective cannot be accepted.")

(2) If one who could and should make a clear statement did not do so, then he himself must bear the consequences ("No convention is secure, if one can deprive it of value through later objections, which should be expressed in the document, if such was the will of the negotiating parties.")

(3) None of the parties has the right to interpret a treaty according to his own fashion ("... for if we may give our obligation on interpretation to our liking, then we shall be able to obligate the other

side arbitrarily against his intention and beyond what he has really obligated himself to").

(4) What has been pronounced in a sufficient manner is accepted as truth ("... this is an incontrovertible principle which we apply to treaties: for if they are not to be an idle game, the negotiating parties must speak honestly and in accordance with their intentions").

(5) Interpretations should be made in accordance with established rules ("... if one does not accord the established rules the meaning in which the statements are to be accepted, then treaties will be only an idle game, one will not be able to have any certainty, and it will be almost ludicrous to expect them to be effective").

▷ Law of Nations: Vattel's Principles, 1758.

E. VATTEL, *Droit des gens ou principes de la loi naturelle appliquée à la conduite et aux affaires des nations et des souverains*, Neuchâtel, 1758; Ch.G. FENWICK, "The Authority of Vattel", in: *American Political Science Review*, No. 7, 1913; A. NUSSBAUM, *Concise History of the Law of Nations*, London, 1956.

V-DAY. Victory Day. An international abbreviation for the day of Germany's unconditional surrender, marking the end of World War II.

"VEGA". Two scientific satellites constructed by the Cosmos Research Institute in Moscow with the co-operation of scientists from Austria, Bulgaria, France, FRG, GDR, Hungary, Poland and USSR, launched on Dec, 15 and 28, 1984 to observe Halley's comet in March 1986.

VEGETARIANISM. International term formed in the 19th century for a system of nutrition with vegetable and also dairy food, the advantages of which were promoted on the turn of the 19th century by many national associations, united in 1908.
Organization reg. with the UIA:

International Vegetarian Union, f. 1908, Quarrytown, UK, branch offices in India and in the USA.

Yearbook of International Organizations.

VEGETATION SCIENCE. Subject of international co-operation. Organization reg. with UIA:

International Organization for Vegetation Science, f. 1938, Göttingen, FRG, Publ.: *Vegetatio*; *The Europa Yearbook 1988. A World Survey*, Vol. I, 1988.

VENDA. One of the South African ▷ Bantu Homelands, declared independent as The Republic of, on Sept. 13, 1979, not recognized by governments other than that of the South African Republic. Area: 6,500 sq km. Population (1980): 513,890.

The Europa Yearbook, Vol. II, London, 1987.

VENEZUELA. Member of the UN. Republic of Venezuela. A state in South America on the Atlantic Ocean and Caribbean Sea. Borders with Guyana, Brazil and Colombia. Area: 912,050 sq. km. Pop.: 1988 est.: 18,770,000 (at the censuses: 1873 – 1,732,000; 1881 – 2,005,000; 1891 – 2,210,000; 1920 – 2,479,000; 1941 – 3,850,000; 1950 – 5,034,000; 1961 – 7,523,000; 1971 – 10,721,000; 1981 – 14,516,735); share of the urban population: 1941 – 31%; 1950 – 48%; 1961 – 62%; 1971 – 73%). Capital: Caracas with suburbs 2,664,225 inhabitants in 1976. Official language: Spanish. Currency: one Bolivar = 100 centimos. GNP per capita in 1986: US $2,930. National Day: July 5, Independence Day, 1811.
Founding member of the UN and all UN special organizations with the exception of the IDA and GATT. Founding member of OAS. 1966–80 a member of ALALC, since 1975 of SELA, and since

1980 of ALADI. Member of OPEC and of the Andean Group.
International relations: a Spanish colony until July 5, 1811; from 1819 to 1830 part of Greater Colombia; since Nov. 28, 1830 an independent state; from 1864 to 1954 known as the United States of Venezuela and since then under the present name. In the 19th and at the beginning of the 20th century in conflicts with Germany, Great Britain, France and the USA on the repayment of debts. Since the 19th century Venezuela has laid claims to about 150,000 sq. km of British Guyana (by an agreement with Guyana in 1971 these claims were laid aside for 12 years). In the 19th and 20th centuries Venezuela participated in all inter-American conferences. In World War I Venezuela was neutral; in World War II on the side of the UN. Member of the League of Nations 1919–38. In Feb.–June and Aug.–Sept. 1960 the OAS examined Venezuela's complaint against the Dominican Republic on acts of aggression. In 1963–64 and 1967 Venezuela charged Cuba in the OAS and in the UN of threatening peace in the Western Hemisphere. A trade agreement of 1939 with the USA was cancelled by Venezuela on Dec. 31, 1971. The US investments in Venezuela at that time were estimated at $4.5 billion, which amounted to 30% of all US investments in Latin America. Also in 1971 the process of regaining its oil fields from American and English–Dutch oil companies began, which was completed in 1975. The rise in the price of crude oil introduced by OPEC, of which Venezuela is a member, enabled Venezuela to establish a special fund for accelerating the development of industry, agriculture, a tanker fleet and a scholarship fund called the Ayacucho Fund for the education in foreign schools in 1975–80 of around 10,000 engineers and technicians. In Feb., 1975, at a meeting in Port of Spain, Trinidad, the heads of government of the states of the Caribbean region were offered special funds for economic co-operation. In 1978/79 Venezuela in the OAS charged Nicaragua's president Somoza with violating human rights and gave assistance to the national liberation forces of Nicaragua. In 1980 with Mexico initiated a special petroleum fund for the Central American States. In 1983–85 participated in the ▷ Contadora Group.

S. MARON, *A History of Venezuela*, London, 1964; E. LIEUVEN, *Venezuela*, New York, 1965; *Las Naciones Unidas en Venezuela*, Caracas, 1965; R. BETANCOURT, *Venezuela, Politica y Petroleo*, México, DF, 1965; F. BRITO FIGUEROA, *Historia Económica y Social de Venezuela*, Caracas, 1966; A. MIJARES, *La evolución politica de Venezuela 1810–1960*, Buenos Aires, 1967; H.B. MEIER, *Der Kapitalmarkt in der Wirtschaftsentwicklung Venezuela*, Zürich, 1969; F. BRITO FIGUEROA, *Venezuela contemporanea pais colonial*, Caracas, 1972; F. TUGWELL, *The Policy of Oil in Venezuela*, Stanford, 1975; C.J. SALAZAR, *Oil in the Economic Development of Venezuela*, New York, 1976; J. LOMBARD, *Venezuelan History. A Comprehensive Working Bibliography*, Boston, 1977; R. BETANCOURT, *Venezuela's Oil*, London, 1978; G.E. BIGLER, *Politic and State Capitalist in Venezuela*, Madrid, 1981; J.A. GIL YEPES, *The Challenge of Venezuelan Democracy*, London, 1981; *The Europa Year Book 1984. A World Survey*, Vol. II, pp. 2666–2682, London, 1984; S. BITAR, E. TRANCOSO, *Venezuela, The Industrial Challenge*, Oxford, 1987.

VENICE. A city in northeast Italy, situated on 118 alluvial islets in the Lagoon of Venice, connected with the mainland by a dike, 4 km long; the islets are separated by 150 canals, and connected by 400 bridges; a monument of world culture; subject of an international rescue operation, organized in 1971 by UNESCO, in connection with the oldest, monumental part of the city with canals and bridges being imperiled by periodic swelling of lagoon waters.

Venice is the headquarters of the European Society of Culture, SEC. The European 'Pro Venetia Viva' Foundation, f. 1974, Strasbourg, by the Parliamentary Assembly of the Council of Europe.

M. MURARO, *Treasures of Venice*, London, 1963; E. MIOZZI, *La verita sagli sprofondamenti di Venezia*, Venezia, 1970; J.J. NORWICH, *A History of Venice*, New York, 1982.

VENICE CHARTER, 1964. The monuments protection program adopted by the Second International Congress of Monuments Architects and Technicians in Venice, 25–31 May 1964; International Charter of Maintenance and Restoration of Monuments and Monumental Places. In 1989 the Italian Government decided to test a sea gate which would seal the entire Venice Lagoon from Adriatic tides.

C. HABERMAN, "Italy Embarks on Bold Effort to Save Fabled City of Venice from Threatening Tides", in: *The New York Times*, January 31, 1989.

VENICE CSCE MEETING ON MEDITER-RANEAN, 1984. Held in Venice, on Oct. 16–26, 1984, with delegations of Egypt and Israel present at the opening session, boycotted by other invited non-European states. The meeting discussed subjects prepared by the UN Economic Commission for Europe.

KEESING's *Contemporary Archive*, 1986, No 12.

VENICE DECLARATION OF INDUSTRIALIZED COUNTRIES, 1980. A declaration adopted on June 23, 1980, in Venice, at the Economic Summit Conference of Industrialized Countries. The Conference of the heads of governments of the seven major industrial capitalistic countries: Canada, France, FRG, Italy, Japan, the UK and the US, called the Venice Summit, pledged to reduce the industrialized world's dependence on oil and to develop alternative energy sources to "break the link between oil consumption and economic growth." The target is to reduce oil consumption from 53% in 1980 to 40% of total energy consumption by 1990. The text reads as follows:

"I. *Introduction.* (1) In this, our first meeting of the 1980's the economic issues that have dominated our thoughts are the price and supply of energy and the implications for inflation and the level of economic activity in our own countries and for the world as a whole. Unless we can deal with the problems of energy, we cannot cope with our problems.

(2) Successive large increases in the price of oil, bearing no relation to market conditions and culminating in the recent decisions by some members of the Organization of Petroleum Exporting Countries (OPEC) at Algiers, have produced the reality of even higher inflation and the imminent threat of severe recession and unemployment in the industrialised countries. At the same time they have undermined and in some cases virtually destroyed the prospects for growth in the developing countries. We believe that these consequences are increasingly coming to be appreciated by some of the oil exporting countries. The fact is that the industrialised countries of the free world, the oil producing countries, and the non-oil developing countries depend upon each other for the realisation of their potential for economic development and prosperity. Each can overcome the obstacles to that development, but only if all work together, and with the interests of all in mind.

(3) In this spirit we have discussed the main problems that confront us in the coming decade. We are confident in the ability of our democratic societies, based on individual freedom and social solidarity, to meet these challenges. These are no quick or easy solutions; sustained efforts are needed to achieve a better future.

II. *Inflation.* (4) The reduction of inflation is our immediate top priority and will benefit all nations. Inflation retards growth and harms all sectors of our societies. Determined fiscal and monetary restraint is required to break inflationary expectations. Continuing dialogue among the social partners is also needed for this purpose. We must retain effective international co-ordination to carry out this policy of restraint, and also to guard against the threat of growing unemployment and worldwide recession.

(5) We are also committed to encouraging investment and innovation, so as to increase productivity, to fostering the movement of resources from declining into expanding sectors so as to provide new job opportunities, and to promoting the most effective use of resources within and among countries. This will require shifting resources from government spending to the private sector and from consumption to investment, and avoiding or carefully limiting actions that shelter particular industries or sectors from the rigors of adjustment. Measures of this kind may be economically and politically difficult in short term, but they are essential to sustained non-inflationary growth and to increasing employment which is our major goal.

(6) In shaping economic policy, we need a better understanding of the long-term effects of global population growth, industrial expansion and economic development generally. A study of trends in these areas is in hand, and our representatives will keep these matters under review.

III. *Energy.* (7) We must break the existing link between economic growth and consumption of oil, and we mean to do so in this decade. This strategy requires conserving oil and substantially increasing production and use of alternative energy sources. To this end, maximum reliance should be placed on the price mechanism, and domestic prices for oil should take into account representative world prices. Market forces should be supplemented, where appropriate, by effective fiscal incentives and administrative measures. Energy investment will contribute substantially to economic growth and employment.

(8) We welcome the recent decisions of the European Community (EC), the International Energy Agency (IEA) and the Organization for Economic Co-operation and Development (OECD) regarding the need for long-term structural changes to reduce oil consumption, continuing procedures to monitor progress, the possible use of oil ceilings to deal with tight market conditions, and co-ordination to stock policies to mitigate the effect of market disruption. We note that the member countries of the IEA have agreed that their energy policies should result in their collective 1985 net oil imports being substantially less than their existing 1985 group objective, and that they will quantify the reduction as part of their continuing monitoring efforts. The potential for reduction has been estimated by the IEA Secretariat, given existing uncertainties, at around 4 million barrels a day (MBD).

(9) To conserve oil in our countries:
– We are agreed that no new base-load, oil-fired generating capacity should be constructed, save in exceptional circumstances, and that the conversion of oil-fired capacity to other fuels should be accelerated.
– We will increase efforts, including fiscal incentives where necessary, to accelerate the substitution of oil in industry.
– We will encourage oil saving investments in residential and commercial buildings, where necessary by financial incentives and by establishing insulation standards. We look to the public sector to set an example.
– In transportation, our objective is the introduction of increasingly fuel efficient vehicles. The demand of consumers and competition among manufacturers are already leading in this direction. We will accelerate this progress, where appropriate, by arrangements or standards for improved automobile fuel efficiency, by gasoline pricing and taxation decisions, by research and development, and by making public transport more attractive.

(10) We must rely on fuels other than oil to meet the energy needs of future economic growth. This will require early, resolute, and wide-ranging actions. Our potential to increase the supply and use of energy sources other than oil over the next ten years is estimated at the equivalent of 15–20 MBD of oil. We intend to make a coordinated and vigorous effort to realise this potential. To this end, we will seek a large increase in the use of coal and enhanced use of nuclear power in the medium-term, and a substantial increase in production of synthetic fuels, in solar energy and other sources of renewable energy over the longer term.

(11) We shall encourage the exploration and development of our indigenous hydrocarbon resources in order to secure maximum production on a long-term basis.

(12) Together we intend to double coal production and use by early 1990. We will encourage long-term commitments by coal producers and consumers. It will be necessary to improve infrastructures in both exporting and importing countries, as far as is economically justified, to ensure the required supply and use of coal. We look forward to the recommendations of the International Coal Industry Advisory Board. They will be considered promptly. We are conscious of the environmental risks associated with increased coal production and combustion. We will do everything in our power to ensure that increased use of fossil fuels, especially coal, does not damage the environment.

(13) We underline the vital contribution of nuclear power to a more secure energy supply. The role of nuclear energy has to be increased if world energy needs are to be met. We shall therefore have to expand our nuclear generating capacity. We will continue to give the highest priority to ensuring the health and safety of the public and to perfecting methods for dealing with spent fuels and disposal of nuclear waste. We reaffirm the importance of ensuring the reliable supply of nuclear fuel and minimizing the risk of nuclear proliferation.

(14) The studies made by the International Nuclear Fuel Cycle Evaluation Group, launched at the London Summit in 1977 are a significant contribution to the use of nuclear energy. We welcome their findings with respect to: increasing predictable supplies; the most effective utilization of uranium sources, including the development of advanced technologies; and the minimization of proliferation risks, including support of International Atomic Energy Agency (IAEA) safeguards. We urge all countries to take these findings into account when developing policies and programmes for the peaceful use of nuclear energy.

(15) We will actively support the recommendations of the International Energy Technology Group, proposed at the Tokyo Summit last year, for bringing new energy technologies into commercial use at the earliest feasible time. As far as national programmes are concerned, we will by mid-1981 adopt a two-phased approach; first, listing the numbers and types of commercial scale plants to be constructed in each of our countries by the mid-1980's, and, second, indicating quantitative projections for expanding production by 1990, 1995 and 2000, as a basis for future actions. As far as international programmes are concerned, we will join others in creating an international team to promote collaboration among interested nations on specific projects.

(16) A high level group of representatives of our countries and of the EEC Commission will review periodically the results achieved in these fields.

(17) Our comprehensive energy strategy is designed to meet the requirements of the coming decade. We are convinced that it can reduce the demand for energy, particularly oil, without hampering economic growth. By carrying out this strategy we expect that, over the coming decade, the ratio between increases in collective energy consumption and economic growth of our countries will be reduced to about 0.6, that the share of oil in our total energy demand will be reduced from 53 per cent now to about 40 per cent by 1990, and that our collective consumption of oil in 1990 will be significantly below present levels so as to permit a balance between supply and demand at tolerable prices.

(18) We continue to believe that international co-operation in energy is essential. All countries have a vital interest in a stable equilibrium between energy supply and demand. We would welcome a constructive dialogue on energy and related issues between energy producers and consumers in order to improve the coherence of their policies.

IV. *Relations with developing countries.* (19) We are deeply concerned about the impact of the oil price increases on the developing countries that have to import oil. The increase in oil prices in the last two years has more than doubled the bill of these countries, which now amounts to over $50 billion. This will drive them into ever increasing indebtness, and put at risk the whole basis of their economic growth and social progress, unless something can be done to help them.

(20) We approach in a positive spirit the prospect of global negotiations in the framework of the United Nations and the formulation of a new International Development Strategy. In particular, our object is to co-operate with the developing countries in energy conservation and development, expansion of exports, enhancement of human skills, and the tackling of underlying food and population problems.

(21) A major international effort to help these countries increase their energy production is required. We believe that this view is gaining ground among oil-exporting countries. We ask the World Bank to examine the adequacy of the resources and the mechanisms now in place for the exploration, development and production of conventional and renewable energy sources in oil importing developing countries, to consider means, including the possibility of establishing a new affiliate or facility by which it might improve and increase its lending programmes for energy assistance, and to explore its findings with both oil-exporting and industrial countries.

(22) We are deeply conscious that extreme poverty and chronic malnutrition afflict hundreds of millions of people of developing countries. The first requirement in these countries is to improve their ability to feed themselves and reduce their dependence on food imports. We are ready to join with them and the International Agencies concerned in their comprehensive long-term strategies to increase food production, and to help to improve national, as well as international research services. We will support and, where appropriate, supplement initiatives of the World Bank and of the Food and Agricultural Organization (FAO) to improve grain storage and food handling facilities. We underline the importance of wider membership of the new Food Aid Convention so as to secure at least 10 million tons of food aid annually and of an equitable replenishment of the International Fund for Agricultural Development.

(23) High priority should be given to efforts to cope with population growth and to existing United Nations and other programmes for supporting these efforts.

(24) We strongly support the general capital increase of the World Bank increases in the funding of the regional development banks, and the sixth replenishment of the International Development Association. We would welcome an increase in the rate of lending of these institutions, within the limits of their present replenishments, as needed to fulfill the programmes described above. It is essential that all members, especially the major donors, provide their full contributions on the agreed schedule.

(25) We welcome the report of the Brandt Commission. We shall carefully consider its recommendations.

(26) The democratic industrialised countries cannot alone carry the responsibility of aid and other different contributions to the developing countries: it must be equitably shared by the oil-exporting countries and the industrialised Communist countries. The Personal Representatives are instructed to review aid policies and procedures and other contributions to developing countries and to report back their conclusions to the next Summit.

V. *Monetary problems.* (27) The situation created by large oil-generated payments imbalances, in particular those of oil-importing developing countries, requires a combination of determined actions by all countries to promote external adjustment and effective mechanisms for balance of payments financing. We look to the international capital market to continue to play the primary role in rechanneling the substantial oil surplus funds on the basis of sound lending standards. We support the work in progress by our monetary authorities and the Bank for International Settlements designed to improve the supervision and security of the international banking system. The private banks could usefully supplement these efforts.

(28) Private lending will need to be supplemented by an expanded role for international institutions, especially the International Monetary Fund (IMF). We are committed to implementing the agreed increase in the IMF quotas, and to supporting appropriate borrowing by the Fund, if needed to meet financing requirements of its members. We encourage the IMF to seek ways in which it could, within its guidelines on conditionality, make it more attractive for countries with financing problems to use its resources. In particular, we support the IMF's examination of possible ways to reduce

charges on credits to low-income developing countries. The IMF and the World Bank should work closely together in responding to these problems. We welcome the Bank's innovative lending scheme for structural adjustment. We urge oil-exporting countries to increase their direct lending to countries with financial problems thus reducing the strain on other recycling mechanisms.

(29) We reaffirm our commitment to stability in the foreign exchange markets. We note that the European Monetary System (EMS) has contributed to this end. We will continue close co-operation in exchange market policies so as to avoid disorderly exchange fluctuations. We will also co-operate with the IMF to achieve more effective surveillance. We support continuing examination by the IMF of arrangements to provide for a more balanced evolution of the world reserve system.

VI. *Trade.* (30) We are resolved further to strengthen the open world trading system. We will resist pressures for protectionist actions, which can only be self-defeating and aggravate inflation.

(31) We endorse the positive conclusion of the multilateral trade negotiations, and commit ourselves to early and effective implementation. We welcome the participation of some of our developing partners in the new non-tariff codes and call upon others to participate. We also call for the full participation of as many countries as possible in strengthening the system of the General Agreement on Tariffs and Trade. We urge the more advanced of our developing partners gradually to open their markets over the coming decade.

(32) We reaffirm our determination to avoid a harmful export credit race. To this end we shall work with the other participants to strengthen the International Arrangement on Export Credits, with a view to reaching a mutually acceptable solution covering all aspects of the Arrangement by 1 December 1980. In particular, we shall seek to bring its terms closer to current market conditions and reduce distortions in export competition, recognising the differentiated treatment of developing countries in the Arrangement.

(33) As a further step in strengthening the international trading system, we commit our governments to work in the United Nations toward an agreement to prohibit illicit payments to foreign government officials in international business transactions. If that effort falters, we will seek to conclude an agreement among our countries, but open to all, with the same objective.

VII. *Conclusions.* (34) The economic message from this Venice Summit is clear. The key to success in resolving the major economic challenges which the world faces is to achieve and maintain a balance between energy supply and demand at reasonable levels and at tolerable prices. The stability of the world economy, on which the prosperity of every individual country relies, depends upon all of the countries concerned, recognising their mutual needs and accepting their mutual responsibilities. Those among us whose countries are members of the European Community intend to make their efforts within this framework. We, who represent seven large industrialised countries of the free world, are ready to tackle our own problems with determination and to work with others to meet the challenges of the coming decade, to our own advantage and to the benefit of the whole world."

Weekly Compilation of Presidential Documents, Vol. 16, No. 26, June 30, 1980. *Recueil des documents*, No. 4–6, 1980, pp. 446–458.

VENICE SEMINAR, 1984. The CSCE Seminar on Economic, Scientific and Cultural Co-operation in the Mediterranean, held in Venice, Oct. 16–24, 1984. ▷ Madrid CSCE Meeting, 1980–83.

VENUS. A planet of the solar system circling the sun at an average distance of 108 million km; located nearest to the earth (*c.* 40 million km at its closest distance); subject of constant, organized research under the auspices of the International Astronomical Union carried out since 1961 by American craft of the Mariner type and Soviet Venus types. On Dec. 9, 1978 probes from the American interplanetary station Venus-Pioneer 2 landed on Venus; the data transmitted introduced essential corrections in the theory of the origin of

the planets of the solar system. Up to 1985 it had been determined that there are no forms of life and no magnetic field on the planet. During the ▷ USA-USSR summit 1987, an agreement on space providing for the exchange of scientific data obtained from unmanned missions to Mars and to ▷ Venus, and ▷ Mars, was signed in Washington DC.

J.O. BRANDT, M.B. MC ELROY (eds.), *The Atmospheres of Venus and Mars*, London, 1968; KEESING's *Record of World Events*, March 1988.

VERACRUZ. A port city in eastern Mexico in the state of Veracruz, on the Gulf of Mexico; in the years 1810–24, site of battles for independence against the Spaniards; 1862–67 against French intervention; 1914/15 against intervention of the USA, which on 21 Apr. 1914 shelled the city from the sea and occupied it with the aim of forcing the resignation of Mexican President, General Huerta.

H. HELD, "Veracruz Zwischenfall", in: *Strupp-Schlochauers Wörterbuch des Völkerrechts*, Berlin, 1962.

VERBRANNTE ERDE. *German* = "burnt earth". An international term introduced by German troops in 1943 during the retreat from the Ukraine, for the total destruction of an abandoned occupied territory; applied in World War II by the German armed forces in accord with the command of H. Himmler of Sept. 7, 1943 for the total destruction of the Donets Basin:

"One should realize a condition in which not one person remains, no cattle, no wheat, no railroad track; that there will be neither a house nor a mine which would not be destroyed for years; that there would be no well which would not be poisoned."

The commands of adopting *"Verbrannte Erde"* in retreat were up to then issued to individual German units retreating from the occupied territories in the east as well as from the north in Norway. On Mar. 19, 1945 A. Hitler issued an order, called by German historians the Nero-edict (*Nero-Befehl*), to completely destroy German lands as well.

A. BULLOCK, *Hitler*, London, 1952; "Verbrannte Erde", in: *Lexicon für Geschichte und Politik im 20 Jahrhundert*, Köln, 1971, Vol. 2, p. 810.

VERDUN. A town in France situated on the Moselle river, site of the greatest battle in World War I (Feb. 21–Sept. 9, 1916), in which the number of casualties exceeded probably one million soldiers.

VERIFICATION. The certification of documents; in international relations the certification of the full powers of diplomats. Within the UN there is a Credentials Committee of the Secretary General.

VERIFICATION TECHNOLOGY IN ARMS CONTROL. One of the key problems of ▷ arms control, partly resolved for the first time in the late 1980's.

A.S. KRASS, *Verification: How Much Is Enough?*, SIPRI, London, 1985; K. TSIPIS, D. HAFEMEISTER, P. JANEWAY eds., *Arms Control Verification: The Technologies That Make It Possible*, Washington DC, 1986; *SIPRI Yearbook 1987*, Oxford 1988, pp. 433–446.

VERONA CONGRESS, 1822. A meeting in Verona, Italy, Oct. 20–Dec. 14, 1822 of Austrian Emperor Francis I, Russian Tsar Alexander I, Prussian King Frederic William III, the King of Naples, the King of Sardinia and diplomats of these countries as well as those of France and Britain. Conflicting interests caused the withdrawal of Prussia, a dispute over the Balkans between Russia and Austria, and a rejection by England of the principle of intervention (which England had already refused to accept at the Laibach Congress, 1821). In practice the Verona Congress meant rejection of the principles of the Holy Alliance. A secret protocol allowed France's anti-revolutionary intervention against Spain.

G.F. MARTENS, *Recueil des traités et conventions conclus par la Russie*, Pétersbourg, 1874–1905, Vol. 4.

VERSAILLES. A city in France on the outskirts of Paris, residence of the Kings of France, seat of the General States of the French Revolution 1789. After the defeat of France at Sedan on Sept. 1, 1870 Versailles was the headquarters of the Prussian forces, and on Jan. 18, 1871 site of the proclamation of the German Empire; on June 28, 1919 the place of signing the Peace Treaty of the Entente states with Germany, the so-called ▷ Versailles Peace Treaty. The Palace and Park are included in the ▷ World Heritage UNESCO List.

UNESCO, *A Legacy for All*, Paris, 1984.

VERSAILLES PEACE TREATY, 1871. Preliminary peace treaty between France and the German Reich, signed in Versailles Feb. 26, 1871. France ceded Alsace-Lorraine to Prussia (art. I) and was obliged to pay over a period of 3 years to the Emperor of Germany the sum of 5 billion gold francs (art. II). After this preliminary treaty, France and Germany signed the ▷ Frankfurt Peace Treaty, 1871.

Major Peace Treaties of Modern History, New York, 1967, Vol. I, pp. 645–649.

VERSAILLES PEACE TREATY, 1919. A Treaty between the Principal Allied and Associated Powers with Germany, signed on June 28, 1919 in Versailles, ▷ Paris Peace Conference, 1919. Highlights of the Treaty:

"The United States of America, the British Empire, France, Italy and Japan, these Powers being described in the present Treaty as the Principal Allied and Associated Powers; Belgium, Bolivia, Brazil, China, Cuba, Ecuador, Greece, Guatemala, Haiti, the Hedjaz, Honduras, Liberia, Nicaragua, Panama, Peru, Poland, Portugal, Romania, the Serb-Croat-Slovene State, Siam, Czechoslovakia and Uruguay, these Powers constituting with the Principal Powers mentioned above the Allied and Associated Powers, of the one part; and Germany, of the other part:

Bearing in mind that on the request of the Imperial German Government an Armistice was granted on November 11, 1918, to Germany by the Principal Allied and Associated Powers in order that a Treaty of Peace might be concluded with her, and The Allied and Associated Powers being equally desirous that the war in which they were successively involved directly or indirectly and which originated in the declaration of war by Austria-Hungary on July 28, 1914, against Serbia, the declaration of war by Germany against Russia on August 1, 1914, and against France on August 3, 1914, and in the invasion of Belgium, should be replaced by a firm, just and durable Peace,

For this purpose the High Contracting Parties represented as follows:

Part I ▷ *League of Nations Covenant, 1919.*

Part II *Boundaries of Germany.*

Art. 27. The boundaries of Germany will be determined as follows:

1. With Belgium:

From the point common to the three frontiers of Belgium, Holland, and Germany and in a southerly direction: the north-eastern boundary of the former territory of neutral Moresnet, then the eastern boundary of the Kreis of Eupen, then the frontier between Belgium and the Kreis of Montjoie, then the north-eastern and eastern boundary of the Kreis of Malmedy to its junction with the frontier of Luxemburg.

2. With Luxemburg:

The frontier of August 3, 1914, to its junction with the frontier of France of the 18th July, 1870.

3. With France:

The frontier of July 18, 1870, from Luxemburg to Switzerland with the reservations made in Article 48 of Section IV (Saar Basin) of Part III.

4. With Switzerland:

The present frontier.

5. With Austria.

The frontier of August 3, 1914, from Switzerland to Czechoslovakia as hereinafter defined.

6. With Czecho-Slovakia:

The frontier of August 3, 1914, between Germany and Austria from its junction with the old administrative boundary separating Bohemia and the province of Upper Austria to the point north of the salient of the old province of Austrian Silesia situated at about 8 kilometres east of Neustadt.

7. With Poland

From the point defined above to a point to be fixed on the ground about 2 kilometres east of Lorzendorf:

the frontier as it will be fixed in accordance with Article 88 of the present Treaty ...

8. With Denmark:

The frontier as it will be fixed in accordance with Articles 109 to 111 of Part III, Section XII (Schleswig).

Art. 28. The boundaries of East Prussia, with the reservations made in Section IX (East Prussia) of Part III, will be determined as follows:

Art. 29. The boundaries as described above are drawn in red on a one-in-a-million map which is annexed to the present Treaty. (See Map page 1267 and Color Map Plate 24). In the case of any discrepancies between the text of the Treaty and this map or any other map which may be annexed, the text will be final.

Art. 30. In the case of boundaries which are defined by a water-way, the terms "course" and "channel" used in the present Treaty signify: in the case of non-navigable rivers, the median line of the water-way or of its principal arm, and, in the case of navigable rivers, the median line of the principal channel of navigation. It will rest with the Boundary Commissions provided by the present Treaty to specify in each case whether the frontier line shall follow any changes of the course or channel which may take place or whether it shall be definitely fixed by the position of the course or channel at the time when the present Treaty comes into force.

Part III. *Political Clauses for Europe.*

Section I. Belgium. Art. 31. Germany, recognizing that the Treaties of April 19, 1839, which established the status of Belgium before the war, no longer conform to the requirements of the situation, consents to the abrogation of the said Treaties and undertakes immediately to recognise and to observe whatever conventions may be entered into by the Principal Allied and Associated Powers, or by any of them, in concert with the Governments of Belgium and of the Netherlands, to replace the said Treaties of 1839. If her formal adhesions should be required to such conventions or to any of their stipulations, Germany undertakes immediately to give it.

Art. 32. Germany recognises the full sovereignty of Belgium over the whole of the contested territory of Moresnet (called Moresnet neutre).

Art. 33. Germany renounces in favour of Belgium all rights and title over the territory of Prussian Moresnet situated on the west of the road from Liège to Aix-la-Chapelle; the road will belong to Belgium where it bounds this territory.

Art. 34. Germany renounces in favour of Belgium all rights and title over the territory comprising the whole of the Kreise of Eupen and of Malmedy ...

Art. 39. The proportion and nature of the financial liabilities of Germany and of Prussia with Belgium will have to bear on account of the territories ceded to her shall be fixed in conformity with Articles 254 and 256 of Part IX (Financial Clauses) of the present Treaty.

Section II. Luxemburg. Art. 40. With regard to the Grand Duchy of Luxemburg, Germany renounces the benefit of all the provisions inserted in her favour in the Treaties of February 8, 1842, April 2, 1847, October 20–25, 1865, August 18, 1866, February 21 and May 11, 1867, May 10, 1871, June 11, 1872, and November 11, 1902, and in all Conventions consequent upon such Treaties.

Germany recognises that the Grand Duchy of Luxemburg ceased to form part of the German Zollverein as from January 1, 1919, renounces all rights to the exploitation of the railways, adheres to the termination of the regime of neutrality of the Grand Duchy, and accepts in advance all international arrangements which may be concluded by the Allied and Associated Powers relating to the Grand Duchy.

Art. 41. Germany undertakes to grant to the Grand Duchy of Luxemburg, when a demand to that effect is made to her by the Principal Allied and Associated Powers, the rights and advantages stipulated in favour of such Powers or their nationals in the present Treaty with regard to economic questions, to questions relative to transport and to aerial navigation.

Section III. Left Bank of the Rhine. Art. 42. Germany is forbidden to maintain or construct any fortifications either on the left bank of the Rhine or on the right bank to the west of a line drawn 50 kilometres to the East of the Rhine.

Art. 43. In the area defined above the maintenance and the assembly of armed forces, either permanently or temporarily, and military manoeuvres of any kind, as well as the upkeep of all permanent works for mobilization, are in the same way forbidden.

Art. 44. In case Germany violates in any manner whatever the provisions of Articles 42 and 43, she shall be regarded as committing a hostile act against the Powers signatory of the present Treaty and as calculated to disturb the peace of the world.

Section IV. Saar Basin. Art. 45. As compensation for the destruction of the coal-mines in the north of France and as part payment towards the total reparation due from Germany for the damage resulting from the war, Germany cedes to France in full and absolute possession, with exclusive rights of exploitation, unencumbered and free from all debts and charges of any kind, the coal-mines situated in the Saar Basin as defined in Article 48.

Art. 48. The boundaries of the territory of the Saar Basin, as dealt with in the present stipulations, will be fixed as follows ...

Section V. Alsace-Lorraine. The High Contracting Parties, recognising the moral obligation to redress the wrong done by Germany in 1871 both to the rights of France and to the wishes of the population of Alsace and Lorraine, which were separated from their country in spite of the solemn protest of their representatives at the Assembly of Bordeaux,

Agree upon the following Articles:

Art. 51. The territories which were ceded to Germany in accordance with the Preliminaries of Peace signed at Versailles on February 26, 1871, and the Treaty of Frankfurt of May 10, 1871, are restored to French sovereignty as from the date of the Armistice of November 11, 1918.

The provisions of the Treaties establishing the delimitation of the frontiers before 1871 shall be restored.

Section VI. Austria. Art. 80. Germany acknowledges and will respect strictly the independence of Austria, within the frontiers which may be fixed in a Treaty between that State and the Principal Allied and Associated Powers; she agrees that this independence shall be inalienable, except with the consent of the Council of the League of Nations.

Section VII. Czecho-Slovak State. Art. 81. Germany, in conformity with the action already taken by the Allied and Associated Powers, recognises the complete independence of the Czecho-Slovak State which will include the autonomous territory of the Ruthenians to the south of the Carpathians. Germany hereby recognises the frontiers of this State as determined by the Principal Allied and Associated Powers and the other interested States.

Provisions as may be deemed necessary by the said Powers to protect the interests of inhabitants of that State who differ from the majority of the population in Race, language or religion.

The Czecho-Slovak State further accepts and agrees to embody in a Treaty with the said Powers such provisions as they may deem necessary to protect freedom of transit and equitable treatment of the commerce of other nations.

The proportion and nature of the financial obligations of Germany and Prussia which the Czecho-Slovak State will have to assume on account of the Silesian territory placed under its sovereignty will be determined in accordance with Article 254 of Part IX (Financial Clauses) of the present Treaty.

Subsequent agreements will decide all questions not decided by the present Treaty which may arise in consequence of the cession of the said territory.

Section VIII. Poland. Art. 87. Germany, in conformity with the action already taken by the Allied and

Associated Powers, recognises the complete independence of Poland, and renounces in her favour all rights and title over the territory bounded by the Baltic Sea, the eastern frontier of Germany as laid down in Article 27 of Part II (Boundaries of Germany) of the present Treaty up to a point situated about 2 kilometres to the east of Lorzendorf, then a line to the acute angle with the northern boundary of Upper Silesia makes about 3 kilometres north-west of Simmenau, then the boundary of Upper Silesia to its meeting point with the old frontier between Germany and Russia, then this frontier to the point where it crosses the course of the Niemen, and then the northern frontier of East Prussia as laid down in Article 28 of Part II aforesaid.

The provisions of this Article do not, however, apply to the territories of East Prussia and the Free City of Danzig, as defined in Article 28 of Part II (Boundaries of Germany) and in Article 100 of Section XI (Danzig) of this Part.

The boundaries of Poland not laid down in the present Treaty will be subsequently determined by the Principal Allied and Associated Powers ...

Art. 88. In the portion of Upper Silesia included within the boundaries described below, the inhabitants will be called upon to indicate by a vote whether they wish to be attached to Germany or to Poland ...

Section IX. East Prussia. Art. 94. In the area between the southern frontier of East Prussia, as described in Article 28 of Part II (Boundaries of Germany) of the present Treaty, and the line described below, the inhabitants will be called upon to indicate by a vote the State to which they wish to belong ...

Section X. Memel. Art. 99. Germany renounces in favour of the Principal Allied and Associated Powers all rights and title over the territories included between the Baltic, the north-eastern frontier of East Prussia as defined in Article 28 of Part II (Boundaries of Germany) of the present Treaty and the former frontier between Germany and Russia. Germany undertakes to accept the settlement made by the Principal Allied and Associated Powers in regard to these territories, particularly in so far as concerns the nationality of the inhabitants.

Section XI. Free City of Danzig. Art. 100. Germany renounces in favour of the Principal Allied and Associated Powers all rights and title over the territory comprised within the following limits:

from the Baltic Sea southwards to the point where the principal channels of navigation of the Nogat and the Vistula (Weichsel) meet:

the boundary of East Prussia as described in Article 28 of Part II (Boundaries of Germany) of the present Treaty; thence the principal channel of navigation of the Vistula downstream to a point about 6 ½ kilometres north of the bridge of Dirschau ...

Art. 101. A Commission composed of three members appointed by the Principal Allied and Associated Powers, including a High Commissioner as President, one member appointed by Germany and one member appointed by Poland, shall be constituted within fifteen days of the coming into force of the present Treaty for the purpose of delimiting on the spot the frontier of the territory as described above, taking into account as far as possible the existing communal boundaries.

Art. 102. The Principal Allied and Associated Powers undertake to establish the town of Danzig, together with the rest of the territory described in Article 100, as a Free City. It will be placed under the protection of the League of Nations.

Art. 103. A constitution for the Free City of Danzig shall be drawn up by the duly appointed representatives of the Free City in agreement with a High Commissioner to be appointed by the League of Nations. This constitution shall be placed under the guarantee of the League of Nations.

The High Commissioner will also be entrusted with the duty of dealing in the first instance with all differences arising between Poland and the Free City of Danzig in regard to this Treaty or any arrangements or agreements made thereunder. The High Commissioner shall reside at Danzig.

Art. 104. The Principal Allied and Associated Powers undertake to negotiate a Treaty between the Polish Government and the Free City of Danzig, which shall come into force at the same time as the establishment of the said Free City, with the following objects:

(1) To effect the inclusion of the Free City of Danzig within the Polish Customs frontiers, and to establish a free area in the port;

(2) To ensure to Poland without any restriction the free use and service of all waterways, docks, basins, wharves and other works within the territory of the Free City necessary for Polish imports and exports;

(3) To ensure to Poland the control and administration of the Vistula and of the whole railway system within the Free City, except such street and other railways as serve primarily the needs of the Free City, and of postal, telegraphic and telephonic communication between Poland and the port of Danzig;

(4) To ensure to Poland the right to develop and improve the waterways, docks, basins, wharves, railways and other works and means of communication mentioned in this Article, as well as to lease or purchase through appropriate processes such land and other property as may be necessary for these purposes;

(5) To provide against any discrimination within the Free City of Danzig to the detriment of citizens of Poland and other persons of Polish origin or speech.

(6) To provide that the Polish Government shall undertake the conduct of the foreign relations of the Free City of Danzig as well as the diplomatic protection of citizens of that city when abroad.

Section XII. Schleswig.

Section XIII. Heligoland. Art. 115. The fortifications, military establishments, and harbours, of the Islands of Heligoland and Dune shall be destroyed under the supervision of the Principal Allied Governments by German labour and at the expense of Germany within a period to be determined by the said Governments ...

Section XIV. Russia and Russian States. Art. 116. Germany acknowledges and agrees to respect as permanent and inalienable the independence of all the territories which were part of the former Russian Empire on August 1, 1914.

In accordance with the provisions of Article 259 of Part IX (Financial Clauses) and Article 292 of Part X (Economic Clauses) Germany accepts definitely the abrogation of the Brest–Litovsk Treaties and of all other treaties, conventions, and agreements entered into by her with the Maximalist Government in Russia. The Allied and Associated Powers formally reserve the rights of Russia to obtain from Germany restitution and reparation based on the principles of the present Treaty.

Art. 117. Germany undertakes to recognise the full force of all treaties or agreements which may be entered into by the Allied and Associated Powers with States now existing or coming into existence in future in the whole or part of the former Empire of Russia as it existed on August 1, 1914, and to recognise the frontiers of any such States as determined therein.

Part IV German Rights and interest outside Germany (art. 118–158).

Art. 119 Germany renounces in favour of the Principal Allied and Associated Powers all her rights and titles over her overseas possessions ...

Art. 128 Germany renounces in favour of China all benefits and privileges resulting from the provisions of the ▷ Boxer Protocol, 1901 ..."

Germany renounced also all rights and privileges in Siam (Art. 135–232), Liberia (art. 138–140), Morocco (art. 141–146), Egypt (art. 147–154), Turkey and Bulgaria (art. 155), Shantung (156–158).

Part V Military, Naval and Air Clause (art. 157–213)

Part VI Prisoners of War and Graves (art. 214–226)

Part VII Penalties (art. 227–230)

"Art. 227. The Allied and Associated Powers publicly arraign William II of Hohenzollern, formerly German Emperor, for a supreme offence against international morality and the sanctity of treaties.

A special tribunal will be constituted to try the accused, thereby assuring him the guarantees essential to the right of defence. It will be composed of five judges, one appointed by each of the following Powers: namely, the United States of America, Great Britain, France, Italy and Japan.

In its decision the tribunal will be guided by the highest motives of international policy, with a view to vindicating the solemn obligations of international undertakings and the validity of international morality. It will be its duty to fix the punishment which it considers should be imposed.

The Allied and Associated Powers will address a request to the Government of the Netherlands for the surrender to them of the ex-Emperor in order that he may be put on trial.

Art. 228. The German Government recognises the right of the Allied and Associated Powers to bring before military tribunals persons accused of having committed acts in violation of the laws and customs of war. Such persons shall, if found guilty, be sentenced to punishments laid down by law. This provision will apply notwithstanding any proceedings or prosecution before a tribunal in Germany or in the territory of her allies. The German Government shall hand over to the Allied and Associated Powers, or to such one of them as shall so request, all persons accused of having committed an act in violation of the laws and customs of war who are specified either by name or by the rank, office or employment which they held under the German authorities.

Art. 229. Persons guilty of criminal acts against the nationals of one of the Allied and Associated Powers will be brought before the military tribunals of that Power.

Persons guilty of criminal acts against the nationals of more than one of the Allied and Associated Powers will be brought before military tribunals composed of members of the military tribunals of the Powers concerned.

In every case the accused will be entitled to name his own counsel.

Art. 230. The German Government undertakes to furnish all documents and information of every kind, the production of which may be considered necessary to ensure the full knowledge of the incriminating acts, the discovery of offenders and the just appreciation of responsibility."

Part VIII. Reparation (art. 231–244 with 7 Annexes)

"Art. 231. The Allied and Associated Governments affirm and Germany accepts the responsibility of Germany and her allies for causing all the loss and damage to which the Allied and Associated Governments and their nations have been subjected as a consequence of the war imposed upon them by the aggression of Germany and her allies."

Part IX. Financial Clauses (art. 248–263)

Part X. Commercial Clauses (art. 264–312)

Part XI. Aerial Navigation (art. 313–320)

Part XII. Posts, Waterways and Railways (art. 321–386), art. 340–342

Part XIII. Labour (art. 387–427)

Part XIV. Guarantees (art. 428–433)

"Art. 428. As a guarantee for the execution of the present Treaty by Germany, the German territory situated to the west of the Rhine, together with the bridgeheads, will be occupied by Allied and Associated troops for a period of fifteen years from the coming into force of the present Treaty.

Art. 433. As a guarantee for the execution of the provisions of the present Treaty, by which Germany accepts definitely the abrogation of the Brest–Litovsk Treaty, and of all treaties, conventions and agreements entered into by her with the Maximalist Government in Russia, and in order to ensure the restoration of peace and good government in the Baltic Provinces and Lithuania, all German troops at present in the said territories shall return to within the frontiers of Germany as soon as the Governments of the Principal Allied and Associated Powers shall think the moment suitable, having regard to the internal situation of these territories. These troops shall abstain from all requisitions and seizures and from any other coercive measures, with a view to obtaining supplies intended for Germany, and shall in no way interfere with such measures for national defence as may be adopted by the Provisional Governments of Esthonia, Latvia, and Lithuania.

No other German troops shall, pending the evacuation or after the evacuation is complete, be admitted to the said territories.

Part XV. Miscellaneous Provisions. Art. 434. Germany undertakes to recognise the full force of the Treaties of Peace and Additional Conventions which may be concluded by the Allied and Associated Powers with the Powers who fought on the side of Germany and to recognise whatever dispositions may be made concerning the territories of the former Austro-Hungarian Monarchy, of the Kingdom of Bulgaria and of the Ottoman Empire, and to recognise the new States within their frontiers as there laid down.

V

Art. 435. The High Contracting Parties, while they recognise the guarantees stipulated by the Treaties of 1815, and especially by the Act of November 20, 1815, in favour of Switzerland, the said guarantees constituting international obligations for the maintenance of peace, declare nevertheless that the provisions of these treaties, conventions, declarations and other supplementary Acts concerning the neutralized zone of Savoy, as laid down in paragraph I of Article 92 of the Final Act of the Congress of Vienna and in paragraph 2 of Article 3 of the Treaty of Paris of November 20, 1815, are no longer consistent with present conditions. For this reason the High Contracting Parties take note of the agreement reached between the French Government and the Swiss Government for the abrogation of the stipulations relating to this zone which are and remain abrogated.

The High Contracting Parties also agree that the stipulations of the Treaties of 1815 and of the other supplementary Acts concerning the free zones of Upper Savoy and the Gex district are no longer consistent with present conditions, and that it is for France and Switzerland to come to an agreement together with a view to settling between themselves the status of these territories under such conditions as shall be considered suitable by both countries.

Art. 440. Germany accepts and recognises as valid and binding all decrees and orders concerning German ships and goods and all orders relating to the payment of costs made by any Prize Court of any of the Allied or Associated Powers, and undertakes not to put forward any claim arising out of such decrees or orders on behalf of any German national ...

The present Treaty, of which the French and English texts are both authentic, shall be ratified.

The deposit of ratifications shall be made at Paris as soon as possible.

In faith whereof the above-named Plenipotentiaries have signed the present Treaty."

LNTS, 1920; E.M. HOUSE, Ch. SEYMOUR (eds.), *What Really Happened in Paris? The Story of the Peace Conference 1918–1919 by American Delegates*, New York, 1921; F.S. MARSTONE, *The Peace Conference 1919. Organization and Procedure*, New York, 1944; US Department of State, *The Treaty of Versailles; Annotation of the Text of the Treaty*, Washington, DC, 1947; B. STEIN, *Ruskii vopros na pariskoi mirovoi konferentsii 1919–1920*, Moscow, 1949; E. WUEST, *Der Vertrag von Versailles im Licht und Schatten der Kritik*, Zürich, 1962; A.F. MAYER, *Politics and Diplomacy of Peacemaking. Containment and Counterrevolution in Versailles, 1918–1919*, New York, 1967.

VESSELS CMEA CHARTERING BUREAU. A
CMEA office est. 1962 at Moscow. The Bureau for Co-ordination of the Chartering of Vessels by the CMEA Countries organizes information concerning the situation in the world chartering market, works out particular problems, organizes joint lines between CMEA member countries and to third countries, collects data on cargoes not provided with tonnage, observes the level of rates fixed for the chartering by particular chartering organization, publ. *Information Bulletin*.

W.E. BUTLER (ed.), *A Source Book on Socialist International Organizations*, Alphen, 1978, pp. 254–257.

VESSELS MEASUREMENT CONVENTION, 1925.
The Convention concerning the Measurement of Vessels employed in Inland Navigation, signed on Nov. 27, 1925 in Paris by Austria, Belgium, Bulgaria, the British Empire, Czechoslovakia, Finland, France, Germany, Greece, Hungary, Italy, Netherlands, Poland, Romania, Serbo-Croat-Slovene State, Spain, Switzerland and USSR.

LNTS, Vol. 67, p. 63.

VESSELS UNDER CONSTRUCTION CONVENTION, 1967.
▷ Maritime Law Conventions, 1882–1978.

VETERINARY MEDICINE. A subject of international co-operation.
Organizations reg. with the UIA:

Commonwealth Veterinary Association, 1974, Ottawa.
East African Veterinary Research Organization, f. 1938, Kilenya, Kenya.
European Union of Veterinary Practitioners, f. 1970, Gressen, FRG.
Federation of Veterinarians of the EEC, f. 1961, London.
International Veterinary Association for Animal Production, f. 1951, Madrid. Publ.: *Zootechnia*.
International Women's Auxiliary to the Veterinary Profession, f. 1949. London Publ.: *IWA Bulletin*.
International Committee on Veterinary Anatomical Nomenclature, f. 1957, Vienna.
Panamerican Veterinary Association, f. 1970, Bogota.
Veterinary CMEA Cooperation, f. 1959, Sofia.
World Association of Veterinary Anatomists, f. 1955, Alfort, Seine, France, Publ.: *Nomina Anatomica Veterinaria*.
World Association of Veterinary Microbiologists, Immunologists and Specialists in Infectious Diseases, f. 1967, Paris.
World Association of Veterinary Pathologists, f. 1959, Madrid.
World Small Animal Veterinary Association, f. 1965, Paris.
World Veterinary Association, f. 1959, Madrid. Consultative status with FAO. Publ.: *News Items*.
World Veterinary Poultry Associations, f. 1959, Madrid.

Yearbook of International Organizations.

VETO IN UN SECURITY COUNCIL. Under the
UN Charter (art. 27) all decisions of the Security Council on all substantive issues (non-procedural) "shall be made by an affirmative vote of nine members including the concurring votes of the permanent members", China, France, the UK, the USSR and the USA. This is the rule of great Power "unanimity", often referred to as the "veto". All permanent members, except China, have exercised the right of veto at one time or another; an abstention is not considered as a veto.

On Dec. 10, 1981 the UN General Assembly Res. 36/122 decided to take no action on a proposal to study Veto rule in the Security Council (62 votes in favor, 32 against, 43 abstentions).

S.B. KRYLOV, *Material po Histori OON*, Moscow, 1948; J. DE PREUX, *Le droit de veto dans la Charte de l'ONU*, Paris, 1949; P.F. BRUGIERE, *Droit de veto*, Paris, 1952; G. DAY, *Le droit de veto dans l'ONU*, Paris, 1952; L. GROSS, "The Double Veto", in *Harvard Law Review*, 1954; *UN Chronicle*, February, 1982, p. 63.

VEXLLOLOGY. From Latin Vexillum = cloth
flag. An international scientific term for the study of the history, symbolism and usage of flags. Subject of international co-operation and research. See ▷ Flag.

W. SMITH, *Flags Through the Ages and Across the World*, New York, 1976.

VÉZELAY. The church and hill of Vézelay, France,
are included in the ▷ World Heritage UNESCO List. The Basilica dominates a magnificent landscape and was one of the greatest centers of pilgrimage in Europe from the 11th to the 13th centuries. The majesty of its sculpted doorways and the variety and exuberance of its carved capitals make it one of the masterpieces of Romanesque art.

UNESCO, *A Legacy for All*, Paris, 1984.

VÉZÈRE VALLEY. A historical site of France
with decorated grottos, included in the ▷ World Heritage UNESCO List. Excavations at 150 sites among the wooded cliffs which run along this river, have brought to light half a million tools and fossils which have made it possible to establish the chronology of the Old Stone Age. They also contain masterpieces in the form of rock paintings and engraving dating back 15,000 years.

UNESCO, *A Legacy for All*, Paris, 1984.

VIBRATION. The vibrations caused mechanically
in the work environment that are dangerous to health are a subject of ILO Conventions.

J.P. DEN HARTOG, *Mechanical Vibrations*, London, 1956.

VICHY. A health resort in France which from July,
1940 to Aug., 1944 was the seat of the French government under the direction of Marshal P. Pétain.

R. ARON, *Histoire de Vichy 1940–1944*, Paris, 1954; B. KLARSFELD, *Vichy-Auschwitz*, Paris, 1983; J.B. DUROSSELLE, *L'Abime 1939–45*; Paris, 1983.

VIDEOGRAMS. ▷ Phonograms and Videograms.

VIEDMA AGREEMENT. A series of bilateral
Argentinian-Brazilian agreements on biotechnology, trade, transportation, and monetary unit (▷ Gaucho), signed in Viedma, Argentina, on Aug. 17, 1987.

KEESING'S *Record of World Events*, 1987.

VIENNA. Capital city of Austria, the seat of the
IAEA, the UNIDO, the OPEC and other international organizations, most of them concentrated in the Vienna UN City. In 1938 and 1940 it was the site of arbitration talks on the Hungarian–Romanian border issue, ▷ Vienna Arbitraments; in 1961–63 it was host to the special UN Conference on international diplomatic and consular law. Vienna is called the "third UN city" after New York and Geneva.

Yearbook of International Organizations.

VIENNA ARBITRAMENTS, 1938 AND 1940.
Two statements on border disputes: (1) concerning the Hungarian–Czechoslovakia border, proclaimed Oct. 29, 1938 in Vienna by mediators forced upon both sides: the ministers of foreign affairs of the Reich and Italy. Hungary received about 12,000 sq. km with 1,064,000 inhabitants, which included five towns. Besides this, Slovakia had to give up two towns to the Transcarpathian Ukraine. The delimitation of the new border took place Nov. 10, 1938. These cessions were annulled as a result of World War II. (2) concerning the Hungarian–Romanian border, proclaimed Aug. 30, 1940 by the same mediators. This was also to the benefit of Hungary, which received the north part of Transylvania, previously lost with the Trianon Treaty. This cession was annulled by the Paris Peace Treaty, 1947.

BRUNS-GRETSCHANINOV, *Politische Verträge*, 5 Vols., Berlin, 1936–42; C.A. COLLARD, *Droit international et histoire diplomatique*, Paris, 1952.

VIENNA CLUB. The name of bank institutions in
Western Europe, participants in International Conferences on Technical Interbancarian Rationalizations held in Vienna annually since 1957.

VIENNA CONFERENCE, CSCE, 1986–1987.
The Conference on Security and Co-operation in Europe (▷ Helsinki Conference 1973–75 and in the 1980's).

VIENNA CONFERENCE MURFAAMCE, 1973.
▷ MURFAAMCE.

VIENNA CONGRESS, 1814–1815. The meeting of
monarchs and statesmen of Europe from Oct., 1814

to June, 1815 following the French Revolution and the fall of Napoleon I; the Final Act signed and ratified 1815–16 by Austria, France, Great Britain, Portugal, Prussia, Russia, Sweden and the German states. Provided for redivision of Poland; the greater part of the Duchy of Warsaw formed the Kingdom of Poland in personal union with Russia; Cracow and its surrounding areas formed a republic, Free City of Cracow, under joint protection of Austria, Russia and Prussia (incorporated by Austria 1846); Prussia received parts of Saxony, the Rhine Province and Westphalia, Szczecin Pomerania with the island of Rugia and departments of Poznań and Bydgoszcz districts; Austria received northern Italy (Piedmont excluded), regions of Tarnopol and of Wieliczka near Cracow; Switzerland was guaranteed neutrality in unchanged borderline; the constitution of the German confederation headed by Austria and of the union of Belgium and Holland were accepted. The Vienna Congress prepared grounds for the Big Powers to sign at Paris on Sept. 26, 1815 the ▷ Holy Alliance.

G.F. DE MARTENS, *Nouveau Recueil Général*, Vol. 2, p. 379, and Supplement Vol., p. 368; *Major Peace Treaties of Modern History*, New York, 1967, Vol. I, pp. 519–575.

VIENNA CONVENTION ON CONSULAR RELATIONS, 1963.
Adopted on Apr. 22, 1963 by the UN Conference on Consular Relations held at the Neue Hofburg in Vienna, from Mar. 4 to Apr. 22, 1963; came into force on Mar. 19, 1967. The text of the Convention and two Optional Protocols is as follows:

"The States Parties to the present Convention,
Recalling that consular relations have been established between peoples since ancient times,
Having in mind the Purposes and Principles of the Charter of the United Nation concerning the sovereign equality of States, the maintenance of international peace and security, and the promotion of friendly relations among nations,
Considering that the United Nations Conference on Diplomatic Intercourse and Immunities adopted the Vienna Convention on Diplomatic Relations which was opened for signature on 18 April, 1961,
Believing that an international convention on consular relations, privileges and immunities would also contribute to the development of friendly relations among nations, irrespective of their differing constitutional and social systems,
Realizing that the purpose of such privileges and immunities is not to benefit individuals but to ensure the efficient performance of functions by consular posts on behalf of their respective States,
Affirming that the rules of customary international law continue to govern matters not expressly regulated by the provisions of the present Convention,
Have agreed as follows:
Art. 1. Definitions
(1) For the purposes of the present Convention, the following expressions shall have the meanings hereunder assigned to them:
(a) 'consular post' means any consulate-general, consulate, vice-consulate or consular agency;
(b) 'consular district' means the area assigned to a consular post for the exercise of consular functions;
(c) 'head of consular post' means the person charged with the duty of acting in that capacity;
(d) 'consular officer' means any person, including the head of a consular post, entrusted in that capacity with the exercise of consular functions;
(e) 'consular employee' means any person employed in the administrative or technical service of a consular post;
(f) 'member of the service staff' means any person employed in the domestic service of a consular post;
(g) 'members of the consular post' means consular officers, consular employees and members of the service staff;
(h) 'members of the consular staff' means consular officers, other than the head of a consular post, consular employees and members of the service staff;

(i) 'member of the private staff' means a person who is employed exclusively in the private service of a member of the consular post;
(j) 'consular premises' means the buildings or parts of buildings and the land ancillary thereto, irrespective of ownership, used exclusively for the purposes of the consular post;
(k) 'consular archives' includes all the papers, documents, correspondence, books, films, tapes and registers of the consular post, together with the ciphers and codes, the card-indexes and any article of furniture intended for their protection or safekeeping.
(2) Consular officers are of two categories, namely career consular officers and honorary consular officers. The provisions of Chapter II of the present Convention apply to consular posts headed by career consular officers; the provisions of Chapter III govern consular posts headed by honorary consular officers.
(3) The particular status of members of the consular posts who are nationals or permanent residents of the receiving State is governed by Article 71 of the present Convention.
Chapter I. *Consular relations in general*
Section I. Establishment and conduct of consular relations
Art. 2. Establishment of consular relations
(1) The establishment of consular relations between States takes place by mutual consent.
(2) The consent given to the establishment of diplomatic relations between two States implies, unless otherwise stated, consent to the establishment of consular relations.
(3) The severance of diplomatic relations shall not ipso facto involve the severance of consular relations.
Art. 3. Exercise of consular functions.
Consular functions are exercised by consular posts. They are also exercised by diplomatic missions in accordance with the provisions of the present Convention.
Art. 4. Establishment of a consular post
(1) A consular post may be established in the territory of the receiving State only with that State's consent.
(2) The seat of the consular post, its classification and the consular district shall be established by the sending State and shall be subject to the approval of the receiving State.
(3) Subsequent changes in the seat of the consular post, its classification or the consular district may be made by the sending State only with the consent of the receiving State.
(4) The consent of the receiving State shall also be required if a consulate-general or a consulate desires to open a vice-consulate or a consular agency in a locality other than that in which it is itself established.
(5) The prior express consent of the receiving State shall also be required for the opening of an office forming part of an existing consular post elsewhere than at the seat thereof.
Art. 5. Consular functions
Consular functions consist in:
(a) protecting in the receiving State the interests of the sending State and of its nationals, both individuals and bodies corporate, within the limits permitted by international law;
(b) furthering the development of commercial, economic, cultural and scientific relations between the sending State and the receiving State and otherwise promoting friendly relations between them in accordance with the provisions of the present Convention;
(c) ascertaining by all lawful means conditions and developments in the commercial, economic, cultural and scientific life of the receiving State, reporting thereon to the Government of the sending State and giving information to persons interested;
(d) issuing passports and travel documents to nationals of the sending State, and visas or appropriate documents to persons wishing to travel to the sending State;
(e) helping and assisting nationals, both individuals and bodies corporate, of the sending State;
(f) acting as notary and civil registrar and in capacities of a similar kind, and performing certain functions of an administrative nature, provided that there is nothing contrary thereto in the laws and regulations of the receiving State;
(g) safeguarding the interests of nationals, both individuals and bodies corporate, of the sending State in cases of succession mortis causa in the territory of the receiving State, in accordance with the laws and regulations of the receiving State;

(h) safeguarding, within the limits imposed by the laws and regulations of the receiving State, the interests of minors and other persons lacking full capacity who are nationals of the sending State, particularly where any guardianship or trusteeship is required with respect to such persons;
(i) subject to the practices and procedures obtaining in the receiving State, representing or arranging appropriate representation for nationals of the sending State before the tribunals and other authorities of the receiving State, for the purpose of obtaining, in accordance with the laws and regulations of the receiving State, provisional measures for the preservation of the rights and interests of these nationals, where, because of absence or any other reason, such nationals are unable at the proper time to assume the defence of their rights and interests;
(j) transmitting judicial and extra-judicial documents or executing letters rogatory or commissions to take evidence for the courts of the sending State in accordance with international agreements in force or, in the absence of such international agreements, in any other manner compatible with the laws and regulations of the receiving State;
(k) exercising rights of supervision and inspection provided for in the laws and regulations of the sending State in respect of vessels having the nationality of the sending State, and of aircraft registered in that State, and in respect of their crews;
(l) extending assistance to vessels and aircraft mentioned in sub-paragraph (k) of this Article and to their crews, taking statements regarding the voyage of a vessel, examining and stamping the ship's papers, and, without prejudice to the powers of the authorities of the receiving State, conducting investigations into any incidents which occurred during the voyage, and settling disputes of any kind between the master, the officers and the seamen in so far as this may be authorized by the laws and regulations of the sending State;
(m) performing any other functions entrusted to a consular post by the sending State which are not prohibited by the laws and regulations of the receiving State or to which no objection is taken by the receiving State or which are referred to in the international agreements in force between the sending State and the receiving State.
Art. 6. Exercise of consular functions outside the consular district.
A consular officer may, in special circumstances, with the consent of the receiving State, exercise his functions outside his consular district.
Art. 7. Exercise of consular functions in a third State.
The sending State may, after notifying the States concerned, entrust a consular post established in a particular State with the exercise of consular functions in another State, unless there is express objection by one of the States concerned.
Art. 8. Exercise of consular functions on behalf of a third State.
Upon appropriate notification to the receiving State, a consular post of the sending State may, unless the receiving objects, exercise consular functions in the receiving State on behalf of a third State.
Art. 9. Classes of heads of consular posts.
(1) Heads of consular posts are divided into four classes, namely:
(a) consuls-general;
(b) consuls;
(c) vice-consuls;
(d) consular agents.
(2) Paragraph 1 of this Article in no way restricts the right of any of the Contracting Parties to fix the designation of consular officers other than the heads of consular posts.
Art. 10. Appointment and admission of heads of consular posts.
(1) Heads of consular posts are appointed by the sending State and are admitted to the exercise of their functions by the receiving State.
(2) Subject to the provisions of the present Convention, the formalities for the appointment and for the admission of the head of a consular post are determined by the laws, regulations and usages of the sending State and of the receiving State respectively.
Art. 11. The consular commission or notification of appointment.
(1) The head of a consular post shall be provided by the sending State with a document, in the form of a commission or similar instrument, made out for each

appointment, certifying his capacity and showing, as a general rule, his full name, his category and class, the consular district and the seat of the consular post.

(2) The sending State shall transmit the commission or similar instrument through the diplomatic or other appropriate channel to the Government of the State in whose territory the head of a consular post is to exercise his functions.

(3) If the receiving State agrees, the sending State may, instead of a commission or similar instrument, send to the receiving State a notification containing the particulars required by paragraph 1 of this Article.

Art. 12. The exequatur

(1) The head of a consular post is admitted to the exercise of his functions by an authorization from the receiving State termed an exequatur, whatever the form of this authorization.

(2) A State which refuses to grant an exequatur is not obliged to give to the sending State reasons for such refusal.

(3) Subject to the provisions of Articles 13 and 15, the head of a consular post shall not enter upon his duties until he has received an exequatur.

Art. 13. Provisional admission of heads of consular posts. Pending delivery of the exequatur, the head of a consular post may be admitted on a provisional basis to the exercise of his functions. In that case, the provisions of the present Convention shall apply.

Art. 14. Notification to the authorities of the consular district.

As soon as the head of a consular post is admitted even provisionally to the exercise of his functions, the receiving State shall immediately notify the competent authorities of the consular district. It shall also ensure that the necessary measures are taken to enable the head of a consular post to carry out the duties of his office and to have the benefit of the provisions of the present Convention.

Art. 15. Temporary exercise of the functions of the head of a consular post.

(1) If the head of a consular post is unable to carry out his functions or the position of head of consular post is vacant, an acting head of post may act provisionally as head of the consular post.

(2) The full name of the acting head of post shall be notified either by the diplomatic mission of the sending State or, if that State has no such mission in the receiving State, by the head of the consular post, or, if he is unable to do so, by any competent authority of the sending State, to the Ministry for Foreign Affairs of the receiving State or to the authority designated by that Ministry. As a general rule, this notification shall be given in advance. The receiving State may make the admission as acting head of post of a person who is neither a diplomatic agent nor a consular officer of the sending State in the receiving State conditional on its consent.

(3) The competent authorities of the receiving State shall afford assistance and protection to the acting head of post. While he is in charge of the post, the provisions of the present Convention shall apply to him on the same basis as to the head of the consular post concerned. The receiving State shall not, however, be obliged to grant to an acting head of post any facility, privilege or immunity which the head of the consular post enjoys only subject to conditions not fulfilled by the acting head of post.

(4) When, in the circumstances referred to in paragraph 1 of this Article, a member of the diplomatic staff of the diplomatic mission of the sending State in the receiving State is designated by the sending State as an acting head of post, he shall, if the receiving State does not object thereto, continue to enjoy diplomatic privileges and immunities.

Art. 16. Precedence as between heads of consular posts.

(1) Heads of consular posts shall rank in each class according to the date of the grant of the exequatur.

(2) If, however, the head of a consular post before obtaining the exequatur is admitted to the exercise of his functions provisionally, his precedence shall be determined according to the date of the provisional admission; this precedence shall be maintained after the granting of the exequatur.

(3) The order of precedence as between two or more heads of consular posts who obtained the exequatur or provisional admission on the same date shall be determined according to the dates on which their commissions or similar instruments or the notifications

referred to in paragraph 3 of Article 11 were presented to the receiving State.

(4) Acting heads of posts shall rank after all heads of consular posts and, as between themselves, they shall rank according to the dates on which they assumed their functions as acting heads of posts as indicated in the notifications given under paragraph 2 of Article 15.

(5) Honorary consular officers who are heads of consular posts shall rank in each class after career heads of consular posts, in the order and according to the rules laid down in the foregoing paragraphs.

(6) Heads of consular posts shall have precedence over consular officers not having that status.

Art. 17. Performance of diplomatic acts by consular officers.

(1) In a State where the sending State has no diplomatic mission and is not represented by a diplomatic mission of a third State, a consular officer may, with the consent of the receiving State, and without affecting his consular status, be authorized to perform diplomatic acts. The performance of such acts by a consular officer shall not confer upon him any right to claim diplomatic privileges and immunities.

(2) A consular officer may, after notification addressed to the receiving State, act as representative of the sending State to any inter-governmental organization. When so acting, he shall be entitled to enjoy any privileges and immunities accorded to such a representative by customary international law or by international agreements; however, in respect of the performance by him of any consular function, he shall not be entitled to any great immunity from jurisdiction than that to which a consular officer is entitled under the present Convention.

Art. 18. Appointment of the same person by two or more States as a consular officer.

Two or more States may, with the consent of the receiving State, appoint the same person as a consular officer in that State.

Art. 19. Appointment of members of consular staff.

(1) Subject to the provisions of Articles 20, 22 and 23, the sending State may freely appoint the members of the consular staff.

(2) The full name, category and class of all consular officers, other than the head of a consular post, shall be notified by the sending State to the receiving State in sufficient time for the receiving State, if it so wishes, to exercise its rights under paragraph 3 of Article 23.

(3) The sending State may, if required by its laws and regulations, request the receiving State to grant an exequatur to a consular officer other than the head of a consular post.

(4) The receiving State may, if required by its laws and regulations, grant an exequatur to a consular officer other than the head of a consular post.

Art. 20. Size of the consular staff.

In the absence of an express agreement as to the size of the consular staff, the receiving State may require that the size of the staff be kept within limits considered by it to be reasonable and normal, having regard to circumstances and conditions in the consular district and to the needs of the particular post.

Art. 21. Precedence as between consular officers of a consular post.

The order of precedence as between the consular officers of a consular post and any change thereof shall be notified by the diplomatic mission of the sending State or, if that State has no such mission in the receiving State, by the head of the consular post, to the Ministry for Foreign Affairs of the receiving State or to the authority designated by that Ministry.

Art. 22. Nationality of consular officers.

(1) Consular officers should, in principle, have the nationality of the sending State.

(2) Consular officers may not be appointed from among persons having the nationality of the receiving State except with the express consent of that State which may be withdrawn at any time.

(3) The receiving State may reserve the same right with regard to nationals of a third State who are not also nationals of the sending State.

Art. 23. Persons declared "non grata".

(1) The receiving State may at any time notify the sending State that a consular officer is persona non grata or that any other member of the consular staff is not acceptable. In that event, the sending State shall, as the case may be, either recall the person concerned or terminate his functions with the consular post.

(2) If the sending State refuses or fails within a reasonable time to carry out its obligations under paragraph 1 of this Article, the receiving State may, as the case may be, either withdraw the exequatur from the person concerned or cease to consider him as a member of the consular staff.

(3) A person appointed as a member of a consular post may be declared unacceptable before arriving in the territory of the receiving State or, if already in the receiving State, before entering on his duties with the consular post. In any such case, the sending State shall withdraw his appointment.

(4) In the cases mentioned in paragraphs 1 and 3 of this Article, the receiving State is not obliged to give to the sending State reasons for its decision.

Art. 24. Notification to the receiving State of appointments, arrivals and departures.

(1) The Ministry for Foreign Affairs of the receiving State or the authority designated by that Ministry shall be notified of:

(a) the appointment of members of a consular post, their arrival after appointment to the consular post, their final departure or the termination of their functions and any other changes affecting their status that may occur in the course of their service with the consular post;

(b) the arrival and final departure of a person belonging to the family of a member of a consular post forming part of his household and, where appropriate, the fact that a person becomes or ceases to be such a member of the family;

(c) the arrival and final departure of members of the private staff and, where appropriate, the termination of their service as such;

(d) the engagement and discharge of persons resident in the receiving State as members of a consular post or as members of the private staff entitled to privileges and immunities.

(2) When possible, prior notification of arrival and final departure shall also be given.

Section II. End of consular functions.

Art. 25. Termination of the functions of a member of a consular post.

The functions of a member of a consular post shall come to an end inter alia:

(a) on notification by the sending State to the receiving State that his functions have come to an end;

(b) on withdrawal of the exequatur;

(c) on notification by the receiving State to the sending State that the receiving State has ceased to consider him as a member of the consular staff.

Art. 26. Departure from the territory of the receiving State.

The receiving State shall, even in case of armed conflict, grant to members of the consular post and members of the private staff, other than nationals of the receiving State, and to members of their families forming part of their household irrespective of nationality, the necessary time and facilities to enable them to prepare their departure and to leave at the earliest possible moment after the termination of the functions of the members concerned. In particular, it shall, in case of need, place at their disposal the necessary means of transport for themselves and their property other than property acquired in the receiving State the export of which is prohibited at the time of departure.

Art. 27. Protection of consular premises and archives and of the interests of the sending State in exceptional circumstances.

(1) In the event of the severance of consular relations between two States:

(a) the receiving State shall, even in case of armed conflict, respect and protect the consular premises, together with the property of the consular post and the consular archives;

(b) the sending State may entrust the custody of the consular premises, together with the property contained therein and the consular archives, to a third State acceptable to the receiving State;

(c) the sending State may entrust the protection of its interests and those of its nationals to a third State acceptable to the receiving State.

(2) In the event of the temporary or permanent closure of a consular post, the provisions of sub-paragraph (a) of paragraph 1 of this Article shall apply. In addition,

(a) if the sending State, although not represented in the receiving State by a diplomatic mission, has another consular post in the territory of that State, that consular

post may be entrusted with the custody of the premises of the consular post which has been closed, together with the property contained therein and the consular archives, and, with the consent of the receiving State, with the exercise of consular functions in the district of that consular post; or
(b) if the sending State has no diplomatic mission and no other consular post in the receiving State, the provisions of sub-paragraphs (b) and (c) of paragraph 1 of this Article shall apply.
Chapter II. *Facilities, privileges and immunities relating to consular posts, career consular officers and other members of a consular post.*
Section I. Facilities, privileges and immunities relating to a consular post.
Art. 28. Facilities for the work of the consular post. The receiving State shall accord full facilities for the performance of the functions of the consular post.
Art. 29. Use of national flag and coat-of-arms.
(1) The sending State shall have the right to the use of its national flag and coat-of-arms in the receiving State in accordance with the provisions of this Article.
(2) The national flag of the sending State may be flown and its coat-of-arms displayed on the building occupied by the consular post and at the entrance door thereof, on the residence of the head of the consular post and on his means of transport when used on official business.
(3) In the exercise of the right accorded by this Article regard shall be had to the laws, regulations and usages of the receiving State.
Art. 30. Accommodation.
(1) The receiving State shall either facilitate the acquisition on its territory, in accordance with its laws and regulations, by the sending State of premises necessary for its consular post or assist the latter in obtaining accommodation in some other way.
(2) It shall also, where necessary, assist the consular post in obtaining suitable accommodation for its members.
Art. 31. Inviolability of the consular premises.
(1) Consular premises shall be inviolable to the extent provided in this Article.
(2) The authorities of the receiving State shall not enter that part of the consular premises which is used exclusively for the purpose of the work of the consular post except with the consent of the head of the consular post or of his designee or of the head of the diplomatic mission of the sending State. The consent of the head of the consular post may, however, be assumed in case of fire or other disaster requiring prompt protective action.
(3) Subject to the provisions of paragraph 2 of this Article, the receiving State is under a special duty to take all appropriate steps to protect the consular premises against any intrusion or damage and to prevent any disturbance of the peace of the consular post or impairment of its dignity.
(4) The consular premises, their furnishings, the property of the consular post and its means of transport shall be immune from any form of requisition for purposes of national defence or public utility. If expropriation is necessary for such purposes, all possible steps shall be taken to avoid impeding the performance of consular functions, and prompt, adequate and effective compensation shall be paid to the sending State.
Art. 32. Exemption from taxation of consular premises.
(1) Consular premises and the residence of the career head of consular post of which the sending State or any person acting on its behalf is the owner or lessee shall be exempt from all national, regional or municipal dues and taxes whatsoever, other than such as represent payment for specific services rendered.
(2) The exemption from taxation referred to in paragraph 1 of this Article shall not apply to such dues and taxes if, under the law of the receiving State, they are payable by the person who contracted with the sending State or with the person acting on its behalf.
Art. 33. Inviolability of the consular archives and documents.
The consular archives and documents shall be inviolable at all times and wherever they may be.
Art. 34. Freedom of movement.
Subject to its laws and regulations concerning zones entry into which is prohibited or regulated for reasons of national security, the receiving State shall ensure freedom of movement and travel in its territory to all members of the consular post.
Art. 35. Freedom of communication.
(1) The receiving State shall permit and protect freedom of communication on the part of the consular post for all official purposes. In communicating with the Government, the diplomatic missions and other consular posts, wherever situated, of the sending State, the consular post may employ all appropriate means, including diplomatic or consular couriers, diplomatic or consular bags and messages in code or cipher. However, the consular post may install and use a wireless transmitter only with the consent of the receiving State.
(2) The official correspondence of the consular post shall be inviolable. Official correspondence means all correspondence relating to the consular post and its functions.
(3) The consular bag shall be neither opened nor detained. Nevertheless, if the competent authorities of the receiving State have serious reason to believe that the bag contains something other than the correspondence, documents or articles referred to in paragraph 4 of this Article, they may request that the bag be opened in their presence by an authorized representative of the sending State. If this request is refused by the authorities of the sending State, the bag shall be returned to its place of origin.
(4) The packages constituting the consular bag shall bear visible external marks of their character and may contain only official correspondence and documents or articles intended exclusively for official use.
(5) The consular courier shall be provided with an official document indicating his status and the number of packages constituting the consular bag. Except with the consent of the receiving State he shall be neither a national of the receiving State, nor, unless he is a national of the sending State, a permanent resident of the receiving State. In the performance of his functions he shall be protected by the receiving State. He shall enjoy personal inviolability and shall not be liable to any form of arrest or detention.
(6) The sending State, its diplomatic missions and its consular posts may designate consular couriers ad hoc. In such cases the provisions of paragraph 5 of this Article shall also apply except that the immunities therein mentioned shall cease to apply when such a courier has delivered to the consignee the consular bag in his charge.
(7) A consular bag may be entrusted to the captain of a ship or of a commercial aircraft scheduled to land at an authorized port of entry. He shall be provided with an official document indicating the number of packages constituting the bag, but he shall not be considered to be a consular courier. By arrangement with the appropriate local authorities, the consular post may send one of its members to take possession of the bag directly and freely from the captain of the ship or of the aircraft.
Art. 36. Communication and contact with nationals of the sending State.
(1) With a view to facilitating the exercise of consular functions relating to nationals of the sending State:
(a) consular officers shall be free to communicate with nationals of the sending State and to have access to them. Nationals of the sending State shall have the same freedom with respect to communication with and access to consular officers of the sending State;
(b) if he so requests, the competent authorities of the receiving State shall, without delay, inform the consular post of the sending State if, within its consular district, a national of that State is arrested or committed to prison or to custody pending trial or is detained in any other manner. Any communication addressed to the consular post by the person arrested, in prison, custody or detention shall also be forwarded by the said authorities without delay. The said authorities shall inform the person concerned without delay of his rights under this sub-paragraph;
(c) consular officers shall have the right to visit a national of the sending State who is in prison, custody or detention, to converse and correspond with him and to arrange for his legal representation. They shall also have the right to visit any national of the sending State who is in prison, custody or detention in their district in pursuance of a judgment. Nevertheless, consular officers shall refrain from taking action on behalf of a national who is in prison, custody or detention if he expressly opposes such action.
(2) The rights referred to in paragraph 1 of this Article shall be exercised in conformity with the laws and regulations of the receiving State, subject to the proviso, however, that the said laws and regulations must enable full effect to be given to the purposes for which the rights accorded under this Article are intended.
Art. 37. Information in cases of deaths, guardianship or trusteeship, wrecks and air accidents.
If the relevant information is available to the competent authorities of the receiving State, such authorities shall have the duty:
(a) in the case of the death of a national of the sending State, to inform without delay the consular post in whose district the death occurred;
(b) to inform the competent consular post without delay of any case where the appointment of a guardian or trustee appears to be in the interests of a minor or other person lacking full capacity who is a national of the sending State. The giving of this information shall, however, be without prejudice to the operation of the laws and regulations of the receiving State concerning such appointments;
(c) if a vessel, having the nationality of the sending State, is wrecked or runs aground in the territorial sea or internal waters of the receiving State, or if an aircraft registered in the sending State suffers an accident on the territory of the receiving State, to inform without delay the consular post nearest to the scene of the occurrence.
Art. 38. Communication with the authorities of the receiving State.
In the exercise of their functions, consular officers may address:
(a) the competent local authorities of their consular district;
(b) the competent central authorities of the receiving State if and to the extent that this is allowed by the laws, regulations and usages of the receiving State or by the relevant international agreements.
Art. 39. Consular fees and charges.
(1) The consular post may levy in the territory of the receiving State the fees and charges provided by the laws and regulations of the sending State for consular acts.
(2) The sums collected in the form of the fees and charges referred to in paragraph 1 of this Article, and the receipts for such fees and charges, shall be exempt from all dues and taxes in the receiving State.
Section II. Facilities, privileges and immunities relating to career consular officers and other members of a consular post.
Art. 40. Protection of consular officers.
The receiving State shall treat consular officers with due respect and shall take all appropriate steps to prevent any attack on their person, freedom or dignity.
Art. 41. Personal inviolability of consular officers.
(1) Consular officers shall not be liable to arrest or detention pending trial, except in the case of a grave crime and pursuant to a decision by the competent judicial authority.
(2) Except in the case specified in paragraph 1 of this Article, consular officers shall not be committed to prison or liable to any other form of restriction on their personal freedom save in execution of a judicial decision of final effect.
(3) If criminal proceedings are instituted against a consular officer, he must appear before the competent authorities. Nevertheless, the proceedings shall be conducted with the respect due to him by reason of his official position and, except in the case specified in paragraph 1 of this Article, in a manner which will hamper the exercise of consular functions as little as possible. When, in the circumstances mentioned in paragraph 1 of this Article, it has become necessary to detain a consular officer, the proceedings against him shall be instituted with the minimum of delay.
Art. 42. Notification of arrest, detention or prosecution. In the event of the arrest or detention, pending trial, of a member of the consular staff, or of criminal proceedings being instituted against him, the receiving State shall promptly notify the head of the consular post. Should the latter be himself the object of any such measure, the receiving State shall notify the sending State through the diplomatic channel.
Art. 43. Immunity from jurisdiction.
(1) Consular officers and consular employees shall not be amenable to the jurisdiction of the judicial or administrative authorities of the receiving State in respect of acts performed in the exercise of consular functions.
(2) The provisions of paragraph 1 of this Article shall not, however, apply in respect of a civil action either:

(a) arising out of a contract concluded by a consular officer or a consular employee in which he did not contract expressly or impliedly as an agent of the sending State; or

(b) by a third party for damage arising from an accident in the receiving State caused by a vehicle, vessel or aircraft.

Art. 44. Liability to give evidence.

(1) Members of a consular post may be called upon to attend as witnesses in the course of judicial or administrative proceedings. A consular employee or a member of the service staff shall not, except in the cases mentioned in paragraph 3 of this Article, decline to give evidence. If a consular officer should decline to do so, no coercive measure or penalty may be applied to him.

(2) The authority requiring the evidence of a consular officer shall avoid interference with the performance of his functions. It may, when possible take such evidence at his residence or at the consular post or accept a statement from him in writing.

(3) Members of a consular post are under no obligation to give evidence concerning matters connected with the exercise of their functions or to produce official correspondence and documents relating thereto. They are also entitled to decline to give evidence as expert witnesses with regard to the law of the sending State.

Art. 45. Waiver of privileges and immunities.

(1) The sending State may waive, with regard to a member of the consular post, any of the privileges and immunities provided for in Articles 41, 43 and 44.

(2) The waiver shall in all cases be express, except as provided in paragraph 3 of this Article, and shall be communicated to the receiving State in writing.

(3) The initiation of proceedings by a consular officer or a consular employee in a matter where he might enjoy immunity from jurisdiction under Article 43 shall preclude him from invoking immunity from jurisdiction in respect of any counterclaim directly connected with the principal claim.

(4) The waiver of immunity from jurisdiction for the purposes of civil or administrative proceedings shall not be deemed to imply the waiver of immunity from the measures of execution resulting from the judicial decision; in respect of such measures, a separate waiver shall be necessary.

Art. 46. Exemption from registration of aliens and residence permits.

(1) Consular officers and consular employees and members of their families forming part of their households shall be exempt from all obligations under the laws and regulations of the receiving State in regard to the registration of aliens and residence permits.

(2) The provisions of paragraph 1 of this Article shall not, however, apply to any consular employee who is not a permanent employee of the sending State or who carries on any private gainful occupation in the receiving State or to any member of the family of any such employee.

Art. 47. Exemption from work permits.

(1) Members of the consular post shall, with respect to services rendered for the sending State, be exempt from any obligations in regard to work permits imposed by the laws and regulations of the receiving State concerning the employment of foreign labour.

(2) Members of the private staff of consular officers and of consular employees shall, if they do not carry on any other gainful occupation in the receiving State, be exempt from the obligations referred to in paragraph 1 of this Article.

Art. 48. Social security exemption.

(1) Subject to the provisions of paragraph 3 of this Article, members of the consular post with respect to services rendered by them for the sending State, and members of their families forming part of their households, shall be exempt from social security provisions which may be in force in the receiving State.

(2) The exemption provided for in paragraph 1 of this Article shall apply also to members of the private staff who are in the sole employ of members of the consular post, on condition:

(a) that they are not nationals of or permanently resident in the receiving State; and

(b) that they are covered by the social security provisions which are in force in the sending State or a third State.

(3) Members of the consular post who employ persons to whom the exemption provided for in paragraph 2 of this Article does not apply shall observe the obligations which the social security provisions of the receiving State impose upon employers.

(4) The exemption provided for in paragraphs 1 and 2 of this Article shall not preclude voluntary participation in the social security system of the receiving State, provided that such participation is permitted by that State.

Art. 49. Exemption from taxation.

(1) Consular officers and consular employees and members of their families forming part of their households shall be exempt from all dues and taxes, personal or real, national, regional or municipal, except:

(a) indirect taxes of a kind which are normally incorporated in the price of goods or services;

(b) dues or taxes on private immovable property situated in the territory of the receiving State, subject to the provisions of Article 32;

(c) estate, succession or inheritance duties, and duties on transfers, levied by the receiving State, subject to the provisions of paragraph (b) of Article 51;

(d) dues and taxes on private income, including capital gains, having its source in the receiving State and capital taxes relating to investments made in commercial or financial undertakings in the receiving State;

(e) charges levied for specific services rendered;

(f) registration, court or record fees, mortgage dues and stamp duties, subject to the provisions of Article 32.

(2) Members of the service staff shall be exempt from dues and taxes on the wages which they receive for their services.

(3) Members of the consular post who employ persons whose wages or salaries are not exempt from income tax in the receiving State shall observe the obligations which the laws and regulations of that State impose upon employers concerning the levying of income tax.

Art. 50. Exemption from customs duties and inspection.

(1) The receiving State shall, in accordance with such laws and regulations as it may adopt, permit entry of and grant exemption from all customs duties, taxes, and related charges other than charges for storage, cartage and similar services, on:

(a) articles for the official use of the consular post;

(b) articles for the personal use of a consular officer or members of his family forming part of his household, including articles intended for his establishment. The articles intended for consumption shall not exceed the quantities necessary for direct utilization by the persons concerned.

(2) Consular employees shall enjoy the privileges and exemptions specified in paragraph 1 of this Article in respect of articles imported at the time of first installation.

(3) Personal baggage accompanying consular officers and members of their families forming part of their households shall be exempt from inspection. It may be inspected only if there is serious reason to believe that it contains articles other than those referred to in subparagraph (b) of paragraph 1 of this Article, or articles the import or export of which is prohibited by the laws and regulations of the receiving State or which are subject to its quarantine laws and regulations. Such inspection shall be carried out in the presence of the consular officer or member of his family concerned.

Art. 51. Estate of a member of the consular post or of a member of his family.

In the event of the death of a member of the consular post or of a member of his family forming part of his household, the receiving State:

(a) shall permit the export of the movable property of the deceased, with the exception of any such property acquired in the receiving State the export of which was prohibited at the time of his death;

(b) shall not levy national, regional or municipal estate, succession or inheritance duties, and duties on transfers, on movable property the presence of which in the receiving State was due solely to the presence in that State of the deceased as a member of the consular post or as a member of the family of a member of the consular post.

Art. 52. Exemption from personal services and contributions. The receiving State shall exempt members of the consular post and members of their families forming part of their households from all personal services, from all public service of any kind whatsoever, and from military obligations such as those connected with requisitioning, military contributions and billeting.

Art. 53. Beginning and end of consular privileges and immunities.

(1) Every member of the consular post shall enjoy the privileges and immunities provided in the present Convention from the moment he enters the territory of the receiving State on proceeding to take up his post or, if already in its territory, from the moment when he enters on his duties with the consular post.

(2) Members of the family of a member of the consular post forming part of his household and members of his private staff shall receive the privileges and immunities provided in the present Convention from the date from which he enjoys privileges and immunities in accordance with paragraph 1 of this Article or from the date of their entry into the territory of the receiving State or from the date of their becoming a member of such family or private staff, whichever is the latest.

(3) When the functions of a member of the consular post have come to an end, his privileges and immunities and those of a member of his family forming part of his household or a member of his private staff shall normally cease at the moment when the person concerned leaves the receiving State or on the expiry of a reasonable period in which to do so, whichever is the sooner, but shall subsist until that time, even in case of armed conflict. In the case of the persons referred to in paragraph 2 of this Article, their privileges and immunities shall come to an end when they cease to belong to the household or to be in the service of a member of the consular post provided, however, that if such persons intend leaving the receiving State within a reasonable period thereafter, their privileges and immunities shall subsist until the time of their departure.

(4) However, with respect to acts performed by a consular officer or a consular employee in the exercise of his functions, immunity from jurisdiction shall continue to subsist without limitation of time.

(5) In the event of the death of a member of the consular post, the members of his family forming part of his household shall continue to enjoy the privileges and immunities accorded to them until they leave the receiving State or until the expiry of a reasonable period enabling them to do so, whichever is the sooner.

Art. 54. Obligations of third State.

(1) If a consular officer passes through or is in the territory of a third State, which has granted him a visa if a visa was necessary, while proceeding to take up or return to his post or when returning to the sending State, the third State shall accord to him all immunities provided for by the other Articles of the present Convention as may be required to ensure his transit or return. The same shall apply in the case of any member of his family forming part of his household enjoying such privileges and immunities who are accompanying the consular officer or travelling separately to join him or to return to the sending State.

(2) In circumstances similar to those specified in paragraph 1 of this Article, third States shall not hinder the transit through their territory of other members of the consular post or of members of their families forming part of their households.

(3) Third States shall accord to official correspondence and to other official communications in transit, including messages in code or cipher, the same freedom and protection as the receiving State is bound to accord under the present Convention. They shall accord to consular couriers who have been granted a visa, if a visa was necessary, and to consular bags in transit, the same inviolability and protection as the receiving State is bound to accord under the present Convention.

(4) The obligations of third States under paragraphs 1, 2 and 3 of this Article shall also apply to the persons mentioned respectively in those paragraphs, and to official communications and to consular bags, whose presence in the territory of the third State is due to force majeure.

Art. 55. Respect for the laws and regulations of the receiving State.

(1) Without prejudice to their privileges and immunities, it is the duty of all persons enjoying such privileges and immunities to respect the laws and regulations of the receiving State. They also have a duty not to interfere in the internal affairs of that State.

(2) The consular premises shall not be used in any manner incompatible with the exercise of consular functions.
(3) The provisions of paragraph 2 of this Article shall not exclude the possibility of offices of other institutions or agencies being installed in part of the building in which the consular premises are situated, provided that the premises assigned to them are separate from those used by the consular post. In that event, the said offices shall not, for the purposes of the present Convention, be considered to form part of the consular premises.
Art. 56. Insurance against third party risks.
Members of the consular post shall comply with any requirement imposed by the laws and regulations of the receiving State in respect of insurance against third party risks arising from the use of any vehicle, vessel or aircraft.
Art. 57. Special provisions concerning private gainful occupation.
(1) Career consular officers shall not carry on for personal profit any professional or commercial activity in the receiving State.
(2) Privileges and immunities provided in this Chapter shall not be accorded:
(a) to consular employees or to members of the service staff who carry on any private gainful occupation in the receiving State;
(b) to members of the family of a person referred to in sub-paragraph (a) of this paragraph or to members of his private staff;
(c) to members of the family of a member of a consular post who themselves carry on any private gainful occupation in the receiving State.
Chapter III. *Regime relating to honorary consular officers and consular posts headed by such officers.*
Art. 58. General provisions relating to facilities, privileges and immunities.
(1) Articles 28, 29, 30, 34, 35, 36, 37, 38 and 39, paragraph 3 of Article 54 and paragraphs 2 and 3 of Article 55 shall apply to consular posts headed by an honorary consular officer. In addition, the facilities, privileges and immunities of such consular posts shall be governed by Articles 59, 60, 61 and 62.
(2) Articles 42 and 43, paragraph 3 of Article 44, Articles 45 and 53 and paragraph 1 of Article 55 shall apply to honorary consular officers. In addition, the facilities, privileges and immunities of such consular officers shall be governed by Articles 63, 64, 65, 66 and 67.
(3) Privileges and immunities provided in the present Convention shall not be accorded to members of the family of an honorary consular officer or of a consular employee employed at a consular post headed by an honorary consular officer.
(4) The exchange of consular bags between two consular posts headed by honorary consular officers in different States shall not be allowed without the consent of the two receiving States concerned.
Art. 59. Protection of the consular premises.
The receiving State shall take such steps as may be necesary to protect the consular premises of a consular post headed by an honorary consular officer against any intrusion or damage and to prevent any disturbance of the peace of the consular post or impairment of its dignity.
Art. 60. Exemption from taxation of consular premises.
(1) Consular premises of a consular post headed by an honorary consular officer of which the sending State is the owner or lessee shall be exempt from all national, regional or municipal dues and taxes whatsoever, other than such as represent payment for specific services rendered.
(2) The exemption from taxation referred to in paragraph 1 of this Article shall not apply to such dues and taxes if, under the laws and regulations of the receiving State, they are payable by the person who contracted with the sending State.
Art. 61. Inviolability of consular archives and documents. The consular archives and documents of a consular post headed by an honorary consular officer shall be inviolable at all times and wherever they may be, provided that they are kept separate from other papers and documents and, in particular, from the private correspondence of the head of a consular post and of any person working with him, and from the materials, books or documents relating to their profession or trade.
Art. 62. Exemption from customs duties.
The receiving State shall, in accordance with such laws and regulations as it may adopt, permit entry of, and grant exemption from all customs duties, taxes, and related charges other than charges for storage, cartage and similar services on the following articles, provided that they are for the official use of a consular post headed by an honorary consular officer: coats-of-arms, flags, signboards, seals and stamps, books, official printed matter, office furniture, office equipment and similar articles supplied by or at the instance of the sending State to the consular post.
Art. 63. Criminal proceedings.
If criminal proceedings are instituted against an honorary consular officer, he must appear before the competent authorities. Nevertheless, the proceedings shall be conducted with the respect due to him by reason of his official position and, except when he is under arrest or detention, in a manner which will hamper the exercise of consular functions as little as possible. When it has become necessary to detain an honorary consular officer, the proceedings against him shall be instituted with the minimum of delay.
Art. 64. Protection of honorary consular officers.
The receiving State is under a duty to accord to an honorary consular officer such protection as may be required by reason of his official position.
Art. 65. Exemption from registration of aliens and residence permits.
Honorary consular officers, with the exception of those who carry on for personal profit any professional or commercial activity in the receiving State, shall be exempt from all obligations under the laws and regulations of the receiving State in regard to the registration of aliens and residence permits.
Art. 66. Exemption from taxation.
An honorary consular officer shall be exempt from all dues and taxes on the remuneration and emoluments which he receives from the sending State in respect of the exercise of consular functions.
Art. 67. Exemption from personal services and contributions.
The receiving State shall exempt honorary consular officers from all personal services and from all public services of any kind whatsoever and from military obligations such as those connected with requisitioning, military contributions and billeting.
Art. 68. Optional character of the institution of honorary consular officers.
Each State is free to decide whether it will appoint or receive honorary consular officers.
Chapter IV. *General provisions.*
Art. 69. Consular agents who are not heads of consular posts.
(1) Each State is free to decide whether it will establish or admit consular agencies conducted by consular agents not designated as heads of consular post by the sending State.
(2) The conditions under which the consular agencies referred to in paragraph 1 of this Article may carry on their activities and the privileges and immunities which may be enjoyed by the consular agents in charge of them shall be determined by agreement between the sending State and the receiving State.
Art. 70. Exercise of consular functions by diplomatic missions.
(1) The provisions of the present Convention apply also, so far as the context permits, to the exercise of consular functions by a diplomatic mission.
(2) The names of members of a diplomatic mission assigned to the consular section or otherwise charged with the exercise of the consular functions of the mission shall be notified to the Ministry for Foreign Affairs of the receiving State or to the authority designated by that Ministry.
(3) In the exercise of consular functions a diplomatic mission may address:
(a) the local authorities of the consular district;
(b) the central authorities of the receiving State if this is allowed by the laws, regulations and usages of the receiving State or by relevant international agreements.
(4) The privileges and immunities of the members of a diplomatic mission referred to in paragraph 2 of this Article shall continue to be governed by the rules of international law concerning diplomatic relations.
Art. 71. Nationals or permanent residents of the receiving State.
(1) Except in so far as additional facilities, privileges and immunities may be granted by the receiving State, consular officers who are nationals of or permanently resident in the receiving State shall enjoy only immunity from jurisdiction and personal inviolability in respect of official acts performed in the exercise of their functions, and the privilege provided in paragraph 3 of Article 44. So far as these consular officers are concerned, the receiving State shall likewise be bound by the obligation laid down in Article 42. If criminal proceedings are instituted against such a consular officer, the proceedings shall, except when he is under arrest or detention, be conducted in a manner which will hamper the exercise of consular functions as little as possible.
(2) Other members of the consular post who are nationals of or permanently resident in the receiving State and members of their families, as well as members of the families of consular officers referred to in paragraph 1 of this Article, shall enjoy facilities, privileges and immunities only in so far as these are granted to them by the receiving State. Those members of the families of members of the consular post and those members of the private staff who are themselves nationals of or permanently resident in the receiving State shall likewise enjoy facilities, privileges and immunities only in so far as these are granted to them by the receiving State. The receiving State shall, however, exercise its jurisdiction over those persons in such a way as not to hinder unduly the performance of the functions of the consular post.
Art. 72. Non-discrimination.
(1) In the application of the provisions of the present Convention the receiving State shall not discriminate as between States.
(2) However, discrimination shall not be regarded as taking place:
(a) where the receiving State applies any of the provisions of the present Convention restrictively because of a restrictive application of that provision to its consular posts in the sending State;
(b) where by custom or agreement States extend to each other more favourable treatment than is required by the provisions of the present Convention.
Art. 73. Relationship between the present Convention and other international agreements.
(1) The provisions of the present Convention shall not affect other international agreements in force as between States parties to them.
(2) Nothing in the present Convention shall preclude States from concluding international agreements confirming or supplementing or extending or amplifying the provisions thereof.
Chapter V. *Final provisions.*
Art. 74. Signature.
The present Convention shall be open for signature by all States Members of the United Nations or of any of the specialized agencies or Parties to the Statute of the International Court of Justice, and by any other State invited by the General Assembly of the United Nations to become a Party to the Convention, as follows until 31 October 1963 at the Federal Ministry for Foreign Affairs of the Republic of Austria and subsequently, until 31 March 1964, at the United Nations Headquarters in New York.
Art. 75. Ratification.
The present Convention is subject to ratification. The instruments of ratification shall be deposited with the Secretary-General of the United Nations.
Art. 76. Accession.
The present Convention shall remain open for accession by any State belonging to any of the four categories mentioned in Article 74. The instruments of accession shall be deposited with the Secretary-General of the United Nations.
Art. 77. Entry into force.
(1) The present Convention shall enter into force on the thirtieth day following the date of deposit of the twenty-second instrument of ratification or accession with the Secretary-General of the United Nations.
(2) For each State ratifying or acceding to the Convention after the deposit of the twenty-second instrument of ratification or accession, the Convention shall enter into force on the thirtieth day after deposit by such State of its instrument of ratification or accession.
Art. 78. Notifications by the Secretary-General.
The Secretary-General of the United Nations shall inform all States belonging to any of the four categories mentioned in Article 74:
(a) of signatures to the present Convention and of the deposit of instruments of ratification or accession, in accordance with Articles 74, 75 and 76;

(b) of the date on which the present Convention will enter into force, in accordance with Article 77.
Art. 79. Authentic texts.
The original of the present Convention, of which the Chinese, English, French, Russian and Spanish texts are equally authentic, shall be deposited with the Secretary-General of the United Nations, who shall send certified copies thereof to all States belonging to any of the four categories mentioned in Article 74.
In witness whereof the undersigned Plenipotentiaries, being duly authorized thereto by their respective Governments, have signed the present Convention.
Done at Vienna, this twenty-fourth day of April, one thousand nine hundred and sixty-three."

Optional Protocol to the Vienna Convention concerning Acquisition of Nationality done at Vienna on Apr. 24, 1963. The art. 2 read as follows:

"Members of the consular post not being national of the receiving State, and members of their families forming part of their households, shall not, solely by the operation of the law of the receiving State, acquire the nationality of that State."

Optional Protocol concerning the Compulsory Settlement of Disputes, done at Vienna on Apr. 24, 1963. The art. 1 read as follows:

"Disputes arising out of the interpretation or application of the Convention shall lie within the compulsory jurisdiction of the International Court of Justice and may accordingly be brought before the Court by an application made by any party to the dispute being a Party to the present Protocol."

Both Protocols came into force also on Mar. 19, 1967.

UNTS, Vol. 569, pp. 262–232, 470–472 and 488–490.

VIENNA CONVENTION ON DIPLOMATIC RELATIONS, 1961. Adopted on Apr. 14, 1961 by the UN Conference on Diplomatic Relations and Immunities held at the Neue Hofburg in Vienna Mar. 2–Apr. 14, 1961; approved by UN General Assembly Res. 2350/XXIV; Came into force on Apr. 24, 1964. The text of the Conventions and of two Optional Protocols is as follows:

"The States Parties to the present Convention,
Recalling that peoples of all nations from ancient times have recognized the status of diplomatic agents,
Having in mind the purposes and principles of the Charter of the United Nations concerning the sovereign equality of States, the maintenance of international peace and security, and the promotion of friendly relations among nations,
Believing that an international convention on diplomatic intercourse, privileges and immunities would contribute to the development of friendly relations among nations, irrespective of their differing constitutional and social systems,
Realizing that the purpose of such privileges and immunities is not to benefit individuals but to ensure the efficient performance of the functions of diplomatic missions as representing States,
Affirming that the rules of customary international law should continue to govern questions not expressly regulated by the provisions of the present Convention,
Have agreed as follows:
Art. 1. For the purpose of the present Convention, the following expression shall have the meanings hereunder assigned to them:
(a) the 'head of the mission' is the person charged by the sending State with the duty of acting in that capacity;
(b) the 'members of the mission' are the head of the mission and the members of the staff of the mission;
(c) the 'members of the staff of the mission' are the members of the diplomatic staff, of the administrative and technical staff and of the service of the mission;
(d) the 'members of the diplomatic staff' are the members of the staff of the mission having diplomatic rank;
(e) a 'diplomatic agent' is the head of the mission or a member of the diplomatic staff of the mission;
(f) the 'members of the administrative and technical staff' are the members of the staff of the mission employed in the administrative and technical service of the mission;
(g) the 'members of the service staff' are the members of the staff of the mission in the domestic service of the mission;
(h) a 'private servant' is a person who is in the domestic service of a member of the mission and who is not an employee of the sending State;
(i) the 'premises of the mission' are the buildings or parts of buildings and the land ancillary thereto, irrespective of ownership, used for the purpose of the mission including the residence of the head of the mission.
Art. 2. The establishment of diplomatic relations between States, and of permanent diplomatic missions, takes place by mutual consent.
Art. 3.(1) The functions of a diplomatic mission consist inter alia in:
(a) representing the sending State in the receiving State;
(b) protecting in the receiving State the interests of the sending State and of its nationals, within the limits permitted by international law;
(c) negotiating with the Government of the receiving State;
(d) ascertaining by all lawful means conditions and developments in the receiving State, and reporting thereon to the Government of the sending State;
(e) promoting friendly relations between the sending State and the receiving State, and developing their economic, cultural and scientific relations.
(2) Nothing in the present Convention shall be construed as preventing the performance of consular functions by a diplomatic mission.
Art. 4.(1) The sending State must certain that the agrément of the receiving State has been given for the person it proposes to accredit as head of the mission to that State.
(2) The receiving State is not obliged to give reasons to the sending State for a refusal of agrément.
Art. 5.(1) The sending State may, after it has given due notification to the receiving States concerned, accredit a head of mission or assign any member of the diplomatic staff, as the case may be, to more than one State, unless there is express objection by any of the receiving States.
(2) If the sending State accredits a head of mission to one or more other States it may establish a diplomatic mission headed by a chargé d'affaires ad interim in each State where the head of mission has not his permanent seat.
(3) A head of mission or any member of the diplomatic staff of the mission may act as representative of the sending State to any international organization.
Art. 6. Two or more States may accredit the same person as head of mission to another State, unless objection is offered by the receiving State.
Art. 7. Subject to the provisions of Art. 5, 8, 9 and 11, the sending State may freely appoint the members of the staff of the mission. In the case of military naval or air attachés, the receiving State may require their names to be submitted beforehand, for its approval.
Art. 8.(1) Members of the diplomatic staff of the mission should in principle be of the nationality of the sending State.
(2) Members of the diplomatic staff of the mission may not be appointed from among persons having the nationality of the receiving State, except with the consent of that State which may be withdrawn at any time.
(3) The receiving State may reserve the same right with regard to nationals of a third State who are not also nationals of the sending State.
Art. 9.(1) The receiving State may at any time and without having to explain its decision, notify the sending State that the head of the mission or any member of the diplomatic staff of the mission is persona non grata or that any other member of the staff of the mission is not acceptable. In any such case, the sending State shall, as appropriate, either recall the person concerned or terminate his functions with the mission. A person may be declared non grata or not acceptable before arriving in the territory of the receiving State.
(2) If the sending State refuses or fails within a reasonable period to carry out its obligations under paragraph 1 of this Article, the receiving State may refuse to recognise the person concerned as a member of the mission.
Art. 10.(1) The Ministry for Foreign Affairs of the receiving State, or such other ministry as may be agreed, shall be notified of:
(a) the appointment of members of the mission, their arrival and their final departure or the termination of their function with the mission;
(b) the arrival and final departure of a person belonging to the family of a member of the mission and, where appropriate, the fact that a person becomes or ceases to be a member of the family of a member of the mission;
(c) the arrival and final departure of private servants in the employ of persons referred to in sub-paragraph (a) of this paragraph and, where appropriate, the fact that they are leaving the employ of such persons;
(d) the engagement and discharge of persons resident in the receiving State as members of the mission or private servants entitled to privileges and immunities.
(2) Where possible, prior notification of arrival and final departure shall also be given.
Art. 11.(1) In the absence of specific agreement as to size of the mission, the receiving State may require that the size of a mission be kept within limits considered by it to be reasonable and normal, having regard to circumstances and conditions in the receiving State and to the needs of the particular mission.
(2) The receiving State may equally, within similar bounds and on a non-discriminatory basis, refuse to accept officials of a particular category.
Art. 12. The sending State may not, without the prior express consent of the receiving State, establish offices forming part of the mission in localities other than those in which the mission itself is established.
Art. 13.(1) The head of the mission is considered as having taken up his functions in the receiving State either when he has presented his credentials or when he has notified his arrival and a true copy of his credentials has been presented to the Ministry for Foreign Affairs of the receiving State, or such other ministry as may be agreed, in accordance with the practice prevailing in the receiving State which shall be applied in a uniform manner.
(2) The order of presentation of credentials or of a true copy thereof will be determined by the date and time of the arrival of the head of the mission.
Art. 14.(1) Heads of mission are divided into three classes, namely:
(a) that of ambassadors or nuncios accredited to Heads of State, and other heads of mission of equivalent rank;
(b) that of envoys, ministers and internuncios accredited to Heads of State;
(c) that of chargés d'affaires accredited to Ministers for Foreign Affairs.
(2) Except as concerns precedence and etiquette, there shall be no differentiation between heads of mission by reason of their class.
Art. 15. The class to which the heads of their missions are to be assigned shall be agreed between States.
Art. 16.(1) Heads of mission shall take precedence in their respective classes in the order of the date and time of taking up their functions in accordance with Art. 13.
(2) Alterations in the credentials of a head of mission not involving any change of class shall not affect his precedence.
(3) This article is without prejudice to any practice accepted by the receiving State regarding the precedence of the representative of the Holy See.
Art. 17. The precedence of the members of the diplomatic staff of the missions shall be notified by the head of the mission to the Ministry for Foreign Affairs or such other ministry as may be agreed.
Art. 18. The procedure to be observed in each State for the reception of heads of mission shall be uniform in respect of each class.
Art. 19.(1) If the post of head of the mission is vacant, or if the head of the mission is unable to perform his functions a chargé d'affaires ad interim shall act provisionally as head of the mission. The name of the chargé d'affaires ad interim shall be notified, either by the head of the mission or, in case he is unable to do so, by the Ministry for Foreign Affairs of the sending State to the Ministry for Foreign Affairs of the receiving State or such other ministry as may agreed.
(2) In cases where no member of the diplomatic staff of the mission is present in the receiving State, a member of the administrative and technical staff may, with the consent of the receiving State, be designated by the sending State to be in charge of the current administrative affairs of the mission.

Art. 20. The mission and its head shall have the right to use the flag and emblem of the sending State on the premises of the mission, including the residence of the head of the mission, and on his means of transport.

Art. 21.(1) The receiving State shall either facilitate the acquisition on its territory, in accordance with its laws, by the sending State of premises necessary for its mission or assist the latter in obtaining accommodation in some other way.

(2) It shall also, where necessary, assist missions in obtaining suitable accommodation for their members.

Art. 22.(1) The premises of the mission shall be inviolable. The agents of the receiving State may not enter them except with the consent of the head of the mission.

(2) The receiving State is under a special duty to take all appropriate steps to protect the premises of the mission against any intrusion or damage and to prevent any disturbance of the peace of the mission or impairment of its dignity.

(3) The premises of the mission, their furnishings and other property thereon and the means of transport of the mission shall be immune from search, requisition, attachment or execution.

Art. 23.(1) The sending State and the head of the mission shall be exempt from all national, regional or municipal dues and taxes in respect of the premises of the mission, whether owned or leased, other than such as represent payment for specific services rendered.

(2) The exemption from taxation referred to in this Article shall not apply to such dues and taxes payable under the law of the receiving State by persons contracting with the sending State or the head of the mission.

Art. 24. The archives and documents of the mission shall be inviolable at any time and wherever they may be.

Art. 25. The receiving State shall accord full facilities for the performance of the functions of the mission.

Art. 26. Subject to its laws and regulations concerning zones entry into which is prohibited or regulated for reasons of national security, the receiving State shall ensure to all members of the mission freedom of movement and travel in its territory.

Art. 27.(1) The receiving State shall permit and protect free communication on the part of the mission for all official purposes. In communicating with the Government and the other missions and consulates of the sending State, wherever situated, the mission may employ all appropriate means, including diplomatic couriers and messages in code or cipher. However, the mission may install and use a wireless transmitter only with the consent of the receiving State.

(2) The official correspondence of the mission shall be inviolable. Official correspondence means all correspondence relating to the mission and its functions.

(3) The diplomatic bag shall not be opened or detained.

(4) The packages constituting the diplomatic bag must bear visible external marks of their character and may contain only diplomatic documents or articles intended for official use.

(5) The diplomatic courier, who shall be provided with an official document indicating his status and the number of packages constituting the diplomatic bag, shall be protected by the receiving State in the performance of his functions. He shall enjoy personal inviolability and shall not be liable to any form of arrest or detention.

(6) The sending State or the mission may designate diplomatic couriers ad hoc. In such cases the provisions of paragraph 5 of this Article shall also apply, except that the immunities therein mentioned shall cease to apply when such a courier has delivered to the consignee the diplomatic bag in his charge.

(7) A diplomatic bag may be entrusted to the captain of a commercial aircraft scheduled to land at an authorized port of entry. He shall be provided with an official document indicating the number of packages constituting the bag but he shall not be considered to be a diplomatic courier. The mission may send one of its members to take possession of the diplomatic bag directly and freely from the captain of the aircraft.

Art. 28. The fees and charges levied by the mission in the course of its official duties shall be exempt from all dues and taxes.

Art. 29. The person of a diplomatic agent shall be inviolable. He shall not be liable to any form of arrest or detention. The receiving State shall treat him with due respect and shall take all appropriate steps to prevent any attack on his person, freedom or dignity.

Art. 30.(1) The private residence of a diplomatic agent shall enjoy the same inviolability and protection as the premises of the mission.

(2) His papers, correspondence and, except as provided in paragraph 3 of Article 31, his property, shall likewise enjoy inviolability.

Art. 31.(1) A diplomatic agent shall enjoy immunity from the criminal jurisdiction of receiving State. He shall also enjoy immunity from its civil and administrative jurisdiction, except in the case of:

(a) a real action relating to private immovable property situated in the territory of the receiving State, unless he holds it on behalf of the sending State for the purposes of the mission;

(b) an action relating to succession in which the diplomatic agent is involved as executor, administrator, heir or legate as a private person and not on behalf of the sending State;

(c) an action relating to any professional or commercial activity exercised by the diplomatic agent in the receiving State outside his official functions.

(2) A diplomatic agent is not obliged to give evidence as a witness.

(3) No measures of execution may be taken in respect of a diplomatic agent except in the cases coming under sub-paragraphs (a), (b) and (c) of paragraph 1 of this Article, and provided that the measures concerned can be taken without infringing the inviolability of his person or of his residence.

(4) The immunity of a diplomatic agent from the jurisdiction of the receiving State does not exempt him from the jurisdiction of the sending State.

Art. 32.(1) The immunity from jurisdiction of diplomatic agents and of persons enjoying immunity under Article 37 may be waived by the sending State.

(2) Waiver must always be express.

(3) The initiation of proceedings by a diplomatic agent or by a person enjoying immunity from jurisdiction under Article 37 shall preclude him from invoking immunity from jurisdiction in respect of any counter-claim directly connected with the principal claim.

(4) Waiver of immunity from jurisdiction in respect of civil or administrative proceedings shall not be held to imply waiver of immunity in respect of the execution of the judgment, for which a separate waiver shall be necessary.

Art. 33.(1) Subject to the provisions of paragraph 3 of this Article, a diplomatic agent shall with respect to services rendered for the sending State be exempt from social security provisions which may be in force in the receiving State.

(2) The exemption provided for in paragraph 1 of this Article shall also apply to private servants who are in the sole employ of a diplomatic agent, on condition:

(a) that they are not nationals of or permanently resident in the receiving State; and

(b) that they are covered by the social security provisions which may be in force in the sending State or a third State.

(3) A diplomatic agent who employs persons to whom the exemption provided for in paragraph 2 of this Article does not apply shall observe the obligations which the social security provisions of the receiving State impose upon employers.

(4) The exemption provided for in paragraph 1 and 2 of this Article shall not preclude voluntary participation in the social security system of the receiving State provided that such participation is permitted by that State.

(5) The provisions of this Article shall not affect bilateral or multilateral agreements concerning social security concluded previously and shall not prevent the conclusion of such agreements in the future.

Art. 34. A diplomatic agent shall be exempt from all dues and taxes, personal or real, national, regional or municipal, except;

(a) indirect taxes of a kind which are normally incorporated in the price of goods or services;

(b) dues and taxes on private immovable property situated in the territory of the receiving State, unless he holds it on behalf of the sending State for the purposes of the mission;

(c) estate, succession or inheritance duties levied by the receiving State, subject to the provisions of paragraph 4 of Article 39;

(d) dues and taxes on private income having its source in the receiving State and capital taxes on investments made in commercial undertakings in the receiving State;

(e) charges levied for specific services rendered;

(f) registration, court or record fees, mortgage dues and stamp duty, with respect to immovable property, subject to the provisions of Article 23.

Art. 35. The receiving State shall exempt diplomatic agents from all personal services, from all public service of any kind whatsoever, and from military obligations such as those connected with requisitioning, military contributions and billeting.

Art. 36.(1) The receiving State shall, in accordance with such laws and regulations as it may adopt, permit entry of and grant exemption from all customs duties taxes, and related charges other than charges for storage, cartage and similar services, on:

(a) articles for the official use of the mission;

(b) articles for the personal use of a diplomatic agent or members of his family forming part of his household, including articles intended for his establishment.

(2) The personal baggage of a diplomatic agent shall be exempt from inspection, unless there are serious grounds for presuming that it contains articles not covered by the exemptions mentioned in paragraph 1 of this Article, or articles the import or export of which is prohibited by the law or controlled by the quarantine regulations of the receiving State. Such inspection shall be conducted only in the presence of the diplomatic agent or of his authorized representative.

Art. 37.(1) The members of the family of a diplomatic agent forming part of his household shall, if they are not nationals of the receiving State, enjoy the privileges and immunities specified in Articles 29 to 36.

(2) Members of the administrative and technical staff of the mission, together with members of their families forming part of their respective households, shall, if they are not nationals of or permanently resident in the receiving State, enjoy the privileges and immunities specified in Articles 29 to 35, except that the immunity from civil and administrative jurisdiction of the receiving State specified in paragraph 1 of Article 31 shall not extend to acts performed outside the course of their duties. They shall also enjoy the privileges specified in Article 36, paragraph 1, in respect of articles imported at the time of first installation.

(3) Members of the service staff of the mission who are not nationals of or permanently resident in the service State shall enjoy immunity in respect of acts performed in the course of their duties, exemption from dues and taxes on the emoluments they receive by reason of their employment and the exemption contained in Article 33.

(4) Private servants of members of the mission shall, if they are not nationals of or permanently resident in the receiving State, be exempt from dues and taxes on the emoluments they receive by reason of their employment. In other respects, they may enjoy privileges and immunities only to the extent admitted by the receiving State. However, the receiving State must exercise its jurisdiction over those persons in such a manner as not to interfere unduly with the performance of the functions of the mission.

Art. 38.(1) Except insofar as additional privileges and immunities may be granted by the receiving State, a diplomatic agent who is a national of or permanently resident in that State shall enjoy immunity from jurisdiction, and inviolability, in respect of official acts performed in the exercise of his functions.

(2) Other members of the staff of the mission and private servants who are nationals of or permanently resident in the receiving State shall enjoy privileges and immunities only to the extent admitted by the receiving State. However the receiving State must exercise its jurisdiction over those persons in such a manner as not to interfere unduly with performance of the function of the mission.

Art. 39.(1) Every person entitled to privileges and immunities shall enjoy them from the moment he enters the territory of the receiving State on proceeding to take up his post or, if already in its territory, from the moment when his appointment is notified to the Ministry of Foreign Affairs or such other ministry as may be agreed.

(2) When the functions of a person enjoying privileges and immunities have come to an end, such privileges and immunities shall normally cease at the moment when he leaves the country, or on expiry of a reasonable period in which to do so, but shall subsist until that time, even in case of armed conflict. However, with

respect to acts performed by such a person in the exercise of his functions as a member of the mission, immunity shall continue to subsist.
(3) In case of the death of a member of the mission, the members of his family shall continue to enjoy the privileges and immunities to which they are entitled until the expiry of a reasonable period in which to leave the country.
(4) In the event of the death of a member of the mission not a national of or permanently resident in the receiving State or a member of his family forming part of his household, the receiving State shall permit the withdrawal of the movable property of the deceased, with the exception of any property acquired in the country of the export of which was prohibited at the time of his death. Estate, succession and inheritance duties shall not be levied on movable property the presence of which in the receiving State was due solely to the presence there of the deceased as a member of the mission or as a member of the family of a member of the mission.
Art. 40.(1) If a diplomatic agent passes through or is in the territory of a third State, which has granted him a passport visa if such visa was necessary, while proceeding to take up or to return to his post, or when returning to his own country, the third State shall accord him inviolability and such other immunities as may be required to ensure his transit or return. The same shall apply in the case of any members of his family enjoying privileges or immunities who are accompanying the diplomatic agent, or travelling separately to join him or to return to their country.
(2) In circumstances similar to those specifed in paragraph 1 of this Article, third States shall not hinder the passage of members of the administrative and technical or service staff of a mission, and of members of their families, through their territories.
(3) Third States shall accord to official correspondence and other official communications in transit, including messages in code or cipher, the same freedom and protection as is accorded by the receiving State. They shall accord to diplomatic couriers, who have been granted a passport visa if such visa was necessary, and diplomatic bags in transit the same inviolability and protection as the receiving State is bound to accord.
(4) The obligations of third States under paragraphs 1, 2 and 3 of this Article shall also apply to the persons mentioned respectively in those paragraphs, and to official communications and diplomatic bags, whose presence in the territory of the third State is due to force majeure.
Art. 41.(1) Without prejudice to their privileges and immunities, it is the duty of all persons enjoying such privileges and immunities to respect the laws and regulations of the receiving State. They also have a duty not to interfere in the internal affairs of that State.
(2) All official business with the receiving State entrusted to the mission by sending State shall be conducted with or through the Ministry for Foreign Affairs of the receiving State or such other ministry as may be agreed.
(3) The premises of the mission must not be used in any manner incompatible with the functions of the mission as laid down in the present Convention or by other rules of general international law or by any special agreements in force between the sending and receiving State.
Art. 42. A diplomatic agent shall not in the receiving State practise for personal profit any professional or commercial activity.
Art. 43. The function of a diplomatic agent comes to an end, inter alia:
(1) on notification by the sending State to the receiving State that the function of the diplomatic agent has come to an end;
(b) on notification by the receiving State to the sending State that, in accordance with paragraph 2 of Article 9, it refuses to recognize the diplomatic agent as a member of the mission.
Art. 44. The receiving State must, even in case of armed conflict, grant facilities in order to enable persons enjoying privileges and immunities, other than nationals of the receiving State, and members of the families of such persons irrespective of their nationality, to leave at the earliest possible moment. It must, in particular, in case of need, place at their disposal the necessary means of transport for themselves and their property.
Art. 45. If diplomatic relations are broken off between two States, or if a mission is permanently or temporarily recalled:
(a) the receiving State must, even in case of armed conflict, respect and protect the premises of the mission, together with its property and archives;
(b) the sending State may entrust the custody of the premises of the mission, together with its property and archives, to a third State acceptable to the receiving State;
(c) the sending State may entrust the protection of its interests and those of its nationals to a third State acceptable to the receiving State.
Art. 46. A sending State may with the prior consent of a receiving State, and at the request of a third State not represented in the receiving State, undertake the temporary protection of the interests of the third State and of its nationals.
Art. 47.(1) In the application of the provisions of the present Convention, the receiving State shall not discriminate as between States.
(2) However, discrimination shall not be regarded as taking place:
(a) where the receiving State applies any of the provisions of the present Convention restrictively because of a restrictive application of that provision to its mission in the sending State;
(b) where by custom or agreement States extend to each other more favourable treatment than is required by the provisions of the present Convention.
Art. 48. The present Convention shall be open for signature by all States Members of the United Nations or of any of the specialized agencies or Parties to the Statute of the International Court of Justice, and by any other State invited by the General Assembly of the United Nations to become a Party to the Convention, as follows: until 31 October 1961 at the Federal Ministry for Foreign Affairs of Austria and subsequently, until 31 March 1962, at the United Nations Headquarters in New York.
Art. 49. The present Convention is subject to ratification. The instruments of ratification shall be deposited with the Secretary-General of the United Nations.
Art. 50. The present Convention shall remain open for accession by any State belonging to any of the four categories mentioned in Article 48. The instruments of accession shall be deposited with the Secretary-General of the United Nations.
Art. 51.(1) The present Convention shall enter into force on the thirtieth day following the date of deposit of the twenty-second instrument of ratification or accession with the Secretary-General of the United Nations.
(2) For each State ratifying or acceding to the Convention after the deposit of the twenty-second instrument of ratification or accession, the Convention shall enter into force on the thirtieth day after deposit by such State of its instrument of ratification or accession.
Art. 52. The Secretary-General of the United Nations shall inform all States belonging to any of the four categories mentioned in Article 48:
(a) of signatures to the present Convention and of the deposit of instruments of ratification or accession, in accordance with Articles 48, 49 and 50;
(b) of the date on which the present Convention will enter into force, in accordance with Article 51.
Art. 53. The original of the present Convention, of which the Chinese, English, French, Russian and Spanish texts are equally authentic, shall be deposited with the Secretary-General of the United Nations, who shall send certified copies thereof to all States belonging to any of the four categories mentioned in Article 48.
In witness whereof the undersigned Plenipotentiaries, being duly authorized thereto by their respective Governments, have signed the present Convention.
Done at Vienna, this eighteenth day of April one thousand nine hundred and sixty-one."

Optional Protocol concerning acquisition of nationality, done at Vienna, on April 18, 1961, read as follows:

"The States Parties to the present Protocol and to the Vienna Convention on Diplomatic Relations, hereinafter referred to as 'the Convention', adopted by the United Nations Conference held at Vienna from 2 March to 14 April 1961,
Expressing their wish to establish rules between them concerning acquisition of nationality by the members of their diplomatic missions and of the families forming part of the household of those members,
Have agreed as follows:
Art. I. For the purpose of the present Protocol, the expression 'members of the mission' shall have the meaning assigned to in Article 1, sub-paragraph (b), of the Convention, namely 'the head of the mission and the members of the staff of the mission'.
Art. II. Members of the mission not being nationals of the receiving State, and members of their families forming part of their household, shall not, solely by the operation of the law of the receiving State, acquire the nationality of that State.
Art. III. The present Protocol shall be open for signature by all States which may become Parties to the Convention, as follows: until 31 October 1961 at the Federal Ministry for Foreign Affairs of Austria and subsequently, until 31 March 1962, at the United Nations Headquarters in New York.
Art. IV. The present Protocol is subject to ratification. The instruments of ratification shall be deposited with the Secretary-General of the United Nations.
Art. V. The present Protocol shall remain open for accession by all States which may become Parties to the Convention. The instruments of accession shall be deposited with the Secretary-General of the United Nations.
Art. VI.(1) The present Protocol shall enter into force on the same day as the Convention or on the thirtieth day following the date of deposit of the second instrument of ratification or accession to the Protocol with the Secretary-General of the United Nations, whichever date is the later.
(2) For each State ratifying or acceding to the present Protocol after its entry into force in accordance with paragraph 1 of this Article, the Protocol shall enter into force on the thirtieth day after deposit by such State of its instrument of ratification or accession.
Art. VII. The Secretary-General of the United Nations shall inform all States which may become Parties to the Convention:
(a) of signatory to the present Protocol and of the deposit of instruments of ratification or accession, in accordance with Articles III, IV and V;
(b) of the date on which the present Protocol will enter into force, in accordance with Article VI."

Optional Protocol concerning the Compulsory Settlement of Disputes, done at Vienna, on Apr. 18, 1961 read as follows:

"The States Parties to the present Protocol and to the Vienna Convention on Diplomatic Relations, hereinafter referred to as 'The Convention', adopted by the United Nations Conference held at Vienna from 2 March to 14 April 1961,
Expressing their wish to resort in all matters concerning them in respect of any dispute arising out of the interpretation or application of the Convention to the Compulsory jurisdiction of the International Court of Justice, unless some other form of settlement has been agreed upon by the parties within a reasonable period,
Have agreed as follows:
Art. I. Disputes arising out of the interpretation or application of the Convention shall lie within the compulsory jurisdiction of the International Court of Justice and may accordingly be brought before the Court by an application made by any party to the dispute being a Party to the present Protocol.
Art. II. The parties may agree, within a period of two months after one party has notified its opinion to the other that a dispute exists, to resort not to the International Court of Justice but on an arbitral tribunal. After the expiry of the said period, either party may bring the dispute before the Court by an application.
Art. III.(1) Within the same period of two months, the parties may agree to adopt a conciliation procedure before resorting to the International Court of Justice.
(2) The conciliation commission shall make its recommendations within five months after its appointment. If its recommendations are not accepted by the parties to the dispute within two months after they have been delivered, either party may bring the dispute before the Court by an application.
Art. IV. States Parties to the Convention, to the Optional Protocol concerning Acquisition of Nationality, and to the present Protocol may at any time declare that

they will extend the provisions of the present Protocol to disputes arising out of the interpretation or application of the Optional Protocol concerning Acquisition of Nationality. Such declarations shall be notified to the Secretary-General of the United Nations.

Art. V. The present Protocol shall be open for signature by all States which may become Parties to the Convention, as follows: until 31 October 1961 at the Federal Ministry for Foreign Affairs of Austria and subsequently, until 31 March 1962, at the United Nations Headquarters in New York.

The present Protocol is subject to ratification. The instruments of ratification shall be deposited with the Secretary-General of the United Nations.

Art. VII. The present Protocol shall remain open for accession by all States which may become Parties to the Convention. The instruments of accession shall be deposited with the Secretary-General of the United Nations.

Art. VIII.(1) The present Protocol shall enter into force on the same day as the Convention or on the thirtieth day following the date of deposit of the second instrument of ratification or accession to the Protocol with the Secretary-General of the United Nations, whichever day is the later.

(2) For each State ratifying or acceding to the present Protocol after its entry into force in accordance with paragraph 1 of this Article, the Protocol shall enter into force on the thirtieth day after deposit by such State of its instrument of ratification or accession.

Art. IX. The Secretary-General of the United Nations shall inform all States which become Parties to the Convention:

(a) of signatures to the present Protocol and of the deposit of instruments of ratification or accession, in accordance with Articles V, VI and VII;

(b) of declarations made in accordance with Article IV of the present Protocol;

(c) of the date on which the present Protocol will enter into force, in accordance with Article VIII."

UNTS, Vol. 500, pp. 96–126, 224–226, 242–246.

VIENNA CONVENTION ON SUCCESSION OF STATES IN RESPECT OF TREATIES, 1978.

Adopted on Aug. 23, 1978 by the UN Conference July 31–Aug. 23, 1978 at Vienna, convened by the UN General Assembly 3496/XXX of Dec. 15, 1975 and Res. 31/18 of Nov. 24, 1976. The text of the Convention read as follows:

"The States Parties to the present Convention,

Considering the profound transformation of the international community brought about by the decolonization process,

Considering also that other factors may lead to cases of succession of States in the future,

Convinced, in these circumstances, of the need for the codification and progressive development of the rules relating to succession of States in respect of treaties as a means for ensuring greater juridical security in international relations,

Noting that the principles of free consent, good faith and pacta sunt servanda are universally recognized,

Emphasizing that the consistent observance of general multilateral treaties which deal with the codification and progressive development of international law and those the object and purpose of which are of interest to the international community as a whole is of special importance for the strengthening of peace and international co-operation,

Having in mind the principles of international law embodied in the Charter of the United Nations, such as the principles of the equal rights and self-determination of peoples, of the sovereign equality and independence of all States, of non-interference in the domestic affairs of States, of the prohibition of the threat or use of force, and of universal respect for, and observance of, human rights and fundamental freedoms for all,

Recalling that respect for the territorial integrity and political independence of any State is required by the Charter of the United Nations,

Bearing in mind the provisions of the Vienna Convention on the Law of Treaties of 1969,

Bearing also in mind art. 73 of that Convention,

Affirming that questions of the law of treaties other than those that may arise from a succession of States are governed by the relevant rules of international law, including those rules of customary international law which are embodied in the Vienna Convention on the Law of Treaties of 1969,

Affirming that the rules of customary international law will continue to govern questions not regulated by the provisions of the present Convention,

Have agreed as follows:

Part I. *General Provisions*

Art. 1. Scope of the present Convention. The present Convention applies to the effects of a succession of States in respect of treaties between States.

Art. 2. Use of terms. (1) For the purposes of the present Convention:

(a) 'treaty' means an international agreement concluded between States in written form and governed by international law, whether embodied in a single instrument or in two or more related instruments and whatever its particular designation;

(b) 'succession of States' means the replacement of one State by another in the responsibility for the international relations of territory;

(c) 'predecessor State' means the State which has been replaced by another State on the occurrence of a succession of States;

(d) 'successor State' means the State which has replaced another State on the occurrence of a succession of States;

(e) 'date of the succession of States' means the date upon which the successor State replaced the predecessor State in the responsibility for the international relations of the territory to which the succession of States relates;

(f) 'newly independent State' means a successor State the territory of which immediately before the date of the succession of States was a dependent territory for the international relations of which the predecessor State was responsible;

(g) 'notification of succession' means in relation to a multilateral treaty any notification, however phrased or named, made by a successor State expressing its consent to be considered as bound by the treaty;

(h) 'full powers' means in relation to a notification of succession or any other notification under the present Convention a document emanating from the competent authority of a State designating a person or persons to represent the State for communicating the notification of succession or, as the case may be, the notification;

(i) 'ratification', 'acceptance' and 'approval' mean in each case the international act so named whereby a State establishes on the international plane its consent to be bound by a treaty;

(j) 'reservation' means a unilateral statement, however phrased or named, made by a State when signing, ratifying, accepting, approving and acceding to a treaty or when making a notification of succession to a treaty, whereby it purports to exclude or to modify the legal effect of certain provisions of the treaty in their application to that State;

(k) 'contracting State' means a State which has consented to be bound by the treaty, whether or not the treaty has entered into force;

(l) 'party' means a State which has consented to be bound by the treaty and for which the treaty is in force;

(m) 'other State party' means in relation to a successor State any party, other than the predecessor State, to a treaty in force at the date of a succession of States in respect of the territory to which that succession of States relates;

(n) 'international organization' means an intergovernmental organization.

(2) The provisions of paragraph 1 regarding the use of terms in the present Convention are without prejudice to the use of those terms or to the meanings which may be given to them in the internal law of any State.

Art. 3. Cases not within the scope of the present Convention. The fact that the present Convention does not apply to the effects of a succession of States in respect of international agreements concluded between States and other subjects of international law or in respect of international agreements not in written form shall not affect:

(a) the application to such cases of any of the rules set forth in the present Convention to which they are subject under international law independently of the Convention;

(b) the application as between States of the present Convention to the effects of a succession of States in respect of international agreements to which other subjects of international law are also parties.

Art. 4. Treaties constituting international organizations and treaties adopted within an international organization. The present Convention applies to the effects of a succession of States in respect of:

(a) any treaty which is the constituent instrument of an international organization without prejudice to the rules concerning acquisition of membership and without prejudice to any other relevant rules of the organization;

(b) any treaty adopted within an international organization without prejudice to any relevant rules of the organization.

Art. 5. Obligations imposed by international law independently of a treaty. The fact that a treaty is not considered to be in force in respect of a State by virtue of the application of the present Convention shall not in any way impair the duty of that State to fulfil any obligation embodied in the treaty to which it is subject under international law independently of the treaty.

Art. 6. Cases of succession of States covered by the present Convention. The present Convention applies only to the effects of a succession of States occurring in conformity with international law and, in particular, the principles of international law embodied in the Charter of the United Nations.

Art. 7. Temporal application of the present Convention (1) Without prejudice to the application of any of the rules set forth in the present Convention to which the effects of a succession of States would be subject under international law independently of the Convention, the Convention applies only in respect of a succession of States which has occurred after the entry into force of the Convention except as may be otherwise agreed.

(2) A successor State may, at the time of expressing its consent to be bound by the present convention or at any time thereafter, make a declaration that it will apply the provisions of the Convention in respect of its own succession of States which has occurred before the entry into force of the Convention in relation to any other contracting State or State Party to the Convention which makes a declaration accepting the declaration of the successor State. Upon the entry into force of the Convention as between the States making the declarations or upon the making of the declaration of acceptance, whichever occurs later, the provisions of the Convention shall apply to the effects of the succession of States as from the date of that succession of States.

(3) A successor State may at the time of signing or of expressing its consent to be bound by the present Convention make a declaration that it will apply the provisions of the Convention provisionally in respect of its own succession of States which has occurred before the entry into force of the Convention in relation to any other signatory or contracting State which makes a declaration accepting the declaration of the successor State; upon the making of the declaration of acceptance, those provisions shall apply provisionally to the effects of the succession of States as between those two States as from the date of that succession of States.

(4) Any declaration made in accordance with paragraph 2 or 3 shall be contained in a written notification communicated to the depositary, who shall inform the Parties and the States entitled to become Parties to the present Convention of the communication to him of that notification and of its terms.

Art. 8. Agreements for the devolution of treaty obligations or rights from a predecessor State to a successor State

(1) The obligations or rights of a predecessor State under treaties in force in respect of a territory at the date of a succession of States do not become the obligations or rights of the successor State towards other States Parties to those treaties by reason only of the fact that the predecessor State and the successor State have concluded an agreement providing that such obligations or rights shall devolve upon the successor State.

(2) Notwithstanding the conclusion of such an agreement, the effects of a succession of States on treaties which, at the date of that succession of States, were in force in respect of the territory in question are governed by the present Convention.

Art. 9. Unilateral declaration by a successor State regarding treaties of the predecessor State. (1) Obligations or rights under treaties in force in respect of a territory at the date of a succession of States do not become the obligations or rights of the successor State

or of other States parties to those treaties by reason only of the fact that the successor State has made a unilateral declaration providing for the continuance in force of the treaties in respect of its territory.
(2) In such a case, the effects of the succession of States on treaties which, at the date of that succession of States, were in force in respect of the territory in question are governed by the present Convention.
Art. 10. Treaties providing for the participation of a successor State. (1) When a treaty provides that, on the occurrence of a succession of States, a successor State shall have the option to consider itself a party to the treaty, it may notify its succession in respect of the treaty in conformity with the provisions of the treaty or, failing any such provisions, in conformity with the provisions of the present Convention.
(2) If a treaty provides that, on the occurrence of a succession of States, a successor State shall be considered as a party to the treaty, that provision takes effect as such only if the successor State expresses accepts in writing to be so considered.
(3) In cases falling under paragraph 1 or 2, a successor State which establishes its consent to be a party to the treaty is considered as a party from the date of the succession of States unless the treaty otherwise provides or it is otherwise agreed.
Art. 11. Boundary regimes. A succession of States does not as such affect:
(a) a boundary established by a treaty; or
(b) obligations and rights established by a treaty and relating to the regime of a boundary.
Art. 12. Other territorial regimes. (1) A succession of States does not as such affect:
(a) obligations relating to the use of any territory, or to restrictions upon its use, established by a treaty for the benefit of any territory of a foreign State and considered as attaching to the territories in question;
(b) rights established by a treaty for the benefit of any territory and relating to the use, or to restrictions upon the use, of any territory of a foreign State and considered as attaching to the territories in question.
(2) A succession of States does not as such affect:
(a) obligations relating to the use of any territory, or to restrictions upon its use, established by a treaty for the benefit of a group of States or of all States and considered as attaching to that territory;
(b) rights established by a treaty for the benefit of a group of States or of all States and relating to the use of any territory, or to restrictions upon its use, and considered as attaching to that territory.
(3) The provisions of the present article do not apply to treaty obligations of the predecessor State providing for the establishment of foreign military bases on the territory to which the succession of States relates.
Art. 13. The present Convention and permanent sovereignty over natural wealth and resources. Nothing in the present Convention shall affect the principles of international law affirming the permanent sovereignty of every people and every State over its natural wealth and resources.
Art. 14. Questions relating to the validity of a treaty. Nothing in the present Convention shall be considered as prejudging in any respect any question relating to the validity of a treaty.
Part II. *Succession in respect of part of territory.*
Art. 15. Succession in respect of part of territory. When part of the territory of a State, or when any territory for the international relations of which a State is responsible, not being part of the territory of that State, becomes part of the territory of another State;
(a) treaties of the predecessor State cease to be in force in respect of the territory to which the succession of States relates from the date of the succession of States; and
(b) treaties of the successor State are in force in respect of the territory to which the succession of States relates from the date of the succession of States, unless it appears from the treaty or is otherwise established that the application of the treaty to that territory would be incompatible with the object and purpose of the treaty or would radically change the conditions for its operation.
Part III. *Newly independent States.*
Section 1. General rule. Art. 16. Position in respect of the predecessor State. A newly independent State is not bound to maintain in force, or to become a party to, any treaty by reason only of the fact that at the date of the succession of States the treaty was in force in respect of the territory to which the succession of States relates.
Section 2. Multilateral treaties.
Art. 17. Participation in treaties in force at the date of the succession of States. (1) Subject to paragraphs 2 and 3, a newly independent State may, by a notification of succession, establish its status as a party to any multilateral treaty which at the date of the succession of States was in force in respect of the territory to which the succession of States relates.
(2) Paragraph 1 does not apply if it appears from the treaty or is otherwise established that the application of the treaty in respect of the newly independent State would be incompatible with the object and purpose of the treaty or would radically change the conditions for its operation.
(3) When, under the terms of the treaty or by reason of the limited number of the negotiating States and the object and purpose of the treaty, the participation of any other State in the treaty must be considered as requiring the consent of all the parties, the newly independent State may establish its status as a party to the treaty only with such consent.
Art. 18. Participation in treaties not in force at the date of the succession of States. (1) Subject to paragraphs 3 and 4, a newly independent State may, by a notification of succession, establish its status as a contracting State to a multilateral treaty which is not in force if at the date of the succession of States the predecessor State was a contracting State in respect of the territory to which that succession of States relates.
(2) Subject to paragraphs 3 and 4, a newly independent State may, by a notification of succession, establish its status as a party to a multilateral treaty which enters into force after the date of the succession of States if at the date of the succession of States the predecessor State was a contracting State in respect of the territory to which that succession of States relates.
(3) Paragraphs 1 and 2 do not apply if it appears from the treaty or is otherwise established that the application of the treaty in respect of the newly independent State would be incompatible with the object and purpose of the treaty or would radically change the conditions for its operation.
(4) When, under the terms of the treaty or by reason of the limited number of the negotiating States and the object and purpose of the treaty, the participation of any other State in the treaty must be considered as requiring the consent of all the parties or of all the contracting States, the newly independent State may establish its status as a party or as a contracting State to the treaty only with such consent.
(5) When a treaty provides that a specified number of contracting States shall be necessary for its entry into force, a newly independent State which establishes its status as a contracting State to the treaty under paragraph 1 shall be counted as a contracting State for the purpose of that provisions unless a different intention appears from the treaty or is otherwise established.
Art. 19. Participation in treaties signed by the predecessor State subject to ratification, acceptance or approval.
(1) Subject to paragraphs 3 and 4, if before the date of the succession of States the predecessor State signed a multilateral treaty subject to ratification, acceptance or approval and by the signature intended that the treaty should extend to the territory to which the succession of States relates, the newly independent State may ratify, accept or approve the treaty as if it had signed that treaty and may thereby become a party or a contracting State to it.
(2) For the purpose of paragraph 1, unless a different intention appears from the treaty or is otherwise established, the signature by the predecessor State of a Treaty is considered to express the intention that the treaty should extend to the entire territory for the international relations of which the predecessor State was responsible.
(3) Paragraph 1 does not apply if it appears from the treaty or is otherwise established that the application of the treaty in respect of the newly independent State would be incompatible with the object and purpose of the treaty or would radically change the conditions for its operation.
(4) When, under the terms of the treaty or by reason of the limited number of the negotiating States and the object and purpose of the treaty, the participation of any other State in the treaty must be considered as requiring the consent of all the parties or of all the contracting States, the newly independent State may become a party or a contracting State to the treaty only with such consent.
Art. 20. Reservations.(1) When a newly independent State establishes its status as a party or as a contracting State to a multilateral treaty by a notification of succession under article 17 or 18, it shall be considered as maintaining any reservation to that treaty which was applicable at the date of the succession of States in respect of the territory to which the succession of States relates unless, when making the notification of succession, it expresses a contrary intention or formulates a reservation which relates to the same subject-matter as that reservation.
(2) When making a notification of succession establishing its status as a party or as a contracting State to a multilateral treaty under article 17 or 18, a newly independent State may formulate a reservation unless the reservation is one the formulation of which would be excluded by the provisions of sub-paragraph (a), (b) or (c) of article 19 of the Vienna Convention on the Law of Treaties.
(3) When a newly independent State formulates a reservation in conformity wih paragraph 2, the rules set out in articles 20 to 23 of the Vienna Convention on the Law of Treaties apply in respect of that reservation.
Art. 21. Consent to be bound by part of a treaty and choice between differing provisions. (1) When making a notification of succession under article 17 or 18 establishing its status as a party or contracting State to a multilateral treaty, a newly independent State may, if the treaty so permits, express its consent to be bound by part of the treaty or make a choice between differing provisions under the conditions laid down in the treaty for expressing such consent or making such choice.
(2) A newly independent State may also exercise, under the same conditions as the other parties or contracting States, any right provided for in the treaty to withdraw or modify any consent expressed or choice made by itself or by the predecessor State in respect of the territory to which the succession of States relates.
(3) If the newly independent State does not in conformity with paragraph 1 express its consent or make a choice, or in conformity with paragraph 2 withdraw or modify the consent or choice of the predecessor State, it shall be considered as maintaining:
(a) the consent of the predecessor State, in conformity with the treaty, to be bound, in respect of the territory to which the succession of States relates, by part of that treaty; or
(b) the choice of the predecessor State, in conformity with the treaty, between differing provisions in the application of the treaty in respect of the territory to which the succession of States relates.
Art. 22. Notification of succession. (1) A notification of succession in respect of a multilateral treaty under art. 17 or 18 shall be made in writing.
(2) If the notification of succession is not signed by the Head of State, Head of Government or Minister for Foreign Affairs, the representative of the State communicating it may be called upon to produce full powers.
(3) Unless the treaty otherwise provides, the notification of succession shall:
(a) be transmitted by the newly independent State to the depositary, or, if there is no depositary, to the parties or the contracting States;
(b) be considered to be made by the newly independent State on the date on which it is received by the depositary or, if there is no depositary, on the date on which it is received by all the parties or, as the case may be, by all the contracting States.
(4) Paragraph 3 does not affect any duty that the depositary may have, in accordance with the treaty or otherwise, to inform the parties or the contracting States of the notification of succession or any communication made in connection therewith by the newly independent State.
(5) Subject to the provisions of the treaty, the notification of succession or the communication made in connection therewith shall be considered as received by the State for which it is intended only when the latter State has been informed by the depositary.
Art. 23. Effects of a notification of succession. (1) Unless the treaty otherwise provides or it is otherwise agreed, a newly independent State which makes a notification of succession under art. 17 or art. 18,

paragraph 2, shall be considered a party to the treaty from the date of the succession of States or from the date of entry into force of the treaty, whichever is the later date.

(2) Nevertheless, the operation of the treaty shall be considered as suspended as between the newly independent State and the other parties to the treaty until the date of making of the notification of succession except in so far as that treaty may be applied provisionally in accordance with art. 27 or as may be otherwise agreed.

(3) Unless the treaty otherwise provides or it is otherwise agreed, a newly independent State which makes a notification of succession under art. 18, paragraph 1, shall be considered a contracting State to the treaty from the date on which the notification of succession is made.

Section 3. Bilateral treaties. Art. 24. Conditions under which a treaty is considered as being in force in the case of a succession of States. (1) A bilateral treaty which at the date of a succession of States was in force in respect of the territory to which the succession of States relates is considered as being in force between a newly independent State and the other State party when:

(a) they expressly so agree; or

(b) by reason of their conduct they are to be considered as having so agreed.

(2) A treaty considered as being in force under paragraph 1 applies in the relations between the newly independent State and the other State party from the date of the succession of States, unless a different intention appears from their agreement or is otherwise established.

Art. 25. the position as between the predecessor State and the newly independent State. A treaty which under art. 24 is considered as being in force between a newly independent State and the other State party is not by reason only of that fact to be considered as being in force also in the relations between the predecessor State and the newly independent State.

Art. 26. Termination, suspension of operation or amendment of the treaty as between the predecessor State and the other State party. (1) When under art. 24 a treaty is considered as being in force between a newly independent State and the other State party, the treaty:

(a) does not cease to be in force between them by reason only of the fact that it has subsequently been terminated as between the predecessor State and the other State party;

(b) is not suspended in operation as between them by reason only of the fact that it has subsequently been suspended in operation as between the predecessor State and the other State party;

(c) is not amended as between them by reason only of the fact that it has subsequently been amended as between the predecessor State and the other State party.

(2) The fact that a treaty has been terminated or, as the case may be, suspended in operation as between the predecessor State and the other State party after the date of the succession of States does not prevent the treaty from being considered to be in force or, as the case may be, in operation as between the newly independent State and the other State party if it is established in accordance with art. 24 that they so agreed.

(3) The fact that a treaty has been amended as between the predecessor State and the other State party after the date of the succession of States does not prevent the unamended treaty from being considered to be in force under art. 24 as between the newly independent State and the other State party, unless it is established that they intended the treaty as amended to apply between them.

Section 4. Provisional application.

Art. 27. Multilateral treaties.(1) If, at the date of the succession of States, a multilateral treaty was in force in respect of the territory to which the succession of States relates and the newly independent State give notice of its intention that the treaty should be applied provisionally in respect of its territory, that treaty shall apply provisionally between the newly independent State and any party which expressly so agrees or by reason of its conduct is to be considered as having so agreed.

(2) Nevertheless, in the case of a treaty which falls within the category mentioned in art. 14, paragraph 3, the consent of all the parties to such provisional application is required.

(3) If, at the date of the succession of States, a multilateral treaty not yet in force was being applied provisionally in respect of the territory to which the succession of States relates and the newly independent State gives notice of its intention that the treaty should continue to be applied provisionally in respect of its territory, that treaty shall apply provisionally between the newly independent State and any contracting State which expressly so agrees or by reason of its conduct is to be considered as having so agreed.

(4) Nevertheless, in the case of a treaty which falls within the category mentioned in art. 17, paragraph 3, the consent of all the contracting States to such continued provisional application is required.

(5) Paragraphs 1 to 4 do not apply if it appears from the treaty or is otherwise established that the application of the treaty in respect of the newly independent State would be incompatible with the object and purpose of the treaty or would radically change the conditions for its operation.

Art. 28. Bilateral treaties. A bilateral treaty which at the date of a succession of States was in force or was being provisionally applied in respect of the territory to which the succession of States relates is considered as applying provisionally between the newly independent State and the other State concerned when:

(a) they expressly so agree; or

(b) by reason of their conduct they are to be considered as having so agreed.

Art. 29. Termination of provisional application. (1) Unless the treaty otherwise provides or it is otherwise agreed, the provisional application of a multilateral treaty under art. 27 may be terminated:

(a) by reasonable notice of termination given by the newly independent State or the party or contracting State provisionally applying the treaty and the expiration of the notice; or

(b) in the case of a treaty which falls within the category mentioned in art. 17, paragraph 3, by reasonable notice of termination given by the newly independent State or all of the parties or, as the case may be, all of the contracting States and the expiration of the notice.

(2) Unless the treaty otherwise provides or it is otherwise agreed, the provisional application of a bilateral treaty under art. 28 may be terminated by reasonable notice of termination given by the newly independent State or the other State concerned and the expiration of the notice.

(3) Unless the treaty provides for a shorter period for its termination or it is otherwise agreed, reasonable notice of termination shall be twelve months' notice from the date on which it is received by the other State or States provisionally applying the treaty.

(4) Unless the treaty otherwise provides or it is otherwise agreed, the provisional application of a multilateral treaty under art. 27 shall be terminated if the newly independent State gives notice of its intention not to become a party to the treaty.

Section 5. Newly independent states formed from two or more territories.

Art. 30. Newly independent States formed from two or more territories. (1) Art. 16 to 29 apply in the case of a newly independent State formed from two or more territories.

(2) When a newly independent State formed from two or more territories is considered as or becomes a party to a treaty by virtue of art. 17, 18 or 24 and at the date of the succession of States the treaty was in force, or consent to be bound had been given, in respect of one or more, but not all, of those territories, the treaty shall apply in respect of the entire territory of that State unless:

(a) it appears from the treaty or is otherwise established that the application of the treaty in respect of the entire territory would be incompatible with the object and purpose of the treaty or would radically change the conditions for its operation;

(b) in the case of a multilateral treaty not falling under art. 17, paragraph 3, or under art. 18, paragraph 4, the notification of succession is restricted to the territory in respect of which the treaty was in force at the date of the succession of States, or in respect of which consent to be bound by the treaty had been given prior to that date;

(c) in the case of a multilateral treaty falling under art. 17, paragraph 3, or under art. 18, paragraph 4, the newly independent State and the other States parties or, as the case may be, the other contracting States otherwise agree; or

(d) in the case of a bilateral treaty, the newly independent State and the other State concerned otherwise agree.

(3) When a newly independent State formed from two or more territories becomes a party to a multilateral treaty under art. 19 and by the signature or signatures of the predecessor State or States it had been intended that the treaty should extend to one or more, but not all, of those territories, the treaty shall apply in respect of the entire territory of the newly independent State unless:

(a) it appears from the treaty or is otherwise established that the application of the treaty in respect of the entire territory would be incompatible with the object and purpose of the treaty or would radically change the conditions for its operation;

(b) in the case of a multilateral treaty not falling under art. 19, paragraph 4, the ratification, acceptance or approval of the treaty is restricted to the territory or territories to which it was intended that the treaty should extend; or

(c) in the case of a multilateral treaty falling under art. 19, paragraph 4, the newly independent State and the other States parties or, as the case may be, the other contracting States otherwise agree.

Part. IV. *Uniting and separation of States.*

Art. 31. Effects of a uniting of States in respect of treaties in force at the date of the succession of States. (1) When two or more States unite and so form one successor State, any treaty in force at the date of the succession of States in respect of any of them continues in force in respect of the successor State unless:

(a) the successor State and the other State party or States parties otherwise agree; or

(b) it appears from the treaty or is otherwise established that the application of the treaty in respect of the successor State would be incompatible with the object and purpose of the treaty or would radically change the conditions for its operation.

(2) Any treaty continuing in force in conformity with paragraph 1 shall apply only in respect of the part of the territory of the successor State in respect of which the treaty was in force at the date of the succession of States unless:

(a) in the case of a multilateral treaty not falling within the category mentioned in art. 17, paragraph 3, the successor State makes a notification that the treaty shall apply in respect of its entire territory;

(b) in the case of a multilateral treaty falling within the category mentioned in art. 17, paragraph 3, the successor State and the other States parties otherwise agree; or

(c) in the case of a bilateral treaty, the successor State and the other State party otherwise agree.

(3) Paragraph 2(a) does not apply if it appears from the treaty or is otherwise established that the application of the treaty in respect of the entire territory of the successor State would be incompatible with the object and purpose of the treaty or would radically change the conditions for its operation.

Art. 32. Effects of a uniting of States in respect of treaties not in force at the date of the succession of States

(1) Subject to paragraphs 3 and 4, a successor State falling under art. 31 may, by making a notification, establish its status as a contracting State to a multilateral treaty which is not in force if, at the date of the succession of States, any of the predecessor States was a contracting State to the treaty.

(2) Subject to paragraphs 3 and 4, a successor State falling under art. 31 may, by making a notification, establish its status as a party to a multilateral treaty which enters into force after the date of the succession of States if, at that date, any of the predecessor States was a contracting State to the treaty.

(3) Paragraphs 1 and 2 do not apply if it appears from the treaty or is otherwise established that the application of the treaty in respect of the successor State would be incompatible with the object and purpose of the treaty or would radically change the conditions for its operation.

(4) If the treaty is one falling within the category mentioned in art. 17, paragraph 3, the successor State may establish its status as a party or as a contracting State to the treaty only with the consent of all the parties or of all the contracting States.

(5) Any treaty to which the successor State becomes a contracting State or a party in conformity with

paragraph 1 or 2 shall apply only in respect of the part of the territory of the successor State in respect of which consent to be bound by the treaty had been given prior to the date of the succession of States unless:

(a) in the case of a multilateral treaty not falling within the category mentioned in art. 17, paragraph 3, the successor State indicates in its notification made under paragraph 1 or 2 that the treaty shall apply in respect of its entire territory; or

(b) in the case of a multilateral treaty falling within the category mentioned in art. 17, paragraph 3, the successor State and all the parties or, as the case may be, all the contracting States otherwise agree.

(6) Paragraph 5(a) does not apply if it appears from the treaty or is otherwise established that the application of the treaty in respect of the entire territory of the successor State would be incompatible with the object and purpose of the treaty or would radically change the conditions for its operation.

Art. 33. Effects of a uniting of States in respect of treaties signed by a predecessor State subject to ratification, acceptance or approval. (1) Subject to paragraphs 2 and 3, if before the date of the succession of States one of the predecessor States had signed a multilateral treaty subject to ratification, acceptance or approval, a successor State falling under art. 31 may ratify, accept or approve the treaty as if it had signed that treaty and thereby become a party or a contracting State to it.

(2) Paragraph 1 does not apply if it appears from the treaty or is otherwise established that the application of the treaty in respect of the successor State would be incompatible with the object and purpose of the treaty or would radically change the conditions for its operation.

(3) If the treaty is one falling within the category mentioned in art. 17, paragraph 3, the successor State may become a party or a contracting State to the treaty only with the consent of all the parties or of all the contracting States.

(4) Any treaty to which the successor State becomes a party or a contracting State in conformity with paragraph 1 shall apply only in respect of the part of the territory of the successor State in respect of which the treaty was signed by one of the predecessor States unless:

(a) in the case of the multilateral treaty not falling within the category mentioned in art. 17, paragraph 3, the successor State when ratifying, accepting or approving the treaty gives notice that the treaty shall apply in respect of its entire territory; or

(b) in the case of a multilateral treaty falling within the category mentioned in art. 17, paragraph 3, the successor State and all the parties or, as the case may be, all the contracting States otherwise agree.

(5) Paragraph 4(a) does not apply if it appears from the treaty or is otherwise established that the application of the treaty in respect of the entire territory of the successor State would be incompatible with the object and purpose of the treaty or would radically change the conditions for its operation.

Art. 34. Succession of States in cases of separation of parts of a State. (1) When a part or parts of the territory of a State separate to form one or more States, whether or not the predecessor State continues to exist:

(a) any treaty in force at the date of the succession of States in respect of the entire territory of the predecessor State continues in force in respect of each successor State so formed;

(b) any treaty in force at the date of the succession of States in respect only of that part of the territory of the predecessor State which has become a successor State continues in force in respect of that successor State alone.

(2) Paragraph 1 does not apply if:

(a) the States concerned otherwise agree; or

(b) it appears from the treaty or is otherwise established that the application of the treaty in respect of the successor State would be incompatible with the object and purpose of the treaty or would radically change the conditions for its operation.

Art. 35. Position if a State continues after separation of part of its territory. When, after separation of any part of the territory of a State, the predecessor State continues to exist, any treaty which at the date of the succession of States was in force in respect of the predecessor State continues in force in respect of its remaining territory unless:

(a) the States concerned otherwise agree;

(b) it is established that the treaty related only to the territory which has separated from the predecessor State; or

(c) it appears from the treaty or is otherwise established that the application of the treaty in respect of the predecessor State would be incompatible with the object and purpose of the treaty or would radically change the conditions for its operation.

Art. 36. Participation in treaties not in force at the date of the succession of States in cases of separation of parts of a State. (1) Subject to paragraphs 3 and 4, a successor State falling under art. 34, paragraph 1, may, by making a notification, establish its status as a contracting State to a multilateral treaty which is not in force if, at the date of the succession of States, the predecessor State was a contracting State to the treaty in respect of the territory to which the succession of States relates.

(2) Subject to paragraphs 3 and 4, a successor State falling under art. 34, paragraph 1, may, by making a notification, establish its status as a party to a multilateral treaty which enters into force after the date of the succession of States if at that date the predecessor State was a contracting State to the treaty in respect of the territory to which the succession of States relates.

(3) Paragraphs 1 and 2 do not apply if it appears from the treaty or is otherwise established that the application of the treaty in respect of the successor State would be incompatible with the object and purpose of the treaty or would radically change the conditions for its operation.

(4) If the treaty is one falling within the category mentioned in art. 17, paragraph 3, the successor State may establish its status as a party or as a contracting State to the treaty only with the consent of all the parties or of all the contracting States.

Art. 37. Participation in cases of separation of parts of a State in treaties signed by the predecessor State subject to ratification, acceptance or approval.

(1) Subject to paragraphs 2 and 3, if before the date of the succession of States the predecessor State had signed a multilateral treaty subject to ratification, acceptance or approval and the treaty, if it had been in force at that date, would have applied in respect of the territory to which the succession of States relates, a successor State falling under art. 34, paragraph 1, may ratify, accept or approve the treaty as if it had signed that treaty and may thereby become a party or a contracting State to it.

(2) Paragraph 1 does not apply if it appears from the treaty or is otherwise established that the application of the treaty in respect of the successor State would be incompatible with the object and purpose of the treaty or would radically change the conditions for its operation.

(3) If the treaty is one falling within the category mentioned in art. 17, paragraph 3, the successor State may become a party or a contracting State to the treaty only with the consent of all the parties or of all the contracting States.

Art. 38. Notifications. (1) Any notification under art. 31, 32 or 36 shall be made in writing.

(2) If the notification is not signed by the Head of State, Head of Government or Minister for Foreign Affairs, the representative of the State communicating it may be called upon to produce full powers.

(3) Unless the treaty otherwise provides, the notification shall:

(a) be transmitted by the successor State to the depositary or, if there is no depositary, to the parties or the contracting States;

(b) be considered to be made by the successor State on the date on which it is received by the depositary or, if there is no depositary, on the date on which it is received by all the parties or, as the case may be, by all the contracting States.

(4) Paragraph 3 does not affect any duty that the depositary may have, in accordance with the treaty or otherwise, to inform the parties or the contracting States of the notification or any communication made in connection therewith by the successor State.

(5) Subject to the provisions of the treaty, such notificaton or communication shall be considered as received by the State for which it is intended only when the latter State has been informed by the depositary.

Part V. *Miscellaneous Provisions*

Art. 39. Cases of State responsibility and outbreak of hostilities. The provisions of the present Convention shall not prejudge any question that may arise in regard

to the effects of a succession of States in respect of a treaty from the international responsibility of a State or from the outbreak of hostilities between States.

Art. 40. Cases of military occupation. The provisions of the present Convention shall not prejudge any question that may arise in regard to a treaty from the military occupation of a territory.

Part. VI. *Settlement of Disputes.* Art. 41. Consultation and negotiation. If a dispute regarding the interpretation or application of the present Convention arises between two or more Parties to the Convention, they shall, upon the request of any of them, seek to resolve it by a process of consultation and negotiation.

Art. 42. Conciliation. If the dispute is not resolved within six months of the date on which the request referred to in art. 41 has been made, any party to the dispute may submit it to the conciliation procedure specified in the Annex to the present Convention by submitting a request to that effect to the Secretary-General of the United Nations and informing the other party or parties to the dispute of the request.

Art. 43. Judicial settlement and arbitration. Any State at the time of signature or ratification of the present Convention or accession thereto or at any time thereafter, may, by notification to the depositary, declare that, where a dispute has not been resolved by the application of the procedures referred to in art. 41 and 42, that dispute may be submitted for a decision to the International Court of Justice by a written application of any party to the dispute, or in the alternative to arbitration, provided that the other party to the dispute has made a like declaration.

Art. 44. Settlement by common consent. Notwithstanding art. 41, 42 and 43, if a dispute regarding the interpretation or application of the present Convention arises between two or more Parties to the Convention, they may by common consent agree to submit it to the International Court of Justice, or to arbitration, or to any other appropriate procedure for the settlement of disputes.

Art. 45. Other provisions in force for the settlement of disputes. Nothing in art. 41 to 44 shall affect the rights or obligations of the Parties to the present Convention under any provisions in force binding them with regard to the settlement of disputes.

Part VII. Final Provisions. Art. 46. Signature. The present Convention shall be open for signature by all States until Feb. 28, 1979 at the Federal Ministry for Foreign Affairs of the Republic of Austria, and subsequently, until Aug. 31, 1979 at United Nations Headquarters in New York.

Art. 47. Ratification. The present Convention is subject to ratification. The instruments of ratification shall be deposited with the Secretary-General of the United Nations.

Art. 48. Accession. The present Convention shall remain open for accession by any State. The instruments of accession shall be deposited with the Secretary-General of the United Nations.

Art. 49. Entry into force. (1) The present Convention shall enter into force on the thirtieth day following the date of deposit of the fifteenth instrument of ratification or accession.

(2) For each State ratifying or acceding to the Convention after the deposit of the fifteenth instrument of ratification or accession, the Convention shall enter into force on the thirtieth day after deposit by such State of its instrument of ratification or accession.

Art. 50. Authentic texts. The original of the present Convention, of which the Arabic, Chinese, English, French, Russian and Spanish texts are equally authentic, shall be deposited with the Secretary-General of the United Nations.

In witness whereof the undersigned Plenipotentiaries, being duly authorized thereto by their respective Governments, have signed the present Convention.

Done at Vienna, this twenty-third day of August, one thousand nine hundred and seventy-eight.

Annex

(1) A list of conciliators consisting of qualified jurists shall be drawn up and maintained by the Secretary-General of the United Nations. To this end, every State which is a Member of the United Nations or a Party to the present Convention shall be invited to nominate two conciliators, and the names of the persons so nominated shall constitute the list. The term of a conciliator, including that of any conciliator nominated to fill a casual vacancy, shall be five years and may be

renewed. A conciliator whose term expires shall continue to fulfil any function for which he shall have been chosen under the following paragraph.

(2) When a request has been made to the Secretary-General under art. 42, the Secretary-General shall bring the dispute before a conciliation commission constituted as follows:

The State or States constituting one of the parties to the dispute shall appoint:

(a) one conciliator of the nationality of that State or of one of those States, who may or may not be chosen from the list referred to in paragraph 1; and

(b) one conciliator not of the nationality of that State or of any of those States, who shall be chosen from the list.

The State or States constituting the other party to the dispute shall appoint two conciliators in the same way. The four conciliators chosen by the parties shall be appointed within sixty days following the date on which the Secretary-General receives the request.

The four conciliators shall, within sixty days following the date of the appointment of the last of them, appoint a fifth conciliator chosen from the list, who shall be chairman.

If the appointment of the chairman or of any of the other conciliators has not been made within the period prescribed above for such appointment, it shall be made by the Secretary-General within sixty days following the expiry of that period. The appointment of the chairman may be made by the Secretary-General either from the list or from the membership of the International Law Commission. Any of the periods within which appointments must be made may be extended by agreement between the parties to the dispute.

Any vacancy shall be filled in the manner prescribed for the initial appointment.

(3) The Conciliation Commission shall decide its own procedure. The Commission, with the consent of the parties to the dispute, may invite any Party to the present Convention to submit to it its views orally or in writing. Decisions and recommendations of the Commission shall be made by a majority vote of the five members.

(4) The Commission may draw the attention of the parties to the dispute to any measures which might facilitate an amicable settlement.

(5) The Commission shall hear the parties, examine the claims and objections, and make proposals to the parties with a view to reaching an amicable settlement of the dispute.

(6) The Commission shall report within twelve months of its constitution. Its report shall be deposited with the Secretary-General and transmitted to the parties to the dispute. The report of the Commission, including any conclusions started therein regarding the facts or questions of law, shall not be binding upon the parties and it shall have no other character than that of recommendations submitted for the consideration of the parties in order to facilitate an amicable settlement of the dispute.

(7) The Secretary-General shall provide the Commission with such assistance and facilities as it may require. The expenses of the Commission shall be borne by the United Nations.

UN Yearbook, 1975, pp. 861-862; 1976, pp. 820–821; UN General Assembly A/Conf. 80/3, August 22, 1978, English, 35 pp.

VIENNA CONVENTION ON THE LAW OF INTERNATIONAL TREATIES, 1969.

Elaborated by the UN Conference on the Law of Treaties in Vienna, Mar. 1968–May 1969, and adopted May 23, 1969. The text is as follows:

"The States Parties to the present Convention,

Considering the fundamental role of treaties in the history of international relations,

Recognizing the ever-increasing importance of treaties as a source of international law and as a means of developing peaceful co-operation among nations, whatever their constitutional and social systems,

Noting that the principles of free consent and of good faith and the pacta sunt servanda rule are universally recognized,

Affirming that disputes concerning treaties, like other international disputes, should be settled by peaceful means and in conformity with the principles of justice and international law,

Recalling the determination of the peoples of the United Nations to establish conditions under which justice and respect for the obligations arising from treaties can be maintained,

Having in mind the principles of international law embodied in the Charter of the United Nations, such as the principles of the equal rights and self-determination of peoples, of the sovereign equality and independence, of all States, of non-interference in the domestic affairs of States, of the prohibition of the threat or use of force and of universal respect for, and observance of, human rights and fundamental freedoms for all,

Believing that the codification and progressive development of the law of treaties achieved in the present Convention will promote the purposes of the United Nations set forth in the Charter, namely, the maintenance of international peace and security, the development of friendly relations and the achievement of co-operation among nations,

Affirming that the rules of customary international law will continue to govern questions not regulated by the provisions of the present Convention,

Have agreed as follows:

Part. I. *Introduction*

Art. 1. Scope of the present Convention

The present Convention applies to treaties between States.

Art. 2. Use of terms

(1) For the purposes of the present Convention:

(a) 'treaty' means an international agreement concluded between States in written form and governed by international law, whether embodied in a single instrument or in two or more related instruments and whatever its particular designation;

(b) 'ratification', 'acceptance', 'approval' and 'accession' mean in each case the international act so named whereby a State establishes on the international plane its consent to be bound by a treaty;

(c) 'full powers' means a document emanating from the competent authority of a State designating a person or persons to represent the State for negotiating, adopting or authenticating the text of a treaty, for expressing the consent of the State to be bound by a treaty, or for accomplishing any other act with respect to a treaty;

(d) 'reservation' means a unilateral statement, however phrased or named, made by a State, when signing, ratifying, accepting, approving or acceding to a treaty, whereby it purports to exclude or to modify the legal effect of certain provisions of the treaty in their application to that State;

(e) 'negotiating State' means a State which took part in the drawing up and adoption of the text of the treaty;

(f) 'contracting State' means a State which has consented to be bound by the treaty, whether or not the treaty has entered into force;

(g) 'party' means a State which has consented to be bound by the treaty and for which the treaty is in force;

(h) 'third State' means a State not a party to the treaty;

(i) 'international organization' means an intergovernmental organization.

(2) The provisions of paragraph 1 regarding the use of terms in the present Convention are without prejudice to the use of those terms or to the meanings which may be given to them in the internal law of any State.

Art. 3. International agreements not within the scope of the present Convention

The fact that the present Convention does not apply to international agreements concluded between States and other subjects of international law or between such other subjects of international law, or to international agreements not in written form, shall not affect:

(a) the legal force of such agreements;

(b) the application to them of any of the rules set forth in the present Convention to which they would be subject under international law independently of the Convention;

(c) the application of the Convention to the relations of States as between themselves under international agreements to which other subjects of international law are also parties.

Art. 4. Non-retroactivity of the present Convention

Without prejudice to the application of any rules set forth in the present Convention to which treaties would be subject under international law independently of the Convention, the convention applies only to treaties which are concluded by States after the entry into force of the present Convention with regard to such States.

Art. 5. Treaties constituting international organizations and treaties adopted within an international organization

The present Convention applies to any treaty which is the constituent instrument of an international organization and to any treaty adopted within an international organization without prejudice to any relevant rules of the organization.

Part II. *Conclusion and Entry into Force of Treaties*
Section 1:
Conclusion of Treaties

Art. 6. Capacity of States to conclude treaties

Every State possesses capacity to conclude treaties.

Art. 7. Full powers

(1) A person is considered as representing a State for the purpose of adopting or authenticating the text of a treaty or for the purpose of expressing the consent of the State to be bound by a treaty if:

(a) he produces appropriate full powers; or

(b) it appears from the practice of the States concerned or from other circumstances that their intention was to consider that person as representing the State for such purposes and to dispense with full powers.

(2) In virtue of their functions and without having to produce full powers, the following are considered as representing their State:

(a) Heads of State, Heads of Government and Ministers for Foreign Affairs, for the purpose of performing all acts relating to the conclusion of a treaty;

(b) heads of diplomatic missions, for the purpose of adopting the text of a treaty between the accrediting State and the State to which they are accredited;

(c) representatives accredited by States to an international conference or to an international organization or one of its organs, for the purpose of adopting the text of a treaty in that conference, organization or organ.

Art. 8. subsequent confirmation of an act performed without authorization

An act relating to the conclusion of a treaty performed by a person who cannot be considered under article 7 as authorized to represent a State for that purpose is without legal effect unless afterwards confirmed by the State.

Art. 9. Adoption of the text

(1) The adoption of the text of a treaty takes place by the consent of all the States participating in its drawing up except as provided in paragraph 2.

(2) The adoption of the text of a treaty at an international conference takes place by the vote of two-thirds of the States present and voting, unless by the same majority they shall decide to apply a different rule.

Art. 10. Authentication of the text

The text of a treaty is established as authentic and definitive:

(a) by such procedure as may be provided for in the text or agreed upon by the States participating in its drawing up; or

(b) failing such procedure, by the signature, signature ad referendum or initialling by the representatives of those States of the text of the treaty or of the Final Act of a conference incorporating the text.

Art. 11. Means of expressing consent to be bound by a treaty

The consent of a State to be bound by a treaty may be expressed by signature, exchange of instruments constituting a treaty, ratification, acceptance, approval or accession, or by any other means if so agreed.

Art. 12. Consent to be bound by a treaty expressed by signature

(1) The consent of a State to be bound by a treaty is expressed by the signature of its representative when:

(a) The treaty provides that signature shall have that effect;

(b) it is otherwise established that the negotiating States were agreed that signature should have that effect; or

(c) the intention of the State to give that effect to the signature appears from the full powers of its representative or was expressed during the negotiation.

(2) For the purposes of paragraph 1:

(a) the initialling of a text constitutes a signature of the treaty when it is established that the negotiating States so agreed;

(b) the signature ad referendum of a treaty by a representative, if confirmed by his State, constitutes a full signature of the treaty.

Art. 13. Consent to be bound by a treaty expressed by an exchange of instruments constituting a treaty
The consent of States to be bound by a treaty constituted by instruments exchanged between them is expressed by that exchange when:
(a) the instruments provide that their exchange shall have that effect; or
(b) it is otherwise established that those States were agreed that the exchange of instruments should have that effect.
Art. 14. Consent to be bound by a treaty expressed by ratification, acceptance or approval
(1) The consent of a State to be bound by a treaty is expressed by ratification when:
(a) the treaty provides for such consent to be expressed by means of ratification;
(b) it is otherwise established that the negotiating States were agreed that ratification should be required;
(c) the representative of the State has signed the treaty subject to ratification; or
(d) the intention of the State to sign the treaty subject to ratification appears from the full powers of its representative or was expressed during the negotiation.
(2) The consent of a State to be bound by a treaty is expressed by acceptance or approval under conditions similar to those which apply to ratification.
Art. 15. Consent to be bound by a treaty expressed by accession. The consent of a State to be bound by a treaty is expressed by accession when:
(a) the treaty provides that such consent may be expressed by that State by means of accession;
(b) it is otherwise established that the negotiating States were agreed that such consent may be expressed by that State by means of accession; or
(c) all the parties have subsequently agreed that such consent may be expressed by that State by means of accession.
Art. 16. Exchange or deposit of instruments of ratification, acceptance, approval or accession
Unless the treaty otherwise provides, instruments of ratification, acceptance, approval or accession establish the consent of a State to be bound by a treaty upon:
(a) their exchange between the contracting States;
(b) their deposit with the depositary; or
(c) their notification to the contracting States or to the depositary, if so agreed.
Art. 17. Consent to be bound by part of a treaty and choice of differing provisions
(1) Without prejudice to articles 19 to 23, the consent of a State to be bound by part of a treaty is effective only if the treaty so permits or the other contracting States so agree.
(2) The consent of a State to be bound by a treaty which permits a choice between differing provisions is effective only if it is made clear to which of the provisions the consent relates.
Art. 18. Obligation not to defeat the object and purpose of a treaty prior to its entry into force
A State is obliged to refrain from acts which would defeat the object and purpose of a treaty when:
(a) it has signed the treaty or has exchanged instruments constituting the treaty subject to ratification, acceptance or approval, until it shall have made its intention clear not to become a party to the treaty; or
(b) it has expressed its consent to be bound by the treaty, pending the entry into force of the treaty and provided that such entry into force is not unduly delayed.
Section 2: Reservations
Art. 19. Formulation of reservations
A State may, when signing, ratifying, accepting, approving or acceding to a treaty, formulate a reservation unless:
(a) the reservation is prohibited by the treaty;
(b) the treaty provides that only specified reservations, which do not include the reservation in question, may be made; or
(c) in cases not falling under sub-paragraphs (a) and (b), the reservation is incompatible with the object and purpose of the treaty.
Art. 20. Acceptance of an objection to reservations
(1) A reservation expressly authorized by a treaty does not require any subsequent acceptance by the other contracting States unless the treaty so provides.
(2) When it appears from the limited number of the negotiating States and the object and purpose of a treaty that the application of the treaty in its entirety between all the parties is an essential condition of the consent of each one to be bound by the treaty, a reservation requires acceptance by all the parties.
(3) When a treaty is a constituent instrument of an international organization and unless it otherwise provides, a reservation requires the acceptance of the competent organ of that organization.
(4) In cases not falling under the preceding paragraphs and unless the treaty otherwise provides:
(a) acceptance by another contracting State of a reservation constitutes the reserving State a party to the treaty in relation to that other State if or when the treaty is in force for those States;
(b) an objection by another contracting State to a reservation does not preclude the entry into force of the treaty as between the objecting and reserving States unless a contrary intention is definitely expressed by the objecting State;
(c) an act expressing a State's consent to be bound by the treaty and containing a reservation is effective as soon as at least one other contracting State has accepted the reservation.
(5) For the purposes of paragraphs 2 and 4 and unless the treaty otherwise provides, a reservation is considered to have been accepted by a State if it shall have raised no objection to the reservation by the end of a period of twelve months after it was notified of the reservation or by the date on which it expressed its consent to be bound by the treaty, whichever is later.
Art. 21. Legal effects of reservations and of objections to reservations
(1) A reservation established with regard to another party in accordance with articles 19, 20 and 23;
(a) modifies for the reserving State in its relations with that other party the provisions of the treaty to which the reservation relates to the extent of the reservation; and
(b) modifies those provisions to the same extent for that other party in its relations with the reserving State.
(2) The reservation does not modify the provisions of the treaty for the other parties to the treaty inter se.
(3) When a State objecting to a reservation has not opposed the entry into force of the treaty between itself and the reserving State, the provisions to which the reservation relates do not apply as between the two States to the extent of the reservation.
Art. 22. Withdrawal of reservations and of objections to reservations.
(1) Unless the treaty otherwise provides, a reservation may be withdrawn at any time and the consent of a State which has accepted the reservation is not required for its withdrawal.
(2) Unless the treaty otherwise provides, an objection to a reservation may be withdrawn at any time.
(3) Unless the treaty otherwise provides, or it is otherwise agreed:
(a) the withdrawal of a reservation becomes operative in relation to another contracting State only when notice of it has been received by that State;
(b) the withdrawal of an objection to a reservation becomes operative only when notice of it has been received by the State which formulated the reservation.
Art. 23. Procedure regarding reservations
(1) A reservation, an express acceptance of a reservation and an objection to a reservation must be formulated in writing and communicated to the contracting States and other States entitled to become parties to the treaty.
(2) If formulated when signing the treaty subject to ratification, acceptance or approval, a reservation must be formally confirmed by the reserving State when expressing its consent to be bound by the treaty. In such a case the reservation shall be considered as having been made on the date of its confirmation.
(3) An express acceptance of, or an objection to, a reservation made previously to confirmation of the reservation does not itself require confirmation.
(4) The withdrawal of a reservation or of an objection to a reservation must be formulated in writing.
Section 3: Entry into Force and Provisional Application of Treaties
Art. 24. Entry into force
(1) A treaty enters into force in such manner and upon such date as it may provide or as the negotiating States may agree.
(2) Failing any such provision of agreement, a treaty enters into force as soon as consent to be bound by the treaty has been established for all the negotiating States.
(3) When the consent of a State to be bound by a treaty is established on a date after the treaty has come into force, the treaty enters into force for that State on that date, unless the treaty otherwise provides.
(4) The provisions of a treaty regulating the authentication of its text, the establishment of the consent of States to be bound by the treaty, the manner or date of its entry into force, reservations, the functions of the depositary and other matters arising necessarily before the entry into force of the treaty apply from the time of the adoption of its text.
Art. 25. Provisional application
(1) A treaty or a part of a treaty is applied provisionally pending its entry into force if:
(a) the treaty itself so provides; or
(b) the negotiating States have in some other manner so agreed.
(2) Unless the treaty otherwise provides or the negotiating State have otherwise agreed, the provisional application of a treaty or a part of a treaty with respect to a State shall be terminated if that State notifies the other States between which the treaty is being applied provisionally of its intention not to become a party to the treaty.
Part III. *Observance, Application and Interpretation of Treaties*
Section 1: Observance of Treaties
Art. 26. Pacta sunt servanda
Every treaty in force is binding upon the parties to it and must be performed by them in good faith.
Art. 27. Internal law and observance of treaties
A party may not invoke the provisions of its internal law as justification for its failure to perform a treaty. This rule is without prejudice to article 46.
Section 2: Application of Treaties
Art. 28. Non-retroactivity of treaties
Unless a different intention appears from the treaty or is otherwise established, its provisions do not bind a party in relation to any act or fact which took place or any situation which ceased to exist before the date of the entry into force of the treaty with respect to that party.
Art. 29. Territorial scope of treaties
Unless a different intention appears from the treaty or is otherwise established, a treaty is binding upon each party in respect of its entire territory.
Art. 30. Application of successive treaties relating to the same subject-matter
(1) Subject to Art. 103 of the Charter of the United Nations, the rights and obligations of States parties to successive treaties relating to the same subject-matter shall be determined in accordance with the following paragraphs.
(2) When a treaty specifies that it is subject to, or that it is not to be considered as incompatible with, an earlier or later treaty, the provisions of that other treaty prevail.
(3) When all the parties to the earlier treaty are parties also to the later treaty but the earlier treaty is not terminated or suspended in operation under article 59, the earlier treaty applies only to the extent that its provisions are compatible with those of the later treaty.
(4) When the parties to the later treaty do not include all the parties to the earlier one:
(a) as between States parties to both treaties the same rule applies as in paragraph 3;
(b) as between a State party to both treaties and a State party to only one of the treaties, the treaty to which both States are parties governs their mutual rights and obligations.
(5) Paragraph 4 is without prejudice to article 41, or to any question of the termination or suspension of the operation of a treaty under article 60 or to any question of responsibility which may arise for a State from the conclusion or application of a treaty the provisions of which are incompatible with its obligations towards another State under another treaty.
Section 3: Interpretation of Treaties
Art. 31. General rule of interpretation
(1) A treaty shall be interpreted in good faith in accordance with the ordinary meaning to be given to the terms of the treaty in their context and in the light of its object and purpose.
(2) The context for the purpose of the interpretation of a treaty shall comprise in addition to the text, including its preamble and annexes:
(a) any agreement relating to the treaty which was made between all the parties in connection with the conclusion of the treaty;

(b) any instrument which was made by one or more parties in connexion with the conclusion of the treaty and accepted by the other parties as an instrument related to the treaty.

(3) There shall be taken into account, together with the context:

(a) any subsequent agreement between the parties regarding the interpretation of the treaty or the application of its provisions;

(b) any subsequent practice in the application of the treaty which establishes the agreement of the parties regarding its interpretation;

(c) any relevant rules of international law applicable in the relations between the parties.

(4) A special meaning shall be given to a term if it is established that the parties so intended.

Art. 32. Supplementary means of interpretation

Recourse may be had to supplementary means of interpretation, including the preparatory work of the treaty and the circumstances of its conclusion, in order to confirm the meaning resulting from the application of art. 31, or to determine the meaning when the interpretation according to art. 31:

(a) leaves the meaning ambiguous or obscure; or

(b) leads to a result which is manifestly absurd or unreasonable.

Art. 33. Interpretation of treaties authenticated in two or more languages

(1) When a treaty has been authenticated in two or more languages, the text is equally authoritative in each language, unless the treaty provides or the parties agree that, in case of divergence, a particular text shall prevail.

(2) A version of the treaty in a language other than one of those in which the text was authenticated shall be considered an authentic text only if the treaty so provides or the parties so agree.

(3) The terms of the treaty are presumed to have the same meaning in each authentic text.

(4) Except where a particular text prevails in accordance with paragraph 1, when a comparison of the authentic texts discloses a difference of meaning which the application of art. 31 and 32 does not remove, the meaning which best reconciles the texts, having regard to the object and purpose of the treaty, shall be adopted.

Section 4: Treaties and Third States

Art. 34. General rule regarding third States

A treaty does not create either obligations or rights for a third State without its consent.

Art. 35. Treaties providing for obligations for third States.

An obligation arises for a third State from a provision of a treaty if the parties to the treaty intend the provision to be the means of establishing the obligation and the third State expressly accepts that obligation in writing.

Art. 36. Treaties providing for rights for third States

(1) A right arises for a third State from a provision of a treaty if the parties to the treaty intend the provision to accord that right either to the third State, or to a group of States to which it belongs, or to all States, and the third State assents thereto. Its assent shall be presumed so long as the contrary is not indicated, unless the treaty otherwise provides.

(2) A State exercising a right in accordance with paragraph 1 shall comply with the conditions for its exercise provided for in the treaty or established in conformity with the treaty.

Art. 37. Revocation or modification of obligations or rights of third States

(1) When an obligation has arisen for a third State in conformity with art. 35, the obligation may be revoked or modified only with the consent of the parties to the treaty and of the third State, unless it is established that they had otherwise agreed.

(2) When a right has arisen for a third State in conformity with art. 36, the right may not be revoked or modified by the parties if it is established that the right was intended not to be revocable or subject to modification without the consent of the third State.

Art. 38. Rules in a treaty becoming binding on third States through international custom

Nothing in articles 34 to 37 precludes a rule set forth in a treaty from becoming binding upon a third State as a customary rule of international law, recognized as such.

Part IV. Amendment and Modification of Treaties

Art. 39. General rule regarding the amendment of treaties

A treaty may be amended by agreement between the parties. The rules laid down in Part II apply to such an agreement except in so far as the treaty may otherwise provide.

Art. 40. Amendment of multilateral treaties

(1) Unless the treaty otherwise provides, the amendment of multilateral treaties shall be governed by the following paragraphs.

(2) Any proposal to amend a multilateral treaty as between all the parties must be notified to all the contracting States, each one of which shall have the right to take part in:

(a) the decision as to the action to be taken in regard to such proposal;

(b) the negotiation and conclusion of any agreement for the amendment of the treaty.

(3) Every State entitled to become a party to the treaty shall also be entitled to become a party to the treaty as amended.

(4) The amending agreement does not bind any State already a party to the treaty which does not become a party to the amending agreement; art. 30, paragraph 4(b), applies in relation to such State.

(5) Any State which becomes a party to the treaty after the entry into force of the amending agreement shall, failing an expression of a different intention by the State:

(a) be considered as a party to the treaty as amended; and

(b) be considered as a party to the unamended treaty in relation to any party to the treaty not bound by the amending agreement.

Art. 41. Agreements to modify multilateral treaties between certain of the parties only

(1) Two or more of the parties to a multilateral treaty may conclude an agreement to modify the treaty as between themselves alone if:

(a) the possibility of such a modification is provided for by the treaty; or

(b) the modification in question is not prohibited by the treaty and;

(c) does not affect the enjoyment by the other parties of their rights under the treaty or the performance of their obligations;

(d) does not relate to a provision, derogation from which is incompatible with the effective execution of the object and purpose of the treaty as a whole.

(2) Unless in a case falling under paragraph 1 (a) the treaty otherwise provides, the parties in question shall notify the other parties of their intention to conclude the agreement and of the modification to the treaty for which it provides.

Part V. Invalidity, Termination and Suspension of the Operation of Treaties

Section 1: General Provisions

Art. 42. Validity and continuance in force of treaties

(1) The validity of a treaty or of the consent of a State to be bound by a treaty may be impeached only through the application of the present Convention.

(2) The termination of a treaty, its denunciation or the withdrawal of a party, may take place only as a result of the application of the provisions of the treaty or of the present Convention. The same rule applies to suspension of the operation of a treaty.

Art. 43. Obligations imposed by international law independently of a treaty

The invalidity, termination or denunciation of a treaty, the withdrawal of a party from it, or the suspension of its operation, as a result of the application of the present Convention or of the provisions of the treaty, shall not in any way impair the duty of any State to fulfil any obligation embodied in the treaty to which it would be subject under international law independently of the treaty.

Art. 44. Separability of treaty provisions

(1) A right of a party, provided for in a treaty or arising under art. 56, to denounce, withdraw from or suspend the operation of the treaty may be exercised only with respect to the whole treaty unless the treaty otherwise provides or the parties otherwise agree.

(2) A ground for invalidating, terminating, withdrawing from or suspending the operation of a treaty recognized in the present Convention may be invoked only with respect to the whole treaty except as provided in the following paragraphs or in art. 60.

(3) If the ground relates solely to particular clauses, it may be invoked only with respect to those clauses where:

(a) the said clauses are separable from the remainder of the treaty with regard to their application;

(b) it appears from the treaty or is otherwise established that acceptance of those clauses was not an essential basis of the consent of the other party or parties to be bound by the treaty as a whole; and

(c) continued performance of the remainder of the treaty would not be unjust.

(4) In cases falling under articles 49 and 50 the State entitled to invoke the fraud or corruption may do so with respect either to the whole treaty or, subject to paragraph 3, to the particular clauses alone.

(5) In cases falling under art. 51, 52 and 53, no separation of the provisions of the treaty is permitted.

Art. 45. Loss of a right to invoke a ground for invalidating, terminating, withdrawing from or suspending the operation of a treaty

A State may no longer invoke a ground for invalidating, terminating, withdrawing from or suspending the operations of a treaty under articles 46 to 50 or articles 60 and 62 if, after becoming aware of the facts:

(a) it shall have expressly agreed that the treaty is valid or remains in force or continues in operation, as the case may be; or

(b) it must by reason of its conduct be considered as having acquiesced in the validity of the treaty or in its maintenance in force or in operation, as the case may be.

Section 2: Invalidity of Treaties

Art. 46. Provisions of internal law regarding competence to conclude treaties

(1) A State may not invoke the fact that its consent to be bound by a treaty has been expressed in violation of a provision of its internal law regarding competence to conclude treaties as invalidating its consent unless that violation was manifest and concerned a rule of its internal law of fundamental importance.

(2) A violation is manifest if it would be objectively evident to any State conducting itself in the matter in accordance with normal practice and in good faith.

Art. 47. Specific restrictions on authority to express the consent of a State

If the authority of a representative to express the consent of a State to be bound by a particular treaty has been made subject to a specific restriction, his omission to observe that restriction may not be invoked as invalidating the consent expressed by him unless the restriction was notified to the other negotiating States prior to his expressing such consent.

Art. 48. Error

(1) A State may invoke an error in a treaty as invalidating its consent to be bound by the treaty if the error relates to a fact or situation which was assumed by that State to exist at the time when the treaty was concluded and formed an essential basis of its consent to be bound by the treaty.

(2) Paragraph 1 shall not apply if the State in question contributed by its own conduct to the error or if the circumstances were such as to put that State on notice of a possible error.

(3) An error relating only to the wording of the text of a treaty does not affect its validity; art. 79 then applies.

Art. 49. Fraud

If a State has been induced to conclude a treaty by the fraudulent conduct of another negotiating State, the State may invoke the fraud as invalidating its consent to be bound by the treaty.

Art. 50. Corruption of a representative of a State

If the expression of a State's consent to be bound by a treaty has been procured through the corruption of its representative directly or indirectly by another negotiating State, the State may invoke such corruption as invalidating its consent to be bound by the treaty.

Art. 51. Coercion of a representative of a State

The expression of a State's consent to be bound by a treaty which has been procured by the coercion of its representative through acts or threats directed against him shall be without any legal effect.

Art. 52. Coercion of a State by the threat or use of force

A treaty is void if its conclusion has been procured by the threat or use of force in violation of the principles of international law embodied in the Charter of the United Nations.

Art. 53. Treaties conflicting with a peremptory norm of general international law (jus cogens)

A treaty is void if, at the time of its conclusion, it conflicts with a peremptory norm of general international law. For the purposes of the present Convention, a peremptory norm of general international law is a norm accepted and recognized by the international community of States as a whole as a norm from which no derogation is permitted and which can be modified only by a subsequent norm of general international law having the same character.

Section 3: Termination and Suspension of the Operation of Treaties

Art. 54. Termination of or withdrawal from a treaty under its provisions or by consent of the parties

The termination of a treaty or the withdrawal of a party may take place:
(a) in conformity with the provisions of the treaty; or
(b) at any time by consent of all the parties after consultation with the other contracting States.

Art. 55. Reduction of the parties to a multilateral treaty below the number necessary for its entry into force

Unless the treaty otherwise provides, a multilateral treaty does not terminate by reason only of the fact that the number of the parties falls below the number necessary for its entry into force.

Art. 56. Denunciation of or withdrawal from a treaty containing no provision regarding termination, denunciation or withdrawal

(1) A treaty which contains no provision regarding its termination and which does not provide for denunciation or withdrawal is not subject to denunciation or withdrawal unless:
(a) it is established that the parties intended to admit the possibility of denunciation or withdrawal; or
(b) a right of denunciation or withdrawal may be implied by the nature of the treaty.
(2) A party shall give not less than twelve months' notice of its intention to denounce or withdraw from a treaty under paragraph 1.

Art. 57. Suspension of the operation of a treaty under its provisions or by consent of the parties

The operation of a treaty in regard to all the parties or to a particular party may be suspended:
(a) in conformity with the provisions of the treaty; or
(b) at any time by consent of all the parties after consultation with the other contracting States.

Art. 58. Suspension of the operation of a multilateral treaty by agreement between certain of the parties only

(1) Two or more parties to a multilateral treaty may conclude an agreement to suspend the operation of provisions of the treaty, temporarily and as between themselves alone; if:
(a) the possibility of such a suspension is provided for by the treaty; or
(b) the suspension in question is not prohibited by the treaty and:
(i) does not affect the enjoyment by the other parties of their rights under the treaty of the performance of their obligations;
(ii) is not incompatible with the object and purpose of the treaty.
(2) Unless in a case falling under paragraph 1(a) the treaty otherwise provides, the parties in question shall notify the other parties of their intention to conclude the agreement and of those provisions of the treaty the operation of which they intend to suspend.

Art. 59. Termination or suspension of the operation of a treaty implied by conclusion of a later treaty

(1) A treaty shall be considered as terminated if all the parties to it conclude a later treaty relating to the same subject-matter and:
(a) it appears from the later treaty or is otherwise established that the parties intended that the matter should be governed by that treaty; or
(b) the provisions of the later treaty are so far incompatible with those of the earlier one that the two treaties are not capable of being applied at the same time.
(2) The earlier treaty shall be considered as only suspended in operation if it appears from the later treaty or is otherwise established that such was the intention of the parties.

Art. 60. Termination or suspension of the operation of a treaty as a consequence of its breach

(1) A material breach of a bilateral treaty by one of the parties entitles the other to invoke the breach as a ground for terminating the treaty or suspending its operation in whole or in part.
(2) A material breach of a multilateral treaty by one of the parties entitles:
(a) the other parties by unanimous agreement to suspend the operation of the treaty in whole or in part or to terminate it either:
(i) in the relations between themselves and the defaulting State, or
(ii) as between all the parties;
(b) a party specially affected by the breach to invoke it as a ground for suspending the operation of the treaty in whole or in part in the relations between itself and the defaulting State;
(c) any party other than the defaulting State to invoke the breach as a ground for suspending the operation if the treaty in whole or in part with respect to itself of the treaty is of such a character that a material breach of its provisions by one party radically changes the position of every party with respect to the further performance of its obligations under the treaty.
(3) A material breach of a treaty, for the purposes of this article, consists in:
(a) a repudiation of the treaty not sanctioned by the present Convention; or
(b) the violation of a provision essential to the accomplishment of the object or purpose of the treaty.
(4) The foregoing paragraphs are without prejudice to any provision in the treaty applicable in the event of a breach.
(5) Paragraphs 1 to 3 do not apply to provisions relating to the protection of the human person contained in treaties of a humanitarian character, in particular to provisions prohibiting any form of reprisals against persons protected by such treaties.

Art. 61. Supervening impossibility of performance

(1) A party may invoke the impossibility of performing a treaty as a ground for terminating or withdrawing from it if the impossibility results from the permanent disappearance or destruction of an object indispensable for the execution of the treaty. If the impossibility is temporary, it may be invoked only as a ground for suspending the operation of the treaty.
(2) Impossibility of performance may not be invoked by a party as a ground for terminating, withdrawing from or suspending the operation of a treaty if the impossibility is the result of a breach by that party either of an obligation under the treaty or of any other international obligation owed to any other party to the treaty.

Art. 62. Fundamental change of circumstances

(1) A fundamental change of circumstances which has occurred with regard to those existing at the time of the conclusion of a treaty, and which was not foreseen by the parties, may not be invoked as a ground for terminating or withdrawing from the treaty unless;
(a) the existence of those circumstances constituted an essential basis of the consent of the parties to be bound by the treaty; and
(b) the effect of the change is radically to transform the extent of obligations still to be performed under the treaty.
(2) A fundamental change of circumstances may not be invoked as a ground for terminating or withdrawing from a treaty;
(a) if the treaty established a boundary; or
(b) if the fundamental change is the result of a breach by the party invoking it either of an obligation under the treaty or of any other international obligation owed to any other party to the treaty.
(3) If, under the foregoing paragraphs, a party may invoke a fundamental change of circumstances as a ground for terminating or withdrawing from a treaty it may also invoke the change as a ground for suspending the operation of the treaty.

Art. 63. Severance of diplomatic or consular relations

The severance of diplomatic or consular relations between parties to a treaty does not affect the legal relations established between them by the treaty except in so far as the existence of diplomatic or consular relations is indispensable for the application of the treaty.

Art. 64. Emergence of a new peremptory norm of general international law (jus cogens)

If a new peremptory norm of general international law emerges, any existing treaty which is in conflict with that norm becomes void and terminates.

Section 4: Procedure

Art. 65. Procedure to be followed with respect to invalidity, termination, withdrawal from or suspension of the operation of a treaty

(1) A party which, under the provisions of the present Convention, invokes either a defect in its consent to be bound by a treaty or a ground for impeaching the validity of a treaty, terminating it, withdrawing from it or suspending its operation, must notify the other parties of its claim. The notification shall indicate the measure proposed to be taken with respect to the treaty and the reasons therefore.
(2) If, after the expiry of a period which, except in cases of special urgency, shall not be less than three months after the receipt of the notification, no party has raised any objection, the party making the notification may carry out in the manner provided in art. 67 the measure which it has proposed.
(3) If, however, objection has been raised by any other party, the parties shall seek a solution through the means indicated in Art. 33 of the Charter of the United Nations.
(4) Nothing in the foregoing paragraphs shall affect the rights or obligations of the parties under any provisions in force binding the parties with regard to the settlement of disputes.
(5) Without prejudice to art. 45, the fact that a State has not previously made the notification prescribed in paragraph 1 shall not prevent it from making such notification in answer to another party claiming performance of the treaty or alleging its violation.

Art. 66. Procedures for judicial settlement, arbitration and conciliation

If, under paragraph 3 of art. 65, no solution has been reached within a period of 12 months following the date on which the objection was raised, the following procedures shall be followed:
(a) any one of the parties to a dispute concerning the application or the interpretation of art. 53 or 64 may, by a written application, submit it to the International Court of Justice for a decision unless the parties by common consent agree to submit the dispute to arbitration;
(b) any one of the parties to a dispute concerning the application or the interpretation of any of the other articles in Part V of the present Convention may set in motion the procedure specified in the Annex to the Convention by submitting a request to that effect to the Secretary-General of the United Nations.

Art. 67. Instruments for declaring invalid, terminating, withdrawing from or suspending the operation of a treaty

(1) The notification provided for under art. 65 paragraph 1 must be made in writing
(2) Any act declaring invalid, terminating, withdrawing from or suspending the operation of a treaty pursuant to the provisions of the treaty or of paragraph 2 or 3 of art. 65 shall be carried out through an instrument communicated to the other parties. If the instrument is not signed by the Head of State, Head of Government or Minister for Foreign Affairs, the representative of the State communicating it may be called upon to produce full powers.

Art. 68. Revocation of notifications and instruments provided for in art. 65 and 67

A notification or instrument provided for in art. 65 or 67 may be revoked at any time before it takes effect.

Section 5: Consequences of the invalidity, Termination or Suspension of the Operation of a Treaty

Art. 69. Consequences of the invalidity of a treaty

(1) A treaty the invalidity of which is established under the present Convention is void. The provisions of a void treaty have no legal force.
(2) If acts have nevertheless been performed in reliance on such a treaty:
(a) each party may require any other party to establish as far as possible in their mutual relations the position that would have existed if the acts had not been performed,
(b) acts performed in good faith before the invalidity was invoked are not rendered unlawful by reason only of the invalidity of the treaty.
(3) In cases failing under art. 49, 50, 51 or 52, paragraph 2 does not apply with respect to the party to which the fraud, the act of corruption or the coercion is imputable.
(4) In the case of the invalidity of a particular State's consent to be bound by a multilateral treaty, the foregoing rules apply in the relations between that State and the parties to the treaty.

Art. 70. Consequences of the termination of a treaty

(1) Unless the treaty otherwise provides or the parties otherwise agree, the termination of a treaty under its

provisions or in accordance with the present Convention:
(a) releases the parties from any obligation further to perform the treaty;
(b) does not affect any right, obligation or legal situation of the parties created through the execution of the treaty prior to its termination.
(2) If a State denounces or withdraws from a multilateral treaty, paragraph 1 applies in the relations between that State and each of the other parties to the treaty from the date when such denunciation or withdrawal takes effect.
Art. 71. Consequences of the invalidity of a treaty which conflicts with a peremptory norm of general international law
(1) In the case of a treaty which is void under art. 53 the parties shall:
(a) eliminate as far as possible the consequences of any act performed in reliance on any provision which conflicts with the peremptory norm of general international law; and
(b) bring their mutual relations into conformity with the peremptory norm of general international law.
(2) In the case of a treaty which becomes void and terminates under art. 64, the termination of the treaty:
(a) releases the parties from any obligation further to perform the treaty;
(b) does not affect any right, obligation or legal situation of the parties created through the execution of the treaty prior to its termination; provided that those rights, obligations or situations may thereafter be maintained only to the extent that their maintenance is not in itself in conflict with the new peremptory norm of general international law.
Art. 72. Consequences of the suspension of the operation of a treaty
(1) Unless the treaty otherwise provides or the parties otherwise agree, the suspension of the operation of a treaty under its provisions or in accordance with the present Convention:
(a) releases the parties between which the operation of the treaty is suspended from the obligation to perform the treaty in their mutual relations during the period of the suspension;
(b) does not otherwise affect the legal relations between the parties established by the treaty.
(2) During the period of the suspension the parties shall refrain from acts tending to obstruct the resumption of the operation of the treaty.
Part VI. *Miscellaneous Provisions*
Art. 73. Cases of State succession, State responsibility and outbreak of hostilities
The provisions of the present Convention shall not prejudge any question that may arise in regard to a treaty from a succession of States or from the international responsibility of a State or from the outbreak of hostilities between States.
Art. 74. Diplomatic and consular relations and the conclusion of treaties
The severance or absence of diplomatic or consular relations between two or more States does not prevent the conclusion of treaties between those States. The conclusion of a treaty does not in itself affect the situation in regard to diplomatic or consular relations.
Art. 75. Case of an aggressor State
The provisions of the present Convention are without prejudice to any obligation in relation to a treaty which may arise for an aggressor State in consequence of measures taken in conformity with the Charter of the United Nations with reference to that State's aggression.
Part VII. Depositaries, Notifications, Corrections and Registration
Art. 76. Depositaries of treaties
(1) The designation of the depositary of a treaty may be made by the negotiating States, either in the treaty itself or in some other manner. The depositary may be one or more States, an international organization or the chief administrative officer of the organization.
(2) The functions of the depositary of a treaty are international in character and the depositary is under an obligation to act impartially in their performance. In particular, the fact that a treaty has not entered into force between certain of the parties or that a difference has appeared between a State and a depositary with regard to the performance of the latter's functions shall not affect that obligation.
Art. 77. Functions of depositaries

(1) The functions of a depositary, unless otherwise provided in the treaty or agreed by the contracting States, comprise in particular:
(a) keeping custody of the original text of the treaty and of any full powers delivered to the depositary;
(b) preparing certified copies of the original text and preparing any further text of the treaty in such additional languages as may be required by the treaty and transmitting them to the parties and to the States entitled to become parties in the treaty;
(c) receiving any signatures to the treaty and receiving and keeping custody of any instruments, notifications and communications relating to it;
(d) examining whether the signature or any instrument, notification or communication relating to the treaty is in due and proper form and, if need be, bringing the matter to the attention of the State in question;
(e) informing the parties and the States entitled to become parties to the treaty of acts, notifications and communications relating to the treaty;
(f) informing the States entitled to become parties to the treaty when the number of signatures or of instruments of ratification, acceptance, approval or accession required for the entry performing the functions specified in other provisions of the present Convention.
(2) In the event of any difference appearing between a State and the depositary as to the performance of the latter's functions, the depositary shall bring the question to the attention of the signatory States and the contracting States or, where appropriate, of the competent organ of the international organization concerned.
Art. 78. Notifications and communications
Except as the treaty or the present Convention otherwise provide, any notification or communication to be made by any State under the present Convention shall:
(a) if there is no depositary, be transmitted direct to the States for which it is intended, or if there is a depositary, to the latter;
(b) be considered as having been made by the State in question only upon its receipt by the State to which it was transmitted or, as the case may be, upon its receipt by the depositary;
(c) if transmitted to a depositary, be considered as received by the State for which it was intended only when the latter State has been informed by the depositary in accordance with art. 77, paragraph 1(e).
Art. 79. Correction of errors in texts or in certified copies of treaties
(1) Where, after the authentication of the text of a treaty, the signatory States and the contracting States are agreed that it contains an error, the error shall, unless they decide upon some other means of correction, be corrected:
(a) by having the appropriate correction made in the text and causing the correction to be initialled by duly authorized representatives;
(b) by executing or exchanging an instrument or instruments setting out the correction which it has been agreed to make; or
(c) by executing a corrected text of the whole treaty by the same procedure as in the case of the original text.
(2) Where the treaty is one for which there is a depositary, the latter shall notify the signatory States and the contracting States of the error and of the proposal to correct it and shall specify an appropriate time-limit within which objection to the proposed correction may be raised. If, on the expiry of the time-limit:
(a) no objection has been raised, the depositary shall make and initial the correction in the text and shall execute a procès-verbal of the rectification of the text and communicate a copy of it to the parties and to the States entitled to become parties to the treaty;
(b) an objection has been raised, the depositary shall communicate the objection to the signatory States and to the contracting States.
(3) The rules in paragraphs 1 and 2 apply also where the text has been authenticated in two or more languages and it appears that there is a lack of concordance which the signatory States and the contracting States agree should be corrected.
(4) The corrected text replaces the defective text ab initio, unless the signatory States and the contracting States otherwise decide.
(5) The correction of the text of a treaty that has been registered shall be notified to the Secretariat of the United Nations.

(6) Where an error is discovered in a certified copy of a treaty, the depositary shall execute a procès-verbal specifying the rectification and communicate a copy of it to the signatory States and to the contracting States.
Art. 80. Registration and publication of treaties
(1) Treaties shall, after their entry into force, be transmitted to the Secretariat of the United Nations for registration or filing and recording, as the case may be, and for publication.
(2) The designation of a depositary shall constitute authorization for it to perform the acts specified in the preceding paragraph.
Part VIII. *Final Provisions*
Art. 81. Signature
The present Convention shall be open for signature by all States Members of the United Nations or of any of the specialized agencies or of the International Atomic Energy Agency or parties to the Statute of the International Court of Justice, and by any other State invited by the General Assembly of the United Nations to become a party to the Convention, as follows: until 30 November 1969, at the Federal Ministry for Foreign Affairs of the Republic of Austria, and subsequently, until 30 April 1970, at United Nations Headquarters, New York.
Art. 82. Ratification
The present Convention is subject to ratification. The instruments of ratification shall be deposited with the Secretary-General of the United Nations.
Art. 83. Accession
The present Convention shall remain open for accession by any State belonging to any of the categories mentioned in art. 81. The instruments of accession shall be deposited with the Secretary-General of the United Nations.
Art. 84. Entry into force
(1) The present Convention shall enter into force on the thirtieth day following the date of deposit of the thirty-fifth instrument of ratification or accession.
(2) For each State ratifying or acceding to the Convention after the deposit of the thirty-fifth instrument of ratification or accession, the Convention shall enter into force on the thirtieth day after deposit by such State of its instrument of ratification or accession.
Art. 85. Authentic texts
The original of the present Convention, of which the Chinese, English, French, Russian and Spanish texts are equally authentic, shall be deposited with the Secretary-General of the United Nations.
In witness Whereof the undersigned Plenipotentiaries, being duly authorized thereto by their respective Governments, have signed the present Convention.
Done at Vienna, this twenty-third day of May, one thousand nine hundred and sixty-nine.
Annex
(1) A list of conciliators consisting of qualified jurists shall be drawn up and maintained by the Secretary-General of the United Nations. To this end, every State which is a Member of the United Nations or a party to the present Convention shall be invited to nominate two conciliators, and the names of the persons so nominated shall constitute the list. The term of a conciliator, including that of any conciliator nominated to fill a casual vacancy, shall be five years and may be renewed. A conciliator whose term expires shall continue to fulfil any function for which he shall have been chosen under the following paragraph.
(2) When a request has been made to the Secretary-General under art. 66, the Secretary-General shall bring the dispute before a conciliation commission constituted as follows:
The State or States constituting one of the parties to the dispute shall appoint:
(a) one conciliator of the nationality of that State or of one of those States, who may or may not be chosen from the list referred to in paragraph 1; and
(b) one conciliator not of the nationality of that State or of any of those States, who shall be chosen from the list.
The State or States constituting the other party to the dispute shall appoint two conciliators in the same way. The four conciliators chosen by the parties shall be appointed within sixty days following the date on which the Secretary-General receives the request.
The four conciliators shall, within sixty days following the date of the last of their own appointments, appoint a fifth conciliator chosen from the list, who shall be chairman.

If the appointment of the chairman or of any of the other conciliators has not been made within the period prescribed above for such appointment, it shall be made by the Secretary-General within sixty days following the expiry of that period. The appointment of the chairman may be made by the Secretary-General either from the list or from the membership of the International Law Commission. Any of the periods within which appointments must be made may be extended by agreement between the parties to the dispute.

Any vacancy shall be filled in the manner prescribed for the initial appointment.

(3) The Conciliation Commission shall decide its own procedure. The Commission, with the consent of the parties to the dispute, may invite any party to the treaty to submit to it its view orally or in writing. Decisions and recommendations of the Commission shall be made by a majority vote of the five members.

(4) The Commission may draw the attention of the parties to the dispute to any measures which might facilitate an amicable settlement.

(5) The Commission shall hear the parties, examine the claims and objections, and make proposals to the parties with a view to reaching an amicable settlement of the dispute.

(6) The Commission shall report within twelve months of its constitution. Its report shall be deposited with the Secretary-General and transmitted to the parties to the dispute. The report of the Commission, including any conclusions stated therein regarding the facts or questions of law, shall not be binding upon the parties and it shall have no other character than that of recommendations submitted for the consideration of the parties in order to facilitate an amicable settlement of the dispute.

(7) The Secretary-General shall provide the Commission with such assistance and facilities as it may require. The expenses of the Commission shall be borne by the United Nations."

"The Treaty of Treaties", in *American Journal of International Law*, No. 3, 1970.

VIENNA CONVENTION ON THE REPRESENTATION OF STATES IN THEIR RELATIONS WITH INTERNATIONAL ORGANIZATIONS OF A UNIVERSAL CHARACTER, 1975.

Adopted on Mar. 14, 1975, at Vienna by the UN Conference, Feb. 4–Mar. 14, 1975, convened by the UN General Assembly Res. 2966/XXVIII of Dec. 14, 1972, and Res. 3072/XXVIII of Nov. 30, 1973, with the participation of 81 states and 16 observers. The text of the convention reads as follows:

"The States Parties to the present Convention,

Recognizing the increasingly important role of multilateral diplomacy in relations between States and the responsibilites of the United Nations, its specialized agencies and other international organizations of a universal character within the international community,

Having in mind the purposes and principles of the Charter of the United Nations concerning the sovereign equality of States, the maintenance of international peace and security and the promotion of friendly relations and co-operation among States,

Recalling the work of codification and progressive development of international law applicable to bilateral relations between States which was achieved by the Vienna Convention on Diplomatic Relations of 1961, the Vienna Convention on Consular Relations of 1963, and the Convention on Special Missions of 1969,

Believing that an international convention on the representation of States in their relations with international organizations of a universal character would contribute to the promotion of friendly relations and co-operation among States, irrespective of their political, economic and social systems,

Recalling the provisions of Article 105 of the Charter of the United Nations,

Recognizing that the purpose of privileges and immunities contained in the present Convention is not to benefit individuals but to ensure the efficient performance of their functions in connexion with organizations and conferences,

Taking account of the Convention on the Privileges and Immunities of the United Nations of 1946, the Convention on the Privileges and Immunities of the Specialized Agencies of 1947 and other agreements in force between States and between States and international organizations,

Affirming that the rules of customary international law continue to govern questions not expressly regulated by the provisions of the present Convention,

Have agreed as follows:

Part I. *Introduction*

Art. 1. Use of terms

1. For the purposes of the present Convention:

(1) 'international organization' means an intergovernmental organization;

(2) 'international organization of a universal character' means the United Nations, its specialized agencies, the International Atomic Energy Agency and any similar organization whose membership and responsibilities are on a world-wide scale;

(3) 'organization' means the international organization in question;

(4) 'organ' means:

(a) any principal or subsidiary organ of an international organization, or

(b) any commission, committee or sub-group of any such organ, in which States are members;

(5) 'conference' means a conference of States convened by or under the auspices of an international organization;

(6) 'mission' means, as the case may be, the permanent mission or the permanent observer mission;

(7) 'permanent mission' means a mission of permanent character, representing the State, sent by a State member of an international organization to the Organization;

(8) 'permanent observer mission' means a mission of permanent character, representing the State, sent to an international organization by a State not a member of the Organization;

(9) 'delegation' means, as the case may be, the delegation to an organ or the delegation to a conference;

(10) 'delegation to an organ' means the delegation sent by a State to participate on its behalf in the proceedings of the organ;

(11) 'delegation to a conference' means the delegation sent by a State to participate on its behalf in the conference;

(12) 'observer delegation' means, as the case may be, the observer delegation to an organ or the observer delegation to a conference;

(13) 'observer delegation to an organ' means the delegation sent by a State to participate on its behalf as an observer in the proceedings of the organ;

(14) 'observer delegation to a conference' means the delegation sent by a State to participate on its behalf as an observer in the proceedings of the conference;

(15) 'host State' means the State in whose territory:

(a) the Organization has its seat or an office, or

(b) a meeting of an organ or a conference is held;

(16) 'sending State' means the State which sends:

(a) a mission to the Organization at its seat or to an office of the Organization, or

(b) a delegation to an organ or a delegation to a conference, or

(c) an observer delegation to an organ or an observer delegation to a conference;

(17) 'head of mission' means, as the case may be, the permanent representative or the permanent observer;

(18) 'permanent representative' means the person charged by the sending State with the duty of acting as the head of the permanent mission;

(19) 'permanent observer' means the person charged by the sending State with the duty of acting as the head of the permanent observer mission;

(20) 'members of the mission' means the head of mission and the members of the staff;

(21) 'head of delegation' means the delegate charged by the sending State with the duty of acting in that capacity;

(22) 'delegate' means any person designated by a State to participate as its representative in the proceedings of an organ or in a conference;

(23) 'members of the delegation' means the delegates and the members of the staff;

(24) 'head of the observer delegation' means the observer delegate charged by the sending State with the duty of acting in that capacity;

(25) 'observer delegate' means any person designated by a State to attend as an observer the proceedings of an organ or of a conference;

(26) 'members of the observer delegation' means the observer delegates and the members of the staff;

(27) 'members of the staff' means the members of the diplomatic staff, the administrative and technical staff and the service staff of the mission, the delegation or the observer delegation;

(28) 'members of the diplomatic staff' means the members of the staffmission, the delegation or the observer delegation who enjoy diplomatic status for the purpose of the mission, the delegation or the observer delegation;

(29) 'members of the administrative and technical staff' means the members of the staff employed in the administrative and technical service of the mission, the delegation or the observer delegation;

(30) 'members of the service staff' means the members of the staff employed by the mission, the delegation or the observer delegation as household workers or for similar tasks;

(31) 'private staff' means persons employed exclusively in the private service of the members of the mission or the delegation;

(32) 'premises of the mission' means the buildings or parts of buildings and the land ancillary thereto, irrespective of ownership, used for the purpose of the mission, including the residence of the head of mission;

(33) 'premises of the delegation' means the buildings or parts of buildings, irrespective of ownership, used solely as the offices of the delegation;

(34) 'rules of the Organization' means, in particular, the constituent instruments, relevant decisions and resolutions, and established practice of the Organization.

2. The provisions of paragraph 1 of this article regarding the use of terms in the present Convention are without prejudice to the use of those terms or to the meanings which may be given to them in other international instruments or the internal law of any State.

Art. 2. Scope of the present Convention.

(1) The present Convention applies to the representation of States in their relations with any international organization of a universal character, and to their representation at conferences convened by or under the auspices of such an organization, when the convention has been accepted by the host State and the Organization has completed the procedure envisaged by article 90.

(2) The fact that the present Convention does not apply to other international organizations is without prejudice to the application to the representation of States in their relations with such other organizations of any of the rules set forth in the Convention which would be applicable under international law independently of the Convention.

(3) The fact that the present Convention does not apply to other conferences is without prejudice to the application to the representation of States at such other conferences of any of the rules set forth in the Convention which would be applicable under international law independently of the Convention.

(4) Nothing in the present Convention shall preclude the conclusion of agreements between States or between States and international organizations making the Convention applicable in whole or in part to international organizations or conferences other than those referred to in paragraph 1 of this article.

Art. 3. Relationship between the present Convention and the relevant rules of international organizations or conferences.

The provisions of the present Convention are without prejudice to any relevant rules of the Organization or to any relevant rules of procedure of the conference.

Art. 4. Relationship between the present Convention and other international agreements.

The provisions of the present Convention:

(a) are without prejudice to other international agreements in force between States or between States and international organizations of a universal character, and

(b) shall not preclude the conclusion of other international agreements regarding the representation of States in their relations with international organizations of a universal character or their representation at conferences convened by or under the auspices of such organizations.

Part II. *Missions to International Organizations.*

Art. 5. Establishment of missions.

(1) Member States may, if the rules of the Organization so permit, establish permanent missions for the performance of the functions mentioned in article 6.

(2) Non-member States may, if the rules of the Organization so permit, establish permanent observer missions for the performance of the functions mentioned in article 7.

(3) The Organization shall notify the host State of the institution of a mission prior to its establishment.

Art. 6. Functions of the permanent mission.

The functions of the permanent mission consist inter alia in:

(a) ensuring the representation of the sending State to the Organization;

(b) maintaining liaison between the sending State and the Organization;

(c) negotiating with and within the Organization;

(d) ascertaining activities in the Organization and reporting thereon to the government of the sending State;

(e) ensuring the participation of the sending State in the activities of the Organization;

(f) protecting the interests of the sending State in relation to the Organization;

(g) promoting the realization of the purposes and principles of the Organization by co-operating with and within the Organization.

Art. 7. Functions of the permanent observer mission.

The functions of the permanent observer mission consist inter alia in:

(a) ensuring the representation of the sending State and safeguarding its interests in relation to the Organization and maintaining liaison with it;

(b) ascertaining activities in the Organization and reporting thereon to the government of the sending State;

(c) promoting co-operation with the Organization and negotiating with it.

Art. 8. Multiple accreditation or appointment.

(1) The sending State may accredit the same person as head of mission to two or more international organizations or appoint a head of mission as a member of the diplomatic staff of another of its missions.

(2) The sending State may accredit a member of the diplomatic staff of the mission as head of mission to other international organizations or appoint a member of the staff of the mission as a member of the staff of another of its missions.

(3) Two or more States may accredit the same person as head of mission to the same international organization.

Art. 9. Appointment of the members of the mission.

Subject to the provisions of articles 14 and 73, the sending State may freely appoint the members of the mission.

Art. 10. Credentials of the head of mission.

The credentials of the head of mission shall be issued by the Head of State, by the Head of Government, by the Minister for Foreign Affairs or, if the rules of the Organization so permit, by another competent authority of the sending State and shall be transmitted to the Organization.

Art. 11. Accreditation to organs of the Organization.

(1) A member State may specify in the credentials issued to its permanent representative that he is authorized to act as a delegate to one or more organs of the Organization.

(2) Unless a member State provides otherwise its permanent representative may act as a delegate to organs of the Organization for which there are no special requirements as regards representation.

(3) A non-member State may specify in the credentials issued to its permanent observer that he is authorized to act as an observer delegate to one or more organs of the Organization when this is permitted by the rules of the Organization or the organ concerned.

Art. 12. Full powers for the conclusion of a treaty with the Organization.

(1) The head of mission, by virtue of his functions and without having to produce full powers, is considered as representing his State for the purpose of adopting the text of a treaty between that State and the Organization.

(2) The head of mission is not considered by virtue of his functions as representing his State for the purpose of signing a treaty, or signing a treaty and referendum,

between that State and the Organization unless it appears from the practice of the Organization, or from other circumstances, that the intention of the parties was to dispense with full powers.

Art. 13. Composition of the mission.

In addition to the head of mission, the mission may include diplomatic staff, administrative and technical staff and service staff.

Art. 14. Size of the mission.

The size of the mission shall not exceed what is reasonable and normal, having regard to the functions of the Organization, the needs of the particular mission and the circumstances and conditions in the host State.

Art. 15. Notifications.

(1) The sending State shall notify the Organization of:

(a) the appointment, position, title and order of precedence of the members of the mission, their arrival, their final departure or the termination of their functions with the mission, and any other changes affecting their status that may occur in the course of their service with the mission;

(b) the arrival and final departure of any person belonging to the family of a member of the mission and forming part of his household and, where appropriate, the fact that a person becomes or ceases to be such a member of the family;

(c) the arrival and final departure of persons employed on the private staff of members of the mission and the termination of their employment as such;

(d) the beginning and the termination of the employment of persons resident in the host State as members of the staff of the mission or as persons employed on the private staff;

(e) the location of the premises of the mission and of the private residences enjoying inviolability under articles 23 and 29, as well as any other information that may be necessary to identify such premises and residences.

(2) Where possible, prior notification of arrival and final departure shall also be given.

(3) The Organization shall transmit to the host State the notifications referred to in paragraphs 1 and 2 of this article.

(4) The sending State may also transmit to the host State the notifications referred to in paragraphs 1 and 2 of this article.

Art. 16. Acting head of mission.

If the post of head of mission is vacant, or if the head of mission is unable to perform his functions, the sending State may appoint an acting head of mission whose name shall be notified to the Organization and by it to the host State.

Art. 17. Precedence

(1) Precedence among permanent representatives shall be determined by the alphabetical order of the names of the States used in the Organization.

(2) Precedence among permanent observers shall be determined by the alphabetical order of the names of the States used in the Organization.

Art. 18. Location of the mission.

Missions should be established in the locality where the Organization has its seat. However, if the rules of the Organization so permit and with the prior consent of the host State, the sending State may establish a mission or an office of a mission in a locality other than that in which the Organization has its seat.

Art. 19. Use of flag and emblem

(1) The mission shall have the right to use the flag and emblem of the sending State on its premises. The head of mission shall have the same right as regards his residence and means of transport.

(2) In the exercise of the right accorded by this article regard shall be had to the laws, regulations and usages of the host State.

Art. 20. General facilities.

(1) The host State shall accord to the mission all necessary facilities for the performance of its functions.

(2) The Organization shall assist the mission in obtaining those facilities and shall accord to the mission such facilities as lie within its own competence.

Art. 21. Premises and accommodation.

(1) The host State and the Organization shall assist the sending State in obtaining on reasonable terms premises necessary for the mission in the territory of the host State. Where necessary, the host State shall facilitate in accordance with its laws the acquisition of such premises.

(2) Where necessary, the host State and the Organization shall also assist the mission in obtaining on reasonable terms suitable accommodation for its members.

Art. 22. Assistance by the Organization in respect of privileges and immunities.

(1) The Organization shall, where necessary, assist the sending State, its mission and the members of its mission in securing the enjoyment of the privileges and immunities provided for under the present Convention.

(2) The Organization shall, where necessary, assist the host State in securing the discharge of the obligations of the sending State, its mission and the members of its mission in respect of the privileges and immunities provided for under the present Convention.

Art. 23. Inviolability of premises.

(1) The premises of the mission shall be inviolable. The agents of the host State may not enter them, except with the consent of the head of mission.

(2)(a) The host State is under a special duty to take all appropriate steps to protect the premises of the mission against any intrusion or damage and to prevent any disturbance of the peace of the mission or impairment of its dignity.

(b) In case of an attack on the premises of the mission, the host State shall take all appropriate steps to prosecute and punish persons who have committed the attack.

(3) The premises of the mission, their furnishings and other property thereon and the means of transport of the mission shall be immune from search, requisition, attachment or execution.

Art. 24. Exemption of the premises from taxation

(1) The premises of the mission of which the sending State or any person acting on its behalf is the owner or the lessee shall be exempt from all national, regional or municipal dues and taxes other than such as represent payment for specific services rendered.

(2) The exemption from taxation referred to in this article shall not apply to such dues and taxes payable under the law of the host State by persons contracting with the sending State or with any person acting on its behalf.

Art. 25. Inviolability of archives and documents.

The archives and documents of the mission shall be inviolable at all times and wherever they may be.

Art. 26. Freedom of movement.

Subject to its laws and regulations concerning zones entry into which is prohibited or regulated for reasons of national security, the host State shall ensure freedom of movement and travel in its territory to all members of the mission and members of their families forming part of their households.

Art. 27. Freedom of communication.

(1) The host State shall permit and protect free communication on the part of the mission for all official purposes. In communicating with the Government of the sending State, its permanent diplomatic missions, consular posts, permanent missions, permanent observer missions, special missions, delegations and observer delegations, wherever situated, the mission may employ all appropriate means, including couriers and messages in code or cipher. However, the mission may install and use a wireless transmitter only with the consent of the host State.

(2) The official correspondence of the mission shall be inviolable. Official correspondence means all corespondence relating to the mission and its functions.

(3) The bag of the mission shall not be opened or detained.

(4) The packages constituting the bag of the mission must bear visible external marks of their character and may contain only documents or articles intended for the official use of the mission.

(5) The courier of the mission, who shall be provided with an official document indicating his status and the number of packages constituting the bag, shall be protected by the host State in the performance of his functions. He shall enjoy personal inviolability and shall not be liable to any form of arrest or detention.

(6) The sending State or the mission may designate couriers ad hoc of the mission. In such cases the provisions of paragraph 5 of this article shall also apply, except that the immunities therein mentioned shall cease to apply when the courier ad hoc has delivered to the consignee the mission's bag in his charge.

(7) The bag of the mission may be entrusted to the captain of a ship or of a commercial aircraft scheduled to land at an authorized port of entry. He shall be

provided with an official document indicating the number of packages constituting the bag, but he shall not be considered to be a courier of the mission. By arrangement with the appropriate authorities of the host State, the mission may send one of its members to take possession of the bag directly and freely from the captain of the ship or of the aircraft.

Art. 28. Personal inviolability.

The persons of the head of mission and of the members of the diplomatic staff of the mission shall be inviolable. They shall not be liable to any form of arrest or detention. The host State shall treat them with due respect and shall take all appropriate steps to prevent any attack on their persons, freedom or dignity and to prosecute and punish persons who have committed such attacks.

Art. 29. Inviolability of residence and property.

(1) The private residence of the head of mission and of the members of the diplomatic staff of the mission shall enjoy the same inviolability and protection as the premises of the mission.

(2) The papers, correspondence and, except as provided in paragraph 2 of article 30, the property of the head of mission or of members of the diplomatic staff of the mission shall also enjoy inviolability.

Art. 30. Immunity from jurisdiction.

(1) The head of mission and the members of the diplomatic staff of the mission shall enjoy immunity from the criminal jurisdiction of the host State. They shall also enjoy immunity from its civil and administrative jurisdiction, except in the case of:

(a) a real action relating to private immovable property situated in the territory of the host State, unless the person in question holds it on behalf of the sending State for the purposes of the mission;

(b) an action relating to succession in which the person in question is involved as executor, administrator, heir or legatee as a private person and not on behalf of the sending State;

(c) an action relating to any professional or commercial activity exercised by the person in question in the host State outside his official functions.

(2) No measures of execution may be taken in respect of the head of mission or a member of the diplomatic staff of the mission except in cases coming under subparagraphs (a), (b) and (c) of paragraph 1 of this article, and provided that the measures concerned can be taken without infringing the inviolability of his person or of his residence.

(3) The head of mission and the members of the diplomatic staff of the mission are not obliged to give evidence as witnesses.

(4) The immunity of the head of mission or of a member of the diplomatic staff of the mission from the jurisdiction of the host State does not exempt him from the jurisdiction of the sending State.

Art. 31. Waiver of immunity.

(1) The immunity from jurisdiction of the head of mission and members of the diplomatic staff of the mission and of persons enjoying immunity under article 36 may be waived by the sending State.

(2) Waiver must always be express.

(3) The initiation of proceedings by any of the persons referred to in paragraph 1 of this article shall preclude him from invoking immunity from jurisdiction in respect of any counter-claim directly connected with the principal claim.

(4) Waiver of immunity from jurisdiction in respect of civil or adminstrative proceedings shall not be held separate waiver shall be necessary.

(5) If the sending State does not waive the immunity of any of the persons mentioned in paragraph 1 of this article in respect of a civil action, it shall use its best endeavours to bring about a just settlement of the case.

Art. 32. Exemption from social security legislation.

(1) Subject to the provisions of paragraph 3 of this article, the head of mission and the members of the diplomatic staff of the mission shall with respect to services rendered for the sending State be exempt from social security provisions which may be in force in the host State.

(2) The exemption provided for in paragraph 1 of this article shall also apply to persons who are in the sole private employ of the head of mission or of a member of the diplomatic staff of the mission, on condition:

(a) that such employed persons are not nationals of or permanently resident in the host State; and

(b) that they are covered by the social security provisions which may be in force in the sending State or a third State.

(3) The head of mission and the members of the diplomatic staff of the mission who employ persons to whom the exemption provided for in paragraph 2 of this article does not apply shall observe the obligations which the social security provisions of the host State impose upon employers.

(4) The exemption provided for in paragraphs 1 and 2 of this article shall not preclude voluntary participation in the social security system of the host State provided that such participation is permitted by that State.

(5) The provisions of this article shall not affect bilateral or multilateral agreements concerning social security concluded previously and shall not prevent the conclusion of such agreements in the future.

Art. 33. Exemption from dues and taxes.

The head of mission and the members of the diplomatic staff of the mission shall be exempt from all dues and taxes, personal or real, national, regional or municipal, except:

(a) indirect taxes of a kind which are normally incorporated in the price of goods or services;

(b) dues and taxes on private immovable property situated in the territory of the host State, unless the person concerned holds it on behalf of the sending State for the purposes of the mission;

(c) estate, succession or inheritance duties levied by the host State, subject to the provisions of paragraph 4 of article 38;

(d) dues and taxes on private income having its source in the host State and capital taxes on investments made in commercial undertakings in the host State;

(e) charges levied for specific services rendered;

(f) registration, court or record fees, mortgage dues and stamp duty, with respect to immovable property, subject to the provisions of article 24.

Art. 34. Exemption from personal services.

The host State shall exempt the head of mission and the members of the diplomatic staff of the mission from all personal services, from all public service of any kind whatsoever, and from military obligations such as those connected with requisitioning, military contributions and billeting.

Art. 35. Exemption from customs duties and inspection.

(1) The host State shall, in accordance with such laws and regulations as it may adopt, permit entry of and grant exemption from all customs duties, taxes and related charges other than charges for storage, cartage and similar services, on:

(a) articles for the official use of the mission;

(b) articles for the personal use of the head of mission or a member of the diplomatic staff of the mission, including articles intended for his establishment.

(2) The personal baggage of the head of mission or a member of the diplomatic staff of the mission shall be exempt from inspection, unless there are serious grounds for presuming that it contains articles not covered by the exemptions mentioned in paragraph 1 of this article, or articles the import or export of which is prohibited by the law or controlled by the quarantine regulations of the host State. In such cases, inspection shall be conducted only in the presence of the person enjoying the exemption or of his authorized representative.

Art. 36. Privileges and immunities of other persons.

(1) The members of the family of the head of mission forming part of his household and the members of the family of a member of the diplomatic staff of the mission forming part of his household shall, if they are not nationals of or permanently resident in the host State, enjoy the privileges and immunities specified in articles 28, 29, 30, 32, 33, 34 and in paragraphs 1(b) and 2 of article 35.

(2) Members of the adminstrative and technical staff of the mission, together with members of their families forming part of their respective households who are not nationals of or permanently resident in the host State, shall enjoy the privileges and immunities specified in articles 28, 29, 30, 32, 33 and 34, except that the immunity from civil and administrative jurisdiction of the host State specified in paragraph 1 of article 30 shall not extend to acts performed outside the course of their duties. They shall also enjoy the privileges specified in paragraph 1(b) of article 35 in respect of articles imported at the time of first installation.

(3) Members of the service staff of the mission who are not nationals of or permanently resident in the host State shall enjoy immunity in respect of acts performed in the course of their duties, exemption from dues and taxes on the emoluments they receive by reason of their employment and the exemption specified in article 32.

(4) Private staff of members of the mission shall, if they are not nationals of or permanently resident in the host State, be exempt from dues and taxes on the emoluments they receive by reason of their employment. In other respects, they may enjoy privileges and immunities only to the extent admitted by the host State. However, the host State must exercise its jurisdiction over those persons in such a manner as not to interfere unduly with the performance of the functions of the mission.

Art. 37. Nationals and permanent residents of the host State.

(1) Except in so far as additional privileges and immunities may be granted by the host State, the head of mission or any member of the diplomatic staff of the mission who is a national of or permanently resident in that State shall enjoy only immunity from jurisdiction and inviolability in respect of official acts performed in the exercise of his functions.

(2) Other members of the staff of the mission who are nationals of or permanently resident in the host State shall enjoy only immunity from jurisdiction in respect of official acts performed in the exercise of their functions. In all other respects, those members, and persons on the private staff who are nationals of or permanently resident in the host State, shall enjoy privileges and immunities only to the extent admitted by the host State. However, the host State must exercise its jurisdiction over those members and persons in such a manner as not to interfere unduly with the performance of the functions of the mission.

Art. 38. Duration of privileges and immunities.

(1) Every person entitled to privileges and immunities shall enjoy them from the moment he enters the territory of the host State on proceeding to take up his post or, if already in its territory, from the moment when his appointment is notified to the host State by the Organization or by the sending State.

(2) When the functions of a person enjoying privileges and immunities have come to an end, such privileges and immunities shall normally cease at the moment when he leaves the territory, or on the expiry of a reasonable period in which to do so. However, with respect to acts performed by such a person in the exercise of his functions as a member of the mission, immunity shall continue to subsist.

(3) In the event of the death of a member of the mission, the members of his family shall continue to enjoy the privileges and immunities to which they are entitled until the expiry of a reasonable period in which to leave the territory.

(4) In the event of the death of a member of the mission not a national of or permanently resident in the host State or of a member of his family forming part of his household, the host State shall permit the withdrawal of the movable property of the deceased, with the exception of any property acquired in the territory the export of which was prohibited at the time of his death. Estate, succession and inheritance duties shall not be levied on movable property which is in the host State solely because of the presence there of the deceased as a member of the mission or of the family of a member of the mission.

Art. 39. Professional or commercial activity.

(1) The head of mission and members of the diplomatic staff of the mission shall not practise for personal profit any professional or commercial activity in the host State.

(2) Except in so far as such privileges and immunities may be granted by the host State, members of the administrative and technical staff and persons forming part of the household of a member of the mission shall not, when they practise a professional or commercial activity for personal profit, enjoy any privilege or immunity in respect of acts performed in the course of or in connexion with the practice of such activity.

Art. 40. End of functions.

The functions of the head of mission or of a member of the diplomatic staff of the mission shall come to an end, inter alia:

(a) on notification of their termination by the sending State to the Organization;

(b) if the mission is finally or temporarily recalled.

Art. 41. Protection of premises, property and archives.

(1) When the mission is temporarily or finally recalled, the host State must respect and protect the premises, property and archives of the mission. The sending State must take all appropriate measures to terminate this special duty of the host State as soon as possible. It may entrust custody of the premises, property and archives of the mission to the Organization if it so agrees, or to a third State acceptable to the host State.

(2) The host State, if requested by the sending State, shall grant the latter facilities for removing the property and archives of the mission from the territory of the host State.

Part. III. *Delegations to Organs and to Conferences.*

Art. 42. Sending of delegations.

(1) A State may send a delegation to an organ or to a conference in accordance with the rules of the Organization.

(2) Two or more States may send the same delegation to an organ or to a conference in accordance with the rules of the Organization.

Art. 43. Appointment of the members of the delegation. Subject to the provisions of articles 46 and 73, the sending State may freely appoint the members of the delegation.

Art. 44. Credentials of delegates.

The credentials of the head of delegation and of other delegates shall be issued by the Head of State, by the Head of Government, by the Minister for Foreign Affairs or, if the rules of the Organization or the rules of procedure of the conference so permit, by another competent authority of the sending State. They shall be transmitted, as the case may be, to the Organization or to the conference.

Art. 45. Composition of the delegation.

In addition to the head of delegation, the delegation may include other delegates, diplomatic staff, administrative and technical staff and service staff.

Art. 46. Size of the delegation.

The size of the delegation shall not exceed what is reasonable and normal, having regard, as the case may be, to the functions of the organ or the object of the conference, as well as the needs of the particular delegation and the circumstances and conditions in the host State.

Art. 47. Notifications.

(1) The sending State shall notify the Organization or, as the case may be, the conference of:

(a) the composition of the delegation, including the position, title and order of precedence of the members of the delegation, and any subsequent changes therein;

(b) the arrival and final departure of members of the delegation and the termination of their functions with the delegation;

(c) the arrival and final departure of any person accompanying a member of the delegation;

(d) the beginning and the termination of the employment of persons resident in the host State as members of the staff of the delegation or as persons employed on the private staff;

(e) the location of the premises of the delegation and of the private accommodation enjoying inviolability under article 59, as well as any other information that may be necessary to identify such premises and accommodation.

(2) Where possible, prior notification of arrival and final departure shall also be given.

(3) The Organization or, as the case may be, the conference shall transmit to the host State the notifications referred to in paragraphs 1 and 2 of this article.

(4) The sending State may also transmit to the host State the notifications referred to in paragraphs 1 and 2 of this article.

Art. 48. Acting head of delegation.

(1) If the head of delegation is absent or unable to perform his functions, an acting head of delegation shall be designated from among the other delegates by the head of delegation or, in case he is unable to do so, by a competent authority of the sending State. The name of the acting head of delegation shall be notified, as the case may be, to the Organization or to the conference.

(2) If a delegation does not have another delegate available to serve as acting head of delegation, another person may be designated for that purpose. In such case credentials must be issued and transmitted in accordance with article 44.

Art. 49. Precedence.

Precedence among delegations shall be determined by the alphabetical order of the names of the States used in the Organization.

Art. 50. Status of the Head of State and persons of high rank.

(1) The Head of State or any member of a collegial body performing the functions of Head of State under the constitution of the State concerned, when he leads the delegation, shall enjoy in the host State or in a third State, in addition to what is granted by the present Convention, the facilities, privileges and immunities accorded by international law to Heads of State.

(2) The Head of Government, the Minister for Foreign Affairs or other person of high rank, when he leads or is a member of the delegation, shall enjoy in the host State or in a third State, in addition to what is granted by the present Convention, the facilities, privileges and immunities accorded by international law to such persons.

Art. 51. General facilities.

(1) The host State shall accord to the delegation all necessary facilities for the performance of its tasks.

(2) The Organization or, as the case may be, the conference shall assist the delegation in obtaining those facilities and shall accord to the delegation such facilities as lie within its own competence.

Art. 52. Premises and accommodation.

If so requested, the host State and, where necessary, the Organization or the conference shall assist the sending State in obtaining on reasonable terms premises necessary for the delegation and suitable accommodation for its members.

Art. 53. Assistance in respect of privileges and immunities.

(1) The Organization or, as the case may be, the Organization and the conference shall, where necessary, assist the sending State, its delegation and the members of its delegation in securing the enjoyment of the privileges and immunities provided for under the present Convention.

(2) The Organization or, as the case may be, the Organization and the conference shall, where necessary, assist the host State in securing the discharge of the obligations of the sending State, its delegation and the members of its delegation in respect of the privileges and immunities provided for under the present Convention.

Art. 54. Exemption of the premises from taxation.

(1) The sending State or any member of the delegation acting on behalf of the delegation shall be exempt from all national, regional or municipal dues and taxes in respect of the premises of the delegation other than such as represent payment for specific services rendered.

(2) The exemption from taxation referred to in this article shall not apply to such dues and taxes payable under the law of the host State by persons contracting with the sending State or with a member of the delegation.

Art. 55. Inviolability of archives and documents.

The archives and documents of the delegation shall be inviolable at all times and wherever they may be.

Art. 56. Freedom of movement.

Subject to its laws and regulations concerning zones entry into which is prohibited or regulated for reasons of national security, the host State shall ensure to all members of the delegation such freedom of movement and travel in its territory as is necessary for the performance of the tasks of the delegation.

Art. 57. Freedom of communication.

(1) The host State shall permit and protect free communication on the part of the delegation for all official purposes. In communicating with the Government of the sending State, its permanent diplomatic missions, consular posts, permanent missions, permanent observer missions, special missions, other delegations, and observer delegations, wherever situated, the delegation may employ all appropriate means, including couriers and messages in code or cipher. However, the delegation may install and use a wireless transmitter only with the consent of the host State.

(2) The official correspondence of the delegation shall be inviolable. Official correspondence means all correspondence relating to the delegation and its tasks.

(3) Where practicable, the delegation shall use the means of communication, including the bag and the courier, of the permanent diplomatic mission, of a consular post, of the permanent mission or of the permanent observer mission of the sending State.

(4) The bag of the delegation shall not be opened or detained.

(5) The packages constituting the bag of the delegation must bear visible external marks of their character and may contain only documents or articles intended for the official use of the delegation.

(6) The courier of the delegation, who shall be provided with an official document indicating his status and the number of packages constituting the bag, shall be protected by the host State in the performance of his functions. He shall enjoy personal inviolability and shall not be liable to any form of arrest or detention.

(7) The sending State or the delegation may designate couriers ad hoc of the delegation. In such cases the provisions of paragraph 6 of this article shall also apply, except that the immunities therein mentioned shall cease to apply when the courier ad hoc has delivered to the consignee the delegation's bag in his charge.

(8) The bag of the delegation may be entrusted to the captain of a ship or of a commercial aircraft scheduled to land at an authorized port of entry. He shall be provided with an official document indicating the number of packages constituting the bag, but he shall not be considered to be a courier of the delegation. By arrangement with the appropriate authorities of the host State, the delegation may send one of its members to take possession of the bag directly and freely from the captain of the ship or of the aircraft.

Art. 58. Personal inviolability.

The persons of the head of delegation and of other delegates and members of the diplomatic staff of the delegation shall be inviolable. They shall not be liable inter alia to any form of arrest or detention. The host State shall treat them with due respect and shall take all appropriate steps to prevent any attack to their persons, freedom or dignity and to prosecute and punish persons who have committed such attacks.

Art. 59. Inviolability of private accommodation and property.

(1) The private accommodation of the head of delegation and of other delegates and members of the diplomatic staff of the delegation shall enjoy inviolability and protection.

(2) The papers, correspondence and, except as provided in paragraph 2 of article 60, the property of the head of delegation and of other delegates or members of the diplomatic staff of the delegation shall also enjoy inviolability.

Art. 60. Immunity from jurisdiction.

(1) The head of delegation and other delegates and members of the diplomatic staff of the delegation shall enjoy immunity from the criminal jurisdiction of the host State, and immunity from its civil and administrative jurisdiction in respect of all acts performed in the exercise of their official functions.

(2) No measures of execution may be taken in respect of such persons unless they can be taken without infringing their rights under articles 58 and 59.

(3) Such persons are not obliged to give evidence as witnesses.

(4) Nothing in this article shall exempt such persons from the civil and administrative jurisdiction of the host State in relation to an action for damages arising from an accident caused by a vehicle, vessel or aircraft, used or owned by the persons in question, where those damages are not recoverable from insurance.

(5) Any immunity of such persons from the jurisdiction of the host State does not exempt them from the jurisdiction of the sending State.

Art. 61. Waiver of immunity.

(1) The immunity from jurisdiction of the head of delegation and of other delegates and members of the diplomatic staff of the delegation and of persons enjoying immunity under article 66 may be waived by the sending State.

(2) Waiver must always be express.

(3) The initiation of proceedings by any of the persons referred to in paragraph 1 of this article shall preclude him from invoking immunity from jurisdiction in respect of any counter-claim directly connected with the principal claim.

(4) Waiver of immunity from jurisdiction in respect of civil or administrative proceedings shall not be held to imply waiver of immunity in respect of the execution of the judgement, for which a separate waiver shall be necessary.

(5) If the sending State does not waive the immunity of any of the persons mentioned in paragraph 1 of this article in respect of a civil action, it shall use its best endeavours to bring about a just settlement of the case.

Art. 62. Exemption from social security legislation.

(1) Subject to the provisions of paragraph 3 of this article, the head of delegation and other delegates and members of the diplomatic staff of the delegation shall with respect to services rendered for the sending State be exempt from social security provisions which may be in force in the host State.

(2) The exemption provided for in paragraph 1 of this article shall also apply to persons who are in the sole private employ of the head of delegation or of any other delegate or member of the diplomatic staff of the delegation, on condition:

(a) that such employed persons are not nationals of or permanently resident in the host State; and

(b) that they are covered by the social security provisions which may be in force in the sending State or a third State.

(3) The head of delegation and other delegates and members of the diplomatic staff of the delegation who employ persons to whom the exemption provided for in paragraph 2 of this article does not apply shall observe the obligations which the social security provisions of the host State impose upon employers.

(4) The exemption provided for in paragraphs 1 and 2 of this article shall not preclude voluntary participation in the social security system of the host State provided that such participation is permitted by that State.

(5) The provisions of this article shall not affect bilateral or multilateral agreements concerning social security concluded previously and shall not prevent the conclusion of such agreements in the future.

Art. 63. Exemption from dues and taxes.

The head of delegation and other delegates and members of the diplomatic staff of the delegation shall be exempt, to the extent practicable, from all dues and taxes, personal or real, national, regional or municipal, except:

(a) indirect taxes of a kind which are normally incorporated in the price of goods and services;

(b) dues and taxes on private immovable property situated in the territory of the host State, unless the person concerned holds it on behalf of the sending State for the purposes of the delegation;

(c) estate, succession or inheritance duties levied by the host State, subject to the provisions of paragraph 4 of article 68;

(d) dues and taxes on private income having its source in the host State and capital taxes on investments made in commercial undertakings in the host State;

(e) charges levied for specific services rendered;

(f) registration, court or record fees, mortgage dues and stamp duty, with respect to immovable property, subject to the provisions of article 54.

Art. 64. Exemption from personal services.

The host State shall exempt the head of delegation and other delegates and members of the diplomatic staff of the delegation from all personal services, from all public service of any kind whatsoever, and from military obligations such as those connected with requisitioning, military contributions and billeting.

Art. 65. Exemption from customs duties and inspection.

(1) The host State shall, in accordance with such laws and regulations as it may adopt, permit entry of and grant exemption from all customs duties, taxes and related charges other than charges for storage, cartage and similar services, on:

(a) articles for the official use of the delegation;

(b) articles for the personal use of the head of delegation or any other delegate or member of the diplomatic staff of the delegation, imported in his personal baggage at the time of his first entry into the territory of the host State to attend the meeting of the organ or conference.

(2) The personal baggage of the head of delegation or any other delegate or member of the diplomatic staff of the delegation shall be exempt from inspection, unless there are serious grounds for presuming that it contains articles not covered by the exemptions mentioned in paragraph 1 of this article, or articles the import or export of which is prohibited by the law or controlled by the quarantine regulations of the host State. In such cases, inspection shall be conducted only in the presence of the person enjoying the exemption or of his authorized representative.

Art. 66. Privileges and immunities of other persons.

(1) The members of the family of the head of delegation who accompany him and the members of the family of any other delegate or member of the diplomatic staff of the delegation who accompany him shall, if they are not nationals of or permanently resident in the host State, enjoy the privileges and immunities specified in articles 58, 60 and 64 and in paragraphs 1(b) and 2 of article 65 and exemption from aliens' registration obligations.

(2) Members of the administrative and technical staff of the delegation shall, if they are not nationals of or permanently resident in the host State, enjoy the privileges and immunities specified in articles 58, 59, 60, 62, 63 and 64. They shall also enjoy the privileges specified in paragraph 1(b) of article 65 in respect of articles imported in their personal baggage at the time of their first entry into the territory of the host State for the purpose of attending the meeting of the organ or conference. Members of the family of a member of the administrative and technical staff who accompany him shall if they are not nationals of or permanently resident in the host State, enjoy the privileges and immunities specified in articles 58, 60 and 64 and in paragraph 1(b) of article 65 to the extent accorded to such a member of the staff.

(3) Members of the service staff of the delegation who are not nationals of or permanently resident in the host State shall enjoy the same immunity in respect of acts performed in the course of their duties as is accorded to members of the administrative and technical staff of the delegation, exemption from dues and taxes on the emoluments they receive by reason of their employment and the exemption specified in article 62.

(4) Private staff of members of the delegation shall, if they are not nationals of or permanently resident in the host State, be exempt from dues and taxes on the emoluments they receive by reason of their employment. In other respects, they may enjoy privileges and immunities only to the extent admitted by the host State. However, the host State must exercise its jurisdiction over those persons in such a manner as not to interfere unduly with the performance of the tasks of the delegation.

Art. 67. Nationals and permanent residents of the host State.

(1) Except in so far as additional privileges and immunities may be granted by the host State the head of delegation or any other delegate or member of the diplomatic staff of the delegation who is a national of or permanently resident in that State shall enjoy only immunity from jurisdiction and inviolability in respect of official acts performed in the exercise of his functions.

(2) Other members of the staff of the delegation and persons on the private staff who are nationals of or permanently resident in the host State shall enjoy privileges and immunities only to the extent admitted by the host State. However, the host State must exercise its jurisdiction over those members and persons in such a manner as not to interfere unduly with the performance of the tasks of the delegation.

Art. 68. Duration of privileges and immunities.

(1) Every person entitled to privileges and immunities shall enjoy them from the moment he enters the territory of the host State for the purpose of attending the meeting of an organ or conference or, if already in its territory, from the moment when his appointment is notified to the host State by the Organization, by the conference or by the sending State.

(2) When the functions of a person enjoying privileges and immunities have come to an end, such privileges and immunities shall normally cease at the moment when he leaves the territory, or on the expiry of a reasonable period in which to do so. However, with respect to acts performed by such a person in the exercise of his functions as a member of the delegation, immunity shall continue to subsist.

(3) In the event of the death of a member of the delegation, the members of his family shall continue to enjoy the privileges and immunities to which they are entitled until the expiry of a reasonable period in which to leave the territory.

(4) In the event of the death of a member of the delegation not a national of or permanently resident in the host State or of a member of his family accompanying him, the host State shall permit the withdrawal of the movable property of the deceased, with the exception of any property acquired in the territory the export of which was prohibited at the time of his death. Estate,

succession and inheritance duties shall not be levied on movable property which is in the host State solely because of the presence there of the deceased as a member of the delegation or of the family of a member of the delegation.

Art. 69. End of functions.

The functions of the head of delegation or of any other delegate or member of the diplomatic staff of the delegation shall come to an end, inter alia:

(a) on notification of their termination by the sending State to the Organization or the conference;

(b) upon the conclusion of the meeting of the organ or the conference.

Art. 70. Protection of premises, property and archives.

(1) When the meeting of an organ or a conference comes to an end, the host State must respect and protect the premises of the delegation so long as they are used by it, as well as the property and archives of the delegation. The sending State must take all appropriate measures to terminate this special duty of the host State as soon as possible.

(2) The host State, if requested by the sending State, shall grant the latter facilities for removing the property and the archives of the delegation from the territory of the host State.

Part. IV. *Observer delegations to organs and to conferences.*

Art. 71. Sending of observer delegations.

A State may send an observer delegation to an organ or to a conference in accordance with the rules of the Organization.

Art. 72. General provision concerning observer delegations.

All the provisions of articles 43 to 70 of the present Convention shall apply to observer delegations.

Part V. *General provisions.*

Art. 73. Nationality of the members of the mission, the delegation or the observer delegation.

(1) The head of mission and members of the diplomatic staff of the mission, the head of delegation, other delegates and members of the diplomatic staff of the delegation, the head of the observer delegation, other observer delegates and members of the diplomatic staff of the observer delegation should in principle be of the nationality of the sending State.

(2) The head of mission and members of the diplomatic staff of the mission may not be appointed from among persons having the nationality of the host State except with the consent of that State, which may be withdrawn at any time.

(3) Where the head of delegation, any other delegate or any member of the diplomatic staff of the delegation or the head of the observer delegation, any other observer delegate or any member of the diplomatic staff of the observer delegation is appointed from among persons having the nationality of the host State, the consent of that State shall be assumed if it has been notified of such appointment of a national of the host State and has made no objection.

Art. 74. Laws concerning acquisition of nationality.

Members of the mission, the delegation or the observer delegation not being nationals of the host State, and members of their families forming part of their household or, as the case may be, accompanying them, shall not, solely by the operation of the law of the host State, acquire the nationality of that State.

Art. 75. Privileges and immunities in case of multiple functions.

When members of the permanent diplomatic mission or of a consular post in the host State are included in a mission, a delegation or an observer delegation, they shall retain their privileges and immunities as members of their permanent diplomatic mission or consular post in addition to the privileges and immunities accorded by the present Convention.

Art. 76. Co-operation between sending States and host States.

Whenever necessary and to the extent compatible with the independent exercise of the functions of the mission, the delegation or the observer delegation, the sending State shall co-operate as fully as possible with the host State in the conduct of any investigation or prosecution carried out pursuant to the provisions of articles 23, 28, 29 and 58.

Art. 77. Respect for the laws and regulations of the host State.

(1) Without prejudice to their privileges and immunities, it is the duty of all persons enjoying such

privileges and immunities to respect the laws and regulations of the host State. They also have a duty not to interfere in the internal affairs of that State.

(2) In case of grave and manifest violation of the criminal law of the host State by a person enjoying immunity from jurisdiction, the sending State shall, unless it waives the immunity of the person concerned, recall him, terminate his functions with the mission, the delegation or the observer delegation or secure his departure, as appropriate. The sending State shall take the same action in case of grave and manifest interference in the internal affairs of the host State. The provisions of this paragraph shall not apply in the case of any act that the person concerned performed in carrying out the functions of the mission or the tasks of the delegation or of the observer delegation.

(3) The premises of the mission and the premises of the delegation shall not be used in any manner incompatible with the exercise of the functions of the mission or the performance of the tasks of the delegation.

(4) Nothing in this article shall be construed as prohibiting the host State from taking such measures as are necessary for its own protection. In that event the host State shall, without prejudice to articles 84 and 85, consult the sending State in an appropriate manner in order to ensure that such measures do not interfere with the normal functioning of the mission, the delegation or the observer delegation.

(5) The measures provided for in paragraph 4 of this article shall be taken with the approval of the Minister for Foreign Affairs or of any other competent minister in conformity with the constitutional rules of the host State.

Art. 78. Insurance against third party risks.

The members of the mission, of the delegation or of the observer delegation shall comply with all obligations under the laws and regulations of the host State relating to third-party liability insurance for any vehicle, vessel or aircraft used or owned by them.

Art. 79. Entry into the territory of the host State.

(1) The host State shall permit entry into its territory of:

(a) members of the mission and members of their families forming part of their respective households, and

(b) members of the delegation and members of their families accompanying them, and

(c) members of the observer delegation and members of their families accompanying them.

(2) Visas, when required, shall be granted as promptly as possible to any person referred to in paragraph 1 of this article.

Art. 80. Facilities for departure.

The host State shall, if requested, grant facilities to enable persons enjoying privileges and immunities, other than nationals of the host State, and members of the families of such persons irrespective of their nationality, to leave its territory.

Art. 81. Transit through the territory of a third State.

(1) If a head of mission or a member of the diplomatic staff of the mission, a head of delegation, other delegate or member of the diplomatic staff of the delegation, a head of an observer delegation, other observer delegate or member of the diplomatic staff of the observer delegation passes through or is in the territory of a third State which has granted him a passport visa if such visa was necessary, while proceeding to take up or to resume his functions, or when returning to his own country, the third State shall accord him inviolability and such other immunities as may be required to ensure his transit.

(2) The provisions of paragraph 1 of this article shall also apply in the case of:

(a) members of the family of the head of mission or of a member of the diplomatic staff of the mission forming part of his household and enjoying privileges and immunities, whether travelling with him or travelling separately to join him or to return to their country;

(b) members of the family of the head of delegation, of any other delegate or member of the diplomatic staff of the delegation who are accompanying him and enjoy privileges and immunities, whether travelling with him or travelling separately to join him or to return to their country;

(c) members of the family of the head of the observer delegation, of any other observer delegate or member of the diplomatic staff of the observer delegation, who are accompanying him and enjoy privileges and im-

munities, whether travelling with him or travelling separately to join him or to return to their country.

(3) In circumstances similar to those specified in paragraphs 1 and 2 of this article, third States shall not hinder the passage of members of the administrative and technical or service staff, and of members of their families, through their territories.

(4) Third States shall accord to official correspondence and other official communications in transit, including messages in code or cipher, the same freedom and protection as the host State is bound to accord under the present Convention. They shall accord to the couriers of the mission, of the delegation or of the observer delegation, who have been granted a passport visa if such visa was necessary, and to the bags of the mission, of the delegation or of the observer delegation in transit the same inviolability and protection as the host State is bound to accord under the present Convention.

(5) The obligations of third States under paragraphs 1, 2, 3 and 4 of this article shall also apply to the persons mentioned respectively in those paragraphs, and to the official communications and bags of the mission, of the delegation or of the observer delegation when they are present in the territory of the third State owing to force majeure.

Art. 82. Non-recognition of States or governments or absence of diplomatic or consular relations

(1) The rights and obligations of the host State and of the sending State under the present Convention shall be affected neither by the non-recognition by one of those States of the other State or of its government nor by the non-existence or the severance of diplomatic or consular relations between them.

(2) The establishment or maintenance of a mission, the sending or attendance of a delegation or of an observer delegation or any act in application of the present Convention shall not by itself imply recognition by the sending State of the host State or its government or by the host State of the sending State or its government.

Art. 83. Non-discrimination.

In the application of the provisions of the present Convention no discrimination shall be made as between States.

Art. 84. Consultations.

If a dispute between two or more States Parties arises out of the application or interpretation of the present Convention, consultations between them shall be held upon the request of any of them. At the request of any of the parties to the dispute, the Organization or the conference shall be invited to join in the consultations.

Art. 85. Conciliation.

(1) If the dispute is not disposed of as a result of the consultations referred to in article 84 within one month from the date of their inception, any State participating in the consultations may bring the dispute before a conciliation commission constituted in accordance with the provisions of this article by giving written notice to the Organization and to the other States participating in the consultations.

(2) Each conciliation commission shall be composed of three members: two members who shall be appointed respectively by each of the parties to the dispute, and a Chairman appointed in accordance with paragraph 3 of this article. Each State Party to the present Convention shall designate in advance a person to serve as a member of such a commission. It shall notify the designation to the Organization, which shall maintain a register of persons so designated. If it does not make the designation in advance, it may do so during the conciliation procedure up to the moment at which the Commission begins to draft the report which it is to prepare in accordance with paragraph 7 of this article.

(3) The Chairman of the Commission shall be chosen by the other two members. If the other two members are unable to agree within one month from the notice referred to in paragraph 1 of this article or if one of the parties to the dispute has not availed itself of its right to designate a member of the Commission, the Chairman shall be designated at the request of one of the parties to the dispute by the chief administrative officer of the Organization. The appointment shall be made within a period of one month from such request. The chief administrative officer of the Organization shall appoint as the Chairman a qualified jurist who is neither an official of the Organization nor a national of any State party to the dispute.

(4) Any vacancy shall be filled in the manner prescribed for the initial appointment.

(5) The Commission shall function as soon as the Chairman has been appointed even if its composition is incomplete.

(6) The Commission shall establish its own rules of procedure and shall reach its decisions and recommendations by a majority vote. It may recommend to the Organization, if the Organization is so authorized in accordance with the Charter of the United Nations, to request an advisory opinion from the International Court of Justice regarding the application or interpretation of the present Convention.

(7) If the Commission is unable to obtain an agreement among the parties to the dispute on a settlement of the dispute within two months from the appointment of its Chairman, it shall prepare as soon as possible a report of its proceedings and transmit it to the parties to the dispute. The report shall include the Commission's conclusions upon the facts and questions of law and the recommendations which it has submitted to the parties to the dispute in order to facilitate a settlement of the dispute. The two months time limit may be extended by decision of the Commission. The recommendations in the report of the Commission shall not be binding on the parties to the dispute unless all the parties to the dispute have accepted them. Nevertheless, any party to the dispute may declare unilaterally that it will abide by the recommendations in the report so far as it is concerned.

(8) Nothing in the preceding paragraphs of this article shall preclude the establishment of any other appropriate procedure for the settlement of disputes arising out of the application or interpretation of the present Convention or the conclusion of any agreement between the parties to the dispute to submit the dispute to a procedure instituted in the Organization or to any other procedure.

(9) This article is without prejudice to provisions concerning the settlement of disputes contained in international agreement in force between States or between States and international organizations.

Part VI. *Final clauses.*

Art. 86. Signature.

The present Convention shall be open for signature by all States until 30 September 1975 at the Federal Ministry for Foreign Affairs of the Republic of Austria and subsequently, until 30 March 1976, at United Nations Headquarters in New York.

Art. 87. Ratification.

The present Convention is subject to ratification. The instrument of ratification shall be deposited with the Secretary-General of the United Nations.

Art. 88. Accession.

The present Convention shall remain open for accession by any State. The instruments of accession shall be deposited with the Secretary-General of the United Nations.

Art. 89. Entry into force.

(1) The present Convention shall enter into force on the thirtieth day following the date of deposit of the thirty-fifth instrument of ratification or accession.

(2) For each State ratifying or acceding to the Convention after the deposit of the thirty-fifth instrument of ratification or accession, the Convention shall enter into force on the thirtieth day after the deposit by such State of its instrument of ratification or accession.

Art. 90. Implementation by organizations.

After the entry into force of the present Convention, the competent organ of an international organization of a universal character may adopt a decision to implement the relevant provisions of the Convention. The Organization shall communicate the decision to the host State and to the depositary of the Convention.

Art. 91. Notifications by the depositary.

(1) As depositary of the present Convention, the Secretary-General of the United Nations shall inform all States:

(a) of signatures to the Convention and of the deposit of instruments of ratification or accession, in accordance with articles 86, 87 and 88;

(b) of the date on which the Convention will enter into force, in accordance with article 89;

(c) of any decision communicated in accordance with article 90.

(2) The Secretary-General of the United Nations shall also inform all States, as necessary, of other acts, notif-

ications or communications relating to the present Convention.

Art. 92. Authentic texts.

The original of the present Convention, of which the Chinese, English, French, Russian and Spanish texts are equally authentic, shall be deposited with the Secretary-General of the United Nations, who shall send certified copies thereof to all States."

UN Conference on the Representation of States in Their Relations with International Organization, Vienna, Austria, Feb. 4–Mar. 14, 1975, Vol. I: *Summary Records,* Vol. II: *Document of the Conference,* New York, 1975.

VIENNA INSTITUTE FOR DEVELOPMENT, f. 1964, Vienna. Members: 20 countries.

Yearbook of International Organizations, 1986/87; The Europa Yearbook 1988. A World Survey, Vol. I, London 1988.

VIENNA PEACE TREATY, 1809. A Treaty between Austria and France, signed in Vienna, Oct. 14, 1809.

Major Peace Treaties of Modern History, New York, 1967, Vol. I, pp. 487–500.

VIENNA PEACE TREATY, 1864. A Treaty between Denmark, Austria and Prussia, signed in Vienna, Oct. 30, 1864; Denmark renounced all its rights to the Duchies of Schleswig, Holstein and Lauenburg.

Major Peace Treaties of Modern History, New York, 1967, Vol. I, pp. 611–628.

VIENNA PEACE TREATY, 1866. A Treaty between Austria and Italy, signed in Vienna, Oct. 3, 1866.

Major Peace Treaties of Modern History, New York, 1967, Vol. I. pp. 635–645.

VIENNA RULES, 1815. The first diplomatic code adopted by the Vienna Congress on Mar. 19, 1815, stating the classes of foreign representation as well as the rules of protocol; substituted by the Vienna Diplomatic Convention of 1961.

VIENNA ULTIMATUM TO SERBIA, 1914. The Austro–Hungarian note to Serbia on July 23, 1914 after the assassination of the Austrian Archduke Francis Ferdinand at Sarajevo on June 28, 1914. Serbia was ready to submit the case to the International Tribunal at The Hague, but Austria–Hungary declared war on July 28, 1914.

"Official Documents Bearing Upon the European War", in: *International Conciliation,* No. 83, October, 1914.

VIET CONG. *Vietnamese* = "Vietnamese communist". A term introduced during the Vietnam war designating all Vietnamese fighting on the North Vietnam side.

VIETNAM. Member of the UN. The Socialist Republic of Vietnam. A state in Southeast Asia on the South China Sea. Area: 329,566 sq. km. Pop. 1989 est.: 61,400,000 (1979 census: 52,741,766. Capital: Hanoi with 2,000,000 inhabitants in 1979). Official language: Vietnamese, Currency: one dong = 10 hao = 100 xu. GUP per capita 1989: US $200. National Day: Sept. 2, anniversary of the proclamation of the Democratic Republic of Vietnam, 1945.

Member of the UN since Sept. 20, 1977 and all specialized agencies with exception of ILO and GATT. Member of the CMEA.

International relations: since the 10th century an independent state (939); since the 18th century under French influence, supported by military intervention from 1858. A French protectorate over Vietnam was formally established in 1884 and the country was administratively divided into three provinces: a northern, named Tonkin (now the region of Bac Bo), a central, named Annam (now Trung Bo) and a southern named Kochinchina (now Nam Bo). In 1887 Vietnam was incorporated into the Indochina Union subject to colonial France and including Laos, Cambodia and Vietnam. Regional uprisings of the peasant population against feudal Vietnam and the French protectors took place in 1913 and 1930, the latter in the province of Nghe An under the communists whose leader, Ho Chi Minh, then initiated an organized national liberation struggle which after 1940/41 developed into a war for independence directed by the Democratic Front for Vietnamese Independence, called in short Viet Minh. The signal for a nationwide partisan liberation struggle was the capitulation of France to the III Reich in June, 1940 and the signing by the French government in Vichy on Sept. 22, 1940 of an understanding with Japan allowing her to militarily occupy North Vietnam and, by the treaty of July 29, 1941, the whole of Indochina, while retaining French colonial administration. As the partisan movement spread to the entire country, Japan, wishing to intercept aspirations for independence, abolished the French colonial administration on Mar. 9, 1945, and on Mar. 11, 1945 Emperor Bao Dai restored the "Annamite Empire" as an "independent state within the Greater East Asian Prosperity Sphere." The government of liberated France on Mar. 24, 1945 announced that after the victory over Japan a federal state would be formed in Indochina within the French Union. Victory was achieved in Aug., 1945 by the National Liberation Committee under the leadership of Ho Chi Minh, who, after the occupation of Saigon and the abdication of Bao Dai, proclaimed the transformation of all of Vietnam into a Democratic Republic of Vietnam. The nationwide general elections on Jan. 6, 1946 convened a National Constitutional Assembly which elected Ho Chi Minh President and Prime Minister. At the same time, from Sept., 1945 a new infiltration of foreign troops was in progress: to North Vietnam, Kuomintang forces and to South Vietnam, French forces under the protection of the British fleet, which led to the occupation of Saigon. The President of the Democratic Republic of Vietnam, Ho Chi Minh, on Mar. 6, 1946 signed in Hanoi a treaty with the designated representative of the French Government, Jean Sainteny. It was agreed as follows:

"(1) The French government recognizes the Republic of Vietnam as a free State having its own government, parliament, army and finances, and forming part of the Indochinese Federation and the French Union.

Concerning the unification of the three "Ky," the French Government agrees to accept (enteriner) the decisions taken by the population consulted by referendum.

(2) The Government of Vietnam declares itself prepared to receive the French army amicably when, in conformity with international agreements, it relieves the Chinese forces. An agreement annexed to this Preliminary Convention will settle the means by which the relief operations will be effected.

(3) The provisions formulated above will enter into force immediately. Immediately after the exchange of signatures each of the High Contracting Parties will take all necessary measures to bring about an immediate cessation of hostilities, to maintain the military forces in their respective positions, and to create the favourable climate necessary to the immediate opening of frank and friendly negotiations. These negotiations will deal in particular with the diplomatic relations of Vietnam with foreign states with the future status of Indochina, and with the French economic and cultural interests in Vietnam."

This agreement was confirmed on Sept. 14, 1946 by a treaty signed in Paris by Ho Chi Minh; albeit France on June 1, 1946 formed the so-called Republic of Kochinchina in South Vietnam with the capital in Saigon and led by the French High Commissioner. In Nov.–Dec., 1946 the French went on the military offensive in North Vietnam, capturing the port of Haiphong on Nov. 19, and Hanoi on Dec. 19. The authorities of the DRV were evacuated to the mountainous region of the country, from where they began military liberation operations and a diplomatic campaign on the international forum; both were crowned with success after 8 years. France was forced to end the war in the spring of 1954 (after the defeat at Dien Bien Phu) and to sign the Indochina Treaties, July 22, 1954 (▷ Indochina Geneva Conference and Agreements, 1954), and to withdraw all of its forces from Vietnam. Simultaneously, as a result of US pressure the division of Vietnam was retained, consisting of the northern region under the authority of the DRV and the southern region under the administration of Emperor Bao Dai, who on July 7, 1954 gave the function of Prime Minister to the US-sponsored Ngo Dinh Diem; the latter immediately revoked the Geneva treaties, did not permit nationwide general elections, and on Oct. 26, 1955 removed Bao Dai and proclaimed the Republic of South Vietnam with himself as President. The terror applied by the dictatorship of Ngo Dinh Diem led in 1957–59 to new partisan activities of various social and religious groupings which on Dec. 20, 1960 formed the National Front for the Liberation of South Vietnam, called by western press ▷ Viet Cong. These protests against the new war in Vietnam, which in following years was to become the subject of protests in the USA and in most countries of the world became also a source of growing diplomatic conflicts in the UN. On Mar. 7, 1968 the democratic candidate for President of the USA, R. Kennedy, referred to the US intervention in Vietnam as "immoral and not to be further tolerated." In Dec., 1968 the government of the USA began negotiations with the DRV which ended in Apr., 1973 with evacuation of all American troops; for the first time since 1858, i.e. in 115 years, there was no foreign soldier on Vietnamese soil. The attempt to maintain the division of Vietnam through ▷ "Vietnamization" ended on Apr. 30, 1974 with the unconditional surrender of the forces of the Saigon administration. The unification of Vietnam formally occurred on July 2, 1976.

In 1978 armed incidents took place on the border with China and Kampuchea, ruled by the pro-Chinese regime of Pol Pot. The government of the Chinese People's Republic demanded the closing of three Vietnamese consulates which had functioned since 1956 in Peking, Nanking and since 1957 in Canton. In Moscow on Nov. 3, 1978 a Treaty of Friendship and Co-operation was signed with the USSR, extended in June, 1983. In Jan., 1979 Vietnam was charged in the Security Council by the Chinese People's Republic of participating in the overthrow of the Pol Pot regime in ▷ Kampuchea (formerly Cambodia). In Mar., 1979 the government of the Chinese People's Republic carried out a military operation against Vietnam referred to as a "punitive expedition." The question of the presence of Vietnamese forces in Cambodia became a subject of debates of the UN General Assembly and the Security Council from 1979 up to 1984. Vietnam and the USSR signed on July 4, 1980 at Moscow an agreement granting the Soviet Union oil-drilling rights of the Vietnamese coast. Drilling of oil on the South Vietnam coast was abandoned by Mobil Oil Company after the 1975 defeat of the Saigon administration. Since July 6, 1983 Member of the Tripartite Commission Kampuchea, Laos,

Vietnam. Until Jan., 1986 the relations with China and the USA have not been normalized. Vietnam withdrew from the ILO on May 31, 1985. Land border tension with China also took place in 1987 and 1988; territorial water conflicts took place in 1988 over the ▷ Spratly Islands.

Conférence de Genève. Procès-verbaux de séances, Paris, 1955; B. FALL, *Le Viêt-Minh 1945–1960*, Paris, 1960; HÔ CHI MINH, *Selected Works*, 4 Vols., Hanoi, 1960–62; W.G. BURCHETT, *Vietnam*, New York, 1965; W.G. BURCHETT, *Vietnam North*, London, 1966; G.G. KADYMOV, *Put' k nezavisimosti Vietnama, Laosa i Kambodzhi 1945–1965*, Moscow, 1966; LE CHAN, *Del feudalismo al socialismo. La economia del Vietnam del Norte*, México, DF, 1967; HÔ CHI MINH, *On Revolution: Selected writings 1922–1966*, London, 1967; L.P. BLOOMITIELO, *The UN and Vietnam*, New York, 1968; J. GERASSI, *North Vietnam. A Documentary*, London, 1968; T. TAYLOR, *Nuremberg and Vietnam: an American Tragedy*, Chicago, 1970; L. LAVALLE, *L'économie du Nord Viêt-nam 1960–1970*, Paris, 1972; J.N.M. CHEN, *Vietnam: A Comprehensive Bibliography*, London, 1973; W.G. BURCHETT, "South Vietnam after the US Evacuation", in: *Far Eastern Economic Review*, October 10, 1975; R.I. GALLUCI, *Neither Peace Nor Honor*, Baltimore, 1975; P.V. NGUYEN GIAP, *To arm the revolutionary masses, to build the People's Army*, Hanoi, 1975; P.V. NGUYEN GIAP, *Guerre du peuple contra guerre aéronaval*, Hanoi, 1975; P. TIEN CHAN, *Vietnamese Communism. A Research Bibliography*, Westport Conn., 1975; R. PIC, *Le Viêtnam d'Hô Chi Minh*, Paris, 1976; C. NGUYEN TIEN HUNG, *Economic Development of Socialist Vietnam 1955–1980*, New York, 1977; LE THANH KHOI, *Socialisme et Développement au Viêt-nam*, Paris, 1978; D. PIKE, *History of Vietnamese Communism, 1925–1976*, Stanford, 1978; A.E. GOODMAN, *The Lost Peace: America's Search for a Negotiated Settlement of the Vietnam War*, Stanford, 1978; G. LEVY, *America in Vietnam*, 1979; S.L. POPKIN, *The Rational Peasant. The Political Economy of Rural Society in Vietnam*, Berkeley, 1979; VIET TRAN, *J'ai choisi l'exil*, Paris, 1979; A.S. VORONIN, L.A. OGNIETOV, *Sotsialisticheskaia Respublica Vietnam. Spravochnik*, Moscow, 1981; T. HODGKIN, *Vietnam. The Revolutionary Path*, London, 1981; M. LEITENBERG, R.D. BURNS, *War in Vietnam*, Oxford, 1982; A. ISAACS, *Without Honor. Defeat in Vietnam and Cambodia*, Baltimore, 1984; S. KARNOW, *Vietnam. A History*, New York, 1984; *The Europa Year Book 1984. A World Survey*, Vol. II, pp. 2683–2696, London, 1984. D. PIKE, *Vietnam and the Soviet Union: Anatomy of an Alliance*, Boulder Col., 1987. K. WILLENSON, *The Bad War*, New York, 1987; N.B. HANNAH, *The Key to Failure: Laos and the Vietnam War*, Lanham, Md., 1987; P. DAVIDSON, *Vietnam at War. The History 1946–1975*, London, 1988; R.B. SMITH, *The International History of the Vietnam War*, Vol. I *Revolution Versus Containment, 1955–61*; Vol. II *The Struggle for South-East Asia, 1961–65*; Vol. III *Limited War, 1965–70*; Vol. IV *The Denouement, 1970–76*, London 1987, 1988, 1990.

VIETNAM AGREEMENT ON ENDING THE WAR AND RESTORING PEACE, 1973. Agreement signed at Paris by the US Secretary of State W.P. Rogers and Vietnamese Minister for Foreign Affairs Tran Van Lam on Jan. 27, 1973; came into force by signature, reads as follows:

"The Parties participating in the Paris Conference on Viet-Nam, With a view to ending the war and restoring peace in Viet-Nam on the basis of respect for the Vietnamese people's fundamental national rights and the South Vietnamese people's right to self-determination, and to contributing to the consolidation of peace in Asia and the world,
Have agreed on the following provisions and undertake to respect and to implement them:

Chapter I. *The Vietnamese People's Fundamental National Rights*

Art. 1. The United States and all other countries respect the independence, sovereignty, unity and territorial integrity of Viet-Nam as recognized by the 1954 Geneva Agreements on Viet-Nam.

Chapter II. *Cessation of Hostilities; Withdrawal of Troops*

Art. 2. A cease-fire shall be observed throughout South Viet-Nam as of 2400 hours G.M.T., on January 27, 1973.
At the same hour, the United States will stop all its military activities against the territory of the Democratic Republic of Viet-Nam by ground, air and naval forces, wherever they may be based, and end the mining of the territorial waters, ports, harbors, and waterways of the Democratic Republic of Viet-Nam. The United States will remove, permanently deactivate or destroy all the mines in the territorial waters, ports, harbors, and waterways of North Viet-Nam as soon as this Agreement goes into effect.
The complete cessation of hostilities mentioned in this Article shall be durable and without limit of time.

Art. 3. The parties undertake to maintain the cease-fire and to ensure a lasting and stable peace.
As soon as the cease-fire goes into effect:
(a) The United States forces and those of the other foreign countries allied with the United States and the Republic of Viet-Nam shall remain in-place pending the implementation of the place of troop withdrawal. The Four-Party Joint Military Commission described in Article 16 shall determine the modalities.
(b) The armed forces of the two South Vietnamese parties shall remain in-place. The Two-Party Joint Military Commission described in Article 17 shall determine the areas controlled by each party and the modalities of stationing.
(c) The regular forces of all services and arms and the irregular forces of the parties in South Viet-Nam shall stop all offensive activities against each other and shall strictly abide by the following stipulations:
– All acts of force on the ground, in the air, and on the sea shall be prohibited;
– All hostile acts, terrorism and reprisals by both sides will be banned.

Art. 4. The United States will not continue its military involvement or intervene in the internal affairs of South Viet-Nam.

Art. 5. Within sixty days of the signing of this Agreement, there will be a total withdrawal from South Viet-Nam of troops, military advisers, and military personnel, including technical military personnel and military personnel associated with the pacification program, armaments, munitions, and war material of the United States and those of the other foreign countries mentioned in Article 3(a). Advisers from the above-mentioned countries to all paramilitary organizations and the police force will also be withdrawn within the same period of time.

Art. 6. The dismantlement of all military bases in South Viet-Nam of the United States and of the other foreign countries mentioned in Article 3(a) shall be completed within sixty days of the signing of this Agreement.

Art. 7. From the enforcement of the cease-fire to the formation of the government provided for in Articles 9(b) and 14 of this Agreement, the two South Vietnamese parties shall not accept the introduction of troops, military advisers, and military personnel including technical military personnel, armaments, munitions, and war material into South Viet-Nam. The two South Vietnamese parties shall be permitted to make periodic replacement of armaments, munitions and war material which have been destroyed, damaged, worn out or used up after the cease-fire, on the basis of piece-for-piece, of the same characteristics and properties, under the supervision of the Joint Military Commission of the two South Vietnamese parties and of the International Commission of Control and Supervision.

Chapter III. *The Return of Captured Military Personnel and Foreign Civilians, and Captured and Detained Vietnamese Civilian Personnel*

Art. 8.(a) The return of captured military personnel and foreign civilians of the parties shall be carried out simultaneously with and completed not later than the same day as the troop withdrawal mentioned in Article 5. The parties shall exchange complete lists of the above-mentioned captured military personnel and foreign civilians on the day of the signing of this Agreement.
(b) The parties shall help each other to get information about those military personnel and foreign civilians of the parties missing in action, to determine the location and take care of the graves of the dead so as to facilitate the exhumation and repatriation of the remains, and to take any such other measures as may be required to get information about those still considered missing in action.
(c) The question of the return of Vietnamese civilian personnel captured and detained in South Viet-Nam will be resolved by the two South Vietnamese parties on the basis of the principles of Article 21(b) of the Agreement on the Cessation of Hostilities in Viet-Nam of July 20, 1954. The two South Vietnamese parties will do so in a spirit of national reconciliation and concord, with a view to ending hatred and enmity, in order to ease suffering and to reunite families. The two South Vietnamese parties will do their utmost to resolve this question within ninety days after the cease-fire comes into effect.

Chapter IV. *The Exercise of the South Vietnamese People's Right to Self-determination*

Art. 9. The Government of the United States of America and the Government of the Democratic Republic of Viet-Nam undertake to respect the following principles for the exercise of the South Vietnamese people's right to self-determination:
(a) The South Vietnamese people's right to self-determination is sacred, inalienable, and shall be respected by all countries.
(b) The South Vietnamese people shall decide themselves the political future of South Viet-Nam through genuinely free and democratic general elections under international supervision.
(c) Foreign countries shall not impose any political tendency or personality on the South Vietnamese people.

Art. 10. The two South Vietnamese parties undertake to respect the cease-fire and maintain peace in South Viet-Nam, settle all matters of contention through negotiations, and avoid all armed conflict.

Art. 11. Immediately after the cease-fire, the two South Vietnamese parties will:
– achieve national reconciliation and concord, end hatred and enmity, prohibit all acts of reprisal and discrimination against individuals or organizations that have collaborated with one side or the other;
ensure the democratic liberties of the people: personal freedom, freedom of speech, freedom of the press, freedom of meeting, freedom of organization, freedom of political activities, freedom of belief, freedom of movement, freedom of residence, freedom of work, right to property ownership, and right to free enterprise.

Art. 12.(a) Immediately after the cease-fire, the two South Vietnamese parties shall hold consultations in a spirit of national reconciliation and concord, mutual respect, and mutual non-elimination to set up a National Council of National Reconciliation and Concord of three equal segments. The Council shall operate on the principle of unanimity. After the National Council of National Reconciliation and Concord has assumed its functions, the two South Vietnamese parties will consult about the formation of councils at lower levels. The two South Vietnamese parties shall sign an agreement on the internal matters of South Viet-Nam as soon as possible and do their utmost to accomplish this within ninety days after the cease-fire comes into effect, in keeping with the South Vietnamese people's aspirations for peace, independence and democracy.
(b) The National Council of National Reconciliation and Concord shall have the task of promoting the two South Vietnamese parties' implementation of this Agreement, achievement of national reconciliation and concord and ensurance of democratic liberties. The National Council of National Reconciliation and Concord will organize the free and democratic general elections provided for in Article 9(b) and decide the procedures and modalities of these general elections. The institutions for which the general elections are to be held will be agreed upon through consultations between the two South Vietnamese parties. The National Council of National Reconciliation and Concord will also decide the procedures and modalities of such local elections as the two South Vietnamese parties agree upon.

Art. 13. The question of Vietnamese armed forces in South Viet-Nam shall be settled by the two South Vietnamese parties in a spirit of national reconciliation and concord, equality and mutual respect, without foreign interference, in accordance with the postwar situation. Among the questions to be discussed by the two South Vietnamese parties are steps to reduce their military effectives and to demobilize the troops being reduced.

The two South Vietnamese parties will accomplish this as soon as possible.

Art. 14. South Viet-Nam will pursue a foreign policy of peace and independence. It will be prepared to establish relations with all countries irrespective of their political and social systems on the basis of mutual respect for independence and sovereignty and accept economic and technical aid from any country with no political conditions attached. The acceptance of military aid by South Viet-Nam in the future shall come under the authority of the government set up after the general elections in South Viet-Nam provided for in Article 9 (b).

Chapter V. *The Reunification of Viet-Nam and the Relationship Between North and South Viet-Nam*

Art. 15. The reunification of Viet-Nam shall be carried out step by step through peaceful means on the basis of discussions and agreements between North and South Viet-Nam, without coercion or annexation by either party, and without foreign interference. The time for reunification will be agreed upon by North and South Viet-Nam.

Pending reunification:

(a) The military demarcation line between the two zones at the 17th parallel is only provisional and not a political or territorial boundary, as provided for in paragraph 6 of the Final Declaration of the 1954 Geneva Conference.

(b) North and South Viet-Nam shall respect the Demilitarized Zone on either side of the Provisional Military Demarcation Line.

(c) North and South Viet-Nam shall promptly start negotiations with a view to re-establishing normal relations in various fields. Among the questions to be negotiated are the modalities of civilian movement across the Provisional Military Demarcation Line.

(d) North and South Viet-Nam shall not join any military alliance or military bloc and shall not allow foreign powers to maintain military bases, troops, military advisers, and military personnel on their respective territories, as stipulated in the 1954 Geneva Agreements on Viet-Nam.

Chapter VI. *The Joint Military Commissions, the International Commission of Control and Supervision, the International Conference*

Art. 16.(a) The Parties participating in the Paris Conference on Viet-Nam shall immediately designate representatives to form a Four-Party Joint Military Commission with the task of ensuring joint action by the parties in implementing the following provisions of this Agreement:

– The first paragraph of Article 2, regarding the enforcement of the cease-fire throughout South Viet-Nam;

– Article 3(a), regarding the cease-fire by US forces and those of the other foreign countries referred to in that Article;

– Article 3(c) regarding the cease-fire between all parties in South Viet-Nam;

– Article 5, regarding the withdrawal from South Viet-Nam of US troops and those of the other foreign countries mentioned in Article 3(a);

– Article 6, regarding the dismantlement of military bases in South Viet-Nam of the United States and those of the other foreign countries mentioned in Article 3(a);

– Article 8(a), regarding the return of captured military personnel and foreign civilians of the parties;

– Article 8(b), regarding the mutual assistance of the parties in getting information about those military personnel and foreign civilians of the parties missing in action.

(b) The Four-Party Joint Military Commission shall operate in accordance with the principle of consultations and unanimity. Disagreements shall be referred to the International Commission of Control and Supervision.

(c) The Four-Party Joint Military Commission shall begin operating immediately after the signing of this Agreement and end its activities in sixty days, after the completion of the withdrawal of US troops and those of the other foreign countries mentioned in Article 3(a) and the completion of the return of captured military personnel and foreign civilians of the parties.

(d) The four parties shall agree immediately on the organization, the working procedure, means of activity, and expenditures of the Four-Party Joint Military Commission.

Art. 17.(a) The two South Vietnamese parties shall immediately designate representatives to form a Two-Party Joint Military Commission with the task of ensuring joint action by the two South Vietnamese parties in implementing the following provisions of this Agreement:

– The first paragraph of Article 2, regarding the enforcement of the cease-fire throughout South Viet-Nam, when the Four-Party Joint Military Commission has ended its activities;

– Article 3(b), regarding the cease-fire between the two South Vietnamese parties,

– Article 3(c), regarding the cease-fire between all parties in South Viet-Nam, when the Four-Party Joint Military Commission has ended its activities;

– Article 7, regarding the prohibition of the introduction of troops into South Viet-Nam and all other provisions of this Article;

– Article 8(c), regarding the question of the return of Vietnamese civilian personnel captured and detained in South Viet-Nam;

– Article 13, regarding the reduction of the military effectives of the two South Vietnamese parties and the demobilization of the troops being reduced.

(b) Disagreements shall be referred to the International Commission of Control and Supervision.

(c) After the signing of this Agreement, the Two-Party Joint Military Commission shall agree immediately on the measures and organization aimed at enforcing the cease-fire and preserving peace in South Viet-Nam.

Art. 18.(a) After the signing of this Agreement, an International Commission of Control and Supervision shall be established immediately.

(b) Until the International Conference provided for in Article 19 makes definitive arrangements, the International Commission of Control and Supervision will report to the four parties on matters concerning the control and supervision of the implementation of the following provisions of this Agreement:

– The first paragraph of Article 2, regarding the enforcement of the cease-fire throughout South Viet-Nam;

– Article 3(a), regarding the cease-fire by US forces and those of the other foreign countries referred to in that Article;

– Article 3(c), regarding the cease-fire between all the parties in South Viet-Nam;

– Article 5, regarding the withdrawal from South Viet-Nam of US troops and those of the other foreign countries mentioned in Article 3(a);

– Article 6, regarding the dismantlement of military bases in South Viet-Nam of the United States and those of the other foreign countries mentioned in Article 3(a);

– Article 8(a), regarding the return of captured military personnel and foreign civilians of the parties.

The International Commission of Control and Supervision shall form control teams for carrying out its tasks. The four parties shall agree immediately on the location and operation of these teams. The parties will facilitate their operation.

(c) Until the International Conference makes definitive arrangements, the International Commission of Control and Supervision will report to the two South Vietnamese parties on matters concerning the control and supervision of the implementation of the following provisions of this Agreement;

– The first paragraph of Article 2, regarding the enforcement of the cease-fire throughout South Viet-Nam, when the Four-Party Joint Military Commission has ended its activities;

– Article 3(b), regarding the cease-fire between the two South Vietnamese parties;

– Article 3(c), regarding the cease-fire between all parties in South Viet-Nam, when the Four-Party Joint Military Commission has ended its activities;

– Article 7, regarding the prohibition of the introduction of troops into South Viet-Nam and all other provisions of this Article;

– Article 8(c), regarding the question of the return of Vietnamese civilian personnel captured and detained in South Viet-Nam;

– Article 9(b), regarding the free and democratic general elections in South Viet-Nam;

– Article 13, regarding the reduction of the military effectives of the two South Vietnamese parties and the demobilization of the troops being reduced.

The International Commission of Control and Supervision shall form control teams for carrying out its tasks. The two South Vietnamese parties shall agree immediately on the location and operation of these teams. The two South Vietnamese parties will facilitate their operation.

(d) The International Commission of Control and Supervision shall be composed of representatives of four countries: Canada, Hungary, Indonesia and Poland. The chairmanship of this Commission will rotate among the members for specific periods to be determined by the Commission.

(e) The International Commission of Control and Supervision shall carry out its tasks in accordance with the principle of respect for the sovereignty of South Viet-Nam.

(f) The International Commission of Control and Supervision shall operate in accordance with the principle of consultations and unanimity.

(g) The International Commission of Control and Supervision shall begin operating when a cease-fire comes into force in Viet-Nam. As regards the provisions in Article 18(b) concerning the four parties, the International Commission of Control and Supervision shall end its activities when the Commission's tasks of control and supervision regarding these provisions have been fulfilled. As regards the provisions in Article 18(c) concerning the two South Vietnamese parties, the International Commission of Control and Supervision shall end its activities on the request of the government formed after the general elections in South Viet-Nam provided for in Article 9(b).

(h) The four parties shall agree immediately on the organization, means of activity, and expenditures of the International Commission of Control and Supervision. The relationship between the International Commission and the International Conference will be agreed upon by the International Commission and the International Conference.

Art. 19. The parties agree on the convening of an International Conference within thirty days of the signing of this Agreement to acknowledge the signed agreements; to guarantee the ending of the war, the maintenance of peace in Viet-Nam, the respect of the Vietnamese people's fundamental national rights, and the South Vietnamese people's right to self-determination; and to contribute to and guarantee peace in Indochina. The United States and the Democratic Republic of Viet-Nam, on behalf of the parties participating in the Paris Conference on Viet-Nam, will propose to the following parties that they participate in this International Conference: the People's Republic of China, the Republic of France, the Union of Soviet Socialist Republics, the United Kingdom, the four countries of the International Commission of Control and Supervision, and the Secretary-General of the United Nations, together with the parties participating in the Paris Conference on Viet-Nam.

Chapter VII. *Regarding Cambodia and Laos*

Art. 20.(a) The parties participating in the Paris Conference on Viet-Nam shall strictly respect the 1954 Geneva Agreements on Cambodia and the 1962 Geneva Agreements on Laos, which recognized the Cambodian and the Lao peoples' fundamental national rights, i.e., the independence, sovereignty, unity, and territorial integrity of these countries. The parties shall respect the neutrality of Cambodia and Laos. The parties participating in the Paris Conference on Viet-Nam undertake to refrain from using the territory of Cambodia and the territory of Laos to encroach on the sovereignty and security of one another and of other countries.

(b) Foreign countries shall put an end to all military activities in Cambodia and Laos, totally withdraw from and refrain from reintroducing into these two countries troops, military advisers and military personnel, armaments, munitions and war material.

(c) The internal affairs of Cambodia and Laos shall be settled by the people of each of these countries without foreign interference.

(d) The problems existing between the Indochinese countries shall be settled by the Indochinese parties on the basis of respect for each other's independence, sovereignty and territorial integrity, and non-interference in each other's internal affairs.

Chapter VIII. *The Relationship Between the United States and the Democratic Republic of Viet-Nam*

Art. 21. The United States anticipates that this Agreement will usher in an era of reconciliation with the Democratic Republic of Viet-Nam as with all the peoples of Indochina. In pursuance of its traditional policy, the United States will contribute to healing the wounds of war and to postwar reconstruction of the Democratic Republic of Viet-Nam and throughout Indochina.

Art. 22. The ending of the war, the restoration of peace in Viet-Nam, and the strict implementation of this Agreement will create conditions for establishing a new, equal and mutually beneficial relationship between the United States and the Democratic Republic of Viet-Nam on the basis of respect for each other's independence and sovereignty, and non-interference in each other's internal affairs. At the same time this will ensure stable peace in Viet-Nam and contribute to the preservation of lasting peace in Indochina and Southeast Asia.

Chapter IX. *Other Provisions*

Art. 23. This Agreement shall enter into force upon signature by plenipotentiary representatives of the parties participating in the Paris Conference on Viet-Nam. All the parties concerned shall strictly implement this Agreement and its Protocols.

Done in Paris this twenty-seventh day of January, one thousand nine hundred and seventy-three, in English and Vietnamese. The English and Vietnamese texts are official and equally authentic."

UNTS, Vol. 935, 1974; pp. 6–16.

VIETNAM AGREEMENTS, 1973. Three separate documents, called also Paris Agreements, concerning Vietnam:

I. The agreement signed on Jan. 27, 1973, in Paris by the struggling Vietnamese parties and the USA on ending the war and restoring peace in Vietnam, annexed by supplementary Protocols.

"The United States and all other countries respect the independence, sovereignty, unity and territorial integrity of Vietnam as recognized by the 1954 Geneva Agreements on Vietnam" (art. I).

The Protocols annexed to the Agreement concerned: (1) removal, permanent discharge or destruction of mines planted in territorial waters, ports and water highways of the Democratic Republic of Vietnam; (2) detailed functions of the International Supervision and Control Commission; (3) ceasefire in Vietnam and Joint Military Commission; (4) return of prisoners of war (military and civilian) and information about dead and missing persons.

II. The Final Act of the International Conference on Vietnam held on Feb. 26–Mar. 2, 1973, in Paris adopted unanimously, was composed of a preamble and nine articles:

"The Government of the United States of America; the Government of the French Republic; the Provisional Revolutionary Government of the Republic of South Viet-Nam; the Government of the Hungarian People's Republic; the Government of the Republic of Indonesia; the Government of the Polish People's Republic; the Government of the Democratic Republic of Viet-Nam; the Government of the Union of Soviet Socialist Republics; the Government of Canada; and the Government of the People's Republic of China; In the presence of the Secretary-General of the United Nations:

With a view to acknowledging the signed Agreements; guaranteeing the ending of the war, the maintenance of peace in Viet-Nam, the respect of the Vietnamese people's fundamental national rights, and the South Vietnamese people's right to self-determination; and contributing to and guaranteeing peace in Indochina; Have agreed on the following provisions, and undertake to respect and implement them;

Art. 1. The Parties to this Act solemnly acknowledge, express their approval of, and support the Paris Agreement on Ending the War and Restoring Peace in Viet-Nam signed in Paris on January 27, 1973, and the four Protocols to the Agreement signed on the same date (hereinafter referred to respectively as the Agreement and the Protocols).

Art. 2. The Agreement responds to the aspirations and fundamental national rights of the Vietnamese people, i.e., the independence, sovereignty, unity, and territorial integrity, of Viet-Nam, to the right of the South-Vietnamese people to self-determination, and to the

earnest desire for peace shared by all countries in the world. The Agreement constitutes a major contribution to peace, self-determination, national independence, and the improvement of relations among countries. The Agreement and the Protocols should be strictly respected and scrupulously implemented.

Art. 3. The Parties to this Act solemnly acknowledge the commitments by the parties to the Agreement and the Protocols to strictly respect and scrupulously implement the Agreement and the Protocols.

Art. 4. The Parties to this Act solemnly recognize and strictly respect the fundamental national rights of the Vietnamese people, i.e., the independence, sovereignty, unity, and territorial integrity of Viet-Nam, as well as the right of the South Vietnamese people to self-determination. The Parties to this Act shall strictly respect the Agreement and the Protocols by refraining from any action at variance with their provisions.

Art. 5. For the sake of a durable peace in Viet-Nam, the Parties to this Act call on all countries to strictly respect the fundamental national rights of the Vietnamese people, i.e., the independence, sovereignty, unity, and territorial integrity of Viet-Nam and the right of the South Vietnamese people to self-determination and to strictly respect the Agreement and the Protocols by refraining from any action at variance with their provisions.

Art. 6.(a) The four parties to the Agreement or the two South Vietnamese parties may, either individually or through joint action, inform the other Parties to this Act about the implementation of the Agreement and the Protocols. Since the reports and views submitted by the International Commission of Control and Supervision concerning the control and supervision of the implementation of those provisions of the Agreement and the Protocols which are within the tasks of the Commission will be sent to either the four parties signatory to the Agreement or to the two South Vietnamese parties, those parties shall be responsible, either individually or through joint action, for forwarding them promptly to the other Parties to this Act.

(b) The four parties to the Agreement or the two South Vietnamese parties shall also, either individually or through joint action, forward this information and these reports and views to the other participant in the International Conference on Viet-Nam for his information.

Art. 7.(a) In the event of a violation of the Agreement or the Protocols which threatens the peace, the independence, sovereignty, unity, or territorial integrity of Viet-Nam, or the right of the South Vietnamese people to self-determination, the parties signatory to the Agreement and the Protocols shall, either individually or jointly, consult with the other Parties to this Act with a view to determining necessary remedial measures.

(b) The International Conference on Viet-Nam shall be reconvened upon a joint request by the Government of the United States of America and the Government of the Democratic Republic of Viet-Nam on behalf of the parties signatory to the Agreement or upon a request by six or more of the Parties to this Act.

Art. 8. With a view to contributing to and guaranteeing peace in Indochina, the Parties to this Act acknowledge the commitment of the parties to the Agreement to respect the independence, sovereignty, unity, territorial integrity, and neutrality of Cambodia and Laos as stipulated in the Agreement, agree also to respect them and to refrain from any action at variance with them, and call on other countries to do the same.

Art. 9. This Act shall enter into force upon signature by plenipotentiary representatives of all twelve Parties and shall be strictly implemented by all the Parties. Signature of this Act does not constitute recognition of any Party in any case in which it has not previously been accorded. Done in twelve copies, in Paris this second day of March, One Thousand Nine Hundred and Seventy-Three, in English, French, Russian, Vietnamese and Chinese. All texts are equally authentic."

III. The third document was the joint Communiqué, signed on June 13, 1973, in Paris by signatories of the Paris Agreement of Jan. 27, 1973, and concerned "strict observance and scrupulous implementation of all provisions contained in the agreement and the supplementary protocols" in order to "secure peace in Vietnam and contribute to

the cause of peace in Indochina and South East Asia."

Recueil des documents, 1973; *The Department of State Bulletin*, No. 1761, Mar. 26, 1973.

VIETNAM GENEVA CONFERENCE, 1954. ▷ Indochina Geneva Conference and Agreements, 1954.

VIETNAMIZATION. An international term introduced by the US President R. Nixon for a program of the US government for replacing its own armed forces in Vietnam with the South Vietnamese army and police of the Saigon administration; subject of sharp international controversy. President R. Nixon on Apr. 7, 1971 announced:

"The day is approaching when the South Vietnamese will be able to take over their own defense. Our purpose is the complete withdrawal of Americans from South Vietnam. We can reach and shall reach this goal through Vietnamization."

After the US forces withdrew, the Saigon administration and its army collapsed.

New York Times, April 8, 1971.

VIETNAM PARIS CONFERENCE, 1973. A Conference on the question of guarantees for Vietnam, held Feb. 26–Mar. 2, 1973 in the French capital in accordance with an agreement reached in Paris, Jan. 27, 1973 on ending the war in Vietnam. Participants, the signatories of the Paris agreement – USA, Democratic Republic of Vietnam, Provisional Revolutionary Government of South Vietnam, and the Saigon administration; four great powers: China, France, the UK, the USSR, as well as four member states of the International Control and Supervision Commission – Canada, Hungary, Indonesia, and Poland. Taking turns in chairing the Conference were the ministers of foreign affairs of Canada and Poland. The agreement was signed Mar. 2, 1973 in Paris by the representatives of the 12 above-mentioned governments in the presence of the UN Secretary-General; prepared in 12 copies in English, Chinese, French, Russian and Vietnamese.

KEESING's *Contemporary Archive*, 1973.

VIKING. The American scientific-research space stations, of which Viking 1 was launched Aug. 20, 1975 and Viking 2 on Sept. 9, 1975 both in the direction of ▷ Mars, at a cost of 1 billion dollars. Viking 1 entered into an elliptical orbit circling Mars June 19, 1976 and landed on Mars July 20, 1976, and Viking 2 on Aug. 7 and Sept. 3, 1976.

VILNIUS. The capital of the Lithuanian SSR, population 1986 census. 555,000, historical capital of Lithuania since the 13th century, together with Lithuania within the boundaries of the Polish Republic since the 14th century up to the partitions of Poland; a subject of an international dispute 1919–39. Proclaimed Jan. 5, 1919 as the capital of Soviet Lithuania, on Apr. 19, 1919 occupied by the Polish army and awarded to Poland Dec. 8, 1919 by a decision of the Supreme Council of the Coalition against the objections of Lithuania supported by Soviet Russia, which on July 14, 1920 occupied Vilnius in the Polish–Soviet war and granted it to Lithuania. Re-occupied on Oct. 9, 1920 by the Polish army, it became the subject of a debate in the LN. On Dec. 1, 1920 the LN Council convened a Plebiscite Commission composed of representatives of Belgium, Great Britain, Italy and Spain, which began its consultations in Warsaw Dec. 20, 1920 and Jan. 15, 1921 in Kovno. Agreement was reached, and on Mar. 11, 1921 the LN Council decided that the plebiscite should be abandoned. The Conference of Ambassadors on Mar. 15, 1923 recognized the incorporation of Vilnius by Poland against the protests of Lithuania and the USSR. From Oct. 10, 1939 again the capital of Lithuania and from July, 1940 of the Lithuanian SSR; occupied by Germany June 23, 1941–July 13, 1944. Poland renounced her claim to Vilnius as part of the treaty with the USSR on the new frontiers of 1945.

Différend polono-lithuanien. Documents. Octobre 1920 – Avril 1921, SdN, Genève, 1921; *Documents Diplomatiques. Conflit polono-lithuanien. Question de Vilna*, 1918–1924, Kaunas, 1924; S. KUTRZEBA, *La Question de Vilna*, Paris, 1928; M. ANYSAS, *Der litauisch-polnische Streit um das Vilnagebiet von seinen Anfängen bis zum Gutachten des Ständigen Internationalen Gerichtshofes vom 15. Oktober 1931*, Berlin, 1934; *Question de Vilna*, Paris, 1938.

VIÑA DEL MAR CHARTER, 1969. The official name of a document unanimously adopted on May 17–29, 1969 in a Chilean seaside resort, Viña del Mar, by the Special Latin American Coordinating Commission, CECLA, further submitted on June 10, 1969 by Chilean minister of foreign affairs, G. Valdes, as a Memorandum of Latin American governments to the US President, R. Nixon. This was a reply to suggestions made by the US to Latin American states which were to work out their own socio-economic program and their postulates toward the USA independently of the program of ▷ Alliance for Progress. The following is an abridged text of the Charter, containing no direct references to the Alliance for Progress, and in the years 1969–70 subject to negotiations between Latin America and the USA:

"The governments of Latin America and the government of the USA, in the Declaration of American Peoples, in the Punta del Este Charter, in the Rio de Janeiro Economic and Social Declaration and in the Declaration of American Presidents, determined obligations and programs of joint activities, including aspirations of Latin American countries to animate development and progress in the region. Such obligations and programs have not been yet effectively implemented. The CECLA member-states reaffirm importance of the aims and principles contained in these documents and the need to effect in full the agreements. Moreover, they support the postulates contained in the Alta Gracia Charter and in the Tequendama Charter whose adoption by the USA and promotion by other industrialized countries shall be a favorable contribution into the effort exerted by Latin American countries directed at just treatment in international coexistence.

Although the solution of developmental problems is a predominant interest of international community, decisions, recommendations, principles and programs of activities applied until now – although they constitute a significant contribution – are insufficient. For this reason the CECLA member-states deem it necessary to determine more effective forms of interamerican and international cooperation. Concepts encumbent in the points below are neither of antagonistic, nor negative character; they are a logical consequence of a historic process of reaffirmation of Latin America's own values and awareness of mutuality of interests. The character and essence of interamerican and international cooperation.

(1) The CECLA member-states confirm self-personality of Latin America. The process of development taking place in the region and in each country combined with changes in the world impose a need to make substantial transformations in the way Latin America develops relations with other members of international community. For this reason it is inevitable for Latin American countries to seek solutions worked out from the point of their interests expressing their national identity.

(2) Determined to eliminate backwardness they affirm their conviction that it is the countries themselves that are responsible for economic growth and social progress ...

(3) The attainment of these goals depends, to a great extent, on the fact whether the international society, and particularly the countries that weigh most heavily on world decisions, shall recognize and assume due responsibility ...

(4) In the recent decade, interamerican and international cooperation in favor of Latin America was considerably far from satisfying aspirations of the countries of the region agreed in the course of important meetings and in interamerican and world documents.

(5) Toward the end of this decade the gap in economic, scientific and technical development between developing and developed countries has widened considerably and continues to widen; external difficulties hampering rapid economic growth of Latin American countries have piled up. Such difficulties persist with particular intensity in the form of e.g. customs, and not only customs, restrictions impeding access to major world markets on mutually advantageous terms with basic raw materials, semi-finished products and ready-made commodities produced in Latin American countries; in the continuously deteriorating volume of export, terms and amount of financial aid being in practice equivalent to the servicing of foreign credits, serious curtailment of import capacity of Latin American countries, disturbances resulting from the functioning of the international monetary system, terms of maritime transportation which impede or add cost to Latin American overseas trade and in difficulties encountered in transfer of modern technology to countries of this region hampering its application and assimilation wherever it is necessary, as well as in modernizing methods of production.

(6) The presented situation requires a new program of interamerican and international cooperation to be worked out for meeting the aspirations of Latin American countries ...

(28) The interamerican financial cooperation should be guided by the following standards: introduction of real transfer. Countries granting credits and international financial establishments should base their cooperation on economic and social foundations mindful of the recipient country's assumption of development.

(29) Foreign credits should be entirely separated from terms acting detrimentally on Latin American economies, such as mandatory use of particular shipping companies, or purchase on the basis of lists of particular composition which grossly raise costs and disturb trade in this region.

(30) It is indispensable to adopt a principle that no specific terms shall be attached to credits ...

(38) It is urgent that economic development should lead to real social transformations ...".

The Charter was negotiated by the USA and Latin American states on June 14–23, 1969, at Port of Spain, Trinidad, during the Sixth Session of the OAS Interamerican Economic and Social Council.

Carta Viña del Mar, CECLA, Santiago de Chile, 1969.

VIOLENCE. The increase in various forms of politically motivated violence, including hijacking, kidnapping, car bombing and assassination was mentioned in the 1984 Report of the UN General Secretary as "a serious threat to order civility and even public life in many parts of the world."

J. PEREZ DE CUELLAR, *Report of the Secretary General on the Work of Organization 1984*, New York, 1984, pp. 14–15.

VIOLENCE IN SPORTS. An international term, subject of international studies. On Nov. 4, 1985 the UNESCO announced it would undertake a study of the increasing problems of violence in sports.

UN Chronicle, 1986, No 1, p. 84.

VIRGINIA BILL OF RIGHTS, 1776. A bill adopted by the Virginia Convention, on June 12, 1776, drafted by George Mason, anticipated the July 4, 1776 United States Declaration of Independence:

"A declaration of rights made by the representatives of the good people of Virginia, assembled in full and free convention; which rights do pertain to them and their posterity, as the basis and foundation of government:

(1) That all men are by nature equally free and independent, and have certain inherent rights, of which, when they enter into a state of society, they cannot by any compact deprive or divest their posterity; namely, the enjoyment of life and liberty, with the means of acquiring and possessing property, and pursuing and obtaining happiness and safety.

(2) That all power is vested in, and consequently derived from, the people; that magistrates are their trustees and servants, and at all times amenable to them.

(3) That government is, or ought to be instituted for the common benefit, protection, and security of the people, nation, or community; of all the various modes and forms of government, that is best which is capable of producing the greatest degree of happiness and safety, and is most effectually secured against the danger of maladministration; and that when any government shall be found inadequate or contrary to these purposes, a majority of the community hath an indubitable, unalienable and indefeasible right to reform, alter or abolish it, in such manner as shall be judged most conductive to the public weal.

(4) That no man, or set of men, are entitled to exclusive or separate emoluments or privileges from the community, but in consideration of public services; which, not being descendible, neither ought the offices of magistrate, legislator or judge to be hereditary.

(5) That the legislative and executive powers of the state should be separate and distinct from the judiciary; and that the members of the two first may be restrained from oppression, by feeling and participating the burthens of the people, they should, at fixed periods, be reduced to a private station, return into that body from which they were originally taken, and the vacancies be supplied by frequent, certain, and regular elections, in which all, or any part of the former members to be again eligible or ineligible, as the laws shall direct.

(6) That elections of members to serve as representatives of the people in assembly, ought to be free; and that all men having sufficient evidence of permanent common interest with, and attachment to the community, have the right to suffrage, and cannot be taxed or deprived of their property for publick uses, without their own consent, or that of their representatives so elected, nor bound by any law to which they have not, in like manner, assented for the public good.

(7) That all power of suspending laws, or the execution of laws, by any authority without consent of the representatives of the people, is injurious to their rights, and ought not to be exercised.

(8) That in all capital or criminal prosecutions a man hath a right to demand the cause and nature of his accusation, to be confronted with the accusers and witnesses, to call for evidence in his favour, and to a speedy trial by an impartial jury of his vicinage, without whose unanimous consent he cannot be found guilty; nor can he be compelled to give evidence against himself; that no man be deprived of his liberty, except by the law of the land or the judgment of his peers.

(9) That excessive bail ought not to be required, nor excessive fines imposed, nor cruel and unusual punishments inflicted.

(10) That general warrants, whereby an officer or messenger may be commanded to search suspected places without evidence of a fact committed, or to seize any person or persons not named, or whose offence is not particularly described and supported by evidence, are grievous and oppressive, and ought not to be granted.

(11) That in controversies respecting property, and in suits between man and man, the ancient trial by jury is preferable to any other, and ought to be held sacred.

(12) That the freedom of the press is one of the great bulwarks of liberty, and can never be restrained but by despotick governments.

(13) That a well-regulated militia, composed of the body of the people trained to arms, is the proper, natural and safe defence of a free state; that standing armies in time of peace should be avoided as dangerous to liberty; and that in all cases the military should be under strict subordination to, and governed by, the civil power.

(14) That the people have a right to uniform government; and, therefore, that no government separate from, or independent of the government of Virginia, ought to be erected or established within the limits thereof.

(15) That no free government, or the blessings of liberty, can be preserved to any people, but by a firm adherence to justice, moderation, temperance, frugality and virtue, and by frequent recurrence to fundamental principles.

(16) That religion, or the duty which we owe to our Creator, and the manner of discharging it, can be directed only by reason and conviction, not by force or violence; and therefore all men are equally entitled to the free exercise of religion, according to the dictates of conscience; and that it is the mutual duty of all to practise Christian forbearance, love, and charity towards each other."

K.M. ROWLAND, *The Life and Writings of George Mason*, Philadelphia, 1882; H.D. HILL, *George Mason: Constitutionalist*, New York, 1938.

VIRGIN ISLANDS, BRITISH. A group of small islands in the Caribbean, east of Puerto Rico. The largest are Tortola, Virgin, Gorda, Anegada and Jost Van Dyke. Area: 158 sq. km. Population: 1980 census 10,985; 1985 estimate 11,858. Under British administration. Official language: English. Currency: US dollar.

I. DOOKHAN, *A History of the British Virgin Islands*, Epping, 1975; *The Europa Year Book 1984. A World Survey*, Vol. II, pp. 1240–1241, London, 1984.

VIRGIN ISLANDS, UNITED STATES. The islands, formerly Danish West Indies, were purchased from Denmark Mar. 31, 1917 for US $25,000,000; a US "unincorporated territory" administered by the US Department of the Interior; since 1954 a limited autonomy. The UN Special (Decolonization) Committee on Sept. 14, 1983 called upon the administering Power to take all necessary steps to expedite the process of decolonization. A group of islands east of Puerto Rico consisting of the islands of St Thomas, St Croix, St John and about 50 small islets or cays. Area: 344 sq. km. Pop.: 96,569, census 1980. The capital Charlotte Amalie on St Thomas with 11,756 inhabitants 1980.

J.A. JARVIS, *The Virgin Islands and Their People*, Philadelphia, 1944; L.H. EVANS, *The Virgin Islands: from Naval Base to New Deal*, Ann Arbor, 1945; *UN Chronicle*, January 1984, p. 64; *The Europa Year Book 1984. A World Survey*, Vol. II, pp. 2635–2636, London, 1984.

VIRUNGA. The National Park of Zaïre, included in the ▷ World Heritage UNESCO List. This park is situated almost entirely in the Kivu region, and includes marshy deltas and lava plains, and savannahs extending up to the volcanoes and eternal snows of the Ruwenzori range. Some 20,000 hippopotami live in its rivers. In winter it is visited by birds from Siberia.

UNESCO, *A Legacy for All*, Paris, 1984.

VISA. An international term for a seal affixed in a passport by a foreign consulate, giving the right of entry or transit in a state; subject of international conventions and bilateral agreements, in the second half of 20th century, frequently manifested by abolition of visas on reciprocal basis. An international Agreement in connection with the economic integration permits citizens of member-states of the European Community to travel inside the community without a visa. In the CMEA region, in the years, 1979–80, citizens of member-states could travel in the same way, but not to the USSR, whose capital is the seat of CMEA HQ. The visa facilities as an international problem were a subject of discussion at the ▷ Berne CSCE Human Contacts Meeting, 1986. The UK and the USA, as well as the USA and Japan came in 1988, to reciprocal agreements to lift visa requirements for their citizens travelling on vacation or business up to 90 days as long as they had a ticket and valid passport. Only those seeking to work or live in the other country would have to get visas. Also on Jan 1, 1988 Austria and Poland signed an agreement on free movement of their citizens.

F.L. AUERBACH, "The Visa Process and Review of Visa Application", in: *US Department of State Bulletin*, No. 63, 1960; KEESING's *Contemporary Archive*, 1986, No. 12; *The International Herald Tribune*, February 28, 1988.

VISION HABITAT. Habitat Film Library, one of the information systems of the UNHCR (▷ Refugees).

VISTULA. A river in Poland, the longest Polish river flowing into the Baltic Sea (1068 km); rising in the Silesia Beskidy Mountains, a western range of the Carpathians, flows through Cracow, Warsaw, Torun to the Gulf of Gdańsk on the Baltic; connected by canals with the rivers Oder, Neman, and Dnieper; subject of international dispute between Poland and Germany (▷ Gdańsk), settled by the Potsdam Agreements, 1945.

J. STYCZYŃSKI, *The Vistula, The Story of a River*, Warsaw, 1973.

VITAL STATISTICS. An international term for all data on birth, death, diseases, suicides, marriages, divorces, etc., registered nationwide in Europe and USA in 19th century censuses, worldwide from 1950 on the basis of UN Population and Vital Statistics Program. UN publ.: *Population and Vital Statistics* (quarterly); WHO, *Annual Epidemiological and Vital Statistics*.

Proceedings of the World Population Conference, 1954, 7 Vols., UN New York, 1955; B. BENJAMIN, *Elements of Vital Statistics*, New York, 1959.

VITTEL SUMMIT CONFERENCE, 1983. A Conference of Heads of State of France and Africa, in Oct., 1983, in Vittel, France.

VLADIVOSTOK. The chief Soviet port on the Pacific, capital of Maritime Territory (Primorsky Kray) of the Far Eastern USSR. Founded 1860, linked with Moscow since 1903 by the Trans-Siberian Rail Road. Occupied 1917–22 by American, British, French and Japanese marines. The Russian Far Eastern Republic, proclaimed 1920 after the withdrawal of Allied troops, was dissolved with the proclamation of the Soviet power on Oct. 25, 1922. During World War II the US Lend-Lease military equipment was sent 1942–45, towards Vladivostok, as towards Archangel and the Persian Bay. Place of a summit meeting on Nov. 23–24, 1974 of the Heads of State, L. Brezhnev and G. Ford. Since June 1986, Vladivostok, the headquarters of the Soviet Union Pacific Fleet and the neighboring port of Nahodka, together with a new commercial deep-water terminus Vostochny Port are 'a major international center, a wide-open window of the USSR on the East' (M.S. Gorbachov).

KEESING's *Contemporary Archive*, 1974.

VNYESHTORGBANK. A USSR state bank for foreign trade and financial international operations, est. 1922 in Moscow.

VOCABULARIES. A subject of international co-operation under the aegis of UNESCO. An international bibliography of standardized vocabularies, registered by the International Information Centre for Terminology (▷ INFOTERM) in co-operation with the Siemens Computer Programme TEAM (Terminologie-Erfassung- und Aswertungs-Methode).

E. WUSTER, *Bibliography of Monolingual Scientific and Technical Glossaries*, National Standards, UNESCO Paris, 1955.

VOICE OF AMERICA ▷ Radio Voice of America.

VOLAPÜK. A "world language", based largely on English, invented 1880 by a German priest J.M. Schleyer (1831–1912).

J.M. SCHLEYER, *Grammar with Vocabularies of Volapük*, London, 1887.

VOLCAMONICA. A natural site of Italy, in the Central Alps in Lombardy, included in the ▷ World Heritage UNESCO List. On the rock faces in this valley in the Central Alps, in Lombardy, are the remains of 150,000 engravings. The most recent were executed in the first century AD, and the oldest 8000 years before. They illustrate 80 centuries of European history.

UNESCO, *A Legacy for All*, Paris, 1984.

VOLCANOLOGY. A subject of international research. Organizations reg. with the UIA:

International Association of Volcanology and Chemistry of the Earth's Interior, f. 1919, Leeds, UK. Recognized by ICAO. Publ.: *Bulletin Volcanologique, Catalogue of Active Volcanoes of the World including Solfatane Fields*.
Nordic Volcanological Institute, f. 1972, Reykjavik, Iceland.

A. RITTMAN, *Volcanoes and their Activity*, London, 1962.

VOLGA. The longest river of Europe (3700 km) rising in the Valday Hills (USSR) flows through the Rybinsk Reservoir, past Gorky, Kazan, Ulyanovsk, Volgograd, Kuybyshev and enters the Caspian Sea below Astrakhan; linked by the ▷ Volga–Baltic Waterway with the Baltic Sea, and with the Baltic–White Sea Canal; by the Volga–Don Canal with the Azov Sea and with the Black Sea; and by the Moscow Canal with the capital of the USSR. During World War II the major battle between Soviet and German troops took place on the Volga (▷ Battle of Stalingrad, 1942–43).

VOLGA–BALTIC WATERWAY. The canal and river system 1100 km long, constructed 1709–1964, linking the Volga River in the USSR with the Baltic Sea in the Leningrad area. The waterway system consists of the Moscow–Volga Canal, the ▷ Volga River, the Rybinsk Reservoir, the Marjinsk system (the Sheksna River, the White Lake Canal, the Kovzha River, the Mariinsk Canal, and the Vytegsa River), the Onega Canal, the Svir River, the Ladoga Canals and the Neva River to Leningrad. Open (since May 1964) to vessels carrying up to 2700 tons of freight.

VOLGOGRAD. City on southeast European USSR and a port on the Volga river, formerly 1925–61, Stalingrad. ▷ Battle of Stalingrad.

VOLHYNIA. A historic European region, divided in 14th century between Lithuania and Poland, called also Volyn; united after the Polish–Lithuanian Union, 1569; province of Poland until the partitions of the Polish state, since 1797 Russian province; divided between Poland and Soviet Ukraine by the Riga Treaty, 1921; the Polish part was formally ceded to the USSR on Aug. 16, 1945 by the Soviet–Polish border agreement.

V

VOLKSDEUTSCHE. German = "people's Germans". A German term coined for German colonists living outside the territory of the German III Reich, as distinct from Germans of the Reich (▷ Reichsdeutsche). After the occupation of Czechoslovakia, 1938, introduced in the legislation of the III Reich developed during World War II. According to that legislation, following a voluntary or terror-forced avowal of being a German national (in line with the rule ▷ Minderheit ist wer will) of foreign state citizens, the given persons were classified in one of five categories of German citizenship, established in the III Reich, with common liability to military service. That concerned, primarily, the areas of adjoining states annexed in 1940 to Germany (such as in France Alsace-Lorraine and in Poland Silesia, Great Poland and Pomerania). The compulsory character of military service in the Wehrmacht for Poles, citizens of the Reich (Reichsdeutsche) of the Polish minority in Germany and of Poles registered on the Volksliste (Volksdeutsche) in the occupied territories is confirmed by the fact that in the years 1943/44 over 200,000 Wehrmacht soldiers of Polish nationality crossed the front line and fought in Polish armed forces in the East and West.

J. SOBCZAK, "The Ethnic Germans as the Subject of the Nazi Resettlement Campaign during the World War II", in: *Polish Western Affairs*, No. 1, 1967, pp. 63–95.

VOLKSKAMMER. German = "People's Chamber". The name of the German Democratic Republic parliament, est. Oct. 7, 1949.

VOLLEYBALL. An Olympic sport since 1964, organized in the International Volleyball Federation, FIVB, est. 1947 and since 1949 sponsoring the world championships. Reg. with the UIA.

Yearbook of International Organizations.

VOLTA GREATER ACCRA. A historic site of Ghana, included in the ▷ World Heritage UNESCO List.

VOLTAIRE DOCTRINE, 1713. The thesis that peace will only be assured when those who start wars are judged as ordinary criminals. This thesis was presented by Voltaire (1694–1778), commenting in 1763 on the classical work of the French cleric de Sainte Pierre (1658–1743), on perpetual peace.

CH. J. SAINT PIERRE, *A Project of Perpetual Peace*, London, 1927.

VOLUNTARY CONTRIBUTIONS. An international term. In the UN system every year the Governments of the Member States declare their contributions to different UN programs and funds at the special meetings of the Ad Hoc Committee of the UN General Assembly for the Announcement of Voluntary Contributions.

UN Chronicle, January 1984, pp. 2 and 28.

VOLUNTARY SERVICES. A subject of international co-operation. Organizations reg. with the UIA:

Association for Volunteer Service in Europe, f. 1972, Lyon. Co-ordinating Committee for International Voluntary Service, f. 1948 under the auspices of UNESCO. Headquarters UNESCO House, Paris. Consultative status with UNESCO, ECOSOC and FAO. Publ.: *Workcamps Programme* (annual in English, French, Spanish), *Voluntary Service Bulletin* (in English and French).
Ex-Volunteers International, f. 1970, London.
International Christian Service for Peace, f. 1957, Königswinter, FRG. Publ.: *Newsletter*.

International Council of Voluntary Agencies, f. 1962, Geneva. Consultative status with ECOSOC, UNESCO, UNICEF and UNCTAD. Publ.: *ICVA News*.
International Voluntary Services, f. 1953, Washington, DC.
Latin American Regional Center of the Voluntary Service, f. 1975, Buenos Aires.
Organization of Youth and Voluntary Work Movements for Africa, f. 1972, Nairobi.
Regional Conference on International Voluntary Service, f. 1964, Brussels. Publ.: *Bulletin*.
United Nations Volunteers, est. 1971 by authority of the UN General Assembly Res. 2659/XXV, as part of the UN Development Programme. Coordinator: Palais des Nations Geneva, Liaison Office UNDP, New York.
Volunteers in Technical Assistance, f. 1959, Mt Rainier, Md. USA.
World Voluntary Service Corps in the event of Natural Disasters, f. 1971, Paris.

Yearbook of International Organizations.

VORARLBERG, 1919. A province of Austria, area 2600 sq. km, population about 140,000 in 1919 (271,000 inhabitants in 1970), subject of international dispute. On Apr. 25, 1919, the Landtag of Vorarlberg decided to carry out a plebiscite for separation of Vorarlberg from Austria and its annexation to Switzerland. The plebiscite held on May 11, 1919 gave 80% of votes for Switzerland, which was confirmed by the Landtag resolution of Aug. 10, 1919. The Supreme Council of the Versailles Conference, which was addressed by the population of Vorarlberg in May 1919, did not declare itself on the question; it was, however, settled by the Saint Germain Treaty of Powers Allied and Associated with Austria, which left Vorarlberg within the boundaries of Austria. The population's complaint submitted to the League of Nations in 1920 remained without reply.

LANDERRAT VON VORARLBERG, *Memorial to the League of Nations*, Bregenz, August 1, 1920.

"VOSTOK". The Russian name of Soviet space ships, whose flights began the era of man in space.

VOTING IN THE UN. The main system in the UN foreseen in arts. 18, 19, 20 and 27 of the UN Charter is very complicated and is not used in any other intergovernmental organization. Of the two systems in common use, one is based on the principle of "One Nation–One Vote," and the second is based on demographic, economic, and other indices, so-called "Weighted Voting." A new system was created whose main feature was granting the Great Powers the right to veto exclusively in the Security Council (but not in the UN General Assembly or other organs), ▷ Veto in UN Security Council. This is a requirement of unanimity of the permanent members of the Council in all but procedural questions (art. 27 para. 3 of the UN Charter). The remaining UN organs make decisions by a simple majority or, in important matters by a two-thirds vote. Without the right to veto neither the USA nor the USSR would have been willing to ratify the UN Charter and thus on this question at the ▷ San Francisco Conference of the United Nations in Apr., 1945 they maintained a joint position. Even in succeeding years, except for the period of the intense "cold war" 1950–53, when the government of the USA considered the possibility of revising the UN Charter, none of the Great Powers has opposed the specific system of voting in the Security Council. On the other hand, the system has been criticized by some of the states of Latin America, Africa, and South Asia, regarding it as a symbol of disrespect for the principle of the equality of all states. Plans were drawn up for increasing the number of permanent members in the Security Council and creating a group of semi-permanent

members. In practice during the decade 1971–80 more and more often the Security Council has taken decisions by ▷ Consensus, which eliminated voting. Some of the states of Latin American noted that the entry into the UN of a large number of states of small demographic potential has resulted in a situation where in the UN General Assembly these states make up c. 50% of the total votes but represent hardly 10% of the world's population; therefore, they considered more equitable the adoption of a system of "weighted voting" in the UN General Assembly. On the other hand, experts of the Department of State made additional studies of 15 various "weighted" voting systems, testing them against many of the votes which had been taken in the UN. The results: none of the systems examined either improved or worsened the position of the USA in the UN. The only change which was made, experimentally in 1964 and since Dec. 7, 1966 on a permanent basis, concerned voting in the UN General Assembly and later in several Committees by electronic voting machines rather than by show of hands, a time-saving procedure. There are supporters of a secret voting system in the UN which would free small states from external pressure, but no state has formally made such a motion. However, the UN General Assembly in 1967 accepted Res. 2323/XXII to change arts. 89 and 129 of the Assembly Rules, introducing two kinds of voting: (1) Recorded Vote; (2) Non-Recorded Vote.
The former head of the US delegation to the UN, P. Moynihan, stated in a CBS television interview, May 28, 1976, that there were cases of buying votes in the UN and that such a vote could be bought for around US $2000 and, in one case, even for US $600. Moynihan refused to reveal who had purchased or sold votes.

A.C. RICHES, *Majority Rule in International Organizations*, London, 1940; W. KOO, *Voting Procedures in International Political Organizations*, London, 1947; E.J. DE ARCHAGA, *Voting and Handling of Disputes in the Security Council*, New York, 1950; L. QUINTANILLA, "El Problema de la Paz. Un nuevo Sistema de votación para la ONU," in: *Excelsior*, México, DF, Aug. 28, 1965; *UN Monthly Chronicle*, No. 11, 1967; J. KOLASA, "'One State – One Vote Rule' in International Universal Organizations", in: *Polish Yearbook of International Law*, 1975, pp. 215–244.

VOTING PROCEDURE IN THE SECURITY COUNCIL. THE GREAT POWERS STATEMENT, 1945. A Joint Statement of the UK, the USA, the USSR and China on June 7, 1945 in San Francisco on the question of unanimity of permanent members in the decisions of the Security Council. The Statement was supplied by France. The main points of the Statement read as follows:
"I.(1) The Yalta voting formula recognizes that the Security Council, in discharging its responsibilities for the maintenance of international peace and security, will have two broad groups of functions. Under Chapter VI and VII the Council will have to make decisions which involve its taking direct measures in connection with settlement of disputes, adjustment of situations likely to lead to disputes, determination of threats to the peace, removal of threats to the peace, and suppression of breaches of the peace. It will also have to make decisions which do not involve the taking of such measures. The Yalta formula provides that the second of these two groups of decisions will be governed by a procedure vote – that is, the vote of any seven members. The first group of decisions will be governed by a qualified vote – that is, the vote of seven members, including the concurring votes of the five permanent members, subject to the proviso that in decisions under Section A and a part of Section C of Chapter VIII parties to a dispute shall abstain from voting ...
...(7) The Yalta voting formula substitutes for the rule of complete unanimity of the League Council a system of qualified majority voting in the Security Council.

Under this system non-permanent members of the Security Council individually would have no 'veto'. As regards the permanent members, there is no question under the Yalta formula of investing them with a new right, namely, the right to veto, a right which the permanent members of the League Council always had. The formula proposed for the taking of action in the Security Council by a majority of seven would make the operation of the Council less subject to obstruction than was the case under the League of Nations rule of complete unanimity.

(8) It should also be remembered that under the Yalta formula the five major powers could not act by themselves, since even under the unanimity requirement any decisions of the Council would have to include the concurring votes of at least two of the non-permanent members. In other words, it would be possible for five non-permanent members as a group to exercise a 'veto'. It is not to be assumed, however, that the permanent members, any more than the non-permanent members, would use their 'veto' power wilfully to obstruct the operation of the Council.

(9) In view of the primary responsibilities of the permanent members, they could not be expected, in the present condition of the world, to assume the obligation to act in so serious matter as the maintenance of international peace and security in consequence of a decision in which they had not concurred. Therefore, if majority voting in the Security Council is to be made possible, the only practicable method is to provide, in respect of non-procedural decisions, for unanimity of the permanent members plus the concurring votes of at least two of the non-permanent members.

(10) For all these reasons, the four sponsoring Governments agreed on the Yalta formula and have presented it to this Conference as essential if an international organization is to be created through which all peace-loving nations can effectively discharge their common responsibilities for the maintenance of international peace and security.

II. In the light of the considerations set forth in Part 1 of this statement, it is clear what the answers to the questions submitted by the subcommittee should be with the exception of Question 19. The answer to that question is as follows:

(1) In the opinion of the Delegations of the Sponsoring Governments, the Draft Charter itself contains an indication of the application of the voting procedures to the various functions of the Council.

(2) In this case, it will be unlikely that there will arise in the future any matters of great importance on which a decision will have to be made as to whether a procedural vote would apply. Should, however, such a matter arise, the decision regarding the preliminary question as to whether or not such a matter is procedural must be taken by a vote of seven members of the Security Council, including the concurring votes of the permanent members."

UNCIO Doc. 852/E/III/1/37/1, pp. 710–714.

VOTUM SEPARATUM. *Latin* = "separate voting". An international term in court practice for the separate opinion of a judge, members of the internal or international tribunal, being in the minority as to their assessment of the discussed case or with their opinion on the rate of penalty. In the past, *votum separatum* was called "contravotum".

VOYAGER. American experimental plane which made a successful attempt to fly around the World without stopping or refueling. Accomplished in 9 days 3 minutes, 44 seconds starting from Edwards Air Force Base, Ca., from Dec 14 to 23, 1986. The Voyager 1 and 2 were used as unmanned American space probes; in 1986 encountered ▷ Saturn.

KEESING's *Record of World Events*, 1986 and 1987.

VYBORG. A Baltic port and city in the USSR, northwest of Leningrad, near the Finnish border. Hanseatic League port in 15th century. In 1710 came to Russia, but 1812 integrated by the Finnish province of Russian Empire, and remained with Finland 1919–40; ceded to the USSR by the Paris Peace Treaty on Feb. 10, 1947.

E. JUTIKKALA, K. PIRINEN, *A History of Finland*, New York, 1979.

W

WADI HADRAMAVI AND SHIBAN. Masterpieces of Yemini architecture, subject of the UNESCO International Campaign for Safeguarding Wadi Hadramavi and Shiban. The skyscraper houses of Shiban built entirely of mud are known as "the Manhattan of the desert".

R. LEWCOCK, *Wadi Hadramavi and the Walled City of Shiban*, UNESCO, Paris, 1986.

WAGER OF WAR. The Third Council of Ministers of Foreign Affairs of the American Republics on Jan. 28, 1942 adopted the following principle:

"In the interests of solidarity the American Republics will not consider as a party waging war any American state which finds itself or will find itself in a state of war with any non-American state."

Under this doctrine the states of Latin America maintaining their neutrality were freed from all limitations in their normal relations with the USA.

Conferencias Internacionales Americanas. Primer Suplemento, 1938–1942, Washington, DC, 1943 (in Spanish and English).

WAGES. An international term, defined by ILO as follows:

". . . – irrespective of name or form of computation – remuneration or earnings (that can be expressed in term of cash and determined upon contracts or national legislation) which by virtue of written or oral contract on hiring services are charged by the employee on the employer, either for work done or which is to be done, or for services rendered or which are to be rendered" (ILO Convention No. 95, Art. 1).

Since 1905 wages are subject to international statistics, the year when the British Board of Trade started a four-year study concerning wages in the building, printing and metal industries in Great Britain, the USA, Belgium, France and Germany and obtained comparative data. Since 1920 the ILO statistical office has carried out permanent research into real wages in major cities and introduced standard statistics concerning wages and work time. Also the UN keeps international records of wages. Wages are subject to the following international conventions:
(1) The ILO Convention Concerning the Protection of Wages, signed on Dec. 1, 1949, in Geneva, stipulating that: "it shall be prohibited for the employer to limit in any way any employee's freedom to dispose of his wages at will (Art. 6); in case of bankruptcy of a firm "wages being a privileged liability shall be paid in full before ordinary creditors may claim their shares" (Art. 11) and "it shall be prohibited to pay wages in stores merchandizing liquors and other similar establishments" (Art. 13).
(2) The ILO Convention Concerning Equal Renumeration for Men and Women Workers for Work of Equal Value, No. 100, signed on June 29, 1951, in Geneva, determined that "the term 'renumeration' indicates wages or ordinary salary, basic or minimum, and any other benefits paid directly in cash or in kind, by the employer to the employees by virtue of hiring this employee" (Art. 1) and "each Member should promote . . . application of the principle of equal wages for men and women workers doing work of equal value."

The British Ministry of Labour announced in Aug., 1972 the results of a study conducted in eight Western European states to determine the percentage of women workers paid equally to men for the same work in industry: nowhere as high as 100%, the highest in Sweden – 83%, in France – 77%, FRG – 70%, Belgium – 68%, the Netherlands – 61%, Great Britain – 59% and the least in Luxembourg – 56%.

Wage statistics are published in: *UN Statistical Yearbook, ILO Yearbook of Labour Statistics*.

La standardisation internationale des statistiques des salaires et des heures du travail, OIT, Genève, 1937.

WAITANGI TREATY, 1840. A treaty between Great Britain and the representatives of the Maori people in New Zealand which ceded the sovereignty over the island to the British Crown, signed on Feb. 6, 1840 at Waitangi on Bay of Islands, New Zealand. The Day of the Waitangi Treaty called New Zealand Day is a National Day of New Zealand.

Oxford New Zealand Encyclopedia, London, 1965.

WAKE ISLAND. The US atoll in the central Pacific with three islets: Wake, Wilkes and Peale. Area: 7.8 sq. km. Pop. 1978 est.: 1,000. Annexed by the United States 1895. Occupied by the Japanese from Dec., 1941 to July, 1945. Now commercial and military US base.

WALLIS AND FUTUNA ISLANDS. The French overseas protectorate in the South Pacific, West of Samoa and North East of Fiji, since 1942. The territory comprises: Wallis Archipelago (96 sq. km) with the main island of Ueva with 6019 inhabitants and Horn Islands (159 sq. km) with the main island of Futuna with 3173 residents (census 1976). The status of the Protectorate changed to an Overseas Territory of France (Territoire d'outre mere) on July 29, 1961.

The Europa Year Book 1984. A World Survey, Vol. II, pp. 1585–1586, London, 1984.

WALLOONS. A people inhabiting the southern provinces of Belgium numbering in 1970 *c.* 4 millions, comprising along with the Flemings the population of that country. The Walloons speak French (Walloon dialect). Claims of the Walloons over linguistic priority in the administration and school system of Belgium were reflected in the State legislation and self-government movements as well as in pronouncements of the European Court for the Protection of Human Rights (The ▷ Flemish).

R. LEJEUNE, *Histoire sommaire de la littérature wallonne*, Brussels, 1942.

WALL STREET. A street in downtown Manhattan, New York City; headquarters of the New York Stock Exchange and the oldest American banks, e.g. Bank of New York est. 1784, First National City Bank est. 1812, Irving Trust Co. est. 1851, US Trust Co. est. 1853, and other symbols of American financiers.
In 1789 the first US Congress met at the Federal Building in Wall Street and nominated the first US President, George Washington.

R. WARSCHOW, *The Story of Wall Street*, New York, 1929.

WANG HIYA PEACE TREATY, 1844. The peace and trade treaty between China and US, signed on July 3, 1844 in Wang Hiya. Art. 3 permitted citizens of the US to frequent the five ports of Kwang-Chas, Amoy, Fuchow, Ningpo and Shanghai.

Major Peace Treaties of Modern History, New York, 1967, Vol. II, pp. 719–732.

WAN-HSIEN TREATY, 1844. ▷ American-Chinese Treaties, 1844–1908.

WANTED NOTICE. An announcement concerning criminals wanted by the court or attorney; introduced in the 19th century in Europe with respect to both criminal and political offenders.

WAR. One of the most ancient international terms for armed conflicts; subject of international studies, agreements on status of war under international law, and "outlawry of war".
The principle of non-use of war for the settlement of international problems was incorporated in the UN Charter, 1945. The UN International Law Commission in 1967 initiated studies on a draft Declaration on War jointly motioned by the governments of Argentina, Chile and Venezuela (Law of war).
According to estimates based on the period from 3600 B.C. until 1960, mankind has known only 292 years of universal peace, and in the remaining 5268 years has faced 14,513 armed conflicts taking 1240 million human lives.

J. BLOCH, *La Guerre*, Paris, 1898; K. VON CLAUSEWITZ, *Vom Kriege*, 3 Vols., Berlin, 1905; S.R. STEINMETZ, *Die Philosophie des Krieges*, Leipzig, 1907; J.T. SHOTWELL, "Plans and Protocols to End War, Historical Outline and Guide", in: *International Conciliation*, No. 208, March., 1925, pp. 79–113; C. MORRISON, *The Outlawry of War*, Chicago, 1927; Q. WRIGHT, *The Role of International Law in Elimination of War*, New York, 1961; R.C. SNYDER, *Theory and Research on the Cause of War*, London, 1969; E. ALVARES-ARENA, *Idea de Guerra*, Madrid, 1984. E. LUARD, *War in International Society*, London, New Haven, 1986.

WAR BOOTIES OR WAR PRIZES. An international term stemming from medieval right of booty, *jus praede*, in time of war granted by the State to ships of its fleet, or even to private ships, allowing them to loot enemy's or neutral merchant ships; however, the Paris Declaration of 1856 issued a ban on plundering neutral ships with the exception of those carrying war contraband, and the First Hague Conference of 1899 adopted a convention (never ratified) on the establishment of an International Booty Court.

R. LAUN, *Die Haager Landskriegsordnung*, Berlin, 1950.

WAR CONTRIBUTIONS. A war custom contrary to international law, usually tribute in kind, money, or work imposed on a country occupied or defeated by enemy forces. (Germany imposed war contribution on France after her defeat on Sept. 1, 1870, to the sum of 5 billion francs in gold, paid by Sept. 1, 1873). After World War I in Saint-Germain-en-Laye on Sept. 10, 1919 a Treaty on Contributions was signed obligating the successor states of the Austria-Hungarian monarchy, Czechoslovakia, Poland, Romania as well as the Serbo-Croatian-Slovenian State to pay one and a half billion francs in gold as a contribution to the expenses connected with the liberation of the territories of the monarchy. In Paris on Dec. 8, 1919 a declaration of the powers was signed, changing the form of contribution.

LNTS, Vol. 2, pp. 35 and 43; H.J. CAHN, *Das Kriegsschädenrecht der Nationen*, Zürich, 1947.

WAR CORRESPONDENTS. The press, radio, TV journalists collecting news in areas of armed conflict; subject of international draft convention by UN expert committee providing for establishment of a special international institution entitled to grant journalists on such dangerous missions, documents stating they are not soldiers, perform no military missions and are under international protection by signatories of the convention.

G. MORITZ, "Kriegsberichterstatter", in: *Strupp-Schlochauer Wörterbuch des Völkerrechts*, Vol.2, pp. 332–333, Berlin, 1961; C. PILLOUD, "Protection des journalistes en mission périlleuse dans les zones de conflit armé", in: *Revue internationale de la Croix Rouge*, No. 1, 1971.

WAR CRIMES. ▷ Voltaire Doctrine, 1713.

WAR CRIMES AND UN RESOLUTIONS, 1946–70. On Feb. 13, 1946 the UN General Assembly called on member states to use extradition and to punish war criminals.

The UN General Assembly in a unanimously passed Res. 95/I, Dec. 11, 1946, recognizing the obligation of supporting the development of international law and its codification, placed on it in Art. 13 of the UN Charter, took note of the agreement to create the ICJ and in connection with this confirmed "the principles of international law recognized by the Statute of the Nuremberg Tribunal and the verdict of this Tribunal." In this same resolution the Assembly instructed the Committee for the Codification of International Law as follows:

"The General Assembly,
Recognizes the obligation laid upon it by Article 13, paragraph 1, sub-paragraph a, of the Charter, to initiate studies and make recommendations for the purpose of encouraging the progressive development of international law and its codification;
Take Note of the Agreement for the establishment of an International Military Tribunal for the prosecution and punishment of the major war criminals of the European Axis signed in London on August 8, 1945, and of the Charter annexed thereto, and of the fact that similar principles have been adopted in the Charter of the International Military Tribunal for the trial of the major war criminals in the Far East, proclaimed at Tokyo on January 19, 1946.
Therefore,
Affirms the principles of international law recognized by the Charter of the Nürnberg Tribunal and the judgement of the Tribunal;
Directs the Committee on the codification of international law established by the resolution of the General Assembly of December 11, 1946, to treat as a matter of primary importance plans for the formulation, in the context of a general codification of offences against the peace and security of mankind, or of an International Criminal Code, of the principles recognized in the Charter of the Nürnberg Tribunal and in the judgement of the Tribunal."

On the recommendation of the Sixth Committee the General Assembly at its 55th plenary meeting on Dec. 11, 1946, unanimously adopted the following resolution related to the crime of ▷ Genocide:

"Genocide is a denial of the right of existence of entire human groups, as homicide is the denial of the right to live of individual human beings: such denial of the right of existence shocks the conscience of mankind, results in great losses to humanity in the form of cultural and other contributions represented by these human groups, and is contrary to moral law and to the spirit and aims of the United Nations. Many instances of such crimes of genocide have occurred when racial, religious, political and other groups have been destroyed, entirely or in part.
The punishment of the crime of genocide is a matter of international concern.
The general assembly, therefore,
Affirms that genocide is a crime under international law, which the civilized world condemns, and for the

commission of which principals and accomplices – whether private individuals, public officials or statesmen, and whether the crime is committed on religious, racial, political or any other grounds – are punishable;
Invites the Member States to enact the necessary legislation for the prevention and punishment of this crime;
Recommends, that international co-operation be organized between States with a view to facilitating the speedy prevention and punishment of the crime of genocide, and, to this end,
Requests the Economic and Social Council to undertake the necessary studies with a view to drawing up a draft convention on the crime of genocide to be submitted to the next regular session of the general assembly."

The Assembly in this same Res. 95/I enjoined the UN member States to introduce the Nuremberg principles to their national codes. This was also reflected in Peace Treaties signed on Feb. 10, 1947 in Paris with Bulgaria, Finland, Hungary, Italy, and Romania, in the Peace Treaty with Japan in San Francisco, Sept. 8, 1951 (Art. 11), and partially in the State Treaty with Austria, May 15, 1955 (Art. 12). The new international instruments against war criminals are: the Convention on the Prevention and Punishment of Genocide, Dec. 9, 1948. ▷ Genocide and the Convention on the Protection of War Victims, Aug. 12, 1949. The UN General Assembly in Res. 177/II, of Nov. 21, 1947, initiated work on a Code of Crimes against the Peace and Security of Humanity, and in Res. 488/V, Dec. 12, 1950, evaluated the work of the UN International Law Commission in this regard.

In 1964 the problem of the expiration of the validity of war crimes arising during the 20 years 1944–64, some 70,000 war criminals had been tried in Western Europe, among which 61,700 were citizens of the German Third Reich, but less than 6115 had been punished; among this number nearly all had been pardoned either by the western allies or by the FRG government. Then the FRG government on Nov. 5, 1964, made a declaration based on the criminal code of the Reich of May 18, 1971, that after 20 years from the ending of the war, i.e. May 8, 1965, the validity of all war crimes should expire. This caused a sharp outcry of world opinion and a split in German opinion. Nevertheless, the FRG government, on Feb. 2, 1965, submitted the required proposal for a law, which was passed Mar. 25, 1965 with the amendment that the 20-year period of expiration could not be counted from May 8, 1945, but from Dec. 31, 1949.

Poland expressed itself against this on Mar. 8, 1965 in a memorandum to the UN requesting the examination of the matter by the Session of the UN ILC, which on Apr. 10, 1965, unanimously stated that war crimes in no case may lose their validity. Then the Commission undertook the task of drafting a Convention on the Non-Applicability of Statutory Limitations to War Crimes and Crimes against Humanity, whose final text was approved by the UN General Assembly, Nov. 26, 1968. ▷ War Crimes, Convention on the Nonapplicability, 1968.

However, the Convention, which was also open to non-UN members, was not joined by the FRG, where on Apr. 26, 1969 the Bundestag passed a reform of penal law, introducing the obligation to investigate murders ("Mord") for 30 years (to Dec. 31, 1979), but not man-slaughter ("Totschlag"). The law evaded the norms of international law contained in the UN Convention of 1968; but the Bundestag on July 3, 1979 passed an additional law stating that murder ("Mord") is not subject to expiration.

On Dec. 15, 1970 the UN General Assembly Res. 2712/XXV, adopted by 55 votes to 4 (Australia,

Portugal, UK, USA) with 33 abstentions, read as follows:

"The General Assembly,
Recalling its resolution 2583/XXIV of 15 December 1969 on the punishment of war criminals and of persons who have committed crimes against humanity,
Welcoming with satisfaction the fact that the Convention on the Non-Applicability of Statutory Limitations to War Crimes and Crimes against Humanity entered into force on 11 November 1970,
Noting with regret that the numerous decisions adopted by the United Nations on the question of the punishment of war criminals and of persons who have committed crimes against humanity are still not being fully complied with,
Expressing deep concern at the fact in present-day conditions, as a result of aggressive wars and the policies and practices of racism, apartheid and colonialism and other similar ideologies and practices, war crimes and crimes against humanity are being committed in various parts of the world;
Convinced that a thorough investigation of war crimes and crimes against humanity, as well as the arrest, extradition and punishment of persons guilty of such crimes – wherever they may have been committed – and the establishment of criteria for determining compensation to the victims of such crimes, are important elements in the prevention of similar crimes now and in the future, and also in the protection of human rights and, fundamentally, the strengthening of confidence and the development of co-operation between peoples and the safeguarding of international peace and security,
(1) Draws attention to the fact that many war criminals and persons who have committed crimes against humanity are continuing to take refuge in the territories of certain States and are enjoying protection;
(2) Calls upon all States to take measures, in accordance with recognized principles of international law, to arrest such persons and extradite them to the countries where they have committed war crimes and crimes against humanity, so that they can be brought to trail and punished in accordance with the laws of those countries;
(3) Condemns the war crimes and crimes against humanity at present being committed as a result of aggressive wars and the policies of racism, apartheid and colonialism and calls upon the States concerned to bring to trial persons guilty of such crimes;
(4) Also calls upon all the States concerned to intensify their co-operation in the collection and exchange of information which will contribute to the detection, arrest, extradition, trial and punishment of persons guilty of war crimes and crimes against humanity;
(5) Once again request the States concerned, if they have not already done so, to take the necessary measures for the thorough investigation of war crimes and crimes against humanity, as defined in Art. I of the Convention on the Non-Applicability of Statutory Limitations to War Crimes and Crimes against Humanity, and for the detection, arrest, extradition and punishment of all war criminals and persons guilty of crimes against humanity who have not yet been brought to trial or punished;
(6) Request States which have not yet become parties to the Convention on the Non-Applicability of Statutory Limitations to War Crimes and Crimes against Humanity to do so as soon as possible;
(7) Appeals to Governments to provide the Secretary-General with information on the measures which they have taken or are taking to become parties to the Convention on the Non-Applicability of Statutory Limitations to War Crimes and Crimes against Humanity;
(8) Also appeals to States which have not yet become parties to the Convention on the Non-Applicability of Statutory Limitations to War Crimes and Crimes against Humanity strictly to observe the provisions of General Assembly Res. 2583/XXIV to the effect that they should refrain from action running counter to the main purposes of that Convention;
(9) Requests the Secretary-General to continue, in the light of the comments and observations submitted by Governments, the study of the question of the punishment of war crimes and crimes against humanity and the criteria for determining compensation to the victims of such crimes, in order to submit a report on this ques-

W

tion to the General Assembly at its twenty-sixth session."

In the Human Rights Commission a debate took place on the protection of humanity against war criminals by: (1) introducing the international obligation to give legal assistance in the pursuit of war criminals; (2) defining the obligation of extradition; introducing the incontestable prohibition on asylum for war criminals; (4) convening a Permanent International Tribunal to judge war criminals. The UN Human Rights Commission on Mar. 25, 1971 passed a plan for a resolution on war crimes and crimes against humanity, referring to UN General Assembly, Res, 2712/XXV. One of the criminal methods used by the German Third Reich régimes in genocidal actions was the forced euthanasia of ill persons (e.g. consumptives) or the handicapped through injections of phenolate. In Oct., 1945 in Wiesbaden in the American occupied zone the first trial of hospital personnel, charged with the murder of 476 women, children and men, was held before an American military court. The victims, of Polish and Russian nationality, were murdered by forced euthanasia in 1944 in the hospital of Hadamar near Wiesbaden.

The UN General Assembly on Dec. 18, 1971 adopted Res. 2840/XXVI on the punishment of war criminals and persons who have committed crimes against humanity. The text read as follows:

"The General Assembly,
Recalling its Res. 3 (I) of Feb. 13, 1946 and 70 (II) of Oct. 31, 1947 on the extradition and punishment of war criminals and its Res. 95 (1) of Dec. 11, 1946 affirming the principles of international law recognized by the Charter of the International Military Tribunal, Nuremberg, and the judgement of that Tribunal,
Recalling further its Res. 2712 (XXV) of Dec. 15, 1970 in which it condemned the war crimes and crimes against humanity at present being committed as a result of aggressive wars and the policies of racism, apartheid and colonialism,
Again noting with regret that the numerous decisions adopted by the United Nations on the question of the punishment of war criminals and of persons who have committed crimes against humanity are still not being fully complied with,
Recalling the Convention on the Non-Applicability of Statutory Limitations to War Crimes and Crimes against Humanity,
Convinced that the effective punishment of war crimes and crimes against humanity is an important element in putting an end to and preventing such crimes, in the protection of human rights and fundamental freedoms, in the strengthening of confidence and in promoting co-operation between peoples as well as peace and international security,
Expressing its deep concern at the fact that many war criminals and persons who have committed crimes against humanity are continuing to take refuge in the territories of certain States and are enjoying their protection,
Affirming that war crimes and crimes against humanity are among the most dangerous crimes under international law,
Firmly convinced of the need for international co-operation in the thorough investigations of war crimes and crimes against humanity, as defined in Art. I of the Convention on the Non-Applicability of Statutory Limitations to War Crimes and Crimes against Humanity, and in bringing about the detection, arrest, extradition and punishment of all war criminals and persons guilty of crimes against humanity who have not yet been brought to trial or punished,
(1) Urges all States to implement the relevant resolutions of the General Assembly and to take measures in accordance with international law to put an end to and prevent war crimes and crimes against humanity and to ensure the punishment of all persons guilty of such crimes, including their extradition to those countries where they have committed such crimes;
(2) Further urges all States to co-operate in particular in the collection and exchange of information which will contribute to the detection, arrest, extradition, trial

and punishment of persons guilty of war crimes and crimes against humanity;
(3) Again calls upon all States which have not yet done so to become as soon as possible parties to the Convention on the Non-Applicability of Statutory Limitations to War Crimes and Crimes against Humanity;
(4) Affirms that refusal by States to co-operate in the arrest, extradition, trial and punishment of persons guilty of war crimes and crimes against humanity is contrary to the purposes and principles of the Charter of the United Nations and to generally recognized norms of international law;
(5) Requests the Commission on Human Rights to consider the principles of international co-operation in the detection, arrest, extradition and punishment of persons guilty of war crimes and crimes against humanity and to submit a report on this question to the General Assembly at its twenty-seventh session."

The central file on war criminals developed by the allies after the war is in Ludwigsburg in FRG. ▷ Arolsen. The UN General Assembly Resolutions 3(I) on the Extradition and punishment of War Criminals, adopted Febr. 13, 1946; the 177(II) on the principles recognized in the Charter of Nuremberg Tribunal and in the Judgement of the Tribunal, adapted Nov. 21, 1947; and the 217A(III) Universal Declaration on Human Rights, adopted Dec. 10, 1948, the 260(III) the Prevention and Punishment of the Crime of Genocide, adopted Dec. 9, 1948 are reprinted in International Organizations III (Febr. 1949).

The Records of the Nuremberg War Crimes Trials were transferred in 1949 to the custody of the UN Archives in New York.

Reports of Trial of War Criminals. Selected and prepared by the UN War Crimes Commission, London 1947; UN International Law Commission, *Historical Survey of the Question of International Criminal Jurisdiction*. Memorandum submitted by the Secretary General (Doc. A/CN 4/7/Rev 1), Lake Success, 1949, pp. 147; UN Archive Section, *Guide to Records of the War Crimes Trials Held in Nuremberg, Germany, 1945–1949*, Lake Success, Oct. 7, 1949 (mimeo); H. MANGHAM, *UNO and War Crimes*, London, 1951; J.S. NEUMANN, *A Bibliography of the European War Crimes Trials*, Carnegie Endowment, New York, 1961; *Question of Punishment of War Criminals*, UN, New York, 1966; J.R. LEWIS, *Uncertain Judgement. A Bibliography of War Crimes Trials*, Oxford, UK, 1979.

WAR CRIMES AND WAR CRIMINALS. Two international terms universally accepted during World Wars I and II, but formulated in the 19th century in the course of drafting the first conventions with the aim of regulating actions during war (Geneva Conventions).
The first international document establishing penal responsibility of heads of State for actions against peace was the Declaration of the Congress of Vienna on Mar. 13, 1815, stating that: "Napoleon Bonaparte placed himself outside social and civic relations as an enemy of Humanity, disturbing the peace of the world, and exposed himself to the responsibility of public repression."
The next international document establishing penal responsibility for crimes against peace or law was the Versailles Treaty (Arts. 227–230), in which the former Emperor of the Reich and King of Prussia, Wilhelm II Hohenzollern, was placed in a state of public indictment "for the highest affront to international morality and to holy inviolability of treaties", and legal proceedings were requested to be undertaken against persons who had committed acts "against law and war practices." In Versailles the so-called Committee for Responsibility in session from Jan. to June, 1919, which prepared the above-mentioned articles of the treaty, defined 32 acts which were war crimes and prepared a list of 895 war criminals, at the head of which, besides Wilhelm II, were i.a. Field Marshals Paul von Hindenburg and A. von Mackensen, Generals A. von

Kluck, E. von Falkenhayn, H.H. von Beseler, E. Ludendorff, B. von Deimling and M. Hoffmann, Admirals E. von Scheer and A. von Tirpitz, the Chancellor of the Reich, T. von Bethmann-Holweg and sons of Wilhelm II: August Wilhelm and Oskar von Preussen. From the list Great Britain demanded that 100 German war criminals be placed before British courts, among them 29 submarine commanders, France and Belgium 334, Poland 53, Romania 41, Italy 29 and Yugoslavia 4. The United States did not make any demands, and President W. Wilson on Apr. 19, 1919 stated his opposition to calling an international tribunal to judge Wilhelm II, who had been granted lifetime political asylum by Holland on Sept. 9, 1919 in the town of Doorn (where he died June 5, 1941 at the age of 81). The government of Holland in July, 1919 had officially refused to hand Wilhelm over to the allies. In order to evade the obligation of extradicting war criminals to the States of the Entente, the Weimar Republic in Jan., 1920 passed a law on the punishment of crimes and war offenses (Gesetz über die Verfolgung von Kriegsverbrechen und Kriegsvergehen) and on Feb. 7, 1920 obtained the consent of those States not to hand over the accused, but to place them before the Court of the Reich in Lepzig. This court in only one trial against lower-ranking officers and non-commissioned officers recognized the guilt of the accused and sentenced them Jan. 10, 1921 to several years of hard labor for robbery at the front. However, on Dec. 20, 1922 it pronounced a verdict exonerating 93 higher officers and simultaneously closing all further proceedings. The LN made efforts to define the crimes of preparing and carrying out armed aggression and the crimes of using gases and chemical and bacteriological weapons.
During World War II the first document of the United Nations raising the question of penal responsibility for war crimes and announcing the punishment of the guilty after the war was the pronouncement of Jan. 13, 1942, drafted by emigrant governments at a conference in London (representatives of Great Britain, China, USA and USSR participated as observers).
This pronouncement was published as the Declaration of Allied Countries Occupied by Germany on the Question of punishing Nazis and their accomplices for crimes committed in occupied Europe. ▷ War Crimes London Declaration, 1942.
The second Document warning German war criminals of the consequences of their actions was the Joint Declaration of the governments of Belgium, Great Britain, Czechoslovakia, Greece, Luxembourg, the Netherlands, Norway, Poland, United States, Yugoslavia, USSR, and the French National Committee concerning the extermination by German authorities of the Jewish population of Europe, published Aug. 18, 1942 in London. Then in London, Moscow and Washington the Declaration of the United Nations was published Jan. 5, 1943 which was directed against the economic plundering of territories occupied by the enemy. Finally, on Nov. 1, 1943 in Moscow the great powers: Great Britain, USA and USSR, in a Declaration on the question of the responsibility for crimes committed, solemnly announced the punishment of war criminals and prepared a list of them from all the occupied territories. ▷ War Crimes Moscow Declaration, 1943. In 1944 the United States received assurance from neutral States (Argentina, Iceland, Portugal, Spain, Sweden, Switzerland and Turkey) that they would not grant asylum to war criminals. In London the UN War Crimes Commission, UNWCC, was created on Oct. 20, 1943, which in 1944 established so-called National Offices and founded the Central Register of War Criminals and Suspected Subjects, CROWCASS, which in Apr., 1945 was transferred to Paris and 1946 to

Berlin under the supervision of the Allied Control Council for Germany. Placed on the roll were the names of persons along with a description of the crimes committed by them, submitted to UNWCC by the prosecuting organs of the territories occupied during the war. Each State, within which a war criminal on the CROWCASS list had operated, had the right to demand his pursuit from the allied occupying authorities and, upon capture, to hand him over to the courts of that State. In the Yalta Declaration on Germany accepted at the Yalta Conference in Feb., 1945 it was recalled that the United Nations had decided ". . . to punish justly and rapidly all war criminals." A conference of the member States of UNWCC was held in London June 1-7, 1945. At the Potsdam Conference (July 17-Aug. 2, 1945) in Chapter II Art. 5 it was stated:

"War Criminals and those who have participated in planning or carrying out Nazi enterprises involving or resulting in atrocities or war crimes shall be arrested and brought to judgement. The three Governments (Great Britain, USSR and the USA) reaffirm their intention to bring the (war) criminals to swift and sure justice."

On Aug. 8, 1945 in London an agreement was signed between the governments of Great Britain, USA, France and the USSR on the subject of prosecution and punishment of the major war criminals of the European axis countries, and the Charter of the International Military Tribunal was approved.

Law No. 10 of the Allied Control Council for Germany on the matter of punishing persons guilty of war crimes, crimes against peace, and crimes against humanity was announced on Dec. 20, 1945 in Berlin.

The Nuremberg Tribunal in sentences handed down in Nov., 1946 stated that crimes against the international law are committed by persons and not by abstract subjects. ▷ Nuremberg Principles; ▷ Nuremberg War Criminals Trial, 1945-46.

On Jan. 19, 1946, the Supreme Commander for the Allied Powers in Japan, the US Army General D. MacArthur proclaimed a Charter of the International Military Tribunal for the Far East. ▷ Tokyo Military Trial, 1946-48. The Tribunal represented Australia, Canada, China, France, India, the Netherlands, New Zealand, the Philippines, the UK, the USA and the USSR.

In many countries national courts tried war criminals, German or Japanese or other nationalities, military or civilian, for war crimes in Europe and the Far East, South Asia and the Pacific area. The number of these trials is estimated in thousands in the years 1945-49 and in hundreds in the next 35 years. ▷ War Crimes, Convention on the Nonapplicability of Statutory Limitations to War Crimes and Crimes Against Humanity, 1968. See also ▷ War Criminals UN Archive.

M. LACHS, *War Crimes, An Attempt to Define the Issue*, London, 1945; *UN Yearbook 1946-47*, pp. 254-256; *The Trial of German Major War Criminals. Proceedings of the International Military Tribunal Sitting at Nuremberg, Germany*, 42 vols., London, 1946-48; H. v. MANGOLDT, "Das Kriegsverbrechen und seine Verfolgung in Vergangenheit und Gegenwart," in: *Jahrbuch für Internationales und Ausländisches Öffentliches Recht*, 1948, pp. 283-334 and 387-399; *History of the UN War Criminals Commission*, 9 Vols., London, 1948-52; *Law Reports of Trials of War Criminals*, 15 vols., London, 1947-52; S. HORWITZ, "The Tokyo Trial", in: *International Conciliation*, No. 465, 1950; R. PAL, *International Military Tribunal for the Far East*, London, 1953; M. MEISER, *Die Bestimmungen über das Kriegsverbrechen und Besatzungstrafrecht in dem Genfer Abkommen zum Schutze der Kriegsopfer von 1949*, Winterthur, 1964; A. KLAFKOWSKI, *L'imprescriptibilité des crimes de guerre et l'Allemagne Fédérale au regard du droit international*, Poznań, 1970; Y. TESNON, S. HEIMAN, *Le masacre des aliénés*, Paris, 1971; Ph. AZIZ, *Les criminels de guerre*, Paris, 1974. R.L. BLEDSOE, B.A. BOCZEK, *The International Law Dictionary*, Oxford, 1987.

WAR CRIMES, CONVENTION ON THE NON-APPLICABILITY OF STATUTORY LIMITATIONS TO WAR CRIMES AND CRIMES AGAINST HUMANITY, 1968.

A Convention adopted by the UN General Assembly Res. 2392/XXIII, Nov. 26, 1968, by 80 votes to 0, with 23 abstentions. The text is as follows:

"Preamble. The States Parties to the present Convention, recalling resolution of the General Assembly of the United Nations 3 (I) of 13 February 1964 and 170 (II) of 31 October 1947 on the extradition and punishment of war criminals, resolution 95 (I) of 11 December 1946 affirming the principles of international law recognized by the Charter of the International Military Tribunal, Nurnberg, and the judgement of the Tribunal, and resolutions 2184 (XXI) of 12 December 1966 and 2202 (XXI) of 16 December 1966 which expressly condemned as crimes against humanity the violation of the economic and political rights of the indigenous population on the one hand and the policies of apartheid on the other,

Recalling resolutions of the Economic and Social Council of the United Nations 1074 D (XXXIX) of 28 July 1965 and 1158 (XLI) of 5 August 1966 on the punishment of war criminals and of persons who have committed crimes against humanity,

Noting that none of the solemn declarations, instruments or conventions relating to the prosecution and punishment of war crimes and crimes against humanity made provision for a period of limitation,

Considering that war crimes and crimes against humanity are among the gravest crimes in international law,

Convinced that the effective punishment of war crimes and crimes against humanity is an important element in the prevention of such crimes, the protection of human rights and fundamental freedoms, the encouragement of confidence, the furtherance of co-operation among peoples and the promotion of international peace and security,

Noting that the application to war crimes and crimes against humanity of the rules of municipal law relating to the period of limitation for ordinary crimes is a matter of serious concern to world public opinion, since it prevents the prosecution and punishment of persons responsible for those crimes,

Recognizing that it is necessary and timely to affirm in international law, through this Convention, the principle that there is no period of limitation for war crimes and crimes against humanity, and to secure its universal application,

Have agreed as follows:

Art. 1. No statutory limitation shall apply to the following crimes, irrespective of the date of their commission:

(a) War crimes as they are defined in the Charter of the International Military Tribunal, Nurnberg, of 8 August 1945 and confirmed by resolutions 3 (I) of 13 February 1946 and 95 (I) of 11 December 1946 of the General Assembly of the United Nations, particularly the 'grave breaches' enumerated in the Geneva Conventions of 12 August 1949 for the protection of war victims;

(b) Crimes against humanity whether committed in time of war or in time of peace as they are defined in the Charter of the International Military Tribunal, Nurnberg, of 8 August 1945 and confirmed by resolutions 3 (I) of 13 February 1946 and 95 (I) of 11 December 1946 of the General Assembly of the United Nations, eviction by armed attack or occupation and inhuman acts resulting from the policy of apartheid, and the crime of genocide as defined in the 1948 Convention on the Prevention and Punishment of the Crime of Genocide, even if such acts do not constitute a violation of the domestic law of the country in which they were committed.

Art. 2. If any of the crimes mentioned in Art. 1 is committed, the provisions of this Convention shall apply to representatives of the State authority and private individuals who, as principals or accomplices, participate in or who directly incite others to the commission of any of those crimes, or who conspire to commit them, irrespective of the degree of completion, and to representatives of the State authority who tolerate their commission.

Art. 3. The States Parties to the present Convention undertake to adopt all necessary domestic measures, legislative or otherwise, with a view to making possible the extradition, in accordance with international law, of the persons referred to in article II of this Convention.

Art. 4. The States Parties to the present Convention undertake to adopt, in accordance with their respective constitutional processes, any legislative or other measures necessary to ensure that statutory or other limitations shall not apply to the prosecution and punishment of the crimes referred to in Arts. 1 and 2 of this Convention and that, where they exist, such limitations shall be abolished.

Art. 5. This Convention shall, until 31 December 1969, be open for signature by any State Member of the United Nations or member of any of its specialized agencies or of the International Atomic Energy Agency, by any State Party to the Statute of the International Court of Justice, and by any other State which has been invited by the General Assembly of the United Nations to become a Party to this Convention.

Art. 6. This Convention is subject to ratification. Instruments of ratification shall be deposited with the Secretary-General of the United Nations.

Art. 7. This Convention shall be open to accession by any State referred to in Art. 5. Instruments of accession shall be deposited with the Secretary-General of the United Nations.

Art. 8(1) This Convention shall enter into force on the ninetieth day after the date of the deposit with the Secretary-General of the United Nations of the tenth instrument of ratification or accession.

(2) For each State ratifying this Convention or acceding to it after the deposit of the tenth instrument of ratification or accession, the Convention shall enter into force on the ninetieth day after the date of the deposit of its own instrument of ratification or accession.

Art. 9.(1) After the expiry of a period of ten years from the date on which this Convention enters into force, a request for the revision of the Convention may be made at any time by any Contracting Party by means of a notification in writing addressed to the Secretary-General of the United Nations.

(2) The General Assembly of the United Nations shall decide upon the steps, if any, to be taken in respect of such a request.

Art. 10.(1) This Convention shall be deposited with the Secretary-General of the United Nations.

(2) The Secretary-General of the United Nations shall transmit certified copies of this Convention to all States referred to in Art. 5.

(3) The Secretary-General of the United Nations shall inform all States referred to in Art. 5 of the following particulars:

(a) Signatures of this Convention and instruments of ratification and accession deposited under articles V, VI and VII;

(b) The date of entry into force of this Convention in accordance with Art. 8.

(c) Communications received under Art. 9.

Art. 11. This Convention, of which the Chinese, English, French, Russian and Spanish texts are equally authentic, shall bear the date of November 1968."

UN Yearbook, 1968, pp. 607-611.

WAR CRIMES, LAW FOR GERMANY, 1945.

The punishment of persons guilty of war crimes against Peace and Humanity, as ordered in occupied Germany by the Four Power Control Council for Germany, as Law No. 10, Dec. 20, 1945, read as follows:

"In order to give effect to the terms of the Moscow Declaration of 30 October 1943 and the London Agreement of 8 August 1945, and the Charter issued pursuant thereto, and in order to establish a uniform legal basis in Germany for the prosecution of war criminals and other similar offenders, other than those dealt with by the International Military Tribunal.

The Control Council enacts as follows:

Art. 1. The Moscow Declaration of 30 October 1943 'Concerning Responsibility of Hitlerites for Committed Atrocities' and the London Agreement of 8 August 1945 'Concerning Prosecution and Punishment of Major War Criminals of the European Axis' are made integral parts of this Law. Adherence to the provisions of the London Agreement by any of the United Nations, as provided for in Article V of that Agreement, shall not entitle such Nation to participate or interfere in the operation of this Law within the Control Council area of authority in Germany.

Art. 2.(1) Each of the following acts is recognized as a crime.

(a) Crimes against peace. Initiation of invasions of other countries and wars of aggression in violation of international laws and treaties, including but not limited to planning, preparation, initiation or waging a war of aggression, or a war of violation of international treaties, agreements or assurances, or participation in a common plan or conspiracy for the accomplishment of any of the foregoing.

(b) War crimes. Atrocities or offenses against persons or property constituting violations of the laws or customs of war, including but not limited to murder, ill treatment or deportation to slave labor, or for any other purpose, of civilian population from occupied territory, murder or ill treatment of prisoners of war or persons on the seas, killing of hostages, plunder of public or private property, wanton destruction of cities, towns or villages, or devastation not justified by military necessity.

(c) Crimes against humanity. Atrocities and offenses, including but not limited to murder, extermination, enslavement, deportation, imprisonment, torture, rape, or other inhumane acts committed against any civilian population, or persecutions on political, racial or religious grounds whether or not in violation of the domestic laws of the country where perpetrated.

(d) Membership in categories of a criminal group or organization declared criminal by the International Military Tribunal.

(e) Any person, without regard to nationality or the capacity in which he acted, is deemed to have committed a crime as defined in paragraph I of this Article, if he

(a) was a principal or

(b) was an accessory to the commission of any such crime or ordered or abetted the same or

(c) took a consenting part therein or

(d) was connected with plans or enterprises involving its commission or

(e) was a member of any organization or group connected with the commission of any such crime or

(f) with reference to paragraph 1(a), if he held a high political, civil or military (including General Staff) position in Germany or in one of its Allies, co-belligerents or satellites or held high position in the financial, industrial or economic life of any such country.

(3) Any person found guilty of any of the Crimes above mentioned may upon conviction be punished as shall be determined by the tribunal to be just. Such punishment may consist of one or more of the following:

(a) Death.

(b) Imprisonment for life or a term of years, with or without hard labor.

(c) Fine, and imprisonment with or without hard labor, in lieu thereof.

(d) Forfeiture of property.

(e) Restitution of property wrongfully acquired.

(f) Deprivation of some or all civil rights.

Any property declared to be forfeited or the restitution of which is ordered by the Tribunal shall be delivered to the Control Council for Germany, which shall decide on its disposal.

(4)(a) The official position of any person, whether as Head of State or as a responsible official in a Government Department, does not free him from responsibility for a crime or entitle him to mitigation of punishment.

(b) The fact that any person acted pursuant to the order of his Government or of a superior does not free him from responsibility for a crime, but may be considered in mitigation.

5. In any trial or prosecution for a crime herein referred to, the accused shall not be entitled to the benefits of any statute of limitation in respect of the period from 30 January 1933 to 1 July 1945, not shall any immunity, pardon or amnesty granted under the Nazi régime be admitted as a bar to trial or punishment.

Art. 3.(1) Each occupying authority, within its Zone of occupation,

(a) shall have the right to cause persons within such Zone suspected of having committed a crime, including those charged with crime by one of the United Nations, to be arrested and shall take under control the property, real and personal, owned or controlled by the said persons, pending decisions as to its eventual disposition.

(b) shall report to the Legal Directorate the names of all suspected criminals, the reasons for and the places of their detention, if they are detained, and the names and location of witnesses.

(c) shall take appropriate measures to see that witnesses and evidence will be available when required.

(d) shall have the right to cause all persons so arrested and charged, and not delivered to another authority, as herein provided, or released, to be brought to trial before an appropriate tribunal. Such tribunal may, in the case of crimes committed by persons of German citizenship or nationality against other persons of German citizenship or nationality or stateless persons, be a German Court, if authorized by the occupying authorities.

(2) The tribunal by which persons charged with offenses hereunder shall be tried and the rules and procedure thereof shall be determined or designated by each Zone Commander for his respective Zone. Nothing herein is intended to, or shall impair or limit the jurisdiction or power of any court or tribunal now or hereafter established in any Zone by the Commander thereof, or of the International Military Tribunal established by the London Agreement of 8 August 1945.

(3) Persons wanted for trial by an International Military Tribunal will not be tried without the consent of the Committee of Chief Prosecutors. Each Zone Commander will deliver such persons who are within his Zone to that Committee upon request and will make witnesses and evidence available to it.

(4) Persons known to be wanted for trial in another Zone or outside Germany will not be tried prior to decision under Article IV unless the fact of their apprehension has been reported in accordance with Section 1(b) of this Article, three months have elapsed thereafter, and no request for delivery of the type contemplated by Article IV has been received by the Zone Commander concerned.

(5) The execution of death sentences may be deferred but not to exceed one month after the sentence has become final when the Zone Commander concerned has reason to believe that the testimony of those under sentence would be of value in the investigation and trial of crimes within or without his Zone.

(6) Each Zone Commander will cause such effect to be given to the judgments of courts of competent jurisdiction, with respect to the property taken under his control pursuant hereto, as he may deem proper in the interest of justice.

Art. 4. I. When any person in a Zone in Germany is alleged to have committed a crime, as defined in Article II, in a country other than Germany or in another Zone, the government of the nation or the Commander of the latter Zone, as the case may be, may request the Commander of the Zone in which the person is located for his arrest and delivery for trial to the country or Zone in which the crime was committed.

Such request for delivery shall be granted by the Commander receiving it unless he believes such person is wanted for trial or as a witness by an International Military Tribunal, or in Germany, or in a nation other than the one making the request, or the Commander is not satisfied that delivery should be made, in any of which cases he shall have the right to forward the said request to the Legal Directorate of the Allied Control Authority. A similar procedure shall apply to witnesses, material exhibits and other forms of evidence.

II. The Legal Directorate shall consider all requests referred to it, and shall determine the same in accordance with the following principles, its determination to be communicated to the Zone Commander.

(a) A person wanted for trial or as a witness by an International Military Tribunal shall not be delivered for trial or required to give evidence outside Germany, as the case may be, except upon approval by the Committee of Chief Prosecutors acting under the London Agreement of 8 August 1945.

(b) A person wanted for trial by several authorities (other than an International Military Tribunal) shall be disposed of in accordance with the following priorities:

(1) If wanted for trial in the Zone in which he is, he should not be delivered unless arrangements are made for his return after trial elsewhere;

(2) If wanted for trial in a Zone other than that in which he is, he should be delivered to that Zone in preference to delivery outside Germany unless arrangements are made for his return to that Zone after trial elsewhere;

(3) If wanted for trial outside Germany by two or more of the United Nations, of one of which he is a citizen, that one should have priority;

(4) If wanted for trial outside Germany by several countries, not all of which are the United Nations, United Nations should have priority;

(5) If wanted for trial outside Germany by two or more of the United Nations, then, subject to Art. 4, 2(b)(3) above, that which has the most serious charge against him, which are moreover supported by evidence, should have priority.

Art. 5. The delivery, under Art. 4 of this Law, of persons for trial shall be made on demands of the Governments or Zone Commanders in such a manner that the delivery of criminals to one jurisdiction will not become the means of defeating or unnecessarily delaying the carrying out of justice in another place.

If within six months the delivered person has not been convicted by the Court of the Zone of country to which he has been delivered, then such person shall be returned upon demand of the Commander of the Zone where the person was located prior to delivery.

Official Gazette of the Control Council for Germany, No. 3, January 31, 1946.

WAR CRIMES LONDON AGREEMENT, 1945. Agreement of the Four Big Powers for the Prosecution and Punishment of the Major War Criminals of the European Axis and an annexed Charter of the International Military Tribunal, signed at London on Aug. 8, 1945.

T. TAYLOR, "The Nuremberg War Crimes Trials," in: *International Conciliation*, No. 450, April, 1949, pp. 253–254.

WAR CRIMES LONDON DECLARATION, 1942. Declaration of Allied Countries Occupied by Germany (Belgium, Czechoslovakia, France, Greece, Luxembourg, the Netherlands, Norway, Poland and Yugoslavia) Concerning Responsibility of Hitlerites for Committed Atrocities, signed at St James's Palace in London on Jan. 13, 1942. The St James's Declaration was not only a protest against crimes committed by the Germans in the course of occupations of nine European countries, but for the first time pointed out that:

"international solidarity is necessary in order to avoid the repression of these acts of violence simply by acts of vengeance on the part of the general public, and in order to satisfy the sense of justice of the civilized world, – and in which the nine powers – place among their principal war aims the punishment, through the channel of organized justice, of those guilty of or responsible for these crimes, whether they have ordered them, perpetrated them or participated in them, (and) resolve to see to it in a spirit of international solidarity, that (a) those guilty or responsible, whatever their nationality, are sought out, handed over to justice and judged, (b) that the sentences pronounced are carried out."

Punishment for War Crimes. The Inter-Allied Declaration signed at St James's Palace, London on 13th January 1942, and relative documents, London, 1942, pp. 3–4.

WAR CRIMES MOSCOW DECLARATION, 1943. Declaration on German Atrocities in Occupied Europe, approved by the Three Power Conference at Moscow on Nov. 1, 1943, warning Germany responsible for war crimes, as follows:

"The United Kingdom, the United States, and the Soviet Union have received from many quarters evidence of atrocities, massacres, and cold blooded mass executions which are being perpetrated by the Hitlerite forces in many of the countries they have overrun and from which they are now being steadily expelled. The brutalities of Hitlerite domination are no new thing, and all peoples or territories in their grip have suffered from the worst form of government by terror.

What is new is that many of these territories are now being redeemed by the advancing armies of the liberating Powers and that, in their desperation, the recoiling Hitlerite Huns are redoubling their ruthless cruelties. This is now evidenced with particular clearness by the monstrous crimes of the Hitlerites on the territory of the Soviet Union which is being liberated from the Hitlerites, and on French and Italian territory.

Accordingly the aforesaid three allied Powers, speaking in the interests of the 32 United Nations, hereby solemnly declare and give full warning of the declaration as follows: At the time of the granting of any armistice to any Government which may be set up in Germany, those German officers and men and members of the Nazi Party who have been responsible for or have taken a consenting part in the above atrocities, massacres, and executions will be sent back to the countries in which their abominable deeds were done in order that they may be judged and punished according to the laws of these liberated countries and of the free Governments which will be erected therein.

Lists will be compiled in all possible detail from all these countries having regard especially to the invaded parts of the Soviet Union, to Poland and Czechoslovakia, to Yugoslavia and Greece, including Crete and other islands, to Norway, Denmark, the Netherlands, Belgium, Luxemberg, France and Italy.

Thus Germans who take part in wholesale shootings of Polish officers or in the execution of French, Dutch, Belgian or Norwegian hostages or of Cretan peasants, or who have shared in the slaughters inflicted on the people of Poland or in the territories of the Soviet Union which are now being swept clear of the enemy, will know that they will be brought back to the scenes of their crimes and judged on the spot by the peoples whom they have outraged. Let those who have hitherto not imbrued their hands with innocent blood beware lest they join the ranks of the guilty, for most assuredly the three allied Powers will pursue them to the uttermost ends of the earth and will deliver them to the accusers in order that justice may be done.

The above declaration is without prejudice to the case of German criminals whose offenses have no particular geographical location and who will be punished by a joint decision of the Governments of the Allies."

UN Information Paper, London, 1943, No. 1, pp. 11–12. *El Libro Negro del terror nazi en Europa*, México, DF, 1945; A. GARCIA-ROBLES, *El Mundo de la Postguerra*, México, DF, 1946, Vol. 2, pp. 263–264; *A Decade of American Foreign Policy. Basic Documents 1941–49*, Washington, DC, 1950, p. 9.

WAR CRIMES, PRINCIPLES OF INTERNATIONAL CO-OPERATION AGAINST WAR CRIMINALS, 1973. Principles of International Co-operation in the Declaration, Arrest, Extradition and Punishment of Persons Guilty of War Crimes and Crimes against Humanity, adopted by the UN General Assembly Res. 3074/XXVIII, Dec. 3, 1973, by 63 votes to 0, with 27 abstentions. The text is as follows:

"The General Assembly,

Recalling its Resolutions 2583/XXIV of Dec. 15, 1969, 2712/XXV of Dec. 15, 1970, 2840/XXVI of Dec. 18, 1971 and 3020/XXVII of Dec. 18, 1972,

Taking into account the special need for international action in order to ensure the prosecution and punishment of persons guilty of war crimes and crimes against humanity,

Having considered the draft principles of international co-operation in the detection, arrest, extradition, and punishment of persons guilty of war crimes and crimes against humanity,

Declares that the United Nations, in pursuance of the principles and purposes set forth in the Charter concerning the promotion of co-operation between peoples and the maintenance of international peace and security, proclaims the following principles of international co-operation in the detection, arrest, extradition and punishment of persons guilty of war crimes and crimes against humanity;

(1) War crimes and crimes against humanity, whenever or wherever they are committed, shall be subject to investigation and the persons against whom there is evidence that they have committed such crimes shall be subject to tracing, arrest, trial and, if found guilty, to punishment.

(2) Every State has the right to try its own nationals for war crimes or crimes against humanity.

(3) States shall co-operate with each other on a bilateral and multilateral basis with a view to halting and preventing war crimes and crimes against humanity, and shall take the domestic and international measures necessary for that purpose.

(4) States shall assist each other in detecting, arresting and bringing to trial persons suspected of having committed such crimes and, if they are found guilty, in punishing them.

(5) Persons against whom there is evidence that they have committed war crimes and crimes against humanity shall be subject to trial and, if found guilty, to punishment, as a general rule in the countries in which they committed those crimes. In that connexion, States shall co-operate on questions of extraditing such persons.

(6) States shall co-operate with each other in the collection of information and evidence which would help to bring to trial the persons indicated in paragraph 5 above and shall exchange such information.

(7) In accordance with Art. 1 of the Declaration on Territorial Asylum of Dec. 14, 1967, States shall not grant asylum to any person with respect to whom there are serious reasons for considering that he has committed a crime against peace, a war crime or a crime against humanity.

(8) States shall not take any legislative or other measures which may be prejudicial to the international obligations they have assumed in regard to the detection, arrest extradition and punishment of persons guilty of war crimes and crimes against humanity.

(9) In co-operating with a view to the detection, arrest and extradition of persons against whom there is evidence that they have committed war crimes and crimes against humanity and, if found guilty, their punishment, States shall act in conformity with the provisions of the Charter of the United Nations and of the Declaration on Principles of International Law concerning Friendly Relations and Co-operation among States in accordance with the Charter of the United Nations."

UN Yearbook, 1973.

WAR CRIMES UN COMMISSION 1943–1948. Established on Oct. 23, 1943 in London by a Diplomatic Conference of representatives of 17 Allied Governments, some in exile in London, and Dominium representatives, invited by British Prime Minister Winston Churchill to discuss the collection, investigation and recording of war crimes, which took place during the II World War (▷ War Crimes and War Criminals). The UN War Crimes Commission, UNWCC, was created with HQ in London by Australia, Belgium, Canada, China, Czechoslovakia, Denmark, France, Greece, India, Luxembourg, the Netherlands, New Zealand, Norway, Poland, UK, USA and Yugoslavia (South Africa participated in the Diplomatic Conference but not in the work of the UNWCC). The Commission's objectives were to gather information on war crimes and report to Governments concerned in cases where the material appeared to disclose a prima facie case. Governments themselves provided summaries of information to the Commission to obtain assistance in identifying and locating specific individuals. Within their own jurisdiction, Governments, and not the Commission, could decide to pursue prosecution of particular individuals charged with crimes on their territories or against their nationals.

The group first met on January 11, 1944, working until the end of March 1948. When the Commission finished, it transferred some 40,000 files to the United Nations, which established rules for access to those records.

Until 1986, the archives located in a Park Avenue office in New York City, were available only to Governments on specific requests, in connection with the investigation and prosecution of war criminals. The United Nations argued that the files should remain sealed because the material on specific individuals had not been submitted to judicial process, or otherwise subjected to legal evaluation. In most cases, the individuals had not been informed of the charges and thus had had no opportunity to reply.

On the initiative of Secretary-General Javier Pérez de Cuéllar, the original 17 members of the United Nations War Crimes Commission, consulted on the issue in September and October 1987, and agreed that some of the secrecy shrouding the archives for 40 years should be dispelled.

As a result, Governements can now conduct general research, and the files may be opened to 'bona fide research by individuals into the history and work of the United Nations War Crimes Commission and into war crimes'.

UN Chronicle, March 1988, p. 91.

WAR CRIMINALS. ▷ War crimes and war criminals.

WAR CRIMINALS UN ARCHIVE. The United Nations War Crimes Commission Archive. It contains files on nearly 25,000 class A (with enough evidence for prosecution) cases. After the Commission wound up its work in 1948, the archive was moved from London to New York and deposited with the United Nations. Only governments have been allowed access to the archive. Until Oct. 1987 it was not opened fully to the public, on the strength of opposition by some former Commission members.

WAR CRIPPLES AGREEMENT, 1955. An agreement on the exchange of War Cripples between Member Countries of the Council of Europe with a view to medical treatment, signed on Dec. 13, 1955 in Paris.

UNTS, Vol. 250, p. 3.

WAR DEBTS. The inter-governmental obligations for war expenditures. During World War I inter-allied debts along with aid for demobilization in 1919–20 reached nearly 21 billion US dollars; during World War II the value of war material lend leased, or donated by the USA under the ▷ Lend-Lease program, exceeded 50 billion US dollars.

H.G. MOULTON, L. PASVOLSKY, *War Debts and World Prosperity*, Washington, DC, 1932; "War Debts", in: *International Conciliation*, No. 294, November, 1933, pp. 481–525.

WAR DECLARATION. The international practice of establishing a state of war with a second country by a formal war declaration, usually preceded by threats in the form of ultimatums fixing the period for fulfilling or not fulfilling conditions on which the commencement of war declared depends; generally strictly adhered to in Europe in the 19th century as well as in World War I and II, but not in Asia (e.g. Japan never declared war on China despite the fact that there was a state of war with China for several years; similarly, the USA never declared war on the Democratic Republic of Vietnam despite waging war there for 12 years). In 1907 the Third Hague Convention established norm as follows: "War measures should not commence without the prior and unambiguous announcement in the form of stating the grounds for declaring war or an ultimatum with a conditional declaration of war." An example of the mechanism of declaring war is the initiation of World War I: The German Reich on Aug. 1 at 17:00 hrs. through its ambassador, Herr de Pourtales, transmitted to the Russian

W

Minister of Foreign Affairs, S.D. Sazanov, a formal declaration of war, referring to the challenge of the Russian order to mobilize its land and sea forces: "His Imperial Highness accepts this challenge in the name of the Reich and regards Ourselves in a state of war with Russia."

On Aug. 3, 1914 in Paris the ambassador of the Reich, Herr Viviana, submitted a declaration in the Quai d'Orsay charging the French airforce with bombing the railway line Karlsruhe–Nuremberg, as a result of which "The German Reich regards itself in a state of war with France." On that same day forces violating Belgian neutrality crossed its territory heading in the direction of France. This caused the ultimatum of Great Britain on Aug. 4, 1914 directed to the government of the German Reich demanding the withdrawal of Germany from Belgium to the north on that same day. In view of the rejection of the ultimatum by the German Reich and the declaration of Wilhelm II that treaties are a "scrap of paper" (▷ Papierfetzen), England also on Aug. 5, 1914 found itself in a formal state of war with Germany. The German Reich on Aug. 2, 1914 concluded an alliance with Turkey, that from the moment of Russian pronouncement against Austria-Hungary, which formally took place Aug. 6, 1914, Turkey would enter the war on the side of the central powers, which did not occur until Nov. 3, 1914, also in the form of an official declaration. The German Reich made a similar alliance on Sept. 6, 1915 with Bulgaria. On Oct. 4, 1915 the Entente sent an ultimatum to Bulgaria demanding the breaking of diplomatic relations with the central powers and, receiving a refusal, severed diplomatic relations with Bulgaria, while the latter on Oct. 14, 1915 formally declared war on Serbia and that same day all of the States of the Entente formally declared war on Bulgaria. In World War II the axis states acted through surprise, ignoring not only the Third Hague Convention, but all of their international obligations. The priority of surprise over the formality of declaration was accepted after World War II by all of the aggressive States, attack initiating invasion.

K. KAUTSKY (ed.),*Die Deutschen Dokumente zum Kriegsausbruch*, 4 Vols., Berlin, 1924; C. MÜHLMANN, "Deutschland und die Turkei", in: *Politische Wissenschaft*, Vol. 7, Berlin, 1929; C. EAGLETON, "The Form and Function of the Declaration of War", in: *American Journal of International Law*, No. 32, 1938; F. SCHLÜTER, "Der Ausbruch des Krieges", in: *Zeitschrift für Ausländisches Öffentliches Recht und Völkerrecht, 1940/41*; L.C. GREEN, "Armed Conflicts, War and Self-Defence", in: *Archiv des Völkerrechts 1955/56*; H. MOSLER, "Kriegsbeginn", in: STRUPP-SCHLOCHAUER *Wörterbuch des Völkerrechts*, Vol. 2, Berlin, 1961, pp. 326–329. R.L. BLEDSOE, B.A. BOCZEK, *The International Law Dictionary*, Oxford, 1987.

WAR DEVASTATION. The war desolation caused by air raids, artillery, or special destruction units. A subject of international conventions and declarations limiting destruction to military necessities, and recognizing as war crimes devastation which threatens the existence of civilization and the human environment in a given country (e.g. destruction of water supplies or ecological desolation).

H.J. CAHN, *Das Kriegsschädenrecht der Nationen*, Zürich, 1947.

WAR FLEETS. A subject of treaties between powers as well as conventions (the Seventh Hague Convention of 1907). The arms race at sea initiated by Kaiser Wilhelm II of Germany led to English–French–Russian Triple Alliance and influenced the outbreak of World War I. The Versailles Treaty of 1919 prohibited Germany from possessing a strong war fleet. The 1922 Washington Disarmament Conference, Geneva Conference of 1927, and the London Conferences of 1930 and 1935 unsuccessfully attempted to introduce limitations of naval armaments among the victorious powers: France, Great Britain, Italy, Japan and USA. On June 7, 1935 Great Britain negotiated a sea treaty allowing Germany to possess submarines equal to the tonnage of the British submarine fleet and the right to construct surface vessels up to 35% of the tonnage of the British Commonwealth. The German Third Reich renounced this treaty on Apr. 28, 1939.

S.E. MORISON, *The Two-Ocean War*, London 1963.

WAR GRAVES. The graves of soldiers killed at the front and war prisoners who have died in captivity; subject of Arts. 225–226 of the Versailles Treaty as well as other multilateral and bilateral treaties negotiated after World Wars I and II; subject of international respect and the practice of preserving the graves of those soldiers killed or deceased during wartime, as well as reciprocal privileges in the exhumation and transportation of corpses.

G.F. DE MARTENS, *Nouveau Recueil Général*, 3 S., Vol. XV, p. 323; *LNTS*, Vol. 167, 1936, pp. 142–149; J. PAESLEE (ed.), *International Governmental Organizations*, Vol. 5, London, 1979.

WAR-HEADS. An international military term, related to the land-based and submarine-launched missiles, a subject of American-Soviet negotiations before the Summit Meeting in Dec. 1987 in Washington DC. Both sides agreed that they should work out a method to count the number of warheads on missles.
See also ▷ Trident..

The New York Times, December 11, 1989.

WAR LOANS CONVENTION, 1922. An agreement between Italy, Poland, Romania, Kingdom of Serbs, Croats and Slovenes and Czechoslovakia regarding investments in War Loans, signed on Apr. 6, 1922 in Rome.

LNTS, Vol. 20, p. 16.

WAR LOSSES. A subject of international statistics. The losses incurred in wars by combatants in terms of people and national wealth. ▷ World War, 1914–18 and ▷ World War 1939–45.

WAR, MEANS OF WAR. A subject of international law which from the second half of the 19th century introduced a series of limitations based on the principle that a party waging war may not employ any and all means for striking and destroying an enemy and his country, but is limited to the norms and prohibitions of international law. The struggle concerning the prohibition of weapons of mass destruction (▷ ABC weapons) became the dominant theme of disarmament negotiations in the forum of the UN.

WARMIA. A historic region of NE Poland. In 1236 occupied by the Teutonic Knights, ceded to Poland by the Torun Peace Treaty 1466; occupied by Prussia after the first partition of Poland 1772; reverted to Poland by the Potsdam Agreement 1945. German name: Ermland.

"Die Polen Ermlands. Ein Geschichtlicher Ueberblick", in: *Kulturwille*, Berlin, No. 1, 1925, pp. 29, 35. T. CIEŚLAK, "Warmia and Mazury in the 19th and 20th Century History of Poland's Territories", in: *Polish Western Affairs*, Poznań, No. 2, 1965, pp. 314–328.

WAR NECESSITY. The warfare that is limited so as to cause only necessary damage on an enemy's territory; subject to international assessment by military courts for war crimes.

WAR OF NERVES. An international term often in use in the 1930s, replaced in the 1950s by ▷ Psychological war.

WAR OF THE CITIES. An international term for a war the aim of which is to destroy by ground-to-ground missiles the capital of the enemy. First evidenced in the Iran-Iraq war in March-April 1988 with Baghdad and Teheran as the targets.

WAR PREVENTION CONVENTION, 1931. The League of Nations Assembly in Sept. 1931 approved a Convention to Improve the Means of Preventing War. Principal aim: to form demilitarized zones in areas of armed conflict and a League of Nations Inspecting Commission whose rights and duties were defined in an Additional Protocol. The Convention was never ratified because in the same year Japan's invasion of Manchuria took place and in the following years Germany and Italy paralysed the League of Nations peaceful functions.

WAR PRIZES. ▷ War booties or War prizes.

WAR PROPAGANDA. The promotion of armed aggression; the problem was examined on Nov. 3 and 5, 1947 by the UN General Assembly which passed a resolution binding all of the UN member States to combat all forms of war propaganda. The text of Res. 110/II adopted unanimously by the UN General Assembly on Nov. 8, 1947 is as follows:

"Whereas in the Charter of the United Nations the peoples express their determination to save succeeding generations from the scourge of war, which twice in our lifetime has brought untold sorrow to mankind, and to practice tolerance and live together in peace with one another as good neighbours, and

Whereas the Charter also calls for the promotion of universal respect for, and observance of, fundamental freedoms which include freedom of expression, all Members having pledged themselves in Article 56 to take joint and separate action for such observance of fundamental freedoms, The General Assembly

(1) Condemns all forms of propaganda, in whatsoever country conducted, which is either designed or likely to provoke or encourage any threat to the peace, breach of the peace, or act of aggression;

(2) Requests the Governments of each Member to take appropriate steps within its constitutional limits:

(a) To promote, by all means of publicity and propaganda available to them, friendly relations among nations based upon the Purposes and Principles of the Charter;

(b) To encourage the dissemination of all information designed to give expression to the undoubted desire of all peoples for peace.

(3) Directs that this resolution be communicated to the forthcoming Conference on Freedom of Inforamtion."

The principles of this resolution were confirmed by a Conference on Freedom of Information 1947, and the UN General Assembly 1948 instructed ECOSOC to draft an international convention on this issue. The Pact ratified on Civil and Political Rights prohibits any propaganda in support of war and any preaching of nationalistic, racial or religious hatred which promotes discrimination, hostile acts, and violence.

UN Yearbook, 1947/48, pp. 83–89, 133–135 and 588–595.

WARRANT. A receipt stating that the product was loaded in the repository and is at the disposal of the owner of the warrant. Credit granted by pledging the warrant as security is called warrant credit, the non-payment of which results in putting the stored article up for auction.

J. WALMSLEY. *A Dictionary of International Finance*, London, 1979.

WAR RENUNCIATION TREATY. ▷ Briand-Kellogg Treaty, 1928.

WAR RESISTERS' INTERNATIONAL, f. 1921, London; encourages refusal to participate in military service. Publ.: Newsletter. Members: individuals; in co-operation with national resisters' organizations, since 1987 also active in Warsaw Pact countries. See also ▷ Military Service.

The Europa Yearbook 1988. A World Survey, Vol. I, London 1988.

WARS, 1918–39. In the period between the two world wars the following major international armed conflicts took place:

1918–20, civil war in Russia with the armed intervention of the Entente, which started Mar. 6, 1918 with the landing of British and French troops in Murmansk, ended in Europe in Nov., 1920 with the liquidation of the last white guard units of General P.N. Wrangel in the Crimea and in 1922 in the Far East, when the Japanese army was pushed out of Eastern Siberia.

1919–20, the Polish-Soviet War began in mid-Feb., 1919 and ended with a cease-fire on Oct. 12, 1920 and the Treaty of Riga on Mar. 18, 1921.

1931–45, the Sino-Japanese War, launched on Sept. 18, 1931 with the occupation of Mukden, ended with the unconditional surrender of Japan, Sept. 2, 1945.

1935–36, the Italian-Abyssinian War, commenced on Oct. 3, 1935 with the invasion of Ethiopia (Abyssinia) by Italian armed forces, ended for Italy on May 10, 1936 with the occupation of all of Ethiopia; in World War II as a result of action in Eastern Africa, Ethiopia was by Apr 5 1941 liberated by the British army and Ethiopian partisan units.

1936–39, the Spanish Civil War which had international repercussions.

WARSAW. *Polish:* Warszawa. The capital city of Poland, the only capital to be almost completely destroyed in World War II as a result of Hitler's orders of Oct. 3, 1944 to raze Warsaw to the ground and wipe it off the map of Europe.

Planned destruction of the city carried out by special Wehrmacht destruction units (Vernichtungskommando) resulted in the ravaging of all its historical buildings, all churches and monuments (among others Chopin's and Copernicus'), libraries and institutions of higher learning. The city received the International Peace Award at the World Peace Congress, on Nov. 22, 1950. Warsaw is the seat of international organizations reg. with the UIA: International Committee of Former Prisoners of Auschwitz Concentration Camp; International Committee of Slavists; International Organizing Committee of World Mining Congress; Organization for Co-operation of Railways of CMEA Countries.

The historic center of Warsaw is included in the ▷ World Heritage UNESCO List.

DUCHESS OF ATHOLL, *The Tragedy of Warsaw and Its Documentation*, London, 1945; A. BOGUSŁAWSKI, *Warsaw, Her Faith, Her Fight, Her Fate*, Warsaw, 1945; S. LORENTZ, *Destruction of Royal Castle in Warsaw*, Warsaw, 1947; T. KLIMASZEWSKI, *Verbrennungskommando Warschau*, Berlin, 1962; W. BARTOSZEWSKI, *Warsaw Death Ring 1939–1944*, Warsaw, 1968. A. CIBOROWSKI, *Warsaw, Destruction and Reconstruction of the City*, Warsaw, 1969.

WARSAW AIR CONVENTION, 1929. ▷ Air Warsaw Convention, 1929.

WARSAW CONFERENCE, 1955. The Second Conference on the Question of Ensuring Peace and Security in Europe which took place in the Polish capital, May 11–14, 1955 (the First took place in Moscow Nov. 29–Dec. 2, 1954), with the participation of the Chiefs of State of Albania, Bulgaria, Czechoslovakia, Hungary, GDR, Poland, Romania, and the USSR and an observer from the People's Republic of China. The Warsaw Pact was signed at this Conference on May 14, 1955. ▷ Warsaw Treaty or Warsaw Pact, 1955.

WARSAW DECLARATION, 1950. A common declaration of the German Democratic Republic and Poland on June 6, 1950 in Warsaw that their governments have agreed "that it is in interest of further deepening and development of good-neighborly relations and friendship between the Polish and German peoples, to delimit the established and existing between them inviolable frontier of peace and friendship on the Oder and Lusitian Neisse rivers." ▷ German-Polish Zgorzelec Agreement, 1950.

WARSAW GHETTO UPRISING, 1943. The armed resistance from Apr. 19 to the middle of July, 1943 in the area sealed off by German occupation authorities as a residential district exclusively for Jews, who were marked by the star of David. German units of police, SS and Wehrmacht under the command of the war criminal, SS General Jürgen Stroop (1895–1951), began on April. 19, 1943 the operation to liquidate the Ghetto, which led to the armed resistance of the Jewish Combat Organization (ZOB). During the uprising 13,000 Jews were killed (among them 6000 who were burned alive in houses set on fire by the SS), while the remainder were transported to the death camp in Treblinka, where on Aug. 2, 1943 an uprising broke out. Following the example of the Warsaw Ghetto, the Polish-Jewish Anti-Fascist Organization in Białystok from Aug. 16–20, 1943 waged a five-day armed struggle. The Białystok uprising was also an answer to the German operation of liquidating the Ghetto and enabled part of the fighting group to break through to partisan units. On Oct. 14, 1943 a rebellion broke out in the death camp in Sobibór. In Warsaw the Germans levelled the remaining ruins of the Ghetto. On the fifth anniversary of the Ghetto Uprising, Apr. 19, 1948, a Memorial to the Heroes of the Ghetto was unveiled at L. Zamenhof Street in Warsaw, the work of the sculptor N. Rapaport and the architect L.M. Suzin, made from the Scandinavian basalt offered by Sweden.

The Trial of German Major War Criminals. Proceedings of the International Military Tribunal Sitting at Nuremberg, Germany, 42 Vols., London, 1946–48, Vol. 1, p. 67, Vol. 2, pp. 408–409, Vol. 11, p. 319, Vol. 22, p. 465; G. REITLINGER, *The Final Solution*, London, 1953; B. MARK, *Der Aufstand in Warschauer Ghetto*, Berlin, 1959; R. HILBERG, *The Destruction of the European Jews*, New York, 1961; W. POTERANSKI, *The Warsaw Ghetto. On the 25th Anniversary of the Uprising*, Warsaw, 1968; K. MOCZARSKI, *Rozmowy z katem*, Warszawa, 1978. German edition: *Gespräche mit Henker (General Jürgen Stroop)*, Frankfurt am Main, 1979; J.J. HEYDECKER, *Das Warschauer Getto*, München, 1983; H. KRALL, *Shielding the Flame, An Intimate Conversation with Dr. Marek Edelman. The Last Surviving Leader of the Warsaw Ghetto Uprising*, New York, 1986; B. MAJEWSKA ed., *The Warsaw Ghetto*, Warsaw, 1988.

WARSAW–OXFORD RULES 1932. The Rules for CIF Contracts elaborated by a Conference of the International Law Association in Warsaw and adopted in Oxford on Aug. 12, 1932.

ILO Report of the Thirty-seventh Conference held at Oxford, 1932, Geneva, 1932.

WARSAW TREATY OR WARSAW PACT, 1955. The Treaty of Friendship, Co-operation and Mutual Assistance between Albania, Bulgaria, Czechoslovakia, Hungary, GDR, Poland, Romania and the USSR, signed on May 14, 1955, at Warsaw; came into force on June 6, 1955. The text is as follows:

"The Contracting Parties, Reaffirming their desire to create a system of collective security in Europe based on the participation of all European States, irrespective of their social and political structure, whereby the said States may be enabled to combine their efforts in the interests of ensuring peace in Europe;

Taking into consideration, at the same time, the situation that has come about in Europe as a result of the ratification of the Paris Agreements, which provide for the consitution of a new military group in the form of a "West European Union", with the participation of a remilitarized West Germany and its inclusion in the North Atlantic bloc, thereby increasing the danger of a new war and creating a threat to the national security of peace-loving States;

Being convinced that in these circumstances the peace-loving States of Europe must take the necessary steps to safeguard their security and to promote the maintenance of peace in Europe;

Being guided by the purposes and principles of the Charter of the United Nations;

In the interests of the further strengthening and development of friendship, co-operation and mutual assistance in accordance with the principles of respect for the independence and sovereignty of States and of non-intervention in their domestic affairs;

Have resolved to conclude the present Treaty of Friendship, Co-operation and Mutual Assistance and have appointed as their plenipotentiaries (follow names) who having exhibited their full powers, found in good and due form, have agreed as follows:

Art. 1. The Contracting Parties undertake, in accordance with the Charter of the United Nations, to refrain in their international relations from the threat or use of force and to settle their international disputes by peaceful means in such a manner that international peace and security are not endangered.

Art. 2. The Contracting Parties declare that they are prepared to participate, in a spirit of sincere co-operation, in all international action for ensuring international peace and security and will devote their full efforts to the realization of these aims.

In this connexion, the Contracting Parties shall endeavour to secure, in agreement with other States desiring to co-operate in this matter, the adoption of effective measures for the general reduction of armaments and the prohibition of atomic, hydrogen and other weapons of mass destruction.

Art. 3. The Contracting Parties shall consult together on all important international questions involving their common interests, with a view to strengthening international peace and security.

Whenever any one of the Contracting Parties considers that a threat of armed attack on one or more of the States Parties to the Treaty has arisen, they shall consult together immediately with a view to providing for their joint defence and maintaining peace and security.

Art. 4. In the event of an armed attack in Europe on one or more of the States Parties to the Treaty by any State or group of States, each State Party to the Treaty shall, in the exercise of the right of individual or collective self-defence, in accordance with Article 51 of the United Nations Charter, afford the State or States so attacked immediate assistance, individually and in agreement with the other State Parties to the Treaty, by all the means it considers necessary, including the use of armed force. The States Parties to the Treaty shall consult together immediately concerning the joint measures necessary to restore and maintain international peace and security.

Measures taken under this article shall be reported to the Security Council in accordance with the provision of the United Nations Charter. These measures shall be discontinued as soon as the Security Council takes the necessary action to restore and maintain international peace and security.

Art. 5. The Contracting Parties have agreed to establish a Unified Command, to which certain elements of their armed forces shall be allocated by agreement between the Parties, and which shall act in accordance with jointly established principles. The Parties shall likewise take such other concerted action as may be necessary to reinforce their defensive strength, in order to defend the peaceful labour of their peoples, guarantee the inviolability of their frontiers and territories and afford protection against possible aggression.

Art. 6. For the purpose of carrying out the consultations provided for in the present Treaty between the States Parties thereto, and for the consideration of matters arising in connexion with the application of the present Treaty, a Political Consultative Committee shall be established, in which each State Party to the Treaty shall be represented by a member of the Government or by some other specially appointed representative.

The Committee may establish such auxiliary organs as may prove to be necessary.

Art. 7. The Contracting Parties undertake not to participate in any coalitions or alliances, and not to conclude any agreements, the purposes of which are compatible with the purposes of the present Treaty.

The Contracting Parties declare that their obligations under international treaties at present in force are not incompatible with the provisions of the present Treaty.

Art. 8. The Contracting Parties declare that they will act in a spirit of friendship and co-operation to promote the further development and strengthening of the economic and cultural ties among them, in accordance with the principles of respect for each other's independence and sovereignty and of non-intervention in each other's domestic affairs.

Art. 9. The present Treaty shall be open for accession by other States, irrespective of their social and political structure, which express their readiness, by participating in the present Treaty, to help in combining the efforts of the peace-loving States to ensure the peace and security of the peoples. Such accessions shall come into effect with the consent of the States Parties to the Treaty after the instruments of accession have been deposited with the Government of the Polish People's Republic.

Art. 10. The present Treaty shall be subject to ratification, and the instruments of ratification shall be deposited with the Government of the Polish People's Republic.

The Treaty shall come into force on the date of deposit of the last instrument of ratification. The Government of the Polish People's Republic shall inform the other States Parties to the Treaty of the deposit of each instrument of ratification.

Art. 11. The present Treaty shall remain in force for twenty years. For Contracting Parties which do not, one year before the expiration of that term, give notice of termination of the Treaty to the Government of the Polish People's Republic, the Treaty shall remain in force for a further ten years (*eo ipso* to June 6, 1995). In the event of the establishment of a system of collective security in Europe and the conclusion for that purpose of a General European Treaty concerning collective security, a goal which the Contracting Parties shall steadfastly strive to achieve, the present Treaty shall cease to have effect as from the date on which the General European Treaty comes into force.

Done at Warsaw, this fourteenth day of May 1955, in one copy, in the Russian, Polish, Czech and German languages, all the texts being equally authentic. Certified copies of the present Treaty shall be transmitted by the Government of the Polish People's Republic to all the other Parties to the Treaty."

The seat of the Organization of Joint Command together with the General Staff and the Political Advisory Committee and its auxiliary organs is Moscow. On Jan. 5, 1983 the Summit Session of the Warsaw Pact States called for a Treaty between NATO and Warsaw Pact States on the use of military forces.

UNTS, Vol. 249, 1955, pp. 24–32. R.W. CLAWSON, L.S. KAPLAN, *Warsaw Pact. Political Purpose and Military Means*, Wilmington, 1982; W.J. LEWIS, *The Warsaw Pact: Doctrine and Strategy*, Maidenhead, 1982; W.R. KINTNER, *Soviet Global Strategy*, Fairfax, Va., 1987; D. ROBERTSON, *Guide to Modern Defense and Strategy*, Detroit, 1988.

WARSAW UPRISING, 1944. The uprising of Polish underground armed forces (Home Army) against the German occupier which commenced Aug. 1, 1944 and ended with the capitulation of the uprising command after 63 days of fighting on Oct. 3, 1944 and the order of A. Hitler to resettle all of the surviving inhabitants, partly to concentration camps, and completely destroy the remaining churches, museums, libraries, monuments and homes by special Wehrmacht destruction units (Vernichtungskommando); in addition to being a Polish national tragedy, it had international significance. The only crime of its kind in the history of modern Europe: the conscious total destruction of the capital of an occupied country. The empty ruins ▷ of Warsaw were liberated by the Soviet Army and the First Polish Army on Jan. 17, 1945.

J. CIECHANOWSKI, *The Warsaw Rising of 1944*, New York, 1974; J.K. ZAWODNY, *Nothing but Honor. The Story of the Warsaw Uprising, 1944*, Stanford, 1978; J.K.M. HANSON, *The Civilian Population and the Warsaw Uprising of 1944*, Cambridge, 1982; W. BARTOSZEWSKI, *Dni Walczącej Warszawy. Kronika Powstania Warszawskiego (Chronicle of the Warsaw Uprising)*, London, 1984.

WARSHIP. A subject of the Geneva Convention (II) on the High Seas, 1958. The Art. 8 p. 2 established that a warship is a ship belonging to the combat fleet of a state and bearing the external markings of the warships of that state. The commander of a warship must be on state service, his name on the list of combat naval officers and its crew under the rules of military discipline. A warship has the sovereign right to inspect only the vessels of its own country on the high seas, or those of the same flag: but in relation to foreign vessels only in three cases defined in Art. 22 of Geneva Convention (II): suspicion that the ship is engaged in piracy; or is engaged in slave-trading; or if the ship conceals its flag and refuses to raise it. In these cases the crew of a warship has the right to board the vessel and, if need be, to conduct a search.

C. BALDONI, "Les navires de guerre dans les eaux territoriales étrangères", in: *Recueil de Cours de l'Académie du Droit International de la Haye, 1965; Jane's Fighting Ships 1984–85*, New York, 1984.

WARS, JUST AND UNJUST. ▷ Bellum justum et injustum.

WARS OF NATIONAL LIBERATION. The armed conflicts whose aim is to liberate a country from military occupation, colonial domination or neo-colonial dependence. After World War II, national liberation movements sprang up in all or most of the dependent countries; in face of the intransigence of the colonial régimes these movements in many countries turned into wars of national liberation. The UN General Assembly on many occasions expressed support for national liberation movements, acting with all means available to them. On Dec. 20, 1976 the UN General Assembly Res. 31/150 concerning Namibia supported the armed struggle of the Namibian people carried on by SWAPO "for the purpose of gaining self-determination, freedom, and national independence in a united Namibia." The resolution was adopted by 107 States, with 12 abstentions and 6 votes against (Belgium, France, FRG, Great Britain, Luxembourg and USA).

The UN General Assembly held a special Session on Namibia, Apr. 24–May 3, 1978, and adopted a Declaration and Program of Action in support of Namibia independence and the armed struggle of the people under SWAPO leadership. ▷ Namibia.

UN Yearbook, 1976, pp. 789–790; and 1978, pp. 912–914.

WAR, STATE OF WAR. The state of relations between states which are in armed conflict with each other, obligating each side to adhere to international conventions both in terms of the rules for conducting war (Hague and Geneva Conventions) as well as in relation to third states maintaining neutrality (Hague Convention) and also with respect to war crimes; ▷ war crimes and war criminals.

WAR TERMINATION. According to customary and conventional international law, the termination of war is usually preceded by an armistice, that is, a formal and general suspension of hostilities or a formal surrender of one side (surrender truce) on established conditions, or an unconditional surrender, as was the case with the Third Reich and Japan, 1945; this is followed by the termination of war through the conclusion of peace or a peace treaty by the belligerents, declaration on the termination of war, the debilitation of the defeated state, or its formal liquidation, as in the case of ▷ Prussia, 1947.

D. OTTENSOOSER, "Termination of War by Unilateral Declaration," in: *The British Yearbook of International Law 1952*; H. MOSLER, "Kriegsende," in: STRUPP-SCHLOCHAUER *Wörterbuch des Völkerrechts*, Vol. 2, Berlin, 1961, pp. 333–337.

WARTIME AND PEACETIME OCCUPATION. The armed occupation of foreign territory for the duration of a war while abiding by the norms established by the Hague Statutes annexed to the Fourth Hague Convention on Military Authority in Enemy Territory as well as by the Geneva Convention on the Protection of Civilians of Aug. 12, 1949; or occupation for a certain postwar period for the purpose of executing the conditions of surrender (e.g. occupation of the Ruhr Valley after World War I to extract reparations), or (in the case of unconditional surrender) for the purpose of securing the peace through measures allowed under international law and recognized as proper by the victors (e.g. occupation of Germany and Japan after World War II). According to the Nuremberg Principles, occupation contrary to international law constitutes a war crime.

CARNEGIE ENDOWMENT. *The Conventions and Declarations of the First and Second Hague Conference*, Washington, DC, 1914; *UNTS*, Vol. 75.

WARTIME COLLABORATION. An international term for collaboration with the enemy during a war.

Les Procès Laval: Compte rendue sténographique, Paris, 1946; *Wartime Collaborators: A Comparative Study of the Effect of Their Trials on the Treason Law of Great Britain, Switzerland and France*, in: *Yale Law Journal*, August, 1947; *Les Procès de collaboration*, Paris, 1948; A. REPACI, *Il processo graziani*, Milano, 1952; J. ROY, *The Trial of Marshal Pétain*, New York, 1972; P.M. HAYES, *Quisling: The Career and Political Ideas of Vidkun Quisling, 1887–1945*, Bloomington, Ind., 1972.

WAR VETERANS. The former members of armed forces who fought in a war, a term commonly used after World War I; after World War II more often – combatants; the latter term comprises both former soldiers of regular armies, guerilla and resistance movements. Organizations reg. with UIA:

Union of Resistance Veterans for a United Europe, Union des resistants pour une Europe unie, est. 1955,

Brussels, Publ.: *La voix internationale de la Résistance,* and *Europe Unie.*
World Veterans Federation, WVF, f. 1950, Paris, through fusion of the Inter-Allied Federation of Verterans, f. 1920 and Rassemblement Internationale des Anciens Combatants, f. 1948. WVF assists war veterans and acts on behalf of peace and development. Publ.: *World Veteran Disarmament, Informative Bulletin* and *Annual of Comparative Legislation.*

Yearbook of International Organizations.

WASHINGTON CONFERENCE, 1921–22. On the situation in the Far East and Pacific as well as the limitation of naval armaments, held in Washington Nov. 12, 1921–Feb. 6, 1922 with the participation of the USA (initiator of the conference), Belgium, China, France, Great Britain, Italy, Japan, the Netherlands and Portugal. The conference negotiated the following:
(1) On Dec. 13, 1921 a treaty between the USA, Great Britain, Japan and France. ▷ Washington Four Power Pacific Treaty, 1921.
(2) On Feb. 4, 1922 a treaty between China and Japan on the withdrawal of Japanese troops from Shantung.
(3) On Feb. 6, 1922 a treaty on chemical weapons, banning the use of poisonous and similar gasses; not ratified by either Japan or the USA;
(4) On Feb. 6, 1922 a treaty between the USA, Great Britain, Japan, France, Italy, Belgium, Holland, Portugal and China which formally declared the principle of the recognition of the sovereignty and territorial integrity of China. ▷ Washington Nine Powers Treaty on the Sovereignty of China, 1922.
(5) On Feb. 6, 1922 a treaty between the USA, Great Britain, Japan, France, and Italy setting the limits of the tonnage of the combat fleets of those states in the proportions: 5–5–3–1.67–1.67 and limiting the tonnage of battleships to 35,000 tons and naval guns to 16 inch caliber.
The Washington Conference was a United States success, since it deprived Great Britain of maritime supremacy and Japan of special rights in China.
"The Contracting Powers agree to limit their respective naval armament . . ." (Art. 1).
"The Treaty shall remain in force until Dec. 31, 1936 . . ." (Art. 23).

"Washington Conference on the Limitation of Armament," in: *International Conciliation,* No. 169, December, 1921, and No. 172, Mar., 1922; *Washington Conference 1921–1922 (Minutes),* Washington, DC, 1922; R.L. BULL, *Washington Conference,* New York, 1922; J.C. SHILOCK, "The Post-War Movements to Reduce Naval Armaments", in: *International Conciliation,* No. 245, December, 1928; *Major Peace Treaties of Modern History,* New York, 1967, pp. 2277–2299; *LNTS,* Vol. 25, p. 201.

WASHINGTON, DC. The Capital of the United States since 1792, where Congress holds its sessions since 1800. Coterminous with the ▷ District of Colombia. Called in 19th century "Uncle Sams company town." British troops occupied and sacked the Capitol and the White House 1814. Seat of UN specialized agencies (World Bank and IMF) and of 70 intergovernmental and international organizations, reg. with the UIA.

C. McLAUGHLIN GREEN, *Washington, DC,* 3 Vols, New York, 1962–68; *Yearbook of International Organizations;* H. SMITH, *The Power Game. How Washington Works,* New York, 1988.

WASHINGTON DECLARATION ON ATOMIC ENERGY, 1945. The tripartite declaration of the President of United States H. Truman, Prime Minister of United Kingdom C.R. Attlee and Prime Minister of Canada W.L. Mackenzie King on atomic energy, on Nov, 15, 1945 in Washington, DC. The text is as follows:

"(1) We recognize that the application of recent scientific discoveries to the methods and practice of war has placed at the disposal of mankind means of destruction hitherto unknown, against which there can be no adequate military defense, and in the employment of which no single nation can in fact have a monopoly.
(2) We desire to emphasize that the responsibility for devising means to insure that the new discoveries shall be used for the benefit of mankind, instead of as a means of destruction, rests not on our nations alone but upon the whole civilized world. Nevertheless, the progress that we have made in the development and use of atomic energy demands that we take an initiative in the matter, and we have accordingly met together to consider the possibility of international action:
(a) To prevent the use of atomic energy for destructive purposes.
(b) To promote the use of recent and future advances in scientific knowledge, particularly in the utilization of atomic energy, for peaceful and humanitarian ends.
(3) We are aware that the only complete protection for the civilized world from the destructive use of scientific knowledge lies in the prevention of war. No system of safeguards that can be devised will of itself provide an effective guarantee against production of atomic weapons by a nation bent on aggression. Nor can we ignore the possibility of the development of other weapons, or of new methods of warfare which may constitute as great a threat to civilization as the military use of atomic energy.
(4) Representing, as we do, the three countries which possess the knowledge essential to the use of atomic energy, we declare at the outset our willingness, as a first contribution, to proceed with the exchange of fundamental scientific information and the interchange of scientists and scientific literature for peaceful ends with any action that will fully reciprocate.
(5) We believe that the fruits of scientific research should be made available to all nations, and that freedom of investigation and free interchange of ideas are essential to the progress of knowledge. In pursuance of the policy, the basic scientific information essential to the development of atomic energy for peaceful purposes has already been made available to the world. It is our intention that all further information of this character that may become available from time to time shall be similarly treated. We trust that other nations will adopt the same policy, thereby creating an atmosphere of reciprocal confidence in which political agreement and co-operation will flourish.
(6) We have considered the question of the disclosure of detailed information concerning the practical industrial application of atomic energy. The military exploitation of atomic energy depends, in large part, upon the same methods and processes as would be required for industrial uses. We are not convinced that the spreading of the specialized information regarding the practical application of atomic energy, before it is possible to devise effective, reciprocal and enforceable safeguards acceptable to all nations, would contribute to a constructive solution of the problem of the atomic bomb.
On the contrary we think it might have the opposite effect. We are, however, prepared to share, on a reciprocal basis with others of the United Nations, detailed information concerning the practical industrial application of atomic energy just as soon as effective enforceable safeguards against its use for destructive purposes can be devised.
(7) In order to attain the most effective means of entirely eliminating the use of atomic energy for destructive purposes and promoting its widest use for industrial and humanitarian purposes, we are of the opinion that at the earliest practicable date a commission should be set up under the United Nations Organization to prepare recommendations for submission to the organization.
The commission should be instructed to proceed with the utmost dispatch and should be authorized to submit recommendations from time to time dealing with separate phases of its work.
In particular the commission should make specific proposals:
(a) For extending between all nations the exchange of basic scientific information for peaceful ends;
(b) For control of atomic energy to the extent necessary to insure its use for peaceful purposes;
(c) For the elimination from national armaments of atomic weapons and of all major weapons adaptable to mass destruction;
(d) For effective safeguards by way of inspection and other means to protect complying States against the hazards of violations and evasions.
(8) The work of the commission should proceed by separate stages, the successful completion of each one of which will develop the necessary confidence of the world before the next stage is undertaken. Specifically, it is considered that the commission might well devote its attention first to the wide exchange of scientists and scientific information, and as a second stage to the development of full knowledge concerning natural resources of raw materials.
(9) Faced with the terrible realities of the application of science to destruction, every nation will realize more urgently than before the overwhelming need to maintain the rule of law among nations and to banish the scourge of war from the earth. This can only be brought about by giving wholehearted support to the United Nations Organization and by consolidating and extending its authority, thus creating conditions of mutual trust in which all peoples will be free to devote themselves to the arts of peace. It is our firm resolve to work without reservation to achieve these ends."

International Conciliation, No. 416, December, 1945, pp. 787–789. *UNTS,* Vol 3, pp. 124–128.

WASHINGTON DOCTRINE OF UNSTABLE ALLIANCES, 1801. The principle of US foreign policy which emerged from the warning of the first President of the United States, G. Washington, against entangling alliances in a speech Sept. 17, 1796; formulated by President T. Jefferson in his inauguration speech to Congress on Jan. 7, 1801. According to this principle, the States should regard their war alliances as temporary and quickly change their alliances, guided solely by their own interests.

D. MALONE, *Jefferson and his Time,* New York, 1948.

WASHINGTON ENERGY CONFERENCE, 1974. The Conference, convened at the initiative of the US President in the context of the world energy crisis, was held Feb. 11–13, 1974 in Washington with the participation of the ministers of foreign affairs, energy, finance and science of nine EEC states, Japan, Canada, Norway and the USA, as well as representatives of EEC and OECD boards. The final communiqué was not approved by France with respect to some important issues (9, 10, 16, 17). The text is as follows:

"(1) The Ministers examined the international energy situation and its implications and charted a course of action to meet this challenge which requires constructive and comprehensive solutions. To this end they agreed on specific steps to provide for effective international co-operation. The Ministers affirmed that solutions to the world's energy problems should be sought in consultation with producer countries and other consumers.
Analysis of the Situation
(2) They noted that during the past three decades progress in improving productivity and standards of living was greatly facilitated by the ready availability of increasing supplies at energy at fairly stable prices. They recognized that the problem of meeting growing demand existed before the current situation and that the needs of the world economy for increased energy supplies require positive long-term solutions.
(3) They concluded that the current energy situation results from an intensification of these underlying factors and from political developments.
(4) They reviewed the problems created by the large rise in oil prices and agreed with the serious concern expressed by the International Monetary Fund's Committee of Twenty at its recent Rome meeting over the abrupt and significant changes in prospect for the world balance of payments structure.
(5) They agreed that present petroleum prices presented the structure of world trade and finance with an unprecedented situation. They recognized that none of

the consuming countries could hope to insulate itself from these developments, or expect to deal with the payments impact of oil prices by the adoption of monetary or trade measures alone. In their view, the present situation, if continued, could lead to a serious deterioration in income and employment, intensify inflationary pressures, and endanger the welfare of nations. They believed that financial measures by themselves will not be able to deal with the strains of the current situation.
(6) They expressed their particular concern about the consequences of the situation for the developing countries and recognized the need for efforts by the entire international community to resolve this problem. At current oil prices the additional energy costs for developing countries will cause a serious setback to the prospect for economic development of these countries.
(7) General Conclusions. They affirmed that, in the pursuit of national policies, whether in trade, monetary or energy fields, efforts should be made to harmonize the interests of each country on the one hand and the maintenance of the world economic system on the other. Concerted international co-operation between all the countries concerned including oil producing countries could help to accelerate an improvement in the supply and demand situation, ameliorate the adverse economic consequences of the existing situation and lay the groundwork for a more equitable and stable international energy relationship.
(8) They felt that these considerations taken as a whole made it essential that there should be a substantial increase of international co-operation in all fields. Each participant in the Conference states its firm intention to do its utmost to contribute to such an aim, in close co-operation both with the other consumer countries and with the producer countries.
(9) They concurred in the need for a comprehensive action program to deal with all facets of the world energy situation by co-operative measures. In so doing they will build on the work of the OECD. They recognized that they may wish to invite, as appropriate, other countries to join with them in these efforts. Such an action program of international co-operation would include, as appropriate, the sharing of means and efforts, while concerting national policies, in such areas as:
The conservation of energy and restraint of demand.
A system of allocating oil supplies in times of emergency and severe shortages.
The acceleration of development of additional energy sources so as to diversify energy supplies.
The acceleration of energy research and development programs through international co-operative efforts.
(10) With respect to monetary and economic questions, they decided to intensify their co-operation and to give impetus to the work being undertaken in the IMF, the World Bank and the OECD on the economic and monetary consequences of the current energy situation, in particular to deal with balance of payments disequilibria. They agreed that:
In dealing with the balance of payments impact of oil prices they stressed the importance of avoiding competitive depreciation and the escalation of restrictions on trade and payments or disruptive actions in external borrowing.
While financial co-operation can only partially alleviate the problems which have recently arisen for the international economic system, they will intensify work on short-term financial measures and possible longer-term mechanisms to reinforce existing official and market credit facilities. They will pursue domestic economic policies which will reduce as much as possible the difficulties resulting from the current energy cost levels.
They will make strenuous efforts to maintain and enlarge the flow of development aid bilaterally and through multilateral institutions, on the basis of international solidarity embracing all countries with appropriate resources.
(11) Further, they have agreed to accelerate wherever practicable their own national programs of new energy sources and technology which will help the overally world-wide supply and demand situation.
(12) They agreed to examine in detail the role of international oil companies.
(13) They stressed the continued importance of maintaining and improving the natural environment as part of developing energy sources and agreed to make this an important goal of their activity.
(14) They further agreed that there was need to develop a co-operative multilateral relationship with producing countries, and other consuming countries, that takes into account the long-term interests of all. They are ready to exchange technical information on the problem of stabilizing energy supplies with regard to quantity and prices.
(15) They welcomed the initiatives in the UN to deal with the larger issues of energy and primary products at world-wide level and particularly for a special session of the UN General Assembly.
Establishment of Follow-on Machinery.
(16) They agreed to establish a co-ordinating group headed by senior officials to direct and to co-ordinate the development of the actions referred to above. The co-ordinating group shall decide how best to organize its work. It should:
Monitor and give focus to the tasks that might be addressed to existing organizations;
Establish such ad hoc working groups as may be necessary to undertake tasks for which there are presently no suitable bodies;
Direct preparations for a conference of consumer and producer countries which will be held at the earliest possible opportunity and which, if necessary, will be preceded by a further meeting of consumer countries.
(17) They agreed that the preparations for such meetings should involve consultations with developing countries and other consumer and producer countries."

US Department of State Bulletin, No. 1810, 1974.

WASHINGTON FOUR POWER PACIFIC TREATY, 1921. Called also the Four Power Pact, signed at Washington, DC, on Dec. 13, 1921. The text is as follows:

"The United States of America, the British Empire, France and Japan,
With a view to the preservation of the general peace and the maintenance of their rights in relation to their insular possessions and insular dominions in the region of the Pacific Ocean,
Have determined to conclude a Treaty to this effect and have appointed as their Plenipotentiaries:
(follow names)
Who, having communicated their Full Powers, found in good and due form, have agreed as follows:
I. The High Contracting Parties agree as between themselves to respect their rights in relation to their insular possessions and insular dominions in the region of the Pacific Ocean.
If there should develop between any of the High Contracting Parties a controversy arising out of any Pacific question and involving their said rights which is not satisfactorily settled by diplomacy and is likely to affect the harmonious accord now happily subsisting between them, they shall invite the other High Contracting Parties to a joint conference to which the whole subject will be referred for consideration and adjustment.
II. If the said rights are threatened by the aggressive action of any other Power, the High Contracting Parties shall communicate with one another fully and frankly in order to arrive at an understanding as to the most efficient measures to be taken, jointly or separately, to meet the exigencies of the particular situation.
III. This Treaty shall remain in force for ten years from the time it shall take effect, and after the expiration of said period it shall continue to be in force subject to the right of any of the High Contracting Parties to terminate it upon twelve months' notice."

The Treaty came into force on Aug. 10, 1923.

UST, 1921: *International Conciliation*, No. 251, June, 1929, pp. 339–340.

WASHINGTON NAVAL TREATY, 1922. ▷ Washington Conference, 1921–22.

WASHINGTON NINE POWERS TREATY ON THE SOVEREIGNTY OF CHINA, 1922. The Treaty of Nine Powers on the Sovereignty, Independence, and Integrity of China, which condemned "zones of influence" but maintained the "open door" policy in relation to Chinese ports, signed on Feb. 6, 1922 at Washington after the Japanese invasion of China: the LN on July 26, 1938 convened a special conference on the crisis in the Far East, which confirmed the validity of the obligations of the Treaty of Nine Powers.

The text of the Nine Powers Treaty is as follows:

"Art. I. The Contracting Powers, other than China, agree:
(1) To respect the sovereignty, the independence, and the territorial and administrative integrity of China;
(2) To provide the fullest and most unembarrassed opportunity to China to develop and maintain for herself an effective and stable government;
(3) To use their influence for the purpose of effectually establishing and maintaining the principle of equal opportunity for the commerce and industry of all nations throughout the territory of China:
(4) To refrain from taking advantage of conditions in China in order to seek special rights or privileges which would abridge the rights of subject or citizens of friendly States, and from countenancing action inimical to the security of such States.
Art. II. The Contracting Powers agree not to enter into any Treaty, agreement, arrangement, or understanding, either with one another, or, individually or collectively, with any Power or Powers, which would infringe or impair the principles stated in Art. I.
Art. III. With a view to applying more effectively the principles of the Open Door or equality of opportunity in China for the trade and industry of all nations, the Contracting Powers, other than China, agree they will not seek, nor support their respective nationals in seeking:
(a) Any arrangement which might purport to establish in favor of their interests any general superiority of rights with respect to commercial or economic development in any designated region of China;
(b) Any such monopoly or preference as would deprive the nationals of any other Power of the right of undertaking any legitimate trade or industry in China, or of participating with the Chinese Government, or with any local authority, in any category of public enterprise, or which by reason of its scope, duration or geographical extent is calculated to frustrate the practical application of the principle of equal opportunity.
It is understood that the foregoing stipulations of this Article are not to be so construed as to prohibit the acquisition of such properties or rights as may be necessary to the conduct of a particular commercial, industrial, or financial undertaking or to the encouragement of invention and research.
China undertakes to be guided by the principles stated in the foregoing stipulations of this Article in dealing with applications for economic rights and privileges from Governments and nationals of all foreign countries, whether parties to the present Treaty or not.
Art IV. The Contracting Powers agree not to support any agreements by their respective nationals with each other designed to create Spheres of Influence or to provide for the enjoyment of mutually exclusive opportunities in designated parts of Chinese territory.
Art. V. China agree that, throughout the whole of the railways in China, she will not exercise or permit unfair discrimination of any kind. In particular there shall be no discrimination whatever, direct or indirect, in respect of charges or of facilities on the ground of the nationality of passengers or the countries from which or to which they are proceeding, or the origin or ownership of goods or the country from which or to which they are consigned, or the nationality or ownership of the ship or other means of conveying such passengers or goods before or after their transport on the Chinese railways.
The Contracting Powers, other than China, assume a corresponding obligation in respect of any of the aforesaid railways over which they or their nationals are in a position to exercise any control in virtue of any concession, special agreement or otherwise.
Art. VI. The Contracting Powers, other than China, agree fully to respect China's rights as a neutral in time of war to which China is not a party; and China declares that when she is a neutral she will observe the obligations of neutrality.
Art. VII. The Contracting Powers agree that, whenever a situation arises which in the opinion of any one of them involves the application of the stipulations of the present Treaty, and renders desirable discussion of such

application, there shall be full and frank communication between the Contracting Powers concerned.

Art. VIII. Powers not signatory to the present Treaty, which have Governments recognized with China, shall be invited to adhere to the present Treaty. To this end the Governments of the United States will make the necessary communications to non-Signatory Powers and will inform the Contracting Powers of the replies received. Adherence by any Power shall become effective on receipt of notice thereof by the Government of the United States."

(Art. IX provides for exchange and deposit of ratifications.)

The Treaty came into force on Dec. 31, 1922.

UST No. 723; *US Department of State, Treaty Information*, December 31, 1922.

WASHINGTON RULES, 1871. Three rules for a neutral government adopted in art. 6 of the American-British Arbitration Treaty signed on May 8, 1871 at Washington, related to the "Alabama" Case as the test of neutral duty that could apply to the case. The first rule was later adopted in art. 8 of the Hague Arbitration Convention 1907.

E. REALE, *L'arbitrage international. Le règlement judiciaire du conflit de l'"Alabama"*, Paris, 1929; C. CAUSHING, *The Treaty of Washington, its Negotiation, Execution and the Discussion Relating Thereto*, Washington, DC, 1973.

WASHINGTON TREATY, 1871. Agreement between Great Britain and the US to provide an amiable settlement of the ▷ "Alabama" claims, signed in Washington, May 8, 1871.

Major Peace Treaties of Modern History, New York, 1967, Vol. II, pp. 803–842.

WASHINGTON TREATY, 1921. ▷ Pacific Ocean Washington Treaty, 1921.

WASP. White Anglo-Saxon Protestants. A name accepted in the USA for the historical American power élite.

WASTE MATERIALS. The secondary raw material, subject of international research and co-operation. Organizations reg. with the UIA:

Common Market Committee on Waste Paper, f. 1960, Brussels.

EEC Section of the Co-ordinating Committee for Textile Salvage, f. 1961, Frankfurt am M, FRG.

International Reclamation Bureau, Bureau international de la recuperation, f. 1948, Brussels. Research institution on all problems concerning secondary raw materials like ferrous scrap, textiles, waste, paperstock etc. Publ.: Documentary Booklets,

International Solid Wastes and Public Cleansing Association, f. 1931, London. Publ.: Information Bulletin.

Yearbook of International Organizations.

WATCH TOWER BIBLE AND TRACT SOCIETY. The Jehovah's Witnesses, f. 1872 as the International Bible Students Association, incorporated 1884 as Zion's Watch Tower Tract Society, present name adopted 1896, organized under the laws of Pennsylvania, USA and Brooklyn, New York. The Society acts as servant of and legal worldwide governing agency for that body of Christian persons known as Jehovah's Witnesses; to preach gospel of God's Kingdom under Christ Jesus to all nations as witness to the name, word and supremacy of the Almighty God Jehovah; to print and distribute the Bible, and disseminate Bible truths in various languages; to establish and maintain gratuitous private Bible schools and classes; teach, train, prepare and equip men and women as ministers, missionaries, evangelists, preachers, teachers and lecturers. Members (1975): 96 branches directing 2,179,256 active workers in 210 countries. Publ.: *Jehovah's Witness in the Divine Purpose*; *The Watch Tower* in 32 languages. Bibles in over 185 languages. Reg. with the UIA.

Yearbook of International Organizations.

WATER. A major problem for the majority of nations, subject of international research, co-operation and conventions. ▷ Water for Peace. Organizations reg. with the UIA:

European Federation for the Protection of Waters, f. 1956, Zurich. Publ.: Information Bulletin.

International Association for Water Law, 1967, Rome. Consultative status with ECOSOC and FAO. Publ.: Reports.

International Association on Water Pollution Research, f. 1962, London, Publ.: *Water Research* (monthly).

International Study Group for Waterworks in the Rhine Catchment Area, f. 1970, Amsterdam.

International Waterproofing Association, f. 1968, Brussels.

International Water Resources Association, f. 1971, Milwaukee. Publ.: *Water International*.

International Water Supply Association, f. 1949, London. Official relations with WHO. Publ.: *Aqua* (quarterly).

Oil Companies International Study Group for Conservation of Clean Air and Water in Europe, f. 1963, The Hague. Publ.: Reports.

Scientific Committee on Water Research, f. 1964, London. Adviser on behalf of the International Council of Scientific Union to UNESCO, WHO, FAO and WMO.

On Nov. 10, 1979, the UN General Assembly proclaimed 1981–90 as the International Drinking Water Supply and Sanitation Decade.

F. MEINCK, K. MOHLE, *Dictionary of Water and Sewage Engineering*, (in German, English, French and Italian), Amsterdam, 1977, p 738; *UN Chronicle*, January, 1980, pp. 28–30; WHO, *Statistical Survey of Water and Sanitation Service*, Geneva, 1983; WHO, *La technologie appropriée au traitement des eaux usées dans les petites localités rurales*, Genève, 1984. *Yearbook of International Organizations.*

WATER DESALINIZATION. Making salt water fit for use, above all sea water for industry and consumption, by the extraction of salt; subject of international co-operation in connection with the growing shortage of drinking and industrial water in a majority of regions of the world. In the second half of the 20th century, the search for methods to desalinate sea water became the subject of extensive international co-operation; particularly the method of hyperfiltration, or reversed osmosis. In 1960 ECOSOC initiated a world UN program on water desalination with the task of discovering the cheapest methods of desalinization (in 1967 the cost of one thousand gallons of drinking water from wells was not more than one cent, while that of desalinated water was more than one dollar). The two great powers, USA and USSR, created special departments for water desalination and began desalinization work with the help of atomic energy. On the assumption of the UN program it is anticipated that this presently important problem for human civilization will be successfully solved.

Water Desalinization in Developing Countries, UN, New York, 1964; "Use of Nuclear Power for the Production of the Fresh Water from Salt Water," Hearing, Joint Committee on Atomic Energy, August 18, 1964, Washington, DC, 1964; *Dessalement de l'eau*, UN, New York, 1965; *Proceedings of the Inter-regional Seminar on the Economic Application of Water Desalination*, New York, 1965; *First UN Desalinization Plant Operation Survey*, New York, 1969; WHO, *Health Effects of the Removal of Substances Occurring Naturally in Drinking-Water, with Special Reference to Demineralized and Desalinated Water*, Copenhagen, 1979.

WATER FOR PEACE. Motto of a UN campaign for protection of the globe against shortage of water resources, formulated 1967 in view of growing demand for water in the 20th century due to expanding industry and population. Water, becoming the key to all world resources, was the main subject in 1951 of the UN Conference on Utilization and Conservation of Natural Resources which started a UN program for global study of problems of drinking water and water for industrial use. The International Center of Water Resources Development, headquarters New York, was est. in 1959; and in 1957 UNESCO launched the International Hydrological Decade. An International Conference on Water for Peace was held in Washington, May–June, 1967. The UN Water Conference was held in Mar del Plata, Mar. 14–15, 1977, to create world-wide awareness of the water resource supply/demand picture. The Conference adopted the Plan of Action of Mar del Plata calling for an International Drinking Water Supply and Sanitation Decade for 1980–90, to provide all people with water of safe quality and adequate quantity and basic sanitary facilities by 1990, according priority to the poor and less privileged. Attending the Conference were representatives of 116 States, 17 intergovernmental and 58 non-governmental organizations.

UN Chronicle, April, 1977, pp. 36–39.

WATERFOWL. A subject of the Convention on the Protection of Marshlands of International Significance, Especially as a Life Environment for Water Birds, signed Feb. 2, 1971.

Organization reg. with the UIA:

International Waterfowl Research Bureau, f. 1954, Stimbridge, England.

Yearbook of International Organizations 1986/87; The Europa Yearbook 1988. A World Survey, Vol. I, London, 1988.

WATERGATE. A complex of residential, office and hotel buildings in the US capital at Virginia Avenue near Kennedy Center, constructed in the 1960s, where on June 17, 1972 a break-in occurred to the electoral campaign staff offices of the Democratic Party and the perpetrators caught in the act turned out to be members of a special task group directly subordinate to White House officials and representing the interests of the US President and Republican Party candidate for a second term, Richard Nixon. After the elections, Nov. 6, 1972 (R. Nixon won with 65% of the votes), investigations of the Watergate affair precipitated a deep internal political crisis in the USA and constitutional disputes between the President and Congress, which in June, 1974 placed President R. Nixon under indictment (▷ Impeachment) and ultimately led to his resignation. In view of its worldwide publicity, Watergate became an international term, a synonym for a minor criminal affair which unexpectedly grows into a deep political crisis.

F. MANKIEWICZ, *Nixon's Road to Watergate*, New York, 1973; MCCRISTAL, *Watergate: the Full Inside Story*, London, 1973; *The Watergate Hearings: Break-in and Cover-up. Proceedings of the Senate Select Committee on Presidential Campaign Activities as Edited by the Staff at the New York Times*, New York, 1973.

WATER LAW, INTERNATIONAL. A branch of international public law comprising the accepted legal norms on all sorts of usable waters, lakes and underground or interstate rivers. The importance of these norms increases with the growing deficit of fresh water in the majority of countries in the world, connected with the problem of pollution of rivers and lakes, with the international protection of flood-threatened regions, with shipping on rivers and international canals and with fishery in fresh waters.

WATERLOO. A Belgian town near Brussels, famous for the Battle of Waterloo on June 18, 1815, in which Napoleon I was finally defeated. An international synonym for defeat.

WATER POLLUTION. A world problem at the end of the 20th century related to industrialization on land, shipment of oil by sea and pollution of rivers with chemicals. Industrialization involves discharge of industrial sewage, often toxic, into rivers and lakes and thereby produces degradation of fish and aquatic plants. Shipment of chemicals by sea, mainly oil, produces spills disastrous to sea waters, often polluting territorial waters and coasts. A definition of pollution of sea waters is provided by the Convention on the Protection of the Marine Environment of the Baltic Sea Area, signed Mar. 22, 1974, in Helsinki:

"Pollution means introduction by man, directly or indirectly of substances or energy into the marine environment, including estuaries, resulting in such deleterious effects as hazard to human health, harm to living resources and marine life, hindrance to legitimate uses of the sea including fishing, impairment of the quality for use of sea water, and reduction of amenities."

In 1970, Canada passed legislation on the protection against pollution of a 100-mile-wide strip of its territorial waters as well as withheld its agreement on the International Court of Justice's jurisdiction over questions of water pollution. This was a manifestation of Canada's expansion of its territorial sea. The government of the Netherlands, June 20, 1972, issued a ban on pollution of the North Sea and the English Channel. In Berlin, June 26, 1972, the governments of the German Democratic Republic and Poland initiated a project on the protection of rivers and the Baltic, as well as air against pollution. In London, Nov. 13, 1972, 57 states (including France, Japan, Great Britain and the USSR) signed the International Treaty on the Protection of Clear Sea and Ocean Waters.

The Baltic Convention, called the Helsinki Convention of 1974 on the Protection of the Baltic Sea against Pollution, provided for close co-operation and reciprocal assistance by the Baltic states in eliminating pollution, co-ordination of scientific research into this area, and also a joint system of monitoring, control and exchange of information; it includes limitations or bans on hazardous substances introduced into the Baltic and specifies the areas which will be particularly protected by member States.

Organizations reg. with the UIA:

International Association on Water Pollution Research, f. 1962, London. Publ.: *Water Research*.
International Commission for the Protection of the Moselle against Pollution, an organ of the Moselle Conference est. Dec. 20, 1961, headquarters in capitals of member States: France, Luxembourg and the FRG.
International Commission for the Protection of the Rhine against Pollution, an organ of the Berne Rhine Convention, est. Apr. 29, 1963, by the governments of France, FRG, Luxembourg, the Netherlands and Switzerland. Headquarters Koblenz, FRG.

In Rome, Mar. 29–Apr. 3, 1974, The Interparliamentary Conference of the Mediterranean Sea Coastal States on eliminating pollution of this sea was held. Bulgaria and the USSR did not participate, since their position is to consider the pollution of the Black Sea together with that of the Mediterranean Sea. It was resolved to prepare an international convention on the protection of the Mediterranean Sea.

During 1954–74 seven extended multinational and seven regional conventions were signed:
The International Convention on the Prevention of Pollution of the Sea by Oil, signed on May 12, 1954, in London; amendments were adopted on Apr. 11, 1962, in London as well as annexes: Oct. 21, 1969, Oct. 12, 1971 and Oct. 15, 1971.
The International Convention Relating to Intervention on the High Seas in Cases of Oil Pollution Casualties, signed on Nov. 29, 1969, in Brussels.
The International Covention on Civil Liability for Oil Pollution Damage, signed on Nov. 29, 1969, in Brussels.
The International Convention on Establishment of an International Fund for Compensation for Oil Pollution Damage, signed on Dec. 18, 1971, in Brussels.
The Convention on the Preservation of Marine Pollution by Dumping Wastes and other Matter, signed on Dec. 29, 1972, in London.
The International Convention for the Prevention of Pollution by Ships, signed on Nov. 2, 1973, in London.
The Protocol on Intervention on High Seas in Cases of Sea Pollution by Substances other than Oil, signed on Nov. 2, 1973, in London.
The regional conventions:
The Agreement for Co-operation in Dealing with Pollution of the North Sea by Oil, signed on June 9, 1969, in Bonn.
The Agreement between Denmark, Finland, Norway and Sweden Concerning Co-operation in Measures to Deal with Pollution of the Sea by Oil, signed on Sept. 16, 1971.
The Convention for the Prevention of Marine Pollution by Dumping from Ship and Aircraft, signed on Feb. 16, 1972, in Oslo.
The Convention for the Prevention of Marine Pollution from Land Based Sources, signed on June 4, 1974, in Paris.
The Convention on the Protection of the Marine Environment of the Baltic Sea Area, signed on Apr. 22, 1974, in Helsinki.
The Convention for the Protection of the Mediterranean Sea against Pollution, signed on Feb. 16, 1976, in Barcelona together with the Protocol on the prevention of pollution of the Mediterranean Sea by dumping from ships and aircraft of Feb. 16, 1976, and the Protocol on co-operation in elimination of pollution of the Mediterranean Sea with oil and other deleterious substances in case of emergency of Feb. 16, 1976.
The Agreement between Denmark and Sweden concerning the protection of the Sund (Oresund) from pollution, signed on Apr. 5, 1974, in Copenhagen.
In 1969 at IMCO, FAO, IAEA, IMCO, UNESCO, WHO and the UN Secretariat formed a Group of Experts for the Scientific Aspects of Marine Pollution, GESAMP.
In 1969 the International Tanker Owners' Pollution Federation Ltd. was founded, headquarters London. The Federation represents shipowners and large oil companies using tankers and therefore prepared the Tanker Owners' Voluntary Agreement Concerning Liability for Oil Pollution called TOVALOP. In addition to this, the Oil Companies' Institute for Marine Pollution Compensation was established, in Bermuda, also headquarters of the International Tanker Association Ltd.
In 1972 in Stockholm a UN Conference on the Protection of Environment adopted recommendations concerning the problem of the protection of seas and oceans against pollution.
A separate regional inter-governmental institution founded to prevent pollution is the Regional Oil Combating Centre for the Mediterranean, est.

under the auspices of IMCO and UNESCO, headquarters Malta.

J.J. FRIED, *Groundwater Pollution*, Amsterdam, 1975; A.W. KNIGHT, M.A. SIMMONS, *Water Pollution. A Guide to Information Sources*, Detroit, 1980; UN. *The Law of the Sea: Pollution by Dumping. Legislative History of the Convention*, New York, 1985.

WATER QUALITY CANADA–USA, AGREEMENT 1972. A bilateral agreement to improve water quality and promote steps against pollution in the Saint Lawrence Sea-way and the Great Lakes.

WATERS, INTERNATIONAL AND WATER LAW. A general international term for high sea, international channels, rivers and gulfs; subject of international treaties, conventions and agreements. The list including 114 such agreements concluded between 1616 to 1962 is given in the work of R.R. Baxter. In 1970, the UN General Assembly Res. 2669/XXV recommended the UN Committee for the Law of the Sea to study the law of the non-navigational uses of international water-courses. The term was defined by art. 8 of the Convention on the Law of the Sea, 1981 as follows: "waters on the land-ward side of the baseline of the territorial sea form part of the internal Waters of the State."

Comptes rendus et textes relatifs à la Convention sur le régime des voies navigables d'interêt international et à la Déclaration portant reconnaissance du droit au pavillon des États depourvus de littoral maritime, Geneve, 1921; B. WINIARSKI, *Principes généraux du droit fluvial international*, La Haye, 1933; J. FRIEDRICH, "The Settlement of Disputes between States concerning Right to the Waters of Interstate Streams", in: *Iowa Law Review*, No. 32, 1946/47; H. THALMAN, "Wasserrecht Internationales", in: *STRUPP SCHLOCHAUER Wörterbuch des Völkerrechts*, Vol. 3, pp. 808–811, Berlin, 1962; R.R. BAXTER, *The Law of International Waterways*, Cambridge, 1964.

WATERWAYS OF INTERNATIONAL CONCERN, BARCELONA CONVENTION, 1921. The Convention and Statute on the Régime of Navigable Waterways of International Concern, signed on Apr. 20, 1921 at Barcelona, realizing the purpose of art. 23 (e) of the League of Nations Covenant by Albania, Austria, Belgium, Bolivia, Brazil, Bulgaria, Czechoslovakia, Chile, China, Colombia, Costa Rica, Cuba, Denmark, Estonia, Finland, France, Greece, Guatemala, Haiti, Honduras, Italy, Japan, Latvia, Lithuania, Luxembourg, the Netherlands, Norway, Panama, Paraguay, Persia, Poland, Portugal, Romania, the Serb–Croat–Slovene State, Spain, Sweden, Switzerland, the UK, Uruguay and Venezuela.
The High Contracting Parties of the Convention, "carrying further the development as regards the international régime of navigation on internal waterways, which began more than a century ago, and which has been solemnly affirmed in numerous treaties," declared "that they accept the Statute (defined by art. 1) on the Régime of Navigable Waterways of International Concern" and this Statute "constitutes an integral part of the Convention."
Signed the same day was the Additional Protocol to the Convention with reservation by Belgium, Czechoslovakia, Denmark, Finland, Spain, Sweden and the UK.

LNTS, Vol. 7, pp. 65 and 67.

WATER WORLD CONFERENCE, 1977. ▷ Mar del Plata, Water World Plan of Action of, 1977.

WAT PHOU. A famous temple of the Khmer Empire in Laos on the Mekong River, included in the World Heritage List, 1987.

UN Chronicle, November, 1987.

WAWEL ARRAS COLLECTION. A tapestry collection of about 350 pieces, purchased by Polish King Sigismund Augustus in Flanders (1548–67). The tapestry consists of biblical scenes, landscapes and other scenes. Of these 156 were saved after the Swedish wars. They were subject of international disputes. In 1795 they were removed to Russia, 136 were returned to Poland by the Soviet authorities 1921–25, in compliance with the Riga Treaty, Mar. 18, 1921. In Sept., 1939 they were brought to France, and in June, 1940 to Montreal, Canada, whose government refused to return the tapestry to Poland until 1961, when they were returned to Wawel Palace in Cracow.

M. MORELOWSKI, *Arrasy Zygmunta Augusta*, Cracow, 1929; S. LORENTZ, *Canada Refuses to Return Polish Cultural Treasures*, Warsaw, 1949.

WEAPONS, INJURIOUS. An international term for all incendiary conventional weapons, landmines, booby-traps and similar devices. Subject of a UN Conference on Excessively Injurious Conventional Weapons held in Geneva from Sept. 16 to Oct. 10, 1980. The Conference called for broad measures of protection for Civilians and the outlawing of especially harmful and inhuman weapons of war.

UN Chronicle, December, 1980, pp. 16–17.

WEATHER FORECASTS. A subject of intergovernmental convention and research. Organization reg. with the UIA:

European Center for Medium Range Weather Forecast, f. Oct. 23, 1973, by a Convention signed by the governments of Belgium, France, Finland, FRG, Greece, Italy, Luxembourg, the Netherlands, Portugal, Spain, Sweden, Switzerland, the UK and Yugoslavia. Headquarters in Bracknell, Berks, UK.

Yearbook of International Organizations.

WEEDS. A subject of international research. Organizations reg. with the UIA:

Asian Pacific Weed Science Society, f. 1967, Honolulu. Publ.: *Newsletter*.
European Weed Research Society, f. 1959, Amsterdam. Publ.: *Weed Research* (bimonthly in English, French and German).

Yearbook of International Organizations.

WEEKLY REST. A subject of an international convention adopted by the ILO General Conference on Nov. 17, 1921, introducing the following principle (art. 2):

"The whole personnel employed in an industrial establishment, public or private, should benefit in each seven-day period from at least 24 hours of uninterrupted rest, under the stipulations provided for in articles that follow. The rest should be granted, if possible, to the whole personnel at a time. It should fall, if possible, on days honored by tradition, national or regional customs."

Exceptions are allowed in the convention for economic and humanitarian reasons, however, upon consultation of competent workers' and employers' organizations where they exist.

Conventions and Recommendations adopted by the ILO Conferences 1919–66, Geneva 1966.

WEHRMACHT. German: "defense force." The official name for the whole of the armed forces of the German Third Reich (except the army of the SS – Waffen SS), introduced Mar. 16, 1935 under the law on universal compulsory military service, which was a unilateral violation of the military clauses of the Versailles Treaty. The predecessor of the Wehrmacht was the 100,000 professional cadre called Reichswehr. From May 21, 1935 to Apr. 30, 1945 the supreme commander of Wehrmacht was A. Hitler, and then until May 8, 1945 Admiral K. von Doenitz. The International Military Tribunal at the Nuremberg Trial confirmed the guilt of accused leaders of Wehrmacht (Marshall Goering, Generals Keitl and Jodl and Admiral Doenitz) without recognizing – against the protest of the Soviet members of the Tribunal – either the Supreme Command or the General Staff as criminal organizations. The Tribunal explained that participation in the work of these institutions did not prejudge participation in criminal actions, but their members could be brought on charges involving individual judicial responsibility. In the trials of war criminals before American military tribunals 1947–48, 24 field-marshals and generals were charged, of whom four were sentenced to life imprisonment and 15 to long jail terms (all of them were released early). Before sentencing, suicide was committed by 64 generals of the land armies, 16 generals of the Luftwaffe, 12 generals of the Waffen SS, and 11 vice-admirals and rear-admirals.

R. ABSALON, *Wehrgesetz und Wehrmacht 1933–1945*, Doppard am Rhein, 1969; S. DATNER, *Crimes against Prisoners of War. Responsibility of the Wehrmacht*, Warsaw, 1980; M. COOPER, *The German Army 1833–1945. Its Political and Military Failure*, New York, 1984.

WEIGHT LIFTING. Olympic sport since 1920, organized by the International Federation of Weight Lifting, Federation Haltérophile Internationale, FHI, founded in 1920.

Yearbook of International Organizations.

WEIGHTS AND MEASURES, INTERNATIONAL BUREAU OF. The Bureau was est. on May 20, 1878, as an organ of the Metric Convention of May 20, 1875, revised and amended by Regulations of Oct. 6, 1921; headquarters in Sèvres near Paris has eight laboratories for comparisons of national standards with international standards of: length, mass, temperature, acceleration of gravity, voltage, resistance, photometry and ionizing radiation. In keeping with art. 6 of the Convention, the International Bureau of Weights and Measures deals with:

"(1) any comparison and checking of new prototypes of meter and kilogram. (2) storage of international standards. (3) periodical comparison of national standards with international prototypes and their copies as well as ordinary thermometers. (4) comparison of new prototypes with basic standards of metric measures used in various countries and sciences. (5) standardizing and comparing land-surveying instruments. (6) comparison of exact standard and scales by request of governments, scientific association or even artists and scholars."

The principal organ of the Convention and the Bureau is the General Conference of Weights and Measurements whose participants are all members of the Convention; the Conference is convened at least once every 6 years and elects the 18 members of the International Committee of Weights and Measurements which meets annually in Sèvres. The committee appoints the Director of the Bureau.

The International Bureau of Weights and Measurements in 1949 concluded an agreement on co-operation with UNESCO in 1961, with Euratom in 1965 and in 1967 with IAEA. Publ.: *Comptes Rendus de Conférences Générales des Poids et Mesures; Procés verbaux des séances du comité International des Poids et Mesures; Travaux et Mémoires du PIPM*. ▷ Metric system.

Ch. E. GUILLAUME, *La création du Bureau International des Poids et Mesures et son oeuvre*, Paris, 1927.

WEI-HAI-WEI. A Chinese seaport in Shantung province, part of the Wei-Hai-Wei Territory, leased 1898–1930 by Great Britain.

WEIMAR. A historical German city in the Erfurt district, GDR, on the Ilm River. The intellectual center of Europe during Goethe's residence in Weimar 1775–1832; the site of Constitutional National Assembly of Germany, 1919, which established the republican system, called the Weimar Republic. Occupied on Apr. 11, 1945 by US troops. The German population of Weimar, men and women aged from 18 to 45, were ordered by American command on Apr. 16, 1945 to make a pilgrimage to the concentration camp of ▷ Buchenwald near Weimar, in which about 56,000 persons were murdered by the Nazis.

W. BARTEL (ed.), *Buchenwald*, Berlin, 1983, pp. 640–641.

WELFARE STATE. An international term for the states with organized assistance for the needy (▷ Social International Welfare); after World War II a common name for the Scandinavian states.

R.R. FRIEDMAN ed., *Modern Welfare States: A Comparative View of Trends and Prospects*, Brighton, UK, 1987; N. JOHNSON, *The Welfare State in Transition: The Theory and Practice of Welfare Pluralism*, Brighton, UK, 1987.

WELLINGTON AIR SERVICES AGREEMENT, 1949. The inter-governmental agreement between Australia, New Zealand and UK for the continued operation of regular air services between Australia and New Zealand by Pasman Empire Airways Ltd., signed on Sept. 15, 1949 in Wellington.

UNTS, Vol. 53, pp. 235–239.

WEST AFRICAN CONFERENCE, 1978. A summit meeting, Mar. 18–19, 1978, in the capital of Liberia, Monrovia, of the heads of government of five West African states: Gambia, Guinea, Liberia, Senegal and the Ivory Coast. At the conference the Ivory Coast, Guinea and Senegal decided to bury their old disagreements and develop broad co-operation in the spirit of the Treaty on the Economic Community of West Africa.

KEESING's *Contemporary Archive*, 1978.

WEST AFRICAN CUSTOMS AND ECONOMIC UNION, 1959. ▷ Economic Community of West African States, ECOWAS.

WEST AFRICAN DEVELOPMENT BANK. Banque ouest africaine de développement, BOAD, f. 1973, Lomé, Togo. The inter-governmental finance institutions of Benin, Ivory Coast (now Côte d'Ivoire), Niger, Senegal, Togo and Upper Volta (now Burkina Faso).

WEST AFRICAN ECONOMIC COMMUNITY, 1959–75. Est. in Ougadougou as the Customs Union of West African Countries (Ivory Coast, Mali, Mauritania, Niger, Senegal and Upper Volta) 1959; new name from May, 1970, after the intergovernmental agreement, signed in Accra May 4, 1967 by the governments of Benin, Gambia, Guinea, Ivory Coast, Liberia, Mali, Mauritania, Niger, Nigeria, Senegal, Sierra Leone, Togo and Upper Volta (now Burkina Faso), to promote through the economic co-operation of the Member States a co-ordinated and equitable development of their economies, especially in industry, agriculture, transport and communications, trade and payments, manpower, energy and natural resources (art. 1a).

The Access agreement revised by the Abidjan Treaty, 1973; came into force Jan. 1, 1974. In May, 1975 members of the Community signed the Lagos Treaty establishing the Economic Community of West African States, ECOWAS.

UNTS, Vol. 595, p. 288.

WEST BANK. A part of Palestine in the Jordan Valley on the West Bank of the Jordan River; since 1967 occupied by Israel; subject of disputes between the Arab States and Israel in the UN General Assembly and UN Security Council; subject of Egyptian-Israeli discussions, after the Camp David talks, 1979–80.

The West Bank was until 1917 part of the Ottoman Empire and since 1922 part of the League of Nations Palestinian mandate, administered until 1948 by Great Britain. On Sept. 20, 1948 an independent West Bank Palestinian Government was proclaimed by the Mufti of Jerusalem, but on Oct. 1, 1948 at the Jericho Conference the Arab West Bank's notables decided to merge with Jordan and proclaimed Jordan's King as the sovereign of Arab Palestine. The decision was affirmed by the Trans-Jordanian Parliament on Dec. 13, 1948. The West Bank was incorporated by Jordan until the 1967 Arab-Israeli War, when Israel occupying the region claimed that the status of the West Bank was never defined in international law and 1948 proclamations were never recognized by the international community.

The Right of Self-Determination of the Palestinian People, UN, New York, 1978; A. GERSON, *Israel, the West Bank and International Law*, London, 1978; *UN Chronicle*, April, 1979, pp. 5–15 and 73–92; *UN Chronicle*, June, 1983, p. 7 and March 1984, p. 26; J. LEDERMAN, Dateline West Bank: Interpreting the Intifada, in: *Foreign Policy, Fall, 1988*.

WESTERN EUROPEAN UNION, WEU. Intergovernmental institution, based on the ▷ Brussels Treaty, 1948, est. in 1955 in London. Members: the Governments of Belgium, France, FRG, Italy, Luxembourg, the Netherlands and the UK. Aims: co-ordinate the defence policy and equipment of the Member States and co-operate in political, social, legal and cultural affairs. Organization: The council of WEU in London (the Foreign Ministers or the Ambassadors resident in London) charged with co-operation with NATO; and in Paris: the Agency for the Control of Armaments, Standing Armaments Committee, Assembly and Permanent Committees of the Assembly (Defence Questions, General Affairs, Budgetary Affairs, Rules of Procedure and Relations with Parliaments). Publ. in English and French *Proceedings of the WEU Assembly*.
On the 30th Anniversary of the WEU, the Foreign Ministers of Member States decided in Rome on Oct. 27, 1984, to reform the structure of the WEU.

Yearbook of International Organizations.

WESTERN SAHARA. An African territory, 1912–76 Spanish protectorate. Area: 266,769 sq. km. Population 1979 est.: 165,000; 1970 census: 76,425 (Saharans 59,777 and European 16,658). Capital: Laayoune with 24,048 inhabitants 1970. International relations: the territory was a subject of dispute between Morocco and Spain from 1957 to 1976; in 1972 Morocco attempted to annex Spanish Sahara. In 1974 the International Court of Justice and the UN Decolonization Committee demanded self-determination right for the Spanish Sahara population. On Nov. 14, 1975 Spain signed in Madrid an agreement with Morocco and Mauritania on the transfer of power to them over Western Sahara. On Jan. 12, 1976 the Spanish Army left Western Sahara, and Morocco and Mauritania on Feb. 28, 1976 took over the country.

Protests against the partition of Western Sahara were made by Algeria and the people of the territory organized by a Liberation Movement called Frente ▷ Polisario, which proclaimed on Feb. 27, 1976 the Sahrawi Arab Democratic Republic. In Aug., 1979 Mauritania ceded its part of Western Sahara, and the area was occupied by Moroccan troops. The military conflict between Morocco and Polisario troops has not been resolved until spring 1985.

UN Chronicle, January, 1979, p. 41; V. THOMPSON, R. ADLOFF, *The Western Saharans. Background to Conflict*, London, 1980; M. BARBIER, *Le conflit du Sahara Occidental*, Paris, 1982; *The Europa Year Book 1984. A World Survey*, Vol. II, pp. 2068–2071, London, 1984.

WESTERN SAMOA. Member of the UN. Western part of a chain of volcanic islands in the South Pacific. ▷ Samoa. Area: 2831 sq. km. Pop. 1981 census: 156,349. Two main islands: Savau'i (1708 sq. km with 43,150 inhabitants). Capital and chief port: Apia in Upolu with 33,170 inhabitants 1981. Official languages: Samoan and English. Currency: one tala = 100 cents. GNP per capita 1976: USA $350. National Day: January 1, Independence Day, 1962.
Member of the UN since Dec. 15, 1976. Member of FAO, UNESCO, IDA, ITU, IFAD, WHO, IBRD, IMF and IFC. Member of the Commonwealth and is an ACP state of the EEC.
International relations: since 1861 under informal protection of Germany, Great Britain and the United States until 1899, during which Samoa was divided into ▷ American Samoa and the German protectorate of Western Samoa, by a tripartite treaty. Occupied by New Zealand in Sept., 1914 and administered by New Zealand 1920–45 under a League of Nations Mandate and, 1946–61, under a UN Trusteeship Agreement of Dec. 13, 1946. In May, 1961 the population voted under UN supervision in favor of independence, which took effect on Jan. 1, 1962.
In monetary union with New Zealand. Under the terms of a treaty with New Zealand, signed on Aug. 1, 1962, New Zealand represents Western Samoa in all foreign and diplomatic relations with exception of the United Nations. A signatory of the Lomé Convention of 1975 and of 1980.

UNTS, Vol. 8, pp. 71–89; J.W. FOX (ed.) *Western Samoa*, Auckland, 1963; *The Economy of Western Samoa*, 1968; *Economic Prospects of Western Samoa*, Auckland, 1978; *The Europa Year Book 1984. A World Survey*, Vol. II, pp. 2697–2700, London, 1984.

WESTERN TASMANIA WILDERNESS. The Australian natural site included in the ▷ World Heritage UNESCO List.

WESTERPLATTE. The trans-shipping port of Gdansk, located on the Bay of Gdansk at the mouth of the Vistula, 1921–39, subject of Polish-German conflicts and disputes. The LN Council on June 22, 1921 granted Poland the right by virtue of the statute of the Free City of Gdansk to install there a trans-shipping ammunition station for Polish warships and to quarter a garrison company, confirmed Dec. 7, 1925. The dispute on the limits of the Polish zone again arose in 1927 and was resolved on the recommendations of the LN Council by an agreement on Aug. 4, 1928. The LN Council on Mar. 14, 1933 granted Poland the right to strengthen its garrison at Westerplatte, which with 182 men, reinforced with heavy infantry weapons, became the objective of the shelling on Sept. 1, 1939 by the German Battleship *Schleswig-Holstein*, which began World War II.

Monthly Summary of the League on Nations, 1921–28 and 1933; Z. FLISOWSKI, *Westerplatte*, Warsaw, 1968.

WEST INDIES. The archipelago between North and South America, from Florida to the coast of Venezuela in the Caribbean Sea and the Gulf of Mexico, 4020 km long, includes the independent states of Barbados, Cuba, Haiti, the Dominican Republic, Jamaica, the Bahama Islands, Trinidad and Tobago; and the dependencies: the Netherlands Antilles, Puerto Rico, the Venezuelan Antilles, the US Virgin Islands and the overseas departments of France.

WEST INDIES ASSOCIATED STATES. A British administrative unit since 1967 of Caribbean self-governing islands: Antigua, St Kitts-Nevis-Anguilla, Dominica, St Lucia, Grenada and St Vincent. Member of the Caribbean Free Trade Area (CARIFTA now CARICOM). Responsibility for defence and foreign policy rests with the British Government.

SIR A. BURNS, *History of the British West Indies*, London, 1965; J. MORDECAI, *The West Indies*, London, 1968; SIR F. PHILIPPS, *Freedom in the Caribbean*, London, 1977.

WEST INDIES COMPANY. The Dutch commercial association for direct trade with the Caribbean, North America, South America and West Africa, 1621–1794; founded in New Amsterdam, presently New York.

WEST INDIES FEDERATION. The Federation of British Territories in the West Indies archipelago: Antigua, St Kitts-Nevis-Anguilla, Dominica, Grenada, Jamaica, St Lucia, St Vincent and Trinidad and Tobago, established on Jan. 3, 1958, dissolved in 1962 after Jamaica and Trinidad and Tobago had opted out of independence.

SIR A. BURNS, *History of the British West Indies*, London, 1965.

WESTMINSTER. The City of Westminster, a division of the historical center of London, after which the Westminster Statutes of British Commonwealth Dominions were named, elaborated by the Imperial Conference which convened in 1926 and 1930, and adopted by the British Parliament in 1931.

WESTMINSTER STATUTE, 1931. An Act of the Commonwealth to give effect to certain resolutions passed by Imperial Conferences held in the years 1926 and 1930. The Statute adopted by the Imperial Conference held at Westminster on Dec. 11, 1930, reads as follows:

"Whereas the delegates of His Majesty's Governments in the United Kingdom, the Dominion of Canada, the Commonwealth of Australia, the Dominion of New Zealand, the Union of South Africa, the Irish Free State and Newfoundland, at Imperial Conferences holden at Westminster in the years of our Lord nineteen hundred and twenty-six and nineteen hundred and thirty did concur in making the declarations and resolutions set forth in the Reports of the said Conferences:
And whereas it is meet and proper to set out by way of preamble to this Act that, inasmuch as the Crown is the symbol of the free association of the members of the British Commonwealth of Nations, and as they are united by a common allegiance to the Crown, it would be in accord with the established constitutional position of all the members of the Commonwealth in relation to one another that any alteration in the law touching the Succession to the Throne or the Royal Style and Titles shall hereafter require the assent as well of the Parliaments of all the Dominions as of the Parliament of the United Kingdom:

And whereas it is in accord with the established constitutional position that no law hereafter made by the Parliament of the United Kingdom shall extend to any of the said Dominions as part of the law of that Dominion otherwise than at the request and with the consent of that Dominion:

And whereas it is necessary for the ratifying, confirming and establishing of certain of the said declarations and resolutions of the said Conferences that a law be made and enacted in due form by authority of the Parliament of the United Kingdom:

And whereas the Dominion of Canada, the Commonwealth of Australia, the Dominion of New Zealand, the Union of South Africa, the Irish Free State and Newfoundland have severally requested and consented to the submission of a measure to the Parliament of the United Kingdom for making such provision with regard to the matters aforesaid as is hereafter in this Act contained:

Now, therefor, be it enacted by the King's Most Excellent Majesty by and with the advice and consent of the Lords Spiritual and Temporal, and Commons, in this present Parliament assembled, and by authority of the same, as follows:

1. In this Act the expression 'Dominion' means any of the following Dominions, that is to say, the Dominion of Canada, the Commonwealth of Australia, the Dominion of New Zealand, the Union of South Africa, the Irish Free State and Newfoundland.

2.(1) The Colonial Law Validity Act, 1865, shall not apply to any law made after the Commencement of this Act by the Parliament of a Dominion.

(2) No law and no provision of any law made after the commencement of this Act by the Parliament of a Dominion shall be void or inoperative on the ground that it is repugnant to the law of England, or to the provisions of any existing or future Act of Parliament of the United Kingdom, or to any order, rule or regulation made and any such Act, and powers of the Parliament of a Dominion shall include the power to repeal or amend any such Act, order, rule or regulation in so far as the same is part of the law of the Dominion.

3. It is hereby declared and enacted that the Parliament of a Dominion has full power to make laws having extra-territorial operation.

4. No Act of Parliament of the United Kingdom passed after the commencement of this Act shall extend, or be deemed to extend, to a Dominion as part of the law of that Dominion, unless it is expressly declared in that Act that that Dominion has requested, and consented to, the enactment thereof.

5. Without prejudice to the generality of the foregoing provisions of this Act, sections seven hundred and thirty-five and seven hundred and thirty-six of the Merchant Shipping Act, 1949, shall be construed as though reference therein to the Legislature of a British possession did not include reference to the Parliament of a Dominion.

6. Without prejudice to the generality of the foregoing provisions of this Act, section four of the Colonial Courts of Admiralty Act, 1890 (which requires certain laws to be reserved for the signification of His Majesty's pleasure or to contain a suspending clause), and so much of section seven of the Act as requires the approval of His Majesty in Council to any rules of Court for regulating the practice and procedure of a Colonial Court of Admiralty, shall cease to have effect in any Dominion as from the commencement of this Act.

7.(1) Nothing in this Act shall be deemed to apply to the repeal, amendment or alteration of the British North American Acts, 1867 to 1930, or any order, rule or regulation made thereunder.

(2) The provisions of section two of this Act shall extend to laws made by any of the Provinces of Canada and to the powers of the legislatures of such Provinces.

(3) The powers conferred by this Act upon the Parliament of Canada or upon the legislatures of the Provinces shall be restricted to the enactment of laws in relation to matters within the competence of the Parliament of Canada or of any of the legislatures of the Provinces respectively.

8. Nothing in this Act shall be deemed to confer any power to repeal or alter the Constitution or the Constitution Act of the Commonwealth of Australia or the Constitution Act of the Dominion of New Zealand otherwise than in accordance with the law existing before the commencement of this Act.

9.(1) Nothing in this Act shall be deemed to authorize the Parliament of the Commonwealth of Australia to make laws on any matter within the authority of the States of Australia, not being a matter within the authority of the Parliament or Government of the Commonwealth of Australia.

(2) Nothing in this Act shall be deemed to require the concurrence of the Parliament of Government of the Commonwealth of Australia in any law made by the Parliament of the United Kingdom with respect to any matter within the authority of the States of Australia, not being a matter within the authority of the Parliament or Government of the Commonwealth of Australia, in any case where it would have commencement of this Act that the Parliament of the United Kingdom should made that law without such concurrence.

(3) In the application of this Act to the Commonwealth of Australia the request and consent referred to in section four shall mean the request and consent of the Parliament and Government of the Commonwealth.

10.(1) None of the following sections of this Act, that is to say, sections two, three, four, five and six, shall extend to a Dominion unless that section is adopted by the Parliament of the Dominion, and any Act of that Parliament adopting any section of this Act may provide that the adoption shall have effect either from the commencement of this Act or from such later date as is specified in the adopting Act.

(2) The Parliament of any such Dominion as aforesaid may at any time revoke the adoption of any section referred to in sub-section (1) of this section.

(3) The Dominions to which this section applies are the Commonwealth of Australia, the Dominion of New Zealand and Newfoundland.

11. Notwithstanding anything in the Interpretation Act, 1889, the expression "Colony" shall not, in any Act of the Parliament of the United Kingdom passed after the commencement of this Act, include a Dominion or any Province or State forming part of a Dominion.

12. This Act may be cited as the Statute of Westminster, 1931."

H.D. HALL, *Commonwealth: A History of the British Commonwealth of Nations*, New York, 1971.

WESTPHALIA PEACE, 1648. A peace negotiated after the Thirty Years War at the Congress of Westphalia in two cities of Westphalia: in Münster – between the German Reich and France; in Osnabrück – between the German Reich and Sweden; composed of two documents: Instrumentum Pacis Osnabrugense and Instrumentum Pacis Monasteriense. The signatories of the peace in Osnabrück were Emperor Ferdinand III and Queen Kristina of Sweden along with her German allies; in Münster, Emperor Ferdinand III and King Louis XIV of France. Also signing both treaties were representatives of France, Spain and Venice. Protesting and condemning both treaties in the name of Pope Innocent X was Cardinal Fabio Chigi. Ratified by the signatories in October and December 1648, it restored religious peace between Catholics and Protestants to the Habsburg Reich which earlier had been established under the Augsburg Religious Peace, 1555; opened a new period of history for Central Europe.

J. DUMONT, *Corps Universel diplomatic du droit des gens*, Amsterdam, 1726–31, Vol. 6, p. 450; *Bullarum Magnum Romanorum*, Turin, 1857, Vol. 15, p. 603.

WEST PRUSSIA. A historical region of North Poland, on the Baltic Sea between Pomerania and East Prussia. After the Polish partition of 1772 and 1793 part of Prussia until 1919. Divided by the Treaty of Versailles into four administrative units: the Free City of Gdansk (Danzig), part of the Prussian new province of Grenzmark–Prosen–Westpreussen, part of Polish province Pomorze, and the district of West Prussia in the province of East Prussia. Unified Sept., 1939 by war annexation of the whole territory, returned to Poland by the Potsdam Agreement on Aug. 2, 1945.

J. ANGEL, *La Pologne et la Prusse–Orientale*, Paris, 1933.

WETBACKS. American term for Mexican seasonal workers the majority of whom come to the USA illegally by crossing the Rio Grande River. See also ▷ Hispanic Population in the USA.

WEU. ▷ Western European Union.

WFC. ▷ World Food Council.

WFP. ▷ World Food Program.

WHALES. A subject of international conventions and co-operation for the protection of whales against destruction by poachers. The First International Convention on Limiting Whale Catches was signed on Sept. 24, 1931 in Geneva. The International agreement for the Regulation of Whaling was signed by Australia, Canada, Denmark, France, the Netherlands, New Zealand, Norway, South Africa, UK and USA on June 8, 1937 in London, amended by two protocols signed on June 24, 1939 and Nov. 26, 1945 in London. The Second International Whaling Convention, signed on Dec. 2, 1946 in Washington came into force Nov. 10, 1948; its organ is the London International Whaling Commission whose members are the governments of Argentina, Australia, Brazil, Denmark, France, Great Britain, Iceland, Japan, the Netherlands, South Africa, Sweden the USA and USSR. The Commission closely co-operates with the International Bureau of Whaling Statistics, est. 1929, in Sanderfjord (Norway), and with the International Council for the Exploitation of the Seas. Publ.: *Annual Report*. The UN Stockholm Conference on Environmental Protection in June 1972 adopted resolutions to suspend whale catches for a period of 10 years. The world whale catch fell from 65,641 in the season 1960–61 to 37,889 in 1970–71. In June, 1975 the XXVII Session of the International Whaling Commission in Washington determined to further limit catches. A ban on commercial whaling was passed in 1982 and 1988. On April 15, 1985 Japan decided to end commercial whaling from April 1, 1988. On July 16, 1985, the USSR announced the end of commercial whaling in the Atlantic for the 1987–1988 season. On May 25, 1987 the USSR has announced that it is halting commercial whaling.

Since the end of the 1987 season Norway stopped commercial whaling, catches would be made only for research purposes.

J.T. JENKINS, *A History of the Whale Fisheries*, London, 1921; *LNTS*, Vol. CXC, p. 79; *LNTS*, Vol. XCVI, p. 131; *UNTS*, Vol. 11, pp. 43–57; N.A. MACKINTOSH, *The Stocks of Whales*, London, 1965; KEESING's *Contemporary Archive*, June 1985, August, 1985; *Yearbook of International Organizations, 1986/87; The Europa Yearbook 1988. A World Survey*, Vol. I, London, 1988; Controversial "Scientific Whaling", in: KEESING's *Record of World Events*, April, 1988.

WHEAT. One of the main food resources of the world, along with rice the main weapon in the World Campaign against Hunger; subject of international conventions. Main producers: USA, China, USSR, Canada, France, Italy, India, Turkey, Argentina, Mexico, Australia, Spain, FRG, Great Britain.

The world annual production in the years 1948–52 averaged 171 million tons, 1960 – 242 million tons, 1970 – 318 million tons. The first International Wheat Conference was held in London, Oct.

28–Nov. 6, 1918. The International Agricultural Conference in Warsaw in Aug., 1930 postulated the need for the institutionalization of special conferences on wheat. In Mar.–Apr., 1931 the International Wheat Conference was held in Rome under LN auspices, and in London in Aug., 1933; and drafted the International Convention on Wheat Levies, Export and Prices, whose organ was the International Wheat Council; modified 1942. After World War II the governments of the wheat exporting states – Argentina, Australia, Canada, France, Italy, Mexico, Spain, Sweden, USA and USSR – as well as 37 importing states participated in an International Wheat Conference in Mar., 1948 in Washington and subsequently 42 states on July 1, 1949 in Washington signed the International Wheat Agreement, prepared under the FAO International Wheat Convention; administered by the International Wheat Council. Since 1956 the Council under UN auspices organizes every three years the UN Wheat Conference in Geneva which modifies the convention for the next three years. In July, 1967, after the signing of the Kennedy round treaties, a new convention was drafted on the initiative of GATT which in 1968 superseded the previous one, modified in 1965. On Feb. 20, 1971 the next conference in Geneva ratified the new International Wheat Agreement for the years 1971–74 between 9 exporting and 39 importing countries; agreement extended together with the Convention on Food Assistance in 1974, 1976, 1978, 1980 and 1983. Headquarters of the Council is London. Publ.: *Review of the World Wheat Situation*, *World Wheat Situation*, and *Annual Report* for the crop year 1949–50 and succeeding years. In Mexico the International Center for Improving Corn and Wheat operating under FAO auspices, Centro Internacional de Mejoramiento de Maiz y Trigo, in the years 1960–63 cultivated a dwarf wheat strain able to bear the weight of unusually heavy ears, resistant to wheat rot and other diseases, yielding more than 60 quintals per hectare. Varieties of this wheat, called Larma, Mayo, Rojo, and Sonora, were sent to India to start the "green revolution" there; in the years 1964–68 the area planted with "Mexican" wheat was increased to 2 million hectares in the main agricultural province of Punjab. Afghanistan, Turkey and Pakistan followed India's example. The American scientist in charge of the Mexican Center, Prof. N. Borland (1966), under whose supervision the "Mexican" strain was cultivated by a system of gamma rays, received the Nobel Prize in 1970. The FAO annual World Catalogue of Genetic Wheat Stocks provides information on the world resources of wheat.
Organization reg. with the UIA:

International Maize and Wheat Improvement Centre, f. 1966, Mexico DF; to develop varieties and techniques for improved production of maize, wheat, triticalo and barley in the developing countries.

UNTS, Vol. 7, pp. 331–341; M. AN-GELARIBE, *La Révolution Agricole*, Paris, 1957; *UN Review*, April, 1959, January, 1962, April, 1962; *Situación y Perspectivas del Trigo en los paises de la ALALC*, Buenos Aires, 1969; W.R. AYKROD, J. DOUGHTY, *What is Human Nutrition?* Rome, 1970; *Notas sobre la economia y el desarrollo de América Latina*, CEPAL, No. 78, Junio 16, 1971; *UN Chronicle*, April, 1978, p. 63. *The International Wheat Agreement*, Washington, DC, 1979; *The Europa Yearbook 1988. A World Survey, Vol. I*, London, 1988.

WHITE BOOK. An international term adopted for collections of documents published for diplomatic purposes, the name depending on the color of the binding; initiated by Great Britain's Blue Books, mid-19th century; France followed with Les Jaune Livres, Germany with Weissbuch, Italy – Libro Verde, etc. In the first years of World War I the

Great Powers started to publish collections of documents, presenting the diplomatic negotiations before entering the war; the German and English with the name White Papers, the Russian Orange Paper, the Gray Paper – Belgium, the Yellow Book – France, Green Book – Italy and Austria. Hungary the Red Book. All the Papers and Books, full text translated from the original, were published in 1915 by the *New York Times*. After the Reichstag fire, Feb. 29, 1933, anti-Nazi centers in France published a Braunesbuch. During World Wars I and II, Korean and Vietnam wars it became a custom to publish documents on war crimes in black covers, as Black Books.

CARNEGIE ENDOWMENT, "Official documents regarding the European War", in: *International Conciliation*, New York, 1914–18.

WHITE HOUSE. A common international term for the home of the US President in Washington, DC (indirectly for US policies), constructed 1792–1800 on Pennsylvania Avenue opposite Lafayette Square, burned down by the British army 1814, and after reconstruction the previously gray building was painted white and since then is commonly called White House. The US President Theodore Roosevelt was the first to introduce, 1901, the term White House as an official name in presidential government documents and also foreign correspondence.

"WHITE RUSSIANS". ▷ Byezhentsy.

WHITING. A fish, *Gadus Merlangus*, protected by international Conventions. (▷ Fishery.)
UNTS, Vol. 231, p. 199.

WHO. World Health Organization; Organisation Mondiale de la Santé, OMS; Organización Mundial de la Salud, OMS; Vsiermirnaya Organizatsya Zdravokhronieniya, VOZ; est. July 22, 1946 by adoption of the ▷ WHO Constitution by the 61 State inter-governmental conference convened by the ECOSOC. On Apr. 7, 1948 the Constitution came into force; WHO on Sept. 1, 1948 took over the functions of Office International d'Hygiene Publique, League of Nations Health Organization, and the peace time aspects of the work of Health Division of UNRRA. The main organs of WHO are the World Health Assembly (annual) composed of delegations representing all member States with the Executive Board and Secretariat in Geneva and Regional Offices in Alexandria, Brazzaville, Copenhagen, Manilla, New Delhi and Washington, DC (Pan American Sanitary Bureau). WHO's headquarters are in Geneva, but the activities of the organization have been largely decentralized to six regional organizations, each having a regional committee composed of government representatives of the countries in the region and a regional office.
Membership in WHO is open to all States. Members of the United Nations join WHO by accepting its Constitution; other States become members when the World Health Assembly has approved their application by a simple majority vote. Territories which are not responsible for the conduct of their international relations may become associate members. As of 1 Jan., 1985, WHO had 162 member states and two associate members.
In 1977 the General Assembly declared the goal of WHO and member nations to be the attainment by all peoples of a level of health that will permit them to lead a socially and economically productive life. A blueprint for health for all by the year 2000 was drawn up with special emphasis on the provision of primary health care, that is essential care made

universally accessible to the people by means acceptable to them, with their full participation and at a cost the community and country can afford. Nutrition, safe water supply, communicable disease control and research in applying the existing knowledge to the health problems of developing countries were identified in the blueprint as priority areas for action. The WHO provides worldwide services to promote health, co-operates with member countries in their health efforts, and co-ordinates biomedical research. Its services, which benefit all countries, include a day-to-day information service on the occurrence of internationally important diseases, publication of the international list of causes of diseases, injury and death, disseminating information on the effect on human health of environmental pollutants and laying global standards for antibiotics, vaccines, etc. Assistance rendered to individual countries at their request includes support for national programs to fight diseases, training health workers and strengthening health services.
In 1967 WHO started a global campaign to eradicate ▷ smallpox within 10 years. That year, 131,418 cases were reported in 43 countries; in 1984 the smallpox plague, according to the WHO, does not exist anymore.
A long-term program to immunize children in the developing countries against six diseases of childhood – diphtheria, tetanus, whooping cough, poliomyelitis, measles and tuberculosis – was developed during 1975 and 1976. WHO supported national tuberculosis control programs by means of regional and national seminars and training courses for key workers and teachers of auxiliary health personnel. Pulmonary tuberculosis is still widespread in the developing countries, there being an annual incidence of 200–350 cases per 100,000 inhabitants in some parts of Africa, Asia and Oceania. Even in some technically-advanced countries, where tuberculosis is considered rare, it causes more deaths than all other notifiable diseases combined.
Cholera continued to spread westward from the Far East, and in 1969 re-established itself in Africa where it had not been reported for about a century. The technique of treating dehydration in cholera and other acute diarrhoeal diseases by giving the patient an easily prepared solution to drink was a major advance. WHO and UNICEF launched campaigns to popularize the new treatment method. Support for research aimed at improving cholera vaccine continued. In 1974 it became clear that the global anti-malaria effort was not making the hoped-for progress. WHO assessed all anti-malaria programs and prepared guidelines for Governments to help them to evaluate and classify their malarious areas. In 1975 different objectives were adopted for different areas in accordance with their malaria situation and technical possibilities.
The International Health Regulations, which superseded the International Sanitary Regulations in 1969, were amended in 1973, to reflect the growth of epidemiological disease surveillance on an international scale, and to promote the development of integrated national surveillance services and better co-operation among countries.
Much of the WHO research program consists of the co-ordination and collaborative research involving research workers of member countries and national institutions, over 500 of which WHO has designated collaborating centres. In 1975–84 a special program for research and training in tropical diseases was initiated. It seeks to develop, through biomedical research, effective new techniques to attack six widespread tropical diseases: malaria, schistosomiasis, filariasis, trepanosomiasis, leprosy and leishmaniasis.

As for cancer, WHO concentrates on basic and clinical research and a standardization of terminology and cancer control services. Epidemiology and environmental research is undertaken by the International Agency for Cancer Research in Lyon, France, an autonomous body within the framework of WHO.

WHO information systems: Appropriate Technology for Health Information System, WHO–ATHIS and Clearing House or Ongoing Research in Cancer Epidemiology, WHO–IARCH/CH.

The WHO has published *Basic Documents* since 1950 in English, French, Russian, Spanish; *International Digest of Health Legislation* (quarterly, since 1948 in English and French), *World Health* (monthly, since 1957 in Arabic, English, French, German, Italian, Persian, Portuguese, Russian and Spanish); WHO Chronicle (monthly, since 1947 in Chinese, English, French, Russian and Spanish); *Manuals, WHO Statistics, Weekly Epidemiological Record* (since 1926 in English and French), *Bibliography of the WHO Publications, World Directories of Medical Schools.*

The First Ten Years of the WHO, Geneva, 1958; *The Second Ten Years of the WHO*, Geneva, 1968; *Everyone's United Nations*, UN, New York, 1979, pp. 360–363.

WHO CONSTITUTION. The Constitution establishing the ⟨?⟩ WHO, World Health Organization, was adopted by the UN Conference on July 22, 1946; entered into force on Sept. 1, 1948. The text amended by the WHO Conferences up to 1960 is as follows:

"The States Parties to this Constitution declare, in conformity with the Charter of the United Nations, that the following principles are basic to the happiness, harmonious relations and security of all peoples:
Health is a state of complete physical, mental and social well-being and not merely the absence of disease or infirmity.
The enjoyment of the highest attainable standard of health is one of the fundamental rights of every human being without distinction of race, religion, political belief, economic or social condition.
The health of all peoples is fundamental to the attainment of peace and security and is dependent upon the fullest co-operation of individuals and States.
The achievement of any State in the promotion and protection of health is of value to all.
Unequal development in different countries in the promotion of health and control of disease, especially communicable disease, is a common danger.
Healthy development of the child is of basic importance; the ability to live harmoniously in a changing total environment is essential to such development.
The extension to all peoples of the benefits of medical psychological and related knowledge is essential to the fullest attainment of health.
Informed opinion and active co-operation on the part of the public are of the utmost importance in the improvement of the health of the people.
Governments have a responsibility for the health of their peoples which can be fulfilled only by the provision of adequate health and social measures.
Accepting these principles, and for the purpose of co-operation among themselves and with others to promote and protect the health of all peoples, the Contracting Parties agree to the present Constitution and hereby establish the World Health Organization as a specialized agency within the terms of art. 57 of the Charter of the United Nations.
Chapter I – *Objective*
Art. 1. The objective of the World Health Organization (hereinafter called the Organization) shall be the attainment by all peoples of the highest possible level of health.
Chapter II – *Functions*
Art. 2. In order to achieve its objective, the functions of the Organization shall be:
(a) to act as the directing and co-ordinating authority on international health work;

(b) to establish and maintain effective collaboration with the United Nations, specialized agencies, governmental health administrations, professional groups and such other organizations as may be deemed appropriate;
(c) to assist Government, upon request, in strengthening health services;
(d) to furnish appropriate technical assistance and, in emergencies, necessary aid upon the request or acceptance of Governments;
(e) to provide or assist in providing, upon the request of the United Nations, health services and facilities to special groups, such as the peoples of trust territories;
(f) to establish and maintain such administrative and technical services as may be required, including epidemiological and statistical services;
(g) to stimulate and advance work to eradicate epidemic, endemic and other diseases;
(h) to promote, in co-operation with other specialized agencies where necessary, the prevention of accidental injuries;
(i) to promote, in co-operation with other specialized agencies where necessary, the improvement of nutrition, housing, sanitation, recreation, economic or working conditions and other aspects of environmental hygiene;
(j) to promote co-operation among scientific and professional groups which contribute to the advancement of health;
(k) to propose conventions, agreements and regulations, and make recommendations with respect to international health matters and to perform such duties as may be assigned thereby to the Organization and are consistent with its objective;
(l) to promote maternal and child health and welfare and to foster the ability to live harmoniously in a changing total environment;
(m) to foster activities in the field of mental health, especially those affecting the harmony of human relations;
(n) to promote and conduct research in the field of health;
(o) to promote improved standards of teaching and training in the health, medical and related professions;
(p) to study and report on, in co-operation with other specialized agencies where necessary, administrative and social techniques affecting public health and medical care from preventive and curative points of view, including hospital services and social security;
(q) to provide information, counsel and assistance in the field of health;
(r) to assist in developing an informed public opinion among all peoples on matters of health;
(s) to establish and revise as necessary international nomenclatures of diseases, of causes of death and of public health practices;
(t) to standardize diagnostic procedures as necessary;
(u) to develop, establish and promote international standards with respect to food, biological, pharmaceutical and similar products;
(v) generally to take all necessary action to attain the objective of the Organization.
Chapter III – *Membership and Associate Membership*
Art. 3. Membership in the Organization shall be open to all States.
Art. 4. Members of the United Nations may become Members of the Organization by signing or otherwise accepting this Constitution in accordance with the provisions of Chapter XIX and in accordance with their constitutional processes.
Art. 5. The States whose Governments have been invited to send observers to the International Health Conference held in New York, 1946, may become Members by signing or otherwise accepting this Constitution in accordance with the provisions of Chapter XIX and in accordance with their constitutional processes provided that such signature or acceptance shall be completed before the first session of the Health Assembly.
Art. 6. Subject to the conditions of any agreement between the United Nations and the Organization, approved pursuant to Chapter XVI, States which do not become Members in accordance with arts. 4 and 5 may apply to become Members and shall be admitted as Members when their application has been approved by a simple majority vote of the Health Assembly.
Art. 7. If a Member fails to meet its financial obligations to the Organization or in other exceptional circumstan-

ces, the Health Assembly may, on such conditions as it thinks proper, suspend the voting privileges and services to which a Member is entitled. The Health Assembly shall have the authority to restore such voting privileges and services.
Art. 8. Territories or groups of territories which are not responsible for the conduct of their international relations may be admitted as Associate Members by the Health Assembly upon application made on behalf of such territory or group of territories by the Member or other authority having responsibility for their international relations. Representatives of Associate Members to the Health Assembly should be qualified by their technical competence in the field of health and should be chosen from the native population. The nature and extent of the rights and obligations of Associate Members shall be determined by the Health Assembly.
Chapter IV – *Organs*
Art. 9. The work of the Organization shall be carried out by:
(a) The World Health Assembly (herein called the Health Assembly);
(b) The Executive Board (hereinafter called the Board);
(c) The Secretariat.
Chapter V – *The World Health Assembly*
Art. 10. The Health Assembly shall be composed of delegates representing Members.
Art. 11. Each Member shall be represented by not more than three delegates, one of whom shall be designated by the Member as chief delegate. These delegates should be chosen from among persons most qualified by their technical competence in the field of health, preferably representing the national health administration of the Member.
Art. 12. Alternates and advisers may accompany delegates.
Art. 13. The Health Assembly shall meet in regular annual session and in such special sessions as may be necessary. Special sessions shall be convened at the request of the Board or of a majority of the Members.
Art. 14. The Health Assembly, at each annual session, shall select the country or region in which the next annual session shall be held, the Board subsequently fixing the place. The Board shall determine the place where a special session shall be held.
Art. 15. The Board, after consultation with the Secretary-General of the United Nations, shall determine the date of each annual and special session.
Art. 16. The Health Assembly shall elect its President and other officers at the beginning of each annual session. They shall hold office until their successors are elected.
Art. 17. The Health Assembly shall adopt its own rules of procedure.
Art. 18. The functions of the Health Assembly shall be:
(a) to determine the policies of the Organization;
(b) to name the members entitled to designate a person to serve on the Board;
(c) to appoint the Director-General;
(d) to review and approve reports and activities of the Board and of the Director-General and to instruct the Board in regard to matters upon which action, study, investigation or report may be considered desirable;
(e) to establish such committees as may be considered necessary for the work of the Organization;
(f) to supervise the financial policies of the Organization and to review and approve the budget;
(g) to instruct the Board and the Director-General to bring to the attention of Members and of international organizations, governmental or non-governmental, any matter with regard to health which the Health Assembly may consider appropriate;
(h) to invite any organization, international or national, governmental or non-governmental, which has responsibilities related to those of the Organization, to appoint representatives to participate, without right of vote, in its meetings or in those of the committees and conferences convened under its authority, on conditions prescribed by the Health Assembly; but in the case of national organizations, invitations shall be issued only with the consent of the Government concerned;
(i) to consider recommendations bearing on health made by the General Assembly, the Economic and Social Council, the Security Council or Trusteeship Council of the United Nations, and to report to them

on the steps taken by the Organization to give effect to such recommendations;

(j) to report to the Economic and Social Council in accordance with any agreement between the Organization and the United Nations;

(k) to promote and conduct research in the field of health by the personnel of the Organization, by the establishment of its own institutions or by co-operation with official or non-official institutions of any Member with the consent of its Government;

(l) to establish such other institutions as it may consider desirable;

(m) to take any other appropriate action to further the objective of the Organization.

Art. 19. The Health Assembly shall have authority to adopt conventions or agreements with respect to any matter within the competence of the Organization. A two-thirds vote of the Health Assembly shall be required for the adoption of such conventions or agreements, which shall come into force for each Member when accepted by it in accordance with its constitutional processes.

Art. 20. Each Member undertakes that it will, within eighteen months after the adoption by the Health Assembly of a convention or agreement, take action relative to the acceptance of such convention or agreement. Each Member shall notify the Director-General of the action taken, and if it does not accept such convention or agreement within the time limit, it will furnish a statement of the reasons for non-acceptance. In case of acceptance, each Member agrees to make an annual report to the Director-General in accordance with Chapter XIV.

Art. 21. The Health Assembly shall have authority to adopt regulations concerning:

(a) sanitary and quarantine requirements and other procedures designed to prevent the international spread of disease;

(b) nomenclatures with respect to diseases, causes of death and public health practices;

(c) standards with respect to diagnostic procedures for international use;

(d) standards with respect to the safety, purity and potency of biological, pharmaceutical and similar products moving in international commerce;

(e) advertising and labelling of biological, pharmaceutical and similar products moving in international commerce.

Art. 22. Regulations adopted pursuant to art. 21 shall come into force for all Members after due notice has been given of their adoption by the Health Assembly except for such Members as may notify the Director-General of rejection or reservations within the period stated in the notice.

Art. 23. The Health Assembly shall have authority to make recommendations to Members with respect to any matter within the competence of the Organization.

Chapter VI – *The Executive Board*

Art. 24. The Board shall consist of twenty-four persons designated by as many Members. The Health Assembly, taking into account an equitable geographical distribution, shall elect the Members entitled to designate a person to serve on the Board. Each of these Members should appoint to the Board a person technically qualified in the field of health, who may be accompanied by alternates and advisers.

Art. 25. These Members shall be elected for three years and may be re-elected, provided that of the twelve Members elected at the first session of the Health Assembly held after the coming into force of the amendment to this Constitution increasing the membership of the Board from eighteen to twenty-four the terms of two Members shall be for one year and the terms of two Members shall be for two years, as determined by lot.

Art. 26. The Board shall meet at least twice a year and shall determine the place of each meeting.

Art. 27. The Board shall elect its Chairman from among its members and shall adopt its own rules of procedure.

Art. 28. The functions of the Board shall be:

(a) to give effect to the decisions and policies of the Health Assembly;

(b) to act as the executive organ of the Health Assembly;

(c) to perform any other functions entrusted to it by the Health Assembly;

(d) to advise the Health Assembly on questions referred to it by that body and on matters assigned to the Organization by conventions, agreements and regulations;

(e) to submit advice or proposals to the Health Assembly on its own initiative;

(f) to prepare the agenda of meetings of the Health Assembly;

(g) to submit to the Health Assembly for consideration and approval a general programme of work covering a specific period;

(h) to study all questions within its competence;

(i) to take emergency measures within the functions and financial resources of the Organization to deal with events requiring immediate action. In particular it may authorize the Director-General to take the necessary steps to combat epidemics, to participate in the organization of health relief to victims of a calamity and to undertake studies and research the urgency of which has been drawn to the attention of the Board by any Member or by the Director-General.

Art. 29. The Board shall exercise on behalf of the whole Health Assembly the powers delegated to it by that body.

Chapter VII – *The Secretariat*

Art. 30. The Secretariat shall comprise the Director-General and such technical and administrative staff as the Organization may require.

Art. 31. The Director-General shall be appointed by the Health Assembly on the nomination of the Board on such terms as the Health Assembly may determine. The Director-General, subject to the authority of the Board, shall be the chief technical and administrative officer of the Organization.

Art. 32. The Director-General shall be ex-officio Secretary of the Health Assembly, of the Board, of all commissions and committees of the Organization and of conferences convened by it. He may delegate these functions.

Art. 33. The Director-General or his representative may establish a procedure by agreement with Members, permitting him, for the purpose of discharging his duties, to have direct access to their various departments, especially to their health administrations and to national health organizations, governmental or non-governmental. He may also establish direct relations with international organizations whose activities come within the competence of the Organization. He shall keep regional offices informed on all matters involving their respective areas.

Art. 34. The Director-General shall prepare and submit annually to the Board the financial statements and budget estimates of the Organization.

Art. 35. The Director-General shall appoint the staff of the Secretariat in accordance with staff regulations established by the Health Assembly. The paramount consideration in the employment of the staff shall be to assure that the efficiency, integrity and internationally representative character of the Secretariat shall be maintained at the highest level. Due regard shall be paid also to the importance of recruiting the staff on as wide a geographical basis as possible.

Art. 36. The conditions of service of the staff of the Organization shall conform as far as possible with those of other United Nations organizations.

Art. 37. In the performance of their duties the Director-General and the staff shall not seek or receive instructions from any government or from any authority external to the Organization. They shall refrain from any action which might reflect on their position as international officers. Each Member of the Organization on its part undertakes to respect the exclusively international character of the Director-General and the staff and not to seek to influence them.

Chapter VIII – *Committees*

Art. 38. The Board shall establish such committees as the Health Assembly may direct and, on its own initiative or on the proposal of the Director-General, may establish any other committees considered desirable to serve any purpose within the competence of the Organization.

Art. 39. The Board, from time to time an in any event annually, shall review the necessity for continuing each committee.

Art. 40. The Board may provide for the creation of or the participation by the Organization in joint or mixed committees with other organizations and for the representation of the Organization in committees established by such other organizations.

Chapter IX – *Conferences*

Art. 41. The Health Assembly or the Board may convene local, general, technical or other special conference to consider any matter within the competence of the Organization and may provide for the representation at such conferences of international organizations and, with the consent of the Government concerned, of national organizations, governmental or non-governmental. The manner of such representation shall be determined by the Health Assembly or the Board.

Art. 42. The Board may provide for representation of the Organization at conferences in which the Board considers that the Organization has an interest.

Chapter X – *Headquarters*

Art. 43. The location of the headquarters of the Organization shall be determined by the Health Assembly after consultation with the United Nations.

Chapter XI – *Regional Arrangements*

Art. 44.(a) The Health Assembly shall from time to time define the geographical areas in which it is desirable to establish a regional organization.

(b) The Health Assembly may, with the consent of a majority of the Members situated within each area so defined, establish a regional organization to meet the special needs of such area.

Art. 45. Each regional organization shall be an integral part of the Organization in accordance with this Constitution.

Art. 46. Each regional organization shall consist of a regional committee and a regional office.

Art. 47. Regional committees shall be composed of representatives of the Member States and Associate Members in the region concerned. Territories or groups of territories within the region, which are not responsible for the conduct of their international relations and which are not Associate Members, shall have the right to be represented and to participate in regional committees. The nature and extent of the rights and obligations of these territories or groups of territories in regional committees shall be determined by the Health Assembly in consultation with the Member or other authority having responsibility for the international relations of these territories and with the Member States in the region.

Art. 48. Regional committees shall meet as often as necessary and shall determine the place of each meeting.

Art. 49. Regional committees shall adopt their own rules of procedure.

Art. 50. The functions of the regional committee shall be:

(a) to formulate policies governing matters of an exclusively regional character;

(b) to supervise the activities of the regional office;

(c) to suggest to the regional office the calling of technical conferences and such additional work or investigation in health matters as in the opinion of the regional committee would promote the objective of the Organization within the region;

(d) to co-operate with the respective regional committees of the United Nations and with those of other specialized agencies and with other regional international organizations having interests in common with the Organization;

(e) to tender advice, through the Director-General, to the Organization on international health matters which is wider than regional significance;

(f) to recommend additional regional appropriations by the Governments of the respective regions if the proportion of the central budget of the Organization allotted to that region is insufficient for the carrying-out of the regional functions;

(g) such other functions as may be delegated to the regional committee by the Health Assembly, the Board or the Director-General.

Art. 51. Subject to the general authority of the Director-General of the Organization, the regional office shall be the administrative organ of the regional committee. It shall, in addition, carry out within the region the decisions of the Health Assembly and of the Board.

Art. 52. The head of the regional office shall be the Regional Director appointed by the Board in agreement with the regional committee.

Art. 53. The staff of the regional office shall be appointed in a manner to be determined by agreement between the Director-General and the Regional Director.

Art. 54. The Pan American Sanitary Organization represented by the Pan American Sanitary Bureau and the Pan American Sanitary Conferences, and all other inter-governmental region health organizations in existence prior to the date of signature of this Constitution, shall in due course be integrated with the Organization. This integration shall be effected as soon as practicable through common action based on mutual consent of the competent authorities expressed through the organizations concerned.

Chapter XII – *Budget and Expenses*

Art. 55. The Director-General shall prepare and submit to the Board the annual budget estimates of the Organization. The Board shall consider and submit to the Health Assembly such budget estimates, together with any recommendations the Board may deem advisable.

Art. 56. Subject to any agreement between the Organization and the United Nations, the Health Assembly shall review and approve the budget estimates and shall apportion the expenses among the Members in accordance with a scale to be fixed by the Health Assembly.

Art. 57. The Health Assembly or the Board acting on behalf of the Health Assembly may accept and administer gifts and bequests made to the Organization provided that the conditions attached to such gifts or bequests are acceptable to the Health Assembly or the Board and are consistent with the objective and policies of the Organization.

Art. 58. A special fund to be used at the discretion of the Board shall be established to meet emergencies and unforeseen contingencies.

Chapter XIII – *Voting*

Art. 59. Each Member shall have one vote in the Health Assembly.

Art. 60.(a) Decisions of the Health Assembly on important questions shall be made by a two-thirds majority of the Members present and voting. These questions shall include: the adoption of conventions or agreements; the approval of agreements bringing the Organization into relation with the United Nations and inter-governmental organizations and agencies in accordance with Articles 69, 70 and 72; amendments to this Constitution.

(b) Decisions on other questions, including the determination of additional categories of questions to be decided by a two-thirds majority, shall be made by a majority of the Members present and voting.

(c) Voting on analogous matters in the Board and in committees of the Organization shall be made in accordance with paragraphs (a) and (b) of this Article.

Chapter XIV – *Reports Submitted by States*

Art. 61. Each Member shall report annually to the Organization on the action taken and progress achieved in improving the health of its people.

Art. 62. Each Member shall report annually on the action taken with respect to recommendations made to it by the Organization and with respect to conventions, agreements and regulations.

Art. 63. Each Member shall communicate promptly to the Organization important laws, regulations, official reports and statistics pertaining to health which have been published in the State concerned.

Art. 64. Each Member shall provide statistical and epidemiological reports in a manner to be determined by the Health Assembly.

Art. 65. Each Member shall transmit upon the request of the Board such additional information pertaining to health as may be practicable.

Chapter XV – *Legal Capacity, Privileges and Immunities*

Art. 66. The Organization shall enjoy in the territory of each Member such legal capacity as may be necessary for the fulfilment of its objective and for the exercise of its functions.

Art. 67.(a) The Organization shall enjoy in the territory of each Member such privileges and immunities as may be necessary for the fulfilment of its objective and for the exercise of its functions.

(b) Representations of Members, persons designated to serve on the Board and technical and administrative personnel of the Organization shall similarly enjoy such privileges and immunities as are necessary for the independent exercise of their functions in connexion with the Organization.

Art. 68. Such legal capacity, privileges and immunities shall be defined in a separate agreement to be prepared by the Organization in consultation with the Secretary-General of the United nations and concluded between the Members.

Chapter XVI – *Relations with Other Organizations*

Art. 69. The Organization shall be brought into relation with the United Nations as one of the specialized agencies referred to in art. 57 of the Charter of the United Nations. The agreement or agreements bringing the Organization into relation with the United Nations shall be subject to approval by a two-thirds vote of the Health Assembly.

Art. 70. The Organization shall establish effective relations and co-operate closely with such other inter-governmental organizations as may be desirable. Any formal agreement entered into with such organizations shall be subject to approval by a two-thirds vote of the Health Assembly.

Art. 71. The Organization may, on matters within its competence, make suitable arrangements for consultation and co-operation with non-governmental international organizations and, with the consent of the Government concerned, with national organizations, governmental or non-governmental.

Art. 72. Subject to the approval by a two-thirds vote of the Health Assembly, the Organization may take over from any other international organization or agency whose purpose and activities lie within the field of competence of the Organization such functions, resources and obligations as may be conferred upon the Organization by international agreement or by mutually acceptable arrangements entered into between the competent authorities of the respective organizations.

Chapter XVII – *Amendments*

Art. 73. Texts of proposed amendments to this Constitution shall be communicated by the Director-General to Members at least six months in advance of their consideration by the Health Assembly. Amendments shall come into force for all Members when adopted by a two-thirds vote of the Health Assembly and accepted by two-thirds of the Members in accordance with their respective constitutional processes.

Chapter XVIII – *Interpretation*

Art. 74. The Chinese, English, French, Russian and Spanish texts of this Constitution shall be regarded as equally authentic.

Art. 75. Any question or dispute concerning the interpretation or application of this Constitution which is not settled by negotiation or by the Health Assembly shall be referred to the International Court of Justice in conformity with the Statute of the Court, unless the parties concerned agree on another mode of settlement.

Art. 76. Upon authorization by the General Assembly of the United Nations or upon authorization in accordance with any agreement between the Organization and the United Nations, the Organization may request the International Court of Justice for an advisory opinion on any legal question arising within the competence of the Organization.

Art. 77. The Director-General may appear before the Court on behalf of the Organization in connexion with any proceedings arising out of such request for an advisory opinion. He shall make arrangements for the presentation of the case before the Court, including arrangements for the argument of different views on the question.

Chapter XIX – *Entry-into-Force*

Art. 78. Subject to the provisions of Chapter III, this Constitution shall remain open to all States for signature or acceptance

Art. 79.(a) States may become parties to this Constitution by:
(i) signature without reservation as to approval;
(ii) signature subject to approval followed by acceptance;
or
(iii) acceptance.
(b) Acceptance shall be effected by the deposit of a formal instrument with the Secretary-General of the United Nations.

Art. 80. This Constitution shall come into force when twenty-six Members of the United Nations have become parties to it in accordance with the provisions of Article 79.

Art. 81. In accordance with art. 102 of the Charter of the United Nations, the Secretary-General of the United Nations will register this Constitution when it has been signed without reservation as to approval on behalf of one State or upon deposit of the first instrument of acceptance.

Art 82. The Secretary-General of the United Nations will inform States parties to this Constitution of the date when it has come into force. He will also inform

them of the dates when other States have become parties to this Constitution.

In faith whereof the undersigned representatives, having been duly authorized for that purpose, sign this Constitution. Done in the City of New York this twenty-second day of July 1946, in a single copy of the Chinese, English, French, Russian and Spanish languages, each text being equally authentic. The original texts shall be deposited in the archives of the United Nations. The Secretary-General of the United Nations will send certified copies to each of the Governments represented at the Conference."

UNTS, Vol. 14, pp. 185–285; *WHO Basic Documents*, Geneva, 1977.

WHO'S WHO IN THE UN. The bibliographical directory of more than 3700 UN and agency personnel as well as of diplomatic representatives of Member and Observer States, was published in 1975 by Arno Press with the co-operation of the Secretariat of the UN. The first *Who's Who in the United Nations?* was published by the *UN Yearbook 1947–1948*, pp. 1046–1093.

Who's Who in the UN and Related Agencies, New York, 1975.

WIDER. ▷ World Institute for Development Economics Research.

WIEDERGUTMACHUNGSGESETZ. German law on compensation: The legal program on compensation paid by the FRG to the victims of Germany's Third Reich racist policy 1933–45. The law did not provide compensation for victims resident in Poland, Czechoslovakia or the USSR.

WIELICZKA. The salt mines in Poland, near Cracow, included in the ▷ World Heritage UNESCO List. Now a museum of mining techniques and skills, these mines, worked since the thirteenth century, contain over 300 km of galleries. On display are tools, equipment and machines used during the last 500 years. There are also works of art in the form of subterranean chapels hewn out of the salt and decorated with statues made of salt.

UNESCO, *A Legacy for All*, Paris, 1984.

WILDERNESS RESERVES. An international term defined by the Inter-American Convention on Nature Protection 1940, as follows: "A region under public control characterized by primitive conditions of flora, fauna, transportation and habitation wherein there is no provision for the passage of motorized transportation and all commercial developments are excluded."

OAS *Treaty Series*, No. 31, Washington, DC, 1964.

WILDLIFE. Subject of international co-operation and convention (▷ European Wildlife and Natural Habitats Convention 1982). Organization reg. with the UIA:

World Wildlife Fund, f. 1961, Gland, Switzerland, Publ.: Monthly Report.

Yearbook of International Organizations 1986/87; The Europa Yearbook 1988. A World Survey, Vol. I, London, 1988.

WILHELMSTRASSE. German: William's Street. A street in the center of Berlin, where until 1945 the building of the Ministry of Foreign Affairs was located at Nos. 74–76; metaphorically, an international term identifying (1871–1945) German foreign policy. ▷ Foggy Bottom, ▷ Foreign Office, ▷ Itamarati, ▷ MID, ▷ Quai d'Orsay.

WILLANDRA LAKES. An Australian natural site included in the ▷ World Heritage UNESCO List. These lakes, in New South Wales, dried up 15,000 years ago, since when the landscape has remained completely unaltered. The fossils of giant marsupials, exterminated long ago by man, are preserved there. Extremely ancient burial places and millstones for wild cereals, 18,000 years old, are also found in this region.

UNESCO, *A Legacy for All*, Paris, 1984.

WILSON DOCTRINE, 1913. An interventionary theory contained in the Declaration on US policy in relation to Latin America, formulated Mar. 1, 1913, by the US President, W. Wilson, as follows: "We do not sympathize with those who establish their government authority in order to satisfy their personal interests and ambitions ... We must teach the Latin Americans to select the right man."
One year later, Apr. 21, 1914, Wilson, on the basis of his doctrine, ordered military intervention in Mexico, and the US marines occupied the port of Veracruz.

A.S. LINK, *Woodrow Wilson and the Progressive Era, 1910–17*, London, 1954; D.G. MUNRO, *Intervention and Dollar-Diplomacy in the Caribbean 1900–21*, Princeton, 1964, pp. 128–129.

WILSON'S FOURTEEN POINTS, 1918. A program contained in 14 points, making precise the conditions of peace and the normalization of international relations after World War I, presented on Jan. 8, 1918 by US President W.T. Wilson in a message to the US Congress. It reads as follows:

"We entered this war because violations of right had occurred which touched us to the quick and made the life of our own people impossible unless they were corrected and the world secured once for all against their recurrence. What we demand in this war, therefore, is nothing peculiar to ourselves. It is that the world be made fit and safe to live in; and particularly that it be made safe for every peace-loving nation which, like our own, wishes to live its own life, determine its own institutions, be assured of justice and fair dealing by the other peoples of the world as against force and selfish aggression. All the peoples of the world are in effect partners in this interest, and for our own part we see very clearly that unless justice be done to others it will not be done to us. The program of the world's peace, therefore, is our program; and that program; the only possible program, as we see it, is this:
I. Open convenants of peace, openly arrived at, after which there shall be no private international understandings of any kind but diplomacy shall proceed always frankly and in the public view.
II. Absolute freedom of navigation upon the seas, outside territorial waters, alike in peace and in war, except as the seas may be closed in whole or in part by international action for the enforcement of international convenants.
III. The removal, so far as possible, of all economic barriers and the establishment of an equality of trade conditions among all the nations consenting to the peace and associating themselves for its maintenance.
IV. Adequate guarantees given and taken that national armaments will be reduced to the lowest point consistent with domestic safety.
V. A free, open-minded, and absolutely impartial adjustment of all colonial claims, based upon a strict observance of the principle that in determining all such questions of sovereignty the interests of the populations concerned must have equal weight with the equitable claims of the government whose title is to be determined.
VI. The evacuation of all Russian territory and such a settlement of all questions affecting Russia as will secure the best and freest cooperation of the other nations of the world in obtaining for her an unhampered and unembarrassed opportunity for the independent determination of her own political development and national policy and assure her of a sincere welcome into the society of free nations under institutions of her own choosing; and, more than a welcome, assistance of every kind that she may need and may herself desire. The treatment accorded Russia by her sister nations in the months to come will be the acid test of their good

will, of their comprehension of her needs as distinguished from their own interests, and of their intelligent and unselfish sympathy.
VII. Belgium, the whole world will agree, must be evacuated and restored, without any attempt to limit the sovereignty which she enjoys in common with all other free nations. No other single act will serve as this will serve to restore confidence among the nations in the laws which they have themselves set and determined for the government of their relations with one another. Without this healing act the whole structure and validity of international law is forever impaired.
VIII. All French territory should be freed and the invaded portions restored, and the wrong done to France by Prussia in 1871 in the matter of Alsace-Lorraine, which has unsettled the peace of the world for nearly fifty years, should be righted, in order that peace may once more be made secure in the interest of all.
IX. A readjustment of the frontiers of Italy should be effected along clearly recognizable lines of nationality.
X. The peoples of Austria-Hungary, whose place among the nations we wish to see safeguarded and assured, should be accorded the freest opportunity of autonomous development.
XI. Rumania, Serbia, and Montenegro should be evacuated; occupied territories restored; Serbia accorded free and secure access to the sea; and the relations of the several Balkan states to one another determined by friendly counsel along historically established lines of allegiance and nationality; and international guarantees of the political and economic independence and territorial integrity of the several Balkan states should be entered into.
XII. The Turkish portions of the present Ottoman Empire should be assured a secure sovereignty, but the other nationalities which are now under Turkish rule should be assured an undoubted security of life and an absolutely unmolested opportunity of autonomous development, and the Dardanelles should be permanently opened as a free passage to the ships and commerce of all nations under international guarantees.
XIII. An independent Polish state should be erected which should include the territories inhabited by indisputably Polish populations, which should be assured a free and secure access to the sea, and whose political and economic independence and territorial integrity should be guaranteed by international convenant.
XIV. A general association of nations must be formed under specific covenants for the purpose of affording mutual guarantees of political independence and territorial integrity to great and small states alike."

The last point was realized at the Versailles Conference, 1919 with the establishment of ▷ League of Nations.

R.S. BAKER, *Woodrow Wilson and World Settlement*, Garden City, 1922.

WIND-ENERGY. An international term for the attempts to convert wind power into mechanical power, using a power station with wind turbines.

L. OBIDNIAK, *Harnessing the Wind*, Quebec, 1988; UNU *Work in Progress*, May, 1988.

WINDWARD CHANNEL. A strait between Cuba and Haiti, 80 km wide, connecting the Atlantic Ocean and Caribbean Sea.

WINDWARD ISLANDS. A group of the Lesser Antilles islands that form the eastern barrier to the Caribbean Sea between Martinique and Trinidad. Together with the ▷ Leeward Islands called the West Indies. Geographically the group consists of French Martinique, Grenada, St Vincent, the Grenadines, St Lucia and Dominica.

WINE. A subject of international co-operation and agreements. In art. 275 of the Versailles Treaty, France prevented Germans from using French names for wines and alcoholic beverages such as champagne or cognac, and later, by agreement with a number of other countries, retained the sole right to use those names. The main wine exporters are

Algeria, France, FRG, Spain, Switzerland, Italy, Portugal, Morocco and Tunisia. Organizations reg. with UIA:
International Federation of Gastronomical and Vinicultural Press, 1962, Paris.
International Union of Wine, Spirits, Brandy and Liqueurs Industrialists and Wholesalers, f. 1951, Paris. It associates national societies of 16 European states and the USA.
International Vine and Wine Office (IWO), Office International de la Vigne et du Vin (OIV), f. 1924, Paris, by intergovernmental agreement, its task is to promote studies on vine and wine culture, exchange experiences and elaborate common trade policy; advisory status with FAO; members are the governments of the main wine-producing countries: Algeria, Argentina, Austria, Belgium, Chile, Cyprus, Czechoslovakia, France, Greece, Israel, Luxemburg, Morocco, the Netherlands, Portugal, Romania, Spain, Switzerland, Tunisia, Ukranian SSR, Yugoslavia, and the USSR. Publ: *Bulletin de l'OIV, Mémento de l'OIV, Registre ampélographique international, Répertoire des stations et laboratoires de viniculture et de l'oenologie, Lexique de la vigne et du vin* (in 7 languages).
International Wine and Food Society, f. 1969, London.
Two Wine and Wine Trade Committees, attached to the EEC, have existed since 1959.

Two international wine adulteration scandals took place in Austria, 1985 and in Italy, 1987 when exporters adulterated wine with chemical mixtures to boost its alcohol content.

Yearbook of International Organisations; A. LICHINE, *Encyclopedia of Wines and Spirits*, London, 1967.

WIPO. World Intellectual Property Organisation; Organisation mondiale de la propriété intelectuelle, OMPI; Organización Mundial de la Propiedad Intelectual, OMPI; Wsiemirnaya organizatsya intelektualnoy sobstviennosti, WOIS; est. July 14, 1967 on signature at Stockholm of a ▷ WIPO Convention.
The origins of what is now WIPO go back to 1883 when the Paris Convention was established and to 1886 when the Berne Convention was organized. These two Conventions brought into being the International Union for the Protection of Industrial Property and the International Union for the Protection of Literary and Artistic Works, generally referred to as the Paris Union and the Berne Union. Both Conventions provided for the establishment of an International Bureau or secretariat. These were united in 1893 and functioned under various names, the last being the United International Bureau for the Protection of Intellectual Property, known by its French acronym BIRPI. BIRPI still has a legal existence for the purpose of those States which are members of the Paris or Berne Unions but have not yet become members of WIPO; in practice, however, WIPO replaces BIRPI and is indistinguishable from it. WIPO became the 14th specialized agency in the United Nations system on Dec. 17, 1974 and is one of the most highly technical. It has 79 members.
WIPO'S objectives are to promote the protection of intellectual property throughout the world through co-operation among States and, where appropriate, in collaboration with other international organizations; and to administer the various "Unions," each founded on a multilateral treaty and dealing with different aspects of intellectual property.
Membership in WIPO is open to any State which is a member of any of the Unions and to any other State fulfilling any one of the three following conditions: first, it is a Member of the United Nations or any of the specialized agencies brought into relationship with the United Nations or the International Atomic Energy Agency; second, it is a party to the Statute of the International Court of Justice; or third, it is invited by the General Assembly of WIPO to become a party to the Convention.

To promote the protection of intellectual property, WIPO encourages the conclusion of new international treaties and the harmonization of national legislation. The protection of intellectual property comprises two main branches: the protection of industrial property, which refers chiefly to inventions, trademarks and industrial designs, and the repression of unfair competition; and copyrights, which protect literary, musical, artistic, photographic and cinematographic works.

WIPO gives legal and technical assistance to developing countries, assembles and disseminates information, and maintains services for international registration or other administrative co-operation among member States.

A substantial part of WIPO's activities and resources is devoted to furthering development by encouraging the transfer or technology, including knowhow, from highly industrialized to developing countries.

WIPO has established the Permanent Program for Development Co-operation related to Industrial Property in order to encourage inventive and innovative activity in developing countries with a view to strengthening their technological capacities. The Program's Permanent Committee plans and guides the execution of projects, drafts model laws, establishes collections of foreign patent documents, trains people in the use of such documentation, and helps establish or modernize government machinery. As for copyright, a Permanent Program for Development Co-operation has been established to encourage literary, scientific and artistic creation there, and to help strengthen national institutions in those fields.

Among other activities, WIPO is examining the Paris Convention to determine the need for providing special rules to benefit developing countries, has recently adopted a treaty on the international recording of scientific discoveries, and is studying problems connected with the avoidance of double taxation of copyright royalties and with the increasing use of cable television and video cassettes.

With regard to technical co-operation in the patent field, a committee has been established to promote standardization of documents and patent office procedures. The International Patent Documentation Centre, established in Vienna in 1972, pursuant to an Agreement between the Government of Austria and WIPO, puts on computer the principal bibliographic data of almost one million patent documents per year and permits retrieval of the data by patent offices, industry, and research and development institutions. WIPO assists the Centre in its contacts with the patent offices of the various countries and with users of such data and technological information contained in patent documents. On Jan 1, 1989 the number of WIPO member countries was 122. The WIPO Office in Geneva is a continuation of the United International Bureau for the Protection of Intellectual Property. Publ.: *Industrial Property* (monthly, in English and French); *Copyright* (monthly, in English and French); *La propiedad intelectual* (quarterly); *Les marques internationales* (monthly) and Manuals.

WIPO information institutions: Patent Information Network–Bibliographic Data Exchange System, WIPO–PIN–BDES and Patent Information Network–Patent Information and Documentation System, WIPO–PIN–PIDS.

Yearbook of International Organizations; KEESING's *Record of World Events*, November 1988.

WIPO CONVENTION ON WORLD INTELLECTUAL PROPERTY, 1967. The Convention establishing the ▷ WIPO was signed at Stockholm on July 14, 1967; entered into force on Apr. 26, 1970. The text reads as follows:

"The Contracting Parties,

Desiring to contribute to better understanding and co-operation among States for their mutual benefit on the basis of respect for their sovereignty and equality,

Desiring, in order to encourage creative activity, to promote the protection of intellectual property throughout the world,

Desiring to modernize and render more efficient the administration of the Unions established in the fields of the protection of industrial property and the protection of literary and artistic works, while fully respecting the independence of each of the Unions,

Agree as follows:

Establishment of the Organization

Art. 1. The World Intellectual Property Organization is hereby established.

Definitions

Art. 2. For the purposes of this Convention:

(i) 'Organization' shall mean the World Intellectual Property Organization (WIPO);

(ii) 'International Bureau' shall mean the International Bureau of Intellectual Property;

(iii) 'Paris Convention' shall mean the Convention for the Protection of Industrial Property signed on March 20, 1883, including any of its revisions;

(iv) 'Berne Convention' shall mean the Convention for the Protection of Literary and Artistic Works signed on September 9, 1889, including any of its revisions;

(v) 'Paris Union' shall mean the International Union established by the Paris Convention;

(vi) 'Berne Union' shall mean the International Union established by the Berne Conventions;

(vii) 'Unions' shall mean the Paris Union, the Special Unions and Agreements established in relation with that Union, the Berne Union, and any other international agreement designed to promote the protection of intellectual property whose administration is assumed by the Organization according to art. 4. (iii);

(viii) 'intellectual property' shall include the rights relating to:

– literary, artistic and scientific works,

– performances of performing artists, phonograms, and broadcasts,

– inventions in all fields of human endeavour,

– scientific discoveries,

– industrial designs,

– trademarks, service marks, and commercial names and designations,

– protection against unfair competition,

and all other rights resulting from intellectual activity in the industrial, scientific, literary or artistic fields.

Objectives of the Organization

Art. 3. The objectives of the Organization are:

(i) to promote the protection of intellectual property throughout the world through co-operation among States and, where appropriate, in collaboration with any other international organization,

(ii) to ensure administrative co-operation among the Unions.

Functions

Art. 4. In order to attain the objectives described in Art. 3, the Organization, through its appropriate organs, and subject to the competence of each of the Unions:

(i) shall promote the development of measures designed to facilitate the efficient protection of intellectual property throughout the world and to harmonize national legislation in this field;

(ii) shall perform the administrative tasks of the Paris Union, the Special Unions established in relation with that Union, and Berne Union;

(iii) may agree to assume, or participate in, the administration of any other international agreement designed to promote the protection of intellectual property;

(iv) shall encourage the conclusion of international agreements designed to promote the protection of intellectual property;

(v) shall offer it co-operation to States requesting legal-technical assistance in the field of intellectual property;

(vi) shall assemble and disseminate information concerning the protection of intellectual property, carry out and promote studies in this field, and publish the results of such studies;

(vii) shall maintain services facilitating the international protection of intellectual property and, where appropriate, provide for registration in this field and the publication of the data concerning the registrations;

(viii) shall take all other appropriate action.

Membership

Art. 5.(1) Membership in the Organization shall be open to any State which is a member of any of the Unions as defined in art. 2 (vii).

(2) Membership in the Organization shall be equally open to any State not a member of any of the Unions, provided that:

(i) it is a member of the United Nations, any of the Specialized Agencies brought into relationship with the United Nations, or the International Atomic Energy Agency, or is a party to the Statute of the International Court of Justice, or

(ii) it is invited by the General Assembly to become a party to this Convention.

General Assembly

Art. 6.(1) (a) There shall be a General Assembly consisting of the States party to this Convention which are members of any of the unions.

(b) The Government of each State shall be represented by one delegate, who may be assisted by alternate delegates, advisors and experts.

(c) The expenses of each delegation shall be borne by the Government which has appointed it.

(2) The General Assembly shall:

(i) appoint the Director General upon nomination by the Coordination Committee;

(ii) review and approve reports of the Director General concerning the Organization and give him all necessary instructions;

(iii) review and approve the reports and activities of the Coordination Committee and give instructions to such Committee;

(iv) adopt the triennial budget of expenses common to the Unions;

(v) approve the measures proposed by the Director General concerning the administration of the international agreements referred to in art. 4 (iii);

(vi) adopt the financial regulations of the Organization;

(vii) determine the working languages of the Secretariat, taking into consideration the practice of the United Nations;

(viii) invite States referred to under art. 5. (2) (ii) to become party to this Convention;

(ix) determine which States are not members of the Organization and which intergovernmental and international non-governmental organizations shall be admitted to its meetings as observers;

(x) exercise such other functions as are appropriate under this Convention.

(3) (a) Each State, whether member of one or more Unions, shall have one vote in the General Assembly.

(b) One half of the States members of the General Assembly shall constitute a quorum.

(c) Notwithstanding the provisions of sub-paragraph (b), if, in any session, the number of States represented is less than one half but equal to or more than one third of the States members of the General Assembly, the General Assembly may make decisions but, with the exception of decisions concerning its own procedure, all such decisions shall take effect only if the following conditions are fulfilled. The International Bureau shall communicate the said decisions to the States members of the General Assembly which were not represented and shall invite them to express in writing their vote or abstention within a period of three months from the date of the communication. If, at the expiration of this period, the number of States having thus expressed their vote or abstention attains the number of States which was lacking for attaining the quorum in the session itself, such decisions shall take effect provided that at the same time the required majority still obtains.

(d) Subject to the provisions of sub-paragraphs (e) and (f), the General Assembly shall make its decisions by a majority of two thirds of the votes cast.

(e) The approval of measures concerning the administration of international agreements referred to in Art. 4 (iii) shall require a majority of three fourths of the votes cast.

(f) The approval of an agreement with the United Nations under art. 57 and 63 of the Charter of the United Nations shall require a majority of nine tenths of the votes cast.

(g) For the appointment of the Director General (paragraph (2) (i)), the approval of measures proposed by the Director General concerning the administration

of international agreements (paragraph (2) (v)), and the transfer of headquarters (art. 10), the required majority must be attained not only in the General Assembly but also in the Assembly of the Paris Union and the Assembly of the Berne Union.
(h) Abstentions shall not be considered as votes.
(i) A delegate may represent, and vote in the name of, one State only.
(4)(a) The General Assembly shall meet once in every third calendar year in ordinary session, upon convocation by the Director General.
(b) The General Assembly shall meet in extraordinary session upon convocation by the Director General either at the request of the Coordination Committee or at the request of one fourth of the States members of the General Assembly.
(c) Meetings shall be held at the headquarters of the Organization.
(5) States party to this Convention which are not members of any of the Unions shall be admitted to the meetings of the General Assembly as observers.
(6) The General Assembly shall adopt its own rules of procedure.
Conference
Art. 7.(1) (a) There shall be a Conference consisting of the States party to this Convention whether or not they are members of any of the Unions.
(b) The Government of each State shall be represented by one delegate, who may be assisted by alternate delegates, advisors, and experts.
(c) The expenses of each delegation shall be borne by the Government which has appointed it.
(2) The Conference shall:
(i) discuss matters of general interest in the field of intellectual property and may adopt recommendations relating to such matters, having regard for the competence and autonomy of the Unions;
(ii) adopt the triennial budget of the Conference;
(iii) within the limits of the budget of the Conference, establish the triennial program of legal-technical assistance;
(iv) adopt to this Convention as provided in art. 17;
(v) determine which States not members of the Organization and which intergovernmental and international non-governmental organizations shall be admitted to its meetings as observers;
(vi) exercise such other functions as are appropriate under this Convention.
(3) (a) Each member State shall have one vote in the Conference.
(b) One third of the member States shall constitute a quorum.
(c) Subject to the provisions of art. 17, the Conference shall make its decisions by a majority of two thirds of the votes cast.
(d) The amounts of the contributions of States party to this Convention not members of any of the Unions shall be fixed by a vote in which only the delegates of such States shall have the right to vote.
(e) Abstentions shall not be considered as votes.
(f) A delegate may represent, and vote in the name of, one State only.
(4) (a) The Conference shall meet in ordinary session, upon convocation by the Director General, during the same period and at the same place as the General Assembly.
(b) The Conference shall meet in extraordinary session, upon convocation by the Director General, at the request of the majority of the member States.
(5) The Conference shall adopt its own rules of procedure.
Coordination Committee
Art. 8.(1) (a) There shall be a Coordination Committee consisting of the States party to this Convention which are members of the Executive Committee of the Paris Union, or the Executive Committee of the Berne Union, or both. However, if either of these Executive Committees is composed of more than one fourth of the number of the countries members of the Assembly which elected it, then such Executive Committee shall designate from among its members the States which will be members of the Coordination Committee, in such a way that their number shall not exceed the one fourth referred to above, it being understood that the country on the territory of which the Organization has its headquarters shall not be included in the computation of the said one fourth.
(b) The Government of each State member of the Coordination Committee shall be represented by one delegate, who may be assisted by alternate delegates, advisors and experts.
(c) Whenever the Coordination Committee considers either matters of direct interest to the program or budget of the Conference and its agenda, or proposals for the amendment of this Convention which would affect the rights or obligations of States party to this Convention not members of any of the Unions, one fourth of such States shall participate in the meetings of the Coordination Committee with the same rights as members of that Committee. The Conference shall, at each of its ordinary sessions, designate these States.
(d) The expenses of each delegation shall be borne by the Government which has appointed it.
(2) If the other Unions administered by the Organization wish to be represented as such in the Coordination Committee, their representatives must be appointed from among the States members of the Coordination Committee.
(3) The Coordination Committee shall:
(i) give advice to the organs of the Unions, the General Assembly, the Conference, and the Director General, on all administrative, financial and other matters of common interest to two or more of the Unions, or to one or more of the Unions and the Organization, and in particular on the budget of expenses common to the Unions;
(ii) prepare the draft agenda and the draft program and budget of the Conference;
(iii) prepare the draft agenda and the draft program and budget of the Conference;
(iv) on the basis of the triennial budget of expenses common to the Unions and the triennial budget of the Conference, as well as on the basis of the triennial program of legal-technical assistance, establish the corresponding annual budgets and programs;
(v) when the term of office of the Director General is about to expire, or when there is a vacancy in the post of the Director General, nominate a candidate for appointment to such position by the General Assembly; if the General Assembly does not appoint its nominee, the Coordination Committee shall nominate another candidate; this procedure shall be repeated until the latest nominee is appointed by the General Assembly;
(vi) if the post of the Director General becomes vacant between two sessions of the General Assembly, appoint an Acting Director General for the term preceding the assuming of office by the new Director General;
(vii) perform such other functions as are allocated to it under this Convention.
(4) (a) The Coordination Committee shall meet once every year in ordinary session, upon convocation by the Director General. It shall normally meet at the headquarters of the Organization.
(b) The Coordination Committee shall meet in extraordinary session upon convocation by the Director General, either on his own initiative, or at the request of its Chairman or one fourth of its members.
(5) (a) Each State, whether a member of one or both of the Executive Committees referred to in paragraph (1) (a), shall have one vote in the Coordination Committee.
(b) One half of the members of the Coordination Committee shall constitute a quorum.
(c) A delegate may represent, and vote in the name of, one State only.
(6) (a) The Coordination Committee shall express its opinion and make its decisions by a simple majority of the votes cast. Abstentions shall not be considered as votes.
(b) Even if a simple majority is obtained, any member of the Coordination Committee may, immediately after the vote, request that the votes be the subject of a special recount in the following manner: two separate lists shall be prepared, one containing the names of the States members of the Executive Committee of the Paris Union and the other the names of the States members of the Executive Committee of the Berne Union; the vote of each State shall be inscribed opposite its name in each list in which it appears. Should this special recount indicate that a simple majority has not been obtained in each of those lists, the proposal shall not be considered as carried.
(7) Any State member of the Organization which is not a member of the Coordination Committee may be represented at the meetings of the Committee by observers having the right to take part in the debates but without the right to vote.
(8) The Coordination Committee shall establish its own rules of procedure.
International Bureau
Art. 9(1) The International Bureau shall be the Secretariat of the Organization.
(2) The International Bureau shall be directed by the Director General, assisted by two or more Deputy Directors General.
(3) The Director General shall be appointed for a fixed term, which shall be not less than six years. He shall be eligible for reappointment for fixed terms. The periods of the initial appointment and possible subsequent appointments, as well as all other conditions of the appointment, shall be fixed by the General Assembly.
(4) (a) The Director General shall be the chief executive of the Organization.
(b) He shall represent the Organization.
(c) He shall report to, and conform to the instruction of, the General Assembly as to the internal and external affairs of the Organization.
(5) The Director General shall prepare the draft programs and budgets and periodical reports on activities. He shall transmit them to the Governments of the interested States and to the competent organs of the Unions and the Organization.
(6) The Director General and any staff member designated by him shall participate, without the right to vote, in all meetings of the General Assembly, the Conference, the Coordination Committee, and any other committee or working group. The Director General or a staff member designated by him shall be ex officio secretary of these bodies.
(7) The Director General shall appoint the staff necessary for the efficient performance of the tasks of the International Bureau. He shall appoint the Deputy Directors General after approval by the Coordination Committee. The conditions of employment shall be fixed by the staff regulations to be approved by the Coordination Committee on the proposal of the Director General. The paramount consideration in the employment of the staff and in the determination of the conditions of service shall be the necessity of securing the highest standards of efficiency, competence, and integrity. Due regard shall be paid to the importance of recruiting the staff on as wide a geographical basis as possible.
(8) The nature of the responsibilities of the Director General and of the staff shall be exclusively international. In the discharge of their duties they shall not seek or receive instructions from any Government or from any authority external to the Organization. They shall refrain from any action which might predudice their position as international officials. Each member State undertakes to respect the exclusively international character of the responsibilities of the Director General and the staff, and not to seek to influence them in the discharge of their duties.
Headquarters
Art. 10.(1) The headquarters of the Organization shall be at Geneva.
(2) Its transfer may be decided as provided for art. 6.(3) (d) and (g).
Finances
Art. 11.(1) The Organization shall have two separate budgets: the budget of expenses common to the Unions, and the budget of the Conference.
(2) (a) The budget of expenses common to the Unions shall include provision for expenses of interest to several Unions.
(b) This budget shall be financed from the following sources:
(i) contributions of the Unions, provided that the amount of the contribution of each Union shall be fixed by the Assembly of that Union, having regard to the interest the Union has in the common expenses;
(ii) charges due for services performed by the International Bureau not in direct relation with any of the Unions or not received for services rendered by the International Bureau in the field of legal-technical assistance;
(iii) sale of, or royalties on, the publications of the International Bureau not directly concerning any of the Unions;
(iv) gifts, bequests, and subventions, given to the Organization, except those referred to in paragraph (3) (b) (iv);
(v) rents, interests, and other miscellaneous income, of the Organization.

(3) (a) The budget of the Conference shall include provision for the expenses of holding sessions of the Conference and for the cost of the legal-technical assistance program.
(b) This budget shall be financed from the following sources:
(i) Contributions of States party to this Convention not members of any of the Unions;
(ii) any sums made available to this budget by the Unions, provided that the amount of the sum made available by each Union shall be fixed by the Assembly of that Union and that each Union shall be free to abstain from contributing to the said budget;
(iii) sums received for services rendered by the International Bureau in the field of legal-technical assistance;
(iv) gifts, bequests, and subventions, given to the Organization for the purposes referred to in sub-paragraph (a).
(4) (a) For the purpose of establishing its contribution towards the budget of the Conference, each State party to this Convention not a member of any of the Unions shall belong to a class, and shall pay its annual contributions on the basis of a number of units fixed as follows:
Class A – 10
Class B – 3
Class C – 1
(b) Each such State shall, concurrently with taking action as provided in art.14(1), indicate the class to which it wishes to belong. Any such State may change class. If it chooses a lower class, the State must announce it the Conference at one of its ordinary sessions. Any such change shall take effect at the beginning of the calendar year following the session.
(c) The annual contribution of each such State shall be an amount in the same proportion to the total sum to be contributed to the budget of the Conference by all such States as the number of its units is to the total of the units of all the said States.
(d) Contributions shall become due on the first of January of each year.
(e) If the budget is not adopted before the beginning of a new financial period, the budget shall be at the same level as the budget of the previous year, in accordance with the financial regulations.
(5) Any State party to this Convention not a member of any of the Unions which is in arrears in the payment of its financial contributions under the present Art., and any State party to this Convention member of any of the Unions which is in arrears in the payment of its contributions to any of the Unions, shall have no vote in any of the bodies of the Organization of which it is a member, if the amount of its arrears equals or exceeds the amount of the contributions due from it for the preceding two full years. However, any of these bodies may allow such a State to continue to exercise its vote in that body if, and as long as, it is satisfied that the delay in payment arises from exceptional and unavoidable circumstances.
(6) The amount of the fees and charges due for services rendered by the International Bureau in the field of legal-technical assistance shall be established, and shall be reported to the Coordination Committee, by the Director General.
(7) The Organization, with the approval of the Coordination Committee, may receive gifts, bequests, and subventions, directly from Governments, public or private institutions, associations or private persons.
(8) (a) The Organization shall have a working capital fund which shall be constituted by a single payment made by the Unions and by each State party to this Convention not member of any Union. If the fund becomes insufficient, it shall be increased.
(b) The amount of the single payment of each Union and its possible participation in any increase shall be decided by its Assembly.
(c) The amount of the single payment of each State party to this Convention not member of any Union and its part in any increase shall be a proportion of the contribution of that State for the year in which the fund is established or the increase decided. The proportion and the terms of payment shall be fixed by the Conference on the proposal of the Director General and after it has heard the advice of the Coordination Committee.
(9) (a) In the headquarters agreement concluded with the State on the territory of which the Organization has its headquarters, it shall be provided that, whenever the working capital fund is insufficient, such State shall grant advances. The amount of these advances and the conditions on which they are granted shall be the subject of separate agreements, in each case, between such State and the Organization. As long as it remains under the obligation to grant advances, such State shall have an ex officio seat on the Coordination Committee.
(b) The State referred to in sub-paragraph (a) and the Organization shall each have the right to denounce the obligation to grant advances, by written notification. Denunciation shall take effect three years after the end of the year in which it has been notified.
(10) The auditing of the accounts shall be effected by one or more member States, or by external auditors, as provided in the financial regulations. They shall be designated, with their agreement, by the General Assembly.

Legal Capacity; Privileges and Immunities

Art. 12.(1) The Organization shall enjoy on the territory of each member State, in conformity with the laws of that State, such legal capacity as may be necessary for the fulfilment of the Organization's objectives and for the exercise of its functions.
(2) The Organization shall conclude a headquarters agreement with the Swiss Confederation and with any other State in which the headquarters may subsequently be located.
(3) The Organization may conclude bilateral or multilateral agreements with the other member States with a view to the enjoyment by the Organization, its officials, and representatives of all member States, of such privileges and immunities as may be necessary for the fulfilment of its objectives and for the exercise of its functions.
(4) The Director General may negotiate and, after approval by the Coordination Committee, shall conclude and sign on behalf of the Organization the agreement referred to in paragraphs 2 and 3.

Relations with Other Organizations

Art. 13.(1) The Organization shall, where appropriate, establish working relations and co-operate with other intergovernmental organizations. Any general agreement to such effect entered into with such organizations shall be concluded by the Director General after approval by the Coordination Committee.
(2) The Organization may, on matters within its competence, make suitable arrangements for consultation and co-operation with international non-governmental organizations and, with the consent of the Governments concerned, with national organizations, governmental or non-governmental. Such arrangements shall be made by the Director General after approval by the Coordination Committee.

Becoming Party to the Convention

Art. 14.(1) States referred to in art. 5 may become party to this Convention and Member of the Organization by:
(i) signature without reservation as to ratification, or
(ii) signature subject to ratification followed by the deposit of an instrument of ratification, or
(iii) deposit of an instrument of accession.
(2) Notwithstanding any other provision of this Convention, a State party to the Paris Convention, the Berne Convention, or both Conventions, may become party to this Convention only if it concurrently ratifies or accedes to, or only after it has ratified or acceded to: either the Stockholm Act of the Paris Convention in its entirety or with only the limitation set forth in art. 20(1) (b) (i) thereof,
or the Stockholm Act of the Berne Convention in its entirety or with only the limitation set forth in art. 28(1) (b) (i) thereof.
(3) Instruments of ratification or accession shall be deposited with the Director General.

Entry into Force of the Convention

Art. 15.(1) This Convention shall enter into force three months after ten States members of the Paris Union and seven States members of the Berne Union have taken action as provided in Art. 14(1), it being understood that, if a State is a member of both Unions, it will be counted in both groups. On that date, this Convention shall enter into force also in respect of States which, not being members of either of two Unions, have taken action as provided in Art. 14(1) three months or more prior to that date.
(2) In respect to any other State, this Conventions shall enter into force three months after the date on which such State takes action as provided in Art. 14(1).

Reservations

Art. 16. No reservations to this Convention are permitted.

Amendments

Art. 17.(1) Proposals for the amendment of this Convention may be initiated by any member State, by the Coordination Committee, or by the Director General. Such proposals shall be communicated by the Director General to the member States at least six months in advance of their consideration by the Conference.
(2) Amendments shall be adopted by the Conference. Whenever amendments would affect the rights and obligations of States party to this Convention not members of any of the Unions, such States shall also vote. On all other amendments proposed only States party to this Convention members of any Union shall vote. Amendments shall be adopted by a simple majority of the votes cast, provided that the Conference shall vote only on such proposals for amendments as have previously been adopted by the Assembly of the Paris Union and the Assembly of the Berne Union according to the rules applicable in each of them regarding the adoption of amendments to the administrative provisions of their respective Conventions.
(3) Any amendment shall enter into force one month after written notifications of acceptance, effected in accordance with their respective constitutional processes, have been received by the Director General from three fourths of the States members of the Organization, entitled to vote on the proposal for amendment pursuant to paragraph (2), at the time the Conference adopted the amendment. Any amendments thus accepted shall bind all the States which are Members of the Organization at the time the amendment enters into force or which become members at a subsequent date, provided that any amendment increasing the financial obligations of member States shall bind only those States which have notified their acceptance of such amendment.

Denunciation

Art. 18.(1) Any member State may denounce this Convention by notification addressed to the Director General.
(2) Denunciation shall take effect six months after the day on which the Director General has received the notification.

Notifications

Art. 19. The Director General shall notify the Governments of all member States of:
(i) the date of entry into force of the Convention,
(ii) signatures and deposits of instruments of ratification or accession,
(iii) acceptances of an amendment to this Convention, and the date upon which the amendment enters into force,
(iv) denunciations of this Convention.

Final Provisions

Art. 20(1) (a) This Convention shall be signed in a single copy in English, French, Russian and Spanish, all texts being equally authentic, and shall be deposited with the Government of Sweden.
(b) This Convention shall remain open for signature at Stockholm until January 13, 1968.
(2) Official texts shall be established by the Director General, after consultation with the interested Governments, in German, Italian and Portuguese, and such other languages as the Conference may designate.
(3) The Director General shall transmit two duly certified copies of this Convention and of each amendment adopted by the Conference to the Governments of the States members of the Paris or Berne Unions, to the Government of any other State when it accedes to this Convention, and, on request, to the Government of any other State. The copies of the signed text of the Convention transmitted to the Governments shall be certified by the Government of Sweden.
(4) The Director General shall register this Convention with the Secretariat of the United Nations.

Transitional Provisions

Art. 21.(1) Until the first Director General assumes office, references in this Convention to the International Bureau or the Director General shall be deemed to be references to the United International Bureaux for the Protection of Industrial, Literary and Artistic Property (also called the United International Bureaux for the Protection of Intellectual Property (BIRPI), or its Director, respectively.

(2) (a) States which are members of any of the Unions but which have not become party to this Convention may, for five years from the date of entry into force of this Convention, exercise, if they so desire, the same rights as if they had become party to this Convention. Any State desiring to exercise such rights shall give written notification to this effect to the Director General; this notification shall be effective on the date of its receipt. Such States shall be deemed to be members of the General Assembly and the Conference until the expiration of the said period.
(b) Upon expiration of this five-year period, such States shall have no right to vote in the General Assembly, the Conference, and the Coordination Committee.
(c) Upon becoming party to this Conventions, such States shall regain such right to vote.
(3) (a) As long as there are States members of the Paris or Berne Unions which have not become party to this Convention, the International Bureau and the Director General shall also function as the United International Bureaux for the Protection of Industrial, Literary and Artistic Property, and its Director, respectively.
(b) The staff in the employment of the said Bureaux on the date of entry into force of this Convention shall, during the transitional period referred to in sub-paragraph (a), be considered as also employed by the International Bureau.
(4) (a) Once all the States members of the Paris Union have become members of the Organization, the rights, obligations, and property, of the Bureau of that Union shall devolve on the International Bureau of the Organization.
(b) Once all the States members of the Berne Union have become members of the Organization, the rights, obligations, and property, of the Bureau of that Union shall devolve on the International Bureau of the Organization."

A.J. PEASLEE (ed.), *International Governmental Organizations. Constitutional Documents*, The Hague, 1979, Parts III–IV, pp. 474–487.

WISMUT SDAG. Wismut Sovietisch-Deutsch Aktion-Gesellschaft. Uranium Soviet German SA, est. 1946 with hq in Moscow, since 1954 Soviet-German hqs in Chemnitz-Siegmar; exploiting the uranium resources in Oberschlensme Sax., German Democratic Republic. The Soviet-German shares since 1954 stand in a relation of 60 to 40.

WMO. World Meteorological Organization; Organisation météorologique mondiale, OMM; Organización Meteorológica Mundial, OMM; Wsiemirnaya mietierologicheskaya organizatsya, WMO; est. Oct., 1947 on adoption of the ▷ WMO Convention, signed by representatives of 42 States, at the conclusion of the 12th Conference of Directors of the ▷ International Meteorological Organization. The Convention came into force on Mar. 23, 1950 and the activities, resources and obligations of IMO were transferred to WMO during the First WMO Congress in Paris, Mar. 19–Apr. 4, 1951. On Dec. 20, 1951 the UN General Assembly approved the agreement between the UN and WMO as a Specialized Agency.
As stated in the preamble to its Convention, WMO was established with a view to co-ordinating, standardizing and improving world meteorological and related activities and to encourage an efficient exchange of meteorological and related information between countries in the aid of human activities.
The purposes of WMO are to facilitate international co-operation in the establishment of networks of stations and centres to provide meteorological services and observations; to promote the establishment and maintenance of systems for the rapid exchange of meteorological and related information; to promote standardization of meteorological observations and ensure the uniform publication of observations and statistics; to further the application of meteorology to aviation, shipping, water problems, agriculture and other human activities; to promote activities in operational

hydrology; and to encourage research and training in meteorology.
The 148 Members of WMO are States and Territories maintaining their own meteorological services.
The seventh World Meteorological Congress of WMO, meeting at its headquarters in Geneva in May, 1975, reorganized the Organization's activities into the following programs: world weather watch; research and development; meteorological applications and environment; hydrology and water resources development; technical co-operation; and education and training. World Weather Watch provides for surface and upper-air observations from a world-wide network of stations, as well as from mobile and fixed ships, commercial aircraft and meteorological satellites. The material gathered, together with processed data obtained by using high-speed computers, is disseminated to all countries over special meteorological networks. In addition, meteorological satellites provide direct read-out of the cloud images and, as far as possible, of other real-time data to all countries equipped with reception facilities for automatic picture transmissions (APT). WMO, with the Inter-governmental Oceanographic Commission, co-sponsors an international program called "Integrated Global Ocean Station System (IGOSS)" which was conceived as an oceanic counterpart of the World Weather Watch to produce and provide oceanographic analyses and predictions. The Research Program includes all activities relating to the improvement of the scientific understanding of atmospheric processes. One of WMO's main research efforts, carried out jointly with the International Council of Scientific Unions, is the Global Atmospheric Research Program (GARP), designed to increase the accuracy of forecasting over periods ranging from one day to several weeks and to obtain a better understanding of the physical basis of climate. WMO's Program on Meteorological Application and the Environment deals with the application of meteorological knowledge to human activities such as agriculture, transport, building climatology, energy, atmospheric and marine pollution and environmental problems in general. The Organization has undertaken and expanded activities to aid food production through strengthening national agro-meteorological services and through closer collaboration with FAO. A global network initiated in 1970 to measure background air pollution has continued to expand and now consists of about 100 stations.
The WMO Hydrology and Water Resources development program seeks to promote world-wide co-operation in the evaluation of water resources and to assist in their development through the co-ordinated establishment of networks and services. Through its Technical Co-operation Program, WMO helps developing countries establish and improve national meteorological and hydrological services by providing experts, fellowships and equipment. Assistance is given in the development of observational and telecommunications networks, data-processing facilities and training and research institutes and in the application of observational data and forecasts to other sectors of the national economy.
The main features of the Education and Training Program comprise, besides the training activities mentioned above, organization of training seminars and preparation of training publications.
A World Climate Program, the purpose of which is to improve the knowledge of the natural variability of climate and the effects of climate changes, due either to natural causes or to man's activities, was submitted to the Eighth WMO Congress

(Apr.–May, 1979) for adoption. It is expected that such knowledge will assist decision-makers in planning and co-ordinationg climate-sensitive activities dealing with agriculture, water resources, energy and so forth.
The WMO has working arrangements with FAO, UNESCO, ICAO, WHO, ITU, IMCO. Publ.: Basic Documents, Final Reports, Manuals, *WMO Bulletin*, Annual Reports. WHO information system: World Weather Watch, WMO–WWW.

Publications of the WMO, 1951–77, Geneva, 1978; WMO. *Publications of the WMO, 1951–80*, Geneva, 1981; *Meteorological Service of the WMO*, Geneva, 1982.

WMO, CONVENTION ON WORLD METEOROLOGICAL ORGANIZATION, 1947. The Convention was adopted and signed at Washington on Oct. 11, 1947; entered into force on Mar. 23, 1950. The text as amended to 1975 reads as follows:

"With a view to co-ordinating, standardizing and improving world meteorological and related activities, and to encouraging an efficient exchange of meteorological and related information between countries in the aid of human activities, the contracting States agree to the present Convention, as follows:
Part I – *Establishment*
Art. 1. The World Meteorological Organization (hereinafter called 'the Organization') is hereby established.
Part II – *Purposes*
Art. 2. The purposes of the Organization shall be:
(a) To facilitate world-wide co-operation in the establishment of networks of stations for the making of meteorological observations as well as hydrological and other geophysical observations related to meteorology, and to promote the establishment and maintenance of centers charged with the provision of meteorological and related services;
(b) To promote the establishment and maintenance of systems for the rapid exchange of meteorological and related information;
(c) To promote standardization of meteorological and related observations and to ensure the uniform publication of observations and statistics;
(d) To further the application of meteorology to aviation, shipping, water problems, agriculture and other human activities;
(e) To promote activities in operational hydrology and to further close co-operation between Meteorological and Hydrological Services; and
(f) To encourage research and training in meteorology and, as appropriate, in related fields and to assist in coordinating the international aspects of such research and training.
Part III – *Membership*
Art. 3. The following may become members of the Organization by the procedure set forth in the present Convention:
(a) Any State represented at the Conference of Directors of the International Meteorological Organization convened at Washington, DC, on 22 September 1947, as listed in Annex I attached hereto and which signs the present Convention and ratifies it in accordance with Art. 32, or which accedes thereto, in accordance with Art. 33;
(b) Any member of the United Nations having a Meteorological Service by acceding to the present Convention in accordance with art. 33;
(c) Any State fully responsible for the conduct of its international relations and having a Meteorological Service, not listed in Annex I of the present Convention and not member of the United Nations, after the submission of a request for membership to the Secretariat of the Organization and after its approval by two thirds of the members of the Organization as specified in paragraphs (a), (b) and (c) of this Art., by acceding to the present Convention in accordance with art. 33;
(d) Any territory or group of territories maintaining its own Meteorological Service and listed in Annex II attached thereto, upon application of the present Convention on its behalf, in accordance with paragraph (a) of Art. 34, by the State or States responsible for its international relations and represented at the Conference of Directors of the International Meteoro-

logical Organization convened at Washington, DC, on 22 September 1947, as listed in Annex I of the present Convention;

(e) Any territory or group of territories not listed in Annex II of the present Convention, maintaining its own Meteorological Service but not responsible for the conduct of its international relations, on behalf of which the present Convention is applied in accordance with paragraph (b) of art. 34; provided that the request for membership is presented by the member responsible for its international relations, and secures approval by two thirds of the members of the Organization as specified in paragraphs (a), (b) and (c) of this Article;

(f) Any trust territory or group of trust territories maintaining its own Meteorological Service, and administered by the United Nations, to which the United Nations applies the present Convention in accordance with art. 34.

Any request for membership in the Organization shall state in accordance with this paragraph of this Article membership is sought.

Part IV – Organization

Art. 4.(a) The Organization shall comprise:
(1) The World Meteorological Congress (hereinafter called 'Congress');
(2) The Executive Committee;
(3) Regional Meteorological Associations (hereinafter called 'the Regional Association');
(4) Technical Commissions;
(5) The Secretariat.

(b) There shall be a President and three Vice-Presidents of the Organization who shall also be President and Vice-Presidents of Congress and of the Executive Committee.

Art. 5. The activities of the Organization and the conduct of its affairs shall be decided by the members of the Organization.

(a) Such decisions shall normally be taken by Congress in session.

(b) However, except on matters reserved in the Convention for decisions by Congress, decisions may also be taken by members by correspondence, when urgent action is required between sessions of Congress. Such a vote shall be taken upon receipt by the Secretary-General of the request of a majority of the members of the Organization, or when so decided by the Executive Committee.

Such votes shall be conducted in accordance with art. 11 and 12 of the Convention and with the General Regulations (hereinafter referred to as 'the Regulations').

Part V – Officers of the Organization and Members of the Executive Committee

Art. 6.(a) Eligibility for election to the offices of President and Vice-Presidents of the Organization, of President and Vice-President of the Regional Associations, and for membership subject to the provisions of Art. 13 (c) (ii) of the Convention, of the Executive Committee, shall be confined to persons who are designated as Directors of their Meteorological or Hydrometeorological Services by the members of the Organization for the purpose of this Convention, as provided for in the Regulations.

(b) In the performance of their duties, all officers of the Organization and members of the Executive Committee shall act as representatives of the Organization and not as representatives of particular members thereof.

Part VI – The World Meteorological Congress

Art. 7.(a) The Congress is the General assembly of delegates representing Members and as such is the supreme body of the Organization.

(b) Each member shall designate one of its delegates, who should be the Director of its Meteorological or Hydrometeorological Service, as its principal delegate at Congress.

(c) With a view to securing the widest possible technical representation, any Director of a Meteorological or Hydrometeorological Service or any other individual may be invited by the President to be present at and to participate in the discussions of Congress in accordance with the provisions of the Regulations.

Functions

Art. 8. In addition to the functions set out in other Articles of the Convention, the primary duties of Congress shall be:
(a) To determine general policies for the fulfilment of the purposes of the Organization as set forth in art. 2;
(b) To make recommendations to members on matters within the purposes of the Organization;
(c) To refer to any body of Organization any matter within the provision of the Convention upon which such a body is empowered to act;
(d) To determine regulations prescribing the procedures of the various bodies of the Organization, in particular the General, Technical, Financial and Staff Regulations;
(e) To consider the reports and activities of the Executive Committee and to take appropriate action in regard thereto;
(f) To establish Regional Associations in accordance with the provisions of art. 18; to determine their geographical limits, co-ordinate their activities, and consider their recommendations;
(g) To establish Technical Commissions in accordance with the provisions of art. 19; to define their terms of reference, co-ordinate their activities, and consider their recommendation;
(h) To establish any additional bodies it may deem necessary;
(i) To determine the location of the Secretariat of the Organization;
(j) To elect the President and Vice-Presidents of the Organization, and members of the Executive Committee other than the Presidents of the Regional Associations.

Congress may also take any other appropriate action on matters affecting the Organization.

Execution of Congress Decisions

Art. 9. (a) All members shall do their utmost to implement the decisions of Congress.

(b) If, however, any member finds it impracticable to give effect to some requirement in a technical resolution adapted by Congress, such member shall inform the Secretary-General of the Organization whether its inability to give effect to it is provisional or final, and state its reasons therefor.

Sessions

Art. 10.(a) Congress shall normally be convened at intervals as near as possible to four years, at a place and on a date to be decided by the Executive Committee.
(b) An extraordinary Congress may be convened by decision of the Executive Committee.
(c) On receipt of requests for an extraordinary Congress from one third of the members of the Organization the Secretary-General shall conduct a vote by correspondence, and if a simple majority of the members are in favor an extraordinary Congress shall be convened.

Voting

Art. 11(a) In a vote in Congress each Member shall have one vote. However, only members of the Organization which are States (hereinafter referred to as 'members which are States') shall be entitled to vote or to take a decision on the following subjects:
(1) Amendment or interpretation of the Convention or proposals for a new Convention;
(2) Request for membership of the Organization;
(3) Relations with the United Nations and other intergovernmental organizations;
(4) Election of the President and Vice-Presidents of the Organization and of the members of the Executive Committee other than the Presidents of the Regional Associations.

(b) Decisions shall be by a two-thirds majority of the votes cast for and against, except that elections of individuals to serve in any capacity in the Organization shall be by simple majority of the votes cast. The provisions of this paragraph, however, shall not apply to decisions taken in accordance with art. 3, 10(c), 25, 26 and 28 of the Convention.

Quorum

Art. 12. The presence of delegates of a majority of the members shall be required to constitute a quorum for meetings of Congress. For those meetings of Congress at which decisions are taken on the subjects enumerated in paragraph (a) of art. 11, the presence of delegates of a majority of the members which are States shall be required to constitute a quorum.

Part VII – The Executive Committee

Composition

Art. 13. The Executive Committee shall consist of:
(a) The President and the Vice-Presidents of the Organization;
(b) The Presidents of Regional Associations who can be replaced at sessions by their alternates, as provided for in the Regulations;
(c) Fourteen Directors of Meteorological or Hydrometeorological Services of members of the Organization, who can be replaced at sessions by alternates provided:
(i) That these alternates shall be as provided for in the Regulations;
(ii) That not more than seven and not less than two members of the Executive Committee, comprising the President and Vice-Presidents of the Organization, the Presidents of Regional Associations and the fourteen elected Directors, shall come from one Region, this Region being determined in the case of each member in accordance with the Regulations.

Functions

Art. 14. The Executive Committee is the executive body of the Organization and is responsible to Congress for the coordination of the program of the Organization and for the utilization of its budgetary resources in accordance with the decisions of Congress.

In addition to functions set out in other Articles of the Convention, the primary functions of the Executive Committee shall be:
(a) To implement the decisions taken by the members of the Organization either in Congress or by means of correspondence and to conduct the activities of the Organization in accordance with the intention of such decisions;
(b) To examine the program and budget estimates for the following financial period prepared by the Secretary-General and to present its observations and its recommendations thereon to Congress;
(c) To consider and, where necessary, take action on behalf of the Organization on resolutions and recommendations of Regional Associations and Technical Commissions in accordance with the procedure laid down in the Regulations;
(d) To provide technical information, counsel and assistance in the fields of activities of the Organization;
(e) To study and make recommendations on any matter affecting international meteorology and related activities of the Organization;
(f) To prepare the agenda for Congress and to give guidance to the Regional Associations and Technical Commissions in the preparation of their agenda;
(g) To report on its activities to each session of Congress;
(h) To administer the finances of the Organization in accordance with the provisions of Part XI of the Convention.

The Executive Committee may also perform such other functions as may be conferred on it by Congress or by members collectively.

Sessions

Art. 15.(a) The Executive Committee shall normally hold a session at least once a year, at a place and on a date to be determined by the President of the Organization after consultation with other members of the Committee.

(b) An extraordinary session of the Executive Committee shall be convened according to the procedures contained in the Regulations, after receipt by the Secretary-General of request from a majority of the members of the Executive Committee. Such a session may also be convened by agreement between the President and the three Vice-Presidents of the Organization.

Voting

Art. 16(a) Decisions of the Executive Committee shall be by two-thirds majority of the votes cast for and against. Each member of the Executive Committee shall have only one vote, notwithstanding that he may be a member in more than one capacity.

(b) Between sessions the Executive Committee may vote to correspondence. Such votes shall be conducted in accordance with art. 16(a) and 17 of the Convention.

Quorum

Art. 17. The presence of two thirds of the members shall be required to constitute a quorum for meetings of the Executive Committee.

Part VIII – *Regional Associations*

Art. 18.(a) Regional Associations shall be composed of the members of the Organization, the networks of which lie in or extend into the Region.

(b) Members of the Organization shall be entitled to attend the meetings of Regional Associations to which they do not belong, to take part in the discussions and to present their views upon questions affecting their own Meteorological or Hydrometeorological Services but shall not have the right to vote.

(c) Regional Associations shall meet as often as necessary. The time and place of the meeting shall be determined by the President of the Regional Associations in agreement with the President of the Organization.

(d) The functions of the Regional Associations shall be:

(i) To promote the execution of the resolutions of Congress and the Executive Committee in their respective Regions;

(ii) To consider matters brought to their attention by the Executive Committee;

(iii) To discuss matters of general interest and to coordinate meteorological and related activities in their respective Regions;

(iv) To make recommendations to Congress and the Executive Committee on matters within the purpose of the Organization;

(v) To perform such other functions as may be conferred on them by Congress.

(e) Each Regional Association shall elect its President and Vice-President.

Part IX – *Technical Commissions*

Art. 19(a) Commissions consisting of technical experts may be established by Congress to study and make recommendations to Congress and the Executive Committee on any subject within the purpose of the Organization.

(b) Members of the Organization have right to be represented on the Technical Commissions.

(c) Each Technical commission shall elect its President and Vice-President.

(d) Presidents of Technical Commissions may participate without vote in the meetings of Congress and of the Executive Committee.

Part X – *The Secretariat*

Art. 20. The permanent Secretariat of the Organization shall be composed of a Secretary-General and such technical and clerical staff as may be required for the work of the Organization.

Art. 21.(a) The Secretary-General shall be appointed by Congress on such terms as Congress may approve.

(b) The staff of the Secretariat shall be appointed by the Secretary-General with the approval of the Executive Committee in accordance with regulations established by the Congress.

Art. 22.(a) The Secretary-General is responsible to the President of the Organization for the technical and administrative work of the Secretariat.

(b) In the performance of their duties, the Secretary-General and the staff shall not seek or receive instructions from any authority external to the Organization. They shall refrain from any action which might reflect on their position as international officers. Each member of the Organization on its part shall respect the exclusively international character of the responsibilities of the Secretary-General and the staff and not seek to influence them in the discharge of their responsibilities to the Organization.

Part XI – *Finances*

Art. 23.(a) Congress shall determine the maximum expenditure which may be incurred by the Organization on the basis of the estimates submitted by the Secretary-General after prior examination by, and with the recommendations of, the Executive Committee.

(b) Congress shall delegate to the Executive Committee such authority as may be required to approve the annual expenditures of the Organization within the limitations determined by Congress.

Art. 24. The expenditures of the Organization shall be apportioned among the members of the Organization in the proportions determined by Congress.

Part XII – *Relations with the United Nations*

Art. 25. The Organization shall be in relationship to the United Nations pursuant to art. 57 of the Charter of the United Nations. Any agreement concerning such relationship shall require approval by two thirds of the members which are States.

Part XIII – *Relations with other Organizations*

Art. 26.(a) The Organization shall establish effective relations and co-operate closely with such other intergovernmental organizations as may be desirable. Any formal agreement entered into with such organizations shall be made by the Executive Committee, subject to approval by two thirds of the members which are States, either in Congress or by correspondence.

(b) The Organization may on matters within its purpose make suitable arrangements for consultation and co-operation with non-governmental international organizations and, with the consent of the government concerned, with national organizations, governmental or non-governmental.

(c) Subject to approval by two thirds of the members which are States, the Organization may take over from any other international organization or agency, the purpose and activities of which lie within the purposes of the Organization, such functions, resources and obligations as may be transferred to the Organization by international agreement or by mutually acceptable arrangements entered into between competent authorities of the respective organizations.

Part XIV – *Legal Status, Privileges and Immunities*

Art. 27.(a) The Organization shall enjoy in the territory of each member such legal capacity as may be necessary for the fulfilment of its purpose and for the exercise of its functions.

(b) (i) The Organization shall enjoy in the territory of each member to which the present Convention applies such privileges and immunities as may be necessary for the fulfilment of its purposes and for the exercise of its functions.

(ii) Representatives of members, officers and officials of the Organization, as well as members of the Executive Committee, shall similarly enjoy such privileges and immunities as are necessary for the independent exercise of their functions in connexion with the Organization.

(c) In the territory of any member which is a State and which has acceded to the Convention on the Privileges and Immunities of the Specialized Agencies adopted by the General Assembly of the United Nations on 21 November 1947, such legal capacity, privileges and immunities shall be those defined in the said Convention.

Part XV – *Amendments*

Art. 28.(a) The text of any proposed amendment to the present Convention shall be communicated by the Secretary-General to members of the Organization at least six months in advance of its consideration by Congress.

(b) Amendments to the present Convention involving new obligations for members shall require approval by Congress, in accordance with the provisions art. 11 of the present Convention, by a two-thirds majority vote, and shall come into force on acceptance by two thirds of the members which are States for each such member accepting the amendment, and thereafter for each remaining such member on acceptance by it. Such amendments shall come into force for any member not responsible for its own international relations upon the acceptance on behalf of such a member by the member responsible for the conduct of its international relations.

(c) Other amendments shall come into force upon approval by two thirds of the members which are States.

Part XVI – *Interpretation and Disputes*

Art. 29. Any question or dispute concerning the interpretation or application of the present Convention which is not settled by negotiation or by Congress shall be referred to an independent arbitrator appointed by the President of the International Court of Justice, unless the parties concerned agree on another mode of settlement.

Part XVII – *Withdrawal*

Art. 30.(a) Any member may withdraw from the Organization on twelve months' notice in writing given by it to the Secretary-General of the Organization, who shall at once inform all the members of the Organization of such notice of withdrawal.

(b) Any member of the Organization not responsible for its own international relations may be withdrawn from the Organization on twelve months' notice in writing given by the member or other authority responsible for its international relations to the Secretary-General of the Organization, who shall at once inform all the members of the Organization of such notice of withdrawal.

Part XVIII – *Suspension*

Art. 31. If any member fails to meet its financial obligations to the Organization or otherwise fails in its obligations under the present Convention, Congress may by resolution suspend it from exercising its rights and enjoying privileges as a member of the Organization until it has met such financial or other obligations.

Part XIX – *Ratification and Accession*

Art. 32. The present Convention shall be ratified by the signatory States and the instruments of ratification shall be deposited with the Government of the United States of America, which will notify each signatory and acceding State of the date deposit thereof.

Art. 33. Subject to the provisions of Art. 3 of the present Convention, accession shall be effected by the deposit of an instrument of accession with the Government of the United States of America, which shall notify each Member of the Organization thereof.

Art. 34. Subject to the provisions of art. 3 of the present Convention:

(a) Any contracting State may declare that its ratification of, or accession to, the present Convention includes any territory or group of territories for the international relations of which it is responsible.

(b) The present Convention may at any time thereafter be applied to any such territory or group of territories upon a notification in writing to the Government of the United States of America and the present Convention shall apply to the territory or group of territories on the date of the receipt of the notification by the Government of the United States of America, which will notify each signatory and acceding State thereof.

(c) The United Nations may apply the present Convention to any trust territory or group of territories for which it is the administering authority. The Government of the United States of America will notify all signatory and acceding States of any such Application.

Part XX – *Entry into Force*

Art. 35. The present Convention shall come into force on the thirtieth day after the date of the deposit of the thirtieth instrument of ratification or accession. The present Convention shall come into force for each State ratifying or acceding after that date on the thirtieth day after the deposit of instruments of ratification or accession. The present Convention shall bear the date on which it is opened for signature and all remain open for signature for a period of one hundred and twenty days therafter.

In witness whereof the undersigned, being duly authorized by their respective governments, have signed the present Convention.

Done at Washington this eleventh day of October 1947, in the English and French languages, each equally authentic, the original of which shall be deposited in the archives of the Government of the United States of America. The Government of the United States of America shall transmit certified copies thereof to all the signatory and acceding States."

WMO *Basic Documents*, Geneva 1975.

WOLGADEUTSCHE. *German* = Germans on the Volga. The name for German colonists who settled on the lower Volga 1770–80 and who in the USSR in 1923–41 were the core of the Autonomous Socialistic Soviet Republic of Volga Germans (28,000 sq. km, 605,000 inhabitants 1940). After the German aggression against the USSR in 1941 the German population (about 400,000) was displaced to the Siberia region and the republic formally dissolved Oct. 25, 1945.

Part of the deported Wolgadeutsche were repatriated to Germany after 1955.

Der Grosse Brockhaus, Vol. 12, Wiesbaden, 1957; I. FLEISCHHAVER, B. FINKUS, *The Soviet Germans. Past and Present*, London, 1986.

WOMEN. The UN research programs on the social status of Women was elaborated in the 1970s, realized during the UN Decade for Women in the 1980's. An International Research and Training Institute for the Advancement of Women, INSTRAW, was inaugurated on Aug. 11, 1983, in Santo Domingo. The ECOSOC adopted a number of resolutions and decisions without a vote:

– It welcomed the entry into force on 3 September 1981 of the Convention on the elimination of All Forms of Discrimination against Women and urged the earliest possible commencement of the work of the Committee on the Elimination of Discrimination against Women provided for in the Convention.

– On the role of women in economic development, the Council recommended that the General Assembly request all specialized agencies and other relevant organizations, in particular the UND Program, to consider including special financial components, within existing budgetary resources, in their technical co-operation programs for the economic development of women.

– On the suppression of the traffic in persons and of the exploitation of the prostitution of others, the Council requested the Secretary-General to appoint a special rapporteur who would make a synthesis of the surveys and studies on the traffic in persons and exploitation of prostitution that had been or were being carried out within or outside the United Nations system.

– On the physical abuse of women and children, including such abuses as kidnapping, abduction, forced child labour battered women and children, violence in the family, rape and prostitution, the council called upon Member States of the United Nations to take immediate and energetic steps to combat those social evils and to inform the Secretary-General of the action taken.

– On the subject of elderly women, the Council urged that the special problems faced by elderly women, such as income security, education, employment, housing, health be given explicit and full attention by the World Assembly on Aging held in Vienna from July 26 to August 6, 1982. It further requested member States to ensure that women were included in the preparations for the World Assembly.

– On women and children refugees, the Council expressed grave concern at the plight of Kampuchean women and children, including the many thousands that had been forced to flee to other countries as refugees, and called upon the international community to continue to share the burden of assisting refugees and displaced persons from Democratic Kampuchea.

– On preparations for the 1985 World Conference to Review and Appraise the Achievements of the United Nations Decade for Women, the Council emphasized the importance of undertaking at the conclusion of the Decade, a critical review and appraisal of progress at international, regional and national levels in the achievement of the goals of the Decade.

– The Council decided that the Commission on the Status of Women would be the preparatory body for the July, 1985 World Conference in Nairobi. The Council recommended that a forward-looking perspective on the status of women to the year 2000 be prepared by the preparatory body and considered by the Conference. In 1984 two women first walked in Space: on July 25, Svetlana Savitskaya and on Oct. 11, Catherine D. Sullivan.

UN Chronicle, February, 1979, p. 74; and June, 1982, pp. 82–86; *Women and Development. Guidelines for Program and Project Planning*, UN, New York, 1982; *UN Chronicle*, January, 1984, p. 47; R. ROACH PERSON, *Women and Peace: Theoretical, Historical and Political Perspectives*, London, 1987; S. JOCKES, *Women in the World Economy*, London, 1987; *Women in the World 1975–85. The Women's Decade*, Oxford, 1987.

WOMEN AND CHILDREN. A term incorporated in the international rights of the child and rights of women, also in the UN Declaration on Protection of Women and Children During the State of Emergency and Armed Conflicts; adopted under the UN General Assembly Res. 3318/XXIX, Dec. 14, 1974.

WOMEN, CONVENTION ON THE ELIMINATION OF ALL FORMS OF DISCRIMINATION AGAINST WOMEN, 1979. A Convention adopted on Dec. 18, 1979, came into force on Sept. 3, 1980. The text is as follows:

"The States Parties to the present Convention.

Noting that the Charter of the United Nations reaffirms faith in fundamental human rights, in the dignity and worth of the human person and in the equal rights of men and women.

Noting that the Universal Declaration of Human Rights affirms the principle of the inadmissibility of discrimination and proclaims that all human beings are born free and equal in dignity and rights and that everyone is entitled to all the rights and freedom set forth therein, without distinction of any kind, including distinction based on sex.

Noting that the States parties to the international Covenants on Human Rights have the obligation to ensure the equal right of men and women to enjoy all economic, social cultural, civil and political rights.

Considering the international conventions concluded under the auspices of the United Nations and the specialized agencies promoting equality of rights of men and women.

Noting also the resolutions, declarations and recommendations adopted by the United Nations and the specialized agencies promoting equality of rights of men and women.

Concerned, however, that despite these various instruments extensive discrimination against women continues to exist. Recalling that discrimination against women violates the principles of equality of rights and respect for human dignity, is an obstacle to the participation of women, on equal terms with men, in the political, social, economic and cultural life of their countries, hampers the growth of the prosperity of society and the family and makes more difficult the full development of the potentialities of women in the service of their countries and of humanity.

Concerned that in situations of poverty women have the least access to food, health, education, training and opportunities for employment and other needs.

Convinced that the establishment of the new international economic order based on equity and justice will contribute significantly towards the promotion of equality between men and women.

Emphasizing that the eradication of apartheid, all forms of racism, racial discrimination, colonialism, neo-colonialism, aggression, foreign occupation and domination and interference in the internal affairs of States is essential to the full enjoyment of the rights of men and women.

Affirming that the strengthening of international peace and security, the relaxation of international tension, mutual co-operation among all States irrespective of their social and economic systems, general and complete disarmament, in particular nuclear disarmament under strict and effective international control, the affirmation of the principles of justice, equality and mutual benefit in relations among countries and the realization of the right of peoples under alien and colonial domination and foreign occupation to self-determination and independence, as well as respect for national sovereignty and territorial integrity, will promote social progress and development and as a consequence will contribute to the attainment of full equality between men and women.

Convinced that the full and complete development of a country, the welfare of the world and the cause of peace require the maximum participation of women on equal terms with men in all fields.

Bearing in mind the great contribution of women to the welfare of the family and to the development of society, so far not fully recognized, the social significance of maternity and the role of both parents in the family and in the upbringing of children, and aware that the role of women in procreation should not be a basis for discrimination but that the upbringing of children requires a sharing of responsibility between men and women and society as a whole.

Aware that a change in the traditional role of men as well as the role of women in society and in the family is needed to achieve full equality between men and women.

Determined to implement the principles set forth in the Declaration on the Elimination of Discrimination against Women and for that purpose, to adopt the measures required for the elimination of such discrimination in all its forms and manifestations.

Have agreed on the following:

Part I. For the purposes of the present Convention, the term 'discrimination against women' shall mean any distinction, exclusion or restriction made on the basis of sex which has the effect or purpose of impairing or nullifying the recognition, enjoyment or exercise by women, irrespective of their marital status, on a basis of equality of men and women, of human rights and fundamental freedoms in the political, economic, social, cultural, civil or any other field.

States Parties condemn discrimination against women in all its forms, agree to pursue by all appropriate means and without delay a policy of eliminating discrimination against women, and, to this end, undertake:

(a) To embody the principle of the equality of men and women in their national constitution or other appropriate legislation if not yet incorporated therein and to ensure, through law and other appropriate means, the practical realization of this principle;

(b) To adopt appropriate legislative and other measures, including sanctions where appropriate, prohibiting all discrimination against women;

(c) To establish legal protection of the rights of women on an equal basis with men and to ensure through competent national tribunals and other public institutions the effective protection of women against any act of discrimination;

(d) To refrain from engaging in any act or practice of discrimination against women and to ensure that public authorities and institutions shall act in conformity with this obligation;

(e) To take all appropriate measures to eliminate discrimination against women by any person, organization or enterprise;

(f) To take all appropriate measures, including legislation, to modify or abolish existing laws, regulations, customs and practices which constitute discrimination against women;

(g) To repeal all national penal provisions which constitute discrimination against women.

States Parties shall take in all fields, in particular in the political, social, economic and cultural fields, all appropriate measures, including legislation, to ensure the full development and advancement of women, for the purpose of guaranteeing them the exercise and enjoyment of human rights and fundamental freedoms on a basis of equality with men.

(1) Adoption by States Parties of temporary special measures aimed at accelerating de facto equality between men and women shall not be considered discrimination as defined in the present Convention, but shall in no way entail as a consequence the maintenance of unequal or separate standards; these measures shall be discontinued when the objectives of equality of opportunity and treatment have been achieved.

(2) Adoption by States Parties of special measures, including those measures contained in the present Convention, aimed at protecting maternity shall not be considered discriminatory. States Parties shall take all appropriate measures:

(a) To modify the social and cultural patterns of conduct of men and women, with a view to achieving the elimination of prejudices and customary and all other practices which are based on the idea of the in-

feriority or the superiority of either of the sexes or on stereotyped roles for men and women;
(b) To ensure that family education includes a proper understanding of maternity as a social function and the recognition of the common responsibility of men and women in the upbringing and development of their children, it being understood that the interest of the children is the primordial consideration in all cases.
States Parties shall take all appropriate measures, including legislation to suppress all forms of traffic in women and exploitation of prostitution of women.
Part. II. Art. 7. States Parties shall take all appropriate measures to eliminate discrimination against women in the political and public life of the country and, in particular, shall ensure to women, on equal terms with men, the right:
(a) To vote in all elections and public referenda and to be eligible for election to all publicly elected bodies;
(b) To participate in the formulation of government policy and the implementation thereof and to hold public office and perform all public functions at all levels of government;
(c) To participate in non-governmental organizations and associations concerned with the public and political life of the country.
Art. 8. States Parties shall take all appropriate measures to ensure to women, on equal terms with men and without any discrimination, the opportunity to represent their Governments at the international level and to participate in the work of international organizations.
Art. 9.(1) States Parties shall grant women equal rights with men to acquire, change or retain their nationality. They shall ensure in particular that neither marriage to an alien nor change of nationality by the husband during marriage shall automatically change the nationality of the wife, render her stateless or force upon her the nationality of the husband.
(2) States Parties shall grant women equal rights with men with respect to the nationality of their children.
Part III. Art. 10. States Parties shall take all appropriate measures to eliminate discrimination against women in order to ensure to them equal rights with men in the field of education and in particular to ensure, on a basis of equality of men and women:
(a) The same conditions for career and vocational guidance, for access to studies and for the achievement of diplomas in educational establishments of all categories in rural as well as in urban areas: this equality shall be ensured in pre-school, general, technical, professional and higher technical education, as well as in all types of vocational training;
(b) Access to the same curricula, the same examinations, teaching staff with qualifications of the same standard and school premises and equipment of the same quality;
(c) The elimination of any stereotyped concept of the roles of men and women at all levels and in all forms of education which will help to achieve this aim and, in particular, by the revision of textbooks and school programmes and the adaptation of teaching methods;
(d) The same opportunities to benefit from scholarships and other study grants;
(e) The same opportunities for access to programmes of continuing education, including adult and functional literacy programmes, particularly those aimed at reducing, at the earliest possible time, any gap in education existing between men and women;
(f) The reduction of female student drop-out rates and the organization of programmes to girls and women who have left school prematurely;
(g) The same opportunities to participate actively in sports and physical education;
(h) Access to specific educational information to help to ensure the health and well-being of families, including information and advice on family planning.
Art. 11.(1) States Parties shall take all appropriate measures to eliminate discrimination against women in the field of employment in order to ensure, on a basis of equality of men and women the same rights, in particular:
(a) The right to work as an inalienable right of all human beings;
(b) The right to the same employment opportunities, including the application of the same criteria for selection in matters of employment;
(c) The right to free choice of profession and employment, the right to promotion, job security and all benefits and conditions of service and the right to receive vocational training and retraining, including apprenticeship, advanced vocational training and reccurrent training;
(d) The right to equal remuneration, including benefits, and to equal treatment in respect of work of equal value, as well as equality of treatment in the evaluation of the quality of work;
(e) The right to social security particularly in cases of retirement, unemployment, sickness, invalidity and old age and other incapacity to work, as well as the right to paid leave;
(f) The right to protection of health and to safety in working conditions, including the safeguarding of the function of reproduction;
(2) In order to prevent discrimination against women on the grounds of marriage or maternity and to ensure their effective right to work, States Parties shall take appropriate measures:
(a) To prohibit, subject to the imposition of sanctions, dismissal on the grounds of pregnancy or of maternity leave and discrimination in dismissals on the basis of material status;
(b) To introduce maternity leave with pay or with comparable social benefits without loss of former employment, seniority or social allowances;
(c) To encourage the provision of the necessary supporting social services to enable parents to combine family obligations with work responsibilities and participation in public life, in particular through promoting the establishment and development of a network of child-care facilities;
(d) To provide special protection to women during pregnancy in types of work proved to be harmful to them.
(3) Protective legislation relating to matters covered in this article shall be reviewed periodically in the light of scientific and technicological knowledge and shall be revised, repealed or extended as necessary.
Art. 12.(1) States Parties shall take all appropriate measures to eliminate discrimination against women in the field of health care in order to ensure, on a basis of equality of men and women, access to health care services, including those related to family planning.
(2) Notwithstanding the provisions of paragraph 1 of this article, States Parties shall ensure to women appropriate services in connexion with pregnancy, confinement and the postnatal period, granting free services where necessary, as well as adequate nutrition during pregnancy and lactation.
Art. 13. States Parties shall take all appropriate measures to eliminate discrimination against women in other spheres of economic and social life in order to ensure, on a basis of equality of men and women, the same rights, in particular:
(a) The right to family benefits;
(b) The right to ban loans, mortgages and other forms of financial credit;
(c) The right to participate in recreational activities, sports and all aspects of cultural life.
Art. 14.(1) States Parties shall take into account the particular problems faced by rural women and significant roles which rural women play in the economic survival of their families, including their work in the non-monetized sectors of the economy, and shall take all appropriate measures to ensure the application of the provisions of the present Convention to women in rural areas.
(2) States Parties shall take all appropriate measures to eliminate discrimination against women in rural areas in order to ensure, on a basis of equality of men and women, that they participate in and benefit from rural development and in particular, shall ensure to such women the right:
(a) To participate in the elaboration and implementation of development planning at all levels;
(b) To have access to adequate health care facilities including information, counselling and services in family planning;
(c) To benefit directly from social security programmes;
(d) To obtain all types of training and education, formal and non-formal, including that relating to functional literacy, as well as, inter alia, the benefit of all community and extension services, in order to increase their technical proficiency;
(e) To organize self-help groups and co-operatives in order to obtain equal access to economic opportunities through employment or self-employment;
(f) To participate in all community activities;
(g) To have access to agricultural credit and loans, marketing facilities, appropriate technology and equal treatment in land and agrarian reform as well as in land resettlement schemes;
(h) To enjoy adequate living conditions, particularly in relation to housing, sanitation, electricity and water supply, transport and communications.
Part. IV. Art. 15.(1) States Parties shall accord to women equality with men before the law.
(2) States Parties shall accord to women, in civil matters, a legal capacity identical to that of men and the same opportunities to exercise that capacity. In particular, they shall give women equal rights to conclude contracts and to administer property and shall treat them equally in all stages of procedure in courts and tribunals.
(3) States Parties agree that all contracts and all other private instruments of any kind with a legal effect which is directed at restricting the legal capacity of women shall be deemed null and void.
(4) States Parties shall accord to men and women the same rights with regard to the law relating to the movement of persons and the freedom to choose their residence and domicile.
Art. 16.(1) States parties shall take all appropriate measures to eliminate discrimination against women in all matters relating to marriage and family relations and in particular shall ensure, on a basis of equality of men and women:
(a) The same right to enter into marriage;
(b) The same right freely to choose a spouse and to enter into marriage only with their free and full consent;
(c) The same rights and responsibilities during marriage and at its dissolution;
(d) The same rights and responsibilities as parents, irrespective of their marital status, in matters relating to their children; in all cases the interests of the children shall be paramount;
(e) The same rights to decide freely and responsibly on the number and spacing of their children and to have access to the information, education and means to enable them to exercise these rights;
(f) The same rights and responsibilities with regard to guardianship, wardship, trusteeship and adoption of children, or similar institutions where these concepts exist in national legislation; in all cases the interests of the children shall be paramount;
(g) The same personal rights as husband and wife, including the right to choose a family name, a profession and an occupation;
(h) The same rights for both in respect of the ownership, acquisition, management, administration, enjoyment and disposition of property, whether free of charge or for a valuable consideration.
(2) The betrothal and the marriage of a child shall have no legal effect, and all necessary action, including legislation, shall be taken, to specify a minimum age for marriage and to make the registration of marriages in an official registry compulsory.
Part V. Art.17(1) For the purpose of considering the progress made in the implementation of the present Convention, there shall be established a Committee on the Elimination of Discrimination against Women (hereinafter referred to as the Committee) consisting, at the time of entry into force of the Convention, of eighteen and, after ratification of or accession to the Convention by the thirty-fifth State Party, of twenty-three experts of high moral standing and competence in the field covered by the Convention. The experts shall be elected by States Paries from among their nationals and shall serve in their personal capacity, consideration being given to equitable geographical distribution and to the representation of the different forms of civilization as well as the principal legal systems.
(2) The members of the Committee shall be elected by secret ballot from a list of persons nominated by States Parties. Each State Party may nominate one person from among its own nationals.
(3) The initial election shall be held six months after the date of the entry into force of the present Convention. At least three months before the date of each election the Secretary-General of the United Nations shall address a letter to the State Parties inviting them to submit their nominations within two months. The

Secretary-General shall prepare a list in alphabetical order of all persons thus nominated, indicating the States Parties which have nominated them, and shall submit it to the States Parties.

(4) Elections of the members of the Committee shall be held at a meeting of States Parties convened by the Secretary-General at United Nations Headquarters. At that meeting, for which two thirds of the States Parties shall constitute a quorum, the persons elected to the Committee shall be those nominees who obtain the largest number of votes and an absolute majority of the votes of the representatives of States parties present and voting.

(5) The members of the Committee shall be elected for a term of four years. However, the terms of nine of the members elected at the first election shall expire at the end of two years; immediately after the first election the names of these nine members shall be chosen by lot by the Chairman of the Committee.

(6) The election of the five additional members of the Committee shall be held in accordance with the provisions of paragraphs 2, 3 and 4 of this article, following the thirty-fifth ratification or accession. The terms of two of the additional members elected on this occasion shall expire at the end of two years, the names of these two members having been chosen by lot by the Chairman of the Committee.

(7) For the filling of casual vacancies, the State party whose expert has ceased to function as a member of the Committee shall appoint another expert from its nationals, subject to the approval of the Committee.

(8) The members of the Committee shall, with the approval of the General Assembly, receive emoluments from United Nations resources on such terms and conditions as the Assembly may decide, having regard to the importance of the Committee's responsibilities.

(9) The Secretary-General of the United Nations shall provide the necessary staff and facilities for the Committee under the present Convention.

Art. 18.(1) States parties undertake to submit to the Secretary-General of the United Nations, for consideration by the Committee, a report on the legislative, judicial, administrative or other measures which they have adopted to give effect to the provisions of the present Convention and on the progress made in this respect:

(a) Within one year after the entry into force for the State concerned;

(b) Thereafter at least every four years and further whenever the Committee so requests.

(2) Reports may indicate factors and difficulties affecting the degree of fulfilment of obligations under the present Convention.

Art. 19.(1) The Committee shall adopt its own rules of procedure.

(2) The Committee shall elect its officers for a term of two years.

Art. 20.(1) The Committee shall normally meet for a period of not more than two weeks annually in order to consider the reports submitted in accordance with art. 18 of the present Convention.

(2) The meetings of the Committee shall normally be held at United Nations Headquarters or at any other convenient place as determined by the Committee.

Art. 21.(1) The Committee shall, through the Economic and Social Council, report annually to the General Assembly of the United Nations on its activities and may make suggestions and general recommendations based on the examination of reports and information received from the States Parties. Such suggestions and general recommendations shall be included in the report of the Committee together with comments, if any, from States Parties.

(2) The Secretary-General of the United Nations shall transmit the reports of the Committee to the Commission on the Status of Women for its information.

Art. 22. The specialized agencies shall be entitled to be represented at the consideration of the implementation of such provisions of the present Convention as fall within the scope of their activities. The Committee may invite the specialized agencies to submit reports on the implementation of the Convention in areas falling within the scope of their activities.

Part VI. Art. 23. Nothing in the present Convention shall affect any provisions that are more conducive to the achievement of equality between men and women which may be contained:

(a) in the legislation of a State Party; or

(b) In any other international Convention, treaty or agreement in force for that State.

Art. 24. States Parties undertake to adopt all necessary measures at the national level aimed at achieving the full realization of the rights recognized in the present Convention.

Art. 25.(1) The present Convention shall be open for signature by all States.

(2) The Secretary-General of the United Nations is designated as the depositary of the present Convention.

(3) The present Convention is subject to ratification; instruments of ratification shall be deposited with the Secretary-General of the United Nations.

(4) The present Convention shall be open to accession by all States. Accession shall be effected by the deposit of an instrument of accession with the Secretary-General of the United Nations.

Art. 26.(1) A request for the revision of the present Convention may be made at any time by any State Party by means of a notification in writing addressed to the Secretary-General of the United Nations.

(2) The General Assembly of the United Nations shall decide upon the steps, if any, to be taken in respect of such a request.

Art.27(1) The present Convention shall enter into force on the thirtieth day after the date of deposit with the Secretary-General of the United Nations of the twentieth instrument of ratification or accession.

(2) For each State ratifying the present Convention or acceding to it after the deposit of twentieth instrument of ratification or accession, the Convention shall enter into force on the thirtieth day after the date of the deposit of its own instrument of ratification or accession.

Art. 28.(1) The Secretary-General of the United Nations shall receive and circulate to all States the text of reservations made by States at the time of ratification or accession.

(2) A reservation incompatible with the object and purpose of the present Convention shall not be permitted.

(3) Reservations may be withdrawn at any time by notification to this effect addressed to the Secretary-General of the United Nations, who shall then inform all States thereof. Such notification shall take effect on the date on which it is received.

Art. 29.(1) Any dispute between two or more States Parties concerning the interpretation or application of the present Convention which is not settled by negotiation shall, at the request of one of them, be submitted to arbitration. If within six months from the date of the request for arbitration the parties are unable to agree on the organization of the arbitration, any one of those parties may refer the dispute to the international Court of Justice by request in conformity with the Statute of the Court.

(2) Each State Party may at the time of signature or ratification of the present Convention or accession thereto declare that it does not consider itself bound by paragraph 1 of this article. The other States Parties shall not be bound by that paragraph with respect to any State Party which has made such a reservation.

(3) Any State Party which has made a reservation in accordance with paragraph 2 of this article may at any time withdraw that reservation by notification to the Secretary-General of the United Nations.

Art. 30. The present Convention, the Arabic, Chinese, English, French, Russian and Spanish texts of which are equally authentic, shall be deposited with the Secretary-General of the United Nations.

In Witness Whereof the undersigned duly authorized, have signed the present Convention."

The GA Resolution 43/100 of Dec. 8, 1988 urges all States that have not yet ratified or acceded to the Convention, to do so as soon as possible.

UN Yearbook, 1979, pp. 895–899; UN Chronicle, January, 1984, p. 47; UN Resolutions and Decisions adopted by the General Assembly during the First Part of its Forty-Third Session, from 20 September to 22 December 1988, New York, 1989, pp. 342–343.

WOMEN, INTER-AMERICAN CONVENTIONS. The Seventh International Conference of American States prepared a Convention on the Nationality of Women, signed by the governments of 21 American Republics on Dec. 26, 1933 at Montevideo; came into force on Aug. 29, 1934; not ratified by Bolivia, the Dominican Republic, El Salvador, Haiti, Paraguay and Peru.

The Ninth Conference prepared the Inter-American Convention on the Granting of Political Rights to Women, signed on May 2, 1948, by the governments of 20 Republics (not signed by Mexico); came into force for each country on the date of its deposit of ratification; not ratified by Chile, the USA and Venezuela.

The Inter-American Convention on the Granting of Civil Rights to Women was also signed on May 2, 1948 at Bogota, by the governments of 21 American Republics; not ratified by Bolivia, Chile, Peru and Venezuela.

CARNEGIE ENDOWMENT, *International Conferences of American States, First Supplement 1933–1940*, Washington, DC, 1940; PAU, *Second Supplement, 1942–1954*, Washington, DC, 1958.

WOMEN'S DAY, INTERNATIONAL. The Women's Day is celebrated on Mar. 8, in keeping with the proclamation of the International Conference of Socialist Women, Aug. 25–27, 1910, held in Copenhagen with delegations from 18 countries attending. On the fiftieth anniversary of the International Women's Day (in Apr., 1960) the World Federation of Democratic Women convened an International Conference of Women, attended by 999 delegates from 73 countries.

WOMEN'S DECADE, 1976–1985. The UN Decade for Women, proclaimed by General Assembly Res. 3520, 1975, terminated with a World Conference to Review and Appraise the Achievements of the Decade, in Nairobi, July 15–27, 1985, attended by over 3,000 delegates from 158 countries.

The United Nations Decade for Women: An End and a Beginning, in: *WHO Chronicle 1985*, No. 5; *UN Chronicle*, 1985, No. 7; KEESING's *Record of World Events*, January, 1986.

WOMEN'S INTERNATIONAL ORGANIZATIONS. Organizations reg. with the UIA:

Africa Women's Committee of the African-American Institute, f. 1959, New York.
All African Women's Conference, f. 1962, Algiers.
All India Women's Conference, f. 1926, New Delhi. Consultative status with ECOSOC, UNESCO, UNICEF and FAO.
All Pakistan Women's Association, f. 1949, Karachi. Consultative status with UNESCO and UNICEF. Publ.: *Newsletter.*
Altrusa Club, f. 1935, Chicago.
European Union of Women, f. 1955, London.
Federation of Asian Women's Association, f. 1969, Manila, Consultative status with UNESCO.
General Federation of Women's Clubs, f. 1890, New York. Publ.: *Clubwoman.*
Inter-American Commission of Women, f. 1928, Washington, DC. Specialized organization of OAS. Publ.: *News Bulletin* (in English and Spanish).
International Alliance of Women Equal Rights and Equal Responsibilities, f. 1904, London. Consultative status with ECOSOC, UNESCO and UNICEF. Publ.: *International Women's News* (bi-monthly).
International Association of Physical Education and Sports for Girls and Women, f. 1953, Paris.
International Association of Women and Home Page Journalists, f. 1964, Brussels.
International Conference of Women Engineers and Scientists, f. 1964, New York.
International Council of Jewish Women, f. 1912, Paris.
International Council of Social Democratic Women, f. 1955, London. Consultative status with ECOSOC and UNESCO; ILO special list. Publ.: *Bulletin.*
International Council of Women, f. 1888, Paris. Consultative status with ECOSOC, UNESCO, UNICEF and FAO; ILO special list. Publ.: *ICW Newsletter.*
International Federation of Business and Professional Women, f. 1930, London.

International Federation of Mazdarnan Women, f. 1951, Stuttgart. Publ.: *Mazdarnan Bulletin.*

International Federation of Women in Legal Careers, f. 1929, Paris. Consultative status with ECOSOC and UNESCO; ILO special list. Publ.: *Bulletin.*

International Federation of Women Lawyers, f. 1944, México, DF. Publ.: *La Abogada News Letters.*

International Federation of University Women, f. 1919, London. Publ.: *Newsletter.*

International Federation of Women's Football, f. 1970, Berne.

International Inner Wheel, f. 1934, London. Rotarians Women's Clubs with the name Inner Wheel Clubs. Publ.: *Magazine.*

International Scientific Institute for Feminine Interpretation, f. 1971, Amsterdam.

International Union of Liberal Christian Women, f. 1910, The Hague. Publ.: *Newsletter.*

International Union of Women Architects, f. 1963, Paris.

International Women's Cricket Circle, f. 1958, London. International Women's Fishing Association, f. 1955, Palm Beach, Florida.

Liaison Committee of Women's International Organizations, f. 1925, New York. Consultative status with UNESCO.

Medical Women's International Association, f. 1919, Geneva.

Open Door International for the Economic Emancipation of the Women Worker, f. 1929, Brussels. Consultative status with ECOSOC. Publ.: *Circular Letter.*

Pan-American Liaison Committee of Women's Organizations, f. 1944, Washington, DC.

Pan-American Medical Women's Alliance, f. 1947, Kansas City.

Pan-Pacific and South-east Asia Women's Association, f. 1928, Seoul.

Quota International, f. 1919, Washington, DC. Business Women's Quota Club in Canada, USA, Australia and New Zealand.

Scandinavian Association of Women Teachers, f. 1931, Malmö.

Sainte Jeanne d'Arc International Alliance, f. 1911, Geneva. Consultative status with ECOSOC and UNESCO; ILO special list. Publ.: *The Catholic Citizen* (English and French).

United Women of Americas, f. 1934, New York.

Women's Corona Society, f. 1950, London.

Women's International Cultural Federation, f. 1961, Paris, Publ.: *Expression.*

Women's International Democratic Federation, f. 1945, Berlin. Consultative status with UNESCO and ECOSOC; ILO special list. Publ.: *Women of the Whole World.*

Women's International League for Peace and Freedom, f. 1915, Geneva. Consultative status with ECOSOC, FAO and UNICEF; ILO special list. Publ.: *Pax et Libertas* (quarterly Bulletin).

Women's International Network, f. 1975, Lexington, Ky., USA. Publ.: *WIN News.*

Women's International Zionist Organization, f. 1920, Tel Aviv. Consultative status with ECOSOC and UNICEF. Publ.: *WIZO Review.*

World Association of Women Executives, f. 1950, Paris.

World Federation of Methodist Women, f. 1939, Aurora Illinois. Publ.: *Newsletter* (quarterly).

World Union of Catholic Women's Organizations, f. 1910, Paris. Consultative status with ECOSOC, UNESCO, UNICEF and FAO; ILO special list. Publ.: *Newsletter.*

World Women's Christian Temperance Union, f. 1883, London. Consultative status with ECOSOC and UNICEF. Publ.: *White Ribbon Bulletin.*

World Young Women's Christian Association ▷ YWCA, f. 1894, Geneva.

Yearbook of International Organizations.

WOMEN'S INTERNATIONAL YEAR, 1975. The Year was proclaimed by the UN General Assembly on Nov. 11, 1972. The first World Conference on Women took place in 1975 in Mexico City with more than 1000 delegates from 133 countries.

WOMEN'S LABOUR. A subject of international ILO conventions excluding women from work that is taxing and dangerous to their health.

WOMEN'S POLITICAL RIGHTS CONVENTION, 1952. A Convention adopted by the UN General Assembly on Dec. 20, 1952, "considering that the peoples of the United Nations are determined to promote equality of rights for men and women, in conformity with the principles embodied in the Charter, believing that an international convention on the political rights of women will constitute an important step towards the universal attainment of equal rights of men and women."
The text is as follows:

"The Contracting Parties,
Desiring to implement the principles of equality of rights for men and women contained in the Charter of the United Nations,
Recognizing that everyone has the right to take part in the government of his country directly or through freely chosen representatives, and has the right to equal access to public service in his country, and desiring to equalize the status of men and women in the enjoyment and exercise of political rights, in accordance with the provisions of the Charter of the United Nations and of the Universal Declaration of Human rights,
Having resolved to conclude a Convention for this purpose,
Hereby agree as hereinafter provided:
Art. I. Women shall be entitled to vote in all elections on equal terms with men, without any discrimination.
Art. II. Women shall be eligible for election to all publicly elected bodies, established by national law, on equal terms with men, without any discrimination.
Art. III. Women shall be entitled to hold public office and to exercise all public functions, established by national law, on equal terms with men, without any discrimination.
Art. IV.(1) This Convention shall be open for signature on behalf of any Member of the United Nations and also on behalf of any other State to which an invitation has been addressed by the General Assembly.
(2) This Convention shall be ratified and the instruments of ratification shall be deposited with the Secretary-General of the United Nations.
Art. V.(1) This Convention shall be open for accession to all States referred to in paragraph 1 of art. IV.
(2) Accession shall be effected by the deposit of an instrument of accession with the Secretary-General of the United Nations.
Art. VI.(1) This Convention shall come into force on the ninetieth day following the date of deposit of the sixth instrument of ratification of accession.
(2) For each State ratifying or acceding to the Convention after the deposit of the sixth instrument of ratification or accession the Convention shall enter into force on the ninetieth day after deposit by such State of its instrument of ratification or accession.
Art. VII. In the event that any State submits a reservation to any of the articles of this Convention at the time of signature, ratification or accession, the Secretary-General shall communicate the text of the reservation to all States which objects to the reservation may, within a period of ninety days from the date of the said communication (or upon the date of its becoming a party to the Convention), notify the Secretary-General that it does not accept it. In such case, the Convention shall not enter into force as between such State and the State making the reservation.
Art. VIII.(1) Any State may denounce this Convention by written notification to the Secretary-General of the United Nations. Denunciation shall take effect one year after the date of receipt of the notification by the Secretary-General.
(2) This Convention shall cease to be in force as from the date when the denunciation which reduces the number of parties to less than six becomes effective.
Art. IX. Any dispute which may arise between any two or more Contracting States concerning the interpretation or application of this Convention, which is not settled by negotiation, shall at the request of any one of the parties to the dispute be referred to the International Court of Justice for decision, unless they agree to another mode of settlement.

Art. X. The Secretary-General of the United Nations shall notify all Members of the United Nations and the non-member States contemplated in paragraph 1 of art. IV of this Convention of the following:
(a) Signatures and instruments of ratification received in accordance with art. IV;
(b) Instruments of accession received in accordance with art. V;
(c) The date upon which this Convention enters into force in accordance with art. VI;
(d) Communications and notifications received in accordance with art. VII;
(e) Notifications of denunciation received in accordance with paragraph 1 of art. VIII;
(f) Abrogation in accordance with paragraph 2 of Art. VIII.
Art. XI.(1) This Convention, of which the Chinese, English, French, Russian and Spanish texts shall be equally authentic, shall be deposited in the Archives of the United Nations.
(2) The Secretary-General of the United Nations shall transmit a certified copy to all Members of the United Nations and to the non-member States contemplated in paragraph 1 of art. IV."

UN Yearbook, 1952.

WOMEN'S RIGHTS. The aim of the struggle waged by the international movement for the emancipation of women in the late 19th century (since 1888); subject of international conventions. The first convention drawn up in The Hague (1902) referred to the marital rights in case of a divorce and the right to exercise custody over minors. The conventions of 1904 and 1910 included the ban on trafficking in women and children. Since 1919 the problem of women's social position and their occupational status have been the topic of conventions prepared by the International Labor Organization, the first of them under the auspices of the League of Nations and later the UN.
The Fifth International Conference of American States, held in Santiago in 1923, voiced their concern over the "legal inequality of women;" the Sixth Conference in Havana in 1928 established an International Women's Commission; the Seventh Conference in Montevideo in 1933 approved the Convention on the Nationality of Women ratified by the majority of American states; the Eighth Conference held in Lima in 1938, declared that "Women have the right to equal political treatment as men" and recommended that governments urgently adopt appropriate legislation. The political right to participate in elections was granted women by New Zealand in 1893, Australia in 1902, Finland in 1906, England (from the age of 30) in 1917, Poland in 1918, Russia in 1919, the USA in 1920, Ecuador in 1929, Brazil in 1932, Cuba in 1934, El Salvador in 1939, Dominica in 1942, Guatemala and Panama in 1945, Argentina and Venezuela in 1947, Chile and Costa Rica in 1949, Haiti in 1950, Bolivia in 1952, Mexico in 1953, Honduras, Nicaragua and Peru in 1955, Colombia in 1957, Paraguay in 1961.
After World War II about 90 new States introduced electoral women's righs into their constitutions. In Europe there is only one state – Liechtenstein – which does not recognize equal rights of women; of the Arab states – Saudi Arabia, Jordan and Kuwait; of the African states – Nigeria. The UN Convention on Political Rights of Women of 1956 has been ratified by all American states except Chile, Uruguay, the USA and Venezuela, and that on Civil Rights of Women by all except for Bolivia, Chile, Haiti, Peru, Uruguay and Venezuela. The 1951 Convention No. 100 of the ILO on equal remuneration for men and women has been ratified only by Argentina, Dominica, Haiti, Honduras, Mexico, Panama and Venezuela. Even fewer African and Asian states have ratified it. In the mid-war period the ILO drafted and adopted three conventions on maternity protection (1919), on the limitation of

employment of women on nightshifts (revised in 1934) and on the ban on employing women in subterranean work (1935). In 1935 the Assembly of the League of Nations resolved to examine the legal and social conditions of women in the matter of civil and political rights. These Studies (the part related to private law was prepared by the Institute of Codification of Private Law in Rome) were discontinued during World War II and later resumed by the UN. Three UN bodies: the General Assembly, the ECOSOC and the Secretariat, jointly with the special Commission on the Status of Women, introduced the problem of women's rights into their programs of activity. The above-mentioned commission was constituted on June 21, 1946, as one of the main functional commissions of ECOSOC. The UN efforts to promote the principle of equal rights of men and women were initially directed towards securing equality of men and women in law. As women achieved legal equality in many member States, emphasis shifted from *de jure* to *de facto* equality. The Commission on the Status of Women and other organs of the United Nations system sought to encourage and to assist governments to give women equal opportunities, as well as equal rights, with men. Expansion of the Commission's program dates back to 1962 when the UN General Assembly called for a study of the possibility of providing new resources for the establishment of a unified long-term United Nations program for the advancement of women. Under such a program, all interested organs and agencies within the UN system and all the methods and techniques available, including technical assistance, would be used to enable women to participate in all aspects of national and international life and to encourage their participation. In 1966 the Commission suggested that basic objectives of such a program should be: to promote the universal recognition of the dignity and worth of the human person and of the equal rights of men and women in accordance with the Charter and the Universal Declaration of Human Rights; to enable women to participate fully in the development of society so that it may benefit from the contribution of all its members; and to stimulate an awareness among both men and women of women's full potential and of the importance of their contribution to the development of society. In 1970, on the recommendations of the Commission, the UN General Assembly adopted a program of concerted international action for the advancement of women. The program set forth general objectives and minimum targets to be achieved during the Second United Nations Development Decade (1970–1980). At the same session, the Assembly adopted a comprehensive strategy for the entire decade, which included the encouragement of "the full integration of women in the total development effort." General objectives of the program included: ratification of or accession to international conventions relating to the status of women; enactment of legislation to bring national laws into conformity with relevant international instruments, in particular the Declaration on the Elimination of Discrimination against Women; assessment of women's contribution to the various economic and social sectors in relation to their countries' overall development plans and programs; and study of the effects of scientific and technological change on the status of women. In 1970 the UN General Assembly adopted the first resolution in its history urging equal opportunities for the employment of women in the UN Secretariat. Related resolutions were adopted by the Assembly in 1972 and 1974. At the suggestion of the Commission on the Status of Women and a number of non-governmental organizations, the UN General Assembly in 1972 proclaimed 1975 as

International Women's Year. The Assembly devoted the Year to promoting equality between men and women; to ensure the full integration of women in the total development effort; and to recognize the importance of women's increasing contribution to the development of friendly relations and co-operation among States and to the strengthening of world peace. The major event of the Year, whose theme was "Equality, Development and Peace," was the World Conference sponsored by the UN, and held in Mexico City from June 19 to July 2. More than 1000 representatives, about 70% of them women, from 133 States attended the first world inter-governmental conference on women ever held. The Conference adopted the Declaration of Mexico on the Equality of Men and Women and their Contribution to Development and Peace, 1975; the World Plan of Action and regional plans for the implementation of the objectives of the year and 34 related resolutions on subjects ranging from improved education and health services to rights of Palestinians. The Declaration contains 17 principles which, among other things, define the meaning of equality between women and men, stress the specific responsibility of the State to find ways and means to enable women to be fully integrated into society and stress the responsibilities of men in the context of family life. The World Plan of Action sets out guidelines for improving the status of women and seeks to stimulate national and international efforts to solve the problems of underdevelopment and of the socio-economic structures which place women in an inferior position. The Plan recommends a series of targets to be achieved as a "minimum" by 1980, including a marked increase in women's literacy and equal access of women to every level of education; vocational training in basic skills; employment opportunities; laws to guarantee equality in political participation, employment and pay; health education and rural services; parity in civil, social and political rights such as those relating to marriage, citizenship and commerce; and recognition of the economic value of women's traditionally unpaid work in the home and in domestic food production. During International Women's Year 1975, the Assembly reaffirmed that the equitable distribution of positions between men and women was a major principle of United Nations recruitment policy, urged member States to recommend women candidates for professional posts, and requested the Secretary-General to intensify the recruitment of women. The Assembly also approved a number of amendments to the regulations of the UN Joint Staff Pension Fund, thereby removing, 30 years after the adoption of the UN Charter, the final element of differential treatment based on sex in the UN staff rules and regulations. In Dec., 1975 the UN General Assembly endorsed the Plan of Action and the Conference resolutions. It adopted a number of related resolutions, among them a call to ratify international conventions and other instruments concerning the protection of women's rights. In 1976 the UN General Assembly adopted criteria for the use of the Voluntary Fund and proposals for its management. The criteria stress that in utilizing the Fund's resources, priority should be given to projects benefiting rural women, poor women in urban areas and similar disadvantaged groups. The first pledging conference for the Decade was held in Nov., 1977. At that Conference, 34 countries pledged the equivalent of $3,837,155 of which $3,301,655 was earmarked for the Voluntary Fund and $535,500 for the International Research and Training Institute for the Advancement of Women. A second pledging conference for voluntary contributions took place in 1978. In 1980 the UN

General Assembly adopted a number of resolutions related to the protection of women's rights. On 15–26 July 1985, the World Conference to Review and Appraise the Achievements of the UN Decade for Women: Equality, Development and Peace took place in Nairobi. GA Res. 43/107 of Dec. 8, 1988 was related to the implementation of the Nairobi Forward-looking Strategies for the Advancement of Women.

Nationality of Married Women, New York, 1955; *The History of the Recognition of the Political Rights of the American Women*, PAU, Washington, DC, 1965; "Women Around the World," in: *The Annals*, Philadelphia, January, 1968; *Employment of Qualified Women*, UN, New York, 1970; *Año Internacional de la Mujer*, México, DF, 1975; *UN Resolutions and Decisions adopted by the General Assembly during the First Part of its Forty-Third Session, from 20 September to 22 December 1988*, New York, 1989, pp. 344–345.

WOMEN'S RIGHTS, UN DECLARATION, 1967.
Elaborated 1963–66 and adopted Nov. 7, 1967 by the UN General Assembly with the title Declaration on Elimination of Discrimination of Women. The text is as follows:

"The General Assembly,
Considering that the peoples of the United Nations have, in the Charter, reaffirmed their faith in fundamental human rights, in the dignity and worth of the human person and in the equal rights of men and women.
Considering that the Universal Declaration of Human Rights asserts the principle of non-discrimination and proclaims that all human beings are born free and equal in dignity and rights and that everyone is entitled to all the rights and freedoms set forth therein, without distinction of any kind, including any distinction as to sex.
Taking into account the resolutions, declarations, conventions and recommendations of the United Nations and the specialized agencies designed to eliminate all forms of discrimination and to promote equal rights for men and women,
Concerned that, despite the Charter of the United Nations, the Universal Declaration of Human Rights, the International Covenants on Human Rights and other instruments of the United Nations and the specialized agencies, and despite the progress made in the matter of equality of rights, there continues to exist considerable discrimination against women,
Considering that discrimination against women is incompatible with human dignity and with the welfare of the family and of society, prevents their participation, on equal terms, with men, in the political, social, economic and cultural life of their countries, and is an obstacle to the full development of the potentialities of women in the service of their countries and of humanity,
Bearing in mind the great contribution made by women to social, political, economic and cultural life and the part they play in the family and particularly in the rearing of children,
Convinced that the full and complete development of a country, the welfare of the world and the cause of peace require the maximum participation of women as well as men in all fields,
Considering that it is necessary to ensure the universal recognition in law and in fact of the principle of equality of men and women.
Solemnly proclaims this Declaration:
Art. 1. Discrimination against women, denying or limiting as it does their equality or rights with men, is fundamentally unjust and constitutes an offence against human dignity.
Art. 2. All appropriate measures shall be taken to abolish existing laws, customs, regulations and practices which are discriminatory against women, and to establish adequate legal protection for equal rights of men and women, in particular:
(a) The principle of equality of rights shall be embodied in the constitution or otherwise guaranteed by law;
(b) The international instruments of the United Nations and the specialized agencies relating to the elimination of discrimination against women shall be

ratified or acceded to and fully implemented as soon as practicable.

Art. 3. All appropriate measures shall be taken to educate public opinion and to direct national aspirations towards the eradication of prejudice and the abolition of customary and all other practices which are based on the idea of the inferiority of women.

Art. 4. All appropriate measures shall be taken to ensure to women on equal terms with men, without any discrimination:

(a) The right to vote in all elections and be eligible for election to all publicly elected bodies;

(b) The right to vote in all public referenda;

(c) The right to hold public office and to exercise all public functions. Such rights shall be guaranteed by legislation.

Art. 5. Women shall have the same rights as men to acquire, change or retain their nationality. Marriage to an alien shall not automatically affect the nationality of the wife either by rendering her stateless or by forcing upon her the nationality of her husband.

Art. 6.(1) Without prejudice to the safeguarding of the unity and the harmony of the family, which remains the basic unit of any society, all appropriate measures, particularly legislative measures, shall be taken to ensure to women, married or unmarried, equal rights with men in the field of civil law, and in particular:

(a) The right to equality in legal capacity and the exercise thereof;

(b) The right to acquire, administer, enjoy, dispose of and inherit property, including property acquired during marriage;

(c) The same rights as men with regard to the law on the movement of persons.

(2) All appropriate measures shall be taken to ensure the principle of equality of status of the husband and wife, and in particular:

(a) Women shall have the right as men to free choice of a spouse and to enter into marriage only with their free and full consent;

(b) Women shall have equal rights with men during marriage and at its dissolution. In all cases the interest of the children shall be paramount.

(c) Parents shall have equal rights and duties in matters relating to their children. In all cases the interest of the children shall be paramount.

(3) Child marriage and the betrothal of young girls before puberty shall be prohibited, and effective action, including legislation, shall be taken to specify a minimum age for marriage and to make the registration of marriages in an official registry compulsory.

Art. 7. All provisions of penal codes which constitute discrimination against women shall be repealed.

Art. 8. All appropriate measures, including legislation, shall be taken to combat all forms of traffic in women and exploitation of prostitution of women.

Art. 9. All appropriate measures shall be taken to ensure to girls and women, married or unmarried, equal rights with men in education at all levels, and in particular:

(a) Equal conditions of access to, and study in, educational institutions of all types, including universities and vocational, technical and professional schools;

(b) The same choice of curricula, the same examinations, teaching staff with qualifications of the same standard, and school premises and equipment of the same quality, whether the institutions are co-educational or not;

(c) Equal opportunities to benefit from scholarships and other study grants;

(d) Equal opportunities for access to programmes of continuing education, including adult literacy programmes;

(e) Access to educational information to help in ensuring the health and well-being of families.

Art. 10.(1) All appropriate measures shall be taken to ensure to women, married or unmarried, equal rights with men in the field of economic and social life, and in particular:

(a) The rights, without discrimination on grounds of marital status or any other grounds, to receive vocational training, to work, to free choice of profession and employment, and to professional and vocational advancement;

(b) The right to equal remuneration with men and to equality of treatment in respect of work of equal value;

(c) The right to leave with pay, retirement privileges and provision for security in respect of unemployment, sickness, old age or other incapacity to work;

(d) The right to receive family allowance on equal terms with men.

(2) In order to prevent discrimination against women on account of marriage or maternity and to ensure their effective right to work, measures shall be taken to prevent their dismissal in the event of marriage or maternity leave, with the guarantee of returning to former employment, and to provide the necessary social services, including child-care facilities.

(3) Measures taken to protect women in certain types of work, for reasons inherent in their physical nature, shall not be regarded as discriminatory.

Art. 11.(1) The principle of equality of rights of men and women, demands implementation in all States in accordance with the principles of the Charter of the United Nations and of the Universal Declaration of Human Rights.

(2) Governments, non-governmental organizations and individuals are urged, therefore, to do all in their power to promote the implementation of the principles contained in this Declaration."

UN Yearbook, 1967.

WOMEN, UN DEVELOPMENT FUND FOR.
Est. on Dec. 14, 1984. A subject of GA Res. 43/102, of Dec. 8, 1988.

UN Resolutions and Decisions adopted by the General Assembly during the First Part of its Forty-Third Session from 20 September to 22 December 1988, New York, 1989, pp. 346–347.

WON. A monetary unit of the Democratic People's Republic of Korea; one won = 100 cheun; issued by the Central Bank of the Democratic People's Republic of Korea.

WOOD AND TIMBER. A subject of international co-operation. Organizations reg. with the UIA:

European Committee of Woodworking Machinery Manufacturers, f. 1960, Neuilly-sur-Seine.
European Confederation of Woodworking Industries, f. 1952, Paris.
European Woodworking Machinery Importers Committee, f. 1974, Paris.
Inter-African Organization for Forestry Economy and Marketing of Timber, est. 1975, Libreville, by the governments of Cameroon, Central African Republic, Congo, Gabon, Ghana, Equatorial Guinea, Ivory Coast, Liberia, Madagascar, Tanzania and Zaire.
International Association of Wood Anatomists, f. 1931, Leiden.
International Wood Collectors Society, f. 1947, Frenton, Michigan, USA.
International Federation of Building and Woodworkers, f. 1891, Geneva.
Latin American Federation of Workers in the Building and Wood Industry, f. 1958, Caracas.
Nordic Federation of Building and Wood Workers' Trade Unions, f. 1952, Stockholm.
Nordic Wood Preservation Council, f. 1969, Stockholm.
Union for Tropical Wood Trade of the EEC, f. 1958, Brussels.
Wood Industries Executive Committee for EFTA, f. 1967, Paris.
Wood Industries Executive Committee for EEC, f. 1958, Paris.
World Federation of Building and Woodworkers Unions, f. 1973, Utrecht.

W. BOERHAVE BEEKMAN, *ELSEVIER'S Wood Dictionary* (*In English/American, French, Spanish, Italian, Swedish, Dutch and German*). Vol. I. *Commercial and Botanical Nomenclature of World Timbers, Sources and Supply*, Amsterdam, 1964, Vol. 2. *Production, Transport, Trade*, Amsterdam, 1966, Vol. 3. *Research, Manufacture, Utilization, Amsterdam*, 1968; *Yearbook of International Organizations*.

WOOL. One of the main clothing raw materials, subject of international conventions and co-operation. The first international agreement was con-

cluded in 1924 by national societies of France and Great Britain, which were joined in 1929 by Belgium, Germany and Italy. The First World London Wool Conference convened in Nov., 1946 in London, and called into being in 1947 the International Wool Study Group with a seat in London, as an inter-governmental organization of countries interested in exports or imports of wool; in constant touch with FAO, GATT, OECD and the International Wool Secretariat and International Wool Textile Organization. It introduced the international wool quality mark, called Woolmark. World production in 1948–52 amounted yearly on average to 1,830,000 t, in 1960–2,540,000 t, in 1970–2,750,000 t. Organizations reg. with the UIA:

International Wool Textile Organization, f. 1929, Bradford, UK, as the organ of the 1924 agreement; it associates national societies of Argentina, Austria, Australian, Belgium, Denmark, Finland, France, Italy, Japan, Mexico, the Netherlands, Norway, Portugal, South Africa, Spain, Switzerland, Sweden, UK, Uruguay, USA and Yugoslavia. Liaison status with FAO.
International Wool Secretariat, f. 1937 in Melbourne, by the Australian, South African and New Zealand Wool Boards, with the seat in London; it associates governmental institutions of Austria, Belgium, Canada, Denmark, France, FRG, India, Japan, the Netherlands, Norway, Spain, Sweden, Switzerland, the UK and USA. Publ.: *IWS News Service, Wool Science Review, World Wool Digest, Fashion News*.
Since 1961 the INTERLAINE Committee for the Wool Industries of the EEC is operating attached to EEC, headquarters in Brussels.

The biggest sheep-farming countries: Australia, USSR, People's Republic of China, India, New Zealand, South Africa, USA, Turkey, Uruguay, Great Britain, Ethiopia, Brazil and Chile.

N. HYDE, *The Europa Yearbook 1988. A World Survey*, Vol. I, London, 1988. Fabric of History. Wool, in: *National Geographic*, May, 1988.

WOOLMARK. The international mark of quality for wool and wool clothing, permitted only for 100% wool products of high quality, introduced 1960 by the International Wool Study Group.

WORKING CLASS UNITED FRONT. An international term for a workers' movement formed after World War I, determining unity of aims and activities of workers organized in a variety of parties and associations, mostly communist and socialist. As a result of existence of working class united fronts, people's fronts and anti-imperialist fronts were created in the 1930s and national fronts during World War II and a number of united front actions in various part of the world after World War II.

WORKING ENVIRONMENT CONVENTION, 1977. A Convention and Recommendation on the Working Environment, approved by the 63rd ILO Conference at Geneva on June 22, 1977, recommending that, as far as possible, the working environment should be kept free of any hazard due to ▷ air pollution, ▷ noise or ▷ vibration.

UN Chronicle, July, 1977, p. 45.

WORK TIME. A subject of international conventions influenced by international workers' Congresses which in 1866, 1867, 1868, 1869, 1872 and 1889 waged a struggle for an 8-hour work day, during which period in Europe and the USA 12–13-hour work days in industry was the practice and in agriculture in the season – 18 hours. The first law on an 8-hour work day for women and children was introduced in 1873 by New Zealand and from 1901 also for men. In Germany the law of 1891 fixed the beginning of work at 5:30 and the end no later than

20:30. Only in the mines was an 8-hour work day introduced in 1899. The legal passage to the 8-hour work day in Europe came only after World War I. In the USA the work day of federal workers was fixed at 10 hours in 1840 and from 1868 – at 8 hours. However, in industry only at the end of the 19th century did labor unions gain an 8-hour work day and not in all branches or in all states, while in the railroad industry only in 1916. The concept of a 40-hour work week was generally accepted in the USA shortly after World War II and in the highly developed European countries around 1955. Up to World War I only one international convention, i.e. the Berne Convention of 1906, concerned work time – specifically – the prohibition of night work for women for more than 11 hours without interruption, changed in 1919 by ordering rest from 22:00 to 5:00. Also accepted was the Convention limiting the extent of night work for youth, modified July 11, 1948. A turning point came after the establishment of the ILO, which acted in accord with one of the principles of the LN, contained in art. 427 of the Versailles Treaty: "the adoption of the 8-hour work day or the 48-hour work week belongs among the particularly important methods and principles."

The first ILO International Conference on Work in Washington, 1919, ratified the convention on the 48-hour work week in industry, leaving it to the individual states to define what they mean by "industry", as well as a 25% bonus for overtime hours. Ratification came slowly; Greece – 1920, Czechoslovakia and Romania – 1921, Bulgaria – 1922, Luxembourg – 1928, Lithuania – 1931, Austria, Belgium, France and Spain ratified with provisos. On May 19, 1925 the convention on night work in the baking industry was accepted, setting night work time at 7 hours: from 22:00 to 5:00. In 1930 the 48-hour work week for workers in merchandising and offices was ratified; on May 28, 1931 the convention on a 7 hours 45 minutes work day in mines, which was modified on Jan. 28, 1935 to an 8-hour work day in particular cases, but did not take effect. On June 25, 1935 the convention on the 40-hour work week for certain branches of industry with high unemployment was ratified but did not take effect. In 1921 ILO adopted a work time convention which included the obligation of a week's vacation.

ILO, *Conventions and Recommendations adopted by the ILO 1919–1966*, Geneva, 1966; R. CUVILLIER, *The Reduction of Working Time: Scope and Implications in Industrialized Market Economies*, ILO, Geneva, 1984.

WORLD BANK OR IBRD/WORLD BANK. The common name of the International Bank for Reconstruction and Development (IBRD), Banque internationale pour la reconstruction et le développement (BIRD), Banca internacional para la reconstrucción y el desarrollo (BIRD), Mezhdunarodnyi bank riekonstruktsyi i razvitiya (Mirovoy Bank). A UN specialized agency, est. on Dec. 27, 1945 in Washington, DC; operations were started June 25, 1946. The World Bank/IBRD was conceived at the ▷ Bretton Woods Conference in 1944 when representatives of 44 nations met to lay plans for international economic and financial co-operation in the postwar years.

Formal relationships between the Bank and the UN are governed by an agreement approved by the Bank's Board of Governors in Sept., 1947 and by the UN General Assembly in Nov., 1947.

Aims: The principal purposes of the Bank are:
(a) to assist in the reconstruction and development of its member States by facilitating the investment of capital for productive purposes, thereby promoting the long-range growth of international trade and the improvement of living standards;

(b) to promote private foreign investment by guarantees of and participations in loans and other investments made by private investors; and
(c) when private capital is not available on reasonable terms, to make loans for productive purposes out of its own resources or from funds borrowed by it;
(d) provide member countries with technical assistance on matters relating to their economic development; try to increase the effectiveness of the international development effort by fostering co-operation with and among other donors of financial and technical assistance.

Organization: The Bank's administration is composed of a Board of Governors, Executive Directors, a President, other officers, and a staff.

All powers of the Bank are vested in the Board of the Governors, which consists of one Governor and one alternate appointed by each member of the Bank. Each member State has 250 votes, plus one vote for each share of capital stock held. Each Governor exercises the voting power of the member he represents. The Board of Governors meets annually, but additional meetings may be held if required. The Board of Governors has delegated most of its powers to the Executive Directors, who normally meet once a month at the Bank's headquarters in Washington. There are eighteen Executive Directors. Five of them are appointed, one by each of the five members having the largest number of shares of capital stock, and the thirteen others are elected by the Governors representing the remaining members. The Executive Directors function as a Board, and each Executive Director is entitled to cast as a unit the number of votes of the member or members by whom he was appointed or elected.

The President is selected by the Executive Directors. He is *ex officio* Chairman of the Executive Directors and Chief Executive Officer of the Bank. Subject to the general direction of the Executive Directors on questions of policy, he is responsible for the conduct of the business of the Bank and for the organization, appointment and dismissal of staff.

Finance: Funds for loans obtained from (a) payments made by members on account of their capital subscriptions, (b) borrowings in the various capital markets of the world, (c) net earnings. In addition, the Bank sells to financial institutions portions of its loans (usually instalments that are due to be repaid within a fairly short time), and thus replenishes its cash resources. The Bank also uses for lending the repayments of principal on earlier loans. Authorized capital, which was originally US $10,000 million, was US $27,000 million in June, 1972, when member countries had subscribed a total of US $26,606 million. Of this total, however, only about one tenth is paid in. The remainder is subject to call only if required by the Bank to meet its obligations on borrowings or on loans guaranteed by it. In Jan., 1980 an increase equivalent to US $40,000 million was approved by the required three-fourths majority. The three-fourths majority was achieved despite the fact that the United States, which controls 21.47% of the vote, abstained during the voting. The increase was needed to permit continued growth of the Bank's lending program, since the total amount loaned out at any one time is limited to the total of its capital stock and reserves, and its loans total was close to the old ceiling. Contributing nations will not have to provide the full 40,000 million dollars, but only 7.5% of that amount, or approximately 3000 million dollars. The other 92.5% as in the past, will be added to "callable capital" which is not actually paid in but is subject to call by the Bank if needed. This "callable capital" serves as backing for the bank and permits it to borrow widely in the interna-

tional market, where it gets more of the funds which it lends to developing countries. Throughout its history the Bank has never had to call in any of this "callable capital."

The World Bank is since 1960 a group of three institutions: the International Bank for Reconstruction and Development (IBRD), the International Development Association (IDA) and the International Finance Corporation (IFC). The common objective of these institutions is to help raise standards of living in developing countries by channeling financial resources from developed countries to the developing world. While the World Bank has traditionally financed all kinds of infrastructure facilities such as roads, railways and power facilities, its present development strategy places a greatly increased emphasis on investments which can directly affect the well-being of the masses of poor people of developing countries by making them more productive and by including them as active participants in the development process. This strategy is increasingly evident in the rural development, agriculture and education projects which the Bank and IDA help finance. The same strategy is also being carried out for the benefit of the urban poor in projects designed to develop water and sewerage facilities as well as low-cost housing, and to increase the productivity of small industries. The Bank has also committed itself to helping member countries with their more intractable development problems. These include questions of income distribution, rural poverty, unemployment, excessive population growth and rapid urbanization. Since the earliest days, technical assistance has been an integral part of the Bank's work, but its importance has increased enormously. Many borrowers look to it for assistance in identifying, preparing, designing and carrying out projects, and in strengthening national institutions with economic development responsibilities. The Bank co-operates closely with the United Nations Development Program (UNDP) and often serves as an executing agency for UNDP projects.

The Bank conducts a large, continuing program of research, both basic and applied, in virtually every aspect of development with which its members are concerned. It plays a leading role in efforts to co-ordinate assistance from a variety of sources to individual countries, and it co-operates with all agencies engaged in development assistance. This has resulted in greater participation in inter-agency policy consultations, joint operations, research and conferences, both within and outside the United Nations system. Under special co-operative agreements, four organizations within the United Nations system provide staff support for Bank operations in their fields of interest. These are the Food and Agriculture Organization (FAO) the United Nations Educational, Scientific and Cultural Organization (UNESCO), the World Health Organization (WHO), and the United Nations Industrial Development Organization (UNIDO). The Bank has almost continuous contact and close working relations with other United Nations agencies and commissions, regional organizations and development banks, and most of the national agencies that provide development finance and technical assistance.

IBRD and IDA have the same officers, directors and staff, which numbers about 5000 people of more than 100 nationalities. Control in both institutions is exercised through a Board of Governors, consisting of one Governor and one alternate appointed by each member country. Most functions of the Governors are delegated to 20 full-time Executive Directors. Five of the Executive Directors are appointed by the largest shareholders (United States, United Kingdom, France, Federal

Republic of Germany and Japan) and the rest are elected by and represent the other members. The IFC has a similar organizational structure and a staff of 234 people from 47 countries.

The Bank's headquarters are in Washington, DC and membership is open to all members of the ▷ IMF.

Publications: *Questions and Answers; Annual Reports; Summary Proceedings of Annual Meetings; Quarterly Financial Statements.* Pamphlets, speeches, sector and technical papers. All publications can be obtained from IBRD/World Bank 1818 H Street NW, Washington DC 20433, USA. ▷ World Bank/IBRD Statute.

Bretton Woods Agreements, A Bibliography April 1943 – December 1945, Washington, 1945; A. BASH, "IBRD, 1944–49", in: *International Conciliation*, No. 455, November, 1949, pp. 787–871; A. CAIRNCROSS, *The IBRD*, Princeton, 1959; A. MORRIS, *La Banque mondiale*, Paris, 1965; J.A. KING Jr., *Economic Development Projects and their Appraisal: Cases and Principles from the Experience of the World Bank*, Washington, DC, 1976; *Everyone's United Nations*, UN, New York, 1979, pp. 363–364; IBRD. *Catalogue of Publications*, Washington, DC, 1982; B.A.de VRIES, *Remaking the World Bank*, Cabin John, Md., 1987.

WORLD BANK ADMINISTRATIVE TRIBUNAL.
A Tribunal est. on July 1, 1980 by the World Bank Group with functions similar to tribunals created at other UN specialized agencies. The seven jurists appointed to the Tribunal are from Egypt, France, India, Nigeria, UK, Uruguay and the US.

WORLD BANK FOR HEALTH.
In the 1980's the World Bank began lending to health projects. The 1985 loans for health totalled US$250 million, 1990 – US$500 million.

WORLD BANK GROUP.
Since 1960 the official name of three associated UN finance institutions: the World Bank, the International Development Association (IDA) and the International Finance Corporation (IFC).

WORLD BANK/IBRD STATUTE.
Articles of Agreement of the International Bank for Reconstruction and Development, called World Bank/IBRD, signed at Washington, DC on Dec. 27, 1945 by Australia, Belgium, Bolivia, Brazil, Canada, Chile, China, Colombia, Costa Rica, Cuba, Czechoslovakia, Denmark, Dominican Republic, Ecuador, Egypt, El Salvador, Ethiopia, France, Greece, Guatemala, Haiti, Honduras, Iceland, India, Iran, Iraq, Liberia, Luxembourg, Mexico, the Netherlands, New Zealand, Nicaragua, Norway, Panama, Paraguay, Peru, Philippine Commonwealth, Poland, Union of South Africa, Union of Soviet Socialist Republics, United Kingdom, United States, Uruguay, Venezuela, Yugoslavia.

The text as amended Dec. 17, 1965, read as follows:

"The Governments on whose behalf the present Agreement is signed agree as follows:

Introductory Article: The International Bank for Reconstruction and Development is established and shall operate in accordance with the following provisions:

Art. I. *Purposes. The purposes of the Bank are:*

(i) To assist in the reconstruction and development of territories of members by facilitating the investment of capital for productive purposes, including the restoration of economies destroyed or disrupted by war, the reconversion of productive facilities to peacetime needs and the encouragement of the development of productive facilities and resources in less developed countries.

(ii) To promote private foreign investment by means of guarantees or participations in loans and other investments made by private investors; and when private capital is not available on reasonable terms, to supplement private investment by providing, on suitable conditions, finance for productive purposes out of its own capital, funds raised by it and its other resources.

(iii) To promote the long-range balanced growth of international trade and the maintenance of equilibrium in balances of payments by encouraging international investment for the development of the productive resources of members, thereby assisting in raising productivity, the standard of living and conditions of labor in their territories.

(iv) To arrange the loans made or guaranteed by it in relation to international loans through other channels so that the more useful and urgent projects, large and small alike, will be dealt with first.

(v) To conduct its operations with due regard to the effect of international investment on business conditions in the territories of members and, in the immediate postwar years, to assist in bringing about a smooth transition from a war-time to a peacetime economy.

Art. II. *Membership in and Capital of the Bank.*

Sec. 1. Membership: (a) The original members of the Bank shall be those members of the International Monetary Fund which accept membership in the Bank before the date specified in Article XI, Section 2 (e).

(b) Membership, shall be open to other members of the Fund, at such times and in accordance with such terms as may be prescribed by the Bank.

Sec. 2. Authorised: (a) The authorised capital stock of the Bank shall be $10,000,000,000, in terms of United States dollars of the weight and fineness in effect on July 1, 1944. The capital stock shall be divided into 100,000 shares having a par value of $100,000 each, which shall be available for subscription only by members.

(b) The capital stock may be increased when the Bank deems it advisable by a three-fourths majority of the total voting power.

Sec. 3. Subscription of shares. (a) Each member shall subscribe shares of the capital stock of the Bank. The minimum number of shares to be subscribed by the original members shall be those set forth in Schedule A. The minimum number of shares to be subscribed by other members shall be determined by the Bank, which shall reserve a sufficient portion of its capital stock for subscription by such members.

(b) The Bank shall prescribe rules laying down the conditions under which members may subscribe shares of the authorized capital stock of the Bank in addition to their minimum subscriptions.

(c) If the authorized capital stock of the Bank is increased, each member shall have a reasonable opportunity to subscribe, under such conditions as the Bank shall decide, a proportion of the increase of stock equivalent to the proportion which its stock theretofore subscribed bears to the total capital stock of the Bank, but no member shall be obligated to subscribe any part of the increased capital.

Sec. 4. Issue price of shares. Shares included in the minimum subscriptions of original members shall be issued at par. Other shares shall be issued at par unless the Bank by a majority of the total voting power decides in special circumstances to issue them on other terms.

Sec. 5. Division and calls of subscribed capital. The subscription of each member shall be divided into two parts as follows:

(i) twenty percent shall be paid or subject to call under Section 7 (i) of this Article as needed by the Bank for its operations;

(ii) the remaining eighty percent shall be subject to call by the Bank only when required to meet obligations of the Bank created under Article IV. Sections 1 (a) (ii) and (iii). Calls on unpaid subscriptions shall be uniform on all shares.

Sec. 6. Limitation on liability.

Liability on shares shall be limited to the unpaid portion of the issue price of the shares.

Sec. 7. Method of payment of subscriptions for shares. Payment of subscriptions for shares shall be made in gold or United States dollars and in the currencies of the members as follows:

(i) under Section 5 (i) of this Article, two percent of the price of each share shall be payable in gold or United States dollars, and, when calls are made, the remaining eighteen percent shall be paid in the currency of the member;

(ii) when a call is made under Section 5 (ii) of this Article, payment may be made at the option of the member either in gold, in United States dollars or in the currency required to discharge the obligations of the Bank for the purpose for which the call is made;

(iii) when a member makes payments in any currency under (i) and (ii) above, such payments shall be made in amounts equal in value to the member's liability under the call. This liability shall be a proportionate part of the subscribed capital stock of the Bank as authorized and defined in Section 2 of this Article.

Sec. 8. Time of payment of subscriptions.

(a) The two percent payable on each share in gold or United States dollars under Section 7 (i) of this Article, shall be paid within sixty days of the date on which the Bank begins operations, provided that:

(i) any original member of the Bank whose metropolitan territory has suffered from enemy occupation or hostilities during the present war shall be granted the right to postpone payment of one-half percent until five years after that date;

(ii) an original member who cannot make such a payment because it has not recovered possession of its gold reserves which are still seized or immobilized as a result of the war may postpone all payment until such date as the Bank shall decided.

(b) The remainder of the price of each share payable under Section 7 (i) of this Article shall be paid as and when called by the Bank, provided that

(i) the Bank shall, within one year of its beginning operations, call not less than eight percent of the price of the share in addition to the payment of two percent referred to in (a) above;

(ii) not more than five percent of the price of the share shall be called in any period of three months.

Sec. 9. Maintenance of value of certain currency holdings of the Bank.

(a) Whenever (i) the par value of a member's currency is reduced, or (ii) the foreign exchange value of a member's currency has, in the opinion of the Bank, depreciated to a significant extent within that member's territories, the member shall pay to the Bank within a reasonable time an additional amount of its own currency sufficient to maintain the value, as of the time of initial subscription, of the amount of the currency of such member which is held by the Bank and derived from currency originally paid in to the Bank by the member under Article II, Section 7 (i), from currency referred to in Article IV, Section 2 (b), or from an additional currency furnished under the provisions of the present paragraph, and which has not been repurchased by the member for gold or for the currency of any member which is acceptable to the Bank.

(b) Whenever the par value of a member's currency is increased, the Bank shall return to such member within a reasonable time an amount of that member's currency equal to the increase in the value of the amount of such currency described in (a) above.

(c) The provisions of the preceding paragraphs may be waived by the Bank when a uniform proportionate change in the par values of the currencies of all its members is made by the International Monetary Fund.

Sec. 10. Restriction on diposal of shares.

Shares shall not be pledged or encumbered in any manner whatever and they shall be transferable only to the Bank.

Art. III. *General Provisions Relating to Loans and Guarantees.*

Sec. 1. Use of resources.

(a) The resources and the facilities of the Bank shall be used exclusively for the benefit of members with equitable consideration to projects for development and projects for reconstruction alike.

(b) For the purpose of facilitating the restoration and reconstruction of the economy of members whose metropolitan territories have suffered great devastation from enemy occupation or hostilities, the Bank, in determining the conditions and terms of loans made to such members, shall pay special regard to lightening the financial burden and expediting the completion of such restoration and reconstruction.

Sec. 2. Dealings between members and the Bank.

Each member shall deal with the Bank only through its Treasury, central bank, stabilization fund or other similar fiscal agency, and the Bank shall deal with members only by or through the same agencies.

Sec. 3. Limitations on guarantees and borrowings of the Bank.

The total amount outstanding of guarantees, participations in loans and direct loans made by the Bank shall not be increased at any time, if by such increase the total would exceed one hundred percent of the unimpaired subscribed capital, reserves and surplus of the Bank.

Sec. 4. Conditions on which the Bank may guarantee or make loans.

The Bank may guarantee, participate in, or make loans to any member or any political sub-division thereof and any business, industrial, and agricultural enterprise in the territories of a member, subject to the following conditions:

(i) When the member in whose territories the project is located is not itself the borrower, the member or the central bank or some comparable agency of the member which is acceptable to the Bank, fully guarantees the repayment of the principal and the payment of interest and other charges on the loan.

(ii) The Bank is satisfied that in the prevailing market conditions the borrower would be unable otherwise to obtain the loan under conditions which in the opinion of the Bank are reasonalbe for the borrower.

(iii) A competent committee, as provided for in Article V, Section 7, has submitted a written report recommending the project after a careful study of the merits of the proposal.

(iv) In the opinion of the Bank the rate of interest and other charges are reasonable and such rate, charges and the schedule for repayment of principal are appropriate to the project.

(v) In making or guaranteeing on loan, the Bank shall pay due regard to the prospects that the borrower, and, if the borrower is not a member, that the guarantor, will be in position to meet its obligations under the loan; and the Bank shall act prudently in the interests both of the particular member in whose territories the project is located and of the members as a whole.

(vi) In guaranteeing a loan made by other investors, the Bank receives suitable compensation for its risk.

(vii) Loans made or guaranteed by the Bank shall, except in special circumstances, be for the purpose of specific projects of reconstruction or development.

Sec. 5. Use of loans guaranteed, participated in or made by the Bank.

(a) The Bank shall impose no conditions that the proceeds of a loan shall be spent in the territories of any particular member or members.

(b) The Bank shall make arrangements to ensure that the proceeds of any loan are used only for the purposes for which the loan was granted, with due attention to considerations of economy and efficiency and without regard to political or other non-economic influences or considerations.

(c) In the case of loans made by the Bank, it shall open an account in the name of the borrower and the amount of the loan shall be credited to this account in the currency or currencies in which the loan is made. The borrower shall be permitted by the Bank to draw on this account only to meet expenses in connection with the project as they are actually incurred.

Sec. 6. Loans to the International Finance Corporation.

(a) The Bank may make, participate in, or guarantee loans to the International Finance Corporation, an affiliate of the Bank, for use in its lending operations. The total amount outstanding of such loans, participation and guarantees shall not be increased if, at the time or as a result thereof, the aggregate amount of debt (including the guarantee of any debt) incurred by the said Corporation from any source and then outstanding shall exceed an amount equal to four times its unimpaired subscribed capital and surplus.

(b) The provisions of Article III, Sections 4 and 5 (c) and of Article IV, Section 3 shall not apply to loans, participations and guarantees authorized by this Section.

Art. IV. *Operations.*

Sec. 1. Methods of making or facilitating loans.

(a) The Bank may make or facilitate loans which satisfy the general conditions of Article III in any of the following ways:

(i) By making or participating in direct loans out of its own funds corresponding to its unimpaired paid-up capital and surplus and, subject to Section 6 of this Article, to its reserves.

(ii) By making or participating in direct loans out of funds raised in the market of a member, or otherwise borrowed by the Bank.

(iii) By guaranteeing in whole or in part loans made by private investors through the usual investment channels.

(b) The bank may borrow funds under (a) and (ii) above or guarantee loans under (a) (iii) above only with the approval of the member in whose markets the funds are raised and the member in whose currency the loan is denominated, and only if those members agree that the proceeds may be exchanged for the currency of any other member without restriction.

Sec. 2. Availability and transferability of currencies.

(a) Currencies paid into the Bank under Article II, Section 7 (i), shall be loaned only with the approval in each case of the member whose currency is involved; provided, however, that if necessary, after the Bank's subscribed capital has been entirely called, such currencies shall, without restriction by the members whose currencies are offered, be used or exchanged for the currencies required to meet contractual payments of interest, other charges or amortization on the Bank's own borrowings, or to meet the Bank's liabilities with respect to such contractual payments on loans guaranteed by the Bank.

(b) Currencies received by the Bank from borrowers or guarantors in payment on account of principal of direct loans made with currencies referred to in (a) above shall be exchanged for the currencies of other members or reloaned only with approval in each case of the members whose currencies are involved; provided, however, that if necessary, after the Bank's subscribed capital has been entirely called, such currencies shall, without restriction by the members whose currencies are offered, be used or exchanged for the currencies required to meet contractual payments of interest, other charges or amortization on the Bank's own borrowings, or to meet the Bank's liabilities with respect to such contractual payments on loans guaranteed by the Bank.

(c) Currencies received by the Bank from borrowers or guarantors in payment on account of principal of direct loans made by the Bank under Section 1 (a) (ii) of this Article, shall be held and used, without restriction by the members, to make amortization payments, or to anticipate payment of or repurchase part or all of the Bank's own obligations.

(d) All other currencies available to the Bank, including those raised in the market or otherwise borrowed under Section 1 (a) (ii) of this Article, those obtained by the sale of gold, those received as payments of interest and other charges for direct loans made under Section 1 (a) (i) and (ii), and those received as payments of commissions and other charges under Section 1 (a) (iii), shall be used or exchanged for other currencies or gold required in the operations of the Bank without restriction by the members whose currencies are offered.

(e) Currencies raised in the markets of members by borrowers on loans guaranteed by the Bank under Section 1(a) (iii) of this Article, shall also be used or exchanged for other currencies without restriction by such members.

Sec. 3. Provision of currencies for direct loans.

The following provisions shall apply to direct loans under Sections 1(a) (i) and (ii) of this Article:

(a) The Bank shall furnish the borrower with such currencies of members, other than the member in whose territories the project is located, as are needed by the borrower for expenditures to be made in the territories of such other members to carry out the purposes of the loan.

(b) The Bank may, in exceptional circumstances when local currency required for the purposes of the loan cannot be raised by the borrower on reasonable terms, provide the borrower as part of the loan with an appropriate amount of that currency.

(c) The Bank, if the project gives rise indirectly to an increased need for foreign exchange by the member in whose territories the project is located, may in exceptional circumstances provide the borrower as part of the loan with an appropriate amount of gold or foreign exchange not in excess of the borrower's local expenditure in connection with the purposes of the loan.

(d) The Bank may, in exceptional circumstances, at the request of a member in whose territories a portion of the loan is spent, repurchase with gold or foreign exchange a part of that member's currency thus spent but in no case shall the part so repurchased exceed the amount by which the expenditure of the loan in those

territories gives rise to an increased need for foreign exchange.

Sec. 4. Payment provisions for direct loans.

Loan contracts under Section 1 (a) (i) or (ii) of this Article shall be made in accordance with the following payment provisions:

(a) The terms and conditions of interest and amortization payments, maturity and dates of payment of each loan shall be determined by the Bank. The Bank shall also determine the rate and any other terms and conditions of commission to be charged in connection with such loan.

In the case of loans made under Section 1 (a) (ii) of this Article during the first ten years of the Bank's operations, this rate of commission shall be not less than one percent per annum, and shall be charged on the outstanding portion of any such loan. At the end of this period of ten years, the rate of commission may be reduced by the Bank with respect both to the outstanding portions of loans already made and to future loans, if the reserves accumulated by the Bank under Section 6 of this Article and out of other earnings are considered by it sufficient to justify a reduction. In the case of future loans the Bank shall also have discretion to increase the rate of commission beyond the above limit, if experience indicates that an increase is advisable.

(b) All loan contracts shall stipulate the currency or currencies in which payments under the contract shall be made to the Bank. At the option of the borrower, however, such payments may be made in gold, or subject to the agreement of the Bank, in the currency of a member other than that prescribed in the contract.

(i) In the case of loans made under Section 1 (a) (i) of this Article, the loan contracts shall provide that payments to the Bank of interest, other charges and amortization shall be made in the currency loaned, unless the member whose currency is loaned agrees that such payments shall be made in some other specified currency or currencies. These payments, subject to the provisions of Article II, Section 9 (c), shall be equivalent to the value of such contractual payments at the time the loans were made, in terms of a currency specified for the purpose by the Bank by a three-fourths majority of the total voting power.

(ii) In the case of loans made under Section 1 (a) (ii) of this Article, the total amount outstanding and payable to the Bank in any one currency shall at no time exceed the total amount of the outstanding borrowings made by the Bank under Section 1 (a) (ii) and payable in the same currency.

(c) If a member suffers from an acute exchange stringency, so that the service of any loan contracted by that member or guaranteed by it or by one of its agencies cannot be provided in the stipulated manner, the member concerned may apply to the Bank for a relaxation of the conditions of payment.

If the Bank is satisfied that some relaxation is in the interest of the particular member and of the operations of the Bank and of its members as a whole, it may take action under either, or both, of the following paragraphs with respect to the whole, or part, of the annual service:

(i) The Bank may, in its direction, make arrangements with the member concerned to accept service payments on the loan in the member's currency for periods not to exceed three years upon appropriate terms regarding the use of such currency and the maintenance of its foreign exchange value; and for the repurchase of such currency on appropriate terms.

(ii) The Bank may modify the terms of amortization or extend the life of the loan, or both.

Sec. 5. Guarantees.

(a) In guaranteeing a loan placed through the usual investment channels, the Bank shall charge a guarantee commission payable periodically on the amount of the loan outstanding at a rate determined by the Bank. During the first ten years of the Bank's operations, this rate shall be not less than one percent per annum and not greater than one and one-half percent per annum. At the end of this period of ten years, the rate of commission may be reduced by the Bank with respect both to the outstanding portions of loans already guaranteed and to future loans if the reserves accumulated by the Bank under Section 6 of this Article and out of other earnings are considered by it sufficient to justify a reduction. In the case of future loans the Bank shall also have discretion to increase the rate of commission

beyond the above limit, if experience indicates that an increase is advisable.
(b) Guarantee commissions shall be paid directly to the Bank by the borrower.
(c) Guarantees by the Bank shall provide that the Bank may terminate its liability with respect to interest if, upon default by the borrower and by the guarantor, if any, the Bank offers to purchase, at par and interest accrued to a date designated in the offer, the bonds or other obligations guaranteed.
(d) The Bank shall have power to determine any other terms and conditions of the guarantee.
Sec. 6. Special reserve.
The amount of commissions received by the Bank under Sections 4 and 5 of this Article shall be set aside as a special reserve, which shall be kept available for meeting liabilities of the Bank in accordance with Section 7 of this Article. The special reserve shall be held in such liquid form, permitted under this agreement, as the Executive Directors may decide.
Sec. 7. Methods of meeting liabilities of the Bank in case of defaults.
In cases of default on loans made, participated in, or guaranteed by the Bank:
(a) The Bank shall make such arrangements as may be feasible to adjust the obligations under the loans, including arrangements under or analogous to those provided in Section 4 (c) of this Article.
(b) The payments in discharge of the Bank's liabilities on borrowings or guarantees under Section 1 (a) (ii) and (iii) of this Article shall be charged:
(i) first, against the special reserve provided in Section 6 of this Article.
(ii) then, to the extent necessary and at the discretion of the Bank, against the other reserves, surplus and capital available to the Bank.
(c) Whenever necessary to meet contractual payments of interest, other charges or amortization on the Bank's own borrowings, or to meet the Bank's liabilities with respect to similar payments on loans guaranteed by it, the Bank may call an appropriate amount of the unpaid subscriptions of members in accordance with Article II, Sections 5 and 7. Moreover, if it believes that a default may be of long duration, the Bank may call an additional amount of such unpaid subscriptions not to exceed in any one year one percent of the total subscriptions of the members for the following purposes:
(i) To redeem prior to maturity, or otherwise discharge its liability on, all or part of the outstanding principal of any loan guaranteed by it in respect of which the debtor is in default.
(ii) to repurchase, or otherwise discharge its liability on, all or part of its own outstanding borrowings.
Sec. 8. Miscellaneous operations.
In addition to the operations specified elsewhere in this Agreement, the Bank shall have the power:
(i) To buy and sell securities it has issued and to buy and sell securities which it has guaranteed or in which it has invested, provided that the Bank shall obtain the approval of the member in whose territories the securities are to be bought or sold.
(ii) To guarantee securities in which it has invested for the purpose of facilitating their sale.
(iii) To borrow the currency of any member with the approval of that member.
(iv) To buy and sell such other securities as the Directors by a three-fourths majority of the total voting power may deem proper for the investment of all or part of the special reserve under Section 6 of this Article.
In exercising the powers conferred by this Section, the Bank may deal with any person, partnership, association, corporation or other legal entity in the territories of any member.
Sec. 9. Warning to be placed on securities.
Every security guaranteed or issued by the Bank shall bear on its face a conspicuous statement to the effect that it is not an obligation of any government unless expressly stated on the security.
Sec. 10. Political activity prohibited.
The Bank and its officers shall not interfere in the political affairs of any member; nor shall they be influenced in their decisions by the political character of the member or members concerned. Only economic consideration shall be relevant to their decisions, and these considerations shall be weighed impartially in order to achieve the purposes stated in Article I.
Art. V. *Organization and Management.*
Sec. 1. Structure of the Bank.
The Bank shall have a Board of Governors, Executive Directors, a President and such other officers and staff to perform such duties as the Bank may determine.
Sec. 2. Board of Governors.
(a) All the powers of the Bank shall be vested in the Board of Governors consisting of one governor and one alternate appointed by each member in such manner as it may determine. Each governor and each alternate shall serve for five years, subject to the pleasure of the member appointing him, and may be reappointed. No alternate may vote except in the absence of his principal. The Board shall select one of the governors as Chairman.
(b) The Board of Governors may delegate to the Executive Directors authority to exercise any powers of the Board, except the power to:
(i) Admit new members and determine the conditions of their admission;
(ii) Increase or decrease the capital stock;
(iii) Suspend a member;
(iv) Decide appeals from interpretations of this Agreement given by the Executive Directors;
(v) Make arrangements to co-operate with other international organizations (other than informal arrangements of a temporary and administrative character);
(vi) Decide to suspend permanently the operations of the Bank and to distribute its assets;
(vii) Determine the distribution of the net income of the Bank.
(c) The Board of Governors shall hold an annual meeting and such other meetings as may be provided for by the Board or called by the Executive Directors. Meetings of the Board shall be called by the Directors whenever requested by five members or by members having one quarter of the total voting power.
(d) A quorum for any meeting of the Board of Governors shall be a majority of the Governors, exercising not less than two thirds of the total voting power.
(e) The Board of Governors may by regulation establish a procedure whereby the Executive Directors, when they deem such action to be in the best interests of the Bank, may obtain a vote of the Govenors on a specific question without calling a meeting of the Board.
(f) The Board of Governors, and the Executive Directors to the extent authorized, may adopt such rules and regulations as may be necessary or appropriate to conduct the business of the Bank.
(g) Governors and alternates shall serve as such without compensation from the Bank, but the Bank shall pay them reasonable expenses incurred in attending meetings.
(h) The Board of Governors shall determine the remuneration to be paid to the Executive Directors and the salary and terms of the contract of service of the President.
Sec. 3. Voting.
(a) Each member shall have two hundred fifty votes plus one additional vote for each share of stock held.
(b) Except as otherwise specifically provided, all matters before the Bank shall be decided by a majority of the votes cast.
Sec. 4. Executive Directors.
(a) The Executive Directors shall be responsible for the conduct of the general operations of the Bank, and for this purpose, shall exercise all the powers delegated to them by the Board of Governors.
(b) There shall be twelve Executive Directors, who need not be governors, and of whom:
(i) five shall be appointed, one by each of the five members having the largest number of shares;
(ii) seven shall be elected according to Schedule B by all the Governors other than those appointed by the five members referred to in (i) above.
For the purpose of this paragraph, 'members' means governments of countries whose names are set forth in Schedule A, whether they are original members or become members in accordance with Article II, Section 1 (b). When governments of other countries become members, the Board of Governors may, by a four-fifths majority of the total voting power, increase the total number of directors by increasing the number of directors to be elected.
Executive directors shall be appointed or elected every two years.
(c) Each executive director shall appoint an alternate with full power to act for him when he is not present. When the executive directors appointing them are present, alternates may participate in meetings but shall not vote.
(d) Directors shall continue in office until their successors are appointed or elected. If the office of an elected director becomes vacant more than ninety days before the end of his term, another director shall be elected for the remainder of the term by the governors who elected the former director. A majority of the votes cast shall be required for election. While the office remains vacant, the alternate of the former director shall exercise his powers, except that of appointing an alternate.
(e) The Executive Directors shall function in continuous session at the principal office of the Bank and shall meet as often as the business of the Bank may require.
(f) A quorum for any meeting of the Executive Directors shall be a majority of the Directors, exercising not less than one half of the total voting power.
(g) Each appointed director shall be entitled to cast the number of votes alloted under Section 3 of this Article to the member appointing him. Each elected director shall be entitled to cast the number of votes which counted toward his election. All the votes which a director is entitled to cast shall be cast as a unit.
(h) The Board of Governors shall adopt regulations under which a member not entitled to appoint a director under (b) above may send a representative to attend any meeting of the Executive Directors when a request made by, or a matter particularly affecting, that member is under consideration.
(i) The executive Directors may appoint such committees as they deem advisable. Membership of such committees need not be limited to governors or directors or their alternates.
Sec. 5. President and staff.
(a) The Executive Directors shall select a President who shall not be a governor or an executive director or an alternate for either. The President shall be Chairman of the Executive Directors, but shall have no vote except a deciding vote in case of an equal division. He may participate in meetings of the Board of Governors, but shall not vote at such meetings.
The President shall cease to hold office when the Executive Directors so decide.
(b) The President shall be chief of the operating staff of the Bank and shall conduct, under the direction of the Executive Directors, the ordinary business of the Bank. Subject to the general control of the Executive Directors, he shall be responsible for the organization, appointment and dismissal of the officers and staff.
(c) The President, officers and staff of the Bank, in the discharge of their offices, owe their duty entirely to the Bank and to no other authority. Each member of the Bank shall respect the international character of this duty and shall refrain from all attempts to influence any of them in the discharge of their duties.
(d) In appointing the officers and staff the President shall, subject to the paramount importance of securing the highest standards of efficiency and of technical competence, pay due regard to the importance of recruiting personnel on as wide a geographical basis as possible.
Sec. 6. Advisory Council.
(a) There shall be an Advisory Council of not less than seven persons selected by the Board of Governors including representatives of banking, commercial, industrial, labor, and agricultural interests, and with as wide a national representative as possible. In those fields where specialized international organizations exist, the members of the Council representative of those fields shall be selected in agreement with such organizations. The Council shall advise the Bank on matters of general policy. The Council shall meet annually and on such other occasions as the Bank may request.
(b) Councillors shall serve for two years and may be reappointed. They shall be paid their resonable expenses incurred on behalf of the Bank.
Sec. 7. Loan committees.
The committees required to report on loans under Article III, Section 4, shall be appointed by the Bank. Each such committee shall include an expert selected by the governor representing the member in whose territories the project is located and one or more members of the technical staff of the Bank.
Sec. 8. Relationship to other international organizations.

(a) The Bank, within the terms of this Agreement, shall co-operate with any general international organization and with public international organizations having specialized responsibilities in related fields. Any arrangements for such co-operation which would involve a modification of any provision of this Agreement may be effected only after amendment to this Agreement under Article VIII.

(b) In making decisions on applications for loans or guarantees relating to matters directly within the competence of any international organization of the types specified in the preceding paragraph and participated in primarily by members of the Bank, the Bank shall give consideration to the views and recommendations of such organization.

Sec. 9. Location of offices.

(a) The principal office of the Bank shall be located in the territory of the member holding the greatest number of shares.

(b) The Bank may establish agencies or branch offices in the territories of any member of the Bank.

Sec. 10. Regional offices and councils.

(a) The Bank may establish regional offices and determine the location of, and the areas to be covered by, each regional office.

(b) Each regional office shall be advised by a regional council representative of the entire area and selected in such manner as the Bank may decide.

Sec. 11. Depositories.

(a) Each member shall designate its central bank as a depository for all the Bank's holdings of its currency or, if it has no central bank, it shall designate such other institution as may be acceptable to the Bank.

(b) The Bank may hold other assets, including gold, in depositories designated by the five members having the largest number of shares and in such other designated depositories as the Bank may select. Initially, at least one half of the gold holdings of the Bank shall be held in the depository designated by the member in whose territory the Bank has its principal office, and at least forty percent shall be held in the depositories designated by the remaining four members referred to above, each of such depositories to hold, initially, not less than the amount of gold paid on the shares of the member designating it. However, all transfers of gold by the Bank shall be made with due regard to the costs of transport and anticipated requirements of the Bank. In an emergency the Executive Directors may transfer all or any part of the Bank's gold holdings to any place where they can be adequately protected.

Sec. 12. Form of holdings of currency.

The Bank shall accept from any member, in place of any part of the member's currency, paid in to the Bank under Article II, Section 7 (i), or to meet amortization payments on loans made with such currency, and not needed by the Bank in its operations, notes or similar obligations issued by the Government of the member or the depository designated by such member, which shall be non-negotiable, non-interest-bearing and payable at their par value on demand by credit to the account of the Bank in the designated depository.

Sec. 13. Publications of report and provision of information.

(a) The Bank shall publish an annual report containing an audited statement of its accounts and shall circulate to members at intervals of three months or less a summary statement of its financial position and a profit and loss statement showing the results of its operations.

(b) The Bank may publish such other reports as it deems desirable to carry out its purposes.

(c) Copies of all reports, statements and publications made under this section shall be distributed to members.

Sec. 14. Allocation of net income.

(a) The Board of Governors shall determine annually what part of the Bank's net income, after making provision for reserves, shall be allocated to surplus and what part, if any, shall be distributed.

(b) If any part is distributed, up to two percent non-cumulative shall be paid, as a first charge against the distribution of any year, to each member on the basis of the average amount of the loans outstanding during the year made under Article IV, Section 1 (a) (i), out of currency corresponding to its subscription. If two percent is paid as a first charge, any balance remaining to be distributed shall be paid to all members in proportion to their shares. Payments to each member shall be made in its own currency, or if that currency is not available in other currency acceptable to the member. If such payments are made in currencies other than the member's own currency, the transfer of the currency and its use by the receiving member after payment shall be without restriction by the members.

Art. VI. *Withdrawal and Suspension of Membership: Suspension of Operations.*

Sec. 1. Right of members to withdraw.

Any member may withdraw from the Bank at any time by transmitting a notice in writing to the Bank at its principal office. Withdrawal shall become effective on the date such notice is received.

Sec. 2. Suspension of membership.

If a member fails to fulfil any of its obligations to the Bank, the Bank may suspend its membership by decision of a majority of the Governors, exercising a majority of the total voting power. The member so suspended shall automatically cease to be a member one year from the date of its suspension unless a decision is taken by the same majority to restore the member to good standing.

While under suspension, a member shall not be entitled to exercise any rights under this Agreement, except the right of withdrawal, but shall remain subject to all obligations.

Sec. 3. Cessation of membership in International Monetary Fund.

Any member which ceases to be a member of the International Monetary Fund shall automatically cease after three months to be a member of the Bank unless the Bank by three fourths of the total voting power has agreed to allow it to remain a member.

Sec. 4. Settlement of accounts with governments ceasing to be members.

(a) When a government ceases to be a member, it shall remain liable for its direct obligations to the Bank and for its contingent liabilities to the Bank so long as any part of the loans or guarantees contracted before it ceased to be a member are outstanding; but it shall cease to incur liabilities with respect to loans and guarantees entered into thereafter by the Bank and to share either in the income or the expenses of the Bank.

(b) At the time a government ceases to be a member, the Bank shall arrange for the repurchase of its shares as a part of the settlement of accounts with such government in accordance with the provisions of (c) and (d) below. For this purpose the repurchase price of the shares shall be the value shown by the books of the Bank on the day the government ceases to be a member.

(c) The payment for shares repurchased by the Bank under this section shall be governed by the following conditions:

(i) Any amount due to the government for its shares shall be withheld so long as the government, its central bank or any of its agencies remains liable, as borrower or guarantor, to the Bank and such amount may, at the option of the Bank, be applied on any such liability as it matures. No amount shall be withheld on account of the liability of the government resulting from its subscription for shares under Article II, Section 5 (ii). In any event, no amount due to a member for its shares shall be paid until six months after the date upon which the government ceases to be a member.

(ii) Payments for shares may be made from time to time, upon their surrender by the government, to the extent by which the amount due as the repurchase price in (b) above exceeds the aggregate of liabilities on loans and guarantees in (c) (i) above until the former member has received the full repurchase price.

(iii) Payments shall be made in the currency of the country receiving payment or at the option of the Bank in gold.

(iv) If losses are sustained by the Bank on any guarantees, participations in loans, or loans which were outstanding on the date when the government ceased to be a member, and the amount of such losses exceeds the amount of the reserve provided against losses on the date when the government ceased to be a member, such government shall be obligated to repay upon demand the amount by which the repurchase price of its shares would have been reduced, if the losses had been taken into account when the repurchase price was determined. In addition, the former member government shall remain liable on any call for unpaid subscriptions under Article II, Section 5 (ii), to the extent that it would have been required to respond if the impairment of capital had occurred and the call had been made at the time the repurchase price of its shares was determined.

(d) If the Bank suspends permanently its operations under Section 5 (b) of this Article within six months of the date upon which any government ceases to be a member, all rights of such government shall be determined by the provisions of Section 5 of this Article.

Sec. 5. Suspension of operations and settlement of obligations.

(a) In an emergency the Executive Directors may suspend temporarily operations in respect of new loans and guarantees pending an opportunity for further consideration and action by the Board of Governors.

(b) The Bank may suspend permanently its operations in respect of new loans and guarantees by vote of a majority of the Governors, exercising a majority of the total voting power. After such suspension of operations the Bank shall forthwith cease all activities, except those incident to the orderly realization, conservation, and preservation of its assets and settlement of its obligations.

(c) The liability of all members for uncalled subscriptions to the capital stock of the Bank and in respect of the depreciation of their own currencies shall continue until all claims of creditors, including all contingent claims, shall have been discharged.

(d) All creditors holding direct claims shall be paid out of the assets of the Bank, and then out of payments to the Banks on calls on upaid subscriptions. Before making any payments to creditors holding direct claims, the Executive Directors shall make such arrangements as are necessary, in their judgement, to insure a distribution to holders of contingent claims rateably with creditors holding direct claims.

(e) No distribution shall be made to members on account of their subscriptions to the capital stock of the Bank until:

(i) all liabilities to creditors have been discharged or provided for, and

(ii) a majority of the Governors, exercising a majority of the total voting power, have decided to make a distribution.

(f) After a decision to make a distribution has been taken under (e) above, the Executive Directors may by a two-thirds majority vote make successive distributions of the assets of the Bank to members until all of the assets have been distributed. This distribution shall be subject to the prior settlement of all outstanding claims of the Bank against each member.

(g) Before any distribution of assets is made, the Executive Directors shall fix the proportionate share of each member according to the ratio of its shareholding to the total outstanding shares of the Bank.

(h) The Executive Directors shall value the assets to be distributed as at the date of distribution and then proceed to distribute in the following manner:

(i) There shall be paid to each member in its own obligations or those of its official agencies or legal entities within its territories, insofar as they are available for distribution, an amount equivalent in value to its proportionate share of the total amount to be distributed.

(ii) Any balance due to a member after payment has been made under (i) above, shall be paid, in its own currency, insofar as it is held by the Bank, up to an amount equivalent in value to such balance.

(iii) Any balance due to a member after payment has been made under (i) and (ii) above shall be paid in gold or currency acceptable to the member, insofar as they are held by the Bank, up to an amount equivalent in value to such balance.

(iv) Any remaining assets held by the Bank after payments have been made to members under (i), (ii), and (iii) above shall be distributed pro rata among the members.

(i) Any member receiving assets distributed by the Bank in accordance with (h) above, shall enjoy the same rights with respect to such assets as the Bank enjoyed prior to their distribution.

Art. VII. *Status, Immunities and Privileges.*

Sec. 1. Purposes of Article.

To enable the Bank to fulfil the functions with which it is entrusted, the status, immunities and privileges set forth in this Article shall be accorded to the Bank in the territories of each member.

Sec. 2. Status of the Bank.

The Bank shall possess full juridical personality, and, in particular, the capacity:

(i) to contract;

(ii) to acquire and dispose of immovable and movable property;

(iii) to institute legal proceedings.

Sec. 3. Position of the Bank with regard to judicial process. Actions may be brought against the Bank only in a court of competent jurisdiction in the territories of a member in which the Bank has an office, has appointed an agent for the purpose of accepting service or notice of process, or has issued or guaranteed securities. No actions shall, however, be brought by members or persons acting for or deriving claims from members. The property and assets of the Bank shall, wheresoever located and by whomsoever held, be immune from all forms of seizure, attachment or execution before the delivery of final judgment against the Bank.

Sec. 4. Immunity of assets from seizure.

Property and assets of the Bank, wherever located and by whomsoever held, shall be immune from search, requisition, confiscation, expropriation or any other form of seizure by executive or legislative action.

Sec. 5. Immunity of archives.

The archives of the Bank shall be inviolable.

Sec. 6. Freedom of assets from restrictions.

To the extent necessary to carry out the operations provided for in this Agreement and subject to the provisions of this Agreement, all property and assets of the Bank shall be free from restrictions, regulations, controls and moratoria of any nature.

Sec. 7. Privilege for communications.

The official communications of the Bank shall be accorded by each member the same treatment that it accords to the official communications of other members.

Sec. 8. Immunities and privileges of officers and employees.

All governors, executive directors, alternates, officers and employees of the Bank:

(i) shall be immune from legal process with respect to acts performed by them in their official capacity except when the Bank waives this immunity;

(ii) not being local nationals, shall be accorded the same immunities from immigration restrictions, alien registration requirements and national service obligations and the same facilities as regards exchange restrictions as are accorded by members to the representatives, officials, and employees of comparable rank of other members;

(iii) shall be granted the same treatment in respect of travelling facilities as is accorded by members to representatives, officials and employees of comparable rank of other members.

Sec. 9. Immunities from taxation.

(a) The Bank, its assets, property, income and its operations and transactions authorized by this Agreement, shall be immune from all taxation and from all customs duties. The Bank shall also be immune from liability for the collection or payment of any tax or duty.

(b) No tax shall be levied on or in respect of salaries and emoluments paid by the Bank to executive directors, alternates, officials or employees of the Bank who are not local citizens, local subjects, or other local nationals.

(c) No taxation of any kind shall be levied on any obligation or security issued by the Bank (including any dividend or interest thereon) by whomsoever held

(i) which discriminates against such obligation or security solely because it is issued by the Bank; or

(ii) if the sole jurisdictional basis for such taxation is the place or currency in which it is issued, made payable or paid, or the location of any office or place of business maintained by the Bank.

(d) No taxation of any kind shall be levied on any obligation or security guaranteed by the Bank (including any dividend or interest thereon) by whomsoever held,

(i) which discriminates against such obligation or security solely because it is guaranteed by the Bank; or

(ii) if the sole jurisdictional basis for such taxation is the location of any office or place of business maintained by the Bank.

Sec. 10. Application of Article.

Each member shall take such action as is necessary in its own territories for the purpose of making effective in terms of its own law the principles set forth in this Article and shall inform the Bank of the detailed action which it has taken.

Art. VIII. *Amendments.*

(a) Any proposal to introduce modifications in this Agreement, whether emanating from a member, a governor or the Executive Directors, shall be communicated to the Chairman of the Board of Governors who shall bring the proposal before the Board. If the proposed amendment is approved by the Board the Bank shall, by circular letter or telegram, ask all members whether they accept the proposed amendment. When three fifths of the members, having four fifths of the total voting power, have accepted the proposed amendments, the Bank shall certify the fact by formal communication addressed to all members.

(b) Notwithstanding (a) above, acceptance by all members is required in the case of any amendment modifying:

(i) the right to withdraw from the Bank provided in art. VI, Section 1;

(ii) the right secured by art. II, Section 3 (c);

(iii) the limitation on liability provided in Art. II, Section 6.

(c) Amendments shall enter into force for all members three months after the date of the formal communication unless a shorter period is specified in the circular letter or telegram.

Art. IX. *Interpretation.*

(a) Any question of interpretation of the provisions of this Agreement arising between any member and the Bank or between any members of the Bank shall be submitted to the Executive Directors for their decision. If the question particularly affects any member not entitled to appoint an executive director, it shall be entitled to representation in accordance with Article V, Section 4 (h).

(b) In any case where the Executive Directors have given a decision under (a) above, any member may require that the question be referred to the Board of Governors, whose decision shall be final. Pending the result of the reference to the Board, the Bank may, so far as it deems necessary, act on the basis of the decision of the Executive Directors.

(c) Whenever a disagreement arises between the Bank and a country which has ceased to be a member, or between the Bank and any member during the permanent suspension of the Bank, such disagreement shall be submitted to arbitration by a tribunal of three arbitrators, one appointed by the Bank, another by the country involved and an umpire who, unless the parties otherwise agree, shall be appointed by the President of the Permanent Court of International Justice or such other authority as may have been prescribed by regulation adopted by the Bank. The umpire shall have full power to settle all questions of procedure in any case where the parties are in disagreement with respect thereto.

Art. X. *Approval Deemed Given.*

Whenever the approval of any member is required before any act may be done by the Bank, except in art. VIII, approval shall be deemed to have been given unless the member presents an objection within such reasonable period as the Bank may fix in notifying the member of the proposed act.

Art. XI. *Final Provisions.*

Sec. 1. Entry in to force.

This Agreement shall enter into force when it has been signed on behalf of governments whose minimum subscriptions comprise not less than sixty-five percent of the total subscriptions set forth in Schedule A, and when the instruments referred to in Section 2 (a) of this Article have been deposited on their behalf, but in no event shall this Agreement enter into force before May 1, 1945.

Sec. 2. Signature.

(a) Each government on whose behalf this Agreement is signed shall deposit with the Government of the United States of America an instrument setting forth that it has accepted this Agreement in accordance with its law and has taken all steps necessary to enable it to carry out all of its obligations under this Agreement.

(b) Each government shall become a member of the Bank as from the date of the deposit on its behalf of the instrument referred to in (a) above, except that no government shall become a member before this Agreement enters into force under Section 1 of this Article.

(c) The Government of the United States of America shall inform the governments of all countries whose names are set forth in Schedule A, and all governments whose membership is approved in accordance with art.

II, Section 1 (b), of all signatures of this Agreement and of the deposit of all instruments referred to in (a) above.

(d) At the time this Agreement is signed on its behalf, each government shall transmit to the Government of the United States of America one one-hundredth of one percent of the price of each share in gold or United States dollars for the purpose of meeting administrative expenses of the Bank. This payment shall be credited on account of the payment to be made in accordance with Article II, Section 8, (a). The Government of the United States of America shall hold such funds in a special deposit account and shall transmit them to the Board of Governors of the Bank when the initial meeting has been called under Section 3 of this Article. If this Agreement has not come into force by December 31, 1945, The Government of the United States of America shall return such funds to the governments that transmitted them.

(e) This agreement shall remain open for signature at Washington on behalf of the governments of the countries whose names are set forth in Schedule A until December 31, 1945.

(f) After December 31, 1945, this Agreement shall be open for signature on behalf of the government of any country whose membership has been approved in accordance with art. II, Section 1 (b).

(g) By their signature of this Agreement, all governments accept it both on their own behalf and in respect of all their colonies, overseas territories, all territories under their protection, suzerainty, or authority and all territories in respect of which they exercise a mandate.

(h) In the case of governments whose metropolitan territories have been under enemy occupation, the deposit of the instrument referred to in (a) above may be delayed until one hundred and eighty days after the date on which these territories have been liberated. If, however, it is not deposited by any such government before the expiration of this period, the signature affixed on behalf of that government shall become void and the portion of its subscription paid under (d) above shall be returned to it.

(i) Paragraphs (d) and (h) shall come into force with regard to each signatory government as from the date of its signature.

Sec. 3. Inauguration of the Bank.

(a) As soon as this Agreement enters into force under Section 1 of this Article, each member shall appoint a governor and the member to whom the largest number of shares is allocated in Schedule A shall call the first meeting of the Board of Governors.

(b) At the first meeting of the Board of Governors, arrangements shall be made for the selection of provisional executive directors. The governments of the five countries, to which the largest number of shares are allocated in Schedule A, shall appoint provisional executive directors. If one or more of such governments have not become members, the executive directorships which they would be entitled to fill shall remain vacant until they become members, or until January 1, 1946, whichever is the earlier. Seven provisional executive directors shall be elected in accordance with the provisions of Schedule B and shall remain in office until the date of the first regular election of executive directors which shall be held as soon as practicable after January 1, 1946.

(c) The Board of Governors may delegate to the provisional executive directors any powers except those which may not be delegated to the Executive Directors.

(d) The Bank shall notify members when it is ready to commence operations."

The Executive Directors mentioned in Art. V. Sec. 4 Schedule A include names of all signatories of the Agreement. The Schedule B reads as follows:

"Election of executive directors: (1) The election of the elective executive directors shall be by ballot of the Governors eligible to vote under Article V, Section 4 (b).

(2) In balloting for the elective executive directors, each governor eligible to vote shall cast for one person all of the votes to which the member appointing him is entitled under Section 3 of art. V. The seven persons receiving the greatest number of votes shall be executive directors, except that no person who receives less than fourteen percent of the total of the votes which can be cast (eligible votes) shall be considered elected.

(3) When seven persons are not elected on the first ballot, a second ballot shall be held in which the person

who received the lowest number of votes shall be ineligible for election and in which there shall vote only (a) those governors who voted in the first ballot for a person not elected and (b) those governors whose votes for a person elected are deemed under 4 below to have raised the votes cast for that person above fifteen percent of the eligible votes.

(4) In determining whether the votes cast by a governor are to be deemed to have raised the total of any person above fifteen percent of the eligible votes, the fifteen percent shall be deemed to include first, the votes of the governor casting the largest number of votes for such person, then the votes of the governor casting the next largest number, and so on until fifteen percent is reached.

(5) Any governor, part of whose votes must be counted in order to raise the total of any person above fourteen percent shall be considered as casting all of his votes for such person even if the total votes for such person thereby exceed fifteen percent.

(6) If, after the second ballot, seven persons have not been elected, further ballots shall be held on the same principles until seven persons have been elected, provided that after six persons are elected, the seventh may be elected by a simple majority of the remaining votes and shall be deemed to have been elected by all such votes."

Articles of Agreement of the International Bank for Reconstruction and Development, World Bank, Washington, DC, January 1970.

WORLD CALENDAR. In 1937 the League of Nations initiated work on reform of the Gregorian calendar in favor of a world calendar. In 1964, work was resumed by ECOSOC, stimulated by the UN General Assembly's initiative, and based on a draft proposed by the International Association for a World Calendar. The provisions of the reform were the following: each year would start on Sunday and each quarter would have 91 days: 31 + 30 + 30; each year would have 364 days, and to make up the difference the day between Dec. 30 and Jan. 1 was to be a "World Day," and every four years the day between June 30 and July 1 – "Universe Day." Simultaneously, it was suggested that all religious holidays should fall on Saturday, Sunday or Monday. The year 1978, according to the calendar's draft, was supposed to initiate a new era of the calendar, as it started on a Sunday. The II Vatican Council, 1963, generally approved the UN reform of the Gregorian calendar. Advocates of the world unified calendar remind us that the Gregorian calendar was also created by an international commission of astronomers appointed in 1576 by Pope Gregory XIII to reform the Julian calendar made by Julius Caesar in 46 B.C. The Gregorian calendar has been in use since 1582.

UN Yearbook, 1947–48, p. 653; *Yearbook of International Organizations*.

WORLD COLUMBIAN EXPOSITION, 1893. An international exposition in Chicago, May–Nov., 1893, on the 400th anniversary of the discovery of America by Christopher Columbus (1446–1506).

WORLD CONFEDERATION OF LABOUR. One of the trade unions organizations, reg. with the UIA, est. 1966 as a successor to the International Confederation of Christian Labour Unions, seat in Brussels. Consultative status with ECOSOC.

Yearbook of International Organizations.

WORLD CONFERENCE OF THE INTERNATIONAL WOMEN'S YEAR, 1975. The conference was held in Mexico City from June 19 to July 2, 1975 under the slogan "equality, development and peace." ▷ Women's rights.

UN Chronicle, July, 1975, pp. 44–49.

WORLD CONFERENCE ON TRADE AND DEVELOPMENT. A conference held from Feb. 25 to June 15, 1964 in Geneva and transformed with the approval of the UN General Assembly on Dec. 30, 1964 into a permanent institution, called for short ▷ UNCTAD.

WORLD CONFERENCE TO END THE ARMS RACE, 1976. Full name: World Conference to End the Arms Race for Disarmament and Detente; held in Helsinki, Finland, Sept. 23–26, 1976. It was organized by the Continuing Liaison Council of the World Congress of Peace Forces. The Conference, with representatives of 90 countries and 51 international organizations, was devoted to the mobilization of world public opinion against the arms race, for disarmament and detente. The conference was attended by the President of Finland, U. Kekkonen.

World Conference to End the Arms Race, Helsinki, 1976.

WORLD CONVENTION. The concept of world integration under one authority, of a World Assembly, World Council or World United States; subject of organized international co-operation of adherents of world integration. Organizations reg. with the UIA:

Campaign for a World Constituent Assembly, Action pour une assemblée constituante mondiale, f. 1962, Brussels.
Universal League, Ligue Universelle, f. 1942, The Hague. Publ.: *La traktiko* (monthly in esperanto).
World Council for the People's World Convention – Conseil Mondial pour l'assemblée constituante des peuples, f. 1951, Paris. Publ.: *Toward World Democracy.*

Yearbook of International Organizations.

WORLD COUNCIL OF CHURCHES. The leading organization of the Ecumenical movement of Christian churches, est. 1948 in Amsterdam, seat in Geneva and New York, reg. with the UIA; has a permanent representative at the UN. Consultative status with ECOSOC, UNESCO, and FAO. In 1954 UN Secretary-General Dag Hammarskjöld made a speech at the Second General Assembly of the World Council of Churches in Evanston, Illinois, USA which is held every six years. Initially it unified only Protestant churches, from 1961 also Orthodox, and from 1962 it expanded contacts with the Roman Catholic Church, which found expression in the visit of Paul VI to the seat of WCC in Geneva in 1969. It groups a total of 267 non-Roman Catholic churches working in some 80 countries. Publ.: *The Ecumenical Review, Study Encounter and Risk* (quarterlies), as well as the *Interchurch Aid Newsletter* (monthly). In 1976 the Council supported the Helsinki Final Act.
The WCC publ.: *Official Reports of the Assembly from 1948; Official Reports of the Faith and Order and other Conferences*, from 1925; *Minutes of the Central Committee*, from 1949; and a *Handbook of Member Churches of the WCC.*
Ecumenical Organizations, co-operating with WCC, reg. with the UIA:
Conference of European Churches, f. 1959, Geneva. Members: Christian, non-Catholic Churches.
Council of Education and Sunday School Association, f. 1907, New York.
European Alliance, f. 1957, Amsterdam.
International Council of Christian Churches, f. 1948, Amsterdam.
World Congress of Faith, f. 1936, London.
World's Christian Endeavour Union, f. 1895, Columbus, Ohio.
World Students Christian Federation, f. 1895, Geneva.
R. ROUSE, S. NEIL, *A History of the Ecumenical Movement 1517–1948*, London, 1954; G. THIL, *Histoire doctrinale du Mouvement oecuménique*, Louvain,

1955; A. CROW, *The Ecumenical Movement in Bibliographical Outline*, New York, 1965; WCC, *From New Delhi to Uppsala, 1961–68*, Geneva, 1968; WCC, *From Uppsala to Nairobi*, 1968–75, Geneva, 1975; D.M. PATTON, *Breaking Barriers*, Nairobi, 1975, London, 1976; A.J. VAN DER BENT, *What in the World is the World Council of Churches*, Geneva, 1978; P. POTTER, *Life in all its Fullness*, Geneva, 1982; L. HOVELL, *Acting Faith. The World Council of Churches since 1975*, London, 1982; *Yearbook of International Organizations*; *Handbook of Member Churches of the World Council of Churches*, Geneva, 1985.

WORLD ECONOMIC AND SOCIAL DEVELOPMENT. A subject of international co-operation under the auspices of the UN in keeping with the UN Charter and UN Declaration on Progress and Development as well as the Development Decade. Secretary-General U Thant in 1962 said:

"... Development should be automatically economic and social. Development means growth plus change, and change in turn is as social and cultural as economic, as qualitative as quantitative."

Since 1946 the UN and specialized agencies have kept record of, observed and researched into economic and social development of UN member States and regions of the World. ECOSOC and its regional Socio-Economic Commissions co-ordinate the work. A separate organization dealing with the study of the Third World is the International Development Center est. in 1964 by the French government in Paris.

According to studies conducted by World Bank, 1972:

"The poorest nations are those whose national income per capita is less than 200 dollars per annum, they account for 67 per cent of the population of the Third World and score annual growth of national income less than 4 per cent. Countries scoring national income per capita from 200 to 500 dollars and being populated by 20 per cent of the Third World, have income growth of about 5 per cent annually. Countries having national income per capita higher than 500 dollars – populated by 9 per cent of the Third World population, obtain 6.2 per cent growth of national income yearly. Developing countries – large oil exporters – populated by less than 4 per cent of world population – score 8.4 per cent national income growth every year."

With reference to these data, President of the World Bank R. McNamara said:

"The state of development of a majority of developing countries is unsatisfactory. Simultaneously the state deteriorates. Their situation does not allow them to satisfy basic needs and also to participate on equal footing in economic development, both of their countries and the whole world."

On July 22, 1974, in Lima President L. Echevaria of Mexico advanced an initiative to form a permanent regional intergovernmental institution to supervise the strategy of development of Latin American economies, called Sistema Económico Latinoamericano ▷ SELA.

US News and World Report, October 16, 1972.

WORLD ECONOMIC CRISIS, 1929–39. The Great Depression caused by the collapse of the world financial system began on Black Friday, Oct. 25, 1929 with inconvertibility into gold of key world currencies which triggered a downturn in prices and production, bankruptcies of many banks, insurance and trading, industrial and farming companies, and mass unemployment. Colonial and dependent regions became cut off from US and European markets because of downturn in imports of raw materials and ceased to develop for lack of profits and foreign credits. In Latin America all insurance companies associated with US insurance business declared insolvency.

W

E. VARGA, *The Great Crisis and its Political Consequences. Economics and Politics 1928–1934*, London, 1935; W. WOYTINSKY, *Les Conséquences sociales de la crise*, Paris, 1936; A. STURMTHAL, *Die grosse Krise*, Zürich, 1937; H.V. HUDSON, *Slump and Recovery 1929–1937. A Survey of World Economic Affairs*, London, 1938; W.A. BROWN Jr., *The International Gold Standard Reinterpreted 1914–1934*, 2 Vols., New York, 1940; J.K. GALBRAITH, *The Great Crash 1929*, London, 1955; L.A. HAHN, *50 Jahre zwischen Inflation und Deflation*, Tübingen, 1963.

WORLD ECONOMIC DESTABILIZATION IN THE 1980's. A permanent destabilization of the World economy caused by underdevelopment and indebtedness of the Third World and of a part of developing countries in Europe (with planned economies) as well as by the retardedness in high technology of non-military industry in the USSR. In the opinion of the World Bank President, Barber B. Conable, Geneva UNCTAD Conference, July 12, 1987.

"Stuttering growth, volatile currencies, high real interest rates, heavy debt load, depressed commodity prices, rising trade barriers and outsize payments imbalances have acted in destructive combination not just to slow earlier rates of advance, but actually to erode many previous gains by developing societies. Now by decision or by default, the nations represented here will set a course either toward renewed global growth or toward stagnation and eventual recession. Those are the choices".

International Herald Tribune July 13, 1987.

WORLD FOOD COUNCIL, WFC. An intergovernmental institution est. in Dec., 1974 by the UN General Assembly following a recommendation of the World Food Conference, 1974. In the Council 36 States are represented according to a regional key, and each year one third of the make-up is changed. Annual sessions of the Council are held at the ministerial level to review major problems and policy issues affecting the world food situation and to develop an integrated approach to their solution.

WORLD FOOD COUNCIL MEXICO DECLARATION, 1978. A Declaration adopted during the Ministerial Session of World Food Council on June 14, 1978 in Mexico City, containing recommendations designed to combat widespread hunger and malnutrition which cause hardships to millions of peoples in developing countries.

"The Council invited interested food priority countries to seek its assistance in formulating basic food and nutrition plans and seeking assistance for them.
The Council called for a 10-year programme to eliminate the blindness inflicted every year by vitamin A deficiency on 100,000 children and to prevent endemic goitre from which an estimated 200 million people suffer.
The Council recommended that developing countries establish specific operational goals for nutritional improvement and consider practical ways to ensure a more equitable pattern of food consumption. The Council asked Governments and international organizations to give priority to projects contributing to nutrition improvement and to try to include such components as education and training, distribution of food supplements and primary health care into the design of development projects. The Council recommended that the United Nations introduce specific nutrition-related goals into its operational programmes and that all countries able to do so increase or initiate substantial assistance in that field. The Council recommended that Governments reaffirm their commitment to world food security and aim at a level of assured food aid of at least 10 million tons. Governments, the Council said, should seek in the new agreement an international system of grain reserves of adequate size to provide world food security and reasonable market and price stability,

which should ensure for food-deficit importing countries assured access to the reserve system during times of shortage."

The Council called on international financial institutions and Governments to consider ways to help developing countries to stockpile grains.
The Council called for at least 10 million tons of cereals as food aid per year.

UN Chronicle, July, 1978, p. 22.

WORLD FOOD DAY. The anniversary day of the FAO founding date on Oct. 16, 1945, since 1981 World Food Day.

WORLD FOOD PROGRAM, WFP. One of the UN institutions, established in 1961 jointly by the UN General Assembly Res. 1714/XVI and FAO Res. 1/61; began three-year experimental operations in Jan., 1963, permanently since Jan., 1966. Provides food assistance and emergency supplies to countries or regions threatened with famine and supplies them with technical assistance in developing their own food base. The basis for its operations are voluntary contributions in cash or kind or in services of UN and FAO members. The main organ of WFP is an inter-governmental committee composed of 24 members, half of whom are selected by ECOSOC and the other half by FAO, to whom the common administrative unit, UN/FAO Administrative Unit, seat in the main headquarters of FAO, Rome, is subject.

WORLD GOLD CURRENCIES. For thousands of years several systems of legal tender, at the time considered most precious metals or products, have existed. From 3000 B.C. until the 19th century it was most often silver, also gold which became the foundation of key currencies in the 19th and early 20th centuries. This is depicted in the table of continuity of these currencies drawn by F. Pick:

Currency	Period	Years
Golden French franc	1814–1914	100
Golden Dutch gulden	1816–1914	98
Golden pound sterling	1831–1924	93
Golden Swiss franc	1850–1936	86
Golden Belgian franc	1832–1914	82
Golden Swedish krona	1875–1913	58
Golden German mark	1875–1914	39
Golden Italian lira	1883–1914	31

F. PICK, *Currency Yearbook*, New York, 1968.

WORLD HERITAGE UNESCO CONVENTION, 1972. The Convention concerning the Protection of the World Cultural and Natural Heritage, normally referred to as the World Heritage UNESCO Convention, was adopted in 1972 and came into force in 1975 after twenty UNESCO Member States had adhered to it. As of Jan. 1, 1984, 82 States had ratified or accepted it. The text of the first two Articles, concerning the definition of the cultural and natural heritage, reads as follows:
"Art. 1. For the purpose of this Convention, the following shall be considered as 'cultural heritage':

monuments: architectural works; works of monumental sculpture and paintings, elements or structures of an archaeological nature, inscriptions, cave dwellings and combinations of features, which are of outstanding universal value from the point of view of history, art or science; groups of buildings: groups of separate or connected buildings which, because of their architecture, their homogeneity or their place in the landscape, are of outstanding universal value from the point of view of history, art or science; sites: works of man or the combined works of nature and of man and areas including archaeological sites which are of outstanding universal value from the historical, aesthetic, ethnological or anthropological points of view.

Art. 2. For the purpose of this Convention, the following shall be considered as 'natural heritage':
natural features consisting of physical and biological formations or groups of such formations, which are of outstanding universal value from the aesthetic or scientific point of view;
geological and physiographical formations and precisely delineated areas which constitute the habitat of threatened species of animals and plants of outstanding universal value from the points of view of science or conservation;
natural sites or precisely delineated natural areas of outstanding universal value from the point of view of science, conservation or natural beauty.
The criteria for the inclusion of 'cultural' properties in the World Heritage List are as follows:
A monument, group of buildings or site – as defined in Art. 1 of the Convention – which is nominated for inclusion in the World Heritage List will be considered to be of outstanding universal value for the purposes of the Convention when the Committee finds that it meets one or more of the following criteria and the test of authenticity. Each property nominated should therefore;
(a) (i) represent a unique artistic achievement, a masterpiece of the creative genius; or
(ii) have exerted great influence, over a span of time or within a cultural area of the world, on developments in architecture, monumental arts or town-planning and land-scaping; or
(iii) bear a unique or at least exceptional testimony to a civilization which has disappeared; or
(iv) be an outstanding example of a type of structure which illustrates a significant stage in history; or
(v) be an outstanding example of a traditional human settlement which is representative of a culture and which has become vulnerable under the impact of irreversible change; or
(vi) be directly and tangibly associated with events or with ideas or beliefs of outstanding universal significance; and
(b) meet the test of authenticity in design, materials, workmanship or setting.
The following additional factors will be kept in mind by the Committee in deciding on the eligibility of a cultural property for inclusion in the List:
(a) The state of preservation of the property should be evaluated relatively, that is, it should be compared with that of other property of the same type dating from the same period; and
(b) Nominations of immovable property which are likely to become movable will not be considered.
The criteria for the inclusion of natural properties in the World Heritage List are as follows:

A natural heritage property – as defined in Art. 2 of the Convention – which is submitted for inclusion in the World Heritage List will be considered to be of outstanding universal value for the purposes of the Convention when the Committee finds that it meets one or more of the following criteria and fulfils the conditions of integrity set out below. Properties nominated should therefore:
(i) be outstanding examples representing the major stages of the earth's evolutionary history. This category would include sites which represent the major 'eras' of geological history such as 'the age of reptiles' where the development of the planet's natural diversity can well be demonstrated, and such as the 'ice age' where early man and his environment underwent major changes; or
(ii) be outstanding examples representing significant ongoing geological processes, biological evolution and man's interaction with his natural environment. As distinct from the periods of the earth's development, this focuses upon ongoing processes in the development of communities of plants and animals, landforms and marine and fresh-water bodies. This category would include for example (a) as geological processes, glaciation and volcanism, (b) as biological evolution such as tropical rainforests, deserts and tundra, (c) as interaction between man and his natural environment, terraced agricultural landscapes; or
(iii) contain superlative natural phenomena, formations or features or areas of exceptional natural beauty, such as superlative examples of the ecosystems most important to man, natural features (for instance, rivers, mountains, water-falls, spectacles presented by great concentrations of animals, sweeping vistas

covered by natural vegetation and exceptional combinations of natural and cultural elements; or
(iv) Contain the foremost natural habitats where threatened species of animals or plants of outstanding universal value from the point of view of science or conservation still survive.
In addition to the above criteria, the sites should also fulfil the conditions of integrity:
(a) The areas described in (i) above should contain all or most of the key interrelated and interdependent elements in their natural relationships; for example, an 'ice age' area would be expected to include the snow field, the glacier itself and samples of cutting patterns, deposition and colonization (striations, moraines, pioneer stages of plant succession, etc.).
(b) The areas described in (ii) above should have sufficient size and contain the necessary elements to demonstrate the key aspects of the process and to be self-perpetuating. For example, an area of 'tropical rain forest' may be expected to include some variation in elevation above sea level, changes in topography and soil types, river banks or oxbow lakes, to demonstrate the diversity and complexity of the system.
(c) The areas described in (iii) above should contain those ecosystem components required for the continuity of the species or of the objects to be conserved. This will vary according to individual cases; for example, the protected area of a waterfall would include all, or as much as possible, of the supporting upstream watershed; or a coral reef area would be provided with control over siltation or pollution through the stream flow or ocean currents which provide its nutrients.
(d) The area containing threatened species as described in (iv) above should be of sufficient size and contain necessary habitat requirements for the survival of the species.
(e) In the case of migratory species, seasonable sites necessary for their survival, wherever they are located, should be adequately protected. If such sites are located in other countries, the Committee must receive assurances that the necessary measures be taken to ensure that the species are adequately protected throughout their full life cycle. If necessary, it is the responsibility of the nominating State to provide the assurances. Agreements made in this connection, either through adherence to international conventions or in the form of other multilateral or bilateral arrangements should be noted in the nomination.
The Convention functions under the guidance of an intergovernmental committee known as the 'World Heritage Committee'. This Committee, composed of representatives of 21 States Parties to the Convention, has the following main responsibilities:
– to identify those national and cultural sites which are to be protected under the World Heritage Convention by inscribing them on the World Heritage List;
– to make the sites known throughout the world and to create an awareness among the public of their responsibility in respecting and safeguarding that universal heritage; and
– to provide technical co-operation for the safeguarding of World Heritage sites from the World Heritage Fund to States whose resources are, for the time being, insufficient.
This Committee normally meets once in the autumn of each year and its members are elected from among the States Parties to the Convention for a period of office of six years. One third of the members change at the end of each General Conference of UNESCO. The States Parties who are members of the Committee are represented by persons possessing specialized knowledge of the conservation of the cultural and natural heritage. The Committee is aided in its tasks by the International Council on Monuments and Sites (ICOMOS), the International Centre for the Study of the Preservation and the Restoration of Cultural Property in Rome (ICCROM), and the International Union for the Conservation of Nature and Natural Resources (IUCN), professional organizations that have been accorded an advisory role by the Convention because they are competent in the fields of conservation of the cultural and natural heritage.
The World Heritage List identifies cultural and natural properties considered to be of outstanding universal value, and, by virtue of this quality, especially worth safeguarding for future generations.
The World Heritage Committee will decide which cultural and natural properties proposed by States Parties will be included in the World Heritage List, by evaluating them against criteria, which it drew up at its first session with the advice of ICOMOS, IUCN and ICCROM. An effort is made furthermore, to keep a reasonable balance between the cultural and natural heritage. The building up of the World Heritage List is an ongoing process; that is, the List will continue to grow as more and more sites are added.
The Committee also prepares and publishes a List of World Heritage in Danger which may include only sites threatened by serious and specific dangers. The List enumerates those endangered properties for the conservation of which major operations are necessary and for which assistance has been requested under the Convention. This List is to contain an estimate of the cost of such operations.
Both Lists are brought up to date and published every two years.
States Parties have themselves to identify and draw up a tentative list of natural and cultural sites in their country which they consider to be of worldwide significance and to warrant inclusion in the List. They then forward their proposals to the Secretariat of the World Heritage Committee using a printed form (available from the Secretariat of UNESCO) that asks for a detailed description of the property, information on its state of preservation, its history, its importance, etc. Nominations submitted by 1st January will be considered within the same year. Those received after 1st January will be considered in the following year.
Under the Convention a Fund, called the World Heritage Fund, has been created, which is a collective endeavour designed to support the individual efforts of States to preserve their cultural and natural heritage, and to meet emergency conservation needs to save a property which is in imminent danger of destruction.
The list of States which have deposited an instrument of ratification, acceptance or accession as at January 1, 1984 is as follows: Afghanistan, Algeria, Antigua and Barbuda, Argentina, Australia, Bangladesh, Benin, Bolivia, Brazil, Bulgaria, Burundi, Cameroon, Canada, Central African Republic, Chile, Colombia, Costa Rica, Cuba, Cyprus, Democratic Yemen, Denmark, Ecuador, Egypt, Ethiopia, France, Fed. Rep. of Germany, Ghana, Greece, Guatemala, Guinea, Guyana, Haiti, Holy See, Honduras, India, Iraq, Islamic Republic of Iran, Italy, Ivory Coast, Jordan, Lebanon, Libya, Luxembourg, Madagascar, Malawi, Mali, Malta, Mauritania, Monaco, Morocco, Mozambique, Nepal, Nicaragua, Niger, Nigeria, Norway, Oman, Pakistan, Panama, Peru, Poland, Portugal, Saudi Arabia, Senegal, Seychelles, Spain, Sri Lanka, Sudan, Switzerland, Syria, Tanzania, Tunisia, Turkey, USA, Yugoslavia, Zaïre, Zimbabwe."

UNESCO. *World Cultural Heritage, Information Bulletin*, No. 20–21, May, 1984.

WORLD HERITAGE UNESCO LIST 1988, CULTURAL AND NATURAL. The contracting states of the 288 properties included in the list as of January 1988 having submitted the nomination of the properties in accordance with the ▷ World Heritage UNESCO Convention, 1972:

Algeria – Al Qal'a of Beni Hammad, Tassili n'Ajjer, M'Zab Valley, Djemila, Tipasa, Timgad.
Argentina – Los Glaciares, Iguazu National Park.
Argentina and Brazil – Jesuit Missions of the Guaranis: San Ignacio Mini, Santa Ana, Nuestra Señora de Loreto and Santa Maria Mayor (Argentina), Ruins of Sao Miguel das Missoes (Brazil).
Australia – Kakadu National Park, Great Barrier Reef, Willandra Lakes Region, Western Tasmania Wilderness National Parks, Lord Howe Island Group, Australian East Coast Temperate and Sub-Tropical Rainforest Parks, Uluru National Park.
Bangladesh – The historic mosque city of Bagerhat, Ruins of the Buddhist Vihara at Paharpur.
Benin – Royal Palaces of Abomey.
Bolivia – City of Potosi.
Brazil – Historic town of Ouro Preto. Historic Centre of the town of Olinda. Historic Centre of Salvador de Bahia, Sanctuary of Bom Jesus do Congonhas, Iguaçu National Park, Brasilia.
Bulgaria – Boyana Church, Madara Rider, Thracian tomb of Kazanlak, Rock-hewn churches of Ivanovo, Ancient City of Nessebar, Rila Monastery, Srebarna Nature Reserve, Pirin National Park, Thracian tomb of Sveshtari.
Cameroon – Dja Faunal Reserve.
Canada – L'Anse aux Meadows National Historic Park, Nahanni National Park, Dinosaur Provincial Park, Anthony Island, Head-Smashed-In Bison Jump Complex, Wood Buffalo National Park, Canadian Rocky Mountains Parks, Quebec (Historic area), Gros Morne National Park.
Canada and United States of America – Kluane National Park/Wrangell–St. Elias National Park and Preserve.
China (People's Republic of) – Mount Taishan, The Great Wall, Imperial Palace of the Ming and Qing Dynasties, Mogao Caves, The Mausoleum of the First Qin Emperor, Peking Man Site at Zhoukoudian.
Colombia – Port, Fortresses and Group of Monuments, Carthagena.
Costa Rica – Talamanca Range–La Amistad Reserves.
Côte d'Ivoire – Tai National Park, Comoé National Park.
Cuba – Old Havana and its Fortifications.
Cyprus – Paphos, Painted churches in the Troodos region.
Democratic Yemen – Old walled City of Shibam.
Ecuador – Galapagos Islands, City of Quito, Sangay National Park.
Egypt – Memphis and its Necropolis, the Pyramid fields from Giza to Dahshur, Ancient Thebes with its Necropolis, Nubian monuments from Abu Simbel to Philae, Islamic Cairo, Abu Mena.
Ethiopia – Simen National Park, Rock-hewn Churches, Lalibela, Fasil Ghebbi, Gondar Region, Lower Valley of the Awash, Tiya, Aksum, Lower Valley of the Omo.
France – Mont-Saint-Michel and its Bay, Chartres Cathedral, Palace and Park of Versailles, Vézelay–Church and Hill, Decorated Grottoes of the Vézere Valley, Palace and Park of Fontainebleau, Chateau and Estate of Chambord, Amiens Cathedral, The Roman Theatre and its surroundings and the 'Triumphal Arch' of Orange, Roman and Romanesque Monuments of Arles, Cistercian Abbey of Fontenay, Royal Saltworks of Arc-et-Senans, Place Stanislas, Place de la Carrière and Place d'Alliance in Nancy, Church of Saint-Savin sur Gartempe, Cape Girolta, Cape Porto and Scandola Nature Reserve in Corsica, Pont du Gard (Roman aqueduct).
Germany (Federal Republic of) – Aachen Cathedral, Speyer Cathedral, Würzburg Residence with the Court Gardens and Residence Square, Pilgrimage Church of Wies, The Castles of Augustusburg and Falkenlust at Brühl, St. Mary's Cathedral and St. Michael's Church at Hildesheim, Monuments of Trier, Hanseatic City of Lübeck.
Ghana – Fort and castles, Volta Greater Accra, Central and Western Regions, Ashanti Traditional Buildings.
Greece – Temple of Apollo Epicurius at Bassae, Archaeological Site of Delphi, The Acropolis–Athens.
Guatemala – Tikal National Park, Antigua Guatemala, Archaeological Park and Ruins of Quirigua.
Guinea and Côte d'Ivoire – Mount Nimba Strict Nature Reserve.
Haiti – National History Park – Citadel, San Souci, Ramiers.
Holy See – Vatican City.
Honduras – Maya Site of Copan, Rio Platano Biosphere Reserve.
Hungary – Budapest, the banks of the Danube with the district of Buda Castle, Hollokö.
India – Ajanta Caves, Ellora Caves, Agra Fort, Taj Mahal, The Sun Temple Konarak, Group of Monuments at Mahabalipuram, Kaziranga National Park, Manas Wildlife Sanctuary, Keoladeo National Park, Churches and convents of Goa, Khajuraho group of monuments, Group of monuments at Hampi, Fatehpur Sikri, Group of monuments at Pattadakal, Elephanta Caves, Brihadisvara Temple Thanjavur, Sundarbans National Park.
Iran – Tchogha Zanbil, Persepolis, Meidan Emam–Esfahan.
Iraq – Hatra.
Italy – Rock drawings in Valcamonica, Historic Centre of Rome, The Church and Dominican Convent of Santa Maria delle Grazie with "The Last Supper" by

Leonardo da Vinci, Historic Centre of Florence, Venice and its lagoon, Piazza del Duomo, Pisa.

Jordan – Old City of Jerusalem and its Walls, Petra, Quseir Amra.

Lebanon – Anjar, Baalbek, Byblos, Tyr.

Libyan Arab Jamahiriya – Archaeological Site of Leptis Magna, Archaeological Site of Sabratha, Archaeological Site of Cyrene, Rock-art sites of Tadrart Acacus, Old Town of Ghadamès.

Malawi – Lake Malawi National Park.

Malta – Hal Saflieni Hypogeum, City of Valetta, Ggantija Temples.

Mexico – Sian Ka'an, Pre-Hispanic City and National Park of Palenque, Historic Centre of Oaxaca and archaeological site of Monte Alban, Historic Centre of Puebla.

Morocco – Medina of Fez, Medina of Marrakesh, Ksar of Ait-Ben-Haddou.

Nepal – Sagarmatha National Park, Kathmandu Valley, Royal Chitwan National Park.

New Zealand – Westland and Mount Cook National Park, Fiordland National Park.

Norway – Urnes Stave Church, Bryggen, Roros, Rock drawings of Alta.

Oman – Bahla Fort.

Pakistan – Archaeological ruins at Moenjodaro, Taxila, Buddhist ruins of Takht-i-Bahi and neighbouring city remains at Sahr-i-Bahlol, Historical Monuments of Thatta, Fort and Shalamar Gardens in Lahore.

Panama – The fortifications on the Caribbean side of Portobelo-San Lorenzo, Darien National Park.

Peru – City of Cuzco, Historic Sanctuary of Machu Picchu, Chavin (Archaeological site), Huascaran National Park, Chan Chan archaeological zone, Manu National Park.

Poland – Cracow's Historic Centre, Wieliczka Salt Mine, Auschwitz Concentration Camp, Bialowieza National Park, Historic Centre of Warsaw.

Portugal – Central Zone of the Town of Angra do Heroismo in the Azores. Monastery of the Hieronymites and Tower of Belem in Lisbon, Monastery of Batalha, Convent of Christ in Tomar, Historic Centre of Evora.

Seychelles – Aldabra Atoll, Vallée de Mai Nature Reserve.

Spain – The Mosque of Cordoba, The Alhambra and the Generalife – Granada, Burgos Cathedral, Monastery and site of the Escurial – Madrid, Parque Güell, Palacio Güell and Casa Mila, in Barcelona, Altamira Cave, Old Town of Segovia and its aqueduct, Churches of the Kingdom of the Asturias, Santiago de Compostela (Old Town), Old Town of Avila with its extramuros churches, Mudejar Architecture of Teruel, Historic City of Toledo, Garajonay National Park, Old Town of Caceres, The Cathedral, the Alcazar and the Archivo de Indias in Seville.

Sri Lanka – Sacred City of Anuradhapura, Ancient City of Polonnaruva, Ancient City of Sigiriya.

Switzerland – Convent of St. Gall, Benedictine Convent of St. John at Müstair, Old City of Berne.

Syrian Arab Republic – Ancient City of Damascus, Ancient City of Bosra, Site of Palmyra, Ancient City of Aleppo.

Tunisia – Medina of Tunis, Site of Carthage, Amphitheatre of El Djem, Ichkeul National Park, Punic town of Kerkuane and its Necropolis.

Turkey – Historic areas of Istanbul, Göreme National Park and the rock sites of Cappadocia, Great Mosque and Hospital of Divrigi, Hattusha, Nemrut Dag.

United Kingdom – The Giant's Causeway and causeway coast, Durham Castle and Cathedral, Ironbridge Gorge, Studley Royal Park including the ruins of Fountains Abbey, Stonehenge, Avebury and associated sites, The Castles and Town Walls of King Edward in Gwynedd, St. Kilda, Blenheim Palace, City of Bath, Hadrian's Wall, Palace of Westminster Abbey of Westminster and Saint Margaret's Church.

United Republic of Tanzania – Ngorongoro Conservation Area, Ruins of Kilwa Kisiwani and Ruins of Songo Mnara, Serengeti National Park, Selous Game Reserve, Kilimanjaro National Park.

United States of America – Mesa Verde, Yellowstone, Grand Canyon National Park, Everglades National Park, Independence Hall, Redwood National Park, Mammoth Cave National Park, Olympic National Park, Cahokia Mounds State Historic Site, Great Smoky Mountains National Park, La Fortaleza and San Juan Historic Site in Puerto Rico, The Statue of Liberty, Yosemite National Park, Chaco Culture National Historical Park, Monticello and University of Virginia in Charlottesville, Hawaii Volcanoes National Park.

Yemen – Old City of Sana'a.

Yugoslavia – Old City of Dubrovnik, Stari Ras and Sopocani, Historical complex of Split with the Palace of Diocletian, Plitvice Lakes National Park, Ohrid region with its cultural and historical aspect and its natural environment, Natural and Culturo-Historical Region of Kotor, Durmitor National Park, Studencia Monastery, Skocjan Caves.

Zaire – Virunga National Park, Garamba National Park, Kahuzi-Biega National Park, Salonga National Park.

Zimbabwe – Mana Pools National Park, Sapi and Chewore Safari Areas, Great Zimbabwe National Monument, Khami Ruins National Monument.

The UNESCO Intergovernmental Committee for the Protection of the World Cultural and Natural Heritage published January 1987 the revised Operational Guidelines for the implementation of the World Heritage Convention.

WORLD INSTITUTE FOR DEVELOPMENT ECONOMIC RESEARCH, WIDER. Est. 1985 by the United Nations University, operated from Helsinki through a worldwide network of scholars and institutions. The WIDER governing board is composed of ten distinguished scholars from various regions of the world. The WIDER started with a 1986/87 budget of $4,845,000. The Government of Finland offered contributions totalling $30 million.

UN Chronicle, 1985, No. 6, pp. 58.

WORLD MARITIME UNIVERSITY, WMU. The WMU established on July 4, 1983, in Malmö, Sweden, under the auspices of the IMLO, to increase the role of developing countries in world shipping. One of the main purposes of the University is to serve as the apex of an international system of training in the maritime field. It will maintain dialogue and collaboration with regional, sub-regional and national maritime training institutions throughout the world, many of which have benefited from IMPO and United Nations Development Program (UNDP) assistance.

As the University develops, it will establish links with other programs, such as the UNDP-supported interregional project for training development in maritime transport (TRAINMAR), executed by the UNCTAD. That project has introduced new and innovative techniques for training port managers and other maritime transport personnel in all regions. Originally involving maritime training institutions in India, Ivory Coast and Kenya, TRAINMAR has made materials available to other countries through its technical co-operation network, which includes 40 developing countries.

The University will also contribute to maintaining international standards for maritime safety and preventing pollution of the seas by ships.

Seventy-five students have been selected from more than 100 applications received from 44 developing countries. Most of the students will pursue two-year courses in general maritime administration, maritime safety administration, maritime education and technical management of shipping companies. One-year courses for technical officers engaged in maritime safety administration and for technical staff of shipping companies will also be offered. Specialized 4–6 week short courses will be offered for personnel serving aboard ships carrying oil, gas and dangerous goods.

Total operating costs of the University are expected to be approximately $3.6 million a year for five years toward operating costs, in addition to contributing $100,000 through UNDP for start-up costs. UNDP contributed $800,000 a year in 1983 and 1984.

UN Chronicle, September, 1983, pp. 80–81.

WORLD MARKETS. An international term for countries whose markets have the largest import absorptive power and export trade. Among the main import world market in the decade 1971–80 in order of size were USA, FRG, Great Britain, France, Japan, Canada, Italy, USSR, Belgium, Luxembourg, the Netherlands and Sweden. The development of integrative regions created regional world markets such as the EEC market or the CMEA market, basically differing from each other in terms of socio-economic systems.

WORLD MEETINGS. An international term for all regional and global meetings organized or sponsored by non-governmental organizations, members of the ▷ UIA. A quarterly "World Meeting: Outside the United States and Canada" is published in New York since 1967.

WORLD METEOROLOGY DAY. The day is celebrated since 1961 by the World Meteorological Organization (WMO) on Mar. 23, in order to commemorate the entry into force of the WMO Convention, Mar. 23, 1950, and to publicize a variety of meteorological issues.

WORLDNET. The first world satellite TV network, est. in November 1983 by the United States Information Agency, USIA.

WORLD OPINION. An international term for widespread opinions in the world, subject of international research carried out by institutes for the study of public opinion.

WORLD PEACE COUNCIL. Organization reg. with the UIA, est. 1950, in Warsaw by the Second World Peace Defenders Congress, with headquarters in Helsinki; consultative status with UNESCO.

Yearbook of International Organizations.

WORLD PEACE FOUNDATION. An American institution reg. with the UIA, f. 1910, Boston, to conduct studies in world affairs, and research into international organizations. Publ.: *International Organization* (quarterly).

Yearbook of International Organizations.

WORLD PEACE THROUGH LAW. A Center for World Peace, f. 1963 in Athens by lawyers, jurists and legal scholars from over 100 nations at the First World Conference on World Peace Through Law as an international voluntary association of the legal profession, composed of the World Association of Judges, World Association of Lawyers, and World Association of Law Professors. Headquarters: Washington, DC. Consultative status with ECOSOC, ILO and Council of Europe. Publ.: *World Jurist, World Law Directory*.

Yearbook of International Organizations.

WORLD POPULATION CENSUS, 1950–80. The first world population census organized by the majority of UN members on the basis of standardized norms recommended by ECOSOC was made in 1950. The results warned of a demographic explosion of the world population. The majority of the UN member states accepted the recommendation of ECOSOC to make censuses every five years, the others every ten years. In 1960 the UN Statistical Committee initiated a program for the evaluation of 236 national censuses which had been made in the decade 1955–64, entitled World Population Census Program. The first censuses on the American continent were made in the US – 1790, since 1860 every 10 years by the "federal standard" method; Colombia – 1851; Chile – 1854. Other countries: 1860 – Uruguay, 1864 – Costa Rica, 1869 – Argentina, 1872 – Brazil, 1873 – Venezuela, 1876 – Peru, 1880 – Guatemala, 1887 – Honduras, 1895 – Mexico, 1899 – Cuba, 1900 – Bolivia, 1901 – Salvador, 1911 – Panama, 1920 – the Dominican Republic and Nicaragua, 1950 – Ecuador and Haiti.

See p. xxiii World Population Statistics 1985–2025

WORLD POPULATION CONFERENCES, 1954–85. The World Population Conferences under the aegis of the UN were held 1954 in Rome, 1965 in Belgrade, 1974 in Bucharest, and 1984 in Mexico.

WORLD POPULATION DISTRIBUTION BY REGION, 1750–1950. According to UN population trends studies the world population distribution by regions has changed during the last 200 years, 1750–1950 as follows (world total 100%):

Year	1750	1950
Asia (excl. Russia)	65.2%	54.9%
Europe and Russia	19.8%	22.7%
Africa	13.0%	8.8%
North America	0.1%	6.6%
Middle America	0.7%	2.1%
South America	0.8%	4.4%
Oceania	0.4%	0.5%

UNITED NATIONS, *Determination and Consequences of Population Trends*, New York, 1952; *UN Demographic Yearbook*.

WORLD POPULATION UN PROGNOSIS, 1984–2025. According to the UN data there were 4,76 billion people 1984, one billion more than in 1970; roughly 75 per cent live in the developing regions of the world. By the year 2025 world population is expected to reach 8,2 billion with 6,8 billion – 83 per cent – in the developing countries. On July 11, 1987 at 8:25 a.m. in Zagreb, Yugoslavia a baby boy Matej, second child of Sanja and Dragutin Gaspas was born, proclaimed by Secretary General Javier Perez de Cuellar as the five billionth person on the planet. The UN report "State of World Population" 1987 expects the population to double in the next hundred years.

UN Chronicle, No. 6, 1984; *UN Chronicle*, May, 1987.

WORLD PRICES. An international term for prices prevailing on the major markets and auctions of raw materials and agricultural-food products as well as in international commercial centers of industrial goods, to some extent imposed by the main producers and exporters. Market and auction quotations, trade bids, as well as indexes of world prices are the object of international analyses and serve as the basis for negotiations in international trade. The capitalist world exerts the main influence in determining world prices, since it is the largest world exporter and importer. The question of determining world prices is one of the main problems of Third World countries. ▷ New International Economic Order.

WORLD SCIENCE INFORMATION SYSTEM. The ▷ UNISYST, est. 1972, in Paris, Maison de l'UNESCO; an inter-governmental institution of the UNESCO member States, a world network of information services in the field of basic sciences,

applied sciences, engineering and technology; reg. with the UIA.

Yearbook of International Organizations.

WORLD'S COURT LEAGUE. An American organization reg. with the UIA, f. 1915, New York; advocated the establishment of a World Court for the settlement of disputes between nations. Publ.: *The World Court Magazine*.

W.E. DERBY, *International Tribunals: a Collection of the Various Schemes since 1815*, London, 1899; *Yearbook of International Organizations*.

WORLD'S MONEY. International term for instruments of international payments.

R. HARROD, *Reforming the World's Money*, New York, 1965; R. TRIFFIN, *The World Money Maze*, New Haven, 1966; A. K. SWOBODA, *The Eurodollar Market*, Princeton, 1968; J. SWIDROWSKI, *Exchange and Trade Controls, Principles and Procedures of International Transactions and Settlements*, Epping, 1975; R. SOLOMON, *The International Monetary System 1945–1976*, New York, 1977; B. TEW, *The Evolution of the International Monetary System 1945–1977*, London, 1978; J. B. COHEN, *Organizing the World's Money, the Political Economy of International Monetary Relations*, London, 1978; S. RACZKOWSKI, *Międzynarodowe Stosunki Finansowe*, Warszawa, 1984.

WORLD'S WARS. An international term for the local and regional wars after World War II. They have killed about 17 million persons in the years 1945–1987. The absolute majority of the wars took place in the Third World countries.

R.L. SIVARD, *World Military and Social Expenditures, 1987–1988*, Washington DC, 1988; The World's Wars, in: *The Economist*, March 12, 1988.

WORLD UNIVERSITY SERVICE. f. 1920, as the World Student Christian Federation, name changed in 1950, Geneva. Aims: promote the social role of university, extend post-secondary institutions to underdeveloped areas, provide scholarships at university level for refugees. Members: national committees in 62 countries. Consultative status: ECOSOC, UNESCO, FAO. Publ.: *WUS News*.

Yearbook of International Organizations, 1986/87; The Europa Yearbook 1988. A World Survey, Vol. I, London, 1988.

WORLD WAR, 1914–18. World War I; armed conflict between two groups of states initiated by the central powers led by Germany and Austria-Hungary against the states of the Entente (Allies), represented by France, Russia, and England; began with the declaration of war against Serbia on July 28, 1914 by Austria-Hungary, followed by declaration of war Aug. 1, against Russia and Aug. 3, against France by the German Reich; Aug. 4, England and its dominions declared war against Germany, and Aug. 6, Austria-Hungary against Russia. On the side of the central powers were: Turkey (in Nov., 1914) and Bulgaria (in Oct., 1915); on the side of the Entente: Montenegro and Japan (in Aug., 1914), Egypt (in Dec., 1914), Italy (in May, 1915), Portugal (in Mar., 1916), Romania (in Aug., 1916); in 1917: Greece (in June), Siam (in July), Liberia and China (in Aug.). Up to Apr., 1917 all of the states of the American continent remained neutral and traded with both combatant sides. The value of US trade with the Allies rose from 824 million dollars in 1914 to 3215 million in 1916, and with the Central Powers in the same time from 169 to 3214 million dollars. Only in the granting of credits the USA failed to be neutral. Up to Apr.,

1917 it granted the Allies 2300 million dollars credit while to the German Reich only 27 million. The President of the USA, W. Wilson, on Apr. 2, 1917 called attention to the "unlimited submarine warfare waged by Germany since February 1917 which does not respect the ships of neutral states. The present German submarine war against trade is a war against humanity. It is a war against all nations. I propose that Congress declare that the war of the imperialist German government is nothing other than a war against the government and nation of the USA".

The Congress on Apr. 6, 1917 ratified the declaration of war against Germany in the House of Representatives by 373 votes to 56, and in the Senate by 86 votes to 6. Under the influence of the USA the same was done by: Brazil, Costa Rica, Cuba, the Dominican Republic, Guatemala, Haiti, Nicaragua, while Bolivia, Ecuador, Peru, and Uruguay only severed diplomatic relations with the central powers: Argentina, Chile, Colombia, Mexico, Paraguay, El Salvador, and Venezuela remained neutral to the end. Besides the armed forces of the USA, among the states which declared war only the Brazilian navy took part in the war. The remaining served the United States as military and raw materials bases. Taking part in the war were 33 states of five continents with around 1.5 billion population. During the period of military action, which spanned three continents (Europe, Africa, and Asia) as well as oceans and seas, 70 million soldiers were mobilized. The losses reached c. 10 million killed and 20 million wounded and the costs 208 billion dollars. Victorious were the Allies, to whom the following states surrendered in successive order: Sept. 29, 1918 Bulgaria, Oct. 30, 1918 Turkey, Nov. 3, 1918 Austria-Hungary, Nov. 11, 1918 Germany. During the time of the Paris Peace Conference 1919–20 the Allies signed: with Germany June 28, 1919 ▷ Versailles Peace Treaty; with Austria Sept. 10, 1919 ▷ Saint-Germain-en-Laye Austria Peace Treaty; with Bulgaria Nov. 27, 1919 ▷ Neuilly Peace Treaty; with Hungary July 26, 1920 ▷ Hungary Peace Treaty; with Turkey Aug. 10, 1920 ▷ Sèvres Peace Treaty.

The political map of Europe was greatly changed. As a result of the October Revolution the Soviet Union arose in place of Tsarist Russia. The Austro-Hungarian monarchy broke up, significant territorial losses were incurred by Germany, Turkey, Bulgaria, and Russia. In Europe new states came into being or acquired independence: Poland, Hungary, Czechoslovakia, Yugoslavia, as well as Latvia, Estonia, Lithuania, and Finland; Germany and Austria became republics. The allies in 1919 formed the first world international organization, the League of Nations. World War I completely changed the European-American financial relationship. From a debtor of Europe in 1914 the USA in 1918 became its creditor. The national income of the USA, which was 33 billion in 1914, reached 72 billion in 1920. In 1927 the foreign investments in the USA were 3.7 billion dollars whereas the investments of the United States in Latin America, Canada, and Europe exceeded 12 billion dollars. The USA became the banker of the capitalist world. The USA, which did not ratify the Versailles Treaty 1919, ended the state of war through bilateral treaties with Austria Aug. 24, 1921, with the German Reich Aug. 25, 1921, and with Hungary Aug. 29, 1921. According to the calculations of the American scholar E.R.A. Seligman, *Essays in Taxation*, 1925, based on the budgets of the states taking part in the war the financial costs of World War I were:

	million dollars
British Empire	46,085
France	32,617
USA	32,261
Russia (to Oct. 31, 1917)	26,522
Italy	15,636
Belgium	1,387
Serbia	635
Total Allies	146,050
Germany	48,616
Austria-Hungary	24,858
Turkey	1,802
Bulgaria	732
Total Central Powers	76,008
Total Allies and Central Powers	232,058

V.J. ESPOSITO, *A Concise History of World War I*, New York, 1964; L. KOELTZ, *La Guerre de 1914–1918*, Paris, 1966; F. FISCHER, *Krieg der Illusionen*, Hamburg, 1969; I. BROZ, *Les causes de la I Guerre Mondiale*, Paris, 1973.

WORLD WAR, 1939–45. World War II began Sept. 1, 1939 with the invasion of Poland by Germany. Entering the war on the side of the German Third Reich were the remaining ▷ Rome-Berlin-Tokyo Axis powers: Italy June 10, 1940 and Japan Dec. 7, 1941, as well as successively: Hungary, Romania, Slovakia (in Nov., 1940), Bulgaria (in Mar., 1941), Finland (in June, 1941); on the side of the states of the anti-Fascist coalition, which from Jan. 1, 1941 took the name United Nations, were 51 states, the later signatories of the Charter of the UN 1945. The nucleus of this coalition were Great Britain (together with the states of the British Commonwealth) and France, and from 1941 USSR and USA. In sum, participating in World War II were more than 60 states from 5 continents with 1.7 billion people, while the military action covered 40 states on 3 continents: Europe, Asia, Africa and the Pacific area. More than 110 million soldiers were mobilized, the general losses in people were more than 50 million killed, murdered by Fascists, died as a result of epidemics, hunger, etc. The greatest losses in people were incurred by the Jewish nation – c. 33%, by Poland – c. 22% of the population, then the USSR and Yugoslavia – more than 11%; the Western powers: France c. 1.5%, Great Britain c. 0.8% and USA c. 0.14%. The estimated total military and civilian death casualties of the USSR were over 18 million, of Poland – 6,000,000, of Germany – 4,200,000, of Japan – 2,000,000, of China – 1,310,000. The greatest material losses were also incurred by Poland, USSR, and Yugoslavia. The direct war expenditures of the warring states were more than 1380 billion dollars.

In the first two years of the war, just as in World War I, all of the republics of America remained neutral in accordance with the Panama Declaration of Oct. 3, 1939. The Japanese air attack on the American naval base Pearl Harbor in Hawaii Dec. 7, 1941 and the declaration of war by Germany and Italy Dec. 10, 1941 against the United States, started the participation of the USA in World War II. The Ministers of Foreign Affairs of the American republics at their second Conference on Jan. 28, 1942 in Rio de Janeiro proposed the severing of diplomatic, consular, and trade relations with the Axis states. The following American republics first severed relations with the Axis states and then declared war on them: Argentina (Jan. 26 and Mar. 27, 1945), Bolivia (Apr. 7 and Dec. 4, 1943), Brazil (Jan. 22 and Oct. 22, 1942), Chile (Jan. 20, 1943 and Feb. 11, 1945), Colombia (Nov. 27, 1943 and Jan. 17, 1944), Ecuador (Jan. 17, 1944 and Feb. 19, 1945), Paraguay (Jan. 26, 1942 and Feb. 8, 1945), Peru (Jan. 24, 1942 and Feb. 12, 1945), Uruguay (Jan. 25, 1942 and Feb. 15, 1945), Venezuela (Dec. 31, 1941 and Feb. 16, 1945). Declaring war without

previously severing relations were: the Dominican Republic, Guatemala, Costa Rica, Cuba, Nicaragua – Dec. 11, 1941; Haiti, Honduras, and El Salvador – Dec. 12, 1941; Mexico – May 25, 1942, Panama – Jan. 13, 1942. The only Latin American state which took military action in the war was Brazil, whose army fought in Italy 1944 and its navy and airforce in the Atlantic. World War II was the bloodiest war in the history of mankind. The Axis states gave it the character of total war, perpetrating war crimes to an extent never before encountered in history. In response, the occupied nations organized mass resistance movements, whose most active form was the partisan units both in Europe as well as in South Asia. Finally the use of the atomic bomb by the USA against Japan in the last phase of the conflict (dropping of the bomb Aug. 6 and 9, 1945 on Hiroshima and Nagasaki) turned the end of World War II in the Far East into the beginning of atomic era.

The heaviest burden of the struggle against Hitler's Germany fell on the USSR, whose armed forces tied down and then destroyed the mass of Hitler's forces. The United Nations forced the unconditional surrender of Germany on May 8–9, 1945. Italy on Sept. 3, 1943, Japan on Sept. 2, 1945.

In view of the disintegration of the German Third Reich and the non-existence of any German authority, the responsibility for Germany was assumed by the four powers; its expression was the ▷ Declaration on the Defeat of Germany on June 5, 1945 as well as resolutions of the Potsdam Conference, July 17–Aug. 2, 1945. As a result of the Paris Peace Conference 1946 peace treaties were signed Feb. 10, 1947 in Paris with Bulgaria, Finland, Italy, and Hungary; the Peace Treaty with Japan was signed Sept. 8, 1951 in San Francisco; the four powers signed a State Treaty with Austria May 15, 1955 in Vienna. On the basis of the UN Charter signed June 16, 1945 in San Francisco the victors established the United Nations Organization on Oct. 24, 1945 with the task of maintaining international peace and security as well as developing international cooperation in all fields. In its consequences World War II brought greater political and social changes than the first.

Population Changes of Europe (without USSR) after World War II:

Years	W. Europe	E. Europe (except USSR)	Germany Austria	Poland
1938	207.9	108.3	85.8	34.8
1947	217.0	91.4	74.7	23.7
Difference	+9.1	−16.9	−11.3	−11.1

Source: Economic Survey of Europe since the War, Geneva, 1953.

Material Losses of Some Countries Occupied by the Germans during World War II:

Country	General (in mil.$)	Per person (in $)
USSR	128	745
Poland	16.8	626
Yugoslavia	9.1	601
Holland	4.4	520
France	21.1	504
Norway	1.2	434
Czechoslovakia	4.2	407
Greece	2.5	368
Belgium	2.2	277

Calculations of the financial expenditure for World War II are only approximate. According to such calculations of the *Encyclopaedia Britannica* (1973) the cost of World War II amounted to

1,166,825,000,000 American dollars, divided as follows among particular countries:

	billion dollars
USA	387
Germany	273
USSR	192
Great Britain	120
Italy	94
Japan	56
Canada	15.6
France	15.0
South America	8
Belgium	3.25
Poland	1.55
Holland	0.925
Czechoslovakia	0.8
Greece	0.22
Yugoslavia	0.2
Mexico	0.2

(In this estimation as far as Poland, Holland, Czechoslovakia, Greece, and Yugoslavia are concerned, the budgetary expenditures from 1935 to the moment of the Nazi invasion were accepted. The financial costs of China were not considered at all.) These costs comprise only part of the real costs of World War II in losses in people and costs of the results of the war.

"The causes of the Peace Failure 1919–39, by the International Consultative Group of Geneva", in: *International Conciliation*, No. 363, October, 1940; J.F.C. FULLER, *The Second World War, 1939–45: a Strategical and Tactical History*, London, 1949; T. HERRE, H. AUERBACH, *Bibliographie zur Zeitgeschichte und zum zweiten Weltkrieg für die Jahre 1945–1950*, München, 1955; A.M. ARMSTRONG, *Unconditional Surrender: the Impact of the Casablanca Policy in World War II*, London, 1961; *Istoriia Velikoi Otchestvennoi voiny Sovetskogo Soiuza 1941–1945*, Moscow, 1962–1965; V.J. ESPOSITO, *A concise History of World War II*, New York, 1964; J.R. SALIS, *Weltchronik 1939–1945*, Zürich, 1966; P. LAZAROFF, G. GROSRICHARD, *Histoire de la Guerre 1939–1945*, Paris, 1967; H. FEIS, *Japan Subdued: the Atomic Bomb and the End of the War in Pacific*, London, 1968; L.B.H. HART, *History of the Second World War*, London, 1970; P. CALVO-CORESSI, G. WINT, *Total War*, London, 1972; *The Second World War: A Guide to Documents in the Public Record Office*, HMSO, London, 1972; D. MASON, *Who's Who in World War II*, London, 1972; S. ASTER, *1939. The Making of the Second World War*, New York, 1974; J. KEEGAN ed., *The Rand McNally Encyclopedia of World War II*, Chicago, New York, 1977; H. SALISBURY, *The Unknown War*, New York, 1978; E.H. CARR, *International Relations between the two World Wars, 1919–1939*, London, 1985; D. KILLINGRAY, R. RATHBONE eds., *Africa and the II World War*, London, 1986; F.H. HINSLEY, *British Intelligence in the Second World War*, HMSO 3 Vls., London, 1979–88.

WORLD WEIGHTS AND MEASURES. The name of a periodically published UN guidebook on systems of measures and weights in force in the member countries, first edition 1955; second edition 1966 includes the International System of Units ▷ SI.

WORLD YEAR OF POPULATION PROBLEMS, 1974. A year declared by the UN General Assembly in 1972, for spreading knowledge of demographic problems of the present-day world, in connection with the Third World Population Conference in Aug., 1974 in Bucharest.

WOUNDED AND SICK GENEVA CONVENTION, 1929. Convention for the amelioration of the condition of the wounded and sick in armies in the field, signed in Geneva, July 27, 1929 by Austria, Belgium, Bolivia, Brazil, Bulgaria, Chile, China, Colombia, Cuba, Czechoslovakia, Denmark, Dominican Republic, Egypt, Estonia, Finland,

France, Germany, Great Britain, Greece, Hungary, Italy, Japan, Latvia, Luxembourg, Mexico, the Netherlands, Nicaragua, Norway, Persia, Poland, Portugal, Romania, Serbo-Croat-Slovene State, Siam, Spain, Sweden, Switzerland, Turkey, Uruguay and Venezuela. The text is as follows:

"Chapter I.
Wounded and Sick.
Art. 1. Officers and soldiers and other persons officially attached to the armed forces who are wounded or sick shall be respected and protected in all circumstances; they shall be treated with humanity and cared for medically, without distinction of nationality, by the belligerent in whose power they may be.
Nevertheless, the belligerent who is compelled to abandon wounded or sick to the enemy, shall, as far as military exigencies permit, leave with them a portion of his medical personnel and material to help with their treatment.
Art. 2. Except as regards the treatment to be provided for them in virtue of the preceding article, the wounded and sick of an army who fall into the hands of the enemy shall be prisoners of war, and the general provisions of international law concerning prisoners of war shall be applicable to them. Belligerents shall, however, be free to prescribe, for the benefit of wounded or sick prisoners such arrangements as they may think fit beyond the limits of the existing obligations.
Art. 3. After each engagement the occupant of the field of battle shall take measures to search for the wounded and dead, and to protect them against pillage and maltreatment.
Whenever circumstances permit, a local armistice or a suspension of fire shall be arranged to permit the removal of the wounded remaining between the lines.
Art. 4. Belligerents shall communicate to each other reciprocally, as soon as possible, the names of the wounded, sick and dead, collected or discovered, together with any indications which may assist in their identification. They shall establish and transmit to each other the certificates of death.
They shall likewise collect and transmit to each other all articles of a personal nature found on the field of battle or on the dead, especially one half of their identity discs, the other half to remain attached to the body.
They shall ensure that the burial or cremation of the dead is preceded by a careful, and if possible medical, examination of the bodies, with a view to confirming death, establishing identity and enabling a report to be made.
They shall further ensure that the dead are honourably interred, that their graves are respected and marked so that they may always be found.
To this end, at the commencement of hostilities, they shall exchange the list of graves and of dead interred in their cemeteries and elsewhere.
Art. 5. The military authorities may appeal to the charitable zeal of the inhabitants to collect and afford medical assistance, under their direction, to the wounded or sick of armies, and may accord to persons who have responded to this appeal special protection and certain facilities.
Chapter II.
Medical Formations and Establishments.
Art. 6. Mobile medical formations, that is to say, those which are intended to accompany armies in the field, and the fixed establishments of the medical service shall be respected and protected by the belligerents.
Art. 7. The protection to which medical formations and establishments are entitled shall cease if they are made use of to commit acts harmful to the enemy.
Art. 8. The following conditions are not considered to be of such a nature as to deprive a medical formation or establishment of the protection guaranteed by article 6:
(1) That the personnel of the formation or establishment is armed, and they they use the arms in their own defence or in that of the sick and wounded in charge;
(2) That in the absence of armed orderlies the formation or establishment is protected by a picket or by sentries;
(3) That small arms and ammunition taken from the wounded and sick, which have not yet been transferred to the proper service, are found in the formation or establishment;
(4) That personnel and material of the veterinary service are found in the formation or establishment, without forming an integral part of the same.
Chapter III.
Personnel.
Art. 9. The personnel engaged exclusively in the collection, transport and treatment of the wounded and sick, and in the administration of medical formations and establishments, and chaplains attached to armies, shall be respected and protected under all circumstances. If they fall into the hands of the enemy they shall not be treated as prisoners of war. Soldiers specially trained to be employed, in case of necessity, as auxiliary nurses or stretch-bearers for the collection, transport and treatment of the wounded and sick, and furnished with a proof of identity, shall enjoy the same treatment as the permanent medical personnel if they are taken prisoners while carrying out these functions.
Art. 10. The personnel of Voluntary Aid Societies, duly recognised and authorised by their Government, who may be employed on the same duties as those of the personnel mentioned in the first paragraph of art. 9, are placed on the same footing as the personnel contemplated in that paragraph, provided that the personnel of such societies are subject to military law and regulations.
Each High Contracting Party shall notify to the other, either in time of peace or at the commencement of or during the course of hostilities, but in every case before actually employing them, the names of the societies which it has authorised, under its responsibility, to render assistance to the regular medical service of its armed forces.
Art. 11. A recognised society of a neutral country can only afford the assistance of its medical personnel and formations to a belligerent with the previous consent of its own Government and the authorisation of the belligerent concerned. The belligerent who accepts such assistance is bound to notify the enemy thereof before making any use of it.
Art. 12. The persons designated in arts. 9, 10 and 11 may not be retained after they have fallen into the hands of the enemy.
In the absence of an agreement to the contrary, they shall be sent back to the belligerent to which they belong as soon as a route for their return shall be open and military considerations permit.
Pending their return they shall continue to carry out their duties under the direction of the enemy; they shall preferably be engaged in the care of the wounded and sick of the belligerent to which they belong.
On their departure, they shall take with them the effects, instruments, arms and means of transport belonging to them.
Art. 13. Belligerents shall secure to the personnel mentioned in arts. 9, 10, 11, while in their hands, the same food, the same lodging, the same allowances and the same pay as are granted to the corresponding personnel of their own armed forces.
At the outbreak of hostilities the belligerents will notify one another of the grades of their respective medical personnel.
Chapter IV. *Buildings and Material.*
Art. 14. Mobile medical formations, of whatsoever kind, shall retain, if they fall into the hands of the enemy, their equipment and stores, their means of transport and the drivers employed.
Nevertheless, the competent military authority shall be free to use the equipment and stores for the care of the wounded and sick; it shall be restored under the conditions laid down for the medical personnel, and as far as possible at the same time.
Art. 15. The buildings and material of the fixed medical establishments of the army shall be subject to the laws of war, but may not be diverted from their purpose so long as they are necessary for the wounded and the sick. Nevertheless, the commanders of troops in the field may make use of them, in case of urgent military necessity, provided that they make previous arrangements for the welfare of the wounded and sick who are being treated therein.
Art. 16. The buildings of aid societies which are admitted to the privileges of the Convention shall be regarded as private property.
The material of these societies, wherever it may be, shall similarly be considered as private property.
The right of requisition recognised for belligerents by the laws and customs of war, shall only be exercised in case of urgent necessity and only after the welfare of the wounded and sick has been secured.
Chapter V.
Medical Transport.
Art. 17. Vehicles equipped for the evacuation of wounded and sick, proceeding singly or in convoy, shall be treated as mobile medical formations, subject to the following special provisions:
A belligerent intercepting vehicles of medical transport, singly or in convoy, may, if military exigencies demand, stop them, and break up the convoy, provided he takes charge in every case of the wounded and sick who are in it. He can only use the vehicles in the sector where they have been intercepted, and exclusively for medical requirements. These vehicles, as soon as they are no longer required for local use, shall be given up in accordance with the conditions laid down in art. 14.
The military personnel in charge of the transport and furnished for this purpose with authority in due form, shall be sent back in accordance with the conditions prescribed in art. 12 for medical personnel, subject to the condition of the last paragraph of art. 18.
All means of transport specially organised for evacuation and the material used in equipping these means of transport belonging to the medical service shall be restored in accordance with the provisions of chapter IV.
Military means of transport other than those of the medical service may be captured, with their teams.
The civilian personnel and all means of transport obtained by requisition shall be subject to the general rules of international law.
Art. 18. Aircraft used as means of medical transport shall enjoy the protection of the Convention during the period in which they are reserved exclusively for the evacuation of wounded and sick and the transport of medical personnel and material.
They shall be painted white and shall bear, clearly marked, the distinctive emblem prescribed in art. 19, side by side with their national colours, on their lower and upper surfaces.
In the absence of special and express permission, flying over the firing line, and over the zone situated in front of clearing or dressing stations, and generally over all enemy territory or territory occupied by the enemy, is prohibited. Medical aircraft shall obey every summons to land. In the event of a landing thus imposed, or of an involuntary landing in enemy territory and territory occupied by the enemy, the wounded and sick, as well as the medical personnel and material, including the aircraft, shall enjoy the privileges of the present Convention.
The pilot, mechanics and wireless telegraph operators captured shall be sent back, on condition that they shall be employed until the close of hostilities in the medical service only.
Chapter VI.
The Distinctive Emblem.
Art. 19. As compliment to Switzerland, the heraldic emblem of the red cross on a white ground, formed by reversing the Federal Colours, is retained as the emblem and distinctive sign of the medical service of armed forces.
Nevertheless, in the case of countries which already use, in place of the Red Cross, the Red Crescent or the Red Lion and Sun on a white ground as a distinctive sign, these emblems are also recognised by the terms of the present Convention.
Art. 20. The emblem shall figure on the flags, armlets, and on all material belonging to the medical service, with the permission of the competent military authority.
Art. 21. The personnel protected in pursuance of articles 9 (paragraph 1), 10 and 11, shall wear, affixed to the left arm, an armlet bearing the distinctive sign, issued and stamped by military authority.
The personnel mentioned in art. 9, paragraphs 1 and 2, shall be provided with a certificate of identity, consisting either of an entry in their small book (paybook) or a special document.
The persons mentioned in arts. 10 and 11 who have no military uniform shall be furnished by the competent military authority with a certificate of identity, with photograph, certifying their status as medical personnel.
The certificates of identity shall be uniform and of the same pattern in each army.
In no case may the medical personnel be deprived of their armlets or the certificates of identity belonging to them. In case of loss they have the right to obtain duplicates.

Art. 22. The distinctive flag of the Convention shall be hoisted only over such medical formations and establishments as are entitled to be respected under the Convention, and with the consent of the military authorities. In fixed establishments it shall be, and in mobile formations it may be, accompanied by the national flag of the belligerent to whom the formation or establishment belongs.

Nevertheless, medical formations which have fallen into the hands of the enemy, so long as they are in that situation, shall not fly any other flag than that of the Convention. Belligerents shall take the necessary steps, so far as military exigencies permit, to make clearly visible to the enemy forces, whether land, air, or sea, the distinctive emblems indicating medical formations and establishments, in order to avoid the possibility of any offensive action.

Art. 23. The medical units belonging to neutral countries which shall have been authorised to lend their services under the conditions laid down in art. 11, shall fly, along with the flag of the Convention, the national flag of the belligerent to whose army they are attached. They shall also have the right, so long as they shall lend their services to a belligerent, to fly their national flag. The provisions of the second paragraph of the preceding article are applicable to them.

Art. 24. The emblem of the red cross on a white ground and the words 'Red Cross' or 'Geneva Cross' shall not be used either in time of peace or in time of war, except to protect or to indicate the medical formations and establishments and the personnel and material protected by the Convention. The same shall apply, as regards the emblem mentioned in art. 19, paragraph 2, in respect of the countries which use them.

The Voluntary Aid Societies mentioned in article 10, may, in accordance with their national legislation, use the distinctive emblem in connexion with their humanitarian activities in time of peace.

As an exceptional measure, and with the express authority of one of the national societies of the Red Cross (Red Crescent, Red Lion and Sun), use may be made of the emblem of the Convention in time of peace to mark the position of aid stations exclusively reserved for the purposes of giving free treatment to the wounded or the sick.

Chapter VII.
Application and Execution of the Convention.

Art. 25. The provisions of the present Convention shall be respected by the High Contracting Parties in all circumstances.

If, in time of war, a belligerent is not a party to the Convention, its provisions shall, nevertheless, be binding as between all the belligerents who are parties thereto.

Art. 26. The Commanders-in-Chief of belligerent armies shall arrange the details for carrying out the preceding articles, as well as for cases not provided for, in accordance with the instructions of their respective Governments and in conformity with the general principles of the present Convention.

Art. 27. The High Contracting Parties shall take the necessary steps to instruct their troops, and in particular the personnel protected, in the provisions of the present Convention and to bring them to the notice of the civil population.

Chapter VIII.
Suppression of Abuses and Infractions.

Art. 28. The Governments of the High Contracting Parties whose legislation is not at present adequate for the purpose shall adopt or propose to their legislatures the measures necessary to prevent at all times:

(a) The use of the emblem or designation 'Red Cross' or 'Geneva Cross' by private individuals or associations, firms or companies, other than those entitled thereto under the present Convention, as well as the use of any sign or designation constituting an imitation, for commercial or any other purposes;

(b) By reason of the compliment paid to Switzerland by the adoption of the reversed federal colours, the use by private individuals or associations, firms or companies of the arms of the Swiss Confederation, or marks constituting an imitation, whether as trademarks or as parts of such marks, for a purpose contrary to commercial honesty, or in circumstances capable of wounding Swiss national sentiment.

The prohibition indicated in (a) of the use of marks or designations constituting an imitation of the emblem or designation of 'Red Cross' or 'Geneva Cross', as well as

the prohibition in (b) of the use of the arms of the Swiss Confederation or marks constituting an imitation, shall take effect as from the date fixed by each legislature, and not later than five years after the coming into force of the present Convention. From the date of such coming into force, it shall no longer be lawful to adopt a trademark in contravention of these rules.

Art. 29. The Governments of the High Contracting Parties shall also propose to their legislatures, should their penal laws be inadequate, the necessary measures for the repression in time of war of any act contrary to the provisions of the present Convention.

They shall communicate to one another, through the Swiss Federal Council, the provisions relative to such repression not later than five years from the ratification of the present Convention.

Art. 30. On the request of a belligerent, an enquiry shall be instituted, in a manner to be decided between the interested parties, concerning any alleged violation of the Convention; when such violation has been established the belligerents shall put an end to and repress it as promptly as possible.

Art. 31. The present Convention, which shall bear this day's date, may be signed, up to the 1st February, 1930, on behalf of all the countries represented at the Conference which opened at Geneva on the 1st July, 1929 as well as by countries not represented at that Conference but which were parties to the Geneva Conventions of 1864 and 1906.''

LNTS, Vol. 118, pp. 315–331.

WOUNDED KNEE. A town in South Dakota, USA, located on the territory of a reservation inhabited by Oglala Pine Ridge Indians. It earned fame for being occupied by an armed group of 200 Sioux Indians, from Feb. 27 to Apr. 5, 1973, protesting against discrimination. This was a follow-up of an action started in Sept., 1972 in Denver, and the march along the "Trail of Broken Treaties" to Washington DC, in Oct., 1972 to commemorate the treaties concluded by Indians with the new settlers (371 in total). The demonstration in Wounded Knee was meant to turn public attention to the problem of American Indians not only in the USA, but worldwide. During the occupation of Wounded Knee on Mar. 3, 1973, delegates of the Oglala Pine Ridge reservation called on the UN headquarters in New York and deposited a petition with UN Secretary-General, K. Waldheim. The selection of Wounded Knee for the site of the demonstration was connected with the final act of the Indian wars, finishing on Dec. 29, 1890, in Wounded Knee by assassination of the chief of the Sioux Indians and the murder of 200 men, women and children survivors.

KEESING's *Contemporary Archive*, 1973.

WRENDA. World Request List for Nuclear Data, one of the information systems of the ▷ IAEA.

WRESTLING. An olympic sport from the 1st Games of 1896, organized by the International Wrestling Federation, Federation Internationale de lutte amateur, FILA, est. 1911, sponsors the annual (with the exception of Olympic years) World Championships.

Yearbook of International Organizations.

WTO. ▷ Warsaw Treaty or Warsaw Pact 1955.

WTO. World Tourism Organization. Organisation mondiale du tourisme, OMT. Organización Mundial del Turismo, OMT. Vsiemirnaya Organizatsya Turisma, WOT. An inter-governmental organization est. Jan. 2, 1975 in Madrid by 88 countries. Aims: to promote tourism with a view to contributing to economic development, international better understanding, peace and prosperity. Consultative status with ECOSOC,

UNESCO, IMCO and ICAO. Publ.: *World Travel Tourism.* Reg. with the UIA.

Yearbook of International Organizations.

WTO STATUTE, 1970. The Statute adopted at the Mexico City Conference on Sept. 27, 1970, entered into force on Nov. 1, 1974, following ratification by 51 States. The text is as follows:

"Establishment
Art. 1. The World Tourism Organization, hereinafter referred to as 'the Organization,' an international organization of inter-governmental character resulting from the transformation of the International Union of Official Travel Organizations (IUOTO), is hereby established.
Headquarters
Art. 2. The headquarters of the Organization shall be determined and may at any time be changed by decision of the General Assembly.
Aims
Art. 3.(1) The fundamental aim of the Organization shall be the promotion and development of tourism with a view to contributing to economic development, international understanding, peace, prosperity, and universal respect for, and observance of, human rights and fundamental freedoms for all without distinction as to race, sex, language or religion. The Organization shall take all appropriate action to attain this objective.
(2) In pursuing this aim, the Organization shall pay particular attention to the interests of the developing countries in the field of tourism.
(3) In order to establish its central role in the field of tourism, the Organization shall establish and maintain effective collaboration with the appropriate organs of the United Nations and its specialized agencies. In this connection the Organization shall seek a co-operative relationship with and participation in the activities of the United Nations Development Program, as a participating and executing agency.
Membership
Art. 4. Membership of the Organization shall be open to:
(a) Full members
(b) Associate members
(c) Affiliate members
Art. 5.(1) Full membership of the Organization shall be open to all sovereign States.
(2) States whose national tourism organizations are full members of IUOTO at the time of adoption of these Statutes by the Extraordinary General Assembly of IUOTO shall have the right to become full members of the Organization, without requirement to vote, on formally declaring that they adopt the Statutes of the Organization and accept the obligation of membership.
(3) Other States may become full members of the Organization if their candidatures are approved by the General Assembly by a majority of two thirds of the full members present and voting provided that said majority is a majority of the full members of the Organization.
Art. 6.(1) Associate membership of the Organization shall be open to all Territories or groups of Territories not responsible for their external relations.
(2) Territories or groups of Territories whose national tourism organizations are full members of IUOTO at the time of adoption of these Statutes by the Extraordinary General Assembly of IUOTO shall have the right to become associate members of the Organization, without requirement of vote, provided that the State which assumes responsibility for their external relations approves their membership and declares on their behalf that such Territories or groups of Territories adopt the Statutes of the Organization and accept the obligations of membership.
(3) Territories or group of Territories may become associate members of the Organization if their candidature has the prior approval of the member State which assumes responsibility for their external relations and declares on their behalf that such Territories or groups of Territories adopt the Statutes of the Organization and accept the obligations of membership. Such candidatures must be approved by the Assembly by a majority of two thirds of the fully members present and voting provided that said majority is a majority of the full members of the Organization.

(4) When an associate member of the Organization becomes responsible for the conduct of its external relations, that associate member shall be entitled to become a full member of the Organization on formally declaring in writing to the Secretary-General that it adopts the Statutes of the Organization and accepts the obligations of full membership.

Art. 7(1) Affiliate membership of the Organization shall be open to international bodies, both inter-governmental and non-governmental, concerned with specialized interests in tourism and commercial bodies and associations whose activities are related to the aims of the Organization or fall within its competence.

(2) Associate members of IUOTO at the time of adoption of these Statutes by the Extraordinary General Assembly of IUOTO shall have the right to become affiliate members of the Organization, without requirement of vote, on declaring that they accept the obligations of affiliate membership.

(3) Other international bodies, both inter-governmental and non-governmental, concerned with specialized interests in tourism, may become affiliate members of the Organization provided the request for membership is presented in writing to the Secretary-General and receives approval by the Assembly by a majority of two thirds of the full members present and voting and provided that said majority is a majority of the full members of the Organization.

(4) Commercial bodies or associations with interests defined in paragraph 1 above may become affiliate members of the Organization provided their requests for membership are presented in writing to the Secretary-General and are endorsed by the State in which the headquarters of the candidate is located. Such candidatures must be approved by the General Assembly by a majority of two thirds of the full members present and voting provided that said majority is a majority of the full members of the Organization.

(5) There may be a Committee of affiliate members which shall establish its own rules and submit them to the General Assembly for approval. The Committee may be represented at meetings of the Organization. It may request the inclusion of questions in the agenda of those meetings. It may also make recommendations to the meetings.

(6) Affiliate members may participate in the activities of the Organization individually or grouped in the Committee of affiliate members.

Organs

Art. 8.(1) The organs of the Organization are:

(a) The General Assembly, hereinafter referred to as the Assembly.

(b) The Executive Council, hereinafter referred to as the Council.

(c) The Secretariat.

(2) Meetings of the Assembly and the Council shall be held at the headquarters of the Organization unless the respective organs decide otherwise.

General Assembly

Art. 9.(1) The Assembly is the supreme organ of the Organization and shall be composed of delegates representing full members.

(2) At each session of the Assembly each full and associate member shall be represented by not more than five delegates, one of whom shall be designated by the member as Chief Delegate.

(3) The Committee of affiliate members may designate up to three observers and each affiliate member may designate one observer, who may participate in the work of the Assembly.

Art. 10. The Assembly shall meet in ordinary session every two years and, as well, in extraordinary session when circumstances require. Extraordinary sessions may be convened at the request of the Council or of a majority of full members of the Organization.

Art. 11. The Assembly shall adopt its own rules of procedure.

Art. 12. The Assembly may consider any question and make recommendations on any matter within the competence of the Organization. Its functions, other than those which have been conferred on it elsewhere in the present Statutes, shall be:

(a) to elect its President and Vice-Presidents;

(b) to elect members of the Council;

(c) to appoint the Secretary-General on the recommendation of the Council;

(d) to approve the Financial Regulations of the Organization;

(e) to lay down general guidelines for the administration of the Organization;

(f) to approve the staff regulations applicable to the personnel of the Secretariat;

(g) to elect the auditors on the recommendation of the Council;

(h) to approve the general program of work of the Organization;

(i) to supervise the financial policies of the Organization and to review and approve the budget;

(j) to establish any technical or regional body which may become necessary;

(k) to consider and approve reports on the activities of the Organization and of its organs and to take all necessary steps to give effect to the measures which arise from them;

(l) to approve or to delegate the power to approve the conclusion of agreements with governments and international organizations;

(m) to approve or to delegate the power to approve the conclusion of agreements with private organizations or private entities;

(n) to prepare and recommend international agreements on any question that falls within the competence of the Organization;

(o) to decide, in accordance with the present Statutes, on applications for membership.

Art. 13.(1) The Assembly shall elect its President and Vice-Presidents at the beginning of each session.

(2) The President shall preside over the Assembly and shall carry out the duties which are entrusted to him.

(3) The President shall be responsible to the Assembly while it is in session.

(4) The President shall represent the Organization for the duration of his term of office on all occasions on which such representation is necessary.

Executive Council

Art. 14.(1) The Council shall consist of full members elected by the Assembly at the ratio of one member for every five full members, in accordance with the Rules of Procedure laid down by the Assembly, with a view to achieving fair and equitable geographical distribution.

(2) One associate member selected by the associate members of the Organization may participate in the work of the Council without the right to vote.

(3) A representative of the Committee of Affiliate Members may participate in the work of the Council without the right to vote.

Art. 15. The term of elected members shall be four years except that the terms of one half of the members of the first Council as determined by the lot, shall be two years. Election for one half of the membership of the Council shall be held every two years.

Art. 16. The Council shall meet at least once a year.

Art. 17. The Council shall elect a Chairman and Vice-Chairman from among its elected members to serve for a term of one year.

Art. 18. The Council shall adopt its own Rules of Procedure.

Art. 19. The functions of the Council, other than those which are elsewhere assigned to it in these Statutes, shall be:

(a) to take all necessary measures, in consultation with the Secretary-General, for the implementation of the decisions and recommendations of the Assembly and to report thereon to the Assembly;

(b) to receive from the Secretary-General reports on the activities of the Organization;

(c) to submit proposals to the Assembly;

(d) to examine the General program of work of the Organization as prepared by the Secretary-General, prior to its submission to the Assembly;

(e) to submit reports and recommendations on the Organization's accounts and budget estimates to the Assembly;

(f) to set up any subsidiary body which may be required by its own activities;

(g) to carry out any other functions which may be entrusted to it by the Assembly.

Art. 20. Between sessions of the Assembly and in the absence of any contrary provisions in these Statutes, the Council shall take such administrative and technical decisions as may be necessary, within the functions and financial resources of the Organization, and shall report the decisions which have been taken to the Assembly at its following session, for approval.

Secretariat

Art. 21. The Secretariat shall consist of the Secretary-General and such staff as the Organization may require.

Art. 22. The Secretary-General shall be appointed by a two-thirds majority of full members present and voting in the Assembly, on the recommendation of the Council, and for term of four years. His appointment shall be renewable.

Art. 23.(1) The Secretary-General shall be responsible to the Assembly and Council.

(2) The Secretary-General shall carry out the direction of the Assembly and Council. He shall submit to the Council reports on the activities of the Organization, its accounts and the draft general program of work and budget estimates of the Organization.

(3) The Secretary-General shall ensure the legal representation of the Organization.

Art. 24.(1) The Secretary-General shall appoint the staff of the Secretariat in accordance with staff regulations approved by the Assembly.

(2) The staff of the Organization shall be responsible to the Secretary-General.

(3) The paramount consideration in the recruitment of staff and in the determination of the conditions of service shall be the necessity of securing the highest standards of efficiency, technical competence and integrity. Subject to this consideration, due regard shall be paid to the importance of recruiting the staff on as wide a geographical basis as possible.

(4) In the performance of their duties the Secretary-General and staff shall not seek or receive instructions from any Government or any other authority external to the Organization. They shall refrain from any action which might reflect on their position as international officials responsible only to the Organization.

Budget and Expenditure

Art. 25.(1) The budget of the Organization, covering its administrative functions and the general program of work, shall be financed by contributions of the full, associate and affiliate members according to a scale of assessment accepted by the Assembly and from other possible sources of receipts for the Organization in accordance with the Financing Rules which are attached to these Statutes and form an integral part thereof.

(2) The budget prepared by the Secretary-General shall be submitted by the Council to the Assembly for examination and approval.

Art. 26.(1) The accounts of the Organization shall be examined by two auditors elected by the Assembly on the recommendation of the Council for a period of two years. The auditors shall be eligible for re-election.

(2) The auditors, in addition to examining the accounts, may make such observations as they deem necessary with respect to the efficiency of the financial procedures and management, the accounting system, the internal financial controls and, in general, the financial consequences of administrative practices.

Quorum

Art. 27.(1) The presence of a majority of the full members shall be necessary to constitute a quorum at meetings of the Assembly.

(2) The presence of a majority of the full members of the Council shall be necessary to constitute a quorum at meetings of the Council.

Voting

Art. 28. Each full member shall be entitled to one vote.

Art. 29.(1) Subject to other provisions of the present Statutes, decisions on all matters shall be taken in the Assembly by a simple majority of full members present and voting.

(2) A two-thirds majority vote of the full members, present and voting, shall be necessary to take decisions on matters involving budgetary and financial obligations of the members, the location of the headquarters of the Organization and other questions deemed of particular importance by a simple majority of the full members present and voting at the Assembly.

Art. 30. Decisions of the Council shall be made by a simple majority of members present and voting except on budgetary and financial recommendations which shall be approved by a two-thirds majority of members present and voting.

Legal Personality, Privileges and Immunities

Art. 31. The Organization shall have legal personality.

Art. 32. The Organization shall enjoy in the territories of its member States the privileges and immunities required for the exercise of its functions. Such privileges and immunities may be defined by agreements concluded by the Organization.

Amendments

Art. 33.(1) Any suggested amendment to the present Statutes and its Annex shall be transmitted to the Secretary-General who shall circulate it to the full members at least six months before being submitted to the consideration of the Assembly.

(2) An amendment shall be adopted by the Assembly by a two-thirds majority of full members present and voting.

(3) An amendment shall come into force for all members when two thirds of the member States have notified the Depository Government of their approval of such amendment.

Suspension and Membership

Art. 34.(1) If any member is found by the Assembly to persist in a policy that is contrary to the fundamental aim of the Organization as mentioned in Art. 3 of these Statutes, the Assembly may, by a resolution adopted by a majority of two thirds of full members present and voting, suspend such member from exercising the rights and enjoying the privileges of membership.

(2) The suspension shall remain in force until a change of such policy is recognized by the Assembly.

Withdrawal from Membership

Art. 35.(1) Any full member may withdraw from the Organization on the expiry of one year's notice in writing to the Depository Government.

(2) Any associate member may withdraw from the Organization on the same conditions of notice, provided the Depository Government has been notified in writing by the full member which is responsible for the external relations of that associate member.

(3) An affiliate member may withdraw from the Organization on the expiry of one year's notice in writing to the Secretary-General.

Entry into Force

Art. 36. The present Statutes shall enter into force one hundred and twenty days after fifty-one States whose official tourism organizations are full members of IUOTO at the time of adoption of these Statutes, have formally signified to the provisional Depository their approval of the Statutes and their acceptance of the obligations of membership.

Depository

Art. 37.(1) The Government of Switzerland shall notify all States entitled to receive such notification of the receipt of such declarations and of the date of entry into force of these Statutes.

Interpretation and Languages

Art. 38. The official languages of the Organization shall be English, French, Russian and Spanish.

Art. 39. The English, French, Russian and Spanish texts of these Statutes shall be regarded as equally authentic.

Transitional Provision

Art. 40. The headquarters shall provisionally be in Geneva, Switzerland, pending a decision by the General Assembly under Art. 2.

Art. 41. During a period of one hundred and eighty days after these Statutes enter into force, states members of the United Nations, the specialized agencies and the International Atomic Energy Agency or parties to the Statute of the International Court of Justice shall have the right to become full members of the Organization, without reqirement of vote, on formally declaring that they adopt the Statutes of the Organization and accept the obligations of membership.

Art. 42. During the year following the entry into force of the present Statutes, States whose national tourism organizations were members of IUOTO at the time of adoption of these Statutes and which have adopted the present Statutes subject to approval may participate in the activities of the Organization with the rights and obligations of a full member.

Art. 43. During the year following the entry into force of the present Statutes, Territories or group of Territories not responsible for their external relations but whose tourism organizations were full members of IUOTO and are therefore entitled to associate members and which have adopted the Statutes subject to approval by the State which assumes responsibility for their external relations may participate in the activities of the Organization with the rights and obligations of an associate member.

Art. 44. When the present Statutes come into force, the rights and obligations of IUOTO shall be transferred to the Organization.

Art. 45. The Secretary-General of IUOTO at the time of the entry into force of the present Statutes shall act as Secretary-General of the Organization until such time as the Assembly has elected the Secretary-General of the Organization."

An Annex on Financial Rules in the first main Articles stated:

"(1) The financial period of the Organization shall be two years.

(2) The financial years shall be from January 1st to December 31st.

(3) The budget shall be financed by the contributions of the members according to a method of apportionment to be determined by the Assembly, based on the level of eonomic development of and the importance of tourism in each country, and by other receipts of the Organization.

(4) The budget shall be formulated in United States dollars. The currency used for the payment of contributions shall be United States dollar. This shall not preclude acceptance by the Secretary-General, to the extent authorized by the Assembly, of other currencies in payment of members' contributions.

(5) A General Fund shall be established. All membership contributions made pursuant to paragraph 3, miscellaneous income and any advances from the Working Capital Fund shall be credited to the General Fund. Expenditure for administration and the general program of work shall be paid out of the General Fund.

(6) A Working Capital Fund shall be established, the amount of which is to be fixed by the Assembly. Advance contributions of members and any other budget receipts which the Assembly decides may be so used, shall be paid into the Working Capital Fund. When required, amounts therefrom shall be transferred to the General Fund.

(7) Funds-in-trust may be established to finance activities not provided for in the budget of the Organization which are of interest to some member countries or groups of countries. Such Funds shall be financed by voluntary contributions. A fee may be charged by the Organization to administer these Funds.

(8) The Assembly shall determine the utilization of gifts, legacies and other extraordinary receipts not included in the budget."

A.J.PEASLEE (ed.), *International Governmental Organizations, Constitutional Documents*, The Hague, 1976, Part V, pp. 647–656.

WÜRZBURG. A Bavarian city on the Main River. The Würzburg Residence, a cultural monument, is included in the ▷ World Heritage UNESCO List. Of all the chateaux built in Europe in the 18th century, the residence of the prince-bishops of Franconia stands out because of its magnificence. It is the high point of the Baroque style which, specifically in Germany, became the dazzling Rococo style.

UNESCO, *A Legacy for All*, Paris, 1984.

WWW. World Weather Watch, information system of the ▷ WMO.

X

X-30. ▷ Spaceplane.

XENOPHOBIA. International term for in-tolerance of foreigners, known in the past century in both East and West. According to a report of the UNHCR Round Table on Refugees, Victims of Xenophobia in Geneva, in Apr., 1984, "the phenomenon of xenophobia is on the upsurge, more visible in Western industrialized societies where xenophobic tendencies contrast with previously tolerant attitudes to foreigners and where liberal admission policies in the past have permitted the growth of sizeable foreign population." In fact with 600,000 ▷ Gastarbeiter in European countries only

one in 710 is a refugee, that means asylum-seeker. In the opinion of the UN High Commissioner for Refugees, P. Hartling, the new phenomenon is a warning signal for the world community.

The European Parliament on Feb. 17, 1986 adopted a Resolution on the growing number of crimes connected with fascism, racism and xenophobia in European Community countries. The text is as follows:

The European Parliament
– having regard to the conclusion and recommen-dations of the Committee of Inquiry into the rise of fascism and racism in Europe,
– having regard to its resolution of January 16, 1986 on the rise of fascism and racism in Europe,
– having regard to the joint declaration of the Com-munity institutions,
(A) shocked by the criminal attack of arson committed by fascist or neo-Nazi organizations on May 17, 1987 in Wuppertal in North Rhine-Westphalia, on a building housing foreigners, mainly Greek workers, resulting in the death of the Liolias couple and their nine-year-old son and causing burns to 18 other residents,
(B) concerned at the fact that similar attacks of arson were reported a few days earlier in the same city aimed this time at a building housing Turkish immigrants,
(C) noting an atmosphere of tolerance towards systematic attempts on the parts of extreme right-wing parties and organizations to foster xenophobic feelings and hostility particularly towards immigrant workers to whom they attribute the chief blame for unemploy-ment in the Community with a view to developing young people, especially those who are unemployed,

(1) Condemns the criminal activities of fascist organizations and calls for them to be disbanded;
(2) Considers that the work of fascist organizations is facilitated by the fostering, on whatever pretext, of xenophobic sentiments and the broadcasting by the mass media of statements likely to arouse such senti-ments, especially in the current economic climate;
(3) Calls on the governments of the Member States to implement without delay the Committee of Inquiry's recommendations in all the sectors provided for (in-stitutional, educational, information, etc.);
(4) Calls on the governments of the Member States to take urgent legal measures and other appropriate steps banning the reporting of statements and demon-strations against immigrant workers which shake con-fidence in democratic institutions and encourage fascism;
(5) Also calls on the governments of the Member States to provide cultural, democratic and workers' organiza-tions with essential resources and facilities in their attempt to alert public opinion to the danger of the revival of fascism;
(6) Instructs its President to forward this resolution to the Council, the Commission and the governments of the Member States.

UNHCR Refugees, May, 1984; Council of Europe, *Human Rights, Information Sheet No. 21,* Strasbourg, 1988, pp. 236.

XHOSA PEOPLE. ▷ Ciskei.

X RAY, LASER. ▷ Space war.

Y

YACHT RACING. Organizations reg. with the UIA:

El Toro International Yacht Racing Association, f. 1947, La Salle, Canada.
International Ice Yacht Racing Association, f. 1953, Shrewsbury, NJ.
International Star Class Yacht Racing Association, f. 1911, New York.
International Yacht Racing Union, f. 1907, London. Recognized by International Olympic Committee. Publ.: *Racing Rules*.

Yearbook of International Organizations.

YALTA. One of the largest USSR holiday resorts in the Crimean peninsula, on the Black Sea. In 1945 site of the Summit Meeting of Churchill, Roosevelt and Stalin.

YALTA CONFERENCE, 1945. The summit meeting of the Heads of State of the UK (W. S. Churchill), the USA (F. D. Roosevelt) and the USSR (J. V. Stalin) on Feb. 4–11, 1945 at Yalta in the Crimea. Besides the military and political problems of Europe and the Far East, the Conference discussed the Dumbarton Oaks draft of the UN Charter and especially the problem of voting in the Security Council. The English language protocols of the Conference were published in 1956.

"Report of Crimea Conference", in: *International Conciliation*, No. 409, March, 1945; US Department of State, *Crimea Conference, Yalta, Russia, 1945*, 3 Vols., Washington, DC, 1955; C. L. SULZBERGER, *Such a Peace: the Roots and Ashes of Yalta*, New York, 1982.

YALTA DECLARATION, 1945. Official name of the Final Act of the Summit Meeting in Yalta (Crimea), Feb. 11, 1945. The text is as follows:

"For the past eight days Winston S. Churchill, Prime Minister of Great Britain, Franklin D. Roosevelt, President of the United States of America, and Marshal J. V. Stalin, Chairman of the Council of People's Commissars of the Union of Soviet Socialist Republics, have met with the Foreign Secretaries, Chiefs of Staff and other advisers in the Crimea.
The following statement is made by the Prime Minister of Great Britain, the President of the United States of America, and the Chairman of the Council of People's Commissars of the Union of Soviet Socialist Republics, on the results of the Crimea Conference.
I. The Defeat of Germany.
We have considered and determined the military plans of the three Allied Powers for the final defeat of the common enemy. The military staffs of the three allied nations have met in daily meetings throughout the Conference. These meetings have been most satisfactory from every point of view and have resulted in closer co-ordination of the military effort of the three Allies than ever before. The fullest information has been interchanged. The timing, scope and co-ordination of new and even more powerful blows to be launched by our armies and air forces into the heart of Germany from the East, West, North and South have been fully agreed and planned in detail.
Our combined military plans will be made known only as we execute them, but we believe that the very close working partnership among the three staffs attained at

this Conference will result in shortening the war. Meetings of the three staffs will be continued in the future whenever the need arises.
Nazi Germany is doomed. The German people will only make the cost of their defeat heavier to themselves by attempting to continue a hopeless resistance.
II. The Occupation and Control of Germany.
We have agreed on common policies and plans for enforcing the unconditional surrender terms which we shall impose together on Nazi Germany after German armed resistance has been finally crushed. These terms will not be made known until the final defeat of Germany has been accomplished. Under the agreed plan, the forces of the Three Powers will each occupy a separate zone of Germany. Co-ordinated administration and control has been provided for under the plan through a central Control Commission consisting of the Supreme Commanders of the Three Powers with headquarters in Berlin. It has been agreed that France should be invited by the Three Powers, if she should so desire, to take over a zone of occupation, and to participate as a fourth member of the Control Commission. The limits of the French zone will be agreed by the four Governments concerned through their representatives on the European Advisory Commission.
It is our inflexible purpose to destroy German militarism and Nazism and to ensure that Germany will never again be able to disturb the peace of the world.
We are determined to disarm and disband all German armed forces; break up for all time the German General Staff that has repeatedly contrived the resurgence of German militarism; remove or destroy all German military equipment; eliminate or control all German industry that could be used for military production; bring all war criminals to just and swift punishment and exact reparation in kind for the destruction wrought by the Germans; wipe out the Nazi party, Nazi laws, organisations and institutions, remove all Nazi and militarist influences from public office and from the cultural and economic life of the German people; and take in harmony such other measures in Germany as may be necessary to the future peace and safety of the world. It is not our purpose to destroy the people of Germany, but only when Nazism and militarism have been extirpated, will there be hope for a decent life for Germans, and place for them in the comity of nations.
III. Reparation by Germany.
We have considered the question of the damage caused by Germany to the Allied Nations in this war and recognised it as just that Germany be obliged to make compensation for this damage in kind to the greatest extent possible. A Commission will be instructed to consider the question of the extent and methods for compensating damage caused by Germany to the Allied countries. The Commission will work in Moscow.
IV. United Nations Conference.
We are resolved upon the earliest possible establishment with our Allies of a general international organisation to maintain peace and security. We believe that this is essential, both to prevent aggression and to remove the political, economic and social causes of war through the close and continuing collaboration of all peace-loving peoples.
The foundations were laid at Dumbarton Oaks. On the important question of voting procedure, however, agreement was not reached. The present Conference has been able to resolve this difficulty.
We have agreed that a Conference of United Nations should be called to meet at San Francisco in the United States on the 25th April, 1945, to prepare the Charter of such an organisation, along the lines proposed in the informal conversations at Dumbarton Oaks.
The Government of China and the Provisional Government of France will be immediately consulted and invited to sponsor invitations to the Conference jointly with the Governments of the United States, Great Britain and the Union of Soviet Socialist Republics. As soon as the consultation with China and France has been completed, the text of the proposals on voting procedure will be made public.
V. Declaration on Liberated Europe.
We have drawn up and subscribed to a declaration on liberated Europe. This declaration provides for concerting the policies of the Three Powers and for joint action by them in meeting the political and economic problems of liberated Europe in accordance with democratic principles.

The text of the Declaration is as follows.
The Premier of the Union of Soviet Socialist Republics, the Prime Minister of the United Kingdom, and the President of the United States of America have consulted with each other in the common interests of the peoples of their countries and those of liberated Europe. They jointly declare their mutual agreement to concert during the temporary period of instability in liberated Europe the policies of their three Governments in assisting the peoples liberated for the domination of Nazi Germany and the peoples of the former Axis satellite States of Europe to solve by democratic means their pressing political and economic problems. The establishment of order in Europe and the rebuilding of national economic life must be achieved by processes which will enable the liberated peoples to destroy the last vestiges of Nazism and Fascism and to create democratic institutions of their own choice.
This is a principle of the Atlantic Charter – the right of all peoples to choose the form of government under which they will live – the restoration of sovereign rights and self-government to those peoples who have been forcibly deprived of them by the aggressor nations.
To foster the conditions in which the liberated peoples may exercise those rights, the three Governments will jointly assist the people in any European liberated State or former Axis satellite State in Europe where in their judgment conditions require: (a) to establish conditions of internal peace; (b) to carry out emergency measures for the relief of distressed peoples; (c) to form interim governmental authorities broadly representative of all democratic elements in the population and pledged to the earliest possible establishment through free elections of Governments responsive to the will of the people; and (d) to facilitate where necessary the holding of such elections.
The three Governments will consult the other United Nations and provisional authorities or other Governments in Europe when matters of direct interest to them are under consideration. When, in the opinion of the three Governments, conditions in any European liberated State or any former Axis satellite State in Europe make such action necessary, they will immediately consult together on the measures necessary to discharge the joint responsibilities set forth in this Declaration.
By this Declaration we reaffirm our faith in the principles of the Atlantic Charter, our pledge in the Declaration by the United Nations, and our determination to build in co-operation with other peace-loving nations a world order under law, dedicated to peace, security, freedom and the general well-being of all mankind.
In issuing this Declaration, the Three Powers express the hope that the Provisional Government of the French Republic may be associated with them in the procedure suggested.
VI. Poland.
We came to the Crimea Conference resolved to settle our differences about Poland. We discussed fully all aspects of the question. We reaffirm our common desire to see established a strong, free, independent and democratic Poland. As a result of our discussions we have agreed on the conditions in which a new Polish Provisional Government of National Unity may be formed in such a manner as to command recognition by the three major Powers.
The agreement reached is as follows:
A new situation has been created in Poland as a result of her complete liberation by the Red Army. This calls for the establishment of a Polish Provisional Government which can be more broadly based than was possible before the recent liberation of western Poland. The Provisional Government which is now functioning in Poland should therefore be re-organised on a broader democratic basis with the inclusion of democratic leaders from Poland itself and from Poles abroad. This new Government should then be called the Polish Provisional Government of National Unity.
M. Molotov, Mr. Harriman and Sir A. Kerr are authorised as a Commission to consult in the first instance in Moscow with members of the present Provisional Government and with other Polish democratic leaders from within Poland and from abroad, with a view to the reorganisation of the present Government along the above lines. This Polish Provisional Government of National Unity shall be pledged to the holding of free and unfettered elections

as soon as possible on the basis of universal suffrage and secret ballot. In these elections all democratic and anti-Nazi parties shall have the right to take part and to put forward candidates.

When a Polish Provisional Government of National Unity has been properly formed in conformity with the above, the Government of the Union of Soviet Socialist Republics, which now maintains diplomatic relations with the present Provisional Government of Poland, and the Government of the United Kingdom and the Government of the United States will establish diplomatic relations with the new Polish Provisional Government of National Unity, and will exchange Ambassadors by whose reports the respective Governments will be kept informed about the situation in Poland.

The three Heads of Government consider that the eastern frontier of Poland should follow the Curzon line with digressions from it in some regions of five to eight kilometres in favour of Poland. They recognise that Poland must receive substantial accessions of territory in the North and West. They feel that the opinion of the new Polish Provisional Government of National Unity should be sought in due course on the extent of these accessions and that the final delimitation of western frontier of Poland should thereafter await the Peace Conference.

VII. Yugoslavia.

We have agreed to recommend to Marshal Tito and Dr. Subasic that the Agreement between them should be put into effect immediately, and that a new Government should be formed on the basis of that Agreement. We also recommend that as soon as the new Government has been formed it should declare that:

(1) The Anti-Fascist Assembly of National Liberation should be extended to include members of the last Yugoslav Parliament (Skupshtina) who have not compromised themselves by collaboration with the enemy, thus forming a body to be known as a temporary Parliament; and

(2) Legislative acts passed by the Assembly of National Liberation will be subject to subsequent ratification by a Constituent Assembly.

There was a general review of other Balkan questions.

VIII. Meetings of Foreign Secretaries.

Throughout the Conference, besides the daily meetings of the Heads of Governments, and the Foreign Secretaries, and their advisers, have also been held daily.

The meetings have proved of the utmost value and the Conference agreed that permanent machinery should be set up for regular consultation between the three Foreign Secretaries. They will, therefore, meet as often as may be necessary, probably about every three or four months. These meetings will be held in rotation in the three Capitals, the first meeting being held in London, after the United Nations Conference on World Organisation.

IX. Unity for Peace as for War.

Our meeting here in the Crimea has reaffirmed our common determination to maintain and strengthen in the peace to come that unity of purpose and of action which has made victory possible and certain for the United Nations in this war. We believe that this is a sacred obligation which our Governments owe to our peoples and to all the peoples of the world. Only with continuing and growing co-operation and understanding among our three countries, and among all the peace-loving nations, can the highest aspiration of humanity be realised – a secure and lasting peace which will, in the words of the Atlantic Charter 'Afford assurance that all men in all the lands may live out their lives in freedom from fear and want'. It is considered that victory in this war and establishment of the proposed International Organisation will provide the greatest opportunity in all history to create in the years to come the essential conditions of such a peace."

A Decade of American Foreign Policy. Basic Documents 1941–1949, Washington, DC, 1950; Z. BRZEZINSKI, "Yalta", in: *Foreign Affairs*, Winter, 1984/1985.

YALTA VOTING FORMULA, 1945. The Yalta Conference decision on the ▷ Voting procedure in the Security Council.

YALU. A river, 805 km long, rising in north-east China and flowing partly as the China–North Korea border, to the Bay of Korea. During the Korean War on Nov. 6, 1950 a one million strong Chinese Voluntary Army crossed the Yalu river.

YANGTZE. The Chinese river, longest in Asia; length 5,550 km; area of river basin 1,942,500 sq. km; navigable to a length of 2,800 km; rising in the Tibetan Highlands and flowing into the East China Sea at Shanghai; accessible to ocean-going vessels up to Wuhan, 970 km upstream; subject of international treaties from 1858, the date Great Britain acquired the right to navigate the Yangtze; the right was also gained at the end of the 19th century by France, Japan, Germany, Russia, and the USA; it expired with the establishment of the People's Republic of China.

MACMURRAY, *Treaties and Agreements with and concerning China*, 2 Vols., London, 1922; *Relations with China*, Washington, DC, 1949.

YAOUNDÉ. The capital of Cameroon since 1961. Seat of the African–Malagasy Industrial Property Office, African–Malagasy Union of Development Banks and of the Organization for the Development of African Tourism; all reg. with the UIA.

Yearbook of International Organizations.

YAOUNDÉ CONVENTIONS, 1965 AND 1970. A name adopted by the European Economic Community for the prolonged and expanded treaties on association of African and Pacific states with the EEC. The first Yaoundé Convention was concluded in the capital of Cameroon for the period from Jan. 1, 1965 to Dec. 31, 1969; the second in July, 1969 for the period from Jan. 1, 1970 to Dec. 31, 1974, with the participation of 18 states, former French, Belgian and Italian colonies. After the acceptance of Great Britain into the European Economic Community on Jan. 1, 1973, a part of the former British colonies expressed their readiness to acquire the status of associated states with the EEC on conditions provided for in the Yaoundé Conventions, so as to guarantee the continuity of their exports to the EEC countries, mainly raw materials and products being their basic commodities. The EEC Committee for African States in Apr., 1973 announced a memorandum specifying the draft of a new Yaoundé Convention to cover the increased number of African states on the basis of an EEC Special Fund, which would regulate the raw materials prices in case of their change on world markets or in case of their bad crop. The draft provided for the following raw materials: peanuts, peanut oil, coffee, cocoa, sugar, cotton, bananas and copper. The bodies of the Yaoundé Conventions were the Association's Council, grouping, inter alia, the economy ministers of the associated states, the Committee, functioning in the capacity of a permanent secretariat, an annual Parliamentary Conference and the Court of Arbitration, composed of a chairman and two judges from Africa and two judges from Europe. Due to the energy crisis and difficulties in raw materials a new situation occurred which formed a subject of debates at the Extraordinary Session of the UN General Assembly in Apr., 1974. In 1975 the Yaoundé Conventions were substituted by the ▷ Lomé Conventions, 1975, 1980 and 1985.

European Communities Yearbook, 1964, 1970 and 1976.

YAP ISLAND. ▷ Japan–USA Agreements, 1908–1922.

YARD. A unit of English and American official measures until 1960 (one English yard = 0.914.399 meters; one American yard = 0.914.401 meters). On the strength of an agreement, signed on Jan. 1, 1960 by Australia, Canada, New Zealand, South Africa, UK and the USA an international yard came into existence: one international yard = 91.44 centimeters.

J. PAXTON, *The Statesman's Yearbook 1973–74*, London, 1973.

YARN FIBRES. A subject of international co-operation. Organizations reg. with the UIA:

International Association of Users of Yarn Man-Made Fibres, f. 1954, Paris.
Common Market Working Party of the International Association of Users of Yarn Man-Made Fibres, f. 1959, Paris.

Yearbook of International Organizations.

YEAR 2000. A subject of international co-operation. Organization reg. with the UIA:

World Association for Celebrating Year 2000, f. 1963, London. Publ.: *WACY News.*

Yearbook of International Organizations.

YEARBOOK OF INTERNATIONAL ORGANIZATIONS. The main publication of the Union of International Associations; the only official documentation containing a register of inter-governmental and non-governmental organizations in accordance with Res. 334/XI ECOSOC of July 20, 1950 and the opinion of the UN Secretary-General of Nov. 17, 1955 (E/2088), that the ECOSOC Committee on Non-Governmental Organizations base itself on the Yearbook.

YEARBOOK OF THE UNITED NATIONS. The proceedings of the UN and its specialized agencies. The first three yearbooks were for the years 1946–47, 1947–48 and 1948–49.

YEARBOOK OF WORLD PROBLEMS AND HUMAN POTENTIALS. A yearbook first published in 1976 in Brussels by the Union of International Associations with Mankind 2000.

YEAR OF THE FOREST 1985. Declared by FAO, as "forests are vital for the environmental stability of our planet and the quality of life on it".

FAO, *Press Release*, 3345.

YEDO TREATY, 1858. A Treaty signed on June 29, 1858 in Tokyo (then Yedo) between Japan and the USA, whose consul, T. Harris, as the first foreign diplomat admitted to the Shogun, gained special rights for the USA: exchange of diplomats with centers in Yedo and Washington; granting the USA the role of arbiter in Japanese disputes with the European powers; anchorage of ships and vessels beyond the ports determined by the ▷ Kanagawa Treaty, 1854, i.e. Yokohama, Nagasaki, Niigata, Kobe; art. 3 also permitted Americans to settle in Yedo and Osaka. In exchange, Japan received the right to purchase ships and military supplies of all kinds and to engage scientists, technicians and military experts from the USA. The Yedo Treaty came into force on May 23, 1860; it was superseded by the Washington Treaty of Nov. 22, 1894. The Yedo Treaty became a model for similar treaties signed by Japan, in turn with Russia on Aug. 10, 1858; the Netherlands on Aug. 18, 1858; Great Britain on Aug. 26, 1858; France on Oct. 7, 1858; and then in 1861 with Prussia, 1869 with Austria–Hungary, Italy, Spain, Portugal, Denmark, Sweden, Belgium and Switzerland.

G.F. de MARTENS, *Nouveau Recueil Général*, Vol. 17, p. 51.

YELLOW DOG CONTRACT. In Anglo-Saxon countries, a derogatory name of an employment contract in which the employee pledges not to enter a trade union; banned in the USA by the so-called Norris–La Guardia Act of 1932.

YELLOW FEVER. A subject of International Health Regulations: "... the incubation period of yellow fever is six days" (art. 72 of IHR).

UNTS, Vol. 764, pp. 60–66.

YELLOW JOURNALISM. An international term since the end of the XIX century for sensational press accounts, hysterical propaganda, manipulation of the news, neglecting real data and facts, libel and publishing reports on ▷ private life.

F. WILLIAMS, *Dangerous Estate an Anatomy of Newspaper*, London, 1957; A.M. SILVERMAN, *The American Newspaper*, New York, 1964.

YELLOW PERIL. An international racist term, popular at the end of the 19th century especially in Australia and on the west coast of the United States, stating that to people of white race the greatest danger in the future would be the dominance in the World of races like the Chinese and Japanese with a yellow or yellowish-brown skin.
The slogan was invented by the Kaiser of the German Reich Wilhelm II at the end of 1895. In German 'Die gelbe Gefahr'.

J.A. DE GOBINEAU, *Essais sur l'inégalité des races humaines*, Paris, 1853; H. GOLLWITZER, *Die Gelbe Gefahr. Geschichte eines Schlagwortes. Studien zum imperialistischen Denken*, Zurich, 1962.

YELLOW RAIN. An international term for a yellowish poisonous substance generated by certain molds or fungi (trichothecene mycotoxins, subject of the Geneva Protocol of 1925 and the Biological and Toxin Weapons Convention of 1972). The rumors about a yellow rain-like material used in Laos and Cambodia were subject of international investigations, 1979–1986.

J.J. NORMAN, J.G. PURDON, Final Summary Report on the Investigation of 'Yellow Rain' Samples from Southeast Asia, *in: Defence Research Establishment Ottawa Report*, No. 912, Febr., 1986; J. ROBINSON, J. GUILLEMIN, M. MESELSON, Yellow Rain: The Story Collapses, *in: Foreign Policy, Fall*, 1987.

YELLOWSTONE. A natural site of the USA, included in the ▷ World Heritage UNESCO List. Twenty-seven fossil forests lie buried under the volcanic ash which engulfed them fifty million years ago. At the foot of the mountains gush hundreds of hot-water springs and geysers. In the deep, multicolored gorge of the Yellowstone River, lava formations have created many waterfalls.

UNESCO, *A Legacy for All*, Paris, 1984.

YEMEN, NORTH. Member of the UN. Yemen Arab Republic. A State in southwest Asia on the Arabian Peninsula on the Red Sea; bordering on Saudi Arabia and the People's Democratic Republic of Yemen, called South Yemen. The boundary with Saudi Arabia was defined by the Treaty of Ta'iz, 1934. Area: 200,000 sq.km. Pop. 1988 est.: 8,600,000 (1975 census: 5,258,530). Capital: San'a with 277,817 inhabitants in 1981. Official language: Arabic. GNP per capita in 1986: US $550. Currency: one riyal = 100 fils. National Day: Sept. 26, Proclamation of the Republic, 1962. Member of the UN since Sept. 30, 1947 and of all UN special organizations except IAEA, IMCO and GATT. Member of the Arab League.
International relations: in the 16th–19th centuries in the Ottoman Empire; during World War I at war with Turkey on the side of the Allies; until 1934 in border disputes with Saudi Arabia, 1934 treaty with

Great Britain. Neutral during World War II; in a dispute with Great Britain 1945–67 over South Yemen; 1958–61 in symbolic union with Egypt (▷ United Arab States). A republic since Sept. 26, 1962; in 1963 Yemen charged Saudi Arabia and Egypt with anti-republican diversionary activity, which led to the sending on June 13, 1963 of an Observer Mission, UNYOM, by the UN, which established a demilitarized zone; it remained in Yemen until Sept. 4, 1964. A treaty signed in Cairo on Oct. 28, 1972 on unification with South Yemen did not enter into force. In 1978/79 in conflict with South Yemen, which ended with the signing of a treaty on the unification of both states; also not implemented. In 1983 one-half of the PLO guerillas evacuated from Lebanon arrived to Yemen, and Y. Arafat set up the military hqs of al-Fatah in the capital of the Yemen Arab Republic.

H. INGRAMS, *The Yemen*, London, 1963; E. MIAESO, *Yemen and the Western World 1871–1964*, London, 1967; R.W. STOOKEY, *Yemen: The Politics of the Yemen Arab Republic*, Boulder, 1978; J.E. PETERSON, *Yemen. The Search for a Modern State*, London, 1982; *The Europa Year Book 1984. A World Survey*, Vol. II, pp. 2701–2708, London, 1984.

YEMEN, SOUTH. Member of the UN. The People's Democratic Republic of Yemen. A State in southwest Asia on the Arabian Peninsula on the Arabian Sea; borders on Saudi Arabia, Oman, Gulf of Aden and Yemen Arab Republic, called North Yemen. Area: 336,869 sq. km. Pop. 1988 est.: 2,345,666 (1973 census: 1,590,275). Capital: Aden with 264,326 inhabitants in 1973. Official language: Arabic. Currency: one dinar = 1000 fils. GNP per capita in 1987: US $420. National Day: Nov. 11, Independence Day, 1967.
Member of the UN since Dec. 12, 1967 and member of all UN special organizations except IAEA, IFC, WIPO and GATT. Member of the Arab League.
International relations: the territory of South Yemen comprised of ▷ Aden and 22 sheikdoms since 1839 was a British colony in part of Aden, and from 1882 to 1914 the sheikdoms accepted a British protectorate; the majority entered the Federation of South Arabia in 1959. After the withdrawal of British troops in 1967, Aden along with the sheikdoms announced their independence on Nov. 26, 1967. Attempts to unite South Yemen with North Yemen were unsuccessful; in June, 1969 a revolutionary council assumed power and in a new constitution changed the name of the Republic of Yemen. In 1969 in a border dispute with Saudi Arabia. In 1971–73 in a dispute with the United Arab Emirates, Bahrain and Qatar. In 1972 a treaty on unification with the Yemen Arab Republic was not implemented; renewed in 1979, also without result. In 1975/76 in armed conflict with Oman, ended in Mar., 1976 with the signing of an armistice. Diplomatic relations re-established with Oman and Saudi Arabia in 1983. With the USSR a 20 year Treaty of Friendship and Co-operation ratified on Oct. 24, 1984.
In December 1988 a Protocol was signed with the USSR to build a 230 km oil pipeline from the Shabwa region to the coast.
See also ▷ World Heritage UNESCO List.

W. THESIGER, *Arabian Lands*, London, 1959; SIR T, HICKINBOTHAM, *Aden*, London, 1959; R.W. STOOKEY, *South Yemen*, Boulder, 1982; *The Europa Year Book 1984. A World Survey*, Vol. II, pp. 2709–2717, London, 1984; KEESING's *Record of World Events*, May, 1988.

YEN. A monetary unit of Japan; one yen = 100 sen; issued by the Bank of Japan. On March 17, 1986 the US dollar dropped to a post World War II low against the yen (124.5 yen to the dollar).

YETI OR ABOMINABLE SNOWMAN. A legendary Himalayan manlike creature, never identified, but the subject of international research expeditions, the last, 1987.

YIDDISH. The language of the Jewish populaton in Central and Eastern Europe (Askhenazim) formed in the Middle Ages on the basis of German and Hebrew. In 1939 spoken by some 11 million persons. After World War II gave way to Hebrew, the official language of Israel. Yiddish is an official language together with Russian in the ▷ Jewish Autonomous Region in the USSR.

U. and B. WEINREICH, *Yiddish Language and Folklore: a Selective Bibliography for Research*, New York, 1959.

YIELD. An international military term for the measurement of the power of nuclear explosions; expressed in terms of megatonnage (▷ Megaton).

D. ROBERTSON, *Guide to Modern Defense and Strategy*, Detroit, 1988.

YIN-CHUEN PEACE TREATY, 1882. A Treaty between the Kingdom of Chosen (Korea) and the United States signed in Yin Chuen May 2, 1882.

Major Peace Treaties of Modern History, New York, 1967, Vol. II, pp. 843–850.

YMCA. ▷ Youth International Organizations.

YOKOHAMA TREATY, 1854. ▷ Kanagawa Treaty, 1854.

YOM KIPPUR. Day of Atonement, the holiest day in the Jewish calendar year (12 lunar months), devoted to fasting, prayer and meditation.

YORDIM. *Hebrew* = "deserters". A pejorative name used in Israel for Jewish inhabitants of that country who left it permanently. In 1977 they were estimated at 300,000.

YORK–ANTWERP RULES. A set of unified rules on maritime accidents, called General Average. The first set elaborated in York in 1864, considerably amended in Antwerp in 1877, since then referred to as the York–Antwerp Rules, YAR. Amended also in 1890, 1924 and 1950. Though these rules are a private code, they are commonly included in a form of a separate clause in transportation agreeements, with the YAR being decisive in the case of general average. The text adopted by the IMCO and the International Law Association, at Copenhagen, Sept. 2, 1950, is as follows:
"In the adjustment of general average the following letter and numbered Rules shall apply to the exclusion of any Law and and Practice inconsistent therewith. Except as provided by the numbered Rules, general average shall be adjusted according to the lettered Rules.
Rule A. There is a general average act, when, and only when, any extraordinary sacrifice or expenditure is intentionally and reasonably made or incurred for the common safety for the purpose of preserving from peril the property involved in a common maritime adventure.
Rule B. General average sacrifices and expenses shall be borne by the different contributing interests on the basis thereinafter provided.
Rule C. Only such losses, damages or expenses which are the direct consequence of the general average act shall be allowed as general average.
Loss or damage sustained by the ship or cargo through delay, whether on the voyage, or subsequently, such as demurrage, and any indirect loss whatsoever, such as loss of market, shall not be admitted as general average.
Rule D. Rights to contributions in general average shall not be affected, though the event which gave rise to the sacrifice or expenditure may have been due to the fault

of one of the parties to the adventure; but this shall not prejudice any remedies which may be open against that party for such fault.

Rule E. The onus of proof is upon the party claiming in general average to show that the loss or expense claimed is properly allowable as general average.

Rule F. Any extra expense incurred in place of another expense which would have been allowable as general average shall be deemed to be general average and so allowed without regard to the saving, if any, to other interests, but only up to the amount of the general average expense avoided.

Rule G. General average shall be adjusted as regards both loss and contribution upon the basis of values at the time and place when and where the adventure ends. This rule shall not affect the determination of the place at which the average statement is to be made up.

Rule I. Jettison of Cargo. No jettison of cargo shall be made good as general average, unless such cargo is carried in accordance with the recognised custom of the trade.

Rule II. Damage by Jettison and Sacrifice for the Common Safety. Damage done to a ship and cargo, or either of them, by or in consequence of a sacrifice made for the common safety, and by water which goes down a ship's hatches opened or other opening made for the purpose of making a jettison for the common safety shall be made good as general average.

Rule III. Extinguishing Fire on Shipboard. Damage done to a ship and cargo, or either of them, by water or otherwise, including damage by beaching or scuttling a burning ship, in extinguishing a fire on board the ship, shall be made good as general average; except that no compensation shall be made for damage to such portions of the ship and bulk cargo, or to such separate packages of cargo, as have been on fire.

Rule IV. Cutting Away Wreck. Loss or damage caused by cutting away the wreck or remains of spars or of other things which have previously been carried away by sea-peril, shall not be made good as general average.

Rule V. Voluntary Stranding. When a ship is intentionally run on shore, and the circumstances are such that if that course were not adopted she would inevitably drive on shore or on rocks, no loss or damage caused to the ship, cargo and freight or any of them by such intentional running on shore shall be made good as general average, but loss or damage incurred in refloating such a ship shall be allowed as general average. In all other cases where a ship is intentionally run on shore for the common safety, the consequent loss or damage shall be allowed as general average.

Rule VI. Carrying Press of Sail – Damage to or Loss of Sails. Damage to or loss of sails and spars, or either of them, caused by forcing a ship off the ground or by driving her higher up the ground, for the common safety, shall be made good as general average; but where a ship is afloat, no loss or damage caused to the ship, cargo and freight, or any of them, by carrying a press of sail, shall be made good as general average.

Rule VII. Damage to Machinery and Boilers. Damage caused to machinery and boilers of a ship which as ashore and in a position of peril, in endeavouring to refloat, shall be allowed in general average when shown to have arisen from an actual intention to float the ship for the common safety at the risk of such damage; but where a ship is afloat no loss or damage caused by working the machinery and boilers, including loss or damage due to compounding of engines or such measures, shall in any circumstances be made good as general average.

Rule VIII. Expenses Lightening a Ship When Ashore, and Consequent Damage. When a ship is ashore and cargo and ship's fuel and stores or any of them are discharged as a general average act, the extra cost of lightening, lighter hire and reshipping (if incurred), and the loss or damage sustained thereby, shall be admitted as general average.

Rule IX. Ship's Materials and Stores Burnt for Fuel. Ship's materials and stores, or any of them, necessarily burnt for fuel for the common safety at a time of peril, shall be admitted as general average, when and only when an ample supply of fuel had been provided; but the estimated quantity of fuel that would have been consumed, calculated at the price current at the ship's last port of departure at the date of her leaving, shall be credited to the general average.

Rule X. Expenses at Port of Refuge, etc. (a) When a ship shall have entered a port or place of refuge, or shall

have returned to her port or place of loading in consequence of accident, sacrifice, or other extraordinary circumstances, which render that necessary for the common safety, the expenses of entering such port or place shall be admitted a general average; and when she shall have sailed thence with her original cargo, or a part of it, the corresponding expenses of leaving such port or place consequent upon such entry or return shall likewise be admitted as general average.

When a ship is at any port or place of refuge and is necessarily removed to another port or place because repairs cannot be carried out in the first port or place, the provisions of this Rule shall be applied to the second port or place as if it were a port or place of refuge. The provisions of Rule XI shall be applied to the prolongation of the voyage occasioned by such removal.

(b) The cost of handling on board or discharging cargo, fuel or stores whether at a port or place of loading, call or refuge shall be admitted as general average when the handling or discharge was necessary for the common safety or to enable damage to the ship caused by sacrifice or accident to be repaired, if the repairs were necessary for the safe prosecution of the voyage.

(c) Whenever the cost of handling or discharging cargo, fuel or stores is admissible as general average, the cost of reloading and stowing such cargo, fuel or stores on board the ship, together with all storage charges (including insurance, if reasonably incurred) on such cargo, fuel or stores, shall likewise be so admitted. But when the ship is condemned or does not proceed on her original voyage, no storage expenses incurred after the date of the ship's condemnation or of the abandonment of the voyage shall be admitted as general average. In the event of the condemnation of the ship or the abandonment of the voyage before completion or discharge of cargo, storage expenses, as above, shall be admitted as general average up to the date of completion of discharge.

(d) If a ship under average be in a port or place at which it is practicable to repair her, so as to enable her to carry on the whole cargo, and if, in order to save expense, either she is towed thence to some other port or place of repair or to her destination, or the cargo or a portion of it is trans shipped by another ship, or otherwise forwarded, then the extra cost of such towage, trans-shipment and forwarding, or any of them (up to the amount of the extra expense saved) shall be payable by the several parties to the adventure in proportion to the extraordinary expense saved.

Rule XI. Wages and Maintenance of Crew and Other Expenses Bearing Up for and in a Port of Refuge, etc.
(a) Wages and maintenance of master, officers and crew reasonably incurred and fuel and stores consumed during the prolongation of the voyage occasioned by a ship entering a port or place of refuge or returning to her port or place of loading shall be admitted as general average when the expenses of entering such port or place are allowable in general average in accordance with Rule X (a).

(b) When a ship shall have entered or been detained in any port or place in consequence of accident, sacrifice or other extraordinary circumstances which render that necessary for the common safety, or to enable damage to the ship caused by sacrifice or accident to be repaired, if the repairs were necessary for the safe prosecution of the voyage, the wages and maintenance of the master, officers and crew reasonably incurred during the extra period of detention in such port or place until the ship shall or should have been made ready to proceed upon her voyage, shall be admitted in general average. When the ship is condemned or does not proceed on her original voyage, the extra period of detention shall be deemed not to extend beyond the date of the ship's condemnation or of the abandonment of the voyage or, if discharge of cargo is not then completed, beyond the date of completion of discharge. Fuel and stores consumed during the extra period of detention shall be admitted as general average, except such fuel and stores as are consumed in effecting repairs not allowable in general average.

Port charges incurred during the extra period of detention shall likewise be admitted as general average except such charges as are incurred solely by reason of repairs not allowable in general average.

(c) For the purpose of this and the other Rules wages shall include all payments made to or for the benefit of the master, officers and crew, whether such payments be

imposed by law upon the shipowners or be made under the terms or articles of employment.

(d) When overtime is paid to the master, officers or crew for maintenance of the ship or repairs, the cost of which is not allowable in general average, such overtime shall be allowed in general average only up to the saving in expense which would have been incurred and admitted as general average had such overtime not been incurred.

Rule XII. Damage to Cargo in Discharging, etc. Damage to or loss of cargo, fuel or stores caused in the act of handling, discharging, storing, reloading and stowing shall be made good as general average, when and only when the cost of those measures respectively is admitted as general average.

Rule XIII. Deductions from Cost of Repairs. In adjusting claims for general average, repairs, to be allowed in general average, shall be subject to deductions in respect of 'new for old' according to the following rules, where old material or parts are replaced by new.

The deduction to be regulated by the age of the ship from date of original register to the date of accident, except for provisions and stores, insulation, life- and similar boats, gyro compass equipment, wireless direction finding, echo sounding and similar apparatus, machinery and boilers for which the deductions shall be regulated by the age of the particular parts to which they apply.

No deduction to be made in respect of provisions, stores and gear which have not been in use.

The deductions shall be made from the cost of new material or parts, including labour and establishment charges, but excluding cost of opening up.

Drydock and slipway dues and costs of shifting the ship shall be allowed in full.

No cleaning and painting of bottom to be allowed, if the bottom has not been painted within six months previous to the date of the accident.

A. Up to 1 year old. All repairs to be allowed in full, except scaling and cleaning and painting or coating of bottom, from one-third is to be deducted.

B. Between 1 and 3 years old. Deductions off scaling, cleaning and painting bottom as above under Clause A. One-third to be deducted off sails, rigging, ropes, sheets and hawsers (other than wire and chain), awnings, covers, provisions and stores and painting.

One-sixth to be deducted off woodwork of hull, including hold ceiling, wooden masts, spars and boats, furniture, upholstery, rockery, metal- and glass-wire, wire rigging, wire ropes and wire hawsers, gyro compass equipment, wireless, direction finding, echo sounding and similar apparatus, chain cables and chains, insulation, auxiliary machinery, steering gear and connections, winches and cranes and connections and electrical machinery and connections other than electric propelling machinery; other repairs to be allowed in full.

Metal sheathing for wooden or composite ships shall be dealt with by allowing in full the cost of a weight equal to the gross weight of metal sheathing stripped off, minus the proceeds of the old metals. Nails, felt and labour metalling are subject to a deduction of one-third.

C. Between 3 and 6 years old. Deductions as above under Clause B, except that one-third be deducted off woodwork of hull, including hold ceiling, wooden masts and boats, furniture, upholstery, and one-sixth be deducted off ironwork of masts and spars and all machinery (inclusive of boilers and their mountings).

D. Between 6 and 10 years old. Deductions as above under Clause C, except that one-third be deducted off all rigging, ropes, sheets and hawsers, ironwork of masts and spars, gyro and similar apparatus, insulation, auxiliary machinery, steering gear, winches, cranes and connections and all other machinery (inclusive of boilers and their mountings).

E. Between 10 and 15 years old. One-third to be deducted off all renewals except ironwork of hull and cementing and chain cables, from which one-sixth to be deducted, and anchors, which are allowed in full.

F. Over 15 years old. One-third to be deducted of all renewals, except chain cables, from which one-sixth to be deducted, and anchors, which are allowed in full.

Rule XIV. Temporary Repairs. Where temporary repairs are affected to a ship at a port of loading, call or refuge, for the common safety, or of damage caused by general average sacrifice, the cost of such repairs shall be admitted as general average.

Where temporary repairs of accidental damage are effected merely to enable the adventure to be completed, the cost of such repairs shall be admitted as general average without regard to the saving, if any, to other interests, but only up to the saving in expense which would have been incurred and allowed in general average if such repairs had not been effected there.

No deductions 'new for old' shall be made from the cost of temporary repairs allowable as general average.

Rule XV. Loss of Freight. Loss of freight arising from damage to or loss of cargo shall be made good as general average, either when caused by a general average act, or when the damage to or loss of cargo is so made good.

Deduction shall be made from the amount of gross freight lost, of the charges which the owner thereof would have incurred to earn such freight, but has, in consequence of the sacrifice, not incurred.

Rule XVI. Amount to Be Made Good for Cargo Lost or Damaged by Sacrifice. The amount to be made good as general average for damage to or loss of goods sacrificed shall be the loss which the owner of the goods has sustained thereby, based on the market values at the last day of discharge of the vessel or at the termination of the adventure where this ends at a place other than the original destination.

Where goods so damaged are sold and the amount of the damage has not been otherwise agreed, the loss to be made good in general average shall be the difference between the net proceeds of sale and the net sound value at the last day of discharge of the vessel or at the termination of the adventure where this ends at a place other than the original destination.

Rule XVII. Contributory Values. The contribution to a general average shall be made upon the actual net values of the property at the termination of the adventure, to which values shall be added the amount made good as general average for property sacrificed, if not already included, deduction being made from the shipowner's freight and passage money at risk, of such charges and crew's wages as would not have been incurred in earning the freight had the ship and cargo been totally lost at the date of the general average act and have not been allowed a general average; deduction being also made from the value of the property of all charges incurred in respect thereof subsequently to the general average act, except such charges as are allowed in general average.

Passenger's luggage and personal effects not shipped under bill of lading shall not contribute in general average.

Rule XVIII. Damage to Ship. The amount to be allowed as general average for damage or loss to the ship, her machinery and/or gear when repaired or replaced shall be the actual reasonable cost of repairing or replacing such damage or loss, subject to deduction in accordance with Rule XIII. When not repaired, the reasonable depreciation shall be allowed, not exceeding the estimated cost of repairs.

Where there is an actual or constructive total loss of the ship the amount to be allowed as general average for damage or loss to the ship caused by a general average act shall be the estimated sound value of the ship after deducting therefrom the estimated cost of repairing damage which is not general average and the proceeds of sale, if any.

Rule XIX. Undeclared or Wrongfully Declared Cargo. Damage or loss caused to goods loaded without the knowledge of the shipowner or his agent or to goods wilfully misdescribed at time of shipment shall not be allowed as general average, but such goods shall remain liable to contribute, if saved. Damage or loss caused to goods which have been wrongfully declared on shipment at a value which is lower than their real value shall be contributed for at the declared value, but such goods shall contribute upon their actual value.

Rule XX. Provision of Funds. A commission of 2 per cent, on general average disbursements, other than the wages and maintenance of master, officers and crew and fuel and stores not replaced during the voyage, shall be allowed in general average, but when the funds are not provided by any of the contributing interests, the necessary cost of obtaining the funds required by means of a bottomry bond or otherwise, or the loss sustained by owners of goods sold for the purpose, shall be allowed in general average.

The cost of insuring money advanced to pay for general average disbursements shall also be allowed in general average.

Rule XXI. Interest on Losses Made Good in General Average. Interest shall be allowed on expenditure, sacrifices and allowances charged to general average at the rate of 5 per cent, per annum, until the date of the general average statement, due allowance being made for any interim reimbursement from the contributory interests or from the general average deposit fund.

Rule XXII. Treatment of Cash Deposits. Where cash deposits have been collected in respect of cargo's liability for general average, salvage or special charges, such deposits shall be paid without any delay into a special account in the joint names of a representative nominated on behalf of the shipowner and a representative nominated on behalf of two depositors in a bank to be approved by both. The sum so deposited, together with accrued interest, if any, shall be held as security for payment to the parties entitled thereto of the general average, salvage or special charges payable by cargo in respect of which the deposits have been collected. Payments on account of refunds of deposits may be made if certified to in writing by the average adjuster. Such deposits and payments or refunds shall be without prejudice to the ultimate liability of the parties."

Register of Texts of Conventions and other Instruments Concerning International Trade Law, 2 Vols., UN, New York, 1973, pp. 185–192; V. DOVER, *A Handbook of Marine Insurance*, London, 1975.

YOUNG PLAN, 1929. A New Plan for the Settlement of German Reparations Obligations formulated by the American delegate to the Paris Conference on Reparations, 1929, O. Young, which significantly reduced German war debts in relation to the ▷ Dawes Plan, 1924, and spread them in installments to 1987. The implementation of the Plan was expressed in eight interwar documents: in the Hague Protocol, Aug. 31, 1929; two Hague Agreements of the Creditor Powers of Germany, Jan. 20, 1930; The Hague Treaty with Austria, Jan. 20, 1930; The Hague Treaty with Bulgaria, Jan. 20, 1930; The Hague Treaty with Czechoslovakia, Jan. 20, 1930; The Hague Agreement on the Joint Memorandum, Jan. 20, 1930. The plan entered into force formally on May 17, 1930, but in fact remained on paper, suspended by the so-called Hoover Memorandum of Aug. 11, 1931 and cancelled at the Lausanne Conference of the Creditor Powers of Germany.

G.F. DE MARTENS, *Nouveau Recueil Général*, 3s., Vol. 24, p. 73; *Reichsgesetzblatt 1930*, Teil II, p. 454, p. 464, p. 1317.

YOUTH. The subject of international conventions concluded since 1919 under the auspices of the ILO and permanent organized international co-operation since 1945 under the guidance of UNESCO. First conventions referred to the ban on work at nightshifts. Since 1919 the ILO has worked out 14 international conventions specifying conditions of work affecting youth. The first established the lowest age-limit for industrial workers at 14; induction into a navy at 15, under the convention of 1936; in mines at 16, under the convention of 1955; for work under hazardous conditions, at 18. Furthermore, the 1937 convention determined that the same principles refer to industrial as well as non-industrial work. In 1951 the UN prepared the I International Youth Program and in 1960 the ILO World Conference on Youth and Labor was held in Geneva; in 1964 in Grenoble the UNESCO International Youth Conference was arranged. Since 1946 educational and cultural patronage over the development of youth is exercised by UNESCO and has included a world campaign against illiteracy. Patronage in the field of health is exercised by the WHO which has carried out a number of sanitary and vaccination programs; and in the field of nutrition by the FAO in its fight against hunger. In 1967 the FAO sponsored a Youth World Food and Development Conference in Toronto. On Dec. 7, 1965 the UN Declaration on the Promotion among Youth of the Ideals of Peace, Mutual Respect and Understanding between Peoples. In 1968 the XV UNESCO General Conference made an assessment of the world situation as regards youth and stated that the majority of young people still lived in difficult, sometimes extremely bad, social conditions and were insufficiently included in the UN Decade of Development, 1961–70.

The World Youth Assembly, the first international youth convocation ever organized by the UN, was held in New York from July 9 to 17, 1970 with some 650 young people from all over the world taking part.

In Feb. 1973, UN Secretary-General Kurt Waldheim, dispatched to ECOSOC a study on the situation with respect to youth. It included a number of suggestions, including the following:

– Youth should play a greater role in the management of schools they attend including universities, secondary and primary schools.
– Youth should participate in decision-making in the UN and other international institutions.
– Social and economic development programs should be prepared to provide equitable division of wealth and services among all categories of youth within society irrespective of race, sex and social background.

According to the report the issue of creating equal opportunity for personal and social fulfilment of youth in face of a dramatic growth in population, posed a grave problem. In 1980, it was estimated, that 55% of the world population was under 25. "The so-called generation gap has become in some fields a source of conflict and a struggle for power between the young and older generations." The conclusions contained in the report were a result of surveys made in 14 countries: the USA, France, United Kingdom, Romania, Yugoslavia, Ghana, Zambia, Iran, India, Ceylon, Japan, Philippines, Mexico and Jamaica. The UN General Assembly, Res. 34/151 of Dec. 17, 1979 designated 1985 as the International Year of Youth and decided to establish an Advisory Committee for the Youth Year.

On Nov. 18, 1985 the General Assembly unanimously adopted Res. 40/14 containing a set of guidelines for future action concerning youth:

On 18 November 1985, the General Assembly, acting as the "World Conference for International Youth Year", unanimously adopted resolution 40/14, containing a set of guidelines for further planning and suitable follow-up in the field of youth. The text had been approved by consensus in Vienna in April by the Advisory Committee for the Year. The guidelines reflect the experience gained at all levels–regional, national and international–during preparations for the Year. A primary objective of the Year has been to bring about widespread awareness of the situation of youth and increase recognition of their problems and aspirations, with a view to further integrating them into the mainstream of development.

"An assessment of the global economic situation, and its regional manifestations, indicate the tenuous position of many young people", the guidelines state. They also provide for specific recommendations for action on behalf of youth at the national, regional and international levels, identifying areas in which Governments may expect support from the United Nations and intergovernmental and non-governmental organizations. Regional and international action is intended to support and complement national action, through such measures as technical assistance, advisory services, dissemination of information and studies on specific youth issues and problems.

National action

Measures at the national level are earmarked for priority action. "Since the situation of youth varies from one country to another, policies and programmes for youth must be geared to the existing realities of each country", the text affirms. The guidelines provide a detailed framework for Governments to develop policies appropriate to national circumstances and traditions. They also stress the importance of encouraging youth participation in all sectors and areas of national life, and underscore the need for continuous advocacy on behalf of youth and improved public awareness of their situation and needs.

Some guidelines relate to specific societal sectors; others to specific groups of vulnerable youth.

Employment, industry and other economic activities: In this context, the guidelines suggest that Governments review labour policies affecting young people and promote policies to eliminate unemployment and create equal job opportunities for them. Measures to encourage self-employment and self-help activities are also recommended, along with development of co-operatives and small-scale industries and services, in order to extend the range of economic roles open to youth.

Education and training: The guidelines encourage a reorientation of education in line with economic, social and cultural realities, including programmes to eradicate illiteracy and guarantee "free, compulsory and relevant" primary school education for all. Also suggested are policies to eliminate discrimination in education, promote lifelong schooling, increase educational and vocational opportunities for marginalized young people, and support non-formal education and training aimed at increasing employment and self-employment. Higher priority is recommended for technical and vocational educational programmes.

Promotion of peace: The guidelines suggest that Governments provide continuous peace education to young people and encourage their participation in activities dedicated to international peace and disarmament. Steps to encourage young people's concern about the plight of their peers victimized by colonialism, racism, *apartheid* and "all forms of aggression and occupation" are also recommended.

Health: Governments are invited to ensure adequate health care for young people, including education programmes, and to provide the necessary training for them to fill the health care gap, especially in rural and semi-urban areas.

Human settlements and environment: Active youth involvement in self-help projects to meet their own housing needs in urban and rural areas is recommended, as is their participation in tree planting and nurturing projects.

Population and family life: Recommendations include measures to promote sex education for young people, discourage early pregnancy and childbearing and assist the family in protecting youth from exploitation and abuse.

Culture, sports and leisure: The guidelines also contain suggestions to stimulate the creativity and artistic endeavours of young people, as well as to provide technical and financial support for youth centres, libraries, recreation and sports centres, and encourage youth to be actively involved in protecting their cultural heritage.

Other guidelines include recommendations for social services, legislation and legal measures for youth and for more active participation of young people in travel and tourism to promote increased intercultural understanding.

Support of specific groups: The guidelines also call for special attention to the specific needs of youth in especially vulnerable groups, such as young women, urban and rural youth, young people living under *apartheid*, students, migrants, refugees, youthful offenders, and young drugs addicts and alcoholics.

T. PATRIKOS, *Droit et responsabilités des jeunes,* Paris, 1972; *Un Chronicle,* January, 1980, p. 71, January, 1982, p. 36, November, 1982, p. 46; *UN Chronicle,* 1986, No. 1, pp. 35–36; *UN Resolutions and Decisions adopted by the General Assembly during the First Part of its Forty-Third Session, from 20 September to 22 December 1988,* pp. 328–330.

YOUTH AND STUDENTS WORLD FESTIVALS.

The meetings organized periodically by the World Federation of Democratic Youth. The First Festival was held in Prague with the participation of 17,000 young people from 17 countries; the Second in Budapest in 1949 with the participation of delegates from 82 countries; the Third in East Berlin, 1951 with delegates from 104 countries; the Fourth in Bucharest in 1953 with the participation of 30,000 delegates from 114 countries; the Fifth in Warsaw in 1955 with 30,000 delegates from 114 countries and 150,000 Polish youth; the Sixth in Moscow in 1957 with the participation of delegates from 131 countries under the slogan "there are ways to understanding for the purpose of avoiding a new war"; the Seventh in Vienna in 1959 expanded by Friendship Sports Competitions; the Eighth in Helsinki in 1962 with delegates from 137 countries, the Ninth in Sofia in 1968; the Tenth in East Berlin in 1973; the Eleventh in Havana in 1978; the Twelfth in Moscow in 1985, the Thirteenth in Pyongyang in 1988.

YOUTH EXCHANGE INTERNATIONAL PROGRAMS.

Promoted by UNESCO, defined in the ▷ Helsinki Final Act (Human Contacts, p. 1, Meetings among Young People), the youth exchange programs initiated by ▷ Scholarship international under the aegis of the League of Nations and later of the United Nations in a system of bilateral (▷ German-American Youth Exchange Program) and multilateral, regional and global agreements (▷ Fulbright Scholarship Program).

C. WELLS, *The UN, UNESCO and the Politics of Knowledge,* London, 1987.

YOUTH INTERNATIONAL ORGANIZATIONS.

Organizations reg. with the UIA:

Atlantic Association of Young Political Leaders, f. 1963, London.

Casablanca Youth Committee on Human Environment, f. 1970, Karabella, Trinidad.

Christian Democratic Youth of Latin America, f. 1959, Lima.

Commonwealth Youth Exchange, f. 1975, London.

Commonwealth Youth Programme, f. 1975, London.

Council of International Programs for Youth Leaders and Social Workers, f. 1957, Cleveland, Ohio.

Democratic Youth Community, f. 1964, Bonn.

Ecumenical Youth Council in Europe, f. 1968, Grenoble.

European Association of Producers of Publications for Youth, f. 1960, Brussels.

European Community of Young Horticulturalists, f. 1965, Paris.

European Co-ordination Bureau for International Youth Organizations, Brussels, 1975.

European Council of the Trade Union Youth, f. 1960, Brussels.

European Council of Young Agriculturists, f. 1958, Brussels.

European Federation of Liberal and Radical Youth, f. 1970, London.

European Federation of Young Managers, f. 1958, Paris.

European Organization of Unions of Homes and Services for Young Workers, f. 1967, Paris.

European Union of Young Christian Democrats, f. 1951, Bonn.

European Youth Centre, f. 1972, Strasbourg.

Federation of Associations for Children's and Youth theatres, f. 1965, Paris.

Federation of International Youth Travel Organizations, f. 1950, Copenhagen.

Federation of Junior Economic Chambers in Francophone Countries, f. 1965, Paris.

International Association for Temperance Education, f. 1954, Leeuwarden, Holland.

International Association of Youth Magistrates, f. 1928, Paris.

International Association of Y's Men's Clubs, Inc., f. 1922, Oak Brook, Illinois.

International Board on Books for Young People, f. 1953, Basel.

International Bureau for Tourism and Youth Exchanges, f. 1961, Budapest.

International Central Institute for Youth and Educational TV, f. 1975, Munich.

International Centre of Films for Children and Young People, f. 1955, Paris.

International Council for the International Christian Youth Exchange, f. 1957, Geneva.

International Falcon Movement, Socialist Educational International, f. 1947, Brussels. Consultative status with UNESCO and ECOSOC.

International Federation of Catholic Parochial Youth Communities, f. 1961, Antwerp.

International Federation of Jeunesses Musicales, f. 1945, Brussels.

International Good Templar Youth Federation, f. 1962, Gothenburg, Sweden.

International Independent Christian Youth, f. 1973, Rome.

International Movement of Catholic Agricultural and Rural Youth, f. 1954, Leuven.

International Union of Socialist Youth, f. 1946, Vienna. Consultative status with ECOSOC, UNESCO, UNICEF, FAO, ILO and Council of Europe.

International Union of Young Christian Democrats, f. 1962, Rome. Consultative status with UNESCO.

International Young Catholic Students, f. 1946, Paris. Consultative status with UNESCO, ECOSOC and Council of Europe.

International Young Christian Workers, f. 1945, Brussels. Consultative status with ECOSOC.

International Youth Confederation, f. 1968, Mexico DF.

International Youth Federation for Environmental Studies and Conservation, f. 1956, Morges.

International Youth Hostel Federation, f. 1932, Amsterdam. Consultative status with UNESCO and ECOSOC.

JAYCEES International, f. 1944, Mexico City. Consultative status with ECOSOC, UNESCO and UNICEF.

Liberal European Youth, f. 1952, Paris.

Maccabi World Union, f. 1921, Ramat Chen, Israel.

Middle European Good Templar Youth Council, f. 1954, Königsfelden, Switzerland.

Organization of Youth and Voluntary Work Movements for Africa, f. 1972, Nairobi.

Nordic Liberal and Radical Youth, f. 1965, Oslo.

Nordic Union of Young Conservatives, f. 1970, Stockholm.

Pan African Youth Movement, f. 1962, Algiers.

Scandinavian Fakon Organization, f. 1970, Stockholm.

Scandinavian Jewish Youth Federation, f. 1909, Göteborg.

Union of Latin American Ecumenical Youth, f. 1941, Lima.

World Assembly of Youth, f. 1948, Brussels. Consultative status with ECOSOC, UNESCO, UNICEF, FAO, ILO and Council of Europe.

World Association of Young People's Friends, f. 1963, Monaco.

World Council of Young Men's Service Clubs, f. 1946, Fredericia, Denmark.

World Federalist Youth, f. 1946, Amsterdam.

World Federation of Catholic Youth, f. 1968, Brussels. Consultative status with ECOSOC, UNESCO, UNICEF, Council of Europe and OAS.

World Federation of Democratic Youth, f. 1945, Budapest. Consultative status with ECOSOC, UNESCO, FAO and ILO.

World Federation of Liberal and Radical Youth, f. 1947, Brussels.

World Federation of Jewish Community Centres, f. 1947, New York.

World Fellowship of Buddhist Youth, f. 1972, Bangkok.

World Organization of Young Esperantists, f. 1938.

World Union of Organizations for the Safeguard of Youth, f. 1956, Paris. Consultative status with ECOSOC and UNESCO.

World Youth Forum, f. 1961, New York.

YMCA, World Alliance of Young Men's Christian Associations, f. 1855, Geneva. Consultative status with ECOSOC, UNESCO, UNICEF and ILO.

YMCA's Center for International Management Studies, f. 1955, Geneva.

YMCA's Latin American Conference, f. 1914, Montevideo.

YMCA's World Federation of Associations of Secretaries, f. 1955, Geneva.

Young Lawyers International Association, f. 1962, Geneva.

Young World Development, f. 1961, Washington, DC.

Youth Environmental Programme for West Africa, f. 1975, Orido, Nigeria.

Youth for Christ International, f. 1975, Wheaton, Illinois.

YWCA, World Young Women's Christian Association, f. 1894, Geneva. Consultative status with ECOSOC, UNESCO, UNICEF, UNHCR, FAO and ILO.

Yearbook of International Organizations.

YOUTH, UN DECLARATION ON, 1965.

Declaration on the Promotion among Youth of the Ideals of Peace, Mutual Respect and Understanding Among Peoples, adopted by the UN General Assembly on Dec. 17, 1965, Res. 2037/XX; proclaimed six principles. The text is as follows:

"The General Assembly,

Recalling that under the terms of the Charter of the United Nations the peoples have declared themselves determined to save succeeding generations from the scourge of war,

Recalling further that the United Nations has affirmed in the Charter its faith in fundamental human rights, in the dignity of the human person and in the equal rights of men and nations.

Reaffirming the principles embodied in the Universal Declaration of Human Rights, the Declaration on the Granting of Independence to Colonial Countries and Peoples, the United Nations Declaration on the Elimination of All Forms of Racial Discrimination, General Assembly resolution 11 (II) of 3 November 1947 condemning all forms of propaganda designed or likely to provoke or encourage any threat to the peace, the Declaration of the Rights of the Child and General Assembly resolution 1572 (XV) of 18 December 1960, which have a particular bearing upon the upbringing of young people in a spirit of peace, mutual respect and understanding among peoples,

Recalling that the purpose of the United Nations Educational, Scientific and Cultural Organization is to contribute to peace and security by promoting collaboration among nations through education, science and culture, and recognizing the role and contributions of that organization towards the education of young people in the spirit of international understanding, co-operation and peace.

Taking into consideration the fact that in the conflagrations which have afflicted mankind it has been the young people who have had to suffer most and who have had the greatest number of victims,

Convinced that young people wish to have an assured future and that peace, freedom and justice are among the chief guarantees that their desire for happiness will be fulfilled,

Bearing in mind the important part being played by young people in every field of human endeavour and the fact that they are destined to guide the fortunes of mankind,

Bearing in mind furthermore that, in this age of great scientific, technological and cultural achievements, the energies, enthusiasm and creative abilities of the young should be devoted to the material and spiritual advancement of all peoples.

Convinced that the young should know, respect and develop the cultural heritage of their own country and that of all mankind.

Convinced furthermore that the education of the young and exchanges of young people and of ideas in a spirit of peace, mutual respect and understanding between peoples can help to improve international relations and to strengthen peace and security,

Proclaims this Declaration on the Promotion among Youth of the Ideals of Peace, Mutual Respect and Understanding between Peoples and calls upon Governments, non-governmental organizations and youth movements to recognize the principles set forth therein and to ensure their observance by means of appropriate measures:

Principle I. Young people shall be brought up in the spirit of peace, justice, freedom, mutual respect and understanding in order to promote equal rights for all human beings and all nations, economic and social progress, disarmament and the maintenance of international peace and security.

Principle II. All means of education, including as of major importance the guidance given by parents or family, instruction and information intended for the young should foster among them the ideals of peace, humanity, liberty and international solidarity and all other ideals which help to bring peoples closer together, and acquaint them with the role entrusted to the United Nations as a means of preserving and maintaining peace and promoting international understanding and cooperation.

Principle III. Young people shall be brought up in the knowledge of the dignity and equality of all men without distinction as to race, colour, ethnic origins or beliefs, and in respect for fundamental human rights and for the right of peoples to self-determination.

Principle IV. Exchanges, travel, tourism, meetings, the study of foreign languages, the twinning of towns and universities without discrimination and similar activities should be encouraged and facilitated among young people of all countries in order to bring them together in educational, cultural and sporting activities in the spirit of this Declaration.

Prinicple V. National and International associations of young people should be encouraged to promote the purposes of the United Nations, particularly international peace and security, friendly relations, among nations based on respect for the equal sovereignty of States, the final abolition of colonialism and of racial discrimination and other violations of human rights.

Youth organizations, in accordance with this Declaration, should take all appropriate measures within their respective fields of activity in order to make their contribution without any discrimination to the work of educating the young generation in accordance with these ideals.

Such organizations, in conformity with the principle of freedom of association, should promote the free exchange of ideas in the spirit of the principles of this Declaration and of the purposes of the United Nations set forth in the Charter. All youth organizations should conform to the principles set forth in this Declaration.

Principle VI. A major aim in educating the young shall be to develop all their faculties and to train them to acquire higher moral qualities, to be deeply attached to the noble ideals of peace, liberty, the dignity and equality of all men, and imbued with respect and love for humanity and its creative achievements. To this end the family has an important role to play.

Young people must become conscious of their responsibilities in the world they will be called upon to manage and should be inspired with confidence in a future of happiness for mankind."

UN Yearbook, 1965.

YPERITE.

The mustard gas, mustard-smelling poisonous gas used for the first time during World War I on July 12, 1917 by Germans near Ypres, Belgium (hence the name); within several hours may cause fatal poisoning of respiratory organs and hard-healing burns. Employed again by Italians in Makale, Ethiopia, in Jan., 1936. The use of yperite as a chemical warfare agent was banned by the 1925 Geneva Protocol.

During the Iraq–Iran war Iran accused Iraq of employing chemical weapons. The UN experts after examining Iranian soldiers in hospitals concluded that they had been affected by Yperite. The Security Council on April 25, 1986, condemned the use of chemical weapons.

W. WARTHIN, *The Medical Aspect of Mustard Gas Poisoning*, London, 1920; *UN Yearbook*, 1986.

Y'S MEN'S CLUBS. ▷ Youth International Organizations.

YUCA's.

Acronym for Young Upscale Cuban-Americans. An international term in the end of the 1980's for the second generation of Cuban exiles in the US, educated in American colleges and universities, the majority of which are lawyers, bankers, businessmen.

J. NORDHEIMER, *Rise of the Young Cuban-Americans, in: International Herald Tribune*, April 14, 1988.

YUGOBANK.

A state bank est. 1955 under the name Yugoslav Bank for Foreign Trade, present name from 1971. A state-owned international commercial bank with 154 branches as well as representatives in Amsterdam, East Berlin, Düsseldorf, Frankfurt am Main, London, Milan, Munich, Moscow, New York, Paris, Prague, Tripoli, Stuttgart and Vienna.

YUGOSLAVIA.

Member of the UN. Socialist Federal Republic of Yugoslavia. A state in southern Europe on the Adriatic. Area: 255,804 sq. km. Pop. 1988 est.: 23,410,000 (census of 1971: 20,522,972). Capital: Belgrade with 1,470,073 inhabitants, 1981. Yugoslavia is a federation of 6 people's republics: Bosnia and Herzegovina (capital: Sarajevo), Croatia (Zagreb), Macedonia (Skopje), Montenegro (Titograd), Slovenia (Ljubljana), Serbia (Belgrade). Frontiers with Italy, Austria, Hungary, Romania, Bulgaria, Greece and Albania. Official languages: Slovene, Macedonian and Serbo-Croatian. Nationalities (1981): Serbs – 8,140,507; Croats – 4,428,043; Slovenes – 1,753,571; Macedonians – 1,341,598; Montenegris – 579,043; Moslems – 1,999,890; of the 18 other ethnic groups: Albanians – 1,730,878; Hungarians – 426,867; and 1,219,024 persons registered as Yugoslavs. GNP per capita in 1986: US $2,300. Currency: one dinar = 100 para. National Day: Nov. 29, National Liberation Manifesto, 1943.

A member of the UN since Oct. 24, 1945 and of all specialized agencies. Special relationship with the CMEA and EEC.

International relations: the process of the integration of Yugoslavia began in the 19th century. The United Kingdom of Serbs, Croats and Slovenes was proclaimed on Dec. 1, 1918, and its boundaries were established by the peace treaties of Saint-Germain, 1919, Neuilly-sur-Seine, 1920, Trianon, 1920, with the exception of frontiers in the region of Trieste despite the Rapallo Treaty, 1920, with Italy. In 1929 the name of the state was changed to the Kingdom of Yugoslavia. A member of the LN, 1919–39, from 1920 a member of the ▷ Entente, Little; from 1934 of the ▷ Balkan Entente. During World War II the regent of Yugoslavia on Mar. 25, 1941 entered into a pact with the Axis states; a *coup d'état* against the regent then changed Yugoslavia's orientation; on Apr. 5, 1941 a treaty of friendship and non-aggression was signed with the USSR; on the following day Nazi Germany attacked Yugoslavia, whose army surrendered on Apr. 17, 1941. The Yugoslav anti-German partisan forces directed by J. Tito, liberated Belgrade on Oct. 20, 1944 together with the Soviet Army. The Federated People's Republic of Yugoslavia, FPRY, was proclaimed on Nov. 29, 1945. Earlier, on Apr. 11, 1945, Yugoslavia signed a Treaty of Friendship, Mutual Assistance and Postwar Co-operation with the USSR; cancelled in 1948 as a result of a crisis in Soviet–Yugoslavian relations. The new constitution of Apr. 7, 1963 changed the name of

Yugoslavia to the Socialist Federal Republic of Yugoslavia, SFRY. The UN Political Committee, Nov. 26–Dec. 1, 1951, debated the Yugoslavian motion on the crisis in relations between the SFRY and the USSR and with other people's democracies; on Dec. 14, 1951 the UN General Assembly passed a resolution on this question, recommending a settlement of the matter in the spirit of the UN Charter, which took place in May, 1955 (Belgrade Declaration on Normalization of Relations between the SFRY and the USSR). A member of the ▷ Balkan Pact since Aug. 9, 1954, the Balkan Consultative Assembly since Mar. 2, 1955, and the ▷ Ankara Treaty since Feb. 28, 1953. Yugoslavia was one of the initiators of the ▷ Nonalignment movement. In 1979 President J. Tito took an active part in the Conference of Non-aligned States in Havana. Diplomatic relations with the Vatican (concordat of July 25, 1935 was not ratified by Yugoslavia) renewed on Oct. 22, 1945, suspended on Jan. 12, 1953, renewed on June 25, 1966. In 1984 a dispute with Albania over the Albanian minority in the Kosovo region. On Nov. 29, 1984 Yugoslavia as the first European state recognized the ▷ Sahrawi Arab Democratic Republic (▷ Polisario and ▷ Western Sahara).

See also ▷ World Heritage UNESCO List. ▷ Ustashes. ▷ Chetniks.

F. KARDEIL, *Put nove Yugoslaviye*, Beograd, 1946; *UN Yearbook*, 1951, 1952; *UN Bulletin*, January, 1952, pp. 33–44; A. FFCHIMOWICH, *Yugoslavia y OON*, Belgrado, 1964; A. RUBINSTEIN, *Yugoslavia and the Non-aligned World*, Princeton, 1970; J.J. HAUVONEN, *Postwar Development in Money and Banking in Yugoslavia*, IMF, Washington, DC, 1970; V. DEDIJER, *History of Yugoslavia*, New York, 1974; B. HORVAT, *The Yugoslav Economic System*, White Planes, 1976; B. HUNTER, *Soviet–Yugoslav Relations 1948–1972. A Bibliography*, New York, 1976; F. SINGLETON, *Twentieth Century Yugoslavia*, London, 1976; D.I. RUSINOV, *The Yugoslav Experiment, 1948–1974*, London, 1977; W.E. BUTLER, *A Source Book on Socialist International Organizations*, Alphen, 1978, pp. 277–284; D. WILSON, *Tito's Yugoslavia*, Cambridge, 1979; S. STANKOVICS, *The End of the Tito Era. Yugoslavia's Dilemmas*, Stanford, 1981; A. CARTER, *Democratic Reform in Yugoslavia. The Changing Role of the Party*, Princeton, 1982; V. MIHAILOWIC, M. MATEJIC, *A Comprehensive Bibliography of Yugoslav Literature in English*, 1593–1980, Columbus, Ohio, 1983; *The Europa Year Book 1984. A World Survey*, Vol. I, pp. 1015–1035, London, 1984; W. ZIMMERMAN, *Open Borders, Nonalignment, and the Political Evolution of Yugoslavia*, Princeton, N.J., 1987.

YUGOSLAV INDEPENDENCE DECLARATION, 1917. A Declaration also called the Corfu Declaration, signed on July 20, 1917 at Corfu, by the President of the Council and Minister of Foreign Affairs of the Kingdom of Serbia, Nicola Pashitch (1845–1926) and the President of the Yugoslav Committee, Anto Trumbic (1864–1938). The text is as follows:

"(1) The State of the Serbs, Croats and Slovenes, who are also known by the name Southern Slavs or Yugoslavs, will be a free and independent kingdom, with an indivisible territory and unity of power. This State will be a constitutional, democratic, and Parliamentary monarchy, with the Karageorgevich dynasty, which has always shared the ideals and feelings of the nation in placing above everything else the national liberty and will at its head.
(2) The name of this State will be the Kingdom of the Serbs, Croats, and Slovenes, and the title of the sovereign will be King of the Serbs, Croats, and Slovenes.
(3) This State will have one coat-of-arms, only one flag, and one crown.
(4) The four different flags of the Serbs, Croats, and Slovenes will have equal rights, and may be hoisted freely on all occasions. The same will obtain for the four different coats-of-arms.
(5) The three national denominations, the Serbs, Croats, and Slovenes, are equal before the law in all the territory of the kingdom, and each may freely use it, on all occasions in public life and before all authorities.
(6) The two Cyrillic and Latin alphabets also have the same rights and every one may freely use them in all territory of the kingdom. The royal and local self-governing authorities have the right and ought to employ the two alphabets according to the desire of the citizens.
(7) All religions are recognized, and may be free and publicly practised. The Orthodox, Roman Catholic, and Mussulman religions, which are most professed in our country, will be equal, and will enjoy the same rights in relation to the State. In view of these principles, the Legislature will be careful to preserve the religious peace in conformity with the spirit and tradition of our entire nation.
(8) The Gregorian calendar will be adopted as soon as possible.
(9) The territory of the Serbs, Croats, and Slovenes will comprise all the territory where our nation lives in compact masses and without discontinuity, and where it could not be mutilated without injuring the vital interests of the community. Our nation does not ask for anything which belongs to others, and only claims that which belongs to it. It desires to free itself and establish its unity. That is why it conscientiously and firmly rejects every partial solution of the problem of its freedom from the Austro–Hungarian domination.
(10) The Adriatic Sea, in the interests of liberty and equal rights of all nations, is to be free and open to all and each.
(11) All citizens throughout the territory of the kingdom are equal, and enjoy the same rights in regard to the State and the Law.
(12) The election of Deputies to the national representation will take place under universal suffrage, which is to equal, direct, and secret. The same will apply to the elections in the communes and other administrative institutions. A vote will be taken in each commune.
(13) The Constitution to be established after the conclusion of peace by the Constituent Assembly elected by universal, direct, and secret suffrage will serve as a basis for the life of the State. It will be the origin and ultimate end of all the powers and all rights by which the whole national life will be regulated. The Constitution will give the people the opportunity of exercising its particular energies in local autonomies, regulated by natural, social, and economic conditions. The Constitutions must be adopted in its entirety by a numerical majority of the Constituent Assembly, and all other laws passed by the Constituent Assembly will not come into force until they have been sanctioned by the King. Thus the united nation of Serbs, Croations, and Slovenes will form a state of twelve million inhabitants. This State will be a guarantee of their national independence and of their general national progress and civilization, and a powerful rampart against the pressure of the Germans, and an inseparable ally of all civilized peoples and States. Having proclaimed the principle of right and liberty and of international justice, it will form a worthy part of the new society of nations."

International Conciliation. Special Bulletin, Jan., 1919, pp. 31–33.

YUPPIES. Young Urban (or Upwardly-Mobile) Professionals, an international term coined in the United States in the mid 1980's for an elite group of young businessmen and bankers.

YWCA. ▷ Youth International Organizations.

Z

ZAÏRE. Member of the UN. Republic of Zaïre. A State of Central Africa bordering on Angola, Congo Republic, Central African Republic, Sudan, Uganda, Rwanda, Burundi, Lake Tanganyika and Zambia. The boundaries were defined in Aug., 1885 and Dec., 1894 by the European colonial powers in agreements on the Belgian Congo and in the Belgian–Portuguese agreement of July 11, 1927. Area: 2,344,885 sq. km. Population, 1985 census: 34,671,607 (1970 census: 21,637,876; 1976: 25,567,400). Capital: Kinshasa, 1985 census: 2,778,281. Official language: French. Currency: one zaïre = 100 makuta. GNP per capita in 1987: US $150. National Day: June 30, Independence Day, 1960.

Member of the UN since Sept. 20, 1960 and of all specialized agencies. Member of the OAU and is an ACP state of the EEC.

International relations: in the 15th–16th centuries in trade relations and armed conflicts with Portugal, then with Holland. In the years 1867–85 the king of Belgium, Leopold II, conquered the entire territory and created a colony entitled the Free State of the Congo, which in 1908 was formally handed over to Belgium. After World War II, the Congo was granted independence on June 30, 1960 and became a member of the UN and its specialized organizations on Sept. 20, 1960. In the face of the threat of Belgian armed military intervention the government of the Congo on July 12, 1960 called in UN armed forces, which remained in the Congo from the middle of July 1960 to June 31, 1964, under the French name: Opération des Nations Unies au Congo, ONUC (United Nations Operation in the Congo). The UN Security Council on July 6, 1967 examined a complaint by J. Mobutu concerning the diversionary activities of mercenary troops supported by Belgium, Spain and Portugal. These forces were finally evacuated from the Congo in May, 1968. In Mar., 1968 the Congo entered into an economic union with Chad and the Central African Republic; the latter soon withdrew. In 1971 armed incidents took place with the Congo (Brazzaville) and with Zambia. The 1977 conflict with Angola was resolved peacefully in 1978. In the summer and fall of 1978 two conferences were held by 9 states interested in economic co-operation with Zaïre (Belgium, France, Canada, Great Britain, Iran, Japan, the FRG, the Netherlands and the USA) with the participation of Zaïre and experts from the IMF, World Bank and the EEC. On Oct. 14, 1979 Zaïre signed a non-aggression pact with Angola and Zambia. A signatory of the Yaoundé Conventions of 1963 and of 1969, as of the Lomé Conventions of 1975, 1980 and 1985. In May 1982 Zaïre restored diplomatic relations with Israel. In July 1983 Zaïre troops supported President H. Habre in Chad. On Nov. 13, 1984 Zaïre and Morocco left the OAU Summit Conference in Addis Ababa in protest the presence of the ▷ Polisario Front; ▷ Western Sahara.

See also ▷ World Heritage UNESCO List.

R.M. SLADE, *Leopold's Congo*, London, 1962; R.R. COMEVIRI, *Histoire de Congo*, Paris, 1963; C. LACLERG, *L'ONU et l'affaire du Congo*, Paris, 1964; E.W. LEFEWER, *Uncertain Mandate. Politics of the UN Congo Operation*, Baltimore, 1967; G. MARTELLI, *Experiment in World Government. The UN Operation in the Congo 1960–64*, London, 1967; K. NKRUMAH, *Challenge of the Congo*, New York, 1967; *Area Handbook for the Democratic Republic of the Kongo (Kinshasa)*, Washington, DC, 1971; R. CORNAVIN, *Le Zaïre*, Paris, 1972; G. GRAN, *Zaïre. The Political Economy of Underdevelopment*, New York, 1979; J. BROWNLIE, *African Boundaries*, London, 1979; *The Europa Year Book 1984. A World Survey*, Vol II, pp. 2718–2730, London, 1984; NZONGOLA-NTALAJA, *The Crisis in Zaire: Myth and Realities*, Trenton, N.J., 1986.

ZAÏRE. A monetary unit of Zaïre: one zaïre = 100 makuta = 10,000 sengi; issued June 23, 1967 by the Banque du Zaïre, replacing the Franc Congolais.

ZAÏRE RIVER OR CONGO RIVER. The river of equatorial Africa, 4,375 km long; drains 3,690,750 sq. km; flows through the Zaïre Republic to the Atlantic Ocean.

ZAMBEZI. The African river, 2,735 km long, rising in north-west Zambia and flowing through Angola, along the Zambia–Zimbabwe border, through Mozambique to the Indian Ocean; subject of international projects of hydro-electric power plants under the aegis of the UNDP.

"ZAJEDNO". The first ecumenical bi-annual journal of the Catholic and Orthodox Churches and Islamic Community, published in Sarajevo, Yugoslavia since July 1987.

ZAMBIA. Member of the UN. Republic of Zambia. A state in Central Africa, bordering on Namibia, Angola, Zaïre, Tanzania, Malawi, Mozambique, Zimbabwe and Botswana. Area: 752,614 sq. km. Pop. 1987 est.: 7,120,000 (1969 census: 4,056,995). Capital: Lusaka with 538,469 inhabitants, 1980. Official language: English. Currency: one kwacha = 100 ngwee. GNP per capita 1986: US $300. National Day: October 24, Independence Day, 1964.

Member of the UN from Dec. 10, 1964 and of all UN specialized agencies with the exception of IMO. Member of the Commonwealth, OAU and is an ACP state of the EEC.

International relations: the region penetrated by British traders and explorers in the middle of 19th century (David Livingstone discovered the Victoria Falls 1855); since 1890 colonized by Cecil Rhodes' British South Africa company, in 1885 called Rhodesia; in 1900 divided into two protectorates of Northwestern and Northeastern Rhodesia; on Aug. 17, 1911 merged into Northern Rhodesia; since Feb. 20, 1924 a British Crown colony. In 1953 integrated by the Federation of Rhodesia and Nyasaland until the dissolution of the Federation on Dec. 31, 1963. The independent Republic of Zambia came into being on Oct. 24, 1964.

In 1971 incidents with the Republic of South Africa troops on the Namibia border; in 1972 with Portuguese troops on the Mozambique border; in 1977–79 in state of war with Rhodesia (Zimbabwe). On Oct. 14, 1979 Zambia signed a pact of non-aggression with Angola and Zaïre. A signatory of the Lomé Conventions of 1975 and of 1980. Since Apr., 1980 diplomatic relations with Zimbabwe. In Apr., 1982 President K. Kaunda met the South African Prime Minister P. Botha.

A border dispute with Malawi 1983–87 ended with a recommendation of a special commission that Zambia should withdraw its claims.

On April 25, 1987 South African commandos conducted a helicopter raid on the town of Livingstone.

K.D. KENNETH, *Zambia Shall be Free*, London, 1962; H. GARM, *History of Northern Rhodesia to 1953*, London, 1964; C. LEGUM, *Zambia Independence and Beyond*, London, 1966; J.J. ZULU, N.A. MUJANDAR, MONLY, *Banking and Economic Development in Zambia*, Lusaka, 1970; W. TORDOFF, *Politics in Zambia*, Manchester, 1974; J. SCHULTZ, *Land use in Zambia*, Munich, 1976; G.C. BOND, *The Politics of Change in a Zambian Community*, Chicago, 1976; A. ROBERTS, *A History of Zambia*, London, 1977; A.A. BEVERIDGE, A.R. OBERSHALL, *African Businessmen and Development in Zambia*, Princeton, 1980; *The Europa Year Book 1984. A World Survey*, Vol. II, pp. 2731–2742, London, 1984; KEESING's *Record of World Events*, No. 6, 1988; M.M. BURDETTE, *Zambia: Between Two Worlds*, Boulder, Colo., 1988.

ZANZIBAR AND PEMBA. An historic region of the United Republic of Tanzania, East Africa, consisting of the Indian Ocean islands of Zanzibar, Tumbatu and Pemba. The islands came under British protectorate, 1890; on Dec. 10, 1963 the sultanate of Zanzibar and Pemba became independent and on Dec. 17, 1963 member of the UN. On Jan. 19, 1964 a republic was proclaimed and on April 27, 1964 Tanganyika merged with Zanzibar and Pemba (▷ Tanzania).

M.F. LOVCHIE, *Zanzibar. Background to Revolution*, Princeton, 1965.

ZERO OPTION AND ZERO-ZERO OPTION.
▷ Double Zero Option.

ZGORZELEC TREATY, 1950. ▷ German–Polish Zgorzelec Agreement, 1950.

ZIMBABWE. Member of the UN. Republic of Zimbabwe. A state in south central Africa bordering on Mozambique, Republic of South Africa, Botswana and Zambia. Area: 390,759 sq. km. Pop. 1987 est.: 9,001,000 (census of 1961: 3,857,466; 1969: 5,107,330). Capital: Harare (formerly Salisbury) with 656,000 inhabitants in 1982. Official language: English. Currency: one dollar of Zimbabwe = 100 cents. GNP per capita in 1987: US $590. National Day: Apr. 18, Independence Day, 1980.

Member of the UN since Aug. 29, 1980 and of all specialized agencies except the IMO. Member of OAU and is an ACP state of the EEC.

International relations: the region gave archeological evidence of organized life from *c.* ad 180; a ruined city named Zimbabwe was discovered by Europeans *c.* 1870. In 1889 the British South Africa Company formed by Cecil Rhodes (1858–1902) initiated the British colonial régime. The resistance of the Ndebelo and Shona tribes was broken 1883–97. Since 1924 a British Crown Colony with self-government granted to the British settlers. In 1953 integrated by the Federation of Rhodesia and Nyasaland, but in 1963 the Africans in Northern Rhodesia and in Nyasaland became independent (▷ Zambia and ▷ Malawi). The colonial racist government in South Rhodesia on Nov. 11, 1965 proclaimed the independence of Rhodesia. The UN Security Council at the request of the British government on Nov. 20, 1965 called upon all UN members to impose economic sanctions against Rhodesia. The country was divided on the basis of a racist law into a "European region" comprising 44,948,000 acres as the property of *c.* 250,000 Europeans and an "African region" of 44,949,000 acres set apart for the 5,220,000 Africans. The remaining area was called a "national region". On May 27, 1977 the UN Security Council again increased sanctions against Rhodesia. At the end of 1979 an armistice was concluded with the Front for the Liberation of Zimbabwe and as a result of two constitutional elections the government of the Republic of Zimbabwe was proclaimed on Apr. 18, 1980. Readmitted into the British Commonwealth. See also ▷ World Heritage UNESCO List.

L.H. GANN, *A History of Southern Rhodesia*, London, 1965; C. PALLEY, *The Constitutional History and Law of Southern Rhodesia 1888–1965*, New York, 1966; D. LARDNER–BURKE, *The Story of Crisis*, London, 1966; J. PARKER, *Rhodesia: Little White Island*, London, 1972; R. GOOD, *The International Politics of the Rhodesian Rebellion*, Princeton, 1973; S.M. DANIELS, *Drums of War: The Continuing Crisis in Rhodesia*, New York, 1974, 190 pp.; M. LONEY, *Rhodesia: White Racism and Imperial Response*, Baltimore, 1975; *UN Monthly Chronicle*, No. 8, 1975; E, WINDRICH, *The Rhodesian Problem: A Documentary Record 1923–1973*, London, 1976; R. PALMER, *Land and Racial Domination in Rhodesia*, London, 1977; D. MARTIN, P. JOHNSON, *The Struggle for Zimbabwe*, London, 1981; *The Europa Year Book 1984. A World Survey*, Vol. II, pp. 2743–2759, London, 1984.

ZIMMERMANN NOTE, 1917. A secret instruction of Jan. 1, 1917 sent in code by the German Minister of Foreign Affairs, Arthur Zimmermann (1864–1940), to his representative in Mexico, proposing to Mexico an alliance against the USA with the promise of regaining the territory of Texas, Arizona and New Mexico, decoded by English intelligence, transmitted to the government of the United States, published in the US press Feb. 24, 1917. The note significantly influenced the change of isolationist sentiments in the USA and the entry of the United States into World War I on the side of the Allies. The arguments of the isolationists that the cable was forged were overturned by Zimmermann himself, who confirmed its contents to correspondents in Berlin.

B.W. TUCHMAN, *The Zimmermann Telegram*, London, 1958.

ZIONISM. From *Hebrew*: Zion, name of a hill in the northwest part of Jerusalem, site of Solomon's Temple. An international term formulated in 1886 by Nathan Birnbaum (Matlas Archer) for a Jewish movement with the aim of reconstructing the Jewish state in Palestine, whose symbol is Mount Zion. It was organized in 1894 in the form of the Jewish Agency. The leading institution of the Zionist movement is the Zionist Congress, which has held periodic meetings since 1897. The First Congress was held in Basel, Switzerland. The Basel Program, adopted on Aug. 29, 1897, reads as follows:

"The aim of Zionism is to create for the Jewish people a home in Palestine secured by public law. The Congress contemplates the following means to the attainment of this end:
(1) The promotion, on suitable lines, of the colonization of Palestine by Jewish agricultural and industrial workers.
(2) The organization and binding together of the whole of Jewry by means of appropriate institutions, local and international, in accordance with the laws of each country.
(3) The strengthening and fostering of Jewish national sentiment and consciousness.
(4) Preparatory steps towards obtaining Government consent, where necessary, to the attainment of the aim of Zionism."

▷ Balfour Declaration 1917, and ▷ Palestine.

In Oct. and Nov., 1975 Zionism was the subject of a debate in the UN and a Resolution passed on Nov. 10, 1975 by the UN General Assembly stating that Zionism is a "form of racism and discrimination". The vote was 72 in favor (Afghanistan, Albania, Algeria, Bahrain, Bangladesh, Brazil, Bulgaria, Burundi, Byelorussia, Cambodia, Cameroon, Cape Verde Isl., Chad, Chinese People's Republic, Congo, Cuba, Cyprus, Czechoslovakia, Dahomey, Egypt, Gambia, GDR, Grenada, Guinea, Guinea-Bissau, Equatorial Guinea, Guyana, Hungary, India, Indonesia, Iraq, Iran, Jordan, Kuwait, Laos, Lebanon, Libya, Madagascar, Malaysia, Maldives, Mali, Malta, Morocco, Mauritania, Mexico, Mongolia, Mozambique, Niger, Nigeria, Oman, Pakistan, Poland, Portugal, Rwanda, Senegal, Saudi Arabia, Somalia, Sri Lanka, Sudan, Syria, Tunisia, Turkey, Uganda, United Arab Emirates, Tanzania, St Thomas and Prince Islands, Yemen South, Yemen North and the USSR); 35 states voted against (Australia, Austria, Bahamas, Belgium, Central African Republic, Costa Rica, Denmark, Fiji, Finland, France, FRG, Great Britain, Italy, Ivory Coast, Liberia, Luxembourg, Malawi, New Zealand, Nicaragua, Norway, Panama, El Salvador, Swaziland, Sweden, Uruguay and the USA), and the following not participating in the voting: Romania, Republic of South Africa and Spain; the remaining 32 states abstained. The UN Resolution was opposed on Nov. 11, 1975 by the World Council of Churches, which stated that:

"there is no evidence that Zionism is racism. Zionism from the historical point of view was a movement connected with liberating the Jewish nation from racist oppression. Zionism is a complicated, involved historical process, an expression of many various aspirations of the Jewish nation and as such can be understood and interpreted in various ways, but no such interpretation allows one to unequivocally include it among forms of racism."

However, in the opinion of communist parties (including the Communist Party of Israel) Zionism and anti-semitism are two forms of nationalism.

N. SOKOLOV, *History of Zionism*, 2 Vols., London, 1919; *Reports of the Palestine Commissions*, London, July 1933; *London October 1938; Statement of Policy on Palestine*, London, 1946; Ch. WEIZMANN, *Trial and Error*, New York, 1949; A.M. HYAMSON, *Palestine under the Mandate 1920–1948*, New York, 1950; R. PATAI (ed.), *Encyclopaedia of Zionism and Israel*, 2 Vols., New York, 1971; *Sionizm: teoriia i praktika*, Moscow, 1973; P. GINIEWSKI, *L'antisionisme*, Bruxelles, 1973; L. HYMAN, *Zionism. It's role in World Politics*, New York, 1973; N.A. ROSE, *The Gentile Zionists: A Study in Anglo-Zionist Diplomacy 1929–1939*, London, 1973; N. GOLDMANN, "Zionist Ideology and the Reality of Israel", in: *Foreign Affairs*, Fall, 1978; Y. GORNY, *Zionism and the Arabs 1882–1948: A Study of Ideology*, Oxford, 1987.

ZIP CODE. The postal zones code, introduced first in the United States during World War II promoted globally by the Universal Post Union, UPU from 1960. In Feb., 1981 the United States introduced the nine-digit ZIP Code, which increased the number of US postal zones from 40,000 to about 20 million.

A.O. SULZBERGER Jr., "The Nine-Digit ZIP Code", in: *New York Times*, October 12, 1980, p. 77.

ZLOTY. The monetary unit of Poland; one zloty = 100 grosze; issued from 1945 by the Narodowy Bank Polski.

ZONE OF PEACE. An international term for denuclearized or demilitarized territorial or maritime regions.
See also ▷ Baltic Sea of Peace; ▷ Denuclearized Zones; ▷ Indian Ocean; ▷ Rapacki Plan; ▷ Tlatelolco Treaty.

UN Chronicle, August, 1981.

ZONTA INTERNATIONAL. International Executive Women's Service Organization, reg. with the UIA, f. 1919, Chicago, Ill. USA. Members: in 47 countries. Publ.: The Zonthan (every 2 months).

Yearbook of International Organizations, 1986/87; The Europa Yearbook 1988. A World Survey, Vol. I, London, 1988.

ZOOLOGY. A subject of international co-operation. Organizations reg. with the UIA:
Iberian Union of Zoological Parks, f. 1970, Barcelona.
International Commission on Zoological Nomenclature, ICZN, f. 1895, London. Publ.: *Official Lists of Zoological Names* and *Official Index of Rejected and Invalid Names*.
International Trust for Zoological Nomenclature, f. 1970, London.
International Union of Directors of Zoological Gardens, f. 1946, Rotterdam.
World Association for Animal Production, f. 1965, Rome.

Yearbook of International Organizations.

ZULULAND. The historical region of the Zulu people in the Natal province of South Africa Republic. Area: 25,900 sq. km; occupied by British colonial forces 1887, denominated 1959. ▷ Kwazulu Bantustan.

J. STUART, *History of the Zulu Rebellion*, 1906, London, 1913; A.T. BRYANT, *Olden Times in Zululand and Natal*, London, 1929; E.J. KRIEGE, *Social System of the Zulu*, London, 1936; D.R. MORRIS, *The Washing of the Spears*, London, 1965; *The Laws of Armed Conflicts*, Leyden, 1973; M. BARTHORP, *The Zulu War*, Poole, UK, 1986.

ZURICH PEACE TREATY, 1859. The Peace Treaty between Austria and Sardinia, signed at Zurich, Switzerland, Nov. 10, 1859.

Major Peace Treaties of Modern History, New York, 1967, Vol. I, pp. 603–610.

ZWINGLIANISM. One of the main doctrines of Protestantism (besides Calvinism and Lutheranism), which was formulated by the Swiss reformer H. Zwingli (1484–1531) in the work, *On True and False Religion* (1525). He professed, i.a., that the eucharist is only a relic of the Last Supper and that there cannot be a separation between religious and secular power.

O. FAMER, *Huldreich Zwingli*, 4 Vols. Zürich, 1943–60; E. KÜNZLI (ed.), *Huldreich Zwingli, Auswahl seiner Schriften*, Zürich, 1962.

ZYKLON B. German name for a poisonous gas produced in Germany since 1934 by two associate firms: *Tesch und Stabenow Internationale Gesellschaft für Schädlingsbekämpfung m.b.H.* and *Degesch, Deutsche Gesellschaft für Schädlingsbekämpfung m.b.H.*, the former in Hamburg and the latter in Frankfurt am Main. The gas was produced on the basis of an American invention intended for the extermination of pests, above all rodents, and was patented (Deutscher Reichspatent No 575293). During World War II the Gestapo with the knowledge of the owners of both these firms used this gas, based on a preparation of hydrocyanic acid, for genocidal operations in gas chambers specially constructed for this purpose in Auschwitz and other concentration camps. According to the testimony of witnesses and Gestapo reports death occurred within 10–15 minutes through a process of asphyxiation accompanied by feelings of terror and hemorrhaging.

According to Pravda of June 8, 1988 the first experiment with Zyklon B Gas in ▷ Auschwitz-Birkenau took place in September 1941. The first victims were 600 Soviet prisoners of war. The first film of the Gas Chamber with reports on Zyklon B was a Soviet war correspondence film made after the liberation of Auschwitz by Soviet troops, January 27, 1945, not containing any information on Soviet prisoners of war killed in Auschwitz. The victims of Zyklon B according to the research of International Commissions were in the first place Jews, then Poles, Russians, Gypsies and other ethnic groups.

Z

The Trial of German Major War Criminals. Proceedings of the International Military Tribunal sitting at Nuremberg, Germany, 42 Vols., London 1946–48, Vol. 2, pp. 365–410; Vol. 3, pp. 259–261; Vol. 5, p. 209; Vol. 7, pp. 44, 96–112, 116–125; J.H. BARRINGTON ed., *The 'Zyklon B' Trial: Trial of Bruno Tesch and Two Others*, London, 1948; *Dokumentation zur Massen-Vergasung*, Bonn, 1955; S. KANIA, *Publications of the Main Commission for Investigation of Nazi Crimes in Poland 1945–1982*, Warsaw, 1983; E. KOGON, H. LANGBEIN, A. RÜCKERL (eds.), *Nationalsozialistische Massentötung durch Giftgas, Eine Dokumentation*, Frankfurt am M., 1983.

APPENDIX

The documents quoted from in the following entries were issued during the 44th session of the General Assembly, the unofficial record of which was published not long prior to the printing of this Encyclopedia, rendering impossible their inclusion into the text proper.

ABOLITION OF THE DEATH PENALTY, SECOND OPTIONAL PROTOCOL TO THE INTERNATIONAL COVENANT ON CIVIL AND POLITICAL RIGHTS AIMING AT THE.

Intended as a supplement to Article 6 of the International Covenant on Civil and Political Rights /▷ Human Rights, International Convention on Civil and Political Rights, 1966/ and adopted by GA Res. 44/128 on 15 December 1989. The text is as follows:

The States parties to the present Protocol,

Believing that abolition of the death penalty contributes to enhancement of human dignity and progressive development of human rights,

Recalling article 3 of the Universal Declaration of Human Rights adopted on 10 December 1948 and article 6 of the International Covenant on Civil and Political Rights adopted on 16 December 1966,

Noting that article 6 of the International Covenant on Civil and Political Rights refers to abolition of the death penalty in terms that strongly suggest that abolition is desirable,

Convinced that all measures of abolition of the death penalty should be considered as progress in the enjoyment of the right to life,

Desirous to undertake hereby an international commitment to abolish the death penalty,

Have agreed as follows:

Article 1

1. No one within the jurisdiction of a State party to the present Optional Protocol shall be executed.
2. Each State party shall take all necessary measures to abolish the death penalty within its jurisdiction.

Article 2

1. No reservation is admissible to the present Protocol, except for a reservation made at the time of ratification or accession that provides for the application of the death penalty in time of war pursuant to a conviction for a most serious crime of a military nature committed during wartime.
2. The State party making such a reservation shall at the time of ratification or accession communicate to the Secretary-General of the United Nations the relevant provisions of its national legislation applicable during wartime.
3. The State party having made such a reservation shall notify the Secretary-General of the United Nations of any beginning or ending of a state of war applicable to its territory.

Article 3

The States parties to the present Protocol shall include in the reports they submit to the Human Rights Committee, in accordance with article 40 of the Covenant, information on the measures that they have adopted to give effect to the present Protocol.

Article 4

With respect to the States parties to the Covenant that have made a declaration under article 41, the competence of the Human Rights Committee to receive and consider communications when a State party claims that another State party is not fulfilling its obligations shall extend to the provisions of the present Protocol, unless the State party concerned has made a statement to the contrary at the moment of ratification or accession.

Article 5

With respect to the States parties to the (First) Optional Protocol to the International Covenant on Civil and Political Rights adopted on 16 December 1966, the competence of the Human Rights Committee to receive and consider communications from individuals subject to its jurisdiction shall extend to the provisions of the present Protocol, unless the State party concerned has made a statement to the contrary at the moment of ratification or accession.

Article 6

1. The provisions of the present Protocol shall apply as additional provisions to the Covenant.
2. Without prejudice to the possibility of a reservation under article 2 of the present Protocol, the right guaranteed in article 1, paragraph 1, of the present Protocol shall not be subject to any derogation under article 4 of the Covenant.

Article 7

1. The present Protocol is open for signature by any State that has signed the Covenant.
2. The present Protocol is subject to ratification by any State that has ratified the Covenant or acceded to it. Instruments of ratification shall be deposited with the Secretary-General of the United Nations.
3. The present Protocol shall be open to accession by any State that has ratified the Covenant or acceded to it.
4. Accession shall be effected by the deposit of an instrument of accession with the Secretary-General of the United Nations.
5. The Secretary-General of the United Nations shall inform all States that have signed the present Protocol or acceded to it of the deposit of each instrument of ratification or accession.

Article 8

1. The present Protocol shall enter into force three months after the date of the deposit with the Secretary-General of the United Nations of the tenth instrument of ratification or accession.
2. For each State ratifying the present Protocol or acceding to it after the deposit of the tenth instrument of ratification or accession, the present Protocol shall enter into force three months after the date of the deposit of its own instrument of ratification or accession.

Article 9

The provisions of the present Protocol shall extend to all parts of federal States without any limitations or exceptions.

Article 10

The Secretary-General of the United Nations shall inform all States referred to in article 48, paragraph 1, of the Covenant of the following particulars:

(*a*) Reservations, communications and notifications under article 2 of the present Protocol;
(*b*) Statements made under its articles 4 or 5;
(*c*) Signatures, ratifications and accessions under its article 7;
(*d*) The date of the entry into force of the present Protocol under its article 8.

Resolutions and Decisions Adopted by the General Assembly during the First Part of its Forty-Fourth Session from 19 September to 29 December 1989, New York, 1990.

DECOLONIZATION.

The General Assembly in the light of the reports of the Committee on Decolonization considered the questions of Western Sahara, New Caledonia, Tokelau, the Cayman Islands, Bermuda, the Turks and Caicos Islands, Anguilla, the British Virgin Islands, Montserrat, American Samoa, Guam and the United States Virgin Islands, reaffirming in all cases "the inalienable right of the people to self-determination and independence in accordance with the Declaration on the Granting of Independence to Colonial Countries and Peoples". It urged the administering powers to "take effective measures to safeguard and guarantee the right of the people to own and dispose of" 'the territories' natural resources, and to "continue to take all necessary measures to accelerate progress in the social and economic life" of the territories.

The Assembly praised the contribution of UN missions in "ascertaining the situation" in given territories and requested that information from the territories continue to be relayed to the UN by the administrative powers.

The Special Committees for Decolonization were asked to continue the examination of the questions of all above-mentioned territories and the items were placed on the agenda of the forty-fifth session.

In addition the General Assembly condemned the "intensified activities of those foreign economic, financial and other interests that continue to exploit the natural and human resources of the colonial Territories and to accumulate and repatriate huge profits to the detriment of the interests of the inhabitants, thereby impeding the realization by the peoples of the Territories of their legitimate aspirations for self-determination and independence" and strongly condemned "the collaboration with the racist minority regime of South Africa of certain Western and other countries as well as transnational corporation that continue to make new investments in South Africa and supply the regime with armaments, nuclear technology and all other materials that are likely to buttress it and thus aggravate the threat to world peace"

"Fully recognizing the need to provide continuing educational opportunities and counselling to a greater number of student refugees from South Africa and Namibia in a wide range of professional, cultural and linguistic disciplines, as well as opportunities for vocational and technical training and for advanced studies at graduate and postgraduate levels in the priority fields of study" the Assembly commended the United Nations Educational and Training Programme for Southern Africa, appealing "to all States, institutions, organizations and individuals to offer greater financial and other support to the Programme in order to secure its continuation and steady expansion"

All States were invited "to make or continue to make generous offers of study and training facilities to the inhabitants of those Territories that have not yet attained self-government of independence"

The matter of Namibia was not discussed explicitly, due to that territory's impending independence (achieved March 20 1990). The GA limited itself to requesting "all specialized agencies and other organizations of the United Nations system to render concrete assistance to the people of Namibia, in particular during the period of transition to and immediately after independence".

Resolutions and Decisions adopted by the General Assembly during the First Part of its Forty-Fourth Session from 19 September to 29 December 1989, New York, 1990.

ENVIRONMENT AND DEVELOPMENT, UNITED NATIONS CONFERENCE ON.

The need for such a conference was recognized in GA Res. 43/196 and 44/228 as well as in UNEP decision 15/3 and ECOSOC resolution 1989/87. It is to be convened "at the highest possible level of participation" in Brazil and will coincide with World Environment Day 'June 5, 1992'. The Conference should address the following issues:

(a) Protection of the atmosphere by combating climate change, depletion of the ozone layer and transboundary air pollution;

(b) Protection of the quality and supply of freshwater resources;

(c) Protection of the oceans and all kinds of seas, including enclosed and semi-enclosed seas, and of coastal areas and the protection, rational use and development of their living resources;

(d) Protection and management of land resources by, *inter alia*, combating deforestation, desertification and drought;

(e) Conservation of biological diversity;

(f) Environmentally sound management of biotechnology;

(g) Environmentally sound management of wastes, particularly hazardous wastes, and of toxic chemicals, as well as prevention of illegal international traffic in toxic and dangerous products and wastes;

(h) Improvement of the living and working environment of the poor in urban slums and rural areas, through eradicating poverty, *inter alia*, by implementing integrated rural and urban development programmes, as well as taking other appropriate measures at all levels necessary to stem the degradation of the environment;

(i) Protection of human health conditions and improvement of the quality of life;

its objectives being:

(a) To examine the state of the environment and changes that have occurred since the 1972 United Nations Conference on the Human Environment and since the adoption of such international agreements as the Plan of Action to Combat Desertification, the Vienna Convention for the Protection of the Ozone Layer, adopted on 22 March 1985, and the Montreal Protocol on Substances that Deplete the Ozone Layer, adopted on 16 September 1987, taking into account the actions taken by all countries and intergovernmental organizations to protect and enhance the environment;

(b) To identify strategies to be co-ordinated regionally and globally, as appropriate, for concerned action to deal with major environmental issues in the socio-economic development processes of all countries within a particular time-frame;

(c) To recommend measures to be taken at the national and international levels to protect and enhance the environment, taking into account the specific needs of developing countries, through the development and implementation of policies for sustainable and environmentally sound development with special emphasis on incorporating environmental concerns in the economic and social development process, and of various sectoral policies and through, *inter alia*, preventive action at the sources of environmental degradation, clearly identifying the sources of such degradation and appropriate remedial measures, in all countries;

(d) To promote the further development of international environmental law, taking into account the Declaration of the United Nations Conference on Human Environment, as well as the special needs and concerns of the developing countries, and to examine, in this context, the feasibility of elaborating general rights and obligations of States, as appropriate, in the field of the environment, also taking into account relevant existing international legal instruments;

(e) To examine ways and means further to improve co-operation in the field of protection and enhancement of the environment between neighbouring countries with a view to eliminating adverse environmental effects;

(f) To examine strategies for national and international action with a view to arriving at specific agreements and commitments by Governments for defined activities to deal with major environmental issues, in order to restore the global ecological balance and to prevent further deterioration of the environment, taking into account the fact that the largest part of the current emission of pollutants into the environment, including toxic and hazardous wastes, originates in developed countries, and therefore recognizing that those countries have the main responsibility for combating such pollution;

(g) To accord high priority to drought and desertification control and to consider all means necessary, including financial, scientific and technological resources, to halt and reverse the process of desertification with a view to preserving the ecological balance of the planet;

(h) To examine the relationship between environmental degradation and the structure of the international economic environment, with a view to ensuring a more integrated approach to environment-and-development problems in relevant international forums without introducing new forms of conditionality;

(i) To examine strategies for national and international action with a view to arriving at specific agreements and commitments by Governments and by intergovernmental organizations for defined activities to promote a supportive international economic environment that would result in sustained and environmentally sound development in all countries, with a view to combating poverty and improving the quality of life, and bearing in mind that the incorporation of environmental concerns and consideration in development planning and policies should not be used to introduce new forms of conditionality in aid or in development financing and should not serve as a pretext for creating unjustified barriers to trade;

(j) To identify ways and means to provide new and additional financial resources, particularly to developing countries, for environmentally sound development programmes and projects in accordance with national development objectives, priorities and plans and to consider ways of establishing effective monitoring of the implementation of the provision of such new and additional financial resources, particularly to developing countries, so as to enable the international community to take further appropriate action on the basis of accurate and reliable data;

(k) To identify ways and means to provide additional financial resources for measures directed towards solving major environmental problems of global concern and especially to support those countries, in particular developing countries, for whom the implementation of such measures would entail a special or abnormal burden, in particular owing to their lack of financial resources, expertise or technical capacity;

(l) To consider various funding mechanisms, including voluntary ones, and to examine the possibility of a special international fund and other innovative approaches, with a view to ensuring the carrying out, on a favourable basis, of the most effective and expeditious

transfer of environmentally sound technologies to developing countries;

(m) To examine with the view to recommending effective modalities for favourable access to, and transfer of, environmentally sound technologies, in particular to the developing countries, including on concessional and preferential terms, and for supporting all countries in their efforts to create and develop their endogenous technological capacities in scientific research and development, as well as in the acquisition of relevant information, and, in this context, to explore the concept of assured access for developing countries to environmentally sound technologies in its relation to proprietary rights with a view to developing effective responses to the needs of developing countries in this area;

(n) To promote the development of human resources, particularly in developing countries, for the protection and enhancement of the environment;

(o) To recommend measures to Governments and the relevant bodies of the United Nations system, with a view to strengthening technical co-operation with the developing countries to enable them to develop and strengthen their capacity for identifying, analysing, monitoring, managing or preventing environmental problems in accordance with their national development plans, objectives and priorities;

(p) To promote open and timely exchange of information on national environmental policies, situations and accidents;

(q) To review and examine the role of the United Nations system in dealing with the environment and possible ways of improving it;

(r) To promote the development or strengthening of appropriate institutions at the national, regional and global levels to address environmental matters in the context of the socio-economic development processes of all countries;

(s) To promote environmental education, especially of the younger generation, as well as other measures to increase awareness of the value of the environment;

(t) To promote international co-operation within the United Nations system in monitoring, assessing and anticipating environmental threats and in rendering assistance in cases of environmental emergency;

(u) To specify the respective responsibilities of and support to be given by the organs, organizations and programmes of the United Nations system for the implementation of the conclusion of the Conference;

(v) To quantify the financial requirements for the successful implementation of Conference decisions and recommendations and to identify possible sources, including innovative ones, of additional resources;

(w) To assess the capacity of the United Nations system to assist in the prevention and settlement of disputes in the environmental sphere and to recommend measures in this field, while respecing exisiting bilateral and international agreements that provide for the settlement of such disputes;

Resolutions and Decisions adopted by the General Assembly during the First Part of its Forty-Fourth Session from 19 September to 29 December 1989, New York, 1990.

FREEZING AND REDUCTION OF MILITARY BUDGETS, PRINCIPLES THAT SHOULD GOVERN FURTHER ACTIONS OF STATES IN THE FIELD OF.

Elaborated by the Defense Commission:

1. Concerned efforts should be made by all States, in particular by those States with the largest military arsenals and by the appropriate negotiating forums, with the objective of concluding international agreements to freeze and reduce military budgets, including adequate verification measures acceptable to all parties. Such agreements should contribute to genuine reductions of armed forces and armaments of States parties, with the aim of strengthening international peace and security at lower levels of armed forces and armaments. Definite agreements on the freezing and reduction of military expenditures are assuming special importance and should be reached within the shortest period of time in order to contribute to the curbing of the arms race, alleviate international tensions and increase the possibilities of reallocation of resources now being used for military purposes to economic and social development, particularly for the benefit of the developing countries.

2. All efforts in the field of the freezing and reduction of military expenditures should take into account the principles and purposes of the Charter of the United Nations and the relevant paragraphs of the Final Document on the Tenth Special Session of the General Assembly.

3. Pending the conclusion of agreements to freeze and reduce military expenditures, all States, in particular the most heavily armed States, should exercise self-restraint in their military expenditures.

4. The reduction of military expenditures on a mutually agreed basis should be implemented gradually and in a balanced manner, either on a percentage or on an absolute basis, so as to ensure that no individual State or group of States may obtain advantages over others at any stage, and without prejudice to the right of all States to undiminished security and sovereignty and to undertake the necessary measures of self-defence.

5. While the freezing and reduction of military budgets is the responsibility of all States, to be implemented in stages in accordance with the principles of greatest responsibility, the process should begin with those nuclear-weapon States with the largest military arsenals and the biggest military expenditures, to be followed immediately by other nuclear-weapon States and militarily significant States. This should not prevent other States from initiating negotiations and reaching agreements on the balanced reduction of their respective military budgets at any time during this process.

6. Human and material resources released through the reduction of military expenditures should be devoted to economic and social development, particularly for the benefit of the developing countries.

7. Meaningful negotiations on the freezing and reduction of military budgets would require that all parties to such negotiations have accepted and implemented transparency and comparability. The elaboration of agreed methods of measuring and comparing military expenditures between specified periods of time and between countries with different budgeting systems would be required. To this end States should utilize the reporting system adopted by the General Assembly in 1980.

8. Armaments and military activities that would be the subject of physical reductions within the limits provided for in any agreement to reduce military expenditures will be identified by every State party to such agreements.

9. The agreements to freeze and reduce military expenditures should contain adequate and efficient measures of verification, satisfactory to all parties, in order to ensure that their provisions are strictly applied and fulfilled by all States parties. The specific methods of verification or other compliance procedure should be agreed upon the process of negotiation depending upon the purposes, scope and nature of the agreement.

10. Unilateral measures undertaken by States concerning the freezing and reduction of military expenditures, especially when they are followed by similar measures adopted by other States on the basis of mutual example, could contribute to favourable conditions for the negotiation and conclusion of international agreements to freeze and reduce military expenditures.

11. Confidence-building measures could help to create a political climate conducive to the freezing and reduction of military expenditures. Conversely, the freezing and reduction of military expenditure could contribute to the increase of confidence among States.

12. The United Nations should play a central role in orienting, stimulating and initiating negotiations on freezing and reducing military expenditures, and all Member States should co-operate with the Organization and among themselves, with a view to solving the problems implied by this process.

13. The freezing and reduction of military expenditures may be achieved, as appropriate, on a global, regional or subregional level, with the agreement of all States concerned.

Resolutions and Decisions Adopted by the General Assembly during the First Part of its Forty-Fourth Session from 19 September to 29 December 1989, New York, 1990.

MERCENARIES, INTERNATIONAL CONVENTION AGAINST THE RECRUITMENT, USE, FINANCING AND TRAINING OF.

Adopted and opened for signature by the General Assembly on Dec. 4, 1989. The text is as follows:

The States Parties to the present Convention,

Reaffirming the purposes and principles enshrined in the Charter of the United Nations and in the Declaration on the Principles of International Law concerning Friendly Relations and Co-operation among States in accordance with the Charter of the United Nations,

Being aware of the recruitment, use, financing and training of mercenaries for activities which violate principles of international law such as those of sovereign equality, political independence, territorial integrity of States and self-determination of peoples,

Affirming that the recruitment, use, financing and training of mercenaries should be considered as offences of grave concern to all States and that any person committing any of these offences should either be prosecuted or extradited,

Convinced of the necessity to develop and enhance international co-operation among States for the prevention, prosecution and punishment of such offences,

Expressing concern at new unlawful international activities linking drug traffickers and mercenaries in the perpetration of violent actions which undermine the constitutional order of States,

Also convinced that the adoption of a convention against the recruitment, use, financing and training of mercenaries would contribute to the eradication of these nefarious activities and thereby to the observance of the purposes and principles enshrined in the Charter of the United Nations,

Cognizant that matters not regulated by such a convention continue to be governed by the rules and principles of international law,

Have agreed as follows:

Article 1

For the purposes of the present Convention,

1. A mercenary is any person who:

(a) Is specially recruited locally or abroad in order to fight in an armed conflict;

(b) Is motivated to take part in the hostilities essentially by the desire for private gain and, in fact, is promised, by or on behalf of a party to the conflict, material compensation substantially in excess of that promised or paid to combatants of similar rank and functions in the armed forces of that party;

(c) Is neither a national of a party to the conflict nor a resident of territory controlled by a party to the conflict;

(d) Is not a member of the armed forces of a party to the conflict; and

(e) Has not been sent by a State which is not a party to the conflict on official duty as a member of its armed forces.

2. A mercenary is also any person who, in any other situation:

(a) Is specially recruited locally or abroad for the purpose of participating in a concerted act of violence aimed at:

(i) Overthrowing a Government or otherwise undermining the constitutional order of a State; or

(ii) Undermining the territorial integrity of a State;

(b) Is motivated to take part therein essentially by the desire for significant private gain and is prompted by the promise or payment of material compensation;

(c) Is neither a national nor a resident of the State against which such an act is directed;

(d) Has not been sent by a State on official duty; and

(e) Is not a member of the armed forces of the State on whose territory the act is undertaken.

Article 2

Any person who recruits, uses, finances or trains mercenaries, as defined in article 1 of the present Convention, commits an offence for the purposes of the Convention.

Article 3

1. A mercenary, as defined in article 1 of the present Convention, who participates directly in hostilities or in a concerted act of violence, as the case may be, commits an offence for the purposes of the Convention.

2. Nothing in this article limits the scope of application of article 4 of the present Convention.

Article 4

An offence is committed by any person who:

(a) Attempts to commit one of the offences set forth in the present Convention;

(b) Is the accomplice of a person who commits or attempts to commit any of the offences set forth in the present Convention.

Article 5

1. States Parties shall not recruit, use, finance or train mercenaries and shall prohibit such activities in accordance with the provisions of the present Convention.

2. States Parties shall not recruit, use, finance or train mercenaries for the purpose of opposing the legitimate exercise of the inalienable right of peoples to self-determination, as recognized by international law, and shall take, in conformity with international law, the appropriate measures to prevent the recruitment, use, financing or training of mercenaries for that purpose.

3. They shall make the offences set forth in the present Convention punishable by appropriate penalties which take into account the grave nature of those offences.

Article 6

States Parties shall co-operate in the prevention of the offences set forth in the present Convention, particularly by:

(a) Taking all practicable measures to prevent preparations in their respective territories for the commission of those offences within or outside their territories, including the prohibition of illegal activities of persons, groups and organizations that encourage, instigate, organize or engage in the perpetration of such offences;

(b) Co-ordinating the taking of administrative and other measures as appropriate to prevent the commission of those offences.

Article 7

States Parties shall co-operate in taking the necessary measures for the implementation of the present Convention.

Article 8

Any State Party having reason to believe that one of the offences set forth in the present Convention has been, is being or will be committed shall, in accordance with its national law, communicate the relevant information, as soon as it comes to its knowledge, directly or through the Secretary-General of the United Nations, to the States Parties affected.

Article 9

1. Each State Party shall take such measures as may be necessary to establish its jurisdiction over any of the offences set forth in the present Convention which are committed:

(a) In its territory or on board a ship or aircraft registered in that State;

(b) By any of its national or, if that State considers it appropriate, by those stateless persons who have their habitual residence in that territory.

2. Each State Party shall likewise take such measures as may be necessary to establish its jurisdiction over the offences set forth in articles 2, 3 and 4 of the present Convention in cases where the alleged offender is present in its territory and it does not extradite him to any of the States mentioned in paragraph 1 of this article.

3. The present Convention does not exclude any criminal jurisdiction exercised in accordance with national law.

Article 10

1. Upon being satisfied that the circumstances so warrant, any State Party in whose territory the alleged offender is present shall, in accordance with its laws, take him into custody or take such other measures to ensure his presence for such time as is necessary to enable any criminal or extradition proceedings to be instituted. The State Party shall immediately make a prelimary inquiry into the facts.

2. When a State Party, pursuant to this article, has taken a person into custody or has taken such other measures referred to in paragraph 1 of this article, it shall notify without delay either directly or through the Secretary-General of the United Nations:

(a) The State Party where the offence was committed;

(b) The State Party against which the offence has been directed or attempted;

(c) The State Party of which the natural or juridical person against whom the offence has been directed or attempted is a national;

(d) The State Party of which the alleged offender is a national or, if he is a stateless person, in whose territory he has his habitual residence;

(e) Any other interested State Party which it considers it appropriate to notify.

3. Any person regarding whom the measures referred to in paragraph 1 of this article are being taken shall be entitled:

(a) To communicate without delay with the nearest appropriate representative of the State of which he is a national or which is otherwise entitled to protect his rights or, if he is a stateless person, the State in whose territory he has his habitual residence;

(b) To be visited by a representative of that State.

4. The provisions of paragraph 3 of this article shall be without prejudice to the right of any State Party having a claim to jurisdiction in accordance with article 9, paragraph 1 (b), to invite the International Committee of the Red Cross to communicate with and visit the alleged offender.

5. The State which makes the preliminary inquiry contemplated in paragraph 1 of this article shall promptly report its findings to the States referred to in paragraph 2 of this article and indicate whether it intends to exercise jurisdiction.

Article 11

Any person regarding whom proceedings are being carried out in connection with any of the offences set forth in the present Convention shall be guaranteed at all stages of the proceedings fair treatment and all the rights and guarantees provided for in the law of the State in question. Applicable norms of international law should be taken into account.

Article 12

The State Party in whose territory the alleged offender is found shall, if it does not extradite him, be obliged, without exception whatsoever and whether or not the offence was committed in its territory, to submit the case to its competent authorities for the purpose of prosecution, through proceedings in accordance with the laws of that State. Those authorities shall take their decision in the same manner as in the case of any other offence of a grave nature under the law of that State.

Article 13

1. States Parties shall afford one another the greatest measure of assistance in connection with criminal proceedings brought in respect of the offences set forth in the present Convention, including the supply of all evidence at their disposal necessary for the proceedings. The law of the State whose assistance is requested shall apply in all cases.

2. The provisions of paragraph 1 of this article shall not affect obligations concerning mutual judicial assistance embodied in any other treaty.

Article 14

The State Party where the alleged offender is prosecuted shall in accordance with its laws communicate the final outcome of the proceedings to the Secretary-General of the United Nations, who shall transmit the information to the other States concerned.

Article 15

1. The offences set forth in articles 2, 3 and 4 of the present Convention shall be deemed to be included as extraditable offences in any extradition treaty existing between States Parties. States Parties undertake to include such offences as extraditable offences in every extradition treaty to be concluded between them.

2. If a State Party which makes extradition conditional on the existence of a treaty receives a request for extradition from another State Party with which it has no extradition treaty, it may at its option consider the present Convention as the legal basis for extradition in respect of those offences. Extradition shall be subject to the other conditions provided by the law of the request State.

3. States Parties which do not make extradition conditional on the existence of a treaty shall recognize those offences as extraditable offences between themselves, subject to the conditions provided by the law of the requested State.

4. The offences shall be treated, for the purpose of extradition between States Parties, as if they had been committed not only in the place in which they occurred

but also in the territories of the States required to establish their jurisdiction in accordance with article 9 of the present Convention.

Article 16

The present Convention shall be applied without prejudice to:

(a) The rules relating to the international responsibility of States;

(b) The law of armed conflict and international humanitarian law, including the provisions relating to the status of combatant or of prisoner of war.

Article 17

1. Any dispute between two or more States Parties concerning the interpretation or application of the present Convention which is not settled by negotiation shall, at the request of one of them, be submitted to arbitration. If, within six months from the date of the request for arbitration, the parties are unable to agree on the organization of the arbitration, any one of those parties may refer the dispute to the International Court of Justice by a request in conformity with the Statute of the Court.

2. Each State may, at the time of signature or ratification of the present Convention or accession thereto, declare that it does not consider itself bound by paragraph 1 of this article. The other States Parties shall not be bound by paragraph 1 of this article with respect to any State Party which has made such a reservation.

3. Any State Party which has made a reservation in accordance with paragraph 2 of this article may at any time withdraw that reservation by notification to the Secretary-General of the United Nations.

Article 18

1. The present Convention shall be open for signature by all States until 31 December 1990 at United Nations Headquarters in New York.

2. The present Convention shall be subject to ratification. The instruments of ratification shall be deposited with the Secretary-General of the United Nations.

3. The present Convention shall remain open for accession by any State. The instruments of accession shall be deposited with the Secretary-General of the United Nations.

Article 19

1. The present Convention shall enter into force on the thirtieth day following the date of deposit of the twenty-second instrument of ratification or accession with the Secretary-General of the United Nations.

2. For each State ratifying or acceding to the Convention after the deposit of the twenty-second instrument of ratification or accession, the Convention shall enter into force on the thirtieth day after deposit by such State of its instrument of ratification or accession.

Article 20

1. Any State Party may denounce the present Convention by written notification to the Secretary-General of the United Nations.

2. Denunciation shall take effect one year after the date on which the notification is received by the Secretary-General of the United Nations.

Article 21

The original of the present Convention, of which the Arabic, Chinese, English, French, Russian and Spanish texts are equally authentic, shall be deposited with the Secretary-General of the United Nations, who shall send certified copies thereof to all States.

Resolutions and Decisions Adopted by the General Assembly During the First Part of its Forty-Fourth Session from 19 September to 29 December 1989. New York, 1990.

NATURAL DISASTER REDUCTION, INTERNATIONAL DECADE AND INTERNATIONAL FRAMEWORK OF ACTION FOR.

The General Assembly "recognizing the necessity for the international community to demonstrate the strong political determination required to mobilize and use existing scientific and techical knowledge to mitigate natural disasters" proclaimed 1990–1999 the International Decade for Natural Disaster Reduction by its Res. 44/236. The second Wednesday of October was designated the International Day for Disaster Reduction to be observed

throughout the Decade and the International Framework for the Decade was adopted with the following objective and goals:

1. The objective of the Decade is to reduce through concerted international action, especially in developing countries, the loss of life, property damage, and social and economic disruption caused by natural disasters, such as earthquakes, windstorms, tsunamis, floods, landslides, volcanic eruptions, wildfires, grasshopper and locust infestations, drought and desertification and other calamities of natural origin.

2. The goals of the Decade are:

(a) To improve the capacity of each country to mitigate the effects of natural disasters expeditiously and effectively, paying special attention to assisting developing countries in the assessment of disaster damage potential and in the establishment of early-warning systems and disaster-resistant structures when and where needed;

(b) To devise appropriate guidelines and strategies for applying existing scientific and technical knowledge, taking into account the cultural and economic diversity among nations;

(c) To foster scientific and engineering endeavours aimed at closing critical gaps in knowledge in order to reduce loss of life and property;

(d) To disseminate existing and new technical information related to measures for the assessment, prediction and mitigation of natural disasters;

(e) To develop measures for the assessment, prediction, prevention and mitigation of natural disasters through programmes of technical assistance and technology transfer, demonstration projects, and education and training, tailored to specific disasters and locations, and to evaluate the effectiveness of those programmes.

Resolutions and Decisions Adopted by the General Assembly during the First Part of its Forty-Fourth Session from 19 September to 29 December 1989, New York, 1990.

PROHIBITION OF THE USE OF NUCLEAR WEAPONS, DRAFT CONVENTION ON.

Annexed to GA Res. 44/117C and intended as the basis for a future "international convention prohibiting the use or threat of use of nuclear weapons under any circumstances" to be elaborated by the UN Conference on Disarmament. The text of the Draft Convention:

The States Parties to this Convention.

Alarmed by the threat to the very survival of mankind posed by the existence of nuclear weapons,

Convinced that any use of nuclear weapons constitutes a violation of the Charter of the United Nations and a crime against humanity,

Convinced that this Convention would be a step towards the complete elimination of nuclear weapons leading to general and complete disarmament under strict and effective international control,

Determined to continue negotiations for the achievement of this goal,

Have agreed as follows:

Article 1

The States Parties to this Convention solemnly undertake not to use or threaten to use nuclear weapons under any circumstances.

Article 2

This Convention shall be of unlimited duration.

Article 3

1. This Convention shall be open to all States for signature. Any State that does not sign the Convention before its entry into force in accordance with paragraph 3 of this article may accede to it at any time.

2. This Convention shall be subject to ratification by signatory States. Instruments of ratification or accession shall be deposited with the Secretary-General of the United Nations.

3. This Convention shall enter into force on the deposit of instruments of ratification by twenty-five Governments, including the Governments of the five nuclear-weapon States, in accordance with paragraph 2 of this article.

4. For States whose instruments of ratification or accession are deposited after the entry into force of the Convention, it shall enter into force on the date of the

deposits of their instruments of ratification or accession.

5. The depositary shall promptly inform all signatory and acceding States of the date of each signature, the date of deposit of each instrument of ratification or accession and the date of the entry into force of this Convention, as well as of the receipt of other notices.

6. This Convention shall be registered by the depositary in accordance with Article 102 of the Charter of the United Nations.

Resolutions and Decisions Adopted by the General Assembly during the First Part of its Forty-Fourth Session from 19 September to 29 December 1989, New York, 1990.

TALLINN GUIDELINES FOR ACTION ON HUMAN RESOURCES DEVELOPMENT IN THE FIELD OF DISABILITY.
The period 1983–1992 was by GA Res. 37/53 proclaimed the United Nations Decade of Disabled Persons, while GA Res. 37/52 adopted the World Programme of Action concerning Disabled Persons. GA Res. 44/70 adopted without a vote on 8 December 1989 reaffirmed the validity of the World Programme of Action and in connection with the need to place emphasis on "the equalization of opportunities for disabled persons" called for the dissemination of the nine-point strategy "to promote the participation, training and employment of disabled persons, especially in developing countries" adopted at the International Meeting on Human Resources in the Field of Disability held at Tallinn, USSR, the text of which follows:

INTRODUCTION
1. The International Meeting on Human Resources in the Field of Disability, convened at Tallinn, Estonian Soviet Socialist Republic, Union of Soviet Socialist Republics, from 14 to 22 August 1989, having considered the situation of human resources development in the field of disability, particularly in developing countries, firmly believes that the reinforcement of existing as well as new and innovative action is required to promote the further development and continued progress of disabled persons.

2. Following the adoption of the World Programme of Action concerning Disabled Persons by the General Assembly, in its resolution 37/52 of 3 December 1982, there has been a growing need for higher priority to be given to the development of the human resources of disabled persons, with specific reference to education and training, employment, and science and technology. In this connection, the General Assembly also, in its resolution 37/53 of 3 December 1982, proclaimed the United Nations Decade of Disabled Persons, 1983–1992, encouraging Member States to utilize that period as one of the means to implement the World Programme of Action.

3. The main objectives of the World Programme of Action are to promote effective measures for the prevention of disability, for rehabilitation and for the realization of the goals of full participation and equality for persons with disabilities. To accomplish these goals, due regard must be paid to education, training and work opportunities.

4. While it is acknowledged that the living conditions of the general population in developing countries urgently need to be improved, the objectives of the World Programme of Action call for the situation of disabled persons to be given special attention during the remainder of the Decade and beyond. Effective implementation of the World Programme of Action will make an important contribution to the development process of societies through the mobilization of more human resources.

5. While it is also acknowledged that a number of countries have already initiated or carried out activities within the framework of the World Programme of Action, further concerted efforts should be made to integrate the human resources development of disabled persons into intersectoral planning at the national level.

GUIDING PHILOSOPHY
6. Human resources development is a human-centred process that seeks to realize the full potential and capabilities of human beings. This process is fundamental to the concept of equalization of opportunities, in keeping with the goals of the World Programme of Action.

7. Through human resources development, disabled persons are able effectively to exercise their rights of full citizenship. As full citizens, they have the same rights and responsibilities as other members of society, including the right to life, as declared in international human rights instruments. They also have the same choices as other citizens in the social, cultural, economic and political life of their communities.

8. Because persons with disabilities are agents of their own destiny rather than objects of care, Governments and organizations need to reflect this perception in their policies and programmes. This means that disabled persons, as individuals and as members of organizations, should be involved in the decision-making process as equal partners.

9. The abilities of disabled persons and their families should be strengthened through community-based supplementary services provided by Governments and non-governmental organizations. These services should promote self-determination and enable disabled persons to participate in the development of society. Governments should recognize and support the role of disabled persons' organizations in enabling persons with disabilities to take charge of their own lives.

STRATEGIES
A. *Participation of persons with disabilities*
10. A statutory basis is required to enable disabled persons to participate as full citizens in decision-making at all levels of the planning, implementation, and monitoring and evaluation of policies and programmes.

11. To facilitate the full participation of disabled persons and enable them to exercise their rights as citizens, access to information is essential. To this end, all information has to be adapted to appropriate formats. These information formats may include Braille script, large print, audio-visual media and sign-language interpretation. Information channels should include television, radio, newspapers and postal services. Governments should work with organizations of disabled persons to identify appropriate information formats and channels to reach disabled citizens.

12. Governments should adopt, enforce and fund legally binding standards and regulations to improve access for persons with disabilities, ensuring that buildings, streets, and road, sea and air transport are barrier-free, architecturally and in all other ways. Communication systems and security and safety measures should be developed and adapted to meet the needs of disabled citizens.

13. To facilitate the recruitment of disabled persons and to assist private-sector industries in hiring them, organizations at the national, regional and international levels, including the United Nations, should identify and maintain listings of qualified disabled candidates.

B. *Strengthening of grass-roots initiatives*
14. Local community initiatives should be especially promoted. Disabled persons and their families should be encouraged to form grass-roots organizations, with governmental recognition of their importance and governmental support in the form of financing and training.

15. Governmental and non-governmental organizations concerned with disability issues should allow disabled persons to participate as equal partners.

16. The efficient functioning of governmental and non-governmental organizations concerned with disability calls for training in organizational and management skills.

C. *Promotion of an integrated approach*
17. Overall national policy frameworks with supporting legislation should be developed.

18. The essence of an integrated approach is the inclusion of disability issues in all ministries and at every level of governmental policy and planning. National co-ordination bodies, with linkages at the local, regional and interregional levels, should be established or strengthened. The membership of those bodies should include all government ministries, legislative committees and non-governmental organizations, particularly organizations of disabled persons. The co-ordination body should review existing policies, plans and programmes, identify existing and projected resources and monitor and evaluate the implementation of national policies.

19. National development programmes should include disability components.

20. Disabled women should be included in the existing national and regional programmes aimed at women.

21. At the level of service delivery, an integrated approach entails co-operation and referral among professionals working in organizational settings that provide educational, vocational, health and social services.

D. *Promotion of education and training*
22. The early years are critical in the overall development of a disabled child and in fostering positive attitudes towards the child. Specific programmes and training materials should be developed to address these needs during the formative infant and pre-school years.

23. Education at the primary, secondary and higher levels should be available to disabled persons within the regular educational system and in regular school settings, as well as in vocational training programmes. When such education is provided to deaf students, teachers and/or interpreters who are proficient in the indigenous sign language must be provided.

24. Special education programmes and schools that promote the indigenous sign language and the indigenous deaf culture must be available to deaf people. Deaf people should be employed in such programmes and schools.

25. Cost-effective alternatives to segregated school facilities should be developed and implemented by Governments at the national and local levels. These alternatives include special education teachers as consultants to regular education teachers, resource rooms with specialized personnel and materials, special classrooms in regular schools and interpreters for deaf students.

26. The education of disabled children should involve the co-operation and concerted efforts of health and social services, as well as teachers and parents. It should provide support measures, such as technical aids, especially adapted pedagogical approaches, and incentives for teachers.

27. The content and quality of education and training should ensure the acquisition of skills that are economically viable and that provide opportunities for work. Career education and vocational training programmes should be available to ensure the transition of disabled students into the economic mainstream.

28. In addition to being offered formal skills training and education, disabled persons should be offered training in social and self-help skills to prepare them for independent living. Special efforts should be made to promote education and skills training for disabled girls and women, in both urban and rural areas.

29. General teacher-training curricula should include a course of study in skills for teaching disabled children and young persons in regular schools.

30. Each Government should have a national plan for training and employing an adequate number of health, education and vocational professionals in rehabilitation. Persons with disabilities should be recruited for such training and employment.

31. In fields such as education, labour, health and social services, law, architecture and technical development, which are often involved in the different aspects of rehabilitation, the professional training should include training on the rights and needs of disabled people. Professionals in these fields should also be made aware of the resources available for disabled persons so that appropriate referrals can be made or services provided.

32. Appropriate technology should be considered essential for the utilization of available resources. This may include simple, universally available equipment, as well as computer technology.

E. *Promotion of employment*
33. Disabled persons have the right to be trained for and to work on equal terms in the regular labour force. Community-based rehabilitation programmes should be encouraged to provide better job opportunities in developing countries. Use should be made of the vocational services, guidance and training, placement, employment and related services that already exist for

workers in general. On-the-job training may be more effective than conventional training.

34. General development programmes that provide loans, training and equipment for income-generating activities should include disabled persons.

35. Employment opportunities can be promoted primarily by measures relating to employment and salary standards that apply to all workers and secondarily by measures offering special support and incentives. In addition to formal employment, opportunities should be broadened to include self-employment, co-operatives and other group income-generating schemes. Where special national employment drives have been launched for youth and unemployed persons, disabled persons should be actively recruited, and when a disabled candidate and a non-disabled candidate are equally qualified, the disabled candidate should be chosen.

36. Employers' and workers' organizations should adopt, in co-operation with organizations of disabled persons, policies that promote the training and employment of disabled and non-disabled persons on an equal basis, including disabled women.

37. Policies for affirmative action should be formulated and implemented to increase the employment of disabled women. Governments and non-governmental organizations should support the creation of income-generating projects involving disabled women.

F. *Provisions for funding*

38. In general, funding should be allocated through regular sectoral budgeting systems. A national rehabilitation fund may be established to facilitate the employment or self-employment of disabled persons. This fund could be used to cover the costs of training, equipment and initial capital outlay.

39. Similarly, funds should be established for loans to small-scale pilot projects at the grass-roots level; such funds could be administered locally using simple procedures.

G. *Promotion of community awareness*

40. To increase community understanding of the rights, needs and potentials of disabled persons, collaborative efforts with disabled persons and their organizations are required to develop and promote a flow of information using mass media, especially film, television, radio and print media. In particular, information for disabled persons and their families on all aspects of living with a disability should be as clear and uncomplicated as possible.

41. Community awareness programmes should include specific strategies for the prevention of disability. Government efforts aimed at early identification, intervention and prevention should be strengthened through community awareness and community involvement in programmes on disability.

42. Persons with mental disability (mental retardation or mental illness) or multiple disabilities are among the most stigmatized groups of citizens. They have the right to make choices, take risks, control their own lives and live in the community. Their adult status, abilities and aspirations must be respected and reinforced by their inclusion in decision-making, although many may need individual advocacy to be clearly understood.

43. It should be acknowledged that people with mental and multiple disabilities benefit from education, skills training and work opportunities. For many of these people, opportunities need to be individualized. Support is required to help them and their families to establish and maintain a positive life-style.

44. The World Programme of Action should be translated into all national languages, through governmental action. Braille, large print and simplified versions should also be made available by the appropriate media to ensure as wide a distribution as possible to all citizens, including disabled persons, their families, and non-governmental and governmental organizations.

H. *Improving the methodology for human resources development*

45. Policies and programmes for human resources development concerning disabled persons should be based on an assessment of their needs and resources as well as on the potential of existing development programmes and services to meet those needs. The implementation of such policies and programmes should be periodically monitored, with adjustments made to ensure effective implementation.

46. Evaluation should be built into programmes at the planning stage so that their overall efficacy in fulfilling policy objectives can be assessed. Persons with disabilities should play an active role in developing the criteria for monitoring and evaluation.

47. Increased attention should be given to services for people with hearing, speech, mental, intellectual or multiple disabilities.

48. The requirements of particular groups, such as disabled children, disabled women, the disabled elderly, disabled migrants and refugees, should also be recognized and met.

49. Governmental and non-governmental organizations should utilize recent developments in education through communications media, also known as distance education, which has been found to be an appropriate methodology in human resources development in the field of disability.

50. The local use of appropriate technologies for producing such items as wheel chairs, prosthetic devices and mobility aids, as well as aids for hearing and seeing, should take into account the technical, socio-economic and cultural conditions in the particular society. Each country should have a national system for the delivery of rehabilitation aids.

I. *Regional and international co-operation*

51. Training programmes in human resources development in the field of disability should be strengthened by collaborative efforts at the regional and/or subregional levels. Such programmes should be co-ordinated through existing intergovernmental and regional organizations, including those of disabled persons.

52. International development aid projects should include a component specifically aimed at supporting organizations of disabled persons and training their members. In addition, employment opportunities should be made available to disabled individuals within these projects.

53. All international development assistance programmes directed at macro-level planning and development, such as those in agriculture or education, should include a specific component ensuring the participation of disabled persons in such schemes.

54. At both the national and interregional levels, Governments should strongly support collaboration with non-governmental agencies in specific areas of disability, to ensure co-ordination and to prevent duplication of services.

55. Linkages between organizations of disabled persons in developed and developing countries should be strengthened. This can be done through the exchange of information, training and meetings to provide forums for disabled persons to share experiences on strategic approaches. Workshops and field studies should be organized to train trainers and the management personnel of organizations of disabled persons.

56. Implementation of these Guidelines relies on effective action at the national level. This action should be supplemented by concerted efforts at the international level, particularly on the part of the United Nations and its focal point for the implementation of the World Programme of Action concerning Disabled Persons, as well as its relevant organizations and specialized agencies. National and international non-governmental organizations, in particular organizations of disabled persons, should be fully involved.

Resolutions and Decisions Adopted by the General Assembly during the First Part of its Forty-Fourth Session from 19 September to 29 December 1989, New York, 1990.

WORLD POPULATION STATISTICS 1985–2025

The world population situation is monitored continuously by the United Nations and reviewed every two years, as recommended in the Plan of Action adopted at the 1974 World Population Conference in Bucharest. The most recent monitoring exercise – the fourth since 1977 – covered the period 1981–1983. The findings, summarized in the "concise report on monitoring of population trends and policies" *(document E/CN.9/1984/2)* were published in *World Population Trends and Policies: 1983 Monitoring Reports, Vols. I and II,* New York, 1985.

The fourth round of monitoring was the last before the 1984 International Conference on Population, held in August in Mexico City. In addition to examining current population trends and projections, it reviewed the most significant demographic events in the decade since the Bucharest Conference.

The demographic information presented here was drawn from the above monitoring report, which reflects the United Nations medium variant projections.

Population Growth. According to the United Nations long-range projections, world population is expected to continue increasing until the end of the 21st century when it may stabilize at 10.5 billion. Population increase in absolute terms – some 77 million persons per year in 1974 and 78 million at present – is expected to peak at almost 90 million by the year 2000 before falling back to 74 million by 2025.

The monitoring reports emphasize, however, that continued expansion of world population in absolute terms should not obscure the fact that the rate of world population growth has steadily declined – from a peak of 2.1% at the end of the 1960s to 1.7% at the beginning of the 1980s. The downward trend is expected to continue, reaching a rate of 1.5% by 2000 and 0.9% by 2025.

Global population trends must be viewed, however, in light of marked differences between developed and developing regions and even within regions, particularly the developing ones. The current annual rate of population increase in the less developed regions is 2.1%; in the developed, 0.6%. Whereas the growth rate of the developing regions peaked at about 2.6% during the late 1960s, that of the developed countries has declined steadily from approximately 1.3% in the early 1950s.

Africa: Among developing regions, Africa alone shows an upward trend in rate of population increase. Its growth rate is estimated at 3.01% for the period 1980–1985, an increase of 2.74% over 1970–1975. Growth rates are even higher in the subregions of Western and Eastern Africa. The only significant declines are on a few small islands.

Latin America: The growth rate in Latin America is an estimated 2.3% for 1980–1985, down from the 1970–1975 rate of 2.51%. Although the general trend is downward, Central America (including Mexico) and Tropical South America still show high growth rates (2.7 and 2.4%, respectively).

Asia: In absolute terms, population increase in the South Asian subregion is anticipated to be the largest of the major regions during the next four decades. The estimated growth rate for 1980–1985 is 2.2%, a slight decrease from the 1970–1975 figure of 2.44%. In East Asia (China, Japan and several other countries), it is expected the growth rate will decline sharply from the 1970–1975 level of 2.25% to 1.14 for 1980–1985, due largely to China's 54.2% drop in fertility (its current growth rate is about 1.2%).

Oceania: The population of Melanesia continues to grow rapidly, while Micronesia exhibits much lower rates of growth. The trend in the developed countries of the region is also downward, but from very low initial levels. Their growth rate – 0.89% in 1970–1975 – is projected at 0.64 for 1980–1985.

Europe: Some countries in Western Europe are showing negative growth rates, and the rate for the subregion as a whole will be only 0.06% in 1980–1985, slightly below Northern Europe's 0.09%. Rates in Eastern and Southern Europe are slightly higher: 0.57 and 0.58 respectively.

Population growth rates at the end of the century are projected to be 1.79% for the developing regions and 0.52 for the developed. Accelerating growth is expected to continue until then in Africa and the Caribbean. In China and Northern Europe, growth is expected to stabilize at current levels.

Due to differing rates of growth among the major regions, the proportional distribution of the world population is changing in important ways. Whereas the population of Europe (excluding the USSR) in 1950 represented 15.6% of the world total, it declined to 10.9% in 1980 and is expected to be 6.3% by the year 2025. East Asia, too, is expected to drop in share of world population – from 26.5% in 1950 to 20.8% by 2025.

In contrast, proportions for Africa, Latin America and South Asia are expected to continue increasing. The biggest change is Africa, which went from 8.9% in 1950 to 10.7 in 1980 and is expected to reach 20.1% of the world's population in 2025.

Mortality. During the past decade, life expectancy in the developing countries has increased from 52.7 years to 56.6, and in the developed, from 71.4 years to 73. Within developing regions, however, life expectancy varies from 49.7 years in Africa to 68 years in East Asia. In Latin America, life expectancy is 64.1 years; in South Asia, 53.6

Progress in East Asia has been "spectacular", according to the report, particularly in China, where it is estimated the between 1970–1975 and 1980–1985 life expectancy will increase by 7.9 years to 68. In Africa, however, the gain has been only 4.2 years (to 49.7) and even less in some subregions. In South Asia, especially in the Indian subcontinent, life expectancy has increased by only 3.8 years, to 51.8.

In the developed countries, mortality trends in the 1970s differed strikingly from those in the 1960s. North America, Western and Northern Europe, and Oceania (Australia and New Zealand) registered a rapid decline in mortality by contrast with the stagnation or regression observed in the previous period. Southern and Eastern Europe showed slower progress than in the 1960s.

The gap between developed and developing countries is expected to continue narrowing, so that by 2025, life expectancy in the developing countries is projected at 68.9 years, against 77.2 in the developed – a difference of 8.9 years. But among the developing countries great diversity is expected to persist: in Africa, life expectancy will be 55.7 years in 2000 and 64.9 in 2025. In East Asia, on the other hand, it will reach 71.4 years in 2000 and 74.6 by 2025.

Females can still expect to live longer than males in a majority of developing and developed countries. The difference is particularly pronounced in some countries of East and Southeastern Asia. On the other hand, female life expectancy is lower than, or at best equal to, male life expectancy in some Southern Asian countries, including Afghanistan, Bangladesh, India, Iran, Nepal and Pakistan.

Infant mortality remains high in the developing regions, although important progress has been made over the past 30 years. The estimated infant mortality rate declined from 164 per 1,000 in 1950–1955 to 100 in 1975–1980. None the less, the disparity between the developed and developing regions remains very large – the estimated infant mortality rate for the developed countries in 1975–1980 was 19 per 1,000.

In 1980–1985 the world infant mortality rate is estimated to be 80.8 deaths per 1,000 births. In the developing regons, that rate is expected to be 91.5 per 1,000; in the developed regions, 16.9 per 1,000. In sub-Saharan Africa, the infant mortality rate is likely to exceed 100 deaths per 1,000 births, with highs of 200 in some countries.

Projected infant deaths per 1,000 births in East Asia for the 1980–1985 period are 36; in Latin America, 63. Developing countries showing sharp drops in infant mortality include China, Cuba and Singapore (41, 20.4 and 11.1 per 1,000 births, respectively). Costa Rica's progress in that area has been remarkable: from 86 per 1,000 births to 20 over the 20-year period to 1981.

In three out of five developed countries, the already very low levels of infant mortality are expected to decline 30% or more between 1970–1975 and 1980–1985, when approximately three quarters of the developed countries are expected to have rates not exceeding 15 per 1,000 and nine countries rates below 10 per 1,000. The best results are observed in Western and Northern Europe.

Fertility. During the 1970s, average births per woman of child-bearing age in the developing countries decreased from 5.5 to 4.1, a drop of 26% (15%, excluding China). The decline in fertility levels varied considerably among developing countries, but China's decrease of 54.2% is an exception. The rate there dropped from 5.09 births per woman in 1970–1975 to 2.33 in 1980–1985. As the Chinese population accounts for roughly 30% of the developing world's population, that decline has had a major impact on global population trends.

In Western and Eastern regions of Africa, which currently have the world's highest fertility levels, fertility rates approaching 7 have been observed – Kenya's went as high as 8.2 in the mid-1970s – and show no signs of slackening.

In the developed countries, the downward trend in fertility that prevailed in the 1960s appears to have slowed during the 1970s. In many countries fertility is tending to stabilize at a very low level. In others, the decline continues or a very slight upturn is observed. Overall, the fertility rate decreased by 9%, from 2.2 births per woman to 2. The countries of Southern and Eastern Europe registered higher total fertility rates (2.12 and 2.17 births per woman respectively) than the rest of Europe. The Soviet Union remains at a relatively high level among developed countries, with a total fertility rate expected to reach 2.36 in 1980–1985.

According to United Nations projections, the fertility rate in the developing regions is expected to drop from 4.8 in 1980–1985 to 3.2 in 1995–2000 and 2.4 in 2020–2025. In the developed countries, where the current level is already quite low, it is assumed the level will increase slightly, to 2.03 births per woman in 1995–2000 and 2.13 in 2020–2025.

Again, regional disparities are expected to be significant. By 1995–2000, Africa is expected to have a total fertility rate of 5.81; Latin America, 3.13; South Asia, 3.19; and East Asia, 1.92. In Europe, the total fertility rate is expected to be 2.07 in 1995–2000 and 2.14 in 2020–2025.

Among the demographic factors affecting fertility levels, the average age of women at first marriage – female nuptiality – is considered to be of particular significance, since it generally determines the length of time they may conceive. (Despite a rise in out-of-wedlock births, discussed below, child-bearing is still for the most part confined within some socially recognized unit.)

The developing countries show a rather broad spectrum of averages ages at first marriage, from 20 and below in most of Africa, South Asia and the Caribbean to more than 22 years in Tunisia, Mauritius and parts of Latin America. In the majority of those countries, however, the trend is towards a higher average age at first marriage.

In the developed countries, average age at first marriage ranges from approximately 21 years in Eastern Europe to more than 25 years in parts of Northern Europe. One reason for the rise in marriage age seems to be the development of new attitudes towards the institution of marriage, notably the proliferation of cohabitation or "trial marriage" – arrangements which lead to postponement of legal union.

A 1975 study of fertility and contraception in 12 developed countries found the following percentages for women aged 20–24 living in cohabiting arrangements: Denmark (30%), France (10), Great Britain (2) and Norway (12). The number of unmarried couples living together in the United States more than tripled between 1970 and 1981; in 1981, 3.5% of couple-households were unmarried.

Child-bearing among unmarried women is increasingly common in Europe and the United States, the monitoring report indicates. In 1980, more than 20% of live births in Denmark, Sweden and the German Democratic Republic were out of wedlock, as were between 10 and 20% in Austria, Bulgaria, Finland, France, Norway, the United Kingdom and the United States. Those figures are part of an upward trend in the 1970s. In Denmark, for example, the percentage of births out of wedlock almost doubled, from 18.8 to 33.2%, over the decade.

Contraception. Increased practice of birth control within marriage has been largely responsible for the recent declines in fertility in developing countries, according to the monitoring reports. However, contraception use varies widely between regions, it was found.

In the developed countries, the level of contraceptive use – already high – further increased during the 1970s. In most countries, approximately two thirds to four fifths of married women of reproductive age were using contraception, according to surveys conducted around 1975. Spain, Yugoslavia and Romania showed lower levels (51, 55 and 58%, respectively), while use in Belgium was 85%.

In some countries of sub-Saharan Africa and Asia, birth control is practiced very infrequently. In most of Africa (except for Tunisia, Egypt and Kenya), less than 70% of the women had even heard of contraception, recent surveys found. In parts of East Asia and Latin America, on the other hand, contraceptive use is nearly as common as in developed countries. In some regions, the number of married couples who practice contraception is increasing by over 2 percentage points per year.

A wide range of birth control methods are used. In developed countries, where contraception began long before the advent of modern methods, those methods co-exist with traditional means such as coitus interruptus, particularly in Southern and Eastern Europe. Overall, however, there is a trend towards greater use of modern methods.

In the developing countries, where contraception has been practiced for only a relatively short time, the pill, the intra-uterine device (IUD) and female sterilization are the most widespread methods. "Without a doubt", states the concise report, "credit for dissemination of these modern methods of contraception must be given to the birth-control programmes."

Sterilization has made considerable advances during the past ten years, it is reported. In a significant number of countries, particularly in parts of Asia and Latin America, more couples are protected from risk of pregnancy by this method than any other. In some developed countries, the proportion of women of child-bearing age who have been sterilized is rising. Sterilization of men, however, is declining.

In countries where birth-control programmes are being implemented, significant disparities exist among population groups regarding the practice of contraception. "In general", says the concise report, "the level of contraceptive use depends on both the overall level of development and the effectiveness of birth-control programmes."

In developing countries, the differences may be very great, as the World Fertility Survey showed. In Western Asia and Latin America, differentials of more than 25% in the rates of contraceptive use between rural women and urban women are found. "This gap could probably be narrowed if birth-control services were made more accessible in rural areas", states the concise report.

Age. The median age of the population – the age at which half the population is younger and half older – varies considerably between countries and regions, reflecting their fertility and mortality rates. In Europe, the median age is already 33 years; it is expected to be more than 40 by the year 2025.

In North America and East Asia, the median age is expected to be 38 years by 2025; in Japan, it will probably exceed 44. In the Soviet Union and Oceania, the median age is expected to be lower: 35.6 and 33.7 years respectively. In Africa and Latin America, the aging of the population will not be experienced until considerably later: in 2025, the median age will be only 21.8 and 29.8 years respectively.

Future trends with respect to the youth population (aged 15–24) will also be very different in the developed and developing regions. In the developed countries, the youth population,

after peaking at approximately 192 million in 1980, will decline to around 173 million by 1995, increasing only slightly thereafter, reaching 179 million by 2025. In the developing regions, however, youth will increase from more than 600 million in 1980 to 890 million in 2000 and 1.1 billion by 2025.

At the other end of the spectrum is the population 60 years and over, which is expected to increase by more than 200 million between 1980 and 2000. The relative size of this group will increase from 8.3% today to 9.7% in that period. The most important changes are expected to occur in the first quarter of the 21st century, when the proportion of elderly in the world population will rise to approximately 14%.

The population of the developed countries already shows a pronounced aging. In 2025, the elderly will account for nearly 25%. In Japan, that number may be as high as 26.4%.

The proportion of elderly in the population of the developing countries as a whole was 5.9% in 1980. Currently, it is approximately 5% in Africa and South Asia and 6.4% in Latin America. In most of the developing world, those proportions are expected to increase, reaching approximately 12% in South Asia and Latin America by 2025. In Africa, however, the increase will be slight – to only 6%.

In China, because of the considerable and rapid decline in fertility, the proportion of elderly is expected to rise from 7.3 to 18.5% between 1980 and 2025. "Such rapid changes in age structure are unprecedented in the history of world demography, and are likely to have a considerable impact in the economic and social spheres", the report points out.

Urbanization. The urbanization of the world's population continued during the 1970s, increasing from 37 to 40%, or 1.4 billion to 1.8 billion people. According to projections, by the year 2010 more than half the people in the world will live in urban areas; by 2025, that figure could be close to two thirds.

In the developing countries, the rate of growth of the urban population is three times higher than in the developed countries (3.6 and 1.1% respectively in 1980). In 1970, only one fourth of the population in developing regions lived in urban areas; in 1980, the proportion had increased to 29% and is projected to pass the 50% mark between 2010 and 2025. But despite a continuing urbanization of the population, the developing countries are not expected over the long term to reach the urbanization level of the developed regions. (In 1980, 71% of the population of developed countries were urban dwellers; by 2025, it is estimated the proportion will rise to 85%.)

Within the developing regions, there are major differences in levels of urbanization. In Latin America – the most urbanized developing region – 65.4% of the population lives in urban areas. In Africa, on the other hand, the urbanization level is still low (28.7% of the total population), but the urban population is rapidly growing (in East Africa, the annual growth rate is the world's highest, at 3.69%).

In some parts of Asia and Africa with intermediate urbanization levels (around 50%), there is relatively slow growth of the urban population (less than 1.5% per year). Middle Africa, China and Melanesia, which continue to be the least urbanized regions of the world, are likely to remain predominantly rural.

The rapid growth rate of the urban population in most developing countries does not, however, imply a stabilization or decrease of the rural population in absolute terms, although the situation varies from region to region. In East Asia and Latin America the growth rates of the rural population are moderate or even negative (in general, below 1% in 1980–1985). In other regions, they remain high (above 2% in 1980–1985 in Melanesia and most of sub-Saharan Africa, for example).

The developed regions, on the other hand, show a marked decline in rural population during the 1970s, except North America. There, the rural population grew by 4 million to 66 million and is projected to continue growing until 1990.

The developed countries are also experiencing substantial variations in the distribution of their urban populations. The recent trend, with a few exceptions, is towards deconcentration of populations from the very large cities to suburban areas and smaller towns.

In 1970, almost half the world's 36 largest cities were in developed countries; ten years later, the situation was about the same. But future projections indicate that by the end of the century, only slightly more than 25% of the 36 largest cities will be in the developed world. The average size of the largest-cities group will increase from 7.9 to 12 million, and Mexico City and São Paulo, Brazil will head the list, with an estimated 26.3 and 24 million residents respectively.

Tokyo–Yokohama (17 million) and New York–Northeastern New Jersey (15.6 million), which now top the list, are expected to drop to third and sixth places respectively by the year 2000. Kinshasa, Zaire; Lagos, Nigeria; and Dacca, Bangladesh are expected to be added to the list.

International Migration. During the past decade, there have been important changes in the migration flows between countries. Of the few countries which are still allowing or encouraging permanent immigration – Australia, Canada, Israel and the United States, for example – only the United States has increased the number admitted over the past decade. The current immigration policies of countries such as Australia, Canada and New Zeland are aimed at ensuring that immigrant flows are tailored to the level of economic activity.

Although permanent migration has in general declined over the past decade, temporary migration has varied from region to region. European countries which received temporary migrants in often considerable numbers in the 1970s subsequently made their immigration policies very restrictive. The last available statistics show that between 1974 and 1980, the number of foreign workers residing in European countries declined by approximately 6%.

Migrant labour has long been important in South Africa. Over the past few years, however, there has been a 30% drop in the number of foreign workers there, as a result of restrictive measures imposed by the countries of emigration and the desire of the South African Government to lessen its dependence on foreign labour.

In other parts of the world, however, the numbers have increased. It is estimated that at the end of the 1970s, more than 2.8 million foreign workers had settled in the oil-producing countries of the Middle East and Northern Africa. In some, foreign workers made up most of the total labour force.

Temporary migration of workers is also substantial in parts of Africa, the Caribbean and South America. In those regions it is not as institutionalized as in Europe, the Middle East and South Africa, and tends therefore to take the form of illegal migration. For example, approximately 500,000 illegal immigrants of Colombian origin were found to be working in Venezuela prior to measures adopted in 1980 to make their stay unlawful. In the United States, estimates of the number of illegal immigrants vary from 2 million to 6 million. Although levels of illegal migration are difficult to evaluate, it appears that they are rising, according to the monitoring reports.

Also contributing to international migration levels are refugees. The United Nations High Commissioner for Refugees indicates that between 1974 and 1981, the numbers tripled from 1.8 to 6.8 million, not including the Palestine refugees, whose number was estimated at 1.9 million in 1981.

According to the latest estimates, 79% of the world population lives in the 25 countries or areas in the table below. Included for comparison are 1975 population totals and annual rates of population growth for the period 1980–1985.

Country (1985 rank)	1975	1985	Annual Growth Rate (%) (1980–1985)
(1) China	933.0 million	1,063.1 million	1.17
(2) India	618.8 million	761.2 million	1.99
(3) Soviet Union	253.4 million	278.4 million	0.95
(4) United States	216.0 million	237.7 million	0.86
(5) Indonesia	135.7 million	164.9 million	1.77
(6) Brazil	108.0 million	135.6 million	2.23
(7) Japan	111.5 million	120.1 million	0.57
(8) Pakistan	75.2 million	101.7 million	3.08
(9) Bangladesh	76.6 million	101.1 million	2.73
(10) Nigeria	67.7 million	95.2 million	3.34
(11) Mexico	60.2 million	79.0 million	2.59
(12) Federal Republic of Germany	61.8 million	61.1 million	−0.18
(14) Viet Nam	47.6 million	59.5 million	2.02
(13) Italy	55.8 million	56.9 million	0.25
(15) United Kingdom	56.0 million	55.6 million	−0.01
(17) Philippines	42.6 million	54.7 million	2.49
(16) France	52.7 million	54.6 million	0.30
(18) Thailand	41.4 million	51.6 million	2.09
(19) Turkey	40.0 million	50.0 million	2.33
(20) Egypt	36.3 million	46.8 million	2.52
(21) Iran	33.3 million	45.1 million	3.02
(22) Republic of Korea	35.3 million	40.9 million	1.39
(23) Spain	35.6 million	39.0 million	0.82
(25) Poland	34.0 million	37.6 million	0.95
(24) Burma	30.8 million	35.5 million	2.52

Country or Area	World Population Estimates (thousands) mid-year			Growth Rate % 1980–1985	Life Expectancy	Infant Mortality Rate (Per 1,000)	% 0–14 years	% 65 + years
	1984	2000	2025	1980–1985			Mid 1984	
World total	4,763,004	6,127,117	8,177,052	1.7	59	81	34	6
More Developed Regions	1,165,611	1,275,655	1,396,673	0.6	73	17	22	11
Less Developed Regions+	3,597,393	4,851,462	6,780,379	2.0	57	92	38	4
AFRICA	536,685	877,439	1,642,903	3.0	50	114	45	3
Eastern Africa	155,447	266,238	531,365	3.2	49	110	47	3
British Indian Ocean Territory	2	2	2	0.0	...	...	...	...
Burundi	4,503	6,951	11,047	2.7	44	137	44	3
Comoros	443	715	1,076	3.0	50	88	46	3
Djibouti	334	604	1,203	3.2	...	...	...	...
Ethiopia	35,420	58,407	111,983	2.6	43	143	46	3
Kenya	19,761	38,534	82,850	4.1	53	82	52	2
Madagascar	9,731	15,552	29,663	2.8	50	67	44	3
Malawi[1]	6,788	11,669	23,187	3.2	45	165	48	2
Mauritius[1]	1,031	1,298	1,606	1.9	67	32	32	3
Mozambique	13,693	21,779	39,705	3.0	49	110	45	3
Reunion	555	685	825	1.4	66	19	31	4
Rwanda	5,903	10,565	22,161	3.5	50	110	49	2
Seychelles	74	127	252	3.2	...	...	...	...
Somalia	5,423	7,079	13,204	3.7	43	143	44	4
Uganda	15,150	26,774	52,334	3.5	52	94	48	3
United Rep. of Tanzania	21,710	39,129	83,805	3.5	51	98	49	2
Zambia	6,445	11,237	23,800	3.3	51	101	47	3
Zimbabwe	8,461	15,132	32,660	3.5	56	70	48	3
Middle Africa	60,819	96,072	183,477	2.7	48	120	44	3
Angola	8,540	13,234	24,473	2.5	42	149	45	3
Central African Rep.	2,508	3,736	6,724	2.3	43	143	42	4
Chad	4,901	7,304	13,115	2.3	32	143	42	4
Congo	1,695	2,646	5,050	2.6	47	124	44	3
Equatorial Guinea	383	559	937	2.2	44	137	41	4
Gabon	1,146	1,611	3,273	1.6	49	112	35	6
Sao Tome and Principe	94	149	284	2.7	...	...	...	...
United Rep. of Cameroon	9,467	14,424	25,234	2.5	48	117	43	4
Zaire	32,084	52,410	104,387	2.9	50	107	45	3
Northern Africa	121,386	185,671	294,994	2.9	56	108	43	4
Algeria	21,272	35,194	57,344	3.3	58	109	46	4
Egypt	45,657	65,200	97,391	2.5	57	113	39	4
Libyan Arab Jamahirlya	3,471	6,072	11,057	3.8	58	92	47	2
Morocco	22,848	36,325	59,859	3.3	58	99	46	3
Sudan	20,945	32,926	55,379	2.9	48	118	45	3
Tunisia	7,042	9,725	13,599	2.4	61	85	40	4
Western Sahara	151	229	365	2.8	...	...	...	...
Southern Africa	36,246	54,456	90,673	2.5	53	94	42	4
Botswana	1,042	1,865	4,057	3.5	54	79	50	2
Lesotho	1,481	2,251	4,055	2.5	49	110	42	4
Namibia	1,507	2,382	4,286	2.8	48	115	44	3
South Africa	31,586	46,918	76,332	2.5	53	92	41	4
Swaziland	630	1,041	1,943	3.0	49	129	46	3

Country or Area	World Population Estimates (thousands) mid-year			Growth Rate % 1980–1985	Life Expectancy	Infant Mortality Rate (Per 1,000)	% 0–14 years	% 65 + years
	1984	2000	2025	1980–1985			Mid 1984	
Western Africa	162,787	275,002	542,394	3.1	47	123	47	3
Benin	3,890	6,381	12,166	2.9	43	149	46	3
Burkina Faso	6,768	10,542	19,488	2.3	42	149	44	3
Cape Verde	317	382	457	1.4	57	77	32	4
Gambia	630	898	1,500	1.9	35	193	42	3
Ghana	13,044	21,923	37,748	3.2	52	98	46	3
Guinea	5,301	7,935	13,906	2.3	40	159	43	3
Guinea-Bissau	875	1,241	2,141	1.9	43	143	41	4
Ivory Coast	9,474	15,581	28,134	3.4	47	122	45	3
Liberia	2,123	3,564	6,763	3.2	49	112	47	3
Mali	7,825	12,363	21,368	2.8	42	149	46	3
Mauritania	1,832	2,999	5,901	2.9	44	137	46	3
Niger	5,940	9,750	18,940	2.8	43	146	47	3
Nigeria	92,037	161,930	338,105	3.3	49	114	48	2
St. Helena[2]	6	10	19	3.1	...	...	...	...
Senegal	6,352	10,036	18,928	2.7	43	141	45	3
Sierra Leone	3,536	4,868	7,805	1.8	34	200	41	3
Togo	2,838	4,599	9,024	2.9	49	113	44	3
AMERICAS	658,258	847,654	1,133,932	1.7	67	50	32	7
Latin America	397,138	549,971	786,584	2.3	64	63	38	4
Caribbean	31,364	40,833	57,685	1.5	64	58	35	6
Antigua and Barbuda	79	99	125	1.3	...	...	...	...
Bahamas	221	276	350	1.3	...	...	...	...
Barbados	262	307	372	0.8	72	23	28	9
British Virgin Islands	13	16	20	1.3	...	...	...	...
Cayman Islands	18	22	29	1.4	...	...	...	...
Cuba	9,966	11,718	13,575	0.6	73	20	27	8
Dominica	77	96	131	1.2	...	...	...	...
Dominican Rep.	6,101	8,407	12,154	2.3	63	64	41	3
Grenada	112	140	190	1.2	...	...	...	...
Guadeloupe	319	338	400	0.1	70	23	31	7
Haiti	6,419	9,860	18,312	2.5	53	108	44	3
Jamaica	2,290	2,849	3,671	1.4	70	28	38	6
Martinique	312	338	396	0.0	71	20	29	8
Montserrat	13	16	20	1.3	...	...	...	...
Netherlands Antilles	260	324	411	1.3	...	...	...	...
Puerto Rico	3,404	4,212	5,219	1.5	74	17	30	8
St. Christopher and Nevis	54	68	86	1.4	...	...	...	...
Saint Lucia	126	158	215	1.2	...	...	...	...
St. Vincent- the Grenadines	104	130	176	1.2	...	...	...	...
Trinidad and Tobago	1,105	1,321	1,656	0.9	70	28	32	6
Turks and Caicos Islands	8	10	12	1.3	...	...	...	...
US Virgin Islands	103	128	163	1.4	...	...	...	...
Central America	102,811	149,557	222,590	2.7	65	57	43	3
Belize	156	201	268	1.7	...	...	...	...
Costa Rica	2,534	3,596	5,099	2.6	73	20	37	4
El Salvador	5,388	8,708	15,048	2.9	65	71	45	3
Guatemala	8,165	12,739	21,717	2.9	61	68	43	3
Honduras	4,232	6,978	13,293	3.4	60	82	47	3
Mexico	77,040	109,180	154,085	2.6	66	53	43	4
Nicaragua	3,162	5,261	9,219	3.3	60	85	47	2
Panama	2,134	2,893	3,862	2.2	71	26	38	4

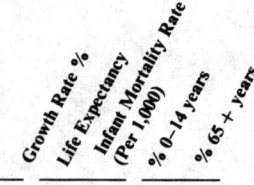

Country or Area	World Population Estimates (thousands) mid-year 1984	2000	2025	Growth Rate % 1980–1985	Life Expectancy Mid 1984	Infant Mortality Rate (Per 1,000) Mid 1984	% 0–14 years Mid 1984	% 65+ years Mid 1984
Temperate South America	44,964	55,496	70,056	1.5	69	37	31	8
Argentina	30,094	37,197	47,421	1.6	70	36	31	8
Chile	11,878	14,934	18,758	1.7	67	40	31	6
Falkland Is. (Malvinas)	2	2	2	0.0	...	...	...	...
Uruguay	2,990	3,364	3,875	0.7	70	38	27	11
Tropical South America	217,999	304,085	436,253	2.4	63	70	38	4
Bolivia	6,200	9,724	18,294	2.7	51	124	44	3
Brazil	132,648	179,487	245,809	2.2	63	71	37	4
Colombia	28,110	37,999	51,718	2.1	64	53	38	4
Ecuador	9,090	14,596	25,725	3.1	63	77	44	3
French Guiana	72	96	129	2.3	...	...	...	...
Guyana	936	1,196	1,562	2.0	68	35	37	4
Paraguay	3,576	5,405	8,552	3.0	65	45	42	4
Peru	19,197	27,952	41,006	2.6	59	99	41	4
Suriname	352	423	612	0.1	69	31	43	4
Venezuela	17,819	27,207	42,846	3.3	68	39	41	3
Northern America	261,120	297,683	347,348	0.9	74	12	22	11
Bermuda	77	103	140	2.2	...	...	...	...
Canada	25,302	29,435	34,447	1.2	75	11	23	9
Greenland	54	60	70	0.8	...	...	...	...
St. Pierre and Miquelon	6	6	6	0.0	...	...	...	...
United States	235,681	268,079	312,686	0.9	74	12	22	11
ASIA	2,777,385	3,543,693	4,466,694	1.7	58	87	36	4
East Asia	1,238,640	1,470,036	1,696,050	1.1	68	36	31	5
China	1,051,551	1,255,656	1,460,086	1.2	67	38	32	5
Japan	119,492	127,683	127,600	0.6	77	8	22	10
Other East Asia	67,597	86,697	108,363	1.8	67	30	33	4
Hong Kong	5,498	6,894	7,877	2.1	74	12	24	7
Korea	59,939	76,742	96,112	1.7	66	30	33	4
Dem. Peo. Rep. of Korea	19,630	27,256	37,556	2.3	65	32	38	4
Rep. of Korea	40,309	49,485	58,556	1.4	68	29	30	4
Macau	309	388	486	1.4	...	...	...	...
Mongolia	1,851	2,673	3,888	2.7	65	50	41	3
South Asia	1,538,745	2,073,657	2,770,644	2.2	54	109	39	3
Southeastern Asia	393,082	519,707	684,721	2.1	57	79	39	3
Brunei	269	386	495	4.0	...	...	...	...
Burma	38,513	55,186	82,153	2.5	55	94	41	4
Democratic Kampuchea	7,149	9,918	12,526	2.9	43	160	33	3
East Timor	638	876	1,144	2.5	40	183	35	2
Indonesia	162,167	204,486	255,334	1.8	53	87	39	3
Lao Peoples' Democratic Rep.	4,315	6,213	9,217	2.5	50	122	43	3
Malaysia	15,204	20,615	26,942	2.3	67	29	37	4
Philippines	53,395	74,810	102,318	2.5	65	50	39	3
Singapore	2,540	2,976	3,207	1.3	72	11	25	5
Thailand	50,584	66,115	86,282	2.1	63	51	37	3
Viet Nam	58,307	78,129	105,103	2.0	59	90	41	4
Southern Asia	1,036,011	1,385,652	1,815,940	2.2	52	120	39	3
Afghanistan	14,292	24,180	35,937	0.0	37	205	44	2
Bangladesh	98,464	145,800	219,383	2.7	48	133	46	3
Bhutan	1,388	1,893	2,662	2.0	46	144	40	3
India	746,742	961,531	1,188,504	2.0	53	118	38	3
Iran	43,799	65,549	96,166	3.0	60	101	43	3
Maldives	173	254	379	2.8	...	...	...	...
Nepal	16,107	23,048	33,946	2.3	46	144	43	3
Pakistan	98,971	142,554	212,811	3.1	50	120	44	3
Sri Lanka	16,076	20,843	26,152	2.0	67	38	35	4

Country or Area	World Population Estimates (thousands) mid-year 1984	2000	2025	Growth Rate % 1980–1985	Life Expectancy Mid 1984	Infant Mortality Rate (Per 1,000) Mid 1984	% 0–14 years Mid 1984	% 65+ years Mid 1984
Western Asia	109,651	168,298	269,984	2.9	61	93	41	4
Arab Countries	55,964	93,695	162,759	3.4	58	86	45	3
Bahrain	414	688	1,056	4.3	68	37	34	2
Democratic Yemen	2,066	3,309	5,629	2.7	46	138	45	3
Gaza Strip (Palestine)	479	000	981	2.2	...	...	...	...
Iraq	15,158	24,926	42,734	3.4	59	72	46	3
Jordan	3,375	6,400	13,366	3.7	64	63	48	3
Kuwait	1,703	2,969	4,796	5.3	71	30	41	1
Lebanon	2,644	3,617	5,221	-0.0	65	48	38	5
Oman	1,181	1,909	3,303	4.5	50	122	44	2
Qatar	291	469	774	4.0	71	45	34	2
Saudi Arabia	10,824	18,864	33,510	3.9	56	103	43	3
Syrian Arab Rep.	10,189	18,102	32,265	3.7	67	57	48	3
United Arab Emirates	1,255	1,916	2,659	5.8	71	45	30	2
Yemen	6,386	9,859	16,465	2.4	44	154	45	3
Non-Arab Countries	53,686	74,602	107,225	2.3	64	104	37	5
Cyprus	659	759	895	1.1	74	17	25	10
Israel	4,216	5,376	7,017	2.1	74	15	33	8
Turkey	48,811	68,466	99,313	2.3	63	110	37	4
Europe	400,456	513,110	520,888	0.3	73	10	21	13
Eastern Europe	112,339	120,970	131,159	0.6	72	20	23	11
Bulgaria	9,182	9,713	10,249	0.5	72	20	22	12
Czechoslovakia	15,588	16,776	18,762	0.4	72	16	24	11
German Dem. Rep.[3]	16,658	16,553	16,130	-0.1	73	12	19	14
Hungary	10,786	10,908	10,946	0.2	71	21	22	13
Poland	37,228	41,391	45,869	0.9	72	21	25	10
Romania	22,897	25,629	29,202	0.8	71	26	25	10
Northern Europe	82,090	83,410	83,577	0.1	74	11	20	15
Channel Islands	137	152	175	0.7	...	...	...	...
Denmark	5,141	5,126	4,756	0.1	75	8	19	15
Faeroe Islands	42	45	50	0.5	...	...	...	...
Finland	4,859	4,970	4,786	0.4	73	7	19	12
Iceland	239	270	296	1.0	77	7	26	10
Ireland	3,555	4,247	5,237	1.1	73	13	31	11
Isle of Man	69	73	79	0.6	...	...	...	...
Norway	4,140	4,227	4,272	0.3	76	8	21	15
Sweden	8,284	8,065	7,537	0.0	76	7	18	17
United Kingdom	55,624	56,235	56,390	-0.0	74	12	20	15
Southern Europe	141,814	153,147	162,831	0.6	73	18	23	12
Andorra	34	40	47	2.4	...	...	...	...
Albania	2,985	4,102	5,772	2.2	71	43	36	5
Gibralter	31	35	40	1.3	...	...	...	...
Greece	9,884	10,734	11,755	0.6	74	19	22	13
Holy See	1	1	1	0.0	...	...	...	...
Italy	56,724	58,155	56,948	0.3	74	14	20	13
Malta	380	419	462	0.7	72	15	24	9
Portugal	10,008	10,995	11,916	0.7	71	25	25	10
San Marino	22	25	30	1.0	...	...	...	...
Spain	38,717	43,442	49,235	0.8	74	12	25	11
Yugoslavia	23,028	25,200	26,626	0.8	71	29	24	9
Western Europe	154,212	155,583	149,322	0.1	74	11	19	13
Austria	7,489	7,498	7,260	-0.0	73	13	19	14
Belgium	9,877	9,925	9,825	0.0	73	11	19	14
France	54,449	57,083	58,530	0.3	75	10	21	13
Germany Federal Rep. of[3]	61,214	59,755	53,802	-0.2	73	13	16	14
Liechtenstein	27	34	43	1.5	...	...	...	...
Luxembourg	363	358	332	-0.1	73	11	18	14
Monaco	27	30	36	0.8	...	...	...	...
Netherlands	14,456	15,011	14,609	0.4	76	8	20	12
Switzerland	6,309	5,889	4,885	-0.3	76	8	16	16

Country or Area	World Population Estimates (thousands) mid-year			Growth Rate % 1980–1985	Life Expectancy	Infant Mortality Rate (Per 1,000)	% 0–14 years Mid 1984	% 65 + years
	1984	2000	2025					
Oceania	24,460	30,403	39,507	1.5	68	39	29	8
Australia– New Zealand	18,783	22,361	27,709	1.2	74	11	25	10
Australia[4]	15,519	18,668	23,508	1.3	74	11	24	10
New Zealand	3,264	3,693	4,201	0.8	73	12	25	10
Melanesia	4,831	6,986	10,527	2.6	57	84	42	3
Fiji	674	821	942	1.7	73	28	36	3
New Caledonia	152	193	232	1.8	...	...	...	...
Papua New Guinea	3,601	5,292	8,205	2.7	53	98	43	3
Solomon Islands	269	457	783	3.8	...	...	...	...
Vanuatu	136	223	365	3.6	...	...	...	...
Micronesia– Polynesia	846	1,056	1,271	1.7	67	39	43	3
Micronesia	348	437	522	1.7	63	58	40	3
Guam	119	133	151	2.3	...	...	...	...
Kiribati[5]	62	75	86	1.7	...	...	...	...
Nauru	8	9	11	2.7	...	...	...	...
Pacific Islands[6]	149	199	250	2.2	...	...	...	...
Tuvalu	8	9	11	2.7	...	...	...	...
Other Micronesia[7]	10	12	13	2.1	...	...	...	...
Polynesia	498	619	749	1.7	71	27	45	3
American Samoa	34	43	51	1.8	...	...	...	...
Cook Islands	19	22	23	0.0	...	...	...	...
French Polynesia	160	218	281	2.2	...	...	...	...
Niue	4	4	4	0.0	...	...	...	...
Samoa	163	182	203	0.9	...	...	...	...
Tonga	107	140	177	2.7	...	...	...	...
Wallis and Futuna Is.	10	10	10	0.0	...	...	...	...
USSR	275,761	314,818	367,127	0.9	71	25	25	9

Source: The UN Chronicle, June, 1984

Words frequently found in United Nations documents, showing the prescribed spelling and hyphening

above-mentioned
abridgement
acknowledgement
advertise
advisable
adviser
aerial
aeroplane
aesthetic
aging
agro-industry
aide-mémoire (invariably in plural)
air-conditioned
aircraft
airline
airspace
allot, allotted, allotment
aluminium
anaemia
analogue (but in computer technology, analog)
analyse
apartheid
appal, appalled, appalling
armour
artwork
attaché
averse

backward (adj.)
backwards (adv.)
balance-of-payments (adj.)
balance of payments (noun)
balance sheet
beforehand
behaviour
belligerent
benifited, benefiting
biased
biannual (twice a year)
biennial (every second year)
biennium (pl. bienniums)
bilateral
bilingual
bimonthly
birth rate
bookkeeping
bottle-neck
break down (verb)
breakdown (noun)
breakthrough
budgeted
bureaux (pl.)
by-product

calibre

cancel, cancelled, cancelling
cannot
canvas (cloth)
canvass (to solicit)
capital (city)
Capitol (building)
case-study
catalogue (but in computer technology, catalog)
catastrophe
cathode-ray tube
cease-fire (noun and adj.)
centre, centred, centring
channelled, channelling
chargé d'affaires
charter-party
check list
chef de cabinet
cheque (bank)
class-room
clue (not clew, except in a nautical sense)
coefficient
coexistence
colour
combated, combating
communiqué
compel, compelled
complexion
connection
consensus
co-operate, co-operation
co-ordinate, co-ordination
councillor
counsellor
countermeasure
coup d'état
cross-reference
cross-section
curriculum vitae (pl. curricula vitae)
cut-back (noun)

deadline
dead weight
death rate
decision maker
decision-making (adj. and noun)
defence (but: Department of Defense (United States of America))
demagogy
demarcation
dependant (noun)
dependent (adj.)
derestricted
desiccate
détente
develop, developed

diktat
disassociate
dispatch
dissension
draft (text)
draught (air)
drier

earmark
élite
embarkation
émigré
enclose
encyclopaedia
endeavour
enrol, enrolment
en route
ensure
equalled
equilibrium
everyday (adj.)
exaggerate
exorbitant
expel, expelled, expelling
expense
exposé
extrabudgetary

fact-finding
fait accompli
fall-out
far-reaching
favour
feedback
field-work
flavour
flow-sheet
focused, focusing
follow-up
foodstuff
footnote
forcible
forego (precede)
for ever
foreword
forfeit
forgo (go without)
forum (pl. forums)
freedom fighter
front line (noun)
front-line (adj.)
fulfil, fulfilment, fulfilled, fulfilling

gauge
goal

1093

Words frequently found in United Nations documents

good will (virtuous intent)
goodwill (kindly feeling, benevolence)
gram
grey
ground-nut
ground water (noun)
ground-water (adj.)
groundwork
guerrilla
guidelines

harbour
heretofore
hierarchy, hierarchical
highlight
homogeneous
honorarium (pl. honorariums)
honorary
honour
honourable
horsepower
hotbed
hygiene
hypocrisy
hydroelectric, hydrosystem, hydropower
hydro-interaction

imperilled
improvise
inasmuch as
incommunicado
in-depth (adj.)
index (pl. indexes (a list in a book); indices (mathematical))
indispensable
infrastructure
initialling
in-migration
inquire
inquiry
in-session
in so far as
install, installation, instalment
instil
insure (take out insurance)
inter-agency
inter alia
inter-American
intercede
interdependence
interdisciplinary
intergovernmental
interim
International Labour Organisation
interregional
interrelate, interrelation
inter-sessional
interspace
inter-state
interstate (within a country)
intra-industry
intraregional
inward

jewellery
judgement (BUT Judgment of the International Court of Justice)

kilogram (kg)
kilometre (km)
kilowatt
kilowatt-hour
know-how

label, labelled
labour
laborious
laissez-passer

land-locked
last-mentioned
layout
learned (past and past participle)
liaison
licence (noun)
license (verb)
life-style
lifetime
litre
liveable
long-term (adj.)
loophole

machine-gun
macro-economics
macrolevel
macroscopic
mainland
man-hour
manoeuvre
manpower
man-made
many-sided
marshal(led) (verb)
meagre
mast-head
matériel
meantime (adv.) *but* in the mean time
meanwhile (adv.) *but* in the mean while
meeting-place
merchandise
metre (unit of length)
meter (instrument)
microfiche
microfilm
microlevel
microwave
midday
midway
misspelt
modelled
moneys
monies (different kinds of currencies)
monopsonistic, monopsy
mould
multilateral
multilingual
multinational
multi-purpose

neighbour
nevertheless
non-administrative
non-committal
non-co-operation
non-existent
non-governmental
none the less
no one
north-east(ern)
north-west(ern)
note verbale (pl. *notes verbales*)
noticeable

occur, occurred, occurrence
offence
offensive
offered
offhand
offprint
offset
offshore
ombudsman (pl. *ombudsmen*)
ongoing
on-line
onward

organization (but International Labour Organisation Organisation for Economic Co-operation and Development)
organize
out-migration
out-of-date (attributive adj.)
out of date (predicative adl.)
overall (noun and adj.)
overall (noun and adj.)
over-emphasize
overestimate
overflight
over-population
over-production
overrate
overriding
overrun
overspending
overstatement
overthrow

paralyse
pay-roll
peace-keeping (adj. and noun)
per annum
per capita
per diem
photocopy
piecemeal
pipeline
plebiscite
policy-making (adj. and noun)
post-graduate (adj. and noun)
post-session (adj.)
pourparler (usually in pl. *pourparlers*)
practice (noun)
practise (verb)
pre-conceive
pre-condition
pre-empt
pre-investment
prerequisite
pre-session
pretence
principal (head person)
principal (adj.)
principle (noun) (a matter of)
print-out
procès-verbal (pl. *procès-verbaux*)
programme (but computer program)
proof-reader

radioactive
rainwater (noun)
raison d'être
rancour
rapprochement
reaffirmation
realize
rearrange
re-establish
refoulment
reflection
reinforce
reinsure
régime
reorganize
re-route
résumé
reversible
rigour
rigorous
river water (noun)
river-water (adj.)
road-block
roll-call
rumour
run-down (noun)

saleable
savour
sceptic(al), scepticism
schoolteacher
sea-bed
sea-level
sea water (noun)
sea-water (adj.)
sectoral
set-back (noun)
sewage (waste matter)
sewerage (system of drains)
shortcoming
sizeable
skilful
slave trade, slave trader (trading)
slow down (verb)
slow-down (noun)
smelt
some time, sometimes
south-east(ern)
south-west(ern)
soybean
spacecraft
spaceship
specialize
spelt (past participle)
spring water (noun)
spring-water (adj.)
staff member
stationary (not moving)
stationery (paper)
stockpile
storey (building)
straightforward
stumbling-block
sub-amendment
sub-area
sub-commission
sub-committee
sub-continent
sub-contract
subdivision
sub-entry
subgroup
subheading
sub-item
subject-matter
subparagraph
subregional

subsection
substructure
subtitle
subtotal
subunit
sulphur
supersede
superstructure
supervise
supervisor
supranational
surface water (noun)
surface-water (adj.)
syllable
symmetry
synchronize
synthesize, synthesis

taxpayer
teen-age (adj.)
teenager (noun)
telegram
terrain
test-ban (adj.)
thermonuclear
time-consuming
time-limit
timetable
title-page
totalling
towards
trade mark
trafficking
tranquility
transatlantic
transferable
trans-ship
travelling
turnkey
turn-round (of ships)
twofold
two thirds (noun)
two-thirds (adj.)
typesetting

underdevelop
underemployment
underestimate
underground
underlie

underprivileged
Under-Secretary-General
underwater (adj.)
under way
updated
upgrade
uproot
up-to-date (attributive adj.)
up to date (predicative adj.)
usable

valour
versus
via
vice versa
viewpoint
vigour
vigorous
vis-à-vis

wagon
warlike
watercourse
weekday
weekend
well-being
well-founded (adj.)
well known (predicative)
well-known (attributive, immediately preceding noun)
well water (noun)
well-water (adj.)
whole-hearted(ly)
widespread
wildlife
wilful, wilfulness
withhold
woollen
word processing (noun)
word-processing (adj.)
work-hour
work-load
world-wide (adj.)
worth while (predicative adj.)
worthwhile project (attributive adj.)

X-ray

Source: *United Nations Manual*, New York, 1983, pp. 355–360.

ACRONYMS

AAPSO   Afro-Asian Peoples' Solidarity Organization

AARRO   Afro-Asian Rural Reconstruction Organization

ABC   Argentina, Brazil, Chile

ABC   Atomic, Bacteriological and Chemical Weapons

ABCD   American, British, Chinese and Dutch Allied Forces

ABM   Anti-Ballistic Missile

ABS   American Bureau of Shipping

ACA   Allied Control Authority

ACAST   Advisory Committee on the Application of Science and Technology for Development

ACCHAN   Allied Command Channel

ACE   Allied Command Europe

ACLANT   Allied Command Atlantic

ACP   African, Caribbean and Pacific Countries

ADELA   Atlantic Development Group for Latin America

ADP   Automatic Data Processing

AEDF   Asian Economic Development Fund

AFSED   Arab Fund for Economic and Social Development

AGM   Air-to-Ground Missile

AGRIS   International Information System for the Agricultural Sciences and Technology

AGROMASH   International Society for Machines for Vegetable Growing, Horticulture and Viticulture

AIFTA   Anglo-Irish Free Trade Agreement

ALADI   Asociación Latinoamericana de Integración

ALAF   Asociación Latinoamericana de Ferrocarriles

ALALC   Asociación Latinoamericana de Libre Comercio

ALAMAR   Asociación Latinoamericana de Armadores

ALCM   Air-Launched Cruise Missile

ALGOL   Algorithmic Language

AMGOT   Allied Military Government of Occupied Territories

AMTORG   Amerykanskaya Torgovla Corporation

AMU   Asian Monetary Unit

ANF   Atlantic Nuclear Forces

ANZAC   Australia and New Zealand Army Corps

ANZUK   Australia, New Zealand, United Kingdom Military Alliance

ANZUS   Australia, New Zealand, USA Security Treaty

APO   Asian Productivity Organization

ARABSAT   League of Arab States Satellite

ARCOS LTD   All Russian Co-Operative Society Limited

ARPEL   Asociación de Asistencia Recíproca Petrolera Estatal Latinoamericana

ASAT   Anti-Satellite System

ASBM   Air-to-Surface Ballistic Missile

ASEAN   Association of Southeast Asian Nations

ASIL   American Society of International Law

ASM   Air-to-Surface Missiles

ASPAC   Asian and Pacific Council

ASW   Anti-Submarine Warfare

ATA   Admission Temporaire – Temporary Admission-Book

AWACS   Airborne Warning and Control System

BAC   British Air Corporation

BADED   Banque arabe pour le développement économique

BAM   Baykalsko-Amurskaya Magistralia

B AND C   Bacteriological and Chemical Weapons

BEAC   Banque des états de l'Afrique centrale

BENELUX   Belgium, Netherlands, Luxembourg

BIS   Bank for International Settlements

BMD   Ballistic Missile Defence

BOAD   Banque ouest-africaine de développement

BRT   Brutto Register Tonnage

BW   Bacteriological Weapons

CARE   Co-operative for American Relief Everywhere

CARICOM   Caribbean Community

CARIFTA   Caribbean Free Trade Association

CBEC   Classification by Broad Economic Categories

CBU   Cluster Bomb Unit

CC   Corps Consulaire

CD   Corps diplomatique

CECON   Comisión Especial de Consulta y Negociación

CEDEL   Centrale de livraison de valeurs mobilières

CELADE   Centro Latinoamericano de Demografía

CELAM   Consejo Episcopal Latinoamericano

CEMLA   Centro de Estudios Monetarios Latinoamericanos

CENTO   Central Treaty Organization

CEPLA   Centro Experimental para Lanzamiento de Proyectiles Autopropulsados

CERN   Centre européenne pour la recherche nucléaire

CETIS   Centre de transformations des informations scientifiques

CFA   Communauté financière africaine

CHANCOM   Channel Command

CHINCOM   China Trade Co-ordinating Committee

CIA   Central Intelligence Agency

CIF   Cost, Insurance, Freight

CIJ   Cour International de Justice

CINA   Commission internationale de la navigation aérienne

CINCCHAN   Commander-in-Chief Channel

CINTERFOR   Centro Interamericano de Investigación y Documentación sobre Formación Profesional

CITEJA   Comité international technique d'experts juridiques aériens

CLADES   Centro Latinoamericano de Documentación Económica y Social

CMEA   Council for Mutual Economic Assistance

CMR   Convention de marchandises par route

COBOL   Common Business-Oriented Language

COCOM   Co-ordinating Committee for East-West Trade Policy

COFACE   Compagnie française d'assurance-crédit pour le commerce extérieur

COMECON   Council for Mutual Economic Assistance

COMEX   Commodity Exchange of New York

COMINFORM   Information Bureau of the Communist and Workers' Parties

COMINTERN   Communist International

COMISCO   Committee of International Socialistic Conferences

COMITEXTIL   Co-ordinating Committee of the Textile Industry

COMSAT   Commercial Satellite Corporation

COMUNBANA   Comercializadora Multinacional de Banana

COPMEC   Committee of Small and Medium Sized Commercial Enterprises

COSPAR   Committee for Space Research

CPJI   Cour permanente de justice internationale

CPUSTAL   Congreso permanente de Unidad Sindical de Trabajadores de América Latina

CREST   Committee of Scientific and Technological Research

CROWCASS   Criminals of War Commission

CSCE   Conference of Security and Co-operation in Europe

CSTD   Committee on Science and Technology for Development

DAC   Development Assistance Committee

DARE   Data Retrieval System for Social Science

DSB   Drug Supervisory Body

EAAFRO   East African Agriculture and Forestry Research Organization

EACSO   East African Common Services Organization

EAGGF   European Agriculture Guidance and Guarantee Fund

ECA   UN Economic Commission for Africa

ECAFE   UN Economic Commission for Asia and the Far East

ECDC   Economic Co-operation Among Developing Countries

ECE   UN Economic Commission for Europe

ECLA   UN Economic Commission for Latin America

ECOSOC   Economic and Social Council

ECOWAS   Economic Community of West African States

ECS   European Communication Satellite

ECSC   European Coal and Steel Community

ECU   European Currency Unit

ECWA   UN Economic Commission for Western Asia

EDC   European Defence Community

EDU   European Democratic Union

EEC   European Economic Community

EFTA   European Free Trade Association

ELACT   Encuentro Latinoamericano Camilo Torres

ELDO   European Space Vehicle Launcher Development Organization

EMA   European Monetary Agreement

EMCOF   European Monetary Co-operation Fund

EMF   European Monetary Fund

EMP   Electro-Magnetic-Pulse Bomb

EMS   European Monetary System

ENMOD   Modification of Environment

ERAP   Entreprise des recherches et d activité pétrolière

ERP   European Recovery Plan

ESA   European Space Agency

ESAPAC   Escuela Superior de Administración Pública de América Central

ESCAP   UN Economic and Social Commission for Asia and the Pacific

ESRO   European Space Research Organization

EUA   European Unit of Account

EURATOM   European Atomic Energy Community

EUREX   Computer Trading and Information System

EUROBANK   Banque commerciale pour l'Europe du Nord

EUROCHEMIC   European Company for Chemical Processing of Irradiated Fuels

EUROCONTROL   European Organization for the Safety of Air Navigation

EUROCULT   European Culture

EUROFER   European Steel Federation

EUROFINA   European Company for the Financing of Railway Equipment

EUROMEDIC   European Company for the Manufacture of Hospital Equipment and the Construction of Hospital Buildings

EURONET   European Information Network

EUROPÊCHE   Association of National Organizations of Fishing Enterprises

EUROSPACE   European Industrial Space Study Group

EUROTOX   European Standing Committee for the Protection of Populations against the Long-Term Risks of Chronic Toxicity

EUROVISION   European Broadcasting Union

EXIMBANK   Export-Import Bank of the USA

FAO   Food and Agriculture Organization of the UN

FAS   Free Alongside Ship

FBI   Federal Bureau of Investigation

FBS   Forward Based System

FDC   First Day Cover

FELABAN   Federación Latinoamericana de Bancos

FINEFTA   Finland — EFTA Association

FLACSO   Facultad Latinoamericana de Ciencias Sociales

FOA   Foreign Operations Administration

FOB   Free on Board

FOR   Free on Rail

FORATOM   Forum atomique européen

FORTRAN   Formula Translating System

FPA   Foreign Policy Association

FRG   Federal Republic of Germany

FUND A   Agriculture Fund

GAB   General Arrangements to Borrow

GANEFO   Games of the New Emerging Forces

GATT   General Agreement on Tariffs and Trade

GCC   Co-operation Council for the Arab States of the Gulf

GDP   Gross Domestic Product

GDR   German Democratic Republic

GEMS   Global Environmental Monitoring System

GESAMP   Group of Experts on the Scientific Aspects of Marine Pollution

GESTAPO   Geheime Staatspolizei

GMT   Greenwich Meridian Time

GNP   Gross National Product

GSP   Generalized System of Preferences

HICOG   Allied High Commission for Germany

IAEA   International Atomic Energy Agency

IA-ECOSOC   Inter-American Economic and Social Council

IAFP   Inter-American Forces of Peace

IANEC   Inter-American Nuclear Energy Commission

IARA   Inter-Allied Reparation Agency

IATA   International Air Transport Association

IBD   Inter-American Development Bank

IBEC   International Bank for Economic Co-operation

IBM   International Business Machines Corporation

IBRD   International Bank for Reconstruction and Development

ICA   International Communication Agency

ICAO   International Civil Aviation Organization

ICBM   Inter-Continental-Ballistic Missiles

ICCS   International Commissions for Control and Supervision

ICFTU   International Confederation of Free Trade Unions

ICJ   International Court of Justice

ICSID   International Centre for Settlement of Investment Disputes

ICSU   International Council of Scientific Unions

IDA   International Development Association

IDI   Institut de droit international

IDS   International Development Strategy

IFAD   International Fund of Agricultural Development

IFC   International Finance Corporation

IFCTU   International Federation of Christian Trade Unions

IGAT   Iranian Gas Trunkline

IID   International Investment Bank

ILAFA   Instituto Latinoamericano del Fierro y el Acero

ILCE   Instituto Latinoamericano de la Communicación Educativa

ILO   International Labour Organisation

ILPES   Instituto Latinoamericano de Planificación Económica y Social

IMCO   Inter-Governmental Maritime Consultative Organization

IMF   International Monetary Fund

IMO   International Maritime Organization

IMO   International Meteorological Organization

IMT   International Military Tribunal

INCB   International Narcotics Control Board

INCIDI   Institute of Differing Civilization

INFORMBIURO   Information Bureau of the Communist and Workers' Parties

INFOTERM   International Information Centre for Technology

INIS   International Nuclear Information System

INMARSAT   International Maritime Satellite Organization

INSEAD   Institut européen d'administration des affaires

INSTRAW   International Research and Training Institute for the Advancement of Women

INTAL   Instituto para la Integración de América Latina

INTELSAT   International Telecommunications Satellite Organization

INTERAMPOL   Inter-American Police

INTERATOMENERGO   International Economic Association for the Organization of Co-operation in Building Nuclear Power Stations

INTERATOMINSTRUMENT   International Economic Association for Nuclear Instrument Building

INTERCHIM   International Organization for Co-operation in Small-Tonnage Chemical Products

INTERCHIMVOLOKNO   International Economic Association for Chemical Fibres

1097

Acronyms

INTERCOSMOS International Space Exploration Program

INTERELEKTRO International Organization for Co-operation in the Electrical Engineering Industry

INTERELEKTROTEST International Organization for Co-operation in Large Capacity and High Voltage Experimental Laboratories

INTERFLORA International Organization for Flowers' Deliveries

INTERLAINE Committee for the Wool Industries

INTERLIGHTER International Interland Shipping Enterprise

INTERMETAL International Organization for Co-operation in the Iron and Steel Industry

INTERPOL International Criminal Police Organization

INTERSHIPNIK International Organization for Co-operation of Bearings Industry

INTERSPUTNIK International System and Organization for Space Communications

INTERSTENO International Federation of Shorthand and Typewriting

INTERTEXTILMASH International Association for Production of Technological Equipment for the Textile Industry

INTERVISION International Television Organization

INTERVODOCHISTKA International Organization for Co-operation in the Field of Rational Utilization and Protection of Water Resources

IOB Inter-Organization Information Board

IPAC Instituto Centroamericano de Administración Pública

IPDC International Program for the Development of Communication

IPL Information Processing Language

IPU Inter-Parliamentary Union

IRA Irish Republican Army

IRI Instituto per la Riconstruzione Industriali

ISBN International Standard Book Number

ITO International Trade Organization

ITU International Telecommunication Union

KOLKHOZ Kolektivnoye Hozyastvo

KOMINFORM Information Bureau of the Communist and Workers' Parties

KOMINTERN Kommunistische Internationale

KRIESTINTERN Krestiansky Internatsional

KWIC Key Word in Context

KWOC Key Word Out of Context

LAFTA Latin American Free Trade Association

LARCEF Latin American Council for Cosmic Radiation and Physical Interplanetary Space

LASER Light Amplification by Stimulated Emission of Radiation

LASO Latin American Solidarity Organization

LIBOR London Inter-Bank Offered Rate

LITBIEL Lithuania and Byelorussia

LNTS League of Nations Treaty Series

LRTNF Long-Range Theatre Nuclear Force

LSD Lysergic Acid Diethylamide

MAB Man and Biosphere

MAD Mutual Assured Destruction

MARSAT International Radiocommunication Satellite System

MARV Maneuvering Reentry Vehicle

MASHRAG Egypt, Jordan, Lebanon, Syria

MBFR Mutual and Balanced Forces Reduction

M.D. M'aider

MFN Most Favoured Nation IMF Clause

MHV Miniature Homing Vehicle

MID Ministierstvo Innostrannykh Diel

MIRV Multiple Independent Reentry Vehicles

MLF Multilateral Force, Multilateral Fleet

MMM Mouvement mondial des mères

MOPR Mezhdunarodnaya Organizatsya Pomoshchi Revolutsyonistom-Red Secours

MSA Mutual Security Agency

MURFAAMCE Mutual Reduction of Forces and Armaments and Associated Measures in Central Europe

NACA National Advisory Committee for Aeronautics

NAM National Association of Manufactures

NAMUCAR Naveira Multinacional del Caribes

NASA National Aeronautics and Space Administration

NATO North Atlantic Treaty Organization

NAUCA Nomenclatura Arancelaria Uniforme de Centroamérica

NAVICERT Navy Certificate

NEP Novaya Ekonomicheskaya Politika

NGO Non-Governmental Organizations

NIEO New International Economic Order

N.N. Nomen Nescio

NORDEC Nordic Economic Union

NORDEK Nordic Economic Union

NORDEL Electric Power Committee Nordic Council

NOR-SHIPPING International Maritime Exhibition in Oslo

NRT Netto Register Tonnage

NSDAP Nationalsozialistische Deutsche Arbeiterpartei

NTB Non-Tariff Barrier

OAMCE Organisation africaine et malgache de coopération économique

OAPEC Organization of Arab Petroleum Exporting Countries

OAS Organization of American States

OAU Organization of African Unity

OCAM Organisation commune africaine et mauricienne

ODA Official Development Assistance

ODECA Organización de los Estados Centroamericanos

OECD Organization for Economic Co-operation and Development

OEEC Organization for European Economic Co-operation

OIRT Organisation internationale de radiodiffusion et télévision

OKW Oberkommando der Wehrmacht

OLADE Organización Latinoamericana de Energía

OLAS Organización Latinoamericana de Solidaridad

OPANAL Organismo para la Prescripción de las Armas Nucleares en América Latina

OPEC Organization of the Petroleum Exporting Countries

ORTRAG Orbital Transport und Raketen Aktiengesellschaft

OSPAAAL Organización de Solidaridad con los Pueblos de África, Asia e América Latina

OSS Office of Strategic Services

OWI Office of War Information

PAHO Pan-American Health Organization

PANA Pan-African Press Agency

PAU Pan-American Union

PLO Palestine Liberation Organization

POLISARIO Frente Popular para la Liberación de Sanguia el Hamra y Río de Oro

POLITRUK Politicheski Rukovoditiyel

POW Prisoner of War

PROFINTERN Krasnyj Internatsional Profsoiuzov

PUAS Postal Union of the Americas and Spain

R AND D Research and Development

RCD Middle East Regional Co-operation for Development

REPCO Reparation Committee of the Big Powers

RPV Remotely Piloted Vehicles

RSFSR Russian Soviet Federated Socialist Republic

RSHS Reichssicherheitshauptamt

SA Sturmabteilungen der NSDAP

SABMIS Seabased Anti-Ballistic Missile Intercept System

SACEUR Supreme Allied Commander Europe

SACLANT Supreme Allied Commander Atlantic

SALT Strategic Armaments Limitation Talks

SARC South Asian Regional Commission

SAS Scandianavian Airlines System

SATO South Atlantic Treaty Organization

SDR Special Drawing Rights

SEAMEO Southeast Asian Ministers of Education Organization

SEATO Southeast Asia Treaty Organization

SEC European Society of Culture

SELA Sistema Económico Latinoamericano

SENEGAMBIA Senegal and Gambia

SHAPE Supreme Headquarters Allied Powers in Europe

SI International System of Units

SIFIDA Société internationale financière pour les investissements et le développement en Afrique

SILA Servicio de Información de América Latina

SIPO Sicherheitspolizei

SIPRI Stockholm International Peace Research Institute

SIS Secret Intelligence Service

SLBM Submarine-Launched Ballistic Missiles

SODEPAX Committee on Society, Development and Peace

SOE Special Operations Executive

SOLAS Safety of Life at Sea

SONATRACH Société Nationale pour le transport et la commercialisation des hydrocarbures

SOS Save our Ship

SOVKHOZ Sovyetskoye Hozyastvo

SPEC South Pacific Bureau for Economic Co-operation

SS Schutz-Staffeln der NSDAP

STABEX Stabilization of Export

STANAFORCHAN Standing Naval Force for Channel

START Strategic Arms Reduction Talks

STAVKA Stavka Glavnego Komendovaniya

STD Sexually Transmitted Diseases

SUMED   Suez-Mediterranée
SUNFED   UN Special Fund
SWAPO   Southwest Africa People's Organization
SWIFT   Society for Worldwide Interbank Financial Telecommunication
TANZAM   Tanzania — Zambia Railroad Line
TDW   Ton Deadweight
TEE   Trans-Europe Express
TELSTAR   Television Satellite of the USA
TEM   Trans-European Motorway
TIAS   Treaties and Other International Acts Series
TIMS   The Institute of Management Sciences
TIR   Transport internationeaux routiers
TIS   UN Treaty Information System
TOVALOP   Tanker Owners' Voluntary Agreement Concerning Liability for Oil Pollution
UAE   United Arab Emirates
UAMCE   Union africaine et malgache de coopération économique
UAMED   Union africaine et malgache de banques pour le développement
UAS   United Arab States
UFO   Unidentified Flying Objects
UIA   Union of International Associations
UK   United Kingdom
UML   Union Monetaria Latina
UMOA   Union monétaire ouest-africaine
UN   United Nations
UNCA   UN Correspondents Association
UNCD   UN Centre for Disarmament
UNCIO   UN Conference of International Organization
UNCITRAL   UN Commission on International Trade Law
UNCTAD   UN Conference on Trade and Development

UNDOF   UN Disengagement Observer Force
UNDP   UN Development Programme
UNDRO   UN Disaster Relief Office
UNEP   UN Environment Programme
UNEPTA   UN Expanded Programme of Technical Assistance
UNESCO   UN Educational, Scientific and Cultural Organization
UNESOB   UN Economic and Social Office in Beirut
UNFDAC   UN Fund for Drug Abuse Control
UNFICYP   UN Peace-Keeping Force in Cyprus
UNFPA   UN Fund for Population Activities
UNHCR   UN High Commissioner for Refugees
UNIAPAC   International Christian Union of Business Executives
UNICEF   UN Children's Fund
UNIDO   UN Industrial Development Organization
UNIFIL   UN Interim Force in Lebanon
UNIPOM   UN India-Pakistan Observation Mission
UNISIST   UN International System of Information on Science and Technology
UNISPACE   UN Conference on the Exploration and Peaceful Uses of Outer Space
UNITAR   UN Institute for Training and Research
UNMOGIP   UN Military Observer Group in India and Pakistan
UNRIP   UN Representative for India and Pakistan
UNRISD   UN Research Institute for Social Development
UNRRA   UN Relief and Rehabilitation Administration
UNRWA   UN Relief and Works Agency for Palestine Refugees in the Near East

UNSCEAR   UN Scientific Committee on the Effects of Atomic Radiation
UNSCOB   UN Special Committee on the Balkans
UNSDRI   UN Social Defence Research Institute
UNSO   UN Sahelian Office
UNTAG   UN Temporary Auxiliary Group
UNTSO   UN Truce Supervision Organization
UPU   Universal Postal Union
URANCO   British-Dutch-West German Consortium for Processing Uranium
USA   United States of America
USIA   US Information Agency
USSR   Union of Soviet Socialist Republics
UTA   Union de transports aériens
UTAL   Universidad de los Trabajadores de América Latina
V1, V2   Vergeltungswaffe
VAT   Value Added Tax
WASP   White Anglo-Saxon Protestants
WCC   World Council of Churches
WEU   Western European Union
WFP   World Food Program
WFU   World Food Council
WHO   World Health Organization
WIPO   World Intellectual Property Organization
WMO   World Meteorological Organization
WMU   World Maritime University
WNIESHTORGBANK   Foreign Trade Bank of the USSR
WPC   World Peace Council
WTO   World Tourism Organization
YMCA   World Alliance of Young Men's Christian Associations
YWCA   World Young Women's Christian Association

Official abbreviations of names of organizations in the UN system

The following is a list of specialized agencies and other organizations in the UN system. The specialized agencies are shown in the order in which they should normally be listed. The order is that of the dates on which they became affiliated with the United Nations.

ILO	International Labour Organization		Reconstruction and Development)	IFAD	International Fund for Agricultural Development
FAO	Food and Agriculture Organization of the United Nations	IMF	International Monetary Fund		
		UPU	Universal Postal Union	IAEA	International Atomic Energy Agency
UNESCO	United Nations Educational, Scientific and Cultural Organization	WMO	World Meteorological Organization	GATT	General Agreement on Tariffs and Trade
		ITU	International Telecommunication Union		
ICAO	International Civil Aviation Organization			IOB	Inter-Organization Board for Information System
		IMO	International Maritime Organization		
WHO	World Health Organization	WIPO	World Intellectual Property Organization		
IBRD	World Bank (International Bank for				

United Nations Editorial Manual, New York, 1983, pp. 415–417.

Abbreviations

Admin. = Administration
Afr. = African
Aggr. = Aggression
Agr. = Agreement
Agricult. = Agriculture
Am., Amer. = American
Arbitr. = Arbitration
Art. = Article
Arm. = Armaments
Assist. = Assistance
Assoc. = Association

Br. = British
Biol. = Biological

Carib. = Caribbean
Cath. = Catholic
Chr. = Christian
Commerc. = Commercial
Cmt. = Committee
Cms. = Commission
Cmq. = Communique
Co. = Company
Comm. = Community
Conf. = Conference
Consult. = Consultative
Cont. = Continental
Conv. = Convention
Co-Op. = Co-operation
Co-ord. = Co-ordination
Corp. = Corporation
Cult. = Cultural
Cl. = Council
Czechosl. = Czechoslovakia

Decl. = Declaration
Dem. = Democratic
Demogr. = Demographic, demography
Denucl. = Denuclarization
Devel. = Development
Disarm. = Disarmament
Doctr. = Doctrine

Ec. = Economic
Educ. = Education
Eng. = English
Est. = Established
Est. = Estimate
Exhib. = Exhibition

Feder. = Federation
Fr. = French
For. = Foreign
Found. = Foundation

Gen. = General
Ger. = German

Hqs. = Headquarters
Hum. = Human

Indep. = Independence
Ind. = Industry
Integr. = Integration
Inter-Am. = Inter-American
Intergov. = Intergovernmental
Int. = International
Interv. = Intervention
Invest. = Investment
Inst. = Institute
Isl. = Island
Ital. = Italian, Italy

Jap. = Japanese

Latin Am. = Latin American
Lat. = Latin
Limit. = Limitation

Malag. = Malagasy
Marit. = Maritime
Med. = Medical
Meteor. = Meteorological
Milit. = Military
Mov. = Movement

Navig. = Navigation
Neutr. = Neutrality
Non-Aggr. = Non-aggression
Non-Alig. = Non-Aligned
Non-Gov. = Non-Governmental
Nucl. = Nuclear

Org. = Organization

Pan-Am. = Pan-American, Pan-Americanism
Pp = Pages
Polit. = Political
Procl. = Proclamation
Protec. = Protection
Prot. = Protocol
Publ. = Publication

Radiocom. = Radiocommunication
Reg. = Registered
Rep. = Republic
Res. = Resolution
Rev. = Revolution
Rus. = Russian

Scand. = Scandinavian
Sec. = Security
Serv. = Service
Settl. = Settlement
Soc. = Social
Solid. = Solidarity
Sov. = Soviet

Telecom. = Telecommunication
Tr. = Treaty
Trib. = Tribunal

Vol. = Volume

Yugosl. = Yugoslavia, Yugoslav

A SELECTIVE INDEX

BAHA'I 140
BAHAMAS 140
BAHRAIN 140
BAHR PLAN, 1969 140
BAHT 140
  BAILIFFS 140
BAILIWICK OF GUERNSEY 74
BAISSE 75
BAJA CALIFORNIA 75
BAKER PLAN 75
BAKERY 75
BALANCE OF PAYMENTS 75
BALANCE OF POWER 75
BALANCE OF TERROR 75
BALANCE OF TRADE 75
BALEARIC ISLANDS 75
BALFOUR DECL., 1917 75
BALKAN 75
BALKAN ALLIANCE 1954 ▷ Balkan Pact
  1954
BALKAN ALLIANCES 1912 AND 1913 75
BALKAN CONFERENCE 75
BALKAN CONFS. 1976 AND 1984 75
BALKAN ENTENTE, 1934 75
BALKAN PACT, 1954 76
BALKAN QUESTION 76
BALKAN RAILROAD 76
BALKANS 76
BALKANS, PROBLEMS IN THE UN 76
  – UNSCOB 965
BALKAN WARS, 1912 - 13 76
BALLET 76
BALLISTIC MISSILE EARLY WARNING
  SYSTEM, BMEWS 76
BALLISTIC MISSILES 76
BALLOON 76
  – Hague Decl. 1907 358
BALLOON AND YACHT
  COMPETITIONS 77
BALLOON INCIDENTS 1953 - 56 77
BALNEOLOGY 77
BALTAFRICA 77
BALTAMERICA 77
BALTIC AND NORTH SEA CONVS., 1907 -
  08 77
BALTIC CLUB 77
BALTIC CODE 77
BALTIC CONFS., 1920 - 25 77
BALTIC CONVS., 1925 - 29 77
BALTIC ENTENTE 77
BALTIC GDANSK CONV., 1973 77
BALTIC GEODETIC CONV. ▷ Baltic Convs.
  1925 - 29
BALTIC HELSINKI CONF., 1974 77
BALTIC HELSINKI CONV., 1974 78
BALTIC INSTITUTE 78
BALTIC MERCANTILE EXCHANGE 79
BALTIC PACT 1934 ▷ Baltic Entente
BALTIC PEOPLES 79
BALTIC SALMON CMS. 79
BALTIC SEA 79
BALTIC SEA OF PEACE 79
BALTIC STATES 79
BALTIC STATES AGR., 1922 79
BALTIC STATES CO-OP. TR. ▷ Baltic
  Entente

BALTIC STATES CONV. ON ARBITR.
  ▷ Baltic Convs. 1925 - 29 79
BALTIC STATES CONV. ON BILLS OF
  EXCHANGE 1938 79
BALTIC STATES CONV. ON CHEQUES,
  1938 79
BALTIC STATES CONV. ON JUDGMENTS,
  1935 79
BALUCHISTAN 79
BALZAN FOUNDATION 79
BAM 79
BAMAKO 80
BAMBOO CURTAIN 80
BANACH MATHEMATICAL CENTER 80
BANANAS 80
  – Comunbana 184
  – United Brands 945
  – United Fruit Co. 945
BANAT 81
BANCO DE DESARROLLO DEL
  CARIBE 81
BANCO DE LA NACION ARGENTINA 81
BANCO DO BRASIL 81
BANCOR 81
BANCROFT TRS., 1867 - 72 81
B AND C ARMS 80
BANDUNG 81
BANDUNG CONF., 1955 81
BANGKOK 83
BANGLADESH 83
BANISHMENT 83
BANJUL 83
BANK 83
  – Afr. Devel. Bank 11
  – Allied Bank Cms. 29
  – Arab Bank for Ec. Devel. in Africa 53
  – Asian Devel. Bank 62
  – Banco de Desarrollo del Caribe 81
  – Banco de la Nacion Argentina 81
  – Banco do Brasil SA 81
  – Banque Commerc. pour l'Europe du
    Nord 86
  – Carib. Devel. Bank 134
  – Central Am. Bank for Ec. Integr. 140
  – Central Bank of the West Afr. States 142
  – Central Banks 142
  – Clearing 172
  – Clearing Houses 172
  – Club of Paris 172
  – Club of Vienna 173
  – Compensation Chambers 183
  – Crash 200
  – Credit Markets 201
  – Deutsche Bundesbank 222
  – Devel. Bank of Central Afr. States 223
  – Devel. Banks 223
  – East Afr. Devel. Bank 245
  – Eur. Clearing Union 275
  – Eur. Invest. Bank 282
  – Euro-yen Bonds 285
  – Export-Import Bank of Japan 287
  – Export-Import Bank of the USA 287
  – Federal Reserve System 295
  – Floating Rate of Exchange 300
  – Foreign Bonds 303
  – Foreign Credits 304
  – Gnomes of Zurich 345
  – Gold Pool Int. 347
  – Gold Standard 347
  – Gosbank SSSR 349
  – Holding 385
  – Hot Money 389
  – IBRD/World Bank 407
  – Int. Bank for Ec. Co-op. 446

  – Int. Invest. Bank 457
  – Inter-Am. Bank 432
  – Inter-Am. Devel. Bank 437
  – Islamic Devel. Bank 469
  – Latin Am. Banking Feder. 501
  – Letter of Credit 519
  – Lombard Street 529
  – Moscow Narodny B. 582
  – Narodowy Bank Polski 596
  – Nordisk B 635
  – Order of Payment 657
  – Overseas China Banking Corp. 664
  – Pawnbroking Institutions 682
  – Pig on Pork 693
  – Point 696
  – Rate of Interest 738
  – Reserve Currencies 797
  – Roll-over Credits 760
  – Roubles Transferable 772
  – Savings Assocs. 793
  – Settl. Multilateral System 871
  – Slavonic Bank 850
  – Swap 887
  – "Third Window" 897
  – Transnational Banks 915
  – Vnyeshtorgbank 1015
  – West Afr. Devel. Bank 1031
  – World Bank-IBRD 1051
BANK DRUG MONEY ACCOUNTS 83
BANK FOR INT. SETTLEMENTS 83
BANK HOLIDAY 83
BANK OF CENTRAL AFR. STATES,
  BEAC 83
BANK OF CHINA 84
BANK OF EUROPE 84
BANK OF GENES 84
BANK OF INDIA 84
BANK OF ISLAM 84
BANK OF JAPAN 84
BANK OF NEW ZEALAND 84
BANK OF THE UNITED STATES 84
BANK PRIVACY 84
BANKRUPTCY 84
BANKS AND BANKERS ORGS. 84
BANKS OF ARGENTINA 84
BANKS OF BELGIUM 84
BANKS OF FRANCE 84
BANKS OF FRG 84
BANKS OF ISRAEL 84
BANKS OF JAPAN 85
BANKS OF LUXEMBOURG 85
BANKS OF SCANDINAVIA 85
BANKS OF SOUTH AFRICA 85
BANKS OF SPAIN 85
BANKS OF SWITZERLAND 85
BANKS OF THE NETHERLANDS 85
BANKS OF THE UK 85
BANKS OF THE USA 85
BANKS OF THE USSR 86
BANNED ARMS 86
BANQUE COMMERC. POUR L'EUROPE DU
  NORD 86
BANTU HOMELANDS 86
BANTU INTERLACUSTRINE 86
BANTU LINE 86
BANTU PEOPLES 86
BANTUSTAN 86
BAPTISTS 86
BARBADOS 86
BARBAROSSA PLAN, 1940 86

INDEX OF AGREEMENTS, CONVENTIONS, TREATIES

INDEX OF NAMES

G

L. GABRIEL ROBINET 101
F. GAD 351
L. GADDIS 191
O. GADO 403
A. GAGUA 834
A. GAIGALATÉ 489
G. GAIL 163
H.A. GAILAY 316
P.H. GAIN 169
P.D. GAITONDE 345
J.K. GALBRAITH 132, 175, 574, 575, 851, 1058
Z. GALICKI 22
L.N. GALIENSKAYA 202
A.A. GALKIN 340
A.D. GALKIN 295
Ch.T. GALLAGHER 578
M.A. GALLARDO 260
L. GALLEY 23
M. GALLO 865
R.I. GALLUCI 1011
G.H. GALLUP 316, 725
W. GALNSON 913
L.N. GALONSKAIA 64
V. GAMBA 290
R. GANATRA 642
J. GANIAGE 10
B.W. GANIUSHKIN 658
L.H. GANN 1077
J.W. GANTENBEIN 194
C. GANZ 385
F. GARAS 922
N. GARAY 675
A. GARBALETTO 791
J.W. GARBER 21
P.N. GARBER 563
F.V. GARCIA-AMADOR 219
L. GARCIA ARIAS 6, 196
F. GARCIA 865
P. GARCIA REYNOSO 503
A. GARCIA ROBLES 33, 97, 141, 145, 176, 219, 221, 229, 244, 249, 273, 309, 391, 404, 437, 500, 563, 601, 634, 676, 677, 758, 790, 801, 831, 836, 890, 895, 903, 935, 951, 969, 1023
C. GARCIA TRELLOS 676
W. GARDNER SMITH 602
J.S. GARLAW 772
J. GARLINSKI 69, 263, 855, 885
H. GARM 1076
F.X. GARNEAU 131
J.W. GARNER 45
R. GARNER 777
R.I. GARNER 409
R.E. GARRAY 743
A. GARRETSON 241
A.H. GARRETSON 612
S.A. GARRETT 697
K.C. GARRIGUE 631
R. GARSIDE 164
R.L. GARTHOFF 2, 204, 222
G. GARVEY 446
G. GASEVI 342
C. GASTEYER 542
K. GASTEYGER 285
Ch. GATI 246, 403
R. GATLIN 883
T.M. GAUDEMET 171
M. GAUDIER 946
J.P. GAULLIER 84
J.C. GAUTEON 840
Ph. GAVI 83
S. GAWEDA 475
W. GAWEDA 430
P. GAXOTTE 307
P.B. GAYENDRAGATKAR 475

H. GEATTE 873
S. GEEL 179
G. GEGAL 164
J. GEHL 45
H.S. GEIS 84
R. GELAROZIER 316
N. GELB 93
L. GELBER 314
L. GELBERG 78, 79
T.M. GELEWSKI 646
S. GELLAR 840
W. GELLHORN 654
R. GENET 832
R. GENOLARME 536
W. GENZER 283
T.J.S. GEORGE 847
F. GERA 734
E. GERADA 544
R.C. GERARD 365
J. GERASSI 1011
M. GERSHEN 586
J. GERSHENBERG 924
A. GERSON 1032
A. GERVAIS 919
F. GHADAR 655
E. GHALEB 893
E. GHAREEB 467
F.W. GHILLANY 90, 749
C. GHIBALBERTI 472
D.C. GIBBONS 58
C. GIBBS-SMITH 77
Ch. GIBBS-SMITH 73
T. GIBNEY 476
J.C.M. GIBSON 724
W.B. GIBSON 239, 734
R. GIBSON-JARVIE 533
G. GIDEL 137
E. GIERAT 100, 480, 489, 526
A. GIEYSZTOR 32, 203, 261, 697
T. GILBERG 760
M. GILBERT 53, 69, 261
O.C. GILES 911
J.A. GIL YEPES 981
P. GINIEWSKI 1077
G. GINSBURG 944
S. GINSBURG 164
G. GINSHARGS 944
L. GIOVATETTIX 384
E. GIRANDZ 838
E. GIRAUD 511, 965
C.C. GIUSESCU 760
O. GJERSTAD 354
S. GLADSTONE 553
M. GLADWELL 326
A. GLAISE-HOLSTENAU 71
M.H. GLANTZ 404
N. GLASER 560
S. GLASER 288
H.F. GLASS 429
E. GLASSER 636
M.J. GLASSPER 504
S. GLASSTONE 67
T. GLAZEBROOK 773
G.P. GLAZERBROOK 131
K. GLEDISH 313
G. GLESS 430
W.H. GLEYSTEEN 490
L.W. GLOWER 520
S. GLUECK 16
V. GLUNIN 164
W.G. GODDARD 306, 887
J. GODECHOT 129, 472, 589
M. GODFREY 935
R. GODSON 430
J. GOEBEL 290
D. GOEDHUIS 21, 24
A. GOELLNER 749
M. GOERTEMAKER 659

J. GOETSCHALCKX 519
I. GOLD 193, 347, 414, 803
J. GOLDBLAT 2, 4, 40, 59, 76, 98, 99, 128, 159, 160, 488, 508, 560, 562, 569, 571, 585, 586, 604, 613, 640, 642, 645, 646, 661, 688, 706, 760, 781, 789, 850, 878, 910, 918, 922
W. GOLDINGER 69
M.I. GOLDMAN 303
N. GOLDMANN 1077
A. GOLDSCHMIDT 495
B. GOLDSCHMIDT 66, 67, 599, 633, 861
B. GOLDSTEIN 343
J. GOLDSTEIN 586
R. GOLDSTEIN 22
W. GOLDSTEIN 884
W. GOLLHOM 881
H. GOLLWITZER 1070
J.M. GOLOVIN 578
S. GOLT 318, 325
M.A. GOMEZ DE LA TORRE 37
S.D. GOMKALE 884
A.M. GOMMAA 509
A.F. GONCHAROV 944
R. GONFIANTINI 470
S.A. GONIONSKIY 501
G.P. GOOCH 333
D. GOOD 57
R. GOOD 1077
A.E. GOODMAN 1011
H. GOODMAN 415
V. GOODMAN 556
L.M. GOODRICH 176, 596, 656, 939, 950
Ch.A. GOODRUM 520
S. GOODSPEED 658
G.S. GOODWIN-GILL 287, 583, 743
W. GOONERATUE 870
J. GOORMAGHTIGH 275
W. GÓRALCZYK 77
M. GORBACHEV 687, 945
A. GORBIEL 331, 661
L. GORDENKER 965
N. GORDIMER 857
G. GORDON-SMITH 438
C.H. GORDON 882
D.C. GORDON 26
H.J. GORDON 744
I. GORDON 143
J. GORDON 778
L. GORDON 246
M.R. GORDON 446
O. GORE 137
W. GÖRLITZ 326
R. GORMAN 743
Y. GORNY 1077
X. GORZUCHOWSKI 526
P. GOSSE 832
R. GOTT 354, 923
M.H. GOTZ 499
Sir C. GOUTH 846
J.W. GOULD 543
W.L. GOULD 458
B. GOUTROS GHALI 152
L.C.B. GOVER 921
J. GOYTISOLO 865
I.N. GRABELSON 299
J. GRADY 85
B. GRAEFRATH 872
H. GRAETZ 481
W.G. GRAEVE 683
L.S. GRAHAM 760
M.W. GRAHAM 740
R. GRAHAM 687
R.A. GRAHAM 760, 981
A. GRAHL-MADSEN 290, 743
G. GRAN 1076
G. GRANDIDIER 536
E.D. GRANE 240
M. GRANET 888

J.M. HURRAULT 311
H.E. HURST 612
S. HURWITZ 654
C. HURY 535
E.S. HUSEBYE 245
A. HUSSEIN 672
D. HUSSEY 441
J.M. HUSSEY 128
A. HUSTON 529
G. HUT 470
B. HUTCHINSON 131
E. HYAMS 895
A.M. HYAMSON 471, 673, 1077
C.C. HYDE 458
F.E. HYDE 77
J. HYDE 684
N. HYDE 1050
L. HYMAN 1077

I

Y. ICHICHASKI 666
R.J. ICKS 888
O. IDSOE 687
S. IENAGA 476
Card. IGINO 981
V. IGNATIEFF 296
D. IKEDA 115
F.W. IKLE 476
M. IKLE 885
J. ILIFFE 10
V. ILLINGWORTH 64
R. ILNYTZKYJ 924
N. IMAMURA 469
J. INCOX 611
R. INFIESTA 695
H. INGRAMS 1070
D.T. INGRAN 180
F.C. INKLÉ 222
N.M. INNES 274
A.D. INN 846
D. INSOR 896
M.E. IONESCU 760
H.P. IPSEN 370
G.E. IRANI 564
G. IRELAND 131, 519
A. IRIYE 175
A. ISAACMAN 583
A. ISAACS 1011
T.Y. ISMAEL 564
J.C. ITSINNG 887
L.A. IVANASHCHENKO 132
W. H. IVERS 246
N.F. IZMIEROFF 22

J

F.A. JAARSVELD 857
D.T. JACK 846
E. JACKEL 340, 800
E. JACKSON 965
G. JACKSON 865
G.D. JACKSON 495
J.H. JACKSON 272
K.F. JACKSON 563
Y.H. JACKSON 305
J. JACOB 728
D. JACOBS 96
H.A. JACOBSEN 331
A. JACOBSON 240
H.A. JACOBSON 870
CH. JACON 355
G. JAENICKE 749
S. JAENICKE 30
O. JAGER 800
M. JAHODA 173, 315
A.M. JAIDAH 655
R. JAIPAL 614

V.M. JAITSMAN 228
N. JAKOVLEV 518
A. JAMES 859
C.L.R. JAMES 343
P. JAMES 544
R. W. JANES 246
P. JANEWAY 983
R. JANIN 245, 552, 658
C.W. JANKS 171
O. JANOWSKI 481
O.J. JANOWSKI 738
G.H. JANSEN 469
M. JANSEN 673
P. JARIN 657
J.A. JARVIS 1015
B. JASANI 260, 661, 793, 864
K. JASPERS 340
R. JAULIN 273
J.K. JAVITS 887
R. JAY LIFTON 328
J. JEDRUCH 842
T. JEDRUSZCZAK 702
W. JEDRZEJEWICZ 697
N. JEE 144
O. JEFFERSON 475
H.B. JEFFREY 355
R. JEFFREY-JONES 430, 659
E.A. JELF 238
O. JELLINEK 756
C.W. JENGS 410, 497
J.T. JENKINS 1033
W.M. JENKINS 96
C.W. JENKS 47, 658, 953
W. JENKS 688
T. JENNING 301
R.Y. JENNINGS 5
R.G. JENSEN 945
B.W. JENTLESON 652
S. JENZOWSKI 108
N.N. JERSHOV 1
L. JERZEWSKI 487
P. JESSUP 273
P.C. JESSUP 313, 353, 458, 490, 603
Ph.C. JESSUP 114, 674, 894
W.S. JEVONS 286
E. JICHEI 612
E. JIMENEZ ARECHAGA 740
J.T. JOCKEL 634
S. JOCKES 1045
H.B. JOHN 204
I. JOHN 285
Sir R. JOHN 731
V. JOHN 110
N.S. JOHN-STEVAS 705
S.B. JOHNES 313
R. JOHNS 793
C. JOHNSON 213, 566, 652
C.H. S. JOHNSON 840
D.H.N. JOHNSON 408
M.W. JOHNSON 651
N. JOHNSON 1031
P. JOHNSON 481, 666, 1077
R.A. JOHNSON 935
S.B. JOHNSON 872
T.H. JOHNSON 878
U.A. JOHNSON 476
W. JOHNSON 33
D.M. JOHNSTON 164, 167
M. JOKL 918
J. JOLL 852
Ch. JONES 246
D. JONES 518
D.L. JONES 679
F.C. JONES 476, 545, 610
G. JONES 543
P.H. JONES 913
T. JONES 343
W. JONES 544

W.M. JONES 420
L. JONHAUX 410
L.C.D. JOOS 857
C. JORDAN 32
Ph. JORDAN 42
R.S. JORDAN 965
Z. JORDAN 651
J.J. JORGENSEN 924
B. JOSEPH 673
A. JOSEY 847
M. JOVANOVIC 81
J.A. JOYCE 391
C.B. JOYNT 273
D. JUDD 180
M.D. JUGLAST 7
W. JUKER 96
Ch.A. JULIEN 26
K. JUNCKERSTORFF 49
T. JUNILLA 298
C.R. JURGELA 526
E. JUTIKKALA 297, 1017

K

N. KAASIK 193
T. KABDEBO 403
G. KACEWICZ 349
J. KACZMAREK 495
S. KADI 673, 674
G.G. KADYMOV 1011
G. KAECKENBEECK 56, 970
W. KAGI 353
M. KAHALIL 511
G. KAHIN 83
J.A. KAHL 424
D. KAHN 170, 430
H. KAHN 476
J. KAHN 263
O. KAHN-FREUND 497
M. KAJIMA 476
M. KALDOR 216
S. KALEGOROPOULOS-STRATIS 483
TH. KALIYARVI 486
G. KALMANOFF 482
F. KALSHOVEN 508, 746
M.J. KAMEL 131
B. KAMINSKI 246
V. KANAPATHY 543
J. KANDELL 563
S. KANIA 1078
I. KANT 685
F. KANTANTAS 526
H. KANTOROWICZ 495
J.I. KAPINSKI 96
F.M. KAPLAN 164
L.S. KAPLAN 599, 1026
M. KAPLAN 483
D. KAPPELER 747
H. KAPUR 278
R. KAPUSCIŃSKI 45, 273, 302
P.P. KARAN 96
V.P. KARAVAYEV 260
E. KARCELA 272
E. KARDEIL 1075
S. KARNOW 1011
K.S. KAROL 164
H.K. KARPAT 660
E. KARSH 466
H.N.S. KARUNATILAKE 870
M. KASER 945
S.C. KASHYAP 83
B. KASME 508
H.L. KASTER 466
G. KATO 844
H. KATOUZIAN 466
A.M. KATZ 645
E. KATZ 112, 297
M. KATZ 945

G.F. DE MARTENS   312, 466, 476, 724, 774, 778, 920
D. MARTIN   160, 1077
M. MARTIN   314
M.R. MARTIN   501
N. MARTIN   722
J. MARTIN-CHAUFFIER   919
R.A. MARTINEZ   676
J. MARTINEZ COBO   903
R. MARTINEZ CORTINA   85
M.E. MARTY   724
J.D. MARTZ   252, 253
K. MARX   183
E. MARY RAMSAY   169
C. MARZANI   89
F. MARZARI   472
J. MASAVALL   865
P. MASFRAND   657
E. MASI   164
D. MASON   1062
R.A. MASON   23
D. MASSE   311
F. MASSEY   243
P.W. MASSING   50
G. MASSIS   656
J.L. MASSO   89
V. MASTNY   104
L. MASUY   652
N. MATEESCO MATTE   21
M. MATEJIC   1075
S. MATEOTTI   295
H.L. MATHEWS   349
T.G. MATHEWS   135
J.A. MATHIESON   224
R.S. MATHIJSEN   276
T. MATHISEN   868
D.J.I. MATKO   945
A. MATNELART   219
J.S.M. MATSEBULA   885
S. MATSUMOTO   108
H.L. MATTHEWS   204
H.T., R.D. MATTHEWS   882
C.C. MATTHIEWS   1
R.P. MATTIONE   501
F.H. MAUGHAM   201
R. MAURACH   868
J. MAURICE   518
A. MAUROIS   956
P. MAURY   1
F. MAUTNER   65
W.H. MAXWELL   180
A.J. MAY   71
A.R. MAY   883
H.L. MAY   243, 596
A. MAYAR   577
M.W. MAYAR   691
D. MAYBURY-LEWIS   679
A. MAYER   23
A.F. MAYER   986
B. MAYER   671
F. MAYER   981
H.W. MAYER   738
O. MAYER   654
H. MAYERS   834
H.M. MAYERZEDT   254
A.J. MAYNE   475
J.A. MAYOBRE   503
A.A. MAZRUI   10
M. MCCARTHY   270
M. McCAULEY   944
R. McCLINTOCK   597
G. McCORMACK   490, 491
C. MCCORRNICK   171
T.K. McCRAW   476
MCCRISTAL   1029
R. McCRUM   262
A. McDERMOTT   255
H. MCDONALD   423

J. MCDONALD   316
M.S. MCDOUGAL   651
M.B. MCELROY   983
R.M. McELROY   172
F.F. MCGARM   58
W.P. MCGREEWEY   176
Z. MCINNIS   131
C. McLAUGHLIN GREEN   1027
S. McLEAN   642
J. MCLELLAN   651
B. McLENNAN   916
E. McLEOD   296
A.H. McLINTOCK   611
W. McMALLOY   563
B. McMASTER   793
C. McMASTER   543
A.D. MCNAIR   874
R. McNAMARA   599, 642
R.H. McNEAL   182, 945
J.T. McNEILL   129
R. McNEIL   262
G. MCTURNAU   15
E. McWHINNEY   22
D. MEAD   564
D.L. MEADOWS   173
J.L. MECHAM   114, 348
J.M. MECKLIN   495
L. MEDARD   317
J.T. MEDINA   428
R. MEDVEDEV   165
Z.A. MEDVEDEV   18
M. MEGRAH   98
B.N. MEHRISH   83
H.B. MEIER   981
M.S. MEIER   161
U. MEIER   85
C. MEILASSOUX   973
F. MEINCK   1029
M. MEISER   1021
A. MEISNER   261
B. MEISSNER   246, 340
L. MEISSNER   476
A. MEISTER   964
S. MEIXLEJOHN TERRY   651, 697
T.P. MELADY   118
A. MELAMID   53
F. MELE   846, 898
J.W. MELLOR   302
D.J. MELNIKOV   340
O. MELTZER   136
F. MENDEL   462, 681
M. MENDELSOHN   944
R. MENDOR   414
J.L. MENDOZA   91
B. MENNE   495
K.M. MENON   345
A.K. MENSAH-BROWN   10
E. MENZEL   221, 545
H.Z. MERINO   163
M. MERINO-RODRIGUEZ   679, 694
F. MERK   545
M. MERLE   775
T. MERON   965
Th. MERON   391
Ch.E. MERRIAM   859
W.S. MERZLIAKOV   544
C. MESA   204
M. MESELSON   1070
F.M. MESSERLI   654
A. MESTAS   260
G.E. METCALFE   343
J. METGE   611
A. METREAUX   245
M. METTATIS   859
A. MEYER   21, 170
H.E. MEYER   203
K. MEYER   89, 204
K.E. MEYER   911

D.T. MEYERS   577
H. MEYERS   552
F. MEYNOND   557
J. MEYRIAT   307
H. MEYROWITZ   682
E. MIAESO   1070
K. MICHAŁOWSKI   3
H. MICHEL   548
Ch. MICOT   922
K. MIDDLEMAS   274
W.E.K. MIDDLETON   89
J. MIDGAARD   636
H.W. MIEBLE   802
R. MIGOT   485
V. MIHAILOWIC   1075
E.B. MIHALY   602
A. MIJARES   981
R.F. MIKESELL   739
S.W. MIKHAILOV   666
M.J. MILAZZO   160
E. MILCENT   840
E.S. MILENKY   502
S.B. MILES   74
M. MILGATE   250
E. MILHAUD   790
J.T. MILIK   216
T. MILJAN   302
T.B. MILLAR   69
O. MILLAS   163
D.H. MILLER   328, 747
D.N. MILLER   110
E. MILLER   220
E.W. MILLER   602
G.E. MILLER   842
H. MILLER   543, 956
J.D.B. MILLER   69
J.E. MILLER   472
J.H. MILLER C.S.C.   253
J.M. MILLER   973
L. MILLER   840
W. MILLER   660
H.A. MILLIS   913
A.C. MILLISPANGH   365
F.C. MILLS   713
M. MILLS   368
A. MILNE   265
R.S. MILNE   543
H.V. MILNER   722
J. MILWETZ   907
J. MINCES   26
MIN-CHUAN KU   946
H. MINEAR   567, 904
N. MINERS   386
MING-MIN PEN   105
J. MINHAS   672
E. MIOZZI   982
I. MIRCHUK   924
B. MIRKIN-GUTZEVITCH   285
G.J. MIRSKI   509
S. MISHAL   673
R.J. MISIUNAS   79, 272
K.P. MISRA   8
J. MISSAKIN   59
L.S. MITCHEL   545
J. MITCHELL   565, 566
T. MIYAOKA   476
Z. MLYNAR   211
J. MOCH   599, 745
J. MOCHOT   354
K. MOCZARSKI   1025
G. MODELSKI   500, 832, 833, 916
S. MODELSKI   499
E.D. MODZHANSKAJA   217
L.A. MODZHORIAN   308, 458
A. MOE   87
K. MOHLE   1029
P. MOHN   480, 920
L. MOJSOV   614

O

E. O'BALLANCE 495
C.C. O'BRIEN 842
P. O'HAGEN 105
D. O'HIGGINS 163
P. O'REILLY 311
R. OAKLEY 895
O.A. OBBE 612
A.R. OBERSHALL 1076
L. OBIDNIAK 1038
H. OCHSNER 160
R. OCHSNER 915
S. ODA 651, 831, 832
P.R. ODELL 652
J. ODUHE 882
D. OEHLER 687
E. OESER 872
R.M. OGELVIE 877
L.A. OGNIETOV 1011
H. OHLENDORF 188
T. OHLSON 897
Th. OHLSON 60, 217
A.T. OJO 612
J.C. OJWA 602
Ch.N. OKEKE 458
J. OKPAKU 612
M. OKSENBURG 165
M. OKUMIYA 565
O. OLALOKU 612
R. OLIVER 10
W.H. OLIVER 611
N. OLLESTADT 295
M. OLSON 596
A. OMARA-OTUNNU 924
J.K. ONDENIJE 805
R.I. ONWUKA 606
J.B. OOI 847
R. OPIE 186, 275
L. OPPENHEIM 169, 458, 675, 881
M. OPPENHEIMER 343
P.E. OPPENHEIMER 349
W. ORAN 262
M. ORELLANA 893
L. ORIZET 307
D. ORLOV 637
J. ORNSTEIN-GALICIA 161
D.W. ORR 248
A. ORTELIUS 33
A.K. ORVIN 868
J. OSENTON 7
R. OSGOOD 635, 680
E. OSMAŃCZYK 30, 193, 219, 760
E.J. OSMAŃCZYK 16, 34, 73, 88, 102, 106,
   261, 367, 501, 522, 651, 676, 855, 944
W. OSTRENG 87
G. OSTROGORSKY 128
M. OSWARD 62
D. OTTENSOOSER 1026
J.K. OUDENDIJK 6
B. OUTZE 220
D.J. OWEN 90
O. OYEDIRAY 612
F. OZBUDUN 923
R.E. OZGOOD 599
O.A. OZGUNT 857

P

E. PACE 204
H. PACHECO 129
R.K. PACHUARI 420
C.N. PACKETT 600, 791
P. PADFIELD 899
G. PADMORE 674
J. PADUA 563
J. PAENSON 893
J. PAESLEE 1024

Ch.H. PAGE 846
H.J. PAGE 296
K.J. PAGE Jr. 265
R.M. PAGE 733
J. PAGET 5
D.S. PAINTER 841
J. PAJEWSKI 570
T. PAKENHAM 101
R. PAL 1021
E. PALACIO 58
C. PALAZZOLI 578
M.G. PALEOLOGUE 792
A. PALIWALA 685
C. PALLENBORG 981
C. PALLEY 1077
H.M. PALMER 747
M. PALMER 857
R. PALMER 1077
L. PALSON 553
A.F. PANASENKOV 642
M. PANDEFF 76
K.M. PANIKKAR 246
H.F. PANKHUYS 170
S. PANNAMBALAM 870
N.C. PANO 25
B.G. PAPACOSTAS 671
N. PAPADOKIS 470
V.eL. PAPALETTERA 555
C. PAPE 868
G.U. PAPI 83
R. PAPINI 631, 935
S.J. PAPROCKI 569, 697
J.M. PARDESSUS 845
W. PARDY 981
A.M. PAREDES 458
J. PARENT 885
I.S. PARETERKU 601
Ch. PARK 831
J.K. PARK 831
Y.S. PARK 63, 278
F.D. PARKER 197
J. PARKER 1077
W.H. PARKER 884
Y.T. PARKER 274
J. PARKES 50, 471
J.W. PARKES 481
F. PARKINSON 501
L. PARKINSON 239
A. PARODI 684
S. PARRIN 10
A. PARRY 276, 458
C. PARRY 458, 567
M. PARTINGTON 108
J. PARTSCH 846
K.J. PARTSCH 327
R. PASCAL 537
H. PASDERMADYIAN 221
G. PASETTI 276
R.A. PASTOR 563
L. PASVOLSKY 1023
R. PATAI 1077
T. PAT COOGAN 467
H. PATRICK 385, 476
T. PATRIKOS 1073
A.D. PATTERSON 180
D.M. PATTON 1057
G. PAUCHOU 657
A. PAUL 485
V. PAVERCHEV 199
V.V. PAVLOVA 888
F.L. PAXTON 470
J. PAXTON 5, 49, 91, 93, 96, 106, 107, 109,
   113, 128, 129, 139, 144, 164, 168, 194, 199,
   213, 215, 239, 274, 275, 276, 278, 282, 285,
   309, 311, 367, 370, 385, 386, 429, 480, 486,
   487, 531, 535, 542, 545, 548, 549, 558, 561,
   568, 680, 710, 713, 776, 870, 887, 979, 1069
A.J. PAYNE 134

R. PAYNES 895
J.A. PAYNO 276
P. PAZ 501
B.M. PEAK 483
C.H. PEAKE 177
R. PEAR 384
A.J. PEARLE 631
M. PEARLMAN 257
Ch. PEARSON 584
A.J. PEASLEE 83, 142, 182, 439, 694, 840, 910,
   1042, 1066
M. PEIL 612
J. PEIRATS 43
P. PELISSIER 271
R. PELISSIER 409, 846
V.V. PELLA 199, 895
M.E. PELLY 44
G. PENDLE 679, 973
M.N. PENKUWER 261
W. PENN 283
D. PENZIG 882
G. PEPIN 2, 73
T. PEPPER 476
E. PEPPIN 21
L. PEREK 331
I.S. PERETERSKI 917
D. PERETZ 464, 471
L.M. PEREZ 883
J. PEREZ DE CUELLAR 1014
D. PERKINS 512, 576, 771
S. PERLMAN 913
J. PERÓN 484
G. PERRIN 885
J. PERRINJAQUED 534
M. PERROT 878
J. PERRY ROBINSON 160
K.S. PETERSEN 958
J.E. PETERSON 654, 1070
M.J. PETERSON 939
J. PETIT 535
R. PETKOVIC 76
T. PETRAN 886
J. PETRAS 163
A. PETROSYANTS 160
R. PETROV 220
V.P. PETROV 575
M.B. PETROVITCH 678
W.E. PEUCKERT 742
CH. PEYREFITTE 657
B. PFAHLBERG 15
D. PFALTZGRAFF 274
H.O. PFANNKUCH 405
L. PFEIFER 840
P.L. PHILLIPS 66
D. PHARAND 57
R.H. PHELPS 50
H. PHILBY 793
G.D. PHILIP 689
W. PHILIPPS 654
D. PHILIPSON 481
A.W. PHILLIPS 386
N. PHILLIPS 857
Sir F. PHILLIPS 45, 1032
T.R. PHILLIPS 848
C.S. PHYLLIPS 612
R. PIC 1011
G. PICARD 136
G. PICCIOTTO 685
O. PICHON 521
F. PICK 206, 306, 847, 1058
J.S. PICTET 721, 741
A. PIECZARSKI 851
J. PIEKALKIEWICZ 257
E. PIENKOS 893
J. PIENKOS 893
B.L. PIERCE 298
A.J. PIERRE 60
D. PIKE 1011

W

J. WACH 745
D.A. WADDELL 91
M. WADE 728
D.N. WADHWA 602
P. WAESTBERG 45
H. WAGNER 55
D.M. WAI 882
D. WAINHOUSE 683
D.W. WAINHOUSE 1, 217, 420, 468, 485, 499, 684, 685, 962
S. WAJDA 790
A. WALASZEK 746
M. WALCZAK 430
H. WALDMAN 803
J. WALENSLEY 98
J.K. WALENSLEY 282
L. WAŁĘSA 697
B.G. WALK 365
A. WALKER 180, 258
B. WALKER 384
F.A. WALKER 98
T.W. WALKER 611, 790
W. WALKER 894
M. WALLACE 658
W.V. WALLACE 199
J.E. WALLACH 800
W.V. WALLAS 211
C.C. WALLEN 172
J. WALMSLEY 139, 275, 282, 574, 681, 693, 696, 923, 1025
D. WALSH 25
M.J. WALSH 15
W.T. WALSH 428
S.M. WALT 29, 65
F.P. WALTERS 512
L.C. WALTON 304
A. WALWORTH 680
M. WALZER 91
S. WAMBAUGH 1, 135, 274, 430, 695, 887, 970
J.C. WAND 44
P. WANDYCZ 212
P.S. WANDYCZ 264, 307, 697
I. WANG 543
B.A. WAPENSKY 846
J.P. WARBURG 175
B. WARD 265, 597
Ch. WARD 39
K. WARD 554
S.J. WARNECKE 278
J.W. WARNOCK 404
R. WARSCHOW 1018
W. WARTHIN 1074
A.H. WASHBARN 101
A. WASILKOWSKI 199
R. WASITA 480
H.A. WASSENBERGH 21
M.J. WASSERMAN 574
S.R. WASSERMAN 873
J. WASSERMAN O'BRIEN 873
B. WASSERSTEIN 481
J. WATERBURY 255, 578
J. WATERHOUSE 132
J.T. WATKINS 707
M.B. WATKINS 8
M.M. WATKINS 747
T. WATLING 739
D. WATSON 956
A. WATT 69
D. WATT 467
A.D. WATTS 458
M. WAXMAN 483
R.C. WEAVER 343
J.D. WEAWER 840
B. WEBB 913
R.C. WEBB 689

S. WEBB 913
F.G. WEBER 923
H. WEBER 611
W. WEBER 526
C.K. WEBSTER 511
J. WECK 306
D. WECTER 470
G. WEDELL 735
D.E. WEDTHERBEE 423
R.P. WEEKS 776
W. WEGENER 215
H. WEHBERG 45, 171, 671, 874
H.W. WEIGERT 566
W. WEIKER 923
M.G. WEINBAUM 255
S.L. WEINBERG 337
C. WEINBERGER 222
N.J. WEINBERGER 886
T. WEINER 599
B. WEINREB 159, 241, 280, 300, 351, 421, 531
U. and B. WEINREICH 1070
B.D. WEINRYB 481
B. WEINSTEIN 316
F.B. WEINSTEIN 423
M. WEINSTEIN 973
W. WEINSTEIN 118
F. WEINTAL 865
P. WEIS 872
J.M. WEISGALL 97
T.G. WEISS 933, 965
L. WEI TSING SING 981
C. WEIZMANN 471
Ch. WEIZMANN 1077
C. WELCH 724
C.E. WELCH 674
D.A. WELCH 204
S. WELLES 673, 911
J.W. WELLINGTON 589
Ph.A. WELLONS 304
C. WELLS 935, 1073
R.A. WELLS 553
S.F. WELLS 897
E.K. WELSH 602
G.L. WENBERG 584
F. WENDEL 129
B.S.J. WENG 164
A.R. WERNER 741
F. WERNER 340
L. WERNER 678
F.L. WERTENSTADT 691
M.S. WERTHEIMER 678
R. WESSON 501
J.F. WEST 294
R.M. WESTEBBE 144, 555
A. WESTING 652
A.H. WESTING 247, 265, 287, 381
G. WETTIG 340
E.M. WEYER 272
L.D. WEYLER 956
W.J. WHALEN 479
K.C. WHEARE 180, 182
H. WHEATON 458
P. WHEATON 351
J.W. WHEELER-BENNET 110, 584
B. WHELPTON 75
F.I. WHIPPLE 694
A.P. WHITAKER 743, 771, 973
J.S. WHITAKER 10
P. WHITAKER 676
A. WHITE 260
E.M. WHITE 922
F. WHITE 661
J. WHITE 83, 438
L.C. WHITE 631, 904
M. WHITE 476
Th. WHITE 272
A. WHITEAKER 676
D. WHITEHEAD 295

R. WHITEHOUSE 57
J.B. WHITTON 671
D.K. WHYNES 897
J. WICKETT 850
H. WICKHAM STEED 69
C.G. WIDSTRAND 313
J. WIDTSOE 578
P.H. WIENFIELD 463
E. WIESEL 481
B. WIEWIÓRA 651
F.J.M. WIJNEKUS 714
U. WIKAN 654
Ch.L. WIKTOR 918
D.N. WILBER 8, 672
A.M. WILBUR 945
C. WILCOX 366
H. WILCOX 173
R.R. WILCOX 687
J. WILCZYNSKI 173
L. WILDHABER 917
N. WILDING 681
R.J. WILHELM 196
J. WILKES 679
H.C. WILKINSON 96
P. WILKINSON 488, 895
N. WILLARD 687
K. WILLENSON 1011
H.T. WILLETS 945
P. WILLETS 614, 630
D. WILLIAMS 612, 866
E. WILLIAMS 919
F. WILLIAMS 1070
G. WILLIAMS 522, 599, 636, 933
G.E. WILLIAMS 286
R. WILLIAMS 197
T.D. WILLIAMS 543
T.H. WILLIAMS 41
W.L. WILLIAMS 962
K. WILLIAMSON 294
F.R. WILLIS 340
H.P. WILLIS 98, 504
A.J. WILSON 870, 887
C.M. WILSON 520
D. WILSON 62, 899, 1075
G.W. WILSON 131
M. WILSON 381
M.C. WILSON 482
R. WILSON 33, 847
R.R. WILSON 462
W.T. WILSON 680
S.E. WIMBUSH 469
S. WINCHESTER 465, 491
E. WINDRICH 1077
G.R. WINHAM 904
B. WINIARSKI 313, 688, 834, 1030
J. WINIECKI 246
J. WINNICKI 687
H.V. WINSTONE 496
G. WINT 30, 1062
E. WINTER 981
M.M. WINTROBE 381
W. WINZER 738
M.S. WIONCZEK 503
R.S. WIRIODJATMODIO 176
E. WIRTH 467
L. WIRTH 343
H. WISEMAN 684
E. WISKEMANN 73, 472, 697, 761, 970
J. WISNIEWSKI 697
R. WISTRICH 601
K. WITHAUER 703
A. WITKOWSKI 553
M. WITTER 475
A.M. WITTFOHT 694
J. WITTLIN 697
A. WITTMAN 425
L.S. WITTNER 671, 685
R. WIXMAN 945

DESCRIPTIVE MAP OF THE UNITED

- ● UNITED NATIONS ORGANS, SPECIALIZED AGENCIES AND OTHER AUTONOMOUS ORGANIZATIONS WITHIN THE SYSTEM
- ■ UNITED NATIONS DEVELOPMENT PROGRAMME OFFICES
- ★ UNITED NATIONS INFORMATION CENTRES SERVICES
- ▲ PEACE-KEEPING OPERATIONS/OBSERVER MISSIONS

Reproduced with kind permission of the United Nations

THE UNITED NATIONS SYSTEM

PRINCIPAL ORGANS OF THE UNITED NATIONS

New York:
General Assembly
Security Council
Economic and Social Council
Trusteeship Council
Secretariat

The Hague:
The International Court of Justice

OTHER UNITED NATIONS ORGANS
(representative list only)

Geneva:
UNCTAD — United Nations Conference on Trade and Development
UNDRO — Office of the United Nations Disaster Relief Co-ordinator
UNHCR — Office of the United Nations High Commissioner for Refugees

Nairobi:
UNCHS — United Nations Centre for Human Settlements (Habitat)
UNEP — United Nations Environment Programme

New York:
UNDP — United Nations Development Programme
UNFPA — United Nations Population Fund
UNICEF — United Nations Children's Fund
UNITAR — United Nations Institute for Training and Research

Rome:
WFC — World Food Council
WFP — Joint UN/FAO World Food Programme

Santo Domingo:
INSTRAW — International Research and Training Institute for the Advancement of Women

Tokyo:
UNU — United Nations University

Vienna:
UNRWA — United Nations Relief and Works Agency for Palestine Refugees in the Near East

PEACE-KEEPING OPERATIONS/OBSERVER MISSIONS

UNAVEM — United Nations Angola Verification Mission
UNDOF — United Nations Disengagement Observer Force
UNFICYP — United Nations Peace-keeping Force in Cyprus
UNIFIL — United Nations Interim Force in Lebanon
UNIIMOG — United Nations Iran-Iraq Military Observer Group
UNMOGIP — United Nations Military Observer Group in India and Pakistan
UNTAG — United Nations Transition Assistance Group
UNTSO — United Nations Truce Supervision Organization

SPECIALIZED AGENCIES AND OTHER AUTONOMOUS ORGANIZATIONS WITHIN THE SYSTEM

Berne:
UPU — Universal Postal Union

Geneva:
GATT — General Agreement on Tariffs and Trade
ILO — International Labour Organisation
ITU — International Telecommunication Union
WHO — World Health Organization
WIPO — World Intellectual Property Organization
WMO — World Meteorological Organization

London:
IMO — International Maritime Organization

Montreal:
ICAO — International Civil Aviation Organization

Paris:
UNESCO — United Nations Educational, Scientific and Cultural Organization

Rome:
FAO — Food and Agriculture Organization of the United Nations
IFAD — International Fund for Agricultural Development

Vienna:
IAEA — International Atomic Energy Agency
UNIDO — United Nations Industrial Development Organization

Washington:
IFC — International Finance Corporation
IMF — International Monetary Fund
The World Bank — International Development Association (IDA) International Bank for Reconstruction and Development (IBRD)

REGIONAL COMMISSIONS

Addis Ababa:
ECA — Economic Commission for Africa

Baghdad:
ESCWA — Economic and Social Commission for Western Asia

Bangkok:
ESCAP — Economic and Social Commission for Asia and the Pacific

Geneva:
ECE — Economic Commission for Europe

Santiago:
ECLAC — Economic Commission for Latin America and the Caribbean

Name of country	Date of admission	Total area (square kilometres)	Estimated population (mid-year 1988)
Afghanistan	19 Nov. 1946	652 090	15 513 000
Albania	14 Dec. 1955	28 748	3 143 200
Algeria	8 Oct. 1962	2 381 741	23 841 000
Angola	1 Dec. 1976	1 246 700	9 481 000
Antigua and Barbuda	11 Nov. 1981	440	84 000
Argentina	24 Oct. 1945	2 766 889	31 963 000
Australia	1 Nov. 1945	7 686 848	16 532 000
Austria	14 Dec. 1955	83 853	7 595 358
Bahamas	18 Sept. 1973	13 878	244 000
Bahrain	21 Sep. 1971	678	481 000
Bangladesh	17 Sep. 1974	143 998	104 532 000
Barbados	9 Dec. 1966	430	254 000
Belgium	27 Dec. 1945	30 519	9 925 000
Belize	25 Sep. 1981	22 965	174 000
Benin	20 Sep. 1960	112 622	4 446 000
Bhutan	21 Sep. 1971	47 000	1 451 000
Bolivia	14 Nov. 1945	1 098 581	6 993 000
Botswana	17 Oct. 1966	581 730	1 212 000
Brazil	24 Oct. 1945	8 511 965	144 428 000
Brunei Darussalam	21 Sep. 1984	5 765	241 400
Bulgaria	14 Dec. 1955	110 912	8 995 000
Burkina Faso	20 Sep. 1960	274 200	8 509 000
Burundi	18 Sep. 1962	27 834	5 149 000
Byelorussian Soviet Socialist Republic	24 Oct. 1945	207 600	10 108 000
Cameroon	20 Sep. 1960	475 442	10 674 000
Canada	9 Nov. 1945	9 976 139	25 949 600
Cape Verde	16 Sep. 1975	4 033	358 000
Central African Republic	20 Sep. 1960	622 984	2 771 000
Chad	20 Sep. 1960	1 284 000	5 401 000
Chile	24 Oct. 1945	756 945	12 748 209
China	24 Oct. 1945	9 596 961	1 103 983 000
Colombia	5 Nov. 1945	1 138 914	30 241 000

Name of country	Date of admission
Comoros	12 Nov. 19..
Congo	20 Sep. 19..
Costa Rica	2 Nov. 19..
Côte d'Ivoire	20 Sep. 19..
Cuba	24 Oct. 19..
Cyprus	20 Sep. 19..
Czechoslovakia	24 Oct. 19..
Democratic Kampuchea	14 Dec. 19..
Democratic Yemen	14 Dec. 19..
Denmark	24 Oct. 19..
Djibouti	20 Sep. 19..
Dominica	18 Dec. 19..
Dominican Republic	24 Oct. 19..
Ecuador	21 Dec. 19..
Egypt	24 Oct. 19..
El Salvador	24 Oct. 19..
Equatorial Guinea	12 Nov. 19..
Ethiopia	13 Nov. 19..
Fiji	13 Oct. 19..
Finland	14 Dec. 19..
France	24 Oct. 19..
Gabon	20 Sep. 19..
Gambia	21 Sep. 19..
German Democratic Republic	18 Sep. 19..
Germany, Federal Republic of	18 Sep. 19..
Ghana	8 Mar. 19..
Greece	25 Oct. 19..
Grenada	17 Sep. 19..
Guatemala	21 Nov. 19..
Guinea	12 Dec. 19..
Guinea-Bissau	17 Sep. 19..
Guyana	20 Sep. 19..